The Oxford Dictionary and Thesaurus

American Edition

The Oxford Dictionary and Thesaurus

American Edition

New York   Oxford

OXFORD UNIVERSITY PRESS · 1996

Oxford University Press

Oxford   New York
Athens   Auckland   Bangkok   Bogota   Bombay
Buenos Aires   Calcutta   Cape Town   Dar es Salaam
Delhi   Florence   Hong Kong   Istanbul   Karachi
Kuala Lumpur   Madras   Madrid   Melbourne
Mexico City   Nairobi   Paris   Singapore
Taipei   Tokyo   Toronto

and associated companies in
Berlin   Ibadan

Published by Oxford University Press, Inc.
198 Madison Avenue, New York, NY 10016

American edition copyright © 1996 Oxford University Press, Inc.

Also published as *Reader's Digest Oxford Complete Wordfinder*
by The Reader's Digest Association, Inc., Pleasantville, New York

Oxford is a registered trademark of Oxford University Press.

First British edition published in 1993 as *The Reader's Digest
Oxford Wordfinder*; and published in a revised edition in 1995 as
The Oxford Dictionary and Thesaurus. Original text from *The Concise
Oxford Dictionary, Eighth Edition*, edited by R. E. Allen © 1990
Oxford University Press. Additional material from *The Oxford Thesaurus*,
First Edition © 1991 Laurence Urdang. Further additions © 1993
Oxford University Press and © 1993 The Reader's Digest Association Limited.

Library of Congress Cataloging-in-Publication Data
The Oxford dictionary and thesaurus.—American ed.
p.   cm.
Americanized version of the Oxford dictionary and thesaurus.
Also published as: "Reader's Digest Oxford complete wordfinder"
by the Reader's Digest Association—Publisher's info.
ISBN 0-19-509949-4
1. English language—United States—Dictionaries.   2. English language—
United States—Synonyms and antonyms.   3. Americanisms—Dictionaries.
I. Title: Reader's Digest Oxford complete wordfinder.
PE2835.092   1996   96-14847
423—dc20   CIP

1 3 5 7 9 8 6 4 2

Printed in the United States of America
on acid-free paper

Contents

Preface

The publication of the *Oxford Dictionary and Thesaurus* marks the beginning of a new era in language reference books. This volume offers, for the first time in the United States, a thoroughly integrated presentation of entries from the two most widely used types of language reference books, the dictionary and the thesaurus. This unified approach, treating meanings and related words within the same entry, offers the user an abundance of information about words, and a far more thorough analysis of the lexical variety and nuances of the English language than is possible in a dictionary or thesaurus alone.

Oxford's American dictionary staff drew on the unparalleled lexical resources of Oxford University Press, the world's most experienced and respected authority on English language and dictionaries. An international team of lexicographers, representing all major varieties of English (the United States and Canada, the United Kingdom, Australia and New Zealand, and South Africa), have contributed to the entries contained herein, making this volume innovative in both presentation and content. No American dictionary or thesaurus to date has been able to offer so much of the richness of "World English" as the *Oxford Dictionary and Thesaurus*. The result is an up-to-date and thoroughly reliable dictionary of American English, amply augmented by integrated thesaurus coverage, with a unique global perspective of English, the lingua franca of the late twentieth century and the new millennium.

The editorial and production staff wish to acknowledge the sagacity and unflagging support of Linda Halvorson Morse, Editorial Director of the Trade Reference Department of Oxford University Press.

F.A.

Project staff

General Project Editor
Frank Abate

Senior Editors
Stephen P. Elliott
Jacquelyn S. Goodwin
Elizabeth J. Jewell

Editors
Katherine M. Isaacs
Ruth Handlin Manley
Christine L. Stevens

Pronunciation Editor
Rima McKinzey

Specialist Editors, Neologisms
Robert Costello
Lois Principe

Proofreaders
Joan Carlson
Robin Fleisig
Larry Hand
Margaret Hand
Chris Kelley
Julie Marsh
Susan Munger

Additional Editorial Support
Elaine Chasse

Production Manager
Ellen Barrie

Production Assistant
Anita Vanca

How to use this book

A great deal of the information given in the entries is self-explanatory, but if you need help in understanding any part of an entry, start here by looking at the "entry maps." In the sample entries, the various types of information in an entry are numbered (❶ ❷ ❸ etc.); find the number preceding whatever is puzzling you, then match it up with the numbered notes around the sample entries. The notes will tell you which type of dictionary information you are looking at.

A Defining sections

❶ **Main entry word**
introduces a new entry

❷ **Pronunciation**
enclosed within oblique strokes / /

❸ **Part(s) of speech**
in *italic* type

New part of speech
signaled by a bullet •

❹ **Variant spellings**
in **bold** type

❺ **Inflected forms**
in **bold** type

❻ **Sense letters and numbers**
in **bold** type subdivide meanings

Definitions
explain meaning

❼ **Grammar notes**
give constructional information

❶ **ambidextrous** ❷ /ámbidékstrəs/ ❸ *adj.* (❾ *Brit.* also ❹ **ambidexterous**) ❻ **1** able to use the right and left hands equally well. **2** working skillfully in more than one medium. ◻◻ **ambidexterity** /-stéritee/ *n.* **ambidextrously** *adv.* **ambidextrousness** *n.* [LL *ambidexter* f. *ambi-* on both sides + *dexter* right-handed]

brief /breef/ *adj., n., & v.* • *adj.* **1** of short duration; fleeting. **2** concise in expression. **3** abrupt; brusque (❽ *was rather brief with me*). **4** scanty; lacking in substance (*wearing a brief skirt*). • *n.* **1** ❼ (in *pl.*) women's or men's brief underpants. **2** *Law* **a** a summary of the facts and legal points of a case drawn up for the court or counsel. **b** *Brit.* a piece of work for a barrister. **3** instructions given for a task, operation, etc. (orig. a bombing plan given to an aircrew). **4** ❾ *RC Ch.* a letter from the Pope to a person or community on a matter of discipline. **5** a short account or summary; a synopsis. • *v.tr.* **1** instruct (an employee, a participant, etc.) in preparation for a task; inform or instruct thoroughly in advance (*briefed him for the interview*) (cf. DEBRIEF). **2** *Brit. Law* instruct (a barrister) by brief. ❿ ⓫ ◻ **be brief** use few words. **hold a brief for 1** argue in favor of. **2** *Brit.* be retained as counsel for. **in brief** in short. **watching brief** *Brit.* **1** a brief held by a barrister following a case for a client not directly involved. **2** a state of interest maintained in a proceeding not directly or immediately concerning one. ⓬ ◻◻ **briefly** *adv.* **briefness** *n.* ⓭ [ME f. AF *bref*, OF *brief*, f. L *brevis* short]

■ *adj.* **1** short, momentary, short-lived; flying, brisk, hasty, speedy, swift; transitory, fleeting, transient, evanescent, passing. **2** short, concise, thumbnail, succinct, compact, to the point, laconic, terse, summary, compendious. **3** curt, abrupt, terse, short, blunt, brusque, direct, unceremonious. **4** see SCANTY.
■ *n.* **1** (*briefs*) bikini briefs, G-string; underpants . . .

broadcast /bráwdkast/ *v., n., adj., & adv.* • *v.* (*past* ❺ **broadcast** or **broadcasted**; *past part.* **broadcast**) **1** *tr.* **a** transmit (programs or information) by radio or television. **b** disseminate (information) widely. **2** *intr.* undertake or take part in a radio or television transmission. **3** *tr.* scatter (seed, etc.) over a large area, esp. by hand. • *n.* a radio or television program or transmission. • *adj.* **1** transmitted by radio or television. **2 a** scattered widely. **b** (of information, etc.) widely disseminated. • *adv.* over a large area. ◻◻ **broadcaster** *n.* **broadcasting** *n.* [BROAD + ⓯ CAST *past part.*]

■ *v.* **1 a** air, transmit, relay; radio; screen, televise, telecast. **b** announce, advertise, circulate, publish, proclaim, pronounce; put *or* give out, report . . .

❽ **Examples**
in *italic* type in parentheses ( )

❾ **Usage labels**
in *italic* type show restricted use

Further notes on usage
signaled by ¶

❿ ⓫ **Phrase list**
signaled by ◻ gives idioms, phrases, compounds

⓬ **Derivative list**
signaled by ◻◻ gives regularly derived forms

⓭ **Etymology**
(word history) in square brackets [ ]

⓯ **Cross-references**
in SMALL CAPITALS to other main entries or *italic* type to phrases, etc.

Further information is to be found on the correspondingly numbered paragraphs on pp. xii–xix. For example, if you want to know more about how usage labels work in defin- ing sections, look at paragraph 9 on p. xiv; if you want to understand synonym ordering, look at paragraphs 6, 7, and 9 on pp. xviii–xix, and so on.

B Synonym sections

❶ Synonyms
introduced by a black box ■

❷ Content
of synonym sections:
a synonyms,
b cross-references, or
c both

❸ Part(s) of speech
in *italic* type

New part of speech
signaled by a bullet ●

❹ Forms
in parentheses ( )

❺ Sense numbers and letters
refer back to defined meanings

❻ ❼ Ordering
of synonyms

❼ Punctuation
is significant

brief /breef/ *adj., n.,* & *v.* ● *adj.* **1** of short duration; fleeting. **2** concise in expression. **3** abrupt; brusque (*was rather brief with me*). **4** scanty; lacking in substance (*wearing a brief skirt*). ● *n.* **1** (in *pl.*) women's or men's brief underpants. **2** *Law* **a** a summary of the facts and legal points of a case drawn up for the court or counsel. **b** *Brit.* a piece of work for a barrister. **3** instructions given for a task, operation, etc. (orig. a bombing plan given to an aircrew). **4** *RC Ch.* a letter from the Pope to a person or community on a matter of discipline. **5** a short account or summary; a synopsis. ● *v.tr.* **1** instruct (an employee, a participant, etc.) in preparation for a task; inform or instruct thoroughly in advance (*briefed him for the interview*) (cf. DEBRIEF). **2** *Brit. Law* instruct (a barrister) by brief. □ **be brief** use few words. **hold a brief for 1** argue in favor of. **2** *Brit.* be retained as counsel for. **in brief** in short. **watching brief** *Brit.* **1** a brief held by a barrister following a case for a client not directly involved. **2** a state of interest maintained in a proceeding not directly or immediately concerning one. □□ **briefly** *adv.* **briefness** *n.* [ME f. AF *bref,* OF *brief,* f. L *brevis* short]

❶ ■ ❸*adj.* ❺ 1 ❷ₐ—❻ short, momentary, short-lived ❼; flying, brisk, hasty, speedy, swift; transitory, fleeting, transient, evanescent, passing. **2** short, concise, thumbnail, succinct, compact, to the point, laconic, terse, summary, compendious. **3** curt, abrupt, terse, short, blunt, brusque, direct, unceremonious.
4 ❷ᵦ see SCANTY. ❸ ● *n.* **1** ❹ (*briefs*) bikini briefs, G-string; underpants, drawers, boxer shorts, shorts, ❾ *Brit.* pants, knickers. **3** instructions, guideline(s), directive(s), orders, directions. **5** summary, outline, digest, précis, résumé, *aperçu,* abstract, abridgment, synopsis. ● *v.* **1** coach, instruct, train, drill, prime, prepare, make *or* get ready; advise, inform, apprise, acquaint, put in the picture, *colloq.* fill in, put a person wise. ❿ ⓫ □ **hold a brief for 1** ⓭ see ADVOCATE *v.* **in brief** in short, briefly, concisely, in sum, in summary, to sum up, succinctly, in a word, to cut a long story short, in a nutshell. ⓬ □□ ❷c **briefly** momentarily, for a few moments *or* seconds *or* minutes, fleetingly, hurriedly, hastily, quickly; see also *in brief* (BRIEF) above.

addictive /ədíktiv/ *adj.* (of a drug, habit, etc.) causing addic- tion or dependence.
■ ❷ₐ habit-forming, compulsive, obsessive, (❽ *of a drug*) hard.

abash /əbásh/ *v.tr.* (usu. as **abashed** *adj.*) embarrass; discon- cert. □□ **abashment** *n.* [ME f. OF *esbaïr* (*es-* = A-⁴ 3, *baïr* astound or *baer* yawn)]
■ ❹ (**abashed**) ⓭ see *embarrassed* (EMBARRASS 1b).

❽ Explanations
in *italic* type

❾ Usage labels
in *italic* type show restricted use

❿ ⓫ Synonym phrase list
signaled by □

⓬ Synonym derivative list
signaled by □□

⓭ Cross-references
in the synonym sections

Visual Cues

The symbols that identify parts of an entry are printed on every other page.

/ / **pronunciation**

● **part of speech**

□ **phrases, idioms, and compounds**

□□ **derivatives**

■ **synonym section**

SMALL CAPITALS or *italics* **cross-references**

A Detailed explanation of defining sections

1 Main entry word

Each main entry is printed in bold roman type, or in bold italic type if the word is not naturalized in English and is usually found in italics in printed matter:

adumbrate /ádumbrayt/ *v.tr.* **1** indicate faintly. **2** represent in outline. **3** foreshadow; typify. **4** overshadow. □□ **adumbration** /-bráyshən/ *n.* **adumbrative** /ədúmbrətiv/ *adj.* [L *adumbrare* (as AD-, *umbrare* f. *umbra* shade)]

bel esprit /bél espree'/ *n.* (*pl.* **beaux esprits** /bŏz espree'/ a witty person. [F, lit. fine mind]

Main entries are arranged in letter-by-letter alphabetical order.

Different words that are spelled the same way (homographs) are distinguished by raised numerals:

bale[1] /bayl/ *n. & v.* ● *n.* **1** a bundle of merchandise or hay, etc., tightly wrapped and bound with cords or hoops. **2** the quantity in a bale as a measure, esp. 500 lb. of cotton. ● *v.tr.* make up into bales. [ME prob. f. MDu., ult. identical with BALL[1]]

■ *n.* **1** see BUNDLE *n.* 1.

bale[2] /bayl/ *n. archaic* or *poet.* evil; destruction; woe; pain; misery. [OE *b(e)alu*]

2 Pronunciation

Guidance on the pronunciation of a main entry will be found in most cases immediately after the main entry, enclosed in oblique strokes / /. In some cases, more than one pronunciation is given: that given first is always the preferred pronunciation; if the variant is preceded by the label *disp.*, this indicates that some people disapprove of it or consider it incorrect. Guidance on the pronunciation of words printed in bold type within an entry (for example, in the derivatives list) is limited to cases in which the main entry pronunciation would be of no help in establishing the correct pronunciation of the derivative.

The dictionary uses a simple respelling system to represent pronunciation. This is meant to be self-explanatory and easily readable by the lay person without constant recourse to a table of special characters. The system includes only one letter that is not found in the English alphabet: the character ə is used to represent the short neutral vowel called *schwa*, used in many unstressed syllables in English in normal speech. This vowel sounds something like the sound *er* or *uh* used by some people when hesitating; it is the sound of the initial *a* in words such as *abode* or *attract*, the *o* of *confide*, the *e* of *condiment*, etc. For speakers of "r-less" dialects of English (as for many natives of eastern New England) it is also the sound of the last syllable of words like *father* or *insular*, the first and last syllables of *particular*, and so on. This is repre-

sented as /ər/ in the transcriptions, since most speakers of General American English pronounce the *r* that follows the vowel.

The respelling system also uses a number of accents and diacritics over letters: an acute accent shows a stressed syllable. The macron (ˉ) is used over certain vowels to show that they are pronounced as long vowels, e.g., o͞o (the vowel sound in *food*), or diphthongs, e.g., ī (the vowel sound in *bright*). A breve mark (˘) shows that a sound is to be pronounced as a short vowel, e.g., o͝o (the vowel in *book* and *put*). An underline character is used to link certain consonants, e.g., to distinguish th (the sound at the beginning of *thin*) from t̲h̲ (the sound at the beginning of *then*). An apostrophe (') is used before vocalic *l* or *n* to show that some speakers articulate the *l*- or *n*-sound without a full vowel sound, as in the final syllables of *candle* and *button*.

For a full explanation of every sound's representation in the respelling system, please see the *Key to the pronunciations* on pp. xx–xxi.

3 Part of speech

The grammatical identity of words as noun, verb, adjective, and so on, is given for all main entries and derivatives, and for compounds and phrases when necessary to aid clarity. The same part-of-speech label is used for groups of more than one word when the group has the function of that part of speech, e.g., *ad hoc, Parthian shot.*

When a main entry has more than one part of speech, a list is given at the beginning of the entry, and the treatment of the successive parts of speech (in the same order as the list) is introduced by a bullet in each case:

accidental /áksidént'l/ *adj. & n.* ● *adj.* **1** happening by chance, unintentionally, or unexpectedly. **2** not essential to a conception; subsidiary. ● *n.* **1** *Mus.* a sign indicating a momentary departure from the key signature by raising or lowering a note. **2** something not essential to a conception. □□ **accidentally** *adv.* [ME f. LL *accidentalis* (as ACCIDENT)]

The standard part-of-speech names are used, and the following additional explanations should be noted:

● Nouns used attributively are designated *attrib.* when their function is not fully adjectival (e.g., *model* in a *model student;* but *the student is very model* is not acceptable usage).

● Adjectives are labeled *attrib.* (= attributive) when they are normally placed before the word they modify (e.g., *acting* in *acting manager*), and *predic.* (= predicative) when they normally occur (usually after a verb) in the predicate of a sentence (e.g., *afraid* in *he was afraid*). When an adjective can occur either attributively or predicatively, the designation *adj.* is used on its own.

- The designation *absol.* (= absolute) refers to uses of transitive verbs with an object implied but not stated (as in *smoking kills* and *let me explain*).

- The designation "in *comb.*" (= in combination), or "also in *comb.*," refers to uses of words (especially adjectives and nouns) as an element joined by a hyphen to another word, as with *crested* (which often appears in forms such as *red-crested, large-crested*) or *footer* (as *six-footer*).

4 Variants

Variant spellings are given before the definition; in all such cases the form given as the main entry is the preferred form. Variant forms are also given at their own places in the dictionary when these are three or more entries away from the main form:

a cappella /aá kəpélə/ *adj.* & *adv.* (also **alla cappella** /álə/) *Mus.* (of choral music) unaccompanied. [It., = in church style]

alla cappella var. of A CAPPELLA.

Variant spellings given at the beginning of an entry normally apply to the whole entry, including any phrases and undefined derivatives.

When variants apply only to certain functions or senses of a word, these are given in parentheses at the relevant point in the entry:

burden /bərdən/ *n.* & *v.* ● *n.* **1** a load, esp. a heavy one. **2** an oppressive duty, obligation, expense, emotion, etc. **3** the bearing of loads (*beast of burden*). **4** (also *archaic* **burthen** /bərthən/) a ship's carrying capacity; tonnage. **5 a** the refrain or chorus of a song. **b** the chief theme or gist of a speech, book, poem, etc. ● *v.tr.* load with a burden; encumber; oppress.

Words that are normally spelled with a capital initial letter are given in this form as the main entry; when they are in some senses spelled with a small initial and in others with a capital initial letter this is indicated by repetition of the full word in the appropriate form within the entry.

Variant British spellings are indicated by the designation *Brit.* These variants are often found in British use in addition to or instead of the main forms given:

apothegm /ápəthem/ (*Brit.* **apophthegm**) a terse saying or maxim; an aphorism. □□ **apothegmatic** /-thegmátik/ *adj.* [F *apophthegme* or mod.L *apothegma* f. Gk *apophthegma -matos* f. *apophtheggomai* speak out]

Pronunciation of variants is given when this differs significantly from the pronunciation of the headword.

abatis /ábətis/ *n.* (also **abattis** /əbátis/) (*pl.* same or **abatises, abattises**) *hist.* a defense made of felled trees with the sharpened branches pointing outward. □□ **abatised** *adj.* [F f. *abatre* fell: see ABATE]

5 Inflection

Inflection of words (i.e., plural, past tenses, etc.) is given after the part of speech concerned:

broadcast /bráwdkast/ *v.*, *n.* *adj.*, & *adv.* ● *v.* (*past* **broadcast** or **broadcasted**; *past part.* **broadcast**) **1** *tr.* **a** transmit (programs or information) by radio or television. **b** disseminate (information) widely. **2** *intr.* undertake or take part in a radio or television transmission. **3** *tr.* scatter (seed, etc.) over a large area, esp. by hand. ● *n.* a radio or television program or transmission. ● *adj.* **1** transmitted by radio or television. **2 a** scattered widely. **b** (of information, etc.) widely disseminated. ● *adv.* over a large area.

The forms given are normally those in use in American English. Variant British forms are identified by the label *Brit.*; these variants are often found in British use in addition to or instead of the main forms given.

Pronunciation of inflected forms is given when this differs significantly from the pronunciation of the main entry. The designation "*pronunc.* same" denotes that the pronunciation, despite a change of form, is the same as that of the main entry.

In general, the inflection of nouns, verbs, adjectives, and adverbs is given when it is irregular (as described further below) or when, though regular, it causes difficulty (as with forms such as *budgeted, coos,* and *taxis*).

Plurals of nouns

Nouns that form their plural regularly by adding -*s* (or -*es* when they end in -*s*, -*x*, -*z*, -*sh*, or soft -*ch*) receive no comment. Other plural forms are given, notably:

- nouns ending in -*i* or -*o*.
- nouns ending in -*y*.
- nouns ending in Latinate forms such as -*a* and -*um*.
- nouns with more than one plural form, e.g., *fish* and *aquarium*.
- nouns with plurals involving a change in the stem, e.g., *foot, feet*.
- nouns with a plural form identical to the singular form, e.g., *sheep*.
- nouns in -*ful*, e.g., *handful*.

Forms of verbs

The following forms are regarded as regular:

- third person singular present forms adding -*s* to the stem (or -*es* to stems ending in -*s*, -*x*, -*z*, -*sh*, or soft -*ch*).
- past tenses and past participles adding -*ed* to the stem, dropping a final silent -*e* (e.g., *changed, danced*).
- present participles adding -*ing* to the stem, dropping a final silent -*e* (e.g., *changing, dancing*).

Other forms are given, notably:

- doubling of a final consonant, e.g., *bat, batted, batting*.
- strong and irregular forms involving a change in the stem, e.g., *come, came, come*, and *go, went, gone*.
- irregular inflections of borrowed words, e.g., *polka'd*.

Comparative and superlative of adjectives and adverbs

Words of one syllable adding -*er* or -*est* and those ending in silent -*e* dropping the -*e* (e.g., *braver, bravest*) are regarded as regular. Most one-syllable words have these forms, but participial adjectives (e.g., *pleased*) do not.

Those that double a final consonant (e.g., *hot, hotter, hottest*) are given, as are two-syllable words that have comparative and superlative forms in -*er* and -*est* (of which very many are forms ending in -*y*, e.g., *lucky, luckier, luckiest*), and their negative forms (e.g., *unluckier, unluckiest*).

It should be noted that specification of these forms indicates only that they are available; it is usually also possible to form comparatives with *more* and superlatives with *most* (as in *more lucky, most unlucky*), which is the standard way of proceeding with adjectives and adverbs that do not admit of inflection.

Adjective in -able formed from transitive verbs

These are given as derivatives when there is sufficient evidence of their currency; in general they are formed as follows:

- verbs drop silent final *-e* except after *c* and *g* (e.g., *movable* but *changeable*).

- verbs of more than one syllable ending in *-y* (preceded by a consonant or *qu*) change *y* to *i* (e.g., *enviable, undeniable*).

- a final consonant is often doubled as in normal inflection (e.g., *conferrable, regrettable*).

6 Definition

Definitions are listed in a numbered sequence in order of comparative familiarity and importance, with the most current and important senses first.

They are subdivided into lettered senses (a, b, etc.) when these are closely related or call for collective treatment.

7 Grammar notes

Definitions are often accompanied by explanations in parentheses of how the word or phrase in question is used in context. Often, the comment refers to words that usually follow (foll. by) or precede (prec. by) the word being explained. For example, at *bridle*:

> . . . consisting of buckled leather straps, a metal bit, and reins. **b** a restraining device or influence (*put a bridle on your tongue*). **2** *Naut.* a mooring cable. **3** *Physiol.* a ligament checking the motion of a part. ● *v.* **1** *tr.* put a bridle on (a horse, etc.). **2** *tr.* bring under control; curb. **3** *intr.* (often foll. by *at* or *up at*) express offense, resentment, etc., esp. by throwing up the head and drawing in the chin. □ **bridle path** (or esp. *Brit.* **road** or **way**) a rough path or road suitable for horseback riding. [OE *brīdel*]

The formula (foll. by *to* + infin.) means that the word is followed by a normal infinitive with *to*, as after *want* in *wanted to leave* and after *ready* in *ready to burst*.

The formula (foll. by *that* + clause) indicates the routine addition of a clause with *that*, as after *say* in *said that it was late* or after *warn* in *warned her that she was being followed*. (For the omission of *that*, as in *said it was late*, see the usage note in the entry for *that*.)

"*pres. part.*" and "*verbal noun*" denote verbal forms in *-ing* that function as adjectives and nouns respectively, as in *set him laughing* and *tired of asking*.

8 Illustrative examples

Many examples of words in use are given to support, and in some cases supplement, the definitions. These appear in italics following the definition, enclosed in parentheses. They are meant to amplify meaning and (especially when following a grammatical point) illustrate how the word is used in context.

(*See examples in the "map" of articles on p. x.*)

9 Usage

If the use of a word is restricted in any way, this is indicated by any of various labels printed in italics, as follows:

Geographical

US indicates that the use is found chiefly in American English (often including Canada) but not in British English except as a conscious Americanism.

Brit. indicates that the use is found chiefly in British English (and often also in Australian and New Zealand English, and in other parts of the British Commonwealth) but not in American English.

Other geographical designations (e.g., *Austral., NZ, S.Afr.*) restrict uses to the areas named.

These usage labels should be distinguished from comments of the type "(in the UK)" preceding definitions, which denote that the thing defined is associated with the country named. For example, *Parliament* is a British institution, but the term is not restricted to British English.

Register

Levels of usage, or registers, are indicated as follows:

- *formal* indicates uses that are normally restricted to formal (esp. written) English, e.g., *commence.*

- *colloq.* (= colloquial) indicates a use that is normally restricted to informal (esp. spoken) English.

- *sl.* (= slang) indicates a use of the most informal kind, unsuited to written English and often restricted to a particular social group, while *coarse sl.* is used to show that an expression is regarded as vulgar or unacceptable even in spoken use in most social contexts.

- *archaic* indicates a word that is restricted to special contexts such as legal or religious use, or is used for special effect.

- *literary* indicates a word or use that is found chiefly in literature.

- *poet.* (= poetic) indicates uses confined to poetry or other contexts with romantic connotations.

- *joc.* (= jocular) indicates uses that are intended to be humorous or playful.

- *derog.* (= derogatory) denotes uses that are intentionally disparaging.

- *offens.* (= offensive) denotes uses that cause offense, whether intentionally or not.

- *disp.* (= disputed) indicates a use that is disputed or controversial. Often this is enough to alert the user to a danger or difficulty; when further explanation is needed a usage note (see below) is used as well or instead. Many uses labeled *disp.* are also treated more fully in Appendix 2, "Some Points of English Usage."

- *hist.* (= historical) denotes a word or use that is confined to historical reference, normally because the thing referred to no longer exists.

- *propr.* (= proprietary) denotes a term that has the status of a trademark (see the Note on Proprietary Status, p. xxiv).

Subject

The many subject labels, e.g., *Law, Math., Naut.*, show that a word or sense is current only in a particular field of activity, and is not in general use.

Usage notes

These are added to give extra information not central to the definition, and to explain points of grammar and usage. They are introduced by the symbol ¶. The purpose of these notes is not to prescribe usage but to alert the user to a difficulty or controversy attached to particular uses. Appendix 2 is devoted to the most important points of difficulty in English usage.

10 Phrases and idioms

These are listed (together with compounds) in alphabetical order after the treatment of the main senses and introduced by the symbol □. The words, *a the, one*, and *person* do not count for purposes of alphabetical order.

They are normally defined under the earliest important word in the phrase, except when a later word is more clearly the key word or is the common word in a phrase with variants (in which case a cross-reference often appears at the entry for the earliest word).

11 Compounds

Compound terms forming one word (e.g., *bathroom*) are listed as main entries; those consisting of two or more words (e.g., *chain reaction*) or joined by a hyphen (e.g., *chain-link*) are entered as phrases under the first word or occasionally as main entries.

12 Derivatives

Words formed by adding a suffix to another word are in many cases listed at the end of the entry for the main word, introduced by the symbol □□. In this position they are not defined since they can be understood from the sense of the main word and that given at the suffix concerned.

When further definition is called for they are given main entries in their own right (e.g., *changeable*).

For derivative words used in combination (e.g., *-crested* in *red-crested*), see 3 above.

13 Etymology

The user is also referred to Appendix 1, "The History of English."

A brief account of the etymology, or origin, of words is given in square brackets at the end of entries. It is not given for compund words of obvious formation (such as *bathroom* and *jellyfish*), for routinely formed derivatives (such as *changeable, muddy,* and *seller*), or for words consisting of clearly identified elements already explained (such as *Anglo-Saxon, overrun,* and many words in *-in, re-, un-*, etc.). It is not always given for every word of a set sharing the same basic origin (such as the group *proprietary* to *propriety*). Noteworthy features, such as an origin in Old English, are however always given.

More detailed information can be found in the *Oxford Dictionary of English Etymology* (ed. C. T. Onions et al., 1966) and the *Concise Oxford Dictionary of English Etymology* (ed. T. F. Hoad, 1986).

The immediate source language is given first. Forms in other languages are not given if they are exactly or nearly the same as the English form given in the headword.

Words of Germanic origin are described as "f. Gmc" or "f. WG" (West Germanic) as appropriate; unrecorded or postulated forms are not normally given.

OE (Old English) is used for words that are known to have been used before AD 1150, and ME (Middle English) for words traceable to the period 1150–1500 (no distinction being made between early and late Middle English).

Words of Romance origin are referred to their immediate source, usually F (French) or OF (Old French before 1400), and then to earlier sources when known.

AF (Anglo-French) denotes a variety of French current in England in the Middle Ages after the Norman Conquest.

Rmc (Romance) denotes the vernacular descendants of Latin that are the source of French, Spanish, Italian, etc. Romanic forms are almost always of the "unrecorded" or "postulated" kind, and are not specified except to clarify a significant change of form. Often the formula "ult. f. L", etc. (ultimately from Latin, etc.) is used to indicate that the route from Latin is via Romanic forms.

(Latin) denotes classical Latin up to about AD 200; OL (Old Latin) Latin before about 75 BC; LL (Late Latin) Latin of about 200–600; med.L (medieval Latin) Latin of about 600–1500; mod.L (modern Latin) Latin in use (mainly for technical purposes) since about 1500.

Similar divisions for "late," "medieval," and "modern" are made for Greek.

Many English words have corresponding forms in both French and Latin, and it cannot always be established which was the immediate source. In such cases the formula "F or L" is used (e.g., *section . . . F section* or *L sectio*); in these cases the Latin form is the source of the French word and (either directly or indirectly) of the English word.

Some words are derived from languages that are not in wide enough use for them to be included as entries in the dictionary. These languages are listed below by regions; further information about them can be found in encyclopedias and other reference books.

- Those spoken in **America** are Surinam Negro (a Creole based on English) and the following Native American languages: Araucan, Aymará, Galibi, Miskito, Nootka, Renape, and Taino.

- Those spoken in **Africa** are Bangi, Fiot, Foulah, Khoisan, Kongo, Lingala, Mandingo, Mbuba, Mende, Nguni, Temne, and Twi.

- Those spoken in **Asia** are Ambonese (spoken in Indonesia), Assamese (in India), Batti (in Tibet), Maldive (in the Maldive Islands), Mishmi (in India), Sundanese (in Indonesia), and Tungus (in Siberia).

- Tongan is a Polynesian language.

When the origin of a word cannot be reliably established, the forms "orig. unkn." (= origin unknown) and "orig. uncert." (= origin uncertain) are used, even if frequently canvassed speculative derivations exist (as with *gremlin* and *gloat*). In these cases the century of the first recorded occurrence of the word in English is given.

An equals sign (=) precedes words in other languages that are parallel formations from a common source (cognates) rather than sources of the English word.

14 Prefixes, suffixes, and combining forms

A large selection of these is given in the main body of the text; prefixes are given in the form **ex-**, **re-**, etc., and suffixes in the form **-ion**, **-ness**, etc. These entries should be consulted to explain the many routinely formed derivatives given at the end of entries (see 12 above).

Combining forms (e.g., *bio-*, *-graphy*) are semantically significant elements that can be attached to words or elements as explained in the usage note at the entry for *combine*.

The pronunciation given for a prefix, suffix, or combining form is an approximate one for purposes of articulating and (in some cases) identifying the main entry; pronunciation and stress may change considerably when they form part of a word.

15 Cross-references

Cross-references in defining sections are introduced in any of a number of ways, as follows:

- "=" denotes that the meaning of the item at which the cross-reference occurs is the same as that of the item referred to.

- "see" indicates that the information sought will be found at the point referred to, and is widely used in the phrase sections of entries to deal with items that can be located at any of a number of words included in a phrase or idiom (see also 10 above).

- "see also" indicates that further information can be found at the point referred to.

- "cf." denotes an item related or relevant to the one being consulted, and the reference often completes or clarifies the exact meaning of the item being treated.

- "opp." refers to a word or sense that is opposite to the one being treated, and again often completes or clarifies the sense.

- References of the kind "*pl.* of" (= plural of) "*past* of" (= past tense of), etc., are given at entries for inflections and other related forms.

Cross-references introduced in any of these ways appear in small capitals if the reference is to a main entry and in italics if the reference is to a compound, idiom, or phrase within an entry.

References in italics to compounds and defined phrases and idioms are to the entry for the first word unless another is specified.

B Detailed explanation of synonym sections

1 Distribution and marking of synonym sections

Synonyms are offered for approximately a third of the entries in the dictionary, covering in all more than 23,000 lexical items. The categories for which no synonyms are normally offered include the following:

- highly technical vocabulary, especially nouns in technical use only (e.g., *eosinophil, habeas corpus, organzine, spirochete, trochoid*);

- words for which there are no true synonyms (e.g., *abbot, pannier, rectangle*);

- main entries that treat word-forming elements such as prefixes, suffixes, and combining forms (e.g., *ad-, hyper-, un-, -acious, -ling, -ness*);

- main entries that are abbreviations made up of initial capitals (e.g., *CEO, FHA, ICU, SAT*), and most other abbreviations;

- main entries providing only a cross-reference for a variant spelling of another main entry (e.g., *ay, baulk, hejira, phantasy*);

- most main entries that are labeled *archaic* in all their uses (e.g., *grimalkin, hitherward, whilom*);

- words and meanings that are labeled *coarse sl.* in their defining sections.

Outside these categories an attempt has been made to provide at least one full synonym list for each semantic group, together with cross-references to the full list from the most important words within the group. In general, nouns that are normally used in literal senses and have developed no metaphorical or extended uses are less likely to have synonyms than adjectives, adverbs, and verbs. Even if no synonyms are offered at the main entry you first look up, it may be worth also looking up the keyword(s) used in its definition, where synonyms or related words could be used. Other ways of finding extra synonyms include looking up the items in synonym sections (which may have synonym sections of their own), and considering the synonyms of related items; as Laurence Urdang has pointed out, users "can easily find synonyms for, say, *abdication* by making nouns out of the verbs listed under *abdicate.*" In this dictionary and thesaurus, this is illustrated by using the synonyms listed, for example, under the words *savage* in order to create a set of synonyms for *savagely*. Moreover, extra information about the synonyms themselves can be found in the defining sections, for in this book the synonym sections and the defining sections complement each other.

A synonym section is always signaled by the symbol ■; the main entry itself is never repeated. Readers will also notice that the synonym sections have a ragged right-hand margin, contrasting with the justified setting of the defining sections; this is designed to aid orientation on the page.

2 Content of synonym sections

A synonym section may consist of one or more lists of synonyms, one or more cross-references to synonym sections under other main entries, or a mixture of the two. A synonym list may also be supplemented by a "see also" reference to another list.

All cross-references in synonym sections are to the appropriate sense(s) of the *synonym section* of another entry, not to its defining section. For a full explanation of the cross-reference styles used in the synonym sections, see 13 below.

3 Parts of speech in synonym sections

The full list of parts of speech included in the entry is not repeated at the beginning of the synonym paragraph. Only those parts of speech for which synonyms are offered are mentioned again in the synonym paragraph; where more than one part of speech has synonyms, the bullet symbol is used as a visual separator between the part-of-speech sections, but not before the first part of speech.

Parts of speech are mentioned within the phrases or derivatives list of a synonym section only when this is necessary to distinguish between synonyms for a single compound or phrase that may have different grammatical functions according to context. In these cases the bullet separator is not used, but the synonym lists for the different parts of speech are labeled with their part of speech in parentheses

4 Forms of synonyms

If the synonyms offered are only substitutable in context for any form other than the exact form of the main entry, the altered form for which the synonyms substitute is given in parentheses at the beginning of the synonym list. The type-style of the form in parentheses follows as closely as possible the information given in the appropriate sense of the defining section. For example, in the entry for *bag*, sense 2a of the synonym section offers a list of synonyms for the main entry in the sense of "a piece of luggage"; after part of the list, there is an italicized note in parentheses "(*bags*)," corresponding to the grammar note in the defining section "(usu. in *pl.*)," followed by synonyms for the plural use *bags* in the collective sense of "luggage." Sense 3 of the noun is used only in the plural, so the whole synonym list for this sense is preceded by "(*bags*)."

How to use this book

bag /bag/ *n. & v.* ● *n.* **1** a receptacle of flexible material with an opening at the top. **2 a** (usu. in *pl.*) a piece of luggage; (*put the bags in the trunk*). **b** a woman's handbag. **3** (in *pl.*; usu. foll. by *of*) *colloq.* a large amount; plenty (*bags of money*). **4** (in *pl.*) *Brit. colloq.* trousers. **5** *sl. derog.* a woman, esp. regarded as unattractive or unpleasant. **6** an animal's sac containing poison, honey, etc. **7** an amount of game shot or allowed. **8** (usu. in *pl.*) baggy folds of skin under the eyes. **9** *sl.* a person's particular interest or preoccupation (*his bag is baroque music*). ● *v.* (**bagged, bagging**) **1** *tr.* put in a bag. **2** *colloq. tr.* **a** secure; get hold of (*bagged the best seat*). **b** *colloq.* steal. **c** shoot (game). **d** (often in phr. **bags I**) *Brit. colloq.* claim on grounds of being the first to do so (*bagged first go; bags I go first*). **3 a** *intr.* hang loosely; bulge; swell. **b** *tr.* cause to do this. **4** *tr. Austral. sl.* criticize; disparage. □ **bag and bagggage** with all one's belongings. . . .

■ *n.* **1** sack, shopping bag, string bag, plastic bag, *Austral.* port, *dial.* poke, *usu. hist.* reticule. **2 a** valise, satchel, grip, suitcase, case, overnight bag, vanity case, carry-on luggage *or* bag, gladstone bag, carpetbag, portmanteau; briefcase, attaché case, dispatch case, (*bags*) baggage, luggage, gear, belongings.
b pocketbook, purse, handbag, evening bag, clutch bag, shoulder bag, wallet. **3** (*bags*) see LOT *n.* 1.
5 crone, (old) hag, ogress, gorgon, dragon, witch, harridan, *archaic* beldam, *colloq.* battleaxe, *sl.* (old) cow, old bag, *sl. derog.* dog. **9** occupation, hobby, avocation, business, vocation, specialty, field, métier, department, concern, affair, passion, specialty, *colloq.* lookout, thing, cup of tea. ● *v.* **2 a** see SECURE *v.* 3. **b** see STEAL *v.* 1. **c** kill, shoot, gun down, pick off, *colloq.* blast, *sl.* plug; catch, trap, ensnare, snare, entrap, capture, land. **3** see SWELL *v.* 3. . . .

In the case of verbs with grammar notes, an alternative form with a following particle is often given in parentheses to show that the synonyms substitute for the phrase rather than the main entry alone:

consist /kənsist/ *v.intr.* **1** (foll. by *of*) be composed; have specified ingredients or elements. **2** (foll. by *in, of*) have its essential features as specified (*its beauty consists in the use of color*). **3** (usu. foll. by *with*) harmonize; be consistent. [L *consistere* exist (as COM-, *sistere* stop)]
■ **1** (*consist of*) contain, comprise, be composed of, include, have in it.

Forms that are given in bold type in the defining section are repeated in bold type in parentheses in the synonym section if the synonyms offered are for that form; for example, the adjective *impoverished* is treated under the verb *to impoverish* by the grammar note "(often as **impoverished** *adj.*)" at the beginning of the entry. In the synonym section, a cross-reference is given for the verb in each of its senses, followed by a list of synonyms for the adjective *impoverished*, in each case introduced by "(**impoverished**)" to show that the synonyms are for this different form.

5 Synonym senses numbering

The sense numbering of synonym sections follows the pattern of the defining section of the entry, so that readers can easily see which synonyms are appropriate to which meanings of the main entry. However, it is not the practice to give synonyms for every sense represented in the defining section, and in some cases it is less repetitious to give a list of synonyms for a number of senses together. Sense numbering in the synonym section may therefore take the form of a list of numbers (and sometimes also letters), as, for example, **1a 2b, 3d,** or show a range of senses to which the synonyms apply as **1–3, 2–5,** etc.

Wherever a single list of synonyms covers all the meanings explained in the defining section, sense numbers are dispensed with and the synonym list is simply introduced by the synonym symbol ■ .

6 Arrangement of synonyms

Within a synonym sense, the synonyms are arranged in conceptual groups separated by semicolons. Each "branch" of meaning has its own group, within which the synonyms are organized loosely in order of association, with labeled synonyms (see 9 below) in their own sequence at the end of the group.

This means that the synonyms that are semantically and stylistically closest to each other are also physically close to each other on the page. For each sense the list of synonyms begins with those closest in meaning to it; then come those less close to it in meaning. In each list of synonyms a comma separates items that are virtually synonyms of each other; a semicolon separates items that are less close to each other in meaning. Sometimes the division is a grammatical rather than a semantic one; for example, synonyms for a meaning of a verb that is labeled both for transitive and intransitive uses in the defining section may have first a group of synonyms that substitute for both types of context, then synonyms limited to one or the other use in their own group(s) after a semicolon.

7 Punctuation and style of synonym lists

Synonyms may be single words or phrases. The individual synonyms within a group are separated by commas, while a new group (and resetting of the label sequence) is signaled by a semicolon within synonym sections. Readers should note the difference in this use of the semicolon from that employed in defining sections (where it introduces a separate piece of defining text with a different nuance of meaning from the part of the definition that precedes it).

Parentheses are sometimes used in synonym lists. Their principal use is to show optional parts of a synonym or phrase, e.g., for single-word synonyms, "content(ed)" (indicating that both "content" and "contented" are appropriate synonyms); for phrases "reflect (on *or* upon)" (indicating that the simple verb "reflect" has phrasal variants "reflect on" and "reflect upon"), etc.

Explanatory matter in italic type is discussed at 8 below. All synonym text is printed in roman type with the exception of unassimilated foreign words that are normally printed in italic in English contexts; these words (which at their own defining sections have the main entry printed in bold italic type) are printed in light italic type in synonym sections.

8 Explanations in synonym lists

Sometimes it is necessary to provide further explanatory text in a synonym list; these are given in italic type to differentiate them from the synonyms themselves. Grammatical notes are explained at 4 above and usage labels at 9 below. Apart from these categories of explanatory matter, the reader will find that the word *or* is frequently used in phrasal synonyms to introduce a variant without repeating the whole phrase, e.g., "make public *or* known" (expandable to "make public" and "make known"), "not worth anything *or* a straw *or* a rap" ("not worth anything," "not worth a straw," "not worth a rap"), etc.

Occasionally it is necessary to limit the application of a synonym to a narrower field than that implied by the definition of the main entry. For example, in the entry *habit*, the compound *habit-forming* is defined as 'causing addiction.' The corresponding synonym list reads "addictive, compulsive, (*of a drug*) hard; see also *obsessive* (OBSESS)," indicating that the synonyms "addictive" and "compulsive" may be used of habit-forming substances in general and of activities, etc., that may cause dependence, whereas the synonym "hard" may only be applied to a habit-forming drug.

9 Usage labels in synonym lists

The same range of subject, regional, and register labels is used in synonym sections as in defining sections: for a full explanation of their meaning, please see 9 on p. xiv above. Labeled synonyms have their own sequence at the end of the unlabeled group (which means that if, for example, you were looking for synonyms of a slang word, you would find the neutral synonyms before those that also are limited to a particular subject, regional variety, or style of language).

The label precedes the synonym or group of synonyms to which it applies and applies to all synonyms listed up to the next label, semicolon, or period (whichever comes first). The order of precedence of the labels themselves is:

   (i) subject (only) in alphabetical order, e.g., *Archaeol., Biol., Law;*

   (ii) region (only) in alphabetical order of the main label (with labels qualified by "esp." preceding the main label and those followed by "*and*" and "*or*" following), e.g, esp. *Austral., Austral., Austral. & NZ, Brit., NZ, S.Afr., US;*

   (iii) combinations of region and subject, e.g., *Brit. Law* fit in after the appropriate regional label on its own;

   (iv) register (only) in alphabetical order, e.g., *archaic, colloq., disp., hist., sl.;*

   (v) combinations of register and region fit in after the appropriate register label on its own, e.g., *colloq., Austral. colloq., Brit. colloq., US colloq., sl., Austral. sl., Brit. sl., US sl.*

10 Synonyms of phrases

Phrase lists in synonym sections are introduced by the same symbol, □ , as is used in the defining section. Those phrases for which synonyms are being offered are shown in bold, followed by their part of speech (if needed: see 3 above), sense number (if needed: see 5 above), and synonyms and/or cross-references. The synonyms of phrases may, of course, include single words as well as other phrases.

11 Synonyms of compounds

The explanation of synonym phrase lists also applies to compounds, which are listed in a single alphabetical sequence with the phrases.

12 Synonyms of derivatives

Synonym derivative lists are introduced by the same symbol, □□ , as is used in the defining section. Those derivatives for which synonyms are being offered are shown in bold, followed by their part of speech (if needed: see 3 above), synonyms and/or cross-references.

13 Synonym cross-references

Essentially the same conventions are used for cross-references in synonym sections as for cross-references elsewhere in the text, with the exception that, when referring to a derivative in a synonym section, the derivative itself is given in italic type, followed by the main entry under which this will be found, in small capitals inside parentheses, e.g., "see *elasticity* (ELASTIC)."

It should be noted that cross-references in synonym sections are to the *synonym section* of the appropriate entry, not to its defining section. Only such information (in the way of parts of speech, sense numbers, etc.) is given as is necessary to enable the reader to find the correct synonym list.

Key to the pronunciations

This book uses a simple respelling system to show how entries are pronounced. As far as possible the phonetic symbols follow the letters of the English alphabet and special symbols have been kept to a minimum.

a, á	*as in*	**pat** /pat/, **fasten** /fásən/
aa, áa	*as in*	**palm** /paam/, **father** /faáthər/, **maharaja** /maáhəraajə/, **barnyard** /baárnyaard/
air, áir	*as in*	**fair** /fair/, **share** /shair/, **heir** /air/, **footwear** /fŏŏtwair/, **fairy** /fáiree/
aw, áw	*as in*	**law** /law/, **caught** /kawt/, **thought** /thawt/, **lawful** /láwfŏŏl/, **horse** /hawrs/
ay, áy	*as in*	**day** /day/, **raid** /rayd/, **made** /mayd/, **prey** /pray/, **gauge** /gayj/, **reign** /rayn/, **graceful** /gráysfŏŏl/
b	*as in*	**bay** /bay/, **ebb** /eb/
ch	*as in*	**church** /chərch/, **itch** /ich/, **picture** /píkchər/, **cello** /chélō/
d	*as in*	**dog** /dog/, **deed** /deed/
e, é	*as in*	**men** /men/, **said** /sed/, **mellow** /mélo/, **merry** /méree/
ee, eé	*as in*	**feet** /feet/, **leave** /leev/, **siege** /seej/, **receive** /riseév/, **city** /sítee/
ə	*as in*	**along** /əlóng/, **soda** /sŏ́də/, **pollen** /pólən/, **civil** /sívəl/, **lemon** /lémən/, **suppose** /səpóz/
ər, ə́r	*as in*	**parade** /pəráyd/, **bitter** /bítər/, **curl** /kərl/, **person** /pə́rsən/, **maternity** /mətə́rnitee/
f	*as in*	**fit** /fit/, **telephone** /télifōn/, **tough** /tuf/, **taffy** /táfee/
g	*as in*	**get** /get/, **ghost** /gōst/, **exhaust** /igzáwst/, **egg** /eg/
h	*as in*	**head** /hed/, **behave** /biháyv/
i, í	*as in*	**pin** /pin/, **guild** /gild/, **decide** /disíd/, **women** /wímin/, **busy** /bízee/, **lyrics** /líriks/
ī, í	*as in*	**time** /tīm/, **fight** /fīt/, **guide** /gīd/, **buy** /bī/, **writing** /rı́ting/, **dial** /díəl/, **sky** /skī/
īr, ír	*as in*	**fire** /fīr/, **choir** /kwīr/, **desire** /dizír/, **thyroid** /thíroyd/
j	*as in*	**judge** /juj/, **carriage** /kárij/, **soldier** /sṓljər/
k	*as in*	**kick** /kik/, **coat** /kōt/, **mix** /miks/, **chaos** /káyos/, **school** /skŏŏl/
kh	*as in*	**loch** /lokh/, **Bach** /baakh/
l	*as in*	**like** /līk/, **lily** /lílee/
'l	*as in*	**bottle** /bót'l/, **candle** /kánd'l/
m	*as in*	**may** /may/, **ham** /ham/
n	*as in*	**nun** /nun/, **runner** /rúnər/
N	*as in*	**en route** /oN root/, **thé dansant** /táy doNsóN/ (used to show that the preceding vowel is nasalized)
'n	*as in*	**wooden** /wŏŏd'n/, **button** /bút'n/
ng	*as in*	**sing** /sing/, **sink** /singk/, **anger** /ánggər/
o, ó	*as in*	**rob** /rob/, **pocket** /pókit/
ō, ṓ	*as in*	**go** /gō/, **boat** /bōt/, **show** /shō/, **toe** /tō/, **hotel** /hōtél/, **promote** /prəmŏ́t/, **rainbow** /ráynbō/
ö, ö́	*as in*	**jeu** /zhö/, **schön** /shön/
ŏŏ, ŏ́ŏ	*as in*	**wood** /wŏŏd/, **could** /kŏŏd/, **push** /pŏŏsh/, **football** /fŏŏtbawl/
ōō, ṓō	*as in*	**food** /fōōd/, **few** /fyōō/, **do** /dōō/, **blue** /blōō/, **music** /myŏ́ōsik/, **review** /rivyŏ́ō/
ow, ów	*as in*	**mouse** /mows/, **coward** /kówərd/, **hour** /owr/
oy, óy	*as in*	**boy** /boy/, **noisy** /nóyzee/
p	*as in*	**pit** /pit/, **hop** /hop/

r	*as in*	**run** /run/, **fur** /fər/, **spirit** /spírit/
s	*as in*	**sit** /sit/, **scent** /sent/, **fix** /fiks/, **pizza** /peétsə/
sh	*as in*	**shut** /shut/, **social** /sőshəl/, **partial** /paárshəl/, **passion** /páshən/, **action** /ákshən/, **machine** /məsheén/
t	*as in*	**taste** /tayst/, **butter** /bútər/
th	*as in*	**thin** /thin/, **truth** /trōōth/
th	*as in*	**then** /then/, **mother** /múthər/
u, ú	*as in*	**cut** /kut/, **blood** /blud/, **enough** /inúf/
v	*as in*	**vet** /vet/, **have** /hav/
w	*as in*	**way** /way/, **quick** /kwik/
y	*as in*	**yet** /yet/, **million** /mílyən/, **queue** /kyōō/, **accuse** /əkyōōz/, **tortilla** /tawrteéyə/
Y	*as in*	**mot juste** /mō zhYst/, **Sprachgefühl** /shpraákhgəfYl/
z	*as in*	**zero** /zeérō/, **phrase** /frayz/, **lenses** /lénziz/, **examine** /igzámin/, **fuzzy** /fúzee/, **xylem** /zíləm/
zh	*as in*	**measure** /mézhər/, **jabot** /zhabő/, **vision** /vizhən/

Hyphen

As an aid to correct pronunciation a hyphen is used within a pronunciation entry to avoid confusion; for example, to distinguish between *t* followed by *h* and *th*, or *s* followed by *h* and *sh*, etc.:

> **gatehouse** /gáyt-hows/, **mishap** /mís-hap/

or where two or more vowels appearing together would be unclear; for example:

> **zoology** /zō-óləjee/, **vehicle** /veé-ikəl/

More than one acceptable pronunciation may be given, with commas between the variants; for example:

> **news** /nōōz, nyōōz/

If the pronunciations of a word differ only in part, then the syllable or syllables affected are shown as follows:

> **bedroom** /bédrōōm, -rōōm/, **forest** /fáwrist, fór-/

The same principle applies to derivative forms that are given within the main entry; for example:

> **complete** /kəmpleét/, **completion** /-pleéshən/

Stress

The mark that appears over the vowel symbol in words of more than one syllable indicates the part of the word that carries the stress. Where a word has two or more stress markers then the main stress may vary according to the context in which a word is used; for example:

> **afternoon** /áftərnōōn/

In the phrase "afternoon tea" the main stress falls on the first syllable /áftər-/, but in the phrase "all afternoon" the main stress falls on the last syllable /-nōōn/.

Abbreviations used in this book

Some abbreviations (especially of language names) occur only in etymologies. Others may appear in italics. Abbreviations in general use (such as etc., i.e., and those for books of the Bible) are explained in the dictionary text itself.

abbr.	abbreviation	Bret.	Breton	dimin.	diminutive
ablat.	ablative	Brit.	British	disp.	disputed (use or
absol.	absolute(ly)	Bulg.	Bulgarian		pronunciation)
acc.	according	Burm.	Burmese	dissim.	dissimilated
accus.	accusative	Byz.	Byzantine	distrib.	distributive
adj.	adjective			Du.	Dutch
adv.	adverb	c.	century		
Aeron.	Aeronautics	*c.*	*circa*	E	English
AF	Anglo-French	Can.	Canada, Canadian	Eccl.	Ecclesiastical
Afr.	Africa, African	Cat.	Catalan	Ecol.	Ecology
Afrik.	Afrikaans	Celt.	Celtic	Econ.	Economics
Akkad.	Akkadian	Ch.	Church	EFris	East Frisian
AL	Anglo-Latin	Chem.	Chemistry	Egypt.	Egyptian
alt.	alteration	Chin.	Chinese	E.Ind.	East Indian, of the
Amer.	America, American	Cinematog.	Cinematography		East Indies
Anat.	Anatomy	class.	classical	Electr.	Electricity
anc.	ancient	coarse sl.	coarse slang	elem.	elementary
Anglo-Ind.	Anglo-Indian	cogn.	cognate	ellipt.	elliptical(ly)
Anthropol.	Anthropology	collect.	collective(ly)	emphat.	emphatic(ally)
Antiq.	Antiquities,	colloq.	colloquial(ly)	Engin.	Engineering
	Antiquity	comb.	combination,	Engl.	England, English
app.	apparently		combining	Entomol.	Entomology
Arab.	Arabic	compar.	comparative	erron.	erroneous(ly)
Aram.	Aramaic	compl.	complement	esp.	especial(ly)
arbitr.	arbitrary, arbitrarily	Conchol.	Conchology	etym.	etymology
Archaeol.	Archaeology	conj.	conjunction	euphem.	euphemism
Archit.	Architecture	conn.	connected	Eur.	Europe, European
Arith.	Arithmetic	constr.	construction	ex.	example
assim.	assimilated	contr.	contraction	exc.	except
assoc.	associated,	Corn.	Cornish	exclam.	exclamation
	association	corresp.	corresponding		
Assyr.	Assyrian	corrupt.	corruption	F	French
Astrol.	Astrology	Criminol.	Criminology	f.	from
Astron.	Astronomy	Crystallog.	Crystallography	fam.	familiar
Astronaut.	Astronautics			fem.	feminine
Attrib.	attributive(ly)	Da.	Danish	fig.	figurative(ly)
attrib.adj.	attributive adjective	decl.	declension	Finn.	Finnish
augment.	augmentative	def.	definite	fl.	flourished
Austral.	Australia,	Demog.	Demography	Flem.	Flemish
	Australian	demons.	demonstrative	foll.	followed, following
aux.	auxiliary	demons.adj.	demonstrative	form.	formation
			adjective	Fr.	French
back-form.	back-formation	demons.pron.	demonstrative	Frank.	Frankish
Bibl.	Biblical		pronoun	frequent.	frequentative(ly)
Bibliog.	Bibliography	deriv.	derivative		
Biochem.	Biochemistry	derog.	derogatory	G	German
Biol.	Biology	dial.	dialect	Gael.	Gaelic
Bot.	Botany	different.	differentiated	Gallo-Rom.	Gallo-Roman
Braz.	Brazil, Brazilian				

gen.	general	M	Middle (with languages)	OIt.	Old Italian		
genit.	genitive	masc.	masculine	OL	Old Latin		
Geog.	Geography	Math.	Mathematics	OLG	Old Low German		
Geol.	Geology	MDa.	Middle Danish	ON	Old Norse		
Geom.	Geometry	MDu.	Middle Dutch	ONF	Old Norman French		
Ger.	German	ME	Middle English	ONorw.	Old Norwegian		
Gk	Greek	Mech.	Mechanics	OPers.	Old Persian		
Gk Hist.	Greek History	Med.	Medicine	OPort.	Old Portuguese		
Gmc	Germanic	med.	medieval	opp.	(as) opposed (to), opposite (of)		
Goth.	Gothic	med.L	medieval Latin				
Gram.	Grammar	metaph.	metaphorical	OProv.	Old Provençal		
		metath.	metathesis	orig.	origin, original(ly)		
Heb.	Hebrew	Meteorol.	Meteorology	Ornithol.	Ornithology		
Hind.	Hindustani	Mex.	Mexican	OS	Old Saxon		
Hist.	History	MFlem.	Middle Flemish	OScand.	Old Scandinavian		
hist.	with historical reference	MHG	Middle High German	OSlav.	Old Slavonic		
				OSp.	Old Spanish		
Horol.	Horology	Mil.	Military	OSw.	Old Swedish		
Hort.	Horticulture	Mineral.	Mineralogy				
Hung.	Hungarian	mistransl.	mistranslation	Paleog.	Palaeography		
		MLG	Middle Low German	Parl.	Parliament, Parliamentary		
Icel.	Icelandic	mod.	modern				
IE	Indo-European	mod.L	modern Latin	part.	participle		
illit.	illiterate	MSw.	Middle Swedish	past part.	past participle		
imit.	imitative	Mus.	Music	Pathol.	Pathology		
immed.	immediate(ly)	Mythol.	Mythology	pejor.	pejorative		
imper.	imperative			perf.	perfect (tense)		
impers.	impersonal	n.	noun	perh.	perhaps		
incept.	inceptive	N.Amer.	North America, North American	Pers.	Persian		
incl.	including, inclusive			pers.	person(al)		
Ind.	of the subcontinent comprising India, Pakistan, and Bangladesh	Nat.	National	Peruv.	Peruvian		
		Naut.	Nautical	Pharm	Pharmacy, Pharmacology		
		neg.	negative(ly)				
		neut.	neuter	Philol.	Philology		
ind.	indirect	N. Engl.	New England	Philos.	Philosophy		
indecl.	indeclinable	No. of Engl.	North of England	Phoen.	Phoenician		
indef.	indefinite	Norm.	Norman	Phonet.	Phonetics		
infin.	infinitive	north.	northern	Photog.	Photography		
infl.	influence(d)	Norw.	Norwegian	phr.	phrase		
instr.	instrumental (case)	n.pl.	noun plural	Phrenol.	Phrenology		
int.	interjection	num.	numeral	Physiol.	Physiology		
interrog.	interrogative(ly)	NZ	New Zealand	pl.	plural		
interrog.adj.	interrogative adjective			poet.	poetical		
		O	Old (with languages)	Pol.	Polish		
interrog.pron.	interrogative pronoun			Polit.	Politics		
		obj.	object, objective	pop.	popular, not technical		
intr.	intransitive	OBret.	Old Breton				
Ir.	Irish (language or usage)	OBrit.	Old British	pop. L.	popular Latin, informal spoken Latin		
		obs.	obsolete				
iron.	ironical(ly)	Obstet.	Obstetrics				
irreg.	irregular(ly)	OBulg.	Old Bulgarian	Port.	Portuguese		
It.	Italian	occas.	occasional(ly)	poss.	possessive		
		OCelt.	Old Celtic	poss.pron.	possessive pronoun		
Jap.	Japan, Japanese	ODa.	Old Danish	prec.	preceded, preceding		
Jav.	Javanese	ODu.	Old Dutch				
joc.	jocular(ly)	OE	Old English	predic.	predicate, predicative(ly)		
		OF	Old French				
		offens.	offensive	predic.adj.	predicative adjective		
L	Latin	OFrank.	Old Frankish	prep.	preposition		
lang.	language	OFris.	Old Frisian	pres.part.	present participle		
LG	Low German	OGael.	Old Gaelic	prob.	probable, probably		
LHeb.	Late Hebrew	OHG	Old High German	pron.	pronoun		
lit.	literal(ly)	OIcel.	Old Icelandic	pronunc.	pronunciation		
LL	Late Latin	OIr.	Old Irish	propr.	proprietary term		

Abbreviations

Prov.	Provençal	Sci.	Science	ult.	ultimate(ly)
Psychol.	Psychology	Shakesp.	Shakespeare	uncert.	uncertain
		sing.	singular	unexpl.	unexplained
		Sinh.	Sinhalese	univ.	university
RC Ch.	Roman Catholic	Skr.	Sanskrit	unkn.	unknown
	Church	sl.	slang	US	American, in
redupl.	reduplicated	Slav.	Slavic, Slavonic		American use, in
ref.	reference	Sociol.	Sociology		the United States
refl.	reflexive(ly)	Sp.	Spanish	usu.	usual(ly)
rel.	related, relative	spec.	special(ly)		
rel.adj.	relative adjective	Stock Exch.	Stock Exchange	v.	verb
Relig.	Religion	subj.	subject, subjunctive	var.	variant(s)
rel.pron.	relative pronoun	superl.	superlative	v.aux.	auxiliary verb
repr.	representing	Sw.	Swedish	Vet.	Veterinary
Rhet.	Rhetoric	syll.	syllable	v.intr.	intransitive verb
rhet.	rhetorical(ly)	symb.	symbol	voc.	vocative
Rmc	Romanic	syn.	synonym	v.refl.	reflexive verb
Rom.	Roman			v.tr.	transitive verb
Rom.Hist.	Roman History				
Russ.	Russian	techn.	technical(ly)		
		Telev.	Television	WFris.	West Frisian
		Teut.	Teutonic	WG	West Germanic
S.Afr.	South Africa,	Theatr.	Theater, Theatrical	W.Ind.	West Indian, of the
	South African	Theol.	Theology		West Indies
S.Amer.	South America,	tr.	transitive	WS	West Saxon
	South American	transf.	in transferred sense	WSlav.	West Slavonic
Sc.	Scottish	transl.	translation		
Scand.	Scandinavia,	Turk.	Turkish		
	Scandinavian	Typog.	Typography	Zool.	Zoology

Note on proprietary status

This book includes some words that are, or are asserted to be, proprietary names or trademarks. Their inclusion does not imply that they have acquired for legal purposes a non-proprietary or general significance, nor is any other judgment implied concerning their legal status. In cases where the editor has some evidence that a word is used as a proprietary name or trademark, this is indicated by the designation *propr.*, but no judgment concerning the legal status of such words is made or implied thereby.

The Oxford Dictionary and Thesaurus

American Edition

A¹ /ay/ *n.* (also **a**) (*pl.* **As** or **A's**) **1** the first letter of the alphabet. **2** *Mus.* the sixth note of the diatonic scale of C major. **3** the first hypothetical person or example. **4** the highest class or category (of academic grades, etc.). **5** (usu. **a**) *Algebra* the first known quantity. **6** a human blood type of the ABO system. □ **A1** /áy wún/ *n. Naut.* a first-class vessel, esp. in Lloyd's Register of Shipping. ● *adj.* **1** *Naut.* (of a ship) first-class. **2** *colloq.* excellent; first-class. **from A to B** from one place to another (*a means of getting from A to B*). **from A to Z** over the entire range; completely.
■ □ **A1** (*adj.*) **2** see *first-class adj.* **from A to Z** see *completely* (COMPLETE).

A² /ay/ *abbr.* (also **A.**) **1** ampere(s). **2** answer. **3** Associate of. **4** atomic (energy, etc.).

a¹ /ə, ay/ *adj.* (also **an** before a vowel) (called the indefinite article) **1** (as an unemphatic substitute) one; some; any. **2** one like (*a Judas*). **3** one single (*not a thing in sight*). **4** the same (*all of a size*). **5** in, to, or for each (*twice a year*; *$20 a person*; *seven a side*). [weakening of OE *ān* one; sense 5 orig. = A²]

a² /ə/ *prep.* (usu. as *prefix*) **1** to; toward (*ashore*; *aside*). **2** (with verb in pres. part. or infin.) in the process of; in a specified state (*a-hunting*; *a-wandering*; *abuzz*; *aflutter*). **3** on (*afire*; *afoot*). **4** in (*nowadays*). [weakening of OE prep. *an, on* (see ON)]

a³ *abbr.* atto-.

Å *abbr.* ångström(s).

a-¹ /ay, ə/ *prefix* not; without (*amoral*; *agnostic*; *apetalous*). [Gk *a-*, or L f. Gk, or F f. L f. Gk]

a-² /ə/ *prefix* implying motion onward or away, adding intensity to verbs of motion (*arise*; *awake*). [OE *a-*, orig. *ar-*]

a-³ /ə/ *prefix* to, at, or into a state (*adroit*; *agree*; *amass*; *avenge*). [ME *a-* (= OF prefix *a-*), (f. F) f. L *ad-* to, at]

a-⁴ /ə/ *prefix* **1** from; away (*abridge*). **2** of (*akin*; *anew*). **3** out; utterly (*abash*; *affray*). **4** in, on, engaged in, etc. (see A²). [sense 1 f. ME *a-*, OF *a-*, f. L *ab*; sense 2 f. ME *a-* f. OE of prep.; sense 3 f. ME, AF *a-* = OF *e-, es-* f. L *ex*]

a-⁵ /ə, a/ *prefix* assim. form of AD- before *sc, sp, st.*

-a¹ /ə/ *suffix* forming nouns from Greek, Latin, and Romance feminine singular, esp.: **1** ancient or Latinized modern names of animals and plants (*amoeba*; *campanula*). **2** oxides (*alumina*). **3** geographical names (*Africa*). **4** ancient or Latinized modern feminine names (*Lydia*; *Hilda*).

-a² /ə/ *suffix* forming plural nouns from Greek and Latin neuter plural, esp. names (often from modern Latin) of zoological groups (*phenomena*; *Carnivora*).

-a³ /ə/ *suffix colloq.* **1** of (*kinda*; *coupla*). **2** have (*mighta*; *coulda*). **3** to (*oughta*).

AA *abbr.* **1** Alcoholics Anonymous. **2** Associate of Arts. **3** *Mil.* antiaircraft.

AAA *abbr.* **1** American Automobile Association. **2** Amateur Athletic Association. **3** antiaircraft artillery.

A. & M. *abbr.* **1** Agricultural and Mechanical (college or university). **2** (Hymns) Ancient and Modern.

A. & R. *abbr.* **1** artists and recording. **2** artists and repertoire.

aardvark /aárdvaark/ *n.* a nocturnal mammal of southern Africa, *Orycteropus afer*, with a tubular snout and a long extensible tongue, that feeds on termites. Also called *ant bear*. [Afrik. f. *aarde* earth + *vark* pig]

aardwolf /aárdwŏolf/ *n.* (*pl.* **aardwolves** /-wŏolvz/) an Af-

rican mammal, *Proteles cristatus*, of the hyena family, with gray fur and black stripes, that feeds on insects. [Afrik. f. *aarde* earth + *wolf* wolf]

Aaron's beard /áirənz, ár-/ *n.* any of several plants, esp. rose of Sharon (*Hypericum calycinum*). [ref. to Ps. 133:2]

Aaron's rod /áirən, ár-/ *n.* any of several tall plants, esp. goldenrod or mullein. [ref. to Num. 17:8]

AAU *abbr.* Amateur Athletic Union.

AB¹ /áybee/ *n.* a human blood type of the ABO system.

AB² *abbr.* **1** able seaman. **2** Bachelor of Arts. [sense 1 f. *ablebodied*; sense 2 f. L *Artium Baccalaureus*]

ab- /əb, ab/ *prefix* off; away; from (*abduct*; *abnormal*; *abuse*). [F or L]

aba /əbaá, aába/ *n.* (also **abba, abaya** /əbáy-yə, əbíyə/) a sleeveless outer garment worn by Arabs. [Arab. '*abā*']

abaca /ábəkaá/ *n.* **1** Manila hemp. **2** the plant, *Musa textilis*, yielding this. [Sp. *abacá*]

aback /əbák/ *adv.* **1** *archaic* backward; behind. **2** *Naut.* (of a sail) pressed against the mast by a head wind. □ **take aback 1** surprise; disconcert (*your request took me aback*; *I was greatly taken aback by the news*). **2** (as **taken aback**) (of a ship) with the sails pressed against the mast by a head wind. [OE *on bæc* (as A², BACK)]
■ □ **take aback 1** astound, astonish, surprise, startle, shock, stun, stagger, dumbfound, confound, nonplus, stupefy, *colloq.* floor, flabbergast, knock sideways, *sl.* knock out; disconcert, puzzle, mystify.

abacus /ábəkəs, əbákəs/ *n.* (*pl.* **abacuses**) **1** an oblong frame with rows of wires or grooves along which beads are slid, used for calculating. **2** *Archit.* the flat slab on top of a capital, supporting the architrave. [L f. Gk *abax abakos* slab, drawing board, f. Heb. '*āḇāḳ* dust]
■ **1** see CALCULATOR.

Abaddon /əbád'n/ *n.* **1** hell. **2** the Devil (Rev. 9:11). [Heb., = destruction]

abaft /əbáft/ *adv.* & *prep. Naut.* ● *adv.* in the stern half of a ship. ● *prep.* nearer the stern than; aft of. [A² + -*baft* f. OE *beæftan* f. *be* BY + *æftan* behind]

abalone /ábəlṓnee/ *n.* any mollusk of the genus *Haliotis*, with a shallow ear-shaped shell having respiratory holes, and lined with mother-of-pearl, e.g., the ormer. [Amer. Sp. *abulón*]

abandon /əbándən/ *v.* & *n.* ● *v.tr.* **1** give up completely or before completion (*abandoned hope*; *abandoned the game*). **2 a** forsake or desert (a person or a post of responsibility). **b** leave or desert (a motor vehicle, ship, building, etc.). **3 a** give up to another's control or mercy. **b** *refl.* yield oneself completely to a passion or impulse. ● *n.* lack of inhibition or restraint; reckless freedom of manner. □□ **abandoner** *n.* **abandonment** *n.* [ME f. OF *abandoner* f. *à bandon* under control ult. f. LL *bannus, -um* BAN]
■ *v.* **1** give up *or* over, relinquish, renounce, leave, quit, abort; withdraw from, pull out of, discontinue, forgo, drop, scrap, scrub, shelve, abstain from, bury, climb

1

down from. **2 a** desert, forsake, leave behind, get out of, abdicate; jilt, walk *or* run out on, throw over, cast off *or* aside, turn one's back on, leave in the lurch, discard, drop, renege, jettison, throw overboard, give over; *colloq.* dump, *sl.* ditch. **b** leave, desert, evacuate, quit, depart from, go away from. **3** give up *or* over, yield, surrender, renounce, deliver (up), resign, cede, concede, let go. ● *n.* recklessness, lack of restraint *or* self-control, uninhibitedness, unrestraint, intemperance, dissipation, profligacy, dissolution, debauchery, wantonness, licentiousness.

abandoned /əbándənd/ *adj.* **1 a** (of a person or animal) deserted; forsaken (*an abandoned child*). **b** (of a building, vehicle, etc.) left empty or unused (*an abandoned cottage; an abandoned ship*). **2** (of a person or behavior) unrestrained; profligate.
  ▪ **1 a** forsaken, deserted, neglected, rejected, shunned, castaway, jilted, forlorn, dropped, outcast, lonely, lonesome, *predic.* left alone, cast-off, cast aside, out of it; stray. **b** deserted, desolate, derelict, uninhabited, vacant, discarded, disused, *predic.* thrown *or* cast aside *or* away, left behind *or* empty *or* unused. **2** unrestrained, uncontrolled, uninhibited, unconstrained, profligate, licentious, unprincipled, disreputable, loose, wanton, debauched, wild, dissolute, dissipated; depraved, lewd, impure, unchaste, promiscuous, lascivious; incorrigible, reprobate, immoral, amoral.

abase /əbáys/ *v.tr. & refl.* humiliate or degrade (another person or oneself). □□ **abasement** *n.* [ME f. OF *abaissier* (as A-³, *baissier* to lower ult. f. LL *bassus* short of stature): infl. by BASE²]
  ▪ see DEGRADE 2.

abash /əbásh/ *v.tr.* (usu. as **abashed** *adj.*) embarrass; disconcert. □□ **abashment** *n.* [ME f. OF *esbaïr* (*es- =* A-⁴ 3, *baïr* astound or *baer* yawn)]
  ▪ (**abashed**) see *embarrassed* (EMBARRASS 1b).

abate /əbáyt/ *v.* **1** *tr. & intr.* make or become less strong, severe, intense, etc. **2** *tr. Law* **a** quash (a writ or action). **b** put an end to (a nuisance). □□ **abatement** *n.* [ME f. OF *abatre* f. Rmc (as A-³, L *batt(u)ere* beat)]
  ▪ **1** see REDUCE 1, WANE *v.*

abatis /ábətis/ *n.* (also **abattis** /əbátis/) (*pl.* same or **abatises**, **abattises**) *hist.* a defense made of felled trees with the sharpened branches pointing outward. □□ **abatised** *adj.* [F f. *abatre* fell: see ABATE]

abattoir /ábətwaar/ *n.* a slaughterhouse. [F (as ABATIS, -ORY¹)]

abaxial /abákseeəl/ *adj. Bot.* facing away from the stem of a plant, esp. of the lower surface of a leaf (cf. ADAXIAL). [AB- + AXIAL]

abaya (also **abba**) var. of ABA.

abbacy /ábəsee/ *n.* (*pl.* **-ies**) the office, jurisdiction, or period of office of an abbot or abbess. [ME f. eccl.L *abbacia* f. *abbat-* ABBOT]

Abbasid /əbásid, ábəsid/ *n. & adj.* ● *n.* a member of a dynasty of caliphs ruling in Baghdad 750–1258. ● *adj.* of this dynasty. [*Abbas*, Muhammad's uncle d. 652]

abbatial /əbáyshəl/ *adj.* of an abbey, abbot, or abbess. [F *abbatial* or med.L *abbatialis* (as ABBOT)]

abbé /abáy, ábay/ *n.* (in France) an abbot; a man entitled to wear ecclesiastical dress. [F f. eccl.L *abbas abbatis* ABBOT]

abbess /ábis/ *n.* a woman who is the head of certain communities of nuns. [ME f. OF *abbesse* f. eccl.L *abbatissa* (as ABBOT)]

Abbevillian /abvíleeən, abə-/ *n. & adj.* ● *n.* the culture of the earliest Paleolithic period in Europe. ● *adj.* of this culture. [F *Abbevillien* f. *Abbeville* in N. France]

abbey /ábee/ *n.* (*pl.* **-eys**) **1** the building(s) occupied by a community of monks or nuns. **2** the community itself. **3** a church or house that was once an abbey. [ME f. OF *abbeie* f. med.L *abbatia* ABBACY]

abbot /ábət/ *n.* a man who is the head of an abbey of monks. □□ **abbotship** *n.* [OE *abbod* f. eccl.L *abbas -atis* f. Gk *abbas* father f. Aram. *'abbā*]

abbr. *abbr.* (also **abbrev.**) abbreviation.

abbreviate /əbre'evee-ayt/ *v.tr.* shorten, esp. represent (a word, etc.) by a part of it. [ME f. LL *abbreviare* shorten f. *brevis* short: cf. ABRIDGE]
  ▪ shorten, compress, telescope, contract, truncate, trim, reduce, curtail, cut (off), cut down *or* short, clip, condense, abridge, abstract, précis, digest, epitomize, summarize, synopsize.

abbreviation /əbre'evee-áyshən/ *n.* **1** an abbreviated form, esp. a shortened form of a word or phrase. **2** the process or result of abbreviating.
  ▪ initialism, acronym, symbol; abridgment, contraction, précis, summary, abstract, synopsis, digest, epitome.

ABC¹ /áybeeseé/ *n.* **1** the alphabet. **2** the rudiments of any subject. **3** an alphabetical guide.

ABC² *abbr.* American Broadcasting Company.

abdicate /ábdikayt/ *v.tr.* **1** (usu. *absol.*) give up or renounce (a throne). **2** renounce (a responsibility, duty, etc.). □□ **abdication** /-káyshən/ *n.* **abdicator** *n.* [L *abdicare abdicat-* (as AB-, *dicare* declare)]
  ▪ give up, renounce, surrender, yield, disclaim, relinquish, vacate, resign (from), quit, waive, disown; (*absol.*) step down; see also ABANDON *v.* 2a.
  □□ **abdication** see RESIGNATION 1.

abdomen /ábdəmən, abdṓ-/ *n.* **1** the part of the body containing the stomach, bowels, reproductive organs, etc. **2** *Zool.* the hind part of an insect, crustacean, spider, etc. □□ **abdominal** /abdóminəl/ *adj.* **abdominally** /abdómin-əlee/ *adv.* [L]

abduct /əbdúkt/ *v.tr.* **1** carry off or kidnap (a person) illegally by force or deception. **2** (of a muscle, etc.) draw (a limb, etc.) away from the middle line of the body. □□ **abduction** /-dúkshən/ *n.* **abductor** *n.* [L *abducere abduct-* (as AB-, *ducere* draw)]
  ▪ **1** kidnap, carry off, make off with, seize, snatch, grab, nab, take (away), spirit away *or* off. □□ **abduction** kidnap(ping), carrying off, seizure, capture.

abeam /əbe'em/ *adv.* **1** on a line at right angles to a ship's or an aircraft's length. **2** (foll. by *of*) opposite the middle of (a ship, etc.). [A² + BEAM]

abed /əbéd/ *adv. archaic* in bed. [OE (as A², BED)]

abele /əbe'el, áybəl/ *n.* the white poplar, *Populus alba*. [Du. *abeel* f. OF *abel*, *aubel* ult. f. L *albus* white]

abelia /əbe'eleeə/ *n.* any shrub of the genus *Abelia*, esp. *A. grandiflora*. [Clarke *Abel*, Engl. botanist d. 1826]

Abenaki /abənaákee/ *n.* (also **Abnaki** /abnaákee/) **1 a** a N. American people native to northern New England and adjoining parts of Quebec. **b** a member of this people. **2** either of the two languages of this people.

Aberdeen Angus /ábərdeen ánggəs/ *n.* **1** an animal of a Scottish breed of hornless black beef cattle. **2** this breed. [*Aberdeen* in Scotland, *Angus* former Scottish county]

aberrant /əbérənt, ábə-/ *adj.* **1** esp. *Biol.* diverging from the normal type. **2** departing from an accepted standard. □□ **aberrance** /-rəns/ *n.* **aberrancy** *n.* [L *aberrare aberrant-* (as AB-, *errare* stray)]
  ▪ see ABNORMAL. □□ **aberrance, aberrancy** see ABNORMALITY 1.

aberration /ábəráyshən/ *n.* **1** a departure from what is normal or accepted or regarded as right. **2** a moral or mental lapse. **3** *Biol.* deviation from a normal type. **4** *Optics* the failure of rays to converge at one focus because of a defect in a lens or mirror. **5** *Astron.* the apparent displacement of a celestial body, meteor, etc., caused by the observer's velocity. □□ **aberrational** *adj.* [L *aberratio* (as ABERRANT)]
  ▪ **1–3** see ABNORMALITY 1.

abet /əbét/ *v.tr.* (**abetted**, **abetting**) (usu. in **aid and abet**) encourage or assist (an offender or offense). □□ **abetment** *n.* [ME f. OF *abeter* f. *à* to + *beter* BAIT¹]
  ▪ encourage, urge, instigate, prompt, incite, provoke, egg on, prod, goad, spur; aid, help, assist, support, back (up); endorse, second, sanction, countenance, connive at *or* with, cooperate in; further, advance, promote, uphold.

abettor /əbétər/ *n.* (also **abetter**) one who abets.
  ▪ see ACCESSORY 3, ACCOMPLICE.

abeyance /əbáyəns/ *n.* (usu. prec. by *in*, *into*) a state of temporary disuse or suspension. □□ **abeyant** /-ənt/ *adj.* [AF *abeiance* f. OF *abeer* f. *à* to + *beer* f. med.L *batare* gape]
■ see PAUSE *n.*; (*in abeyance*) pending, abeyant, reserved, in reserve, shelved, pushed *or* shoved *or* shunted aside, postponed, deferred, put off, suspended, on the shelf, in (the) deep freeze, in cold storage, in limbo; temporarily inactive, dormant, latent, on hold, tabled, laid on the table, *colloq.* on ice, on the back burner, hanging fire. □□ **abeyant** see *in abeyance* (ABEYANCE) above.

abhor /əbháwr/ *v.tr.* (**abhorred**, **abhorring**) detest; regard with disgust and hatred. □□ **abhorrer** *n.* [ME f. F *abhorrer* or f. L *abhorrēre* (as AB-, *horrēre* shudder)]
■ hate, loathe, detest, abominate, execrate; regard *or* view with horror *or* dread *or* fright *or* repugnance *or* loathing *or* disgust *or* hatred, despise, shudder at, recoil *or* shrink from, be *or* stand aghast at, have no use for; *literary* contemn.

abhorrence /əbháwrəns, -hór-/ *n.* **1** disgust; detestation. **2** a detested thing.
■ **1** detestation, hatred, loathing, contempt, execration, abomination, disgust, horror, dread, repugnance. **2** abomination.

abhorrent /əbháwrənt, -hór-/ *adj.* **1** (often foll. by *to*) (of conduct, etc.) inspiring disgust; repugnant; hateful; detestable. **2** (foll. by *to*) not in accordance with; strongly conflicting with (*abhorrent to the spirit of the law*). **3** *archaic* (foll. by *from*) inconsistent with.
■ **1** hateful, detestable, abominable, contemptible, odious, loathsome, horrid, heinous, hideous, awful, execrable, repugnant, vile; repulsive, repellent, revolting, offensive, disgusting, distasteful, disagreeable, horrifying, frightful, obnoxious, *sl.* yucky. **2** (*abhorrent to*) against, in conflict with, contrary to, opposed to, averse to, resistant to, remote *or* distant from.

abide /əbíd/ *v.* (*past* **abode** /əbṓd/ or **abided**) **1** *tr.* (usu. in *neg.* or *interrog.*) tolerate; endure (*can't abide him*). **2** *intr.* (foll. by *by*) **a** act in accordance with (*abide by the rules*). **b** remain faithful to (a promise). **3** *intr. archaic* **a** remain; continue. **b** dwell. **4** *tr. archaic* sustain; endure. □□ **abidance** *n.* [OE *ābīdan* (as A-², *bidan* BIDE)]
■ **1** stand, endure, tolerate, suffer, support, bear, put up with, stomach, accept, *literary* brook. **2** (*abide by*) comply with, observe, obey, heed, follow, fulfill, conform to, stick to *or* with, keep to, consent to, agree to, acknowledge, submit to, remain true to, stand by, adhere to, hold to. **3 a** remain, stay, continue, stop, linger, rest, *archaic or literary* tarry. **b** live, stay, reside, sojourn, *archaic or dial.* bide, *literary* dwell.

abiding /əbíding/ *adj.* enduring; permanent (*an abiding sense of loss*). □□ **abidingly** *adv.*
■ lasting, permanent, constant, steadfast, everlasting, unending, eternal, enduring, indestructible, timeless; unchanging, (hard and) fast, fixed, firm, immutable, changeless, invariable.

ability /əbílitee/ *n.* (*pl.* **-ies**) **1** (often foll. by *to* + infin.) capacity or power (*has the ability to write songs*). **2** cleverness; talent; mental power (*a person of great ability; has many abilities*). [ME f. OF *ablete* f. L *habilitas -tatis* f. *habilis* able]
■ **1** capacity, power, adeptness, aptitude, facility, faculty, knack, proficiency, strength, competence. **2** talent(s), skill(s), gift(s), faculties; genius, cleverness, capacity, wit, qualification, skillfulness, capability, flair, adroitness, savoir faire, know-how.

-ability /əbílitee/ *suffix* forming nouns of quality from, or corresponding to, adjectives in *-able* (*capability*; *vulnerability*). [F *-abilité* or L *-abilitas*: cf. -ITY]

ab initio /áb inísheeṓ/ *adv.* from the beginning. [L]
■ see *primarily* (PRIMARY).

abiogenesis /áybīōjénisis/ *n.* **1** the formation of living organisms from inanimate substances. **2** the supposed spontaneous generation of living organisms. □□ **abiogenic** /-jénik/ *adj.* [A-¹ + Gk *bios* life + GENESIS]

abject /ábjekt, abjékt/ *adj.* **1** miserable; wretched. **2** degraded; self-abasing; humble. **3** despicable. □□ **abjectly** *adv.* **abjectness** *n.* [ME f. L *abjectus* past part. of *abicere* (as AB-, *jacere* throw)]
■ **1** see MISERABLE. **2** see SERVILE. **3** see LOW¹ *adj.* 11.

abjection /əbjékshən/ *n.* a state of misery or degradation. [ME f. OF *abjection* or L *abjectio* (as ABJECT)]
■ see MISERY 1.

abjure /əbjŏŏr/ *v.tr.* **1** renounce under oath (an opinion, cause, claim, etc.). **2** swear perpetual absence from (one's country, etc.). □□ **abjuration** /-ráyshən/ *n.* [L *abjurare* (as AB-, *jurare* swear)]
■ **1** see RENOUNCE 1.

ablation /abláyshən/ *n.* **1** the surgical removal of body tissue. **2** *Geol.* the wasting or erosion of a glacier, iceberg, or rock by melting, evaporation, or the action of water. **3** *Astronaut.* the evaporation or melting of part of the outer surface of a spacecraft through heating by friction with the atmosphere. □□ **ablate** *v.tr.* [F *ablation* or LL *ablatio* f. L *ablat-* (as AB-, *lat-* past part. stem of *ferre* carry)]

ablative /áblətiv/ *n. & adj. Gram.* ● *n.* the case (esp. in Latin) of nouns and pronouns (and words in grammatical agreement with them) indicating an agent, instrument, or location. ● *adj.* of or in the ablative. □ **ablative absolute** an absolute construction in Latin with a noun and participle or adjective in the ablative case (see ABSOLUTE). [ME f. OF *ablatif -ive* or L *ablativus* (as ABLATION)]

ablaut /áblowt/ *n.* a change of vowel in related words or forms, esp. in Indo-European languages, arising from differences of accent and stress in the parent language, e.g., in *sing, sang, sung*. [G]

ablaze /əbláyz/ *predic.adj. & adv.* **1** on fire (*set it ablaze; the house was ablaze*). **2** (often foll. by *with*) glittering; glowing; radiant. **3** (often foll. by *with*) greatly excited.
■ *adj.* **1** aflame, afire, burning, on fire, in flames, alight, blazing, fiery. **2** lit up, alight, brilliantly *or* brightly lit, glittering, sparkling, gleaming, aglow, glowing, bright, brilliant, luminous, illuminated, radiant. **3** see FERVENT 1.

able /áybəl/ *adj.* (**abler**, **ablest**) **1** (often foll. by *to* + infin.; used esp. in *is able, will be able, was able*, etc., replacing tenses of *can*) having the capacity or power (*was not able to come*). **2** having great ability; clever; skillful. □ **able-bodied** fit; healthy. **able-bodied seaman** *Naut.* one able to perform all duties. [ME f. OF *hable, able* f. L *habilis* handy f. *habēre* to hold]
■ **1** (*able to*) capable of, qualified to, competent to, equal to, up to, fit to, free to, prepared to. **2** talented, capable, competent, clever, brainy, knowledgeable, quick, skilled, masterful, masterly, adept, skillful, proficient, gifted, superior, expert, adroit, deft, accomplished. □ **able-bodied** see FIT¹ *adj.* 2.

-able /əbəl/ *suffix* forming adjectives meaning: **1** that may or must be (*eatable; forgivable; payable*). **2** that can be made the subject of (*dutiable; objectionable*). **3** that is relevant to or in accordance with (*fashionable; seasonable*). **4** (with active sense, in earlier word formations) that may (*comfortable; suitable*). [F *-able* or L *-abilis* forming verbal adjectives f. verbs of first conjugation]

abled /áybəld/ *adj.* having a full range of physical and mental abilities; able-bodied. □ **differently abled** *euphem.* disabled.
■ see FIT¹ *adj.* 2.

ableism /áybəlizəm/ *n.* (also **ablism**, **ablebodiedism**) discrimination in favor of the able-bodied.

abloom /əblṓm/ *predic.adj.* blooming; in flower.

ablush /əblúsh/ *predic.adj.* blushing.

ablution /əblṓshən/ *n.* (usu. in *pl.*) **1** the ceremonial washing of parts of the body or sacred vessels, etc. **2** *colloq.* the or-

---

dinary washing of the body. **3** *Brit.* a building containing toilet or bathing facilities, etc., in a military camp, ship, etc. □□ **ablutionary** *adj.* [ME f. OF *ablution* or L *ablutio* (as AB-, *lutio* f. *luere* lut- wash)]

ably /áyblee/ *adv.* capably; cleverly; competently.
▪ see WELL[1] *adv.* 3.

-ably /əblee/ *suffix* forming adverbs corresponding to adjectives in *-able*.

ABM *abbr.* antiballistic missile.

abnegate /ábnigayt/ *v.tr.* **1** give up or deny oneself (a pleasure, etc.). **2** renounce or reject (a right or belief). □□ **abnegator** *n.* [L *abnegare* abnegat- (as AB-, *negare* deny)]

abnegation /ábnigáyshən/ *n.* **1** denial; the rejection or renunciation of a doctrine. **2** = SELF-ABNEGATION. [OF *abnegation* or LL *abnegatio* (as ABNEGATE)]

abnormal /abnáwrməl/ *adj.* **1** deviating from what is normal or usual; exceptional. **2** relating to or dealing with what is abnormal (*abnormal psychology*). □□ **abnormally** *adv.* [earlier and F *anormal*, *anomal* f. Gk *anōmalos* ANOMALOUS, assoc. with L *abnormis*: see ABNORMITY]
▪ **1** peculiar, unusual, odd, strange, curious, unconventional, divergent, exceptional, unnatural, extraordinary, singular, weird, eccentric, bizarre, quirky, wayward, anomalous, aberrant, queer, freakish, deformed, perverse, deviant, deviating, irregular, offbeat, *colloq.* oddball, kinky, far-out, way-out, *sl.* bent.

abnormality /ábnawrmálitee/ *n.* (*pl.* -**ies**) **1 a** an abnormal quality, occurrence, etc. **b** the state of being abnormal. **2** a physical irregularity.
▪ **1** oddity, peculiarity, irregularity, curiosity, deviation, aberration, idiosyncrasy, freak, perversion; nonconformity, unconformity, unusualness, singularity, eccentricity, oddness, queerness, unconventionality, uncommonness. **2** distortion, irregularity, malformation, deformity, anomaly.

abnormity /abnáwrmitee/ *n.* (*pl.* -**ies**) an abnormality or irregularity. [L *abnormis* (as AB-, *normis* f. *norma* rule)]
▪ **1** see ABNORMALITY 1.

Abo /ábō/ *n.* & *adj.* (also **abo**) *Austral. offens. sl.* ● *n.* (*pl.* **Abos**) an Aborigine. ● *adj.* Aboriginal. [abbr.]

aboard /əbáwrd/ *adv.* & *prep.* **1** on or into (a ship, aircraft, train, etc.). **2** alongside. □ **all aboard!** a call that warns of the imminent departure of a ship, train, etc. [ME f. A[2] + BOARD & F *à bord*]

abode[1] /əbód/ *n.* **1** a dwelling; one's home. **2** *archaic* a stay or sojourn. [verbal noun of ABIDE: cf. *ride*, *rode*, *road*]
▪ **1** residence, house, home, domicile, habitat, habitation, seat, quarters, rooms, lodging(s), place, accommodation, *Mil.* billet; *colloq.* pad, *Brit. colloq.* digs, diggings, *formal* dwelling (place).

abode[2] *past of* ABIDE.

abolish /əbólish/ *v.tr.* put an end to the existence or practice of (esp. a custom or institution). □□ **abolishable** *adj.* **abolisher** *n.* **abolishment** *n.* [ME f. F *abolir* f. L *abolēre* destroy]
▪ eliminate, end, put an end to, terminate, stop, *colloq.* knock on the head; destroy, annihilate, annul, set aside, (make) void, demolish, do away with, dispense with, nullify, repeal, revoke, cancel, rescind, abrogate, vitiate, obliterate, blot out, liquidate, stamp out, quash, extinguish, erase, delete, expunge, eradicate, extirpate, uproot; *colloq.* chop; *literary* deracinate.

abolition /ábəlíshən/ *n.* **1** the act or process of abolishing or being abolished. **2** an instance of this. [F *abolition* or L *abolitio* (as ABOLISH)]
▪ elimination, end, ending, termination, abolishment, repeal, removal, rescindment, rescission, annulment, abrogation, nullification, repudiation, cancellation; vitiation, obliteration, eradication, dissolution, destruction, annihilation, liquidation, erasure, extirpation.

abolitionist /ábəlíshənist/ *n.* one who favors the abolition of a practice or institution, esp. of capital punishment or slavery. □□ **abolitionism** *n.*

abomasum /ábəmáysəm/ *n.* (*pl.* **abomasa** /-sə/) the fourth stomach of a ruminant. [mod.L f. AB- + OMASUM]

A-bomb /áybom/ *n.* = *atomic bomb.* [A (for ATOMIC) + BOMB]

abominable /əbóminəbəl/ *adj.* **1** detestable; loathsome; morally reprehensible. **2** *colloq.* very bad or unpleasant (*abominable weather*). □ **abominable snowman** an unidentified humanoid or bearlike animal said to exist in the Himalayas; a yeti. □□ **abominably** *adv.* [ME f. OF f. L *abominabilis* f. *abominari* deprecate (as AB-, *ominari* f. OMEN)]
▪ **1** offensive, repugnant, repulsive, vile, monstrous, outrageous, loathsome, odious, execrable, detestable, reprehensible, despicable, base, disgusting, revolting, nauseous, nauseating, sickening, gruesome, foul, abhorrent, horrid, deplorable; see also EVIL *adj.* 1. **2** atrocious, distasteful, unpleasant, disagreeable, horrible, desperate, woeful, miserable, *colloq.* terrible, dreadful, awful, lousy, shocking, frightful, wicked, beastly, abysmal, *Brit. colloq.* chronic, *sl.* yucky.

abominate /əbóminayt/ *v.tr.* detest; loathe. □□ **abominator** *n.* [L *abominari* (as ABOMINABLE)]
▪ see DETEST.

abomination /əbómin
áyshən/ *n.* **1** loathing. **2** an odious or degrading habit or act. **3** (often foll. by *to*) an object of disgust. [ME f. OF (as ABOMINATE)]
▪ **1** see REVULSION 1.

aboral /abáwrəl/ *adj.* away from or opposite the mouth. [AB- + ORAL]

aboriginal /ábəríjinəl/ *adj.* & *n.* ● *adj.* **1** (of peoples and natural phenomena) inhabiting or existing in a land from the earliest times or from before the arrival of colonists. **2** (usu. **Aboriginal**) of the Australian Aborigines. ● *n.* **1** an aboriginal inhabitant. **2** (usu. **Aboriginal**) an aboriginal inhabitant of Australia. □□ **Aboriginality** /-nálitee/ *n.* **aboriginally** *adv.* [as ABORIGINE + -AL]
▪ *adj.* **1** see NATIVE *adj.* 2, 5. ● *n.* **1** native, aborigine, local, autochthon. **2** *Austral.* Aborigine, bushman, *Austral. offens. sl.* Abo.

aborigine /ábəríjinee/ *n.* (usu. in *pl.*) **1** an aboriginal inhabitant. **2** (usu. **Aborigine**) an aboriginal inhabitant of Australia. **3** an aboriginal plant or animal. [back-form. f. pl. *aborigines* f. L, prob. f. phr. *ab origine* from the beginning]
▪ see ABORIGINAL 1.

abort /əbáwrt/ *v.* & *n.* ● *v.* **1** *intr.* **a** (of a woman) undergo abortion; miscarry. **b** (of a fetus) suffer abortion. **2** *tr.* **a** effect the abortion of (a fetus). **b** effect abortion in (a mother). **3 a** *tr.* cause to end fruitlessly or prematurely; stop in the early stages. **b** *intr.* end unsuccessfully or prematurely. **4 a** *tr.* abandon or terminate (a space flight or other technical project) before its completion, usu. because of a fault. **b** *intr.* terminate or fail to complete such an undertaking. **5** *Biol.* **a** *intr.* (of an organism) remain undeveloped; shrink away. **b** *tr.* cause to do this. ● *n.* **1** a prematurely terminated space flight or other undertaking. **2** the termination of such an undertaking. [L *aboriri* miscarry (as AB-, *oriri* ort- be born)]
▪ *v.* **1** see MISCARRY. **3a, 4a** see PREVENT 1, TERMINATE 1, 2. **3b, 4b** see FAIL *v.* 1, 2a, MISCARRY.

abortifacient /əbáwrtifáyshənt/ *adj.* & *n.* ● *adj.* effecting abortion. ● *n.* a drug or other agent that effects abortion.

abortion /əbáwrshən/ *n.* **1** the expulsion of a fetus (naturally or esp. by medical induction) from the womb before it is able to survive independently, esp. in the first 28 weeks of a human pregnancy. **2** a stunted or deformed creature or thing. **3** the failure of a project or an action. **4** *Biol.* the arrest of the development of an organ. [L *abortio* (as ABORT)]
▪ **1** miscarriage, termination. **2** see MONSTER 3, 4. **3** see MISCARRIAGE 2.

abortionist /əbáwrshənist/ *n.* a person who carries out abortions, esp. illegally.

abortive /əbáwrtiv/ *adj.* **1** fruitless; unsuccessful; unfinished. **2** resulting in abortion. **3** *Biol.* (of an organ, etc.) rudimentary; arrested in development. □□ **abortively** *adv.* [ME f. OF *abortif* -*ive* f. L *abortivus* (as ABORT)]
▪ **1** see UNSUCCESSFUL.

ABO system /áybee-ṓ/ *n.* a system of four types (A, AB, B, and O) by which human blood may be classified, based on the presence or absence of certain inherited antigens.

aboulia var. of ABULIA.

abound /əbównd/ v.intr. **1** be plentiful. **2** (foll. by in, with) be rich; teem or be infested. [ME f. OF abunder, etc., f. L abundare overflow (as AB-, undare f. unda wave)]

■ **1** prevail, thrive, flourish, be prolific or plentiful, proliferate. **2** (abound in, abound with) be well supplied or furnished with, be crowded or packed or crammed or filled or jammed with, be abundant or rich in, teem or swarm or throng with, be infested with, overflow with, colloq. be jam-packed or stuffed with.

about /əbówt/ prep. & adv. ● prep. **1 a** on the subject of; in connection with (a book about birds; what are you talking about?; argued about money). **b** relating to (something funny about this). **c** in relation to (symmetry about a plane). **d** so as to affect (can do nothing about it; what are you going to do about it?). **2** at a time near to (come about four). **3 a** in; around; surrounding (wandered about the town; a scarf about her neck). **b** all around from a center (look about you). **4** here and there in; at points throughout (toys lying about the house). **5** at a point or points near to (fighting going on about us). ● adv. **1 a** approximately (costs about a dollar; is about right). **b** colloq. used to indicate understatement (just about had enough; it's about time they came). **2** here and there; at points nearby (a lot of flu about; I've seen him about recently). **3** all around; in every direction (look about; wandered about; scattered all about). **4** on the move; in action (out and about). **5** in partial rotation or alteration from a given position (the wrong way about). **6** in rotation or succession (turn and turn about). **7** Naut. on or to the opposite tack (go about; put about). □ **be about to** be on the point of (doing something) (was about to laugh). [OE onbūtan (on = A², būtan BUT¹)]

■ prep. **1 a, b, d** concerning, concerned or connected or dealing with, on, involving, in or with reference to, in or with regard to, regarding, affecting, in the matter of, on the subject of, in connection with, with respect to, respecting, relative to, relating to, apropos, anent, literary touching. **2** around, round about, close to, archaic or dial. nigh on. **3** around, surrounding, encircling, encompassing, enfolding, enveloping, all around, round about, in, all over, Brit. round. **5** around, all around, near (to), nearby, adjacent to, beside, alongside, close by or to, adjacent to, archaic or dial. nigh. **6** with, on, on one's person, in one's possession. ● adv. **1 a** approximately, around, nearly, roughly, more or less, almost, close to or upon, in the region of, in the neighborhood of, something like, . . . or so; colloq. in the ballpark of. **b** really, honestly, archaic or rhet. wellnigh. **2** around, close by, nearby; in the area or vicinity, round about; going on or around, in the air, abroad. **3** (all) around, around, all over, on every side, to and fro, up and down, back and forth, here and there, far and wide, hither and thither, helter-skelter, colloq. every which way, literary & dial. hither and yon. **5** around, up. **6** around, again. □ **be about to** be just going to, be on the point or verge or brink of, be preparing to; be within an ace of.

about-face /əbówtfáys/ n., v., & int. ● n. **1** a turn made so as to face the opposite direction. **2** a change of opinion or policy, etc. ● v.intr. make an about-face. ● int. Mil. a command to make an about-face. [orig. as int.]

■ n. **1, 2** volte-face, reversal, reverse, turnabout, turnaround, U-turn, about-turn. **2** change of heart or tune, (complete) switch.

about-turn /əbówt-túrn/ n., v., & int. Brit. = ABOUT-FACE.

above /əbúv/ prep., adv., adj., & n. ● prep. **1** over; on the top of; higher (vertically, up a slope or stream, etc.) than; over the surface of (head above water; above the din). **2** more than (above average). **3** higher in rank, position, importance, etc., than (thwarted by those above him). **4 a** too great or good for (above one's station; is not above cheating at cards). **b** beyond the reach of; not affected by (above my understanding; above suspicion). **5** archaic to an earlier time than (not traced above the third century). ● adv. **1** at or to a higher point; overhead (the floor above; the clouds above). **2 a** upstairs (lives above). **b** esp. Brit. upstream. **3** (of a text reference) further back on

a page or in a book (as noted above). **4** on the upper side (looks similar above and below). **5** in addition (over and above). **6** rhet. in heaven (Lord above!). ● adj. mentioned earlier; preceding (the above argument). ● n. (prec. by the) what is mentioned above (the above shows). □ **above all** most of all; more than anything else. **above one's head** see HEAD.

above oneself conceited; arrogant. [A² + OE bufan f. be = BY + ufan above]

■ prep. **1** on, on (the) top of, upon, over, atop, higher than. **2** over, more than, exceeding, in excess of, beyond, greater than, surpassing. **4 b** beyond, insusceptible to, unaffected by, not subject to, not liable to, out of reach of, not open to, not susceptible or vulnerable or exposed to, not in danger of, superior to. ● adv. **1** overhead, on high, aloft, in the sky, esp. poet. in the heavens. **2 a** upstairs. **3** earlier, before, previously, formerly, further back. **4** on (the) top, on the front. ● adj. earlier, former, previous, prior. ● adj. & n. preceding, abovementioned, aforementioned, above-stated, aforestated, above-named. □ **above all** before or beyond everything, first or most of all, chiefly, primarily, in the first place, mainly, principally, especially, essentially, at bottom.

aboveboard /əbúvbawrd/ adj. & adv. without concealment; fair or fairly; open or openly.

■ open, candid, fair, frank, straight, direct, honorable, straightforward, forthright, guileless, undeceiving, artless, ingenuous, undeceptive, undeceitful, straight from the shoulder; respectable, honest, genuine, sincere, colloq. on the level, upfront; openly, candidly, fairly, freely, publicly, frankly, straightforwardly, plainly, for all to see, (out) in the open, in plain or full view.

aboveground /əbúvgrownd/ **1** alive. **2** not secret or underground.

ab ovo /ab ṓvō/ adv. from the very beginning. [L, = from the egg]

Abp. abbr. Archbishop.

abracadabra /ábrəkədábrə/ int. & n. ● int. a supposedly magic word used by magicians in performing a trick. ● n. **1** a spell or charm. **2** jargon or gibberish. [a mystical word engraved and used as a charm: L f. Gk]

abrade /əbráyd/ v.tr. scrape or wear away (skin, rock, etc.) by rubbing. □□ **abrader** n. [L f. radere ras- scrape]

■ see ERODE, SCRAPE v. 3b.

abrasion /əbráyzhən/ n. **1** the scraping or wearing away (of skin, rock, etc.). **2** a damaged area resulting from this. [L abrasio (as ABRADE)]

■ **1** see EROSION. **2** see SCRAPE n. 2.

abrasive /əbráysiv/ adj. & n. ● adj. **1 a** tending to rub or abrade. **b** capable of polishing by rubbing or grinding. **2** harsh or hurtful in manner. ● n. an abrasive substance. [as ABRADE + -IVE]

■ **1** see gritty (GRIT). **2** see ABRUPT 2.

abreact /ábreeákt/ v.tr. Psychol. release (an emotion) by abreaction. [back-form. f. ABREACTION]

abreaction /ábreeákshən/ n. Psychol. the free expression and consequent release of a previously repressed emotion. □□ **abreactive** adj. [AB- + REACTION after G Abreagierung]

abreast /əbrést/ adv. **1** side by side and facing the same way. **2 a** (often foll. by with) up to date. **b** (foll. by of) well-informed (abreast of all the changes). [ME f. A² + BREAST]

abridge /əbríj/ v.tr. **1** shorten (a book, movie, etc.) by using fewer words or making deletions. **2** curtail (liberty). □□ **abridgable** or **abridgeable** adj. **abridger** n. [ME f. OF abreg(i)er f. LL abbreviare ABBREVIATE]

■ **1** shorten, reduce, condense, abbreviate, cut (back or down or off or short), trim, clip, curtail, pare down,

---

/.../ pronunciation	● part of speech
□ phrases, idioms, and compounds	
□□ derivatives	■ synonym section
cross-references appear in SMALL CAPITALS or italics	

contract, compress, telescope, digest, summarize, epitomize, abstract, précis, synopsize. **2** curtail.

abridgment /əbríjmənt/ *n.* (also **abridgement**) **1 a** a shortened version, esp. of a book; an abstract. **b** the process of producing this. **2** a curtailment (of rights). [F *abrégement* (as ABRIDGE)]
■ **1 a** digest, condensation, epitome, compendium, concise edition *or* version, cut edition *or* version; synopsis, abstract, summary, précis, outline, résumé. **b** reduction, abbreviation, condensation, contraction, truncation. **2** curtailment.

abroad /əbráwd/ *adv.* **1** in or to a foreign country or countries. **2** over a wide area; in different directions; everywhere (*scatter abroad*). **3** at large; freely moving about; in circulation (*there is a rumor abroad*). **4** in or into the open; out of doors. **5** *archaic* wide of the mark; erring. □ **from abroad** from another country. [ME f. A² + BROAD]
■ **1** overseas, in *or* to foreign lands *or* parts, out of the country. **2** about, around, everywhere, all over, broadly, widely, at large, near and far, far and wide, extensively, publicly, *colloq.* here there and everywhere, *colloq.* every which way. **3** at large, about, in circulation, spread around, in the air. **4** outside, out, out of doors, away, out and about. □ **from abroad** foreign, nonnative, exotic, alien; imported.

abrogate /ábrəgayt/ *v.tr.* repeal, annul, or abolish (a law or custom). □□ **abrogation** /-gáyshən/ *n.* **abrogator** *n.* [L *abrogare* (as AB-, *rogare* propose a law)]
■ see REPEAL *v.*

abrupt /əbrúpt/ *adj.* **1** sudden and unexpected; hasty (*his abrupt departure*). **2** (of speech, manner, etc.) uneven; lacking continuity; curt. **3** steep; precipitous. **4** *Bot.* truncated. **5** *Geol.* (of strata) suddenly appearing at the surface. □□ **abruptly** *adv.* **abruptness** *n.* [L *abruptus* past part. of *abrumpere* (as AB-, *rumpere* break)]
■ **1** sudden, hasty, quick, precipitate, immediate, summary, snap, rapid, swift; unexpected, unannounced, unplanned, unforeseen, unanticipated, impetuous. **2** broken, uneven, jerky, discontinuous, disconnected, irregular, inelegant; curt, short, brusque, blunt, terse, sharp, bluff, gruff, abrasive, offhand, uncivil, moody, rude, short- *or* quick-tempered, discourteous, impolite, unceremonious, ungracious, snappish, snappy. **3** precipitous, steep, sheer, sudden, sharp; declivitous, acclivitous. □□ **abruptly** see *suddenly* (SUDDEN). **abruptness** see SPEED *n.* 1.

ABS *abbr.* antilock brake (or braking) system.

abs- /abs, abs/ *prefix* = AB-. [var. of L *ab-* used before *c, q, t*]

abscess /ábses/ *n.* a swollen area accumulating pus within a body tissue. □□ **abscessed** *adj.* [L *abscessus* a going away (as AB-, *cedere cess-* go)]
■ see ULCER 1.

abscisic acid /absízik/ *n.* a plant hormone which promotes leaf detachment and bud dormancy and inhibits germination. [L *abscis-* past part. stem of *abscindere* (as AB-, *scindere* to cut)]

abscissa /əbsísə/ *n.* (*pl.* **abscissae** /-ee/ or **abscissas**) *Math.* **1** (in a system of coordinates) the shortest distance from a point to the vertical or *y*-axis, measured parallel to the horizontal or *x*-axis; the Cartesian *x*-coordinate of a point (cf. ORDINATE). **2** the part of a line between a fixed point on it and an ordinate drawn to it from any other point. [mod.L *abscissa* (*linea*) fem. past part. of *abscindere absciss-* (as AB-, *scindere* cut)]

abscission /əbsízhən/ *n.* **1** the act or an instance of cutting off. **2** *Bot.* the natural detachment of leaves, branches, flowers, etc. [L *abscissio* (as ABSCISSA)]

abscond /əbskónd/ *v.intr.* depart hurriedly and furtively, esp. unlawfully or to avoid arrest. □□ **absconder** *n.* [L *abscondere* (as AB-, *condere* stow)]
■ see DEPART 1, FLEE 1.

abseil /áapzil, ábsayl/ esp. *Brit.* = RAPPEL.

absence /ábsəns/ *n.* **1** the state of being away from a place or person. **2** the time or duration of being away. **3** (foll. by

of) the nonexistence or lack of. □ **absence of mind** inattentiveness. [ME f. OF f. L *absentia* (as ABSENT)]
■ **1, 2** nonattendance, nonappearance, truancy; leave, holiday. **3** lack, want, deficiency, nonexistence, unavailability; insufficiency, scantiness, exiguousness, exiguity, paucity, scarcity, dearth, poverty.

absent *adj. & v.* ● *adj.* /ábsənt/ **1** not present. **b** (foll. by *from*) not present at or in. **2** not existing. **3** inattentive to the matter in hand. ● *v.refl.* /absént/ **1** stay away. **2** withdraw. □□ **absently** *adv.* (in sense 3 of *adj.*). [ME ult. f. L *absent-* pres. part. of *abesse* be absent]
■ *adj.* **1** out, off, elsewhere, not present, not here, away, on leave, on holiday, missing, gone, truant, *colloq.* AWOL. **2** missing, lacking, nonexistent, wanting, deficient. **3** see ABSENTMINDED. ● *v.* (*absent oneself*) **1** keep *or* stay away. **2** withdraw, retire, take one's leave, remove oneself, slip away, take oneself off. □□ **absently** see *absentmindedly* (ABSENTMINDED).

absentee /ábsəntée/ *n.* a person not present, esp. one who is absent from work or school. □ **absentee ballot** a ballot, usu. returned by mail, for a voter who cannot be present at the polls. **absentee landlord** a landlord who rents out a property while living elsewhere.
■ see TRUANT *n.*

absenteeism /ábsəntéeizəm/ *n.* the practice of absenting oneself from work or school, etc., esp. frequently or illicitly.
■ truancy, malingering, playing hooky.

absentminded /ábsəntmíndid/ *adj.* habitually forgetful or inattentive; with one's mind on other things. □□ **absentmindedly** *adv.* **absentmindedness** *n.*
■ forgetful, preoccupied, inattentive, absorbed, unmindful, absent, withdrawn, careless, unheeding, heedless, unheedful, inadvertent; distracted, abstracted, daydreaming, in a brown study, in the clouds, unaware, oblivious, in a trance, distrait, mooning, faraway, stargazing, woolgathering. □□ **absentmindedly** absently, vaguely, inattentively, forgetfully, distractedly, unthinkingly, carelessly, abstractedly, obliviously, in a brown study, with one's head in the clouds. **absentmindedness** forgetfulness, obliviousness, carelessness, heedlessness, inattentiveness, unawareness, lack of awareness, blankness, vacantness, abstraction.

absinthe /ábsinth/ *n.* (also **absinth**) **1** a shrubby plant, *Artemisia absinthium*, or its essence. Also called WORMWOOD. **2** a green aniseed flavored potent liqueur based on wormwood and turning milky when water is added. [F *absinthe* f. L *absinthium* f. Gk *apsinthion*]

absolute /ábsəlōot/ *adj. & n.* ● *adj.* **1** complete; utter; perfect (*an absolute fool*; *absolute bliss*). **2** unconditional; unlimited (*absolute authority*). **3** despotic; ruling arbitrarily or with unrestricted power (*an absolute monarch*). **4** (of a standard or other concept) universally valid; not admitting exceptions; not relative or comparative. **5** *Gram.* **a** (of a construction) syntactically independent of the rest of the sentence, as in *dinner being over, we left the table*; *let us toss for it, loser to pay*. **b** (of an adjective or transitive verb) used or usable without an expressed noun or object (e.g., *the deaf*; *guns kill*). **6** (of a legal decree, etc.) final. ● *n. Philos.* **1** a value, standard, etc., which is objective and universally valid, not subjective or relative. **2** (prec. by *the*) **a** *Philos.* that which can exist without being related to anything else. **b** *Theol.* ultimate reality; God. □ **absolute alcohol** *Chem.* ethanol free from water or other impurities. **absolute magnitude** the magnitude, i.e., brightness, of a celestial body as seen at a standard distance of 10 parsecs (opp. *apparent magnitude*). **absolute majority 1** a majority over all others combined. **2** more than half. **absolute pitch** *Mus.* **1** the ability to recognize the pitch of a note or produce any given note. **2** a fixed standard of pitch defined by the rate of vibration. **absolute temperature** one measured from absolute zero. **absolute zero** a theoretical lowest possible temperature, at which the particle motion that constitutes heat is minimal, calculated as −273.15 °C (or 0 °K). □□ **absoluteness** *n.* [ME f. L *absolutus* past part.: see ABSOLVE]

■ *adj.* **1** perfect, complete, utter, unmitigated, categorical, unqualified, total, outright, sheer, out-and-out, all-out, veritable, downright, genuine, unmistakable, rank, pure, real, thorough, thoroughgoing, consummate, entire, unreserved, flawless, faultless, unadulterated, unmixed, unalloyed, undiluted. **2** unconditional, unlimited, limitless, unconditioned, untrammeled, unrestrained, unrestricted, unconstrained; total. **3** unrestrained, unconstrained, arbitrary, despotic, dictatorial, totalitarian, supreme, almighty, autocratic, tyrannical, autarchic, authoritarian. **4** positive, certain, sure, unambiguous, clear, fixed, definite, definitive, decided, categorical, unequivocal, conclusive, universal, infallible, unquestionable, indubitable, authoritative, incontrovertible, inevitable, stark, uncompromising.

absolutely /ábsəlo͞otlee/ *adv.* **1** completely; utterly; perfectly (*absolutely marvelous*; *he absolutely denies it*). **2** independently; in an absolute sense. **3** (foll. by *neg.*) (no or none) at all (*absolutely no chance of winning*; *absolutely nowhere*). **4** *colloq.* in actual fact; positively (*it absolutely exploded*). **5** *Gram.* in an absolute way, esp. (of a verb) without a stated object. **6** *colloq.* (used in reply) quite so; yes.
■ **1** totally, utterly, completely, perfectly, entirely, fully, quite, altogether, wholly; unqualifiedly, unconditionally, unreservedly, unequivocally, unquestionably, positively, manifestly, definitely, really, genuinely, decidedly, surely, truly, certainly, categorically. **3** (*absolutely no* or *none*) no . . . whatever *or* whatsoever *or* at all, none whatever *or* whatsoever *or* at all. **6** quite so, yes, certainly, assuredly, positively, definitely, of course, naturally, indubitably, without a doubt, (yes) indeed, to be sure, right you are, *colloq.* you bet, I'll say, sure, OK, sure thing.

absolution /ábsəlo͞oshən/ *n.* **1** a formal release from guilt, obligation, or punishment. **2** an ecclesiastical declaration of forgiveness of sins. **3** a remission of penance. **4** forgiveness. [ME f. OF f. L *absolutio -onis* (as ABSOLVE)]
■ **1, 4** see FORGIVENESS 1, PARDON *n.* 1.

absolutism /ábsəlo͞otizəm/ *n.* the acceptance of or belief in absolute principles in political, philosophical, ethical, or theological matters. □□ **absolutist** *n.* & *adj.*

absolve /əbzólv, -sólv/ *v.tr.* **1** (often foll. by *from*, *of*) a set or pronounce free from blame or obligation, etc. **b** acquit; pronounce not guilty. **2** pardon or give absolution for (a sin, etc.). □□ **absolver** *n.* [L *absolvere* (as AB-, *solvere* solut- loosen)]
■ see FORGIVE, PARDON *v.*

absorb /əbsáwrb, -záwrb/ *v.tr.* **1** include or incorporate as part of itself or oneself (*the country successfully absorbed its immigrants*). **2** take in; suck up (liquid, heat, knowledge, etc.) (*she quickly absorbed all she was taught*). **3** reduce the effect or intensity of; deal easily with (an impact, sound, difficulty, etc.). **4** consume (income, time, resources, etc.) (*his debts absorbed half his income*). **5** engross the attention of (*television absorbs them completely*). □□ **absorbable** *adj.* **absorbability** /-bəbílitee/ *n.* **absorber** *n.* [ME f. F *absorber* or L *absorbēre absorpt-* (as AB-, *sorbēre* suck in)]
■ **1** see INCLUDE 1. **2** see SOAK *v.* 3. **5** see OCCUPY 6.

absorbed /əbsáwrbd, -záwrbd/ *adj.* intensely engaged or interested (*he was absorbed in his work*). □□ **absorbedly** /-bid-lee/ *adv.*
■ engrossed, involved, lost, wrapped up, deep, occupied, interested, engaged, immersed, buried, preoccupied, rapt, in a brown study.

absorbent /əbsáwrbənt, -záwr-/ *adj.* & *n.* • *adj.* having a tendency to absorb (esp. liquids). • *n.* **1** an absorbent substance. **2** any of the vessels in plants and animals (e.g., root tips) that absorb nutriment. □□ **absorbency** /-bənsee/ *n.* [L *absorbent-* f. *absorbēre* ABSORB]

absorbing /əbsáwrbing, -záwr-/ *adj.* engrossing; intensely interesting. □□ **absorbingly** *adv.*
■ engrossing, engaging, interesting, riveting, captivating, fascinating, spellbinding, gripping.

absorption /əbsáwrpshən, -záwrp-/ *n.* **1** the process or action of absorbing or being absorbed. **2** disappearance through incorporation into something else. **3** mental engrossment. □□ **absorptive** *adj.* [L *absorptio* (as ABSORB)]

abstain /əbstáyn/ *v.intr.* **1** **a** (usu. foll. by *from*) restrain oneself; refrain from indulging in (*abstained from cake and candy*; *abstained from mentioning it*). **b** refrain from drinking alcohol. **2** formally decline to use one's vote. □□ **abstainer** *n.* [ME f. AF *astener* f. OF *abstenir* t. L *abstinēre abstent-* (as AB-, *tenēre* hold)]
■ **1 a** (*abstain from*) see LEAVE[1] *v.* 9a, REFRAIN[1].

abstemious /əbstéemeeəs/ *adj.* (of a person, habit, etc.) moderate, not self-indulgent, esp. in eating and drinking. □□ **abstemiously** *adv.* **abstemiousness** *n.* [L *abstemius* (as AB-, *temetum* strong drink)]
■ see TEMPERATE 4.

abstention /əbsténshən/ *n.* the act or an instance of abstaining, esp. from voting. [F *abstention* or LL *abstentio -onis* (as ABSTAIN)]

abstinence /ábstinəns/ *n.* **1** the act of abstaining, esp. from food, alcohol, or sexual relations. **2** the habit of abstaining from pleasure, food, etc. [ME f. OF f. L *abstinentia* (as ABSTINENT)]
■ see SELF-DENIAL, TEMPERANCE 2.

abstinent /ábstinənt/ *adj.* practicing abstinence. □□ **abstinently** *adv.* [ME f. OF f. L (as ABSTAIN)]
■ see TEMPERATE 4.

abstract *adj.*, *v.*, & *n.* • *adj.* /ábstrakt/ **1 a** to do with or existing in thought rather than matter, or in theory rather than practice; not tangible or concrete (*abstract questions rarely concerned him*). **b** (of a word, esp. a noun) denoting a quality or condition or intangible thing rather than a concrete object. **2** (of art) achieving its effect by grouping shapes and colors in satisfying patterns rather than by the recognizable representation of physical reality. • *v.* /əbstrákt/ **1** *tr.* (often foll. by *from*) take out of; extract; remove. **2 a** *tr.* summarize (an article, book, etc.). **b** *intr.* do this as an occupation. **3** *tr.* & *refl.* (often foll. by *from*) disengage (a person's attention, etc.); distract. **4** *tr.* (foll. by *from*) consider abstractly or separately from something else. **5** *tr.* *euphem.* steal. • *n.* /ábstrakt/ **1** a summary or statement of the contents of a book, scholarly paper, etc. **2** an abstract work of art. **3** an abstraction or abstract term. □ **abstract expressionism** a development of abstract art which aims at a subjective emotional expression of an ideal rather than a picture of a physical object. **in the abstract** in theory rather than in practice. □□ **abstractly** *adv.* **abstractor** *n.* (in sense 2 of *v.*). [ME f. OF *abstract* or L *abstractus* past part. of *abstrahere* (as AB-, *trahere* draw)]
■ *adj.* **1 a** theoretical, unapplied, pure, notional, ideational, conceptual, metaphysical, transcendental, unpractical, intellectual, academic, noetic; intangible. **2** nonrepresentational. • *v.* **1** extract, take out *or* away, remove, draw out. **2** epitomize, abbreviate, digest, summarize, précis, condense, compress, shorten, abridge, cut (down), synopsize, telescope. **4** see DISSOCIATE. **5** see STEAL *v.* 1. • *n.* **1** summary, epitome, synopsis, essence, digest, condensation, survey, conspectus, extract, abridgment; outline, précis, résumé; *Law* brief. **2** abstraction.

abstracted /əbstráktid/ *adj.* inattentive to the matter at hand; preoccupied. □□ **abstractedly** *adv.*
■ see INATTENTIVE.

abstraction /əbstrákshən/ *n.* **1** the act or an instance of abstracting or taking away. **2 a** an abstract or visionary idea. **b** the formation of abstract ideas. **3 a** abstract qualities (esp. in art). **b** an abstract work of art. **4** absentmindedness. [F *abstraction* or L *abstractio* (as ABSTRACT)]
■ **1** see DEDUCTION 1a. **4** see *absentmindedness* (ABSENTMINDED).

/. . ./ **pronunciation**	● **part of speech**
□ **phrases, idioms, and compounds**	
□□ **derivatives**	■ **synonym section**
cross-references appear in SMALL CAPITALS or *italics*	

abstractionism /əbstrákshənizəm/ n. **1** the principles and practice of abstract art. **2** the pursuit or cult of abstract ideas. □□ **abstractionist** n.

abstruse /abstrōōs/ adj. hard to understand; obscure; profound. □□ **abstrusely** adv. **abstruseness** n. [F abstruse or L abstrusus (as AB-, trusus past part. of trudere push)]
▪ see PROFOUND adj. 1b.

absurd /əbsə́rd/ adj. **1** (of an idea, suggestion, etc.) wildly unreasonable, illogical, or inappropriate. **2** (of a person) unreasonable or ridiculous in manner. **3** (of a thing) ludicrous; incongruous (an absurd hat; the situation was becoming absurd). □□ **absurdly** adv. **absurdness** n. [F absurde or L absurdus (as AB-, surdus deaf, dull)]
▪ ridiculous, silly, nonsensical, senseless, outlandish, preposterous, farcical, mad, stupid, foolish, idiotic, imbecilic, imbecile, moronic, childish, asinine, senseless, illogical, irrational, unreasoned, unreasonable, incongruous, inappropriate, paradoxical, unsound, meaningless; laughable, ludicrous, risible, inane, daft, colloq. crazy, sl. nutty, nuts, batty, sl. kooky. □□ **absurdly** see MADLY 1. **absurdness** see ABSURDITY 1, 2.

absurdism /əbsə́rdizm/ n. a philosophical belief that the universe is without meaning or rationality and that humankind exists in isolation.

absurdity /əbsə́rditee/ n. (pl. **-ies**) **1** wild inappropriateness or incongruity. **2** extreme unreasonableness. **3** an absurd statement or act. [F absurdité or LL absurditas (as ABSURD)]
▪ **1, 2** folly, silliness, ridiculousness, foolishness, ludicrousness, nonsense, senselessness, meaninglessness, illogicality, peculiarity, irrationality, unreasonableness, incongruity, stupidity, daftness, colloq. craziness, sl. nuttiness. **3** paradox, self-contradiction, fallacy; triviality, idiocy.

abulia /əbōōleeə/ n. (also **aboulia**) the loss of willpower as a mental disorder. □□ **abulic** /-bōōlik/ adj. [Gk a- not + boulē will]

abundance /əbúndəns/ n. **1** a very great quantity, usu. considered to be more than enough. **2** wealth; affluence. **3** wealth of emotion (abundance of heart). **4** a call in solo whist undertaking to make nine tricks. [ME f. OF abundance f. L abundantia (as ABUNDANT)]
▪ **1** overflow, superfluity, overabundance, superabundance, excess, surplus, too much, oversupply, glut, satiety, oversufficiency; plethora, quantities, wealth, amplitude, ampleness, cornucopia, copiousness, profusion, mine, flush, literary plenitude; colloq. pile, stack, heap, mountain, esp. Brit. colloq. lashings; (in abundance) à gogo, galore. **2** see RICHES.

abundant /əbúndənt/ adj. **1** existing or available in large quantities; plentiful. **2** (foll. by in) having an abundance of (a country abundant in fruit). □□ **abundantly** adv. [ME f. L (as ABOUND)]
▪ **1** plentiful, overflowing, ample, generous, copious, lavish, liberal, opulent, rich, luxuriant, oversufficient, superabundant, profuse, inexhaustible, replete, full, bountiful, colloq. wall-to-wall, poet. bounteous, plenteous. **2** (abundant in) abounding in, full of, filled or replete with, rich in, teeming with, overflowing or spilling over or well-supplied or well-furnished or well-stocked or bristling with, colloq. jam-packed or stuffed with. □□ **abundantly** plentifully, copiously, prolifically, amply, generously, lavishly; absolutely, completely, very, quite.

abuse v. & n. ● v.tr. /əbyōōz/ **1 a** use to bad effect or for a bad purpose; misuse (abused his position of power). **b** take (a drug) for a purpose other than a therapeutic one; be addicted to (a substance). **2** insult verbally. **3** maltreat; assault (esp. sexually). ● n. /əbyōōs/ **1 a** incorrect or improper use (the abuse of power). **b** an instance of this. **2** insulting language (a torrent of abuse). **3** unjust or corrupt practice. **4** maltreatment of a person (child abuse). □□ **abused** /əbyōōzd/ adj. **abuser** /əbyōōzər/ n. [ME f. OF abus (n.), abuser (v.) f. L abusus, abuti (as AB-, uti us- USE)]
▪ v. **1 a** misuse, take advantage of, misemploy, pervert,

misapply, exploit. **b** take, use, be addicted to or dependent on, sl. do. **2** malign, insult, call a person names, revile, censure, upbraid, assail, berate, rebuke, scold, reproach, disparage, traduce, defame, swear at, curse (at), execrate, calumniate, slander, libel, decry, deprecate, vilify, bespatter, blackguard, rail at or against, rubbish, colloq. lambaste, literary objurgate, sl. dump on. **3** maltreat, ill-use, injure, wrong, hurt, mistreat, walk (all) over, molest, ill-treat, treat like dirt, colloq. manhandle; assault, beat (up), batter, hit, thrash, knock about or around, damage; rape, violate, esp. Brit. euphem. interfere with. ● n. **1** misuse, misusage, misemployment, perversion, misapplication, misappropriation; catachresis, solecism, anacoluthon, abusiveness; addiction, dependence, use (of drugs, etc.). **2** revilement, mudslinging, reviling, execration, vituperation, malediction, imprecation, tongue-lashing, calumny, calumniation, vilification, obloquy, scurrility, invective, maligning, aspersion, upbraiding, berating, scolding, (bad) language, name-calling, literary objurgation. **3** injustice, unjustness, wrong, wrongdoing, fault, corruption, misdeed. **4** maltreatment, ill-treatment, ill-usage, molestation; battering, battery, beating; rape, violation. □□ **abused** misused, maltreated, ill-treated, mistreated, battered, beaten, molested, hurt; raped, violated. **abuser** maltreater, wife or husband or baby or child batterer, (child) molester; addict, dependent, user.

abusive /əbyōōsiv/ adj. **1** using or containing insulting language. **2** (of language) insulting. **3** involving or given to physical abuse. □□ **abusively** adv. **abusiveness** n.
▪ **1, 2** insulting, scurrilous, vituperative, calumnious, calumniatory, offensive, slanderous, libelous, defamatory, censorious, opprobrious, disparaging, deprecatory, depreciatory, derogatory, pejorative, derisory, derisive, reviling, vilifying; profane, rude, foul, vulgar, obscene, vile. **3** brutal, cruel, injurious, hurtful, harmful, destructive; perverted, exploitive, exploitative, exploitatory. □□ **abusiveness** see ABUSE n. 2.

abut /əbút/ v. (**abutted, abutting**) **1** intr. (foll. by on) (of land, countries, etc.) adjoin (another). **2** intr. (foll. by on, against) (of part of a building) touch or lean on (another) with a projecting end or point (the shed abutted on the side of the house). **3** tr. abut on. [OF abouter (BUTT¹) and AL abuttare f. OF but end]
▪ see BORDER v. 3a.

abutment /əbútmənt/ n. **1** the lateral supporting structure of a bridge, arch, etc. **2** the point of junction between such a support and the thing supported.

abutter /əbútər/ n. Law the owner of an adjoining property.

abuzz /əbúz/ adv. & adj. in a 'buzz' (see BUZZ n. 3); in a state of excitement or activity.

abysmal /əbízməl/ adj. **1** colloq. extremely bad (abysmal weather; the standard is abysmal). **2** profound; utter (abysmal ignorance). □□ **abysmally** adv. [archaic or poet. abysm = ABYSS, f. OF abi(s)me f. med.L abysmus]
▪ **1** awful, appalling, dreadful, terrible, abominable, fearful, wretched, foul, egregious, colloq. lousy, dire, vile. **2** abyssal, bottomless, profound, unfathomable, unfathomed; utter, complete, perfect, absolute, incredible, astounding. □□ **abysmally** see BADLY 1.

abyss /əbís/ n. **1** a deep or seemingly bottomless chasm. **2 a** an immeasurable depth (abyss of despair). **b** a catastrophic situation as contemplated or feared (his loss brought him a step nearer the abyss). **3** (prec. by the) primal chaos; hell. [ME f. LL abyssus f. Gk abussos bottomless (as A-¹, bussos depth)]
▪ **1** deep, gulf, (yawning) chasm, (gaping) void, (impenetrable or unfathomable or bottomless) depths. **2 a** see DEPTH 5a. **b** see CATASTROPHE 3. **3** see HELL 1.

abyssal /əbísəl/ adj. **1** at or of the ocean depths or floor. **2** Geol. plutonic.

AC abbr. **1** (also **ac**) alternating current. **2** air conditioning. **3** before Christ. **4** Brit. aircraftman. [sense 3 f. L ante Christum]

Ac symb. Chem. the element actinium.

a/c *abbr.* account. [*account current*: see ACCOUNT *n.* 2, 3]

ac- /ək/ *prefix* assim. form of AD- before *c*, *k*, *q*.

-ac /ak/ *suffix* forming adjectives which are often also (or only) used as nouns (*cardiac*; *maniac*) (see also -ACAL). [F *-aque* or L *-acus* or Gk *-akos* adj. suffix]

acacia /əkáyshə/ *n.* **1** any tree of the genus *Acacia*, with yellow or white flowers, esp. *A. senegal*, yielding gum arabic. **2** (also **false acacia**) the locust tree, *Robinia pseudoacacia*, grown for ornament. [L f. Gk *akakia*]

academe /ákədeem/ *n.* **1 a** the world of learning. **b** universities collectively. **c** the academic community in general. **2** *literary* a college or university. □ **grove** (or **groves**) **of Academe** a university environment. [Gk *Akadēmos* (see ACADEMY): used by Shakesp. (*Love's Labour's Lost* I. i. 13) and Milton (*Paradise Regained* iv. 244)]

academia /ákədeémeeə/ *n.* the academic world; scholastic life. [mod.L: see ACADEMY]

academic /ákədémik/ *adj. & n.* ● *adj.* **1 a** scholarly; to do with learning. **b** of or relating to a scholarly institution (*academic dress*). **2** abstract; theoretical; not of practical relevance. **3** *Art* conventional; overly formal. **4 a** of or concerning Plato's philosophy. **b** skeptical. ● *n.* a teacher or scholar in a university or institute of higher education. □ **academic year 1** the customary period of instruction in schools, colleges, and universities, usu. from September to June. **2** *Brit.* a period of nearly a year reckoned usu. from the beginning of the autumn term to the end of the summer term. □□ **academically** *adv.* [F *académique* or L *academicus* (as ACADEMY)]

■ *adj.* **1 a** scholarly, learned, lettered, erudite, intellectual, highbrow, cerebral, well-read, studious, bookish. **b** scholastic, collegiate, academical, educational. **2** abstract, theoretical, hypothetical, conjectural, speculative; ivory-tower, visionary, idealistic; impractical, unrealistic, unpractical, doctrinaire. ● *n.* lecturer, teacher, tutor, professor, fellow, doctor, instructor, esp. *Brit.* reader, don; intellectual, scholar, researcher, *usu. derog.* bluestocking.

academical /ákədémikəl/ *adj. & n.* ● *adj.* belonging to a college or university. ● *n.* (in *pl.*) academic costume.

■ *adj.* see ACADEMIC *adj.* 1.

academician /ákədəmíshən, əkádə-/ *n.* **1** a member of an Academy. **2** = ACADEMIC. [F *académicien* (as ACADEMIC)]

academicism /ákədémisizəm/ *n.* (also **academism** /əkádəmizəm/) academic principles or their application in art.

academy /əkádəmee/ *n.* (*pl.* **-ies**) **1 a** a place of study or training in a special field (*military academy*; *academy of dance*). **b** *hist.* a place of study. **2** (usu. **Academy**) a society or institution of distinguished scholars, artists, scientists, etc. (*Royal Academy*). **3** a secondary school, esp. one that is private. **4** the community of scholars, academe. **5 a** Plato's followers or philosophical system. **b** the garden near Athens where Plato taught. [F *académie* or L *academia* f. Gk *akadēmeia* f. *Akadēmos* the hero after whom Plato's garden was named]

Acadian /əkáydeeən/ *n. & adj.* ● *n.* **1** a native or inhabitant of Acadia in Nova Scotia, esp. a French-speaking descendant of the early French settlers in Canada. **2** a descendant of French-speaking Nova Scotian immigrants in Louisiana. ● *adj.* of or relating to Acadians. [F *Acadie* Nova Scotia]

-acal /əkəl/ *suffix* forming adjectives, often used to distinguish them from nouns in *-ac* (*heliacal*; *maniacal*).

acanthus /əkánthəs/ *n.* **1** any herbaceous plant or shrub of the genus *Acanthus*, with spiny leaves. **2** *Archit.* a conventionalized representation of an acanthus leaf, used esp. as a decoration for Corinthian column capitals. [L f. Gk *akanthos* f. *akantha* thorn perh. f. *akē* sharp point]

a cappella /aá kəpélə/ *adj. & adv.* (also **alla cappella** /álə/) *Mus.* (of choral music) unaccompanied. [It., = in church style]

acaricide /əkárisīd/ *n.* a preparation for destroying mites.

acarid /ákərid/ *n.* any small arachnid of the order Acarina, including mites and ticks. [mod.L *acarida* f. *acarus* f. Gk *akari* mite]

acarpous /əkaárpəs/ *adj. Bot.* (of a plant, etc.) without fruit or that does not produce fruit. [A-¹ + Gk *karpos* fruit]

Accadian var. of AKKADIAN.

accede /aksee´d/ *v.intr.* (often foll. by *to*) **1** assent or agree (*acceded to the proposal*). **2** take office, esp. become monarch. **3** (foll. by *to*) formally subscribe to a treaty or other agreement. [ME f. L *accedere* (as AC-, *cedere cess-* go)]

■ **1, 3** see AGREE 2.

accelerando /əksélərándō, aachéləraán-/ *adv., adj., & n. Mus.* ● *adv. & adj.* with a gradual increase of speed. ● *n.* (*pl.* **accelerandos** or **accelerandi** /-dee/) a passage performed accelerando. [It.]

accelerate /əksélərayt/ *v.* **1** *intr.* **a** (of a moving body) move or begin to move more quickly; increase speed. **b** (of a process) happen or reach completion more quickly. **2** *tr.* **a** cause to increase speed. **b** cause (a process) to happen more quickly. [L *accelerare* (as AC-, *celerare* f. *celer* swift)]

■ see QUICKEN 1, HURRY 1.

acceleration /əkséləráyshən/ *n.* **1** the process or act of accelerating or being accelerated. **2** an instance of this. **3** (of a vehicle, etc.) the capacity to gain speed (*the car has good acceleration*). **4** *Physics* the rate of change of velocity measured in terms of a unit of time. [F *accélération* or L *acceleratio* (as ACCELERATE)]

accelerative /əksé/ərəytiv, -ərətiv/ *adj.* tending to increase speed; quickening.

accelerator /əkséləraytər/ *n.* **1** a device for increasing speed, esp. the pedal that controls the speed of a vehicle's engine. **2** *Physics* an apparatus for imparting high speeds to charged particles. **3** *Chem.* a substance that speeds up a chemical reaction.

accelerometer /əkséləròmitər/ *n.* an instrument for measuring acceleration. [ACCELERATE + -METER]

accent *n. & v.* ● *n.* /áksent/ **1** a particular mode of pronunciation, esp. one associated with a particular region or group (*Boston accent*; *German accent*; *upper-crust accent*). **2** prominence given to a syllable by stress or pitch. **3** a mark on a letter or word to indicate pitch, stress, or the quality of a vowel. **4** a distinctive feature or emphasis (*an accent on comfort*). **5** *Mus.* emphasis on a particular note or chord. ● *v.tr.* also /aksént/ **1** pronounce with an accent; emphasize (a word or syllable). **2** write or print accents on (words, etc.). **3** accentuate. **4** *Mus.* play (a note, etc.) with an accent. □□ **accentual** /aksénchōōəl/ *adj.* [L *accentus* (as AC-, *cantus* song) repr. Gk *prosōidia* (PROSODY), or through F *accent*, *accenter*]

■ *n.* **1** pronunciation, articulation, intonation, speech pattern, inflection. **2, 4** emphasis, stress, force, prominence, accentuation, weight; intensity, inflection; cadence, beat. **3** diacritic, (diacritical) mark, accent mark. ● *v.* **1, 3** accentuate, emphasize, stress, lay stress on, give prominence *or* weight to, place *or* put emphasis on, mark, underline, underscore, distinguish, highlight, focus on, spotlight, set off *or* apart.

accentor /akséntər/ *n.* any bird of the genus *Prunella*, e.g., the hedge sparrow. [med.L *accentor* f. L *ad* to + *cantor* singer]

accentuate /aksénchōōayt/ *v.tr.* emphasize; make prominent. □□ **accentuation** /-áyshən/ *n.* [med.L *accentuare accentuat-* (as ACCENT)]

■ see ACCENT *v.*

accept /aksépt/ *v.tr.* **1** (also *absol.*) consent to receive (a thing offered). **2** (also *absol.*) give an affirmative answer to (an offer or proposal). **3** regard favorably; treat as welcome (*her mother-in-law never accepted her*). **4 a** believe; receive (an opinion, explanation, etc.) as adequate or valid. **b** be prepared to subscribe to (a belief, philosophy, etc.). **5** receive as suitable (*the hotel accepts traveler's checks*; *the machine only accepts tokens*). **6 a** tolerate; submit to (*accepted the umpire's*

/.../ **pronunciation**	● **part of speech**
□ **phrases, idioms, and compounds**	
□□ **derivatives**	■ **synonym section**
cross-references appear in SMALL CAPITALS or *italics*	

decision). **b** (often foll. by *that* + clause) be willing to believe (*we accept that you meant well*). **7** undertake (an office or responsibility). **8** agree to meet (an obligation) or pay (a bill of exchange, etc.). □ **accepted opinion** one generally held to be correct. □□ **accepter** *n.* [ME f. OF *accepter* or L *acceptare* f. *accipere* (as AC-, *capere* take)]

■ **1** receive, take, be the recipient of. **2** accede *or* agree *or* say yes *or* assent *or* consent to, acknowledge, admit *or* allow that, recognize; (*absol.*) assent, consent, accede, agree, say yes. **3** be favorably disposed toward, favor, embrace, understand, warm to; receive, welcome, take in, be hospitable to. **4** see BELIEVE 1. **5** take, allow, permit; do, deal in. **6 a** submit to, tolerate, reconcile oneself to, resign oneself to, go along with, put up with, live with; suffer, undergo, experience, stand, withstand, stomach, endure, bear, allow, take, *literary* brook. **7** assume, undertake, take on *or* up, agree to bear.

acceptable /akséptəbəl/ *adj.* **1 a** worthy of being accepted. **b** pleasing; welcome. **2** adequate; satisfactory. **3** tolerable (*an acceptable risk*). □□ **acceptability** /-bílitee/ *n.* **acceptableness** *n.* **acceptably** *adv.* [ME f. OF f. LL *acceptabilis* (as ACCEPT)]

■ **1 a** worthy, deserving, suitable, appropriate, apt; competent, able, commendable. **b** agreeable, pleasing, welcome, satisfying, delightful, pleasant. **2** satisfactory, adequate, tolerable, all right, not (too) bad, fair, middling, respectable, sufficient, admissible, passable, *colloq.* OK, okay. **3** reasonable, tolerable, understandable, allowable. □□ **acceptability** suitability, aptness, acceptableness, worthiness; reasonableness, appropriateness, tolerableness, tolerability, bearableness, bearability. **acceptableness** see *acceptability* above. **acceptably** adequately, satisfactorily, reasonably, passably, tolerably, bearably; allowably.

acceptance /əkséptəns/ *n.* **1** willingness to receive (a gift, payment, duty, etc.). **2** an affirmative answer to an invitation or proposal. **3** (often foll. by *of*) a willingness to accept (conditions, a circumstance, etc.). **4 a** approval; belief (*found wide acceptance*). **b** willingness or ability to tolerate. **5 a** agreement to meet a bill of exchange. **b** a bill so accepted. [F f. *accepter* (as ACCEPT)]

■ **3** see CONSENT *n.* **4 a** see APPROVAL. **b** see RESIGNATION 3.

acceptant /əkséptənt/ *adj.* (foll. by *of*) willingly accepting. [F (as ACCEPTANCE)]

acceptation /ákseptáyshən/ *n.* a particular sense, or the generally recognized meaning, of a word or phrase. [ME f. OF f. med.L *acceptatio* (as ACCEPT)]

acceptor /akséptər/ *n.* **1** *Commerce* a person who accepts a bill. **2** *Physics* an atom or molecule able to receive an extra electron, esp. an impurity in a semiconductor. **3** *Chem.* a molecule or ion, etc., to which electrons are donated in the formation of a bond. **4** *Electr.* a circuit able to accept a given frequency.

access /ákses/ *n.* & *v.* ● *n.* **1** a way of approaching or reaching or entering (*a building with rear access*). **2 a** (often foll. by *to*) the right or opportunity to reach or use or visit; admittance (*has access to secret files; was granted access to the prisoner*). **b** the condition of being readily approached; accessibility. **3** (often foll. by *of*) an attack or outburst (*an access of anger*). **4** (*attrib.*) (of broadcasting) allowed to special interest groups to undertake (*community access*). ● *v.tr.* **1** *Computing* gain access to (data, a file, etc.). **2** accession. □ **access road 1** a road giving access to a highway. **2** a road giving access only to the properties along it. **access time** *Computing* the time taken to retrieve data from storage. [ME f. OF *acces* or L *accessus* f. *accedere* (as AC-, *cedere* cess- go)]

■ *n.* **2 a** see ADMISSION 2a, ADMITTANCE. **3** see OUTBURST.

accessary var. of ACCESSORY.

accessible /aksésibəl/ *adj.* (often foll. by *to*) **1** that can readily be reached, entered, or used. **2** (of a person) readily available (esp. to subordinates). **3** (in a form) easy to understand. □□ **accessibility** /-bílitee/ *n.* **accessibly** *adv.* [F *accessible* or LL *accessibilis* (as ACCEDE)]

■ **1** open, available, attainable, obtainable, reachable, at *or* to hand, handy, at one's fingertips, within (arm's) reach, *colloq.* getatable. **2** approachable, accommodating, available, obtainable, on hand. **3** simple, understandable, comprehensible.

accession /akséshən/ *n.* & *v.* ● *n.* **1** entering upon an office (esp. the throne) or a condition (as adulthood). **2** (often foll. by *to*) a thing added (e.g., a book to a library); increase; addition. **3** *Law* the incorporation of one item of property into another. **4** assent; the formal acceptance of a treaty, etc. ● *v.tr.* record the addition of (a new item) to a library or museum. [F *accession* or L *accessio -onis* (as ACCEDE)]

■ *n.* **1** see SUCCESSION 2b.

accessorize /aksésəriz/ *v.tr.* provide (clothing, etc.) with accessories.

■ see ORNAMENT *v.*

accessory /aksésəree/ *n.* & *adj.* (also **accessary**) ● *n.* (*pl.* **-ies**) **1** an additional or extra thing. **2** (usu. in *pl.*) **a** a small attachment or fitting. **b** a small item of (esp. a woman's) dress (e.g., shoes, gloves, belt, etc.). **3** (often foll. by *to*) a person who helps in or knows the details of an (esp. illegal) act, without taking part in it. ● *adj.* additional; contributing or aiding in a minor way; dispensable. □ **accessory before** (or **after**) **the fact** a person who incites (or assists) another to commit a crime. □□ **accessorial** /áksesáwreeəl/ *adj.* [med.L *accessorius* (as ACCEDE)]

■ *n.* **1** extra, addition, adjunct, attachment, add-on, component, frill, doodad. **2** (*accessories*) extras, trappings, frills, trimmings, trim, adornments, *colloq.* bells and whistles. **3** accomplice, helper, assistant, confederate, colleague, abetter, aide, collaborator, coconspirator, conspirator, fellow criminal, associate *or* partner in crime. ● *adj.* extra, subordinate, auxiliary, additional, ancillary, supplemental, supplementary, secondary; see also DISPENSABLE.

acciaccatura /əchaákətŏŏrə/ *n. Mus.* a grace note performed as quickly as possible before an essential note of a chord or melody. [It.]

accidence /áksidəns/ *n.* the part of grammar that deals with the variable parts or inflections of words. [med.L sense of L *accidentia* (transl. Gk *parepomena*) neut. pl. of *accidens* (as ACCIDENT)]

accident /áksidənt/ *n.* **1** an event that is without apparent cause, or is unexpected (*their early arrival was just an accident*). **2** an unfortunate event, esp. one causing physical harm or damage, brought about unintentionally. **3** occurrence of things by chance; the working of fortune (*accident accounts for much in life*). **4** *colloq.* an occurrence of involuntary urination or defecation. **5** an irregularity in structure. □ **accident-prone** (of a person) subject to frequent accidents. **by accident** unintentionally. [ME f. OF f. LL *accidens* f. L *accidere* (as AC-, *cadere* fall)]

■ **1, 3** chance, coincidence, fortune, luck, fortuity, fluke; serendipity. **2** mishap, misfortune, mischance, misadventure, bit of bad luck, blunder, mistake; casualty, disaster, catastrophe, calamity; crash, collision, *colloq.* smashup, pileup, *Brit. sl.* prang. □ **by accident** accidentally, by chance, fortuitously, unintentionally, inadvertently, unwittingly, by mistake, unknowingly, unexpectedly.

accidental /áksidént'l/ *adj.* & *n.* ● *adj.* **1** happening by chance, unintentionally, or unexpectedly. **2** not essential to a conception; subsidiary. ● *n.* **1** *Mus.* a sign indicating a momentary departure from the key signature by raising or lowering a note. **2** something not essential to a conception. □□ **accidentally** *adv.* [ME f. LL *accidentalis* (as ACCIDENT)]

■ *adj.* **1** chance, fortuitous, lucky, unlucky, serendipitous, incidental; undesigned, unpremeditated, uncalculated, unintended, unintentional, unwitting, inadvertent; unexpected, unplanned, unlooked-for, unforeseen, unanticipated, adventitious; casual, random, fluky. **2** see INCIDENTAL *adj.* 1a, b. ● *n.* **2** incidental,

inessential, extra, addition. □□ **accidentally** see *by accident* (ACCIDENT).
accidie /áksidee/ var of ACEDIA.
acclaim /əkláym/ *v. & n.* ● *v.tr.* **1** welcome or applaud enthusiastically; praise publicly. **2** (foll. by compl.) hail as (*acclaimed him king*; *was acclaimed the winner*). ● *n.* **1** applause; welcome; public praise. **2** a shout of acclaim. □□ **acclaimer** *n.* [ME f. L *acclamare* (as AC-, *clamare* shout: spelling assim. to *claim*)]
■ *v.* **1** see PRAISE *v.* 1. ● *n.* **1** occ PRAISE *n.*
acclamation /ákləmáyshən/ *n.* **1** loud and eager assent to a proposal. **2** (usu. in *pl.*) shouting in a person's honor. **3** the act or process of acclaiming. □ **by acclamation** *Polit.* (elected or enacted) by overwhelming vocal approval and not formal ballot. [L *acclamatio* (as ACCLAIM)]
■ **3** see PRAISE *n.*
acclimate /áklimayt, əklímit/ *v.tr.* acclimatize. [F *acclimater* f. *à* to + *climat* CLIMATE]
■ (*acclimate to*) see ACCUSTOM.
acclimation /ákləmáyshən/ *n.* acclimatization. [irreg. f. ACCLIMATE]
■ see ACCOMMODATION 3, ORIENTATION 3.
acclimatize /əklímətiz/ *v.* **1** *tr.* accustom to a new climate or to new conditions. **2** *intr.* become acclimatized. □□ **acclimatization** /-tizáyshən/ *n.* [F *acclimater*: see ACCLIMATE]
■ **1** see ACCUSTOM. **2** see ADJUST 5. □□ **acclimatization** see ACCOMMODATION 3, ORIENTATION 3.
acclivity /əklívitee/ *n.* (*pl.* **-ies**) an upward slope. □□ **acclivitous** *adj.* [L *acclivitas* f. *acclivis* (as AC-, *clivis* f. *clivus* slope)]
■ see RISE *n.* 2.
accolade /ákəláyd/ *n.* **1** the awarding of praise; an acknowledgement of merit. **2** a touch made with a sword at the bestowing of a knighthood. [F f. Prov. *acolada* (as AC-, L *collum* neck)]
■ **1** see HONOR *n.* 1, PRAISE *n.*
accommodate /əkómədayt/ *v.tr.* **1** provide lodging or room for (*the apartment accommodates three people*). **2** adapt; harmonize; reconcile (*must accommodate ourselves to new surroundings*; *cannot accommodate your needs to mine*). **3 a** do a service or favor to; oblige (a person). **b** (foll. by *with*) supply (a person) with. [L *accommodare* (as AC-, *commodus* fitting)]
■ **1** put up, house, lodge, shelter, quarter, *Mil.* billet; hold, admit, have capacity for, carry, seat, sleep, contain. **2** (*accommodate a thing to*) harmonize with, make consistent with, reconcile to, adapt to, fit to *or* with, adjust to; (*accommodate oneself to*) become accustomed *or* acclimatized to, get used to, adapt to, adjust to. **3 a** suit, oblige, do a person a favor, favor, convenience, serve; aid, assist. **b** equip, supply, provide, furnish.
accommodating /əkómədayting/ *adj.* obliging; compliant. □□ **accommodatingly** *adv.*
■ obliging, cooperative, helpful, hospitable; considerate, conciliatory, easy to deal with, adaptable, pliant, yielding, compliant, polite, friendly, accessible, complaisant, kind, kindly.
accommodation /əkómədáyshən/ *n.* **1** (in *pl.*) **a** lodgings; a place to live. **b** room and board. **2 a** an adjustment or adaptation to suit a special or different purpose. **b** a convenient arrangement; a settlement or compromise. **3** the act or process of accommodating or being accommodated. **4** (in *pl.*) a seat, berth, or other facilities or services provided for a passenger of a public vehicle. □ **accommodation address** *Brit.* an address used on letters to a person who is unable or unwilling to give a permanent address. **accommodation bill** a bill to raise money on credit. **accommodation ladder** a ladder up the side of a ship for access to or from a small boat. **accommodation road** *Brit.* a road for access to a place not on a public road. [F *accommodation* or L *accommodatio -onis* (as ACCOMMODATE)]
■ **1 a** lodging(s), room(s), quarters, shelter, housing, house, home, residence, domicile, abode, *Mil.* billet, *colloq.* pad, *Brit. colloq.* digs, diggings, *formal* dwelling (place). **2 a** adaptation, adjustment, modification,

change, alteration, conformation. **b** settlement, treaty, compromise, arrangement, terms, contract, deal; loan, (financial) assistance *or* aid, grant, grant-in-aid. **3** see sense 2a above; *also* conformity, orientation, acclimatization, acclimation. **4** (*accommodations*) seat, place.
accompaniment /əkúmpənimənt/ *n.* **1** *Mus.* an instrumental or orchestral part supporting or partnering a solo instrument, voice, or group. **2** an accompanying thing; an appendage. [F *accompagnement* (as ACCOMPANY)]
accompanist /əkúmpənist/ *n.* (also **accompanyist** /-nee-ist/) a person who provides a musical accompaniment.
accompany /əkúmpənee/ *v.tr.* (**-ies, -ied**) **1** go with; escort; attend. **2** (usu. in *passive*; foll. by *with*, *by*) **a** be done or found with; supplement (*speech accompanied with gestures*). **b** have as a result (*pills accompanied by side-effects*). **3** *Mus.* support or partner with accompaniment. [ME f. F *accompagner* f. *à* to + OF *compaing* COMPANION[1]: assim. to COMPANY]
■ **1** attend, escort, chaperon, go (along) with, keep a person *or* thing company, usher, guide, conduct, squire; *Naut.* convoy. **2** go (along) with, come with, occur with, be associated with, belong with, go together with, be linked with, be an adjunct to, be part of.
accomplice /əkómplis, əkúm-/ *n.* a partner or helper, esp. in a crime or wrongdoing. [ME and F *complice* (prob. by assoc. with ACCOMPANY), f. LL *complex complicis* confederate: cf. COMPLICATE]
■ accessory, partner in crime, confederate; participator, henchman, collaborator, conspirator, coconspirator, abetter, fellow criminal; ally, partner, helper, aide, right-hand man *or* woman, assistant, associate, colleague, fellow, *colloq.* sidekick, cohort.
accomplish /əkómplish/ *v.tr.* perform; complete; succeed in doing. □□ **accomplishable** *adj.* [ME f. OF *acomplir* f. L *complēre* COMPLETE]
■ fulfill, perform, achieve, carry out, execute, bring about, produce, carry off, do, complete, carry through, finish, conclude, effect, effectuate, bring off, pull off, bring to an end, conclude, wind up, end; attain, reach, gain; *colloq.* knock off, swing, *sl.* hack.
accomplished /əkómplisht/ *adj.* clever; skilled; well trained or educated.
■ clever, consummate, expert, masterly, masterful, capable, competent, adept, skillful, proficient, practiced, polished, gifted, talented, skilled, professional; qualified, well-trained, well-educated, experienced, complete.
accomplishment /əkómplishmənt/ *n.* **1** the fulfillment or completion (of a task, etc.). **2** an acquired skill, esp. a social one. **3** a thing done or achieved.
■ **1** fulfillment, consummation, completion, realization, attainment, achievement, conclusion. **2** skill, talent, gift, ability. **3** achievement, attainment, acquirement, coup, feat, deed, act, stroke, exploit, triumph, tour de force.
accord /əkáwrd/ *v. & n.* ● *v.* **1** *intr.* (often foll. by *with*) (esp. of a thing) be in harmony; be consistent. **2** *tr.* **a** grant (permission, a request, etc.). **b** give (a welcome, etc.). ● *n.* **1** agreement; consent. **2** harmony or harmonious correspondence in pitch, tone, color, etc. **3** a formal treaty or agreement. □ **in accord** of one mind; united; in harmony. **of one's own accord** on one's own initiative; voluntarily. **with one accord** unanimously; in a united way. [ME f. OF *acord, acorder* f. L *cor cordis* heart]
■ *v.* **1** agree, harmonize, concur, be at one, correspond, be in harmony *or* accord, be consistent, go (together), coincide, conform, chime (in), *colloq.* jibe. **2 a** see GIVE

v. **4. b** see EXTEND 5. ● *n.* **1** agreement, consent, unanimity, concord, harmony, mutual understanding, conformity, accordance, unison, rapport, concert. **2** agreement, harmony, sympathy, congruence, concord, concordance. **3** agreement, treaty, pact, compact, contract. □ **in accord** see UNITED 3. **of one's own accord** see *voluntarily* (VOLUNTARY). **with one accord** unanimously, uniformly, with one voice, in unison, unitedly, solidly, as one man, *Polit.* by acclamation.

accordance /əkáwrd'ns/ *n.* harmony; agreement. □ **in accordance with** in a manner corresponding to (*we acted in accordance with your wishes*). [ME f. OF *acordance* (as ACCORD)]
■ see ACCORD *n.* 2.

accordant /əkáwrd'nt/ *adj.* (often foll. by *with*) in tune; agreeing. □□ **accordantly** *adv.* [ME f. OF *acordant* (as ACCORD)]
■ see CONSISTENT 1.

according /əkáwrding/ *adv.* **1** (foll. by *to*) **a** as stated by or in (*according to my sister; according to their statement*). **b** in a manner corresponding to; in proportion to (*he lives according to his principles*). **2** (foll. by *as* + clause) in a manner or to a degree that varies as (*he pays according as he is able*).
■ **1** (*according to*) **a** on the authority of, in conformity or agreement with, as said or stated or believed or maintained by. **b** by, in keeping or line or step or conformity or harmony or agreement with, in proportion to.

accordingly /əkáwrdinglee/ *adv.* **1** as suggested or required by the (stated) circumstances (*silence is vital so please act accordingly*). **2** consequently; therefore (*accordingly, he left the room*).
■ **1** correspondingly, in accordance, suitably, in conformity, appropriately, compliantly. **2** hence, therefore, consequently, (and) so, that being so or the case, *formal* thus, in consequence whereof.

accordion /əkáwrdeeən/ *n.* a portable musical instrument with reeds blown by bellows and played by means of keys and buttons. □ **accordion pleat, wall,** etc., one folding like the bellows of an accordion. □□ **accordionist** *n.* [G *Akkordion* f. It. *accordare* to tune]

accost /əkáwst, əkóst/ *v.tr.* **1** approach and address (a person), esp. boldly. **2** (of a prostitute) solicit. [F *accoster* f. It. *accostare* ult. f. L *costa* rib: see COAST]
■ **1** see ADDRESS *v.* 3, HAIL² *v.* 1, 2. **2** see PROPOSITION *v.*

accouchement /ákōōshmón/ *n.* **1** childbirth. **2** the period of childbirth. [F f. *accoucher* act as midwife]

accoucheur /ákōōshőr/ *n.* one, esp. a doctor, who assists at childbirth. [F (as ACCOUCHEMENT)]

account /əkównt/ *n.* & *v.* ● *n.* **1** a narration or description (*gave a long account of the ordeal*). **2 a** an arrangement or facility at a bank, etc., for commercial or financial transactions, esp. for depositing and withdrawing money (*opened an account*). **b** the assets credited by such an arrangement (*has a large account; paid the money into her account*). **c** an arrangement at a store for buying goods on credit (*has an account at the hardware store*). **3 a** (often in *pl.*) a record or statement of money, goods, or services received or expended, with the balance (*firms must keep detailed accounts*). **b** (in *pl.*) the practice of accounting or reckoning (*is good at accounts*). **4** a statement of the administration of money in trust (*demand an account*). **5** *Brit.* the period during which transactions take place on a stock exchange; the period from one account day to the next. **6** counting; reckoning. **7** estimation; importance; consideration. ● *v.tr.* (foll. by *to be* or compl.) consider; regard as (*account it a misfortune; account him wise; account him to be guilty*). ¶ Use with *as* (*we accounted him as wise*) is considered incorrect. □ **account day** *Brit.* a day of periodic settlement of stock exchange accounts. **account for 1** serve as or provide an explanation or reason for (*that accounts for their misbehavior*). **2 a** give a reckoning of or answer for (money, etc., entrusted). **b** answer for (one's conduct). **3** succeed in killing, destroying, disposing of, or defeating. **4** supply or make up a specified amount or proportion of (*rent accounts for 50% of expenditures*). **account**

rendered a bill which has been sent but is not yet paid. **by all accounts** in everyone's opinion. **call to account** require an explanation from (a person). **give a good** (or **bad**) **account of oneself** make a favorable (or unfavorable) impression; be successful (or unsuccessful). **keep account of** keep a record of; follow closely. **leave out of account** fail or decline to consider. **money of account** denominations of money used in reckoning, but not necessarily in circulation, as coins or paper money. **of no account** unimportant. **of some account** important. **on account 1** (of goods or services) to be paid for later. **2** (of money) in part payment. **on account of** because of. **on no account** under no circumstances; certainly not. **on one's own account** for one's own purposes; at one's own risk. **settle** (or **square**) **accounts with 1** receive or pay money, etc., owed to. **2** have revenge on. **take account of** (or **take into account**) consider along with other factors (*took their age into account*). **turn to account** (or **good account**) turn to one's advantage. [ME f. OF *acont, aconter* (as AC-, *conter* COUNT¹)]
■ *n.* **1** explanation, narration, narrative, statement, description, report, version, relation, recital, commentary; history, chronicle, story, sketch, tale. **3 a** books, (financial) statement; invoice, bill, *colloq.* tab. **b** (*accounts*) accounting, accountancy, bookkeeping. **6** counting, reckoning, calculation, computation; enumeration. **7** consideration, use, worth, importance, import, consequence, note, value, merit; standing, significance, estimation, esteem. ● *v.* regard as, consider, count (as), view as, look upon as, rate (as), judge. □ **account for 1** explain, serve as an explanation, justify. **2 b** give or render a reckoning for, answer for, make plausible or believable or understandable, justify, excuse, explain (away), vindicate. **3** kill, destroy, do away with, dispose of, defeat. **4** make up, supply, constitute, form, *disp.* comprise. **of no account** unimportant, insignificant, paltry, inconsequential, trifling, trivial, negligible, nonessential, inessential, minor, nugatory, *colloq.* piddling. **of some account** see IMPORTANT 1. **on account 1** on credit, *colloq.* on (one's) tab, esp. *Brit. colloq.* on tick. **on account of** see OWING 2. **on no account** see *by no means* (MEANS). **settle** (or **square**) **accounts with 2** see REVENGE *v.* 1, 2. **take account of** (or **take into account**) notice, take note of, consider, take into consideration, allow for. **turn to account** (or **good account**) turn to one's advantage or benefit or profit; benefit or profit from.

accountable /əkówntəbəl/ *adj.* **1** responsible; required to account for (one's conduct) (*accountable for one's actions*). **2** explicable, understandable. □□ **accountability** /-bílitee/ *n.* **accountableness** *n.* **accountably** *adv.*
■ **1** answerable, responsible, liable, chargeable. **2** explicable; understandable, explainable, interpretable, comprehensible, decipherable. □□ **accountability, accountableness** answerability, responsibility, liability, culpability. **accountably** understandably, discernibly, clearly.

accountancy /əkównt'nsee/ *n.* the profession or duties of an accountant.

accountant /əkównt'nt/ *n.* a professional keeper or inspector of accounts. [legal F f. pres. part. of OF *aconter* ACCOUNT]
■ see BOOKKEEPER.

accounting /əkównting/ *n.* **1** the process of or skill in keeping and verifying accounts. **2** in senses of ACCOUNT *v.*
■ **1** see ACCOUNT *n.* 3b.

accoutre /əkōōtər/ *v.tr.* (also **accouter**) (usu. as **accoutred** *adj.*) attire, equip, esp. with a special costume. [F *accoutrer* f. OF *acoustrer* (as A-³, *couture* sewing: cf. SUTURE)]
■ see EQUIP.

accoutrement /əkōōtrəmənt, -tərmənt/ *n.* (also **accouterment** /-tərmənt/) (usu. in *pl.*) **1** equipment; trappings. **2** *Mil.* a soldier's outfit other than weapons and garments. [F (as ACCOUTRE)]
■ (*accoutrements*) see EQUIPMENT.

accredit /əkrédit/ *v.tr.* (**accredited, accrediting**) **1** (foll. by

to) attribute (a saying, etc.) to (a person). **2** (foll. by *with*) credit (a person) with (a saying, etc.). **3** (usu. foll. by *to* or *at*) send (an ambassador, etc.) with credentials; recommend by documents as an envoy (*was accredited to the president*). **4** gain belief or influence for or make credible (an adviser, a statement, etc.). **5** certify (esp. an educational institution) as maintaining professional standards. □□ **accreditation** /-táyshən/ *n.* [F *accréditer* (as AC-, *crédit* CREDIT)]
■ **1** see ATTRIBUTE *v.* **3** see DELEGATE *v.* 2. **4** see CONFIRM 1, 2.

accredited /əkréditid/ *adj.* **1 a** (of a person or organization) officially recognized. **b** (of an educational institution) having credentials that indicate the maintenance of professional standards. **2** (of a belief) generally accepted; orthodox. **3** (of cattle, milk, etc.) having guaranteed quality.
■ **1 a** see OFFICIAL *adj.* 3, 4.

accrete /əkréet/ *v.* **1** *intr.* grow together or into one. **2** *intr.* (often foll. by *to*) form around or on, as around a nucleus. **3** *tr.* attract (such additions). [L *accrescere* (as AC-, *crescere cret-* grow)]

accretion /əkréeshən/ *n.* **1** growth by organic enlargement. **2 a** the growing of separate things into one. **b** the product of such growing. **3 a** extraneous matter added to anything. **b** the adhesion of this. **4** *Law* **a** = ACCESSION. **b** the increase of a legacy, etc., by the share of a failing co-legatee. □□ **accretive** *adj.* [L *accretio* (as ACCRETE)]

accrue /əkróo/ *v.intr.* (**accrues, accrued, accruing**) (often foll. by *to*) come as a natural increase or advantage, esp. financial. □□ **accrual** *n.* **accrued** *adj.* **accruement** *n.* [ME f. AF *acru(e)*, past part. of *acreistre* increase f. L *accrescere* ACCRETE]

acct. *abbr.* **1** account. **2** accountant.

acculturate /əkúlchərayt/ *v.* **1** *intr.* adapt to or adopt a different culture. **2** *tr.* cause to do this. □□ **acculturation** /-ráyshən/ *n.* **acculturative** /-rətiv/ *adj.*
■ □□ **acculturative** see ADAPTABLE 1.

accumulate /əkyōomyəlayt/ *v.* **1** *tr.* **a** acquire an increasing number or quantity of; heap up. **b** produce or acquire (a resulting whole) in this way. **2** *intr.* grow numerous or considerable; form an increasing mass or quantity. [L *accumulare* (as AC-, *cumulus* heap)]
■ **1** collect, gather, amass, mass, pile or heap up, aggregate, cumulate; assemble, store, stock, hoard, stockpile, put or lay away. **2** collect, pile up.

accumulation /əkyōomyəláyshən/ *n.* **1** the act or process of accumulating or being accumulated. **2** an accumulated mass. **3** the growth of capital by continued interest. [L *accumulatio* (as ACCUMULATE)]
■ **1** collecting, amassing, gathering, accretion, accruement, aggregation, piling or heaping or building up; growth, increase, buildup. **2** heap, pile, mass, mound, stack, mountain, collection, hoard, store, stockpile, stock, aggregation, assemblage, *colloq.* stash.

accumulative /əkyōomyəlaytiv, -lətiv/ *adj.* **1** arising from accumulation; cumulative (*accumulative evidence*). **2** arranged so as to accumulate. **3** acquisitive; given to hoarding. □□ **accumulatively** *adv.*

accumulator /əkyōomyəlaytər/ *n.* **1** a person who accumulates things. **2** a register in a computer used to contain the results of an operation. **3** *Brit.* a storage battery. **4** *Brit.* a bet placed on a sequence of events, the winnings and stake from each being placed on the next.
■ **1** see COLLECTOR.

accuracy /ákyərəsee/ *n.* exactness or precision, esp. arising from careful effort.
■ exactness, correctness, accurateness, exactitude, precision, preciseness.

accurate /ákyərət/ *adj.* **1** careful; precise; lacking errors. **2** conforming exactly with a qualitative standard, physical or quantitative target, etc. □□ **accurately** *adv.* **accurateness** *n.* [L *accuratus* done carefully, past part. of *accurare* (as AC-, *cura* care)]
■ careful, precise, meticulous, nice, with an eye to or for detail, scrupulous, conscientious; exact, correct, perfect, true, right, truthful, faithful, unerring, on

target, faultless, flawless, defectless, error-free, *colloq.* on the mark, *formal* veracious. □□ **accurately** see EXACTLY 1, TRULY 4.

accursed /əkə́rsid, əkə́rst/ *adj.* (*archaic* **accurst** /əkúrst/) **1** being under a curse; ill-fated. **2** *colloq.* detestable; annoying. [past part. of *accurse*, f. A-² + CURSE]
■ **1** see *doomed* (DOOM *v.* 2). **2** see DAMNABLE.

accusal /əkyōozəl/ *n.* accusation.
■ see ACCUSATION.

accusation /ákyəzáyshən/ *n.* **1** the act or process of accusing or being accused. **2** a statement charging a person with an offense or crime. [ME f. OF f. L *accusatio -onis* (as ACCUSE)]
■ accusal, charge, allegation, indictment, citation, arraignment, complaint; imputation, incrimination, denunciation, impeachment; reproach, reproof; *Brit. Law* plaint, *US Law* complaint.

accusative /əkyōozətiv/ *n.* & *adj. Gram.* ● *n.* the case of nouns, pronouns, and adjectives expressing the object of an action or the goal of motion. ● *adj.* of or in this case. □□ **accusatival** /-tívəl/ *adj.* **accusatively** *adv.* [ME f. OF *accusatif -ive* or L (*casus*) *accusativus*, transl. Gk (*ptōsis*) *aitiatikē*]

accusatorial /əkyōozətáwreeəl/ *adj. Law* (of proceedings) involving accusation by a prosecutor and a verdict reached by an impartial judge or jury (opp. INQUISITORIAL). [L *accusatorius* (as ACCUSE)]

accusatory /əkyōozətawree/ *adj.* (of language, manner, etc.) of or implying accusation.

accuse /əkyōoz/ *v.tr.* **1** (foll. by *of*) charge (a person, etc.) with a fault or crime; indict (*accused them of murder*; *was accused of stealing a car*). **2** lay the blame on. □ **the accused** the person or persons charged with a crime. □□ **accuser** *n.* **accusingly** *adv.* [ME *acuse* f. OF *ac(c)user* f. L *accusare* (as AC-, CAUSE)]
■ **1** (*accuse of*) charge with, indict or impeach or arraign for, incriminate in, *Law* implead in, cite for, *archaic* delate of. **2** blame, censure, hold responsible or accountable, charge, denounce, lay a thing at the door of, call to account, call down, *colloq.* stick or pin a thing on, point the finger at, *sl.* put the finger on. □□ **accuser** prosecutor, indicter, informer, *Law* plaintiff, prosecution, *archaic* delator. **accusingly** censoriously.

accustom /əkústəm/ *v.tr.* & *refl.* (foll. by *to*) make (a person or thing or oneself) used to (*the army accustomed him to discipline*; *was accustomed to their strange ways*). [ME f. OF *acostumer* (as AD-, *costume* CUSTOM)]
■ (*accustom to*) familiarize with, make or become familiar with, acquaint with, habituate to, inure to, train to, season to; adapt to, acclimatize to, make or get or become used to, acclimate to.

accustomed /əkústəmd/ *adj.* **1** (usu. foll. by *to*) used to (*accustomed to hard work*). **2** customary; usual.
■ **1** (*accustomed to*) used or inured or habituated or acclimatized to, familiar or acquainted with. **2** customary, habitual, usual, traditional, normal, regular, set, routine, mundane, ordinary, familiar, wonted, common, *colloq.* common or garden.

ace /ays/ *n.* & *adj.* ● *n.* **1 a** a playing card, domino, etc., with a single spot and generally having the value "one" or in card games the highest value in each suit. **b** a single spot on a playing card, etc. **2 a** a person who excels in some activity. **b** *Mil.* a pilot who has shot down many enemy aircraft. **3 a** (in tennis) a service too good for the opponent to touch. **b** a point scored in this way. **4** *Golf* a hole in one. ● *adj. sl.* excellent. □ **ace up one's sleeve** (or **in the hole**) something effective kept in reserve. **play one's ace** use one's best resource. **within an ace of** on the verge of. [ME f. OF f. L *as* unity, AS²]
■ *n.* **2 a** see EXPERT *n.* ● *adj.* see SUPERLATIVE *adj.*

-acea /áyshə/ *suffix* forming the plural names of orders and

---

/.../ **pronunciation**	● **part of speech**
□ **phrases, idioms, and compounds**	
□□ **derivatives**	■ **synonym section**
cross-references appear in SMALL CAPITALS or *italics*	

classes of animals (*Crustacea*) (cf. -ACEAN). [neut. pl. of L adj. suffix -*aceus* of the nature of]

-aceae /áysi-ee/ *suffix* forming the plural names of families of plants (*Rosaceae*). [fem. pl. of L adj. suffix -*aceus* of the nature of]

-acean /áyshən/ *suffix* **1** forming adjectives, = -ACEOUS. **2** forming nouns as the sing. of names in -*acea* (*crustacean*). [L -*aceus*: see -ACEA]

acedia /əseédiə/ *n.* laziness; sloth; apathy. [LL *acedia* f. Gk *akēdia* listlessness]

acellular /aysélyoolər/ *adj. Biol.* **1** having no cells; not consisting of cells. **2** (esp. of protozoa) consisting of one cell only; unicellular.

-aceous /áyshəs/ *suffix* forming adjectives, esp. from nouns in -*acea*, -*aceae* (*herbaceous*; *rosaceous*). [L -*aceus*: see -ACEA]

acephalous /əséfələs, əkéf-/ *adj.* **1** headless. **2** having no chief. **3** *Zool.* having no part of the body specially organized as a head. **4** *Bot.* with a head aborted or cut off. **5** *Prosody* lacking a syllable or syllables in the first foot. [med.L *acephalus* f. Gk *akephalos* headless (as A-[1], *kephalē* head)]

acerb /əsérb/ *adj.* = ACERBIC.

acerbic /əsérbik/ *adj.* **1** astringently sour; harsh-tasting. **2** bitter in speech, manner, or temper. □□ **acerbically** *adv.* **acerbity** *n.* (*pl.* -**ies**). [L *acerbus* sour-tasting]
■ **1** see TART³ 1. **2** see TART³ 2.

acetabulum /ásitábyooləm/ *n.* (*pl.* **acetabulums** or **acetabula** /-lə/) *Zool.* **1** the socket for the head of the thighbone, or of the leg in insects. **2** a cup-shaped sucker of various organisms, including tapeworms and cuttlefish. [ME f. L, = vinegar cup f. *acetum* vinegar + -*abulum* dimin. of -*abrum* holder]

acetal /ásital/ *n. Chem.* any of a class of organic compounds formed by the condensation of two alcohol molecules with an aldehyde molecule. [as ACETIC + -AL]

acetaldehyde /ásitáldihīd/ *n.* a colorless volatile liquid aldehyde. Also called ETHANAL. ¶ Chem. formula: CH_3CHO. [ACETIC + ALDEHYDE]

acetaminophen /əseetəmínəfən/ *n.* a crystalline substance, $C_8H_9NO_2$, that is used medically to reduce fever and relieve pain. [*acet* +*amino* + *phenol*]

acetate /ásitayt/ *n.* **1** a salt or ester of acetic acid, esp. the cellulose ester used to make textiles, phonograph records, etc. **2** a fabric made from cellulose acetate. □ **acetate fiber** (or **silk**) fiber (or silk) made artificially from cellulose acetate. [ACETIC + -ATE¹ + -AL]

acetic /əseétik/ *adj.* of or like vinegar. □ **acetic acid** the clear liquid acid that gives vinegar its characteristic taste. ¶ Chem. formula: CH_3COOH. [F *acétique* f. L *acetum* vinegar]

aceto- /ásitō/ *comb. form Chem.* acetic, acetyl.

acetone /ásitōn/ *n.* a colorless, volatile liquid ketone valuable as a solvent of organic compounds, esp. paints, varnishes, etc. Also called PROPANONE. ¶ Chem. formula: CH_3COCH_3. [ACETO- + -ONE]

acetous /ásitəs, əseé-/ *adj.* **1** having the qualities of vinegar. **2** producing vinegar. **3** sour. [LL *acetosus* sour (as ACETIC)]

acetyl /ásitil, -tīl/ *n. Chem.* the univalent radical of acetic acid. ¶ Chem. formula: CH_3CO-. □ **acetyl silk** = *acetate silk*. [ACETIC + -YL]

acetylcholine /ásitilkōleen, ásitil-/ *n.* a compound serving to transmit impulses from nerve fibers. [ACETYL + CHOLINE]

acetylene /əsétileen/ *n.* a colorless hydrocarbon gas, burning with a bright flame, used esp. in welding and formerly in lighting. ¶ Chem. formula: C_2H_2. [ACETIC + -YL + -ENE]

acetylide /əsétilīd/ *n.* any of a class of salts formed from acetylene and a metal.

acetylsalicylic acid /ásitilsálisílik/ *n.* = ASPIRIN. [ACETYL + SALICYLIC ACID]

Achaean /əkeéən/ *adj. & n.* ● *adj.* **1** of or relating to Achaea in ancient Greece. **2** *literary* (esp. in Homeric contexts) Greek. ● *n.* **1** an inhabitant of Achaea. **2** *literary* (usu. in *pl.*) a Greek. [L *Achaeus* f. Gk *Akhaios*]

Achaemenid /əkeémənid/ *adj. & n.* (also **Achaemenian** /ákimeéneeən/) ● *adj.* of or relating to the dynasty ruling in Persia from Cyrus I to Darius III (553–330 BC). ● *n.* a

member of this dynasty. [L *Achaemenius* f. Gk *Akhaimenēs*, ancestor of the dynasty]

acharnement /áshaarnmóN/ *n.* **1** bloodthirsty fury; ferocity. **2** gusto. [F]

ache /ayk/ *n. & v.* ● *n.* **1** a continuous or prolonged dull pain. **2** mental distress. ● *v.intr.* **1** suffer from or be the source of an ache (*I ached all over*; *my left leg ached*). **2** (foll. by *to* + infin.) desire greatly (*we ached to be at home again*). □□ **achingly** *adv.* [ME f. OE *æce*, *acan*]
■ *n.* **1** pain, pang, throbbing, pounding, smarting, soreness; discomfort. **2** pang, pain; sorrow, grief, distress; longing, yearning, craving. ● *v.* **1** hurt, pain, smart, throb, pound, be sore *or* painful, sting. **2** yearn, long, hunger, hanker, pine; crave.

achene /əkeén/ *n. Bot.* a small, dry, one-seeded fruit that does not open to liberate the seed (e.g., a strawberry pip). [mod.L *achaenium* (as A-[1], Gk *khainō* gape)]

Acheulian /əshŏŏliən/ *adj. & n.* (also **Acheulean**) ● *adj.* & *n.* of the Paleolithic period in Europe, etc., following the Abbevillian and preceding the Mousterian. ● *n.* the culture of this period. [F *acheuléen* f. St-*Acheul* in N. France, where remains of it were found]

achieve /əcheév/ *v.tr.* **1 a** reach or attain by effort (*achieved victory*). **b** acquire; gain; earn (*achieved notoriety*). **2** accomplish or carry out (a feat or task). **3** *absol.* be successful; attain a desired level of performance. □□ **achievable** *adj.* **achiever** *n.* [ME f. OF *achever* f. *a chief* to a head]
■ **1** attain, reach, gain, get, manage, acquire, earn, win, obtain, accomplish, carry off, bring *or* pull off. **2** accomplish, carry out, execute, succeed in, complete, do, fulfill, bring off *or* about; realize, effect, effectuate, engineer, produce. **3** succeed, triumph, ride high, come through, perform (well), prosper, get ahead, give a good account of oneself, flourish, make a hit, *colloq.* go places, make it, click. □□ **achievable** see POSSIBLE *adj.* 2. **achiever** high-flyer, success story, *colloq.* golden boy *or* girl, whiz kid, whiz, *colloq.* hotshot.

achievement /əcheévmənt/ *n.* **1** something achieved; an instance of achieving. **2** the act or process of achieving. **3** *Psychol.* performance in a standardized test. **4** *Heraldry* **a** an escutcheon with adjuncts, or bearing, esp. in memory of a distinguished feat. **b** = HATCHMENT.
■ **1** see ACCOMPLISHMENT 3, ACT *n.* 1. **2** see CONSUMMATION 1.

achillea /ákileéə, əkíl-/ *n.* any plant of the genus *Achillea*, comprising hardy perennial, usu. aromatic plants with flower heads (often white or yellow) usu. in corymbs. [L f. Gk *Akhilleios* a plant supposed to have been used medicinally by Achilles]

Achilles heel /əkíleez/ *n.* a person's weak or vulnerable point. [L *Achilles* f. Gk *Akhilleus*, a hero in the *Iliad*, invulnerable except in the heel]
■ see WEAKNESS 2.

Achilles tendon /əkíleez/ *n.* the tendon connecting the heel with the calf muscles.

achiral /aykírəl/ *adj. Chem.* (of a crystal or molecule) not chiral.

achromat /ákrōmat/ *n.* a lens made achromatic by correction.

achromatic /ákrōmátik/ *adj. Optics* **1** that transmits light without separating it into constituent colors (*achromatic lens*). **2** without color (*achromatic fringe*). □□ **achromatically** *adv.* **achromaticity** /əkrōmətísitee/ *n.* **achromatism** /əkrōmətizəm/ *n.* [F *achromatique* f. Gk *akhromatos* (as A-[1], CHROMATIC)]

achy /áykee/ *adj.* (**achier**, **achiest**) full of or suffering from aches.
■ see PAINFUL 1, 2.

acid /ásid/ *n. & adj.* ● *n.* **1** *Chem.* **a** any of a class of substances that liberate hydrogen ions in water, are usu. sour and corrosive, turn litmus red, and have a pH of less than 7. **b** any compound or atom donating protons. **2** (in general use) any sour substance. **3** *sl.* the drug LSD. ● *adj.* **1** sharp-tasting; sour. **2** biting; sharp (*an acid wit*). **3** *Chem.* having the essential properties of an acid. **4** *Geol.* containing much

silica. **5** (of a color) intense; bright. □ **acid radical** one formed by the removal of hydrogen ions from an acid. **acid rain** acid formed in the atmosphere, esp. from industrial waste gases, and falling with rain. **acid test 1** a severe or conclusive test. **2** a test in which acid is used to test for gold, etc. **put the acid on** *Austral. sl.* seek to extract a loan or favor, etc., from. □□ **acidic** /əsídik/ *adj.* **acidimeter** /ásidímitər/ *n.* **acidimetry** /ásidímitree/ *n.* **acidly** *adv.* **acidness** *n.* [F *acide* or L *acidus* f. *acēre* be sour]
■ *adj.* **1** see TART³ 1. **2** see TART³ 2.

acidhead /ásidhed/ *n. sl.* a user of the drug LSD.

acidify /əsídifī/ *v.tr. & intr.* (**-ies, -ied**) make or become acid. □□ **acidification** /-fikáyshən/ *n.*

acidity /əsíditee/ *n.* (*pl.* **-ies**) an acid quality or state, esp. an excessively acid condition of the stomach.

acidosis /ásidṓsis/ *n.* an overacid condition of the body fluids or tissues. □□ **acidotic** /-dótik/ *adj.*

acidulate /əsídyoolayt/ *v.tr.* make somewhat acid. □□ **acidulation** /-láyshən/ *n.* [L *acidulus* dimin. of *acidus* sour]

acidulous /əsídyooləs/ *adj.* somewhat acid.
■ see TART³.

acinus /ásinəs/ *n.* (*pl.* **acini** /-nī/) **1** any of the small elements that make up a compound fruit of the blackberry, raspberry, etc. **2** the seed of a grape or berry. **3** *Anat.* **a** any multicellular gland with saclike secreting ducts. **b** the terminus of a duct in such a gland. [L, = berry, kernel]

-acious /áyshəs/ *suffix* forming adjectives meaning 'inclined to, full of' (*vivacious; pugnacious; voracious; capacious*). [L *-ax -acis*, added chiefly to verbal stems to form adjectives + *-ous*]

-acity /ásitee/ *suffix* forming nouns of quality or state corresponding to adjectives in *-acious*. [F *-acité* or L *-acitas -tatis*]

ack-ack /ákák/ *adj. & n. colloq.* ● *adj.* antiaircraft. ● *n.* an antiaircraft gun, etc. [formerly Brit. signalmen's name for the letters *AA*]

ackee var. of akee

acknowledge /əknólij/ *v.tr.* **1 a** recognize; accept; admit the truth of (*acknowledged the failure of the plan*). **b** (often foll. by *to be* + compl.) recognize as (*acknowledged it to be a great success*). **c** (often foll. by *that* + clause or *to* + infin.) admit that something is so (*acknowledged that he was wrong; acknowledged him to be wrong*). **2** confirm the receipt of (*acknowledged her letter*). **3 a** show that one has noticed (*acknowledged my arrival with a grunt*). **b** express appreciation of (a service, etc.). **4** own; recognize the validity of (*the acknowledged king*). □□ **acknowledgeable** *adj.* [obs. KNOWLEDGE *v.* after obs. *acknow* (as A-⁴, KNOW), or f. obs. noun *acknowledge*]
■ **1** admit, accept, confess to, own up to, allow (for), concede, recognize, accede to, acquiesce in, homologate, own, grant. **2** answer, reply to, respond to, react to. **3 a** greet, mark, note, observe, salute, honor. **b** thank a person for, give thanks for, honor, reward, celebrate. **4** own, grant, accept.
□□ **acknowledgeable** admittable, confessable; answerable; rewardable.

acknowledgment /əknólijmənt/ *n.* (also **acknowledgement**) **1** the act or an instance of acknowledging. **2 a** a thing given or done in return for a service, etc. **b** a letter confirming receipt of something. **3** (usu. in *pl.*) an author's statement of indebtedness to others.
■ **1** admission, confession, avowal, assent, affirmation, endorsement, confirmation, approval, acceptance; greeting, salutation, honoring, recognition. **2 a** reward, tribute, (show of) appreciation, honoring, thanks, thank you. **b** recognition, reply, response, answer; receipt.

aclinic line /əklínik/ *n.* = *magnetic equator*. [Gk *aklinēs* (as A-¹, *klinō* bend)]

ACLU *abbr.* American Civil Liberties Union.

acme /ákmee/ *n.* the highest point or period (of achievement, success, etc.); the peak of perfection (*displayed the acme of good taste*). [Gk, = highest point]
■ climax, culmination; peak, apex, top, height(s), high point, summit, pinnacle, zenith, ne plus ultra.

acne /áknee/ *n.* a skin condition, usu. of the face, characterized by red pimples. □□ **acned** *adj.* [mod.L f. erron. Gk *aknas* for *akmas* accus. pl. of *akmē* facial eruption: cf. ACME]
■ see SPOT *n.* 1c.

acolyte /ákəlit/ *n.* **1** a person assisting a priest in a service or procession; an altar boy or girl. **2** an assistant; a beginner. [ME f. OF *acolyt* or eccl.L *acolytus* f. Gk *aholouthos* follower]
■ **2** see ASSISTANT 1, APPRENTICE *n.*

aconite /ákənit/ *n.* **1 a** any poisonous plant of the genus *Aconitum*, esp. monkshood or wolfsbane. **b** the drug obtained from this. Also called ACONITINE. **2** (in full **winter aconite**) any ranunculaceous plant of the genus *Eranthis*, with yellow flowers. □□ **aconitic** /-nítik/ *adj. Chem.* [F *aconit* or L *aconitum* f. Gk *akoniton*]

aconitine /əkóniteen/ *n. Pharm.* a poisonous alkaloid obtained from the aconite plant.

acorn /áykorn/ *n.* the fruit of the oak, with a smooth nut in a rough cuplike base. □ **acorn barnacle** a multivalve marine cirriped, *Balanus balanoides*, living on rocks. **acorn worm** any marine wormlike animal of the phylum Hemichordata, having a proboscis and gill slits, and inhabiting seashores. [OE *æcern*, rel. to *æcer* ACRE, later assoc. with OAK and CORN¹]

acotyledon /əkótileéd'n/ *n.* a plant with no distinct seed leaves. □□ **acotyledonous** *adj.* [mod.L *acotyledones* pl. (as A-¹, COTYLEDON)]

acoustic /əkoóstik/ *adj. & n.* ● *adj.* **1** relating to sound or the sense of hearing. **2** (of a musical instrument, phonograph, or recording) not having electrical amplification (*acoustic guitar*). **3** (of building materials) used for soundproofing or modifying sound. **4** *Mil.* (of a mine) that can be exploded by sound waves transmitted under water. ● *n.* **1** (usu. in *pl.*) the properties or qualities (esp. of a room or hall, etc.) in transmitting sound (*good acoustics; a poor acoustic*). **2** (in *pl.*; usu. treated as *sing.*) the science of sound (*acoustics is not widely taught*). □ **acoustic coupler** *Computing* a modem that converts digital signals into audible signals and vice versa, so that the former can be transmitted and received over telephone lines. □□ **acoustical** *adj.* **acoustically** *adv.* [Gk *akoustikos* f. *akouō* hear]

acoustician /ákoostíshən/ *n.* an expert in acoustics.

acquaint /əkwáynt/ *v.tr. & refl.* (usu. foll. by *with*) make (a person or oneself) aware of or familiar with (*acquaint me with the facts*). □ **be acquainted with** have personal knowledge of (a person or thing); have made the acquaintance of (a person). [ME f. OF *acointier* f. LL *accognitare* (as AC-, *cognoscere cognit-* come to know)]
■ (*acquaint with*) familiarize with, inform of or about, make aware of, verse in, tell of or about, apprise of, advise of, notify of, introduce to, *colloq.* fill in on.
□ **be acquainted with** be familiar with or aware of or informed of or knowledgeable of or conversant with; know, be on speaking terms with.

acquaintance /əkwáyntəns/ *n.* **1** (usu. foll. by *with*) slight knowledge (of a person or thing). **2** the fact or process of being acquainted (*our acquaintance lasted a year*). **3** a person one knows slightly. □ **make a person's acquaintance** first meet or introduce oneself to another person; come to know. □□ **acquaintanceship** *n.* [ME f. OF *acointance* (as ACQUAINT)]
■ **1** familiarity, knowledge, acquaintanceship, understanding, awareness; experience. **2** association, friendship, acquaintanceship, companionship, relationship. **3** associate, fellow, colleague, companion, nodding acquaintance. □ **make a person's acquaintance** introduce oneself to, make oneself known to, meet; come or get to know, become friendly or familiar with. □□ **acquaintanceship** see ACQUAINTANCE 1, 2 above.

acquiesce /ákwee-és/ *v.intr.* **1** agree, esp. tacitly. **2** raise no

/.../ **pronunciation**	● **part of speech**
□ **phrases, idioms, and compounds**	
□□ **derivatives**	■ **synonym section**
cross-references appear in SMALL CAPITALS or *italics*	

objection. **3** (foll. by *in*) accept (an arrangement, etc.). □□ **acquiescence** *n.* **acquiescent** *adj.* [L *acquiescere* (as AC-, *quiescere* rest)]
■ **1** see AGREE 1. **2** see AGREE 2. □□ **acquiescent** see YIELDING 1.

acquire /əkwír/ *v.tr.* **1** gain by and for oneself; obtain. **2** come into possession of (*acquired fame*; *acquired much property*). □ **acquired characteristic** *Biol.* a characteristic caused by the environment, not inherited. **acquired immune deficiency syndrome** *Med.* see AIDS. **acquired taste 1** a liking gained by experience. **2** the object of such a liking. □□ **acquirable** *adj.* [ME f. OF *aquerre* ult. f. L *acquirere* (as AC-, *quaerere* seek)]
■ **1** get, obtain, gain, win, earn, make, take, procure, secure, get *or* lay one's hands on, get hold of, pull in, gather; buy, purchase. **2** come by *or* into, receive, come into possession of, amass, pick up; inherit. □□ **aquirable** obtainable, gettable, procurable, securable, winnable, gainable.

acquirement /əkwírmənt/ *n.* **1** something acquired, esp. a mental attainment. **2** the act or an instance of acquiring.
■ **1** see ACCOMPLISHMENT 3. **2** see ACQUISITION 2.

acquisition /ákwizíshən/ *n.* **1** something acquired, esp. if regarded as useful. **2** the act or an instance of acquiring. [L *acquisitio* (as ACQUIRE)]
■ **1** possession(s), belongings, property, purchase; object. **2** gain, acquirement, procurement, purchase, inheritance.

acquisitive /əkwízitiv/ *adj.* eager to acquire things; avaricious; materialistic. □□ **acquisitively** *adv.* **acquisitiveness** *n.* [F *acquisitive* or LL *acquisitivus* (as ACQUIRE)]
■ see *avaricious* (AVARICE). □□ **acquisitiveness** see AVARICE.

acquit /əkwít/ *v.* (**acquitted, acquitting**) **1** *tr.* (often foll. by *of*) declare (a person) not guilty (*were acquitted of the offense*). **2** *refl.* **a** conduct oneself or perform in a specified way (*we acquitted ourselves well*). **b** (foll. by *of*) discharge (a duty or responsibility). [ME f. OF *aquiter* f. med.L *acquitare* pay a debt (as AC-, QUIT)]
■ **1** see FORGIVE 1. **2** see CONDUCT *v.* 5.

acquittal /əkwít'l/ *n.* **1** the process of freeing or being freed from a charge, esp. by a judgment of not guilty. **2** performance of a duty.

acquittance /əkwít'ns/ *n.* **1** payment of or release from a debt. **2** a written receipt attesting settlement of a debt. [ME f. OF *aquitance* (as ACQUIT)]

acre /áykər/ *n.* **1** a measure of land, 4,840 sq. yds., 4047 sq. m. **2** *archaic* a piece of land; a field. **3** (in *pl.*) a large area. □□ **acred** *adj.* (also in *comb.*). [OE *æcer* f. Gmc]

acreage /áykərij, áykrij/ *n.* **1** a number of acres. **2** an extent of land.
■ **2** see AREA 1.

acrid /ákrid/ *adj.* (**acrider, acridest**) **1** bitterly pungent; irritating; corrosive. **2** bitter in temper or manner. □□ **acridity** /-ríditee/ *n.* **acridly** *adv.* [irreg. f. L *acer acris* keen + -ID¹, prob. after *acid*]
■ **1** see BITTER *adj.* 1, TART³ 1. **2** see TART³ 2.

acridine /ákrideen/ *n.* a colorless crystalline compound used in the manufacture of dyes and drugs. [ACRID + -INE⁴]

acriflavine /ákrifláyvin, -veen/ *n.* a reddish powder used as an antiseptic. [irreg. f. ACRIDINE + FLAVINE]

acrimonious /ákrimốneeəs/ *adj.* bitter in manner or temper. □□ **acrimoniously** *adv.* [F *acrimonieux*, *-euse* f. med.L *acrimoniosus* f. L *acrimonia* ACRIMONY]
■ see TART³ 2.

acrimony /ákrimōnee/ *n.* (*pl.* **-ies**) bitterness of temper or manner; ill feeling. [F *acrimonie* or L *acrimonia* pungency (as ACRID)]
■ see ANIMOSITY.

acrobat /ákrəbat/ *n.* **1** a performer of spectacular gymnastic feats. **2** a person noted for constant change of mind, allegiance, etc. □□ **acrobatic** /-bátik/ *adj.* **acrobatically** *adv.* [F *acrobate* f. Gk *akrobatēs* f. *akron* summit + *bainō* walk]

acrobatics /ákrəbátiks/ *n.pl.* **1** acrobatic feats. **2** (as *sing.*)

the art of performing these. **3** a skill requiring ingenuity (*mental acrobatics*).

acrogen /ákrəjən/ *n. Bot.* any nonflowering plant having a perennial stem with the growing point at its apex, e.g., a fern or moss. □□ **acrogenous** /əkrójinəs/ *adj.* [Gk *akron* tip + -GEN]

acromegaly /ákrəmégəlee/ *n. Med.* the abnormal growth of the hands, feet, and face, caused by excessive activity of the pituitary gland. □□ **acromegalic** /-migálik/ *adj.* [F *acromégalie* f. Gk *akron* extremity + *megas megal-* great]

acronym /ákrənim/ *n.* a word, usu. pronounced as such, formed from the initial letters of other words (e.g., *laser*, *NATO*). [Gk *akron* end + -*onum-* = *onoma* name]

acropetal /əkrópit'l/ *adj. Bot.* developing from below upwards. □□ **acropetally** *adv.* [Gk *akron* tip + L *petere* seek]

acrophobia /ákrəfốbeeə/ *n. Psychol.* an abnormal dread of heights. □□ **acrophobic** /-fốbik/ *adj.* [Gk *akron* peak + -PHOBIA]

acropolis /əkrópəlis/ *n.* **1** a citadel or upper fortified part of esp. an ancient Greek city. **2** (**Acropolis**) the ancient citadel at Athens. [Gk *akropolis* f. *akron* summit + *polis* city]

across /əkráws/ *prep. & adv.* ● *prep.* **1** to or on the other side of (*walked across the road*; *lives across the river*). **2** from one side to another side of (*the cover stretched across the opening*; *a bridge across the river*). **3** at or forming an angle (esp. a right angle) with (*deep cuts across his legs*). ● *adv.* **1** to or on the other side (*ran across*; *shall soon be across*). **2** from one side to another (*a blanket stretched across*). **3** forming a cross (*with cuts across*). **4** (of a crossword clue or answer) read horizontally (*cannot do nine across*). □ **across the board** general; generally; applying to all. [ME f. OF *a croix*, *en croix*, later regarded as f. A² + CROSS]
■ *prep.* **1, 2** see OVER *prep.* 3, 4. ● *adv.* **1, 2** see OVER *adv.* 4.

acrostic /əkráwstik, əkrós-/ *n.* **1** a poem or other composition in which certain letters in each line form a word or words. **2** a word puzzle constructed in this way. □ **double acrostic** one using the first and last letters of each line. **single acrostic** one using the first letter only. **triple acrostic** one using the first, middle, and last letters. [F *acrostiche* or Gk *akrostikhis* f. *akron* end + *stikhos* row, line of verse, assim. to -IC]

acrylic /əkrílik/ *adj. & n.* ● *adj.* **1** of material made with a synthetic polymer derived from acrylic acid. **2** *Chem.* of or derived from acrylic acid. ● *n.* an acrylic fiber. □ **acrylic acid** a pungent liquid organic acid. ¶ *Chem.* formula: $C_3H_4O_2$. **acrylic resin** any of various transparent colorless polymers of acrylic acid. [*acrolein* f. L *acer acris* pungent + *olēre* to smell + -IN + -YL + -IC]

ACT *abbr.* **1** American College Test. **2** Australian Capital Territory.

act /akt/ *n. & v.* ● *n.* **1** something done; a deed; an action. **2** the process of doing something (*caught in the act*). **3 a** a piece of entertainment, usu. one of a series in a program. **b** the performer(s) of this. **4** a pretense; behavior intended to deceive or impress (*it was all an act*). **5** a main division of a play or opera. **6 a** a written ordinance of a legislature or other legislative body. **b** a document attesting a legal transaction. **7** (often in *pl.*) the recorded decisions or proceedings of a committee, an academic body, etc. **8** (**Acts**) (in full **Acts of the Apostles**) the New Testament book relating the growth of the early Church. ● *v.* **1** *intr.* behave (*see how they act under stress*). **2** *intr.* perform actions or functions; operate effectively; take action (*act as referee*; *we must act quickly*). **3** *intr.* (also foll. by *on*) exert energy or influence (*the medicine soon began to act*; *alcohol acts on the brain*). **4** *intr.* **a** perform a part in a play, movie, etc. **b** pretend. **5** *tr.* **a** perform the part of (*acted Othello*; *acts the fool*). **b** perform (a play, etc.). **c** portray (an incident) by actions. **d** feign (*we acted indifference*). □ **act for** be the (*Brit.*, esp. legal) representative of. **act of God** the operation of uncontrollable natural forces. **act of grace** a privilege or concession that cannot be claimed as a right. **act on** (or **upon**) perform or carry out; put into operation (*acted on my advice*). **act out 1** translate (ideas, etc.) into action. **2** *Psychol.* represent (one's subconscious desires, etc.) in action. **3** perform (a drama). **act**

up *colloq.* misbehave; give trouble (*my car is acting up again*). **get one's act together** *sl.* become properly organized; make preparations for an undertaking, etc. **get into** (or **in on**) **the act** *sl.* become a participant (esp. for profit). **put on an act** *colloq.* carry out a pretense. □□ **actable** *adj.* (in sense 5 of *v.*). **actability** /áktəbílitee/ *n.* (in sense 5 of *v.*). [ME ult. f. L *agere act-* do]

■ *n.* **1** deed, action, undertaking, operation, step, move; feat, exploit; accomplishment, achievement. **2** see PERFORMANCE 1. **3 a** performance, show, skit, stand, routine, turn, sketch, *sl.* shtick. **b** see CAST *n.* 6. **4** performance, pretense, posture, pose, stance, feigning, front, fake, dissimulation, show, sham, trick, deception, hoax, affectation. **6** bill, law, decree, edict, statute, order, ordinance, command, mandate, resolution, measure, enactment. ● *v.* **1** behave (oneself), carry on, deport oneself, conduct oneself, bear oneself, carry oneself, *literary* comport oneself. **3** take effect, work, operate, function, be effective *or* efficacious, perform. **4 a** perform, appear. **b** feign, pretend, counterfeit, fake, dissemble, make believe, sham, simulate, dissimulate, posture, pose. **5 a** portray, play, be, represent, impersonate, personify, take *or* play the part *or* role of, personate. **b** put on, do, play, act out. **d** pretend, feign, profess, make a show *or* pretense of, give the impression of, affect, put on an act *or* air of, simulate. □ **act for** see REPRESENT 10. **act on** see DEAL¹ *v.* 1. **act out** see ACT *v.* 5b above. **act up** see MISBEHAVE. **get one's act together** pull oneself together, rally oneself; hurry up, *colloq.* get moving, get a move on. **put on an act** see ACT *v.* 4b above. □□ **actable** performable, playable, portrayable.

ACTH *abbr. Med.* adrenocorticotrophic hormone.

acting /ákting/ *n. & attrib. adj.* ● *n.* **1** the art or occupation of performing parts in plays, movies, etc. **2** in senses of ACT *v.* ● *attrib.adj.* serving temporarily or on behalf of another or others (*acting manager; Acting President*).
■ *attrib. adj.* see TEMPORARY *adj.*

actinia /aktíneeə/ *n.* (*pl.* **actiniae** /-nee-ee/) any sea anemone, esp. of the genus *Actinia.* [mod.L f. Gk *aktis -inos* ray]

actinide /áktinïd/ *n. Chem.* any of the series of 15 radioactive elements having increasing atomic numbers from actinium to lawrencium. □ **actinide series** this series of elements. [ACTINIUM + -IDE as in *lanthanide*]

actinism /áktinizəm/ *n.* the property of shortwave radiation that produces chemical changes, as in photography. □□ **actinic** /aktínik/ *adj.* [Gk *aktis -inos* ray]

actinium /aktíneeəm/ *n. Chem.* a radioactive metallic element of the actinide series, occurring naturally in pitchblende. ¶ Symb.: **Ac**.

actinometer /áktinómitər/ *n.* an instrument for measuring the intensity of radiation, esp. ultraviolet radiation. [Gk *aktis -tinos* ray + -METER]

actinomorphic /áktinəmáwrfik/ *adj. Biol.* radially symmetrical. [as ACTINOMETER + Gk *morphē* form]

actinomycete /áktinōmíseet, -míseet/ *n.* any of the usu. nonmotile filamentous anerobic bacteria of the order Actinomycetales. [as ACTINOMORPHIC + -*mycetes* f. Gk *mukēs -ētos* mushroom]

action /ákshən/ *n. & v.* ● *n.* **1** the fact or process of doing or acting (*demanded action; put ideas into action*). **2** forcefulness or energy as a characteristic (*a woman of action*). **3** the exertion of energy or influence (*the action of acid on metal*). **4** something done; a deed or act (*not aware of his own actions*). **5 a** a series of events represented in a story, play, etc. **b** *sl.* exciting activity (*arrived late and missed the action; want some action*). **6 a** armed conflict; fighting (*killed in action*). **b** an occurrence of this, esp. a minor military engagement. **7 a** the way in which a machine, instrument, etc., works (*explain the action of an air pump*). **b** the mechanism that makes a machine, instrument, etc. (e.g., a musical instrument, a gun, etc.), work. **c** the mode or style of movement of an animal or human (usu. described in some way) (*a runner with good action*). **8** a legal process; a lawsuit (*bring an action*). **9** (in *imper.*) a word of command to begin, esp. used

by a film director, etc. ● *v.tr.* bring a legal action against. □ **action committee** (or **group**, etc.) a body formed to take active steps or lobby, esp. in politics. **action-packed** full of action or excitement. **action painting** an aspect of abstract expressionism with paint applied by the artist's random or spontaneous gestures. **action point** a proposal for action, esp. arising from a discussion, etc. **action replay** *Brit.* a playback of part of a television broadcast, esp. a sporting event, often in slow motion. **action stations** esp. *Brit.* positions taken up by troops, etc., ready for battle. **go into action** start work. **out of action** not working. **take action** begin to act (esp. energetically in protest). [ME f. OF f. L *actio -onis* (as ACT)]

■ *n.* **1** activity, performance, movement, motion; operation, execution, enactment, practice. **2** forcefulness, energy, liveliness, vim, vigor, spirit, vitality, go, animation, *colloq.* get-up-and-go, *sl.* feistiness; enterprise, initiative. **3** influence, effect, power, force, strength; effectiveness, activity, performance, reaction. **4** deed, act, undertaking, operation, feat, exertion; (*actions*) behavior, conduct, deportment, demeanor, ways, manner(s). **5 b** excitement, interest, adventure, thrills. **6 a** fighting, combat, conflict; battle, war. **b** fight, battle, engagement, encounter, clash, fray, sortie, skirmish, affray. **7 a, b** see MOVEMENT 2, MECHANISM 1. **8** lawsuit, suit, litigation, proceeding, process, case; remedy. ● *v.* proceed against, institute proceedings against. □ **out of action** see DEFUNCT 1, 2.

actionable /ákshənəbəl/ *adj.* giving cause for legal action. □□ **actionably** *adv.*
■ see ILLEGAL 2.

activate /áktivayt/ *v.tr.* **1** make active; bring into action. **2** *Chem.* cause reaction in; excite (a substance, molecules, etc.). **3** *Physics* make radioactive. □ **activated carbon** (or **charcoal**) carbon, esp. charcoal, treated to increase its adsorptive power. **activated sludge** aerated sewage containing aerobic bacteria. □□ **activation** /-váyshən/ *n.* **activator** *n.*
■ **1** move, actuate, set in motion, get started, energize, get *or* set going, start, initiate, switch *or* turn on, trigger, bring into play, motivate, rouse, arouse, prompt, stimulate, stir, mobilize, animate, impel, galvanize. □□ **activation** operation, movement, actuation, ignition. **activator** initiator, starter.

active /áktiv/ *adj. & n.* ● *adj.* **1 a** consisting in or marked by action; energetic; diligent (*leads an active life; an active helper*). **b** able to move about or accomplish practical tasks (*infirmity made him less active*). **2** working; operative (*an active volcano*). **3** originating action; not merely passive or inert (*active support; active ingredients*). **4** radioactive. **5** *Gram.* designating the voice that attributes the action of a verb to the person or thing from which it logically proceeds (e.g., of the verbs in *guns kill; we saw him*). ● *n. Gram.* the active form or voice of a verb. □ **active carbon** = *activated carbon* (see ACTIVATE). **active citizen** a person who takes an active role in the community through crime prevention, etc. **active list** *Mil.* a list of officers available for service. **active service** service in the armed forces during a war. □□ **actively** *adv.* **activeness** *n.* [ME f. OF *actif -ive* or L *activus* (as ACT *v.*)]

■ *adj.* **1 a** strenuous, vigorous, full, dynamic, physical, hectic; diligent, tireless, industrious, hard-working, untiring, energetic, lively, hyperactive, animated, busy, brisk, bustling, occupied, on the move, *colloq.* on the go. **b** agile, spry, nimble, quick, sprightly. **2, 3** effective, efficacious, effectual, working, functioning, operative, potent, influential; powerful.

/.../ **pronunciation**	● **part of speech**
□ **phrases, idioms, and compounds**	
□□ **derivatives**	■ **synonym section**
cross-references appear in SMALL CAPITALS or *italics*	

activism /áktivizəm/ *n.* a policy of vigorous action in a cause, esp. in politics. ▫▫ **activist** *n.*

activity /aktívitee/ *n.* (*pl.* **-ies**) **1 a** the condition of being active or moving about. **b** the exertion of energy; vigorous action. **2** (often in *pl.*) a particular occupation or pursuit (*outdoor activities*). **3** = RADIOACTIVITY. [F *activité* or LL *activitas* (as ACTIVE)]
■ **1** action, movement, motion, operation, function, work(ing); liveliness, busyness, (hustle and) bustle; exertion, vigor, vim, energy, effort. **2** pursuit, occupation, vocation, work, employment, function, operation, job, labor, endeavor, enterprise, project, undertaking, venture, interest.

actor /áktər/ *n.* **1** the performer of a part in a play, movie, etc. **2** a person whose profession is performing such parts. ▫ **Actors' Equity Association** stage actors' labor union. [L, = doer, actor (as ACT, -OR¹)]
■ **1** see PLAYER 3.

actress /áktris/ *n.* a female actor.
■ see PLAYER 3.

actual /ákchōōəl/ *adj.* (usu. *attrib.*) **1** existing in fact; real (often as distinct from ideal). **2** existing now; current. ¶ Redundant use, as in *tell me the actual facts*, is *disp.*, but common. ▫▫ **actualize** *v.tr.* **actualization** /-lizáyshən/ *n.* [ME f. OF *actuel* f. LL *actualis* f. *agere* ACT]
■ **1** real, genuine, factual, true (to life), authentic, verifiable, manifest, realized, realistic, tangible, physical, hard, solid. **2** existing, existent, present, current, extant. ▫▫ **actualize** see REALIZE 4.
actualization see *realization* 2 (REALIZE).

actuality /ákchōō-álitee/ *n.* (*pl.* **-ies**) **1** reality; what is the case. **2** (in *pl.*) existing conditions. [ME f. OF *actualité* entity or med.L *actualitas* (as ACTUAL)]
■ **1** see CASE¹ 2, 9, REALITY 1.

actually /ákchōōəlee/ *adv.* **1** as a fact; really (*I asked for ten, but actually got nine*). **2** as a matter of fact; even (strange as it may seem) (*he actually refused!*). **3** at present; for the time being.
■ **1** really, in reality, in fact, in actuality, in point of fact, as a matter of fact, truly, literally, *literary* in truth. **2** even, as a matter of fact, strange as it may seem, *colloq.* believe it or not. **3** at (the) present (time), for the time being, currently, (just) now.

actuary /ákchōōeree/ *n.* (*pl.* **-ies**) an expert in statistics, esp. one who calculates insurance risks and premiums. ▫▫ **actuarial** /-chōōáireeəl/ *adj.* **actuarially** *adv.* [L *actuarius* bookkeeper f. *actus* past part. of *agere* ACT]

actuate /ákchōō-ayt/ *v.tr.* **1** communicate motion to (a machine, etc.). **2** cause the operation of (an electrical device, etc.). **3** cause (a person) to act. ▫▫ **actuation** /-áyshən/ *n.* **actuator** *n.* [med.L *actuare* f. L *actus*: see ACTUAL]
■ see ACTIVATE.

acuity /əkyōoitee/ *n.* sharpness; acuteness (of a needle, senses, understanding). [F *acuité* or med.L *acuitas* f. *acuere* sharpen: see ACUTE]

aculeate /əkyōoleeət, -ayt/ *adj.* **1** *Zool.* having a sting. **2** *Bot.* prickly. **3** pointed; incisive. [L *aculeatus* f. *aculeus* sting, dimin. of *acus* needle]

acumen /ákyəmən, əkyōō-/ *n.* keen insight or discernment; penetration. [L *acumen -minis* anything sharp f. *acuere* sharpen: see ACUTE]
■ see DISCRIMINATION 2, 3, *profundity* (PROFOUND).

acuminate /əkyōominət, -nayt/ *adj.* *Biol.* tapering to a point. [L *acuminatus* pointed (as ACUMEN)]

acupressure /ákyəpreshər/ *n.* a form of therapy in which symptoms are relieved by applying pressure with the thumbs or fingers to specific points on the body. [alt. of ACUPUNCTURE]

acupuncture /ákyəpungkchər/ *n.* a method (orig. Chinese) of treating various conditions by pricking the skin or tissues with needles. ▫▫ **acupuncturist** *n.* [L *acu* with a needle + PUNCTURE]

acutance /əkyōōt'ns/ *n.* sharpness of a photographic or printed image; a measure of this. [ACUTE + -ANCE]

acute /əkyōōt/ *adj.* & *n.* ● *adj.* (**acuter, acutest**) **1 a** (of senses, etc.) keen; penetrating. **b** (of pain) intense; severe; sharp or stabbing rather than dull, aching, or throbbing. **2** shrewd; perceptive (*an acute critic*). **3** (of a disease) coming sharply to a crisis; severe, not chronic. **4** (of a difficulty or controversy) critical; serious. **5 a** (of an angle) less than 90°. **b** sharp; pointed. **6** (of a sound) high; shrill. ● *n.* = *acute accent*. ▫ **acute accent** a mark (´) placed over letters in some languages to show quality, vowel length, pronunciation (e.g., *maté*), etc. ▫▫ **acutely** *adv.* **acuteness** *n.* [L *acutus* past part. of *acuere* sharpen f. *acus* needle]
■ *adj.* **1 a** keen, sharp, penetrating, sensitive, discriminating, exquisite, fine, fine-honed. **b** sharp, cutting, intense, keen, severe, violent, excruciating, exquisite, fierce, shooting, stabbing, piercing, sudden. **2** keen, sharp-witted, shrewd, clever, ingenious, astute, quick, sharp, canny, bright, incisive, discerning, perceptive, perspicacious, intelligent, penetrating, insightful, percipient, wise, sensitive, subtle, discriminating; alert, aware, on the qui vive, *colloq.* on the ball. **3** severe, intense, critical, dangerous, grave, serious, life-threatening. **4** see SERIOUS 2, 3, 7.
5 b sharp, pointed, narrow. ▫▫ **acutely** see *severely* (SEVERE), VERY *adv.* **acuteness** see GRAVITY 3a, *penetration* (PENETRATE).

-acy /əsee/ *suffix* forming nouns of state or quality (*accuracy*; *piracy*; *supremacy*), or an instance of it (*conspiracy*; *fallacy*) (see also -CRACY). [a branch of the suffix -CY from or after F *-acie* or L *-acia* or *-atia* or Gk *-ateia*]

acyl /ásil/ *n.* *Chem.* the univalent radical of an organic acid. [G (as ACID, -YL)]

AD *abbr.* (of a date) of the Christian era. ¶ Strictly, AD should precede a date (e.g., AD 410), but uses such as *the tenth century* AD are well established. [*Anno Domini*, 'in the year of the Lord']

ad /ad/ *n.* *colloq.* an advertisement. [abbr.]
■ see ADVERTISEMENT 1.

ad- /əd, ad/ *prefix* (also **a-** before *sc*, *sp*, *st*, **ac-** before *c*, *k*, *q*, **af-** before *f*, **ag-** before *g*, **al-** before *l*, **an-** before *n*, **ap-** before *p*, **ar-** before *r*, **as-** before *s*, **at-** before *t*) **1** with the sense of motion or direction to, reduction or change into, addition, adherence, increase, or intensification. **2** formed by assimilation of other prefixes (*accurse*; *admiral*; *advance*; *affray*). [(sense 1) (through OF *a-*) f. L *ad* to: (sense 2) *a-* repr. various prefixes other than *ad-*]

-ad¹ /əd, ad/ *suffix* forming nouns: **1** in collective numerals (*myriad*; *triad*). **2** in fem. patronymics (*Dryad*). **3** in names of poems and similar compositions (*Iliad*; *Dunciad*; *jeremiad*). [Gk *-as -ada*]

-ad² /əd/ *suffix* forming nouns (*ballad*; *salad*) (cf. -ADE¹). [F *-ade*]

adage /ádij/ *n.* a traditional maxim; a proverb. [F f. L *adagium* (as AD-, root of *aio* say)]
■ see MAXIM.

adagio /ədáazheeō/ *adv.*, *adj.*, & *n.* *Mus.* ● *adv.* & *adj.* in slow time. ● *n.* (*pl.* **-os**) an adagio movement or passage. [It.]

Adam¹ /ádəm/ *n.* the first man, in the Biblical and Koranic traditions. ▫ **Adam's ale** water. **Adam's apple** a projection of the thyroid cartilage of the larynx, esp. as prominent in men. **not know a person from Adam** be unable to recognize the person in question. [Heb. *'ādām* man]

Adam² /ádəm/ *adj.* of the style of architecture, furniture, and design created by the Scottish brothers Robert and James Adam (18th c.).

adamant /ádəmənt/ *adj.* & *n.* ● *adj.* stubbornly resolute; resistant to persuasion. ● *n.* *archaic* diamond or other hard substance. ▫▫ **adamance** *n.* **adamantine** /-mántin/ *adj.* **adamantly** *adv.* [OF *adamaunt* f. L *adamas adamant-* untamable f. Gk (as A-¹, *damaō* to tame)]
■ *adj.* see RESOLUTE.

adapt /ədápt/ *v.* **1** *tr.* **a** (foll. by *to*) fit; adjust (one thing to another). **b** (foll. by *to, for*) make suitable for a purpose. **c** alter or modify (esp. a text). **d** arrange for broadcasting, etc. **2** *intr.* & *refl.* (usu. foll. by *to*) become adjusted to new conditions. □□ **adaptive** *adj.* **adaptively** *adv.* [F *adapter* f. L *adaptare* (as AD-, *aptare* f. *aptus* fit)]

■ **1 a** (*adapt to*) fit to *or* with, adjust to, align to, coordinate with, attune to. **b** gear, suit, fit (out), adjust, make suitable, tailor, design, fashion, equip, outfit, get *or* make ready, prepare, revamp, regulate; qualify. **c, d** edit, rewrite, modify, alter, change, revise, correct, amend, emend, reword, restyle, convert, remodel, reshape, rework, remold, shape, fashion, polish, touch up, retouch, arrange. **2** (*adapt oneself to*) adjust (oneself) to, accommodate *or* accustom *or* acclimatize *or* habituate *or* inure *or* orient *or* orientate oneself to, get used to, acclimate oneself to; comply with, conform to *or* with, follow, observe, respect.

adaptable /ədáptəbəl/ *adj.* **1** able to adapt oneself to new conditions. **2** that can be adapted. □□ **adaptability**/-bílitee/ *n.* **adaptably** *adv.*

■ **1** flexible, versatile, cooperative, amenable; acculturative, obliging, accommodating, compliant, tractable. **2** modifiable, alterable, changeable, adjustable; pliable, pliant, tractable, malleable, ductile. □□ **adaptability** see *flexibility* (FLEXIBLE).

adaptation /ádaptáyshən/ *n.* **1** the act or process of adapting or being adapted. **2** a thing that has been adapted. **3** *Biol.* the process by which an organism or species becomes suited to its environment. [F f. LL *adaptatio -onis* (as ADAPT)]

■ **1** modification, change, adjustment, accommodation, customization, conversion. **2** modification, adjustment, conversion, alteration; see also VERSION 2, 3.

adapter /ədáptor/ *n.* (also **adaptor**) **1** a device for making equipment compatible. **2** *Brit.* a device for connecting several electrical plugs to one socket. **3** a person who adapts.

adaxial /adákseeəl/ *adj. Bot.* facing toward the stem of a plant, esp. of the upper side of a leaf (cf. ABAXIAL). [AD- + AXIAL]

add /ad/ *v.tr.* **1** join (one thing to another) as an increase or supplement (*add your efforts to mine*; *add insult to injury*). **2** put together (two or more numbers) to find a number denoting their combined value. **3** say in addition (*added a remark*; *added that I was wrong*; *"What's more, I don't like it,"* he *added*). □ **add in** include. **add-on** something added to an existing object or quantity. **add to** increase; be a further item among (*this adds to our difficulties*). **add up 1** find the total of. **2** (foll. by *to*) amount to; constitute (*adds up to a disaster*). **3** *colloq.* make sense; be understandable. □□ **added** *adj.* [ME f. L *addere* (as AD-, *dare* put)]

■ **1** join, unite, aggregate, combine, annex, attach, affix, append, tack on, *archaic* adjoin. **2** add up, total, sum (up), combine, count up, reckon (up), tot (up). **3** continue, go on. □ **add to** increase, enlarge, amplify, augment, supplement, complement; extend, expand, lengthen. **add up 1** see ADD 2 above. **2** amount to, constitute, be equivalent to, signify, mean. **3** make sense, hang together, cohere, be coherent *or* understandable, tie in. □□ **added** see EXTRA *adj.*

addax /ádaks/ *n.* a large antelope, *Addax nasomaculatus*, of North Africa, with twisted horns. [L f. an African word]

addendum /ədéndəm/ *n.* (*pl.* **addenda** /-də/) **1** a thing (usu. something omitted) to be added, esp. (in *pl.*) as additional matter at the end of a book. **2** an appendix; an addition. [L, gerundive of *addere* ADD]

■ see ADDITION 2.

adder /ádər/ *n.* **1** any of various small venomous snakes, esp. the common European viper, *Vipera berus*. **2** any of various small N. American snakes similar to the viper. □ **adder's tongue** any fern of the genus *Ophioglossum*. [OE *nædre*: *n* lost in ME by wrong division of *a naddre*: cf. APRON, AUGER, UMPIRE]

addict *v. & n.* ● *v.tr. & refl.* /ədíkt/ (usu. foll. by *to*) devote or apply habitually or compulsively; make addicted. ● *n.* /ádikt/ **1** a person addicted to a habit, esp. one dependent on a (specified) drug (*drug addict*; *heroin addict*). **2** *colloq.* an enthusiastic devotee of a sport or pastime (*movie addict*). [L *addicere* assign (as AD-, *dicere* dict- say)]

■ *v.* (*be(come) addicted*) be(come) dependent, *sl.* be(come) hooked, have a monkey on one's back. ● *n.* **1** (habitual) user, drug addict, drug abuser, *colloq.* druggy, freak, tripper, pill popper, *sl.* junkie, doper, head, hype, pothead, acidhead, mainliner, hophead. **2** devotee, aficionado, fan, admirer, follower, adherent, supporter, enthusiast, hound, *colloq.* buff, maniac, *sl.* nut, freak, fiend, groupie.

addicted /ədíktid/ *adj.* (foll. by *to*) **1** dependent on as a habit; unable to do without (*addicted to heroin*; *addicted to smoking*). **2** devoted (*addicted to football*).

■ (*addicted to*) **1** dependent on, *sl.* hooked on. **2** see KEEN¹ 2.

addiction /ədíkshən/ *n.* the fact or process of being addicted, esp. the condition of taking a drug habitually and being unable to give it up without incurring adverse effects. [L *addictio*: see ADDICT]

■ see HABIT *n.* 2, 5.

addictive /ədíktiv/ *adj.* (of a drug, habit, etc.) causing addiction or dependence.

■ habit-forming, compulsive, obsessive, (*of a drug*) hard.

Addison's disease /ádisənz/ *n.* a disease characterized by progressive anemia and debility and brown discoloration of the skin. [T. *Addison*, Engl. physician d. 1860, who first recognized it]

addition /ədíshən/ *n.* **1** the act or process of adding or being added. **2** a person or thing added (*a useful addition to the team*). □ **in addition** moreover; furthermore; as well. **in addition to** as well as; as something added to. [ME f. OF *addition* or f. L *additio* (as ADD)]

■ **1** increase, augmentation, union, combination, attachment, annexation, extension; reckoning, calculation, computation. **2** addendum, appendix, appendage, supplement, increment; extra, add-on; annex, extension, wing. □ **in addition** moreover, furthermore, additionally, to boot, in *or* into the bargain, too, also, as well, *archaic* withal. **in addition to** as well as, besides, beyond, over and above, on top of.

additional /ədíshənəl/ *adj.* added; extra; supplementary. □□ **additionally** *adv.*

■ see EXTRA *adj.*

additive /áditiv/ *n. & adj.* ● *n.* a thing added, esp. a substance added to another so as to give it specific qualities (*food additive*). ● *adj.* **1** characterized by addition (*additive process*). **2** to be added. [LL *additivus* (as ADD)]

addle /ád'l/ *v. & adj.* ● *v.* **1** *tr.* muddle; confuse. **2** *intr.* (of an egg) become addled. ● *adj.* **1** muddled; unsound (*addlebrained*). **2** empty; vain. **3** (of an egg) addled. [OE *adela* filth, used as adj., then as verb]

addled /ád'ld/ *adj.* **1** (of an egg) rotten, producing no chick. **2** muddled. [ADDLE *adj.*, assim. to past part. form]

addn. *abbr.* addition.

address /ədrés/ *n. & v.* ● *n.* **1** (also /ádres/) **a** the place where a person lives or an organization is situated. **b** particulars of this, esp. for postal purposes. **c** *Computing* the location of an item of stored information. **2** a discourse delivered to an audience. **3** skill; dexterity; readiness. **4** (in *pl.*) a courteous approach; courtship (*pay one's addresses to*). **5** *archaic* manner in conversation. ● *v.tr.* **1** write directions for delivery (esp. the name and postal location of the intended recipient) on (an envelope, package, etc.). **2** direct in speech or writing (remarks, a protest, etc.). **3** speak or write to, esp. formally (*addressed the audience*; *asked me how to address the ambassador*). **4** direct one's attention to. **5** *Golf* take aim at or prepare to hit (the ball). □ **address oneself to 1** speak or write to. **2** attend to. □□ **addresser** *n.* [ME f. OF *adresser* ult. f. L (as AD-, *directus* DIRECT): (n.) perh. f. F *adresse*]

/.../ pronunciation	● part of speech
□ phrases, idioms, and compounds	
□□ derivatives	■ synonym section
cross-references appear in SMALL CAPITALS or *italics*	

■ *n.* **1 a** location, whereabouts, position, site, situation. **2** speech, talk, oration, lecture, paper, declaration; sermon, *literary* discourse. ● *v.* **2** direct, send, post, mail; aim, focus, level, point, train, turn. **3** speak *or* talk *or* write to, deliver *or* give a speech to, present a paper to, lecture; greet, hail, accost, approach, salute, introduce oneself to, address oneself to. **4** focus on, aim at, turn to, concentrate on, converge on, zero in on; come *or* get to grips with. □ **address oneself to 1** see ADDRESS *v.* 3 above. **2** devote *or* direct *or* apply oneself to, take care of, occupy oneself with, concentrate on, concern oneself with; see also ADDRESS *v.* 4 above, ATTEND 4.

addressee /ádreseé/ *n.* the person to whom something (esp. a letter) is addressed.

Addressograph /ədrésəgraf/ *n. propr.* a machine for printing addresses on envelopes.

adduce /ədoõs, ədyoõs/ *v.tr.* cite as an instance or as proof or evidence. □□ **adducible** *adj.* [L *adducere adduct-* (as AD-, *ducere* lead)]

adduct /ədúkt/ *v.tr.* draw toward a middle line, esp. draw (a limb) toward the middle line of the body. □□ **adduction** /-dúkshən/ *n.*

adductor /ədúktər/ *n.* (in full **adductor muscle**) any muscle that moves one part of the body toward another or toward the middle line of the body.

-ade[1] /ayd/ *suffix* forming nouns: **1** an action done (*blockade*; *tirade*). **2** the body concerned in an action or process (*cavalcade*). **3** the product or result of a material or action (*arcade*; *lemonade*; *masquerade*). [from or after F -*ade* f. Prov., Sp., or Port. -*ada* or It. -*ata* f. L -*ata* fem. sing. past part. of verbs in -*are*]

-ade[2] /ayd/ *suffix* forming nouns (*decade*) (cf. -AD[1]). [F -*ade* f. Gk -*as* -*ada*]

-ade[3] /ayd/ *suffix* forming nouns: **1** = -ADE[1] (*brocade*). **2** a person concerned (*renegade*). [Sp. or Port. -*ado*, masc. form of -*ada*: see -ADE[1]]

adenine /ád'neen, -in/ *n.* a purine derivative found in all living tissue as a component base of DNA or RNA. [G *Adenin* formed as ADENOIDS: see -INE[4]]

adenoids /ád'noydz/ *n.pl. Med.* a mass of enlarged lymphatic tissue between the back of the nose and the throat, often hindering speaking and breathing in the young. □□ **adenoidal** /-nóyd'l/ *adj.* **adenoidally** *adv.* [Gk *adēn* -*enos* gland + -OID]

adenoma /ád'nómə/ *n.* (*pl.* **adenomas** or **adenomata** /-mətə/) a glandlike benign tumor. [mod.L f. Gk *adēn* gland + -OMA]

adenosine /ədénəseen/ *n.* a nucleoside of adenine and ribose present in all living tissue in a combined form (see ADP, AMP, ATP). [ADENINE + RIBOSE]

adept *adj. & n.* ● *adj.* /ədépt/ (foll. by *at*, *in*) thoroughly proficient. ● *n.* /ádept/ a skilled performer; an expert. □□ **adeptly** *adv.* **adeptness** *n.* [L *adeptus* past part. of *adipisci* attain]

■ *adj.* versed, proficient, skilled, well-skilled, expert, accomplished, talented, skillful, adroit, dexterous, able, masterful, masterly, polished. ● *n.* expert, master, specialist, authority, proficient, old hand, esp. *Brit. colloq.* dab hand. □□ **adeptly** see WELL[1] *adv.* 3. **adeptness** see *proficiency* (PROFICIENT).

adequate /ádikwət/ *adj.* **1** sufficient; satisfactory. **2** (foll. by *to*) proportionate. **3** barely sufficient. □□ **adequacy** *n.* **adequately** *adv.* [L *adaequatus* past part. of *adaequare* make equal (as AD-, *aequus* equal)]

■ sufficient, enough; satisfactory, fitting, fitted, equal, suitable, proper, qualified, competent, good enough, up to par, *colloq.* up to snuff; passable, fair, fair to middling, middling, average, tolerable, (barely) acceptable, (barely) satisfactory, all right, not (at all) bad, so-so, *comme ci comme ça*, *colloq.* OK, not that *or* too bad, no great shakes. □□ **adequacy** see *fitness* (FIT[1]). **adequately** see FAIRLY 2.

à deux /aa dő/ *adv. & adj.* **1** for two. **2** between two. [F]

ad fin. /ad fín/ *abbr.* at or near the end. [L *ad finem*]

adhere /ədheér/ *v.intr.* **1** (usu. foll. by *to*) (of a substance) stick fast to a surface, another substance, etc. **2** (foll. by *to*) behave according to; follow in detail (*adhered to our plan*). **3** (foll. by *to*) give support or allegiance. [F *adhérer* or L *adhaerēre* (as AD-, *haerēre haes-* stick)]

■ **1** see STICK[2] 4. **2** (*adhere to*) see FOLLOW 5.

adherent /ədheérənt, -hér-/ *n. & adj.* ● *n.* **1** a supporter of a party, person, etc. **2** a devotee of an activity. ● *adj.* **1** (foll. by *to*) faithfully observing a rule, etc. **2** (often foll. by *to*) (of a substance) sticking fast. □□ **adherence** /-rəns/ *n.* [F *adhérent* (as ADHERE)]

■ *n.* **1** see SUPPORTER. **2** see FOLLOWER. □□ **adherence** see DEDICATION 1.

adhesion /ədheézhən/ *n.* **1** the act or process of adhering. **2** the capacity of a substance to stick fast. **3** *Med.* an unnatural union of surfaces due to inflammation. **4** the maintenance of contact between the wheels of a vehicle and the road. **5** the giving of support or allegiance. ¶ More common in physical senses (e.g., *the glue has good adhesion*), with *adherence* used in abstract senses (e.g., *adherence to principles*). [F *adhésion* or L *adhaesio* (as ADHERE)]

■ **2** see *tenacity* (TENACIOUS). **4** see TRACTION 3. **5** see DEVOTION 1.

adhesive /ədheésiv, -ziv/ *adj. & n.* ● *adj.* sticky; enabling surfaces or substances to adhere to one another. ● *n.* an adhesive substance, esp. one used to stick other substances together. □□ **adhesively** *adv.* **adhesiveness** *n.* [F *adhésif* -*ive* (as ADHERE)]

■ *adj.* see STICKY *adj.* 1. ● *n.* see GLUE *n.*

adhibit /ədhíbit/ *v.tr.* (**adhibited**, **adhibiting**) **1** affix. **2** apply or administer (a remedy). □□ **adhibition** /ádhibíshən/ *n.* [L *adhibēre adhibit-* (as AD-, *habēre* have)]

ad hoc /ád hók/ *adv. & adj.* for a particular (usu. exclusive) purpose (*an ad hoc appointment*). [L, = to this]

ad hominem /ad hóminem, hó-/ *adv. & adj.* **1** relating to or associated with a particular person. **2** (of an argument) appealing to the emotions and not to reason. [L, = to the person]

adiabatic /ádeeəbátik, áydīə-/ *adj. & n. Physics* ● *adj.* **1** impassable to heat. **2** occurring without heat entering or leaving the system. ● *n.* a curve or formula for adiabatic phenomena. □□ **adiabatically** *adv.* [Gk *adiabatos* impassable (as A-[1], *diabainō* pass)]

adiantum /ádeeántəm/ *n.* **1** any fern of the genus *Adiantum*, e.g., maidenhair. **2** (in general use) a spleenwort. [L f. Gk *adianton* maidenhair (as A-[1], *diantos* wettable)]

adieu /ədyőő, ədőő/ *int. & n.* ● *int.* good-bye. ● *n.* (*pl.* **adieus** or **adieux** /ədyőőz, ədőőz/) a good-bye. [ME f. OF f. *à* to + *Dieu* God]

ad infinitum /ad ínfinítəm/ *adv.* without limit; for ever. [L]

ad interim /ad íntərim/ *adv. & adj.* for the meantime. [L]

adios /áadee-ős, ádee-/ *int.* good-bye. [Sp. *adiós* f. *a* to + *Dios* God]

adipocere /ádipōseér/ *n.* a grayish fatty or soapy substance generated in dead bodies subjected to moisture. [F *adipocire* f. L *adeps adipis* fat + F *cire* wax f. L *cera*]

adipose /ádipōs/ *adj.* of or characterized by fat; fatty. □ **adipose tissue** fatty connective tissue in animals. □□ **adiposity** /-pósitee/ *n.* [mod.L *adiposus* f. *adeps adipis* fat]

adit /ádit/ *n.* **1** a horizontal entrance or passage in a mine. **2** a means of approach. [L *aditus* (as AD-, *itus* f. *ire it-* go)]

adjacent /əjáysənt/ *adj.* (often foll. by *to*) lying near or adjoining. □□ **adjacency** /-sənsee/ *n.* [ME f. L *adjacēre* (as AD-, *jacēre* lie)]

■ see *adjoining* (ADJOIN 1).

adjective /ájiktiv/ *n. & adj.* ● *n.* a word or phrase naming an attribute, added to or grammatically related to a noun to modify it or describe it. ● *adj.* additional; not standing by itself; dependent. □□ **adjectival** /ájiktív'l/ *adj.* **adjectivally** *adv.* [ME f. OF *adjectif* -*ive* ult. f. L *adjicere adject-* (as AD-, *jacere* throw)]

adjoin /əjóyn/ *v.tr.* **1** (often as **adjoining** *adj.*) be next to and joined with. **2** *archaic* = ADD 1. [ME f. OF *ajoindre*, *ajoign-* f. L *adjungere adjunct-* (as AD-, *jungere* join)]

■ **1** see BORDER *v.* 3a; (**adjoining**) neighboring, contiguous, adjacent, abutting, bordering, next.

adjourn /əjə́rn/ *v.* **1** *tr.* **a** put off; postpone. **b** break off (a meeting, discussion, etc.) with the intention of resuming later. **2** *intr.* of persons at a meeting: **a** break off proceedings and disperse. **b** (foll. by *to*) transfer the meeting to another place. [ME f. OF *ajorner* (as AD-, *jorn* day ult. f. L *diurnus* DIURNAL): cf. JOURNAL, JOURNEY]
■ **1 a** see POSTPONE. **b** see DISSOLVE *v.* 3a.

adjournment /əjə́rnmənt/ *n.* adjourning or being adjourned.

adjudge /əjúj/ *v.tr.* **1** adjudicate (a matter). **2** (often foll. by *that* + clause, or *to* + infin.) pronounce judicially. **3** (foll. by *to*) award judicially. **4** *archaic* condemn. [ME f. OF *ajuger* f. L *adjudicare*: see ADJUDICATE]
■ **1** see JUDGE *v.* 5b. **2 a** see JUDGE *v.* 1a, 3.

adjudicate /əjṓodikayt/ *v.* **1** *intr.* act as judge in a competition, court, tribunal, etc. **2** *tr.* **a** decide judicially regarding (a claim, etc.). **b** (foll. by *to be* + compl.) pronounce (*was adjudicated to be bankrupt*). □□ **adjudication** /-dikáyshən/ *n.* **adjudicative** *adj.* **adjudicator** *n.* [L *adjudicare* (as AD-, *judicare* f. *judex -icis* judge)]
■ **1** see JUDGE *v.* 5b. **2 a** see JUDGE *v.* 1a, 3.

adjunct /ájungkt/ *n.* **1** (foll. by *to, of*) a subordinate or incidental thing. **2** an assistant; a subordinate person, esp. one with temporary appointment only. **3** *Gram.* a word or phrase used to explain or amplify the predicate, subject, etc. □□ **adjunctive** /əjúngktiv/ *adj.* **adjunctively** /əjúngktivlee/ *adv.* [L *adjunctus*: see ADJOIN]
■ **1** see ACCESSORY *n.* 1, EXTENSION 4. **2** see ASSISTANT 2.

adjure /əjṓor/ *v.tr.* (usu. foll. by *to* + infin.) charge or request (a person) solemnly or earnestly, esp. under oath. □□ **adjuration** /ájṓoráyshən/ *n.* **adjuratory** /-rətawree/ *adj.* [ME f. L *adjurare* (as AD-, *jurare* swear) in LL sense 'put a person to an oath']

adjust /əjúst/ *v.* **1** *tr.* **a** arrange; put in the correct order or position. **b** regulate, esp. by a small amount. **2** *tr.* (usu. foll. by *to*) make suitable. **3** *tr.* harmonize (discrepancies). **4** *tr.* assess (loss or damages). **5** *intr.* (usu. foll. by *to*) make oneself suited to; become familiar with (*adjust to one's surroundings*). □□ **adjustable** *adj.* **adjustability** /əjústəbílitee/ *n.* **adjuster** *n.* **adjustment** *n.* [F *adjuster* f. OF *ajoster* ult. f. L *juxta* near]
■ **1** put in (working) order, put *or* set to rights, (fine-)tune, fix, arrange, rearrange, reset, set, reposition, change, alter, modify, regulate, calibrate; repair. **2** see ADAPT 1b. **3** set right, arrange, settle, harmonize, reconcile, resolve, set *or* put to rights; redress, rectify, correct, patch up. **4** see EVALUATE 1. **5** (*adjust to*) adapt to, accommodate oneself to, accustom oneself to, familiarize oneself with, inure oneself to; get used to, acclimatize to, reconcile oneself to, acclimate to. □□ **adjustable** see ADAPTABLE 2. **adjustability** see *flexibility* (FLEXIBLE). **adjustment** alteration, setting, regulation, correction, calibration, tuning; arrangement, coordination, alignment, harmonization.

adjutant /ájət'nt/ *n.* **1 a** *Mil.* an officer who assists superior officers by communicating orders, conducting correspondence, etc. **b** an assistant. **2** (in full **adjutant stork** or **bird**) a giant Indian stork. □ **Adjutant General** a high-ranking Army or National Guard administrative officer. □□ **adjutancy** /-t'nsee/ *n.* [L *adjutare* frequent. of *adjuvare*: see ADJUVANT]

adjuvant /ájəvənt/ *adj.* & *n.* ● *adj.* helpful; auxiliary. ● *n.* an adjuvant person or thing. [F *adjuvant* or L *adjuvare* (as AD-, *juvare jut-* help)]

Adlerian /adléereeən/ *adj.* of or relating to A. Adler, Austrian psychologist d. 1937, or his system of psychology.

ad lib /ád líb/ *v., adj., adv.,* & *n.* ● *v.intr.* (**ad libbed, ad libbing**) speak or perform without formal preparation; improvise. ● *adj.* improvised. ● *adv.* as one pleases; to any desired extent. ● *n.* something spoken or played extempore. [abbr. of AD LIBITUM]
■ *v.* see IMPROVISE 1. ● *adj.* see EXTEMPORANEOUS.

ad libitum /ad líbitəm/ *adv.* = AD LIB *adv.* [L, = according to pleasure]

ad litem /ad lítem/ *adj.* (of a guardian, etc.) appointed for a lawsuit. [L]

ad loc *abbr.* to or at that place. [L *ad locum*]

Adm. *abbr.* (preceding a name) Admiral.

adman /ádman/ *n.* (*pl.* **admen**) *colloq.* a person who produces advertisements commercially.

admass /ádmas/ *n.* esp. *Brit.* the section of the community that is regarded as readily influenced by advertising and mass communication.

admeasure /admézhər/ *v.tr.* apportion; assign in due shares. □□ **admeasurement** *n.* [ME f. OF *amesurer* f. med.L *admensurare* (as AD-, MEASURE)]

admin /ádmin/ *n. Brit. colloq.* administration. [abbr.]

adminicle /ədmínikəl/ *n.* **1** a thing that helps. **2** (in Scottish law) collateral evidence of the contents of a missing document. □□ **adminicular** /ádminíkyōōlər/ *adj.* [L *adminiculum* prop]

administer /ədmínistər/ *v.* **1** *tr.* attend to the running of (business affairs, etc.); manage. **2** *tr.* **a** be responsible for the implementation of (the law, justice, punishment, etc.). **b** *Eccl.* give out, or perform the rites of (a sacrament). **c** (usu. foll. by *to*) direct the taking of (an oath). **3** *tr.* **a** provide; apply (a remedy). **b** give; deliver (a rebuke). **4** *intr.* act as administrator. □□ **administrable** *adj.* [ME f. OF *aministrer* f. L *administrare* (as AD-, MINISTER)]
■ **1** administrate, manage, control, run, direct, conduct, superintend, supervise, oversee, preside over, head, look after. **2 a** execute, carry out, discharge, deal out, dispense; apply, implement. **3 a** dispense, apply, supply, furnish, give (out), provide (with), distribute, deliver, deal, hand out, *literary* mete out. **b** see DELIVER 7. □□ **administrable** manageable, controllable; executable, dischargeable, dispensable.

administrate /ədmínistrayt/ *v.tr.* & *intr.* administer (esp. business affairs); act as an administrator. [L *administrare* (as ADMINISTER)]
■ see ADMINISTER 1.

administration /ədmínistráyshən/ *n.* **1** management of a business. **2** the management of public affairs; government. **3** the government in power. **4 a** a President's period of office. **b** a President's advisers, cabinet officials, and their subordinates. **5** *Law* the management of another person's estate. **6** (foll. by *of*) **a** the administering of justice, an oath, etc. **b** application of remedies. [ME f. OF *administration* or L *administratio* (as ADMINISTRATE)]
■ **1** management, direction, conduct, supervision, oversight, superintendence, regulation, charge. **2, 3** authority, management, ministry, government, leadership, *derog.* regime. **4 a** presidency, term, office, rule. **6** dispensation, provision, delivery, distribution, application.

administrative /ədmínistráytiv, -trətiv/ *adj.* concerning or relating to the management of affairs. □□ **administratively** *adv.* [F *administratif -ive* or L *administrativus* (as ADMINISTRATION)]

administrator /ədmínistraytər/ *n.* **1** a person who administers a business or public affairs. **2** a person capable of organizing (*is no administrator*). **3** *Law* a person appointed to manage the estate of a person who has died intestate. **4** a person who performs official duties in some sphere, e.g., in religion. □□ **administratorship** *n.* **administratrix** *n.* [L (as ADMINISTER)]

admirable /ádmərəbəl/ *adj.* **1** deserving admiration. **2** excellent. □□ **admirably** *adv.* [F f. L *admirabilis* (as ADMIRE)]
■ **1** see PRAISEWORTHY. **2** wonderful, awe-inspiring, excellent, estimable, splendid, superb, marvelous, superior, first-rate, first-class, of the first water, fine, *colloq.* top-drawer, ripsnorting, A1, smashing, magic; see also GREAT *adj.* 5. □□ **admirably** marvelously,

---

/.../ **pronunciation**	● **part of speech**
□ **phrases, idioms, and compounds**	
□□ **derivatives**	■ **synonym section**
cross-references appear in SMALL CAPITALS or *italics*	

wonderfully, superbly, excellently, splendidly, very *or* really well.

admiral /ádmərəl/ *n.* **1 a** the commander in chief of a country's navy. **b** a naval officer of high rank, the commander of a fleet or squadron. **2** any of various butterflies (*red admiral*; *white admiral*). □ **Admiral of the Fleet** an admiral of the highest rank in the British navy. **Fleet Admiral** an admiral of the highest rank in the US navy. □□ **admiralship** *n.* [ME f. OF *a*(*d*)*mira*(*i*)*l*, etc. f. med.L *a*(*d*)*miralis*, etc., f. Arab. *'amīr* commander (cf. AMIR), assoc. with ADMIRABLE]

Admiralty /ádmərəltee/ *n.* (*pl.* **-ies**) **1** (*hist.* except in titles) (in the UK) the department administering the Royal Navy. **2** (**admiralty**) *Law* trial and decision of maritime questions and offenses. □ **Admiralty Board** *hist.* (in the UK) a committee of the Ministry of Defence superintending the Royal Navy. [ME f. OF *admiral*(*i*)*té* (as ADMIRAL)]

admiration /ádmiráyshən/ *n.* **1** pleased contemplation. **2** respect; warm approval. **3** an object of this (*was the admiration of the whole town*). [F *admiration* or L *admiratio* (as ADMIRE)]
■ **1** wonder, awe, delight, pleasure. **2** esteem, (high) regard, appreciation, respect, approval, high opinion, approbation. **3** focus *or* center of attention, delight, sensation, cynosure.

admire /ədmír/ *v.tr.* **1** regard with approval, respect, or satisfaction. **2** express one's admiration of. [F *admirer* or L *admirari* (as AD-, *mirari* wonder at)]
■ **1** respect, approve of, esteem, regard *or* rate highly, look up to, revere, idolize, venerate, worship. **2** wonder at, delight in, *literary* marvel (at).

admirer /ədmírər/ *n.* **1** a woman's suitor. **2** a person who admires, esp. a fan of a famous person.
■ **1** beau, suitor, wooer; lover, sweetheart, boyfriend, darling, *poet.* swain. **2** devotee, aficionado, fan, supporter, enthusiast, adorer, adherent, follower, idolator, *sl.* groupie, wanna-be.

admiring /ədmíring/ *adj.* showing or feeling admiration (*an admiring follower*; *admiring glances*). □□ **admiringly** *adv.*

admissible /ədmísibəl/ *adj.* **1** (of an idea or plan) worth accepting or considering. **2** *Law* allowable as evidence. **3** (foll. by *to*) capable of being admitted. □□ **admissibility** /-bílitee/ *n.* [F *admissible* or med.L *admissibilis* (as ADMIT)]
■ see PERMISSIBLE.

admission /ədmíshən/ *n.* **1** an acknowledgment (*admission of error*; *admission that he was wrong*). **2 a** the process or right of entering or being admitted. **b** a charge for this (*admission is $5*). **3** a person admitted to a hospital. ¶ Has more general application in senses of ADMIT than *admittance*. [ME f. L *admissio* (as ADMIT)]
■ **1** acknowledgment, confession, concession, avowal, allowance, profession, declaration, disclosure, affirmation, divulgence, divulgement, revelation. **2 a** access, admittance, entrée, entry, entrance; reception, acceptance, appointment, institution, induction, installation, investiture. **b** ticket, (entry *or* entrance) fee, tariff, charge.

admit /ədmít/ *v.* (**admitted**, **admitting**) **1** *tr.* **a** (often foll. by *to be*, or *that* + clause) acknowledge; recognize as true. **b** accept as valid or true. **2** *intr.* **a** (foll. by *to*) acknowledge responsibility for (a deed, fault, etc.). **b** (foll. by *of*) allow for something to exist, have influence, etc. **3** *tr.* **a** allow (a person) entrance or access. **b** allow (a person) to be a member of (a class, group, etc.) or to share in (a privilege, etc.). **c** (of a hospital, etc.) bring in (a person) for inpatient treatment. **4** *tr.* (of an enclosed space) have room for; accommodate. **5** *intr.* (foll. by *of*) allow as possible. □□ **admittable** *adj.* [ME f. L *admittere admiss-* (as AD-, *mittere* send)]
■ **1** acknowledge, accept, concede, allow, grant, recognize, take cognizance of, *formal* aver. **2 a** (*admit to*) confess, own (up to); concede, divulge, reveal, acknowledge, declare. **b** (*admit of*) allow, permit, grant, tolerate, *literary* brook. **3** let in, allow to enter, give access to, take *or* allow in; accept, receive. **4** accommodate, hold, receive, embrace.

admittance /ədmít'ns/ *n.* **1** the right or process of admitting or being admitted, usu. to a place (*no admittance except on*

business). **2** *Electr.* the reciprocal of impedance. ¶ A more formal and technical word than *admission*.
■ **1** leave *or* permission to enter, entry, admission, entrance, access, entrée.

admittedly /ədmítidlee/ *adv.* as an acknowledged fact (*admittedly there are problems*).

admix /admíks/ *v.* **1** *tr.* & *intr.* (foll. by *with*) mingle. **2** *tr.* add as an ingredient.

admixture /admíkschər/ *n.* **1** a thing added, esp. a minor ingredient. **2** the act of adding this. [L *admixtus* past part. of *admiscēre* (as AD-, *miscēre* mix)]

admonish /ədmónish/ *v.tr.* **1** reprove. **2** (foll. by *to* + infin., or *that* + clause) urge. **3** give earnest advice to. **4** (foll. by *of*) warn. □□ **admonishment** *n.* **admonition** /ádməníshən/ *n.* **admonitory** *adj.* [ME f. OF *amonester* ult. f. L *admonēre* (as AD-, *monēre monit-* warn)]
■ **1** see REPRIMAND *v.* **2** see URGE *v.* 2. **3** see ADVISE 1, 2. **4** see WARN.

ad nauseam /ad náwzeeəm/ *adv.* to an excessive or disgusting degree. [L, = to sickness]

adnominal /adnóminəl/ *adj. Gram.* attached to a noun. [L *adnomen -minis* (added name)]

ado /ədōō/ *n.* (*pl.* **ados**) fuss; busy activity; trouble; difficulty. □ **without more** (or **further**) **ado** immediately. [orig. in *much ado* = much to do, f. north. ME *at do* (= to do) f. ON *at* AT as sign of infin. + DO[1]]

-ado /áadō/ *suffix* forming nouns (*desperado*) (cf. -ADE[3]). [Sp. or Port. *-ado* f. L *-atus* past part. of verbs in *-are*]

adobe /ədōbee/ *n.* **1** a sun-dried brick of clay and straw. **2** the clay used for making such bricks. **3** a structure of such bricks. [Sp. f. Arab.]

adolescent /ádəlésənt/ *adj.* & *n.* ● *adj.* between childhood and adulthood. ● *n.* an adolescent person. □□ **adolescence** /-səns/ *n.* [ME f. OF f. L *adolescere* grow up]
■ *adj.* teenage(d), young, youthful, maturing, pubescent; immature, callow, puerile, juvenile, jejune.
● *n.* teenager, juvenile, minor, stripling, youngster, teen, *colloq.* teenybopper, kid; see also YOUTH 4.
□□ **adolescence** puberty, teenage years, the awkward age.

Adonis /ədónis, ədó-/ *n.* a handsome young man. □ **Adonis blue** a kind of butterfly, *Lysandra bellargus*. [the name of a youth loved by Venus: L f. Gk f. Phoen. *adōn* lord]

adopt /ədópt/ *v.tr.* **1** take (a person) into a relationship, esp. another's child as one's own. **2** choose to follow (a course of action, etc.). **3** take over (a name, idea, etc.) and use as one's own. **4** *Brit.* choose as a candidate for office. **5** esp. *Brit.* (of a local authority) accept responsibility for the maintenance of (a road, etc.). **6** accept; formally approve (a report, accounts, etc.). □□ **adoption** /-dópshən/ *n.* [F *adopter* or L *adoptare* (as AD-, *optare* choose)]
■ **1** take (in), accept, take *or* accept as one's own. **2, 4** choose, select, take on, assume, embrace. **3** take (up *or* on *or* over), espouse; arrogate, appropriate. **6** see ACCEPT 2.

adoptive /ədóptiv/ *adj.* due to adoption (*adoptive son*; *adoptive father*). □□ **adoptively** *adv.* [ME f. OF *adoptif -ive* f. L *adoptivus* (as ADOPT)]

adorable /ədáwrəbəl/ *adj.* **1** deserving adoration. **2** *colloq.* delightful; charming. □□ **adorably** *adv.* [F f. L *adorabilis* (as ADORE)]
■ **1** lovable, wonderful, estimable, honorable, praiseworthy; beloved, loved, cherished, prized. **2** delightful, appealing, attractive, charming, lovely, enchanting, gorgeous, captivating, fetching; darling, sweet, dear, cunning, *colloq.* cute. □□ **adorably** delightfully, charmingly, enchantingly, gorgeously, attractively.

adore /ədáwr/ *v.tr.* **1** regard with honor and deep affection. **2 a** worship as divine. **b** *RC Ch.* offer reverence to. **3** *colloq.* like very much. □□ **adoration** /ádəráyshən/ *n.* **adoring** *adj.* **adoringly** *adv.* [ME f. OF *aourer* f. L *adorare* worship (as AD-, *orare* speak, pray)]
■ **1** esteem, honor, respect, admire; love, idolize, dote on. **2 a** worship, venerate, reverence, revere, exalt;

hallow. **3** cherish, fancy, revere, adulate; carry the *or a* torch for; be mad on *or* about, be addicted to, be crazy about; *colloq.* love, be in love with, be hooked on, have a crush on. □□ **adoration** see LOVE *n.* 1, REVERENCE *n.*

adorer /ədáwrər/ *n.* **1** a worshiper. **2** an ardent admirer.

adorn /ədáwrn/ *v.tr.* **1** add beauty or luster to; be an ornament to. **2** furnish with ornaments; decorate. □□ **adornment** *n.* [ME f. OF *ao(u)rner* f. L *adornare* (as AD-, *ornare* furnish, deck)]
■ see EMBELLISH 1.

ADP *abbr.* **1** adenosine diphosphate. **2** automatic data processing.

ad rem /ad rém/ *adv. & adj.* to the point; to the purpose. [L, = to the matter]

adrenal /ədréenəl/ *adj. & n.* ● *adj.* **1** at or near the kidneys. **2** of the adrenal glands. ● *n.* (in full **adrenal gland**) either of two ductless glands above the kidneys, secreting adrenaline. [AD- + RENAL]

adrenaline /ədrénəlin/ = EPINEPHRINE.

adrenocorticotrophic hormone /ədre͞enōkáwrtikōtrófik, -trŏ́fik/ *n.* (also **adrenocorticotropic** /-trópik, -trŏ́-/) a hormone secreted by the pituitary gland and stimulating the adrenal glands. ¶ Abbr.: **ACTH**. [ADRENAL + CORTEX + -TROPHIC, -TROPIC]

adrenocorticotrophin /ədre͞enōkáwrtikōtrófin, -trŏ́fin/ *n.* (also **adrenocorticotropin** /-trópin, -trŏ́-/) = ADRENOCORTICOTROPHIC HORMONE. [ADRENOCORTICOTROPHIC (HORMONE) + -IN]

adrift /ədríft/ *adv. & predic.adj.* **1** drifting. **2** at the mercy of circumstances. **3** *Brit. colloq.* **a** unfastened. **b** out of touch. **c** absent without leave. **d** (often foll. by *of*) failing to reach a target. **e** out of order. **f** ill-informed. [A² + DRIFT]

adroit /ədróyt/ *adj.* dexterous; skillful. □□ **adroitly** *adv.* **adroitness** *n.* [F f. *à droit* according to right]
■ see SKILLFUL.

adsorb /adsáwrb, -záwrb/ *v.tr.* (usu. of a solid) hold (molecules of a gas or liquid or solute) to its surface, causing a thin film to form. □□ **adsorbable** *adj.* **adsorbent** *adj. & n.* **adsorption** *n.* (also **adsorbtion**). [AD-, after ABSORB]

adsorbate /adsáwrbayt, -bit, -záwr-/ *n.* a substance adsorbed.

adsuki var. of ADZUKI.

adulate /ájəlayt/ *v.tr.* flatter obsequiously. □□ **adulation** /-láyshən/ *n.* **adulator** *n.* **adulatory** /-lətáwree/ *adj.* [L *adulari adulat-* fawn on]
■ see IDOLIZE.

adult /ədúlt, ádult/ *adj. & n.* ● *adj.* **1** mature; grown-up. **2 a** of or for adults (*adult education*). **b** *euphem.* sexually explicit; indecent (*adult films*). ● *n.* **1** an adult person. **2** *Law* a person who has reached the age of majority. □□ **adulthood** *n.* **adultly** *adv.* [L *adultus* past part. of *adolescere* grow up: cf. ADOLESCENT]
■ *adj.* **1** mature, grown(-up), full-grown, matured, of age, having reached the age of discretion. **2 b** see INDECENT. ● *n.* **1** grown-up. □□ **adulthood** see *maturity* (MATURE). **adultly** maturely, sensibly.

adulterant /ədúltərənt/ *adj. & n.* ● *adj.* used in adulterating. ● *n.* an adulterant substance.

adulterate *v. & adj.* ● *v.tr.* /ədúltərayt/ debase (esp. foods) by adding other or inferior substances. ● *adj.* /ədúltərət/ spurious; debased; counterfeit. □□ **adulteration** /-ráyshən/ *n.* **adulterator** *n.* [L *adulterare adulterat-* corrupt]
■ *v.* falsify, corrupt, alloy, debase, spoil, water (down), weaken, dilute, bastardize, contaminate, pollute, taint, doctor, cut. ● *adj.* see SPURIOUS. □□ **adulteration** see *pollution* (POLLUTE).

adulterer /ədúltərər/ *n.* (*fem.* **adulteress** /-təris/) a person who commits adultery. [obs. *adulter* (v.) f. OF *avoutrer* f. L *adulterare*: see ADULTERATE]

adulterine /ədúltərin, -reen/ *adj.* **1** illegal; unlicensed. **2** spurious. **3** born of adultery. [L *adulterinus* f. *adulter*: see ADULTERY]

adulterous /ədúltərəs/ *adj.* of or involved in adultery. □□ **adulterously** *adv.* [ME f. *adulter*: see ADULTERER]

adultery /ədúltəree/ *n.* voluntary sexual intercourse between a married person and a person (married or not) other than his or her spouse. [ME f. OF *avoutrie*, etc., f. *avoutre* adulterer f. L *adulter*, assim. to L *adulterium*]

adumbrate /ádumbrayt/ *v.tr.* **1** indicate faintly. **2** represent in outline. **3** foreshadow; typify. **4** overshadow. □□ **adumbration** /-bráyshən/ *n.* **adumbrative** /ədúmbrətiv/ *adj.* [L *adumbrare* (as AD-, *umbrare* f. *umbra* shade)]

ad valorem /ad vəláwrəm/ *adv. & adj.* (of taxes) in proportion to the estimated value of the goods concerned. [L, = according to the value]

advance /ədváns/ *v., n., & adj.* ● *v.* **1** *tr. & intr.* move or put forward. **2** *intr.* make progress. **3** *tr.* **a** pay (money) before it is due. **b** lend (money). **4** *tr.* give active support to; promote (a person, cause, or plan). **5** *tr.* put forward (a claim or suggestion). **6** *tr.* cause (an event) to occur at an earlier date (*advanced the meeting three hours*). **7** *tr.* raise (a price). **8** *intr.* rise (in price). **9** *tr.* (as **advanced** *adj.*) **a** far on in progress (*the work is well advanced*). **b** ahead of the times (*advanced ideas*). ● *n.* **1** an act of going forward. **2** progress. **3** a payment made before the due time. **4** a loan. **5** (esp. in *pl.*; often foll. by *to*) an amorous or friendly approach. **6** a rise in price. ● *attrib.adj.* done or supplied beforehand (*advance warning*; *advance copy*). □ **advance guard** a body of soldiers preceding the main body of an army. **advance on** approach threateningly. **in advance** ahead in place or time. □□ **advancer** *n.* [ME f. OF *avancer* f. LL *abante* in front f. L *ab* away + *ante* before: (n.) partly through F *avance*]
■ *v.* **1, 2** move, move *or* put *or* push *or* go forward(s), move *or* send on(ward), go *or* push *or* press on, proceed, get ahead, make progress, gain ground, forge ahead, continue, keep going; move up, promote, be promoted, rise. **3** prepay; lend, loan. **4** support, further, promote, forward, help, aid, abet, assist; benefit, improve; contribute to. **5** see *put forward* (PUT¹). **6** bring forward. **7** see RAISE *v.* 3. **8** see RISE *v.* 7. **9** (**advanced**) **a** well-ahead, far on; nearing completion, nearly finished. **b** see PROGRESSIVE *adj.* 3. ● *n.* **1, 2** progress, progression, forward movement, development; headway; improvement, betterment, furtherance; breakthrough, step forward. **3, 4** prepayment, deposit; loan. **5** see APPROACH *n.* 4. **6** rise, increase, appreciation, gain, addition, hike. □ **advance guard** avant-garde; see also SPEARHEAD *n.* **in advance** beforehand, ahead (of time), before, previously, early, earlier; in front, ahead, beyond.

advancement /ədvánsmənt/ *n.* the promotion of a person, cause, or plan. [ME f. F *avancement* f. *avancer* (as ADVANCE)]
■ see *promotion* (PROMOTE).

advantage /ədvántij/ *n. & v.* ● *n.* **1** a beneficial feature; a favorable circumstance. **2** benefit; profit (*is not to your advantage*). **3** (often foll. by *over*) a better position; superiority in a particular respect. **4** (in tennis) the next point won after deuce. ● *v.tr.* **1** be beneficial or favorable to. **2** further; promote. □ **have the advantage of** be in a better position in some respect than. **take advantage of 1** make good use of (a favorable circumstance). **2** exploit or outwit (a person), esp. unfairly. **3** *euphem.* seduce. **to advantage** in a way which exhibits the merits (*was seen to advantage*). **turn to advantage** benefit from. □□ **advantageous** /ádvəntáyjəs/ *adj.* **advantageously** *adv.* [ME f. OF *avantage*, *avantager* f. *avant* in front f. LL *abante*: see ADVANCE]
■ *n.* **1, 3** strength, benefit, feature, attraction, selling point, asset, plus, bonus, added extra, convenience, improvement, boon, appeal, pull, beauty; superiority, upper hand, dominance, edge, head start, odds on one's side, trump (card); sway; *archaic* vantage. **2** gain, profit, benefit, interest, betterment, advancement; use, usefulness, utility, help, service. ● *v.* **1, 2** see BENEFIT *v.* 1. □ **take advantage of 1** see PROFIT *v.* 2. **2** see

EXPLOIT *v*. **3** see SEDUCE 1. **to advantage** in a good light, (more) favorably, advantageously. **turn to advantage** see PROFIT *v*. 2. □□ **advantageous** profitable, worthwhile, gainful, opportune, beneficial, helpful, favorable, propitious, useful, valuable. **advantageously** see *favorably* (FAVORABLE).

advection /ədvékshən/ *n*. **1** *Meteorol.* transfer of heat by the horizontal flow of air. **2** horizontal flow of air or water. □□ **advective** *adj*. [L *advectio* f. *advehere* (as AD-, *vehere vect-* carry)]

Advent /ádvent/ *n*. **1** the season before Christmas, including the four preceding Sundays. **2** the coming or second coming of Christ. **3** (**advent**) the arrival, esp. of an important person or thing. □ **Advent calendar** a calendar for Advent, usu. of cardboard with flaps to open each day revealing a picture or scene. **Advent Sunday** the first Sunday in Advent. [OE f. OF *advent*, *auvent* f. L *adventus* arrival f. *advenire* (as AD-, *venire vent-* come)]
■ **3** see ARRIVAL 1.

Adventist /ádvéntist/ *n*. a member of a Christian sect that believes in the imminent second coming of Christ. □□ **Adventism** *n*.

adventitious /ádventíshəs/ *adj*. **1** accidental; casual. **2** added from outside. **3** *Biol.* formed accidentally or under unusual conditions. **4** *Law* (of property) coming from a stranger or by collateral succession rather than directly. □□ **adventitiously** *adv*. [L *adventicius* (as ADVENT)]

adventure /ədvénchər/ *n*. & *v*. ● *n*. **1** an unusual and exciting experience. **2** a daring enterprise; a hazardous activity. **3** enterprise (*the spirit of adventure*). **4** a commercial speculation. ● *v.intr.* **1** (often foll. by *into*, *upon*) dare to go or come. **2** (foll. by *on*, *upon*) dare to undertake. **3** incur risk; engage in adventure. □ **adventure playground** *Brit.* a playground where children are provided with functional materials for climbing on, building with, etc. □□ **adventuresome** *adj*. [ME f. OF *aventure*, *aventurer* f. L *adventurus* about to happen (as ADVENT)]
■ *n*. **1** experience, incident, event, occurrence, happening, episode. **2** exploit, escapade, affair, undertaking, feat, deed, enterprise; danger, peril, risk. **3** enterprise. **4** speculation, hazard, chance, risk, venture, enterprise. ● *v*. **1** (*adventure into* or *upon*) venture into *or* upon, brave. **2, 3** try one's luck (on *or* at), take a risk (on), gamble (on), wager (on), bet (on), *sl.* punt (on); dare. □□ **adventuresome** see ADVENTUROUS 1.

adventurer /ədvénchərər/ *n*. (*fem.* **adventuress** /-chəris/) **1** a person who seeks adventure, esp. for personal gain or enjoyment. **2** a financial speculator. [F *aventurier* (as ADVENTURE)]
■ **1** adventuress, soldier of fortune, swashbuckler, hero, heroine, daredevil. **2** speculator, punter, opportunist; adventuress, *colloq.* fortune hunter, *sl.* gold-digger.

adventurism /ədvénchərizəm/ *n*. a tendency to take risks, esp. in foreign policy. □□ **adventurist** *n*.

adventurous /ədvénchərəs/ *adj*. **1** rash; venturesome; enterprising. **2** characterized by adventures. □□ **adventurously** *adv*. **adventurousness** *n*. [ME f. OF *aventuros* (as ADVENTURE)]
■ **1** daring, bold, venturesome, adventuresome, audacious, fearless, intrepid, enterprising, undaunted, dauntless, unafraid, brave, courageous, valiant, heroic; rash, reckless, devil-may-care, foolhardy, hazardous, risky, daredevil, *literary* temerarious. **2** see EVENTFUL. □□ **adventurously** daringly, boldly, intrepidly, enterprisingly, fearlessly, undauntedly, dauntlessly, bravely, valiantly. **adventurousness** see DARING *n*.

adverb /ádvərb/ *n*. a word or phrase that modifies or qualifies another word (esp. an adjective, verb, or other adverb) or a group of words, expressing a relation of place, time, circumstance, manner, cause, degree, etc. (e.g., *gently, quite, then, there*). □□ **adverbial** /ədvə́rbeeəl/ *adj*. [F *adverbe* or L *adverbium* (as AD-, VERB)]

adversarial /ádvərsáireeəl/ *adj*. **1** involving conflict or opposition. **2** opposed; hostile. [ADVERSARY + -IAL]

■ **2** see ADVERSARY *adj*.

adversary /ádvərseree/ *n*. & *adj*. ● *n*. (*pl.* **-ies**) **1** an enemy. **2** an opponent in a sport or game; an antagonist. ● *adj*. opposed; antagonistic. [ME f. OF *adversarie* f. L *adversarius* f. *adversus*: see ADVERSE]
■ *n*. **1** enemy, opponent, antagonist; opposition, other side, esp. *poet.* or *formal* foe. **2** opponent, antagonist, competitor, rival, challenger, contender; opposition, other side, competition. ● *adj*. opposed, hostile, antagonistic, competitive, adversarial.

adversative /ədvə́rsətiv/ *adj*. (of words, etc.) expressing opposition or antithesis. □□ **adversatively** *adv*. [F *adversatif* -*ive* or LL *adversativus* f. *adversari* oppose f. *adversus*: see ADVERSE]

adverse /ádvərs, ád-/ *adj*. (often foll. by *to*) **1** contrary; hostile. **2** harmful; injurious. □□ **adversely** *adv*. **adverseness** *n*. [ME f. OF *advers* f. L *adversus* past part. of *advertere* (as AD-, *vertere vers-* turn)]
■ **1** see HOSTILE 2. **2** see INJURIOUS 1.

adversity /ədvə́rsitee/ *n*. (*pl.* **-ies**) **1** the condition of adverse fortune. **2** a misfortune. [ME f. OF *adversité* f. L *adversitas* -*tatis* (as ADVERSE)]
■ **1** see MISFORTUNE 1. **2** see MISFORTUNE 2.

advert[1] /ədvə́rt/ *v.intr.* (foll. by *to*) *literary* refer in speaking or writing. [ME f. OF *avertir* f. L *advertere*: see ADVERSE]
■ see REFER 7, 8.

advert[2] /ádvərt/ *n*. *Brit. colloq.* an advertisement. [abbr.]

advertise /ádvərtiz/ (also **advertize**) *v*. **1** *tr.* draw attention to or describe favorably (goods or services) in a public medium to promote sales. **2** *tr.* make generally or publicly known. **3** *intr.* (foll. by *for*) seek by public notice, esp. in a newspaper. **4** *tr.* (usu. foll. by *that* + clause) notify. □□ **advertiser** *n*. [ME f. OF *avertir* (stem *advertiss-*): see ADVERT[2]]
■ **1, 2** see PUBLICIZE. **4** see NOTIFY 2.

advertisement /ádvərtizmənt, ədvə́rtis-, -tiz-/ *n*. **1** a public notice or announcement, esp. one advertising goods or services in newspapers, on posters, or in broadcasts. **2** the act or process of advertising. **3** *archaic* a notice to readers in a book, etc. [earlier *avert-* f. F *avertissement* (as ADVERTISE)]
■ **1** notice, handbill, blurb, broadside, bill, circular, junk mail, jingle, brochure, poster, placard, classified advertisement, commercial, spot, puff, announcement, flyer, *colloq.* ad, plug, *Brit. colloq.* advert. **2** advertising, promotion, marketing; publicity; propaganda, ballyhoo, *colloq.* promo, plugging, boost, *sl.* hype.

advice /ədvís/ *n*. **1** words given or offered as an opinion or recommendation about future action or behavior. **2** information given; news. **3** formal notice of a transaction. **4** (in *pl.*) communications from a distance. □ **take advice** act according to advice given. [ME f. OF *avis* f. L *ad* to + *visum* past part. of *vidēre* see]
■ **1** counsel, guidance, recommendation, suggestion, tip, hint, opinion, view; warning, admonition. **2** information, news, intelligence, notice, notification; communication.

advisable /ədvízəbəl/ *adj*. **1** (of a course of action, etc.) to be recommended. **2** expedient. □□ **advisability** /-bílitee/ *n*. **advisably** *adv*.
■ recommendable, expedient, prudent, practical, sensible, sound, seemly, well, judicious, wise, intelligent, smart, proper, politic. □□ **advisability** see *prudence* (PRUDENT).

advise /ədvíz/ *v*. **1** *tr.* (also *absol.*) give advice to. **2** *tr.* recommend; offer as advice (*they advise caution; advised me to rest*). **3** *tr.* (usu. foll. by *of*, or *that* + clause) inform; notify. **4** *intr.* **a** (foll. by *with*) consult. **b** offer advice. [ME f. OF *aviser* f. L *ad* to + *visare* frequent. of *vidēre* see]
■ **1, 2** counsel, guide, take under one's wing, direct, steer; caution, admonish, warn; recommend, suggest, commend, tell; urge, exhort, encourage, *archaic* rede. **3** tell, notify, announce to, inform, apprise, make known to, intimate to, give news *or* word to, acquaint, *colloq.* let on to.

advised /ədvízd/ *adj*. **1** judicious (*well-advised*). **2** deliberate; considered. □□ **advisedly** /-zidlee/ *adv*.

adviser /ədvízər/ n. (also **advisor**) **1** a person who advises, esp. one appointed to do so and regularly consulted. **2** a person who advises students on education, careers, etc.
■ **1** counselor, mentor, guide, counsel, consultant, confidant(e), director, *Law* amicus curiae.

advisory /ədvízəree/ adj. & n. ● adj. **1** giving advice; constituted to give advice (*an advisory body*). **2** consisting in giving advice. ● n. (pl. **-ies**) an advisory statement, esp. a warning about bad weather, potential danger, etc.
■ adj. consultative, counseling, hortatory, hortative, admonitory, *literary* monitory. ● n. bulletin, notice, warning, admonition, announcement, prediction.

advocaat /ádvəkaat/ n. a liqueur of eggs, sugar, and brandy. [Du., = ADVOCATE (being orig. an advocate's drink)]

advocacy /ádvəkəsee/ n. **1** (usu. foll. by *of*) verbal support or argument for a cause, policy, etc. **2** the function of an advocate. [ME f. OF *a(d)vocacie* f. med.L *advocatia* (as ADVOCATE)]

advocate n. & v. ● n. /ádvəkət/ **1** (foll. by *of*) a person who supports or speaks in favor. **2** a person who pleads for another. **3** a professional pleader in a court of justice. ● v.tr. /ádvəkayt/ **1** recommend or support by argument (a cause, policy, etc.). **2** plead for; defend. □□ **advocateship** n. **advocatory** /advókətáwree, ádvəkə-, ádvəkaytəree/ adj. [ME f. OF *avocat* f. L *advocatus* past part. of *advocare* (as AD-, *vocare* call)]
■ n. **1** supporter, champion, apostle, backer, upholder, second, exponent, proponent, patron, defender, apologist, *disp.* protagonist. **2, 3** lawyer, counsel, counselor; intercessor; attorney, counselor-at-law *Brit.* barrister, solicitor. ● v. support, champion, back, endorse, uphold, defend, recommend, stand behind *or* by, second, favor, speak *or* plead *or* argue for *or* in favor of, hold a brief for; urge; preach, teach.

advowson /ədvówzən/ n. *Brit. Eccl.* (in ecclesiastical law) the right of recommending a member of the clergy for a vacant benefice, or of making the appointment. [ME f. AF *a(d)voweson* f. OF *avoeson* f. L *advocatio -onis* (as ADVOCATE)]

advt. abbr. advertisement.

adytum /áditəm/ n. (pl. **adyta** /-tə/) the innermost part of an ancient temple. [L f. Gk *aduton* neut. of *adutos* impenetrable (as A-¹, *duō* enter)]

adze /adz/ n. & v. (also **adz**) ● n. a tool for cutting away the surface of wood, like an axe with an arched blade at right angles to the handle. ● v.tr. dress or cut with an adze. [OE *adesa*]

adzuki /ədzóōkee/ n. (also **adsuki, azuki**) **1** an annual leguminous plant, *Vigna angularis*, native to China and Japan. **2** the small round dark red edible bean of this plant. [Jap. *azuki*]

-ae /ee/ suffix forming plural nouns, used in names of animal and plant families, tribes, etc., (*Felidae; Rosaceae*) and instead of *-as* in the plural of many nonnaturalized or unfamiliar nouns in *-a* derived from Latin or Greek (*larvae; actiniae*). [pl. *-ae* of L nouns in *-a* or pl. *-ai* of some Gk nouns]

aedile /éedīl/ n. either of a pair of Roman magistrates who administered public works, maintenance of roads, public games, the grain supply, etc. □□ **aedileship** n. [L *aedilis* concerned with buildings f. *aedes* building]

aegis /éejis/ n. a protection; an impregnable defense. □ **under the aegis of** under the auspices of. [L f. Gk *aigis* mythical shield of Zeus or Athene]
■ see AUSPICE 1.

aegrotat /éegrōtat/ n. *Brit.* **1** a certificate that a university student is too ill to attend an examination. **2** an examination pass awarded in such circumstances. [L, = is sick f. *aeger* sick]

-aemia esp. *Brit.* var. of -EMIA.

aeolian /eeṓleeən/ *Brit.* = EOLIAN. □ **aeolian harp** a stringed instrument or toy that produces musical sounds when the wind passes through it. [L *Aeolius* f. *Aeolus* god of the winds f. Gk *Aiolos*]

Aeolian mode /eeṓleeən/ n. *Mus.* the mode represented by the natural diatonic scale A–A. [L *Aeolius* f. *Aeolis* in Asia Minor f. Gk *Aiolis*]

aeon var. of **eon**.

aerate /áirayt/ v.tr. **1** expose to the mechanical or chemical action of the air. **2** oxygenate, esp. the blood. **3** *Brit.* = CARBONATE. □□ **aeration** /-ráyshən/ n. **aerator** n. [L *aer* AIR + -ATE³, after F *aérer*]

aerenchyma /aréngkəmə/ n. *Bot.* a soft plant tissue containing air spaces found esp. in many aquatic plants. [Gk *aēr* air + *egkhuma* infusion]

aerial /áireeəl/ n. & adj. ● n. *Brit.* = ANTENNA. ● adj. **1** by or from or involving aircraft (*aerial navigation; aerial photography*). **2 a** existing, moving, or happening in the air. **b** of or in the atmosphere, atmospheric. **3** operated or powered by elevated cables or rails (*aerial ski lift*). **4 a** thin as air; ethereal. **b** immaterial; imaginary. **c** of air; gaseous. □□ **aeriality** /-reeálitee/ n. **aerially** adv. [L *aerius* f. Gk *aerios* f. *aēr* air]

aerialist /áireeəlist/ n. a high-wire or trapeze artist.

aerie /áiree, áree/ n. (also **eyrie**) **1** a nest of a bird of prey, esp. an eagle, built high up. **2** a house, etc., porched high up. [med. L. *aeria, aerea*, etc., prob. f. OF *aire* lair ult. f. L *agrum* piece of ground]
■ **1** nest, roost, perch.

aeriform /áirifawrm/ adj. **1** of the form of air; gaseous. **2** unsubstantial; unreal. [L *aer* AIR + -FORM]

aero- /áirō/ comb. form **1** air. **2** aircraft. [Gk *aero-* f. *aēr* air]

aerobatics /áirəbátiks/ n.pl. **1** feats of expert and usu. spectacular flying and maneuvering of aircraft. **2** (as *sing.*) a performance of these. [AERO- + ACROBATICS]

aerobe /áirōb/ n. a microorganism usu. growing in the presence of oxygen, or needing oxygen for growth. [F *aérobie* (as AERO-, Gk *bios* life)]

aerobic /airṓbik/ adj. **1** existing or active only in the presence of oxygen. **2** of or relating to aerobes. **3** of or relating to aerobics.

aerobics /airṓbiks/ n.pl. vigorous exercises designed to increase the body's heart rate and oxygen intake.

aerobiology /áirōbīóləjee/ n. the study of airborne microorganisms, pollen, spores, etc., esp. as agents of infection.

aerodrome /áirədrōm/ n. *Brit.* a small airport or airfield.

aerodynamics /áirōdínámiks/ n.pl. (usu. treated as *sing.*) the study of the interaction between the air and solid bodies moving through it. □□ **aerodynamic** adj. **aerodynamically** adv. **aerodynamicist** /-misist/ n.

aeroembolism /áirōémbəlizəm/ n. a condition caused by the sudden lowering of air pressure and formation of bubbles in the blood: also called *caisson disease, decompression sickness, the bends* (see BEND¹ n. 4).

aero-engine /áirōenjin/ n. *Brit.* an engine used to power an aircraft.

aerofoil esp. *Brit.* var. of AIRFOIL.

aerogram /áirəgram/ n. (also **aerogramme**) an air letter in the form of a single sheet that is folded and sealed.

aerolite /áirəlīt/ n. a stony meteorite.

aerology /airóləjee/ n. the study of the upper levels of the atmosphere. □□ **aerological** /airəlójikəl/ adj.

aeronautics /áirənáwtiks/ n.pl. (usu. treated as *sing.*) the science or practice of motion or travel in the air. □□ **aeronautic** adj. **aeronautical** adj. [mod.L *aeronautica* (as AERO-, NAUTICAL)]

aeronomy /airónəmee/ n. the science, esp. the physics and chemistry, of the upper atmosphere.

aeroplane esp. *Brit.* var. of AIRPLANE.

aerosol /áirəsawl, -sol/ n. **1 a** a container used to hold a substance packed under pressure with a device for releasing it as a fine spray. **b** the releasing device. **c** the substance contained in an aerosol. **2** a system of colloidal particles dispersed in a gas (e.g., fog or smoke). [AERO- + SOL²]
■ **1 a, b** see SPRAY¹ n. 3.

/.../ **pronunciation**	● **part of speech**
□ **phrases, idioms, and compounds**	
□□ **derivatives**	■ **synonym section**
cross-references appear in SMALL CAPITALS or *italics*	

aerospace /áirōspays/ *n.* **1** the earth's atmosphere and outer space. **2** the technology of aviation in this region.

aerotrain /áirōtrayn/ *n.* an experimental train that is supported on an air cushion and guided by a track. [F *aérotrain* (as AERO-, TRAIN)]

aeruginous /iróōjinəs/ *adj.* of the nature or color of verdigris. [L *aeruginosus* f. *aerugo* -*inis* verdigris f. *aes aeris* bronze]

Aesculapian /éskyaláypeeən/ *adj.* of or relating to medicine or physicians. [L *Aesculapius* f. Gk *Asklēpios* god of medicine]

aesthete /és-theet/ *n.* (also **esthete**) a person who has or professes to have a special appreciation of beauty. [Gk *aisthētēs* one who perceives, or f. AESTHETIC]
■ connoisseur, art lover, lover of beauty.

aesthetic /es-thétik/ *adj. & n.* (also **esthetic**) ● *adj.* **1** concerned with beauty or the appreciation of beauty. **2** having such appreciation; sensitive to beauty. **3** in accordance with the principles of good taste. ● *n.* **1** (in *pl.*) the philosophy of the beautiful, esp. in art. **2** a set of principles of good taste and the appreciation of beauty. □□ **aesthetically** *adv.* **aestheticism** /-tisizəm/ *n.* [Gk *aisthētikos* f. *aisthanomai* perceive]
■ *adj.* **1** artistic, *colloq.* arty. **2** sensitive, artistic, refined, discriminating, cultivated, cultured; *colloq.* arty. **3** artistic, tasteful, beautiful, in good *or* excellent taste; elegant, polished, refined, cultured. □□ **aesthetically** artistically; sensitively, tastefully, beautifully, elegantly. **aestheticism** beauty; sensitivity, tastefulness, artistry, elegance.

aestival esp. *Brit.* var. of ESTIVAL.

aestivate esp. *Brit.* var. of ESTIVATE.

aestivation esp. *Brit.* var. of ESTIVATION.

aet. *abbr.* (also **aetat.**) aetatis.

aetatis /ītaátis, eetáy-/ *adj.* of or at the age of.

aether var. of ETHER 2, 3.

aetiology esp. *Brit.* var. of ETIOLOGY.

AF *abbr.* **1** Air Force. **2** audio frequency.

af- /əf/ *prefix* assim. form of AD- before *f*.

afar /əfaár/ *adv.* at or to a distance. □ **from afar** from a distance. [ME f. A-², A-⁴ + FAR]

AFB *abbr.* Air Force Base.

AFC *abbr.* **1** American Football Conference. **2** *Brit.* Association Football Club.

affable /áfəbəl/ *adj.* **1** (of a person) approachable and friendly. **2** kind and courteous. □□ **affability** /-bílitee/ *n.* **affably** *adv.* [F f. L *affabilis* f. *affari* (as AD-, *fari* speak)]
■ see FRIENDLY *adj.* 1.

affair /əfaár/ *n.* **1** a concern; a business; a matter to be attended to (*that is my affair*). **2 a** a celebrated or notorious happening or sequence of events. **b** *colloq.* a noteworthy thing or event (*was a puzzling affair*). **3** = *love affair*. **4** (in *pl.*) **a** ordinary pursuits of life. **b** business dealings. **c** public matters (*current affairs*). [ME f. AF *afere* f. OF *afaire* f. *à faire* to do: cf. ADO]
■ **1** business, concern, interest, area. **2 b** event, occasion, episode, business, occurrence, happening, proceeding, incident, experience, operation. **3** affaire, love affair, amour, romance, fling, liaison, relationship, flirtation, affaire de cœur, *archaic* intrigue, *sl.* carrying-on. **4** (*affairs*) **a, b** concerns, undertakings, activity, activities, interests, matters, business, dealings; transactions, operation(s), finances, ventures, enterprise(s). **c** topics, issues, matters, concerns.

affaire /afáir/ *n.* (also **affaire de cœur** /afáir də kőr/) a love affair. [F]

affect¹ /əfékt/ *v.tr.* **1 a** produce an effect on. **b** (of a disease, etc.) attack (*his liver is affected*). **2** move; touch the feelings of (*affected me deeply*). ¶ Often confused with *effect*, which as a verb means 'bring about; accomplish.' □□ **affecting** *adj.* **affectingly** *adv.* [F *affecter* or L *afficere* affect- influence (as AD-, *facere* do)]
■ **1 a** influence, act *or* play *or* work on; sway, change, transform, modify, alter. **b** attack, act upon, damage, lay hold of, strike. **2** move, stir, impress, touch, strike; perturb, upset, disturb, trouble, agitate, bother.

affect² /əfékt/ *v.tr.* **1** pretend to have or feel (*affected indifference*). **2** (foll. by *to* + infin.) pretend. **3** assume the character or manner of; pose as (*affect the freethinker*). **4** make a show of liking or using (*she affects fancy hats*). [F *affecter* or L *affectare* aim at, frequent. of *afficere* (as AFFECT¹)]
■ **1** assume, adopt, put on, pretend, feign, sham, fake, counterfeit. **3** see POSE¹ *v.* 2. **4** choose, select; use, wear, adopt.

affect³ /áfekt/ *n.* *Psychol.* a feeling, emotion, or desire, esp. as leading to action. [G *Affekt* f. L *affectus* disposition f. *afficere* (as AFFECT¹)]

affectation /áfektáyshən/ *n.* **1** an assumed or contrived manner of behavior, esp. in order to impress. **2** (foll. by *of*) a studied display. **3** pretense. [F *affectation* or L *affectatio* (as AFFECT²)]
■ **1** affectedness, pretentiousness, pretension, airs (and graces), artificiality, insincerity, posturing. **2, 3** pose, false display, act, show, front, façade; pretense, pretension.

affected /əféktid/ *adj.* **1** in senses of AFFECT¹, AFFECT². **2** artificially assumed or displayed; pretended (*an affected air of innocence*). **3** (of a person) full of affectation; artificial. **4** (prec. by *adv.*; often foll. by *toward*) disposed, inclined. □□ **affectedly** *adv.* **affectedness** *n.*
■ **1** (AFFECT¹) attacked, seized, afflicted, diseased, gripped, laid hold of, *archaic* stricken; moved, touched, stirred, distressed, troubled, upset, hurt; influenced, swayed, impressed, struck, played *or* worked *or* acted upon; altered, modified, changed, transformed. **2** unnatural, artificial, specious, stilted, stiff, studied, awkward, nonnatural, contrived, overstudied, mannered, euphuistic; pretended, simulated, hollow, assumed, feigned, fake, false, counterfeit, synthetic, spurious, sham, bogus, *colloq.* phony. **3** pretentious, pompous, insincere, artificial, high-sounding, theatrical, mincing, minikin, chichi, niminy-piminy, lackadaisical, *colloq.* la-di-da. **4** see *inclined* (INCLINE *v.*).

affection /əfékshən/ *n.* **1** (often foll. by *for, toward*) goodwill; fond or tender feeling. **2** a disease; a diseased condition. **3** a mental state; an emotion. **4** a mental disposition. **5** the act or process of affecting or being affected. □□ **affectional** *adj.* (in sense 3). **affectionally** *adv.* [ME f. OF f. L *affectio* -*onis* (as AFFECT¹)]
■ **1** goodwill, (high) regard, liking, fondness, fond *or* kindly feeling, (loving) attachment, tenderness, warmth, love. **2** see ILLNESS.

affectionate /əfékshənət/ *adj.* loving; tender; showing love or tenderness. □□ **affectionately** *adv.* [F *affectionné* or med.L *affectionatus* (as AFFECTION)]
■ fond, loving, tender, caring, devoted, doting, warm, warm-hearted, tender-hearted. □□ **affectionately** see *fondly* (FOND).

affective /əféktiv/ *adj.* **1** concerning the affections; emotional. **2** *Psychol.* relating to affects. □□ **affectivity** /áfektívitee/ *n.* [F *affectif* -*ive* f. LL *affectivus* (as AFFECT¹)]
■ **1** see EMOTIONAL 4.

affenpinscher /áfənpinshər/ *n.* **1** a dog of a small breed resembling the griffon. **2** this breed. [G f. *Affe* monkey + *Pinscher* terrier]

afferent /áfərənt/ *adj.* *Physiol.* conducting inwards or toward (*afferent nerves*; *afferent vessels*) (opp. EFFERENT). [L *afferre* (as AD-, *ferre* bring)]

affiance /əfíəns/ *v.tr.* (usu. in *passive*) *literary* promise solemnly to give (a person) in marriage. [ME f. OF *afiancer* f. med.L *affidare* (as AD-, *fidus* trusty)]

affidavit /áfidáyvit/ *n.* a written statement confirmed under oath, for use as evidence in court. [med.L, = has stated on oath, f. *affidare*: see AFFIANCE]

affiliate *v. & n.* ● *v.* /əfíleeayt/ **1** *tr.* (usu. in *passive*; foll. by *to, with*) attach or connect (a person or society) with a larger organization. **2** *tr.* (of an institution) adopt (persons as members, societies as branches, etc.). **3** *intr.* **a** (foll. by *to*) associate oneself with a society. **b** (foll. by *with*) associate oneself with a political party. ● *n.* /əfíleeət, -leeayt/ an affiliated person or organization. [med.L *affiliare* adopt (as AD-, *filius* son)]

■ *v.* **1, 2** associate; attach, connect, combine, unite, join.

affiliation /əfíleeáyshən/ *n.* the act or process of affiliating or being affiliated. □ **affiliation order** *Brit.* a legal order that the man judged to be the father of an illegitimate child must help to support it. [F f. med.L *affiliatio* f. *affiliare*: see AFFILIATE]

■ see ASSOCIATION 2–4.

affined /əfínd/ *adj.* related; connected. [*affine* (adj.) f. L *affinis* related: see AFFINITY]

affinity /əfínitee/ *n.* (*pl.* **-ies**) **1** (often foll. by *between*, or *disp.* *to*, *for*) a spontaneous or natural liking for or attraction to a person or thing. **2** relationship, esp. by marriage. **3** resemblance in structure between animals, plants, or languages. **4** a similarity of character suggesting a relationship. **5** *Chem.* the tendency of certain substances to combine with others. [ME f. OF *afinité* f. L *affinitas -tatis* f. *affinis* related, lit. bordering on (as AD- + *finis* border)]

■ **1** friendliness, fondness, liking, taste, penchant, partiality, attractiveness, attraction, rapport, sympathy, agreement. **2–4** relationship, kinship, closeness, alliance, connection, affiliation, association, link, tie, interconnection, correspondence; similarity, similitude, resemblance; conformity.

affirm /əfə́rm/ *v.* **1** *tr.* assert strongly; state as a fact. **2** *intr.* **a** *Law* make an affirmation. **b** make a formal declaration. **3** *tr.* *Law* confirm; ratify (a judgment). □□ **affirmatory** *adj.* **affirmer** *n.* [ME f. OF *afermer* f. L *affirmare* (as AD-, *firmus* strong)]

■ **1** see DECLARE 3. **2 b** see DECLARE 1, 2.

affirmation /áfərmáyshən/ *n.* **1** the act or process of affirming or being affirmed. **2** *Law* a solemn declaration by a person who conscientiously declines to take an oath. [F *affirmation* or L *affirmatio* (as AFFIRM)]

■ **1** see DECLARATION 1, 2a.

affirmative /əfə́rmətiv/ *adj.* & *n.* ● *adj.* **1** affirming; asserting that a thing is so. **2** (of a vote) expressing approval. ● *n.* **1** an affirmative statement, reply, or word. **2** (prec. by *the*) a positive or affirming position. □ **affirmative action** action favoring those who often suffer or have previously suffered from discrimination. **in the affirmative** with affirmative effect; so as to accept or agree to a proposal; yes (*the answer was in the affirmative*). □□ **affirmatively** *adv.* [ME f. OF *affirmatif -ive* f. LL *affirmativus* (as AFFIRM)]

■ *adj.* **2** see FAVORABLE 1b.

affix *v.* & *n.* ● *v.tr.* /əfíks/ **1** (usu. foll. by *to*, *on*) attach; fasten. **2** add in writing (a signature or postscript). **3** impress (a seal or stamp). ● *n.* /áfiks/ **1** an appendage; an addition. **2** *Gram.* an addition or element placed at the beginning (*prefix*) or end (*suffix*) of a root, stem, or word, or in the body of a word (*infix*), to modify its meaning. □□ **affixal** or **affixial** *adj.* **affixation** /áfiksáyshən/ *n.* **affixture** /əfíkschər/ *n.* [F *affixer*, *affixe* or med.L *affixare* frequent. of L *affigere* (as AD-, *figere fix-* fix)]

afflatus /əfláytəs/ *n.* a divine creative impulse; inspiration. [L f. *afflare* (as AD-, *flare flat-* to blow)]

afflict /əflíkt/ *v.tr.* inflict bodily or mental suffering on. □ **afflicted with** suffering from. □□ **afflictive** *adj.* [ME f. L *afflictare*, or *afflict-* past part. stem of *affligere* (as AD-, *fligere flict-* dash)]

■ affect, bother, distress, oppress, trouble, torment, plague, disturb, agitate; weaken, enfeeble, debilitate, incapacitate, *archaic* ail.

affliction /əflíkshən/ *n.* **1** physical or mental distress, esp. pain or illness. **2** a cause of this. [ME f. OF f. L *afflictio -onis* (as AFFLICT)]

■ **1** hardship, misery, misfortune, distress, ordeal, trial, tribulation, adversity, suffering, trouble, illness, agony, pain, grief, torment, torture, wretchedness, *archaic or literary* woe. **2** curse, calamity, catastrophe, disaster, plague, scourge, tribulation, trouble, sea of troubles; see also ILLNESS 1.

affluence /áflōōəns/ *n.* an abundant supply of money, com-

modities, etc.; wealth. [ME f. F f. L *affluentia* f. *affluere*: see AFFLUENT]

■ see WEALTH 1, 2.

affluent /áflōōənt/ *adj.* & *n.* ● *adj.* **1** wealthy; rich. **2** abundant. **3** flowing freely or copiously. ● *n.* a tributary stream. □ **affluent society** a society in which material wealth is widely distributed. □□ **affluently** *adv.* [ME f. OF f. L *affluere* (as AD-, *fluere flux-* flow)]

■ *adj.* **1** see WEALTHY. **2** see ABUNDANT 1.

afflux /áfluks/ *n.* a flow toward a point; an influx. [med.L *affluxus* f. L *affluere*: see AFFLUENT]

afford /əfáwrd/ *v.tr.* **1** (prec. by *can* or *be able to*; often foll. by *to* + infin.) **a** have enough money, means, time, etc., for; be able to spare (*can afford $50; could not afford a vacation; can we afford to buy a new television?*). **b** be in a position to do something (esp. without risk of adverse consequences) (*can't afford to let him think so*). **2** yield a supply of. **3** provide (*affords a view of the sea*). □□ **affordable** *adj.* **affordability** *n.* [ME f. OE *geforthian* promote (as Y-, FORTH), assim. to words in AF-]

■ **1 a** have the *or* sufficient means, be able *or* rich enough, manage, find the means *or* money, *colloq.* have the wherewithal; bear *or* meet the expense of, pay for. **2** yield, give, supply, produce, provide, furnish, grant, offer; give forth. **3** see PROVIDE 1. □□ **affordable** reasonably priced, inexpensive; reasonable, fair, acceptable, within reason, economical, cheap.

afforest /əfáwrist, əfór-/ *v.tr.* **1** convert into forest. **2** plant with trees. □□ **afforestation** /-stáyshən/ *n.* [med.L *afforestare* (as AD-, *foresta* FOREST)]

affranchise /əfránchīz/ *v.tr.* release from servitude or an obligation. [OF *afranchir* (as ENFRANCHISE, with prefix A-³)]

affray /əfráy/ *n.* a breach of the peace by fighting or rioting in public. [ME f. AF *afrayer* (v.) f. OF *esfreer* f. Rmc]

affricate /áfrikət/ *n.* *Phonet.* a combination of a stop, or plosive, with an immediately following fricative or spirant, e.g., *ch*. [L *affricare* (as AD-, *fricare* rub)]

affront /əfrúnt/ *n.* & *v.* ● *n.* an open insult (*feel it an affront; offer an affront to*). ● *v.tr.* **1** insult openly. **2** offend the modesty or self respect of. **3** face, confront. [ME f. OF *afronter* slap in the face; insult, ult. f. L *frons frontis* face]

■ *n.* see INSULT *n.* 1. ● *v.* **1** see INSULT *v.* 1. **2** see INSULT *v.* 2.

Afghan /áfgan/ *n.* & *adj.* ● *n.* **1 a** a native or inhabitant of Afghanistan. **b** a person of Afghan descent. **2** the official language of Afghanistan (also called PASHTO). **3** (**afghan**) a knitted or crocheted and sewn woolen blanket or shawl. **4** *Brit.* (in full **Afghan coat**) a kind of sheepskin coat with the skin outside and usu. with a shaggy border. ● *adj.* of or relating to Afghanistan or its people or language. □ **Afghan hound** a tall hunting dog with long silky hair. [Pashto *afghānī*]

aficionado /əfísheeənaádō, əfísee-/ *n.* (*pl.* **-os**) a devotee of a sport or pastime (orig. of bullfighting). [Sp.]

afield /əféeld/ *adv.* **1** away from home; to or at a distance (esp. *far afield*). **2** in the field. [OE (as A², FIELD)]

afire /əfír/ *adv.* & *predic.adj.* **1** on fire. **2** intensely roused or excited.

aflame /əfláym/ *adv.* & *predic.adj.* **1** in flames. **2** = AFIRE 2.

aflatoxin /áflətóksin/ *n.* *Chem.* any of several related toxic compounds produced by the fungus *Aspergillus flavus*, which cause tissue damage and cancer. [*A*spergillus + *flavus* + TOXIN]

afloat /əflṓt/ *adv.* & *predic.adj.* **1** floating in water or on air. **2** at sea; on board ship. **3** out of debt or difficulty. **4** in general circulation; current. **5** full of or covered with a liquid. **6** in full swing. [OE (as A², FLOAT)]

afoot /əfŏŏt/ *adv.* & *predic.adj.* **1** in operation; progressing. **2** astir; on the move.

/.../ **pronunciation**	● **part of speech**
□ **phrases, idioms, and compounds**	
□□ **derivatives**	■ **synonym section**
cross-references appear in SMALL CAPITALS or *italics*	

afore /əfáwr/ *prep.* & *adv. archaic* & *dial.* before; previously; in front (of). [OE *onforan* (as A², FORE)]

afore- /əfáwr/ *comb. form* before; previously (*aforementioned*; *aforesaid*).

aforethought /əfáwrthawt/ *adj.* premeditated (following a noun: *malice aforethought*).

a fortiori /aa fawrtiáwrī/ *adv.* & *adj.* with a yet stronger reason (than a conclusion already accepted); more conclusively. [L]

afoul /əfówl/ *adv.* foul. □ **run afoul of** come into conflict with.

■ □ **run afoul of** run foul of, become entangled with, be in trouble *or* conflict with, be at odds with.

afraid /əfráyd/ *predic.adj.* **1** (often foll. by *of*, or *that* or *lest* + clause) alarmed; frightened. **2** (foll. by *to* + infin.) unwilling or reluctant for fear of the consequences (*was afraid to go in*). □ **be afraid** (foll. by *that* + clause) *colloq.* admit or declare with (real or politely simulated) regret (*I'm afraid there's none left*). [ME, past part. of obs. *affray* (v.) f. AF *afrayer* f. OF *esfreer*]

■ fearful, frightened, scared, alarmed, intimidated, apprehensive, lily-livered, white-livered, terrified, panic-stricken, fainthearted, weak-kneed, timid, timorous, hesitant, unwilling, reluctant, nervous, anxious, jittery, on edge, edgy, jumpy; cowardly, pusillanimous, craven, *colloq.* yellow, chicken. □ **be afraid** be sorry *or* unhappy *or* regretful *or* apologetic *or* rueful; regret (to say), admit.

afreet /áfreet/ *n.* (also **afrit**) a demon in Muslim or Arabic mythology. [Arab. *'ifrīt*]

afresh /əfrésh/ *adv.* anew; with a fresh beginning. [A-² + FRESH]

African /áfrikən/ *n.* & *adj.* ● *n.* **1** a native of Africa (esp. a black person). **2** a person of African descent. ● *adj.* of or relating to Africa. □ **African-American** *n.* an American citizen of African origin or descent, esp. a black American. ● *adj.* of or relating to American blacks or their culture. **African elephant** the elephant, *Loxodonta africana*, of Africa, which is larger than the Indian elephant. **African violet** a tropical plant, *Saintpaulia ionantha*, with heart-shaped velvety leaves and blue, purple, or pink flowers. [L *Africanus*]

Africana /áfrikáanə/ *n.pl.* things connected with Africa.

Africander /áfrikándər/ *n.* (also **Afrikander**) one of a S. African breed of sheep or longhorn cattle. [Afrik. *Afrikaander* alt. of Du. *Afrikaner* after *Hollander*, etc.]

Afrikaans /áfrikáans/ *n.* the language of the Afrikaner people developed from Cape Dutch, an official language of the Republic of South Africa. [Du., = African]

Afrikander var. of AFRICANDER.

Afrikaner /áfrikáanər/ *n.* **1** an Afrikaans-speaking white person in S. Africa, esp. one of Dutch descent. **2** *Bot.* a S. African species of *Gladiolus* or *Homoglossum*. [Afrik., formed as AFRICANDER]

afrit var. of AFREET.

Afro /áfrō/ *adj.* & *n.* ● *adj.* (of a hairstyle) full and bushy, as naturally grown originally by blacks. ● *n.* (*pl.* **-os**) an Afro hairstyle. [AFRO-, or abbr. of AFRICAN]

Afro- /áfrō/ *comb. form* African (*Afro-Asian*). [L *Afer Afr-* African]

Afro-American /áfrōəmérikən/ *adj.* & *n.* = *African-American*.

Afro-Caribbean /áfrōkáribéeən, -kəríbeeən/ *n.* & *adj.* ● *n.* a person of African descent in or from the Caribbean. ● *adj.* of or relating to the Afro-Caribbeans or their culture.

afrormosia /áfrawrmṓzeeə, -zhə/ *n.* **1** an African tree, *Pericopsis* (formerly *Afrormosia*) *elata*, yielding a hard wood resembling teak and used for furniture. **2** this wood. [mod.L f. AFRO- + *Ormosia* genus of trees]

aft /aft/ *adv. Naut.* & *Aeron.* at or toward the stern or tail. [prob. f. ME *baft*: see ABAFT]

after /áftər/ *prep., conj., adv.,* & *adj.* ● *prep.* **1 a** following in time; later than (*after six months*; *after midnight*; *day after day*). **b** in specifying time (*a quarter after eight*). **2** (with causal force) in view of (something that happened shortly

before) (*after your behavior tonight what do you expect?*). **3** (with concessive force) in spite of (*after all my efforts I'm no better off*). **4** behind (*shut the door after you*). **5** in pursuit or quest of (*run after them*; *inquire after him*; *hanker after it*; *is after a job*). **6** about; concerning (*asked after her*; *asked after her health*). **7** in allusion to (*named him William after his uncle*). **8** in imitation of (a person, word, etc.) (*a painting after Rubens*). **9** next in importance to (*the best book on the subject after mine*). **10** according to (*after a fashion*). ● *conj.* in or at a time later than that when (*left after we arrived*). ● *adv.* **1** later in time (*soon after*; *a week after*). **2** behind in place (*followed on after*). ● *adj.* **1** later; following (*in after years*). **2** *Naut.* nearer the stern (*after cabins*; *after mast*). □ **after all 1** in spite of all that has happened or has been said, etc. (*after all, what does it matter?*). **2** in spite of one's exertions, expectations, etc. (*they tried for an hour and failed after all*; *so you have come after all!*). **after one's own heart** see HEART. **after you** a formula used in offering precedence. [OE after f. Gmc]

afterbirth /áftərbərth/ *n. Med.* the placenta and fetal membranes discharged from the womb after childbirth.

afterburner /áftərbərnər/ *n.* an auxiliary burner in a jet engine to increase thrust.

aftercare /áftərkair/ *n.* -ker/ *n.* care of a patient after a stay in the hospital or of a person on release from prison.

afterdamp /áftərdamp/ *n.* choking gas left after an explosion of firedamp in a mine.

aftereffect /áftərəfékt/ *n.* an effect that follows after an interval or after the primary action of something.

afterglow /áftərglō/ *n.* a light or radiance remaining after its source has disappeared or been removed.

afterimage /áftərímij/ *n.* an image retained by a sense organ, esp. the eye, and producing a sensation after the cessation of the stimulus.

afterlife /áftərlif/ *n.* **1** life after death. **2** life at a later time.

aftermarket /áftərmaarkit/ *n.* **1** a market in spare parts and components. **2** *Stock Exch.* a market in shares after their original issue.

aftermath /áftərmath/ *n.* **1** consequences; aftereffects (*the aftermath of war*). **2** new grass growing after mowing or after a harvest. [AFTER *adj.* + *math* mowing f. OE *mæth* f. Gmc]

■ **1** see OUTCOME.

aftermost /áftərmōst/ *adj.* **1** last. **2** *Naut.* farthest aft. [AFTER *adj.* + -MOST]

afternoon /áftərnṓn/ *n.* & *int.* ● *n.* **1** the time from noon or lunchtime to evening (*this afternoon*; *during the afternoon*). **2** this time spent in a particular way (*had a lazy afternoon*). **3** a time compared with this, esp. the later part of something (*the afternoon of life*). ● *int.* = good afternoon (see GOOD *adj.* 14).

afterpains /áftərpaynz/ *n.pl.* pains caused by contraction of the womb after childbirth.

afters /áftərz/ *n.pl. Brit. colloq.* the course following the main course of a meal.

aftershave /áftərshayv/ *n.* an astringent lotion for use after shaving.

aftershock /áftərshok/ *n.* a lesser shock following the main shock of an earthquake.

aftertaste /áftərtáyst/ *n.* a taste remaining or recurring after eating or drinking.

after-tax /áftərtáks/ *adj.* (of income) after the deduction of taxes.

afterthought /áftərthawt/ *n.* an item or thing that is thought of or added later.

afterward /áftərwərd/ *adv.* (also **afterwards**) later; subsequently. [OE *æftanwearde* adj. f. *æftan* AFT + -WARD]

■ see *subsequently* (SUBSEQUENT).

afterword /áftərwərd/ *n.* concluding remarks in a book, esp. by a person other than its author.

Ag *symb. Chem.* the element silver. [L *argentum*]

ag- /əg/ *prefix* assim. form of AD- before *g*.

aga /áagə/ *n.* (in Muslim countries) a commander; a chief. □ **Aga Khan** the spiritual leader of the Ismaili Muslims. [Turk. *ağa* master]

again /əgén/ *adv.* **1** another time; once more. **2** as in a previous position or condition (*back again*; *home again*; *healthy again*). **3** in addition (*as much again*; *half as many again*). **4** further; besides (*again, what about the children?*). **5** on the other hand (*I might, and again I might not*). □ **again and again** repeatedly. [orig. a northern form of ME *ayen*, etc., f. OE *ongēan*, *ongǽgn*, etc., f. Gmc]

■ **1** see OVER *adv.* 7b. **3** see EXTRA *adv.* 2.

against /əgénst/ *prep.* **1** in opposition to (*fight against the invaders*; *arson is against the law*). **2** into collision or in contact with (*ran against a rock*; *lean against the wall*; *up against a problem*). **3** to the disadvantage of (*his age is against him*). **4** in contrast to (*against a dark background*; *99 as against 102 yesterday*). **5** in anticipation of or preparation for (*against his coming*; *against a rainy day*; *protected against the cold*; *warned against pickpockets*). **6** as a compensating factor to (*income against expenditure*). **7** in return for (*issued against a later payment*). □ **against the clock** see CLOCK[1] **3**. **against the grain** see GRAIN. **against time** see TIME. [ME *ayenes*, etc., f. *ayen* AGAIN + -*t* in *amongst*: see AMONG]

■ **1, 4** opposed to, anti, averse to, resistant toward.

agama /ágəmə, əgáy-/ *n.* any Old World lizard of the genus *Agama*. [Carib]

agamic /əgámik/ *adj.* characterized by the absence of sexual reproduction. [as AGAMOUS + -IC]

agamogenesis /ágáməjénisis, ágəmō-/ *n.* Biol. asexual reproduction. □□ **agamogenetic** /-jinétik/ *adj.* [as AGAMOUS + Gk *genesis* birth]

agamous /ágəməs/ *adj.* Biol. without (distinguishable) sexual organs. [LL *agamus* f. Gk *agamos* (as A-[1], *gamos* marriage)]

agapanthus /ágəpánthəs/ *n.* any African plant of the genus *Agapanthus*, esp. the ornamental African lily, with blue or white flowers. [mod.L f. Gk *agapē* love + *anthos* flower]

agape[1] /əgáyp/ *adv.* & *predic.adj.* gaping, openmouthed, esp. with wonder or expectation.

agape[2] /əgaápay, ágə-/ *n.* **1** a Christian feast in token of fellowship, esp. one held by early Christians in commemoration of the Last Supper. **2** love for one's fellow humans, esp. as distinct from erotic love. [Gk, = brotherly love]

agar /áygaar/ *n.* (also **agar-agar** /áygaaráygaar/) a gelatinous substance obtained from any of various kinds of red seaweed and used in food, microbiological media, etc. [Malay]

agaric /ágərik, əgár-/ *n.* any fungus of the family Agaricaceae, with cap and stalk, including the common edible mushroom. [L *agaricum* f. Gk *agarikon*]

agate /ágət/ *n.* **1** any of several varieties of hard usu. streaked chalcedony. **2** a colored toy marble resembling this. [F *agate, -the*, f. L *achates* f. Gk *akhatēs*]

agave /əgaávee, əgáy-/ *n.* any plant of the genus *Agave*, with rosettes of narrow spiny leaves and tall inflorescences, e.g., the aloe. [L f. Gk *Agauē*, proper name in myth f. *agauos* illustrious]

agaze /əgáyz/ *adv.* gazing.

age /ayj/ *n.* & *v.* ● *n.* **1 a** the length of time that a person or thing has existed or is likely to exist. **b** a particular point in or part of one's life, often as a qualification (*old age*; *voting age*). **2 a** colloq. (often in *pl.*) a long time (*took an age to answer*; *have been waiting for ages*). **b** a distinct period of the past (*golden age*; *Bronze age*; *Middle Ages*). **c** Geol. a period of time. **d** a generation. **3** the latter part of life; old age (*the infirmity of age*). ● *v.* (*pres. part.* **aging**, **ageing**) **1** *intr.* show signs of advancing age (*has aged a lot recently*). **2** *intr.* grow old. **3** *intr.* mature. **4** *tr.* cause or allow to age. □ **age of consent** see CONSENT. **age of discretion** see DISCRETION. **age-old** having existed for a very long time. **come of age** reach adult status. **of age** old enough; of adult status. [ME f. OF ult. f. L *aetas -atis* age]

■ *n.* **1** a lifetime, duration, (length of) existence; lifespan, period. **b** period, time, point; see also STAGE *n.* 1. **2** a long time, eon; years, weeks, months, colloq. for ever, donkey's years. **b** era, epoch, period, time(s), day(s), *Hinduism* & *Buddhism* kalpa. **3** old age, later *or* declining years, senescence; senility, dotage; *archaic or poet.* eld. ● *v.* **1, 2** grow *or* get *or* become old(er), get on (in years), senesce; decline. **3, 4** mature, ripen, mellow. □ **age of consent** maturity, years *or* age of

discretion; majority, adulthood, seniority. **age-old** see ANCIENT[1] *adj.* 2. **come of age** see MATURE *v.* 1a, c.

-age /ij/ *suffix* forming nouns denoting: **1** an action (*breakage*; *spillage*). **2** a condition or function (*bondage*). **3** an aggregate or number of (*coverage*; *acreage*). **4** fees payable for; the cost of using (*postage*). **5** the product of an action (*dosage*; *wreckage*). **6** a place; an abode (*anchorage*; *orphanage*; *parsonage*). [OF ult. f. L *-aticum* neut. of adj. suffix *-aticus* -ATIC]

aged *adj.* **1** /ayjd/ **a** of the age of (*aged ten*). **b** that has been subjected to aging. **c** (of a horse) over six years old. **d** allowed to reach maturity or ripeness in storage (*aged cheese*). **2** /áyjid/ having lived long; old.

■ **1 b** mature(d), ripe(ned), mellow(ed). **2** old, elderly, superannuated, ancient, gray, decrepit, hoary, advanced in years, immemorial, old as the hills, having or with one foot in the grave, colloq. over the hill, antediluvian.

ageism /áyjizəm/ *n.* (also **agism**) prejudice or discrimination on the grounds of age. □□ **ageist** *adj.* & *n.* (also **agist**).

ageless /áyjlis/ *adj.* **1** never growing or appearing old or outmoded. **2** eternal; timeless.

■ **2** see TIMELESS.

agelong /áyjlong/ *adj.* lasting for a very long time.

■ see EVERLASTING. *adj.*

agency /áyjənsee/ *n.* (*pl.* **-ies**) **1 a** the business or establishment of an agent (*employment agency*). **b** the function of an agent. **2 a** active operation; action. **b** intervening action; means (*fertilized by the agency of insects*). **c** action personified (*an invisible agency*). **3** a specialized department, as of a government. [med.L *agentia* f. L *agere* do]

■ **1 a** see BUSINESS 8. **2 a** activity, action, working(s), operation, performance, energy. **b** means, medium, instrumentality, ways and means, way, channel(s); intervention, intercession, intermediation, hand(s); operation, mechanism, force, power.

agenda /əjéndə/ *n.* **1** (*pl.* **agendas**) **a** a list of items of business to be considered at a meeting. **b** a series of things to be done. **2** (as *pl.*) **a** items to be considered. **b** things to be done. **3** an ideology or underlying motivation. ¶ Now very common as a countable noun in sense 1 (cf. DATA, MEDIA). [L, neut. pl. of gerundive of *agere* do]

■ **1 a** see LIST[1] *n.* 1.

agent /áyjənt/ *n.* **1 a** a person who acts for another in business, politics, etc. (*insurance agent*). **b** a spy. **2 a** a person or thing that exerts power or produces an effect. **b** the cause of a natural force or effect on matter (*oxidizing agent*). **c** such a force or effect. □ **agent-general** a representative of an Australian state or Canadian province, usu. in England. **Agent Orange** a dioxin-containing herbicide used as a defoliant by the US during the Vietnam War; so-called from the orange stripe on storage drums. □□ **agential** /əjénshəl/ *adj.* [L *agent-* part. stem of *agere* do]

■ **1 a** representative, intermediary, mediator, go-between, middleman, broker, negotiator, proxy, emissary, delegate, spokesman, spokeswoman, spokesperson, deputy, substitute, surrogate, advocate, envoy, messenger, factor, dealer. **b** secret *or* undercover *or* double agent, spy, informer, emissary; FBI *or* CIA *or* MI6 *or* KGB agent, apparatchik, fifth columnist, Mata Hari, *archaic* lurcher, colloq. mole, G-man, *hist.* beagle, *sl.* spook. **2 a** see INFLUENCE *n.* **b** factor, agency, cause, means, medium, channel, force, instrument, power, vehicle, ingredient. □□ **agential** instrumental, causal, influential; mediating, intermediary.

agent provocateur /aázhon prəvókətˈor/ *n.* (*pl.* **agents provocateurs** *pronunc.* same) a person employed to detect suspected offenders by tempting them to overt self-incriminating action. [F, = provocative agent]

agglomerate *v.*, *n.*, & *adj.* ● *v.tr.* & *intr.* /əglómərayt/

/.../ **pronunciation**	● **part of speech**
□ **phrases, idioms, and compounds**	
□□ **derivatives**	■ **synonym section**
cross-references appear in SMALL CAPITALS or *italics*	

1 collect into a mass. **2** accumulate in a disorderly way. ● *n.* /əglómərət/ **1** a mass or collection of things. **2** *Geol.* a mass of large volcanic fragments bonded under heat (cf. CONGLOMERATE). ● *adj.* /əglómərət/ collected into a mass. □□ **agglomeration** /-ráyshən/ *n.* **agglomerative** /əglómərətiv, -raytiv/ *adj.* [L *agglomerare* (as AD-, *glomerare* f. *glomus -meris* ball)]

agglutinate /əglŏot'nayt/ *v.* **1** *tr.* unite as with glue. **2** *tr. & intr. Biol.* cause or undergo adhesion (of bacteria, erythrocytes, etc.). **3** *tr.* (of language) combine (simple words) without change of form to express compound ideas. □□ **agglutination** /-náyshən/ *n.* **agglutinative** /əglŏot'nətiv, -aytiv/ *adj.* [L *agglutinare* (as AD-, *glutinare* f. *gluten -tinis* glue)]

agglutinin /əglŏot'nin/ *n. Biol.* a substance or antibody causing agglutination. [AGGLUTINATE + -IN]

aggrandize /əgrándīz/ *v.tr.* **1** increase the power, rank, or wealth of (a person or nation). **2** cause to appear greater than is the case. □□ **aggrandizement** /-dizmənt/ *n.* **aggrandizer** *n.* [F *agrandir* (stem *agrandiss-*), prob. f. It. *agrandire* f. L *grandis* large: assim. to verbs in -IZE]

aggravate /ágrəvayt/ *v.tr.* **1** increase the seriousness of (an illness, offense, etc.). **2** *disp.* annoy; exasperate (a person). □□ **aggravation** /-váyshən/ *n.* [L *aggravare aggravat-* make heavy f. *gravis* heavy]
■ **1** worsen, intensify, exacerbate, heighten, magnify, increase, inflame. **2** exasperate, frustrate, infuriate, irritate, irk, nettle, vex, annoy, pique, rankle; harass, hector, goad, bother; anger, incense, madden; get on a person's nerves, rub (a person) the wrong way, *colloq.* peeve, needle, rile, get under a person's skin, niggle, wind up, get a person's goat. □□ **aggravation** see ANNOYANCE.

aggregate *n., adj., & v.* ● *n.* /ágrigət/ **1** a collection of, or the total of, disparate elements. **2** pieces of crushed stone, gravel, etc., used in making concrete. **3 a** *Geol.* a mass of minerals formed into solid rock. **b** a mass of particles. ● *adj.* /ágrigət/ **1** (of disparate elements) collected into one mass. **2** constituted by the collection of many units into one body. **3** *Bot.* **a** (of fruit) formed from several carpels derived from the same flower (e.g., raspberry). **b** (of a species) closely related. ● *v.* /ágrigayt/ **1** *tr. & intr.* collect together; combine into one mass. **2** *tr. colloq.* amount to (a specified total). **3** *tr. Brit.* unite (*was aggregated to the group*). □ **in the aggregate** as a whole. □□ **aggregation** /-gáyshən/ *n.* **aggregative** /-gáytiv/ *adj.* [L *aggregare aggregat-* herd together (as AD-, *grex gregis* flock)]
■ *n.* **1** see TOTAL *n.*, MASS[1] *n.* 1, 2. ● *v.* **1** see AMASS. **3** see ADD 1, UNITE 1, 5.

aggression /əgréshən/ *n.* **1** the act or practice of attacking without provocation, esp. beginning a fight or war. **2** an unprovoked attack. **3** self-assertiveness; forcefulness. **4** *Psychol.* hostile or destructive tendency or behavior. [F *agression* or L *aggressio* attack f. *aggredi aggress-* (as AD-, *gradi* walk)]
■ **1** aggressiveness, hostility, belligerence, belligerency, combativeness, bellicosity, pugnacity, *Brit. sl.* aggro. **2** attack, assault, onslaught, invasion, encroachment. **3** (self-)assertion, (self-)assertiveness, forcefulness, boldness.

aggressive /əgrésiv/ *adj.* **1** of a person: **a** given to aggression; openly hostile. **b** forceful; self-assertive. **2** (of an act) offensive; hostile. **3** of aggression. □□ **aggressively** *adv.* **aggressiveness** *n.*
■ **1 a** combative, antagonistic, warlike, martial, belligerent, bellicose, truculent, pugnacious, quarrelsome, disputatious, litigious; hostile, unfriendly. **b** forward, (self-)assertive, forceful, bold, brash, loud, pushing, pushful, *colloq.* pushy, *sl.* feisty. **2** offensive, hostile, unfriendly, threatening, provocative, combative. □□ **aggressively** forcefully, assertively, belligerently, quarrelsomely, disputatiously; antagonistically, hostilely, threateningly, combatively, pugnaciously, truculently, angrily. **aggressiveness** see AGGRESSION 1.

aggressor /əgrésər/ *n.* a person who attacks without provocation. [L (as AGGRESSION)]

■ assailant, attacker, assaulter; instigator, initiator, provoker; belligerent, enemy, adversary, esp. *poet. or formal* foe.

aggrieved /əgreévd/ *adj.* having a grievance. □□ **aggrievedly** /-vidlee/ *adv.* [ME, past part. of *aggrieve* f. OF *agrever* make heavier (as AD-, GRIEVE[1])]

aggro /ágrō/ *n. Brit. sl.* **1** aggressive troublemaking. **2** trouble; difficulty. [abbr. of *aggravation* (see AGGRAVATE) or AGGRESSION]

aghast /əgást/ *adj.* (usu. *predic.*; often foll. by *at*) filled with dismay, shock, or consternation. [ME, past part. of obs. *agast, gast* frighten: see GHASTLY]

agile /ájəl, ájīl/ *adj.* quick-moving; nimble; active. □□ **agilely** *adv.* **agility** /əjílitee/ *n.* [F f. L *agilis* f. *agere* do]
■ nimble, quick, quick-moving, brisk, swift, active, lively, lithe, limber, spry, sprightly; dexterous, resourceful; keen, sharp, alert, acute. □□ **agility** see DEXTERITY 2.

agin /əgín/ *prep. colloq.* or *dial.* against. [corrupt. of AGAINST or synonymous *again* obs. prep.]

aging /áyjing/ *n.* (also **ageing**) **1** growing old. **2** giving the appearance of advancing age. **3** a change of properties occurring in some metals after heat treatment or cold working.

agism var. of AGEISM.

agitate /ájitayt/ *v.* **1** *tr.* (often as **agitated** *adj.*) disturb or excite (a person or feelings). **2** *intr.* (often foll. by *for, against*) stir up interest or concern, esp. publicly (*agitated for tax reform*). **3** *tr.* shake or move, esp. briskly. □□ **agitatedly** *adv.* **agitative** *adj.* [L *agitare agitat-* frequent. of *agere* drive]
■ **1** excite, arouse, rouse, move, perturb, disturb, stir up, disquiet, fluster, ruffle, disconcert, discomfit, discompose, unsettle, upset, rock, unnerve, bother, shake (up), *colloq.* rattle, *joc.* discombobulate; (**agitated**) excited, aroused, roused, *etc.*; nervous, jittery, jumpy, uneasy, ill at ease, fidgety. **2** push, press, campaign, fight, work; (*agitate for*) promote. **3** stir (up), churn, disturb, shake (up), roil, jolt, convulse.

agitation /ájitáyshən/ *n.* **1** the act or process of agitating or being agitated. **2** mental anxiety or concern. [F *agitation* or L *agitatio* (as AGITATE)]
■ **1** shaking, disturbance, churning, stirring, turbulence, convulsion; rabble-rousing, provocation, stirring up, incitement, trouble; excitement, arousal, stimulation, overstimulation, commotion, ferment. **2** see ANXIETY 1, 2.

agitato /ájitaátō/ *adv. & adj. Mus.* in an agitated manner. [It.]

agitator /ájitaytər/ *n.* **1** a person who agitates, esp. publicly for a cause, etc. **2** an apparatus for shaking or mixing liquid, etc. [L (as AGITATE)]
■ **1** activist, rabble-rouser, incendiary, militant, agent provocateur, insurrectionist, troublemaker, demagogue, firebrand. **2** mixer, blender, churn, beater, whisk; (food) processor.

agitprop /ájitprop/ *n.* the dissemination of Communist political propaganda, esp. in plays, movies, books, etc. [Russ. (as AGITATION, PROPAGANDA)]

aglet /áglit/ *n.* **1** a metal or plastic tag attached to each end of a shoelace, etc. **2** = AIGUILLETTE. [ME f. F *aiguillette* small needle, ult. f. L *acus* needle]

agley /əgláy, əglee/ *adv. Sc.* askew; awry. [A[2] + Sc. *gley* squint]

aglow /əglō/ *adv. & adj.* ● *adv.* glowingly. ● *predic.adj.* glowing.

agma /ágmə/ *n.* **1** the sound represented by the pronunciation /ng/. **2** a symbol (ŋ) used for this sound. [Gk, lit. 'fragment']

agnail /ágnayl/ = HANGNAIL.

agnate /ágnayt/ *adj. & n.* ● *adj.* **1** descended esp. by male line from the same male ancestor (cf. COGNATE). **2** descended from the same forefather; of the same clan or nation. **3** of the same nature; akin. ● *n.* one who is descended, esp. by male line, from the same male ancestor. □□ **agnatic** /-nátik/ *adj.* **agnation** /-náyshən/ *n.* [L *agnatus* f. *ad* to + *gnasci* be born f. stem *gen-* beget]

agnosia /agnṓzhə/ *n. Med.* the loss of the ability to interpret sensations. [mod.L f. Gk *agnōsia* ignorance]

agnostic /agnóstik/ *n*. & *adj*. ● *n*. a person who believes that nothing is known, or can be known, of the existence or nature of God or a god or of anything beyond material phenomena. ● *adj*. of or relating to agnostics. □□ **agnosticism** *n*. [A-¹ + GNOSTIC]
■ *n*. see NONBELIEVER.

Agnus Dei /ágnəs dáyee, dee-ī, aányōōs/ *n*. **1** a figure of a lamb bearing a cross or flag, as an emblem of Christ. **2** the prayer in the Mass beginning with the words "Lamb of God." [L, = lamb of God]

ago /əgṓ/ *adv*. earlier; before the present (*ten years ago*; *long ago*). [ME (*ago, agone*), past part. of obs. *ago* (v.) (as A-², GO¹)]

agog /əgóg/ *adv*. & *adj*. ● *adv*. eagerly; expectantly. ● *predic.adj*. eager; expectant. [F *en gogues* f. *en* in + pl. of *gogue* fun]
■ *adv*. eagerly, expectantly, avidly, keenly, with bated breath, impatiently, breathlessly. ● *predic.adj*. eager, avid, keen, enthusiastic, expectant, waiting, itching, impatient, breathless, anxious, on tenterhooks, on the edge of one's seat, on pins and needles.

à gogo /əgṓgṓ/ *adv*. in abundance (*whiskey à gogo*). [F]

agonic /əgónik/ *adj*. having or forming no angle. □ **agonic line** a line passing through the two poles, along which a magnetic needle points directly north or south. [Gk *agōnios* without angle (as A-¹, *gōnia* angle)]

agonistic /ágənístik/ *adj*. polemical; combative. □□ **agonistically** *adv*. [LL *agonisticus* f. Gk *agōnistikos* f. *agōnistēs* contestant f. *agōn* contest]

agonize /ágənīz/ *v*. **1** *intr*. (often foll. by *over*) undergo (esp. mental) anguish; suffer agony. **2** *tr*. (often as **agonizing** *adj*.) cause agony or mental anguish to. **3** *tr*. (as **agonized** *adj*.) expressing agony (*an agonized look*). **4** *intr*. struggle; contend. □□ **agonizingly** *adv*. [F *agoniser* or LL *agonizare* f. Gk *agōnizomai* contend f. *agōn* contest]
■ **1** see WORRY *v*. 1. **2** see TORMENT *v*. 1; (**agonizing**) painful, distressful, distressing, harrowing, torturous, racking, excruciating.

agony /ágənee/ *n*. (*pl*. **-ies**) **1** extreme mental or physical suffering. **2** a severe struggle. □ **agony aunt** *Brit. colloq*. a person (esp. a woman) who answers letters in an agony column. **agony column** *colloq*. **1** *Brit*. a column in a newspaper or magazine offering personal advice to those who write in. **2** = *personal column*. **agony uncle** *Brit. colloq*. the male equivalent of an agony aunt. [ME f. OF *agonie* or LL f. Gk *agōnia* f. *agōn* contest]
■ **1** anguish, trouble, distress, suffering, misery, wretchedness, pain, pangs, torment, hurt, throes, torture, affliction, *archaic or literary* woe. **2** see STRUGGLE *n*. 1, 3.

agoraphobe /ágərəfōb/ *n*. a person who suffers from agoraphobia.

agoraphobia /ágərəfṓbeeə/ *n*. *Psychol*. an abnormal fear of open spaces or public places. □□ **agoraphobic** *adj*. & *n*. [mod.L f. Gk *agora* place of assembly, marketplace + -PHOBIA]

agouti /əgōōtee/ *n*. (also **aguti**) (*pl*. **agoutis**) any burrowing rodent of the genus *Dasyprocta* or *Myoprocta* of Central and S. America, related to the guinea pig. [F *agouti* or Sp. *aguti* f. Tupi *aguti*]

agrarian /əgráireeən/ *adj*. & *n*. ● *adj*. **1** of or relating to the land or its cultivation. **2** relating to the ownership of land. ● *n*. a person who advocates a redistribution of land ownership. [L *agrarius* f. *ager agri* field]

agree /əgree/ *v*. (**agrees, agreed, agreeing**) **1** *intr*. hold a similar opinion (*I agree with you about that*; *they agreed that it would rain*). **2** *intr*. (often foll. by *to*, or *to* + infin.) consent (*agreed to the arrangement*; *agreed to go*). **3** *intr*. (often foll. by *with*) **a** become or be in harmony. **b** suit; be good for (*caviar didn't agree with him*). **c** *Gram*. have the same number, gender, case, or person as. **4** *tr*. *Brit*. reach agreement about (*agreed a price*). **5** *tr*. *Brit*. consent to or approve of (terms, a proposal, etc.). **6** *tr*. *Brit*. bring (things, esp. accounts) into harmony. **7** *intr*. (foll. by *on*) decide by mutual consent (*agreed on a compromise*). □ **agree to differ** leave a difference

of opinion, etc., unresolved. **be agreed** have reached the same opinion. [ME f. OF *agreer* ult. f. L *gratus* pleasing]
■ **1** concur, see eye to eye, be as one man, be at one, understand each other *or* one another, acquiesce, consent, assent; concede, grant, admit, allow, accept. **2** consent, acquiesce, approve, accede, assent. **3 a** concur, conform, come *or* go *or* blend together, coincide, be consonant, be in harmony *or* accord, correspond, harmonize, chime, accord, tally, match, *colloq*. jibe. **b** suit, go well, prove suitable, assort. **7** see SETTLE¹ 5–7, 8b.

agreeable /əgreeəbəl/ *adj*. **1** (often foll. by *to*) pleasing. **2** (often foll. by *to*) (of a person) willing to agree (*was agreeable to going*). **3** (foll. by *to*) conformable; consonant with. □□ **agreeability** /-bílitee/ *n*. **agreeableness** *n*. **agreeably** *adv*. [ME f. OF *agreable* f. *agreer* AGREE]
■ **1** pleasing, pleasant, enjoyable, pleasurable, favorable, delightful, satisfying, satisfactory, good, nice, acceptable, appealing; to one's liking *or* taste *or* fancy. **2** in favor, willing, consenting, acquiescent, compliant, in agreement *or* accord, concurring, amenable, sympathetic, well-disposed; accommodating. □□ **agreeably** see *willingly* (WILLING), *favorably* (FAVORABLE).

agreement /əgreemənt/ *n*. **1** the act of agreeing; the holding of the same opinion. **2** mutual understanding. **3** an arrangement between parties as to a course of action, etc. **4** *Gram*. having the same number, gender, case, or person. **5** mutual conformity of things; harmony. [ME f. OF (as AGREE)]
■ **1, 2** concord, accord, concordance, accordance, consensus, harmony, compatibility, unity, concurrence, unanimity, understanding. **3** understanding, arrangement, covenant, treaty, pact, accord, compact, settlement, concordat, contract, bargain, capitulation, *colloq*. deal. **5** see HARMONY 3.

agribusiness /ágribiznis/ *n*. **1** agriculture conducted on strictly commercial principles, esp. using advanced technology. **2** an organization engaged in this. **3** the group of industries dealing with the produce of, and services to, farming. □□ **agribusinessman** *n*. (*pl*. **-men**; *fem*. **agribusinesswoman**, *pl*. **-women**). [AGRICULTURE + BUSINESS]

agriculture /ágrikulchər/ *n*. the science or practice of cultivating the soil, raising crops, and rearing animals. □□ **agricultural** /-kúlchərəl/ *adj*. **agriculturalist** *n*. **agriculturally** *adv*. **agriculturist** *n*. [F *agriculture* or L *agricultura* f. *ager agri* field + *cultura* CULTURE]

agrimony /ágrimōnee/ *n*. (*pl*. **-ies**) any perennial plant of the genus *Agrimonia*, esp. *A. eupatoria* with small yellow flowers. [ME f. OF *aigremoine* f. L *agrimonia* alt. of *argemonia* f. Gk *argemōnē* poppy]

agro- /ágrō/ *comb. form* agricultural (*agrochemical*; *agro-ecological*). [Gk *agros* field]

agrochemical /ágrōkémikəl/ *n*. a chemical used in agriculture, esp. an insecticide or herbicide.

agronomy /əgrónəmee/ *n*. the science of soil management and crop production. □□ **agronomic** /ágrənómik/ *adj*. **agronomical** *adj*. **agronomically** *adv*. **agronomist** /-grón-/ *n*. [F *agronomie* f. *agronome* agriculturist f. Gk *agros* field + -*nomos* f. *nemō* arrange]

aground /əgrównd/ *predic.adj*. & *adv*. (of a ship) on or on to the bottom of shallow water (*be aground*; *run aground*). [ME f. A² + GROUND¹]

ague /áygōō/ *n*. **1** *hist*. a malarial fever, with cold, hot, and sweating stages. **2** a shivering fit. □□ **agued** *adj*. **aguish** *adj*. [ME f. OF f. med.L *acuta* (*febris*) acute (fever)]

aguti var. of AGOUTI.

AH *abbr*. in the year of the Hegira (AD 622); of the Muslim era. [L *anno Hegirae*]

ah /aa/ *int*. expressing surprise, pleasure, sudden realization,

---

/.../ **pronunciation**	● **part of speech**
□ **phrases, idioms, and compounds**	
□□ **derivatives**	■ **synonym section**
cross-references appear in SMALL CAPITALS or *italics*	

resignation, etc. ¶ The sense depends much on intonation. [ME f. OF *a*]

aha /aaha´a, əha´a/ *int.* expressing surprise, triumph, mockery, irony, etc. ¶ The sense depends much on intonation. [ME f. AH + HA]

ahead /əhéd/ *adv.* **1** further forward in space or time. **2** in the lead; further advanced (*ahead on points*). **3** in the line of one's forward motion (*road construction ahead*). **4** straight forward. □ **ahead of 1** further forward or advanced than. **2** in the line of the forward motion of. **3** prior to. [orig. *Naut.*, f. A² + HEAD]
■ **1** at the front, in front, in advance, in the lead *or* vanguard, up ahead, before, to the fore. **2** winning, in the lead, in front. **4** onward(s), forward(s), on, straight (on). □ **ahead of 1** in front of, in advance of, before; beating, defeating, winning over, outdoing, routing, surpassing. **3** see BEFORE *prep.* 2.

ahem /əhém/ (not usu. clearly articulated) *int.* used to attract attention, gain time, or express disapproval. [lengthened form of HEM²]

ahimsa /əhímsaa/ *n.* (in the Hindu, Buddhist, and Jainist tradition) respect for all living things and avoidance of violence toward others both in thought and deed. [Skr. f. *a* without + *himsa* injury]

-aholic /əhólik/ *suffix* (also **-oholic**) denoting one addicted to or compulsively in need of what is specified in the initial element (*workaholic, chocoholic*). [extracted f. *alcoholic*]

ahoy /əhóy/ *int. Naut.* a call used in hailing. [AH + HOY¹]

AI *abbr.* **1** artificial insemination. **2** artificial intelligence.

ai /áa-ee/ *n.* (*pl.* **ais**) the three-toed sloth of S. America, of the genus *Bradypus*. [Tupi *ai*, repr. its cry]

AID *abbr.* **1** Agency for International Development. **2** *Brit.* artificial insemination by donor.

aid /ayd/ *n. & v.* ● *n.* **1** help. **2** financial or material help, esp. given by one country to another. **3** a material source of help (*teaching aid*). **4** a person or thing that helps. **5** *hist.* a grant of subsidy or tax to a king. ● *v.tr.* **1** (often foll. by *to* + infin.) help. **2** promote or encourage (*sleep will aid recovery*). □ **in aid of** in support of. **what's this** (or **all this**) **in aid of?** *Brit. colloq.* what is the purpose of this? [ME f. OF *aïde, aïdier*, ult. f. L *adjuvare* (as AD-, *juvare jut-* help)]
■ *n.* **1** help, support, assistance, backing, relief, benefit, service, succor, comfort. **2** funding, subsidy, subvention, grant money, grant, grant-in-aid, relief money, donation; scholarship, *Brit.* bursary. **3** see EQUIPMENT. **4** see AIDE, AUXILIARY *n.* ● *v.* **1** help, support, assist, facilitate, back, abet, uphold, promote; succor, relieve, subsidize. **2** see PROMOTE 2.

-aid /ayd/ *comb. form* esp. *Brit.*denoting an organization or event that raises money for charity (*school aid*). [20th c.: orig. in *Band Aid*, rock musicians campaigning for famine relief]

aide /ayd/ *n.* **1** an aide-de-camp. **2** an assistant. **3** an unqualified assistant to a social worker, teacher, etc. [abbr.]
■ **1, 2** aide-de-camp; aid, assistant, helper, help, helpmate, coadjutor; good *or* strong right arm, right hand, right-hand man *or* woman; colleague, partner, ally, comrade, comrade in arms, man Friday, girl Friday, cohort, *colloq.* sidekick.

aide-de-camp /áyd-dəkámp/ *n.* (*pl.* **aides-de-camp** *pronunc.* same) an officer acting as a confidential assistant to a senior officer. [F]

aide-mémoire /áydmemwaár/ *n.* (*pl.* **aides-mémoire** *pronunc.* same) **1 a** an aid to the memory. **b** a book or document meant to aid the memory. **2** *Diplomacy* a memorandum. [F f. *aider* to help + *mémoire* memory]

AIDS /aydz/ *n.* acquired immune deficiency syndrome, a fatal disorder caused by a virus transmitted in the blood and other bodily fluids, marked by severe loss of resistance to infection. □ **AIDS-related complex** the symptoms of a person affected with the AIDS virus who has not developed the disease. [abbr.]

aigrette /áygret, aygrét/ *n.* **1** a tuft of feathers or hair, esp. the plume of an egret. **2** a spray of gems or similar ornament. [F]

aiguille /aygweél/ *n.* a sharp peak of rock, esp. in the Alps. [F: see AGLET]

aiguillette /áygwilét/ *n.* a tagged braid or cord hanging from the shoulder on the breast of some uniforms. [F: see AGLET]

aikido /íkeedō/ *n.* a Japanese form of self-defense making use of the attacker's own movements without causing injury. [Jap. f. *ai* mutual + *ki* mind + *dō* way]

ail /ayl/ *v.* **1** *tr. archaic* (only in 3rd person interrog. or indefinite constructions) trouble or afflict in mind or body (*what ails him?*). **2** *intr.* (usu. **be ailing**) be ill. [OE *egl(i)an* f. *egle* troublesome]
■ **1** trouble, afflict, affect, bother, distress, upset, worry, make ill *or* sick, pain, hurt. **2** suffer, be *or* feel ill *or* poorly *or* unwell *or* indisposed *or* off color, be sick, decline, feel strange *or* wretched, be out of sorts, *Brit. colloq.* be a bit off.

ailanthus /aylánthəs/ *n.* a tall deciduous tree of the genus *Ailanthus*, esp. *A. altissima*, native to China and Australasia. [mod.L *ailantus* f. Ambonese *aylanto*]

aileron /áyləron/ *n.* a hinged surface in the trailing edge of an airplane wing, used to control lateral balance and to initiate banking for turns, etc. [F, dimin. of *aile* wing f. L *ala*]

ailing /áyling/ *adj.* **1** ill, esp. chronically. **2** in poor condition.
■ **1** see ILL *adj.* 1.

ailment /áylmənt/ *n.* an illness, esp. a minor or chronic one.
■ illness, sickness, affliction, affection, disease, disorder, indisposition, malady, complaint, condition, infection, trouble, *sl.* bug; disability, infirmity; malaise, queasiness, nausea.

aim /aym/ *v. & n.* ● *v.* **1** *intr.* (foll. by *at* + verbal noun, or *to* + infin.) intend or try (*aim at winning; aim to win*). **2** *tr.* (usu. foll. by *at*) direct or point (a weapon, remark, etc.). **3** *intr.* take aim. **4** *intr.* (foll. by *at, for*) seek to attain or achieve. ● *n.* **1** a purpose; a design; an object aimed at. **2** the directing of a weapon, missile, etc., at an object. □ **take aim** direct a weapon, etc., at an object. [ME f. OF ult. f. L *aestimare* reckon]
■ *v.* **1, 4** (*aim at, aim for*) focus on, try for, strive for, have designs on, aspire to, plan on, set one's sights on; (*aim to*) seek to, intend to, plan to, mean to, propose to, strive to, try to, wish to, want to. **2** direct, point, focus, train, level. ● *n.* **1** purpose, goal, design, ambition, desire, aspiration, object, end, objective, target, intent, intention, plan. □ **take aim** aim; (*take aim at*) draw a bead on, zero in on, focus on.

aimless /áymlis/ *adj.* without aim or purpose. □□ **aimlessly** *adv.* **aimlessness** *n.*
■ purposeless, pointless, undirected, erratic, haphazard, random, vagrant, wayward; wanton, frivolous. □□ **aimlessly** pointlessly, purposelessly, erratically, unsystematically, haphazardly, randomly.

ain't /aynt/ *contr. colloq.* **1** am not; are not; is not (*you ain't doing it right; she ain't nice*). **2** has not; have not (*we ain't seen him*). ¶ Although often regarded as an uneducated use *ain't* is used jocularly and to show informality in spoken and written English. [contr. of *are not*]

air /air/ *n. & v.* ● *n.* **1** an invisible gaseous substance surrounding the earth, a mixture mainly of oxygen and nitrogen. **2 a** the earth's atmosphere. **b** the free or unconfined space in the atmosphere (*birds of the air; in the open air*). **c** the atmosphere as a place where aircraft operate. **3 a** a distinctive impression or characteristic (*an air of absurdity*). **b** one's manner or bearing, esp. a confident one (*with a triumphant air; does things with an air*). **c** (esp. in *pl.*) an affected manner; pretentiousness (*gave himself airs; airs and graces*). **4** *Mus.* a tune or melody; a melodious composition. **5** a breeze or light wind. ● *v.tr.* **1** esp. *Brit.* warm (washed laundry) to dry, esp. at a fire or in a heated closet. **2** expose (a room, etc.) to the open air; ventilate. **3** express publicly (an opinion, grievance, etc.). **4** parade; show ostentatiously (esp. qualities). **5** broadcast, esp. a radio or television program. **6** *refl.* go out in the fresh air. □ **air bag** a safety device that fills with nitrogen on impact to protect the occupants of a vehicle in a collision. **air bed** *Brit.* = air mattress. **air bladder** a bladder or sac filled with air in fish or some plants (cf. *swim bladder*). **air brake 1** a brake worked by air pressure. **2** a movable flap or spoiler on an aircraft to reduce its speed. **air brick** a brick perforated with small holes for ventilation. **air-conditioned** (of a room, building, etc.) equipped with air-conditioning. **air conditioner** an air-conditioning apparatus. **air-conditioning 1** a system for regulating the humidity, ventilation, and temperature in a building. **2** the apparatus for this. **air-cooled** cooled by means of a current of air. **air corridor** = CORRIDOR 4. **air cushion 1** an inflatable cushion. **2** the layer of air supporting a hovercraft or similar vehicle. **air force** a branch of the armed forces concerned with fighting or defense in the air. **air gun** a gun using compressed air to propel pellets. **air lane** a path or course regularly used by aircraft (cf. LANE 4). **air letter** a sheet of light paper forming a letter for sending by airmail. **air line** a pipe or tube supplying air, esp. to a diver. **air mattress** an inflatable mattress. **air plant** a plant growing naturally without soil, esp. an epiphyte. **air pocket** an apparent downdraft in the air causing an aircraft to drop suddenly. **air power** the ability to defend and attack by means of aircraft, missiles, etc. **air pump** a device for pumping air into or out of a vessel. **air raid** an attack by aircraft. **air rifle** a rifle using compressed air to propel pellets. **air sac** an extension of the lungs in birds or the tracheae in insects. **air-sea rescue** rescue from the sea by aircraft. **air-to-air** from one aircraft to another in flight. **air-traffic controller** an airport official who controls air traffic by giving radio instructions to pilots concerning route, altitude, takeoff, and landing. **by air** by aircraft; in an aircraft. **in the air** (of opinions, feelings, etc.) prevalent; gaining currency. **on** (or **off**) **the air** in (or not in) the process of broadcasting. **take the air** go outdoors. **up in the air** (of projects, etc.) uncertain; not decided. **walk** (or **tread**) **on air** feel elated. [ME f. F and L f. Gk *aēr*]

■ *n.* **3 a** atmosphere, ambience, aura, climate, feeling, sense, mood, impression, quality. **b** manner, style, appearance, aura, attitude, demeanor, aspect, feeling, bearing, look, quality, flavor, *literary* mien. **c** (*airs*) pretension(s), pretense, pretentiousness, show, affectedness, affectation, posing; haughtiness, hauteur, arrogance, superiority, superciliousness. **4** melody, tune, song, music, ditty, strain. **5** breeze, current, draft, breath, puff, whiff, waft, wafting, wind, *literary* zephyr. ● *v.* **2** ventilate, freshen, refresh, aerate. **3** publish, broadcast, circulate, publicize, make public *or* known, disseminate, vent, reveal, expose, disclose, divulge, express, declare. **4** show off, parade, display, exhibit, flaunt; boast of, brag about, *colloq.* talk big about, *colloq.* blow about, *literary* vaunt. □ **by air** by aircraft, by airplane, *or* esp. *Brit.* aeroplane, *colloq.* by plane; by airmail. **in the air** see ABOUT *adv.* 2. **take the air** go out, go for a walk *or* stroll, get some fresh air. **up in the air** see UNCERTAIN 1. **walk** (or **tread**) **on air** be elated; (see ELATE 1).

air base /áir bays/ *n.* a base for the operation of military aircraft.

airborne /áirbawrn/ *adj.* **1** transported by air. **2** (of aircraft) in the air after taking off.

airbrush /áirbrush/ *n. & v.* ● *n.* an artist's device for spraying paint by means of compressed air. ● *v.tr.* paint with an airbrush.

Airbus /áirbus/ *n.* (also **airbus**) *propr.* a passenger aircraft serving routes of relatively short distance.

aircraft /áirkraft/ *n.* (*pl.* same) a machine capable of flight, esp. an airplane or helicopter. □ **aircraft carrier** a warship that carries and serves as a base for airplanes.

aircrew /áirkrōō/ *n.* **1** the crew manning an aircraft. **2** (*pl.* **aircrew**) a member of such a crew.

Airedale /áirdayl/ *n.* **1** a large terrier of a rough-coated breed. **2** this breed. [*Airedale* in Yorkshire, England]

airer /áirər/ *n. Brit.* a frame or stand for airing or drying clothes, etc.

airfare /áirfair/ *n.* the price of a passenger ticket for travel by aircraft.

airfield /áirfeeld/ *n.* an area of land where aircraft take off and land, are maintained, etc.

airfoil /áirfoyl/ *n.* a structure with curved surfaces (e.g., a wing, fin, or horizontal stabilizer) designed to give lift in flight. [AIR + FOIL²]

airframe /áirfraym/ *n.* the body of an aircraft as distinct from its engine(s).

airfreight /áirfrayt/ *n. & v.* ● *n.* cargo carried by an aircraft. ● *v.tr.* transport by air.

airglow /áirglō/ *n.* radiation from the upper atmosphere, detectable at night.

airhead /áirhed/ *n.* **1** *Mil.* a forward base for aircraft in enemy territory. **2** *sl.* a silly or stupid person.

airing /áiring/ *n.* **1** exposure to fresh air, esp. for exercise or an excursion. **2** esp. *Brit.* exposure (of laundry, etc.) to warm air. **3** public expression of an opinion, etc. (*the idea will get an airing at tomorrow's meeting*). **4** a broadcast, esp. of a radio or television program.

airless /áirlis/ *adj.* **1** stuffy; not ventilated. **2** without wind or breeze; still. □□ **airlessness** *n.*

■ **1** see STUFFY 1.

airlift /áirlift/ *n. & v.* ● *n.* the transport of troops, supplies, or passengers by air, esp. in a blockade or other emergency. ● *v.tr.* transport in this way.

airline /áirlīn/ *n.* an organization providing a regular public service of air transport on one or more routes.

airliner /áirlinər/ *n.* a passenger aircraft, esp. a large one.

■ see PLANE¹ *n.* 3.

airlock /áirlok/ *n.* **1** a stoppage of the flow in a pump or pipe, caused by an air bubble. **2** a compartment with controlled pressure and parallel sets of doors, to permit movement between areas at different pressures.

airmail /áirmayl/ *n. & v.* ● *n.* **1** a system of transporting mail by air. **2** mail carried by air. ● *v.tr.* send by airmail.

airman /áirmən/ *n.* (*pl.* **-men**) **1** a pilot or member of the crew of an aircraft. **2** a member of the USAF or RAF below commissioned rank.

airmiss /áirmis/ *n. Brit.* a circumstance in which two or more aircraft in flight on different routes are less than a prescribed distance apart.

airmobile /áirmōbəl, -beel, -bil/ *adj.* (of troops) that can be moved about by air.

airplane /áirplayn/ *n.* a powered heavier-than-air flying vehicle with fixed wings. [F *aéroplane* (as AERO-, PLANE¹)]

■ see PLANE¹ 3.

airplay /áirplay/ *n.* broadcasting (of recorded music).

airport /áirpawrt/ *n.* a complex of runways and buildings for the takeoff, landing, and maintenance of civil aircraft, with facilities for passengers.

airscrew /áirskrōō/ *n. Brit.* an aircraft propeller.

airship /áirship/ *n.* a power-driven aircraft that is lighter than air.

airsick /áirsik/ *adj.* affected with nausea due to travel in an aircraft. □□ **airsickness** *n.*

airspace /áirspays/ *n.* the air available to aircraft to fly in, esp. the part subject to the jurisdiction of a particular country.

airspeed /áirspeed/ *n.* the speed of an aircraft relative to the air through which it is moving.

airstrip /áirstrip/ *n.* a strip of ground suitable for the takeoff and landing of aircraft but usu. without other facilities.

airtight /áirtīt/ *adj.* **1** not allowing air to pass through. **2** having no visible or apparent weaknesses (*an airtight alibi*).

■ see TIGHT *adj.* 4.

airtime /áirtīm/ *n.* time allotted for a broadcast.

airwaves /áirwayvz/ *n.pl. colloq.* radio waves used in broadcasting.

airway /áirway/ *n.* **1 a** a recognized route followed by aircraft. **b** (often in *pl.*) = AIRLINE. **2** a ventilating passage in a mine.

/.../ **pronunciation**	● **part of speech**
□ **phrases, idioms, and compounds**	
□□ **derivatives**	■ **synonym section**
cross-references appear in SMALL CAPITALS or *italics*	

3 *Med.* (often in *pl.*) the passage(s) through which air passes into the lungs.

airwoman /áirwŏŏmən/ *n.* (*pl.* **-women**) **1** a woman pilot or member of the crew of an aircraft. **2** a member of the USAF or WRAF below commissioned rank.

airworthy /áirwərthee/ *adj.* (of an aircraft) fit to fly.

airy /áiree/ *adj.* (**airier, airiest**) **1** well ventilated; breezy. **2** flippant; superficial. **3 a** light as air. **b** graceful; delicate. **4** insubstantial; ethereal; immaterial. □ **airy-fairy** esp. *Brit. colloq.* unrealistic; impractical; foolishly idealistic. □□ **airily** *adv.* **airiness** *n.*

■ **1** see BREEZY 1. **2** see BREEZY 3. **3 b** see DELICATE 1a. **4** see IMMATERIAL 2.

aisle /īl/ *n.* **1** part of a church, esp. one parallel to and divided by pillars from the nave, choir, or transept. **2** a passage between rows of pews, seats, etc. **3** a passageway in a supermarket, department store, etc. □□ **aisled** *adj.* [ME *ele, ile* f. OF *ele* f. L *ala* wing: confused with *island* and F *aile* wing]

ait /ayt/ *n.* (also **eyot**) *Brit.* a small island, esp. in a river. [OE *iggath,* etc. f. *īeg* ISLAND + dimin. suffix]

aitch /aych/ *n.* the name of the letter H. □ **drop one's aitches** esp. *Brit.* fail to pronounce the initial *h* in words. [ME f. OF *ache*]

aitchbone /áychbōn/ *n.* **1** the buttock or rump bone. **2** a cut of beef lying over this. [ME *nage-, nache-bone* buttock, ult. f. L *natis, -es* buttock(s): for loss of *n* cf. ADDER, APRON]

ajar[1] /əjáar/ *adv. & predic.adj.* (of a door) slightly open. [A[2] + obs. *char* f. OE *cerr* a turn]

■ see OPEN *adj.* 1–4, 13, 20.

ajar[2] /əjáar/ *adv.* out of harmony. [A[2] + JAR[2]]

AK *abbr.* Alaska (in official postal use).

a.k.a. *abbr.* also known as.

AKC *abbr.* American Kennel Club.

akee /əkée/ *n.* (also **ackee**) **1** a tropical tree, *Blighia sapida.* **2** its fruit, edible when cooked. [Kru *ākee*]

akela /əkéelə, aakáylə/ *n.* the adult leader of a group of Cub Scouts. [name of the leader of a wolf pack in Kipling's *Jungle Book*]

akimbo /əkímbō/ *adv.* (of the arms) with hands on the hips and elbows turned outwards. [ME *in kenebowe,* prob. f. ON]

akin /əkín/ *predic.adj.* **1** related by blood. **2** (often foll. by *to*) of similar or kindred character. [A-[4] + KIN]

■ **1** see KIN *adj.* **2** kindred; see also ALIKE *adj.*; (*akin to*) related to, allied *or* connected *or* affiliated to *or* with, associated with, germane to, like, similar to.

Akkadian /əkáydeeən/ (also **Accadian**) *adj. & n. hist.* ● *adj.* of Akkad in ancient Babylonia. ● *n.* **1** the Semitic language of Akkad. **2** an inhabitant of Akkad.

akvavit var. of AQUAVIT.

AL *abbr.* Alabama (in official postal use).

Al *symb. Chem.* the element aluminum.

al- /al, əl/ *prefix* assim. form of AD- before *-l.*

-al /əl/ *suffix* **1** forming adjectives meaning 'relating to; of the kind of': **a** from Latin or Greek words (*central; regimental; colossal; tropical*) (cf. -IAL, -ICAL). **b** from English nouns (*tidal*). **2** forming nouns, esp. of verbal action (*animal; rival; arrival; proposal; trial*). [sense 1 f. F *-el* or L *-alis* adj. suffix rel. to *-aris* (-AR[1]); sense 2 f. F *-aille* or f. (or after) L *-alis,* etc., used as noun]

Ala. *abbr.* Alabama.

à la /áa laa/ *prep.* after the manner of (*à la russe*). [F, f. À LA MODE]

alabaster /áləbastər/ *n. & adj.* ● *n.* a translucent usu. white form of gypsum, often carved into ornaments. ● *adj.* **1** of alabaster. **2** like alabaster in whiteness or smoothness. □□ **alabastrine** /-bástrin/ *adj.* [ME f. OF *alabastre* f. L *alabaster, -trum,* f. Gk *alabast(r)os*]

à la carte /áa laa kaárt/ *adv. & adj.* ordered as separately priced item(s) from a menu, not as part of a set meal. [F]

alack /əlák/ *int.* (also **alack-a-day** /əlákəday/) *archaic* an expression of regret or surprise. [prob. f. AH + LACK]

alacrity /əlákritee/ *n.* briskness or cheerful readiness. [L *alacritas* f. *alacer* brisk]

■ see DISPATCH *n.* 4.

Aladdin's cave /əlád'nz/ *n.* a place of great riches. [*Aladdin* in the *Arabian Nights' Entertainments*]

Aladdin's lamp *n.* a talisman enabling its holder to gratify any wish.

à la mode /áa laa mṓd/ *adv. & adj.* **1** in fashion; fashionable. **2 a** served with ice cream. **b** (of beef) braised in wine. [F, = in the fashion]

■ **1** see FASHIONABLE 1, 2.

alar /áylər/ *adj.* **1** relating to wings. **2** winglike or wing-shaped. **3** axillary. [L *alaris* f. *ala* wing]

alarm /əláarm/ *n. & v.* ● *n.* **1** a warning of danger, etc. (*gave the alarm*). **2 a** a warning sound or device (*the burglar alarm was set off accidentally*). **b** = *alarm clock.* **3** frightened expectation of danger or difficulty (*were filled with alarm*). ● *v.tr.* **1** frighten or disturb. **2** arouse to a sense of danger. □ **alarm clock** a clock with a device that can be made to sound at a time set in advance. [ME f. OF *alarme* f. It. *allarme* f. *all'arme!* to arms]

■ *n.* **1** warning, alert, danger signal, distress signal. **2 a** tocsin, bell, gong, siren, whistle, horn; red *or* warning light; call. **3** fear, fright, apprehension, dismay, trepidation, terror, dread, anxiety, angst, excitement, panic, consternation, distress, nervousness, uneasiness, concern, discomfort. ● *v.* **1** frighten, scare, daunt, startle, terrify, panic; unnerve, dismay, disturb, upset. **2** alert, warn, rouse, put on the alert.

alarming /əláarming/ *adj.* disturbing; frightening. □□ **alarmingly** *adv.*

■ see *frightening* (FRIGHTEN).

alarmist /əláarmist/ *n. & adj.* ● *n.* a person given to spreading needless alarm. ● *adj.* creating needless alarm. □□ **alarmism** *n.*

alarum /əláarəm/ *n. archaic* = ALARM. □ **alarums and excursions** confused noise and activity.

Alas. *abbr.* Alaska.

alas /əlás/ *int.* an expression of grief, pity, or concern. [ME f. OF *a las(se)* f. *a* ah + *las(se)* f. L *lassus* weary]

alate /áylayt/ *adj.* having wings or winglike appendages. [L *alatus* f. *ala* wing]

alb /alb/ *n.* a usu. white vestment reaching to the feet, worn by some Christian priests at church ceremonies. [OE *albe* f. eccl.L *alba* fem. of L *albus* white]

albacore /álbəkawr/ *n.* **1** a long-finned tuna, *Thunnus alalunga.* **2** any of various other related fish. [Port. *albacor, -cora,* f. Arab. *al* the + *bakr* young camel or *bakūr* premature, precocious]

Albanian /albáyneeən, awl-/ *n. & adj.* ● *n.* **1 a** a native or inhabitant of Albania in SE Europe. **b** a person of Albanian descent. **2** the language of Albania. ● *adj.* of or relating to Albania or its people or language.

albata /albáatə/ *n. Brit.* German silver; an alloy of nickel, copper, and zinc. [L *albata* whitened f. *albus* white]

albatross /álbətraws, -tros/ *n.* **1 a** any long-winged stout-bodied bird of the family Diomedeidae related to petrels, inhabiting the Pacific Ocean. **b** a source of frustration or guilt; an encumbrance. **2** *Brit. Golf* = *double eagle.* [alt. (after L *albus* white) of 17th-c. *alcatras,* applied to various seabirds, f. Sp. and Port. *alcatraz,* var. of Port. *alcatruz* f. Arab. *alk̄adūs* the pitcher]

albedo /albéedō/ *n.* (*pl.* **-os**) the proportion of light or radiation reflected by a surface, esp. of a planet or moon. [eccl.L, = whiteness, f. L *albus* white]

albeit /áwlbéeit/ *conj. formal* though (*he tried, albeit without success*).

albescent /albésənt/ *adj.* growing or shading into white. [L *albescere albescent-* f. *albus* white]

Albigenses /álbijénseez/ *n.pl.* the members of a heretic sect in S. France in the 12th–13th c. □□ **Albigensian** *adj.* [L f. *Albi* in S. France]

albino /albínō/ *n.* (*pl.* **-os**) **1** a person or animal having a congenital absence of pigment in the skin and hair (which are white), and the eyes (which are usu. pink). **2** a plant lacking normal coloring. □□ **albinism** /álbinizəm/ *n.* **albinotic** /álbinótik/ *adj.* [Sp. & Port. f. *albo* L f. *albus* white + *-ino* = -INE[1]]

Albion /álbeeən/ n. literary (also **perfidious Albion**) Britain or England. [OE f. L f. Celt. Albio (unrecorded): F la perfide Albion with ref. to alleged treachery to other nations]

albite /álbīt/ n. Mineral. a feldspar, usu. white, rich in sodium. [L albus white + -ITE¹]

album /álbəm/ n. **1** a blank book for the insertion of photographs, stamps, etc. **2 a** a long-playing phonograph, audio cassette, or compact disc recording. **b** a set of these. [L, = a blank tablet, neut. of albus white]

albumen /álbyo͞omin/ n. **1** egg white. **2** Bot. the substance found between the skin and embryo of many seeds, usu. the edible part; = ENDOSPERM. [L albumen -minis white of egg f. albus white]

albumin /álbyo͞omin/ n. any of a class of water-soluble proteins found in egg white, milk, blood, etc. □□ **albuminous** adj. [F albumine f. L albumin-: see ALBUMEN]

albuminoid /álbyo͞ominoyd/ n. = SCLEROPROTEIN.

albuminuria /álbyo͞omino͝oreeə, -nyo͝or-/ n. the presence of albumin in the urine, usu. as a symptom of kidney disease.

alburnum /albэ́rnəm/ n. = SAPWOOD. [L f. albus white]

alcahest var. of ALKAHEST.

alcaic /alkáyik/ adj. & n. ● adj. of the verse meter invented by Alcaeus, lyric poet of Mytilene c.600 BC, occurring in four line stanzas. ● n. (in pl.) alcaic verses. [LL alcaicus f. Gk alkaikos f. Alkaios Alcaeus]

alcalde /aalkaálday/ n. a magistrate or mayor in a Spanish, Portuguese, or Latin American town. [Sp. f. Arab. al-ḳāḍī the judge: see CADI]

alchemy /álkəmee/ n. (pl. **-ies**) **1** the medieval forerunner of chemistry, esp. seeking to turn base metals into gold or silver. **2** a miraculous transformation or the means of achieving this. □□ **alchemic** /alkémik/ adj. **alchemical** /-kémikəl/ adj. **alchemist** n. **alchemize** v.tr. [ME f. OF alkemie, alkamie f. med.L alchimia, -emia, f. Arab. alkīmiyā' f. al the + kīmiyā' f. Gk khēmia, -meia art of transmuting metals]

alcheringa /álchərínggə/ n. (in the mythology of some Australian Aboriginals) the "golden age" when the first ancestors were created. [Aboriginal, = dreamtime]

alcohol /álkəhawl, -hol/ n. **1** (in full **ethyl alcohol**) a colorless volatile flammable liquid forming the intoxicating element in wine, beer, liquor, etc., and also used as a solvent, as fuel, etc. Also called ETHANOL. ¶ Chem. formula: C_2H_5OH. **2** any liquor containing this. **3** Chem. any of a large class of organic compounds that contain one or more hydroxyl groups attached to carbon atoms. [F or med.L f. Arab. al-kuḥl f. al the + kuḥl KOHL]
■ **2** spirits, liquor, (strong) drink, colloq. booze, firewater, grog, hooch, sl. rotgut, hard stuff, moonshine, lush.

alcoholic /álkəháwlik, -hól-/ adj. & n. ● adj. of, relating to, containing, or caused by alcohol. ● n. a person suffering from alcoholism.
■ adj. intoxicating, intoxicant, inebriating.
● n. drunkard, drunk, dipsomaniac, sot, drinker, winebibber, serious or hard or problem drinker, tippler, archaic or literary toper, colloq. barfly, soak, boozer, dipso, sl. wino, lush.

alcoholism /álkəhawlízəm, -ho-/ n. **1** an addiction to the consumption of alcoholic liquor. **2** the diseased condition resulting from this. [mod.L alcoholismus (as ALCOHOL)]

alcoholometer /álkəhawlómitər, -ho-/ n. an instrument for measuring alcoholic concentration in a liquid. □□ **alcoholometry** n.

alcove /álkōv/ n. a recess, esp. in the wall of a room or of a garden. [F f. Sp. alcoba f. Arab. al-ḳubba f. al the + ḳubba vault]
■ see RECESS n. 1.

aldehyde /áldihīd/ n. Chem. any of a class of compounds formed by the oxidation of alcohols (and containing the group -CHO). □□ **aldehydic** /áldihīdik/ adj. [abbr. of mod.L alcohol dehydrogenatum alcohol deprived of hydrogen]

al dente /aal déntay, al déntee/ adj. (of pasta, etc.) cooked so as to be still firm when bitten. [It., lit. 'to the tooth']

alder /áwldər/ n. any tree of the genus Alnus, related to the birch, with catkins and toothed leaves. □ **alder buckthorn**

a shrub, Frangula alnus, related to the buckthorn. [OE alor, aler, rel. to L alnus, with euphonic d]

alderman /áwldərmən/ n. (pl. **-men**; fem. **alderwoman**, pl. **-women**) **1** an elected municipal official serving on the governing council of a city. **2** esp. hist. a co-opted member of an English county or borough council, next in dignity to the mayor. □□ **aldermanic** /-mánik/ adj. **aldermanship** n. [OE aldor patriarch f. ald old + MAN]

aldrin /áwldrin/ n. a white crystalline chlorinated hydrocarbon used as an insecticide. [K. Alder, Ger. chemist d. 1958 + -IN]

ale /ayl/ n. **1** beer. **2** a similar beverage with a more pronounced, often bitter taste. [OE alu, = ON öl]

aleatoric /áyleeətáwrik, -tór-/ adj. **1** depending on the throw of a die or on chance. **2** Mus. & Art involving random choice by a performer or artist; improvisational. [L aleatorius aleator dice player f. alea die]

aleatory /áyleeətawree/ adj. = ALEATORIC. [as ALEATORIC]

alec /álik/ n. (also **aleck**) Austral. sl. a stupid person. [shortening of SMART ALEC]

alee /əlee'/ adv. & predic.adj. **1** on the lee or sheltered side of a ship. **2** to leeward. [ME, f. A² + LEE]

alehouse /áylhows/ n. a tavern.

alembic /əlémbik/ n. **1** hist. an apparatus formerly used in distilling. **2** a means of refining or extracting. [ME f. OF f. med.L alembicus f. Arab. al-'anbīḳ f. al the + 'anbīḳ still f. Gk ambix, -ikos cup, cap of a still]

aleph /áalif/ n. the first letter of the Hebrew alphabet. [Heb. 'āleṗ, lit. 'ox']

alert /əlέrt/ adj., n., & v. ● adj. **1** watchful or vigilant; ready to take action. **2** quick (esp. of mental faculties); attentive. ● n. **1** a warning call or alarm. **2 a** warning of an air raid, weather emergency, etc. **b** the duration of this. ● v.tr. (often foll. by to) make alert; warn (were alerted to the danger). □ **on the alert** on the lookout against danger or attack. □□ **alertly** adv. **alertness** n. [F alerte f. It. all' erta to the watchtower]
■ adj. **1** awake, wide awake, watchful, vigilant, attentive, heedful, wary, cautious, aware, observant, open-eyed, on one's toes, on one's guard, colloq. on the ball. **2** active, nimble, lively, agile, quick, spry, sprightly, vivacious, alive; attentive, colloq. all there, with it, bright-eyed and bushy-tailed, Brit. sl. fly. ● n. **1** alarm, warning, signal, call, siren, danger signal, distress signal. ● v. warn, caution, alarm, forewarn; (alert to) advise of, notify of, point out. □ **on the alert** on the qui vive, on guard, on the lookout, watchful, on one's toes. □□ **alertness** see VIGILANCE, INTELLIGENCE 1b.

-ales /áyleez/ suffix forming the plural names of orders of plants (Rosales). [pl. of L adj. suffix -alis: see -AL]

aleurone /ályo͝orōn/ n. (also **aleuron** /-ron/) Biochem. a protein found as granules in the seeds of plants, etc. [Gk aleuron flour]

Aleut /aleeo͝ot, əlo͝ot/ n. **1 a** a N. American people native to the Aleutian Islands and the western Alaskan Peninsula. **b** a member of this people. **2** the language of this people. □□ **Aleutian** adj.

alewife /áylwīf/ n. (pl. **alewives**) any of several species of fish related to the herring. [corrupt. of 17th-c. aloofe: orig. uncert.]

alexanders /áligzándərz/ n. **1** an umbelliferous plant, Smyrnium olusatrum, with yellow flowers formerly used in salads. **2** a white-flowered tall plant, Angelica atropurpurea, of the parsley family. [OE f. med.L alexandrum]

Alexandrian /áligzándreeən/ adj. **1** of or characteristic of Alexandria in Egypt. **2 a** belonging to or akin to the schools of literature and philosophy of Alexandria. **b** (of a writer) derivative or imitative; fond of recondite learning.

alexandrine /áligzándrin, -dreen/ adj. & n. ● adj. (of a line of verse) having six iambic feet. ● n. an alexandrine line.

/.../ pronunciation	● part of speech
□ phrases, idioms, and compounds	
□□ derivatives	■ synonym section
cross-references appear in SMALL CAPITALS or italics	

[F *alexandrin* f. *Alexandre* Alexander (the Great), the subject of an Old French poem in this meter]

alexandrite /áligzándrīt/ *n. Mineral.* a green variety of chrysoberyl. [Tsar *Alexander* I of Russia + -ITE¹]

alexia /əlékseeə/ *n.* the inability to see words or to read, caused by a condition of the brain. [mod.L, A-¹ + Gk *lexis* speech f. *legein* to speak, confused with L *legere* to read]

alfalfa /alfálfə/ *n.* a leguminous plant, *Medicago sativa*, with clover-like leaves and flowers used for fodder. Also called LUCERNE. [Sp. f. Arab. *al-faṣfaṣa*, a green fodder]

alfresco /alfréskō/ *adv. & adj.* in the open air (*we lunched alfresco; an alfresco lunch*). [It. *al fresco* in the fresh (air)]

alga /álgə/ *n.* (*pl.* **algae** /áljee/ also **algas**) (usu. in *pl.*) a non-flowering stemless water plant, esp. seaweed and phytoplankton. □□ **algal** *adj.* **algoid** *adj.* [L]

algebra /áljibrə/ *n.* **1** the branch of mathematics that uses letters and other general symbols to represent numbers and quantities in formulae and equations. **2** a system of this based on given axioms (*linear algebra; the algebra of logic*). □□ **algebraic** /áljibráyik/ *adj.* **algebraical** *adj.* **algebraically** *adv.* **algebraist** *n.* [It. & Sp. & med.L, f. Arab. *al-jabr* f. *al* the + *jabara* reunion of broken parts f. *jabara* reunite]

-algia /áljə/ *comb. form Med.* denoting pain in a part specified by the first element (*neuralgia*). □□ **-algic** *comb. form* forming adjectives. [Gk f. *algos* pain]

algicide /álgisīd/ *n.* a preparation for destroying algae.

algid /áljid/ *adj. Med.* cold; chilly. □□ **algidity** /aljíditee/ *n.* [L *algidus* f. *algēre* be cold]

alginate /áljinayt/ *n.* a salt or ester of alginic acid. [ALGA + -IN + -ATE¹]

alginic acid /aljínik/ *n.* an insoluble carbohydrate found (chiefly as salts) in many brown seaweeds. [ALGA + -IN + -IC]

algoid see ALGA.

Algol /álgawl, -gol/ *n.* (also **ALGOL**) a high-level computer programming language. [*algorithmic* (see ALGORITHM) + LANGUAGE]

algolagnia /álgəlágneeə/ *n.* sexual pleasure derived from inflicting pain on oneself or others; masochism or sadism. □□ **algolagnic** *adj. & n.* [mod.L f. G *Algolagnie* f. Gk *algos* pain + *lagneia* lust]

algology /algóləjee/ *n.* the study of algae. □□ **algological** /-lójikəl/ *adj.* **algologist** *n.*

Algonquian /algóngkweeən/ *n.* any of the languages or dialects used by the Algonquin peoples.

Algonquin /algóngkwən/ *n.* **1** a N. American people native to the Ottawa River valley and the northern St. Lawrence River valley. **2** a member of this people.

algorithm /álgərithəm/ *n.* **1** *Math.* a process or set of rules used for calculation or problem-solving, esp. with a computer. **2** (also **algorism** /álgərizəm/) the Arabic or decimal notation of numbers. □□ **algorithmic** /álgəríthmik/ *adj.* [*algorism* ME ult. f. Pers. *al-Ḵuwārizmī* 9th-c. mathematician: *algorithm* infl. by Gk *arithmos* number (cf. F *algorithme*)]

alguacil /álgwəsil/ *n.* (also **alguazil** /-zil/) **1** a mounted official at a bullfight. **2** a constable or an officer of justice in Spain or Spanish-speaking countries. [Sp. f. Arab. *al-wazīr* f. *al* the + *wazir*: see VIZIER]

alias /áyleeəs/ *adv. & n.* ● *adv.* also named or known as. ● *n.* a false or assumed name. [L, = at another time, otherwise]

■ *n.* see PSEUDONYM.

alibi /álibī/ *n. & v.* (*pl.* **alibis**) ● *n.* **1** a claim, or the evidence supporting it, that when an alleged act took place one was elsewhere. **2** an excuse of any kind; a pretext or justification. ● *v.* (**alibis, alibied, alibiing**) *colloq.* **1** *tr.* provide an alibi or offer an excuse for (a person). **2** *intr.* provide an alibi. [L, = elsewhere]

■ *n.* excuse, explanation; justification, reason; *colloq.* story, side of the story, line. ● *v.* excuse, explain, justify; give an explanation or excuse.

alicyclic /álisíklik, -síklík/ *adj. Chem.* of, denoting, or relating to organic compounds combining a cyclic structure with aliphatic properties, e.g., cyclohexane. [G *alicyclisch* (as ALIPHATIC, CYCLIC)]

alidade /álidayd/ *n. Surveying & Astron.* an instrument for determining directions or measuring angles. [F f. med.L f. Arab. *al-'iḍāda* the revolving radius f. *'aḍud* upper arm]

alien /áyleeən/ *adj. & n.* ● *adj.* **1 a** (often foll. by *to*) unfamiliar; not in accordance or harmony; unfriendly; hostile; unacceptable or repugnant (*army discipline was alien to him; struck an alien note*). **b** (often foll. by *to* or *from*) different or separated. **2** foreign; from a foreign country. **3** of or relating to beings supposedly from other worlds. **4** *Bot.* (of a plant) introduced from elsewhere and naturalized in its new home. ● *n.* **1** a foreigner, esp. one who is not a naturalized citizen of the country where he or she is living. **2** a being supposedly from another world. **3** *Bot.* an alien plant. □□ **alienness** *n.* [ME f. OF f. L *alienus* belonging to another (*alius*)]

■ *adj.* **1 a** foreign, strange, odd, weird, bizarre, peculiar, abnormal; exotic, remote, outlandish, unfamiliar, unknown, unrelated, unconnected; see also UNACCEPTABLE, HOSTILE 2. **b** different, separate(d), unlike, unalike, dissimilar, differing. **2** see FOREIGN 1. **3** extraterrestrial, unearthly. ● *n.* **1** foreigner, stranger, denizen, outlander, outsider, nonnative, immigrant, newcomer. **2** extraterrestrial, E.T.; martian.

alienable /áyleeənəbəl/ *adj. Law* able to be transferred over ownership. □□ **alienability** /-bílitee/ *n.*

alienage /áyleeənij/ *n.* the state or condition of being an alien.

alienate /áyleeənayt/ *v.tr.* **1 a** cause (a person) to become unfriendly or hostile. **b** (often foll. by *from*) cause (a person) to feel isolated or estranged from (friends, society, etc.). **2** transfer ownership of (property) to another person, etc. □□ **alienator** *n.* [ME f. L *alienare alienat-* (as ALIEN)]

■ **1** estrange, isolate, detach, distance, put at a distance; antagonize; (*alienate from*) turn away from, wean away from.

alienation /áyleeənáyshən/ *n.* **1** the act or result of alienating. **2** (*Theatr.* **alienation effect**) a theatrical effect whereby an audience remains objective, not identifying with the characters or action of a play.

alienist /áyleeənist/ *n.* a psychiatrist, esp. a legal adviser on psychiatric problems. [F *aliéniste* (as ALIEN)]

aliform /áylifawrm/ *adj.* wing-shaped. [mod.L *aliformis* f. L *ala* wing: see -FORM]

alight¹ /əlít/ *v.intr.* **1** esp. *Brit.* **a** (often foll. by *from*) descend from a vehicle. **b** dismount from a horse. **2** descend and settle; come to earth from the air. **3** (foll. by *on*) find by chance; notice. [OE *ālīhtan* (as A-², *līhtan* LIGHT² *v.*)]

alight² /əlít/ *predic.adj.* **1** on fire; burning (*they set the old shed alight; is the fire still alight?*). **2** lighted up; excited (*eyes alight with expectation*). [ME, prob. f. phr. *on a light* (= lighted) *fire*]

■ **1** see ABLAZE *adj.* 1. **2** see ABLAZE 2, FERVENT 1.

align /əlín/ *v.tr.* (also **aline**) **1** put in a straight line or bring into line (*three books were neatly aligned on the shelf*). **2** esp. *Polit.* (usu. foll. by *with*) bring (oneself, etc.) into agreement or alliance with (a cause, policy, political party, etc.). □□ **alignment** *n.* [F *aligner* f. phr. *à ligne* into line: see LINE¹]

alike /əlík/ *adj. & adv.* ● *adj.* (usu. *predic.*) similar; like one another; indistinguishable. ● *adv.* in a similar way or manner (*all were treated alike*). [ME f. OE *gelīc* and ON *glíkr* (LIKE¹)]

■ *adj.* similar, akin, resembling or like one another, akin to one another, similar to one another, showing *or* exhibiting a resemblance, much of a muchness; agnate, allied, related; indistinguishable, identical, undifferentiated, like two peas in a pod; (like) Tweedledum and Tweedledee. ● *adv.* in like manner, in the same manner *or* way, similarly, the same, equally, uniformly, identically.

aliment /álimənt/ *n. formal* **1** food. **2** support or mental sustenance. □□ **alimental** /álimént'l/ *adj.* [ME f. F *aliment* or L *alimentum* f. *alere* nourish]

alimentary /áliméntəree/ *adj.* of, relating to, or providing nourishment or sustenance. □ **alimentary canal** *Anat.* the passage along which food is passed from the mouth to the anus during digestion. [L *alimentarius* (as ALIMENT)]

alimentation /álimentáyshən/ *n.* **1** nourishment; feeding. **2**

maintenance; support; supplying with the necessities of life. [F *alimentation* or med.L *alimentatio* f. *alimentare* (as ALI-MENT)]

alimony /álimōnee/ *n.* the money payable by a man to his wife or former wife or by a woman to her husband or former husband after they are separated or divorced. [L *alimonia* nutriment f. *alere* nourish]
■ maintenance.

A-line /áylīn/ *adj.* (of a garment) having a narrow waist or shoulders and somewhat flared skirt.

aliphatic /álifátik/ *adj. Chem.* of, denoting, or relating to organic compounds in which carbon atoms form open chains, not aromatic rings. [Gk *aleiphar -atos* fat]

aliquot /álikwot/ *adj. & n.* ● *adj.* (of a part or portion) contained by the whole an integral or whole number of times (*4 is an aliquot part of 12*). ● *n.* **1** an aliquot part; an integral factor. **2** (in general use) any known fraction of a whole; a sample. [F *aliquote* f. L *aliquot* some, so many]

alive /əlīv/ *adj.* (usu. *predic.*) **1** (of a person, animal, plant, etc.) living; not dead. **2 a** (of a thing) existing; continuing; in operation or action (*kept his interest alive*). **b** under discussion; provoking interest (*the topic is still very much alive today*). **3** (of a person or animal) lively; active. **4** charged with an electric current; connected to a source of electricity. **5** (foll. by *to*) aware of; alert or responsive to. **6** (foll. by *with*) **a** swarming or teeming with. **b** full of. □ **alive and kicking** *colloq.* very active; lively. **alive and well** still alive or active (esp. despite contrary assumptions or rumors). □□ **aliveness** *n.* [OE *on līfe* (as A[2], LIFE)]
■ **1** living, live, breathing, *archaic* quick, *joc.* in the land of the living, among the living. **2** in operation *or* action; existing, continuing, in existence; discussed, under discussion, on the agenda. **3** alert, active, lively, vivacious, vibrant, quick, spirited, animated, brisk, spry, sprightly, vigorous, energetic, dynamic, vitalized, *colloq.* alive and kicking. **5** (*alive to*) sensitive *or* alert *or* responsive to, aware *or* conscious *or* mindful of, in touch with, cognizant *or* apprised of, *colloq.* wise to. **6 a** astir, teeming, swarming, thronging, crowded, packed, buzzing, crawling, jumping, bustling, humming, *colloq.* lousy. □ **alive and kicking** *colloq.* full of beans, full of pep *or* go *or* life, full of vim and vigor; see also ALIVE 3 above.

alizarin /əlízərin/ *n.* **1** the red coloring matter of madder root, used in dyeing. **2** (*attrib.*) (of a dye) derived from or similar to this pigment. [F *alizarine* f. *alizari* madder f. Arab. *al-'iṣara* pressed juice f. 'aṣara to press fruit]

alkahest /álkəhest/ *n.* (also **alchaest**) the universal solvent sought by alchemists. [sham Arab., prob. invented by Paracelsus]

alkali /álkəlī/ *n.* (*pl.* **alkalis**) **1 a** any of a class of substances that liberate hydroxide ions in water, usu. form caustic or corrosive solutions, turn litmus blue, and have a pH of more than 7, e.g., sodium hydroxide. **b** any other substance with similar but weaker properties, e.g., sodium carbonate. **2** *Chem.* any substance that reacts with or neutralizes hydrogen ions. □ **alkali metals** any of the univalent group of metals, lithium, sodium, potassium, rubidium, and cesium, whose hydroxides are alkalis. □□ **alkalimeter** /álkəlímitər/ *n.* **alkalimetry** /álkəlímitree/ *n.* [ME f. med.L, f. Arab. *al-ḳalī* calcined ashes f. *ḳala* fry]

alkaline /álkəlīn/ *adj.* of, relating to, or having the nature of an alkali; rich in alkali. □ **alkaline earth** (or **alkaline earth metal**) **1** any of the bivalent group of metals, beryllium, magnesium, calcium, strontium, barium, and radium. **2** an oxide of the lime group. □□ **alkalinity** /álkəlínitee/ *n.*

alkaloid /álkəloyd/ *n.* any of a series of nitrogenous organic compounds of plant origin, many of which are used as drugs, e.g., morphine, quinine. [G (as ALKALI)]

alkalosis /álkəlōsis/ *n. Med.* an excessive alkaline condition of the body fluids or tissues.

alkane /álkayn/ *n. Chem.* any of a series of saturated aliphatic hydrocarbons having the general formula C_nH_{2n+2}, including methane, ethane, and propane. [ALKYL + -ANE[2]]

alkanet /álkənet/ *n.* **1 a** any plant of the genus *Alkanna*, esp.

A. tinctoria, yielding a red dye from its roots. **b** the dye itself. **2** any of various similar plants. [ME f. Sp. *alcaneta* dimin. of *alcana* f. Arab. *al-ḥinnā'* the henna shrub]

alkene /álkeen/ *n. Chem.* any of a series of unsaturated aliphatic hydrocarbons containing a double bond and having the general formula C_nH_{2n}, including ethylene. [ALKYL + -ENE]

alkyd /álkid/ *n.* any of the group of synthetic resins derived from various alcohols and acids. [ALKYL + ACID]

alkyl /álkil/ *n.* (in full **alkyl radical**) *Chem.* any radical derived from an alkane by the removal of a hydrogen atom. [G *Alkohol* ALCOHOL + -YL]

alkylate /álkilayt/ *v.tr. Chem.* introduce an alkyl radical into (a compound).

alkyne /álkin/ *n. Chem.* any of a series of unsaturated aliphatic hydrocarbons containing a triple bond and having the general formula C_nH_{2n-2}, including acetylene. [ALKYL + -YNE]

all /awl/ *adj., n., & adv.* ● *adj.* **1 a** the whole amount, quantity, or extent of (*waited all day; all his life; we all know why; take it all*). **b** (with *pl.*) the entire number of (*all the others left; all ten men; the children are all boys; movie stars all*). **2** any whatever (*beyond all doubt*). **3** greatest possible (*with all speed*). **4** *dial.* consumed; entirely finished. ● *n.* **1 a** all the persons or things concerned (*all were present; all were thrown away*). **b** everything (*all is lost; that is all*). **2** (foll. by *of*) **a** the whole of (*take all of it*). **b** every one of (*all of us*). **c** *colloq.* as much as (*all of six feet tall*). **d** *colloq.* affected by; in a state of (*all of a dither*). **3** one's whole strength or resources (*prec. by my, your, etc.*). **4** (in games) on both sides (*the score was two all*). ¶ Widely used with *of* in sense 2a, b, esp. when followed by a pronoun or by a noun implying a number of persons or things, as in *all of the children are here*. However, use with mass nouns (as in *all of the bread*) is often avoided. ● *adv.* **1 a** entirely; quite (*dressed all in black; all around the room; the all-important thing*). **b** as an intensifier (*a book all about ships; stop all this grumbling*). **2** *colloq.* very (*went all shy*). **3** (foll. by *the* + compar.) **a** by so much; to that extent (*if they go, all the better*). **b** in the full degree to be expected (*that makes it all the worse*). □ **all along** all the time (*he was joking all along*). **all-American 1** representing the whole of (or only) America or the US. **2** truly American (*all-American boy*). **3** *Sports* recognized as one of the best in a particular sport. **all and sundry** everyone. **all-around 1** in all respects (*a good performance all around*). **2** for each person (*he bought drinks all around*). **3** (*attrib.*) (of a person) versatile. **all but** very nearly (*it was all but impossible; he was all but drowned*). **all clear** a signal that danger or difficulty is over. **All Fools' Day** esp. *Brit.* April 1. **all for** *colloq.* strongly in favor of. **All Hallows** see HALLOW. **all-important** crucial; vitally important. **all in** *colloq.* exhausted. **all-in** (*attrib.*) *Brit.* inclusive of all. **all in all** everything considered. **all-in wrestling** esp. *Brit.* wrestling with few or no restrictions. **all manner of** see MANNER. **all of a sudden** see SUDDEN. **all one** (or **the same**) (usu. foll. by *to*) a matter of indifference (*it's all one to me*). **all out** involving all one's strength; at full speed (also (with hyphen) *attrib.*: *an all-out effort*). **all over 1** completely finished. **2** in or on all parts of (esp. the body) (*went hot and cold all over; mud all over the carpet*). **3** *colloq.* typically (*that is you all over*). **4** *sl.* effusively attentive to (a person). **all-purpose** suitable for many uses. **all right** (*predic.*) **1** satisfactory; safe and sound; in good condition. **2** satisfactorily; as desired (*it worked out all right*). **3 a** an interjection expressing consent or assent to a proposal or order. **b** as an intensifier (*that's the one all right*). **all-right** *attrib.adj. colloq.* fine; acceptable (*an all-right guy*). **all round** (also **all-round**) *Brit.* = *all-around*. **all-rounder** *Brit.* a versatile person. **All Saints' Day** Nov. 1. **all the same** nevertheless, in spite of this (*he was innocent but was punished*

/.../ **pronunciation**	● **part of speech**
□ **phrases, idioms, and compounds**	
□□ **derivatives**	■ **synonym section**
cross-references appear in SMALL CAPITALS or *italics*	

all the same). **all set** *colloq.* ready to start. **All Souls' Day** Nov. 2. **all there** *colloq.* mentally alert. **all-time** (of a record, etc.) hitherto unsurpassed. **all the time** see TIME. **all together** all at once; all in one place or in a group (*they came all together*) (cf. ALTOGETHER). **all told** in all. **all-up weight** *Brit.* the total weight of an aircraft with passengers, cargo, etc., when airborne. **all very well** *colloq.* an expression used to reject or to imply skepticism about a favorable or consoling remark. **all the way** the whole distance; completely. **at all** (with *neg.* or *interrog.*) in any way; to any extent (*did not swim at all; did you like it at all?*). **in all** in total number; altogether (*there were 10 people in all*). **on all fours** see FOUR. **one and all** everyone. [OE *all*, *eall*, prob. f. Gmc]
■ *n.* **1 a** see EVERYONE, EVERYTHING 1. **b** see EVERYTHING 1. **2 a** see WHOLE *n.* 2. □ **all and sundry** see EVERYONE. **all-around** see VERSATILE 1. **all but** see NEARLY 1. **all-important** see IMPORTANT 1. **all in** see *exhausted* (EXHAUST *v.* 2). **all in all** see *on the whole* (WHOLE). **all out** see BREAKNECK, THOROUGH 1. **all over 2** see EVERYWHERE. **all-purpose** see VERSATILE 2. **all right 2** see OK[1] *adv.* **all-right** see SATISFACTORY 1. **all the same** see NEVERTHELESS. **all set** see READY *adj.* 1, 2. **all there** see ALERT *adj.* 2. **all together** see *at one time* 2 (TIME). **all the way** see *hook, line, and sinker* (HOOK), WIDE *adv.* 2. **at all** see SCARCELY 2. **in all** see ALTOGETHER 3. **one and all** see EVERYONE.

alla breve /álə brév, aálaa brévay/ *n.* *Mus.* a time signature indicating 2 or 4 half note beats in a bar. [It., = at the BREVE]

alla cappella var. of A CAPPELLA.

Allah /álə, aálaa/ *n.* the name of God in Islam. [Arab. *'allāh* contr. of *al-'ilāh* f. *al* the + *ilāh* god]

allantois /əlántōis/ *n.* (*pl.* **allantoides** /áləntō-ideez/) *Zool.* one of several membranes that develop in embryonic reptiles, birds, or mammals. □□ **allantoic** /áləntō-ik/ *adj.* [mod.L f. Gk *allantoeidēs* sausage-shaped]

allay /əláy/ *v.tr.* **1** diminish (fear, suspicion, etc.). **2** relieve or alleviate (pain, hunger, etc.). [OE *ālecgan* (as A-[2], LAY[1])]
■ **2** see RELIEVE 2.

allegation /áligáyshən/ *n.* **1** an assertion, esp. an unproved one. **2** the act or an instance of alleging. [ME f. F *allégation* or L *allegatio* f. *allegare* allege]
■ assertion, avowal, asseveration, claim, declaration, deposition; charge, accusation, indictment, statement, complaint.

allege /əléj/ *v.tr.* **1** (often foll. by *that* + clause, or *to* + infin.) declare to be the case, esp. without proof. **2** advance as an argument or excuse. □□ **alleged** *adj.* [ME f. AF *alegier*, OF *esligier* clear at law; confused in sense with L *allegare*: see ALLEGATION]
■ declare, claim, profess, state, assert, charge, hold, affirm, avow, asseverate, *formal* aver; maintain, contend, report, say. □□ **alleged** claimed, avowed, professed, ostensible, stated; purported, so-called, suspected, supposed, assumed, presumed, reputed; hypothetical, conjectural.

allegedly /əléjidlee/ *adv.* as is alleged or said to be the case.

allegiance /əléejəns/ *n.* **1** loyalty (to a person or cause, etc.). **2** the duty of a subject to his or her sovereign or government. [ME f. AF f. OF *ligeance* (as LIEGE): perh. assoc. with ALLIANCE]
■ see LOYALTY.

allegorical /áligáwrikəl, -gór-/ *adj.* (also **allegoric** /-rik/) consisting of or relating to allegory; by means of allegory. □□ **allegorically** *adv.*

allegorize /áligəríz/ *v.tr.* treat as or by means of an allegory. □□ **allegorization** /-rizáyshən/ *n.*

allegory /áligawree/ *n.* (*pl.* **-ies**) **1** a story, play, poem, picture, etc., in which the meaning or message is represented symbolically. **2** the use of such symbols. **3** a symbol. □□ **allegorist** *n.* [ME f. OF *allegorie* f. L *allegoria* f. Gk *allēgoria* f. *allos* other + *-agoria* speaking]

allegretto /áligrétō/ *adv.*, *adj.*, & *n.* *Mus.* ● *adv.* & *adj.* in a fairly brisk tempo. ● *n.* (*pl.* **-os**) an allegretto passage or movement. [It., dimin. of ALLEGRO]

allegro /əléggrō, əláy-/ *adv.*, *adj.*, & *n.* *Mus.* ● *adv.* & *adj.*

in a brisk tempo. ● *n.* (*pl.* **-os**) an allegro passage or movement. [It., = lively]

allele /əleél/ *n.* one of the (usu. two) alternative forms of a gene. □□ **allelic** /əleélik/ *adj.* [G *Allel*, abbr. of ALLELOMORPH]

allelomorph /əleéləmawrf, əlél-/ *n.* = ALLELE. □□ **allelomorphic** /-mórfik/ *adj.* [Gk *allēl-* one another + *morphē* form]

alleluia /álilōōyə/ *int.* & *n.* (also **alleluya**, **hallelujah** /hál-/) ● *int.* God be praised. ● *n.* **1** praise to God. **2** a song of praise to God. **3** *RC Ch.* the part of the mass including this. [ME f. eccl.L f. (Septuagint) Gk *allēlouia* f. Heb. *hallĕlûyāh* praise ye the Lord]

allemande /álemánd, -maánd/ *n.* **1** a figure in a country dance. **2 a** the name of several German dances. **b** the music for any of these, esp. as a movement of a suite. [F, = German (dance)]

Allen screw /álən/ *n.* a screw with a hexagonal socket in the head.

Allen wrench /álən/ *n.* a hexagonal wrench designed to fit into and turn an Allen screw. [*Allen*, name of the manufacturer]

allergen /álərjən/ *n.* any substance that causes an allergic reaction. □□ **allergenic** /-jénik/ *adj.* [ALLERGY + -GEN]

allergic /əlórjik/ *adj.* **1** (foll. by *to*) **a** having an allergy to. **b** *colloq.* having a strong dislike for (a person or thing). **2** caused by or relating to an allergy.

allergy /álərjee/ *n.* (*pl.* **-ies**) **1** *Med.* a condition of reacting adversely to certain substances, esp. particular foods, pollen, fur, or dust. **2** *colloq.* an antipathy or dislike. □□ **allergist** *n.* [G *Allergie*, after *Energie* ENERGY, f. Gk *allos* other]

alleviate /əleéveeayt/ *v.tr.* lessen or make less severe (pain, suffering, etc.). □□ **alleviation** /-áyshən/ *n.* **alleviative** *adj.* **alleviator** *n.* **alleviatory** /-veeátawree/ *adj.* [LL *alleviare* lighten f. L *allevare* (as AD-, *levare* raise)]
■ see EASE *v.* 1a, 2a.

alley[1] /álee/ *n.* (*pl.* **-eys**) **1** (also **alleyway**) **a** a narrow street. **b** a narrow passageway, esp. between or behind buildings. **2** a path or walk in a park or garden. **3** an enclosure for bowling, etc. **4** (in tennis) either of the two side strips of a doubles court. □ **alley cat** a stray cat often mangy or half wild. **up** (or **right up**) **one's alley** (or **street**) *colloq.* **1** within a person's range of interest or knowledge. **2** to a person's liking. [ME f. OF *alee* walking, passage f. *aler* go f. L *ambulare* walk]
■ **up** (or **right up**) **one's alley** (or **street**) suiting a person to a T, *colloq.* one's cup of tea.

alley[2] /álee/ *n.* (also **ally**) (*pl.* **-eys** or **-ies**) a choice playing marble made of marble, alabaster, or glass. [perh. dimin. of ALABASTER]

alliaceous /álee-áyshəs/ *adj.* **1** of or relating to the genus *Allium*. **2** tasting or smelling like onion or garlic. [mod.L *alliaceus* f. L *allium* garlic]

alliance /əlíəns/ *n.* **1 a** a union or agreement to cooperate, esp. of nations by treaty or families by marriage. **b** the parties involved. **2** (**Alliance**) a political party formed by the allying of separate parties. **3** a relationship resulting from an affinity in nature or qualities, etc. (*the old alliance between logic and metaphysics*). **4** *Bot.* a group of allied families. [ME f. OF *aliance* (as ALLY[1])]
■ **1** union, confederation, federation, league, association, coalition, affiliation; axis, pact, connection, bond. **3** affinity, connection, marriage, closeness; see also KINSHIP 2.

allied /əlíd, álid/ *adj.* **1 a** united or associated in an alliance. **b** (**Allied**) of or relating to the US and its allies in World War I and World War II. **2** connected or related (*studied medicine and allied subjects*).

alligator /áligaytər/ *n.* **1** a large reptile of the crocodile family native to the Americas and China, with upper teeth that lie outside the lower teeth and a head broader and shorter than that of the crocodile. **2** (in general use) any of several large members of the crocodile family. **3 a** the skin of such an animal or material resembling it. **b** (in *pl.*) shoes of this. □ **alligator clip** a clip with teeth for gripping. **alligator pear** an avocado. **alligator snapper** (or **snapping turtle**

or *Brit.* **tortoise**) a large freshwater snapping turtle. [Sp. *el lagarto* the lizard f. L *lacerta*]

alliterate /əlítərayt/ *v.* **1** *intr.* **a** contain alliteration. **b** use alliteration in speech or writing. **2** *tr.* **a** construct (a phrase, etc.) with alliteration. **b** speak or pronounce with alliteration. □□ **alliterative** /əlítəraytiv, -rətiv/ *adj.* [back-form. f. ALLITERATION]

alliteration /əlítəráyshən/ *n.* the occurrence of the same letter or sound at the beginning of adjacent or closely connected words (e.g., *calm, cool, and collected*). [mod.L *alliteratio* (as AD-, *littera* letter)]

allium /áleeəm/ *n.* any plant of the genus *Allium*, usu. bulbous and strong smelling, e.g., onion and garlic. [L, = garlic]

allo- /álō, əló/ *comb. form* other (*allophone*; *allogamy*). [Gk *allos* other]

allocate /áləkayt/ *v.tr.* (usu. foll. by *to*) assign, apportion, or devote to (a purpose, person, or place). □□ **allocable** /-kəbəl/ *adj.* **allocation** /-káyshən/ *n.* **allocator** *n.* [med.L *allocare* f. *locus* place]

■ see ALLOT, ALLOW 2, ASSIGN 1a.

allocution /áləkyōōshən/ *n.* formal or hortatory speech or manner of address. [L *allocutio* f. *alloqui allocut-* speak to]

allogamy /álógəmee/ *n. Bot.* cross-fertilization in plants. [ALLO- + Gk *-gamia* f. *gamos* marriage]

allomorph /áləmawrf/ *n. Linguistics* any of two or more alternative forms of a morpheme. □□ **allomorphic** *adj.* [ALLO- + MORPHEME]

allopath /áləpath/ *n.* one who practices allopathy. [F *allopathe* back-form. f. *allopathie* = ALLOPATHY]

allopathy /əlópəthee/ *n.* the treatment of disease with drugs or other agents having opposite effects to the symptoms (cf. HOMEOPATHY). □□ **allopathic** /áləpáthik/ *adj.* **allopathist** *n.* [G *Allopathie* (as ALLO-, -PATHY)]

allophone /áləfōn/ *n. Linguistics* any of the variant sounds forming a single phoneme. □□ **allophonic** /-fónik/ *adj.* [ALLO- + PHONEME]

allot /əlót/ *v.tr.* (**allotted**, **allotting**) **1** give or apportion to (a person) as a share or task; distribute officially to (*they allotted us each a pair of boots*; *the men were allotted duties*). **2** (foll. by *to*) give or distribute officially (*a sum was allotted to each charity*). [OF *aloter* f. *a* to + LOT]

■ apportion, allocate, allow, assign, give, hand, deal, earmark for; (*allot to*) divide among(st), share (out) among(st), distribute to, hand or deal out to, parcel or dole out to, deal (out) to, dispense to.

allotment /əlótmənt/ *n.* **1** a share allotted. **2** *Brit.* a small piece of land rented (usu. from a local authority) for cultivation. **3** the action of allotting.

■ **1** share, apportionment, ration, portion, quota, lot, allowance, measure. **3** see DISTRIBUTION 1, 2a.

allotrope /álətrōp/ *n.* any of two or more different physical forms in which an element can exist (*graphite, charcoal, and diamond are all allotropes of carbon*). [back-form. f. ALLOTROPY]

allotropy /əlótrəpee/ *n.* the existence of two or more different physical forms of a chemical element. □□ **allotropic** /álətrópik/ *adj.* **allotropical** *adj.* [Gk *allotropos* of another form f. *allos* different + *tropos* manner f. *trepō* to turn]

allottee /əlotée/ *n.* a person to whom something is allotted.

allow /əlów/ *v.* **1** *tr.* permit (a practice, a person to do something, a thing to happen, etc.) (*smoking is not allowed*; *we allowed them to speak*). **2** *tr.* give or provide; permit (a person) to have (a limited quantity or sum) (*we were allowed $500 a year*). **3** *tr.* provide or set aside for a purpose; add or deduct in consideration of something (*allow 10% for inflation*). **4** *tr.* **a** admit; agree; concede (*he allowed that it was so*; *"You know best," he allowed*). **b** assert; be of the opinion. **5** *refl.* permit oneself; indulge oneself in (conduct) (*allowed herself to be persuaded*; *allowed myself a few angry words*). **6** *intr.* (foll. by *of*) admit of. **7** *intr.* (foll. by *for*) take into consideration or account; make addition or deduction corresponding to (*allowing for waste*). □□ **allowable** *adj.* **allowably** *adv.* [ME, orig. = 'praise,' f. OF *alouer* f. L *allaudare* to praise, and med.L *allocare* to place]

■ **1** agree to, permit, give leave or permission for,

authorize, admit, entertain, consent to, give the go-ahead or *colloq.* green light to; tolerate, suffer, stand (for), sanction, countenance, consider, put up with, *literary* brook; (*allow to*) let. **2** give, let have, grant, allot, allocate, assign, approve; provide or furnish with. **3** make allowance(s) or concession(s) for, set apart or aside, put aside, take into account or consideration; add (in), include; deduct, take away, exclude. **4 a** agree, acknowledge, admit, grant, concede, own, confess. **5** permit oneself, give oneself, grant oneself; (*allow oneself to*) let oneself. **7** see CONSIDER 4.

□□ **allowable** see PERMISSIBLE. **allowably** see *acceptably* (ACCEPTABLE).

allowance /əlówəns/ *n. & v.* ● *n.* **1** an amount or sum allowed to a person, esp. regularly for a stated purpose. **2** an amount allowed in reckoning. **3** a deduction or discount. **4** (foll. by *of*) tolerance of. ● *v.tr.* **1** make an allowance to (a person). **2** supply in limited quantities. □ **make allowances** (often foll. by *for*) **1** take into consideration (mitigating circumstances) (*made allowances for his demented state*). **2** look with tolerance upon; make excuses for (a person, bad behavior, etc.). [ME f. OF *alouance* (as ALLOW)]

■ *n.* **1** stipend, grant, dole, pin or pocket money, perquisite, quota, ration; remittance, remuneration; pension, annuity, quarterage, per diem. **3** deduction, discount, reduction, rebate, payment, recompense, compensation, remuneration, reimbursement, remittal; tare; *hist.* tret. **4** tolerance, toleration, sufferance, concession, sanction, support, approval. □ **make allowances** (*make allowances for*) **1** take into consideration or account, consider, bear in mind, have regard for. **2** be patient or tolerant with, excuse, make concessions for.

allowedly /əlówidlee/ *adv.* as is generally allowed or acknowledged.

alloy /áloy, əlóy/ *n. & v.* ● *n.* **1** a mixture of two or more chemical elements, at least one of which is a metal, e.g., brass (a mixture of copper and zinc). **2** an inferior metal mixed esp. with gold or silver. ● *v.tr.* **1** mix (metals). **2** debase (a pure substance) by admixture. **3** moderate. [F *aloi* (n.), *aloyer* (v.) f. OF *aloier, aleier* combine f. L *alligare* bind]

■ *n.* **1** mixture, mix, combination, compound, composite, blend, amalgam. **2** admixture. ● *v.* **1** see MIX *v.* 1, 3. **2** contaminate, pollute, adulterate, debase, diminish, impair, vitiate. **3** change, modify, temper, alter, moderate, reduce, diminish.

allspice /áwlspīs/ *n.* **1** the aromatic spice obtained from the ground berry of the pimento plant, *Pimenta dioica*. **2** the berry of this. **3** any of various other aromatic shrubs.

allude /əlōōd/ *v.intr.* (foll. by *to*) **1** refer, esp. indirectly, covertly, or briefly to. **2** mention. [L *alludere* (as AD-, *ludere* lus-play)]

■ **1** see REFER 7, 8.

allure /əlōōr/ *v. & n.* ● *v.tr.* attract, charm, or fascinate. ● *n.* attractiveness; personal charm; fascination. □□ **allurement** *n.* **alluring** *adj.* **alluringly** *adv.* [ME f. OF *alurer* attract (as AD-, *luere* LURE *v.* 1)]

■ *v.* see ATTRACT 2, CAPTIVATE. ● *n.* see CHARM *n.* 1a, b.

allusion /əlōōzhən/ *n.* (often foll. by *to*) a reference, esp. a covert, passing, or indirect one. ¶ Often confused with *illusion*. [F *allusion* or LL *allusio* (as ALLUDE)]

■ see REFERENCE *n.* 3b.

allusive /əlōōsiv/ *adj.* **1** (often foll. by *to*) containing an allusion. **2** containing many allusions. □□ **allusively** *adv.* **allusiveness** *n.*

alluvial /əlōōveeəl/ *adj. & n.* ● *adj.* of or relating to alluvium. ● *n.* alluvium, esp. containing a precious metal.

alluvion /əlōōveeən/ *n.* **1** the wash of the sea against the shore, or of a river against its banks. **2 a** a large overflow of

/.../ **pronunciation**	● **part of speech**
□ **phrases, idioms, and compounds**	
□□ **derivatives**	■ **synonym section**
cross-references appear in SMALL CAPITALS or *italics*	

water. **b** matter deposited by this, esp. alluvium. **3** the formation of new land by the movement of the sea or of a river. [F f. L *alluvio -onis* f. *luere* wash]

alluvium /əlóōveeəm/ *n.* (*pl.* **alluviums** or **alluvia** /-ə/) a deposit of usu. fine fertile soil left during a time of flood, esp. in a river valley or delta. [L neut. of *alluvius* adj. f. *luere* wash]

ally[1] /álī/ *n.* & *v.* ● *n.* (*pl.* **-ies**) **1** a government formally cooperating or united with another for a special purpose, esp. by a treaty. **2** a person or organization that cooperates with or helps another. ● *v.tr.* /also əlí/ (**-ies, -ied**) (often foll. by *with*) combine or unite in alliance. [ME f. OF *al(e)ier* f. L *alligare* bind: cf. ALLOY]

ally[2] var. of ALLEY[2].

-ally /əlee/ *suffix* forming adverbs from adjectives in *-al* (cf. -AL, -LY[2], -ICALLY).

allyl /álil/ *n. Chem.* the unsaturated univalent radical $CH_2=CH-CH_2'$. [L *allium* garlic + -YL]

alma mater /aálmə maátər, álmə máytər/ *n.* (also **Alma Mater**) **1** the university, school, or college one attends or attended. **2** the official anthem or song of a university, school, or college. [L, = bounteous mother]

almanac /áwlmənak, ál-/ *n.* an annual calendar of months and days, usu. with astronomical data and other information. [ME f. med.L *almanac(h)* f. Gk *almenikhiaka*]

almandine /álməndeen, -dīn/ *n.* (also **almandite** /-dīt/) a kind of garnet with a violet tint. [F, alt. of obs. *alabandine* f. med.L *alabandina* f. *Alabanda*, ancient city in Asia Minor]

almighty /áwlmītee/ *adj.* & *adv.* ● *adj.* **1** having complete power; omnipotent. **2** (**the Almighty**) God. **3** *sl.* very great (*an almighty crash*). ● *adv. sl.* extremely; very much. [OE *ælmihtig* (as ALL, MIGHTY)]

almond /aámənd, ám-/ *n.* **1** the oval nutlike seed (kernel) of the fruit from the tree *Prunus dulcis*, of which there are sweet and bitter varieties. **2** the tree itself, of the rose family and related to the peach and plum. □ **almond eyes** narrow almond-shaped eyes. **almond oil** the oil expressed from the seed (esp. the bitter variety), used for cosmetic preparations, flavoring, and medicinal purposes. [ME f. OF *alemande*, etc. f. med.L *amandula* f. L *amygdala* f. Gk *amugdalē*: assoc. with words in AL-]

almoner /aámənər, álmə-/ *n.* **1** *Brit.* a social worker attached to a hospital. ¶ Now usu. called *medical social worker*. **2** *hist.* an official distributor of alms. [ME f. AF *aumoner*, OF *aumonier*, ult. f. med.L *eleēmosynarius* (as ALMS)]

almost /áwlmōst/ *adv.* all but; very nearly. [OE *ælmæst* for the most part (as ALL, MOST)]

■ nearly, (just) about, practically, virtually, bordering on, on the brink of, verging on, on the verge of, more or less, little short of, not quite, all but, *archaic* near, *archaic or rhet.* wellnigh, *colloq.* damn(ed) near.

alms /aamz/ *n.pl. hist.* the charitable donation of money or food to the poor. [OE *ælmysse, -messe*, f. Gmc ult. f. Gk *eleēmosunē* compassionateness f. *eleēmōn* (adj.) f. *eleos* compassion]

almshouse /aámz-hows/ *n.* esp. *Brit. hist.* a house founded by charity for the poor.

aloe /álō/ *n.* **1** any plant of the genus *Aloe*, usu. having toothed fleshy leaves. **2** (in *pl.*) (in full **bitter aloes**) a strong laxative obtained from the bitter juice of various species of aloe. **3** (also **American aloe**) an agave native to Central America. **4** (also **aloe vera**) a species of aloe whose leaves yield an emollient juice. [OE *al(e)we* f. L *aloē* f. Gk]

aloetic /álō-étik/ *adj.* & *n.* ● *adj.* of or relating to an aloe. ● *n.* a medicine containing aloes. [Gk *aloē* aloe, on the false analogy of *diuretic*, etc.]

aloft /əláwft, əlóft/ *predic.adj.* & *adv.* **1** high up; overhead. **2** upwards. [ME f. ON *á lopt(i)* f. *á* in, on, to + *lopt* air: cf. LIFT, LOFT]

■ **1** high up, above, overhead, (up) in the air, in flight, up (above), on high. **2** upwards, up, heavenwards, skywards.

alogical /áylójikəl/ *adj.* **1** not logical. **2** opposed to logic.

aloha /əlōhaa, aa-/ *int.* a Hawaiian salutation at meeting or parting. [Hawaiian, *aloha* love]

alone /əlṓn/ *predic.adj.* & *adv.* **1 a** without others present (*they wanted to be alone*; *the tree stood alone*). **b** without others' help (*succeeded alone*). **c** lonely and isolated (*felt alone*). **2** (often foll. by *in*) standing by oneself in an opinion, quality, etc. (*was alone in thinking this*). **3** only; exclusively (*you alone can help me*). □ **go it alone** act by oneself without assistance. □□ **aloneness** *n.* [ME f. ALL + ONE]

■ **1 a** unaccompanied, unescorted, solitar(il)y, by oneself *or* itself, on one's *or* its own, by *or* on one's lonesome, solo, solus, unattended, isolated. **b** unassisted, unaided, unhelped, single-handed; by oneself *or* itself, single-handedly, independently, individually, personally, under one's own steam. **c** lonely, wretched, friendless, abandoned, forsaken, desolate, remote, deserted. **2** unique, on one's own, without parallel; unequaled, unparalleled, nonpareil, unrivaled, unsurpassed, without equal, untypical, peerless, matchless. **3** only, solely, exclusively; simply, just, merely. □ **go it alone** act independently *or* by oneself, do it under one's own steam. □□ **aloneness** see *loneliness* (LONELY), SOLITUDE 1.

along /əláwng, əlóng/ *prep.* & *adv.* ● *prep.* **1** from one end to the other end of (*a handkerchief with lace along the edge*). **2** on or through any part of the length of (*was walking along the road*). **3** beside or through the length of (*shelves stood along the wall*). ● *adv.* **1** onward; into a more advanced state (*come along*; *getting along nicely*). **2** at or to a particular place or time; arriving (*I'll be along soon*). **3** in company with a person, esp. oneself (*bring a book along*). **4** beside or through part or the whole length of a thing. □ **along with** in addition to; together with. [OE *andlang* f. WG, rel. to LONG[1]]

alongshore /əláwngshawr, əlóng-/ *adv.* along or by the shore.

alongside /əláwngsíd, əlóng-/ *adv.* & *prep.* ● *adv.* at or to the side (of a ship, pier, etc.). ● *prep.* close to the side of; next to. □ **alongside of** side by side with; together or simultaneously with.

■ *prep.* see BESIDE 1.

aloof /əlóōf/ *adj.* & *adv.* ● *adv.* distant; unsympathetic. ● *adv.* away; apart (*he kept aloof from his colleagues*). □□ **aloofly** *adv.* **aloofness** *n.* [orig. Naut., f. A[2] + LUFF]

■ *adj.* distant, remote, cold, cool, chilly, unresponsive, undemonstrative, reserved, indifferent, unapproachable, indrawn, withdrawn; unsympathetic, haughty, superior, supercilious, standoffish, antisocial, unsociable, unfriendly, unsocial, *colloq.* offish, stuck-up. ● *adv.* apart, away, at a distance, separate, at arm's length. □□ **aloofness** see DISTANCE 4.

alopecia /áləpeéshə/ *n. Med.* the absence (complete or partial) of hair from areas of the body where it normally grows; baldness. [L f. Gk *alōpekia* fox mange f. *alōpēx* fox]

aloud /əlówd/ *adv.* **1** audibly; not silently or in a whisper. **2** *archaic* loudly. [A[2] + LOUD]

alow /əlṓ/ *adv.* & *predic.adj. Naut.* in or into the lower part of a ship. [A[2] + LOW[1]]

alp /alp/ *n.* **1 a** a high mountain. **b** (**the Alps**) the high range of mountains in Switzerland and adjoining countries. **2** (in Switzerland) pastureland on a mountainside. [orig. pl., f. F f. L *Alpes* f. Gk *Alpeis*]

alpaca /alpákə/ *n.* **1** a S. American mammal, *Lama pacos*, related to the llama, with long shaggy hair. **2** the wool from the animal. **3** fabric made from the wool, with or without other fibers. [Sp. f. Aymará or Quechua]

alpenhorn /álpənhawrn/ *n.* a long wooden horn used by Alpine herdsmen to call their cattle. [G, = Alp horn]

alpenstock /álpənstok/ *n.* a long iron-tipped staff used in hiking and mountain climbing. [G, = Alp stick]

alpha /álfə/ *n.* **1** the first letter of the Greek alphabet (A, α). **2** a beginning; something that is primary or first. **3** *Brit.* a first-class mark given for a piece of work or on an examination. **4** *Astron.* the chief star in a constellation. □ **alpha and omega** the beginning and the end; the most important features. **alpha particle** (or **ray**) a helium nucleus emitted by a radioactive substance, orig. regarded as a ray. [ME f. L f. Gk]

alphabet /álfəbet/ n. **1** the set of letters used in writing a language (*the Cyrillic alphabet*). **2** a set of symbols or signs representing letters. [LL *alphabetum* f. Gk *alpha*, *bēta*, the first two letters of the alphabet]

alpha-beta brass /álfəbaytə brás/ n. = MUNTZ METAL.

alphabetical /álfəbétikəl/ adj. (also **alphabetic** /-bétik/) **1** of or relating to an alphabet. **2** in the order of the letters of the alphabet. □□ **alphabetically** adv.

alphabetize /álfəbətiz/ v.tr. arrange (words, names, etc.) in alphabetical order. □□ **alphabetization** /-izáyshən/ n.

alphanumeric /álfənoomérik, -nyoo-/ adj. (also **alphameric** /álfəmérik/, **alphanumerical**) containing both alphabetical and numerical symbols. [ALPHABETIC (see ALPHABETICAL) + NUMERICAL]

alpine /álpīn/ adj. & n. ● adj. **1 a** of or relating to high mountains. **b** growing or found on high mountains. **2** (**Alpine**) of or relating to the Alps. ● n. a plant native or suited to a high mountain habitat. [L *Alpinus*: see ALP]

Alpinist /álpinist/ n. (also **alpinist**) a climber of high mountains, esp. the Alps. [F *alpiniste* (as ALPINE; see -IST)]

already /áwlrédee/ adv. **1** before the time in question (*I knew that already*). **2** as early or as soon as this (*already at the age of six*). [ALL adv. + READY]

alright /áwlrít/ adj., adv., & int. disp. = all right.

ALS abbr. AMYOTROPHIC LATERAL SCLEROSIS.

Alsatian /alsáyshən/ n. **1** a native of Alsace, a region of E. France. **2** esp. *Brit.* = German shepherd. [*Alsatia* (= Alsace) + -AN]

alsike /álsik/ n. a European species of clover, *Trifolium hybridum*. [*Alsike* in Sweden]

also /áwlsō/ adv. in addition; likewise; besides. □ **also-ran 1** a horse or dog, etc., not among the winners in a race. **2** one who does not win a competition. **3** an undistinguished person. [OE *alswā* (as ALL adv., SO[1])]
■ see *in addition* (ADDITION).

alt. abbr. **1** alternate. **2** altimeter. **3** altitude.

Alta. abbr. Alberta.

altar /áwltər/ n. **1** a table or flat-topped block, often of stone, for sacrifice or offering to a deity. **2** a raised surface or table at which a Christian service, esp. the Eucharist, is celebrated. □ **altar boy** (or **girl**) a child who serves as a priest's assistant in a service. [OE *altar -er*, Gmc adoption of LL *altar*, *altarium* f. L *altaria* (pl.) burnt offerings, altar, prob. rel. to *adolēre* burn in sacrifice]

altarpiece /áwltərpees/ n. a piece of art, esp. a painting, set above or behind an altar.

altazimuth /altáziməth/ n. a telescope or other instrument mounted so as to allow both vertical and horizontal movement, esp. one used for measuring the altitude and azimuth of celestial bodies. [ALTITUDE + AZIMUTH]

alter /áwltər/ v. **1** tr. & intr. make or become different; change. **2** tr. castrate or spay. □□ **alterable** adj. **alteration** /-ráyshən/ n. [ME f. OF *alterer* f. LL *alterare* f. L *alter* other]
■ **1** change, revise, modify, vary, transform; adjust, adapt, convert, remodel, restyle, refashion, remold, revamp; correct, amend, emend. **2** neuter, castrate, spay, desex, doctor, fix, geld. □□ **alterable** see CHANGEABLE 2. **alteration** change, modification, shift, switch, revision, amendment, emendation, transformation; adjustment, adaptation, conversion, remodeling, reworking; correction.

alterative /áwltəráytiv, -rətiv/ adj. & n. ● adj. **1** tending to alter. **2** (of a medicine) that alters bodily processes. ● n. an alterative medicine or treatment. [ME f. med.L *alterativus* (as ALTER)]

altercate /áwltərkayt/ v.intr. (often foll. by *with*) dispute hotly; wrangle. □□ **altercation** /-káyshən/ n. [L *altercari altercat-*]
■ see ARGUE 1.

alter ego /áwltər ée gō, égō/ n. (pl. **alter egos**) **1** an intimate and trusted friend. **2** a person's secondary or alternative personality. [L, = other self]

alternate v., adj., & n. ● v. /áwltərnayt, ál-/ **1** intr. (often foll. by *with*) (of two things) succeed each other by turns (*rain and sunshine alternated*; *elation alternated with depression*). **2** intr. (foll. by *between*) change repeatedly (between two conditions) (*the patient alternated between hot and cold fevers*). **3** tr. (often foll. by *with*) cause (two things) to succeed each other by turns (*the band alternated fast and slow tunes*; *we alternated criticism with reassurance*). ● adj. /áwltərnət, ál-/ **1** (with noun in *pl.*) every other (*comes on alternate days*). **2** (of things of two kinds) each following and succeeded by one of the other kind (*alternate joy and misery*). **3** (of a sequence, etc.) consisting of alternate things. **4** *Bot.* (of leaves, etc.) placed alternately on the two sides of the stem. **5** = ALTERNATIVE. ● n. /áwltərnət, ál-/ something or someone that is an alternative; a deputy or substitute. □ **alternate angles** two angles, not adjoining one another, that are formed on opposite sides of a line that intersects two other lines. **alternating current** an electric current that reverses its direction at regular intervals. □□ **alternately** adv. [L *alternatus* past part. of *alternare* do things by turns f. *alternus* every other f. *alter* other]
■ v. **1** succeed *or* follow each other, be in alternation *or* succession *or* rotation; be interspersed. **2** see OSCILLATE. **3** rotate, exchange, interchange, switch (around), take in turn *or* by turns, intersperse. ● adj. **1** every other, every second. **2** successive, alternating, rotating, in rotation. **5** alternative, second, (an)other, additional, substitute. ● n. alternative, second (choice), substitute, deputy, delegate, proxy, representative, relief, reserve, stand-in, standby, backup, understudy, pinch hitter, *Austral.* offsider. □□ **alternately** by turns, reciprocally, in rotation.

alternation /áwltərnáyshən, ál-/ n. the action or result of alternating. □ **alternation of generations** reproduction by alternate processes, e.g., sexual and asexual.
■ rotation; interspersion, exchange, interchange, substitution.

alternative /áwltérnətiv, al-/ adj. & n. ● adj. **1** (of one or more things) available or usable instead of another (*an alternative route*). ¶ Use with reference to more than two options (e.g., *many alternative methods*) is common and acceptable. **2** (of two things) mutually exclusive. **3** of or relating to practices that offer a substitute for established or conventional ones (*alternative medicine*; *alternative theater*). ● n. **1** any of two or more possibilities. **2** the freedom or opportunity to choose between two or more things (*I had no alternative but to go*). □ **the alternative society** esp. *Brit.* a group of people dissociating themselves from conventional society and its values. □□ **alternatively** adv. [F *alternatif -ive* or med.L *alternativus* (as ALTERNATE)]
■ adj. **1** second, (an)other, additional, substitute, alternate. **3** see DIFFERENT 3. ● n. **1** see ALTERNATE n. **2** see CHOICE 4, OPTION 1, 2.

alternator /áwltərnaytər, ál-/ n. a generator that produces an alternating current.

althorn /ált-hawrn/ n. *Mus.* an instrument of the saxhorn family, esp. the alto or tenor saxhorn in E flat. [G f. *alt* high f. L *altus* + HORN]

although /awlthō/ conj. = THOUGH conj. 1–3. [ME f. ALL adv. + THOUGH]

altimeter /altimitər, áltimeetər/ n. an instrument for showing height above sea or ground level, esp. one fitted in an aircraft. [L *altus* high + -METER]

altitude /áltitood, -tyood/ n. **1** the height of an object in relation to a given point, esp. sea level or the horizon. **2** *Geom.* the length of the perpendicular from a vertex to the opposite side of a figure. **3** a high or exalted position (*a social altitude*). □ **altitude sickness** a sickness experienced at high altitudes due to a lack of oxygen. □□ **altitudinal** /-tood'n'l, -tyoo-/ adj. [ME f. L *altitudo* f. *altus* high]

/.../	pronunciation	●	part of speech
□	phrases, idioms, and compounds		
□□	derivatives	■	synonym section
cross-references appear in SMALL CAPITALS or *italics*			

■ **1** height, elevation, level.

alto /áltō/ n. (pl. **-os**) **1** = CONTRALTO. **2** = COUNTERTENOR. **3 a** (attrib.) denoting the member of a family of instruments pitched next below a soprano of its type. **b** an alto instrument. □ **alto clef** a clef placing middle C on the middle line of the staff, used chiefly for viola music. [It. alto (canto) high (singing)]

altocumulus /áltōkyŏ́ōmyələs/ n. (pl. **altocumuli** /-lī/) Meteorol. a cloud formation at medium altitude consisting of rounded masses with a level base. [mod.L f. L altus high + CUMULUS]

altogether /áwltəgéthər/ adv. **1** totally; completely (you are altogether wrong). **2** on the whole (altogether it had been a good day). **3** in total (there are six bedrooms altogether). ¶ Note that all together is used to mean 'all at once' or 'all in one place,' as in there are six bedrooms all together. □ **in the altogether** colloq. naked. [ME f. ALL + TOGETHER]

■ **1** entirely, utterly, completely, wholly, totally, fully, in all respects, absolutely, perfectly, quite. **2** on the whole, by and large, in the main, generally, for the most part, on balance; (all) in all. **3** in total, in all, all included. □ **in the altogether** see NAKED 1.

alto-relievo /áltōrileévō/ n. (also **altorilievo** /áltōrilyáyvō/) (pl. **-os**) Sculpture **1** a form of relief in which the sculptured shapes stand out from the background to at least half their actual depth. **2** a sculpture characterized by this. [ALTO + RELIEVO]

altostratus /áltōstráytəs, -strátəs/ n. (pl. **altostrati** /-tī/) a continuous and uniformly flat cloud formation at medium altitude. [mod.L f. L altus high + STRATUS]

altricial /áltríshəl/ adj. & n. ● adj. (esp. of a bird) whose young require care and feeding by the parents after hatching or birth. ● n. an altricial bird or animal (cf. PRECOCIAL). [L altrix altricis (fem.) nourisher f. altor f. alere altus nourish]

altruism /áltrōōīzəm/ n. **1** regard for others as a principle of action. **2** unselfishness; concern for other people. □□ **altruist** n. **altruistic** /-ístik/ adj. **altruistically** adv. [F altruisme f. It. altrui somebody else (infl. by L alter other)]

■ **2** selflessness, self-sacrifice, unselfishness, philanthropy, beneficence, generosity, charity, charitableness, humanitarianism, humaneness, benevolence, largesse, humanity, public-spiritedness. □□ **altruist** see philanthropist (PHILANTHROPY). **altruistic** see SELFLESS.

alum /áləm/ n. **1** a double sulfate of aluminum and potassium. **2** any of a group of compounds of double sulfates of a monovalent metal (or group) and a trivalent metal. [ME f. OF f. L alumen aluminis]

alumina /əlŏ́ōminə/ n. the compound aluminum oxide occurring naturally as corundum and emery. [L alumen alum, after soda, etc.]

aluminize /əlŏ́ōminīz/ v.tr. coat with aluminum. □□ **aluminization** /-izáyshən/ n.

aluminum /əlŏ́ōminəm/ n. (Brit. **aluminium** /ályəmíneeəm/) a silvery light and malleable metallic element resistant to tarnishing by air. ¶ Symb.: **Al**. □ **aluminum bronze** an alloy of copper and aluminum. [earlier aluminium f. ALUM + -IUM]

alumnus /əlúmnəs/ n. (pl. **alumni** /-nī/; fem. **alumna**, pl. **alumnae** /-nee, nī/) a former pupil or student of a particular school, college, or university. [L, = nursling, pupil f. alere nourish]

alveolar /alveéələr/ adj. **1** of an alveolus. **2** Phonet. (of a consonant) pronounced with the tip of the tongue in contact with the ridge of the upper teeth, e.g., n, s, t. [ALVEOLUS + -AR[1]]

alveolus /alveéələs/ n. (pl. **alveoli** /-lī/ **1** a small cavity, pit, or hollow. **2** any of the many tiny air sacs of the lungs which allow for rapid gaseous exchange. **3** the bony socket for the root of a tooth. **4** the cell of a honeycomb. □□ **alveolate** adj. [L dimin. of alveus cavity]

always /áwlwayz/ adv. **1** at all times; on all occasions (they are always late). **2** whatever the circumstances (I can always sleep on the floor). **3** repeatedly; often (they are always complaining). **4** for ever; for all time (I am with you always). [ME, prob. distrib. genit. f. ALL + WAY + -´S[1]]

42

■ **1** at all times, again and again, on all occasions, every or each time, each and every time, without exception, archaic aye. **2** in any case or event, as a last resort, if necessary. **3** repeatedly, usually; see also OFTEN. **4** for ever, continually, ever, perpetually; unceasingly, unendingly, eternally, evermore, ever after, everlastingly, for all time, till the end of time, in perpetuity, archaic for aye.

alyssum /álisəm/ n. any plant of the genus Alyssum, widely cultivated and usu. having yellow or white flowers. [L f. Gk alusson]

Alzheimer's disease /aálts-hímərz, álts-, áwlts-, áwlz-/ n. a serious disorder of the brain manifesting itself in premature senility. [A. Alzheimer, Ger. neurologist d. 1915]

AM abbr. **1** amplitude modulation. **2** Master of Arts. **3** Member of the Order of Australia. [(sense 2) L artium Magister]

Am symb. Chem. the element americium.

am 1st person sing. present of BE.

a.m. abbr. (also **A.M.** or **AM**) between midnight and noon. [L ante meridiem]

AMA abbr. American Medical Association.

amadou /ámədŏō/ n. a spongy and combustible tinder prepared from dry fungi. [F f. mod.Prov., lit. = lover (because quickly kindled) f. L (as AMATEUR)]

amah /aámə, aámaa/ n. (in Asia) a nursemaid or maid. [Port. ama nurse]

amalgam /əmálgəm/ n. **1** a mixture or blend. **2** an alloy of mercury with one or more other metals, used esp. in dentistry. [ME f. F amalgame or med.L amalgama f. Gk malagma an emollient]

■ **1** mixture, blend, combination, alloy, mix, composite, admixture, amalgamation, compound.

amalgamate /əmálgəmayt/ v. **1** tr. & intr. combine or unite to form one structure, organization, etc. **2** intr. (of metals) alloy with mercury. □□ **amalgamation** /-máyshən/ n. [med.L amalgamare amalgamat- (as AMALGAM)]

■ **1** blend, combine, unite, mix, join, merge, fuse; consolidate, compound, integrate, put together, marry. □□ **amalgamation** blend, fusion, alloy, combination, mix(ture), amalgam, composite, compound, union, unification, marriage, consolidation, coalescence, integration, merger.

amanuensis /əmányŏō-énsis/ n. (pl. **amanuenses** /-seez/) **1** a person who writes from dictation or copies manuscripts. **2** a literary assistant. [L f. (servus) a manu secretary + -ensis belonging to]

amaranth /áməranth/ n. **1** any plant of the genus Amaranthus, usu. having small green, red, or purple tinted flowers, e.g., prince's feather and pigweed. **2** an imaginary flower that never fades. **3** a purple color. □□ **amaranthine** /-əránthin, -thīn/ adj. [F amarante or mod.L amaranthus f. L f. Gk amarantos everlasting f. a- not + maraino wither, alt. after polyanthus, etc.]

amaretto /amərétō/ n. an almond-flavored liqueur. [It. dimin. of amaro bitter f. L amarus]

amaryllis /ámərílis/ n. **1** a plant genus with a single species, Amaryllis belladonna, a bulbous lily-like plant native to S. Africa with white, pink, or red flowers (also called belladonna lily). **2** any of various related plants formerly of this genus now transferred to other genera, notably Hippeastrum. [L f. Gk Amarullis, name of a country girl]

amass /əmás/ v.tr. **1** gather or heap together. **2** accumulate (esp. riches). □□ **amasser** n. **amassment** n. [F amasser or med.L amassare ult. f. L massa MASS[1]]

■ accumulate, mass, pile or heap up or rack up, collect, gather (together), assemble, muster, aggregate, cumulate, stock or store up, put away, stockpile, hoard, set aside.

amateur /ámachŏōr, -chər, -tər, -tér/ n. & adj. ● n. **1 a** a person who engages in a pursuit (e.g., an art or sport) as a pastime rather than a profession. **b** derog. a person who does something unskillfully, in the manner of an amateur rather than a professional. **2** (foll. by of) a person who is fond of (a thing). ● adj. for or done by amateurs; amateurish; unskillful (*amateur athletics*; *did an amateur job*). □□ **amateurism** *n.* [F f. It. *amatore* f. L *amator -oris* lover f. *amare* love]

■ *n.* **1** layman, nonprofessional, nonspecialist; tyro; dabbler, dilettante, tinkerer. ● *adj.* lay, nonprofessional, nonspecialist, untrained, unpaid; dilettante, amateurish, unprofessional, unskilled, inexpert, inept, incompetent, unskillful, clumsy, mediocre, inferior, bungling, second-rate, sloppy, shoddy, poor. □□ **amateurism** unprofessionalism, dilettantism, inexpertness; ineptitude, incompetence; mediocrity, inferiority, sloppiness, shoddiness.

amateurish /ámǝchŏŏr, -chǝrish, tǝr-, -tǝr-/ *adj.* characteristic of an amateur, esp. unskillful or inexperienced. □□ **amateurishly** *adv.* **amateurishness** *n.*

amatory /ámǝtawree/ *adj.* of or relating to sexual love or desire. [L *amatorius* f. *amare* love]

amaurosis /ámǝrōsis/ *n.* the partial or total loss of sight, from disease of the optic nerve, retina, spinal cord, or brain. □□ **amaurotic** /-rótik/ *adj.* [mod.L f. Gk f. *amauroō* darken f. *amauros* dim]

amaze /ǝmáyz/ *v.tr.* (often foll. by *at*, or *that* + clause, or *to* + infin.) surprise greatly; overwhelm with wonder (*am amazed at your indifference*; *was amazed to find them alive*). □□ **amazement** *n.* **amazing** *adj.* **amazingly** *adv.* **amazingness** *n.* [ME f. OE *āmasod* past part. of *āmasian*, of uncert. orig.]

■ astound, astonish, surprise, awe, stun, stagger, take aback, dumbfound, confound, nonplus, stupefy, *colloq.* floor, flabbergast; (*be amazed*) be thunderstruck *or* dumbstruck. □□ **amazement** astonishment, surprise, awe, wonder, wonderment, stupefaction. **amazing** astonishing, astounding, awe-inspiring, surprising, remarkable, extraordinary, spectacular, stupendous, marvelous, fabulous, wonderful, staggering, prodigious, awesome, far-out, *colloq.* incredible, stunning, *sl.* unreal. **amazingly** astonishingly, astoundingly, surprisingly, remarkably, extraordinarily, marvelously, spectacularly, stupendously, fabulously, prodigiously, unexpectedly, *colloq.* incredibly, stunningly, like nobody's business.

Amazon /ámǝzon, -zǝn/ *n.* **1** a member of a mythical race of female warriors in Scythia and elsewhere. **2** (**amazon**) a very tall, strong, or athletic woman. □□ **Amazonian** /-zṓneeǝn/ *adj.* [ME f. L f. Gk: expl. by the Greeks as 'breastless' (as if A-¹ + *mazos* breast), but prob. of foreign orig.]

ambassador /ambásǝdǝr, -dawr/ *n.* **1** an accredited diplomat sent by a nation on a mission to, or as its permanent representative in, a foreign country. **2** a representative or promoter of a specified thing (*an ambassador of peace*). □ **ambassador-at-large** an ambassador with special duties, not appointed to a particular country. □□ **ambassadorial** /-dáwreeǝl/ *adj.* **ambassadorship** *n.* [ME f. F *ambassadeur* f. It. *ambasciator*, ult. f. L *ambactus* servant]

■ **1, 2** envoy, delegate, emissary, minister, plenipotentiary, diplomat, *archaic* legate; agent, deputy, representative, (papal) nuncio, high commissioner; messenger, herald. □□ **ambassadorial** ministerial, diplomatic, plenipotentiary, agential.

ambassadress /ambásǝdris/ *n.* **1** a female ambassador. **2** an ambassador's wife.

ambatch /ámbach/ *n.* an African tree, *Aeschynomene elaphroxylon*, with very light spongy wood. [Ethiopic]

amber /ámbǝr/ *n.* & *adj.* ● *n.* **1 a** a yellowish translucent fossilized resin deriving from extinct (esp. coniferous) trees and used in jewelry. **b** the honey-yellow color of this. **2** a yellow traffic signal meaning caution, showing between red for "stop" and green for "go." ● *adj.* made of or colored like amber. [ME f. OF *ambre* f. Arab. *'anbar* ambergris, amber]

ambergris /ámbǝrgris, -grees/ *n.* a strong-smelling waxlike secretion of the intestine of the sperm whale, found floating in tropical seas and used in perfume manufacture. [ME f. OF *ambre gris* gray AMBER]

amberjack /ámbǝrjak/ *n.* any large brightly-colored marine fish of the genus *Seriola* found in tropical and subtropical Atlantic waters.

ambiance var. of AMBIENCE.

ambidextrous /ámbidékstrǝs/ *adj.* (*Brit.* also **ambidexterous**) **1** able to use the right and left hands equally well. **2** working skillfully in more than one medium. □□ **ambidexterity** /-stéritee/ *n.* **ambidextrously** *adv.* **ambidextrousness** *n.* [LL *ambidexter* f. *ambi-* on both sides + *dexter* right handed]

ambience /ámbeeǝns, aaNbeeáaNs/ *n.* (also **ambiance**) the surroundings or atmosphere of a place. [AMBIENT + -ENCE or F *ambiance*]

■ see ATMOSPHERE 2a.

ambient /ámbeeǝnt/ *adj.* surrounding. [F *ambiant* or L *ambiens -entis* pres. part. of *ambire* go round]

ambiguity /ámbigyŏŏitee/ *n.* (*pl.* **-ies**) **1 a** a double meaning which is either deliberate or caused by inexactness of expression. **b** an example of this. **2** an expression able to be interpreted in more than one way (e.g., *fighting dogs should be avoided*). [ME f. OF *ambiguité* or L *ambiguitas* (as AMBIGUOUS)]

■ **1 a** equivocalness, equivocality, ambiguousness, equivocacy, amphibology; vagueness, indistinctness, uncertainty, indefiniteness, imprecision, inexactness, inexactitude, inconclusiveness; equivocation, doubletalk, doublespeak, wordplay. **b** pun, equivoque, equivocation, double entendre, amphibology, play on words, quibble, paronomasia.

ambiguous /ambígyŏŏǝs/ *adj.* **1** having an obscure or double meaning. **2** difficult to classify. □□ **ambiguously** *adv.* **ambiguousness** *n.* [L *ambiguus* doubtful f. *ambigere* f. *ambi-* both ways + *agere* drive]

■ equivocal, obscure, indistinct, inconclusive, vague, unclear, indefinite, indeterminate, inexact, uncertain, undefined, misty, foggy; cryptic, enigmatic(al), mysterious, Delphic, Delphian, oracular, puzzling, confusing, misleading, confusable; unreliable, undependable. □□ **ambiguously** equivocally; see also *vaguely* (VAGUE). **ambiguousness** see AMBIGUITY 1a.

ambit /ámbit/ *n.* **1** the scope, extent, or bounds of something. **2** precincts or environs. [ME f. L *ambitus* circuit f. *ambire*: see AMBIENT]

■ see RANGE *n.* 1.

ambition /ambíshǝn/ *n.* **1** (often foll. by *to* + infin.) the determination to achieve success or distinction, usu. in a chosen field. **2** the object of this determination. **3** energy; interest in activity, etc. **4** aggressive self-centeredness. [ME f. OF f. L *ambitio -onis* f. *ambire* ambit- canvass for votes: see AMBIENT]

■ **1** drive, enterprise, energy, initiative, push, vigor, enthusiasm, determination, motivation, zeal, eagerness, keenness, *colloq.* get-up-and-go. **2** goal, object, aim, end, aspiration, hope, desire, dream, objective, intent, wish, purpose. **4** arrivism, pushiness, self-seeking.

ambitious /ambíshǝs/ *adj.* **1 a** full of ambition. **b** showing ambition (*an ambitious attempt*). **2** (foll. by *of*, or *to* + infin.) strongly determined. □□ **ambitiously** *adv.* **ambitiousness** *n.* [ME f. OF *ambitieux* f. L *ambitiosus* (as AMBITION)]

■ **1 a** energetic, enterprising, go-ahead, vigorous, zealous, keen, enthusiastic, eager, aspiring, determined, (highly) motivated, high-flying, pushing, *colloq.* pushy, go-getting; greedy, avaricious, overzealous, overambitious, self-seeking. **b** enterprising, grandiose, *colloq.* big. **2** see DETERMINED 1. □□ **ambitiousness** see DRIVE *n.* 2a.

ambivalence /ambívǝlǝns/ *n.* (also **ambivalency** /-lǝnsee/) **1** the coexistence in one person's mind of opposing feelings, esp. love and hate, in a single context. **2** uncertainty over a course of action or decision. □□ **ambivalent** *adj.* **ambiva-**

/.../ **pronunciation**	● **part of speech**
□ **phrases, idioms, and compounds**	
□□ **derivatives**	■ **synonym section**
cross-references appear in SMALL CAPITALS or *italics*	

lently adv. [G Ambivalenz f. L ambo both, after equivalence, -ency]

ambivert /ámbivert/ n. Psychol. a person who fluctuates between being an introvert and an extrovert. □□ **ambiversion** /-vérzhən/ n. [L ambi- on both sides + -vert f. L vertere to turn, after EXTROVERT, INTROVERT]

amble /ámbəl/ v. & n. ● v.intr. **1** move at an easy pace, in a way suggesting an ambling horse. **2** (of a horse, etc.) move by lifting the two feet on one side together. **3** ride an ambling horse; ride at an easy pace. ● n. an easy pace; the gait of an ambling horse. [ME f. OF ambler f. L ambulare walk]
■ v. **1** see STROLL v.

amblyopia /ámbleeŏpeeə/ n. dimness of vision without obvious defect or change in the eye. □□ **amblyopic** /-leeópik/ adj. [Gk f. ambluōpos (adj.) f. amblus dull + ōps, ōpos eye]

ambo /ámbō/ n. (pl. **-os** or **ambones** /-bŏneez/) a stand for reading lessons in an early Christian church, etc. [med.L f. Gk ambōn rim (in med.Gk = pulpit)]

amboyna /ambóynə/ n. the decorative wood of the SE Asian tree Pterocarpus indicus. [Amboyna Island in Indonesia]

ambrosia /ambrŏzhə/ n. **1** (in Greek and Roman mythology) the food of the gods; the elixir of life. **2** anything very pleasing to taste or smell. **3** the food of certain bees and beetles. □□ **ambrosial** adj. **ambrosian** adj. [L f. Gk, = elixir of life f. ambrotos immortal]

ambry var. of AUMBRY.

ambulance /ámbyələns/ n. **1** a vehicle specially equipped for conveying the sick or injured to and from a hospital, esp. in emergencies. **2** hist. a mobile hospital following an army. [F (as AMBULANT)]

ambulant /ámbyələnt/ adj. Med. **1** (of a patient) able to walk about; not confined to bed. **2** (of treatment) not confining a patient to bed. [L ambulare ambulant- walk]
■ **1** see MOBILE adj. 1, 3.

ambulatory /ámbyələtawree/ adj. & n. ● adj. **1** = AMBULANT. **2** of or adapted for walking. **3** a movable. **b** not permanent. ● n. (pl. **-ies**) a place for walking, esp. an aisle or cloister in a church or monastery. [L ambulatorius f. ambulare walk]
■ adj. **3 a** see MOVABLE adj. 1.

ambuscade /ámbəskáyd/ n. & v. ● n. an ambush. ● v. **1** tr. attack by means of an ambush. **2** intr. lie in ambush. **3** tr. conceal in an ambush. [F embuscade f. It. imboscata or Sp. emboscada f. L imboscare: see AMBUSH, -ADE[1]]

ambush /ámbŏosh/ n. & v. ● n. **1** a surprise attack by persons (e.g., troops) in a concealed position. **2 a** the concealment of troops, etc., to make such an attack. **b** the place where they are concealed. **c** the troops, etc., concealed. ● v.tr. **1** attack by means of an ambush. **2** lie in wait for. [ME f. OF embusche, embuschier, f. a Rmc form = 'put in a wood': rel. to BUSH[1]]
■ n. **1** trap, ambuscade. ● v. **1** trap, waylay, ensnare, entrap, ambuscade, intercept, jump, bushwhack. **2** lie in wait for, bushwhack.

ameba var. of AMOEBA.

ameer var. of EMIR.

ameliorate /əmeélyərayt/ v.tr. & intr. make or become better; improve. □□ **amelioration** /-ráyshən/ n. **ameliorative** adj. **ameliorator** n. [alt. of MELIORATE after F améliorer]
■ see IMPROVE 1a.

amen /áamén, áy-/ int. & n. ● int. **1** uttered at the end of a prayer or hymn, etc., meaning 'so be it.' **2** (foll. by to) expressing agreement or assent (amen to that). ● n. an utterance of 'amen' (sense 1). [ME f. eccl.L f. Gk f. Heb. 'āmēn certainly]

amenable /əmeénəbəl, əmén-/ adj. **1** responsive; tractable. **2** (often foll. by to) (of a person) responsible to law. **3** (foll. by to) (of a thing) subject or liable. □□ **amenability** /-bílitee/ n. **amenableness** n. **amenably** adv. [AF (Law) f. F amener bring to f. a- to + mener bring f. LL minare drive animals f. L minari threaten]
■ **1** see TRACTABLE 1.

amend /əménd/ v.tr. **1** make minor improvements in (a text or a written proposal). **2** correct an error or errors in (a document). **3** make better; improve. **4** modify formally, as a legal document or legislative bill. ¶ Often confused with

emend, a more technical word used in the context of textual correction. □□ **amendable** adj. **amender** n. [ME f. OF amender ult. f. L emendare EMEND]
■ **1** enhance, revise, edit, refine, polish (up), improve. **2** correct, emend, rectify, put or set to rights, right, fix, revise, Printing read. **3** reform, mend, change for the better, improve, (make) better, formal ameliorate, literary meliorate. □□ **amendable** correctable, emendable, rectifiable, rightable.

amende honorable /əménd ónərəbəl, amáaᴎd awnawráablə/ n. (pl. **amendes honorables** pronunc. same) a public or open apology, often with some form of reparation. [F, = honorable reparation]

amendment /əméndmənt/ n. **1** a minor change in a document (esp. a legal or statutory one). **2** an article added to the US Constitution. [AMEND + -MENT]
■ **1** correction, emendation, change, alteration, modification, adjustment, insertion, rectification, revision, reform, enhancement, improvement, formal amelioration.

amends /əméndz/ n. □ **make amends** (often foll. by for) compensate or make up (for). [ME f. OF amendes penalties, fine, pl. of amende reparation f. amender AMEND]
■ □ **make amends** (make amends for) make reparation or restitution for, atone for, compensate for, expiate, repair, make good; (make amends to) make it up to, pay, repay, recompense, indemnify, redress, remedy, requite.

amenity /əménitee, əmeé-/ n. (pl. **-ies**) **1** (usu. in pl.) a pleasant or useful feature. **2** pleasantness (of a place, person, etc.). □ **amenity-bed** Brit. a bed available in a hospital to give more privacy for a small payment. [ME f. OF amenité or L amoenitas f. amoenus pleasant]

amenorrhea /ayménəreéə/ n. (Brit. **amenorrhoea**) Med. an abnormal absence of menstruation. [A-[1] + MENO- + Gk -rrhoia f. rheō flow]

ament /əmént/ n. (also **amentum** /-təm/) (pl. **aments** or **amenta** /-tə/) a catkin. [L, = thong]

amentia /əménshə/ n. Med. severe congenital mental deficiency. [L f. amens ament- mad (as A-[1], mens mind)]

Amerasian /aməráyzhən/ n. a person of American and Asian descent.

amerce /əmárs/ v.tr. **1** Law punish by fine. **2** punish arbitrarily. □□ **amercement** n. **amerciable** /-seeəbəl/ adj. [ME amercy f. AF amercier f. a at + merci MERCY]

American /əmérikən/ adj. & n. ● adj. **1** of, relating to, or characteristic of the United States or its inhabitants. **2** (usu. in comb.) of or relating to the continents of America (Latin-American). ● n. **1** a native or citizen of the United States. **2** (usu. in comb.) a native or inhabitant of the continents of America (North Americans). **3** (also **American English**) the English language as it is used in the United States. □ **American dream** the traditional social ideals of the American people, such as equality, democracy, and material prosperity. **American Indian** a member of the aboriginal peoples of America or their descendants. [mod.L Americanus f. America f. Latinized name of Amerigo Vespucci, It. navigator d. 1512]

Americana /əmérikánə, -káanə, -káynə/ n.pl. things connected with America, esp. with the United States.

Americanism /əmérikənizəm/ n. **1 a** a word, sense, or phrase peculiar to or originating from the United States. **b** a thing or feature characteristic of or peculiar to the United States. **2** attachment to or sympathy for the United States.

Americanize /əmérikəniz/ v. **1** tr. **a** make American in character. **b** naturalize as an American. **2** intr. become American in character. □□ **Americanization** /-nizáyshən/ n.

americium /ámərísheeəm/ n. Chem. an artificially made transuranic radioactive metallic element. ¶ Symb.: **Am**. [America (where first made) + -IUM]

Amerindian /ámərindeeən/ adj. & n. (also **Amerind** /ámərínd/) = American Indian. □□ **Amerindic** /-ríndik/ adj. [portmanteau word]

amethyst /ámithist/ n. a precious stone of a violet or purple variety of quartz. □□ **amethystine** /-thísteen/ adj. [ME f.

OF *ametiste* f. L *amethystus* f. Gk *amethustos* not drunken, the stone being supposed to prevent intoxication]

Amharic /amhárik/ *n. & adj.* ● *n.* the official and commercial language of Ethiopia. ● *adj.* of this language. [*Amhara*, Ethiopian province + -IC]

amiable /áymeeəbəl/ *adj.* friendly and pleasant in temperament; likable. □□ **amiability** /-bílitee/ *n.* **amiableness** *n.* **amiably** *adv.* [ME f. OF f. LL *amicabilis* amicable: confused with F *aimable* lovable]

■ friendly, likable, amicable, agreeable, cordial, congenial, genial, affable, pleasant, obliging, winsome, winning, tractable, approachable, benign, well-disposed; warm, kindly, kind, good-natured, good-hearted, kindhearted, affectionate.

amianthus /ámee-ánthəs/ *n.* (also **amiantus** /-təs/) any fine silky-fibered variety of asbestos. [L f. Gk *amiantos* undefiled f. *a*- not + *miainō* defile, i.e. purified by fire, being incombustible: for -*h*- cf. AMARANTH]

amicable /ámikəbəl/ *adj.* showing or done in a friendly spirit (*an amicable meeting*). □□ **amicability** /-bílitee/ *n.* **amicableness** *n.* **amicably** *adv.* [LL *amicabilis* f. *amicus* friend]

■ friendly, amiable, congenial, harmonious, brotherly, kind-hearted; warm, courteous, cordial, polite, civil, pleasant; peaceful, peaceable.

amice[1] /ámis/ *n.* a white linen cloth worn on the neck and shoulders by a priest celebrating the Eucharist. [ME f. med.L *amicia*, *-sia* (earlier *amit* f. OF), f. L *amictus* outer garment]

amice[2] /ámis/ *n.* a cap, hood, or cape worn by members of certain religious orders. [ME f. OF *aumusse* f. med.L *almucia*, etc., of unkn. orig.]

amicus curiae /ameékəs kyōŏree-ee, kyōŏree-ī/ *n.* (*pl.* **amici curiae** /ameékī, -kee/) *Law* an impartial adviser in a court of law. [mod.L, = friend of the court]

amid /əmíd/ *prep.* (also **amidst** /əmídst/) **1** in the middle of. **2** in the course of. [ME *amidde(s)* f. OE *on* ON + MID[1]]

■ **1** in the middle or midst or center or thick of, amongst, among, *poet.* mid, midst; surrounded by. **2** in the middle of, during, in the course of.

amide /áymīd, ám-/ *n. Chem.* a compound formed from ammonia by replacement of one (or sometimes more than one) hydrogen atom by a metal or an acyl radical. [AMMONIA + -IDE]

amidships /əmídships/ *adv.* (also **amidship**) in or into the middle of a ship. [MIDSHIP after AMID]

amidst var. of AMID.

amigo /əmeégō/ *n.* (*pl.* **-os**) (often as a form of address) a friend or comrade, esp. in Spanish-speaking areas. [Sp.]

amine /əmeén, ámeen/ *n. Chem.* a compound formed from ammonia by replacement of one or more hydrogen atoms by an organic radical or radicals. [AMMONIA + -INE[4]]

amino /əmeénō/ *n.* (*attrib.*) *Chem.* of, relating to, or containing the monovalent group -NH$_2$. [AMINE]

amino acid /əmeénō/ *n. Biochem.* any of a group of organic compounds containing both the carboxyl (COOH) and amino (NH$_2$) groups, occurring naturally in plant and animal tissues and forming the basic constituents of proteins. [AMINE + ACID]

amir var. of EMIR.

Amish /aámish, ám-/ *adj. & n.* ● *adj.* belonging to a strict Mennonite sect in the US. ● *n.* a follower of this sect. [prob. f. G *Amisch* f. J. *Amen* 17th-c. Swiss preacher]

amiss /əmís/ *predic.adj. & adv.* ● *predic.adj.* wrong; out of order; faulty (*knew something was amiss*). ● *adv.* wrong; wrongly; inappropriately (*everything went amiss*). □ **take amiss** be offended by (*took my words amiss*). [ME prob. f. ON *à mis* so as to miss f. *à* on + *mis* rel. to MISS[1]]

■ *predic.adj.* wrong, at fault, awry, out of order, out of kilter, faulty, defective; untoward, astray, erroneous, fallacious, confused, incorrect, off. ● *adv.* wrong(ly), awry, badly, poorly, imperfectly, incorrectly; inopportunely, unfavorably, unpropitiously; inappropriately, out of place or turn, inopportunely, unsuitably, improperly. □ **take amiss** (also *take it*

amiss) be offended (by), take offense (at), take (it) the wrong way, mistake, misinterpret, misunderstand.

amitosis /ámitōsis/ *n. Biol.* a form of nuclear division that does not involve mitosis. [A-[1] + MITOSIS]

amitriptyline /ámitríptileen/ *n. Pharm.* an antidepressant drug that has a mild tranquilizing action. [AMINE + TRI- + *heptyl* (see HEPTANE) + -INE[4]]

amity /ámitee/ *n.* friendship; friendly relations. [ME f. OF *amitié* ult. f. L *amicus* friend]

■ see FRIENDSHIP 1.

ammeter /ám-meetər/ *n.* an instrument for measuring electric current in amperes. [AMPERE + -METER]

ammo /ámō/ *n. colloq.* ammunition. [abbr.]

ammonia /əmṓnyə/ *n.* **1** a colorless strongly alkaline gas with a characteristic pungent smell. ¶ Chem. formula: NH$_3$. **2** (in full **ammonia water**) (in general use) a solution of ammonia gas in water. [mod.L f. SAL AMMONIAC]

ammoniacal /ámənī́əkəl/ *adj.* of, relating to, or containing ammonia or sal ammoniac. [ME *ammoniac* f. OF (*arm-, amm-*) f. L f. Gk *ammōniakos* of Ammon (cf. SAL AMMONIAC) + -AL]

ammoniated /əmṓneeaytid/ *adj.* combined or treated with ammonia.

ammonite /ámənīt/ *n.* any extinct cephalopod mollusk of the order Ammonoidea, with a flat coiled spiral shell found as a fossil. [mod.L *ammonites*, after med.L *cornu Ammonis*, = L *Ammonis cornu* (Pliny), horn of (Jupiter) Ammon]

ammonium /əmṓneeəm/ *n.* the univalent ion NH$_4$$^+$, formed from ammonia. [mod.L (as AMMONIA)]

ammunition /ámyəníshən/ *n.* **1** a supply of projectiles (esp. bullets, shells, and grenades). **2** points used or usable to advantage in an argument. [obs. F *amunition*, corrupt. of (*la*) *munition* (the) MUNITION]

■ **2** see FUEL *n.* 4.

amnesia /amneézhə/ *n.* a partial or total loss of memory. □□ **amnesiac** /-zeeak, -zheeak/ *n.* **amnesic** *adj. & n.* [mod.L f. Gk, = forgetfulness]

amnesty /ámnistee/ *n. & v.* ● *n.* (*pl.* **-ies**) a general pardon, esp. for political offenses. ● *v.tr.* (**-ies**, **-ied**) grant an amnesty to. □ **Amnesty International** an independent international organization in support of human rights, esp. for prisoners of conscience. [F *amnestie* or L f. Gk *amnēstia* oblivion]

■ *n.* see PARDON *n.* ● *v.* see PARDON *v.*

amniocentesis /ámneeōsenteésis/ *n.* (*pl.* **amniocenteses** /-seez/) *Med.* the sampling of amniotic fluid by insertion of a hollow needle to determine the sex of or certain abnormalities in an embryo. [AMNION + Gk *kentēsis* pricking f. *kentō* to prick]

amnion /ámneeən/ *n.* (*pl.* **amnia**) *Zool. & Physiol.* the innermost membrane that encloses the embryo of a reptile, bird, or mammal. □□ **amniotic** /ámneeótik/ *adj.* [Gk, = caul (dimin. of *amnos* lamb)]

amoeba /əmeébə/ *n.* (also **ameba**) (*pl.* **amoebas** or **amoebae** /-bee/) any usu. aquatic protozoan of the genus *Amoeba*, esp. *A. proteus*, capable of changing shape. □□ **amoebic** *adj.* **amoeboid** *adj.* [mod.L f. Gk *amoibē* change]

amok /əmúk, əmók/ *adv.* (also **amuck** /əmúk/) □ **run amok** run about wildly in an uncontrollable violent rage. [Malay *amok* rushing in a frenzy]

among /əmúng/ *prep.* (also esp. *Brit.* **amongst** /əmúngst/) **1** surrounded by; in the company of (*lived among the trees; be among friends*). **2** in the number of (*among us were those who disagreed*). **3** an example of; in the class or category of (*is among the richest men alive*). **4 a** between; within the limits of (collectively or distributively); shared by (*had $5 among us; divide it among you*). **b** by the joint action or from the joint resources of (*among us we can manage it*). **5** with one

---

/.../ **pronunciation**	● **part of speech**
□ **phrases, idioms, and compounds**	
□□ **derivatives**	■ **synonym section**
cross-references appear in SMALL CAPITALS or *italics*	

another; by the reciprocal action of (*was decided among the participants*; *talked among themselves*). **6** as distinguished from; preeminent in the category of (*she is one among many*). [OE *ongemang* f. *on* ON + *gemang* assemblage (cf. MINGLE): *-st* = adverbial genitive *-s* + *-t* as in AGAINST]

■ **1** amid, amidst, in the midst *or* middle *or* center of, surrounded by, in the company of, *poet.* mid, midst. **3** one of, an example of. **4 a** to each *or* all (of), between. **6** out of, from.

amontillado /əmóntiláadō, -tee-aádō/ *n.* (*pl.* **-os**) a medium dry sherry. [Sp. f. *Montilla* in Spain + *-ado* = -ATE²]

amoral /áymáwrəl, -mór-/ *adj.* **1** not concerned with or outside the scope of morality (cf. IMMORAL). **2** having no moral principles. □□ **amoralism** *n.* **amoralist** *n.* **amorality** /-rálitee/ *n.*

amoretto /ámərétō/ *n.* (*pl.* **amoretti** /-tee/) a Cupid. [It., dimin. of *amore* love f. L (as AMOUR)]

amorist /ámərist/ *n.* a person who professes or writes of (esp. sexual) love. [L *amor* or F *amour* + -IST]

amoroso¹ /ámərṓsō/ *adv.* & *adj. Mus.* in a loving or tender manner. [It.]

amoroso² /áamərṓsō/ *n.* (*pl.* **-os**) a full rich type of sherry. [Sp., = amorous]

amorous /ámərəs/ *adj.* **1** showing, feeling, or inclined to sexual love. **2** of or relating to sexual love. □□ **amorously** *adv.* **amorousness** *n.* [ME f. OF f. med.L *amorosus* f. L *amor* love]

■ *see* PASSIONATE.

amorphous /əmáwrfəs/ *adj.* **1** shapeless. **2** vague; ill-organized; unclassifiable. **3** *Mineral.* & *Chem.* noncrystalline; having neither definite form nor structure. □□ **amorphously** *adv.* **amorphousness** *n.* [med.L *amorphus* f. Gk *amorphos* shapeless f. *a-* not + *morphē* form]

■ **1** *see* SHAPELESS. **2** *see* VAGUE 1.

amortize /ámərtiz, əmáwr-/ *v.tr. Commerce* **1** gradually extinguish (a debt) by money regularly put aside. **2** gradually write off the initial cost of (assets). **3** transfer (land) to a corporation in mortmain. □□ **amortization** /-tizáyshən/ *n.* [ME f. OF *amortir* (stem *amortiss-*) ult. f. L *ad* to + *mors mort-* death]

amount /əmównt/ *n.* & *v.* ● *n.* **1** a quantity, esp. the total of a thing or things in number, size, value, extent, etc. (*a large amount of money*; *came to a considerable amount*). **2** the full effect or significance. ● *v.intr.* (foll. by *to*) **1** be equivalent to in number, size, significance, etc. (*amounted to $100*; *amounted to a disaster*). **2** (of a person) develop into; become (*might one day amount to something*). □ **any amount of** a great deal of. **no amount of** not even the greatest possible amount of. [ME f. OF *amunter* f. *amont* upward, lit. uphill, f. L *ad montem*]

■ *n.* **1** quantity, extent, volume, mass, expanse, area, bulk, quantum, portion; number, total, aggregate. **2** *see* SIGNIFICANCE 2. ● *v.* (*amount to*) **1** add up to, total, aggregate, come (up) to; be equivalent *or* equal to. **2** become, develop into, be capable of. □ **any amount of** *see* LOT *n.* 1.

amour /əmōōr/ *n.* a love affair, esp. a secret one. [F, = love, f. L *amor amoris*.]

■ *see* *love affair.*

amour propre /áamōōrr práwprə/ *n.* self-respect. [F]

■ *see* SELF-RESPECT.

AMP *abbr.* adenosine monophosphate.

amp¹ /amp/ *n. Electr.* an ampere. [abbr.]

amp² /amp/ *n. colloq.* an amplifier. [abbr.]

ampelopsis /ámpilópsis/ *n.* (*pl.* same) any plant of the genus *Ampelopsis* or *Parthenocissus*, usu. a climber supporting itself by twining tendrils, e.g., Virginia creeper. [mod.L f. Gk *ampelos* vine + *opsis* appearance]

amperage /ámpərij/ *n. Electr.* the strength of an electric current in amperes.

ampere /ámpeer/ *n. Electr.* the SI base unit of electric current. ¶ Symb.: **A**. [A. M. *Ampère*, Fr. physicist d. 1836]

ampersand /ámpərsand/ *n.* the sign & (= *and*). [corrupt. of *and per se and* ('&' by itself is 'and')]

amphetamine /amfé'təmeen, -min/ *n.* a synthetic drug used

esp. as a stimulant. [abbr. of chemical name *alpha methyl phenethylamine*]

amphi- /ámfee/ *comb. form* **1** both. **2** of both kinds. **3** on both sides. **4** around. [Gk]

amphibian /amfíbeeən/ *adj.* & *n.* ● *adj.* **1** living both on land and in water. **2** *Zool.* of or relating to the class Amphibia. **3** (of a vehicle) able to operate on land and water. ● *n.* **1** *Zool.* any vertebrate of the class Amphibia, with a life history of an aquatic gill-breathing larval stage followed by a terrestrial lung-breathing adult stage, including frogs, toads, newts, and salamanders. **2** (in general use) a creature living both on land and in water. **3** an amphibian vehicle.

amphibious /amfíbeeəs/ *adj.* **1** living both on land and in water. **2** of or relating to or suited for both land and water. **3** *Mil.* **a** (of a military operation) involving forces landed from the sea. **b** (of forces) trained for such operations. **4** having a twofold nature; occupying two positions. □□ **amphibiously** *adv.*

amphibology /ámfibólləjee/ *n.* (*pl.* **-ies**) **1** a quibble. **2** an ambiguous wording. [ME f. OF *amphibologie* f. LL *amphibologia* for L f. Gk *amphibolia* ambiguity]

■ *see* AMBIGUITY 1.

amphimixis /ámfimíksis/ *n. Biol.* true sexual reproduction with the fusion of gametes from two individuals (cf. APOMIXIS). □□ **amphimictic** /-míktik/ *adj.* [mod.L, formed as AMPHI- + Gk *mixis* mingling]

amphioxus /ámfeeóksəs/ *n.* any lancelet of the genus *Branchiostoma* (formerly *Amphioxus*). [mod.L, formed as AMPHI- + Gk *oxus* sharp]

amphipathic /ámfipáthik/ *adj. Chem.* **1** of a substance or molecule that has both a hydrophilic and a hydrophobic part. **2** consisting of such parts. [AMPHI- Gk *pathikos* (as PATHOS)]

amphipod /ámfipod/ *n.* any crustacean of the largely marine order Amphipoda, having a laterally compressed abdomen with two kinds of limb, e.g., the freshwater shrimp (*Gammarus pulex*). [AMPHI- + Gk *pous podos* foot]

amphiprostyle /amfíprəstil, amfiprṓ-/ *n.* & *adj.* ● *n.* a classical building with a portico at each end. ● *adj.* of or in this style. [L *amphiprostylus* f. Gk *amphiprostulos* (as AMPHI-, *prostulos* PRO-² + STYLE)]

amphisbaena /ámfisbeénə/ *n.* **1** *Mythol.* & *poet.* a mythical serpent with a head at each end. **2** *Zool.* any burrowing wormlike lizard of the family Amphisbaena, having no apparent division of head from body, making both ends look similar. [ME f. L f. Gk *amphisbaina* f. *amphis* both ways + *bainō* go]

amphitheater /ámfitheeətər/ *n.* (*Brit.* **amphitheatre**) **1** a round, usu. unroofed building with tiers of seats surrounding a central space. **2** a semicircular gallery in a theater. **3** a large circular hollow. **4** the scene of a contest. [L *amphitheatrum* f. Gk *amphitheatron* (as AMPHI-, THEATER)]

amphora /ámfərə/ *n.* (*pl.* **amphorae** /-ree/ or **amphoras**) a Greek or Roman vessel with two handles and a narrow neck. [L f. Gk *amphoreus*]

amphoteric /ámfətérik/ *adj. Chem.* able to react as a base and an acid. [Gk *amphoteros* compar. of *amphō* both]

ampicillin /ámpisílin/ *n. Pharm.* a semisynthetic penicillin used esp. in treating infections of the urinary and respiratory tracts. [*amino* + *penicillin*]

ample /ámpəl/ *adj.* (**ampler, amplest**) **1** plentiful; abundant; extensive. **b** *euphem.* (esp. of a person) large; stout. **2** enough or more than enough. □□ **ampleness** *n.* **amply** *adv.* [F f. L *amplus*]

■ **1 a** abundant, full, complete, plentiful, copious, generous, substantial, lavish; extensive, wide-ranging, broad, expansive, great, large; liberal, unsparing, unstinted, unstinting. **b** *see* STOUT *adj.* 1. **2** sufficient, adequate, enough, satisfactory. □□ **ampleness** *see* ABUNDANCE 1. **amply** to a great extent, largely, extensively, fully, completely, abundantly, broadly, copiously; well, liberally, unstintingly, generously, richly, substantially, lavishly; sufficiently, adequately, satisfactorily.

amplifier /ámplifiər/ *n.* an electronic device for increasing the strength of electrical signals, esp. for conversion into sound in radio, etc., equipment.

amplify /ámplifī/ v. (**-ies, -ied**) **1** tr. increase the volume or strength of (sound, electrical signals, etc.). **2** tr. enlarge upon or add detail to (a story, etc.). **3** intr. expand what is said or written. □□ **amplification** /-fikáyshən/ n. [ME f. OF amplifier f. L amplificare (as AMPLE, -FY)]

■ **1** magnify, increase, add to, augment, make larger or greater or louder or bigger, supplement, colloq. boost; broaden, widen, extend, enlarge (on). **2** enlarge (on), elaborate (on), expand (on), develop, expound on, stretch, lengthen, broaden, widen, extend, detail, expatiate on, embellish, embroider, overstate, exaggerate. **3** elaborate, go into detail, explain, exaggerate, expatiate. □□ **amplification** see elaboration (ELABORATE), INCREASE n. 1, 2.

amplitude /ámplitōōd, -tyōōd/ n. **1 a** Physics the maximum extent of a vibration or oscillation from the position of equilibrium. **b** Electr. the maximum departure of the value of an alternating current or wave from the average value. **2 a** spaciousness; breadth; wide range. **b** abundance. □ **amplitude modulation** Electr. **1** the modulation of a wave by variation of its amplitude. **2** the system using such modulation. [F amplitude or L amplitudo (as AMPLE)]

■ **2 a** see BREADTH 1, 3. **b** see ABUNDANCE 1.

ampoule /ámpyōōl, -pōōl/ n. (also **ampule** or **ampul**) a small capsule in which measured quantities of liquids or solids, esp. for injecting, are sealed ready for use. [F f. L AMPULLA]

ampster /ámstər/ n. (also **amster**) Austral. sl. the accomplice of a sideshow operator who acts as a purchaser in an attempt to persuade others to follow his example. [f. Amsterdam, rhyming sl. for RAM n. 6]

ampulla /ampōōlə/ n. (pl. **ampullae** /-ee/) **1 a** a Roman globular flask with two handles. **b** a vessel for sacred uses. **2** Anat. the dilated end of a vessel or duct. [L]

amputate /ámpyətayt/ v.tr. cut off by surgical operation (a part of the body, esp. a limb), usu. because of injury or disease. □□ **amputation** /-táyshən/ n. **amputator** n. [L amputare f. amb- about + putare prune]

amputee /ámpyətee/ n. a person who has lost a limb, etc., by amputation.

amtrac /ámtrak/ n. (also **amtrack**) an amphibious tracked vehicle used for landing assault troops on a shore. [amphibious + tractor]

Amtrak /ámtrak/ n. propr. US passenger railroad system.

amu abbr. atomic mass unit.

amuck var. of AMOK.

amulet /ámyəlit/ n. **1** an ornament or small piece of jewelry worn as a charm against evil. **2** something which is thought to give such protection. [L amuletum, of unkn. orig.]

■ charm, talisman, good-luck piece, periapt, phylactery, juju, Austral. churinga; toadstone, horseshoe, rabbit's foot.

amuse /əmyōōz/ v. **1** tr. cause (a person) to laugh or smile. **2** tr. & refl. (often foll. by with, by) interest or occupy; keep (a person) entertained. □□ **amusing** adj. **amusingly** adv. [ME f. OF amuser cause to muse (see MUSE[2]) f. causal a to + muser stare]

■ **1** make laugh or smile, delight, tickle, cheer, colloq. get. **2** divert, entertain, please, beguile, interest, occupy, distract. □□ **amusing** see ENTERTAINING.

amusement /əmyōōzmənt/ n. **1** something that amuses, esp. a pleasant diversion, game, or pastime. **2 a** the state of being amused. **b** the act of amusing. **3** Brit. a mechanical device (e.g., a merry-go-ground) for entertainment at a fairground, etc. □ **amusement arcade** Brit. an indoor area for entertainment with video games, pinball machines, etc. **amusement park** a park with rides such as a merry-go-round, Ferris wheel, roller coaster, etc., and usu. booths with games of chance or skill, foods, etc. [F f. amuser: see AMUSE, -MENT]

■ **1** entertainment, diversion, divertissement, recreation, distraction, pastime, activity, game, sport, joke, colloq. lark. **2** entertainment, diversion, recreation, pleasure, relaxation, distraction, beguilement, enjoyment, fun

(and games), play, gaiety, jollity, sport, Brit. beer and skittles; mirth.

amygdaloid /əmígdəloyd/ adj. shaped like an almond. □ **amygdaloid nucleus** a roughly almond-shaped mass of gray matter deep inside each cerebral hemisphere. [L amygdala f. Gk amugdalē almond]

amyl /ámil/ n. (used attrib.) Chem. the monovalent group C_5H_{11}-, derived from pentane. Also called PENTYL. [L amylum starch, from which oil containing it was distilled]

amylase /ámilays, -layz/ n. Biochem. any of several enzymes that convert starch and glycogen into simple sugars. [AMYL + -ASE]

amylopsin /ámilópsin/ n. Biochem. an enzyme of the pancreas that converts starch into maltose. [AMYL after pepsin]

amyotrophic lateral sclerosis /aymīətrṓfik, -tró-/ n. an incurable degenerative disease of the nervous system marked by increasing muscle weakness and eventual paralysis. Also called **Lou Gehrig's disease**. [A-[1] + MYO- + -TROPHIC]

Amytal /ámitawl, -tal/ n. propr. a trade name for amobarbital, a barbiturate drug used as a sedative and a hypnotic. [chem. name amylethyl barbituric acid]

an /an, ən/ adj. the form of the indefinite article (see A[1]) used before words beginning with a vowel sound (an egg; an hour). ¶ Now less often used before aspirated words beginning with h and stressed on a syllable other than the first (so a hotel, not an hotel).

an-[1] /ən, an/ prefix not; without (anarchy) (cf. A-[1]). [Gk an-]

an-[2] /ən, an/ assim. form of AD- before n.

-an /ən/ suffix (also **-ean, -ian**) forming adjectives and nouns, esp. from names of places, systems, zoological classes or orders, and founders (Mexican; Anglican; crustacean; European; Lutheran; Georgian; theologian). [ult. f. L adj. endings -(i)anus, -aeus: cf. Gk -aios, -eios]

ana /áanə/ n. **1** (as pl.) anecdotes or literary gossip about a person. **2** (as sing.) a collection of a person's memorable sayings. [= -ANA]

ana- /ánə/ prefix (usu. **an-** before a vowel) **1** up (anadromous). **2** back (anamnesis). **3** again (anabaptism). [Gk ana up]

-ana /ánə, áanə, áynə/ suffix forming plural nouns meaning 'things associated with' (Victoriana; Americana). [neut. pl. of L adj. ending -anus]

Anabaptism /ánəbáptizəm/ n. the doctrine that baptism should only be administered to believing adults. □□ **Anabaptist** n. [eccl.L anabaptismus f. Gk anabaptismos (as ANA-, BAPTISM)]

anabas /ánəbas/ n. any of the freshwater fish of the climbing perch family native to Asia and Africa, esp. the genus Anabas, able to breathe air and move on land. [mod.L f. Gk Anabas past part. of anabainō walk up]

anabasis /ənábəsis/ n. (pl. **anabases** /-seez/) **1** a march from a coast into the interior, as that of the younger Cyrus into Asia in 401 BC narrated by Xenophon in his work Anabasis. **2** a military advance. [Gk, = ascent f. anabainō (as ANA-, bainō go)]

anabatic /ánəbátik/ adj. Meteorol. (of a wind) caused by air flowing upwards (cf. KATABATIC). [Gk anabatikos ascending (as ANABASIS)]

anabiosis /ánəbīṓsis/ n. (pl. **anabioses** /-seez/) revival after apparent death. □□ **anabiotic** /-bíotik/ adj. [med.L f. Gk anabiōsis f. anabioō return to life]

anabolic /ánəbólik/ adj. Biochem. of or relating to anabolism. □ **anabolic steroid** any of a group of synthetic steroid hormones used to increase muscle size.

anabolism /ənábəlizəm/ n. Biochem. the synthesis of complex molecules in living organisms from simpler ones together with the storage of energy; constructive metabolism (opp. CATABOLISM). [Gk anabolē ascent (as ANA-, ballō throw)]

/.../ pronunciation   ● part of speech
□ phrases, idioms, and compounds
□□ derivatives   ■ synonym section
cross-references appear in SMALL CAPITALS or italics

anabranch /ánəbranch/ *n.* a stream that leaves a river and reenters it lower down. [ANASTOMOSE + BRANCH]

anachronic /ánəkrónik/ *adj.* **1** out of date. **2** involving anachronism. [ANACHRONISM after *synchronic*, etc.]
■ **1** see *old-fashioned*.

anachronism /ənákrənizəm/ *n.* **1 a** the attribution of a custom, event, etc., to a period to which it does not belong. **b** a thing attributed in this way. **2 a** anything out of harmony with its period. **b** an old-fashioned or out-of-date person or thing. □□ **anachronistic** /-nístik/ *adj.* **anachronistically** *adv.* [F *anachronisme* or Gk *anakhronismos* (as ANA-, *khronos* time)]
■ **1** misdating, misapplication, prochronism, parachronism. **2 b** (old) fogy, conservative, *colloq.* stick-in-the-mud, geriatric, *sl.* fuddy-duddy, square, back number; dodo, *colloq.* fossil, *derog.* museum piece, troglodyte. □□ **anachronistic** see *old-fashioned*.

anacoluthon /ánəkəlóōthon/ *n.* (*pl.* **anacolutha** /-thə/) a sentence or construction that lacks grammatical sequence (e.g., *while in the garden the door banged shut*). □□ **anacoluthic** *adj.* [LL f. Gk *anakolouthon* (as AN-¹, *akolouthos* following)]

anaconda /ánəkóndə/ *n.* a large nonpoisonous snake living mainly in water or in trees that kills its prey by constriction. [alt. of *anacondaia* f. Sinh. *henakandayā* whipsnake f. *hena* lightning + *kanda* stem: orig. of a snake in Sri Lanka]

anacreontic /ənákree-óntik/ *n.* & *adj.* ● *n.* a poem written after the manner of Anacreon, a Greek lyric poet (d. 478 BC). ● *adj.* **1** after the manner of Anacreon. **2** convivial and amatory in tone. [LL *anacreonticus* f. Gk *Anakreōn*]

anacrusis /ánəkróōsis/ *n.* (*pl.* **anacruses** /-seez/) **1** (in poetry) an unstressed syllable at the beginning of a verse. **2** *Mus.* an unstressed note or notes before the first bar line. [Gk *anakrousis* (as ANA-, *krousis* f. *krouō* strike)]

anadromous /ənádrəməs/ *adj.* (of a fish, e.g., the salmon) that swims up a river from the sea to spawn (opp. CATADROMOUS). [Gk *anadromos* (as ANA-, *dromos* running)]

anaemia *Brit.* var. of ANEMIA.

anaemic *Brit.* var. of ANEMIC.

anaerobe /ánərōb, anáirōb/ *n.* an organism that grows without air, or requires oxygen-free conditions to live. □□ **anaerobic** *adj.* [F *anaérobie* formed as AN-¹ + AEROBE]

anaesthesia *Brit.* var. of ANESTHESIA.

anaesthetic *Brit.* var. of ANESTHETIC.

anaesthetist *Brit.* var. of ANESTHETIST.

anaesthetize *Brit.* var. of ANESTHETIZE.

anaglyph /ánəglif/ *n.* **1** *Photog.* a composite stereoscopic photograph printed in superimposed complementary colors. **2** an embossed object cut in low relief. □□ **anaglyphic** /-glífik/ *adj.* [Gk *anagluphē* (as ANA-, *gluphē* f. *gluphō* carve)]

anagram /ánəgram/ *n.* a word or phrase formed by transposing the letters of another word or phrase. □□ **anagrammatic** /-mátik/ *adj.* **anagrammatical** *adj.* **anagrammatize** /-grámətiz/*v.tr.* [F *anagramme* or mod.L *anagramma* f. Gk ANA- + *gramma -atos* letter: cf. -GRAM]

anal /áynəl/ *adj.* **1** relating to or situated near the anus. **2** = *anal retentive*. □□ **anal retentive** (of a person) excessively orderly and fussy (supposedly owing to aspects of toilet training in infancy). □□ **anally** *adv.* [mod.L *analis* (as ANUS)]

analects /ánəlekts/ *n.pl.* (also **analecta** /ánəléktə/) a collection of short literary extracts. [L f. Gk *analekta* things gathered f. *analegō* pick up]

analeptic /ánəléptik/ *adj.* & *n.* ● *adj.* (of a drug, etc.) restorative; stimulating the central nervous system. ● *n.* a restorative medicine or drug. [Gk *analēptikos* f. *analambanō* take back]

analgesia /ánəljeézeeə, -seeə/ *n.* the absence or relief of pain. [mod.L Gk, = painlessness]

analgesic /ánəljeézik, -sik/ *adj.* & *n.* ● *adj.* relieving pain. ● *n.* an analgesic drug.
■ *n.* see PAINKILLER.

analog /ánəlog/ *n.* **1** an analogous or parallel thing. **2** (*attrib.*) (of a computer or electronic process) using physical variables, e.g., voltage, weight, or length, to represent numbers (cf. DIGITAL). [F f. Gk *analogon* neut. adj.: see ANALOGOUS]

■ **1** see METAPHOR, PARALLEL *n.* 1.

analogize /ənálojiz/ *v.* **1** *tr.* represent or explain by analogy. **2** *intr.* use analogy.

analogous /ənáləgəs/ *adj.* (usu. foll. by *to*) partially similar or parallel; showing analogy. □□ **analogously** *adv.* [L *analogus* f. Gk *analogos* proportionate]
■ see LIKE¹ *adj.* 1a.

analogue var. of ANALOG.

analogy /ənálojee/ *n.* (*pl.* **-ies**) **1** (usu. foll. by *to, with, between*) correspondence or partial similarity. **2** *Logic* a process of arguing from similarity in known respects to similarity in other respects. **3** *Philol.* the imitation of existing words in forming inflections or constructions of others, without the existence of corresponding intermediate stages. **4** *Biol.* the resemblance of function between organs essentially different. **5** = ANALOG 1. □□ **analogical** /ánəlójikəl/ *adj.* **analogically** *adv.* [F *analogie* or L *analogia* proportion f. Gk (as ANALOGOUS)]
■ **1** see METAPHOR. **5** see METAPHOR, PARALLEL *n.*

analysand /ənálisand/ *n.* a person undergoing psychoanalysis.

analyse *Brit.* var. of ANALYZE.

analysis /ənálisis/ *n.* (*pl.* **analyses** /-seez/) **1 a** a detailed examination of the elements or structure of a substance, etc. **b** a statement of the result of this. **2 a** *Chem.* the determination of the constituent parts of a mixture or compound. **b** the act or process of breaking something down into its constituent parts. **3** psychoanalysis. **4** *Math.* the use of algebra and calculus in problem solving. □ **in the final** (or **last** or **ultimate**) **analysis** after all due consideration; in the end. [med.L f. Gk *analusis* (as ANA-, *luō* set free)]
■ **1** examination, investigation, study, scrutiny, inquiry, dissection, anatomy, assessment; interpretation, criticism, critique; review. **2** assay, breakdown, division. **3** see THERAPY 2. □ **in the final** (or **last** or **ultimate**) **analysis** see *ultimately* (ULTIMATE).

analyst /ánəlist/ *n.* **1** a person skilled in (esp. chemical) analysis. **2** a psychoanalyst. [F *analyste*]

analytic /ánəlítik/ *adj.* **1** of or relating to analysis. **2** *Philol.* analytical. **3** *Logic* (of a statement, etc.) such that its denial is self-contradictory; true by definition (see SYNTHETIC). [LL f. Gk *analutikos* (as ANALYSIS)]

analytical /ánəlítikəl/ *adj.* **1** using analytic methods. **2** *Philol.* using separate words instead of inflections (cf. SYNTHETIC). □ **analytical geometry** geometry using coordinates. □□ **analytically** *adv.*

analyze /ánəliz/ *v.tr.* **1** examine in detail the constitution or structure of. **2 a** *Chem.* ascertain the constituents of (a sample of a mixture or compound). **b** take apart; break (something) down into its constituent parts. **3** find or show the essence or structure of (a book, music, etc.). **4** *Gram.* resolve (a sentence) into its grammatical elements. **5** psychoanalyze. □□ **analyzable** *adj.* **analyzer** *n.* [obs. *analyse* (n.) or F *analyser* f. *analyse* (n.) f. med.L ANALYSIS]
■ **1** examine, investigate, study, scrutinize, inquire *or* look into, dissect. **2 b** take apart *or* to pieces, separate, dissect, break down, anatomize. **3** interpret, assess, evaluate, critique, criticize, review. **5** psychoanalyze, give therapy to, put in therapy, *colloq.* psych.

anamnesis /ánəmneésis/ *n.* (*pl.* **anamneses** /-seez/) **1** recollection (esp. of a supposed previous existence). **2** a patient's account of his or her medical history. **3** *Eccl.* the part of the anaphora recalling the Passion, Resurrection, and Ascension of Christ. [Gk, = remembrance]

anandrous /ənándrəs/ *adj. Bot.* having no stamens. [Gk *anandros* without males f. *an-* not + *anēr andros* male]

Anangu /áanaangōō/ *n.* (*pl.* same) *Austral.* an Aborigine, esp. one from Central Australia. [Western Desert language, = person]

anapest /ánəpest/ *n. Prosody* a foot consisting of two short or unstressed syllables followed by one long or stressed syllable. □□ **anapestic** /-péstik/ *adj.* [L *anapaestus* f. Gk *anapaistos* reversed (because the reverse of a dactyl)]

anaphase /ánəfayz/ *n. Biol.* the stage of meiotic or mitotic cell division when the chromosomes move away from one another to opposite poles of the spindle. [ANA- + PHASE]

anaphora /ənáfərə/ *n.* **1** *Rhet.* the repetition of a word or phrase at the beginning of successive clauses. **2** *Gram.* the use of a word referring to or replacing a word used earlier in a sentence, to avoid repetition (e.g., *do* in *I like it and so do they*). **3** *Eccl.* the part of the Eucharist which contains the consecration, anamnesis, and communion. □□ **anaphoric** /ánəfórik/ *adj.* [L f. Gk, = repetition (as ANA-, *pherō* to bear)]

anaphrodisiac /anáfrədeézeeak, -díz-/ *adj.* & *n.* ● *adj.* tending to reduce sexual desire. ● *n.* an anaphrodisiac drug.

anaphylaxis /ánəfiláksis/ *n.* (*pl.* **anaphylaxes** /-seez/) *Med.* hypersensitivity of tissues to a dose of antigen, as a reaction against a previous dose. □□ **anaphylactic** /-láktik/ *adj.* [mod.L f. F *anaphylaxie* (as ANA- + Gk *phulaxis* guarding)]

anaptyxis /ánəptíksis/ *n.* (*pl.* **anaptyxes** /-seez/) *Phonet.* the insertion of a vowel between two consonants to aid pronunciation (as in *went thataway*). □□ **anaptyctic** /-tíktik/ *adj.* [mod.L f. Gk *anaptuxis* (as ANA-, *ptussō* fold)]

anarchism /ánərkizəm/ *n.* the doctrine that all government should be abolished. [F *anarchisme* (as ANARCHY)]

anarchist /ánərkist/ *n.* an advocate of anarchism or of political disorder. □□ **anarchistic** *adj.* [F *anarchiste* (as ANARCHY)]

anarchy /ánərkee/ *n.* **1** disorder, esp. political or social. **2** lack of government in a society. □□ **anarchic** /ənáarkik/ *adj.* **anarchical** *adj.* **anarchically** *adv.* [med.L f. Gk *anarkhia* (as AN-[1], *arkhē* rule)]

Anasazi /onəsáazee/ *n.* **1 a** a prehistoric N. American people native to the southwestern US. **b** a member of this people. **2** the language of this people.

anastigmat /ánástigmat/ *n.* a lens or system of lenses made free from astigmatism by correction. [G f. *anastigmatisch* ANASTIGMATIC]

anastigmatic /ánəstigmátik/ *adj.* free from astigmatism.

anastomose /ənástəmōz, -mōs/ *v.intr.* link by anastomosis. [F *anastomoser* (as ANASTOMOSIS)]

anastomosis /ənástəmṓsis/ *n.* (*pl.* **anastomoses** /-seez/) a cross-connection of arteries, branches, rivers, etc. [mod.L f. Gk f. *anastomoō* furnish with a mouth (as ANA-, *stoma* mouth)]

anastrophe /ənástrəfee/ *n. Rhet.* the inversion of the usual order of words or clauses. [Gk *anastrophē* turning back (as ANA-, *strephō* to turn)]

anat. *abbr.* **1** anatomical. **2** anatomy.

anathema /ənáthəmə/ *n.* (*pl.* **anathemas**) **1** a detested thing or person (*is anathema to me*). **2 a** an ecclesiastical curse, excommunicating a person or denouncing a doctrine. **b** a cursed thing or person. **c** a strong curse. [eccl.L, = excommunicated person, excommunication, f. Gk *anathema* thing devoted, (later) accursed thing, f. *anatithēmi* set up]

■ **1** see HATEFUL.

anathematize /ənáthəmətiz/ *v.tr.* & *intr.* curse. [F *anathématiser* f. L *anathematīzāre* f. Gk *anathematizo* (as ANATHEMA)]

■ see CURSE *v.* 1a.

anatomical /ánətómikəl/ *adj.* **1** of or relating to anatomy. **2** structural. □□ **anatomically** *adv.* [F *anatomique* or LL *anatomicus* (as ANATOMY)]

anatomist /ənátəmist/ *n.* a person skilled in anatomy. [F *anatomiste* or med.L *anatomista* (as ANATOMIZE)]

anatomize /ənátəmiz/ *v.tr.* **1** examine in detail. **2** dissect. [F *anatomiser* or med.L *anatomizare* f. *anatomia* (as ANATOMY)]

■ see ANALYZE 2b.

anatomy /ənátəmee/ *n.* (*pl.* **-ies**) **1** the science of the bodily structure of animals and plants. **2** this structure. **3** *colloq.* a human body. **4** analysis. **5** the dissection of the human body, animals, or plants. [F *anatomie* or LL *anatomia* f. Gk (as ANA-, -TOMY)]

■ **2** see FORM *n.* 1a. **3** see FORM *n.* 1b, BODY *n.* 1.

anatta (also **anatto**) var. of ANNATTO.

ANC *abbr.* African National Congress.

-ance /əns/ *suffix* forming nouns expressing: **1** a quality or state or an instance of one (*arrogance*; *protuberance*; rele-

vance; resemblance). **2** an action (*assistance*; *furtherance*; *penance*). [from or after F -*ance* f. L -*antia*, -*entia* (cf. -ENCE) f. pres. part. stem -*ant*-, -*ent*-]

ancestor /ánsestər/ *n.* (*fem.* **ancestress** /-stris/) **1** any (esp. remote) person from whom one is descended. **2** an early type of animal or plant from which others have evolved. **3** an early prototype or forerunner (*ancestor of the computer*). [ME f. OF *ancestre* f. L *antecessor* -*oris* f. *antecedere* (as ANTE-, *cedere cess-* go)]

■ **1** forebear, forefather, progenitor, primogenitor, predecessor, grandam, *archaic* grandsire. **3** forerunner, precursor, antecedent, progenitor; prototype, archetype; harbinger.

ancestral /ánséstrəl/ *adj.* belonging to or inherited from one's ancestors. [F *ancestrel* (as ANCESTOR)]

ancestry /ánsestree/ *n.* (*pl.* **-ies**) **1** one's (esp. remote) family descent. **2** one's ancestors collectively. [ME alt. of OF *ancesserie* (as ANCESTOR)]

anchor /ángkər/ *n.* & *v.* ● *n.* **1** a heavy metal weight used to moor a ship to the seafloor or a balloon to the ground. **2** a thing affording stability. **3** a source of confidence. **4** (in full **anchorman, anchorperson, anchorwoman**) **a** a person who plays a vital part, as the end member of a tug-of-war team, the last member of a relay team, etc. **b** a news broadcaster who introduces segments and reads the main portion of the news. ● *v.* **1** *tr.* secure (a ship or balloon) by means of an anchor. **2** *tr.* fix firmly. **3** *intr.* cast anchor. **4** *intr.* be moored by means of an anchor. □ **anchor light** a light shown by a ship at anchor. **at anchor** moored by means of an anchor. **cast** (or **come to**) **anchor** let the anchor down. **weigh anchor** take the anchor up. [OE *ancor* f. L *anchora* f. Gk *agkura*]

■ *n.* **1** mooring, sheet anchor. **2** mainstay, support, stabilizer, sheet anchor, holdfast; hold, grasp, grip. **4 b** presenter, announcer, newsreader, newscaster, reporter, broadcaster; master of ceremonies, MC, *colloq.* emcee. ● *v.* **1, 2** attach, affix, secure, moor, fix, fasten, make fast; pin, rivet, glue. **3, 4** drop or cast anchor, harbor, moor, be moored, be at anchor.

anchorage /ángkərij/ *n.* **1** a place where a ship may be anchored. **2** the act of anchoring or lying at anchor. **3** anything dependable.

anchorite /ángkərit/ *n.* (also **anchoret** /-rit/) (*fem.* **anchoress** /-ris/) **1** a hermit; a religious recluse. **2** a person of secluded habits. □□ **anchoretic** /-rétik/ *adj.* **anchoritic** /-rítik/ *adj.* [ME f. med.L *anc(h)orita*, eccl.L *anchoreta* f. eccl.Gk *anakhōrētēs* f. *anakhōreō* retire]

anchorman /ángkərmən/ *n.* (*pl.* **-men**) = ANCHOR *n.* 4.

anchoveta /ánchəvétə/ *n.* (also **anchovetta**) a small Pacific anchovy caught for use as bait or to make fishmeal. [Sp., dimin. of *anchova*: cf. ANCHOVY]

anchovy /ánchōvee/ *n.* (*pl.* **-ies**) any of various small silvery fish of the herring family usu. preserved in salt and oil and having a strong taste. □ **anchovy pear** a W. Indian fruit like a mango. [Sp. & Port. *ancho(v)a*, of uncert. orig.]

anchusa /ankyóōzə, anchóōzə/ *n.* any plant of the genus *Anchusa*, akin to borage. [L f. Gk *agkhousa*]

anchylose var. of ANKYLOSE.

anchylosis var. of ANKYLOSIS.

ancien régime /onsyáN rezheém/ *n.* (*pl.* **anciens régimes** *pronunc.* same) **1** the political and social system in France before the Revolution of 1789. **2** any superseded regime. [F, = old rule]

ancient[1] /áynshənt/ *adj.* & *n.* ● *adj.* **1** of long ago. **2** having lived or existed long. ● *n. archaic* an old man. □ **ancient history 1** the history of the ancient civilizations of the Mediterranean area and the Near East before the fall of the Western Roman Empire in 476. **2** something already long familiar. **ancient monument** *Brit.* an old building, etc.,

---

/.../ pronunciation	● part of speech
□ phrases, idioms, and compounds	
□□ derivatives	■ synonym section
cross-references appear in SMALL CAPITALS or *italics*	

49

preserved usu. under government control. **the ancients** the people of ancient times, esp. the Greeks and Romans. □□ **ancientness** n. [ME f. AF auncien f. OF ancien, ult. f. L ante before]
■ adj. **1** old, archaic, antique, bygone, past, former, earlier, antediluvian, primitive, prehistoric, primeval, primordial, immemorial, archaic olden. **2** old, timeworn, aged, aging, age-old, obsolescent, antiquated, antique, elderly, venerable, gray, hoary, superannuated, obsolete, fossil, fossilized, colloq. antediluvian. ● n. Methuselah, archaic graybeard.

ancient[2] /áynshənt/ n. archaic = ENSIGN. [corrupt. of form ensyne, etc., by assoc. with ancien = ANCIENT[1]]

anciently /áynshəntlee/ adv. long ago.

ancillary /ánsələree/ adj. & n. ● adj. **1** (of a person, activity, or service) providing essential support to a central service or industry, esp. the medical service. **2** (often foll. by to) subordinate; subservient. ● n. (pl. **-ies**) **1** an ancillary worker. **2** something which is ancillary; an auxiliary or accessory. [L ancillaris f. ancilla maidservant]
■ adj. see AUXILIARY adj. ● n. see AUXILIARY n.

ancon /ángkən/ n. (pl. **-es** /angkôneez/) Archit. **1** a console, usu. of two volutes, supporting or appearing to support a cornice. **2** each of a pair of projections on either side of a block of stone, etc., for lifting or repositioning. [L f. Gk agkōn elbow]

-ancy /ənsee/ suffix forming nouns denoting a quality (constancy; relevancy) or state (expectancy; infancy) (cf. -ANCE). [from or after L -antia: cf. -ENCY]

and /and, ənd/ conj. **1 a** connecting words, clauses, or sentences, that are to be taken jointly (cakes and pastries; white and brown bread; buy and sell; two hundred and forty). **b** implying progression (better and better). **c** implying causation (do that and I'll hit you; she hit him and he cried). **d** implying great duration (he cried and cried). **e** implying a great number (miles and miles). **f** implying addition (two and two are four). **g** implying variety (there are books and books). **h** implying succession (walking two and two). **2** colloq. to (try and open it). **3** in relation to (Britain and the US). □ **and/or** either or both of two stated possibilities (usually restricted to legal and commercial use). [OE and]

-and /and/ suffix forming nouns meaning 'a person or thing to be treated in a specified way' (ordinand). [L gerundive ending -andus]

andante /aandaantay, andántē/ adv., adj., & n. Mus. ● adv. & adj. in a moderately slow tempo. ● n. an andante passage or movement. [It., part. of andare go]

andantino /aandaanteénō, ándan-/ adv., adj., & n. Mus. ● adv. & adj. somewhat quicker (orig. slower) than andante. ● n. (pl. **-os**) an andantino passage or movement. [It., dimin. of ANDANTE]

andesite /ándizit/ n. a fine-grained brown or grayish intermediate volcanic rock. [Andes mountain chain in S. America + -ITE[1]]

andiron /ándirn/ n. a metal stand (usu. one of a pair) for supporting burning wood in a fireplace; a firedog. [ME f. OF andier, of unkn. orig.: assim. to IRON]

androecium /andreéseeəm/ n. (pl. **androecia** /-seeə/) Bot. the stamens taken collectively. [mod.L f. Gk andro- male + oikion house]

androgen /ándrəjən/ n. a male sex hormone or other substance capable of developing and maintaining certain male sexual characteristics. □□ **androgenic** /-jénik/ adj. [Gk andro- male + -GEN]

androgyne /ándrəjin/ adj. & n. ● adj. hermaphrodite. ● n. a hermaphroditic person. [OF androgyne or L androgynus f. Gk androgunos (anēr andros male, gunē woman)]

androgynous /andrójinəs/ adj. **1** hermaphroditic. **2** not clearly male or female; exhibiting the appearance or attributes of both sexes. **3** Bot. with stamens and pistils in the same flower or inflorescence.

androgyny /andrójinee/ n. hermaphroditism.

android /ándroyd/ n. a robot with a human form or appearance. [Gk andro- male, man + -OID]

-androus /ándrəs/ comb. form Bot. forming adjectives meaning 'having specified male organs or stamens' (monandrous). [mod.L f. Gk -andros f. anēr andros male + -OUS]

-ane[1] /ayn/ suffix var. of -AN; usu. with distinction of sense (germane; humane; urbane) but sometimes with no corresponding form in -an (mundane).

-ane[2] /ayn/ suffix Chem. forming names of saturated hydrocarbons (methane; propane). [after -ene, -ine, etc.]

anecdotage /ánikdôtij/ n. **1** joc. garrulous old age. **2** anecdotes. [ANECDOTE + -AGE: sense 1 after DOTAGE]

anecdote /ánikdōt/ n. a short account (or painting, etc.) of an entertaining or interesting incident. □□ **anecdotal** /-dôt'l/ adj. **anecdotalist** /-dôt'list/ n. **anecdotic** /-dótik/ adj. **anecdotist** n. [F anecdote or mod.L f. Gk anekdota things unpublished (as AN-[1], ekdotos f. ekdidōmi publish)]
■ see STORY 1.

anechoic /ánikóik/ adj. free from echo.

anemia /əneémeeə/ n. a deficiency in the blood, usu. of red cells or their hemoglobin, resulting in pallor and weariness. □ **pernicious anemia** a defective formation of red blood cells through a lack of vitamin B_{12} or folic acid. [mod.L f. Gk anaimia (as AN-[1], -AEMIA)]

anemic /əneémik/ adj. **1** relating to or suffering from anemia. **2** pale; lacking in vitality.
■ **2** see PALE[1] adj. 1, 4, WEAK 2.

anemograph /ənémməgraf/ n. an instrument for recording on paper the direction and force of the wind. □□ **anemographic** /-gráfik/ adj. [Gk anemos wind + -GRAPH]

anemometer /ánimómitər/ n. an instrument for measuring the force of the wind. [Gk anemos wind + -METER]

anemometry /ánimómitree/ n. the measurement of the force, direction, etc., of the wind. □□ **anemometric** /-məmétrik/ adj. [Gk anemos wind + -METRY]

anemone /ənémmənee/ n. **1** any plant of the genus Anemone, akin to the buttercup, with flowers of various vivid colors. **2** = PASQUEFLOWER. [L f. Gk anemōnē wind flower f. anemos wind]

anemophilous /ánimófiləs/ adj. wind-pollinated. [Gk anemos wind + -philous (see -PHILIA)]

anent /ənént/ prep. concerning. [OE on efen on a level with]

-aneous /áyneeəs/ suffix forming adjectives (cutaneous; miscellaneous). [L -aneus + -ous]

aneroid /ánəroyd/ adj. & n. ● adj. (of a barometer) that measures air pressure by its action on the elastic lid of an evacuated box, not by the height of a column of fluid. ● n. an aneroid barometer. [F anéroïde f. Gk a- not + nēros water]

anesthesia /ánis-theéezhə/ n. the absence of sensation, esp. artificially induced insensitivity to pain usu. achieved by the administration of gases or the injection of drugs. □□ **anesthesiology** /-zeeóləjee/ n. [mod.L f. Gk anaisthēsia (as AN-[1], aisthēsis sensation)]

anesthetic /ánis-thétik/ adj. & n. ● n. a substance that produces insensibility to pain, etc. ● adj. producing partial or complete insensibility to pain, etc. □ **general anesthetic** an anesthetic that affects the whole body, usu. with loss of consciousness. **local anesthetic** an anesthetic that affects a restricted area of the body. [Gk anaisthētos insensible (as AN-ESTHESIA)]
■ n. see PAINKILLER. ● adj. see NARCOTIC adj.

anesthetist /ənés-thətist/ n. a specialist in the administration of anesthetics.

anesthetize /ənés-thətīz/ v.tr. **1** administer an anesthetic to. **2** deprive of physical or mental sensation. □□ **anesthetization** /-tizáyshən/ n.
■ **2** see NUMB v.

aneurin /ányərin/ n. = THIAMINE. [anti + polyneuritis + vitamin]

aneurysm /ányərizəm/ n. (also **aneurism**) an excessive localized enlargement of an artery. □□ **aneurysmal** /-rízməl/ adj. (also **aneurismal**). [Gk aneurusma f. aneurunō widen out f. eurus wide]

anew /ənōo, ənyōo/ adv. **1** again. **2** in a different way. [ME, f. A-[4] + NEW]

anfractuosity /anfráktōo-ósitee/ n. **1** circuitousness. **2** intricacy. [F anfractuosité f. LL anfractuosus f. L anfractus a bending]

anfractuous /anfrákchŏŏəs/ adj. winding; sinuous; round-about; circuitous. [f. late L anfractuosus, f. L anfractus a bending]

angary /ánggəree/ n. Law the right of a belligerent (subject to compensation for loss) to seize or destroy neutral property under military necessity. [F angarie ult. f. Gk aggareia f. aggaros courier]

angel /áynjəl/ n. **1 a** an attendant or messenger of God. **b** a conventional representation of this in human form with wings. **c** an attendant spirit (evil angel; guardian angel). **d** a member of the lowest order of the ninefold celestial hierarchy (see ORDER). **2 a** a very virtuous person. **b** an obliging person (be an angel and answer the door). **3** Brit. an old English coin bearing the figure of the archangel Michael piercing the dragon. **4** sl. a financial backer of an enterprise, esp. in the theater. **5** an unexplained radar echo. □ **angel dust** sl. the hallucinogenic drug phencyclidine hydrochloride. **angel food cake** (also Brit. **angel cake**) a very light sponge cake. **angel shark** = MONKFISH 2. **angels-on-horseback** Brit. a dish of oysters wrapped in slices of bacon. [ME f. OF angele f. eccl.L angelus f. Gk aggelos messenger]

angelfish /áynjəlfish/ n. any of various fish, esp. Pterophyllum scalare, with large dorsal and ventral fins.

angelic /anjélik/ adj. **1** like or relating to angels. **2** having characteristics attributed to angels, esp. sublime beauty or innocence. □□ **angelical** adj. **angelically** adv. [ME f. F angélique or LL angelicus f. Gk aggelikos (as ANGEL)]

angelica /anjélikə/ n. **1** an aromatic umbelliferous plant, Angelica archangelica, used in cooking and medicine. **2** its candied stalks. [med.L (herba) angelica angelic herb]

angelus /ánjiləs/ n. **1** a Roman Catholic devotion commemorating the Incarnation, said at morning, noon, and sunset. **2** a bell rung to announce this. [opening words Angelus domini (L, = the angel of the Lord)]

anger /ánggər/ n. & v. ● n. extreme or passionate displeasure. ● v.tr. make angry; enrage. [ME f. ON angr grief, angra vex]
  ■ n. rage, fury, pique, spleen, colloq. dander, literary wrath, ire, poet. or archaic choler; antagonism, irritation, vexation, indignation, displeasure, ill or bad feeling, annoyance, irritability, resentment, outrage. ● v. enrage, infuriate, madden, pique, incense, make a person's hackles rise, make a person's blood boil, rile, gall, empurple; annoy, irritate, vex, nettle, displease, exasperate, provoke, get or put a person's back up, mad.

Angevin /ánjivin/ n. & adj. ● n. **1** a native or inhabitant of the Anjou region of France. **2** a Plantagenet, esp. any of the English kings from Henry II to John. ● adj. **1** of Anjou. **2** of the Plantagenets. [F]

angina /anjínə, ánjənə/ n. **1** an attack of intense constricting pain often causing suffocation. **2** (in full **angina pectoris** /péktəris/) pain in the chest brought on by exertion, owing to an inadequate blood supply to the heart. [L, = spasm of the chest f. angina quinsy f. Gk agkhonē strangling]

angiogram /ánjeeəgram/ n. an X-ray taken by angiography. [Gk aggeion vessel + -GRAM]

angiography /anjeeáagrəfee/ n. the visualization by X-ray of blood vessels following injection with a substance that is radiopaque. [Gk aggeion vessel + -GRAPHY]

angioma /ánjeeṓmə/ n. (pl. **angiomata** /-mətə/) a tumor produced by the dilatation or new formation of blood vessels. [mod.L f. Gk aggeion vessel]

angiosperm /ánjeeəspərm/ n. any plant producing flowers and reproducing by seeds enclosed within a carpel, including herbaceous plants, herbs, shrubs, grasses, and most trees (opp. GYMNOSPERM). □□ **angiospermous** /-spérməs/ adj. [Gk aggeion vessel + sperma seed]

Angle /ánggəl/ n. (usu. in pl.) a member of a tribe from Schleswig, Germany, that settled in Eastern Britain in the 5th c. □□ **Anglian** adj. [L Anglus f. Gmc (OE Engle: cf. ENGLISH) f. Angul a district of Schleswig (now in N. Germany) (as ANGLE²)]

angle¹ /ánggəl/ n. & v. ● n. **1 a** the space between two meeting lines or surfaces. **b** the inclination of two lines or surfaces to each other. **2 a** a corner. **b** a sharp projection. **3 a** the direction from which a photograph, etc., is taken. **b** the aspect from which a matter is considered. **c** an approach, technique, etc. ● v. **1** tr. & intr. move or place obliquely; point in a particular direction. **2** tr. present (information) from a particular point of view (was angled in favor of the victim). □ **angle brackets** brackets in the form < > (see BRACKET n. 3). **angle iron** a piece of iron or steel with an L-shaped cross section, used to strengthen a framework. **angle of repose** the angle beyond which an inclined body will not support another on its surface by friction. [ME f. OF angle or f. L angulus]
  ■ n. **1 b** slant, inclination. **2** bend, corner, intersection, cusp, point, apex, tip; sharp end, projection, protrusion. **3** direction, slant, point of view, aspect, viewpoint, standpoint, approach, position, side, perspective, bias. ● v. **1** slant, bend, point, direct, aim. **2** see SLANT v. 3.

angle² /ánggəl/ v. & n. ● v.intr. **1** (often foll. by for) fish with hook and line. **2** (foll. by for) seek an objective by devious or calculated means (angled for a pay raise). ● n. archaic a fishhook. [OE angul]
  ■ v. **2** (angle for) fish (for); look or hope for, seek, be or go after, try or aim for, hunt for.

angled /ánggəld/ adj. **1** placed at an angle to something else. **2** presented to suit a particular point of view. **3** having an angle.

angler /ángglər/ n. **1** a person who fishes with a hook and line. **2** = ANGLERFISH.

anglerfish /ángglərfish/ n. any of various fishes that prey upon small fish, attracting them by filaments arising from the dorsal fin: also called FROGFISH.

Anglican /ángglikən/ adj. & n. ● adj. of or relating to the Church of England or any Church in communion with it. ● n. a member of an Anglican Church. □□ **Anglicanism** n. [med.L Anglicanus (Magna Carta) f. Anglicus (Bede) f. Anglus ANGLE]

anglice /ángglisee/ adv. in English. [med.L]

Anglicism /ángglisizəm/ n. **1** a peculiarly English word or custom. **2** Englishness. **3** preference for what is English. [L Anglicus (see ANGLICAN) + -ISM]

Anglicist /ánggləsist/ n. a student of or scholar in English language or literature. □□ **Anglistics** /angglístiks/ n. [G f. L Anglus English]

Anglicize /ánggləsiz/ v.tr. **1** make English in form or character. **2** (**anglicize**) adopt (a foreign word) into English.

Anglist /ángglist/ var. of ANGLICIST.

Anglo /ánggO/ n. (pl. **-os**) **1** a person of British or northern European origin. **2** a white, English-speaking person not of Hispanic descent. [abbr. of ANGLO-SAXON]

Anglo- /ánggO/ comb. form **1** English (Anglo-Catholic). **2** of English origin (an Anglo-American). **3** English or British and (an Anglo-American agreement). [f. mod.L f. L Anglus English]

Anglo-Catholic /ánggOkáthəlik, -káthlik/ adj. & n. ● adj. of a High Church Anglican group that emphasizes its Roman Catholic tradition. ● n. a member of this group.

Anglocentric /ánggOséntrik/ adj. centered on or considered in terms of England.

Anglo-French /ánggOfrénch/ adj. & n. ● adj. **1** English (or British) and French. **2** of Anglo-French. ● n. the French language as retained and separately developed in England after the Norman Conquest.

Anglo-Indian /ánggO-índeeən/ adj. & n. ● adj. **1** of or relating to England and India. **2 a** of British descent or birth but living or having lived long in India. **b** of mixed British and Indian parentage. **3** (of a word) adopted into English from an Indian language. ● n. an Anglo-Indian person.

/.../ **pronunciation**   ● **part of speech**
  □ **phrases, idioms, and compounds**
  □□ **derivatives**   ■ **synonym section**
  cross-references appear in SMALL CAPITALS or italics

Anglo-Latin /ángglōlát'n/ adj. & n. ● adj. of Latin as used in medieval England. ● n. this form of Latin.

Anglomania /ánggIōmáyneeə/ n. excessive admiration of English customs.

Anglo-Norman /ángglōnáwrmən/ adj. & n. ● adj. 1 English and Norman. 2 of the Normans in England after the Norman Conquest. 3 of the dialect of French used by them. ● n. the Anglo-Norman dialect.

Anglophile /ánggləfīl/ n. & adj. (also **Anglophil** /-fil/) ● n. a person who is fond of or greatly admires England or the English. ● adj. being or characteristic of an Anglophile.

Anglophobe /ánggləfōb/ n. & adj. ● n. a person who greatly hates or fears England or the English. ● adj. being or characteristic of an Anglophobe.

Anglophobia /ángglǝfōbeeǝ/ n. intense hatred or fear of England or the English.

anglophone /ángglǝfōn/ adj. & n. ● adj. English-speaking. ● n. an English-speaking person. [ANGLO-, after FRANCO-PHONE]

Anglo-Saxon /ángglōsáksǝn/ adj. & n. ● adj. 1 of the English Saxons (as distinct from the Old Saxons of the European continent, and from the Angles) before the Norman Conquest. 2 of the Old English people as a whole before the Norman Conquest. 3 of English descent. ● n. 1 an Anglo-Saxon person. 2 the Old English language. 3 colloq. plain (esp. crude) English. [mod.L Anglo-Saxones, med.L Angli Saxones after OE Angulseaxe, -an]

angora /anggáwrǝ/ n. 1 a fabric made from the hair of the angora goat or rabbit. 2 a long-haired variety of cat, goat, or rabbit. □ **angora wool** a mixture of sheep's wool and angora rabbit hair. [Angora (Ankara) in Turkey]

angostura /ánggǝstŏōrǝ, -styŏōrǝ/ n. (in full **angostura bark**) an aromatic bitter bark used as a flavoring, and formerly used as a medicinal tonic and to reduce fever. □ **Angostura Bitters** propr. a kind of tonic first made in Angostura. [Angostura, a town in Venezuela on the Orinoco, now Ciudad Bolívar]

angry /ánggree/ adj. (**angrier, angriest**) 1 feeling or showing anger; extremely displeased or resentful. 2 (of a wound, sore, etc.) inflamed; painful. 3 suggesting or seeming to show anger (an angry sky). □□ **angrily** adv. [ME, f. ANGER + -Y[1]]

  ■ 1 enraged, furious, irate, ireful, piqued, incensed, infuriated, fuming; irritated, annoyed, vexed, cross, provoked, indignant, exasperated, hot under the collar, in a bad or foul temper or mood, out of temper, up in arms, in high dudgeon, as cross as two sticks, archaic wroth, colloq. livid, on the warpath, (all) steamed up, mad, ratty, fit to be tied, Austral. & NZ colloq. crook, literary wrathful, colloq. mad as a hornet, mad as a wet hen. 2 inflamed, irritated, sore, smarting, painful, stinging. 3 black, lowering, dark, savage, glowering. □□ **angrily** furiously, irately, crossly, hotly, in high dudgeon, literary wrathfully; gloweringly, blackly, darkly, savagely.

angst /aangkst/ n. 1 anxiety. 2 a feeling of guilt or remorse. [G]

  ■ 1 see ANXIETY 1, 2.

angstrom /ángstrǝm/ n. (also **ångström** /áwngström/) a unit of length equal to 10^{-10} meter. ¶ Symb.: Å. [A.J. Ångström, Swedish physicist d. 1874]

anguine /ánggwin/ adj. of or resembling a snake. [L anguinus f. anguis snake]

anguish /ánggwish/ n. & v. ● n. severe misery or mental suffering. ● v.tr. (often as **anguished** adj.) cause to suffer physical or mental pain. [ME f. OF anguisse choking f. L angustia tightness f. angustus narrow]

  ■ n. suffering, pain, angst, distress, agony, torment, torture, anxiety, misery, throe, heartache, grief, archaic or literary woe, archaic or poet. bale. ● v. disturb, upset, distress, afflict, trouble; torment, torture.

anguished /ánggwisht/ adj. suffering or expressing anguish. [past part. of anguish (v.) f. OF anguissier f. eccl.L angustiare to distress, formed as ANGUISH]

  ■ see worried (WORRY v. 4).

angular /ánggyǝlǝr/ adj. 1 a having angles or sharp corners. b (of a person) having sharp features; lean and bony. c awkward in manner. 2 forming an angle. 3 measured by angle (angular distance). □ **angular momentum** the quantity of rotation of a body, the product of its moment of inertia and angular velocity. **angular velocity** the rate of change of angular position of a rotating body. □□ **angularity** /-láritee/ n. **angularly** adv. [L angularis f. angulus ANGLE[1]]

anhedral /anheédrǝl/ n. & adj. Aeron. ● n. the angle between the wing and horizontal when the wing is inclined downwards. ● adj. of or having an anhedral. [AN-[1] + -hedral (see -HEDRON)]

anhydride /anhídrid/ n. Chem. a substance obtained by removing the elements of water from a compound, esp. from an acid. [as ANHYDROUS + -IDE]

anhydrite /anhídrit/ n. a naturally occurring usu. rock-forming anhydrous mineral form of calcium sulfate. [as ANHYDROUS + -ITE[1] 2]

anhydrous /anhídrǝs/ adj. Chem. without water, esp. water of crystallization. [Gk anudros (as AN-[1], hudōr water)]

aniline /ánillin, -lin/ n. a colorless oily liquid, used in the manufacture of dyes, drugs, and plastics. □ **aniline dye 1** any of numerous dyes made from aniline. 2 any synthetic dye. [G Anilin f. Anil indigo (from which it was orig. obtained), ult. f. Arab. an-nīl]

anima /ánimǝ/ n. Psychol. 1 the inner personality (opp. PERSONA). 2 Jung's term for the feminine part of a man's personality (opp. ANIMUS). [L, = mind, soul]

animadvert /ánimadvért/ v.intr. (foll. by on) criticize; censure (conduct, a fault, etc.). □□ **animadversion** /-vérzhǝn/ n. [L animadvertere f. animus mind + advertere (as AD-, vertere vers- turn)]

animal /ánimǝl/ n. & adj. ● n. 1 a living organism which feeds on organic matter, usu. one with specialized sense organs and a nervous system, and able to respond rapidly to stimuli. 2 such an organism other than human beings. 3 a brutish or uncivilized person. 4 colloq. a person or thing of any kind (there is no such animal). ● adj. 1 characteristic of animals. 2 of animals as distinct from vegetables (animal charcoal). 3 characteristic of the physical needs of animals; carnal; sensual. □ **animal husbandry** the science of breeding and caring for farm animals. **animal magnetism 1** hist. mesmerism. 2 sex appeal. **animal rights** (a movement upholding) the natural right of animals to live free from human exploitation. **animal spirits** natural exuberance. [L f. animale neut. of animalis having breath f. anima breath]

  ■ n. 1 creature, (sentient) being, organism, living thing. 3 beast, brute, barbarian, savage, monster. ● adj. 1 zoological, biological. 3 physical, fleshly, sensual, gross, coarse, unrefined, uncultured, uncultivated, rude, carnal, crude, bestial, beastlike, subhuman. □ **animal spirits** see exuberance (EXUBERANT).

animalcule /ánimálkyŏōl/ n. a microscopic animal. □□ **animalcular** adj. [mod.L animalculum (as ANIMAL, -CULE)]

animalism /ánimǝlizǝm/ n. 1 the nature and activity of animals. 2 the belief that humans are not superior to other animals. 3 concern with physical matters; sensuality.

animality /ánimálitee/ n. 1 the animal world. 2 the nature or behavior of animals. [F animalité f. animal (adj.)]

animalize /ánimǝliz/ v.tr. 1 make (a person) bestial; sensualize. 2 convert to animal substance. □□ **animalization** /-li-záyshǝn/ n.

animate adj. & v. ● adj. /ánimǝt/ 1 having life. 2 lively. ● v.tr. /ánimayt/ 1 enliven; make lively. 2 give life to. 3 inspire; actuate. 4 encourage. 5 produce using animation. [L animatus past part. of animare give life to f. anima life, soul]

  ■ adj. 1 alive, living, animated, moving, breathing, archaic quick. 2 lively, spirited, vivacious, animated, vigorous. ● v. 1, 2 activate, enliven, invigorate, stimulate, inspirit, excite, stir, vitalize, spark, vivify, revitalize, energize, breathe life into, ginger up. 3, 4 inspire, inspirit, stimulate, actuate, move, motivate, incite, rouse, arouse, excite, fire (up), ginger up, encourage, spur (on or onwards).

animated /ánimaytid/ adj. 1 lively; vigorous. 2 having life. 3

(of a movie, etc.) using techniques of animation. □□ **animatedly** *adv.* **animator** *n.* (in sense 3).

■ **1** lively, alive, quick, spirited, active, vivacious, energetic, vigorous, excited, ebullient, enthusiastic, dynamic, vibrant, ardent, enlivened, passionate, impassioned, fervent, animate. **2** see ANIMATE *adj.* 1. □□ **animatedly** see *vigorously* (VIGOROUS). **animator** cartoonist.

animation /ánimáyshən/ *n.* **1** vivacity; ardor. **2** the state of being alive. **3** *Cinematog.* the technique of filming successive drawings or positions of puppets, etc., to create an illusion of movement when the film is shown as a sequence.

■ **1** vivacity, vivaciousness, spirit, spiritedness, vitality, dash, élan, zest, verve, liveliness, exhilaration, energy, go, dynamism, enthusiasm, eagerness, excitement, vigor, *colloq.* pep; fire, ardor, fervor, feeling, zeal, intensity, ardency.

animé /ánimay/ *n.* any of various resins, esp. a W. Indian resin used in making varnish. [F, of uncert. orig.]

animism /ánimizəm/ *n.* **1** the attribution of a living soul to plants, inanimate objects, and natural phenomena. **2** the belief in a supernatural power that organizes and animates the material universe. □□ **animist** *n.* **animistic** /-místik/ *adj.* [L *anima* life, soul + -ISM]

animosity /ánimósitee/ *n.* (*pl.* **-ies**) a spirit or feeling of strong hostility. [ME f. OF *animosité* or LL *animositas* f. *animosus* spirited, formed as ANIMUS]

■ hostility, antagonism, antipathy, ill will, bad *or* ill feeling, malevolence, enmity, hatred, animus, loathing, detestation, contempt; bad *or* ill blood, malice, bitterness, acrimony, resentment, rancor.

animus /ániməs/ *n.* **1** a display of animosity. **2** ill feeling. **3** a motivating spirit or feeling. **4** *Psychol.* Jung's term for the masculine part of a woman's personality (opp. ANIMA). [L, = spirit, mind]

anion /ánīən/ *n.* a negatively charged ion; an ion that is attracted to the anode in electrolysis (opp. CATION). [ANA- + ION]

anionic /ánīónik/ *adj.* **1** of an anion or anions. **2** having an active anion.

anise /ánis/ *n.* an umbelliferous plant, *Pimpinella anisum*, having aromatic seeds (see ANISEED). [ME f. OF *anis* f. L f. Gk *anison* anise, dill]

aniseed /ániseed/ *n.* the seed of the anise, used to flavor liqueurs and candy. [ME f. ANISE + SEED]

anisette /ánisét, -zét/ *n.* a liqueur flavored with aniseed. [F, dimin. of *anis* ANISE]

anisotropic /ánisətrópik, -trō-/ *adj.* having physical properties that are different in different directions, e.g., the strength of wood along the grain differing from that across the grain (opp. ISOTROPIC). □□ **anisotropically** *adv.* **anisotropy** /-sótrəpee/ *n.* [AN-¹ + ISOTROPIC]

ankh /angk/ *n.* a device consisting of a looped bar with a shorter crossbar, used in ancient Egypt as a symbol of life. [Egypt., = life, soul]

ankle /ángkəl/ *n.* & *v.* ● *n.* **1** the joint connecting the foot with the leg. **2** the part of the leg between this and the calf. ● *v.intr. Brit. sl.* walk. □ **ankle-biter** esp. *Austral. colloq.* a child. **ankle sock** esp. *Brit.* = ANKLET 2. [ME f. ON *ankul-* (unrecorded) f. Gmc: rel. to ANGLE¹]

anklebone /ángkəlbōn/ *n.* a bone forming the ankle.

anklet /ángklit/ *n.* **1** an ornament or fetter worn around the ankle. **2** a short sock just covering the ankle. [ANKLE + -LET, after BRACELET]

ankylose /ángkilōs/ *v.tr.* & *intr.* (also **anchylose**) (of bones or a joint) stiffen or unite by ankylosis. [back-form. f. ANKYLOSIS after *anastomose*, etc.]

ankylosis /ángkilósis/ *n.* (also **anchylosis**) **1** the abnormal stiffening and immobility of a joint by fusion of the bones. **2** such fusion. □□ **ankylotic** /-lótik/ *adj.* [mod.L f. Gk *agkulōsis* f. *agkuloō* crook]

anna /aanə/ *n.* a former monetary unit of India and Pakistan, one-sixteenth of a rupee. [Hind. *ānā*]

annal /ánəl/ *n.* **1** the annals of one year. **2** a record of one item in a chronicle. [back-form. f. ANNALS]

annalist /ánəlist/ *n.* a writer of annals. □□ **annalistic** /-lístik/ *adj.* **annalistically** /-lístikəlee/ *adv.*

annals /ánəlz/ *n.pl.* **1** a narrative of events year by year. **2** historical records. [F *annales* or L *annales* (*libri*) yearly (books) f. *annus* year]

annatto /ənátō/ *n.* (also **anatta** /-tə/, **anatto**) an orangish red dye from the pulp of a tropical fruit, used for coloring foods. [Carib name of the fruit tree]

anneal /əneél/ *v.* & *n.* ● *v.tr.* **1** heat (metal or glass) and allow it to cool slowly, esp. to toughen it. **2** toughen. ● *n.* treatment by annealing. □□ **annealer** *n.* [OE *onǣlan* f. *on* + *ǣlan* burn, bake f. *āl* fire]

annectent /ənéktənt/ *adj. Biol.* connecting (*annectent link*). [L *annectere annectent-* bind (as ANNEX)]

annelid /án'lid/ *n.* any segmented worm of the phylum Annelida, e.g., earthworms, lugworms, etc. [F *annélide* or mod.L *annelida* (pl.) f. F *annelés* ringed animals f. OF *anel* ring f. L *anellus* dimin. of *anulus* ring]

annelidan /ənélid'n/ *adj.* & *n.* ● *adj.* of the annelids. ● *n.* an annelid.

annex *v.* & *n.* /anéks, áneks/ ● *v.tr.* **1 a** add as a subordinate part. **b** (often foll. by *to*) append to a book, etc. **2** incorporate (territory of another) into one's own. **3** add as a condition or consequence. **4** *colloq.* take without right. ● *n.* (*Brit.* also **annexe**) /áneks, ániks/ **1** a separate or added building, esp. for extra accommodation. **2** an addition to a document. □□ **annexation** /-sáyshən/ *n.* [ME f. OF *annexer* f. L *annectere* (as AN-², *nectere nex-* bind)]

■ **1** see ADD 1. **2** see CONQUER 1a. **3** see TACK¹ *v.* 3. **4** see APPROPRIATE *v.* 1. ● *n.* **1** extension, addition; wing. **2** see ADDITION 2.

annihilate /ənīəlayt/ *v.tr.* **1** completely destroy. **2** defeat utterly; make insignificant or powerless. □□ **annihilator** *n.* [LL *annihilare* (as AN-², *nihil* nothing)]

■ **1** see DESTROY 1, 2. **2** see DEFEAT *v.* 1.

annihilation /ənīəláyshən/ *n.* **1** the act or process of annihilating. **2** *Physics* the conversion of a particle and an antiparticle into radiation. [F *annihilation* or LL *annihilatio* (as AN-NIHILATE)]

anniversary /ánivírsəree/ *n.* (*pl.* **-ies**) **1** the date on which an event took place in a previous year. **2** the celebration of this. [ME f. L *anniversarius* f. *annus* year + *versus* turned]

Anno Domini /ánō dóminī, -nee/ *adv.* & *n.* ● *adv.* in the year of our Lord; in the year of the Christian era. ● *n. Brit. colloq.* advancing age (*suffering from Anno Domini*). [L, = in the year of the Lord]

annotate /ánōtayt/ *v.tr.* add explanatory notes to (a book, document, etc.). □□ **annotatable** *adj.* **annotation** /-táyshən/ *n.* **annotative** *adj.* **annotator** *n.* [L *annotare* (as AD-, *nota* mark)]

■ see GLOSS² *v.* 1a.

announce /ənówns/ *v.* **1** *tr.* (often foll. by *that*) make publicly known. **2** *tr.* make known the arrival or imminence of (a guest, dinner, etc.). **3** *intr.* declare one's candidacy for office. **4** *tr.* make known (without words) to the senses or the mind; be a sign of. [ME f. OF *annoncer* f. L *annuntiare* (as AD-, *nuntius* messenger)]

■ **1** proclaim, make public, make known, set forth, put out, publish, advertise, publicize, promulgate, broadcast, herald, bill, *formal* put forth; circulate; reveal, disclose, divulge, declare, state, assert, affirm, asseverate, confirm, *formal* aver. **2** introduce, present, make known. **4** intimate, suggest, hint at; signal; foretell, betoken, augur, portend, presage, harbinger, herald, proclaim; precede.

announcement /ənównsmənt/ *n.* **1** the action of announcing; something announced. **2** an official communication or statement. **3** an advertisement or other piece of promotional material.

/. . ./ **pronunciation** ● **part of speech**
□ **phrases, idioms, and compounds**
□□ **derivatives** ■ **synonym section**
cross-references appear in SMALL CAPITALS or *italics*

1 declaration, pronouncement, proclamation, statement, annunciation, rescript; notification, notice, word. **2** report, bulletin, communiqué, disclosure. **3** see ADVERTISEMENT 1.

announcer /ənównsər/ n. a person who announces, esp. introducing programs or describing sports events in broadcasting.
■ presenter, anchor, anchorman, anchorperson, anchorwoman, newscaster, reporter, broadcaster; esp. *Brit.* newsreader, master of ceremonies, MC, *colloq.* emcee.

annoy /ənóy/ v.tr. **1** cause slight anger or mental distress to. **2** (in *passive*) be somewhat angry (*am annoyed with you; was annoyed at my remarks*). **3** molest; harass repeatedly. □□ **annoyer** n. **annoying** adj. [ME f. OF *anuier, anui, anoi*, etc., ult. f. L *in odio* hateful]
■ **1** irritate, bother, irk, vex, nettle, spite, get on a person's nerves, exasperate, provoke, rile, madden, get *or* put a person's back up, ride, ballyrag, *colloq.* peeve, get in a person's hair, get under a person's skin, get, *disp.* aggravate. **3** pester, harass, harry, badger, keep on at, nag, plague, molest, bedevil, *colloq.* needle, hassle, get under a person's skin, *sl.* bug. □□ **annoying** irritating, maddening, infuriating, irksome, vexing, vexatious, exasperating, galling, grating, bothersome, pestilential, *colloq.* pestilent, pesky, *disp.* aggravating, *Austral. sl.* on the nose.

annoyance /ənóyəns/ n. **1** the action of annoying or the state of being annoyed; irritation; vexation. **2** something that annoys; a nuisance.
■ **1** irritation; bother, vexation, exasperation, pique, *colloq.* botheration, *disp.* aggravation, *Brit. sl.* aggro. **2** nuisance, pest, irritant, bore, *colloq.* pain, bind, pain in the neck, *disp.* aggravation, *sl.* pain in the butt.

annual /ányoॊəl/ adj. & n. ● adj. **1** reckoned by the year. **2** occurring every year. **3** living or lasting for one year. ● n. **1** a book, etc., published once a year; a yearbook. **2** a plant that lives only for a year or less. □ **annual meeting** a yearly meeting of members or shareholders, esp. for holding elections and reporting on the year's events. **annual ring** a ring in the cross section of a plant, esp. a tree, produced by one year's growth. □□ **annually** adv. [ME f. OF *annuel* f. LL *annualis* f. L *annalis* f. *annus* year]
■ adj. **2** yearly, once a year, regular.

annualized /ányoॊəlizd/ adj. (of rates of interest, inflation, etc.) calculated on an annual basis, as a projection from figures obtained for a shorter period.

annuitant /ənoॊoit'nt, ənyoॊo-/ n. a person who holds or receives an annuity. [ANNUITY + -ANT, by assim. to *accountant*, etc.]

annuity /ənoॊoitee, ənyoॊo-/ n. (pl. **-ies**) **1** a yearly grant or allowance. **2** an investment of money entitling the investor to a series of equal annual sums. **3** a sum payable in respect of a particular year. [ME f. F *annuité* f. med.L *annuitas -tatis* f. L *annuus* yearly (as ANNUAL)]
■ **1** see ALLOWANCE n. 1.

annul /ənúl/ v.tr. (**annulled, annulling**) **1** declare (a marriage, etc.) invalid. **2** cancel; abolish. □□ **annulment** n. [ME f. OF *anuller* f. LL *annullare* (as AD-, *nullus* none)]
■ **2** see CANCEL v. 4.

annular /ányələr/ adj. ring-shaped; forming a ring. □ **annular eclipse** an eclipse of the sun in which the moon leaves a ring of sunlight visible around it. □□ **annularly** adv. [F *annulaire* or L *annularis* f. *an(n)ulus* ring]

annulate /ányələt, -layt/ adj. having rings; marked with or formed of rings. □□ **annulation** /-láyshən/ n. [L *annulatus* (as ANNULUS)]

annulet /ányəlit/ n. **1** *Archit.* a small fillet or band encircling a column. **2** a small ring. [L *annulus* ring + -ET¹]

annulus /ányələs/ n. (pl. **annuli** /-li/) esp. *Math. & Biol.* a ring. [L *an(n)ulus*]

annunciate /ənúnseeayt/ v.tr. **1** proclaim. **2** indicate as coming or ready. [LL *annunciare* f. L *annuntiare annuntiat-* announce]

annunciation /ənúnseeáyshən/ n. **1** (**Annunciation**) **a** the

announcing of the Incarnation, made by the angel Gabriel to Mary, related in Luke 1:26-38. **b** the festival commemorating this on March 25. **2 a** the act or process of announcing. **b** an announcement. [ME f. OF *annonciation* f. LL *annuntiatio -onis* (as ANNUNCIATE)]

annunciator /ənúnseeaytər/ n. **1** a device giving an audible or visible indication of which of several electrical circuits has been activated, of the position of a train, etc. **2** an announcer. [LL *annuntiator* (as ANNUNCIATE)]

annus mirabilis /ánəs mirábilis/ n. a remarkable or auspicious year. [mod.L, = wonderful year]

anoa /ənóə/ n. any of several small deerlike water buffalo of the genus *Bubalus*, native to Sulawesi. [name in Sulawesi]

anode /ánōd/ n. *Electr.* **1** the positive electrode in an electrolytic cell or electronic tube. **2** the negative terminal of a primary cell such as a battery (opp. CATHODE). □ **anode ray** a beam of particles emitted from the anode of a high vacuum tube. □□ **anodal** adj. **anodic** /ənódik/ adj. [Gk *anodos* way up f. *ana* up + *hodos* way]

anodize /ánədīz/ v.tr. coat (a metal, esp. aluminum) with a protective oxide layer by electrolysis. □□ **anodizer** n. [ANODE + -IZE]

anodyne /ánədīn/ adj. & n. ● adj. **1** able to relieve pain. **2** mentally soothing. ● n. an anodyne drug or medicine. [L *anodynus* f. Gk *anōdunos* painless (as AN-¹, *odunē* pain)]
■ n. see PAINKILLER.

anoesis /ánō-eesis/ n. *Psychol.* consciousness with sensation but without thought. □□ **anoetic** /-étik/ adj. [A-¹ + Gk *noēsis* understanding]

anoint /ənóynt/ v.tr. **1** apply oil or ointment to, esp. as a religious ceremony (e.g., at baptism, or the consecration of a priest or king, or in ministering to the sick). **2** (usu. foll. by *with*) smear; rub. □□ **anointer** n. [ME f. AF *anoint* (adj.) f. OF *enoint* past part. of *enoindre* f. L *inungere* (as IN-², *ungere unct-* smear with oil)]

anomalistic /ənóməlistik/ adj. *Astron.* of the anomaly or angular distance of a planet from its perihelion. □ **anomalistic month** a month measured between successive perigees of the moon. **anomalistic year** a year measured between successive perihelia of the earth.

anomalous /ənómələs/ adj. having an irregular or deviant feature; abnormal. □□ **anomalously** adv. **anomalousness** n. [LL *anomalus* f. Gk *anōmalos* (as AN-¹, *homalos* even)]
■ see ABNORMAL.

anomaly /ənóməlee/ n. (pl. **-ies**) **1** an anomalous circumstance or thing; an irregularity. **2** irregularity of motion, behavior, etc. **3** *Astron.* the angular distance of a planet or satellite from its last perihelion or perigee. [L f. Gk *anōmalia* f. *anōmalos* ANOMALOUS]
■ **1** see ODDITY 1. **2** see ODDITY 3.

anomie /ánəmee/ n. (also **anomy**) lack of the usual social or ethical standards in an individual or group. □□ **anomic** /ənómik/ adj. [Gk *anomia* f. *anomos* lawless: *-ie* f. F]

anon /ənón/ adv. *archaic or literary* soon; shortly (*will say more of this anon*). [OE f. *ān* into one, *on āne* in one]

anon. /ənón/ abbr. anonymous; an anonymous author.

anonym /ánənim/ n. **1** an anonymous person or publication. **2** a pseudonym. [F *anonyme* f. Gk *anōnumos*: see ANONYMOUS]

anonymous /ənóniməs/ adj. **1** of unknown name. **2** of unknown or undeclared source or authorship. **3** without character; featureless; impersonal. □□ **anonymity** /ánənímitee/ n. **anonymously** adv. [LL *anonymus* f. Gk *anōnumos* nameless (as AN-¹, *onoma* name)]
■ **1** see NAMELESS 1, 3, 5.

anopheles /ənófileez/ n. any of various mosquitoes of the genus *Anopheles*, many of which are carriers of the malarial parasite. [mod.L f. Gk *anōphelēs* unprofitable]

anorak /ánərak/ n. a waterproof jacket of cloth or synthetic material, usu. with a hood, of a kind orig. used in polar regions; a parka. [Greenland Eskimo *anoraq*]

anorectic var. of ANOREXIC.

anorexia /ánərékseeə/ n. **1** a lack or loss of appetite for food. **2** (in full **anorexia nervosa** /nərvōsə/) a psychological illness, esp. in young women, characterized by an obsessive desire to lose weight by refusing to eat. [LL f. Gk f. *an-* not + *orexis* appetite]

anorexic /ánəréksik/ *adj. & n.* (also **anorectic** /-réktik/)
● *adj.* **1** involving, producing, or characterized by a lack of appetite, esp. in anorexia nervosa. **2** *colloq.* extremely thin. ● *n.* **1** an anorexic agent. **2** a person with anorexia. [F *anorexique*; *anorectic* f. Gk *anorektos* without appetite (as ANOREXIA)]

anosmia /anózmeeə/ *n.* the loss of the sense of smell. □□ **anosmic** *adj.* [LL f. Gk f. *an-* not + *osmē* smell]

another /ənúthər/ *adj. & pron.* ● *adj.* **1** an additional; one more (*have another piece of cake; after another six months*). **2** a person like or comparable to (*another Lincoln*). **3** a different one (*quite another matter*). **4** some or any other (*will not do another person's work*). ● *pron.* **1** an additional one (*have another*). **2** a different one (*take this book away and bring me another*). **3** some or any other one (*I love another*). **4** *Brit.* an unnamed additional party to a legal action (*X versus Y and another*). **5** *Brit.* (also **A. N. Other** /áy en úthər/) a player unnamed or not yet selected. □ **another place** *Brit.* the other House of Parliament (used in the Commons to refer to the Lords, and vice versa). **such another** another of the same sort. [ME f. AN + OTHER]

anovulant /anóvyələnt/ *n. & adj. Pharm.* ● *n.* a drug preventing ovulation. ● *adj.* preventing ovulation. [AN-¹ + *ovulation* (see OVULATE) + -ANT]

anoxia /ənókseeə/ *n. Med.* an absence or deficiency of oxygen reaching the tissues; severe hypoxia. □□ **anoxic** *adj.* [mod.L, formed as AN-¹ + OXYGEN + -IA¹]

anschluss /áanshlõõs/ *n.* a unification, esp. the annexation of Austria by Germany in 1938. [G f. *anschliessen* join]

anserine /ánsərin, -rin/ *adj.* **1** of or like a goose. **2** silly. [L *anserinus* f. *anser* goose]
■ **2** see SILLY *adj.* 1.

answer /ánsər/ *n. & v.* ● *n.* **1** something said or done to deal with or in reaction to a question, statement, or circumstance. **2** the solution to a problem. ● *v.* **1** *tr.* make an answer to (*answer me; answer my question*). **2** *intr.* (often foll. by *to*) make an answer. **3** *tr.* respond to the summons or signal of (*answer the door; answer the telephone*). **4** *tr.* be satisfactory for (a purpose or need). **5** *intr.* **a** (foll. by *for, to*) be responsible (*you will answer to me for your conduct*). **b** (foll. by *for*) vouch (for a person, conduct, etc.). **6** *intr.* (foll. by *to*) correspond, esp. to a description. **7** *intr.* be satisfactory or successful. □ **answer back** answer a rebuke, etc., impudently. **answering machine** a tape recorder which supplies a recorded answer to a telephone call and usu. records incoming messages. **answering service** a business that receives and answers telephone calls for its clients. **answer to the name of** be called. [OE *andswaru, andswarian* f. Gmc, = swear against (charge)]
■ *n.* **1** reply, response, rejoinder, retort, riposte, reaction, explanation, *sl.* comeback; *Law* defense, counterstatement, plea, rejoinder, surrejoinder, rebutter, surrebutter. **2** solution, explanation, explication; key. ● *v.* **1** reply to, respond to. **2** reply, respond; (make a) retort, riposte. **4** satisfy, fulfill, suffice for, meet, suit, serve, fit, fill, conform to, correlate with. **5** be accountable *or* responsible *or* answerable; (*answer for*) take *or* accept the blame for; take *or* undertake responsibility for, suffer the consequences of; vouch for, sponsor, support, guarantee the conduct of. **6** see CORRESPOND 1.
□ **answer back** talk back. **answer to the name of** be named *or* called.

answerable /ánsərəbəl/ *adj.* **1** (usu. foll. by *to, for*) responsible (*answerable to them for any accident*). **2** that can be answered. □□ **answerability** /-bílitee/ *n.*
■ **1** see RESPONSIBLE 1, 2.

ant /ant/ *n.* any small insect of a widely distributed hymenopterous family, living in complex social colonies, wingless (except for adults in the mating season), and proverbial for industry. □ **ant bear** = AARDVARK. **ant** (or **ant's**) **eggs** pupae of ants. **ant lion** any of various dragonfly-like insects, the larvae of which dig pits in which to trap ants and other in-

sects for food. **have ants in one's pants** *colloq.* be fidgety; be restless. **white ant** = TERMITE. [OE *æmet(t)e, ēmete* (see EMMET) f. WG]

ant- /ant/ assim. form of ANTI- before a vowel or *h* (*Antarctic*).

-ant /ənt/ *suffix* **1** forming adjectives denoting attribution of an action (*pendant; repentant*) or state (*arrogant; expectant*). **2** forming nouns denoting an agent (*assistant; celebrant; deodorant*). [F *-ant* or L *-ant-, -ent-*, pres. part. stem of verbs: cf. -ENT]

antacid /antásid/ *n. & adj.* ● *n.* a substance that prevents or corrects acidity, esp. in the stomach. ● *adj.* having these properties.

antagonism /antágənizəm/ *n.* active opposition or hostility. [F *antagonisme* (as ANTAGONIST)]
■ opposition, animosity, enmity, rancor, hostility, antipathy; conflict, rivalry, discord, dissension, friction, strife; contention.

antagonist /antágənist/ *n.* **1** an opponent or adversary. **2** *Biol.* a substance, muscle, or organ that partially or completely opposes the action of another. □□ **antagonistic** *adj.* **antagonistically** *adv.* [F *antagoniste* or LL *antagonista* f. Gk *antagōnistēs* (as ANTAGONIZE)]
■ **1** adversary, opponent, enemy, contender, competitor, esp. *poet.* or *formal* foe; *collect.* competition, opposition, other side. □□ **antagonistic** see HOSTILE 2.

antagonize /antágəniz/ *v.tr.* **1** evoke hostility or opposition or enmity in. **2** (of one force, etc.) counteract or tend to neutralize (another). □□ **antagonization** /-nizáyshən/ *n.* [Gk *antagōnizomai* (as ANTI-, *agōnizomai* f. *agōn* contest)]
■ **1** see ALIENATE 1.

antalkali /antálkəli/ *n.* (*pl.* **antalkalis**) any substance that counteracts an alkali.

Antarctic /antaárktik/ *adj. & n.* ● *adj.* of the south polar regions. ● *n.* this region. □ **Antarctic Circle** the parallel of latitude 66° 32′ S., forming an imaginary line around this region. [ME f. OF *antartique* or L *antarcticus* f. Gk *antarktikos* (as ANTI-, *arktikos* ARCTIC)]

ante /ántee/ *n. & v.* ● *n.* **1** a stake put up by a player in poker, etc., before receiving cards. **2** an amount to be paid in advance. ● *v.tr.* (**antes, anted**) **1** put up as an ante. **2 a** bet; stake. **b** (foll. by *up*) pay. [L, = before]

ante- /ántee/ *prefix* forming nouns and adjectives meaning 'before; preceding' (*anteroom; antenatal*). [L *ante* (prep. & adv.), = before]

anteater /ánteetər/ *n.* any of various mammals feeding on ants and termites, e.g., a tamandua.

antebellum /ánteebéləm/ *adj.* occurring or existing before a particular war, esp. the US Civil War. [L f. *ante* before + *bellum* war]

antecedent /ántiseéd'nt/ *n. & adj.* ● *n.* **1** a preceding thing or circumstance. **2** *Gram.* a word, phrase, clause, or sentence, to which another word (esp. a relative pronoun, usu. following) refers. **3** (in *pl.*) past history, esp. of a person. **4** *Logic* the statement contained in the 'if' clause of a conditional proposition. ● *adj.* **1** (often foll. by *to*) previous. **2** presumptive; a priori. □□ **antecedence** /-d'ns/ *n.* **antecedently** *adv.* [ME f. F *antecedent* or L *antecedere* (as ANTE-, *cedere* go)]
■ *n.* **1** see ANCESTOR 3, ROOT¹ *n.* 5a, 6. ● *adj.* **1** see PREVIOUS *adj.* 1.

antechamber /ánteechaymbər/ *n.* a small room leading to a main one. [earlier *anti-*, f. F *antichambre* f. It. *anticamera* (as ANTE-, CHAMBER)]

antechapel /ánteechapəl/ *n.* an anteroom to a church or chapel.

antedate /ántidáyt/ *v. & n.* ● *v.tr.* **1** exist or occur at a date earlier than. **2** assign an earlier date to (a document, event, etc.), esp. one earlier than its actual date. ● *n.* a date earlier than the actual one.

/.../ **pronunciation**	● **part of speech**
□ **phrases, idioms, and compounds**	
□□ **derivatives**	■ **synonym section**
cross-references appear in SMALL CAPITALS or *italics*	

55

■ *v.* **1** see PRECEDE 1.

antediluvian /ánteedilŏoveeən/ *adj.* **1** of or belonging to the time before the Biblical flood. **2** *colloq.* very old or out of date. [ANTE- + L *diluvium* DELUGE + -AN]

antelope /ántilōp/ *n.* (*pl.* same or **antelopes**) **1 a** any of various deerlike ruminants of the family Bovidae, esp. abundant in Africa and typically tall, slender, graceful, and swift-moving with smooth hair and upward-pointing horns, e.g. gazelles, gnus, kudus, and impala. **b** a pronghorn. **2** leather made from the skin of any of these. [ME f. OF *antelop* or f. med.L *ant(h)alopus* f. late Gk *antholops*, of unkn. orig.]

antenatal /ánteenáyt'l/ *adj.* **1** existing or occurring before birth; prenatal. **2** relating to the period of pregnancy.

antenna /anténə/ *n.* (*pl.* **antennae** /-ee/) **1** *Zool.* one of a pair of mobile appendages on the heads of insects, crustaceans, etc., sensitive to touch and taste; a feeler. **2** (*pl.* **antennas**) a metal rod, wire, or other structure by which signals are transmitted or received as part of a radio or television transmission or receiving system. □□ **antennal** *adj.* (in sense 1). **antennary** *adj.* (in sense 1). [L, = sail yard]

■ **1** feeler, tentacle, palp.

antenuptial /ánteenúpshəl/ *adj.* = PRENUPTIAL.

antependium /ánteepéndeeəm/ *n.* (*pl.* **antependia** /-deeə/) a veil or hanging for the front of an altar, podium, etc. [med.L (as ANTE-, *pendēre* hang)]

antepenult /ánteepinúlt/ *n.* the last syllable but two in a word as "te" in "antepenult." [abbr. of LL *antepaenultimus* (as ANTE-, *paenultimus* PENULT)]

antepenultimate /ánteepinúltimət/ *adj.* & *n.* ● *adj.* last but two; third from the end. ● *n.* anything that is last but two.

anterior /antéereeər/ *adj.* **1** nearer the front. **2** (often foll. by *to*) earlier; prior. □□ **anteriority** /-reeáwritee/ *n.* **anteriorly** *adv.* [F *antérieur* or L *anterior* f. *ante* before]

■ **1** see FRONT *attrib.adj.* **2** see FOREGOING.

anteroom /ánteerŏom, -rŏom/ *n.* a small room leading to a main one.

antheap /ánt-heep/ *n.* = ANTHILL.

anthelion /ant-héeleeən, anthée-/ *n.* (*pl.* **anthelia** /-liə/) a luminous halo projected on a cloud or fog bank opposite to the sun. [Gk, neut. of *anthēlios* opposite to the sun (as ANTI-, *hēlios* sun)]

anthelmintic /ánt-helmíntik, ánthel-/ (also **anthelminthic** /-thik/) *n.* & *adj.* ● *n.* any drug or agent used to destroy parasitic, esp. intestinal, worms, e.g., tapeworms, roundworms, and flukes. ● *adj.* having the power to eliminate or destroy parasitic worms. [ANTI- + Gk *helmins helminthos* worm]

anthem /ánthəm/ *n.* **1** an elaborate choral composition usu. based on a passage of scripture for church use. **2** a solemn hymn of praise, etc., esp. = *national anthem.* **3** a composition sung antiphonally. [OE *antefn, antifne* f. LL *antiphona* ANTIPHON]

anthemion /anthéemeeən/ *n.* (*pl.* **anthemia** /-meeə/) a flower-like ornament used in art. [Gk, = flower]

anther /ánthər/ *n. Bot.* the apical portion of a stamen containing pollen. □□ **antheral** *adj.* [F *anthère* or mod.L *anthera*, in L 'medicine extracted from flowers' f. Gk *anthēra* flowery, fem. adj. f. *anthos* flower]

antheridium /ánthərídeeəm/ *n.* (*pl.* **antheridia** /-deeə/) *Bot.* the male sex organ of algae, mosses, ferns, etc. [mod.L f. *anthera* (as ANTHER) + -*idion* dimin. suffix]

anthill /ánt-hil/ *n.* **1** a moundlike nest built by ants or termites. **2** a community teeming with people.

anthologize /anthóləjīz/ *v.tr.* & *intr.* compile or include in an anthology.

anthology /anthóləjee/ *n.* (*pl.* **-ies**) a published collection of passages from literature, songs, reproductions of paintings, etc. □□ **anthologist** *n.* [F *anthologie* or med.L f. Gk *anthologia* f. *anthos* flower + -*logia* collection f. *legō* gather]

■ see COLLECTION 2.

anthozoan /ánthəzŏən/ *n.* & *adj.* ● *n.* any of the sessile marine coelenterates of the class Anthozoa, including sea anemones and corals. ● *adj.* of or relating to this class. [mod.L *Anthozoa* f. Gk *anthos* flower + *zōia* animals]

anthracene /ánthrəseen/ *n.* a colorless crystalline aromatic hydrocarbon obtained by the distillation of crude oils and used in the manufacture of chemicals. [Gk *anthrax -akos* coal + -ENE]

anthracite /ánthrəsīt/ *n.* coal of a hard variety burning with little flame and smoke. □□ **anthracitic** /-sítik/ *adj.* [Gk *anthrakitis* a kind of coal (as ANTHRACENE)]

anthrax /ánthraks/ *n.* a disease of sheep and cattle transmissible to humans. [LL f. Gk, = carbuncle]

anthropo- /ánthrəpō/ *comb. form* human; humankind. [Gk *anthrōpos* human being]

anthropocentric /ánthrəpōséntrik/ *adj.* regarding humankind as the center of existence. □□ **anthropocentrically** *adv.* **anthropocentrism** *n.*

anthropogenesis /ánthrəpōjénisis/ *n.* = ANTHROPOGENY.

anthropogeny /ánthrəpójinee/ *n.* the study of the origin of humans. □□ **anthropogenic** /ánthrəpōjénik/ *adj.*

anthropoid /ánthrəpoyd/ *adj.* & *n.* ● *adj.* **1** resembling a human being in form. **2** *colloq.* (of a person) apelike. ● *n.* a being that is human in form only, esp. an anthropoid ape. [Gk *anthrōpoeidēs* (as ANTHROPO-, -OID)]

anthropology /ánthrəpólⱥjee/ *n.* **1** the study of humankind, esp. of its societies and customs. **2** the study of the structure and evolution of human beings as animals. □□ **anthropological** /-pəlójikəl/ *adj.* **anthropologist** *n.*

anthropometry /ánthrəpómitree/ *n.* the scientific study of the measurements of the human body. □□ **anthropometric** /-pəmétrik/ *adj.*

anthropomorphic /ánthrəpəmáwrfik/ *adj.* of or characterized by anthropomorphism. □□ **anthropomorphically** *adv.* [as ANTHROPOMORPHOUS + -IC]

anthropomorphism /ánthrəpəmáwrfizəm/ *n.* the attribution of a human form or personality to a god, animal, or thing. □□ **anthropomorphize** *v.tr.*

anthropomorphous /ánthrəpəmáwrfəs/ *adj.* human in form. [Gk *anthrōpomorphos* (as ANTHROPO-, *morphē* form)]

anthroponymy /ánthrəpónimee/ *n.* the study of personal names. [ANTHROPO- + Gk *ōnumia* f. *onoma* name: cf. TOPONYMY]

anthropophagy /ánthrəpófəjee/ *n.* cannibalism. □□ **anthropophagous** *adj.* [Gk *anthrōpophagia* (as ANTHROPO-, *phagō* eat)]

anthroposophy /ánthrəpósəfee/ *n.* a movement inaugurated by Rudolf Steiner (1861–1925) to develop the faculty of cognition and the realization of spiritual reality. [ANTHROPO- + Gk *sophia* wisdom f. *sophos* wise]

anti /ántee, -tī/ *prep.* & *n.* ● *prep.* (also *absol.*) opposed to (*is anti everything; seems to be rather anti*). ● *n.* (*pl.* **antis**) a person opposed to a particular policy, etc. [ANTI-]

■ *prep.* see AVERSE.

anti- /ántee/ *prefix* (also **ant-** before a vowel or *h*) forming nouns and adjectives meaning: **1** opposed to; against (*antivivisectionism*). **2** preventing (*antiscorbutic*). **3** the opposite of (*anticlimax*). **4** rival (*antipope*). **5** unlike the conventional form (*antihero; antinovel*). **6** *Physics* the antiparticle of a specified particle (*antineutrino; antiproton*). [from or after Gk *anti-* against]

antiabortion /ánteeəbáwrshən, ántī-/ *adj.* opposing abortion. □□ **antiabortionist** *n.*

antiaircraft /ánteeáirkraft, ántī-/ *adj.* (of a gun, missile, etc.) used to attack enemy aircraft.

antiar /ántiaar/ *n.* = UPAS 1a, 2. [Jav. *antjar*]

antiballistic missile /ánteebəlístik, ántī-/ *n.* a missile designed for intercepting and destroying a ballistic missile while in flight.

antibiosis /ánteebīósis, ántī-/ *n.* an antagonistic association between two organisms (esp. microorganisms), in which one is adversely affected (cf. SYMBIOSIS). [mod.L f. F *antibiose* (as ANTI-, SYMBIOSIS)]

antibiotic /ántibiótik, ántī-/ *n.* & *adj. Pharm.* ● *n.* any of various substances (e.g., penicillin) produced by microorganisms or made synthetically, that can inhibit or destroy susceptible microorganisms. ● *adj.* functioning as an antibiotic. [F *antibiotique* (as ANTI-, Gk *biōtikos* fit for life f. *bios* life)]

antibody /ántibodee, ánti-/ n. (pl. **-ies**) any of various blood proteins produced in response to and then counteracting antigens. [transl. of G *Antikörper* (as ANTI-, *Körper* body)]

antic /ántik/ n. & adj. ● n. **1** (usu. in *pl.*) absurd or foolish behavior. **2** an absurd or silly action; a prank. ● adj. *archaic* grotesque; bizarre. [It. *antico* ANTIQUE, used as = grotesque] ■ n. **2** see CAPER[1] n. 2a.

anticathode /ánteekúthōd, ánti-/ n. the target (or anode) of an X-ray tube on which the electrons from the cathode impinge and from which X-rays are emitted.

Antichrist /ánteekrīst, ánti-/ n. **1** an archenemy of Christ. **2** a postulated personal opponent of Christ expected by some denominations of the Christian church to appear before the end of the world. [ME f. OF *antecrist* f. eccl.L *antichristus* f. Gk *antikhristos* (as ANTI-, *Khristos* CHRIST)]

antichristian /ánteekríschən, ánti-/ adj. **1** opposed to Christianity. **2** concerning the Antichrist.

anticipate /antísipayt/ v.tr. **1** deal with or use before the proper time. **2** *disp.* expect; foresee; regard as probable (*did not anticipate any difficulty*). **3** forestall (a person or thing). **4** look forward to. □□ **anticipative** adj. **anticipator** n. **anticipatory** adj. [L *anticipare* f. *anti-* for ANTE- + *-cipare* f. *capere* take]
■ **2** foretell, forecast, predict, prophesy, foretaste, foresee, see, expect; bank *or* reckon *or* count on. **3** forestall, preempt, intercept, head off, preclude, obviate, prevent, be beforehand with; nullify. **4** look forward to, prepare for, wait for, await. □□ **anticipative, anticipatory** preemptive, forward-looking, interceptive, preclusive, preventative, preventive, precautionary; see also EXPECTANT adj. 1.

anticipation /antísipáyshən/ n. **1** the act or process of anticipating. **2** *Mus.* the introduction beforehand of part of a chord which is about to follow. [F *anticipation* or L *anticipatio* (as ANTICIPATE)]
■ **1** expectation, expectancy; hope; foreknowledge, precognition, presentiment; foreboding; compare ANTICIPATE.

anticlerical /ánteeklérikəl, ánti-/ adj. & n. ● adj. opposed to the influence of the clergy, esp. in politics. ● n. an anticlerical person. □□ **anticlericalism** n.

anticlimax /ánteeklímaks, ánti-/ n. a trivial conclusion to something significant or impressive, esp. where a climax was expected. □□ **anticlimactic** /-máktik/ adj. **anticlimactically** adv.
■ see NONEVENT.

anticline /ántiklīn/ n. *Geol.* a ridge or fold of stratified rock in which the strata slope down from the crest (opp. SYNCLINE). □□ **anticlinal** adj. [ANTI- + Gk *klīnō* lean, after INCLINE]

anticlockwise /ánteeklókwīz, ánti-/ adv. & adj. *Brit.* = COUNTERCLOCKWISE.

anticoagulant /ánteekō-ágyələnt, ánti-/ n. & adj. ● n. any drug or agent that retards or inhibits coagulation, esp. of the blood. ● adj. retarding or inhibiting coagulation.

anticodon /ánteekōdon, ánti-/ n. *Biochem.* a sequence of three nucleotides forming a unit of genetic code in a transfer RNA molecule that corresponds to a complementary codon in messenger RNA.

anticonvulsant /ánteekənvúlsənt, ánti-/ n. & adj. ● n. any drug or agent that prevents or reduces the severity of convulsions, esp. as in epilepsy. ● adj. preventing or reducing convulsions.

anticyclone /ánteesíklōn, ánti-/ n. a system of winds rotating outwards from an area of high barometric pressure, clockwise in the Northern hemisphere and counterclockwise in the Southern hemisphere. □□ **anticyclonic** /-klónik/ adj.

antidepressant /ánteediprésənt, ánti-/ n. & adj. ● n. any drug or agent that alleviates depression. ● adj. alleviating depression.

antidiuretic hormone /ánteedíyərétik, ánti-/ n. = VASOPRESSIN. [ANTI- + DIURETIC]

antidote /ántidōt/ n. **1** a medicine, etc., taken or given to counteract poison. **2** anything that counteracts something unpleasant or evil. □□ **antidotal** adj. [F *antidote* or L *anti-*

dotum f. Gk *antidoton* neut. of *antidotos* given against (as ANTI- + stem of *didonai* give)]
■ **1** antitoxin, antiserum, antivenene, counterirritant; cure, remedy. **2** countermeasure, corrective, correction, remedy, cure, solution; (counter)balance. □□ **antidotal** antitoxic; counteractive, corrective, remedial.

antifreeze /ántifreez, ántee-/ n. a substance (usu. ethylene glycol) added to water to lower its freezing point, esp. in the radiator of a motor vehicle.

antigen /ántijən/ n. a foreign substance (e.g., toxin) that causes the body to produce antibodies. □□ **antigenic** /-jénik/ adj. [G (as ANTIBODY, -GEN)]

antigravity /ánteegrávitee, ánti-/ n. *Physics* a hypothetical force opposing gravity.

antihero /ánteeheerō, ánti-/ n. (pl. **-oes**) a central character in a story or drama who noticeably lacks conventional heroic attributes.

antihistamine /ánteehístəmin, -meen, ántī-/ n. a substance that counteracts the effects of histamine, used esp. in the treatment of allergies.

anti-inflammatory /anteeinflámətōree, ántī-/ adj. & n. ● adj. reducing or counteracting inflammation (*aspirin is an anti-inflammatory drug*). ● n. (pl. **-ies**) an anti inflammatory medication.

antiknock /ánteenók, ántī-/ n. a substance added to motor fuel to prevent premature combustion.

antilock /ánteelók, ántī-/ n. & attrib. adj. (of brakes) designed so as to prevent locking and skidding when applied suddenly.

antilog /ánteelawg, -log, ántī-/ n. colloq. = ANTILOGARITHM. [abbr.]

antilogarithm /ánteeláwgərithəm, -lóg-, ántī-/ n. the number to which a logarithm belongs (*100 is the common antilogarithm of 2*).

antilogy /antíləjee/ n. (pl. **-ies**) a contradiction in terms. [F *antilogie* f. Gk *antilogia* (as ANTI-, -LOGY)]

antimacassar /ánteeməkásər/ n. a covering put over furniture, esp. over the back of a chair as protection or as an ornament. [ANTI- + MACASSAR]

antimatter /ánteematər, ántī-/ n. *Physics* matter composed solely of antiparticles.

antimetabolite /ánteemitábəlīt, ántī-/ n. *Pharm.* a drug that interferes with the normal metabolic processes within cells, usu. by combining with enzymes.

antimony /ántimōnee/ n. *Chem.* a brittle silvery white metallic element used esp. in alloys. ¶ Symb.: **Sb**. □□ **antimonial** /-mōneeal/ adj. **antimonic** adj. **antimonious** /-mōneeəs/ adj. [ME f. med.L *antimonium* (11th c.), of unkn. orig.]

antinode /ánteenōd, ántī-/ n. *Physics* the position of maximum displacement in a standing wave system.

antinomian /ántinōmeeən/ adj. & n. ● adj. of or relating to the view that Christians are released from the obligation of observing the moral law. ● n. (**Antinomian**) hist. a person who holds this view. □□ **antinomianism** n. [med.L *Antinomi*, name of a sect in Germany (1535) alleged to hold this view (as ANTI-, Gk *nomos* law)]

antinomy /antínəmee/ n. (pl. **-ies**) **1** a contradiction between two beliefs or conclusions that are in themselves reasonable; a paradox. **2** a conflict between two laws or authorities. [L *antinomia* f. Gk (as ANTI-, *nomos* law)]

antinovel /ánteenovəl, ántī-/ n. a novel in which the conventions of the form are studiously avoided.

antinuclear /ánteenōōkleeər, -nyōō-, ántī-/ adj. opposed to the development of nuclear weapons or nuclear power.

antioxidant /ántee-óksid'nt, ántī-/ n. an agent that inhibits oxidation, esp. used to reduce deterioration of products stored in air.

antiparticle /ánteepaartikəl, ántī-/ n. *Physics* an elementary particle having the same mass as a given particle but opposite electric or magnetic properties.

antipasto /ánteepaástō/ n. (pl. **-os** or **antipasti** /-tee/) an hors d'oeuvre, esp. in an Italian meal. [It.]
■ see HORS D´OEUVRE.

antipathetic /ántipəthétik/ adj. (usu. foll. by to) having a strong aversion or natural opposition. □□ **antipathetical** adj. **antipathetically** adv. [as ANTIPATHY after PATHETIC]
■ see AVERSE.

antipathic /ántipáthik/ adj. of a contrary nature or character.

antipathy /antípəthee/ n. (pl. **-ies**) (often foll. by to, for, between) a strong or deep-seated aversion or dislike. [F antipathie or L antipathia f. Gk antipatheia f. antipathēs opposed in feeling (as ANTI-, pathos -eos feeling)]
■ see AVERSION 1.

antipersonnel /ánteepórsənél, ántī-/ adj. (of a bomb, mine, etc.) designed to kill or injure people rather than to damage buildings or equipment.

antiperspirant /ánteepórspirənt, ántī-/ n. & adj. ● n. a substance applied to the skin to prevent or reduce perspiration. ● adj. that acts as an antiperspirant.

antiphlogistic /ánteeflәjístik, ántī-/ n. & adj. ● n. any drug or agent that alleviates or reduces inflammation. ● adj. alleviating or reducing inflammation.

antiphon /ántifon/ n. **1** a hymn or psalm, the parts of which are sung or recited alternately by two groups. **2** a versicle or phrase from this. **3** a sentence sung or recited before or after a psalm or canticle. **4** a response. [eccl.L antiphona f. Gk (as ANTI-, phōnē sound)]

antiphonal /antífənəl/ adj. & n. ● adj. **1** sung or recited alternately by two groups. **2** responsive; answering. ● n. a collection of antiphons. □□ **antiphonally** adv.

antiphonary /antífənéree/ n. (pl. **-ies**) a book of antiphons. [eccl.L antiphonarium (as ANTIPHON)]

antiphony /antífənee/ n. (pl. **-ies**) **1** antiphonal singing or chanting. **2** a response or echo.

antipode /ántipōd/ n. (usu. foll. by of, to) the exact opposite. [see ANTIPODES]

antipodes /antípədeez/ n.pl. **1 a** (also **Antipodes**) a place diametrically opposite another, esp. Australasia as the region on the opposite side of the earth from Europe. **b** places diametrically opposite each other. **2** (usu. foll. by of, to) the exact opposite. □□ **antipodal** adj. **antipodean** /-deéən/ adj. & n. [F or LL f. Gk antipodes having the feet opposite (as ANTI-, pous podos foot)]

antipole /ántipōl/ n. **1** the direct opposite. **2** the opposite pole.

antipope /ánteepōp, ántī-/ n. a person set up as pope in opposition to one (held by others to be) canonically chosen. [F antipape f. med.L antipapa, assim. to POPE[1]]

antiproton /ánteeprŏton, ántī-/ n. Physics the negatively charged antiparticle of a proton.

antipruritic /ánteeprōōritik, ántī-/ adj. & n. ● adj. relieving itching. ● n. an antipruritic drug or agent. [ANTI- + PRURITUS + -IC]

antipyretic /ánteepīrétik, ántī-/ adj. & n. ● adj. preventing or reducing fever. ● n. an antipyretic drug or agent.

antiquarian /ántikwáireeən/ adj. & n. ● adj. **1** of or dealing in antiques or rare books. **2** of the study of antiquities. ● n. an antiquary. □□ **antiquarianism** n. [see ANTIQUARY]

antiquary /ántikweree/ n. (pl. **-ies**) a student or collector of antiques or antiquities. [L antiquarius f. antiquus ancient]

antiquated /ántikwaytid/ adj. old-fashioned; out of date. [eccl.L antiquare antiquat- make old]
■ old, old-fashioned, outmoded, passé, out-of-date, dated, archaic, obsolescent, antique, obsolete, quaint, colloq. old hat, medieval, antediluvian; primitive; extinct.

antique /anteék/ n., adj., & v. ● n. an object of considerable age, esp. an item of furniture or the decorative arts having a high value. ● adj. **1** of or existing from an early date. **2** old-fashioned; archaic. **3** of ancient times. ● v.tr. (**antiques, antiqued, antiquing**) give an antique appearance to (furniture, etc.) by artificial means. [F antique or L antiquus, anticus former, ancient f. ante before]

■ n. collectible, collector's item, bibelot, objet d'art, object or article of virtu, heirloom, curio, rarity, treasure. ● adj. **1** old, age-old, ancient, historic(al), timeworn. **2** old-fashioned, archaic, antiquated, outmoded, passé, out-of-date, dated, obsolete. **3** see ANCIENT[1] adj. 1.

antiquity /antíkwitee/ n. (pl. **-ies**) **1** ancient times, esp. the period before the Middle Ages. **2** great age (a city of great antiquity). **3** (usu. in pl.) physical remains or relics from ancient times, esp. buildings and works of art. **4** (in pl.) customs, events, etc., of ancient times. **5** the people of ancient times regarded collectively. [ME f. OF antiquité f. L antiquitas -tatis f. antiquus: see ANTIQUE]
■ **1** see HISTORY 2c.

antiracism /ánteeráysizəm, ántī-/ n. the policy or practice of opposing racism and promoting racial tolerance. □□ **antiracist** n. & adj.

antirrhinum /ántirīnəm/ n. any plant of the genus Antirrhinum, esp. the snapdragon. [L f. Gk antirrhinon f. anti counterfeiting + rhis rhinos nose (from the resemblance of the flower to an animal's snout)]

antiscorbutic /ánteeskawrbyŏōtik, ántī-/ adj. & n. ● adj. preventing or curing scurvy. ● n. an antiscorbutic agent or drug.

anti-Semite /ánteesémit, ántī-/ n. a person hostile to or prejudiced against Jews. □□ **anti-Semitic** /-simítik/ adj. **anti-Semitism** /-sémitizəm/ n.

antisepsis /ántisépsis/ n. the process of using antiseptics to eliminate undesirable microorganisms such as bacteria, viruses, and fungi that cause disease. [mod.L (as ANTI-, SEPSIS)]

antiseptic /ántiséptik/ adj. & n. ● adj. **1** counteracting sepsis, esp. by preventing the growth of disease-causing microorganisms. **2** sterile or free from contamination. **3** lacking character. ● n. an antiseptic agent. □□ **antiseptically** adv.
■ adj. **2** see STERILE 3. ● n. see DISINFECTANT n.

antiserum /ántiseerəm/ n. (pl. **antisera** /-rə/) a blood serum containing antibodies against specific antigens, injected to treat or protect against specific diseases.

antisocial /ánteesōshəl, ántī-/ adj. **1** opposed or contrary to normal social instincts or practices. **2** not sociable. **3** opposed or harmful to the existing social order.
■ **2** see UNSOCIAL.

antistatic /ánteestátik, ántī-/ adj. that counteracts the effects of static electricity.

antistrophe /antístrəfee/ n. the second section of an ancient Greek choral ode or of one division of it (see STROPHE). [LL f. Gk antistrophē f. antistrephō turn against]

antithesis /antíthisis/ n. (pl. **antitheses** /-seez/) **1** (foll. by of, to) the direct opposite. **2** (usu. foll. by of, between) contrast or opposition between two things. **3** a contrast of ideas expressed by parallelism of strongly contrasted words. [LL f. Gk antitithēmi set against (as ANTI-, tithēmi place)]
■ **1** see OPPOSITE n.

antithetical /ántithétikəl/ adj. (also **antithetic**) **1** contrasted; opposite. **2** connected with, containing, or using antithesis. □□ **antithetically** adv. [Gk antithetikos (as ANTITHESIS)]

antitoxin /ánteetóksin/ n. an antibody that counteracts a toxin. □□ **antitoxic** adj.

antitrades /ántitráydz/ n.pl. winds that blow in the opposite direction to (and usu. above) a trade wind.

antitrust /ánteetrúst, ántī-/ adj. (of a law, etc.) opposed to or controlling trusts or other monopolies.

antitype /ánteetīp/ n. **1** that which is represented by a type or symbol. **2** a person or thing of the opposite type. □□ **antitypical** /-típikəl/ adj. [Gk antitupos corresponding as an impression to the die (as ANTI-, tupos stamp)]

antivenin /ánteevénin, ántī-/ n. an antiserum containing antibodies against specific poisons in the venom of esp. snakes, spiders, scorpions, etc. [ANTI- + VENOM.]

antiviral /ánteevīrəl, ántī-/ adj. effective against viruses.

antivivisectionism /ánteevívisékshənizəm, ántī-/ n. opposition to vivisection. □□ **antivivisectionist** n.

antler /ántlər/ n. **1** each of the branched horns of a stag or other (usu. male) deer. **2** a branch of this. □□ **antlered** adj. [ME f. AF, var. of OF antoillier, of unkn. orig.]

antonomasia /ántənəmáyzhə/ n. **1** the substitution of an epithet or title, etc., for a proper name (e.g., the Maid of Orleans for Joan of Arc). **2** the use of a proper name to express a general idea (e.g., a Scrooge for a miser). [L f. Gk f. antonomazō name instead (as ANTI-, + onoma name)]

antonym /ántənim/ n. a word opposite in meaning to another in the same language (e.g., bad and good) (opp. SYNONYM). □□ **antonymous** /antóniməs/ adj. [F antonyme (as ANTI-, SYNONYM)]

antrum /ántrəm/ n. (pl. **antra** /-trə/) Anat. a natural chamber or cavity in the body, esp. in a bone. □□ **antral** adj. [L f. Gk antron cave]

antsy /ántsee/ adj. colloq. irritated; impatient; fidgety; restless. [ants, pl. of ANT + -Y¹]
■ see ANXIOUS 1.

anuran /ənŏŏrən, ənyŏŏr-/ n. & adj. ● n. any tailless amphibian of the order Anura, including frogs and toads. ● adj. of or relating to this order. [mod.L Anura (AN-¹ + Gk oura tail)]

anus /áynəs/ n. Anat. the excretory opening at the end of the alimentary canal. [L]

anvil /ánvil/ n. **1** a block (usu. of iron) with a flat top, concave sides, and often a pointed end, on which metals are worked in forging. **2** Anat. a bone of the ear; the incus. [OE anfilte, etc.]

anxiety /angzíətee/ n. (pl. **-ies**) **1** the state of being anxious. **2** concern about an imminent danger, difficulty, etc. **3** (foll. by for, or to + infin.) anxious desire. **4** a thing that causes anxiety. **5** Psychol. a nervous disorder characterized by a state of excessive uneasiness. [F anxieté or L anxietas -tatis (as ANXIOUS)]
■ **1, 2** solicitude, concern, uneasiness, disquiet, nervousness, worry, dread, angst, agitation, apprehension, foreboding; neurosis, depression; see also STRESS n. 2. **3** desire, longing, yearning, ache, avidity, concern; appetite, hunger, thirst. **4** see WORRY n. 1.

anxious /ángkshəs/ adj. **1** troubled; uneasy in the mind. **2** causing or marked by anxiety (an anxious moment). **3** (foll. by for, or to + infin.) earnestly or uneasily wanting or trying (anxious to please; anxious for you to succeed). □□ **anxiously** adv. **anxiousness** n. [L anxius f. angere choke]
■ **1** troubled, uneasy, disquieted, uncertain, apprehensive, depressed, neurotic; solicitous, concerned, worried, distressed, disturbed, nervous, tense, fretful, on edge, restless, edgy, perturbed, upset, colloq. antsy; wary, cautious, careful, watchful. **3** desirous, eager, keen, enthusiastic, ardent, avid, yearning, longing, aching, impatient. □□ **anxiousness** see ANXIETY 1, 2.

any /énee/ adj., pron., & adv. ● adj. **1** (with interrog., neg., or conditional expressed or implied) **a** one, no matter which, of several (cannot find any answer). **b** some, no matter how much or many or of what sort (if any books arrive; have you any sugar?). **2** a minimal amount of (hardly any difference). **3** whichever is chosen (any fool knows that). **4 a** an appreciable or significant (did not stay for any length of time). **b** a very large (has any amount of money). ● pron. **1** any one (did not know any of them). **2** any number (are any of them yours?). **3** any amount (is there any left?). ● adv. (usu. with neg. or interrog.) at all; in some degree (is that any good?; do not make it any larger; without being any the wiser). **any time** (or **day** or **minute**, etc.) **now** colloq. at any time in the near future. **not having any** colloq. unwilling to participate. [OE ænig f. Gmc (as ONE, -Y¹)]

anybody /éneebudee, -bodee/ n. & pron. **1 a** a person, no matter who. **c** whatever person is chosen. **2** a person of importance (are you anybody?). □ **anybody's** (of a contest) evenly balanced (it was anybody's game). **anybody's guess** see GUESS.

anyhow /éneehow/ adv. **1** anyway. **2** in a disorderly manner or state (does his work anyhow).
■ **1** see HOWEVER 1a, 2.

anymore /eneemáwr/ adv. to any further extent (don't like you anymore).

anyone /éneewun/ pron. anybody. ¶ Written as two words to imply a numerical sense, as in any one of us can do it.
■ see ONE pron. 1, 2.

anyplace /éneeplays/ adv. anywhere.

anything /éneething/ pron. **1** a thing, no matter which. **2** a thing of any kind. **3** whatever thing is chosen. □ **anything but** not at all (was anything but honest). **like anything** colloq. with great vigor, intensity, etc.

anytime /éneetīm/ adv. colloq. at any time.

anyway /éneeway/ adv. (also dial. **anyways** /éneewayz/) **1** in any way or manner. **2** at any rate. **3** in any case. **4** to resume (anyway, as I was saying).
■ **2, 3** see at any rate (RATE¹).

anywhere /éneehwair, -wair/ adv. & pron. ● adv. in or to any place. ● pron. any place (anywhere will do).

anywise /éneewīz/ adv. in any manner. [OE on ænige wīsan in any wise]

Anzac /ánzak/ n. **1** a soldier in the Australian and New Zealand Army Corps (1914–18). **2** any person, esp. a member of the armed services, from Australia or New Zealand. □ **Anzac Day** April 25, commemorating the Anzac landing at Gallipoli in 1915. [acronym]

Anzus /ánzəs/ n. (also **ANZUS**) Australia, New Zealand, and the US, as an alliance for the Pacific area.

A-OK abbr. colloq. excellent; in good order. [all systems OK]

aorist /áyərist/ n. & adj. Gram. ● n. an unqualified past tense of a verb (esp. in Greek), without reference to duration or completion. ● adj. of or designating this tense. □□ **aoristic** adj. [Gk aoristos indefinite f. a- not + horizō define, limit]

aorta /ayáwrtə/ n. (pl. **aortas**) the main artery, giving rise to the arterial network through which oxygenated blood is supplied to the body from the heart. □□ **aortic** adj. [Gk aortē f. a(e)irō raise]

à outrance /aa ōōtróns/ adv. **1** to the death. **2** to the bitter end. [F, = to the utmost]

ap-¹ /ap/ prefix assim. form of AD- before p.

ap-² /ap/ prefix assim. form of APO- before a vowel or h.

apace /əpáys/ adv. literary swiftly; quickly. [OF à pas at (a considerable) pace]

Apache /əpáchee/ n. **1** a member of a N. American Indian tribe of the southwestern US. **2** (**apache**) (/əpásh/) a violent street ruffian, orig. in Paris. [Mex. Sp.]

apanage var. of APPANAGE.

apart /əpáart/ adv. **1** separately; not together (stand apart from the crowd). **2** into pieces (came apart in my hands). **3 a** to or on one side. **b** out of consideration (placed after noun: joking apart). **4** to or at a distance. □ **apart from** excepting; not considering. **2** in addition to (apart from roses we grow irises). [ME f. OF f. à to + part side]
■ **1** separately, individually, singly, alone, independently. **2** to or into pieces, to bits, in two or archaic twain, literary asunder. **3 a** aside, to one side, by oneself or itself, at a distance, separate, separately. **b** aside. □ **apart from 1** except (for), excepting, separately from, besides, but (for), bar, not including, excluding, not counting, aside from. **2** see BESIDES prep.

apartheid /əpáart-hayt, -hīt/ n. **1** (esp. as formerly in S. Africa) a policy or system of segregation or discrimination on grounds of race. **2** segregation in other contexts. [Afrik. (as APART, -HOOD)]

apartment /əpáartmənt/ n. **1** a set of rooms, usu. on one floor, used as a residence. **2** (in pl.) a suite of rooms, usu. rented. □ **apartment building** (or **house**) a building containing a number of separate apartments. [F appartement f. It. appartamento f. appartare to separate f. a parte apart]
■ **1** set or suite of rooms, Brit. flat.

/. . ./ **pronunciation**	● **part of speech**
□ **phrases, idioms, and compounds**	
□□ **derivatives**	■ **synonym section**
cross-references appear in SMALL CAPITALS or italics	

apathetic /ápəthétik/ *adj.* having or showing no emotion or interest. □□ **apathetically** *adv.* [APATHY, after PATHETIC]
■ see UNMOVED 3.

apathy /ápəthee/ *n.* (often foll. by *toward*) lack of interest or feeling; indifference. [F *apathie* f. L *apathia* f. Gk *apatheia* f. *apathēs* without feeling f. *a-* not + *pathos* suffering]
■ see INDIFFERENCE 1.

apatite /ápətīt / *n.* a naturally occurring crystalline mineral of calcium phosphate and fluoride, used in the manufacture of fertilizers. [G *Apatit* f. Gk *apatē* deceit (from its deceptive forms)]

apatosaurus /əpátəsáwrəs/ *n.* = BRONTOSAURUS.

ape /ayp/ *n. & v.* ● *n.* **1** any of the various primates of the family Pongidae characterized by the absence of a tail, e.g., the gorilla, chimpanzee, orangutan, or gibbon. **2** (in general use) any monkey. **3 a** an imitator. **b** an apelike person. ● *v.tr.* imitate; mimic. □ **ape-man** (*pl.* **-men**) any of various apelike primates held to be forerunners of present-day human beings. **go ape** *sl.* **1** become crazy. **2** be emotional or enthusiatic. **naked ape** present-day humans. [OE *apa* f. Gmc]
■ *n.* **1, 2** monkey, simian, primate. ● *v.* see IMITATE 2.

aperçu /aapersý/ *n.* **1** a summary or survey. **2** an insight. [F, past part. of *apercevoir* perceive]

aperient /əpeéreeənt/ *adj. & n.* ● *adj.* laxative. ● *n.* a laxative medicine. [L *aperire aperient-* to open]
■ *adj.* see PURGATIVE *adj.* 2. ● *n.* see PURGATIVE *n.* 2.

aperiodic /áypeereeódik/ *adj.* **1** not periodic; irregular. **2** *Physics* (of a potentially oscillating or vibrating system, e.g., an instrument with a pointer) that is adequately damped to prevent oscillation or vibration. **3** (of an oscillation or vibration) without a regular period. □□ **aperiodicity** /-reeədísitee/ *n.*

aperitif /əpéritéef/ *n.* an alcoholic drink taken before a meal to stimulate the appetite. [F *apéritif* f. med.L *aperitivus* f. L *aperire* to open]

aperture /ápərchər/ *n.* **1** an opening; a gap. **2** a space through which light passes in an optical or photographic instrument, esp. a variable space in a camera. [L *apertura* (as APERITIF)]
■ **1** opening, space, gap, cleft, chink, crevice, crack, fissure, hole, chasm.

apery /áypəree/ *n.* (*pl.* **-ies**) **1** mimicry. **2** a prank or trick.
■ **1** see IMITATION *n.* 1.

apetalous /aypét'ləs/ *adj. Bot.* (of flowers) having no petals. [mod.L *apetalus* f. Gk *apetalos* leafless f. *a-* not + *petalon* leaf]

Apex /áypeks/ *n.* (also **APEX**) (often *attrib.*) a system of reduced fares for scheduled airline flights when paid for before a certain period in advance of departure. [*Advance Purchase Excursion*]

apex /áypeks/ *n.* (*pl.* **apexes** or **apices** /áypiseez/) **1** the highest point. **2** a climax; a high point of achievement, etc. **3** the vertex of a triangle or cone. **4** a tip or pointed end. [L, = peak, tip]
■ **1, 3, 4** see VERTEX. **1, 2** see ACME.

aphaeresis /əférisis/ *n.* (also **apheresis**) (*pl.* **aphaereses**, **aphereses** /-seez/) the omission of a letter or syllable at the beginning of a word as a morphological development (e.g., in the derivation of *adder* from *naddre*). [LL f. Gk *aphairesis* (as APO-, *haireō* take)]

aphasia /əfáyzhə/ *n. Med.* the loss of ability to understand or express speech, owing to brain damage. □□ **aphasic** /-zik/ *adj. & n.* [mod.L f. Gk f. *aphatos* speechless f. *a-* not + *pha-* speak]

aphelion /əféeleeən, ap-héeleeən/ *n.* (*pl.* **aphelia** /-leeə/) the point in a body's orbit where it is furthest from the sun (opp. PERIHELION). ¶ Symb.: **Q**. [f. mod.L *aphelium* f. Gk *aph' hēliou* from the sun]

aphesis /áfisis/ *n.* (*pl.* **apheses** /-seez/) the gradual loss of an unstressed vowel at the beginning of a word (e.g., of *e* from *esquire* to form *squire*). □□ **aphetic** /əfétik/ *adj.* **aphetically** *adv.* [Gk, = letting go (as APO-, *hiēmi* send)]

aphid /áyfid, áfid/ *n.* any small homopterous insect which feeds by sucking sap from leaves, stems, or roots of plants; a plant louse. [back-form. f. *aphides*: see APHIS]

aphis /áyfis, áfis/ *n.* (*pl.* **aphides** /áyfideez/) an aphid, esp. of the genus *Aphis* including the greenfly. [mod.L (Linnaeus) f. Gk (1523), perh. a misreading of *koris* bug]

aphonia /ayfṓneeə/ *n.* (also **aphony** /áfənee/) *Med.* the loss or absence of the voice through a disease of the larynx or mouth. [mod.L *aphonia* f. Gk f. *aphōnos* voiceless f. *a-* not + *phōnē* voice]

aphorism /áfərizəm/ *n.* **1** a short pithy maxim. **2** a brief statement of a principle. □□ **aphorist** *n.* **aphoristic** *adj.* **aphoristically** *adv.* **aphorize** *v.intr.* [F *aphorisme* or LL f. Gk *aphorismos* definition f. *aphorizō* (as APO-, *horos* boundary)]
■ **1** see MAXIM.

aphrodisiac /áfrədeézeeak, -díz-/ *adj. & n.* ● *adj.* that arouses sexual desire. ● *n.* an aphrodisiac drug. [Gk *aphrodisiakos* f. *aphrodisios* f. *Aphroditē* Gk goddess of love]
■ *adj.* see EROTIC.

aphyllous /ayfíləs/ *adj. Bot.* (of plants) having no leaves. [mod.L f. Gk *aphullos* f. *a-* not + *phullon* leaf]

apian /áypeeən/ *adj.* of or relating to bees. [L *apianus* f. *apis* bee]

apiary /áypee-eree/ *n.* (*pl.* **-ies**) a place where bees are kept. □□ **apiarist** *n.* [L *apiarium* f. *apis* bee]

apical /áypikəl, áp-/ *adj.* of, at, or forming an apex. □□ **apically** *adv.* [L *apex apicis*: see APEX]

apices *pl.* of APEX.

apiculture /áypikulchər/ *n.* beekeeping. □□ **apicultural** /-kúlchərəl/ *adj.* **apiculturist** *n.* [L *apis* bee, after AGRICULTURE]

apiece /əpeés/ *adv.* for each one; severally; individually (*had five dollars apiece*). [A[2] + PIECE]

apish /áypish/ *adj.* **1** of or like an ape. **2** silly; affected. □□ **apishly** *adv.* **apishness** *n.*
■ **2** see SILLY *adj.* 1.

aplanat /áplənat/ *n.* a reflecting or refracting surface made aplanatic by correction. [G]

aplanatic /áplənátik/ *adj.* (of a reflecting or refracting surface) free from spherical aberration. [Gk *aplanētos* free from error f. *a-* not + *planaō* wander]

aplasia /əpláyzhə/ *n. Med.* total or partial failure of development of an organ or tissue. □□ **aplastic** /əplástik/ *adj.* [mod.L f. Gk f. *a-* not + *plasis* formation]

aplenty /əpléntee/ *adv.* in plenty.
■ see GALORE.

aplomb /əplóm, əplóm/ *n.* assurance; self-confidence. [F, = perpendicularity, f. *à plomb* according to a plummet]
■ see ASSURANCE 5a.

apnea /ápneeə, apnéeə/ *n.* (*Brit.* **apnoea**) *Med.* a temporary cessation of breathing. [mod.L f. Gk *apnoia* f. *apnous* breathless]

APO *abbr.* US Army post office.

apo- /ápə/ *prefix* **1** away from (*apogee*). **2** separate (*apocarpous*). [Gk *apo* from, away, un-, quite]

Apoc. *abbr.* **1** Apocalypse (New Testament). **2** Apocrypha.

apocalypse /əpókəlips/ *n.* **1** (**the Apocalypse**) Revelation, the last book of the New Testament, recounting a divine revelation to St John. **2** a revelation, esp. of the end of the world. **3** a grand or violent event resembling those described in the Apocalypse. [ME f. OF ult. f. eccl.L *apocalypsis* f. Gk *apokalupsis* f. *apokaluptō* uncover, reveal]

apocalyptic /əpókəlíptik/ *adj.* **1** of or resembling the Apocalypse. **2** revelatory; prophetic. □□ **apocalyptically** *adv.* [Gk *apokaluptikos* (as APOCALYPSE)]

apocarpous /ápəkaárpəs/ *adj. Bot.* (of ovaries) having distinct carpels not joined together (opp. SYNCARPOUS). [APO- + Gk *karpos* fruit]

apochromat /ápəkrōmát/ *n.* a lens or lens system that reduces spherical and chromatic aberrations. □□ **apochromatic** *adj.* [APO- + CHROMATIC]

apocope /əpókəpee/ *n.* the omission of a letter or letters at the end of a word as a morphological development (e.g., in the derivation of *curio* from *curiosity*). [LL f. Gk *apokopē* (as APO-, *koptō* cut)]

Apocr. *abbr.* Apocrypha.

apocrine /ápəkrin, -krīn/ *adj. Biol.* (of a multicellular gland, e.g., the mammary gland) releasing some cytoplasm when secreting. [APO- + Gk *krinō* to separate]

Apocrypha /əpókrifə/ *n.pl.* **1** the books included in the Septuagint and Vulgate versions of the Old Testament but not in the Hebrew Bible. ¶ Modern Bibles sometimes include them in the Old Testament or as an appendix, and sometimes omit them. **2** (**apocrypha**) writings or reports not considered genuine. [ME f. eccl.L *apocrypha* (*scripta*) hidden writings f. Gk *apokruphos* f. *apokruptō* hide away]

apocryphal /əpókrifəl/ *adj.* **1** of doubtful authenticity. **2** invented; mythical (*an apocryphal story*). **3** of or belonging to the Apocrypha.
■ **2** see FICTITIOUS 1.

apodal /ápəd'l/ *adj.* **1** without (or with undeveloped) feet. **2** (of fish) without ventral fins. [*apod* apodal creature f. Gk *apous* footless f. *a-* not + *pous podos* foot]

apodictic /ápədíktik/ *adj.* (also **apodeictic** /-díktik/) **1** clearly established. **2** of clear demonstration. [L *apodicticus* f. Gk *apodeiktikos* (as APO-, *deiknumi* show)]

apodosis /əpódəsis/ *n.* (*pl.* **apodoses** /-seez/) the main (consequent) clause of a conditional sentence (e.g., *I would agree* in *if you asked me I would agree*). [LL f. Gk f. *apodidōmi* give back (as APO-, *didōmi* give)]

apogee /ápəjee/ *n.* **1 a** the point in a celestial body's orbit where it is farthest from the earth (opp. PERIGEE). **b** the point in a celestial body's orbit where it is farthest from the body being orbited. **2** the most distant or highest point. □□ **apogean** /ápəjeeən/ *adj.* [F *apogée* or mod.L *apogaeum* f. Gk *apogeion* away from earth (as APO-, *gē* earth)]

apolitical /áypəlítikəl/ *adj.* not interested in or concerned with politics.

Apollonian /ápəlṓneeən/ *adj.* **1** of or relating to Apollo, the Greek and Roman sun god, patron of music and poetry. **2** orderly; rational; self-disciplined. [L *Apollonius* f. Gk *Apollōnios*]

apologetic /əpóləjétik/ *adj. & n.* ● *adj.* **1** regretfully acknowledging or excusing an offense or failure. **2** diffident. **3** of reasoned defense or vindication. ● *n.* (usu. in *pl.*) a reasoned defense, esp. of Christianity. □□ **apologetically** *adv.* [F *apologétique* f. LL *apologeticus* f. Gk *apologētikos* f. *apologeomai* speak in defense]
■ *adj.* **1** regretful, sorry, contrite, remorseful, penitent, rueful, repentant, conscience-stricken. **2** diffident, retiring, meek, self-effacing, modest, unassuming, reticent, hesitant, shy, timid, cowering.
□□ **apologetically** contritely, sorrily, remorsefully, regretfully, penitently; diffidently, self-effacingly, meekly, shyly, timidly, reticently, hesitantly, modestly.

apologia /ápəlṓjeeə/ *n.* a formal defense of one's opinions or conduct. [L: see APOLOGY]

apologist /əpóləjist/ *n.* a person who defends something by argument. [F *apologiste* f. Gk *apologizomai* render account f. *apologos* account]

apologize /əpóləjiz/ *v.intr.* **1** (often foll. by *for*) make an apology for an offense or failure; express regret. **2** (foll by *for*) seek to explain or justify. [Gk *apologizomai*: see APOLOGIST]
■ **1** beg or ask pardon, express regret(s), say sorry, make an apology. **2** (*apologize for*) make or give excuses or explanation(s) for, defend, justify, vindicate.

apologue /ápəlawg, -log/ *n.* a moral fable. [F *apologue* or L *apologus* f. Gk *apologos* story (as APO-, *logos* discourse)]

apology /əpóləjee/ *n.* (*pl.* **-ies**) **1** a regretful acknowledgement of an offense or failure. **2** an assurance that no offense was intended. **3** an explanation or defense. **4** (foll. by *for*) a poor or scanty specimen of (*this apology for a letter*). [F *apologie* or LL *apologia* f. Gk (as APOLOGETIC)]
■ **1** see EXCUSE *n.* 1, 2. **3** see EXCUSE *n.* 1, 2, DEFENSE 4a. **4** excuse, farce, mockery, travesty.

apolune /ápəlōōn/ *n.* the point in a body's lunar orbit where it is furthest from the moon's center (opp. PERILUNE). [APO- + L *luna* moon, after *apogee*]

apomixis /ápəmíksis/ *n.* (*pl.* **-seez**) *Biol.* a form of asexual reproduction (cf. AMPHIMIXIS). □□ **apomictic** /-míktik/ *adj.* [mod.L, formed as APO- + Gk *mixis* mingling]

apophthegm *Brit.* var. of APOTHEGM.

apoplectic /ápəpléktik/ *adj.* **1** of, causing, suffering, or liable to apoplexy. **2** *colloq.* enraged. □□ **apoplectically** *adv.* [F

apoplectique or LL *apoplecticus* f. Gk *apoplēktikos* f. *apoplēssō* strike completely (as APO-, *plēssō* strike)]

apoplexy /ápəpleksee/ *n.* a sudden loss of consciousness, voluntary movement, and sensation caused by blockage or rupture of a brain artery; a stroke. [ME f. OF *apoplexie* f. LL *apoplexia* f. Gk *apoplēxia* (as APOPLECTIC)]

aposematic /ápəsimátik/ *adj. Zool.* (of coloration, markings, etc.) serving to warn or repel. [APO- + Gk *sēma sēmatos* sign]

apostasy /əpóstəsee/ *n.* (*pl.* **-ies**) **1** renunciation of a belief or faith, esp. religious. **2** abandonment of principles or of a party. **3** an instance of apostasy. [ME f. eccl.L f. NT Gk *apostasia* f. *apostasis* defection (as APO-, *stat-* stand)]
■ **2, 3** see SECESSION.

apostate /əpóstayt/ *n. & adj.* ● *n.* a person who renounces a former belief, adherence, etc. ● *adj.* engaged in apostasy. □□ **apostatical** /ápəstátikəl/ *adj.* [ME f. OF *apostate* or eccl.L *apostata* f. Gk *apostatēs* deserter (as APOSTASY)]
■ *n.* see RENEGADE *n.* ● *adj.* see DISLOYAL.

apostatize /əpóstətiz/ *v.intr.* renounce a former belief, adherence, etc. [med.L *apostatizare* f. *apostata*: see APOSTATE]
■ see SECEDE.

a posteriori /áy posteeóre-áwree, -áwrī/ *adj. & adv.* ● *adj.* (of reasoning) inductive; empirical; proceeding from effects to causes. ● *adv.* inductively; empirically; from effects to causes (opp. A PRIORI). [L, = from what comes after]

apostle /əpósəl/ *n.* **1** (**Apostle**) **a** any of the chosen twelve first sent out to preach the Christian Gospel. **b** the first successful Christian missionary in a country or to a people. **2** a leader or outstanding figure, esp. of a reform movement (*apostle of temperance*). **3** a messenger or representative. □ **apostle bird** any of various Australian birds, forming flocks of about a dozen. **Apostles' Creed** an early statement of the Christian creed, ascribed to the Apostles. □□ **apostleship** [OE *apostol* f. eccl.L *apostolus* f. Gk *apostolos* messenger (as APO-, *stellō* send forth)]
■ **2** see ADVOCATE *n.* 1.

apostolate /əpóstələt, -layt/ *n.* **1** the position or authority of an Apostle. **2** leadership in reform. [eccl.L *apostolatus* (as APOSTLE)]

apostolic /ápəstólik/ *adj.* **1** of or relating to the Apostles. **2** of the Pope regarded as the successor of St Peter. **3** of the character of an Apostle. □ **Apostolic Fathers** the Christian leaders immediately succeeding the Apostles. **apostolic succession** the uninterrupted transmission of spiritual authority from the Apostles through successive popes and bishops. [F *apostolique* or eccl.L *apostolicus* f. Gk *apostolikos* (as APOSTLE)]

apostrophe[1] /əpóstrəfee/ *n.* a punctuation mark used to indicate: **1** the omission of letters or numbers (e.g., *can't*; *he's*; *Class of '92*). **2** the possessive case (e.g., *Harry's book*; *boys' coats*). [F *apostrophe* or LL *apostrophus* f. Gk *apostrophos* accent of elision f. *apostrephō* turn away (as APO-, *strephō* turn)]

apostrophe[2] /əpóstrəfee/ *n.* an exclamatory passage in a speech or poem, addressed to a person (often dead or absent) or thing (often personified). □□ **apostrophize** *v.tr. & intr.* [L f. Gk, lit. 'turning away' (as APOSTROPHE[1])]

apothecary /əpóthəkeree/ *n.* (*pl.* **-ies**) *archaic* a pharmacist or pharmacy licensed to dispense medicines and drugs. □ **apothecaries' measure** (or **weight**) units of weight and liquid volume formerly used in pharmacy. [ME f. OF *apotecaire* f. LL *apothecarius* f. L *apotheca* f. Gk *apothēkē* storehouse]
■ see PHARMACIST.

apothegm /ápəthem/ (*Brit.* **apophthegm**) a terse saying or maxim; an aphorism. □□ **apothegmatic** /-thegmátik/ *adj.* [F *apophthegme* or mod.L *apothegma* f. Gk *apophthegma -matos* f. *apophtheggomai* speak out]

apothem /ápəthem/ *n. Geom.* a line from the center of a reg-

/. . ./ **pronunciation**	● **part of speech**
□ **phrases, idioms, and compounds**	
□□ **derivatives**	■ **synonym section**
cross-references appear in SMALL CAPITALS or *italics*	

ular polygon at right angles to any of its sides. [Gk *apotithēmi* put aside (as APO-, *tithēmi* place)]

apotheosis /əpóthee-ōsis/ *n.* (*pl.* **apotheoses** /-seez/) **1** elevation to divine status; deification. **2** a glorification of a thing; a sublime example (*apotheosis of the dance*). **3** a deified ideal. [eccl.L f. Gk *apotheoō* make a god of (as APO-, *theos* god)]

apotheosize /əpóthee·əsiz/ *v.tr.* **1** make divine; deify. **2** idealize; glorify.

apotropaic /ápətrōpáyik/ *adj.* supposedly having the power to avert an evil influence or bad luck. [Gk *apotropaios* (as APO-, *trepō* turn)]

appall /əpáwl/ *v.tr.* (also **appal**) (**appalled, appalling**) **1** greatly dismay or horrify. **2** (as **appalling** *adj.*) *colloq.* shocking; unpleasant; bad. □□ **appallingly** *adv.* [ME f. OF *apalir* grow pale]
  ■ **1** dismay, shock, horrify, alarm, outrage, scandalize; revolt, disgust, repel, repulse, sicken, offend. **2** (**appalling**) see ATROCIOUS 1. □□ **appallingly** horrifically, shockingly, outrageously; badly, terribly, awfully, horrendously, atrociously, abysmally, dreadfully.

Appaloosa /ápəlōōsə/ *n.* **1** a horse of a N. American breed having dark spots on a light background. **2** this breed. [*Opelousa* in Louisiana, or *Palouse*, a river in Idaho]

appanage /ápənij/ *n.* (also **apanage**) **1** government provision for the maintenance of members of a royal family, etc. **2** a perquisite. **3** a natural accompaniment or attribute. [F ult. f. med.L *appanare* endow with the means of subsistence (as APO-, *panis* bread)]
  ■ see PERQUISITE.

apparat /ápərát, áapəráat/ *n.* the administrative system of a political party, esp. of a Communist party in a Communist country. [Russ. f. G, = apparatus]

apparatchik /áapəráatchik/ *n.* (*pl.* **apparatchiks** or *Russ.* **apparatchiki** /-kee/) **1 a** a member of a Communist apparat. **b** a Communist agent or spy. **2 a** a member of a political party in any country who blindly executes policy; a zealous functionary. **b** an official of a public or private organization. [Russ.: see APPARAT]

apparatus /ápərátəs, -ráytəs/ *n.* **1** the equipment needed for a particular purpose or function, esp. scientific or technical. **2** a political or other complex organization. **3** *Anat.* the organs used to perform a particular process. **4** (in full **apparatus criticus**) a collection of variants and annotations accompanying a printed text and usu. appearing below it. [L f. *apparare apparat-* make ready for]
  ■ **1** equipment, gear, gadgetry, paraphernalia, tackle, machinery; requisites, tools, instruments, utensils, implements; machine, appliance, gadget, device, outfit, *derog. or joc.* contraption.

apparel /əpárəl/ *n.* & *v.* ● *n.* **1** clothing; dress. **2** embroidered ornamentation on some ecclesiastical vestments. ● *v.tr.* (**appareled, appareling** or **apparelled, apparelling**) clothe. [ME *aparailen* (v.) f. OF *apareillier* f. Rmc *appariculare* (unrecorded) make equal or fit, ult. f. L *par* equal]
  ■ *n.* **1** clothing, clothes, dress, garments, outfit, *archaic* raiment, *colloq.* gear, glad rags, *formal* attire, *sl.* duds, threads. ● *v.* see CLOTHE 1.

apparent /əpárənt/ *adj.* **1** readily visible or perceivable. **2** seeming. □ **apparent magnitude** the magnitude, i.e., brightness, of a celestial body as seen from the earth (opp. *absolute magnitude*). **apparent time** solar time (see SOLAR *adj.*). □□ **apparently** *adv.* [ME f. OF *aparant* f. L (as APPEAR)]
  ■ **1** evident, plain, clear, obvious, patent, unmistakable; conspicuous, marked, manifest, visible, perceivable, discernible. **2** seeming, ostensible, superficial, surface, outward; see also PROFESSED 2. □□ **apparently** evidently, plainly, clearly, obviously, patently, manifestly, demonstrably; seemingly, ostensibly, superficially, outwardly, on the face of it, to all (outward) appearances; purportedly, allegedly, professedly.

apparition /ápəríshən/ *n.* a sudden or dramatic appearance, esp. of a ghost or phantom; a visible ghost. [ME f. F *apparition* or f. L *apparitio* attendance (as APPEAR)]
  ■ see PHANTOM *n.* 1.

appeal /əpeél/ *v.* & *n.* ● *v.* **1** *intr.* make an earnest or formal request; plead (*appealed for calm; appealed to us not to leave*). **2** *intr.* (usu. foll. by *to*) be attractive or of interest; be pleasing. **3** *intr.* (foll. by *to*) resort to or cite for support. **4** *Law* a *intr.* (often foll. by *to*) apply (to a higher court) for a reconsideration of the decision of a lower court. **b** *tr.* refer to a higher court to review (a case). **c** *intr.* (foll. by *against*) apply to a higher court to reconsider (a verdict or sentence). **5** *intr. Sports* call on an umpire or referee to reverse a decision. ● *n.* **1** the act or an instance of appealing. **2** a formal or urgent request for public support, esp. financial, for a cause. **3** *Law* the referral of a case to a higher court. **4** attractiveness; appealing quality (*sex appeal*). □□ **appealer** *n.* [ME f. OF *apel, apeler* f. L *appellare* to address]
  ■ *v.* **1** plead, supplicate, solicit, petition, pray, beg, cry; (*appeal to*) entreat, beseech, implore, invoke, ask, request. **2** be attractive *or* alluring *or* of interest; (*appeal to*) attract, allure, please, charm, fascinate, interest. **3** see RESORT *v.* 1. ● *n.* **1** entreaty, call, clamor, request, supplication, solicitation, petition, plea, application, suit, SOS, cri de coeur, cry (from the heart), prayer. **3** referral. **4** attraction, attractiveness, allurement, allure, (personal) charm, charisma, lure, fascination, interest, draw, pull.

appealable /əpeéləbəl/ *adj. Law* (of a case) that can be referred to a higher court for review.

appealing /əpeéling/ *adj.* attractive; likable. □□ **appealingly** *adv.*
  ■ see ATTRACTIVE 1.

appear /əpeér/ *v.intr.* **1** become or be visible. **2** be evident (*a new problem then appeared*). **3** seem; have the appearance of being (*appeared unwell; you appear to be right*). **4** present oneself publicly or formally, esp. on stage or as the accused or counsel in a court of law. **5** be published (*it appeared in the papers; a new edition will appear*). [ME f. OF *apareir* f. L *apparēre apparit-* come in sight]
  ■ **1** come forth, become visible *or* manifest, put in an appearance, show oneself *or* itself, arrive, show up. **2** materialize, surface, emerge, rise, arise, come up, enter (into) the picture, turn up, arrive, come, crop *or* show up, be revealed, become plain, show oneself *or* itself, manifest oneself *or* itself. **3** see SEEM. **4** (*appear as*) play, perform *or* act *or* take the part *or* role of. **5** be published, come out; become available.

appearance /əpeérəns/ *n.* **1** the act or an instance of appearing. **2** an outward form as perceived (whether correctly or not), esp. visually (*neaten up one's appearance*; *gives the appearance of trying hard*). **3** a semblance. □ **keep up appearances** maintain an impression or pretense of virtue, affluence, etc. **make** (or **put in**) **an appearance** be present, esp. briefly. **to all appearances** as far as can be seen; apparently. [ME f. OF *aparance, -ence* f. LL *apparentia* (as APPEAR, -ENCE)]
  ■ **1** arrival, advent, coming, emergence, debut; presence; publication; compare APPEAR. **2** aspect, look(s), form; air, demeanor, *literary* mien; bearing, manner. **3** semblance, show, hint, indication, suggestion; illusion; pretense. □ **to all appearances** see *apparently* (APPARENT).

appease /əpeéz/ *v.tr.* **1** make calm or quiet, esp. conciliate (a potential aggressor) by making concessions. **2** satisfy (an appetite, scruples). □□ **appeasement** *n.* **appeaser** *n.* [ME f. AF *apeser*, OF *apaisier* f. *à* to + *pais* PEACE]
  ■ **1** see CALM *v.* **2** meet, comply with, answer, serve; see also FULFILL 4.

appellant /əpélənt/ *n. Law* a person who appeals to a higher court. [ME f. F (as APPEAL, -ANT)]
  ■ see *supplicant n.* (SUPPLICATE).

appellate /əpélət/ *adj. Law* (esp. of a court) concerned with or dealing with appeals. [L *appellatus* (as APPEAL, -ATE²)]

appellation /ápəláyshən/ *n. formal* a name or title; nomenclature. [ME f. OF f. L *appellatio -onis* (as APPEAL, -ATION)]

■ see NAME *n.* 1, 2.

appellative /əpélətiv/ *adj.* **1** naming. **2** *Gram.* (of a noun) that designates a class; common. [LL *appellativus* (as AP-PEAL, -ATIVE)]

append /əpénd/ *v.tr.* (usu. foll. by *to*) attach, affix, add, esp. to a written document, etc. [L *appendere* hang]

■ see TACK¹ *v.* 3.

appendage /əpéndij/ *n.* **1** something attached; an addition. **2** *Zool.* a limb or other projecting part of a body.

■ **1** see ATTACHMENT 1.

appendant /əpéndənt/ *adj. & n.* ● *adj.* (usu. foll. by *to*) attached in a subordinate capacity. ● *n.* an appendant person or thing. [OF *apendant* f. *apendre* formed as APPEND, -ANT]

appendectomy /ápəndéktəmee/ *n.* (also **appendicectomy** /-diséktəmee/) (*pl.* **-ies**) the surgical removal of the appendix. [APPENDIX + -ECTOMY]

appendicitis /əpéndisítis/ *n.* inflammation of the appendix. [APPENDIX + -ITIS]

appendix /əpéndiks/ *n.* (*pl.* **appendices** /-diseez/; **appendixes**) **1** (in full **vermiform appendix**) *Anat.* a small outgrowth of tissue forming a tube-shaped sac attached to the lower end of the large intestine. **2** subsidiary matter at the end of a book or document. [L *appendix -icis* f. *appendere* APPEND]

■ **2** see ADDITION 2.

apperceive /ápərseév/ *v.tr.* **1** be conscious of perceiving. **2** *Psychol.* compare (a perception) to previously held ideas so as to extract meaning from it. □□ **apperception** /-sépshən/ *n.* **apperceptive** *adj.* [ME (in obs. sense 'observe') f. OF *aperceveir* ult. f. L *percipere* PERCEIVE]

appertain /ápərtáyn/ *v.intr.* (foll. by *to*) **1** relate. **2** belong as a possession or right. **3** be appropriate. [ME f. OF *apertenir* f. LL *appertinēre* f. *pertinēre* PERTAIN]

■ **1** see RELATE 4.

appetence /ápitəns/ *n.* (also **appetency** /-tənsee/) (foll. by *for*) longing or desire. [F *appétence* or L *appetentia* f. *appetere* seek after]

■ see APPETITE 2.

appetite /ápitīt/ *n.* **1** a natural desire to satisfy bodily needs, esp. for food or sexual activity. **2** (usu. foll. by *for*) an inclination or desire. □□ **appetitive** /ápitítiv/ *adj.* [ME f. OF *apetit* f. L *appetitus* f. *appetere* seek after]

■ **1** see HUNGER *n.* 2. **2** desire, inclination, proclivity, tendency, disposition, bent, preference, liking, predilection, zest, fondness, love, zeal, enthusiasm, taste; craving, hunger, thirst, keenness, hankering, yearning, longing, passion, demand; appetence.

appetizer /ápitīzər/ *n.* a small amount, esp. of food or drink served before a meal, to stimulate an appetite. [*appetize* (back-form. f. APPETIZING)]

■ see HORS D´OEUVRE.

appetizing /ápitīzing/ *adj.* stimulating an appetite, esp. for food. □□ **appetizingly** *adv.* [F *appétissant* irreg. f. *appétit*, formed as APPETITE]

■ see TEMPTING.

applaud /əpláwd/ *v.* **1** *intr.* express strong approval or praise, esp. by clapping. **2** *tr.* express approval of (a person or action). [L *applaudere applaus-* clap hands]

■ **1** approve, express approval *or* approbation, clap, cheer. **2** clap, cheer, *colloq.* give a person a (big) hand, *sl.* root for; express approval *or* approbation of, praise, hail, acclaim, sing the praises of, extol, congratulate, compliment, pay tribute *or* homage to; eulogize, commend, laud.

applause /əpláwz/ *n.* **1** an expression of approbation, esp. from an audience, etc., by clapping. **2** emphatic approval. [med.L *applausus* (as APPLAUD)]

■ **1** clapping, (standing) ovation, plaudit; cheering, cheers, hurrah, salvo, *Brit.* Kentish fire, *colloq.* hand. **2** acclamation, acclaim, congratulation, éclat, approval, commendation, approbation, praise, extolment, plaudit(s), *colloq.* kudos, *formal* laudation.

apple /ápəl/ *n.* **1** the fruit of a tree of the genus *Malus*, rounded in form and with a crisp flesh. **2** the tree bearing this. □ **apple of one's eye** a cherished person or thing. **ap-**

ple-pie bed a bed made (as a joke) with the sheets folded short, so that the legs cannot be accommodated. **apple-pie order** perfect order; extreme neatness. **she's apples** *Austral. sl.* everything is fine. **upset the applecart** spoil careful plans. [OE *æppel* f. Gmc]

applejack /ápəljak/ *n.* an alcoholic beverage made by distilling or freezing fermented apple cider. [APPLE + JACK¹]

appliance /əplíəns/ *n.* a device or piece of equipment used for a specific task, esp. a household device for washing, drying, cooking, etc. [APPLY + -ANCE]

■ see DEVICE 1a.

applicable /áplikəbəl, əplíkə-/ *adj.* (often foll. by *to*) **1** that may be applied. **2** having reference; appropriate. □□ **applicability** *n.* **applicably** *adv.* [OF *applicable* or med.L *applicabilis* (as APPLY, -ABLE)]

■ **2** fit, fitting, suitable, suited, appropriate, proper, apropos, befitting, pertinent, apt, germane, right, seemly, relevant, apposite. □□ **applicability** see *relevance* (RELEVANT).

applicant /áplikənt/ *n.* a person who applies for something, esp. a job. [APPLICATION + -ANT]

■ candidate, job seeker, job-hunter; applier, auditioner, petitioner, solicitor, requester.

application /áplikáyshən/ *n.* **1** the act or an instance of applying. **2** a formal request, usu. in writing, for employment, membership, etc. **3 a** relevance. **b** the use to which something can or should be put. **4** sustained or concentrated effort; diligence. [ME f. F f. L *applicatio -onis* (as APPLY, -ATION)]

■ **1** utilization; administration, rubbing in, putting on. **2** request, solicitation; appeal, petition, submission, claim. **3 a** relevance, relevancy, reference, pertinence, germaneness, appositeness, aptness, importance; bearing. **b** use, purpose, function, employment, utilization, practice, operation. **4** attention, diligence, industriousness, industry, effort, perseverance, persistence, assiduity, assiduousness, devotion, dedication, commitment, attentiveness, *colloq.* guts.

applicator /áplikaytər/ *n.* a device for applying a substance to a surface. [APPLICATION + -OR¹]

applied /əplíd/ *adj.* (of a subject of study) put to practical use as opposed to being theoretical (cf. PURE *adj.* 10). □ **applied mathematics** see MATHEMATICS.

■ see PRACTICAL 1.

appliqué /áplikáy/ *n., adj., & v.* ● *n.* ornamental work in which fabric is cut out and attached, usu. sewn, to the surface of another fabric to form pictures or patterns. ● *adj.* executed in appliqué. ● *v.tr.* (**appliqués, appliquéd, appliquéing**) decorate with appliqué; make using appliqué technique. [F, past part. of *appliquer* apply f. L *applicare*: see APPLY]

apply /əplí/ *v.* (**-ies, -ied**) **1** *intr.* (often foll. by *for, to*, or *to* + infin.) make a formal request for something to be done, given, etc. (*apply for a job*; *apply for help to the governors*; *applied to be sent overseas*). **2** *intr.* have relevance (*does not apply in this case*). **3** *tr.* **a** make use of as relevant or suitable; employ (*apply the rules*). **b** operate (*apply the hand brake*). **4** *tr.* (often foll. by *to*) **a** put or spread on (*applied the ointment to the cut*). **b** administer (*applied the remedy*). **c** apply common sense to the problem). **5** *refl.* (often foll. by *to*) devote oneself (*applied myself to the task*). □□ **applier** *n.* [ME f. OF *aplier* f. L *applicare* fold, fasten to]

■ **1** make application, register, bid, put in; audition; (*apply for*) seek, go after, appeal for; (*apply to*) petition, solicit, appeal to, request. **2** have bearing, be relevant, pertain; (*apply to*) involve, include, suit; bear on, refer to, appertain to, relate to. **3 a** use, utilize, employ, put to use, administer, implement, exercise, execute, practice, carry out. **b** engage, operate, put *or* turn on,

/.../ pronunciation	● part of speech
□ phrases, idioms, and compounds	
□□ derivatives	■ synonym section
cross-references appear in SMALL CAPITALS or *italics*	

activate, work. **4 a** administer, rub in *or* on, spread in *or* on; put, place, fix, set. **b** administer, direct. **5** devote, dedicate, commit, give, address; (*apply oneself*) focus, concentrate, pay attention, attend, buckle *or* knuckle down; (*apply oneself to*) work at, do.

appoggiatura /əpójətōŏrə/ *n. Mus.* a grace note performed before an essential note of a melody and normally taking half or less than half its time value. [It.]

appoint /əpóynt/ *v.tr.* **1** assign a post or office to (*appoint him governor*; *appoint her to govern*; *appointed to the post*). **2** (often foll. by *for*) fix; decide on (a time, place, etc.) (*Wednesday was appointed for the meeting*; *8:30 was the appointed time*). **3** prescribe; ordain. **4** *Law* **a** (also *absol.*) declare the destination of (property, etc.). **b** declare (a person) as having an interest in property, etc. (*Jones was appointed in the will*). **5** (as **appointed** *adj.*) equipped; furnished (*a badly appointed hotel*). □□ **appointee** /-tée/ *n.* **appointer** *n.* **appointive** *adj.* [ME f. OF *apointer* f. *à point* to a point]
■ **1** name, designate, nominate, elect, *Mil.* detail; assign, delegate, commission; select, choose. **2** fix, set, settle, determine, decide on, ordain, authorize, establish, destine, arrange, assign, prescribe, decree. **5** (**appointed**) equipped, fitted out, furnished, decorated, presented, *colloq.* done up. □□ **appointee** see APPOINTMENT 2b.

appointment /əpóyntmənt/ *n.* **1** an arrangement to meet at a specific time and place. **2 a** a post or office, esp. one available for applicants, or recently filled (*took up the appointment on Monday*). **b** a person appointed. **c** the act or an instance of appointing, esp. to a post. **3** (usu. in *pl.*) **a** furniture; fittings. **b** equipment. [ME f. OF *apointement* (as APPOINT, -MENT)]
■ **1** meeting, rendezvous, engagement; time, slot; assignation, *archaic* tryst, *colloq.* date. **2 a** job, position, post, situation, office, place, assignment, *colloq.* berth. **b** appointee, choice, successful candidate. **c** nomination, election; assignment, designation; selection, choice. **3** (*appointments*) see FITTING *n.*

apportion /əpáwrshən/ *v.tr.* (often foll. by *to*) share out; assign as a share. □□ **apportionable** *adj.* **apportionment** *n.* [F *apportionner* or f. med.L *apportionare* (as AD-, PORTION)]
■ see ASSIGN *v.* 1a.

apposite /ápəzit/ *adj.* (often foll. by *to*) **1** apt; well chosen. **2** well expressed. □□ **appositely** *adv.* **appositeness** *n.* [L *appositus* past part. of *apponere* (as AD-, *ponere* put)]
■ see APPLICABLE 2.

apposition /ápəzíshən/ *n.* **1** placing side by side; juxtaposition. **2** *Gram.* the placing of a word next to another, esp. the addition of one noun to another, in order to qualify or explain the first (e.g., *William the Conqueror*; *my friend Sue*). □□ **appositional** *adj.* [ME f. F *apposition* or f. LL *appositio* (as APPOSITE, -ITION)]

appraisal /əpráyzəl/ *n.* the act or an instance of appraising.
■ see *evaluation* (EVALUATE), PRICE *n.* 1b, SURVEY *n.* 1, 3.

appraise /əpráyz/ *v.tr.* **1** estimate the value or quality of (*appraised her skills*). **2** (esp. officially or expertly) set a price on; value. □□ **appraisable** *adj.* **appraiser** *n.* **appraisive** *adj.* [APPRIZE by assim. to PRAISE]
■ **1** evaluate, assess, value.

appreciable /əpréeshəbəl/ *adj.* large enough to be noticed; significant; considerable (*appreciable progress has been made*). □□ **appreciably** *adv.* [F f. *apprécier* (as APPRECIATE)]
■ see CONSIDERABLE 1, 2.

appreciate /əpréeshee·áyt/ *v.* **1** *tr.* **a** esteem highly; value. **b** be grateful for (*we appreciate your sympathy*). **c** be grateful to (*appreciate the nuances*). **2** *tr.* (often foll. by *that* + clause) understand; recognize (*I appreciate that I may be wrong*). **3 a** *intr.* (of property, etc.) rise in value. **b** *tr.* raise in value. □□ **appreciative** /-shətiv, -shee-áytiv/ *adj.* **appreciatively** *adv.* **appreciativeness** *n.* **appreciator** *n.* **appreciatory** /-sheeətáwree/ *adj.* [LL *appretiare* appraise (as AD-, *pretium* price)]
■ **1 a** value, find worthwhile *or* valuable, esteem, cherish, admire, rate *or* regard highly, think highly *or* much *or* well of, prize, treasure, respect. **b** be grateful *or*

thankful for. **c** be sensitive to, perceive, detect, discern, recognize, feel. **2** understand, comprehend, recognize, realize, perceive, know, be aware *or* cognizant *or* conscious (of) *or* that. **3 a** increase *or* rise *or* gain in value *or* worth, go up, rise. □□ **appreciative**, **appreciatory** understanding, aware, cognizant, perceptive; see also THANKFUL. **appreciatively** in appreciation *or* recognition *or* admiration, respectfully; thankfully, gratefully. **appreciativeness** see APPRECIATION 1, SENSITIVITY.

appreciation /əpréeshee-áyshən/ *n.* **1** favorable or grateful recognition. **2** an estimation or judgment; sensitive understanding of or reaction to (*a quick appreciation of the problem*). **3** an increase in value. **4** a (usu. favorable) review of a book, movie, etc. [F f. LL *appretiatio -onis* (as APPRECIATE, -ATION)]
■ **1** gratitude, thankfulness, gratefulness, thanks; acknowledgment, recognition. **2** estimation, evaluation, judgment, assessment, valuation, appraisal; understanding, comprehension, perception, recognition, detection, knowledge, awareness, realization. **3** increase, rise, advance, growth, escalation, enhancement, gain. **4** review, critique, notice; tribute, acknowledgment, *formal* laudation.

apprehend /áprihénd/ *v.tr.* **1** understand; perceive (*apprehend your meaning*). **2** seize; arrest (*apprehended the criminal*). **3** anticipate with uneasiness or fear (*apprehending the results*). [F *appréhender* or L *apprehendere* (as AD-, *prehendere* lay hold of)]
■ **1** see PERCEIVE 1, 2. **2** see ARREST *v.* 1a. **3** see DREAD *v.*

apprehensible /áprihénsibəl/ *adj.* capable of being apprehended by the senses or the intellect (*an apprehensible theory*; *an apprehensible change in her expression*). □□ **apprehensibility** /-bílitee/ *n.* [LL *apprehensibilis* (as APPREHEND, -IBLE)]
■ see SENSIBLE 1, 3, INTELLIGIBLE 1.

apprehension /áprihénshən/ *n.* **1** uneasiness; dread. **2** understanding; perception. **3** arrest; capture (*apprehension of the suspect*). **4** an idea; a conception. [F *appréhension* or LL *apprehensio* (as APPREHEND, -ION)]
■ **1** see DREAD *n.* 1, 2. **2** see UNDERSTANDING 1, 2. **3** see ARREST *n.* 1. **4** see IDEA 1, 2a, b.

apprehensive /áprihénsiv/ *adj.* **1** (often foll. by *of*, *for*, *over*, *about*) uneasily fearful; dreading. **2** relating to perception by the senses or the intellect. **3** perceptive; intelligent. □□ **apprehensively** *adv.* **apprehensiveness** *n.* [F *appréhensif* or med.L *apprehensivus* (as APPREHEND, -IVE)]
■ **1** see FEARFUL 1.

apprentice /əpréntis/ *n.* & *v.* ● *n.* **1** a person who is learning a trade by being employed in it for an agreed period usu. at low wages. **2** a beginner; a novice. ● *v.tr.* (usu. foll. by *to*) engage or bind as an apprentice (*was apprenticed to a builder*). □□ **apprenticeship** *n.* [ME f. OF *aprentis* f. *apprendre* learn (as APPREHEND), after words in *-tis*, *-tif*, f. L *-tivus*: see -IVE]
■ *n.* trainee, novice, probationer, tyro, learner, starter, beginner, acolyte, greenhorn, tenderfoot, neophyte, novitiate, cub, punk, *sl.* rookie. ● *v.* article, contract, bind, tie, *hist.* indenture; (*be apprenticed to*) be enrolled *or* employed *or* taken on by. □□ **apprenticeship** training, probation, novitiate, *hist.* indentureship.

apprise /əpríz/ *v.tr.* inform. □ **be apprised of** be aware of. [F *appris -ise* past part. of *apprendre* learn, teach (as APPREHEND)]
■ see INFORM 1. □ **be apprised of** be aware *or* conscious *or* cognizant *or* sensible of, be sensitive *or* awake *or* alert to, be informed *or* seized of, *colloq.* be wise to.

apprize /əpríz/ *v.tr.* **1** esteem highly. **2** appraise. [ME f. OF *apriser* f. *à* to + *pris* PRICE]

appro /áprō/ *n. Brit. colloq.* □ **on appro** = *on approval* (see APPROVAL). [abbr. of *approval* or *approbation*]

approach /əprōch/ *v.* & *n.* ● *v.* **1** *tr.* come near or nearer to (a place or time). **2** *intr.* come near or nearer in space or time (*the hour approaches*). **3** *tr.* make a tentative proposal or suggestion to (*approached me about a loan*). **4** *tr.* **a** be similar in character, quality, etc., to (*doesn't approach her for artistic skill*). **b** approximate to (*a population approaching 5 million*). **5** *tr.* attempt to influence or bribe. **6** *tr.* set about, tackle (a

task, etc.). **7** *intr. Golf* play an approach shot. **8** *intr. Aeron.* prepare to land. **9** *tr. archaic* bring near. ● *n.* **1** an act or means of approaching (*made an approach; an approach lined with trees*). **2** an approximation (*an approach to an apology*). **3** a way of dealing with a person or thing (*needs a new approach*). **4** (usu. in *pl.*) a sexual advance. **5** *Golf* a stroke from the fairway to the green. **6** *Aeron.* the final descent of a flight before landing. **7** *Bridge* a bidding method with a gradual advance to a final contract. □ **approach road** *Brit.* a road by which traffic enters a highway. [ME f. OF *aproch(i)er* f. eccl.L *appropiare* draw near (as AD-, *propius* compar. of *prope* near)]
■ *v.* **1, 2** near, draw *or* come near *or* nearer *or* close *or* closer (to), *archaic or dial.* come nigh. **2** advance, creep up *or* on, loom. **3** make a proposal to, make advances *or* overtures to, proposition, sound out, *Brit. colloq.* chat up. **4 a** see COMPARE *v.* 3, 4. **b** approximate to, near, nearly equal *or* reach, come close to. **6** see TACKLE *v.* 1. ● *n.* **1** access, entrance, passage, way, path, drive, driveway, course; entry, advance, advancement. **3** method, procedure, modus operandi, way, technique, style, manner; attitude, angle, point of view, viewpoint, standpoint, position. **4** (*approaches*) advances, overtures, attentions, proposal, proposition, suit.

approachable /əprṓchəbəl/ *adj.* **1** friendly; easy to talk to. **2** able to be approached. □□ **approachability** /-bílitee/ *n.*
■ **1** see FRIENDLY *adj.* 1. **2** see ACCESSIBLE 2.

approbate /áprəbayt/ *v.tr.* approve formally; sanction. [ME f. L *approbare* (as AD-, *probare* test f. *probus* good)]

approbation /áprəbáyshən/ *n.* approval; consent. □□ **approbative** *adj.* **approbatory** /áprŏbətawree/ *adj.* [ME f. OF f. L *approbatio -onis* (as APPROBATE, -ATION)]
■ see APPROVAL.

appropriate *adj. & v.* ● *adj.* /əprṓpreeət/ (often foll. by *to, for*) **1** suitable or proper. **2** belonging or particular to. ● *v.tr.* /əprṓpreeayt/ **1** take possession of, esp. without authority. **2** devote (money, etc.) to special purposes. □□ **appropriately** *adv.* **appropriateness** *n.* **appropriator** *n.* [LL *appropriatus* past part. of *appropriare* (as AD-, *proprius* own)]
■ *adj.* **1** suitable, apt, fitting, fit, proper, right, deserved, becoming, befitting, seemly, suited, apropos, correct, germane, pertinent, happy, felicitous, *archaic* meet. ● *v.* **1** take (over), seize, expropriate, usurp, commandeer, arrogate, impound; steal, pilfer, filch, carry away, snatch, thieve, make off with, *colloq.* lift, bag, swipe, walk off with, *Brit. colloq.* snaffle, *euphem.* abstract, *formal or joc.* purloin, *sl.* pinch, hook, knock off, crib, glom, knock down, nip, snitch, *Brit. sl.* nick. **2** set aside *or* apart, devote, assign, earmark, allot, apportion. □□ **appropriately** fittingly, aptly, suitably, properly, correctly, rightly, becomingly, befittingly, deservedly, meetly. **appropriateness** see *fitness* (FIT¹), *relevance* (RELEVANT).

appropriation /əprṓpreeáyshən/ *n.* **1** an act or instance of appropriating. **2** something appropriated, as money officially set aside for a specific use.

approval /əprṓŏvəl/ *n.* **1** the act of approving. **2** an instance of this; consent; a favorable opinion (*with your approval; looked at him with approval*). □ **on approval** (of goods supplied) to be returned if not satisfactory.
■ sanction, approbation, blessing, consent, agreement, backing, concurrence; endorsement, acceptance, imprimatur, seal of approval, affirmation, éclat, confirmation, mandate, authorization; license, leave, permission, rubber stamp, go-ahead, thumbs up, *colloq.* OK, okay, green light.

approve /əprṓŏv/ *v.* **1** *tr.* confirm; sanction (*approved her application*). **2** *intr.* give or have a favorable opinion. **3** *tr.* commend (*approved the new hat*). **4** *tr. archaic* (usu. *refl.*) demonstrate oneself to be (*approved himself a coward*). □ **approved school** *Brit. hist.* a residential school for delinquents. **approve of 1** pronounce or consider good or satisfactory; commend. **2** agree to. □□ **approver** *n.* **approvingly** *adv.* [ME f. OF *aprover* f. L (as APPROBATE)]
■ **1, 3** confirm, affirm, support, ratify, uphold, subscribe

to, second, give the stamp of approval to, approve of, approbate; allow, carry, countenance, condone, permit, sanction, authorize, endorse, commend, put one's imprimatur on, agree (to), accept, assent to, go along with, give the go-ahead *or* one's blessing to, rubber-stamp, *colloq.* OK, okay, give the green light to. □ **approve of 1** sanction, commend, consider fair *or* good *or* right, think highly of, esteem, value, give one's blessing to, accept, favor, respect, have regard for, be partial to, like. **2** see APPROVE 1, 3 above.

approx. *abbr.* **1** approximate. **2** approximately.

approximate *adj. & v.* ● *adj.* /əprŏksimət/ **1** fairly correct or accurate; near to the actual (*the approximate time of arrival; an approximate guess*). **2** near or next to (*your approximate neighbor*). ● *v.tr. & intr.* /əprŏksimayt/ bring or come near (esp. in quality, number, etc.), but not exactly (*approximates to the truth; approximates the amount required*). □□ **approximately** /-mətlee/ *adv.* **approximation** /-máyshən/ *n.* [LL *approximatus* past part. of *approximare* (as AD-, *proximus* very near)]
■ *adj.* **1** rough, inexact, loose, imprecise, estimated; (*attrib.*) *colloq.* ballpark. ● *v.* near, approach, come close to, verge *or* border on; resemble, look *or* seem like; simulate. □□ **approximately** approaching; nearly, almost, close to, about, around, more or less, give or take a few, in the region of, roughly, generally, *colloq.* in the ballpark of, in the right ballpark. **approximation** guess, (rough) estimate, estimation, rounding up *or* down, *colloq.* ballpark figure; approach.

appurtenance /əpɔ́rt'nəns/ *n.* (usu. in *pl.*) a belonging; an appendage; an accessory. [ME f. AF *apurtenaunce*, OF *apertenance* (as APPERTAIN, -ANCE)]
■ see EQUIPMENT.

appurtenant /əpɔ́rt'nənt/ *adj.* (often foll. by *to*) belonging or appertaining; pertinent. [ME f. OF *apartenant* pres. part. (as APPERTAIN)]

APR *abbr.* annual or annualized percentage rate (esp. of interest on loans or credit).

Apr. *abbr.* April.

après-ski /ápraykée, áapray-/ *n. & adj.* ● *n.* the evening, esp. its social activities, following a day's skiing. ● *attrib.adj.* (of clothes, drinks, etc.) appropriate to social activities following skiing. [F]

apricot /áprikot, áypri-/ *n. & adj.* ● *n.* **1 a** a juicy soft fruit, smaller than a peach, of an orange-yellow color. **b** the tree, *Prunus armeniaca*, bearing it. **2** the ripe fruit's orange-yellow color. ● *adj.* orange-yellow (*apricot dress*). [Port. *albricoque* or Sp. *albaricoque* f. Arab. *al* the + *barkuk* f. late Gk *praikokion* f. L *praecoquum* var. of *praecox* early ripe: *apri-* after L *apricus* ripe, *-cot* by assim. to F *abricot*]

April /áypril/ *n.* the fourth month of the year. □ **April fool** a person successfully tricked on April 1. **April Fool's** (or **Fools') Day** April 1. [ME f. L *Aprilis*]

a priori /áa pree-áwree, áy pri-áwri/ *adj. & adv.* ● *adj.* **1** (of reasoning) deductive; proceeding from causes to effects (opp. A POSTERIORI). **2** (of concepts, knowledge, etc.) logically independent of experience; not derived from experience (opp. EMPIRICAL). **3** not submitted to critical investigation (*an a priori conjecture*). ● *adv.* **1** in an a priori manner. **2** as far as one knows; presumptively. □□ **apriorism** /ay-prī́orizəm/ *n.* [L, = from what is before]

apron /áyprən/ *n.* **1 a** a garment covering and protecting the front of a person's clothes, either from chest or waist level, and tied at the back. **b** official clothing of this kind. **c** anything resembling an apron in shape or function. **2** *Theatr.* the part of a stage in front of the curtain. **3** the paved area of an airfield used for maneuvering or loading aircraft. **4** an endless conveyor belt. □ **tied to a person's apron strings** dominated by or dependent on that person (usu. a woman).

/. . ./ **pronunciation**	● **part of speech**
	□ **phrases, idioms, and compounds**
□□ **derivatives**	■ **synonym section**
cross-references appear in SMALL CAPITALS or *italics*	

□□ **aproned** *adj.* **apronful** *n.* (*pl.* **-fuls**). [ME *naperon*, etc., f. OF dimin. of *nape* tablecloth f. L *mappa*: for loss of *n* cf. ADDER]

apropos /ápropṓ/ *adj., adv., & prep.* ● *adj.* to the point or purpose; appropriate (*his comment was apropos*). ● *adv.* **1** appropriately (*spoke apropos*). **2** (*absol.*) by the way; incidentally (*apropos, she's not going*). ● *prep.* (foll. by *of*) in respect to; concerning. [F *à propos* f. *à* to + *propos* PURPOSE] ■ *adj.* see APPROPRIATE *adj.* ● *prep.* see CONCERNING.

apse /aps/ *n.* **1** a large semicircular or polygonal recess, arched or with a domed roof, esp. at the eastern end of a church. **2** = APSIS. □□ **apsidal** /ápsid'l/ *adj.* [L APSIS]

apsis /ápsis/ *n.* (*pl.* **apsides** /-sīdeez/) either of two points in the orbit of a planet or satellite that are nearest to or farthest from the body around which it moves. □□ **apsidal** /ápsid'l/ *adj.* [L f. Gk (h)*apsis, -idos* arch, vault]

apt /apt/ *adj.* **1** appropriate; suitable. **2** (foll. by *to* + infin.) having a tendency (*apt to lose his temper*). **3** clever; quick to learn (*an apt pupil*; *apt at the work*). □□ **aptly** *adv.* **aptness** *n.* [ME f. L *aptus* fitted, past part. of *apere* fasten]
■ **1** see APPROPRIATE *adj.* see PRONE 2. **3** see QUICK *adj.* 4. □□ **aptness** see APTITUDE 2.

apt. *abbr.* **1** apartment. **2** aptitude.

apterous /áptərəs/ *adj.* **1** *Zool.* (of insects) without wings. **2** *Bot.* (of seeds or fruits) having no winglike expansions. [Gk *apteros* f. *a-* not + *pteron* wing]

apteryx /áptəriks/ *n.* = KIWI. [mod.L f. Gk *a-* not + *pterux* wing]

aptitude /áptitōōd, -tyōōd/ *n.* **1** a natural propensity or talent (*shows an aptitude for drawing*). **2** ability or suitability, esp. to acquire a particular skill. [F f. LL *aptitudo -inis* (as APT, -TUDE)]
■ **1** talent, gift, ability, capability, facility, faculty, flair; tendency, propensity, disposition, predilection, bent, proclivity. **2** fitness, suitability, appropriateness, relevance, applicability, suitableness, aptness; quick-wittedness, intelligence.

aqua /ákwə/ *n.* the color aquamarine. [abbr.]

aquaculture /ákwəkulchər, aakwə-/ *n.* (also **aquiculture**) the cultivation or rearing of aquatic plants or animals. □□ **aquacultural** *adj.* **aquaculturist** *n.* [L *aqua* water + CULTURE, after *agriculture*]

aqua fortis /ákwə fáwrtis, aakwə/ *n. Chem.* nitric acid. [L, = strong water]

Aqua-Lung /ákwəlung, aakwə-/ *n. & v. propr.* (*Brit.* **aqualung**) ● *n.* a portable breathing apparatus for divers, consisting of cylinders of compressed air strapped on the back, feeding air automatically through a mask or mouthpiece. ● *v.intr.* use an Aqua-Lung. [L *aqua* water + LUNG]

aquamarine /ákwəməreen, aakwə-/ *n.* **1** a light bluish green beryl. **2** its color. [L *aqua marina* sea water]

aquanaut /ákwənawt, aakwə-/ *n.* an underwater swimmer or explorer. [L *aqua* water + Gk *nautēs* sailor]

aquaplane /ákwəplayn, aakwə-/ *n. & v.* ● *n.* a board for riding on the water, pulled by a speedboat. ● *v.intr.* **1** ride on an aquaplane. **2** *Brit.* = HYDROPLANE *v.* 2 [L *aqua* water + PLANE[1]]

aqua regia /ákwə reéjeə, reéjə, aakwə/ *n. Chem.* a mixture of concentrated nitric and hydrochloric acids, a highly corrosive liquid attacking many substances unaffected by other reagents. [L, = royal water]

aquarelle /ákwərél/ *n.* a painting in thin, usu. transparent watercolors. [F f. It. *acquarella* watercolor, dimin. of *acqua* f. L *aqua* water]

aquarium /əkwáireeəm/ *n.* (*pl.* **aquariums** or **aquaria** /-reeə/) **1** an artificial environment designed for keeping live aquatic plants and animals for study or exhibition, esp. a tank of water with transparent sides. **2** an institution in which live aquatic plants and animals are kept for study and exhibition. [neut. of L *aquarius* of water (*aqua*) after *vivarium*]

Aquarius /əkwáireeəs/ *n.* **1** a constellation, traditionally regarded as portraying the figure of a water carrier. **2 a** the eleventh sign of the zodiac (the Water Carrier). **b** a person

born when the sun is in this sign. □□ **Aquarian** *adj. & n.* [ME f. L (as AQUARIUM)]

aquatic /əkwátik, əkwótik/ *adj. & n.* ● *adj.* **1** growing or living in or near water. **2** (of a sport) played in or on water. ● *n.* **1** an aquatic plant or animal. **2** (in *pl.*) aquatic sports. [ME f. F *aquatique* or L *aquaticus* f. *aqua* water]

aquatint /ákwətint, aákwə-/ *n.* **1** a print resembling a watercolor, produced from a copper plate etched with nitric acid. **2** the process of producing this. [F *aquatinte* f. It. *acqua tinta* colored water]

aquavit /aákwəveet, ákwə-/ (also **akvavit** /ákvə-/) *n.* an alcoholic liquor made from potatoes, etc., and usu. flavored with caraway seeds. [Scand.]

aqua vitae /aákwə vítee, veé-/ *n.* a strong alcoholic liquor, esp. brandy. [L = water of life]

aqueduct /ákwidukt/ *n.* **1** an artificial channel for conveying water, esp. in the form of a bridge supported by tall columns across a valley. **2** *Physiol.* a small canal or passage for liquids in the body. [L *aquae ductus* conduit f. *aqua* water + *ducere duct-* to lead]

aqueous /áykweeəs, ák-/ *adj.* **1** of, containing, or like water. **2** *Geol.* produced by water (*aqueous rocks*). □ **aqueous humor** *Anat.* the clear fluid in the eye between the lens and the cornea. [med.L *aqueus* f. L *aqua* water]
■ **1** see FLUID *adj.* 1.

aquifer /ákwifər/ *n. Geol.* a layer of rock or soil able to hold or transmit much water. [L *aqui-* f. *aqua* water + *-fer* bearing f. *ferre* bear]

aquilegia /ákwileéjə/ *n.* any (often blue-flowered) plant of the genus *Aquilegia*. Also called COLUMBINE. [mod. use of a med.L word: orig. unkn.]

aquiline /ákwilīn/ *adj.* **1** of or like an eagle. **2** (of a nose) curved like an eagle's beak. [L *aquilinus* f. *aquila* eagle]

AR *abbr.* Arkansas (in official postal use).

Ar *symb. Chem.* the element argon.

ar- /ər/ *prefix* assim. form of AD- before *r*.

-ar[1] /ər/ *suffix* **1** forming adjectives (*angular; linear; nuclear; titular*). **2** forming nouns (*scholar*). [OF *-aire* or *-ier* or L *-aris*]

-ar[2] /ər/ *suffix* forming nouns (*pillar*). [F *-er* or L *-ar, -are*, neut. of *-aris*]

-ar[3] /ər/ *suffix* forming nouns (*bursar; exemplar; mortar; vicar*). [OF *-aire* or *-ier* or L *-arius, -arium*]

-ar[4] /ər/ *suffix* assim. form of -ER[1], -OR[1] (*liar; beggar*).

Arab /árəb/ *n. & adj.* ● *n.* **1** a member of a Semitic people inhabiting originally Saudi Arabia and the neighboring countries, now the Middle East generally. **2** = ARABIAN 2. ● *adj.* of Arabia or the Arabs (esp. with ethnic reference). [F *Arabe* f. L *Arabs Arabis* f. Gk *Araps -abos* f. Arab. *'arab*]

arabesque /árəbésk/ *n.* **1** *Ballet* a posture with one leg extended horizontally backward, torso extended forward, and arms outstretched. **2** a design of intertwined leaves, scrolls, etc. **3** *Mus.* a florid melodic section or composition. **4** an elaborate, florid, or intricate design. [F f. It. *arabesco* f. *arabo* Arab]

Arabian /əráybeeən/ *adj. & n.* ● *adj.* of or relating to Arabia (esp. with geographical reference) (*the Arabian desert*). ● *n.* **1** a native of Arabia. ¶ Now less common than *Arab* in this sense. **2** (in full **Arabian horse**) a horse of a breed orig. native to Arabia. □ **Arabian camel** a domesticated camel, *Camelus dromedarius*, native to the deserts of N. Africa and the Near East, with one hump: also called DROMEDARY. [ME f. OF *arabi* prob. f. Arab. *'arabī*, or f. L *Arabus, Arabius* f. Gk *Arabios*]

Arabic /árəbik/ *n. & adj.* ● *n.* the Semitic language of the Arabs, now spoken in much of N. Africa and the Middle East. ● *adj.* of or relating to Arabia (esp. with reference to language or literature). □ **Arabic numeral** any of the numerals 0, 1, 2, 3, 4, 5, 6, 7, 8, and 9 (cf. *Roman numeral*). [ME f. OF *arabic* f. L *arabicus* f. Gk *arabikos*]

arabis /árəbis/ *n.* esp. *Brit.* = rock cress. [med.L f. Gk, = Arabian]

Arabist /árəbist/ *n.* **1** a student of Arabic civilization, language, etc. **2** an advocate of Arabic interests, etc.

arable /árəbəl/ *adj. & n.* ● *adj.* **1** (of land) plowed, or suitable for plowing and crop production. **2** (of crops) that can be grown on arable land. ● *n. Brit.* arable land or crops. [F *arable* or L *arabilis* f. *arare* to plow]

Araby /árəbee/ *n. poet.* Arabia. [OF *Arabie* f. L *Arabia* f. Gk]

arachnid /əráknid/ *n.* any arthropod of the class Arachnida, having four pairs of walking legs and characterized by simple eyes, e.g., scorpions, spiders, mites, and ticks. □□ **arachnid** *adj.* **arachnidan** *adj. & n.* [F *arachnide* or mod.L *arachnida* f. Gk *urakhnē* spidει]

arachnoid /əráknoyd/ *n. & adj.* ● *n. Anat.* (in full **arachnoid membrane**) one of the three membranes (see MENINX) that surround the brain and spinal cord of vertebrates. ● *adj. Bot.* covered with long cobweb-like hairs. [mod.L *arachnoides* f. Gk *arakhnoeidēs* like a cobweb f. *arakhnē*: see ARACHNID]

arachnophobia /əráknəfṓbeeə/ *n.* an abnormal fear of spiders. □□ **arachnophobe** /əráknəfṓb/ *n.* [mod. L. f. Gk *arakhnē* spider + -PHOBIA]

arak var. of ARRACK.

Aramaic /árəmáyik/ *n. & adj.* ● *n.* a branch of the Semitic family of languages, esp. the language of Syria used as a lingua franca in the Near East from the sixth century BC, later dividing into varieties one of which included Syriac and Mandaean. ● *adj.* of or in Aramaic. [L *Aramaeus* f. Gk *Aramaios* of Aram (bibl. name of Syria)]

Arapaho /ərápəhṓ/ *n.* **1 a** a N. American people native to the central plains of Canada and the US. **b** a member of this people. **2** the language of this people.

arational /áyráshənəl/ *adj.* that does not purport to be rational.

araucaria /árawkáireeə/ *n.* any evergreen conifer of the genus *Araucaria*, e.g., the monkey puzzle tree. [mod.L f. *Arauco*, name of a province in Chile]

arb /aarb/ *n. colloq.* = ARBITRAGEUR.

arbalest /áarbələst/ *n.* (also **arbalist** or *Brit.* **arblast** /áarblast/) *hist.* a crossbow with a mechanism for drawing the string. [OE *arblast* f. OF *arbaleste* f. LL *arcubalista* f. *arcus* bow + BALLISTA]

arbiter /áarbitər/ *n.* **1 a** an arbitrator in a dispute. **b** a judge; an authority (*arbiter of taste*). **2** (often foll. by *of*) a person who has entire control of something. □ **arbiter elegantiarum** (or **elegantiae**) /élegáanteeáərəm, élegáanshee-ee/ a judge of artistic or social taste and etiquette. [L]

■ **1 a** see JUDGE *n.* 2, *negotiator* (NEGOTIATE). **b** see JUDGE *n.* 3b, AUTHORITY 3c.

arbitrage /áarbitraazh, -trij/ *n.* the buying and selling of stocks or bills of exchange to take advantage of varying prices in different markets. [F f. *arbitrer* (as ARBITRATE)]

arbitrageur /áarbitraazhőr/ *n.* (also **arbitrager** /áarbitraazhər/) a person who engages in arbitrage. [F]

arbitral /áarbitrəl/ *adj.* concerning arbitration. [F *arbitral* or LL *arbitralis*: see ARBITER]

arbitrament /aarbítrəmənt/ *n.* **1** the deciding of a dispute by an arbiter. **2** an authoritative decision made by an arbiter. [ME f. OF *arbitrement* f. med.L *arbitramentum* (as ARBITRATE, -MENT)]

■ **1** see SETTLEMENT 3.

arbitrary /áarbitreree/ *adj.* **1** based on or derived from uninformed opinion or random choice; capricious. **2** despotic. □□ **arbitrarily** *adv.* **arbitrariness** *n.* [L *arbitrarius* or F *arbitraire* (as ARBITER, -ARY¹)]

■ **1** capricious, erratic, uncertain, inconsistent, unpredictable, whimsical, irrational, varying, chance, random, subjective, unreasoned. **2** absolute, tyrannical, despotic, authoritarian, tyrannous, imperious, magisterial, summary, peremptory, autocratic, dogmatic, uncompromising, inconsiderate, highhanded, dictatorial. □□ **arbitrarily** inconsistently, despotically, tyrannically, tyrannously, autocratically, magisterially, dictatorially, dogmatically; see also *at random* (RANDOM). **arbitrariness** inconsistency, irrationality, randomness; see also TYRANNY.

arbitrate /áarbitrayt/ *v.tr. & intr.* decide by arbitration. [L *arbitrari* judge]

■ see DECIDE 2b, JUDGE *v.* 5b.

arbitration /áarbitráyshən/ *n.* the settlement of a dispute by an arbitrator. [ME f. OF f. L *arbitratio -onis* (as ARBITER, -ATION)]

■ see SETTLEMENT 3.

arbitrator /áarbitraytər/ *n.* a person appointed to settle a dispute; an arbiter. □□ **arbitratorship** *n.* [ME f. LL (as ARBITRATION, -OR¹)]

■ see JUDGE *n.* 2, *negotiator* (NEGOTIATE).

arblast var. of ARBLEST.

arbor¹ /áarbər/ *n.* **1** an axle or spindle on which something revolves. **2** a device holding a tool in a lathe, etc. [F *arbre* tree, axis, f. L *arbor*: refashioned on L]

arbor² /áarbər/ *n.* (*Brit.* **arbour**) a shady alcove with the sides and roof formed by trees or climbing plants; a bower. □□ **arbored** *adj.* [ME f. AF *erber* f. OF *erbier* f. *erbe* herb f. L *herba*: phonetic change to *ar-* assisted by assoc. with L *arbor* tree]

arboraceous /áarbəráyshəs/ *adj.* **1** treelike. **2** wooded. [L *arbor* tree + -ACEOUS]

Arbor Day /áarbər/ *n.* a day dedicated annually to tree planting in the US, Australia, and other countries. [L *arbor* tree]

arboreal /aarbáwreeəl/ *adj.* of, living in, or connected with trees. [L *arboreus* f. *arbor* tree]

arboreous /aarbáwreeəs/ *adj.* **1** wooded. **2** arboreal.

arborescent /áarbərésənt/ *adj.* treelike in growth or general appearance. □□ **arborescence** *n.* [L *arborescere* grow into a tree (*arbor*)]

arboretum /áarbəréetəm/ *n.* (*pl.* **arboretums** or **arboreta** /-tə/) a botanical garden devoted to trees, shrubs, etc. [L f. *arbor* tree]

arboriculture /áarbərikúlchər, aarbáwri-/ *n.* the cultivation of trees and shrubs. □□ **arboricultural** *adj.* **arboriculturist** *n.* [L *arbor -oris* tree, after *agriculture*]

arborization /áarbərizáyshən/ *n.* a treelike arrangement, esp. in anatomy.

arbor vitae /áarbər vítee/ *n.* any of the evergreen conifers of the genus *Thuja*, native to N. Asia and N. America, usu. of pyramidal shape with flattened shoots bearing scale-leaves. [L, = tree of life]

arbour *Brit.* var. of ARBOR².

arbutus /aarbyóotəs/ *n.* **1** any evergreen ericaceous tree or shrub of the genus *Arbutus*, having white or pink clusters of flowers and strawberry-like berries. Also called **strawberry tree**. **2** = *trailing arbutus*. □ **trailing arbutus** the mayflower, *Epigaea repens*, a creeping plant of the heath family with pink or white flowers. [L]

ARC *abbr.* AIDS-related complex.

arc /aark/ *n. & v.* ● *n.* **1** part of the circumference of a circle or any other curve. **2** *Electr.* a luminous discharge between two electrodes. ● *v.intr.* (**arced** /aarkt/; **arcing** /áarking/) form an arc or follow an arc-shaped trajectory. □ **arc lamp** (or **light**) a light source using an electric arc. □ **arc welding** a method of using an electric arc to melt metals to be welded. [ME f. OF f. L *arcus* bow, curve]

arcade /aarkáyd/ *n.* **1** a passage with an arched roof. **2** any covered walk, esp. with shops along one or both sides. **3** *Archit.* a series of arches supporting or set along a wall. **4** an entertainment establishment with coin-operated games, etc. □□ **arcaded** *adj.* [F f. Prov. *arcada* or It. *arcata* f. Rmc: rel. to ARCH¹]

Arcadian /aarkáydeeən/ *n. & adj.* ● *n.* an idealized peasant or country dweller, esp. in poetry. ● *adj.* simple and poetically rural. □□ **Arcadianism** *n.* [L *Arcadius* f. Gk *Arkadia* mountain district in Peloponnese]

Arcady /áarkədee/ *n.* (also **Arcadia** /aarkáydeeə/) *poet.* an ideal rustic paradise. [Gk *Arkadia*: see ARCADIAN]

arcane /aarkáyn/ *adj.* mysterious; secret; understood by few. □□ **arcanely** *adv.* [F *arcane* or L *arcanus* f. *arcēre* shut up f. *arca* chest]

■ see MYSTERIOUS.

/. . ./ **pronunciation**	● **part of speech**
□ **phrases, idioms, and compounds**	
□□ **derivatives**	■ **synonym section**
cross-references appear in SMALL CAPITALS or *italics*	

arcanum /aarkáynəm/ *n.* (*pl.* **arcana** /-nə/) (usu. in *pl.*) a mystery; a profound secret. [L neut. of *arcanus*: see ARCANE]
■ see MYSTERY 1.

arch[1] /aarch/ *n. & v.* ● *n.* **1 a** a curved structure as an opening or a support for a bridge, roof, floor, etc. **b** an arch used in building as an ornament. **2** any arch-shaped curve, e.g., as on the inner side of the foot, the eyebrows, etc. ● *v.* **1** *tr.* provide with or form into an arch. **2** *tr.* span like an arch. **3** *intr.* form an arch. [ME f. OF *arche* ult. f. L *arcus* arc]

arch[2] /aarch/ *adj.* self-consciously or affectedly playful or teasing. □□ **archly** *adv.* **archness** *n.* [ARCH-, orig. in *arch rogue*, etc.]

arch- /aarch/ *comb. form* **1** chief; superior (*archbishop*; *archduke*). **2** preeminent of its kind (esp. in unfavorable senses) (*archenemy*). [OE *arce-* or OF *arche-*, ult. f. Gk *arkhos* chief]
■ **2** chief, principal, prime, primary, preeminent, foremost, first, greatest, major.

Archaean *Brit.* var. of ARCHEAN.

archaeology /aarkee-ólə jee/ *n.* (also **archeology**) the study of human history and prehistory through the excavation of sites and the analysis of physical remains. □□ **archaeologic** /-keeəlójik/ *adj.* **archaeological** *adj.* **archaeologist** *n.* **archaeologize** *v.intr.* [mod.L *archaeologia* f. Gk *arkhaiologia* ancient history (as ARCHEAN, -LOGY)]

archaeopteryx /aarkee-óptəriks/ *n.* the oldest known fossil bird, *Archaeopteryx lithographica*, with teeth, feathers, and a reptilian tail. [Gk *arkhaios* ancient + *pteryx* wing]

archaic /aarkáyik/ *adj.* **1 a** antiquated. **b** (of a word, etc.) no longer in ordinary use, though retained for special purposes. **2** primitive. **3** of an early period of art or culture, esp. the 7th–6th c. BC in Greece. □□ **archaically** *adv.* [F *archaïque* f. Gk *arkhaïkos* (as ARCHEAN)]
■ **1** see ANTIQUATED, OBSOLETE. **2, 3** see ANCIENT[1] *adj.* 1.

archaism /aarkeeizəm, -kay-/ *n.* **1** the retention or imitation of the old or obsolete, esp. in language or art. **2** an archaic word or expression. □□ **archaist** *n.* **archaistic** *adj.* [mod.L f. Gk *arkhaïsmos* f. *arkhaïzō* (as ARCHAIZE, -ISM)]

archaize /aarkeeiz, -kay-/ *v.* **1** *intr.* imitate the archaic. **2** *tr.* make (a work of art, literature, etc.) imitate the archaic. [Gk *arkhaïzō* be old-fashioned f. *arkhaios* ancient]

archangel /aarkaynjəl/ *n.* **1** an angel of the highest rank. **2** a member of the eighth order of the nine ranks of heavenly beings (see ORDER). □□ **archangelic** /-anjélik/ *adj.* [OE f. AF *archangele* f. eccl.L *archangelus* f. eccl.Gk *arkhaggelos* (as ARCH-, ANGEL)]

archbishop /aarchbíshəp/ *n.* the chief bishop of a province. [OE (as ARCH-, BISHOP)]

archbishopric /aarchbíshəprik/ *n.* the office or diocese of an archbishop. [OE (as ARCH-, BISHOPRIC)]

archdeacon /aarchdeékən/ *n.* a cleric in various churches ranking below a bishop. □□ **archdeaconry** *n.* (*pl.* **-ies**). **archdeaconship** *n.* [OE *arce-, ercediacon,* f. eccl.L *archidiaconus* f. eccl.Gk *arkhidiakonos* (as ARCH-, DEACON)]
■ □□ **archdeaconry, archdeaconship** archidiaconate.

archdiocese /aarchdíəsis, -sees, -seez/ *n.* the diocese of an archbishop. □□ **archdiocesan** /aarchdíósisən/ *adj.*

archduke /aarchdook, -dyook/ *n.* (*fem.* **archduchess** /-dúchis/) *hist.* the chief duke (esp. as the title of a son of the Emperor of Austria). □□ **archducal** *adj.* **archduchy** /-dúchee/ *n.* (*pl.* **-ies**). [OF *archeduc* f. med.L *archidux -ducis* (as ARCH-, DUKE)]

Archean /aarkeéən/ *adj. & n.* (*Brit.* **Archaean**) ● *adj.* of or relating to the earlier part of the Precambrian era. ● *n.* this time. [Gk *arkhaios* ancient f. *arkhē* beginning]

archegonium /aarkigốneeəm/ *n.* (*pl.* **archegonia** /-eeə/) *Bot.* the female sex organ in mosses, ferns, conifers, etc. [L, dimin. of Gk *arkhegonos* f. *arkhe-* chief + *gonos* race]

archenemy /aarchénəmee/ *n.* (*pl.* **-ies**) **1** a chief enemy. **2** the Devil.

archeology var. of ARCHAEOLOGY.

archer /aarchər/ *n.* **1** a person who shoots with a bow and arrows. **2** (**the Archer**) the zodiacal sign or constellation Sagittarius. [AF f. OF *archier* ult. f. L *arcus* bow]

archerfish /aarchərfish/ a SE Asian fish that catches flying insects by shooting water at them from its mouth.

archery /aarchəree/ *n.* shooting with a bow and arrows, esp. as a sport. [OF *archerie* f. *archier* (as ARCHER, -ERY)]

archetype /aarkitip/ *n.* **1 a** an original model; a prototype. **b** a typical specimen. **2** (in Jungian psychology) a primitive mental image inherited from man's earliest ancestors, and supposed to be present in the collective unconscious. **3** a recurrent symbol or motif in literature, art, etc. □□ **archetypal** *adj.* **archetypical** /-típikəl/ *adj.* [L *archetypum* f. Gk *arkhetupon* (as ARCH-, *tupos* stamp)]
■ **1 a** see PROTOTYPE 1.

archidiaconal /aarkidiákənəl/ *adj.* of or relating to an archdeacon. □□ **archidiaconate** /-nət, -nayt/ *n.* [med.L *archidiaconalis* (as ARCH-, DIACONAL)]
■ □□ **archidiaconate** archdeaconry, archdeaconship.

archiepiscopal /aarkee-ipískəpəl/ *adj.* of or relating to an archbishop. □□ **archiepiscopate** /-pət, -payt/ *n.* [eccl.L *archiepiscopus* f. Gk *arkhiepiskopos* archbishop]

archil var. of ORCHIL.

archimandrite /aarkimándrit/ *n.* **1** the superior of a large monastery or group of monasteries in the Orthodox Church. **2** an honorary title given to a monastic priest. [F *archimandrite* or eccl.L *archimandrita* f. eccl. Gk *arkhimandrites* (as ARCH-, *mandra* monastery)]

Archimedean /aarkimeédeeən/ *adj.* of or associated with the Greek mathematician Archimedes (d. 212 BC). □ **Archimedean screw** a device of ancient origin for raising water by means of a spiral inside a tube.

Archimedes' principle /aarkimeédeez/ *n.* the law that a body totally or partially immersed in a fluid is subject to an upward force equal in magnitude to the weight of fluid it displaces.

archipelago /aarkipélagō/ *n.* (*pl.* **-os** or **-oes**) **1** a group of islands. **2** a sea with many islands. [It. *arcipelago* f. Gk *arkhi-* chief + *pelagos* sea (orig. = the Aegean Sea)]

architect /aarkitekt/ *n.* **1** a designer who prepares plans for buildings, ships, etc., and supervises their construction. **2** (foll. by *of*) a person who brings about a specified thing (*the architect of the tax reform bill*). [F *architecte* f. It. *architetto*, or L *architectus* f. Gk *arkhitektōn* (as ARCH-, *tektōn* builder)]
■ **1** see DESIGNER 1. **2** see AUTHOR *n.* 2.

architectonic /aarkitektónik/ *adj. & n.* ● *adj.* **1** of or relating to architecture or architects. **2** of or relating to the systematization of knowledge. ● *n.* (in *pl.*; usu. treated as *sing.*) **1** the scientific study of architecture. **2** the study of the systematization of knowledge. [L *architectonicus* f. Gk *arkhitektonikos* (as ARCHITECT)]

architecture /aarkitekchər/ *n.* **1** the art or science of designing and constructing buildings. **2** the style of a building as regards design and construction. **3** buildings or other structures collectively. □□ **architectural** /-tékchərəl/ *adj.* **architecturally** *adv.* [F *architecture* or L *architectura* f. *architectus* (as ARCHITECT)]

architrave /aarkitrayv/ *n.* **1** (in classical architecture) a main beam resting across the tops of columns. **2** the molded frame around a doorway or window. **3** a molding around the exterior of an arch. [F f. It. (as ARCH-, *trave* f. L *trabs trabis* beam)]

archive /aarkiv/ *n. & v.* ● *n.* (usu. in *pl.*) **1** a collection of esp. public or corporate documents or records. **2** the place where these are kept. ● *v.tr.* **1** place or store in an archive. **2** *Computing* transfer (data) to a less frequently used file or less easily accessible medium, e.g., from disk to tape. □□ **archival** /aarkívəl/ *adj.* [F *archives* (pl.) f. L *archi(v)a* f. Gk *arkheia* public records f. *arkhē* government]
■ *n.* **1** see CHRONICLE *n.* ● *v.* **1** see CHRONICLE *v.*

archivist /aarkivist, aarkí-/ *n.* a person who maintains and is in charge of archives.

archivolt /aarkivōlt/ *n.* **1** a band of moldings around the lower curve of an arch. **2** the lower curve itself from impost to impost of the columns. [F *archivolte* or It. *archivolto* (as ARC, VAULT)]

archlute /aarchlōōt/ *n.* a bass lute with an extended neck and unstopped bass strings. [F *archiluth* (as ARCH-, LUTE[1])]

archon /aarkon, -kən/ *n.* each of the nine chief magistrates in ancient Athens. □□ **archonship** n. [Gk *arkhōn* ruler, = pres. part. of *arkhō* rule]

archway /aʹarchway/ n. **1** a vaulted passage. **2** an arched entrance.

Arctic /aʹarktik, aʹartik/ adj. & n. ● adj. **1** of the north polar regions. **2** (**arctic**) *colloq.* (esp. of weather) very cold. ● n. **1** the Arctic regions. **2** (**arctic**) a thick waterproof overshoe. □ **Arctic Circle** the parallel of latitude 66° 33′ N, forming an imaginary line around this region. [ME f. OF *artique* f. L *ar(c)ticus* f. Gk *arktikos* f. *arktos* bear, Ursa Major]
■ adj. **2** see POLAR 6.

arcuate /aʹarkyōōət, -ayt/ adj. shaped like a bow; curved. [L *arcuatus* past part. of *arcuare* curve f. *arcus* bow, curve]

arcus senilis /aʹarkəs sənilis/ n. a narrow opaque band commonly encircling the cornea in old age. [L, lit. 'senile bow']

-ard /ərd/ suffix **1** forming nouns in depreciatory senses (*drunkard*; *sluggard*). **2** forming nouns in other senses (*Spaniard*; *wizard*). [ME & OF f. G *-hard* hardy (in proper names)]

ardent /aʹard'nt/ adj. **1** eager; zealous; (of persons or feelings) fervent; passionate. **2** burning. □□ **ardency** /-d'nsee/ n. **ardently** adv. [ME f. OF *ardant* f. L *ardens -entis* f. *ardēre* burn]
■ **1** eager, intense, zealous, keen, enthusiastic, fervent, fervid, passionate, avid, fierce, impassioned, hot, burning, warm, *literary* perfervid; earnest, sincere, deep. □□ **ardency** see ARDOR, DEVOTION 1.

ardor /aʹardər/ (*Brit.* **ardour**) n. zeal; burning enthusiasm; passion. [ME f. OF f. L *ardor -oris* f. *ardēre* burn]
■ desire, zeal, fervency, ardency, burning desire, fervor, passion, full-heartedness, heat, warmth; enthusiasm, animation, eagerness, keenness.

arduous /aʹardōōəs/ adj. **1** (of a task, etc.) hard to achieve or overcome; difficult; laborious. **2** (of an action, etc.) energetic; strenuous. □□ **arduously** adv. **arduousness** n. [L *arduus* steep, difficult]
■ laborious, difficult, hard, tough, strenuous, energetic, onerous, burdensome, backbreaking, painful; tiring, exhausting, wearisome, fatiguing, taxing, grueling, trying, formidable. □□ **arduously** see HARD adv. 1. **arduousness** see DIFFICULTY 1.

are[1] *2nd sing. present & 1st, 2nd, 3rd pl. present* of BE.

are[2] /aar/ n. a metric unit of measure, equal to 100 square meters. [F f. L AREA]

area /aʹireeə/ n. **1** the extent or measure of a surface (*over a large area*; *3 acres in area*; *the area of a triangle*). **2** a region or tract (*the southern area*). **3** a space allocated for a specific purpose (*dining area*; *camping area*). **4** the scope or range of an activity or study. **5** = AREAWAY. □ **area code** a three-digit number that identifies one of the telephone service regions into which the US, Canada, etc., are divided and which is dialed when calling from one area to another. □□ **areal** adj. [L, = vacant piece of level ground]
■ **1** extent, limit, compass, size, space, square footage, acreage; measure. **2** region, tract, territory, district, zone, stretch; section, quarter, precinct, arrondissement, neighborhood, locality, bailiwick, block. **3** space, room, ground, zone. **4** scope, range, compass, margin, sphere; section, part; subject.

areaway /aʹireeəway/ n. a space below ground level in front of the basement of a building.
■ court, courtyard, enclosure, close, yard.

areca /əreʹekə, aʹrikə/ n. any tropical palm of the genus *Areca*, native to Asia. □ **areca nut** the astringent seed of a species of areca, *A. catechu*: also called *betel nut*. [Port. f. Malayalam *áḍekka*]

areg pl. of ERG[2].

arena /əreʹenə/ n. **1** the central part of an amphitheater, etc., where contests take place. **2** a scene of conflict; a sphere of action or discussion. □ **arena theater** (or **stage**) a stage situated with the audience all around it. [L *(h)arena* sand, sand-strewn place of combat]

arenaceous /árinayʹshəs/ adj. **1** (of rocks) containing sand; having a sandy texture. **2** sandlike. **3** (of plants) growing in sand. [L *arenaceus* (as ARENA, -ACEOUS)]

aren't /aarnt, aʹarənt/ contr. **1** are not. **2** (in *interrog.*) am not (*aren't I coming too?*).

areola /əreʹeələ/ n. (pl. **areolae** /-lee/) **1** *Anat.* a circular pigmented area, esp. that surrounding a nipple. **2** any of the spaces between lines on a surface, e.g., of a leaf or an insect's wing. □□ **areolar** adj. [L, dimin. of *area* AREA]

arête /əráyt/ n. a sharp mountain ridge. [F f. L *arista* ear of wheat, fishbone, spine]

argali /aʹargəlee/ n. (pl. same) a large Asiatic wild sheep, *Ovis ammon*, with massive horns. [Mongol]

argent /aʹarjənt/ n. & adj. *Heraldry* silver; silvery white. [F f. L *argentum*]

argentiferous /aʹarjəntífərəs/ adj. containing natural deposits of silver. [L *argentum* + -FEROUS]

Argentine /aʹarjənteen, -tin/ adj. & n. (also **Argentinian** /-tíneeən/) ● adj. of or relating to Argentina in S. America. ● n. **1** a native or citizen of Argentina. **2** a person of Argentine descent. □ **the Argentine** Argentina. [Sp. *Argentina* (as ARGENTINE)]

argentine /aʹarjəntin, -teen/ adj. of silver; silvery. [F *argentin* f. *argent* silver]

argil /aʹarjil/ n. clay, esp. that used in pottery. □□ **argillaceous** /-jiláyshəs/ adj. [F *argille* f. L *argilla* f. Gk *argillos* f. *argos* white]

arginine /aʹarjineen/ n. an amino acid present in many animal proteins and an essential nutrient in the vertebrate diet. [G *Arginin*, of uncert. orig.]

Argive /aʹargīv/ adj. & n. ● adj. **1** of Argos in ancient Greece. **2** *literary* (esp. in Homeric contexts) Greek. ● n. **1** a citizen of Argos. **2** *literary* (usu. in *pl.*) a Greek. [L *Argivus* f. Gk *Argeios*]

argol /aʹargawl/ n. crude potassium hydrogen tartar. [ME f. AF *argoile*, of unkn. orig.]

argon /aʹargon/ n. *Chem.* an inert gaseous element, of the noble gas group and forming almost 1% of the earth's atmosphere. ¶ Symb.: **Ar**. [Gk, neut. of *argos* idle f. *a-* not + *ergon* work]

argosy /aʹargəsee/ n. (pl. **-ies**) *poet.* **1** a large merchant ship, orig. esp. from Ragusa (now Dubrovnik) or Venice. **2** an opulent or abundant supply. [prob. It. *Ragusea (nave)* Ragusan (vessel)]

argot /aʹargō, -gət/ n. the jargon of a group or class, formerly esp. of criminals. [F: orig. unkn.]
■ see JARGON[1] 1, 2.

arguable /aʹargyōōəbəl/ adj. **1** that may be argued; open to dispute. **2** reasonable; supported by argument. □□ **arguably** adv.
■ **2** see REASONABLE 2.

argue /aʹargyōō/ v. (**argues, argued, arguing**) **1** intr. (often foll. by *with, about,* etc.) exchange views or opinions, especially heatedly or contentiously (with a person). **2** tr. & intr. (often foll. by *that* + clause) indicate; maintain by reasoning. **3** intr. (foll. by *for, against*) reason (*argued against joining*). **4** tr. treat by reasoning (*argue the point*). **5** tr. (foll. by *into, out of*) persuade (*argued me into going*). □ **argue the toss** *Brit. colloq.* dispute a decision or choice already made. □□ **arguer** n. [ME f. OF *arguer* f. L *argutari* prattle, frequent. of *arguere* make clear, prove, accuse]
■ **1** bicker, wrangle, quarrel, squabble, spar, fight, debate, discuss, reason, dispute, disagree, remonstrate, altercate, *colloq.* row, scrap, spat. **2** reason, assert, hold, maintain, claim, contend; indicate, suggest, signify, show, prove, demonstrate, establish. **3** reason, make or put a case, speak, plead. **4** see DEBATE v. 1. **5** persuade, talk, prevail (up)on, convince; dissuade; see also COAX.

argufy /aʹargyəfī/ v.intr. (**-ies, -ied**) *colloq.* argue excessively or tediously. [fanciful f. ARGUE: cf. SPEECHIFY]

argument /aʹargyəmənt/ n. **1** an exchange of views, esp. a contentious or prolonged one. **2** (often foll. by *for, against*)

/.../	**pronunciation**	●	**part of speech**
□	**phrases, idioms, and compounds**		
□□	**derivatives**	■	**synonym section**
cross-references appear in SMALL CAPITALS or *italics*			

a reason advanced; a reasoning process (*an argument for abolition*). **3** a summary of the subject matter or line of reasoning of a book. **4** *Math.* an independent variable determining the value of a function. [ME f. OF f. L *argumentum* f. *arguere* (as ARGUE, -MENT)]

■ **1** debate, dispute, disagreement, quarrel, controversy, polemic, wrangle, squabble, tiff, altercation; conflict, fight, fracas, affray, fray, skirmish, donnybrook, feud, falling out, *colloq.* row, scrap, miff, run-in, barney, spat. **2** (line of) reasoning, case, assertion, contention, plea, claim, pleading; defense; reason, explanation, excuse, justification, rationalization, vindication. **3** line (of reasoning), thread; see also THEME 1.

argumentation /aárgyəməntáyshən/ *n.* **1** methodical reasoning. **2** debate or argument. [F f. L *argumentatio* f. *argumentari* (as ARGUMENT, -ATION)]

■ **2** see DEBATE *n.* 2.

argumentative /aárgyəméntətiv/ *adj.* **1** fond of arguing; quarrelsome. **2** using methodical reasoning. □□ **argumentatively** *adv.* **argumentativeness** *n.* [F *argumentatif -ive* or LL *argumentativus* (as ARGUMENT, -ATIVE)]

■ **1** quarrelsome, cantankerous, contentious, disputatious, belligerent, combative, pugnacious, disagreeable, contrary; litigious.

Argus /aárgəs/ *n.* **1** a watchful guardian. **2** an Asiatic pheasant having markings on its tail resembling eyes. **3** a butterfly having markings resembling eyes. □ **Argus-eyed** vigilant. [ME f. L f. Gk *Argos* mythical person with a hundred eyes]

■ □ **Argus-eyed** see VIGILANT.

argy-bargy /aárjeebaárjee/ *n.* & *v. Brit. joc.* ● *n.* (*pl.* **-ies**) a dispute or wrangle. ● *v.intr.* (**-ies**, **-ied**) quarrel, esp. loudly. [orig. Sc.]

aria /aáreeə/ *n. Mus.* a long accompanied song for solo voice in an opera, oratorio, etc. [It.]

Arian /áireeən/ *n.* & *adj.* ● *n.* an adherent of the doctrine of Arius of Alexandria (4th c.), who denied the divinity of Christ. ● *adj.* of or concerning this doctrine. □□ **Arianism** *n.*

-arian /áireeən/ *suffix* forming adjectives and nouns meaning '(one) concerned with or believing in' (*agrarian; antiquarian; humanitarian; vegetarian*). [L *-arius* (see -ARY¹)]

arid /árid/ *adj.* **1 a** (of ground, climate, etc.) dry; parched. **b** too dry to support vegetation; barren. **2** uninteresting (*arid verse*). □□ **aridity** /əríditee/ *n.* **aridly** *adv.* **aridness** *n.* [F *aride* or L *aridus* f. *arēre* be dry]

■ **1** see DRY *adj.* 1c. **2** see BORING, DRY *adj.* 3b.

Aries /áireez/ *n.* (*pl.* same) **1** a constellation, traditionally regarded as portraying the figure of a ram. **2 a** the first sign of the zodiac (the Ram). **b** a person born when the sun is in this sign. □□ **Arian** /-reeən/ *adj.* & *n.* [ME f. L, = ram]

aright /ərít/ *adv.* rightly. [OE (as A², RIGHT)]

aril /áril/ *n. Bot.* an extra seed covering, often colored and hairy or fleshy, e.g., the red fleshy cup around a yew seed. □□ **arillate** *adj.* [mod.L *arillus*: cf. med.L *arilli* dried grape stones]

-arious /áireeəs/ *suffix* forming adjectives (*gregarious; vicarious*). [L *-arius* (see -ARY¹) + -OUS]

arise /əríz/ *v.intr.* (*past* **arose** /ərőz/; *past part.* **arisen** /ərízən/) **1** begin to exist; originate. **2** (usu. foll. by *from, out of*) result (*accidents can arise from carelessness*). **3** come to one's notice; emerge (*the question of payment arose*). **4** rise. [OE *árīsan* (as A-², RISE)]

■ **1** spring up, begin, start (up *or* off), originate, come up, come into existence, *formal* commence. **2** see DERIVE 2. **3** come up, be brought up, be mentioned, emerge, surface, *colloq.* crop up. **4** rise, get up, stand up, get to one's feet; wake up, get out of bed, awake, waken; be resurrected, be raised.

aristocracy /áristókrəsee/ *n.* (*pl.* **-ies**) **1 a** the highest class in society; the nobility. **b** the nobility as a ruling class. **2 a** government by a privileged group. **b** a nation governed in this way. **3** (often foll. by *of*) those considered to be the best representatives or upper echelons (*aristocracy of intellect; aristocracy of labor*). [F *aristocratie* f. Gk *aristokratia* f. *aristos* best + *kratia* (as -CRACY)]

aristocrat /ərístəkrat, áris-/ *n.* **1** a member of the aristocracy. **2** something believed to be the best of its kind. [F *aristocrate* (as ARISTOCRATIC)]

■ see NOBLE *n.*

aristocratic /árístəkrátik/ *adj.* **1** of or relating to the aristocracy. **2 a** distinguished in manners or bearing. **b** grand; stylish. □□ **aristocratically** *adv.* [F *aristocratique* f. Gk *aristokratikos* (as ARISTOCRACY)]

■ **1** see NOBLE *adj.* 1. **2** see NOBLE *adj.* 3, 4.

Aristotelian /áristəteéleeən, əris-/ *n.* & *adj.* ● *n.* a disciple or student of the Greek philosopher Aristotle (d. 322 BC). ● *adj.* of or concerning Aristotle or his ideas.

Arita /əreéetə/ *n.* (usu. *attrib.*) a type of Japanese porcelain characterized by asymmetric decoration. [*Arita* in Japan]

arithmetic *n.* & *adj.* ● *n.* /əríthmətik/ **1 a** the science of numbers. **b** esp. *Brit.* one's knowledge of this (*have improved my arithmetic*). **2** the use of numbers; computation (*a problem involving arithmetic*). ● *adj.* /árithmétik/ (also **arithmetical** /-métikəl/) of or concerning arithmetic. □ **arithmetic mean** an average calculated by adding quantities and dividing the total by the number of quantities. **arithmetic progression 1** an increase or decrease by a constant quantity (e.g., 1, 2, 3, 4, etc., 9, 7, 5, 3, etc.). **2** a sequence of numbers showing this. □□ **arithmetician** /ərithmətishən/ *n.* [ME f. OF *arismetique* f. L *arithmetica* f. Gk *arithmetike* (*tekhne*) art of counting f. *arithmos* number]

-arium /áireeəm/ *suffix* forming nouns usu. denoting a place (*aquarium; planetarium*). [L, neut. of adjs. in *-arius*: see -ARY¹]

Ariz. *abbr.* Arizona.

Ark. *abbr.* Arkansas.

ark /aark/ *n.* **1** = NOAH'S ARK 1. **2** *archaic* a chest or box. **3** a refuge. □ **Ark of the Covenant** a chest or box containing the tablets of the Ten Commandments, kept in the Temple at Jerusalem until the destruction of the Temple. **out of the ark** *colloq.* very antiquated. [OE *ærc* f. L *arca* chest]

arm¹ /aarm/ *n.* **1** each of the upper limbs of the human body from the shoulder to the hand. **2 a** the forelimb of an animal. **b** the flexible limb of an invertebrate animal (e.g., an octopus). **3 a** the sleeve of a garment. **b** the side part of a chair, etc., used to support a sitter's arm. **c** a thing resembling an arm in branching from a main stem (*an arm of the sea*). **d** a large branch of a tree. **4** a control; a means of reaching (*arm of the law*). **5** a branch or division of a larger group (*the pacifist arm of the movement*). □ **an arm and a leg** a large sum of money. **arm in arm** (of two or more persons) with arms linked. **arm-twisting** *colloq.* (persuasion by) the use of physical force or moral pressure. **arm wrestling** a trial of strength in which each party tries to force the other's arm down onto a table on which their elbows rest. **as long as your** (or **my**) **arm** *colloq.* very long. **at arm's length 1** as far as an arm can reach. **2** far enough to avoid undue familiarity. **in arms** (of a baby) too young to walk. **in a person's arms** embraced. **on one's arm** supported by one's arm. **under one's arm** between the arm and the body. **within arm's reach** reachable without moving one's position. **with open arms** cordially. □□ **armful** *n.* (*pl.* **-fuls**). **armless** *adj.* [OE f. Gmc]

■ **3 d** see BRANCH *n.* 1. □ **arm-twisting** see FORCE¹ *n.* 2, PRESSURE *n.* 4.

arm² /aarm/ *n.* & *v.* ● *n.* **1** (usu. in *pl.*) **a** a weapon. **b** = FIREARM. **2** (in *pl.*) the military profession. **3** a branch of the military (e.g., infantry, cavalry, artillery, etc.). **4** (in *pl.*) heraldic devices (*coat of arms*). ● *v.tr.* & *refl.* **1** supply with weapons. **2** supply with tools or other requisites or advantages (*armed with the truth*). **3** make (a bomb, etc.) able to explode. □ **arms control** international disarmament or arms limitation, esp. by mutual agreement. **arms race** a contest for superiority, esp. in nuclear weapons between the US and the former Soviet Union. **in arms** armed. **lay down one's arms** cease fighting. **take up arms** begin fighting. **under arms** ready for war or battle. **up in arms** (usu. foll. by *against, about*) actively rebelling. □□ **armless** *adj.* [ME f. OF *armes* (pl.), *armer*, f. L *arma* arms, fittings]

■ *n.* **1** see HARDWARE 2. **4** (*arms*) see SYMBOL *n.*

armada /aarmaáadə/ n. a fleet of warships, esp. that sent by Spain against England in 1588. [Sp. f. Rmc *armata* army]

armadillo /aȧrmədílō/ n. (pl. **-os**) any nocturnal insect-eating mammal of the family Dasypodidae, native to Central and S. America, with large claws for digging and a body covered in bony plates, often rolling itself into a ball when threatened. [Sp. dimin. of *armado* armed man f. L *armatus* past part. of *armare* ARM²]

Armageddon /aȧrməgéd'n/ n. **1 a** (in the New Testament) the last battle between good and evil before the Day of Judgment. **b** the place where this will be fought. **2** a bloody battle or struggle on a huge scale. [Gk f. Heb. *har megiddōn* hill of Megiddo: see Rev. 16:16]

armament /aȧrməmənt/ n. **1** (often in pl.) military weapons and equipment, esp. guns on a warship. **2** the process of equipping for war. **3** a force equipped for war. [L *armamentum* (as ARM², -MENT)]
■ **1** see HARDWARE 2.

armamentarium /aȧrməmentáireeəm/ n. (pl. **armamentaria** /-reeə/) **1** a set of medical equipment or drugs. **2** the resources available to a person engaged in a task. [L, = arsenal]

armature /aȧrməchŏŏr/ n. **1 a** the rotating coil or coils of a generator or electric motor. **b** any moving part of an electrical machine in which a voltage is induced by a magnetic field. **2** a piece of soft iron placed in contact with the poles of a horseshoe magnet to preserve its power. Also called KEEPER. **3** *Biol.* the protective covering of an animal or plant. **4** a metal framework on which a sculpture is molded with clay or similar material. **5** *archaic* arms; armor. [F f. L *armatura* armor (as ARM², -URE)]

armband /aȧrmband/ n. a band worn around the upper arm to hold up a shirtsleeve or as a form of identification, etc.

armchair n. /aȧrmcháir/ **1** a comfortable, usu. upholstered, chair with side supports for the arms. **2** (*attrib.*) theoretical rather than active or practical (*an armchair critic*).

Armenian /aȧrmeéneeən/ n. & adj. ● n. **1 a** a native of Armenia, an ancient kingdom corresponding to an area in modern Armenia, Turkey, and Iran. **b** a person of Armenian descent. **2** the language of Armenia. ● adj. of or relating to Armenia, its language, or the Christian Church established there *c*.300.

armhole /aȧrmhōl/ n. each of two holes in a garment through which the arms are put, usu. into a sleeve.

armiger /aȧrmijər/ n. a person entitled to heraldic arms. □□ **armigerous** /-míjərəs/ adj. [L, = bearing arms, f. *arma* arms + *gerere* bear]

armillary /aȧrmíleree/ adj. relating to bracelets. □ **armillary sphere** *hist.* a representation of the celestial globe constructed from metal rings and showing the celestial equator, the celestial tropics, etc. [mod.L *armillaris* f. L *armilla* bracelet]

Arminian /aȧrmíneeən/ adj. & n. ● adj. relating to the doctrine of Arminius, a Dutch Protestant theologian (d. 1609), who opposed the views of Calvin, esp. on predestination. ● n. an adherent of this doctrine. □□ **Arminianism** n.

armistice /aȧrmistis/ n. a stopping of hostilities by common agreement of the opposing sides; a truce. □ **Armistice Day** former name of Veteran's Day, the anniversary of the World War I armistice of Nov. 11, 1918. [F *armistice* or mod.L *armistitium*, f. *arma* arms (ARM²) + *-stitium* stoppage]
■ see TRUCE.

armlet /aȧrmlit/ n. **1** a band worn around the arm. **2** a small inlet of the sea, or branch of a river.

armoire /aarmwaȧr/ n. a tall, upright, often ornate cupboard or wardrobe. [F, f. L *armarium* chest]

armor n. /aȧrmər/ n. & v. (*Brit.* **armour**) ● n. **1** a defensive covering, usu. of metal, formerly worn to protect the body in fighting. **2 a** (in full **armor plate**) a protective metal covering for an armed vehicle, ship, etc. **b** armored fighting vehicles collectively. **3** a protective covering or shell on certain animals and plants. **4** heraldic devices. ● v.tr. (usu. as **armored** adj.) provide with a protective covering, and often with guns (*armored car*; *armored train*). [ME f. OF *armure* f. L *armatura*: see ARMATURE]

armorer n. /aȧrmərər/ n. (*Brit.* **armourer**) **1** a maker or repairer of arms or armor. **2** an official in charge of a ship's or a regiment's arms. [AF *armurer*, OF *-urier* (as ARMOR, -ER⁵)]

armory¹ /aȧrmoree/ n. (*Brit.* **armoury**) (pl. **-ies**) **1 a** a place where arms are kept; an arsenal. **b** a place where military reservists are trained or headquartered. **2** an array of weapons, defensive resources, usable material, etc. **3** a place where arms are manufactured. [ME f. OF *armoirie*, *armoterie* f. *armoier* to blazon f. *arme* ARM²: assim. to ARMORY]

armory² /aȧrmoree/ n. (pl. **-ies**) heraldry. □□ **armorial** /aarmóreeəl/ adj. [OF *armoierie*: see ARMORY¹]

armour *Brit.* var. of ARMOR.

armourer *Brit.* var. of ARMORER.

armoury *Brit.* var. of ARMORY¹.

armpit /aȧrmpit/ n. **1** the hollow under the arm at the shoulder. **2** *colloq.* a place or part considered disgusting or contemptible (*the armpit of the world*).

armrest /aȧrmrest/ n. = ARM¹ 3b.

army /aȧrmee/ n. (pl. **-ies**) **1** an organized force armed for fighting on land. **2** (prec. by *the*) the military profession. **3** (often foll. by *of*) a very large number (*an army of locusts*; *an army of helpers*). **4** an organized body regarded as working for a particular cause. □ **army ant** any ant of the subfamily Dorylinae, foraging in large groups. [ME f. OF *armee* f. Rmc *armata* fem. past part. of *armare* arm]
■ **1** troops, soldiers, armed forces; legion, *archaic* host. **2** see MILITARY n. **3** see HOST¹.

armyworm /aȧrmeewərm/ n. any of various moth or fly larvae occurring in destructive swarms.

arnica /aȧrnikə/ n. **1** any composite plant of the genus *Arnica*, having erect stems bearing yellow daisy-like flower heads. **2** a medicine prepared from this, used for bruises, etc. [mod.L: orig. unkn.]

aroid /áiroyd/ adj. of or relating to the family Araceae, including arums. [ARUM + -OID]

aroma /ərṓmə/ n. **1** a fragrance; a distinctive and pleasing smell, often of food. **2** a subtle pervasive quality. [L f. Gk *arōma* *-atos* spice]
■ **1** smell, odor, fragrance, scent, perfume, bouquet, redolence, *archaic* savor. **2** aura, atmosphere, flavor, character, redolence, savor, hint, suggestion.

aromatherapy /ərṓmethérəpee/ n. the use of plant extracts and essential oils in massage. □□ **aromatherapeutic** /-pyŏŏtik/ adj. **aromatherapist** n.

aromatic /árəmátik/ adj. & n. ● adj. **1** fragrant; (of a smell) pleasantly pungent. **2** *Chem.* of organic compounds having an unsaturated ring, esp. containing a benzene ring. ● n. an aromatic substance. □□ **aromatically** adv. **aromaticity** /árəmətísitee/ n. [ME f. OF *aromatique* f. LL *aromaticus* f. Gk *arōmatikos* (as AROMA, -IC)]
■ adj. **1** fragrant, spicy, pungent, perfumy, perfumed, sweet-smelling, balmy. □□ **aromaticity** see FRAGRANCE 2.

aromatize /ərṓmetīz/ v.tr. *Chem.* convert (a compound) into an aromatic structure. □□ **aromatization** /-tizáyshən/ n.

arose past of ARISE.

around /ərównd/ adv. & prep. ● adv. **1** on every side; on all sides. **2** in various places; here and there; at random (*fool around*; *shop around*). **3** *colloq.* **a** in existence; available (*has been around for weeks*). **b** near at hand (*it's good to have you around*). **4** approximately (*around 400 people attended*). **5** with circular motion (*wheels go around*). **6** with return to the starting point or an earlier state (*summer soon comes around*). **7 a** with rotation, or change to an opposite position (*he turned around to look*). **b** with change to an opposite opinion, etc. (*they were angry but I soon won them around*). **8** to, at, or affecting all or many points of a circumference or an area or the members of a company, etc. (*tea was then handed around*;

/.../ **pronunciation**	● **part of speech**
□ **phrases, idioms, and compounds**	
□□ **derivatives**	■ **synonym section**
cross-references appear in SMALL CAPITALS or *italics*	

may I look around?). **9** in every direction from a center or within a radius (*spread destruction around; everyone for a mile around*). **10** by a circuitous way (*will you jump over or go around?; go a long way around*). **11 a** to a person's house, etc. (*ask him around; will be around soon*). **b** to a more prominent or convenient position (*brought the car around*). **12** measuring a (specified distance) in girth. ● *prep.* **1** on or along the circuit of. **2** on every side of; enveloping. **3** here and there; in or near (*chairs around the room*). **4** (of amount, time, etc.) about; at a time near to (*come around four o'clock; happened around June*). **5** so as to encircle or enclose (*tour around the world; has a blanket around him*). **6** at or to points on the circumference of (*sat around the table*). **7** with successive visits to (*hawks them around the cafés*). **8** in various directions from or with regard to (*towns around; shells bursting around them*). **9** having as an axis of revolution or as a central point (*turns around its center of gravity; write a book around an event*). **10 a** so as to double or pass in a curved course (*go around the corner*). **b** having passed in this way (*around the corner*). **c** in the position that would result from this (*find them around the corner*). **11** so as to come close from various sides but not into contact. **12** at various places in or around (*had lots of clocks around the house to always know the time*). ● □ **around the bend** see BEND¹. **have been around** *colloq.* be widely experienced. [A² + ROUND]
■ *adv.* **1** all around *or* around, everywhere, in every direction, on all sides *or* every side, round about, all over. **2** about, all about, everywhere, all over, back and forth, up and down, to and fro, here and there, hither and thither, far and wide, *Brit.* round, *literary & dial.* hither and yon; at random. **3** see ABOUT *adv.* 1, AVAILABLE 2. **7 a** about. **8** about. **9** about, in the neighborhood *or* vicinity, in the area, on all sides. **10** in a circle *or* circuit, in *or* by a circular route *or* path, in *or* by a circuitous route *or* path, circuitously. **12** in perimeter *or* periphery. ● *prep.* **1** on, along. **2** about, surrounding, encompassing, enveloping, encircling, on all sides of, in all directions from, enclosing, *Brit.* round. **4 b** about, (at) approximately, (at) roughly, (at) nearly, (at) almost, circa; sometime in *or* during. **5** about, encircling, enclosing; orbiting. **6** about, near. **8** about, near, in the neighborhood *or* vicinity of, in the area of. **12** here and there, in, about, throughout, all over, everywhere in. □ **have been around** know the ropes *or* setup, know one's stuff, be an old hand, esp. *Brit. colloq.* be a dab hand.

arouse /ərówz/ *v.tr.* **1** induce; call into existence (esp. a feeling, emotion, etc.). **2** awake from sleep. **3** stir into activity. **4** stimulate sexually. □□ **arousable** *adj.* **arousal** *n.* **arouser** *n.* [A-² + ROUSE]
■ **1** initiate, excite, stir up, call forth, stimulate, kindle, awaken, induce, summon up, spark (off), provoke, encourage, inspire, foster, foment. **2** awaken, raise (up), wake up, waken, rouse, revive, stir (up). **3** rouse, activate, stir up, animate, enliven, vivify, quicken, impassion, move. **4** excite, stimulate, *colloq.* turn on. □□ **arousal** excitement, stimulation, incitement, encouragement, fomentation, awakening, revival; activation, animation, enlivenment, vivification. **arouser** stimulator, inciter, encourager, fomenter, reviver, animator; stimulus, inspiration.

arpeggio /aarpéjeeō/ *n.* (*pl.* **-os**) *Mus.* the notes of a chord played in succession, either ascending or descending. [It. f. *arpeggiare* play the harp f. *arpa* harp]

arquebus var. of HARQUEBUS.

arr. *abbr.* **1** *Mus.* arranged by. **2** arrives.

arrack /árək/ *n.* (also **arak** /ərák/) an alcoholic liquor, esp. distilled from coco sap or rice. [Arab. ʿaraḳ sweat, alcoholic liquor from grapes or dates]

arraign /əráyn/ *v.tr.* **1** indict before a court; formally accuse. **2** find fault with; call into question (an action or statement). □□ **arraignment** *n.* [ME f. AF *arainer* f. OF *araisnier* (ult. as AD-, L *ratio -onis* reason, discourse)]
■ **1** see INDICT.

arrange /əráynj/ *v.* **1** *tr.* put into the required or suitable or-

---

der; classify. **2** *tr.* plan or provide for; cause to occur (*arranged a meeting*). **3** *tr.* settle beforehand the order or manner of. **4** *intr.* take measures; make plans; give instructions (*arrange to be there at eight; arranged for a taxi to come*). **5** *intr.* come to an agreement (*arranged with her to meet later*). **6** *tr.* a *Mus.* adapt (a composition) for performance with instruments or voices other than those originally specified. **b** *Brit.* adapt (a play, etc.) for broadcasting. **7** *tr.* settle (a dispute, etc.). □□ **arrangeable** *adj.* **arranger** *n.* (esp. in sense 6). [ME f. OF *arangier* f. *à* to + *rangier* RANGE]
■ **1** classify, (put in) order, dispose, array, organize, sort (out), systematize, methodize, marshal, group, set up, rank, line up, align, position. **2, 3** settle, convene, plan, set (up), organize, fix, call, prearrange; predetermine, decide on, prepare, determine, map out; orchestrate, choreograph. **5** agree, consent. **6 a** orchestrate, score, adapt, transcribe. □□ **arranger** organizer, planner, settler, convener, orchestrator; transcriber, adapter.

arrangement /əráynjmənt/ *n.* **1** the act or process of arranging or being arranged. **2** the condition of being arranged; the manner in which a thing is arranged. **3** something arranged. **4** (in *pl.*) plans; preparations (*make your own arrangements*). **5** *Mus.* a composition arranged for performance by different instruments or voices (see ARRANGE 6a). **6** settlement of a dispute, etc. [F (as ARRANGE, -MENT)]
■ **1-3** classification, ordering, organization, grouping, disposition, structuring, planning, groundwork; configuration, combination, construction; order, array, display, structure, alignment, lineup, setup. **4** (*arrangements*) preparations, plans, measures, program, schedule, itinerary. **5** orchestration, instrumentation, adaptation, transcription; interpretation, version. **6** settlement, agreement, terms, plan, contract, covenant, compact.

arrant /árənt/ *attrib.adj.* downright; utter; notorious (*arrant liar; arrant nonsense*). □□ **arrantly** *adv.* [ME, var. of ERRANT, orig. in phrases like *arrant* (= outlawed, roving) *thief*]
■ see BLATANT 1.

arras /árəs/ *n. hist.* a rich tapestry, often hung on the walls of a room, or to conceal an alcove. [*Arras*, a town in NE France famous for the fabric]

array /əráy/ *n. & v.* ● *n.* **1** an imposing or well-ordered series or display. **2** an ordered arrangement, esp. of troops (*battle array*). **3** an outfit or dress (*in fine array*). **4 a** *Math.* an arrangement of quantities or symbols in rows and columns; a matrix. **b** *Computing* an ordered set of related elements. **5** *Law* a list of jurors impaneled. ● *v.tr.* **1** deck; adorn. **2** set in order; marshal (forces). **3** *Law* impanel (a jury). [ME f. AF *araier*, OF *areer* ult. f. a Gmc root, = prepare]
■ *n.* **1** see DISPLAY *n.* 2. **2** see ARRANGEMENT 1-3. ● *v.* **1** see DRESS *v.* 1a, 3. **2** see ARRANGE 1.

arrears /əreérz/ *n.pl.* an amount still outstanding or uncompleted, esp. work undone or a debt unpaid. □ **in arrears** (or **arrear**) behindhand, esp. in payment. □□ **arrearage** *n.* [ME (orig. as *adv.*) f. OF *arere* f. med.L *adretro* (as AD-, *retro* backward): first used in phr. *in arrear*]

arrest /ərést/ *v. & n.* ● *v.tr.* **1 a** seize (a person) and take into custody, esp. by legal authority. **b** seize (a ship) by legal authority. **2** stop or check (esp. a process or moving thing). **3 a** attract (a person's attention). **b** attract the attention of (a person). ● *n.* **1** the act of arresting or being arrested. **2** the legal seizure of a person. **3** a stoppage or check (*cardiac arrest*). □ **under arrest** in custody; deprived of liberty. □□ **arresting** *adj.* **arrestingly** *adv.* **arrestment** *n.* [ME f. OF *arester* ult. f. L *restare* remain, stop]
■ *v.* **1 a** catch, capture, seize, apprehend, take (in), take into custody *or* charge, pick up, detain, collar, *colloq.* run *or* pull in, bust, *sl.* nab, cop, pinch, esp. *Brit. sl.* lag, *Brit. sl.* snare. **2** stop, halt, check, stall, retard, slow, forestall, hold up, detain, delay, hinder, restrain, obstruct, block, interrupt, freeze, abort. **3 a** attract, draw, catch, get hold of, secure. ● *n.* **1** seizure, capture, apprehension, detention, restraint, *colloq.* bust. **2** stop, stoppage, check, cessation; retardation, slowness; blockage, obstruction; abortion. □ **under**

arrest in custody, under legal restraint, in the hands of the law, imprisoned, arrested. □□ **arresting** striking, shocking, remarkable, impressive, electrifying, extraordinary, surprising, dazzling, *colloq.* stunning.

arrestable /əréstəbəl/ *adj.* **1** susceptible to arrest. **2** *Brit. Law* (esp. of an offense) such that the offender may be arrested without a warrant.

arrière-pensée /áryairpoNsáy/ *n.* **1** an undisclosed motive. **2** a mental reservation. [F, = behind thought]
■ **1** see MOTIVE *n.*

arris /áris/ *n. Archit.* a sharp edge formed by the meeting of two flat or curved surfaces. [corrupt. f. F *areste*, mod. ARÊTE]

arrival /ərívəl/ *n.* **1 a** the act of arriving. **b** an appearance on the scene. **2** a person or thing that has arrived. □ **new arrival** *colloq.* a newborn child. [ME f. AF *arrivaille* (as ARRIVE, -AL)]
■ **1** coming, advent, appearance, entry, entrance, incoming; dawn; beginning, *formal* commencement. **2** newcomer; immigrant; traveler, passenger; tourist; migrant.

arrive /əˈrív/ *v.intr.* (often foll. by *at, in*) **1** reach a destination; come to the end of a journey or a specified part of a journey (*arrived in Tibet; arrived at the station; arrived late*). **2** (foll. by *at*) reach (a conclusion, decision, etc.). **3** *colloq.* establish one's reputation or position. **4** *colloq.* (of a child) be born. **5** (of a thing) be brought (*the flowers have arrived*). **6** (of a time) come (*her birthday arrived at last*). [ME f. OF *ariver*, ult. as AD- + L *ripa* shore]
■ **1** come, make one's *or* its appearance, come on the scene, appear, show, turn up, draw *or* pull *or* roll *or* walk in, check in, *colloq.* show *or* roll up, blow in, fetch up; (*arrive at*) make, hit, reach. **2** (*arrive at*) come *or* get to, reach, attain (to), hit, make. **3** succeed, be successful, prosper, get ahead (in the world), reach the top, establish oneself, come through, *colloq.* make it, make the grade, get somewhere, get there.

arrivism /árəvízəm/ *n.* the behavior and condition of an arriviste.

arriviste /áreevéest/ *n.* **1** an ambitious or ruthlessly self-seeking person. **2** a person who is newly arrived in social status, wealth, etc. [F f. *arriver* f. OF (as ARRIVE, -IST)]
■ see UPSTART *n.*

arrogant /árəgənt/ *adj.* (of a person, attitude, etc.) aggressively assertive or presumptuous; overbearing. □□ **arrogance** *n.* **arrogantly** *adv.* [ME f. OF (as ARROGATE, -ANT)]
■ presumptuous, assuming, (self-)assertive, conceited, egotistical, pompous, superior, bumptious, hubristic; haughty, overbearing, imperious, high-handed, overweening, disdainful, opinionated, contemptuous, scornful, snobbish, supercilious, lofty, swaggering, cavalier, *colloq.* uppity, stuck-up, high and mighty, snotty, uppish, esp. *Brit. colloq.* jumped-up, esp. *Brit. sl.* toffee-nosed. □□ **arrogance** self-assertion, impertinence, insolence, presumption, nerve, effrontery, presumptuousness, opinionatedness, self-importance, conceit, egotism, hauteur, haughtiness, loftiness, pride, hubris, pompousness, pomposity, pretension, pretentiousness, bluster, snobbery, snobbishness, *colloq.* snottiness, *sl.* gall, *Brit. sl.* side.

arrogate /árəgayt/ *v.tr.* **1** (often foll. by *to* oneself) claim (power, responsibility, etc.) without justification. **2** (often foll. by *to*) attribute unjustly (to a person). □□ **arrogation** /-gáyshən/ *n.* [L *arrogare arrogat-* (as AD-, *rogare* ask)]
■ **1** see TAKE *v.* 2.

arrondissement /aróNdeesmóN/ *n.* **1** a subdivision of a French department, for local government administration purposes. **2** an administrative district of a large city, esp. Paris. [F]
■ see AREA 2.

arrow /árō/ *n.* **1** a sharp pointed wooden or metal stick shot from a bow as a weapon. **2** a drawn or printed, etc., representation of an arrow indicating a direction; a pointer. □ **broad arrow** *Brit.* a mark formerly used on British prison clothing and other government stores. □□ **arrowy** *adj.* [OE *ar(e)we* f. ON *ör* f. Gmc]

■ **1** see BOLT[1] *n.* 5. **2** see POINTER 1.

arrowhead /árōhed/ *n.* **1** the pointed end of an arrow. **2** an aquatic plant, *Sagittaria sagittaria*, with arrow-shaped leaves. **3** a decorative device resembling an arrowhead.

arrowroot /árōrōōt, -rŏŏt/ *n.* a plant of the family Marantaceae from which a starch is prepared and used for nutritional and medicinal purposes.

arrowworm /árōwerm/ *n.* = CHAETOGNATH.

arroyo /ərŏyō/ *n.* (*pl.* -os) **1** a brook or stream, esp. in an arid region. **2** a gully. [Sp.]

arse esp. *Brit.* var. of ASS[2].

arsenal /áarsənəl/ *n.* **1** a store of weapons. **2** a government establishment for the storage and manufacture of weapons and ammunition. **3** resources regarded collectively. [obs. F *arsenal* or It. *arzanale* f. Arab. *dārşinā'a* f. *dār* house + *sinā'a* art, industry f. *şana'a* fabricate]

arsenic *n. & adj.* ● *n.* /áarsənik/ **1** a nonscientific name for arsenic trioxide, a highly poisonous white powdery substance used in weed killers, rat poison, etc. **2** *Chem.* a brittle semimetallic element, used in semiconductors and alloys. ¶ Symb.: **As**. ● *adj.* /aarsénik/ **1** of or concerning arsenic. **2** *Chem.* containing arsenic with a valence of five. □ **red arsenic** = REALGAR. **white arsenic** = sense 1. □□ **arsenious** /aarseéniəs/ *adj.* [ME f. OF f. L *arsenicum* f. Gk *arsenikon* yellow orpiment, identified with *arsenikos* male, but in fact f. Arab. *al-zarnĭk* f. *al* the + *zarnĭk* orpiment f. Pers. f. *zar* gold]

arsenical /aarsénikəl/ *adj. & n.* ● *adj.* of or containing arsenic. ● *n.* a drug containing arsenic.

arsine /áarseen/ *n. Chem.* arsenic trihydride, a colorless poisonous gas smelling slightly of garlic. [ARSENIC after *amine*]

arsis /áarsis/ *n.* (*pl.* **arses** /-seez/) a stressed syllable or part of a metrical foot in Greek or Latin verse (opp. THESIS). [ME f. LL f. Gk, = lifting f. *airō* raise]

arson /áarson/ *n.* the act of maliciously setting fire to property. □□ **arsonist** *n.* [legal AF, OF, f. med.L *arsio -onis* f. L *ardēre ars-* burn]

arsphenamine /aarsfénəmeen/ *n.* a drug formerly used in the treatment of syphilis and parasitic diseases. [ARSENIC + PHENYL + AMINE]

art[1] /aart/ *n.* **1 a** human creative skill or its application. **b** work exhibiting this. **2 a** (in *pl.*; prec. by *the*) the various branches of creative activity concerned with the production of imaginative designs, sounds, or ideas, e.g., painting, music, writing, considered collectively. **b** any one of these branches. **3** creative activity, esp. painting and drawing, resulting in visual representation (*interested in music but not art*). **4** human skill or workmanship as opposed to the work of nature (*art and nature had combined to make her a great beauty*). **5** (often foll. by *of*) a skill, aptitude, or knack (*the art of writing clearly; keeping people happy is quite an art*). **6** (in *pl.*; usu. prec. by *the*) those branches of learning (esp. languages, literature, and history) associated with creative skill as opposed to scientific, technical, or vocational skills. **7** crafty or wily behavior; an instance of this. □ **art and mystery** *Brit.* any of the special skills or techniques in a specified area. **art deco** /dékō/ the predominant decorative art style of the period 1910–30, characterized by precise and boldly delineated geometric motifs, shapes, and strong colors. **art form 1** any medium of artistic expression. **2** an established form of composition (e.g., the novel, sonata, sonnet, etc.). **art nouveau** /aart nōōvó/ an art style of the late 19th century characterized by flowing lines and natural organic forms. **art paper** *Brit.* smooth coated high-quality paper. **arts and crafts** decorative design and handcrafts. [ME f. OF f. L *ars artis*]
■ **1** creativity, creativeness, creative power(s), artistry, inventiveness, imagination, imaginativeness; creation. **2, 3** visual art(s). **4** skill, skillfulness, ingenuity, talent,

/.../ pronunciation	● part of speech
□ phrases, idioms, and compounds	
□□ derivatives	■ synonym section
cross-references appear in SMALL CAPITALS or *italics*	

artistry, craftsmanship, workmanship; knowledge, expertise; craft, technique, adroitness, dexterity, know-how. **5** skill, talent, craft, knack, aptitude, faculty, technique. **6** (*the arts*) humanities, nonsciences; letters, belles lettres, fine arts, aesthetics, literae humaniores. **7** trickery, craftiness, cunning, wiliness, slyness, guile, deceit, duplicity, artfulness, cleverness, astuteness; wile, scheme, stratagem, artifice, subterfuge, trick, deception, dodge, maneuver.

art² /aart/ *archaic* or *dial.* 2nd *sing. present* of BE.

art. /aart/ *abbr.* article.

artefact *Brit.* var. of ARTIFACT.

artel /aartél/ *n.* an association of craftsmen, peasants, etc., in the former USSR. [Russ.]

arterial /aarteéereeəl/ *adj.* **1** of or relating to an artery (*arterial blood*). **2** (esp. of a road) main, important, esp. linking large cities or towns. [F *artériel* f. *artère* artery]

arterialize /aarteéereeəlīz/ *v.tr.* **1** convert venous into arterial (blood) by reoxygenation esp. in the lungs. **2** provide with an arterial system. □□ **arterialization** *n.*

arteriole /aarteéereeōl/ *n.* a small branch of an artery leading into capillaries. [F *artériole*, dimin. of *artère* ARTERY]

arteriosclerosis /aarteéereeōsklərṓsis/ *n.* the loss of elasticity and thickening of the walls of the arteries, esp. in old age; hardening of the arteries. □□ **arteriosclerotic** /-rótik/ *adj.* [ARTERY + SCLEROSIS]

artery /aartəree/ *n.* (*pl.* **-ies**) **1** any of the muscular-walled tubes forming part of the blood circulation system of the body, carrying oxygen-enriched blood from the heart (cf. VEIN). **2** a main road or railroad line. □□ **arteritis** /-rítis/ *n.* [ME f. L *arteria* f. Gk *artēria* prob. f. *airō* raise]

artesian well /aarteézhən/ *n.* a well bored perpendicularly, esp. through rock, into water-bearing strata lying at an angle, so that natural pressure produces a constant supply of water with little or no pumping. [F *artésien* f. *Artois*, an old French province]

artful /aartfool/ *adj.* **1** (of a person or action) crafty; deceitful. **2** skillful; clever. □□ **artfully** *adv.* **artfulness** *n.*
■ **1** scheming, wily, sly, cunning, foxy, crafty, deceitful, underhand, underhanded, double-dealing, guileful, disingenuous. **2** ingenious, clever, astute, shrewd, dexterous, skillful. □□ **artfully** see *astutely* (ASTUTE). **artfulness** see ART¹ 7, ARTIFICE 2a.

arthritis /aarthrítis/ *n.* inflammation of a joint or joints. □□ **arthritic** /-thrítik/ *adj.* & *n.* [L f. Gk f. *arthron* joint]

arthropod /aarthrəpod/ *n. Zool.* any invertebrate animal of the phylum Arthropoda, with a segmented body, jointed limbs, and an external skeleton, e.g., an insect, spider, or crustacean. [Gk *arthron* joint + *pous podos* foot]

arthroscope /aarthrəskōp/ *n.* an endoscope for viewing the interior of a joint, as the knee. □□ **arthroscopic** *adj.* **arthroscopy** *n.* [Gk *arthron* joint + -SCOPE]

Arthurian /aarthōóreeən/ *adj.* relating to or associated with King Arthur, the legendary British ruler, or his court.

artichoke /aartichōk/ *n.* **1** a European plant, *Cynara scolymus*, allied to the thistle. **2** (in full **globe artichoke**) the flower head of the artichoke, the bracts of which have edible bases **3** = JERUSALEM ARTICHOKE. [It. *articiocco* f. Arab. *al-karšūfa*]

article /aartikəl/ *n.* & *v.* ● *n.* **1** (often in *pl.*) an item or commodity, usu. not further distinguished (*a collection of odd articles*). **2** a nonfictional essay, esp. one included with others in a newspaper, magazine, journal, etc. **3 a** a particular part (*an article of faith*). **b** a separate clause or portion of any document (*articles of apprenticeship*). **4** *Gram.* the definite or indefinite article. ● *v.tr.* bind by articles of apprenticeship. □ **articles of agreement** the terms on which seamen take service on a ship. **definite article** *Gram.* the word (*the* in English) preceding a noun and implying a specific or known instance (as in *the book on the table*; *the art of government*; *the famous university at Oxford*). **indefinite article** *Gram.* the word (e.g., *a*, *an*, *some* in English) preceding a noun and implying lack of specificity (as in *bought me a book*; *government is an art*; *went to a state university*). [ME f. OF f. L *articulus* dimin. of *artus* joint]

■ *n.* **1** see THING 2, 3, ITEM 1, 2. **2** see ESSAY *n.* 1. **3** see ITEM *n.* 1, 2. ● *v.* see APPRENTICE *v.*

articular /aartíkyələr/ *adj.* of or relating to the joints. [ME f. L *articularis* (as ARTICLE, -AR¹)]

articulate *adj.* & *v.* ● *adj.* /aartíkyələt/ **1** able to speak fluently and coherently. **2** (of sound or speech) having clearly distinguishable parts. **3** having joints. ● *v.* /aartíkyəlayt/ **1** *tr.* **a** pronounce (words, syllables, etc.) clearly and distinctly. **b** express (an idea, etc.) coherently. **2** *intr.* speak distinctly (*was quite unable to articulate*). **3** *tr.* (usu. in *passive*) connect by joints. **4** *tr.* mark with apparent joints. **5** *intr.* (often foll. by *with*) form a joint. □ **articulated lorry** *Brit.* a truck consisting of two or more trailers connected by a flexible joint. □□ **articulacy** *n.* **articulately** *adv.* **articulateness** *n.* **articulator** *n.* [L *articulatus* (as ARTICLE, -ATE²)]
■ *adj.* **1** see FLUENT, COHERENT. **3** articulated, jointed, hinged. ● *v.* **1 a** see ENUNCIATE 1, PRONOUNCE 1. **b** see EXPRESS¹ 1, 2.

articulation /aartíkyəláyshən/ *n.* **1 a** the act of speaking. **b** articulate utterance; speech. **2 a** the act or a mode of jointing. **b** a joint. [F *articulation* or L *articulatio* f. *articulare* joint (as ARTICLE, -ATION)]

artifact /aartifakt/ *n.* (*Brit.* **artefact**) **1** a product of human art and workmanship. **2** *Archaeol.* a product of prehistoric or aboriginal workmanship as distinguished from a similar object naturally produced. **3** *Biol.*, etc., a feature not naturally present, introduced during preparation or investigation (e.g., as in the preparation of a slide). □□ **artifactual** /-fákchōoəl/ *adj.* (in senses 1 and 2). [L *arte* (ablat. of *ars* art) + *factum* (neut. past part. of *facere* make)]
■ **1** product, commodity, item, article, object.

artifice /aartifis/ *n.* **1** a clever device; a contrivance. **2 a** cunning. **b** an instance of this. **3** skill; dexterity. **4** the products of human skill; man-made objects. [F f. L *artificium* f. *ars artis* art, *-ficium* making f. *facere* make]
■ **1** stratagem, device, maneuver, trick, contrivance, wile, ruse, subterfuge, expedient, dodge. **2 a** cunning, trickery, craft, craftiness, artfulness, guile, duplicity, deception, chicanery, underhandedness, shrewdness, slyness, wiliness, trickiness. **3** see DEXTERITY 1.

artificer /aartífisər/ *n.* **1** an inventor. **2** a craftsman. [ME f. AF, prob. alt. of OF *artificien*]

artificial /aartifíshəl/ *adj.* **1** produced by human art or effort rather than originating naturally (*an artificial lake*). **2** not real; imitation; fake (*artificial flowers*). **3** affected; insincere (*an artificial smile*). □ **artificial insemination** the injection of semen into the vagina or uterus other than by sexual intercourse. **artificial intelligence** the application of computers to areas normally regarded as requiring human intelligence. **artificial kidney** an apparatus that performs the functions of the human kidney (outside the body), when one or both organs are damaged. **artificial respiration** the restoration or initiation of breathing by manual or mechanical or mouth-to-mouth methods. **artificial silk** rayon. □□ **artificiality** /-sheeálitee/ *n.* **artificially** *adv.* [ME f. OF *artificiel* or L *artificialis* (as ARTIFICE, -AL)]
■ **1, 2** synthetic, man-made, manufactured, fabricated; imitation, simulated, plastic; made-up, concocted, bogus, fake, sham, false, counterfeit, *colloq.* phony. **3** affected, unnatural, forced, pretended, high-sounding, feigned, synthetic, assumed, contrived, factitious; insincere, sham, false, meretricious, hollow, faked, *colloq.* phony. □□ **artificiality** see AFFECTATION 1.

artillery /aartílaree/ *n.* (*pl.* **-ies**) **1** large-caliber guns used in warfare on land. **2** a branch of the armed forces that uses these. □□ **artillerist** *n.* [ME f. OF *artillerie* f. *artiller* alt. of *atillier*, *atirier* equip, arm]

artilleryman /aartílareeman/ *n.* (*pl.* **-men**) a member of the artillery.

artisan /aartizən, -sən/ *n.* **1** a skilled, esp. manual, worker or craftsman. **2** *Brit.* a mechanic. □□ **artisanship** *n.* [F f. It. *artigiano*, ult. f. L *artitus* past part. of *artire* instruct in the arts]
■ **1** see WORKER.

artist /aartist/ *n.* **1** a painter. **2** a person who practices any of the arts. **3** a professional performer, esp. a singer or dancer. **4** a person who works with the dedication and attributes associated with an artist (*an artist in crime*). **5** *colloq.* a devotee; a habitual or skillful practicer of a specified activity (*con artist*). □□ **artistry** *n.* [F *artiste* f. It. *artista* (as ART[1], -IST)]

■ **1, 2** see DESIGNER 1. **3** see *performer* (PERFORM). **4, 5** see SPECIALIST 2. □□ **artistry** see SKILL.

artiste /aarteést/ *n.* esp. *Brit. n.* = ARTIST 3.

artistic /aartístik/ *adj.* **1** having natural skill in art. **2** made or done with art. **3** of art or artists. □□ **artistically** *adv.*

■ **1** see CREATIVE.

artless /aártlis/ *adj.* **1** guileless; ingenuous. **2** not resulting from or displaying art. **3** clumsy. □□ **artlessly** *adv.* **artlessness** *n.*

■ **1** innocent, sincere, guileless, ingenuous, true, natural, open, genuine, simple, direct, candid, frank, honest, straightforward, aboveboard, uncomplicated, undevious, undeceptive, *colloq.* on the up-and-up; unassuming, unaffected, unpretentious, naive, unsophisticated, plain, ordinary, humble. **2** unartistic, unimaginative, uncreative, talentless. **3** clumsy, inept, unskilled, untalented, unskillful, awkward, bungling, unpracticed, inexperienced, inexpert, primitive, unproficient, incompetent, crude.

artsy-craftsy /aártsee-kráftsee/ *adj.* quaintly artistic; (of furniture, etc.) seeking stylistic effect rather than usefulness or comfort.

artwork /aártwərk/ *n.* **1** an artistic work, esp. in the visual arts. **2** the illustrations in a printed work.

■ see ILLUSTRATION 1.

arty /aártee/ *adj.* (**artier, artiest**) *colloq.* pretentiously or affectedly artistic. □□ **artiness** *n.*

arum /áirəm/ *n.* any plant of the genus *Arum*, usu. stemless with arrow-shaped leaves. □ **arum lily** = CALLA 1. [L f. Gk *aron*]

arvo /aárvō/ *n. Austral. sl.* afternoon. [abbr.]

-ary[1] /eree/ *suffix* **1** forming adjectives (*budgetary; contrary; primary; unitary*). **2** forming nouns (*dictionary; fritillary; granary; January*). [F *-aire* or L *-arius* 'connected with']

-ary[2] /eree/ *suffix* forming adjectives (*military*). [F *-aire* or f. L *-aris* 'belonging to']

Aryan /áireeən/ *n. & adj.* ● *n.* **1** a member of the peoples speaking any of the languages of the Indo-European (esp. Indo-Iranian) family. **2** the parent language of this family. **3** *improperly* (in Nazi ideology) a Caucasian not of Jewish descent. ● *adj.* of or relating to Aryan or the Aryans. [Skr. *āryas* noble]

aryl /áril/ *n. Chem.* any radical derived from or related to an aromatic hydrocarbon by removal of a hydrogen atom. [G *Aryl* (as AROMATIC, -YL)]

AS *abbr.* **1** Anglo-Saxon. **2** American Samoa (in official postal usu).

As *symb. Chem.* the element arsenic.

as[1] /az, *unstressed* əz/ *adv., conj., & pron.* ● *adv. & conj.* (*adv.* as antecedent in main sentence; *conj.* in relative clause expressed or implied) . . . to the extent to which . . . is or does, etc. (*I am as tall as he; am as tall as he is; am not so tall as he;* (*colloq.*) *am as tall as him; as many as six; as recently as last week; it is not as easy as you think*). ● *conj.* (with relative clause expressed or implied) **1** (with antecedent *so*) expressing result or purpose (*came early so as to meet us; we so arranged matters as to avoid a long wait; so good as to exceed all hopes*). **2** (with antecedent adverb) having concessive force (*good as it is* = although it is good; *try as he might* = although he might try). **3** (without antecedent adverb) **a** in the manner in which (*do as you like; was regarded as a mistake; they rose as one*). **b** in the capacity or function of (*I speak as your friend; Olivier as Hamlet; as a matter of fact*). **c** during or at the time that (*came up as I was speaking; fell just as I reached the door*). **d** for the reason that; seeing that (*as you are here, we can talk*). **e** for instance (*composers, as Monteverdi*). ● *rel.pron.* (with verb of relative clause expressed or implied) **1** that; who; which (*I had the same trouble as you; he is a writer, as is his wife; such money as you have; such*

countries as France). **2** (with sentence as antecedent) a fact that (*he lost, as you know*). □ **as and when** to the extent and at the time that (*I'll do it as and when I want to*). **as for** with regard to (*as for you, I think you are wrong*). **as from** esp. *Brit.* = *as of* 1. **as if** (or **though**) as would be the case if (*acts as if she were in charge; as if you didn't know!; looks as though we've won*). **as it is** (or **as is**) in the existing circumstances or state. **as it were** in a way; to a certain extent (*he is, as it were, infatuated*). **as long as** see LONG[1]. **as much** see MUCH. **as of 1** on and after (a specified date). **2** as at (a specified time). **as per** see PER. **as regards** see REGARD. **as soon as** see SOON. **as such** see SUCH. **as though** see *as if.* **as to** with respect to; concerning (*said nothing as to money; as to you, I think you are wrong*). **as was** in the previously existing circumstances or state. **as well** see WELL[1]. **as yet** until now or a particular time in the past (usu. with *neg.* and with implied reserve about the future: *have received no news as yet*). [reduced form of OE *alswá* ALSO]

as[2] /as/ *n.* (*pl.* **asses**) a Roman copper coin. [L]

as- /əs/ *prefix* assim. form of AD- before *s.*

asafetida /ásəfétidə/ *n.* (also **asafoetida**) a resinous plant gum with a fetid ammoniac smell, formerly used in medicine, now as an herbal remedy and in Indian cooking. [ME f. med.L f. *asa* f. Pers. *azā* mastic + *fetida* (as FETID)]

a.s.a.p. *abbr.* (also **ASAP**) as soon as possible.

asbestos /ásbéstəs, áz-/ *n.* **1** a fibrous silicate mineral that is not flammable. **2** this used as a heat-resistant or insulating material. □□ **asbestine** /-tin/ *adj.* [ME f. OF *albeston*, ult. f. Gk *asbestos* unquenchable f. *a-* not + *sbestos* f. *sbennumi* quench]

asbestosis /ásbestósis, áz-/ *n.* a lung disease resulting from the inhalation of asbestos particles.

ascarid /áskərid/ *n.* (also **ascaris** /-ris/) a parasitic nematode worm of the genus *Ascaris*, e.g., the intestinal roundworm of humans and other vertebrates. [mod.L *ascaris* f. Gk *askaris*]

ascend /əsénd/ *v.* **1** *intr.* move upwards; rise. **2** *intr.* **a** slope upwards. **b** lie along an ascending slope. **3** *tr.* climb; go up. **4** *intr.* rise in rank or status. **5** *tr.* mount upon. **6** *intr.* (of sound) rise in pitch. **7** *tr.* go along (a river) to its source. **8** *intr. Printing* (of a letter) have part projecting upwards. □ **ascend the throne** become king or queen. [ME f. L *ascendere* (as AD-, *scandere* climb)]

■ **1** see *go up* 1. **2 a** see RISE *v.* 2. **3** see CLIMB *v.* 1. **4** see RISE *v.* 9. **5** mount, climb *or* get *or* clamber (up) on; scale.

ascendancy /əséndənsee/ *n.* (also **ascendency**) (often foll. by *over*) a superior or dominant condition or position.

■ see SUPREMACY 1.

ascendant /əséndənt/ *adj. & n.* ● *adj.* **1** rising. **2** *Astron.* rising toward the zenith. **3** *Astrol.* just above the eastern horizon. **4** predominant. ● *n. Astrol.* the point of the sun's apparent path that is ascendant at a given time. □ **in the ascendant 1** supreme or dominating. **2** rising; gaining power or authority. [ME f. OF f. L (as ASCEND, -ANT)]

■ *adj.* **4** see PREDOMINANT 1.

ascender /əséndər/ *n.* **1 a** a part of a letter that extends above the main part (as in *b* and *d*). **b** a letter having this. **2** a person or thing that ascends.

ascension /əsénshən/ *n.* **1** the act or an instance of ascending. **2** (**Ascension**) the ascent of Christ into heaven on the fortieth day after the Resurrection. □ **Ascension Day** Thursday on which this is celebrated annually. **right ascension** *Astron.* longitude measured along the celestial equator. □□ **ascensional** *adj.* [ME f. OF f. L *ascensio -onis* (as ASCEND, -ION)]

ascent /əsént/ *n.* **1** the act or an instance of ascending. **2 a** an upward movement or rise. **b** advancement or progress

---

/. . ./ **pronunciation**	● **part of speech**
□ **phrases, idioms, and compounds**	
□□ **derivatives**	■ **synonym section**
cross-references appear in SMALL CAPITALS or *italics*	

(*the ascent of mammals*). **3** a way by which one may ascend; an upward slope. [ASCEND, after *descent*]

ascertain /ásərtáyn/ *v.tr.* **1** find out as a definite fact. **2** get to know. □□ **ascertainable** *adj.* **ascertainment** *n.* [ME f. OF *acertener*, stem *acertain*- f. *à* to + CERTAIN]
■ **1** see DETERMINE 1. **2** see LEARN 5.

ascesis /əséesis/ *n.* the practice of self-discipline. [Gk *askēsis* training f. *askeō* exercise]

ascetic /əsétik/ *n. & adj.* ● *n.* a person who practices severe self-discipline and abstains from all forms of pleasure, esp. for religious or spiritual reasons. ● *adj.* relating to or characteristic of ascetics or asceticism; abstaining from pleasure. □□ **ascetically** *adv.* **asceticism** /-tisizəm/ *n.* [med.L *asceticus* or Gk *askētikos* f. *askētēs* monk f. *askeō* exercise]
■ *adj.* see SPARTAN *adj.*

ascidian /əsídeeən/ *n.* Zool. any tunicate animal of the class Ascidiacea, often found in colonies, the adults sedentary on rocks or seaweeds, e.g., the sea squirt. [mod.L *Ascidia* f. Gk *askidion* dimin. of *askos* wineskin]

ASCII /áskee/ *abbr.* Computing American Standard Code for Information Interchange.

ascites /əsíteez/ *n.* (*pl.* same) Med. the accumulation of fluid in the abdominal cavity, causing swelling. [ME f. LL f. Gk f. *askitēs* f. *askos* wineskin]

ascorbic acid /əskáwrbik/ *n.* a vitamin found in citrus fruits and green vegetables, essential in maintaining healthy connective tissue, a deficiency of which results in scurvy. Also called *vitamin C.*

ascot /áskot, -kət/ *n.* a scarf-like item of neckwear with broad ends worn looped to lie flat one over the other against the chest. [f. its being worn traditionally by men attending the races at Ascot, England]

ascribe /əskríb/ *v.tr.* (usu. foll. by *to*) **1** attribute or impute (*ascribes his well-being to a sound constitution*). **2** regard as belonging. □□ **ascribable** *adj.* [ME f. L *ascribere* (as AD-, *scribere script-* write)]
■ see ATTRIBUTE *v.*

ascription /əskrípshən/ *n.* **1** the act or an instance of ascribing. **2** a preacher's words ascribing praise to God at the end of a sermon. [L *ascriptio -onis* (as ASCRIBE)]

asdic /ázdik/ *n.* = SONAR. [initials of *A*llied *S*ubmarine *D*etection *I*nvestigation *C*ommittee]

-ase /ays/ *suffix* Biochem. forming the name of an enzyme (*amylase*). [DIASTASE]

ASEAN /áseeən/ *abbr.* Association of South East Asian Nations.

asepsis /aysépsis/ *n.* **1** the absence of harmful bacteria, viruses, or other microorganisms. **2** a method of achieving asepsis in surgery.

aseptic /ayséptik/ *adj.* **1** free from contamination caused by harmful bacteria, viruses, or other microorganisms. **2** (of a wound, instrument, or dressing) surgically sterile or sterilized. **3** (of a surgical method, etc.) aiming at the elimination of harmful microorganisms, rather than counteraction (cf. ANTISEPTIC).
■ **2** see STERILE 3.

asexual /aysékshōōəl/ *adj.* Biol. **1** without sex or sexual organs. **2** (of reproduction) not involving the fusion of gametes. **3** without sexuality. □□ **asexuality** /-shōōálitee/ *n.* **asexually** *adv.*

ash[1] /ash/ *n.* **1** (often in *pl.*) the powdery residue left after the burning of any substance. **2** (*pl.*) the remains of the human body after cremation or disintegration. **3** ashlike material thrown out by a volcano. □ **ash blond** (or **blonde**) **1** a very pale blond color. **2** a person with hair of this color. **Ash Wednesday** the first day of Lent (from the custom of marking the foreheads of penitents with ashes on that day). [OE *æsce*]

ash[2] /ash/ *n.* **1** any tree of the genus *Fraxinus*, with silvery-gray bark, compound leaves, and hard, tough, pale wood. **2** its wood. **3** an Old English runic letter, = æ (named from a word of which it was the first letter). [OE *æsc* f. Gmc]

ashamed /əsháymd/ *adj.* (usu. *predic.*) **1** (often foll. by *of* (= with regard to), *for* (= on account of), or *to* + infin.) embarrassed or disconcerted by shame (*ashamed of his aunt*;

ashamed of having lied; *ashamed for you*; *ashamed to be seen with him*). **2** (foll. by *to* + infin.) hesitant; reluctant (but usu. not actually refusing or declining) (*am ashamed to admit that I was wrong*). □□ **ashamedly** /-midlee/ *adv.* [OE *āscamod* past part. of *āscamian* feel shame (as A-[2], SHAME)]
■ **1** embarrassed, conscience-stricken, remorseful, abashed, disconcerted, humiliated, chagrined, mortified, blushing, shamefaced, sheepish, red-faced. **2** afraid, sorry.

ashbin /áshbin/ *n.* Brit. a receptacle for the disposal of ashes.

ash can /áshkan/ *n.* a container for household trash.

ashen[1] /áshən/ *adj.* **1** of or resembling ashes. **2** ash colored; gray or pale.
■ **2** see PALE[1] *adj.* 1, 2.

ashen[2] /áshən/ *adj.* **1** of or relating to the ash tree. **2** *archaic* made of ash wood.

Ashkenazi /áashkənáazee/ *n.* (*pl.* **Ashkenazim** /-zim/) **1** an eastern European Jew. **2** a Jew of eastern European ancestry (cf. SEPHARDI). □□ **Ashkenazic** *adj.* [mod.Heb., f. *Ashkenaz* (Gen. 10:3)]

ashlar /áshlər/ *n.* **1** a large square-cut stone used in building. **2** masonry made of ashlars. **3** such masonry used as a facing on a rough rubble or brick wall. [ME f. OF *aisselier* f. L *axilla* dimin. of *axis* board]

ashlaring /áshləring/ *n.* **1** ashlar masonry. **2** the short upright boarding in a garret which cuts off the acute angle between the roof and the floor.

ashore /əsháwr/ *adv.* toward or on the shore or land (*sailed ashore*; *stayed ashore*).

ashram /áashrəm/ *n. Ind.* a place of religious retreat for Hindus; a hermitage. [Skr. *āshrama* hermitage]

ashtray /áshtray/ *n.* a small receptacle for cigarette ashes, butts, etc.

ashy /áshee/ *adj.* (**ashier, ashiest**) **1** = ASHEN[1]. **2** covered with ashes.

Asian /áyzhən, -shən/ *n. & adj.* ● *n.* **1** a native of Asia. **2** a person of Asian descent. ● *adj.* of or relating to Asia or its people, customs, or languages. [L *Asianus* f. Gk *Asianos* f. *Asia*]

Asiatic /áyzheeátik, -shee-, -zee-/ *n. & adj.* ● *n. offens.* an Asian. ● *adj.* Asian. [L *Asiaticus* f. Gk *Asiatikos*]

A-side /áysīd/ *n.* the side of a phonograph record regarded as the main one.

aside /əsíd/ *adv. & n.* ● *adv.* **1** to or on one side; away. **2** out of consideration (placed after noun: *joking aside*). ● *n.* **1** words spoken in a play for the audience to hear, but supposed not to be heard by the other characters. **2** an incidental remark. □ **aside from** apart from. **set aside 1** put to one side. **2** keep for a special purpose or future use. **3** reject or disregard. **4** annul. **5** remove (land) from agricultural production for fallow, forestry, or other use. **take aside** engage (a person) esp. in a private conversation. [orig. *on side*: see A[2]]
■ *adv.* see APART 3. □ **aside from** see *apart from* 1. **set aside** annul, cancel, nullify, declare *or* render null and void, reverse, repudiate, abrogate, quash, overturn, overrule, discard.

asinine /ásinīn/ *adj.* **1** stupid. **2** of or concerning asses; like an ass. □□ **asininity** /-nínitee/ *n.* [L *asininus* f. *asinus* ass]
■ see STUPID *adj.* 1, 5.

-asis /əsis/ *suffix* (usu. as **-iasis**) forming the names of diseases (*psoriasis*; *satyriasis*). [L f. Gk *-asis* in nouns of state f. verbs in *-aō*]

ask /ask/ *v.* **1** *tr.* call for an answer to or about (*ask her about it*; *ask him his name*; *ask a question of him*). **2** *tr.* seek to obtain from another person (*ask a favor of*; *ask to be allowed*). **3** *tr.* (usu. foll. by *out* or *over*, or *to* (a function, etc.)) invite; request the company of (*must ask them over*; *asked her to dinner*). **4** *intr.* (foll. by *for*) **a** seek to obtain, meet, or be directed to (*ask for a donation*; *ask for the post office*; *asking for you*). **b** invite; provoke (trouble, etc.) by one's behavior; bring upon oneself (*they were asking for all they got*). **5** *tr. archaic* require (a thing). □ **ask after** inquire about (esp. a person). **ask for it** *sl.* invite trouble. **asking price** the price of an object set by the seller. **ask me another** *colloq.* I do

not know. **for the asking** (obtainable) for nothing. **I ask you!** an exclamation of disgust, surprise, etc. **if you ask me** *colloq.* in my opinion. □□ **asker** *n.* [OE *āscian*, etc. f. WG]
■ **1** question, interrogate, quiz; inquire of. **2** request, beg, seek, demand, apply *or* appeal *or* solicit *or* petition *or* plead for; beseech, pray, entreat, implore. **3** invite, summon, *archaic or literary* bid. **4** (*ask for*) **a** request, demand, seek, beg, beg *or* apply *or* appeal for, seek, petition *or* plead *or* pray for. **b** invite, attract, encourage, provoke, court, promote, bring upon oneself. □ **ask after** inquire after *or* about. **ask me another** I don't know, I haven't a clue, it beats me, *colloq.* dunno, I haven't the faintest *or* foggiest (idea), no idea, search me, I wouldn't know. **for the asking** see FREE *adv.* 2. **if you ask me** see PERSONALLY 2.

askance /əskáns/ *adv.* (also **askant** /-skánt/) sideways or squinting. □ **look askance at** regard with suspicion or disapproval. [16th c.: orig. unkn.]

askari /askaáree/ *n.* (*pl.* same or **askaris**) an East African soldier or policeman. [Arab. ´*askarī* soldier]

askew /əskyōō/ *adv.* & *predic.adj.* ● *adv.* obliquely; awry. ● *predic.adj.* oblique; awry. [A² + SKEW]
■ *adv.* awry, obliquely, aslant, crookedly. ● *predic.adj.* awry, bent, oblique, crooked, one-sided, lopsided, off-center.

aslant /əslánt/ *adv.* & *prep.* ● *adv.* obliquely or at a slant. ● *prep.* obliquely across (*lay aslant the path*).

asleep /əsleép/ *predic.adj.* & *adv.* **1 a** in or into a state of sleep (*he fell asleep*). **b** inactive; inattentive (*the nation is asleep*). **2** (of a limb, etc.) numb. **3** *euphem.* dead.
■ **1 b** see UNPREPARED. **2** see NUMB *adj.*

aslope /əslṓp/ *adv.* & *predic.adj.* sloping; crosswise. [ME: orig. uncert.]

ASM *abbr.* air-to-surface missile.

asocial /áysṓshəl/ *adj.* **1** not social; antisocial. **2** *colloq.* inconsiderate of or hostile to others.

asp /asp/ *n.* **1** a small viper, *Vipera aspis*, native to southern Europe, resembling the adder. **2** a small venomous snake, *Naja haje*, native to North Africa and Arabia. [ME f. OF *aspe* or L *aspis* f. Gk]

asparagus /əspárəgəs/ *n.* **1** any plant of the genus *Asparagus*. **2** one species of this, *A. officinalis*, with edible young shoots and leaves; this as food. □ **asparagus fern** a decorative plant, *Asparagus setaceus*. [L f. Gk *asparagos*]

aspartame /əspaártaym/ *n.* a very sweet, low-calorie substance used as a sweetener instead of sugar or saccharin. [chem. name *1-methyl* N-L-*aspartyl*-L-*phenylalanine*, f. *aspartic acid* (invented name)]

aspect /áspekt/ *n.* **1 a** a particular component or feature of a matter (*only one aspect of the problem*). **b** a particular way in which a matter may be considered. **2 a** a facial expression; a look (*a cheerful aspect*). **b** the appearance of a person or thing, esp. as presented to the mind of the viewer (*has a frightening aspect*). **3** the side of a building or location facing a particular direction (*southern aspect*). **4** *Gram.* a verbal category or form expressing inception, duration, or completion. **5** *Astrol.* the relative position of planets, etc., measured by angular distance. □ **aspect ratio 1** *Aeron.* the ratio of the span to the mean chord of an airfoil. **2** *Telev.* the ratio of picture width to height. □□ **aspectual** /aspékchōōəl/ *adj.* (in sense 4). [ME f. L *aspectus* f. *adspicere adspect-* look at (as AD-, *specere* look)]
■ **1 a** part, component, constituent, ingredient, feature, attribute, characteristic, quality, detail, bit, facet, side, manifestation, element. **b** viewpoint, point of view, position, standpoint, approach, side, angle, perspective; light, interpretation. **2 a** look, expression, face. **b** appearance, look(s), complexion, face, countenance; bearing, manner, air, *literary* mien. **3** perspective, prospect, outlook, orientation.

aspen /áspən/ *n.* a poplar tree, *Populus tremula*, with especially tremulous leaves. [earlier name *asp* f. OE *æspe* + -EN² forming adj. taken as noun]

asperity /əspéritee/ *n.* (*pl.* **-ies**) **1** harshness or sharpness of

temper or tone. **2** roughness. **3** a rough excrescence. [ME f. OF *asperité* or L *asperitas* f. *asper* rough]
■ **1** see *bitterness* (BITTER).

asperse /əspérs/ *v.tr.* (often foll. by *with*) attack the reputation of; calumniate. □□ **aspersive** *adj.* [ME, = besprinkle, f. L *aspergere aspers-* (as AD-, *spargere* sprinkle)]
■ see DISCREDIT *v.* 1.

aspersion /əspérzhən/ *n.* a slander; a false insinuation. □ **cast aspersions on** attack the reputation or integrity of. [L *as persio* (as ASPERSE, -ION)]
■ slander, libel, false insinuation, calumny, imputation, allegation, detraction, slur, obloquy, defamation, disparagement. □ **cast aspersions on** see BLACKEN 2.

asphalt /ásfalt/ *n.* & *v.* ● *n.* **1** a dark bituminous pitch occurring naturally or made from petroleum. **2** a mixture of this with sand, gravel, etc., for surfacing roads, etc. ● *v.tr.* surface with asphalt. □□ **asphalter** *n.* **asphaltic** /-fáltik/ *adj.* [ME, ult. f. LL *asphalton, -um*, f. Gk *asphalton*]

asphodel /ásfədel/ *n.* **1** any plant of the genus *Asphodelus*, of the lily family. **2** *poet.* an immortal flower growing in Elysium. [L *asphodelus* f. Gk *asphodelos*: cf. DAFFODIL]

asphyxia /asfíkseeə/ *n.* a lack of oxygen in the blood, causing unconsciousness or death; suffocation. □□ **asphyxial** *adj.* **asphyxiant** *adj.* & *n.* [mod.L f. Gk *asphuxia* f. *a-* not + *sphuxis* pulse]

asphyxiate /asfíkseeayt/ *v.tr.* cause (a person) to have asphyxia; suffocate. □□ **asphyxiation** /-áyshən/ *n.* **asphyxiator** *n.*
■ see SMOTHER *v.* 1.

aspic /áspik/ *n.* a savory meat jelly used as a garnish or to contain game, eggs, etc. [F, = ASP, from the colors of the jelly (compared to those of the asp)]

aspidistra /áspidístrə/ *n.* a foliage plant of the genus *Aspidistra*, with broad tapering leaves, often grown as a houseplant. [mod.L f. Gk *aspis -idos* shield (from the shape of the leaves)]

aspirant /áspirənt, əspírənt/ *adj.* & *n.* (usu. foll. by *to, after, for*) ● *adj.* aspiring. ● *n.* a person who aspires. [F *aspirant* or f. L *aspirant-* (as ASPIRE, -ANT)]

aspirate /áspirət/ *adj., n.,* & *v. Phonet.* ● *adj.* **1** pronounced with an exhalation of breath. **2** blended with the sound of *h*. ● *n.* **1** a consonant pronounced in this way. **2** the sound of *h*. ● *v.* /also áspiráyt/ **1 a** *tr.* pronounce with a breath. **b** *intr.* make the sound of *h*. **2** *tr.* draw (fluid) by suction from a vessel or cavity. **3** *tr.* draw (air, fluid, etc.) into the lungs, as by breathing. [L *aspiratus* past part. of *aspirare*: see ASPIRE]

aspiration /áspiráyshən/ *n.* **1** a strong desire to achieve an end; an ambition. **2** the act or process of drawing breath. **3** the action of aspirating. [ME f. OF *aspiration* or L *aspiratio* (as ASPIRATE, -ATION)]
■ **1** ambition, aim, goal, objective, end, purpose, intention, plan, scheme; desire, longing, yearning, craving, hankering, wish, dream, hope.

aspirator /áspiraytər/ *n.* an apparatus for aspirating fluid. [L *aspirare* (as ASPIRATE, -OR)]

aspire /əspír/ *v.intr.* (usu. foll. by *to* or *after*, or *to* + infin.) **1** have ambition or strong desire. **2** *poet.* rise high. [ME f. F *aspirer* or L *aspirare* f. *ad* to + *spirare* breathe]
■ **1** desire, hope, long, wish, aim, yearn; (*aspire to*) dream of, hanker after, have designs on, set one's sights on, go after.

aspirin /ásprin/ *n.* (*pl.* same or **aspirins**) **1** a white powder, acetylsalicylic acid, used to relieve pain and reduce fever. **2** a tablet of this. [G, formed as ACETYL + *spiraeic* (= salicylic) *acid* + -IN]

asquint /əskwínt/ *predic.adj.* & *adv.* (usu. **look asquint**). **1** to one side; from the corner of an eye. **2** with a squint. [ME perh. f. Du. *schuinte* slant]

/.../ **pronunciation**	● **part of speech**
□ **phrases, idioms, and compounds**	
□□ **derivatives**	■ **synonym section**
cross-references appear in SMALL CAPITALS or *italics*	

ass[1] /as/ *n.* **1 a** either of two kinds of four-legged long-eared mammals of the horse genus *Equus*, *E. africanus* of Africa and *E. hemionus* of Asia. **b** (in general use) a donkey. **2 a** stupid person. □ **asses' bridge** = *pons asinorum*. **make an ass of** make (a person) look absurd or foolish. [OE *assa* thr. OCelt. f. L *asinus*]
■ *n.* **2** see DOLT.

ass[2] /as/ *n. & v.* (*Brit.* **arse** /aars/) *coarse sl.* ● *n.* **1** the buttocks. **2** the anus. ● *v.intr.* (usu. foll. by *about*, *around*) play the fool. □ **ass-kisser** = *ass-licker*. **ass-kissing** *n. & adj.* = *ass-licking*. **ass-licker** a toady. **ass-licking** *n. & adj.* obsequious(ness) for the purpose of gaining favor; toadying. ¶ Usually considered a taboo word. [OE *ærs*]
■ *n.* see BUTTOCK. □ **ass-kisser, ass-licker** see *yes-man*. **ass-kissing, ass-licking** (*adj.*) see OBSEQUIOUS.

assagai var. of ASSEGAI.

assai /así/ *adv. Mus.* very (*adagio assai*). [It.]

assail /əsáyl/ *v.tr.* **1** make a strong or concerted attack on. **2** make a resolute start on (a task). **3** make a strong or constant verbal attack on (*was assailed with angry questions*). □□ **assailable** *adj.* [ME f. OF *asaill-* stressed stem of *asalir* f. med.L *assalire* f. L *assilire* (as AD-, *salire salt-* leap)]
■ **1** see ATTACK *v.* 1. **2** see ATTACK *v.* 5.

assailant /əsáylənt/ *n.* a person who attacks another physically or verbally. [F (as ASSAIL)]
■ attacker, assaulter, mugger, aggressor; enemy, adversary, antagonist, opponent, esp. *poet. or formal* foe; detractor, critic.

assassin /əsásin/ *n.* **1** a killer, esp. of a political or religious leader. **2** *hist.* any of a group of Muslim fanatics sent on murder missions in the time of the Crusades. [F *assassin* or f. med.L *assassinus* f. Arab. *ḥaššāš* hashish eater]
■ **1** see KILLER 1.

assassinate /əsásinayt/ *v.tr.* kill (esp. a political or religious leader) for political, fanatical, or religious motives. □□ **assassination** /-náyshən/ *n.* **assassinator** *n.* [med.L *assassinare* f. *assassinus*: see ASSASSIN]
■ see KILL[1] *v.* 1.

assault /əsáwlt/ *n. & v.* ● *n.* **1** a violent physical or verbal attack. **2 a** *Law* an act that threatens physical harm to a person (whether or not actual harm is done). **b** *euphem.* an act of rape. **3** (*attrib.*) relating to or used in an assault (*assault craft*; *assault troops*). **4** a vigorous start made to a lengthy or difficult task. **5** a final rush on a fortified place, esp. at the end of a prolonged attack. ● *v.tr.* **1** make an assault on. **2** *euphem.* rape. □ **assault and battery** *Law* a threatening act that results in physical harm done to a person. **assault course** esp. *Brit.* an obstacle course used in training soldiers, etc. □□ **assaulter** *n.* **assaultive** *adj.* [ME f. OF *asaut*, *assauter* ult. f. L (*salire salt-* leap)]
■ *n.* **1, 5** attack, beating, battering, holdup, mugging, *Law* battery; onslaught, onset, charge, offensive, blitzkrieg, strike, raid, incursion, sortie, invasion, rush, *colloq.* blitz. **2 b** rape, sexual assault, violation, molestation. **4** see ATTEMPT *n.* ● *v.* **1** attack, assail, set or fall or descend upon, pounce upon, storm, come at, beset, charge, rush, lay into; beat (up), batter, harm, hit, strike, punch, *archaic or literary* smite; mug. **2** rape, violate, molest, sexually assault. □□ **assaulter** see AGGRESSOR.

assay /əsáy, ásay/ *n. & v.* ● *n.* **1** the testing of a metal or ore to determine its ingredients and quality. **2** *Chem.*, etc., the determination of the content or strength of a substance. ● *v.* **1** *tr.* make an assay of (a metal or ore). **2** *tr. Chem.* etc., perform a concentration on (a substance). **3** *tr.* show (content) on being assayed. **4** *intr.* make an assay. **5** *tr. archaic* attempt. □ **assay office** an establishment which assays and registers prospectors' claims, gold sales, etc. □□ **assayer** *n.* [ME f. OF *assaier*, *assai*, var. of *essayer*, *essai*: see ESSAY]
■ *v.* **5** see ATTEMPT *v.*

assegai /ásigī/ *n.* (also **assagai** /ásəgī/) a slender iron-tipped spear of hard wood, esp. as used by S. African peoples. [obs. F *azagaie* or Port. *azagaia* f. Arab. *az-zaġāyah* f. *al* the + *zaġāyah* spear]

assemblage /əsémblij/ *n.* **1** the act or an instance of bringing or coming together. **2** a collection of things or gathering of people. **3 a** the act or an instance of fitting together. **b** an object made of pieces fitted together. **4** a work of art made by grouping found or unrelated objects.
■ **1, 2** see ASSEMBLY 1, 2a. **3** see FABRICATION 1.

assemble /əsémbəl/ *v.* **1** *tr. & intr.* gather together; collect. **2** *tr.* arrange in order. **3** *tr.* esp. *Mech.* fit together the parts of. [ME f. OF *asembler* ult. f. L *ad* to + *simul* together]
■ **1** convene, gather, meet, call or get or meet together, summon, muster, marshal, rally, levy, round up, collect, congregate, forgather, *formal* convoke; accumulate, amass, collect, bring or group or lump together, pile or heap up, compile, join or draw together, aggregate. **2** see ARRANGE 1. **3** construct, put together, erect, set up, fit or join or piece together, connect, fabricate, manufacture, make.

assembler /əsémblər/ *n.* **1** a person who assembles a machine or its parts. **2** *Computing* **a** a program for converting instructions written in low-level symbolic code into machine code. **b** the low-level symbolic code itself; an assembly language.

assembly /əsémblee/ *n.* (*pl.* **-ies**) **1** the act or an instance of assembling or gathering together. **2 a** a group of persons gathered together, esp. as a deliberative or legislative body. **b** a gathering of the entire membership of a school. **3** the assembling of a machine or structure or its parts. **4** *Mil.* a call to assemble, given by drum or bugle. □ **assembly language** *Computing* the low-level symbolic code converted by an assembler. **assembly line** machinery arranged in stages by which a product is progressively assembled. **assembly room** (or **shop**) a place where a machine or its components are assembled. **assembly rooms** esp. *Brit.* public rooms in which meetings or social functions are held. [ME f. OF *asemblee* fem. past part. of *asembler*: see ASSEMBLE]
■ **1, 2a** gathering, group, meeting, assemblage, collection, body, circle, company, congregation, flock, crowd, audience, throng, multitude, host; convocation, council, convention, congress, association, caucus, committee, conclave; diet, synod. **3** construction, putting or fitting or joining or piecing together, fabrication, manufacture, making. □ **assembly rooms** see CHAMBER 1a.

assent /əsént/ *v. & n.* ● *v.intr.* (usu. foll. by *to*) **1** express agreement (*assented to my view*). **2** consent (*assented to my request*). ● *n.* **1** mental or inward acceptance or agreement (*a nod of assent*). **2** consent or sanction, esp. official. □ **royal assent** *Brit.* assent of the sovereign to a bill passed by Parliament. □□ **assentor** *n.* (also **assenter**, *as(s)ente* ult. f. L *assentari* (*ad* to, *sentire* think)]
■ *v.* **1** see AGREE 1. **2** see AGREE 2. ● *n.* **1** see CONSENT *n.* **2** see CONSENT *n.*, SANCTION *n.* 1.

assert /əsórt/ *v.* **1** *tr.* declare; state clearly (*assert one's beliefs*; *assert that it is so*). **2** *refl.* insist on one's rights or opinions; demand recognition. **3** *tr.* vindicate a claim to (*assert one's rights*). □□ **assertor** *n.* [L *asserere* (as AD-, *serere sert-* join)]
■ **1** see DECLARE 1.

assertion /əsórshən/ *n.* **1** a declaration; a forthright statement. **2** the act or an instance of asserting. **3** (also **self-assertion**) insistence on the recognition of one's rights or claims. [ME f. F *assertion* or L *assertio* (as ASSERT, -ION)]
■ **1, 2** statement, declaration, claim, affirmation, contention, asseveration, averment, avowal, announcement, pronouncement, allegation, attestation, *Law* affidavit, deposition. **3** insistence, proclamation, representation, affirmation, confirmation; see also *assertiveness* (ASSERTIVE).

assertive /əsórtiv/ *adj.* **1** tending to assert oneself; forthright; positive. **2** dogmatic. □□ **assertively** *adv.* **assertiveness** *n.*
■ **1** declaratory, affirmative, asseverative; forthright, definite, certain, sure, positive, confident, firm, emphatic, bold; aggressive, insistent, forceful. **2** dogmatic, self-assertive, doctrinaire, domineering, opinionated, peremptory, bumptious, pushful, officious, *colloq.* bossy, pushy. □□ **assertively** forcefully, boldly, firmly, confidently, insistently, positively,

emphatically; dogmatically, domineeringly, *colloq.* bossily, pushily; see also *aggressively* (AGGRESSIVE). **assertiveness** forcefulness, boldness, firmness, forthrightness, (self-)assertion, self-assertiveness, dogmatism.

asses *pl.* of AS², ASS¹, ASS².

assess /əsés/ *v.tr.* **1 a** estimate the size or quality of. **b** estimate the value of (a property) for taxation. **2 a** (usu. foll. by *on*) fix the amount of (a tax, etc.) and impose it on a person or community. **b** (usu. foll. by *in, at*) fine or tax (a person, community, etc.) in or at a specific amount (*assessed them at $100*). □□ **assessable** *adj.* **assessment** *n.* [ME f. F *assesser* f. L *assidēre* (as AD-, *sedēre* sit)]

■ **1** see ESTIMATE *v.* 2–4. **2** see TAX *v.* 1. □□ **assessment** SEE MEASUREMENT 1, REVIEW *n.* 1.

assessor /əsésər/ *n.* **1** a person who assesses taxes or estimates the value of property for taxation purposes. **2** a person called upon to advise a judge, committee of inquiry, etc., on technical questions. □□ **assessorial** /ásesáwreeəl/ *adj.* [ME f. OF *assessour* f. L *assessor -oris* assistant judge (as ASSESS, -OR¹): sense 1 f. med.L]

asset /áset/ *n.* **1 a** a useful or valuable quality. **b** a person or thing possessing such a quality or qualities (*is an asset to the firm*). **2** (usu. in *pl.*) **a** property and possessions, esp. regarded as having value in meeting debts, commitments, etc. **b** any possession having value. □ **asset stripping** *Commerce* the practice of taking over a company and selling off its assets to make a profit. [*assets* (taken as pl.), f. AF *asetz* f. OF *asez* enough, ult. f. L *ad* to + *satis* enough]

■ **1 a** talent, strength, advantage, resource, benefit, attraction, selling point, appeal. **b** see PLUS *n.* 3. **2 a** (*assets*) property, resources, possessions, holdings, effects, capital, means, valuables, money, wealth.

asseverate /əsévərayt/ *v.tr.* declare solemnly. □□ **asseveration** /-ráyshən/ *n.* **asseverative** /-rətiv/ *adj.* [L *asseverare* (as AD-, *severus* serious)]

■ see ATTEST 1, 3.

asshole /ás-hōl/ *n.* **1** the anus. **2** *offens.* a term of contempt for a person.

assibilate /əsíbilayt/ *v.tr. Phonet.* **1** pronounce (a sound) as a sibilant or affricate ending in a sibilant. **2** alter (a syllable) to become this. □□ **assibilation** /-láyshən/ *n.* [L *assibilare* (as AD-, *sibilare* hiss)]

assiduity /ásidōŏitee, -dyōō-/ *n.* (*pl.* **-ies**) **1** constant or close attention to what one is doing. **2** (usu. in *pl.*) constant attentions to another person. [L *assiduitas* (as ASSIDUOUS, -ITY)]

■ **1** see APPLICATION 4.

assiduous /əsíjōōəs/ *adj.* **1** persevering; hardworking. **2** attending closely. □□ **assiduously** *adv.* **assiduousness** *n.* [L *assiduus* (as ASSESS)]

■ see DILIGENT. □□ **assiduousness** see APPLICATION 4.

assign /əsín/ *v. & n.* ● *v.tr.* **1** (usu. foll. by *to*) **a** allot as a share, task, or responsibility. **b** appoint to a position, task, etc. **2** fix (a time, place, etc.) for a specific purpose. **3** (foll. by *to*) ascribe or refer to (a reason, date, etc.) (*assigned the manuscript to 1832*). **4** (foll. by *to*) transfer formally (esp. personal property) to (another). ● *n.* a person to whom property or rights are legally transferred. □□ **assignable** *adj.* **assigner** *n.* **assignor** *n.* (in sense 4 of *v.*). [ME f. OF *asi(g)ner* f. L *assignare* mark out to (as AD-, *signum* sign)]

■ *v.* **1 a** allot, allocate, apportion, consign, appropriate, distribute, give (out), grant, hand (out), deal (out), dispense. **b** appoint, designate, order; name, delegate, nominate, attach. **2** fix (on), set apart *or* aside, settle on, determine on, allot, appoint, authorize, designate, ordain, prescribe, specify; choose, select. **3** attribute, ascribe, refer, accredit, put down, impute.

□□ **assignable** attributable, ascribable, imputable.

assignation /ásignáyshən/ *n.* **1 a** an appointment to meet. **b** a secret appointment, esp. between illicit lovers. **2** the act or an instance of assigning or being assigned. [ME f. OF f. L *assignatio -onis* (as ASSIGN, -ATION)]

■ **1** see APPOINTMENT 1.

assignee /ásineé/ *n.* **1** a person appointed to act for another. **2** an assign. [ME f. OF *assigné* past part. of *assigner* ASSIGN]

assignment /əsínmənt/ *n.* **1** something assigned, esp. a task allotted to a person. **2** the act or an instance of assigning or being assigned. **3 a** a legal transfer. **b** the document effecting this. [ME f. OF *assignement* f. med.L *assignamentum* (as ASSIGN, -MENT)]

■ **1** task, obligation, responsibility, chore, duty, position, post, charge, job, mission, commission; lesson, homework. **2** allotment, allocation, apportionment, distribution, dispensation; appointment, designation, nomination, delegation; attribution, specification, ascription.

assimilate /əsímilayt/ *v.* **1** *tr.* **a** absorb and digest (food, etc.) into the body. **b** absorb (information, etc.) into the mind. **c** absorb (people) into a larger group. **2** *tr.* (usu. foll. by *to, with*) make like; cause to resemble. **3** *tr. Phonet.* make (a sound) more like another in the same or next word. **4** *intr.* be absorbed into the body, mind, or a larger group. □□ **assimilable** /əsímələbəl/ *adj.* **assimilation** /-láyshən/ *n.* **assimilative** *adj.* **assimilator** *n.* **assimilatory** /-lətáwree/ *adj.* [ME f. L *assimilare* (as AD-, *similis* like)]

■ **1 b** see DIGEST *v.* 2.

Assiniboin /əsínəboyn/ *n.* **1 a** a N. American people native to northeastern Montana and adjoining parts of Canada. **b** a member of this people. **2** the language of this people.

assist /əsíst/ *v. & n.* ● *v.* **1** *tr.* (often foll. by *in* + verbal noun) help (a person, process, etc.) (*assisted them in running the playgroup*). **2** *intr.* (often foll. by *in, at*) attend or be present (*assisted in the ceremony*). ● *n.* **1** an act of helping. **2** *Sports* a player's action of helping a teammate to put out a runner (as in baseball) or score (as in basketball). □□ **assistance** *n.* **assister** *n.* [ME f. F *assister* f. L *assistere* take one's stand by (as AD-, *sistere* take one's stand)]

■ *v.* **1** aid, help, support, work for *or* with, lend *or* give a hand, back (up), succor; further, promote, abet, advance, benefit, facilitate. **2** take part, have *or* take a hand, be present, attend, be in attendance. □□ **assistance** help, aid, support, succor; backing, reinforcement, relief, benefit.

assistant /əsístənt/ *n.* **1** a helper. **2** (often *attrib.*) a person who assists, esp. as a subordinate in a particular job or role. **3** *Brit.* = *shop assistant.* [ME *assistent* f. med.L *assistens assistent-* present (as ASSIST, -ANT, -ENT)]

■ **1** helper, mate, aide, right-hand man *or* woman, acolyte, amanuensis, PA, girl *or* gal *or* man Friday, *Austral.* offsider, *sl.* gofer; aide-de-camp, adjutant; see also ACCOMPLICE. **2** deputy, subordinate, subsidiary, auxiliary, underling, *colloq.* vice.

assize /əsíz/ *n.* (usu. in *pl.*) *Brit. hist.* a court sitting at intervals in each county of England and Wales to administer the civil and criminal law. [ME f. OF *as(s)ise*, fem. past part. of *aseeir* sit at, f. L *assidēre*: cf. ASSESS]

assn. *abbr.* association.

Assoc. *abbr.* (as part of a title) Association.

associable /əsṓshəbəl/ *adj.* (usu. foll. by *with*) capable of being connected in thought. □□ **associability** *n.* [F f. *associer* (as ASSOCIATE, -ABLE)]

associate *v., n., & adj.* ● *v.* /əsṓsheeayt, -see-/ **1** *tr.* connect in the mind (*associate fireworks with Independence Day*). **2** *tr.* join or combine. **3** *refl.* make oneself a partner; declare oneself in agreement (*associate myself in your endeavor; did not want to associate ourselves with the plan*). **4** *intr.* combine for a common purpose. **5** *intr.* (usu. foll. by *with*) meet frequently or have dealings; be friends. ● *n.* /əsṓsheeət, -see-/ **1** a business partner or colleague. **2** a friend or companion. **3** a subordinate member of a body, institute, etc. **4** a thing connected with another. ● *adj.* /əsṓshiət, əsṓsee-/ **1** joined in companionship, function, or dignity. **2** allied; in the same

---

/. . ./ **pronunciation**	● **part of speech**
□ **phrases, idioms, and compounds**	
□□ **derivatives**	■ **synonym section**
cross-references appear in SMALL CAPITALS or *italics*	

group or category. **3** of less than full status (*associate member*). □□ **associateship** *n.* **associator** *n.* **associatory** /-shee-ətawree, -see-/ *adj.* [E f. L *associatus* past part. of *associare* (as AD-, *socius* sharing, allied)]

■ *v.* **1** link, connect, make a connection between; affiliate, relate. **2** ally, join (up *or* together), unite, combine, couple, confederate, conjoin. **3** (*associate oneself*) ally, align, affiliate, connect, link. **4** unite, join (up *or* together), join ranks *or* forces, make a combined effort. **5** (*associate with*) see, be seen with, socialize *or* fraternize with, mix *or* mingle with, go (out *or* about *or* around) with, consort with, have to do with, hang about *or* around with, *colloq.* pal up with, *sl.* hang out with. ● *n.* **1** colleague, partner, fellow, fellow worker, workmate, coworker, comrade; see also ACCOMPLICE. **2** comrade, companion, friend, mate, confidant(e), *colloq.* pal, buddy. **3** junior member. ● *adj.* **2** allied, affiliate, affiliated, associated; sister, related, connected. **3** subsidiary, secondary; deputy, auxiliary, supplementary, accessory.

association /əsṓseeáyshən/ *n.* **1** a group of people organized for a joint purpose; a society. **2** the act or an instance of associating. **3** fellowship; human contact or cooperation. **4** a mental connection between ideas. **5** *Chem.* a loose aggregation of molecules. **6** *Ecol.* a group of associated plants. □ **Association Football** *Brit.* = SOCCER. □□ **associational** *adj.* [F *association* or med.L *associatio* (as ASSOCIATE, -ATION)]

■ **1** society, organization, confederation, confederacy, federation, league, union, alliance, guild, coalition, group; syndicate, combine, consortium, cooperative. **2** combination, alliance, marriage, union, amalgamation, integration, coalition, confederation. **3** fellowship, companionship, intimacy, friendship, amity, camaraderie, comradeship, relationship, liaison; affiliation, alliance, connection, contact, partnership, cooperation. **4** connection, interconnection, link, affiliation, relationship, bond, tie, thread, linkage, conjunction, correspondence.

associative /əsṓsheeətiv, -see-/ *adj.* **1** of or involving association. **2** *Math.* & *Computing* involving the condition that a group of quantities connected by operators (see OPERATOR 4) gives the same result whatever their grouping, as long as their order remains the same, e.g., $(a \times b) \times c = a \times (b \times c)$.

assonance /ásənəns/ *n.* the resemblance of sound between two syllables in nearby words, arising from the rhyming of two or more accented vowels, but not consonants, or the use of identical consonants with different vowels, e.g., *sonnet*, *porridge*, and *killed*, *cold*, *culled*. □□ **assonant** *adj.* **assonate** /-nayt/ *v.intr.* [F f. L *assonare* respond to (as AD-, *sonus* sound)]

assort /əsáwrt/ *v.* **1** *tr.* (usu. foll. by *with*) classify or arrange in groups. **2** *intr.* suit; fit into; harmonize with (*assort well with*). [OF *assorter* f. *à* to + *sorte* SORT]

■ **1** see CATEGORIZE.

assortative /əsáwrtətiv/ *adj.* assorting. □ **assortative mating** *Biol.* selective mating based on the similarity of the partners' characteristics, etc.

assorted /əsáwrtid/ *adj.* **1** of various kinds put together; miscellaneous. **2** sorted into groups. **3** matched (*ill-assorted*; *poorly assorted*).

■ **1** see MISCELLANEOUS.

assortment /əsáwrtmənt/ *n.* a set of various kinds of things or people put together; a mixed collection.

■ collection, mixture, miscellany, jumble, medley, mélange, array, agglomeration, conglomeration, group, grouping, lot, farrago, hodgepodge, olio, variety, potpourri, salmagundi, gallimaufry, mishmash, mixed bag *or* bunch.

ASSR *abbr. hist.* Autonomous Soviet Socialist Republic.

Asst. *abbr.* Assistant.

assuage /əswáyj/ *v.tr.* **1** calm or soothe (a person, pain, etc.). **2** appease or relieve (an appetite or desire). □□ **assuagement** *n.* **assuager** *n.* [ME f. OF *as(s)ouagier* ult. f. L *suavis* sweet]

■ **1** see STILL[1] *v.* **2** see SLAKE.

assume /əsṓm/ *v.tr.* **1** (usu. foll. by *that* + clause) take or accept as being true, without proof, for the purpose of argument or action. **2** simulate or pretend (ignorance, etc.). **3** undertake (an office or duty). **4** take or put on oneself or itself (an aspect, attribute, debt, etc.) (*the problem assumed immense proportions*). **5** (usu. foll. by *to*) arrogate, usurp, or seize (credit, power, etc.) (*assumed to himself the right of veto*). □□ **assumable** *adj.* **assumedly** /-midlee/ *adv.* [ME f. L *assumere* (as AD-, *sumere* sumpt- take)]

■ **1** presume, suppose, believe, fancy, expect, think, presuppose, take it (for granted *or* as read), accept; surmise, guess. **2** pretend, feign, simulate, affect, fake, counterfeit; profess. **3** take over *or* up, take control of, undertake, accept, adopt; arrogate, claim, appropriate. **4** take on *or* upon oneself *or* itself, don, adopt, acquire. **5** see take over.

assumed /əsṓmd/ *adj.* **1** false; adopted (*went under an assumed name*). **2** supposed; accepted (*assumed income*).

■ **1** sham, false, feigned, affected, adopted, counterfeit, simulated, pretend, spurious, bogus, fake; pseudonymous, made-up, *colloq.* phony. **2** presumed, supposed, accepted, expected, presupposed, taken (for granted); hypothetical, theoretical, suppositional.

assuming /əsṓming/ *adj.* (of a person) taking too much for granted; arrogant; presumptuous.

■ see ARROGANT.

assumption /əsúmpshən/ *n.* **1** the act or an instance of assuming. **2 a** the act or an instance of accepting without proof. **b** a thing assumed in this way. **3** arrogance. **4** (**Assumption**) **a** the reception of the Virgin Mary bodily into heaven, according to Roman Catholic and Orthodox Christian belief. **b** the feast in honor of this (August 15). [ME f. OF *asompsion* or L *assumptio* (as ASSUME, -ION)]

■ **1, 2** see PRESUMPTION 2. **3** see PRESUMPTION 1.

assumptive /əsúmptiv/ *adj.* **1** taken for granted. **2** arrogant. [L *assumptivus* (as ASSUME, -IVE)]

assurance /əshṓrəns/ *n.* **1** a positive declaration that a thing is true. **2** a solemn promise or guarantee. **3** esp. *Brit.* insurance, esp. life insurance. **4** certainty. **5 a** self-confidence. **b** impudence. [ME f. OF *aseürance* f. *aseürer* (as ASSURE, -ANCE)]

■ **1** see DECLARATION 2a. **2** promise, pledge, guarantee, word (of honor), oath, vow, warranty, undertaking, commitment, bond, surety. **3** (life) insurance, indemnity. **4** certainty, sureness, positiveness, fixedness, definiteness, assuredness, certitude, conviction, *archaic* surety. **5 a** self-confidence, self-reliance, confidence, steadiness, intrepidity, self-possession, poise, aplomb, coolness, control, self-control, resolve, *colloq.* gumption; conviction. **b** audacity, impudence, presumption, boldness, brazenness, nerve, cheek, effrontery, insolence, impertinence, *colloq.* brass, *sl.* gall, chutzpah.

assure /əshṓr/ *v.tr.* **1** (often foll. by *of*) **a** make (a person) sure; convince (*assured him of my sincerity*). **b** tell (a person) confidently (*assured him the bus went to Baltimore*). **2 a** make certain of; ensure the happening, etc., of (*will assure her success*). **b** make safe (against overthrow, etc.). **3** confirm; encourage. **4** *Brit.* insure (esp. a life). **5** (as **assured** *adj.*) **a** guaranteed. **b** self-confident. □ **rest assured** remain confident. □□ **assurable** *adj.* **assurer** *n.* [ME f. OF *aseürer* ult. f. L *securus* safe, SECURE]

■ **1 a** convince, persuade, reassure. **b** promise, reassure; assert *or* affirm *or* state *or* asseverate to, *archaic or literary* avouch to, *formal* aver to. **2** ensure, confirm, secure, stabilize, settle, establish, certify, guarantee, make safe, make sure, make certain; see also PROTECT. **3** confirm, encourage, inspirit, hearten. **5** (**assured**) **a** guaranteed, warranted, certain, sure, inevitable, definite, firm, fixed, confirmed, *colloq.* surefire. **b** see CONFIDENT *adj.* 1. □□ **assurable** insurable, warrantable. **assurer** insurer, guarantor, warranter, indemnifier.

assuredly /əshṓridlee/ *adv.* certainly.

■ see *undoubtedly* (UNDOUBTED).

assuredness /əshṓridnis/ *n.* certainty; (self-)assurance.

Assyrian /əsíreeən/ *n. & adj. hist.* • *n.* **1** an inhabitant of Assyria, an ancient kingdom in Mesopotamia. **2** the Semitic language of Assyria. • *adj.* of or relating to Assyria. [L *Assyrius* f. Gk *Assurios* of Assyria]

Assyriology /əsíreeóləjee/ *n.* the study of the language, history, and antiquities of Assyria. □□ **Assyriologist** *n.*

AST *abbr.* Atlantic Standard Time.

astatic /áystátik/ *adj.* **1** not static; unstable or unsteady. **2** *Physics* not tending to keep one position or direction. □ **astatic galvanometer** one in which the effect of the earth's magnetic field on the meter needle is greatly reduced. [Gk *astatos* unstable f. *a-* not + *sta-* stand]

astatine /ástəteen, -tin/ *n. Chem.* a radioactive element, the heaviest of the halogens, which occurs naturally and can be artificially made by nuclear bombardment of bismuth. ¶ Symb.: **At**. [formed as ASTATIC + -INE⁴]

aster /ástər/ *n.* any composite plant of the genus *Aster*, with bright daisy-like flowers, e.g., the Michaelmas daisy. □ **China aster** a related plant, *Callistephus chinensis*, cultivated for its bright and showy flowers. [L f. Gk *astēr* star]

-aster /ástər/ *suffix* **1** forming nouns denoting poor quality (*criticaster; poetaster*). **2** *Bot.* denoting incomplete resemblance (*oleaster; pinaster*). [L]

asterisk /ástərisk/ *n. & v.* • *n.* a symbol (*) used in printing and writing to mark words, etc., for reference, to stand for omitted matter, to signify a hypothetical linguistic form, etc. • *v.tr.* mark with an asterisk. [ME f. LL *asteriscus* f. Gk *asteriskos* dimin. (as ASTER)]

asterism /ástərizəm/ *n.* **1** a cluster of stars. **2** a group of three asterisks (⁂) calling attention to following text. [Gk *asterismos* (as ASTER, -ISM)]

astern /əstə́rn/ *adv. Naut. & Aeron.* (often foll. by *of*) **1** aft; away to the rear. **2** backward. [A² + STERN²]

asteroid /ástəroyd/ *n.* **1** any of the small celestial bodies revolving around the sun, mainly between the orbits of Mars and Jupiter. **2** *Zool.* a starfish. □□ **asteroidal** /ástəróyd'l/ *adj.* [Gk *asteroeidēs* (as ASTER, -OID)]

asthenia /astheéneeə/ *n. Med.* loss of strength; debility. [mod.L f. Gk *astheneia* f. *asthenēs* weak]

asthenic /asthénik/ *adj. & n.* • *adj.* **1** of a lean or long-limbed build; ectomorphic. **2** *Med.* of or characterized by asthenia. • *n.* a lean long-limbed person; an ectomorph.

asthma /ázmə, ás-/ *n.* a usu. allergic respiratory disease, often with paroxysms of difficult breathing. [ME f. Gk *asthma -matos* f. *azō* breathe hard]

asthmatic /azmátik, as-/ *adj. & n.* • *adj.* relating to or suffering from asthma. • *n.* a person suffering from asthma. □□ **asthmatically** *adv.* [L *asthmaticus* f. Gk *asthmatikos* (as ASTHMA, -IC)]

Asti /áastee/ *n.* (*pl.* **Astis**) an Italian white wine. □ **Asti spumante** /spoōmáantee/ a sparkling form of this. [*Asti* in Piedmont]

astigmatism /əstígmətizəm/ *n.* a defect in the eye or in a lens resulting in distorted images, as light rays are prevented from meeting at a common focus. □□ **astigmatic** /ástigmátik/ *adj.* [A-¹ + Gk *stigma -matos* point]

astilbe /əstílbee/ *n.* any plant of the genus *Astilbe*, with plumelike heads of tiny white or red flowers. [mod.L f. Gk *a-* not + *stilbē* fem. of *stilbos* glittering, from the inconspicuous (individual) flowers]

astir /əstə́r/ *predic.adj. & adv.* **1** in motion. **2** awake and out of bed (*astir early; already astir*). **3** excited. [A² + STIR¹ *n.*]

astonish /əstónish/ *v.tr.* amaze; surprise greatly. □□ **astonishing** *adj.* **astonishingly** *adv.* **astonishment** *n.* [obs. *astone* f. OF *estoner* f. Gallo-Roman: see -ISH²]

■ amaze, surprise, shock, astound, stun, stagger, take aback, dumbfound, stupefy, daze, *colloq.* flabbergast, knock the (or one's) socks off, bowl over, floor.
□□ **astonishing** see *amazing* (AMAZE). **astonishingly** see *amazingly* (AMAZE). **astonishment** amazement, surprise, shock, awe, stupefaction, wonder, wonderment.

astound /əstównd/ *v.tr.* shock with alarm or surprise; amaze. □□ **astounding** *adj.* **astoundingly** *adv.* [obs. *astound* (adj.) = *astoned* past part. of obs. *astone*: see ASTONISH]

■ amaze, surprise, shock, astonish, stun, stagger, take aback, dumbfound, stupefy, bewilder, overwhelm, daze, *colloq.* flabbergast, bowl over, floor.
□□ **astounding** see *amazing* (AMAZE). **astoundingly** see *amazingly* (AMAZE).

astraddle /əstrád'l/ *adv.* & *predic.adj.* in a straddling position.

astragal /ástrəgəl/ *n. Archit.* a small semicircular molding around the top or bottom of a column. [ASTRAGALUS]

astragalus /əstrágələs/ *n.* (*pl.* **-li** /-lī/) **1** *Anat.* = TALUS¹. **2** *Bot.* a leguminous plant of the genus *Astragalus*, e.g., the milk vetch. [L f. Gk *astragalos* ankle bone, molding, a plant]

astrakhan /ástrəkán/ *n.* **1** the dark curly fleece of young lambs from Astrakhan. **2** a cloth imitating astrakhan. [*Astrakhan* in Russia]

astral /ástrəl/ *adj.* **1** of or connected with the stars. **2** consisting of stars; starry. **3** *Theosophy* relating to or arising from a supposed ethereal existence, esp. of a counterpart of the body, associated with oneself in life and surviving after death. [LL *astralis* f. *astrum* star]

astray /əstráy/ *adv. & predic.adj.* **1** in or into error or sin (esp. *lead astray*). **2** out of the right way. □ **go astray** be lost or mislaid. [ME f. OF *estraié* past part. of *estraier* ult. f. L *extra* out of bounds + *vagari* wander]

■ **1** (*lead astray*) lead on, mislead, misguide, misdirect, deceive; fool, decoy, hoodwink, *colloq.* bamboozle.

astride /əstríd/ *adv. & prep.* • *adv.* **1** (often foll. by *of*) with a leg on each side. **2** with legs apart. • *prep.* with a leg on each side of; extending across.

astringent /əstrínjənt/ *adj. & n.* • *adj.* **1** causing the contraction of body tissues. **2** checking bleeding. **3** severe; austere. • *n.* an astringent substance or drug. □□ **astringency** /-jənsee/ *n.* **astringently** *adv.* [F f. L *astringere* (as AD-, *stringere* bind)]

■ *adj.* **2** styptic. **3** see KEEN¹ 4.

astro- /ástrō/ *comb. form* **1** relating to the stars or celestial bodies. **2** relating to outer space. [Gk f. *astron* star]

astrochemistry /ástrōkémistree/ *n.* the study of molecules and radicals in interstellar space.

astrodome /ástrədōm/ *n.* a domed window in an aircraft for astronomical observations.

astrohatch /ástrəhach/ *n.* = ASTRODOME.

astrolabe /ástrəlayb/ *n.* an instrument, usu. consisting of a disk and pointer, formerly used to make astronomical measurements, esp. of the altitudes of celestial bodies, and as an aid in navigation. [ME f. OF *astrelabe* f. med.L *astrolabium* f. Gk *astrolabon*, neut. of *astrolabos* star taking]

astrology /əstróləjee/ *n.* the study of the movements and relative positions of celestial bodies interpreted as an influence on human affairs. □□ **astrologer** *n.* **astrological** /ástrəlójikəl/ *adj.* **astrologist** *n.* [ME f. OF *astrologie* f. L *astrologia* f. Gk (as ASTRO-, -LOGY)]

astronaut /ástrənawt/ *n.* a person who is trained to travel in a spacecraft. □□ **astronautical** /-náwtikəl/ *adj.* [ASTRO-, after *aeronaut*]

astronautics /ástrənáwtiks/ *n.* the science of space travel.

astronomical /ástrənómikəl/ *adj.* (also **astronomic**) **1** of or relating to astronomy. **2** extremely large; too large to contemplate. □ **astronomical unit** a unit of measurement in astronomy equal to the mean distance from the center of the earth to the center of the sun, 1.496×10^{11} meters or 92.9 million miles. **astronomical year** see YEAR *n.* 1. □□ **astronomically** *adv.* [L *astronomicus* f. Gk *astronomikos*]

■ **2** see INFINITE *adj.* 1–3.

astronomy /əstrónəmee/ *n.* the scientific study of celestial bodies and other matter beyond earth's atmosphere. □□ **astronomer** *n.* [ME f. OF *astronomie* f. L f. Gk *astronomia* f. *astronomos* (adj.) star arranging f. *nemō* arrange]

astrophysics /ástrōfíziks/ *n.* a branch of astronomy concerned with the physics and chemistry of celestial bodies

---

/.../ **pronunciation**   • **part of speech**
□ **phrases, idioms, and compounds**
□□ **derivatives**   ■ **synonym section**
cross-references appear in SMALL CAPITALS or *italics*

and phenomena. □□ **astrophysical** *adj.* **astrophysicist** /-zisist/ *n.*

Astroturf /ástrōtərf/ *n. propr.* an artificial grass surface, esp. for sports fields. [*Astrodome*, name of a sports stadium in Texas where it was first used, + TURF]

astute /əstóot, əstyóot/ *adj.* **1** shrewd; sagacious. **2** crafty. □□ **astutely** *adv.* **astuteness** *n.* [obs. F *astut* or L *astutus* f. *astus* craft]

■ **1** sharp, keen, perceptive, observant, shrewd, alert, quick, quick-witted, sage, sagacious, wise, intelligent, insightful, perspicacious, penetrating, discerning, knowledgeable, *colloq.* on the ball. **2** shrewd, subtle, clever, ingenious, adroit, wily, cunning, calculating, canny, crafty, artful, arch, sly, foxy, guileful, underhand, underhanded. □□ **astutely** perceptively, insightfully, perspicaciously, penetratingly, adroitly; shrewdly, sagaciously; artfully; craftily. **astuteness** shrewdness, subtleness, adroitness, sharpness, keenness, perceptiveness, perspicacity, discernment, alertness, quick-wittedness, sagacity; artfulness; see also ART[1] 7.

asunder /əsúndər/ *adv. literary* apart. [OE *on sundran* into pieces: cf. SUNDER]

■ see APART 2.

asylum /əsíləm/ *n.* **1** sanctuary; protection, esp. for those pursued by the law (*seek asylum*). **2** *hist.* any of various kinds of institution offering shelter and support to distressed or destitute individuals, esp. the mentally ill. □ **political asylum** protection given by a government to a political refugee from another country. [ME f. L f. Gk *asulon* refuge f. *a-* not + *sulon* right of seizure]

■ **1** see SANCTUARY 4, 5a. **2** see HOME *n.* 4.

asymmetry /aysímitree/ *n.* lack of symmetry. □□ **asymmetric** /-métrik/ *adj.* **asymmetrical** *adj.* **asymmetrically** /-métrikəlee/ *adv.* [Gk *asummetria* (as A-[1], SYMMETRY)]

■ see DISPROPORTION.

asymptomatic /áysimptəmátik/ *adj.* producing or showing no symptoms.

asymptote /ásimptōt/ *n.* a line that continually approaches a given curve but does not meet it at a finite distance. □□ **asymptotic** /-tótik/ *adj.* **asymptotically** *adv.* [mod.L *asymptota* (*linea* line) f. Gk *asumptōtos* not falling together f. *a-* not + *sun* together + *ptōtos* falling f. *piptō* fall]

asynchronous /aysíngkrənəs/ *adj.* not synchronous. □□ **asynchronously** *adv.*

asyndeton /əsínditən/ *n.* (*pl.* **asyndeta** /-tə/) the omission of a conjunction. □□ **asyndetic** /ásindétik/ *adj.* [mod.L f. Gk *asundeton* (neut. adj.) f. *a-* not + *sundetos* bound together]

At *symb. Chem.* the element astatine.

at /at, unstressed ət/ *prep.* **1** expressing position, exact or approximate (*wait at the corner*; *at the top of the hill*; *is at school*; *at a distance*). **2** expressing a point in time (*see you at three*; *went at dawn*). **3** expressing a point in a scale or range (*at boiling point*; *at his best*). **4** expressing engagement or concern in a state or activity (*at war*; *at work*; *at odds*). **5** expressing a value or rate (*sell at $10 each*). **6 a** with or with reference to; in terms of (*at a disadvantage*; *annoyed at losing*; *good at soccer*; *play at fighting*; *sick at heart*; *came at a run*; *at short notice*; *work at it*). **b** by means of (*starts at a touch*; *drank it at a gulp*). **7** expressing: **a** motion toward (*arrived at the station*; *went at them*). **b** aim toward or pursuit of (physically or conceptually) (*aim at the target*; *work at a solution*; *guess at the truth*; *laughed at us*; *has been at the milk again*). □ **at all** see ALL. **at hand** see HAND. **at home** see HOME. **at it** **1** engaged in an activity; working hard. **2** *colloq.* repeating a habitual (usu. disapproved of) activity (*found them at it again*). **at once** see ONCE. **at that** moreover (*found one, and a good one at that*). **at times** see TIME. [OE *æt*, rel. to L *ad* to]

at- /ət/ *prefix* assim. form of AD- before *t.*

Atabrine /átəbreen/ *n.* (also **Atebrin** /-brin/) *propr.* = QUIN-ACRINE. [-ATE[1] 2 + BRINE]

ataractic /átəráktik/ *adj. & n.* (also **ataraxic** /-ráksik/) ● *adj.* calming or tranquilizing. ● *n.* a tranquilizing drug. [Gk *ataraktos* calm: cf. ATARAXY]

ataraxy /átəraksee/ *n.* (also **ataraxia** /-rákseeə/) calmness or tranquility; imperturbability. [F *ataraxie* f. Gk *ataraxia* impassiveness]

atavism /átəvizəm/ *n.* **1** a resemblance to remote ancestors rather than to parents in plants or animals. **2** reversion to an earlier type. □□ **atavistic** *adj.* **atavistically** *adv.* [F *atavisme* f. L *atavus* great-grandfather's grandfather]

ataxia /ətákseeə/ *n.* (also **ataxy** /-see/) *Med.* the loss of full control of bodily movements. □□ **ataxic** *adj.* [mod.L *ataxia* f. Gk f. *a-* not + *taxis* order]

ATC *abbr.* **1** air traffic control. **2** Air Training Corps.

ate *past* of EAT.

-ate[1] /ət, ayt/ *suffix* **1** forming nouns denoting: **a** status or office (*doctorate*; *episcopate*). **b** state or function (*curate*; *magistrate*; *mandate*). **2** *Chem.* forming nouns denoting the salt of an acid with a corresponding name ending in *-ic* (*chlorate*; *nitrate*). **3** forming nouns denoting a group (*electorate*). **4** *Chem.* forming nouns denoting a product (*condensate*; *filtrate*). [from or after OF *-at* or *é(e)* or f. L *-atus* noun or past part.: cf. -ATE[2]]

-ate[2] /ət, ayt/ *suffix* **1** forming adjectives and nouns (*associate*; *delegate*; *duplicate*; *separate*). **2** forming adjectives from Latin or English nouns and adjectives (*cordate*; *insensate*; *Italianate*). [from or after (F *-é* f.) L *-atus* past part. of verbs in *-are*]

-ate[3] /ayt/ *suffix* forming verbs (*associate*; *duplicate*; *fascinate*; *hyphenate*; *separate*). [from or after (F *-er* f.) L *-are* (past part. *-atus*): cf. -ATE[2]]

Atebrin var. of ATABRINE.

atelier /átəlyáy/ *n.* a workshop or studio, esp. of an artist or designer. [F]

a tempo /aa témpō/ *adv. Mus.* in the previous tempo. [It., lit. 'in time']

Athanasian Creed /áthənáyzhən/ *n.* an affirmation of Christian faith formerly thought to have been drawn up by Athanasius, bishop of Alexandria d. 373.

atheism /áytheeizəm/ *n.* the theory or belief that God does not exist. □□ **atheist** *n.* **atheistic** *adj.* **atheistical** *adj.* [F *athéisme* f. Gk *atheos* without God f. *a-* not + *theos* god]

■ □□ **atheist** see NONBELIEVER.

atheling /áthəling/ *n. hist.* a prince or nobleman in Anglo-Saxon England. [OE *ætheling* = OHG *ediling* f. WG: see -ING[3]]

athematic /áytheemátik/ *adj.* **1** *Mus.* not based on the use of themes. **2** *Gram.* (of a verb form) having a suffix attached to the stem without a correcting (thematic) vowel.

athenaeum /áthinéeəm/ *n.* (also **atheneum**) **1** an institution for literary or scientific study. **2** a library. [LL *Athenaeum* f. Gk *Athēnaion* temple of Athene (used as a place of teaching)]

Athenian /ətheeneeən/ *n. & adj.* ● *n.* a native or inhabitant of ancient or modern Athens. ● *adj.* of or relating to Athens. [L *Atheniensis* f. *Athenae* f. Gk *Athēnai* Athens, principal city of Greece]

atherosclerosis /áthərōsklərōsis/ *n.* a form of arteriosclerosis characterized by the degeneration of the arteries because of a buildup of fatty deposits. □□ **atherosclerotic** /-rótik/ *adj.* [G *Atherosklerose* f. Gk *athērē* gruel + SCLEROSIS]

athirst /əthúrst/ *predic. adj. poet.* **1** (usu. foll. by *for*) eager (*athirst for knowledge*). **2** thirsty. [OE *ofthyrst* for *ofthyrsted* past part. of *ofthyrstan* be thirsty]

athlete /áthleet/ *n.* **1** a skilled performer in sports and physical activities, esp. *Brit.* in track and field events. **2** a person with natural athletic ability. □ **athlete's foot** a fungal foot condition affecting esp. the skin between the toes. [L *athleta* f. Gk *athlētēs* f. *athleō* contend for a prize (*athlon*)]

athletic /athlétik/ *adj.* **1** of or relating to athletes or athletics (*an athletic competition*). **2** muscular or physically powerful. □□ **athletically** *adv.* **athleticism** /-tisizəm/ *n.* [F *athlétique* or L *athleticus* f. Gk *athlētikos* (as ATHLETE, -IC)]

athletics /athlétiks/ *n.pl.* (usu. treated as *sing.*) **1 a** physical exercises, esp. *Brit.* track and field events. **b** the practice of these. **2** physical sports and games of any kind.

athwart /əthwáwrt/ *adv. & prep.* ● *adv.* **1** across from side to side (usu. obliquely). **2** perversely or in opposition.

● *prep.* **1** from side to side of. **2** in opposition to. [A² + THWART]

-atic /átik/ *suffix* forming adjectives and nouns (*aquatic*; *fanatic*; *idiomatic*). [F -*atique* or L -*aticus*, often ult. f. Gk -*atikos*]

atilt /ətílt/ *adv.* tilted and nearly falling. [A² + TILT]

-ation /áyshən/ *suffix* **1** forming nouns denoting an action or an instance of it (*alteration*; *flirtation*; *hesitation*). **2** forming nouns denoting a result or product of action (*plantation*; *starvation*; *vexation*) (see also -FICATION). [from or after F -*ation* or L -*atio* -*ationis* f. verbs in -*are*: see -ION]

-ative /ətiv, aytiv/ *suffix* forming adjectives denoting a characteristic or propensity (*authoritative*; *imitative*; *pejorative*; *qualitative*; *talkative*). [from or after F -*atif* -*ative* or f. L -*ativus* f. past part. stem -*at*- of verbs in -*are* + -*ivus* (see -IVE): cf. -ATIC]

Atlantean /ətlánteeən/ *adj. literary* of or like Atlas, esp. in physical strength. [L *Atlanteus* (as ATLAS)]

atlantes /ətlánteez/ *n.pl. Archit.* male figures carved in stone and used as columns to support the entablature of a Greek or Greek-style building. Also called TELAMON. [Gk, pl. of *Atlas*: see ATLAS]

Atlantic /ətlántik/ *n. & adj.* ● *n.* the ocean between Europe and Africa to the east, and North and South America to the west. ● *adj.* of or adjoining the Atlantic. □ **Atlantic Time** the standard time used in the most eastern parts of Canada and in parts of the Caribbean. [ME f. L *Atlanticus* f. Gk *Atlantikos* (as ATLAS, -IC): orig. of the Atlas Mountains, then of the sea near the W. African coast]

atlas /átləs/ *n.* **1** a book of maps or charts. **2** *Anat.* the cervical vertebra of the backbone articulating with the skull at the neck. [L f. Gk *Atlas* -*antos* a Titan who held up the pillars of the universe, whose picture appeared at the beginning of early atlases]

ATM *abbr.* automatic teller machine.

atm *abbr. Physics* atmosphere(s).

atman /áatmən/ *n. Hinduism* **1** the real self. **2** the supreme spiritual principle. [Skr. *ātmán* essence, breath]

atmosphere /átməsfeer/ *n.* **1 a** the envelope of gases surrounding the earth, any other planet, or any substance. **b** the air in any particular place, esp. if unpleasant. **2 a** the pervading tone or mood of a place or situation, esp. with reference to the feelings or emotions evoked. **b** the feelings or emotions evoked by a work of art, a piece of music, etc. **3** *Physics* a unit of pressure equal to mean atmospheric pressure at sea level, 101,325 pascals or 14.7 pounds per square inch. ¶ Abbr.: **atm.** □□ **atmospheric** /-férik, -feér-/ *adj.* **atmospherical** *adj.* **atmospherically** *adv.* [mod.L *atmosphaera* f. Gk *atmos* vapor: see SPHERE]
  ■ **1** air, gases, heaven(s), sky, ether. **2 a** air, ambience, environment, climate, mood, feeling, aura, feel, sense, spirit, tone, quality, *colloq.* vibes. □□ **atmospheric, atmospherical** aerial, meteorological; aural, auric. **atmospherically** meteorologically, climatically, environmentally.

atmospherics /átməsfériks, -feér-/ *n.pl.* **1** electrical disturbance in the atmosphere, esp. caused by lightning. **2** interference with telecommunications caused by this.

atoll /átawl, átol, áy-/ *n.* a ring-shaped coral reef enclosing a lagoon. [Maldive *atolu*]

atom /átəm/ *n.* **1 a** the smallest particle of a chemical element that can take part in a chemical reaction. **b** this particle as a source of nuclear energy. **2** (usu. with *neg.*) the least portion of a thing or quality (*not an atom of pity*). □ **atom bomb** a bomb involving the release of energy by nuclear fission = *fission bomb.* **atom smasher** *colloq.* = ACCELERATOR 2. [ME f. OF *atome* f. L *atomus* f. Gk *atomos* indivisible]
  ■ **1 a** particle, molecule. **2** see PARTICLE 2.

atomic /ətómik/ *adj.* **1** concerned with or using atomic energy or atomic bombs. **2** of or relating to an atom or atoms. □ **atomic bomb** = *atom bomb.* **atomic clock** a clock in which the periodic process (time scale) is regulated by the vibrations of an atomic or molecular system, such as cesium or ammonia. **atomic energy** nuclear energy. **atomic mass** the mass of an atom measured in atomic mass units. **atomic**

mass unit a unit of mass used to express atomic and molecular weights that is equal to one twelfth of the mass of an atom of carbon-12. ¶ Abbr.: **amu. atomic number** the number of protons in the nucleus of an atom, which is characteristic of a chemical element and determines its place in the periodic table. ¶ Symb.: Z. **atomic particle** any one of the particles of which an atom is constituted. **atomic philosophy** atomism. **atomic physics** the branch of physics concerned with the structure of the atom and the characteristics of the elementary particles of which it is composed. **atomic pile** a nuclear reactor. **atomic power** nuclear power. **atomic spectrum** the emission or absorption spectrum arising from electron transitions inside an atom and characteristic of the element. **atomic structure** the structure of an atom as being a central positively charged nucleus surrounded by negatively charged orbiting electrons. **atomic theory 1** the concept of an atom as being composed of elementary particles. **2** the theory that all matter is made up of small indivisible particles called atoms, and that the atoms of any one element are identical in all respects but differ from those of other elements and only unite to form compounds in fixed proportions. **3** *Philos.* atomism. **atomic warfare** warfare involving the use of atom bombs. **atomic weight** the ratio of the average mass of one atom of an element to one twelfth of the mass of an atom of carbon-12: also called *relative atomic mass.* □□ **atomically** *adv.* [mod.L *atomicus* (as ATOM, -IC)]
  ■ **1** see NUCLEAR.

atomicity /átəmísitee/ *n.* **1** the number of atoms in the molecules of an element. **2** the state or fact of being composed of atoms.

atomism /átəmizəm/ *n. Philos.* **1** the theory that all matter consists of tiny individual particles. **2** *Psychol.* the theory that mental states are made up of elementary units. □□ **atomist** *n.* **atomistic** /-místik/ *adj.*

atomize /átəmíz/ *v.tr.* **1** reduce to atoms or fine particles. **2** fragment or divide into small units. □□ **atomization** *n.*
  ■ break apart, fragment; separate, disperse, scatter.

atomizer /átəmīzər/ *n.* an instrument for emitting liquids as a fine spray.

atomy /átəmee/ *n.* (*pl.* -**ies**) *archaic* **1** a skeleton. **2** an emaciated body. [ANATOMY taken as *an atomy*]

atonal /áytōn'l/ *adj. Mus.* not written in any key or mode. □□ **atonality** /-nálitee/ *n.*

atone /ətōn/ *v.intr.* (usu. foll. by *for*) make amends; expiate for (a wrong). [back-form. f. ATONEMENT]
  ■ make amends, pay, repay, answer, compensate; (*atone for*) expiate, make up for, make good, remedy, redress, redeem, condone, *Law* purge.

atonement /ətōnmənt/ *n.* **1** expiation; reparation for a wrong or injury. **2** (in Christianity) the reconciliation of God and humans. □ **the Atonement** the expiation by Christ of humankind's sin. **Day of Atonement** the most solemn religious fast of the Jewish year, eight days after the Jewish New Year. [*at one* + -MENT, after med.L *adunamentum* and earlier *onement* f. obs. *one* (v.) unite]
  ■ **1** expiation, reparation, repayment, compensation, satisfaction, payment, restitution, recompense, propitiation.

atonic /ətónik/ *adj.* **1** without accent or stress. **2** *Med.* lacking bodily tone. □□ **atony** /átənee/ *n.*

atop /ətóp/ *adv. & prep.* ● *adv.* (often foll. by *of*) on the top. ● *prep.* on the top of. ● *prep.* see ABOVE *prep.* 1.

-ator /áytər/ *suffix* forming agent nouns, usu. from Latin words (sometimes via French) (*agitator*; *creator*; *equator*; *escalator*). See also -OR¹. [L -*ator*]

-atory /ətáwree/ *suffix* forming adjectives meaning 'relating to

/.../ **pronunciation**	● **part of speech**
□ **phrases, idioms, and compounds**	
□□ **derivatives**	■ **synonym section**
cross-references appear in SMALL CAPITALS or *italics*	

or involving (a verbal action)' (*amatory*; *explanatory*; *predatory*). See also -ORY². [L -*atorius*]

ATP *abbr.* adenosine triphosphate.

atrabilious /átrəbílyəs/ *adj.* melancholy; ill-tempered. [L *atra bilis* black bile, transl. Gk *melagkholia* MELANCHOLY]

atrium /áytreeəm/ *n.* (*pl.* **atriums** or **atria** /-treeə/) **1 a** the central court of an ancient Roman house. **b** a usu. skylit central court rising through several stories with galleries and rooms opening off at each level. **c** (in a modern house) a central hall or courtyard with rooms opening off it. **2** *Anat.* a cavity in the body, esp. one of the two upper cavities of the heart, receiving blood from the veins. □□ **atrial** *adj.* [L]

atrocious /ətróshəs/ *adj.* **1** very bad or unpleasant (*atrocious weather*; *their manners were atrocious*). **2** extremely savage or wicked (*atrocious cruelty*). □□ **atrociously** *adv.* **atrociousness** *n.* [L *atrox -ocis* cruel]

■ **1** bad, disagreeable, unpleasant, horrible, objectionable, woeful, horrendous, *colloq.* awful, terrible, appalling, dreadful, abysmal, lousy, horrid, frightful, desperate, hellish, ghastly, beastly, *sl.* rotten. **2** cruel, wicked, iniquitous, villainous, fiendish, execrable, appalling, abominable, monstrous, inhuman, savage, barbaric, brutal, barbarous, heinous, dreadful, flagrant, flagitious, gruesome, grisly, ghastly, unspeakable, horrifying, horrible, awful, infernal, satanic, hellish.

atrocity /ətrósitee/ *n.* (*pl.* **-ies**) **1** an extremely evil or cruel act, esp. one involving physical violence or injury. **2** extreme wickedness. [F *atrocité* or L *atrocitas* (as ATROCIOUS, -ITY)]

■ **1** outrage, crime, villainy, offense, violation, evil, enormity. **2** enormity, wickedness, flagitiousness, iniquity, infamy, cruelty, heinousness, horror, horribleness, evil, inhumanity, barbarity, savagery, monstrousness, brutality.

atrophy /átrəfee/ *v.* & *n.* ● *v.* (**-ies, -ied**) **1** *intr.* waste away through undernourishment, aging, or lack of use; become emaciated. **2** *tr.* cause to atrophy. ● *n.* the process of atrophying; emaciation. [F *atrophie* or LL *atrophia* f. Gk f. *a-* not + *trophē* food]

■ *v.* see WASTE *v.* 4.

atropine /átrəpeen, -pin/ *n.* a poisonous alkaloid found in deadly nightshade, used in medicine to treat renal and biliary colic, etc. [mod.L *Atropa belladonna* deadly nightshade f. Gk *Atropos* inflexible, the name of one of the Fates]

attach /ətách/ *v.* **1** *tr.* fasten; affix; join. **2** *tr.* (in *passive*; foll. by *to*) be very fond of or devoted to (*am deeply attached to her*). **3** *tr.* attribute; assign (some function, quality, or characteristic) (*can you attach a name to it?*; *attaches great importance to it*). **4 a** *tr.* include; enclose (*attach no conditions to the agreement*; *attach particulars*). **b** *intr.* (foll. by *to*) be an attribute or characteristic (*great prestige attaches to the job*). **5** *refl.* (usu. foll. by *to*) (of a thing) adhere; (of a person) join; take part (*the sticky stamps attached themselves to his fingers*; *climbers attached themselves to the expedition*). **6** *tr.* appoint for special or temporary duties. **7** *tr.* *Law* seize (a person or property) by legal authority. □□ **attachable** *adj.* **attacher** *n.* [ME f. OF *estachier* fasten f. Gmc: in Law sense thr. OF *atachier*]

■ **1** fasten, join, connect, secure, fix, affix, unite. **2** (*be attached to*) be fond of, be devoted *or* close *or* attracted to, love, adore, dote on, have a liking *or* fondness *or* penchant for, be affectionate toward, be partial to, *sl.* be hooked on; like. **3** ascribe, assign, attribute, apply, associate, connect; fix, affix, pin, put, place. **4 a** see INCLUDE 1. **b** (*attach to*) see ACCOMPANY 2. **5** adhere, stick, *literary* cleave; see also JOIN *v.* 3, 4. **6** appoint, assign, affiliate, enlist, engage; transfer, *Brit.* second. **7** seize, lay hold of, take into custody, confiscate, appropriate, commandeer, take possession of, impound. □□ **attachable** joinable, connectable, securable, fixable; attributable, assignable, ascribable.

attaché /atasháy/ *n.* a person appointed to an ambassador's staff, usu. with a special sphere of activity (*military attaché*; *press attaché*). □ **attaché case** a small flat rectangular case

for carrying documents, etc. [F, past part. of *attacher*: see ATTACH]

attached /ətácht/ *adj.* **1** fixed; connected; enclosed. **2** (of a person) involved in a long-term relationship, esp. engagement or marriage.

■ **1** connected, joined, (af)fixed, secured, enclosed. **2** spoken for, married, unavailable, engaged, betrothed, *literary* affianced.

attachment /ətáchmənt/ *n.* **1** a thing attached or to be attached, esp. to a machine, device, etc., for a special function. **2** affection; devotion. **3** a means of attaching. **4** the act of attaching or the state of being attached. **5** legal seizure. **6** a temporary position in an organization. [ME f. F *attachement* f. *attacher* (as ATTACH, -MENT)]

■ **1** affixture, fixture; adjunct, addition, accessory, device, appliance, (added) extra, accoutrement, appendage, part, gadget; ornament, decoration. **2** affection, devotion, liking, fondness, warmth, regard, fidelity, faithfulness, affinity, friendliness, loyalty, admiration, tenderness, partiality, friendship, love. **3** see FASTENING, BOND *n.* 2a. **4** linkage, connection. **5** see SEIZURE 1. **6** assignment, posting, appointment, *Brit.* secondment.

attack /əták/ *v.* & *n.* ● *v.* **1** *tr.* act against with (esp. armed) force. **2** *tr.* seek to hurt or defeat. **3** *tr.* criticize adversely. **4** *tr.* act harmfully upon (*a virus attacking the nervous system*). **5** *tr.* vigorously apply oneself to; begin work on (*attacked his meal with gusto*). **6** *intr.* make an attack. **7** *intr.* be in a mode of attack. ● *n.* **1** the act or process of attacking. **2 a** an offensive operation or mode of behavior. **b** severe criticism. **3** *Mus.* the action or manner of beginning a piece, passage, etc. **4** gusto; vigor. **5** a sudden occurrence of an illness. **6** a player or players seeking to score goals, etc.; offensive players. □□ **attacker** *n.* [F *attaque, attaquer* f. It. *attacco* attack, *attaccare* ATTACH]

■ *v.* **1** assail, assault, fall *or* set *or* pounce (up)on, lay into, beset, throw oneself on *or* upon; charge, rush, raid, strike (at), storm; engage (in battle), fight; mug, jump; *colloq.* weigh into. **3** criticize, censure, berate, come down on, have a go at, rap, abuse, revile, inveigh against, denounce, condemn, malign, denigrate, decry, flay, disparage, deprecate, vilify, bad-mouth, *colloq.* lay into, lambaste, put down, jump on, bitch (about), slate, *sl.* knock, slam, dump on, bomb. **4** affect, afflict, harm, damage, injure, infect, invade, destroy; waste, devour, eat, erode, corrode, decompose, dissolve. **5** launch into, embark on *or* upon, set off *or* out on, get going on, begin, start (off); approach, undertake. **6** charge, pounce; engage in battle, fight. ● *n.* **1** assault, bombardment, onset, offensive, onslaught, incursion, raid, charge, strike, blitzkrieg, inroad, invasion; destruction, wasting, erosion, corrosion. **2 b** criticism, censure, abuse, denunciation, condemnation, revilement, denigration, decrial, disparagement, deprecation, vilification. **4** gusto, vigor. **5** seizure, spell, spasm, paroxysm; fit, bout, outbreak, outburst, eruption, flare-up. □□ **attacker** see AGGRESSOR.

attain /ətáyn/ *v.* **1** *tr.* arrive at; reach (a goal, etc.). **2** *tr.* gain; accomplish (an aim, distinction, etc.). **3** *intr.* (foll. by *to*) arrive at by conscious development or effort. □□ **attainable** *adj.* **attainability** *n.* **attainableness** *n.* [ME f. AF *atain-, atein-*, OF *ataign-* stem of *ataindre* f. L *attingere* (as AD-, *tangere* touch)]

■ **1** see REACH *v.* 5, 7. **2** see GAIN *v.* 1. **3** (*attain to*) see ARRIVE 2.

attainder /ətáyndər/ *n.* *hist.* the forfeiture of land and civil rights suffered as a consequence of a sentence of death for treason or felony. □ **act** (or **bill**) **of attainder** an item of legislation inflicting attainder without judicial process. [ME f. AF, = OF *ateindre* ATTAIN used as noun: see -ER⁶]

attainment /ətáynmənt/ *n.* **1** (often in *pl.*) something attained or achieved; an accomplishment. **2** the act or an instance of attaining.

■ **1** see ACCOMPLISHMENT 3. **2** see ACCOMPLISHMENT 1.

attaint /ətáynt/ *v.tr.* **1** *hist.* subject to attainder. **2 a** (of disease, etc.) strike; affect. **b** *archaic* taint. [ME f. obs. *attaint* (adj.) f. OF *ataint, ateint* past part. formed as ATTAIN: confused in meaning with TAINT]

attar /átaar/ *n.* (also **otto** /ótō/) a fragrant essential oil, esp. from rose petals. [Pers. *'atar* f. Arab. f. *'iṭr* perfume]

attempt /ətémpt/ *v. & n.* ● *v.tr.* (often foll. by *to* + infin.) seek to achieve, complete, or master (a task, action, challenge, etc.) (*attempted the exercise; attempted to explain; attempted Everest*). ● *n.* (often foll. by *at, on,* or *to* + infin.) an act of attempting; an endeavor (*made an attempt at winning; an attempt to succeed; an attempt on his life*). □ **attempt the life of** *archaic* try to kill. □□ **attemptable** *adj.* [OF *attempter* f. L *attemptare* (as AD-, *temptare* TEMPT)]

■ *v.* try, undertake, take on, venture, *archaic* assay, *colloq.* have *or* take a crack at, have a go *or* shot *or* stab at, *formal* essay; (*attempt to*) endeavor *or* strive *or* struggle *or* make an effort to. ● *n.* endeavor, try, effort, undertaking, attack, assault, *colloq.* crack, go, shot, stab, bid, whirl, *formal* essay, *Brit. sl.* bash.

attend /əténd/ *v.* **1** *tr.* **a** be present at (*attended the meeting*). **b** go regularly to (*attends the local school*). **2** *intr.* **a** be present (*many members failed to attend*). **b** be present in a serving capacity; wait on. **3 a** *tr.* escort; accompany (*the king was attended by soldiers*). **b** *intr.* (foll. by *on*) wait on; serve. **4** *intr.* **a** (usu. foll. by *to*) turn or apply one's mind; focus one's attention (*attend to what I am saying; was not attending*). **b** (foll. by *to*) deal with; take care of (*shall attend to the matter myself; attend to the older people*). **5** *tr.* (usu. in *passive*) follow as a result from (*the error was attended by serious consequences*). □□ **attender** *n.* [ME f. OF *atendre* f. L *attendere* (as AD-, *tendere tent-* stretch)]

■ **1a, 2a** be present (at), go (to), appear (at), put in an appearance (at), turn up (at), sit in (on), assist (at); be at; be there. **1 b** go to, be at, take, be enrolled *or* registered at, be a member of, haunt, frequent, audit. **2 b** see WAIT *v.* 6b. **3 a** escort, accompany, serve, conduct, convoy, squire, follow, usher, wait (up)on; chaperon. **4** (*attend to*) **a** pay attention to, heed, listen to, take notice *or* account of, mind, concentrate on. **b** take care of, deal with, handle, look after, see to, reckon with, occupy oneself with, devote oneself to; turn *or* come to; tend, watch over, wait on *or* upon, care for, minister to, look out for. **5** accompany, be associated with, go along *or* together with, come with; result in *or* from, give rise to, lead to; bring on *or* about, produce, create, generate. □□ **attender** member, frequenter, participant, attendee; see also ATTENDANT *n.*

attendance /əténdəns/ *n.* **1** the act of attending or being present. **2** the number of people present (*a high attendance*). □ **attendance allowance** (in the UK) a government benefit paid to disabled people in need of constant care at home. **attendance center** *Brit.* a place where young offenders report by order of a court as a minor penalty. **in attendance** on hand; available for service. [ME f. OF *atendance* (as ATTEND, -ANCE)]

■ **1** presence, appearance, being. **2** turnout, gate, audience; gathering, crowd, assembly, assemblage, *Austral. sl.* muster. □ **in attendance** on hand, available, serving.

attendant /əténdənt/ *n. & adj.* ● *n.* a person employed to wait on others or provide a service (*cloakroom attendant; museum attendant*). ● *adj.* **1** accompanying (*attendant circumstances*). **2** waiting on; serving (*ladies attendant on the queen*). [ME f. OF (as ATTEND, -ANT)]

■ *n.* escort, servant, menial, helper, steward, stewardess, valet, usher, usherette, chaperon; aide, subordinate, underling, boy, page, assistant, henchman, second; waiter, waitress, garçon, butler, *Brit. Mil.* batman, batwoman, esp. *Brit.* commissionaire, scout, *archaic* pursuivant, servitor, *derog.* lackey, flunky, *hist.* squire, varlet. ● *adj.* **1** accompanying, following; resultant, related, consequent, concomitant, dependent, accessory, associated. **2** serving, waiting on, ministering to.

attendee /átendeé/ *n.* a person who attends (a meeting, etc.). ■ see *attender* (ATTEND).

attention /əténshən/ *n. & int.* ● *n.* **1** the act or faculty of applying one's mind (*give me your attention; attract his attention*). **2 a** consideration (*give attention to the problem*). **b** care (*give special attention to your handwriting*). **c** notice; publicity (*only needs a bit of attention; labeled an attention seeker*). **3** (in *pl.*) **a** ceremonious politeness (*he paid his attentions to her*). **b** wooing; courting (*he was the subject of her attentions*). **4** *Mil.* an erect attitude of readiness (*stand at attention*). ● *int.* (in full **stand to attention!**) an order to assume an attitude of attention. [ME f. L *attentio* (as ATTEND, -ION)]

■ *n.* **1** awareness, consciousness, attentiveness. **2 a** heed, regard, notice, concentration. **b** see CARE *n.* 3. **c** notice, publicity, distinction, acclaim, prominence, notoriety; limelight. **3** (*attentions*) **a** see RESPECT *n.* 1. **b** suit, courtship.

attentive /əténtiv/ *adj.* **1** concentrating; paying attention. **2** assiduously polite. **3** heedful. □□ **attentively** *adv.* **attentiveness** *n.* [ME f. F *attentif -ive* f. attente, OF *atente*, fem. past part. of *atendre* ATTEND]

■ **1** observant, awake, alert, on the qui vive, aware, intent, watchful, assiduous, *colloq.* on the ball. **2** polite, courteous, courtly, gallant, gracious, accommodating, considerate, thoughtful, solicitous, civil, respectful, deferential. **3** see MINDFUL. □□ **attentively** intently, closely, carefully, observantly, watchfully, vigilantly, alertly, heedfully, mindfully, assiduously, concentratedly; politely, courteously, graciously, considerately, solicitously, civilly. **attentiveness** attention, awareness, consciousness, concentration; see also RESPECT *n.* 1.

attenuate *v. & adj.* ● *v.tr.* /ətényooayt/ **1** make thin. **2** reduce in force, value, or virulence. **3** *Electr.* reduce the amplitude of (a signal or current). ● *adj.* /ətényooət/ **1** slender. **2** tapering gradually. **3** rarefied. □□ **attenuated** *adj.* **attenuation** /-áyshən/ *n.* **attenuator** *n.* [L *attenuare* (as AD-, *tenuis* thin)]

■ *adj.* attenuated; slender, tapering, rarefied. □□ **attenuated** see NARROW *adj.* 1a, THIN *adj.* 2.

attest /ətést/ *v.* **1** *tr.* certify the validity of. **2** *tr. Brit.* enroll (a recruit) for military service. **3** *intr.* (foll. by *to*) bear witness to. **4** *intr. Brit.* enroll oneself for military service. □□ **attestable** *adj.* **attestor** *n.* [F *attester* f. L *attestari* (as AD-, *testis* witness)]

■ **1, 3** confirm, verify, substantiate, vouch for, validate, assert, asseverate, affirm, vow, declare, *Law* depose, *formal* aver; (*attest to*) bear witness to, bear out, swear to, testify to, certify.

attestation /átestáyshən/ *n.* **1** the act of attesting. **2** a testimony. [F *attestation* or LL *attestatio* (as ATTEST, -ATION)]

Attic /átik/ *adj. & n.* ● *adj.* of ancient Athens or Attica, or the form of Greek spoken there. ● *n.* the form of Greek used by the ancient Athenians. □ **Attic salt** (or **wit**) refined or dry wit. [L *Atticus* f. Gk *Attikos*]

attic /átik/ *n.* **1** the uppermost story in a house, usu. under the roof. **2** a room in the attic area. [F *attique*, as ATTIC: orig. (Archit.) a small order above a taller one]

atticism /átisizəm/ *n.* **1** extreme elegance of speech. **2** an instance of this. [Gk *Attikismos* (as ATTIC, -ISM)]

attire /ətír/ *v. & n. formal* ● *v.tr.* dress, esp. in fine clothes or formal wear. ● *n.* clothes, esp. fine or formal. [ME f. OF *atir(i)er* equip f. *à tire* in order, of unkn. orig.]

■ *v.* see DRESS *v.* 1a. ● *n.* see CLOTHES.

attitude /átitōōd, -tyōōd/ *n.* **1 a** a settled opinion or way of thinking. **b** behavior reflecting this (*I don't like his attitude*). **2 a** a bodily posture. **b** a pose adopted in a painting or a play, esp. for dramatic effect (*strike an attitude*). **3** the position of an aircraft, spacecraft, etc., in relation to specified directions. □ **attitude of mind** a settled way of thinking.

/. . ./ **pronunciation** ● **part of speech**
□ **phrases, idioms, and compounds**
□□ **derivatives** ■ **synonym section**
cross-references appear in SMALL CAPITALS or *italics*

□□ **attitudinal** /-tōod'nəl, -tyōod-/ *adj.* [F f. It. *attitudine* fitness, posture, f. LL *aptitudo -dinis* f. *aptus* fit]
■ **1** position, opinion, feeling, view, point of view, viewpoint, outlook, approach, leaning, thought, inclination, bent, tendency, orientation; disposition, demeanor. **2** pose, posture, position, stance, aspect; form, shape. □□ **attitudinal** postural, positional, aspectual.

attitudinize /átitōod'nīz, -tyōod-/ *v.intr.* **1** practice or adopt attitudes, esp. for effect. **2** speak, write, or behave affectedly. [It. *attitudine* f. LL (as ATTITUDE) + -IZE]
■ **2** see POSE[1] *v.* 3.

attn. *abbr.* **1** attention. **2** for the attention of.

atto- /átō/ *comb. form Math.* denoting a factor of 10⁻¹⁸ (*attometer*). [Da. or Norw. *atten* eighteen + -O-]

attorney /ətə́rnee/ *n.* (*pl.* **-eys**) **1** a person, esp. a lawyer, appointed to act for another in business or legal matters. **2** a qualified lawyer, esp. one representing a client in a court of law. □ **attorney general** the chief legal officer in the US, England, and other countries. **district attorney** see DISTRICT. **power of attorney** the authority to act for another person in legal or financial matters. □□ **attorneyship** *n.* [ME f. OF *atorné* past part. of *atorner* assign f. *à* to + *torner* turn]
■ see LAWYER.

attract /ətrákt/ *v.tr.* **1** (also *absol.*) draw or bring to oneself or itself (*attracts many admirers; attracts attention*). **2** be attractive to; fascinate. **3** (of a magnet, gravity, etc.) exert a pull on (an object). □□ **attractable** *adj.* **attractor** *n.* [L *attrahere* (as AD-, *trahere tract-* draw)]
■ **1** draw, catch, capture, bring in *or* out *or* forth, *colloq.* pull. **2** entice, lure, allure, appeal to, charm, captivate, fascinate, *colloq.* turn on. □□ **attractor** drawer, *colloq.* puller; charmer.

attractant /ətráktənt/ *n. & adj.* ● *n.* a substance which attracts (esp. insects). ● *adj.* attracting.

attraction /ətrákshən/ *n.* **1 a** the act or power of attracting (*the attraction of foreign travel*). **b** a person or thing that attracts by arousing interest (*the fair is a big attraction*). **2** *Physics* the force by which bodies attract or approach each other (opp. REPULSION). **3** *Gram.* the influence exerted by one word on another which causes it to change to an incorrect form, e.g., *the wages of sin is death.* [F *attraction* or L *attractio* (as ATTRACT, -ION)]
■ **1 a** draw, appeal, lure, magnetism, (personal) charm, attractiveness, seductiveness, allure, fascination, captivation, pull, winsomeness. **b** draw, lure, enticement, pull, inducement, allurement, *sl.* come-on; show, entertainment, presentation, performance, crowd puller, crowd pleaser. **2** magnetism, polarity; gravitation.

attractive /ətráktiv/ *adj.* **1** attracting or capable of attracting; interesting (*an attractive proposition*). **2** aesthetically pleasing or appealing. □□ **attractively** *adv.* **attractiveness** *n.* [F *attractif -ive* f. LL *attractivus* (as ATTRACT, -IVE)]
■ **1** captivating, appealing, luring, catching, taking, inviting, seductive, engaging, enchanting, interesting, pleasing, pleasant, winning, winsome, alluring. **2** good-looking, pretty, handsome, fetching, comely, beautiful, *Sc. & No. of Engl.* bonny; aesthetic. □□ **attractiveness** SEE ATTRACTION 1a, BEAUTY 1.

attribute *v. & n.* ● *v.tr.* /ətríbyōot/ (usu. foll. by *to*) **1** regard as belonging or appropriate (*a poem attributed to Shakespeare*). **2** ascribe; regard as the effect of a stated cause (*the delays were attributed to the heavy traffic*). ● *n.* /átribyōot/ **1 a** a quality ascribed to a person or thing. **b** a characteristic quality. **2** a material object recognized as appropriate to a person, office, or status (*a large car is an attribute of seniority*). **3** *Gram.* an attributive adjective or noun. □□ **attributable** /ətríbyōotəbəl/ *adj.* **attribution** /-byōoshən/ *n.* [ME f. L *attribuere attribut-* (as AD-, *tribuere* assign): (n.) f. OF *attribut* or L *attributum*]
■ *v.* ascribe, impute, assign, put down, trace, charge, credit. ● *n.* **1** quality, character, characteristic, property, feature, trait, virtue. **2** see INDICATION 1b.

□□ **attributable** assignable, ascribable, imputable; traceable, chargeable; connectable. **attribution** assignment, ascription, imputation, credit, tracing; connection, association, linkage.

attributive /ətríbyətiv/ *adj. Gram.* (of an adjective or noun) preceding the word described and expressing an attribute, as *old* in *the old dog* (but not in *the dog is old*) and *expiration* in *expiration date* (opp. PREDICATIVE). □□ **attributively** *adv.* [F *attributif -ive* (as ATTRIBUTE, -IVE)]

attrit /ətrít/ *v.tr. colloq.* wear (an enemy or opponent) down by attrition. [back-form. f. ATTRITION]

attrition /ətríshən/ *n.* **1 a** the act or process of gradually wearing out, esp. by friction. **b** abrasion. **2** a gradual reduction, as by retirement, etc., in a work force. **3** *Theol.* sorrow for sin, falling short of contrition. □ **war of attrition** a war in which one side wins by gradually wearing the other down with repeated attacks, etc. □□ **attritional** *adj.* [ME f. LL *attritio* f. *atterere attrit-* rub]
■ **1** see EROSION.

attune /ətōon, ətyōon/ *v.tr.* **1** (usu. foll. by *to*) adjust (a person or thing) to a situation. **2** bring (an orchestra, instrument, etc.) into musical accord. [AT- + TUNE]
■ **1** (*attune to*) see ADAPT 1a. **2** see TUNE *v.* 1

atty. *abbr.* attorney.

Atty. Gen. *abbr.* Attorney General.

ATV *abbr.* all-terrain vehicle.

atypical /áytípikəl/ *adj.* not typical; not conforming to a type. □□ **atypically** *adv.*
■ see PECULIAR *adj.* 1.

AU *abbr.* **1** (also **au.**) astronomical unit. **2** ångström unit.

Au *symb. Chem.* the element gold. [L *aurum*]

aubade /ōbaád/ *n.* a poem or piece of music appropriate to the dawn or early morning. [F f. Sp. *albada* f. *alba* dawn]

auberge /ōbáirzh/ *n.* an inn. [F]

aubergine /ōbərzheen/ *n.* esp. *Brit.* = EGGPLANT. [F f. Cat. *alberginia* f. Arab. *al-bādinjān* f. Pers. *bādingān* f. Skr. *vātimgaṇa*]

auburn /áwbərn/ *adj.* reddish brown (usu. of a person's hair). [ME, orig. yellowish white, f. OF *auborne, alborne,* f. L *alburnus* whitish f. *albus* white]

AUC *abbr.* (of a date) from the foundation of the city (of Rome). [L *ab urbe condita*]

au courant /ō kōorón/ *predic.adj.* (usu. foll. by *with, of*) knowing what is going on; well-informed. [F, = in the (regular) course]

auction /áwkshən/ *n. & v.* ● *n.* **1** a sale of goods, usu. in public, in which articles are sold to the highest bidder. **2** the sequence of bids made in auction bridge or other card games. ● *v.tr.* sell at auction. □ **auction bridge** a form of bridge in which players bid for the right to name trumps. **Dutch auction** a sale, usu. public, of goods in which the price is reduced by the auctioneer until a buyer is found. [L *auctio* increase, auction f. *augēre auct-* increase]

auctioneer /áwkshəneér/ *n.* a person who conducts auctions professionally, by calling for bids and declaring goods sold. □□ **auctioneering** *n.*

audacious /awdáyshəs/ *adj.* **1** daring; bold. **2** impudent. □□ **audaciously** *adv.* **audaciousness** *n.* **audacity** /awdásitee/ *n.* [L *audax -acis* f. *audēre* dare]
■ **1** daring, bold, confident, intrepid, brave, courageous, adventurous, fearless, unafraid, venturesome, mettlesome, *archaic or joc.* doughty, *colloq.* gutsy; reckless, rash, foolhardy, daredevil, devil-may-care. **2** presumptuous, shameless, bold, impudent, defiant, impertinent, insolent, brazen, unabashed, rude, disrespectful, cheeky, forward. □□ **audaciousness**, **audacity** see GUT *n.* 3, GALL[1] 1.

audible /áwdibəl/ *adj.* capable of being heard. □□ **audibility** *n.* **audibleness** *n.* **audibly** *adv.* [LL *audibilis* f. *audire* hear]

audience /áwdeeəns/ *n.* **1 a** the assembled listeners or spectators at an event, esp. a stage performance, concert, etc. **b** the people addressed by a movie, book, play, etc. **2** a formal interview with a person in authority. **3** *archaic* a hearing (*give audience to my plea*). [ME f. OF f. L *audientia* f. *audire* hear]

■ **1 a** see ATTENDANCE 2. **2** see INTERVIEW *n.* 3.

audile /áwdīl/ *adj.* of or referring to the sense of hearing. [irreg. f. L *audire* hear, after *tactile*]

audio /áwdeeō/ *n.* (usu. *attrib.*) sound or the reproduction of sound. □ **audio frequency** a frequency capable of being perceived by the human ear. [AUDIO-]

audio- /áwdeeō/ *comb. form* hearing or sound. [L *audire* hear + -o-]

audiocassette /áwdeeōkəsét/ *n.* an audiotape enclosed within a cassette.

audiology /áwdeeóləjee/ *n.* the science of hearing. □□ **audiologist** *n.*

audiometer /áwdeeómitər/ *n.* an instrument for testing hearing.

audiophile /áwdeeōfīl/ *n.* a high-fidelity sound enthusiast.

audiotape /áwdeeōtayp/ *n.* & *v.* ● *n.* **1 a** magnetic tape on which sound can be recorded. **b** a length of this. **2** a sound recording on tape. ● *v.tr.* record (sound, speech, etc.) on tape.

audiovisual /áwdeeōvízhyōōəl/ *adj.* (esp. of teaching methods) using both sight and sound.

audit /áwdit/ *n.* & *v.* ● *n.* an official examination of accounts. ● *v.tr.* (**audited, auditing**) **1** conduct an audit of. **2** attend (a class) informally, without working for a grade or credit. [ME f. L *auditus* hearing f. *audire audit-* hear]

■ *v.* **1** see MONITOR *v.* **2** see ATTEND 1b.

audition /awdíshən/ *n.* & *v.* ● *n.* **1** an interview for a role as a singer, actor, dancer, etc., consisting of a practical demonstration of suitability. **2** the power of hearing or listening. ● *v.* **1** *tr.* interview (a candidate at an audition). **2** *intr.* be interviewed at an audition. [F *audition* or L *auditio* f. *audire audit-* hear]

auditive /áwditiv/ *adj.* concerned with hearing. [F *auditif -ive* (as AUDITION, -IVE)]

■ auditory, aural, auricular.

auditor /áwditər/ *n.* **1** a person who audits accounts. **2** a person who audits a class. **3** a listener. □□ **auditorial** /-táwreeəl/ *adj.* [ME f. AF *auditour* f. L *auditor -oris* (as AUDITIVE, -OR¹)]

auditorium /áwditáwreeəm/ *n.* (*pl.* **auditoriums** or **auditoria** /-reeə/) **1** a large room or building for meetings, etc. **2** the part of a theater, etc., in which the audience sits. [L neut. of *auditorius* (adj.): see AUDITORY, -ORIUM]

auditory /áwditawree/ *adj.* **1** concerned with hearing. **2** received by the ear. [L *auditorius* (as AUDITOR, -ORY²)]

■ **1** auditive, aural, auricular. **2** aural.

au fait /ō fáy/ *predic.adj.* (usu. foll. by *with*) having current knowledge; conversant (*fully au fait with the arrangements*). □ **put** (or **make**) **au fait with** esp. *Brit.* instruct in. [F]

■ see AWARE 2.

au fond /ō fáwn/ *adv.* basically; at bottom. [F]

■ see *in essence* (ESSENCE).

Aug. *abbr.* August.

Augean /awjéeən/ *adj.* **1** filthy; extremely dirty. **2** extremely difficult and unpleasant. [L *Augeas* f. Gk *Augeias* (in Gk mythology, the owner of stables cleaned by Hercules by diverting a river through them)]

■ **1** see DIRTY *adj.* 1.

auger /áwgər/ *n.* **1** a tool resembling a large corkscrew, for boring holes in wood. **2** a similar larger tool for boring holes in the ground. [OE *nafogār* f. *nafu* NAVE², + *gār* pierce: for loss of *n* cf. ADDER]

aught¹ /awt/ *n.* (also **ought**) *archaic* (usu. implying *neg.*) anything at all. [OE *āwiht* f. Gmc]

aught² /awt/ *n.* (also **ought**) *colloq.* a figure denoting nothing; zero. [perh. f. *an aught* for a NAUGHT]

augite /áwjīt/ *n. Mineral.* a complex calcium magnesium aluminous silicate occurring in many igneous rocks. [L *augites* f. Gk *augitēs* f. *augē* luster]

augment *v.* & *n.* ● *v.tr.* & *intr.* /awgmént/ **1** make or become greater; increase. **2** add to; supplement. ● *n.* /áwgment/ *Gram.* a vowel prefixed to the past tenses in the older Indo-European languages. □ **augmented interval** *Mus.* a perfect or major interval that is increased by a halfstep. □□ **aug-**

menter *n.* [ME f. OF *augment* (n.), F *augmenter* (v.), or LL *augmentum, augmentare* f. L *augēre* increase]

■ *v.* see INCREASE *v.* 1.

augmentation /áwgməntáyshən/ *n.* **1** enlargement; growth; increase. **2** *Mus.* the lengthening of the time values of notes in melodic parts. [ME f. F f. LL *augmentatio -onis* f. *augmentare* (as AUGMENT)]

■ **1** see INCREASE *n.* 1, 2.

augmentative /awgméntətiv/ *adj.* **1** having the property of increasing. **2** *Gram.* (of an affix or derived word) reinforcing the idea of the original word. [F *augmentatif -ive* or med.L *augmentativus* (as AUGMENT)]

au gratin /ō gratáN/ *adj. Cookery* cooked with a crisp brown crust, usu. of breadcrumbs or melted cheese. [F f. *gratter*, = by grating, f. GRATE¹]

augur /áwgər/ *v.* & *n.* ● *v.* **1** *intr.* **a** (of an event, circumstance, etc.) suggest a specified outcome (usu. *augur well* or *ill*). **b** portend; bode (*all augured well for our success*). **2** *tr.* **a** foresee; predict. **b** portend. ● *n.* an ancient Roman religious official who observed natural signs, esp. the behavior of birds, interpreting these as an indication of divine approval or disapproval of a proposed action. □□ **augural** *adj.* [L]

■ *v.* **1 b** see PROMISE *v.* 2a. **2 a** see FORESEE. **b** see FORESHADOW. ● *n.* see SEER¹.

augury /áwgyəree/ *n.* (*pl.* **-ies**) **1** an omen; a portent. **2** the work of an augur; the interpretation of omens. [ME f. OF *augurie* or L *augurium* f. AUGUR]

■ **1** see OMEN *n.* **2** see PROPHECY 2.

August /áwgəst/ *n.* the eighth month of the year. [OE f. L *Augustus* Caesar, the first Roman emperor]

august /awgúst/ *adj.* inspiring reverence and admiration; venerable; impressive. □□ **augustly** *adv.* **augustness** *n.* [F *auguste* or L *augustus* consecrated, venerable]

■ see VENERABLE.

Augustan /awgústən/ *adj.* & *n.* ● *adj.* **1** connected with, occurring during, or influenced by the reign of the Roman emperor Augustus, esp. as an outstanding period of Latin literature. **2** (of a nation's literature) refined and classical in style (as the literature of the 17th–18th c. in England). ● *n.* a writer of the Augustan age of any literature. [L *Augustanus* f. *Augustus*]

Augustine /awgústeen/ *n.* an Augustinian friar. [ME f. OF *augustin* f. L *Augustinus*: see AUGUSTINIAN]

Augustinian /áwgəstíneeən/ *adj.* & *n.* ● *adj.* **1** of or relating to St. Augustine, a Doctor of the Church (d. 430), or his doctrines. **2** belonging to a religious order observing a rule derived from St. Augustine's writings. ● *n.* **1** an adherent of the doctrines of St. Augustine. **2** one of the order of Augustinian friars. [L *Augustinus* Augustine]

auk /awk/ *n.* any sea diving bird of the family Alcidae, with heavy body, short wings, and black and white plumage, e.g., the guillemot, puffin, and razorbill. □ **great auk** an extinct flightless auk, *Alca impennis*. **little auk** a small Arctic auk, *Plautus alle*. [ON *álka*]

auld /awld/ *adj. Sc.* old. [OE *ald*, Anglian form of OLD]

auld lang syne /áwld lang zīn, sín/ *n.* times long past. [Sc., = old long since: also as the title and refrain of a song]

aumbry /áwmbree/ *n.* (also **ambry** /ámbree/) (*pl.* **-ies**) **1** a small recess in the wall of a church. **2** *Brit. hist.* a small cupboard. [ME f. OF *almarie, armarie* f. L *armarium* closet, chest f. *arma* utensils]

au naturel /ō nachərél/ *predic.adj.* & *adv.* **1** *Cookery* uncooked; (cooked) in the most natural or simplest way. **2** naked. [F, = in the natural state]

aunt /ant, aant/ *n.* **1** the sister of one's father or mother. **2** an uncle's wife. **3** *colloq.* an unrelated woman friend of a child or children. □ **Aunt Sally** *Brit.* **1** a game in which players throw sticks or balls at a wooden dummy. **2** the object of an unreasonable attack. **my** (or **my sainted**, etc.) **aunt**

/.../ pronunciation	● part of speech
□ phrases, idioms, and compounds	
□□ derivatives	■ synonym section
cross-references appear in SMALL CAPITALS or *italics*	

esp. *Brit. sl.* an exclamation of surprise, disbelief, etc. [ME f. AF *aunte*, OF *ante*, f. L *amita*]

auntie /ántee, aántee/ *n.* (also **aunty**) (*pl.* **-ies**) *colloq.* **1** = AUNT. **2** *Brit.* (**Auntie**) an institution considered to be conservative or cautious, esp. the BBC.

au pair /ō páir/ *n.* a young foreign person, esp. a woman, helping with housework, etc., in exchange for room, board, and pocket money, esp. as a means of learning a language. [F]

aura /áwrə/ *n.* (*pl.* **aurae** /-ree/ or **auras**) **1** the distinctive atmosphere diffused by or attending a person, place, etc. **2** (in mystic or spiritualistic use) a supposed subtle emanation, visible as a sphere of white or colored light, surrounding the body of a living creature. **3** a subtle emanation or aroma from flowers, etc. **4** *Med.* premonitory symptom(s) in epilepsy, etc. [ME f. L f. Gk, = breeze, breath]
■ **1** air, atmosphere, feeling, ambience, spirit, sense, mood, character, quality. **3** odor, aroma, emanation, fragrance, scent, perfume; see also HINT *n.* 3.

aural[1] /áwrəl/ *adj.* of or relating to or received by the ear. □□ **aurally** *adv.* [L *auris* ear]
■ auditive, auditory, auricular.

aural[2] /áwrəl/ *adj.* of, relating to, or resembling an aura; atmospheric. [as AURA]
■ auric, atmospheric.

aureate /áwreeət/ *adj.* **1** golden, gold colored. **2** resplendent. **3** (of a language) highly ornamented. [ME f. LL *aureatus* f. L *aureus* golden f. *aurum* gold]

aureole /áwreeōl/ *n.* (also **aureola** /awreéələ/) **1** a halo or circle of light, esp. around the head or body of a portrayed religious figure. **2** a corona around the sun or moon. [ME f. L *aureola* (*corona*), = golden (crown), fem. of *aureolus* f. *aureus* f. *aurum* gold: *aureole* f. OF f. L *aureola*]

Aureomycin /áwreeōmísin/ *n. propr.* an antibiotic used esp. in lung diseases. [L *aureus* golden + Gk *mukēs* fungus + -IN]

au revoir /ō rəvwaár/ *int.* & *n.* good-bye (until we meet again). [F]

auric[1] /áwrik/ *adj.* of or relating to trivalent gold. [L *aurum* gold]

auric[2] /áwrik/ *adj.* = AURAL[2].

auricle /áwrikəl/ *n. Anat.* **1 a** a small muscular pouch on the surface of each atrium of the heart. **b** the atrium itself. **2** the external ear of animals. Also called PINNA. **3** an appendage shaped like the ear. [AURICULA]

auricula /awríkyələ/ *n.* a primrose, *Primula auricula*, with leaves shaped like bears' ears. [L, dimin. of *auris* ear]

auricular /awríkyələr/ *adj.* **1** of or relating to the ear or hearing. **2** of or relating to the auricle of the heart. **3** shaped like an auricle. □□ **auricularly** *adv.* [LL *auricularis* (as AURICULA)]

auriculate /awríkyələt, -layt/ *adj.* having one or more auricles or ear-shaped appendages. [L]
■ auditive, auditory, aural.

auriferous /awrífərəs/ *adj.* naturally bearing gold. [L *aurifer* f. *aurum* gold]

Aurignacian /áwrignáyshən/ *n.* & *adj.* ● *n.* a flint culture of the Paleolithic period in Europe following the Mousterian and preceding the Solutrean. ● *adj.* of this culture. [F *Aurignacien* f. *Aurignac* in SW France, where remains of it were found]

aurochs /áwroks, ówroks/ *n.* (*pl.* same) an extinct wild ox, *Bos primigenius*, ancestor of domestic cattle and formerly native to many parts of the world. Also called URUS. [G f. OHG *ūrohso* f. *ūr-* urus + *ohso* ox]

aurora /awráwrə/ *n.* (*pl.* **auroras** or **aurorae** /-ree/) **1** a luminous electrical atmospheric phenomenon, usu. of streamers of light in the sky above the northern or southern magnetic pole. **2** *poet.* the dawn. □ **aurora australis** /awstráylis/ a southern occurrence of aurora. **aurora borealis** /báwree-ális/ a northern occurrence of aurora. □□ **auroral** *adj.* **aurorean** *adj.* [L, = dawn, goddess of dawn]

auscultation /áwskəltáyshən/ *n.* the act of listening, esp. to sounds from the heart, lungs, etc., as a part of medical diagnosis. □□ **auscultatory** /-kúltətawree/ *adj.* [L *auscultatio* f. *auscultare* listen to]

auspice /áwspis/ *n.* **1** (in *pl.*) patronage (esp. *under the auspices of*). **2** a forecast. [orig. 'observation of bird flight in divination': F *auspice* or L *auspicium* f. *auspex* observer of birds f. *avis* bird]
■ **1** (*auspices*) aegis, sponsorship, authority, protection, support, backing, supervision, guidance, patronage, sanction, approval, control, influence. **2** see FORECAST *n.*

auspicious /awspíshəs/ *adj.* **1** of good omen; favorable. **2** prosperous. □□ **auspiciously** *adv.* **auspiciousness** *n.* [AUSPICE + -OUS]
■ **1** see PROPITIOUS 1.

Aussie /áwsee, -zee/ *n.* & *adj.* (also **Ossie, Ozzie**) *colloq.* ● *n.* **1** an Australian. **2** Australia. ● *adj.* Australian. [abbr.]

austere /awsteér/ *adj.* (**austerer, austerest**) **1** severely simple. **2** morally strict. **3** harsh; stern. □□ **austerely** *adv.* [ME f. OF f. L *austerus* f. Gk *austēros* severe]
■ **1** see SIMPLE *adj.* 2. **2** see STRICT 2a. **3** see STERN[1].

austerity /awstéritee/ *n.* (*pl.* **-ies**) **1** sternness; moral severity. **2** severe simplicity, e.g., of economies. **3** (esp. in *pl.*) an austere practice (*the austerities of a monk's life*).
■ **1** see *severity* (SEVERE). **3** rigors, asceticism; see also HARDSHIP.

Austin /áwstin/ *n.* = AUGUSTINIAN. [contr. of AUGUSTINE]

austral /áwstrəl/ *adj.* **1** southern. **2** (**Austral**) of Australia or Australasia (*Austral English*). [ME f. L *australis* f. *Auster* south wind]

Australasian /áwstrəláyzhən, -shən/ *adj.* of or relating to Australasia, a region consisting of Australia and islands of the SW Pacific. [*Australasia* f. F *Australasie*, formed as *Australia* + *Asia*]

Australian /awstráylyən/ *n.* & *adj.* ● *n.* **1** a native or inhabitant of Australia. **2** a person of Australian descent. **3** any of the aboriginal languages of Australia. ● *adj.* of or relating to Australia. □ **Australian Rules Football** a form of football played with a rugby ball by teams of 18. **Australian terrier** a wirehaired Australian breed of terrier. □□ **Australianism** *n.* **Australianize** *v.* [F *australien* f. L (as AUSTRAL)]

Australiana /awstráyleeánə, -aánə/ *n. pl.* objects relating to or characteristic of Australia.

Australoid /áwstrəloyd/ *adj.* of the ethnological type of the Australian aborigines.

australopithecus /áwstrəlōpíthikəs/ *n.* any extinct bipedal primate of the genus *Australopithecus* having apelike and human characteristics, or its fossilized remains. □□ **australopithecine** /-píthiseen/ *n.* & *adj.* [mod.L f. L *australis* southern + Gk *pithēkos* ape]

Austro- /áwstrō/ *comb. form* Austrian; Austrian and (*Austro-Hungarian*).

autarchy /áwtaarkee/ *n.* (*pl.* **-ies**) **1** absolute sovereignty. **2** despotism. **3** an autarchic country or society. □□ **autarchic** /-taárkik/ *adj.* **autarchical** *adj.* [mod.L *autarchia* (as AUTO-, Gk -*arkhia* f. *arkhō* rule)]
■ **1** see SUPREMACY 2. **2** see DESPOTISM.

autarky /áwtaarkee/ *n.* (*pl.* **-ies**) **1** self-sufficiency, esp. as an economic system. **2** a government, etc., run according to such a system. □□ **autarkic** /-taárkik/ *adj.* **autarkical** *adj.* **autarkist** *n.* [Gk *autarkeia* (as AUTO-, *arkeō* suffice)]

auth. *abbr.* **1** authentic. **2** author. **3** authority. **4** authorized.

authentic /awthéntik/ *adj.* **1 a** of undisputed origin; genuine. **b** reliable or trustworthy. **2** *Mus.* (of a mode) containing notes between the final and an octave higher (cf. PLAGAL). □□ **authentically** *adv.* **authenticity** /áwthentisitee/ *n.* [ME f. OF *autentique* f. LL *authenticus* f. Gk *authentikos* principal, genuine]
■ **1** genuine, real, actual, bona fide, sterling, factual, accurate, true, exact, legitimate, valid, echt, *colloq.* honest-to-goodness, kosher; authoritative, reliable, incontrovertible, veritable, trustworthy, dependable, faithful, undisputed, indubitable. □□ **authentically** genuinely, bona fide; reliably, authoritatively, faithfully. **authenticity** reality, realness, fact, truth, genuineness, accuracy, legitimacy, validity; reliability,

trustworthiness, dependability, authoritativeness, incontrovertibility.

authenticate /awthéntikayt/ *v.tr.* **1** establish the truth or genuineness of. **2** validate. □□ **authentication** /-káyshən/ *n.* **authenticator** *n.* [med.L *authenticare* f. LL *authenticus*: see AUTHENTIC]
■ verify, validate, certify, endorse, vouch for, confirm; clinch, seal; corroborate, substantiate, prove, sustain, make good, justify, support. □□ **authentication** verification, validation, certification, confirmation; corroboration; see also PROOF *n.* 3.

author /áwthər/ *n. & v.* ● *n.* (*fem.* **authoress** /áwthris, áwthərés/) **1** a writer, esp. of books. **2** the originator of an event, a condition, etc. (*the author of all my woes*). ● *v.tr.* be the author of (a book, the universe, a child, etc.). □□ **authorial** /awtháwriəl/ *adj.* [ME f. AF *autour*, OF *autor* f. L *auctor* f. *augēre auct-* increase, originate, promote]
■ *n.* **1** writer, man *or* woman of letters, penman, littérateur, wordsmith, *often derog.* scribbler; novelist, playwright, dramatist, essayist, poet; journalist, columnist. **2** creator, originator, inventor, father, founder, framer, initiator, maker, producer, begetter, prime mover, instigator, architect, designer, engineer; cause. ● *v.* see CREATE 1, WRITE 7.

authoritarian /ətháwritáireeən, əthór-/ *adj. & n.* ● *adj.* **1** favoring, encouraging, or enforcing strict obedience to authority, as opposed to individual freedom. **2** tyrannical or domineering. ● *n.* a person favoring absolute obedience to a constituted authority. □□ **authoritarianism** *n.*
■ *adj.* dictatorial, imperious, totalitarian, autocratic, tyrannical, despotic, autarchic(al), arbitrary, absolute, dogmatic, domineering, high-handed, overweening, strict, rigid, inflexible, severe, tough, unyielding. ● *n.* disciplinarian, absolutist. □□ **authoritarianism** strictness, inflexibility, rigidity, severity; see also TYRANNY.

authoritative /ətháwritáytiv, əthór-/ *adj.* **1** being recognized as true or dependable. **2** (of a person, behavior, etc.) commanding or self-confident. **3** official; supported by authority (*an authoritative document*). **4** having or claiming influence through recognized knowledge or expertise. □□ **authoritatively** *adv.* **authoritativeness** *n.*
■ **1** dependable, reliable, trustworthy, authentic, definitive, valid, sound, veritable, verifiable, accurate, factual, faithful, true, truthful. **2** see DOMINANT *adj.*, *self-assured* (SELF-ASSURANCE). **3** official, approved, valid, authentic, documented, certified, validated, legitimate, lawful, accredited, sanctioned, recognized, accepted. **4** influential, scholarly, learned, knowledgeable, well-informed, *colloq.* in the know. □□ **authoritatively** officially, learnedly, knowledgeably; reliably, dependably, definitively, soundly, faithfully, truthfully; self-confidently, confidently, self-assuredly, with certainty *or* conviction, convincingly. **authoritativeness** authority, knowledgeability, scholarliness, learnedness; reliability, dependability, soundness, faithfulness, truthfulness; legitimacy; see also CONFIDENCE 2b.

authority /ətháwritee, əthór-/ *n.* (*pl.* **-ies**) **1 a** the power or right to enforce obedience. **b** (often foll. by *for*, or *to* + infin.) delegated power. **2** (esp. in *pl.*) a person or body having authority, esp. political or administrative. **3 a** an influence exerted on opinion because of recognized knowledge or expertise. **b** such an influence expressed in a book, quotation, etc. (*an authority on vintage cars*). **c** a person whose opinion is accepted, esp. an expert in a subject. **4** the weight of evidence. [ME f. OF *autorité* f. L *auctoritas* f. *auctor*: see AUTHOR]
■ **1 a** power, jurisdiction, dominion, right, control, prerogative. **b** authorization, license; see also PERMISSION. **2** (*authorities*) government, establishment, officials, officialdom, powers that be. **3 a** see INFLUENCE *n.* **c** expert, specialist, scholar, sage, judge, arbiter, connoisseur, *colloq.* maven. **4** word, testimony,

evidence, attestation, averment, asseveration, *colloq.* say-so.

authorize /áwthəriz/ *v.tr.* **1** sanction. **2** (foll. by *to* + infin.) **a** give authority. **b** commission (a person or body) (*authorized to trade*). □ **Authorized Version** an English translation of the Bible made in 1611 and used in Protestant worship. Also called *King James Version.* □□ **authorization** /-rizáyshən/ *n.* [ME f. OF *autoriser* f. med.L *auctorizare* f. *auctor*: see AUTHOR]
■ **1** sanction, approve, countenance, consent *or* subscribe to, permit, allow, license, endorse, give the go-ahead to, *colloq.* OK, give the green light to; legalize, legitimatize, legitimize. **2 a** permit, give leave *or* permission, allow, license, entitle, empower. **b** commission, license. □□ **authorization** see LICENSE, PERMISSION.

authorship /áwthərship/ *n.* **1** the origin of a book or other written work (*of unknown authorship*). **2** the occupation of writing.

autism /áwtizəm/ *n. Psychol.* a mental condition, usu. present from childhood, characterized by complete self-absorption and a reduced ability to respond to or communicate with the outside world. □□ **autistic** /awtístik/ *adj.* [mod.L *autismus* (as AUTO-, -ISM)]

auto /áwtō/ *n.* (*pl.* **-os**) *colloq.* an automobile. [abbr. of AUTOMOBILE]

auto- /áwtō/ *comb. form* (usu. **aut-** before a vowel) **1** self (*autism*). **2** one's own (*autobiography*). **3** by oneself or spontaneous (*autosuggestion*). **4** by itself or automatic (*automobile*). [from or after Gk *auto-* f. *autos* self]

autobahn /áwtōbaan/ *n.* (*pl.* **autobahns** or **autobahnen** /-nən/) a German, Austrian, or Swiss highway. [G f. *Auto* car + *Bahn* path, road]

autobiography /áwtōbīógrəfee/ *n.* (*pl.* **-ies**) **1** a personal account of one's own life, esp. for publication. **2** this as a process or literary form. □□ **autobiographer** *n.* **autobiographic** /-bíəgráfik/ *adj.* **autobiographical** *adj.*

autocephalous /áwtōséfələs/ *adj.* **1** (esp. of an Eastern church) appointing its own head. **2** (of a bishop, church, etc.) independent. [Gk *autokephalos* (as AUTO-, *kephalē* head)]

autochthon /awtókthən/ *n.* (*pl.* **autochthons** or **autochthones** /-thəneez/) (in *pl.*) the original or earliest known inhabitants of a country; aboriginals. □□ **autochthonal** *adj.* **autochthonic** /-thónik/ *adj.* **autochthonous** *adj.* [Gk, = sprung from the earth (as AUTO-, *khthōn*, *-onos* earth)]
■ see ABORIGINAL *n.* 1.

autoclave /áwtōklayv/ *n.* **1** a strong vessel used for chemical reactions at high pressures and temperatures. **2** a sterilizer using high pressure steam. [AUTO- + L *clavus* nail or *clavis* key]

autocracy /awtókrəsee/ *n.* (*pl.* **-ies**) **1** absolute government by one person. **2** the power exercised by such a person. **3** an autocratic country or society. [Gk *autokrateia* (as AUTOCRAT)]
■ **1** see TYRANNY. **3** tyranny, dictatorship.

autocrat /áwtəkrat/ *n.* **1** an absolute ruler. **2** a dictatorial person. □□ **autocratic** /-krátik/ *adj.* **autocratically** *adv.* [F *autocrate* f. Gk *autokratēs* (as AUTO-, *kratos* power)]
■ **1** see DICTATOR 1, 2. **2** see DICTATOR 3.

autocross /áwtōkraws, -kros/ *n.* automobile racing across country or on unpaved roads or to display driving skill. [AUTOMOBILE + CROSS- 1]

Autocue /áwtōkyōō/ *n. Brit. propr.* a device, unseen by the audience, displaying a television script to a speaker or performer as an aid to memory (cf. TELEPROMPTER).

auto-da-fé /áwtōdaafáy/ *n.* (*pl.* **autos-da-fé** /áwtōz-/) **1** a sentence of punishment by the Spanish Inquisition. **2** the

---

/.../ pronunciation	● part of speech
□ phrases, idioms, and compounds	
□□ derivatives	■ synonym section
cross-references appear in SMALL CAPITALS or *italics*	

execution of such a sentence, esp. the burning of a heretic. [Port., = act of the faith]

autodidact /áwtōdídakt, -dákt/ *n.* a self-taught person. □□ **autodidactic** /-dáktik/ *adj.* [AUTO- + *didact* as DIDACTIC]

autoerotism /áwtō-érətizəm/ *n.* (also **autoeroticism** /-irótisizəm/) *Psychol.* sexual excitement generated by stimulating one's own body; masturbation. □□ **autoerotic** /-irótik/ *adj.*

autofocus /áwtōfōkəs/ *n.* a device for focusing a camera, etc., automatically.

autogamy /awtōgəmee/ *n. Bot.* self-fertilization in plants. □□ **autogamous** *adj.* [AUTO- + Gk *-gamia* f. *gamos* marriage]

autogenous /awtójinəs/ *adj.* self-produced. □ **autogenous welding** a process of joining metal by melting the edges together without adding material.

autogiro /áwtōjírō/ *n.* (also **autogyro**) (*pl.* **-os**) an early form of helicopter with freely rotating horizontal vanes and a propeller. [Sp. (as AUTO-, *giro* gyration)]

autograft /áwtōgraft/ *n. Surgery* a graft of tissue from one point to another of the same person's body.

autograph /áwtəgraf/ *n. & v.* ● *n.* **1 a** a signature, esp. that of a celebrity. **b** handwriting. **2** a manuscript in an author's own handwriting. **3** a document signed by its author. ● *v.tr.* **1** sign (a photograph, autograph album, etc.). **2** write (a letter, etc.) by hand. [F *autographe* or LL *autographum* f. Gk *autographon* neut. of *autographos* (as AUTO-, -GRAPH)]
■ *n.* **2** holograph. ● *v.* **1** see SIGN *v.* 1.

autography /awtógrəfee/ *n.* **1** writing done with one's own hand. **2** the facsimile reproduction of writing or illustration. □□ **autographic** /-təgráfik/ *adj.*

autogyro var. of AUTOGIRO.

Autoharp /áwtōhaarp/ *n. propr.* a kind of zither with a mechanical device to allow the playing of chords.

autoimmune /áwtōimyŏŏn/ *adj. Med.* (of a disease) caused by antibodies produced against substances naturally present in the body. □□ **autoimmunity** *n.*

autointoxication /áwtōintóksikáyshən/ *n. Med.* poisoning by a toxin formed within the body itself.

autolysis /awtólisis/ *n.* the destruction of cells by their own enzymes. □□ **autolytic** /áwtəlítik/ *adj.* [G *Autolyse* (as AUTO-, -LYSIS)]

Automat /áwtəmat/ *n. propr.* a cafeteria containing coin-operated machines dispensing food and drink. [G f. F *automate*, formed as AUTOMATION]

automate /áwtəmayt/ *v.tr.* convert to or operate by automation (*the ticket office has been automated*). □ **automated teller machine** electronic machine that allows customers to insert a card, punch in an identification number, and then perform banking transactions such as depositing or withdrawing funds, etc. ¶Abbr.: **ATM.** [back-form. f. AUTOMATION]
■ automatize. □ **automated teller machine** *colloq.* cash machine, automatic teller machine.

automatic /áwtəmátik/ *adj. & n.* ● *adj.* **1** (of a machine, device, etc., or its function) working by itself, without direct human intervention. **2 a** done spontaneously; without conscious thought or intention (*an automatic reaction*). **b** necessary and inevitable (*an automatic penalty*). **3** *Psychol.* performed unconsciously or subconsciously. **4** (of a firearm) that continues firing until the ammunition is exhausted or the pressure on the trigger is released. **5** (of a motor vehicle or its transmission) using gears that change automatically according to speed and acceleration. ● *n.* **1** an automatic device, esp. a gun or transmission. **2** *colloq.* a vehicle with automatic transmission. □ **automatic pilot** a device for keeping an aircraft on a set course. □□ **automatically** *adv.*

automaticity /áwtəmətísitee/ *n.* [formed as AUTOMATON + -IC]
■ *adj.* **1** self-acting, self-governing, self-regulating, self-executing, mechanical, robotic, automated. **2 a** mechanical, involuntary, instinctive, instinctual, natural, spontaneous, impulsive, immediate, conditioned, unconscious, subconscious, intuitive, reflex, knee-jerk, gut, robotlike, robotic, unbidden. **b** unavoidable, inevitable, inescapable, ineluctable;

mandatory, compulsory; assured, definite. **3** see sense 2a above. ● *n.* **1** (*spec.*) *Mil.* machine-gun, MG, tommy gun, pom-pom, Bren, Gatling (gun), Lewis gun, Sten gun, *sl.* chopper. □ **automatic pilot** autopilot, *Brit. sl.* George. □□ **automatically** mechanically, by itself *or* oneself, on its *or* one's own; involuntarily, instinctively, instinctually, intuitively, spontaneously, impulsively, immediately, unconsciously, unthinkingly; see also NECESSARILY.

automation /áwtəmáyshən/ *n.* **1** the use of automatic equipment to save mental and manual labor. **2** the automatic control of the manufacture of a product through its successive stages. [irreg. f. AUTOMATIC + -ATION]

automatism /awtómətizəm/ *n.* **1** *Psychol.* the performance of actions unconsciously or subconsciously; such action. **2** involuntary action. **3** unthinking routine. [F *automatisme* f. *automate* AUTOMATON]

automatize /awtómətīz/ *v.tr.* **1** make (a process, etc.) automatic. **2** subject (a business, enterprise, etc.) to automation. □□ **automatization** *n.* [AUTOMATIC + -IZE]
■ automate.

automaton /awtómətən, -ton/ *n.* (*pl.* **automata** /-tə/ *or* **automatons**) **1** a piece of mechanism with concealed motive power. **2** a person who behaves mechanically, like an automaton. [L f. Gk, neut. of *automatos* acting of itself: see AUTO-]
■ **1** see ROBOT 1, 2. **2** see ROBOT 3.

automobile /áwtəməbeel/ *n.* a motor vehicle for road use with an enclosed passenger compartment; a car. [F (as AUTO-, MOBILE)]
■ see CAR 1.

automotive /áwtəmőtiv/ *adj.* concerned with motor vehicles.

autonomic /áwtənómik/ *adj.* esp. *Physiol.* functioning involuntarily. □ **autonomic nervous system** the part of the nervous system responsible for control of the bodily functions not consciously directed, e.g., heartbeat. [AUTONOMY + -IC]

autonomous /awtónəməs/ *adj.* **1** having self-government. **2** acting independently or having the freedom to do so. □□ **autonomously** *adv.* [Gk *autonomos* (as AUTONOMY)]
■ **1** see INDEPENDENT *adj.* 1b.

autonomy /awtónəmee/ *n.* (*pl.* **-ies**) **1** the right of self-government. **2** personal freedom. **3** freedom of the will. **4** a self-governing community. □□ **autonomist** *n.* [Gk *autonomia* f. *autos* self + *nomos* law]
■ **1** see SELF-GOVERNMENT 1. **2** see FREEDOM 1, 2. **3** freedom, independence, self-determination.

autopilot /áwtōpilət/ *n.* an automatic pilot. [abbr.]

autopsy /áwtopsee/ *n.* (*pl.* **-ies**) **1** a postmortem examination to determine cause of death, etc. **2** any critical analysis. **3** a personal inspection. [F *autopsie* or mod.L *autopsia* f. Gk f. *autoptēs* eyewitness]
■ **1** postmortem, necropsy. **2** *colloq.* postmortem; see also ANALYSIS 1.

autoradiograph /áwtōráydeeəgraf/ *n.* a photograph of an object, produced by radiation from radioactive material in the object. □□ **autoradiographic** *adj.* **autoradiography** /áwtōráydiógrəfee/ *n.*

autosuggestion /áwtōsəgjéschən/ *n.* a hypnotic or subconscious suggestion made by a person to himself or herself and affecting behavior.

autotelic /áwtōtélik/ *adj.* having or being a purpose in itself. [AUTO- + Gk *telos* end]

autotomy /awtótəmee/ *n. Zool.* the casting off of a part of the body when threatened, e.g., the tail of a lizard.

autotoxin /áwtōtóksin/ *n.* a poisonous substance originating within an organism. □□ **autotoxic** *adj.*

autotrophic /áwtətrófik, -trṓ-/ *adj. Biol.* able to form complex nutritional organic substances from simple inorganic substances such as carbon dioxide (cf. HETEROTROPHIC). [AUTO- + Gk *trophos* feeder]

autotype /áwtətīp/ *n.* **1** a facsimile. **2 a** a photographic printing process for monochrome reproduction. **b** a print made by this process.

autoxidation /awtōksidáyshən/ *n. Chem.* oxidation by exposure to air at room temperature.

autumn /áwtəm/ n. **1** the third season of the year, when crops and fruits are gathered, and leaves fall, in the N. hemisphere from September to November and in the S. hemisphere from March to May. Also called FALL. **2** *Astron.* the period from the autumnal equinox to the winter solstice. **3** a time of maturity or incipient decay. □ **autumn crocus** any plant of the genus *Colchicum*, esp. meadow saffron, of the lily family and unrelated to the true crocus. [ME f. OF *autompne* f. L *autumnus*]
■ **1** fall.

autumnal /awtúmnəl/ adj. **1** of, characteristic of, or appropriate to autumn (*autumnal colors*). **2** occurring in autumn (*autumnal equinox*). **3** maturing or blooming in autumn. **4** past the prime of life. [L *autumnalis* (as AUTUMN, -AL)]

auxiliary /awgzílyəree/ adj. & n. ● adj. **1** (of a person or thing) that gives help. **2** (of services or equipment) subsidiary; additional. ● n. (pl. **-ies**) **1** an auxiliary person or thing. **2** (in pl.) *Mil.* auxiliary troops. **3** *Gram.* an auxiliary verb. □ **auxiliary troops** *Mil.* foreign or allied troops in a belligerent nation's service. **auxiliary verb** *Gram.* one used in forming tenses, moods, and voices of other verbs. [L *auxiliarius* f. *auxilium* help]
■ adj. supportive, support; additional, accessory, supplementary, supplemental, subsidiary, ancillary, secondary, extra, reserve. ● n. **1** help, assistance, aid, support, accessory; helper, assistant, aide, supporter, helpmate, man Friday, girl or gal Friday; subordinate, deputy.

auxin /áwksin/ n. a plant hormone that regulates growth. [G f. Gk *auxō* increase + -IN]

AV abbr. **1** audiovisual (teaching aids, etc.). **2** Authorized Version (of the Bible).

avail /əváyl/ v. & n. ● v. **1** tr. help; benefit. **2** refl. (foll. by *of*) profit by; take advantage of. **3** intr. **a** provide help. **b** be of use, value, or profit. ● n. (usu. in neg. or interrog. phrases) use; profit (*to no avail; without avail; of what avail?*). [ME f. obs. *vail* (v.) f. OF *valoir* be worth f. L *valēre*]
■ v. **2** (*avail oneself of*) see PROFIT v. 2. ● n. see PROFIT n. 1.

available /əváyləbəl/ adj. (often foll. by *to, for*) **1** capable of being used; at one's disposal. **2** within one's reach. **3** (of a person) **a** free. **b** able to be contacted. □□ **availability** n. **availableness** n. **availably** adv. [ME f. AVAIL + -ABLE]
■ **1** at one's disposal, free, unoccupied, unengaged, not busy; on the market, in stock, on sale. **2** at or to hand, close at hand, accessible, handy, present, ready, (readily) obtainable, nearby, close by, within (easy) reach, on hand, at one's elbow, colloq. getatable, on tap. **3** free, unoccupied, at liberty, not busy, on hand, in attendance; contactable, accessible.

avalanche /ávəlanch/ n. & v. ● n. **1** a mass of snow and ice tumbling rapidly down a mountain. **2** a sudden appearance or arrival of anything in large quantities (*faced with an avalanche of work*). ● v. **1** intr. descend like an avalanche. **2** tr. carry down like an avalanche. [F, alt. of dial. *lavanche* after *avaler* descend]

avant-garde /avón-gaárd/ n. & adj. ● n. pioneers or innovators, esp. in art and literature. ● adj. (of ideas, etc.) new; progressive. □□ **avant-gardism** n. **avant-gardist** n. [F, = vanguard]
■ n. vanguard, innovators, pioneers, trendsetters. ● adj. innovative, advanced, progressive, experimental, original, new, trendsetting, pioneering; unconventional, eccentric, far-out, unusual, unorthodox, offbeat, colloq. way-out; revolutionary, extreme, extremist. □□ **avant-gardist** innovator, pioneer, trendsetter, experimenter; eccentric; extremist, revolutionary.

avarice /ávəris/ n. extreme greed for money or gain; cupidity. □□ **avaricious** /-ríshəs/ adj. **avariciously** adv. **avariciousness** /-ríshəsnis/ n. [ME f. OF f. L *avaritia* f. *avarus* greedy]
■ avariciousness, greed, greediness, acquisitiveness, cupidity, covetousness, graspingness, rapacity, selfishness, Brit. itching palm. □□ **avaricious** greedy, acquisitive, grasping, covetous, mercenary, selfish, rapacious. **avariciously** greedily, covetously,

acquisitively, graspingly. **avariciousness** see AVARICE above.

avast /əvást/ int. Naut. stop; cease. [Du. *houd vast* hold fast]

avatar /ávətaar/ n. **1** (in Hindu mythology) the descent of a deity or released soul to earth in bodily form. **2** incarnation; manifestation. **3** a manifestation or phase. [Skr. *avatāra* descent f. *ava* down + *tr̥-* pass over]

avaunt /əváwnt, əvaánt/ int. archaic begone. [ME f. AF f. OF *avant* ult. f. L *ab* from + *ante* before]

Ave. abbr. Avenue.

ave /aávay/ int. & n. ● int. **1** welcome. **2** farewell. ● n. **1** (in full **Ave Maria**) a prayer to the Virgin Mary, the opening line from Luke 1:28. Also called *Hail Mary*. **2** a shout of welcome or farewell. [ME f. L, 2nd sing. imper. of *avēre* fare well]

avenge /əvénj/ v.tr. **1** inflict retribution on behalf of (a person, a violated right, etc.). **2** take vengeance for (an injury). □ **be avenged** avenge oneself. □□ **avenger** n. [ME f. OF *avengier* f. *à* to + *vengier* f. L *vindicare* vindicate]
■ **2** see REVENGE v. 2.

avens /ávənz/ n. any of various plants of the genus *Geum*. □ **mountain avens** a related plant (*Dryas octopetala*). [ME f. OF *avence* (med.L *avencia*), of unkn. orig.]

aventurine /əvénchəreen, -rin/ n. Mineral. **1** brownish glass or mineral containing sparkling gold colored particles usu. of copper or gold. **2** a variety of spangled quartz resembling this. [F f. It. *avventurino* f. *avventura* chance (because of its accidental discovery)]

avenue /ávənoō, -nyoō/ n. **1 a** a broad road or street, often with trees at regular intervals along its sides. **b** esp. Brit. a tree-lined approach to a country house. **2** a way of approaching or dealing with something (*explored every avenue to find an answer*). [F, fem. past part. of *avenir* f. L *advenire* come to]
■ **1 a** see ROAD¹ 1. **2** see ROUTE n.

aver /əvór/ v.tr. (**averred, averring**) formal assert; affirm. [ME f. OF *averer* (as AD-, L *verus* true)]
■ see DECLARE 3.

average /ávərij, ávrij/ n., adj., & v. ● n. **1 a** the usual amount, extent, or rate. **b** the ordinary standard. **2** an amount obtained by dividing the total of given amounts by the number of amounts in the set. **3** Law the distribution of loss resulting from damage to a ship or cargo. ● adj. **1 a** usual; typical. **b** mediocre; undistinguished. **2** estimated or calculated by average. ● v.tr. **1** amount on average to (*the sale of the product averaged one hundred a day*). **2** do on average (*averages six hours' work a day*). **3 a** estimate or calculate the average of. **b** estimate the general standard of. □ **average out** result in an average. **average out at** result in an average of. **batting average 1** Baseball a batter's safe hits per official times at bat. **2** Cricket a batsman's runs scored per completed innings. **law of averages** the principle that if one of two extremes occurs the other will also tend to so as to maintain the normal average. **on** (or **on an**) **average** as an average rate or estimate. □□ **averagely** adv. [F *avarie* damage to ship or cargo (see sense 3), f. It. *avaria* f. Arab. *ʿawārīya* damaged goods f. *ʿawār* damage at sea, loss: *-age* after *damage*]
■ n. **1** standard, usual, mean, norm, (happy) medium. ● adj. **1 a** normal, common, usual, customary, general, typical, ordinary, regular, standard. **b** mediocre, middling, run-of-the-mill, commonplace, undistinguished, unexceptional, indifferent, so-so, colloq. no great shakes. **2** mean. □ **on average** in the main, generally, in general, normally, usually, ordinarily, typically, commonly, customarily, as a rule, for the most part. □□ **averagely** see QUITE 2.

averment /əvórmənt/ n. a positive statement; an affirmation,

/.../ pronunciation	● part of speech
□ phrases, idioms, and compounds	
□□ derivatives	■ synonym section
cross-references appear in SMALL CAPITALS or *italics*	

esp. *Law* one with an offer of proof. [ME f. AF, OF *aver(r)ement* (as AVER, -MENT)]
■ see PROFESSION 3.

averse /əvɔ́rs/ *predic.adj.* (usu. foll. by *to*; also foll. by *from*) opposed; disinclined (*was not averse to helping me*). ¶ Construction with *to* is now more common. [L *aversus* (as AVERT)]
■ disinclined, unwilling, reluctant, resistant, loath, opposed, antipathetic, ill-disposed, indisposed, hostile, antagonistic; anti, against.

aversion /əvɔ́rzhən, -shən/ *n.* **1** (usu. foll. by *to, from, for*) a dislike or unwillingness (*has an aversion to hard work*). **2** an object of dislike (*my pet aversion*). □ **aversion therapy** therapy designed to make a subject averse to an existing habit. [F *aversion* or L *aversio* (as AVERT, -ION)]
■ **1** dislike, abhorrence, repugnance, antipathy, antagonism, animosity, hostility, loathing, hatred, odium, horror; disinclination, unwillingness, resistance, reluctance, distaste. **2** dislike, bugbear, bête noire, *colloq.* hate, peeve.

avert /əvɔ́rt/ *v.tr.* (often foll. by *from*) **1** turn away (one's eyes or thoughts). **2** prevent or ward off (an undesirable occurrence). □□ **avertable** *adj.* **avertible** *adj.* [ME f. L *avertere* (as AB-, *vertere vers-* turn): partly f. OF *avertir* f. Rmc]
■ **1** see DEFLECT. **2** see PREVENT 1.

Avesta /əvéstə/ *n.* (usu. prec. by *the*) the sacred writings of Zoroastrianism (cf. ZEND). [Pers.]

Avestan /əvéstən/ *adj. & n.* ● *adj.* of or relating to the Avesta. ● *n.* the ancient Iranian language of the Avesta.

avg. *abbr.* average.

avian /áyveeən/ *adj.* of or relating to birds. [L *avis* bird]
■ ornithological.

aviary /áyvee-eree/ *n.* (*pl.* **-ies**) a large enclosure or building for keeping birds. [L *aviarium* (as AVIAN, -ARY¹)]

aviate /áyveeayt/ *v.* **1** *intr.* fly in an airplane. **2** *tr.* pilot (an airplane). [back-form. f. AVIATION]

aviation /áyveeáyshən/ *n.* **1** the skill or practice of operating aircraft. **2** aircraft manufacture. [F f. L *avis* bird]

aviator /áyveeaytər/ *n.* (*fem.* **aviatrix** /áyveeáytriks/) a person who pilots an aircraft. [F *aviateur* f. L *avis* bird]

aviculture /áyvikulchər/ *n.* the rearing and keeping of birds. □□ **aviculturist** /-kúlchərist/ *n.* [L *avis* bird, after AGRICULTURE]

avid /ávid/ *adj.* (usu. foll. by *of, for*) eager; greedy. □□ **avidity** /əvíditee/ *n.* **avidly** *adv.* [F *avide* or L *avidus* f. *avēre* crave]
■ see EAGER.

avifauna /áyvifawnə/ *n.* birds of a region or country collectively. [L *avis* bird + FAUNA]

avionics /áyveeóniks/ *n.pl.* (treated as *sing.*) electronics as applied to aviation.

avitaminosis /ayvitəminṓsis/ *n.* *Med.* a condition resulting from a deficiency of one or more vitamins.

avizandum /ávizándəm/ *n.* *Sc. Law* a period of time for further consideration of a judgment. [med.L, gerund of *avizare* consider (as ADVISE)]

avocado /ávəkaádō, aávə-/ *n.* (*pl.* **-os**) **1** (in full **avocado pear**) a pear-shaped fruit with rough leathery skin, a smooth oily edible flesh, and a large stone. **2** the tropical evergreen tree, *Persea americana*, native to Central America, bearing this fruit. Also called *alligator pear*. **3** the light green color of the flesh of this fruit. [Sp., = advocate (substituted for Aztec *ahuacatl*)]

avocation /ávōkáyshən/ *n.* **1** a minor occupation. **2** *colloq.* a vocation or calling. [L *avocatio* f. *avocare* call away]
■ calling, vocation; see also INTEREST *n.* 2.

avocet /ávəset/ *n.* any wading bird of the genus *Recurvirostra* with long legs and a long slender upward-curved bill and usu. black and white plumage. [F *avocette* f. It. *avosetta*]

Avogadro's constant /ávōgaádrōz, aávō-/ *n.* (also **Avogadro's number**) *Physics* the number of atoms or molecules in one mole of a substance; 6.02×10^{23}. [A. *Avogadro*, It. physicist d. 1856]

Avogadro's law /ávōgaádrōz, aávō-/ *n.* *Physics* the law that equal volumes of all gases at the same temperature and pressure contain the same number of molecules.

avoid /əvóyd/ *v.tr.* **1** refrain or keep away from (a thing, person, or action). **2** escape; evade. **3** *Law* **a** nullify (a decree or contract). **b** quash (a sentence). □□ **avoidable** *adj.* **avoidably** *adv.* **avoidance** *n.* **avoider** *n.* [AF *avoider*, OF *evuider* clear out, get quit of, f. *vuide* empty, VOID]
■ **1** shun, keep *or* stay (away) from, keep off, leave alone, keep *or* steer clear of, keep at arm's length, fight shy of, give a wide berth to, refrain from, abstain from, miss, *literary* eschew. **2** escape, evade, get away from *or* without, miss; dodge, circumvent, sidestep, elude, skirt (around), keep *or* steer clear of, fight shy of; ward *or* fend *or* stave off, keep away. □□ **avoidable** escapable, evadable. **avoidance** see EVASION 1.

avoirdupois /ávərdəpóyz/ *n.* (in full **avoirdupois weight**) **1** a system of weights based on a pound of 16 ounces or 7,000 grains. **2** weight; heaviness. [ME f. OF *aveir de peis* goods of weight f. *aveir* f. L *habēre* have + *peis* (see POISE¹)]

avouch /əvówch/ *v.tr. & intr.* guarantee; affirm; confess. □□ **avouchment** *n.* [ME f. OF *avochier* f. L *advocare* (as AD-, *vocare* call)]
■ see DECLARE 3.

avow /əvów/ *v.tr.* **1** admit; confess. **2 a** *refl.* admit that one is (*avowed himself the author*). **b** (as **avowed** *adj.*) admitted (*the avowed author*). □□ **avowal** *n.* **avowedly** /əvówidlee/ *adv.* [ME f. OF *avouer* acknowledge f. L *advocare* (as AD-, *vocare* call)]
■ **1** see CONFESS 1a.

avulsion /əvúlshən/ *n.* **1** a tearing away. **2** *Law* a sudden removal of land by a flood, etc., to another person's property. [F *avulsion* or L *avulsio* f. *avellere avuls-* pluck away]

avuncular /əvúngkyələr/ *adj.* like or of an uncle; kind and friendly, esp. toward a younger person. [L *avunculus* maternal uncle, dimin. of *avus* grandfather]

AWACS /áywaks/ *n.* a long-range radar system for detecting enemy aircraft. [abbr. of *airborne warning and control system*]

await /əwáyt/ *v.tr.* **1** wait for. **2** (of an event or thing) be in store for (*a surprise awaits you*). [ME f. AF *awaitier*, OF *aguaitier* (as AD-, *waitier* WAIT)]

awake /əwáyk/ *v. & adj.* ● *v.* (*past* **awoke** /əwṓk/; *past part.* **awoken** /əwṓkən/) **1** *intr.* **a** cease to sleep. **b** become active. **2** *intr.* (foll. by *to*) become aware of. **3** *tr.* rouse, esp. from sleep. ● *predic.adj.* **1 a** not asleep. **b** vigilant. **2** (foll. by *to*) aware of. [OE *āwæcnan, āwacian* (as A-², WAKE¹)]
■ *v.* **1 a** wake (up), awaken, get up, rouse *or* bestir oneself, come to, *colloq.* surface. **b** see STIR¹ *v.* 2c. **2** (*awake to*) awaken to, wake up to, realize, understand, become aware *or* conscious of, become sensitive *or* alive to, become informed *or* knowledgeable about, *colloq.* get wise to, get on to. **3** awaken, animate, arouse, rouse, stimulate, revive, incite, excite, activate, alert; stir up, fan, kindle, ignite, fire. ● *predic.adj.* **1 a** up (and about), aroused, roused, astir, wide awake, open-eyed, conscious. **b** vigilant, alert, on the alert, on the qui vive, watchful, on one's guard *or* toes, on the spot, attentive, aware, conscious, alive; heedful. **2** see AWARE 1.

awaken /əwáykən/ *v.tr. & intr.* **1** = AWAKE *v.* **2** (often foll. by *to*) make aware. [OE *onwæcnan*, etc. (as A-², WAKEN)]
■ **1** see AWAKE *v.* **2** arouse, rouse, alert; (*awaken to*) make aware *or* conscious *or* apprised of, arouse *or* alert to, inform *or* apprise *or* advise of.

award /əwáwrd/ *v. & n.* ● *v.tr.* **1** give or order to be given as a payment, compensation, or prize (*awarded her a scholarship; was awarded damages*). **2** grant; assign. ● *n.* **1 a** a payment, compensation, or prize awarded. **b** the act or process of awarding. **2** a judicial decision. □□ **awarder** *n.* [ME f. AF *awarder*, ult. f. Gmc: see WARD]
■ *v.* grant, give (out), donate; confer on, bestow on, present to, furnish with, endow with; assign, apportion, accord. ● *n.* **1 a** a prize, trophy, reward, honor(s); payment, subsidy, grant, donation, gift, compensation, damages, subvention. **b** grant, bestowal, presentation, endowment, conferral. **2** see DECISION 2, 3.

aware /əwáir/ *predic.adj.* **1** (often foll. by *of*, or *that* + clause) conscious; not ignorant; having knowledge. **2** well-informed. ¶ Also found in *attrib.* use in sense 2, as in *a very aware person*; this is *disp.* □□ **awareness** *n.* [OE *gewær*]

■ **1** awake, alert, on the qui vive, *colloq.* switched-on, *poet.* ware; (*aware of*) conscious *or* cognizant *or* sensible of, sensitive *or* awake *or* alert to, informed *or* apprised *or* seized of, *colloq.* wise to. **2** well-informed, knowledgeable, knowing, posted, in the know, enlightened, au fait, au courant, *colloq.* switched-on, *sl.* hip. □□ **awareness** see SENSITIVITY, UNDERSTANDING *n.* 1, 5.

awash /əwósh, əwáwsh/ *predic.adj.* **1** level with the surface of water, so that it just washes over. **2** carried or washed by the waves; flooded or as if flooded.

away /əwáy/ *adv., adj., & n.* ● *adv.* **1** to or at a distance from the place, person, or thing in question (*go away*; *give away*; *look away*; *they are away*; *5 miles away*). **2** toward or into nonexistence (*sounds die away*; *explain it away*; *idled their time away*). **3** constantly; persistently; continuously (*work away*; *laugh away*). **4** without delay (*ask away*). ● *adj.* **1** *Sports* played at an opponent's field, etc. (*away game*; *away win*). **2** absent or distant. **3** *Baseball* out. ● *n. Sports* an away game or win. □ **away with** (as *imper.*) take away; let us be rid of. [OE *onweg, aweg* on one's way f. A² + WAY]

■ □ **away with** down with.

awe /aw/ *n. & v.* ● *n.* reverential fear or wonder (*stand in awe of*). ● *v.tr.* inspire with awe. □ **awe-inspiring** causing awe or wonder; amazing; magnificent. □□ **awe-inspiringly** *adv.* [ME *age* f. ON *agi* f. Gmc]

■ *n.* see WONDER *n.* 1. □□ **awe-inspiring** see AWESOME 1.

aweary /əweéree/ *predic.adj. poet.* (often foll. by *of*) weary. [aphetic *a* + WEARY]

aweigh /əwáy/ *predic.adj. Naut.* (of an anchor) clear of the sea or river bed; hanging. [A² + WEIGH¹]

awesome /áwsəm/ *adj.* **1** inspiring awe. **2** *sl.* excellent; superb. □□ **awesomely** *adv.* **awesomeness** *n.* [AWE + -SOME¹]

■ **1** awe-inspiring, imposing, overwhelming, formidable, daunting, dreadful, fearsome, fearful, frightening, horrifying, terrifying, terrible; breathtaking, amazing, wonderful, marvelous, moving, stirring, affecting, *poet.* awful, wondrous; unbelievable, incredible; alarming, shocking, stupefying, astounding, astonishing, *colloq.* stunning. **2** see GREAT *adj.* 10.

awestricken /áwstrikən/ *adj.* (also **awestruck** /-struk/) struck or affected by awe.

awful /áwfŏŏl/ *adj.* **1** *colloq.* **a** unpleasant or horrible (*awful weather*). **b** poor in quality; very bad (*has awful writing*). **c** (*attrib.*) excessive; remarkably large (*an awful lot of money*). **2** *poet.* inspiring awe. □□ **awfulness** *n.* [AWE + -FUL]

■ **1 a, b** unpleasant, horrible, atrocious, horrendous, disagreeable, nasty, abhorrent, repellent, gruesome, desperate, detestable, woeful, unspeakable, grotesque, execrable, *colloq.* terrible, horrid, ghastly, hideous, dreadful, abominable, lousy, shocking, frightful, wicked, accursed, infernal, *Brit. colloq.* chronic, *sl.* rotten, gross; bad, inferior, base. **c** see EXCESSIVE, LARGE *adj.* 1, 2. **2** see AWESOME 1.

awfully /áwfəlee, -flee/ *adv.* **1** *colloq.* in an unpleasant, bad, or horrible way (*he played awfully*). **2** *colloq.* very (*she's awfully pleased*). **3** *poet.* reverently.

■ **1** terribly, woefully, atrociously, shockingly, poorly, ineptly, *colloq.* lousily, dreadfully, abominably, abysmally; see also BADLY 1. **2** very, extremely, really, greatly, remarkably, exceedingly, excessively, fearfully, inordinately, incomparably, *colloq.* terribly, dreadfully, real, *Brit. colloq.* beastly; very much, a lot, *Brit. colloq.* ever so (much).

awhile /əhwíl, əwíl/ *adv.* for a short time. [OE *āne hwīle* a while]

awkward /áwkwərd/ *adj.* **1** ill-adapted for use; causing difficulty in use. **2** clumsy or bungling. **3 a** embarrassed (*felt awkward about it*). **b** embarrassing (*an awkward situation*). **4** difficult to deal with (*an awkward customer*). □ **the awkward age** adolescence. □□ **awkwardly** *adv.* **awkwardness** *n.*

[obs. *awk* backhanded, untoward (ME f. ON *afugr* turned the wrong way) + -WARD]

■ **1** unwieldy, cumbersome, cumbrous; unfriendly, ill-adapted; tricky. **2** clumsy, ungainly, left-handed, heavy-handed, blundering, lumbersome, bungling, maladroit, uncoordinated, ungraceful, graceless, ungainly, inelegant, gawky, wooden, artless, blockish, cloddish, lumpish, inexpert, gauche, unhandy, inept, oafish, unskilled, unskillful, all thumbs, *colloq.* ham-fisted, ham-handed. **3 a** embarrassed, shamefaced, uncomfortable, ill at ease, uneasy, out of place, discomfited, disconcerted, self-conscious. **b** embarrassing, uncomfortable, humiliating. **4** difficult, touchy, sensitive, embarrassing, delicate, unpleasant, uncomfortable, ticklish, tricky, trying, troublesome, problematic, problematical, scabrous, knotty, *colloq.* sticky. □ **the awkward age** adolescence, puberty, (the) teenage years.

awl /awl/ *n.* a small pointed tool used for piercing holes, esp. in leather. [OE *æl*]

awn /awn/ *n.* a stiff bristle growing from the grain sheath of grasses, or terminating a leaf, etc. □□ **awned** *adj.* [ME f. ON *ögn*]

awning /áwning/ *n.* a sheet of canvas or similar material stretched on a frame and used to shade a window, doorway, ship's deck, or other area from the sun or rain. [17th c. (Naut.): orig. uncert.]

■ see SHADE *n.* 7, 8.

awoke *past* of AWAKE.

awoken *past part.* of AWAKE.

AWOL /áywawl/ *abbr.* absent without leave.

awry /ərí/ *adv. & adj.* ● *adv.* **1** crookedly or askew. **2** improperly or amiss. ● *predic.adj.* crooked; deviant or unsound (*his theory is awry*). □ **go awry** go or do wrong. [ME f. A² + WRY]

■ *adv.* **1** see ASKEW *adv.* **2** see AMISS *adv.* ● *adj.* see CROOKED 1, WRONG *adj.* 4.

ax /aks/ *n. & v.* (also **axe**) ● *n.* **1** a chopping tool, usu. of iron with a steel edge at a right angle to a wooden handle. **2** the drastic cutting or elimination of expenditure, staff, etc. ● *v.tr.* (**axing**) **1** use an ax. **2** cut (esp. costs or services) drastically. **3** remove or dismiss. □ **an ax to grind** private or selfish purpose to serve. [OE *æx* f. Gmc]

axel /áksəl/ *n.* a jumping movement in skating, similar to a loop (see LOOP *n.* 7) but from one foot to the other. [*Axel* R. Paulsen, Norw. skater d. 1938]

axes *pl.* of AXIS¹.

axial /ákseeəl/ *adj.* **1** forming or belonging to an axis. **2** around or along an axis (*axial rotation*; *axial symmetry*). □□ **axiality** /-seeálitee/ *n.* **axially** *adv.*

axil /áksil/ *n.* the upper angle between a leaf and the stem it springs from, or between a branch and the trunk. [L *axilla*: see AXILLA]

axilla /aksílə/ *n.* (*pl.* **axillae** /-ee/) **1** *Anat.* the armpit. **2** an axil. [L, = armpit, dimin. of *ala* wing]

axillary /áksiléree/ *adj.* **1** *Anat.* of or relating to the armpit. **2** *Bot.* in or growing from the axil.

axiom /ákseeəm/ *n.* **1** an established or widely accepted principle. **2** esp. *Geom.* a self-evident truth. [F *axiome* or L *axioma* f. Gk *axiōma axiōmat-* f. *axios* worthy]

■ **1** see PRINCIPLE 1.

axiomatic /ákseeəmátik/ *adj.* **1** self-evident. **2** relating to or containing axioms. □□ **axiomatically** *adv.* [Gk *axiōmatikos* (as AXIOM)]

■ **1** see SELF-EVIDENT. **2** see PROVERBIAL 2.

axis¹ /áksis/ *n.* (*pl.* **axes** /-seez/) **1 a** an imaginary line about which a body rotates or about which a plane figure is conceived as generating a solid. **b** a line which divides a regular figure symmetrically. **2** *Math.* a fixed reference line for the

---

/.../ **pronunciation**	● **part of speech**
□ **phrases, idioms, and compounds**	
□□ **derivatives**	■ **synonym section**
cross-references appear in SMALL CAPITALS or *italics*	

measurement of coordinates, etc. **3** *Bot.* the central column of an inflorescence or other growth. **4** *Anat.* the second cervical vertebra. **5** *Physiol.* the central part of an organ or organism. **6 a** an agreement or alliance between two or more countries forming a center for an eventual larger grouping of nations sharing an ideal or objective. **b** (**the Axis**) the alliance of Germany and Italy formed before and during World War II, later extended to include Japan and other countries; these countries as a group. [L, = axle, pivot]

axis² /áksis/ *n.* a white spotted deer, *Cervus axis*, of S. Asia. Also called CHITAL. [L]

axle /áksəl/ *n.* a rod or spindle (either fixed or rotating) on which a wheel or group of wheels is fixed. [orig. *axletree* f. ME *axeltre* f. ON *öxulltré*]

Axminster /áksminstər/ *n.* (in full **Axminster carpet**) a kind of machine-woven patterned carpet with a cut pile. [*Axminster* in S. England]

axolotl /áksəlot'l/ *n.* an aquatic newtlike salamander, *Ambystoma mexicanum*, from Mexico, which in natural conditions retains its larval form for life but is able to breed. [Nahuatl f. *atl* water + *xolotl* servant]

axon /ákson/ *n. Anat. & Zool.* a long threadlike part of a nerve cell, conducting impulses from the cell body. [mod.L f. Gk *axōn* axis]

ay var. of AYE.

ayah /íə/ *n.* a native nurse or maidservant, esp. in India and other former British overseas territories. [Anglo-Ind. f. Port. *aia* nurse]

ayatollah /íətŏlə/ *n.* a Shiite religious leader in Iran. [Pers. f. Arab., = token of Gŏd]

aye¹ /í/ *adv. & n.* (also **ay**) ● *adv.* **1** *archaic* or *dial.* yes. **2** (in voting) I assent. **3** (as **aye aye**) *Naut.* a response accepting an order. ● *n.* an affirmative answer or assent, esp. in voting. □ **the ayes have it** the affirmative votes are in the majority. [16th c.: prob. f. first pers. personal pron. expressing assent]

■ yes, *archaic* yea.

aye² /ay/ *adv.* (also **ay**) *archaic* ever; always. □ **for aye** for ever. [ME f. ON *ei, ey* f. Gmc]

■ see ALWAYS 1. □ **for aye** see ALWAYS 4.

aye-aye /í-í/ *n.* an arboreal nocturnal lemur, *Daubentonia madagascariensis*, native to Madagascar. [F f. Malagasy *aiay*]

Aylesbury /áylzbəree/ *n.* (*pl.* **Aylesburys**) **1** a bird of a breed of large white domestic ducks. **2** this breed. [*Aylesbury* in S. England]

Ayrshire /áirshər, -sheer/ *n.* **1** one of a mainly white breed of dairy cattle. **2** this breed. [name of a former Scottish county]

AZ *abbr.* Arizona (in official postal use).

azalea /əzáylyə/ *n.* any of various flowering deciduous shrubs of the genus *Rhododendron*, with large pink, purple, white, or yellow flowers. [mod.L f. Gk, fem. of *azaleos* dry (from the dry soil in which it was believed to flourish)]

azeotrope /əzéeətrōp, áyzee-/ *n. Chem.* a mixture of liquids in which the boiling point remains constant during distillation at a given pressure, without change in composition. □□ **azeotropic** /əzéeətrópik/ *adj.* [A-¹ + Gk *zeō* boil + *tropos* turning]

azide /áyzīd/ *n. Chem.* any compound containing the radical N₃.

Azilian /əzíleeən/ *n. & adj. Archaeol.* ● *n.* the transitional culture between the Paleolithic and neolithic ages in Europe. ● *adj.* of or relating to this culture. [Mas d'*Azil* in the French Pyrenees, where remains of it were found]

azimuth /ázimə th/ *n.* **1** the angular distance from a north or south point of the horizon to the intersection with the horizon of a vertical circle passing through a given celestial body. **2** the horizontal angle or direction of a compass bearing. □□ **azimuthal** /-múthəl/ *adj.* [ME f. OF *azimut* f. Arab. *as-sumūt* f. *al* the + *sumūt* pl. of *samt* way, direction]

azine /ázeen, áy-/ *n. Chem.* any organic compound with two or more nitrogen atoms in a six atom ring. [AZO- + -INE⁴]

azo- /ázō, áy-/ *prefix Chem.* containing two adjacent nitrogen atoms between carbon atoms. [F *azote* nitrogen f. Gk *azōos* without life]

azoic /ayzóik/ *adj.* **1** having no trace of life. **2** *Geol.* (of an age, etc.) having left no organic remains. [Gk *azōos* without life]

AZT *n.* a drug used against the AIDS virus. [chem. name *azidothymidine*]

Aztec /áztek/ *n. & adj.* ● *n.* **1** a member of the native people dominant in Mexico before the Spanish conquest of the 16th century. **2** the language of the Aztecs. ● *adj.* of the Aztecs or their language (see also NAHUATL). [F *Aztèque* or Sp. *Azteca* f. Nahuatl *aztecatl* men of the north]

azuki var. of ADZUKI.

azure /ázhər/ *n. & adj.* ● *n.* **1 a** a deep sky-blue color. **b** *Heraldry* blue. **2** *poet.* the clear sky. ● *adj.* **1 a** of the color azure. **b** *Heraldry* blue. **2** serene; untroubled. [ME f. OF *asur, azur*, f. med.L *azzurum, azolum* f. Arab. *al* the + *lāzaward* f. Pers. *lāžward* lapis lazuli]

■ *adj.* **1 a** see BLUE¹ *adj.* 1. **2** see SERENE *adj.*

azygous /ayzígəs/ *adj. & n. Anat.* ● *adj.* (of any organic structure) single; not existing in pairs. ● *n.* an organic structure occurring singly. [Gk *azugos* unyoked f. *a-* not + *zugon* yoke]

Bb

B¹ /bee/ n. (also **b**) (pl. **Bs** or **B's**) **1** the second letter of the alphabet. **2** Mus. the seventh note of the diatonic scale of C major. **3** the second hypothetical person or example. **4** the second highest class or category (of roads, academic marks, etc.). **5** Algebra (usu. **b**) the second known quantity. **6** a human blood type of the ABO system. □ **B movie** a supporting, usu. less well-known movie in a theater's program.

B² symb. **1** Chem. the element boron. **2** Physics magnetic flux density.

B³ abbr. (also **B.**) **1** Bachelor. **2** bel (s). **3** bishop. **4** black (pencil lead). **5** Blessed. **6** Baseball base; baseman.

b symb. Physics barn.

b. abbr. **1** born. **2** billion.

BA abbr. **1** Bachelor of Arts. **2** British Academy. **3** British Airways. **4** batting average.

Ba symb. Chem. the element barium.

BAA abbr. Bachelor of Applied Arts.

baa /baa/ v. & n. ● v.intr. (**baas, baaed** or **baa'd**) (esp. of a sheep) bleat. ● n. (pl. **baas**) the cry of a sheep or lamb. [imit.]

baas /baas/ n. S.Afr. boss; master (often as a form of address). [Du.: cf. BOSS¹]

baasskap /báaskaap/ n. S.Afr. domination, esp. of nonwhites by whites. [Afrik. f. baas master + -skap condition]

baba /baábaa/ n. (in full **baba au rhum** /ō rúm/) a small rich sponge cake, usu. soaked in rum syrup. [F f. Pol.]

babacoote /baábəkōōt/ n. = INDRI. [Malagasy babakoto]

Babbitt¹ /bábit/ n. (also **babbitt**) **1** (in full **Babbitt metal**) any of a group of soft alloys of tin, antimony, copper, and usu. lead, used for lining bearings, etc., to diminish friction. **2** (**babbitt**) a bearing lining made of this. [I. Babbitt, Amer. inventor d. 1862]

Babbitt² /bábit/ n. a materialistic, complacent businessman. □□ **Babbittry** n. [George Babbitt, a character in the novel Babbitt (1922) by S. Lewis]
■ see PHILISTINE 2.

babble /bábəl/ v. & n. ● v. **1** intr. **a** talk in an inarticulate or incoherent manner. **b** chatter excessively or irrelevantly. **c** (of a stream, etc.) murmur; trickle. **2** tr. repeat foolishly; divulge through chatter. ● n. **1 a** incoherent speech. **b** foolish, idle, or childish talk. **2** the murmur of voices, water, etc. **3** Teleph. background disturbance caused by interference from conversations on other lines. □□ **babblement** n. [ME f. MLG babbelen, or imit.]
■ v. **1 a, b** burble, gabble, gurgle, jabber, gibber, blab, blabber; prattle, twaddle, chatter, prate, blather, tattle, tittle-tattle, gossip, clack, colloq. gab, natter, colloq. or dial. yammer, yatter (on), Brit. colloq. mag, sl. yak. **c** murmur, trickle, whisper, gurgle, purl, burble, bubble. **2** divulge, tell, disclose, broadcast, repeat, reveal, blurt (out), burst out with, give away, blab, let out, colloq. let on. ● n. **1 a** gibberish, gibber, jabber, gabble. **b** twaddle, prattle, chatter, burble, prate, blather, tattle, tittle-tattle, gossip, colloq. chitchat, gab, natter, colloq. or dial. yatter, yak; sl. yak; nonsense, drivel, rubbish; baby talk. **2** murmur, gurgle, whisper, purl, literary susurration; buzz.

babbler /báblər/ n. **1** a chatterer. **2** a person who reveals secrets. **3** any of a large group of passerine birds with loud chattering voices.

babe /bayb/ n. **1** esp. literary a baby. **2** an innocent or helpless person (babes in the wood). **3** sometimes derog. sl. a young woman (often as a form of address). [ME: imit. of child's ba, ba]
■ **1** see BABY n. 1.

babel /báybəl, báb-/ n. **1** a confused noise, esp. of voices. **2** a noisy assembly. **3** a scene of confusion. □ **Tower of Babel** a visionary or unrealistic plan. [ME f. Heb. Bābel Babylon f. Akkad. bab ili gate of god (with ref. to the biblical account of the tower that was built to reach heaven but ended in chaos when God confused the builders' speech: see Gen. 11)]
■ **1** see DIN n.

Babis /bábis/ n. a member of a Persian eclectic sect founded in 1844 whose doctrine includes Muslim, Christian, Jewish, and Zoroastrian elements. □□ **Babism** n. [Pers. Bab-ed-Din, gate (= intermediary) of the Faith]

baboon /babōōn/ n. **1** any of various large Old World monkeys of the genus Papio, having a long doglike snout, large teeth, and naked callosities on the buttocks. **2** an ugly or uncouth person. [ME f. OF babuin or med.L babewynus, of unkn. orig.]

babu /baábōō/ n. (also **baboo**) Ind. **1** a title of respect, esp. to Hindus. **2** derog. formerly, an English-writing Indian clerk. [Hindi bābū]

babushka /bəbōōshkə/ n. **1** a headscarf tied under the chin. **2** an elderly or grandmotherly Russian woman. [Russ., = grandmother]

baby /báybee/ n. & v. ● n. (pl. **-ies**) **1** a very young child or infant, esp. one not yet able to walk. **2** an unduly childish person (is a baby about injections). **3** the youngest member of a family, team, etc. **4** (often attrib.) **a** a young or newly born animal. **b** a thing that is small of its kind (baby car; baby rose). **5** sl. a young woman; a sweetheart (often as a form of address). **6** sl. a person or thing regarded with affection or familiarity. **7** one's own responsibility, invention, concern, achievement, etc., regarded in a personal way. ● v.tr. (**-ies, -ied**) **1** treat like a baby. **2** pamper. □ **baby boom** colloq. a temporary marked increase in the birthrate. **baby boomer** a person born during a baby boom, esp. after World War II. **baby-bouncer** Brit. a frame supported by elastic or springs, into which a child is harnessed for exercise and entertainment. **Baby Buggy** (pl. **-ies**) Brit. propr. a kind of child's collapsible stroller. **baby carriage** a four-wheeled carriage for a baby, pushed by a person on foot. **baby grand** the smallest size of grand piano. **baby-sit** look after a child or children while the parents are out. **baby talk** childish talk used by or to young children. **carry** (or **hold**) **the baby** bear unwelcome responsibility. **throw out the baby with the bath water** reject the essential with the inessential. □□ **babyhood** n. **baby-sitter** n. [ME, formed as BABE, -Y²]
■ n. **1** infant, neonate, child, toddler, tot, Sc. & No. of Engl. bairn, colloq. new arrival, literary babe (in arms).

/.../ **pronunciation**	● **part of speech**
□ **phrases, idioms, and compounds**	
□□ **derivatives**	■ **synonym section**
cross-references appear in SMALL CAPITALS or italics	

3 youngest, smallest, littlest. **5** see DARLING *n*. 1. ● *v*. cosset, coddle, pamper, mollycoddle, indulge, spoil, pet, dandle. □ **baby talk** see BABBLE *n*. 1b. **baby-sit** see MIND *v*. 3. □□ **babyhood** infancy, early childhood, early *or* initial stage(s) *or* days. **baby-sitter** sitter, nanny, au pair, governess, esp. *Brit*. minder.

Babygro /báybeegrō/ *n*. (*pl*. **-os**) *Brit. propr*. a kind of all-in-one stretch garment for babies. [BABY + GROW]

babyish /báybeeish/ *adj*. **1** childish; simple. **2** immature. □□ **babyishly** *adv*. **babyishness** *n*.
■ **2** see CHILDISH 2.

Babylonian /bábilṓneeən/ *n. & adj*. ● *n*. an inhabitant of Babylon, an ancient city and kingdom in Mesopotamia. ● *adj*. of or relating to Babylon. [L *Babylonius* f. Gk *Babulonios* f. *Babulon* f. Heb. *Bābel*]

Bacardi /bəkaárdee/ *n*. (*pl*. **Bacardis**) *propr*. a West Indian rum produced orig. in Cuba. [name of the company producing it]

baccalaureate /bákəláwreeət/ *n*. **1** the college or university degree of bachelor. **2** an examination intended to qualify successful candidates for higher education. **3** a religious service held for a graduating class. [F *baccalauréat* or med.L *baccalaureatus* f. *baccalaureus* bachelor]

baccarat /baakəraá, bá-/ *n*. a gambling card game played against the dealer. [F]

baccate /bákayt/ *adj. Bot*. **1** bearing berries. **2** of or like a berry. [L *baccatus* berried f. *bacca* berry]

bacchanal /bakənál, bákənəl/ *n. & adj*. ● *n*. **1** a wild and drunken revelry. **2** a drunken reveler. **3** a priest, worshiper, or follower of Bacchus. ● *adj*. **1** of or like Bacchus, the Greek or Roman god of wine, or his rites. **2** riotous; roistering. [L *bacchanalis* f. *Bacchus* god of wine f. Gk *Bakkhos*]
■ *n*. **1** see REVEL *n*.

Bacchanalia /bákənáylyə/ *n.pl*. **1** the Roman festival of Bacchus. **2** (**bacchanalia**) a drunken revelry. □□ **Bacchanalian** *adj. & n*. [L, neut. pl. of *bacchanalis*: see BACCHANAL]
■ **2** see ORGY 1.

bacchant /bəkánt, -kaánt, bákənt/ *n. & adj*. ● *n*. (*pl*. **bacchants** or **bacchantes** /bəkánteez/; *fem*. **bacchante** /bəkántee, -kaánt-/) **1** a priest, worshiper, or follower of Bacchus. **2** a drunken reveller. ● *adj*. **1** of or like Bacchus or his rites. **2** riotous; roistering. □□ **bacchantic** *adj*. [F *bacchante* f. L *bacchari* celebrate Bacchanal rites]

Bacchic /bákik/ *adj*. = BACCHANAL *adj*. [L *bacchicus* f. Gk *bakkhikos* of Bacchus]

baccy /bákee/ *n*. (*pl*. **-ies**) *Brit. colloq*. tobacco. [abbr.]

bachelor /báchələr, báchlər/ *n*. **1** an unmarried man. **2** a man or woman who has taken the degree of Bachelor of Arts or Science, etc. **3** *hist*. a young knight serving under another's banner. □ **bachelor girl** an independent unmarried young woman. **bachelor's buttons** any of various buttonlike flowers, esp. the double buttercup. □□ **bachelorhood** *n*. **bachelorship** *n*. [ME & OF *bacheler* aspirant to knighthood, of uncert. orig.]
■ **2** graduate. □ **bachelor girl** see MISS[2].

bacillary /básəleree, bəsíləree/ *adj*. relating to or caused by bacilli.

bacilliform /bəsílifawrm/ *adj*. rod-shaped.

bacillus /bəsíləs/ *n*. (*pl*. **bacilli** /-lī/) **1** any rod-shaped bacterium. **2** (usu. in *pl*.) any pathogenic bacterium. [LL, dimin. of L *baculus* stick]

back /bak/ *n., adv., v., & adj*. ● *n*. **1 a** the rear surface of the human body from the shoulders to the hips. **b** the corresponding upper surface of an animal's body. **c** the spine (*fell and broke his back*). **d** the keel of a ship. **2 a** any surface regarded as corresponding to the human back, e.g., of the head or hand, or of a chair. **b** the part of a garment that covers the back. **3 a** the less active or visible or important part of something functional, e.g., of a knife or a piece of paper (*write it on the back*). **b** the side or part normally away from the spectator or the direction of motion or attention, e.g., of a car, house, or room (*stood at the back*). **4 a** a defensive player in some games. **b** this position. ● *adv*. **1** to the rear; away from what is considered to be the front (*go back a little*; *ran off without looking back*). **2 a** in or into an

earlier or normal position or condition (*came back late*; *went back home*; *ran back to the car*; *put it back on the shelf*). **b** in return (*pay back*). **3** in or into the past (*back in June*; *three years back*). **4** at a distance (*stand back from the road*). **5** in check (*hold him back*). **6** (foll. by *of*) behind (*was back of the house*). ● *v*. **1** *tr*. **a** help with moral or financial support. **b** bet on the success of (a horse, etc.). **2** *tr. & intr*. move, or cause (a vehicle, etc.) to move, backward. **3** *tr*. **a** put or serve as a back, background, or support to. **b** *Mus*. accompany. **4** *tr*. lie at the back of (*a beach backed by steep cliffs*). **5** *intr*. (of the wind) move around to a counterclockwise direction. ● *adj*. **1** situated behind, esp. as remote or subsidiary (*back street*; *back teeth*; *back entrance*). **2** of or relating to the past; not current (*back pay*; *back issue*). **3** reversed (*back flow*). □ **at a person's back** in pursuit or support. **at the back of one's mind** remembered but not consciously thought of. **back and forth** to and fro. **back bench** *Brit*. a back-bencher's seat in the House of Commons. **back-bencher** *Brit*. a member of Parliament not holding a senior office. **back-crawl** = BACKSTROKE. **back door** a secret or ingenious means of gaining an objective. **back down** withdraw one's claim or point of view, etc.; concede defeat in an argument, etc. **back-formation 1** the formation of a word from its seeming derivative (e.g., *laze* from *lazy*). **2** a word formed in this way. **back number 1** an issue of a periodical earlier than the current one. **2** *sl*. an out-of-date person or thing. **the back of beyond** a very remote or inaccessible place. **back off 1** draw back; retreat. **2** abandon one's intention, stand, etc. **back on to** have its back adjacent to (*the house backs on to a field*). **back out** (often foll. by *of*) withdraw from a commitment. **back passage** *Brit. colloq*. the rectum. **back projection** the projection of a picture from behind a translucent screen for viewing or filming. **back room** (often, with hyphen, *attrib.*) a place where secret work is done. **back slang** slang using words spelled backward (e.g., *yob*). **back street 1** a street in a quiet part of a town, away from the main streets. **2** (*attrib.*) denoting illicit, secretive, or illegal activity (*a back street drug deal*). **back talk** *colloq*. the practice of replying rudely or impudently. **back to back** with backs adjacent and opposite each other (*we stood back to back*). **back-to-back** *adj*. esp. *Brit*. (of houses) with a party wall at the rear. **back to front 1** with the back at the front and the front at the back. **2** in disorder. **back-to-nature** (usu. *attrib.*) applied to a movement or enthusiast for the reversion to a simpler way of life. **back up 1** give (esp. moral) support to. **2** *Computing* make a spare copy of (data, a disk, etc.). **3** (of running water) accumulate behind an obstruction. **4** reverse (a vehicle) into a desired position. **5** form a line or mass of vehicles, etc., esp. in congested traffic. **back water** reverse a boat's forward motion using oars. **get** (or **put**) **a person's back up** annoy or anger a person. **get off a person's back** stop troubling a person. **go back on** fail to honor (a promise or commitment). **know like the back of one's hand** be entirely familiar with. **on one's back** injured or ill in bed. **on the back burner** see BURNER. **put one's back into** approach (a task, etc.) with vigor. **see the back of** see SEE[1]. **turn one's back on 1** abandon. **2** disregard; ignore. **with one's back to** (or **up against**) **the wall** in a desperate situation; hard-pressed. □□ **backer** *n*. (in sense 1 of *v*.). **backless** *adj*. [OE *bæc* f. Gmc]
■ *n*. **1, 2** rear; spine. **3 a** reverse, rear, other *or* opposite side, wrong side, verso, underside, *colloq*. flip side. **b** rear, far side *or* corner. **4** defense, fullback, halfback, *Soccer* sweeper, stopper, *Rugby* three-quarter (back), *colloq*. half. ● *adv*. **1** to *or* toward(s) the rear, rearward(s), backward(s), behind; away, off. **b** again, re-. **b** in return *or* repayment *or* requital *or* retaliation; again. **3** in the past, ago, in time(s) past, earlier, before. **4** away, at a distance, at arm's length; aside, to one side. **5** in check, under control. **6** (*back of*) behind, on the other side of, at the rear of. ● *v*. **1 a** back up, support, stand behind, encourage, help, second, side with, aid, abet, assist; uphold, endorse, promote; sponsor, subsidize, fund, underwrite, finance, *colloq*. bankroll, stake. **b** invest in, wager *or* bet on, lay *or* stake

or place a bet on. **2** back up, reverse, go *or* move in reverse, go *or* move backward. **3 b** accompany, provide the backing *or* harmony *or* accompaniment for. ● *adj.* **1** rear, side; service, servants'. **2** in arrears, overdue, past due, late; behindhand; old, past, out-of-date, outdated. **3** reversed, backward. □ **at a person's back** behind, following, pursuing, in (hot) pursuit, chasing, in back of; supporting, seconding. **back and forth** see AROUND *adv.* 2. **back down** see *give in,* WITHDRAW 2. **back number 2** see FOGY. **the back of beyond** see BACKCOUNTRY. **back off 1** see RETREAT *v.* 1a. **2** see *give in.* **back out** see RENEGE 1a. **back talk** see *impudence* (IMPUDENT). **back to front 1** inside out, wrong way around, wrong side out. **2** see DISORDERLY 1. **back up 1** see BACK *v.* 1a. see BACK *v.* 2 above. **get a person's back up** get on a person's nerves, *colloq.* get under a person's skin, get in a person's hair; see also ANNOY 1. **go back on** renege on, back out of, back down from *or* on, backtrack on, retract, take back, default on, fail to honor, break, repudiate, forsake; *colloq.* chicken out of. **know like the back of one's hand** know backward and forwards *or* inside out. **on one's back** see ILL *adj.* 1. **put one's back into** put (some *or* a lot of) elbow grease into, put effort into, throw oneself into. **turn one's back on 1** abandon, forsake, reject, repudiate, cast off, disown, deny. **2** disregard, overlook; see also IGNORE 2. **with one's back to** (or **up against**) **the wall** hard-pressed, struggling (against odds), without hope, with little *or* no hope, helpless, in dire straits, in (serious) trouble. □□ **backer** investor, benefactor, benefactress, underwriter, patron, advocate, promoter, sponsor, *sl.* angel; better, punter; see also SUPPORTER.

backache /bákayk/ *n.* a (usu. prolonged) pain in one's back.

backbite /bákbīt/ *v.tr.* slander; speak badly of. □□ **backbiter** *n.*
■ see DISPARAGE 1.

backblocks /bákbloks/ *n.pl. Austral. & NZ* land in the remote and sparsely inhabited interior. □□ **backblocker** *n.*

backboard /bákbawrd/ *n.* **1 a** a board worn to support or straighten the back. **2 a** a board placed at or forming the back of anything. **b** *Basketball* the board behind the basket.

backbone /bákbōn/ *n.* **1** the spine. **2** the main support of a structure. **3** firmness of character. **4** the spine of a book.
■ **1** spine, spinal column, vertebrae. **2** mainstay, chief *or* main support, buttress, pillar. **3** resoluteness, sturdiness, firmness, determination, strength (of character), mettle, purposefulness, resolution, perseverance, tenacity, tenaciousness, courage, fortitude, resolve, will, willpower, stability, stamina, staying power, *colloq.* guts, grit.

backbreaking /bákbrayking/ *adj.* (esp. of manual work) extremely hard.
■ see *exhausting* (EXHAUST).

backchat /bákchat/ *n. Brit.* = *back talk.*

backcloth /bák-klawth, -kloth/ *n. Brit.* = BACKDROP.

backcountry /bák-kuntree/ *n.* an area away from settled districts.
■ bush, backwater, interior, wilds, back of beyond, backwoods, hinterland, esp. *Austral.* outback, *colloq.* middle of nowhere, sticks, *sl.* boondocks.

backcross /bák-kraws/ *v. & n. Biol.* ● *v.tr.* cross a hybrid with one of its parents. ● *n.* an instance or the product of this.

backdate /bákdáyt/ *v.tr.* **1** put an earlier date on (an agreement, etc.) than the actual one. **2** *Brit.* make retrospectively valid.

backdoor /bákdáwr/ *adj.* (of an activity) clandestine; underhand (*backdoor deal*).
■ covert, clandestine, secret, hidden, backstage, secretive, private, hugger-mugger; underhand, furtive, shady, sneaky, deceitful, conspiratorial, cloak-and-dagger, dishonest, under-the-counter.

backdrop /bákdrop/ *n. Theatr.* a painted cloth at the back of the stage as a main part of the scenery.

backfill /bákfil/ *v.tr. & intr.* refill an excavated hole with the material dug out of it.

backfire /bákfīr/ *v. & n.* ● *v.intr.* **1** undergo a mistimed explosion in the cylinder or exhaust of an internal combustion engine. **2** (of a plan, etc.) rebound adversely on the originator; have the opposite effect to what was intended. ● *n.* an instance of backfiring.
■ *v.* **2** see BOOMERANG *v.* ● *n.* see REPORT *n.* 6.

backgammon /bákgámən/ *n.* **1** a game for two played on a board with pieces moved according to throws of the dice. **2** the most complete form of win in this. [BACK + GAMMON[2]]

background /bákgrownd/ *n.* **1** part of a scene, picture, or description that serves as a setting to the chief figures or objects and foreground. **2** an inconspicuous or obscure position (*kept in the background*). **3** a person's education, knowledge, or social circumstances. **4** explanatory or contributory information or circumstances. **5** *Physics* low intensity ambient radiation from radioisotopes present in the natural environment. **6** *Electronics* unwanted signals, such as noise in the reception or recording of sound. □ **background music** music intended as an unobtrusive accompaniment to some activity, or to provide atmosphere in a movie, etc.
■ **1** backing, surroundings, surround; field, distance, horizon, obscurity. **2** (*in the background*) inconspicuous, unnoticed, unobtrusive, behind the scenes, out of the limelight *or* spotlight, unseen, out of *or* away from the public eye, backstage; see also *hidden* (HIDE[1]). **3** history, experience, qualifications, credentials, grounding, training, knowledge; circumstances, breeding, upbringing, past, life, story, family; curriculum vitae, c.v. □ **background music** incidental music, *usu. derog.* Muzak.

backhand /bák-hand/ *n. Tennis,* etc. **1** a stroke played with the back of the hand turned toward the opponent. **2** (*attrib.*) of or made with a backhand (*backhand volley*).
■ **1** backhander. **2** (*attrib.*) backhanded.

backhanded /bák-hándid/ *adj.* **1** (of a blow, etc.) delivered with the back of the hand, or in a direction opposite to the usual one. **2** indirect; ambiguous (*a backhanded compliment*). **3** = BACKHAND *attrib.*

backhander /bák-hándər/ *n.* **1 a** a backhand stroke. **b** a backhanded blow. **2** *colloq.* an indirect attack. **3** *Brit. sl.* a bribe.

backing /báking/ *n.* **1 a** support. **b** a body of supporters. **c** material used to form a back or support. **2** musical accompaniment, esp. to a singer; backup.
■ **1 a** support, help, aid, assistance, succor, backup, reinforcement; approval, endorsement, patronage, sponsorship, promotion, financing; grant, contribution, subsidy, investment, money, funds, funding. **b** backers, supporters, helpers, campaigners, patrons, sponsors, benefactors, investors, financiers. **c** lining, interlining, underlay, reinforcement, support, mount, mounting, background, setting, coating. **2** accompaniment, harmony.

backlash /báklash/ *n.* **1** an excessive or marked adverse reaction. **2 a** a sudden recoil or reaction between parts of a mechanism. **b** excessive play between such parts.
■ **1** reaction, retaliation, retort, reprisal, repercussion, counteraction, rebound, *sl.* comeback; revenge, retribution. **2** recoil, counteraction, rebound, backfire, boomerang, *colloq.* kickback.

backlist /báklist/ *n.* a publisher's list of books published before the current season and still in print.

backlit /báklit/ *adj.* (esp. in photography) illuminated from behind.

backlog /báklawg, -log/ *n.* **1** accumulation of uncompleted work, etc. **2** a reserve; reserves (*a backlog of goodwill*).

/.../ **pronunciation**	● **part of speech**
□ **phrases, idioms, and compounds**	
□□ **derivatives**	■ **synonym section**
cross-references appear in SMALL CAPITALS or *italics*	

backmarker /bákmaarkər/ *n. Brit.* a competitor who has the least favorable handicap in a race, etc.

backmost /bákmōst/ *adj.* furthest back.

backpack /bákpak/ *n. & v.* ● *n.* a bag slung by straps from both shoulders and resting on the back. ● *v.intr.* travel or hike with a backpack. □□ **backpacker** *n.*
  ■ *n.* see PACK[1] *n.* 1.

backpedal /bákped'l/ *v.* (**-pedaled, -pedaling**) **1** pedal backward on a bicycle, etc. **2** reverse one's previous action or opinion.
  ■ back up, backtrack, go backward, *Naut.* make sternway.

backrest /bákrest/ *n.* a support for the back.

backscatter /bákskatər/ *n.* the scattering of radiation in a reverse direction.

backscratcher /bákskrachər/ *n.* **1** a rod terminating in a clawed hand for scratching one's own back. **2** a person who performs mutual services with another for gain.

backseat /bákseét/ *n.* **1** a seat in the rear. **2** an inferior position or status. □ **backseat driver** a person who is eager to advise without responsibility (orig. of a passenger in a car, etc.).

backsheesh var. of BAKSHEESH.

backside /báksíd/ *n. colloq.* the buttocks.
  ■ see BUTTOCK[2].

backsight /báksit/ *n.* **1** the sight of a rifle, etc., that is nearer the stock. **2** *Surveying* a sight or reading taken backward or toward the point of starting.

backslapping /bákslaping/ *adj.* vigorously hearty.

backslash /bákslash/ *n.* a backward-sloping diagonal line; a reverse slash (\ ).

backslide /bákslíd/ *v.intr.* (*past* **-slid** /-slíd/; *past part.* **-slid** or **-slidden** /-slíd'n/) relapse into bad ways or error. □□ **backslider** *n.*
  ■ see RELAPSE *v.*

backspace /bákspays/ *v.intr.* move a typewriter carriage, computer cursor, etc., back one or more spaces.

backspin /bákspin/ *n.* a backward spin imparted to a ball causing it to fly off at an angle on hitting a surface.

backstage /bákstáyj/ *adv. & adj.* ● *adv.* **1** *Theatr.* out of view of the audience, esp. in the wings or dressing rooms. **2** not known to the public. ● *adj.* that is backstage; concealed.
  ■ *adv.* see *in the background* (BACKGROUND 2). ● *adj.* see BACKDOOR.

backstairs /bákstairz/ *n.pl.* **1** stairs at the back or side of a building. **2** (also **backstair**) (*attrib.*) denoting underhand or clandestine activity.
  ■ **2** (*attrib.*) see STEALTHY.

backstay /bákstay/ *n.* a rope, etc., leading downwards and aft from the top of a mast.
  ■ see STAY[2] *n.*

backstitch /bákstich/ *n. & v.* ● *n.* a stitch bringing thread back to the preceding stitch. ● *v.tr. & intr.* sew using backstitch.

backstop /bákstaap/ *n.* **1** *Baseball.* a fence or screen positioned behind home plate. **2** something that provides support or reinforcement.

backstroke /bákstrōk/ *n.* a swimming stroke performed on the back with the arms lifted alternately out of the water in a backward circular motion and the legs extended in a kicking action.
  ■ back-crawl.

backtrack /báktrak/ *v.intr.* **1** retrace one's steps. **2** reverse one's previous action or opinion.
  ■ **1** see REVERSE 3.

backup /bákup/ *n.* **1** moral or technical support (*called for extra backup*). **2** a reserve. **3** *Computing* (often *attrib.*) **a** the procedure for making security copies of data (*backup facilities*). **b** the copy itself (*made a backup*). **4** a line or mass of vehicles, etc., esp. in congested traffic. **5** musical accompaniment. □ **backup light** a white light at the rear of a vehicle operated when the vehicle is in reverse gear.
  ■ **1** see SUPPORT *n.* 1. **2** see RESERVE 6.

backveld /bákvelt/ *n. S.Afr.* remote country districts, esp. those strongly conservative. □□ **backvelder** *n.*

backward /bákwərd/ *adv. & adj.* ● *adv.* (also **backwards**) **1** away from one's front (*lean backward; look backward*). **2 a** with the back foremost (*walk backward*). **b** in reverse of the usual way (*count backward; spell backward*). **3 a** into a worse state (*new policies are taking us backward*). **b** into the past (*looked backward over the years*). **c** (of a thing's motion) back toward the starting point (*rolled backward*). ● *adj.* **1** directed to the rear or starting point (*a backward look*). **2** reversed. **3 a** mentally retarded or slow. **b** slow to progress; late. **4** reluctant; shy; unassertive. □ **backward and forward** in both directions alternately; to and fro. **bend** (or **fall** or **lean**) **over backward** (often foll. by *to* + infin.) *colloq.* make every effort, esp. to be fair or helpful. **know backward and forward** be entirely familiar with. □□ **backwardness** *n.* [earlier *abackward*, assoc. with BACK]
  ■ *adv.* **1** see BACK *adv.* 1. **2** rearward(s), in reverse, regressively, retrogressively, backward; in the wrong direction *or* way; against the sun, anticlockwise, counterclockwise; back to front. **3 a** (*go backward*) see DETERIORATE. **b** into the past, into an earlier time, back. **c** back. ● *adj.* **1** rearward, to the rear, behind; to the past. **2** reversed, reverse, contrariwise, in the opposite way *or* direction; retrograde, retrogressive, regressive. **3 a** (mentally) retarded, retardate; slow, dull, stupid, slow-witted, simple, simple-minded, soft-headed, feeble-minded, thick-witted, *colloq.* dim, dumb, dimwitted, esp. *Brit. colloq.* gormless. **b** slow, late, behindhand, retarded. **4** bashful, shy, reticent, diffident, retiring, unassertive, coy, timid, unwilling, loath, chary, reluctant, averse. □ **backward and forward** back and forth, to and fro, up and down; see also AROUND *adv.* 2. **bend over backward** do one's utmost *or* best, make every effort. **know backward and forward** know inside out, know like the back of one's hand.

backwash /bákwosh, -wawsh/ *n.* **1 a** receding waves created by the motion of a ship, etc. **b** a backward current of air created by a moving aircraft. **2** repercussions.
  ■ **1** see WAKE[2] 1. **2** see UPSHOT.

backwater /bákwawtər, -wotər/ *n.* **1** a place or condition remote from the center of activity or thought. **2** stagnant water or water not fed by a main current.

backwoods /bákwŏŏdz/ *n.pl.* **1** remote uncleared forest land. **2** any remote or sparsely inhabited region.
  ■ **2** see STICK[1] 11.

backwoodsman /bákwŏŏdzmən/ *n.* (*pl.* **-men**) **1** an inhabitant of backwoods. **2** an uncouth person.
  ■ **1** see BOOR 3.

backyard /bakyaárd/ *n.* a yard at the back of a house, etc.
  □ **in one's own backyard** *colloq.* near at hand.

baclava var. of BAKLAVA.

bacon /báykən/ *n.* cured meat from the back or sides of a pig. □ **bring home the bacon** *colloq.* **1** succeed in one's undertaking. **2** supply material provision or support. [ME f. OF f. Frank. *bako* = OHG *bahho* ham, flitch]

Baconian /baykṓneeən/ *adj. & n.* ● *adj.* of or relating to the English philosopher Sir Francis Bacon (d. 1626), or to his inductive method of reasoning and philosophy. ● *n.* **1** a supporter of the view that Bacon was the author of Shakespeare's plays. **2** a follower of Bacon.

bacteria *pl.* of BACTERIUM.

bactericide /bakté̄erisíd/ *n.* a substance capable of destroying bacteria. □□ **bactericidal** /-risíd'l/ *adj.*

bacteriology /bákteereeóləjee/ *n.* the study of bacteria. □□ **bacteriological** /-reeəlójikəl/ *adj.* **bacteriologically** *adv.* **bacteriologist** /-ólǝjist/ *n.*

bacteriolysis /baktéereeólisis/ *n.* the rupture or destruction of bacterial cells.

bacteriolytic /baktéereeəlítik/ *adj.* capable of rupturing bacteria.

bacteriophage /bakté̄ereeəfayj/ *n.* a virus parasitic on a bacterium. [BACTERIUM + Gk *phagein* eat]

bacteriostasis /baktéereeōstáysis/ *n.* the inhibition of the growth of bacteria without destroying them. □□ **bacterio-static** /-státik/ *adj.*

bacterium /bakteéreeəm/ *n.* (*pl.* **bacteria** /-reeə/) a member of a large group of unicellular microorganisms lacking organelles and an organized nucleus, some of which can cause disease. □□ **bacterial** *adj.* [mod.L f. Gk *baktērion* dimin. of *baktron* stick]
■ see MICROBE.

Bactrian /báktreeən/ *adj.* of or relating to Bactria in central Asia. □ **Bactrian camel** a camel, *Camelus bactrianus,* native to central Asia, with two humps. [L *Bactrianus* f. Gk *Baktrianos*]

bad /bad/ *adj., n.,* & *adv.* ● *adj.* (**worse** /wərs/; **worst** /wərst/) **1** inferior; inadequate; defective (*bad work; a bad driver; bad light*). **2 a** unpleasant; unwelcome (*bad weather; bad news*). **b** unsatisfactory; unfortunate (*bad business*). **3** harmful (*is bad for you*). **4 a** (of food) decayed; putrid. **b** polluted (*bad air*). **5** ill; injured (*am feeling bad today; a bad leg*). **6** *colloq.* regretful; guilty; ashamed (*feels bad about it*). **7** (of an unwelcome thing) serious; severe (*a bad headache; a bad mistake*). **8 a** morally unsound or offensive (*a bad man; bad language*). **b** disobedient; badly behaved (*a bad child*). **9** worthless; not valid (*a bad check*). **10** (**badder, baddest**) *sl.* good; excellent. ● *n.* **1 a** ill fortune (*take the bad with the good*). **b** ruin; a degenerate condition (*go to the bad*). **2** the debit side of an account (*$500 to the bad*). **3** (as *pl.*; prec. by *the*) bad or wicked people. ● *adv. colloq.* badly (*took it bad*). □ **bad blood** ill feeling. **bad books** see BOOK. **bad breath** unpleasant smelling breath. **bad debt** a debt that is not recoverable. **bad egg** see EGG[1]. **bad faith** see FAITH. **bad form** see FORM. **a bad job** *Brit. colloq.* an unfortunate state of affairs. **bad-mannered** having bad manners; rude. **bad-mouth** *v.tr.* subject to malicious gossip or criticism. **bad news** *colloq.* an unpleasant or troublesome person or thing. **from bad to worse** into an even worse state. **in a bad way** ill; in trouble (*looked in a bad way*). **not** (or **not so**) **bad** *colloq.* fairly good. **too bad** *colloq.* (of circumstances, etc.) regrettable but now beyond retrieval. □□ **baddish** *adj.* **badness** *n.* [ME, perh. f. OE *bæddel* hermaphrodite, womanish man: for loss of *l* cf. MUCH, WENCH]
■ *adj.* **1** poor, inferior, defective, worthless, substandard, shoddy, second-rate, second-class, not up to par *or* scratch *or* standard, low-quality, unsatisfactory, disappointing, inadequate, indifferent, insufficient, wretched, *colloq.* not up to snuff, lousy, crummy, *sl.* rotten, *Brit. sl.* grotty, bum; see also AWFUL 1a, b. **2 a** unpleasant, unwelcome, unwanted, offensive, disagreeable, inclement, unfavorable, adverse, undesirable, *colloq.* lousy, *sl.* rotten; see also AWFUL 1a, b. **b** unsatisfactory; unfavorable, unlucky, untoward, unpropitious, unfortunate, inauspicious, inopportune; troubled, sad, wretched, unhappy, grim, distressing, lamentable, regrettable, discouraging, unpleasant. **3** injurious, dangerous, harmful, hurtful, detrimental, pernicious, deleterious, ruinous, inimical; unhealthful, unhealthy, noxious, mephitic, poisonous, baleful, destructive, evil, malignant, pestilent, *archaic* miasmic, miasmatic, *literary* nocuous, noisome. **4 a** off, spoiled, moldy, stale, rotten, decayed, putrefied, putrid, addled, contaminated, tainted. **b** corrupt, polluted, vitiated, debased, base, vile, foul, rotten. **5** injured, wounded, diseased, lame, game, *Brit. sl.* gammy; see also ILL *adj.* 1. **6** sorry, regretful, apologetic, guilty, ashamed, conscience-stricken, remorseful, contrite; rueful, sad, unhappy, depressed, upset, distressed, dejected, downhearted, disconsolate, melancholy, inconsolable. **7** distressing, severe, grave, serious, critical, terrible, awful, dreadful, dire, dangerous. **8 a** evil, ill, immoral, wicked, vicious, vile, sinful, depraved, awful, villainous, corrupt, amoral, criminal, wrong, unspeakable; see also OFFENSIVE *adj.* 1. **b** naughty, ill-behaved, badly behaved, disobedient, unruly, wild, mischievous, rebellious, recalcitrant, *Brit.* unbiddable. **9** see INVALID[2]. **10** see EXCELLENT. ● *adv.* see BADLY. □ **bad blood** see *ill will.* **bad-mouth** criticize, attack, *colloq.*

pan, trash. **in a bad way** see ILL *adj.* 1, *in trouble* 1 (TROUBLE). **not bad** see OK[1] *adj.* **too bad** see REGRETTABLE. □□ **badness** see EVIL *n.* 2, *misbehavior* (MISBEHAVE).

baddie /bádee/ *n.* (also **baddy**) (*pl.* **-ies**) *colloq.* a villain or criminal, esp. in a story, movie, etc.

bade see BID.

badge /baj/ *n.* **1** a distinctive emblem worn as a mark of office, membership, achievement, licensed employment, etc. **2** any feature or sign which reveals a characteristic condition or quality. [ME: orig. unkn.]
■ **1** see EMBLEM 1, 3.

badger /bájər/ *n.* & *v.* ● *n.* **1** an omnivorous gray-coated nocturnal mammal of the family Mustelidae with a white stripe flanked by black stripes on its head, which lives in sets. **2** a fishing fly, brush, etc., made of its hair. ● *v.tr.* pester; harass; tease. [16th c.: perh. f. BADGE, with ref. to its white forehead mark]
■ *v.* see HARASS 1.

badinage /bád'naazh/ *n.* humorous or playful ridicule. [F f. *badiner* to joke]
■ see CHAFF *n.* 3.

badlands /bádlandz/ *n.* extensive uncultivable eroded tracts in arid areas. [transl. F *mauvaises terres*]

badly /bádlee/ *adv.* (**worse** /wərs/; **worst** /wərst/) **1** in a bad manner (*works badly*). **2** *colloq.* very much (*wants it badly*). **3** *colloq.* (*was badly defeated*).
■ **1** poorly, defectively, incorrectly, shoddily, deficiently, faultily, inaccurately, erroneously, unacceptably, insufficiently, inadequately, unfavorably, unsatisfactorily, unsuccessfully, carelessly, ineptly, inartistically, amateurishly, abysmally, *colloq.* awfully, lousily, crummily, terribly; unkindly, cruelly, wickedly, harshly, severely, damagingly, critically, wretchedly, dreadfully, improperly, immorally, viciously, mischievously, naughtily, shamefully, villainously; atrociously, horribly, unspeakably, *colloq.* bad. **2** very much, greatly, seriously, *colloq.* bad. **3** severely, gravely, critically, grievously, seriously, dangerously.

badminton /bádmint'n/ *n.* **1** a game with rackets in which a shuttlecock is volleyed back and forth across a net. **2** *Brit.* a summer drink of claret, soda, and sugar. [*Badminton* in S. England]

bad-tempered /bádtémpərd/ *adj.* having a bad temper; irritable; easily annoyed. □□ **bad-temperedly** *adv.*
■ see IRRITABLE 1.

Baedeker /báydikər/ *n.* any of various travel guidebooks published by the firm founded by the German Karl *Baedeker* (d. 1859).

baffle /báfəl/ *v.* & *n.* ● *v.tr.* **1** confuse or perplex (a person, one's faculties, etc.). **2 a** frustrate or hinder (plans, etc.). **b** restrain or regulate the progress of (fluids, sounds, etc.). ● *n.* (also **baffle-board, baffle-plate**) a device used to restrain or deflect the flow of fluid, gas, sound, etc., often found in microphones, loudspeakers, etc., to regulate spreading or the emission of sound. □□ **bafflement** *n.* **baffling** *adj.* **bafflingly** *adv.* [perh. rel. to F *bafouer* ridicule, OF *beffer* mock]
■ *v.* **1** see PERPLEX 1. **2** see FRUSTRATE *v.* 2.

baffler /báflər/ *n.* = BAFFLE *n.*

bag /bag/ *n.* & *v.* ● *n.* **1** a receptacle of flexible material with an opening at the top. **2 a** (usu. in *pl.*) a piece of luggage (*put the bags in the trunk*). **b** a woman's handbag. **3** (in *pl.*; usu. foll. by *of*) *colloq.* a large amount; plenty (*bags of money*). **4** (in *pl.*) *Brit. colloq.* trousers. **5** *sl. derog.* a woman, esp. regarded as unattractive or unpleasant. **6** an animal's sac containing poison, honey, etc. **7** an amount of game shot or allowed. **8** (usu. in *pl.*) baggy folds of skin under the eyes. **9** *sl.* a person's particular interest or preoccupation (*his bag*

─────────────────────────────

/.../ **pronunciation**	● **part of speech**
□ **phrases, idioms, and compounds**	
□□ **derivatives**	■ **synonym section**
cross-references appear in SMALL CAPITALS or *italics*	

is baroque music). ● *v.* (**bagged, bagging**) **1** *tr.* put in a bag. **2** *colloq. tr.* **a** secure; get hold of (*bagged the best seat*). **b** *colloq.* steal. **c** shoot (game). **d** (often in phr. **bags I**) *Brit. colloq.* claim on grounds of being the first to do so (*bagged first go; bags I go first*). **3 a** *intr.* hang loosely; bulge; swell. **b** *tr.* cause to do this. **4** *tr. Austral. sl.* criticize; disparage. □ **bag and baggage** with all one's belongings. **bag lady** a homeless woman who carries her possessions around in shopping bags. **bag** (or **whole bag**) **of tricks** *colloq.* everything; the whole lot. **in the bag** *colloq.* achieved; as good as secured. □□ **bagful** *n.* (*pl.* **-fuls**). [ME, perh. f. ON *baggi*]

■ *n.* **1** sack, shopping bag, string bag, plastic bag, *Austral.* port, *dial.* poke, *usu. hist.* reticule. **2 a** valise, satchel, grip, suitcase, case, overnight bag, vanity case, carry-on luggage *or* bag, gladstone bag, carpetbag, portmanteau; briefcase, attaché case, dispatch case, (*bags*) baggage; luggage, gear, belongings. **b** pocketbook, purse, handbag, evening bag, clutch bag, shoulder bag, wallet. **3** (*bags*) see LOT *n.* 1. **5** crone, (old) hag, ogress, gorgon, dragon, witch, harridan, *archaic* beldam, *colloq.* battleaxe, *sl.* (old) cow, old bag, *sl. derog.* dog. **9** occupation, hobby, avocation, business, vocation, specialty, field, métier, department, concern, affair, passion, specialty, *colloq.* lookout, thing, cup of tea. ● *v.* **2 a** see SECURE *v.* 3. **b** see STEAL *v.* 1. **c** kill, shoot, gun down, pick off, *colloq.* blast, *sl.* plug; catch, trap, ensnare, snare, entrap, capture, land. **3** see SWELL *v.* 3. □ **whole bag of tricks** see EVERYTHING 1.

bagasse /bəgás/ *n.* the dry pulpy residue left after the extraction of juice from sugar cane, usable as fuel or to make paper, etc. [F f. Sp. *bagazo*]

bagatelle /bágətél/ *n.* **1** a game in which small balls are struck into numbered holes on a board, with pins as obstructions. **2** a mere trifle; a negligible amount. **3** *Mus.* a short piece of music, esp. for the piano. [F f. It. *bagatella* dimin., perh. f. *baga* BAGGAGE]

■ **2** see TRIFLE *n.* 1.

bagel /báygəl/ *n.* a hard bread roll in the shape of a ring. [Yiddish *beygel*]

baggage /bágij/ *n.* **1** everyday belongings packed up in suitcases, etc., for traveling; luggage. **2** the portable equipment of an army. **3** *derog.* a girl or woman. □ **baggage car** a car on a passenger train used for luggage, etc. [ME f. OF *bagage* f. *baguer* tie up or *bagues* bundles: perh. rel. to BAG]

■ **1** see LUGGAGE. **3** see WOMAN *n.* 1.

baggy /bágee/ *adj.* (**baggier, baggiest**) **1** hanging in loose folds. **2** puffed out. □□ **baggily** *adv.* **bagginess** *n.*

■ **1** see LOOSE *adj.* 3–5.

bagman /bágmən/ *n.* (*pl.* **-men**) **1** *sl.* an agent who collects or distributes illicitly gained money. **2** *Brit. sl.* a traveling salesman. **3** *Austral.* a tramp.

bagnio /baanyō/ *n.* (*pl.* **-os**) **1** a brothel. **2** *hist.* a prison in the Orient. [It. *bagno* f. L *balneum* bath]

■ **1** see BROTHEL.

bagpipe /bágpīp/ *n.* (usu. in *pl.*) a musical instrument consisting of a windbag connected to two kinds of reeded pipes: drone pipes which produce single sustained notes and a fingered melody pipe or 'chanter'. □□ **bagpiper** *n.*

baguette /bagét/ *n.* **1** a long narrow French loaf. **2** a gem cut in a long rectangular shape. **3** *Archit.* a small molding, semicircular in section. [F f. It. *bacchetto* dimin. of *bacchio* f. L *baculum* staff]

bah /baa/ *int.* an expression of contempt or disbelief. [prob. F]

Baha'i /bəhaá-ee, -hí/ *n.* (*pl.* **Baha'is**) a member of a monotheistic religion founded in 1863 as a branch of Babism (see BABIS), emphasizing religious unity and world peace. □□ **Baha'ism** *n.* [Pers. *bahá* splendor]

Bahamian /bəháymeeən, -haá-/ *n.* & *adj.* ● *n.* **1** a native or inhabitant of the Bahamas in the W. Indies. **2** a person of Bahamian descent. ● *adj.* of or relating to the Bahamas.

Bahasa Indonesia /baahaásə indənéezhə/ *n.* the official language of Indonesia. [Indonesian *bahasa* language f. Skr. *bhāṣā* f. *bhāṣate* he speaks: see INDONESIAN]

bail¹ /bayl/ *n.* & *v.* ● *n.* **1** money, etc., required as security for the temporary release of a prisoner pending trial. **2** a person or persons giving such security. ● *v.tr.* (usu. foll. by *out*) **1** release or secure the release of (a prisoner) on payment of bail. **2** release from a difficulty; come to the rescue of. □ **forfeit** (*colloq.* **jump**) **bail** fail to appear for trial after being released on bail. **go** (or **stand**) **bail** (often foll. by *for*) act as or provide surety (for an accused person). □□ **bailable** *adj.* [ME f. OF *bail* custody, *bailler* take charge of, f. L *bajulare* bear a burden]

■ *n.* **1** see PAWN² *n.* ● *v.* (*bail out*) see SAVE *v.* 1.

bail² /bayl/ *n.* & *v.* ● *n.* **1** the bar on a typewriter holding the paper against the platen. **2** *Cricket* either of the two crosspieces bridging the stumps. **3** an arched usu. wire handle, as of a pail. **4** a bar separating horses in an open stable. **5** *Austral. & NZ* a framework for securing the head of a cow during milking. ● *v. Austral. & NZ* (usu. foll. by *up*) **1** *tr.* secure (a cow) during milking. **2 a** *tr.* make (a person) hold up his or her arms to be robbed. **b** *intr.* surrender by throwing up one's arms. **c** *tr.* buttonhole (a person). [ME f. OF *bail(e)*, perh. f. *bailler* enclose]

bail³ /bayl/ *v.tr.* **1** (usu. foll. by *out*) scoop water out of (a boat, etc.). **2** scoop (water, etc.) out. □ **bail out** (of a pilot, etc.) make an emergency parachute descent from an aircraft. □□ **bailer** *n.* [obs. *bail* (n.) bucket f. F *baille* ult. f. L *bajulus* carrier]

■ (*bail out*) scoop out, spoon out.

bailee /baylee/ *n.* *Law* a person or party to whom goods are committed for a purpose, e.g., custody or repair, without transfer of ownership. [BAIL¹ + -EE]

bailey /báylee/ *n.* (*pl.* **-eys**) **1** the outer wall of a castle. **2** a court enclosed by it. [ME, var. of BAIL²]

Bailey bridge /báylee/ *n.* a temporary bridge of lattice steel designed for rapid assembly from prefabricated standard parts, used esp. in military operations. [Sir D. *Bailey* (d. 1985), its designer]

bailie /báylee/ *n.* esp. *hist.* a municipal officer and magistrate in Scotland. [ME, f. OF *bailli(s)* BAILIFF]

bailiff /báylif/ *n.* **1** an official in a court of law who keeps order, looks after prisoners, etc. **2** esp. *Brit.* a sheriff's officer who executes writs and processes and carries out distraints and arrests. **3** *Brit.* the agent or steward of a landlord. **4** *Brit.* (*hist.* except in formal titles) the sovereign's representative in a district, esp. the chief officer of a hundred. **5** *Brit.* the first civil officer in the Channel Islands. [ME f. OF *baillif* ult. f. L *bajulus* carrier, manager]

bailiwick /báyliwik/ *n.* **1** *Law* the district or jurisdiction of a bailie or bailiff. **2** *joc.* a person's sphere of operations or particular area of interest. [BAILIE + WICK²]

■ **1** see JURISDICTION 2. **2** see AREA 4.

bailment /báylmənt/ *n.* the act of delivering goods, etc., for a (usu. specified) purpose.

bailor /báylər/ *n.* *Law* a person or party that entrusts goods to a bailee. [BAIL¹ + -OR]

bailout /báylowt/ *n.* a rescue from a dire situation (*a financial bailout for an ailing company*).

bailsman /báylzmən/ *n.* (*pl.* **-men**) a person who stands bail for another. [BAIL¹ + MAN]

bain-marie /bánmaree/ *n.* (*pl.* **bains-marie** *pronunc.* same) **1** a cooking utensil consisting of a vessel of hot water in which a receptacle containing a sauce, etc., can be slowly and gently heated. **2** esp. *Brit.* a double boiler. [F, transl. med.L *balneum Mariae* bath of Maria (an alleged Jewish alchemist)]

bairn /bairn/ *n. Sc. & No. of Engl.* a child. [OE *bearn*]

bait¹ /bayt/ *n.* & *v.* ● *n.* **1** food used to entice a prey, esp. a fish or an animal. **2** an allurement; something intended to tempt or entice. **3** *archaic* a halt on a journey for refreshment or a rest. **4** = BATE². ● *v.* **1** *tr.* **a** harass or annoy (a person). **b** torment (a chained animal). **2** *tr.* put bait on (a hook, trap, etc.) to entice a prey. **3** *archaic* **a** *tr.* give food to (horses on a journey). **b** *intr.* stop on a journey to take food or a rest. [ME f. ON *beita* hunt or chase]

■ *n.* **1, 2** see *enticement* (ENTICE). ● *v.* **1 a** see HARASS 1. **b** see TANTALIZE.

bait² var. of BATE².

baize /bayz/ *n.* a coarse usu. green woolen material resembling felt used as a covering or lining, esp. on the tops of billiard and card tables. [F *baies* (pl.) fem. of *bai* chestnut colored (BAY⁴), treated as sing.: cf. BODICE]

bake /bayk/ *v. & n.* ● *v.* **1 a** *tr.* cook (food) by dry heat in an oven or on a hot surface, without direct exposure to a flame. **b** *intr.* undergo the process of being baked. **2** *intr. colloq.* **a** (usu. as **be baking**) (of weather, etc.) be very hot. **b** (of a person) become hot. **3 a** *tr.* harden (clay, etc.) by heat. **b** *intr.* (of clay, etc.) be hardened by heat. **4 a** *tr.* (of the sun) affect by its heat, e.g., ripen (fruit). **b** *intr.* (e.g., of fruit) be affected by the sun's heat. ● *n.* **1** the act or an instance of baking. **2** a batch of baking. **3** a social gathering at which baked food is eaten. □ **baked Alaska** sponge cake and ice cream with a meringue covering browned in an oven. **baking powder** a mixture of sodium bicarbonate, cream of tartar, etc., used instead of yeast in baking. **baking soda** sodium bicarbonate. [OE *bacan*]
■ *v.* **2 a** (**be baking**) see BOIL¹ *v.* 3c.

bakehouse /báyk-hows/ *n.* = BAKERY.

Bakelite /báykəlit, báyklit/ *n. propr.* any of various thermosetting resins or plastics made from formaldehyde and phenol and used for cables, buttons, plates, etc. [G *Bakelit* f. L.H. *Baekeland* its Belgian-born inventor d. 1944]

Baker /báykər/ *n.* □ **Baker day** *Brit. colloq.* a day set aside for in-service training of teachers in England and Wales. [Kenneth *Baker*, government official responsible for introducing them]

baker /báykər/ *n.* a person who bakes and sells bread, cakes, etc., esp. professionally. □ **baker's dozen** thirteen (so called from the former bakers' custom of adding an extra loaf to a dozen sold; the exact reason for this is unclear). [OE *bæcere*]

bakery /báykəree/ *n.* (*pl.* **-ies**) a place where bread and cakes are made or sold.

Bakewell tart /báykwel/ *n. Brit.* a baked open pie consisting of a pie crust lined with jam and filled with a rich almond paste. [*Bakewell* in Derbyshire]

baklava /baákləvaá/ *n.* (also **baclava**) a rich dessert of flaky pastry, honey, and nuts. [Turk.]

baksheesh /bákshee'sh/ *n.* (also **backsheesh**) (in some eastern countries) a small sum of money given as a gratuity or as alms. [ult. f. Pers. *bakšīš* f. *bakšīdan* give]
■ see TIP³ *n.* 1.

balaclava /báləklaávə/ *n.* (in full **balaclava helmet**) a tight woolen garment covering the whole head and neck except for the eyes, nostrils, and mouth, worn orig. by soldiers on active service in the Crimean War. [*Balaclava* in the Crimea, the site of a battle in 1854]

balalaika /báləlíkə/ *n.* a guitar-like musical instrument having a triangular body and 2–4 strings, popular in Russia and other Slav countries. [Russ.]

balance /báləns/ *n. & v.* ● *n.* **1** an apparatus for weighing, esp. one with a central pivot, beam, and two scales. **2 a** a counteracting weight or force. **b** (in full **balance wheel**) the regulating device in a clock, etc. **3 a** an even distribution of weight or amount. **b** stability of body or mind (*regained his balance*). **4** a preponderating weight or amount (*the balance of opinion*). **5 a** an agreement between or the difference between credits and debits in an account. **b** the difference between an amount due and an amount paid (*will pay the balance next week*). **c** an amount left over; the rest. **6 a** *Art* harmony of design and proportion. **b** *Mus.* the relative volume of various sources of sound (*bad balance between violins and trumpets*). **c** proportion. **7** (**the Balance**) the zodiacal sign or constellation Libra. ● *v.* **1** *tr.* (foll. by *with, against*) offset or compare (one thing) with another (*must balance the advantages with the disadvantages*). **2** *tr.* counteract, equal, or neutralize the weight or importance of. **3 a** *tr.* bring into or keep in equilibrium (*balanced a book on her head*). **b** *intr.* be in equilibrium (*balanced on one leg*). **4** *tr.* (usu. as **balanced** *adj.*) establish equal or appropriate proportions of elements in (*a balanced diet; balanced opinion*). **5** *tr.* weigh up (arguments, etc.) against each other. **6 a** *tr.* compare and esp. equalize debits and credits of (an account). **b** *intr.* (of an account) have credits and debits equal. □ **balance of**

payments the difference in value between payments into and out of a country. **balance of power 1** a situation in which the chief nations of the world have roughly equal power. **2** the power held by a small group when larger groups are of equal strength. **balance of trade** the difference in value between imports and exports. **balance sheet** a statement giving the balance of an account. **in the balance** uncertain; at a critical stage. **on balance** all things considered. **strike a balance** choose a moderate course or compromise. □□ **balanceable** *adj.* **balancer** *n.* [ME f. OF, ult. f. LL (*libra*) *bilanx bilancis* two-scaled (balance)]
■ *n.* **1** (weighing) scale(s), pair of scales, steelyard, spring balance, trebuchet, weigher. **3 a** even spread *or* cover, evenness, symmetry, equality, harmony. **b** equilibrium, equilibration, stability, steadiness, footing; poise, control, composure, self-possession. **4** weight, preponderance; control, command, authority. **5 a** bank balance. **b, c** difference, remainder, residue, rest; extra, excess, surplus. **6** see PROPORTION *n.* 2. ● *v.* **1** weigh, estimate, consider, assess, measure, compare, evaluate, offset, counterbalance; compensate, make up; (*balance with* or *against*) put *or* place *or* set against. **2** counteract, neutralize, cancel (out), offset; match (up with), equal, counterbalance, countervail, compensate (for), counterpoise, equipoise. **3 a** equilibrate, steady, poise. **b** be steadied *or* steady *or* poised, poise; stabilize, level (up *or* out), even out *or* up. **4** proportion, equilibrate, moderate, regulate, stabilize, equalize; (**balanced**) well-balanced; delicately balanced. **5** weigh up, compare, set side by side, contrast, measure. □ **in the balance** see UNCERTAIN 1. **on balance** see *on the whole* (WHOLE). **strike a balance** find a happy medium, strike *or* take a middle course, compromise. □□ **balancer** harmonizer, steadier.

balata /balótə/ *n.* **1** any of several latex-yielding trees of Central America, esp. *Manilkara bidentata.* **2** the dried sap of this used as a substitute for gutta-percha. [ult. f. Carib]

balbriggan /balbrígən/ *n.* a knitted cotton fabric used for underwear, etc. [*Balbriggan* in Ireland, where it was orig. made]

balcony /bálkənee/ *n.* (*pl.* **-ies**) **1 a** a usu. balustraded platform on the outside of a building, with access from an upper floor window or door. **b** such a balustraded platform inside a building; a gallery. **2 a** a tier of seats in a gallery in a theater, etc. **b** the upstairs seats in a movie theater, etc. □□ **balconied** *adj.* [It. *balcone*]

bald /bawld/ *adj.* **1** (of a person) with the scalp wholly or partly lacking hair. **2** (of an animal, plant, etc.) not covered by the usual hair, feathers, leaves, etc. **3** *colloq.* with the surface worn away (*a bald tire*). **4 a** blunt; unelaborated (*a bald statement*). **b** undisguised (*the bald effrontery*). **5** meager or dull (*a bald style*). **6** marked with white, esp. on the face (*a bald horse*). □ **bald eagle** a white-headed eagle (*Haliaeetus leucocephalus*), used as the emblem of the United States. □□ **balding** *adj.* (in senses 1–3). **baldly** *adv.* (in sense 4). **baldness** *n.* [ME *ballede*, orig. 'having a white blaze,' prob. f. an OE root *ball-* 'white patch']
■ **1, 2** see *hairless* (HAIR). **4 b** see OUTRIGHT *adj.* 1.

baldachin /báwldəkin/ *n.* (also **baldachino** /-kee'nō/, **baldaquin**) **1** a ceremonial canopy over an altar, throne, etc. **2** a rich brocade. [It. *baldacchino* f. *Baldacco* Baghdad, its place of origin]

balderdash /báwldərdash/ *n.* senseless talk or writing; nonsense. [earlier = 'mixture of drinks': orig. unkn.]
■ see NONSENSE.

baldhead /báwldhed/ *n.* a person with a bald head.

baldric /báwldrik/ *n. hist.* a belt for a sword, bugle, etc., hung from the shoulder across the body to the opposite hip. [ME *baudry* f. OF *baudrei*: cf. MHG *balderich*, of unkn. orig.]

/. . ./ **pronunciation**	● **part of speech**
□ **phrases, idioms, and compounds**	
□□ **derivatives**	■ **synonym section**
cross-references appear in SMALL CAPITALS *or italics*	

bale[1] /bayl/ *n. & v.* ● *n.* **1** a bundle of merchandise or hay, etc., tightly wrapped and bound with cords or hoops. **2** the quantity in a bale as a measure, esp. 500 lb. of cotton. ● *v.tr.* make up into bales. [ME prob. f. MDu., ult. identical with BALL[1]]
■ *n.* **1** see BUNDLE *n.* 1.

bale[2] /bayl/ *n. archaic* or *poet.* evil; destruction; woe; pain; misery. [OE *b(e)alu*]

baleen /bəleen/ *n.* whalebone. □ **baleen whale** any of various whales of the suborder Mysticeti, having plates of baleen fringed with bristles for straining plankton from the water. [ME f. OF *baleine* f. L *balaena* whale]

baleful /báylfoŏl/ *adj.* **1** (esp. of a manner, look, etc.) gloomy; menacing. **2** harmful; malignant; destructive. □□ **balefully** *adv.* **balefulness** *n.* [BALE[2] + -FUL]
■ **2** see HARMFUL.

baler /báylər/ *n.* a machine for making bales of hay, straw, metal, etc.

Balinese /báalineéz/ *n. & adj.* ● *n. (pl.* same) **1** a native of Bali, an island in Indonesia. **2** the language of Bali. ● *adj.* of or relating to Bali or its people or language.

balk /bawk/ *v. & n.* ● *v.* **1** *intr.* **a** refuse to go on. **b** (often foll. by *at*) hesitate. **2** *tr.* **a** thwart; hinder. **b** disappoint. **3** *tr.* **a** miss; let slip (a chance, etc.). **b** ignore; shirk. ● *n.* **1 a** hindrance; a stumbling block. **2 a** a roughly-squared timber beam. **b** a tie beam of a house. **3** *Billiards*, etc., the area on a billiard table from which a player begins a game. **4** *Baseball* an illegal action made by a pitcher. **5** a ridge left unplowed between furrows. □□ **balker** *n.* [OE *balc* f. ON *bálkr* f. Gmc]
■ *v.* **1** see RECOIL *v.* 1, 2. **2a** see HINDER[1]. ● *n.* **1** see *prevention* (PREVENT). **2** see BEAM *n.* 1.

Balkan /báwlkən/ *adj. & n.* ● *adj.* **1** of or relating to the region of SE Europe bounded by the Adriatic, the Aegean, and the Black Sea. **2** of or relating to its peoples or countries. ● *n.* **(the Balkans)** the Balkan countries. [Turk.]

balky /báwkee/ *adj.* **(-ier, -iest)** reluctant; perverse. □□ **balkiness** *n.* [BALK + -Y[1]]

ball[1] /bawl/ *n. & v.* ● *n.* **1 a** a solid or hollow sphere, esp. for use in a game. **b** a game played with such a sphere. **2 a** a ball-shaped object; material forming the shape of a ball (*ball of snow; ball of wool; rolled himself into a ball*). **b** a rounded part of the body (*ball of the foot*). **3** a solid nonexplosive missile for a cannon, etc. **4** a single delivery of a ball in cricket, etc., or passing of a ball in soccer. **5** *Baseball* a pitched ball that is not swung at by the batter and that does not pass through the strike zone. **6** (in *pl.*) *coarse sl.* **a** the testicles. **b** *Brit.* (usu. as an exclam. of contempt) nonsense; rubbish. **c** *Brit.* = *balls-up.* **d** courage; guts. ¶ Sense 6 is usually considered a taboo use. ● *v.* **1** *tr.* squeeze or wind into a ball. **2** *intr.* form or gather into a ball or balls. **3** *tr. & intr. coarse sl.* have sexual intercourse. □ **ball-and-socket joint** *Anat.* a joint in which a rounded end lies in a concave cup or socket, allowing freedom of movement. **ball bearing 1** a bearing in which the two halves are separated by a ring of small metal balls which reduce friction. **2** one of these balls. **ball cock** a floating ball on a hinged arm, whose movement up and down controls the water level in a cistern, etc. **ball game 1** any game played with a ball, esp. a game of baseball. **2** *colloq.* a particular affair or concern (*a whole new ball game*). **the ball is in your**, etc., **court** you, etc., must be next to act. **ball lightning** a rare globular form of lightning. **balls** (or **ball**) **up** *Brit. coarse sl.* bungle; make a mess of. **balls-up** *n. Brit. coarse sl.* a mess; a confused or bungled situation. **have the ball at one's feet** *Brit.* have one's best opportunity. **keep the ball rolling** maintain the momentum of an activity. **on the ball** *colloq.* alert. **play ball 1** start or continue a ballgame. **2** *colloq.* cooperate. **start**, etc., **the ball rolling** set an activity in motion; make a start. [ME f. ON *böllr* f. Gmc]
■ *n.* **1a, 2a** see ORB *n.* 3 see SHOT[1] 3. □ **ball game 2** see SITUATION 2. **on the ball** see ALERT *adj.* 1. **play ball 2** cooperate, agree, work together, work hand in glove, play along.

ball[2] /bawl/ *n.* **1** a formal social gathering for dancing. **2** *sl.* an enjoyable time (esp. *have a ball*). [F *bal* f. LL *ballare* to dance]
■ **1** see DANCE *n.*

ballad /bálad/ *n.* **1** a poem or song narrating a popular story. **2** a slow sentimental or romantic song. □ **ballad stanza** (also **meter**) esp. *Brit.* = *common measure.* [ME f. OF *balade* f. Prov. *balada* dancing song f. *balar* to dance]
■ see LAY[3].

ballade /baláad/ *n.* **1** a poem of one or more triplets of stanzas with a repeated refrain and an envoy. **2** *Mus.* a short lyrical piece, esp. for piano. [earlier spelling and pronunc. of BALLAD]
■ **1** see LAY[3].

balladeer /báladeér/ *n.* a singer or composer of ballads.
■ see *singer* (SING).

balladry /bálədree/ *n.* ballad poetry.

ballast /báləst/ *n. & v.* ● *n.* **1** any heavy material placed in a ship or the basket of a balloon, etc., to secure stability. **2** coarse stone, etc., used to form the bed of a railroad track or road. **3** *Electr.* any device used to stabilize the current in a circuit. **4** anything that affords stability or permanence. ● *v.tr.* **1** provide with ballast. **2** afford stability or weight to. [16th c.: f. LG or Scand., of uncert. orig.]

ballboy /báwlboy/ *n. (fem.* **ballgirl** /-gərl/) a boy or girl who retrieves balls that go out of play during a game.

ballerina /bálər   ́eenə/ *n.* a female ballet dancer. [It., fem. of *ballerino* dancing master f. *ballare* dance f. LL: see BALL[2]]

ballet /baláy, bá, lay/ *n.* **1 a** a dramatic or representational style of dancing and mime, using set steps and techniques and usu. (esp. in classical ballet) accompanied by music. **b** a particular piece or performance of ballet. **c** the music for this. **2** a company performing ballet. □ **ballet dancer** a dancer who specializes in ballet. □□ **balletic** /balétik/ *adj.* [F f. It. *balletto* dimin. of *ballo* BALL[2]]

balletomane /balétəmayn/ *n.* a devotee of ballet. □□ **balletomania** /-máyneeə/ *n.*

ballista /bəlístə/ *n. (pl.* **ballistae** /-stee/) a catapult used in ancient warfare for hurling large stones, etc. [L f. Gk *ballō* throw]

ballistic /bəlístik/ *adj.* **1** of or relating to projectiles. **2** moving under the force of gravity only. □ **ballistic missile** a missile which is initially powered and guided but falls under gravity on its target. **go ballistic** *colloq.* become frantically overwrought or furiously angry. □□ **ballistically** *adv.* [BALLISTA + -IC]
■ □ **ballistic missile** see MISSILE.

ballistics /bəlístiks/ *n.pl.* (usu. treated as *sing.*) the science of projectiles and firearms.

ballocks var. of BOLLOCKS.

balloon /bəloŏn/ *n. & v.* ● *n.* **1** a small inflatable rubber pouch with a neck, used as a child's toy or as decoration. **2** a large usu. round bag inflatable with hot air or gas to make it rise in the air, often carrying a basket for passengers. **3** a balloon shape enclosing the words or thoughts of characters in a comic strip or cartoon. **4** a large globular drinking glass, usu. for brandy. ● *v.* **1** *intr. & tr.* swell out or cause to swell out like a balloon. **2** *intr.* travel by balloon. **3** *tr. Brit.* hit or kick (a ball, etc.) high in the air. □ **when the balloon goes up** *colloq.* when the action or trouble starts. □□ **balloonist** *n.* [F *ballon* or It. *ballone* large ball]
■ *v.* **1** see SWELL *v.* 3.

ballot /bálət/ *n. & v.* ● *n.* **1** a process of voting, in writing and usu. secret. **2** the total of votes recorded in a ballot. **3** the drawing of lots. **4** a paper or ticket, etc., used in voting. **5** the right to vote. ● *v.* (**balloted, balloting**) **1** *intr.* (usu. foll. by *for*) **a** hold a ballot; give a vote. **b** draw lots for precedence, etc. **2** *tr.* take a ballot of (*the union balloted its members*). □ **ballot box** a sealed box into which voters put completed ballot papers. **ballot paper** a slip of paper used to register a vote. [It. *ballotta* dimin. of *balla* BALL[1]]
■ *n.* **1** see VOTE *n.* 1. ● *v.* **1 a** see VOTE *v.* 1.

ballpark /báwlpaark/ *n.* **1** a baseball field. **2** (*attrib.*) *colloq.* approximate; rough (*a ballpark figure*). □ **in the (right) ballpark** *colloq.* close to one's objective; approximately correct.

■ **2** see APPROXIMATE *adj.*

ballpoint /báwlpoynt/ *n.* (in full **ballpoint pen**) a pen with a tiny ball as its writing point.
■ see PEN¹ *n.*

ballroom /báwlrōom, -rŏŏm/ *n.* a large room or hall for dancing. □ **ballroom dancing** formal social dancing as a recreation.

bally /bálee/ *adj. & adv. Brit. sl.* a mild form of *bloody* (see BLOODY *adj.* 3) (*tooh the bally lot*). [alt. of BLOODY]

ballyhoo /báleehŏŏ/ *n.* **1** a loud noise or fuss; a confused state or commotion. **2** extravagant or sensational publicity. [19th or 20th c.: orig. unkn.]
■ **1** see NOISE *n.* **2** see FANFARE 2.

ballyrag var. of BULLYRAG.

balm /baam/ *n.* **1** an aromatic ointment for anointing, soothing, or healing. **2** a fragrant and medicinal exudation from certain trees and plants. **3** a healing or soothing influence or consolation. **4** an Asian and N. African tree yielding balm. **5** any aromatic herb, esp. one of the genus *Melissa*. **6** a pleasant perfume or fragrance. □ **balm of Gilead** (cf. Jer. 8:22) **1 a** a fragrant resin formerly much used as an unguent. **b** a plant of the genus *Commiphora* yielding such resin. **2** the balsam fir or poplar. [ME f. OF *ba(s)me* f. L *balsamum* BALSAM]
■ **1** see OINTMENT.

balmoral /balmáwrəl, -mór-/ *n.* **1** a type of brimless boat-shaped cocked hat with a cockade or ribbons attached, usu. worn by certain Scottish regiments. **2** a heavy leather walking shoe with laces up the front. [*Balmoral* Castle in Scotland]

balmy /baámee/ *adj.* (**balmier, balmiest**) **1** mild and fragrant; soothing. **2** yielding balm. **3** esp. *Brit. sl.* = BARMY. □□ **balmily** *adv.* **balminess** *n.*
■ **1** see MILD 3.

balneology /bálneeólajee/ *n.* the scientific study of bathing and medicinal springs. □□ **balneological** /-neeəlójikəl/ *adj.* **balneologist** *n.* [L *balneum* bath + -LOGY]

baloney /bəlŏnee/ *n.* (also **boloney**) (*pl.* **-eys**) *sl.* **1** humbug; nonsense. **2** = BOLOGNA. [20th c.: alt. of BOLOGNA]
■ **1** see NONSENSE.

balsa /báwlsə/ *n.* **1** (in full **balsa wood**) a type of tough lightweight wood used for making models, etc. **2** the tropical American tree, *Ochroma lagopus*, from which it comes. [Sp., = raft]

balsam /báwlsəm/ *n.* **1** any of several aromatic resinous exudations, such as balm, obtained from various trees and shrubs and used as a base for certain fragrances and medical preparations. **2** an ointment, esp. one composed of a substance dissolved in oil or turpentine. **3** any of various trees or shrubs which yield balsam. **4** any of several flowering plants of the genus *Impatiens*. **5** a healing or soothing agency. □ **balsam apple** any of various gourdlike plants of the genus *Momordica*, having warty orange-yellow fruits. **balsam fir** a N. American tree (*Abies balsamea*) which yields pulpwood and balsam. **balsam poplar** any of various N. American poplars, esp. *Populus balsamifera*, yielding balsam. □□ **balsamic** /-sámik/ *adj.* [OE f. L *balsamum*]
■ □□ **balsamic** see *soothing* (SOOTHE).

Baltic /báwltik/ *n. & adj.* ● *n.* **1** (**the Baltic**) **a** an almost landlocked sea of NE Europe. **b** the nations bordering this sea. **2** an Indo-European branch of languages comprising Old Prussian, Lithuanian, and Latvian. ● *adj.* of or relating to the Baltic or the Baltic branch of languages. [med.L *Balticus* f. LL *Balthae* dwellers near the Baltic Sea]

baluster /báləstər/ *n.* each of a series of often ornamental short posts or pillars supporting a rail or coping, etc. ¶ Often confused with *banister*. [F *balustre* f. It. *balaustro* f. L f. Gk *balaustion* wild pomegranate flower]
■ see RAIL¹ *n.* 1.

balustrade /báləstráyd/ *n.* a railing supported by balusters, esp. forming an ornamental parapet to a balcony, bridge, or terrace. [F (AS BALUSTER)]
■ see RAIL¹ *n.* 1.

bama /bámə, pámə/ *n.* (also **pama**) *Austral.* an Aboriginal

person, esp. one from northern Queensland. [f. many north Qld. languages *bama* person or man]

bambino /bambeénō/ *n.* (*pl.* **bambini** /-nee/) *colloq.* **1** a young child. **2** an image of the Christ child. [It., dimin. of *bambo* silly]

bamboo /bambŏŏ/ *n.* **1** a mainly tropical giant woody grass of the subfamily Bambusidae. **2** its hollow jointed stem, used as a stick or to make furniture, etc. [Du. *bamboes* f. Port. *mambu* f. Malay]

bamboozle /bambŏŏzəl/ *v.tr. colloq.* cheat; hoax; mystify. □□ **bamboozlement** *n.* **bamboozler** *n.* [c.1700: prob. of cant orig.]
■ see CHEAT *v.* 1.

ban /ban/ *v. & n.* ● *v.tr.* (**banned, banning**) forbid; prohibit (an action, etc.), esp. formally; refuse admittance to (a person). ● *n.* **1** a formal or authoritative prohibition (*a ban on smoking*). **2** a tacit prohibition by public opinion. **3** *hist.* a sentence of outlawry. **4** *archaic* a curse or execration. [OE *bannan* summon f. Gmc]
■ *v.* prohibit, forbid, outlaw, interdict, stop, prevent, bar, disallow; debar, proscribe, banish, exile. ● *n.* **1, 2** prohibition, taboo, proscription, interdiction, interdict; embargo, boycott. **4** see CURSE *n.* 1.

banal /bənál, báynəl, bənaál/ *adj.* trite; feeble; commonplace. □□ **banality** /-nálitee/ *n.* (*pl.* **-ies**). **banally** *adv.* [orig. in sense 'compulsory,' hence 'common to all,' f. F f. *ban* (as BAN)]
■ trite, hackneyed, stereotyped, clichéd, stereotypical, commonplace, stock, common, everyday, ordinary, pedestrian, humdrum, tired, well-worn, feeble, threadbare, unoriginal, unimaginative, uninspired, bourgeois, platitudinous; petty, jejune, *archaic* trivial, *colloq.* corny, old hat. □□ **banality** triteness, pedestrianism, tiredness, feebleness, unimaginativeness, triviality, corniness; see also CLICHÉ. **banally** tritely, stereotypically, unimaginatively, unoriginally, *colloq.* cornily.

banana /bənánə/ *n.* **1** a long curved fruit with soft pulpy flesh and yellow skin when ripe, growing in clusters. **2** (in full **banana tree**) the tropical and subtropical treelike plant, *Musa sapientum*, bearing this. □ **banana republic** *derog.* a small nation, esp. in Central America, dependent on one crop or the influx of foreign capital. **banana skin 1** the skin of a banana. **2** a cause of upset or humiliation; a blunder. **banana split** a dessert made with split bananas, ice cream, sauce, whipped cream, etc. **go bananas** *sl.* become crazy or angry. [Port. or Sp., f. a name in Guinea]

banausic /bənáwsik/ *adj.* usu. *derog.* **1 a** uncultivated. **b** materialistic. **2** utilitarian. [Gk *banausikos* for artisans]

banc /bangk/ *n.* a judge's seat in court. □ **in banc** *Law* sitting as a full court. [AF (= bench) f. med.L (as BANK²)]

band¹ /band/ *n. & v.* ● *n.* **1** a flat, thin strip or loop of material (e.g., paper, metal, or cloth) put around something esp. to hold it together or decorate it (*headband; rubber band*). **2 a** a strip of material forming part of a garment (*hatband; waistband*). **b** a stripe of a different color or material in or on an object. **3 a** a range of frequencies or wavelengths in a spectrum (esp. of radio frequencies). **b** a range of values within a series. **4** a plain or simple ring, esp. without a gem, etc. **5** *Mech.* a belt connecting wheels or pulleys. **6** (in *pl.*) a collar having two hanging strips, worn by some lawyers, ministers, and academics in formal dress. **7** *archaic* a thing that restrains, binds, connects, or unites; a bond. ● *v.tr.* **1** put a band on. **2** mark with stripes. **b** (as **banded** *adj.*) *Bot. & Zool.* marked with colored bands or stripes. □ **banded anteater** = NUMBAT. **band saw** a mechanical saw with a blade formed by an endless toothed band. [ME f. OF *bande, bende* (sense 7 f. ON *band*) f. Gmc]
■ *n.* **1** strip, ribbon, headband, belt, bandeau, fillet, tie,

string, *literary* cincture. **2 b** strip, stripe, line, streak, bar, border, edging, edge, frame, fringe, *Heraldry* bordure, orle. **3 a** frequency, wavelength. ● *v.* **1** tie (up), keep, bind, fasten, secure; encircle, belt, *literary* gird. **2 a** line, stripe, border, streak, striate; edge, frame, fringe.

band² /band/ *n. & v.* ● *n.* **1** an organized group of people having a common object, esp. of a criminal nature (*band of cutthroats*). **2 a** a group of musicians, esp. playing wind instruments and percussion (*brass band*; *military band*). **b** a group of musicians playing jazz, pop, or dance music. **c** *colloq.* an orchestra. **3** a herd or flock. ● *v.tr. & intr.* form into a group for a purpose (*band together for mutual protection*). □ **Band of Hope** *Brit.* an association promoting total abstinence from alcohol. [ME f. OF *bande, bander*, med.L *banda*, prob. of Gmc orig.]
  ■ *n.* **1** company, troop, platoon, corps, group, body, gang, horde, party, pack, *colloq.* bunch, crew, mob. **2** group, ensemble, combination, orchestra, *sl.* combo. ● *v.* (*band together*) unite, confederate, ally, gather *or* join *or* league together, team *or* join up, affiliate, merge, federate.

bandage /bándij/ *n. & v.* ● *n.* **1** a strip of material for binding up a wound, etc. **2** a piece of material used as a blindfold. ● *v.tr.* bind (a wound, etc.) with a bandage. [F f. *bande* (as BAND¹)]
  ■ *v.* see BIND *v.* 10a.

Band-Aid /bándayd/ *n.* **1** *propr.* an adhesive bandage with a gauze pad in the center for covering minor wounds. **2** (**band-aid**) a stopgap solution to a problem.

bandanna /bandánə/ *n.* a large handkerchief or neckerchief, usu. of silk or cotton, and often having a colorful pattern. [prob. Port. f. Hindi]

b. & b. *abbr.* (also **B & B**) bed and breakfast.
  ■ see HOTEL 1.

bandbox /bándboks/ *n.* a usu. circular cardboard box for carrying hats. □ **out of a bandbox** extremely neat. [BAND¹ + BOX¹]

bandeau /bandṓ/ *n.* (*pl.* **bandeaux** /-dōz/) **1** a narrow band worn around the head. **2** a narrow covering for the breasts. [F]
  ■ see BAND¹ *n.* 1.

banderilla /bándəréeə, -rílyə/ *n.* a decorated dart thrust into a bull's neck or shoulders during a bullfight. [Sp.]

banderole /bándərṓl/ *n.* (also **banderol**) **1 a** a long narrow flag with a cleft end, flown at a masthead. **b** an ornamental streamer on a knight's lance. **2 a** a ribbon-like scroll. **b** a stone band resembling a banderole, bearing an inscription. [F *banderole* f. It. *banderuola* dimin. of *bandiera* BANNER]
  ■ **1** see STREAMER.

bandicoot /bándikōōt/ *n.* **1** any of the insect- and plant-eating marsupials of the family Peramelidae. **2** (in full **bandicoot rat**) *Ind.* a destructive rat, *Bandicota benegalensis*. [Telugu *pandikokku* pig-rat]

bandit /bándit/ *n.* (*pl.* **bandits** or **banditti** /-dítee/) **1** a robber or murderer, esp. a member of a band. **2** an outlaw. □□ **banditry** *n.* [It. *bandito* (pl. *-iti*), past part. of *bandire* ban, = med.L *bannire* proclaim: see BANISH]
  ■ see OUTLAW *n.*

bandmaster /bándmastər/ *n.* the conductor of a (esp. military or brass) band. [BAND² + MASTER]

bandolier /bándəleér/ *n.* (also **bandoleer**) a shoulder belt with loops or pockets for cartridges. [Du. *bandelier* or F *bandoulière*, prob. formed as BANDEROLE]

bandsman /bándzmən/ *n.* (*pl.* **-men**) a player in a (esp. military or brass) band.

bandstand /bándstand/ *n.* a covered outdoor platform for a band to play on, usu. in a park.

bandwagon /bándwagən/ *n.* a wagon used for carrying a band in a parade, etc. □ **climb** (or **jump**) **on the bandwagon** join a party, cause, or group that seems likely to succeed.

bandwidth /bándwidth, -with/ *n.* the range of frequencies within a given band (see BAND¹ *n.* 3a).

bandy¹ /bándee/ *adj.* (**bandier, bandiest**) **1** (of the legs) curved so as to be wide apart at the knees. **2** (also **bandy-legged** /-légəd, -legd/) (of a person) having bandy legs. [perh. f. obs. *bandy* curved stick]

bandy² /bándee/ *v.tr.* (**-ies, -ied**) **1** (often foll. by *about*) a pass (a story, rumor, etc.) to and fro. **b** throw or pass (a ball, etc.) to and fro. **2** (often foll. by *about*) discuss disparagingly (*bandied his name about*). **3** (often foll. by *with*) exchange (blows, insults, etc.) (*don't bandy words with me*). [perh. f. F *bander* take sides f. *bande* BAND²]

bane /bayn/ *n.* **1** the cause of ruin or trouble; the curse (esp. *the bane of one's life*). **2** ruin; woe. **3** *archaic* (except in *comb.*) poison (*ratsbane*). □□ **baneful** *adj.* **banefully** *adv.* [OE *bana* f. Gmc]
  ■ **1** see CURSE *n.* 4. **2** see RUIN *n.* 1–3a. **3** see POISON *n.* 1.

baneberry /báynberee/ *n.* (*pl.* **-ies**) **1** a plant of the genus *Actaea*. **2** the bitter poisonous berry of this plant.

bang /bang/ *n., v., & adv.* ● *n.* **1 a** a loud short sound. **b** an explosion. **c** the report of a gun. **2 a** a sharp blow. **b** the sound of this. **3** (esp. in *pl.*) a fringe of hair cut straight across the forehead. **4** *coarse sl.* **a** an act of sexual intercourse. **b** a partner in sexual intercourse. **5** *sl.* a drug injection (cf. BHANG). **6** *sl.* a thrill (*got a bang from going fast*). ● *v.* **1** *tr. & intr.* strike or shut noisily (*banged the door shut*; *banged on the table*). **2** *tr. & intr.* make or cause to make the sound of a blow or an explosion. **3** *tr.* cut (hair) in bangs. **4** *coarse sl.* **a** *intr.* have sexual intercourse. **b** *tr.* have sexual intercourse with. ● *adv.* **1** with a bang or sudden impact. **2** esp. *Brit. colloq.* exactly (*bang in the middle*). □ **bang off** *Brit. sl.* immediately. **bang on** *Brit. colloq.* exactly right. **bang up** damage. **2** *Brit. sl.* lock up; imprison. **bang-up** *sl.* first-class, excellent (esp. *bang-up job*). **go bang 1** (of a door, etc.) shut noisily. **2** explode. **3** *colloq.* be suddenly destroyed (*bang went their chances*). **go with a bang** go successfully. [16th c.: perh. f. Scand.]
  ■ *n.* **1** see EXPLOSION 2. **2a** see HIT *n.* 1a. ● *v.* **1** see HIT *v.* 1a, BEAT *v.* 2a. **2** see BOOM¹ *v.*

banger /bángər/ *n. Brit.* **1** *sl.* a sausage. **2** *sl.* an old car, esp. a noisy one. **3** a loud firework.

bangle /bánggəl/ *n.* a rigid ornamental band worn around the arm or occas. the ankle. [Hindi *bangri* glass bracelet]

bangtail /bángtayl/ *n. & v.* ● *n.* a horse, esp. with its tail cut short and straight across. ● *v.tr. Austral.* cut the tails of (horses or cattle) as an aid to counting or identification. □ **bangtail muster** *Austral.* the counting of cattle involving cutting across the tufts at the tail ends as each is counted.

banian var. of BANYAN.

banish /bánish/ *v.tr.* **1** formally expel (a person), esp. from a country. **2** dismiss from one's presence or mind. □□ **banishment** *n.* [ME f. OE *banir* ult. f. Gmc]
  ■ **1** exile, expatriate, deport, extradite, transport, eject, oust, proscribe, expel, drive out *or* away, dismiss, outlaw, ban, ostracize, rusticate, relegate, *Eccl.* excommunicate. **2** drive out *or* away, expel, cast out, dismiss, push out, reject. □□ **banishment** see EXILE *n.* 1.

banister /bánistər/ *n.* (also **bannister**) **1** the uprights and handrail at the side of a staircase. **2** an upright supporting a handrail. ¶ Often confused with *baluster*. [earlier *barrister*, corrupt. of BALUSTER]
  ■ **1** (*banisters*) see RAIL¹ 1.

banjo /bánjō/ *n.* (*pl.* **-os** or **-oes**) a stringed musical instrument with a neck and head like a guitar and an open-backed body consisting of parchment stretched over a metal hoop. □□ **banjoist** *n.* [prob. ult. of African origin, akin to Kimbundu (a Banta language) *mbanza* a similar stringed instrument]

bank¹ /bangk/ *n. & v.* ● *n.* **1 a** the sloping edge of land by a river. **b** the area of ground alongside a river (*had a picnic on the bank*). **2** a raised shelf of ground; a slope. **3** an elevation in the sea or a river bed. **4** the artificial slope of a road, etc., enabling vehicles to maintain speed round a curve. **5** a mass of cloud, fog, snow, etc. **6** the edge of a hollow place (e.g., the top of a mine shaft). ● *v.* **1** *tr. & intr.* (often foll. by *up*) heap or rise into banks. **2** *tr.* heap up (a fire) tightly so that it burns slowly. **3 a** *intr.* (of a vehicle or aircraft or its oc-

cupant) travel with one side higher than the other in rounding a curve. **b** *tr.* cause (a vehicle or aircraft) to do this. **4** *tr.* contain or confine within a bank or banks. **5** *tr.* build (a road, etc.) higher at the outer edge of a bend to enable fast cornering. □ **bank swallow** a swallowlike bird, *Riparia riparia*, nesting in the side of a sandy bank, etc. [ME f. Gmc f. ON *banki* (unrecorded: cf. OIcel. *bakki*): rel. to BENCH]
■ *n.* **1a, 2, 4** see SLOPE *n.* 1–3. **3** see SHALLOW *n.* ● *v.* **1** see HEAP *v.* 1.

bank² /bangk/ *n.* & *v.* ● *n.* **1 a** a financial establishment which uses money deposited by customers for investment, pays it out when required, makes loans at interest, exchanges currency, etc. **b** a building in which this business takes place. **2** = *piggy bank.* **3 a** the money or tokens held by the banker in some gambling games. **b** the banker in such games. **4** a place for storing anything for future use (*blood bank*; *data bank*). ● *v.* **1** *tr.* deposit (money or valuables) in a bank. **2** *intr.* engage in business as a banker. **3** *intr.* (often foll. by *at, with*) keep money (at a bank). **4** *intr.* act as banker in some gambling games. □ **bank balance** the amount of money held in a bank account at a given moment. **bank bill 1** *Brit.* a bill drawn by one bank on another. **2** = BANKNOTE. **bank holiday** a day on which banks are officially closed, (in the UK) usu. kept as a public holiday. **bank manager** a person in charge of a local branch of a bank. **the Bank of England** the central bank of England and Wales, issuing banknotes and having the government as its main customer. **bank on** rely on (*I'm banking on your help*). **bank statement** a printed statement of transactions and balance issued periodically to the holder of a bank account. [F *banque* or It. *banca* f. med.L *banca, bancus,* f. Gmc: rel. to BANK¹]
■ *n.* **4** see STOREHOUSE. ● *v.* **1** see DEPOSIT *v.* 2. □ **bank on** see RELY.

bank³ /bangk/ *n.* **1** a row of similar objects, esp. of keys, lights, or switches. **2** a tier of oars. **3** a row or set of elevators, pay telephones, etc. [ME f. OF *banc* f. Gmc: rel. to BANK¹, BENCH]

bankable /bángkəbəl/ *adj.* **1** acceptable at a bank. **2** reliable (*a bankable reputation*). **3** certain to bring profit; good for the box office (*Hollywood's most bankable stars*).

bankbook /bángkbŏŏk/ *n.* = PASSBOOK.

bankcard /bángk-kard/ *n.* a bank-issued credit card or automatic teller machine card.

banker¹ /bángkər/ *n.* **1** a person who manages or owns a bank or group of banks. **2 a** a keeper of the bank or dealer in some gambling games. **b** a card game involving gambling. **3** *Brit.* a result forecast identically (while other forecasts differ) in several soccer pool entries on one coupon. [F *banquier* f. *banque* BANK²]

banker² /bángkər/ *n.* **1 a** a fishing boat off Newfoundland. **b** a Newfoundland fisherman. **2** *Austral. colloq.* a river flooded to the top of its banks. [BANK¹ + -ER¹]

banking /bángking/ *n.* the business transactions of a bank.

banknote /bángknōt/ *n.* a banker's promissory note, esp. from a central bank, payable to the bearer on demand, and serving as money.

bankroll /bángkrōl/ *n.* & *v.* ● *n.* **1** a roll of paper currency. **2** funds. ● *v.tr. colloq.* support financially.

bankrupt /bángkrupt/ *adj., n.,* & *v.* ● *adj.* **1 a** insolvent; declared in law unable to pay debts. **b** undergoing the legal process resulting from this. **2** (often foll. by *of*) exhausted or drained (of some quality, etc.); deficient; lacking. ● *n.* **1 a** an insolvent person whose estate is administered and disposed of for the benefit of the creditors. **b** an insolvent debtor. **2** a person exhausted of or deficient in a certain attribute (*a moral bankrupt*). ● *v.tr.* make bankrupt. □□ **bankruptcy** /-ruptsee/ *n.* (*pl.* **-ies**). [16th c.: f. It *banca rotta* broken bench (as BANK², L *rumpere rupt-* break), assim. to L]
■ *adj.* **1** see INSOLVENT *adj.* ● *n.* **1** see PAUPER. ● *v.* see RUIN *v.* 1a.

banksia /bángkseeə/ *n.* any evergreen flowering shrub of the genus *Banksia*, native to Australia. □ **banksia rose** a Chi-

nese climbing rose with small flowers. [Sir J. *Banks*, Engl. naturalist d. 1820]

banner /bánər/ *n.* **1 a** a large rectangular sign bearing a slogan or design and usu. carried on two side poles or a crossbar in a demonstration or procession. **b** a long strip of cloth, etc., hung across a street or along the front of a building, etc., and bearing a slogan. **2** a flag on a pole used as the standard of a king, knight, etc., esp. in battle. **3** (*attrib.*) excellent; outstanding (*a banner year in sales*). □ **banner headline** a large newspaper headline, esp. one across the top of the front page. **join** (or **follow**) **the banner of** adhere to the cause of. **under the banner of** associated with the cause of, esp. by the use of the same slogans as, adherence to the same principles as, etc. □□ **bannered** *adj.* [ME f. AF *banere,* OF *baniere* f. Rmc ult. f. Gmc]
■ **1, 2** standard, flag, pennant, ensign, burgee, gonfalon, pennon, streamer, color, banderole, *Eccl.* vexillium, *Naut.* jack, house flag. **3** (*attrib.*) outstanding, celebrated, exceptional, momentous, memorable, notable, important, noteworthy, distinguished; see also EXCELLENT. □ **under the banner of** in association with, using the slogan(s) *or* rallying cry *or* motto *or* catchword(s) of.

banneret /bánəret/ *n.* **1** a small banner. **2** (also /-rit/) *hist.* a knight who commanded his own troops in battle under his own banner. **3** *hist.* a knighthood given on the battlefield for courage. [ME & OF *baneret* f. *baniere* BANNER + -*et* as -ATE¹]

bannister var. of BANISTER.

bannock /bánək/ *n. Sc.* & *No. of Engl.* a round flat griddle cake, usu. unleavened. [OE *bannuc,* perh. f. Celt.]

banns /banz/ *n.pl.* a notice read out, esp. on three successive Sundays in a parish church, announcing an intended marriage and giving the opportunity for objections. □ **forbid the banns** raise an objection to an intended marriage, esp. in church following the reading of the banns. [pl. of BAN]

banquet /bángkwit/ *n.* & *v.* ● *n.* **1** an elaborate usu. extensive feast. **2** a dinner for many people followed by speeches in favor of a cause or in celebration of an event. ● *v.* (**banqueted, banqueting**) **1** *intr.* hold a banquet; feast. **2** *tr.* entertain with a banquet. □□ **banqueter** *n.* [F, dimin. of *banc* bench, BANK²]
■ *n.* feast, dinner, sumptuous meal, ceremonial dinner, lavish dinner, function, *formal* sumptuous repast. ● *v.* feast, indulge, wine and dine, carouse; regale. □□ **banqueter** diner, feaster.

banquette /bangkét/ *n.* **1** an upholstered bench along a wall, esp. in a restaurant or bar. **2** a raised step behind a rampart. [F f. It. *banchetta* dimin. of *banca* bench, BANK²]

banshee /bánshee, -sheé/ *n.* a female spirit whose wailing warns of a death in a house. [Ir. *bean sídhe* f. OIr. *ben síde* woman of the fairies]

bantam /bántəm/ *n.* **1** any of several small breeds of domestic fowl, of which the male is very aggressive. **2** a small but aggressive person. [app. f. *Banten* in Java, although the fowl is not native there]

bantamweight /bántəmwayt/ *n.* **1** a weight in certain sports intermediate between flyweight and featherweight. **2** a sportsman of this weight.

banter /bántər/ *n.* & *v.* ● *n.* good-humored teasing. ● *v.* **1** *tr.* ridicule in a good-humored way. **2** *intr.* talk humorously or teasingly. □□ **banterer** *n.* [17th c.: orig. unkn.]
■ *n.* raillery, badinage, persiflage, pleasantries, jesting, jests, joking, repartee; teasing, chaff, *colloq.* kidding, ribbing, *Austral.* & *NZ sl.* borak. ● *v.* **1** tease, kid, joke, poke fun at, jolly, chaff, ridicule, *colloq.* have on, rib, *sl.* josh, razz. **2** kid, joke (around), jest, fool (about *or* around).

Bantu /bántōō/ *n.* & *adj.* ● *n.* (*pl.* same or **Bantus**) **1** often *offens.* **a** a large group of Negroid peoples of central and

/.../ **pronunciation**	● **part of speech**
□ **phrases, idioms, and compounds**	
□□ **derivatives**	■ **synonym section**
cross-references appear in SMALL CAPITALS or *italics*	

southern Africa. **b** a member of any of these peoples. **2** the group of languages spoken by them. ● *adj.* of or relating to these peoples or languages. [Bantu, = people]

Bantustan /bántōōstan/ *n. S.Afr. hist.* often *offens.* any of several partially self-governing areas formerly reserved for black South Africans (see also HOMELAND). [BANTU + -*stan* as in *Hindustan*]

banyan /bányən/ *n.* (also **banian**) **1** an Indian fig tree, *Ficus benghalensis*, the branches of which hang down and root themselves. **2** a Hindu trader. **3** a loose flannel jacket, shirt, or gown worn in India. [Port. *banian* f. Gujarati *vāṇiyo* man of trading caste, f. Skr.: applied orig. to one such tree under which banyans had built a pagoda]

banzai /baanzí/ *int.* **1** a Japanese battle cry. **2** a form of greeting used to the Japanese emperor. [Jap., = ten thousand years (of life to you)]

baobab /báyōbab, baa-/ *n.* an African tree, *Adansonia digitata*, with an enormously thick trunk and large fruit containing edible pulp. [L (1592), prob. f. an Afr. lang.]

bap /bap/ *n. Brit.* a soft flattish bread roll. [16th c.: orig. unkn.]

baptism /báptizəm/ *n.* **1 a** the religious rite, symbolizing admission to the Christian Church, of sprinkling the forehead with water, or (usu. only with adults) by immersion, generally accompanied by name giving. **b** the act of baptizing or being baptized. **2** any similar non-Christian rite. **3** an initiation, e.g., into battle. **4** the naming of ships, church bells, etc. □ **baptism of fire 1** initiation into battle. **2** a painful new undertaking or experience. □□ **baptismal** /-tízməl/ *adj.* [ME f. OF *ba(p)te(s)me* f. eccl.L *baptismus* f. eccl.Gk *baptismos* f. *baptizō* BAPTIZE]

baptist /báptist/ *n.* **1** a person who baptizes, esp. John the Baptist. **2** (**Baptist**) a Christian advocating baptism by total immersion, esp. of adults, as a symbol of membership of and initiation into the Church. [ME f. OF *baptiste* f. eccl.L *baptista* f. eccl.Gk *baptistēs* f. *baptizō* BAPTIZE]

baptistery /báptistree/ *n.* (also **baptistry**) (*pl.* **-ies**) **1 a** the part of a church used for baptism. **b** *hist.* a building next to a church, used for baptism. **2** (in a Baptist chapel) a sunken receptacle used for total immersion. [ME f. OF *baptisterie* f. eccl.L *baptisterium* f. eccl.Gk *baptistērion* bathing place f. *baptizō* BAPTIZE]

baptize /báptíz/ *v.tr.* **1** (also *absol.*) administer baptism to. **2** give a name or nickname to; christen. [ME f. OF *baptiser* f. eccl.L *baptizare* f. Gk *baptizō* immerse, baptize]
■ **1** christen. **2** see CALL *v.* 7.

bar¹ /baar/ *n., v.,* & *prep.* ● *n.* **1** a long rod or piece of rigid wood, metal, etc., esp. used as an obstruction, confinement, fastening, weapon, etc. **2 a** something resembling a bar in being (thought of as) straight, narrow, and rigid (*bar of soap*; *bar of chocolate*). **b** a band of color or light, esp. on a flat surface. **c** the heating element of an electric heater. **d** = CROSSBAR. **e** *Brit.* a metal strip below the clasp of a medal, awarded as an extra distinction. **f** a sandbank or shoal as at the mouth of a harbor or an estuary. **g** *Brit.* a rail marking the end of each chamber in the Houses of Parliament. **h** *Heraldry* a narrow horizontal stripe across a shield. **3 a** a barrier of any shape. **b** a restriction (*color bar*; *a bar to promotion*). **4 a** a counter in a restaurant, etc., across which alcohol or refreshments are served. **b** a room in which alcohol is served and customers may sit and drink. **c** an establishment selling alcoholic drinks to be consumed on the premises. **d** a small store or stall serving refreshments (*snack bar*). **5 a** an enclosure in which a defendant stands in a court of law. **b** a public standard of acceptability, before which a person is said to be tried (*bar of conscience*). **c** a plea arresting an action or claim in a law case. **d** a particular court of law. **6** *Mus.* **a** any of the sections of usu. equal time value into which a musical composition is divided by vertical lines across the staff. **b** = *bar line.* **7** (**the Bar**) *Law* a lawyers collectively. **b** the profession of lawyers. ● *v.tr.* (**barred,** **barring**) **1 a** fasten (a door, window, etc.) with a bar or bars. **b** (usu. foll. by *in, out*) shut or keep in or out (*barred him in*). **2** obstruct; prevent (*bar his progress*). **3 a** (usu. foll. by *from*) prohibit; exclude (*bar them from attending*). **b** ex-

clude from consideration (cf. BARRING). **4** mark with stripes. **5** *Law* prevent or delay (an action) by objection. ● *prep.* **1** except (*all were there bar a few*). **2** *Brit. Racing* except (the horses indicated: used in stating the odds, indicating the number of horses excluded) (*33–1 bar three*). □ **bar chart** a chart using bars to represent quantity. **bar code** a machine-readable code in the form of a pattern of stripes printed on and identifying a commodity, used esp. for inventory control. **bar line** *Mus.* a vertical line used to mark divisions between bars. **bar none** with no exceptions. **bar sinister** = *bend sinister* (see BEND²). **bar tracery** tracery with strips of stone across an aperture. **be called to the Bar** be admitted as a lawyer or barrister. **behind bars** in prison. [ME f. OF *barre, barrer,* f. Rmc]
■ *n.* **1** rod, shaft, pole, stick, stake, beam, railing, rail. **2 a** see BLOCK *n.* 1. **b** strip, stripe, band, belt, streak, line. **f** sand bar, shallow, shoal, bank, sandbank. **3** barrier, obstacle, obstruction, barricade, hindrance, block, deterrent, impediment, restriction, control, check, restraint, constraint; ban, embargo, boycott. **4 a** counter. **b, c** barroom, saloon, café, lounge (bar), cocktail lounge, wine bar, taproom, inn, *Austral.* & *NZ* hotel, *Brit.* beerhouse, public house, *archaic or literary* hostelry, *literary* tavern, *Brit. colloq.* local, pub, *hist.* alehouse. **d** counter, kiosk, stall, booth, store, shop. **5 d** tribunal, court (of justice), courtroom, law court, court of law, bench. ● *v.* **1 a** fasten, close up, secure, make fast, shut up, barricade, lock, lock up, padlock. **b** (*bar in*) see *keep in* 2; (*bar out*) see *shut out* 1. **2** block, obstruct, stop, hinder, prevent, impede, hamper, inhibit, frustrate, check, retard, balk, *archaic or literary* stay. **3** keep (out), shut out, exclude, forbid, prohibit, outlaw, disallow, prevent; ban. **4** stripe, band, line. ● *prep.* **1** except (for), excepting, excluding, barring, outside (*disp.* of), but (for), apart from, other than aside from, *archaic or poet.* save (for). □ **behind bars** in prison *or* jail, *colloq.* doing time, in hock, *sl.* inside, in clink *or* jug *or* stir, in the can *or* cooler *or* nick *or* slammer, in hoosegow, in the slam, *Brit. sl.* in the choky.

bar² /baar/ *n.* esp. *Meteorol.* a unit of pressure, 10^5 newton per square meter, approx. one atmosphere. [Gk *baros* weight]

barathea /bárəthee̮ə/ *n.* a fine woolen cloth, sometimes mixed with silk or cotton, used esp. for coats, suits, etc. [19th c.: orig. unkn.]

barb /baarb/ *n.* & *v.* ● *n.* **1** a secondary, backward facing projection from an arrow, fishhook, etc., angled to make extraction difficult. **2** a deliberately hurtful remark. **3** a beardlike filament at the mouth of some fish, e.g., barbel and catfish. **4** any one of the fine hairlike filaments growing from the shaft of a feather, forming the vane. ● *v.tr.* **1** provide (an arrow, a fishhook, etc.) with a barb or barbs. **2** (as **barbed** *adj.*) (of a remark, etc.) deliberately hurtful. □ **barb bolt** a bolt with barbs to keep it tight when it has been driven in. **barbed wire** wire bearing sharp pointed spikes close together and used in fencing, or in warfare as an obstruction. [ME f. OF *barbe* f. L *barba* beard]
■ *n.* **1** see SPINE 2. **2** see WISECRACK *n.* ● *v.* **2** (**barbed**) see TART³ 3.

Barbadian /baarbáydeeən/ *n.* & *adj.* ● *n.* **1** a native or inhabitant of Barbados in the W. Indies. **2** a person of Barbadian descent. ● *adj.* of or relating to Barbados or its people.

barbarian /baarbáireeən/ *n.* & *adj.* ● *n.* **1** an uncultured or brutish person; a lout. **2** a member of a primitive community or tribe. ● *adj.* **1** rough and uncultured. **2** uncivilized. [orig. of any foreigner not of a different language or customs: F *barbarien* f. *barbare* (as BARBAROUS)]
■ *n.* **1** boor, lowbrow, lout, oaf, clod, lubber, churl, philistine, ignoramus, yahoo; hooligan, vandal, ruffian, tough, hoodlum, *Austral.* larrikin, *Brit.* skinhead, *colloq.* hobbledehoy, *derog.* peasant, *sl.* lug, rube, *Brit sl.* yob, yobbo. **2** savage, brute, native. ● *adj.* uncivilized, uncultivated, uncultured, philistine, savage; barbarous,

barbaric, coarse, vulgar, uncouth, rude; boorish, loutish, oafish, crude, rough, insensitive, churlish, uncivil.

barbaric /baarbárik/ *adj.* **1** brutal; cruel (*flogging is a barbaric punishment*). **2** rough and uncultured; unrestrained. **3** of or like barbarians and their art or taste; primitive. □□ **barbarically** *adv.* [ME f. OF *barbarique* or L *barbaricus* f. Gk *barbarikos* f. *barbaros* foreign]
■ **1** see BRUTAL. **2, 3** see SAVAGE *adj.* 2.

barbarism /baárbərizəm/ *n.* **1 a** the absence of culture and civilized standards; ignorance and rudeness. **b** an example of this. **2** a word or expression not considered correct; a solecism. **3** anything considered to be in bad taste. [F *barbarisme* f. L *barbarismus* f. Gk *barbarismos* f. *barbarizō* speak like a foreigner f. *barbaros* foreign]
■ **1 b** see OUTRAGE *n.* 1, INSULT *n.* 2 see SOLECISM.

barbarity /baarbáritee/ *n.* (*pl.* **-ies**) **1** savage cruelty. **2** an example of this.
■ **1** cruelty, inhumanity, ruthlessness, savagery, brutishness, barbarousness, heartlessness, viciousness, cold-bloodedness, bloodthirstiness. **2** atrocity, outrage, villainy.

barbarize /baárbərīz/ *v.tr.* & *intr.* make or become barbarous. □□ **barbarization** *n.*

barbarous /baárbərəs/ *adj.* **1** uncivilized. **2** cruel. **3** coarse and unrefined. □□ **barbarously** *adv.* **barbarousness** *n.* [orig. of any foreign language or people: f. L f. Gk *barbaros* foreign]
■ **1** see UNCIVILIZED 1. **2** see CRUEL *adj.* **3** see UNGRACEFUL.

Barbary ape /baárbəree/ *n.* a macaque, *Macaca sylvanus*, of N. Africa and Gibraltar. [*Barbary*, an old name of the western part of N. Africa, ult. f. Arab. *barbar* BERBER]

barbecue /baárbikyōō/ *n.* & *v.* ● *n.* **1 a** a meal cooked on an open fire out of doors, esp. meat grilled on a metal appliance. **b** a party at which such a meal is cooked and eaten. **c** marinated or seasoned meat prepared for cooking as such a meal. **2 a** the metal appliance used for the preparation of a barbecue. **b** a fireplace, usu. of brick, containing such an appliance. ● *v.tr.* (**barbecues, barbecued, barbecuing**) cook (esp. meat) on a barbecue. □ **barbecue sauce** a highly seasoned sauce, usu. containing chilies, in which meat, etc., may be cooked. [Sp. *barbacoa* f. Haitian *barbacòa* wooden frame on posts]

barbel /baárbəl/ *n.* **1** any large European freshwater fish of the genus *Barbus*, with fleshy filaments hanging from its mouth. **2** such a filament growing from the mouth of any fish. [ME f. OF f. LL *barbellus* dimin. of *barbus* barbel f. *barba* beard]

barbell /baárbel/ *n.* an iron bar with a series of weighted disks at each end, used for weightlifting exercises. [BAR¹ + BELL¹]

barber /baárbər/ *n.* & *v.* ● *n.* a person who cuts men's hair and shaves or trims beards as an occupation; a men's hairdresser. ● *v.tr.* **1** cut the hair, shave or trim the beard of. **2** cut or trim closely (*barbered the grass*). □ **barber pole** a spirally painted striped red and white pole hung outside barbers' shops as a business sign. [ME & AF f. OF *barbeor* f. med.L *barbator -oris* f. *barba* beard]
■ *v.* see TRIM *v.* 1b.

barberry /baárberee/ *n.* (*pl.* **-ies**) **1** any shrub of the genus *Berberis*, with spiny shoots, yellow flowers, and ovoid red berries, often grown as hedges. **2** its berry. [ME f. OF *berberis*, of unkn. orig.: assim. to BERRY]

barbershop /baárbərshop/ *n.* a barber's place of business. □ **barbershop quartet** a popular style of close harmony singing for four male voices.

barbet /baárbit/ *n.* any small brightly colored tropical bird of the family Capitonidae, with bristles at the base of its beak. [F f. *barbe* beard]

barbette /baarbét/ *n.* a platform in a fort or ship from which guns can be fired over a parapet, etc., without an embrasure. [F, dimin. of *barbe* beard]

barbican /baárbikən/ *n.* the outer defense of a city, castle, etc., esp. a double tower above a gate or drawbridge. [ME f. OF *barbacane*, of unkn. orig.]

barbie /baárbee/ *n. Austral. colloq.* a barbecue. [abbr.]

barbital /baárbitawl, -tal/ *n.* (*Brit.* **barbitone** /baárbitōn/) a sedative drug. [as BARBITURIC ACID + *-al* as in *veronal*]

barbiturate /baarbítchərət, -rayt/ *n.* any derivative of barbituric acid used in the preparation of sedative and sleep-inducing drugs. [BARBITURIC + -ATE¹]
■ see SEDATIVE *n.*

barbituric acid /baárbitōōrik, -tyōōr-/ *n. Chem.* an organic acid from which various sedatives and sleep-inducing drugs are derived. [F *barbiturique* f. G *Barbitursäure* (*Säure* acid) f. the name *Barbara*]

barbule /baárbyōōl/ *n.* a minute filament projecting from the barb of a feather. [L *barbula*, dimin. of *barba* beard]

barbwire /baárbwír/ *n.* = barbed wire (see BARB).

barcarole /baárkərōl/ *n.* (also **barcarolle**) **1** a song sung by Venetian gondoliers. **2** music in imitation of this. [F *barcarolle* f. Venetian It. *barcarola* boatman's song f. *barca* boat]

Barcoo /baarkōō/ *adj. Austral.* of or relating to a remote area of the country. □ **Barcoo rot** scurvy. **Barcoo sickness** illness marked by attacks of vomiting. **Barcoo sore** an ulcer characteristic of Barcoo rot. [river in W. Qld.]

bard¹ /baard/ *n.* **1 a** *hist.* a Celtic minstrel. **b** the winner of a prize for Welsh verse at an Eisteddfod. **2** a poet, esp. one treating heroic themes. **3** a composer or singer of epic poetry. □ **the Bard** (or **the Bard of Avon**) Shakespeare. □□ **bardic** *adj.* [Gael. & Ir. *bárd*, Welsh *bard*, f. OCelt.]
■ **1 a** see MINSTREL.

bard² /baard/ *n.* & *v.* ● *n.* a strip of fat placed on meat or game before roasting. ● *v.tr.* cover (meat, etc.) with bards. [F *barde*, orig. = horse's breastplate, ult. f. Arab.]

bare /bair/ *adj.* & *v.* ● *adj.* **1** (esp. of part of the body) unclothed or uncovered (*with bare head*). **2** without appropriate covering or contents: **a** (of a tree) leafless. **b** unfurnished; empty (*bare rooms; the cupboard was bare*). **c** (of a floor) uncarpeted. **3 a** undisguised (*the bare truth*). **b** unadorned (*bare facts*). **4** (*attrib.*) **a** scanty (*a bare majority*). **b** mere (*bare necessities*). ● *v.tr.* **1** uncover; unsheathe (*bared his teeth*). **2** reveal (*bared his soul*). □ **bare bones** the minimum essential facts, ingredients, etc. **bare of** without. **with one's bare hands** without using tools or weapons. □□ **bareness** *n.* [OE *bær, barian* f. Gmc]
■ *adj.* **1** unclothed, naked, nude, stark naked, unclad, exposed, uncovered, undressed, in a state of nature, in the raw, *colloq.* in the altogether, in the buff, *joc.* in one's birthday suit, *Brit. sl.* starkers. **2 a** denuded, stripped, leafless, defoliated, shorn, barren. **b** unfurnished, undecorated, vacant, stripped; empty, uninhabited, unoccupied, deserted. **3** unconcealed, undisguised, open, revealed, literal, bald, manifest, out-and-out, overt, uncovered, straightforward, direct, unvarnished, unembellished, unadulterated, cold, hard, plain, unadorned, basic, simple. **4** plain, mere, simple, minimal, essential, absolute, basic; meager, scant, scanty. ● *v.* **1** expose, lay bare, uncover, unsheathe, reveal; unveil, strip, divest, denude; defoliate. **2** disclose, reveal, lay bare, uncover, divulge, unfold, unveil, tell, expose, betray, unmask, bring to light, show. □ **bare of** without, minus, less. □□ **bareness** nakedness, nudity; see also *emptiness* (EMPTY), SIMPLICITY.

bareback /báirbak/ *adj.* & *adv.* on an unsaddled horse, donkey, etc.

barefaced /báirfáyst/ *adj.* undisguised; impudent (*barefaced lie*). □□ **barefacedly** /-fáysidlee/ *adv.* **barefacedness** *n.*
■ unconcealed, open, undisguised, blatant, manifest, unmitigated, outright, downright, arrant, out-and-out, sheer, unalloyed, undiluted; audacious, impudent, shameless, insolent, impertinent, immodest, bold, unabashed, forward, brazen, brassy, saucy, cocky, pert,

---

/ . . . / **pronunciation**   ● **part of speech**
□ **phrases, idioms, and compounds**
□□ **derivatives**   ■ **synonym section**
cross-references appear in SMALL CAPITALS or *italics*

unblushing, *archaic* malapert. □□ **barefacedness** see *impudence* (IMPUDENT).

barefoot /báirfŏŏt/ *adj. & adv.* (also **barefooted** /-fŏŏtid/) with nothing on the feet. □ **barefoot doctor** a paramedical worker with basic medical training, esp. in China.

barège /bərézh/ *n.* a silky gauze made from wool or other material. [F f. *Barèges* in SW France, where it was orig. made]

bareheaded /báirhédid/ *adj. & adv.* without a covering for the head.

barely /báirlee/ *adv.* **1** only just; scarcely (*barely escaped*). **2** scantily (*barely furnished*). **3** *archaic* openly; explicitly.
■ **1** scarcely, only, just, not quite, hardly, only just, no more than. **2** scantily, sparsely, sparely, austerely, simply, plainly.

barf /baarf/ *v. & n. sl.* ● *v.intr.* vomit or retch. ● *n.* vomit. [20th c.: orig. unkn.]
■ *v.* see VOMIT *v.* 1.

barfly /báarflī/ *n.* (*pl.* **-flies**) *colloq.* a person who frequents bars.

bargain /báargin/ *n. & v.* ● *n.* **1 a** an agreement on the terms of a transaction or sale. **b** this seen from the buyer's viewpoint (*a bad bargain*). **2** something acquired or offered cheaply. ● *v.intr.* (often foll. by *with, for*) discuss the terms of a transaction (*expected him to bargain, but he paid up; bargained with her; bargained for the table*). □ **bargain away** part with for something worthless (*had bargained away the estate*). **bargain basement** (also *attrib.*) the basement of a store where bargains are displayed. **bargain for** (or *colloq.* **on**) (usu. with *neg.* actual or implied) be prepared for; expect (*didn't bargain for bad weather; more than I bargained for*). **bargain on** rely on. **drive a hard bargain** pursue one's own profit in a transaction keenly. **in** (also **into**) **the bargain** moreover; in addition to what was expected. **make** (or **strike**) **a bargain** agree to or on a transaction. **bargainer** *n.* [ME f. OF *bargaine, bargaignier*, prob. f. Gmc]
■ *n.* **1** agreement, contract, understanding, arrangement, covenant, pact, compact, settlement, transaction, deal. **2** good deal, best buy, bargain steal, *Brit.* snip, *colloq.* giveaway, steal. ● *v.* negotiate, trade, haggle, barter, chaffer, huckster, dicker. □ **bargain for** expect, be prepared for, count on *or* upon, reckon on *or* upon, envisage, envision, foresee, take into account, allow for, *disp.* anticipate. **bargain on** see *count on*. **in the bargain** see MOREOVER. **make a bargain** agree to terms.

barge /baarj/ *n. & v.* ● *n.* **1** a long flat-bottomed boat for carrying freight on canals, rivers, etc. **2** a long ornamental boat used for pleasure or ceremony. **3** a boat used by the chief officers of a flagship, etc. ● *v.intr.* **1** (often foll. by *around*) lurch or rush clumsily about. **2** (foll. by *in, into*) **a** intrude or interrupt rudely or awkwardly (*barged in while we were kissing*). **b** collide with (*barged into her*). [ME f. OF perh. f. med.L *barica* f. Gk *baris* Egyptian boat]
■ *v.* **2 a** see INTRUDE 1.

bargeboard /báarjbawrd/ *n.* a board (often ornamental) fixed to the gable end of a roof to hide the ends of the roof timbers. [perh. f. med.L *bargus* gallows]

bargee /baarjée/ *n. Brit.* a person in charge of or working on a barge.

bargepole /báarjpōl/ *n.* a long pole used for punting barges, etc., and for fending off obstacles. □ **would not touch with a bargepole** *Brit.* refuse to be associated or concerned with (a person or thing).

barilla /bəreé·ə, -rílə/ *n.* **1** any plant of the genus *Salsola* found chiefly in Spain and Sicily. **2** an impure alkali made by burning either this or kelp. [Sp.]

barite /báirit, bár-/ *n.* a mineral form of barium sulfate. [Gk *barus* heavy, partly assim. to mineral names in *-ite*]

baritone /báritōn/ *n. & adj.* ● *n.* **1 a** the second-lowest adult male singing voice. **b** a singer with this voice. **c** a part written for it. **2 a** an instrument that is second-lowest in pitch in its family. **b** its player. ● *adj.* of the second-lowest range. [It. *baritono* f. Gk *barutonos* f. *barus* heavy + *tonos* TONE]

barium /báireeəm, bár-/ *n. Chem.* a white reactive soft metallic element of the alkaline earth group. ¶ Symb.: **Ba**. □ **barium meal** (or **enema**) a mixture of barium sulfate and water, which is opaque to X-rays, and is given to patients requiring radiological examination of the stomach and intestines. [BARYTA + -IUM]

bark[1] /baark/ *n. & v.* ● *n.* **1** the sharp explosive cry of a dog, fox, etc. **2** a sound resembling this cry. ● *v.* **1** *intr.* (of a dog, fox, etc.) give a bark. **2** *tr. & intr.* speak or utter sharply or brusquely. **3** *intr.* cough fiercely. **4** *tr.* sell or advertise publicly by calling out. □ **one's bark is worse than one's bite** one is not as ferocious as one appears. **bark up the wrong tree** be on the wrong track; make an effort in the wrong direction. [OE *beorcan*]
■ *n.* **1** see YAP *n.* 1. **2** see WHOOP *n.* ● *v.* **1, 2** see YAP *v.* 1.

bark[2] /baark/ *n. & v.* ● *n.* **1** the tough protective outer sheath of the trunks, branches, and twigs of trees or woody shrubs. **2** this material used for tanning leather or dyeing material. ● *v.tr.* **1** graze or scrape (one's shin, etc.). **2** strip bark from (a tree, etc.). **3** tan or dye (leather, etc.) using the tannins found in bark. [ME f. OIcel. *börkr bark-*: perh. rel. to BIRCH]
■ *v.* **1** see SCRAPE *v.* 3b.

bark[3] /baark/ *n.* a ship or boat. [= BARQUE]
■ see VESSEL 2.

barkeeper /báarkeepər/ *n.* (also **barkeep**) a person who owns or serves drinks in a bar.

barkentine /báarkənteen/ *n.* (also **barquentine, barquantine**) a sailing ship with the foremast square-rigged and the remaining (usu. two) masts fore-and-aft rigged. [BARQUE after *brigantine*]

barker /báarkər/ *n.* a tout at an auction, sideshow, etc., who calls out to passersby as advertising. [BARK[1] + -ER[1]]

barley /báarlee/ *n.* **1** any of various hardy awned cereals of the genus *Hordeum* widely used as food and in malt liquors and spirits such as whiskey. **2** the grain produced from this (cf. *pearl barley*). □ **barley sugar** an amber-colored candy made of boiled sugar, traditionally shaped as a twisted stick. **barley water** a drink made from water and a boiled barley mixture. [OE *bærlic* adj. f. *bære, bere* barley]

barleycorn /báarleekawrn/ *n.* **1** the grain of barley. **2** a former unit of measure (about a third of an inch) based on the length of a grain of barley.

barleymow /báarleemow/ *n. Brit.* a stack of barley.

barm /baarm/ *n.* **1** the froth on fermenting malt liquor. **2** *archaic* or *dial.* yeast or leaven. [OE *beorma*]

barmaid /báarmayd/ *n.* a woman serving drinks in a bar, restaurant, etc.

barman /báarmən/ *n.* (*pl.* **-men**) esp. *Brit.* = BARTENDER.

Barmecide /báarmisīd/ *adj. & n.* (also **Barmecidal** /-sīd'l/) ● *adj.* illusory; imaginary; such as to disappoint. ● *n.* a giver of benefits that are illusory or disappointing. [the name of a wealthy man in the *Arabian Nights' Entertainments* who gave a beggar a feast consisting of ornate but empty dishes]

bar mitzvah /baar mítsvə/ *n.* **1** the religious initiation ceremony of a Jewish boy who has reached the age of 13. **2** the boy undergoing this ceremony. □□ **bar mitzvah** *v.* [Heb., = 'son of the commandment']

barmy /báarmee/ *adj.* (**barmier, barmiest**) **1** frothy; foamy. **2** esp. *Brit. sl.* crazy; stupid. □□ **barmily** *adv.* **barminess** *n.* [earlier = frothy, f. BARM]

barn[1] /baarn/ *n.* **1** a large farm building for storing grain, housing livestock, etc. **2** a large plain or unattractive building. **3** a large shed for storing road or railroad vehicles, etc. □ **barn burner** (or **barnburner**) *colloq.* something or someone that has a sensational effect or stirs excited interest. **barn dance 1** an informal social gathering for country dancing, orig. in a barn. **2** a dance for a number of couples forming a line or circle, with couples moving along it in turn. **barn owl** a kind of owl, *Tyto alba*, frequenting barns. [OE *bern, beren* f. *bere* barley + *ern, ærn* house]
■ **1** see STALL[1] *n.* 2.

barn[2] /baarn/ *n. Physics* a unit of area, 10^{-28} square meters, used esp. in particle physics. ¶ Symb.: **b**. [perh. f. phrase 'as big as a barn']

barnacle /báarnəkəl/ *n.* **1** any of various species of small marine crustaceans of the class Cirripedia which in adult form cling to rocks, ships' hulls, etc. **2** a tenacious attendant or follower who cannot easily be shaken off. □ **barnacle goose** an Arctic goose, *Branta leucopsis*. □□ **barnacled** *adj.* [ME *bernak* (= med.L *bernaca*), of unkn. orig.]

barney / baárnee/ *n.* (*pl.* **-eys**) esp. *Brit. colloq.* a noisy quarrel. [perh. dial.]

barnstorm /baárnstawrm/ *v.intr.* **1** tour rural districts giving theatrical performances (formerly often in barns). **2** make a rapid tour esp. for political meetings. **3** *Aeron.* give informal flying exhibitions; do stunt flying. □□ **barnstormer** *n.*

barnyard /baárnyaard/ *n.* the area around a barn.

barograph /bárəgraf/ *n.* a barometer equipped to record its readings. [Gk *baros* weight + -GRAPH]

barometer /bərómitər/ *n.* **1** an instrument measuring atmospheric pressure, esp. in forecasting the weather and determining altitude. **2** anything which reflects changes in circumstances, opinions, etc. □□ **barometric** /bárəmétrik/ *adj.* **barometrical** /bárəmétrikəl/ *adj.* **barometry** *n.*

baron /bárən/ *n.* **1 a** a member of the lowest order of the British nobility. **b** a similar member of a foreign nobility. **2** an important businessman or other powerful or influential person (*sugar baron; newspaper baron*). **3** *hist.* a person who held lands or property from the sovereign or a powerful overlord. □ **baron of beef** chiefly *Brit.* a double sirloin cut of beef. [ME f. AF *barun*, OF *baron* f. med.L *baro, -onis* man, of unkn. orig.]

baronage /bárənij/ *n.* **1** barons or nobles collectively. **2** an annotated list of barons or peers. [ME f. OF *barnage* (as BARON)]

baroness /bárənis/ *n.* **1** a woman holding the rank of baron. **2** the wife or widow of a baron. [ME f. OF *baronesse* (as BARON)]

baronet /bárənit, -nét/ *n.* a member of the lowest hereditary titled British order. [ME f. AL *baronettus* (as BARON)]

baronetage /bárənitij, -nét-/ *n.* **1** baronets collectively. **2** an annotated list of baronets.

baronetcy /bárənitsee, -nét-/ *n.* (*pl.* **-ies**) the domain, rank, or tenure of a baronet.

baronial /bərṓneeəl/ *adj.* of, relating to, or befitting barons.

barony /bárənee/ *n.* (*pl.* **-ies**) **1** the domain, rank, or tenure of a baron. **2** (in Ireland) a division of a county. **3** (in Scotland) a large manor or estate. [ME f. OF *baronie* (as BARON)]

baroque /bərók/ *adj.* & *n.* ● *adj.* **1** highly ornate and extravagant in style, esp. of European art, architecture, and music of the 17th and 18th c. **2** of or relating to this period. ● *n.* **1** the baroque style. **2** baroque art collectively. [F (orig. = 'irregular pearl') f. Port. *barroco*, of unkn. orig.]
■ *adj.* **1** see ORNATE.

barouche /bərṓosh/ *n.* a horse-drawn carriage with four wheels and a collapsible hood over the rear half, used esp. in the 19th c. [G (dial.) *Barutsche* f. It. *baroccio* ult. f. L *birotus* two-wheeled]

barque /baark/ *n.* (also **bark**) **1** a sailing ship with the rear mast fore-and-aft rigged and the remaining (usu. two) masts square-rigged. **2** *poet.* any boat. [ME f. F prob. f. Prov. *barca* f. L *barca* ship's boat]
■ see VESSEL 2.

barquentine var. of BARKENTINE.

barrack[1] /bárək/ *n.* & *v.* ● *n.* (usu. in *pl.*, often treated as *sing.*) **1** a building or building complex used to house soldiers. **2** any building used to accommodate large numbers of people. **3** a large building of a bleak or plain appearance. ● *v.tr.* place (soldiers, etc.) in barracks. □ **barrack-room lawyer** *Brit.* a pompously argumentative person. [F *baraque* f. It. *baracca* or Sp. *barraca* soldier's tent, of unkn. orig.]

barrack[2] /bárək/ *v. Brit.* **1** *tr.* shout or jeer at (players in a game, a performer, speaker, etc.). **2** *intr.* (of spectators at games, etc.) shout or jeer. [app. f. BORAK]

barracouta /bárəkṓotə/ *n.* (*pl.* same or **barracoutas**) **1** a long slender fish, *Thyrsites atun*, usu. found in southern oceans. **2** *NZ* a small narrow loaf of bread. [var. of BARRACUDA]

barracuda /bárəkṓodə/ *n.* (*pl.* same or **barracudas**) a large

and voracious tropical marine fish of the family Sphyraenidae. [Amer. Sp. *barracuda*]

barrage /bəraázh/ *n.* **1** a concentrated artillery bombardment over a wide area. **2** a rapid succession of questions or criticisms. **3** /baárij/ an artificial barrier, esp. in a river. □ **barrage balloon** a large anchored balloon, often with netting suspended from it, used (usu. as one of a series) as a defense against low-flying aircraft. [F f. *barrer* (as BAR[1])]
■ **1** see VOLLEY *n.* 1. **2** see STREAM *n.* 2.

barramundi /bárəmúndee/ *n.* (*pl.* same or **barramundis**) any of various Australian freshwater fishes, esp. *Lates calcarifer*, used as food. [Aboriginal]

barrator /bárətər/ *n.* **1** a malicious person causing discord. **2** one who commits barratry. [ME f. AF *baratour*, OF *barateor* trickster, f. *barat* deceit]

barratry /bárətree/ *n.* **1** fraud or gross negligence of a ship's master or crew at the expense of its owners or users. **2** frivolous or groundless litigation or incitement to it. **3** *hist.* trade in the sale of church or state appointments. □□ **barratrous** *adj.* [ME f. OF *baraterie* (as BARRATOR)]

barre /baar/ *n.* a horizontal bar at waist level used in dance exercises. [F]

barré /baaráy/ *n. Mus.* a method of playing a chord on the guitar, etc., with a finger laid across the strings at a particular fret, raising their pitch. [F, past part. of *barrer* bar]

barrel /bárəl/ *n.* & *v.* ● *n.* **1** a cylindrical container usu. bulging out in the middle, traditionally made of wooden staves with metal hoops around them. **2** the contents of this. **3** a measure of capacity, usu. varying from 30 to 40 gallons. **4** a cylindrical tube forming part of an object such as a gun or a pen. **5** the trunk of a four-legged animal, e.g., a horse. ● *v.* (**barreled, barreling** or **barrelled, barrelling**) **1** *tr.* put into a barrel or barrels. **2** *intr. sl.* drive or move fast. □ **barrel-chested** having a large rounded chest. **barrel organ** a mechanical musical instrument in which a rotating pin-studded cylinder acts on a series of pipe valves, strings, or metal tongues. **barrel roll** an aerobatic maneuver in which an aircraft follows a single turn of a spiral while rolling once about its longitudinal axis. **barrel vault** *Archit.* a vault forming a half cylinder. **over a barrel** *colloq.* in a helpless or awkward position; at a person's mercy. [ME f. OF *baril* perh. f. Rmc.: rel to BAR[1]]
■ **n. 1, 2** see KEG.

barren /bárən/ *adj.* & *n.* ● *adj.* (**barrener, barrenest**) **1 a** unable to bear young. **b** unable to produce fruit or vegetation. **c** devoid of vegetation or other signs of life. **2** meager; unprofitable. **3** dull; unstimulating. **4** (foll. by *of*) lacking in (*barren of wit*). ● *n.* (also in *pl.*) a barren tract or tracts of land. □□ **barrenly** *adv.* **barrenness** *n.* [ME f. AF *barai(g)ne*, OF *barhaine*, etc., of unkn. orig.]
■ *adj.* **1 a** sterile, childless, infertile. **b** unproductive, sterile, infertile, fruitless, unfruitful. **c** bare, dry, bleak, desolate, deserted, uninhabited, empty, unpeopled, trackless, waste, austere. **2** unprofitable, unrewarding, poor, meager, profitless, deficient. **3** see DREARY.
● *n.* (barrens) see WILD *n.* □□ **barrenness** sterility, childlessness, infertility, fruitlessness, unfruitfulness; unprofitability, poverty; bareness, desolation, waste, emptiness, tracklessness, bleakness, austerity; dullness, tedium, dreariness, drabness, tediousness, changelessness.

barrette /bərét/ *n.* a typically bar-shaped clip or ornament for the hair. [F, dimin. of *barre* BAR[1]]

barricade /bárikáyd/ *n.* & *v.* ● *n.* a barrier, esp. one improvised across a street, etc. ● *v.tr.* block or defend with a barricade. [F f. *barrique* cask f. Sp. *barrica*, rel. to BARREL]
■ *n.* see BAR[1] *n.* 3. ● *v.* see BAR[1] *v.* 1a.

barrier /báreeər/ *n.* **1** a fence, mountain range, or other obstacle that bars advance or access. **2** an obstacle or circum-

/ . . . / **pronunciation**   ● **part of speech**
□ **phrases, idioms, and compounds**
□□ **derivatives**   ■ **synonym section**
cross-references appear in SMALL CAPITALS or *italics*

stance that keeps people or things apart, or prevents communication (*class barriers*; *a language barrier*). **4** anything that prevents progress or success. **4** a gate at a parking lot, toll booth, etc., that controls access. **5** *colloq.* = *sound barrier*. □ **barrier island** a sandy island running parallel to shore and protecting it from storms, etc. **barrier reef** a coral reef separated from the shore by a broad deep channel. [ME f. AF *barrere*, OF *barriere*]
■ **1** bar, fence, railing, wall, barrage, barricade. **2, 3** obstacle, bar, obstruction, block, impediment, hindrance, encumbrance. **4** gate, toll.

barring /baáring/ *prep.* except; not including. [BAR¹ + -ING²]
■ excluding, exclusive of, bar, omitting, not including, leaving out, excepting, except (for), save for, besides, but, aside from.

barrio /baáreeō, bár-/ *n.* (*pl.* **-os**) **1** (in Spanish-speaking countries) a division or district of a city or town. **2** (in the US) the Spanish-speaking quarter or neighborhood of a town or city. [Sp., = district of a town]

barrister /báristər/ *n.* (in full **barrister-at-law**) **1** *Brit.* a person called to the bar and entitled to practice as an advocate in the higher courts. **2** a lawyer. [16th c.: f. BAR¹, perh. after *minister*]
■ see LAWYER.

barroom /bárōōm, -rŏŏm/ *n.* an establishment specializing in serving alcoholic drinks.

barrow¹ /bárō/ *n.* **1** a metal frame with two wheels used for transporting luggage, etc. **2** = WHEELBARROW. **3** *Brit.* a two-wheeled handcart used esp. by street vendors. □ **barrow boy** *Brit.* a boy who sells wares from a barrow. [OE *bearwe* f. Gmc]
■ **1, 3** see CART *n.* 2.

barrow² /bárō/ *n.* *Archaeol.* an ancient grave mound or tumulus. [OE *beorg* f. Gmc]
■ see MOUND¹ *n.* 1, 2.

Bart. /baart/ *abbr.* Baronet.

bartender /baártendər/ *n.* a person serving behind the bar of a tavern, bar, etc.

barter /baártər/ *v.* & *n.* ● *v.* **1** *tr.* exchange (goods or services) without using money. **2** *intr.* make such an exchange. ● *n.* trade by exchange of goods. □□ **barterer** *n.* [prob. OF *barater*: see BARRATOR]
■ *v.* see EXCHANGE *v.* ● *n.* see EXCHANGE *n.* 1.

bartizan /baártizən, -zán/ *n.* *Archit.* a battlemented parapet or an overhanging corner turret at the top of a castle or church tower. □□ **bartizaned** *adj.* [var. of *bertisene*, erron. spelling of *bratticing*: see BRATTICE]

baryon /báreeon/ *n.* *Physics* an elementary particle that is of equal mass to or greater mass than a proton (i.e., is a nucleon or a hyperon). □□ **baryonic** /-ónik/ *adj.* [Gk *barus* heavy + -ON]

barysphere /bárisfeer/ *n.* the dense interior of the earth, including the mantle and core, enclosed by the lithosphere. [Gk *barus* heavy + *sphaira* sphere]

baryta /bəritə/ *n.* barium oxide or hydroxide. □□ **barytic** /-rítik/ *adj.* [BARYTES, after *soda*, etc.]

barytes /bəriteez/ *n.* *Brit.* = BARITE.

basal /báysəl, -zəl/ *adj.* **1** of, at, or forming a base. **2** fundamental. □ **basal metabolism** the chemical processes occurring in an organism at complete rest. [BASE¹ + -AL]

basalt /bəsáwlt, báysawlt/ *n.* **1** a dark basic volcanic rock whose strata sometimes form columns. **2** a kind of black stoneware resembling basalt. □□ **basaltic** /-sáwltik/ *adj.* [L *basaltes* var. of *basanites* f. Gk f. *basanos* touchstone]

bascule bridge /báskyōōl/ *n.* a type of drawbridge that is raised and lowered using counterweights. [F, earlier *bacule* seesaw f. *battre* bump + *cul* buttocks]

base¹ /bays/ *n.* & *v.* ● *n.* **1 a** a part that supports from beneath or serves as a foundation for an object or structure. **b** a notional structure or entity on which something draws or depends (*power base*). **2** a principle or starting point; a basis. **3** esp. *Mil.* a place from which an operation or activity is directed. **4 a** a main or important ingredient of a mixture. **b** a substance, e.g., water, in combination with which pigment forms paint, etc. **c** a substance used as a foundation

for makeup. **6** *Chem.* a substance capable of combining with an acid to form a salt and water and usu. producing hydroxide ions when dissolved in water. **7** *Math.* a number in terms of which other numbers or logarithms are expressed (see RADIX). **8** *Archit.* the part of a column between the shaft and pedestal or pavement. **9** *Geom.* a line or surface on which a figure is regarded as standing. **10** *Surveying* a known line used as a geometrical base for trigonometry. **11** *Electronics* the middle part of a transistor separating the emitter from the collector. **12** *Linguistics* a root or stem as the origin of a word or a derivative. **13** *Baseball*, etc., one of the four stations that must be reached in turn to score a run. **14** *Bot.* & *Zool.* the end at which an organ is attached to the trunk. **15** *Heraldry* the lowest part of a shield. ● *v.tr.* **1** (usu. foll. by *on*, *upon*) found or establish (*a theory based on speculation*; *his opinion was soundly based*). **2** (foll. by *at*, *in*, etc.) station (*troops were based in Malta*). □ **base hit** *Baseball* a fair ball that enables the batter to get on base without benefit of an opponent's error and without forcing out another player already on base. **base hospital** esp. *Austral.* a hospital in a rural area, or (in warfare) removed from the field of action. **base on balls** *Baseball* advancement to first base by a player who has been pitched four balls while at bat. **base pairing** *Biochem.* complementary binding by means of hydrogen bonds of a purine to a pyrimidine base in opposite strands of nucleic acids. **base rate** *Brit.* the interest rate set by the Bank of England, used as the basis for other English banks' rates. **base unit** a unit that is defined arbitrarily and not by combinations of other units. [F *base* or L *basis* stepping f. Gk]
■ *n.* **1 a** bottom, foot, support, stand, pedestal. **b** center, hub, focus, nucleus, focal point. **2** basis, starting point, point of departure, groundwork, background, (fundamental *or* underlying) principle, foundation, underpinning, infrastructure. **3** home, station, camp, starting point, point of departure, post, center, headquarters, (G)HQ. **12** root, stem, theme, radical, core. ● *v.* **1** establish, found, secure, build, ground, anchor, fix, hinge, form, bottom; derive, draw. **2** establish, post, station, position, place, quarter.

base² /bays/ *adj.* **1** lacking moral worth; cowardly; despicable. **2** menial. **3** not pure; alloyed (*base coin*). **4** (of a metal) low in value (opp. NOBLE, PRECIOUS). **5** cheap; shoddy. **6** mean; degraded. □□ **basely** *adv.* **baseness** *n.* [ME in sense 'of small height,' f. F *bas* f. med.L *bassus* short (in L as a cognomen)]
■ **1** low, undignified, cowardly, mean, despicable, abject, contemptible, dastardly, evil, sordid, ignoble, dishonorable, disreputable, degenerate, vile, scurrilous, wicked, iniquitous, corrupt, depraved, shameful, currish, loathsome, scurvy, insufferable, villainous, verminous, sordid, offensive, lewd, lascivious, obscene, profane, rude, ribald, unseemly, vulgar, coarse, dirty, indecent, evil-minded, filthy, pornographic, *poet. or archaic* caitiff, whoreson, *literary* recreant. **2** degrading, menial, inferior, mean, unworthy, lowly, low, groveling, servile, slavish, subservient, *colloq.* infra dig. **3** see IMPURE 1. **5** mean, poor, common, low-quality, low-grade, second-rate, shoddy, shabby, cheap, tawdry, fake, pinchbeck, inferior, counterfeit, fraudulent, debased, forged, spurious, worthless, bad, *colloq.* two-bit. **6** mean, degraded, poor, downtrodden, abject, miserable, wretched, undignified.

baseball /báysbawl/ *n.* **1** a game played with two teams of nine, a bat and ball, and a circuit of four bases that must be completed to score. **2** the ball used in this game.

baseboard /báysbawrd/ *n.* a narrow board, etc., along the bottom of the wall of a room.

baseless /báyslis/ *adj.* unfounded; groundless. □□ **baselessly** *adv.* **baselessness** *n.*
■ see UNFOUNDED.

baseline /báyslīn/ *n.* **1** a line used as a base or starting point. **2** (in tennis, basketball, etc.) the line marking each end of a court. **3** *Baseball* either of the lines leading from home plate and determining the boundaries of fair territory.

baseload /báyslōd/ *n. Brit. Electr.* the permanent load on power supplies, etc.

baseman /báysmən/ *n.* (*pl.* **-men**) *Baseball* a fielder stationed near a base.

basement /báysmənt/ *n.* the lowest floor of a building, usu. at least partly below ground level. [prob. Du., perh. f. It. *basamento* column base]
■ see CELLAR *n.*

bases *pl.* of BASE[1], BASIS.

bash /bash/ *v. & n.* ● *v.* **1** *tr.* **a** strike bluntly or heavily. **b** (often foll. by *up*) *colloq.* attack or criticize violently. **c** (often foll. by *down, in*, etc.) damage or break by striking forcibly. **2** *intr.* (foll. by *into*) collide with. ● *n.* **1** a heavy blow. **2** *Brit. sl.* an attempt (*had a bash at painting*). **3** *sl.* a party or social event. □□ **basher** *n.* [imit., perh. f. *bang, smash, dash,* etc.]
■ *v.* **1 a, b** see STRIKE *v.* 1. ● *n.* **3** see PARTY[1] *n.* 1.

bashful /báshfŏŏl/ *adj.* **1** shy; diffident; self-conscious. **2** sheepish. □□ **bashfully** *adv.* **bashfulness** *n.* [obs. *bash* (v.), = ABASH]
■ shy, retiring, embarrassed, meek, abashed, shamefaced, sheepish, timid, timorous, diffident, coy, demure, self-effacing, reserved, restrained; ill at ease, uneasy, uncomfortable, nervous, self-conscious, awkward.

BASIC /báysik/ *n.* a computer programming language using familiar English words and designed for beginners. [*Beginner's All-purpose Symbolic Instruction Code*]

basic /báysik/ *adj. & n.* ● *adj.* **1** forming or serving as a base. **2** fundamental. **3 a** simplest or lowest in level (*basic pay; basic requirements*). **b** vulgar (*basic humor*). **4** *Chem.* having the properties of or containing a base. **5** *Geol.* (of volcanic rocks, etc.) having less than 50 percent silica. **6** *Metallurgy* of or produced in a furnace, etc., which is made of a basic material. ● *n.* (usu. in *pl.*) the fundamental facts or principles. □ **basic dye** a dye consisting of salts of organic bases. **Basic English** a simplified form of English limited to 850 selected words intended for international communication. **basic industry** an industry of fundamental economic importance. **basic slag** fertilizer containing phosphates formed as a by-product during steel manufacture. □□ **basically** *adv.* [BASE[1] + -IC]
■ *adj.* **2** fundamental, essential, key, underlying, prime, primary, root, principal, central, focal, vital. **3 a** elementary, elemental, primary, simple. **b** see VULGAR 1. ● *n.* (*basics*) see ELEMENT 6. □□ **basically** see *in essence* (ESSENCE).

basicity /baysísitee/ *n. Chem.* the number of protons with which a base will combine.

basidium /bəsídeeəm/ *n.* (*pl.* **basidia** /-deeə/) a microscopic spore-bearing structure produced by certain fungi. [mod.L f. Gk *basidion* dimin. of BASIS]

basil /bázəl, báyzəl/ *n.* an aromatic herb of the genus *Ocimum*, esp. *O. basilicum* (in full **sweet basil**), whose leaves are used as a flavoring in cooking. [ME f. OF *basile* f. med.L *basilicus* f. Gk *basilikos* royal]

basilar /básilər/ *adj.* of or at the base (esp. of the skull). [mod.L *basilaris* (as BASIS)]

basilica /bəsílikə/ *n.* **1** an ancient Roman public hall with an apse and colonnades, used as a court of law and place of assembly. **2** a similar building used as a Christian church. **3** a church having special privileges from the Pope. □□ **basilican** *adj.* [L f. Gk *basilikē* (*oikia, stoa*) royal (house, portico) f. *basileus* king]

basilisk /básilisk, báz-/ *n.* **1** a mythical reptile with a lethal breath and look. **2** any small American lizard of the genus *Basiliscus*, with a crest from its back to its tail. **3** *Heraldry* a cockatrice. [ME f. L *basiliscus* f. Gk *basiliskos* kinglet, serpent]

basin /báysən/ *n.* **1** a wide, shallow, open container, esp. a fixed one for holding water. **2** a hollow, rounded depression. **3** any sheltered area of water where boats can moor safely. **4** a round valley. **5** an area drained by rivers and tributaries. **6** *Geol.* **a** a rock formation where the strata dip toward the center. **b** an accumulation of rock strata formed in this dip as a result of subsidence and sedimentation. □□ **basinful** *n.*

(*pl.* **-fuls**). [ME f. OF *bacin* f. med.L *ba(s)cinus*, perh. f. Gaulish]
■ **2** see HOLLOW *n.* 1. **4** see HOLLOW *n.* 2.

basipetal /baysípit'l/ *adj. Bot.* (of each new part produced developing nearer the base than the previous one did. □□ **basipetally** *adv.* [BASIS + L *petere* seek]

basis /báysis/ *n.* (*pl.* **bases** /-seez/) **1** the foundation or support of something, esp. an idea or argument. **2** the main or determining principle or ingredient (*on a purely friendly basis*). **3** the starting point for a discussion, etc. [L f. Gk, = BASE[1]]
■ **1, 2** foundation, base, support, footing, grounding, (fundamental *or* underlying) principle, main ingredient *or* constituent, underpinning, infrastructure; essence, bottom, heart, center, focus; grounds, background, reason, explanation, justification, motive. **3** starting point, base, point of departure, beginning.

bask /bask/ *v.intr.* **1** sit or lie back lazily in warmth and light (*basking in the sun*). **2** (foll. by *in*) derive great pleasure (from) (*basking in glory*). □ **basking shark** a very large shark, *Cetorhinus maximus*, which often lies near the surface. [ME, app. f. ON: rel. to BATHE]
■ **1** see SUN *v.* 1, 3. **2** see REVEL *v.* 2.

basket /báskit/ *n.* **1** a container made of interwoven cane, etc. **2** a container resembling this. **3** the amount held by a basket. **4** the goal in basketball, or a goal scored. **5** *Econ.* a group or range (of currencies) **6** *Brit. euphem. colloq.* bastard. **basket case 1** a person who has had all four limbs amputated. **2** a person who cannot function because of tension, stress, etc. □ **basket weave** a weave resembling that of a basket. □□ **basketful** *n.* (*pl.* **-fuls**). [AF & OF *basket*, AL *baskettum*, of unkn. orig.]

basketball /báskitbawl/ *n.* **1** a game between two teams, usu. of five, in which points are scored by making the ball drop through hooped nets fixed high up at each end of the court. **2** the ball used in this game.

basketry /báskitree/ *n.* **1** the art of making baskets. **2** baskets collectively.

basketwork /báskitwərk/ *n.* **1** material woven in the style of a basket. **2** the art of making this.

basmati /baasmaátee/ *n.* (in full **basmati rice**) a long-grained aromatic kind of Indian rice. [Hindi, = fragrant]

bas mitzvah /bas mítsvə/ *n.* (also **bat mitzvah**) **1** an initiation ceremony for a Jewish girl who has reached the age of 12 or 13 and is ready to assume adult religious responsibilities. **2** a girl confirmed by this ceremony. [Heb. *bath miṣwāh*, lit. daughter of the divine law]

Basque /bask/ *n. & adj.* ● *n.* **1** a member of a people of the Western Pyrenees. **2** the language of this people. ● *adj.* of or relating to the Basques or their language. [F f. L *Vasco -onis*]

basque /bask/ *n.* a close-fitting bodice extending from the shoulders to the waist and often with a short continuation below waist level. [BASQUE]

bas-relief /baá-rileef, bás-/ *n.* sculpture or carving in which the figures project slightly from the background. Also called **low relief**. [earlier *basse relieve* f. It. *basso rilievo* low relief: later altered to F form]

bass[1] /bays/ *n. & adj.* ● *n.* **1 a** the lowest adult male singing voice. **b** a singer with this voice. **c** a part written for it. **2** the lowest part in harmonized music. **3 a** an instrument that is the lowest in pitch in its family. **b** its player. **4** *colloq.* **a** a bass guitar or double bass. **b** its player. **5** the low-frequency output of a radio, CD player, turntable, etc., corresponding to the bass in music. ● *adj.* **1** lowest in musical pitch. **2** deep sounding. □ **bass clef** a clef placing F below middle C on the second highest line of the staff. **bass viol 1 a** a viola da gamba. **b** its player. **2** a double bass. □□ **bassist** *n.* (in sense 4b). [alt. of BASE[2] after It. *basso*]

/.../ **pronunciation**	● **part of speech**
□ **phrases, idioms, and compounds**	
□□ **derivatives**	■ **synonym section**
cross-references appear in SMALL CAPITALS or *italics*	

bass² /bas/ *n.* (*pl.* same or **basses**) any of various edible fishes including the common European perch and several N. American marine and freshwater fishes, esp. *Morone saxatilis* and *Micropterus salmoides*. [earlier *barse* f. OE *bærs*]

bass³ /bas/ *n.* = BAST. [alt. f. BAST]

basset /básit/ *n.* (in full **basset hound**) **1** a sturdy hunting dog of a breed with a long body, short legs, and big ears. **2** this breed. [F, dimin. of *bas basse* low: see BASE²]

basset horn /básit hawrn/ *n.* an alto horn in F, with a dark tone. [G, transl. of F *cor de bassette* f. It. *corno di bassetto* f. *corno* horn + *bassetto* dimin. of *basso* BASE²]

bassinet /básinét/ *n.* a child's wicker cradle, usu. with a hood. [F, dimin. of *bassin* BASIN]

basso /básō, baá-/ *n.* (*pl.* **-os** or **bassi** /-see/) a singer with a bass voice. □ **basso profundo** /prōfóōndō/ a bass singer with an exceptionally low range. [It., = BASS¹; *profondo* deep]

bassoon /bəsōōn/ *n.* **1 a** a bass instrument of the oboe family, with a double reed. **b** its player. **2** an organ stop with the quality of a bassoon. □□ **bassoonist** *n.* (in sense 1b). [F *basson* f. *bas* BASS¹]

basso-relievo /básō-rileévō/ *n.* (also **basso-rilievo** /básō-reelyáyvō/) (*pl.* **-os**) = BAS-RELIEF. [It. *basso-rilievo* = BAS-RELIEF]

basswood /báswŏŏd/ *n.* **1** the American linden, *Tilia americana.* **2** the wood of this tree. [BASS³ + WOOD]

bast /bast/ *n.* the inner bark of linden, or other flexible fibrous bark, used as fiber in matting, etc. [OE *bæst* f. Gmc]

bastard /bástərd/ *n.* & *adj.* ● *n.* **1** a person born of parents not married to each other. **2** *sl.* **a** an unpleasant or despicable person. **b** a person of a specified kind (*poor bastard*; *lucky bastard*). **3** *sl.* a difficult or awkward thing, undertaking, etc. ● *adj.* **1** born of parents not married to each other; illegitimate. **2** (of things): **a** unauthorized; counterfeit. **b** hybrid. □□ **bastardy** *n.* (in sense 1 of *n.*). [ME f. OF f. med.L *bastardus*, perh. f. *bastum* packsaddle]

■ *n.* **2 a** son of a bitch, *sl.* bummer; person, chap, fellow, man, boy, lad, child, *colloq.* guy, devil, beggar, *sl.* geezer, *Brit. sl.* bloke; *sl.* jerk; fool, idiot. ● *adj.* **1** see ILLEGITIMATE *adj.* 1.

bastardize /bástərdīz/ *v.tr.* **1** declare (a person) illegitimate. **2** corrupt, debase. □□ **bastardization** *n.*

■ **2** see ADULTERATE *v.*

baste¹ /bayst/ *v.tr.* moisten (meat) with gravy or melted fat during cooking. [16th c.: orig. unkn.]

baste² /bayst/ *v.tr.* stitch loosely together in preparation for sewing; tack. [ME f. OF *bastir* sew lightly, ult. f. Gmc]

■ see TACK¹ *v.* 2.

baste³ /bayst/ *v.tr.* beat soundly; thrash. [perh. figurative use of BASTE¹]

■ see CLUB *v.* 1.

bastille /basteél/ *n. hist.* a fortress or prison. [ME f. OF *bastille* f. Prov. *bastir* build: orig. of the fortress and prison in Paris, destroyed in 1789]

bastinado /bástináydō, -naá-/ *n.* & *v.* ● *n.* punishment by beating with a stick on the soles of the feet. ● *v.tr.* (**-oes**, **-oed**) punish (a person) in this way. [Sp. *bastonada* f. *baston* BATON]

bastion /báschən, -teeən/ *n.* **1** a projecting part of a fortification built at an angle of, or against the line of, a wall. **2** a thing regarded as protecting (*bastion of freedom*). **3** a natural rock formation resembling a bastion. [F f. It. *bastione* f. *bastire* build]

■ **1, 2** see STRONGHOLD 1, 3.

basuco /bəsōōkō/ *n.* a cheap impure form of cocaine smoked for its stimulating effect. [Colombian Sp.]

bat¹ /bat/ *n.* & *v.* ● *n.* **1** an implement with a handle, usu. of wood and with a flat or curved surface, used for hitting balls in games. **2** *Cricket* a turn at using this. **3** a batsman, esp. in cricket, etc., usu. described in some way (*an excellent bat*). **4** (usu. in *pl.*) an object like a table tennis paddle used to guide aircraft when taxiing. ● *v.* (**batted, batting**) **1** *tr.* hit with or as with a bat. **2** *intr.* take a turn at batting. **3** have a batting average of. □ **bat around 1** *sl.* drift or putter aimlessly. **2** discuss (an idea or proposal). **3** *Baseball* have each player in a lineup bat in the course of a single inning. **off**

one's own bat *Brit.* unprompted; unaided. **right off the bat** immediately. [ME f. OE *batt* club, perh. partly f. OF *batte* club f. *battre* strike]

■ *v.* **1** see HIT *v.* 1a. □ **right off the bat** see *rapidly* (RAPID).

bat² /bat/ *n.* any mouselike nocturnal mammal of the order Chiroptera, capable of flight by means of membranous wings extending from its forelimbs. □ **have bats in the belfry** be eccentric or crazy. **like a bat out of hell** very fast. [16th c., alt. of ME *bakke* f. Scand.]

bat³ /bat/ *v.tr.* (**batted, batting**) wink (one's eye) (now usu. in phr.). □ **not** (or **never**) **bat an eye** *colloq.* show no reaction or emotion. [var. of obs. *bate* flutter]

batch /bach/ *n.* & *v.* ● *n.* **1** a number of things or persons forming a group or dealt with together. **2** an installment (*have sent off the latest batch*). **3** the loaves produced at one baking. **4** (*attrib.*) using or dealt with in batches, not as a continuous flow (*batch production*). **5** *Computing* a group of records processed as a single unit. ● *v.tr.* arrange or deal with in batches. [ME f. OE *bæcce* f. *bacan* BAKE]

■ *n.* **1, 2** set, group, number, quantity, assortment, lot, bunch, pack, bundle, collection, assemblage; consignment, installment. ● *v.* group, sort, bunch, pack, bundle, collect, assemble.

bate¹ /bayt/ *v.* **1** *tr.* moderate; restrain. **2** *tr.* diminish; deduct. **3** *intr.* diminish; abate.

■ see ABATE.

bate² /bayt/ *n.* (also **bait**) *Brit. sl.* a rage; a cross mood (*is in an awful bate*). [BAIT¹ = state of baited person]

bateau /batō/ *n.* (*pl.* **bateaux** /-tōz/) a light riverboat, esp. of the flat-bottomed kind used in Canada and the southern US. [F, = boat]

bated /báytid/ *adj.* □ **with bated breath** very anxiously. [past part. of obs. *bate* (v.) restrain, f. ABATE]

■ □ **with bated breath** see EXPECTANT *adj.* 1.

bateleur /bátəlŏr/ *n.* a short-tailed African eagle, *Terathopius ecaudatus.* [F, = juggler]

bath /bath/ *n.* & *v.* ● *n.* (*pl.* **baths** /bathz, baths/) **1 a** = BATHTUB. **b** a bathtub with its contents (*your bath is ready*). **2** the act or process of immersing the body for washing or therapy (*take a bath*). **3 a** a vessel containing liquid in which something is immersed, e.g., a film for developing, for controlling temperature, etc. **b** this with its contents. **4** esp. *Brit.* (usu. in *pl.*) a building with baths or a swimming pool, usu. open to the public. ● *v. Brit.* **1** *tr.* wash (esp. a person) in a bath. **2** *intr.* take a bath. □ **bath cube** *Brit.* a cube of compacted bath salts. **bath salts** soluble salts used for softening or scenting bathwater. **take a bath** *sl.* suffer a large financial loss. [OE *bæth* f. Gmc]

■ *n.* **2** see WASH *n.* 1.

Bath bun /bath/ *n. Brit.* a round spiced kind of sweet bun with currants, often with icing. [*Bath* in S. England, named from its hot springs]

Bath chair /bath/ *n.* esp. *Brit.* a wheelchair for invalids.

bathe /bayth/ *v.* & *n.* ● *v.* **1** *intr.* immerse oneself in water, esp. (Brit.) to swim or wash oneself. **2** *tr.* immerse in or wash or treat with liquid, esp. for cleansing or medicinal purposes. **3** *tr.* (of sunlight, etc.) suffuse or envelop with. ● *n. Brit.* an immersion in liquid, esp. to swim. □ **bathing suit** (or *Brit.* **costume**) (or **-suit**) a garment worn for swimming. [OE *bathian* f. Gmc]

■ *v.* **1** see CLEAN *v.* 4. **2** see DIP *v.* 1. **3** see SUFFUSE.

bather /báythər/ *n.* **1** a person who bathes. **2** (in *pl.*) *Austral.* a bathing suit.

bathhouse /báth-hows/ *n.* **1** a building with baths for public use. **2** a building with changing rooms, as at the beach.

batholith /báthəlith/ *n.* a dome of igneous rock extending inwards to an unknown depth. [G f. Gk *bathos* depth + -LITH]

bathometer /bəthómitər/ *n.* an instrument used to measure the depth of water. [Gk *bathos* depth + -METER]

bathos /báythaws, -thos/ *n.* an unintentional lapse in mood from the sublime to the absurd or trivial; a commonplace or ridiculous feature offsetting an otherwise sublime situation; an anticlimax. □□ **bathetic** /bəthétik/ adj. **bathotic** /bəthótik/ adj. [Gk, = depth]

bathrobe /báthrōb/ n. a loose robe, often of toweling, worn before and after taking a bath.
■ see WRAPPER 4.

bathroom /báthrōōm, -rŏŏm/ n. **1** a room containing a toilet. **2** a room containing a bath and usu. other washing facilities.
■ **2** see LAVATORY.

bathtub /báthtəb/ n. a container for liquid, usu. water, used for immersing and washing the body.

bathyscaphe /báthiskaf/ n. a manned vessel controlled by ballast for deep-sea diving. [Gk bathus deep + skaphos ship]

bathysphere /báthisfeer/ n. a spherical vessel connected to a surface vessel by cables, used for deep-sea observation. [Gk bathus deep + SPHERE]

batik /bətéek, bátik/ n. a method (orig. used in Indonesia) of producing colored designs on textiles by applying wax to the parts to be left uncolored; a piece of cloth treated in this way. [Jav., = painted]

batiste /batéest/ n. & adj. ● n. a fine linen or cotton cloth. ● adj. made of batiste. [F (earlier batiche), perh. rel. to battre BATTER[1]]

batman /bátmən/ n. (pl. **-men**) Brit. Mil. an attendant serving an officer. [OF bat, bast f. med.L bastum packsaddle + MAN]

bat mitzvah /bat mítsvə/ var. of BAS MITZVAH.

baton /bətón, ba-, bát'n/ n. **1** a thin stick used by a conductor to direct an orchestra, choir, etc. **2** Sports a short stick or tube carried and passed on by the runners in a relay race. **3** a long stick carried and twirled by a drum major. **4** a staff of office or authority, esp. Brit. a Field Marshal's. **5** esp. Brit. a policeman's truncheon. **6** Heraldry a narrow truncated bend. **7** Horol. a short bar replacing some figures on dials. □ **baton round** Brit. a rubber or plastic bullet. [F bâton, baston ult. f. LL bastum stick]
■ **1–5** see STAFF[1] n. 1a, b.

batrachian /bətráykeeən/ n. & adj. ● n. any of the amphibians that discard gills and tails, esp. the frog and toad. ● adj. of or relating to the batrachians. [Gk batrakhos frog]

bats /bats/ predic.adj. sl. crazy. [f. phr. (have) bats in the belfry: see BAT[2]]
■ see CRAZY 1.

batsman /bátsmən/ n. (pl. **-men**) **1** a person who bats or is batting, esp. in cricket. **2** esp. Brit. a signaler using bats to guide aircraft on the ground. □□ **batsmanship** n. (in sense 1).

battalion /bətályən/ n. **1** a large body of men ready for battle, esp. an infantry unit forming part of a brigade. **2** a large group of people pursuing a common aim or sharing a major undertaking. [F bataillon f. It. battaglione f. battaglia BATTLE]
■ **1** see CORPS.

batten[1] /bát'n/ n. & v. ● n. **1** a long flat strip of squared lumber or metal, esp. used to hold something in place or as a fastening against a wall, etc. **2** a strip of wood used for clamping the boards of a door, etc. **3** Naut. a strip of wood or metal for securing a tarpaulin over a ship's hatchway. ● v.tr. strengthen or fasten with battens. □ **batten down the hatches 1** Naut. secure a ship's tarpaulins. **2** prepare for a difficulty or crisis. [OF batant part. of batre beat f. L battuere]

batten[2] /bát'n/ v.intr. (foll. by on) thrive or prosper at another's expense. [ON batna get better f. bati advantage]

batter[1] /bátər/ v. **1 a** tr. strike repeatedly with hard blows, esp. so as to cause visible damage. **b** intr. (often foll. by against, at, etc.) strike repeated blows; pound heavily and insistently (batter at the door). **2** tr. (often in passive) **a** handle roughly, esp. over a long period. **b** censure or criticize severely. □ **battered child** a child that has suffered repeated violence from adults, esp. its parents. **battered wife** a wife subjected to repeated violence by her husband. **battering ram** hist. a heavy beam, orig. with an end in the form of a carved ram's head, used in breaching fortifications. □□ **batterer** n. **battering** n. [ME f. AF baterer f. OF batre beat f. L battuere]
■ **1 a** beat, beat up, knock about, hit, strike, clout, belabor, pound, buffet, pummel, pelt, bash, bang,

thrash, sl. wallop, clobber, archaic or literary smite; bombard. **b** pound, beat, strike, bang, thrash. **2 a** maltreat, mistreat, ill-treat, abuse, mishandle, harm; maul, bruise, mangle. **b** attack, blast, flay, cut up, roast, colloq. pan, lambaste, esp. Brit. colloq. slate, sl. knock, clobber, slam, take to the cleaners; censure, criticize, damn, condemn, reprobate. □□ **batterer** maltreater, abuser, (child) molester.

batter[2] /bátər/ n. **1** a fluid mixture of flour, egg, and milk or water, used in cooking, esp. for cakes, etc., and for coating food before frying. **2** Printing an area of damaged type. [ME f. AF batour f. OF bateüre f. batre: see BATTER[1]]

batter[3] /bátər/ n. Sports a player batting, esp. in baseball.

batter[4] /bátər/ n. & v. ● n. **1** a wall, etc., with a sloping face. **2** a receding slope. ● v.intr. have a receding slope. [ME: orig. unkn.]

battered /bátərd/ adj. coated in batter and deep-fried.

battery /bátəree/ n. (pl. **-ies**) **1** a usu. portable container of a cell or cells carrying an electric charge, as a source of current. **2** (often attrib.) esp. Brit. a series of cages for the intensive breeding and rearing of poultry or cattle. **3** a set of similar units of equipment, esp. connected. **4** a series of tests, esp. psychological. **5 a** a fortified emplacement for heavy guns. **b** an artillery unit of guns, soldiers, and vehicles. **6** Law an act inflicting unlawful personal violence on another (see ASSAULT). **7** Baseball the pitcher and the catcher. [F batterie f. batre, battre strike f. L battuere]

batting /báting/ n. **1** the action of hitting with a bat. **2** cotton wadding prepared in sheets for use in quilts, etc. □ **batting order** the order in which people act or take their turn, esp. of batters in baseball or batsmen in cricket.

battle /bát'l/ n. & v. ● n. **1 a** a prolonged fight between large organized armed forces. **b** a fight between two individuals. **2** a contest; a prolonged or difficult struggle (life is a constant battle; a battle of wits). ● v. **1** intr. struggle; fight persistently (battled against the elements; battled for women's rights). **2** tr. fight (one's way, etc.). **3** tr. engage in battle with. □ **battle-ax 1** a large ax used in ancient warfare. **2** colloq. a formidable or domineering older woman. **battle cruiser** a heavily armed ship faster and more lightly armored than a battleship. **battle cry** a cry or slogan of participants in a battle or contest. **battle dress** the field uniform of a soldier, often camouflaged. **battle fatigue** = combat fatigue. **battle royal 1** a battle in which several combatants or all available forces engage; a free fight. **2** a heated argument. **half the battle** the key to the success of an undertaking. □□ **battler** n. [ME f. OF bataille ult. f. LL battualia gladiatorial exercises f. L battuere beat]
■ n. **1** fight, conflict, combat, war, action, encounter, clash, engagement, struggle, donnybrook, fray. **2** contest, competition, match, tournament, game, encounter; struggle, fight, war, conflict, crusade, campaign; brawl, fracas, melee; duel, hand-to-hand, Law affray; argument, dispute, altercation, quarrel. ● v. **1** fight, struggle, combat, wage war, war, wrestle, crusade, campaign, lobby; (battle with or against) oppose, stand against, engage with, grapple with, strive or contend with or against, take up arms against. **3** see FIGHT v. 1a. □ **battle-ax** see WITCH n. 2. **battle cry** see SLOGAN. **battle royal 1** see BRAWL n. **2** see ROW[3] n. 2. □□ **battler** fighter, soldier, pugilist, warrior, militant, combatant, campaigner.

battledore /bát'ldawr/ n. hist. **1 a** (in full **battledore and shuttlecock**) a game similar to badminton played with a shuttlecock and rackets. **b** the racket used in this. **2** a kind of wooden utensil like a paddle, formerly used in washing, baking, etc. [15th c., perh. f. Prov. batedor beater f. batre beat]

/.../ pronunciation	● **part of speech**
□ **phrases, idioms, and compounds**	
□□ **derivatives**	■ **synonym section**
cross-references appear in SMALL CAPITALS or italics	

battlefield /bát'lfeeld/ *n.* (also **battleground** /-grownd/) the piece of ground on which a battle is or was fought.

battlement /bát'lmənt/ *n.* (usu. in *pl.*) **1** a parapet with recesses along the top of a wall, as part of a fortification. **2** a section of roof enclosed by this (*walking on the battlements*). □□ **battlemented** *adj.* [OF *bataillier* furnish with ramparts + -MENT]

battleship /bát'lship/ *n.* a warship with the heaviest armor and the largest guns.

battue /batōō, -tyōō/ *n.* **1 a** the driving of game toward hunters by beaters. **b** a hunt arranged in this way. **2** wholesale slaughter. [F, fem. past part. of *battre* beat f. L *battuere*]

batty /bátee/ *adj.* (**battier, battiest**) *sl.* crazy. □□ **battily** *adv.* **battiness** *n.* [BAT² + -Y¹]
■ see CRAZY 1.

batwing /bátwing/ *adj.* (esp. of a sleeve or a flame) shaped like the wing of a bat.

batwoman /bátwŏŏmən/ *n.* (*pl.* **-women**) *Brit.* a female attendant serving an officer in the women's services. [as BATMAN + WOMAN]

bauble /báwbəl/ *n.* **1** a showy trinket or toy of little value. **2** a baton formerly used as an emblem by jesters. [ME f. OF *ba(u)bel* child's toy, of unkn. orig.]
■ **1** gewgaw, trinket, bijou, ornament, trifle, gimcrack, kickshaw, bagatelle, knickknack, falderal, frippery, toy, plaything.

baud /bawd/ *n.* (*pl.* same or **bauds**) *Computing*, etc. **1** a unit used to express the speed of electronic code signals, corresponding to one information unit per second. **2** (loosely) a unit of data transmission speed of one bit per second. [J. M. E. *Baudot*, Fr. engineer d. 1903]

Bauhaus /bówhows/ *n.* **1** a German school of architectural design (1919–33). **2** its principles, based on functionalism and development of existing skills. [G f. *Bau* building + *Haus* house]

baulk *Brit.* var. of BALK.

baulky *Brit.* var. of BALKY.

bauxite /báwksīt/ *n.* a claylike mineral containing varying proportions of alumina, the chief source of aluminum. □□ **bauxitic** /-sítik/ *adj.* [F f. *Les Baux* near Arles in S. France + -ITE¹]

bawd /bawd/ *n.* a woman who runs a brothel. [ME *bawdstrot* f. OF *baudetrot, baudestroyt* procuress]
■ see PROCURER.

bawdy /báwdee/ *adj.* & *n.* ● *adj.* (**bawdier, bawdiest**) (esp. humorously) indecent; raunchy. ● *n.* bawdy talk or writing. □ **bawdy house** a brothel. □□ **bawdily** *adv.* **bawdiness** *n.* [BAWD + -Y¹]
■ *adj.* lewd, obscene, taboo, vulgar, dirty, smutty, saucy, randy, filthy, coarse, earthy, gross, scatological, rude, lascivious, lubricious, salacious, indelicate, indecent, indecorous, broad, crude, ribald, risqué, suggestive, Rabelaisian, uninhibited, unrestrained, *Gk Hist.* ithyphallic. ● *n.* scatology, obscenity, smut, filth, pornography, ribaldry, *colloq.* porn. □ **bawdy house** see BROTHEL. □□ **bawdily** lewdly, obscenely, rudely, dirtily, filthily, smuttily, saucily, coarsely, grossly, lasciviously, salaciously, indelicately, crudely, indecorously, suggestively. **bawdiness** see RIBALDRY.

bawl /bawl/ *v.* **1** *tr.* speak or call out noisily. **2** *intr.* weep loudly. □ **bawl out** *colloq.* reprimand angrily. □□ **bawler** *n.* [imit.: cf. med.L *baulare* bark, Icel. *baula* (Sw. *böla*) to low]
■ **1** shout, bellow, vociferate, roar, yell, cry, trumpet, thunder, *colloq.* holler. **2** cry, wail, weep, howl, keen, sob, squall, blubber, whimper, *Sc.* greet, *colloq. or dial.* yammer. □ **bawl out** see REPRIMAND *v.* □□ **bawler** shouter, bellower, roarer; weeper, crybaby, sobber, howler, wailer, blubberer, *colloq. or dial.* yammerer.

bay¹ /bay/ *n.* **1** a broad inlet of the sea where the land curves inwards. **2** a recess in a mountain range. □ **Bay State** Massachusetts. [ME f. OF *baie* f. OSp. *bahia*]
■ **1** see GULF *n.* 1.

bay² /bay/ *n.* **1** (in full **bay laurel**) a laurel, *Laurus nobilis*, having deep green leaves and purple berries. Also called *sweet bay.* **2** (in *pl.*) a wreath made of bay leaves, for a victor or poet. □ **bay leaf** the aromatic (usu. dried) leaf of the bay tree, used in cooking. **bay rum** a perfume, esp. for the hair, distilled orig. from bayberry leaves in rum. [OF *baie* f. L *baca* berry]
■ **2** (*bays*) see TROPHY 1.

bay³ /bay/ *n.* **1** a space created by a window line projecting outwards from a wall. **2** a recess; a section of wall between buttresses or columns, esp. in the nave of a church, etc. **3** a compartment (*bomb bay*). **4** an area specially allocated or marked off (*sick bay; loading bay*). **5** *Brit.* the terminus of a branch line at a railroad station also having through lines, usu. at the side of an outer platform. □ **bay window** a window built into a bay. [ME f. OF *baie* f. *ba(y)er* gape f. med.L *batare*]
■ **1, 2** see RECESS *n.* 1.

bay⁴ /bay/ *adj.* & *n.* ● *adj.* (esp. of a horse) dark reddish brown. ● *n.* a bay horse with a black mane and tail. [OF *bai* f. L *badius*]

bay⁵ /bay/ *v.* & *n.* ● *v.* **1** *intr.* (esp. of a large dog) bark or howl loudly and plaintively. **2** *tr.* bay at. ● *n.* the sound of baying, esp. in chorus from hounds in close pursuit. □ **at bay 1** cornered; apparently unable to escape. **2** in a desperate situation. **bring to bay** gain on in pursuit; trap. **hold** (or **keep**) **at bay** hold off (a pursuer). **stand at bay** turn to face one's pursuers. [ME f. OF *bai, baiier* bark f. It. *baiare*, of imit. orig.]
■ *v.* **1** see HOWL *v.* 1.

bayberry /báyberee/ *n.* (*pl.* **-ies**) any of various N. American plants of the genus *Myrica*, having aromatic leaves and bearing berries covered in a wax coating. [BAY² + BERRY]

bayonet /báyənét/ *n.* & *v.* ● *n.* **1** a stabbing blade attachable to the muzzle of a rifle. **2** an electrical or other fitting engaged by being pushed into a socket and twisted. ● *v.tr.* (**bayoneted, bayoneting**) stab with a bayonet. [F *baïonnette*, perh. f. *Bayonne* in SW France, where they were first made]

bayou /bí-ōō/ *n.* a marshy offshoot of a river, etc., in the southern US. [Amer. F: cf. Choctau *bayuk*]

bazaar /bəzaár/ *n.* **1** a market in an Eastern or Middle Eastern country. **2** a fund-raising sale of goods, esp. for charity. **3** a large store selling fancy goods, etc.; a department store. [Pers. *bāzār*, prob. through Turk. and It.]
■ **1, 3** see MARKET *n.* 2. **2** see FAIR² 2.

bazooka /bəzōōkə/ *n.* **1** a tubular short-range rocket launcher used against tanks. **2** a crude trombone-like musical instrument. [app. f. *bazoo* mouth, of unkn. orig.]

BB *abbr.* **1** a shot pellet about .18 inch in diameter, for use in a BB gun or air gun. **2** *Brit.* double-black (pencil lead).

BBC *abbr.* British Broadcasting Corporation. □ **BBC English** English as supposedly pronounced by BBC announcers.

bbl. *abbr.* barrels (esp. of oil).

BC *abbr.* **1** (of a date) before Christ. **2** British Columbia.

BCD /béeseedeé/ *n. Computing* a code representing decimal numbers as a string of binary digits. [abbr. for *binary coded decimal*]

BCE *abbr.* (of a date) before the Common Era.

BCG *abbr.* Bacillus Calmette-Guérin, an anti-tuberculosis vaccine.

BD *abbr.* Bachelor of Divinity.

Bde *abbr.* Brigade.

bdellium /déleeəm/ *n.* **1** any of various trees, esp. of the genus *Commiphora*, yielding resin. **2** this fragrant resin used in perfumes. [L f. Gk *bdellion* f. Heb. *bᵉdhōlaḥ*]

bdrm. *abbr.* bedroom.

BE *abbr.* **1** Bachelor of Education. **2** Bachelor of Engineering. **3** bill of exchange.

Be *symb. Chem.* the element beryllium.

be /bee/ *v.* & *v.aux.* (*sing. present* **am** /am, əm/; **are** /aar, ər/; **is** /iz/; *pl. present* **are**; *1st and 3rd sing. past* **was** /wuz, woz, wəz/; *2nd sing. past and pl. past* **were** /wər/; *present subj.* **be**; *past subj.* **were**; *pres. part.* **being**; *past part.* **been** /bin/)
● *v.intr.* **1** (often prec. by *there*) exist; live (*I think, therefore I am; there is a house on the corner; there is no God*). **2 a** occur; take place (*dinner is at eight*). **b** occupy a position in space (*he is in the garden; have you been to Paris?*). **3** remain; con-

tinue (*let it be*). **4** linking subject and predicate, expressing: **a** identity (*she is the person*; *today is Thursday*). **b** condition (*he is ill today*). **c** state or quality (*he is very kind*; *they are my friends*). **d** opinion (*I am against hanging*). **e** total (*two and two are four*). **f** cost or significance (*it is $5 to enter*; *it is nothing to me*). ● *v.aux.* **1** with a past participle to form the passive mood (*it was done*; *it is said*; *we shall be helped*). **2** with a present participle to form continuous tenses (*we are coming*; *it is being cleaned*). **3** with an infinitive to express duty or commitment, intention, possibility, destiny, or hypothesis (*I am to tell you*; *we are to wait here*; *he is to come at four*; *it was not to be found*; *they were never to meet again*; *if I were to die*). **4** *archaic* with the past participle of intransitive verbs to form perfect tenses (*the sun is set*; *Babylon is fallen*). □ **be about** occupy oneself with (*is about his business*). **be-all and end-all** *colloq.* (often foll. by *of*) the whole being or essence. **be at** occupy oneself with (*mice have been at the food*). **been** (or **been and gone**) and esp. *Brit. sl.* an expression of protest or surprise (*he's been and taken my car!*). **2 be off** *colloq.* go away; leave. **be that as it may** see MAY. **-to-be** of the future (in *comb.*: *bride-to-be*). [OE *beo(m)*, *(e)am*, *is*, *(e)aron*; past f. OE *wæs* f. *wesan* to be; there are numerous Gmc cognates]
■ *v.* **1** see EXIST 1, 2a. □ **be-all and end-all** see TOTALITY.

be- /bee/ *prefix* forming verbs: **1** (from transitive verbs) **a** all over; all around (*beset*; *besmear*). **b** thoroughly; excessively (*begrudge*; *belabor*). **2** (from intransitive verbs) expressing transitive action (*bemoan*; *bestride*). **3** (from adjectives and nouns) expressing transitive action (*befool*; *befoul*). **4** (from nouns) **a** affect with (*befog*). **b** treat as (*befriend*). **c** (forming adjectives in *-ed*) having; covered with (*bejeweled*; *bespectacled*). [OE *bi-*, weak form of *bī* BY as in *bygone*, *byword*, etc.]

beach /beech/ *n.* & *v.* ● *n.* a pebbly or sandy shore esp. of the sea between high- and low-water marks. ● *v.tr.* run or haul up (a boat, etc.) on to a beach. □ **beach ball** a large inflated ball for games on the beach. **beach buggy** esp. *Brit.* = *dune buggy*. **beach plum 1** a maritime N. American shrub, *Prunus maritima*. **2** its edible fruit. [16th c.: orig. unkn.]
■ *n.* shore, lakeshore, bank, seashore, seaside, plage, lido, coast, margin, littoral, *rhet. or poet.* strand.
● *v.* ground, run aground, strand; land.

beachcomber /beechkōmər/ *n.* **1** a vagrant who lives by searching beaches for articles of value. **2** a long wave rolling in from the sea.
■ **1** see TRAMP *n.* 1.

beachhead /beech-hed/ *n. Mil.* a fortified position established on a beach by landing forces. [after *bridgehead*]

Beach-la-mar /beechləmaár/ *n. Brit.* an English-based Creole language spoken in the W. Pacific. [corrupt. f. Port. *bicho do mar* BÊCHE-DE-MER]

beacon /beekən/ *n.* **1 a** a fire or light set up in a high or prominent position as a warning, etc. **b** *Brit.* (now often in place-names) a hill suitable for this. **2** a visible warning or guiding point or device (e.g., a lighthouse, navigation buoy, etc.). **3** a radio transmitter whose signal helps fix the position of a ship or aircraft. [OE *bēacn* f. WG]
■ **1a, 2** fire, light, bonfire, flare, signal fire, Very light, rocket; signal, sign, guide, guiding light; lighthouse, pharos.

bead /beed/ *n.* & *v.* ● *n.* **1 a** a small usu. rounded and perforated piece of glass, stone, etc., for threading with others to make jewelry, or sewing on to fabric, etc. **b** (in *pl.*) a string of beads; a rosary. **2** a drop of liquid; a bubble. **3** a small knob in the foresight of a gun. **4** the inner edge of a pneumatic tire that grips the rim of the wheel. **5** *Archit.* **a** a molding like a series of beads. **b** a narrow molding with a semicircular cross section. ● *v.* **1** *tr.* furnish or decorate with beads. **2** *tr.* string together. **3** *intr.* form or grow into beads. □ **draw a bead on** take aim at. **tell one's beads** use the beads of a rosary, etc., in counting prayers. □□ **beaded** *adj.* [orig. = 'prayer' (for which the earliest use of beads arose): OE *gebed* f. Gmc, rel. to BID]
■ *n.* **1a** see ROUND *n.* 1. **2** see DROP *n.* 1. **5** see BORDER *n.* 3.

beading /beeding/ *n.* **1** decoration in the form of or resembling a row of beads, esp. lacelike looped edging. **2** *Archit.* a bead molding. **3** the bead of a tire.

beadle /beed'l/ *n.* **1** *Brit.* a ceremonial officer of a church, college, etc. **2** *Sc.* a church officer attending on the minister. **3** *Brit. hist.* a minor parish officer dealing with petty offenders, etc. □□ **beadleship** *n.* [ME f. OF *bedel* ult. f. Gmc]

beadsman /beedzmən/ *n.* (*pl.* **-men**) *hist.* **1** a pensioner provided for by a benefactor in return for prayers. **2** an inmate of an almshouse.

beady /beedee/ *adj.* (**beadier, beadiest**) **1** (of the eyes) small, round, and bright. **2** covered with beads or drops. □ **beady-eyed** with beady eyes. □□ **beadily** *adv.* **beadiness** *n.*

beagle /beegəl/ *n.* & *v.* ● *n.* **1 a** a small hound of a breed with a short coat, orig. used for hunting hares. **b** this breed. **2** *hist.* an informer or spy; a constable. ● *v.intr.* (often as **beagling** *n.*) esp. *Brit.* hunt with beagles. □□ **beagler** *n.* [ME f. OF *beegueule* noisy person, prob. f. *beer* open wide + *gueule* throat]

beak¹ /beek/ *n.* **1 a** a bird's horny projecting jaws; a bill. **b** the similar projecting jaw of other animals, e.g., a turtle. **2** *sl.* a hooked nose. **3** *Naut. hist.* the projection at the prow of a warship. **4** a spout. □□ **beaked** *adj.* **beaky** *adj.* [ME f. OF *bec* f. L *beccus*, of Celt. orig.]
■ **1** see BILL² *n.* 1, 2.

beak² /beek/ *n. Brit. sl.* **1** a magistrate. **2** a schoolmaster. [19th c.: prob. f. thieves' cant]

beaker /beekər/ *n.* **1** a tall drinking vessel, usu. of plastic and tumbler-shaped. **2** a lipped cylindrical glass vessel for scientific experiments. **3** *archaic* or *literary* a large drinking vessel with a wide mouth. □ **Beaker Folk** *Archaeol.* a people thought to have come to Britain from Central Europe in the early Bronze Age, named after beaker-shaped pottery found in their graves. [ME f. ON *bikarr*, perh. f. Gk *bikos* drinking bowl]
■ **1, 3** see GLASS *n.* 2a.

beam /beem/ *n.* & *v.* ● *n.* **1** a long sturdy piece of squared timber or metal spanning an opening or room, usu. to support the structure above. **2 a** a ray or shaft of light. **b** a directional flow of particles or radiation. **3** a bright look or smile. **4 a** a series of radio or radar signals as a guide to a ship or aircraft. **b** the course indicated by this (*off beam*). **5** the crossbar of a balance. **6 a** a ship's breadth at its widest point. **b** the width of a person's hips (esp. *broad in the beam*). **7** (in *pl.*) the horizontal cross-timbers of a ship supporting the deck and joining the sides. **8** the side of a ship (*land on the port beam*). **9** the chief timber of a plow. **10** the cylinder in a loom on which the warp or cloth is wound. **11** the main stem of a stag's antlers. **12** the lever in an engine connecting the piston rod and crank. **13** the shank of an anchor. ● *v.* **1** *tr.* emit or direct (light, radio waves, etc.). **2** *intr.* **a** shine. **b** look or smile radiantly. □ **beam compass** (or **compasses**) compasses with a beam connecting sliding sockets, used for large circles. **a beam in one's eye** a fault that is greater in oneself than in the person one is finding fault with (see Matt. 7:3). **off** (or **off the**) **beam** *colloq.* mistaken. **on the beam** *colloq.* on the right track. **on the beam-ends** (of a ship) on its side; almost capsizing. **on one's beam-ends** near the end of one's resources. [OE *bēam* tree f. WG]
■ *n.* **1** timber, balk, pile, purlin, collar beam, tie beam, crosspiece, summer, summertree, hammerbeam, scantling, girder, rafter, cantilever; bar, brace, plank, board, stud, trestle, *Archit.* breastsummer. **2 a** ray, gleam, shaft. ● *v.* **1** emit, radiate, shed, give off *or* out, send out; direct, shine, train, aim, focus. **2 a** radiate, shine (out *or* forth), pour out *or* forth, emanate, gleam, glow, blaze. **b** smile, grin. □ **off** (or **off the**) **beam** see WRONG *adj.* 1. **on the beam** on the right track, along

---

the right lines, close, *colloq.* warm. **on one's beam-ends** see BROKE.

beamer /beemər/ *n. Cricket colloq.* a ball bowled at a batsman's head.

beamy /beemee/ *adj.* (of a ship) broad-beamed.
■ broad-beamed, broad, wide, broad in the beam.

bean /been/ *n. & v.* ● *n.* **1 a** any kind of leguminous plant with edible usu. kidney-shaped seeds in long pods. **b** one of these seeds. **2** a similar seed of coffee and other plants. **3** *sl.* the head, esp. as a source of common sense. **4** (in *pl.*; with *neg.*) *sl.* anything at all (*doesn't know beans about it*). ● *v.tr. sl.* hit on the head. □ **bean counter** a person, esp. an accountant, who is regarded as concerned with financial details to the exclusion of other factors. **bean curd** soft cheese-like cake or paste made from soybeans, used esp. in Asian cooking. **bean sprout** a sprout of a bean seed, esp. of the mung bean, used as food. **full of beans** *colloq.* **1** lively; in high spirits. **2** mistaken. **not a bean** *Brit. sl.* no money. **old bean** *Brit. sl.* a friendly form of address, usu. to a man. **spill the beans** see SPILL. [OE *bēan* f. Gmc]
■ *n.* **3** see HEAD *n.* 1.

beanbag /beenbag/ *n.* **1** a small bag filled with dried beans and used esp. in children's games. **2** (in full **beanbag chair**) a large cushion filled usu. with polystyrene beads and used as a seat.

beanery /beenəree/ *n.* (*pl.* **-ies**) *sl.* a cheap restaurant.

beanfeast /beenfeest/ *n. Brit.* **1** *colloq.* a celebration; a merry time. **2** an employer's annual dinner given to employees. [BEAN + FEAST, beans and bacon being regarded as an indispensable dish]

beanie /beenee/ *n.* a small close-fitting cap worn on the back of the head. [perh. f. BEAN 'head' + -IE]

beano /beenō/ *n.* (*pl.* **-os**) **1** bingo. **2** *Brit. sl.* a celebration; a party. [abbr. of BEANFEAST]

beanpole /beenpōl/ *n.* **1** a stick for supporting bean plants. **2** *colloq.* a tall thin person.

beanstalk /beenstawk/ *n.* the stem of a bean plant.

bear[1] /bair/ *v.* (*past* **bore** /bor/; *past part.* **borne, born** /bawrn/) ¶ In the passive *born* is used with reference to birth (e.g., *was born in July*), except for *borne by* foll. by the name of the mother (e.g., *was borne by Sarah*). **1** *tr.* carry, bring, or take (esp. visibly) (*bear gifts*). **2** *tr.* show; be marked by; have as an attribute or characteristic (*bear marks of violence*; *bears no relation to the case*; *bore no name*). **3** *tr.* **a** produce; yield (fruit, etc.). **b** give birth to (*has borne a son*; *was born last week*). **4** *tr.* **a** sustain (a weight, responsibility, cost, etc.). **b** stand; endure (an ordeal, difficulty, etc.). **5** *tr.* (usu. with *neg.* or *interrog.*) **a** tolerate; put up with (*can't bear him*; *how can you bear it?*). **b** admit of; be fit for (*does not bear thinking about*). **6** *tr.* carry in thought or memory (*bear a grudge*). **7** *intr.* veer in a given direction (*bear left*). **8** *tr.* bring or provide (something needed) (*bear him company*). **9** *refl.* behave (in a certain way). □ **bear arms 1** carry weapons; serve as a soldier. **2** *Brit.* wear or display heraldic devices. **bear away** (or **off**) win (a prize, etc.). **bear down** exert downward pressure. **bear down on** approach rapidly or purposefully. **bear fruit** have results. **bear hard on** oppress. **bear in mind** take into account having remembered. **bear on** (or **upon**) be relevant to. **bear out** support or confirm (an account or the person giving it). **bear repeating** be worth repetition. **bear up 1** raise one's spirits; not despair. **2** (often foll. by *against, under*) endure; survive. **bear with** treat forbearingly; tolerate patiently. **bear witness** testify. [OE *beran* f. Gmc]
■ **1** carry, transport, convey, move, take, deliver, bring, *colloq.* schlep, tote, *sl.* cart. **2** have, carry, show, hold, exhibit, display, be marked by. **3** produce, yield, develop, breed, generate; give birth to, spawn, bring forth, have, *archaic* engender; (*be born*) come into the world, *colloq.* arrive. **4** carry, support, sustain, shoulder, take, uphold; endure, stand, withstand, hold *or* stand up under, hold out against, weather, suffer, cope with, undergo, go through with, experience. **5 a** stand, put up with, abide, tolerate, endure, submit (oneself) to, reconcile oneself to, *literary* brook. **b** merit, admit of,

be worthy of, warrant, be fit for, deserve, rate; invite. **6** carry, harbor, keep, hold, retain, maintain, foster, have; entertain. **7** turn, veer, swing, shift, wheel, incline. **9** (*bear oneself*) see ACT *v.* □ **bear away** see WIN *v.* 1. **bear down on** travel headlong toward, head toward, approach, home in on. **bear hard on** see OPPRESS 1, 2. **bear in mind** remember, keep in mind, do not forget *or* overlook, recollect, recall, be aware *or* cognizant *or* mindful of; see also CONSIDER 4. **bear on** (or **upon**) relate to, have relevance to, be relevant to, pertain to, be *or* have to do with, touch on *or* upon, affect, concern, have a bearing on *or* upon, appertain to. **bear out** confirm, support, corroborate, substantiate, uphold, back up, authenticate, verify, bear witness to. **bear up 1** cheer up, be encouraged, raise *or* lift one's spirits, buoy oneself up, uplift *or* hearten *or* comfort oneself. **2** endure, survive, hold out *or* up, stand up, withstand. **bear with** put up with, be patient *or* tolerant with, tolerate, make allowance(s) *or* concessions for, excuse. **bear witness** see TESTIFY 1.

bear[2] /bair/ *n. & v.* ● *n.* **1** any large heavy mammal of the family Ursidae, having thick fur and walking on its soles. **2** a rough, unmannerly, or uncouth person. **3** *Stock Exch.* a person who sells shares hoping to buy them back later at a lower price. **4** = TEDDY. **5** (**the Bear**) *colloq.* Russia. ● *v. Stock Exch.* **1** *intr.* speculate for a fall in price. **2** *tr.* produce a fall in the price of (stocks, etc.). □ **bear hug** a tight embrace. **bear market** *Stock Exch.* a market with falling prices. **bear's breech** a kind of acanthus, *Acanthus mollis*. **bear's ear** auricula. **bear's foot** a hellebore, *Helleborus fetidus*. **the Great Bear** *Brit.* = Big Dipper. **the Little Bear** *Brit.* = *Little Dipper.* **like a bear with a sore head** *Brit. colloq.* very irritable. [OE *bera* f. WG]

bearable /báirəbəl/ *adj.* that may be endured or tolerated. □□ **bearability** /-bílitee/ *n.* **bearableness** *n.* **bearably** *adv.*
■ tolerable, supportable, endurable, acceptable, manageable, sufferable. □□ **bearability, bearableness** see *acceptability* (ACCEPTABLE). **bearably** see *acceptably* (ACCEPTABLE)

bearbaiting /báirbāting/ *n. hist.* an entertainment involving setting dogs to attack a captive bear.

beard /beerd/ *n. & v.* ● *n.* **1** hair growing on the chin and lower cheeks of the face. **2** a similar tuft or part on an animal (esp. a goat). **3** the awn of a grass, sheath of barley, etc. ● *v.tr.* oppose openly; defy. □□ **bearded** *adj.* **beardless** *adj.* [OE f. WG]
■ □□ **bearded** see HAIRY 1.

beardie /beerdee/ *n. Brit. colloq.* a bearded man.

bearer /báirər/ *n.* **1** a person or thing that bears, carries, or brings. **2** a carrier of equipment on an expedition, etc. **3** a person who presents a check or other order to pay money. **4** (*attrib.*) payable to the possessor (*bearer stock*). **5** *hist.* (in India, etc.) a personal servant.

beargarden /báirgaard'n/ *n.* a rowdy or noisy scene.

bearing /báiring/ *n.* **1** a person's bodily attitude or outward behavior. **2** (foll. by *on, upon*) relation or relevance to (*his comments have no bearing on the subject*). **3** endurability (*beyond bearing*). **4** a part of a machine that supports a rotating or other moving part. **5** direction or position relative to a fixed point, measured esp. in degrees. **6** (in *pl.*) **a** one's position relative to one's surroundings. **b** awareness of this; a sense of one's orientation (*get one's bearings*; *lose one's bearings*). **7** *Heraldry* a device or charge. **8** = *ball bearing* (see BALL[1]). □ **bearing rein** a fixed rein from bit to saddle that forces a horse to arch its neck.
■ **1** carriage, deportment, manner, behavior, conduct, aspect, demeanor, posture, stance, air, attitude, presence, *literary* mien. **2** relation, reference, relationship, correlation, pertinence, relevance, connection, relevancy, applicability, application, germaneness, significance. **3** endurance, endurability, tolerance, tolerability, acceptance, acceptability, sufferance, manageability. **5** see POSITION *n.* 1. **6** (*bearings*) (sense of) direction, orientation, (relative) position.

bearish /báirish/ *adj.* **1** like a bear, esp. in temper. **2** *Stock Exch.* causing or associated with a fall in prices.
■ **1** see *short-tempered*.

Béarnaise sauce /báirnáyz/ *n.* a rich sauce thickened with egg yolks and flavored with tarragon. [F, fem. of *béarnais* of *Béarn* in SW France]

bearskin /báirskin/ *n.* **1 a** the skin of a bear. **b** a wrap, etc., made of this. **2** a tall furry hat worn ceremonially by some regiments.

beast /beest/ *n.* **1** an animal other than a human being, esp. a wild quadruped. **2 a** a brutal person. **b** *colloq.* an objectionable or unpleasant person or thing (*a beast of a problem*). **3** (prec. by *the*) a human being's brutish or uncivilized characteristics (*saw the beast in him*). □ **beast of burden** an animal, e.g., an ox, used for carrying or pulling loads. **beast of prey** see PREY. [ME f. OF *beste* f. Rmc *besta* f. L *bestia*]
■ **1** animal, creature, living thing; being. **2 a** brute, savage, animal, monster, fiend, ogre, barbarian, demon. **b** see STINKER.

beastie /béestee/ *n.* a small animal.

beastly /béestlee/ *adj.* & *adv.* ● *adj.* (**beastlier, beastliest**) **1** *colloq.* objectionable; unpleasant. **2** like a beast; brutal. ● *adv. Brit. colloq.* very; extremely. □□ **beastliness** *n.*
■ *adj.* **1** objectionable, horrible, awful, unpleasant, atrocious, disagreeable, intolerable, offensive, hateful, execrable, vile, nasty, unspeakable, woeful, *colloq.* terrible, horrid, hideous, dreadful, abominable, lousy, shocking, frightful, ghastly, wicked, accursed, infernal, foul, *sl.* rotten. **2** uncivilized, uncultivated, uncivil, rude, crude, uncouth, insensitive, vulgar, boorish, unrefined, coarse; cruel, inhuman, savage, barbaric, barbarous, bestial, brutal. □□ **beastliness** see *brutality* (BRUTAL).

beat /beet/ *v., n.,* & *adj.* ● *v.* (*past* **beat**; *past part.* **beaten** /béet'n/) **1** *tr.* **a** strike (a person or animal) persistently or repeatedly, esp. to harm or punish. **b** strike (a thing) repeatedly, e.g., to remove dust from (a carpet, etc.), or to sound (a drum, etc.). **2** *intr.* (foll. by *against, at, on,* etc.) a pound or knock repeatedly (*waves beat against the shore*; *beat at the door*). **b** = *beat down* 3. **3** *tr.* **a** overcome; surpass; win a victory over. **b** complete an activity before (another person, etc.). **c** be too hard for; perplex. **4** *tr.* (often foll. by *up*) stir (eggs, etc.) vigorously into a frothy mixture. **5** *tr.* (often foll. by *out*) fashion or shape (metal, etc.) by blows. **6** *intr.* (of the heart, a drum, etc.) pulsate rhythmically. **7** *tr.* (often foll. by *out*) **a** indicate (a tempo or rhythm) by gestures, tapping, etc. **b** sound (a signal, etc.) by striking a drum or other means (*beat a tattoo*). **8 a** *intr.* (of a bird's wings) move up and down. **b** *tr.* cause (wings) to move in this way. **9** *tr.* make (a path, etc.) by trampling. **10** *tr.* strike (bushes, etc.) to rouse game. **11** *intr. Naut.* sail in the direction from which the wind is blowing. ● *n.* **1 a** a main accent or rhythmic unit in music or verse (*three beats to the bar*; *missed a beat and came in early*). **b** the indication of rhythm by a conductor's movements (*watch the beat*). **c** the tempo or rhythm of a piece of music as indicated by the repeated fall of the main beat. **d** (in popular music) a strong rhythm. **e** (*attrib.*) characterized by a strong rhythm (*beat music*). **2 a** a stroke or blow (e.g., on a drum). **b** a measured sequence of strokes (*the beat of the waves on the rocks*). **c** a throbbing movement or sound (*the beat of his heart*). **3 a** a route or area allocated to a police officer, etc. **b** a person's habitual round. **4** *Physics* a pulsation due to the combination of two sounds or electric currents of similar but not equivalent frequencies. **5** *colloq.* = BEATNIK. **6** *Naut.* an instance of beating. ● *adj.* **1** (*predic.*) *sl.* exhausted; tired out. **2** (*attrib.*) of the beat generation or its philosophy. □ **beat about** (often foll. by *for*) search (for an excuse, etc.). **beat around** (or **about**) **the bush** discuss a matter without coming to the point. **beat the bounds** *Brit.* mark parish boundaries by striking certain points with rods. **beat one's breast** strike one's chest in anguish or sorrow. **beat the clock** complete a task within a stated time. **beat down 1 a** bargain with (a seller) to lower the price. **b** cause a seller to lower (the price). **2** strike (a resisting object) until it falls (*beat the door down*). **3** (of the sun, rain, etc.)

radiate heat or fall continuously and vigorously. **beat the drum for** publicize; promote. **beaten at the post** defeated at the last moment. **beat generation** the members of a movement of young people esp. in the 1950s who rejected conventional society in their dress, habits, and beliefs. **beat in** crush. **beat it** *sl.* go away. **beat off** drive back (an attack, etc.). **beat a retreat** withdraw; abandon an undertaking. **beat time** indicate or follow a musical tempo with a baton or other means. **beat a person to it** arrive or achieve something before another person. **beat up** give a beating to, esp. with punches and kicks. **beat-up** *adj. colloq.* dilapidated; in a state of disrepair. **it beats me** I do not understand (it). □□ **beatable** *adj.* [OE *bēatan* f. Gmc]
■ *v.* **1** strike, pound, bash, batter, baste, pummel, pommel, belabor, pelt, clout, thrash, trounce, give a person a thrashing *or* beating, drub, thump, cane, scourge, whip, flail, strap, bludgeon, club, cudgel, leather, flog, lash, welt, *archaic or literary* smite, *colloq.* manhandle, whack, thwack, give a person a good hiding *or* licking, lambaste, whale, *sl.* clobber, whop, wallop, belt, paste, tan a person's hide, give a person a going-over. **2 a** pound, knock, dash, strike, hit, rap, bang, hammer; (*beat against*) break against. **3 a** defeat, worst, win (out) over, trounce, rout, break, outdo, subdue, overcome, overwhelm, surpass, outstrip, conquer, crush, master, get the better *or* best of, thrash, scalp, *archaic* confound, *colloq.* lick, best, slaughter, pull the plug on, knock *or* take the stuffing out of, take apart, cream, *literary* vanquish, *sl.* crucify, clobber, whip, whop, skunk, shellac. **b** preempt. **c** see PERPLEX 1. **4** mix, whip (up), stir (up), blend (together). **5** hammer (out), forge, shape, form, fashion, make, mold, work. **6** throb, pulsate, pulse, palpitate, pound, thump, hammer. **8** flap, flutter. **9** tread, wear, trample. **11** *Naut.* tack. ● *n.* **1 a** accent, stress; throb, pulsation. **c** rhythm, tempo, measure, cadence, time, timing, pulse. **2 a** stroke, blow, rap. **b** rhythm, cadence. **c** throb, thump, pulse, pulsation, palpitation, throbbing. **3** course, round, tour, route, circuit, run, path; area, zone, territory, *Law* bailiwick. ● *adj.* **1** exhausted, spent, beaten, drained, worn out, played out, weary, bone-tired, dog-tired, tired out, fatigued, ragged, shattered, esp. *Brit.* whacked, *colloq.* all in, done in, dead beat, shot, fagged (out), frazzled, pooped, tuckered (out), *Brit. sl.* knackered. □ **beat about** see SEARCH *v.* 4. **beat around the bush** see PUSSYFOOT 2. **beat one's breast** see GRIEVE¹ 2. **beat down 1** knock *or* bring down. **2** knock *or* batter *or* pound *or* bash down. **3** blaze, shine, burn. **beat the drum for** see PROMOTE 3. **beat it** go away, depart, leave, abscond, run off *or* away, take oneself off, hit the road, *colloq.* push off, be off, clear off *or* out, scram, *sl.* buzz off, shove off, kiss off, get lost, *sl.* go on the lam, vamoose, skiddoo. **beat off** drive off *or* away *or* back, rout, put to rout, repel, fight off, ward off, *Mil.* repulse. **beat a retreat** see WITHDRAW 5. **beat-up** see DILAPIDATED. **it beats me** see *ask me another*.

beaten /béet'n/ *adj.* **1** outwitted; defeated. **2** exhausted; dejected. **3** (of gold or any other metal) shaped by a hammer. **4** (of a path, etc.) well-trodden; much used. □ **off the beaten track** (or **path**) **1** in or into an isolated place. **2** unusual. [past part. of BEAT]

beater /béetər/ *n.* **1** a person employed to rouse game for shooting. **2** an implement used for beating (esp. a carpet or eggs). **3** a person who beats metal.
■ **2** see WHISK *n.* 2.

beatific /béeətifik/ *adj.* **1** *colloq.* blissful (*a beatific smile*). **2 a** of or relating to blessedness. **b** making blessed. □□ **beatifically** *adv.* [F *béatifique* or L *beatificus* f. *beatus* blessed]

/.../ **pronunciation**	● **part of speech**
□ **phrases, idioms, and compounds**	
□□ **derivatives**	■ **synonym section**
cross-references appear in SMALL CAPITALS or *italics*	

■ **1** see ECSTATIC 3. **2** see SAINTLY.

beatification /beeátifikáyshən/ *n.* **1** *RC Ch.* the act of formally declaring a dead person "blessed," often a step toward canonization. **2** making or being blessed. [F *béatification* or eccl.L *beatificatio* (as BEATIFY)]

beatify /beeátifī/ *v.tr.* (**-ies, -ied**) **1** *RC Ch.* announce the beatification of. **2** make happy. [F *béatifier* or eccl.L *beatificare* f. L *beatus* blessed]

■ **1** see SANCTIFY 1.

beating /beéting/ *n.* **1** a physical punishment or assault. **2** a defeat. □ **take some** (or **a lot of**) **beating** be difficult to surpass.

beatitude /beeátitōōd, -tyōōd/ *n.* **1** blessedness. **2** (in *pl.*) the declarations of blessedness in Matt. 5:3–11. **3** a title given to patriarchs in the Orthodox Church. [F *béatitude* or L *beatitudo* f. *beatus* blessed]

beatnik /beétnik/ *n.* a member of the beat generation (see BEAT). [BEAT + *-nik* after *sputnik*, perh. infl. by US use of Yiddish *-nik* agent suffix]

beau /bō/ *n.* (*pl.* **beaux** or **beaus** /bōz, bō/) **1** an admirer; a boyfriend. **2** a fop; a dandy. [F, = handsome, f. L *bellus*]

■ **1** see ADMIRER 1. **2** see DANDY *n.* 1.

Beaufort scale /bṓfərt/ *n.* a scale of wind speed ranging from 0 (calm) to 12 (hurricane). [Sir F. *Beaufort*, Engl. admiral d. 1857]

beau geste /bō zhést/ *n.* (*pl.* **beaux gestes** *pronunc.* same) a generous or gracious act. [F, = splendid gesture]

■ see FAVOR *n.* 1.

beau ideal /bṓ ideéəl/ *n.* (*pl.* **beau ideals** /bṓ ideéəlz/) the highest type of excellence or beauty. [F *beau idéal* = ideal beauty: see BEAU, IDEAL]

■ see PARAGON.

Beaujolais /bṓzhəlay/ *n.* a red or white burgundy wine from the Beaujolais district of France. □ **Beaujolais nouveau** /nōōvṓ/ Beaujolais wine sold in the first year of a vintage.

beau monde /bō mónd, máwnd/ *n.* fashionable society. [F]

■ see SOCIETY 5a.

beaut /byōōt/ *n. & adj. sl.* ● *n.* an excellent or beautiful person or thing. ● *adj. Austral. & NZ* excellent; beautiful. [abbr. of BEAUTY]

beauteous /byōōteeəs/ *adj. poet.* beautiful. [ME f. BEAUTY + -OUS, after *bounteous, plenteous*]

■ see FAIR¹ *adj.* 6.

beautician /byōōtíshən/ *n.* **1** a person who gives beauty treatment. **2** a person who runs or owns a beauty salon.

beautiful /byōōtifŏŏl/ *adj.* **1** delighting the aesthetic senses (*a beautiful voice*). **2** pleasant; enjoyable (*had a beautiful time*). **3** excellent (*a beautiful specimen*). □□ **beautifully** *adv.*

■ **1** attractive, charming, comely, lovely, good-looking, fair, pretty, alluring, appealing, exquisite, handsome, radiant, gorgeous, divine, aesthetic, *Sc. & No. of Engl.* bonny, *colloq.* smashing, *literary* pulchritudinous, *poet.* beauteous; scenic, picturesque. **2** see PLEASANT. **3** excellent, first-rate, unequaled, fine, skillful, admirable, ideal, superb, spectacular, splendid, beyond comparison, first-class, marvelous, remarkable, superlative, wonderful, rip-roaring, incomparable, superior, sovereign, exquisite, elegant, *colloq.* smashing, swinging, magnificent, tremendous, grand, terrific, out of sight, out of this world, way-out, A1, divine, capital, swell, *literary* beyond compare, *sl.* cool, bang-up, wicked, copacetic, cracking, beaut, *archaic sl.* spiffing, *Austral. sl.* bonzer, *sl. esp. Brit.* wizard, *Brit. archaic sl.* topping. □□ **beautifully** attractively, exquisitely, gorgeously, charmingly, prettily, alluringly, handsomely, radiantly, divinely, appealingly, fashionably, delightfully, elegantly, chicly; scenically, picturesquely; splendidly, admirably, superbly, excellently, wonderfully, marvelously, remarkably, superlatively, elegantly, *Sc. & No. of Engl.* bonnily, *colloq.* smashingly, brilliantly, fantastically, magnificently, tremendously, capitally.

beautify /byōōtifī/ *v.tr.* (**-ies, -ied**) make beautiful; adorn. □□ **beautification** /-fikáyshən/ *n.* **beautifier** /-fīər/ *n.*

■ adorn, embellish, decorate, ornament, elaborate, garnish, deck (out), bedeck, smarten (up), *colloq.* titivate. □□ **beautification** see *embellishment* (EMBELLISH). **beautifier** embellisher, decorator, elaborator.

beauty /byōōtee/ *n.* (*pl.* **-ies**) **1 a** a combination of qualities such as shape, color, etc., that pleases the aesthetic senses, esp. the sight. **b** a combination of qualities that pleases the intellect or moral sense (*the beauty of the argument*). **2** *colloq.* **a** an excellent specimen (*what a beauty!*). **b** an attractive feature; an advantage (*that's the beauty of it!*). **3** a beautiful woman. □ **beauty is only skin-deep** a pleasing appearance is not a guide to character. **beauty parlor** (or **salon** or **shop**) an establishment in which manicure, hairdressing, makeup, etc., are offered to women. **beauty queen** the woman judged most beautiful in a competition. **beauty sleep 1** sleep before midnight, supposed to be health-giving. **2** any sleep, esp. extra sleep. **beauty spot 1** a place known for its beauty. **2** a small natural or artificial mark such as a mole on the face, considered to enhance another feature. **beauty treatment** cosmetic treatment received in a beauty parlor. [ME f. AF *beuté*, OF *bealté*, *beauté*, ult. f. L (as BEAU)]

■ **1** loveliness, attractiveness, handsomeness, comeliness, fairness, prettiness, gorgeousness, charm(s), *literary* pulchritude; picturesqueness, aestheticism, elegance, exquisiteness, grandeur, fineness, splendor, radiance, splendidness, gracefulness, delicacy, glory, glamour. **2 a** perfect specimen, jewel, pearl, gem, dream, winner, crème de la crème, treasure, prize, chef d'œuvre, masterpiece, *colloq.* stunner, smasher, knockout, *sl.* corker, gasser, beaut. **b** attraction, appeal, charm, allure, draw, lure, seductiveness, pull; strength, advantage, asset, benefit, boon, selling point, plus, added extra. **3** belle, vision, beauty queen, picture, good-looker, peach, *archaic* fair, *colloq.* looker, knockout, smasher, dreamboat, a fair treat, stunner, beaut, *poet.* Venus, *sl.* bombshell, fox, dish, *Brit. sl.* cracker, bit of all right. □ **beauty is only skin-deep** all that glitters is not gold.

beaux *pl.* of BEAU.

beaux arts /bōz aár/ *n.pl.* **1** fine arts. **2** (*attrib.*) relating to the rules and conventions of the École des Beaux-Arts in Paris (later called Académie des Beaux Arts). [F *beaux-arts*]

beaver¹ /beévər/ *n. & v.* ● *n.* (*pl.* same or **beavers**) **1 a** any large amphibious broad-tailed rodent of the genus *Castor*, native to N. America, Europe, and Asia, and able to cut down trees and build dams. **b** its soft light-brown fur. **c** a hat of this. **2** (in full **beaver cloth**) a heavy woolen cloth like beaver fur. ● *v.intr. Brit. colloq.* (usu. foll. by *away*) work hard. □ **eager beaver** *colloq.* an over-zealous person. [OE *be(o)for* f. Gmc]

■ □ **eager beaver** fanatic, zealot, workaholic, *colloq.* buff, freak, maniac, *sl.* fiend, nut.

beaver² /beévər/ *n. hist.* the lower face-guard of a helmet. [OF *baviere* bib f. *baver* slaver f. *beve* saliva f. Rmc]

beaver³ /beévər/ *n. Brit. sl.* a bearded man. [20th c.: orig. uncert.]

Beaverboard /beévərbawrd/ *n. propr.* a kind of fiberboard. [BEAVER¹ + BOARD]

bebop /beébop/ *n.* a type of jazz originating in the 1940s and characterized by complex harmony and rhythms. □□ **bebopper** *n.* [imit. of the typical rhythm]

becalm /bikaám/ *v.tr.* (usu. in *passive*) deprive (a ship) of wind.

became *past* of BECOME.

because /bikáwz, -kúz/ *conj.* for the reason that; since. □ **because of** on account of; by reason of. [ME f. BY *prep.* + CAUSE, after OF *par cause de* by reason of]

■ for, since, as, inasmuch as, seeing that, owing or due to the fact that.

béchamel /béshəmel/ *n.* a kind of thick white sauce. [invented by the Marquis de *Béchamel*, Fr. courtier d. 1703]

bêche-de-mer /béshdəmáir/ *n.* (*pl.* same or **bêches-de-mer** *pronunc.* same) **1** = TREPANG. **2** = BEACH-LA-MAR. [F, alt. of *biche de mer* f. Port. *bicho do mar* sea worm]

beck[1] /bek/ *n. No. of Engl.* a brook; a mountain stream. [ME f. ON *bekkr* f. Gmc]

beck[2] /bek/ *n.* a gesture requesting attention, e.g., a nod, wave, etc. □ **at a person's beck and call** having constantly to obey a person's orders. [*beck* (v.) f. BECKON]
■ □ **at a person's beck and call** see UNDER *prep.* 3a.

becket /békit/ *n. Naut.* a contrivance such as a hook, bracket, or rope loop, for securing loose ropes, tackle, or spars. [18th c.: orig. unkn.]

beckon /békən/ *v.* **1** *tr.* attract the attention of; summon by gesture. **2** *intr.* (usu. foll. by *to*) make a signal to attract a person's attention; summon a person by doing this. [OE *bīecnan, bēcnan* ult. f. WG *baukna* BEACON]
■ **1** summon, call, *archaic or literary* bid. **2** signal, gesture, motion, sign, gesticulate.

becloud /biklówd/ *v.tr.* **1** obscure (*becloud the argument*). **2** cover with clouds.
■ see OBSCURE *v.* 1, 2.

become /bikúm/ *v.* (*past* **became** /bikáym/; *past part.* **become**) **1** *intr.* (foll. by compl.) begin to be; come to be; turn into (*became president; will become famous; tadpoles become frogs*). **2** *tr.* **a** look well on; suit (*blue becomes him*). **b** befit (*it ill becomes you to complain*). **3** *intr.* (as **becoming** *adj.*) **a** flattering the appearance. **b** suitable; decorous. □ **become of** happen to (*what will become of me?*). □□ **becomingly** *adj.* **becomingness** *n.* [OE *becuman* f. Gmc: cf. BE-, COME]
■ **1** be; turn, grow, get, fall; turn *or* change *or* transform *or* metamorphose into, grow *or* develop *or* evolve into, mature *or* ripen into. **2** look good *or* well on, suit; fit, befit, be proper *or* appropriate *or* suitable, *formal* behoove. **3** (**becoming**)**a** flattering, seemly; attractive, fetching, chic, stylish, fashionable, tasteful. **b** appropriate, apt, fitting, fit, befitting, proper, suitable, well-suited, *archaic* meet; see also DECOROUS. □ **become of** come of, happen to, *archaic* hap to, *poet.* befall, betide. □□ **becomingly** flatteringly, attractively, fetchingly, stylishly, tastefully. **becomingness** see PROPRIETY 1.

B.Ed. *abbr.* Bachelor of Education.

bed /bed/ *n. & v.* ● *n.* **1 a** a piece of furniture used for sleeping in, usu. a framework with a mattress and coverings. **b** such a mattress, with or without coverings. **2** any place used by a person or animal for sleep or rest; a litter. **3 a** a garden plot, esp. one used for planting flowers. **b** a place where other things may be grown (*osier bed*). **4** the use of a bed: **a** *colloq.* for sexual intercourse. **b** for rest. **5** something flat, forming a support or base as in: **a** the bottom of the sea or a river. **b** the foundations of a road or railroad. **c** the slates, etc., on a billiard table. **6** a stratum, such as a layer of oysters, etc. ● *v.* (**bedded, bedding**) **1** *tr. & intr.* (usu. foll. by *down*) put or go to bed. **2** *tr. colloq.* have sexual intercourse with. **3** *tr.* (usu. foll. by *out*) plant in a garden bed. **4** *tr.* cover up or fix firmly in something. **5 a** *tr.* arrange as a layer. **b** *intr.* be or form a layer. □ **bed and board 1** lodging and food. **2** marital relations. **bed and breakfast 1** one night's lodging and breakfast in a hotel, etc. **2** an establishment that provides this. **bed linen** *n.* sheets and pillowcases. **bed rest** confinement of an invalid to bed. **bed of roses** a life of ease. **bed table** a portable table or tray with legs used by a person sitting up in bed. **brought to bed** (often foll. by *of*) *archaic* delivered of a child. **get out of bed on the wrong side** be bad-tempered all day long. **go to bed 1** retire for the night. **2** have sexual intercourse. **3** (of a newspaper) go to press. **keep one's bed** *Brit.* stay in bed because of illness. **make the bed** arrange the bed for use. **make one's bed and lie in it** accept the consequences of one's acts. **put to bed 1** cause to go to bed. **2** make (a newspaper) ready for press. **take to one's bed** stay in bed because of illness. [OE *bed(d), beddian* f. Gmc]
■ *n.* **3 a** see BORDER *n.* 4. **5 a** see BOTTOM *n.* 4. **6** see SEAM *n.* 4. ● *v.* **2** see LAY[1] *v.* 16. **3** see PLANT *v.* 1.

bedabble /bidábəl/ *v.tr.* stain or splash with dirty liquid, blood, etc.
■ see DABBLE 3.

bedad /bidád/ *int. Ir.* by God! [corrupt.: cf. GAD[2]]

bedaub /bidáwb/ *v.tr.* smear or daub with paint, etc.; decorate gaudily.
■ see SMEAR *v.* 1.

bedazzle /bidázəl/ *v.tr.* **1** dazzle. **2** confuse (a person). □□ **bedazzlement** *n.*
■ see DAZE *v.*

bedbug /bédbug/ *n.* either of two flat, wingless, evil-smelling insects of the genus *Cimex* infesting beds and houses and sucking blood.

bedchamber /bédchaymbər/ *n. archaic* a bedroom.

bedclothes /bédklōthz, -klōz/ *n.pl.* coverings for a bed, such as sheets, blankets, etc.
■ see COVER *n.* 1f.

beddable /bédəbəl/ *adj. colloq.* sexually attractive; able to be seduced. [BED + -ABLE]

bedder /bédər/ *n.* **1** a plant suitable for a garden bed. **2** a bedmaker.

bedding /béding/ *n.* **1** a mattress and bedclothes. **2** litter for cattle, horses, etc. **3** a bottom layer. **4** *Geol.* the stratification of rocks, esp. when clearly visible. □ **bedding plant** a plant suitable for a garden bed.
■ **1** see COVER *n.* 1f.

bedeck /bidék/ *v.tr.* adorn.
■ see DECORATE 1, 3.

bedeguar /bédigaar/ *n.* a mosslike growth on rose bushes produced by a gall wasp. [F *bédegar* f. Pers. *bād-āwar* wind brought]

bedel /beed'l, bidél/ *n.* (also **bedell**) *Brit.* a university official with chiefly processional duties. [= BEADLE]

bedevil /bidévəl/ *v.tr.* (**bedeviled, bedeviling**) **1** plague; afflict. **2** confound; confuse. **3** possess as if with a devil; bewitch. **4** treat with diabolical violence or abuse. □□ **bedevilment** *n.*
■ **1** see PESTER. **3** see OBSESS.

bedew /bidōō, -dyōō/ *v.tr.* **1** cover or sprinkle with dew or drops of water. **2** *poet.* sprinkle with tears.
■ **1** see DAMPEN 1.

bedfellow /bédfelō/ *n.* **1** a person who shares a bed. **2** an associate.

Bedford cord /bédfərd/ *n.* a tough woven fabric having prominent ridges, similar to corduroy. [*Bedford* in S. England]

bedight /bidít/ *adj. archaic* arrayed; adorned. [ME past part. of *bedight* (v.) (as BE-, DIGHT)]

bedim /bidím/ *v.tr.* (**bedimmed, bedimming**) *poet.* make (the eyes, mind, etc.) dim.
■ see OBSCURE *v.* 1, 2.

bedizen /bidíz'n, -dízən/ *v.tr. poet.* deck out gaudily. [BE- + obs. *dizen* deck out]

bedjacket /bédjakit/ *n.* a jacket worn when sitting up in bed.

bedlam /bédləm/ *n.* **1** a scene of uproar and confusion. **2** *archaic* a madhouse; an asylum. [hospital of St. Mary of *Bethlehem* in London]
■ **1** pandemonium, uproar, chaos, hubbub, commotion, confusion, tumult, turmoil, furor, *colloq.* madhouse, *sl.* snafu. **2** (mental) asylum, (mental) institution, mental home *or* hospital, *archaic or colloq.* madhouse, *hist.* lunatic asylum, *sl.* loony bin, nuthouse, funny farm, booby hatch.

Bedlington terrier /bédlingtən/ *n.* **1** a terrier of a breed with narrow head, long legs, and curly gray hair. **2** this breed. [*Bedlington* in Northumberland]

bedmaker /bédmaykər/ *n.* **1** a person who makes beds. **2** *Brit.* a person employed to clean students' rooms in a college.

Bedouin /bédōōin/ *n. & adj.* (also **Beduin**) (*pl.* same) ● *n.* **1** a nomadic Arab of the desert. **2** a wanderer; a nomad. ● *adj.* **1** of or relating to the Bedouin. **2** wandering; nomadic.

/. . . ./ **pronunciation**	● **part of speech**
□ **phrases, idioms, and compounds**	
□□ **derivatives**	■ **synonym section**
cross-references appear in SMALL CAPITALS or *italics*	

[ME f. OF *beduin* ult. f. Arab. *badwiyyīn* (oblique case) dwellers in the desert f. *badw* desert]

bedpan /bédpan/ *n.* a receptacle used by a bedridden patient for urine and feces.

bedplate /bédplayt/ *n.* a metal plate forming the base of a machine, etc.

bedpost /bédpōst/ *n.* any of the four upright supports of a bedstead. □ **between you and me and the bedpost** *colloq.* in strict confidence.

bedraggle /bidrágəl/ *v.tr.* **1** (often as **bedraggled** *adj.*) wet (a dress, etc.) by trailing it, or so that it hangs limp. **2** (as **bedraggled** *adj.*) untidy; disheveled. [BE- + DRAGGLE]
■ (**bedraggled**) **1** wet, sloppy, soaking (wet), sopping (wet), wringing wet, soaked, drenched. **2** untidy, disheveled, scruffy, messy, unkempt, rumpled, disorderly, ragged, raggedy, ungroomed; soiled, dirty, muddy, muddied.

bedridden /bédrid'n/ *adj.* **1** confined to bed by infirmity. **2** decrepit. [OE *bedreda* f. *ridan* ride]

bedrock /bédrok/ *n.* **1** solid rock underlying alluvial deposits, etc. **2** the underlying principles or facts of a theory, character, etc.

bedroll /bédrōl/ *n.* portable bedding rolled into a bundle, esp. a sleeping bag.

bedroom /bédrōōm, -rŏŏm/ *n.* **1** a room for sleeping in. **2** (*attrib.*) of or referring to sexual relations (*bedroom comedy*).
■ **1** see CHAMBER 3. **2** (*attrib.*) see SEXY 1.

bedside /bédsīd/ *n.* **1** the space beside esp. a patient's bed. **2** (*attrib.*) of or relating to the side of a bed (*bedside lamp*). □ **bedside manner** (of a doctor) an approach or attitude to a patient.

bedsitter /bédsítər/ *n.* (also **bedsit**) *Brit. colloq.* = BEDSITTING ROOM. [contr.]

bedsitting room /bédsíting/ *n. Brit.* a one-room unit of accommodation usu. consisting of combined bedroom and sitting room with cooking facilities.

bedsock /bédsok/ *n.* each of a pair of thick socks worn in bed.

bedsore /bédsawr/ *n.* a sore developed by an invalid because of pressure caused by lying in bed.

bedspread /bédspred/ *n.* an often decorative cloth used to cover a bed when not in use.
■ see SPREAD *n.* 10.

bedstead /bédsted/ *n.* the framework of a bed.

bedstraw /bédstraw/ *n.* **1** any herbaceous plant of the genus *Galium*, once used as straw for bedding. **2** (in full **Our Lady's bedstraw**) a bedstraw, *G. verum*, with yellow flowers.

bedtime /bédtīm/ *n.* **1** the usual time for going to bed. **2** (*attrib.*) of or relating to bedtime (*bedtime story*).

Beduin var. of BEDOUIN.

bedwetting /bédweting/ *n.* involuntary urination during the night.

bee /bee/ *n.* **1** any four-winged insect of the superfamily Apoidea which collects nectar and pollen, produces wax and honey, and lives in large communities. **2** any insect of a similar type. **3** (usu. **busy bee**) a busy person. **4** a meeting for communal work or amusement. □ **bee dance** a dance performed by worker bees to inform the colony of the location of food. **bee-eater** any brightly plumaged insect-eating bird of the family Meropidae with a long slender curved bill. **a bee in one's bonnet** an obsession. **bee orchid** a kind of European orchid, *Ophrys apifera*, with bee-shaped flowers. **the bee's knees** *old-fashioned sl.* something outstandingly good (*thinks he's the bee's knees*). [OE *bēo* f. Gmc]

beebread /bébred/ *n.* honey or pollen used as food by bees.

beech /beech/ *n.* **1** any large forest tree of the genus *Fagus*, having smooth gray bark and glossy leaves. **2** (also **beechwood**) its wood. **3** *Austral.* any of various similar trees in Australia. □ **beech fern** one of two ferns, *Thelypteris phagopteris* and *T. hexagonoptera*, found in damp woods. **beech marten** a white-breasted marten, *Martes foina*, of S. Europe and Asia. **beech mast** the small rough-skinned fruit of the beech tree. □□ **beechy** *adj.* [OE *bēce* f. Gmc]

beef /beef/ *n. & v.* ● *n.* **1** the flesh of the ox, bull, or cow for eating. **2** *colloq.* well-developed male muscle. **3** (*pl.*

beeves /beevz/ or **beefs**) a cow, bull, or ox fattened for beef; its carcass. **4** (*pl.* **beefs**) *sl.* a complaint; a protest. ● *v.intr. sl.* complain. □ **beef tea** esp. *Brit.* boiled extract of beef, given to invalids. **beef up** *sl.* strengthen; reinforce; augment. [ME f. AF, OF *boef* f. L *bos bovis* ox]
■ *n.* **4** see PROTEST *n.* 1. ● *v.* see COMPLAIN 1.

beefburger /beéfbərgər/ *n.* = HAMBURGER.

beefcake /beéfkayk/ *n. sl.* well-developed male muscles, esp. when photographed and displayed for admiration.

beefeater /beéfeetər/ *n.* a warder in the Tower of London; a Yeoman of the Guard. [f. obs. sense 'well-fed menial']

beefsteak /beéfstáyk/ *n.* a thick slice of lean beef, esp. from the rump, usu. for grilling or frying. □ **beefsteak fungus** a red edible fungus, *Fistulina hepatica*, resembling beef.

beefwood /beéfwŏŏd/ *n.* **1** any of various Australian and W. Indian hardwood trees. **2** the close-grained red timber of these.

beefy /beéfee/ *adj.* (**beefier, beefiest**) **1** like beef. **2** solid; muscular. □□ **beefily** *adv.* **beefiness** *n.*
■ **2** see BRAWNY.

beehive /beéhīv/ *n.* **1** an artificial habitation for bees. **2** a busy place. **3** anything resembling a wicker beehive in being domed.

beekeeper /beékeepər/ *n.* a keeper of bees.

beekeeping /beékeeping/ *n.* the occupation of keeping bees.

beeline /beélīn/ *n.* a straight line between two places. □ **make a beeline for** hurry directly to.

Beelzebub /bee-élzibub/ *n.* the Devil. [OE f. L f. Gk *beelzeboub* & Heb. *ba'al zᵉbûb* lord of the flies, name of a Philistine god]
■ see DEVIL *n.* 1, 2.

been *past part.* of BE.

beep /beep/ *n. & v.* ● *n.* **1** the sound of an automobile horn. **2** any similar high-pitched noise. ● *v.intr.* emit a beep. [imit.]

beeper /beépər/ *n.* an electronic device that receives signals and emits a beep to summon the person carrying it to the telephone, etc.

beer /beer/ *n.* **1 a** an alcoholic drink made from yeast-fermented malt, etc., flavored with hops. **b** a glass, can, or bottle of this, esp. (*Brit.*) a pint or half-pint. **2** any of several other fermented drinks, e.g., ginger beer, birch beer. □ **beer and skittles** *Brit.* amusement (*life is not all beer and skittles*). **beer-cellar** an underground room for storing beer. **2** a basement or cellar for selling or drinking beer. **beer engine** *Brit.* = **beer pump**. **beer garden** a garden or outdoor bar where beer is sold and drunk. **beer hall** a large room where beer is sold and drunk. **beer pump** a machine that draws up beer from a barrel or keg. **beer-up** *Austral. colloq.* a beer-drinking party or session. [OE *bēor* f. LL *biber* drink f. L *bibere*]
■ **1 a** ale, lager, stout.

beerhouse /beérhows/ *n. Brit.* a bar licensed to sell beer, ale, etc., but not hard liquor.

beery /beéree/ *adj.* (**beerier, beeriest**) **1** showing the influence of drink in one's appearance or behavior. **2** smelling or tasting of beer. □□ **beerily** *adv.* **beeriness** *n.*

beestings /beéstingz/ *n.pl.* (also treated as *sing.*) the first milk (esp. of a cow) after giving birth. [OE *bēsting* (implied by *bēost*), of unkn. orig.]

beeswax /beézwaks/ *n. & v.* ● *n.* **1** the wax secreted by bees to make honeycombs. **2** this wax refined and used to polish wood. ● *v.tr.* polish (furniture, etc.) with beeswax.

beeswing /beézwing/ *n.* a filmy second crust on old port.

beet /beet/ *n.* any plant of the genus *Beta* with an edible root (see BEETROOT, *sugar beet*). [OE *bēte* f. L *beta*, perh. of Celt. orig.]

beetle¹ /beét'l/ *n. & v.* ● *n.* **1** any insect of the order Coleoptera, with modified front wings forming hard protective cases closing over the back wings. **2** *colloq.* any similar, usu. black, insect. **3** *sl.* a type of compact rounded Volkswagen car. ● *v.intr. colloq.* (foll. by *about, away,* etc.) *Brit.* hurry; scurry. □ **beetle-crusher** *Brit. colloq.* a large boot or foot. [OE *bitula* biter f. *bītan* BITE]
■ **1, 2** see BUG *n.* 1.

beetle[2] /beet'l/ *n.* & *v.* ● *n.* **1** a tool with a heavy head and a handle, used for ramming, crushing, driving wedges, etc. **2** a machine used for heightening the luster of cloth by pressure from rollers. ● *v.tr.* **1** ram, crush, drive, etc., with a beetle. **2** finish (cloth) with a beetle. [OE *bētel* f. Gmc]

beetle[3] /beet'l/ *adj.* & *v.* ● *adj.* (esp. of the eyebrows) projecting; shaggy; scowling. ● *v.intr.* (usu. as **beetling** *adj.*) (of brows, cliffs, etc.) projecting; overhanging threateningly. □ **beetle-browed** with shaggy, projecting, or scowling eyebrows. [ME: orig. unkn.]
■ *v.* see PROJECT *v.* 2.

beetroot /beet'root, -ŏŏt/ *n.* esp. *Brit.* **1** a beet, *Beta vulgaris*, with an edible spherical dark red root. **2** this root used as a vegetable.

beeves *pl.* of BEEF.

BEF *abbr. hist.* British Expeditionary Force.

befall /bifáwl/ *v.* (*past* **befell** /bifél/; *past part.* **befallen** /bifáwlən/) *poet.* **1** *intr.* happen (*so it befell*). **2** *tr.* happen to (a person, etc.) (*what has befallen her?*). [OE *befeallan* (as BE-, *feallan* FALL)]
■ **1** see HAPPEN *v.* 1. **2** see HAPPEN *v.* 3.

befit /bifít/ *v.tr.* (**befitted**, **befitting**) **1** be fitted or appropriate for; suit. **2** be incumbent on. □□ **befitting** *adj.* **befittingly** *adv.*
■ be appropriate *or* suitable *or* fitting *or* apt for, suit; be required of, be incumbent on, be proper to *or* for, *formal* behoove. □□ **befitting** fitting, becoming, due, suitable, appropriate, apt, apropos, proper, seemly, correct, right, *archaic* meet. **befittingly** see *appropriately* (APPROPRIATE).

befog /bifáwg, -fóg/ *v.tr.* (**befogged**, **befogging**) **1** confuse; obscure. **2** envelop in fog.

befool /bifŏŏl/ *v.tr.* make a fool of; delude.

before /bifáwr/ *conj.*, *prep.*, & *adv.* ● *conj.* **1** earlier than the time when (*crawled before he walked*). **2** rather than that (*would starve before he stole*). ● *prep.* **1 a** in front of (*before her in the queue*). **b** ahead of (*crossed the line before him*). **c** under the impulse of (*recoil before the attack*). **d** awaiting (*the future before them*). **2** earlier than; preceding (*Lent comes before Easter*). **3** rather than (*death before dishonor*). **4 a** in the presence of (*appear before the judge*). **b** for the attention of (*a plan put before the committee*). ● *adv.* **1 a** earlier than the time in question; already (*heard it before*). **b** in the past (*happened long before*). **2** ahead (*go before*). **3** on the front (*hit before and behind*). □ **Before Christ** (of a date) reckoned backward from the birth of Christ. **before God** a solemn oath meaning 'as God sees me'. **before time** see TIME. [OE *beforan* f. Gmc]
■ *conj.* **1** previous to *or* preceding the time when, earlier than. ● *prep.* **1 a, b** ahead of, in advance of, in front of, forward of. **d** awaiting, waiting for, ahead of. **2** earlier than, at an earlier time than; preceding, previous to, anterior to, prior to, ahead of; on the eve of; ante-, pre-. **3** in preference to, rather than, sooner than, more willingly than; instead of, in place of, in lieu of. ● *adv.* **1** previously, earlier, already, beforehand. **b** formerly, in the past, in time(s) past, ago, back; once. **2** (up) ahead, in advance, in (the) front, in the forefront, first, in the lead *or* vanguard, *colloq.* up front.

beforehand /bifáwrhand/ *adv.* in anticipation; in advance; in readiness (*had prepared the meal beforehand*). □ **be beforehand with** anticipate; forestall. [ME f. BEFORE + HAND: cf. AF *avant main*]
■ see *in advance* (ADVANCE).

befoul /bifówl/ *v.tr. poet.* **1** make foul or dirty. **2** degrade; defile.
■ **1** see DIRTY *v.* **2** see DESECRATE.

befriend /bifrénd/ *v.tr.* act as a friend to; help.
■ see *fall in with* 1.

befuddle /bifúd'l/ *v.tr.* **1** make drunk. **2** confuse. □□ **befuddlement** *n.*
■ **1** see INTOXICATE 1. **2** see CONFUSE 1a.

beg /beg/ *v.* (**begged**, **begging**) **1 a** *intr.* ask for (esp. food, money, etc.) (*begged for alms*). **b** *tr.* ask for (food, money, etc.) as a gift. **c** *intr.* live by begging. **2** *tr.*

& *intr.* (usu. foll. by *for*, or *to* + infin.) ask earnestly or humbly (*begged for forgiveness; begged to be allowed out; please, I beg of you; beg your indulgence for a time*). **3** *tr.* ask formally for (*beg leave*). **4** *intr.* (of a dog, etc.) sit up with the front paws raised expectantly. **5** *tr.* take or ask leave (to do something) (*I beg to differ; beg to enclose*). □ **beg one's bread** live by begging. **begging bowl 1** a bowl, etc., held out for food or alms. **2** an earnest appeal for help. **beg off 1** decline to take part in or attend. **2** get (a person) excused from a penalty, etc. **beg pardon** see PARDON. **beg the question 1** assume the truth of an argument or proposition to be proved, without arguing it. **2** *disp.* pose the question. **3** *colloq.* evade a difficulty. **go begging** (or *Brit.* **a-begging**) (of a chance or a thing) not be taken; be unwanted. [ME prob. f. OE *bedecian* f. Gmc: rel. to BID]
■ **1 a** (*beg for*) see ASK 4. **b, c** beg one's bread, solicit, sponge, cadge, *colloq.* scrounge, panhandle, mooch, *sl.* bum, freeload. **2** entreat, beseech, plead (with), ask for, request, call on *or* upon, crave, implore, press, importune, appeal to, invoke, supplicate, pray, petition. **3** see ASK 4. □ **beg off 1** abstain from, decline to, take a rain check on, *colloq.* cry off. **go begging** be unwanted, be available, be there for the taking *or* asking.

begad /bigád/ *int. archaic colloq.* by God! [corrupt.: cf. GAD[2]]

began *past* of BEGIN.

begat *archaic past* of BEGET.

beget /bigét/ *v.tr.* (**begetting**; *past* **begot** /bigót/; *archaic* **begat** /bigát/; *past part.* **begotten** /bigót'n/) *literary* **1** (usu. of a father, sometimes of a father and mother) procreate. **2** give rise to; cause (*beget strife*). □□ **begetter** *n.* [OE *begietan*, formed as BE- + GET = procreate]
■ **1** see CREATE 1.

beggar /bégər/ *n.* & *v.* ● *n.* **1** a person who begs, esp. one who lives by begging. **2** a poor person. **3** *colloq.* a person; a fellow (*poor beggar*). ● *v.tr.* **1** reduce to poverty. **2** *Brit.* outshine. **3** exhaust the resources of (*beggar description*). □ **beggar-my-neighbor** (also **-your-**) **1** a card game in which a player seeks to capture an opponent's cards. **2** (*attrib.*) (esp. of national policy) self-aggrandizing at the expense of competitors. **beggars cannot** (or **must not**) **be choosers** those without other resources must take what is offered. [ME f. BEG + -AR[3]]
■ *n.* **1, 2** mendicant, sponger, tramp, vagrant, pauper, down-and-out, cadger, *colloq.* scrounger, have-not, panhandler, hobo, *sl.* schnorrer, freeloader, bum; supplicant, suppliant. **3** fellow, man, person, *Sc.* carl, *colloq.* chap, guy, codger, devil, lad, scout, *Brit. colloq.* johnny, *sl.* joker, dude, *sl. often derog.* gink, *Brit. sl.* bloke, old cock, josser, *Brit. sl. archaic* cove. ● *v.* **3** see EXCEED.

beggarly /bégərlee/ *adj.* **1** poverty-stricken; needy. **2** intellectually poor. **3** mean; sordid. **4** ungenerous. □□ **beggarliness** *n.*
■ **1** see PENURIOUS 1. **3** see PITIFUL 2. **4** see PALTRY.

beggary /bégəree/ *n.* extreme poverty.
■ see POVERTY 1.

begin /bigín/ *v.* (**beginning**; *past* **began** /bigán/; *past part.* **begun** /bigún/) **1** *tr.* perform the first part of; start (*begin work; begin crying; begin to understand*). **2** *intr.* come into being; arise: **a** in time (*the season began last week*). **b** in space (*your jurisdiction begins beyond the river*). **3** *tr.* (usu. foll. by *to* + infin.) start at a certain time (*then began to feel ill*). **4** *intr.* be begun (*the meeting will begin at 7*). **5** *intr.* a start speaking (*'No,' he began*). **b** take the first step; be the first to do something (*who wants to begin?*). **6** *intr. colloq.* (usu. with *neg.*) show any attempt or likelihood (*can't begin to compete*). □ **begin at** start from. **begin on** (or **upon**) set to work at. **begin school** attend school for the first time. **begin with** take (a

---

/.../ **pronunciation**	● **part of speech**
□ **phrases, idioms, and compounds**	
□□ **derivatives**	■ **synonym section**
cross-references appear in SMALL CAPITALS or *italics*	

subject, task, etc.) first or as a starting point. **to begin with** in the first place; as the first thing. [OE *beginnan* f. Gmc]

■ **1** start (out *or* off *or* in *or* on), initiate, enter on *or* upon, set out *or* about, set out on *or* upon, *formal* commence; inaugurate, get going, get off the ground, put into operation *or* motion. **2, 4** arise, start, originate, come into being, emerge, open, get under way, be inaugurated *or* initiated, get going, get off the ground, be put into operation *or* motion, *colloq.* kick off, *formal* commence. **5 b** take the first step, be first, set the ball rolling, *colloq.* get cracking, take the first crack *or* shot at. □ **to begin with** see *originally* (ORIGINAL).

beginner /bigínər/ *n.* a person just beginning to learn a skill, etc. □ **beginner's luck** good luck supposed to attend a beginner at games, etc.

beginning /bigíning/ *n.* **1** the time or place at which anything begins. **2** a source or origin. **3** the first part. □ **the beginning of the end** the first clear sign of a final result.

■ **1, 2** start, outset, onset, inception, dawn, dawning, birth, genesis, origin, creation, day one, *formal* commencement, *rhet.* birth; origination, source, well spring. **3** opening, start, inception, *formal* commencement; first part.

begone /bigáwn, -gón/ *int. poet.* go away at once!

■ see SHOO *int.*

begonia /bigónyə/ *n.* any plant of the genus *Begonia* with brightly colored sepals and no petals, and often having brilliant glossy foliage. [M. *Bégon*, Fr. patron of science d. 1710]

begorra /bigáwrə, -górə/ *int. Ir.* by God! [corrupt.]

begot *past* of BEGET.

begotten *past part.* of BEGET.

begrime /bigrím/ *v.tr.* make grimy.

■ see DIRTY *v.*

begrudge /bigrúj/ *v.tr.* **1** resent; be dissatisfied at. **2** envy (a person) the possession of. **3** be reluctant or unwilling to give (a thing to a person). □□ **begrudgingly** *adv.*

■ **1, 2** resent, feel envious *or* jealous about, feel embittered *or* bitter about, have hard feelings about, be disgruntled *or* dissatisfied at; envy, grudge. **3** grudge, give (be)grudgingly *or* unwillingly *or* reluctantly, deny, refuse. □□ **begrudgingly** unwillingly, grudgingly, under protest, reluctantly, without good grace; jealously, enviously.

beguile /bigíl/ *v.tr.* **1** charm; amuse. **2** divert attention pleasantly from (work, etc.). **3** (often foll. by *of*, *out of*, or *into* + verbal noun) delude; cheat (*beguiled him into paying*). □□ **beguilement** *n.* **beguiler** *n.* **beguiling** *adj.* **beguilingly** *adv.* [BE- + obs. *guile* to deceive]

■ **1** charm, divert, amuse, distract, fascinate, allure, seduce; captivate, enchant, enthral, entrance, enrapture, engross, engage, occupy, absorb. **3** delude, deceive, cheat, swindle, dupe, gull, fool, mislead, entrap, hoodwink, seduce, jockey, take in, have, *archaic* chicane, *colloq.* pull a fast one on, bamboozle, *literary* cozen, *sl.* con, bilk, chisel, cross, gyp, snow, bunco; (*beguile out of*) defraud of, deprive of. □□ **beguilement** see AMUSEMENT 2, TRICKERY. **beguiler** see *charmer* (CHARM), *swindler* (SWINDLE). **beguiling** see *enchanting* (ENCHANT). **beguilingly** charmingly, enchantingly, seductively, enticingly, winsomely, winningly, alluringly, engagingly.

beguine /bigéen/ *n.* **1** a popular dance of W. Indian origin. **2** its rhythm. [Amer. F f. F *béguin* infatuation]

begum /báygəm/ *n.* on the Indian subcontinent: **1** a Muslim lady of high rank. **2** (**Begum**) the title of a married Muslim woman, equivalent to Mrs. [Urdu *begam* f. E.Turk. *bīgam* princess, fem. of *big* prince: cf. BEY]

begun *past part.* of BEGIN.

behalf /biháf/ *n.* □ **on** (also **in**) **behalf of** (or **on a person's behalf**) **1** in the interests of (a person, principle, etc.). **2** as representative of (*acting on behalf of my client*). [mixture of earlier phrases *on his halve* and *bihalve him*, both = on his side: see BY, HALF]

■ in the interest of, for the benefit *or* advantage of, for, as a representative of, in place of, instead of, in the name of, on the part of.

behave /biháyv/ *v.* **1** *intr.* **a** act or react (in a specified way) (*behaved well*). **b** (esp. to or of a child) conduct oneself properly. **c** (of a machine, etc.) work well (or in a specified way) (*the computer is not behaving today*). **2** *refl.* (esp. of or to a child) show good manners (*behaved herself*). □ **behave toward** treat (in a specified way). **ill-behaved** having bad manners or conduct. **well-behaved** having good manners or conduct. [BE- + HAVE]

■ **1 a** act, react, function, operate, perform, work, do, conduct *or* deport *or* bear *or* demean *or* acquit oneself, *colloq.* play, *literary* comport oneself. **b** act obediently, act properly, be good, *sl.* keep one's nose clean. **c** work, operate, function. **2** see BEHAVE 1b above. □ **ill-behaved** see NAUGHTY 1, IMPOLITE. **well-behaved** good, orderly, well-mannered, obedient, well-bred, polite, proper, correct, decorous, seemly, civil, respectful, courteous, mannerly, *colloq.* house broken, *Brit. colloq.* house-trained, *joc.* couth.

behavior /biháyvyər/ *n.* (*Brit.* **behaviour**) **1 a** the way one conducts oneself; manners. **b** the treatment of others; moral conduct. **2** the way in which a ship, machine, chemical substance, etc., acts or works. **3** *Psychol.* the response (of a person, animal, etc.) to a stimulus. □ **behavior therapy** the treatment of neurotic symptoms by training the patient's reactions (see BEHAVIORISM). **be on one's good** (or **best**) **behavior** behave well when being observed. [BEHAVE after *demeanor* and obs. *haviour* f. *have*]

■ **1 a** conduct, demeanor, deportment, bearing, manners, action(s), *literary* comportment. **2** operation, action, performance, working, functioning.

behavioral /biháyvyərəl/ *adj.* (*Brit.* **behavioural**) of or relating to behavior. □ **behavioral science** the scientific study of human behavior (see BEHAVIORISM). □□ **behavioralist** *n.*

behaviorism /biháyvyərizəm/ *n.* (*Brit.* **behaviourism**) *Psychol.* **1** the theory that human behavior is determined by conditioning rather than by thoughts or feelings, and that psychological disorders are best treated by altering behavior patterns. **2** such study and treatment in practice. □□ **behaviorist** *n.* **behavioristic** /-rístik/ *adj.*

behead /bihéd/ *v.tr.* **1** cut off the head of (a person), esp. as a form of execution. **2** kill by beheading. [OE *behēafdian* (as BE-, *hēafod* HEAD)]

■ decapitate, guillotine, *formal* decollate.

beheld *past* and *past part.* of BEHOLD.

behemoth /biheeməth, beeə-/ *n.* an enormous creature or thing. [ME f. Heb. *bʰĕhēmôt* intensive pl. of *bʰēmāh* beast, perh. f. Egyptian *p-ehe-mau* water ox]

■ see JUMBO *n.*

behest /bihést/ *n. literary* a command; an entreaty (*went at his behest*). [OE *behǣs* f. Gmc]

■ see COMMAND *n.* 1.

behind /bihínd/ *prep., adv., & n.* ● *prep.* **1 a** in, toward, or to the rear of. **b** on the farther side of (*behind the bush*). **c** hidden by (*something behind that remark*). **2 a** in the past in relation to (*trouble is behind me now*). **b** late in relation to (*behind schedule*). **3** inferior to; weaker than (*behind the others in math*). **4 a** in support of (*she's right behind us*). **b** responsible for; giving rise to (*the person behind the project; the reasons behind his resignation*). **5** in the tracks of; following. ● *adv.* **1 a** in or to or toward the rear; farther back (*the street behind; glance behind*). **b** on the farther side (*a high wall with a field behind*). **2** remaining after departure (*leave behind; stay behind*). **3** (usu. foll. by *with*) **a** in arrears (*behind with the rent*). **b** late in accomplishing a task, etc. (*working too slowly and getting behind*). **4** in a weak position; backward (*behind in Latin*). **5** following (*his dog running behind*). ● *n.* **1** *colloq.* the buttocks. **2** (in Australian Rules Football) a kick, etc., scoring one point. □ **behind a person's back** without a person's knowledge. **behind the scenes** see SCENE. **behind time** late. **behind the times** old-fashioned; antiquated. **come from behind** win after being behind in scoring. **fall** (or **lag**) **behind** see FALL. **put behind one 1** refuse to consider. **2** get over (an unhappy experience, etc.).

[OE *behindan*, *bihindan* f. *bi* BY + *hindan* from behind, *hinder* below]

■ *prep.* **1 a, b** around the back of, in *or* at *or* to the rear of, on *or* to the other side of. **c** hidden *or* concealed by. **3** below, inferior to, weaker *or* worse *or* lower than. **4 a** in support of; at a person's back, supporting, seconding; see also *in favor* (FAVOR). **b** responsible for; for, explaining. **5** see *at a person's back* (BACK). ● *adv.* **1 a** see BACK *adv.* 1. **b** see BACK *adv.* 6. **3** in arrear(s), late, overdue, behindhand, belated, delinquent. ● *n.* **1** see BUTTOCK. □ **behind a person's back** surreptitiously, secretly, in secret, covertly, clandestinely, privately, furtively, sneakily, slyly, on the sly, *colloq.* on the q.t.; underhandedly, treacherously, traitorously, perfidiously, deceitfully, insidiously. **behind time** see LATE *adj.* 1. **behind the times** antiquated, old-fashioned, outdated, out-of-date, dated, outmoded, passé, obsolete, outworn, antique, rusty, moldy, *colloq.* fossilized, old hat, medieval, prehistoric, antediluvian. **put behind one 2** see *get over* 1.

behindhand /bihíndhand/ *adv. & predic.adj.* **1** (usu. foll. by *with, in*) late (in discharging a duty, paying a debt, etc.). **2** slow; backwards. [BEHIND + HAND: cf. BEFOREHAND]
■ see LATE *adj.* 1.

behold /bihóld/ *v.tr.* (*past & past part.* **beheld** /bihéld/) *literary* (esp. in *imper.*) see; observe. □□ **beholder** *n.* [OE *bihaldan* (as BE-, *haldan* hold)]
■ see, look at *or* upon, observe, regard, set *or* lay eyes on, gaze at *or* upon, watch, notice, note, spy, perceive, view, *colloq.* clap eyes on, *literary* descry, espy. □□ **beholder** see OBSERVER.

beholden /bihóldən/ *predic.adj.* (usu. foll. by *to*) under obligation. [past part. (obs. except in this use) of BEHOLD, = bound]
■ obliged, obligated, indebted, bound, grateful, in debt, under (an) obligation.

behoof /bihóof/ *n. archaic* (prec. by *to, for, on*; foll. by *of*) benefit; advantage. [OE *behōf*]
■ see PROFIT *n.* 1.

behoove /bihóov/ *v.tr.* (*Brit.* **behove** /-hóv/) (prec. by *it* as subject; foll. by *to* + infin.) **1** be incumbent on. **2** (usu. with *neg.*) befit (*ill behooves him to protest*). [OE *behōfian* f. *behōf*: see BEHOOF]
■ be required of, be incumbent on, be proper to *or* for, be fitting of *or* for, befit; be appropriate *or* suitable *or* apt for, suit; be advisable for, be worthwhile for, be expeditious for *or* of, be advantageous to *or* for, be useful to *or* for, be beneficial to *or* for.

beige /bayzh/ *n. & adj.* ● *n.* a pale sandy fawn color. ● *adj.* of this color. [F: orig. unkn.]
■ *adj.* see NEUTRAL *adj.* 3, 5.

being /beéing/ *n.* **1** existence. **2** the nature or essence (of a person, etc.) (*his whole being revolted*). **3** a human being. **4** anything that exists or is imagined. □ **in being** existing.
■ **1** see EXISTENCE 1. **2** see ESSENCE 1. **3** see PERSON. **4** see ENTITY 1.

bejabers /bijáybərz/ *int.* (also **bejabbers** /-jábərz/) *Ir.* by Jesus! [corrupt.]

bejeweled /bijóoəld/ *adj.* adorned with jewels.

bel /bel/ *n.* a unit used in the comparison of power levels in electrical communication or intensities of sound, corresponding to an intensity ratio of 10 to 1 (cf. DECIBEL). [A. G. Bell, inventor of telephone d. 1922]

belabor /biláybər/ *v.tr.* **1 a** thrash; beat. **b** attack verbally. **2** argue or elaborate (a subject) in excessive detail. [BE- + LABOR = exert one's strength]
■ **1 a** see BEAT *v.* 1. **b** see BERATE. **2** dissect, scrutinize, go over *or* through again, look at again; elaborate (on), enlarge *or* expand *or* expatiate on.

belated /biláytid/ *adj.* **1** coming late or too late. **2** *archaic* overtaken by darkness. □□ **belatedly** *adv.* **belatedness** *n.* [past part. of obs. *belate* delay (as BE-, LATE)]
■ **1** late; behind time, behindhand, out of date, overdue,

behind; delayed, detained. □□ **belatedly** see LATE *adv.* 1. **belatedness** lateness, tardiness.

belay /biláy/ *v. & n.* ● *v.* **1** *tr.* fix (a running rope) around a cleat, pin, rock, etc., to secure it. **2** *tr. & intr.* (usu. in *imper.*) *Naut. sl.* stop; enough! (esp. *belay there!*). ● *n.* **1** an act of belaying. **2** a spike of rock, etc., used for belaying. □ **belaying pin** a fixed wooden or iron pin used for fastening a rope around. [Du. *beleggen*]

bel canto /bel kántō, kaàn-/ *n.* **1** a lyrical style of operatic singing using a full rich broad tone and smooth phrasing. **2** (*attrib.*) (of a type of aria or voice) characterized by this type of singing. [It., = fine song]

belch /belch/ *v. & n.* ● *v.* **1** *intr.* emit wind noisily from the stomach through the mouth. **2** *tr.* **a** (of a chimney, volcano, gun, etc.) send (smoke, etc.) out or up. **b** utter forcibly. ● *n.* an act of belching. [OE *belcettan*]

beldam /béldəm, -dam/ *n.* (also **beldame**) *archaic* **1** an old woman; a hag. **2** a virago. [ME & OF *bel* beautiful + DAM², DAME]
■ see HAG¹.

beleaguer /bilé'egər/ *v.tr.* **1** besiege. **2** vex; harass. [Du. *belegeren* camp around (as BE-, *leger* a camp)]
■ **1** see BESIEGE 1. **2** see MOLEST 1.

belemnite /béləmnīt/ *n.* any extinct cephalopod of the order Belemnoidea, having a bullet-shaped internal shell often found in fossilized form. [mod.L *belemnites* f. Gk *belemnon* dart + -ITE¹]

bel esprit /bél espre'e/ *n.* (*pl.* **beaux esprits** /bőz espre'e/) a witty person. [F, lit. fine mind]

belfry /bélfree/ *n.* (*pl.* **-ies**) **1** a bell tower or steeple housing bells, esp. forming part of a church. **2** a space for hanging bells in a church tower. □ **bats in the belfry** see BAT². [ME f. OF *berfrei* f. Frank.: altered by assoc. with *bell*]
■ **1** see TOWER *n.* 1.

Belgian /béljən/ *n. & adj.* ● *n.* **1** a native or inhabitant of Belgium in W. Europe. **2** a person of Belgian descent. ● *adj.* of or relating to Belgium. □ **Belgian hare** a dark red long-eared breed of domestic rabbit.

Belgic /béljik/ *adj.* **1** of the ancient Belgae of N. Gaul. **2** of the Low Countries. [L *Belgicus* f. *Belgae*]

Belial /beéleeəl/ *n.* the Devil. [Heb. *bᵉliyya'al* worthless]
■ see DEVIL *n.* 1, 2.

belie /bilí/ *v.tr.* (**belying**) **1** give a false notion of; fail to corroborate (*its appearance belies its age*). **2 a** fail to fulfill (a promise, etc.). **b** fail to justify (a hope, etc.). [OE *belēogan* (as BE-, *lēogan* LIE²)]
■ **1** see MISREPRESENT.

belief /bile'ef/ *n.* **1 a** a person's religion; religious conviction (*has no belief*). **b** a firm opinion (*my belief is that he did it*). **c** an acceptance (of a thing, fact, statement, etc.) (*belief in the afterlife*). **2** (usu. foll. by *in*) trust or confidence. □ **beyond belief** incredible. **to the best of my belief** in my genuine opinion. [ME f. OE *gelēafa* (as BELIEVE)]
■ **1** religion, faith, conviction, creed, doctrine, dogma, principle(s), axiom, maxim, opinion, judgment, persuasion, tenet, view, idea, sentiment, intuition; acceptance, credence; assent. **2** trust, confidence, faith, conviction, certitude, certainty, sureness; reliance, security, assurance. □ **beyond belief** see INCREDIBLE 1. **to the best of my belief** as far as I know *or* can see *or* can tell, a priori.

believe /bilé'ev/ *v.* **1** *tr.* accept as true or as conveying the truth (*I believe it*; *don't believe him*; *believes what he is told*). **2** *tr.* think; suppose (*I believe it's raining*; *Mr. Smith, I believe?*). **3** *intr.* (foll. by *in*) **a** have faith in the existence of (*believes in God*). **b** have confidence in (a remedy, a person, etc.) (*believes in alternative medicine*). **c** have trust in the advisability of (*believes in telling the truth*). **4** *intr.* have (esp. religious) faith. □ **believe one's ears** (or **eyes**) accept that what one apparently hears or sees, etc., is true. **believe it or not** *colloq.* it is true though surprising. **make believe** (often foll. by *that* + clause, or *to* + infin.) pretend (*let's make believe that we're young again*). **would you believe it?** *colloq.* = *believe it or not.* □□ **believable** *adj.* **believability** /-leevabílitee/ *n.* [OE *belȳfan, belēfan,* with change of prefix f. *gelēfan* f. Gmc: rel. to LIEF]

■ **1** accept, put faith *or* credence in *or* into, find credible *or* believable, be convinced *or* assured of, take (it) as given *or* read. **2** think, suppose, assume, hold, maintain, feel, take it, allow, fancy, imagine. **3** (*believe in*) trust to *or* in, rely upon *or* on, have faith *or* confidence in, put one's trust in, be convinced *or* assured of, swear by, credit. **4** have faith; have found faith, have seen the light. □ **make believe** pretend, suppose, imagine, fancy, conjecture, assume, make out; playact. □□ **believable** see PLAUSIBLE 1.
believability credibility, feasibility, likelihood, conceivability, plausibility, tenability, dependability, reliability, trustworthiness, cogency.

believer /bileévər/ *n.* **1** an adherent of a specified religion. **2** a person who believes, esp. in the efficacy of something (*a great believer in exercise*).

belittle /bilít'l/ *v.tr.* **1** disparage; depreciate. **2** make small; dwarf. □□ **belittlement** *n.* **belittler** *n.* **belittlingly** *adv.*

■ disparage, decry, cry down, detract from, depreciate, trivialize, deprecate, degrade, denigrate, downgrade, discredit, criticize, pooh-pooh, put down, run down, undervalue, underestimate, underrate, slight, *colloq.* play down, trash, *formal* derogate; minimize, diminish, reduce, lessen. □□ **belittlement** disparagement, deprecation, depreciation, denigration, derogation; diminution. **belittler** decrier, deprecator, denigrator. **belittlingly** deprecatingly, disparagingly, depreciatingly, slightingly.

bell¹ /bel/ *n.* & *v.* ● *n.* **1** a hollow usu. metal object in the shape of a deep upturned cup usu. widening at the lip, made to sound a clear musical note when struck (either externally or by means of a clapper inside). **2 a** a sound or stroke of a bell, esp. as a signal. **b** (prec. by a numeral) *Naut.* the time as indicated every half hour of a watch by the striking of the ship's bell one to eight times. **3** anything that sounds like or functions as a bell, esp. an electronic device that rings, etc., as a signal. **4 a** any bell-shaped object or part, e.g., of a musical instrument. **b** the corolla of a flower when bell-shaped. **5** (in *pl.*) *Mus.* a set of cylindrical metal tubes of different lengths, suspended in a frame and played by being struck with a hammer. ● *v.tr.* **1** provide with a bell or bells; attach a bell to. **2** (foll. by *out*) form into the shape of the lip of a bell. □ **bell-bottom 1** a marked flare below the knee (of a pants leg). **2** (in *pl.*) pants with bell-bottoms. **bell-bottomed** having bell-bottoms. **bell buoy** a buoy equipped with a warning bell rung by the motion of the sea. **bell founder** a person who casts large bells in a foundry. **bell glass** a bell-shaped glass cover for plants. **bell jar** a bell-shaped glass cover or container for use in a laboratory. **bell metal** an alloy of copper and tin for making bells (the tin content being greater than in bronze). **bell pepper** a sweet pepper of the genus *Capsicum,* with a bell shape. **bell push** a button that operates an electric bell when pushed. **bell-ringer** a person who rings church bells or handbells. **bell-ringing** this as an activity. **bells and whistles** *colloq.* attractive but unnecessary additional features, esp. in computing. **bell the cat** perform a daring feat. **clear** (or **sound**) **as a bell** perfectly clear or sound. **give a person a bell** *Brit. colloq.* telephone a person. **ring a bell** *colloq.* revive a distant recollection; sound familiar. **saved by the bell 1** *Boxing* spared a knockout or further blows by the ringing of the bell signalling the end of a round. **2** spared trouble, an unwanted task, etc., by another claim on one's attention. **with bells on** eagerly and prepared for enjoyment (*I'll be there with bells on*). [OE *belle:* perh. rel. to BELL²]

■ *n.* **2 a** see ALARM *n.* 2a.

bell² /bel/ *n.* & *v.* ● *n.* the cry of a stag or buck at rutting time. ● *v.intr.* make this cry. [OE *bellan* bark, bellow]

belladonna /béladónə/ *n.* **1** *Bot.* a poisonous plant, *Atropa belladonna,* with purple flowers and purple-black berries. Also called *deadly nightshade.* **2** *Med.* a drug prepared from this. □ **belladonna lily** a S. African amaryllis with white or pink flowers, *Amaryllis belladonna.* [mod.L f. It., = fair lady, perh. from its use as a cosmetic]

bellbird /bélbərd/ *n.* any of various birds with a bell-like song, esp. any Central or S. American bird of the genus *Procnias,* a New Zealand honey eater, *Anthornis melanura,* and an Australian bird, *Oreoica gutturalis.*

bellboy /bélboy/ *n. Brit.* = BELLHOP.

belle /bel/ *n.* **1** a beautiful woman. **2** a woman recognized as the most beautiful or most charming (*the belle of the ball*). [F f. L *bella* fem. of *bellus* beautiful]

■ see BEAUTY 3.

belle époque /bél epúk/ *n.* the period of settled and comfortable life preceding World War I. [F, = fine period]

belles lettres /bel-létrə/ *n.pl.* (also treated as *sing.*) writings or studies of a literary nature, esp. essays and criticisms. □□ **belletrism** /bel-létrizəm/ *n.* **belletrist** /bel-létrist/ *n.* **belletristic** /bél-letrístik/ *adj.* [F, = fine letters]

■ see WRITING 3.

bellflower /bélflowr/ *n.* = CAMPANULA.

bellhop /bélhop/ *n.* a person who carries luggage, runs errands, etc., in a hotel or club.

■ see PAGE² *n.*

bellicose /bélikōs/ *adj.* eager to fight; warlike. □□ **bellicosity** /-kósitee/ *n.* [ME f. L *bellicosus* f. *bellum* war]

■ see WARLIKE 1.

belligerence /bilíjərəns/ *n.* (also **belligerency** /-rənsee/) **1** aggressive or warlike behavior. **2** the status of a belligerent.

■ **1** see AGGRESSION 1.

belligerent /bilíjərənt/ *adj.* & *n.* ● *adj.* **1** engaged in war or conflict. **2** given to constant fighting; pugnacious. ● *n.* a nation or person engaged in war or conflict. □□ **belligerently** *adv.* [L *belligerare* wage war f. *bellum* war + *gerere* wage]

■ *adj.* **1** warring, militant, warmongering, hawkish, jingoistic, bellicose, martial. **2** quarrelsome, pugnacious, contentious, disputatious, truculent, aggressive, hostile, combative, antagonistic, bellicose, argumentative, cantankerous, contrary; *sl.* feisty. ● *n.* warring party, fighter, antagonist, adversary, contender, contestant; opposition, other side; quarreler, squabbler; aggressor.

bellman /bélmən/ *n.* (*pl.* **-men**) *hist.* a town crier.

bellow /bélō/ *v.* & *n.* ● *v.* **1** *intr.* **a** emit a deep loud roar. **b** cry or shout with pain. **2** *tr.* utter loudly and usu. angrily. ● *n.* a bellowing sound. [ME: perh. rel. to BELL²]

■ *v.* roar, yell, shout, cry, blare, trumpet, thunder, howl, bawl, halloo, hallo, vociferate, sing out, *colloq.* holler. ● *n.* roar, yell, shout, cry, call, blare, hallo, howl, *colloq.* holler.

bellows /bélōz/ *n.pl.* (also treated as *sing.*) **1** a device with an air bag that emits a stream of air when squeezed, esp.: **a** (in full **pair of bellows**) a kind with two handles used for blowing air onto a fire. **b** a kind used in a harmonium or small organ. **2** an expandable component, e.g., joining the lens to the body of a camera. [ME prob. f. OE *belga* pl. of *belig* belly]

bellpull /bélpŏŏl/ *n.* a cord or handle which rings a bell when pulled.

bellwether /bélwethər/ *n.* **1** the leading sheep of a flock, with a bell on its neck. **2** a ringleader.

belly /bélee/ *n.* & *v.* ● *n.* (*pl.* **-ies**) **1** the part of the human body below the chest, containing the stomach and bowels. **2** the stomach, esp. representing the body's need for food. **3** the front of the body from the waist to the groin. **4** the underside of a four-legged animal. **5 a** a cavity or bulging part of anything. **b** the surface of an instrument of the violin family, across which the strings are placed. ● *v.tr.* & *intr.* (**-ies, -ied**) (often foll. by *out*) swell or cause to swell; bulge. □ **belly button** *colloq.* the navel. **belly dance** a Middle Eastern dance performed by a woman, involving voluptuous movements of the belly. **belly dancer** a woman who performs belly dances, esp. professionally. **belly dancing** the performance of belly dances. **belly landing** a crash-landing of an aircraft on the underside of the fuselage, without lowering the undercarriage. **belly laugh** a loud unrestrained laugh. **go belly up** *colloq.* fail financially. [OE *belig* (orig. = bag) f. Gmc]

■ *n.* **1–3** see STOMACH *n.* 2a. ● *v.* see SWELL *v.* 3. □ **belly button** see NAVEL 1. **go belly up** see FAIL *v.* 7.

bellyache /béleeayk/ *n.* & *v.* ● *n.* *colloq.* a stomach pain. ● *v.intr.* *sl.* complain noisily or persistently. □□ **bellyacher** *n.*

■ *n.* see GRIPE *n.* 1. ● *v.* see GRIPE *v.*

bellyband /béleeband/ *n.* a band placed round a horse's belly, holding the shafts of a cart, etc.

bellyflop /béleeflop/ *n.* & *v.* *colloq.* ● *n.* a dive into water in which the body lands with the belly flat on the water. ● *v.intr.* (**-flopped, -flopping**) perform this dive.

bellyful /béleefŏŏl/ *n.* (*pl.* **-fuls**) **1** enough to eat. **2** *colloq.* enough or more than enough of anything (esp. unwelcome).

belong /biláwng, -lóng/ *v.intr.* **1** (foll. by *to*) **a** be the property of. **b** be rightly assigned to as a duty, right, part, member, characteristic, etc. **c** be a member of (a club, family, group, etc.). **2** have the right personal or social qualities to be a member of a particular group (*he's nice but just doesn't belong*). **3** (foll. by *in, under*) **a** be rightly placed or classified. **b** fit a particular environment. □□ **belongingness** *n.* [ME f. intensive BE- + *longen* belong f. OE *langian* (*gelang* at hand)]

■ **1** (*belong to*) **a** be owned by, be the property or possession of. **b** be assigned or allocated to. **c** be a member of, be affiliated or associated or connected with, be attached or bound to, be a part of. **2** fit, be suited, have a (proper) place, be suitable, be clubbable, be one of us, have the right stuff.

belonging /biláwnging, -lóng-/ *n.* **1** (in *pl.*) one's movable possessions or luggage. **2** membership; relationship; esp. a person's membership of, and acceptance by, a group or society.

■ **1** (*belongings*) (personal) property, effects, possessions, goods, chattels, goods and chattels, *colloq.* gear, stuff, things; baggage, luggage, cases. **2** association, connection, alliance, relationship, affinity, relation; membership, acceptance.

Belorussian /bélōrúshən/ *n.* & *adj.* (also **Byelorussian** /byélō-/) ● *n.* **1** a native of Belorussia, now officially the Republic of Belarus. **2** the East Slavonic language of Belorussia. ● *adj.* of or relating to Belorussia or its people or language. [Russ. *Belorussiya* f. *belyi* white + *Russiya* Russia]

beloved /bilúvid, -lúvd/ *adj.* & *n.* ● *adj.* much loved. ● *n.* a much loved person. [obs. *belove* (v.)]

■ *adj.* loved, cherished, adored, dear, dearest, darling, precious, treasured; admired, worshipped, revered, esteemed, idolized, respected, valued, prized. ● *n.* sweetheart, darling, dearest, love, sweet, truelove, *colloq.* honey, girl, young lady or man, *sl.* baby; lover, boyfriend, girlfriend, inamorata, inamorato, gallant, lady, queen, *archaic* paramour, leman, *colloq.* flame.

below /bilṓ/ *prep.* & *adv.* ● *prep.* **1 a** lower in position (vertically, down a slope or stream, etc.) than. **b** (from the map position) south of. **2** beneath the surface of; at or to a greater depth than (*head below water*; *below 500 feet*). **3** lower or less than in amount or degree (*below freezing*). **4** lower in rank, position, or importance than. **5** unworthy of. ● *adv.* **1** at or to a lower point or level. **2 a** downstairs (*lives below*). **b** downstream. **3** (of a text reference) further forward on a page or in a book (*as noted below*). **4** on the lower side (*looks similar above and below*). **5** *rhet.* on earth; in hell. **6** below zero; esp. below freezing. □ **below stairs** *Brit.* in the basement of a house, esp. as the part occupied by servants. [BE- + LOW[1]]

■ *prep.* **1, 2** under, underneath, (submerged) beneath. **3** less or lower or cheaper than; under. **4** inferior or secondary or subordinate to, lower than, under, beneath. **5** beneath, unworthy of, unbefitting (of).
● *adv.* **1** lower down, further or farther down, beneath. **2 a** beneath, underneath; downstairs, below stairs, in

the basement, *Naut.* below deck(s). **3** further on or down, infra. **4** on the other or lower side, on the back; behind. **5** on earth, here (below), in this world, beneath or under the sun, in this sublunary world; see also HELL 1.

Bel Paese /bél paa-áyzay/ *n. propr.* a rich white mild creamy cheese of a kind orig. made in Italy. [It., = fair country]

belt /belt/ *n.* & *v.* ● *n.* **1** a strip of leather or other material worn around the waist or across the chest, esp. to retain or support clothes or to carry weapons or as a safety belt. **2** a belt worn as a sign of rank or achievement. **3 a** a circular band of material used as a driving medium in machinery. **b** a conveyor belt. **c** a flexible strip carrying machine gun cartridges. **4** a strip of color or texture, etc., differing from that on each side. **5** a distinct region or extent (*cotton belt*; *commuter belt*). **6** *sl.* a heavy blow. ● *v.* **1** *tr.* put a belt around. **2** *tr.* (often foll. by *on*) fasten with a belt. **3** *tr.* **a** beat with a belt. **b** *sl.* hit hard. **4** *intr.* *sl.* rush; hurry (usu. with compl.: *belted along*; *belted home*). □ **below the belt** unfair or unfairly; disregarding the rules. **belt and braces** *Brit.* (of a policy, etc.) of twofold security. **belt out** *sl.* sing or utter loudly and forcibly. **belt up 1** *Brit.* *sl.* be quiet. **2** *colloq.* put on a seat belt. **tighten one's belt** live more frugally. **under one's belt 1** (of food) eaten. **2** securely acquired (*has a degree under her belt*). □□ **belter** *n.* (esp. in sense of *belt out*). [OE f. Gmc f. L *balteus*]

■ *n.* **1** sash, girdle, cord, *archaic* zone, *literary* cincture. **4** see BAND[1] *n.* 2b. **5** zone, band, sector, strip, area, region, district, quarter, swath, tract, stretch, sphere. **6** see BLOW[2] 1. ● *v.* **3** see BEAT *v.* 1. **4** see HURRY *v.* 1. □ **below the belt** unfair, unjust, unsporting, unsportsmanlike, underhand(ed), improper, dirty, unscrupulous, unprincipled, wrong; unfairly, unjustly, unsportingly, underhandedly, improperly, dirtily, unscrupulously. **belt out** sing or perform stridently or loudly; put over or across loudly. **tighten one's belt** see ECONOMIZE 1.

Beltane /béltayn, -tən/ *n.* an ancient Celtic festival celebrated on May Day. [Gael. *bealltainn*]

beltman /béltman/ *n.* (*pl.* **-men**) *Austral.* a member of a lifesaving team of surfers; a lifeguard.

beltway /béltway/ *n.* **1** a highway skirting a metropolitan region. **2** (**the Beltway**) the highway skirting Washington DC, viewed as encompassing a parochial, self-interested world of federal politics.

beluga /bəlōōgə/ *n.* **1 a** a large kind of sturgeon, *Huso huso*. **b** caviar obtained from it. **2** a white whale. [Russ. *beluga* f. *belyi* white]

belvedere /bélvideer/ *n.* a summerhouse or open-sided gallery, usu. at rooftop level. [It. f. *bel* beautiful + *vedere* see]

belying *pres. part.* of BELIE.

BEM *abbr.* British Empire Medal.

bemire /bimír/ *v.tr.* **1** cover or stain with mud. **2** (in *passive*) be stuck in mud. [BE- + MIRE]

bemoan /bimṓn/ *v.tr.* **1** express regret or sorrow over; lament. **2** complain about. [BE- + MOAN]

■ **1** bewail, mourn (for or over), grieve or weep or sorrow or moan for or over; see also LAMENT. **2** moan or grumble or complain about, *colloq.* gripe or grouse about, bitch about, *sl.* beef about.

bemuse /bimyōōz/ *v.tr.* stupefy or bewilder (a person). □□ **bemusedly** /-zidlee/ *adv.* **bemusement** *n.* [BE- + MUSE[2]]

■ confuse, mystify, perplex, bewilder, puzzle, baffle, muddle, mix up, addle, befuddle, confound, bedazzle, bedevil, maze, *archaic* wilder, *colloq.* tie in knots, flummox, *joc.* discombobulate; stupefy, benumb, numb, dizzy, paralyze.

ben[1] /ben/ *n. Sc.* a high mountain or mountain peak, esp. in names (*Ben Nevis*). [Gael. *beann*]

ben[2] /ben/ *n. Sc.* an inner room, esp. of a two-room cottage. [ellipt. use of *ben* (adv.), = within (OE *binnan*)]

bench /bench/ *n. & v.* ● *n.* **1** a long seat of wood or stone for seating several people. **2** a worktable, e.g., for a carpenter, mechanic, or scientist. **3** (*prec. by the*) **a** the office of judge or magistrate. **b** a judge's seat in a court of law. **c** a court of law. **d** judges and magistrates collectively. **4** *Sports* **a** an area to the side of a field with seating where coaches and players not taking part can watch the game. **b** those players not taking part in a game. **5** *Brit. Parl.* a seat appropriated as specified (*front bench*). **6** a level ledge in masonry or an earthwork, on a hillside, etc. ● *v.tr.* **1** exhibit (a dog) at a show. **2** *Sports* **a** keep (a player) on the bench. **b** withdraw (a player) from the field to the bench or court. □ **bench test** esp. *Computing n.* a test made by benchmarking. ● *v.tr.* run a series of tests on (a computer, etc.) before its use. **King's** (or **Queen's**) **Bench** (in the UK) a division of the High Court of Justice. **on the bench** appointed a judge or magistrate. [OE *benc* f. Gmc]

■ *n.* **1** see SEAT *n.* 1.

bencher /bénchər/ *n. Brit.* **1** *Law* a senior member of any of the Inns of Court. **2** (in *comb.*) *Parl.* an occupant of a specified bench (*backbencher*).

benchmark /bénchmaark/ *n. & v.* ● *n.* **1** a surveyor's mark cut in a wall, pillar, building, etc., used as a reference point in measuring altitudes. **2** a standard or point of reference. **3** a means of testing a computer, usu. by a set of programs run on a series of different machines. ● *v.tr.* evaluate (a computer) by a benchmark. □ **benchmark test** a test using a benchmark.

■ *n.* **2** see STANDARD *n.* 1, 8.

bend[1] /bend/ *v. & n.* ● *v.* (*past* **bent**; *past part.* **bent** exc. in *bended knee*) **1 a** *tr.* force or adapt (something straight) into a curve or angle. **b** *intr.* (of an object) be altered in this way. **2** *intr.* move or stretch in a curved course (*the road bends to the left*). **3** *intr. & tr.* (often foll. by *down, over,* etc.) incline or cause to incline from the vertical (*bent down to pick it up*). **4** *tr.* interpret or modify (a rule) to suit oneself. **5** *tr. & refl.* (foll. by *to, on*) direct or devote (oneself or one's attention, energies, etc.). **6** *tr.* turn (one's steps or eyes) in a new direction. **7** *tr.* (in *passive*; foll. by *on*) have firmly decided; be determined (*was bent on revenge; on pleasure bent*). **8 a** *intr.* stoop or submit (*bent before his master*). **b** *tr.* force to submit. **9** *tr. Naut.* attach (a sail or cable) with a knot. ● *n.* **1** a curve in a road, stream, etc. **2** a departure from a straight course. **3** a bent part of anything. **4** (in *pl.*; prec. by *the*) *colloq.* sickness due to too rapid decompression underwater. □ **around the bend** *colloq.* crazy; insane. **bend over backward** see BACKWARD. □□ **bendable** *adj.* [OE *bendan* f. Gmc]

■ *v.* **1** arch, bow, curve, crook. **2** incline, turn, curve, wind, deflect, veer, swing, bear. **3** see STOOP *v.* 1. **4** change, modify, adapt, revise, adjust, interpret; see also TWIST *v.* 5. **5, 6** incline, channel, focus, direct, steer, set, fix, turn, train. **7** (*be bent on*) see BENT[1] *adj.* 4. **8 a** bow, curtsy, make *or* drop a curtsy; kowtow, salaam; kneel, genuflect; submit, yield, give way *or* in, be pliant *or* subservient *or* tractable. ● *n.* **1, 3** curve, turn, turning, corner; angle, crook, hook, bow, curvature, flexure. □ **around the bend** see CRAZY 1. □□ **bendable** see PLASTIC *adj.* 1a.

bend[2] /bend/ *n.* **1** *Naut.* any of various knots for tying ropes (*fisherman's bend*). **2** *Heraldry* **a** a diagonal stripe from top right to bottom left of a shield. **b** (**bend sinister**) a diagonal stripe from top left to bottom right, as a sign of bastardy. [OE *bend* band, bond f. Gmc]

bender /béndər/ *n. sl.* a wild drinking spree. [BEND[1] + -ER[1]]

■ drinking bout, drinking spree, revel, carousal, carouse, bacchanal, *Sc.* skite, *archaic* wassail, *colloq.* bust, pub crawl, *sl.* binge, jag, drunk, esp. *Brit.* booze-up, *Brit. sl.* blind.

bendy /béndee/ *adj.* (**bendier, bendiest**) *colloq.* capable of bending; soft and flexible. □□ **bendiness** *n.*

■ see PLIABLE 1.

beneath /bineéth/ *prep. & adv.* ● *prep.* **1** not worthy of; too demeaning for (*it was beneath him to reply*). **2** below; under. ● *adv.* below; under; underneath. □ **beneath contempt** see CONTEMPT. [OE *binithan, bineothan* f. *bi* BY + *nithan,* etc., below f. Gmc]

■ *prep.* **1** below, unworthy of, unbefitting of, undeserving of, too demeaning for, lower than. **2** under, underneath, below, behind. ● *adv.* low *or* lower down, below, under, underneath; underground.

benedicite /bénidísitee/ *n.* a blessing, esp. a grace said at table in religious communities. [ME f. L, = bless ye: see BENEDICTION]

Benedictine /bénidíktin, (in sense 2) -teen/ *n. & adj.* ● *n.* **1** a monk or nun of an order following the rule of St. Benedict established *c.*540. **2** *propr.* a liqueur based on brandy, orig. made by Benedictines in France. ● *adj.* of St. Benedict or the Benedictines. [F *bénédictine* or mod.L *benedictinus* f. *Benedictus* Benedict]

benediction /bénidíkshən/ *n.* **1** the utterance of a blessing, esp. at the end of a religious service or as a special church service. **2** the state of being blessed. [ME f. OF f. L *benedictio -onis* f. *benedicere -dict-* bless]

■ **1** see BLESSING 1.

benedictory /bénidíktəree/ *adj.* of or expressing benediction. [L *benedictorius* (as BENEDICTION)]

Benedictus /bénidíktəs/ *n.* **1** the section of the Latin Mass beginning *Benedictus qui venit in nomine Domini* (Blessed is he who comes in the name of the Lord). **2** a canticle beginning *Benedictus Dominus Deus* (Blessed be the Lord God) from Luke 1:68–79. [L, = blessed: see BENEDICTION]

benefaction /bénifákshən/ *n.* **1** a donation or gift. **2** an act of giving or doing good. [LL *benefactio* (as BENEFIT)]

■ **1** see GIFT *n.* 1.

benefactor /bénifaktər/ *n.* (*fem.* **benefactress** /-tris-/) a person who gives support (esp. financial) to a person or cause. [ME f. LL (as BENEFIT)]

■ patron, supporter, sponsor, donor, philanthropist; backer, investor, underwriter, *sl.* angel.

benefice /bénifis/ *n.* **1** an income from a church office. **2** the property attached to a church office, esp. that bestowed on a cleric. □□ **beneficed** *adj.* [ME f. OF f. L *beneficium* favor f. *bene* well + *facere* do]

beneficent /binéfisənt/ *adj.* doing good; generous; actively kind. □□ **beneficence** /-səns/ *n.* **beneficently** *adv.* [L *beneficent-* (as BENEFICE)]

■ see GENEROUS 2. □□ **beneficence** see KINDNESS 1.

beneficial /bénifíshəl/ *adj.* **1** advantageous; having benefits. **2** *Law* relating to the use or benefit of property; having rights to this use or benefit. □□ **beneficially** *adv.* [ME f. F *bénéficial* or LL *beneficialis* (as BENEFICE)]

■ **1** advantageous, serviceable, useful, profitable, valuable, helpful, supportive, favorable, constructive, worthwhile, good, gainful, propitious, efficacious, effective; healthful, healthy, salutary, salubrious.

beneficiary /bénifíshee-e-ree, -físhəree/ *n.* (*pl.* **-ies**) **1** a person who receives benefits, esp. under a person's will, insurance policy, etc. **2** a holder of a benefice. [L *beneficiarius* (as BENEFICE)]

■ **1** see HEIR.

benefit /bénifit/ *n. & v.* ● *n.* **1** a favorable or helpful factor or circumstance; advantage; profit. **2** (often in *pl.*) payment made under insurance, social security, welfare, etc. **3** a public performance or game of which the proceeds go to a particular charitable cause. ● *v.* (**benefited, benefiting**; also **benefitted, benefitting**) **1** *tr.* do good to; bring advantage to. **2** *intr.* (often foll. by *from, by*) receive an advantage or gain. □ **benefit of clergy 1** *hist.* exemption of the English tonsured clergy and nuns from the jurisdiction of the ordinary civil courts. **2** ecclesiastical sanction or approval (*marriage without benefit of clergy*). **the benefit of the doubt** a concession that a person is innocent, correct, etc., although doubt exists. **benefit society** a society for mutual insurance against illness or the effects of old age. [ME f. AF *benfet,* OF *bienfet,* f. L *benefactum* f. *bene facere* do well]

■ *n.* **1** advantage, profit, good, gain, aid, help, service;

strength, attraction, asset, added extra, boon, plus, appeal, pull, beauty, selling point; sake. **2** payment, payout; sick pay; *Brit. colloq.* dole; (*benefits*) perquisites, emoluments, allowance(s), extras, fringe benefits, *colloq.* perks. **3** charity event. ● *v.* **1** do good to; improve, aid, help, better, promote, further, advance, forward, advantage. **2** profit, gain.

Benelux /béniluks/ *n.* Belgium, the Netherlands, and Luxembourg in association as a regional economic group. [*Bel*gium + *Netherlands* + *Lux*embourg]

benevolent /binévələnt/ *adj.* **1** wishing to do good; actively friendly and helpful. **2** charitable (*benevolent fund*; *benevolent society*). □□ **benevolence** /-ləns/ *n.* **benevolently** *adv.* [ME f. OF *benivolent* f. L *bene volens -entis* well wishing f. *velle* wish]

■ **1** well-disposed, gracious, good, kind, kindly, friendly, cordial, genial, congenial, humane, helpful, humanitarian, altruistic, philanthropic, well-wishing, thoughtful, considerate, sympathetic, caring, kind-hearted, warm-hearted, compassionate, benign, benignant; liberal, generous, magnanimous, open-handed. **2** charitable, good, philanthropic, eleemosynary. □□ **benevolence** charity, kindness, kindliness, kindheartedness, warmheartedness, friendliness, humanity, humanitarianism, compassion, beneficence, charitableness, goodness, altruism, good will, unselfishness, philanthropy, generosity, magnanimity, openhandedness, helpfulness, thoughtfulness, considerateness.

Bengali /benggáwlee, -gaálee/ *n.* & *adj.* ● *n.* **1** a native of Bengal, a former Indian province now consisting of Bangladesh and the Indian state of W. Bengal. **2** the language of this people. ● *adj.* of or relating to Bengal or its people or language.

Bengal light /benggáwl, bénggəl/ *n.* a kind of flare giving off a blue flame, used for signals.

benighted /binítid/ *adj.* **1** intellectually or morally ignorant. **2** overtaken by darkness. □□ **benightedness** *n.* [obs. *benight* (v.)]

■ **1** unenlightened, naive, uninformed, ignorant, in the dark, unknowing, unaware, unversed, uneducated, uninformed, *literary* nescient.

benign /binín/ *adj.* **1** gentle; mild; kind **2** fortunate; salutary. **3** (of the climate, soil, etc.) mild; favorable. **4** *Med.* (of a disease, tumor, etc.) not malignant. □□ **benignly** *adv.* [ME f. OF *benigne* f. L *benignus* f. *bene* well + *-genus* born]

■ **1** kindly, gracious, good, kind, kindhearted, benevolent, benignant, warm, mild, warmhearted, cordial, genial, congenial, tender, gentle, tenderhearted, compassionate, sympathetic, caring, softhearted. **2** salutary, congenial, propitious, beneficial, helpful, wholesome, healthful, healthy; fortunate, advantageous, favorable, auspicious, benignant. **3** mild, temperate, moderate, clement, gentle, mellow, kind, salubrious, favorable, advantageous, promising. **4** nonfatal, nonmalignant, nonvirulent, curable, harmless, benignant.

benignant /binígnənt/ *adj.* **1** kindly, esp. to inferiors. **2** salutary; beneficial. **3** *Med.* = BENIGN 4. □□ **benignancy** /-nənsee/ *n.* **benignantly** *adv.* [f. BENIGN or L *benignus*, after *malignant*]

■ **1** see BENEVOLENT 1, BENIGN 1. **2** see BENIGN 2. **3** see BENIGN 4.

benignity /binígnitee/ *n.* (*pl.* **-ies**) **1** kindliness. **2** *archaic* an act of kindness. [ME f. OF *benignité* or L *benignitas* (as BENIGN)]

■ **1** see KINDNESS 1.

benison /bénizən, -sən/ *n.* a blessing. [ME f. OF *beneiçun* f. L *benedictio -onis*]

bent[1] /bent/ *past* and *past part.* of BEND[1] *v.* ● *adj.* **1** curved or having an angle. **2** *Brit. sl.* dishonest; illicit. **3** esp. *Brit. sl.* **a** sexually deviant. **b** strange; weird; warped. **4** (foll. by *on*) determined to do or have. ● *n.* **1** an inclination or bias. **2** (foll. by *for*) a talent for something specified (*a bent for mimicry*).

■ *adj.* **1** curved, deflected, bowed, crooked, distorted, contorted, twisted, warped, gnarled. **4** (*bent on*) determined about *or* to, intent on, set on, resolved about *or* to, resolute about, decided on *or* to, fixed on. ● *n.* **1** inclination, direction, disposition, predisposition, tendency, bias, leaning, proclivity, propensity, partiality, prejudice. **2** ability, aptitude, talent, gift, skill, faculty, facility, flair, feel, knack, genius.

bent[2] /bent/ *n.* **1 a** any stiff grass of the genus *Agrostis.* **b** any of various grasslike reeds, rushes, or sedges. **2** a stiff stalk of a grass usu. with a flexible base. **3** esp. *Brit. archaic* or *dial.* a heath or unenclosed pasture. [ME repr. OE *beonet-* (in place-names), f. Gmc]

Benthamism /bénthəmizəm/ *n.* the utilitarian philosophy of Jeremy Bentham, Engl. philosopher d. 1832. □□ **Benthamite** *n.* & *adj.*

benthos /bénthos/ *n.* the flora and fauna found at the bottom of a sea or lake. □□ **benthic** /-thik/ *adj.* [Gk, = depth of the sea]

bentonite /béntənīt/ *n.* a kind of absorbent clay used esp. as a filler. [Fort *Benton* in Montana]

ben trovato /bén trōváatō/ *adj.* **1** well invented. **2** characteristic if not true. [It., = well found]

bentwood /béntwŏŏd/ *n.* wood that is artificially shaped for use in making furniture.

benumb /binúm/ *v.tr.* **1** make numb; deaden. **2** paralyze (the mind or feelings). [orig. = deprived, as past part. of ME *benimen* f. OE *beniman* (as BE-, *niman* take)]

■ see DEADEN 2.

Benzedrine /bénzidreen/ *n. propr.* amphetamine. [BENZOIC + EPHEDRINE]

benzene /bénzeen/ *n.* a colorless carcinogenic volatile liquid found in coal tar, petroleum, etc., and used as a solvent and in the manufacture of plastics, etc. ¶ Chem. formula: C_6H_6. □ **benzene ring** the hexagonal unsaturated ring of six carbon atoms in the benzene molecule. □□ **benzenoid** /-zənoyd/ *adj.* [BENZOIC + -ENE]

benzine /bénzeen/ *n.* (also **benzin** /-zin/) a mixture of liquid hydrocarbons obtained from petroleum. [BENZOIN + -INE[4]]

benzoic /benzóik/ *adj.* containing or derived from benzoin or benzoic acid. □ **benzoic acid** a white crystalline substance used as a food preservative. ¶ Chem. formula: $C_7H_6O_2$. [BENZOIN + -IC]

benzoin /bénzōin/ *n.* **1** a fragrant gum resin obtained from various E. Asian trees of the genus *Styrax*, and used in the manufacture of perfumes and incense. **2** the white crystalline constituent of this. Also called *gum benjamin.* [earlier *benjoin* ult. f. Arab. *lubān jāwī* incense of Java]

benzol /bénzawl, -zol/ *n.* (also **benzole** /-zōl/) benzene, esp. unrefined and used as a fuel.

benzoyl /bénzōil/ *n.* (usu. *attrib.*) *Chem.* the radical C_6H_5CO. □ **benzoyl peroxide** a white crystalline compound, $C_{14}H_{10}O_4$, used as a bleaching agent and medicinally for acne.

benzyl /bénzil, -zeel/ *n.* (usu. *attrib.*) *Chem.* the radical $C_6H_5CH_2$.

bequeath /bikwéeth, -kwéeth/ *v.tr.* **1** leave (a personal estate) to a person by a will. **2** hand down to posterity. □□ **bequeathal** *n.* **bequeather** *n.* [OE *becwethan* (as BE-, *cwethan* say: cf. QUOTH)]

■ leave, make over, will, pass on, hand down *or* on, transmit, *Law* devise.

bequest /bikwést/ *n.* **1** the act or an instance of bequeathing. **2** a thing bequeathed. [ME f. BE- + obs. *quiste* f. OE *-cwiss*, *cwide* saying]

■ **2** legacy, inheritance, heritage, patrimony, *Law* hereditament; heirloom.

berate /biráyt/ *v.tr.* scold; rebuke. [BE- + RATE[2]]

■ scold, reprimand, rebuke, rate, upbraid, chastise,

/. . ./ **pronunciation**	● **part of speech**
□ **phrases, idioms, and compounds**	
□□ **derivatives**	■ **synonym section**
cross-references appear in SMALL CAPITALS or *italics*	

reprove, reproach, reprehend, revile, abuse, rail at, excoriate, castigate, keelhaul, belabor, harangue, rap a person's knuckles, slap a person's wrist, take to task, *archaic* lesson, *archaic or literary* chide, *colloq.* dress down, tell off, lay into, *literary* objurgate, *sl.* chew out, rip into, ballyrag.

Berber /bárbər/ *n. & adj.* ● *n.* **1** a member of the indigenous mainly Muslim peoples of N. Africa. **2** the language of these peoples. ● *adj.* of the Berbers or their language. [Arab. *barbar*]

berberis /bárbəris/ *n.* = BARBERRY. [med.L & OF, of unkn. orig.]

berceuse /báirsőz/ *n.* (*pl.* **berceuses** *pronunc.* same) **1** a lullaby. **2** an instrumental piece in the style of a lullaby. [F]

bereave /bireév/ *v.tr.* (esp. as **bereaved** *adj.*) (foll. by *of*) deprive of a relation, friend, etc., esp. by death. □□ **bereavement** *n.* [OE *berēafian* (as BE-, REAVE)]
■ deprive, strip, rob, dispossess; widow.
□□ **bereavement** see LOSS 1, MOURNING 1.

bereft /biréft/ *adj.* (foll. by *of*) deprived (esp. of a non-material asset) (*bereft of hope*). [past part. of BEREAVE]

beret /bəráy/ *n.* a round flattish visorless cap of felt or cloth. [F *béret* Basque cap f. Prov. *berret*]

berg[1] /bərg/ *n.* = ICEBERG. [abbr.]

berg[2] /bərg/ *n. S.Afr.* a mountain or hill. □ **berg wind** a hot dry northerly wind blowing from the interior to coastal districts. [Afrik. f. Du.]

bergamot[1] /bárgəmot/ *n.* **1** an aromatic herb, esp. *Mentha citrata.* **2** an oily perfume extracted from the rind of the fruit of the citrus tree *Citrus bergamia,* a dwarf variety of the Seville orange tree. **3** the tree itself. [*Bergamo* in N. Italy]

bergamot[2] /bárgəmot/ *n.* a variety of fine pear. [F *bergamotte* f. It. *bergamotta* f. Turk. *begarmūdi* prince's pear f. *beg* prince + *armudi* pear]

bergschrund /báirkshroont/ *n.* a crevasse or gap at the head of a glacier or névé. [G]

beriberi /béreebéree/ *n.* a disease causing inflammation of the nerves due to a deficiency of vitamin B₁. [Sinh., f. *beri* weakness]

berk /bərk/ *n.* (also **burk**) *Brit. sl.* a fool; a stupid person. ¶ Usu. not considered *offens.* despite the etymology. [abbr. of *Berkeley* or *Berkshire Hunt*, rhyming sl. for *cunt*]

berkelium /bərkeéleeəm, bárkleeəm/ *n. Chem.* a transuranic radioactive metallic element produced by bombardment of americium. ¶ Symb.: **Bk.** [mod.L f. *Berkeley,* California (where first made) + -IUM]

Berliner /bərlínər/ *n.* a native or citizen of Berlin in Germany. [G]

berm /bərm/ *n.* **1** a narrow path or grass strip beside a road, canal, etc. **2** a narrow ledge, esp. in a fortification between a ditch and the base of a parapet. [F *berme* f. Du. *berm*]

Bermuda onion /bərmyŏŏdə/ *n.* a large, yellow-skinned onion with a mild flavor.

Bermuda shorts /bərmyŏŏdə/ *n.pl.* (also **Bermudas**) shorts reaching almost to the knees. [*Bermuda* in the W. Atlantic]

Bermuda triangle *n.* an area of the western Atlantic where ships and aircraft are reported to have disappeared without a trace.

berry /béree/ *n. & v.* ● *n.* (*pl.* **-ies**) **1** any small roundish juicy fruit without a stone. **2** *Bot.* a fruit with its seeds enclosed in a pulp (e.g., a banana, tomato, etc.). **3** any of various kernels or seeds (e.g., coffee bean, etc.). **4** a fish egg or roe of a lobster, etc. ● *v.intr.* (**-ies, -ied**) **1** (usu. as **berrying** *n.*) go gathering berries. **2** form a berry; bear berries. □□ **berried** *adj.* (also in *comb.*). [OE *berie* f. Gmc]

berserk /bərsárk, -zárk/ *adj. & n.* ● *adj.* (esp. in **go berserk**) wild; frenzied; in a violent rage. ● *n.* (also **berserker** /-kər/) an ancient Norse warrior who fought with a wild frenzy. [Icel. *berserkr* (n.) prob. f. *bern-* BEAR² + *serkr* coat]
■ *adj.* mad, violent, wild, crazy, deranged, crazed, frenzied, maniacal, manic, insane, hysterical, frantic, raving, out of control, out of one's mind, *sl.* loopy, loony, bonkers, out of one's skull; fuming, irate, enraged, incensed, furious, angry.

berth /bərth/ *n. & v.* ● *n.* **1** a fixed bunk on a ship, train, etc., for sleeping in. **2** a ship's place at a wharf. **3** room for a ship to swing at anchor. **4** adequate sea room. **5** *colloq.* a situation or appointment. **6** the proper place for anything. ● *v.* **1** *tr.* moor (a ship) in its berth. **2** *tr.* provide a sleeping place for. **3** *intr.* (of a ship) come to its mooring place. □ **give a wide berth to** stay away from. [prob. f. naut. use of BEAR¹ + -TH²]
■ *n.* **1** see CABIN *n.* 2. **5** see APPOINTMENT 2a. ● *v.* **1, 3** see MOOR².

bertha /bárthə/ *n.* **1** a deep falling collar often of lace. **2** a small cape on a dress. [F *berthe* f. *Berthe* Bertha (the name)]

beryl /béril/ *n.* **1** a kind of transparent precious stone, esp. pale green, blue, or yellow, and consisting of beryllium aluminum silicate in a hexagonal form. **2** a mineral species which includes this, emerald, and aquamarine. [ME f. OF f. L *beryllus* f. Gk *bērullos*]

beryllium /bəríleeəm/ *n. Chem.* a hard white metallic element used in the manufacture of light corrosion-resistant alloys. ¶ Symb.: **Be.** [BERYL + -IUM]

beseech /biseéch/ *v.tr.* (*past* and *past part.* **besought** /-sáwt/ or **beseeched**) **1** (foll. by *for,* or *to* + infin.) entreat. **2** ask earnestly for. □□ **beseeching** *adj.* [ME f. BE- + *secan* SEEK]
■ supplicate, entreat, implore, plead (with), beg, importune, appeal to or for, pray, petition.

beset /bisét/ *v.tr.* (**besetting**; *past* and *past part.* **beset**) **1** attack or pursue persistently (*beset by worries*). **2** surround or hem in (a person, etc.). **3** *archaic* cover with (*beset with pearls*). □ **besetting sin** the sin that especially or most frequently tempts one. □□ **besetment** *n.* [OE *besettan* f. Gmc]
■ **1** assail, attack, harass, beleaguer, besiege, bedevil, harry, hector, bother, nag, afflict, trouble, distress, oppress, torment, hound, badger, *colloq.* plague, crowd in. **2** encompass, surround, besiege, hem in, encircle.

beside /bisíd/ *prep.* **1** at the side of; near. **2** compared with. **3** irrelevant to (*beside the point*). **4** = BESIDES. □ **beside oneself** overcome with worry, anger, etc. [OE *be sīdan* (as BY, SIDE)]
■ **1** alongside, near, next to, with, close to, hard by, by. **3** irrelevant to, away from, wide of, apart from, unconnected with, off. □ **beside oneself** out of one's mind *or* wits, at the end of one's tether, overwrought, agitated, distracted, distraught, upset, crazy, mad; excited, worked up, wound up, *colloq.* in a tizzy, in a flap *or* fluster, all of a dither, in a state.

besides /bisídz/ *prep. & adv.* ● *prep.* in addition to; apart from. ● *adv.* also; as well; moreover.
■ *prep.* over and above, above and beyond, in addition to, additionally to, as well as; barring, bar, excepting, except (for), excluding, exclusive of, not counting *or* including, leaving out, beyond, apart from, other than, but for, aside from, *archaic or poet.* save for. ● *adv.* in addition, additionally, also; further, furthermore, moreover, as well, too, more than that; to boot, on top of everything else, into the bargain.

besiege /biseéj/ *v.tr.* **1** lay siege to. **2** crowd around oppressively. **3** harass with requests. □□ **besieger** *n.* [ME f. *assiege* by substitution of BE-, f. OF *asegier* f. Rmc]
■ **1** lay siege to, beleaguer, invest. **2** blockade, block (off *or* up), hem in, cut off; surround, crowd around, encircle. **3** beleaguer, harass, bedevil, beset, assail, pressurize, press, hound, badger, *colloq.* plague; overwhelm, inundate.

besmear /bismeér/ *v.tr.* **1** smear with greasy or sticky stuff. **2** sully (a reputation, etc.). [OE *bismierwan* (as BE-, SMEAR)]

besmirch /bismɜ́rch/ *v.tr.* **1** soil; discolor. **2** dishonor; sully the reputation or name of. [BE- + SMIRCH]
■ **1** see DIRTY *v.* **2** see SULLY.

besom /beézəm/ *n.* **1** a broom made of twigs tied round a stick. **2** esp. *No. of Engl. derog.* or *joc.* a woman. [OE *besema*]
■ **1** see BRUSH *n.* 1.

besotted /bisótid/ *adj.* **1** intoxicated; stupefied. **2** foolish; confused. **3** infatuated. [*besot* (v.) (as BE-, SOT)]
■ **1** see DRUNK *adj.* 1. **3** see INFATUATED.

besought *past* and *past part.* of BESEECH.

bespangle /bispánggəl/ v.tr. adorn with spangles.

bespatter /bispátər/ v.tr. **1** spatter (an object) all over. **2** spatter (liquid, etc.). **3** overwhelm with abuse, slander, etc.
■ **1, 2** see SPATTER v. 1.

bespeak /bispeék/ v.tr. (past **bespoke** /-spók/; past part. **bespoken** /-spókən/ or as adj. **bespoke**) **1** engage in advance. **2** order (goods). **3** suggest; be evidence of (his gift bespeaks a kind heart). **4** literary speak to. [OE bisprecan (as BE-, SPEAK)]
■ **1** see ENGAGE 5. **3** see INDICATE 2.

bespectacled /bispéktəkəld/ adj. wearing spectacles.

bespoke past and past part. of BESPEAK. ● adj. Brit. **1** (of goods, esp. clothing) made to order. **2** (of a tradesman) making goods to order.

bespoken past part. of BESPEAK.

besprinkle /bispríngkəl/ v.tr. sprinkle or strew all over with liquid, etc. [ME f. BE- + sprengen in the same sense]
■ see SPATTER v. 1a.

Bessemer converter /bésimər/ n. a special furnace used to purify pig iron using the Bessemer process. [Sir H. Bessemer, Engl. engineer d. 1898]

Bessemer process /bésimər/ n. a process once widely used, in which air is blown through molten pig iron to remove carbon, silicon, and other impurities in order to render it suitable for making steel.

best /best/ adj., adv., n., & v. ● adj. (superl. of GOOD) the most excellent or outstanding or desirable kind (my best work; the best solution; the best thing to do would be to confess). ● adv. (superl. of WELL¹). **1** in the best manner (does it best). **2** to the greatest degree (like it best). **3** most usefully (is best ignored). ● n. **1** that which is best (the best is yet to come). **2** the chief merit or advantage; the best aspect or side; a person's best performance, achievement, etc. (brings out the best in him; gave their best to the task). **3** (foll. by of) a winning majority of (a certain number of games, etc., played) (the best of five). **4** = Sunday best. ● v.tr. colloq. defeat, outwit, outbid, etc. □ **all the best** an expression used to wish a person good fortune. **as best one can** (or **may**) as effectively as possible under the circumstances. **at best** on the most optimistic view. **at one's best** in peak condition, etc. **at the best of times** even in the most favorable circumstances. **be for** (or **all for**) **the best** be desirable in the end. **best end of neck** Brit. the rib end of a neck of lamb, etc., for cooking. **best man** the bridegroom's chief attendant at a wedding. **the best part** of most of. **best seller 1** a book or other item that has sold in large numbers. **2** esp. Brit. the author of such a book. **do one's best** do all one can. **get the best of** defeat; outwit. **give a person the best** Brit. admit the superiority of that person. **had best** would find it wisest to. **make the best of** derive what limited advantage one can from (something unsatisfactory or unwelcome); put up with. **to the best of one's ability, knowledge,** etc., as far as one can do, know, etc. **with the best of them** as well as anyone. [OE betest (adj.), bet(o)st (adv.), f. Gmc]
■ adj. top, superlative, unexcelled, unrivaled, finest, preeminent, first, superb, unsurpassed, peerless, superior, excellent, paramount, first-rate, foremost, choicest, colloq. A1; first-class, upper-class, colloq. upper-crust. ● adv. **2** most, to the greatest extent or degree. **3** better. ● n. **1, 2** finest, first, prime, cream, pearl, winner, choice, flower, crème de la crème; utmost, sl. the most. **3** majority. **4** finery, best clothes, best bib and tucker, colloq. glad rags, joc. Sunday best. ● v. win (out) over, conquer, beat, surpass, get the better of, subdue, defeat, worst, trounce, rout, crush, master, outdo, overwhelm, overcome, outwit, literary vanquish; outbid; see also BEAT v. 3a. □ **all the best** see REGARD n. 5. **at best** see ideally (IDEAL). **at one's best** on or in top form, in the best of health, in good or great shape, colloq. in tiptop condition. **the best part** of most of, the majority of, the better part of, the greater part of. **get the best of** see BEAT v. 3a. **had best** had better, ought to, must, should. **make the best of** see put up with.

bestial /béschəl, beés-/ adj. **1** brutish; cruel; savage. **2** sex-

ually depraved; lustful. **3** of or like a beast. □□ **bestialize** v.tr. **bestially** adv. [ME f. OF f. LL bestialis f. bestia beast]
■ **1** see SAVAGE adj. 1, 2. **2** see LIBERTINE adj. 1.

bestiality /béscheeálitee, beés-/ n. (pl. **-ies**) **1** bestial behavior or an instance of this. **2** sexual intercourse between a person and an animal. [F bestialité (as BESTIAL)]

bestiary /béschee-eree, beés-/ n. (pl. **-ies**) a moralizing medieval treatise on real and imaginary beasts. [med.L bestiarium f. L bestia beast]

bestir /bistɔ́r/ v.refl. (**bestirred, bestirring**) exert or rouse (oneself).
■ see ROUSE 2a.

bestow /bistó/ v.tr. **1** (foll. by on, upon) confer (a gift, right, etc.). **2** deposit. □□ **bestowal** n. [ME f. BE- + OE stow a place]
■ **1** confer, give, award, present, donate, grant, cede, afford. □□ **bestowal** see AWARD n. 1b.

bestrew /bistróo/ v.tr. (past part. **bestrewed** or **bestrewn** /-stróon/) **1** (foll. by with) cover or partly cover (a surface). **2** scatter (things) about. **3** lie scattered over. [OE bestrēowian (as BE-, STREW)]
■ **1, 2** see STREW.

bestride /bistríd/ v.tr. (past **bestrode** /-stród/; past part. **bestridden** /-stríd'n/) **1** sit astride on. **2** stand astride over. **3** dominate. [OE bestrīdan]

bet /bet/ v. & n. ● v. (**betting**; past and past part. **bet** or **betted**) **1** intr. (foll. by on or against with ref. to the outcome) risk a sum of money, etc., against another's on the basis of the outcome of an unpredictable event (esp. the result of a race, game, etc., or the outcome in a game of chance). **2** tr. risk (an amount) on such an outcome or result (bet $10 on a horse). **3** tr. risk a sum of money against (a person). **4** tr. colloq. feel sure (bet they've forgotten it). ● n. **1** the act of betting (make a bet). **2** the money, etc., staked (put a bet on). **3** colloq. an opinion, esp. a quickly formed or spontaneous one (my bet is that he won't come). **4** colloq. a choice or course of action (she's our best bet). □ **you bet** colloq. you may be sure. [16th c.: perh. a shortened form of ABET]
■ v. **1, 2** wager, stake, gamble, risk, hazard, play, lay (down), put, chance, venture, try one's luck, colloq. punt. ● n. **1, 2** wager, stake, risk, colloq. flier, Brit. sl. flutter. **4** see OPTION 1. □ **you bet** see ABSOLUTELY 6.

bet. abbr. between.

beta /báytə, beé-/ n. **1** the second letter of the Greek alphabet (Β, β). **2** Brit. a second-class grade given for a piece of work or in an examination. **3** Astron. the second brightest star in a constellation. **4** the second member of a series. □ **beta-blocker** Pharm. a drug that prevents the stimulation of increased cardiac action, used to treat angina and reduce high blood pressure. **beta particle** (or **ray**) a fast-moving electron emitted by radioactive decay of substances (orig. regarded as rays). [ME f. L f. Gk]

betake /bitáyk/ v.refl. (past **betook** /bitóok/; past part. **betaken** /bitáykən/) (foll. by to) go to (a place or person).

betatron /báytətron, beé-/ n. Physics an apparatus for accelerating electrons in a circular path by magnetic induction. [BETA + -TRON]

betel /beét'l/ n. the leaf of the Asian evergreen climbing plant Piper betle, chewed in parts of Asia with parings of the areca nut. □ **betel nut** the areca nut. [Port. f. Malayalam veṭṭila]

bête noire /bet nwaár/ n. (pl. **bêtes noires** pronunc. same) a person or thing one particularly dislikes or fears. [F, = black beast]
■ see AVERSION 2.

bethink /bithíngk/ v.refl. (past and past part. **bethought** /-tháwt/) (foll. by of, how, or that + clause) formal **1** reflect; stop to think. **2** be reminded by reflection. [OE bithencan f. Gmc (as BE-, THINK)]

/.../ **pronunciation**	● **part of speech**
□ **phrases, idioms, and compounds**	
□□ **derivatives**	■ **synonym section**
cross-references appear in SMALL CAPITALS or italics	

betide /bitíd/ v. poet. (only in infin. and 3rd sing. subj.) **1** tr. happen to (woe betide him). **2** intr. happen (whate'er may betide). [ME f. obs. tide befall f. OE tīdan]
■ **1** see HAPPEN v. 3. **2** see HAPPEN v. 1.

betimes /bitímz/ adv. literary **1** early; in good time. **2** occasionally. [ME f. obs. betime (as BY, TIME)]
■ see EARLY adj. & adv. 1.

bêtise /baytéez/ n. **1** a foolish or ill-timed remark or action. **2** a piece of folly. [F]

betoken /bitókən/ v.tr. **1** be a sign of; indicate. **2** augur. [OE (as BE-, tācnian signify: see TOKEN)]
■ **1** see INDICATE 2. **2** see BODE.

betony /bét'nee/ n. **1** a purple-flowered plant, Stachys officinalis. **2** any of various similar plants. [ME f. OF betoine f. L betonica]

betook past of BETAKE.

betray /bitráy/ v.tr. **1** place (a person, one's country, etc.) in the hands or power of an enemy. **2** be disloyal to (another person, a person's trust, etc.). **3** reveal involuntarily or treacherously; be evidence of (his shaking hand betrayed his fear). **4** lead astray or into error. □□ **betrayal** n. **betrayer** n. [ME f. obs. tray, ult. f. L tradere hand over]
■ **2** be or prove false or disloyal to, sell out, break faith with, let down, fail, inform on, stab in the back, double-cross, give away, colloq. sell down the river, rat on, Brit. sl. shop, grass (on). **3** reveal, disclose, divulge, display, demonstrate, make known, expose, lay bare, evidence. **4** lead astray, mislead, misguide, deceive, take in, dupe, beguile, fool, hoodwink. □□ **betrayal** treachery, treason, disloyalty, perfidy, traitorousness, faithlessness, bad faith, breach of faith, stab in the back, sellout; revelation, exposure, disclosure, divulgence, colloq. giveaway.

betroth /bitróth, -tráwth/ v.tr. (usu. as **betrothed** adj.) bind with a promise to marry. □□ **betrothal** n. [ME f. BE- + trouthe, treuthe TRUTH, later assim. to TROTH]
■ (**betrothed**) see ENGAGED 1. □□ **betrothal** see MATCH¹ n. 3.

better¹ /bétər/ adj., adv., n., & v. ● adj. (compar. of GOOD). **1** of a more excellent or outstanding or desirable kind (a better product; it would be better to go home). **2** partly or fully recovered from illness (feeling better). ● adv. (compar. of WELL¹). **1** in a better manner (she sings better). **2** to a greater degree; more (like it better; took us better than an hour to finish). **3** more usefully or advantageously (is better forgotten). ● n. **1** that which is better (the better of the two; had the better of me). **2** (usu. in pl.; prec. by my, etc.) one's superior in ability or rank (take notice of your betters). ● v. **1** tr. improve on; surpass (I can better his offer). **2** tr. make better; improve. **3** refl. improve one's position, etc. **4** intr. become better; improve. □ **better half** colloq. one's wife or husband. **better off** in a better (esp. financial) position. **the better part of** most of. **for better or for worse** on terms accepting all results; whatever the outcome. **get the better of** defeat; outwit; win an advantage over. **go one better 1** outbid, etc., by one. **2** (go one better than) outdo another person. **had better** would find it wiser to. [OE betera f. Gmc]
■ adj. **1** superior; preferable. **2** healthier, haler, heartier, less sick or ill, improved; cured, recovered. ● adv. **3** best. ● n. **1** advantage, mastery, superiority, control; the edge. **2** (betters) superiors, masters, elders. ● v. **1** surpass, excel, outdo, outstrip, beat, improve on, outmatch, exceed, eclipse, colloq. lick, best. **2** improve, advance, raise, elevate, upgrade, enhance, lift, extend, increase, formal ameliorate, literary meliorate. **3** improve, advance, promote. **4** see IMPROVE 1a. □ **better half** see PARTNER n. 4. **better off** improved; wealthier, richer. **the better part of** the best part of, most of, the greater part of, the majority of. **get the better of** see DEFEAT v. 1. **go one better 2** see OUTDO. **had better** had best, ought to, should, must.

better² var. of BETTOR.

betterment /bétərmənt/ n. **1** making better; improvement. **2** Econ. enhanced value (of real property) arising from local improvements.

betting /béting/ n. **1** gambling by risking money on an unpredictable outcome. **2** the odds offered in this. □ **betting shop** Brit. a bookmaker's shop or office. **what's the betting?** Brit. colloq. it is likely or to be expected (what's the betting he'll be late?).

bettor /bétər/ n. (also **better**) a person who bets.
■ gambler, speculator, gamester, punter.

between /bitwéen/ prep. & adv. ● prep. **1 a** at or to a point in the area or interval bounded by two or more other points in space, time, etc. (broke down between Boston and Providence; we must meet between now and Friday). **b** along the extent of such an area or interval (there are five shops between here and the main road; works best between five and six; the numbers between 10 and 20). **2** separating, physically or conceptually (the distance between here and the moon; the difference between right and wrong). **3 a** by combining the resources of (great potential between them; between us we could afford it). **b** shared by; as the joint resources of ($5 between them). **c** by joint or reciprocal action (an agreement between us; sorted it out between themselves). ¶ Use in sense 3 with reference to more than two people or things is established and acceptable (e.g., relations between the United States, Canada, and Mexico). **4** to and from (runs between New York and Philadelphia). **5** taking one and rejecting the other of (decide between eating here and going out). ● adv. (also **in between**) at a point or in the area bounded by two or more other points in space, time, sequence, etc. (not fat or thin but in between). □ **between ourselves** (or **you and me**) in confidence. **between times** (or Brit. **whiles**) in the intervals between other actions; occasionally. [OE betwēonum f. Gmc (as BY, TWO)]

betwixt /bitwíkst/ prep. & adv. archaic between. □ **betwixt and between** colloq. neither one thing nor the other. [ME f. OE betwēox f. Gmc: cf. AGAINST]

BeV abbr. a billion (=10⁹) electron-volts. Also called GeV.

bevatron /bévətron/ n. a synchrotron used to accelerate protons to energies in the billion electron-volt range. [BeV + -TRON]

bevel /bévəl/ n. & v. ● n. **1** a slope from the horizontal or vertical in carpentry and stonework; a sloping surface or edge. **2** (in full **bevel square**) a tool for marking angles in carpentry and stonework. ● v. (**beveled, beveling** or **bevelled, bevelling**) **1** tr. reduce (a square edge) to a sloping edge. **2** intr. slope at an angle; slant. □ **bevel gear** a gear working another gear at an angle to it by means of bevel wheels. **bevel wheel** a toothed wheel whose working face is oblique to the axis. [OF bevel (unrecorded) f. baïf f. baer gape]
■ n. **1** see SLOPE 1–3. ● v. see SLANT 1, 2.

beverage /bévərij, bévrij/ n. a drink (hot beverage; alcoholic beverage). [ME f. OF be(u)vrage, ult. f. L bibere drink]
■ see DRINK n. 1a.

bevvy /bévee/ n. (also **bevy**) Brit. sl. (a) drink, esp. (of) beer or another alcoholic beverage. [shortened f. BEVERAGE]

bevy /bévee/ n. (pl. **-ies**) **1** a flock of quails or larks. **2** a company of persons (orig. of women). [15th c.: orig. unkn.]
■ **1** see FLIGHT¹ n. 3a. **2** see GROUP n. 1.

bewail /biwáyl/ v.tr. **1** greatly regret or lament. **2** wail over; mourn for. □□ **bewailer** n.
■ lament (for or over), regret, mourn (for or over), bemoan, rue; sorrow for or over, sorrow for or over, moan over, weep or cry or keen or wail over, beat one's breast over, archaic or poet. plain for.

beware /biwáir/ v. (only in imper. or infin.) **1** intr. (often foll. by of, or that, lest, etc. + clause) be cautious; take heed (beware of the dog; told us to beware; beware that you don't fall). **2** tr. be cautious of (beware the Ides of March). [BE + WARE³]
■ take heed, be careful, be wary, be cautious, be on one's guard, exercise caution, watch out, look out, take care; (beware of) mind, watch for, heed.

bewilder /biwíldər/ v.tr. utterly perplex or confuse. □□ **bewilderedly** adv. **bewildering** adj. **bewilderingly** adv. **bewilderment** n. [BE- + obs. wilder lose one's way]
■ confuse, confound, perplex, puzzle, mystify, befuddle, nonplus, baffle, bemuse, maze, bedazzle, bedevil,

distract, gravel, *archaic* wilder, *colloq.* flummox.
□□ **bewildering** see *perplexing* (PERPLEX).

bewitch /biwích/ *v.tr.* **1** enchant; greatly delight. **2** cast a
spell on. □□ **bewitching** *adj.* **bewitchingly** *adv.* [ME f. BE-
+ OE *wiccian* enchant f. *wicca* WITCH]
■ **1** enchant, entrance, spellbind, charm, fascinate,
beguile, captivate, enrapture, enthral, seduce, *archaic*
witch, *poet.* glamour; delight, thrill, excite. **2** cast a
spell on *or* over, charm, bedevil, voodoo, hex, hoodoo,
archaic witch; *colloq.* jinx.

bey /bay/ *n. hist.* (in the Ottoman Empire) the title of a governor of a province. [Turk.]

beyond /biyónd/ *prep., adv., & n.* ● *prep.* **1** at or to the farther side of (*beyond the river*). **2** outside the scope, range, or
understanding of (*beyond repair; beyond a joke; it is beyond
me*). **3** more than. ● *adv.* **1** at or to the farther side. **2** farther
on. ● *n.* (prec. by *the*) the unknown after death. □ **the back
of beyond** see BACK. **beyond words** inexpressible. [OE
beg(e)ondan (as BY, YON, YONDER)]
■ *prep.* **1** see OVER *prep.* 3, 4. **2** see ABOVE *prep.* 4b. **3** see
OVER *prep.* 10. ● *adv.* **1** see OVER *adv.* 4. □ **beyond
words** see INEXPRESSIBLE.

bezant /bézənt, bizánt/ *n.* **1** *hist.* a gold or silver coin orig.
minted at Byzantium. **2** *Heraldry* a gold roundel. [ME f. OF
besanz -ant f. L *Byzantius* Byzantine]

bezel /bézəl/ *n.* **1** the sloped edge of a chisel. **2** the oblique
faces of a cut gem. **3 a** a groove holding a watch crystal or
gem. **b** a rim holding a glass, etc., cover. [OF *besel* (unrecorded: cf. F *béseau, bizeau*) of unkn. orig.]

bezique /bizeék/ *n.* **1** a card game for two with a double pack
of 64 cards, including the ace to seven only in each suit. **2**
a combination of the queen of spades and the jack of diamonds in this game. [F *bésigue*, perh. f. Pers. *bāzīgar* juggler]

bezoar /beézawr/ *n.* a small stone that may form in the stom-
achs of certain animals, esp. ruminants, and which was once
used as an antidote for various ills. [ult. f. Pers. *pādzahr*
antidote, Arab. *bāzahr*]

b.f. *abbr.* **1** (also **bf**) *Printing* bold face. **2** brought forward. **3**
Brit. colloq. bloody fool.

bhang /bang/ *n.* the leaves and flower tops of hemp used as
a narcotic; cannabis. [Port. *bangue*, Pers. *bang*, & Urdu, etc.,
bhāng f. Skr. *bhangā*]

bharal /búrəl/ *n.* (also **burhel**) a Himalayan wild sheep,
Pseudois nayaur, with a blue-black coat and horns curved
rearward. [Hindi]

b.h.p. *abbr.* brake horsepower.

Bi *symb. Chem.* the element bismuth.

bi- /bi/ *comb. form* (often **bin-** before a vowel) forming nouns
and adjectives meaning: **1** having two; a thing having two
(*bilateral; binaural; biplane*). **2 a** occurring twice in every one
or once in every two (*biweekly*). **b** lasting for two (*biennial*).
3 doubly; in two ways (*biconcave*). **4** *Chem.* a substance having a double proportion of the acid, etc., indicated by the
simple word (*bicarbonate*). **5** *Bot. & Zool.* (of division and
subdivision) twice over (*bipinnate*). [L]

biannual /bí-ányōōəl/ *adj.* occurring, appearing, etc., twice a
year (cf. BIENNIAL). □□ **biannually** *adv.*

bias /bíəs/ *n. & v.* ● *n.* **1** (often foll. by *toward, against*) a
predisposition or prejudice. **2** *Statistics* a systematic distortion of a statistical result due to a factor not allowed for in
its derivation. **3** an edge cut obliquely across the weave of a
fabric. **4** *Electr.* a steady voltage, magnetic field, etc., applied
to an electronic system or device. ● *v.tr.* (**biased, biasing;
biassed, biassing**) **1** (esp. as **biased** *adj.*) influence (usu.
unfairly); prejudice. **2** give a bias to. □ **bias binding** a strip
of fabric cut obliquely and used to bind edges. **on the bias**
obliquely; diagonally. [F *biais*, of unkn. orig.]
■ *n.* **1** prejudice, predisposition, partiality, inclination,
leaning, bent, disposition, propensity, tendency,
predilection, proclivity. **2** skew, skewness, distortion. **3**
angle, slant, diagonal. ● *v.* **1** affect unduly *or* unfairly,
prejudice, color, taint, predispose, influence, sway,
incline; skew; (**biased**) prejudiced, partial; warped,
distorted, one-sided, subjective, jaundiced; skewed.

biathlon /bi-áthlon, -lən/ *n. Sports* an athletic contest in skiing and shooting. □□ **biathlete** *n.* [BI-, after PENTATHLON]

biaxial /bí-ákseeəl/ *adj.* (esp. of crystals) having two axes
along which polarized light travels with equal velocity.

bib¹ /bib/ *n.* **1** a piece of cloth or plastic fastened round a
child's neck to keep the clothes clean while eating. **2** the top
front part of an apron, overalls, etc. **3** the edible marine fish
Trisopterus luscus of the cod family. Also called POUT². □ **best
bib and tucker** best clothes. **stick** (or **poke**, etc.) **one's
bib in** *Austral. sl.* interfere. [perh. f. BIB²]

bib² /bib/ *v.intr.* (**bibbed, bibbing**) *archaic* drink much or
often. □□ **bibber** *n.* [ME, perh. f. L *bibere* drink]
■ □□ **bibber** see DRUNK *n.* 1.

bibcock /bíbkok/ *n.* a faucet with a bent nozzle fixed at the
end of a pipe. [perh. f. BIB¹ + COCK¹]

bibelot /beéblō/ *n.* a small curio or artistic trinket. [F]

bibl. *abbr.* (also **Bibl.**) biblical.

Bible /bíbəl/ *n.* **1 a** the Christian scriptures consisting of the
Old and New Testaments. **b** the Jewish scriptures. **c** (**bible**)
any copy of these (*three bibles on the table*). **d** a particular
edition of the Bible (*New English Bible*). **2** (**bible**) *colloq.* any
authoritative book (*the woodworker's bible*). **3** the scriptures
of any non-Christian religion. □ **Bible belt** the area of the
southern and central US where fundamentalist Protestant
beliefs prevail. **Bible oath** a solemn oath taken on the Bible.
Bible-thumper (or **-basher**, etc.) *sl.* a person given to Bible-thumping. **Bible-thumping** (or **-bashing**, etc.) *sl.* aggressive fundamentalist preaching. [ME f. OF f. eccl.L *biblia*
f. Gk *biblia* books (pl. of *biblion*), orig. dimin. of *biblos, bublos*
papyrus]
■ **1, 3** see SCRIPTURE.

biblical /bíblikəl/ *adj.* **1** of, concerning, or contained in the
Bible. **2** resembling the language of the Authorized Version
of the Bible. □□ **biblically** *adv.*

biblio- /bíbleeō/ *comb. form* denoting a book or books. [Gk f.
biblion book]

bibliog. *abbr.* bibliography.

bibliography /bíbleeógrəfee/ *n.* (*pl.* **-ies**) **1 a** a list of the
books referred to in a scholarly work, usu. printed as an
appendix. **b** a list of the books of a specific author or publisher, or on a specific subject, etc. **2 a** the history or description of books, including authors, editions, etc. **b** any
book containing such information. □□ **bibliographer** *n.*
bibliographic /-leeəgráfik/ *adj.* **bibliographical** *adj.* **bib-
liographically** *adv.* **bibliographize** /-leeógrəfiz/ *v.tr.* [F
bibliographie f. mod.L *bibliographia* f. Gk (as BIBLE, -GRA-
PHY)]

bibliomancy /bíbleeōmansee/ *n.* foretelling the future by the
analysis of a randomly chosen passage from a book, esp. the
Bible.

bibliomania /bíbleeōmáyneeə/ *n.* an extreme enthusiasm for
collecting and possessing books. □□ **bibliomaniac** /-neeak/
n. & adj.

bibliophile /bíbleeōfil/ *n.* a person who collects or is fond of
books. □□ **bibliophilic** /-fílik/ *adj.* **bibliophily** /-leeófilee/
n. [F *bibliophile* (as BIBLIO-, -PHILE)]
■ see BOOKWORM.

bibliopole /bíbleeōpōl/ *n.* a seller of (esp. rare) books.
□□ **bibliopoly** /-leeópəlee/ *n.* [L *bibliopola* f. Gk *bibliopōlēs* f.
biblion book + *pōlēs* seller]

bibulous /bíbyələs/ *adj.* given to drinking alcoholic beverages. □□ **bibulously** *adv.* **bibulousness** *n.* [L *bibulus* freely
drinking f. *bibere* drink]
■ □□ **bibulousness** see *drunkenness* (DRUNKEN).

bicameral /bíkámərəl/ *adj.* (of a parliament or legislative
body) having two chambers. □□ **bicameralism** *n.* [BI- + L
camera chamber]

bicarb /bika'árb/ *n. colloq.* = BICARBONATE 2. [abbr.]

bicarbonate /bīka'árbənit/ *n.* **1** *Chem.* any acid salt of car-

/.../ **pronunciation**	● **part of speech**
□ **phrases, idioms, and compounds**	
□□ **derivatives**	■ **synonym section**
cross-references appear in SMALL CAPITALS or *italics*	

bonic acid. **2** (in full **bicarbonate of soda**) sodium bicarbonate used as an antacid or in baking powder.

bice /bīs/ *n. Brit.* **1** any of various pigments made from blue or green basic copper carbonate. **2** any similar pigment made from smalt. **3** a shade of blue or green given by these. □ **blue bice** a shade of blue between ultramarine and azure derived from smalt. **green bice** a yellowish green color derived by adding yellow orpiment to smalt. [orig. = brownish gray, f. OF *bis* dark gray, of unkn. orig.]

bicentenary /bīsenténəree, bīséntəneree/ *n. & adj. esp. Brit.* = BICENTENNIAL.

bicentennial /bīsenténeeəl/ *n. & adj. esp. US* ● *n.* **1** a two-hundredth anniversary. **2** a celebration of this. ● *adj.* **1** lasting two hundred years or occurring every two hundred years. **2** of or concerning a bicentennial.

bicephalous /bīséfələs/ *adj.* having two heads.

biceps /bíseps/ *n.* a muscle having two heads or attachments, esp. the one which bends the elbow. [L, = two-headed, formed as BI- + -*ceps* f. *caput* head]

bicker /bíkər/ *v.intr.* **1** quarrel pettily; wrangle. **2** *poet.* **a** (of a stream, rain, etc.) patter (over stones, etc.). **b** (of a flame, light, etc.) flash; flicker. □□ **bickerer** *n.* [ME *biker, beker*, of unkn. orig.]
■ **1** squabble, quarrel, dispute, wrangle, argue, disagree, tiff, *colloq.* row, spat, esp. *Brit. joc.* argy-bargy. **2 a** see PATTER¹ *v.* 1. **b** see FLASH *v.* 1, 3.

bickie /bíkee/ *n.* (also **bikkie**) *Brit. & Austral. colloq.* a biscuit. □ **big bickies** *Austral. colloq.* a large sum of money. [abbr.]

bicolor /bíkúlər/ *adj. & n.* ● *adj.* having two colors. ● *n.* a bicolor blossom or animal.

biconcave /bīkónkayv, bíkonkáyv/ *adj.* (esp. of a lens) concave on both sides.

biconvex /bīkónveks, bíkonvéks/ *adj.* (esp. of a lens) convex on both sides.

bicultural /bíkúlchərəl/ *adj.* having or combining two cultures.

bicuspid /bíkúspid/ *adj. & n.* ● *adj.* having two cusps or points. ● *n.* **1** the premolar tooth in humans. **2** a tooth with two cusps. □□ **bicuspidate** *adj.* [BI- + L *cuspis -idis* sharp point]

bicycle /bísikəl, -sīkəl/ *n. & v.* ● *n.* a vehicle of two wheels held in a frame one behind the other, propelled by pedals and steered with handlebars attached to the front wheel. ● *v.intr.* ride a bicycle. □ **bicycle chain** a chain transmitting power from the bicycle pedals to the wheels. **bicycle clip** either of two metal clips used to confine a cyclist's pants at the ankle. **bicycle pump** a portable pump for inflating bicycle tires. □□ **bicycler** *n.* **bicyclist** /-klist/ *n.* [F f. BI- + Gk *kuklos* wheel]
■ *n.* see CYCLE *n.* 4.

bid /bid/ *v. & n.* ● *v.* (**bidding**; *past* **bid**, *archaic* **bade** /bayd, bad/; *past part.* **bid**, *archaic* **bidden** /bíd'n/) **1** *tr. & intr.* (*past* and *past part.* **bid**) (often foll. by *for, against*) **a** (esp. at an auction) offer (a certain price) (*did not bid for the vase; bid against the dealer; bid $20*). **b** offer to do work, etc., for a stated price. **2** *tr. archaic* or *literary* **a** command; order (*bid the soldiers to shoot*). **b** invite (*bade her to start*). **3** *tr. archaic* or *literary* **a** utter (greeting or farewell) to (*I bade him welcome*). **b** proclaim (defiance, etc.). **4** (*past* and *past part.* **bid**) *Cards* **a** *intr.* state before play how many tricks one intends to make. **b** *tr.* state (one's intended number of tricks). ● *n.* **1 a** (esp. at an auction) an offer (of a price) (*a bid of $5*). **b** an offer (to do work, supply goods, etc.) at a stated price; a tender. **2** *Cards* a statement of the number of tricks a player proposes to make. **3** an attempt; an effort (*a bid for power*). □ **bid fair to** seem likely to. **make a bid for** try to gain (*made a bid for freedom*). □□ **bidder** *n.* [OE *biddan* ask f. Gmc, & OE *bēodan* offer, command]
■ *v.* **1** (*tr.*) offer, make an offer of, tender, proffer, put up, put forward; (*bid for*) make an offer for, tender for. **2 a** command *or* order *or* direct *or* tell *or* enjoin to. **b** invite *or* summon *or* ask *or* request *or* entreat *or* beg to. ● *n.* **1** offer, tender, *literary* proffer. **3** see ATTEMPT *n.*
□ **bid fair to** see LIKELY *adj.* 2.

biddable /bídəbəl/ *adj.* **1** obedient. **2** *Cards* (of a hand or suit) suitable for being bid. □□ **biddability** *n.*
■ **1** see TRACTABLE 1.

bidden *archaic past part.* of BID.

bidding /bíding/ *n.* **1** the offers at an auction. **2** *Cards* the act of making a bid or bids. **3** a command, request, or invitation. □ **bidding prayer** *Anglican Ch.* one inviting the congregation to join in.
■ **3** invitation, summons, call, *colloq.* invite; command, order, dictate, direction, instruction, demand, requisition, *archaic* hest, *formal* pleasure, *literary* behest; request, entreaty, solicitation, plea, petition, supplication, appeal, obsecration.

biddy /bídee/ *n.* (*pl.* **-ies**) *sl. derog.* a woman (esp. *old biddy*). [pet form of the name *Bridget*]

bide /bid/ *v.intr. archaic* or *dial.* remain; stay. □ **bide one's time** await one's best opportunity. [OE *bīdan* f. Gmc]
■ see STAY¹ *v.* 1. □ **bide one's time** see WAIT *v.* 1a.

bidet /beedáy/ *n.* a low oval basinlike bathroom fixture used esp. for washing the genital area. [F, = pony]

Biedermeier /béedərmīər/ *attrib.adj.* **1** (of styles, furnishings, etc.) characteristic of the period 1815–48 in Germany. **2** *derog.* conventional; bourgeois. [*Biedermaier* a fictitious German poet (1854)]

biennial /bī-éneeəl/ *adj. & n.* ● *adj.* **1** lasting two years. **2** recurring every two years (cf. BIANNUAL). ● *n.* **1** *Bot.* a plant that takes two years to grow from seed to fruition and die (cf. ANNUAL, PERENNIAL). **2** an event celebrated or taking place every two years. □□ **biennially** *adv.* [L *biennis* (as BI-, *annus* year)]

biennium /bī-éneeəm/ *n.* (*pl.* **bienniums** or **biennia** /-neeə/) a period of two years. [L (as BIENNIAL)]

bier /beer/ *n.* a movable frame on which a coffin or a corpse is placed, or taken to a grave. [OE *bēr* f. Gmc]

biff /bif/ *n. & v. sl.* ● *n.* a sharp blow. ● *v.tr.* strike (a person). [imit.]
■ *n.* see PUNCH¹ *n.* 1. ● *v.* see PUNCH¹ *v.* 1.

biffin /bífin/ *n. Brit.* a deep-red cooking apple. [= *beefing* f. BEEF + -ING¹, with ref. to the color]

bifid /bífid/ *adj.* divided by a deep cleft into two parts. [L *bifidus* (as BI-, *fidus* f. stem of *findere* cleave)]

bifocal /bífókəl/ *adj. & n.* ● *adj.* having two focuses, esp. of a lens with a part for distant vision and a part for near vision. ● *n.* (in *pl.*) bifocal eyeglasses.
■ *n.* (*bifocals*) see GLASS *n.* 3a.

bifurcate /bífərkayt/ *v. & adj.* ● *v.tr. & intr.* divide into two branches; fork. ● *adj.* forked; branched. [med.L *bifurcare* f. L *bifurcus* two-forked (as BI-, *furca* fork)]
■ *v.* see BRANCH *v.* 2.

bifurcation /bífərkáyshən/ *n.* **1 a** a division into two branches. **b** either or both of such branches. **2** the point of such a division.

big /big/ *adj. & adv.* ● *adj.* (**bigger, biggest**) **1 a** of considerable size, amount, intensity, etc. (*a big mistake; a big helping*). **b** of a large or the largest size (*big toe; big drum*). **c** (of a letter) capital, uppercase. **2 a** important; significant; outstanding (*the big race; my big chance*). **b** *colloq.* of (*a person*) famous, important, esp. in a named field. **3 a** grown up (*a big boy now*). **b** elder (*big sister*). **4** *colloq.* **a** boastful (*big words*). **b** often *iron.* generous (*big of him*). **c** ambitious (*big ideas*). **d** popular (*when disco was big*). **5** (usu. foll. by *with*) advanced in pregnancy; fecund (*big with child; big with consequences*). ● *adv. colloq.* in a big manner, esp.: **1** effectively (*went over big*). **2** boastfully (*talk big*). **3** ambitiously (*think big*). □ **Big Apple** *sl.* New York City. **big band** a large jazz or swing orchestra. **big bang theory** the theory that the universe began with the explosion of dense matter. **Big Ben** the great clock tower of the Houses of Parliament in London and its bell. **Big Board** *colloq.* the New York Stock Exchange. **Big Brother** an all-powerful supposedly benevolent dictator (as in Orwell's *1984*). **big bud** a plant disease caused by the gall mite. **big bug** *Brit. sl.* = BIGWIG. **big business** large-scale financial dealings and the businesses involved in them. **Big Daddy** (or **Chief**) *sl.* = BIGWIG. **big deal!** *sl. iron.* I am not impressed. **big dipper** *Brit.* = *roller*

coaster. **Big Dipper** a constellation of seven bright stars in Ursa Major in the shape of a dipper. **big end** (in a motor vehicle) the end of the connecting rod that encircles the crankpin. **Bigfoot** = SASQUATCH. **big game** large animals hunted for sport. **big gun** *sl.* = BIGWIG. **big house 1** esp. *Brit.* the principal house in a village, etc. **2** *sl.* a prison. **big idea** often *iron.* the important intention or scheme. **big lie** (also **Big Lie**) a gross distortion of the truth promulgated blatantly despite its falsity, esp. as propaganda. **big money** large amounts; high profit; high pay. **big mouth** *colloq.* loquacity; talkativeness. **big name** a famous person. **big noise** (or **shot**) *colloq.* = BIGWIG. **big smoke** *Brit. sl.* **1** London. **2** any large town. **big stick** a display of force. **Big Three** (or **Four**, etc.) the predominant few. **the big time** *sl.* success in a profession, esp. show business. **big-timer** *sl.* a person who achieves success. **big top** the main tent in a circus. **big tree** a giant evergreen conifer, *Sequoiadendron giganteum*, usu. with a trunk of large girth. **big wheel 1** a Ferris wheel. **2** *sl.* = BIGWIG. **come** (or **go**) **over big** make a great effect. **in a big way 1** on a large scale. **2** *colloq.* with great enthusiasm, display, etc. **talk big** boast. **think big** be ambitious. **too big for one's boots** (or **breeches**) *sl.* conceited. ▫▫ **biggish** *adj.* **bigness** *n.* [ME: orig. unkn.]

■ *adj.* **1 a** large, great, grand, huge, enormous, immense, gigantic, giant, monstrous, tremendous, colossal, gargantuan, elephantine, mammoth, king-size, hefty, *colloq.* jumbo, hulking, *sl.* humongous. **c** capital, large, upper case, majuscule. **2** important, significant, outstanding, weighty, consequential, major, momentous, critical, *disp.* vital, *colloq. disp.* crucial; prominent, leading, foremost, noted, noteworthy, notable, renowned, well-known, illustrious, distinguished, esteemed, mighty, powerful, popular, famous, successful. **3 a** grown, mature, grown-up. **b** elder, older. **4 b** generous, magnanimous, charitable, unselfish, good, high-minded. **c** ambitious, grandiose, showy, overambitious, inflated, overblown, puffed up, exaggerated; above one's station. ● *adv.* **1** successfully, well, effectively, outstandingly, like a charm *or* dream, perfectly, wonderfully, like clockwork, without a hitch. **2** pompously, boastfully, conceitedly, arrogantly, pretentiously. **3** ambitiously, determinedly, enterprisingly, enthusiastically. ▫ **big deal** *colloq.* so what?, so?, I could (couldn't) care less. **big house 2** see PRISON *n.* 1. **the big time** success, good fortune, the jackpot, the top. **big-timer** see SOMEBODY *n.* **in a big way 1** on a large *or* grand scale. **2** extravagantly, showily, ostentatiously, grandly, pretentiously, lavishly, unstintingly; wholeheartedly, enthusiastically, zealously, energetically; to the fullest extent, to the utmost. **talk big** see BOAST *v.* 1. **too big for one's boots** see CONCEITED.

bigamy /bígəmee/ *n.* (*pl.* **-ies**) the crime of marrying when one is lawfully married to another person. ▫▫ **bigamist** *n.* **bigamous** *adj.* [ME f. OF *bigamie* f. *bigame* bigamous f. LL *bigamus* (as BI-, Gk *gamos* marriage)]

bighead /bíghed/ *n. colloq.* a conceited person.

bigheaded /bighédid/ *adj. colloq.* conceited.

■ see CONCEITED.

bigheadedness /bighédidnəs/ *n. colloq.* conceitedness.

■ see VANITY 1.

bighearted /bighártid/ *adj.* generous.

■ see GENEROUS 1.

bighorn /bíghawrn/ *n.* (in full **bighorn sheep**) an American sheep, *Ovis canadensis*, esp. native to the Rocky Mountains.

bight /bit/ *n.* **1** a curve or recess in a coastline, river, etc. **2** a loop of rope. [OE *byht*, MLG *bucht* f. Gmc: see BOW[2]]

■ **1** see GULF *n.* 1.

bigmouth /bígmowth/ *n. colloq.* a boastful or talkative person; a gossipmonger.

bigot /bígət/ *n.* an obstinate and intolerant believer in a religion, political theory, etc. ▫▫ **bigotry** *n.* [16th c. f. F: orig. unkn.]

■ dogmatist, partisan, sectionalist, intransigent. ▫▫ **bigotry** prejudice, intolerance, narrow-mindedness, partiality, partisanship, dogmatism; discrimination.

bigoted /bígətid/ *adj.* unreasonably prejudiced and intolerant.

■ intolerant, narrow-minded, uncompromising, inflexible, rigid, set, dogmatic, opinionated; prejudiced, biased, jaundiced, one-sided, partial; distorted, warped, twisted.

bigwig /bígwig/ *n. colloq.* an important person

■ kingpin, king, queen, nabob, chief, VIP, *Austral.* joss, *colloq.* boss, big shot, big noise, brass hat, hotshot, *sl.* (big) cheese, big gun, big daddy, big wheel, honcho, *Brit. sl.* nob.

bijou /beézhōō/ *n.* & *adj.* ● *n.* (*pl.* **bijoux** *pronunc.* same) a jewel; a trinket. ● *attrib.adj.* small and elegant. [F]

■ *n.* see JEWEL *n.* 1a.

bijouterie /beezhōōtəree/ *n.* jewelry; trinkets. [F (as BIJOU, -ERY)]

■ see JEWELRY.

bike /bīk/ *n.* & *v.* ● *n.* **1** *colloq.* a bicycle or motorcycle. **2** *Austral. sl.* a promiscuous woman (*the town bike*). ● *v.intr.* ride a bicycle or motorcycle. [abbr.]

■ *n.* **1** see CYCLE *n.* 4.

biker /bíkər/ *n.* a cyclist, esp. a motorcyclist.

bikie /bíkee/ *n. colloq.* a member of a gang of motorcyclists.

bikini /bikéenee/ *n.* a two-piece swimsuit for women. ▫ **bikini briefs** men's or women's scanty briefs. [*Bikini*, an atoll in the Marshall Islands in the Pacific where an atomic bomb was exploded in 1946, from the supposed 'explosive' effect]

bikkie var. of BICKIE.

bilabial /bīláybeeəl/ *adj. Phonet.* (of a sound, etc.) made with closed or nearly closed lips.

bilateral /bīlátərəl/ *adj.* **1** of, on, or with two sides. **2** affecting or between two parties, countries, etc. (*bilateral negotiations*). ▫ **bilateral symmetry** symmetry about a plane. ▫▫ **bilaterally** *adv.*

bilberry /bílberee/ *n.* (*pl.* **-ies**) **1** a hardy dwarf shrub, *Vaccinium myrtillus*, of N. Europe, growing on heaths and mountains, and having red drooping flowers and dark blue berries. **2** the small blue edible berry of this species. **3** any of various shrubs of the genus *Vaccinium* having dark blue berries. [orig. uncert.: cf. Da. *böllebær*]

bilbo /bílbō/ *n.* (*pl.* **-os** or **-oes**) *hist.* a sword noted for the temper and elasticity of its blade. [*Bilboa* = Bilbao in Spain]

bilboes /bílbōz/ *n.pl. hist.* an iron bar with sliding shackles for a prisoner's ankles. [16th c.: orig. unkn.]

■ see SHACKLE 2.

Bildungsroman /bíldōōngzrōmaan/ *n.* a novel dealing with one person's early life and development. [Gf. *Bildung* formation + *Roman* novel]

bile /bīl/ *n.* **1** a bitter greenish brown alkaline fluid which aids digestion and is secreted by the liver and stored in the gallbladder. **2** bad temper; peevish anger. ▫ **bile duct** the duct which conveys bile from the liver and the gallbladder to the duodenum. [F f. L *bilis*]

■ **2** see GALL[1] 2, 3.

bilge /bilj/ *n.* & *v.* ● *n.* **1 a** the almost flat part of a ship's bottom, inside or out. **b** (in full **bilgewater**) filthy water that collects inside the bilge. **2** *sl.* nonsense; worthless ideas (*don't talk bilge*). ● *v.* **1** *tr.* stave in the bilge of (a ship). **2** *intr.* spring a leak in the bilge. **3** *intr.* swell out; bulge. ▫ **bilge keel** a plate or timber fastened under the bilge to prevent rolling. [prob. var. of BULGE]

■ *n.* **1 b** see MUCK *n.* 1, 2. **2** see NONSENSE.

bilharzia /bilhaártzeeə/ *n.* **1** a tropical flatworm of the genus *Schistosoma* (formerly *Bilharzia*) which is parasitic in blood vessels in the human pelvic region. Also called SCHISTOSOME. **2** the chronic tropical disease produced by its presence. Also

/. . ./ **pronunciation** ● **part of speech**
▫ **phrases, idioms, and compounds**
▫▫ **derivatives** ■ **synonym section**
cross-references appear in SMALL CAPITALS or *italics*

called BILHARZIASIS, SCHISTOSOMIASIS. [mod.L f. T. *Bilharz*, Ger. physician d. 1862]

bilharziasis /bílhaarzíəsis/ *n.* the disease of bilharzia. Also called SCHISTOSOMIASIS.

biliary /bílee-eree/ *adj.* of the bile. [F *biliaire*: see BILE, -ARY²]

bilingual /bílinggwəl/ *adj. & n.* ● *adj.* **1** able to speak two languages, esp. fluently. **2** spoken or written in two languages. ● *n.* a bilingual person. □□ **bilingualism** *n.* [L *bilinguis* (as BI-, *lingua* tongue)]

bilious /bílyəs/ *adj.* **1** affected by a disorder of the bile. **2** bad-tempered. □□ **biliously** *adv.* **biliousness** *n.* [L *biliosus* f. *bilis* bile]

■ **2** ill-tempered, bad-tempered, ill-natured, ill-humored, peevish, irritable, crotchety, splenetic, testy, cross, petulant, irascible, tetchy, crabbed, crabby, choleric, angry, cranky, *literary* wrathful.

bilirubin /bíleerōōbin/ *n.* the orangish yellow pigment occurring in bile and causing jaundice when accumulated in blood. [G f. L *bilis* BILE + *ruber* red]

bilk /bilk/ *v.tr. sl.* **1** cheat. **2** give the slip to. **3** avoid paying (a creditor or debt). □□ **bilker** *n.* [orig. uncert., perh. = BALK: earliest use (17th c.) in cribbage, = spoil one's opponent's score]

■ **1** see CHEAT *v.* 1a.

bill¹ /bil/ *n. & v.* ● *n.* **1 a** a printed or written statement of charges for goods supplied or services rendered. **b** the amount owed (*ran up a bill of $300*). **2** a draft of a proposed law. **3 a** a poster; a placard. **b** = HANDBILL. **4 a** a printed list, esp. a theater program. **b** the entertainment itself (*top of the bill*). **5** a piece of paper money, esp. of a specified value (*ten dollar bill*). **6** *sl.* one hundred dollars. ● *v.tr.* **1** put in the program; announce. **2** (foll. by *as*) advertise. **3** send a note of charges to (*billed him for the books*). □ **bill of exchange** *Econ.* a written order to pay a sum of money on a given date to the drawer or to a named payee. **bill of fare 1** a menu. **2** a program (for a theatrical event). **bill of goods 1** a shipment of merchandise, often for resale. **2** *colloq.* an article that is misrepresented, fraudulent, etc. (*at first it seemed a bargain, but we were being sold a bill of goods*). **bill of health 1** *Naut.* a certificate regarding the state of infectious disease on a ship or in a port at the time of sailing. **2** (**clean bill of health**) **a** such a certificate stating that there is no disease. **b** a declaration that a person or thing examined has been found to be free of illness or in good condition. **bill of indictment** a written accusation as presented to a grand jury. **bill of lading** *Naut.* **1** a shipmaster's detailed list of the ship's cargo. **2** = WAYBILL. **Bill of Rights 1** *Law* (in the US) the original constitutional amendments of 1791, affirming basic civil rights. **2** *Law* the English constitutional settlement of 1689. **3** a statement of the rights of a class of people. **bill of sale** *Econ.* a certificate of transfer of personal property, esp. as a security against debt. □□ **billable** *adj.* [ME f. AF *bille*, AL *billa*, prob. alt. of med.L *bulla* seal, sealed documents, BULL²]

■ *n.* **1** statement, invoice, account, tally, reckoning, tabulation, (restaurant) check, *colloq.* tab. **3 a** see POSTER 1. **b** handbill, flyer, dodger. **4** a playbill, program, bill of fare. **5** banknote; (*bills*) paper money, greenbacks, *colloq.* folding money, *sl.* green, wad, kale. ● *v.* **1, 2** see ANNOUNCE 1, PROMOTE 3. **3** invoice, charge, debit. □ **bill of fare 1** menu; wine list. **2** see BILL¹ *n.* 4 above.

bill² /bil/ *n. & v.* ● *n.* **1** the beak of a bird, esp. when it is slender, flattened, or weak, or belongs to a web-footed bird or a bird of the pigeon family. **2** the muzzle of a platypus. **3** a narrow promontory. **4** the point of an anchor fluke. **5** the visor of a cap. ● *v.intr.* (of doves, etc.) stroke a bill with a bill. □ **bill and coo** exchange caresses. □□ **billed** *adj.* (usu. in *comb.*). [OE *bile*, of unkn. orig.]

■ **1, 2** beak; jaws. **3** promontory, headland, bluff, cape, foreland, head, ness, point, tongue. □ **bill and coo** see CUDDLE *v.* 2.

bill³ /bil/ *n.* **1** *hist.* a weapon like a halberd with a hook instead of a blade. **2** = BILLHOOK. [OE *bil*, ult. f. Gmc]

billabong /bíləbawng, -bong/ *n. Austral.* **1** a branch of a river forming a backwater or a stagnant pool. **2** a watercourse holding water only seasonally. [Aboriginal *Billibang* Bell River f. *billa* water]

billboard /bílbawrd/ *n.* a large outdoor board for advertisements, etc.

billet¹ /bílit/ *n. & v.* ● *n.* **1 a** a place where troops, etc., are lodged, usu. with civilians. **b** a written order requiring a householder to lodge the bearer, usu. a soldier. **2** *colloq.* a situation; a job. ● *v.tr.* (**billeted, billeting**) **1** (usu. foll. by *on, in, at*) quarter (soldiers, etc.). **2** (of a householder) provide (a soldier, etc.) with board and lodging. □□ **billetee** /-teé/ *n.* **billeter** *n.* [ME f. AF *billette*, AL *billetta*, dimin. of *billa* BILL¹]

■ *n.* **1 a** see QUARTER *n.* 9b. **2** see POSITION *n.* 8. ● *v.* **1** see QUARTER *v.* **2** see ACCOMMODATE 1.

billet² /bílit/ *n.* **1** a thick piece of firewood. **2** a small metal bar. **3** *Archit.* each of a series of short rolls inserted at intervals in some decorative moldings. [ME f. F *billette* small log, ult. prob. of Celtic orig.]

billet-doux /bílaydōō/ *n.* (*pl.* **billets-doux** /-dōōz/) often *joc.* a love letter. [F, = sweet note]

■ see NOTE *n.* 3.

billfold /bílfōld/ *n.* a wallet for keeping paper money.

■ see WALLET.

billhead /bílhed/ *n.* a printed account form.

billhook /bílhŏok/ *n.* a sickle-shaped tool with a sharp inner edge, used for pruning, lopping, etc.

billiards /bílyərdz/ *n.* **1** any of several games played on an oblong cloth-covered table, esp. one with three balls struck with cues into pockets round the edge of the table. **2** (**billiard**) (in *comb.*) used in billiards (*billiard ball*; *billiard table*). [orig. pl., f. F *billard* billiards, cue, dimin. of *bille* log: see BILLET²]

billion /bílyən/ *n. & adj.* ● *n.* (*pl.* same or (in sense 3) **billions**) (in *sing.* prec. by *a* or *one*) **1** a thousand million (1,000,000,000 or 10⁹). **2** *Brit.* a million million (1,000,000,000,000 or 10¹²). **3** (in *pl.*) *colloq.* a very large number (*billions of years*). ● *adj.* that amount to a billion. □□ **billionth** *adj. & n.* [F (as BI-, MILLION)]

■ *n.* **3** (*billions*) see LOT *n.* 1.

billionaire /bílyənáir/ *n.* a person possessing over a billion dollars, pounds, etc. [after MILLIONAIRE]

■ see TYCOON.

billon /bílən/ *n.* an alloy of gold or silver with a predominating admixture of a base metal. [F f. *bille* BILLET²]

billow /bílō/ *n. & v.* ● *n.* **1** a wave. **2** a soft upward-curving flow. **3** any large soft mass. ● *v.intr.* move, swell, or build up in billows. □□ **billowy** *adj.* [ON *bylgja* f. Gmc]

■ *n.* **1** see WAVE *n.* 1, 2. ● *v.* see WAVE *v.* 2.

billposter /bílpōstər/ *n.* (also **billsticker** /-stikər/) a person who pastes up advertisements. □□ **billposting** *n.*

billy¹ /bílee/ *n.* (*pl.* -ies) (in full **billycan**) esp. *Austral.* a tin or enamel pot with a lid and wire handle, for use in cooking outdoors. [perh. f. Aboriginal *billa* water]

billy² /bílee/ *n.* (*pl.* -ies) **1** = BILLY GOAT. **2** (in full **billy club**) a bludgeon.

billy goat /bíligōt/ *n.* a male goat. [*Billy*, pet form of the name *William*]

billy-oh /bíleeō/ *n. Brit.* □ **like billy-oh** *sl.* very much, hard, strongly, etc. (*raining like billy-oh*). [19th c.: orig. unkn.]

bilobate /bílōbayt/ *adj.* (also **bilobed** /-lōbd/) having or consisting of two lobes.

biltong /bíltong/ *n. S.Afr.* boneless meat salted and dried in strips. [Afrik., of uncert. orig.]

bimanal /bímənəl/ *adj.* (also **bimanous** /-nəs/) having two hands. [BI- + L *manus* hand]

bimbo /bímbō/ *n.* (*pl.* -os or -oes) *sl.* usu. *derog.* **1** a person. **2** a woman, esp. a young empty-headed one. **3** a promiscuous woman. [It., = little child]

■ **2** see MISS².

bimetallic /bímitálik/ *adj.* **1** made of two metals. **2** of or relating to bimetallism. □ **bimetallic strip** a sensitive element in some thermostats made of two bands of different metals that expand at different rates when heated, causing the strip to bend. [F *bimétallique* (as BI-, METALLIC)]

bimetallism /bĭmét'lĭzəm/ *n.* a system of allowing the unrestricted currency of two metals (e.g., gold and silver) at a fixed ratio to each other, as coined money. □□ **bimetallist** *n.*

bimillenary /bĭmíləneree, -milénəree/ *adj.* & *n.* (also **bimillenial** /-léneeəl/) ● *adj.* of or relating to a two-thousandth anniversary. ● *n.* (*pl.* **-ies**) a bimillenary year or festival.

bimonthly /bĭmúnthlee/ *adj.*, *adv.*, & *n.* ● *adj.* occurring twice a month or every two months. ● *adv.* twice a month or every two months. ● *n.* (*pl.* **-ies**) a periodical produced bimonthly. ¶ Often avoided, because of the ambiguity of meaning, in favor of *every two months* and *twice a month.*

bin /bĭn/ *n.* & *v.* ● *n.* a large receptacle for storage or for depositing trash, garbage, etc. ● *v.tr. colloq.* (**binned, binning**) store or put in a bin. □ **bin end** *Brit.* one of the last bottles from a bin of wine, usu. sold at a reduced price. **bin-liner** *Brit.* a bag (usu. of plastic) for lining a garbage can. [OE *bin(n), binne*]

bin- /bĭn, bĭn/ *prefix* var. of BI- before a vowel.

binary /bíneree/ *adj.* & *n.* ● *adj.* **1 a** dual. **b** of or involving pairs. **2** of the arithmetical system using 2 as a base. ● *n.* (*pl.* **-ies**) **1** something having two parts. **2** a binary number. **3** a binary star. □ **binary code** *Computing* a coding system using the binary digits 0 and 1 to represent a letter, digit, or other character in a computer. **binary compound** *Chem.* a compound having two elements or radicals. **binary fission** the division of a cell or organism into two parts. **binary number** (or **digit**) one of two digits (usu. 0 or 1) in a binary system of notation. **binary star** a system of two stars orbiting each other. **binary system** a system in which information can be expressed by combinations of the digits 0 and 1 (corresponding to 'off' and 'on' in computing). **binary tree** a data structure in which a record is branched to the left when greater and to the right when less than the previous record. [LL *binarius* f. *bini* two together]

binate /bínayt/ *adj. Bot.* **1** growing in pairs. **2** composed of two equal parts. [mod.L *binatus* f. L *bini* two together]

binaural /bĭnáwrəl/ *adj.* **1** of or used with both ears. **2** (of sound) recorded using two microphones and usu. transmitted separately to the two ears.

bind /bīnd/ *v.* & *n.* ● *v.* (*past* and *past part.* **bound** /bownd/) (see also BOUNDEN). **1** *tr.* (often foll. by *to, on, together*) tie or fasten tightly. **2** *tr.* **a** restrain; put in bonds. **b** (as **-bound** *adj.*) constricted; obstructed (*snowbound*). **3** *tr.* esp. *Cookery* cause (ingredients) to cohere using another ingredient. **4** *tr.* fasten or hold together as a single mass. **5** *tr.* compel; impose an obligation or duty on. **6** *tr.* **a** edge (fabric, etc.) with braid, etc. **b** fix together and fasten (the pages of a book) in a cover. **7** *tr.* constipate. **8** *tr.* ratify (a bargain, agreement, etc.). **9** *tr.* (in *passive*) be required by an obligation or duty (*am bound to answer*). **10** *tr.* (often foll. by *up*) **a** put a bandage or other covering around. **b** fix together with something put around (*bound her hair*). **11** *tr.* indenture as an apprentice. **12** *intr.* (of snow, etc.) cohere; stick. **13** *intr.* be prevented from moving freely. **14** *intr. Brit. sl.* complain. ● *n.* **1** *colloq.* **a** a nuisance; a restriction. **b** a tight or difficult situation. **2** an act or instance of being bound. **3** = BINE. □ **be bound up with** be closely associated with. **bind over** *Law* order (a person) to do something, esp. keep the peace. **bind up** bandage. **I'll be bound** a statement of assurance, or guaranteeing the truth of something. [OE *bindan*] ■ *v.* **1** tie (up), fasten, make fast, secure, attach, join; cement, stick, fuse. **2 a** see TIE *v.* 1a, 3. **3** mix, blend, combine. **5** constrain, restrain, confine, restrict; commit, hold, oblige, obligate, pledge; compel, force, require, impel, drive; burden. **6 a** edge, border, band, frame, fringe. **9** see sense 5 above. **10 a** bind up, swathe, bandage, swaddle, wrap, cover. **b** see TIE *v.* 1a; encircle, wreathe, surround, encompass, ring, circle, hem in, enclose, *literary* gird. **11** apprentice, indenture, *archaic* prentice. ● *n.* **1 a** nuisance, annoyance, irritant, bother, bore, pest, trial, irritation, vexation, *colloq.* pain (in the neck), *joc.* menace, *sl.* bummer, pain in the butt; restriction, restraint, difficulty, problem,

snag, hindrance, obstacle. **b** predicament, tight corner or place or spot, (difficult) situation, *colloq.* pickle, fix, jam, *disp.* dilemma; (*in a bind*) *Brit.* in a cleft stick.

binder /bíndər/ *n.* **1** a cover for sheets of paper, for a book, etc. **2** a substance that acts cohesively. **3** a reaping machine that binds grain into sheaves. **4** a bookbinder. **5** a temporary agreement providing insurance coverage until a policy is issued.

bindery /bíndəree/ *n.* (*pl.* **-ies**) a workshop or factory for binding books.

binding /bínding/ *n.* & *adj.* ● *n.* something that binds, esp. the covers, glue, etc., of a book. ● *adj.* (often foll. by *on*) obligatory.
■ *n.* see COVER *n.* 1b. ● *adj.* see INCUMBENT *adj.* 1.

bindweed /bíndweed/ *n.* **1** convolvulus. **2** any of various species of climbing plants such as honeysuckle.

bine /bīn/ *n.* **1** the twisting stem of a climbing plant, esp. the hop. **2** a flexible shoot. [orig. a dial. form of BIND]

Binet-Simon test /bĭnáysímən/ *adj.* (also **Binet test, scale**) *Psychol.* a test used to measure intelligence, esp. of children. [A. *Binet* d. 1911 and T. *Simon* d. 1961, Fr. psychologists]

binge /bĭnj/ *n.* & *v. sl.* ● *n.* a spree; a period of uncontrolled eating, drinking, etc. ● *v.intr.* go on a spree; indulge in uncontrolled eating, drinking, etc. [prob. orig. dial., = soak]
■ *n.* see SPREE *n.* 2. ● *v.* see DRINK *v.* 2.

bingle /bínggəl/ *n. Austral. colloq.* a collision. [Brit. dial. *bing* thump, blow]

bingo /bínggō/ *n.* & *int.* ● *n.* a game for any number of players, each having a card of squares with numbers which are marked off as numbers are randomly drawn by a caller. ● *int.* expressing sudden surprise, satisfaction, etc., as in winning at bingo. [prob. imit.: cf. dial. *bing* 'with a bang']

bingy /bínjee/ *n.* (also **bingie**) *Austral. colloq.* the stomach; the belly. [Dharuk *bindhi* belly]

binman /bínman/ *n.* (*pl.* **-men**) *Brit. colloq.* a garbage collector.

binnacle /bínəkəl/ *n.* a built-in housing for a ship's compass. [earlier *bittacle*, ult. f. L *habitaculum* habitation f. *habitare* inhabit]

binocular /bĭnókyələr/ *adj.* adapted for or using both eyes. [BIN- + L *oculus* eye]

binoculars /bĭnókyələrz/ *n.pl.* an optical instrument with a lens for each eye, for viewing distant objects.

binomial /bĭnṓmeeəl/ *n.* & *adj.* ● *n.* **1** an algebraic expression of the sum or the difference of two terms. **2** a two-part name, esp. in taxonomy. ● *adj.* consisting of two terms. □ **binomial distribution** a frequency distribution of the possible number of successful outcomes in a given number of trials in each of which there is the same probability of success. **binomial nomenclature** a system of nomenclature using two terms, the first one indicating the genus and the second the species. **binomial theorem** a formula for finding any power of a binomial without multiplying at length. □□ **binomially** *adv.* [F *binôme* or mod.L *binomium* (as BI-, Gk *nomos* part, portion)]

bint /bĭnt/ *n. Brit. sl. offens.* a girl or woman. [Arab., = daughter, girl]

binturong /bĭntŏŏrawng, -rong/ *n.* a civet, *Arctictis binturong*, of S. Asia, with a shaggy black coat and a prehensile tail. [Malay]

bio /bí-ō/ *n.* & *adj.* ● *n.* **1** biology. **2** (*pl.* **bios**) biography. ● *adj.* biological. [abbr.]

bio- /bí-ō/ *comb. form* **1** life (*biography*). **2** biological (*biomathematics*). **3** of living beings (*biophysics*). [Gk *bios* (course of) human life]

biochemistry /bí-ōkémistree/ *n.* the study of the chemical and physicochemical processes of living organisms. □□ **biochemical** *adj.* **biochemist** *n.*

biocenosis /bí-ōseenṓsĭs/ *n.* (also **biocoenosis**) (*pl.* **-noses**

/. . . /	**pronunciation**	● **part of speech**
	□ **phrases, idioms, and compounds**	
	□□ **derivatives**	■ **synonym section**
	cross-references appear in SMALL CAPITALS or *italics*	

135

/-seez/) **1** an association of different organisms forming a community. **2** the relationship existing between such organisms. □□ **biocenology** /-nólǝjee/ *n.* **biocenotic** /-nótik/ *adj.* [mod.L f. BIO- + Gk *koinōsis* sharing f. *koinos* common]

biodegradable /bí-ōdigráydǝbǝl/ *adj.* capable of being decomposed by bacteria or other living organisms. □□ **biodegradability** *n.* **biodegradation** /-bí-ōdégrǝdáyshǝn/ *n.*

bioengineering /bí-ō-énjineéring/ *n.* **1** the application of engineering techniques to biological processes. **2** the use of artificial tissues, organs, or organ components to replace damaged or absent parts of the body, e.g., artificial limbs, heart pacemakers, etc. □□ **bioengineer** *n.* & *v.*

bioethics /bí-ō-éthiks/ *n.pl.* (treated as *sing.*) the ethics of medical and biological research. □□ **bioethicist** *n.*

biofeedback /bí-ōfeédbak/ *n.* the technique of using the feedback of a normally automatic bodily response to a stimulus in order to acquire voluntary control of that response.

bioflavonoid /bí-ōfláyvǝnoyd/ *n.* = CITRIN. [BIO- + *flavonoid* f. FLAVINE + -OID]

biog. *abbr.* **1** biographer. **2** biographical. **3** biography.

biogenesis /bí-ōjénisis/ *n.* **1** the synthesis of substances by living organisms. **2** the hypothesis that a living organism arises only from another similar living organism. □□ **biogenetic** /-jinétik/ *adj.*

biogenic /bí-ōjénik/ *adj.* produced by living organisms.

biogeography /bí-ōjeeógrǝfee/ *n.* the scientific study of the geographical distribution of plants and animals. □□ **biogeographical** /-jeeǝgráfikǝl/ *adj.*

biography /bíógrǝfee/ *n.* (*pl.* **-ies**) **1 a** a written account of a person's life, usu. by another. **b** such writing as a branch of literature. **2** the course of a living (usu. human) being's life. □□ **biographer** *n.* **biographic** /bíǝgráfik/ *adj.* **biographical** *adj.* [F *biographie* or mod.L *biographia* f. med.Gk]

■ **1a** see LIFE 10.

biol. *abbr.* **1** biologic. **2** biological. **3** biologist. **4** biology.

biological /bíǝlójikǝl/ *adj.* **1** of or relating to biology or living organisms. **2** related genetically, not by marriage, adoption, etc. □ **biological clock** an innate mechanism controlling the rhythmic physiological activities of an organism. **biological control** the control of a pest by the introduction of a natural enemy. **biological warfare** warfare involving the use of toxins or microorganisms. □□ **biologically** *adv.*

biology /bíólǝjee/ *n.* **1** the study of living organisms. **2** the plants and animals of a particular area. □□ **biologist** *n.* [F *biologie* f. G *Biologie* (as BIO-, -LOGY)]

bioluminescence /bí-ōlōōminésǝns/ *n.* the emission of light by living organisms such as the firefly and glowworm. □□ **bioluminescent** *adj.*

biomass /bí-ōmas/ *n.* the total quantity or weight of organisms in a given area or volume. [BIO- + MASS¹]

biomathematics /bí-ōmáthimátiks/ *n.* the science of the application of mathematics to biology.

biome /bí-ōm/ *n.* **1** a large naturally occurring community of flora and fauna adapted to the particular conditions in which they occur, e.g., tundra. **2** the geographical region containing such a community. [BIO- + -OME]

biomechanics /bí-ōmikániks/ *n.* the study of the mechanical laws relating to the movement or structure of living organisms.

biometry /bíómitree/ *n.* (also **biometrics** /bí-ǝmétriks/) the application of statistical analysis to biological data. □□ **biometric** /bí-ǝmétrik/ *adj.* **biometrical** *adj.* **biometrician** /bí-ōmitríshǝn/ *n.*

biomorph /bí-ōmawrf/ *n.* a decorative form based on a living organism. □□ **biomorphic** /-ǝmáwrfik/ *adj.* [BIO- + Gk *morphē* form]

bionic /bíónik/ *adj.* **1** having artificial body parts or the superhuman powers resulting from these. **2** relating to bionics. □□ **bionically** *adv.* [BIO- after ELECTRONIC]

bionics /bíóniks/ *n.pl.* (treated as *sing.*) the study of mechanical systems that function like living organisms or parts of living organisms.

bionomics /bíǝnómiks/ *n.pl.* (treated as *sing.*) the study of the mode of life of organisms in their natural habitat and their adaptations to their surroundings; ecology. □□ **bionomic** *adj.* [BIO- after ECONOMICS]

biophysics /bí-ōfíziks/ *n.pl.* (treated as *sing.*) the science of the application of the laws of physics to biological phenomena. □□ **biophysical** *adj.* **biophysicist** *n.*

biopsy /bíopsee/ *n.* (*pl.* **-ies**) the examination of tissue removed from a living body to discover the presence, cause, or extent of a disease. [F *biopsie* f. Gk *bios* life + *opsis* sight, after *necropsy*]

biorhythm /bí-ōrithǝm/ *n.* **1** any of the recurring cycles of biological processes thought to affect a person's emotional, intellectual, and physical activity. **2** any periodic change in the behavior or physiology of an organism. □□ **biorhythmic** /-ǝríthmik/ *adj.* **biorhythmically** *adv.*

bioscope /bíǝskōp/ *n. S.Afr. sl.* a movie theater.

biosphere /bí-ōsfeer/ *n.* the regions of the earth's crust and atmosphere occupied by living organisms. [G *Biosphäre* (as BIO-, SPHERE)]

biosynthesis /bí-ōsínthisis/ *n.* the production of organic molecules by living organisms. □□ **biosynthetic** /-thétik/ *adj.*

biota /bí-ṓtǝ/ *n.* the animal and plant life of a region. [mod.L: cf. Gk *biotē* life]

biotechnology /bí-ōteknólǝjee/ *n.* the exploitation of biological processes for industrial and other purposes, esp. genetic manipulation of microorganisms (for the production of antibiotics, hormones, etc.).

biotic /bíótik/ *adj.* **1** relating to life or to living things. **2** of biological origin. [F *biotique* or LL *bioticus* f. Gk *biōtikos* f. *bios* life]

biotin /bíǝtin/ *n.* a vitamin of the B complex, found in egg yolk, liver, and yeast, and involved in the metabolism of carbohydrates, fats, and proteins. [G f. Gk *bios* life + -IN]

biotite /bíǝtīt/ *n. Mineral.* a black, dark brown, or green micaceous mineral occurring as a constituent of metamorphic and igneous rocks. [J. B. *Biot*, Fr. physicist d. 1862]

bipartisan /bípaártizǝn, -sǝn/ *adj.* of or involving two (esp. political) parties. □□ **bipartisanship** *n.*

bipartite /bípaártīt/ *adj.* **1** consisting of two parts. **2** shared by or involving two parties. **3** *Law* (of a contract, treaty, etc.) drawn up in two corresponding parts or between two parties. [L *bipartitus* f. *bipartire* (as BI-, *partire* PART)]

biped /bíped/ *n.* & *adj.* ● *n.* a two-footed animal. ● *adj.* two-footed. □□ **bipedal** *adj.* [L *bipes -edis* (as BI-, *pes pedis* foot)]

bipinnate /bípinayt/ *adj.* (of a pinnate leaf) having leaflets that are further subdivided in a pinnate arrangement.

biplane /bíplayn/ *n.* a type of airplane having two sets of wings, one above the other.

bipolar /bípṓlǝr/ *adj.* having two poles or extremities. □ **bipolar disorder** *Psychol.* a disorder characterized by alternating periods of mania and depression. □□ **bipolarity** /-láritee/ *n.*

birch /bǝrch/ *n.* & *v.* ● *n.* **1** any tree of the genus *Betula*, having thin peeling bark, bearing catkins, and found predominantly in northern temperate regions. **2** (in full **birchwood**) the hard fine-grained pale wood of these trees. **3** *NZ* any of various similar trees. **4** (in full **birch rod**) a bundle of birch twigs used for flogging. ● *v.tr.* beat with a birch (in sense 4). □ **birch bark 1** the bark of *Betula papyrifera* used to make canoes. **2** such a canoe. □□ **birchen** *adj.* [OE *bi(e)rce* f. Gmc]

■ *n.* **4** see ROD 3a. ● *v.* see SWITCH *v.* 6.

bird /bǝrd/ *n.* **1** a feathered vertebrate with a beak, two wings, and two feet, egg-laying and usu. able to fly. **2** a game bird. **3** *Brit. sl.* a young woman. **4** *colloq.* a person (*a wily old bird*). **5** *Brit. sl.* **a** a prison. **b** *rhyming sl.* a prison sentence (short for *birdlime* = time). □ **bird call 1** a bird's natural call. **2** an instrument imitating this. **bird cherry** a wild cherry *Prunus padus*. **bird fancier** a person who knows about, collects, breeds, or deals in birds. **a bird in the hand** something secured or certain. **the bird is** (or **has**) **flown** the prisoner, quarry, etc., has escaped. **bird-** (or **birds'-**) **nesting** hunting for birds' nests, usu. to get eggs. **bird of paradise** any bird of the family Paradiseidae found chiefly in New

Guinea, the males having very beautiful brilliantly colored plumage. **bird of passage 1** a migrant. **2** any transient visitor. **bird of prey** see PREY. **bird sanctuary** an area where birds are protected and encouraged to breed. **the birds and the bees** euphem. sexual activity and reproduction. **bird's-eye** • n. **1** any of several plants having small bright round flowers, such as the germander speedwell. **2** a pattern with many small spots. • adj. of or having small bright round flowers (bird's-eye primrose). **bird's-eye view** a general view from above. **bird's-foot** (pl. **bird's-foots**) any plant like the foot of a bird, esp. of the genus Lotus, having claw-shaped pods. **bird's nest soup** soup made (esp. in Chinese cooking) from the dried gelatinous coating of the nests of swifts and other birds. **birds of a feather** people of like character. **bird-strike** a collision between a bird and an aircraft. **bird table** a raised platform on which food for birds is placed. **bird-watcher** a person who observes birds in their natural surroundings. **bird-watching** this occupation. **for** (or **strictly for**) **the birds** colloq. trivial; uninteresting. **get the bird** Brit. sl. **1** be dismissed. **2** be hissed at or booed. **like a bird** without difficulty or hesitation. **a little bird** an unnamed informant. [OE brid, of unkn. orig.]
■ □ **bird of passage 1** see MIGRANT n.

birdbath /bárdbath/ n. a basin in a garden, etc., with water for birds to bathe in.

birdbrain /bárdbrayn/ n. colloq. a stupid or flighty person. □□ **birdbrained** adj.
■ see HALFWIT. □□ **birdbrained** see FRIVOLOUS 2.

birdcage /bárdkayj/ n. **1** a cage for birds usu. made of wire or cane. **2** an object of a similar design.

birder /bárdər/ n. a bird-watcher. □□ **birding** n.

birdie /bárdee/ n. & v. • n. **1** colloq. a little bird. **2** Golf a score of one stroke less than par at any hole. • v.tr. (**birdies, birdied, birdying**) Golf play (a hole) in a birdie.

birdlime /bárdlīm/ n. sticky material painted on twigs to trap small birds.

birdseed /bárdseed/ n. a blend of seed for feeding caged or wild birds.

birdsong /bárdsawng, -song/ n. the musical cry of a bird or birds.

birefringent /bírifrínjənt/ adj. Physics having two different refractive indices. □□ **birefringence** /-jəns/ n.

bireme /bíreem/ n. hist. an ancient Greek warship, with two banks of oarsmen on each side. [L biremis (as BI-, remus oar)]

biretta /birétə/ n. a square box- or black cap with three flat projections on top, worn by (esp. Roman Catholic) clergymen. [It. berretta or Sp. birreta f. LL birrus cape]

biriani var. of BIRYANI.

Biro /bírō/ n. (pl. **-os**) Brit. propr. a kind of ballpoint pen. [L. Biró, Hung. inventor d. 1985]

birth /bərth/ n. & v. • n. **1** the emergence of a (usu. fully developed) infant or other young from the body of its mother. **2** rhet. the beginning or coming into existence of something (the birth of civilization; the birth of socialism). **3 a** origin; descent; ancestry (of noble birth). **b** high or noble birth; inherited position. • v.tr. colloq. **1** to give birth to. **2** to assist (a woman) to give birth. □ **birth certificate** an official document identifying a person by name, place, date of birth, and parentage. **birth control** the control of the number of children one conceives, esp. by contraception. **birth control pill** the contraceptive pill. **birth defect** a physical, mental, or biochemical abornality present at birth. **birth rate** the number of live births per thousand of population per year. **give birth** bear a child, etc. **give birth to 1** produce (young) from the womb. **2** cause to begin; found. [ME f. ON byrth f. Gmc: see BEAR¹, -TH²]
■ n. **1** childbirth, delivery, nativity, formal parturition. **2** origin, creation, emergence, genesis, beginning, start, origination, dawn, dawning. **3** origin, extraction, parentage, line, lineage, ancestry, descent, family, blood. • v. **1** give birth to, have, deliver, bear, bring forth or into the world, mother, derog. whelp. □ **birth control** family planning, contraception. **give birth to 1** see BIRTH v. above. **2** see FOUND² 1.

birthday /bárthday/ n. **1** the day on which a person, etc., was

born. **2** the anniversary of this. □ **birthday honors** Brit. titles, etc., given on a sovereign's official birthday. **in one's birthday suit** joc. naked.
■ □ **in one's birthday suit** see NAKED 1.

birthmark /bárthmaark/ n. an unusual brown or red mark on one's body at or from birth.

birthplace /bárthplays/ n. the place where a person was born.

birthright /bárthrīt/ n. a right of possession or privilege one has from birth.
■ see INHERITANCE 1.

birthstone /bárthstōn/ n. a gemstone popularly associated with the month of one's birth.

biryani /bíree-aánee/ n. (also **biriani**) an Indian dish made with highly seasoned rice, and meat or fish, etc. [Urdu]

biscuit /bískit/ n. & adj. • n. **1** a small bread or cake leavened with baking soda or baking powder. **2** Brit. **a** = cookie. **b** CRACKER. **3** fired unglazed pottery. **4** a light brown color. • adj. biscuit colored. [ME f. OF bescoit, etc. ult. f. L bis twice + coctus past part. of coquere cook]

bisect /bísékt/ v.tr. divide into two (equal) parts. □□ **bisection** /-sékshən/ n. **bisector** n. [BI- + L secare sect- cut]
■ see CLEAVE¹ 1a.

bisexual /bísékshōōəl/ adj. & n. • adj. **1** sexually attracted to persons of both sexes. **2** Biol. having characteristics of both sexes. **3** of or concerning both sexes. • n. a bisexual person. □□ **bisexuality** /-sékshoo-álitee, -séksyoo-álitee/ n.
■ adj. **2** hermaphrodite, hermaphroditical, hermaphroditic, androgynous, Zool. monoecious.
• n. androgyne, hermaphrodite.

bish /bish/ n. Brit. sl. a mistake. [20th c.: orig. uncert.]

bishop /bíshəp/ n. **1** a senior member of the Christian clergy usu. in charge of a diocese, and empowered to confer holy orders. **2** a chess piece with the top sometimes shaped like a miter. **3** mulled and spiced wine. [OE biscop, ult. f. Gk episkopos overseer (as EPI-, -skopos -looking)]

bishopric /bíshəprik/ n. **1** the office of a bishop. **2** a diocese. [OE bisceoprīce (as BISHOP, rīce realm)]

bismuth /bízməth/ n. Chem. **1** a brittle reddish white metallic element, occurring naturally and used in alloys. ¶ Symb.: **Bi**. **2** any compound of this element used medicinally. [mod.L bisemutum, Latinization of G Wismut, of unkn. orig.]

bison /bísən/ n. (pl. same) either of two wild humpbacked shaggy-haired oxen of the genus Bison, native to N. America (B. bison) or Europe (B. bonasus). [ME f. L f. Gmc]

bisque¹ /bisk/ n. a rich shellfish soup, made esp. from lobster. [F]

bisque² /bisk/ n. Tennis, Croquet, & Golf an advantage of scoring one free point, or taking an extra turn or stroke. [F]

bisque³ /bisk/ n. = BISCUIT 2.

bistable /bístáybəl/ adj. (of an electrical circuit, etc.) having two stable states.

bister /bístər/ n. & adj. (Brit. **bistre**) • n. **1** a brownish pigment made from the soot of burned wood. **2** the brownish color of this. • adj. of this color. [F, of unkn. orig.]

bistort /bístawrt/ n. an herb, Polygonum bistorta, with a twisted root and a cylindrical spike of flesh-colored flowers. [F bistorte or med.L bistorta f. bis twice + torta fem. past part. of torquēre twist]

bistoury /bístəree/ n. (pl. **-ies**) a surgical scalpel. [F bistouri, bistorie, orig. = dagger, of unkn. orig.]

bistre Brit. var. of BISTER.

bistro /béestrō, bís-/ n. (pl. **-os**) a small restaurant. [F]
■ see CAFÉ 1.

bisulfate /bísúlfayt/ n. Chem. a salt or ester of sulfuric acid.

bit¹ /bit/ n. **1** a small piece or quantity (a bit of cheese; give me another bit; that bit is too small). **2** (prec. by a) **a** a fair amount (sold quite a bit; needed a bit of persuading). **b** colloq. somewhat (am a bit tired). **c** (foll. by of) colloq. rather (a bit

/.../ **pronunciation**	● **part of speech**
□ **phrases, idioms, and compounds**	
□□ **derivatives**	■ **synonym section**
cross-references appear in SMALL CAPITALS or italics	

of an idiot). **d** (foll. by *of*) *colloq.* only a little; a mere (*a bit of a boy*). **3** a short time or distance (*wait a bit; move up a bit*). **4** *sl.* an amount equal to 12 $^1/_2$ cents (esp. in the phrase *two bits*). □ **bit by bit** gradually. **bit of all right** *Brit. sl.* a pleasing person or thing, esp. a woman. **bit of fluff** (or **skirt** or **stuff**) see FLUFF, SKIRT, STUFF. **bit on the side** *sl.* an extramarital sexual relationship. **bit part** a minor part in a play or a movie. **bits and pieces** (or *Brit.* **bobs**) an assortment of small items. **do one's bit** *colloq.* make a useful contribution to an effort or cause. **every bit as** see EVERY. **not a bit** (or *Brit.* **not a bit of it**) not at all. **to bits** into pieces. [OE *bita* f. Gmc, rel. to BITE]

■ **1** piece, segment, share, portion, part, fraction; morsel, scrap, fragment, shred, sliver, particle, grain, crumb, drop, sippet, snippet, mite, pinch, spot, *colloq.* smidgen; jot, tittle, whit, rap, iota, speck, atom, *colloq.* tad, *Austral. colloq.* skerrick; touch, trifle, scintilla, trace, hint, suggestion, suspicion. **2 b, c** see RATHER 4. **d** slip. **3** moment, minute, second, little while, flash, two shakes of a lamb's tail, *colloq.* mo, sec; (*in a bit*) very soon, very quickly, in a wink, *colloq.* before you can say Jack Robinson, *joc.* in less than no time; little, inch. □ **bit by bit** see *gradually* (GRADUAL). **bit on the side** see AFFAIR 3. **bits and pieces** odds and ends, oddments, bits. **not a bit** see *by no means* (MEANS).
to bits see APART 2.

bit[2] *past of* BITE.

bit[3] /bit/ *n. & v.* ● *n.* **1** a metal mouthpiece on a bridle, used to control a horse. **2** a (usu. metal) tool or piece for boring or drilling. **3** the cutting or gripping part of a plane, pliers, etc. **4** the part of a key that engages with the bolt. **5** the copper head of a soldering iron. ● *v.tr.* **1** put a bit into the mouth of (a horse). **2** restrain. □ **take the bit between one's teeth 1** take decisive personal action. **2** escape from control. [OE *bite* f. Gmc, rel. to BITE]

bit[4] /bit/ *n. Computing* a unit of information expressed as a choice between two possibilities; a 0 or 1 in binary notation. [BINARY + DIGIT]

bitch /bich/ *n. & v.* ● *n.* **1** a female dog or other canine animal. **2** *sl. offens.* a malicious or spiteful woman. **3** *sl.* a very unpleasant or difficult thing or situation. ● *v. colloq.* **1** *intr.* (often foll. by *about*) **a** speak scathingly. **b** complain. **2** *tr.* be spiteful or unfair to. **3** *tr.* spoil; botch. [OE *bicce*]

■ *n.* **2** shrew, hag, termagant, ogress, witch, virago, harpy, fury, *archaic* scold, beldam, *sl.* cow, (old) bag. **3** *colloq.* beast, pig, swine, pain, *sl.* bastard, stinker, bummer. ● *v.* **1 a** (*bitch about*) criticize, censure, find fault with, malign, come down on, have a go at, lay into, carp at, *colloq.* put down, knock, jump on, *sl.* diss; gossip about. **b** complain, object, protest, grumble, whine, bleat, carp, *colloq.* gripe, grouse, whine, moan, *sl.* beef, bellyache. **2** see ATTACK *v.* 3. **3** bungle, botch, ruin, spoil.

bitchy /bichee/ *adj.* (**bitchier, bitchiest**) *sl.* spiteful; bad-tempered. □□ **bitchily** *adv.* **bitchiness** *n.*

■ see VICIOUS 1. □□ **bitchiness** see SPITE *n.* 1.

bite /bit/ *v. & n.* ● *v.* (*past* **bit** /bit/; *past part.* **bitten** /bit′n/) **1** *tr.* cut or puncture using the teeth. **2** *tr.* (often foll. by *off*, etc.) detach with the teeth. **3** *tr.* (of an insect, snake, etc.) wound with a sting, fangs, etc. **4** *intr.* (of a wheel, screw, etc.) grip; penetrate. **5** *intr.* accept bait or an inducement. **6** *intr.* have a (desired) adverse effect. **7** *tr.* (in *passive*) **a** take in; swindle. **b** (foll. by *by, with*, etc.) be infected by (enthusiasm, etc.). **8** *tr.* (as **bitten** *adj.*) cause a glowing or smarting pain to (*frostbitten*). **9** *intr.* (foll. by *at*) snap at. ● *n.* **1** an act of biting. **2** a wound or sore made by biting. **3 a** a mouthful of food. **b** a snack or light meal. **4** the taking of bait by a fish. **5** pungency (esp. of flavor). **6** incisiveness; sharpness. **7** = OCCLUSION 3. □ **bite back** restrain (one's speech, etc.) by or as if by biting the lips. **bite** (or *Brit.* **bite on**) **the bullet** *sl.* behave bravely or stoically. **bite the dust** *sl.* **1** die. **2** fail; break down. **bite the hand that feeds one** hurt or offend a benefactor. **bite one's lip** see LIP. **bite off more than one can chew** take on a commitment one can-

not fulfill. **once bitten twice shy** an unpleasant experience induces caution. **put the bite on** *sl.* borrow or extort money from. **what's biting you?** *Brit. sl.* what is worrying you? □□ **biter** *n.* [OE *bītan* f. Gmc]

■ *v.* **1, 2** nip, chew, gnaw, nibble; savage. **3** sting. **7 a** see SWINDLE *v.* 1. ● *n.* **1** nibble, chew. **2** sting. **3 a** mouthful; taste; morsel, bit, piece. **b** snack, meal, lunch, *Austral. & NZ* crib, *Brit. colloq.* tiffin, *sl.* nosh. **5** see SPICE *n.* 3a. **6** see EDGE *n.* 7a. □ **bite back** hold back, keep back, suppress, restrain, check, control. **bite the bullet** brave it, bear up, steel oneself, face up to it, grit one's teeth, grin and bear it, screw *or* pluck up one's courage. **bite the dust 1** see DIE[1] 1. **2** stop, break down, fail, stall, die, *colloq.* conk (out).

biting /biting/ *adj.* **1** stinging; intensely cold (*a biting wind*). **2** sharp; effective (*biting wit; biting sarcasm*). □□ **bitingly** *adv.*

■ **1** cold, wintry, freezing, icy, raw, chilling, *colloq.* arctic, perishing, polar, *literary* chill; severe, harsh, cutting, piercing, stinging, penetrating, keen, sharp, bitter, *archaic* shrewd. **2** cutting, piercing, keen, sharp, effective, trenchant, incisive, mordant, rapier-like, penetrating, pungent; acid, acerbic, bitter, caustic, searing, astringent.

bitten *past part.* of BITE.

bitter /bitər/ *adj. & n.* ● *adj.* **1** having a sharp pungent taste; not sweet. **2 a** caused by or showing mental pain or resentment (*bitter memories; bitter rejoinder*). **b** painful or difficult to accept (*bitter disappointment*). **3 a** harsh; virulent (*bitter animosity*). **b** piercingly cold. ● *n.* **1** *Brit.* beer strongly flavored with hops and having a bitter taste. **2** (in *pl.*) liquor with a bitter flavor used as an additive in cocktails. □ **bitter apple** = COLOCYNTH. **bitter orange** = SEVILLE ORANGE. **bitter pill** something unpleasant that has to be accepted. **to the bitter end** to the very end in spite of difficulties. □□ **bitterly** *adv.* **bitterness** *n.* [OE *biter* prob. f. Gmc: *to the bitter end* may be assoc. with a Naut. word *bitter* = 'last part of a cable': see BITTS]

■ *adj.* **1** harsh, acerbic, acrid, sharp. **2 a** disturbing, dispiriting, distressing, disquieting, upsetting, grievous, cruel, distressful, painful, agonizing, severe, harrowing, excruciating, heartbreaking, heartrending, hurtful; aggrieved, pained, wronged, resentful, embittered, rancorous, sour. **b** painful, unwelcome, unpalatable, disagreeable, unappetizing, distasteful, unsavory, unpleasant, hard (to swallow), hurtful. **3 a** stinging, cutting, biting, acerbic, caustic, searing, harsh, vicious, acrimonious, virulent, venomous, vindictive, malicious, spiteful, malevolent, cruel, unkind, unpleasant, nasty. **b** see BITING 1. □□ **bitterness** harshness, acerbity, spleen, gall, gall and wormwood, causticity, asperity; viciousness, virulence, venomousness, animosity, acrimony, acrimoniousness, vindictiveness, maliciousness, spitefulness, cruelty, unkindness, nastiness; hatred, resentment, hostility, antagonism, venom, rancor, hate, malice.

bitterling /bitərling/ *n.* a small brightly colored freshwater fish, *Rhodeus amarus*, from Central Europe. [BITTER + -LING[1]]

bittern /bitərn/ *n.* **1** any of a group of wading birds of the heron family, esp. of the genus *Botaurus* with a distinctive booming call. **2** *Chem.* the liquid remaining after the crystallization of common salt from sea water. [ME f. OF *butor* ult. f. L *butio* bittern + *taurus* bull; -*n* perh. f. assoc. with HERON]

bittersweet /bitərswēt/ *adj.* **1** sweet with a bitter aftertaste. **2** arousing pleasure tinged with pain or sorrow. ● *n.* **1 a** sweetness with a bitter aftertaste. **b** pleasure tinged with pain or sorrow. **2 a** = *woody nightshade* (see NIGHTSHADE). **b** a climbing plant, *Celastrus scandens*, of N. America having red seeds contained in orange capsules.

bitts /bits/ *n.pl. Naut.* a pair of posts on the deck of a ship, for fastening cables, etc. [ME prob. f. LG: cf. LG & Du. *beting*]

bitty /bitee/ *adj.* **1** *colloq.* tiny. **2** *Brit.* (**bittier, bittiest**) made up of unrelated bits; scrappy. □□ **bittily** *adv.* **bittiness** *n.*

bitumen /bítŏŏmin, -tyŏŏ-, bi-/ n. **1** any of various tarlike mixtures of hydrocarbons derived from petroleum naturally or by distillation and used for road surfacing and roofing. **2** Austral. colloq. an asphalt road. [L bitumen -minis]
■ **1** see PITCH² n.

bituminize /bítŏŏminīz, -tyŏŏ-, bi-/ v.tr. convert into, impregnate with, or cover with bitumen. □□ **bituminization** /-izáyshən/ n.

bituminous /bitŏŏminəs, -tyŏŏ-, bi-/ adj. of, relating to, or containing bitumen. □ **bituminous coal** a form of coal burning with a smoky flame.

bitzer /bítsər/ n. (also **bitser**) Austral. colloq. **1** a contraption made from previously unrelated parts. **2** a mongrel dog. [prob. abbr. of bits and pieces]

bivalent /bíváylənt/ adj. & n. ● adj. **1** Chem. having a valence of two. **2** Biol. (of homologous chromosomes) associated in pairs. ● n. Biol. any pair of homologous chromosomes. □□ **bivalence** /-ləns/ n. **bivalency** n. [BI- + valent- pres. part. stem formed as VALENCE¹]

bivalve /bívalv/ n. & adj. ● n. any of a group of aquatic mollusks of the class Bivalvia, with laterally compressed bodies enclosed within two hinged shells, e.g., oysters, mussels, etc. ● adj. **1** with a hinged double shell. **2** Biol. having two valves, e.g., of a peapod.

bivouac /bívŏŏ-ak, bívwak/ n. & v. ● n. a temporary open encampment without tents, esp. of soldiers. ● v.intr. (**bivouacked, bivouacking**) camp in a bivouac, esp. overnight. [F, prob. f. Swiss G Beiwacht additional guard at night]
■ n. see CAMP¹ n. 2. ● v. see CAMP¹ v.

biweekly /bíwėklee/ adv., adj., & n. ● adv. **1** every two weeks. **2** twice a week. ● adj. produced or occurring biweekly. ● n. (pl. **-ies**) a biweekly periodical. ¶ See the note at bimonthly.

biyearly /bíyėerlee/ adv. & adj. ● adv. **1** every two years. **2** twice a year. ● adj. produced or occurring biyearly. ¶ See the note at bimonthly.

biz /biz/ n. colloq. business. [abbr.]

bizarre /bizáar/ adj. strange in appearance or effect; eccentric; grotesque. □□ **bizarrely** adv. **bizarreness** n. [F, = handsome, brave, f. Sp. & Port. bizarro f. Basque bizarra beard]
■ eccentric, unusual, strange, weird, odd, peculiar, queer, different, curious, offbeat, fantastic, unconventional, idiosyncratic, outlandish, outré, fantastic, incongruous, deviant, kinky, extravagant, whimsical; grotesque, freakish, irregular.

bizarrerie /bizáarəree/ n. a bizarre quality; bizarreness. [F]

Bk symb. Chem. the element berkelium.

bk. abbr. book.

BL abbr. **1** Bachelor of Law. **2** Bachelor of Letters. **3** British Library. **4** bill of lading.

bl. abbr. **1** barrel. **2** black. **3** block. **4** blue.

blab /blab/ v. & n. ● v. (**blabbed, blabbing**) **1** intr. **a** talk foolishly or indiscreetly. **b** reveal secrets. ● **2** tr. reveal (a secret, etc.) by indiscreet talk. ● n. a person who blabs. [ME prob. f. Gmc]
■ v. **1** gossip, prattle, chatter, (tittle-)tattle, blather, blether; see also BABBLE v. 1a, b. **2** broadcast, betray, reveal, disclose, divulge, expose; see also BABBLE v. 2.
● n. see BLABBER n.

blabber /blábər/ n. & v. ● n. (also **blabbermouth** /blábərmowth/) a person who blabs. ● v.intr. (often foll. by on) talk foolishly or inconsequentially, esp. at length.
■ n. tattletale, telltale, babbler, chatterer, gossip, chatterbox, gossipmonger, blatherskite, blab, archaic rattle, colloq. bigmouth, esp. Austral. colloq. mag. ● v. see BABBLE v. 1a, b.

black /blak/ adj., n., & v. ● adj. **1** very dark; having no color from the absorption of all or nearly all incident light (like coal or soot). **2** completely dark from the absence of a source of light (black night). **3 a** of the human group having dark-colored skin, esp. of African or Aboriginal descent. **b** of or relating to black people (black rights; historically black colleges). **4** (of the sky, a cloud, etc.) dusky; heavily overcast. **5** angry; threatening (a black look). **6** implying disgrace or condemnation (in his black books). **7** wicked; sinister; deadly (black-hearted). **8** gloomy; depressed; sullen (a black mood). **9** portending trouble or difficulty (things looked black). **10** (of hands, clothes, etc.) dirty; soiled. **11** (of humor or its representation) with sinister or macabre, as well as comic, import (black comedy). **12** (of coffee or tea) without milk. **13** Brit. **a** (of industrial labor or its products) boycotted, esp. by a trade union, in an industrial dispute. **b** (of a person) doing work or handling goods that have been boycotted. **14** dark in color as distinguished from a lighter variety (black bear; black pine). ● n. **1** a black color or pigment. **2** black clothes or material (dressed in black). **3 a** (in a game or sport) a black piece, ball, etc. **b** the player using such pieces. **4** the credit side of an account (in the black). **5** a member of a dark-skinned race, esp. one of African or Aboriginal descent. ● v.tr. **1** make black (blacked his face). **2** polish with blacking. **3** Brit. declare (goods, etc.) 'black'. □ **beyond the black stump** Austral. colloq. in the remote outback. **Black Africa** the area of Africa, generally south of the Sahara, where blacks predominate. **black and blue** discolored by bruises. **Black and Tans** an armed force recruited to fight Sinn Fein in Ireland in 1921, wearing a mixture of military and constabulary uniforms. **black and white 1** recorded in writing or print (down in black and white). **2** (of film, etc.) not in color. **3** consisting of extremes only; oversimplified (interpreted the problem in black and white terms). **the black art** = black magic. **black beetle** Brit. the common cockroach, Blatta orientalis. **black belt 1** a black belt worn by an expert in judo, karate, etc. **2** a person qualified to wear this. **black box 1** a flight recorder in an aircraft. **2** any complex piece of equipment, usu. a unit in an electronic system, with contents which are mysterious to the user. **black bread** a coarse dark-colored type of rye bread. **black bryony** a rooted climber, Tamus communis, with clusters of red berries. **black buck** a small Indian gazelle, Antilope cervicapra, with a black back and white underbelly. Also called SASIN. **black damp** = CHOKEDAMP. **Black Death** (usu. prec. by the) a widespread epidemic of bubonic plague in Europe in the 14th c. **black diamond** (in pl.) coal. **black disk** Brit. a long-playing phonograph record, as distinct from a compact disc. **black economy** unofficial economic activity. **black English** the form of English spoken by many African-Americans, esp. as an urban dialect of the US. **black eye** bruised skin around the eye resulting from a blow. **black-eyed pea** (or Brit. **black-eye bean**) a variety of bean, Vigna sinensis, with seeds often dried and stored prior to eating (so called from its black hilum). **black-eyed Susan** any of several flowers, esp. of the genus Rudbeckia, with yellow colored petals and a dark center. **black flag** see FLAG¹. **black forest cake** a chocolate cake with layers of morello cherries or cherry jam and whipped cream and topped with chocolate icing, orig. from S. Germany. **Black Friar** a Dominican friar. **black frost** see FROST. **black grouse** (or Brit. **game**) a European grouse, Lyrurus tetrix. **black hole 1** a region of space possessing a strong gravitational field from which matter and radiation cannot escape. **2** a place of confinement for punishment, esp. in the armed services. **black ice** thin hard transparent ice, esp. on a road surface. **black in the face** livid with strangulation, exertion, or passion. **black leopard** = PANTHER. **black letter** an old heavy style of type. **black light** Physics the invisible ultraviolet or infrared radiations of the electromagnetic spectrum. **black lung** a chronic lung disease caused by the inhalation of coal dust. **black magic** magic involving supposed invocation of evil spirits. **Black Maria** sl. a police vehicle for transporting prisoners. **black mark** a mark of discredit. **black market** an illicit traffic in officially controlled or scarce commodities. **black marketeer** a person who engages in a black market. **Black Mass**

/.../ **pronunciation**	● **part of speech**
□ **phrases, idioms, and compounds**	
□□ **derivatives**	■ **synonym section**
cross-references appear in SMALL CAPITALS or italics	

a travesty of the Roman Catholic Mass allegedly in worship of Satan. **Black Monk** a Benedictine monk. **Black Muslim** a member of an exclusively African-American Islamic sect proposing a separate African-American community. **Black Nationalism** advocacy of civil rights and separatism for African-Americans and occas. blacks in other countries. **black nightshade** see NIGHTSHADE. **black out 1 a** effect a blackout on. **b** undergo a blackout. **2** obscure windows, etc., or extinguish all lights for protection esp. against an air attack. **Black Panther** one of a group of extremist activists for African-American civil rights in the US. **black pepper** pepper made by grinding the whole dried berry, including the husk, of the pepper plant. **Black Power** a movement in support of rights and political power for blacks in various Western countries. **black pudding** a black sausage containing pork, dried pig's blood, suet, etc. **black raspberry 1** a N. American shrub, *Rubus occidentalis.* **2** the edible fruit of this shrub. **Black Rod** *Brit.* the principal usher of the Lord Chamberlain's department, House of Lords, etc. **black sheep** *colloq.* an unsatisfactory or disreputable member of a family, group, etc.; a scoundrel. **black spot** *Brit.* a place of danger or difficulty, esp. on a road (*an accident black spot*). **black stump** *Austral. colloq.* a mythical marker of distance in the outback. **black swan** *Brit.* **1** something extremely rare. **2** an Australian swan, *Cygnus atratus,* with black plumage. **black tea** tea that is fully fermented before drying. **black tie 1** a black bow tie worn with a dinner jacket. **2** *colloq.* formal evening dress. **black velvet** a drink of stout and champagne. **Black Watch** (usu. prec. by *the*) (in the UK) the Royal Highland Regiment (so called from its dark tartan uniform). **black widow** a venomous spider, *Latrodectus mactans,* of which the female has an hourglass-shaped red mark on her abdomen. □□ **blackish** *adj.* **blackly** *adv.* **blackness** *n.* [OE *blæc*]

■ *adj.* **1** jet, jet-black, coal-black, inky, sooty, swarthy, raven, ebony, *archaic* swart, *literary* ebon. **2** dark, pitch-black, jet-black, coal-black, *literary* stygian; starless, moonless. **3** nonwhite, colored, dark-skinned, negroid, *often offens.* Negro; African, African-American, Afro-American, Afro-Caribbean; Aboriginal; Melanesian. **4** dark, somber, overcast, dusky, murky, gloomy, menacing, glowering, lowering, threatening, funereal. **5** angry, furious, frowning, bad-tempered, sulky, resentful, clouded, threatening, glowering, *literary* wrathful. **7** bad, foul, iniquitous, wicked, evil, diabolical, infernal, hellish, atrocious, awful, malicious, abominable, outrageous, vicious, villainous, flagitious, vile, disgraceful, unscrupulous, unconscionable, unprincipled, blackguardly, knavish, perfidious, insidious, nefarious, dastardly, treacherous, unspeakable, disgraceful, shameful, scurvy, criminal, felonious. **8** see GLOOMY 2. **9** malignant, baleful, baneful, deadly, deathly, sinister, grim, dismal, hateful, disastrous. **10** dirty, soiled, sullied, filthy, grubby, unclean, dingy. ● *v.* **1** blacken. **2** polish. □ **black and blue** bruised (all over), contused, a mass of bruises. **black and white** (*in black and white*) **1** written, printed, in writing *or* print, in written *or* printed form, typewritten, typeset, on paper. **2** in monochrome, not in color. **3** oversimplified, simplistic. **black eye** *colloq.* shiner, *sl.* mouse. **black magic** see MAGIC *n.* 1. **black out 1b** see FAINT *v.* 1. **2** see SHADE *v.* 1–3. **black sheep** scoundrel, wastrel, slacker, good-for-nothing, ne'er-do-well; odd man out, pariah, outcast, persona non grata.

blackamoor /blákəmoor/ *n. archaic* a dark-skinned person, esp. a black person. [BLACK + MOOR]

blackball /blákbawl/ *v.tr.* **1** reject (a candidate) in a ballot (orig. by voting with a black ball). **2** exclude; ostracize.

blackberry /blákberee/ *n. & v.* ● *n.* (*pl.* -ies) **1** a climbing thorny rosaceous shrub, *Rubus fruticosus,* bearing white or pink flowers. Also called BRAMBLE. **2** a black fleshy edible fruit of this plant. ● *v.intr.* (-ies, -ied) gather blackberries.

blackbird /blákbərd/ *n.* **1** a common Eurasian thrush, *Turdus merula,* of which the male is black with an orange beak. **2** any of various birds, esp. a grackle, with black plumage. **3** *hist.* a kidnapped African or Polynesian on a slave ship.

blackboard /blákbawrd/ *n.* a board with a smooth usu. dark surface for writing on with chalk.

blackbody /blákbaadē/ *n. Physics* a hypothetical perfect absorber and radiator of energy, with no reflecting power.

blackboy /blákboy/ *n.* any tree of the genus *Xanthorrhea,* native to Australia, with a thick dark trunk and a head of grasslike leaves. Also called *grass tree.*

blackcap /blák-kap/ *n.* **1** a small European warbler, *Sylvia atricapilla,* the male of which has a black-topped head. **2** a chickadee.

blackcurrant /blák-kərənt, -kúr-/ *n.* **1** a widely cultivated shrub, *Ribes nigrum,* bearing flowers in racemes. **2** the small dark edible berry of this plant.

blacken /blákən/ *v.* **1** *tr. & intr.* make or become black or dark. **2** *tr.* speak evil of; defame (*blacken someone's character*).

■ **1** black, darken, smudge, begrime. **2** slander, libel, asperse, cast aspersions on, traduce, smear, sully, soil, besmirch, taint, tarnish, defame, revile, malign, vilify, discredit, denigrate, defile, drag through the mire, heap dirt on.

blackface /blákfays/ *n.* **1** a variety of sheep with a black face. **2** the makeup used by a non-black performer playing a black role.

blackfellow /blákfelō/ *n.* usu. *offens.* an Australian Aboriginal.

blackfish /blákfish/ *n.* **1** any of several species of dark-colored fish. **2** any of several dark whales of the genus *Globicephala.*

blackfly /blákflī/ *n.* (*pl.* -flies) **1** any of various small biting flies of the family Simuliidae. **2** any of various thrips or aphids, esp. *Aphis fabae,* infesting plants.

Blackfoot /blákfŏŏt/ *n.* **1 a** a N. American people native to Montana and adjoining parts of Canada. **b** a member of this people. **2** the language of this people.

blackguard /blágaard, -ərd/ *n. & v.* ● *n.* a villain; a scoundrel; an unscrupulous, unprincipled person. ● *v.tr.* abuse scurrilously. □□ **blackguardly** *adj.* [BLACK + GUARD: orig. applied collectively to menials, etc.]

■ *n.* see SCOUNDREL.

blackhead /blák-hed/ *n.* a black-topped pimple on the skin.

■ see PIMPLE.

blacking /bláking/ *n.* any black paste or polish, esp. for shoes.

blackjack[1] /blákjak/ *n.* **1** a card game in which players try to acquire cards with a face value totaling 21 and no more. **2** *US* a flexible leaded bludgeon. [BLACK + JACK[1]]

■ **2** see CLUB *n.* 1.

blackjack[2] /blákjak/ *n.* a pirates' black flag. [BLACK + JACK[1]]

blackjack[3] /blákjak/ *n.* a tarred-leather vessel for beer, ale, etc. [BLACK + JACK[2]]

blacklead /blákled/ *n. & v.* esp. *Brit.* ● *n.* graphite. ● *v.tr.* polish with graphite.

blackleg /blákleg/ *n. & v.* ● *n.* (often *attrib.*) *Brit. derog.* a person who fails or declines to take part in industrial action. ● *v.intr.* (-legged, -legging) act as a blackleg.

blacklist /bláklist/ *n. & v.* ● *n.* a list of persons under suspicion, in disfavor, etc. ● *v.tr.* put the name of (a person) on a blacklist.

■ *n.* see BOYCOTT *n.* ● *v.* see BOYCOTT *v.*

blackmail /blákmayl/ *n. & v.* ● *n.* **1 a** an extortion of payment in return for not disclosing discreditable information, a secret, etc. **b** any payment extorted in this way. **2** the use of threats or moral pressure. ● *v.tr.* **1** extort or try to extort money, etc., from (a person) by blackmail. **2** threaten; coerce. □□ **blackmailer** *n.* [BLACK + obs. *mail* rent, OE *māl* f. ON *mál* agreement]

■ *n.* **1** bribe, protection money, hush money, protection, ransom, tribute. **2** extortion, bribery, exaction, milking. ● *v.* **1** see *shake down* 4. **2** threaten, force, coerce, compel, make, *colloq.* put the thumbscrews on.

blackout /blákowt/ *n.* **1** a temporary or complete loss of vision, consciousness, or memory. **2** a temporary loss of power, radio reception, etc. **3** a compulsory period of dark-

ness as a precaution against air raids. **4** a temporary suppression of the release of information, esp. from police or government sources. **5** a sudden darkening of a theater stage.
■ **1** see FAINT *n.*

blackshirt /blákshərt/ *n.* a member of a fascist organization. [f. the color of the It. Fascist uniform]

blacksmith /bláksmith/ *n.* a smith who works in iron.

blackthorn /blákthawrn/ *n.* **1** a thorny rosaceous shrub, *Prunus spinosa*, bearing white flowers before small blue-black fruits. Also called SLOE. **2** a cudgel or walking stick made from its wood. □ **blackthorn winter** *Brit.* the time when the plant flowers in England, usu. marked by cold NE winds.

blacktop /bláktop/ *n.* a type of surfacing material for roads.

blackwater fever /blákwawtər/ *n.* a complication of malaria in which blood cells are rapidly destroyed, resulting in dark urine.

bladder /bládər/ *n.* **1 a** any of various membranous sacs in some animals, containing urine (**urinary bladder**), bile (**gallbladder**), or air (**swim bladder**). **b** this or part of it or a similar object prepared for various uses. **2** an inflated pericarp or vesicle in various plants. **3** anything inflated and hollow. [OE *blǣdre* f. Gmc]

bladderwort /bládərwərt, -wawrt/ *n.* any insectivorous aquatic plant of the genus *Utricularia*, with leaves having small bladders for trapping insects.

bladder wrack /bládərak/ *n.* a common brown seaweed, *Fucus vesiculosus*, with fronds containing air bladders which give buoyancy to the plant.

blade /blayd/ *n.* **1 a** the flat part of a knife, chisel, etc., that forms the cutting edge. **b** a flat piece of metal with a sharp edge or edges used in a razor. **2** the flattened functional part of an oar, spade, propeller, skate, snowplow, etc. **3 a** the flat, narrow, usu. pointed leaf of grass and cereals. **b** the whole of such plants before the ear is formed (*in the blade*). **c** *Bot.* the broad thin part of a leaf apart from the petiole. **4** (in full **bladebone**) a flat bone, e.g., in the shoulder. **5** *Archaeol.* a long narrow flake (see FLAKE[1] 3). **6** *poet.* a sword. **7** *colloq.* (usu. *archaic*) a carefree young fellow. □□ **bladed** *adj.* (also in *comb.*). [OE *blǣd* f. Gmc]
■ **1 a** knife, cutting edge, cutter. **3** leaf, leaflet, frond, shoot. **6** sword, rapier, saber, dagger, stiletto, cutlass, bayonet, knife, penknife, jackknife, *hist.* skean, *literary* poniard, *poet.* brand. **7** playboy, ladies' man, man about town, fop, dandy, beau, gallant, lady-killer, rake, *colloq.* swell.

blaeberry /bláyberee/ *n.* (*pl.* **-ies**) *Brit.* = BILBERRY. [ME f. *blae* (Sc. and No. of Engl. dial. f. ME *blo* or ON *blár* f. Gmc: see BLUE[1]) + BERRY]

blag /blag/ *n. & v. Brit. sl.* ● *n.* robbery, esp. with violence; theft. ● *v.tr. & intr.* (**blagged**, **blagging**) rob (esp. with violence); steal. □□ **blagger** *n.* [19th c.: orig. unkn.]

blah /blaa/ *n. colloq.* **1** (also **blah-blah**) pretentious nonsense. **2** (in *pl.*) a lethargic, dissatisfied feeling of malaise. [imit.]

blain /blayn/ *n.* an inflamed swelling or sore on the skin. [OE *blegen* f. WG]

blakey /bláykee/ *n. Brit.* (also **Blakey**) (*pl.* **-eys**) a metal cap on the heel or toe of a shoe or boot. [*Blakey*, name of the manufacturer]

blame /blaym/ *v. & n.* ● *v.tr.* **1** assign fault or responsibility to. **2** (foll. by *on*) assign the responsibility for (an error or wrong) to a person, etc. (*blamed his death on a poor diet*). ● *n.* **1** responsibility for a bad result; culpability (*shared the blame equally*; *put the blame on the bad weather*). **2** the act of blaming or attributing responsibility; censure (*she got all the blame*). □ **be to blame** (often foll. by *for*) be responsible; deserve censure (*she is not to blame for the accident*). **have only oneself to blame** be solely responsible (for something one suffers). **I don't blame you**, etc. I think your, etc., action was justifiable. □□ **blamable** or **blameable** *adj.* [ME f. OF *bla(s)mer* (v.), *blame* (n.) f. pop.L *blastemare* f. eccl.L *blasphemare* reproach f. Gk *blasphēmeō* blaspheme]
■ *v.* **1** find fault with, hold responsible, censure, criticize, fault; accuse, charge, indict, condemn, point (the

finger) at, rebuke, reprimand, reproach, scold, reprehend, reprove, denounce, incriminate. **2** fix (the) responsibility upon *or* on, put *or* place *or* lay (the) blame on, lay at the door of. ● *n.* **1** culpability, responsibility; guilt. **2** censure, criticism, reproof, rebuke, recrimination, disapproval, disapprobation, reproach, condemnation, reprehension, *literary* objurgation, *sl.* rap.

blameful /bláymfool/ *adj.* deserving blame; guilty. □□ **blamefully** *adv.*

blameless /bláymlis/ *adj.* innocent; free from blame. □□ **blamelessly** *adv.* **blamelessness** *n.*
■ faultless, guiltless, innocent, irreproachable, unimpeachable, virtuous, not guilty, in the clear, spotless, unblemished, above suspicion, above reproach, *sl.* clean.

blameworthy /bláymwərthee/ *adj.* deserving blame. □□ **blameworthiness** *n.*
■ see GUILTY 1, 4.

blanch /blanch/ *v.* **1** *tr.* make white or pale by extracting color. **2** *intr. & tr.* grow or make pale from shock, fear, etc. **3** *tr. Cookery* **a** peel (almonds, etc.) by scalding. **b** immerse (vegetables or meat) briefly in boiling water. **4** *tr.* whiten (a plant) by depriving it of light. □ **blanch over** give a deceptively good impression of (a fault, etc.) by misrepresentation. [ME f. OF *blanchir* f. *blanc* white, BLANK]
■ **1** see BLEACH *v.* **2** see PALE[1] *v.* 1.

blancmange /bləmáanj/ *n.* a sweet opaque gelatinous dessert made with flavored cornstarch and milk. [ME f. OF *blancmanger* f. *blanc* white, BLANK + *manger* eat f. L *manducare* MANDUCATE]

bland /bland/ *adj.* **1 a** mild; not irritating. **b** tasteless; unstimulating; insipid. **2** gentle in manner; smooth. □□ **blandly** *adv.* **blandness** *n.* [L *blandus* soft, smooth]
■ **1** gentle, soothing, smooth, mild. **b** insipid, boring, dull, unstimulating, uninteresting, uninspiring, uninspired, unexciting, characterless, vapid, neutral, prosaic, tasteless, flavorless, watery, flat, tame, wishy-washy. **2** gentle; suave, urbane, cool, unruffled, calm, composed, unemotional, nonchalant, insouciant.

blandish /blándish/ *v.tr.* flatter; coax; cajole. [ME f. OF *blandir* (-ISH[2]) f. L *blandiri* f. *blandus* soft, smooth]
■ see ENTICE.

blandishment /blándishmənt/ *n.* (usu. in *pl.*) flattery; cajolery.
■ see *cajolery* (CAJOLE).

blank /blangk/ *adj., n., & v.* ● *adj.* **1 a** (of paper) not written or printed on. **b** (of a document) with spaces left for a signature or details. **2 a** not filled; empty (*a blank space*). **b** unrelieved; plain; undecorated (*a blank wall*). **3 a** having or showing no interest or expression (*a blank face*). **b** void of incident or result. **c** puzzled; nonplussed. **d** having (temporarily) no knowledge or understanding (*my mind went blank*). **4** (with neg. import) complete; downright (*a blank refusal*; *blank despair*). **5** *euphem.* used in place of an adjective regarded as coarse or abusive. ● *n.* **1 a** a space left to be filled in a document. **b** a document having blank spaces to be filled. **2** (in full **blank cartridge**) a cartridge containing gunpowder but no bullet, used for training, etc. **3** an empty space or period of time. **4 a** a coin disk before stamping. **b** a metal or wooden block before final shaping. **5 a** a dash written instead of a word or letter, esp. instead of an obscenity. **b** *euphem.* used in place of a noun regarded as coarse. **6** a domino with one or both halves blank. **7** a lottery ticket that gains no prize. **8** the white center of the target in archery, etc. ● *v.tr.* **1** (usu. foll. by *off*, *out*) screen; obscure (*clouds blanked out the sun*). **2** (usu. foll. by *out*) cut (a metal blank). **3** defeat without allowing to score. □ **blank check 1** a check with the amount left for the payee to fill in. **2**

/.../ **pronunciation**	● **part of speech**
□ **phrases, idioms, and compounds**	
□□ **derivatives**	■ **synonym section**
cross-references appear in SMALL CAPITALS or *italics*	

colloq. unlimited freedom of action (cf. CARTE BLANCHE).
blank test *Chem.* a scientific test done without a specimen,
to verify the absence of the effects of reagents, etc. **blank
verse** unrhymed verse, esp. iambic pentameters. **draw a
blank** elicit no response; fail. □□ **blankly** *adv.* **blankness** *n.*
[ME f. OF *blanc* white, ult. f. Gmc]

■ *adj.* **1 a** unused, plain, virgin, clean, clear, unfilled. **2 a**
empty, plain, bare, vacant, unfilled. **b** unornamented,
unadorned, undecorated, unrelieved, void. **3 a** passive,
impassive, expressionless, emotionless, vacuous,
mindless, unexpressive. **c** disconcerted, discomfited,
nonplussed, confused, helpless, resourceless,
perplexed, dazed, puzzled, bewildered. **4** unrelieved,
stark, sheer, utter, pure, unmixed, complete,
downright, absolute, unqualified. ● *n.* **1 a** space; line,
box. **3** nothing, zero, nil, *sl.* zilch; void, emptiness,
nothingness, vacuum.

blanket /bláNGkit/ *n., adj., & v.* ● *n.* **1** a large piece of woolen
or other material used esp. as a bed covering or to wrap up
a person or an animal for warmth. **2** (usu. foll. by *of*) a thick
mass or layer that covers something (*blanket of fog; blanket
of silence*). **3** *Printing* a rubber surface transferring an impression from a plate to paper, etc., in offset printing. ● *adj.*
covering all cases or classes; inclusive (*blanket condemnation;
blanket agreement*). ● *v.tr.* (**blanketed, blanketing**) **1**
cover with or as if with a blanket (*snow blanketed the land*).
2 stifle; keep quiet (*blanketed all discussion*). **3** *Naut.* take
wind from the sails of (another craft) by passing to windward. □ **blanket stitch** a stitch used to neaten the edges of
a blanket or other material too thick for hemming. **born on
the wrong side of the blanket** illegitimate. **electric blanket** an electrically wired blanket used for heating a bed. **wet
blanket** *colloq.* a gloomy person preventing the enjoyment
of others. [ME f. OF *blancquet, blanchet* f. *blanc* white,
BLANK]

■ *n.* **1** see COVER *n.* 1f. **2** see MANTLE *n.* 2. ● *adj.* see
INCLUSIVE 3. ● *v.* **1** see COVER *v.* 2. **2** see SMOTHER *v.* 1.

blankety /bláNGkǝtee/ *adj. & n.* (also **blanky** /bláNGkee/) col-
loq. = BLANK *adj.* n. 5.

blanquette /bloNkét/ *n.* *Cookery* a dish consisting of white
meat, e.g., veal, in a white sauce. [F (as BLANKET)]

blare /blair/ *v. & n.* ● *v.* **1** *tr. & intr.* sound or utter loudly.
2 *intr.* make the sound of a trumpet. ● *n.* a loud sound
resembling that of a trumpet. [ME f. MDu. *blaren, bleren*,
imit.]

■ *v.* blast, bellow, trumpet, ring, boom, thunder, roar,
bray; resound, echo, reverberate, resonate. ● *n.* blast,
bellow, ring, roar, boom, noise, sound, clamor.

blarney /bláarnee/ *n. & v.* ● *n.* **1** cajoling talk; flattery. **2**
nonsense. ● *v.* (**-eys, -eyed**) **1** *tr.* flatter (a person) with
blarney. **2** *intr.* talk flatteringly. [*Blarney*, an Irish castle near
Cork with a stone said to confer a cajoling tongue on whoever kisses it]

blasé /blaazáy/ *adj.* **1** unimpressed or indifferent because of
over-familiarity. **2** tired of pleasure; surfeited. [F]

■ **1** indifferent, cool, superior, supercilious, sophisticated,
unmoved, unimpressed, nonchalant, emotionless,
phlegmatic, apathetic, carefree, lighthearted,
insouciant; cavalier. **2** bored, jaded, weary, jaundiced;
surfeited.

blaspheme /blasfeém, blásfeem/ *v.* **1** *intr.* talk profanely,
making use of religious names, etc. **2** *tr.* talk profanely
about; revile. □□ **blasphemer** *n.* [ME f. OF *blasfemer* f.
eccl.L *blasphemare* f. Gk *blasphēmeō*: cf. BLAME]

■ **1** curse, swear, execrate, damn. **2** abuse, malign,
calumniate, defame, disparage, revile, put down, decry,
deprecate, depreciate, belittle.

blasphemy /blásfǝmee/ *n.* (*pl.* **-ies**) **1** profane talk. **2** an
instance of this. □□ **blasphemous** *adj.* **blasphemously**
adv. [ME f. OF *blasfemie* f. eccl.L f. Gk *blasphēmia* slander,
blasphemy]

■ see PROFANITY 2. □□ **blasphemous** profane, impious,
irreverent, disrespectful, sacrilegious, irreligious, sinful,
wicked, evil, iniquitous.

blast /blast/ *n., v., & int.* ● *n.* **1** a strong gust of wind. **2 a**

a destructive wave of highly compressed air spreading outwards from an explosion. **b** such an explosion. **3** the single
loud note of a wind instrument, car horn, whistle, etc. **4**
colloq. a severe reprimand. **5** a strong current of air used in
smelting, etc. **6** *sl.* a party; a good time. ● *v.* **1** *tr.* blow up
(rocks, etc.) with explosives. **2** *tr.* wither, shrivel, or blight
(a plant, animal, limb, etc.) (*blasted oak*). **b** destroy; ruin
(*blasted her hopes*). **c** strike with divine anger; curse. **3** *intr.*
& tr. make or cause to make a loud or explosive noise (*blasted
away on his trumpet*). **4** *tr. colloq.* reprimand severely. **5** *colloq.*
a *tr.* shoot; shoot at. **b** *intr.* shoot. ● *int. Brit.* expressing
annoyance. □ **at full blast** *colloq.* working at maximum
speed, etc. **blast furnace** a smelting furnace into which
compressed hot air is driven. **blast hole** a hole containing
an explosive charge for blasting. **blast off** (of a rocket, etc.)
take off from a launching site. [OE *blǣst* f. Gmc]

■ *n.* **1** blow, gust, wind, gale. **2** explosion, burst,
eruption, discharge; detonation. **3** blare, sound, noise,
racket, din, bellow, roar; boom, report. ● *v.* **1** blow
up, explode, dynamite, demolish, destroy, ruin, waste,
lay waste, shatter, devastate. **2 b** see DESTROY 2. **c**
curse, damn. **4** defame, discredit, denounce, impugn,
put down, criticize, attack, *colloq.* lambaste, pan, knock,
slate. **5 a** fire at, shoot (at), bombard, shell. **b** open
fire, fire, shoot. □ **at full blast** fully, at full tilt, at *or* to
the maximum, completely, thoroughly, entirely,
maximally, *sl.* to the max.

-blast /blast/ *comb. form Biol.* **1** an embryonic cell (*erythroblast*) (cf. -CYTE). **2** a germ layer of an embryo (*epiblast*). [Gk
blastos sprout]

blasted /blástid/ *adj. & adv.* ● *attrib.adj.* **1** damned; annoying (*that blasted dog!*). **2** damaged by or as by a blast. ● *adv.*
Brit. colloq. damned; extremely (*it's blasted cold*).

blaster /blástǝr/ *n.* **1** in senses of BLAST *v.* **2** *Brit. Golf* a heavy
lofted club for playing from a bunker.

blastoff /blástawf/ *n.* **1** the launching of a rocket, etc. **2** the
initial thrust for this.

blastula /bláschǝlǝ/ *n.* (*pl.* **blastulas** or **blastulae** /-lee/)
Biol. an animal embryo at an early stage of development
when it is a hollow ball of cells. [mod.L f. Gk *blastos* sprout]

blatant /bláyt'nt/ *adj.* **1** flagrant; unashamed (*blatant attempt
to steal*). **2** offensively noisy or obtrusive. □□ **blatancy**
/-t'nsee/ *n.* **blatantly** *adv.* [a word used by Spenser (1596),
perh. after Sc. *blatand* = bleating]

■ **1** obvious, flagrant, palpable, obtrusive, arrant,
shameless, unashamed, brazen, overt, glaring. **2** noisy,
clamorous, loud, bellowing, strident, vociferous,
rowdy, boisterous, obstreperous, uproarious; obtrusive.

blather /bláthǝr/ *n. & v.* (also **blether** /bléthǝr/) ● *n.* foolish
chatter. ● *v.intr.* chatter foolishly. [ME *blather*, Sc. *blether*,
f. ON *blathra* talk nonsense f. *blathr* nonsense]

■ *n.* prattle, verbiage, twaddle. ● *v.* jabber (on),
prattle(on), prate.

blatherskite /bláthǝrskīt/ (also **bletherskate** /bléthǝr-
skayt/) *n.* **1** a person who blathers. **2** = BLATHER *n.* [BLATHER
+ *skite*, corrupt. of derog. use of SKATE²]

■ **1** see BLABBER *n.*

blaze¹ /blayz/ *n. & v.* ● *n.* **1** a bright flame or fire. **2 a** a
bright glaring light (*the sun set in a blaze of orange*). **b** a full
light (*a blaze of publicity*). **3** a violent outburst (of passion,
etc.) (*a blaze of patriotic fervor*). **4 a** a glow of color (*roses
were a blaze of scarlet*). **b** a bright display (*a blaze of glory*).
● *v.intr.* **1** burn with a bright flame. **2** be brilliantly lit. **3** be
consumed with anger, excitement, etc. **4 a** show bright colors (*blazing with jewels*). **b** emit light (*stars blazing*). □ **blaze
away** (often foll. by *at*) **1** fire continuously with rifles, etc.
2 work enthusiastically. **blaze up 1** burst into flame. **2** burst
out in anger. **like blazes** *sl.* **1** with great energy. **2** very fast.
what the blazes! esp. *Brit. sl.* what the hell! □□ **blazing** *adj.*
blazingly *adv.* [OE *blǣse* torch, f. Gmc: ult. rel. to BLAZE²]

■ *n.* **1** flame, fire, holocaust, inferno, conflagration. **2, 4**
brightness, brilliance, brilliancy, glow. **3** outburst,
eruption, flare-up, explosion, outbreak. ● *v.* **1** burn,
flare (up), flame. **2, 4** glow, glare, dazzle, sparkle,
shine, gleam, coruscate, twinkle, shimmer, glitter; see

also FLASH *v.* 1, 3; 2. □ **blaze away 1** fire, shoot, open fire, blast; (*blaze away at*) bombard, shell.

blaze[2] /blayz/ *n. & v.* ● *n.* **1** a white mark on an animal's face. **2** a mark made on a tree by slashing the bark esp. to mark a route. ● *v.tr.* mark (a tree or a path) by chipping bark. □ **blaze a trail 1** mark out a path or route. **2** be the first to do, invent, or study something; pioneer. [17th c.: ult. rel. to BLAZE[1]]

blaze[3] /blayz/ *v.tr.* proclaim as with a trumpet. □ **blaze abroad** spread (news) about. [ME f. LG or Du. *blāzen* blow, f. Gmc *blēsan*]

blazer /bláyzər/ *n.* **1** a man's or woman's sports jacket not worn with matching trousers. **2** a colored summer jacket worn by schoolchildren, sportsmen, etc., as part of a uniform. [BLAZE[1] + -ER[1]]

blazon /bláyzən/ *v. & n.* ● *v.tr.* **1** proclaim (esp. *blazon abroad*). **2** *Heraldry* **a** describe or paint (arms). **b** inscribe or paint (an object) with arms, names, etc. ● *n.* **1** *Heraldry* **a** a shield, coat of arms, bearings, or a banner. **b** a correct description of these. **2** a record or description, esp. of virtues, etc. □□ **blazoner** *n.* **blazonment** *n.* [ME f. OF *blason* shield, of unkn. orig.; verb also f. BLAZE[3]]

blazonry /bláyzənree/ *n. Heraldry* **1** a the art of describing or painting heraldic devices or armorial bearings. **b** such devices or bearings. **2** brightly colored display.

bldg. *abbr.* building.

bleach /bleech/ *v. & n.* ● *v.tr. & intr.* whiten by exposure to sunlight or by a chemical process. ● *n.* **1** a bleaching substance. **2** the process of bleaching. □ **bleaching powder** a powder containing calcium hypochlorite used esp. to remove color from materials. [OE *blǣcan* f. Gmc]

■ *v.* whiten, lighten, fade, blanch. ● *n.* **1** whitener, chlorine.

bleacher /bleechər/ *n.* **1** a a person who bleaches (esp. textiles). **b** a vessel or chemical used in bleaching. **2** (usu. in *pl.*) a bench seat at a sports field or arena, esp. one in an outdoor uncovered stand usu. arranged in tiers and very cheap.

bleak[1] /bleek/ *adj.* **1** bare; exposed; windswept. **2** unpromising; dreary (*bleak prospects*). **3** cold; raw. □□ **bleakly** *adv.* **bleakness** *n.* [16th c.: rel. to obs. adjs. *bleach, blake* (f. ON *bleikr*) pale, ult. f. Gmc: cf. BLEACH]

■ **1** austere, inhospitable, grim, harsh, barren, bare, exposed, windswept, desolate. **2** cheerless, dreary, unpromising, disheartening, forebidding, inauspicious, unpropitious, depressing, dismal, gloomy, somber, melancholy, sad, unhappy, mournful.

bleak[2] /bleek/ *n.* any of various species of small European river fish, esp. *Alburnus alburnus*. [ME prob. f. ON *bleikja*, OHG *bleicha* f. Gmc]

blear /bleer/ *adj. & v.* ● *adj.* **1** (of the eyes or the mind) dim; dull; filmy. **2** indistinct. ● *v.tr.* make dim or obscure; blur. [ME, of uncert. orig.]

bleary /bleeree/ *adj.* (**blearier, bleariest**) **1** (of the eyes or mind) dim; blurred. **2** indistinct. □ **bleary-eyed** having dim sight or wits. □□ **blearily** *adv.* **bleariness** *n.*

■ **1** see FILMY 2. **2** see INDISTINCT 2.

bleat /bleet/ *v. & n.* ● *v.* **1** *intr.* (of a sheep, goat, or calf) make a weak, wavering cry. **2** *intr. & tr.* (often foll. by *out*) speak or say feebly, foolishly, or plaintively. ● *n.* **1** the sound made by a sheep, goat, etc. **2** a weak, plaintive, or foolish cry. □□ **bleater** *n.* **bleatingly** *adv.* [OE *blǣtan* (imit.)]

bleb /bleb/ *n.* **1** esp. *Med.* a small blister on the skin. **2** a small bubble in glass or on water. [var. of BLOB]

bleed /bleed/ *v. & n.* ● *v.* (*past* and *past part.* **bled** /bled/) **1** *intr.* emit blood. **2** *tr.* draw blood from surgically. **3** **a** *tr.* extort money from. **b** *intr.* part with money lavishly; suffer extortion. **4** *intr.* (often foll. by *for*) suffer wounds or violent death (*bled for the Revolution*). **5** *intr.* **a** (of a plant) emit sap. **b** (of dye) come out in water. **6** *tr.* **a** allow (fluid or gas) to escape from a closed system through a valve, etc. **b** treat (such a system) in this way. **7** *Printing* **a** *intr.* (of a printed area) be cut into when pages are trimmed. **b** *tr.* cut into the printed area of when trimming. **c** *tr.* extend (an illustration)

to the cut edge of a page. ● *n.* an act of bleeding (cf. NOSEBLEED). □ **one's heart bleeds** usu. *iron.* one is very sorrowful. [OE *blēdan* f. Gmc]

■ **3** see FLEECE *v.* 1.

bleeder /bleedər/ *n.* **1** *colloq.* a hemophiliac. **2** *Brit. coarse sl.* a person (esp. as a term of contempt or disrespect) (*you bleeder; lucky bleeder*).

bleeding /bleeding/ *adj. & adv. Brit. coarse sl.* expressing annoyance or antipathy (*a bleeding nuisance*). □ **bleeding heart 1** *colloq.* a dangerously or foolishly soft-hearted person. **2** any of various plants, esp. *Dicentra spectabilis* having heart-shaped crimson flowers hanging from an arched stem.

bleep /bleep/ *n. & v.* ● *n.* an intermittent high-pitched sound made electronically. ● *v.intr. & tr.* **1** make or cause to make such a sound, esp. as a signal. **2** alert or summon by a bleep or bleeps. [imit.]

bleeper /bleepər/ *n. Brit.* = BEEP.

blemish /blémish/ *n. & v.* ● *n.* a physical or moral defect; a stain; a flaw (*not a blemish on his character*). ● *v.tr.* spoil the beauty or perfection of; stain (*spots blemished her complexion*). [ME f. OF *ble(s)mir* (-ISH[2]) make pale, prob. of Gmc orig.]

■ *n.* disfigurement, scar, mark, impairment, stain, smear, blot; defect, flaw, error, fault, imperfection, erratum.
● *v.* deface, mar, scar, impair, disfigure, tarnish, stain, spoil, flaw, harm, damage, scar, injure, bruise, besmirch, *poet.* sully.

blench /blench/ *v.intr.* flinch; quail. [ME f. OE *blencan*, ult. f. Gmc]

■ see FLINCH[1] *v.*

blend /blend/ *v. & n.* ● *v.* **1** *tr.* mix (esp. sorts or grades) together to produce a desired flavor, etc. **b** produce by this method (*blended whiskey*). **2** *intr.* form a harmonious compound; become one. **3 a** *tr. & intr.* (often foll. by *with*) mingle or be mingled (*truth blended with lies; blends well with the locals*). **b** *tr.* (often foll. by *in, with*) mix thoroughly. **4** *intr.* (esp. of colors): **a** pass imperceptibly into each other. **b** go well together; harmonize. ● *n.* **1 a** a mixture, esp. of various sorts or grades of a substance. **b** a combination (of different abstract or personal qualities). **2** a portmanteau word. [ME prob. f. ON *blanda* mix]

■ *v.* **1 a** mix, mingle, combine, meld, intermingle, *literary* commingle. **2** join, amalgamate, merge, integrate, fuse, unite. **4 a** shade, grade, gradate, graduate, merge, coalesce, fuse, unite. ● *n.* **1 a** amalgamation, mixture, mix, combination. **b** fusion, composite, amalgam, compound, combination.

blende /blend/ *n.* **1** (in full **zinc blende**) = SPHALERITE. **2** any of various other sulfides. [G f. *blenden* deceive, so called because while often resembling galena it yielded no lead]

blender /bléndər/ *n.* **1** a mixing machine used in food preparation for liquefying, chopping, or puréeing. **2 a** a thing that blends. **b** a person who blends.

Blenheim /blénim/ *n.* **1** a small spaniel of a red and white breed. **2** this breed. [the Duke of Marlborough's seat at Woodstock in S. England, named after his victory at Blenheim in Bavaria (1704)]

blenny /blénee/ *n.* (*pl.* **-ies**) any of a family of small spiny-finned marine fish, esp. of the genus *Blennius*, having scaleless skins. [L *blennius* f. Gk *blennos* mucus, with reference to its mucous coating]

blent /blent/ *poet. past* and *past part.* of BLEND.

blepharitis /bléfarítis/ *n.* inflammation of the eyelids. [Gk *blepharon* eyelid + -ITIS]

blesbok /blésbok/ *n.* (also **blesbuck** /-buk/) a subspecies of bontebok, native to southern Africa, having small lyre-shaped horns. [Afrik. f. *bles* BLAZE[2], (from the white mark on its forehead) + *bok* goat]

bless /bles/ *v.tr.* (*past* and *past part.* **blessed,** *poet.* **blest**

/.../ **pronunciation**	● **part of speech**
□ **phrases, idioms, and compounds**	
□□ **derivatives**	■ **synonym section**
cross-references appear in SMALL CAPITALS or *italics*	

/blest/) **1** (of a priest, etc.) pronounce words, esp. in a religious rite, asking for divine favor; ask God to look favorably on (*bless this house*). **2 a** consecrate (esp. bread and wine). **b** sanctify by the sign of the cross. **3** call (God) holy; adore. **4** attribute one's good fortune to (an auspicious time, one's fate, etc.); thank (*bless the day I met her*; *bless my stars*). **5** (usu. in *passive*; often foll. by *with*) **a** make happy or successful (*blessed with children*; *they were truly blessed*). **b** be endowed with. **6** *euphem.* curse; damn (*bless the boy!*). □ **(God) bless me** (or **my soul**) an exclamation of surprise, pleasure, indignation, etc. **(God) bless you! 1** an exclamation of endearment, gratitude, etc. **2** an exclamation made to a person who has just sneezed. **I'm** (or **well, I'm**) **blessed** an exclamation of surprise, etc. **not have a penny to bless oneself with** *Brit.* be impoverished. [OE *blǣdsian, blēdsian, blētsian,* f. *blōd* blood (hence mark with blood, consecrate): meaning infl. by its use at the conversion of the English to translate L *benedicare* praise]

■ **2** consecrate, hallow, sanctify, dedicate. **3** extol, glorify, praise, revere, adore, exalt, honor, venerate, *archaic* magnify. **4** thank, pay homage to, pay respect to. **5** make happy *or* fortunate, endow, favor, furnish, provide, supply, grace. **6** curse, damn, confound.

blessed /blésid, blest/ *adj.* (also *poet.* **blest**) **1 a** consecrated (*Blessed Sacrament*). **b** revered. **2** /blest/ (usu. foll. by *with*) often *iron.* fortunate (in the possession of) (*blessed with good health*; *blessed with children*). **3** *euphem.* cursed; damned (*blessed nuisance!*). **4 a** in paradise. **b** *RC Ch.* a title given to a dead person as an acknowledgment of his or her holy life; beatified. **5** bringing happiness; blissful (*blessed ignorance*). □□ **blessedly** *adv.*

■ **2** see FORTUNATE 1.

blessedness /blésidnis/ *n.* **1** happiness. **2** the enjoyment of divine favor. □ **single blessedness** *joc.* the state of being unmarried (perversion of Shakesp. *Midsummer Night's Dream* I. i. 78).

■ **1** see BLISS 1.

blessing /blésing/ *n.* **1** the act of declaring, seeking, or bestowing (esp. divine) favor (*sought God's blessing*; *mother gave them her blessing*). **2** grace said before or after a meal. **3** a gift of God, nature, etc.; a thing one is glad of (*what a blessing he brought it!*). □ **blessing in disguise** an apparent misfortune that eventually has good results.

■ **1** benediction, prayer, consecration, sanction, approbation, endorsement, imprimatur, favor; see also APPROVAL. **3** boon, favor, advantage, good fortune, godsend, luck, profit, gain, help, asset, gift, bounty.

blest /blest/ *poet.* var. of BLESSED.

blether var. of BLATHER.

bletherskate *Brit.* var. of BLATHERSKITE.

blew *past* of BLOW¹, BLOW³.

blewits /blo͞oits/ *n.* any fungus of the genus *Tricholoma*, with edible lilac-stemmed mushrooms. [prob. f BLUE¹]

blight /blit/ *n. & v.* ● *n.* **1** any plant disease caused by mildews, rusts, smuts, fungi, or insects. **2** any insect or parasite causing such a disease. **3** any obscure force which is harmful or destructive. **4** an unsightly or neglected urban area. ● *v.tr.* **1** affect with blight. **2** harm; destroy. **3** spoil. [17th c.: orig. unkn.]

■ *n.* **1** disease, plague, infestation. **3** affliction, disease, plague, pestilence, misfortune, curse, trouble, calamity, bane, *archaic or literary* woe, scourge. **4** eyesore, wasteland, blot, taint, stain. ● *v.* **1** afflict, infest, plague, scourge. **2** wither, blast, wreck, ruin, destroy, harm, spoil. **3** mar, taint, deface, mutilate, damage, disfigure, blot.

blighter /blitər/ *n. Brit. colloq.* a person (esp. as a term of contempt or disparagement). [BLIGHT + -ER¹]

Blighty /blitee/ *n.* (*pl.* **-ies**) *Brit. sl.* (used by soldiers, esp. during World War I) England; home. [Anglo-Ind. corrupt. of Hind. *bilāyatī, wilāyatī* foreign, European]

blimey /blimee/ *int.* (also **cor blimey** /kawr/) *Brit. sl.* an expression of surprise, contempt, etc. [corrupt. of (*God*) *blind me!*]

blimp /blimp/ *n.* **1 a** a small nonrigid airship. **b** a barrage

balloon. **2** *Brit.* (also **(Colonel) Blimp**) a proponent of reactionary establishment opinions. **3** *Brit.* a soundproof cover for a movie camera. **4** *derog. sl.* a fat person. □□ **blimpery** *n.* **blimpish** *adj.* [20th. c., of uncert. orig.: in sense 2, a pompous, obese, elderly character invented by cartoonist David Low (d. 1963), and used in anti-German or anti-government drawings before and during World War II]

blind /blind/ *adj., v., n., & adv.* ● *adj.* **1** lacking the power of sight. **2 a** without foresight, discernment, intellectual perception, or adequate information (*blind effort*). **b** (often foll. by *to*) unwilling or unable to appreciate (a factor, circumstance, etc.) (*blind to argument*). **3** not governed by purpose or reason (*blind forces*). **4** reckless (*blind hitting*). **5 a** concealed (*blind ditch*). **b** (of a door, window, etc.) walled up. **c** closed at one end. **6** *Aeron.* (of flying) without direct observation, using instruments only. **7** *Cookery* (of a flan case, pie crust, etc.) baked without a filling. **8** esp. *Brit. sl.* drunk. ● *v.* **1** *tr.* deprive of sight, permanently or temporarily (*blinded by tears*). **2** *tr.* (often foll. by *to*) rob of judgment; deceive (*blinded them to the danger*). **3** *intr. Brit. sl.* go very fast and dangerously, esp. in a motor vehicle. ● *n.* **1 a** a screen for a window, esp. (*Brit.*) on a roller, or with slats (*roller blind*; *Venetian blind*). **b** *Brit.* an awning over a shop window. **2 a** something designed or used to hide the truth; a pretext. **b** *Brit.* a legitimate business concealing a criminal enterprise (*he's a spy, and his job is just a blind*). **3** any obstruction to sight or light. **4** *Brit. sl.* a heavy drinking bout. **5** *Cards* a stake put up by a poker player before the cards dealt are seen. **6** a camouflaged shelter used for observing wildlife or hunting animals. ● *adv.* blindly (*fly blind*; *bake it blind*). □ **blind alley 1** a cul-de-sac. **2** a course of action leading nowhere. **blind as a bat** completely blind. **blind coal** *Brit.* coal burning without a flame. **blind corner** a corner around which a motorist, etc., cannot see. **blind date 1** a social engagement between two people who have not previously met. **2** either of the couple on a blind date. **blind drunk** extremely drunk. **blind gut** the cecum. **blind man's buff** a game in which a blindfold player tries to catch others while being pushed about by them. **blind side** a direction in which one cannot see the approach of danger, etc. **blind spot 1** *Anat.* the point of entry of the optic nerve on the retina, insensitive to light. **2** an area in which a person lacks understanding or impartiality. **3** a point of unusually weak radio reception. **blind stamping** (or **tooling**) embossing a book cover without the use of color or gold leaf. **blind-stitch** *n.* sewing visible on one side only. ● *v.tr. & intr.* sew with this stitch. **blind to** incapable of appreciating. **blind with science** esp. *Brit.* overawe with a display of (often spurious) knowledge. **go it blind** act recklessly or without proper consideration. **not a blind bit of** (or **not a blind**) *Brit. sl.* not the slightest; not a single (*took not a blind bit of notice*; *not a blind word out of him*). **turn a** (or **one's**) **blind eye to** pretend not to notice. □□ **blindly** *adv.* **blindness** *n.* [OE f. Gmc]

■ *adj.* **1** sightless, eyeless, visionless, unseeing, unsighted, purblind; partially sighted, visually handicapped. **2 a** imperceptive, unwise, myopic, heedless, inconsiderate, thoughtless, insensitive, thick, dense, obtuse, stupid, weak-minded, dull-witted, slow-witted, dim-witted, esp. *Brit. colloq.* gormless. **b** (*blind to*) unaware *or* unconscious of, impervious *or* insensible to, unaffected *or* untouched *or* unmoved by, heedless of, oblivious to *or* of. **3** indiscriminate, undiscriminating, unreasoning, mindless, senseless, irrational. **4** wild, reckless, rash, impetuous, unthinking. ● *v.* **1** put *or* poke a person's eyes out, cause a person's eyes to fog *or* mist over, dazzle, blindfold; see also DAZZLE *v.* 1. **2** deceive, blindfold, blinker; hoodwink, fool, *colloq.* bamboozle. ● *n.* **1** window shade, shade, curtain, screen, cover, shutter(s), covering; awning. **2** pretense, pretext, front, cover, smokescreen, stratagem, subterfuge, ruse, trick, deception, dodge; *sl.* scam. □ **turn a blind eye to** see IGNORE 2. □□ **blindly** recklessly, heedlessly, deludedly, indiscriminately, rashly, impetuously, irrationally, thoughtlessly, mindlessly, senselessly, unthinkingly.

blinder /blíndər/ n. colloq. **1** (in pl.) either of a pair of screens or flaps attached to a horse's bridle to prevent it from seeing sideways. **2** Brit. an excellent piece of play in a game.

blindfold /blíndfōld/ v., n., adj., & adv. • v.tr. **1** deprive (a person) of sight by covering the eyes, esp. with a tied cloth. **2** deprive of understanding; hoodwink. • n. **1** a bandage or cloth used to blindfold. **2** any obstruction to understanding. • adj. & adv. **1** with eyes bandaged. **2** without care or circumspection (went into it blindfold). **3** Chess without sight of board and pieces. [replacing (by assoc. with FOLD¹) ME blindfellen, past part. blindfelled (FELL¹) strike blind]
■ v. **1** see BLIND v. 1. **2** see BLIND v. 2.

blinding /blíndɪng/ n. **1** the process of covering a newly made road, etc., with grit to fill cracks. **2** such grit.

blindside /blíndsīd/ v.tr. **1** strike or attack unexpectedly from one's blind side. **2** spring a disagreeable surprise upon.

blindworm /blíndwərm/ n. = SLOWWORM.

blink /blingk/ v. & n. • v. **1** intr. shut and open the eyes quickly and usu. involuntarily. **2** intr. (often foll. by at) look with eyes opening and shutting. **3** tr. a (often foll. by back) prevent (tears) by blinking. b (often foll. by away, from) clear (dust, etc.) from the eyes by blinking. **4** tr. & (foll. by at) intr. shirk consideration of; ignore; condone. **5** intr. a shine with an unsteady or intermittent light. b cast a momentary gleam. **6** tr. blink with (eyes). • n. **1** an act of blinking. **2** a momentary gleam or glimpse. **3** = ICEBLINK. □ **on the blink** sl. out of order, esp. intermittently. [partly var. of blenk = BLENCH, partly f. MDu. blinken shine]
■ v. **1** wink, flicker, flutter, nictitate, bat one's eyelid. **2** squint, screw up one's eyes; be shocked, be surprised, be startled, flinch, wince, shrink, quail, blench, recoil, start, move. **4** (blink at) wink at, ignore, overlook, disregard; condone, turn a blind eye to. **5** twinkle, flicker, gleam, glimmer, shimmer, flash, sparkle, scintillate, coruscate. • n. **1** wink, flicker, flutter, waver. **2** flash, sparkle, twinkle, shimmer, flicker, gleam, glimmer. □ **on the blink** out of order, broken, in disrepair, not working or operating, not operational, down, sl. out of whack, on the fritz.

blinker /blíngkər/ n. & v. • n. **1** a device that blinks, esp. a vehicle's turn indicator. **2** Brit. = BLINDER 1. • v.tr. **1** obscure with blinkers. **2** (as **blinkered** adj.) having narrow and prejudiced views.
■ v. **2** (blinkered) see NEARSIGHTED.

blinking /blíngkɪng/ adj. & adv. Brit. sl. an intensive, esp. expressing disapproval (a blinking idiot; a blinking awful time). [BLINK + -ING² (euphem. for BLOODY)]

blip /blɪp/ n. & v. • n. **1** a quick popping sound, as of dripping water or an electronic device. **2** a small image of an object on a radar screen. **3** a minor deviation or error. • v. (**blipped, blipping**) **1** intr. make a blip. **2** tr. strike briskly. [imit.]
■ n. **3** see MISTAKE n.

bliss /blɪs/ n. **1 a** perfect joy or happiness. **b** enjoyment; gladness. **2 a** being in heaven. **b** a state of blessedness. [OE blíths, bliss f. Gmc blíthsjō f. blíthiz BLITHE: sense infl. by BLESS]
■ **1** happiness, gladness, joy, blessedness, delight, felicity, glee, enjoyment, pleasure, joyousness, cheer, exhilaration, gaiety, blissfulness, rapture, ecstasy, poet. blitheness. **2** paradise, nirvana; see also HEAVEN 2.

blissful /blísfōol/ adj. perfectly happy; joyful. □ **blissful ignorance** fortunate unawareness of something unpleasant. □□ **blissfully** adv. **blissfulness** n.
■ see ELATE v.

blister /blístər/ n. & v. • n. **1** a small bubble on the skin filled with serum and caused by friction, burning, etc. **2** a similar swelling on any other surface. **3** Med. anything applied to raise a blister. **4** Brit. sl. an annoying person. • v. **1** tr. raise a blister on. **2** intr. come up in a blister or blisters. **3** tr. attack sharply (blistered them with his criticisms). **4** (as **blistering** adj.) causing blisters; severe; hot. □ **blister copper** copper which is almost pure. **blister gas** a poison gas causing blisters on the skin. **blister pack** a bubble pack.

□□ **blistery** adj. [ME perh. f. OF blestre, blo(u)stre swelling, pimple]
■ n. **1, 2** see LUMP¹ n. 3. • v. **4** see SEVERE 3, 4, HOT adj. 1.

blithe /blith/ adj. **1** poet. gay; joyous. **2** careless; casual (with blithe indifference). □□ **blithely** adv. **blitheness** n. **blithesome** /blíthsəm/ adj. [OE blīthe f. Gmc]
■ **1** blithesome, blissful, happy, cheerful, joyous, merry, lighthearted, well-pleased, delighted, gay, joyful, elated, jubilant. **2** happy-go-lucky, insouciant, heedless, carefree, unconcerned, blasé, casual, detached, indifferent, uncaring, careless, blithesome.

blithering /blíthəring/ adj. colloq. **1** senselessly talkative. **2 a** (attrib.) utter; hopeless (blithering idiot). **b** contemptible. [blither, var. of BLATHER + -ING²]

B.Litt. abbr. Bachelor of Letters. [L Baccalaureus Litterarum]

blitz /blɪts/ n. & v. colloq. • n. **1 a** an intensive or sudden (esp. aerial) attack. **b** an energetic intensive attack, or a specific task (must have a blitz on this room). **2 (the Blitz)** the German air raids on London in 1940 during World War II. **3** Football a charge of the passer by the defensive linebackers just after the ball is snapped. • v.tr. attack, damage, or destroy by a blitz. [abbr. of BLITZKRIEG]
■ n. **1 a** see RAID n. 1. • v. see SHELL v. 2.

blitzkrieg /blítskreeg/ n. an intense military campaign intended to bring about a swift victory. [G, = lightning war]
■ see PUSH n. 4.

blizzard /blízərd/ n. **1** a severe snowstorm with high winds. **2** an overabundance; a deluge. ['violent blow' (1829), 'snowstorm' (1859), perh. imit.]
■ see STORM n. 1.

bloat /blōt/ v. **1** tr. & intr. inflate; swell (wind bloated the sheets; bloated with gas). **2** tr. (as **bloated** adj.) **a** swollen; puffed. **b** puffed up with pride or excessive wealth (bloated plutocrat). **3** tr. cure (a herring) by salting and smoking lightly. [obs. bloat swollen, soft and wet, perh. f. ON blautr soaked, flabby]
■ **1** see SWELL v. 3. **2** (bloated) **a** swollen, distended, full, puffy, bulging, puffed up, tumescent. **b** puffed up, overgrown, inflated, pompous, conceited, bigheaded, self-important, arrogant.

bloater /blōtər/ n. a herring cured by bloating.

blob /blob/ n. **1** a small roundish mass; a drop of matter. **2** a drop of liquid. **3** a spot of color. [imit.: cf. BLEB]
■ **1** gobbet, globule, drop, droplet, bit, lump, dab, glob, gob, archaic gout, colloq. smidgen. **2** drop, droplet, raindrop, bead, drip, spot, archaic gout.

bloc /blok/ n. a combination of parties, governments, groups, etc., sharing a common purpose. □ **bloc vote** = block vote. [F, = block]
■ see COMBINATION 3.

block /blok/ n., v., & adj. • n. **1** a solid hewn or unhewn piece of hard material, esp. of rock, stone, or wood (block of ice). **2** a flat-topped block used as a base for chopping, beheading, standing something on, hammering on, or for mounting a horse from. **3 a** esp. Brit. a large building, esp. when subdivided (block of apartments). **b** a compact mass of buildings bounded by (usu. four) streets. **4** an obstruction; anything preventing progress or normal working (a block in the pipe). **5** a chock for stopping the motion of a wheel, etc. **6** a pulley or system of pulleys mounted in a case. **7** (in pl.) any of a set of solid cubes, etc., used as a child's toy. **8** Printing a piece of wood or metal engraved for printing on paper or fabric. **9** a head-shaped mold used for shaping hats or wigs. **10** sl. the head (knock his block off). **11 a** the area between streets in a town or suburb. **b** the length of such an area, esp. as a measure of distance (lives three blocks away). **12** a stolid, unimaginative, or hard-hearted person. **13** a large quantity or allocation of things treated as a unit,

---

/.../ **pronunciation**   • **part of speech**
□ **phrases, idioms, and compounds**
□□ **derivatives**   ■ **synonym section**
cross-references appear in SMALL CAPITALS or italics

esp. shares, seats in a theater, etc. **14** esp. *Brit.* a set of sheets of paper used for writing, or esp. drawing, glued along one edge. **15** *Cricket* a spot on which a batsman blocks the ball before the wicket, and rests the bat before playing. **16** *Track & Field* = *starting block*. **17** *Football* a blocking action. **18** *Austral.* **a** a tract of land offered to an individual settler by a government. **b** a large area of land. • *v.tr.* **1 a** (often foll. by *up, off*) obstruct (a passage, etc.) (*the road was blocked*; *you are blocking my view*). **b** put obstacles in the way of (progress, etc.). **2** restrict the use or conversion of (currency or any other asset). **3** use a block for making (a hat, wig, etc.). **4** emboss or impress a design on (a book cover). **5** *Sports* stop (a ball, hockey puck, etc.) with a bat, racket, hand, etc., defensively. **6** *Football* impede the progress of (an opponent) with one's body. **7** *Theatr.* design or plan the on stage movements of actors in a play, etc. • *attrib.adj.* treating (many similar things) as one unit (*block booking*). □ **block and tackle** a system of pulleys and ropes, esp. for lifting. **block capitals** (or **letters**) letters printed without serifs, or written with each letter separate and in capitals. **block diagram** a diagram showing the general arrangement of parts of an apparatus. **block in 1** sketch roughly; plan. **2** confine. **block mountain** *Geol.* a mountain formed by natural faults. **block out 1 a** shut out (light, noise, etc.). **b** exclude from memory, as being too painful. **2** sketch roughly; plan. **block system** a system by which no railroad train may enter a section that is not clear. **block tin** refined tin cast in ingots. **block up 1** confine; shut (a person, etc.) in. **2** fill in (a window, doorway, etc.) with bricks, etc. **block vote** a vote proportional in power to the number of people a delegate represents. **mental** (or **psychological**) **block** a particular mental inability due to subconscious emotional factors. **on the block** being auctioned; for sale. **put the blocks on** prevent from proceeding. □□ **blocker** *n.* [ME f. OF *bloc, bloquer* f. MDu. *blok*, of unkn. orig.]

■ *n.* **1** piece, chunk, hunk, lump, slab; stump; brick, cube. **2** plinth. **4** bar, obstacle, obstruction, hindrance, stumbling block, deterrent, impediment, barrier, blockage. **7** (*blocks*) *Brit.* bricks. **10** head, *archaic joc.* costard, *archaic sl.* crumpet, noddle, *sl.* loaf, nut, dome, noodle, bean, noggin, *Brit. sl.* bonce, chump. • *v.* **1 a** obstruct, clog, close off, barricade; bar, shut off; stuff (up), congest, bung up. **b** hinder, hamper, balk, impede, prevent, thwart. □ **block out 1 a** shut out, mask, screen, blank (out), erase, eliminate, exclude, blot out. **b** deny, repress, suppress. **2** rough out, design, outline, sketch, lay out, plan. **block up 1** lock up, imprison, confine, shut in. **2** stuff (up), congest, clog, bung up; infill, fill in, close up, brick up.

blockade /blokáyd/ *n. & v.* • *n.* **1** the surrounding or blocking of a place, esp. a port, by an enemy to prevent entry and exit of supplies, etc. **2** anything that prevents access or progress. • *v.tr.* **1** subject to a blockade. **2** obstruct (a passage, a view, etc.). □ **blockade-runner 1** a vessel which runs or attempts to run into a blockaded port. **2** the owner, master, or one of the crew of such a vessel. **run a blockade** enter or leave a blockaded port by evading the blockading force. □□ **blockader** *n.* [BLOCK + -ADE¹, prob. after *ambuscade*]

blockage /blókij/ *n.* **1** an obstruction. **2** a blocked state.

■ **1** see JAM¹ *n.* 4.

blockbuster /blókbustər/ *n. sl.* **1** something of great power or size, esp. an epic or extremely popular movie or a book. **2** a huge bomb capable of destroying a whole block of buildings.

blockhead /blókhed/ *n.* a stupid person. □□ **blockheaded** *adj.*

■ see CLOD 2. □□ **blockheaded** see FOOLISH.

blockhouse /blókhows/ *n.* **1** a reinforced concrete shelter used as an observation point, etc. **2** *hist.* a one-story timber building with loopholes, used as a fort. **3** a house made of squared logs.

blockish /blókish/ *adj.* **1** resembling a block. **2** excessively dull; stupid; obtuse. **3** clumsy; rude; roughly hewn. □□ **blockishly** *adv.* **blockishness** *n.*

■ **2** see SLOW *adj.* 5.

bloke /blōk/ *n. Brit. sl.* a man; a fellow. [Shelta]

blond /blond/ *adj. & n.* • *adj.* **1** (of hair) light-colored; fair. **2** (of the complexion, esp. as an indication of race) light-colored. **3** (of wood, etc.) light in color or tone. • *n.* a person with fair hair and skin. □□ **blondish** *adj.* **blondness** *n.* [ME f. F f. med.L *blondus, blundus* yellow, perh. of Gmc orig.]

■ *adj.* **1** see FAIR¹ *adj.* 2.

blonde /blond/ *adj. & n.* • *adj.* (of a woman or a woman's hair) blond. • *n.* a blond-haired woman. [F fem. of *blond*; see BLOND]

■ *adj.* see FAIR¹ *adj.* 2.

blood /blud/ *n. & v.* • *n.* **1** a liquid, usually red and circulating in the arteries and veins of vertebrates, that carries oxygen to and carbon dioxide from the tissues of the body. **2** a corresponding fluid in invertebrates. **3** bloodshed, esp. killing. **4** passion; temperament. **5** race; descent; parentage (*of the same blood*). **6** a relationship; relations (*own flesh and blood*; *blood is thicker than water*). **7** a dandy; a man of fashion. • *v.tr.* **1** give (a hound) a first taste of blood. **2** initiate (a person) by experience. □ **bad blood** ill feeling. **blood-and-thunder** (*attrib.*) *colloq.* sensational; melodramatic. **blood bank** a place where supplies of blood or plasma for transfusion are stored. **blood bath** a massacre. **blood brother** a brother by birth or by the ceremonial mingling of blood. **blood count 1** the counting of the number of corpuscles in a specific amount of blood. **2** the number itself. **blood donor** a person who gives blood for transfusion. **blood feud** a feud between families involving killing or injury. **blood group** any one of the various types of human blood determining compatibility in transfusion. **blood-heat** the normal body temperature of a healthy human being, on average about 98.6 °F or 37 °C. **blood horse** a thoroughbred. **one's blood is up** one is in a fighting mood. **blood lust** the desire for shedding blood. **blood money 1** money paid to the next of kin of a person who has been killed. **2** money paid to a hired murderer. **3** money paid for information about a murder or murderer. **4** money gained through the suffering of others. **blood orange** an orange with red or red-streaked pulp. **blood poisoning** a diseased state caused by the presence of microorganisms in the blood. **blood pressure** the pressure of the blood in the circulatory system, often measured for diagnosis since it is closely related to the force and rate of the heartbeat and the diameter and elasticity of the arterial walls. **blood red** red as blood. **blood relation** (or **relative**) a relative by blood, not by marriage or adoption. **blood royal** a royal family. **blood serum** see SERUM. **blood sport** sport involving the wounding or killing of animals, esp. hunting. **blood sugar** the amount of glucose in the blood. **blood test** a scientific examination of blood, esp. for diagnosis. **blood transfusion** the injection of a volume of blood, previously taken from a healthy person, into a patient. **blood type** see *blood group*. **blood vessel** a vein, artery, or capillary carrying blood. **first blood 1** the first shedding of blood, esp. in boxing. **2** the first point gained in a contest, etc. **in one's blood** inherent in one's character. **make a person's blood boil** infuriate. **make a person's blood run cold** horrify. **new** (or **fresh**) **blood** new members admitted to a group, esp. as an invigorating force. **of the blood** esp. *Brit.* royal. **out for a person's blood** set on getting revenge. **taste blood** be stimulated by an early success. **young blood 1** a younger member or members of a group. **2** a rake or fashionable young man. [OE *blōd* f. Gmc]

■ *n.* **3** see GORE¹. **5** see RACE² 7. **6** see *one's own flesh and blood* (FLESH). **7** see DANDY *n.* □ **blood-and-thunder** see *melodramatic* (MELODRAMA). **blood bath** see MASSACRE *n.* 1. **blood vessel** vein, *Anat.* venule.

bloodcurdling /blúdkərdling/ *adj.* horrifying.

■ see HORRIBLE 1.

blooded /blúdid/ *adj.* **1** (of horses, etc.) of good pedigree. **2** (in *comb.*) having blood or a disposition of a specified kind (*cold-blooded*; *red-blooded*).

bloodhound /blúdhownd/ *n.* **1** a large hound of a breed used in tracking and having a very keen sense of smell. **2** this breed.

bloodless /blúdlis/ *adj.* **1** without blood. **2** unemotional; cold. **3** pale. **4** without bloodshed (*a bloodless coup*). **5** feeble; lifeless. □□ **bloodlessly** *adv.* **bloodlessness** *n.*
■ **3** see PALE¹ *adj.* 1, 4.

bloodletting /blúdleting/ *n.* **1** the surgical removal of some of a patient's blood. **2** bloodshed.
■ **2** see BLOODSHED.

bloodline /blúdlīn/ *n.* a line of descent; pedigree; descent.

bloodmobile /blúdmōbeel/ *n.* a van, truck, or bus equipped and staffed to take blood from donors.

bloodshed /blúdshed/ *n.* **1** the spilling of blood. **2** slaughter.
■ **2** slaughter, carnage, butchery, killing, murder, *joc.* bloodletting; violence; genocide.

bloodshot /blúdshot/ *adj.* (of an eyeball) inflamed; tinged with blood.

bloodstain /blúdstayn/ *n.* a discoloration caused by blood.

bloodstained /blúdstaynd/ *adj.* **1** stained with blood. **2** guilty of bloodshed.

bloodstock /blúdstok/ *n.* thoroughbred horses.

bloodstone /blúdstōn/ *n.* a type of green chalcedony spotted or streaked with red, often used as a gemstone.

bloodstream /blúdstreem/ *n.* blood in circulation.

bloodsucker /blúdsukər/ *n.* **1** an animal or insect that sucks blood, esp. a leech. **2** an extortioner. **3** a person who lives off others; a parasite. □□ **bloodsucking** *adj.*
■ **2, 3** leech, extortionist, extortioner, blackmailer; parasite, barnacle, sponge(r), scrounger, *colloq.* moocher, *sl.* freeloader.

bloodthirsty /blúdthərstee/ *adj.* (**bloodthirstier, bloodthirstiest**) eager for bloodshed. □□ **bloodthirstily** *adv.* **bloodthirstiness** *n.*
■ murderous, slaughterous, homicidal, savage, feral, cruel, ruthless, pitiless, vicious, brutal, sadistic, ferocious, fierce, sanguinary, *poet. or rhet.* fell.

bloodworm /blúdwərm/ *n.* **1** any of a variety of bright red midge larvae. **2** a small tubifex worm used as food for aquarium fish.

bloody /blúdee/ *adj., adv., & v.* ● *adj.* (**bloodier, bloodiest**) **1 a** of or like blood. **b** running or smeared with blood (*bloody bandage*). **2 a** involving, loving, or resulting from bloodshed (*bloody battle*). **b** sanguinary; cruel (*bloody butcher*). **3** esp. *Brit. coarse sl.* expressing annoyance or antipathy, or as an intensive (*a bloody shame*; *a bloody sight better*; *not a bloody chocolate left*). **4** red. ● *adv.* esp. *Brit. coarse sl.* as an intensive (*a bloody good job*; *I'll bloody pound him*). ● *v.tr.* (**-ies, -ied**) make bloody; stain with blood. □ **bloody hand** *Heraldry* the armorial device of a baronet. **Bloody Mary** a drink composed of vodka and tomato juice. **bloody-minded** *Brit. colloq.* deliberately uncooperative. **bloody-mindedly** *Brit. colloq.* in a perverse or uncooperative manner. **bloody-mindedness** *Brit. colloq.* perversity; contrariness. □□ **bloodily** *adv.* **bloodiness** *n.* [OE *blōdig* (as BLOOD, -Y¹)]
■ *adj.* **2 a** see GORY. **b** see MURDEROUS 1.

bloom¹ /bloom/ *n. & v.* ● *n.* **1 a** a flower, esp. one cultivated for its beauty. **b** the state of flowering (*in bloom*). **2** a state of perfection or loveliness; the prime (*in full bloom*). **3 a** (of the complexion) a flush; a glow. **b** a delicate powdery surface deposit on plums, grapes, leaves, etc., indicating freshness. **c** a cloudiness on a shiny surface. **4** an overgrowth of algae, plankton, etc. ● *v.* **1** *intr.* bear flowers; be in flower. **2** *intr.* **a** come into, or remain in, full beauty. **b** flourish; be in a healthy, vigorous state. **3** *intr.* become overgrown with algae, plankton, etc. (esp. of a lake or stream). **4** *tr. Photog.* coat (a lens) so as to reduce reflection from its surface. □ **take the bloom off** make stale. **water bloom** scum formed by algae on the surface of standing water. [ME f. ON *blóm*, *blómi*, etc. f. Gmc: cf. BLOSSOM]
■ *n.* **1** see FLOWER *n.* **3** see FLUSH¹ *n.* 1. ● *v.* **1** see FLOWER *v.* 1. **2 b** see THRIVE 3.

bloom² /bloom/ *n. & v.* ● *n.* a mass of puddled iron hammered or squeezed into a thick bar. ● *v.tr.* make into bloom. [OE *blōma*]

bloomer¹ /bloomər/ *n. Brit. sl.* a blunder. [= BLOOMING *error*]

bloomer² /bloomər/ *n. Brit.* an oblong loaf with a rounded diagonally slashed top. [20th c.: orig. uncert.]

bloomer³ /bloomər/ *n.* a plant or person that blooms (in a specified way) (*early autumn bloomer; late bloomer*).

bloomers /bloomərz/ *n.pl.* **1** women's loose almost knee-length underpants. **2** *colloq.* any women's underpants. **3** *hist.* women's loose trousers, gathered at the knee or (orig.) the ankle. [Mrs. A. *Bloomer*, Amer. social reformer d. 1894, who advocated a similar costume]
■ **1, 2** see PANTS 1.

bloomery /blooməree/ *n.* (*pl.* **-ies**) a factory that makes puddled iron into blooms.

blooming /blooming/ *adj. & adv.* ● *adj.* **1** flourishing; healthy. **2** *Brit. sl.* an intensive (*a blooming miracle*). ● *adv. Brit. sl.* an intensive (*was blooming difficult*). [BLOOM¹ + -ING²: euphem. for BLOODY]
■ *adj.* **1** see SOUND² *adj.* 1.

Bloomsbury /bloomzbəree, -bree/ *n. & adj.* ● *n.* (in full **Bloomsbury Group**) a group of writers, artists, and philosophers living in or associated with Bloomsbury in London in the early 20th c. ● *adj.* **1** associated with or similar to the Bloomsbury Group. **2** intellectual; highbrow.

blooper /bloopər/ *n. colloq.* an embarrassing error. [imit. *bloop* + -ER¹]
■ see MISTAKE *n.*

blossom /blósəm/ *n. & v.* ● *n.* **1** a flower or a mass of flowers, esp. of a fruit tree. **2** the stage or time of flowering (*the cherry tree in blossom*). **3** a promising stage (*the blossom of youth*). ● *v.intr.* **1** open into flower. **2** reach a promising stage; mature; thrive. □□ **blossomy** *adj.* [OE *blōstm(a)* prob. formed as BLOOM¹]
■ *n.* **1** see FLOWER *n.* ● *v.* **1** see FLOWER *v.* 1.

blot /blot/ *n. & v.* ● *n.* **1** a spot or stain esp. of ink, etc. **2** a moral defect in an otherwise good character; a disgraceful act or quality. **3** any disfigurement or blemish. ● *v.* (**blotted, blotting**) **1 a** *tr.* spot or stain esp. with ink; smudge. **b** *intr.* (of a pen, ink, etc.) make blots. **2** *tr.* **a** use blotting paper or other absorbent material to absorb excess liquid, esp. ink. **b** (of blotting paper, etc.) soak up (esp. ink). **3** *tr.* disgrace (*blotted his reputation*). □ **blot one's copybook** *Brit.* damage one's reputation. **blot on the escutcheon** a disgrace to the family name. **blot out 1 a** obliterate (writing). **b** obscure (a view, sound, etc.). **2** obliterate (from the memory) as too painful. **3** destroy. **blotting paper** unsized absorbent paper used for soaking up excess ink. [ME prob. f. Scand.: cf. Icel. *blettr* spot, stain]
■ *n.* **1** stain, spot, mark, smudge, blotch, discoloration, *colloq.* splotch. **2, 3** blemish, smear, smirch, scar, taint, flaw, fault, imperfection, black mark, failing, weakness. ● *v.* **1 a** stain, spot, spatter, smudge, mark, blur. **3** spoil, discredit, dishonor, disgrace, shame. □ **blot out 1a, 2** obscure, conceal, cover (up), hide, eclipse, dim, cloud, block out; obliterate, erase, efface, annihilate, delete, rub *or* wipe out, block out, expunge, eradicate, eliminate.

blotch /bloch/ *n. & v.* ● *n.* **1** a discolored or inflamed patch on the skin. **2** an irregular patch of ink or color. ● *v.tr.* cover with blotches. □□ **blotchy** *adj.* (**blotchier, blotchiest**). [17th c.: f. obs. *plotch* and BLOT]
■ *n.* see SPOT *n.* 1a, b. ● *v.* see STAIN *v.* 1.

blotter /blótər/ *n.* **1** a sheet or sheets of blotting paper, usu. inserted into a frame. **2** a temporary record book, esp. a police charge sheet.

blotto /blótō/ *adj. sl.* very drunk, esp. unconscious from drinking. [20th c.: perh. f. BLOT]
■ see DRUNK *adj.* 1.

blouse /blows, blowz/ *n. & v.* ● *n.* **1 a** a woman's loose, usu. lightweight, upper garment, usu. buttoned and collared. **b** the upper part of a military uniform. **2** a worker's or peas-

---

/.../ **pronunciation**	● **part of speech**
□ **phrases, idioms, and compounds**	
□□ **derivatives**	■ **synonym section**
cross-references appear in SMALL CAPITALS or *italics*	

ant's loose linen or cotton garment, usu. belted at the waist. ● *v.tr.* make (a shirt, etc.) fall loosely like a blouse. [F, of unkn. orig.]

blouson /blówson, blŏozon/ *n.* a short blouse-shaped jacket. [F]

blow[1] /blō/ *v. & n.* ● *v.* (*past* **blew** /blōo/; *past part.* **blown** /blōn/) **1 a** *intr.* (of the wind or air, or impersonally) move along; act as an air current (*it was blowing hard*). **b** *intr.* be driven by an air current (*paper blew along the gutter*). **c** *tr.* drive with an air current (*blew the door open*). **2 a** *tr.* send out (esp. air) by breathing (*blew cigarette smoke*; *blew a bubble*). **b** *intr.* send a directed air current from the mouth. **3** *tr. & intr.* sound or be sounded by blowing (*the whistle blew*; *they blew the trumpets*). **4** *tr.* **a** direct an air current at (*blew the embers*). **b** (foll. by *off*, *away*, etc.) clear of by means of an air current (*blew the dust off*). **5** *tr.* (*past part.* **blowed**) esp. *Brit. sl.* (esp. in *imper.*) curse; confound (*blow it!*; *I'll be blowed!*). **6** *tr.* **a** clear (the nose) of mucus by blowing. **b** remove contents from (an egg) by blowing through it. **7 a** *intr.* puff; pant. **b** *tr.* (esp. in *passive*) exhaust of breath. **8** *sl.* **a** *tr.* depart suddenly from (*blew the town yesterday*). **b** *intr.* depart suddenly. **9** *tr.* shatter or send flying by an explosion (*the bomb blew the tiles off the roof*; *blew them to smithereens*). **10** *tr.* make or shape (glass or a bubble) by blowing air in. **11** *tr. & intr.* melt or cause to melt from overloading (*the fuse has blown*). **12** *intr.* (of a whale) eject air and water through a blowhole. **13** *tr.* break into (a safe, etc.) with explosives. **14** *tr. sl.* **a** squander; spend recklessly (*blew $20 on a meal*). **b** spoil; bungle (an opportunity, etc.) (*he's blown his chances of winning*). **c** reveal (a secret, etc.). **15** *intr.* (of a can of food, gasket, etc.) burst from internal pressure. **16** *tr.* work the bellows of (an organ). **17** *tr.* (of flies) deposit eggs in. **18** *intr. colloq.* boast. ● *n.* **1 a** an act of blowing (e.g., one's nose, a wind instrument). **b** *colloq.* a turn or spell of playing jazz (on any instrument); a musical session. **2 a** a violent wind or storm. **b** a gust of wind or air. **c** exposure to fresh air. **3** = FLYBLOW. □ **be blowed if one will** *sl.* be unwilling to. **blow-dry** arrange (the hair) while drying it with a hand-held dryer. **blow-dryer** a dryer used for this. **blow the gaff** *Brit.* reveal a secret inadvertently. **blow hot and cold** *colloq.* vacillate. **blow in 1** break inwards by an explosion. **2** *colloq.* arrive unexpectedly. **blow job** *coarse sl.* fellatio. **blow a kiss** kiss one's hand and wave it or blow it toward a distant person. **blow a person's mind** *sl.* **1** cause a person to have drug-induced hallucinations or a similar experience. **2** amaze; astonish. **blow off 1** escape or allow (steam, pressure, etc.) to escape forcibly. **2** *sl.* renege on (an obligation) (*I decided to blow off studying so I could go to the party*). **3** *Brit. sl.* break wind noisily. **blow out 1 a** extinguish by blowing. **b** send outwards by an explosion. **2** (of a tire) burst. **3** (of a fuse, etc.) melt. **blow over** (of trouble, etc.) fade away without serious consequences. **blow one's own trumpet** praise oneself. **blow one's top** (or **stack**) *colloq.* explode in rage. **blow up 1 a** shatter or destroy by an explosion. **b** explode; erupt. **2** *colloq.* rebuke strongly. **3** inflate (a tire, etc.). **4** *colloq.* **a** enlarge (a photograph). **b** exaggerate. **5** *colloq.* come to notice; arise. **6** *colloq.* lose one's temper. **blow-up** *n.* **1** *colloq.* an enlargement (of a photograph, etc.). **2** an explosion. **blow the whistle on** see WHISTLE. [OE *blāwan* f. Gmc]

■ *v.* **1 a, b** waft, puff, whistle, whine, blast. **2** breathe, puff, exhale; expel. **7a** see PUFF *v.* 4. **8 b** see ESCAPE *v.* 1. **9** blast, shatter. **11** short-circuit, burn out. **14 a** spend, lavish, squander, waste, throw away. **b** bungle, botch, mess up, make a mess of, muff, spoil, wreck, mismanage, *Brit. colloq.* muck up, fluff, *sl.* louse up, goof (up), screw up. **c** see REVEAL 2. ● *n.* **1 a** exhalation, breath, expiration. **2 a** breeze, gust, wind, blast, puff, gale, storm, tempest, whirlwind, tornado, cyclone, hurricane, typhoon. □ **blow hot and cold** vacillate, be inconsistent, be fickle, shilly-shally. **blow out 1** extinguish, snuff (out), smother, put out. **b** explode, burst, blast. **3** short-circuit, burn out. **blow one's top** (**stack**) become angry, become furious *or* infuriated, rage, rant, lose one's temper, *sl.* blow *or* lose

one's cool, get hot under the collar. **blow up 1 a** puncture, rupture, shatter, *colloq.* bust; dynamite, destroy, blast. **b** fly apart, go off, explode, burst; erupt. **3** inflate, dilate, pump up, puff up. **4 a** enlarge, magnify. **b** amplify, expand, exaggerate, inflate, overstate. **6** become furious *or* angry *or* enraged, flare up, lose one's temper, *colloq.* lose one's cool, blow one's top, blow one's stack, *sl.* blow a gasket, flip one's lid.

blow[2] /blō/ *n.* **1** a hard stroke with a hand or weapon. **2** a sudden shock or misfortune. □ **at one blow** by a single stroke; in one operation. **blow-by-blow** (of a description, etc.) giving all the details in sequence. **come to blows** end up fighting. **strike a blow for** (or **against**) help (or oppose). [15th c.: orig. unkn.]

■ **1** cuff, rap, smack, stroke, punch, clout, hit, knock, thump, *colloq.* whack, thwack, bust, *sl.* wallop, belt. **2** shock, surprise, bombshell, jolt, bolt from the blue, revelation, setback, disappointment, frustration, letdown.

blow[3] /blō/ *v. & n. archaic* ● *v.intr.* (*past* **blew** /blōo/; *past part.* **blown** /blōn/) burst into or be in flower. ● *n.* blossoming; bloom (*in full blow*). [OE *blōwan* f. Gmc]

blowball /blóbawl/ *n.* the globular seed head of a dandelion, etc.

blower /blóər/ *n.* **1** in senses of BLOW[1] *v.* **2** a device for creating a current of air. **3** esp. *Brit. colloq.* a telephone.

blowfish /blófish/ *n.* any of several kinds of fish able to inflate their bodies when frightened, etc.

blowfly /blófli/ *n.* (*pl.* **-flies**) a meat fly; a bluebottle.

blowgun /blógun/ *n.* a tube used esp. by primitive peoples for propelling arrows or darts by blowing.

blowhard /blóhaard/ *n. & adj. colloq.* ● *n.* a boastful person. ● *adj.* boastful; blustering.

■ *n.* see *show-off* (SHOW).

blowhole /blóhōl/ *n.* **1** the nostril of a whale or other cetacean, on the top of its head. **2** a hole (esp. in ice) for breathing or fishing through. **3** a vent for air, smoke, etc., in a tunnel, etc.

blowlamp /blólamp/ *n. Brit.* = BLOWTORCH.

blown *past part.* of BLOW[1], BLOW[3].

blowout /blŏ-owt/ *n. colloq.* **1** a burst tire. **2** a melted fuse. **3** a huge meal. **4** a large party. **5** *Sports* victory by a wide margin.

blowpipe /blópīp/ *n.* **1** = BLOWGUN. **2** a tube used to intensify the heat of a flame by blowing air or other gas through it at high pressure. **3** a tube used in glass blowing.

blowtorch /blótawrch/ *n.* a portable device with a very hot flame used for burning off paint, soldering, etc.

blowy /blóee/ *adj.* (**blowier, blowiest**) windy; windswept. □□ **blowiness** *n.*

■ see WINDY 1.

blowzy /blówzee/ *adj.* (**blowzier, blowziest**) **1** coarse looking; red-faced. **2** disheveled; slovenly. □□ **blowzily** *adv.* **blowziness** *n.* [obs. *blowze* beggar's wench, of unkn. orig.]

■ **2** see UNKEMPT.

BLT *abbr.* (*pl.* **BLT's** or **BLTs**) a bacon, lettuce, and tomato sandwich.

blub /blub/ *v.intr.* (**blubbed, blubbing**) *Brit. sl.* sob. [abbr. of BLUBBER[1]]

blubber[1] /blúbər/ *n. & v.* ● *n.* **1 a** whale fat. **b** thick or excessive fat. **2** a spell of weeping. ● *v.* **1** *intr.* sob loudly. **2** *tr.* sob out (words). □□ **blubberer** *n.* **blubberingly** *adv.* **blubbery** *adj.* [ME perh. imit. (obs. meanings 'foaming, bubble')]

■ *v.* see SOB *v.*

blubber[2] /blúbər/ *adj.* (of the lips) swollen; protruding. [earlier *blabber*, *blobber*, imit.]

bluchers /blŏokərz/ *n.pl. hist.* strong leather half boots or high shoes. [G. L. von *Blücher*, Prussian general d. 1819]

bludge /bluj/ *v. & n. Austral. & NZ sl.* ● *v.intr.* avoid work. ● *n.* an easy job or assignment. □ **bludge on** impose on. [back-form. f. BLUDGER]

bludgeon /blújən/ *n. & v.* ● *n.* a club with a heavy end.

● *v.tr.* **1** beat with a bludgeon. **2** coerce. [18th c.: orig. unkn.]

■ *n.* see CLUB *n.* 1. ● *v.* **1** see BEAT *v.* 1.

bludger /blújər/ *n. Austral. & NZ sl.* **1** a hanger-on. **2** a loafer. [orig. E sl., = pimp, f. obs. *bludgeoner* f. BLUDGEON]

blue¹ /bloō/ *adj., n.,* & *v.* ● *adj.* **1** having a color like that of a clear sky. **2** sad; depressed; (of a state of affairs) gloomy; dismal (*feel blue; blue times*). **3** indecent; pornographic (*a blue film*). **4** with bluish skin through cold, fear, anger, etc. **5** *Brit.* politically conservative. **6** having blue as a distinguishing color (*blue jay*). ● *n.* **1** a blue color or pigment. **2** blue clothes or material (*dressed in blue*). **3** (usu. **Blue**) **a** a soldier in the Union army in the US Civil War. **b** the Union army. **4** *Brit.* **a** a person who has represented a university in a sport, esp. Oxford or Cambridge. **b** this distinction. **5** *Brit.* a supporter of the Conservative party. **6** any of various small blue-colored butterflies of the family Lycaenidae. **7** = BLUING. **8** *Austral. sl.* **a** an argument or row. **b** (as a nickname) a red-headed person. **9** a blue ball, piece, etc., in a game or sport. **10 a** (prec. by *the*) the clear sky. **b** the sea. ● *v.tr.* (**blues, blued, bluing** or **blueing**) **1** make or turn blue. **2** treat with laundering blue. □ **blue baby** a baby with a blue complexion from lack of oxygen in the blood due to a congenital defect of the heart or major vessels. **blue bag** *Brit.* a lawyer's briefcase. **blue blood** noble birth. **blue-blooded** of noble birth. **blue book 1** a listing of socially prominent people. **2** a blank book used for college examinations. **3** (**Blue Book**) a reference book listing the prices of used cars. **4** (**Blue Book**) **a** a report issued by the government. **b** *Brit.* a report issued by Parliament or the Privy Council. **blue cheese** cheese produced with veins of blue mold, e.g., Stilton and Danish Blue. **blue-chip** (*attrib.*) of stock of reliable investment, though less secure than gilt-edged stock. **blue-collar** (*attrib.*) of workers who wear work clothes or specialized protective clothing, as miners, mechanics, etc. **blue crab** an edible bluish-green crab, *Callinectes sapidus*, of the Atlantic and Gulf coasts. **blue ensign** see ENSIGN. **blue-eyed boy** esp. *Brit. colloq.* usu. *derog.* a favored person; a favorite. **blue funk** *sl.* a state of great terror or panic. **blue-green alga** = CYANOBACTERIUM. **blue ground** = KIMBERLITE. **blue in the face** in a state of extreme anger or exasperation. **blue jay** a crested jay, *Cyanocitta cristata*, common to N. America, with a blue back and head and a gray breast. **blue jeans** pants made of blue denim. **blue metal** *Brit.* broken blue vitrid used for making roads. **blue mold** a bluish fungus growing on food and other organic matter. **blue-pencil** (**-penciled, -penciling**; also **-pencilled, -pencilling**) censor or make cuts in (a manuscript, movie, etc.). **Blue Peter** a blue flag with a white square raised on board a ship leaving port. **blue ribbon 1** a high honor. **2** *Brit.* the ribbon of the Order of the Garter. **blue-ribbon jury** jury whose members are selected for their education, experience, etc. **blue rinse** a preparation for tinting gray hair. **blue roan** see ROAN¹. **blue rock** = *rock dove* (see ROCK¹). **blue vitriol** (or *Brit.* **stone**) copper sulfate crystals. **blue tit** a common European tit, *Parus caeruleus*, with a distinct blue crest on a black and white head. **blue water** open sea. **blue whale** a rorqual, *Balaenoptera musculus*, the largest known living mammal. **once in a blue moon** very rarely. **out of the blue** unexpectedly. □□ **blueness** *n.* [ME f. OF *bleu* f. Gmc]

■ *adj.* **1** azure, sapphire, aquamarine, turquoise, ultramarine, lapis lazuli, navy, indigo, cyan, hyacinth, lavender, cobalt, saxe, teal, Wedgewood. **2** depressed, low-spirited, dispirited, sad, dismal, gloomy, unhappy, glum, downcast, crestfallen, chapfallen, dejected, melancholy, despondent, downhearted, morose, *colloq.* down in the mouth. **3** obscene, vulgar, indecent, pornographic, dirty, filthy, lewd, smutty, risqué, bawdy, sexy, X-rated), *euphem.* adult; indelicate, suggestive, erotic, coarse, offensive, improper, off color.

blue² /bloō/ *v.tr.* (**blues, blued, bluing** or **blueing**) *Brit. sl.* squander (money). [perh. var. of BLOW¹]

Bluebeard /bloōbeerd/ *n.* **1** a man who murders several wives in succession. **2** a person with a horrible secret. [a character in a fairy tale told orig. in F (*Barbe-Bleue*) by Perrault]

bluebell /bloōbel/ *n.* **1** a liliaceous plant, *Hyacinthoides non-scripta*, with clusters of bell-shaped blue flowers on a stem arising from a rhizome. Also called *wild hyacinth, wood hyacinth* (see HYACINTH). **2** a plant, *Campanula rotundifolia*, with solitary bell-shaped blue flowers on long stalks. Also called HAREBELL. **3** any of several plants with blue bell-shaped flowers, as of the genus *Mertensia*.

blueberry /bloōberee/ *n.* (*pl.* **-ies**) **1** any of several plants of the genus *Vaccinium*, with an edible fruit. **2** the small blue-black fruit of these plants.

bluebird /bloōbərd/ *n.* any of various N. American songbirds of the thrush family, esp. of the genus *Sialia*, with distinctive blue plumage usu. on the back or head.

bluebottle /bloōbot'l/ *n.* **1** a large buzzing fly, *Calliphora vomitoria*, with a metallic blue body. Also called BLOWFLY. **2** *Austral.* a Portuguese man-of-war. **3** a dark blue cornflower. **4** *Brit. colloq.* a policeman.

bluefish /bloōfish/ *n.* a voracious marine fish, *Pomatomus saltatrix*, inhabiting tropical and temperate waters and popular as a game fish.

bluegrass /bloōgras/ *n.* **1** any of several bluish green grasses, esp. Kentucky bluegrass, *Poa pratensis*. **2** a kind of unamplified country music characterized by virtuosic playing of banjos, guitars, etc., and close usu. high harmony.

bluegum /bloōgum/ *n.* any tree of the genus *Eucalyptus*, esp. *E. regnans* with blue-green aromatic leaves.

bluejacket /bloōjakit/ *n.* a sailor in the navy.

■ see SAILOR.

blueprint /bloōprint/ *n.* & *v.* ● *n.* **1** a photographic print of the final stage of engineering or other plans in white on a blue background. **2** a detailed plan, esp. in the early stages of a project or idea. ● *v.tr.* work out (a program, plan, etc.).

■ *n.* see PLAN *n.* 2.

blues /bloōz/ *n.pl.* **1** (prec. by *the*) a bout of depression (*had a fit of the blues*). **2 a** (prec. by *the*; often treated as *sing.*) melancholic music of African-American folk origin, often in a twelve-bar sequence. **b** (*pl.* same) (as *sing.*) a piece of such music. □□ **bluesy** *adj.* (in sense 2).

bluestocking /bloōstoking/ *n.* usu. *derog.* an intellectual or literary woman. [from the (less formal) blue stockings worn by one man at a literary society meeting *c.*1750]

■ see ACADEMIC *n.*

bluet /bloōit/ *n.* a blue-flowered plant of the genus *Houstonia*.

bluey /bloōee/ *n.* (*pl.* **-eys**) *Austral. colloq.* **1** a bundle carried by a bushman. **2** = BLUE¹ n. 8b.

bluff¹ /bluf/ *v.* & *n.* ● *v.* **1** *intr.* make a pretense of strength or confidence to gain an advantage. **2** *tr.* mislead by bluffing, esp. in a card game. ● *n.* an act of bluffing; a show of confidence or assertiveness intended to deceive. □ **call a person's bluff** challenge a person thought to be bluffing. □□ **bluffer** *n.* [19th c. (orig. in poker) f. Du. *bluffen* brag]

■ *v.* **1** pretend, fake, feign, bluster, boast, brag. **2** deceive, hoodwink, dupe, mislead, delude, trick, fool, cheat, pull the wool over a person's eyes, *colloq.* bamboozle, *literary* cozen. ● *n.* bombast, bravado, sham, boasting, bragging, bluster, show, puffery; deception, rodomontade; *sl.* hot air.

bluff² /bluf/ *adj.* & *n.* ● *adj.* **1** (of a cliff, or a ship's bows) having a vertical or steep broad front. **2** (of a person or manner) blunt; frank; hearty. ● *n.* a steep cliff or headland. □□ **bluffly** *adv.* (in sense 2 of *adj.*). **bluffness** *n.* (in sense 2 of *adj.*). [17th-c. Naut. word: orig. unkn.]

■ *adj.* **1** steep, abrupt, sheer, perpendicular, acclivitous, precipitous. **2** blustering, gruff, rough, abrupt, blunt, curt, short, crude, frank, open, hearty, straightforward, plain, plainspoken, outspoken; affable, approachable,

---

/.../ **pronunciation**	● **part of speech**
□ **phrases, idioms, and compounds**	
□□ **derivatives**	■ **synonym section**
cross-references appear in SMALL CAPITALS or *italics*	

good-natured, friendly. ● *n.* cliff, precipice, scarp, *Geol.* escarpment; headland, promontory, palisades.

bluing /blóoing/ *n.* (also **blueing**) blue powder used to whiten laundry.

bluish /blóoish/ (also **blueish**) *adj.* somewhat blue.

blunder /blúndər/ *n. & v.* ● *n.* a clumsy or foolish mistake, esp. an important one. ● *v.* **1** *intr.* make a blunder; act clumsily or ineptly. **2** *tr.* deal incompetently with; mismanage. **3** *intr.* move about blindly or clumsily; stumble. □□ **blunderer** *n.* **blunderingly** *adv.* [ME prob. f. Scand.: cf. MSw *blundra* shut the eyes]

■ *n.* mistake, error, gaffe, faux pas, impropriety, slip, accident, bungle, solecism, bull, *colloq.* (bad) break, slipup, howler, fluff, blooper, *sl.* bloomer, fluff, goof, boner, screwup, clinker *Brit. sl.* clanger. ● *v.* **1** make a mess *or* mistake *or* gaffe *or* faux pas, *sl.* fluff. **2** botch, bungle, make a mess of, mess up, muff, mismanage, *Brit. colloq.* muck up, fluff, *sl.* louse up, goof (up), screw up. **3** stumble, flounder, grope about, stagger, lurch.

blunderbuss /blúndərbus/ *n. hist.* a short large-bored gun firing balls or slugs. [alt. of Du. *donderbus* thunder gun, assoc. with BLUNDER]

blunge /blunj/ *v.tr.* (in ceramics, etc.) mix (clay, etc.) with water. □□ **blunger** *n.* [after *plunge, blend*]

blunt /blunt/ *adj. & v.* ● *adj.* **1** (of a knife, pencil, etc.) lacking in sharpness; having a worn-down point or edge. **2** (of a person or manner) direct; uncompromising; outspoken. ● *v.tr.* make blunt or less sharp. □□ **bluntly** *adv.* (in sense 2 of *adj.*). **bluntness** *n.* [ME perh. f. Scand.: cf. ON *blunda* shut the eyes]

■ *adj.* **1** dull, blunted, obtuse, unpointed, worn (down). **2** abrupt, curt, rough-spoken, plainspoken, short, direct, candid, frank, unceremonious, undiplomatic, inconsiderate, thoughtless, brusque, outspoken, bluff, brash, indelicate, rude, uncivil, ungracious, discourteous, impolite; straightforward, straight, uncomplicated, uncompromising. ● *v.* dull, take the edge off, soften, mitigate, mollify, soothe.

blur /blər/ *n. & v.* ● *v.* (**blurred, blurring**) **1** *tr. & intr.* make or become unclear or less distinct. **2** *tr.* smear; partially efface. **3** *tr.* make (one's memory, perception, etc.) dim or less clear. ● *n.* something that appears or sounds indistinct or unclear. □□ **blurry** *adj.* (**blurrier, blurriest**). [16th c.: perh. rel. to BLEAR]

■ *v.* **1** obscure, hide, conceal, veil, mask; muddle, jumble, mix up, confuse, muffle, muddy. **2** smudge; smear. **3** dim, befog, obscure, cloud, becloud, *poet.* bedim. ● *n.* indistinctness, dimness, haziness, cloudiness, fogginess; cloud, mist, veil, smudge, fog, haze.

blurb /blərb/ *n.* a (usu. eulogistic) description of a book, esp. printed on its jacket, as promotion by its publishers. [coined by G. Burgess, Amer. humorist d. 1951]

■ see LITERATURE 5.

blurt /blərt/ *v.tr.* (usu. foll. by *out*) utter abruptly, thoughtlessly, or tactlessly. [prob. imit.]

■ (*blurt out*) burst out with, utter, tattle; reveal, disclose, give away, divulge, blab.

blush /blush/ *v. & n.* ● *v.intr.* **1 a** develop a pink tinge in the face from embarrassment or shame. **b** (of the face) redden in this way. **2** feel embarrassed or ashamed. **3** be or become red or pink. ● *n.* **1** the act of blushing. **2** a pink tinge. □ **at first blush** on the first glimpse or impression. **spare a person's blushes** refrain from causing embarrassment esp. by praise. [ME f. OE *blyscan*]

■ *v.* **1, 3** redden, flush, color, be *or* become red-faced, burn. **2** be *or* feel shamefaced, be red-faced *or* sheepish *or* mortified.

blusher /blúshər/ *n.* a cosmetic used to give a usu. reddish or pinkish color to the face.

bluster /blústər/ *v. & n.* ● *v.intr.* **1** behave pompously and boisterously; utter empty threats. **2** (of the wind, etc.) blow fiercely. ● *n.* **1** noisily self-assertive talk. **2** empty threats. □□ **blusterer** *n.* **blustery** *adj.* [16th c.: ult. imit.]

■ *v.* **1** swagger, strut, boast, brag, blow one's own trumpet, show off, *colloq.* talk big. **2** storm, rage. ● *n.* **1** swagger, rhetoric, bombast, puffery, bravado, grandiloquence, rodomontade, *sl.* hot air.

blvd. *abbr.* boulevard.

BM *abbr.* **1** Bachelor of Medicine. **2** Bachelor of Music. **3** British Museum. **4** basal metabolism. **5** bowel movement.

B.Mus. *abbr.* Bachelor of Music.

BMX /bee-eméks/ *n.* **1** organized bicycle racing on a dirt track, esp. for youngsters. **2** a kind of bicycle used for this. **3** (*attrib.*) of or related to such racing or the equipment used (*BMX gloves*). [abbr. of bicycle moto*cross*]

Bn. *abbr.* **1** Baron. **2** Battalion.

BO *abbr. colloq.* body odor.

boa /bóə/ *n.* **1** any large nonpoisonous snake from tropical America esp. of the genus *Boa*, which kills its prey by crushing and suffocating it in its coils. **2** any snake which is similar in appearance, such as Old World pythons. **3** a long scarf made of feathers or fur. □ **boa constrictor** a large snake, *Boa constrictor*, native to tropical America and the West Indies, which crushes its prey. [L]

■ **3** see STOLE[1].

boar /bawr/ *n.* **1** (in full **wild boar**) the tusked wild pig, *Sus scrofa*, from which domestic pigs are descended. **2** an uncastrated male pig. **3** its flesh. **4** a male guinea pig, etc. [OE *bār* f. WG]

board /bawrd/ *n. & v.* ● *n.* **1 a** a flat thin piece of sawn lumber, usu. long and narrow. **b** a piece of material resembling this, made from compressed fibers. **c** a thin slab of wood or a similar substance, often with a covering, used for any of various purposes (*chessboard; ironing board*). **d** thick stiff cardboard used in bookbinding. **2** the provision of regular meals, usu. with accommodation, for payment. **3** *archaic* a table spread for a meal. **4** the directors of a company; any other specially constituted administrative body, e.g., a committee or group of councilors, examiners, etc. **5** (in *pl.*) the stage of a theater (cf. *tread the boards*). **6** *Naut.* the side of a ship. ● *v.* **1** *tr.* **a** go on board (a ship, train, aircraft, etc.). **b** force one's way on board (a ship, etc.) in attack. **2 a** *intr.* receive regular meals or meals and lodging, for payment. **b** *tr. esp. Brit.* (often foll. by *out*) arrange accommodation away from home for (esp. a schoolchild). **c** *tr.* provide (a lodger, etc.) with regular meals. **3** *tr.* (usu. foll. by *up*) cover with boards; seal or close. □ **board game** a game played on a board. **go by the board** be neglected, omitted, or discarded. **on board** on or on to a ship, aircraft, oil rig, etc. **take on board** *esp. Brit.* consider (a new idea, etc.). [OE *bord* f. Gmc]

■ *n.* **1 a** plank, lumber. **2** food, meals, provisions. **4** council, committee, directors, directorship, management, cabinet, panel, trustees, advisers, delegates. ● *v.* **1 a** go aboard; enter. **2 a** eat, take meals. **3** see SEAL *v.* 1. □ **go by the board** see STOP *v.* 2. **on board** aboard, on; on to. **take on board** see CONSIDER 4.

boarder /báwrdər/ *n.* **1** a person who boards (see BOARD *v.* 2a), esp. a pupil at a boarding school. **2** a person who boards a ship, esp. an enemy.

boardinghouse /báwrdinghows/ *n.* an establishment providing board and lodging.

boarding school /báwrding skōōl/ *n.* a school where pupils reside during the school term.

boardroom /báwrdrōōm, -rōōm/ *n.* a room in which a board of directors, etc., meets regularly.

boardsailing /báwrdsayling/ *n.* = WINDSURFING. □□ **boardsailor** *n.*

boardwalk /báwrdwawk/ *n.* **1** a wooden walkway across sand, marsh, etc. **2** a promenade, esp. of wooden planks, along a beach.

■ see WALK *n.* 3a.

boart var. of BORT.

boast /bōst/ *v. & n.* ● *v.* **1** *intr.* declare one's achievements, possessions, or abilities with indulgent pride and satisfaction. **2** *tr.* own or have as something praiseworthy, etc. (*the hotel boasts magnificent views*). ● *n.* **1** an act of boasting. **2**

something one is proud of. ◻◻ **boaster** *n.* **boastingly** *adv.* [ME f. AF *bost*, of unkn. orig.]

■ *v.* **1** brag, blow one's (own) trumpet, crow, rodomontade, talk tall, vapor, *colloq.* talk big, show off, *Austral.* & *NZ colloq.* skite, *literary* vaunt. **2** see PROVIDE 1. ● *n.* **1** brag, buck, fanfaronade, rodomontade, braggadocio, *literary* vaunt, *sl.* hot air. ◻◻ **boaster** see BRAGGART *n.*

boastful /bóstfŏŏl/ *adj.* **1** given to boasting. **2** characterized by boasting (*boastful talk*). ◻◻ **boastfully** *adv.* **boastfulness** *n.*

■ braggart, magniloquent, grandiloquent, ostentatious, puffed up, swanky, rodomontade, bragging, egotistical, vain, pompous, conceited, *colloq.* loudmouthed, blowhard, *literary* vainglorious.

boat /bōt/ *n.* & *v.* ● *n.* **1** a small vessel propelled on water by an engine, oars, or sails. **2** (in general use) a ship of any size. **3** an elongated boat-shaped jug used for holding sauce, gravy, etc. ● *v.intr.* travel or go in a boat, esp. for pleasure. ◻ **boat hook** a long pole with a hook and a spike at one end, for moving boats. **boat people** refugees who have left a country by sea. **boat train** a train scheduled to meet or go on a boat. **in the same boat** sharing the same adverse circumstances. **push the boat out** *Brit. colloq.* celebrate lavishly. ◻◻ **boatful** *n.* (*pl.* **-fuls**). [OE *bāt* f. Gmc]

■ *n.* **1** vessel, craft, skiff, motor boat, speedboat, powerboat, launch, yacht, sailboat, rowboat, yawl, *Brit.* rowing-boat, sailing-boat, *colloq.* ship. ● *v.* sail, go boating, cruise.

boater /bótər/ *n.* a flat-topped straw hat with a stiff brim.

boathouse /bót-hows/ *n.* a house or shed at the edge of a river, lake, etc., for housing boats.

boating /bóting/ *n.* rowing or sailing in boats as a sport or form of recreation.

boatload /bótlōd/ *n.* **1** enough to fill a boat. **2** *colloq.* a large number of people.

boatman /bótmən/ *n.* (*pl.* **-men**) a person who hires out boats or provides transport by boat.

boatswain /bós'n/ *n.* (also **bo'sun, bosun, bo's'n**) a ship's officer in charge of equipment and the crew. ◻ **boatswain's chair** a seat suspended from ropes for work on the side of a ship or building. [OE *bātswegen* (as BOAT, SWAIN)]

bob[1] /bob/ *v.* & *n.* ● *v.intr.* (**bobbed, bobbing**) **1** move quickly up and down; dance. **2** (usu. foll. by *back, up*) **a** bounce buoyantly. **b** emerge suddenly; become active or conspicuous again after a defeat, etc. **3** curtsy. **4** (foll. by *for*) try to catch with the mouth alone (an apple, etc., floating or hanging). ● *n.* **1** a jerking or bouncing movement, esp. upward. **2** a curtsy. **3** one of several kinds of change in long peals in bell ringing. [14th c.: prob. imit.]

■ *v.* **1** see WAG[1] *v.*

bob[2] /bob/ *n.* & *v.* ● *n.* **1** a short hairstyle for women and children. **2 a** a weight on a pendulum, plumb line, or kite tail. **b** a cork or quill on a fishing line as an indicator of a fish biting. **3** = BOBSLED. **4** a horse's docked tail. **5** a short line at or toward the end of a stanza. **6** a knot of hair; a tassel or curl. ● *v.* (**bobbed, bobbing**) **1** *tr.* cut (a woman's or child's hair) so that it hangs clear of the shoulders. **2** *intr.* ride on a bobsled. [ME: orig. unkn.]

■ *v.* **1** see TRIM *v.* 1b.

bob[3] /bob/ *n.* (*pl.* same) *Brit. sl.* a former shilling (now = 5 decimal pence). [19th c.: orig. unkn.]

bob[4] /bob/ *n.* ◻ **bob's your uncle** *Brit. sl.* an expression of completion or satisfaction. [pet form of the name *Robert*]

bobbin /bóbin/ *n.* **1** a cylinder or cone holding thread, yarn, wire, etc., used esp. in weaving and machine sewing. **2** a spool or reel. ◻ **bobbin lace** lace made by hand with thread wound on bobbins. [F *bobine*]

bobbinet /bóbinet/ *n.* machine-made cotton, etc., net (imitating lace made with bobbins on a pillow). [BOBBIN + NET[1]]

bobble /bóbəl/ *n.* **1** a small woolly or tufted ball as a decoration or trimming. **2** a fumble, esp. of a baseball or football. [dimin. of BOB[2]]

bobby[1] /bóbee/ *n.* (*pl.* **-ies**) *Brit. colloq.* a police officer. [Sir

Robert Peel, Engl. statesman d. 1850, founder of the metropolitan police force]

bobby[2] /bóbee/ *n.* (*pl.* **-ies**) (in full **bobby calf**) *Austral.* & *NZ* an unweaned calf slaughtered for veal. [Eng. dial.]

bobby-dazzler /bóbeedazlər/ *n. Brit. colloq.* a remarkable or excellent person or thing. [dial., rel. to DAZZLE]

bobby pin /bóbeepin/ *n.* a flat, closed hairpin. [BOB[2] + -Y[2]]

bobby socks *n.pl.* (also **bobby sox**) short socks reaching just above the ankle.

bobcat /bóbkat/ *n.* a small N. American lynx, *Felix rufus*, with a spotted reddish brown coat and a short tail. [BOB[2] + CAT]

bobolink /bóbəlingk/ *n.* a N. American songbird, *Dolichonyx oryzivorus*. [orig. *Bob (o') Lincoln*: imit. of its call]

bobsled /bóbsled/ (also *Brit.* **bobsleigh** /bóbslay/) *n.* & *v.* ● *n.* a mechanically steered and braked sled used for racing down a steep ice-covered run. ● *v.intr.* race in a bob-sled. [BOB[2] + SLED]

bobstay /bóbstay/ *n.* the chain or rope holding down a ship's bowsprit. [prob. BOB[1] + STAY[2]]

bobtail /bóbtayl/ *n.* a docked tail; a horse or a dog with a bobtail. [BOB[2] + TAIL[1]]

bobwhite /bóbhwīt, bóbwit/ *n.* an American quail of the genus *Colinus*. [imit. of the bird's call]

Boche /bosh, bawsh/ *n.* & *adj. sl. derog.* ● *n.* **1** a German, esp. a soldier. **2** (prec. by *the*) Germans, esp. German soldiers, collectively. ● *adj.* German. [F sl., orig. = rascal: applied to Germans in World War I]

bock /bok/ *n.* a strong dark German beer. [F f. G abbr. of *Eimbockbier* f. *Einbeck* in Hanover]

bod /bod/ *n.* **1** a person's physique. **2** *Brit. colloq.* a person. [abbr. of BODY]

bode /bōd/ *v.* **1** *tr.* portend; foreshow. **2** *tr.* foresee; foretell (evil). ◻ **bode well** (or **ill**) show good (or bad) signs for the future. ◻◻ **boding** *n.* [OE *bodian* f. *boda* messenger]

■ portend, promise, augur, betoken, omen, forebode, presage, foreshadow, foreshow, foretell; foresee.

bodega /bōdáygə/ *n.* **1** a grocery store in a Spanish-speaking neighborhood. **2** a wineshop. [Sp. f. L *apotheca* f. Gk *apothēkē* storehouse]

bodge *Brit.* var. of BOTCH.

bodhisattva /bódisútvə/ *n.* in Mahayana Buddhism, one who is able to reach nirvana but delays doing so through compassion for suffering beings. [Skr., = one whose essence is perfect knowledge]

bodice /bódis/ *n.* **1** the part of a woman's dress above the waist. **2** a woman's vest, esp. a laced vest worn as an outer garment. [orig. *pair of bodies* = stays, corsets]

bodiless /bódeelis/ *adj.* **1** lacking a body. **2** incorporeal; insubstantial.

■ **2** see INSUBSTANTIAL 2.

bodily /bód'lee/ *adj.* & *adv.* ● *adj.* of or concerning the body. ● *adv.* **1** with the whole bulk; as a whole (*threw them bodily*). **2** in the body; as a person.

■ *adj.* physical, corporal.

bodkin /bódkin/ *n.* **1** a blunt thick needle with a large eye used esp. for drawing tape, etc., through a hem. **2** a long pin for fastening hair. **3** a small pointed instrument for piercing cloth, removing a piece of type for correction, etc. [ME perh. f. Celt.]

■ **3** see PUNCH[2].

body /bódee/ *n.* & *v.* ● *n.* (*pl.* **-ies**) **1** the physical structure, including the bones, flesh, and organs, of a person or an animal, whether dead or alive. **2** the trunk apart from the head and the limbs. **3 a** the main or central part of a thing (*body of the car*; *body of the attack*). **b** the bulk or majority; the aggregate (*body of opinion*). **4 a** a group of persons regarded collectively, esp. as having a corporate function (*governing body*). **b** (usu. foll. by *of*) a collection (*body of*

/ . . . / **pronunciation**   ● **part of speech**
◻ **phrases, idioms, and compounds**
◻◻ **derivatives**   ■ **synonym section**
cross-references appear in SMALL CAPITALS or *italics*

facts). **5** a quantity (*body of water*). **6** a piece of matter (*heavenly body*). **7** *colloq.* a person. **8** a full or substantial quality of flavor, tone, etc., e.g., in wine, musical sounds, etc. ● *v.tr.* (**-ies, -ied**) (usu. foll. by *forth*) give body or substance to. □ **body blow 1** *Boxing* a blow to the body, esp. the upper torso. **2** a severe setback. **body check** *Sports* a deliberate obstruction of one player by another. **body clock** an internal biological mechanism that is thought to regulate one's circadian rhythms. **body English** a twisting or other movement of one's body in an attempt to control the path of an object, as a ball, that one has thrown, kicked, etc. **body language** the process of communicating through conscious or unconscious gestures and poses. **body odor** the smell of the human body, esp. when unpleasant. **body politic** the nation or government as a corporate body. **body shop** a workshop where repairs to the bodies of vehicles are carried out. **body stocking** a woman's undergarment, usually made of nylon, which covers the torso. **in a body** all together. **keep body and soul together** keep alive, esp. barely. **over my dead body** *colloq.* entirely without my assent. □□ **-bodied** *adj.* (in *comb.*) (*able-bodied*). [OE *bodig*, of unkn. orig.]

■ *n.* **1** (*dead body*) corpse, remains, carcass, esp. *Med.* cadaver, *archaic* corse, *sl.* stiff. **2** trunk, torso, carcass. **3 a** main part *or* portion, hull, fuselage, bodywork, chassis; substance, essentials, essence, heart, center, core. **b** majority, bulk, main part *or* portion, better *or* best part, most, mass(es), greater number; aggregate, whole, sum, (grand *or* sum) total, totality. **4 a** association, league, band, organization, corps, union, confederation, federation, confederacy, fraternity, society; committee, council; group, assemblage, assembly, congress, company. **b** see COLLECTION 2. **5** see AMOUNT *n.* 1. **7** see SOUL 4. **8** richness, substance, firmness, consistency, fullness, solidity, thickness, density, viscosity. ● *v.* (*body forth*) embody. □ **body blow 2** see *setback* 2 (SET¹). **in a body** all together, together, as a group, as one. **keep body and soul together** see SURVIVE 1.

bodybuilding /bódeebílding/ *n.* the practice of strengthening the body, esp. shaping and enlarging the muscles, by exercise.

bodycheck /bódeechek/ *v.tr. Sports* obstruct or impede another player with one's own body.

bodyguard /bódeegaard/ *n.* a person or group of persons escorting and protecting another person (esp. a dignitary).
■ see ESCORT *n.* 1.

bodysuit /bódeesoot/ *n.* a close-fitting one-piece stretch garment for women, used mainly for sport.

bodywork /bódeewərk/ *n.* **1** the outer shell of a vehicle. **2** the repairing of automobile bodies.

Boer /bōr, bawr/ *n.* & *adj.* ● *n.* a South African of Dutch descent. ● *adj.* of or relating to the Boers. [Du.: see BOOR]

boffin /bófin/ *n.* esp. *Brit. colloq.* a person engaged in scientific (esp. military) research. [20th c.: orig. unkn.]

Bofors gun /bṓfərz/ *n.* a type of light antiaircraft gun. [*Bofors* in Sweden]

bog /bog, bawg/ *n.* & *v.* ● *n.* **1 a** wet spongy ground. **b** a stretch of such ground. **2** *Brit. sl.* a toilet. ● *v.tr.* (**bogged, bogging**) (foll. by *down*; usu. in *passive*) impede (*was bogged down by difficulties*). □ **bog myrtle** a deciduous shrub, *Myrica gale*, which grows in damp open places and has short upright catkins and aromatic gray-green leaves: also called *sweet gale* (see GALE²). **bog oak** an ancient oak which has been preserved in peat. **bog spavin** see SPAVIN. □□ **boggy** *adj.* (**boggier, boggiest**). **bogginess** *n.* [Ir. or Gael. *bogach* f. *bog* soft]

■ *n.* **1** swamp, fen, marsh, quagmire, mire, slough, ooze, sink, moor, *literary* morass. ● *v.* (*bog down*) impede, slow (down), hamper, encumber, stay, inhibit, interfere with; set back, hold back *or* up, delay.

bogey¹ /bṓgee/ *n.* & *v. Golf* ● *n.* (*pl.* **-eys**) **1** a score of one stroke more than par at any hole. **2** esp. *Brit.* (formerly) a score that a good player should do a hole or course in; par.

● *v.tr.* (**-eys, -eyed**) play (a hole) in one stroke more than par. [perh. f. *Bogey* as an imaginary player]

bogey² /bṓgee/ *n.* (also **bogy**) (*pl.* **-eys** or **-ies**) **1** an evil or mischievous spirit; a devil. **2** an awkward thing or circumstance. **3** *Brit. sl.* a piece of dried nasal mucus. [19th c., orig. as a proper name: cf. BOGLE]
■ **1** see DEVIL *n.* 1, 2. **2** see JINX *n.*

bogey³ /bṓgee/ *n.* & *v.* (also **bogie**) *Austral.* ● *n.* a swim or bathe; a bath. ● *v.intr.* swim; bathe. [Dharuk *bugi* to bathe or dive]

bogeyman /boʊ́geeman, bṓgee-, bōʊgee-/ *n.* (also **bogyman, boogeyman, boogieman**) (*pl.* **-men**) a person (real or imaginary) causing fear or difficulty.
■ see MONSTER 1.

boggle /bógəl/ *v.intr. colloq.* **1** be startled or baffled (esp. *the mind boggles*). **2** (usu. foll. by *about, at*) hesitate; demur. [prob. f. dial. *boggle* BOGEY²]
■ **2** see HESITATE 2.

bogie /bṓgee/ *n.* esp. *Brit.* **1** a wheeled undercarriage pivoted below the end of a rail vehicle. **2** a small cart used for carrying coal, rubble, etc. [19th-c. north. dial. word: orig. unkn.]

bogle /bṓgəl/ *n.* **1** = BOGEY². **2** a phantom. **3** a scarecrow. [orig. Sc. (16th c.), prob. rel. to BOGEY²]

bogus /bṓgəs/ *adj.* sham; fictitious; spurious. □□ **bogusly** *adv.* **bogusness** *n.* [19th-c. US word: orig. unkn.]
■ counterfeit, spurious, fake, false, fraudulent, sham, imitation, fictitious, *colloq.* phony.

bogy var. of BOGEY².

bogyman var. of BOGEYMAN.

bohea /bōhéé/ *n.* a black tea, the last crop of the season and usu. regarded as of low quality. [*Bu-i* (Wuyi) Hills in China]

Bohemian /bōhéémeeən/ *n.* & *adj.* ● *n.* **1** a native of Bohemia, a former kingdom in central Europe corresponding to part of the modern Czech Republic; Czech. **2** (also **bohemian**) a socially unconventional person, esp. an artist or writer. ● *adj.* **1** of, relating to, or characteristic of Bohemia or its people. **2** socially unconventional. □□ **bohemianism** *n.* (in sense 2). [*Bohemia* + -AN: sense 2 f. F *bohémien* gypsy]
■ *n.* **2** eccentric, nonconformist, dissident, individualist, avant-gardist; *colloq.* hippie. ● *adj.* **2** alternative, radical, experimental, avant-garde; nonconformist, unconventional, unorthodox, casual, free and easy; *colloq.* arty.

boil¹ /boyl/ *v.* & *n.* ● *v.* **1** *intr.* **a** (of a liquid) start to bubble up and turn into vapor; reach a temperature at which this happens. **b** (of a vessel) contain boiling liquid (*the kettle is boiling*). **2 a** *tr.* bring (a liquid or vessel) to a temperature at which it boils. **b** *tr.* cook (food) by boiling. **c** *intr.* (of food) be cooked by boiling. **d** *tr.* subject to the heat of boiling water, e.g., to clean. **3** *intr.* **a** (of the sea, etc.) undulate or seethe like boiling water. **b** (of a person or feelings) be greatly agitated, esp. by anger. **c** *colloq.* (of a person or the weather) be very hot. ● *n.* the act or process of boiling; boiling point (*at a boil*). □ **boil down 1** reduce volume by boiling. **2** reduce to essentials. **3** (foll. by *to*) amount to; signify basically. **boiled shirt** a dress shirt with a starched front. **boiled sweet** *Brit.* a candy made of boiled sugar. **boil over 1** spill over in boiling. **2** lose one's temper; become overexcited. **make one's blood boil** see BLOOD. [ME f. AF *boiller*, OF *boillir*, f. L *bullire* to bubble f. *bulla* bubble]

■ *v.* **1** a bubble, seethe, simmer; evaporate. **2 b, c** simmer, stew, steam. **3 a** undulate, seethe, foam, fret; ferment, sputter, splutter. **b** seethe, fume, foam at the mouth, rage, storm, rant and rave, bristle, smolder, chafe, *colloq.* sizzle, *sl.* burn up. **c** swelter, roast, broil, *colloq.* bake, sizzle, fry, scorch. □ **boil down 2** see TELESCOPE *v.* 3. **3** (*boil down to*) amount to, come down to, mean, signify. **boil over 2** see EXPLODE 2.

boil² /boyl/ *n.* an inflamed pus-filled swelling caused by infection of a hair follicle, etc. [OE *bȳl(e)* f. WG]
■ abscess, carbuncle, pustule, lump, pimple, spot, *Med.* furuncle.

boiler /bóylər/ *n.* **1** a fuel-burning apparatus for heating a hot water supply. **2** a tank for heating water, esp. for turning it to steam under pressure. **3** *Brit.* a metal tub for boiling laundry, etc. **4** a fowl, vegetable, etc., suitable for cooking only by boiling. □ **boiler room** a room with a boiler and other heating equipment, esp. in the basement of a large building. **boiler suit** *Brit.* a one-piece suit worn as overalls for heavy manual work.

boiling /bóyling/ *adj.* (also **boiling hot**) *colloq.* very hot.
■ see HOT *adj.* 1.

boiling point /bóyling poynt/ *n.* **1** the temperature at which a liquid starts to boil. **2** high excitement (*feelings reached boiling point*).

boisterous /bóystərəs/ *adj.* **1** (of a person) rough; noisily exuberant. **2** (of the sea, weather, etc.) stormy; rough. □□ **boisterously** *adv.* **boisterousness** *n.* [var. of ME *boist(u)ous*, of unkn. orig.]
■ **1** rowdy, noisy, clangorous, uproarious, riproaring, tumultuous, roistering, lively, exuberant, clamorous, unruly, stormy, wild, riotous, undisciplined, uncontrolled, irrepressible, knockabout, *Sc.* randy, *colloq.* rambunctious. **2** rough, tempestuous, stormy, turbulent, blustery, wild, raging, roaring, howling.

bok choy /bok chóy/ *n.* a Chinese vegetable resembling cabbage. [f. Chin. *baahk-choi* white cabbage]

boko /bókō/ *n. & adj.* *Austral.* ● *n.* an animal or person who is blind in one eye. ● *adj.* blind. [perh. f. an Aboriginal language]

bolas /bóləs/ *n.* (as *sing.* or *pl.*) (esp. in S. America) a missile consisting of a number of balls connected by strong cord, which when thrown entangles the limbs of the quarry. [Sp. & Port., pl. of *bola* ball]

bold /bōld/ *adj.* **1** confidently assertive; adventurous; courageous. **2** forthright; impudent. **3** vivid; distinct; well-marked (*bold colors*; *a bold imagination*). **4** *Printing* (in full **boldface** or **-faced**) printed in a thick black typeface. □ **as bold as brass** excessively bold or self-assured. **make** (or **be**) **so bold as to** presume to; venture to. □□ **boldly** *adv.* **boldness** *n.* [OE *bald* dangerous f. Gmc]
■ **1** courageous, brave, gallant, adventurous, plucky, spirited, confident, stouthearted, assertive, lionhearted, daring, enterprising, audacious, fearless, unafraid, intrepid, resolute, dauntless, undaunted, valiant, stout, staunch, valorous, stalwart, venturesome, heroic, *colloq.* gutsy, *sl.* feisty; reckless, foolhardy, incautious, daredevil, rash, *literary* temerarious. **2** audacious, forthright, self-assertive, outspoken, presumptuous, familiar, forward, aggressive, brazen, brash, impudent, impertinent, insolent, immodest, shameless, barefaced, *colloq.* fresh, pushy. **3** pronounced, prominent, well-marked, strong, vivid, distinct, striking, loud, noisy, vigorous, clear, conspicuous, glaring, outstanding. □ **make so bold as to** see PRESUME 2. □□ **boldly** see *adventurously* (ADVENTUROUS), *assertively* (ASSERTIVE).

bole[1] /bōl/ *n.* the stem or trunk of a tree. [ME f. ON *bolr*, perh. rel. to BALK]
■ see TRUNK 1.

bole[2] /bōl/ *n.* fine compact earthy clay. [LL BOLUS]

bolero /bōláirō, bə-/ *n.* (*pl.* **-os**) **1 a** a Spanish dance in simple triple time. **b** music for or in the time of a bolero. **2** a woman's short open jacket. [Sp.]

boll /bōl/ *n.* a rounded capsule containing seeds, esp. flax or cotton. □ **boll weevil** a small American or Mexican weevil, *Anthonomus grandis*, whose larvae destroy cotton bolls. [ME f. MDu. *bolle*: see BOWL[1]]

bollard /bólərd/ *n.* **1** a short post on a wharf or ship for securing a rope. **2** *Brit.* a short metal, concrete, or plastic post in the road, esp. as part of a traffic island. [ME perh. f. ON *bolr* BOLE[1] + -ARD]

bollocking /bóləking/ *n. Brit. coarse sl.* a severe reprimand.

bollocks /bóləks/ *n.* (also **ballocks**) *Brit. coarse sl.* ¶ Usually considered a taboo word. **1** the testicles. **2** (usu. as an exclam. of contempt) nonsense; rubbish. [OE *bealluc*, rel. to BALL[1]]

bollocky /bóləkee/ *adj. Austral. sl.* naked.

bologna /bəlőnee, -nyə/ *n.* a large smoked sausage made of beef, veal, pork, and other meats, and sold ready for eating. [*Bologna* in Italy]

bolometer /bōlómitər/ *n.* a sensitive electrical instrument for measuring radiant energy. □□ **bolometry** *n.* **bolometric** /bōləmétrik/ *adj.* [Gk *bolē* ray + -METER]

boloney var. of BALONEY.

Bolshevik /bólshəvik, ból-/ *n. & adj.* ● *n.* **1** *hist.* a member of the radical faction of the Russian Social Democratic party, which became the Communist party in 1918. **2** a Russian communist. **3** (in general use) any revolutionary socialist. ● *adj.* **1** of, relating to, or characteristic of the Bolsheviks. **2** communist. □□ **Bolshevism** *n.* **Bolshevist** *n.* [Russ., = a member of the majority, from the fact that this faction formed the majority group of the Russian Social Democratic party in 1903, f. *bol'she* greater]
■ *n.* **3** see *left-winger*. □□ **Bolshevist** see *left-winger*.

Bolshie /bólshee/ *adj. & n.* (also *Brit.* **Bolshy**) *sl.* ● *adj.* (usu. **bolshie**) **1** uncooperative; rebellious; awkward; bad-tempered. **2** left-wing; socialist. ● *n.* (*pl.* **-ies**) a Bolshevik. □□ **bolshiness** *n.* (in sense 1 of *adj.*). [abbr.]
■ ● *n.* see *left-winger*.

bolster[1] /bólstər/ *n. & v.* ● *n.* **1** a long thick pillow. **2** a pad or support, esp. in a machine. **3** *Building* a short timber cap over a post to increase the bearing of the beams it supports. ● *v.tr.* (usu. foll. by *up*) **1** encourage; reinforce (*bolstered our morale*). **2** support with a bolster; prop up. □□ **bolsterer** *n.* [OE f. Gmc]
■ *v.* support, prop up, shore up, buttress, hold up, uphold, back (up), reinforce, strengthen; aid, help, assist, encourage, further, advance, *colloq.* boost.

bolster[2] /bólstər/ *n.* a chisel for cutting bricks. [20th c.: orig. uncert.]

bolt[1] /bōlt/ *n., v., & adv.* ● *n.* **1** a sliding bar and socket used to fasten or lock a door, gate, etc. **2** a large usu. metal pin with a head, usu. riveted or used with a nut, to hold things together. **3** a discharge of lightning. **4** an act of bolting (cf. sense 4 of *v.*); a sudden escape or dash for freedom. **5** *hist.* an arrow for shooting from a crossbow. **6** a roll of fabric, wallpaper, etc. (orig. as a measure). ● *v.* **1** *tr.* fasten or lock with a bolt. **2** *tr.* (foll. by *in, out*) keep (a person, etc.) from leaving or entering by bolting a door. **3** *tr.* fasten together with bolts. **4** *intr.* **a** a dash suddenly away, esp. to escape. **b** (of a horse) suddenly gallop out of control. **5** *tr.* gulp down (food) unchewed; eat hurriedly. **6** *intr.* (of a plant) run to seed. ● *adv.* (usu. in **bolt upright**) rigidly; stiffly. □ **a bolt from the blue** a complete surprise. **bolt-hole** esp. *Brit.* **1** a place of escape, esp. a hole in the ground into which a pursued animal can flee. **2** a secret refuge. **shoot one's bolt** do all that is in one's power. □□ **bolter** *n.* (in sense 4 of *v.*). [OE *bolt* arrow]
■ *n.* **1** pin, bar, rod, catch, latch. **3** lightning flash, thunderbolt, streak (of lightning), shaft, fulmination, *archaic* levin. **4** see DASH *n.* **1. 5** arrow, dart, projectile, missile, shaft, *hist.* quarrel. **6** roll, length. ● *v.* **1** fasten, lock, latch, secure. **2** (*bolt in*) see LOCK *v.* 2; (*bolt out*) see *lock out*. **3** fix, attach, fasten, connect. **4 a** dart off, race off, shoot off, run (away *or* off), rush (off *or* away), dash (off *or* away), take off, take to one's heels, vanish, do a disappearing act, flee, decamp, abscond, escape, take flight, *colloq.* skedaddle, scram, hightail (it), make oneself scarce, *Brit. colloq.* flit, *sl.* cut and run, *Brit. sl.* take a powder, scarper, do a bunk. **b** break away, go out of control. **5** gulp (down), swallow whole, ingurgitate; gobble, guzzle, wolf down, stuff down, *colloq.* pig (down), scoff. ● *adv.* (**bolt upright**) erect, straight; rigidly, stiffly, woodenly, fixedly. □ **bolt from the blue** surprise, shock, bombshell, blow, jolt, revelation. **shoot one's bolt** exhaust *or* use up one's resources, run out of steam *or* gas, burn oneself out.

bolt² /bōlt/ *v.tr.* sift (flour, etc.). □□ **bolter** *n.* [ME f. OF *bulter, buleter*, of unkn. orig.]

bolus /bṓləs/ *n.* (*pl.* **boluses**) **1** a soft ball, esp. of chewed food. **2** a large pill. [LL f. Gk *bōlos* clod]
■ **2** see PILL 1a.

bomb /bom/ *n. & v.* ● *n.* **1 a** a container with explosive, incendiary material, smoke, gas, etc., designed to explode on impact or by means of a time mechanism, remote-control device, or lit fuse. **b** an ordinary object fitted with an explosive device (*letter bomb*). **2** (prec. by *the*) the atomic or hydrogen bomb considered as a weapon with supreme destructive power. **3** a small pressurized container that sprays liquid, foam, or gas (*an aerosol bomb*). **4** a mass of solidified lava thrown from a volcano. **5** *colloq.* a failure (esp. a theatrical one). **6** *sl.* an old car. **7** *Football* a long forward pass. **8** *Brit. sl.* a drugged cigarette. **9** *Brit. sl.* a large sum of money (*cost a bomb*). ● *v.* **1** *tr.* attack with bombs; drop bombs on. **2** *tr.* (foll. by *out*) drive (a person, etc.) out of a building or refuge by using bombs. **3** *intr.* throw or drop bombs. **4** *intr. sl.* fail badly. **5** *intr. colloq.* move or go very quickly. **6** *tr. sl.* criticize fiercely. □ **bomb bay** a compartment in an aircraft used to hold bombs. **go down a bomb** *Brit. colloq.*, often *iron.* be very well received. **like a bomb** *Brit. colloq.* **1** often *iron.* very successfully. **2** very fast. [F *bombe* f. It. *bomba* f. L *bombus* f. Gk *bombos* hum]
■ *n.* **1** bombshell, shell, explosive, device, torpedo, esp. *Brit.* maroon. **5** see FLOP *n.* ● *v.* **1** bombard, shell, blow up, drop bombs on. **4** see FAIL *v.* 1, 2a. **5** see RUSH¹ *v.* 1. **6** see SLAM *v.* 1.

bombard /bombaárd/ *v.tr.* **1** attack with a number of heavy guns or bombs. **2** (often foll. by *with*) subject to persistent questioning, abuse, etc. **3** *Physics* direct a stream of high-speed particles at (a substance). □□ **bombardment** *n.* [F *bombarder* f. *bombarde* f. med.L *bombarda* a stone throwing engine: see BOMB]
■ **1, 2** bomb, shell, gun; hail, pelt, shower, pepper, volley, assail, attack, assault, set upon; see also BESIEGE 3. □□ **bombardment** see ATTACK *n.* 1.

bombardier /bómbərdeér/ *n.* **1** a member of a bomber crew responsible for sighting and releasing bombs. **2** *Brit.* a non-commissioned officer in the artillery. [F (as BOMBARD)]

bombardon /bombaárdən, bómbərdən/ *n. Mus.* **1** a type of valved bass tuba. **2** an organ stop imitating this. [It. *bombardone* f. *bombardo* bassoon]

bombasine var. of BOMBAZINE.

bombast /bómbast/ *n.* pompous or extravagant language. □□ **bombastic** /-bástik/ *adj.* **bombastically** *adv.* [earlier *bombace* cotton wool f. F f. med.L *bombax -acis* alt. f. *bombyx*; see BOMBAZINE]
■ pretentious language, fustian, pomposity, turgidity, bluster, show, wind, bluff, grandiloquence, magniloquence, bravado, boast, braggadocio, rodomontade, fanfaronade, flatulence, *sl.* hot air; burlesque, rhetoric. □□ **bombastic** high-flown, extravagant, rhetorical, pompous, pretentious, highfalutin, high-sounding, grandiose, grandiloquent, magniloquent, euphuistic, flowery, inflated, fustian, flatulent, turgid, tumid, mouthy.

Bombay duck /bómbay dúk/ *n.* a dried fish, esp. bummalo, usu. eaten in Indian cuisine with curried dishes. [corrupt. of *bombil*: see BUMMALO]

bombazine /bómbəzeén/ (also **bombasine**) *n.* a twilled dress material of worsted with or without an admixture of silk or cotton, esp. when black, formerly used for mourning. [F *bombasin* f. med.L *bombacinum* f. LL *bombycinus* silken f. *bombyx -ycis* silk or silkworm f. Gk *bombux*]

bombe /boNb/ *n. Cookery* a round or dome-shaped dish or confection, freq. frozen. [F, = BOMB]

bomber /bómər/ *n.* **1** an aircraft equipped to carry and drop bombs. **2** a person using bombs, esp. illegally. □ **bomber jacket** a short esp. leather jacket tightly gathered at the waist and cuffs.

bombora /bombáwrə/ *n. Austral.* a dangerous sea area where waves break over a submerged reef. [Aboriginal]

bombproof /bómprōōf/ *adj.* strong enough to resist the effects of blast from a bomb.

bombshell /bómshel/ *n.* **1** an overwhelming surprise or disappointment. **2** an artillery bomb. **3** *sl.* a very attractive woman (*blonde bombshell*).
■ **1** surprise, shock, bomb, blow, jolt, revelation, bolt from *or* out of the blue. **3** see BEAUTY 3.

bombsight /bómsīt/ *n. Brit.* a device in an aircraft for aiming bombs.

bona fide /bṓnə fīd, fīdee, bónə/ *adj. & adv.* ● *adj.* genuine; sincere. ● *adv.* genuinely; sincerely. [L, ablat. sing. of BONA FIDES]
■ *adj.* genuine, authentic, attested, real, veritable, undisputed, legitimate, true, valid; reliable, trustworthy, dependable, solid, indubitable, sincere, honest. ● *adv.* see *authentically* (AUTHENTIC).

bona fides /bṓnaa feédes, fídeez, bónə, (esp. for 2) bṓnə fídz/ *n.* **1** esp. *Law* an honest intention; sincerity. **2** (as *pl.*) *colloq.* documentary evidence of acceptability (*his bona fides are in order*). [L, = good faith]

bonanza /bənánzə/ *n.* **1** a source of wealth or prosperity. **2** a large output (esp. of a mine). **3 a** prosperity; good luck. **b** a run of good luck. [orig. US f. Sp., = fair weather, f. L *bonus* good]
■ *n.* **3** see WINDFALL.

bonbon /bónbon/ *n.* a piece of confectionery; a candy, esp. with a chocolate or fondant coating. [F f. *bon* good f. L *bonus*]
■ see SWEET *n.* 1.

bonce /bons/ *n. Brit.* **1** *sl.* the head. **2** a large playing marble. [19th c.: orig. unkn.]

bond /bond/ *n. & v.* ● *n.* **1 a** a thing that ties another down or together. **b** (usu. in *pl.*) a thing restraining bodily freedom (*broke his bonds*). **2** (often in *pl.*) **a** a uniting force (*sisterly bond*). **b** a restraint; a responsibility (*bonds of duty*). **3** a binding engagement; an agreement (*his word is his bond*). **4** *Commerce* a certificate issued by a government or a public company promising to repay borrowed money at a fixed rate of interest at a specified time; a debenture. **5** adhesiveness. **6** *Law* a deed by which a person is bound to make payment to another. **7** *Chem.* linkage between atoms in a molecule or a solid. **8** *Building* the laying of bricks in one of various patterns in a wall in order to ensure strength (*English bond; Flemish bond*). ● *v.* **1** *tr.* **a** lay (bricks) overlapping. **b** bind together (resin with fibers, etc.). **2** *intr.* adhere; hold together. **3** *tr.* connect with a bond. **4** *tr.* place (goods) in bond. **5** *intr.* become emotionally attached. □ **bond paper** high-quality writing paper. **in bond** (of goods) stored until the importer pays the duty owing. [ME var. of BAND¹]
■ *n.* **1 a** cement, adhesive; glue, mortar; fastening. **b** (*bonds*) tie(s), shackles, chains, fetters, manacles, handcuffs, trammels, thongs, cord(s), rope(s); restraint(s), constraint(s), check(s), control(s), rein(s). **2 a** connection, tie, attachment, link, linkage, union, relationship, alliance. **b** responsibility, charge, duty, trust, obligation, commitment, burden; see also sense 1b above. **3** covenant, pact, contract, agreement, engagement, compact, treaty, arrangement, settlement, *colloq.* deal; word (of honor), assurance, guarantee, warrant, pledge, vow, oath, promise. ● *v.* **2, 3** adhere, hold together; cement, bind, glue, weld, connect, splice, stick, cohere, attach, put together, solder, marry, join, fuse, combine.

bondage /bóndij/ *n.* **1** serfdom; slavery. **2** subjection to constraint, influence, obligation, etc. **3** sadomasochistic practices, including the use of physical restraints or mental enslavement. [ME f. AL *bondagium*: infl. by BOND]
■ **1** slavery, servitude, serfdom, subjection, enslavement, enthralment, *hist.* vassalage, villeinage, peonage, *literary* thralldom, thrall. **2** subjection, subjugation, oppression, repression, suppression; confinement, yoke, restraint, constraint; bonds, fetters, chains, shackles; imprisonment, captivity, *archaic* durance.

bonded /bóndid/ *adj.* **1** (of goods) placed in bond. **2** (of material) reinforced by or cemented to another. **3** (of a debt) secured by bonds. □ **bonded warehouse** a government controlled warehouse for the retention of imported goods until the duty owed is paid.

bondi /bóndi/ *n. Austral.* a heavy club with a knob on the end. □ **give a person bondi** attack savagely. [Wiradhuri *bundi*]

bondsman /bóndzmən/ *n.* (also **bondman**) (*pl.* **-men**) **1** a slave. **2** a person in thrall to another. [var. of *bondman* (f. archaic *bond* in serfdom or slavery) as though f. *bond's* genitive of BOND]

bone /bōn/ *n. & v.* ● *n.* **1** any of the pieces of hard tissue making up the skeleton in vertebrates. **2** (in *pl.*) **a** the skeleton, esp. as remains after death. **b** the body, esp. as a seat of intuitive feeling (*felt it in my bones*). **3 a** the material of which bones consist. **b** a similar substance such as ivory, dentine, or whalebone. **4** a thing made of bone. **5** (in *pl.*) the essential part of a thing (*the bare bones*). **6** (in *pl.*) **a** dice. **b** flat bone or wood clappers held between the fingers and used as a simple rhythm instrument. **7** a strip of stiffening in a corset, etc. ● *v.* **1** *tr.* take out the bones from (meat or fish). **2** *tr.* stiffen (a garment) with bone, etc. **3** *tr. Brit. sl.* steal. □ **bone china** fine china made of clay mixed with the ash from bones. **bone-dry** quite dry. **bone lazy** (or **idle**) esp. *Brit.* utterly lazy or idle. **bone of contention** a source or ground of dispute. **bone spavin** see SPAVIN. **bone tired** extremely weary. **bone up** (often foll. by *on*) *colloq.* study (a subject) intensively. **close to** (or **near**) **the bone 1** tactless to the point of offensiveness. **2** destitute; hard up. **have a bone to pick** (usu. foll. by *with*) have a cause for dispute (with another person). **make no bones about 1** admit or allow without fuss. **2** not hesitate or scruple. **point the bone** (usu. foll. by *at*) *Austral.* **1** wish bad luck on. **2** cast a spell on in order to kill. **to the bone 1** to the bare minimum. **2** penetratingly. **work one's fingers to the bone** work very hard, esp. thanklessly. □□ **boneless** *adj.* [OE *bān* f. Gmc] ■ □ **bone up** see STUDY *v.* 1.

bonefish /bōnfish/ *n.* any of several species of large game fish, esp. *Albula vulpes*, having many small bones.

bonehead /bōnhed/ *n. sl.* a stupid person. □□ **boneheaded** *adj.* ■ see DOLT. □□ **boneheaded** see STUPID *adj.* 1, 5.

bonemeal /bōnmeel/ *n.* crushed or ground bones used esp. as a fertilizer.

boner /bōnər/ *n. sl.* a stupid mistake. [BONE + -ER[1]] ■ see BLUNDER *n.*

bonesetter /bōnsetər/ *n.* a person who sets broken or dislocated bones, esp. without being a qualified physician.

bonfire /bónfir/ *n.* a large open-air fire for burning trash, as part of a celebration, or as a signal. □ **Bonfire Night** *Brit.* Nov. 5, on which fireworks are displayed and an effigy of Guy Fawkes burned (see GUY[1]). **make a bonfire of** destroy by burning. [earlier *bonefire* f. BONE (bones being the chief material formerly used) + FIRE]

bong /bong, bawng/ *n.* a water pipe for smoking marijuana or the like. [Thai *bhaung*]

bongo[1] /bónggō/ *n.* (*pl.* **-os** or **-oes**) either of a pair of small connected drums usu. held between the knees and played with the fingers. [Amer. Sp. *bongó*]

bongo[2] /bónggō/ *n.* (*pl.* same or **-os**) a rare antelope, *Tragelaphus euryceros*, native to the forests of central Africa, having spiraled horns and a chestnut-red coat with narrow white vertical stripes. [cf. Bangi *mbangani*, Lingala *mongu*]

bonhomie /bónomée/ *n.* geniality; good-natured friendliness. [F f. *bonhomme* good fellow]

bonhomous /bónəməs/ *adj.* full of bonhomie.

bonito /bənéetō/ *n.* (*pl.* **-os**) any of several fish similar to the tuna and striped like mackerel. [Sp.]

bonk /bongk/ *v. & n.* ● *v.* **1** *tr.* hit resoundingly. **2** *intr.* bang; bump. **3** *Brit. coarse sl.* **a** *intr.* have sexual intercourse. **b** *tr.* have sexual intercourse with. ● *n.* an instance of bonking (*a bonk on the head*). □□ **bonker** *n.* [imit.: cf. BANG, BUMP, CONK[2]] ■ *v.* **1** see BUMP *v.* 1, 2. ● *n.* see BUMP *n.* 1.

bonkers /bóngkərz/ *adj. sl.* crazy. [20th c.: orig. unkn.] ■ see CRAZY 1.

bon mot /bawN mṓ/ *n.* (*pl.* **bons mots** *pronunc.* same or /-mṓz/) a witty saying. [F] ■ see WITTICISM.

bonnet /bónit/ *n.* **1 a** a woman's or child's hat tied under the chin and usu. with a brim framing the face. **b** a soft round brimless hat like a beret worn by men and boys in Scotland (cf. TAM-O´-SHANTER). **c** *colloq.* any hat. **2** *Brit.* a hinged cover over the engine of a motor vehicle; a hood. **3** the ceremonial feathered headdress of a Native American. **4** the cowl of a chimney, etc. **5** a protective cap in various machines. **6** *Naut.* additional canvas laced to the foot of a sail. □ **bonnet monkey** an Indian macaque, *Macaca radiata*, with a bonnet-like tuft of hair. □□ **bonneted** *adj.* [ME f. OF *bonet* short for *chapel de bonet* cap of some kind of material (med.L *bonetus*)]

bonnethead /bónit-hed/ *n.* = SHOVELHEAD.

bonny /bónee/ *adj.* (**bonnier, bonniest**) esp. *Sc. & No. of Engl.* **1 a** physically attractive. **b** healthy looking. **2** good; fine; pleasant. □□ **bonnily** *adv.* **bonniness** *n.* [16th c.: perh. f. F *bon* good]

bonsai /bónsī, -zī/ *n.* (*pl.* same) **1** the art of cultivating ornamental artificially dwarfed varieties of trees and shrubs. **2** a tree or shrub grown by this method. [Jap.]

bonspiel /bónspeel/ *n.* a curling match (usu. between two clubs). [16th c.: perh. f. LG]

bontebok /bónteebuk/ *n.* (also **bontbok** /bóntbuk/) (*pl.* same or **-boks**) a large chestnut antelope, *Damaliscus dorcas*, native to southern Africa, having a white tail and a white patch on its head and rump. [Afrik. f. *bont* spotted + *bok* BUCK[1]]

bonus /bōnəs/ *n.* **1** an unsought or unexpected extra benefit. **2 a** a usu. seasonal gratuity to employees beyond their normal pay. **b** an extra dividend or issue paid to the shareholders of a company. [L *bonus*, *bonum* good (thing)] ■ **1** see BENEFIT *n.* **2** reward, perquisite, extra, gratuity, allowance, tip, remuneration, compensation, appanage, largesse, *colloq.* perk.

bon vivant /báwN veevaáN/ *n.* (*pl.* **bon vivants** or **bons vivants** *pronunc.* same) a person indulging in good living; a gourmand. [F, lit. good liver f. *vivre* to live] ■ see GOURMET.

bon voyage /báwN vwaayaázh/ *int. & n.* an expression of good wishes to a departing traveler. [F]

bony /bōnee/ *adj.* (**bonier, boniest**) **1** (of a person) thin with prominent bones. **2** having many bones. **3** of or like bone. **4** (of a fish) having bones rather than cartilage. □□ **boniness** *n.* ■ **1** see THIN *adj.* 4.

bonze /bonz/ *n.* a Japanese or Chinese Buddhist monk. [F *bonze* or Port. *bonzo* perh. f. Jap. *bonzō* f. Chin. *fanseng* religious person, or f. Jap. *bō-zi* f. Chin. *fasi* teacher of the law]

bonzer /bónzər/ *adj. Austral. sl.* excellent; first-rate. [perh. f. BONANZA]

boo /bōō/ *int., n., & v.* ● *int.* **1** an expression of disapproval or contempt. **2** a sound, made esp. to a child, intended to surprise. ● *n.* an utterance of *boo*, esp. as an expression of disapproval or contempt made to a performer, etc. ● *v.* (**boos, booed**) **1** *intr.* utter a boo or boos. **2** *tr.* jeer at (a performer, etc.) by booing. □ **can't** (or **wouldn't**) **say boo to a goose** is very shy or timid. [imit.] ■ *v.* see JEER *v.* 1.

boob[1] /bōōb/ *n. & v. sl.* ● *n.* **1** a simpleton. **2** *Brit.* an embarrassing mistake. ● *v.intr. Brit.* make an embarrassing mistake. [abbr. of BOOBY]

boob[2] /bōōb/ *n. sl.* a woman's breast. □ **boob tube** *sl.* **1** (usu. prec. by *the*) television; one's television set. **2** *Brit.* a woman's low-cut, close-fitting, usu. strapless top. [earlier *bubby, booby,* of uncert. orig.] ■ see BREAST *n.* 1a. □ **boob tube 1** see TELEVISION 2, 3.

/.../ **pronunciation**	● **part of speech**
□ **phrases, idioms, and compounds**	
□□ **derivatives**	■ **synonym section**
cross-references appear in SMALL CAPITALS or *italics*	

booboo /bōōbōō/ *n. sl.* **1** a mistake. **2** (esp. by or to a child) a minor injury. [BOOB¹]

■ **1** see MISTAKE *n.*

boobook /bōōbŏŏk/ *n. Austral.* a brown spotted owl, *Ninox novaeseelandiae*, native to Australia and New Zealand. [imit. of its call]

booby /bōōbee/ *n.* (*pl.* **-ies**) **1** a stupid or childish person. **2** a small gannet of the genus *Sula.* □ **booby hatch** *sl.* a mental hospital. **booby prize** a prize given to the least successful competitor in any contest. **booby trap 1** a trap intended as a practical joke, e.g., an object placed on top of a door ajar. **2** *Mil.* an apparently harmless explosive device intended to kill or injure anyone touching it. **booby-trap** *v.tr.* place a booby trap or traps in or on. [prob. f. Sp. *bobo* (in both senses) f. L *balbus* stammering]

■ **1** see SILLY *n.* □ **booby hatch** see BEDLAM 2. **booby trap 1** see TRAP¹ *n.* 3.

boodle /bōōd'l/ *n. sl.* money, esp. when gained or used dishonestly, e.g., as a bribe. [Du. *boedel* possessions]

■ see MONEY 1.

boofhead /bōōfhed/ *n. Austral. sl.* a fool. [prob. f. *bufflehead* fool]

boogeyman var. of BOGEYMAN.

boogie /bōōgee/ *v. & n.* ● *v.intr.* (**boogies, boogied, boogying**) *sl.* **1** dance enthusiastically to rock music. **2** leave, esp. quickly. ● *n.* **1** = BOOGIE-WOOGIE. **2** *sl.* a dance to rock music. [BOOGIE-WOOGIE]

boogieman var. of BOGEYMAN.

boogie-woogie /bōōgeewŏŏgee, bŏŏgeewŏŏgee/ *n.* a style of playing blues or jazz on the piano, marked by a persistent bass rhythm. [20th c.: orig. unkn.]

book /bŏŏk/ *n. & v.* ● *n.* **1 a** a written or printed work consisting of pages glued or sewn together along one side and bound in covers. **b** a literary composition intended for publication (*is working on her book*). **2** a bound set of blank sheets for writing or keeping records in. **3** a set of tickets, stamps, matches, checks, samples of cloth, etc., bound up together. **4** (in *pl.*) a set of records or accounts. **5** a main division of a literary work, or of the Bible (*the Book of Deuteronomy*). **6 a** a libretto, script of a play, etc. **b** a set of rules or regulations. **7** *colloq.* a magazine. **8** a telephone directory (*my number's in the book*). **9** a record of bets made and money paid out at a racetrack by a bookmaker. **10** a set of six tricks collected together in a card game. **11 a** an imaginary record or list (*the book of life*). **b** a source of information or knowledge. ● *v.* **1** *tr.* **a** engage (a seat, etc.) in advance; make a reservation for. **b** engage (a guest, supporter, musical act, etc.) for some occasion. **2** *tr.* **a** take the personal details of (esp. a criminal offender). **b** enter in a book or list. **3** *tr.* issue an airline, etc., ticket to. **4** *intr.* make a reservation (*no need to book*). □ **book club** an enterprise that sells its members selected books on special terms. **book in** esp. *Brit.* register one's arrival at a hotel, etc. **book learning** theory, as opposed to practical knowledge. **book up 1** *Brit.* buy tickets in advance for a theater, concert, vacation, etc. **2** (as **booked up**) with all places reserved. **book value** the value of a commodity as entered in a book of accounts (opp. *market value*). **bring to book** call to account. **closed** (or **sealed**) **book** a subject of which one is ignorant. **go by the book** proceed according to the rules. **the good Book** the Bible. **in a person's bad** (or **good**) **books** in disfavor (or favor) with a person. **like a book** completely; thoroughly. **in my book** in my opinion. **make book** take bets and pay out winnings on a race, game, etc. **not in the book** disallowed. **off the books** (of business) conducted on a cash basis, without keeping accounting records. **one for the books** an event worthy of being recorded. **on the books** contained in a list of members, etc. **suits my book** *Brit.* is convenient to me. **take a leaf out of a person's book** imitate a person. **throw the book at** *colloq.* charge or punish to the utmost. [OE *bōc*, *bōcian*, f. Gmc, usu. taken to be rel. to BEECH (the bark of which was used for writing on)]

■ *n.* **1** volume, tome, work, publication; paperback, hardback; composition, creation, writing. **4** (*books*) records, accounts, documents. **6 a** libretto, words,

lyrics, script, play; continuity. **b** rules, laws, regulations; *colloq.* bible. **7** see MAGAZINE 1. ● *v.* **1** engage, reserve, earmark, save, set *or* put aside, take, ticket; order. **2 b** register, enroll, list, log, record, post. **4** *Brit.* book up. □ **book up 2** (**booked up**) full up, all taken, fully booked. **bring to book** see *take to task* (TASK). **go by the book** follow the rules *or* regulations, abide by the law *or* rules *or* regulations, stick to the rules. **not in the book** see UNLAWFUL. **off the books** under the table. **take a leaf out of a person's book** see IMITATE 1. **throw the book at** see ACCUSE 2, PUNISH 1.

bookbinder /bŏŏkbīndər/ *n.* a person who binds books professionally. □□ **bookbinding** *n.*

bookcase /bŏŏk-kays/ *n.* a set of shelves for books in the form of a cabinet.

bookend /bŏŏkend/ *n.* a usu. ornamental prop used to keep a row of books upright.

bookie /bŏŏkee/ *n. colloq.* = BOOKMAKER.

booking /bŏŏking/ *n.* the act or an instance of booking or reserving a seat, a room in a hotel, etc.; a reservation (see BOOK *v.* 1). □ **booking clerk** *Brit.* an official selling tickets at a railroad station. **booking hall** (or **office**) *Brit.* a room or area at a railroad station in which tickets are sold.

■ reservation, order, arrangement.

bookish /bŏŏkish/ *adj.* **1** studious; fond of reading. **2** acquiring knowledge from books rather than practical experience. **3** (of a word, language, etc.) literary; not colloquial. □□ **bookishly** *adv.* **bookishness** *n.*

■ **1** see STUDIOUS 1.

bookkeeper /bŏŏk-keepər/ *n.* a person who keeps accounts for a business, etc. □□ **bookkeeping** *n.*

■ clerk, accountant, cashier, CPA, certified public accountant, *Brit.* chartered accountant, *Can. & Sc.* CA.

booklet /bŏŏklit/ *n.* a small book consisting of a few sheets, usu. with paper covers.

bookmaker /bŏŏkmaykər/ *n.* a person who takes bets, esp. on horse races, calculates odds, and pays out winnings. □□ **bookmaking** *n.*

■ *Brit.* turf accountant, *colloq.* bookie.

bookman /bŏŏkmən/ *n.* (*pl.* **-men**) a literary person, esp. one involved in the business of books.

bookmark /bŏŏkmaark/ *n.* (also **bookmarker**) a strip of leather, cardboard, etc., used to mark one's place in a book.

bookmobile /bŏŏkmōbeel/ *n.* a mobile library. [after AUTOMOBILE]

bookplate /bŏŏkplayt/ *n.* a decorative label stuck in the front of a book bearing the owner's name.

bookseller /bŏŏkselər/ *n.* a dealer in books.

bookshop /bŏŏkshop/ *n.* esp. *Brit.* = BOOKSTORE.

bookstall /bŏŏkstawl/ *n.* esp. *Brit.* a stand for selling books, newspapers, etc., esp. out of doors.

bookstore /bŏŏkstawr/ *n.* a store where books are sold.

booksy /bŏŏksee/ *adj. Brit. colloq.* having literary or bookish pretensions.

bookwork /bŏŏkwərk/ *n.* the study of books (as opposed to practical work).

■ see STUDY *n.* 1, 2.

bookworm /bŏŏkwərm/ *n.* **1** *colloq.* a person devoted to reading. **2** the larva of a moth or beetle which feeds on the paper and glue used in books.

■ **1** bibliophile, booklover, inveterate *or* ardent reader.

Boolean /bōōleeən/ *adj.* denoting a system of algebraic notation to represent logical propositions. □ **Boolean algebra** an algebraic system applied to symbolic logic and computer operations. **Boolean logic** the use of the logical operators 'and,' 'or,' and 'not' in retrieving information from a computer database. [G. *Boole*, Engl. mathematician d. 1864]

boom¹ /bōōm/ *n. & v.* ● *n.* a deep resonant sound. ● *v.intr.* make or speak with a boom. □ **boom box** *sl.* a portable radio, often with a cassette and/or CD player. [imit.]

■ *n.* rumble, roar, blare, report, peal, blast. ● *v.* sound, resound, resonate, rumble, thunder, roar, bellow; blast, bang.

boom² /bōōm/ *n. & v.* ● *n.* a period of prosperity or sudden activity in commerce, etc. ● *v.intr.* (esp. of commercial ventures) be suddenly prosperous or successful. □ **boom town** a town undergoing sudden growth due to a boom. □□ **boomlet** *n.* [19th-c. US word, perhaps f. BOOM¹ (cf. *make things hum*)]

■ *n.* growth, increase, development, *archaic* flourish, *colloq.* bulge; prosperity, profitability. ● *v.* prosper, thrive, flourish, bloom, blossom, succeed, progress, make progress, grow, increase, be on the upgrade, *Brit. colloq.* be on the up and up, *literary* burgeon.

boom³ /boom/ *n.* **1** *Naut.* a pivoted spar to which the foot of a sail is attached, allowing the angle of the sail to be changed. **2** a long pole over a movie or television stage set, carrying microphones and other equipment. **3** a floating barrier across the mouth of a harbor or river, or enclosing an oil spill. [Du., = BEAM *n.*]

boomer /boomər/ *n.* **1** a transient construction worker, esp. a bridge builder. **2** a N. American mountain beaver, *Aplodontia rufa*. **3** a large male kangaroo. **4** a large wave.

boomerang /boomərang/ *n.* & *v.* ● *n.* **1** a curved flat hardwood missile orig. used by Australian Aboriginals to kill prey, and often of a kind able to return in flight to the thrower. **2** a plan or scheme that recoils on its originator. ● *v.intr.* **1** act as a boomerang. **2** (of a plan or action) backfire. [Aboriginal name, perh. modified]

■ *v.* **2** rebound, recoil, backfire, redound; miscarry, go wrong, fail.

boomslang /boomslang/ *n.* a large venomous tree snake, *Dispholidus typus*, native to southern Africa. [Afrik. f. *boom* tree + *slang* snake]

boon¹ /boon/ *n.* **1** an advantage; a blessing. **2 a** a thing asked for; a request. **b** a gift; a favor. [ME, orig. = prayer, f. ON *bón* f. Gmc]

■ **1** blessing, godsend, stroke of good fortune, piece *or* bit of luck, benefit, advantage, asset, plus, added extra, *colloq.* break, *Austral.* & *NZ sl.* spin. **2 a** see REQUEST *n.* 1, 2. **b** gift, award, reward, gratuity, present, offering, donation; service, favor, kindness, courtesy, good deed, *beau geste*.

boon² /boon/ *adj.* close; intimate; favorite (usu. *boon companion*). [ME (orig. = jolly, congenial) f. OF *bon* f. L *bonus* good]

boondocks /boondoks/ *n. sl.* rough, remote, or isolated country. [Tagalog *bundok* mountain]

boondoggle /boondogəl, -daw-/ *n.* & *v.* ● *n.* **1** work or activity that is wasteful or pointless but gives the appearance of having value. **2** a public project of questionable merit that typically involves political patronage and graft. ● *v.intr.* participate in a boondoggle. [f. *boondoggle*, a braided leather cord worn by Boy Scouts]

boong /boong/ *n. Austral. sl. offens.* an Aborigine. [orig. uncert.]

boonies /booneez/ *n.pl.* (prec. by *the*) *sl.* = BOONDOCKS.

boor /boor/ *n.* **1** a rude, unmannerly person. **2** a clumsy person. **3** a peasant; a yokel. □□ **boorish** *adj.* **boorishly** *adv.* **boorishness** *n.* [LG *būr* or Du. *boer* farmer]

■ **1** barbarian, yahoo, lout, brute, churl, hoodlum, philistine, *Austral.* larrikin, *colloq.* slob, pig, hobbledehoy, *derog.* peasant, *sl.* lug, *Austral. sl.* ocker, *Brit. sl.* yob, yobbo. **2** oaf, lubber, clown, *colloq.* galoot, hobbledehoy, lummox, *sl.* klutz, goop, clod. **3** rustic, peasant, yokel, (country) bumpkin, provincial, backwoodsman, *archaic* churl, kern, villain, esp. *colloq.* hick, hayseed, hillbilly, *hist.* hind. □□ **boorish** rustic, barbarian, rude, crude, ill-mannered, uncultured, coarse, uncivilized, uncouth, churlish, uncivil, loutish, vulgar, ill-bred, *colloq.* slobbish; oafish, clownish, lubberly, gawky, clumsy, *sl.* cloddish.

boost /boost/ *v.* & *n.* ● *v.* **1 a** promote or increase the reputation of (a person, scheme, commodity, etc.) by praise or advertising; push; increase or assist (*boosted his spirits*; *boost sales*). **b** push from below; assist (*boosted me up into the tree*). **2 a** raise the voltage of (an electric circuit, etc.). **b** amplify (a radio signal). ● *n.* **1** an act, process, or result of boosting (*asked for a boost up the hill*). **2 a** *Brit.* an

advertising campaign. **b** the resulting advance in value, reputation, etc. [19th-c. US word: orig. unkn.]

■ *v.* **1 a** encourage, promote, help, kick-start, aid, support, assist, strengthen, bolster, build up, improve, enhance, exalt; increase, raise, swell, extend, lift, *sl.* crank up; inspire, push. **b** lift, shove *or* push (up *or* upward(s)); give a person a leg up; raise; help, assist. **2 b** see AMPLIFY 1. ● *n.* **1** lift, shove, push, leg up, kick-start; raise; help, hand, encouragement, support, furtherance, tonic; increase, rise, jump, leap, revival, (up)surge, raise, hike.

booster /boostər/ *n.* **1** a device for increasing electrical power or voltage. **2** an auxiliary engine or rocket used to give initial acceleration. **3** (also **booster shot**) *Med.* a dose of an immunizing agent increasing or renewing the effect of an earlier one. **4** *colloq.* a person who boosts by helping or encouraging. □ **booster cables** = *jumper cables*.

■ **4** see FAN².

boot¹ /boot/ *n.* & *v.* ● *n.* **1** an outer covering for the foot, esp. of leather, rubber, etc., reaching above the ankle, often to the knee. **2** a covering or sheath to protect a mechanical connection, etc. **3** *colloq.* a firm kick. **4** (prec. by *the*) *colloq.* dismissal, esp. (*Brit.*) from employment (*gave them the boot*). **5** *Mil.* a navy or marine recruit. **6** (also **Denver Boot**) a device attached to the wheel of a parked car that prevents it being driven; used by police against those who park illegally, ignore fines, etc. **7** *hist.* an instrument of torture encasing and crushing the foot. **8** *Brit.* the luggage compartment of an automobile; the trunk. ● *v.tr.* **1** kick, esp. hard. **2** (often foll. by *out*) dismiss (a person) forcefully. **3** (usu. foll. by *up*) put (a computer) in a state of readiness (cf. BOOTSTRAP 2). □ **boot camp** *Mil.* a camp for training navy or marine recruits. **the boot is on the other foot** (or **leg**) *Brit.* the truth or responsibility is reversed. **die with one's boots on** (of a soldier, etc.) die fighting. **put the boot in** *Brit.* **1** kick brutally. **2** act decisively against a person. **you bet your boots** *sl.* it is quite certain. □□ **booted** *adj.* [ME f. ON *bóti* or f. OF *bote*, of unkn. orig.]

■ *n.* **3** see KICK¹ *n.* 1. **4** see SACK¹ *n.* 2. ● *v.* **1** see KICK¹ *v.* 1. **2** (*boot out*) eject, expel, throw *or* cast *or* turn out, push *or* drive *or* force *or* fling out, *colloq.* kick out, *Brit. colloq.* turf out, *sl.* bounce; see also DISMISS 2. □ **you bet your boots** see *of course* (COURSE).

boot² /boot/ *n.* □ **to boot** as well; to the good; in addition. [orig. = 'advantage': OE *bōt* f. Gmc]

■ □ **to boot** in addition, into the bargain, besides, moreover, as well, also, too, additionally, for good measure, on top of everything else, as a bonus, *archaic* withal.

bootblack /bootblak/ *n.* a person who polishes boots and shoes.

bootee /bootee/ *n.* (also **bootie**) **1** a soft shoe worn by a baby. **2** a woman's short boot.

booth /booth/ *n.* (*pl.* **booths** /boothz, booths/) **1** a small temporary roofed structure of canvas, wood, etc., used esp. for the sale or display of goods at a market, fair, etc. **2** an enclosure or compartment for various purposes, e.g., telephoning, broadcasting, or voting. **3** a set of a table and benches in a restaurant or bar. [ME f. Scand.]

■ **1** stall, stand, table. **2** compartment, cubicle, box, kiosk, alcove, carrel, enclosure.

bootjack /bootjak/ *n.* a device for holding a boot by the heel to ease withdrawal of the leg.

bootlace /bootlays/ *n.* **1** a cord or leather thong for lacing boots. **2** *Brit.* = SHOELACE.

■ see LACE *n.* 2.

bootleg /bootleg/ *adj.* & *v.* ● *adj.* (esp. of liquor) smuggled; illicitly sold. ● *v.tr.* (**-legged**, **-legging**) make, distribute, or smuggle (illicit goods, esp. alcohol, computer software,

/.../ pronunciation	● part of speech
□ phrases, idioms, and compounds	
□□ derivatives	■ synonym section
cross-references appear in SMALL CAPITALS or *italics*	

etc.). ▫▫ **bootlegger** *n.* [f. the smugglers' practice of concealing bottles in their boots]
- *v.* see RUN *v.* 24.

bootless /bŏŏtlis/ *adj.* unavailing; useless. [OE *bōtlēas* (as BOOT², LESS)]
- pointless, unavailing, vain, purposeless, hopeless, useless, futile, worthless, unproductive, nonproductive, ineffective, ineffectual, inefficacious, fruitless, idle, unprofitable, profitless, unremunerative, unrewarding, wasteful, time-wasting, Sisyphean.

bootlicker /bŏŏtlikər/ *n. colloq.* a person who behaves obsequiously or servilely; a toady. ▫▫ **bootlick** *v.intr.* **bootlicking** *n.* & *adj.*
- see *flatterer* (FLATTER).

boots /bŏŏts/ *n. Brit.* a hotel employee who cleans boots and shoes, carries luggage, etc.

bootstrap /bŏŏtstrap/ *n.* **1** a loop at the back of a boot used to pull it on. **2** *Computing* a technique of loading a program into a computer by means of a few initial instructions which enable the introduction of the rest of the program from an input device. ▫ **pull oneself up by one's bootstraps** better oneself by one's own efforts.

booty /bŏŏtee/ *n.* **1** plunder gained esp. in war or by piracy. **2** *colloq.* something gained or won. [ME f. MLG *būte*, *buite* exchange, of uncert. orig.]
- **1** plunder, gain, spoil(s), contraband, takings, loot, *sl.* swag, boodle, (hot) goods. **2** gain, pickings, takings, winnings, take; prize, haul.

booze /bŏŏz/ *n.* & *v. colloq.* ● *n.* **1** alcohol, esp. hard liquor. **2** the drinking of this (*on the booze*). ● *v.intr.* drink alcohol esp. excessively or habitually. ▫ **booze-up** esp. *Brit. sl.* a drinking bout; a spree. [earlier *bouse*, *bowse*, f. MDu. *būsen* drink to excess]
- *n.* **1** drink, (hard) liquor, spirit(s), alcohol, *Ir.* poteen, *colloq.* firewater, hooch, esp. *Brit. colloq.* plonk, *sl.* rotgut, hard stuff, lush, red-eye, juice. **2** (*on the booze*) on the drink, *sl.* on a bender *or* a binge *or* the hard stuff, on the bottle. ● *v.* drink, tipple, imbibe, fuddle, sot, carouse, *archaic or literary* tope, *sl.* hit the bottle, *sl.* knock a few back, lush. ▫ **booze-up** see BENDER.

boozer /bŏŏzər/ *n. colloq.* **1** a person who drinks alcohol, esp. to excess. **2** *Brit.* a place for drinking; a tavern or bar.
- **1** see DRUNK *n.* 1.

boozy /bŏŏzee/ *adj.* (**boozier**, **booziest**) *colloq.* intoxicated; addicted to drink. ▫▫ **boozily** *adv.* **booziness** *n.*
- see DRUNK *adj.* 1.

bop¹ /bop/ *n.* & *v. colloq.* ● *n.* **1** = BEBOP. **2** *Brit.* **a** an interval of dancing, esp. to pop music. **b** an organized social occasion for this. ● *v.intr.* (**bopped, bopping**) *Brit.* dance, esp. to pop music. ▫▫ **bopper** *n.* [abbr. of BEBOP]

bop² /bop/ *v.* & *n. colloq.* ● *v.tr.* (**bopped, bopping**) hit; punch lightly. ● *n.* a light blow or hit. [imit.]

bo-peep /bōpéep/ *n.* = PEEKABOO. [*bo* BOO + PEEP¹]

bor. *abbr.* borough.

bora¹ /báwrə/ *n.* a strong cold dry NE wind blowing in the upper Adriatic. [It. dial. f. L *boreas* north wind: see BOREAL]

bora² /báwrə/ *n. Austral.* an Aboriginal rite in which boys are initiated into manhood. [Aboriginal]

boracic /bərásik/ *adj.* of borax; containing boron. ▫ **boracic acid** = *boric acid.* [med.L *borax -acis*]

borage /báwrij, bór-/ *n.* any plant of the genus *Borago*, esp. *Borago officinalis*, native to Europe, with bright blue flowers and leaves used as flavoring. [OF *bourrache* f. med.L *borrago* f. Arab. *'abu 'āraḳ* father of sweat (from its use as a diaphoretic)]

borak /báwrak/ *n. Austral.* & *NZ sl.* banter; ridicule; nonsense. ▫ **poke borak at** make fun of. [Aboriginal Austral.]

borane /báwrayn/ *n. Chem.* any hydride of boron.

borate /báwrayt/ *n.* a salt or ester of boric acid.

borax /báwraks/ *n.* **1** the mineral salt sodium borate, occurring in alkaline deposits as an efflorescence or as crystals. **2** the purified form of this salt, used in making glass and china, and as an antiseptic. [ME f. OF *boras* f. med.L *borax* f. Arab. *būraḳ* f. Pers. *būrah*]

Borazon /báwrəzon/ *n. propr.* a hard form of boron nitride, resistant to oxidation. [BORON + AZO- nitrogen + *-on*]

borborygmus /báwrbərígməs/ *n.* (*pl.* **borborygmi** /-mī/) a rumbling of gas in the intestines. ▫▫ **borborygmic** *adj.* [mod.L f. Gk]
- see WIND¹ *n.* 4.

Bordeaux /bawrdố/ *n.* (*pl.* same /-dốz/) any of various red, white, or rosé wines from the district of Bordeaux in SW France. ▫ **Bordeaux mixture** a fungicide for vines, fruit trees, etc., composed of equal quantities of copper sulfate and calcium oxide in water.

bordello /bawrdélō/ *n.* (*pl.* **-os**) a brothel. [ME (f. It. *bordello*) f. OF *bordel* small farm, dimin. of *borde* ult. f. Frank.: see BOARD]
- see BROTHEL.

border /báwrdər/ *n.* & *v.* ● *n.* **1** the edge or boundary of anything, or the part near it. **2 a** the line separating two political or geographical areas, esp. countries. **b** the district on each side of this. **3** a distinct edging around anything, esp. for strength or decoration. **4** a long narrow bed of flowers or shrubs in a garden (*herbaceous border*). ● *v.* **1** *tr.* be on or along a border. **2** *tr.* provide with a border. **3** *intr.* (usu. foll. by *on*, *upon*) **a** adjoin; come close to being. **b** approximate; resemble. ▫ **Border collie** a common working sheepdog of British origin. **Border terrier 1** a small terrier of a breed with rough hair. **2** this breed. [ME f. OF *bordure*: cf. BOARD]
- *n.* **1** boundary, edge, fringe, verge, rim; periphery, outskirts, margin, extremity. **2 a** boundary, frontier, borderline, divide, dividing line. **b** hinterland(s). **3** edge, margin, hem, band, binding, trimming, trim, edging, fringe, *archaic* purfle, purfling; frame, frieze, mount, molding. **4** bed, flower bed, herbaceous border. ● *v.* **1, 2** edge, trim, bind, fringe, purfle; ring. **3 a** (*border on*) lie alongside, adjoin, line, abut (*on or upon*), butt on to, verge upon *or* on, touch, be adjacent to, flank, join on to; approach (closely), near, come close to. **b** (*border on*) approximate (to), resemble (closely), seem *or* be similar to, be like, verge upon *or* on.

borderer /báwrdərər/ *n.* a person who lives near a border.

borderland /báwrdərland/ *n.* **1 a** the district near a border. **b** the fringes. **2** an intermediate condition between two extremes. **3** an area for debate.

borderline /báwrdərlīn/ *n.* & *adj.* ● *n.* **1** the line dividing two (often extreme) conditions. **2** a line marking a boundary. ● *adj.* **1** on the borderline. **2** verging on an extreme condition; only just acceptable.
- *n.* see LINE¹ *n.* 8a. ● *adj.* **2** see MARGINAL 2b.

bordure /báwrjər/ *n. Heraldry* a border round the edge of a shield. [ME form of BORDER]

bore¹ /bawr/ *v.* & *n.* ● *v.* **1** *tr.* make a hole in, esp. with a revolving tool. **2** *tr.* hollow out (a tube, etc.). **3** *tr.* **a** make (a hole) by boring or excavation. **b** make (one's way) through a crowd, etc. **4** *intr.* drill a well, mine, etc. ● *n.* **1** the hollow of a firearm barrel or of a cylinder in an internal combustion engine. **2** the diameter of this; the caliber. **3** = BOREHOLE. [OE *borian* f. Gmc]
- *v.* **1–3 a** pierce, drill, perforate, penetrate, puncture, punch; tunnel, excavate, sink, dig (out), gouge (out), ream, burrow out; hollow *or* scoop out. **3 b** (*bore one's way*) barge, make *or* thread *or* pick one's way, plow, push one's way. **4** drill, excavate, dig. ● *n.* **2** see CALIBER 1.

bore² /bawr/ *n.* & *v.* ● *n.* a tiresome or dull person or thing. ● *v.tr.* weary by tedious talk or dullness. ▫ **bore a person to tears** weary (a person) in the extreme. [18th c.: orig. unkn.]
- *n.* see NUISANCE. ● *v.* weary, wear out, tire, exhaust, jade, stultify; make a person yawn, make a person fed up.

bore³ /bawr/ *n.* a high tidal wave rushing up a narrow estuary. *Brit.* Also called EAGRE. [ME, perh. f. ON *bára* wave]

bore⁴ *past* of BEAR¹.

boreal /báwreeəl/ *adj.* **1** of the north or northern regions. **2**

of the north wind. [ME f. F *boréal* or LL *borealis* f. L *Boreas* f. Gk *Boreas* god of the north wind]

boredom /báwrdəm/ *n.* the state of being bored; ennui.
■ dullness, dreariness, ennui, tedium, monotony.

borehole /báwrhōl/ *n.* **1** a deep narrow hole, esp. one made in the earth to find water, oil, etc. **2** *Austral.* a water hole for cattle.
■ **1** see WELL[2] *n.* 1.

borer /báwrər/ *n.* **1** any of several worms, mollusks, insects, or insect larvae which bore into wood, other plant material, or rock. **2** a tool for boring.

boric /báwrik/ *adj.* of or containing boron. □ **boric acid** an acid derived from borax, used as a mild antiseptic and in the manufacture of heat-resistant glass and enamels.

boring /báwring/ *adj.* that makes one bored; uninteresting; tedious; dull. □□ **boringly** *adv.* **boringness** *n.*
■ dull, monotonous, tedious, humdrum, routine, mundane, tiresome, dreary, flat, dead, uninteresting, unexciting, uninspiring; wearisome, soporific.

born /bawrn/ *adj.* **1** existing as a result of birth. **2 a** being such or likely to become such by natural ability or quality (*a born leader*). **b** (usu. foll. by *to* + infin.) having a specified destiny or prospect (*born lucky; born to lead*). **3** (in *comb.*) of a certain status by birth (*French-born; well-born*). □ **born-again** (*attrib.*) converted (esp. to fundamentalist Christianity). **born and bred** by birth and upbringing. **in all one's born days** *colloq.* in one's life so far. **not born yesterday** *colloq.* not stupid; shrewd. [past part. of BEAR[1]]

borne /bawrn/ **1** *past part.* of BEAR[1]. **2** (in *comb.*) carried or transported by (*airborne*).

boro- /báwrō/ *comb. form* indicating salts containing boron.

boron /báwron/ *n. Chem.* a nonmetallic yellow crystalline or brown amorphous element extracted from borax and boric acid and mainly used for hardening steel. ¶ Symb.: B. [BORAX + *-on* f. *carbon* (which it resembles in some respects)]

borosilicate /báwrōsílikit, -kayt/ *n.* any of many substances containing boron, silicon, and oxygen generally used in glazes and enamels and in the production of glass.

borough /bə́rō, búrō/ *n.* **1** an incorporated municipality in certain states. **2** each of five political divisions of New York City. **3** (in Alaska) a county equivalent. **4** *Brit.* **a** a town represented in the House of Commons. **b** a town or district granted the status of a borough. **5** *Brit. hist.* a town with a municipal corporation and privileges conferred by a royal charter. [OE *burg, burh* f. Gmc: cf. BURGH]

borrow /bórō, báwrō/ *v.* **1 a** *tr.* acquire temporarily with the promise or intention of returning. **b** *intr.* obtain money in this way. **2** *tr.* use (an idea, invention, etc.) originated by another; plagiarize. □ **borrowed time** an unexpected extension esp. of life. □□ **borrower** *n.* **borrowing** *n.* [OE *borgian* give a pledge]
■ **1** be lent *or* loaned; cadge, sponge, hire, *sl.* touch a person for, bum. **2** see TAKE *v.* 14a.

borscht /bawrsht/ *n.* (also **borsch** /bawrsh, bawrshch/) a highly seasoned Russian or Polish soup made primarily with beets and cabbage and served with sour cream. [Russ. *borshch*]

Borstal /báwrstəl/ *n. Brit. hist.* an institution for reforming and training juvenile delinquents. [*Borstal* in S. England, where the first of these was established]

bort /bawrt/ *n.* (also **boart**) **1** an inferior or malformed diamond, used for cutting. **2** fragments of diamonds used in cutting or abrasion. [Du. *boort*]

borzoi /báwrzoy/ *n.* **1** a large Russian wolfhound of a breed with a narrow head and silky, usu. white, coat. **2** this breed. [Russ. f. *borzyi* swift]

boscage /bóskij/ *n.* (also **boskage**) **1** a mass of trees or shrubs. **2** a wood or thicket. [ME f. OF *boscage* f. Gmc: cf. BUSH[1]]
■ see BRUSH *n.* 6.

bosh /bosh/ *n. & int. sl.* nonsense; foolish talk. [Turk. *boş* empty]
■ see NONSENSE.

bosky /bóskee/ *adj.* (**boskier, boskiest**) wooded; bushy. [ME *bosk* thicket]

■ see WOODED.

bo's'n var. of BOATSWAIN.

bosom /bŏŏzəm/ *n. & adj.* ● *n.* **1 a** a person's breast or chest, esp. a woman's. **b** *colloq.* each of a woman's breasts. **c** the enclosure formed by a person's breast and arms. **2** the seat of the emotions; an emotional center, esp. as the source of an enfolding relationship (*in the bosom of one's family*). **3** the part of a woman's dress covering the breast. ● *adj.* (esp. in **bosom friend**) close; intimate. [OE *bōsm* f. Gmc]
■ *n.* **1** breast, chest, bust; (*bosoms*) *sl.* boobs, *coarse sl.* knockers, tits, jugs. **2** soul, heart (of hearts); blood; midst, interior, core, center. ● *adj.* close, intimate, dear, beloved, cherished, boon, special, confidential; (**bosom friend**) best friend, intimate, second self, crony; see also FRIEND *n.* 1.

bosomy /bŏŏzəmee/ *adj.* (of a woman) having large breasts.
■ busty, buxom, *colloq.* chesty, well-endowed.

boson /bŏson/ *n. Physics* any of several elementary particles obeying the relations stated by Bose and Einstein, with a zero or integral spin, e.g., photons (cf. FERMION). [S. N. Bose, Ind. physicist d. 1974]

boss[1] /baws, bos/ *n. & v.* ● *n.* **1** a person in charge; an employer, manager, or overseer. **2** a person who controls or dominates a political organization. ● *v.tr.* **1** (usu. foll. by *around*) treat domineeringly; give constant peremptory orders to. **2** be the master or manager of. [orig. US: f. Du. *baas* master]
■ *n.* **1** chief, supervisor, head, administrator, manager, foreman, superintendent, overseer, employer, leader, director, managing director, kingpin, president, esp. *Ir.* himself, esp. *Brit. colloq.* super, *Brit. colloq.* gaffer, *sl.* big cheese, big chief *or* daddy, honcho, Mr. Big, *Brit. sl.* prex, governor, gov. ● *v.* **1** push *or* shove around *or* about, dominate, order about *or* around, lord it over, dictate to. **2** supervise, head, manage, run, oversee, watch *or* preside over, overlook, direct, control, superintend, command, have charge of, be in charge of, govern.

boss[2] /baws, bos/ *n.* **1** a round knob, stud, or other protuberance, esp. in the center of a shield or in ornamental work. **2** *Archit.* a piece of ornamental carving, etc., covering the point where the ribs in a vault or ceiling cross. **3** *Geol.* a large mass of igneous rock. **4** *Mech.* an enlarged part of a shaft. [ME f. OF *boce* f. Rmc]

bossa nova /bósə nŏ́və, báwsə/ *n.* **1** a dance like the samba, originating in Brazil. **2** a piece of music for this or in its rhythm. [Port., = new flair]

boss-eyed /báwsíd, bós-/ *adj. Brit. colloq.* **1** having only one good eye; cross-eyed. **2** crooked; out of true. [dial. *boss* miss, bungle]

boss-shot /báws-shot, bós-/ *n. Brit. dial. & sl.* **1** a bad shot or aim. **2** an unsuccessful attempt. [as BOSS-EYED]

bossy /báwsee, bós-/ *adj.* (**bossier, bossiest**) *colloq.* domineering; tending to boss. □ **bossy-boots** *Brit. colloq.* a domineering person. □□ **bossily** *adv.* **bossiness** *n.*
■ overbearing, domineering, high-handed, dictatorial, authoritarian, tyrannical, despotic, imperious, lordly, *colloq.* pushy.

bosun (also **bo'sun**) var. of BOATSWAIN.

bot /bot/ *n.* (also **bott**) any of various parasitic larvae of flies of the family Oestridae, infesting horses, sheep, etc. [prob. of LG orig.]

bot. *abbr.* **1** bottle. **2** botanic; botanical; botany. **3** bought.

botanize /bót'nīz/ *v.intr.* study plants, esp. in their habitat.

botany /bót'nee/ *n.* **1** the study of the physiology, structure, genetics, ecology, distribution, classification, and economic importance of plants. **2** the plant life of a particular area or time. □□ **botanic** /bətánik/ *adj.* **botanical** *adj.* **botanically**

adv. **botanist** /bót'nist/ *n.* [*botanic* f. F *botanique* or LL *botanicus* f. Gk *botanikos* f. *botanē* plant]

botch /boch/ *v. & n.* (also *Brit.* **bodge**) • *v.tr.* **1** bungle; do badly. **2** patch or repair clumsily. • *n.* bungled or spoiled work (*made a botch of it*). □□ **botcher** *n.* [ME: orig. unkn.]
■ *v.* **1** bungle, mismanage, spoil, mess up, muff, make a mess of, *colloq.* make a hash of, muck up, flub, foul up, fluff, *sl.* screw up, louse up, blow, goof (up), *Brit. sl.* cock up. **2** patch up. ■ *n.* mess, hash.

botfly /bótfli/ *n.* (*pl.* **flies**) any dipterous fly of the genus *Oestrus*, with stout hairy bodies.

both /bōth/ *adj., pron., & adv.* • *adj. & pron.* the two; not only one (*both boys; both the boys; both of the boys; the boys are both here*). ¶ Widely used with *of*, esp. when followed by a pronoun (e.g., *both of us*) or a noun implying separate rather than collective consideration, e.g., *both of the boys* suggests *each boy* rather than the two together. • *adv.* with equal truth in two cases (*both the boy and his sister are here; are both here and hungry*). □ **both ways** = *each way.* **have it both ways** alternate between two incompatible points of view to suit the needs of the moment. [ME f. ON *báthir*]

bother /bóthər/ *v., n., & int.* • *v.* **1** *tr.* **a** give trouble to; worry; disturb. **b** *refl.* be anxious or concerned. **2** *intr.* **a** (often foll. by *to* + infin.) worry or trouble oneself (*don't bother about that; didn't bother to tell me*). **b** (foll. by *with*) be concerned. • *n.* **1 a** a person or thing that bothers or causes worry. **b** a minor nuisance. **2** trouble; worry; fuss; a state of worry. • *int.* expressing annoyance or impatience. □ **cannot be bothered** will not make the effort needed. [Ir. *bodhraim* deafen]
■ *v.* **1 a** annoy, pester, keep on at, irritate, trouble, hector, harass, hound, dog, nag, badger, plague, *colloq.* hassle, get at; inconvenience; perturb, disturb, worry, upset, unsettle, make uneasy, disquiet, disconcert, concern, aggravate, distress, discomfit, *archaic* ail, *sl.* bug. **b** see sense 2 below. **2** worry, trouble (oneself), be anxious, fret, concern oneself, upset oneself, lose sleep, burden oneself, get worked up *or* upset, *colloq.* get het up; fuss, make a fuss; be concerned *or* interested. • *n.* **1** nuisance, pest, annoyance, inconvenience, vexation, irritation, bore, burden, *colloq.* bind, headache, hassle, drag, pain, pain in the neck, thorn in the side *or* flesh, pain in the butt, bummer. **2** trouble, worry, inconvenience, discomfort, *colloq.* hassle; disturbance, ado, commotion, fuss, disorder; dither, flutter, *colloq.* tizzy, pet, stew, lather, sweat. • *int.* blast, damn, hang it all, *colloq.* hell, *Brit. colloq.* dash (it), dash it all, *euphem.* sugar, *sl.* blow (it), rats, doggone it, *Brit. sl.* flaming heck. □ **cannot be bothered** cannot be fussed *or Brit. colloq.* fagged.

botheration /bóthəráyshən/ *n. & int. colloq.* = BOTHER *n., int.*

bothersome /bóthərsəm/ *adj.* causing bother; troublesome.
■ see TROUBLESOME 2.

bothy /bóthee, báw-/ *n.* (also **bothie**) (*pl.* **-ies**) *Sc.* a small hut or cottage. [18th c.: orig. unkn.: perh. rel. to BOOTH]

bo-tree /bótree/ *n.* the Indian fig tree, *Ficus religiosa*, regarded as sacred by Buddhists. Also called PIPAL or PEEPUL. [repr. Sinh. *bogaha* tree of knowledge (Buddha's enlightenment having occurred beneath such a tree)]

bott var. of BOT.

bottle /bót'l/ *n. & v.* • *n.* **1** a container, usu. of glass or plastic and with a narrow neck, for storing liquid. **2** the amount that will fill a bottle. **3** a container used in feeding a baby (esp. formula or milk). **4** = *hot-water bottle.* **5** *Brit. sl.* courage; confidence. • *v.tr.* **1** put into bottles or jars. **2** (foll. by *up*) **a** conceal or restrain for a time (esp. a feeling). **b** keep (an enemy force, etc.) contained or entrapped. **3** *Brit.* preserve (fruit, etc.) in jars. **4** (as **bottled** *adj.*) *Brit. sl.* drunk. □ **bottle bank** *Brit.* a place where used bottles may be deposited for recycling. **bottle-feed** feed (a baby) with milk, formula, etc., by means of a bottle. **bottle green** a dark shade of green. **bottle party** a party to which guests bring their own (esp. alcoholic) drink. **bottle tree** any of various Australian trees of the genus *Brachychiton* with a

swollen bottle-shaped trunk. **hit the bottle** *sl.* drink heavily. **on the bottle** *sl.* drinking (alcohol) heavily. □□ **bottleful** *n.* (*pl.* **-fuls**). [ME f. OF *botele, botaille* f. med.L *butticula* dimin. of LL *buttis* BUTT⁴]
■ *n.* **1** flask, container; decanter. • *v.* **2** (*bottle up*) **a** contain, restrain, hold back, control, suppress, repress, hold *or* keep in check, stifle; conceal, hide, cover (up); mask, bury. **b** entrap, trap, contain, confine, hem in, box *or* shut in *or* up, coop (up); surround. □ **hit the bottle** see BOOZE *v.* **on the bottle** see BOOZE *n.* 2.

bottlebrush /bót'lbrush/ *n.* **1** a cylindrical brush for cleaning inside bottles. **2** any of various plants with a flower of this shape.

bottleneck /bót'lnek/ *n.* **1** a point at which the flow of traffic, production, etc., is constricted. **2** a narrow place causing constriction.

bottlenose /bót'lnōz/ *n.* (also **bottlenosed**) a swollen nose.

bottle-nosed dolphin /bót'l-nōzd/ *n.* a dolphin, *Tursiops truncatus*, with a bottle-shaped snout.

bottler /bót'lər/ *n.* **1** a person who bottles drinks, etc. **2** *Austral. & NZ sl.* an excellent person or thing.

bottom /bótəm/ *n., adj., & v.* • *n.* **1 a** the lowest point or part (*bottom of the stairs*). **b** the part on which a thing rests (*bottom of a frying pan*). **c** the underneath part (*scraped the bottom of the car*). **d** the farthest or innermost part (*bottom of the yard*). **2** *colloq.* **a** the buttocks. **b** the seat of a chair, etc. **3 a** the less honorable, important, or successful end of a table, a class, etc. (*at the bottom of the list of requirements*). **b** a person occupying this place (*he's always the bottom of the class*). **c** *Baseball* the second half of an inning. **4** the ground under the water of a lake, a river, etc. (*swam until she touched the bottom*). **5** the basis; the origin (*he's at the bottom of it*). **6** the essential character; reality. **7** *Naut.* **a** the keel or hull of a ship. **b** a ship, esp. a cargo ship. **8** staying power; endurance. • *adj.* **1** lowest (*bottom button*). **2** last (*got the bottom score*). • *v.* **1** *tr.* put a bottom on (a chair, pot, etc.). **2** *intr.* (of a ship) reach or touch the bottom. **3** *tr.* find the extent or real nature of; work out. **4** *tr.* (usu. foll. by *on*) base (an argument, etc.) (*reasoning bottomed on logic*). **5** *tr.* touch the bottom or lowest point of. □ **at bottom** basically; essentially. **be at the bottom of** have caused. **bet one's bottom dollar** *sl.* stake everything. **bottom dog** = UNDERDOG. **bottom drawer** *Brit.* = *hope chest.* **bottom falls out** collapse occurs. **bottom gear** *Brit.* see GEAR. **bottom line** *colloq.* the underlying or ultimate truth; the ultimate, esp. financial, criterion. **bottom out** reach the lowest level. **bottoms up!** a call to drain one's glass. **bottom up** *Brit.* upside down. **get to the bottom of** fully investigate and explain. **knock the bottom out of** prove (a thing) worthless. □□ **bottommost** /bótəm-mōst/ *adj.* [OE *botm* f. Gmc]
■ *n.* **1 a, b** base, foot, foundation. **c** underneath, underside. **d** (far) end, foot. **2 a** seat, buttocks, rump, posterior, hindquarters, hams, *Anat.* nates, gluteus maximus, *archaic* breech, *colloq.* backside, behind, rear, esp. *Brit. colloq.* sit-upon, *colloq. euphem.* derrière, *joc.* fundament, *sl.* prat, cheeks, butt, keister, fanny, can, *Brit. sl.* bum. **4** bed, floor, ground, depths, *sl.* Davy Jones's locker. **5** root, basis, base, foundation, source, origin, cause, heart, seat, center, nub, hub, crux. • *v.* **2** sink, ground, run aground. **4** see BASE¹ *v.* 1. □ **at bottom** basically, fundamentally, in the final *or* last analysis, really, in reality, truly, in fact, actually, essentially, in essence, *au fond, literary* in truth. **be at the bottom of** be behind, be responsible for, have caused, be involved with, be implicated in. **bottoms up!** (to) your (very good) health, here's to &em., skoal, prosit, *colloq.* here's mud in your eye, *colloq.* cheers, *sl.* down the hatch.

bottomless /bótəmlis/ *adj.* **1** without a bottom. **2** (of a supply, etc.) inexhaustible.
■ **1** unfathomed, unfathomable, abyssal, unplumbable, unsounded. **2** inexhaustible, unlimited, boundless, limitless, illimitable; interminable, never-ending, endless, unending, undying, everlasting, inestimable, measureless, immeasurable, infinite.

botulism /bóchəlizəm/ *n.* poisoning caused by a toxin produced by the bacillus *Clostridium botulinum* growing in spoiled food. [G *Botulismus* f. L *botulus* sausage]

bouclé /bōōkláy/ *n.* **1** a looped or curled yarn (esp. wool). **2** a fabric, esp. knitted, made of this. [F, = buckled, curled]

boudoir /bōōdwaar/ *n.* a woman's private room or bedroom. [F, lit. sulking place f. *bouder* sulk]

bouffant /bōōfaànt/ *adj.* (of a dress, hair, etc.) puffed out. [F]

bougainvillea /bōōgənvílyə, -ve'ə/ *n.* (also **bougainvillaea**) any tropical widely cultivated plant of the genus *Bougainvillaea*, with large colored bracts (usu. purple, red, or cream) almost concealing the inconspicuous flowers. [L. A. de *Bougainville*, Fr. navigator d. 1811]

bough /bow/ *n.* a branch of a tree, esp. a main one. [OE *bōg, bōh* f. Gmc]
■ see BRANCH *n.* 1.

bought *past* and *past part.* of BUY.

boughten /báwt'n/ *adj. dial.* bought at a store; not homemade. [var. of past part. of BUY]

bougie /bōōzhee/ *n.* **1** *Med.* a thin flexible surgical instrument for exploring, dilating, etc. the passages of the body. **2** a wax candle. [F f. Arab. *Bujiya* Algerian town with a wax trade]

bouillabaisse /bōōyəbés, bōōlyəbáys/ *n. Cookery* a rich, spicy fish stew, orig. from Provence. [F]

bouillon /bōōlyən, -yon, bōōyóN/ *n.* a clear soup; broth. [F f. *bouillir* to boil]
■ see BROTH.

boulder /bṓldər/ *n.* a large stone worn smooth by erosion. □ **boulder clay** *Geol.* a mixture of boulders, etc., formed by deposition from massive bodies of melting ice, to give distinctive glacial formations. [short for *boulderstone*, ME f. Scand.]
■ see ROCK[1] 4.

boule[1] /bōōl/ *n.* (also **boules** *pronunc.* same) a French form of lawn bowling, played on rough ground with usu. metal balls. [F, = BOWL[2]]

boule[2] /bōōlee/ *n.* a legislative body of an ancient Greek city or of modern Greece. [Gk *boulē* senate]

boule[3] var. of BUHL.

boules var. of BOULE[1].

boulevard /bōōləvaard/ *n.* **1** a broad tree-lined avenue. **2** a broad main road. [F f. G *Bollwerk* BULWARK, orig. of a promenade on a demolished fortification]
■ see STREET 1.

boulle var. of BUHL.

boult var. of BOLT[2].

bounce /bowns/ *v. & n.* ● *v.* **1 a** *intr.* (of a ball, etc.) rebound. **b** *tr.* cause to rebound. **c** *tr. & intr.* bounce repeatedly. **2** *intr. sl.* (of a check) be returned by a bank when there are insufficient funds to meet it. **3** *intr.* **a** (foll. by *about, up*) (of a person, dog, etc.) jump or spring energetically. **b** (foll. by *in, out,* etc.) rush noisily, angrily, enthusiastically, etc. (*bounced into the room; bounced out in a temper*). **4** *tr. colloq.* (usu. foll. by *into* + verbal noun) hustle; persuade (*bounced him into signing*). **5** *intr. colloq.* talk boastfully. **6** *tr. sl.* eject forcibly (from a dancehall, club, etc.). ● *n.* **1 a** a rebound. **b** the power of rebounding (*this ball has a good bounce*). **2** *colloq.* **a** swagger; self-confidence (*has a lot of bounce*). **b** liveliness. **c** resilience. **3** *sl.* (often prec. by *the*) dismissal or ejection. □ **bounce back** regain one's good health, spirits, prosperity, etc. [ME *bunsen* beat, thump, (perh. imit.), or f. LG *bunsen*, Du. *bons* thump]
■ *v.* **1** bound, rebound, ricochet, glance, *Billiards* carom; (*bounce back*) recoil, spring *or* jump back, resile. **3** see SPRING *v.* 1. **4** see HUSTLE *v.* 2. **5** see BOAST *v.* 1. **6** see *throw out* 3. ● *n.* **1** bound, leap, hop; recoil, ricochet, rebound. **2 a** see SELF-ASSURANCE. **b** vitality, energy, verve, zest, vivacity, vivaciousness, liveliness, animation, dynamism, vigor, life, spirit, *colloq.* pep, zip, go, get-up-and-go. **3** see EXPULSION.

bouncer /bównsər/ *n.* **1** *sl.* a person employed to eject troublemakers from a dancehall, club, etc. **2** *Cricket* = BUMPER.

bouncing /bównsing/ *adj.* **1** (esp. of a baby) big and healthy. **2** boisterous.

bouncy /bównsee/ *adj.* (**bouncier, bounciest**) **1** (of a ball, etc.) that bounces well. **2** cheerful and lively. **3** resilient; springy (*a bouncy sofa*). □□ **bouncily** *adv.* **bounciness** *n.*
■ **1** see ELASTIC *adj.* 1, 2. **2** see LIVELY 1. □□ **bounciness** see SPRING *n.* 3.

bound[1] /bownd/ *v. & n.* ● *v.intr.* **1 a** spring; leap (*bounded out of bed*). **b** walk or run with leaping strides. **2** (of a ball, etc.) recoil from a wall or the ground; bounce. ● *n.* **1** a springy movement upward or outward; a leap. **2** a bounce. □ **by leaps and bounds** see LEAP. [F *bond, bondir* (orig. of sound) f. LL *bombitare* f. L *bombus* hum]
■ *v.* **1** leap, jump, hop, spring, vault, bounce; gambol, caper, romp, frolic, skip, prance, *colloq.* galumph, *sl.* cavort. **2** see BOUNCE *v.* 1. ● *n.* **1** leap, jump, vault, spring, hop.

bound[2] /bownd/ *n. & v.* ● *n.* (usu. in *pl.*) **1** a limitation; a restriction (*beyond the bounds of possibility*). **2** a border of a territory; a boundary. ● *v.tr.* **1** (esp. in *passive*; foll. by *by*) set bounds to; limit (*views bounded by prejudice*). **2** be the boundary of. □ **out of bounds 1 a** outside the part of a school, etc., in which one is allowed to be. **b** *Sports* outside the limits of the court, field, etc. (*the ball was out of bounds*). **2** beyond what is acceptable; forbidden. [ME f. AF *bounde*, OF *bonde*, etc., f. med.L *bodina*, earlier *butina*, of unkn. orig.]
■ *n.* **1** (*bounds*) limit(s), extent, confines, margin(s), pale, compass, parameter; limitation, restriction, constraint. **2** (*bounds*) boundary, boundary line, border(s), margins, circuit, pale, edge, line, mete, rim. ● *v.* limit, restrict, confine, enclose, surround, delimit, define, circumscribe, control, restrain, constrain, hem in, *archaic* compass. □ **out of bounds 1 a** off limits. **2** forbidden, prohibited, proscribed, verboten, taboo; inadmissible, unacceptable, beyond the pale, out of order, below the belt.

bound[3] /bownd/ *adj.* **1** (usu. foll. by *for*) ready to start or having started (*bound for stardom*). **2** (in *comb.*) moving in a specified direction (*northbound; outward bound*). [ME f. ON *búinn* past part. of *búa* get ready: *-d* euphonic, or partly after BIND]
■ **1** destined, headed, directed, en route, on the way.

bound[4] /bownd/ *past* and *past part.* of BIND. □ **bound to** certain to (*he's bound to come*).
■ □ **bound to** certain to, sure to.

boundary /bówndəree, -dree/ *n.* (*pl.* **-ies**) a real or notional line marking the limits of an area, territory, etc.; the limit itself or the area near it (*the fence is the boundary; boundary between liberty and license*). □ **boundary layer** the fluid immediately surrounding an object that is immersed and moving. **boundary rider** *Austral. & NZ* a person employed to ride around the fences, etc., of a cattle or sheep station and keep them in good order. [dial. *bounder* f. BOUND[2] + -ER[1] perh. after *limitary*]
■ **1** border, frontier, boundary line, line, borderline, dividing line; parameter, limit, extent, compass; division; edge, bound(s), confines, perimeter, fringe, margin.

bounden /bówndən/ *adj. archaic* obligatory. □ **bounden duty** solemn responsibility. [archaic past part. of BIND]

bounder /bówndər/ *n. Brit. colloq.* or *joc.* a cad; an ill-bred person.

boundless /bówndlis/ *adj.* unlimited; immense (*boundless enthusiasm*). □□ **boundlessly** *adv.* **boundlessness** *n.*
■ limitless, unbounded, unlimited, illimitable, endless, unending, never-ending, infinite, immeasurable, incalculable, measureless, untold, unrestricted, unchecked, inexhaustible, bottomless, unstoppable,

---

/.../ **pronunciation**	● **part of speech**
□ **phrases, idioms, and compounds**	
□□ **derivatives**	■ **synonym section**
cross-references appear in SMALL CAPITALS or *italics*	

unbridled, uncontrolled; vast, immense, enormous, tremendous, great.

bounteous /bównteeəs/ *adj. poet.* **1** generous; liberal. **2** freely given (*bounteous affection*). □□ **bounteously** *adv.* **bounteousness** *n.* [ME f. OF *bontif* f. *bonté* BOUNTY after *plenteous*]
■ generous, beneficent, munificent, liberal, ungrudging, bighearted, openhanded, charitable, eleemosynary, magnanimous, bountiful; free, unsparing, unstinting.

bountiful /bówntifŏŏl/ *adj.* **1** = BOUNTEOUS. **2** ample. □ **Lady Bountiful** a charitable but patronizing lady of a neighborhood (after a character in Farquhar's *Beaux' Stratagem*, 1707). □□ **bountifully** *adv.* [BOUNTY + -FUL]
■ **2** ample, abundant, plentiful, copious, generous, substantial, lavish, princely, profuse, prodigal, opulent, *poet.* bounteous, plenteous.

bounty /bówntee/ *n.* (*pl.* **-ies**) **1** liberality; generosity. **2** a gift or reward, made usu. by a government, esp.: **a** a sum paid for capturing an outlaw, killing destructive wild animals, etc. **b** a sum paid to encourage a business, etc. **c** a sum paid to army or navy recruits on enlistment. □ **bounty hunter** a person who pursues a criminal or seeks an achievement for the sake of the reward. **king's** (or **queen's**) **bounty** *Brit. hist.* a grant made to a mother of triplets. [ME f. OF *bonté* f. L *bonitas -tatis* f. *bonus* good]
■ **1** generosity, liberality, munificence, prodigality, charitableness, philanthropy, charity, unselfishness, beneficence, largesse, goodness, *poet.* bounteousness. **2** gift, present, reward, gratuity, prize, premium, tribute, honor, award, favor, return, recompense; largesse.

bouquet /bōōkáy, bō-/ *n.* **1** a bunch of flowers, esp. for carrying at a wedding or other ceremony. **2** the scent of wine, etc. **3** a favorable comment; a compliment. □ **bouquet garni** /gaarnée/ *Cookery* a bunch of herbs used for flavoring stews, etc. [F f. dial. var. of OF *bos, bois* wood]
■ **1** nosegay, posy, bunch, arrangement, spray. **2** aroma, scent, odor, fragrance, perfume, smell, redolence. **3** compliment(s), honor, tribute, homage, commendation, eulogy, plaudit, encomium, accolade, paean; praise.

bourbon /bárbən/ *n.* whiskey distilled from corn and rye. [*Bourbon* County, Kentucky, where it was first made]
■ see WHISKEY.

Bourbon /bŏŏrbən, bŏŏbáwn/ *n.* a reactionary, esp. a conservative Southern Democrat. [the Bourbon family, whose descendants founded dynasties in France and Spain]

bourdon /bŏŏrdən/ *n. Mus.* **1** a low-pitched stop in an organ, etc. **2** the lowest bell in a peal of bells. **3** the drone pipe of a bagpipe. [F, = bagpipe drone, f. Rmc, imit.]

bourgeois /bŏŏrzhwaá/ *adj. & n. often derog.* ● *adj.* **1 a** conventionally middle class. **b** humdrum; unimaginative. **c** selfishly materialistic. **2** upholding the interests of the capitalist class; noncommunist. ● *n.* a bourgeois person. [F: see BURGESS]
■ *adj.* **1 a** middle-class, conventional, conservative, conformist; propertied, capitalist; see also NARROW-MINDED, PHILISTINE *adj.* **b** see BANAL. **c** materialistic, capitalistic, greedy, selfish, acquisitive, *archaic or joc.* esurient, *colloq.* money-grubbing, *colloq. usu. derog.* yuppie. **2** capitalistic, capitalist; noncommunist. ● *n.* capitalist, materialist, professional, *colloq. usu. derog.* yuppie.

bourgeoisie /bŏŏrzhwaazée/ *n.* **1** the capitalist class. **2** the middle class. [F]

bourn¹ /bawrn, bŏŏrn/ *n.* (also **bourne**) a small stream. [ME: S. Engl. var. of BURN²]

bourn² /bawrn, bŏŏrn/ *n.* (also **bourne**) *archaic* **1** a goal; a destination. **2** a limit. [F *borne* f. OF *bodne* BOUND²]
■ **2** see EDGE *n.* 1.

bourrée /bŏŏráy/ *n.* **1** a lively French dance like a gavotte. **2** the music for this dance. [F]

bourse /bŏŏrs/ *n.* **1** a stock exchange, esp. on the European continent. **2** a money market. [F, = purse, f. med.L *bursa*: cf. PURSE]
■ see EXCHANGE *n.* 4.

boustrophedon /bŏŏstrəféed'n, bów-/ *adj. & adv.* (of writ-

ten words) from right to left and from left to right in alternate lines. [Gk (adv.) = as an ox turns in plowing f. *bous* ox + *-strophos* turning]

bout /bowt/ *n.* (often foll. by *of*) **1 a** a limited period (of intensive work or exercise). **b** a drinking session. **c** a period (of illness) (*a bout of flu*). **2 a** a wrestling or boxing match. **b** a trial of strength. [16th c.: app. the same as obs. *bought* bending]
■ **1 a, c** spell, period, session, stint, term, stretch; round; attack, fit, outburst, burst. **b** see BENDER. **2 a** fight, contest, match, boxing match, wrestling match, prizefight, meet, fist fight, spar, fall, encounter, engagement, *colloq.* set-to, *sl.* mill.

boutique /bōōteék/ *n.* a small shop or department of a store, esp. one selling fashionable clothes or accessories. [F, = small shop, f. L (as BODEGA)]
■ shop, store.

boutonniere /bŏŏtəneér, -tənyáir/ *n.* (also **boutonnière**) a spray of flowers worn in a buttonhole. [F]
■ buttonhole, corsage.

bouzouki /bōōzŏŏkee/ *n.* a Greek form of mandolin. [mod. Gk]

bovate /bṓvayt/ *n. hist.* a measure of land, as much as one ox could plow in a year, varying from 10 to 18 acres. [med.L *bovata* f. L *bos bovis* ox]

bovine /bṓvīn, -veen/ *adj.* **1** of or relating to cattle. **2** stupid; dull. □□ **bovinely** *adv.* [LL *bovinus* f. L *bos bovis* ox]
■ **2** see DULL *adj.* 1.

bovver /bóvər/ *n. Brit. sl.* deliberate troublemaking. □ **bovver boot** a heavy laced boot worn typically by skinheads. **bovver boy** a violent hoodlum. [cockney pronunc. of BOTHER]

bow¹ /bō/ *n. & v.* ● *n.* **1 a** a slipknot with a double loop. **b** a ribbon, shoelace, etc., tied with this. **c** a decoration (on clothing, or painted, etc.) in the form of a bow. **2** a device for shooting arrows with a taut string joining the ends of a curved piece of wood, etc. **3 a** a rod with horsehair stretched along its length, used for playing the violin, cello, etc. **b** a single stroke of a bow across the strings. **4 a** a shallow curve or bend. **b** a rainbow. **5** = SADDLEBOW. **6** a metal ring forming the handle of scissors, a key, etc. **7** the sidepiece of an eyeglass frame. **8** *Archery* = BOWMAN¹. ● *v.tr.* (also *absol.*) use a bow on (a violin, etc.) (*he bowed vigorously*). □ **bow compass** (or **compasses**) compasses with jointed legs. **bow saw** *Carpentry* a narrow saw stretched like a bowstring on a light frame. **bow tie** a necktie in the form of a bow (sense 1). **bow window** a curved bay window. [OE *boga* f. Gmc: cf. BOW²]

bow² /bow/ *v. & n.* ● *v.* **1** *intr.* incline the head or trunk, esp. in greeting or assent or acknowledgment of applause. **2** *intr.* submit (*bowed to the inevitable*). **3** *tr.* cause to incline or submit (*bowed his head; bowed his will to hers*). **4** *tr.* express (thanks, assent, etc.) by bowing (*bowed agreement to the plan*). **5** *tr.* (foll. by *in, out*) usher or escort obsequiously (*bowed us out of the restaurant*). ● *n.* an inclining of the head or body in greeting, assent, or in the acknowledgment of applause, etc. □ **bow and scrape** be obsequious; fawn. **bow down 1** bend or kneel in submission or reverence (*bowed down before the king*). **2** (usu. in *passive*) make stoop; crush (*was bowed down by care*). **bowing acquaintance** a person one acknowledges but does not know well enough to speak to. **bow out 1** make one's exit (esp. formally). **2** retreat; withdraw; retire gracefully. **make one's bow** make a formal exit or entrance. **take a bow** acknowledge applause. [OE *būgan*, f. Gmc: cf. BOW¹]
■ *v.* **1** nod; curtsy, salaam, genuflect, prostrate oneself, make (an) obeisance, *archaic* show reverence, *hist.* kowtow. **2** defer, yield, submit, give in, give way, bow down, capitulate, surrender, succumb; (*bow to*) see OBEY. **3** bend, incline, lower, drop; make submit *or* surrender *or* yield. **5** usher, conduct, escort, guide, show (the way). ● *n.* nod; salaam, genuflection, prostration, obeisance, *archaic* reverence, *hist.* kowtow. □ **bow and scrape** fawn, kowtow, kiss a person's feet, grovel, prostrate oneself, demean *or* lower oneself, toady, lick a person's boots, cringe, dance to a person's

tune, truckle, *colloq.* crawl, creep, bootlick. **bow down
1** bend, kneel, salaam, prostrate oneself, make
obeisance, *hist.* kowtow. **2** weigh down, crush,
overload, load (down), wear *or* press down;
overburden, burden, oppress, overwhelm. **bowing
acquaintance** nodding acquaintance. **bow out 1** make
one's exit, take one's leave. **2** see WITHDRAW 5.

bow³ /bow/ *n. Naut.* **1** the forward end of a boat or ship. **2**
= BOWMAN². □ **bow wave** a wave generated at the bow of a
moving ship or in front of a body moving in air, caused by
the forward motion of the moving body. **on the bow** within
45° of the point directly ahead. **a shot across the bows** a
warning. [LG *boog*, Du. *boeg*, ship's bow, orig. shoulder: see
BOUGH]

bowdlerize /bówdlərīz/ *v.tr.* expurgate (a book, etc.).
□□ **bowdlerism** *n.* **bowdlerization** /-rizáyshən/ *n.* [T.
Bowdler (d. 1825), expurgator of Shakespeare.]
■ see EDIT *v.* 5a.

bowel /bówəl/ *n.* **1** the part of the alimentary canal below the
stomach; the intestine. **2** (in *pl.*) the depths; the innermost
parts (*the bowels of the earth*). □ **bowel movement 1** discharge from the bowels; defecation. **2** the feces discharged
from the body. [ME f. OF *buel* f. L *botellus* little sausage]
■ **1** intestine, gut, guts; (*bowels*) viscera, vitals, belly,
colloq. innards. **2** (*bowels*) interior, inside(s), depths,
innermost reaches, heart, center, core. □ **bowel
movement 1** defecation, movement, evacuation, *Brit.*
motion, *sl.* pooh. **2** feces, excrement, excreta, stool(s),
Brit. motion(s), *sl.* pooh.

bower¹ /bówər/ *n. & v.* ● *n.* **1 a** a secluded place, esp. in a
garden, enclosed by foliage; an arbor. **b** a summer house or
cottage. **2** *poet.* an inner room; a boudoir. ● *v.tr. poet.* embower. □□ **bowery** *adj.* [OE *būr* f. Gmc]

bower² /bówər/ *n.* (in full **bower anchor**) either of two anchors carried at a ship's bow. □ **best bower** the starboard
bower. **bower cable** the cable attached to a bower anchor.
small bower the port bower. [BOW³ + -ER¹]

bowerbird /bówərbərd/ *n.* **1** any of various birds of the Pti-
lonorhynchidae family, native to Australia and New Guinea,
the males of which construct elaborate bowers of feathers,
grasses, shells, etc., during courtship. **2** *Brit.* a person who
collects bric-à-brac.

bowery /bówəree, bówree/ *n.* (also **Bowery**) (*pl.* **-ies**) a district known as a neighborhood of drunks and derelicts.
[orig. the Bowery, a street in New York City, f. Du. *bouwerij*
farm]

bowfin /bófin/ *n.* a voracious American freshwater fish, *Amia
calva.* [BOW¹ + FIN]

bowhead /bóhed/ *n.* an Arctic whale, *Balaena mysticetus.*

bowie /bóōee, bó-/ *n.* (in full **bowie knife**) a long knife with
a blade double-edged at the point, used as a weapon by
American pioneers. [J. *Bowie*, Amer. soldier d. 1836]

bowl¹ /bōl/ *n.* **1 a** a usu. round deep basin used for food or
liquid. **b** the quantity (of soup, etc.) a bowl holds. **c** the
contents of a bowl. **2 a** any deep-sided container shaped like
a bowl (*toilet bowl*). **b** the bowl-shaped part of a tobacco
pipe, spoon, balance, etc. **3** a bowl-shaped region or building, esp. an amphitheater (*Hollywood Bowl*). **4** *Sports* a post-
season football game between invited teams or as a championship. □□ **bowlful** *n.* (*pl.* **-fuls**). [OE *bolle*, *bolla*, f. Gmc]
■ **1 a** dish, plate; basin, pan.

bowl² /bōl/ *n. & v.* ● *n.* **1 a** a wooden or hard rubber ball,
slightly asymmetrical so that it runs on a curved course, used
in the game of bowls. **b** a wooden ball or disk used in playing
skittles. **c** *Brit.* = *bowling ball.* **2** esp. *Brit.* (in *pl.*; usu. treated
as *sing.*) **a** a game played with bowls (sense 1a) on grass;
lawn bowling. **b** *Brit.* tenpin bowling. **c** *Brit.* skittles. **3** a
spell or turn of bowling in cricket. ● *v.* **1 a** *tr.* roll (a ball,
a hoop, etc.) along the ground. **b** *intr.* play bowls or skittles.
2 *intr.* (often foll. by *along*) go along rapidly by revolving,
esp. on wheels (*the cart bowled along the road*). **3** *tr.* (also
absol.) *Cricket*, etc. **a** deliver (a ball, an over, etc.) (*bowled
six overs; bowled well*). **b** (often foll. by *out*) dismiss (a batsman) by knocking down the wicket with a ball (*soon bowled
him out*). **c** (often foll. by *down*) knock (a wicket, pin, etc.)

over. □ **bowl over 1** knock down. **2** *colloq.* **a** impress greatly.
b overwhelm (*bowled over by her energy*). [ME & F *boule* f. L
bulla bubble]
■ *v.* **2** move, trundle, wheel, roll, spin, whirl; hurtle.
□ **bowl over 1** knock down *or* over, bring down, fell,
floor, cut *or* strike down, flatten. **2** see OVERWHELM 3.

bowlegged /bólegid/ *adj.* having legs that curve outward at
the knee.

bowlegs /bólegz/ *n.* legs that curve outward at the knee.

bowler¹ /bólər/ *n.* **1** a player at bowls or bowling. **2** *Cricket*,
etc., a member of the fielding side who bowls or is bowling.

bowler² /bólər/ *n.* (in full **bowler hat**) a man's hard felt hat
with a round dome-shaped crown. □ **bowler-hat (-hatted,
-hatting)** *Brit. sl.* retire (a person) from the army, etc. (*he's
been bowler-hatted*). [*Bowler*, a hatter, who designed it in
1850]

bowline /bólin/ *n. Naut.* **1** a rope attaching the weather side
of a square sail to the bow. **2** a simple knot for forming a
nonslipping loop at the end of a rope. [ME f. MLG *bōline*
(as BOW³, LINE¹)]

bowling /bóling/ *n.* the games of tenpins, skittles, or bowls
as a sport or recreation. □ **bowling alley 1** a long enclosure
for skittles or tenpin bowling. **2** a building containing these.
bowling ball a hard ball with holes drilled in it for gripping,
used in tenpin bowling. **bowling crease** *Cricket* the line
from behind which a bowler delivers the ball. **bowling
green** a lawn used for playing bowls.

bowman¹ /bómən/ *n.* (*pl.* **-men**) an archer.

bowman² /bówmən/ *n.* (*pl.* **-men**) the rower nearest the
bow of esp. a racing boat.

bowshot /bóshot/ *n.* the distance to which a bow can send
an arrow.

bowsprit /bówsprit/ *n. Naut.* a spar running out from a
ship's bow to which the forestays are fastened. [ME f. Gmc
(as BOW³, SPRIT)]

Bow Street runner /bō/ *n.* (also **Bow Street officer**) *hist.*
a London policeman. [*Bow Street* in London, containing the
chief metropolitan police court]

bowstring /bóstring/ *n. & v.* ● *n.* the string of an archer's
bow. ● *v.tr.* strangle with a bowstring (a former Turkish
method of execution).
■ *v.* see CHOKE *v.* 1.

bow-wow /bów-wów/ *int. & n.* ● *int.* an imitation of a dog's
bark. ● *n.* **1** *colloq.* a dog. **2** a dog's bark. [imit.]

bowyer /bó-yər/ *n.* a maker or seller of archers' bows.

box¹ /boks/ *n. & v.* ● *n.* **1** a container, usu. with flat sides
and of firm material such as wood or cardboard, esp. for
holding solids. **2 a** the amount that will fill a box. **b** *Brit.* a
gift of a kind formerly given to delivery people, etc., at
Christmas. **3** a separate compartment for any of various purposes, e.g., for a small group in a theater, for witnesses in a
court, for horses in a stable or vehicle. **4** an enclosure or
receptacle for a special purpose (often in *comb.*: *cash box*).
5 a facility at a newspaper office for receiving replies to an
advertisement. **6** (prec. by *the*) *colloq.* television; one's television set (*what's on the box?*). **7** an enclosed area or space.
8 a space or area of print on a page, enclosed by a border.
9 *Brit.* a small country house for use when shooting, fishing,
or for other sporting activity. **10** a protective casing for a
piece of mechanism. **11** *Brit.* a light shield for protecting the
genitals in sports. **12** (prec. by *the*) *Soccer colloq.* the penalty
area. **13** *Baseball* one of several areas occupied by the batter,
catcher, pitcher, and first and third base coaches. **14** a
coachman's seat. ● *v.tr.* **1** put in or provide with a box. **2**
(foll. by *in*, *up*) confine; restrain from movement. **3** (foll. by
up) *Austral. & NZ* mix up (different flocks of sheep). □ **box
camera** a simple box-shaped hand camera. **box the compass** *Naut.* recite the points of the compass in the correct
order. **box girder** a hollow girder square in cross-section.

/.../ pronunciation	● part of speech
□ phrases, idioms, and compounds	
□□ derivatives	■ synonym section
cross-references appear in SMALL CAPITALS or *italics*	

box junction *Brit.* a road area at a junction marked with a yellow grid, which a vehicle should enter only if its exit from it is clear. **box kite** a kite in the form of a long box open at each end. **box lunch** a lunch packed in a box. **box number** a number by which replies are made to a private advertisement in a newspaper. **box office 1** an office for booking seats and buying tickets at a theater, movie theater, etc. **2** the commercial aspect of the arts and entertainment (often *attrib.*: *a box-office failure*). **box pleat** a pleat consisting of two parallel creases forming a raised band. **box score** *Sports* printed information about a game in which players for both teams are listed with statistics about their performances, as goals, assists, errors, etc. **box seat** a seat in a box enclosure, as at a theater, sports arena, etc. **box spanner** *Brit.* = *box wrench*. **box spring** each of a set of vertical springs housed in a frame, e.g., in a mattress. **box stall** a compartment for a horse, in a stable or vehicle, in which it can move around. **box wrench** a wrench with a box-shaped end fitting over the head of a nut. □□ **boxful** *n.* (*pl.* **-fuls**). **boxlike** *adj.* [OE f. LL *buxis* f. L PYXIS]
■ *n.* **1, 2a** case, receptacle, crate, carton, container, casket, coffer, caddy, chest. **3** compartment, stall, booth, cubicle, enclosure. **6** television, TV, *colloq.* tube, *Brit. colloq.* goggle-box, telly, *sl.* boob tube. ● *v.* **1** crate, encase, package, pack, containerize, case, wrap up. **2** (*box in* or *up*) trap, confine, hem *or* block in, shut up *or* in, coop up, bound, enclose, surround.

box² /boks/ *v. & n.* ● *v.* **1** *a tr.* fight (an opponent) at boxing. **b** *intr.* practice boxing. **2** slap (esp. a person's ears). ● *n.* a slap with the hand, esp. on the ears. [ME: orig. unkn.]
■ *v.* **1** *a* fight (with), come to blows with, spar with, *sl.* mill. **b** fight, engage in fisticuffs, spar, battle. **2** strike, slap, smack, rap, punch, hit, clout, thump, cuff, slug, *colloq.* sock, whack, thwack *sl.* mill, belt, clobber, wallop, whop. ● *n.* blow, slap, smack, rap, punch, hit, strike, clout, thump, cuff, buffet, slug, *colloq.* sock, whack, thwack, *sl.* belt, clobber, whop, wallop.

box³ /boks/ *n.* **1** any small evergreen tree or shrub of the genus *Buxus*, esp. *B. sempervirens*, a slow-growing tree with glossy dark green leaves that is often used in hedging. **2** its wood, used for carving, turning, engraving, etc. **3** any of various trees in Australasia that have similar wood or foliage, esp. those of several species of *Eucalyptus*. □ **box elder** the American ash-leaved maple, *Acer negundo*. [OE f. L *buxus*, Gk *puxos*]

Box and Cox /boks ənd koks/ *n. & v. Brit.* ● *n.* (often *attrib.*) two persons sharing a room, apartment, etc., and using it at different times. ● *v.intr.* share accommodations, duties, etc., by a strictly timed arrangement. [the names of characters in a play (1847) by J. M. Morton]

boxcar /bókskaar/ *n.* an enclosed railroad freight car, usu. with sliding doors on the sides.

boxer /bóksər/ *n.* **1** a person who practices boxing, esp. for sport. **2 a** a medium-sized dog of a breed with a smooth brown coat and puglike face. **b** this breed. □ **boxer shorts** men's underpants similar to shorts worn in boxing, with an elastic waist.
■ **1** see PUGILIST. □ **boxer shorts** undershorts, underpants, trunks, briefs.

Boxer /bóksər/ *n. hist.* a member of a fiercely nationalistic Chinese secret society that flourished in the 19th c. [transl. of Chin. *i ho chuan*, lit. 'righteous harmony fists']

boxing /bóksing/ *n.* the practice of fighting with the fists, esp. in padded gloves as a sport. □ **boxing glove** each of a pair of heavily padded gloves used in boxing.
■ see *pugilism* (PUGILIST).

Boxing Day /bóksing/ *n.* esp. *Brit.* the first weekday after Christmas. [from the custom of giving delivery people gifts or money: see BOX¹ *n.* 2b]

boxroom /bóksrōōm, -rŏŏm/ *n. Brit.* a room or large closet for storing boxes, luggage, etc.

boxwood /bókswŏŏd/ *n.* **1** the wood of the box used esp. by engravers for the fineness of its grain and for its hardness. **2** = BOX³ 1.

boxy /bóksee/ *adj.* (**boxier, boxiest**) reminiscent of a box; (of a room or space) very cramped.

boy /boy/ *n. & int.* ● *n.* **1** a male child or youth. **2** a young man, esp. regarded as not yet mature. **3** a male servant, attendant, etc. **4** (**the boys**) *colloq.* a group of men mixing socially. ● *int.* expressing pleasure, surprise, etc. □ **boy scout 1** (also **Boy Scout**) a member of an organization of boys, esp. the Boy Scouts of America, that promotes character, outdoor activities, community service, etc. **2** a boy or man who demonstrates the qualities associated with a Boy Scout. **boys in blue** esp. *Brit.* policemen. □□ **boyhood** *n.* **boyish** *adj.* **boyishly** *adv.* **boyishness** *n.* [ME = servant, perh. ult. f. L *boia* fetter]
■ *n.* **1, 2** lad, youth, young man, stripling, youngster, schoolboy, juvenile, minor, *colloq.* kid, laddie, (little) shaver, fellow, chap, bub, *usu. derog.* brat, esp. *joc.* little man. **3** servant, house servant, attendant, *hist.* varlet; lackey, slave; waiter, garçon. ● *int.* wow, (my) god, Lord, golly, goodness, gosh, whew, ooh, *archaic* marry, *sl.* jeepers, *Brit. sl.* coo, cor. □□ **boyish** young, youthful, adolescent, childlike; childish, puerile, juvenile, immature, infantile, sophomoric.

boyar /bō-yaár/ *n. hist.* a member of the old aristocracy in Russia. [Russ. *boyarin* grandee]

boycott /bóykot/ *v. & n.* ● *v.tr.* **1** combine in refusing social or commercial relations with (a person, group, country, etc.) usu. as punishment or coercion. **2** refuse to purchase or handle (goods) to this end. ● *n.* such a refusal. [Capt. C. C. *Boycott*, Irish land agent d. 1897, so treated from 1880]
■ *v.* blacklist, embargo, ostracize; avoid, refuse, shun, reject, pass over *or* by, *Brit.* black, *literary* eschew. ● *n.* embargo, blacklist, ban; interdiction, prohibition.

boyfriend /bóyfrend/ *n.* a person's regular male companion or lover.
■ see SWEETHEART 1.

Boyle's law /boylz/ *n.* the law that the pressure of a given mass of gas is inversely proportional to its volume at a constant temperature. [Robert *Boyle*, Irish scientist d. 1691]

boyo /bóyō/ *n.* (*pl.* **-os**) *Welsh & Ir. colloq.* boy; fellow (esp. as a form of address).

boysenberry /bóyzənberee/ *n.* (*pl.* **-ies**) **1** a hybrid of several species of bramble. **2** the large red edible fruit of this plant. [R. *Boysen*, 20th-c. Amer. horticulturalist]

BP *abbr.* **1** boiling point. **2** blood pressure. **3** before the present (era). **4** British Petroleum.

Bp. *abbr.* Bishop.

B.Phil. *abbr.* Bachelor of Philosophy.

bps *abbr.* (also **BPS**) *Computing* bits per second.

Br *symb. Chem.* the element bromine.

Br. *abbr.* **1** British. **2** Brother.

bra /braa/ *n.* (*pl.* **bras**) *colloq.* = BRASSIERE. [abbr.]

brace /brays/ *n. & v.* ● *n.* **1 a** a device that clamps or fastens tightly. **b** a strengthening piece of iron or lumber in building. **2** (in *pl.*) *Brit.* = SUSPENDER 1. **3** (in *pl.*) a wire device for straightening the teeth. **4** (*pl.* same) a pair (esp. of game). **5** a rope attached to the yard of a ship for trimming the sail. **6 a** a connecting mark { or } used in printing. **b** *Mus.* a similar mark connecting staves to be performed at the same time. ● *v.tr.* **1** fasten tightly; give strength to. **2** make steady by supporting. **3** (esp. as **bracing** *adj.*) invigorate; refresh. **4** (often *refl.*) prepare for a difficulty, shock, etc. □ **brace and bit** a revolving tool with a D-shaped central handle for boring. □□ **bracingly** *adv.* **bracingness** *n.* [ME f. OF *brace* two arms, *bracier* embrace, f. L *bra(c)chia* arms]
■ *n.* **1 a** clasp, clamp, vice, fastener, staple, clip, holdfast, catch, coupler, coupling. **b** bracket, reinforcement, reinforcer, support, buttress, prop, stay, strut, truss. **4** pair, couple, set, team (of two). ● *v.* **1** see SECURE *v.* 2. **2** steady, stabilize, reinforce, support, secure, strengthen, prop *or* shore *or* hold up, bolster, buttress, strut. **3** (**bracing**) invigorating, tonic, stimulating, refreshing, exhilarating, fortifying, strengthening, restorative, vitalizing; brisk, fresh. **4** (*brace oneself*) steady *or* gird *or* prepare oneself, gird one's loins, *colloq.*

gear oneself up; get *or* make ready, prepare, hold on, hold tight, *colloq.* get fired *or* geared up, hang on. □ **brace and bit** see DRILL[1] *n.* 1.

bracelet /bráyslit/ *n.* **1** an ornamental band, hoop, or chain worn on the wrist or arm. **2** *sl.* a handcuff. [ME f. OF, dimin. of *bracel* f. L *bracchiale* f. *bra(c)chium* arm]

bracer /bráysər/ *n. colloq.* a tonic, esp. an alcoholic drink. ■ see TONIC *n.*

brachial /bráykeeəl, brák-/ *adj.* **1** of or relating to the arm (*brachial artery*). **2** like an arm. [L *brachialis* f. *bra(c)chium* arm]

brachiate /bráykeeit, -ayt, brák-/ *v. & adj.* ● *v.intr.* (of certain apes and monkeys) move by using the arms to swing from branch to branch. ● *adj. Biol.* **1** having arms. **2** having paired branches on alternate sides. □□ **brachiation** /-áyshən/ *n.* **brachiator** *n.* [L *bra(c)chium* arm]

brachiopod /bráykeeəpod, brák-/ *n.* any marine invertebrate of the phylum Brachiopoda (esp. a fossil one) having a bivalved chalky shell and a ciliated feeding arm. [mod.L f. Gk *brakhiōn* arm + *pous podos* foot]

brachiosaurus /bráykeeəsáwrəs, brák-/ *n.* any huge plant-eating dinosaur of the genus *Brachiosaurus* with forelegs longer than its hind legs. [mod.L f. Gk *brakhiōn* arm + *sauros* lizard]

brachistochrone /brakístəkrōn/ *n.* a curve between two points along which a body can move in a shorter time than for any other curve. [Gk *brakhistos* shortest + *khronos* time]

brachy- /brákee/ *comb. form* short. [Gk *brakhus* short]

brachycephalic /brákeesifálik/ *adj.* having a broad short head. □□ **brachycephalous** /-séfələs/ *adj.* [BRACHY- + Gk *kephalē* head]

brachylogy /brəkíləjee/ *n.* (*pl.* **-ies**) **1** conciseness of expression. **2** an instance of this.

brack /brak/ *n. Ir.* cake or bread containing dried fruit, etc. [abbr. of *barmbrack* f. Ir. *bairgen breac* speckled cake]

bracken /brákən/ *n.* **1** any large coarse fern, esp. *Pteridium aquilinum*, abundant in tropical and temperate areas. **2** a mass of such ferns. Also called BRAKE[5]. [north. ME f. ON]

bracket /brákit/ *n. & v.* ● *n.* **1** a right-angled or other support attached to and projecting from a vertical surface. **2** a shelf fixed with such a support to a wall. **3 a** each of a pair of marks [ ] (**square brackets**) or < > (**angle brackets**) used to enclose words or figures. **b** PARENTHESIS 1b. **c** BRACE 6a. **4** a group classified as containing similar elements or falling between given limits (*income bracket*). **5** *Mil.* the distance between two artillery shots fired either side of the target to establish range. ● *v.tr.* (**bracketed, bracketing**) **1 a** combine (names, etc.) within brackets. **b** imply a connection or equality between. **2 a** enclose in brackets as parenthetic or spurious. **b** *Math.* enclose in brackets as having specific relations to what precedes or follows. **c** include in a bracket. **3** *Mil.* establish the range of (a target) by firing two preliminary shots, one short of and the other beyond it. [F *braguette* or Sp. *bragueta* codpiece, dimin. of F *brague* f. Prov. *braga* f. L *braca*, pl. *bracae* breeches] ■ *n.* **1** support, console, cantilever, gusset, *Archit.* corbel. **2** shelf. **3** parenthesis, brace. **4** category, class, set, group, grouping, classification, division, level, stratum; range, span; order, grade, rank. ● *v.* **1** couple, join, link, connect, put together, place side by side, ally, attach, unite, combine; classify, rank, group, class, order, bunch together; associate, affiliate, relate.

brackish /brákish/ *adj.* (of water, etc.) slightly salty. □□ **brackishness** *n.* [obs. *brack* (adj.) f. MLG, MDu. *brac*] ■ see SALT *adj.*

bract /brakt/ *n.* a modified and often brightly colored leaf, with a flower or an inflorescence in its axil. □□ **bracteal** *adj.* **bracteate** /-tee-it, -ayt/ *adj.* [L *bractea* thin plate, gold leaf]

brad /brad/ *n.* a thin flat nail with a head in the form of slight enlargement at the top. [var. of ME *brod* goad, pointed instrument, f. ON *broddr* spike]

bradawl /brádawl/ *n.* a small tool with a pointed end for boring holes by hand. [BRAD + AWL]

bradycardia /brádikaárdeeə/ *n. Med.* abnormally slow heart action. [Gk *bradus* slow + *kardia* heart]

brae /bray/ *n. Sc.* a steep bank or hillside. [ME f. ON *brá* eyelash]

brag /brag/ *v. & n.* ● *v.* (**bragged, bragging**) **1** *intr.* talk boastfully. **2** *tr.* boast about. ● *n.* **1** a card game like poker. **2** a boastful statement; boastful talk. □□ **bragger** *n.* **braggingly** *adv.* [ME, orig. adj., = spirited, boastful: orig. unkn.] ■ *v.* **1** boast, crow, swagger, rodomontade, blow one's (own) trumpet, *colloq.* show off, bounce, gas, talk big, *Austral.* & *NZ colloq.* skite, *literary* vaunt. **2** boast of, trumpet, *literary* vaunt. ● *n.* **2** see BOAST *n.* □□ **bragger** see BRAGGART *n.*

braggadocio /brágədósheeō/ *n.* empty boasting; a boastful manner of speech and behavior. [*Braggadochio*, a braggart in Spenser's *Faerie Queene*, f. BRAG or BRAGGART + It. augment. suffix *-occio*] ■ see BRAVADO.

braggart /brágərt/ *n. & adj.* ● *n.* a person given to bragging. ● *adj.* boastful. [F *bragard* f. *braguer* BRAG] ■ *n.* boaster, bragger, peacock, gascon, *archaic* scaramouch, *colloq.* show-off, bigmouth, loudmouth, blowhard, *sl.* flannelmouth, *Austral. sl.* lair. ● *adj.* see BOASTFUL.

Brahma /braámə/ *n.* **1** the Hindu Creator. **2** the supreme divine reality in Hindu belief. [Skr., = creator]

Brahman[1] /braámən/ *n.* (also **brahman**) (*pl.* **-mans**) **1** a member of the highest Hindu caste, whose members are traditionally eligible for the priesthood. **2** = BRAHMA 2. □□ **Brahmanic** /-mánik/ *adj.* **Brahmanical** *adj.* **Brahmanism** *n.* [Skr. *brāhmaṇas* f. *brahman* priest]

Brahman[2] /bráymən, braámən/ *n.* (also **brahman**) a breed of humped, heat-resistant, grayish cattle developed from the Indian Zebu and common in the southern US.

brahmaputra /braáməpōótrə/ *n.* (also **brahma**) **1** any bird of a large Asian breed of domestic fowl. **2** this breed. [*Brahmaputra* River in India, from where it was brought]

Brahmin /braámin/ *n.* **1** = BRAHMAN. **2** (esp. in New England) a socially or culturally superior person. [var. of BRAHMAN]

braid /brayd/ *n. & v.* ● *n.* **1** a woven band of silk or thread used for edging or trimming. **2** a length of hair, straw, etc. in three or more interlaced strands. ● *v.tr.* **1** weave or intertwine (hair or thread). **2** trim or decorate with braid. □□ **braider** *n.* [OE *bregdan* f. Gmc] ■ *n.* **1** trimming, trim, fillet, ribbon, twine, soutache, edging, piping, lace, lacing, rickrack, passementerie, thread, ruche, welt, *archaic* purfle; band. **2** plait. ● *v.* **1** intertwine, interlace, weave, twist, twine, interweave, plait. **2** trim, edge, pipe, lace, fringe; see also DECORATE 1, 3.

braiding /bráyding/ *n.* **1** various types of braid collectively. **2** braided work.

Braille /brayl/ *n. & v.* ● *n.* a system of writing and printing for the blind, in which characters are represented by patterns of raised dots. ● *v.tr.* print or transcribe in Braille. [L. *Braille*, Fr. teacher d. 1852, its inventor]

brain /brayn/ *n. & v.* ● *n.* **1** an organ of soft nervous tissue contained in the skull of vertebrates, functioning as the coordinating center of sensation and of intellectual and nervous activity. **2** (in *pl.*) the substance of the brain, esp. as food. **3 a** a person's intellectual capacity (*has a weak brain*). **b** (often in *pl.*) intelligence; high intellectual capacity (*has a brain*; *has brains*). **c** *colloq.* a clever person. **4** (in *pl.*; prec. by *the*) *colloq.* **a** the cleverest person in a group. **b** a person who originates a complex plan or idea (*the brains behind the robbery*). **5** an electronic device with functions comparable to those of a brain. ● *v.tr.* **1** dash out the brains of. **2** strike hard on the head. □ **brain-dead** suffering from brain death. **brain death** irreversible brain damage causing the end of independent respiration and a flat electroencephalogram, regarded as indicative of death. **brain drain** *colloq.* the loss of skilled personnel by emigration. **brain fever** inflammation of the brain. **brain stem** the central trunk of the brain, upon which the cerebrum and cerebellum are set, and which continues downward to form the spinal cord. **brain trust** a group of experts, official or unofficial, who advise on policy and strategy. **brains trust** *Brit.* **1** = *brain trust.* **2** a group of experts on radio or television who give impromptu answers to questions posed by the audience. **brain wave 1** (usu. in *pl.*) an electrical impulse in the brain. **2** *colloq.* a sudden bright idea; inspiration. **on the brain** *colloq.* obsessively in one's thoughts. [OE *brægen* f. WG]

■ *n.* **3a, b** intelligence, intellect, brainpower, understanding, cleverness, brightness, smartness, sense, thought, imagination, capacity, perspicacity, perspicaciousness, perceptiveness, perception, percipience, braininess, *Philos.* nous; head, mind, *archaic* headpiece, *colloq.* gray matter, *Brit. sl.* loaf; wisdom, sagacity, wit(s), discernment, acumen; knowledge, cognition. **3c, 4** (*brains*) genius, mastermind, intellectual, thinker, maestro, authority, *colloq.* whiz kid, highbrow, *Brit. colloq.* boffin; leader, planner. ● *v.* **1** see MURDER *v.* 1. **2** clout, cuff, *colloq.* sock, whack, thwack, *sl.* clobber, whop, wallop. □ **brain wave 2** see INSPIRATION 2.

brainchild /bráynchīld/ *n.* (*pl.* **-children**) *colloq.* an idea, plan, or invention regarded as the result of a person's mental effort.

brainless /bráynlis/ *adj.* stupid; foolish.
■ see STUPID *adj.* 1, 5.

brainpan /bráynpan/ *n. colloq.* the skull.

brainpower /bráynpowr/ *n.* mental ability or intelligence.
■ see INTELLIGENCE 1b.

brainstorm /bráynstawrm/ *n. & v.* ● *n.* **1** a violent or excited outburst often as a result of a sudden mental disturbance. **2** *colloq.* mental confusion. **3** a brain wave. **4** a concerted intellectual treatment of a problem by discussing spontaneous ideas about it. ● *v.intr.* **1** discuss ideas spontaneously and openly. **2** *tr.* discuss (an issue) in this way. □□ **brainstorming** *n.* (in sense 4).
■ **3** see THOUGHT[1] 4.

brainteaser /bráyntēzər/ *n.* (or **braintwister** /-twístər/) *colloq.* a puzzle or problem.
■ **brainteaser** see PUZZLE *n.* 2.

brainwash /bráynwosh, -wawsh/ *v.tr.* subject (a person) to a prolonged process by which ideas other than and at variance with those already held are implanted in the mind. □□ **brainwashing** *n.*
■ see INDOCTRINATE.

brainy /bráynee/ *adj.* (**brainier, brainiest**) intellectually clever or active. □□ **brainily** *adv.* **braininess** *n.*
■ see INTELLECTUAL 2.

braise /brayz/ *v.tr.* fry lightly and then stew slowly with a little liquid in a closed container. [F *braiser* f. *braise* live coals]

brake[1] /brayk/ *n. & v.* ● *n.* **1** (often in *pl.*) a device for checking the motion of a mechanism, esp. a wheel or vehicle, or for keeping it at rest. **2** anything that has the effect of hindering or impeding (*shortage of money was a brake on their enthusiasm*). ● *v.* **1** *intr.* apply a brake. **2** *tr.* retard or stop with a brake. □ **brake drum** a cylinder attached to a wheel on which the brake shoe presses to brake. **brake fluid** fluid used in a hydraulic brake system. **brake horsepower** the power of an engine reckoned in terms of the force needed to brake it. **brake lining** a strip of material which increases the friction of the brake shoe. **brake shoe** a long curved block which presses on the brake drum to brake. **brake van** *Brit.* a railroad car or vehicle from which the train's brakes can be controlled; a caboose. □□ **brakeless** *adj.* [prob. obs. *brake* in sense 'machine handle, bridle']
■ *n.* **2** curb, check, restraint, restriction, constraint, control, rein. ● *v.* **1** put on *or* apply the brakes. **2** slow, slow up *or* down, pull up, reduce the speed of,

decelerate, slacken, hold up; stop, halt, bring to a stop *or* halt.

brake[2] /brayk/ *n. Brit.* a large station wagon. [var. of BRAKE[2]]

brake[3] /brayk/ *n. & v.* ● *n.* **1** a toothed instrument used for crushing flax and hemp. **2** (in full **brake harrow**) a heavy kind of harrow for breaking up large lumps of earth. ● *v.tr.* crush (flax or hemp) by beating it. [ME, rel. to BREAK[1]]

brake[4] /brayk/ *n.* **1** a thicket. **2** brushwood. [ME f. OF *bracu,* MLG *brake* branch, stump]

brake[5] /brayk/ *n.* bracken. [ME, perh. shortened f. BRACKEN, *-en* being taken as a pl. ending]

brake[6] *archaic past* of BREAK[1].

brakeman /bráykmən/ *n.* (*pl.* **-men**) **1** a railroad worker responsible for maintenance on a journey. **2** a person in charge of brakes. [BRAKE[1] + MAN]

brakesman /bráyksmən/ *n.* (*pl.* **-men**) *Brit.* = BRAKEMAN 2.

bramble /brámbəl/ *n.* **1** any of various thorny shrubs bearing fleshy red or black berries, esp. (*Brit.*) the blackberry bush, *Rubus fructicosus.* **2** *Brit.* the edible berry of these shrubs. **3** any of various other rosaceous shrubs with similar foliage, esp. the dog rose (*Rosa canina*). □□ **brambly** *adj.* [OE *bræmbel* (earlier *bræmel*): see BROOM]
■ □□ **brambly** see THORNY 1.

brambling /brámbling/ *n.* the speckled finch, *Fringilla montifringilla,* native to northern Eurasia, the male having a distinctive red breast. [G *Brämling* f. WG (cf. BRAMBLE)]

bran /bran/ *n.* grain husks separated from the flour. [ME f. OF. of unkn. orig.]

branch /branch/ *n. & v.* ● *n.* **1** a limb extending from a tree or bough. **2** a lateral extension or subdivision, esp. of a river, or railroad. **3** a conceptual extension or subdivision, as of a family, knowledge, etc. **4** a local division or office, etc., of a large business, as of a bank, library, etc. ● *v.intr.* (often foll. by *off*) **1** diverge from the main part. **2** divide into branches. **3** (of a tree) bear or send out branches. □ **branch out** extend one's field of interest. □□ **branched** *adj.* **branchlet** *n.* **branchlike** *adj.* **branchy** *adj.* [ME f. OF *branche* f. LL *branca* paw]
■ *n.* **1** offshoot, arm; limb, bough. **2, 3** extension, offshoot; wing, side; department, section, subsection, division, subdivision, ramification, part, area, sphere, field. **4** office, bureau; affiliate, subsidiary. ● *v.* **1** (*branch off*) diverge, deviate, turn off *or* away, separate, depart, divaricate. **2** divide, subdivide, fork, separate, split, ramify, break up. □ **branch out** diversify, spread *or* stretch one's wings.

branchia /brángkeeə/ *n.pl.* (also **branchiae** /-kee-ee/) gills. □□ **branchial** *adj.* **branchiate** /-eeit, -eeayt/ *adj.* [L *branchia,* pl. *-ae,* f. Gk *bragkhia* pl.]

brand /brand/ *n. & v.* ● *n.* **1 a** a particular make of goods. **b** an identifying trademark, label, etc. **2** (usu. foll. by *of*) a special or characteristic kind (*brand of humor*). **3** an identifying mark burned on livestock or (formerly) prisoners, etc., with a hot iron. **4** an iron used for this. **5** a piece of burning, smoldering, or charred wood. **6** a stigma; a mark of disgrace. **7** *poet.* **a** a torch. **b** a sword. ● *v.tr.* **1** mark with a hot iron. **2** stigmatize; mark with disgrace (*they branded him a liar; was branded for life*). **3** impress unforgettably on one's mind. **4** assign a trademark or label to. □ **brand-name** having an identifying trademark, label, etc., esp. one that is well-known. **brand-new** completely or obviously new. □□ **brander** *n.* [OE f. Gmc]
■ *n.* **1 a** kind, make, type, sort, variety. **b** brand name, trade *or* proprietary name, trademark, label, mark, marque, name brand, *Brit. archaic* chop. **2** see TYPE *n.* 1. **6** see STIGMA 1. **7 a** see TORCH *n.* **b** see BLADE 6.
● *v.* **2** discredit, disgrace, dishonor, besmirch, smear, tarnish, taint, blacken; accuse of being, stigmatize as, pronounce; label, characterize as, mark (down) as. **3** see IMPRESS[1] *v.* 3, 4. **4** mark, stamp, identify, tag, label; register (as a trademark). □ **brand-new** new, unused, fresh, firsthand, mint, virgin; latest, today's, up-to-date, up-to-the-minute, just out, hot, hot off the press, red-hot.

brandish /brándish/ *v.tr.* wave or flourish as a threat or in display. □□ **brandisher** n. [OF brandir ult. f. Gmc, rel. to BRAND]

■ see FLOURISH v. 4.

brandling /brándling/ n. a red earthworm, Eisenia foetida, with rings of a brighter color, which is often found in manure and used as bait. [BRAND + -LING[1]]

brandy /brándee/ n. (pl. -ies) a strong alcoholic spirit distilled from wine or fermented fruit juice. □ **brandy-ball** Brit. a kind of brandy-flavored candy. **brandy butter** Brit. a rich, sweet, hard sauce made with brandy, butter, and sugar. [earlier brand(e)wine f. Du. brandewijn burned (distilled) wine]

brant /brant/ n. (Brit. **brent**) a small migratory goose, Branta bernicla. [16th c.: orig. unkn.]

brash[1] /brash/ adj. **1** vulgarly or overly self-assertive. **2** hasty; rash. **3** impudent. □□ **brashly** adv. **brashness** n. [orig. dial., perh. f. RASH[1]]

■ **1** see BOLD 2. **2** hasty, rash, abrupt, impetuous, precipitate, impulsive, unpremeditated, unplanned, unreflective, unreasoned, headlong, reckless. **3** impudent, rude, impertinent, disrespectful, insolent, cheeky, uncivil, discourteous, impolite, forward, self-assertive, audacious, presumptuous, pushing, loud, brassy, brazen, bold, cocksure, cocky, tactless, undiplomatic, colloq. fresh, pushy.

brash[2] /brash/ n. **1** loose broken rock or ice. **2** clippings from hedges, shrubs, etc. [18th c.: orig. unkn.]

brass /bras/ n. & adj. ● n. **1** a yellow alloy of copper and zinc. **2 a** an ornament or other decorated piece of brass. **b** brass objects collectively. **3** Mus. brass wind instruments (including trumpet, horn, trombone) forming a band or a section of an orchestra. **4** Brit. sl. money. **5** (in full **top brass**) colloq. persons in authority or of high (esp. military) rank. **6** esp. Brit. an inscribed or engraved memorial tablet of brass. **7** colloq. effrontery; gall (then had the brass to demand money). **8** a brass block or die used for making a design on a book binding. ● adj. made of brass. □ **brass band** a group of musicians playing brass instruments, sometimes also with percussion. **brassed off** Brit. sl. fed up. **brass hat** colloq. an officer of high rank, usu. with gold braid on the cap. **brass knuckles** a metal guard worn over the knuckles in fighting, esp. to increase the effect of the blows. **brass monkey** coarse sl. used in various phrases to indicate extreme cold. **brass neck** Brit. colloq. cheek; effrontery; = BRASS 7 above. **brass ring** sl. an opportunity for wealth or success; a rich prize. **brass-rubbing 1** the rubbing of charcoal, etc., over paper laid on an engraved brass to take an impression of its design. **2** the impression obtained by this. **brass tacks** sl. actual details; real business (get down to brass tacks). **not have a brass farthing** Brit. colloq. have no money or assets at all. [OE bræs, of unkn. orig.]

■ n. **5** see MANAGEMENT 2b, c. **7** effrontery, nerve, cheek, audacity, presumption, brazenness, brashness, barefacedness, shamelessness, cockiness, temerity, impudence, insolence, rudeness, colloq. nerve, sauce, sl. gall, chutzpah. □ **brass hat** see BIGWIG. **brass tacks** see DETAIL n. 1.

brassard /brəsaárd, brásaard/ n. a band with an identifying mark worn on the sleeve, esp. with a uniform. [F bras arm + -ARD]

brasserie /brásəree/ n. a restaurant, orig. one serving beer with food. [F, = brewery]

■ see CAFÉ 1.

brassica /brásikə/ n. any cruciferous plant of the genus Brassica, having tap roots and erect branched stems, including cabbage, rutabaga, broccoli, brussels sprout, mustard, rape, cauliflower, kohlrabi, kale, and turnip. [L, = cabbage]

brassie /brásee/ n. (also **brassy**) (pl. -ies) a wooden-headed golf club with a brass sole.

brassiere /brəzeér/ n. an undergarment worn by women to support the breasts. [F, = child's vest]

brassy[1] /brásee/ adj. (**brassier**, **brassiest**) **1** impudent. **2** pretentious; showy. **3** loud and blaring. **4** of or like brass. □□ **brassily** adv. **brassiness** n.

■ **1** impudent, forward, self-assertive, insolent, saucy,

brash, rude, cheeky, brazen, bold, pert, shameless, barefaced, cocky, cocksure, loud, coarse, colloq. fresh, pushy. **2** pretentious, showy, ostentatious, flashy, florid, flamboyant. **3** harsh, blaring, loud, strident, tinny, grating, jarring, dissonant, discordant, unharmonious, coarse, raucous, shrill.

brassy[2] var. of BRASSIE.

brat /brat/ n. usu. derog. a child, esp. a badly-behaved one. □ **brat pack** a rowdy or ostentatious group of young celebrities, esp. movie stars. □□ **bratty** adj. [perh. abbr. of Sc. bratchart hound, or f. brat rough garment]

■ see IMP n. 1.

brattice /brátis/ n. a wooden partition or shaft lining in a mine. [ME ult. f. OE brittisc BRITISH]

bratwurst /brátwərst, -voŏrst/ n. a type of small pork sausage. [G f. braten fry, roast + Wurst sausage]

bravado /brəvaádō/ n. a bold manner or a show of boldness intended to impress. [Sp. bravata f. bravo: cf. BRAVE, -ADO]

■ boldness, bluster, boasting, bluff, braggadocio, swagger, boastfulness, self-assurance, rodomontade, Austral. & NZ colloq. skite, Brit. sl. side; machismo.

brave /brayv/ adj., n., & v. ● adj. **1** able or ready to face and endure danger or pain. **2** splendid; spectacular (make a brave show). ● n. a Native American warrior. ● v.tr. defy; encounter bravely. □ **brave it out** behave defiantly under suspicion or blame; see a thing through to the end. □□ **bravely** adv. **braveness** n. [ME f. F, ult. f. L barbarus BARBAROUS]

■ adj. **1** fearless, intrepid, bold, courageous, daring, gallant, stout, stout-hearted, lionhearted, valiant, valorous, stalwart, plucky, staunch, undaunted, dauntless, unafraid, mettlesome, indomitable, heroic, archaic or joc. doughty, colloq. gutsy. **2** fine, handsome, grand, splendid, showy, dramatic, colorful, spectacular, awe-inspiring, Sc. braw. ● v. brazen out, weather, face (up to), confront, encounter, meet head on, come or go up against, withstand, put up with; challenge, defy, stand up to, dare; (brave it) see bite the bullet. □ **brave it out** brave it, weather the storm, brazen it out, sit or stick it out, stay till the bitter end.

bravery /bráyvəree/ n. **1** brave conduct. **2** a brave nature. [F braverie or It. braveria (as BRAVE)]

■ daring, courage, valor, heroism, gallantry, fortitude, fearlessness, intrepidity, intrepidness, determination, staunchness, firmness, resolution, resolution, indomitability, stalwartness, stout-heartedness, manliness, manhood; pluck, nerve, mettle, colloq. grit, guts.

bravo[1] /braávō/ int. & n. ● int. expressing approval of a performer, etc. ● n. (pl. -os) a cry of bravo. [F f. It.]

bravo[2] /braávō/ n. (pl. -oes or -os) a hired thug or killer. [It.: see BRAVE]

bravura /brəvoŏrə, -vyoŏrə/ n. (often attrib.) **1** a brilliant or ambitious action or display. **2 a** a style of (esp. vocal) music requiring exceptional ability. **b** a passage of this kind. **3** bravado. [It.]

■ **1** see VIRTUOSO 1b.

braw /braw/ adj. Sc. fine; good. [var. of brawf BRAVE]

brawl /brawl/ n. & v. ● n. a noisy quarrel or fight. ● v.intr. **1** quarrel noisily or roughly. **2** (of a stream) run noisily. □□ **brawler** n. [ME f. OProv., rel. to BRAY[1]]

■ n. fight, fistfight, mêlée, scrimmage, scuffle, battle, battle royal, donnybrook, fray, free-for-all, Brit. maul, ruckus, colloq. scrap, rumpus, shindy, ruction, set-to, dustup, punch-up, spat, sl. roughhouse; riot, unrest, disturbance, commotion, uproar, fracas, rout; wrangle, dispute, quarrel, squabble, colloq. row. ● v. **1** fight, scuffle, wrangle, clash, quarrel, squabble, dispute, colloq. scrap, row; riot.

/.../ **pronunciation**   ● **part of speech**
□ **phrases, idioms, and compounds**
□□ **derivatives**   ■ **synonym section**
cross-references appear in SMALL CAPITALS or italics

brawn /brawn/ *n.* **1** muscular strength. **2** muscle; lean flesh. **3** *Brit.* a jellied preparation of the chopped meat from a boiled pig's head. [ME f. AF *braun*, OF *braon* f. Gmc]
■ **1** muscle(s), strength, robustness, brawniness, might, power, toughness, huskiness, *archaic* puissance. **2** muscle, sinew, flesh.

brawny /bráwnee/ *adj.* (**brawnier, brawniest**) muscular; strong. □□ **brawniness** *n.*
■ muscular, well-muscled, muscly, strong, tough, robust, mighty, powerful, burly, sturdy, strapping, beefy, hefty, bulky, husky. □□ **brawniness** see BRAWN 1.

bray[1] /bray/ *n. & v.* ● *n.* **1** the cry of a donkey. **2** a sound like this cry, e.g., that of a harshly played brass instrument, a laugh, etc. ● *v.* **1** *intr.* make a braying sound. **2** *tr.* utter harshly. [ME f. OF *braire*, perh. ult. f. Celt.]
■ *v.* see BLARE *v.*

bray[2] /bray/ *v.tr.* pound or crush to small pieces, esp. with a pestle and mortar. [ME f. AF *braier*, OF *breier* f. Gmc]

braze[1] /brayz/ *v. & n.* ● *v.tr.* solder with an alloy of brass and zinc at a high temperature. ● *n.* **1** a brazed joint. **2** the alloy used for brazing. [F *braser* solder f. *braise* live coals]
■ *v.* see WELD[1] *v.* 1.

braze[2] /brayz/ *v.tr.* **1 a** make of brass. **b** cover or ornament with brass. **2** make hard like brass. [OE *bræsen* f. *bræs* BRASS]

brazen /bráyzən/ *adj. & v.* ● *adj.* **1** (also **brazen-faced**) flagrant and shameless; insolent. **2** made of brass. **3** of or like brass, esp. in color or sound. ● *v.tr.* (foll. by *out*) face or undergo defiantly. □ **brazen it out** be defiantly unrepentant esp. under censure. □□ **brazenly** *adv.* **brazenness** *n.* [OE *bræsen* f. *bræs* brass]
■ *adj.* **1** brassy, shameless, barefaced, unashamed, shameless, unabashed, audacious, flagrant, blatant, outright, out-and-out; outspoken, forward, bold, brash, immodest, presumptuous, candid, open; rude, impertinent, insolent, impudent, cheeky, saucy, cocksure, cocky, *colloq.* fresh, pushy, sassy. ● *v.* (*brazen out*) see BRAVE *v.* □ **brazen it out** see *brave it out.* □□ **brazenness** see BRASS *n.* 7.

brazier[1] /bráyzhər/ *n.* a portable heater consisting of a pan or stand for holding lighted coals. [F *brasier* f. *braise* hot coals]

brazier[2] /bráyzhər/ *n.* a worker in brass. □□ **braziery** *n.* [ME prob. f. BRASS + -IER, after *glass, glazier*]

Brazil /brəzíl/ *n.* **1** a tall tree, *Bertholletia excelsa*, forming large forests in S. America. **2** (in full **Brazil nut**) a large three-sided nut with an edible kernel from this tree. [the name of a S.Amer. country, named from *brazilwood*, ult. f. med.L *brasilium*]

brazilwood /brəzílwŏŏd/ *n.* a hard red wood from any tropical tree of the genus *Caesalpina*, that yields dyes.

breach /breech/ *n. & v.* ● *n.* **1** (often foll. by *of*) the breaking of or failure to observe a law, contract, etc. **2 a** a breaking of relations; an estrangement. **b** a quarrel. **3 a** a broken state. **b** a gap, esp. one made by artillery or batting in fortifications. ● *v.tr.* **1** break through; make a gap in. **2** break (a law, contract, etc.). □ **breach of the peace** an infringement or violation of the public peace by any disturbance or riot, etc. **breach of promise** the breaking of a promise, esp. a promise to marry. **stand in the breach** bear the brunt of an attack. **step into the breach** give help in a crisis, esp. by replacing someone who has dropped out. [ME f. OF *breche*, ult. f. Gmc]
■ *n.* **1** break, violation, nonobservance, infringement, contravention, *Law* infraction, *archaic* delict; betrayal. **2 a** break, rift, gulf, split, breakup, separation, rupture, severance, schism, split, alienation, estrangement, *colloq.* bust-up. **b** see QUARREL *n.* 1. **3 b** gap, fissure, crack, hole, opening, aperture. ● *v.* **1** rupture, burst, break through, force oneself *or* itself through; split, fracture, break, *colloq.* bust. **2** see BREAK[1] *v.* 3.

bread /bred/ *n. & v.* ● *n.* **1** baked dough made of flour usu. leavened with yeast and moistened, eaten as a staple food. **2 a** necessary food. **b** (also **daily bread**) one's livelihood. **3** *sl.* money. ● *v.tr.* coat with breadcrumbs for cooking. □ **bread and butter 1** bread spread with butter. **2 a** one's

livelihood. **b** routine work to ensure an income. **bread-and-butter letter** a letter of thanks for hospitality. **bread and circuses** the public provision of subsistence and entertainment, esp. as a palliative to divert attention or avert discontent. **bread and wine** the Eucharist. **bread basket 1** a basket for bread or rolls. **2** *sl.* the stomach. **bread box** a container for keeping bread in. **bread mold** any of various molds, esp. *Rhizopus nigricans*, found esp. on bread. **cast one's bread upon the waters** do good without expecting gratitude or reward. **know which side one's bread is buttered on** know where one's advantage lies. **take the bread out of a person's mouth** take away a person's living, esp. by competition, etc. [OE *brēad* f. Gmc]
■ *n.* **2 a** see FOOD 1. **3** see MONEY 1. □ **bread basket 2** see STOMACH *n.* 2.

breadboard /brédbawrd/ *n.* **1** a board for cutting bread on. **2** a board for making an experimental model of an electric circuit.

breadcrumb /brédkrum/ *n.* **1** a small fragment of bread. **2** (in *pl.*) bread crumbled for use in cooking.

breadfruit /brédfrŏŏt/ *n.* **1** a tropical evergreen tree, *Artocarpus altilis*, bearing edible usu. seedless fruit. **2** the fruit of this tree which when roasted becomes soft like new bread.

breadline /brédlin/ *n.* a line of people waiting to receive free food from a charity or government agency.

breadth /bredth/ *n.* **1** the distance or measurement from side to side of a thing; broadness. **2** a piece (of cloth, etc.) of standard or full breadth. **3** extent; distance; room. **4** (usu. foll. by *of*) capacity to respect other opinions; freedom from prejudice or intolerance (esp. *breadth of mind* or *view*). **5** *Art* unity of the whole, achieved by the disregard of unnecessary details. □□ **breadthways** *adv.* **breadthwise** *adv.* [obs. *brede*, OE *brǣdu*, f. Gmc, rel. to BROAD]
■ **1** width, wideness, broadness, span, spread, thickness, *Naut.* beam. **3** extent, magnitude, degree, amount, area, expanse, depth, range, scope, room, leeway; distance, stretch, measurement. **4** liberality, largeness, catholicity, latitude, width, broadness, wideness.

breadwinner /brédwinər/ *n.* a person who earns the money to support a family.

break[1] /brayk/ *v. & n.* ● *v.* (*past* **broke** /brōk/ or *archaic* **brake** /brayk/; *past part.* **broken** /brōkən/ or *archaic* **broke**) **1** *tr. & intr.* **a** separate into pieces vidently, as from a blow or strain; shatter. **b** make or become inoperative, esp. from damage (*the toaster has broken*). **c** break a bone in or dislocate (part of the body). **d** break the skin of (the head or crown). **2 a** *tr.* cause or effect an interruption in (*broke our journey; the spell was broken; broke the silence*). **b** *intr.* have an interval between periods of work (*let's break now; we broke for coffee*). **3** *tr.* fail to observe or keep (a law, promise, etc.). **4 a** *tr. & intr.* make or become subdued or weakened; yield or cause to yield (*broke his spirit; he broke under the strain*). **b** *tr.* weaken the effect of (a fall, blow, etc.). **c** *tr.* tame or discipline (an animal); accustom (a horse) to saddle and bridle, etc. **d** *tr.* defeat; destroy (*broke the enemy's power*). **e** *tr.* defeat the object of (a strike, e.g., by hiring other personnel). **5** *tr.* surpass (a record, time, score, etc.). **6** *tr.* (foll. by *with*) **a** quarrel or cease association with (another person, etc.). **b** repudiate; depart from (a tradition, practice, etc.) **7** *tr.* **a** be no longer subject to (a habit). **b** (foll. by *of*) cause (a person) to be free of a habit (*broke them of their addiction*). **8** *tr. & intr.* reveal or be revealed; (cause to) become known (*broke the news; the story broke on Friday*). **9** *intr.* **a** (of the weather) change suddenly, esp. after a long period without change. **b** (of waves) curl over and dissolve into foam. **c** (of the day) dawn. **d** (of clouds) move apart; show a gap. **e** (of a storm) begin violently. **10** *tr. Electr.* disconnect (a circuit). **11** *intr.* **a** (of the voice) change with emotion. **b** (of a boy's voice) change in register, etc., at puberty. **12** *tr.* **a** (often foll. by *up*) divide (a set, etc.) into parts, e.g., by selling to different buyers. **b** change (a bill, etc.) for coins or smaller denominations. **13** *tr.* ruin (an individual or institution) financially (see also BROKE *adj.*). **14** *tr.* penetrate (e.g., a safe) by force. **15** *tr.* decipher (a code). **16** *tr.* make (a way, path, etc.) by separating obstacles. **17** *intr.*

burst forth (*the sun broke through the clouds*). **18** *Mil.* **a** *intr.* (of troops) disperse in confusion. **b** *tr.* make a rupture in (ranks). **19 a** *intr.* (usu. foll. by *free, loose, out,* etc.) escape from constraint by a sudden effort. **b** *tr.* escape or emerge from (prison, cover, etc.). **20** *tr. Tennis,* etc., win a game against (an opponent's service). **21** *intr. Boxing,* etc. (of two fighters, usu. at the referee's command) come out of a clinch. **22** *tr. Mil.* demote (an officer). **23** *intr. esp. Stock Exch.* (of prices) fall sharply. **24** *intr.* (of a thrown or bowled ball) change direction abruptly. **25** *intr. Billiards,* etc., disperse the balls at the beginning of a game. **26** *tr.* unfurl (a flag, etc.). **27** *tr. Phonet.* subject (a vowel) to fracture. **28** *tr.* fail to rejoin (one's ship) after absence on leave. **29** *tr.* disprove (an alibi). ● *n.* **1 a** an act or instance of breaking. **b** a point where something is broken; a gap; a split. **2** an interval; an interruption; a pause in work; a vacation. **3** a sudden dash (esp. to escape). **4** *colloq.* **a** a piece of good luck; a fair chance. **b** (also **bad break**) an unfortunate remark or action; a blunder. **c** (in *pl.,* prec. by *the*) fate. **5** a change in direction of a thrown or bowled ball. **6** *Billiards,* etc. **a** a series of points scored during one turn. **b** the opening shot that disperses the balls. **7** *Mus.* (in jazz, etc.) a short unaccompanied passage for a soloist, usu. improvised. **8** *Electr.* a discontinuity in a circuit. □ **bad break** *colloq.* **1** a piece of bad luck. **2** a mistake or blunder. **break away** make or become free or separate (see also BREAKAWAY). **break the back of 1** do the hardest or greatest part of; crack (a problem, etc.). **2** overburden (a person) physically or mentally; crush; defeat. **break bread** have a meal (with someone). **break dancing** an energetic style of street-dancing, developed by African-Americans. **break down 1 a** fail in mechanical action; cease to function. **b** (of human relationships, etc.) fail; collapse. **c** (of health) fail; deteriorate; (of a person) fail in (esp. mental) health. **d** be overcome by emotion; collapse in tears. **2 a** demolish; destroy. **b** suppress (resistance). **c** force (a person) to yield under pressure. **3** analyze into components (see also BREAKDOWN). **break even** emerge from a transaction, etc., with neither profit nor loss. **break ground** begin construction. **break a person's heart** see HEART. **break the ice 1** begin to overcome formality or shyness, esp. between strangers. **2** make a start. **break in 1** enter premises by force, esp. with criminal intent. **2** interrupt. **3 a** accustom to a habit, etc. **b** wear, etc., until comfortable. **c** = *break* 4c. **4** *Austral. & NZ* bring (virgin land) into cultivation. **break-in** *n.* an illegal forced entry into premises, esp. with criminal intent. **breaking and entering** the illegal entering of a building with intent to commit a felony. **breaking point** the point of greatest strain, at which a thing breaks or a person gives way. **break in on** disturb; interrupt. **break into 1** enter forcibly or violently. **2 a** suddenly begin; burst forth with (a song, laughter, etc.). **b** suddenly change one's pace for (a faster one) (*broke into a gallop*). **3** interrupt. **break a leg** *Theatr.* phrase to wish a performer good luck. **break line** *Printing* the last line of a paragraph (usu. not of full length). **break new ground** innovate; start on something new. **break of day** dawn. **break off 1** detach by breaking. **2** bring to an end. **3** cease talking, etc. **break open** open forcibly. **break out 1** escape by force, esp. from prison. **2** begin suddenly; burst forth (*then violence broke out*). **3** (foll. by *in*) become covered in (a rash, etc.). **4** exclaim. **5** unfurl (a flag, etc.). **6 a** open up (a receptacle) and remove its contents. **b** remove (articles) from a place of storage. **break point 1** a place or time at which an interruption or change is made. **2** *Computing* (usu. **breakpoint**) a place in a computer program where the sequence of instructions is interrupted, esp. by another program. **3 a** (in tennis) a point which would win the game for the player(s) receiving service. **b** the situation at which the receiver(s) may break service by winning such a point. **4** = *breaking point.* **break step** get out of step. **break up 1** break into small pieces. **2** disperse; disband. **3** *Brit.* end the school term. **4 a** terminate a relationship; disband. **b** cause to do this. **5** esp. *Brit.* (of the weather) change suddenly (esp. after a fine spell). **6 a** upset or be upset. **b** excite or be excited. **c** convulse or be

convulsed (see also BREAKUP). **break wind** release gas from the anus. **break one's word** see WORD. [OE *brecan* f. Gmc]
■ *v.* **1 a** break apart *or* up, fracture, rupture, break into bits, fall to bits *or* apart *or* in two, come apart, shatter, shiver, crack, snap, splinter, fragment, comminute, split, burst, explode, collapse, *colloq.* break, *literary* break *or* fall asunder. **b** (*tr.*) stop, *colloq.* bust; (*intr.*) break down, stop working *or* functioning, go wrong, give out, die, *archaic or colloq.* give up the ghost, *colloq.* conk out, pack up *or* in, *Brit. colloq.* crock up, *sl.* bite the dust. **2 a** break off, discontinue, suspend, interrupt, hold up, delay, disrupt, punctuate; sever, cut off *or* short. **b** have *or* take a break, stop, pause. **3** violate, transgress, disobey, overstep, go counter to *or* against, contravene, defy, infringe, breach, fail to observe, go beyond, ignore, disregard, flout, fly in the face of. **4 a** weary, exhaust, subdue, sap, drain, wear out, weaken, enfeeble, debilitate, cripple, demoralize, undermine, crush, quash, overcome, defeat, cow; see also YIELD *v.* 3a. **b** lessen, soften, mitigate, cushion, pad, allay, alleviate, take the edge off. **c** tame, discipline, train, condition, domesticate. **d** demolish, smash, destroy, crush, ruin, defeat, quell, overcome, put down, quash, foil, frustrate, *literary* vanquish. **5** see EXCEED 1, 3. **6** (*break with*) **a** see LEAVE[1] *v.* 1b, 3, 4, QUARREL *v.* 2. **b** renounce, repudiate, disavow, dispense with, depart from. **7 a** give up, put an end to, relinquish, *sl.* kick. **8** reveal, announce, disclose, divulge, let *or* put out, release, tell, make public *or* known, spread about, bruit about *or* abroad. **9 a** change, fail; shift, switch, vary. **c** dawn, begin, start. **d** break up, move apart, part, spread out *or* apart, divide, disperse, scatter, dissipate. **e** break forth *or* out, burst forth, erupt. **11 a** see QUAVER *v.* **13** ruin, bankrupt, reduce to penury *or* destitution, put out of business, put into receivership. **14** break *or* force open, get *or* break into. **15** decipher, decode, decrypt. **17** burst forth, emerge, come out, appear. **19 a** see ESCAPE *v.* 1. **22** demote, downgrade, degrade, reduce to the ranks, relegate, *colloq.* bust. **23** see FALL *v.* 1. **29** see DISPROVE. ● *n.* **1 a** fracture, split, separation, rupture, cutoff, severance, burst, breach, rift, schism, *Prosody* caesura, *archaic* discerption. **b** gap, opening, hole, space, aperture, breach, chink, crack, slit. **2** interruption, interval, discontinuity, discontinuation, disruption, hesitation, delay, lapse, lull, wait, suspension, hiatus, gap, lacuna, *colloq.* letup; stop, pause, cease, cessation, *literary* surcease; rest, respite, rest period, time off, time-out, holiday, leave (of absence), vacation; coffee break, tea break, intermission, interlude, entr'acte, recess, *Sport* halftime, *colloq.* breather, *Austral. & NZ colloq.* smoko. **3** see DASH *n.* 1, ESCAPE *n.* 1. **4 a** chance, stroke of luck, opportunity, opening, foot in the door. **b** see BLUNDER *n.* □ **bad break 1** see MISFORTUNE 2. **2** see BLUNDER *n.* **break away** leave, depart, separate (oneself *or* itself); branch off, diverge, turn away, separate off; split. **break the back of 1** overcome, master, get the better of, *colloq.* crack. **2** overburden, overload; weaken, enfeeble, cripple, disable, put out of action; overcome, crush, smash, ruin, destroy, defeat, quell, put down, quash, *literary* vanquish. **break down 1 a** see BREAK[1] *v.* 1b above. **b** see FAIL 1, 2a. **c** see DETERIORATE, *go to pieces* (PIECE). **d** be overcome; burst *or* dissolve into tears. **2 a** see DESTROY 1. **b** see SUPPRESS 1. **3** separate, dissect, anatomize, take apart *or* to pieces, break up, reduce; analyze, examine, sort, classify, codify, organize. **break the ice 2** see *break new ground* below. **break in 1** force one's way in, intrude, *Brit. sl.* crack a crib. **2** see INTERRUPT 1. **3 a** train, educate, prepare;

/ . . . / pronunciation	● part of speech
□ **phrases, idioms, and compounds**	
□□ **derivatives**	■ synonym section
cross-references appear in SMALL CAPITALS or *italics*	

accustom, condition, habituate. **b** wear in. **break in on** see INTERRUPT 1. **break into 1** force one's way into, burst into, irrupt into. **2 a** burst *or* erupt *or* explode into, burst forth with. **3** see INTERRUPT 1. **break new ground** be innovative, innovate, take the initiative *or* lead, take the first steps, make the first move, make a start, make great strides, break the ice, blaze a trail, start the ball rolling, *colloq.* take the plunge. **break of day** see DAWN *n.* 1. **break off 1** see SNAP *v.* 1. **2** see STOP *v.* 1a, b. **3** discontinue; come to a stop, stop, cease, end, halt. **break out 1** see ESCAPE *v.* 1. **2** burst forth *or* out, erupt, come forth, flare up. **3** (*break out in*) come out in. **4** see EXCLAIM 1. **break up 1** see BREAK[1] *v.* 1a above, DISINTEGRATE. **2** see DISPERSE 2. **4 a** see SPLIT *v.* 3a. **6 a** see UPSET *v.* 2. **b** see EXCITE 1. **break wind** *Brit. colloq.* let off, *coarse sl.* fart.

break[2] /brayk/ *n.* **1** a carriage frame without a body, for breaking in young horses. **2** = BRAKE[2]. [perh. = *brake* framework: 17th c., of unkn. orig.]

breakable /bráykəbəl/ *adj. & n.* ● *adj.* that may or is apt to be broken easily. ● *n.* (esp. in *pl.*) a breakable thing.
■ *adj.* see FRAGILE 1.

breakage /bráykij/ *n.* **1 a** a broken thing. **b** damage or loss caused by breaking. **2** an act or instance of breaking.
■ **2** see FRACTURE *n.* 1.

breakaway /bráykəway/ *n.* **1 a** the act or an instance of breaking away or seceding. **b** *Sports* the act or instance of moving forward from a group, as in cycling. **2** (*attrib.*) that breaks away or has broken away; separate.

breakdown /bráykdown/ *n.* **1 a** a mechanical failure. **b** a loss of (esp. mental) health and strength. **2 a** a collapse or disintegration (*breakdown of communication*). **b** physical or chemical decomposition. **3** a detailed analysis (of statistics, chemical components, etc.).
■ **1 a** collapse, failure, failing, *Computing* crash. **b** (mental) collapse, nervous breakdown, trauma, *colloq.* crack-up. **2 a** collapse, disintegration, failure, downfall, decline, deterioration, degeneration. **b** decomposition, dissolution, corruption, degeneration. **3** analysis, review, rundown; itemization, classification, listing, dissection, distillation, fractionation; examination, investigation.

breaker /bráykər/ *n.* **1** a person or thing that breaks something, esp. (*Brit.*) disused machinery. **2** a person who breaks in a horse. **3** a heavy wave that breaks.
■ **3** see WAVE *n.* 1, 2.

breakfast /brékfəst/ *n. & v.* ● *n.* the first meal of the day. ● *v.intr.* have breakfast. □□ **breakfaster** *n.* [BREAK[1] interrupt + FAST[2]]
■ *n.* see MEAL[1].

breakneck /bráyknek/ *adj.* (of speed) dangerously fast.
■ reckless, dangerous, daredevil, careless; excessive, headlong, rash; (*at breakneck speed*) at full speed *or* gallop, headlong, flat out, (at) full tilt, all out, hell for leather, *colloq.* lickety-split.

breakout /bráykowt/ *n.* a forcible escape or emergence.
break-out see ESCAPE *n.* 1.

breakthrough /bráykthrōō/ *n.* **1** a major advance or discovery. **2** an act of breaking through an obstacle, etc.

breakup /bráykup/ *n.* **1** disintegration; collapse. **2** dispersal.
■ **1** see DISSOLUTION 1. **2** see DISSOLUTION 3.

breakwater /bráykwawtər, -wotər/ *n.* a barrier built out into the sea to break the force of waves.

bream[1] /breem/ *n.* (*pl.* same) **1** a yellowish arch-backed European freshwater fish, *Abramis brama.* **2** (in full **sea bream**) a similarly shaped marine fish of the family Sparidae. [ME f. OF *bre(s)me* f. WG]

bream[2] /breem/ *v.tr. Naut. hist.* clean (a ship's bottom) by burning and scraping. [prob. f. LG: rel. to BROOM]

breast /brest/ *n. & v.* ● *n.* **1 a** either of two milk-secreting organs on the upper front of a woman's body. **b** the corresponding usu. rudimentary part of a man's body. **2 a** the upper front part of a human body; the chest. **b** the corresponding part of an animal. **3** the part of a garment that covers the breast. **4** the breast as a source of nourishment

or emotion. ● *v.tr.* **1** face; meet in full opposition (*breast the wind*). **2** contend with; face (*prepared to breast the difficulties of the journey*). **3** climb; reach the top of (a hill).
□ **breast-feed** (*past* and *past part.* **-fed**) feed (a baby) from the breast. **breast the tape** see TAPE. **make a clean breast of** confess fully. □□ **breasted** *adj.* (also in *comb.*). **breastless** *adj.* [OE *brēost* f. Gmc]
■ *n.* **1 a** teat, mamma, mammary gland; (*breasts*) *colloq.* bosoms, *sl.* boobs, *coarse sl.* tits, knockers, jugs. **2** chest, bust, front. **4** soul, core, heart (of hearts); see also BOSOM 2. ● *v.* **1, 2** see FACE *v.* 3a. □ **make a clean breast of** see CONFESS 1a.

breastbone /bréstbōn/ *n.* a thin flat vertical bone and cartilage in the chest connecting the ribs.

breastplate /bréstplayt/ *n.* a piece of armor covering the breast.

breaststroke /bréststrōk/ *n.* a stroke made while swimming face down by extending arms forward and sweeping them back in unison.

breastsummer /brésəmər, -umər/ *n. Archit.* a beam across a broad opening, sustaining a superstructure. [BREAST + SUMMER[2]]

breastwork /bréstwərk/ *n.* a low temporary defense or parapet.
■ see RAMPART.

breath /breth/ *n.* **1 a** the air taken into or expelled from the lungs. **b** one respiration of air. **c** an exhalation of air that can be seen, smelled, or heard (*breath steamed in the cold air*; *bad breath*). **2 a** a slight movement of air; a breeze. **b** a whiff of perfume, etc. **3** a whisper; a murmur (esp. of a scandalous nature). **4** the power of breathing; life (*is there breath in him?*). □ **below** (or **under**) **one's breath** in a whisper. **breath of fresh air 1** a small amount of or a brief time in the fresh air. **2** a refreshing change. **breath of life** a necessity. **breath test** a test of a person's alcohol consumption, using a Breathalyzer. **catch one's breath 1** cease breathing momentarily in surprise, suspense, etc. **2** rest after exercise to restore normal breathing. **draw breath** breathe; live. **hold one's breath 1** cease breathing temporarily. **2** *colloq.* wait in eager anticipation. **in the same breath** (esp. of saying two contradictory things) within a short time. **out of breath** gasping for air, esp. after exercise. **take a person's breath away** astound; surprise; awe; delight. **waste one's breath** talk or give advice without effect. [OE *brǣth* f. Gmc]
■ **1** see EXHALATION 1. **2 a** gust, breeze, puff, stirring, stir, draft, waft, wind, air, *literary* zephyr. **b** smell, whiff, aroma, sniff, scent, waft, wind. **3** murmur, whisper, suggestion, hint, suspicion, indication, intimation, undercurrent, undertone; touch, dash, drop, trace, tinge, soupçon. **4** life. □ **breath of fresh air 2** see TONIC *n.*; (*like a breath of fresh air*) see REFRESHING. **breath of life** see NECESSITY 1a. **draw breath** see LIVE[1] *v.* 1-4. **in the same breath** see *at once* 2 (ONCE). **out of breath** see BREATHLESS 1. **take a person's breath away** astound, astonish, surprise, dazzle, startle, shock, stagger, stun, take aback, *colloq.* bowl over, knock sideways, floor, *Brit.* knock for six, *sl.* knock out, KO; awe, amaze, overawe; delight, excite, thrill.

Breathalyzer /bréthəlizər/ *n.* (also *Brit.* **Breathalyser**) *propr.* an instrument for measuring the amount of alcohol in the breath (and hence in the blood) of a driver. □□ **breathalyze** *v.tr.* [BREATH + ANALYZE + -ER[1]]

breathe /breeth/ *v.* **1** *intr.* take air into and expel it from the lungs. **2** *intr.* be or seem alive (*is she breathing?*). **3** *tr.* **a** utter; say (esp. quietly) (*breathed her forgiveness*). **b** express; display (*breathed defiance*). **4** *intr.* take a breath; pause. **5** *tr.* send out or take in (as if) with breathed air (*breathed enthusiasm into them*; *breathed whiskey*). **6** *intr.* (of wine, fabric, etc.) be exposed to fresh air. **7** *intr.* **a** sound; speak (esp. quietly). **b** (of wind) blow softly. **8** *tr.* allow (a horse, etc.) to breathe; give rest after exertion. □ **breathe again** (or **freely**) recover from a shock, fear, etc., and be at ease. **breathe down a person's neck** follow or check up on a person, esp. menacingly. **breathe new life into** revitalize; refresh. **breathe one's last** die. **breathe upon** *Brit.* tarnish; taint. **not**

breathe a word keep silent. **not breathe a word of** keep secret. [ME f. BREATH]

■ **1** inhale and exhale, respire, draw breath. **2** live, be alive *or* living, exist, draw breath, *joc.* be in the land of the living. **3 a** whisper, murmur, mutter, say under one's breath, hint (at); suggest; tell, speak, say, utter. **4** see REST[1] *v.* 1. **5** exhale, breathe out, expel, puff, blow, send out, emit, give forth, pour out *or* forth, spew forth. □ **breathe new life into** see REFRESH 1. **breathe one's last** see *pass away* 1. **breathe upon** see TAINT *v.* 1. **not breathe a word** see *play one's cards close to one's chest* (CHEST), *dummy up.*

breather /breéthər/ *n.* **1** *colloq.* **a** a brief pause for rest. **b** a short interval of exercise. **2** a safety vent in the crankcase of a motor vehicle, etc.

■ **1 a** see BREAK[1] *n.* 2.

breathing /breéthing/ *n.* **1** the process of taking air into and expelling it from the lungs. **2** *Phonet.* a sign in Greek indicating that an initial vowel is aspirated (**rough breathing**) or not aspirated (**smooth breathing**). □ **breathing space** (also **room**) time to breathe; a pause.

■ □ **breathing space** see PAUSE *n.*

breathless /bréthlis/ *adj.* **1** panting; out of breath. **2** (as if) holding the breath because of excitement, suspense, etc. (*a state of breathless expectancy*). **3** unstirred by wind; still. □□ **breathlessly** *adv.* **breathlessness** *n.*

■ **1** panting, short *or* out of breath, winded, short-winded, gasping (for air *or* breath), puffed (out), puffy; exhausted, spent, worn out, tired out. **2** eager, agog, feverish, excited, keen, expectant, impatient, anxious, frenzied, restive; with bated breath, speechless, surprised, amazed, astonished, astounded, awestruck, thunderstruck, staggered, *poet.* athirst. **3** see STILL[1] *adj.* 1.

breathtaking /bréthtayking/ *adj.* astounding; awe-inspiring. □□ **breathtakingly** *adv.*

■ see TERRIFIC 1b.

breathy /bréthee/ *adj.* (**breathier, breathiest**) (of a singing voice, etc.) containing the sound of breathing. □□ **breathily** *adv.* **breathiness** *n.*

breccia /brécheeə/ *n.* & *v.* ● *n.* a rock of angular stones, etc., cemented by finer material. ● *v.tr.* form into breccia. □□ **brecciate** /-eeayt/ *v.tr.* **brecciation** *n.* [It., = gravel, f. Gmc, rel. to BREACH[1]]

bred /bred/ *past* and *past part.* of BREED.

breech /breech/ *n.* & *v.* ● *n.* **1 a** the part of a cannon behind the bore. **b** the back part of a rifle or gun barrel. **2** the buttocks. ● *v.tr. archaic* put (a boy) into breeches. □ **breech birth** (or **delivery**) the delivery of a baby with the buttocks or feet foremost. **breech-loading** (of a gun) loaded at the breech, not through the muzzle. [OE *brōc*, pl. *brēc* (treated as sing. in ME), f. Gmc]

■ *n.* **2** see BOTTOM *n.* 2a.

breechblock /breéchblok/ *n.* a metal block that closes the breech aperture in a gun.

breeches /bríchiz/ *n.pl.* (also **pair of breeches** *sing.*) **1** short trousers, esp. fastened below the knee, now used esp. for riding. **2** *colloq.* any trousers. □ **breeches buoy** a lifebuoy suspended from a rope which has canvas breeches for the user's legs. **too big for one's breeches** *colloq.* too assertive or forward for one's status, position, abilities, etc. [pl. of BREECH]

breechloader /breéchlōdər/ *n.* a gun loaded at the breech, not through the muzzle.

breed /breed/ *v.* & *n.* ● *v.* (*past* and *past part.* **bred** /bred/) **1** *tr.* & *intr.* bear; generate (offspring); reproduce. **2** *tr.* & *intr.* propagate or cause to propagate; raise (livestock). **3** *tr.* **a** yield; produce; result in (*war breeds famine*). **b** spread (*discontent bred by rumor*). **4** *intr.* arise; spread (*disease breeds in poor sanitation*). **5** *tr.* bring up; train (*bred to the law*; *Hollywood breeds stars*). **6** *tr. Physics* create (fissile material) by nuclear reaction. ● *n.* **1** a stock of animals or plants within a species, having a similar appearance, and usu. developed by deliberate selection. **2** a race; a lineage. **3** a sort; a kind. □ **bred and born** = *born and bred.* **bred in the bone** he-

reditary. **breeder reactor** a nuclear reactor that can create more fissile material than it consumes. **breed in** mate with or marry a close relation. □□ **breeder** *n.* [OE *brēdan*: rel. to BROOD]

■ *v.* **1** produce, generate, bring forth, give birth to, create, spawn, hatch, bear, develop, *archaic* engender, get, *literary* beget; see also REPRODUCE 3. **2** raise, rear, cultivate, propagate, farm; mate, couple, pair (up). **3 a** yield, produce, make, generate, create, bring forth *or* out *or* about, give rise to, spark *or* trigger (off), set off; result in, lead to, cause, bring, *literary* beget. **b** see SPREAD *v.* 3. **4** arise, originate, appear, begin, start (off *or* up), spring up; develop, grow, increase, multiply, spread, proliferate, *literary* burgeon. **5** see *bring up* 1, TRAIN *v.* 1a. ● *n.* **1** stock, strain. **2** race, lineage, stock, family, tribe, strain, blood, extraction, ancestry, descent, parentage, birth. **3** kind, sort, type, form, variety, species, class, group, category, brand, make, stamp, stripe, manner, description, *disp.* ilk. □ **bred in the bone** see HEREDITARY 1.

breeding /breéding/ *n.* **1** the process of developing or propagating (animals, plants, etc.). **2** generation; childbearing. **3** the result of training or education; behavior. **4** good manners (*has no breeding*).

■ **1** rearing, bringing up, raising, cultivation, development, propagation. **2** generation, (re)production, creation, making, bearing, childbearing. **3** see UPBRINGING. **4** (good) upbringing, (good) manners, civility, politeness, politesse, gentility, (good) behavior; decorum, etiquette, social code *or* graces, propriety; refinement, class, sophistication, discernment, taste, urbanity, urbaneness, savoir faire.

breeks /breeks/ *n.pl.* Sc. var. of BREECHES.

breeze[1] /breez/ *n.* & *v.* ● *n.* **1** a gentle wind. **2** *Meteorol.* a wind of 4–31 m.p.h. and between force 2 and force 6 on the Beaufort scale. **3** a wind blowing from land at night or sea during the day. **4** *colloq.* an easy task. **5** esp. *Brit. colloq.* a quarrel or display of temper. ● *v.intr.* (foll. by *in, out, along*, etc.) *colloq.* come or go in a casual or lighthearted manner. [prob. f. OSp. & Port. *briza* NE wind]

■ *n.* **1** breath, puff, stir, waft, wind, draft, gust, air, *Naut.* cat's-paw, *literary* zephyr. **4** easy *or* simple job *or* task, child's play, nothing, five-finger exercise, *Bridge* pianola, *colloq.* cinch, cakewalk, gift, cushy number, steal, piece of cake, picnic, kids' stuff, *sl.* snap, duck soup. ● *v.* drift, waft, float; saunter, cruise, roam, wander.

breeze[2] /breez/ *n.* small cinders. □ **breeze block** *Brit.* = *cinder block.* [F *braise* live coals]

breeze[3] /breez/ *n. Brit.* a gadfly or horsefly. [OE *briosa*, of unkn. orig.]

breezy /breézee/ *adj.* (**breezier, breeziest**) **1** windswept. **b** pleasantly windy. **2** *colloq.* lively; jovial. **3** *colloq.* careless (*with breezy indifference*). □□ **breezily** *adv.* **breeziness** *n.*

■ **1** airy, fresh, windy, blowy, brisk, gusty, drafty; windswept. **2** carefree, lighthearted, free and easy, sunny, easy, easygoing, jovial, cheerful, jaunty, perky, cheery, lively, bright, spirited, buoyant, animated, energetic, *poet.* blithesome. **3** casual, careless, heedless, thoughtless, offhand.

bremsstrahlung /brémshtraálang/ *n. Physics* the electromagnetic radiation produced by the acceleration or esp. the deceleration of a charged particle after passing through the electric and magnetic fields of a nucleus. [G, = braking radiation]

Bren /bren/ *n.* (in full **Bren gun**) a lightweight quick-firing machine gun. [*Brno* in the Czech Republic (where orig. made) + *Enfield* in England (where later made)]

brent *Brit.* var. of BRANT.

/.../ **pronunciation**	● **part of speech**
□ **phrases, idioms, and compounds**	
□□ **derivatives**	■ **synonym section**
cross-references appear in SMALL CAPITALS or *italics*	

brethren see BROTHER.

Breton /brétən, brətáwn/ n. & adj. ● n. **1** a native of Brittany. **2** the Celtic language of Brittany. ● adj. of or relating to Brittany or its people or language. [OF, = BRITON]

breve /brev, breev/ n. **1** Mus. a note, now rarely used, having the time value of two whole notes. **2** a written or printed mark (˘) indicating a short or unstressed vowel. **3** hist. an authoritative letter from a sovereign or pope. [ME var. of BRIEF]

brevet /brəvét, brévit/ n. & v. ● n. (often attrib.) a document conferring a privilege from a sovereign or government, esp. a rank in the army, without the appropriate pay (was promoted by brevet; brevet major). ● v.tr. (**brevetted, brevetting** or **breveted, breveting**) confer brevet rank on. [ME f. OF dimin. of bref BRIEF]

breviary /breevee-eree, brév-/ n. (pl. **-ies**) RC Ch. a book containing the service for each day, to be recited by those in holy orders. [L breviarium summary f. breviare abridge: see ABBREVIATE]

brevity /brévitee/ n. **1** economy of expression; conciseness. **2** shortness (of time, etc.) (the brevity of happiness). [AF breveté, OF brieveté f. bref BRIEF]

■ conciseness, concision, terseness, succinctness, pithiness, compactness, laconicism, laconism, economy; shortness, briefness.

brew /broo/ v. & n. ● v. **1** tr. **a** make (beer, etc.) by infusion, boiling, and fermentation. **b** make (tea, coffee, etc.) by infusion or (punch, etc.) by mixture. **2** intr. undergo either of these processes (the tea is brewing). **3** intr. (of trouble, a storm, etc.) gather force; threaten (mischief was brewing). **4** tr. bring about; set in motion; concoct (brewed their fiendish scheme). ● n. **1 a** an amount (of beer, etc.) brewed at one time (this year's brew). **b** a serving (of beer, etc.). **2** what is brewed (esp. with regard to its quality) (a good strong brew). **3** the action or process of brewing. □ **brew up** Brit. **1** make tea. **2** = BREW v. 2 above. **3** = BREW v. 4 above. **brew-up** n. Brit. an instance of making tea. □□ **brewer** n. [OE brēowan f. Gmc]

■ v. **1, 2** ferment, cook, boil; infuse. **3** gather force, impend, approach, brew up, be (close) at hand or near or imminent or forthcoming or in the wind or in prospect or in store or in the offing or on the horizon, hatch, develop, take shape, begin, form, be upcoming, colloq. cook; threaten, loom, menace. **4** brew up, concoct, devise, plan, plot, contrive, conceive, prepare, develop, formulate, colloq. cook up; bring about, cause, produce, hatch; set in train or motion, set going, institute, launch. ● n. **2** see POTION.

brewery /broo͞oaree, broo͞oree/ n. (pl. **-ies**) a place where beer, etc., is brewed commercially.

briar[1] var. of BRIER[1].

briar[2] var. of BRIER[2].

bribe /brīb/ v. & n. ● v.tr. (often foll. by to + infin.) persuade (a person, etc.) to act improperly in one's favor by a gift of money, services, etc. (bribed the guard to release the suspect). ● n. money or services offered in the process of bribing. □□ **bribable** adj. **briber** n. **bribery** n. [ME f. OF briber, brimber beg, of unkn. orig.]

■ v. pay or buy off, buy (over), oil a person's palm or hand, colloq. fix, grease the palm of, square; corrupt, suborn. ● n. inducement, payoff, colloq. kickback, graft, sweetener, payola, plugola, sl. drop, Brit. sl. backhander. □□ **bribery** extortion, blackmail, subornation, corruption, colloq. graft.

bric-à-brac /bríkəbrak/ n. (also **bric-a-brac, bricabrac**) miscellaneous, often old, ornaments, trinkets, furniture, etc., of no great value. [F f. obs. à bric et à brac at random]

■ curiosities, knickknacks, bits and pieces, sundries, collectibles, trinkets, gewgaws, gimcracks, falderals, kickshaws, bijoux, bibelots, curios, objets d'art; rummage, lumber, junk, Brit. jumble.

brick /brik/ n., v., & adj. ● n. **1 a** a small, usu. rectangular, block of fired or sun-dried clay, used in building. **b** the material used to make these. **c** a similar block of concrete, etc. **2** a brick-shaped solid object (a brick of ice cream). **3** sl. a

generous or loyal person. **4** Brit. a child's toy building block. ● v.tr. (foll. by in, up, over) close, pave, or block with brickwork. ● adj. **1** built of brick (brick wall). **2** of a dull red color. □ **bang** (or **knock** or **run**) **one's head against a brick wall** attempt the impossible. **brick red** the color of bricks. **like a load** (or **ton**) **of bricks** colloq. with crushing weight, force, or authority. **see through a brick wall** have miraculous insight. □□ **bricky** adj. [ME f. MLG, MDu. bri(c)ke, of unkn. orig.]

■ n. **2** block, cube, chunk, hunk, slab, lump, square. **3** the salt of the earth, good chap, colloq. good sort, trump, Brit. colloq. topper. ● v. see WALL v. 2a.

brickbat /bríkbat/ n. **1** a piece of brick, esp. when used as a missile. **2** an uncomplimentary remark.

■ **1** see MISSILE. **2** see TAUNT n.

brickfield Brit. = BRICKYARD.

brickfielder /bríkfeeldər/ n. Austral. a hot, dry north wind.

brickie /brikee/ n. Brit. sl. a bricklayer.

bricklayer /bríklayər/ n. a worker who builds with bricks. □□ **bricklaying** n.

brickwork /bríkwərk/ n. **1** building in brick. **2** a wall, building, etc., made of brick.

brickyard /bríkyaard/ n. a place where bricks are made.

bridal /bríd'l/ adj. of or concerning a bride or a wedding. □□ **bridally** adv. [orig. as noun, = wedding feast, f. OE brȳdealu f. brȳd BRIDE + ealu ale drinking]

■ nuptial, wedding, marriage, literary hymeneal.

bride /brīd/ n. a woman on her wedding day and for some time before and after it. □ **bride-price** money or goods given to a bride's family in some cultures. [OE brȳd f. Gmc]

■ see WIFE.

bridegroom /brídgroom, -groom/ n. a man on his wedding day and for some time before and after it. [OE brȳdguma (as BRIDE, guma man, assim. to GROOM)]

■ see HUSBAND.

bridesmaid /brídzmayd/ n. a girl or woman attending a bride on her wedding day. [earlier bridemaid, f. BRIDE + MAID]

bridewell /brídwəl, -wel/ n. Brit. archaic a prison; a reformatory. [St. Bride's Well in London, near which such a building stood]

bridge[1] /brij/ n. & v. ● n. **1 a** a structure carrying a road, path, railroad, etc., across a stream, ravine, road, railroad, etc. **b** anything providing a connection between different things (English is a bridge between nations). **2** the superstructure on a ship from which the captain and officers direct operations. **3** the upper bony part of the nose. **4** Mus. an upright piece of wood on a violin, etc., over which the strings are stretched. **5** = BRIDGEWORK. **6** Billiards, etc. **a** a long stick with a structure at the end which is used to support a cue for a difficult shot. **b** a support for a cue formed by a raised hand. **7** = land bridge. **8** = bridge passage. ● v.tr. **1 a** be a bridge over (a fallen tree bridges the stream). **b** make a bridge over; span. **2** span as if with a bridge (bridged their differences with understanding). □ **bridge roll** a small soft bread roll. **bridge of asses** = pons asinorum. **bridge of boats** a bridge formed by mooring boats together abreast across a river, etc. **bridge passage** Mus. a transitional piece between main themes. **bridge** (also Brit. **bridging**) **loan** a loan from a bank, etc., to cover the short interval between buying a house, etc., and selling another. **cross a** (or **that**) **bridge when one comes to it** deal with a problem when and if it arises. □□ **bridgeable** adj. [OE brycg f. Gmc]

■ n. **1 a** viaduct. **b** link, connection, tie, bond. ● v. **1** span, cross (over), go or pass or stretch or extend or reach over, traverse, go across. **2** overcome, reconcile.

bridge[2] /brij/ n. a card game derived from whist, in which one player's cards are exposed and are played by his or her partner (cf. auction bridge, contract bridge). [19th c.: orig. unkn.]

bridgehead /bríjhed/ n. Mil. a fortified position held on the enemy's side of a river or other obstacle.

bridgework /bríjwərk/ n. Dentistry a dental structure used to cover a gap, joined to and supported by the teeth on either side.

bridle /bríd'l/ n. & v. ● n. **1 a** the headgear used to control a horse, consisting of buckled leather straps, a metal bit, and reins. **b** a restraining device or influence (*put a bridle on your tongue*). **2** *Naut.* a mooring cable. **3** *Physiol.* a ligament checking the motion of a part. ● *v.* **1** *tr.* put a bridle on (a horse, etc.). **2** *tr.* bring under control; curb. **3** *intr.* (often foll. by *at* or *up at*) express offense, resentment, etc., esp. by throwing up the head and drawing in the chin. □ **bridle path** (or esp. *Brit.* **road** or **way**) a rough path or road suitable for horseback riding. [OE *brīdel*]

■ *n.* **1 b** restraint, curb, check, control, brake, rein; command. ● *v.* **2** curb, check, restrain, hold in (check), control, subdue; command, master, hold sway over, govern. **3** (*bridle* (*up*) *at*) bristle at, draw oneself up at, be or become indignant at or with, take offense or umbrage or affront at, be affronted or offended by.

Brie /bree/ *n.* a kind of soft ripened cheese. [*Brie* in N. France]

brief /breef/ *adj., n., & v.* ● *adj.* **1** of short duration; fleeting. **2** concise in expression. **3** abrupt; brusque (*was rather brief with me*). **4** scanty; lacking in substance (*wearing a brief skirt*). ● *n.* **1** (in *pl.*) women's or men's brief underpants. **2** *Law* **a** a summary of the facts and legal points of a case drawn up for the court or counsel. **b** *Brit.* a piece of work for a barrister. **3** instructions given for a task, operation, etc. (orig. a bombing plan given to an aircrew). **4** *RC Ch.* a letter from the Pope to a person or community on a matter of discipline. **5** a short account or summary; a synopsis. ● *v.tr.* **1** instruct (an employee, a participant, etc.) in preparation for a task; inform or instruct thoroughly in advance (*briefed him for the interview*) (cf. DEBRIEF). **2** *Brit. Law* instruct (a barrister) by brief. □ **the brief** use few words. **hold a brief for 1** argue in favor of. **2** *Brit.* be retained as counsel for. **in brief** in short. **watching brief** *Brit.* **1** a brief held by a barrister following a case for a client not directly involved. **2** a state of interest maintained in a proceeding not directly or immediately concerning one. □□ **briefly** *adv.* **briefness** *n.* [ME f. AF *bref*, OF *brief*, f. L *brevis* short]

■ *adj.* **1** short, momentary, short-lived; flying, brisk, hasty, speedy, swift; transitory, fleeting, transient, evanescent, passing. **2** short, concise, thumbnail, succinct, compact, to the point, laconic, terse, summary, compendious. **3** curt, abrupt, terse, short, blunt, brusque, direct, unceremonious. **4** see SCANTY. ● *n.* **1** (*briefs*) bikini briefs, G-string; underpants, drawers, boxer shorts, shorts, *Brit.* pants, knickers. **3** instructions, guideline(s), directive(s), orders, directions. **5** summary, outline, digest, précis, résumé, *aperçu*, abstract, abridgment, synopsis. ● *v.* **1** coach, instruct, train, drill, prime, prepare, make or get ready; advise, inform, apprise, acquaint, put in the picture, *colloq.* fill in, put a person wise. □ **hold a brief for 1** see ADVOCATE *v.* **in brief** in short, briefly, concisely, in sum, in summary, to sum up, succinctly, in a word, to cut a long story short, in a nutshell. □□ **briefly** momentarily, for a few moments or seconds or minutes, fleetingly, hurriedly, hastily, quickly; see also *in brief* (BRIEF) above.

briefcase /breefkays/ *n.* a flat rectangular case for carrying documents, etc.

■ see BAG *n.* 2a.

briefing /breefing/ *n.* **1** a meeting for giving information or instructions. **2** the information or instructions given; a brief. **3** the action of informing or instructing.

■ see ORIENTATION 3.

briefless /breeflis/ *adj. Brit. Law* (of a barrister) having no clients.

brier[1] /brīer/ *n.* (also **briar**) any prickly bush, esp. of a wild rose. □ **brier rose** dog rose. □□ **briery** *adj.* [OE *brēr*, *brēr*, of unkn. orig.]

brier[2] /brīer/ *n.* (also **briar**) **1** a white heath, *Erica arborea*, native to S. Europe. **2** a tobacco pipe made from its root. [19th-c. *bruyer* f. F *bruyère* heath]

■ **2** see PIPE *n.* 2a.

brig /brig/ *n.* **1** a two-masted square-rigged ship with an additional lower fore-and-aft sail on the gaff and a boom to

the mainmast. **2** a prison, esp. in the navy. [abbr. of BRIGANTINE]

■ **2** see PRISON *n.* 1.

Brig. *abbr.* Brigadier.

brigade /brigáyd/ *n. & v.* ● *n.* **1** *Mil.* **a** a subdivision of an army. **b** an infantry unit consisting usu. of 3 battalions and forming part of a division. **c** a corresponding armored unit. **2** an organized or uniformed band of workers (*fire brigade*). **3** *colloq.* any group of people with a characteristic in common (*the couldn't-care-less brigade*). ● *v.tr.* form into a brigade. [F f. It. *brigata* company f. *brigare* be busy with f. *briga* strife]

■ *n.* **1 a** see CORPS.

brigadier /brígadéer/ *n. Mil.* **1** *Brit.* an officer commanding a brigade. **2 a** *Brit.* a staff officer of similar standing, above a colonel and below a major general. **b** the titular rank granted to such an officer. □ **brigadier general** an officer ranking between colonel and major general. [F (as BRIGADE, -IER)]

brigand /brígand/ *n.* a member of a robber band living by pillage and ransom, usu. in wild terrain. □□ **brigandage** *n.* **brigandish** *adj.* **brigandism** *n.* **brigandry** *n.* [ME f. OF f. It. *brigante* f. *brigare*: see BRIGADE]

■ see ROBBER.

brigantine /brígantéen/ *n.* a two-masted sailing ship with a square-rigged foremast and a fore-and-aft rigged mainmast. [OF *brigandine* or It. *brigantino* f. *brigante* BRIGAND]

bright /brīt/ *adj. & adv.* ● *adj.* **1** emitting or reflecting much light; shining. **2** (of color) intense; vivid. **3** clever; talented; quick-witted (*a bright idea; a bright child*). **4 a** (of a person) cheerful; vivacious. **b** (of prospects, the future, etc.) promising; hopeful. ● *adv.* esp. *poet.* brightly (*the moon shone bright*). □ **bright and early** very early in the morning. **bright-eyed and bushy-tailed** *colloq.* alert and energetic. **the bright lights** the glamour and excitement of the city. **look on the bright side** be optimistic. □□ **brightish** *adj.* **brightly** *adv.* **brightness** *n.* [OE *beorht*, (adv.) *beorhte*, f. Gmc]

■ *adj.* **1** light, shining, gleaming, radiant, brilliant, luminous, resplendent, glittering, sparkling, *formal* splendent, *literary* refulgent, effulgent, *poet. or rhet.* fulgent; alight, aglow, beaming, dazzling, glowing, lambent, incandescent, ablaze; shiny, polished, lustrous, glossy, sheeny. **2** brilliant, vivid, intense, bold, strong, striking, loud, fluorescent, *prop.* Day-Glo. **3** intelligent, clever, quick, quick-witted, brilliant, keen, sharp-witted, sharp, brainy, astute, receptive, alert, smart, *colloq.* on the ball; precocious; talented; gifted. **4 a** cheerful, gay, happy, cheery, exuberant, bubbly, lively, active, dynamic, animated, vivacious, spirited, vibrant, perky, perk, energetic, enthusiastic, eager. **b** hopeful, optimistic, favorable, propitious, auspicious, promising, rosy. ● *adv.* brightly, radiantly, brilliantly, luminously, resplendently, *literary* refulgently, effulgently, lambently. □ **bright and early** see EARLY *adj. & adv.* **1. bright-eyed and bushy-tailed** see ALERT *adj.* 2, PERKY 2. □□ **brightly** see BRIGHT *adv.* above.

brighten /brīt'n/ *v.tr. & intr.* (often foll. by *up*) **1** make or become brighter. **2** make or become more cheerful or hopeful.

■ **1** see LIGHTEN[2]. **2** enliven, lighten, cheer (up), liven up, perk or lift up, hearten.

Bright's disease /brīts/ *n.* inflammation of the kidney from any of various causes; nephritis. [R. *Bright*, Engl. physician d. 1858]

brill[1] /bril/ *n.* a European flatfish, *Scophthalmus rhombus*, resembling a turbot. [15th c.: orig. unkn.]

brill[2] /bril/ *adj. Brit. colloq.* = BRILLIANT *adj.* 4. [abbr.]

/. . ./ **pronunciation**	● **part of speech**
□ **phrases, idioms, and compounds**	
□□ **derivatives**	■ **synonym section**
cross-references appear in SMALL CAPITALS or *italics*	

brilliance /brílyəns/ *n.* (also **brilliancy** /-ənsee/) **1** great brightness; sparkling or radiant quality. **2** outstanding talent or intelligence.

■ **1** brightness, radiance, lustrousness, luster, luminosity, resplendence, refulgence, lambency, incandesence, splendor, magnificence, pomp, glory, sparkle, dazzle, glitter, *literary* effulgence. **2** intelligence, cleverness, brightness, wit, intellect, keenness, sharpness, smartness, acuteness, quickness, genius, excellence, talent, flair, ability, aptitude; precocity.

brilliancy var. OF BRILLIANCE.

brilliant /brílyənt/ *adj. & n.* ● *adj.* **1** very bright; sparkling. **2** outstandingly talented or intelligent. **3** showy; outwardly impressive. **4** esp. *Brit. colloq.* excellent; superb. ● *n.* a diamond of the finest cut with many facets. □□ **brilliantly** *adv.* [F *brillant* part. of *briller* shine f. It. *brillare*, of unkn. orig.]

■ *adj.* **1** bright, shining, lustrous, radiant, resplendent, dazzling, luminous; incandescent, glittering, sparkling, gleaming, scintillating, coruscating, twinkling, *formal* splendent, *literary* effulgent, refulgent, *poet. or rhet.* fulgent. **2** intelligent, clever, gifted, bright, smart, quick-witted, sharp-witted; outstanding, exceptional, excellent, superior, superlative; talented, expert, masterful, masterly, accomplished, ingenious, imaginative, creative, enlightened; resourceful, discerning, able, competent. **3** showy, glittering, dazzling, sparkling, scintillating, gaudy, garish, impressive, pyrotechnic.

brilliantine /brílyənteen/ *n.* **1** an oily liquid ointment for making the hair glossy. **2** a lustrous dress fabric. [F *brillantine* (as BRILLIANT)]

brim /brim/ *n. & v.* ● *n.* **1** the edge or lip of a cup or other vessel, or of a hollow. **2** the projecting edge of a hat. ● *v.tr. & intr.* (**brimmed**, **brimming**) fill or be full to the brim. □ **brim over** overflow. □□ **brimless** *adj.* **brimmed** *adj.* (usu. in *comb.*). [ME *brimme*, of unkn. orig.]

■ *n.* **1** edge, margin, lip, rim, side; brink. ● *v.* be full *or* filled. □ **brim over** overflow, spill *or* slosh over, bubble over.

brimful /brímfŏŏl/ *adj.* (also **brimfull**) (often foll. by *of*) filled to the brim.

■ see FULL¹ *adj.* 1.

brimstone /brímstōn/ *n.* **1** the element sulfur. **2** a butterfly, *Gonepteryx rhamni*, or moth, *Opisthograptis luteolata*, having yellow wings. **3** see *fire and brimstone* under *fire*. [ME prob. f. OE *bryne* burning + STONE]

brindled /bríndʼld/ *adj.* (also **brindle**) brownish or tawny with streaks of other color(s) (esp. of domestic animals). [earlier *brinded*, *brended* f. *brend*, perh. of Scand. orig.]

■ see *speckled* (SPECKLE *v.*).

brine /brin/ *n. & v.* ● *n.* **1** water saturated with or strongly impregnated with salt. **2** sea water. ● *v.tr.* soak in or saturate with brine. [OE *brīne*, of unkn. orig.]

bring /bring/ *v.tr.* (*past* and *past part.* **brought** /brawt/) **1 a** come conveying esp. by carrying or leading. **b** come with. **2** cause to come or be present (*what brings you here?*). **3** cause or result in (*war brings misery*). **4** be sold for; produce as income. **5 a** prefer (a charge). **b** initiate (legal action). **6** cause to become or to reach a particular state (*brings me alive*; *brought them to their senses*; *cannot bring myself to agree*). **7** adduce (evidence, an argument, etc.). □ **bring about 1** cause to happen. **2** turn (a ship) around. **bring-and-buy sale** *Brit.* a kind of charity sale at which participants bring items for sale and buy what is brought by others. **bring around 1** restore to consciousness. **2** persuade. **bring back** call to mind. **bring down 1** cause to fall. **2** lower (a price). **3** *sl.* make unhappy or less happy. **4** *colloq.* damage the reputation of; demean. **bring forth 1** give birth to. **2** produce; emit; cause. **bring forward 1** move to an earlier date or time. **2** transfer from the previous page or account. **3** draw attention to; adduce. **bring home to** cause to realize fully (*brought home to me that I was wrong*). **bring the house down** receive rapturous applause. **bring in 1** introduce (legislation, a custom, fashion, topic, etc.). **2** yield or earn

as income or profit. **bring into play** cause to operate; activate. **bring low** overcome. **bring off** achieve successfully. **bring on 1** cause to happen or appear. **2** accelerate the progress of. **bring out 1** emphasize; make evident. **2** publish. **bring over** convert to one's own side. **bring through** aid (a person) through adversity, esp. illness. **bring to 1** restore to consciousness (*brought him to*). **2** check the motion of. **bring to bear** (usu. foll. by *on*) direct and concentrate (forces). **bring to light** reveal; disclose. **bring to mind** recall; cause one to remember. **bring to pass** cause to happen. **bring under** subdue. **bring up 1** rear (a child). **2** vomit; regurgitate. **3** call attention to; broach. **4** (*absol.*) stop suddenly. **bring upon oneself** be responsible for (something one suffers). □□ **bringer** *n.* [OE *bringan* f. Gmc]

■ **1 a** bring along, carry, bear, transport, fetch, take (along), convey, *colloq.* tote. **b** bring along, escort, invite, accompany, take (along); see, usher, show, conduct, lead. **2** lead, draw, direct, attract, lure, allure, entice. **3** result in, lead to, bring on, bring about, occasion, give rise to, be the source *or* cause of, create, cause, spark *or* trigger (off), set off, produce, *archaic* engender; contribute to. **4** see *bring in* 2 below. **5 a** see PREFER 2. **b** see INITIATE *v.* 1. **7** see QUOTE *v.* 1. □ **bring about 1** occasion, cause, give rise to, bring (on), spark *or* trigger (off), set off, induce; accomplish, effect, effectuate, achieve, engineer, produce. **bring down 1** overthrow, depose, oust, unseat, dethrone, overturn; see also TOPPLE 1b. **2** decrease, reduce, lower, drop, mark down, diminish, cut, cut back *or* down (on), slash, *colloq.* knock down. **3** see DEPRESS 2. **4** see MORTIFY 1. **bring forth 1** bear, give birth to, bring into the world, spawn, procreate, have, deliver, *archaic* engender, *literary* beget; yield, produce, generate, put out *or* forth. **2** produce, set forth, bring out *or* in *or* up, introduce, present, put out, submit, offer, advance; see also CAUSE *v.* 1, EMIT 1. **bring forward 1** advance. **3** see *bring up* 3 below. **bring home to** make a person realize *or* be aware, impress upon, drive home to, make clear to, stress *or* emphasize to. **bring in 1** see INTRODUCE 3, 7. **2** earn, reap, make, pocket, return, net, yield, produce; fetch, sell for, get, bring, pick up. **bring into play** see ACTIVATE 1, USE *v.* 1a. **bring low** see PROSTRATE *v.* 3. **bring off** succeed (in), achieve, accomplish, do, carry out *or* off, perform, pull off; put over. **bring on 1** produce, introduce, bring in *or* out; see also *bring about* 1 above. **2** see HASTEN 2. **bring out 1** emphasize, focus on, make noticeable *or* conspicuous *or* evident, display, feature, illuminate, reveal, show up, throw up. **2** publish, issue, release, put *or* turn out, come out with, make known *or* public, produce, launch; put on, stage. **bring around 1** revive, resuscitate, bring to; restore. **2** persuade, win over, sway, convince, convert. **bring to 1** see *bring around* 1 above. **bring to bear** see EXERT 1. **bring to mind** see RECALL *v.* 2. **bring up 1** rear, raise, care for, look after, nurture, breed, mother, parent; educate, teach, train, tutor. **2** vomit, throw up, regurgitate, disgorge, spew up, *Brit. colloq.* sick up, *sl.* puke (up). **3** introduce, broach, bring in, raise, call attention to, mention, touch on, talk about, voice, discuss, suggest, allude to, moot, set forth. **bring upon oneself** be responsible *or* to blame for, ask for, invite, attract, provoke, court; bring about one's ears; be at fault for.

brinjal /brínjəl/ *n.* (in India and Africa) an eggplant. [ult. Port. *berinjela* formed as AUBERGINE]

brink /bringk/ *n.* **1** the extreme edge of land before a precipice, river, etc., esp. when a sudden drop follows. **2** the furthest point before something dangerous or exciting is discovered. □ **on the brink** of about to experience or suffer; in imminent danger of. [ME f. ON: orig. unkn.]

■ **1** edge, brim, rim, margin, lip, border. □ **on the brink of** on the threshold *or* point *or* verge of, within an ace of, close *or* near to, approaching; about to, at *or* on the point of.

brinkmanship /bríngkmənship/ *n.* the art or policy of pursuing a dangerous course to the brink of catastrophe before desisting.

briny /brínee/ *adj. & n.* ● *adj.* (**brinier, briniest**) of brine or the sea; salty. ● *n.* (prec. by *the*) *Brit. sl.* the sea. □□ **brininess** *n.*
■ *adj.* see SALT *adj.* ● *n.* see SEA 1.

brio /brée-ō/ *n.* dash; vigor; vivacity. [It.]
■ see VERVE.

brioche /brēe´ōsh, bré´e ōōsh, ōōsh/ *n.* a small rounded sweet roll made with a light yeast dough. [F]

briquette /brikét/ *n.* (also **briquet**) a block of compressed coal dust or charcoal used as fuel. [F *briquette*, dimin. of *brique* brick]

brisk /brisk/ *adj. & v.* ● *adj.* **1** quick; lively (*a brisk pace; brisk trade*). **2** enlivening; fresh (*a brisk wind*). **3** curt; peremptory (*a brisk manner*). ● *v.tr. & intr.* (often foll. by *up*) make or grow brisk. □□ **briskly** *adv.* **briskness** *n.* [prob. F *brusque* BRUSQUE]
■ *adj.* **1** active, lively, busy, vigorous, bustling, vibrant; quick, fast, prompt, rapid, smart, snappy, speedy, swift, keen, expeditious; animated, sprightly, spry, energetic, spirited, jaunty. **2** breezy, strong, steady, fresh, refreshing, bracing, invigorating, stimulating, enlivening, vitalizing, energizing; crisp, biting, keen, sharp, chilly, cool, cold, *colloq.* nippy, *literary* chill. □□ **briskly** see FAST¹ *adv.* 1.

brisket /brískit/ *n.* an animal's breast, esp. as a cut of meat. [AF f. OF *bruschet*, perh. f. ON]

brisling /brízling, brís-/ *n.* a small herring or sprat. [Norw. & Da., = sprat]

bristle /brísəl/ *n. & v.* ● *n.* **1** a short stiff hair, esp. one of those on an animal's back. **2** this, or an artificial substitute, used in clumps to make a brush. ● *v.* **1 a** *intr.* (of the hair) stand upright, esp. in anger or pride. **b** *tr.* make (the hair) do this. **2** *intr.* show irritation or defensiveness. **3** *intr.* (usu. foll. by *with*) be covered or abundant (in). [ME *bristel, brestel* f. OE *byrst*]
■ *n.* **1** hair, whisker(s); *Bot. & Zool.* seta. ● *v.* **1** rise, stand up. **2** draw oneself up, take offense *or* umbrage (at); seethe, foam at the mouth, be angry *or* infuriated *or* furious *or* maddened, get *or* have one's hackles up, boil, flare up, rage, storm, see red, bridle. **3** teem, crawl, swarm, throng, be thick *or* crowded *or* packed *or* jammed, be infested, be alive, abound, be abundant *or* rich *or* covered.

bristletail /brísəltayl/ *n.* = SILVERFISH.

bristly /bríslee/ *adj.* (**bristlier, bristliest**) full of bristles; rough; prickly.
■ see PRICKLY 1.

Bristol board /bríst´l/ *n.* a kind of fine smooth pasteboard for drawing on. [*Bristol* in S. England]

Bristol fashion /bríst´l/ *n.* (functioning as *predic.adj.*) *Brit.* (in full **shipshape and Bristol fashion**) orig. *Naut.* with all in good order.

bristols /brístəlz/ *n.pl. Brit. coarse sl.* a woman's breasts. [rhyming sl. f. *Bristol cities* = titties]

Brit /brit/ *n. colloq.* a British person. [abbr.]

Brit. *abbr.* **1** British. **2** Britain.

Britannia /britányə/ *n.* the personification of Britain, esp. as a helmeted woman with shield and trident. □ **Britannia metal** a silvery alloy of tin, antimony, and copper. [L f. Gk *Brettania* f. *Brettanoi* Britons]

Britannic /británik/ *adj.* (esp. in **His (or Her) Britannic Majesty**) of Britain. [L *Britannicus* (as BRITANNIA)]

Briticism /brítisizəm/ *n.* (also **Britishism** /-tishizəm/) an idiom used in Britain but not in other English-speaking countries. [BRITISH, after GALLICISM]

British /brítish/ *adj. & n.* ● *adj.* **1** of or relating to Great Britain or the United Kingdom, or to its people or language. **2** of the British Commonwealth or (formerly) the British Empire (*British subject*). ● *n.* **1** (prec. by *the*; treated as *pl.*) the British people. **2** = *British English*. □ **British English** English as used in Great Britain, as distinct from that used elsewhere. **British thermal unit** see THERMAL. □□ **Britishness** *n.* [OE *Brettisc*, etc., f. *Bret* f. L *Britto* or OCelt.]

Britisher /brítishər/ *n.* a British subject, esp. of British descent. ¶ Not used in British English.

Britishism var. of BRITICISM.

Briton /brítən/ *n.* **1** one of the people of S. Britain before the Roman conquest. **2** a native or inhabitant of Great Britain or (formerly) of the British Empire. [ME & OF *Breton* f. L *Britto -onis* f. OCelt.]

brittle /brít´l/ *adj. & n.* ● *adj.* **1** hard and fragile; apt to break. **2** frail; weak; unstable. ● *n.* a brittle confection made from nuts and hardened melted sugar. □ **brittle-bone disease** = OSTEOPOROSIS. **brittle star** an echinoderm of the class Ophiuroidea, with long brittle arms radiating from a small central body. □□ **brittlely** *adv.* **brittleness** *n.* **brittly** *adv.* [ME ult. f. a Gmc root rel. to OE *brēotan* break up]
■ *adj.* **1** fragile, frangible, breakable, delicate; friable. **2** frail, weak, delicate, sensitive, insecure, unstable.

bro. *abbr.* brother.

broach /brōch/ *v. & n.* ● *v.tr.* **1** raise (a subject) for discussion. **2** pierce (a cask) to draw liquor, etc. **3** open and start using contents of (a box, bale, bottle, etc.). **4** begin drawing (liquor, etc.). ● *n.* **1** a bit for boring. **2** a roasting spit. □ **broach spire** an octagonal church spire rising from a square tower without a parapet. [ME f. OF *broche* (n.), *brocher* (v.) f. L *brocc(h)us* projecting]
■ *v.* **1** introduce, raise, open (up), venture, put *or* bring forward, suggest, mention, moot, voice, hint at, touch on *or* upon, bring up *or* in, talk about, advance.

broad /brawd/ *adj. & n.* ● *adj.* **1** large in extent from one side to the other; wide. **2** (following a measurement) in breadth (*2 meters broad*). **3** spacious or extensive (*broad acres; a broad plain*). **4** full and clear (*broad daylight*). **5** explicit; unmistakable (*broad hint*). **6** general; not taking account of detail (*broad intentions; a broad inquiry; in the broadest sense of the word*). **7** chief or principal (*the broad facts*). **8** tolerant; liberal (*take a broad view*). **9** somewhat coarse (*broad humor*). **10** (of speech) markedly regional (*broad Brooklyn accent*). ● *n.* **1** the broad part of something (*broad of the back*). **2** *sl.* a woman. **3** *Brit.* (**the Broads**) large areas of fresh water in E. Anglia, formed where rivers widen. □ **broad arrow** see ARROW. **broad bean 1** a kind of bean, *Vicia faba*, with pods containing large edible flat seeds. **2** one of these seeds. **Broad Church** esp. *Brit.* a group within the Anglican Church favoring a liberal interpretation of doctrine. **broad-gauge** a railway track with a gauge wider than the standard one. **broad-leaved** (of a tree) deciduous and hard-timbered. **broad-minded** tolerant or liberal in one's views. **broad pennant** a short swallow-tailed pennant distinguishing the commodore's ship in a squadron. **broad spectrum** (of a medicinal substance) effective against a large variety of microorganisms. □□ **broad-mindedly** *adv.* **broad-mindedness** *n.* **broadness** *n.* **broadways** *adv.* **broadwise** *adv.* [OE *brād* f. Gmc]
■ *adj.* **2** in breadth, in width, wide. **3** wide, expansive, wide-ranging, large, extensive, spacious, sweeping, sizable, spread out, far-reaching, ample. **4** clear, bright, plain, open, full, complete, undiminished, pure, total. **5** plain, clear, obvious, unmistakable, explicit, direct, unconcealed, undisguised, unsubtle, overt, bald, bald-faced, self-evident. **6** general, generalized, basic, overall, sweeping, rough, approximate; imprecise, unspecific, nonspecific, unfocused. **7** see MAIN¹ *adj.* 1. **8** liberal, tolerant, catholic, ecumenical, latitudinarian, open-minded, broad-minded, unprejudiced, undogmatic, enlightened. **9** dirty, blue, coarse, rude, indecent, vulgar, improper, indelicate, gross, obscene, lewd, lascivious, filthy, pornographic; inelegant, unrefined, unladylike, ungentlemanly. ● *n.* **2** woman, girl, *sl.* chick, doll, petticoat, dame, cookie, babe, *Austral. & NZ sl.* sheila, *Brit. sl.* bird, *sl. offens.* (bit of)

/.../ **pronunciation**	● **part of speech**
□ **phrases, idioms, and compounds**	
□□ **derivatives**	■ **synonym section**
cross-references appear in SMALL CAPITALS or *italics*	

skirt, *derog. sl.* piece (of baggage). □ **broad-minded** see LIBERAL *adj.* 3.

broadcast /bráwdkast/ *v., n., adj.,* & *adv.* ● *v.* (*past* **broadcast** or **broadcasted**; *past part.* **broadcast**) **1** *tr.* **a** transmit (programs or information) by radio or television. **b** disseminate (information) widely. **2** *intr.* undertake or take part in a radio or television transmission. **3** *tr.* scatter (seed, etc.) over a large area, esp. by hand. ● *n.* **a** radio or television program or transmission. ● *adj.* **1** transmitted by radio or television. **2 a** scattered widely. **b** (of information, etc.) widely disseminated. ● *adv.* over a large area. □□ **broadcaster** *n.* **broadcasting** *n.* [BROAD + CAST *past part.*]
■ *v.* **1 a** air, transmit, relay; radio; screen, televise, telecast. **b** announce, advertise, circulate, publish, proclaim, pronounce; put *or* give out, report; disseminate. **3** sow, scatter, strew, seed, litter, sprinkle, disperse, disseminate. ● *n.* program, show; transmission, telecast. □□ **broadcaster** see ANNOUNCER.
broadcloth /bráwdklawth, -kloth/ *n.* a fine cloth of wool, cotton, or silk. [orig. with ref. to width and quality]
broaden /bráwdən/ *v.tr.* & *intr.* make or become broader.
■ see WIDEN.
broadloom /bráwdlōōm/ *adj.* (esp. of carpet) woven in broad widths.
broadly /bráwdlee/ *adv.* in a broad manner; widely (*grinned broadly*). □ **broadly speaking** disregarding minor exceptions.
■ □ **broadly speaking** see GENERALLY 2.
broadsheet /bráwdsheet/ *n.* **1** a large sheet of paper printed on one side only, esp. with information. **2** *Brit.* a newspaper with a large format.
broadside /bráwdsīd/ *n.* **1** the firing of all guns from one side of a ship. **2** a vigorous verbal onslaught. **3** the side of a ship above the water between the bow and quarter. **4** = BROADSHEET. □ **broadside on** sideways on.
broadsword /bráwdsawrd/ *n.* a sword with a broad blade, for cutting rather than thrusting.
broadtail /bráwdtayl/ *n.* **1** the karakul sheep. **2** the fleece or wool from its lamb.
broadway /bráwdway/ *n.* **1** a large open or main road. **2** (as **Broadway**) a principal thoroughfare in New York City, noted for its theaters, and the center of U.S. commercial theater production.
brocade /brōkáyd/ *n.* & *v.* ● *n.* a rich fabric with a silky finish woven with a raised pattern, and often with gold or silver thread. ● *v.tr.* weave with this design. [Sp. & Port. *brocado* f. It. *broccato* f. *brocco* twisted thread]
broccoli /brókəlee/ *n.* **1** a vegetable related to cabbage with a loose cluster of greenish flower buds. **2** the flower stalk and head used as a vegetable. [It., pl. of *broccolo* dimin. of *brocco* sprout]
broch /brok, brokh, brukh/ *n.* (in Scotland) a prehistoric circular stone tower. [ON *borg* castle]
brochette /brōshét/ *n.* a skewer on which chunks of meat are cooked, esp. over an open fire. [F, dimin. of *broche* BROACH]
brochure /brōshōōr/ *n.* a pamphlet or leaflet, esp. one giving descriptive information. [F, lit. 'stitching,' f. *brocher* stitch]
■ pamphlet, leaflet, booklet, insert, catalog, folder.
brock /brok/ *n. Brit.* (esp. in rural use) a badger. [OE *broc(c)* f. OBrit. *brokkos*]
brocket /brókit/ *n.* any small deer of the genus *Mazama,* native to Central and S. America, having short straight antlers. [ME f. AF *broque* (= *broche* BROACH)]
brogue¹ /brōg/ *n.* **1** a strong outdoor shoe with ornamental perforated bands. **2** a rough shoe of untanned leather. [Gael. & Ir. *brōg* f. ON *brók*]
brogue² /brōg/ *n.* a marked dialect or accent, esp. Irish. [18th c.: orig. unkn.: perh. allusively f. BROGUE¹]
■ see DIALECT 1.
broil¹ /broyl/ *v.* **1** *tr.* cook (meat) on a rack or a grill. **2** *tr.* & *intr.* make or become very hot, esp. from the sun. [ME f. OF *bruler* burn f. Rmc]
■ **1** grill, barbecue, griddle, frizzle; cook. **2** swelter, roast, *colloq.* bake, sizzle, boil, fry, scorch.

broil² /broyl/ *n.* a brawl; a tumult. [obs. *broil* to muddle: cf. EMBROIL]
broiler /bróylər/ *n.* **1** a young chicken raised for broiling or roasting. **2 a** a device or oven setting on a stove for radiating heat downward. **b** a grill, griddle, etc., for broiling. **3** *colloq.* a very hot day.
broke /brōk/ *past* of BREAK¹. ● *predic.adj. colloq.* having no money; financially ruined. □ **go for broke** *sl.* risk everything in a strenuous effort. [(adj.) archaic past part. of BREAK¹]
■ penniless, indigent, down and out, poverty-stricken, penurious, impoverished, insolvent, destitute, poor, needy, bankrupt, ruined, on one's beam-ends, close to the bone, hard up, *Austral.* unfinancial, *colloq.* on one's uppers, strapped (for cash), flat broke, stony-broke, up against it, on the skids, *Brit. sl.* skint, stone- *or* (be *broke*) not have a penny to one's name, not have a shot in one's locker, not have a (red) cent, *Brit. colloq.* not have a brass farthing. □ **go for broke** throw caution to the wind, take one's life in one's hands, give one's all, *colloq.* go for it, go all out.
broken /brōkən/ *past part.* of BREAK¹. ● *adj.* **1** that has been broken; out of order. **2** (of a person) reduced to despair; beaten. **3** (of a language or of speech) spoken falteringly and with many mistakes, as by a foreigner (*broken English*). **4** disturbed; interrupted (*broken time*). **5** uneven (*broken ground*). **6** (of an animal) trained to obey; tamed. **7** transgressed; not observed (*broken rules*). □ **broken chord** *Mus.* a chord in which the notes are played successively. **brokendown 1** worn out by age, use, or maltreatment. **2** out of order. **broken home** a family in which the parents are divorced or separated. **broken reed** a person who has become unreliable or ineffective. **broken wind** heaves (see HEAVE *n.* 3). **broken-winded** (of a horse) disabled by ruptured air cells in the lungs. □□ **brokenly** *adv.* **brokenness** *n.*
■ **1** fragmented, shattered, shivered, splintered, ruptured, cracked, fractured, split, smashed; broken-down, out of order *or* commission, not working *or* functioning, in (a state of) disrepair, in pieces, inoperative, faulty, malfunctioning, out of kilter, failed, *colloq.* bust, busted, *sl.* on the blink, kaput, dud, *sl.* on the fritz, out of whack. **2** enfeebled, weakened, crushed, defeated, beaten, ruined; dispirited, dejected, discouraged, demoralized, subdued, debilitated, *colloq.* licked. **3** shaky, unsteady, faltering, wobbly, hesitant, halting, stumbling; poor, faulty. **4** interrupted, disturbed, discontinuous, disjointed, disconnected, fragmented, fragmentary, intermittent, erratic, sporadic. **5** see BUMPY 1. **6** tamed, trained, disciplined, obedient, docile, domesticated, subdued; housebroken, esp. *Brit.* house-trained; conditioned. **7** violated, transgressed, disobeyed, contravened, defied, flouted, disregarded, ignored, infringed. □ **broken-down 1** worn out, worn, decrepit, aging, effete, raddled, toilworn, timeworn, *Brit. sl.* clapped-out; delapidated, ramshackle, tumbledown, crumbling, run-down, down at heel; see also BEAT *adj.*, BROKEN 2 above. **2** see BROKEN 1 above.
brokenhearted /brōkənhaártid/ *adj.* overwhelmed with sorrow or grief. □□ **brokenheartedness** *n.*
■ heartbroken, depressed, downhearted, dejected, devastated, crushed, desolate, overwhelmed, heartsick, downcast, cast down, upset, forlorn, sorrowful, disconsolate, inconsolable, grief-stricken, miserable, wretched, melancholy, heavyhearted, sad, doleful, woeful, woebegone, gloomy, morose, glum, cheerless, down, *archaic* stricken, *literary or joc.* dolorous.
□□ **brokenheartedness** see GRIEF 1.
broker /brōkər/ *n.* **1** an agent who buys and sells for others; an intermediary. **2** a member of the stock exchange dealing in stocks and bonds. **3** *Brit.* an official appointed to sell or appraise distrained goods. [ME f. AF *brocour,* of unkn. orig.]
■ **1** agent, dealer, merchant, trader, factor, wholesaler, middleman, intermediary, mediator, go-between, contact, negotiator, jobber, *Brit.* stockjobber, scrivener. **2** broker-dealer, stockbroker, *derog.* stockjobber, *Brit.derog.* jobber.

brokerage /brṓkərij/ *n.* **1** a broker's fee or commission. **2** a broker's business.

brokering /brṓkəring/ *n.* (also *Brit.* **broking** /brṓking/) the trade or business of a broker.

brolga /brólgə/ *n. Austral.* a large Australian crane, *Grus rubicunda*, with a booming call. [Aboriginal]

brolly /brólee/ *n.* (*pl.* **-ies**) *Brit.* **1** *colloq.* an umbrella. **2** *sl.* a parachute. [abbr.]

bromate /brṓmayt/ *n. Chem.* a salt or ester of bromic acid.

brome /brōm/ *n.* (also **bromegrass**) any oatlike grass of the genus *Bromus*, having slender stems with flowering spikes. [mod.L *Bromus* f. Gk *bromos* oat]

bromeliad /brōmeéleead/ *n.* any plant of the family Bromeliaceae (esp. of the genus *Bromelia*), native to the New World, having short stems with rosettes of stiff usu. spiny leaves, e.g., pineapple. [O. *Bromel,* Sw. botanist d. 1705]

bromic /brṓmik/ *adj. Chem.* of or containing bromine. □ **bromic acid** a strong acid used as an oxidizing agent.

bromide /brṓmīd/ *n.* **1** *Chem.* any binary compound of bromine. **2** *Pharm.* a preparation of usu. potassium bromide, used as a sedative. **3** a trite remark. □ **bromide paper** a photographic printing paper coated with silver bromide emulsion.

■ **2** see TRANQUILIZER. **3** see TRUISM.

bromine /brṓmeen/ *n. Chem.* a dark fuming liquid element with a choking irritating smell, extracted from bittern and used in the manufacture of chemicals for photography and medicine. ¶ Symb.: **Br.** □□ **bromism** *n.* [F *brome* f. Gk *brōmos* stink]

bromo- /brṓmō/ *comb. form Chem.* bromine.

bronc /brongk/ *n. colloq.* = BRONCO. [abbr.]

bronchi *pl.* of BRONCHUS.

bronchial /bróngkeeəl/ *adj.* of or relating to the bronchi or bronchioles. □ **bronchial tree** the branching system of bronchi and bronchioles conducting air from the windpipe to the lungs. **bronchial tube** a bronchus or any tube branching from it.

bronchiole /bróngkeeōl/ *n.* any of the minute divisions of a bronchus. □□ **bronchiolar** /-ṓlər, -kíə-/ *adj.*

bronchitis /brongkítis/ *n.* inflammation of the mucous membrane in the bronchial tubes. □□ **bronchitic** /-kítik/ *adj.* & *n.*

broncho- /bróngkō/ *comb. form* bronchi.

bronchocele /bróngkəseel/ *n.* a goiter.

bronchopneumonia /bróngkōnōōmṓnyə, -nyōō-/ *n.* inflammation of the lungs, arising in the bronchi or bronchioles.

bronchoscope /bróngkəskōp/ *n.* a usu. fiber-optic instrument for inspecting the bronchi. □□ **bronchoscopy** /-kóskəpee/ *n.*

bronchus /bróngkəs/ *n.* (*pl.* **bronchi** /-ki/) any of the major air passages of the lungs, esp. either of the two main divisions of the windpipe. [LL f. Gk *brogkhos* windpipe]

bronco /bróngkō/ *n.* (*pl.* **-os**) a wild or half-tamed horse of western N. America. [Sp., = rough]

broncobuster /bróngkōbustər/ *n.* a person who breaks wild horses.

brontosaurus /bróntəsáwrəs/ *n.* (also **brontosaur** /bróntəsawr/) a large plant-eating dinosaur of the genus *Brontosaurus*, with a long whiplike tail and trunk-like legs. Now more correctly APATOSAURUS. [Gk *brontē* thunder + *sauros* lizard]

Bronx cheer /brongks/ *n. colloq.* = RASPBERRY 3a. [*Bronx*, a borough of New York City]

bronze /bronz/ *n., adj.,* & *v.* ● *n.* **1** any alloy of copper and tin. **2** its brownish color. **3** a thing made of bronze, esp. as a work of art. ● *adj.* made of or colored like bronze. ● *v.* **1** *tr.* give a bronzelike surface to. **2** *tr.* & *intr.* make or become brown; tan. □ **Bronze Age** *Archaeol.* the period preceding the Iron Age, when weapons and tools were usu. made of bronze. **bronze medal** a medal usu. awarded to a competitor who comes in third in a meet, etc. □□ **bronzy** *adj.* [F f. It. *bronzo*, prob. f. Pers. *birinj* copper]

■ *n.* **3** see SCULPTURE. ● *v.* **2** see SUN *v.*

brooch /brōch, brōōch/ *n.* an ornament fastened to clothing with a hinged pin. [ME *broche* = BROACH *n.*]

■ clasp, pin, badge; fastening, clip.

brood /brōōd/ *n.* & *v.* ● *n.* **1** the young of an animal (esp. a bird) produced at one hatching or birth. **2** *colloq.* the children in a family. **3** a group of related things. **4** bee or wasp larvae. **5** (*attrib.*) kept for breeding (*broodmare*). ● *v.* **1** *intr.* (often foll. by *on, over,* etc.) worry or ponder (esp. resentfully). **2 a** *intr.* sit as a hen on eggs to hatch them. **b** *tr.* sit on (eggs) to hatch them. **3** *intr.* (usu. foll. by *over*) (of silence, a storm, etc.) hang or hover closely. □□ **broodingly** *adv.* [OE *brōd* f. Gmc]

■ *n.* **1** young, offspring, litter, progeny, issue, progeniture, *archaic* seed, *derog.* spawn. **2** children, family, *colloq.* kids, *derog.* spawn. **3** see SET² *n.* 1, 2, 7. ● *v.* **1** ponder, deliberate, reflect, meditate, ruminate, *literary* muse; mope, sulk, be sullen or moody or resentful, harbor a grudge, get or be worked up, eat one's heart out, fret, worry; (*brood over*) mull over. **2 b** incubate, hatch, sit on, cover. **3** see LOOM² *v.* 2.

brooder /brṓōdər/ *n.* **1** a heated house for chicks, piglets, etc. **2** a person who broods.

broody /brṓōdee/ *adj.* (**broodier, broodiest**) **1** (of a hen) wanting to brood. **2** sullenly thoughtful or depressed. **3** *Brit. colloq.* (of a woman) wanting to have a baby. □□ **broodily** *adv.* **broodiness** *n.*

■ **2** see MOODY *adj.*

brook¹ /brŏŏk/ *n.* a small stream. □ **brook trout** the speckled trout (*Salvelinus fontinalis*), a game fish of N. America. □□ **brooklet** /-lət/ *n.* [OE *brōc*, of unkn. orig.]

■ stream, rivulet, brooklet, streamlet, runlet, runnel, rill, run, creek, bourn, *Brit.* gill, *No. of Engl.* beck, *Sc.* burn.

brook² /brŏŏk/ *v.tr.* (usu. with *neg.*) *formal* tolerate; allow. [OE *brūcan* f. Gmc]

■ endure, tolerate, stand, abide, put up with, support, bear, stomach; see also ALLOW 1.

brooklime /brŏŏklīm/ *n.* a kind of speedwell, *Veronica beccabunga*, growing in wet areas.

brookweed /brŏŏkweed/ *n.* a small herb, *Samolus valerandi*, having slender stems with tiny white flowers and growing in wet places.

broom /brōōm, brŏŏm/ *n.* **1** a long-handled brush of bristles, twigs, etc., for sweeping (orig. one made of twigs of broom). **2** any of various shrubs, esp. *Cytisus scoparius* bearing bright yellow flowers. □ **new broom** a newly appointed person eager to make changes. [OE *brōm*]

■ **1** brush, besom.

broomrape /brŏŏmrayp, brōōm-/ *n.* any parasitic plant of the genus *Orobanche*, with tubular flowers on a leafless brown stem, and living on the roots of broom and similar plants. [BROOM + L *rapum* tuber]

broomstick /brŏŏmstik, brōōm-/ *n.* the handle of a broom, esp. as allegedly ridden on through the air by witches.

Bros. *abbr.* Brothers (esp. in the name of a business).

brose /brōz/ *n.* esp. *Sc. Cookery* a dish of oatmeal with boiling water or milk poured on it. [Sc. form of *brewis* broth: ME f. OF *bro(u)ez*, ult. f. Gmc]

broth /brawth, broth/ *n.* **1** *Cookery* **a** a thin soup of meat or fish stock. **b** unclarified meat, fish or vegetable stock. **2** *Biol.* meat stock as a nutrient medium for bacteria. [OE f. Gmc: rel. to BREW]

■ **1** stock, consommé, decoction, liquor; soup, bouillon, chowder, potage, pot-au-feu, *archaic* pottage.

brothel /bróthəl/ *n.* a house, etc., where prostitution takes place. [orig. *brothel house* f. ME *brothel* worthless man, prostitute, f. OE *brēothan* go to ruin]

■ whorehouse, bawdy house, bagnio, bordello, house, sporting house, *archaic* house of ill fame or ill repute, stews, *euphem.* massage parlor.

/. . ./ **pronunciation**	● **part of speech**
□ **phrases, idioms, and compounds**	
□□ **derivatives**	■ **synonym section**
cross-references appear in SMALL CAPITALS or *italics*	

brother /brúthər/ n. **1** a man or boy in relation to other sons and daughters of his parents. **2 a** (often as a form of address) a close male friend or associate. **b** a male fellow member of a labor union, etc. **3** (pl. also **brethren** /bréthrin/) **a** a member of a male religious order, esp. a monk. **b** a fellow member of a congregation, a religion, or (formerly) a guild, etc. **4** a fellow human being. □ **brother german** see GERMAN. **brother-in-law** (pl. **brothers-in-law**) **1** the brother of one's wife or husband. **2** the husband of one's sister. **3** the husband of one's sister-in-law. **brother uterine** see UTERINE 2. □□ **brotherless** adj. **brotherly** adj. & adv. **brotherliness** n. [OE brōthor f. Gmc]

■ **1** sibling; cousin, relation, relative, kin, kinsman. **2, 4** fellow, fellowman, fellow citizen, fellow countryman, fellow creature; associate, colleague, confrère, comrade, comrade in arms, fellow worker, coworker, companion; mate, friend, colloq. pal, chum, buddy, homeboy, amigo, Austral. & NZ colloq. cobber. **3 a** see MONK. □□ **brotherly** fraternal, neighborly, comradely, loyal, devoted, kind, affectionate, cordial, friendly, amicable, amiable, congenial, convivial, loving, esp. Brit. matey, colloq. chummy, pally.

brotherhood /brúthərhŏŏd/ n. **1 a** the relationship between brothers. **b** brotherly friendliness; companionship. **2 a** an association, society, or community of people linked by a common interest, religion, business, etc. **b** its members collectively. **3** a labor union. **4** community of feeling between all human beings. [ME alt. f. brotherrede f. OE brōthor-ræden (cf. KINDRED) after words in -HOOD, -HEAD]

■ **1 b** brotherliness, fellowship, companionship, alliance, friendship, comradeship, camaraderie, kinship, amity. **2** fraternity, confraternity, guild, society, association, order, league, union, organization, syndicate, club, clan, community, circle, set, clique. **3** union, labor union, Brit. trade(s) union. **4** harmony, love, affinity, sympathy, togetherness, communality, accord, unity.

brougham /brŏŏəm, brŏŏm, brŏəm/ n. hist. **1** a horse-drawn closed carriage with a driver perched outside in front. **2** an automobile with an open driver's seat. [Lord Brougham, d. 1868]

brought past and past part. of BRING.

brouhaha /brŏŏhaahaa/ n. commotion; sensation; hubbub; uproar. [F]

■ see UPROAR.

brow /brow/ n. **1** the forehead. **2** (usu. in pl.) an eyebrow. **3** the summit of a hill or pass. **4** the edge of a cliff, etc. **5** colloq. intellectual level. □□ **browed** adj. [OE brū f. Gmc]

browbeat /brówbeet/ v.tr. (past **-beat**; past part. **-beaten**) intimidate with stern looks and words. □□ **browbeater** n.

■ bully, persecute, torment, intimidate, threaten, badger, cow, frighten, tyrannize, terrorize, hector, harass, hound, dog, plague, keep after, nag, colloq. hassle.

brown /brown/ adj., n., & v. ● adj. **1** having the color produced by mixing red, yellow, and black, as of dark wood or rich soil. **2** dark-skinned or suntanned. **3** (of bread) made from a dark flour such as whole wheat. **4** (of species or varieties) distinguished by brown coloration. ● n. **1** a brown color or pigment. **2** brown clothes or material (dressed in brown). **3** (in a game or sport) a brown ball, piece, etc. **4** (prec. by the) Brit. a brown mass of flying game birds. ● v.tr. & intr. make or become brown by cooking, sunburn, etc. □ **brown ale** Brit. a dark, mild, bottled beer. **brown bagging 1** taking one's lunch to work, etc., in a brown paper bag. **2** taking one's own liquor, wine etc., into a restaurant that is not licensed to serve alcohol. **brown bear** a large N. American brown bear, Ursus arctos. **brown bread 1** a bread made with a dark flour, as whole-wheat or rye. **2** a steamed bread made of cornmeal, molasses, flour, etc. **brown coal** = LIGNITE. **brown dwarf** a dark dwarf star with insufficient mass for nuclear fusion. **browned off** sl. fed up; disheartened. **brown fat** a dark-colored adipose tissue with a rich supply of blood vessels. **brown holland** see HOLLAND. **brown owl 1** any of various owls, esp. the tawny owl. **brown rat** = NORWAY RAT. **brown rice** unpolished rice with only the husk of the grain removed. **Brown shirt** a Nazi; a

member of a fascist organization. **brown sugar** unrefined or partially refined sugar. **brown trout** a common trout, Salmo trutta, of northern Europe. **in a brown study** see STUDY. □□ **brownish** adj. **brownness** n. **browny** adj. [OE brūn f. Gmc]

■ adj. **2** see DARK adj. 3. ● v. see SUN v.

Brownian motion /brównian/ n. (also **Brownian movement**) Physics the erratic random movement of microscopic particles in a liquid, gas, etc., as a result of continuous bombardment from molecules of the surrounding medium. [R. Brown, Sc. botanist d. 1858]

Brownie /brównee/ n. **1** a member of the junior branch of the Girl Scouts. **2** (**brownie**) Cookery **a** a small square of rich, usu. chocolate, cake with nuts. **b** Austral. & NZ a sweet currant bread. **3** (**brownie**) a benevolent elf said to haunt houses and do household work secretly. □ **Brownie point** colloq. a notional credit for something done to please or win favor.

browning /brówning/ n. Brit. Cookery browned flour or any other additive to color gravy.

brownnose /brównnōz/ v. tr. coarse sl. ingratiate oneself; be servile.

brownnoser /brównnōzər/ n. coarse sl. a toady; a yes-man.

brownout /brównowt/ n. a period during which electrical voltage is reduced to avoid a blackout, resulting in lowered illumination.

brownstone /brównstōn/ n. **1** a kind of reddish brown sandstone used for building. **2** a building faced with this.

browse /browz/ v. & n. ● v. **1** intr. & tr. read or survey desultorily. **2** intr. (often foll. by on) feed (on leaves, twigs, or scanty vegetation). **3** tr. crop and eat. ● n. **1** twigs, young shoots, etc., as fodder for cattle. **2** an act of browsing. □□ **browser** n. [(n.) f. earlier brouse f. OF brost young shoot, prob. f. Gmc; (v.) f. F broster]

■ v. **1** (tr.) look over or through, skim (through), scan, run one's eye over, thumb or flip or flick or leaf through, dip into. **2, 3** graze, pasture; feed. ● n. **2** look, scan, skim, glance, Brit. sl. dekko.

brucellosis /brŏŏsəlōsis/ n. a disease caused by bacteria of the genus Brucella, affecting esp. cattle and causing undulant fever in humans. [Brucella f. Sir D. Bruce, Sc. physician d. 1931 + -OSIS]

brucite /brŏŏsīt/ n. a mineral form of magnesium hydroxide. [A. Bruce, US mineralogist d. 1818]

bruin /brŏŏin/ n. a bear. [ME f. Du., = BROWN: used as a name in Reynard the Fox]

bruise /brŏŏz/ n. & v. ● n. **1** an injury appearing as an area of discolored skin on a human or animal body, caused by a blow or impact. **2** a similar area of damage on a fruit, etc. ● v. **1** tr. **a** inflict a bruise on. **b** hurt mentally. **2** intr. be susceptible to bruising. **3** tr. crush or pound. [ME f. OE brȳsan crush, reinforced by AF bruser, OF bruisier break]

■ n. injury, hurt, contusion, bump, welt, weal; blotch, blemish, mark, spot, discoloration. ● v. **1** contuse, hurt, harm, wound, damage; see also INJURE 1, 2. **3** see POUND[2] v. 1.

bruiser /brŏŏzər/ n. colloq. **1** a large tough-looking person. **2** Brit. a professional boxer.

■ **1** tough, ruffian, bodyguard, thug, hoodlum, bouncer, gangster, hooligan, bullyboy, enforcer, Austral. larrikin, colloq. tough guy, toughie, roughneck, hood, lug, plugugly, Brit. sl. yob, yobbo, bovver boy. **2** prizefighter, boxer, fighter, pugilist, welter, slugger, sl. pug.

bruit /brŏŏt/ v. & n. ● v.tr. (often foll. by abroad, about) spread (a report or rumor). ● n. archaic a report or rumor. [F, = noise f. bruire roar]

■ v. see RUMOR v.

brumby /brúmbee/ n. (pl. **-ies**) Austral. a wild or unbroken horse. [19th c.: orig. unkn.]

brume /brŏŏm/ n. mist; fog. [F f. L bruma winter]

brummagem /brúmajəm/ adj. **1** cheap and showy (brummagem goods). **2** counterfeit. [dial. form of Birmingham, England, with ref. to counterfeit coins and plated goods once made there]

■ **1** see GARISH 2.

brunch /brunch/ *n. & v.* ● *n.* a late-morning meal eaten as the first meal of the day. ● *v.intr.* eat brunch. [BR(EAKFAST) + (L)UNCH]

brunette /brŏōnét/ *n. & adj.* (also *masc.* **brunet**) ● *n.* a woman with dark hair. ● *adj.* (of a woman) having dark hair. [F, fem. of *brunet*, dimin. of *brun* BROWN]
■ *adj.* see DARK *adj.* 3.

brunt /brunt/ *n.* the chief or initial impact of an attack, task, etc. (esp. *bear the brunt of*). [ME: orig. unkn.]
■ (full) force, burden, onus, weight, impact, thrust; effect, repercussion(s), consequence(s), responsibility.

brush /brush/ *n. & v.* ● *n.* **1** an implement with bristles, hair, wire, etc., varying in firmness set into a block or projecting from the end of a handle, for any of various purposes, esp. cleaning or scrubbing, painting, arranging the hair, etc. **2** the application of a brush; brushing. **3 a** (usu. foll. by *with*) a short esp. unpleasant encounter (*a brush with the law*). **b** a skirmish. **4 a** the bushy tail of a fox. **b** a brushlike tuft. **5** *Electr.* **a** a piece of carbon or metal serving as an electrical contact esp. with a moving part. **b** (in full **brush discharge**) a faint brushlike electrical discharge without sparks. **6 a** undergrowth; thicket; small trees and shrubs. **b** such wood cut or broken. **c** land covered with brush. **d** *Austral.* dense forest. **7** *Austral. & NZ sl.* a girl or young woman. ● *v.* **1** *tr.* **a** sweep or scrub or put in order with a brush. **b** treat (a surface) with a brush so as to change its nature or appearance. **2** *tr.* **a** remove (dust, etc.) with a brush. **b** apply (a liquid preparation) to a surface with a brush. **3** *tr. & intr.* graze or touch in passing. **4** *intr.* perform a brushing action or motion. □ **brush aside** dismiss or dispose of (a person, idea, etc.) curtly or lightly. **brushed aluminum** aluminum with a lusterless surface. **brushed fabric** fabric brushed so as to raise the nap. **brush off** rebuff; dismiss abruptly. **brush-off** *n.* a rebuff; an abrupt dismissal. **brush over** paint lightly. **brush turkey** *Austral.* a large mound-building bird, *Alectura lathami*. **brush up** (often foll. by *on*) revive one's former knowledge of (a subject). **2** *Brit.* clean up or smarten. **brush-up** *n. Brit.* the process of cleaning up. □□ **brushlike** *adj.* **brushy** *adj.* [ME f. OF *brosse*]
■ *n.* **1** broom, besom. **2** groom; sweep. **3** encounter, altercation, exchange, incident, to-do, clash, collision, wrangle, tussle, run-in, confrontation, quarrel, disagreement, dispute, engagement, *colloq.* set-to, esp. *Brit. joc.* argy-bargy; see also SKIRMISH *n.* 1. **6** brushwood, shrubs, branches, scrub, bracken, brambles, boscage, coppice; thicket, undergrowth, underbrush, chaparral, underwood, brake, cover, thickset, copsewood, *Brit.* spinney. ● *v.* **1, 4** sweep, dust, scrub, clean, wipe; groom, curry. **3** graze, touch, rub *or* press against. □ **brush aside** disregard, discount, discard, dismiss, put *or* push aside, dispose of, shrug off, reject, laugh away *or* off, pooh-pooh; make light of, write off, gloss over, blink at, ridicule, play down, belittle, minimize, trivialize, de-emphasize, underrate, underestimate, undervalue. **brush off** give a person the brush-off, dismiss, ignore, spurn, snub, rebuff, turn one's back on, send off *or* away *or* packing, show a person the door, tell a person where to go *or* get off, cut, give a person the cold shoulder, *colloq.* give a person his *or* her walking papers *or* marching orders, give a person the boot, *sl.* tell a person to get lost. **brush-off** see REBUFF *n.* **brush up 2** (*brush up on*) polish up, review, restudy, go over, study, *archaic* con (over), *colloq.* bone up (on)., *Brit. colloq.* swot up (on).

brushless /brúshlis/ *adj.* not requiring the use of a brush.

brushwood /brúshwŏod/ *n.* **1** cut or broken twigs, etc. **2** undergrowth; a thicket.
■ see BRUSH *n.* 6.

brushwork /brúshwərk/ *n.* **1** manipulation of the brush in painting. **2** a painter's style in this.

brusque /brusk/ *adj.* abrupt or offhand in manner or speech. □□ **brusquely** *adv.* **brusqueness** *n.* **brusquerie** /brúskəree/ *n.* [F f. It. *brusco* sour]
■ blunt, gruff, abrupt, short, curt, sharp, terse, brash, bluff, rough, indelicate, tactless, undiplomatic, overbearing; offhand(ed), unceremonious, cursory, careless, rude, impolite, uncivil, discourteous, ungracious, ill-mannered, unmannerly.

Brussels carpet /brúsəlz/ *n.* a carpet with a wool pile and a strong linen back. [*Brussels* in Belgium]

Brussels lace /brúsəlz/ *n.* an elaborate needlepoint or pillow lace.

brussels sprout /brúsəlz/ *n.* **1** a vegetable related to cabbage with small compact cabbagelike buds borne close together along a tall single stem. **2** any of these buds used as a vegetable.

brut /brŏōt/ *adj.* (of wine) very dry; unsweetened. [F]

brutal /brŏōt'l/ *adj.* **1** savagely or viciously cruel. **2** harsh; merciless. □□ **brutality** /-tálitee/ *n.* (*pl.* **-ies**). **brutally** *adv.* [F *brutal* or med.L *brutalis* f. *brutus* BRUTE]
■ inhuman, savage, cruel, pitiless, merciless, unmerciful, harsh, severe, draconian, barbaric, barbarous, beastly, bestial, sadistic; inhumane, heartless, callous, hardhearted, fierce, stonyhearted, insensitive, unfeeling, cold-blooded, unsympathetic, remorseless, ruthless, ferocious, deadly, *poet. or rhet.* fell; oppressive, tyrannical, repressive, tyrannous, despotic, unjust. □□ **brutality** bestiality, cruelty, savagery, barbarousness, barbarity, inhumanity, beastliness, monstrousness, horribleness, fiendishness, wildness; vulgarity, crudeness, coarseness, boorishness, grossness, insensitivity.

brutalism /brŏōt'lizəm/ *n.* **1** brutality. **2** a heavy plain style of architecture, etc.

brutalize /brŏōt'līz/ *v.tr.* **1** make brutal. **2** treat brutally. □□ **brutalization** /-lizáyshən/ *n.*
■ **2** see MISTREAT.

brute /brŏōt/ *n. & adj.* ● *n.* **1 a** a brutal or violent person or animal. **b** *colloq.* an unpleasant person. **2** an animal as opposed to a human being. ● *adj.* **1** not possessing the capacity to reason. **2 a** animal-like; cruel. **b** stupid; sensual. **3** unthinking; merely physical (*brute force*; *brute matter*). □□ **brutehood** *n.* **brutish** *adj.* **brutishly** *adv.* **brutishness** *n.* [F f. L *brutus* stupid]
■ *n.* **1 a** see BEAST 2a. **b** see STINKER. **2** animal, creature, beast. ● *adj.* **2 a** see CRUEL *adj.* **b** see CARNAL 1, SIMPLE 5. **3** brutish, unfeeling, unthinking, senseless, blind, unintelligent, insensate, thoughtless, mindless, unreasoning, irrational, instinctive, unconscious, physical, material, bodily. □□ **brutish** see BRUTE *adj.* above.

bruxism /brúksizəm/ *n.* the involuntary or habitual grinding or clenching of the teeth. [Gk *brukhein* gnash the teeth]

bryology /brī-óləjee/ *n.* the study of bryophytes. □□ **bryological** /brīəlójikəl/ *adj.* **bryologist** *n.* [Gk *bruon* moss]

bryony /bríənee/ *n.* (*pl.* **-ies**) any climbing plant of the genus *Bryonia*, esp. *B. dioica* bearing greenish white flowers and red berries. □ **black bryony** a similar unrelated plant, *Tamus communis*, bearing poisonous berries. [L *bryonia* f. Gk *bruōnia*]

bryophyte /bríəfit/ *n.* any plant of the phylum Bryophyta, including mosses and liverworts. □□ **bryophytic** /-fítik/ *adj.* [mod.L *Bryophyta* f. Gk *bruon* moss + *phuton* plant]

bryozoan /bríəzŏən/ *n. & adj.* ● *n.* any aquatic invertebrate animal of the phylum Bryozoa, forming colonies attached to rocks, seaweeds, etc. Also called POLYZOAN. ● *adj.* of or relating to the phylum Bryozoa. □□ **bryozoology** /-zō-óləjee, -zōō-/ *n.* [Gk *bruon* moss + *zōia* animals]

Brythonic /brithónik/ *n. & adj.* ● *n.* the language of the Celts of southern Britain and Brittany. ● *adj.* of or relating to this people or their language. [W *Brython* Britons f. OCelt.]

BS *abbr.* **1** Bachelor of Science. **2** Bachelor of Surgery. **3** Blessed Sacrament. **4** *coarse sl.* bullshit.

B.Sc. *abbr.* Bachelor of Science.

/ . . . / **pronunciation**   ● **part of speech**
□ **phrases, idioms, and compounds**
□□ **derivatives**   ■ **synonym section**
cross-references appear in SMALL CAPITALS or *italics*

B-side /béesíd/ *n.* the side of a phonograph record regarded as less important.

BTU *abbr.* (also **B.t.u.**, esp. *Brit.* **B.th.u.**, **B.Th.U.**) British thermal unit(s).

bu. *abbr.* bushel(s).

bub /bub/ *n. colloq.* a boy or a man, often used as a form of address. [earlier *bubby*, perh. a childish form of BROTHER or f. G *Bube* boy]

bubal /byóobəl/ *n.* = HARTEBEEST. [L *bubalus* f. Gk *boubalos* oxlike antelope]

bubble /búbəl/ *n. & v.* ● *n.* **1 a** a thin sphere of liquid enclosing air, etc. **b** an air-filled cavity in a liquid or a solidified liquid such as glass or amber. **c** (in *pl.*) froth; foam. **2** the sound or appearance of boiling. **3** a semicylindrical or domed cavity or structure. **4** a visionary or unrealistic project or enterprise. ● *v.intr.* **1** rise in or send up bubbles. **2** make the sound of boiling. **3** be lively or cheerful. □ **bubble and squeak** *Brit.* cooked cabbage fried with cooked potatoes or meat. **bubble bath 1** a preparation for adding to bath water to make it foam. **2** a bath with this added. **bubble car** *Brit.* a small automobile with a transparent dome. **bubble chamber** *Physics* an apparatus designed to make the tracks of ionizing particles visible as a row of bubbles in a liquid. **bubble gum** chewing gum that can be blown into bubbles. **bubble memory** *Computing* a type of memory which stores data as a pattern of magnetized regions in a thin layer of magnetic material. **bubble over** (often foll. by *with*) be exuberant with laughter, excitement, anger, etc. **bubble pack** a small package enclosing goods in a transparent material on a backing. **bubble wrap** a clear plastic wrap with air bubbles in it, used esp. to protect breakable objects in shipping. [ME: prob. imit.]

■ *n.* **1 a, b** blister, air pocket, globule, droplet. **c** (*bubbles*) froth, foam, suds, lather, spume, *Technical* barm; effervescence, carbonation, fizz. **4** pipe dream, fantasy, illusion, daydream, castle in the air *or* Spain, pie in the sky, harebrained scheme. ● *v.* foam, froth, boil, seethe, fizz, simmer. □ **bubble over** see GUSH *v.* 2.

bubbly /búblee/ *adj. & n.* ● *adj.* (**bubblier, bubbliest**) **1** having or resembling bubbles. **2** exuberant. ● *n. colloq.* champagne. □ **bubbly-jock** *Sc.* a turkeycock.

■ *adj.* **1** effervescent, foamy, frothy, spumy, sudsy, lathery, fizzy, sparkling, sparkly. **2** effervescent, exuberant, merry, gay, buoyant, ebullient, bouncy, animated, vivacious, dynamic, vibrant, radiant, sunny, bright, cheerful, cheery, perky, perk, lively, spirited, energetic, excited. ● *n.* champagne, sparkling wine, (Asti) spumante, *colloq.* fizz, *Brit. sl.* champers.

bubo /byóobō, bóo-/ *n.* (*pl.* **-oes**) a swollen inflamed lymph node in the armpit or groin. [med.L *bubo -onis* swelling f. Gk *boubōn* groin]

bubonic /byóobónik, bóo-/ *adj.* relating to or characterized by buboes. □ **bubonic plague** a contagious bacterial disease characterized by fever, delirium, and the formation of buboes.

buccal /búkəl/ *adj.* **1** of or relating to the cheek. **2** of or in the mouth. [L *bucca* cheek]

buccaneer /búkəneér/ *n. & v.* ● *n.* **1** a pirate, orig. off the American coast in the late 17th c. **2** an unscrupulous adventurer. ● *v.intr.* be a buccaneer. □□ **buccaneering** *n. & adj.* **buccaneerish** *adj.* [F *boucanier* f. *boucaner* cure meat on a barbecue f. *boucan* f. Tupi *mukem*]

■ *n.* **1** see PIRATE *n.* 1a.

buccinator /búksinaytər/ *n.* a flat thin cheek muscle. [L f. *buccinare* blow a trumpet (*buccina*)]

buck[1] /buk/ *n. & v.* ● *n.* **1** the male of various animals, esp. the deer, hare, or rabbit. **2** *archaic* a fashionable young man. **3** (*attrib.*) **a** *sl.* male (*buck antelope*). **b** *Mil.* of the lowest rank (*buck private*). ● *v.* **1** *intr.* (of a horse) jump upwards with back arched and feet drawn together. **2** *tr.* **a** (usu. foll. by *off*) throw (a rider or burden) in this way. **b** oppose; resist. **3** *tr. & intr.* (usu. foll. by *up*) *colloq.* **a** make or become more cheerful. **b** *Brit.* hurry. **4** *tr.* (as **bucked** *adj.*) *Brit. colloq.* encouraged; elated. □ **buck fever** nervousness when called on to act. **buck rarebit** *Brit.* Welsh rarebit with a poached

egg on top. □□ **bucker** *n.* [OE *buc* male deer, *bucca* male goat, f. ON]

■ *v.* **3 a** see CHEER *v.* 3.

buck[2] /buk/ *n. sl.* a dollar. □ **big bucks** a great deal of money. **a fast buck** easy money. [19th c.: orig. unkn.]

buck[3] /buk/ *n. sl.* an article placed as a reminder before a player whose turn it is to deal at poker. □ **pass the buck** *colloq.* shift responsibility (to another). [19th c.: orig. unkn.]

buck[4] /buk/ *n.* **1** a sawhorse. **2** a vaulting horse. [Du. (*zaag*)*boc*]

buck[5] /buk/ *n.* the body of a cart. [perh. f. obs. *bouk* belly, f. OE *būc* f. Gmc]

buck[6] /buk/ *n. Brit.* conversation; boastful talk. [Hindi *buk buk*]

buckbean /búkbeen/ *n.* a bog plant, *Menyanthes trifoliata*, with white or pinkish hairy flowers. Also called *bog-bean*.

buckboard /búkbawrd/ *n.* a horse-drawn vehicle with the body formed by a plank fixed to the axles. [BUCK[5] + BOARD]

bucket /búkit/ *n. & v.* ● *n.* **1 a** a roughly cylindrical open container, esp. of metal, with a handle, used for carrying, catching, or holding water, etc. **b** the amount contained in this (*need three buckets to fill the tub*). **2** (in *pl.*) large quantities of liquid, esp. rain or tears (*wept buckets*). **3** a compartment on the outer edge of a waterwheel. **4** the scoop of a dredger or a grainelevator. ● *v.* (**bucketed, bucketing**) **1** *intr.* (often foll. by *down*) (of liquid, esp. rain) pour heavily. **2** *intr. & tr.* (often foll. by *along*) *Brit.* move or drive jerkily or bumpily. □ **bucket seat** a seat with a rounded back to fit one person, esp. in a car. **bucket shop** a brokerage office that sells stocks very aggressively, esp. an illegal or dishonest one. □□ **bucketful** *n.* (*pl.* **-fuls**). [ME & AF *buket, buquet*, perh. f. OE *būc* pitcher]

■ *n.* **1** pail, scuttle. ● *v.* **1** see POUR 3.

buckeye /búkī/ *n.* **a** any shrub of the genus *Aesculus* of the horse chestnut family, with large sticky buds and showy red or white flowers. **b** the shiny brown nutlike seed of this plant.

buckhorn /búkhawrn/ *n.* horn of a buck as a material for knife handles, etc.

buckhound /búkhownd/ *n.* a small kind of staghound.

buckle /búkəl/ *n. & v.* ● *n.* **1** a flat often rectangular frame with a hinged pin, used for joining the ends of a belt, strap, etc. **2** a similarly shaped ornament, esp. on a shoe. ● *v.* **1** *tr.* (often foll. by *up, on,* etc.) fasten with a buckle. **2** *tr. & intr.* give way or cause to give way under longitudinal pressure; crumple. □ **buckle down** make a determined effort. **buckle to** (or **down to**) prepare for; set about (work, etc.). **buckle to** get to work; make a vigorous start. [ME f. OF *boucle* f. L *buccula* cheek strap of a helmet f. *bucca* cheek: sense 2 of *v.* f. F *boucler* bulge]

■ *n.* **1** clasp, fastener, clip, fastening, hook, catch. **2** brooch, pin, badge. ● *v.* **1** clasp, fasten, bracket, strap, lash, clip, pin, hook. **2** collapse, cave in, give way, crumple (up), knuckle under, fall *or* come apart, bend, warp, distort, twist, bulge. □ **buckle down** see *put one's shoulder to the wheel* (SHOULDER). **buckle to** (or **down to**) get down to, work at, knuckle down to, set to work on, set to, set out on, get going on, launch into, get cracking on, concentrate on, focus on, apply oneself to.

buckler /búklər/ *n.* **1** *hist.* a small round shield held by a handle. **2** *Bot.* any of several ferns of the genus *Dryopteris*, having buckler-shaped indusia. Also called *shield fern*. [ME f. OF *bocler* lit. 'having a boss' f. *boucle* BOSS[2]]

Buckley's /búkleez/ *n.* (in full **Buckley's chance**) *Austral. & NZ colloq.* little or no chance. [19th c.: orig. uncert.]

bucko /búkō/ *n. & adj. sl.* ● *n.* (*pl.* **-oes**) a swaggering or domineering fellow. ● *adj.* blustering; swaggering; bullying. [BUCK[1] + -o]

buckram /búkrəm/ *n. & adj.* ● *n.* **1** a coarse linen or other cloth stiffened with gum or paste, and used as interfacing or in bookbinding. **2** *archaic* stiffness in manner. ● *adj. archaic* starchy; formal. □ **men in buckram** nonexistent persons; figments (Shakesp. *1 Henry IV* II. iv. 210–50). [ME f. AF *bukeram*, OF *boquerant*, perh. f. *Bokhara* in central Asia]

Bucks. /buks/ *abbr.* Buckinghamshire.

bucksaw /búksaw/ *n.* a two-handed saw set in an H-shaped frame and used for sawing wood.

Buck's Fizz /buks/ *n. Brit.* a cocktail of champagne or sparkling white wine and orange juice. [*Buck's* Club in London + FIZZ]

buckshee /búkshéé/ *adj. & adv. Brit. sl.* free of charge. [corrupt. of BAKSHEESH]

buckshot /búkshot/ *n.* large-sized lead shot.
■ see SHOT¹ 3.

buckskin /búkskin/ *n.* **1 a** the skin of a buck. **b** leather made from a buck's skin. **2** a thick smooth cotton or wool cloth.

buckthorn /búkthawrn/ *n.* any thorny shrub of the genus *Rhamnus*, esp. *R. cathartica* with berries formerly used as a cathartic.

bucktooth /búktooth/ *n.* an upper tooth that projects.

buckwheat /búkhweet, -weet/ *n.* any cereal plant of the genus *Fagopyrum*, esp. *F. esculentum* with seeds used for fodder and for flour to make bread and pancakes. [MDu. *boecweite* beech wheat, its grains being shaped like beechnuts]

bucolic /byookólik/ *adj. & n.* ● *adj.* of or concerning shepherds, the pastoral life, etc.; rural. ● *n.* **1** (usu. in *pl.*) a pastoral poem or poetry. **2** a peasant. □□ **bucolically** *adv.* [L *bucolicus* f. Gk *boukolikos* f. *boukolos* herdsman f. *bous* OX]
■ *adj.* see PASTORAL *adj.* 1. ● *n.* 2 see PEASANT.

bud¹ /bud/ *n. & v.* ● *n.* **1 a** an immature knoblike shoot from which a stem, leaf, or flower develops. **b** a flower or leaf that is not fully open. **2** *Biol.* an asexual outgrowth from a parent organism that separates to form a new individual. **3** anything still undeveloped. ● *v.* (**budded, budding**) **1** *intr. Bot. & Zool.* form a bud. **2** *intr.* begin to grow or develop (*a budding violinist*). **3** *tr. Hort.* graft a bud (of a plant) on to another plant. □ **in bud** having newly formed buds. [ME: orig. unkn.]
■ *n.* 1 see SHOOT. ● *v.* 1 see SPROUT *v.* 2.

bud² /bud/ *n. colloq.* (as a form of address) = BUDDY. [abbr.]

Buddha /bóóda, bóóda/ *n.* **1** a title given to successive teachers of Buddhism, esp. to its founder, Gautama. **2** a statue or picture of the Buddha. [Skr., = enlightened, past part. of *budh* know]

Buddhism /bóódizəm, bóód-/ *n.* a widespread Asian religion or philosophy, founded by Gautama Buddha in India in the 5th c. BC, which teaches that elimination of the self and earthly desires is the highest goal (cf. NIRVANA). □□ **Buddhist** *n. & adj.* **Buddhistic** *adj.* **Buddhistical** *adj.*

buddleia /búdleeə/ *n.* any shrub of the genus *Buddleia*, with fragrant lilac, yellow, or white flowers attractive to butterflies. [A. *Buddle*, Engl. botanist d. 1715]

buddy /búdee/ *n. & v. colloq.* ● *n.* (*pl.* **-ies**) (often as a form of address) a close friend or companion. ● *v.intr.* (**-ies, -ied**) (often foll. by *up*) become friendly. [perh. corrupt. of *brother*, or var. of BUTTY¹]
■ *n.* see MATE¹ 1.

budge /buj/ *v.* (usu. with *neg.*) **1** *intr.* **a** make the slightest movement. **b** change one's opinion (*he's stubborn, he won't budge*). **2** *tr.* cause or compel to budge (*nothing will budge him*). □ **budge up** (or **over**) *Brit.* make room for another person by moving. [F *bouger* stir ult. f. L *bullire* boil]
■ **1a, 2** see SHIFT *v.* 1.

budgerigar /búja reegaar/ *n.* a small green parrot, *Melopsittacus undulatus*, native to Australia, and bred in colored varieties which are often kept as cage birds. [Aboriginal, = good cockatoo]

budget /bújit/ *n. & v.* ● *n.* **1** the amount of money needed or available (for a specific item, etc.) (*a budget of $200; mustn't exceed the budget*). **2 a** the usu. annual estimate of national revenue and expenditure. **b** an estimate or plan of expenditure in relation to income for a business, etc. **c** a private person's or family's similar estimate. **3** (*attrib.*) inexpensive. **4** *archaic* a quantity of material, etc., esp. written or printed. ● *v.tr. & intr.* (**budgeted, budgeting**) (often foll. by *for*) allow or arrange for in a budget (*have budgeted for a new car; can budget $60*). □ **budget account** (or **plan**) a bank account, or account with a utility company, etc., into which one makes regular, usu. monthly, payments to cover bills. **on a budget** avoiding expense; cheap. □□ **budgetary**

adj. [ME = pouch, f. OF *bougette* dimin. of *bouge* leather bag f. L *bulga* (f. Gaulish) knapsack: cf. BULGE]
■ *n.* 3 (*attrib.*) see CHEAP *adj.* 1, 2. ● *v.* see RATION 1.
□□ **budgetary** see ECONOMIC 1.

budgie /bújee/ *n. colloq.* = BUDGERIGAR. [abbr.]

buff /buf/ *adj., n., & v.* ● *adj.* of a yellowish beige color. ● *n.* **1** a yellowish beige color. **2** *colloq.* an enthusiast, esp. for a particular hobby (*railroad buff*). **3** *colloq.* the human skin unclothed. **4** a velvety dull yellow ox leather. **b** (*attrib.*) (of a garment, etc.) made of this (*buff gloves*). **5** *Brit.* (**the Buffs**) the former East Kent Regiment (from the color of its uniform facings). ● *v.tr.* **1** polish (metal, fingernails, etc.). **2** make (leather) velvety like buff, by removing the surface. □ **buff stick** a stick covered with buff and used for polishing. **in the buff** *colloq.* naked. [orig. sense 'buffalo,' prob. f. F *buffle*; sense 2 of *n.* orig. f. buff uniforms formerly worn by New York volunteer firemen, applied to enthusiastic fire watchers]
■ *n.* 2 see ENTHUSIAST. ● *v.* 1 see POLISH *v.* 1. □ **in the buff** see NAKED 1.

buffalo /búfəlō/ *n. & v.* ● *n.* (*pl.* same or **-oes**) **1** a N. American bison, *Bison bison*. **2** either of two species of ox, *Synceros caffer*, native to Africa, or *Bubalus arnee*, native to Asia with heavy backswept horns. ● *v.tr.* (**-oes, -oed**) *sl.* overawe; outwit. □ **buffalo grass 1** a grass, *Buchloe dactyloides*, of the N. American plains. **2** a grass, *Stenotaphrum secundatum*, of Australia and New Zealand. [prob. f. Port. *bufalo* f. LL *bufalus* f. L *bubalus* f. Gk *boubalos* antelope, wild ox]
■ *v.* see OVERAWE, SWINDLE *v.*

buffer¹ /búfər/ *n. & v.* ● *n.* **1 a** a device that protects against or reduces the effect of an impact, etc. **b** such a device (usu. one of a pair) on the front and rear of a railroad vehicle or at the end of a track. **2** *Biochem.* a substance that maintains the hydrogen ion concentration of a solution when an acid or alkali is added. **3** *Computing* a temporary memory area or queue for data to aid its transfer between devices or programs operating at different speeds, etc. ● *v.tr.* **1** act as a buffer to. **2** *Biochem.* treat with a buffer. □ **buffer state** a small nation situated between two larger ones potentially hostile to one another and regarded as reducing the likelihood of open hostilities. **buffer stock** a reserve of commodity to offset price fluctuations. **buffer zone 1** a neutral area between two warring groups. **2** any area separating those in conflict. [prob. f. obs. *buff* (v.), imit. of the sound of a soft body struck]
■ *n.* 1 see PROTECTION 1b, c. ● *v.* 1 see CUSHION *v.* 3.

buffer² /búfər/ *n. Brit. sl.* a silly or incompetent old man (esp. *old buffer*). [18th c.: prob. formed as BUFFER¹ or with the sense 'stutterer']

buffet¹ /bóófáy, bə-/ *n.* **1** a meal consisting of several dishes set out on a table from which guests serve themselves (*buffet lunch*). **2** esp. *Brit.* a restaurant or counter where light meals or snacks may be bought (*station buffet*). **3** a sideboard or recessed cupboard for china, etc. □ **buffet car** a railroad car serving light meals or snacks. [F f. OF *bufet* stool, of unkn. orig.]

buffet² /búfit/ *v. & n.* ● *v.* (**buffeted, buffeting**) **1** *tr.* **a** strike or knock repeatedly (*wind buffeted the trees*). **b** strike, esp. repeatedly, with the hand or fist. **2** *tr.* (of fate, etc.) treat badly; plague (*cheerful though buffeted by misfortune*). **3 a** *intr.* struggle; fight one's way (through difficulties, etc.). **b** *tr.* contend with (waves, etc.). ● *n.* **1** a blow, esp. of the hand or fist. **2** a shock. [ME f. OF dimin. of *bufe* blow]
■ *v.* 1 see STRIKE *v.* 1. ● *n.* 1 see BUMP *n.* 1.

buffeting /búfiting/ *n.* **1** a beating; repeated blows. **2** *Aeron.* an irregular oscillation, caused by air eddies, of any part of an aircraft.

bufflehead /búfəlhed/ *n.* a duck, *Bucephala albeola*, native to

/. . ./ **pronunciation**	● **part of speech**
□ **phrases, idioms, and compounds**	
□□ **derivatives**	■ **synonym section**
cross-references appear in SMALL CAPITALS or *italics*	

N. America, with a head that appears overlarge. [obs. *buffle* buffalo + HEAD]

buffo /bŏofō/ *n. & adj.* ● *n.* (*pl.* **-os**) a comic actor, esp. in Italian opera. ● *adj.* comic; burlesque. [It.]

buffoon /bəfŏon/ *n.* **1** a jester; a mocker. **2** a stupid person. □□ **buffoonery** *n.* **buffoonish** *adj.* [F *bouffon* f. It. *buffone* f. med.L *buffo* clown f. Rmc]
■ **1** see FOOL¹ *n.* 2. see FOOL¹ *n.* 1.

bug /bug/ *n. & v.* ● *n.* **1 a** any of various hemipterous insects with oval flattened bodies and mouthparts modified for piercing and sucking. **b** *colloq.* any small insect. **2** *sl.* a microorganism, esp. a bacterium, or a disease caused by it. **3** a concealed microphone. **4** *sl.* an error in a computer program or system, etc. **5** *sl.* **a** an obsession, enthusiasm, etc. **b** an enthusiast. ● *v.* (**bugged**, **bugging**) **1** *tr.* conceal a microphone in (esp. a building or room). **2** *tr. sl.* annoy; bother. **3** *intr.* (often foll. by *out*) *sl.* leave quickly. □ **bug-eyed** with bulging eyes. [17th c.: orig. unkn.]
■ *n.* **1** insect, beetle, fly, midge, no-see-um, *colloq.* creepy-crawly *joc.* beastie. **2** microbe, microorganism, germ, virus, bacterium; disease, affliction, illness, sickness, ailment, disorder, malady, infection, complaint. **3** microphone, transmitter. **4** fault, error, mistake, failing, shortcoming, irregularity, flaw, *colloq.* glitch. **5 a** obsession, enthusiasm, craze, fad, mania, rage, passion, *colloq.* thing, *sl.* bag; hobby, interest, pastime. **b** enthusiast, faddist, fan, fanatic, hobbyist, *colloq.* buff. ● *v.* **1** tap, wiretap. **2** see ANNOY 1, BOTHER *v.* 1a. **3** see BOLT¹ *v.* 4a.

bugaboo /búgəbōo/ *n.* a bogey (see BOGEY²) or bugbear. [prob. of dial. orig.: cf. Welsh *bwcibo* the Devil, *bwci* hobgoblin]
■ see AVERSION 2.

bugbear /búgbair/ *n.* **1** a cause of annoyance or anger; a bête noire. **2** an object of baseless fear. **3** *archaic* a sort of hobgoblin or any being invoked to intimidate children. [obs. *bug* + BEAR²]
■ **1** see AVERSION 2. **3** see DEVIL *n.* 1, 2.

bugger /búgər/ *n., v., & int. coarse sl.* (except in sense 2 of *n.* and 3 of *v.*) ¶ Usually considered a taboo word. ● *n.* **1** esp. *Brit.* **a** an unpleasant or awkward person or thing (*the bugger won't fit*). **b** a person of a specified kind (*he's a miserable bugger*). **2** a person who commits buggery. ● *v.tr.* **1** as an exclamation of annoyance (*bugger the thing!*). **2** (often foll. by *up*) *Brit.* **a** ruin; spoil (*really buggered it up*; *no good, it's buggered*). **b** exhaust; tire out. **3** commit buggery with. ● *int.* expressing annoyance. □ **bugger about** (or **around**) *Brit.* **1** (often foll. by *with*) fool around. **2** mislead; persecute; make things awkward for. **bugger-all** *Brit.* nothing. **bugger off** *Brit.* (often in *imper.*) go away. [ME f. MDu. f. OF *bougre*, orig. 'heretic' f. med.L *Bulgarus* Bulgarian (member of the Greek Church)]

buggery /búgəree/ *n.* **1** esp. *Brit.* anal intercourse. **2** = BESTIALITY 2. [ME f. MDu. *buggerie* f. OF *bougerie*: see BUGGER]

buggy¹ /búgee/ *n.* (*pl.* **-ies**) **1** a light, horse-drawn vehicle for one or two people. **2** a small, sturdy, esp. open, motor vehicle (*beach buggy*; *dune buggy*). **3** a baby carriage. [18th c.: orig. unkn.]
■ **2** see CAR 1.

buggy² /búgee/ *adj.* (**buggier**, **buggiest**) infested with bugs.

bugle¹ /byŏogəl/ *n. & v.* ● *n.* (also **bugle horn**) a brass instrument like a small trumpet, used esp. for military signals. ● *v.* **1** *intr.* sound a bugle. **2** *tr.* sound (a note, a call, etc.) on a bugle. □□ **bugler** /byŏoglər/ *n.* **buglet** /byŏoglit/ *n.* [ME, orig. = 'buffalo,' f. OF f. L *buculus* dimin. of *bos* ox]

bugle² /byŏogəl/ *n.* a blue-flowered mat-forming European plant, *Ajuga reptans*. [ME f. LL *bugula*]

bugle³ /byŏogəl/ *n.* a tube-shaped bead sewn on a dress, etc., for ornament. [16th c.: orig. unkn.]

bugloss /byŏoglaws, -glos/ *n.* **1** any of various bristly plants related to borage, esp. of the genus *Anchusa* with bright blue tubular flowers. **2** = *viper's bugloss* (see VIPER). [F *buglosse* or L *buglossus* f. Gk *bouglōssos* ox-tongued]

buhl /bŏol/ *n.* (also **boule**, **boulle**) **1** pieces of brass, tortoiseshell, etc., cut to make a pattern and used as decorative inlays esp. on furniture. **2** work inlaid with buhl. **3** (*attrib.*) inlaid with buhl. [(*buhl* Germanized) f. A. C. *Boule*, Fr. wood carver d. 1732]

build /bild/ *v. & n.* ● *v.tr.* (*past* and *past. part.* **built** /bilt/) **1 a** construct (a house, vehicle, fire, road, model, etc.) by putting parts or material together. **b** commission, finance, and oversee the building of (*the board has built two new schools*). **2 a** (often foll. by *up*) establish, develop, make, or accumulate gradually (*built the business up from nothing*). **b** (often foll. by *on*) base (hopes, theories, etc.) (*ideas built on a false foundation*). **3** (as **built** *adj.*) having a specified build (*sturdily built*; *brick-built*). ● *n.* **1** the proportions of esp. the human body (*a slim build*). **2** a style of construction; a make. □ **build in** incorporate as part of a structure. **build on** add (an extension, etc.). **build up 1** increase in size or strength. **2** praise; boost. **3** gradually become established. **build up** (or *Brit.* **in** or **round**) surround with houses, etc. **built-in 1** forming an integral part of a structure. **2** forming an integral part of a person's character (*built-in integrity*). **built on sand** unstable. **built-up 1** (of a locality) densely covered by houses, etc. **2** increased in height, etc., by the addition of parts. **3** composed of separately prepared parts. [OE *byldan* f. *bold* dwelling f. Gmc: cf. BOWER¹, BOOTH]
■ *v.* **1** construct, erect, raise, set up, assemble, put together, fabricate, shape, make, produce. **2** build up, develop, expand, extend, cultivate, increase, intensify, enlarge, strengthen; establish, base, found, secure, create, set up, constitute. **3** (**built**) made, constructed. ● *n.* **1** physique, figure, body, shape, form, frame, makeup, proportions, size. **2** see MOLD¹ *n.* 3. □ **build on** add (on), annex, append, attach, tag on, tack on, *colloq.* stick on or up, *Brit. sl.* bung on. **build up 1** see BUILD *v.* 2 above. **2** see BOOST *v.* 1a. **build up** (or *Brit.* **in** or **round**) incorporate, include. **built-in 1, 2** see INHERENT. **built on sand** see UNSOUND 2. **built-up 1** populous, (heavily) populated.

builder /bíldər/ *n.* **1** a contractor for building houses, etc.; a master builder. **2** a person engaged as a construction worker, etc., on a building site.

building /bílding/ *n.* **1** a permanent fixed structure forming an enclosure and providing protection from the elements, etc. (e.g., a house, school, factory, or stable). **2** the constructing of such structures. □ **building line** a limit or boundary between a house and a street beyond which the owner may not build. **building site** an area before or during the construction of a house, etc. **building society** *Brit.* a public finance company which accepts investments at interest and lends capital for mortgages on houses, etc.
■ edifice, structure; construction, erection, fabrication, manufacture, production, assemblage, assembly.
□ **building site** construction site, hard hat area.

buildup /bíldəp/ *n.* **1** a favorable description in advance; publicity. **2** a gradual approach to a climax or maximum (*the buildup was slow but sure*).
■ **2** see INCREASE *n.* 1, 2.

built *past* and *past part.* of BUILD.

bulb /bulb/ *n.* **1 a** an underground fleshy-leaved storage organ of some plants (e.g., lily, onion) sending roots downwards and leaves upwards. **b** a plant grown from this, e.g., a daffodil. **2** = LIGHTBULB (see LIGHT¹). **3** any object or part shaped like a bulb. [L *bulbus* f. Gk *bolbos* onion]
■ **1 a** see SEED *n.* 1a.

bulbous /búlbəs/ *adj.* **1** shaped like a bulb; fat or bulging. **2** having a bulb or bulbs. **3** (of a plant) growing from a bulb.
■ **1** see PROTUBERANT.

bulbul /bŏolbŏol/ *n.* **1** any songbird of the family Pycnonotidae, of dull plumage with contrasting bright patches. **2** a singer or poet. [Pers. f. Arab., of imit. orig.]

Bulgar /búlgaar/ *n.* **1** a member of a tribe who settled in what is now Bulgaria in the 7th c. **2** a Bulgarian. [med.L *Bulgarus* f. OBulg. *Blŭgarinŭ*]

bulgar var. of BULGUR.

Bulgarian /bulgáireeən/ *n. & adj.* ● *n.* **1 a** a native or inhabitant of Bulgaria. **b** a person of Bulgarian descent. **2** the language of Bulgaria. ● *adj.* of or relating to Bulgaria or its people or language. [med.L *Bulgaria* f. *Bulgarus*: see BUL-GAR]

bulge /bulj/ *n. & v.* ● *n.* **1 a** a convex part of an otherwise flat or flatter surface. **b** an irregular swelling; a lump. **2** *colloq.* a temporary increase in quantity or number. **3** *Naut.* the bilge of a ship. **4** *Mil.* a salient. ● *v.* **1** *intr.* swell outwards. **2** *intr.* be full or replete. **3** *tr.* swell (a bag, cheeks, etc.) by stuffing. □□ **bulgingly** *adv.* **bulgy** *adj.* [ME f. OF *boulge, bouge* †. L *bulga*: see BUDGET]

■ *n.* **1** lump, hump, protuberance, bump, swelling, projection, protrusion, excrescence, knob, knop, tumescence, *Anat.* node. **2** see BOOM² 1. ● *v.* **1** protrude, stick out, swell (out); bag, sag, belly out, project, flare out, stand out, *Brit.* knob out. *Naut.* bilge. **2** (*bulging*) see REPLETE 1. **3** see SWELL *v.* 3.

bulgur /búlgər/ *n.* (also **bulgar, bulghur**) whole wheat that has been partially boiled then dried. [Turk.]

bulimarexia /boolimərékseeə, -leemə-, byoo-/ *n.* = BULIMIA 2. □□ **bulimarexic** *adj. & n.* [BULIMIA + ANOREXIA]

bulimia /booleemeeə, -li-, byoo-/ *n. Med.* **1** insatiable over-eating. **2** (in full **bulimia nervosa**) an emotional disorder in which bouts of extreme overeating are followed by de-pression and self-induced vomiting, purging, or fasting. □□ **bulimic** *adj. & n.* [mod.L f. Gk *boulimia* f. *bous* ox + *limos* hunger]

bulk /bulk/ *n. & v.* ● *n.* **1 a** size; magnitude (esp. large). **b** a large mass. **c** a large quantity. **2** a large shape, body, or person (*jacket barely covered his bulk*). **3** (usu. prec. by *the*; treated as *pl.*) the greater part or number (*the bulk of the applicants are women*). **4** roughage. **5** *Naut.* cargo, esp. un-packaged. ● *v.* **1** *intr.* seem in respect to size or importance (*bulks large in his reckoning*). **2** *tr.* (often foll. by *out*) make (a book, a textile yarn, etc.) seem thicker by suitable treat-ment (*bulked it with irrelevant stories*). **3** *tr.* combine (con-signments, etc.). □ **bulk-buy** *Brit.* buy in bulk; engage in bulk-buying. **bulk-buying** *Brit.* **1** buying in large amounts at a discount. **2** the purchase by one buyer of all or most of a producer's output. **in bulk 1** in large quantities. **2** (of a cargo) loose, not packaged. [sense 'cargo' f. OIcel. *búlki*; sense 'mass,' etc., perh. alt. f. obs. *bouk* (cf. BUCK³)]

■ *n.* **1 a** volume, magnitude, mass, size, weight, quantity, amount, extent; largeness, hugeness, immensity, vastness, enormousness, massiveness; fatness, obesity. **3** see MAJORITY 1. **4** fiber, roughage. **5** see CARGO 1a, 2a. ● *v.* see LOOM² *v.* 1. **2** see PAD *v.* 2. □ **bulk-buying 1** wholesale buying. **in bulk 1** wholesale, *en bloc*, by the gross.

bulkhead /búlk-hed/ *n.* **1** an upright partition separating the compartments in a ship, aircraft, vehicle, etc. **2** an embank-ment or retaining wall, esp. along a water front. [*bulk* stall f. ON *bálkr* + HEAD]

■ see WALL *n.* 2.

bulky /búlkee/ *adj.* (**bulkier, bulkiest**) **1** taking up much space; large. **2** awkwardly large; unwieldy. □□ **bulkily** *adv.* **bulkiness** *n.*

■ large, voluminous, unwieldy, awkward, ungainly, cumbersome, weighty, *colloq.* hulking; heavy, chunky, large, big, fat, hefty, brawny, husky, burly, beefy, mighty, stout, obese, overweight, corpulent.

bull¹ /bool/ *n., adj., & v.* ● *n.* **1 a** an uncastrated male bovine animal. **b** a male of the whale, elephant, and other large animals. **2** (**the Bull**) the zodiacal sign or constellation Taurus. **3** *Brit.* the bull's-eye of a target. **4** *Stock Exch.* a person who buys shares hoping to sell them at a higher price later (cf. BEAR²). ● *adj.* like that of a bull (*bull neck*). ● *v.* **1** *tr. & intr.* act or treat violently. **2** *Stock Exch.* **a** *intr.* spec-ulate for a rise in stock prices. **b** *tr.* raise price of (stocks, etc.). □ **bull ant** *Austral.* = *bulldog ant.* **bull at a gate** a hasty or rash person. **bull fiddle** *colloq.* a double bass. **bull in a china shop** a reckless or clumsy person. **bull market** a market with shares rising in price. **bull nose** (or **nosed**) with rounded end. **bull pen** (also **bullpen**) **1** *Baseball* **a** an area in which relief pitchers warm up during a game. **b** the relief pitchers on a team. **2** a large holding cell for prisoners awaiting court appearances. **3** *colloq.* an open, unpartitioned

area for several workers. **bull session** an informal group discussion. **bull's-eye 1** the center of a target; a shot that hits this. **2** a large hard peppermint-flavored candy. **3** a hemisphere or thick disk of glass in a ship's deck or side to admit light. **4** a small circular window. **5 a** a hemispherical lens. **b** a lantern fitted with this. **6** a boss of glass at the center of a blown glass sheet. **bull terrier 1** a short-haired dog of a breed that is a cross between a bulldog and a terrier. **2** this breed. **take the bull by the horns** face danger or challenge boldly. □□ **bullish** *adj.* [ME f. ON *boli* = MLG, MDu *bulle*]

■ □ **bull session** see DISCUSSION 1. **bull's-eye 1** see MIDDLE *n.* 1. **3, 4** see PANE.

bull² /bool/ *n.* a papal edict. [ME f. OF *bulle* f. L *bulla* rounded object, in med.L 'seal']

bull³ /bool/ *n.* **1** (also **Irish bull**) an expression containing a contradiction in terms or implying ludicrous inconsistency. **2** *sl.* **a** unnecessary routine tasks or discipline. **b** nonsense. **c** trivial or insincere talk or writing. **d** a bad blunder in speech (cf. BULLSHIT). [17th c.: orig. unkn.]

■ **2 b** see NONSENSE.

bullace /boolis/ *n.* a thorny European shrub, *Prunus insititia*, bearing globular yellow or purple-black fruits, of which the damson plum is the cultivated form. [ME f. OF *buloce, beloce*]

bulldog /booldawg, -dog/ *n.* **1 a** a dog of a sturdy powerful breed with a large head and smooth hair. **b** this breed. **2 a** tenacious and courageous person. □ **bulldog ant** *Austral.* a large ant with a powerful sting. **bulldog clip** a strong sprung clip for papers.

bulldoze /booldōz/ *v.tr.* **1** clear with a bulldozer. **2** *colloq.* **a** intimidate. **b** make (one's way) forcibly. [perh. fr. BULL¹ + alter. of DOSE]

■ **1** see LEVEL *v.* 2. **2** see FORCE¹ *v.* 2.

bulldozer /booldōzər/ *n.* **1** a powerful tractor with a broad curved vertical blade at the front for clearing ground. **2** a forceful and domineering person.

bullet /boolit/ *n.* **1** a small round or cylindrical missile with a pointed end, fired from a rifle, revolver, etc. **2** *Printing* a round black dot used as a marker (.). [F *boulet, boulette* dimin. of *boule* ball f. L *bulla* bubble]

■ see PROJECTILE *n.*

bulletin /boolitin/ *n.* **1** a short official statement of news. **2** a regular periodical issued by an organization or society. □ **bulletin board 1** a board for posting notices, information, etc. **2** *Computing* a public computer file serving the function of a bulletin board. [F f. It. *bullettino* dimin. of *bulletta* pass-port, dimin. of *bulla* seal, BULL²]

■ **1** report, account, flash, news item, newsflash, update, announcement, communiqué, dispatch, statement, advisory; see also WORD *n.* 7. **2** newsletter, pamphlet, leaflet, message, notice, communication, *Brit.* news sheet.

bulletproof /boolitproof/ *adj. & v.* ● *adj.* (of a material) de-signed to resist the penetration of bullets. ● *v.tr.* make bul-letproof.

bullfight /boolfīt/ *n.* a sport of baiting and (usu.) killing bulls as a public spectacle, esp. in Spain. □□ **bullfighter** *n.* **bull-fighting** *n.*

bullfinch /boolfinch/ *n.* a European finch, *Pyrrhula pyrrhula*, with a short stout beak and bright plumage.

bullfrog /boolfrawg, -frog/ *n.* a large frog, *Rana catesbiana*, native to eastern N. America, with a deep croak.

bullhead /boolhed/ *n.* any of various marine fishes with large flattened heads.

bullheaded /boolhédid/ *adj.* obstinate; impetuous; blunder-ing. □□ **bullheadedly** *adv.* **bullheadedness** *n.*

■ see STUBBORN.

bullhorn /boolhawrn/ *n.* an electronic device for amplifying the sound of the voice so it can be heard at a distance.

/. . ./ **pronunciation**	● **part of speech**
□ **phrases, idioms, and compounds**	
□□ **derivatives**	■ **synonym section**
cross-references appear in SMALL CAPITALS or *italics*	

bullion /bŏŏlyən/ n. a metal (esp. gold or silver) in bulk before coining, or valued by weight. [AF = mint, var. of OF *bouillon* ult. f. L *bullire* boil]

bullish /bŏŏlish/ adj. **1** like a bull, esp. in size or temper. **2 a** *Stock Exch.* causing or associated with a rise in prices. **b** optimistic.
▪ **2** see *optimistic* (OPTIMISM).

bullock /bŏŏlək/ n. & v. ● n. a castrated bull. ● v.intr. (often foll. by *at*) *Austral. colloq.* work very hard. [OE *bulluc*, dimin. of BULL[1]]

bullocky /bŏŏləkee/ n. *Austral. & NZ colloq.* a bullock driver.

bullring /bŏŏlring/ n. an arena for bullfights.

bullshit /bŏŏlshit/ n. & v. *coarse sl.* ● n. **1** (often as *int.*) nonsense; foolish talk. **2** trivial or insincere talk or writing. ● v.intr. (**-shitted, -shitting**) talk nonsense; bluff. □□ **bullshitter** n. [BULL[3]SHIT]
▪ n. **1** see RUBBISH 3. **2** see TALK n. 4c. ● v. see BLUFF[1] v. 1.

bulltrout /bŏŏltrowt/ n. *Brit.* a salmon trout.

bully[1] /bŏŏlee/ n. & v. ● n. (*pl.* **-ies**) a person who uses strength or power to coerce others by fear. ● v.tr. (**-ies, -ied**) **1** persecute or oppress by force or threats. **2** (foll. by *into* + verbal noun) pressure or coerce (a person) to do something (*bullied him into agreeing*). [orig. as a term of endearment, prob. f. MDu. *boele* lover]
▪ n. hooligan, bullyboy, rowdy, thug, ruffian, rough, *colloq.* roughneck, bruiser, tough guy, *sl.* hood; persecutor, oppressor, intimidator, tyrant, hector, swashbuckler. ● v. **1** persecute, victimize, intimidate, tyrannize, torment, browbeat, terrorize, oppress, hector, menace, harass, pick on, push around, *colloq.* heavy, bulldoze. **2** see RAILROAD v.

bully[2] /bŏŏlee/ adj. & int. *colloq.* ● adj. very good; first-rate. ● int. (foll. by *for*) expressing admiration or approval, or *iron.* (*bully for them!*). [perh. f BULLY[1]]
▪ adj. see *first-rate*. ● int. (*bully for you!*) bravo, great, fantastic, fabulous, marvelous, spectacular, good for you, dandy; (*iron.*) big deal, so (what?), what of it?

bully[3] /bŏŏlee/ n. & v. (in full **bully off**) ● n. (*pl.* **-ies**) the start of play in field hockey in which two opponents strike each other's sticks or the ground three times and then go for the ball. ● v.intr. (**-ies, -ied**) start play in this way. [19th c.: perh. f. *bully* scrum in Eton football, of unkn. orig.]

bully[4] /bŏŏlee/ n. (in full **bully beef**) corned beef. [F *bouilli* boiled beef f. *bouillir* BOIL[1]]

bullyboy /bŏŏleeboy/ n. a hired thug.
▪ see BULLY[1] n.

bullyrag /bŏŏleerag/ v.tr. (also **ballyrag** /bál-/) (**-ragged, -ragging**) *sl.* play tricks on; intimidate; harass. [18th c.: orig. unkn.]

bully tree /bŏŏlee/ n. = BALATA. [corrupt.]

bulrush /bŏŏlrush/ n. **1** *Brit.* = CATTAIL. **2** a rushlike water plant, *Scirpus lacustris*, used for weaving. **3** *Bibl.* a papyrus plant. [perh. f. BULL[1] = large, coarse, as in *bullfrog, bulltrout,* etc.]

bulwark /bŏŏlwərk/ n. & v. ● n. **1** a defensive wall, esp. of earth; a rampart; a mole or breakwater. **2** a person, principle, etc., that acts as a defense. **3** (usu. in *pl.*) a ship's side above deck. ● v.tr. serve as a bulwark to; defend; protect. [ME f. MLG, MDu. *bolwerk*: see BOLE[1], WORK]
▪ n. **1** see RAMPART n. 1a. **2** defense, safeguard, protection, shield, shelter, cover, guard, security, provision, buffer, barrier, fortification. ● v. defend, protect, shelter.

bum[1] /bum/ n. esp. *Brit. sl.* the buttocks. □ **bum-bag** *Brit.* = *fanny pack.* **bum-sucker** *Brit. sl.* a toady. **bum-sucking** *sl.* toadying. [ME *bom*, of unkn. orig.]

bum[2] /bum/ n., v., & adj. *sl.* ● n. a habitual loafer or tramp; a lazy dissolute person. ● v. (**bummed, bumming**) **1** *intr.* (often foll. by *about, around*) loaf or wander around; be a bum. **2** *tr.* get by begging; cadge. ● attrib.adj. **1** of poor quality; bad; worthless. **2** false; fabricated. **3** not entirely functional (*bum ankle*). □ **bum rap** imprisonment on a false charge. **bum's rush** forcible ejection. **bum steer** false in-

formation. **on the bum** vagrant; begging. [prob. abbr. or back-form. f. BUMMER]
▪ n. tramp, beggar, down-and-out, vagrant, loafer, drifter, esp. *Brit.* traveler, vagabond, derelict, pauper, grubber, gypsy, hobo, (shopping-)bag lady, esp. *Brit. Austral.* bagman, *Sc. & Ir.* tinker, *colloq.* panhandler, have-not; sponge, sponger, cadger, scrounger, scrounge, slob, moocher, *sl.* freeloader, lug. ● v. **1** see LOAF[2] v. 1. **2** borrow, beg, sponge, cadge, solicit, *colloq.* scrounge, panhandle, mooch; (*bum off*) *sl.* touch, put the touch on, freeload. ● attrib.adj. **1** see BAD adj. 1. **2** improper, unjustified, false, trumped up, untrue, fabricated, made-up, bogus. □ **bum's rush** see EXPULSION. **bum steer** bad *or* poor tip, bad *or* false information. **on the bum** begging, *colloq.* on the scrounge; see also MIGRANT adj.

bumble /búmbəl/ v.intr. **1** (foll. by *on*) speak in a rambling incoherent way. **2** (often as **bumbling** adj.) move or act ineptly; blunder. **3** make a buzz or hum. □□ **bumbler** n. [BOOM[1] + -LE[4]: partly f. *bumble* = blunderer]
▪ **2** (**bumbling**) see INEPT 1.

bumblebee /búmbəlbee/ n. any large loud humming bee of the genus *Bombus*. [as BUMBLE]

bumboat /búmbōt/ n. any small boat selling provisions, etc., to ships.

bumf /bumf/ n. (also **bumph**) *Brit. colloq.* **1** usu. *derog.* papers; documents. **2** toilet paper. [abbr. of *bum fodder*]

bummalo /búmələō/ n. (*pl.* same) a small fish, *Harpodon nehereus*, of S. Asian coasts, dried and used as food (see BOMBAY DUCK). [perh. f. Marathi *bombīl(a)*]

bummer /búmər/ n. *sl.* **1** a bum; a loafer. **2** an unpleasant occurrence. [19th c.: perh. f. G *Bummler*]

bump /bump/ n., v., & adv. ● n. **1** a dull-sounding blow or collision. **2** a swelling or dent caused by this. **3** an uneven patch on a road, field, etc. **4** *Phrenol.* any of various prominences on the skull thought to indicate different mental faculties. **5** *Aeron.* **a** an irregularity in an aircraft's motion. **b** a rising air current causing this. ● v. **1 a** *tr.* hit or come against with a bump. **b** *intr.* (of two objects) collide. **2** *intr.* (foll. by *against, into*) hit with a bump; collide with. **3** *tr.* (often foll. by *against, on*) hurt or damage by striking (*bumped my head on the ceiling; bumped the car while parking*). **4** *intr.* (usu. foll. by *along*) move or travel with much jolting (*we bumped along the road*). **5** *tr.* displace, esp. by seniority. ● adv. with a bump; suddenly; violently. □ **bump into** *colloq.* meet by chance. **bump off** *sl.* murder. **bump up** *colloq.* increase (prices, etc.). [16th c., imit.: perh. f. Scand.]
▪ n. **1** blow, collision, thud, thump, hit, knock, buffet, clunk, jerk, jolt, plump, *colloq.* whack, jar, wallop. **2** lump, protuberance, welt, swelling, tumescence, knob, bulge, protrusion, excrescence, irregularity; dent, indentation, depression, impression, mark, nick. ● v. **1, 2** knock (against), strike, hit, bang, bash, dash, smack, slam, collide (with), run into, drive into, ram, smash, crash, *sl.* wallop. **3** hurt, injure, bruise, hit; scrape, damage. **4** lurch, jerk, jolt, jostle, jog, bounce, jump, *Brit.* bucket. **5** see SUPPLANT. ● adv. crash, *colloq.* smack, plump; suddenly, all of a sudden; violently, hard. □ **bump into** meet, encounter, run into *or* across, come across, stumble over *or* upon *or* across, chance upon, fall in with, rencounter. **bump off** see MURDER v. 1. **bump up** see INCREASE v. 1.

bumper /búmpər/ n. **1** a horizontal bar or strip fixed across the front or back of a vehicle, at the end of a track, etc., to reduce damage in a collision or as a trim. **2** (usu. *attrib.*) an unusually large or fine example (*a bumper crop*). **3** a brimful glass of wine, etc. □ **bumper car** each of a number of small electrically-driven cars in an enclosure at an amusement park, driven around and bumped into each other. **bumper sticker** a strip of paper backed with adhesive that may be affixed to an automobile bumper, usu. bearing a joke, political slogan, tourism advertisement, etc.
▪ **2** (*attrib.*) see PLENTIFUL.

bumph var. of BUMF.

bumpkin /búmpkin/ n. a rustic or socially inept person.

[perh. Du. *boomken* little tree or MDu. *bommekijn* little barrel]

■ see RUSTIC *n.*

bumptious /búmpshəs/ *adj.* offensively self-assertive or conceited. □□ **bumptiously** *adv.* **bumptiousness** *n.* [BUMP, after FRACTIOUS]

■ see PUSHY.

bumpy /búmpee/ *adj.* (**bumpier, bumpiest**) **1** having many bumps (*a bumpy road*). **2** affected by bumps (*a bumpy ride*). □□ **bumpily** *adv.* **bumpiness** *n.*

■ **1** lumpy, rough, uneven, irregular, broken, knobby, knobbly, pitted; potholed, rutted, rocky. **2** rough, bouncy, jarring, jerky, jolty.

bun /bun/ *n.* **1** a small often sweet bread roll, often with dried fruit. **2** *Sc.* a rich fruit cake or currant bread. **3** hair worn in the shape of a bun. **4** (in *pl.*) *sl.* the buttocks. □ **bun fight** *Brit. sl.* a tea party. **have a bun in the oven** *sl.* be pregnant. **hot cross bun** a bun marked with a cross, traditionally eaten on Good Friday. [ME: orig. unkn.]

■ **1** bread roll, brioche.

Buna /bōōnə, byōōnə/ *n. propr.* a synthetic rubber made by polymerization of butadiene. [G (as BUTADIENE, *natrium* sodium)]

bunch /bunch/ *n. & v.* ● *n.* **1** a cluster of things growing or fastened together (*bunch of grapes*; *bunch of keys*). **2** a collection; a set or lot (*best of the bunch*). **3** *colloq.* a group; a gang. ● *v.* **1** *tr.* make into a bunch or bunches; gather into close folds. **2** *intr.* form into a group or crowd. □ **bunch grass** a N. American grass that grows in clumps. **bunch of fives** *Brit. sl.* a fist; hence also, a punch. □□ **bunchy** *adj.* [ME: orig. unkn.]

■ *n.* **1** bundle, cluster, batch, clump; bouquet, nosegay, posy, spray. **2** collection, group, lot, set, clutch, batch, number. **3** group, body, band, gathering, company, cluster, assemblage, assembly, assortment, mass, crowd, huddle, knot; gang, pack, party, *colloq.* crew. ● *v.* sort, class, classify, categorize, organize, arrange, group, bracket, order; gather, collect, band, crowd, group, cluster, assemble, mass, huddle, knot, congregate, accumulate.

bunco /búngkō/ *n. & v.* (also **bunko**) *sl.* ● *n.* (*pl.* **-os**) a swindle, esp. by card sharping or a confidence trick. ● *v.tr.* (**-oes, -oed**) swindle; cheat. [perh. f. Sp. *banca* a card game]

■ *n.* see SWINDLE *n.* 1, 3. ● *v.* see SWINDLE *v.*

buncombe var. of BUNKUM.

Bundesrat /bōōndəsraat/ *n.* the Upper House of Parliament in Germany or in Austria. [G f. *Bund* federation + *Rat* council]

Bundestag /bōōndəstaag/ *n.* the Lower House of Parliament in Germany. [G f. *Bund* federation + *tagen* confer]

bundle /búndəl/ *n. & v.* ● *n.* **1** a collection of things tied or fastened together. **2** a set of nerve fibers, etc., banded together. **3** *sl.* a large amount of money. ● *v.* **1** *tr.* **a** (usu. foll. by *up*) tie in or make into a bundle (*bundled up my exercise things*). **b** sell (a product) together with another one in a single transaction. **2** *tr.* (usu. foll. by *into*) throw or push, esp. quickly or confusedly (*bundled the papers into the drawer*). **3** *tr.* (usu. foll. by *out, off, away,* etc.) send (esp. a person) away hurriedly or unceremoniously (*bundled them off the premises*). **4** *intr. archaic* sleep clothed with another person, esp. a fiancé(e), as a local custom. □ **be a bundle of nerves** (or **prejudices,** etc.) be extremely nervous (or prejudiced, etc.). **bundle up** dress warmly or cumbersomely. **go a bundle on** *Brit. sl.* be very fond of. □□ **bundler** *n.* [ME, perh. f. OE *byndelle* a binding, but also f. LG, Du *bundel*]

■ *n.* **1** bunch, collection, assemblage, cluster, group, package, parcel, packet, pack, *Austral.* shiralee, *Austral. sl.* Matilda; bale, sheaf. **3** (*make a bundle*) make a killing *or* a pretty penny *or* big money *or* a mint *or* a fortune, *colloq.* make a packet *or* a pile, *sl.* make big bucks. ● *v.* **1** tie up; collect, gather (together), pack (up), package. **2** throw, push, thrust, stuff, cram, squeeze, ram, *colloq.* shove. **3** (*bundle off*) dispatch,

pack off, hustle *or* hurry off *or* away, send away *or* off, dismiss, drive off, order off *or* out *or* away. □ **be a bundle of nerves** see WORRY *v.* 1.

bung[1] /bung/ *n. & v.* ● *n.* a stopper for closing a hole in a container, esp. a cask. ● *v.tr.* **1** stop with a bung. **2** *Brit. sl.* throw; toss. □ **bunged up** closed; blocked. [MDu. *bonghe*]

■ *n.* see STOPPER *n.* ● *v.* **1** see PLUG *v.* 1.

bung[2] /bung/ *adj. Austral. & NZ sl.* dead; ruined; useless. □ **go bung 1** die. **2** fail; go bankrupt. [Aboriginal]

bungalow /búnggəlō/ *n.* a one-storied house. [Gujarati *bangalo* f. Hind. *baṅglā* belonging to Bengal]

■ see CABIN *n.* 1.

bungee /búnjee/ *n.* (in full **bungee cord**) elasticized cord used for securing baggage and in bungee jumping. □ **bungee jumping** the sport of jumping from a height while secured by a bungee from the ankles or a harness. [20th c.: orig. unkn.]

bunghole // *n.* a hole for filling or emptying a cask, etc.

bungle /búnggəl/ *v. & n.* ● *v.* **1** *tr.* blunder over, mismanage, or fail at (a task). **2** *intr.* work badly or clumsily. ● *n.* a bungled attempt; bungled work. □□ **bungler** *n.* [imit.: cf. BUMBLE]

■ *v.* **1** see BOTCH *v.* 1. **2** bumble, fumble, make a blunder *or* faux pas, blunder, *colloq.* slip up, drop a brick, flub, *sl.* screw *or* louse up, mess up, goof, make a mess, *Brit. colloq.* drop a clanger, boob. ● *n.* see MISTAKE *n.*

bunion /búnyən/ *n.* a swelling on the foot, esp. at the first joint of the big toe. [OF *buignon* f. *buigne* bump on the head]

bunk[1] /bungk/ *n. & v.* ● *n.* a sleeping berth, esp. a shelflike bed against a wall, e.g., in a ship. ● *v. intr.* **1** sleep in a bunk. **2** share a bunk bed (*bunked together in the army*). □ **bunk bed** each of two or more beds one above the other, forming a unit. [18th c.: orig. unkn.]

bunk[2] /bungk/ *n.* □ **do a bunk** *Brit. sl.* leave or abscond hurriedly. [19th c.: orig. unkn.]

bunk[3] /bungk/ *n. sl.* nonsense; humbug. [abbr. of BUNKUM]

■ see NONSENSE.

bunker /búngkər/ *n. & v.* ● *n.* **1** a large container or compartment for storing fuel. **2** a reinforced underground shelter, esp. for use in wartime. **3** a hollow filled with sand, used as an obstacle in a golf course. ● *v.tr.* **1** fill the fuel bunkers of (a ship, etc.). **2** (usu. in *passive*) **a** trap in a bunker (in sense 3). **b** *Brit.* bring into difficulties. [19th c.: orig. unkn.]

bunkhouse /búngkhows/ *n.* a house where workers, ranch hands, etc., are lodged.

bunkum /búngkəm/ *n.* (also **buncombe**) nonsense; humbug. [orig. *buncombe* f. *Buncombe* county in N. Carolina, mentioned in a nonsense speech by its congressman, c.1820]

■ see NONSENSE.

bunny /búnee/ *n.* (*pl.* **-ies**) **1** a child's name for a rabbit. **2** *Austral. sl.* a victim or dupe. **3** a club hostess, waitress, etc., wearing a skimpy costume with ears and a tail suggestive of a rabbit. [dial. *bun* rabbit]

Bunsen burner /búnsən/ *n.* a small adjustable gas burner used in scientific work as a source of intense heat. [R. W. Bunsen, Ger. chemist d. 1899]

bunt[1] /bunt/ *n.* the baggy center of a fishing net, sail, etc. [16th c.: orig. unkn.]

bunt[2] /bunt/ *n.* a disease of wheat caused by the fungus *Tilletia caries*. [18th c.: orig. unkn.]

bunt[3] /bunt/ *v. & n.* ● *v.* **1** *tr. & intr.* push with the head or horns; butt. **2** *tr. Baseball* to tap or push (a ball) with the bat without swinging. ● *n.* an act of bunting. [19th c.: cf. BUTT[1]]

bunting[1] /búnting/ *n.* any of numerous seed-eating birds of the family Emberizidae, related to the finches and sparrows. [ME: orig. unkn.]

/.../ **pronunciation**	● **part of speech**
□ **phrases, idioms, and compounds**	
□□ **derivatives**	■ **synonym section**
cross-references appear in SMALL CAPITALS or *italics*	

bunting[2] /búnting/ n. **1** flags and other decorations. **2** a loosely woven fabric used for these. [18th c.: orig. unkn.]

bunting[3] /búnting/ n. a baby's hooded sleeping bag made of soft fabric. [prob. f. the term in the nursery rhyme "Bye, baby bunting"]

buntline /búntlin, -lin/ n. a line for confining the bunt (see BUNT[1]) when furling a sail.

bunya /búnyə/ n. (also **bunya bunya**) *Austral.* a tall coniferous tree, *Araucaria bidwillii*, bearing large nutritious cones. [Aboriginal]

bunyip /búnyip/ n. *Austral.* **1** a fabulous monster inhabiting swamps and lagoons. **2** an impostor. [Aboriginal]

buoy /bóō-ee, boy/ n. & v. ● n. **1** an anchored float serving as a navigation mark or to show reefs, etc. **2** a lifebuoy. ● v.tr. **1** (usu. foll. by *up*) **a** keep afloat. **b** sustain the courage or spirits of (a person, etc.); uplift; encourage. **2** (often foll. by *out*) mark with a buoy or buoys. [ME prob. f. MDu. *bo(e)ye*, ult. f. L *boia* collar f. Gk *boeiai* ox hides]

■ n. **1** (navigational *or* channel) marker, float, beacon, dolphin, drogue. **2** lifebuoy, lifebelt. ● v. **1** keep afloat, keep a person's head above water; uplift, lift (up), raise, keep up, elevate, support, sustain, hearten, cheer (up), comfort, enliven, gladden.

buoyancy /bóyənsee/ n. **1** the capacity to be or remain buoyant. **2** resilience; recuperative power. **3** cheerfulness.

buoyant /bóyənt/ adj. **1 a** able or apt to keep afloat or rise to the top of a liquid or gas. **b** (of a liquid or gas) able to keep something afloat. **2** lighthearted; resilient. □□ **buoyantly** adv. [F *buoyant* or Sp. *boyante* part. of *boyar* float f. *boya* BUOY]

■ **1 a** afloat, floating, floatable. **2** light, lively, vivacious, bubbly, bright, cheerful, happy, carefree, animated, jaunty, bouncy, cheery, sunny, ebullient, lighthearted, easygoing, *colloq.* peppy; resilient, robust, tough, strong, *poet.* blithe.

bur /bər/ n. var. of BURR. □ **bur oak** a N. American oak, *Quercus macrocarpa*, with large fringed acorn cups. [ME: cf. Da. *burre* bur, burdock, Sw. *kard-borre* burdock]

bur. *abbr.* bureau.

burble /bórbəl/ v. & n. ● v.intr. **1** speak ramblingly; make a murmuring noise. **2** *Aeron.* (of an airflow) break up into turbulence. ● n. **1** a murmuring noise. **2** rambling speech. □□ **burbler** n. [19th c.: imit.]

■ v. **1** see BABBLE v. 1a, b. ● n. **1** see GURGLE n. 2 see BABBLE n. 1b.

burbot /bórbət/ n. an eellike, flat-headed, bearded freshwater fish, *Lota lota*. [ME: cf. OF *barbote*]

burden /bórdən/ n. & v. ● n. **1** a load, esp. a heavy one. **2** an oppressive duty, obligation, expense, emotion, etc. **3** the bearing of loads (*beast of burden*). **4** (also *archaic* **burthen** /bórthən/) a ship's carrying capacity; tonnage. **5 a** the refrain or chorus of a song. **b** the chief theme or gist of a speech, book, poem, etc. ● v.tr. load with a burden; encumber; oppress. □ **burden of proof** the obligation to prove one's case. □□ **burdensome** adj. **burdensomeness** n. [OE *byrthen*: rel. to BIRTH]

■ n. **1, 2** load, weight, onus; strain, stress, pressure, trouble, trial, tribulation, hardship, imposition, trouble, responsibility, anxiety, worry, charge, millstone, cross, albatross, encumbrance; brunt, force, impact; see also BOTHER n. 1. **5 a** refrain, chorus, reprise. **b** see THEME 1. ● v. load (down), weigh down, saddle, encumber, bow *or* press *or* wear down, crush, overload, lumber; tax, oppress, trouble, pressure, overwhelm.

□□ **burdensome** onerous, cumbersome, oppressive, weighty, troublesome, wearisome, exhausting, bothersome, distressing, worrying, worrisome, vexatious, irksome, trying; arduous, difficult, exacting, hard, heavy, punishing, toilsome, grueling, backbreaking.

burdock /bórdok/ n. any plant of the genus *Arctium*, with prickly flowers and docklike leaves. [BUR + DOCK[3]]

bureau /byōōrō/ n. (pl. **bureaus** or **bureaux** /-rōz/) **1 a** a chest of drawers. **b** *Brit.* a writing desk with drawers and usu. an angled top opening downwards to form a writing

surface. **2 a** an office or department for transacting specific business. **b** a government department. [F, = desk, orig. its baize covering, f. OF *burel* f. *bure*, *buire* dark brown ult. f. Gk *purros* red]

■ **1 a** chest of drawers, chest, commode, dresser, highboy, tallboy. **2** office, agency, department, division, section, subdivision, subsection, desk; ministry.

bureaucracy /byōōrókrəsee/ n. (pl. **-ies**) **1 a** government by central administration. **b** a nation or organization so governed. **2** the officials of such a government, esp. regarded as oppressive and inflexible. **3** conduct typical of such officials. [F *bureaucratie*: see BUREAU]

■ **2, 3** officialdom, officialism, red tape, rigmarole, formalities, punctiliousness, punctilio.

bureaucrat /byōōrəkrat/ n. **1** an official in a bureaucracy. **2** an inflexible or insensitive administrator. □□ **bureaucratic** /-krátik/ adj. **bureaucratically** adv. [F *bureaucrate* (as BUREAUCRACY)]

■ **1** see FUNCTIONARY.

bureaucratize /byōōrókrətiz/ v.tr. govern by or transform into a bureaucratic system. □□ **bureaucratization** /-tizáyshən/ n.

burette /byōōrét/ n. (also **buret**) a graduated glass tube with a stopcock for measuring small volumes of liquid in chemical analysis. [F]

burg /bərg/ n. *colloq.* a town or city. [see BOROUGH]

■ see CITY 1a.

burgage /bórgij/ n. *hist.* (in England and Scotland) tenure of land in a town on a yearly rent. [ME f. med.L *burgagium* f. *burgus* BOROUGH]

burgee /bórjee/ n. a triangular or swallow-tailed flag bearing the colors or emblem of a yacht club. [18th c.: perh. = (ship)owner, ult. F *bourgeois*: see BURGESS]

■ see PENNANT.

burgeon /bórjən/ v. & n. *literary* ● v.intr. **1** begin to grow rapidly; flourish. **2** put forth young shoots; bud. ● n. a bud or young shoot. [ME f. OF *bor-*, *burjon* ult. f. LL *burra* wool]

■ v. **1** see FLOURISH v. 1a, d. **2** see SHOOT v. 5.

burger /bórgər/ n. **1** *colloq.* a hamburger. **2** (in *comb.*) a certain kind of hamburger or variation of it (*beefburger*; *veggieburger*). [abbr.]

burgess /bórjis/ n. **1** *Brit.* an inhabitant of a town or borough, esp. of one with full municipal rights. **2** *Brit. hist.* a Member of Parliament for a borough, corporate town, or university. **3** *hist.* a borough magistrate or legislator in colonial Maryland or Virginia. [ME f. OF *burgeis* ult. f. LL *burgus* BOROUGH]

burgh /bərg, búrə/ n. *hist.* a Scottish borough or chartered town. □□ **burghal** /bórgəl/ adj. [Sc. form of BOROUGH]

■ see TOWN 1.

burgher /bórgər/ n. **1** a citizen or freeman, esp. of a town on the European continent. **2** *S.Afr. hist.* a citizen of a Boer republic. **3** a descendant of a Dutch or Portuguese colonist in Sri Lanka. [G *Burger* or Du. *burger* f. *Burg*, *burg* BOROUGH]

burglar /bórglər/ n. a person who commits burglary. □□ **burglarious** /-gláireeəs/ adj. [legal AF *burgler*, rel. to OF *burgier* pillage]

■ housebreaker, thief, robber, cat burglar, picaroon, *archaic* lurcher, *sl.* cracksman, yegg.

burglarize /bórglərīz/ v. **1** tr. commit burglary against (a building or person). **2** intr. commit burglary.

■ see ROB 1.

burglary /bórgləree/ n. (pl. **-ies**) **1** entry into a building illegally with intent to commit theft, do bodily harm, or do damage. **2** an instance of this. [legal AF *burglarie*: see BURGLAR]

burgle /bórgəl/ v.tr. & intr. = BURGLARIZE. [back-form. f BURGLAR]

burgomaster /bórgəmastər/ n. the mayor of a Dutch or Flemish town. [Du. *burgemeester* f. *burg* BOROUGH: assim. to MASTER]

burgrave /bórgrayv/ n. *hist.* the ruler of a town or castle. [G *Burggraf* f. *Burg* BOROUGH + *Graf* COUNT[2]]

burgundy /bórgəndee/ n. (pl. **-ies**) **1 a** the wine (usu. red) of Burgundy in E. France. **b** a similar wine from another place. **2** the dark red color of Burgundy wine.

burhel var. of BHARAL.

burial /béreeəl/ *n.* **1 a** the burying of a dead body. **b** a funeral. **2** *Archaeol.* a grave or its remains. □ **burial ground** a cemetery. [ME, erron. formed as sing. of OE *byrgels* f. Gmc: rel. to BURY]
■ **1** interment, entombment, *literary* sepulture; funeral, obsequies. **2** grave, tomb, burial vault *or* chamber *or* mound, sepulcher, tumulus, *Archaeol.* barrow. □ **burial ground** see GRAVEYARD.

burin /byŏŏrin, bár-/ *n.* **1** a steel tool for engraving on copper or wood. **2** *Archaeol.* a flint tool with a chisel point. [F]

burk var. of BERK.

burka /bárkə/ *n.* a long enveloping garment worn in public by Muslim women. [Hind. f. Arab. *burka'*]

Burkitt's lymphoma /bárkits/ *n. Med.* a malignant tumor of the lymphatic system, esp. affecting children of Central Africa. [D. P. *Burkitt*, Brit. surgeon b. 1911]

burl /bərl/ *n.* **1** a knot or lump in wool or cloth. **2** a rounded knotty growth on a tree. [ME f. OF *bourle* tuft of wool, dimin. of *bourre* coarse wool f. LL *burra* wool]

burlap /bárlap/ *n.* **1** coarse canvas esp. of jute used for sacking, etc. **2** a similar lighter material for use in dressmaking or furnishing. [17th c.: orig. unkn.]

burlesque /bərlésk/ *n., adj., & v.* ● *n.* **1 a** comic imitation, esp. in parody of a dramatic or literary work. **b** a performance or work of this kind. **c** bombast; mock-seriousness. **2** a variety show, often including striptease. ● *adj.* of or in the nature of burlesque. ● *v.tr.* (**burlesques, burlesqued, burlesquing**) make or give a burlesque of. □□ **burlesquer** *n.* [F f. It. *burlesco* f. *burla* mockery]
■ *n.* **1** imitation, caricature, satirization, mimicry, lampoonery, ridicule, derision, *colloq.* spoofery; lampoon, parody, satire, mockery, travesty, *colloq.* spoof, takeoff, send-up; see also BOMBAST. **2** variety show, vaudeville, *Brit.* music hall, striptease, strip show, *colloq.* girlie show. ● *adj.* satirical, derisive, mocking, sardonic, ironic, ironical, mock-heroic, mock-serious, mock-pathetic. ● *v.* satirize, lampoon, parody, caricature, imitate, travesty, ridicule, mock, mimic, *colloq.* spoof, take off, send up.

burly /bárlee/ *adj.* (**burlier, burliest**) of stout sturdy build; big and strong. □□ **burliness** *n.* [ME *borli* prob. f. an OE form = 'fit for the bower' (BOWER¹)]
■ stout, sturdy, corpulent, large, big, hefty, stocky, thickset, brawny, chunky, heavy, beefy, muscular, muscly, strong, strapping, rugged, tough, husky.

Burmese /bármeez/ *n. & adj.* ● *n.* (*pl.* same) **1 a** a native or inhabitant of Burma (also called Myanmar) in SE Asia. **b** a person of Burmese descent. **2** a member of the largest ethnic group of Burma. **3** the language of this group. ● *adj.* of or relating to Burma or its people or language.

burn¹ /bərn/ *v. & n.* ● *v.* (*past* and *past part.* **burned** or **burnt**) **1** *tr. & intr.* be or cause to be consumed or destroyed by fire. **2** *intr.* **a** blaze or glow with fire. **b** be in the state characteristic of fire. **3** *tr. & intr.* be or cause to be injured or damaged by fire or great heat or by radiation. **4** *tr. & intr.* use or be used as a source of heat, light, or other energy. **5** *tr. & intr.* char or scorch in cooking (*burned the vegetables; the vegetables are burning*). **6** *tr.* produce (a hole, a mark, etc.) by fire or heat. **7** *tr.* **a** subject (clay, chalk, etc.) to heat for a purpose. **b** harden (bricks) by fire. **c** make (lime or charcoal) by heat. **8** *tr.* color, tan, or parch with heat or light (*we were burned brown by the sun*). **9** *tr. & intr.* put or be put to death by fire or electrocution. **10** *tr.* **a** cauterize; brand. **b** (foll. by *in*) imprint by burning. **11** *tr. & intr.* make or be hot; give or feel a sensation or pain of or like heat. **12 a** *tr. & intr.* (often foll. by *with*) make or be passionate; feel or cause to feel great emotion (*burn with shame*). **b** *intr.* (usu. foll. by *to* + infin.) desire passionately; long. **13** *intr. sl.* drive fast. **14** *tr. sl.* anger; infuriate. **15** *intr.* (foll. by *into*) (of acid, etc.) gradually penetrate (into) causing disintegration. ● *n.* **1** a mark or injury caused by or as if by burning. **2** the ignition of a rocket engine in flight, giving extra thrust. **3** a

forest area cleared by burning. **4** *Brit. sl.* a cigarette. **5** *Brit. sl.* a car race. □ **burn one's bridges** (or *Brit.* **boats**) commit oneself irrevocably. **burn the candle at both ends** exhaust one's strength or resources by undertaking too much. **burn down 1 a** destroy (a building) by burning. **b** (of a building) be destroyed by fire. **2** burn less vigorously as fuel fails. **burn one's fingers** suffer for meddling or rashness. **burn a hole in one's pocket** (of money) be quickly spent. **burning glass** a lens for concentrating the sun's rays on an object to burn it. **burn in** darken (part of a photograph) by masking other parts of it and giving more exposure to the unmasked portion during printing. **burn low** (of fire) be nearly out. **burn off** be dissipated by the sun, as fog or mist. **burn the midnight oil** read or work late into the night. **burn out 1** be reduced to nothing by burning. **2** fail or cause to fail by burning. **3** (usu. *refl.*) suffer physical or emotional exhaustion. **4** consume the contents of by burning. **5** make (a person) homeless by burning his or her house. **burnt ocher** (or **sienna** or **umber**) a pigment darkened by burning. **burnt offering 1** an offering burned on an altar as a sacrifice. **2** *joc.* overcooked food. **burned-out** (also **burnt-out**) physically or emotionally exhausted. **burn up 1** get rid of by fire. **2** begin to blaze. **3** *sl.* be or make furious. **have money to burn** have more money than one needs. [OE *birnan, bærnan* f. Gmc]
■ *v.* **1** ignite, set on fire, set alight, set fire to, burn up, fire, light, kindle, incinerate, *sl.* torch. **2** blaze, flame, flare (up), glow, smolder, be on fire *or* ablaze *or* in flames, burn up. **5** overcook, blacken, char, singe, scorch. **8** tan, color, suntan; bake, parch, scorch, char, wither, dry out *or* up, *archaic* sear. **11** see BROIL¹ 2. **12 a** see FLUSH¹ *v.* 1a, PULSATE, SMART *v.* **b** desire, yearn, wish, long, itch. **13** see RACE *v.* 6a. **14** see INFURIATE *v.* ● *n.* **1** scorch, scar, brand. □ **burn the candle at both ends** see *overdo* it. **burn the midnight oil** see STUDY *v.* 2. **burn out 3** see EXHAUST *v.* 2. **burned-out** see *spent* (SPEND 3). **burn up 2** see BURN¹ *v.* 1, 2 above. **3** see MADDEN.

burn² /bərn/ *n. Sc.* a small stream. [OE *burna*, etc., f. Gmc]

burner /bárnər/ *n.* the part of a gas stove, lamp, etc., that emits and shapes the flame. □ **on the back** (or **front**) **burner** *colloq.* receiving little (or much) attention.

burnet /bərnét, bárnit/ *n.* **1** any rosaceous plant of the genus *Sanguisorba*, with pink or red flowers. **2** any of several diurnal moths of the family Zygaenidae, with crimson spots on greenish black wings. [obs. *burnet* (adj.) dark brown f. OF *burnete*]

burning /bárning/ *adj.* **1** ardent; intense (*burning desire*). **2** hotly discussed; exciting (*burning question*). **3** flagrant (*burning shame*). **4** that burns; on fire; very hot. □ **burning bush 1** any of various shrubs with red fruits or red autumn leaves (with ref. to Exod. 3:2). **2** fraxinella. □□ **burningly** *adv.*
■ **1** vehement, ardent, excited, passionate, impassioned, fervent, fervid, avid, intense, fiery, fierce, strong, violent, raging, towering, enthusiastic, *literary* perfervid. **2** see *thrilling* (THRILL). **3** see FLAGRANT. **4** flaming, blazing, fiery; ablaze, aflame, afire, on fire; see also HOT *adj.* 1.

burnish /bárnish/ *v.tr.* polish by rubbing. □□ **burnisher** *n.* [ME f. OF *burnir* = *brunir* f. *brun* BROWN]
■ see POLISH *v.* 1.

burnoose /bərnōōs/ *n.* (also **burnous**) an Arab or Moorish hooded cloak. [F f. Arab. *burnus* f. Gk *birros* cloak]

burnout /bárnowt/ *n.* **1** physical or emotional exhaustion, esp. caused by stress. **2** depression; disillusionment.
■ **1** see EXHAUSTION 2. **2** see DEPRESSION 1b.

burnt see BURN¹.

burp /bərp/ *v. & n. colloq.* ● *v.* **1** *intr.* belch. **2** *tr.* make (a

/.../	**pronunciation**	● **part of speech**
□	**phrases, idioms, and compounds**	
□□	**derivatives**	■ **synonym section**
cross-references appear in SMALL CAPITALS or *italics*		

baby) belch, usu. by patting its back. ● *n.* a belch. □ **burp gun** *sl.* a lightweight machine gun. [imit.]

burr /bər/ *n. & v.* ● *n.* **1 a** a whirring sound. **b** a rough sounding of the letter *r.* **2 a** a rough edge left on cut or punched metal or paper. **b** a surgeon's or dentist's small drill. **3 a** a siliceous rock used for millstones. **b** a whetstone. **4 a** a prickly clinging seedcase or flowerhead. **b** any plant producing these. **5** a person hard to shake off. **6** the coronet of a deer's antler. ● *v.* **1** *tr.* pronounce with a burr. **2** *intr.* speak indistinctly. **3** *intr.* make a whirring sound. [var. of BUR]

burrito /bəreˈetō/ *n.* (*pl.* **-os**) a tortilla rolled around a usu. meat or bean filling. [Amer. Sp., dimin. of *burro* BURRO]

burro /bə́rō, boŏ́rō, bú́rō/ *n.* (*pl.* **-os**) a small donkey used as a pack animal. □ **burro's tail** a succulent plant of Mexico *Sedum morganianum*, with plump hanging stems and clustered pale green leaves. [Sp.]

burrow /bə́rō, bú́rō/ *n. & v.* ● *n.* a hole or tunnel dug by a small animal, esp. a rabbit, as a dwelling. ● *v.* **1** *intr.* make or live in a burrow. **2** *tr.* make (a hole, etc.) by digging. **3** *intr.* hide oneself. **4** *intr.* (foll. by *into*) investigate; search. □□ **burrower** *n.* [ME, app. var. of BOROUGH]
■ *n.* excavation, hole, warren, tunnel; den, set, lair. ● *v.* **1, 2** dig, tunnel, bore, root (around *or* about), *poet.* delve; excavate. **3** see HIDE[1] *v.* 2. **4** (*burrow into*) see INVESTIGATE.

bursa /bə́rsə/ *n.* (*pl.* **bursae** /-see/ or **bursas**) *Anat.* a fluid-filled sac or saclike cavity to lessen friction. □□ **bursal** *adj.* [med.L = bag: cf. PURSE]

bursar /bə́rsər/ *n.* **1** a treasurer, esp. the person in charge of the funds and other property of a college. **2** *Brit.* the holder of a bursary. □□ **bursarship** *n.* [F *boursier* or (in sense 1) med.L *bursarius* f. *bursa* bag]

bursary /bə́rsəree/ *n.* (*pl.* **-ies**) **1** the post or room of a bursar. **2** *Brit.* a grant, esp. a scholarship. □□ **bursarial** /-sáireeəl/ *adj.* [med.L *bursaria* (as BURSAR)]

bursitis /bərsítis/ *n.* inflammation of a bursa.

burst /bərst/ *v. & n.* ● *v.* (*past* and *past part.* **burst**) **1 a** *intr.* break suddenly and violently apart by expansion of contents or internal pressure. **b** *tr.* cause to do this. **c** *tr.* send (a container, etc.) violently apart. **2 a** *tr.* open forcibly. **b** *intr.* come open or be opened forcibly. **3 a** *intr.* (usu. foll. by *in, out*) make one's way suddenly, dramatically, or by force. **b** *tr.* break away from or through (*the river burst its banks*). **4** *tr. & intr.* fill or be full to overflowing. **5** *intr.* appear or come suddenly (*burst into flame; burst upon the scene; sun burst out*). **6** *intr.* (foll. by *into*) suddenly begin to shed or utter (esp. *burst into tears* or *laughter* or *song*). **7** *intr.* be as if about to burst because of effort, excitement, etc. **8** *tr.* suffer bursting of (*burst a blood vessel*). **9** *tr.* separate (continuous stationery) into single sheets. ● *n.* **1** the act of or an instance of bursting; a split. **2** a sudden issuing forth (*burst of flame*). **3** a sudden outbreak (*burst of applause*). **4 a** a short sudden effort; a spurt. **b** a gallop. **5** an explosion. □ **bursting at the seams** being fuller or more crowded than expected. **burst out 1** suddenly begin (*burst out laughing*). **2** exclaim. [OE *berstan* f. Gmc]
■ *v.* **1** break (apart), rupture, split, shatter, come apart, explode, blow up, *colloq.* bust, *literary* break asunder; puncture, pop. **2** break *or* force open. **3 a** force *or* break *or* push *or* drive *or* thrust one's way. **5** break (out *or* forth), erupt; (*burst out*) emerge, come out *or* forth, appear, show *or* manifest (oneself *or* itself), be revealed. **6** (*burst into*) burst out in, break into, burst forth with, erupt *or* collapse *or* dissolve into. **7** (*bursting*) see TENSE *adj.* 1. ● *n.* **1** see SPLIT *n.* 2. **3** see OUTBURST. **4** see SPURT *n.* 2. **5** see BLAST *n.* 2. □ **burst out 1** break out, erupt *or* explode into. **2** see BLURT, EXCLAIM 1.

burthen *archaic* var. of BURDEN *n.* 4.

burton[1] /bə́rt'n/ *n.* □ **go for a burton** *Brit. sl.* be lost or destroyed or killed. [20th c.: perh. *Burton* ale f. *Burton-on-Trent* in England]

burton[2] /bə́rt'n/ *n.* a light two-block tackle for hoisting. [ME *Breton tackles*: see BRETON]

bury /béree/ *v.tr.* (**-ies, -ied**) **1** place (a dead body) in the earth, in a tomb, or in the sea. **2** lose by death (*has buried three husbands*). **3 a** put under ground (*bury alive*). **b** hide (treasure, a bone, etc.) in the earth. **c** cover up; submerge. **4 a** put out of sight (*buried his face in his hands*). **b** consign to obscurity (*the idea was buried after brief discussion*). **c** put away; forget. **5** involve deeply (*buried himself in his work; was buried in a book*). □ **bury the hatchet** cease to quarrel. **burying beetle** a sexton beetle. **burying ground** (or **place**) a cemetery. [OE *byrgan* f. WG: cf. BURIAL]
■ **1** inter, lay to rest, *literary* inhume. **3 b, c** conceal, hide, secrete, cache, keep secret, *colloq.* stash (away); cover (up), submerge, obscure, cloak, veil, shroud, screen, wrap, enclose, envelop. **4 b, c** see ABANDON *v.* 2a, DISREGARD *v.* 1. **5** see IMMERSE 2. □ **bury the hatchet** see *make up* 4. **burying ground** see GRAVEYARD.

bus /bus/ *n. & v.* ● *n.* (*pl.* **buses** or **busses**) **1** a large passenger vehicle, esp. one serving the public on a fixed route. **2** *colloq.* an automobile, airplane, etc. **3** *Computing* a defined set of conductors carrying data and control signals within a computer. ● *v.* (**buses** or **busses, bused,** or **bussed, busing** or **bussing**) **1** *intr.* go by bus. **2** *tr.* transport by bus, esp. children to more distant schools to promote racial integration. □ **bus lane** a part of a roadway marked off mainly for use by buses. **bus shelter** a shelter from rain, etc., beside a bus stop. **bus station** a center, esp. in a town, where (esp. long-distance) buses depart and arrive. **bus stop 1** a regular stopping place for a bus. **2** a sign marking this. [abbr. of OMNIBUS]
■ *n.* **1** see COACH *n.* 1. □ **bus station** see STATION *n.* 1.

bus. *abbr.* business.

busbar /búsbaar/ *n. Electr.* a system of conductors in a generating or receiving station on which power is concentrated for distribution.

busboy /búsboy/ *n.* an assistant to a restaurant waiter who performs such chores as filling water glasses and removing dirty dishes from diners' tables. [f. *omnibus*]

busby /búzbee/ *n.* (*pl.* **-ies**) (not in official use) a tall fur hat worn by some military, esp. British, units. [18th c.: orig. unkn.]

bush[1] /boŏsh/ *n.* **1** a shrub or clump of shrubs with stems of moderate length. **2** a thing resembling this, esp. a clump of hair or fur. **3** (esp. in Australia and Africa) a wild uncultivated or settled district; woodland or forest. **4** *hist.* a bunch of ivy as a vintner's sign. □ **bush baby** (*pl.* **-ies**) a small African tree-climbing lemur, a galago. **bush basil** a culinary herb, *Ocimum minimum.* **bush jacket** a light cotton jacket with a belt. **bush lawyer 1** *Austral. & NZ* a person claiming legal knowledge without qualifications for it. **2** *NZ* a bramble. **bush pilot** a pilot who flies a small plane into remote areas. **bush sickness** a disease of animals due to a lack of cobalt in the soil. **bush telegraph** rapid spreading of information, a rumor, etc. **go bush** *Austral.* leave one's usual surroundings; run wild. [ME f. OE & ON, ult. f. Gmc]
■ **3** see STICK[1] *n.* 12.

bush[2] /boŏsh/ *n. Brit.* = BUSHING. [MDu. *busse* BOX[1]]

bushbuck /boŏshbuk/ *n.* a small antelope, *Tragelaphus scriptus*, of southern Africa, having a chestnut coat with white stripes. [BUSH[1] + BUCK[1], after Du. *boschbok* f. *bosch* bush]

bushed /boŏsht/ *adj. colloq.* **1** tired out. **2** *Austral. & NZ* a lost in the bush. **b** bewildered.
■ **1** see TIRED 1.

bushel /boŏshəl/ *n.* a measure of capacity for grain, fruit, etc. (64 pints; *Brit.* 8 gallons, or 36.4 liters). □□ **bushelful** *n.* (*pl.* **-fuls**). [ME f. OF *buissiel*, etc., perh. of Gaulish orig.]

bushfire /boŏshfīr/ *n.* esp. *Austral.* a fire in a forest or in scrub often spreading widely.

bushido /boŏsheedō/ *n.* the code of honor and morals evolved by the Japanese samurai. [Jap., = military knight's way]

bushing /boŏshing/ *n.* **1** a metal lining for a round hole enclosing a revolving shaft, etc. **2** a sleeve providing electrical insulation.

bushman /boŏshmən/ *n.* (*pl.* **-men**) **1** a person who lives or travels in the Australian bush. **2** (**Bushman**) **a** a member of an aboriginal people in S. Africa. **b** the language of this people. [BUSH¹ + MAN: sense 2 after Du. *boschjesman* f. *bosch* bush]

bushmaster /bŏŏshmastər/ *n.* a venomous viper, *Lachesis muta*, of Central and S. America. [perh. f. Du. *boschmeester*]

bushranger /bŏŏshraynjər/ *n. hist.* an Australian outlaw living in the bush.

bushveld /bŏŏshfelt/ *n.* open country consisting largely of bush. [BUSH¹ + VELD, after Afrik. *bosveld*]

bushwhack /bŏŏsh-hwak, -wak/ *v.* **1** *intr.* **a** clear woods and bush country. **b** live or travel in bush country. **2** *tr.* ambush.
■ **2** see AMBUSH *v.*

bushwhacker /bŏŏsh-hwakər, -wakər/ *n.* **1 a** a person who clears woods and bush country. **b** a person who lives or travels in bush country. **2** a guerrilla fighter (orig. in the American Civil War).

bushy¹ /bŏŏshee/ *adj.* (**bushier, bushiest**) **1** growing thickly like a bush. **2** having many bushes. **3** covered with bush. □□ **bushily** *adv.* **bushiness** *n.*
■ **1** see THICK *adj.* 3c.

bushy² /bŏŏshee/ *n.* (*pl.* **-ies**) *Austral. & NZ colloq.* a person who lives in the bush (as distinct from in a town).

busily /bízilee/ *adv.* in a busy manner.

business /bíznis/ *n.* **1** one's regular occupation, profession, or trade. **2** a thing that is one's concern. **3 a** a task or duty. **b** a reason for coming (*what is your business?*). **4** serious work or activity (*get down to business*). **5** *derog.* an affair; a matter (*sick of the whole business*). **6** a thing or series of things needing to be dealt with (*the business of the day*). **7** business; relations; dealings, esp. of a commercial nature (*good stroke of business*). **8** a commercial house or firm. **9** *Theatr.* action on stage. **10** a difficult matter (*what a business it is!*; *made a great business of it*). □ **business card** a card printed with one's name and professional details. **the business end** *colloq.* the functional part of a tool or device. **business park** an office park or industrial park. **business person** a businessman or businesswoman. **business reply mail** a system of sending business mail in envelopes prepaid by the addressee. **business studies** training in economics, management, etc. **business suit 1** a man's suit consisting of a jacket, trousers, and sometimes a vest. **2** a woman's suit, consisting of a jacket and usu. a skirt. **has no business to** has no right to. **in business 1** trading or dealing. **2** able to begin operations. **in the business of 1** engaged in. **2** intending to (*we are not in the business of surrendering*). **like nobody's business** *colloq.* extraordinarily. **make it one's business to** undertake to. **mind one's own business** not meddle. **on business** with a definite purpose, esp. one relating to one's regular occupation. **send a person about his or her business** dismiss a person; send a person away. [OE *bisignis* (as BUSY, -NESS)]

■ **1** occupation, calling, vocation, trade, profession, career, métier, (line of) work, field, job, employment. **2** concern, affair, interest, responsibility, province, area, job. **3** duty, function, task, job, responsibility, role, charge, obligation. **4** work, serious business, *sl.* brass tacks, nitty-gritty. **5** affair, matter, topic, subject, question, problem, situation, thing; see also PALAVER *n.* 4. **6** concern(s), agenda, matter(s) (in hand), job, assignment, charge, task, subject, question, problem, issue, proceeding(s), point, affair. **7** dealing(s), relations, transaction(s), truck, exchange; trade, commerce, industry, traffic; custom. **8** concern, establishment, operation, practice, organization, company, firm, house, enterprise, *colloq.* outfit; corporation, partnership, proprietorship. **10** see PALAVER *n.* 4. □ **has no business to** see LICENSE *n.* 2. **like nobody's business** see *amazingly* (AMAZE). **make it one's business to** see UNDERTAKE 2. **mind one's own business** stop butting in or prying or interfering, stick to one's last, keep off or out, *colloq.* keep one's paws off, stop poking or sticking one's nose in. **send a person about his or her business** see DISMISS 2.

businesslike /bíznislīk/ *adj.* efficient; systematic; practical.
■ see SYSTEMATIC 1.

businessman /bíznismən/ *n.* (*pl.* **-men**; *fem.* **businesswoman**, *pl.* **-women**) a man or woman engaged in business or commerce, esp. at a senior level (see also *business person*).
■ dealer, merchant, broker, distributor, seller, salesman, salesperson, saleswoman, vendor, buyer, purchaser, supplier, retailer, wholesaler.

busk /busk/ *v.intr.* perform (esp. music) for voluntary donations, usu. in the street or in subways. □□ **busker** *n.* **busking** *n.* [*busk* peddle, etc. (perh. f. obs. F *busquer* seek)]

buskin /búskin/ *n.* **1** either of a pair of thick-soled laced boots worn by an ancient Athenian tragic actor to gain height. **2** (usu. prec. by *the*) tragic drama; its style or spirit. **3** *hist.* either of a pair of calf- or knee-high boots of cloth or leather worn in the Middle Ages. □□ **buskined** *adj.* [prob. f. OF *bouzequin*, var. of *bro(u)sequin*, of unkn. orig.]

busman /búsmən/ *n.* (*pl.* **-men**) the driver of a bus. □ **busman's holiday** leisure time spent in an activity similar to one's regular work.

buss /bus/ *n. & v. colloq.* ● *n.* a kiss. ● *v.tr.* kiss. [earlier *bass* (n. & v.): cf. F *baiser* f. L *basiare*]
■ *n.* see KISS *n.* ● *v.* see KISS *v.* 1.

bust¹ /bust/ *n.* **1 a** the human chest, esp. that of a woman; the bosom. **b** the circumference of the body at bust level (*a 36-inch bust*). **2** a sculpture of a person's head, shoulders, and chest. [F *buste* f. It. *busto*, of unkn. orig.]
■ **1** see BOSOM *n.* 1. **2** see STATUE.

bust² /bust/ *v., n., & adj. colloq.* ● *v.* (*past* and *past part.* **busted** or **bust**) **1** *tr. & intr.* burst; break. **2** *tr.* reduce (a soldier, etc.) to a lower rank; dismiss. **3** *tr.* **a** raid; search. **b** arrest. ● *n.* **1** a sudden failure; a bankruptcy. **2 a** a police raid. **b** an arrest. **3** a drinking bout. **4** a punch; a hit. **5** a worthless thing. **6** a bad hand at cards. ● *adj.* (also **busted**) **1** broken; burst; collapsed. **2** bankrupt. **3** arrested. □ **bust a gut** make every possible effort. **bust up 1** bring or come to collapse; explode. **2** (of esp. a married couple) separate. **bust-up** *n.* **1** *esp. Brit.* a quarrel. **2** a collapse; a breakup; an explosion. **go bust** become bankrupt; fail. [orig. a (dial.) pronunc. of BURST]
■ *v.* **1** see BREAK¹ *v.* 1b. **2** see DOWNGRADE *v.* 1. **3 a** see RAID *v.* 2. **b** see ARREST *v.* 1a. ● *n.* **2** raid, search; see also ARREST *n.* 1. **3** see ORGY 1. **4** see HIT *n.* 1a. ● *adj.* **1** see DUD *adj.* 1. **2** see INSOLVENT *adj.* □ **bust a gut** see *strain every nerve*.

bustard /bústərd/ *n.* any large terrestrial bird of the family Otididae, with long neck, long legs, and stout tapering body. [ME f. OF *bistarde* f. L *avis tarda* slow bird (? = slow on the ground; but possibly a perversion of a foreign word)]

buster /bústər/ *n.* **1** *sl.* buddy; fellow (used esp. as a disrespectful form of address). **2** a violent gale.

bustier /bŏŏstáy, bústeeay/ *n.* a strapless close-fitting bodice, usu. boned. [F]

bustle¹ /búsəl/ *v. & n.* ● *v.* **1** *intr.* (often foll. by *about*) **a** work, etc., showily, energetically, and officiously. **b** hasten (*bustled about the kitchen banging saucepans*). **2** *tr.* make (a person) hurry or work hard (*bustled him into his overcoat*). **3** *intr.* (as **bustling** *adj.*) *colloq.* full of activity. ● *n.* excited activity; a fuss. □□ **bustler** *n.* [perh. f. *buskle* frequent. of *busk* prepare]
■ *v.* **1** see RUSH¹ *v.* 1. **3** (**bustling**) see ACTIVE *adj.* 1a. ● *n.* rush, hustle (and bustle), hurry; haste.

bustle² /búsəl/ *n. hist.* a pad or frame worn under a skirt and puffing it out behind. [18th c.: orig. unkn.]

busty /bústee/ *adj.* (**bustier, bustiest**) (of a woman) having a prominent bust. □□ **bustiness** *n.*
■ see BUXOM.

busy /bízee/ *adj., & v.* ● *adj.* (**busier, busiest**) **1** (often foll. by *in, with, at*, or pres. part.) occupied or engaged in work,

---

/.../ **pronunciation**	● **part of speech**
□ **phrases, idioms, and compounds**	
□□ **derivatives**	■ **synonym section**
cross-references appear in SMALL CAPITALS or *italics*	

etc., with the attention concentrated (*busy at their needle-work*; *he was busy packing*). **2** full of activity or detail; fussy (*a busy evening*; *a picture busy with detail*). **3** employed continuously; unresting (*busy as a bee*). **4** meddlesome; prying. **5** (of a telephone line) in use. ● *v.tr.* (**-ies**, **-ied**) (often *refl.*) keep busy; occupy (*the work busied him for many hours*; *busied herself with the accounts*). □ **busy signal** an intermittent buzzing sound indicating that a telephone line is in use. □□ **busily** /bízilee/ *adv.* **busyness** /bízeenis/ *n.* (cf. BUSINESS). [OE *bisig*]

■ *adj.* **1** occupied, engaged, tied up, wrapped up. **2** hectic, frantic, active, full, brisk, eventful; fancy, fussy, ornate, elaborate, detailed, complicated, complex, (over)decorated, intricate, baroque, rococo. **3** working, industrious, active, tireless, hardworking; bustling, hectic, unresting, frantic, lively, hustling, energetic. **4** see NOSY *adj.* ● *v.* occupy, involve, employ, divert, absorb, engross, preoccupy, hold a person's attention.

busybody /bízeebodee, -budee/ *n.* (*pl.* **-ies**) **1** a meddlesome person. **2** a mischief maker.

■ **1** snoop(er), gossip, meddler, *colloq.* kibitzer, Nosy Parker, *Austral.* & *NZ sl.* stickybeak. **2** see TROUBLEMAKER.

but[1] /but, bət/ *conj., prep., adv., pron., n.,* & *v.* ● *conj.* **1 a** nevertheless; however (*tried hard but did not succeed*; *I am old, but I am not weak*). **b** on the other hand; on the contrary (*I am old but you are young*). **2** (*prec. by can,* etc.; in *neg.* or *interrog.*) except; other than; otherwise than (*cannot choose but do it*; *what could we do but run?*). **3** without the result that (*it never rains but it pours*). **4** prefixing an interruption to the speaker's train of thought (*the weather is ideal—but is that a cloud on the horizon?*). ● *prep.* except; apart from; other than (*everyone went but me*; *nothing but trouble*). ● *adv.* **1** only; no more than; only just (*we can but try*; *is but a child*; *had but arrived*; *did it but once*). **2** introducing emphatic repetition; definitely (*wanted to see nobody, but nobody*). **3** *Austral., NZ,* & *Sc.* though; however (*didn't like it, but*). ● *rel.pron.* who not; that not (*there is not a man but feels pity*). ● *n.* an objection (*ifs and buts*). ● *v.tr.* (in phr. **but me no buts**) do not raise objections. □ **but for** without the help or hindrance, etc., of (*but for you I'd be rich by now*). **but one** (or **two,** etc.) excluding one (or two, etc.) from the number (*next door but one*; *last but one*). **but that** (prec. by *neg.*) that (*I don't deny but that it's true*). **but that** (or *colloq.* **what**) other than that; except that (*who knows but that it is true?*). **but then** (or **yet**) however; on the other hand (*I won, but then the others were beginners*). [OE *be-ūtan, būtan, būta* outside, without]

■ *conj.* **1 a** see NEVERTHELESS. **b** however, on the other hand, on the contrary, contrariwise. ● *prep.* see EXCEPT *prep.*

but[2] /but/ *n. Sc.* □ **but and ben** the outer and inner rooms of a two-roomed house (see BEN[2]). [BUT[1] = outside]

butadiene /byōōtədíeen/ *n. Chem.* a colorless gaseous hydrocarbon used in the manufacture of synthetic rubbers. ¶ Chem. formula: C_4H_6. [BUTANE + DI-[2] + -ENE: cf. BUNA]

butane /byōōtayn/ *n. Chem.* a gaseous hydrocarbon of the alkane series used in liquefied form as fuel. ¶ Chem. formula: C_4H_{10}. [BUTYL + -ANE[2]]

butch /bŏŏch/ *adj.* & *n. sl.* ● *adj.* masculine; tough-looking. ● *n.* **1** (often *attrib.*) **a** a mannish woman. **b** a mannish lesbian. **2** a tough, usu. muscular, youth or man. [perh. abbr. of BUTCHER]

butcher /bŏŏchər/ *n.* & *v.* ● *n.* **1 a** a person whose trade is dealing in meat. **b** a person who slaughters animals for food. **2** a person who kills or has people killed indiscriminately or brutally. ● *v.tr.* **1** slaughter or cut up (an animal) for food. **2** kill (people) wantonly or cruelly. **3** ruin (esp. a job or a musical composition) through incompetence. □ **the butcher, the baker, the candlestick maker** people of all kinds or trades. **butcher-bird** a shrike of the genus *Lanius*, native to Australia and New Guinea, with a long hook-tipped bill for catching prey. **butcher's** *Brit. rhyming sl.* a look (short for *butcher's hook*). **butcher's-broom** a low

spiny-leaved evergreen shrub, *Ruscus aculeatus* native to Europe. □□ **butcherly** *adj.* [ME f. OF *bo(u)chier* f. *boc* BUCK[1]]

■ *n.* **2** murderer, slaughterer, killer, ripper, cutthroat, executioner, annihilator. ● *v.* **2** slaughter, massacre, murder, exterminate, annihilate, kill, liquidate, mow down, cut down, wipe out; cut *or* hack *or* hew to pieces, mutilate, dismember, cut up, disembowel. **3** see RUIN *v.* 1b.

butchery /bŏŏchəree/ *n.* (*pl.* **-ies**) **1** needless or cruel slaughter (of people). **2** the butcher's trade. **3** a slaughterhouse. [ME f. OF *boucherie* (as BUTCHER)]

■ **1** see SLAUGHTER *n.* 2. **2** slaughter, butchering.

butle var. of BUTTLE.

butler /bútlər/ *n.* the principal manservant of a household, usu. in charge of the wine cellar, pantry, etc. [ME f. AF *buteler*, OF *bouteillier*: see BOTTLE]

butt[1] /but/ *v.* & *n.* ● *v.* **1** *tr.* & *intr.* push with the head or horns. **2 a** *intr.* (usu. foll. by *against, upon*) place with one end flat against; meet end to end with; abut. **b** *tr.* (usu. foll. by *against*) place (lumber, etc.) with the end flat against a wall, etc. ● *n.* **1** a push with the head. **2** a join of two edges. □ **butt in** interrupt; meddle. [ME f. AF *buter*, OF *boter* f. Gmc: infl. by BUTT[2] & ABUT]

■ *v.* **1** ram, prod, poke, jab, charge. **2 a** (*butt on to*) join, meet, abut (on *or* against), come up against, border (on *or* upon), touch, adjoin. ● *n.* **1** poke, jab, prod, dig, stab, jog, nudge, push. □ **butt in** interfere, intrude, intervene, meddle, put *or* stick one's oar in, trespass on a person's preserves, *colloq.* poke one's nose in, kibitz; interrupt, cut in, break in, burst out, *colloq.* chip in.

butt[2] /but/ *n.* **1** (often foll. by *of*) an object (of ridicule, etc.) (*the butt of his jokes*; *made him their butt*). **2 a** a mound behind a target. **b** (in *pl.*) a shooting range. **c** a target. **3** a bird hunter's blind screened by low turf or a stone wall. [ME f. OF *but* goal, of unkn. orig.]

■ **1** target, end, object; prey, victim, quarry, scapegoat, dupe, gull, pigeon, cat's-paw, esp. *Brit.* Aunt Sally, *sl.* sucker, fall guy, patsy.

butt[3] /but/ *n.* **1** (also **butt end**) the thicker end, esp. of a tool or a weapon (*gun butt*). **2 a** the stub of a cigar or a cigarette. **b** (also **butt end**) a remnant (*the butt of the evening*). **3** *sl.* the buttocks. **4** (also **butt end**) the square end of a plank meeting a similar one. **5** the trunk of a tree, esp. the part just above the ground. □ **butt weld** a weld in which the pieces are joined end to end. [Du. *bot* stumpy]

butt[4] /but/ *n.* a cask, esp. as a measure of wine or ale. [AL *butta, bota,* AF *but,* f. OF *bo(u)t* f. LL *buttis*]

butt[5] /but/ *n.* a flatfish (e.g., a sole, plaice, or turbot). [MLG, MDu. *but* flatfish]

butte /byōōt/ *n.* a high, isolated, steep-sided hill. [F, = mound]

butter /bútər/ *n.* & *v.* ● *n.* **1 a** a pale yellow edible fatty substance made by churning cream and used as a spread or in cooking. **b** a substance of a similar consistency or appearance (*peanut butter*). **2** excessive flattery. ● *v.tr.* spread, cook, or serve with butter (*butter the bread*; *buttered rum*). □ **butter-and-eggs** any of several plants having two shades of yellow in the flower, e.g., toadflax. **butter bean 1** the flat, dried, white lima bean. **2** a yellow-podded bean. **butter cream** (or **icing**) a mixture of butter, confectioner's sugar, etc., used as a filling or a topping for a cake. **butter knife** a blunt knife used for cutting butter at table. **butter muslin** *Brit.* a thin, loosely woven cloth with a fine mesh, orig. for wrapping butter. **butter up** *colloq.* flatter excessively. **look as if butter wouldn't melt in one's mouth** seem demure or innocent, probably deceptively. [OE *butere* f. L *butyrum* f. Gk *bouturon*]

butterball /bútərbawl/ *n.* **1** a piece of butter shaped into a ball. **2** = BUFFLEHEAD (because it is very fat in autumn). **3** *sl.* a fat person.

butterbur /bútərbər/ *n.* any of several plants of the genus *Petasites* with large soft leaves, formerly used to wrap butter.

buttercup /bútərkup/ *n.* any common yellow-flowered plant of the genus *Ranunculus*.

butterfat /bútərfat/ *n.* the essential fats of pure butter.

butterfingers /bútərfingərz/ n. colloq. a clumsy person prone to drop things.

butterfish /bútərfish/ n. = GUNNEL¹.

butterfly /bútərfli/ n. (pl. **-flies**) **1** any diurnal insect of the order Lepidoptera, with knobbed antennae, a long thin body, and four usu. brightly colored wings erect when at rest. **2** a showy or frivolous person. **3** (in pl.) colloq. a nervous sensation felt in the stomach. □ **butterfly net** a fine net on a ring attached to a pole, used for catching butterflies. **butterfly nut** a kind of wing nut. **butterfly stroke** a stroke in swimming, with both arms raised out of the water and lifted forward together. **butterfly valve** a valve with hinged semicircular plates. [OE buttor-flēoge (as BUTTER, FLY²)]

buttermilk /bútərmilk/ n. a slightly acid liquid left after churning butter.

butternut /bútərnut/ n. **1** a N. American tree, Juglans cinerea. **2** the oily nut of this tree.

butterscotch /bútərskoch/ n. **1** a brittle candy made from butter, brown sugar, etc. **2** this flavor in dessert toppings, puddings, etc. [SCOTCH]

butterwort /bútərwərt, -wawrt/ n. any bog plant of the genus Pinguicula, esp. P. vulgaris with violet-like flowers and fleshy leaves that secrete a fluid to trap small insects for food.

buttery¹ /bútəree/ n. (pl. **-ies**) **1** Brit. a room, esp. in a college, where provisions are kept and supplied to students, etc. **2** a pantry. [ME f. AF boterie butt-store (as BUTT⁴)]

buttery² /bútəree/ adj. like, containing, or spread with butter. □□ **butteriness** n.

buttle /bútəl/ v.intr. (also **butle**) joc. work as a butler. [back-form. f. BUTLER]

buttock /bútək/ n. (usu. in pl.) **1** each of two fleshy protuberances on the lower rear part of the human trunk. **2** the corresponding part of an animal. [butt ridge + -OCK]

■ (buttocks) seat, posterior, rump, hindquarters, hams, Anat. nates, gluteus maximus, colloq. backside, behind, bottom, rear, esp. Brit. colloq. sit-upon, colloq. euphem. derrière, joc. fundament, sl. butt, fanny, can, keister, prat, cheeks, esp. Brit. sl. bum.

button /bút'n/ n. & v. ● n. **1** a small disk or knob sewn or pinned on to a garment, either to fasten it by being pushed through a buttonhole, or as an ornament or badge. **2** a knob on a piece of esp. electronic equipment which is pressed to operate it. **3 a** a small round object (chocolate buttons). **b** (attrib.) anything resembling a button (button nose). **4 a** a bud. **b** a button mushroom. **5** Fencing a terminal knob on a foil making it harmless. ● v. **1** tr. & intr. = button up 1. **2** tr. supply with buttons. □ **buttonball tree** (or **button-wood**) a plane tree, Platanus occidentalis. **button chrysanthemum** a variety of chrysanthemum with small spherical flowers. **buttoned up** colloq. **1** formal and inhibited in manner. **2** silent. **button one's lip** sl. remain silent. **button mushroom** a young unopened mushroom. **button through** Brit. (of a dress) fastened with buttons from neck to hem like a coat. **button up 1** fasten with buttons. **2** colloq. complete (a task, etc.) satisfactorily. **3** colloq. become silent. **4** fasten or close securely. **not worth a button** Brit. worthless. **on the button** sl. precisely. □□ **buttoned** adj. **buttonless** adj. **buttony** adj. [ME f. OF bouton, ult. f. Gmc]

buttonhole /bút'nhōl/ n. & v. ● n. **1** a slit made in a garment to receive a button for fastening. **2** Brit. a flower or spray worn in a lapel buttonhole; a boutonniere. ● v.tr. **1** colloq. accost and detain (a reluctant listener). **2** make buttonholes in. □ **buttonhole stitch** a looped stitch used for making buttonholes.

■ v. **1** corner, detain, hold up, accost, importune, waylay, Austral. & NZ bail (up).

buttonhook /bút'nhŏok/ n. a hook formerly used esp. for pulling the buttons on tight boots, gloves, etc., into place for fastening.

buttons /bút'nz/ n. Brit. colloq. a liveried page boy; a bellhop. [from the rows of buttons on his jacket]

buttress /bútris/ n. & v. ● n. **1 a** a projecting support of stone or brick, etc., built against a wall. **b** a source of help or encouragement (she was a buttress to him in his trouble). **2** a projecting portion of a hill or mountain. ● v.tr. (often foll. by up) **1** support with a buttress. **2** support by argument, etc. (claim buttressed by facts). [ME f. OF (ars) bouterez thrusting (arch) f. bouteret f. bouter BUTT¹]

■ n. **1** support, prop, stay, reinforcement, reinforcer, strengthener, bolster, brace, bracket. ● v. sustain, support, bolster, strengthen, reinforce, fortify, prop (up), hold up, brace, shore up, archaic stay; back up, provide backing for, consolidate, firm up, secure; aid, help, assist, encourage, further, advance, colloq. boost.

butty¹ /bútee/ n. (pl. **-ies**) Brit. **1** colloq. or dial. a friend; a companion. **2** hist. a middleman negotiating between a mine owner and the miners. **3** a barge or other craft towed by another. □ **butty-gang** a gang of men contracted to work on a large job and sharing the profits equally. [19th c.: perh. f. BOOTY in phr. play booty join in sharing plunder]

butty² /bútee/ n. (pl. **-ies**) No. of Engl. **1** a sandwich (bacon butty). **2** a slice of bread and butter. [BUTTER + -Y²]

butyl /byōōt'l/ n. Chem. the univalent alkyl radical C_4H_9. □ **butyl rubber** a synthetic rubber used in the manufacture of tire inner tubes. [BUTYRIC (ACID) + -YL]

butyric acid /byōōtírik/ n. Chem. either of two colorless syrupy liquid organic acids found in rancid butter or arnica oil. □□ **butyrate** /byōōtirayt/ n. [L butyrum BUTTER + -IC]

buxom /búksəm/ adj. (esp. of a woman) plump and healthy-looking; large and shapely; busty. □□ **buxomly** adv. **buxomness** n. [earlier sense pliant: ME f. stem of OE būgan BOW² + -SOME¹]

■ hearty, healthy, vigorous, solid, sizable, large, plump, stout, substantial, lusty, voluptuous, attractive, comely, shapely, hefty; busty, bosomy, colloq. curvaceous, well-endowed, chesty.

buy /bī/ v. & n. ● v. (**buys, buying;** past and past part. **bought** /bawt/) **1** tr. **a** obtain in exchange for money, etc. **b** (usu. in neg.) serve to obtain (money can't buy happiness). **2** tr. **a** procure (the loyalty, etc.) of a person by bribery, promises, etc. **b** win over (a person) in this way. **3** tr. get by sacrifice, great effort, etc. (dearly bought; bought with our sweat). **4** tr. sl. accept; believe in; approve of (it's a good scheme, I'll buy it; he bought it, he's so gullible). **5** absol. be a buyer for a store, etc. (buys for Macy's; are you buying or selling?). ● n. colloq. a purchase (that sofa was a good buy). □ **best buy** the purchase giving the best value in proportion to its price; a bargain. **buy the farm** die. **buy in 1** buy a supply of. **2** withdraw (an item) at auction because of failure to reach the reserve price. **buy into** obtain a share in (an enterprise) by payment. **buy it** (usu. in past) sl. be killed. **buy off** get rid of (a claim, a claimant, a blackmailer) by payment. **buy oneself out** obtain one's release (esp. from the armed services) by payment. **buy out** pay (a person) to give up an ownership, interest, etc. **buy time** delay an event, conclusion, etc., temporarily. **buy up 1** buy as much as possible of. **2** absorb (another business, etc.) by purchase. [OE bycgan f. Gmc]

■ v. **1** purchase; acquire, obtain, get, procure, gain, come by, secure, get or lay one's hands on, get hold of, pick up. **2 b** bribe, pay off, buy off or over, colloq. fix, grease the palm of, square; suborn, corrupt. **4** accept, allow, take, believe (in), find credible or believable, be convinced or assured of, take as given or read, trust, swallow, go for. **5** see TRADE v. 1. ● n. purchase, acquisition, deal. □ **best buy** bargain, good deal or buy, square deal, Brit. snip, colloq. steal, giveaway. **buy it** be or get killed, sl. bite the dust; see also DIE¹ v. 1. **buy off** see BUY v. 2b above. **buy time** see STALL² v. 1.

buyer /bíər/ n. **1** a person employed to select and purchase stock for a large store, etc. **2** a purchaser; a customer. □ **buyer's** (or **buyers'**) **market** an economic position in which

---

/. . ./ **pronunciation**	● **part of speech**
□ **phrases, idioms, and compounds**	
□□ **derivatives**	■ **synonym section**
cross-references appear in SMALL CAPITALS or italics	

goods are plentiful and cheap and buyers have the advantage.

■ **2** customer, consumer, client, purchaser, patron, *colloq.* regular; (*buyers*) see CLIENTELE.

buyout /bíowt/ *n.* the purchase of a controlling share in a company, etc.

buzz /buz/ *n. & v.* ● *n.* **1** the hum of a bee, etc. **2** the sound of a buzzer. **3 a** a confused low sound as of people talking; a murmur. **b** a stir; hurried activity (*a buzz of excitement*). **c** *colloq.* a rumor. **4** *sl.* a telephone call. **5** *sl.* a thrill; a euphoric sensation. ● *v.* **1** *intr.* make a humming sound. **2 a** *tr. & intr.* signal or signal to with a buzzer. **b** *tr. sl.* telephone. **3** *intr.* **a** (often foll. by *about*) move or hover busily. **b** (of a place) have an air of excitement or purposeful activity. **4** *tr. colloq.* throw hard. **5** *tr. Aeron. colloq.* fly fast and very close to (another aircraft, the ground, etc.). □ **buzz off** *sl.* go or hurry away. **buzz saw** a circular saw. [imit.]

■ *n.* **1** hum, drone. **3 a** murmur, undercurrent, undertone, background noise, mumble, murmuring, drone, hum, burble, whispering, *literary* susurration, susurrus. **b** see STIR *n.* 2. **c** rumor, a piece of gossip *or* hearsay; see also WORD *n.* 7. **4** telephone call, phone call, call, *colloq.* ring, *Brit. colloq.* tinkle. **5** thrill, feeling of excitement, sensation, stimulation, *colloq.* kick, *sl.* high, bang, hit. ● *v.* **1** hum, murmur, drone. **2 a** summon, signal, buzz *or* ring for. **b** telephone, call (up), esp. *Brit.* ring (up), *colloq.* phone, give a person a ring, *Brit. colloq.* give a person a tinkle. **3 a** bustle, fuss (about), rush about *or* around; flutter, hover, fly. **b** be alive, bristle, swarm, hum. **4** see THROW *v.* 1, 2. **5** fly close to, fly down on, zoom on to. □ **buzz off** see *beat it.*

buzzard /búzərd/ *n.* **1** a turkey vulture. **2** *Brit.* any of a group of predatory birds of the hawk family, esp. of the genus *Buteo*, with broad wings well adapted for soaring flight. [ME f. OF *busard, buson* f. L *buteo -onis* falcon]

buzzer /búzər/ *n.* **1** an electrical device, similar to a bell, that makes a buzzing noise. **2** a whistle or siren.

buzzword /búzwərd/ *n. sl.* **1** a fashionable piece of esp. technical or computer jargon. **2** a catchword; a slogan.

■ **2** see SLOGAN.

BVM *abbr.* Blessed Virgin Mary.

bwana /bwáanə/ *n. Afr.* master; sir. [Swahili]

BWI *abbr. hist.* British West Indies.

by /bī/ *prep., adv., & n.* ● *prep.* **1** near; beside; in the region of (*stand by the door; sit by me; path by the river*). **2** through the agency, means, instrumentality, or causation of (*by proxy; bought by a millionaire; a poem by Frost; went by bus; succeeded by persisting; divide four by two*). **3** not later than; as soon as (*by next week; by now; by the time he arrives*). **4 a** past; beyond (*drove by the zoo; came by us*). **b** passing through; via (*went by Paris*). **5** in the circumstances of (*by day; by daylight*). **6** to the extent of (*missed by a foot; better by far*). **7** according to; using as a standard or unit (*judge by appearances; paid by the hour*). **8** with the succession of (*worse by the minute; day by day; one by one*). **9** concerning; in respect of (*did our duty by them; Smith by name; all right by me*). **10** used in mild oaths (orig. = as surely as one believes in) (*by God; by gum; swear by all that is sacred*). **11** placed between specified lengths in two directions (*three feet by two*). **12** avoiding; ignoring (*pass by him; passed us by*). **13** inclining to (*north by northwest*). ● *adv.* **1** near (*sat by, watching; lives close by*). **2** aside; in reserve (*put $5 by*). **3** past (*they marched by*). ● *n.* = BYE. □ **by and by** before long; eventually. **by and large** on the whole; everything considered. **by the by** (or **bye**) incidentally; parenthetically. **by oneself 1 a** unaided. **b** without prompting. **2** alone; without company. [OE *bī, bi, be* f. Gmc]

■ *prep.* **1** near, beside, next to, close to, alongside, with, hard by, *archaic or dial.* nigh. **2** by means of, through. **3** before, not later than, sooner than, as soon as. **4 b** via, by way of, through. **5** during, at. **7** see ACCORDING 1b. **9** see CONCERNING. ● *adv.* **1** near, nearby, at hand, close, about, around, *archaic or dial.* nigh. **2** away,

aside, in reserve, on one side. □ **by and by** see PRESENTLY 1. **by and large** see *on the whole* (WHOLE). **by the by** see INCIDENTALLY 1. **by oneself 1** see ALONE 1b. **2** see ALONE 1a.

by- /bī/ *prefix* (also **bye-**) subordinate; incidental; secondary (*by-effect; byroad*).

by-blow /bíblō/ *n.* esp. *Brit.* **1** a side blow not at the main target. **2** an illegitimate child.

bye¹ /bī/ *n.* **1** the status of an unpaired competitor in a sport, who proceeds to the next round as if having won. **2** *Golf* one or more holes remaining unplayed after the match has been decided. □ **by the bye** = *by the by.* [BY as noun]

bye² /bī/ *int. colloq.* = GOOD-BYE. [abbr.]

bye- *prefix* var. of BY-.

bye-bye¹ /bíbī, bəbí/ *int. colloq.* = GOOD-BYE. [childish corrupt.]

bye-bye² /bíbī/ *n.* (also **bye-byes** /-bīz/) (a child's word for) sleep. [ME, f. the sound used in lullabies]

by-election /bí-ilekshən/ *n. Brit.* the election of an MP in a single constituency to fill a vacancy arising during a government's term of office.

Byelorussian var. of BELORUSSIAN.

by-form /bífawrm/ *n.* a collateral form of a word, etc.

bygone /bígawn, -gon/ *adj. & n.* ● *adj.* past; antiquated (*bygone years*). ● *n.* (in *pl.*) past offenses (*let bygones be bygones*).

■ *adj.* past, former, antiquated, ancient, *archaic* olden, *colloq.* antediluvian, medieval; of old, *literary* of yore. ● *n.* (*bygones*) past indiscretions *or* offenses; (*let bygones be bygones*) let sleeping dogs lie, bury the hatchet, bury *or* forget one's differences, call a truce.

bylaw /bílaw/ *n.* (also **byelaw**) **1** a regulation made by a local authority or corporation. **2** a rule made by a company or society for its members. [ME prob. f. obs. *byrlaw* local custom (ON *býjar* genitive sing. of *býr* town, but assoc. with BY)]

byline /bílin/ *n.* **1** a line in a newspaper, etc., naming the writer of an article. **2** a secondary line of work.

byname /bínaym/ *n.* a sobriquet; a nickname.

bypass /bípas/ *n. & v.* ● *n.* **1** a road passing around a town or its center to provide an alternative route for through traffic. **2 a** a secondary channel or pipe, etc., to allow a flow when the main one is closed or blocked. **b** an alternative passage for the circulation of blood during a surgical operation on the heart. ● *v.tr.* **1** avoid; go around. **2** provide with a bypass. **3** neglect or intentionally ignore.

■ *n.* **1** detour, alternative way *or* route, diversion. ● *v.* **1** avoid, evade, circumvent, sidestep, skirt, go *or* get round, steer *or* keep clear of, keep away from, fight shy of, detour; pass over, skip, skip *or* jump over, leave out; ignore, gloss over, overlook, brush over.

bypath /bípath/ *n.* **1** a secluded path. **2** a minor or obscure branch of a subject.

byplay /bíplay/ *n.* a secondary action or sequence of events, esp. in a play.

by-product /bíprodəkt/ *n.* **1** an incidental product of the manufacture of something else. **2** a secondary often unforeseen result.

■ see DERIVATIVE *n.* 1.

byre /bīr/ *n. Brit.* a cowshed. [OE *býre*: perh. rel. to BOWER¹]

byroad /bírōd/ *n.* a minor road.

Byronic /bīrónik/ *adj.* **1** characteristic of Lord Byron, English poet d. 1824, or his romantic poetry. **2** (of a man) handsomely dark, mysterious, or moody.

byssinosis /bísinōsis/ *n. Med.* a lung disease caused by prolonged inhalation of textile fiber dust. [mod.L f. Gk *bussinos* made of byssus + -OSIS]

byssus /bísəs/ *n. hist.* (*pl.* **byssuses** or **byssi** /-sī/) **1** *hist.* a fine textile fiber and fabric of flax. **2** a tuft of tough silky filaments by which some mollusks adhere to rocks, etc. [ME f. L f. Gk *bussos*]

bystander /bístandər/ *n.* a person who stands by but does not take part; a mere spectator.

■ spectator, onlooker, looker-on, observer, witness, passerby, eyewitness.

byte /bīt/ *n.* *Computing* a group of eight binary digits, often used to represent one character. [20th c.: perh. based on BIT[4] and BITE]

byway /bíway/ *n.* **1** a small seldom-traveled road. **2** a minor activity.
■ **1** byroad, bypath, minor road, lane, track, side or little-known street.

byword /bíwərd/ *n.* **1** a person or thing cited as a notable example (*is a byword for luxury*). **2** a familiar saying; a proverb.

■ **2** proverb, proverbial saying, maxim, adage, motto, slogan, apothegm, aphorism, catchword, catchphrase.

Byzantine /bízənteen, -tin, bizántin/ *adj.* & *n.* ● *adj.* **1** of Byzantium or the E. Roman Empire. **2** (of a political situation, etc.): **a** extremely complicated. **b** inflexible. **c** carried on by underhand methods. **3** *Archit.* & *Painting* of a highly decorated style developed in the Eastern Empire. ● *n.* a citizen of Byzantium or the E. Roman Empire. □□ **Byzantinism** *n.* **Byzantinist** *n.* [F *byzantin* or L *Byzantinus* f. *Byzantium*, later Constantinople and now Istanbul]

/. . . ./ pronunciation	● part of speech
□ phrases, idioms, and compounds	
□□ derivatives	■ synonym section
cross-references appear in SMALL CAPITALS or *italics*	

Cc

C¹ /see/ *n.* (also **c**) (*pl.* **Cs** or **C's**) **1** the third letter of the alphabet. **2** *Mus.* the first note of the diatonic scale of C major (the major scale having no sharps or flats). **3** the third hypothetical person or example. **4** the third highest class or category (of academic marks, etc.). **5** *Algebra* (usu. **c**) the third known quantity. **6** (as a Roman numeral) 100. **7** (**c**) the speed of light in a vacuum. **8** (also ©) copyright.

C² *symb. Chem.* the element carbon.

C³ *abbr.* (also **C.**) **1** Cape. **2** Conservative. **3** Celsius; centigrade. **4** Coulomb(s); capacitance.

c. *abbr.* **1** century; centuries. **2** chapter. **3** cent(s). **4** cold. **5** cubic. **6** colt. **7** *Baseball* catcher. **8** centi-. **9** circa; about.

CA *abbr.* **1** California (in official postal use). **2** *Sc. & Can.* chartered accountant.

Ca *symb. Chem.* the element calcium.

ca. *abbr.* circa, about.

CAA *abbr.* Civil Aeronautics Administration.

Caaba var. of KAABA.

CAB *abbr.* Civil Aeronautics Board.

cab /kab/ *n.* **1** a taxi. **2** the driver's compartment in a truck, train, crane, etc. **3** *hist.* a hackney carriage. [abbr. of CABRIOLET]
- taxi, hackney (coach), hack, *Brit.* minicab.

cabal /kəbál/ *n. & v.* ● *n.* **1** a secret intrigue. **2** a political clique or faction. **3** *hist.* a committee of five ministers under Charles II, whose surnames happened to begin with C, A, B, A, and L. ● *v.intr.* (**caballed, caballing**) (often foll. by *together, against*) plot; intrigue. [F *cabale* f. med.L *cabala*, CABBALA]
- *n.* **1** intrigue, plot, conspiracy, scheme, machination. **2** junta, clique, faction, set, sect, coterie, body, band, camarilla, league, pressure group; ring, gang, mafia; unit, party, caucus, club. ● *v.* intrigue, plot, conspire, connive, machinate, scheme, collude.

cabala /kábələ, kəbáálə/ *n.* (also **cabbala, kabbala**) **1** the Jewish mystical tradition. **2** mystic interpretation; any esoteric doctrine or occult lore. □□ **cabalism** *n.* **cabalist** *n.* **cabalistic** /-lístik/ *adj.* [med.L f. Rabbinical Heb. *ḳabbālâ* tradition]
- **2** see *the occult* (OCCULT). □□ **cabalistic** see OCCULT *adj.* 2.

caballero /kábəlyáirō, -bəláirō, kaábaayáirō/ *n.* (*pl.* **-os**) a Spanish gentleman. [Sp.: see CAVALIER]

cabana /kəbánə, -baányə/ *n.* a shelter, bathhouse, etc., at a beach or swimming pool. [Sp. *cabaña* f. LL (as CABIN)]

cabaret /kabəráy/ *n.* **1** an entertainment in a nightclub or restaurant while guests eat or drink at tables. **2** such a nightclub, etc. [F, = wooden structure, tavern]
- **1** floor show, show, entertainment, performance, amusement. **2** nightclub, club, nightspot.

cabbage /kábij/ *n.* **1 a** any of several cultivated varieties of *Brassica oleracea*, with thick green or purple leaves forming a round heart or head. **b** this head usu. eaten as a vegetable. **2** *Brit. colloq. derog.* a person who is inactive or lacks interest. □ **cabbage palm** a palm tree, *Cordyline australis*, with edible cabbagelike terminal buds. **cabbage rose** a double rose with a large round compact flower. **cabbage tree** = *cabbage palm*. **cabbage white** a butterfly, *Pieris brassicae*, whose caterpillars feed on cabbage leaves. □□ **cabbagy** *adj.* [earlier

cabache, -oche f. OF (Picard) *caboche* head, OF *caboce*, of unkn. orig.]

cabbala var. of CABALA.

cabby /kábee/ *n.* (also **cabbie**) (*pl.* **-ies**) *colloq.* a cabdriver. [CAB + -Y²]

cabdriver /kábdrīvər/ *n.* the driver of a cab.

caber /káybər/ *n.* a roughly trimmed tree trunk used in the Scottish Highland sport of tossing the caber. [Gael. *cabar* pole]

cabin /kábin/ *n. & v.* ● *n.* **1** a small shelter or house, esp. of wood. **2** a room or compartment in an aircraft or ship for passengers or crew. **3** a driver's cab. ● *v.tr.* (**cabined, cabining**) confine in a small place; cramp. □ **cabin boy** a boy who waits on a ship's officers or passengers. **cabin class** the intermediate class of accommodation in a ship. **cabin crew** the crew members on an airplane attending to passengers and cargo. **cabin cruiser** a large motorboat with living accommodation. **cabin fever** a state of restlessness and irritability from having been confined or in a remote location for an extended period. [ME f. OF *cabane* f. Prov. *cabana* f. LL *capanna, cavanna*]
- *n.* **1** hut, shack, cottage, crib, shanty, shelter, *poet.* cot; bungalow, lodge, chalet. **2** compartment, berth, room. ● *v.* see IMPRISON 2.

cabinet /kábinit/ *n.* **1 a** a cupboard or case with drawers, shelves, etc., for storing or displaying articles. **b** a piece of furniture housing a radio or television set, etc. **2** (**Cabinet**) the committee of senior advisers responsible for counseling the head of state on government policy. **3** *archaic* a small private room. □ **cabinet minister** esp. *Brit.* a member of a government cabinet. **cabinet pudding** a steamed pudding with dried fruit. [CABIN + -ET¹, infl. by F *cabinet*]
- **1** cupboard, bureau, commode, chiffonier, chest (of drawers), tallboy, highboy, lowboy. **2** council, ministry, committee, board, advisers, senate. **3** closet, cell, cubby, den, antechamber, anteroom, boudoir, *Brit.* snug, *poet. or archaic* chamber.

cabinetmaker /kábinitmáykər/ *n.* a skilled craftsman of wood furniture, etc.

cabinetry /kábinitree/ *n.* finished woodwork, esp. of professional quality. [CABINET + -RY]

cable /káybəl/ *n. & v.* ● *n.* **1** a thick rope of wire or hemp. **2** an encased group of insulated wires for transmitting electricity or electrical signals. **3** a cablegram. **4** *Naut.* **a** the chain of an anchor. **b** (in full **cable length**) a measure of 720 feet (US Navy) or 608 feet (Brit. Navy). **5** (in full **cable-stitch**) a knitted stitch resembling twisted rope. **6** *Archit.* a rope-shaped ornament. ● *v.* **1 a** *tr.* transmit (a message) by cablegram. **b** *tr.* inform (a person) by cablegram. **c** *intr.* send a cablegram. **2** *tr.* furnish or fasten with a cable or cables. **3** *Archit. tr.* furnish with cables. □ **cable car 1** a small cabin (often one of a series) suspended on an endless cable and drawn up and down a mountainside, etc., by an engine at one end. **2** a vehicle drawn along a cable railway. **cable-laid** (of rope) having three triple strands. **cable railway** a railroad along which cars are drawn by a continuous cable. **cable-ready** (of a TV, VCR, etc.) designed for direct connection to a coaxial cable TV system. **cable television** a broadcasting system with signals transmitted by cable to

subscribers' sets. [ME f. OF *chable*, ult. f. LL *capulum* halter f. Arab. *ḥabl*.
■ *n.* **1** wire, line, rope, lead, chain, strand, twine, guy, *Naut.* hawser, stay. **2** lead, cord, wire, *Brit.* flex. **3** telegram, cablegram, radiogram, *colloq.* wire. ● *v.* **1** telegraph, radio, *colloq.* wire; see also TRANSMIT 1a.

cablegram /káybəlgram/ *n.* a telegraph message sent by undersea cable, etc.
■ see TELEGRAM.

cableway /káybəlway/ *n.* a transporting system with a usu. elevated cable.

cabman /kábmən/ *n.* (*pl.* **-men**) a cabdriver.

cabochon /kábəshon/ *n.* a gem polished but not faceted. [F dimin. of *caboche*: see CABBAGE]

caboodle /kəbood'l/ *n.* □ **the whole (kit and) caboodle** *sl.* the whole lot (of persons or things). [19th c. US: perh. f. phr. *kit and boodle*]

caboose /kəboos/ *n.* **1** a car on a freight train for workers, often the final car. **2** esp. *Brit.* a kitchen on a ship's deck. [Du. *cabūse*, of unkn. orig.]

cabotage /kábətaazh, -tij/ *n.* **1** *Naut.* coastal navigation and trade. **2** esp. *Aeron.* the reservation to a country of (esp. air) traffic operation within its territory. [F f. *caboter* to coast, perh. f. Sp. *cabo* CAPE²]

cabriole /kábreeōl/ *n.* a kind of curved leg characteristic of Queen Anne and Chippendale furniture. [F f. *cabrioler*, *caprioler* f. It. *capriolare* to leap in the air; from the resemblance to a leaping animal's foreleg: see CAPRIOLE]

cabriolet /kábreeōláy/ *n.* **1** a light, two-wheeled carriage with a hood, drawn by one horse. **2** an automobile with a folding top. [F f. *cabriole* goat's leap (cf. CAPRIOLE), applied to its motion]

ca'canny /kaakánee/ *n. Brit.* **1** the practice of 'going slow' at work; a labor union policy of limiting output. **2** extreme caution. [Sc., = proceed warily]

cacao /kəkaa-ō, -káyō/ *n.* (*pl.* **-os**) **1** a seed pod from which cocoa and chocolate are made. **2** a small, widely cultivated evergreen tree, *Theobroma cacao*, bearing these. [Sp. f. Nahuatl *cacauatl* (*uatl* tree)]

cachalot /káshəlot, -lō/ *n.* a sperm whale. [F f. Sp. & Port. *cachalote*, of unkn. orig.]

cache /kash/ *n. & v.* ● *n.* **1** a hiding place for treasure, provisions, ammunition, etc. **2** what is hidden in a cache.
● *v.tr.* put in a cache. [F f. *cacher* to hide]
■ *n.* **1** hiding place, hole, vault, repository, *colloq.* hideyhole, stash. **2** store, hoard, supply, reserve, stock, fund, nest egg, stockpile, *Law* (treasure) trove, *colloq.* stash. ● *v.* hide, store, conceal, hoard, put *or* stow away, squirrel away, secrete, bury, *colloq.* stash (away).

cachectic /kəkéktik/ *adj.* relating to or having the symptoms of cachexia.

cachet /kasháy/ *n.* **1** a distinguishing mark or seal. **2** prestige. **3** *Med.* a flat capsule enclosing a dose of unpleasant-tasting medicine. [F f. *cacher* press ult. f. L *coactare* constrain]
■ **1** stamp, seal, sign, hallmark, (distinguishing) mark, identification (mark), tag. **2** distinction, importance, prestige, status, stature, reputation, renown, prominence, preeminence, superiority, merit, value, dignity, style.

cachexia /kəkékseeə/ *n.* (also **cachexy** /-kéksee/) a condition of weakness of body or mind associated with chronic disease. [F *cachexie* or LL *cachexia* f. Gk *kakhexia* f. *kakos* bad + *hexis* habit]

cachinnate /kákinayt/ *v.intr. literary* laugh loudly. □□ **cachinnation** /-náyshən/ *n.* **cachinnatory** /-nətáwree/ *adj.* [L *cachinnare cachinnat-*]

cachou /káshoo/ *n.* **1** a lozenge to sweeten the breath. **2** var. of CATECHU. [F f. Port. *cachu* f. Malay *kāchu*: cf. CATECHU]

cachucha /kəchoochə/ *n.* a Spanish solo dance. [Sp.]

cacique /kəseék/ *n.* **1** a native tribal chief of the West Indies or Mexico. **2** a political boss in Spain or Latin America. [Sp., of Carib orig.]

cack-handed /kák-hándid/ *adj. Brit. colloq.* **1** awkward; clumsy. **2** left-handed. □□ **cack-handedly** *adv.* **cack-handedness** *n.* [dial. *cack* excrement]

cackle /kákəl/ *n. & v.* ● *n.* **1** a clucking sound as of a hen or a goose. **2** a loud, silly laugh. **3** noisy inconsequential talk. ● *v.* **1** *intr.* emit a cackle. **2** *intr.* talk noisily and inconsequentially. **3** *tr.* utter or express with a cackle. □ **cut the cackle** esp. *Brit. colloq.* stop talking aimlessly and come to the point. [ME prob. f. MLG, MDu. *kākelen* (imit.)]
■ *n.* **2** see LAUGH *n.* 1. **3** see PRATTLE *n.* ● *v.* **1, 3** see SQUAWK *v.* **2** see JABBER *v.*1.

cacodemon /kákədeémən/ *n.* (also **cacodaemon**) **1** an evil spirit. **2** a malignant person. [Gk *kakodaimōn* f. *kakos* bad + *daimōn* spirit]
■ **1** see DEMON¹ 1a.

cacodyl /kákədil/ *n.* a malodorous, toxic, spontaneously flammable liquid, tetramethyldiarsine. □□ **cacodylic** /-dílik/ *adj.* [Gk *kakōdēs* stinking f. *kakos* bad]

cacoethes /kákō-eétheez/ *n.* an urge to do something inadvisable. [L f. Gk *kakoēthes* neut. adj. f. *kakos* bad + *ēthos* disposition]
■ see MANIA 2.

cacography /kəkógrəfee/ *n.* **1** bad handwriting. **2** bad spelling. □□ **cacographer** *n.* **cacographic** /kákəgráfik/ *adj.* **cacographical** *adj.* [Gk *kakos* bad, after *orthography*]

cacology /kəkóləjee/ *n.* **1** bad choice of words. **2** bad pronunciation. [LL *cacologia* f. Gk *kakologia* vituperation f. *kakos* bad]

cacomistle /kákəmisəl/ *n.* any raccoonlike animal of several species of the genus *Bassariscus*, native to Central America, having a dark-ringed tail. [Amer. Sp. *cacomixtle* f. Nahuatl *tlacomiztli*]

cacophony /kəkófənee/ *n.* (*pl.* **-ies**) **1** a harsh discordant mixture of sound. **2** dissonance; discord. □□ **cacophonous** *adj.* [F *cacophonie* f. Gk *kakophōnia* f. *kakophōnos* f. *kakos* bad + *phōnē* sound]
■ □□ **cacophonous** see DISCORDANT 2.

cactus /káktəs/ *n.* (*pl.* **cacti** /-tī/ or **cactuses**) any succulent plant of the family Cactaceae, with a thick fleshy stem, usu. spines but no leaves, and brilliantly colored flowers. □ **cactus dahlia** any kind of dahlia with quilled petals resembling a cactus flower. □□ **cactaceous** /-táyshəs/ *adj.* [L f. Gk *kaktos* cardoon]

cacuminal /kakyoominəl/ *adj. Phonet.* = RETROFLEX 2. [L *cacuminare* make pointed f. *cacumen -minis* treetop]

CAD /kad/ *abbr.* computer-aided design.

cad /kad/ *n.* a person (esp. a man) who behaves dishonorably. □□ **caddish** *adj.* **caddishly** *adv.* **caddishness** *n.* [abbr. of CADDIE in sense 'odd-job man']
■ see ROGUE *n.* 1.

cadastral /kədástrəl/ *adj.* of or showing the extent, value, and ownership, of land for taxation. [F f. *cadastre* register of property f. Prov. *cadastro* f. It. *catast(r)o*, earlier *catastico* f. late Gk *katastikhon* list, register f. *kata stikhon* line by line]

cadaver /kədávər/ *n.* esp. *Med.* a corpse. □□ **cadaveric** /-dávərik/ *adj.* [ME f. L *cadere* fall]
■ corpse, (dead) body, remains, *archaic* corse, *sl.* stiff.

cadaverous /kədávərəs/ *adj.* **1** corpselike. **2** deathly pale. [L *cadaverosus* (as CADAVER)]

caddie /kádee/ *n. & v.* (also **caddy**) ● *n.* (*pl.* **-ies**) a person who assists a golfer during a match, by carrying clubs, etc. ● *v.intr.* (**caddies, caddied, caddying**) act as caddie. [orig. Sc. f. F CADET]

caddis fly /kádisflī/ *n.* (*pl.* **flies**) any small, hairy-winged nocturnal insect of the order Trichoptera, living near water. [17th c.: orig. unkn.]

caddish see CAD.

caddisworm /kádiswərm/ *n.* (also **caddis**) a larva of the caddis fly, living in water and making protective cylindrical cases of sticks, leaves, etc., and used as fishing bait. [as CADDIS FLY]

/.../ pronunciation	● part of speech
□ phrases, idioms, and compounds	
□□ derivatives	■ synonym section
cross-references appear in SMALL CAPITALS or *italics*	

caddy[1] /kádee/ *n.* (*pl.* **-ies**) a small container, esp. a box for holding tea. [earlier *catty* weight of 1⅓ lb., f. Malay *kātī*]
■ see BOX[1] *n.* 1.

caddy[2] var. of CADDIE.

cadence /káyd'ns/ *n.* **1** a fall in pitch of the voice, esp. at the end of a phrase or sentence. **2** intonation; tonal inflection. **3** *Mus.* the close of a musical phrase. **4** rhythm; the measure or beat of sound or movement. □□ **cadenced** *adj.* [ME f. OF f. It. *cadenza*, ult. f. L *cadere* fall]
■ **2** see INTONATION 1. **4** measure, beat, rhythm, tempo, accent, pulse, meter; lilt, swing.

cadential /kədénshəl/ *adj.* of a cadence or cadenza.

cadenza /kədénzə/ *n. Mus.* a virtuosic passage for a solo instrument or voice, usu. near the close of a movement of a concerto, sometimes improvised. [It.: see CADENCE]
■ improvisation, bravura.

cadet /kədét/ *n.* **1** a young trainee in the armed services or police force. **2** a business trainee. **3** a younger son. □□ **cadetship** *n.* [F f. Gascon dial. *capdet*, ult. f. L *caput* head]

cadge /kaj/ *v.* **1** *tr.* get or seek by begging. **2** *intr.* beg. □□ **cadger** *n.* [19th c., earlier = ? bind, carry: orig. unkn.]
■ see BEG 1b, c.

cadi /ka'adee, káydee/ *n.* (also **kadi**) (*pl.* **-is**) a judge in a Muslim country. [Arab. *ḳāḍī* f. *ḳaḍā* to judge]

Cadmean /kadmeé·ən/ *adj.* = PYRRHIC[1]. [L *Cadmeus* f. Gk *Kadmeios* f. *Kadmos* Cadmus: see CADMIUM]

cadmium /kádmeeəm/ *n.* a soft, bluish-white metallic element occurring naturally with zinc ores, and used in the manufacture of solders and in electroplating. ¶ Symb.: **Cd**. □ **cadmium yellow** an intense yellow pigment containing cadmium sulfide and used in paints, etc. [obs. *cadmia* calamine f. L *cadmia* f. Gk *kadm(e)ia* (*gē*) Cadmean (earth), f. *Cadmus* legendary founder of Thebes: see -IUM]

cadre /kádree, ka'adray/ *n.* **1** a basic unit, esp. of servicemen, forming a nucleus for expansion when necessary. **2 a** a group of activists in a communist or any revolutionary party. **b** a member of such a group. [F f. It. *quadro* f. L *quadrus* square]
■ **1** see CORPS. **2 a** see FACTION[1] 1.

caduceus /kədōóseeəs, -shəs, -dyōó-/ *n.* (*pl.* **caducei** /-see-ī/) an ancient Greek or Roman herald's wand, esp. as carried by the messenger god Hermes or Mercury. [L f. Doric Gk *karuk(e)ion* f. Gk *kērux* herald]
■ see STAFF[1] *n.* 1a, b.

caducous /kədōókəs, -dyōó-/ *adj. Biol.* (of organs and parts) easily detached or shed at an early stage. □□ **caducity** /-sitee/ *n.* [L *caducus* falling f. *cadere* fall]

caecilian /səsíleeən/ *n.* any burrowing wormlike amphibian of the order Gymnophiona, having poorly developed eyes and no limbs. [L *caecilia* kind of lizard]

caecum *Brit.* var. of CECUM.

Caenozoic var. of CENOZOIC.

Caerphilly /kairfílee, kaar-/ *n.* a kind of mild white cheese orig. made in Caerphilly in Wales.

Caesar /seézər/ *n.* **1** the title of the Roman emperors, esp. from Augustus to Hadrian. **2** an autocrat. □□ **Caesarean**, **Caesarian** /-záireeən/ *adj.* family name of Gaius Julius *Caesar*, Roman statesman d. 44 BC]

Caesarean (also **Caesarian**) var. of CESAREAN.

caesium *Brit.* var. of CESIUM.

caesura /sizhōórə, -zōórə/ *n.* (*pl.* **caesuras** or **caesurae** /-zhōóree, -zōóree/) *Prosody* **1** (in Greek and Latin verse) a break between words within a metrical foot. **2** (in modern verse) a pause near the middle of a line. □□ **caesural** *adj.* [L f. *caedere caes-* cut]
■ see PAUSE *n.*

CAF *abbr.* cost and freight.

café /kafáy/ *n.* (also **cafe**) **1** a small coffeehouse; a simple restaurant. **2** a bar. □ **café au lait** /ō láy/ **1** coffee with milk. **2** the color of this. **café noir** /nwaar/ black coffee. **café society** the regular patrons of fashionable restaurants and nightclubs. [F, = coffee, coffeehouse]
■ **1** coffeehouse, coffee bar, coffee shop, bistro, snack bar, brasserie; tearoom, lunchroom, restaurant, eating

house, canteen, diner, cafeteria, esp. *Brit.* teashop, *Brit.* pull-in, *colloq.* eatery. **2** see BAR[1] *n.* 4b, c.

cafeteria /káfiteéreeə/ *n.* a restaurant in which customers collect their meals on trays at a counter and usu. pay before sitting down to eat. [Amer. Sp. *cafetería* coffee shop]

caff /kaf/ *n. Brit. sl.* = CAFÉ. [abbr.]

caffeine /káfeen, kafeén/ *n.* an alkaloid drug with stimulant action found in tea leaves and coffee beans. [F *caféine* f. *café* coffee]

caftan /káftan/ *n.* (also **kaftan**) **1** a long, usu. belted tunic worn in countries of the Near East. **2 a** a long, loose dress. **b** a loose shirt or top. [Turk. *ḳaftān*, partly through F *cafetan*]
■ see SHIFT *n.* 4a.

cage /kayj/ *n. & v.* ● *n.* **1** a structure of bars or wires, esp. for confining animals or birds. **2** any similar open framework, as an enclosed platform for passengers in a freight elevator, etc. **3** *colloq.* a camp for prisoners of war. ● *v.tr.* place or keep in a cage. □ **cage bird** a bird of the kind customarily kept in a cage. [ME f. OF f. L *cavea*]
■ *n.* **1** crate, enclosure, pen, pound, coop, hutch. ● *v.* cage up *or* in, confine, enclose, pen, impound, shut up *or* in, coop (up), lock up *or* in, fence in, close in, imprison; hem in.

cagey /káyjee/ *adj.* (also **cagy**) (**cagier**, **cagiest**) *colloq.* cautious and uncommunicative; wary. □□ **cagily** *adv.* **caginess** *n.* (also **cageyness**). [20th-c. US: orig. unkn.]
■ see WARY.

cahoots /kəhōóts/ *n.pl.* □ **in cahoots** (often foll. by *with*) *sl.* in collusion. [19th c.: orig. uncert.]
■ □ **in cahoots** see *in* league (LEAGUE[1]).

CAI *abbr.* computer-assisted (or -aided) instruction.

caiman /káymən/ *n.* (also **cayman**) any of various S. American alligatorlike reptilians, esp. of the genus *Caiman*. [Sp. & Port. *caiman*, f. Carib *acayuman*]

Cain /kayn/ *n.* □ **raise Cain** *colloq.* make a disturbance; create trouble. [*Cain*, eldest son of Adam (Gen. 4)]

Cainozoic var. of CENOZOIC.

caïque /kī-eék/ *n.* **1** a light rowboat on the Bosporus. **2** a Levantine sailing ship. [F f. It. *caicco* f. Turk. *kayik*]

cairn /kairn/ *n.* **1** a mound of rough stones as a monument or landmark. **2** (in full **cairn terrier**) **a** a small terrier of a breed with short legs, a longish body, and a shaggy coat (perhaps so called from its being used to hunt among cairns). **b** this breed. [Gael. *carn*]
■ **1** see LANDMARK 1.

cairngorm /káirngawrm/ *n.* a yellow or wine-colored semi-precious form of quartz. [found on *Cairngorm*, a mountain in Scotland f. Gael. *carn gorm* blue cairn]

caisson /káyson, -sən/ *n.* **1** a watertight chamber in which underwater construction work can be done. **2** a floating vessel used as a floodgate in docks. **3** an ammunition chest or wagon. □ **caisson disease** = AEROEMBOLISM. [F (f. It. *cassone*) assim. to *caisse* CASE[2]]

caitiff /káytif/ *n. & adj. poet.* or *archaic* ● *n.* a base or despicable person; a coward. ● *adj.* base; despicable; cowardly. [ME f. OF *caitif, chaitif* ult. f. L *captivus* CAPTIVE]
■ *n.* see WRETCH 2. ● *adj.* see BASE[2] 1.

cajole /kəjōl/ *v.tr.* (often foll. by *into, out of*) persuade by flattery, deceit, etc. □□ **cajolement** *n.* **cajoler** *n.* **cajolery** *n.* [F *cajoler*]
■ wheedle, coax, beguile, seduce, inveigle, persuade, entice, bring around *or* round, *colloq.* soft-soap, jolly (along), cozy (along), butter (up), sweet-talk, smooth-talk; (*cajole into*) talk into; (*cajole out of*) talk out of. □□ **cajolery** wheedling, coaxing, blandishment, beguilement, persuasion, seduction, palaver, inveiglement, blarney, *colloq.* soft soap, buttering up, sweet talk.

cake /kayk/ *n. & v.* ● *n.* **1 a** a mixture of flour, butter, eggs, sugar, etc., baked in the oven. **b** a quantity of this baked in a flat round or ornamental shape and often iced and decorated. **2** other food in a flat round shape (*fish cake*). **3** a flattish compact mass (*a cake of soap*). **4** *Sc.* & *No. of Engl.* thin oaten bread. ● *v.* **1** *tr.* & *intr.* form into a compact

mass. **2** *tr.* (usu. foll. by *with*) cover (with a hard or sticky mass) (*boots caked with mud*). □ **cakes and ale** merrymaking. **have one's cake and eat it too** *colloq.* enjoy both of two mutually exclusive alternatives. **a piece of cake** *colloq.* something easily achieved. **a slice of the cake** esp. *Brit.* participation in benefits. [ME f. ON *kaka*]
■ *n.* **1** pastry, bun, gateau. **2** burger, patty, pat. **3** piece, chunk, bar, block, cube, lump, loaf, slab, hunk. ● *v.* **1** harden, solidify, thicken, congeal, dry, coagulate, set. **2** encrust, coat, cover, layer. □ **cakes and ale** see *revelry* (REVEL). **have one's cake and eat it too** get the best of both worlds. **piece of cake** see BREEZE[1] *n.* **4. slice of the cake** see SHARE[1] *n.*

cakewalk /káykwawk/ *n.* **1** a dance developed from a black American contest in graceful walking with a cake as a prize. **2** *colloq.* an easy task.

CAL *abbr.* computer-assisted learning.

Cal *abbr.* large calorie(s).

Cal. *abbr.* California.

cal *abbr.* small calorie(s).

Calabar bean /kálәbaar/ *n.* a poisonous seed of the tropical African climbing plant *Physostigma venosum*, yielding a medicinal extract. [*Calabar* in Nigeria]

calabash /kálәbash/ *n.* **1 a** an evergreen tree, *Crescentia cujete*, native to tropical America, bearing fruit in the form of large gourds. **b** a gourd from this tree. **2** the shell of this or a similar gourd used as a vessel for water, to make a tobacco pipe, etc. [F *calebasse* f. Sp. *calabaza* perh. f. Pers. *karbuz* melon]

calaboose /kálәbo͞os/ *n. sl.* a prison. [black F *calabouse* f. Sp. *calabozo* dungeon]
■ see PRISON *n.* 1.

calamanco /kálәmángko/ *n.* (*pl.* **-oes**) *hist.* a glossy woolen cloth checkered on one side. [16th c.: orig. unkn.]

calamander /kálәmandәr/ *n.* a fine-grained, red-brown ebony streaked with black, from the Asian tree *Diospyros qualsita*, used in furniture. [19th c.: orig. unkn.: perh. conn. with Sinh. word for the tree *kalu-madīriya*]

calamari /kaalәmáaree, ka-/ *n.* (*pl.* **-ies**) any cephalopod mollusk with a long, tapering, penlike horny internal shell, esp. a squid of the genus *Loligo*. [med.L *calamarium* pen case f. L *calamus* pen]

calamine /kálәmin/ *n.* **1** a pink powder consisting of zinc carbonate and ferric oxide used as a lotion or ointment. **2** a zinc mineral usu. zinc carbonate. [ME f. F f. med.L *calamina* alt. f. L *cadmia*: see CADMIUM]

calamint /kálәmint/ *n.* any aromatic herb or shrub of the genus *Calamintha*, esp. *C. officinalis* with purple or lilac flowers. [ME f. OF *calament* f. med.L *calamentum* f. LL *calaminthe* f. Gk *kalaminthē*]

calamity /kәlámitee/ *n.* (*pl.* **-ies**) **1** a disaster, a great misfortune. **2 a** adversity. **b** deep distress. □□ **calamitous** *adj.* **calamitously** *adv.* [ME f. F *calamité* f. L *calamitas -tatis*]
■ **1** disaster, catastrophe, cataclysm, devastation, tragedy, blight, crisis, misfortune, reverse, accident, misadventure, mischance, mishap. **2** distress, affliction, trouble, tragedy, misfortune, adversity, hardship, misery, grief, suffering, unhappiness, ruin, ruination, desolation, despair, wretchedness, gloom, *archaic or literary* woe. □□ **calamitous** disastrous, cataclysmic, catastrophic, distressful, dire, tragic, troublesome, woeful, sad, grievous, destructive, ruinous, unfortunate, awful, dreadful, terrible, devastating, desperate, pernicious.

calando /kәlaandó/ *adv. Mus.* gradually decreasing in speed and volume. [It., = slackening]

calash /kәlásh/ *n. hist.* **1 a** a light, low-wheeled carriage with a removable folding hood. **b** the folding hood itself. **2** a two-wheeled, horse-drawn vehicle. **3** a woman's hooped silk hood. [F *calèche* f. G *Kalesche* f. Pol. *kolaska* or Czech *kolesa*]

calc- /kalk/ *comb. form* lime or calcium. [G *Kalk* f. L CALX]

calcaneus /kalkáyneeәs/ *n.* (also **calcaneum** /-neeәm/) (*pl.* **calcanei** /-nee-ī/ or **calcanea** /-neeә/) the bone forming the heel. [L]

calcareous /kalkáireeәs/ *adj.* (also **calcarious**) of or containing calcium carbonate; chalky. [L *calcarius* (as CALX)]

calceolaria /kálseeәláireeә/ *n. Bot.* any plant of the genus *Calceolaria*, native to S. America, with slipper-shaped flowers. [mod.L f. L *calceolus* dimin. of *calceus* shoe + *-aria* fem. = -ARY[1]]

calceolate /kálseeәlayt/ *adj. Bot.* slipper-shaped.

calces *pl.* of CALX.

calciferol /kalsífәrol, -rol/ *n.* one of the D vitamins, routinely added to dairy products, essential for the deposition of calcium in bones. Also called ERGOCALCIFEROL, *vitamin D₂*. [CALCIFEROUS + -OL[1]]

calciferous /kalsífәrәs/ *adj.* yielding calcium salts, esp. calcium carbonate. [L CALX lime + -FEROUS]

calcify /kálsifī/ *v.tr. & intr.* (**-ies, -ied**) **1** harden or become hardened by deposition of calcium salts; petrify. **2** convert or be converted to calcium carbonate. □□ **calcific** /-sífik/ *adj.* **calcification** *n.*

calcine /kálsin, -sin/ *v.* **1** *tr.* **a** reduce, oxidize, or desiccate by strong heat. **b** burn to ashes; consume by fire; roast. **c** reduce to calcium oxide by roasting or burning. **2** *tr.* consume or purify as if by fire. **3** *intr.* undergo any of these. □□ **calcination** /-sináyshәn/ *n.* [ME f. OF *calciner* or med.L *calcinare* f. LL *calcina* lime f. L CALX]

calcite /kálsīt/ *n.* natural crystalline calcium carbonate. [G *Calcit* f. L CALX lime]

calcium /kálseeәm/ *n.* a soft, gray metallic element of the alkaline earth group occurring naturally in limestone, marble, chalk, etc., that is important in industry and essential for normal growth in living organisms. ¶ Symb.: **Ca**. □ **calcium carbide** a grayish solid used in the production of acetylene. **calcium carbonate** a white, insoluble solid occurring naturally as chalk, limestone, marble, and calcite, and used in the manufacture of lime and cement. **calcium hydroxide** a white crystalline powder used in the manufacture of plaster and cement; slaked lime. **calcium oxide** a white crystalline solid from which many calcium compounds are manufactured: also called LIME, CALX. **calcium phosphate** the main constituent of animal bones and used as bone ash fertilizer. **calcium sulfate** a white crystalline solid occurring as anhydrite and gypsum. [L CALX lime + -IUM]

calc-spar /kálkspaar/ *n.* = CALCITE. [CALC- + SPAR[3]]

calculable /kálkyәlәbәl/ *adj.* able to be calculated or estimated. □□ **calculability** *n.* **calculably** *adv.*

calculate /kálkyәlayt/ *v.* **1** *tr.* ascertain or determine beforehand, esp. by mathematics or by reckoning. **2** *tr.* plan deliberately. **3** *intr.* (foll. by *on, upon*) rely on; make an essential part of one's reckoning (*calculated on a quick response*). **4** *tr. dial.* suppose; believe. □□ **calculative** /-lәtiv/ *adj.* [LL *calculare* (as CALCULUS)]
■ **1** compute, work out, determine, ascertain, reckon, assess, evaluate, figure (out), measure, estimate, gauge, calibrate. **3** (*calculate on* or *upon*) see RECKON 6, RELY.

calculated /kálkyәlaytid/ *adj.* **1** (of an action) done with awareness of the likely consequences. **2** (foll. by *to* + infin.) designed or suitable; intended. □□ **calculatedly** *adv.*
■ **2** arranged, intended, designed, planned, prepared, adjusted, adapted, fit, fitted, suited, suitable; deliberate, purposeful, purposive, intentional, premeditated; studied, well-thought-out, conscious.

calculating /kálkyәlayting/ *adj.* (of a person) shrewd; scheming. □□ **calculatingly** *adv.*
■ shrewd, conniving, crafty, sly, wily, scheming, designing, Machiavellian, manipulative, canny, cunning, artful, astute.

calculation /kálkyәláyshәn/ *n.* **1** the act or process of calculating. **2** a result got by calculating. **3** a reckoning or forecast. [ME f. OF f. LL *calculatio* (as CALCULATE)]

/.../ **pronunciation**	● **part of speech**
□ **phrases, idioms, and compounds**	
□□ **derivatives**	■ **synonym section**
cross-references appear in SMALL CAPITALS or *italics*	

1 computation, reckoning, estimation, determining, measurement. **2** answer, product, result, figure, count, tally, estimate, amount. **3** estimate, forecast, projection, expectation, prediction.

calculator /kálkyəlaytər/ *n.* **1** a device (esp. a small electronic one) used for making mathematical calculations. **2** a person or thing that calculates. **3** a set of tables used in calculation. [ME f. L (as CALCULATE)]

■ **1** computer, adding machine; abacus.

calculus /kálkyələs/ *n.* (*pl.* **calculi** /-lī/ or **calculuses**) **1** *Math.* **a** a particular method of calculation or reasoning (*calculus of probabilities*). **b** the infinitesimal calculi of integration or differentiation (see *integral calculus, differential calculus*). **2** *Med.* a stone or concretion of minerals formed within the body. □□ **calculous** *adj.* (in sense 2). [L, = small stone used in reckoning on an abacus]

caldera /kaldáirə/ *n.* a large volcanic depression. [Sp. f. LL *caldaria* boiling-pot]

caldron var. of CAULDRON.

Caledonian /kálidṓneeən/ *adj. & n.* ● *adj.* **1** of or relating to Scotland. **2** *Geol.* of a mountain-forming period in Europe in the Paleozoic era. ● *n.* a Scotsman. [L *Caledonia* northern Britain]

calefacient /kálifáyshənt/ *n. & adj. Med.* ● *n.* a substance producing or causing a sensation of warmth. ● *adj.* of this substance. [L *calefacere* f. *calēre* be warm + *facere* make]

calendar /kálindər/ *n. & v.* ● *n.* **1** a system by which the beginning, length, and subdivisions of the year are fixed. **2** a chart or series of pages showing the days, weeks, and months of a particular year, or giving special seasonal information. **3** a timetable or program of appointments, special events, etc. ● *v.tr.* register or enter in a calendar or timetable, etc. □ **calendar month** (or **year**) see MONTH, YEAR. □□ **calendric** /-léndrik/ *adj.* **calendrical** *adj.* [ME f. AF *calender*, OF *calendier* f. L *calendarium* account book (as CALENDS)]

■ *n.* **2** almanac, chronicle, annal(s), yearbook; appointment book, journal, diary, *law* docket. **3** schedule, timetable, program, register, diary, listing.

calender /kálindər/ *n. & v.* ● *n.* a machine in which cloth, paper, etc., is pressed by rollers to glaze or smooth it. ● *v.tr.* press in a calender. [F *calendre(r)*, of unkn. orig.]

■ *n.* see ROLLER 1a. ● *v.* see SMOOTH *v.* 1.

calends /kálendz/ *n.pl.* (also **kalends**) the first of the month in the ancient Roman calendar. [ME f. OF *calendes* f. L *kalendae*]

calendula /kəlénjələ/ *n.* any plant of the genus *Calendula*, with large yellow or orange flowers. [mod.L dimin. of *calendae* (as CALENDS), perh. = little clock]

calenture /kálenchər/ *n. hist.* a tropical delirium of sailors, who think the sea is green fields. [F f. Sp. *calentura* fever f. *calentar* be hot ult. f. L *calēre* be warm]

calf[1] /kaf/ *n.* (*pl.* **calves** /kavz/) **1** a young bovine animal, used esp. of domestic cattle. **2** the young of other animals, e.g., elephant, deer, and whale. **3** *Naut.* a floating piece of ice detached from an iceberg. □ **calf-love** = *puppy love*. **in** (or **with**) **calf** (of a cow) pregnant. □□ **calfhood** *n.* **calfish** *adj.* **calflike** *adj.* [OE *cælf* f. WG]

calf[2] /kaf/ *n.* (*pl.* **calves** /kavz/) the fleshy hind part of the human leg below the knee. □□ **-calved** /kavd/ *adj.* (in *comb.*). [ME f. ON *kálfi*, of unkn. orig.]

calfskin /káfskin/ *n.* calf leather, esp. in bookbinding and shoemaking.

caliber /kálibər/ *n.* (*Brit.* **calibre**) **1 a** the internal diameter of a gun or tube. **b** the diameter of a bullet or shell. **2** strength or quality of character; ability; importance (*we need someone of your caliber*). □□ **calibered** *adj.* (also in *comb.*). [F *caliber* or It. *calibro*, f. Arab. *ḳālib* mold]

■ **1** diameter, size, bore, gauge, width, breadth. **2** merit, ability, talent, capability, competence, proficiency, capacity, quality, strength, stature, importance.

calibrate /kálibrayt/ *v.tr.* **1** mark (a gauge) with a standard scale of readings. **2** correlate the readings of (an instrument) with a standard. **3** determine the caliber of (a gun). **4** de-

termine the correct capacity or value of. □□ **calibration** /-bráyshən/ *n.* **calibrator** *n.* [CALIBER + -ATE[3]]

■ **1, 2** adjust, tune (up), regulate, attune, align, set; graduate, mark, scale, grade; standardize. **4** see CALCULATE 1.

calibre *Brit.* var. of CALIBER.

caliche /kəleéchee/ *n.* a mineral deposit of gravel, sand, and nitrates, esp. found in Chile and Peru. [Amer. Sp.]

calico /kálikō/ *n. & adj.* ● *n.* (*pl.* **-oes** or **-os**) **1** a printed cotton fabric. **2** *Brit.* a cotton cloth, esp. plain white or unbleached. ● *adj.* **1** made of calico. **2** multicolored; piebald. [earlier *calicut* f. *Calicut* in India]

Calif. *abbr.* California.

californium /kálifáwrneeəm/ *n. Chem.* a transuranic radioactive metallic element produced artificially from curium. ¶ Symb.: **Cf.** [*California* (where it was first made) + -IUM]

caliper /kálipər/ *n. & v.* ● *n.* **1** (in *pl.*) (also **caliper compasses**) compasses with bowed legs for measuring the diameter of convex bodies, or with out-turned points for measuring internal dimensions. **2** (in full **caliper splint**) a metal splint to support the leg. ● *v.tr.* measure with calipers. [app. var. of CALIBER]

caliph /káylif, kál-/ *n. esp. hist.* the chief Muslim civil and religious ruler, regarded as the successor of Muhammad. □□ **caliphate** *n.* [ME f. OF *caliphe* f. Arab. *ḳalīfa* successor]

calisthenics /kálisthéniks/ *n.pl.* (also esp. *Brit.* **callisthenics**) gymnastic exercises to achieve bodily fitness and grace of movement. □□ **calisthenic** *adj.* [Gk *kallos* beauty + *sthenos* strength]

■ see EXERCISE *n.* 3.

calk var. of CAULK.

call /kawl/ *v. & n.* ● *v.* **1** *intr.* **a** (often foll. by *out*) cry; shout; speak loudly. **b** (of a bird or animal) emit its characteristic note or cry. **2** *tr.* communicate or converse with by telephone or radio. **3** *tr.* **a** bring to one's presence by calling; summon (*will you call the children?*). **b** arrange for (a person or thing) to come or be present (*called a taxi*). **4** *intr.* (often foll. by *at, on*) pay a brief visit (*called at the house; come and call on me*). **5** *tr.* **a** order to take place; fix a time for (*called a meeting*). **b** direct to happen; announce (*call a halt*). **6 a** *intr.* require one's attention or consideration (*duty calls*). **b** *tr.* urge; invite; nominate (*call to run for office*). **7** *tr.* name; describe as (*call her Jennifer*). **8** *tr.* consider; regard or estimate as (*I call that silly*). **9** *tr.* rouse from sleep (*call me at 8*). **10** *intr.* guess the outcome of tossing a coin, etc. **11** *intr.* (foll. by *for*) order; require; demand (*called for silence*). **12** *tr.* (foll. by *over*) read out (a list of names to determine those present). **13** *intr.* (foll. by *on, upon*) invoke; appeal to; request or require (*called on us to be quiet*). **14** *tr. Cricket* (of an umpire) disallow a ball from (a bowler). **15** *tr. Cards* specify (a suit or contract) in bidding. **16** *tr. Sc.* drive (an animal, vehicle, etc.). ● *n.* **1** a shout or cry; an act of calling. **2 a** the characteristic cry of a bird or animal. **b** an imitation of this. **c** an instrument for imitating it. **3** a brief visit (*paid them a call*). **4 a** an act of telephoning. **b** a telephone conversation. **5 a** an invitation or summons to appear or be present. **b** an appeal or invitation (from a specific source or discerned by a person's conscience, etc.) to follow a certain profession, set of principles, etc. **6** (foll. by *for*, or *to* + infin.) a duty, need, or occasion (*no call to be rude; no call for violence*). **7** (foll. by *for, on*) a demand (*not much call for it these days; a call on one's time*). **8** a signal on a bugle, etc.; a signaling whistle. **9** *Stock Exch.* an option of buying stock at a fixed price at a given date. **10** *Cards* a player's right or turn to make a bid. **b** a bid made. □ **at call** = *on call*. **call away** divert; distract. **call down 1** invoke. **2** reprimand. **call forth** elicit. **call girl** a female prostitute who accepts appointments by telephone. **call in** *tr.* **1** withdraw from circulation. **2** seek the advice or services of. **calling card 1** a card with a person's name, etc., sent or left in lieu of a formal visit. **2** evidence of someone's presence; an identifying mark, etc., left behind (by someone). **3** a card used to charge a telephone call to a number other than that from which the call is placed. **call in** (or **into**) **question** dispute; doubt the validity of. **call into play** give scope for; make use of. **call**

a person names abuse a person verbally. **call off 1** cancel (an arrangement, etc.). **2** order (an attacker or pursuer) to desist. **call of nature** a need to urinate or defecate. **call out 1** summon (troops, etc.) to action. **2** order (workers) to strike. **call-over** *Brit.* **1** a roll call. **2** reading aloud of a list of betting prices. **call the shots** (or **tune**) be in control; take the initiative. **call sign** (or **signal**) a broadcast signal identifying the radio transmitter used. **call to account** see ACCOUNT. **call to mind** recollect; cause one to remember. **call to order 1** request to be orderly. **2** declare (a meeting) open. **call up 1** reach by telephone. **2** imagine; recollect. **3** summon, esp. to serve on active military duty. **call-up** *n.* the act or process of calling up (sense 3). **on call 1** (of a doctor, etc.) available if required but not formally on duty. **2** (of money lent) repayable on demand. **within call** near enough to be summoned by calling. [OE *ceallian* f. ON *kalla*]

■ *v.* **1 a** shout, cry (out), hail, yell, roar, bellow, call out, bawl, howl, *colloq.* holler. **2** call up, telephone, dial, esp. *Brit.* ring (up), *colloq.* buzz, phone, give a person a ring, *Brit. colloq.* give a person a tinkle; radio. **3 a** summon, collect, muster, rally, assemble, convene, *formal* convoke; page, send for. **4** call at *or* on, visit, attend, pay a visit, look in, stop in *or* by, pop in *or* by, come by, *colloq.* drop in *or* by. **5 a** see ARRANGE 2, 3. **b** see ORDER *v.* 1, 2, 5, 6. **6 a** beckon, summon. **7** name, designate, denominate, term, style, nickname, label, title, tag, identify, dub, christen, baptize, *archaic* entitle; (*be called*) answer to the name of. **8** see CONSIDER 6. **9** awake, awaken, wake up, rouse, get up, *Brit.* knock up. **11** (*call for*) see DEMAND *v.* 1. **13** (*call on*) invoke, appeal to, request, entreat, ask. ● *n.* **1** shout, cry, yell, hail, whoop, *colloq.* holler. **2** song, cry. **3** visit. **4** telephone call, phone call, *colloq.* ring, *Brit. colloq.* tinkle, *sl.* buzz. **5** summons, bidding, notice, notification, order, demand, command, dictate, instruction, requisition, *archaic* hest, *literary* behest; invitation; request, appeal, entreaty, plea, petition; subpoena; vocation, calling. **6** reason, justification, case, pretext, ground(s), cause, motive, need, occasion, right, excuse; requirement; duty, responsibility. **7** see DEMAND *n.* 2. □ **call away** see DISTRACT 1. **call down 1** invoke, summon (up), call forth, conjure up, muster. **2** see BERATE. **call forth** summon (up), invoke, draw on *or* upon, evoke, conjure up, muster, call down; elicit, bring *or* draw forth, bring *or* draw out, attract; excite, inspire, incite, occasion, bring about. **call girl** see PROSTITUTE *n.* 1a. **calling card 1** visiting card. **call in** (or **into**) **question** see CHALLENGE *v.* 2. **call into play** see USE *v.* 1a. **call a person names** see ABUSE *v.* 2. **call off 1** cancel; see also POSTPONE. **call the shots** (or **tune**) be in charge *or* command *or* control, rule the roost, be in the driver's seat, be in the saddle, be at the wheel, pull the strings, take the initiative, run *or* direct *or* manage *or* administer *or* control things, *colloq.* run the show. **call to mind** see RECALL *v.* 2, REMIND *v.* 1. **call up 1** see CALL *v.* 2 above. **2** see IMAGINE 1, *call forth* above. **3** summon, enlist, recruit, conscript, draft. **call-up** enlistment, conscription, recruitment, induction, draft, *Brit. hist.* national service, *hist.* selective service. **on call 1** ready, on duty, standing by, on standby, awaiting orders. **within call** within earshot *or* hearing *or* (easy) reach; nearby, close by, close at hand, in the vicinity, about, around.

calla /kálə/ *n.* **1** (in full **calla lily**) a tall, lilylike plant, *Zantedeschia aethiopica*, with white spathe and spadix. **2** an aquatic plant, *Calla palustris*. [mod.L]

callboy /káwlboy/ *n.* **1** a theater attendant who summons actors when needed on stage. **2** a bellhop. **3** (also **call boy**) a male prostitute who accepts appointments by telephone.

caller /káwlər/ *n.* **1** a person who calls, esp. one who pays a visit or makes a telephone call. **2** *Austral.* a racing commentator.

■ **1** see VISITOR.

calligraphy /kəlígrəfee/ *n.* **1** handwriting, esp. when fine or

pleasing. **2** the art of handwriting. □□ **calligrapher** *n.* **calligraphic** /káligráfik/ *adj.* **calligraphist** *n.* [Gk *kalligraphia* f. *kallos* beauty]

■ see WRITING 2.

calling /káwling/ *n.* **1** a profession or occupation. **2** an inwardly felt call or summons; a vocation.

■ **1** profession, occupation, business, trade, employment, work, line, job, métier, pursuit, career, craft, area, province, (area of) expertise, specialty, *colloq.* racket. **2** vocation, mission, purpose, call, summons.

calliope /kəlíəpee/ *n.* a keyboard instrument resembling an organ, with a set of steam whistles producing musical notes. [Gk *Kalliopē* muse of epic poetry (lit. 'beautiful-voiced')]

■ steam organ.

calliper *Brit.* var. of CALIPER.

callisthenics esp. *Brit.* var. of CALISTHENICS.

callop /kálə p/ *n. Austral.* a gold-colored freshwater fish, *Plectroplites ambiguus*, used as food. Also called *golden perch.* [Aboriginal]

callosity /kəlósitee/ *n.* (*pl.* **-ies**) a hard, thick area of skin usu. occurring in parts of the body subject to pressure or friction. [F *callosité* or L *callositas* (as CALLOUS)]

callous /káləs/ *adj.* **1** unfeeling; insensitive. **2** (of skin) hardened or hard. □□ **callously** *adv.* (in sense 1). **callousness** *n.* [ME f. L *callosus* (as CALLUS) or F *calleux*]

■ **1** thick-skinned, unfeeling, uncaring, insensitive, hard, hard-hearted, cold, coldhearted, stonyhearted, heartless, cruel, ruthless, indifferent, unsympathetic, *colloq.* hard-nosed, hardbitten. **2** hard, hardened, tough, leathery.

callow /kálō/ *adj.* inexperienced; immature. □□ **callowly** *adv.* **callowness** *n.* [OE *calu*]

■ inexperienced, immature, juvenile, young, naive, green, fresh, new, tender, guileless, unsophisticated, innocent, raw, unfledged, untried, (still) wet behind the ears.

callus /káləs/ *n.* **1** a hard thick area of skin or tissue. **2** a hard tissue formed around bone ends after a fracture. **3** *Bot.* a new protective tissue formed over a wound. [L]

calm /kaam/ *adj., n., & v.* ● *adj.* **1** tranquil; quiet; windless (*a calm sea; a calm night*). **2** (of a person or disposition) settled; not agitated (*remained calm throughout the ordeal*). **3** self-assured; confident (*his calm assumption that we would wait*). ● *n.* **1** a state of being calm; stillness; serenity. **2** a period without wind or storm. ● *v.tr. & intr.* (often foll. by *down*) make or become calm. □□ **calmly** *adv.* **calmness** *n.* [ME ult. f. LL *cauma* f. Gk *kauma* heat]

■ *adj.* **1** quiet, still, tranquil, serene, peaceful, balmy, halcyon, undisturbed, windless, placid, pacific; motionless, smooth, even. **2** composed, cool, controlled, coolheaded, levelheaded, self-controlled, impassive, dispassionate, unimpassioned, unmoved, nonchalant, unexcited, unexcitable, unruffled, unbothered, unhurried, settled, equable, collected, serene, quiet, tranquil, sedate, stoical, *colloq.* laid-back, together. **3** see CONFIDENT *adj.* 1. ● *n.* **1** calmness, quiet, tranquillity, quietness, serenity, peacefulness, composure, placidity, placidness, sangfroid, coolness, self-control, equanimity, self-possession; stillness, motionlessness. **2** hush, peace; see also LULL *n.* ● *v.* quiet, still, soothe, hush, lull, pacify, quell; mollify, appease, placate, *Brit.* quieten (down); relax, take it easy, cool off *or* down, wind down, *colloq.* unwind; subside, abate, moderate, let up, ease up, die down, slacken (off), diminish, lessen.

calmative /káamətiv, kálm-/ *adj. & n. Med.* ● *adj.* tending to calm or sedate. ● *n.* a calmative drug, etc.

■ *adj.* see SEDATIVE *adj.* ● *n.* see SEDATIVE *n.*

calomel /káləmel/ *n.* a compound of mercury, esp. when

/. . ./ **pronunciation**	● **part of speech**
□ **phrases, idioms, and compounds**	
□□ **derivatives**	■ **synonym section**
cross-references appear in SMALL CAPITALS or *italics*	

used medicinally as a cathartic. [mod.L perh. f. Gk *kalos* beautiful + *melas* black]

caloric /kəláwrik, -lór-/ *adj. & n.* ● *adj.* of heat or calories. ● *n. hist.* a supposed material form or cause of heat. [F *calorique* f. L *calor* heat]

calorie /káləree/ *n.* (also **calory**) (*pl.* **-ies**) a unit of quantity of heat: **1** (in full **small calorie**) the amount needed to raise the temperature of 1 gram of water through 1 °C. ¶ Abbr.: **cal. 2** (in full **large calorie**) the amount needed to raise the temperature of 1 kilogram of water through 1 °C, often used to measure the energy value of foods. ¶ Abbr.: **Cal.** [F, arbitr. f. L *calor* heat + *-ie*]

calorific /kálərifik/ *adj.* producing heat. □ **calorific value** the amount of heat produced by a specified quantity of fuel, food, etc. □□ **calorifically** *adv.* [L *calorificus* f. *calor* heat]

calorimeter /kálərimitər/ *n.* any of various instruments for measuring quantity of heat, esp. to find calorific values. □□ **calorimetric** /-métrik/ *adj.* **calorimetry** *n.* [L *calor* heat + -METER]

calory var. of CALORIE.

calque /kalk/ *n. Philol.* = *loan translation.* [F, = copy, tracing f. *calquer* trace ult. f. L *calcare* tread]

caltrop /káltrəp/ *n.* (also **caltrap**) **1** *hist.* a four-spiked iron ball thrown on the ground to impede cavalry horses. **2** *Heraldry* a representation of this. **3** any creeping plant of the genus *Tribulus*, with woody carpels usu. having hard spines. [(sense 3) OE *calcatrippe* f. med.L *calcatrippa*: (senses 1–2) ME f. OF *chauchetrape* f. *chauchier* tread, *trappe* trap: ult. the same word]

calumet /kályəmét/ *n.* a Native American ceremonial peace pipe. [F, ult. f. L *calamus* reed]

calumniate /kəlúmneeayt/ *v.tr.* slander. □□ **calumniation** /-neeáyshən/ *n.* **calumniator** *n.* **calumniatory** /-ətáwree/ *adj.* [L *calumniari*]
■ see SLANDER *v.*

calumny /káləmnee/ *n. & v.* ● *n.* (*pl.* **-ies**) **1** slander; malicious representation. **2** an instance of this. ● *v.tr.* (**-ies**, **-ied**) slander. □□ **calumnious** /-lúmneeəs/ *adj.* [L *calumnia*]
■ *n.* see SLANDER *n.* ● *v.* see SLANDER *v.* □□ **calumnious** see *slanderous* (SLANDER).

calvados /kálvədōs/ *n.* (also **Calvados**) an apple brandy. [*Calvados* in France]

Calvary /kálvəree/ *n.* the place where Christ was crucified. [ME f. LL *calvaria* skull, transl. Gk *golgotha*, Aram. *gûlgûltâ* (Matt. 27:33)]

calve /kav/ *v.* **1 a** *intr.* give birth to a calf. **b** *tr.* (esp. in *passive*) give birth to (a calf). **2** *tr.* (also *absol.*) (of an iceberg) break off or shed (a mass of ice). [OE *calfian*]

calves *pl.* of CALF[1], CALF[2].

Calvinism /kálvinizəm/ *n.* the theology of the French theologian J. Calvin (d. 1564) or his followers, in which predestination and justification by faith are important elements. □□ **Calvinist** *n.* **Calvinistic** *adj.* **Calvinistical** *adj.* [F *calvinisme* or mod.L *calvinismus*]

calx /kalks/ *n.* (*pl.* **calxes** or **calces** /kálseez/) **1** a powdery metallic oxide formed when an ore or mineral has been heated. **2** calcium oxide. [L *calx calcis* lime prob. f. Gk *khalix* pebble, limestone]

calypso /kəlípsō/ *n.* (*pl.* **-os**) a W. Indian song in African rhythm, usu. improvised on a topical theme. [20th c.: orig. unkn.]

calyx /káyliks, kál-/ *n.* (*pl.* **calyxes** or **calyces** /-liseez/) **1** *Bot.* the sepals collectively, forming the protective layer of a flower in bud. **2** *Biol.* any cuplike cavity or structure. [L f. Gk *kalux* case of bud, husk: cf. *kaluptō* hide]

cam /kam/ *n.* a projection on a rotating part in machinery, shaped to impart reciprocal or variable motion to the part in contact with it. [Du. *kam* comb: cf. Du. *kamrad* cogwheel]

camaraderie /kaaməraádəree/ *n.* mutual trust and sociability among friends. [F]
■ see COMPANIONSHIP.

camarilla /kámərílə/ *n.* a cabal or clique. [Sp., dimin. of *camara* chamber]
■ see FACTION[1] 1.

Camb. *abbr.* Cambridge.

camber /kámbər/ *n. & v.* ● *n.* **1** the slightly convex or arched shape of the surface of a ship's deck, aircraft wing, etc. **2** the slight sideways inclination of the front wheel of a motor vehicle. ● *v.* **1** *intr.* (of a surface) have a camber. **2** *tr.* give a camber to; build with a camber. [F *cambre* arched f. L *camurus* curved inward]
■ *n.* **1** see SLANT *n.* 1.

cambium /kámbeeəm/ *n.* (*pl.* **cambiums** or **cambia** /-beeə/) *Bot.* a cellular plant tissue responsible for the increase in girth of stems and roots. □□ **cambial** *adj.* [med.L, = change, exchange]

Cambodian /kambōdeeən/ *n. & adj.* ● *n.* **1 a** a native or national of Cambodia (Kampuchea) in SE Asia. **b** a person of Cambodian descent. **2** the language of Cambodia. ● *adj.* of or relating to Cambodia or its people or language. Also called KAMPUCHEAN.

Cambrian /kámbreeən/ *adj. & n.* ● *adj.* **1** Welsh. **2** *Geol.* of or relating to the first period in the Paleozoic era, marked by the occurrence of many forms of invertebrate life (including trilobites and brachiopods). ¶ Cf. Appendix VII. ● *n.* this period or system. [L *Cambria* var. of *Cumbria* f. Welsh *Cymry* Welshman or *Cymru* Wales]

cambric /kámbrik/ *n.* a fine white linen or cotton fabric. [*Kamerijk*, Flem. form of *Cambrai* in N. France, where it was orig. made]

camcorder /kámkawrdər/ *n.* a combined video camera and sound recorder. [*camera* + re*corder*]

came *past* of COME.

camel /káməl/ *n.* **1** either of two kinds of large, cud-chewing mammals having slender, cushion-footed legs and one hump (**Arabian camel**, *Camelus dromedarius*) or two humps (**Bactrian camel**, *Camelus bactrianus*). **2** a fawn color. **3** an apparatus for providing additional buoyancy to ships, etc.; a pontoon. **4** (in full **camel spin**) an arabesque spin in figure skating. □ **camel** (or **camel's**) **hair 1** the hair of a camel. **2 a** a fine, soft hair used in artists' brushes. **b** a fabric made of this. [OE f. L *camelus* f. Gk *kamēlos*, of Semitic orig.]

cameleer /káməleér/ *n.* a camel driver.

camellia /kəméelyə/ *n.* any evergreen shrub of the genus *Camellia*, native to E. Asia, with shiny leaves and showy flowers. [J. *Camellus* or *Kamel*, 17th-c. Jesuit botanist]

camelopard /kəméləpaard/ *n. archaic* a giraffe. [L *camelopardus* f. Gk *kamēlopardalis* (as CAMEL, PARD)]

camelry /káməlree/ *n.* (*pl.* **-ies**) troops mounted on camels.

Camembert /káməmbair/ *n.* a kind of soft, creamy cheese, usu. with a strong flavor. [*Camembert* in N. France, where it was orig. made]

cameo /kámeeō/ *n.* (*pl.* **-os**) **1 a** a small piece of onyx or other hard stone carved in relief with a background of a different color. **b** a similar relief design using other materials. **2 a** a short descriptive literary sketch or acted scene. **b** a small character part in a play or film, usu. brief and played by a distinguished actor. [ME f. OF *camahieu* and med.L *cammaeus*]

camera /kámrə, kámərə/ *n.* **1** an apparatus for taking photographs, consisting of a lightproof box to hold light-sensitive film, a lens, and a shutter mechanism, either for still photographs or for motion-picture film. **2** *Telev.* a piece of equipment that forms an optical image and converts it into electrical impulses for transmission or storage. □ **camera obscura** /obskyoŏrə/ an internally darkened box with an aperture for projecting the image of an external object on a screen inside it. **camera-ready** *Printing* (of copy) in a form suitable for immediate photographic reproduction. **in camera 1** *Law* in a judge's private room. **2** privately; not in public. **on camera** (esp. of an actor or actress) being filmed or televised at a particular moment. [orig. = chamber f. L *camera* f. Gk *kamara* vault, etc.]
■ □ **in camera** see *in private* (PRIVATE).

cameraman /kámrəmən/ *n.* (*pl.* **-men**) a person who operates a camera professionally, esp. in filmmaking or television.
■ see *photographer* (PHOTOGRAPH).

camiknickers /kámənikərz/ *n.pl. Brit.* a one-piece close-fitting undergarment formerly worn by women. [CAMISOLE + KNICKERS]

camisole /kámisōl/ *n.* an upper-body undergarment, often embroidered. [F f. It. *camiciola* or Sp. *camisola*: see CHEMISE]

camomile var. of CHAMOMILE.

camouflage /kámaflaazh/ *n., adj., & v.* ● *n.* **1 a** the disguising, by the military, of people, vehicles, aircraft, ships, and installations by painting them or covering them to make them blend with their surroundings. **b** such a disguise. **2** the natural coloring of an animal that enables it to blend in with its surroundings. **3** a misleading or evasive precaution or expedient. ● *adj.* (usu. of clothing) of a mottled green, brown, etc., pattern similar to military camouflage. ● *v.tr.* hide or disguise by means of camouflage. [F f. *camoufler* disguise f. It. *camuffare* disguise, deceive]

■ *n.* **1** disguise, concealment. **2** *Zool.* cryptic coloring *or* coloration. **3** smokescreen, cover-up, cover, guise, cloak, mask, screen, blind, (false) front, show, façade. ● *v.* disguise, cloak, mask, cover (up), hide, obscure, conceal, screen, veil, shroud, dress up; bury, dissemble, dissimulate, misrepresent, falsify.

camp[1] /kamp/ *n. & v.* ● *n.* **1 a** a place where troops are lodged or trained. **b** the military life (*court and camp*). **2** temporary overnight lodging in tents, etc., in the open. **3 a** temporary accommodation of various kinds, usu. consisting of huts or tents, for detainees, homeless persons, and other emergency use. **b** a complex of buildings for vacation accommodation, usu. with extensive recreational facilities. **4** the adherents of a particular party or doctrine regarded collectively (*the Conservative camp was jubilant*). **5** *S.Afr.* a portion of veld fenced off for pasture on farms. **6** *Austral. & NZ* an assembly place of sheep or cattle. ● *v.intr.* **1** set up or spend time in a camp (in senses 1 and 2 of *n.*). **2** (often foll. by *out*) lodge in temporary quarters or in the open. **3** *Austral. & NZ* (of sheep or cattle) flock together, esp. for rest. □ **camp bed** *Brit.* a folding portable bed of a kind used in camping. **camp follower 1** a civilian worker in a military camp. **2** a civilian, esp. a prostitute, who follows or lives near a military camp for the purpose of exploiting military personnel. **3** a disciple or adherent. □□ **camping** *n.* [F f. It. *campo* f. L *campus* level ground]

■ *n.* **1 a** base, station, barrack(s), cantonment, encampment. **2** bivouac. **4** faction, wing, front, set, coterie, clique, side, group, party, body, band, lobby. ● *v.* **1** encamp, pitch camp, tent, lodge, bivouac. **2** (*camp out*) tent, bivouac, stay (over), *sl.* crash. □ **camp follower 3** follower, disciple; see also DEVOTEE.

camp[2] /kamp/ *adj., n., & v. colloq.* ● *adj.* **1** done in an exaggerated way for effect. **2** affected; effeminate. ● *n.* a camp manner or style. ● *v.intr.* behave or do in a camp way. □ **camp it up** overact; behave affectedly. □□ **campy** *adj.* (**campier, campiest**). **campily** *adv.* **campiness** *n.* [20th c.: orig. uncert.]

■ *adj.* **1** outré, outrageous, outlandish, exaggerated, affected, extravagant, artificial, theatrical, mannered, flamboyant, showy, ostentatious, flashy. **2** affected, effeminate, mincing, niminy-piminy, minikin, chichi, *colloq.* campy. ● *v.* exaggerate, overact, go too far, overdo it, go overboard, overshoot the mark, *colloq.* camp it up; show off, strut, flaunt, flounce, prance, posture, *sl.* ham. □ **camp it up** see CAMP[2] *v.* above.

campaign /kampáyn/ *n. & v.* ● *n.* **1** an organized course of action for a particular purpose, esp. to arouse public interest (e.g., before a political election). **2 a** a series of military operations in a definite area or to achieve a particular objective. **b** military service in the field (*on campaign*). ● *v.intr.* conduct or take part in a campaign. □□ **campaigner** *n.* [F *campagne* open country f. It. *campagna* f. LL *campania*]

■ *n.* **1** drive, offensive, push, effort, crusade; move, strategy, scheme, movement, plan. **2** operation(s), maneuver(s), movement, crusade, action, offensive; battle, conflict, engagement. ● *v.* run, electioneer, canvass, compete, vie, contend, stump, *Brit.* stand; agitate, push, press, fight, work; (*campaign for*)

promote, support, back, advocate, champion, speak up for *or* on behalf of.

campanile /kámpanéelee, -néel/ *n.* a bell tower (usu. freestanding), esp. in Italy. [It. f. *campana* bell]

■ see TOWER *n.* 1.

campanology /kámpanólajee/ *n.* **1** the study of bells. **2** the art or practice of bell ringing. □□ **campanologer** *n.* **campanological** /-nəlójikəl/ *adj.* **campanologist** *n.* [mod.L *campanologia* f. LL *campana* bell]

campanula /kampányələ/ *n.* any plant of the genus *Campanula*, with bell-shaped usu. blue, purple, or white flowers. Also called BELLFLOWER. [mod.L dimin. of L *campana* bell]

campanulate /kampányələt, -layt/ *adj. Bot. & Zool.* bell-shaped.

Campeachy wood /kampéechee/ *n.* = LOGWOOD. [*Campeche* in Mexico, from where it was first exported]

camper /kámpər/ *n.* **1** a person who camps out or lives temporarily in a tent, hut, etc., esp. for recreation. **2** a large motor vehicle with accommodation for camping out.

campfire /kámpfir/ *n.* an open-air fire in a camp, etc.

camphor /kámfər/ *n.* a white, translucent, crystalline volatile substance with aromatic smell and bitter taste, used to make celluloid and in medicine. □□ **camphoric** /-fórik/ *adj.* [ME f. OF *camphore* or med.L *camphora* f. Arab. *kāfūr* f. Skr. *karpūram*]

camphorate /kámfərayt/ *v.tr.* impregnate or treat with camphor.

campion /kámpeeən/ *n.* **1** any plant of the genus *Silene*, with usu. pink or white notched flowers. **2** any of several similar cultivated plants of the genus *Lychnis*. [perh. f. obs. *campion* f. OF, = CHAMPION: transl. of Gk *lukhnis stephanōmatikē* a plant used for (champions') garlands]

campsite /kámpsit/ *n.* a place suitable for camping; a site used by campers.

campus /kámpəs/ *n.* (*pl.* **campuses**) **1** the grounds of a university or college. **2** a college or university, esp. as a teaching institution. [L, = field]

camshaft /kámshaft/ *n.* a shaft with one or more cams attached to it.

Can. *abbr.* Canada; Canadian.

can[1] /kan, kən/ *v.aux.* (*3rd sing. present* **can**; *past* **could** /kood/) (foll. by infin. without *to*, or *absol.*; present and past only in use) **1 a** be able to; know how to (*I can run fast; can he?; can you speak German?*). **b** be potentially capable of (*you can do it if you try*). **2** be permitted to (*can we go to the party?*). [OE *cunnan* know]

can[2] /kan/ *n. & v.* ● *n.* **1** a metal vessel for liquid. **2** a metal container in which food or drink is hermetically sealed to enable storage over long periods. **3** (prec. by *the*) *sl.* **a** prison (*sent to the can*). **b** *sl.* toilet. **4** *sl.* the buttocks. ● *v.tr.* (**canned, canning**) **1** put or preserve in a can. **2** record on film or tape for future use. □ **can of worms** *colloq.* a complicated problem. **can opener** a device for opening cans (in sense 2 of *n.*). **in the can** *colloq.* completed; ready (orig. of filmed or recorded material). □□ **canner** *n.* [OE *canne*]

■ *n.* **1, 2** see RECEPTACLE. **3 a** see PRISON *n.* 1. **b** see TOILET. ● *v.* **1** see PRESERVE *v.* 4a. □ **can of worms** see PROBLEM 1, 2.

Canaan /káynən/ *n.* **1** a promised land (orig. that west of the Jordan River, the Promised Land of the Israelites). **2** heaven. [eccl.L f. eccl.Gk *Khanaan* f. Heb. *kᵉna'an*]

Canada balsam /kánədə/ *n. Biol.* a yellow resin obtained from the balsam fir and used for mounting preparations on microscope slides (its refractive index being similar to that of glass).

Canada goose *n.* a wild goose, *Branta canadensis*, of N. America, with a brownish-gray body and white cheeks and breast.

/.../ **pronunciation**	● **part of speech**
□ **phrases, idioms, and compounds**	
□□ **derivatives**	■ **synonym section**
cross-references appear in SMALL CAPITALS or *italics*	

canaille /kənaá-ee, -náyl/ n. the rabble; the populace. [F f. It. *canaglia* pack of dogs f. *cane* dog]
■ see RABBLE[1] 3.

canal /kənál/ n. **1** an artificial waterway for inland navigation or irrigation. **2** any of various tubular ducts in a plant or animal, for carrying food, liquid, or air. **3** *Astron.* any of a network of apparent linear markings on the planet Mars. □ **canal boat** a long, narrow boat for use on canals. [ME f. OF (earlier *chanel*) f. L *canalis* or It. *canale*]
■ **1** see CHANNEL[1] n. 5a, 6. **2** see VESSEL 3.

canalize /kánəlīz/ v.tr. **1** make a canal through. **2** convert (a river) into a canal. **3** provide with canals. **4** give the desired direction or purpose to. □□ **canalization** n. [F *canaliser*: see CANAL]

canapé /kánəpay, -pee/ n. **1** a small piece of bread or pastry with a savory food on top, often served as an hors d'oeuvre. **2** a sofa. [F]

canard /kənaárd/ n. **1** an unfounded rumor or story. **2** an extra surface attached to an airplane forward of the main lifting surface, for extra stability or control. [F, = duck]

Canarese var. of KANARESE.

canary /kənáiree/ n. (pl. **-ies**) **1** any of various small finches of the genus *Serinus*, esp. *S. canaria*, a songbird native to the Canary Islands, with mainly yellow plumage. **2** *hist.* a sweet wine from the Canary Islands. □ **canary grass** a Mediterranean plant *Phalaris canariensis*, grown as a crop plant for birdseed. **canary yellow** bright yellow. [*Canary* Islands f. F *Canarie* f. Sp. & L *Canaria* f. *canis* dog, one of the islands being noted in Roman times for large dogs]

canarybird flower /kənáireebərd/ n. a climbing plant, *Tropaeolium peregrinum*, with flowers of bright yellow, deeply toothed petals, which give the appearance of a small bird in flight. Also called **canarybird vine**.

canasta /kənástə/ n. **1** a card game using two packs and resembling rummy, the aim being to collect sets (or melds) of cards. **2** a set of seven cards in this game. [Sp., = basket]

canaster /kənástər/ n. tobacco made from coarsely broken dried leaves. [orig. the container: Sp. *canastro* ult. f. Gk *kanastron*]

cancan /kánkan/ n. a lively stage dance with high kicking, performed by women in ruffled skirts and petticoats. [F]

cancel /kánsəl/ v. & n. ● v. (**canceled, canceling**; esp. *Brit.* **cancelled, cancelling**) **1** tr. **a** withdraw or revoke (a previous arrangement). **b** discontinue (an arrangement in progress). **2** tr. obliterate or delete (writing, etc.). **3** tr. mark or pierce (a ticket, stamp, etc.) to invalidate it. **4** tr. annul; make void; abolish. **5** (often foll. by *out*) **a** tr. (of one factor or circumstance) neutralize or counterbalance (another). **b** *intr.* (of two factors or circumstances) neutralize each other. **6** tr. *Math.* strike out (an equal factor) on each side of an equation or from the numerator and denominator of a fraction. ● n. **1** a countermand. **2** the cancellation of a postage stamp. **3** *Printing* a new page or section inserted in a book to replace the original text, usu. to correct an error. □□ **canceler** n. [ME f. F *canceller* f. L *cancellare* f. *cancelli* crossbars, lattice]
■ v. **1 a** revoke, call off, retract, withdraw, rescind, countermand, do away with, dispense with, *colloq.* scrub, *sl.* nix. **b** see STOP v. 1c. **2** delete, obliterate, cross *or* strike *or* blot *or* scratch out, rub out, erase, *Printing* dele; expunge, efface, eradicate; eliminate, do away with, get rid of, dispense with, take away, omit. **3** stamp, clip; postmark. **4** void, annul, declare null and void, invalidate, nullify, quash, recall, set aside, wipe off, wash out, write off, remit, dissolve, repeal, abolish, undo, unmake, *Law* defeat, repeal, reverse, vacate, discharge. **5** neutralize, nullify, counterbalance, countervail, counter, compensate (for), make up for, offset, counteract.

cancellate /kánsilət, -layt/ adj. (also **cancellated** /-laytid/) *Biol.* marked with crossing lines. [L *cancelli* lattice]

cancellation /kánsəláyshən/ n. (also **cancelation**) **1** the act or an instance of canceling or being canceled. **2** something that has been canceled, esp. a booking or reservation. [L *cancellatio* (as CANCEL)]

■ **1** annulment, nullification, abrogation, invalidation, rescission, rescindment, reversal, recall, repeal, abandonment, withdrawal, revocation; deletion, elimination; discontinuance, termination, stoppage, cessation.

cancellous /kánsiləs/ adj. (of a bone) with pores. [L *cancelli* lattice]

cancer /kánsər/ n. **1 a** any malignant growth or tumor from an abnormal and uncontrolled division of body cells. **b** a disease caused by this. **2** an evil influence or corruption spreading uncontrollably. **3** (**Cancer**) **a** a constellation, traditionally regarded as contained in the figure of a crab. **b** the fourth sign of the zodiac (the Crab). **c** a person born when the sun is in this sign. □ **cancer stick** *sl.* a cigarette. **Tropic of Cancer** see TROPIC. □□ **Cancerian** /-séreeən/ n. & adj. (in sense 3). **cancerous** adj. [ME f. L, = crab, cancer, after Gk *karkinos*]
■ **1** see TUMOR. **2** see POISON n. 2.

cancroid /kángkroyd/ adj. & n. ● adj. **1** crablike. **2** resembling cancer. ● n. a disease resembling cancer.

candela /kandeélə, -délə/ n. the SI unit of luminous intensity. ¶ Abbr.: **cd**. [L, = candle]

candelabrum /kándəlaábrəm/ n. (also **candelabra** /-brə/) (pl. **candelabra, candelabrums, candelabras**) a large branched candlestick or lamp holder. [L f. *candela* CANDLE]

candescent /kandésənt/ adj. glowing with or as with white heat. □□ **candescence** n. [L *candēre* be white]

candid /kándid/ adj. **1** frank; not hiding one's thoughts. **2** (of a photograph) taken informally, usu. without the subject's knowledge. □ **candid camera** a small camera for taking candid photographs. □□ **candidly** adv. **candidness** n. [F *candide* or L *candidus* white]
■ **1** frank, open, plain, sincere, ingenuous, straight, straightforward, truthful, forthright, direct, unequivocal, plainspoken, round, blunt, outspoken, honest, artless, guileless, aboveboard, undeceitful, undeceiving, *colloq.* upfront, on the level. **2** unposed, informal, impromptu, extemporaneous, extemporary, unofficial, natural, spontaneous.

candida /kándidə/ n. any yeastlike parasitic fungus of the genus *Candida*, esp. *C. albicans* causing thrush. [mod.L fem. of L *candidus*: see CANDID]

candidate /kándidət, -dayt/ n. **1** a person who seeks or is nominated for an office, award, etc. **2** a person or thing likely to gain some distinction or position. **3** a person entered for an examination. □□ **candidacy** /-dəsee/ n. **candidature** /-dəchər/ n. *Brit.* [F *candidat* or L *candidatus* white-robed (Roman candidates wearing white)]
■ **1, 3** runner, nominee; aspirant, seeker, pretender; applicant, entrant, interviewee, examinee. **2** prospect, possibility.

candle /kánd'l/ n. & v. ● n. **1** a cylinder or block of wax or tallow with a central wick, for giving light when burning. **2** = CANDLEPOWER. ● v.tr. test (an egg) for freshness by holding it to the light. □ **cannot hold a candle to** cannot be compared with; is much inferior to. **not worth the candle** not justifying the cost or trouble. □□ **candler** n. [OE *candel* f. L *candela* f. *candēre* shine]
■ n. **1** see LIGHT[1] n. 4a.

candlelight /kánd'l-lit/ n. **1** light provided by candles. **2** dusk. □□ **candlelit** adj.
■ **1** see LIGHT[1] n. 2.

Candlemas /kánd'lməs/ n. a feast with blessing of candles (Feb. 2), commemorating the Purification of the Virgin Mary and the presentation of Christ in the Temple. [OE *Candelmæsse* (as CANDLE, MASS[2])]

candlepower /kánd'lpowr/ n. a unit of luminous intensity.

candlestick /kánd'lstik/ n. a holder for one or more candles.

candlewick /kánd'lwik/ n. **1** a thick soft cotton yarn. **2** material made from this, usu. with a tufted pattern.

candor /kándər/ n. (*Brit.* **candour**) candid behavior or action; frankness. [F *candeur* or L *candor* whiteness]
■ candidness, openness, frankness, straightness, straightforwardness, ingenuousness, simplicity, naïveté, outspokenness, unreservedness, forthrightness,

honesty, truthfulness, sincerity, directness, bluntness, unequivocalness.

C. & W. *abbr.* country-and-western.

candy /kándee/ *n. & v.* ● *n.* (*pl.* **-ies**) **1** a sweet confection, usu. containing sugar, chocolate, etc. **2** (in full **sugar candy**) sugar crystallized by repeated boiling and slow evaporation. ● *v.tr.* (**-ies, -ied**) (usu. as **candied** *adj.*) preserve by coating and impregnating with a sugar syrup (*candied fruit*). □ **candy floss** *Brit.* = *cotton candy*. **candy stripe** a pattern consisting of alternate stripes of white and a color (usu. pink). **candy-striped** having such a pattern. **candy striper** a hospital volunteer, esp. a teenager, who wears a candy-striped uniform. [F *sucre candi* candied sugar f. Arab. *ḳand* sugar]
■ *n.* **1** sweet(s), bonbon(s), sweetmeat(s), confectionery.
● *v.* (**candied**) sugar-coated, preserved, crystallized.

candytuft /kándeetuft/ *n.* any of various plants of the genus *Iberis*, native to W. Europe, with white, pink, or purple flowers in tufts. [obs. *Candy* (*Candia* Crete) + TUFT]

cane /kayn/ *n. & v.* ● *n.* **1 a** the hollow jointed stem of giant reeds or grasses (*bamboo cane*). **b** the solid stem of slender palms (*malacca cane*). **2** = *sugar cane*. **3** a raspberry cane. **4** material of cane used for wickerwork, etc. **5 a** a cane used as a walking stick or a support for a plant or an instrument of punishment. **b** any slender walking stick. ● *v.tr.* **1** beat with a cane. **2** weave cane into (a chair, etc.). □ **cane chair** a chair with a seat made of woven cane strips. **cane sugar** sugar obtained from sugar cane. □□ **caner** *n.* (in sense 2 of *v.*). **caning** *n.* [ME f. OF f. L *canna* f. Gk *kanna*]
■ *n.* **1** see STEM¹ 2. **5** see STICK¹ 1b. ● *v.* **1** see BEAT *v.* 1.

canebrake /káynbrayk/ *n.* a tract of land overgrown with canes.

canine /káynin/ *adj. & n.* ● *adj.* **1** of a dog or dogs. **2** of or belonging to the family Canidae, including dogs, wolves, foxes, etc. ● *n.* **1 a** dog. **2** (in full **canine tooth**) a pointed tooth between the incisors and premolars. [ME f. *canin -ine* or f. L *caninus* f. *canis* dog]

canister /kánistər/ *n.* **1** a small container, usu. of metal and cylindrical, for storing sugar, etc. **2 a** a cylinder of shot, tear gas, etc., that explodes on impact. **b** such cylinders collectively. [L *canistrum* f. Gk f. *kanna* CANE]

canker /kángkər/ *n. & v.* ● *n.* **1 a** a destructive fungus disease of trees and plants. **b** an open wound in the stem of a tree or plant. **2** *Zool.* an ulcerous ear disease of animals, esp. cats and dogs. **3** *Med.* an ulceration, esp. of the lips. **4** a corrupting influence. ● *v.tr.* **1** consume with canker. **2** corrupt. **3** (as **cankered** *adj.*) soured; malignant; crabbed. □□ **cankerous** *adj.* [OE *cancer* & ONF *cancre*, OF *chancre* f. L *cancer* crab]
■ *n.* **2, 3** see ULCER 1. **4** see POISON *n.* 2. ● *v.* **3** (**cankered**) see MALIGNANT 2.

cankerworm /kángkərwərm/ *n.* any caterpillar of various wingless moths that consume the buds and leaves of shade and fruit trees in N. America.

canna /kánə/ *n.* any tropical plant of the genus *Canna* with bright flowers and ornamental leaves. [L: see CANE]

cannabis /kánəbis/ *n.* **1** any hemp plant of the genus *Cannabis*, esp. Indian hemp. **2** a preparation of parts of this used as an intoxicant or hallucinogen. □ **cannabis resin** a sticky product, esp. from the flowering tops of the female cannabis plant. [L f. Gk]

canned /kand/ *adj.* **1** prerecorded (*canned laughter*; *canned music*). **2** supplied in a can (*canned beer*). **3** *sl.* drunk.

cannel /kánəl/ *n.* (in full **cannel coal**) a bituminous coal burning with a bright flame. [16th c.: orig. No. of Engl.]

cannelloni /kánəlōnee/ *n.pl.* tubes or rolls of pasta stuffed with meat or a vegetable mixture. [It. f. *cannello* stalk]

cannery /kánəree/ *n.* (*pl.* **-ies**) a factory where food is canned.

cannibal /kánibəl/ *n. & adj.* ● *n.* **1** a person who eats human flesh. **2** an animal that feeds on flesh of its own species. ● *adj.* of or like a cannibal. □□ **cannibalism** *n.* **cannibalistic** *adj.* **cannibalistically** *adv.* [orig. pl. *Canibales* f. Sp.: var. of *Caribes* name of a W.Ind. nation]

cannibalize /kánibəliz/ *v.tr.* use (a machine, etc.) as a source of spare parts for others. □□ **cannibalization** *n.*

cannikin /kánikin/ *n.* a small can. [Du. *kanneken* (as CAN², -KIN)]

cannon /kánən/ *n. & v.* ● *n.* **1** *hist.* (*pl.* same) a large, heavy gun installed on a carriage or mounting. **2** an automatic aircraft gun firing shells. **3** *Billiards Brit.* CAROM. **4** (in full **cannon bit**) a smooth round bit for a horse. ● *v.intr. Brit.* (usu. foll. by *against, into*) collide heavily or obliquely. □ **cannon bone** the tube-shaped bone between the hock and fetlock of a horse. **cannon fodder** soldiers regarded merely as material to be expended in war. [F *canon* f. It. *cannone* large tube f. *canna* CANE: in Billiards sense f. older CAROM]

cannonade /kánənáyd/ *n. & v.* ● *n.* a period of continuous heavy gunfire. ● *v.tr.* bombard with a cannonade. [F f. It. *cannonata*]
■ *n.* see VOLLEY *n.* 1. ● *v.* see SHELL *v.* 2.

cannonball /kánənbawl/ *n., adj., & v.* ● *n.* **1** a large, usu. metal ball fired by a cannon. **2** *Tennis* a very rapid serve. **3** a very fast vehicle, etc., esp. an express train. **4** a jump into water in which the knees are held tight against the chest. ● *adj.* **1** moving at great speed. **2** of a jump into water in a curled-up position (*a cannonball dive*). ● *v.intr.* travel with great force, momentum, and speed.
■ *n.* **1** see SHOT¹ 3.

cannot /kánot, kanót/ *v.aux.* can not.

cannula /kányələ/ *n.* (*pl.* **cannulas** or **cannulae** /-lee/) *Surgery* a small tube for inserting into the body to allow fluid to enter or escape. [L, dimin. of *canna* cane]

cannulate /kányəlayt/ *v.tr. Surgery* introduce a cannula into.

canny /kánee/ *adj.* (**cannier, canniest**) **1 a** shrewd; worldly-wise. **b** thrifty. **c** circumspect. **2** sly; dryly humorous. **3** *Sc. & No. of Engl.* pleasant; agreeable. □□ **cannily** *adv.* **canniness** *n.* [CAN¹ (in sense 'know') + -Y¹]
■ **1 a** see SHREWD. **b** see THRIFTY 1.

canoe /kənōo/ *n. & v.* ● *n.* a small, narrow boat with pointed ends usu. propelled by paddling. ● *v.intr.* (**canoes, canoed, canoeing**) travel in a canoe. □□ **canoeist** *n.* [Sp. and Haitian *canoa*]

canola oil /kənōlə/ *n.* a type of cooking oil derived from the seed of a variety of the rape plant. [Canada oil low acid]

canon /kánən/ *n.* **1 a** a general law, rule, principle, or criterion. **b** a church decree or law. **2** (*fem.* **canoness**) **a** a member of a cathedral chapter. **b** a member of certain Roman Catholic orders. **3 a** a collection or list of sacred books, etc., accepted as genuine. **b** the recognized genuine works of a particular author; a list of these. **c** literary works as part of a school or university curriculum. **4** *Eccl.* the part of the Mass containing the words of consecration. **5** *Mus.* a piece with different parts taking up the same theme successively, either at the same or at a different pitch. □ **canon law** ecclesiastical law. **canon regular** (or **regular canon**) see REGULAR *adj.* 9b. [OE f. L f. Gk *kanōn*, in ME also f. AF & OF *canun, -on*; in sense 2 ME f. OF *canonie* f. eccl.L *canonicus*: cf. CANONICAL]
■ **1** see LAW 1a. **2** see CLERGYMAN.

canonic /kənónik/ *adj.* = CANONICAL *adj.* [OE f. OF *canonique* or L *canonicus* f. Gk *kanonikos*]

canonical /kənónikəl/ *adj. & n.* ● *adj.* **1 a** according to or ordered by canon law. **b** included in the canon of Scripture. **2** authoritative; standard; accepted. **3** of a cathedral chapter or a member of it. **4** *Mus.* in canon form. ● *n.* (in *pl.*) the canonical dress of the clergy. □ **canonical hours** *Eccl.* the times fixed for a formal set of prayers or for the celebration of marriage. □□ **canonically** *adv.* [med.L *canonicalis* (as CANONIC)]

canonicity /kánənísitee/ *n.* the status of being canonical. [L *canonicus* canonical]

/. . ./ **pronunciation**	● **part of speech**
□ **phrases, idioms, and compounds**	
□□ **derivatives**	■ **synonym section**
cross-references appear in SMALL CAPITALS or *italics*	

canonist /kánənist/ n. an expert in canon law. [ME f. F *canoniste* or f. med.L *canonista*: see CANON]

canonize /kánəniz/ v.tr. **1 a** declare officially to be a saint, usu. with a ceremony. **b** regard as a saint. **2** admit to the canon of Scripture. **3** sanction by church authority. □□ **canonization** n. [ME f. med.L *canonizare*: see CANON]
■ **2, 3** see SANCTIFY 3.

canonry /kánənree/ n. (pl. **-ies**) the office or benefice of a canon.

canoodle /kənóõd'l/ v.intr. colloq. kiss and cuddle amorously. [19th-c. US: orig. unkn.]
■ see KISS v. 3.

canopic /kənṓpik, -nóp-/ adj. □ **canopic jar** (or **vase**) an urn used for holding the entrails of an embalmed body in an ancient Egyptian burial. [L *Canopicus* f. *Canopus* in ancient Egypt]

canopy /kánəpee/ n. & v. ● n. (pl. **-ies**) **1 a** a covering hung or held up over a throne, bed, person, etc. **b** the sky. **c** an overhanging shelter. **2** *Archit.* a rooflike projection over a niche, etc. **3** the uppermost layers of foliage, etc., in a forest. **4 a** the expanding part of a parachute. **b** the cover of an aircraft's cockpit. ● v.tr. (**-ies, -ied**) supply or be a canopy to. [ME f. med.L *canopeum* f. L *conopeum* f. Gk *kōnōpeion* couch with mosquito netting f. *kōnōps* gnat]
■ **1** see MANTLE n. 2.

canorous /kənáwrəs/ adj. melodious; resonant. [L *canorus* f. *canere* sing]

canst /kanst/ archaic 2nd person sing. of CAN[1].

Cant. abbr. Canticles (Old Testament).

cant[1] /kant/ n. & v. ● n. **1** insincere pious or moral talk. **2** ephemeral or fashionable catchwords. **3** language peculiar to a class, profession, sect, etc.; jargon. ● v.intr. use cant. □ **canting arms** *Heraldry* arms containing an allusion to the name of the bearer. [earlier of musical sound, of intonation, and of beggars' whining; perh. from the singing of religious mendicants: prob. f. L *canere* sing]
■ n. **1** hypocrisy, insincerity, sham, pretense, humbug, sanctimony, sanctimoniousness, piety, lip service, pretension. **3** jargon, language, argot, vernacular, idiom, slang, dialect, patois, colloq. lingo.

cant[2] /kant/ n. & v. ● n. **1 a** a slanting surface, e.g., of a bank. **b** a bevel of a crystal, etc. **2** an oblique push or movement that upsets or partly upsets something. **3** a tilted or sloping position. ● v. **1** tr. push or pitch out of level; tilt. **2** intr. take or lie in a slanting position. **3** tr. impart a bevel to. **4** intr. *Naut.* swing around. □ **cant dog** (or **hook**) an iron hook at the end of a long handle, used for rolling logs. [ME f. MLG *kant, kante*, MDu. *cant*, point, side, edge, ult. f. L *cant(h)us* iron tire]

can't /kant/ contr. can not.

Cantab. /kántab/ abbr. Cantabrigian; of Cambridge University. [L *Cantabrigiensis*]

cantabile /kantaábilay/ adv., adj., & n. *Mus.* ● adv. & adj. in a smooth singing style. ● n. a cantabile passage or movement. [It., = singable]

Cantabrigian /kántəbríjeeən/ adj. & n. ● adj. of Cambridge or Cambridge University. ● n. **1** a member of Cambridge University. **2** a native of Cambridge. [L *Cantabrigia* Cambridge]

cantaloupe /kánt'lōp/ n. a small, round ribbed variety of melon with orange flesh. [F *cantaloup* f. *Cantaluppi* near Rome, where it was first grown in Europe]

cantankerous /kántángkərəs/ adj. bad-tempered; quarrelsome. □□ **cantankerously** adv. **cantankerousness** n. [perh. f. Ir. *cant* outbidding + *rancorous*]
■ ill-natured, quarrelsome, cross, grumpy, choleric, cross-grained, crabby, curmudgeonly, crusty, surly, irascible, snappish, bad-tempered, moody, ill-tempered, bearish, bilious, splenetic, peevish, testy, irritable, crotchety, touchy, disagreeable, tetchy, contrary, cranky, colloq. grouchy, literary atrabilious.

cantata /kəntaátə/ n. *Mus.* a short narrative or descriptive composition with vocal solos and usu. chorus and orchestral accompaniment. [It. *cantata* (*aria*) sung (air) f. *cantare* sing]

canteen /kanteén/ n. **1 a** a restaurant for employees in an office or factory, etc. **b** a store selling provisions or liquor in a barracks or camp. **2** *Brit.* a case or box of cutlery. **3 a** soldier's or camper's water flask or set of eating or drinking utensils. [F *cantine* f. It. *cantina* cellar]
■ **1** see CAFÉ 1.

canter /kántər/ n. & v. ● n. a gentle gallop. ● v. **1** intr. (of a horse or its rider) go at a canter. **2** tr. make (a horse) canter. [short for *Canterbury pace*, from the supposed easy pace of medieval pilgrims to Canterbury]

canterbury /kántərberee/ n. (pl. **-ies**) a piece of furniture with partitions for holding music, etc. [*Canterbury* in Kent]

Canterbury bell /kántərbəree/ n. a cultivated campanula with large flowers. [after the bells of Canterbury pilgrims' horses: see CANTER]

cantharides /kanthárideez/ n.pl. a preparation made from dried bodies of a beetle *Lytta vesicatoria*, causing blistering of the skin and formerly used in medicine and as an aphrodisiac. Also called *Spanish fly*. [L f. Gk *kantharis* Spanish fly]

canthus /kánthəs/ n. (pl. **canthi** /-thī/) the outer or inner corner of the eye, where the upper and lower lids meet. [L f. Gk *kanthos*]

canticle /kántikəl/ n. **1** a song or chant with a Biblical text. **2** (also **Canticle of Canticles**) the Song of Solomon. [ME f. OF *canticle* (var. of *cantique*) or L *canticulum* dimin. of *canticum* f. *canere* sing]
■ **1** see CHANT n.

cantilena /kánt'leénə/ n. *Mus.* a simple or sustained melody. [It.]

cantilever /kánt'leevər, -evər/ n. & v. ● n. **1** a long bracket or beam, etc., projecting from a wall to support a balcony, etc. **2** a beam or girder fixed at only one end. ● v.intr. **1** project as a cantilever. **2** be supported by cantilevers. □ **cantilever bridge** a bridge made of cantilevers projecting from the piers and connected by girders. [17th c.: orig. unkn.]

cantillate /kánt'layt/ v.tr. & intr. chant or recite with musical tones. □□ **cantillation** /-láyshən/ n. [L *cantillare* sing low: see CHANT]

cantina /kanteénə/ n. esp. *SW US* a tavern, bar, etc. [Sp. & It.]

canto /kántō/ n. (pl. **-os**) a division of a long poem. [It., = song, f. L *cantus*]
■ see PASSAGE[1] 6.

canton n. & v. ● n. **1** /kánton/ **a** a subdivision of a country. **b** a state of the Swiss confederation. **2** /kántən/ *Heraldry* a square division, less than a quarter, in the upper (usu. dexter) corner of a shield. ● v.tr. **1** /kántón, -tốn/ *Brit.* put (troops) into quarters. **2** /kántón/ divide into cantons. □□ **cantonal** /kánt'nəl, kantónəl/ adj. [OF, = corner (see CANT[2]): (v.) also partly f. F *cantonner*]

Cantonese /kántəneéz/ adj. & n. ● adj. of Canton or the Cantonese dialect of Chinese. ● n. (pl. same) **1** a native of Canton. **2** the dialect of Chinese spoken in SE China and Hong Kong. [*Canton* in China]

cantonment /kantónmənt, -tốn-/ n. **1** quarters assigned to troops. **2** a permanent military station in India. [F *cantonnement*: see CANTON]
■ **1** see QUARTER n. 9b.

cantor /kántər/ n. **1** the leader of the singing in church; a precentor. **2** the precentor in a synagogue. [L, = singer f. *canere* sing]
■ see VOCALIST.

cantorial /kantáwreeəl/ adj. **1** of or relating to the cantor. **2** of the north side of the choir in a church (cf. DECANAL).

cantoris /kantáwris/ adj. *Mus.* to be sung by the cantorial side of the choir in antiphonal singing (cf. DECANI). [L, genit. of CANTOR precentor]

cantrip /kántrip/ n. *Sc.* **1** a witch's trick. **2** esp. *Brit.* a piece of mischief; a playful act. [18th c.: orig. unkn.]

Canuck /kənúk/ n. & adj. sl. often derog. ● n. **1** a Canadian, esp. a French Canadian. **2** a Canadian horse or pony. ● adj. Canadian, esp. French Canadian. [app. f. *Canada*]

canvas /kánvəs/ n. & v. ● n. **1 a** a strong coarse kind of cloth made from hemp or flax or other coarse yarn and used for sails and tents, etc., and as a surface for oil painting. **b**

a piece of this. **2** a painting on canvas, esp. in oils. **3** an open kind of canvas used as a basis for tapestry and embroidery. **4** *sl.* the floor of a boxing or wrestling ring. ● *v.tr.* (**canvased, canvasing**; esp. *Brit.* **canvassed, canvassing**) cover with canvas. □ **under canvas 1** in a tent or tents. **2** with sails spread. [ME & ONF *canevas*, ult. f. L *cannabis* hemp]

canvasback /kánvəsbak/ *n.* a wild duck, *Aythya valisineria*, of N. America, with back feathers the color of unbleached canvas.

canvass /kánvəs/ *v. & n.* ● *v.* **1 a** *intr.* solicit votes. **b** *tr.* solicit votes from (electors in a constituency). **2** *tr.* **a** ascertain opinions of. **b** seek business from. **c** discuss thoroughly. **3** *tr. Brit.* propose (an idea or plan, etc.). ● *n.* the process of or an instance of canvassing, esp. of electors. □□ **canvasser** *n.* [orig. = toss in a sheet, agitate, f. CANVAS]

■ *v.* **1 a** electioneer, campaign, stump, *Brit.* stand. **b** solicit. **2 a** survey, poll, study, examine, investigate, interview, question, sound (out). ● *n.* solicitation, campaign; survey, study, investigation, poll, examination, analysis.

canyon /kányən/ *n.* a deep gorge, often with a stream or river. [Sp. *cañón* tube, ult. f. L *canna* CANE]

■ gorge, ravine, gully, pass, defile, coulée, gulch, pass, arroyo, *Brit.* gill.

canzonet /kánzənét/ *n.* **1** a short, light song. **2** a kind of madrigal. [It., dimin. of *canzone* song f. L *cantio -onis* f. *canere* sing]

caoutchouc /kówchŏŏk/ *n.* raw rubber. [F f. Carib *cahuchu*]

CAP *abbr.* Civil Air Patrol.

cap /kap/ *n. & v.* ● *n.* **1 a** a covering for the head, often soft and with a visor. **b** a head covering worn in a particular profession (*nurse's cap*). **c** esp. *Brit.* a cap awarded as a sign of membership of a sports team. **d** an academic mortarboard or soft hat. **e** a special hat as part of Highland costume. **2 a** a cover like a cap in shape or position (*kneecap*; *toecap*). **b** a device to seal a bottle or protect the point of a pen, lens of a camera, etc. **3** = MOBCAP. **4** = *percussion cap.* **5** = CROWN *n.* 9b. ● *v.tr.* (**capped, capping**) **1 a** put a cap on. **b** cover the top or end of. **c** set a limit to (*rate-capping*). **2 a** esp. *Brit.* award a sports cap to. **b** *Sc. & NZ* confer a university degree on. **3 a** lie on top of; form the cap of. **b** surpass; excel. **c** improve on (a story, quotation, etc.), esp. by producing a better or more apposite one. □ **cap in hand** humbly. **cap rock** a hard rock or stratum overlying a deposit of oil, gas, coal, etc. **cap sleeve** a sleeve extending only a short distance from the shoulder. **set one's cap for** try to attract as a suitor. □□ **capful** *n.* (*pl.* **-fuls**). **capping** *n.* [OE *cæppe* f. LL *cappa*, perh. f. L *caput* head]

■ *n.* **1 a** hat, head covering. **d** mortarboard. **2 b** lid, top, cover, covering. ● *v.* **1 a, b** cover, protect, shelter, shield, screen, sheathe. **c** curb, check, restrain; see also CONTROL *v.* 3. **3 a** see COVER *v.* 2a. **b, c** surpass, exceed, break, top, improve on, outdo, outmatch, outshine, eclipse, outstrip, better, beat, excel, *colloq.* lick, best. □ **cap in hand** humbly, meekly, servilely, submissively, subserviently, docilely, respectfully. **set one's cap for** see COURT *v.* 1b.

cap. *abbr.* **1** capital. **2** capital letter. **3** chapter. [L *capitulum* or *caput*]

capability /káypəbílitee/ *n.* (*pl.* **-ies**) **1** (often foll. by *of, for, to*) ability; power; the condition of being capable. **2** an undeveloped or unused faculty.

■ ability, power, capacity, means, faculty, talent, gift, touch, proficiency, aptitude, facility, adeptness, skill, competence, prowess, caliber, *colloq.* wherewithal; potential, promise.

capable /káypəbəl/ *adj.* **1** competent; able; gifted. **2** (foll. by *of*) **a** having the ability or fitness or necessary quality for. **b** susceptible of admitting of (explanation or improvement, etc.). □□ **capably** *adv.* [F f. LL *capabilis* f. L *capere* hold]

■ **1** able, competent, efficient, proficient, qualified, experienced, talented, gifted, skilled, skillful, expert, masterly, masterful, accomplished, apt, adept, clever, effective, effectual. **2 a** (*capable of*) disposed to,

inclined to, predisposed to; up to; (*be capable of*) have the potential to, have it in one to, *colloq.* have what it takes to.

capacious /kəpáyshəs/ *adj.* roomy; able to hold much. □□ **capaciously** *adv.* **capaciousness** *n.* [L *capax -acis* f. *capere* hold]

■ see ROOMY.

capacitance /kəpásit'ns/ *n. Electr.* **1** the ability of a system to store an electric charge. **2** the ratio of the change in an electric charge in a system to the corresponding change in its electric potential. ¶ Symb.: C. [CAPACITY + -ANCE]

capacitate /kəpásitayt/ *v.tr.* **1** (usu. foll. by *for*, or to + infin.) render capable. **2** make legally competent.

■ see ENABLE 1.

capacitor /kəpásitər/ *n. Electr.* a device of one or more pairs of conductors separated by insulators used to store an electric charge.

capacity /kəpásitee/ *n.* (*pl.* **-ies**) **1 a** the power of containing, receiving, experiencing, or producing (*capacity for heat, pain*, etc.). **b** the maximum amount that can be contained or produced, etc. **c** the volume, e.g., of the cylinders in an internal combustion engine. **d** (*attrib.*) fully occupying the available space, resources, etc. (*a capacity audience*). **2 a** mental power. **b** a faculty or talent. **3** a position or function (*in a civil capacity*; *in my capacity as a critic*). **4** legal competence. **5** *Electr.* capacitance. □ **to capacity** fully; using all resources (*working to capacity*). □□ **capacitative** /-táytiv/ *adj.* (also **capacitive**) (in sense 5). [ME f. F f. L *capacitas -tatis* (as CAPACIOUS)]

■ **1 a** see POTENTIAL *n.* 1. **b** volume, content, size, dimensions, measurements, proportions, magnitude; range, scope, extent, reach, limit; room, space. **2 a** potential, ability, power, capability, competence, intelligence, brainpower, cleverness, brightness, wit, brain(s), acumen, understanding, sense, judgment, perspicacity, perspicaciousness, perceptiveness, imagination, perception, discernment, mother wit, intellect, genius, talent, flair, instinct. **b** genius, skill, gift, faculty, talent, flair, knack, instinct, power. **3** position, function, condition, character, place, post, role, job, office, duty, responsibility. **4** *Law* competency, qualification. □ **to capacity** see *completely* (COMPLETE).

caparison /kəpárisən/ *n. & v.* ● *n.* **1** (usu. in *pl.*) a horse's trappings. **2** equipment; finery. ● *v.tr.* put caparisons on; adorn richly. [obs. F *caparasson* f. Sp. *caparazón* saddlecloth f. *capa* CAPE[1]]

■ *n.* see TRAPPINGS. ● *v.* see DECORATE 1, 3.

cape[1] /kayp/ *n.* **1** a sleeveless cloak. **2** a short, sleeveless cloak as a fixed or detachable part of a longer cloak or coat. [F f. Prov. *capa* f. LL *cappa* CAP]

■ **1** cloak; mantle, shawl, stole, wrap, *hist.* mantelet.

cape[2] /kayp/ *n.* **1** a headland or promontory. **2** (**the Cape**) **a** the Cape of Good Hope. **b** the S. African province containing it. **c** Cape Cod, Massachusetts. □ **Cape Coloured** *adj. S.Afr.* of the Colored (see COLORED 2) population of Cape Province. ● *n.* a member of this population. **Cape Dutch** *archaic* Afrikaans. **Cape gooseberry 1** an edible, soft, roundish yellow berry enclosed in a lanternlike husk. **2** the plant, *Physalis peruviana*, bearing these. [ME f. OF *cap* f. Prov. *cap* ult. f. L *caput* head]

■ **1** headland, promontory, neck, point, tip, ness, bluff, bill, foreland, head, point, tongue.

capelin /kápəlin, káplin/ *n.* (also **caplin** /káplin/) a small smeltlike fish, *Mallotus villosus*, of the N. Atlantic, used as food and as bait for catching cod, etc. [F f. Prov. *capelan*: see CHAPLAIN]

caper[1] /káypər/ *v. & n.* ● *v.intr.* jump or run about playfully. ● *n.* **1** a playful jump or leap. **2 a** a fantastic proceeding; a

/.../ pronunciation	● part of speech
□ phrases, idioms, and compounds	
□□ derivatives	■ synonym section
cross-references appear in SMALL CAPITALS or *italics*	

205

prank. **b** *sl.* any activity or occupation. □ **cut a caper** (or **capers**) act friskily. □□ **caperer** *n.* [abbr. of CAPRIOLE]
■ *v.* skip, hop, frolic, leap, jump, frisk, romp, bound, spring, gambol, prance, *colloq.* galumph, *sl.* cavort; curvet. ● *n.* **1** skip, leap, jump, spring, frolic, hop, gambol, frisk, bound, curvet, gambado. **2 a** escapade, stunt, trick, prank, gambado, high jinks, antic, nonsense, *colloq.* shenanigans, lark, dido. **b** affair, matter, thing, *colloq.* palaver, *derog.* business.

caper[2] /káypər/ *n.* **1** a bramblelike S. European shrub, *Capparis spinosa.* **2** (in *pl.*) its flower buds cooked and pickled for use as flavoring, esp. for a savory sauce. [ME *capres* & F *câpres* f. L *cappari*s f. Gk *kapparis*, treated as pl.: cf. CHERRY, PEA]

capercaillie /kápərkáylee/ *n.* (also **capercailzie** /-káylzee/) a large European grouse, *Tetrao urogallus.* [Gael. *capull coille* horse of the wood]

capeskin /káypskin/ *n.* a soft leather made from S. African sheepskin.

capias /káypeeəs/ *n. Law* a writ ordering the arrest of the person named. [L, = you are to seize, f. *capere* take]

capillarity /kápiláritee/ *n.* a phenomenon at liquid boundaries resulting in the rise or depression of liquids in narrow tubes. Also called *capillary action.* [F *capillarité* (as CAPILLARY)]

capillary /kápəleree/ *adj.* & *n.* ● *adj.* **1** of or like a hair. **2** (of a tube) of hairlike internal diameter. **3** of one of the delicate ramified blood vessels intervening between arteries and veins. ● *n.* (*pl.* **-ies**) **1** a capillary tube. **2** a capillary blood vessel. □ **capillary action** = CAPILLARITY. [L *capillaris* f. *capillus* hair]

capital[1] /kápit'l/ *n., adj.,* & *int.* ● *n.* **1** the most important town or city of a country, state, or region, usu. its seat of government and administrative center. **2 a** the money or other assets with which a company starts in business. **b** accumulated wealth, esp. as used in further production. **c** money invested or lent at interest. **3** capitalists generally. **4** a capital letter. ● *adj.* **1 a** principal; most important; leading. **b** *colloq.* excellent; first-rate. **2 a** involving or punishable by death (*capital punishment; a capital offense*). **b** (of an error, etc.) vitally harmful; fatal. **3** (of letters of the alphabet) large in size and of the form used to begin sentences and names, etc. ● *int.* expressing approval or satisfaction. □ **capital gain** a profit from the sale of investments or property. **capital goods** goods, esp. machinery, plant, etc., used or to be used in producing commodities (opp. *consumer goods*). **capital levy 1** the appropriation by the government of a fixed proportion of the wealth in the country. **2** a wealth tax. **capital sum** a lump sum of money, esp. payable to an insured person. **make capital out of** use to one's advantage. **with a capital —** emphatically such (*art with a capital A*). □□ **capitally** *adv.* [ME f. OF f. L *capitalis* f. *caput* -*itis* head]
■ *n.* **2** money, assets, funds, stocks, finance(s), riches, cash, *colloq.* wherewithal, shekels, *derog. or joc.* pelf, *sl.* dough, scratch, *Brit. sl.* lolly; wealth, means, property, resources, savings, principal. **4** capital letter, upper case letter, initial. ● *adj.* **1 a** chief, main, major, important, cardinal, central, principal, prime, primary, paramount, preeminent, foremost, leading. **b** see BRILLIANT 2. **2 b** see GRAVE[2] *adj.* 2. **3** upper case, initial, large, big. □ **make capital out of** see PROFIT *v.* 2.

capital[2] /kápit'l/ *n. Archit.* the head or cornice of a pillar or column. [ME f. OF *capitel* f. LL *capitellum* dimin. of L *caput* head]
■ head, top, crown, cap, cornice.

capitalism /kápit'lizəm/ *n.* **1 a** an economic system in which the production and distribution of goods depend on invested private capital and profit making. **b** the possession of capital or wealth. **2** *Polit.* the dominance of private owners of capital and production for profit.

capitalist /kápit'list/ *n.* & *adj.* ● *n.* **1** a person using or possessing capital; a rich person. **2** an advocate of capitalism. ● *adj.* of or favoring capitalism. □□ **capitalistic** *adj.* **capitalistically** *adv.*

capitalize /kápit'līz/ *v.* **1** *tr.* **a** convert into or provide with

capital. **b** calculate or realize the present value of an income. **c** reckon (the value of an asset) by setting future benefits against the cost of maintenance. **2** *tr.* **a** write (a letter of the alphabet) as a capital. **b** begin (a word) with a capital letter. **3** *intr.* (foll. by *on*) use to one's advantage; profit from. □□ **capitalization** *n.* [F *capitaliser* (as CAPITAL[1])]

capitation /kápitáyshən/ *n.* **1** a tax or fee at a set rate per person. **2** the levying of such a tax or fee. [F *capitation* or LL *capitatio* poll-tax f. *caput* head]

Capitol /kápit'l/ *n.* **1** the building in Washington, D.C., in which the U.S. Congress meets. **2** (as **capitol**) a building in which a state legislature meets.

capitular /kəpíchələr/ *adj.* **1** of or relating to a cathedral chapter. **2** *Anat.* of or relating to a terminal protuberance of a bone. [LL *capitularis* f. L *capitulum* CHAPTER]

capitulary /kəpíchələree/ *n.* (*pl.* **-ies**) a collection of ordinances, esp. of the Frankish kings. [LL *capitularius* (as CAPITULAR)]

capitulate /kəpíchəlayt/ *v.intr.* surrender, esp. on stated conditions. □□ **capitulator** *n.* **capitulatory** /-lətáwree/ *adj.* [med.L *capitulare* draw up under headings f. L *caput* head]
■ surrender, yield, give up *or* in *or* way, bow (down), submit, succumb, throw in the towel.

capitulation /kəpíchəláyshən/ *n.* **1** the act of capitulating; surrender. **2** a statement of the main divisions of a subject. **3** an agreement or set of conditions.

capitulum /kəpíchələm/ *n.* (*pl.* **capitula** /-lə/) *Bot.* an inflorescence with flowers clustered together like a head, as in the daisy family. [L, dimin. of *caput* head]

caplin var. of CAPELIN.

cap'n /káp'm/ *n. sl.* captain. [contr.]

capo /káypō/ *n.* (in full **capotasto** /-tástō/) (*pl.* **capos** or **capotastos**) *Mus.* a device secured across the neck of a fretted instrument to raise equally the tuning of all strings by the required amount. [It. *capo tasto* head stop]

capon /káypon, -pən/ *n.* a domestic cock castrated and fattened for eating. □□ **caponize** *v.tr.* [OE f. AF *capun*, OF *capon*, ult. f. L *capo* -*onis*]
■ □□ **caponize** see NEUTER *v.*

caponier /kápəneér/ *n.* a covered passage across a ditch around a fort. [Sp. *caponera*, lit. 'capon pen']

capot /kəpót/ *n.* & *v.* ● *n.* (in piquet) the winning of all the tricks by one player. ● *v.tr.* (**capotted, capotting**) score a capot against (an opponent). [F]

capote /kəpốt, kapō/ *n. hist.* a long cloak with a hood, formerly worn by soldiers and travelers, etc. [F, dimin. of *cape* CAPE[1]]

cappuccino /kápoōcheénō/ *n.* (*pl.* **-os**) espresso coffee with milk made frothy with pressurized steam. [It., = CAPUCHIN]

capriccio /kəpreécheeō/ *n.* (*pl.* **-os**) **1** a lively and usu. short musical composition. **2** a painting, etc., representing a fantasy or a mixture of real and imaginary features. [It., = sudden start, orig. 'horror']

capriccioso /kəpreecheeōsō/ *adv., adj.,* & *n. Mus.* ● *adv.* & *adj.* in a free and impulsive style. ● *n.* (*pl.* **-os**) a capriccioso passage or movement. [It., = capricious]

caprice /kəprees/ *n.* **1 a** an unaccountable or whimsical change of mind or conduct. **b** a tendency to this. **2** a work of lively fancy in painting, drawing, or music; a capriccio. [F f. It. CAPRICCIO]
■ **1** see FANCY *n.* 2.

capricious /kəpríshəs, -prée-/ *adj.* **1** guided by or given to caprice. **2** irregular; unpredictable. □□ **capriciously** *adv.* **capriciousness** *n.* [F *capricieux* f. It. CAPRICCIOSO]
■ erratic, unsteady, variable, fitful, unstable, wayward, unpredictable, undependable, inconsistent, irregular, changeable, unreliable, inconstant; giddy, mercurial, volatile, temperamental, wanton, fickle, impulsive, quirky, whimsical, flighty, fanciful.

Capricorn /káprikawrn/ *n.* (also **Capricornus** /-káwrnəs/) **1** a constellation, traditionally regarded as contained in the figure of a goat's horns. **2 a** the tenth sign of the zodiac (the Goat). **b** a person born when the sun is in this sign. □□ **Capricornian** *n.* & *adj.* [ME f. OF *capricorne* f. L *capricornus* f. *caper* -*pri* goat + *cornu* horn]

caprine /káprīn, -rin/ adj. of or like a goat. [ME f. L caprinus f. caper -pri goat]

capriole /kápreeōl/ n. & v. ● n. 1 a leap or caper. 2 a trained horse's high leap and kick without advancing. ● v. 1 intr. (of a horse or its rider) perform a capriole. 2 tr. make (a horse) capriole. [F f. It. capriola leap, ult. f. caper -pri goat]
■ v. 1 see PRANCE v.

capris /kəpréez/ n.pl. (also **capri pants**) women's close-fitting tapered trousers that end above the ankle. [Capri, an island in the bay of Naples]

caps. abbr. capital letters.

Capsian /kápseeən/ adj. & n. ● adj. of or relating to a paleolithic culture of N. Africa and S. Europe. ● n. this culture. [L Capsa = Gafsa in Tunisia]

capsicum /kápsikəm/ n. 1 any plant of the genus Capsicum, having edible capsular fruits containing many seeds, esp. C. annuum yielding several varieties of pepper. 2 the fruit of any of these plants, which vary in size, color, and pungency. [mod.L, perh. f. L capsa box]

capsid[1] /kápsid/ n. any bug of the family Capsidae, esp. one that feeds on plants. [mod.L Capsus a genus of them]

capsid[2] /kápsid/ n. the protein coat or shell of a virus. [F capside f. L capsa box]

capsize /kápsīz, -sīz/ v. 1 tr. upset or overturn (a boat). 2 intr. be capsized. □□ **capsizal** /-sīzəl/ n. [cap- as in Prov. capvirar, F chavirer: -size unexpl.]
■ keel, overturn, turn upside down, turn over, invert, tip over; upset; turn turtle.

capstan /kápstən/ n. 1 a thick revolving cylinder with a vertical axis, for winding an anchor cable or a halyard, etc. 2 a revolving spindle on a tape recorder, that guides the tape past the head. [Prov. cabestan, ult. f. L capistrum halter f. capere seize]

capstone /kápstōn/ n. 1 coping; a coping stone. 2 a crowning achievement.

capsule /kápsəl, -sool/ n. 1 a small gelatinous case enclosing a dose of medicine and swallowed with it. 2 a detachable compartment of a spacecraft or nose cone of a rocket. 3 an enclosing membrane in the body. 4 a a dry fruit that releases its seeds when ripe. b the spore-producing part of mosses and liverworts. 5 Biol. an enveloping layer surrounding certain bacteria. 6 (attrib.) concise; highly condensed (a capsule history of jazz). □□ **capsular** adj. **capsulate** adj. [F f. L capsula f. capsa CASE[2]]
■ 1 see PILL 1a.

capsulize /kápsəlīz, -syoo-/ v.tr. put (information, etc.) in compact form.

Capt. abbr. Captain.

captain /káptin/ n. & v. ● n. 1 a a chief or leader. b the leader of a team, esp. in sports. c a powerful or influential person (captain of industry). 2 a the person in command of a merchant or passenger ship. b the pilot of a civil aircraft. 3 a an army or air force officer next above lieutenant. b a navy officer in command of a warship; one ranking below commodore or rear admiral and above commander. c a police officer in charge of a precinct, ranking below chief. 4 a supervisor of waiters or bellboys. 5 a a great soldier or strategist. b an experienced commander. ● v.tr. be captain of; lead. □□ **captaincy** n. (pl. **-ies**). **captainship** n. [ME & OF capitain f. LL capitaneus chief f. L caput capit- head]
■ n. 1, 4, 5 see CHIEF n. 2 see SKIPPER[1] n. ● v. see LEAD[1] v. 6, 7a.

caption /kápshən/ n. & v. ● n. 1 a title or brief explanation appended to an illustration, cartoon, etc. 2 wording appearing on a motion-picture or television screen as part of a movie or broadcast. 3 the heading of a chapter or article, etc. 4 Law a certificate attached to or written on a document. ● v.tr. provide with a caption. [ME f. L captio f. capere capt- take]
■ n. 1, 3 see TITLE n. 2. 2 see TITLE n. 4.

captious /kápshəs/ adj. given to finding fault or raising petty objections. □□ **captiously** adv. **captiousness** n. [ME f. OF captieux or L captiosus (as CAPTION)]
■ see OVERCRITICAL.

captivate /káptivayt/ v.tr. 1 overwhelm with charm or af-

fection. 2 fascinate. □□ **captivating** adj. **captivatingly** adv.

captivation /-váyshən/ n. [LL captivare take captive (as CAPTIVE)]
■ beguile, charm, delight, enamor, enchant, bewitch, enrapture, dazzle, infatuate, transport, attract, allure, seduce, win (over), take or draw in, regale, take by storm; intrigue, fascinate, enthrall, hypnotize, entrance.

captive /káptiv/ n. & adj. ● n. a person or animal that has been taken prisoner or confined. ● adj. 1 a taken prisoner. b kept in confinement or under restraint. 2 a unable to escape. b in a position of having to comply (captive audience; captive market). 3 of or like a prisoner (captive state). [ME f. L captivus f. capere capt- take]
■ n. prisoner, hostage, detainee, internee; capture, catch; slave, bondsman. ● adj. 1 imprisoned, incarcerated, confined, caged, locked up, chained, shackled, fettered, under lock and key, behind bars; under restraint.

captivity /káptívitee/ n. (pl. **-ies**) 1 a the condition or circumstances of being a captive. b a period of captivity. 2 (the Captivity) the captivity of the Jews in Babylon in the 6th c. BC.
■ 1 confinement, imprisonment, internment, detention, custody, incarceration, restraint, duress, archaic durance; bondage, slavery, enslavement, enthrallment, servitude, literary thralldom.

captor /káptər, -tawr/ n. a person who captures (a person, place, etc.). [L (as CAPTIVE)]

capture /kápchər/ v. & n. ● v.tr. 1 a take prisoner; seize as a prize. b obtain by force or trickery. 2 portray in permanent form (could not capture the likeness). 3 Physics absorb (a subatomic particle). 4 (in board games) make a move that secures the removal of (an opposing piece) from the board. 5 (of a stream) divert the upper course of (another stream) by encroaching on its basin. 6 cause (data) to be stored in a computer. ● n. 1 the act of capturing. 2 a thing or person captured. □□ **capturer** n. [F f. L captura f. capere capt- take]
■ v. 1 seize, take, take captive or prisoner, catch, lay or take hold of, grab, ensnare, entrap, snare, hook, apprehend, arrest, collar, sl. pinch, nab, Brit. sl. nick; kidnap, take as hostage; carry off or away, secure, snap up, snatch, take possession of, take over, get, net, conquer, take away, make off with, snag, colloq. bag, land. 2 see CHARACTERIZE 1, 2. ● n. 1 seizure, taking, arrest, apprehension, sl. pinch; kidnap. 2 see CAPTIVE n., CATCH n. 2b.

capuchin /kápyəchin, -shin, kəpyoo-/ n. 1 (Capuchin) a Franciscan friar of the new rule of 1529. 2 a cloak and hood formerly worn by women. 3 a any monkey of the genus Cebus of S. America, with cowllike head hair. b a variety of pigeon with head and neck feathers resembling a cowl. [F f. It. cappuccino f. cappuccio cowl f. cappa CAPE[1]]

capybara /kápəbáarə/ n. a very large semiaquatic rodent, Hydrochoerus hydrochaeris, native to S. America. [Tupi]

car /kaar/ n. 1 a road vehicle with an enclosed passenger compartment, powered by an internal-combustion engine; an automobile. 2 a vehicle that runs on rails, esp. a railroad car or a streetcar. 3 a railroad car of a specified type (dining car). 4 the passenger compartment of an elevator, cable railway, balloon, etc. 5 poet. a wheeled vehicle; a chariot. □ **car bomb** a terrorist bomb concealed in or under a parked car. **car-boot sale** Brit. an outdoor sale at which participants sell unwanted possessions from the trunks (Brit. boots) of their cars. **car coat** a short coat designed esp. for car drivers. **car park** esp. Brit. an area for parking cars. **car phone** a cellular telephone for use in an automobile. □□ **carful** n. (pl. **-fuls**). [ME f. AF & ONF carre ult. f. L carrum, carrus, of OCelt. orig.]
■ 1 automobile, (motor) vehicle, motor car, passenger car, Brit. motor, archaic horseless carriage, colloq. auto,

---

/.../ **pronunciation**	● **part of speech**	
□ **phrases, idioms, and compounds**		
□□ **derivatives**	■ **synonym section**	
cross-references appear in SMALL CAPITALS or italics		

machine, buggy, bus, wagon, *sl.* wheels. **2, 3** (railroad) car, streetcar, coach, caboose, *Brit.* (railway) carriage, van, wagon.

carabineer /kárəbineér/ *n.* (also **carabinier**) *hist.* **1** a soldier whose principal weapon is a carbine. **2** (**the Carabineers**) the Royal Scots Dragoon Guards. [F *carabinier* f. *carabine* CARBINE]

carabiniere /kaáraabeenyére, kárəbinyáiree/ *n.* (*pl.* **carabinieri** *pronunc.* same) an Italian gendarme. [It.]

caracal /kárəkal/ *n.* a lynx, *Felis caracal*, native to N. Africa and SW Asia. [F or Sp. f. Turk. *karakulak* f. *kara* black + *kulak* ear]

caracole /kárəkōl/ *n.* & *v.* ● *n.* a horse's half turn to the right or left. ● *v.* **1** *intr.* (of a horse or its rider) perform a caracole. **2** *tr.* make (a horse) caracole. [F]

caracul var. of KARAKUL.

carafe /kəráf/ *n.* a glass container for water or wine, esp. at a table or bedside. [F f. It. *caraffa*, ult. f. Arab. *ġarrāfa* drinking vessel]

■ see JUG *n.* 1, 2.

carambola /kárəmbōlə/ *n.* **1** a small tree, *Averrhoa carambola*, native to SE Asia, bearing golden-yellow ribbed fruit. **2** this fruit. Also called **starfruit**. [Port., prob. of Indian or E. Indian orig.]

caramel /kárəmel, -məl, kaárməl/ *n.* **1 a** a sugar or syrup heated until it turns brown, then used as a flavoring or to color spirits, etc. **b** a kind of soft toffee made with sugar, butter, etc., melted and further heated. **2** the light-brown color of caramel. [F f. Sp. *caramelo*]

caramelize /kárəməlīz, kaármə-/ *v.* **1 a** *tr.* convert (sugar or syrup) into caramel. **b** *intr.* (of sugar or syrup) be converted into caramel. **2** *tr.* coat or cook (food) with caramelized sugar or syrup. □□ **caramelization** /-lizáyshən/ *n.*

carapace /kárəpays/ *n.* the hard upper shell of a turtle or a crustacean. [F f. Sp. *carapacho*]

carat /kárət/ *n.* **1** a unit of weight for precious stones, now equivalent to 200 milligrams. **2** *Brit.* var. of KARAT. [F f. It. *carato* f. Arab. *ḳīrāṭ* weight of four grains, f. Gk *keration* fruit of the carob (dimin. of *keras* horn)]

caravan /kárəvan/ *n.* & *v.* ● *n.* **1 a** a covered or enclosed wagon or truck; van. **b** *Brit.* a vehicle equipped for living in and usu. towed by a motor vehicle or a horse; trailer. **2 a** company of merchants or pilgrims, etc., traveling together, esp. across a desert in Asia or N. Africa. **3** a covered cart or carriage. ● *v.intr.* (**caravaned, caravaning** or **caravanned, caravanning**) travel or live in a caravan. □ **caravan site** (or **park**) *Brit.* = *trailer park.* □□ **caravanner** *n.* [F *caravane* f. Pers. *kārwān*]

caravansary /kárəvánsəree, -rī/ *n.* (also **caravanserai**) **1** a Near Eastern inn with a central court where caravans (see CARAVAN 2) may rest. **2** a hotel. [Pers. *kārwānsarāy* f. *sarāy* palace]

caravel /kárəvel/ *n.* (also **carvel** /kaárvəl/) *hist.* a small, light, fast ship, chiefly Spanish and Portuguese of the 15th–17th c. [F *caravelle* f. Port. *caravela* f. Gk *karabos* horned beetle, light ship]

caraway /kárəway/ *n.* an umbelliferous plant, *Carum carvi*, bearing clusters of tiny white flowers. □ **caraway seed** its fruit used as flavoring and as a source of oil. [prob. OSp. *alcarahueya* f. Arab. *alkarāwiyā*, perh. f. Gk *karon, kareon* cumin]

carb /kaarb/ *n. colloq.* a carburetor. [abbr.]

carbamate /kaárbəmayt/ *n. Chem.* a salt or ester of an amide of carbonic acid. [CARBONIC + AMIDE]

carbide /kaárbīd/ *n. Chem.* **1** a binary compound of carbon. **2** = *calcium carbide*.

carbine /kaárbeen, -bīn/ *n.* a lightweight firearm, usu. a rifle, orig. for cavalry use. [F *carabine* (this form also earlier in Engl.), weapon of the *carabin* mounted musketeer]

carbo- /kaárbō/ *comb. form* carbon (*carbohydrate*; *carbolic*; *carboxyl*).

carbohydrate /kaárbəhídrayt, -bō-/ *n. Biochem.* any of a large group of energy-producing organic compounds containing carbon, hydrogen, and oxygen, e.g., starch, glucose, and other sugars.

carbolic /kaarbólik/ *n.* (in full **carbolic acid**) phenol, esp. when used as a disinfectant. □ **carbolic soap** soap containing this. [CARBO- + -OL¹ + -IC]

carbon /kaárbən/ *n.* **1** a nonmetallic element occurring naturally as diamond, graphite, and charcoal, and in all organic compounds. ¶ Symb.: **C**. **2 a** = *carbon copy.* **b** = *carbon paper.* **3** a rod of carbon in an arc lamp. □ **carbon black** a fine carbon powder made by burning hydrocarbons in insufficient air. **carbon copy 1** a copy made with carbon paper. **2** a person or thing identical or similar to another (*is a carbon copy of his father*). **carbon cycle** *Biol.* the cycle in which carbon compounds are interconverted, usu. by living organisms. **carbon dating** the determination of the age of an organic object from the ratio of isotopes, which changes as carbon 14 decays. **carbon dioxide** a colorless, odorless gas occurring naturally in the atmosphere and formed by respiration. ¶ Chem. formula: CO_2. **carbon disulfide** a colorless liquid used as a solvent. ¶ Chem. formula: CS_2. **carbon fiber** a thin, strong crystalline filament of carbon used as strengthening material in resins, ceramics, etc. **carbon 14** a long-lived radioactive carbon isotope of mass 14, used in radiocarbon dating, and as a tracer in biochemistry. **carbon monoxide** a colorless, odorless toxic gas formed by the incomplete burning of carbon. ¶ Chem. formula: CO. **carbon paper** a thin carbon-coated paper used between two sheets of paper when writing to make a copy onto the bottom sheet. **carbon steel** a steel with properties dependent on the percentage of carbon present. **carbon tetrachloride** a colorless, volatile liquid used as a solvent. ¶ Chem. formula: CCl_4. **carbon 12** a carbon isotope of weight 12, used in calculations of atomic weight. [F *carbone* f. L *carbo -onis* charcoal]

■ □ **carbon copy 1** see DUPLICATE *n.*

carbonaceous /kaárbənáyshəs/ *adj.* **1** consisting of or containing carbon. **2** of or like coal or charcoal.

carbonado /kaárbənáydō/ *n.* (*pl.* **-os**) a dark opaque or impure kind of diamond used as an abrasive, for drills, etc. [Port.]

carbonate /kaárbənayt/ *n.* & *v.* ● *n. Chem.* a salt of carbonic acid. ● *v.tr.* **1** impregnate with carbon dioxide; aerate. **2** convert into a carbonate. □□ **carbonation** /-náyshən/ *n.* [F *carbonat* f. mod.L *carbonatum* (as CARBON)]

carbonic /kaarbónik/ *adj. Chem.* containing carbon. □ **carbonic acid** a very weak acid formed from carbon dioxide dissolved in water. **carbonic acid gas** *archaic* carbon dioxide.

carboniferous /kaárbənífərəs/ *adj.* & *n.* ● *adj.* **1** producing coal. **2** (**Carboniferous**) *Geol.* of or relating to the fifth period in the Paleozoic era, with evidence of the first reptiles and extensive coal-forming swamp forests. ¶ Cf. Appendix VII. ● *n.* (**Carboniferous**) *Geol.* this period or system.

carbonize /kaárbənīz/ *v.tr.* **1** convert into carbon by heating. **2** reduce to charcoal or coke. **3** coat with carbon. □□ **carbonization** /-nizáyshən/ *n.*

carbonyl /kaárbənil/ *n.* (used *attrib.*) *Chem.* the divalent radical CO.

carborundum /kaárbərúndəm/ *n.* a compound of carbon and silicon used esp. as an abrasive. [CARBON + CORUNDUM]

carboxyl /kaarbóksil/ *n. Chem.* the univalent acid radical (-COOH), present in most organic acids. □□ **carboxylic** /-boksílik/ *adj.* [CARBON + OXYGEN + -YL]

carboy /kaárboy/ *n.* a large bottle often protected by a frame, used for containing liquids. [Pers. *ḳarāba* large glass flagon]

carbuncle /kaárbungkəl/ *n.* **1** a severe abscess in the skin. **2** a bright red gem. □□ **carbuncular** /-búngkyələr/ *adj.* [ME f. OF *charbucle*, etc. f. L *carbunculus* small coal f. *carbo* coal]

■ **1** see BOIL².

carburation /kaárbəráyshən, -byə-/ *n.* the process of charging air with a spray of liquid hydrocarbon fuel, esp. in an internal combustion engine. [as CARBURET]

carburet /kaárbəráyt, -rét, -byə-/ *v.tr.* (**carbureted, carbureting**; esp. *Brit.* **carburetted, carburetting**) combine (a gas, etc.) with carbon. [earlier *carbure* f. F f. L *carbo* (as CARBON)]

carburetor /kaárbəráytter, -byə-/ *n.* (also **carburator**, esp.

Brit. **carburettor, carburetter**) an apparatus for carburation of fuel and air in an internal combustion engine. [as CARBURET + -OR¹]

carcajou /kaárkəjōō, -kəzhōō/ *n.* = WOLVERINE. [F, app. of Algonquian orig.]

carcass /kaárkəs/ *n.* (also *Brit.* **carcase**) **1** the dead body of an animal, esp. a trunk for cutting up as meat. **2** the bones of a cooked bird. **3** *derog.* the human body, living or dead. **4** the skeleton, framework of a building, ship, etc. **5** worthless remains. □ **carcass meat** *Brit.* raw meat, not preserved. [ME f. AF *carcois* (OF *charcois*) & f. F *carcasse*: ult. orig. unkn.]
■ **1** see BODY *n.* 1.

carcinogen /kaarsínəjən, kaársinəjen/ *n.* any substance that produces cancer. [as CARCINOMA + -GEN]

carcinogenesis /kaársinəjénisis/ *n.* the production of cancer.

carcinogenic /kaársinəjénik/ *adj.* producing cancer. □□ **carcinogenicity** /-nísitee/ *n.*

carcinoma /kaársinōmə/ *n.* (*pl.* **carcinomas** or **carcinomata** /-mətə/) a cancer, esp. one arising in epithelial tissue. □□ **carcinomatous** *adj.* [L f. Gk *karkinōma* f. *karkinos* crab]
■ see TUMOR.

Card. *abbr.* Cardinal.

card¹ /kaard/ *n. & v.* ● *n.* **1** thick, stiff paper or thin pasteboard. **2 a** a flat piece of this, esp. for writing or printing on. **b** = POSTCARD. **c** a card used to send greetings, issue an invitation, etc. (*birthday card*). **d** = *calling card*. **e** = *business card*. **f** a ticket of admission or membership. **3 a** = PLAYING CARD. **b** a similar card in a set designed for board games, etc. **c** (in *pl.*) card playing; a card game. **4** (in *pl.*) *Brit. colloq.* an employee's documents, esp. for tax and national insurance, held by the employer. **5 a** a program of events at boxing matches, races, etc. **b** a scorecard. **c** a list of holes on a golf course, on which a player's scores are entered. **6** *colloq.* a person, esp. an odd or amusing one (*what a card!; a knowing card*). **7** a plan or expedient (*sure card*). **8** a printed or written notice, set of rules, etc., for display. **9** a small rectangular piece of plastic issued by a bank, retail establishment, etc., with personal (often machine-readable) data on it, chiefly to obtain cash or credit (*credit card; do you have a card?*). ● *v.tr.* **1** fix to a card. **2** write on a card, esp. for indexing. **3** ask for proof of age, as at a bar. □ **ask for** (or **get**) **one's cards** *Brit.* ask (or be told) to leave one's employment. **card-carrying** being a registered member of an organization, esp. a political party or trade union. **card game** a game in which playing cards are used. **card index** an index in which each item is entered on a separate card. **card-index** *v.tr.* make a card index of. **card playing** the playing of card games. **card table** a table for card playing, esp. a folding one. **in the cards** possible or likely. **put** (or **lay**) **one's cards on the table** reveal one's resources, intentions, etc. [ME f. OF *carte* f. L *charta* f. Gk *khartēs* papyrus-leaf]
■ *n.* **6** character, eccentric, original; joker, prankster, practical joker, wag, wit, humorist, comedian, comedienne, *archaic* droll, *colloq.* scream, laugh, *Austral. & NZ sl.* dag. □ **in the cards** likely, probable, possible, expected, in the offing, on the horizon, in view *or* prospect *or* store, to come, *disp.* liable. **put** (or **lay**) **one's cards on the table** act openly, play fair, reveal all, be open *or* honest *or* straight, show one's cards *or* hand, *colloq.* come clean.

card² /kaard/ *n. & v.* ● *n.* a toothed instrument; wire brush, etc., for raising a nap on cloth or for disentangling fibers before spinning. ● *v.tr.* brush, comb, cleanse, or scratch with a card. □ **carding wool** short-stapled wool. □□ **carder** *n.* [ME f. OF *carde* f. Prov. *carda* f. *cardar* tease, comb, ult. f. L *carere* card]

cardamom /kaárdəməm/ *n.* (also **cardamum**) **1** an aromatic SE Asian plant, *Elettaria cardamomum*. **2** the seed capsules of this used as a spice. [L *cardamomum* or F *cardamome* f. Gk *kardamōmon* f. *kardamon* cress + *amōmon* a spice plant]

Cardan joint /kaárd'n/ *n. Engin.* a universal joint. [G. *Cardano*, It. mathematician d. 1576]

cardboard /kaárdbawrd/ *n. & adj.* ● *n.* pasteboard or stiff paper, esp. for making cards or boxes. ● *adj.* **1** made of cardboard. **2** flimsy; insubstantial. □ **cardboard city** esp. *Brit.* a place where homeless people gather at night using cardboard boxes, etc., for shelter.

cardiac /kaárdeeak/ *adj. & n.* ● *adj.* **1** of or relating to the heart. **2** of or relating to the part of the stomach nearest the esophagus. ● *n.* a person with heart disease. [F *cardiaque* or L *cardiacus* f. Gk *kardiakos* f. *kardia* heart]
■ *adj.* cardio-.

cardigan /kaárdigən/ *n.* a knitted sweater fastening down the front, usu. with long sleeves. [named after the 7th Earl of *Cardigan* d. 1868]

cardinal /kaárd'nəl/ *n. & adj.* ● *n.* **1** (as a title **Cardinal**) a leading dignitary of the RC Church, one of the college electing the Pope. **2** any small American songbird of the genus *Richmondena*, the males of which have scarlet plumage. **3** *hist.* a woman's cloak, orig. of scarlet cloth with a hood. ● *adj.* **1** chief; fundamental; on which something hinges. **2** of deep scarlet (like a cardinal's cassock). □ **cardinal flower** the scarlet lobelia. **cardinal numbers** those denoting quantity (one, two, three, etc.), as opposed to ordinal numbers (first, second, third, etc.). **cardinal points** the four main points of the compass (N., S., E., W.). **cardinal virtues** the chief moral attributes: justice, prudence, temperance, and fortitude. □□ **cardinalate** /-nəlayt/ *n.* (in sense 1 of *n.*). **cardinally** *adv.* **cardinalship** *n.* (in sense 1 of *n.*). [ME f. OF f. L *cardinalis* f. *cardo -inis* hinge: in Eng. first applied to the four virtues on which conduct 'hinges']
■ *adj.* **1** important, chief, major, key, special, main, central, principal, prime, primary, essential, necessary, fundamental; supreme, paramount, highest, first, foremost, leading, preeminent. **2** scarlet, cinnabar, vermilion, *poet.* vermeil.

cardio- /kaárdeeō/ *comb. form* heart (*cardiogram; cardiology*). [Gk *kardia* heart]

cardiogram /kaárdeeəgram/ *n.* a record of muscle activity within the heart, made by a cardiograph.

cardiograph /kaárdeeəgraf/ *n.* an instrument for recording heart muscle activity. □□ **cardiographer** /-deeógrəfər/ *n.* **cardiography** *n.*

cardiology /kaárdeeóləjee/ *n.* the branch of medicine concerned with diseases and abnormalities of the heart. □□ **cardiologist** *n.*

cardiopulmonary resuscitation /kardeeōpōólmənəree/ *n.* emergency medical procedures for restoring normal heartbeat and breathing to victims of heart failure, drowning, etc. ¶ Abbr.: **CPR**.

cardiovascular /kaárdeeōváskyələr/ *adj.* of or relating to the heart and blood vessels.

cardoon /kaardōōn/ *n.* a thistlelike plant, *Cynara cardunculus*, allied to the globe artichoke, with leaves used as a vegetable. [F *cardon* ult. f. L *cardu(u)s* thistle]

cardphone /kaárdfōn/ *n. Brit.* a public telephone operated by the insertion of a prepaid plastic machine-readable card instead of money.

cardsharp /kaárdshaarp/ *n.* (also **cardsharper**) a swindler at card games.

care /kair/ *n. & v.* ● *n.* **1** worry; anxiety. **2** an occasion for this. **3** serious attention; heed; caution; pains (*assembled with care; handle with care*). **4 a** protection; charge. **b** *Brit.* = *child care*. **5** a thing to be done or seen to. ● *v.intr.* **1** (usu. foll. by *about, for, whether*) feel concern or interest. **2** (usu. foll. by *for, about*) feel liking, affection, regard, or deference (*don't care for jazz; she cares for him a great deal*). **3** (foll. by *to* + infin.) wish or be willing (*do not care to be seen with him; would you care to try them?*). □ **care for** provide for; look after. **care label** a label attached to clothing, with instructions for washing, etc. **care of** at the address of (*sent it care*

/.../ pronunciation	● part of speech
□ phrases, idioms, and compounds	
□□ derivatives	■ synonym section
cross-references appear in SMALL CAPITALS or *italics*	

of his sister). **for all one cares** *colloq.* denoting uninterest or unconcern (*for all I care they can leave tomorrow; I could be dying for all you care*). **have a care** take care; be careful. **I** (etc.) **couldn't** (freq. **could**) **care less** *colloq.* an expression of complete indifference. **in care** *Brit.* (of a child) taken into the care of a local authority. **take care 1** be careful. **2** (foll. by *to* + infin.) not fail nor neglect. **take care of 1** look after; keep safe. **2** deal with. **3** dispose of. [OE *caru, carian*, f. Gmc]

■ *n.* **1, 2** anxiety, worry, trouble, anguish, uneasiness, disquiet, distress, grief, sorrow, sadness, suffering, misery, tribulation, *archaic or literary* woe, *literary* dolor; see also BURDEN *n.* 1, 2. **3** heedfulness, attention, thought, consideration, deliberation, awareness, pains, heed, carefulness, meticulousness, punctiliousness; caution, cautiousness, vigilance, mindfulness, circumspection, watchfulness. **4 a** responsibility, charge, protection, guardianship, custody, custodianship, keeping, safekeeping, trust; control, direction, supervision, management, authority. **5** see RESPONSIBILITY 2. ● *v.* **1** be concerned *or* bothered, trouble oneself, feel interest, worry, fret, trouble, mind. **2** see LIKE² *v.* 1. **3** see WISH *v.* 1. □ **care for** look after, tend, attend (to), watch over, mind, protect, take care of, provide for, nurse, minister to, wait on; be responsible for. **have a care** see BEWARE. **take care 1** see BEWARE. **take care of 1** look after, attend to, be responsible for, take charge of, take responsibility for, be careful of; tend, nurse, minister to, care for; watch over, mind; keep safe, safeguard, protect, conserve. **2** see DEAL¹ *v.* 1a. **3** see *dispose of* (DISPOSE) 1a, c.

careen /kəreén/ *v.* **1** *tr.* turn (a ship) on one side for cleaning, caulking, or repair. **2 a** *intr.* tilt; lean over. **b** *tr.* cause to do this. **3** *intr.* swerve about; career. ¶ Sense 3 is infl. by *career* (v.). □□ **careenage** *n.* [earlier as noun, = careened position of ship, f. F *carène* f. It. *carena* f. L *carina* keel]

■ **2** see TILT *v.* 1. **3** career, sway, veer, swerve, lurch, reel, totter, swing.

career /kəreér/ *n. & v.* ● *n.* **1 a** one's advancement through life, esp. in a profession. **b** the progress through history of a group or institution. **2** a profession or occupation, esp. as offering advancement. **3** (*attrib.*) **a** pursuing or wishing to pursue a career (*career woman*). **b** working permanently in a specified profession (*career diplomat*). **4** swift course; impetus (*in full career*). ● *v.intr.* **1** move or swerve about wildly. **2** go swiftly. [F *carrière* f. It. *carriera* ult. f. L *carrus* CAR]

■ *n.* **1 a** life's work *or* journey. **b** see PROGRESS *n.* 2. **2** occupation, profession, job, trade, craft, métier, (line of) work, business, livelihood, calling, vocation, pursuit. **4** see PROGRESS *n.* 1, IMPETUS 1. ● *v.* **1** see SWERVE *v.* **2** speed, race, rush, dash, dart, zip, sprint, fly, whirl, roar, zoom, hurtle, bolt, shoot, *colloq.* tear, hightail.

careerist /kəreérist/ *n.* a person predominantly concerned with personal advancement.

carefree /káirfree/ *adj.* free from anxiety or responsibility; lighthearted. □□ **carefreeness** *n.*

■ nonchalant, easy, easygoing, insouciant, lighthearted, blithe, debonair, happy-go-lucky, gay, breezy, airy, unworried, careless, trouble-free, worry-free, relaxed, contented, happy.

careful /káirfŏŏl/ *adj.* **1** painstaking; thorough. **2** cautious. **3** done with care and attention. **4** (usu. foll. by *that* + clause, or *to* + infin.) taking care; not neglecting. **5** (foll. by *for, of*) concerned for; taking care of. □□ **carefully** *adv.* **carefulness** *n.* [OE *carful* (as CARE, -FUL)]

■ **1, 3** meticulous, painstaking, attentive, punctilious, (well-)organized, systematic, precise, accurate, fastidious, thorough, scrupulous, nice, conscientious, assiduous, diligent, particular, finicky, finical, fussy, *colloq.* persnickety; sedulous, deliberate, measured, judicious, studious, ceremonious. **2** cautious, wary, circumspect, guarded, chary, prudent, watchful, aware, alert, vigilant, sharp-eyed, on one's guard *or* toes;

suspicious, distrustful, *sl.* leery. **4** (*be careful*) see BEWARE. **5** (*be careful of*) see *take care of* 1 (CARE).

caregiver /káirgivər/ *n.* a person who provides care for children, the sick, the elderly, etc.

careless /káirlis/ *adj.* **1** not taking care nor paying attention. **2** unthinking; insensitive. **3** done without care; inaccurate. **4** lighthearted. **5** (foll. by *of*) not concerned about; taking no heed of. **6** effortless; casual. □□ **carelessly** *adv.* **carelessness** *n.* [OE *carlēas* (as CARE, -LESS)]

■ **1** inattentive, negligent, thoughtless, foolhardy, absentminded, neglectful, remiss, slapdash, devil-may-care, irresponsible, lackadaisical, perfunctory, derelict; unobservant, unthinking, unmindful, incautious, unwary, reckless, rash. **2** unconcerned, unthinking, insensitive, thoughtless, casual, blithe, indifferent, inconsiderate, uncaring. **3** casual, cursory; inaccurate, imprecise, inexact, incorrect, wrong, error-ridden, erroneous, sloppy. **4** see CAREFREE. **5** see *heedless* (HEED). **6** unstudied, ingenuous, artless, casual, nonchalant; effortless.

carer /káirər/ *n. Brit.* a person who cares for a sick or elderly person.

caress /kərés/ *v. & n.* ● *v.tr.* **1** touch or stroke gently or lovingly; kiss. **2** treat fondly or kindly. ● *n.* a loving or gentle touch or kiss. [F *caresse* (n.), *caresser* (v.), f. It. *carezza* ult. f. L *carus* dear]

■ *v.* **1** touch, stroke, pet, fondle, pat, cuddle, embrace, hug, nuzzle; kiss, *colloq.* neck. ● *n.* touch, stroke, pat; cuddle, embrace, hug; kiss.

caret /kárət/ *n.* a mark (˄) indicating a proposed insertion in printing or writing. [L, = is lacking]

caretaker /káirtaykər/ *n.* **1 a** a person employed to look after something, esp. a house in the owner's absence. **b** *Brit.* a janitor. **2** (*attrib.*) exercising temporary authority (*caretaker government*).

careworn /káirwawrn/ *adj.* showing the effects of prolonged worry.

■ see HAGGARD *adj.*

carfare /káarfair/ *n.* a passenger's fare to travel by public transport (orig. streetcar).

cargo /káargō/ *n.* (*pl.* **-oes** or **-os**) **1 a** goods carried on a ship or aircraft. **b** a load of such goods. **2 a** goods carried in a motor vehicle. **b** a load of such goods. □ **cargo cult** (orig. in the Pacific Islands) a belief in the forthcoming arrival of ancestral spirits bringing cargoes of food and other goods. [Sp. (as CHARGE)]

■ **1a, 2a** freight, goods, merchandise, freightage, *Naut.* bulk. **1b, 2b** shipment, consignment, shipload, truckload, wagonload, load, trainload.

carhop /káarhop/ *n. colloq.* a waiter at a drive-in restaurant.

cariama var. of SERIEMA.

Carib /kárib/ *n. & adj.* ● *n.* **1** an aboriginal inhabitant of the southern W. Indies or the adjacent coasts. **2** the language of this people. ● *adj.* of or relating to this people. [Sp. *Caribe* f. Haitian]

Caribbean /káribeeən, kəríbeeən/ *n. & adj.* ● *n.* the part of the Atlantic between the southern W. Indies and Central America. ● *adj.* **1** of or relating to this region. **2** of the Caribs or their language or culture.

caribou /káribōō/ *n.* (*pl.* same) a N. American reindeer. [Can. F, prob. f. Algonquian]

caricature /kárikəchər, -chŏŏr/ *n. & v.* ● *n.* **1** a grotesque usu. comic representation of a person by exaggeration of characteristic traits, in a picture, writing, or mime. **2** a ridiculously poor or absurd imitation or version. ● *v.tr.* make or give a caricature of. □□ **caricatural** /-chŏŏrəl/ *adj.* **caricaturist** *n.* [F f. It. *caricatura* f. *caricare* load, exaggerate: see CHARGE]

■ *n.* **1** cartoon, parody, satire, satirization, burlesque, lampoon, pasquinade, *colloq.* takeoff, spoof, send-up. **2** see JOKE *n.* 2. ● *v.* parody, satirize, lampoon, burlesque, guy; ridicule, mock, distort, *colloq.* take off, send up.

caries /káireez/ *n.* (*pl.* same) decay and crumbling of a tooth or bone. [L]

carillon /kárilon, -lən/ *n.* **1** a set of bells sounded either from a keyboard or mechanically. **2** a tune played on bells. **3** an organ stop imitating a peal of bells. [F f. OF *quarregnon* peal of four bells, alt. of Rmc *quaternio* f. L *quattuor* four]
■ **1** see PEAL *n.*

carina /kəreénə/ *n.* (*pl.* **carinas** or **carinae** /-nee/) *Biol.* a keel-shaped structure, esp. the ridge of a bird's breastbone.
□□ **carinal** *adj.* [L, = keel]

carinate /kárinayt/ *adj.* (of a bird) having a keeled breastbone (opp. RATITE). [L *carinatus* keeled f. *carina* keel]

caring /káiring/ *adj.* **1** compassionate. **2** involving the care of the sick, elderly, or disabled.
■ **1** see SYMPATHETIC *adj.* 1.

carioca /káreeṓkə/ *n.* **1 a** a Brazilian dance like the samba. **b** the music for this. **2** a native of Rio de Janeiro. [Port.]

cariogenic /káreeōjénik/ *adj.* causing caries.

cariole /káreeōl/ *n.* **1** a small open carriage for one. **2** a covered light cart. **3** a Canadian sleigh. [F f. It. *carriuola*, dimin. of *carro* CAR]

carious /káireeəs/ *adj.* (of bones or teeth) decayed. [L *cariosus*]
■ see MOLDY 1.

carjacking /kárjaking/ *n.* theft of an automobile whose driver is forced to leave the vehicle or is kept captive while the thief drives.

carking /káarking/ *adj. archaic* burdensome (*carking care*). [part. of obs. *cark* (v.) f. ONF *carkier* f. Rmc, rel. to CHARGE]

carl /kaarl/ *n. Sc.* a man; a fellow. [OE f. ON *karl*, rel. to CHURL]

carline /káarlin/ *n.* any plant of the genus *Carlina*, esp. the thistlelike *C. vulgaris*. [F f. med.L *carlina* perh. for *cardina* (L *carduus* thistle), assoc. with *Carolus Magnus* Charlemagne]

carload /káarlōd/ *n.* **1** a quantity that can be carried in a car. **2** the minimum quantity of goods for which a lower rate is charged for transport.

Carlovingian var. of CAROLINGIAN.

Carmelite /káarmilit/ *n. & adj.* ● *n.* **1** a friar of the Order of Our Lady of Mount Carmel, following a rule of extreme asceticism. **2** a nun of a similar order. ● *adj.* of or relating to the Carmelites. [F *Carmelite* or med.L *carmelita* f. Mt. *Carmel* in Palestine, where the order was founded in the 12th c.]

carminative /kaarmínətiv, káarminaytiv/ *adj. & n.* ● *adj.* relieving flatulence. ● *n.* a carminative drug. [F *carminatif* -*ive* or med.L *carminare* heal (by incantation): see CHARM]

carmine /káarmin, -mīn/ *adj. & n.* ● *adj.* of a vivid crimson color. ● *n.* **1** this color. **2** a vivid crimson pigment made from cochineal. [F *carmin* or med.L *carminium* perh. f. *carmesinum* crimson + *minium* cinnabar]

carnage /káarnij/ *n.* great slaughter, esp. of human beings in battle. [F f. It. *carnaggio* f. med.L *carnaticum* f. L *caro carnis* flesh]
■ bloodshed, slaughter, butchery, massacre, killing, mass murder, genocide, holocaust, blood bath, *joc.* bloodletting.

carnal /káarnəl/ *adj.* **1** of the body or flesh; worldly. **2** sensual; sexual. □ **carnal knowledge** *Law* sexual intercourse. □□ **carnality** /-áalitee/ *n.* **carnalize** *v.tr.* **carnally** *adv.* [ME f. LL *carnalis* f. *caro carnis* flesh]
■ **1** bodily, physical, corporeal, fleshly, animal, brute; worldly, earthly, material, nonspiritual. **2** sensual, sexual, fleshly, erotic, voluptuous, libidinous, lustful, lecherous, lascivious, licentious, lewd, prurient, *formal* concupiscent. □ **carnal knowledge** see *sexual intercourse*.

carnassial /kaarnáseeəl/ *adj. & n.* ● *adj.* (of a carnivore's upper premolar and lower molar teeth) adapted for shearing flesh. ● *n.* such a tooth. Also called SECTORIAL. [F *carnassier* carnivorous]

carnation[1] /kaarnáyshən/ *n.* **1** any of several cultivated varieties of clove-scented pink, with variously colored showy flowers (see also CLOVE[1] 2). **2** this flower. [orig. uncert.: in early use varying with *coronation*]

carnation[2] /kaarnáyshən/ *n. & adj.* ● *n.* a rosy pink color.

● *adj.* of this color. [F f. It. *carnagione* ult. f. L *caro carnis* flesh]

carnauba /kaarnṓwbə, -náwbə, -nṓōbə/ *n.* **1** a fan palm, *Copernicia cerifera*, native to NE Brazil. **2** (in full **carnauba wax**) the yellowish leaf wax of this tree used as a polish, etc. [Port.]

carnelian /kaarneélyən/ *n.* (also **cornelian** /kawr-/) **1** a dull red or reddish-white variety of chalcedony. **2** this color. [ME f. OF *corneline*; *car-* after L *caro carnis* flesh]

carnet /kaarnáy/ *n.* **1** a customs permit to take a motor vehicle across a frontier for a limited period. **2** a permit allowing use of a campsite. [F, = notebook]

carnival /káarnivəl/ *n.* **1 a** the festivities usual during the period before Lent in Roman Catholic countries. **b** any festivities, esp. those occurring at a regular date. **2** merrymaking; revelry. **3** a traveling fair or circus. [It. *carne-*, *carnovale* f. med.L *carnelevarium*, etc. Shrovetide f. L *caro carnis* flesh + *levare* put away]
■ **1b, 2** see JAMBOREE.

carnivore /káarnivawr/ *n.* **1 a** any mammal of the order Carnivora, with powerful jaws and teeth adapted for stabbing, tearing, and eating flesh, including cats, dogs, and bears. **b** any other flesh-eating mammal. **2** any flesh-eating plant.

carnivorous /kaarnívərəs/ *adj.* **1** (of an animal) feeding on flesh. **2** (of a plant) digesting trapped insects or other animal substances. **3** of or relating to the order Carnivora. □□ **carnivorously** *adv.* **carnivorousness** *n.* [L *carnivorus* f. *caro carnis* flesh + -VOROUS]

carob /kárəb/ *n.* **1** an evergreen tree, *Ceratonia siliqua*, native to the Mediterranean, bearing edible pods. **2** its bean-shaped edible seed pod sometimes used as a substitute for chocolate. [obs. F *carobe* f. med.L *carrubia*, -*um* f. Arab. *ḵarrūba*]

carol /kárəl/ *n. & v.* ● *n.* a joyous song, esp. a Christmas hymn. ● *v.* (**caroled, caroling**; esp. *Brit.* **carolled, carolling**) **1** *intr.* sing carols, esp. outdoors at Christmas. **2** *tr. & intr.* sing joyfully. □□ **caroler** *n.* (also esp. *Brit.* **caroller**). [ME f. OF *carole, caroler*, of unkn. orig.]
■ *n.* see SONG. ● *v.* see SING *v.* 1, 2.

Caroline /kárəlin/ *adj.* **1** (also **Carolean** /-leéən/) of the time of Charles I or II of England. **2** = CAROLINGIAN *adj.* 2. [L *Carolus* Charles]

Carolingian /kárəlínjən, -jeeən/ *adj. & n.* (also **Carlovingian** /káarləvínjeeən/) ● *adj.* **1** of or relating to the second Frankish dynasty, founded by Charlemagne (d. 814). **2** of a style of script developed in France at the time of Charlemagne. ● *n.* **1** a member of the Carolingian dynasty. **2** the Carolingian style of script. [F *carlovingien* f. *Karl* Charles after *mérovingien* (see MEROVINGIAN): re-formed after L *Carolus*]

carom /kárəm/ *n. & v. Billiards* ● *n.* the hitting of two balls by the one ball on one shot. ● *v.intr.* **1** make a carom. **2** (usu. foll. by *off*) strike and rebound. [abbr. of *carambole* f. Sp. *carambola*]
■ *v.* see BOUNCE *v.* 1.

carotene /káröteen/ *n.* any of several orange-colored plant pigments found in carrots, tomatoes, etc., acting as a source of vitamin A. [G *Carotin* f. L *carota* CARROT]

carotenoid /kərót'noyd/ *n.* any of a group of yellow, orange, or brown pigments giving characteristic color to plant organs, e.g., ripe tomatoes, carrots, autumn leaves, etc.

carotid /kərótid/ *n. & adj.* ● *n.* each of the two main arteries carrying blood to the head and neck. ● *adj.* of or relating to either of these arteries. [F *carotide* or mod.L *carotides* f. Gk *karōtides* (pl.) f. *karoō* stupefy (compression of these arteries being thought to cause stupor)]

carouse /kərówz/ *v. & n.* ● *v.intr.* **1** have a noisy or lively drinking party. **2** drink heavily. ● *n.* a noisy or lively drink-

---

/.../ **pronunciation**	● **part of speech**
□ **phrases, idioms, and compounds**	
□□ **derivatives**	■ **synonym section**
cross-references appear in SMALL CAPITALS or *italics*	

ing party. □□ **carousal** *n.* **carouser** *n.* [orig. as adv. = right
out, in phr. *drink carouse* f. G *gar aus trinken*]
■ *v.* **1** make merry, revel, party, *archaic* wassail, *colloq.* go
on a spree, make whoopee, paint the town red. **2** see
BOOZE *v.* ● *n.* revel, party, carousal, bacchanal, orgy,
Austral. corroboree, *archaic* wassail, *colloq.* (drinking)
spree, shindig, pub crawl, *Brit.* rave, rave-up, *Brit.*
colloq. knees-up, *sl.* jag, bender, drunk, binge, esp. *Brit.*
sl. booze-up.
carousel /kárəsél, -zél/ *n.* (also **carrousel**) **1** a merry-go-
round. **2** a rotating delivery or conveyor system, esp. for
passengers' luggage at an airport. **3** *hist.* a kind of equestrian
tournament. [F *carrousel* f. It. *carosello*]
■ **1** merry-go-round, whirligig, *Brit.* roundabout.
carp[1] /kaarp/ *n.* (*pl.* same) any freshwater fish of the family
Cyprinidae, esp. *Cyprinus carpio*, often bred for use as food.
[ME f. OF *carpe* f. Prov. or f. LL *carpa*]
carp[2] /kaarp/ *v.intr.* (usu. foll. by *at*) find fault; complain pettily. □□ **carper** *n.* [obs. ME senses 'talk, say, sing' f. ON
karpa to brag: mod. sense (16th c.) from or infl. by L *carpere*
pluck at, slander]
■ find fault, cavil, complain, grumble, niggle, *colloq.*
gripe; (*carp at*) criticize, fault, pick at *or* on, nag (at),
peck at, put down, pick holes in, *sl.* knock.
carpal /kaárpəl/ *adj.* & *n.* ● *adj.* of or relating to the bones
in the wrist. ● *n.* any of the bones forming the wrist. □ **carpal tunnel syndrome** a condition caused by pressure on a
nerve in the wrist, characterized by numbness, tingling,
weakness, and pain in the hand. [CARPUS + -AL]
carpel /kaárpəl/ *n. Bot.* the female reproductive organ of a
flower, consisting of a stigma, style, and ovary. □□ **carpel-
lary** *adj.* [F *carpelle* or mod.L *carpellum* f. Gk *karpos* fruit]
carpenter /kaárpintər/ *n.* & *v.* ● *n.* a person skilled in woodwork, esp. of a structural kind (cf. JOINER). ● *v.* **1** *intr.* do
carpentry. **2** *tr.* make by means of carpentry. **3** *tr.* (often foll.
by *together*) construct; fit together. □ **carpenter ant** any
large ant of the genus *Camponotus*, boring into wood to nest.
carpenter bee any of various solitary bees that bore into
wood. [ME & AF; OF *carpentier* f. LL *carpentarius* f. *carpen-
tum* wagon f. Gaulish]
carpentry /kaárpintree/ *n.* **1** the work or occupation of a
carpenter. **2** work constructed by a carpenter. [ME f. OF
carpenterie f. L *carpentaria*: see CARPENTER]
carpet /kaárpit/ *n.* & *v.* ● *n.* **1 a** a thick fabric for covering a
floor or stairs. **b** a piece of this fabric. **2** an expanse or layer
resembling a carpet in being smooth, soft, bright, or thick
(*carpet of snow*). ● *v.tr.* **1** cover with or as with a carpet. **2**
colloq. reprimand; reprove. □ **carpet bombing** intensive
bombing. **carpet slipper** a kind of slipper with the upper
made orig. of carpetlike material. **carpet sweeper** a household implement with a revolving brush or brushes for
sweeping carpets. **on the carpet 1** *colloq.* being reprimanded. **2** under consideration. **sweep under the carpet**
conceal (a problem or difficulty) in the hope that it will be
forgotten. [ME f. OF *carpite* or med.L *carpita*, f. obs. It.
carpita woolen counterpane, ult. f. L *carpere* pluck, pull to
pieces]
■ *v.* **2** see REPRIMAND *v.*
carpetbag /kaárpitbag/ *n.* a traveling bag of a kind orig. made
of carpetlike material.
■ see BAG *n.* 2a.
carpetbagger /kaárpitbagər/ *n.* **1** a political candidate in an
area where the candidate has no local connections (orig. a
Northerner in the South after the Civil War). **2** an unscrupulous opportunist, esp. an outsider.
carpeting /kaárpiting/ *n.* **1** material for carpets. **2** carpets
collectively.
carpology /kaarpóləjee/ *n.* the study of the structure of fruit
and seeds. [Gk *karpos* fruit]
carpool /kárpŏŏl/ *n.* & *v.* ● *n.* (also **car pool**) **1** an arrangement by which a group of commuters travel to and from
their destination in a single vehicle, often with the members
taking turns as driver. **2** the commuters taking part in such
an arrangement (*there are four people in our carpool*). ● *v.intr.*
(also **car-pool**) participate in or organize a carpool.

carport /kaárpawrt/ *n.* a shelter with a roof and open sides
for a car, usu. beside a house.
carpus /kaárpəs/ *n.* (*pl.* **carpi** /-pī/) the small bones between the forelimb and metacarpus in terrestrial vertebrates,
forming the wrist in humans. [mod.L f. Gk *karpos* wrist]
carrack /kárək/ *n. hist.* a large armed merchant ship. [ME f.
F *caraque* f. Sp. *carraca* f. Arab. *ḳarāḳir*]
carrageen /kárəgeen/ *n.* (also **carragheen**) an edible red
seaweed, *Chondrus crispus*, of the N. hemisphere. Also called
Irish moss. [orig. uncert.: perh. f. Ir. *cosáinín carraige* carrageen, lit. 'little stem of the rock']
carrel /kárəl/ *n.* **1** a small cubicle for a reader in a library. **2**
hist. a small enclosure or study in a cloister. [OF *carole*,
med.L *carola*, of unkn. orig.]
carriage /kárij/ *n.* **1** a wheeled vehicle, esp. one with four
wheels and pulled by horses. **2** *Brit.* a railroad passenger
coach. **3** *Brit.* **a** the conveying of goods. **b** the cost of this
(*carriage paid*). **4** the part of a machine (e.g., a typewriter)
that carries other parts into the required position. **5** a gun
carriage. **6** a manner of carrying oneself; one's bearing or
deportment. □ **carriage and pair** a carriage with two
horses pulling it. **carriage clock** a portable clock in a rectangular case with a handle on top. **carriage dog** a dalmatian. [ME f. ONF *cariage* f. *carier* CARRY]
■ **6** bearing, air, deportment, demeanor, attitude,
posture, stance, presence, *literary* comportment.
carriageway /kárijway/ *n. Brit.* the part of a road intended
for vehicles; highway.
carrick bend /kárik/ *n. Naut.* a kind of knot used to join
ropes. [BEND[2]: *carrick* perh. f. CARRACK]
carrier /káreeər/ *n.* **1** a person or thing that carries. **2** a person
or company undertaking to convey goods or passengers for
payment. **3** = *carrier bag.* **4** a part of a bicycle, etc., for carrying luggage or a passenger. **5** an insurance company. **6** a
person or animal that may transmit a disease or a hereditary
characteristic without suffering from or displaying it. **7** =
aircraft carrier. **8** a substance used to support or convey a
pigment, a catalyst, radioactive material, etc. **9** *Physics* a mobile electron or hole that carries a charge in a semiconductor. □ **carrier bag** *Brit.* a disposable plastic or paper bag
with handles. **carrier pigeon** a pigeon trained to carry messages tied to its neck or leg. **carrier wave** a high-frequency
electromagnetic wave modulated in amplitude or frequency
to convey a signal.
■ **1, 2** bearer, porter, conveyor, transporter, carter,
shipper, carman; hauler, *Brit.* haulier. **6** transmitter,
Immunology vector.
carrion /káriən/ *n.* & *adj.* ● *n.* **1** dead putrefying flesh. **2**
something vile or filthy. ● *adj.* rotten; loathsome. □ **carrion
crow** a black crow, *Corvus corone*, native to Europe, feeding
mainly on carrion. **carrion flower** = STAPELIA. [ME f. AF
& ONF *caroine*, *-oigne*, OF *charoigne* ult. f. L *caro* flesh]
carrot /kárət/ *n.* **1 a** an umbelliferous plant, *Daucus carota*,
with a tapering orange-colored root. **b** this root as a vegetable. **2** a means of enticement or persuasion. **3** (in *pl.*) *sl.*
a red-haired person. □□ **carroty** *adj.* [F *carotte* f. L *carota* f.
Gk *karōton*]
■ **2** see INCENTIVE *n.* 1.
carrousel var. of CAROUSEL.
carry /káree/ *v.* & *n.* ● *v.* (**-ies**, **-ied**) **1** *tr.* support or hold
up, esp. while moving. **2** *tr.* convey with one from one place
to another. **3** *tr.* have on one's person (*carry a watch*). **4** *tr.*
conduct or transmit (*pipe carries water*; *wire carries electric
current*). **5** *tr.* take (a process, etc.) to a specified point (*carry
into effect*; *carry a joke too far*). **6** *tr.* (foll. by *to*) continue or
prolong (*carry modesty to excess*). **7** *tr.* involve; imply; have
as a feature or consequence (*carries a two-year guarantee*;
principles carry consequences). **8** *tr.* (in reckoning) transfer (a
figure) to a column of higher value. **9** *tr.* hold in a specified
way (*carry oneself erect*). **10** *tr.* **a** (of a newspaper or magazine) publish; include in its contents, esp. regularly. **b** (of a
radio or television station) broadcast, esp. regularly. **11** *tr.*
(of a retailing outlet) keep a regular stock of (particular
goods for sale) (*have stopped carrying that brand*). **12** *intr.* **a**
(of sound, esp. a voice) be audible at a distance. **b** (of a

missile) travel; penetrate. **13** *tr.* (of a gun, etc.) propel to a specified distance. **14** *tr.* **a** win victory or acceptance for (a proposal, etc.). **b** win acceptance from (*carried the audience with them*). **c** win; capture (a prize, a fortress, etc.). **d** gain (a state or district) in an election. **e** *Golf* cause the ball to pass beyond (a bunker, etc.). **15** *tr.* **a** endure the weight of; support (*columns carry the dome*). **b** be the chief cause of the effectiveness of; be the driving force in (*you carry the sales department*). **16** *tr.* be pregnant with (*is carrying twins*). **17** *tr.* **a** (of a motive, money, etc.) cause or enable (a person) to go to a specified place. **b** (of a journey) bring (a person) to a specified point. ● *n.* (*pl.* **-ies**) **1** an act of carrying. **2** *Golf* the distance a ball travels before reaching the ground. **3** a portage between rivers, etc. **4** the range of a gun, etc. □ **carry all before one** succeed; overcome all opposition. **carry away 1** remove. **2** inspire; affect emotionally or spiritually. **3** deprive of self-control (*got carried away*). **4** *Naut.* **a** lose (a mast, etc.) by breakage. **b** break off or away. **carry back** take (a person) back in thought to a past time. **carry the can** *Brit. colloq.* bear the responsibility or blame. **carry conviction** be convincing. **carry-cot** *Brit.* a portable crib for a baby. **carry the day** be victorious or successful. **carry forward** transfer to a new page or account. **carrying-on** (or **carryings-on**) *sl.* **1** a state of excitement or fuss. **2** a questionable piece of behavior. **3** a flirtation or love affair. **carry it off** (or **carry it off well**) do well under difficulties. **carry off 1** take away, esp. by force. **2** win (a prize). **3** (esp. of a disease) kill. **4** render acceptable or passable. **carry on 1** continue (*carry on eating; carry on, don't mind me*). **2** engage in (a conversation or a business). **3** *colloq.* behave strangely or excitedly. **4** (often foll. by *with*) *Brit. colloq.* flirt or have a love affair. **5** advance (a process) by a stage. **carry out** put (ideas, instructions, etc.) into practice. **carry over 1** = *carry forward*. **2** postpone (work, etc.). **3** *Stock Exch.* keep over to the next settling day. **carry through 1** complete successfully. **2** bring safely out of difficulties. **carry weight** be influential or important. **carry with one** bear in mind. [ME f. AF & ONF *carier* (as CAR)]

■ *v.* **1, 2** transport, convey, bear, deliver, bring, haul, lug, cart, ship, move, *colloq.* schlep, hump, tote; drive, take; hold. **4** conduct, transmit, convey, take, transport, transfer, bear. **7** see INCLUDE 1. **9** bear, deport, hold (up), maintain, keep. **10** publish, put out; broadcast, air, screen; disseminate, communicate, present, announce, offer, give, release. **11** stock, keep, have in stock, sell, offer, trade in, deal in, take, have. **14 c** win, take, sweep, carry off *or* away, capture, gain, secure, pick up, *colloq.* walk away *or* off with. **15** see SUPPORT *v.* 1, 2. **16** be pregnant with, be expecting, *literary or Zool.* be gravid with. □ **carry away 1** see REMOVE *v.* 2a. **2** see INSPIRE 1, 2. **carry back** take back, remind. **carry conviction** be convincing, hold up, stand up, carry weight, bear scrutiny, hold water. **carry the day** see TRIUMPH *v.* 1. **carrying-on** (or **carryings-on**) **1** see PALAVER *n.* 1. **3** see AFFAIR 3. **carry off 1** abscond with, take (away), make away *or* off with, run off with, spirit off *or* away, whisk away *or* off, cart off, drag away, kidnap, abduct. **2** win, gain, capture, secure, pick up, take, *colloq.* walk away *or* off with. **3** kill (off), be *or* cause the death of, cause to die, put out of one's misery, *colloq.* finish off. **4** accomplish, achieve, perform, effect, effectuate, do, execute, succeed in *or* with, handle, manage, work, bring off, carry out *or* through, pull off. **carry on 1** continue, go on, keep on; keep (on) going, last, remain; persist, persevere, push *or* press on. **2** engage in, be involved *or* busy *or* absorbed in, occupy oneself with; follow, pursue, prosecute; manage, conduct, operate, run, administer, proceed with, transact. **carry out** perform, carry on *or* through, continue, implement, administer, transact, put into practice, see through, execute, discharge, prosecute, effect, complete, accomplish, conclude. **carry over 2** see POSTPONE. **carry through 1** see ACCOMPLISH, *carry out* above.

carryall /káreeawl/ *n.* **1** a large bag or case. **2** a light carriage (cf. CARIOLE). **3** a car with seats placed sideways.
■ **3** see CASE[2] *n.* 4.

carryout /káreeowt/ *n. & adj.* ● *n.* **1** food prepared and packaged for consumption elsewhere than the place of sale. **2** an establishment that sells such food. ● *adj.* of or designating such foods.

carryover /káreeōvər/ *n.* **1** something carried over. **2** *Stock Exch.* postponement to the next settling day.

carse /kaars/ *n. Sc.* fertile lowland beside a river. [ME, perh. f. *carrs* swamps]

carsick /káarsik/ *adj.* affected with nausea caused by the motion of a car. □□ **carsickness** *n.*

cart /kaart/ *n. & v.* ● *n.* **1** a strong vehicle with two or four wheels for carrying loads, usu. drawn by a horse. **2** a light vehicle for pulling by hand. **3** a light vehicle with two wheels for driving in, drawn by a single horse. ● *v.tr.* **1** convey in or as in a cart. **2** *sl.* carry (esp. a cumbersome thing) with difficulty or over a long distance (*carted it all the way home*). □ **cart horse** a thickset horse suitable for heavy work. **cart off** remove, esp. by force. **cartwright** a maker of carts. **put the cart before the horse 1** reverse the proper order or procedure. **2** take an effect for a cause. □□ **carter** *n.* **cartful** *n.* (*pl.* **-fuls**). [ME f. ON *kartr* cart & OE *cræt*, prob. infl. by AF & ONF *carete* dimin. of *carre* CAR]

■ *n.* **1** dray, trailer, wagon, *hist.* tumbrel. **2** handcart, pushcart, trolley, *Brit.* barrow. **3** cariole, *Brit.* float.
● *v.* **2** carry, lug, drag, haul, transport, *colloq.* schlep, hump, tote. □ **cart off** see *carry off* 1.

cartage /káartij/ *n.* the price paid for carting.

carte var. of QUART 4.

carte blanche /kaart blónsh, blánch/ *n.* full discretionary power given to a person. [F, = blank paper]
■ license, free rein, permission, sanction, warrant, freedom, free hand, liberty, power, authority, discretion, *colloq.* blank check.

cartel /kaartél/ *n.* **1** an informal association of manufacturers or suppliers to maintain prices at a high level, and control production, marketing arrangements, etc. **2** a political combination between parties. □□ **cartelize** /káartəliz/ *v.tr.* & *intr.* [G *Kartell* f. F *cartel* f. It. *cartello* dimin. of *carta* CARD[1]]
■ **1** see SYNDICATE *n.*

Cartesian /kaarteézhən/ *adj. & n.* ● *adj.* of or relating to R. Descartes, 17th-c. French philosopher and mathematician. ● *n.* a follower of Descartes. □ **Cartesian coordinates** a system for locating a point by reference to its distance from two or three axes intersecting at right angles. □□ **Cartesianism** *n.* [mod.L *Cartesianus* f. *Cartesius*, name of *Descartes*]

Carthusian /kaarthōōzhən/ *n. & adj.* ● *n.* a monk of a contemplative order founded by St. Bruno in 1084. ● *adj.* of or relating to this order. [med.L *Carthusianus* f. L *Cart(h)usia* Chartreuse, near Grenoble]

cartilage /káart'lij/ *n.* gristle; a firm flexible connective tissue forming the infant skeleton, which is mainly replaced by bone in adulthood. □□ **cartilaginoid** /-lájinoyd/ *adj.* **cartilaginous** /-lájinəs/ *adj.* [F f. L *cartilago* -*ginis*]
■ □□ **cartilaginoid, cartilaginous** see TOUGH *adj.* 1.

cartload /káartlōd/ *n.* **1** an amount filling a cart. **2** esp. *Brit.* a large quantity of anything.
■ **2** see LOT *n.* 1.

cartogram /káartəgram/ *n.* a map with diagrammatic statistical information. [F *cartogramme* f. *carte* map, card]

cartography /kaartógrəfee/ *n.* the science or practice of map drawing. □□ **cartographer** *n.* **cartographic** /-təgráfik/ *adj.* **cartographical** *adj.* [F *cartographie* f. *carte* map, card]

cartomancy /káartəmansee/ *n.* fortune-telling by interpreting a random selection of playing cards. [F *cartomancie* f. *carte* CARD[1]]

/. . . / **pronunciation**	● **part of speech**
□ **phrases, idioms, and compounds**	
□□ **derivatives**	■ **synonym section**
cross-references appear in SMALL CAPITALS or *italics*	

carton /kaárt'n/ *n.* a light box or container, esp. one made of cardboard. [F (as CARTOON)]
■ see BOX¹ *n.* 1, 2a.

cartoon /kaartŏŏn/ *n. & v.* ● *n.* **1** a humorous drawing in a newspaper, magazine, etc., esp. as a topical comment. **2** a sequence of drawings, often with speech indicated, telling a story; comic strip. **3** a filmed sequence of drawings using the technique of animation. **4** a full-size drawing as an artist's preliminary design for a painting, tapestry, mosaic, etc. ● *v.* **1** *tr.* draw a cartoon of. **2** *intr.* draw cartoons. □□ **cartoonist** *n.* [It. *cartone* f. *carta* CARD¹]

cartouche /kaartŏŏsh/ *n.* **1 a** *Archit.* a scroll-like ornament, e.g., the volute of an Ionic capital. **b** a tablet imitating, or a drawing of, a scroll with rolled-up ends, used ornamentally or bearing an inscription. **c** an ornate frame. **2** *Archaeol.* an oval ring enclosing Egyptian hieroglyphs, usu. representing the name and title of a king. [F, = cartridge, f. It. *cartoccio* f. *carta* CARD¹]
■ **2** see SIGN *n.* 2.

cartridge /kaártrij/ *n.* **1** a case containing a charge of propelling explosive for firearms or blasting, with a bullet or shot if for small arms. **2** a spool of film, magnetic tape, etc., in a sealed container ready for insertion. **3** a component carrying the stylus on the pickup head of a record player. **4** an ink container for insertion in a pen. □ **cartridge belt** a belt with pockets or loops for cartridges (in sense 1). [corrupt. of CARTOUCHE (but recorded earlier)]
■ **1** see SHELL *n.* 2.

cartwheel /kaárt-hweel, -weel/ *n.* **1** the (usu. spoked) wheel of a cart. **2** a circular sideways handspring with the arms and legs extended.

caruncle /kərúngkəl, kárung-/ *n.* **1** *Zool.* a fleshy excrescence, e.g., a male turkey's wattles or the red prominence at the inner angle of the eye. **2** *Bot.* an outgrowth from a seed near the micropyle. □□ **caruncular** /kərúngkyələr/ *adj.* [obs. F f. L *caruncula* f. *caro carnis* flesh]

carve /kaarv/ *v.* **1** *tr.* produce or shape (a statue, representation in relief, etc.) by cutting into a hard material (*carved a figure out of rock*; *carved it in wood*). **2** *tr.* **a** cut patterns, designs, letters, etc., in (hard material). **b** (foll. by *into*) form a pattern, design, etc., from (*carved it into a bust*). **c** (foll. by *with*) cover or decorate (material) with figures or designs cut in it. **3** *tr.* (*absol.*) cut (meat, etc.) into slices for eating. □ **carve out 1** take from a larger whole. **2** establish (a career, etc.) purposefully (*carved out a name for themselves*). **carve up** divide into several pieces; subdivide (territory, etc.). **carve-up** *n. Brit. sl.* a sharing, esp. of spoils. **carving knife** a knife with a long blade, for carving meat. [OE *ceorfan* cut f. WG]
■ **1, 2** hew, cut, sculpt, sculpture, shape, chisel, model, fashion, whittle, chip; engrave, incise, inscribe, *archaic* grave; chase, enchase. **3** slice, cut. □ **carve out 2** see ESTABLISH 1, FORGE¹ 3. **carve up** divide (up), cut (up), subdivide, partition, split (up); share (out), apportion, parcel out, allot.

carvel /kaárvəl/ *n.* var. of CARAVEL. □ **carvel-built** (of a boat) made with planks flush, not overlapping (cf. CLINKER-BUILT). [as CARAVEL]

carven /kaárvən/ *archaic past part.* of CARVE.

Carver /kaárvər/ *n.* (in full **Carver chair**) a chair with arms, a rush seat, and a back having horizontal and vertical spindles. [J. *Carver*, first governor of Plymouth Colony, d. 1621, for whom a prototype was allegedly made]

carver /kaárvər/ *n.* **1** a person who carves. **2 a** a carving knife. **b** (in *pl.*) a knife and fork for carving. **3** *Brit.* the principal chair, with arms, in a set of dining chairs, intended for the person who carves. ¶ To be distinguished (in sense 3) from *Carver.*

carvery /kaárvəree/ *n.* (*pl.* **-ies**) esp. *Brit.* a buffet or restaurant with cuts of meat displayed, and carved as required, in front of customers.

carving /kaárving/ *n.* a carved object, esp. as a work of art.

caryatid /káreeátid/ *n.* (*pl.* **caryatids** or **caryatides** /-deez/) *Archit.* a pillar in the form of a draped female figure,

supporting an entablature. [F *caryatide* f. It. *cariatide* or L f. Gk *karuatis -idos* priestess at Caryae (*Karuai*) in Laconia]
■ see STATUE.

caryopsis /káreeópsis/ *n.* (*pl.* **caryopses** /-seez/) *Bot.* a dry, one-seeded indehiscent fruit, as in wheat and corn. [mod.L f. Gk *karuon* nut + *opsis* appearance]

Casanova /kásənōvə/ *n.* a man notorious for seducing women. [G. J. *Casanova* de Seingalt, It. adventurer d. 1798]
■ see *philanderer* (PHILANDER).

Casbah /kázbaa, kaáz-/ *n.* (also **Kasbah**) **1** the citadel of a N. African city. **2** an Arab quarter near this. [F *casbah* f. Arab. *Kas(a)ba* citadel]

cascade /kaskáyd/ *n. & v.* ● *n.* **1** a small waterfall, esp. forming one in a series or part of a large broken waterfall. **2** a succession of electrical devices or stages in a process. **3** a quantity of material, etc., draped in descending folds. ● *v.intr.* fall in or like a cascade. [F f. It. *cascata* f. *cascare* to fall ult. f. L *casus*: see CASE¹]
■ *n.* **1** see WATERFALL. ● *v.* see STREAM *v.* 1.

cascara /kaskárə/ *n.* (in full **cascara sagrada** /səgraádə/) the bark of a California buckthorn, *Rhamnus purshiana*, used as a purgative. [Sp., = sacred bark]

case¹ /kays/ *n.* **1** an instance of something occurring. **2** a state of affairs, hypothetical or actual. **3 a** an instance of a person receiving professional guidance, e.g., from a doctor or social worker. **b** this person or the circumstances involved. **4** a matter under official investigation, esp. by the police. **5** *Law* **a** a cause or suit for trial. **b** a statement of the facts in a cause sub judice, drawn up for a higher court's consideration (*judge states a case*). **c** a cause that has been decided and may be cited (*leading case*). **6 a** the sum of the arguments on one side, esp. in a lawsuit (*that is our case*). **b** a set of arguments, esp. in relation to persuasiveness (*have a good case*; *have a weak case*). **c** a valid set of arguments (*have no case*). **7** *Gram.* **a** the relation of a word to other words in a sentence. **b** a form of a noun, adjective, or pronoun expressing this. **8** *colloq.* a comical person. **9** the position or circumstances in which one is. □ **as the case may be** according to the situation. **case history** information about a person for use in professional treatment, e.g., by a doctor. **case law** the law as established by the outcome of former cases (cf. *common law, statute law*). **case study 1** an attempt to understand a person, institution, etc., from collected information. **2** a record of such an attempt. **3** the use of a particular instance as an exemplar of general principles. **in any case** whatever the truth is; whatever may happen. **in case 1** in the event that; if. **2** lest; in provision against a stated or implied possibility (*take an umbrella in case it rains*; *took it in case*). **in case of** in the event of. **in the case of** as regards. **in no case** under no circumstances. **in that case** if that is true; should that happen. **is** (or **is not**) **the case** is (or is not) so. [ME f. OF *cas* f. L *casus* fall f. *cadere* cas-to fall]
■ **1** instance, example, specimen, illustration. **2, 9** happening, occasion, event, occurrence, (set of) circumstance(s), state (of affairs), situation, eventuality, contingency, position. **3 b** patient, client; subject. **5 a** action, suit, lawsuit, dispute; cause. **6 a, b** see ARGUMENT 2. □ **in any case** in any event, come what may, at all events, at any rate, anyhow, anyway, regardless, just the same, for all that; always. **in case 1** if, in the event that, if it happens *or* proves *or* turns out that. **2** lest, for fear that. **in the case of** as regards, regarding, in the matter of, with respect *or* regard to, re. **in no case** see NEVER 1b, 2. **is** (or **is not**) **the case** is (not) so, is (not) the fact *or* actuality *or* truth *or* reality, is (not) what really happened *or* happens *or* took place *or* takes place.

case² /kays/ *n. & v.* ● *n.* **1** a container or covering serving to enclose or contain. **2** a container with its contents. **3** the outer protective covering of a watch, book, seed vessel, sausage, etc. **4** an item of luggage, esp. a suitcase. **5** *Printing* a partitioned receptacle for type. **6** a glass box for showing specimens, curiosities, etc. ● *v.tr.* **1** enclose in a case. **2** (foll. by *with*) surround. **3** *sl.* reconnoiter (a house, etc.), esp. with a view to robbery. □ **case-harden 1** harden the surface of, esp. give a steel surface to (iron) by carbonizing. **2** make callous. **case knife** a knife carried in a sheath. **case shot 1** bullets in an iron case fired from a cannon. **2** shrapnel. [ME f. OF *casse, chasse,* f. L *capsa* f. *capere* hold]

■ *n.* **1, 3** box, container, carton, crate, chest, holder, receptacle, casket, caddy; shell, husk, skin, shuck; covering, cover, casing, housing, outside, envelope, wrapper, protection, shield. **4** piece of luggage *or* baggage, bag, trunk, carryall, suitcase, grip, valise, esp. *Brit.* hold-all, *sl.* keister. ● *v.* **1** encase, box; crate, pack, package, containerize, contain; house, cover, wrap, envelop, enclose. **3** see RECONNOITER *v.*

casebook /káysbook/ *n.* a book containing a record of legal or medical cases.

casebound /káysbownd/ *adj.* (of a book) in a hard cover.

casein /káyseen, káyseein/ *n.* the main protein in milk, esp. in coagulated form as in cheese. [L *caseus* cheese]

caseinogen /kaysínəjən/ *n.* the soluble form of casein as it occurs in milk.

caseload /káyslōd/ *n.* the cases with which a lawyer, doctor, etc., is concerned at one time.

casemate /káysmayt/ *n.* **1** a chamber in the thickness of the wall of a fortress, with embrasures. **2** an armored enclosure for guns on a warship. [F *casemate* & It. *casamatta* or Sp. *-mata,* f. *camata,* perh. f. Gk *khasma -atos* gap]

casement /káysmənt/ *n.* **1** a window or part of a window hinged vertically to open like a door. **2** *poet.* a window. [ME f. AL *cassimentum* f. *cassa* CASE²]

casework /káyswərk/ *n.* social work concerned with individuals, esp. involving understanding of the client's family and background. □□ **caseworker** *n.*

cash¹ /kash/ *n. & v.* ● *n.* **1** money in coins or bills, as distinct from checks or orders. **2** (also **cash down**) money paid as full payment at the time of purchase, as distinct from credit. **3** *colloq.* wealth. ● *v.tr.* give or obtain cash for (a note, check, etc.). □ **cash and carry 1** a system in which goods are paid for in cash and taken away by the purchaser. **2** a store where this system operates. **cash cow** a business, product, etc., generating steady profits that are usu. used to fund other enterprises. **cash crop** a crop produced for sale, not for use as food, etc. **cash desk** *Brit.* a counter or compartment in a shop where goods are paid for; checkout counter. **cash flow** the movement of money into and out of a business, as a measure of profitability, or as affecting liquidity. **cash in 1** obtain cash for. **2** *colloq.* (usu. foll. by *on*) profit (from); take advantage (of). **3** *Brit.* pay into a bank, etc. **4** (in full **cash in one's chips**) *colloq.* die. **cash machine** = *automated teller machine.* **cash on delivery** a system of paying the carrier for goods when they are delivered. **cash register** a machine in a store, etc., with a drawer for money, recording the amount of each sale, totaling receipts, etc. **cash up** *Brit.* count and check cash takings at the end of a day's trading. □□ **cashable** *adj.* **cashless** *adj.* [obs. F *casse* box or It. *cassa* f. L *capsa* CASE²]

■ *n.* **1** money, currency, funds, bills, change, hard cash, specie, coin of the realm, purse, *colloq.* shekels, *derog. or joc.* pelf, *sl.* moolah, dough, bread, loot, spondulicks, ready, scratch, stuff, doubloons, green(s), jack, kale, rock, *Brit.* notes, banknotes, *Brit. sl.* lolly, brass, tin. **3** see WEALTH 1. ● *v.* cash in, redeem, exchange; realize. □ **cash in 1** see CASH *v.* above. **2** see PROFIT *v.* 2. **4** see DIE¹ 1. **cash register** register, till, money box, cash box.

cash² /kash/ *n.* (*pl.* same) *hist.* any of various small coins of China or the E. Indies. [ult. f. Port. *ca(i)xa* f. Tamil *kāsu* f. Skr. *karsha*]

cashbook /kashbook/ *n.* a book in which receipts and payments of cash are recorded.

cashew /káshōō, kashōō/ *n.* **1** a bushy evergreen tree, *Anacardium occidentale,* native to Central and S. America, bearing kidney-shaped nuts attached to fleshy fruits. **2** (in full **cashew nut**) the edible nut of this tree. □ **cashew apple** the edible fleshy fruit of this tree. [Port. f. Tupi *(a)caju*]

cashier¹ /kasheér/ *n.* a person dealing with cash transactions

in a store, bank, etc. □ **cashier's check** a check drawn by a bank on its own funds and signed by a cashier of the bank. [Du. *cassier* or F *caissier* (as CASH¹)]

■ see BOOKKEEPER.

cashier² /kasheér/ *v.tr.* dismiss from service, esp. from the armed forces with disgrace. [Flem. *kasseren* disband, revoke, f. F *casser* f. L *quassare* QUASH]

■ see DISMISS 2.

cashmere /kázhmeer, kásh-/ *n.* **1** a fine soft wool, esp. that of a Kashmir goat. **2** a material made from this. [*Kashmir* in Asia]

casing /káysing/ *n.* **1** a protective or enclosing cover or shell. **2** the material for this.

■ **1** see HOUSING¹ 3.

casino /kəseenō/ *n.* (*pl.* **-os**) a public room or building for gambling. [It., dimin. of *casa* house f. L *casa* cottage]

cask /kask/ *n.* **1** a large barrellike container made of wood, metal, or plastic, esp. one for alcoholic liquor. **2** its contents. **3** its capacity. [F *casque* or Sp. *casco* helmet]

■ see KEG.

casket /káskit/ *n.* **1 a** a coffin, esp. a rectangular one. **b** a small wooden box for cremated ashes. **2** a small, often ornamental box or chest for jewels, letters, etc. [perh. f. AF form of OF *cassette* f. It. *cassetta* dimin. of *cassa* f. L *capsa* CASE²]

■ **1** chest, box, container, case, coffer, receptacle.

casque /kask/ *n.* **1** *hist.* or *poet.* a helmet. **2** *Zool.* a helmetlike structure, e.g., the process on the bill of the cassowary. [F f. Sp. *casco*]

Cassandra /kəsándrə/ *n.* a prophet of disaster, esp. one who is disregarded. [L f. Gk *Kassandra,* daughter of Priam King of Troy: she was condemned by Apollo to prophesy correctly but not be believed]

■ see KILLJOY.

cassation /kasáyshən/ *n. Mus.* an informal instrumental composition of the 18th c., similar to a divertimento and orig. often for outdoor performance. [It. *cassazione*]

cassava /kəsaávə/ *n.* **1 a** any plant of the genus *Manihot,* esp. the cultivated varieties *M. esculenta* (**bitter cassava**) and *M. dulcis* (**sweet cassava**), having starchy tuberous roots. **b** the roots themselves. **2** a starch or flour obtained from these roots. Also called TAPIOCA, MANIOC. [earlier *cas(s)avi,* etc., f. Taino *casavi,* infl. by F *cassave*]

casserole /káserōl/ *n. & v.* ● *n.* **1** a covered dish, usu. of earthenware or glass, in which food is cooked, esp. slowly in the oven. **2** food cooked in a casserole. ● *v.tr.* cook in a casserole. [F f. *cassole* dimin. of *casse* f. Prov. *casa* f. LL *cattia* ladle, pan f. Gk *kuathion* dimin. of *kuathos* cup]

■ *n.* **1** see PAN¹ *n.* 1. **2** see STEW¹ *n.* 1. ● *v.* see STEW¹ *v.* 1.

cassette /kəsét, ka-/ *n.* a sealed case containing a length of tape, ribbon, etc., ready for insertion in a machine, esp.: **1** a length of magnetic tape wound on to spools, ready for insertion in a tape recorder. **2** a length of photographic film, ready for insertion in a camera. [F, dimin. of *casse* CASE²]

■ **1** see TAPE *n.* 4.

cassia /káshə/ *n.* **1** any tree of the genus *Cassia,* bearing leaves from which senna is extracted. **2** the cinnamonlike bark of this tree used as a spice. [L f. Gk *kasia* f. Heb. *k̤ṣî'āh* bark like cinnamon]

cassis /kaseés/ *n.* a syrupy usu. alcoholic black-currant flavoring for drinks, etc. [F, = black currant]

cassiterite /kəsítərit/ *n.* a naturally occurring ore of tin dioxide, from which tin is extracted. Also called TINSTONE. [Gk *kassiteros* tin]

cassock /kásək/ *n.* a long, close-fitting, usu. black or red garment worn by clergy, members of choirs, etc. □□ **cassocked** *adj.* [F *casaque* long coat f. It. *casacca* horseman's coat, prob. f. Turkic: cf. COSSACK]

/.../ pronunciation	● **part of speech**
□ **phrases, idioms, and compounds**	
□□ **derivatives**	■ **synonym section**
cross-references appear in SMALL CAPITALS or *italics*	

cassoulet /kasŏŏláy/ *n.* a stew of meat and beans. [F, dimin. of dial. *cassolo* stew pan]

cassowary /kásəwairee/ *n.* (*pl.* **-ies**) any large flightless Australasian bird of the genus *Casuarius*, with heavy body, stout legs, a wattled neck, and a bony crest on its forehead. [Malay *kasuārī, kasavārī*]

cast /kast/ *v. & n.* ● *v.* (*past* and *past part.* **cast**) **1** *tr.* throw, esp. deliberately or forcefully. **2** *tr.* (often foll. by *on, over*) **a** direct or cause to fall (one's eyes, a glance, light, a shadow, a spell, etc.). **b** express (doubts, aspersions, etc.). **3** *tr.* throw out (a fishing line) into the water. **4** *tr.* let down (an anchor, etc.). **5** *tr.* **a** throw off, get rid of. **b** shed (skin, etc.) esp. in the process of growth. **c** (of a horse) lose (a shoe). **6** *tr.* record, register, or give (a vote). **7** *tr.* **a** shape (molten metal or plastic material) in a mold. **b** make (a product) in this way. **8** *tr. Printing* make (type). **9** *tr.* **a** (usu. foll. by *as*) assign (an actor) to play a particular character. **b** allocate roles in (a play, motion picture, etc.). **10** *tr.* (foll. by *in, into*) arrange or formulate (facts, etc.) in a specified form. **11** *tr. & intr.* reckon; add up; calculate (accounts or figures). **12** *tr.* calculate and record details of (a horoscope). ● *n.* **1 a** the throwing of a missile, etc. **b** the distance reached by this. **2** a throw or a number thrown at dice. **3** a throw of a net, fishing line, etc. **4** *Fishing* **a** that which is cast, esp. the line with hook and fly. **b** a place for casting (*a good cast*). **5 a** an object of metal, clay, etc., made in a mold. **b** a molded mass of solidified material, esp. plaster protecting a broken limb. **6** the actors taking part in a play, motion picture, etc. **7** form, type, or quality (*cast of features*; *cast of mind*). **8** a tinge or shade of color. **9 a** (in full **cast in the eye**) a slight squint. **b** a twist or inclination. **10 a** a mass of earth excreted by a worm. **b** a mass of indigestible food thrown up by a hawk, owl, etc. **11** the form into which any work is thrown or arranged. **12 a** a wide area covered by a dog or pack to find a trail. **b** *Austral. & NZ* a wide sweep made by a sheepdog in mustering sheep. □ **cast about** (or **around**) make an extensive search (actually or mentally) (*cast about for a solution*). **cast adrift** leave to drift. **cast ashore** (of waves, etc.) throw to the shore. **cast aside** give up using; abandon. **cast away 1** reject. **2** (in *passive*) be shipwrecked (cf. CAST-AWAY). **cast one's bread upon the waters** see BREAD. **cast down** depress; deject (cf. DOWNCAST). **casting vote** (or **voice**) a deciding vote usu. given by the chairperson when the votes on two sides are equal. ¶ From an obsolete sense of *cast* = turn the scale. **cast iron** a hard alloy of iron, carbon, and silicon cast in a mold. **cast-iron** *adj.* **1** made of cast iron. **2** hard; unchallengeable; unchangeable. **cast loose** detach; detach oneself. **cast lots** see LOT. **cast off 1** abandon. **2** *Knitting* take the stitches off the needle by looping each over the next to finish the edge. **3** *Naut.* **a** set a ship free from a mooring, etc. **b** loosen and throw off (rope, etc.). **4** *Printing* estimate the space that will be taken in print by manuscript copy. **cast-off** abandoned; discarded. **cast on** *Knitting* make the first row of loops on the needle. **cast out** expel. **cast up 1** (of the sea) deposit on the shore. **2** add up (figures, etc.). [ME f. ON *kasta*]

■ *v.* **1** throw, toss, pitch, fling, let fly, sling, hurl, bowl, launch, discharge, dash, send, shoot, shy, *colloq.* chuck. **2 a** see DIRECT *v.* 4, SHED² 5. **5 a** see *throw off*. **b** see SHED² 1. **7** shape, mold, form, fashion. **9 a** give *or* assign the part; appoint, designate, name, nominate, choose, pick, select. **10** see FORMULATE 1. **11** see CALCULATE 1. ● *n.* **1 a** throw, toss, pitch, shy, lob, hurl, *colloq.* chuck. **5 a** model, casting, mold, plaster cast. **6** actors and actresses, players, performers, troupe, company, act. **7** form, shape, mold, cut, figure; stamp, type, quality, character, nature, kind, sort, brand, style, genre, class, variety, strain, fiber; turn, inclination, bent. **8** tinge, tint, shade, tone, coloring, color; hint, touch, suggestion. **9 b** twist, turn, inclination, bend, kink, tilt, bias, irregularity, warp. **11** organization, structure, pattern, formation, formulation, arrangement, grouping, form, layout, makeup, composition, array, categorization, systematization, classification. □ **cast about** (*cast about*

for) search for, look (around) for, seek. **cast aside** reject, discard, cast *or* throw away, cast *or* throw out, dispense with, get rid of, dispose of, abandon; see also REJECT *v.* 1. **cast away 1** see REJECT *v.* 3 **2** (*be cast away*) be marooned *or* shipwrecked. **cast down** see DEPRESS 2. **cast-iron 2** see SOLID *adj.* 4, 6a. **cast loose** see DETACH 1. **cast off 1** see ABANDON *v.* 2a. **cast-off** (*adj.*) see ABANDONED 1a; (*n.*) see REJECT *n.* **cast out** expel, drive *or* force *or* throw *or* fling *or* push *or* turn out, kick *or* boot out, evict, eject, oust, exile, banish, remove, *colloq.* chuck out, *sl.* bounce. **cast up 1** throw *or* bring up, deposit. **2** see ADD 2.

castanet /kástənét/ *n.* (usu. in *pl.*) a small concave piece of hardwood, ivory, etc., in pairs held in the hands and clicked together by the fingers as a rhythmic accompaniment, esp. by Spanish dancers. [Sp. *castañeta* dimin. of *castaña* f. L *castanea* chestnut]

castaway /kástəway/ *n. & adj.* ● *n.* a shipwrecked person. ● *adj.* **1** shipwrecked. **2** cast aside; rejected.
■ *adj.* **1** shipwrecked, marooned, stranded. **2** see ABANDONED 1a.

caste /kast/ *n.* **1** any of the Hindu hereditary classes, distinguished by relative degrees of purity or pollution, whose members are socially equal with one another and often follow the same occupations. **2** a more or less exclusive social class. **3** a system of such classes. **4** the position it confers. **5** *Zool.* a form of social insect having a particular function. □ **caste mark** a symbol usu. on the forehead denoting a person's caste. **lose caste** descend in the social order. [Sp. and Port. *casta* lineage, race, breed, fem. of *casto* pure, CHASTE]
■ **1, 2** (social) class, order, level, stratum, rank, station, *archaic or literary* estate. **4** standing, position, status, rank.

casteism /kástizəm/ *n.* often *derog.* the caste system.

castellan /kástələn/ *n. hist.* the governor of a castle. [ME f. ONF *castelain* f. med.L *castellanus*: see CASTLE]

castellated /kástəlaytid/ *adj.* **1** having battlements. **2** castlelike. □□ **castellation** /-láyshən/ *n.* [med.L *castellatus*: see CASTLE]

caster /kástər/ *n.* (also *Brit.* **castor**) **1** a small swiveled wheel (often one of a set) fixed to a leg (or the underside) of a piece of furniture. **2** a small container with holes in the top for sprinkling the contents. **3** a person who casts. **4** a machine for casting type. □ **caster action** swiveling of vehicle wheels to ensure stability. **caster sugar** finely granulated white sugar.

castigate /kástigayt/ *v.tr.* rebuke or punish severely. □□ **castigation** /-gáyshən/ *n.* **castigator** *n.* **castigatory** /-gətáwree/ *adj.* [L *castigare* reprove f. *castus* pure]
■ chastise, rebuke, scold, reprimand, berate, upbraid, reproach, call down, drop on, pull up, read the riot act to, lecture, tear into, keelhaul, haul *or* call over the coals, rap a person's knuckles, give a rating to, give a piece of one's mind to, strafe, criticize, *archaic or literary* chide, *colloq.* tell off, dress down, bawl out, blast, carpet, haul *or* call on the carpet, give a person an earful, give a person a dressing-down *or* talking-to *or* telling-off *or Brit.* wigging, give a person what for, slap (down), esp. *Brit.* tick off, row, *colloq.* chew out; punish, discipline, chasten, correct, penalize.

castile soap /kasteél/ *n.* a fine, hard, white or mottled soap made with olive oil and soda. [as CASTILIAN]

Castilian /kəstílyən/ *n. & adj.* ● *n.* **1** a native of Castile in Spain. **2** the language of Castile, standard spoken and literary Spanish. ● *adj.* of or relating to Castile.

casting /kásting/ *n.* an object made by casting, esp. of molten metal.
■ see STATUE.

castle /kásəl/ *n. & v.* ● *n.* **1 a** a large fortified building or group of buildings; a stronghold. **b** a formerly fortified mansion. **2** *Chess* = ROOK². ● *v. Chess* **1** *intr.* make a special move (once only in a game on each side) in which the king is moved two squares along the back rank and the nearer rook is moved to the square passed over by the king. **2** *tr.*

move (the king) by castling. □ **castles in the air** (or **in Spain**) a visionary unattainable scheme; a daydream. □□ **castled** adj. [AF & ONF castel, chastel f. L castellum dimin. of castrum fort]

■ n. **1 a** fortress, stronghold, citadel, fastness, tower. **b** mansion, palace, manor house, manor, hall, château, Brit. stately home. □ **castles in the air** (or **in Spain**) see daydream n.

castoff /kástawf/ n. a cast-off thing, esp. a garment.

castor[1] Brit. var. of CASTER 1 & 2.

castor[2] /kástər/ n. **1** an oily substance secreted by beavers and used in medicine and perfumes. **2** a beaver. [F or L f. Gk kastōr beaver]

castor oil /kástər/ n. **1** an oil from the seeds of a plant, Ricinus communis, used as a purgative and lubricant. **2** (in full **castor-oil plant**) this plant. □ **castor-oil bean** (or **castor bean**) a seed of the castor-oil plant. [18th c.: orig. uncert.: perh. so called as having succeeded CASTOR[2] in the medical sense]

castrate /kástrayt/ v.tr. **1** remove the testicles of; geld. **2** deprive of vigor. □□ **castration** /-tráyshən/ n. **castrator** n. [L castrare]

■ **1** see NEUTER v.

castrato /kastraátō/ n. (pl. **castrati** /-tee/) hist. a male singer castrated in boyhood so as to retain a soprano or alto voice. [It., past part. of castrare: see CASTRATE]

casual /kázhōōəl/ adj. & n. ● adj. **1** accidental; due to chance. **2** not regular nor permanent; temporary; occasional (casual work; a casual affair). **3 a** unconcerned; uninterested (was very casual about it). **b** made or done without great care or thought (a casual remark). **c** acting carelessly or unmethodically. **4** (of clothes) informal. ● n. **1** a casual worker. **2** (usu. in pl.) casual clothes or shoes. □□ **casually** adv. **casualness** n. [ME f. OF casuel & L casualis f. casus CASE[1]]

■ adj. **1** accidental, chance, coincidental, adventitious, aleatoric, aleatory, random, incidental, spontaneous, fortuitous, unexpected, impromptu, unforeseen, unpremeditated, unplanned, unlooked-for, unforeseeable, unpredictable, serendipitous, haphazard. **2** occasional, temporary, part-time, impermanent, makeshift, stopgap, irregular, intermittent; superficial, passing, transient, fleeting. **3 a** indifferent, nonchalant, offhand, lax, insouciant, apathetic, cool, unconcerned, unbothered, uninterested, dispassionate, blasé, blithe, relaxed, lackadaisical, indiscriminate, colloq. laid-back. **b** thoughtless, unthinking, offhand, extempore, careless, cursory, passing, stray, ill-considered, ill-judged, inadvertent, unguarded, unpremeditated, hasty, colloq. off the cuff. **c** unmethodical, unsystematic, unsystematized, disorderly, disordered, disorganized, unorganized, haphazard, sporadic, erratic, chaotic, confused, careless, hit-or-miss, colloq. slaphappy. **4** see INFORMAL. ● n. **1** freelance, freelancer; temporary, colloq. temp.

casualty /kázhōōəltee/ n. (pl. **-ies**) **1** a person killed or injured in a war or accident. **2** a thing lost or destroyed. **3** (in full **casualty department**) Brit. a hospital emergency room. **4** an accident, mishap, or disaster. [ME f. med.L casualitas (as CASUAL), after ROYALTY, etc.]

■ **1** victim, fatality, death; (casualties) wounded, injured, dead, Mil. missing in action, losses. **4** disaster, catastrophe, calamity, tragedy; accident, mischance, misfortune, misadventure, mishap.

casuarina /kázhōōərínə/ n. any tree of the genus Casuarina, native to Australia and SE Asia, having tiny, scalelike leaves on slender, jointed branches, resembling gigantic horsetails. [mod.L casuarius cassowary (from the resemblance between branches and feathers)]

casuist /kázhōōist/ n. **1** a person, esp. a theologian, who resolves problems of conscience, duty, etc., often with clever but false reasoning. **2** a sophist or quibbler. □□ **casuistic** adj. **casuistical** adj. **casuistically** adv. **casuistry** /kázhōōə-stree/ n. [F casuiste f. Sp. casuista f. L casus CASE[1]]

■ □□ **casuistic, casuistical** see SPECIOUS.

casus belli /káysəs bélī, kaásəs bélee/ n. an act or situation provoking or justifying war. [L]

CAT /kat/ abbr. **1** Med. computerized axial tomography. **2** clear-air turbulence.

cat /kat/ n. & v. ● n. **1** a small, soft-furred, four-legged domesticated animal, Felis catus or F. domestica. **2 a** any wild animal of the genus Felis, e.g., a lion, tiger, or leopard. **b** = WILDCAT 2. **3** a catlike animal of any other species (civet cat). **4** colloq. a malicious or spiteful woman. **5** sl. a jazz enthusiast. **6** Naut. = CATHEAD. **7** = cat-o'-nine-tails. **8** Brit. a short, tapered stick in the game of tipcat. ● v.tr. (also absol.) (**catted, catting**) Naut. raise (an anchor) from the surface of the water to the cathead. □ **cat-and-dog** (of a relationship, etc.) full of quarrels. **cat-and-mouse** of or similar to behavior like that of a cat toying with a mouse, in which the prey is uncertain of when the predator will strike. **cat burglar** a burglar who enters by climbing to an upper story. **cat door** a small swinging flap in an outer door, for a cat to pass in and out. **cat-o'-nine-tails** hist. a rope whip with nine knotted lashes for flogging sailors, soldiers, or criminals. **cat's cradle** a child's game in which a loop of string is held between the fingers and patterns are formed. **cat's-eye** a precious stone of Sri Lanka and Malabar. **cat's-foot** any small plant of the genus Antennaria, having soft woolly leaves and growing on the surface of the ground. **cat's-paw 1** a person used as a tool by another. **2** a slight breeze rippling the surface of the water. **let the cat out of the bag** reveal a secret, esp. involuntarily. **rain cats and dogs** colloq. rain very hard. [OE catt(e) f. LL cattus]

■ □ **cat-o'-nine-tails** see WHIP n. **cat's-paw 1** see BUTT[2].

cata- /kátə/ prefix (usu. **cat-** before a vowel or h) **1** down; downward (catadromous). **2** wrongly; badly (catachresis). [Gk kata down]

catabolism /kətábəlizəm/ n. Biochem. the breakdown of complex molecules in living organisms to form simpler ones with the release of energy; destructive metabolism (opp. ANABOLISM). □□ **catabolic** /kátəbólik/ adj. [Gk katabolē descent f. kata down + bolē f. ballō throw]

catachresis /kátəkréesis/ n. (pl. **catachreses** /-seez/) an incorrect use of words. □□ **catachrestic** /-kréstik/ adj. [L f. Gk katakhrēsis f. khraomai use]

■ see MISUSE n.

cataclasis /kátəkláysis/ n. (pl. **cataclases** /-seez/) Geol. the natural process of fracture, shearing, or breaking up of rocks. □□ **cataclastic** /-klástik/ adj. [mod.L f. Gk kataklasis breaking down]

cataclasm /kátəklazəm/ n. a violent break; a disruption. [Gk kataklasma (as CATA-, klaō to break)]

cataclysm /kátəklizəm/ n. **1 a** a violent, esp. social or political, upheaval or disaster. **b** a great change. **2** a great flood or deluge. □□ **cataclysmal** /-klízməl/ adj. **cataclysmic** adj. **cataclysmically** adv. [F cataclysme f. L cataclysmus f. Gk kataklusmos f. klusmos flood f. kluzō wash]

■ **1** see DISASTER 1.

catacomb /kátəkōm/ n. (often in pl.) **1** an underground cemetery, esp. a Roman subterranean gallery with recesses for tombs. **2** a similar underground construction; a cellar. [F catacombes f. LL catacumbas (name given in the 5th c. to the cemetery of St. Sebastian near Rome), of unkn. orig.]

■ **1** see CRYPT.

catadromous /kətádrəməs/ adj. (of a fish, e.g., the eel) that swims down rivers to the sea to spawn (cf. ANADROMOUS). [Gk katadromos f. kata down + dromos running]

catafalque /kátəfawk, -fawlk/ n. a decorated wooden framework for supporting the coffin of a distinguished person during a funeral or while lying in state. [F f. It. catafalco, of unkn. orig.: cf. SCAFFOLD]

Catalan /kát'lan/ n. & adj. ● n. **1** a native of Catalonia in

Spain. **2** the language of Catalonia. ● *adj.* of or relating to Catalonia or its people or language. [F f. Sp.]

catalase /kát'lays, -layz/ *n. Biochem.* an enzyme that catalyzes the reduction of hydrogen peroxide. [CATALYSIS]

catalepsy /kát'lepsee/ *n.* a state of trance or seizure with loss of sensation and consciousness accompanied by rigidity of the body. □□ **cataleptic** /-léptik/ *adj.* & *n.* [F *catalepsie* or LL *catalepsia* f. Gk *katalēpsis* (as CATA-, *lēpsis* seizure)]

catalog /kát'lawg, -log/ *n.* & *v.* (also **catalogue**) ● *n.* **1** a list of items (e.g., articles for sale, books held by a library), usu. in alphabetical or other systematic order and often with a description of each. **2** an extensive list (*a catalog of crimes*). **3** a listing of a university's courses, etc. ● *v.tr.* (**catalogs, cataloged, cataloging; catalogues, catalogued, cataloguing**) **1** make a catalog of. **2** enter in a catalog. □□ **cataloger** *n.* (also **cataloguer**). [F f. LL *catalogus* f. Gk *katalogos* f. *katalegō* enroll (as CATA-, *legō* choose)]

■ *n.* see LIST[1] *n.* ● *v.* see LIST[1] *v.*

catalogue raisonné /kát'lawg ráyzənáy, -log/ *n.* a descriptive catalog with explanations or comments. [F, = explained catalog]

■ see LIST[1] *n.* 1.

catalpa /kətálpə/ *n.* any tree of the genus *Catalpa*, with heart-shaped leaves, trumpet-shaped flowers, and long pods. [Creek]

catalyse *Brit.* var. of CATALYZE.

catalysis /kətálisis/ *n.* (*pl.* **catalyses** /-seez/) *Chem.* & *Biochem.* the acceleration of a chemical or biochemical reaction by a catalyst. [Gk *katalusis* dissolution (as CATA-, *luō* set free)]

catalyst /kát'list/ *n.* **1** *Chem.* a substance that, without itself undergoing any permanent chemical change, increases the rate of a reaction. **2** a person or thing that precipitates a change. [as CATALYSIS after *analyst*]

catalytic /kát'lítik/ *adj. Chem.* relating to or involving catalysis. □ **catalytic converter** a device incorporated in the exhaust system of a motor vehicle, with a catalyst for converting pollutant gases into harmless products. **catalytic cracker** a device for cracking (see CRACK *v.* 9) petroleum oils by catalysis.

catalyze /kát'alīz/ *v.tr.* (*Brit.* **catalyse**) *Chem.* produce (a reaction) by catalysis. [as CATALYSIS after *analyze*]

catamaran /kátəmərán/ *n.* **1** a boat with twin hulls in parallel. **2** a raft of yoked logs or boats. **3** *colloq.* a quarrelsome woman. [Tamil *kaṭṭumaram* tied wood]

catamite /kátəmīt/ *n.* **1** a boy kept for homosexual practices. **2** the passive partner in sodomy. [L *catamitus* through Etruscan f. Gk *Ganumēdēs* Ganymede, cupbearer of Zeus]

■ see PROSTITUTE *n.* 1b.

catamountain /kátəmowntin/ *n.* (also **cat-a-mountain, catamount**) **1** a lynx, leopard, puma, or other wild cat. **2** *Brit.* a wild quarrelsome person. [ME f. *cat of the mountain*]

catananche /kátənángkee/ *n.* any composite plant of the genus *Catananche*, with blue or yellow flowers. [mod.L f. L *catanancē* plant used in love potions f. Gk *katanagkē* (as CATA-, *anagkē* compulsion)]

cataplexy /kátəpleksee/ *n.* sudden temporary paralysis due to fright, etc. □□ **cataplectic** /-pléktik/ *adj.* [Gk *katáplēxis* stupefaction]

catapult /kátəpult, -pōōlt/ *n.* & *v.* ● *n.* **1** a mechanical device for launching a glider, an aircraft from the deck of a ship, etc. **2** *hist.* a military machine worked by a lever and ropes for hurling large stones, etc. **3** *Brit.* = SLINGSHOT. ● *v.* **1** *tr.* **a** hurl from or launch with a catapult. **b** fling forcibly. **2** *intr.* leap or be hurled forcibly. [F *catapulte* or L *catapulta* f. Gk *katapeltēs* (as CATA-, *pallō* hurl)]

■ *v.* see LAUNCH[1] *v.* 2.

cataract /kátərakt/ *n.* **1** **a** a large waterfall or cascade. **b** a downpour; a rush of water. **2** *Med.* a condition in which the lens of the eye becomes progressively opaque resulting in blurred vision. [L *cataracta* f. Gk *katarrhaktēs* downrushing; in med. sense prob. f. obs. sense 'portcullis']

■ **1** **a** see WATERFALL. **b** see STREAM *n.* 2.

catarrh /kətaár/ *n.* **1** inflammation of the mucous membrane of the nose, air passages, etc. **2** a watery discharge in the nose or throat due to this. □□ **catarrhal** *adj.* [F *catarrhe* f. LL *catarrhus* f. Gk *katarrhous* f. *katarrheō* flow down]

catarrhine /kátərin/ *adj.* & *n. Zool.* ● *adj.* (of primates) having nostrils close together, and directed downward, e.g., a baboon, chimpanzee, or human. ● *n.* such an animal (cf. PLATYRRHINE). [CATA- + *rhis rhinos* nose]

catastrophe /kətástrəfee/ *n.* **1** a great and usu. sudden disaster. **2** the denouement of a drama. **3** a disastrous end; ruin. **4** an event producing a subversion of the order of things. □□ **catastrophic** /kátəstrófik/ *adj.* **catastrophically** /kátəstrófikəlee/ *adv.* [L *catastropha* f. Gk *katastrophē* (as CATA-, *strophē* turning f. *strephō* turn)]

■ **1** disaster, calamity, cataclysm, casualty, misfortune, tragedy, reverse, affliction, visitation; fiasco. **3** ruin, disaster, destruction, devastation, downfall, havoc, collapse, disintegration, ruination, failure, debacle; the abyss.

catastrophism /kətástrəfizəm/ *n. Geol.* the theory that changes in the earth's crust have occurred in sudden violent and unusual events. □□ **catastrophist** *n.*

catatonia /kátətóneeə/ *n.* **1** schizophrenia with intervals of catalepsy and sometimes violence. **2** catalepsy. □□ **catatonic** /-tónik/ *adj.* & *n.* [G *Katatonie* (as CATA-, TONE)]

Catawba /kətáwbə/ *n.* **1** a variety of grape. **2** a white wine made from it. [*Catawba* River in S. Carolina, named for a Native American people of the Carolinas]

catboat /kátbōt/ *n.* a sailboat with a single mast placed well forward and carrying only one sail. [perh. f. *cat* a former type of coaler in NE England, + BOAT]

catcall /kátkawl/ *n.* & *v.* ● *n.* a shrill whistle of disapproval made at sporting events, stage performances, meetings, etc. ● *v.* **1** *intr.* make a catcall. **2** *tr.* make a catcall at.

■ *n.* see JEER *n.* ● *v.* **1** see JEER *v.* 1. **2** see JEER *v.* 2.

catch /kach/ *v.* & *n.* ● *v.* (*past* and *past part.* **caught** /kawt/) **1** *tr.* **a** lay hold of so as to restrain or prevent from escaping; capture in a trap, in one's hands, etc. **b** (also **catch hold of**) get into one's hands so as to retain, operate, etc. (*caught hold of the handle*). **2** *tr.* detect or surprise (a person, esp. in a wrongful or embarrassing act) (*caught me in the act; caught him smoking*). **3** *tr.*intercept and hold (a moving thing) in the hands, etc. (*failed to catch the ball; a bowl to catch the drips*). **4** *tr.* **a** contract (a disease) by infection or contagion. **b** acquire (a quality or feeling) from another's example (*caught her enthusiasm*). **5** *tr.* **a** reach in time and board (a train, bus, etc.). **b** be in time to see, etc. (a person or thing about to leave or finish) (*if you hurry you'll catch them; caught the end of the performance*). **6** *tr.* **a** apprehend with the senses or the mind (esp. a thing occurring quickly or briefly) (*didn't catch what he said*). **b** (of an artist, etc.) reproduce faithfully. **7** *a intr.* become fixed or entangled; be checked (*the bolt began to catch*). **b** *tr.* cause to do this (*caught her tights on a nail*). **c** *tr.* (often foll. by *on*) hit; deal a blow to (*caught him on the nose; caught his elbow on the table*). **8** *tr.* draw the attention of; captivate (*caught his eye; caught her fancy*). **9** *intr.* begin to burn. **10** *tr.* (often foll. by *up*) reach or overtake (a person, etc., ahead). **11** *tr.* check suddenly (*caught his breath*). **12** *tr.* (foll. by *at*) grasp or try to grasp. ● *n.* **1** **a** an act of catching. **b** *Baseball* a chance or act of catching the ball. **2** **a** an amount of a thing caught, esp. of fish. **b** a thing or person caught or worth catching, esp. in marriage. **3** **a** a question, trick, etc., intended to deceive, incriminate, etc. **b** an unexpected or hidden difficulty or disadvantage. **4** a device for fastening a door or window, etc. **5** *Mus.* a round, esp. with words arranged to produce a humorous effect. □ **catch-as-catch-can 1** a style of wrestling with few holds barred. **2** using any method available. **catch basin 1** a receptacle at the entrance to a sewer designed to catch objects too large to pass through the sewer. **2** a reservoir into which surface water can be drained. **catch crop** a crop grown between two staple crops (in position or time). **catch one's death** see DEATH. **catch fire** see FIRE. **catch it** *sl.* be punished or in trouble. **catch on** *colloq.* **1** (of a practice, fashion, etc.) become popular. **2** (of a person) understand what is meant. **catch out** *Brit.* **1** detect in a mistake, etc. **2** take unawares; cause to be bewildered or confused. **catch the**

sun 1 be in a sunny position. **2** *Brit.* become sunburned.
catch up 1 a (often foll. by *with*) reach a person, etc., ahead (*he caught up in the end; he caught up with us*). **b** (often foll. by *with, on*) make up arrears (of work, etc.) (*must catch up with my correspondence*). **2** snatch or pick up hurriedly. **3** (often in *passive*) **a** involve; entangle (*caught up in suspicious dealings*). **b** fasten up (*hair caught up in a ribbon*). □□ **catchable** *adj.* [ME f. AF & ONF *cachier*, OF *chacier*, ult. f. L *captare* try to catch]

■ *v.* **1 a** capture, seize, apprehend, take *or* get (hold of), grab, take captive, arrest, take prisoner, collar, *sl.* nab, pinch, *Brit. sl.* nick; trap, ensnare, entrap, snare, net, bag, hook, land. **b** grab (hold of), grip, grasp, seize, clasp, clutch, take *or* lay *or* get hold of, fasten on *or* upon. **2** surprise, discover, find, detect, uncover, take unawares. **3** intercept, field, stop; grab, seize, snatch, take possession of. **4 a** contract, get, develop, be seized by, be taken hold of by *or* with, come down with, pick up, acquire, be afflicted by *or* with, suffer from, *Brit.* go down with, *archaic* be stricken by *or* with. **5 a** make; take, get, get on (to), board, *colloq.* hop. **6 a** understand, comprehend, ascertain, grasp, apprehend, follow, take in, hear, gather, fathom, perceive, discern, *colloq.* get, catch on to, get the drift of, cotton on to, *Brit. colloq.* twig. **7 a** tangle, be enmeshed, stick, lodge, become entangled *or* stuck *or* trapped *or* fixed *or* hooked *or* wedged. **b** snag, wedge, fix, entangle, hook; tear, rip. **c** see BOX² *v.* 2. **8** attract, draw, capture; appeal to, engage, captivate, bewitch. **9** ignite, light, flare up. **10** reach, draw level *or* even with, get to, come to, make it to, catch up (with); overtake, pass, go past, overhaul. **11** restrain, control, stop, check, curb. ● *n.* **2 a** take, bag, haul, yield, harvest. **b** find; conquest. **3 a** trick, trap, wile, dodge, *colloq.* ploy, *sl.* con. **b** disadvantage, hitch, snag, problem, drawback, difficulty, twist, rub, fly in the ointment, complication, small print, stumbling block, joker (in the pack). **4** clasp, bolt, hook, pin, clip, buckle, fastening, fastener. □ **catch it** be in trouble *or* deep water, *colloq.* get it in the neck, get a dressing-down *or* telling-off, get a piece of a person's mind. **catch on 1** take hold, become popular *or* fashionable. **2** understand, comprehend, see daylight, *colloq.* get it, cotton on, get the drift, *Brit. colloq.* twig. **catch up 1 a** see CATCH *v.* 10 above. **b** clear the backlog (of); make up time. **3 a** absorb, involve, enthrall, immerse, engross, preoccupy, wrap up; engage, occupy; mix up, bind up, entangle, embroil, implicate, draw in, enmesh, ensnare.

catchall /káchawl/ *n.* (often *attrib.*) **1** something designed to be all-inclusive. **2** a container for odds and ends.
■ (*attrib.*) see INCLUSIVE 3.

catcher /káchər/ *n.* **1** a person or thing that catches. **2** *Baseball* a fielder positioned behind home plate.

catchfly /káchflī/ *n.* (*pl.* **-ies**) any plant of the genus *Silene* or *Lychnis* with a sticky stem.

catching /káching/ *adj.* **1 a** (of a disease) infectious. **b** (of a practice, habit, etc.) likely to be imitated. **2** attractive; captivating.
■ **1 a** contagious, infectious, transmissible, transmittable, communicable. **2** attractive, captivating, fascinating, enchanting, bewitching, entrancing, engaging, winning, enticing, alluring, fetching, winsome.

catchline /káchlīn/ *n. Printing* a short line of type, esp. at the head of copy or as a running headline.

catchment /káchmənt/ *n.* **1** the collection of rainfall. **2** an opening or basin for storm water, etc. □ **catchment area 1** the area from which rainfall flows into a river, etc. **2** the area served by a school, hospital, etc.

catchpenny /káchpenee/ *adj.* intended merely to sell quickly; superficially attractive.

catchphrase /káchfrayz/ *n.* a phrase in frequent use.

catch-22 /káchtwenteetoō/ *n.* (often *attrib.*) *colloq.* a circumstance that presents a dilemma because of mutually conflicting or dependent conditions. [title of a novel by J. Heller (1961) featuring a dilemma of this kind]

■ see DILEMMA 1.

catchup var. of KETCHUP.

catchweight /káchwayt/ *adj.* & *n.* ● *adj.* unrestricted as regards weight. ● *n.* unrestricted weight, as a weight category in sports.

catchword /káchwərd/ *n.* **1** a word or phrase in common (often temporary) use; a topical slogan. **2** a word so placed as to draw attention. **3** *Theatr.* an actor's cue. **4** *Printing* the first word of a page given at the foot of the previous one.
■ **1, 2** see SLOGAN.

catchy /káchee/ *adj.* (**catchier, catchiest**) **1** (of a tune) easy to remember; attractive. **2** that snares or entraps; deceptive. **3** (of the wind, etc.) fitful; spasmodic. □□ **catchily** *adv.* **catchiness** *n.* [CATCH + -Y¹]
■ **1** see MEMORABLE.

cate /kayt/ *n. archaic* (usu. in *pl.*) choice food; delicacies. [obs. *acate* purchase f. AF *acat*, OF *achat* f. *acater, achater* buy: see CATER]

catechetical /kátikétikəl/ *adj.* (also **catechetic**) **1** of or by oral teaching. **2** according to the catechism of a church. **3** consisting of or proceeding by question and answer. □□ **catechetically** *adv.* **catechetics** *n.* [eccl.Gk *katēkhētikos* f. *katēkhētēs* oral teacher: see CATECHIZE]

catechism /kátikizəm/ *n.* **1 a** a summary of the principles of a religion in the form of questions and answers. **b** a book containing this. **2** a series of questions put to anyone. □□ **catechismal** /-kízməl/ *adj.* [eccl.L *catechismus* (as CATECHIZE)]
■ **2** see EXAMINATION 5.

catechist /kátikist/ *n.* a religious teacher, esp. one using a catechism.

catechize /kátikīz/ *v.tr.* **1** instruct by means of question and answer, esp. from a catechism. **2** put questions to; examine. □□ **catechizer** *n.* [LL *catechizare* f. eccl.Gk *katēkhizō* f. *katēkheō* make hear (as CATA-, *ēkheō* sound)]
■ **2** see EXAMINE 5.

catechu /kátichoō/ *n.* (also **cachou** /káshoō/) gambier or similar vegetable extract, containing tannin. [mod.L f. Malay *kachu*]

catechumen /kátikyoōmən/ *n.* a Christian convert under instruction before baptism. [ME f. OF *catechumene* or eccl.L *catechumenus* f. Gk *katēkheō*: see CATECHIZE]
■ see INITIATE *n.*

categorical /kátigáwrikəl, -gór-/ *adj.* (also **categoric**) unconditional; absolute; explicit; direct (*a categorical refusal*). □ **categorical imperative** *Ethics* an unconditional moral obligation derived from pure reason; the bidding of conscience as ultimate moral law. □□ **categorically** *adv.* [F *catégorique* or LL *categoricus* f. Gk *katēgorikos*: see CATEGORY]
■ direct, explicit, express, unconditional, firm, positive, absolute, unmitigated, unqualified, definitive, unequivocal, unambiguous, specific, unreserved, unrestricted, outright, downright, flat, point-blank, emphatic, apodictic.

categorize /kátigərīz/ *v.tr.* place in a category or categories. □□ **categorization** *n.*
■ compartmentalize, classify, class, sort, organize, group, assort, rank, order, section, departmentalize, compartmentalize, file, label, arrange.

category /kátigawree, -goree/ *n.* (*pl.* **-ies**) **1** a class or division. **2** *Philos.* **a** one of a possibly exhaustive set of classes among which all things might be distributed. **b** one of the a priori conceptions applied by the mind to sense-impressions. **c** any relatively fundamental philosophical concept. □□ **categorial** /-gáwreeəl/ *adj.* [F *catégorie* or LL *categoria* f. Gk *katēgoria* statement f. *katēgoros* accuser]
■ **1** class, type, sort, kind, variety, species, form, order, breed, nature, manner, description; division, section, sector, league, bracket, genre, set, group, area, sphere,

---

/.../ **pronunciation**	● **part of speech**
□ **phrases, idioms, and compounds**	
□□ **derivatives**	■ **synonym section**
cross-references appear in SMALL CAPITALS or *italics*	

realm, domain, grouping, grade, department, head, heading.

catena /kəteenə/ *n.* (*pl.* **catenae** /-nee/ or **catenas**) **1** a connected series of patristic comments on Scripture. **2** a series or chain. [L, = chain: orig. *catena patrum* chain of the Fathers (of the Church)]

catenary /kát'neree, kəteenəree/ *n. & adj.* ● *n.* (*pl.* **-ies**) a curve formed by a uniform chain hanging freely from two points not in the same vertical line. ● *adj.* of or resembling such a curve. □ **catenary bridge** a suspension bridge hung from such chains. [L *catenarius* f. *catena* chain]

catenate /kát'nayt/ *v.tr.* connect like links of a chain. □□ **catenation** /-náyshən/ *n.* [L *catenare catenat-* (as CATENARY)]

cater /káytər/ *v.* **1 a** *intr.* (often foll. by *for*) provide food. **b** *tr.* provide food and service (*cater a party*). **2** *intr.* (foll. by *for, to*) provide what is desired or needed by. **3** *intr.* (foll. by *to*) pander to (esp. low tastes). [obs. noun *cater* (now *caterer*), f. *acater* f. AF *acatour* buyer f. *acater* buy f. Rmc]

■ **1 a** (*cater for*) provision, victual, provide. **2** (*cater for* or *to*) provide (services) for, accommodate, be host to, host, entertain, receive, deal with, handle, see to; care for, look after, minister to; make allowances for, take into consideration *or* account, consider, bear in mind, have regard for. **3** (*cater to*) indulge, pander to, minister to, humor, serve.

cateran /kátərən/ *n. Sc.* a Highland irregular fighting man; a marauder. [ME f. med.L *cateranus* & Gael. *ceathairne* peasantry]

catercornered /kátərkáwrnərd/ *adj. & adv.* (also **catercorner, catty-cornered** /kátee-/, **kitty-corner** /kítee-/) ● *adj.* placed or situated diagonally. ● *adv.* diagonally. [dial. adv. *cater* diagonally (cf. obs. *cater* the four on dice f. F *quatre* f. L *quattuor* four)]

caterer /káytərər/ *n.* a person who supplies food for social events, esp. professionally.

catering /káytəring/ *n.* the profession or work of a caterer.

caterpillar /kátərpilər/ *n.* **1 a** the larva of a butterfly or moth. **b** (in general use) any similar larva of various insects. **2** (**Caterpillar**) **a** (in full **Caterpillar track** or **tread**) *propr.* a continuous belt of linked pieces passing around the wheels of a tractor, etc., for travel on rough ground. **b** a vehicle with these tracks, e.g., a tractor or tank. [perh. AF var. of OF *chatepelose* lit. hairy cat, infl. by obs. *piller* ravager]

caterwaul /kátərwawl/ *v. & n.* ● *v.intr.* make the shrill howl of a cat. ● *n.* a caterwauling noise. [ME f. CAT + *-waul*, etc. imit.]

■ *v.* see SCREAM *v.* 1, 2. ● *n.* see SCREAM *n.* 1.

catfish /kátfish/ *n.* any of various esp. freshwater fish, usu. having whiskerlike barbels around the mouth.

catgut /kátgut/ *n.* a material used for the strings of musical instruments and surgical sutures, made of the twisted intestines of the sheep, horse, or ass (but not the cat).

Cath. *abbr.* **1** cathedral. **2** Catholic.

Cathar /káthaar/ *n.* (*pl.* **Cathars** or **Cathari** /-rī/) a member of a medieval sect that sought to achieve great spiritual purity. □□ **Catharism** *n.* **Catharist** *n.* [med.L *Cathari* (pl.) f. Gk *katharoi* pure]

catharsis /kətháarsis/ *n.* (*pl.* **catharses** /-seez/) **1** an emotional release in drama or art. **2** *Psychol.* the process of freeing repressed emotion by association with the cause, and elimination by abreaction. **3** *Med.* purgation. [mod.L f. Gk *katharsis* f. *kathairō* cleanse: sense 1 f. Aristotle's *Poetics*]

cathartic /kətháartik/ *adj. & n.* ● *adj.* **1** effecting catharsis. **2** purgative. ● *n.* a cathartic drug. □□ **cathartically** *adv.* [LL *catharticus* f. Gk *kathartikos* (as CATHARSIS)]

■ *adj.* see PURGATIVE *adj.* 1, 2. ● *n.* see PURGATIVE *n.* 2.

Cathay /katháy/ *n. archaic* or *poet.* the country China. [med.L *Cataya*]

cathead /kát-hed/ *n. Naut.* a horizontal beam from each side of a ship's bow for raising and carrying the anchor.

cathectic see CATHEXIS.

cathedral /kətheédrəl/ *n.* the principal church of a diocese, containing the bishop's throne. □ **cathedral city** a city in which there is a cathedral. [ME (as adj.) f. OF *cathedral* or f. LL *cathedralis* f. L f. Gk *kathedra* seat]

Catherine wheel /káthrin/ *n.* **1** a firework in the form of a flat coil that spins when fixed and lit. **2** a circular window with radial divisions. [mod.L *Catharina* f. Gk *Aikaterina* name of a saint martyred c. 310 on a spiked wheel]

catheter /káthitər/ *n. Med.* a tube for insertion into a body cavity for introducing or removing fluid. [LL f. Gk *kathetēr* f. *kathiēmi* send down]

catheterize /káthitəriz/ *v.tr. Med.* insert a catheter into.

cathetometer /káthitómitər/ *n.* a telescope mounted on a graduated scale along which it can slide, used for accurate measurement of small vertical distances. [L *cathetus* f. Gk *kathetos* perpendicular line (as CATHETER + -METER)]

cathexis /kəthéksis/ *n.* (*pl.* **cathexes** /-seez/) *Psychol.* concentration of mental energy in one channel. □□ **cathectic** *adj.* [Gk *kathexis* retention]

cathode /káthōd/ *n. Electr.* **1** the negative electrode in an electrolytic cell or electronic valve or tube. **2** the positive terminal of a primary cell such as a battery (opp. ANODE). □ **cathode ray** a beam of electrons emitted from the cathode of a high-vacuum tube. **cathode-ray tube** a high-vacuum tube in which cathode rays produce a luminous image on a fluorescent screen. ¶ Abbr.: CRT. □□ **cathodal** *adj.* **cathodic** /kəthódik/ *adj.* [Gk *kathodos* descent f. *kata* down + *hodos* way]

catholic /káthəlik, káthlik/ *adj. & n.* ● *adj.* **1** of interest or use to all; universal. **2** all-embracing; of wide sympathies or interests (*has catholic tastes*). **3** (**Catholic**) **a** of the Roman Catholic religion. **b** including all Christians. **c** including all of the Western Church. ● *n.* (**Catholic**) a Roman Catholic. □□ **catholically** /kəthólikléë/ *adv.* **Catholicism** /kəthólisizəm/ *n.* **catholicity** /káthəlísitee/ *n.* **catholicly** *adv.* [ME f. OF *catholique* or LL *catholicus* f. Gk *katholikos* universal f. *kata* in respect of + *holos* whole]

■ *adj.* **1** universal, general, widespread. **2** inclusive, all-inclusive, broad, wide, wide-ranging, comprehensive, widespread, all-embracing, extensive, eclectic, liberal, tolerant, open-minded, broad-minded, unprejudiced, unbigoted, latitudinarian, enlightened. **3 b** ecumenical, Christian.

catholicize /kəthólisiz/ *v.tr. & intr.* **1** make or become catholic. **2** (**Catholicize**) make or become a Roman Catholic.

cation /kátīən/ *n.* a positively charged ion; an ion that is attracted to the cathode in electrolysis (opp. ANION). [CATA- + ION]

cationic /kátiónik/ *adj.* **1** of a cation or cations. **2** having an active cation.

catkin /kátkin/ *n.* a spike of usu. downy or silky male or female flowers hanging from a willow, hazel, etc. [obs. Du. *katteken* kitten]

catlick /kátlik/ *n. Brit. colloq.* a perfunctory wash.

catlike /kátlīk/ *adj.* **1** like a cat. **2** stealthy.

catnap /kátnap/ *n. & v.* ● *n.* a short sleep. ● *v.intr.* (**-napped, -napping**) have a catnap.

■ *n.* see DOZE *n.* ● *v.* see DOZE *v.*

catnip /kátnip/ *n.* a white-flowered plant, *Nepeta cataria*, having a pungent smell attractive to cats. [CAT + dial. *nip* catnip, var. of dial. *nep*]

catoptric /kətóptrik/ *adj.* of or relating to a mirror, a reflector, or reflection. □□ **catoptrics** *n.* [Gk *katoptrikos* f. *katoptron* mirror]

CAT scan /kat/ *n.* an X-ray image made using computerized axial tomography. □□ **CAT scanner** *n.* [Computerized *A*xial *T*omography]

catsup /kátsəp, kéchəp, kách-/ var. of KETCHUP.

cattail /kát-tayl/ *n.* any tall, reedlike marsh plant of the genus *Typha*, esp. *T. latifola*, with long, flat leaves and brown, velvety flower spikes. (Also called **bulrush** and **reed mace**.)

cattery /kátəree/ *n.* (*pl.* **-ies**) a place where cats are boarded or bred.

cattish /kátish/ *adj.* = CATTY. □□ **cattishly** *adv.* **cattishness** *n.*

cattle /kát'l/ *n.pl.* **1** bison, buffalo, yaks, or domesticated bovine animals, esp. of the genus *Bos*. **2** *archaic* livestock. □ **cattle guard** a grid covering a ditch, allowing vehicles to

pass over but not cattle, sheep, etc. **cattle plague** rinderpest. [ME & AF *catel* f. OF *chatel* CHATTEL]
■ **1, 2** cows, bulls, bullocks, steers, oxen; stock, livestock.

cattleduffer /kát'ldúfər/ *n. Austral.* a cattle thief.

cattleman /kát'lmən/ *n.* (*pl.* **-men**) a person who breeds or rears cattle.

cattleya /kátleeə/ *n.* any epiphytic orchid of the genus *Cattleya*, with handsome violet, pink, or yellow flowers. [mod.L f. W. *Cattley*, Engl. patron of botany d. 1832]

catty /kátee/ *adj.* (**cattier, cattiest**) **1** sly; spiteful; deliberately hurtful in speech. **2** catlike. □□ **cattily** *adv.* **cattiness** *n.*

catty-cornered var. of CATERCORNERED.

CATV *abbr.* community antenna television.

catwalk /kátwawk/ *n.* **1** a narrow footway along a bridge, above a theater stage, etc. **2** a narrow platform or gangway used in fashion shows, etc.

Caucasian /kawkáyzhən/ *adj. & n.* ● *adj.* **1** of or relating to the white or light-skinned division of mankind. **2** of or relating to the Caucasus. ● *n.* a Caucasian person. [*Caucasus*, mountains between the Black and Caspian Seas, the supposed place of origin of this people]
■ *adj.* **1** see WHITE *adj.* 4.

Caucasoid /káwkəsoyd/ *adj.* of or relating to the Caucasian division of mankind.
■ see WHITE *adj.* 4.

caucus /káwkəs/ *n.* **1 a** a meeting of the members of a political party, esp. in a legislature or convention, to decide policy. **b** a bloc of such members. **c** this system as a political force. **2** often *derog.* (esp. in the UK) **a** a usu. secret meeting of a group within a larger organization or party. **b** such a group. [18th-c. US, perh. f. Algonquian *cau'-cau-as'u* adviser]
■ **1a, 2a** see MEETING 2, 5. **1b, 2b** see PARTY¹ *n.* 3.

caudal /káwd'l/ *adj.* **1** of or like a tail. **2** of the posterior part of the body. □□ **caudally** *adv.* [mod.L *caudalis* f. L *cauda* tail]

caudate /káwdayt/ *adj.* having a tail. [see CAUDAL]

caudillo /kawdeélyō, -deéyō, kowtheélyō, -theéyō/ *n.* (*pl.* **-os**) (in Spanish-speaking countries) a military or political leader. [Sp. f. LL *capitellum* dimin. of *caput* head]

caught *past* and *past part.* of CATCH.

caul /kawl/ *n.* **1 a** the inner membrane enclosing a fetus. **b** part of this occasionally found on a child's head at birth, thought to bring good luck. **2** *hist.* **a** a woman's close-fitting indoor headdress. **b** the plain back part of a woman's indoor headdress. **3** the omentum. [ME perh. f. OF *cale* small cap]

cauldron /káwldrən/ *n.* (also **caldron**) a large, deep, bowl-shaped vessel for boiling over an open fire; an ornamental vessel resembling this. [ME f. AF & ONF *caudron*, ult. f. L *caldarium* hot bath f. *calidus* hot]
■ see POT¹ *n.* 1.

cauliflower /káwliflowr, kól-/ *n.* **1** a variety of cabbage with a large immature flower head of small usu. creamy-white flower buds. **2** the flower head eaten as a vegetable. □ **cauliflower ear** an ear deformed by repeated blows, esp. in boxing. [earlier *cole-florie*, etc., f. obs. F *chou fleuri* flowered cabbage, assim. to COLE and FLOWER]

caulk /kawk/ *v.tr.* (also **calk**) **1** stop up (the seams of a boat, etc.) with oakum, etc., and waterproofing material, or by driving plate junctions together. **2** make (esp. a boat) watertight by this method. □□ **caulker** *n.* [OF dial. *cauquer* tread, press with force, f. L *calcare* tread f. *calx* heel]
■ **1** see STOP *v.* 7.

causal /káwzəl/ *adj.* **1** of, forming, or expressing a cause or causes. **2** relating to, or of the nature of, cause and effect. □□ **causally** *adv.* [LL *causalis*: see CAUSE]

causality /kawzálitee/ *n.* **1** the relation of cause and effect. **2** the principle that everything has a cause.

causation /kawzáyshən/ *n.* **1** the act of causing or producing an effect. **2** = CAUSALITY. [F *causation* or L *causatio* pretext, etc., in med.L the action of causing, f. *causare* CAUSE]

causative /káwzətiv/ *adj.* **1** acting as cause. **2** (foll. by *of*) producing; having as effect. **3** *Gram.* expressing cause.

□□ **causatively** *adv.* [ME f. OF *causatif* or f. LL *causativus*: see CAUSATION]

cause /kawz/ *n. & v.* ● *n.* **1 a** that which produces an effect, or gives rise to an action, phenomenon, or condition. **b** a person or thing that occasions something. **c** a reason or motive; a ground that may be held to justify something (*no cause for complaint*). **2** a reason adjudged adequate (*show cause*). **3** a principle, belief, or purpose that is advocated or supported (*faithful to the cause*). **4 a** a matter to be settled at law. **b** an individual's case offered at law (*plead a cause*). **5** the side taken by any party in a dispute. ● *v.tr.* **1** be the cause of; produce; make happen (*caused a commotion*). **2** (foll. by *to* + infin.) induce (*caused me to smile*; *caused it to be done*). □ **in the cause of** to maintain, defend, or support (*in the cause of justice*). **make common cause with** join the side of. □□ **causable** *adj.* **causeless** *adj.* **causer** *n.* [ME f. OF f. L *causa*]
■ *n.* **1 a** origin, derivation, basis, source, root, rise, genesis, agent, reason, occasion, prime mover, wellspring. **b** source, originator, creator, producer, agent, agency, initiator, instigator. **c** reason, ground(s), motive, justification, basis, call, occasion; right, excuse, pretext, case. **3** see PRINCIPLE 1. **4 b** see CASE¹ 5a. **5** see SIDE *n.* 5b. ● *v.* **1** effect, bring (on *or* about *or* forth), give rise to, result in, produce, create, precipitate, occasion, lead to, spark (off), trigger *or* set off, excite, set in motion, touch off, induce, generate, breed, provoke, promote, engender. **2** induce, compel, motivate, prompt, stimulate, encourage; (*cause to*) make. □ **make common cause with** join forces with.

'cause /kawz, kuz/ *conj. & adv. colloq.* = BECAUSE. [abbr.]

cause célèbre /káwz selébrə/ *n.* (*pl.* **causes célèbres** *pronunc.* same) a trial or case that attracts much attention. [F]

causerie /kōzree/, kōzə-/ *n.* (*pl.* **causeries** *pronunc.* same) an informal article or talk, esp. on a literary subject. [F f. *causer* talk]

causeway /káwzway/ *n.* **1** a raised road or track across low or wet ground or a stretch of water. **2** a raised path by a road. [earlier *cauce*, *causeway* f. ONF *caucié* ult. f. L CALX lime, limestone]

causey /káwzee/ *n. archaic* or *Brit. dial.* = CAUSEWAY.

caustic /káwstik/ *adj. & n.* ● *adj.* **1** that burns or corrodes organic tissue. **2** sarcastic; biting. **3** *Chem.* strongly alkaline. **4** *Physics* formed by the intersection of reflected or refracted parallel rays from a curved surface. ● *n.* **1** a caustic substance. **2** *Physics* a caustic surface or curve. □ **caustic potash** potassium hydroxide. **caustic soda** sodium hydroxide. □□ **caustically** *adv.* **causticity** /-tísitee/ *n.* [L *causticus* f. Gk *kaustikos* f. *kaustos* burned f. *kaiō* burn]
■ *adj.* **1** burning, corrosive, destructive, mordant. **2** sarcastic, biting, acrimonious, sharp, bitter, mordant, sardonic, cutting, trenchant, critical, scathing, acidic, astringent, stinging, acerbic, searing, harsh, pungent, virulent.

cauterize /káwtəriz/ *v.tr. Med.* burn or coagulate (tissue) with a heated instrument or caustic substance, esp. to stop bleeding. □□ **cauterization** *n.* [F *cautériser* f. LL *cauterizare* f. Gk *kautēriazō* f. *kautērion* branding iron f. *kaiō* burn]

cautery /káwtəree/ *n.* (*pl.* **-ies**) *Med.* **1** an instrument or caustic for cauterizing. **2** the operation of cauterizing. [L *cauterium* f. Gk *kautērion*: see CAUTERIZE]

caution /káwshən/ *n. & v.* ● *n.* **1** attention to safety; prudence; carefulness. **2 a** esp. *Brit.* a warning, esp. a formal one in law. **b** a formal warning and reprimand. **3** *colloq.* an amusing or surprising person or thing. ● *v.tr.* **1** (often foll. by *against*, or *to* + infin.) warn or admonish. **2** esp. *Brit.* issue a caution to. [ME f. OF f. L *cautio -onis* f. *cavēre caut-* take heed]
■ *n.* **1** wariness, prudence, care, cautiousness,

/.../ pronunciation	● part of speech
□ phrases, idioms, and compounds	
□□ derivatives	■ synonym section
cross-references appear in SMALL CAPITALS or *italics*	

carefulness, vigilance, forethought, heed, heedfulness, watchfulness, alertness, circumspection, discretion, consideration. **3** *Austral.* doer, *colloq.* hoot, scream, riot, laugh, card, giggle, *sl.* gas, yell. ● *v.* **1** see WARN.

cautionary /káwshəneree/ *adj.* that gives or serves as a warning (*a cautionary tale*).

cautious /káwshəs/ *adj.* careful; prudent; attentive to safety. □□ **cautiously** *adv.* **cautiousness** *n.* [ME f. OF f. L: see CAUTION]
■ wary, heedful, careful, prudent, circumspect, watchful, vigilant, alert, discreet, guarded, measured, *sl.* leery.

cavalcade /kávəlkáyd/ *n.* a procession or formal company of riders, motor vehicles, etc. [F f. It. *cavalcata* f. *cavalcare* ride ult. f. L *caballus* packhorse]
■ see PROCESSION 1.

cavalier /kávəleér/ *n. & adj.* ● *n.* **1** *hist.* (**Cavalier**) a supporter of Charles I in the English Civil War. **2** a courtly gentleman, esp. as a lady's escort. **3** *archaic* a horseman. ● *adj.* offhand; supercilious; blasé. □□ **cavalierly** *adv.* [F f. It. *cavaliere*: see CHEVALIER]
■ *adj.* see OFFHAND *adj.*

cavalry /kávəlree/ *n.* (*pl.* **-ies**) (usu. treated as *pl.*) soldiers on horseback or in armored vehicles. □ **cavalry twill** a strong fabric in a double twill. [F *cavallerie* f. It. *cavalleria* f. *cavallo* horse f. L *caballus*]

cavalryman /kávəlrimən/ *n.* (*pl.* **-men**) a soldier of a cavalry regiment.

cavatina /kávəteénə/ *n.* **1** a short simple song. **2** a similar piece of instrumental music, usu. slow and emotional. [It.]

cave /kayv/ *n. & v.* ● *n.* **1** a large hollow in the side of a cliff, hill, etc., or underground. **2** *Brit. hist.* a dissident political group. ● *v.intr.* explore caves, esp. interconnecting or underground. □ **cave bear** an extinct kind of large bear, whose bones have been found in caves. **cave dweller 1** = CAVE-MAN. **2** *sl.* a person who lives in an apartment building in a big city. **cave in 1 a** (of a wall, earth over a hollow, etc.) subside; collapse. **b** cause (a wall, earth, etc.) to do this. **2** yield or submit under pressure; give up. **cave-in** *n.* a collapse, submission, etc. □□ **cavelike** *adj.* **caver** *n.* [ME f. OF f. L *cava* f. *cavus* hollow: *cave in* prob. f. E. Anglian dial. *calve in*]
■ *n.* **1** cavern, grotto, hollow, hole, cavity; den, lair. □ **cave in 1 a** collapse, give (way), subside, buckle, fall in *or* inward, crumple, crumble. **b** knock *or* break down, pull down, tear down, push down, collapse. **2** yield, submit, give way *or* in *or* up, surrender, knuckle under, capitulate. **cave-in** see BREAKDOWN 2a, SUBMISSION 1a.

caveat /kávee-aat, kaá-, -at/ *n.* **1** a warning or proviso. **2** *Law* a process in court to suspend proceedings. [L, = let a person beware]
■ **1** see QUALIFICATION 3a, WARNING 1.

caveat emptor /émptawr/ *n.* the principle that the buyer alone is responsible if dissatisfied. [L, = let the buyer beware]

caveman /káyvman/ *n.* (*pl.* **-men**) **1** a prehistoric human living in a cave. **2** a primitive or crude person, esp. a man who behaves roughly toward women.

cavern /kávərn/ *n.* **1** a cave, esp. a large or dark one. **2** a dark, cavelike place, e.g., a room. □□ **cavernous** *adj.* **cavernously** *adv.* [ME f. OF *caverne* or f. L *caverna* f. *cavus* hollow]

caviar /kávee-aár/ *n.* (also **caviare**) the pickled roe of sturgeon or other large fish, eaten as a delicacy. [early forms repr. It. *caviale*, Fr. *caviar*, prob. f. med.Gk *khaviari*]

cavil /kávil/ *v. & n.* ● *v.intr.* (**caviled, caviling**; esp. *Brit.* **cavilled, cavilling**) (usu. foll. by *at, about*) make petty objections; carp. ● *n.* a trivial objection. □□ **caviler** *n.* [F *caviller* f. L *cavillari* f. *cavilla* mockery]
■ *v.* carp, quibble, split hairs, complain, find fault, object, demur, niggle, pick holes, *colloq.* nitpick, gripe. ● *n.* quibble, complaint, criticism, niggle, *colloq.* gripe.

caving /káyving/ *n.* exploring caves as a sport or pastime.
■ speleology, spelunking, *Brit.* potholing.

cavitation /kávitáyshən/ *n.* **1** the formation of a cavity in a

structure. **2** the formation of bubbles, or of a vacuum, in a liquid.

cavity /kávitee/ *n.* (*pl.* **-ies**) **1** a hollow within a solid body. **2** a decayed part of a tooth. □ **cavity wall** a wall formed from two skins of brick or blockwork with a space between. [F *cavité* or LL *cavitas* f. L *cavus* hollow]
■ pit, hole, hollow, gap, space, opening, crater, pan.

cavort /kəváwrt/ *v.intr. sl.* caper excitedly; gambol; prance. [US, perh. f. CURVET]
■ prance, caper, frisk, bound, gambol, frolic, romp, skip, leap, jump, bound, spring, dance, trip, sport, *colloq.* galumph; curvet.

cavy /káyvee/ *n.* (*pl.* **-ies**) any small rodent of the family Caviidae, native to S. America and having a sturdy body and vestigial tail, including guinea pigs. [mod.L *cavia* f. Galibi *cabiai*]

caw /kaw/ *n. & v.* ● *n.* the harsh cry of a rook, crow, etc. ● *v.intr.* utter this cry. [imit.]

cay /kee, kay/ *n.* a low insular bank or reef of coral, sand, etc. (cf. KEY²). [Sp. *cayo* shoal, reef f. F *quai*: see QUAY]
■ see ISLAND 1.

cayenne /kī-én, kay-/ *n.* (in full **cayenne pepper**) a pungent red powder obtained from various plants of the genus *Capsicum* and used for seasoning. [Tupi *kyynha* assim. to *Cayenne* capital of French Guiana]

cayman var. of CAIMAN.

Cayuga /kayoṓgə, kī-/ *n.* **1 a** a N. American people native to New York. **b** a member of this people. **2** the language of this people.

CB *abbr.* **1** citizens' band. **2** (in the UK) Companion of the Order of the Bath.

Cb *symb. Chem.* the element columbium.

CBC *abbr.* **1** Canadian Broadcasting Corporation. **2** complete blood count.

CBE *abbr.* Commander of the Order of the British Empire.

CBI *abbr.* computer-based instruction.

CBS *abbr.* Columbia Broadcasting System.

CC *abbr.* **1** city council. **2** county clerk. **3** circuit court.

cc *abbr.* (also **c.c.**) **1** cubic centimeter(s). **2** (carbon) copy; copies.

CCTV *abbr.* closed-circuit television.

CCU *abbr.* **1** cardiac care unit. **2** coronary care unit. **3** critical care unit.

CD *abbr.* **1** compact disc. **2** certificate of deposit. **3** congressional district. **4** civil defense. **5** diplomatic corps (*corps diplomatique*).

Cd *symb. Chem.* the element cadmium.

cd *abbr.* candela(s).

CDC *abbr.* Centers for Disease Control (and Prevention).

Cdr. *abbr. Mil.* commander.

Cdre. *abbr.* commodore.

CD-ROM /seédeeróm/ *abbr.* compact disc read-only memory, a medium for data storage and distribution.

CDT *abbr.* central daylight time.

CE *abbr.* **1** Church of England. **2** civil engineer. **3** (with dates) Common Era.

Ce *symb. Chem.* the element cerium.

ceanothus /seéənóthəs/ *n.* any shrub of the genus *Ceanothus*, with small blue or white flowers. [mod.L f. Gk *keanōthos* kind of thistle]

cease /sees/ *v. & n.* ● *v.tr. & intr.* stop; bring or come to an end (*ceased breathing*). ● *n.* (in **without cease**) unendingly. □ **cease fire** *Mil.* stop firing. **cease-fire** *n.* **1** the order to do this. **2** a period of truce; a suspension of hostilities. [ME f. OF *cesser*, L *cessare* frequent. of *cedere cess-* yield]
■ *v.* stop, end, finish, terminate, halt, discontinue, break *or* leave off (from), refrain (from), *literary* desist (from); abandon, cut off, bring to a close *or* an end *or* a halt, suspend, drop, sever; die away, come to a close *or* an end, grind to a halt, expire, die a natural death. ● *n.* (**without cease**) ceaselessly, endlessly, unendingly, incessantly, interminably, continuously, continually, constantly, ad infinitum, infinitely, perpetually, for ever, eternally, everlastingly, nonstop, unremittingly,

without respite, *colloq.* without (a) letup. □ **cease-fire 2** see TRUCE.

ceaseless /séeslis/ *adj.* without end; not ceasing. □□ **ceaselessly** *adv.*

cecitis /sikítis/ *n.* inflammation of the cecum.

cecum /séekəm/ *n.* (*Brit.* **caecum**) (*pl.* **-ca** /-kə/) a blind-ended pouch at the junction of the small and large intestines. □□ **cecal** *adj.* [L for *intestinum caecum* f. *caecus* blind, transl. of Gk *tuphlon enteron*]

cedar /séedər/ *n.* **1** any spreading evergreen conifer of the genus *Cedrus*, bearing tufts of small needles and cones of papery scales. **2** any of various similar conifers yielding timber. **3** (in full **cedar wood**) the fragrant durable wood of any cedar tree. □□ **cedarn** *adj. poet.* [ME f. OF *cedre* f. L *cedrus* f. Gk *kedros*]

cede /seed/ *v.tr.* give up one's rights to or possession of. [F *céder* or L *cedere* yield]

■ yield, give up, grant, surrender, deliver up, turn *or* make *or* hand over, *archaic* render; relinquish, forgo, abandon, renounce, abdicate, forfeit, resign, *colloq.* pass up.

cedilla /sidílə/ *n.* **1** a mark written under the letter *c*, esp. in French, to show that it is sibilant (as in *façade*). **2** a similar mark under *s* in Turkish and other Eastern languages. [Sp. *cedilla* dimin. of *zeda* f. Gk *zēta* letter Z]

ceilidh /káylee/ *n.* orig. *Ir. & Sc.* an informal gathering for conversation, music, dancing, songs, and stories. [Gael.]

ceiling /séeling/ *n.* **1 a** the upper interior surface of a room or other similar compartment. **b** the material forming this. **2** an upper limit on prices, wages, performance, etc. **3** *Aeron.* the maximum altitude a given aircraft can reach. **4** *Naut.* the inside planking of a ship's bottom and sides. [ME *celynge, siling,* perh. ult. f. L *caelum* heaven or *celare* hide]

celadon /sélədon/ *n. & adj.* ● *n.* **1** a willow-green color. **2** a gray-green glaze used on some pottery. **3** Chinese pottery glazed in this way. ● *adj.* of a gray-green color. [F, f. the name of a character in d'Urfé's *L'Astrée* (1607–27)]

celandine /séləndin, -deen/ *n.* either of two yellow-flowered plants, the greater celandine, *Chelidonium majus*, and the lesser celandine, *Ranunculus ficaria*. [ME and OF *celidoine* ult. f. Gk *khelidōn* swallow: the flowering of the plant was associated with the arrival of swallows]

-cele /seel/ *comb. form* (also **-coele**) *Med.* swelling; hernia (*gastrocele*). [Gk *kēlē* tumor]

celeb /siléb/ *n. colloq.* a celebrity; a star.

celebrant /sélibrənt/ *n.* a person who performs a rite, esp. a priest at the Eucharist. [F *célébrant* or L *celebrare celebrant-*: see CELEBRATE]

■ officiant, officiator, celebrator; priest.

celebrate /sélibrayt/ *v.* **1** *tr.* mark (a festival or special event) with festivities, etc. **2** *tr.* perform publicly and duly (a religious ceremony, etc.). **3 a** *tr.* officiate at (the Eucharist). **b** *intr.* officiate, esp. at the Eucharist. **4** *intr.* engage in festivities, usu. after a special event, etc. **5** *tr.* (esp. as **celebrated** *adj.*) honor publicly; make widely known. □□ **celebration** /-bráyshən/ *n.* **celebrator** *n.* **celebratory** /-brətáwree, sélébrətáwree/ *adj.* [L *celebrare* f. *celeber -bris* frequented, honored]

■ **1** mark, memorialize, commemorate, solemnize, honor; hold, keep, observe, recognize. **2** perform, solemnize, ritualize, officiate at; sanctify, hallow, consecrate, dedicate. **4** have a party, have a good time, revel, rejoice, make merry, *archaic* wassail, *colloq.* party, paint the town red, whoop it up, make whoopee. **5** extol, praise, exalt, glorify, laud, eulogize, honor, immortalize, lionize; publicize, advertise, broadcast; (**celebrated**) acclaimed; famous, renowned, well-known, famed, legendary, great, memorable, prominent, noted, notable, eminent, noteworthy, distinguished, illustrious; notorious. □□ **celebration** commemoration, memorialization, observance, solemnization, sanctification, ritualization, dedication, consecration; performance, officiation; party, function, festival, fete, gala, revel; festivities, revelry, merrymaking, merriment.

celebrity /silébritee/ *n.* (*pl.* **-ies**) **1** a well-known person. **2** fame. [F *célébrité* or L *celebritas* f. *celeber*: see CELEBRATE]

■ **1** notable, dignitary, star, luminary, personage, name, personality, superstar, somebody, success story. **2** renown, fame, repute, reputation, prominence, eminence, distinction, prestige, famousness, popularity, notability, acclaim, glory; notoriety.

celeriac /siléereeak, silér-/ *n.* a variety of celery with a swollen turniplike stem base used as a vegetable. [CELERY: *-ac* is unexplained]

celerity /siléritee/ *n. archaic* or *literary* swiftness (esp. of a living creature). [ME f. F *célérité* f. L *celeritas -tatis* f. *celer* swift]

■ see SPEED *n.* 1.

celery /séləree/ *n.* an umbelliferous plant, *Apium graveolens*, with closely packed succulent leafstalks used as a vegetable. [F *céleri* f. It. dial. *selleri* f. L *selinum* f. Gk *selinon* parsley]

celesta /siléstə/ *n. Mus.* a small keyboard instrument resembling a glockenspiel, with hammers striking steel plates suspended over wooden resonators, giving an ethereal bell-like sound. [pseudo-L f. F *céleste*: see CELESTE]

celeste /silést/ *n. Mus.* **1** an organ and harmonium stop with a soft tremulous tone. **2** = CELESTA. [F *céleste* heavenly f. L *caelestis* f. *caelum* heaven]

celestial /siléschəl/ *adj.* **1** heavenly; divinely good or beautiful; sublime. **2 a** of the sky; of the part of the sky commonly observed in astronomy, etc. **b** of heavenly bodies. □ **celestial equator** the great circle of the sky in the plane perpendicular to the earth's axis. **celestial horizon** see HORIZON 1c. **celestial navigation** navigation by the stars, etc. □□ **celestially** *adv.* [ME f. OF f. med.L *caelestialis* f. L *caelestis*: see CELESTE]

■ **1** heavenly, divine, spiritual, godly, godlike, holy, paradisiacal, paradisal, sublime, empyrean, empyreal, elysian, ethereal, immortal, supernatural, unearthly; perfect, ideal, exquisite, blissful, idyllic. **2 a** astronomical. **b** astral, stellar, solar, planetary, nebular, *attrib.* star.

celiac /séeleeak/ *adj.* (esp. *Brit.* **coeliac**) of or affecting the belly. □ **celiac disease** a digestive disease of the small intestine brought on by contact with dietary gluten. [L *coeliacus* f. Gk *koiliakos* f. *koilia* belly]

celibate /sélibət/ *adj. & n.* ● *adj.* **1** committed to abstention from sexual relations and from marriage, esp. for religious reasons. **2** abstaining from sexual relations. ● *n.* a celibate person. □□ **celibacy** /-bəsee/ *n.* [F *célibat* or L *caelibatus* unmarried state f. *caelebs -ibis* unmarried]

■ *adj.* **1** abstinent, abstemious, continent, ascetic, temperate, self-restrained, self-disciplined; unmarried, single, unwed. **2** virgin, virginal, pure, chaste, unsullied, undefiled, virtuous, immaculate. □□ **celibacy** abstemiousness, self-denial, continence, (self-)restraint, abstinence, temperance, asceticism; chastity, virginity, purity, virtue, maidenhead, maidenhood.

cell /sel/ *n.* **1** a small room, esp. in a prison or monastery. **2** a small compartment, e.g., in a honeycomb. **3** a small group as a nucleus of political activity, esp. of a subversive kind. **4** *hist.* a small monastery or nunnery dependent on a larger one. **5** *Biol.* **a** the structural and functional usu. microscopic unit of an organism, consisting of cytoplasm and a nucleus enclosed in a membrane. **b** an enclosed cavity in an organism, etc. **6** *Electr.* a vessel for containing electrodes within an electrolyte for current generation or electrolysis. □□ **celled** *adj.* (also in *comb.*). [ME f. OF *celle* or f. L *cella* storeroom, etc.]

■ **1** room, closet, cubby(hole), den, cubicle, stall, apartment, *archaic* cabinet, *poet. or archaic* chamber. **2** see COMPARTMENT *n.* 1. **3** set, circle, ring, gang, band,

---

/. . ./ **pronunciation**   ● **part of speech**
□ **phrases, idioms, and compounds**
□□ **derivatives**   ■ **synonym section**
cross-references appear in SMALL CAPITALS or *italics*

team, confederacy, federation, clique, coterie, fraternity, brotherhood, secret society.

cellar /sélər/ *n. & v.* ● *n.* **1** a room below ground level in a house, used for storage, etc. **2** a stock of wine in a cellar (*has a good cellar*). ● *v.tr.* store or put in a cellar. [ME f. AF *celer*, OF *celier* f. LL *cellarium* storehouse]
■ *n.* **1** basement, vault. ● *v.* see STORE *v.* 1.

cellarage /sélərij/ *n.* **1** cellar accommodation. **2** the charge for the use of a cellar or storehouse.

cellarer /sélərər/ *n.* a monastic officer in charge of wine.

cellaret /sélərét/ *n.* a case, cabinet, etc., for holding wine bottles in a dining room.

cello /chélō/ *n.* (*pl.* **-os**) a bass instrument of the violin family, held upright on the floor between the legs of the seated player. □□ **cellist** *n.* [abbr. of VIOLONCELLO]

cellophane /sélofayn/ *n. formerly propr.* a thin transparent wrapping material made from viscose. [CELLULOSE + *-phane* (cf. DIAPHANOUS)]

cellphone /sélfōn/ *n.* a small, portable radiotelephone having access to a cellular telephone system.

cellular /sélyələr/ *adj.* **1** of or having small compartments or cavities. **2** of open texture; porous. **3** *Physiol.* of or consisting of cells. □ **cellular telephone** (or **phone**) a system of mobile radiotelephone transmission with an area divided into "cells" each served by its own small transmitter. □□ **cellularity** /-láritee/ *n.* **cellulate** *adj.* **cellulation** /-láyshən/ *n.* **cellulous** *adj.* [F *cellulaire* f. mod.L *cellularis*: see CELLULE]

cellule /sélyōōl/ *n. Biol.* a small cell or cavity. [F *cellule* or L *cellula* dimin. of *cella* CELL]

cellulite /sélyəlīt/ *n.* a lumpy form of fat, esp. on the hips and thighs of women, causing puckering of the skin. [F (as CELLULE)]

cellulitis /sélyəlítis/ *n.* inflammation of cellular tissue.

celluloid /sélyəloyd/ *n.* **1** a transparent flammable plastic made from camphor and cellulose nitrate. **2** motion-picture film. [irreg. f. CELLULOSE]

cellulose /sélyəlōs, -lōz/ *n.* **1** *Biochem.* a carbohydrate forming the main constituent of plant cell walls, used in the production of textile fibers. **2** (in general use) a paint or lacquer consisting of esp. cellulose acetate or nitrate in solution. □□ **cellulosic** /-lōsik/ *adj.* [F (as CELLULE)]

celom var. of COELOM.

Celsius /sélseeəs/ *adj.* of or denoting a temperature on the Celsius scale. □ **Celsius scale** a scale of temperature on which water freezes at 0° and boils at 100° under standard conditions. [A. *Celsius*, Sw. astronomer d. 1744]

Celt /kelt, selt/ *n.* (also **Kelt**) a member of a group of W. European peoples, including the pre-Roman inhabitants of Britain and Gaul and their descendants, esp. in Ireland, Wales, Scotland, Cornwall, Brittany, and the Isle of Man. [L *Celtae* (pl.) f. Gk *Keltoi*]

celt /kelt/ *n. Archaeol.* a stone or metal prehistoric implement with a chisel edge. [med.L *celtes* chisel]

Celtic /kéltik, séltik/ *adj. & n.* ● *adj.* of or relating to the Celts. ● *n.* a group of languages spoken by Celtic peoples, including Gaelic, Welsh, Cornish, and Breton. □ **Celtic cross** a Latin cross with a circle around the center. □□ **Celticism** /-tisizəm/ *n.* [L *celticus* (as CELT) or F *celtique*]

cembalo /chémbəlō/ *n.* (*pl.* **-os**) a harpsichord. [abbr. of CLAVICEMBALO]

cement /simént/ *n. & v.* ● *n.* **1** a powdery substance made by calcining lime and clay, mixed with water to form mortar or used in concrete (see also PORTLAND CEMENT). **2** any similar substance that hardens and fastens on setting. **3** a uniting factor or principle. **4** a substance for filling cavities in teeth. **5** (also **cementum**) *Anat.* a thin layer of bony material that fixes teeth to the jaw. ● *v.tr.* **1 a** unite with or as with cement. **b** establish or strengthen (a friendship, etc.). **2** apply cement to. **3** line or cover with cement. □ **cement mixer** a machine (usu. with a revolving drum) for mixing cement with water. □□ **cementer** *n.* [ME f. OF *ciment* f. L *caementum* quarry stone f. *caedere* hew]
■ *n.* **2** mortar, bond, glue, gum, paste, solder, adhesive. ● *v.* **1 a** stick, glue, paste, solder, weld, braze, bond; join, bind, combine, unite, fuse. **b** see REINFORCE.

cementation /seémentáyshən/ *n.* **1** the act or process of cementing or being cemented. **2** the heating of iron with charcoal powder to form steel.

cemetery /sémiteree/ *n.* (*pl.* **-ies**) a burial ground, esp. one not in a churchyard. [LL *coemeterium* f. Gk *koimētērion* dormitory f. *koimaō* put to sleep]
■ see GRAVEYARD.

cenobite /seénəbit/ *n.* (esp. *Brit.* **coenobite**) a member of a monastic community. □□ **cenobitic** /-bítik/ *adj.* **cenobitical** *adj.* [OF *cenobite* or eccl.L *coenobita* f. LL *coenobium* f. Gk *koinobion* convent f. *koinos* common + *bios* life]
■ see MONK.

cenotaph /sénətaf/ *n.* a tomblike monument, esp. a war memorial, to a person whose body is elsewhere. [F *cénotaphe* f. LL *cenotaphium* f. Gk *kenos* empty + *taphos* tomb]
■ see MONUMENT 1–3.

Cenozoic /seénəzṓik, sén-/ (also **Cainozoic** /kínə-/, **Caenozoic** /seénə-/) *adj. & n. Geol.* ● *adj.* of or relating to the most recent era of geological time, marked by the evolution and development of mammals, birds, and flowers. ¶ Cf. Appendix VII. ● *n.* this era (cf. MESOZOIC, PALEOZOIC). [Gk *kainos* new + *zōion* animal]

censer /sénsər/ *n.* a vessel in which incense is burned, esp. during a religious procession or ceremony. [ME f. AF *censer*, OF *censier* aphetic of *encensier* f. *encens* INCENSE[1]]

censor /sénsər/ *n. & v.* ● *n.* **1** an official authorized to examine printed matter, movies, news, etc., before public release, and to suppress any parts on the grounds of obscenity, a threat to security, etc. **2** *Rom.Hist.* either of two annual magistrates responsible for holding censuses and empowered to supervise public morals. **3** *Psychol.* an impulse that is said to prevent certain ideas and memories from emerging into consciousness. ● *v.tr.* **1** act as a censor of. **2** make deletions or changes in. ¶ As a verb, often confused with *censure*. □□ **censorial** /-sáwreeəl/ *adj.* **censorship** *n.* [L f. *censēre* assess: in sense 3 mistransl. of G *Zensur* censorship]
■ *v.* see EDIT *v.* 5b.

censorious /sensáwreeəs/ *adj.* severely critical; faultfinding; quick or eager to criticize. □□ **censoriously** *adv.* **censoriousness** *n.* [L *censorius*: see CENSOR]
■ see CRITICAL 1.

censure /sénshər/ *v. & n.* ● *v.tr.* criticize harshly; reprove. ¶ Often confused with *censor*. ● *n.* harsh criticism; expression of disapproval. □□ **censurable** *adj.* [ME f. OF f. L *censura* f. *censēre* assess]
■ *v.* see CRITICIZE 1. ● *n.* see CRITICISM 1a.

census /sénsəs/ *n.* (*pl.* **censuses**) the official count of a population or of a class of things, often with various statistics noted. [L f. *censēre* assess]
■ see POLL *n.* 2.

cent /sent/ *n.* **1 a** a monetary unit valued at one-hundredth of a dollar or other metric unit. **b** a coin of this value. **2** *colloq.* a very small sum of money. **3** see PERCENT. [F *cent* or It. *cento* or L *centum* hundred]

cent. *abbr.* century.

centaur /séntawr/ *n.* a creature in Greek mythology with the head, arms, and torso of a man and the body and legs of a horse. [ME f. L *centaurus* f. Gk *kentauros*, of unkn. orig.]

centaury /séntawree/ *n.* (*pl.* **-ies**) any plant of the genus *Centaurium*, esp. *C. erythraea*, formerly used in medicine. [LL *centaurea* ult. f. *kentauros* CENTAUR: from the legend that it was discovered by the centaur Chiron]

centavo /sentaavō/ *n.* a small coin of Spain, Portugal, and some Latin American countries, worth one-hundredth of the standard unit. [Sp. f. L *centum* hundred]

centenarian /séntináireeən/ *n. & adj.* ● *n.* a person a hundred or more years old. ● *adj.* a hundred or more years old.

centenary /séntənaree, séntəneree/ *n. & adj.* ● *n.* (*pl.* **-ies**) = CENTENNIAL *n.* ● *adj.* **1** of or relating to a centenary. **2** occurring every hundred years. [L *centenarius* f. *centeni* hundred each f. *centum* a hundred]

centennial /sénteeeəl/ *adj. & n.* ● *adj.* **1** lasting for a hundred years. **2** occurring every hundred years. ● *n.* **1** a hundredth anniversary. **2** a celebration of this. [L *centum* a hundred, after BIENNIAL]

center /séntər/ *n. & v.* (*Brit.* **centre**) ● *n.* **1** the middle point, esp. of a line, circle, or sphere, equidistant from the ends or from any point on the circumference or surface. **2** a pivot or axis of rotation. **3 a** a place or group of buildings forming a central point in a district, city, etc., or a main area for an activity (*shopping center; town center*). **b** (with preceding word) a piece or set of equipment for a number of connected functions (*music center*). **4** a point of concentration or dispersion; a nucleus or source. **5** a political party or group holding moderate opinions. **6** the filling in a chocolate, candy, etc. **7** *Sports* **a** the middle player in a line or group in many games. **b** a kick or hit from the side to the center of the playing area. **8** (in a lathe, etc.) a conical adjustable support for the workpiece. **9** (*attrib.*) of or at the center. ● *v.* **1** *intr.* (foll. by *in, on; disp.* foll. by *around*) have as its main center. **2** *tr.* place in the center. **3** *tr.* mark with a center. **4** *tr.* (foll. by *in*, etc.) concentrate. **5** *tr. Sports* kick or hit (the ball) from the side to the center of the playing area. □ **center bit** a boring tool with a center point and side cutters. **center of attention 1** a person or thing that draws general attention. **2** *Physics* the point to which bodies tend by gravity. **center of gravity** (or **mass**) the point at which the weight of a body may be considered to act. **center spread** the two facing middle pages of a newspaper, etc. □□ **centered** *adj.* (often in *comb.*). **centermost** *adj.* **centric** *adj.* **centrical** *adj.* **centricity** /-trísitee/ *n.* [ME f. OF *centre* or L *centrum* f. Gk *kentron* sharp point]

■ **1** middle; midpoint, halfway point *or* line; bull's-eye. **2** pivot, axis, fulcrum, nave, hub. **3 a** focal point, hub, focus. **4** nucleus, source, nub, core, heart, kernel, navel, bosom; midst, interior, bowels. **6** filling, inside, middle. **9** (*attrib.*) see CENTRAL 1. ● *v.* **1** (*center on* or *in*) cluster *or* collect *or* congregate around, converge on. **4** focus, concentrate, direct, train, turn.

centerboard /séntərbawrd/ *n.* (*Brit.* **centreboard**) a retractable keel, as for a small sailboat.

centerfold /séntərfōld/ *n.* (*Brit.* **centrefold**) a printed and usu. illustrated sheet folded to form the center spread of a magazine, etc.

centering /séntəring/) *n.* a temporary frame used to support an arch, dome, etc., while under construction.

centerpiece /séntərpees/ *n.* **1** an ornament for the middle of a table. **2** a principal item.

centesimal /sentésiməl/ *adj.* reckoning or reckoned by hundredths. □□ **centesimally** *adv.* [L *centesimus* hundredth f. *centum* hundred]

centi- /séntee/ *comb. form* **1** one-hundredth, esp. of a unit in the metric system (*centigram; centiliter*). **2** hundred. ¶ Abbr.: **c**. [L *centum* hundred]

centigrade /séntigrayd/ *adj.* **1** = CELSIUS. **2** having a scale of a hundred degrees. ¶ In sense 1 *Celsius* is usually preferred in technical use. [F f. L *centum* hundred + *gradus* step]

centigram /séntigram/ *n.* (also *Brit.* **centigramme**) a metric unit of mass, equal to one-hundredth of a gram.

centiliter /séntileetər/ *n.* (*Brit.* **centilitre**) a metric unit of capacity, equal to one-hundredth of a liter.

centime /sonNteém/ *n.* **1** a monetary unit valued at one-hundredth of a franc. **2** a coin of this value. [F f. L *centum* a hundred]

centimeter /séntimeetər/ *n.* (*Brit.* **centimetre**) a metric unit of length, equal to one-hundredth of a meter. □ **centimeter-gram-second system** the system using these as basic units of length, mass, and time. ¶ Abbr.: **cgs system**.

centipede /séntipeed/ *n.* any arthropod of the class Chilopoda, with a wormlike body of many segments each with a pair of legs. [F *centipède* or L *centipeda* f. *centum* hundred + *pes pedis* foot]

cento /séntō/ *n.* (*pl.* **-os**) a composition made up of quotations from other authors. [L, = patchwork garment]

central /séntrəl/ *adj.* **1** of, at, or forming the center. **2** from the center. **3** chief; essential; most important. □ **Central America** the isthmus joining N. and S. America, usually comprising the countries from Guatemala and Belize south to Panama. **central bank** a national bank issuing currency, etc. **central heating** a method of warming a building by

pipes, radiators, etc., fed from a central source of heat. **central nervous system** *Anat.* the complex of nerve tissues that controls the activities of the body, in vertebrates the brain and spinal cord. **central processor** (or **processing unit**) the principal operating part of a computer. □□ **centrality** /-trálitee/ *n.* **centrally** *adv.* [F *central* or L *centralis* f. *centrum* CENTER]

■ **1** middle, center, medial, median, mid, *Anat.* mesial; inner, inside. **3** chief, main, principal, major, key, leading, dominant, prime, primary, preeminent; important, significant; essential, vital, crucial, critical, fundamental, cardinal, pivotal, capital, basic.

centralism /séntrəlizəm/ *n.* a system that centralizes (esp. an administration) (see also *democratic centralism*). □□ **centralist** *n.*

centralize /séntrəlīz/ *v.* **1** *tr. & intr.* bring or come to a center. **2** *tr.* **a** concentrate (administration) at a single center. **b** subject (a government) to this system. □□ **centralization** *n.*

■ **1** see CONCENTRATE *v.* 2, CONVERGE.

centre *Brit.* var. of CENTER.

centreboard *Brit.* var. of CENTERBOARD.

centrefold *Brit.* var. of CENTERFOLD.

-centric /séntrik/ *comb. form* forming adjectives with the sense 'having a (specified) center' (*anthropocentric; eccentric*). [after *concentric*, etc., f. Gk *kentrikos*: see CENTER]

centrifugal /sentrífyəgəl, -trífə-/ *adj.* moving or tending to move from a center (cf. CENTRIPETAL). □ **centrifugal force** an apparent force that acts outward on a body moving about a center. □□ **centrifugally** *adv.* [mod.L *centrifugus* f. L *centrum* center + *fugere* flee]

centrifuge /séntrifyōōj/ *n. & v.* ● *n.* a machine with a rapidly rotating device designed to separate liquids from solids or other liquids (e.g., cream from milk). ● *v.tr.* **1** subject to the action of a centrifuge. **2** separate by centrifuge. □□ **centrifugation** /-fyəgáyshən, -fə-/ *n.*

centriole /séntreeōl/ *n. Biol.* a minute organelle usu. within a centrosome involved esp. in the development of spindles in cell division. [med.L *centriolum* dimin. of *centrum* center]

centripetal /sentrípit'l/ *adj.* moving or tending to move toward a center (cf. CENTRIFUGAL). □ **centripetal force** the force acting on a body causing it to move about a center. □□ **centripetally** *adv.* [mod.L *centripetus* f. L *centrum* center + *petere* seek]

centrist /séntrist/ *n. Polit.* often *derog.* a person who holds moderate views. □□ **centrism** *n.*

■ see MODERATE *n.*

centromere /séntrəmeer/ *n. Biol.* the point on a chromosome to which the spindle is attached during cell division. [L *centrum* center + Gk *meros* part]

centrosome /séntrəsōm/ *n. Biol.* a distinct part of the cytoplasm in a cell, usu. near the nucleus, that contains the centriole. [G *Centrosoma* f. L *centrum* center + Gk *sōma* body]

centuple /séntəpəl, séntyə-/ *n., adj., & v.* ● *n.* a hundredfold amount. ● *adj.* increased a hundredfold. ● *v.tr.* multiply by a hundred; increase a hundredfold. [F *centuple* or eccl.L *centuplus, centuplex* f. L *centum* hundred]

centurion /sentyōóreeən, -tyŏŏr-/ *n.* the commander of a century in the ancient Roman army. [ME f. L *centurio -onis* (as CENTURY)]

century /sénchəree/ *n.* (*pl.* **-ies**) **1 a** a period of one hundred years. **b** any of the centuries calculated from the birth of Christ (*twentieth century* = 1901–2000; *fifth century* BC = 500–401 BC). ¶ In modern use often calculated as, e.g., 1900–1999. **2 a** a score, etc., of a hundred in a sporting event, esp. a hundred runs by one batsman in cricket. **b** a group of a hundred things. **3 a** a company in the ancient Roman army, orig. of 100 men. **b** an ancient Roman political division for voting. □ **century plant** a plant, *Agave americana*, flowering once in many years and yielding sap

---

/.../ **pronunciation**	● **part of speech**
□ **phrases, idioms, and compounds**	
□□ **derivatives**	■ **synonym section**
cross-references appear in SMALL CAPITALS or *italics*	

from which tequila is distilled: also called *American aloe* (see ALOE). [L *centuria* f. *centum* hundred]

CEO *abbr.* chief executive officer.

cep /sep/ *n.* an edible mushroom, *Boletus edulis*, with a stout stalk and brown smooth cap. [F *cèpe* f. Gascon *cep* f. L *cippus* stake]

cephalic /sifálik/ *adj.* of or in the head. □ **cephalic index** *Anthropol.* a number expressing the ratio of a head's greatest breadth to its greatest length. [F *céphalique* f. L *cephalicus* f. Gk *kephalikos* f. *kephalē* head]

-cephalic /sifálik/ *comb. form* = -CEPHALOUS.

cephalopod /séfələpod/ *n.* any mollusk of the class Cephalopoda, having a distinct tentacled head, e.g., octopus, squid, and cuttlefish. [Gk *kephalē* head + *pous podos* foot]

cephalothorax /séfəlōtháwraks/ *n.* (*pl.* **-thoraxes** or **-thoraces** /-tháwrəseez/) *Anat.* the fused head and thorax of a spider, crab, or other arthropod.

-cephalous /séfələs/ *comb. form* -headed (*brachycephalous*; *dolichocephalic*). [Gk *kephalē* head]

Cepheid /séefeeid, séf-/ *n.* (in full **Cepheid variable**) *Astron.* any of a class of variable stars with a regular cycle of brightness that can be used to measure distances. [L *Cepheus* f. Gk *Kēpheus*, a mythical king whose name was given to a constellation]

ceramic /sirámik/ *adj. & n.* ● *adj.* **1** made of (esp.) clay and permanently hardened by heat (*a ceramic bowl*). **2** of or relating to ceramics (*the ceramic arts*). ● *n.* **1** a ceramic article or product. **2** a substance, esp. clay, used to make ceramic articles. [Gk *keramikos* f. *keramos* pottery]

ceramics /sirámiks/ *n.pl.* **1** ceramic products collectively (*exhibition of ceramics*). **2** (usu. treated as *sing.*) the art of making ceramic articles.
■ **1** see POTTERY.

ceramist /sirámist, -sérə/ *n.* a person who makes ceramics.

cerastes /sirásteez/ *n.* any viper of the genus *Cerastes*, esp. *C. cerastes*, having a sharp, upright spike over each eye and moving forward in a lateral motion. [L f. Gk *kerastēs* f. *keras* horn]

cerastium /sirásteeəm/ *n.* any plant of the genus *Cerastium*, with white flowers and often horn-shaped capsules. [mod.L f. Gk *kerastes* horned f. *keras* horn]

cere /seer/ *n.* a waxy fleshy covering at the base of the upper beak in some birds. [L *cera* wax]

cereal /séereeəl/ *n. & adj* ● *n.* **1** (usu. in *pl.*) **a** any kind of grain used for food. **b** any grass producing this, e.g., wheat, corn, rye, etc. **2** a breakfast food made from a cereal and requiring no cooking. ● *adj.* of edible grain or products of it. [L *cerealis* f. *Ceres* goddess of agriculture]
■ *n.* **1 a** see GRAIN *n.* 2.

cerebellum /séribéləm/ *n.* (*pl.* **cerebellums** or **cerebella** /-lə/) the part of the brain at the back of the skull in vertebrates, which coordinates and regulates muscular activity. □□ **cerebellar** *adj.* [L dimin. of CEREBRUM]

cerebral /séribrəl, sərée-/ *adj.* **1** of the brain. **2** intellectual rather than emotional. **3** = CACUMINAL. □ **cerebral hemisphere** each of the two halves of the vertebrate cerebrum. **cerebral palsy** *Med.* spastic paralysis from brain damage before or at birth, with jerky or uncontrolled movements. □□ **cerebrally** *adv.* [L *cerebrum* brain]
■ **2** see INTELLECTUAL *adj.* 1.

cerebration /séribráyshən/ *n.* working of the brain. □ **unconscious cerebration** action of the brain with results reached without conscious thought. □□ **cerebrate** /-brayt/ *v.intr.*
■ see THOUGHT[1] 1, 3a.

cerebro- /séribrō, sərée-/ *comb. form* brain (*cerebrospinal*).

cerebrospinal /séribrōspínəl, sərée-/ *adj.* of the brain and spine.

cerebrovascular /séribrōváskyələr, sərée-/ *adj.* of the brain and its blood vessels.

cerebrum /séribrəm, sərée-/ *n.* (*pl.* **cerebrums** or **cerebra** /-brə/) the principal part of the brain in vertebrates, located in the front area of the skull, which integrates complex sensory and neural functions. [L, = brain]

cerecloth /séerklawth, -kloth/ *n. hist.* waxed cloth used as a

waterproof covering or (esp.) as a shroud. [earlier *cered cloth* f. *cere* to wax f. L *cerare* f. *cera* wax]
■ see SHROUD *n.* 1.

cerement /séermənt/ *n.* (usu. in *pl.*) *literary* graveclothes; cerecloth. [first used by Shakesp. in *Hamlet* (1602): app. f. CERECLOTH]
■ see SHROUD *n.* 1.

ceremonial /sérimōneeəl/ *adj. & n.* ● *adj.* **1** with or concerning ritual or ceremony. **2** formal (*a ceremonial bow*). ● *n.* **1** a system of rites, etc., to be used esp. at a formal or religious occasion. **2** the formalities or behavior proper to any occasion (*the ceremonial of a presidential appearance*). **3** *RC Ch.* a book containing an order of ritual. □□ **ceremonialism** *n.* **ceremonialist** *n.* **ceremonially** *adv.* [LL *caerimonialis* (as CEREMONY)]
■ *adj.* **1** ritual, celebratory, commemorative, state. **2** formal, solemn, stately, official, dignified, ceremonious, ritual, ritualistic, august, grand. ● *n.* **1** rite, ritual, service. **2** formality, ceremony, observance, form.

ceremonious /sérimōneeəs/ *adj.* **1** excessively polite; punctilious. **2** having or showing a fondness for ritualistic observance or formality. □□ **ceremoniously** *adv.* **ceremoniousness** *n.* [F *cérémonieux* or LL *caerimoniosus* (as CEREMONY)]
■ **1** punctilious, nice, courtly, overnice, exact, precise, correct, proper, prim, scrupulous, formal, stuffy, stiff, starchy, conventional, meticulous, careful. **2** ceremonial, formal, dignified, solemn, ritual, ritualistic, stately, official.

ceremony /sérimōnee/ *n.* (*pl.* **-ies**) **1** a formal religious or public occasion, esp. celebrating a particular event or anniversary. **2** formalities, esp. of an empty or ritualistic kind (*ceremony of exchanging compliments*). **3** excessively polite behavior (*bowed low with great ceremony*). □ **master of ceremonies 1** (also **MC** or **emcee**) a person introducing speakers at a banquet, entertainers in a variety show, contestants in a game show, etc. **2** a person in charge of ceremonies at a state or public occasion. **stand on ceremony** insist on the observance of formalities. **without ceremony** informally. [ME f. OF *ceremonie* or L *caerimonia* religious worship]
■ **1** rite(s), solemnity, service, ceremonial, ritual; function, celebration, pageant; formality, observance. **2** formalities, formality, pageantry, pomp, convention(s), niceties, proprieties, social graces or conventions, convenances, form, protocol; rigmarole. **3** punctiliousness, courtesy, etiquette, decorum, politeness, politesse, civility. □ **without ceremony** informally, casually, familiarly; unceremoniously.

Cerenkov radiation /chiréngkawf/ *n.* (also **Cherenkov**) the electromagnetic radiation emitted by particles moving in a medium at speeds faster than that of light in the same medium. [P. A. *Cherenkov*, Russian physicist b. 1904]

ceresin /sérisin/ *n.* a hard, whitish wax used with or instead of beeswax. [mod.L *ceres* f. L *cera* wax + -IN]

cerise /sərées, -réez/ *adj. & n.* ● *adj.* of a light, clear red. ● *n.* this color. [F, = CHERRY]
■ *adj.* see ROSY 1.

cerium /séereeəm/ *n.* *Chem.* a silvery metallic element of the lanthanide series occurring naturally in various minerals and used in the manufacture of lighter flints. ¶ Symb.: **Ce**. [named after the asteroid *Ceres*, discovered (1801) about the same time as this]

cermet /sérmet/ *n.* a heat-resistant material made of ceramic and sintered metal. [*ceramic* + *metal*]

CERN /sərn/ *abbr.* European Organization for Nuclear Research. [F *Conseil Européen pour la Recherche Nucléaire*, its former title]

cero- /séerō/ *comb. form* wax (cf. CEROGRAPHY, CEROPLASTIC). [L *cera* or Gk *kēros* wax]

cerography /seerógrəfee/ *n.* the technique of engraving or designing on or with wax.

ceroplastic /séerōplástik/ *adj.* **1** modeled in wax. **2** of or concerning wax modeling.

cert. /sərt/ *abbr.* **1** a certificate. **2** certified.

certain /sárt'n/ *adj. & pron.* ● *adj.* **1 a** (often foll. by *of*, or

that + clause) confident; convinced (*certain that I put it here*). **b** (often foll. by *that* + clause) indisputable; known for sure (*it is certain that he is guilty*). **2** (often foll. by *to* + infin.) **a** that may be relied on to happen (*it is certain to rain*). **b** destined (*certain to become a star*). **3** definite; unfailing; reliable (*a certain indication of the coming storm*; *his touch is certain*). **4** (of a person, place, etc.) that might be specified, but is not (*a certain lady*; *of a certain age*). **5** some though not much (*a certain reluctance*). **6** (of a person, place, etc.) existing, though probably unknown to the reader or hearer (*a certain John Smith*). ● *pron.* (as *pl.*) some but not all (*certain of them were wounded*). □ **for certain** without doubt. **make certain** = make sure (see SURE). [ME f. OF ult. f. L *certus* settled]
■ *adj.* **1 a** confident, convinced, sure, positive, satisfied, assured, persuaded. **b** sure, definite, indubitable, indisputable, undisputed, undoubted, clear, unequivocal, incontestable, undeniable, incontrovertible, irrefutable, unquestionable, unarguable; inevitable, inescapable, ineluctable, inexorable, unavoidable. **2 a** bound, sure. **b** destined, predestined, fated. **3** definite, firm, sure, decided, settled, stable, invariable, established, standard, constant, unchanging, steady, unfluctuating, nonfluctuating, final; unerring, dependable, unfailing, infallible, reliable, assured, guaranteed, necessary. **4** unnamed, unspecified, nonspecified, undefined; particular. **5** some, a few; a bit of, a little. **6** see ONE *adj.* 3a. ● *pron.* some, a number. □ **for certain** see *for a certainty* (CERTAINTY).

certainly /sə́rt'nlee/ *adv.* **1** undoubtedly; definitely. **2** confidently. **3** (in affirmative answer to a question or command) yes; by all means.
■ **1** see *undoubtedly* (UNDOUBTED). **3** see ABSOLUTELY 6.

certainty /sə́rt'ntee/ *n.* (*pl.* **-ies**) **1 a** an undoubted fact. **b** a certain prospect (*his return is a certainty*). **2** (often foll. by *of*, or *that* + clause) an absolute conviction (*has a certainty of his own worth*). **3** (often foll. by *to* + infin.) a thing or person that may be relied on (*a certainty to win the Derby*). □ **for a certainty** beyond the possibility of doubt. [ME f. AF *certainté*, OF *-eté* (as CERTAIN)]
■ **1 a** fact, actuality, reality, truth, *archaic* surety. **b** sure thing, moral certainty, *colloq.* cinch. **2** assurance, self-assurance, assuredness, definiteness, confidence, conviction, faith, authoritativeness, positiveness, certitude, sureness, fixedness. □ **for a certainty** for certain, assuredly, definitely, certainly, surely, positively; undoubtedly, indubitably, without (a) doubt, beyond *or* without a shadow of a doubt, undeniably, unquestionably, absolutely, *colloq.* for sure.

certifiable /sə́rtifíəbəl/ *adj.* **1** able or needing to be certified. **2** *colloq.* insane.
■ **2** see INSANE 1.

certificate *n. & v.* ● *n.* /sərtífikət/ a formal document attesting a fact, esp. birth, marriage, death, a medical condition, a level of achievement, a fulfillment of requirements, ownership of shares, etc. ● *v.tr.* /sərtífikayt/ (esp. as **certificated** *adj.*) provide with or license or attest by a certificate. □ **certificate of deposit** a certificate issued by a bank to a depositor, stating the amount of money on deposit, usu. at a specified rate of interest and for a specified time period. □□ **certification** /sə́rtifikáyshən/ *n.* [F *certificat* or med.L *certificatum* f. *certificare*: see CERTIFY]
■ *n.* see DOCUMENT *n.*

certify /sə́rtifī/ *v.tr.* (**-ies, -ied**) **1** make a formal statement of; attest; attest to (*certified that he had witnessed the crime*). **2** declare by certificate (that a person is qualified or competent) (*certified as a trained bookkeeper*). **3** officially declare insane (*he should be certified*). □ **certified check** a check the validity of which is guaranteed by a bank. **certified mail** a postal service in which the dispatch and receipt of a letter or package are recorded. **certified milk** milk guaranteed free from the tuberculosis bacillus. **certified public accountant** a member of an officially accredited professional body of accountants. [ME f. OF *certifier* f. med.L *certificare* f. L *certus* certain]

■ **1** confirm, attest (to), verify, vouch for, testify (to), bear witness to, affirm, declare, asseverate, corroborate, substantiate, endorse, guarantee, warrant, *formal* aver; swear.

certiorari /sə́rsheeəráiree, -raírī/ *n. Law* a writ from a higher court requesting the records of a case tried in a lower court. [LL passive of *certiorare* inform f. *certior* compar. of *certus* certain]

certitude /sə́rtitōōd, -tyōōd/ *n.* a feeling of absolute certainty or conviction. [ME f. LL *certitudo* f. *certus* certain]
■ see CONVICTION 2a.

cerulean /sərōōleeən/ *adj. & n. literary* ● *adj.* deep blue like a clear sky. ● *n.* this color. [L *caeruleus* sky blue f. *caelum* sky]

cerumen /sərōōmen/ *n.* the yellow waxy substance in the outer ear. □□ **ceruminous** *adj.* [mod.L f. L *cera* wax]

ceruse /sirōōs, seerōōs/ *n.* white lead. [ME f. OF f. L *cerussa*, perh. f. Gk *kēros* wax]

cervelat /sə́rvəlaa, -lat/ *n.* a kind of smoked pork or beef sausage. [obs. F f. It. *cervellata*]

cervical /sə́rvikəl/ *adj. Anat.* **1** of or relating to the neck (*cervical vertebrae*). **2** of or relating to the cervix. □ **cervical screening** examination of a large number of apparently healthy women for cervical cancer. **cervical smear** a specimen of cellular material from the neck of the womb for detection of cancer. [F *cervical* or mod.L *cervicalis* f. L *cervix -icis* neck]

cervine /sə́rvīn/ *adj.* of or like a deer. [L *cervinus* f. *cervus* deer]

cervix /sə́rviks/ *n.* (*pl.* **cervices** /-viseez/ or **cervixes**) *Anat.* **1** the neck. **2** any necklike structure, esp. the neck of the womb. [L]

Cesarean /sizáireeən/ *adj. & n.* (also **Cesarian**, **Caesarean**, **Caesarian**) ● *adj.* (of a birth) effected by cesarean section. ● *n.* a cesarean section. □ **cesarean section** (also **C-section**) an operation for delivering a child by cutting through the wall of the abdomen (Julius Caesar supposedly having been born this way). [L *Caesarianus*]

cesarevitch /sizáirivich, -zaár-/ *n. hist.* the eldest son of the emperor of Russia (cf. TSAREVICH). [Russ. *tsesarevich*]

cesium /sée'zeeəm/ *n.* (*Brit.* **caesium**) a soft, silver-white element of the alkali metal group, occurring naturally in a number of minerals, and used in photoelectric cells. ¶ Symb.: **Cs.** □ **cesium clock** an atomic clock that uses cesium. [L *caesius*)]

cess[1] /ses/ *n.* (also **sess**) *Sc., Ir., & Ind.*, etc., a tax; a levy. [properly *sess* for obs. *assess* n.: see ASSESS]

cess[2] /ses/ *n. Ir.* □ **bad cess to** may evil befall (*bad cess to their clan*). [perh. f. CESS[1]]

cessation /sesáyshən/ *n.* **1** a ceasing (*cessation of the truce*). **2** a pause (*resumed fighting after the cessation*). [ME f. L *cessatio* f. *cessare* CEASE]
■ **1** see END *n.* 3a, b. **2** see REST[1] *n.* 3.

cession /séshən/ *n.* **1** (often foll. by *of*) the ceding or giving up (of rights, property, and esp. of territory by a nation). **2** the territory, etc., so ceded. [ME f. OF *cession* or L *cessio* f. *cedere cess-* go away]
■ **1** see SURRENDER *n.*

cessionary /séshəneree/ *n.* (*pl.* **-ies**) *Law* an assignee.

cesspit /séspit/ *n.* **1** a pit for the disposal of refuse. **2** = CESSPOOL. [*cess* in CESSPOOL + PIT[1]]

cesspool /séspōol/ *n.* **1** an underground container for the temporary storage of liquid waste or sewage. **2** a center of corruption, depravity, etc. [perh. alt., after POOL[1], f. earlier *cesperalle*, f. *suspiral* vent, water pipe, f. OF *souspirail* air-hole f. L *suspirare* breathe up, sigh (as SUB-, *spirare* breathe)]

cestode /séstōd/ *n.* (also **cestoid** /séstoyd/) any flatworm of the class Cestoda, including tapeworms. [L *cestus* f. Gk *kestos* girdle]

/.../ **pronunciation**   ● **part of speech**
□ **phrases, idioms, and compounds**
□□ **derivatives**   ■ **synonym section**
cross-references appear in SMALL CAPITALS or *italics*

cetacean /sitáyshən/ *n. & adj.* ● *n.* any marine mammal of the order Cetacea with streamlined hairless body and dorsal blowhole for breathing, including whales, dolphins, and porpoises. ● *adj.* of cetaceans. □□ **cetaceous** /-táyshəs/ *adj.* [mod.L *Cetacea* f. L *cetus* f. Gk *kētos* whale]

cetane /séetayn/ *n. Chem.* a colorless liquid hydrocarbon of the alkane series used in standardizing ratings of diesel fuel. □ **cetane number** a measure of the ignition properties of diesel fuel. [f. SPERMACETI after *methane*, etc.]

ceteris paribus /sétəris páribəs, káytəres paáribōōs/ *adv.* other things being equal. [L]

Ceylon moss /silón, say-/ *n.* a red seaweed, *Gracilaria lichenoides*, from E. India. [*Ceylon*, now Sri Lanka]

Cf *symb. Chem.* the element californium.

cf. *abbr.* compare. [L *confer* imper. of *conferre* compare]

c.f. *abbr.* **1** carried forward. **2** *Baseball* center fielder.

CFA *abbr.* chartered financial analyst.

CFC *abbr. Chem.* chlorofluorocarbon, any of various usu. gaseous compounds of carbon, hydrogen, chlorine, and fluorine, used in refrigerants, aerosol propellants, etc., and thought to be harmful to the ozone layer in the earth's atmosphere.

cfm *abbr.* cubic feet per minute.

cfs *abbr.* cubic feet per second.

cg *abbr.* centigram(s).

cgs *abbr.* centimeter-gram-second.

ch. *abbr.* **1** church. **2** chapter. **3** *Chess* check.

c.h. *abbr.* (also **C.H.**) **1** clearing house. **2** courthouse.

cha var. of CHAR³.

Chablis /shableé, shábleé/ *n.* (*pl.* same /-leez/) a type of dry white wine. [*Chablis* in E. France]

cha-cha /chaáchaa/ (also **cha-cha-cha** /chaáchaachaá/) *n. & v.* ● *n.* **1** a ballroom dance with a Latin-American rhythm. **2** music for or in the rhythm of a cha-cha. ● *v.intr.* (**cha-chas, cha-chaed** /-chaad/, **cha-chaing** /-chaa-ing/) dance the cha-cha. [Amer. Sp.]

chaconne /shakáwn, -kón/ *n. Mus.* **1 a** a musical form consisting of variations on a ground bass. **b** a musical composition in this style. **2** *hist.* a dance performed to this music. [F f. Sp. *chacona*]

chador /chaadáwr/ *n.* (also **chadar, chuddar**) a large piece of cloth worn in some countries by Muslim women, wrapped around the body to leave only the face exposed. [Pers. *chador*, Hindi *chador*]

chaetognath /kéetəgnath/ *n.* any dart-shaped worm of the phylum Chaetognatha, usu. living among marine plankton, and having a head with external thorny teeth. [mod.L *Chaetognatha* f. Gk *khaitē* long hair + *gnathos* jaw]

chafe /chayf/ *v. & n.* ● *v.* **1** *tr. & intr.* make or become sore or damaged by rubbing. **2** *tr.* rub (esp. the skin to restore warmth or sensation). **3** *tr. & intr.* make or become annoyed; fret (*was chafed by the delay*). ● *n.* **1 a** an act of chafing. **b** a sore resulting from this. **2** a state of annoyance. [ME f. OF *chaufer* ult. f. L *calefacere* f. *calēre* be hot + *facere* make]
■ *v.* **1** rub, abrade, fret, gall, irritate, make sore. **3** fume, rage, seethe, fret, foam at the mouth, storm, rant and rave, smolder, *sl.* burn up; see also IRRITATE 2. ● *n.* **1 b** sore, abrasion, bruise, soreness, irritation. **2** see RAGE *n.* 2.

chafer /cháyfər/ *n.* any of various large, slow-moving beetles of the family Scarabeidae, esp. the cockchafer. [OE *ceafor, cefer* f. Gmc]

chaff /chaf/ *n. & v.* ● *n.* **1** the husks of corn or other seed separated by winnowing or threshing. **2** chopped hay and straw used as fodder. **3** lighthearted joking; banter. **4** worthless things; rubbish. **5** strips of metal foil released in the atmosphere to obstruct radar detection. ● *v.tr.* **1** tease; banter. **2** chop (straw, etc.). □ **separate the wheat from the chaff** distinguish good from bad. □□ **chaffy** *adj.* [OE *ceaf, cæf* prob. f. Gmc: sense 3 of *n.* & 1 of *v.* perh. f. CHAFE]
■ *n.* **3** banter, raillery, ridicule, badinage, joking, teasing, jest, persiflage, *colloq.* ribbing, *Austral. & NZ* chiack(ing), *Austral. & NZ sl.* borak. **4** see RUBBISH *n.* 1, 2. ● *v.* **1** banter, poke fun (at), gibe (at), jeer (at); tease, jolly, kid, twit, pull a person's leg, mock,

ridicule, *Austral. & NZ* chiack, *colloq.* have on, rib, rag, *sl.* josh, *Austral. & NZ sl.* poke borak at.

chaffer /cháfər/ *v. & n.* ● *v.intr.* haggle; bargain. ● *n.* bargaining; haggling. □□ **chafferer** *n.* [ME f. OE *ceapfaru* f. *ceap* bargain + *faru* journey]
■ *v.* see HAGGLE *v.* ● *n.* see DISPUTE *n.* 1, 2.

chaffinch /cháfinch/ *n.* a common European finch, *Fringilla coelebs*, the male of which has a blue-gray head with pinkish cheeks. [OE *ceaffinc*: see CHAFF, FINCH]

chafing dish /cháyfing/ *n.* **1** a cooking pot with an outer pan of hot water, used for keeping food warm. **2** a dish with an alcohol lamp, etc., for cooking at table. [obs. sense of CHAFE = warm]

Chagas' disease /shaágəs/ (also **Chagas's disease**) *n.* a kind of sleeping sickness caused by a protozoan transmitted by bloodsucking bugs. [C. *Chagas*, Braz. physician d. 1934]

chagrin /shəgrín/ *n. & v.* ● *n.* acute vexation or mortification. ● *v.tr.* affect with chagrin. [F *chagrin(er)*, of uncert. orig.]
■ *n.* see *embarrassment* (EMBARRASS). ● *v.* see MORTIFY *v.* 1.

chain /chayn/ *n. & v.* ● *n.* **1 a** a connected flexible series of esp. metal links as decoration or for a practical purpose. **b** something resembling this (*formed a human chain*). **2** (in *pl.*) **a** fetters used to confine prisoners. **b** any restraining force. **3** a sequence, series, or set (*chain of events; mountain chain*). **4** a group of associated hotels, shops, newspapers, etc. **5** esp. *Brit.* a badge of office in the form of a chain worn around the neck (*mayoral chain*). **6 a** a jointed measuring line consisting of linked metal rods. **b** its length (66 or 100 ft.). **7** *Chem.* a group of (esp. carbon) atoms bonded in sequence in a molecule. **8** a figure in a quadrille or similar dance. **9** (in *pl.*) *Naut.* channels (see CHANNEL²). **10** (also **chain shot**) *hist.* two cannonballs or half balls joined by a chain and used in sea battles for bringing down a mast, etc. ● *v.tr.* **1** (often foll. by *up*) secure or confine with a chain. **2** confine or restrict (a person) (*is chained to the office*). □ **chain bridge** a suspension bridge on chains. **chain drive** a system of transmission by endless chains. **chain gang** a team of convicts chained together and forced to work in the open air. **chain gear** a gear transmitting motion by means of an endless chain. **chain letter** one of a sequence of letters the recipient of which is requested to send copies to a specific number of other people. **chain-link** made of wire in a diamond-shaped mesh (*chain-link fencing*). **chain mail** armor made of interlaced rings. **chain reaction 1** *Physics* a self-sustaining nuclear reaction, esp. one in which a neutron from a fission reaction initiates a series of these reactions. **2** *Chem.* a self-sustaining molecular reaction in which intermediate products initiate further reactions. **3** a series of events, each caused by the previous one. **chain saw** a motor-driven saw with teeth on an endless chain. **chain-smoker** a person who smokes continually, esp. one who lights a cigarette, etc., from the stub of the last one smoked. **chain stitch** an ornamental embroidery or crochet stitch resembling chains. **chain store** one of a series of stores owned by one company and selling the same kind of goods. **chain-wale** (or **chain wale**) = CHANNEL². [ME f. OF *cha(e)ine* f. L *catena*]
■ *n.* **2** (*chains*) **a** see BOND *n.* 1b. **b** restriction(s), restraint, constraint(s), checks, trammels, control, confinement. **3** string, series, set, stream, combination; sequence, succession, procession, concatenation, train, course; range, line, row. ● *v.* **1** shackle, secure, fasten, bind (up), fetter, tie up, manacle, trammel; leash, tether, lash, hitch; confine, restrain. **2** restrict, tie, limit.

chainwheel /cháynhweel, -weel/ *n.* a wheel transmitting power by a chain fitted to its edges; a sprocket.

chair /chair/ *n. & v.* ● *n.* **1** a separate seat for one person, of various forms, usu. having a back and four legs. **2 a** a professorship (*offered the chair in physics*). **b** a seat of authority, esp. on a board of directors. **c** *Brit.* a mayoralty. **3 a** a chairperson. **b** the seat or office of a chairperson (*will you take the chair?*; *I'm in the chair*). **4** = *electric chair*. **5** esp. *Brit.* an iron or steel socket holding a railroad rail in place. **6** *hist.* = *sedan chair*. ● *v.tr.* **1** act as chairperson of or preside over

(a meeting). **2** *Brit.* carry (a person) aloft in a chair or in a sitting position, in triumph. **3** install in a chair, esp. as a position of authority. □ **chair bed** a chair that unfolds into a bed. **chair car** a railroad car with chairs instead of long seats; a parlor car. **take a chair** sit down. [ME f. AF *chaere*, OF *chaiere* f. L *cathedra* f. Gk *kathedra*: see CATHEDRAL]
■ *n.* **2 a, b** professorship; seat, position, place; directorship. **3 a** chairperson, chairman, chairwoman, chairlady, presiding officer, leader, moderator. ● *v.* **1** preside over, head (up), lead, moderate, run, direct, manage, oversee. □ **take a chair** see SIT *v.* 1.

chairborne /cháirbawrn/ *adj.* **1** (of an administrator) not active. **2** (of military personnel) assigned to a desk job rather than field duty.
■ **1** see INACTIVE 1, 2.

chairlady /cháirlaydee/ *n.* (*pl.* **-ies**) = *chairwoman* (see CHAIRMAN).

chairlift /cháirlift/ *n.* a series of chairs on an endless cable for carrying passengers up and down a mountain, etc.

chairman /cháirmən/ *n.* (*pl.* **-men**; *fem.* **chairwoman**, *pl.* **-women**) **1** a person chosen to preside over a meeting. **2** the permanent president of a committee, a board of directors, (*Brit.*) a firm, etc. **3** the master of ceremonies at an entertainment, etc. **4** *hist.* either of two sedan bearers.
□□ **chairmanship** *n.*
■ **1, 2** see HEAD *n.* 6a.

chairperson /cháirpərsən/ *n.* a chairman or chairwoman (used as a neutral alternative).
■ see HEAD *n.* 6a.

chaise /shayz/ *n.* **1** esp. *hist.* a horse-drawn carriage for one or two persons, esp. one with an open top and two wheels. **2** = *post chaise* (see POST²). [F var. of *chaire*, formed as CHAIR]

chaise longue /sháyz lóng, shéz/ *n.* a reclining chair with a lengthened seat forming a leg rest. [F, lit. long chair]

chalaza /kəláyzə/ *n.* (*pl.* **chalazae** /-zee/ or **chalazas**) each of two twisted membranous strips joining the yolk to the ends of an egg. [mod.L f. Gk, = hailstone]

chalcedony /kalséd'nee/ *n.* a type of quartz occurring in several different forms, e.g., onyx, agate, tiger's eye, etc.
□□ **chalcedonic** /kálsidónik/ *adj.* [ME f. L *c(h)alcedonius* f. Gk *khalkēdōn*]

chalcolithic /kálkəlíthik/ *adj.* *Archaeol.* of a prehistoric period in which both stone and bronze implements were used. [Gk *khalkos* copper + *lithos* stone]

chalcopyrite /kálkəpírit/ *n.* a yellow mineral of copper-iron sulfide, which is the principal ore of copper. [Gk *khalkos* copper + PYRITE]

Chaldean /kaldée'ən/ *n.* & *adj.* ● *n.* **1 a** a native of ancient Chaldea or Babylonia. **b** the language of the Chaldeans. **2** an astrologer. **3** a member of the Uniat (formerly Nestorian) sect in Iran, etc. ● *adj.* **1** of or relating to ancient Chaldea or its people or language. **2** of or relating to astrology. **3** of or relating to the Uniat sect. [L *Chaldaeus* f. Gk *Khaldaios* f. Assyr. *Kaldu*]

Chaldee /kaldée/ *n.* **1** the language of the Chaldeans. **2** a native of ancient Chaldea. **3** the Aramaic language as used in Old Testament books. [ME, repr. L *Chaldaei* (pl.) (as CHALDEAN)]

chalet /shaláy, shálay/ *n.* **1** a small suburban house or bungalow, esp. with an overhanging roof. **2** a small, usu. wooden hut or house at a ski resort, beach, etc. **3** a Swiss cowherd's hut, or wooden cottage, with overhanging eaves. [Swiss F]
■ **1** see COTTAGE. **2, 3** see CABIN *n.* 1.

chalice /chális/ *n.* **1** a wine cup used in the Communion service. **2** *literary* a goblet. [ME f. OF f. L *calix -icis* cup]

chalk /chawk/ *n.* & *v.* ● *n.* **1** a white, soft, earthy limestone (calcium carbonate) formed from the skeletal remains of sea creatures. **2 a** a similar substance (calcium sulfate), sometimes colored, used for writing or drawing. **b** a piece of this (*a box of chalk*). **3** a series of strata consisting mainly of chalk. **4** = *French chalk.* ● *v.tr.* **1** rub, mark, draw, or write with chalk. **2** (foll. by *up*) **a** write or record with chalk. **b** register (a success, etc.). **c** *Brit.* charge (to an account). □ as

different as chalk and (or **from**) **cheese** *Brit.* fundamentally different. **by a long chalk** *Brit.* by far (from the use of chalk to mark the score in games). **chalk out** sketch or plan a thing to be accomplished. **chalk stripe** a pattern of thin white stripes on a dark background. **chalk-striped** having chalk stripes. [OE *cealc* ult. f. WG f. L CALX]

chalkboard /cháwkbawrd/ *n.* = BLACKBOARD.

chalkie /cháwkee/ *n.* *Austral. colloq.* a schoolteacher.

chalkstone /cháwkstōn/ *n.* a concretion of urates like chalk in tissues and joints, esp. of hands and feet.

chalky /cháwkee/ *adj.* (**chalkier, chalkiest**) **1 a** abounding in chalk. **b** white as chalk. **2** like or containing chalk stones.
□□ **chalkiness** *n.*
■ **1 b** see WHITE *adj.* 1.

challenge /chálinj/ *n.* & *v.* ● *n.* **1 a** a summons to take part in a contest or a trial of strength, etc., esp. to a duel. **b** a summons to prove or justify something. **2** a demanding or difficult task (*rose to the challenge of the new job*). **3** an act of disputing or denying a statement, claim, etc. **4** *Law* an objection made to a jury member. **5** a call to respond, esp. a sentry's call for a password, etc. **6** an invitation to a sporting contest, esp. one issued to a reigning champion. **7** *Med.* a test of immunity after immunization treatment. ● *v.tr.* **1** (often foll. by *to* + infin.) **a** invite to take part in a contest, game, debate, duel, etc. **b** invite to prove or justify something. **2** dispute; deny (*I challenge that remark*). **3 a** stretch; stimulate (*challenges him to produce his best*). **b** (as **challenging** *adj.*) demanding; stimulatingly difficult. **4** (of a sentry) call to respond. **5** claim (attention, etc.). **6** *Law* object to (a jury member, evidence, etc.). **7** *Med.* test by a challenge.
□□ **challengeable** *adj.* **challenger** *n.* [ME f. OF *c(h)alenge*, *c(h)alenger* f. L *calumnia* calumny, *calumniari* calumny]
■ *n.* **1** defiance, gage, gauntlet, invitation, dare, summons; provocation; ultimatum; (*take up a challenge*) throw one's hat in the ring, take up the glove, enter the lists. **2** demand(s), needs, requirement(s); test, trial, examination; difficulties, problems. **3** question, impeachment, dispute, doubt, refutation, contradiction, objection, protest, opposition, remonstration. ● *v.* **1a** invite, dare, summon, call out; provoke, *archaic* defy; take on; (*challenge a person*) throw down the glove *or* gauntlet, enter the lists. **b** defy. **2** question, dispute, object to, take exception to, cast doubt upon, query, contest, contend, doubt, call into doubt, call in *or* into question, impugn, impeach; deny, disagree with, *disp.* refute; oppose. **3 a** stretch, test; stimulate, drive. **b** (**challenging**) demanding, formidable, difficult, exacting, hard; stimulating. **5** see CLAIM *v.* 1a.

challis /shálee/ *n.* a lightweight, soft clothing fabric. [perh. f. a surname]

chalybeate /kəlíbeeət/ *adj.* (of mineral water, etc.) impregnated with iron salts. [mod.L *chalybeatus* f. L *chalybs* f. Gk *khalups -ubos* steel]

chamaephyte /kámifit/ *n.* a plant whose buds are on or near the ground. [Gk *khamai* on the ground + -PHYTE]

chamber /cháymbər/ *n.* **1 a** a hall used by a legislative or judicial body. **b** the body that meets in it. **c** any of the houses of a legislature (*the House chamber*). **2** (in *pl.*) a judge's room used for hearing cases not needing to be taken in court. **3** *poet.* or *archaic* a room, esp. a bedroom. **4** *Mus.* (*attrib.*) of or for a small group of instruments (*chamber orchestra; chamber music*). **5** an enclosed space in machinery, etc. (esp. the part of a gun bore that contains the charge). **6 a** a cavity in a plant or in the body of an animal. **b** a compartment in a structure. **7** = *chamber pot.* □ **chamber of commerce** an association to promote local commercial interests. **chamber pot** a receptacle for urine, etc., used in a bedroom. [ME f. OF *chambre* f. L CAMERA]

/. . ./ **pronunciation**	● **part of speech**
□ **phrases, idioms, and compounds**	
□□ **derivatives**	■ **synonym section**
cross-references appear in SMALL CAPITALS or *italics*	

■ **1 a** hall, meeting hall, assembly room. **b, c** assembly, body, legislature, judicature, judiciary, diet, caucus, *Brit.* convocation; house, congress, senate. **3** room, apartment; bedroom, bedchamber; (*chambers*) (living) quarters, rooms. **5** enclosure, magazine, *Mech.* manifold. **6 a** *Anat.* antrum, vestibule. **b** compartment, cell, cavity, space, hole, hollow, niche, nook, recess, alcove. □ **chamber pot** chamber, commode, *colloq.* potty, *Brit. sl.* jerry.

chambered /cháymbərd/ *adj.* (of a tomb) containing a burial chamber.

chamberlain /cháymbərlin/ *n.* **1** an officer managing the household of a sovereign or a great noble. **2** *Brit.* the treasurer of a corporation, etc. □□ **chamberlainship** *n.* [ME f. OF *chamberlain*, etc., f. Frank. f. L *camera* CAMERA]

chambermaid /cháymbərmayd/ *n.* **1** a housemaid at a hotel, etc. **2** a housemaid.
■ see MAID 1.

Chambertin /shoNbertáN/ *n.* a high-quality, dry, red wine. [*Gevrey Chambertin* region in E. France]

chambray /shámbray/ *n.* a cotton, silk, or linen gingham cloth with a white weft and a colored warp. [irreg. f. *Cambrai*: see CAMBRIC]

chameleon /kəmeélyən/ *n.* **1** any of a family of small lizards having grasping tails, long tongues, protruding eyes, and the power of changing color. **2** a variable or inconstant person. □□ **chameleonic** /-leeónik/ *adj.* [ME f. L f. Gk *khamaileōn* f. *khamai* on the ground + *leōn* lion]
■ □□ **chameleonic** see VARIABLE 2.

chamfer /chámfər/ *v. & n.* ● *v.tr.* bevel symmetrically (a right-angled edge or corner). ● *n.* a beveled surface at an edge or corner. [back-form. f. *chamfering* f. F *chamfrain* f. *chant* edge (CANT²) + *fraint* broken f. OF *fraindre* break f. L *frangere*]

chamois /shámee/ *n.* (*pl.* same /-eez/) **1** an agile goat antelope, *Rupicapra rupicapra*, native to the mountains of Europe and Asia. **2** (in full **chamois leather**) **a** a soft pliable leather from sheep, goats, deer, etc. **b** a piece of this for polishing, etc. [F: cf. Gallo-Roman *camox*]

chamomile /káməmil, -meel/ *n.* (also **camomile**) any aromatic plant of the genus *Anthemis* or *Matricaria*, with daisylike flowers. □ **chamomile tea** an infusion of its dried flowers used as a tonic. [ME f. OF *camomille* f. LL *camomilla* or *chamomilla* f. Gk *khamaimēlon* earth apple (from the apple smell of its flowers)]

champ¹ /champ/ *v. & n.* ● *v.* **1** *tr. & intr.* munch or chew noisily. **2** *tr.* (of a horse, etc.) work (the bit) noisily between the teeth. **3** *intr.* fret with impatience (*is champing to be away*). ● *n.* a chewing noise or motion. □ **champ at the bit** be restlessly impatient. [prob. imit.]
■ *v.* 1 see MUNCH.

champ² /champ/ *n. sl.* a champion. [abbr.]
■ see WINNER 1.

champagne /shampáyn/ *n.* **1 a** a white sparkling wine from Champagne. **b** a similar wine from elsewhere. ¶ Use in sense b is strictly incorrect. **2** a pale cream or straw color. [*Champagne*, former province in E. France]
■ **1** *colloq.* bubbly, *Brit. colloq.* fizz, champers.

champaign /shampáyn/ *n. literary* **1** open country. **2** an expanse of open country. [ME f. OF *champagne* f. LL *campania*: cf. CAMPAIGN]

champers /shámpərz/ *n. Brit. sl.* champagne.

champerty /chámpərtee/ *n.* (*pl.* **-ies**) *Law* an illegal agreement in which a person not naturally interested in a lawsuit finances it with a view to sharing the disputed property. □□ **champertous** *adj.* [ME f. AF *champartie* f. OF *champart* feudal lord's share of produce, f. L *campus* field + *pars* part]

champion /chámpeeən/ *n. & v.* ● *n.* **1** (often *attrib.*) a person (esp. in a sport or game), an animal, plant, etc., that has defeated or surpassed all rivals in a competition, etc. **2 a** a person who fights or argues for a cause or on behalf of another person. **b** *hist.* a knight, etc., who fought in single combat on behalf of a king, etc. ● *v.tr.* support the cause of; defend; argue in favor of. [ME f. OF f. med.L *campio -onis* fighter f. L *campus* field]

■ *n.* **1** victor, winner, conqueror, titleholder, prizewinner, gold medallist, *sl.* champ; (*attrib.*) prize, winning, prizewinning, victorious. **2 a** defender, guardian, protector, hero, savior, knight in shining armor, supporter, backer, advocate, proponent, upholder, apologist, patron, *disp.* protagonist; fighter, campaigner, lobbyist. **b** fighter, combatant, hero, warrior, campaigner. ● *v.* defend, protect, guard; support, back, stand up for, speak *or* plead *or* argue in favor of, hold a brief for, fight for, lobby for *or* on behalf of, maintain, sustain, uphold; espouse, forward, promote, advocate, urge.

championship /chámpeeənship/ *n.* **1** (often in *pl.*) a contest for the position of champion in a sport, etc. **2** the position of champion over all rivals. **3** the advocacy or defense (of a cause, etc.).
■ **1** see CONTEST *n.* 1. **2** see TITLE *n.* 6. **3** see FURTHERANCE.

champlevé /shónləváy/ *n. & adj.* ● *n.* a type of enamelwork in which hollows made in a metal surface are filled with colored enamels. ● *adj.* of or relating to champlevé (cf. CLOISONNÉ). [F, = raised field]

chance /chans/ *n., adj., & v.* ● *n.* **1 a** a possibility (*just a chance we will catch the train*). **b** (often in *pl.*) probability (*the chances are against it*). **2 a** a risk (*have to take a chance*). **3 a** an undesigned occurrence (*just a chance that they met*). **b** the absence of design or discoverable cause (*here merely because of chance*). **4** an opportunity (*didn't have a chance to speak to him*). **5** the way things happen; fortune; luck (*we'll just leave it to chance*). **6** (often **Chance**) the course of events regarded as a power; fate (*blind Chance rules the universe*). ● *adj.* fortuitous; accidental (*a chance meeting*). ● *v.* **1** *tr. colloq.* risk (*we'll chance it and go*). **2** *intr.* (often foll. by *that* + clause, or *to* + infin.) happen without intention (*it chanced that I found it; I chanced to find it*). □ **by any chance** as it happens; perhaps. **by chance** without design; unintentionally. **chance one's arm** *Brit.* make an attempt though unlikely to succeed. **chance on** (or **upon**) happen to find, meet, etc. **game of chance** a game decided by luck, not skill. **the off chance** the slight possibility. **on the chance** (often foll. by *of*, or *that* + clause) in view of the possibility. **stand a chance** have a prospect of success, etc. **take a chance** (or **chances**) behave riskily; risk failure. **take a** (or **one's**) **chance on** (or **with**) consent to take the consequences of; trust to luck. [ME f. AF *ch(e)aunce*, OF *chéance chéoir* fall ult. f. L *cadere*]
■ *n.* **1** conceivability, possibility; eventuality; (*chances*) likelihood, odds, probability, prospect(s). **2** risk, gamble, venture. **3** accident, coincidence, fluke, fortuity, happenstance. **4** opportunity, time, turn, occasion, moment; window, opening, start, hearing, say, *colloq.* break, show; see also SHOT¹ 5b. **5, 6** fortune, luck, fate, destiny, fortuity, fortuitousness, kismet. ● *adj.* fortuitous, casual, accidental, coincidental, adventitious, aleatoric, aleatory, incidental, arbitrary; unintentional, inadvertent, unplanned, unpremeditated; unexpected, unforeseen, unlooked-for. ● *v.* **1** risk, hazard, venture. **2** happen, occur, come to pass, take place, come about, *poet.* betide, befall. □ **by any chance** see POSSIBLY 2. **by chance** accidentally, coincidentally, fortuitously, adventitiously, incidentally, unexpectedly, unintentionally, inadvertently. **take a chance on** see TRUST *v.* 1.

chancel /chánsəl/ *n.* the part of a church near the altar, reserved for the clergy, the choir, etc., usu. enclosed by a screen or separated from the nave by steps. [ME f. OF f. L *cancelli* lattice]

chancellery /chánsələree, chánslə-/ *n.* (*pl.* **-ies**) **1 a** the position, office, staff, department, etc., of a chancellor. **b** the official residence of a chancellor. **2** an office attached to an embassy or consulate. [ME f. OF *chancellerie* (as CHANCELLOR)]

chancellor /chánsələr, chánslər/ *n.* **1** a government official of various kinds; the head of the government in some European countries, e.g., Germany. **2** the president of a chan-

cery court. **3 a** the chief administrator at certain universities. **b** *Brit.* the nonresident honorary head of a university. **4 a** bishop's law officer. □ **Chancellor of the Exchequer** the finance minister of the United Kingdom. □□ **chancellorship** *n.* [OE f. AF *c(h)anceler*, OF *-ier* f. LL *cancellarius* porter, secretary, f. *cancelli* lattice]
■ **1** see PREMIER *n.*

chance-medley /chánsmédlee/ *n.* (*pl.* **-eys**) **1** *Law* a fight, esp. homicidal, beginning unintentionally. **2** inadvertency. [AF *chance medlee* (see MEDDLE) mixed chance]

chancery /chánsree/ *n.* (*pl.* **-ies**) **1** (in full **court of chancery**) a court of equity. **2** the administrative office for a diocese. **3** *Brit. Law* (**Chancery**) the Lord Chancellor's court, a division of the High Court of Justice. **4** *hist.* the records office of an order of knighthood. **5** *hist.* the court of a bishop's chancellor. **6** an office attached to an embassy or consulate. **7** a public record office. □ **in chancery** *sl.* (of a boxer or wrestler) with the head held under the opponent's arm and being pummeled. [ME, contracted f. CHANCELLERY]

chancre /shángkər/ *n.* a painless ulcer developing in venereal disease, etc. [F f. L CANCER]
■ see ULCER 1.

chancroid /shángkroyd/ *n.* ulceration of lymph nodes in the groin, from venereal disease.

chancy /chánsee/ *adj.* (**chancier**, **chanciest**) subject to chance; uncertain; risky. □□ **chancily** *adv.* **chanciness** *n.*
■ see RISKY.

chandelier /shándəleér/ *n.* an ornamental branched hanging support for several candles or electric lightbulbs. [F (*chandelle* f. as CANDLE)]

chandler /chándlər/ *n.* a dealer in candles, oil, soap, paint, groceries, etc. □ **ship** (or **ship's**) **chandler** a dealer in cordage, canvas, etc. [ME f. AF *chaundeler*, OF *chandelier* (as CANDLE)]

chandlery /chándləree/ *n.* **1** the warehouse or store of a chandler. **2** the goods sold by a chandler.

change /chaynj/ *n. & v.* ● *n.* **1 a** the act or an instance of making or becoming different. **b** an alteration or modification (*the change in her expression*). **2 a** money given in exchange for money in larger units or a different currency. **b** money returned as the balance of that given in payment. **c** = *small change.* **3** a new experience; variety (*fancied a change; for a change*). **4 a** the substitution of one thing for another; an exchange (*change of scene*). **b** a set of clothes, etc., put on in place of another. **5** (in full **change of life**) *colloq.* the menopause. **6** (usu. in *pl.*) the different orders in which a peal of bells can be rung. **7** (**Change**) (also **'Change**) *Brit. hist.* a place where merchants, etc., met to do business. **8** (of the moon) arrival at a fresh phase, esp. at the new moon. ● *v.* **1** *tr. & intr.* undergo, show, or subject to change; make or become different (*the toupee changed his appearance; changed from an introvert into an extrovert*). **2** *tr.* **a** take or use another instead of; go from one to another (*change one's socks; changed his doctor; changed trains*). **b** (usu. foll. by *for*) give up or get rid of in exchange (*changed the car for a van*). **3** *tr.* **a** give or get change in smaller denominations for (*can you change a ten-dollar bill?*). **b** (foll. by *for*) exchange (a sum of money) for (*changed his dollars for pounds*). **4** *tr. & intr.* put fresh clothes or coverings on (*changed the baby as he was wet; changed into something loose*). **5** *tr.* (often foll. by *with*) give and receive; exchange (*changed places with him; we changed places*). **6** *intr.* change trains, etc. (*changed at Grand Central Station*). **7** *intr.* (of the moon) arrive at a fresh phase, esp. become new. □ **change color** blanch or flush. **change gear** engage a different gear in a vehicle. **change hands 1** pass to a different owner. **2** substitute one hand for another. **change one's mind** adopt a different opinion or plan. **change of air** a different climate; variety. **change of heart** a conversion to a different view. **change over** change from one system or situation to another; effect a changeover. **change step** begin to keep step with the opposite leg when marching, etc. **change the subject** begin talking of something different, esp. to avoid embarrassment. **change one's tune 1** voice a different opinion

from that expressed previously. **2** change one's style of language or manner, esp. from an insolent to a respectful tone. **get no change out of** *Brit. sl.* **1** fail to get information from. **2** fail to get the better of (in business, etc.). **ring the changes (on)** vary the ways of expressing, arranging, or doing something. □□ **changeful** *adj.* **changer** *n.* [ME f. AF *chaunge*, OF *change, changer* f. LL *cambiare*, L *cambire* barter, prob. of Celt. orig.]
■ *n.* **1** alteration, transformation, mutation, shift, fluctuation, swing, modulation, metamorphosis, revolution, conversion; modification, adjustment, amendment; transition, flux, movement, motion, upheaval. **2 c** small change, coin(s), silver, cash, specie, *Brit.* coppers. **3** variation, difference, variety, novelty. **4** substitution, switch, interchange, replacement, exchange, changeover, trade. ● *v.* **1** modify, alter, modulate, sway, transmute, transfigure, convert, adapt, change over, ring the changes; mutate, transform, metamorphose, *joc.* transmogrify; fluctuate, shift, vary; influence, affect, have an impact on; distort, warp, deform, disfigure; (*change to* or *into*) turn into; become; make into. **2, 5** exchange, interchange, switch, swap, trade; replace, substitute. □ **change color** see FLUSH[1] *v.* 1a, PALE[1] *v.* 1. **change one's mind** think twice or again, have a change of heart, change one's position or plan(s); (*change one's mind about*) think better of. **change of air** see VARIETY 1. **change over** change, convert, switch, shift.

changeable /cháynjəbəl/ *adj.* **1** irregular; inconstant. **2** that can change or be changed. □□ **changeability** *n.* **changeableness** *n.* **changeably** *adv.* [ME f. OF, formed as CHANGE]
■ **1** variable, protean, inconstant, unstable, unsettled, shifting, fluctuating, uncertain, irregular, erratic, inconsistent, uneven, unsteady, unpredictable, *Chem.* labile, *archaic* versatile, *literary* mutable; capricious, erratic, fickle, flighty, fitful, unreliable, undependable, mercurial, volatile. **2** alterable, modifiable, transformable, convertible, variable, adaptable, flexible.

changeless /cháynjlis/ *adj.* unchanging. □□ **changelessly** *adv.* **changelessness** *n.*
■ unchanging, unvaried, constant, unvarying, invariable, steadfast, firm, unwavering, fixed, stable, static, unchangeable, immutable, unalterable; see also ABIDING.

changeling /cháynjling/ *n.* a child believed to be substituted for another by stealth, esp. an elf child left by fairies.

changeover /cháynjōvər/ *n.* a change from one system or situation to another.
■ change, conversion, switch, shift, revolution; transition, move.

channel[1] /chánəl/ *n. & v.* ● *n.* **1 a** a length of water wider than a strait, joining two larger areas, esp. seas. **b** (**the Channel**) the English Channel between Britain and France. **2** a medium of communication; an agency for conveying information (*through the usual channels*). **3** *Broadcasting* **a** a band of frequencies used in radio and television transmission, esp. as used by a particular station. **b** a service or station using this. **4** the course in which anything moves; a direction. **5 a** a natural or artificial hollow bed of water. **b** the navigable part of a waterway. **6** a tubular passage for liquid. **7** *Electronics* a lengthwise strip on recording tape, etc. **8** a groove or a flute, esp. in a column. ● *v.tr.* (**channeled**, **channeling**; esp. *Brit.* **channelled**, **channelling**) **1** guide; direct (*channeled them through customs*). **2** form channels in; groove. [ME f. OF *chanel* f. L *canalis* CANAL]
■ *n.* **2** avenue, path, course, passage, route, artery, conduit; means, agency, vehicle, method, device, way, approach. **5a, 6** watercourse, canal, waterway, stream, ditch, drain, duct, aqueduct, sluice, conduit, flume,

---

/. . ./ **pronunciation**   ● **part of speech**
□ **phrases, idioms, and compounds**
□□ **derivatives**   ■ **synonym section**
cross-references appear in SMALL CAPITALS or *italics*

chute, race, pipe, trench, trough, gutter, moat. **8** furrow, groove, slot, chase, gouge, *Anat.* sulcus, *Anat.* & *Bot.* vallecula, *Archit.* flute, glyph. ● *v.* **1** direct, convey, pass, guide, lead, conduct, channelize; focus, train, turn, concentrate, center, bend; divert, sublimate.

channel[2] /chánəl/ *n. Naut.* any of the broad thick planks projecting horizontally from a ship's side abreast of the masts, used to widen the basis for the shrouds. [for *chain-wale*: cf. *gunnel* for *gunwale*]

channelize /chánəlīz/ *v.tr.* convey in, or as if in, a channel; guide.

chanson de geste /shoNsáwN də zhést/ *n.* (*pl.* **chansons** *pronunc.* same) any of a group of medieval French epic poems. [F, = song of heroic deeds]

chant /chant/ *n. & v.* ● *n.* **1 a** a spoken singsong phrase, esp. one performed in unison by a crowd, etc. **b** a repetitious singsong way of speaking. **2** *Mus.* **a** a short musical passage in two or more phrases used for singing unmetrical words, e.g., psalms, canticles. **b** the psalm or canticle so sung. **c** a song, esp. monotonous or repetitive. **3** a musical recitation, esp. of poetry. ● *v.tr. & intr.* **1** talk or repeat monotonously (*a crowd chanting slogans*). **2** sing or intone (a psalm, etc.). [ME (orig. as verb) f. OF *chanter* sing f. L *cantare* frequent. of *canere cant-* sing]

■ *n.* **2 b** song, psalm, canticle, plainsong, plainchant, mantra. ● *v.* **1** singsong, recite, repeat; shout (out), cry out, yell (out), *sl.* belt out. **2** sing, intone, cantillate.

chanter /chántər/ *n. Mus.* the melody pipe, with finger holes, of a bagpipe.

chanterelle /chántərél/ *n.* an edible fungus, *Cantharellus cibarius*, with a yellow, funnel-shaped cap and smelling of apricots. [F f. mod.L *cantharellus* dimin. of *cantharus* f. Gk *kantharos* a kind of drinking vessel]

chanteuse /shaantʉ̄z/ *n.* a female singer of popular songs. [F]

■ see *singer* (SING).

chantey /shántee, chán-/ *n.* (also **chanty, shanty**) (*pl.* **chanteys, -ies**) (in full **sea chantey**) a song with alternating solo and chorus, of a kind orig. sung by sailors while hauling ropes, etc. [prob. F *chantez*, imper. pl. of *chanter* sing: see CHANT]

chanticleer /chántikleėr, shán-/ *n. literary* a name given to a domestic cock, esp. in fairy tales, etc. [ME f. OF *chantecler* (as CHANT, CLEAR), a name in *Reynard the Fox*]

Chantilly /shantílee, shónteeyeė/ *n.* **1** a delicate kind of bobbin lace. **2** sweetened or flavored whipped cream. [*Chantilly* near Paris]

chantry /chántree/ *n.* (*pl.* **-ies**) **1** an endowment for a priest or priests to celebrate Masses for the founder's soul. **2** the priests, chapel, altar, etc., endowed. [ME f. AF *chaunterie*, OF *chanterie* f. *chanter* CHANT]

chanty var. of CHANTEY.

Chanukkah var. of HANUKKAH.

chaos /káyos/ *n.* **1 a** utter confusion. **b** *Math.* the unpredictable and apparently random behavior of a deterministic system that is extremely sensitive to infinitesimal changes in initial parameters. **2** the formless matter supposed to have existed before the creation of the universe. □ **chaos theory** *Math.* the study of the apparently random behavior of deterministic systems. □□ **chaotic** /kayótik/ *adj.* **chaotically** *adv.* [F or L f. Gk *khaos*: -*otic* after *erotic*, etc.]

■ **1** pandemonium, bedlam, havoc, mayhem, babel, turmoil, disarray, tumult, uproar, maelstrom, tailspin, pell-mell, topsy-turvy, higgledy-piggledy, hugger-mugger, *sl.* snafu; disorder, confusion, disorganization. **2** formlessness; the abyss. □□ **chaotic** formless, shapeless, incoherent, disordered, disorderly, disorganized, unorganized, unsystematic, unsystematized, unmethodical, haphazard, irregular, helter-skelter, confused, topsy-turvy, all over the place, at sixes and sevens, jumbled, turbulent, tumultuous, higgledy-piggledy, hugger-mugger, *sl.* snafu.

chap[1] /chap/ *v. & n.* ● *v.* (**chapped, chapping**) **1** *intr.* (esp. of the skin; also dry ground, etc.) crack in fissures, esp.

because of exposure and dryness. **2** *tr.* (of the wind, cold, etc.) cause to chap. ● *n.* (usu. in *pl.*) **1** a crack in the skin. **2** an open seam. □ **Chap Stick** *propr.* a cylinder of a cosmetic substance used to prevent chapping of the lips. [ME, perh. rel. to MLG, MDu. *kappen* chop off]

chap[2] /chap/ *n.* esp. *Brit. colloq.* a man; a boy; a fellow. [abbr. of CHAPMAN]

■ fellow, lad, man, boy, customer, *colloq.* guy, *Brit. colloq.* blighter, johnny, *sl.* geezer, dude, *Brit. sl.* bloke, josser, *sl. often derog.* gink.

chap[3] /chap/ *n.* the lower jaw or half of the cheek, esp. of a pig as food. [16th c.: var. of CHOP[2], of unkn. orig.]

chap. *abbr.* chapter.

chaparral /shápərál, cháp-/ *n.* dense, tangled brushwood; undergrowth. □ **chaparral cock** (or **bird**) = ROADRUNNER. [Sp. f. *chaparra* evergreen oak]

chapati /chəpáatee/ *n.* (also **chapatti**) (*pl.* **-is**) *Ind.* a flat thin cake of unleavened whole-wheat bread. [Hindi *capāti*]

chapbook /chápbŏŏk/ *n. hist.* a small pamphlet containing tales, ballads, tracts, etc., hawked by chapmen. [19th c.: see CHAPMAN]

chape /chayp/ *n.* **1** the metal cap of a scabbard point. **2** the back piece of a buckle attaching it to a strap, etc. **3** a sliding loop on a belt or strap. [ME f. OF, = cope, hood, formed as CAP]

chapeau bras /shápōbraa/ *n.* (*pl.* **chapeaux bras** *pronunc.* same) a three-cornered, flat silk hat often carried under the arm. [F f. *chapeau* hat + *bras* arm]

chapel /chápəl/ *n.* **1 a** a place for private Christian worship in a large church or esp. a cathedral, with its own altar and dedication. **b** a place of Christian worship attached to a private house or institution. **2** a building or room in which funeral services are held. **3** *Brit.* **a** a place of worship for certain Protestant denominations. **4** an Anglican church subordinate to a parish church. **5** *Printing* **a** the members or branch of a labor union at a specific place of work. **b** a meeting of them. □ **chapel of ease** a chapel for the convenience of remote parishioners. [ME f. OF *chapele* f. med.L *cappella* dimin. of *cappa* cloak: the first chapel was a sanctuary in which St. Martin's sacred cloak (*cappella*) was preserved]

■ **1** see SANCTUARY 1.

chaperon /shápərōn/ *n. & v.* (also **chaperone**) ● *n.* **1** a person, esp. an older woman, who ensures propriety by accompanying a young unmarried woman on social occasions. **2** a person who takes charge of esp. young people in public. ● *v.tr.* act as a chaperon to. □□ **chaperonage** /shápərōnij/ *n.* [F, = hood, chaperon, dimin. of *chape* cope, formed as CAP]

■ *n.* see ESCORT *n.* 1. ● *v.* see ACCOMPANY 1.

chapfallen /chápfawlən/ *adj.* dispirited; dejected (with the lower jaw hanging).

chaplain /cháplin/ *n.* a member of the clergy attached to a private chapel, institution, ship, regiment, etc. □□ **chaplaincy** *n.* (*pl.* **-ies**). [ME f. AF & OF *c(h)apelain* f. med.L *cappellanus*, orig. custodian of the cloak of St. Martin: see CHAPEL]

■ see CLERGYMAN.

chaplet /cháplit/ *n.* **1** a garland or circlet for the head. **2** a string of 55 beads (one-third of the rosary number) for counting prayers, or as a necklace. **3** a bead molding. □□ **chapleted** *adj.* [ME f. OF *chapelet*, ult. f. LL *cappa* CAP]

■ **1** see GARLAND *n.* 1. **2** see STRING *n.* 6.

chapman /chápmən/ *n.* (*pl.* **-men**) *Brit. hist.* a peddler. [OE *cēapman* f. *cēap* barter]

chappie /chápee/ *n. Brit. colloq.* = CHAP[2].

chappy /chápee/ *adj. Brit.* full of chaps; chapped (*chappy knuckles*).

chaps /chaps/ *n.pl.* a cowboy's leather leggings worn over the trousers as protection for the front of the legs. [Mex. Sp. *chaparejos*]

chapter /cháptər/ *n.* **1** a main division of a book. **2** a period of time (in a person's life, a nation's history, etc.). **3** a series or sequence (*a chapter of misfortunes*). **4 a** the canons of a cathedral or other religious community or knightly order. **b** a meeting of these. **5** *Brit.* an Act of Parliament numbered

as part of a session's proceedings. **6** a local branch of a society. □ **chapter and verse** an exact reference or authority. **chapter house 1** a building used for the meetings of a chapter. **2** the place where a college fraternity or sorority meets. [ME f. OF *chapitre* f. L *capitulum* dimin. of *caput -itis* head]
■ **1** see EPISODE 2. **2** see ERA. **6** see LODGE *n*. 5, 6.

char[1] /chaar/ *v.tr. & intr.* (**charred, charring**) **1** make or become black by burning; scorch. **2** burn or be burned to charcoal. [app. back-form. f. CHARCOAL]
■ **1** see SCORCH *v*. 1, 2.

char[2] /chaar/ *n. & v. Brit. colloq.* ● *n.* = CHARWOMAN. ● *v.intr.* (**charred, charring**) work as a charwoman. [earlier *chare* f. OE *cerr* a turn, *cierran* to turn]

char[3] /chaar/ *n.* (also **cha** /chaa/) *Brit. sl.* tea. [Chin. *cha*]

char[4] /chaar/ *n.* (also **charr**) (*pl.* same) any small troutlike fish of the genus *Salvelinus*. [17th c.: orig. unkn.]

charabanc /shárəbang/ *n. Brit. hist.* an early form of tour bus. [F *char à bancs* seated carriage]

character /káriktər/ *n. & v.* ● *n.* **1** the collective qualities or characteristics, esp. mental and moral, that distinguish a person or thing. **2 a** moral strength (*has a weak character*). **b** reputation, esp. good reputation. **3 a** a person in a novel, play, etc. **b** a part played by an actor; a role. **4** *colloq.* a person, esp. an eccentric or outstanding individual (*he's a real character*). **5 a** a printed or written letter, symbol, or distinctive mark (*Chinese characters*). **b** *Computing* any of a group of symbols representing a letter, etc. **6** a written description of a person's qualities; a testimonial. **7** a characteristic (esp. of a biological species). ● *v.tr. archaic* inscribe; describe. □ **character actor** an actor who specializes in playing eccentric or unusual persons. **character assassination** a malicious attempt to harm or destroy a person's good reputation. **in** (or **out of**) **character** consistent (or inconsistent) with a person's character. □□ **characterful** *adj.* **characterfully** *adv.* **characterless** *adj.* [ME f. OF *caractere* f. L *character* f. Gk *kharaktēr* stamp, impress]
■ *n.* **1** personality, nature, temperament, disposition, temper, makeup, complexion, spirit; qualities, features, properties, attributes, traits; aroma, feel, feeling, atmosphere, aura, quality, air, tone, flavor, tenor; sort, kind, type, description. **2 a** morality, (moral) fiber, honesty, integrity, uprightness, decency, principle, respectability, rectitude, honor, courage, goodness, nobility. **b** see REPUTATION 2. **3 b** role, part, personality; (*characters*) dramatis personae. **4** eccentric, original, individual, individualist, *colloq.* card. **5** mark, symbol, monogram, sign; letter, number, figure, type, sort, rune, hieroglyphic, hieroglyph. **6** see TESTIMONIAL 1. **7** see CHARACTERISTIC *n*. ● *v*. see DESCRIBE 1a. □ **in** (or **out of**) **character** (*in character*) in keeping, typical, normal, expected, characteristic; fitting, proper, suitable; (*out of character*) untypical, atypical, uncharacteristic, abnormal, unexpected, unfitting, unbecoming.

characteristic /káriktərístik/ *adj. & n.* ● *adj.* typical; distinctive (*with characteristic expertise*). ● *n.* **1** a characteristic feature or quality. **2** *Math.* the whole number or integral part of a logarithm. □ **characteristic curve** a graph showing the relationship between two variable but interdependent quantities. **characteristic radiation** radiation the wavelengths of which are peculiar to the element that emits them. □□ **characteristically** *adv.* [F *caractéristique* or med.L *characterizare* f. Gk *kharaktērizō*]
■ *adj.* typical, representative; emblematic, symbolic, distinctive, symptomatic; in character. ● *n.* **1** mark, trait, attribute, feature, quality, property, character, aspect, peculiarity, idiosyncrasy; hallmark, indication, sign, symbol, emblem, symptom.

characterize /káriktərīz/ *v.tr.* **1 a** describe the character of. **b** (foll. by *as*) describe as. **2** be characteristic of. **3** impart character to. □□ **characterization** *n.* [F *caractériser* or med.L *characterizare* f. Gk *kharaktērizō*]
■ **1, 2** describe, define, categorize; delineate, portray, depict, represent, paint, identify, mark. **3** see TYPIFY.

charade /shəráyd/ *n.* **1 a** (usu. in *pl.*, treated as *sing.*) a game

of guessing a word from a written or acted clue given for each syllable and for the whole. **b** one such clue. **2** an absurd pretense. [F f. mod.Prov. *charrado* conversation f. *charra* chatter]
■ **2** travesty, absurdity, mockery, farce, parody, nonsense.

charas /chaárəs/ *n.* a narcotic resin from the flower heads of hemp; cannabis resin. [Hindi]

charcoal /chaárkōl/ *n.* **1 a** an amorphous form of carbon consisting of a porous black residue from partially burned wood, bones, etc. **b** (usu. in *pl.*) a piece of this used for drawing. **2** a drawing in charcoal. **3** (in full **charcoal gray**) a dark gray color. [ME COAL = charcoal: first element perh. *chare* turn (cf. CHAR[1], CHAR[2])]

chard /chaard/ *n.* (in full **Swiss chard**) a kind of beet, *Beta vulgaris cicla*, with edible broad, white leafstalks and green leaves. [F *carde*, and *chardon* thistle: cf. CARDOON]

Chardonnay /shaárd'náy/ *n.* **1** a variety of white grape used for making champagne and other wines. **2** the vine on which this grape grows. **3** a wine made from Chardonnay grapes. [F]

charge /chaarj/ *v. & n.* ● *v.* **1** *tr.* **a** ask (an amount) as a price (*charges $5 a ticket*). **b** ask (a person) for an amount as a price (*you forgot to charge me*). **2** *tr.* **a** (foll. by *to, up to*) debit the cost of to (a person or account) (*charge it to my account*; *charge it up to me*). **b** debit (a person or an account) (*bought a new car and charged the company*). **3** *tr.* **a** (often foll. by *with*) accuse (of an offense) (*charged him with theft*). **b** (foll. by *that* + clause) make an accusation that. **4** *tr.* (foll. by *to* + infin.) instruct or urge. **5** (foll. by *with*) **a** *tr.* entrust with. **b** *refl.* undertake. **6 a** *intr.* make a rushing attack; rush headlong. **b** *tr.* make a rushing attack on; throw oneself against. **7** *tr.* (often foll. by *up*) **a** give an electric charge to (a body). **b** store energy in (a battery). **8** *tr.* (often foll. by *with*) load or fill (a vessel, gun, etc.) to the full or proper extent. **9** *tr.* (usu. as **charged** *adj.*) **a** (foll. by *with*) saturated with (*air charged with vapor*). **b** (usu. foll. by *with*) pervaded (with strong feelings, etc.) (*atmosphere charged with emotion*; *a charged atmosphere*). ● *n.* **1 a** a price asked for goods or services. **b** a financial liability or commitment. **2** an accusation, esp. against a prisoner brought to trial. **3 a** a task, duty, or commission. **b** care, custody, responsible possession. **c** a person or thing entrusted; a minister's congregation. **4 a** an impetuous rush or attack, esp. in a battle. **b** the signal for this. **5** the appropriate amount of material to be put into a receptacle, mechanism, etc., at one time, esp. of explosive for a gun. **6 a** a property of matter that is a consequence of the interaction between its constituent particles and exists in a positive or negative form, causing electrical phenomena. **b** the quantity of this carried by a body. **c** energy stored chemically for conversion into electricity. **d** the process of charging a battery. **7** an exhortation; directions; orders. **8** a burden or load. **9** *Heraldry* a device; a bearing. □ **charge account** a credit account at a store, etc. **charge card** a credit card for which the account must be paid in full when a statement is issued. **charge-hand** *Brit.* a worker, ranking below a foreman, in charge of others on a particular job. **charge-nurse** *Brit.* a nurse in charge of a ward, etc. **charge-sheet** *Brit.* a record of cases and charges made at a police station. **free of charge** gratis. **give a person in charge** *Brit.* hand a person over to the police. **in charge** having command. **return to the charge** begin again, esp. in argument. **take charge** (often foll. by *of*) assume control or direction. □□ **chargeable** *adj.* [ME f. OF *charger* f. LL *car(ri)care* load f. L *carrus* CAR]
■ *v.* **1 a** ask, demand, claim, require, expect. **b** bill, invoice. **2 a** (*charge to*) put on a person's account, put down *or* write to a person's account, chalk up to, *Brit.* put on the slate of. **3** accuse, indict, impeach, arraign, incriminate, inculpate; allege; assert, claim, hold,

asseverate, maintain, contend. **4** instruct, command, order, direct, tell, enjoin, exhort, urge, press, push, beg, call on, *archaic or literary* bid. **5 a** entrust, trust. **b** (*charge oneself with*) see UNDERTAKE 1. **6 a** bear down; see also RUSH[1] *v.* 1. **b** rush at, attack, assault, storm, assail, set upon, come at, descend upon. **9** fill, imbue, load, instill, saturate, steep, suffuse, infuse, surcharge, impregnate, permeate. ● *n.* **1 a** price, fee, cost, payment, rate, tariff, fare, toll, *sl.* damage. **b** debt, debit, expense, assessment, liability. **2** accusation, imputation, indictment, allegation, complaint, *Law* information, *Brit. Law* plaint. **3 a** see OBLIGATION 2. **b** care, custody, protection, safekeeping, keeping, trust, guardianship, wardship, custodianship; supervision, jurisdiction, control, guidance, leadership, direction. **c** concern, responsibility; protégé; flock, congregation. **4 a** attack, onset, assault, sally, sortie, going forth, raid, foray. **7** order(s), mandate, injunction, precept, command, dictate, direction, instruction, demand, exhortation. **8** see LOAD *n.* 1. □ **free of charge** see FREE *adj.* 7. **in charge** (*be in charge*) see *call the shots*, *have the initiative* (INITIATIVE). **take charge** see HEAD *v.* 2.

chargé d'affaires /shaarzháy dafáir/ *n.* (also **chargé**) (*pl.* **chargés** *pronunc.* same) **1** an ambassador's deputy. **2** an envoy to a minor country. [F, = in charge (of affairs)]
∎ see MINISTER *n.* 1, 3.

charger[1] /chaárjər/ *n.* **1 a** a cavalry horse. **b** *poet.* any horse. **2** an apparatus for charging a battery. **3** a person or thing that charges.
∎ see MOUNT[1] *n.* 3.

charger[2] /chaárjər/ *n.* a large, flat dish; a platter. [ME f. AF *chargeour*]
∎ see PLATE *n.* 1a.

chariot /cháreeət/ *n. & v.* ● *n.* **1** *hist.* **a** a two-wheeled vehicle drawn by horses, used in ancient warfare and racing. **b** a four-wheeled carriage with back seats only. **2** *poet.* a stately or triumphal vehicle. ● *v.tr. literary* convey in or as in a chariot. [ME f. OF, augment. of *char* CAR]

charioteer /cháreeəteér/ *n.* a chariot driver.

charisma /kərízmə/ *n.* (*pl.* **charismata** /-mətə/) **1 a** the ability to inspire followers with devotion and enthusiasm. **b** an attractive aura; great charm. **2** a divinely conferred power or talent. [eccl.L f. Gk *kharisma* f. *kharis* favor, grace]
∎ **1** see APPEAL *n.* 4.

charismatic /kárizmátik/ *adj.* **1** having charisma; inspiring enthusiasm. **2** (of Christian worship) characterized by spontaneity, ecstatic utterances, etc. □ **charismatic movement** a Christian movement emphasizing ecstatic religious experience, speaking in tongues, etc. □□ **charismatically** *adv.*
∎ **1** see MAGNETIC.

charitable /cháritəbəl/ *adj.* **1** generous in giving to those in need. **2** of, relating to, or connected with a charity or charities. **3** apt to judge favorably of persons, acts, and motives. □□ **charitableness** *n.* **charitably** *adv.* [ME f. OF f. *charité* CHARITY]
∎ **1** generous, liberal, bountiful, munificent, beneficent, unselfish, openhanded, magnanimous, philanthropic, public-spirited, well-meaning, good, eleemosynary, *poet.* bounteous; free, unsparing, unstinting, ungrudging. **3** sympathetic, magnanimous, well-disposed, lenient, tolerant, forgiving, indulgent, understanding, compassionate, humane, considerate, nonjudgmental, uncritical.

charity /cháritee/ *n.* (*pl.* **-ies**) **1 a** giving voluntarily to those in need; almsgiving. **b** the help, esp. money, so given. **2** an institution or organization for helping those in need. **3 a** kindness; benevolence. **b** tolerance in judging others. **c** love of one's fellow men. [OE f. OF *charité* f. L *caritas -tatis* f. *carus* dear]
∎ **1 b** help, aid, support, assistance; relief, benefit, welfare, *Brit. colloq.* dole; donation, contribution, largesse, *hist.* alms. **3 a** generosity, benevolence, kindness, charitableness, kindheartedness, munificence, liberality, openhandedness, magnanimity, beneficence, largesse, bounty, philanthropy, unselfishness, altruism,

humanity, humanitarianism, goodwill. **b** leniency, tolerance, bigheartedness, magnanimity, indulgence, considerateness, consideration, compassion, understanding, sympathy.

charivari /shívərée/ *n.* (also **shivaree**) **1** a serenade of banging saucepans, etc., to a newly married couple. **2** a medley of sounds; a hubbub. [F, = serenade with pans, trays, etc., to an unpopular person]
∎ **2** see NOISE *n.* 1, 2.

charlady /chaárlaydee/ *n.* (*pl.* **-ies**) = CHARWOMAN.

charlatan /shaárlətən/ *n.* a person falsely claiming a special knowledge or skill. □□ **charlatanism** *n.* **charlatanry** *n.* [F f. It. *ciarlatano* f. *ciarlare* babble]
∎ see FRAUD 3.

Charles' Law /chaárlz/ (also **Charles's Law** /chaárlziz/) *n. Chem.* the law stating that the volume of an ideal gas at constant pressure is directly proportional to the absolute temperature. [J. A. C. *Charles*, Fr. scientist d. 1823]

Charles's Wain /chaárlziz wáyn/ *n.* esp. *Brit.* the constellation Ursa Major or its seven bright stars; the *Big Dipper.* Also called (esp. *Brit.*) *Plough.* [OE *Carles wægn* the wain of Carl (Charles the Great, Charlemagne), perh. by assoc. of the star Arcturus with legends of King Arthur and Charlemagne]

Charleston /chaárlstən/ *n. & v.* ● *n.* a lively American dance of the 1920s with side kicks from the knee. ● *v.intr.* dance the charleston. [*Charleston* in S. Carolina]

charley horse /chaárlee/ *n. sl.* stiffness or cramp in an arm or leg. [19th c.: orig. uncert.]

charlie /chaárlee/ *n. Brit. sl.* **1** a fool. **2** (in *pl.*) a woman's breasts. [dimin. of the name *Charles*]

charlock /chaárlok/ *n.* a wild mustard, *Sinapis arvensis*, with yellow flowers. Also called *field mustard.* [OE *cerlic*, of unkn. orig.]

charlotte /shaárlət/ *n.* a dessert made of stewed fruit with a casing or layers or covering of bread, sponge cake, cookies, or breadcrumbs (*apple charlotte*). □ **charlotte russe** /roos/ custard, etc., enclosed in sponge cake or a casing of ladyfingers. [F]

charm /chaarm/ *n. & v.* ● *n.* **1 a** the power or quality of giving delight or arousing admiration. **b** fascination; attractiveness. **c** (usu. in *pl.*) an attractive or enticing quality. **2** a trinket on a bracelet, etc. **3 a** an object, act, or word(s) supposedly having occult or magic power; a spell. **b** a thing worn to avert evil, etc.; an amulet. **4** *Physics* a property of matter manifested by some elementary particles. ● *v.tr.* **1** delight; captivate (*charmed by the performance*). **2** influence or protect as if by magic (*leads a charmed life*). **3 a** gain by charm (*charmed agreement out of him*). **b** influence by charm (*charmed her into consenting*). **4** cast a spell on; bewitch. □ **charm bracelet** a bracelet hung with small trinkets. **like a charm** perfectly; wonderfully (*worked like a charm; fits like a charm*). □□ **charmer** *n.* [ME f. OF *charme*, *charmer* f. L *carmen* song]
∎ *n.* **1 a, b** attractiveness, appeal, fascination, attraction, allure, magnetism, draw, pull, desirability, winsomeness, seductiveness. **3 a** spell, incantation, conjuration. **b** amulet, talisman, good-luck piece, periapt, phylactery, juju, churinga; horseshoe, toadstone, rabbit's foot. ● *v.* **1** see CAPTIVATE, DELIGHT *v.* 1. **3 b** influence, seduce, coax, disarm, wheedle, hypnotize, mesmerize; see also BEGUILE 1. **4** put *or* cast a spell on, bewitch, bedevil, voodoo, possess, hoodoo, hex, *archaic* witch. □ **like a charm** successfully, perfectly, wonderfully, marvelously, especially well; like a dream, like clockwork, without a hitch *or* hiccup. □□ **charmer** enchanter, enchantress, sorcerer, sorceress, magician; vamp, siren, temptress, seductress; seducer, Romeo, Don Juan, lothario, Casanova, lady-killer, ladies' man; smooth talker, beguiler, flatterer, wheedler, *colloq.* smoothie.

charmeuse /shaarmőz/ *n.* a soft, smooth, silky dress fabric. [F, fem. of *charmeur* (as CHARM)]

charming /chaárming/ *adj.* **1** delightful; attractive; pleasing.

2 (often as *int.*) *iron.* expressing displeasure or disapproval. □□ **charmingly** *adv.*
■ **1** see DELIGHTFUL.

charmless /chaármlis/ *adj.* lacking charm; unattractive. □□ **charmlessly** *adv.* **charmlessness** *n.*

charnel house /chaárnəlhows/ *n.* a house or vault in which dead bodies or bones are piled. [ME & OF *charnel* burying place f. med.L *carnale* f. LL *carnalis* CARNAL]

Charolais /shárəláy/ *n.* (also **Charolaise**) (*pl.* same) **1** an animal of a breed of large, white beef cattle. **2** this breed. [Monts du *Charollais* in E. France]

charpoy /chaárpoy/ *n. Ind.* a light bedstead. [Hind. *chārpāi*].

charr var. of CHAR⁴.

chart /chaart/ *n. & v.* ● *n.* **1** a geographical map or plan, esp. for navigation by sea or air. **2** a sheet of information in the form of a table, graph, or diagram. **3** (usu. in *pl.*) *colloq.* a listing of the currently most popular music recordings. ● *v.tr.* make a chart of, map. [F *charte* f. L *charta* CARD¹]
■ *n.* **1** plan, map. **2** map, table, tabulation, graph, diagram. ● *v.* plot, map (out), chart out, draw, mark (out); delineate, sketch (out), trace, rough out, outline, frame, draft, particularize, spell out.

chartbuster /chaártbustər/ *n. colloq.* a best-selling popular song, recording, etc.

charter /chaártər/ *n. & v.* ● *n.* **1 a** a written grant of rights, by the sovereign or legislature, esp. the creation of a borough, company, university, etc. **b** a written constitution or description of an organization's functions, etc. **2** a contract to hire an aircraft, ship, etc., for a special purpose. **3** (in full **charter party**) a deed between a shipowner and a merchant for the hire of a ship and the delivery of cargo. ● *v.tr.* **1** grant a charter to. **2** hire (an aircraft, ship, etc.). □ **chartered accountant, engineer, librarian, surveyor,** etc. *Brit.* a member of a professional body that has a royal charter. **chartered libertine** *Brit.* a person allowed to do as he or she pleases. **charter flight** a flight by a chartered aircraft. **charter member** an original member of a society, corporation, etc. **Great Charter** = MAGNA CARTA. □□ **charterer** *n.* [ME f. OF *chartre* f. L *chartula* dimin. of *charta* CARD¹]
■ *n.* **1 a** document, contract, compact, agreement, covenant, accord, bill of rights; permit, permission, license, grant, franchise, diploma, patent. **b** constitution, rules, code, law. **2** lease, contract. ● *v.* **1** license, authorize, commission, franchise, approve, certify, qualify, sanction. **2** let, lease, rent, hire, engage, contract, reserve, secure.

Chartism /chaártizəm/ *n. hist.* the principles of the UK Parliamentary reform movement of 1837–48. □□ **Chartist** *n.* [L *charta* charter + -ISM: name taken from the manifesto 'People's Charter']

chartreuse /shaartr̄ooz, -tr̄oos/ *n.* **1** (Chartreuse) a pale green or yellow liqueur of brandy and aromatic herbs, etc. **2** the pale yellow or pale green color of this. [La Grande *Chartreuse* (Carthusian monastery near Grenoble)]

charwoman /chaárwŏomən/ *n.* (*pl.* **-women**) a woman employed as a cleaner in houses or offices.
■ see SERVANT 1.

chary /chaíree/ *adj.* (**charier, chariest**) **1** cautious; wary (*chary of employing such people*). **2** sparing; ungenerous (*chary of giving praise*). **3** shy. □□ **charily** *adv.* **chariness** *n.* [OE *cearig*]
■ **1** see WARY. **3** see SHY *adj.* 2.

Charybdis see SCYLLA AND CHARYBDIS.

Chas. *abbr.* Charles.

chase¹ /chays/ *v. & n.* ● *v.* **1** *tr.* pursue in order to catch. **2** *tr.* (foll. by *from, out of, to*, etc.) drive. **3** *intr.* **a** (foll. by *after*) hurry in pursuit of (a person). **b** (foll. by *around*, etc.) *colloq.* act or move about hurriedly. **4** *tr. Brit.* (usu. foll. by *up*) *colloq.* pursue (overdue work, payment, etc., or the person responsible for it). **5** *tr. colloq.* **a** try to attain. **b** court persistently and openly. ● *n.* **1** pursuit. **2** *Brit.* unenclosed hunting land. **3** (prec. by *the*) hunting, esp. as a sport. **4** an animal, etc., that is pursued. **5** = STEEPLECHASE. □ **go and chase oneself** (usu. in *imper.*) *Brit. colloq.* depart. [ME f. OF *chace chacier*, ult. f. L *capere* take]

■ *v.* **1** chase after, run after, follow, pursue, track, hunt, go (out) after, take off after, trail, *colloq.* tail. **2** drive, hound; expel, throw *or* cast out; (*chase away* or *off*, etc.) rout, put to rout, put to flight, *colloq.* send packing. **3 a** (*chase after*) see CHASE¹ *v.* 1, 4 above. **b** see RUSH¹ *v.* 1. **5 a** see PURSUE 1, 5. **b** see COURT *v.* 1b.
● *n.* **1** search, hunt, tracking, stalking; pursuance.

chase² /chays/ *v.tr.* emboss or engrave (metal). [app. f. earlier *enchase* f. F *enchâsser* (as EN-¹, CASE²)]

chase³ /chays/ *n. Printing* a metal frame holding composed type. [F *châsse* f. L *capsa* CASE²]

chase⁴ /chays/ *n.* **1** the part of a gun enclosing the bore. **2** a trench or groove cut to receive a pipe, etc. [F *chas* enclosed space f. Prov. *ca(u)s* f. med.L *capsum* thorax]

chaser /chaýsər/ *n.* **1** a person or thing that chases. **2** a horse for steeplechasing. **3** *colloq.* a drink taken after another of a different kind, e.g., beer after liquor.

chasm /kázəm/ *n.* **1** a deep fissure or opening in the earth, rock, etc. **2** a wide difference of feeling, interests, etc.; a gulf. **3** *archaic* a hiatus. □□ **chasmic** *adj.* [L *chasma* f. Gk *khasma* gaping hollow]
■ **1** see GORGE *n.* 1. **3** see SPLIT *n.* 2.

chassé /shasáy/ *n. & v.* ● *n.* a gliding step in dancing. ● *v.intr.* (**chasséd; chasséing**) make this step. [F, = chassing]

chassis /shásee, chás-/ *n.* (*pl.* same /-siz/) **1** the base frame of a motor vehicle, carriage, etc. **2** a frame to carry radio, etc., components. [F *châssis* ult. f. L *capsa* CASE²]
■ see FRAME *n.* 2.

chaste /chayst/ *adj.* **1** abstaining from extramarital, or from all, sexual intercourse. **2** (of behavior, speech, etc.) pure, virtuous, decent. **3** (of artistic, etc., style) simple; unadorned. □ **chaste tree** an ornamental shrub, *Vitex agnus-castus*, with blue or white flowers. □□ **chastely** *adv.* **chasteness** *n.* [ME f. OF f. L *castus*]
■ **1** pure, virginal, virgin, vestal, immaculate, celibate, abstinent, continent, virtuous, undefiled, stainless, unstained, unsullied, unblemished, *archaic or poet.* maiden, maidenly. **2** pure, innocent, platonic, uncorrupted, sinless, blameless, immaculate, spotless, stainless, unstained, unsullied, unblemished, untarnished, untainted, undefiled, virtuous, decent, clean, flawless, faultless, irreproachable, pristine, good, wholesome, moral, honest, *colloq.* white. **3** simple, unadorned, undecorated, unembellished, subdued, restrained, austere, severe, pure, clean.

chasten /chaýsən/ *v.tr.* **1** (esp. as **chastening, chastened** *adjs.*) subdue; restrain (*a chastening experience; chastened by his failure*). **2** discipline; punish. **3** moderate. □□ **chastener** *n.* [obs. *chaste* (v.) f. OF *chastier* f. L *castigare* CASTIGATE]
■ **1** subdue, humble, bring *or* pull down, take down a peg, shame, mortify; curb, restrain, control, check, repress, suppress. **2** discipline, correct, chastise, punish, penalize; see also CASTIGATE. **3** temper, tame, quieten *or* tone down, mellow, soften; see also MODERATE *v.* 1.

chastise /chastíz, chástiz/ *v.tr.* **1** rebuke or reprimand severely. **2** punish, esp. by beating. □□ **chastisement** *n.* **chastiser** *n.* [ME, app. irreg. formed f. obs. verbs *chaste, chasty*: see CHASTEN]
■ **1** see REBUKE *v.* **2** punish, beat, thrash, belabor, spank, whip, flog, scourge, birch, cane, flail, strap, give a person a thrashing *or* beating, *colloq.* give a person a good hiding *or* licking, *sl.* tan a person's hide; discipline, chasten, castigate, correct.

chastity /chástitee/ *n.* **1** being chaste. **2** sexual abstinence; virginity. **3** simplicity of style or taste. □ **chastity belt** *hist.* a garment designed to prevent a woman from having sexual

---

/.../ **pronunciation**	● **part of speech**
□ **phrases, idioms, and compounds**	
□□ **derivatives**	■ **synonym section**
cross-references appear in SMALL CAPITALS or *italics*	

intercourse. [ME f. OF chasteté f. L castitas -tatis f. castus CHASTE]

■ **1, 2** purity, continence, virginity, maidenhood, maidenhead, virtue, honor, celibacy, abstinence, abstention, abstemiousness, restraint, self-restraint, forbearance. **3** see SIMPLICITY.

chasuble /cházəbəl, cházyə-, chás-/ n. a loose, sleeveless, often ornate outer vestment worn by a priest celebrating Mass or the Eucharist. [ME f. OF chesible, later -uble, ult. f. L casula hooded cloak, little cottage, dimin. of casa cottage]

chat¹ /chat/ v. & n. ● v.intr. (**chatted, chatting**) talk in a light familiar way. ● n. **1** informal conversation or talk. **2** an instance of this. □ **chat show** Brit. = talk show. **chat up** Brit. colloq. chat to, esp. flirtatiously or with an ulterior motive. [ME: shortening of CHATTER]

■ v. converse, gossip, talk, chatter, palaver, confabulate, visit, colloq. natter, chitchat, jaw, colloq. yatter, sl. chew the fat or rag, rap. ● n. **1** small talk, gossip, palaver, bavardage, colloq. chitchat, gab, colloq. yatter. **2** conversation, colloquy, talk, gossip, confabulation, bull session, visit, colloq. confab, natter, sl. chinwag, rap.

chat² /chat/ n. any of various small birds with harsh calls, esp. a stonechat or yellow-breasted chat. [prob. imit.]

château /sható/ n. (pl. **châteaus** or **châteaux** /-tōz/) a large French country house or castle, often giving its name to wine made in its neighborhood. [F f. OF chastel CASTLE]

■ see CASTLE n. 1b.

chateaubriand /shatṓbree-ón/ n. a thick fillet of beef steak usu. served with a béarnaise sauce. [Vicomte de Chateaubriand d. 1848, Fr. writer and statesman]

chatelaine /shát'layn/ n. **1** the mistress of a large house. **2** hist. a set of short chains attached to a woman's belt, for carrying keys, etc. [F châtelaine, fem. of -ain lord of a castle, f. med.L castellanus CASTELLAN]

chattel /chát'l/ n. (usu. in pl.) a moveable possession; any possession or piece of property other than real estate or a freehold. □ **chattel mortgage** the conveyance of chattels by mortgage as security for a debt. **goods and chattels** personal possessions. [ME f. OF chatel: see CATTLE]

■ (chattels) see EFFECT n. 4.

chatter /chátər/ v. & n. ● v.intr. **1** talk quickly, incessantly, trivially, or indiscreetly. **2** (of a bird) emit short, quick notes. **3** (of the teeth) click repeatedly together (usu. from cold). **4** (of a tool) clatter from vibration. ● n. **1** chattering talk or sounds. **2** the vibration of a tool. □□ **chatterer** n. **chattery** adj. [ME: imit.]

■ v. **1** prattle, gabble, jabber, prate, twaddle, blather, tattle, tittle-tattle, patter, gibber, clack, blab, blabber, drivel on, run or go on, talk the hind leg off a mule, shoot the breeze, Brit. talk nineteen to the dozen, colloq. gab, jaw, natter, witter, yap, yatter, yammer, esp. Austral. colloq. mag, Brit. colloq. waffle, sl. run off at the mouth, sl. derog. yak. **3** clatter, rattle, shake, shiver, vibrate, jiggle. ● n. **1** prattle, prate, prating, patter, gossip, palaver, chattering, babble, twaddle, blather, tattle, rattle, tittle-tattle, bavardage, colloq. chitchat, gab, natter, colloq. yatter, sl. gas, sl. derog. yak.

chatterbox /chátərboks/ n. a talkative person.

■ blabber(mouth), babbler, natterer, chatterer, prater, gossip, colloq. blab, bigmouth.

chatty /chátee/ adj. (**chattier, chattiest**) **1** fond of chatting; talkative. **2** resembling chat; informal and lively (a chatty letter). □□ **chattily** adv. **chattiness** n.

■ **1** see TALKATIVE.

Chaucerian /chawsee'reeən/ adj. & n. ● adj. of or relating to the English poet Chaucer (d. 1400) or his style. ● n. a student of Chaucer.

chaudfroid /shṓfrwaá/ n. a dish of cold cooked meat or fish in jelly or sauce. [F f. chaud hot + froid cold]

chauffeur /shṓfər, -fṓr/ n. & v. ● n. (fem. **chauffeuse** /-fṓz/) a person employed to drive a private or hired automobile or limousine. ● v.tr. drive (a car or a person) as a chauffeur. [F, = stoker]

chaulmoogra /chawlmo͞ogrə/ n. any tree of the genus Hyd-

nocarpus, esp. H. wightiana, with seeds yielding an oil formerly used in the treatment of leprosy. [Bengali]

chautauqua /shətáwkwə, chə-/ n. (also **Chautauqua**) a cultural and educational program of lectures, performances, etc., usu. held outdoors in the summer. [Chautauqua in New York State, where these originated in 1874]

chauvinism /shṓvinizəm/ n. **1** exaggerated or aggressive patriotism. **2** excessive or prejudiced support or loyalty for one's cause or group or sex (male chauvinism). [Chauvin, a Napoleonic veteran in the Cogniards' Cocarde Tricolore (1831)]

■ **1** see jingoism (JINGO).

chauvinist /shṓvinist/ n. **1** a person exhibiting chauvinism. **2** (in full **male chauvinist**) a man showing excessive loyalty to men and prejudice against women. □□ **chauvinistic** /-nístik/ adj. **chauvinistically** /-nístikəlee/ adv.

Ch.E. abbr. chemical engineer.

cheap /cheep/ adj. & adv. ● adj. **1** low in price; worth more than its cost (a cheap vacation; cheap labor). **2** charging low prices; offering good value (a cheap restaurant). **3** of poor quality; inferior (cheap housing). **4 a** costing little effort or acquired by discreditable means and hence of little worth (cheap popularity; a cheap joke). **b** contemptible; despicable (a cheap criminal). ● adv. cheaply (got it cheap). □ **dirt cheap** very cheap. **feel cheap** feel ashamed or contemptible. **on the cheap** cheaply. □□ **cheapish** adj. **cheaply** adv. **cheapness** n. [obs. phr. good cheap f. cheap a bargain f. OE cēap barter, ult. f. L caupo innkeeper]

■ adj. **1, 2** inexpensive, low-priced, low-cost, cut-rate, reasonable, budget, esp. Brit. cut-price, sl. cheapo. **3** shoddy, shabby, tawdry, tatty, seedy, base, pinchbeck, cheapjack; inferior, low-grade, poor, second-rate, trashy, worthless, chintzy, Brit. tinpot, colloq. two-bit, tacky, Brit. colloq. twopenny, sl. cheesy, tinhorn. **4** see LOW¹ adj. 11. ● adv. inexpensively, cheaply, on the cheap, colloq. for a song, for peanuts. □ **on the cheap** see CHEAP adv. above.

cheapen /chee'pən/ v.tr. & intr. make or become cheap or cheaper; depreciate; degrade.

■ see DEPRECIATE 1.

cheapjack /chee'pjak/ n. & adj. ● n. a seller of inferior goods at low prices. ● adj. inferior; shoddy. [CHEAP + JACK¹]

■ n. see PEDDLER. ● adj. see SHODDY adj. 1.

cheapo /chee'pō/ attrib.adj. sl. cheap.

cheapskate /chee'pskayt/ n. colloq. a stingy person.

■ see MISER.

cheat /cheet/ v. & n. ● v. **1** tr. **a** (often foll. by into, out of) deceive or trick (cheated into parting with his savings). **b** (foll. by of) deprive of (cheated of a chance to reply). **2** intr. gain unfair advantage by deception or breaking rules, esp. in a game or examination. **3** tr. avoid (something undesirable) by luck or skill (cheated the bad weather). **4** tr. archaic divert attention from; beguile (time, tedium, etc.). ● n. **1** a person who cheats. **2** a trick, fraud, or deception. **3** an act of cheating. □ **cheat on** colloq. be sexually unfaithful to. □□ **cheatingly** adv. [ME chete f. achete, var. of ESCHEAT]

■ v. **1 a** swindle, deceive, trick, fleece, defraud, euchre, hoodwink, take in, beguile, dupe, rook, flimflam, archaic chicane, colloq. finagle, diddle, rip off, bamboozle, two-time, take for a ride, do, literary cozen, sl. con, fiddle, bilk, chisel, cross, double-cross, clip, bunco. **b** (cheat of) deny, refuse, deprive of, strip or divest of, rob of, do out of. **2** move the goalposts, break the rules. ● n. **1** cheater, swindler, deceiver, impostor, faker, trickster, confidence man, charlatan, mountebank, rogue, cardsharp(er), sharper, flimflammer, four-flusher, colloq. shark, sharp, two-timer, sl. con man, bilker, Austral. sl. shicer, spieler, magsman. **2** see TRICK n. 1. □ **cheat on** be unfaithful to, colloq. two-time.

cheater /chee'tər/ n. **1** a person who cheats. **2** (in pl.) sl. eyeglasses.

check¹ /chek/ v., n., & int. ● v. **1** tr. (also absol.) **a** examine the accuracy, quality, or condition of. **b** (often foll. by that + clause) make sure; verify; establish to one's satisfaction (*checked that the doors were locked*; *checked the train times*). **2** *tr.* **a** stop or slow the motion of; curb; restrain (*progress was checked by bad weather*). **b** *colloq.* find fault with; rebuke. **3** *tr.* *Chess* move a piece into a position that directly threatens (the opposing king). **4** *intr.* agree or correspond when compared. **5** *tr.* mark with a check mark, etc. **6** *tr.* deposit (luggage, etc.) for storage or dispatch. **7** *intr.* (of hounds) pause to ensure or regain scent. ● *n.* **1** a means or act of testing or ensuring accuracy, quality, satisfactory condition, etc. **2 a** a stopping or slowing of motion; a restraint on action. **b** a rebuff or rebuke. **c** a person or thing that restrains. **3** *Chess* (also as *int.*) **a** the exposure of a king to direct attack from an opposing piece. **b** an announcement of this by the attacking player. **4** a bill in a restaurant. **5** a token of identification for left luggage, etc. **6** *Cards* a counter used in various games, esp. a poker chip. **7** a temporary loss of the scent in hunting. **8** a crack or flaw in lumber. **9** = *check mark*. ● *int.* expressing assent or agreement. □ **check in 1** arrive or register at a hotel, airport, etc. **2** record the arrival of. **check-in** *n.* the act or place of checking in. **check into** register one's arrival at (a hotel, etc.). **check mark** a mark (√) to denote correctness, check items in a list, etc. **check off** mark on a list, etc., as having been examined or dealt with. **check on** examine carefully or in detail; ascertain the truth about; keep a watch on (a person, work done, etc.). **check out 1** (often foll. by *of*) leave a hotel, etc., with due formalities. **2** *colloq.* investigate; examine for authenticity or suitability. **check over** examine for errors; verify. **check through** inspect or examine exhaustively; verify successive items of. **check up** ascertain; verify; make sure. **check up on** = *check on*. **check valve** a valve allowing flow in one direction only. **in check** under control; restrained. □□ **checkable** *adj.* [ME f. OF *eschequier* play chess, give check to, and OF *eschec*, ult. f. Pers. *šāh* king]

■ *v.* **1** authenticate, verify, confirm, substantiate, validate, corroborate, look into, check over *or* through, check up on, test out, *colloq.* check out; examine, investigate, inspect, scrutinize, make sure of, look at *or* over, pass one's eye over, keep an eye on, monitor, check on, keep track of, oversee, watch; make sure *or* certain, check up, ascertain. **2 a** stop, arrest, halt, hold up, stall; limit, interfere with, stunt; retard, slow, brake, stanch, stem, curb, *archaic or literary* stay; obstruct, block, hinder, hamper, impede, inhibit, thwart, dampen, frustrate; restrain, control, repress, contain, restrict, bridle, rein in, govern, hold in *or* down. **b** see REBUKE *v.* **4** correspond, coincide, agree, tally, accord, concur, match, conform, fit, mesh, chime, *colloq.* jibe; compare. **5** check off, tick (off), mark. **6** see LEAVE[1] *v.* 10a. ● *n.* **1** control, test, verification, substantiation, authentication, confirmation, validation, corroboration; investigation, examination, inspection, inquiry, look. **2 a** stop, arrest, halt, cessation, discontinuation, discontinuance, *literary* surcease; break, pause, hesitation, interruption, suspension, delay. **b** see REBUKE *n.* **c** restraint, curb, restriction, bridle, control, constraint, hindrance, brake, deterrent, obstruction, impediment, damper, limitation, stint, inhibitor. **4** bill, *colloq.* tab. **5** token, receipt, stub, *Brit.* counterfoil; voucher, chit, certificate. **6** chip, counter, token. □ **check in 1** register, sign in, enroll; see also ARRIVE 1. **check off** tick (off), mark, check. **check on** see CHECK[1] *v.* 1 above. **check out 1** depart, leave; go. **2** investigate, research, explore, inquire into, look into *or* at *or* over, scrutinize, examine, inspect, probe, sound out, survey, check (up) on, follow up, check, check into, check over, *colloq.* vet, size up; see also CHECK[1] 1 above. **check over** see CHECK[1] *v.* 1 above. **check through** see CHECK[1] *v.* 1 above. **check up** see CHECK[1] *v.* 1 above. **check up on** see CHECK[1] *v.* 1 above. **in check** under control *or* restraint, back, down; restrained.

check[2] /chek/ *n.* **1** a pattern of small squares. **2** fabric having this pattern.

check[3] /chek/ *n.* (*Brit.* **cheque**) **1** a written order to a bank to pay the stated sum from the drawer's account. **2** the printed form on which such an order is written. **3** *Austral.* the total sum received by a rural worker at the end of a seasonal contract. [special use of CHECK[1] to mean 'device for checking the amount of an item']

■ **1, 2** see DRAFT *n.* 2a.

checkbook /chékbŏŏk/ *n.* a book of blank checks with a register for recording checks written. □ **checkbook journalism** the payment of large sums for exclusive rights to material for (esp. personal) newspaper stories.

checked /chekt/ *adj.* having a pattern of small squares.

checker[1] /chékər/ *n.* **1** a person or thing that verifies or examines, esp. in a factory, etc. **2** a cashier in a supermarket, etc.

checker[2] /chékər/ *n. & v.* (*Brit.* **chequer**) ● *n.* **1** (often in *pl.*) a pattern of squares often alternately colored. **2 a** (in *pl.*) a game for two played with 12 pieces each on a checkerboard. **b** each of the usu. red or black disk-shaped playing pieces in a game of checkers. ● *v.tr.* **1** mark with checkers. **2** variegate; break the uniformity of. **3** (as **checkered** *adj.*) with varied fortunes (*a checkered career*). [ME *checker* chessboard]

■ *v.* **3** (**checkered**) variable, varied, varying, mixed, changeable, unsettled, up-and-down, diversified, heterogeneous; uncertain.

checkerberry /chékərberee/ *n.* (*pl.* **-ies**) **1** a wintergreen, *Gaultheria procumbens*. **2** the fruit of this plant. [*checkers* berries of service tree]

checkerboard /chékərbawrd/ *n.* **1** a checkered board, identical to a chessboard, used in the game of checkers. **2** a pattern or design resembling it.

checking account /chéking/ *n.* an account at a bank against which checks can be drawn by the account depositor. [CHECK[3]]

checklist /chéklist/ *n.* a list for reference and verification.

checkmate /chékmayt/ *n. & v.* ● *n.* **1** (also as *int.*) *Chess* **a** check from which a king cannot escape. **b** an announcement of this. **2** a final defeat or deadlock. ● *v.tr.* **1** *Chess* put into checkmate. **2** defeat; frustrate. [ME f. OF *eschec mat* f. Pers. *šāh māt* the king is dead]

checkout /chékowt/ *n.* **1** an act of checking out. **2** a point at which goods are paid for in a supermarket, etc.

checkpoint /chékpoynt/ *n.* a place, esp. a barrier or manned entrance, where documents, vehicles, etc., are inspected.

checkrein /chékrayn/ *n.* a rein attaching one horse's rein to another's bit, or preventing a horse from lowering its head.

checkroom /chékrŏŏm, -rŏŏm/ *n.* **1** a cloakroom in a hotel or theater. **2** an office for left luggage, etc.

checkup /chékup/ *n.* a thorough (esp. medical) examination.

■ examination, *colloq.* going-over.

cheddar /chédər/ *n.* (in full **cheddar cheese**) a kind of firm smooth cheese orig. made in Cheddar in S. England.

cheek /cheek/ *n. & v.* ● *n.* **1 a** the side of the face below the eye. **b** the sidewall of the mouth. **2** esp. *Brit.* **a** impertinent speech. **b** impertinence; cool confidence (*had the cheek to ask for more*). **3** *sl.* either buttock. **4 a** either of the side posts of a door, etc. **b** either of the jaws of a vice. **c** either of the sidepieces of various parts of machines arranged in lateral pairs. ● *v.tr.* speak impertinently to. □ **cheek by jowl** close together; intimate. **turn the other cheek** accept attack, etc., meekly; refuse to retaliate. [OE *cē(a)ce, cēoce*]

■ **cheek by jowl** see *side by side*.

cheekbone /cheekbōn/ *n.* the bone below the eye.

cheeky /cheekee/ *adj.* (**cheekier, cheekiest**) impertinent; impudent. □□ **cheekily** *adv.* **cheekiness** *n.*

■ impudent, impertinent, insolent, audacious, disrespectful, rude, uncivil, forward, brazen, pert, saucy, cocky, cocksure, nervy, *colloq.* fresh, lippy, sassy.

/.../ pronunciation	● part of speech
□ phrases, idioms, and compounds	
□□ derivatives	■ synonym section
cross-references appear in SMALL CAPITALS or *italics*	

cheep /cheep/ n. & v. ● n. the weak shrill cry of a young bird. ● v.intr. make such a cry. [imit.: cf. PEEP²]
■ n. see PEEP² n. 1. ● v. see PEEP² v.

cheer /cheer/ n. & v. ● n. 1 a shout of encouragement or applause. 2 mood; disposition (*full of good cheer*). 3 cheerfulness; joy. 4 (in *pl.*; as *int.*) *colloq.* a expressing good wishes on parting. b expressing good wishes before drinking. c expressing gratitude. ● v. 1 tr. a applaud with shouts. b (usu. foll. by *on*) urge or encourage with shouts. 2 *intr.* shout for joy. 3 tr. gladden; comfort. □ **Bronx cheer** = RASPBERRY 3a. **cheer up** make or become less depressed. **three cheers** three successive hurrahs for a person or thing honored. [ME f. AF *chere* face, etc., OF *chiere* f. LL *cara* face f. Gk *kara* head]
■ n. 1 shout, cry, whoop, hurrah, hooray. 2 temper, spirit(s), humor, feelings, sentiments, temperament, nature, disposition, frame of mind, mood. 3 cheerfulness, gladness, mirth, joy, gaiety, happiness, buoyancy, lightheartedness, merrymaking, *poet.* blitheness. 4 (*cheers!*) a see GOOD-BYE int. b see *bottoms up!* (BOTTOM). c thank you, thanks, much obliged, *Brit. colloq.* ta. ● v. 1 a applaud, clap, *colloq.* give a person a (big) hand, hail. b (*cheer on*) urge (on), encourage, egg on, spur on, goad on; halloo. 2 shout, hurrah, clap; see also APPLAUD 1. 3 gladden, comfort, enliven, cheer up, hearten, console, buoy up, brighten, uplift, encourage, lift up, raise a person's spirits, relieve, *colloq.* buck up. □ **cheer up** brighten, perk up, liven up, *colloq.* buck up; see also CHEER v. 3 above.

cheerful /cheerfool/ adj. 1 in good spirits; noticeably happy (*a cheerful disposition*). 2 bright; pleasant (*a cheerful room*). 3 willing; not reluctant. □□ **cheerfully** adv. **cheerfulness** n.
■ 1 happy, cheery, jolly, merry, gay, lighthearted, breezy, optimistic, positive, sunny, upbeat, bubbly, joyous, glad, joyful, exuberant, *poet.* gladsome, blithesome, blithe. 2 cheering, bright, enlivening, genial, cheery, gay; pleasant, charming, agreeable, attractive.

cheerio /cheereeō/ int. Brit. colloq. expressing good wishes on parting or before drinking.

cheerleader /cheerleedər/ n. a person who leads cheers of applause, etc., esp. at a sports event.

cheerless /cheerlis/ adj. gloomy; dreary; miserable. □□ **cheerlessly** adv. **cheerlessness** n.
■ see GLOOMY 2.

cheerly /cheerlee/ adv. & adj. ● adv. esp. Naut. heartily; with a will. ● adj. archaic cheerful.

cheery /cheeree/ adj. (**cheerier, cheeriest**) lively; in good spirits; genial; cheering. □□ **cheerily** adv. **cheeriness** n.
■ see GENIAL¹ 1.

cheese¹ /cheez/ n. 1 a a food made from the pressed curds of milk. b a complete cake of this with rind. 2 Brit. a conserve having the consistency of soft cheese (*lemon cheese*). 3 Brit. a round flat object, e.g., the heavy, flat, wooden disk used in skittles. □ **cheese knife** (or **slicer**) 1 a knife with a broad curved blade. 2 a device for cutting cheese by pulling a wire through it. **hard cheese** Brit. sl. bad luck. [OE *cēse*, etc. ult. f. L *caseus*]

cheese² /cheez/ v.tr. Brit. sl. (as **cheesed** adj.) (often foll. by *off*) bored; fed up. □ **cheese it 1** look out. **2** run away. [19th c.: orig. unkn.]

cheese³ /cheez/ n. (also **big cheese**) sl. an important person. [perh. f. Hind. *chīz* thing]

cheeseboard /cheezbawrd/ n. 1 a board from which cheese is served. 2 a selection of cheeses.

cheeseburger /cheezbərgər/ n. a hamburger with cheese on it.

cheesecake /cheezkayk/ n. 1 a rich dessert cake made with cream cheese, etc. 2 sl. the portrayal of women in a sexually attractive manner.

cheesecloth /cheezklawth, -kloth/ n. thin loosely woven cloth, used orig. for wrapping cheese.

cheesemonger /cheezmunggər, -monggər/ n. Brit. a dealer in cheese, butter, etc.

cheeseparing /cheezpairing/ adj. & n. ● adj. stingy. ● n. stinginess.

■ see MISERLY.

cheesewood /cheezwŏŏd/ n. 1 an Australian tree of the genus *Pittosporum*. 2 its hard yellowish wood.

cheesy /cheezee/ adj. (**cheesier, cheesiest**) 1 like cheese in taste, smell, appearance, etc. 2 sl. inferior; cheap and nasty. □□ **cheesiness** n.
■ 2 see INFERIOR adj. 2.

cheetah /cheetə/ n. a swift-running feline, *Acinonyx jubatus*, with a leopardlike spotted coat. [Hindi *cītā*, perh. f. Skr. *citraka* speckled]

chef /shef/ n. a cook, esp. the chief cook in a restaurant, etc. [F, = head]

chef d'oeuvre /shaydŏvrə/ n. (*pl.* **chefs d'oeuvre** pronunc. same) a masterpiece. [F]
■ see MASTERPIECE.

cheiro- comb. form var. of CHIRO-.

chela¹ /keelə/ n. (*pl.* **chelae** /-lee/) a prehensile claw of crabs, lobsters, scorpions, etc. [mod.L f. L *chele*, or Gk *khēlē* claw]

chela² /cháylə/ n. 1 (in esoteric Buddhism) a novice qualifying for initiation. 2 a disciple; a pupil. [Hindi, = servant]

chelate /keelayt/ n., adj., & v. ● n. Chem. a usu. organometallic compound containing a bonded ring of atoms including a metal atom. ● adj. 1 Chem. of a chelate. 2 Zool. & Anat. of or having chelae. ● v.intr. Chem. form a chelate. □□ **chelation** /-láyshən/ n.

Chellean /shéleeən/ adj. Archaeol. = ABBEVILLIAN. [F *chelléen* f. *Chelles* near Paris]

chelonian /kilóneeən/ n. & adj. ● n. any reptile of the order Chelonia, including turtles, terrapins, and tortoises, having a shell of bony plates covered with horny scales. ● adj. of or relating to this order. [mod.L *Chelonia* f. Gk *khelōnē* tortoise]

chem. abbr. 1 chemical. 2 chemist. 3 chemistry.

chemi- comb. form var. of CHEMO-.

chemical /kémikəl/ adj. & n. ● adj. of, made by, or employing chemistry or chemicals. ● n. a substance obtained or used in chemistry. □ **chemical bond** the force holding atoms together in a molecule or crystal. **chemical engineer** one engaged in chemical engineering, esp. professionally. **chemical engineering** the design, manufacture, and operation of industrial chemical plants. **chemical reaction** a process that involves change in the structure of atoms, molecules, or ions. **chemical warfare** warfare using poison gas and other chemicals. □□ **chemically** adv. [chemic alchemic f. F *chimique* or mod.L *chimicus, chymicus,* f. med.L *alchymicus*: see ALCHEMY]

chemico- /kémikō/ comb. form chemical; chemical and (*chemico-physical*).

chemiluminescence /kémilŏŏminésəns/ n. the emission of light during a chemical reaction. □□ **chemiluminescent** /-nésənt/ adj. [G *Chemilumineszenz* (as CHEMI-, LUMINESCENCE)]

chemin de fer /shəmáN də fáir/ n. a form of baccarat. [F, = railway, lit. road of iron]

chemise /shəmeez/ n. hist. a woman's loose-fitting undergarment or dress hanging straight from the shoulders. [ME f. OF f. LL *camisia* shirt]
■ see SHIFT n. 4.

chemisorption /kémisáwrpshən/ n. adsorption by chemical bonding. [CHEMI- + *adsorption* (see ADSORB)]

chemist /kémist/ n. 1 a person practicing or trained in chemistry. 2 Brit. a a dealer in medicinal drugs, usu. also selling other medical goods and toiletries. b an authorized dispenser of medicines. [earlier *chymist* f. F *chimiste* f. mod.L *chimista* f. *alchimista* alchemist (see ALCHEMY)]

chemistry /kémistree/ n. (*pl.* **-ies**) 1 the study of the elements and the compounds they form and the reactions they undergo. 2 any complex (esp. emotional) change or process (*the chemistry of fear*). 3 colloq. a person's personality or temperament.

chemo- /keemō/ comb. form (also **chemi-** /kémee/) chemical.

chemosynthesis /keemōsínthisis/ n. the synthesis of organic compounds by energy derived from chemical reactions.

chemotherapy /keemōthérəpee/ *n.* the treatment of disease, esp. cancer, by use of chemical substances. □□ **chemotherapist** *n.*

chemurgy /kémərjee, kimɔ́r-/ *n.* the chemical and industrial use of organic raw materials. □□ **chemurgic** /-ɔ́rjik/ *adj.* [CHEMO-, after *metallurgy*]

chenille /shəneél/ *n.* **1 a** tufty, velvety cord or yarn, used in trimming furniture, etc. **2** fabric made from this. [F, = hairy caterpillar f. L *canicula* dimin. of *canis* dog]

cheongsam /chawngsám/ *n.* a Chinese woman's garment with a high neck and slit skirt. [Chin.]

cheque *Brit.* var. of CHECK[3].

chequer *Brit.* var. of CHECKER[2].

Cherenkov radiation /chiréngkawf/ var. of CERENKOV RADIATION.

cherish /chérish/ *v.tr.* **1** protect or tend (a child, plant, etc.) lovingly. **2** hold dear; cling to (hopes, feelings, etc.). [ME f. OF *cherir* f. *cher* f. L *carus* dear]
■ **1** foster, tend, cultivate, protect, preserve, sustain, nurture, nourish, nurse, cosset. **2** treasure, hold *or* keep dear, prize, cling to, hold to.

chernozem /chérnəzem, chírnəzyáwm/ *n.* a fertile, black soil rich in humus, found in temperate regions, esp. S. Russia. Also called *black earth*. [Russ. f. *chernyĭ* black + *zemlya* earth]

Cherokee /chérəkee/ *n. & adj.* ● *n.* **1 a** a N. American people formerly inhabiting much of the southern US. **b** an individual of this people. **2** the language of this people. ● *adj.* of or relating to the Cherokees or their language. □ **Cherokee rose** a fragrant white rose, *Rosa laevigata*, of the southern US. [Cherokee *Tsálăgĭ*]

cheroot /shərōōt/ *n.* a cigar with both ends open. [F *cheroute* f. Tamil *shuruṭṭu* roll]

cherry /chéree/ *n. & adj.* ● *n.* (*pl.* **-ies**) **1 a** a small, soft, round stone fruit. **b** any of several trees of the genus *Prunus* bearing this or grown for its ornamental flowers. **2** (in full **cherry wood**) the wood of a cherry. **3** *coarse sl.* **a** a hymen. **b** virginity. ● *adj.* of a light red color. □ **cherry brandy** a dark-red liqueur of brandy in which cherries have been steeped. **cherry laurel** *Brit.* a small evergreen tree, *Prunus laurocerasus*, with white flowers and cherrylike fruits. **cherry picker** *colloq.* a crane for raising and lowering people. **cherry pie 1** a pie made with cherries. **2** a garden heliotrope. **cherry plum 1** a tree, *Prunus cerasifera*, native to SW Asia, with solitary white flowers and red fruits. **2** the fruit of this tree. **cherry tomato** a miniature tomato. [ME f. ONF *cherise* (taken as pl.: cf. PEA) f. med.L *ceresia* perh. f. L f. Gk *kerasos*]
■ *adj.* see ROSY 1.

chersonese /kársəneez, -nees/ *n.* a peninsula, esp. the Thracian peninsula west of the Hellespont. [L *chersonesus* f. Gk *khersonēsos* f. *khersos* dry + *nēsos* island]

chert /chərt/ *n.* a flintlike form of quartz composed of chalcedony. □□ **cherty** *adj.* [17th c.: orig. unkn.]

cherub /chérəb/ *n.* **1** (*pl.* **cherubim** /-bim/) an angelic being of the second order of the celestial hierarchy. **2** (*pl.* usu. **cherubs**) **a** a representation of a winged child or the head of a winged child. **b** a beautiful or innocent child. □□ **cherubic** /chirōōbik/ *adj.* **cherubically** /chirōōbikəlee/ *adv.* [ME f. OE *cherubin* and f. Heb. *kᵉrūb*, pl. *kᵉrūbīm*]

chervil /chárvil/ *n.* an umbelliferous plant, *Anthriscus cerefolium*, with small white flowers, used as an herb for flavoring soup, salads, etc. [OE *cerfille* f. L *chaerephylla* f. Gk *khairephullon*]

Cheshire /chéshər/ *n.* (in full **Cheshire cheese**) a kind of firm crumbly cheese, orig. made in Cheshire. □ **like a Cheshire cat** with a broad fixed grin. [*Cheshire*, a county in England]

chess /ches/ *n.* a game for two with 16 pieces each, played on a chessboard. [ME f. OF *esches* pl. of *eschec* CHECK[1]]

chessboard /chésbawrd/ *n.* a checkered board of 64 squares on which chess and checkers are played.

chessman /chésman, -mən/ *n.* (*pl.* **-men**) any of the 32 pieces with which chess is played.

chest /chest/ *n.* **1** a large strong box, esp. for storage or transport, e.g., of blankets, tea, etc. **2 a** the part of a human or animal body enclosed by the ribs. **b** the front surface of the body from neck to waist. **3** a small cabinet for medicines, etc. **4 a** the treasury or financial resources of an institution. **b** the money available from it. □ **chest of drawers** a piece of furniture consisting of a set of drawers in a frame. **get a thing off one's chest** *colloq.* disclose a fact, secret, etc., to relieve one's anxiety about it. **play (one's cards, a thing,** etc.) **close to one's chest** *colloq.* be cautious or secretive about. □□ **-chested** *adj.* (in *comb.*). [OE *cest, cyst* f. Gmc f. L f. Gk *kistē*]
■ **1** box, coffer, trunk, strongbox, crate, caddy, case, receptacle, container. **2** breast, front; *Anat. & Zool.* thorax. **4** coffers, treasury, exchequer; funds, resources, cache. □ **chest of drawers** chiffonier, commode, dresser, bureau, highboy, tallboy, lowboy. **get a thing off one's chest** get a load *or* weight off one's mind, unburden oneself of a thing, say one's piece about a thing, say what is on one's mind. **play one's cards** (or **a thing,** etc.) **close to one's chest** give nothing away, not give the game away, keep quiet, say nothing; play it cool *or* safe, keep one's powder dry; be unforthcoming *or* tight-lipped.

chesterfield /chéstərfeeld/ *n.* **1** a sofa with arms and back of the same height and curved outward at the top. **2** (also **Chesterfield**) a plain overcoat usu. with a velvet collar. [19th-c. Earl of *Chesterfield*]

chestnut /chésnut/ *n. & adj.* ● *n.* **1 a** a glossy, hard, brown edible nut. **b** the tree *Castanea sativa*, bearing flowers in catkins and nuts enclosed in a spiny fruit. Also called *Spanish chestnut* or *sweet chestnut*. **2** any other tree of the genus *Castanea*, esp. the American chestnut *C. dentata*. **3** = *horse chestnut*. **4** (in full **chestnut wood**) the heavy wood of any chestnut tree. **5** a horse of a reddish-brown or yellowish-brown color. **6** *colloq.* a stale joke or anecdote. **7** a small hard patch on a horse's leg. **8** a reddish-brown color. ● *adj.* of the color chestnut. □ **liver chestnut** a dark kind of chestnut horse. [obs. *chesten* f. OF *chastaine* f. L *castanea* f. Gk *kastanea*]
■ *n.* **6** see JOKE *n.* 1.

chesty /chéstee/ *adj.* (**chestier, chestiest**) **1** *colloq.* having a large chest or prominent breasts. **2** *sl.* arrogant. **3** *Brit. colloq.* inclined to or symptomatic of chest disease. □□ **chestily** *adv.* **chestiness** *n.*
■ **1** see BUXOM.

Chetnik /chétnik/ *n. hist.* a member of a guerrilla force in the Balkans, esp. during World Wars I and II. [Serbian *četnik* f. *četa* band, troop]

cheval glass /shəválglas/ *n.* a tall mirror swung on an upright frame. [F *cheval* horse, frame]

chevalier /shévəleér/ *n.* **1 a** a member of certain orders of knighthood, and of modern French orders, as the Legion of Honor. **b** *archaic or hist.* a knight. **2** *Brit. hist.* the title of James and Charles Stuart, pretenders to the British throne. **3** a chivalrous man; a cavalier. [ME f. AF *chevaler*, OF *chevalier* f. med.L *caballarius* f. L *caballus* horse]

chevet /shəváy/ *n.* the apsidal end of a church, sometimes with an attached group of apses. [F, = pillow, f. L *capitium* f. *caput* head]

cheviot /chéveeət, chéev-, shév-/ *n.* **1** (also **Cheviot**) **a** a large sheep of a breed with short thick wool. **b** this breed. **2** the wool or cloth obtained from this breed. [*Cheviot* Hills in Northern England and Scotland]

chèvre /shévrə/ *n.* a variety of goat cheese. [F, = goat, she-goat]

chevron /shévrən/ *n.* **1** a badge in a V shape on the sleeve of

---

/.../ **pronunciation**	● **part of speech**
□ **phrases, idioms, and compounds**	
□□ **derivatives**	■ **synonym section**
cross-references appear in SMALL CAPITALS or *italics*	

a uniform indicating rank or length of service. **2** *Heraldry* & *Archit.* a bent bar of an inverted V shape. **3** any V-shaped line or stripe. [ME f. OF ult. f. L *caper* goat: cf. L *capreoli* pair of rafters]

chevrotain /shévrətayn / (also **chevrotin** /-tin/) *n.* any small deerlike animal of the family Tragulidae, native to Africa and SE Asia, having small tusks. Also called *mouse deer*. [F, dimin. of OF *chevrot* dimin. of *chèvre* goat]

chevy var. of CHIVVY.

chew /choō/ *v.* & *n.* ● *v.tr.* (also *absol.*) work (food, etc.) between the teeth; crush or indent with the teeth. ● *n.* **1** an act of chewing. **2** something for chewing, esp. a chewy candy. □ **chew the cud** reflect; ruminate. **chew the fat** (or **rag**) *sl.* **1** chat. **2** grumble. **chewing gum** flavored gum, esp. chicle, for chewing. **chew on 1** work continuously between the teeth (*chewed on a piece of string*). **2** think about; meditate on. **chew out** *colloq.* reprimand. **chew over 1** discuss; talk over. **2** think about; meditate on. □□ **chewable** *adj.* **chewer** *n.* [OE *cēowan*]

■ *v.* **1** masticate, munch, grind, champ, *literary* manduce; bite, gnaw. □ **chew the cud** see MEDITATE 1. **chew the fat** (or **rag**) **1** see CHAT¹ *v.* **2** see COMPLAIN 1. **chew on 2** think about *or* on *or* over, reflect on, consider, review, ponder, ruminate on, meditate on *or* over, mull over, deliberate on *or* over, give thought to. **chew out** see REPRIMAND *v.* **chew over 1** see DISCUSS 1. **2** see *chew on* above.

chewy /choōee/ *adj.* (**chewier**, **chewiest**) **1** needing much chewing. **2** suitable for chewing. □□ **chewiness** *n.*

■ **1** see TOUGH *adj.* 1.

Cheyenne /shīán, -én/ *n.* & *adj.* ● *n.* **1 a** a N. American people formerly living between the Missouri and Arkansas rivers. **b** a member of this people. **2** the language of this people. ● *adj.* of or relating to the Cheyenne or their language. [Canadian F f. Dakota *Sahiyena*]

chez /shay/ *prep.* at the house or home of. [F f. OF *chiese* f. L *casa* cottage]

chi /kī/ *n.* the twenty-second letter of the Greek alphabet (X, χ). □ **Chi-Rho** /rō/ a monogram of chi and rho as the first two letters of Greek *Khristos* Christ. **chi-square test** a method of comparing observed and theoretical values in statistics. [ME f. Gk *khi*]

chiack / chíak/ *v.* & *n.* (also **chyack**) *Austral.* & *NZ* ● *v.tr.* jeer; taunt. ● *n.* jeering; banter. □□ **chiacking** *n.* [19th c.: orig. unkn.]

Chianti /keeaántee, keeán-/ *n.* (*pl.* **Chiantis**) a dry, red Italian wine. [*Chianti*, an area in Tuscany, Italy]

chiaroscuro /keeaárəskōōrō/ *n.* **1** the treatment of light and shade in drawing and painting. **2** the use of contrast in literature, etc. **3** (*attrib.*) half-revealed. [It. f. *chiaro* CLEAR + *oscuro* dark, OBSCURE]

chiasma /kiázmə/ *n.* (*pl.* **chiasmata** /-mətə/) *Biol.* the point at which paired chromosomes remain in contact after crossing over during meiosis. [mod.L f. Gk *chiasma* a cross-shaped mark]

chiasmus /kiázməs/ *n.* inversion in the second of two parallel phrases of the order followed in the first (e.g., *to stop too fearful and too faint to go*). □□ **chiastic** /-ástik/ *adj.* [mod.L f. Gk *khiasmos* crosswise arrangement f. *khiazō* mark with letter CHI]

chibouk /chibōōk, shi-/ *n.* (also **chibouque**) a long Turkish tobacco pipe. [Turk. *çubuk* tube]

■ see PIPE *n.* 2a.

chic /sheek/ *adj.* & *n.* ● *adj.* (**chicer**, **chicest**) stylish; elegant (in dress or appearance). ● *n.* stylishness; elegance. □□ **chicly** *adv.* [F]

■ *adj.* stylish, fashionable, à la mode, modish, in fashion *or* vogue, smart, snappy, tasteful, elegant, sophisticated, glamorous, becoming, in, swish, swell, *colloq. often derog.* trendy; exclusive. ● *n.* good taste, tastefulness, elegance, stylishness, style, fashion, modishness.

□□ **chicly** see *beautifully* (BEAUTIFUL).

chicane /shikáyn/ *n.* & *v.* ● *n.* **1** chicanery. **2** an artificial barrier or obstacle on an automobile racecourse. **3** *Bridge* a hand without trumps, or without cards of one suit. ● *v.*

archaic **1** *intr.* use chicanery. **2** *tr.* (usu. foll. by *into, out of*, etc.) cheat (a person). [F *chicane*(r) quibble]

■ *n.* **1** see CHICANERY 2. ● *v.* see CHEAT *v.* 1a.

chicanery /shikáynəree/ *n.* (*pl.* **-ies**) **1** clever but misleading talk; a false argument. **2** trickery; deception. [F *chicanerie* (as CHICANE)]

■ **1** sophistry, equivocation, humbug, flimflam. **2** trickery, deception, chicane, deceit, sharp practice, cheating, deviousness, duplicity, pettifoggery, double-dealing, legerdemain, artifice, skulduggery, underhandedness, cunning, artfulness, dissimulation, foul play, esp. *Brit. colloq.* jiggery-pokery, *sl.* funny business.

Chicano /chikaánō/ *n.* (*pl.* **-os**; *fem.* **chicana**, *pl.* **-as**) an American of Mexican origin. [Sp. *mejicano* Mexican]

chichi /sheéshee/ *adj.* & *n.* ● *adj.* **1** (of a thing) frilly; showy. **2** (of a person or behavior) fussy; affected. ● *n.* **1** overrefinement; pretentiousness; fussiness. **2** a frilly, showy, or pretentious object. [F]

■ *adj.* **1** see SWANKY 1. **2** see AFFECTED 3.

chick¹ /chik/ *n.* **1** a young bird, esp. one newly hatched. **2** *sl.* **a** a young woman. **b** a child. [ME: shortening of CHICKEN]

■ **2 a** see GIRL 2.

chick² /chik/ *n. Ind.* a screen for a doorway, etc., made from split bamboo and twine. [Hindi *chik*]

chickadee /chíkədee/ *n.* any of various small birds of the titmouse family, esp. *Parus atricapillus* with a distinctive black crown and throat. [imit.]

Chickasaw /chíkəsaw/ *n.* **1 a** a N. American people native to Mississippi and Alabama. **b** a member of this people. **2** the language of this people.

chicken /chíkin/ *n., adj.,* & *v.* ● *n.* (*pl.* same or **chickens**) **1** a common breed of domestic fowl. **2 a** a domestic fowl prepared as food. **b** its flesh. **3** *colloq.* a pastime testing courage, usu. recklessly. ● *adj. colloq.* cowardly. ● *v.intr.* (foll. by *out*) *colloq.* withdraw from or fail in some activity through fear or lack of nerve. □ **chicken-and-egg problem** (or **dilemma**, etc.) the unresolved question as to which of two things caused the other. **chicken cholera** see CHOLERA. **chicken feed 1** food for poultry. **2** *colloq.* an unimportant amount, esp. of money. **chicken-livered** = CHICKENHEARTED. **chicken pox** an infectious disease, esp. of children, with a rash of small blisters. (Also called VARICELLA.) **chicken wire** a light wire netting with a hexagonal mesh. [OE *cīcen, cȳcen* f. Gmc]

■ *adj.* see TIMID. □ **chicken feed 2** see PITTANCE.

chickenhearted /chíkinhaartəd/ *adj.* easily frightened; lacking nerve or courage.

■ see COWARDLY *adj.*

chickpea /chíkpee/ *n.* **1** a leguminous plant, *Cicer arietinum*, with short, swollen pods containing yellow, beaked seeds. **2** this seed used as a vegetable. [orig. *ciche pease* f. L *cicer*: see PEASE]

chickweed /chíkweed/ *n.* any of numerous small plants, esp. *Stellaria media*, a garden weed with slender stems and tiny white flowers.

chicle /chíkəl/ *n.* the milky juice of the sapodilla tree, used in the manufacture of chewing gum. [Amer. Sp. f. Nahuatl *tzietli*]

chicory /chíkəree/ *n.* (*pl.* **-ies**) **1** a blue-flowered plant, *Cichorium intybus*, cultivated for its salad leaves and its root. **2** its root, roasted and ground for use with or instead of coffee. **3** = ENDIVE. [ME f. obs. F *cicorée* endive f. med.L *cic(h)orea* f. L *cichorium* f. Gk *kikhorion* SUCCORY]

chide /chid/ *v.tr.* & *intr.* (*past* **chided** or **chid** /chid/; *past part.* **chided** or **chid** or **chidden** /chíd'n/) *archaic* or *literary* scold; rebuke. □□ **chider** *n.* **chidingly** *adv.* [OE *cīdan*, of unkn. orig.]

■ see SCOLD *v.*

chief /cheef/ *n.* & *adj.* ● *n.* **1 a** a leader or ruler. **b** the head of a tribe, clan, etc. **2** the head of a department; the highest official. **3** *Heraldry* the upper third of a shield. ● *adj.* (usu. *attrib.*) **1** first in position, importance, influence, etc. (*chief engineer*). **2** prominent; leading. □ **chief executive officer** the highest ranking executive in a corporation, organization, etc. ¶ Abbr.: **CEO. chief justice 1** the presiding judge in a court having several judges. **2** (**Chief Justice of the United States**) the presiding judge of the US Supreme Court. **chief of staff** the senior staff officer of a service or command. **in chief** supreme (*commander in chief*). □□ **chiefdom** n. [ME f. OF *ch(i)ef* ult. f. L *caput* head]

■ n. **1, 2** head, leader, principal, employer, manager, managing director, superior, director, supervisor, superintendent, overseer, captain, master, kingpin, king, ruler, supremo, dictator, ringleader, *Ir.* himself, *colloq.* boss, man, super, top dog, brass hat, *Brit. colloq.* gaffer, *sl.* big cheese, big gun, big chief *or* daddy, governor, (head *or* chief) honcho, Mr. Big; chieftain, headman. ● *adj.* **1** head, superior, supreme, foremost, premier, first, greatest, leading, ranking. **2** principal, leading, prominent, most important, outstanding, key, paramount, dominant, overriding, predominant, primary, prime, main, major. □ **in chief** see SUPREME *adj.* 1.

chiefly /chéeflee/ *adv.* above all; mainly but not exclusively.
■ mainly, in particular, especially, primarily, particularly, above all, most of all, preeminently, principally, primarily, mostly, for the most part, predominantly, largely, by and large, on the whole, in the main.

chieftain /chéeftən/ *n.* (*fem.* **chieftainess** /-tənis/) the leader of a tribe, clan, etc. □□ **chieftaincy** /-tənsee/ *n.* (*pl.* **-ies**). **chieftainship** *n.* [ME f. OF *chevetaine* f. LL *capitaneus* CAPTAIN: assim. to CHIEF]
■ see LEADER 1.

chiffchaff /chífchaf/ *n.* a small European bird, *Phylloscopus collybita*, of the warbler family. [imit.]

chiffon /shifón, shífon/ *n.* & *adj.* ● *n.* a light, diaphanous fabric of silk, nylon, etc. ● *adj.* **1** made of chiffon. **2** (of a pie filling, dessert, etc.) light-textured. [F f. *chiffe* rag]

chiffonier /shífəneér/ *n.* a movable low cupboard with a sideboard top. [F *chiffonnier*, *-ière* ragpicker, chest of drawers for odds and ends]

chigger /chígər/ *n.* **1** = CHIGOE. **2** any harvest mite of the genus *Leptotrombidium* with parasitic larvae. [var. of CHIGOE]

chignon /shéenyon, sheenyón/ *n.* a coil or knot of hair worn at the back of the head. [F, orig. = nape of the neck]

chigoe /chígō/ *n.* a tropical flea, *Tunga penetrans*, the females of which burrow beneath the skin causing painful sores. Also called CHIGGER. [Carib]

chihuahua /chiwaáwə/ *n.* **1** a very small dog of a smooth-haired, large-eyed breed originating in Mexico. **2** this breed. [*Chihuahua* state and city in Mexico]

chilblain /chílblayn/ *n.* a painful, itchy swelling of the skin, usu. on a hand, foot, etc., caused by exposure to cold and by poor circulation. □□ **chilblained** *adj.* [CHILL + BLAIN]

child /chīld/ *n.* (*pl.* **children** /chíldrən/) **1 a** a young human being below the age of puberty. **b** an unborn or newborn human being. **2** one's son or daughter (at any age). **3** (foll. by *of*) a descendant, follower, adherent, or product of (*children of Israel; child of God; child of nature*). **4** a childish person. □ **child abuse** maltreatment of a child, esp. by physical violence or sexual molestation. **child care** the care of children, esp. by someone other than a parent, as at a day-care center, etc. **child's play** an easy task. □□ **childless** *adj.* **childlessness** *n.* [OE *cild*]

■ **1 a** toddler, youngster, little one, juvenile, minor, chit, whippersnapper, adolescent, teenager, teen, *Sc. & No. of Engl.* bairn, *colloq.* kid, *Brit. colloq.* nipper, young 'un; boy, young man *or* gentleman, lad, youth, stripling, *colloq.* laddie, (little) shaver; girl, young woman *or* lady, *Sc. & No. of Engl. or poet.* lass, *colloq.* lassie. **b** neonate, infant, baby, tot, *colloq.* new arrival, *literary* babe (in arms). **2** descendant, son, daughter; (*children*) offspring, family, progeny, *Law* issue, *colloq.* brood, *derog.* spawn. **3** descendant; adherent, follower, disciple, votary, devotee, student; product, consequence, issue, result. □ **child's play** see BREEZE[1] *n.* 4.

childbearing /chíldbairing/ *n.* the act of giving birth to a child or children.

childbed /chíldbed/ *n. archaic* = CHILDBIRTH.

childbirth /chíldbərth/ *n.* the act of giving birth to a child.
■ see LABOR *n.* 3.

Childe /chīld/ *n. archaic* a youth of noble birth (*Childe Harold*). [var. of CHILD]

Childermas /chíldərmas/ *n. archaic* the feast of the Holy Innocents, Dec. 28. [OE *cildramæsse* f. *cildra* genit. pl. of *cild* CHILD + *mæsse* MASS[2]]

childhood /chíldhŏŏd/ *n.* the state or period of being a child. □ **second childhood** a person's dotage. [OE *cildhād*]
■ boyhood, girlhood, youth, prepubescence, puberty, minority, adolescence, teens; infancy, babyhood, juvenescence.

childish /chíldish/ *adj.* **1** of, like, or proper to a child. **2** immature, silly. □□ **childishly** *adv.* **childishness** *n.*
■ **1** childlike, boyish, girlish, youthful. **2** juvenile, puerile, adolescent, infantile, babyish; immature, inexperienced, naive, silly, sophomoric.

childlike /chíldlīk/ *adj.* having the good qualities of a child as innocence, frankness, etc.
■ youthful, young, innocent, trustful, ingenuous, unsophisticated, naive, trusting, credulous, open, undissembling, unassuming, guileless, artless, undeceitful, truthful, simple, natural, unaffected.

childminder /chíldmīndər/ *n. Brit.* a person who looks after children for payment; baby-sitter.
■ nanny, au pair, minder.

childproof /chíldprōōf/ *adj.* that cannot be damaged nor operated by a child.

children *pl.* of CHILD.

Chilean /chíleeən, chiláyən/ *n.* & *adj.* ● *n.* **1** a native or national of Chile in S. America. **2** a person of Chilean descent. ● *adj.* of or relating to Chile.

Chile pine /chílee, cheélay/ *n.* a monkey puzzle tree.

Chile saltpeter /chílee/ *n.* (also **Chile niter**) naturally occurring sodium nitrate.

chili /chílee/ *n.* (*pl.* **-ies**) a small, hot-tasting dried red pod of a capsicum, *Capsicum frutescens*, used as seasoning and in curry powder, cayenne pepper, etc. □ **chili con carne** /kon kaárnee/ a stew of chili-flavored ground meat and usu. beans. **chili powder** a powder made of dried chilies, garlic, herbs, spices, etc., used as a seasoning. **chili sauce** a hot sauce made with tomatoes, chilies, and spices. [Sp. *chile*, *chili*, f. Aztec *chilli*]

chiliad /kíleead/ *n.* **1** a thousand. **2** a thousand years. [LL *chilias chiliad-* f. Gk *khilias -ados*]

chiliasm /kíleeazəm/ *n.* the doctrine of or belief in Christ's prophesied reign of 1,000 years on earth (see MILLENNIUM). [Gk *khiliasmos:* see CHILIAD]

chiliast /kíleeast/ *n.* a believer in chiliasm. □□ **chiliastic** /-ástik/ *adj.* [LL *chiliastes:* see CHILIAD, CHILIASM]
■ millenarian, millennialist.

chill /chil/ *n., v.,* & *adj.* ● *n.* **1 a** an unpleasant cold sensation; lowered body temperature. **b** a feverish cold (*catch a chill*). **2** unpleasant coldness (of air, water, etc.). **3 a** a depressing influence (*cast a chill over*). **b** a feeling of fear or dread accompanied by coldness. **4** coldness of manner. ● *v.* **1** *tr.* & *intr.* make or become cold. **2** *tr.* depress; dispirit. **3** *tr.* cool (food or drink); preserve by cooling. **4** *intr. sl.* = chill out. **5** *tr.* harden (molten metal) by contact with cold material. ● *adj.* = CHILLY. □ **chill out** become calm or less agitated. **take the chill off** warm slightly. □□ **chiller** *n.* **chillingly** *adv.* **chillness** *n.* **chillsome** *adj. literary.* [OE *cele, ciele,* etc.: in mod. use the verb is the oldest (ME), and is of obscure orig.]
■ *n.* **1 b** cold, sniffle(s), influenza, ague, *Med.* coryza, *archaic or colloq.* grippe, *colloq.* flu. **2** coldness, cold, nip, chilliness, chillness, coolness; sharpness, keenness, rawness. **3 a** pall, black *or* dark cloud, dampener. **4**

/. . ./ **pronunciation**   ● **part of speech**
□ **phrases, idioms, and compounds**
□□ **derivatives**   ■ **synonym section**
cross-references appear in SMALL CAPITALS or *italics*

chillness, chilliness, coolness, iciness, frostiness, frigidity, aloofness, stiffness; unfriendliness; hostility.
● *v.* **1** cool, refrigerate, freeze, ice; numb. **2** see DEPRESS 2. **3** cool, refrigerate, freeze, ice. ● *adj.* see CHILLY.

chilly /chílee/ *adj.* (**chillier, chilliest**) **1** (of the weather or an object) somewhat cold. **2** (of a person or animal) feeling somewhat cold; sensitive to the cold. **3** unfriendly; unemotional. □□ **chilliness** *n.*
■ **1** cool, coldish, cold, frosty, icy, wintry, crisp, chill, *colloq.* nippy. **3** unemotional, emotionless, unfeeling, passionless, lukewarm, unresponsive, unforthcoming, unreceptive, frosty, stiff, crisp, cool, cold, icy, cold-blooded, stony, flinty, steely, unfriendly, unwelcoming, chill; distant, aloof, remote, formal; hostile.

Chiltern Hundreds /chíltərn/ *n.pl.* (in the UK) a Crown manor, whose administration is a nominal office for which a member of Parliament applies as a way of resigning from the House of Commons. [*Chiltern* Hills in S. England]

chimaera var. of CHIMERA.

chime[1] /chīm/ *n. & v.* ● *n.* **1 a** a set of attuned bells. **b** the series of sounds given by this. **c** (usu. in *pl.*) a set of attuned bells as a door bell. **2** agreement; correspondence; harmony. ● *v.* **1 a** *intr.* (of bells) ring. **b** *tr.* sound (a bell or chime) by striking. **2** *tr.* show (the hour) by chiming. **3** *intr.* (usu. foll. by *together, with*) be in agreement; harmonize. □ **chime in 1** interject a remark. **2** join in harmoniously. **3** (foll. by *with*) agree with. □□ **chimer** *n.* [ME, prob. f. *chym(b)e* bell f. OE *cimbal* f. L *cymbalum* f. Gk *kumbalon* CYMBAL]
■ *n.* **1 a** carillon, ring, peal. **b** ringing, ring, peal, chiming, tolling, tintinnabulation, clanging, dingdong; tinkle, jingle, jangle. **2** see HARMONY 3. ● *v.* **1** ring, toll, sound, clang, strike; see also PEAL *v.* **2** sound, mark, denote, indicate, announce. **3** see ACCORD *v.* 1.
□ **chime in 1** interrupt, intercede, interfere, interpose, interject, break in, cut in, butt in, pipe up, *colloq.* chip in. **2** join in, come in. **3** see ACCORD *v.* 1.

chime[2] /chīm/ *n.* (also **chimb**) the projecting rim at the end of a cask. [ME: cf. MDu., MLG *kimme*]

chimera /kimeérə, kee-/ (also **chimaera**) *n.* **1** (in Greek mythology) a fire-breathing female monster with a lion's head, a goat's body, and a serpent's tail. **2** a fantastic or grotesque product of the imagination; a bogey. **3** any fabulous beast with parts taken from various animals. **4** *Biol.* **a** an organism containing genetically different tissues, formed by grafting, mutation, etc. **b** a nucleic acid formed by laboratory manipulation. **5** any cartilaginous fish of the family Chimaeridae, usu. having a long tapering caudal fin. □□ **chimeric** /-mérik/ *adj.* **chimerical** *adj.* **chimerically** *adv.* [L f. Gk *khimaira* she-goat, chimera]
■ **2** see PHANTOM *n.* 2. □□ **chimerical** see IMAGINARY.

chimney /chímnee/ *n.* (*pl.* **-eys**) **1** a vertical channel conducting smoke or combustion gases, etc., up and away from a fire, furnace, etc. **2** the part of this that projects above a roof. **3** a glass tube protecting the flame of a lamp. **4** a narrow vertical crack in a rock face, often used by mountaineers to ascend. □ **chimney breast** a projecting interior wall surrounding a chimney. **chimney pot** an earthenware or metal pipe at the top of a chimney, narrowing the aperture and increasing the up draft. **chimney sweep** a person whose job is removing soot from inside chimneys. [ME f. OF *cheminée* f. LL *caminata* having a fireplace, f. L *caminus* f. Gk *kaminos* oven]
■ **1** see STACK *n.* 4.

chimneypiece /chímneepees/ *n.* esp. *Brit.* an ornamental structure around an open fireplace; a mantelpiece.

chimp /chimp/ *n. colloq.* = CHIMPANZEE. [abbr.]

chimpanzee /chímpanzee, chimpánzee/ *n.* a small African anthropoid ape, *Pan troglodytes*. [F *chimpanzé* f. Kongo]

chin /chin/ *n.* the front of the lower jaw. □ **chin strap** a strap for fastening a hat, etc., under the chin. **chin up** *colloq.* cheer up. **chin-up** an exercise in which the chin is raised up to the level of an overhead horizontal bar that one grasps. **keep one's chin up** *colloq.* remain cheerful, esp. in adversity. **take on the chin 1** suffer a severe blow from (a misfortune,

etc.). **2** endure courageously. □□ **-chinned** *adj.* (in *comb.*). [OE *cin(n)* f. Gmc]

china /chínə/ *n. & adj.* ● *n.* **1 a** a kind of fine white or translucent ceramic ware, porcelain, etc. **2** things made from ceramic, esp. household tableware. **3** *Brit. rhyming sl.* one's 'mate,' i.e., husband or wife (short for *china plate*). ● *adj.* made of china. □ **china clay** kaolin. **China tea** smoke-cured tea from a small-leaved tea plant grown in China. [orig. *China ware* (from China in Asia): name f. Pers. *chīnī*]
■ **1, 2** see POTTERY.

Chinagraph /chínəgraf/ *n. propr.* a waxy colored pencil used to write on china, glass, etc.

Chinaman /chínəmən/ *n.* (*pl.* **-men**) *archaic* or *derog.* (now usu. *offens.*) a native of China.

Chinatown /chínətown/ *n.* a district of any non-Chinese city in which the population is predominantly Chinese.

chinch /chinch/ *n.* (in full **chinch bug**) **1** a small insect, *Blissus leucopterus*, that destroys the shoots of grasses and grains. **2** a bedbug. [Sp. *chinche* f. L *cimex -icis*]

chincherinchee /chínchərinchee, chíngkə-/ *n.* a white-flowered bulbous plant, *Ornithogalum thyrsoides*, native to S. Africa. [imit. of the squeaky rubbing of its stalks]

chinchilla /chinchílə/ *n.* **1 a** any small rodent of the genus *Chinchilla*, native to S. America, having soft, silver-gray fur and a bushy tail. **b** its highly valued fur. **2** a breed of cat or rabbit. [Sp. prob. f. S. Amer. native name]

chin-chin /chínchín/ *int. Brit. colloq.* a toast; a greeting or farewell. [Chin. *qingqing* (pr. ch-)]

Chindit /chíndit/ *n. hist.* a member of the Allied forces behind the Japanese lines in Burma (now Myanmar) in 1943–45. [Burm. *chinthé*, a mythical creature]

chine[1] /chīn/ *n. & v.* ● *n.* **1 a** a backbone, esp. of an animal. **b** a joint of meat containing all or part of this. **2** a ridge or arête. ● *v.tr.* cut (meat) across or along the backbone. [ME f. OF *eschine* f. L *spina* SPINE]

chine[2] /chīn/ *n. Brit. dial.* a deep, narrow ravine formed by running water. [OE *cinu* chink, etc., f. Gmc]

chine[3] /chīn/ *n.* the joint between the side and the bottom of a ship, etc. [var. of CHINE[2]]

Chinese /chíneéz/ *adj. & n.* ● *adj.* **a** of or relating to China. **b** of Chinese descent. ● *n.* **1** the Chinese language. **2** (*pl.* same) **a** a native or national of China. **b** a person of Chinese descent. □ **Chinese cabbage 1** = BOK CHOY. **2** a lettucelike cabbage, *Brassica chinensis*. **Chinese gooseberry** = *kiwi fruit*. **Chinese lantern 1** a collapsible paper lantern. **2** a solanaceous plant, *Physalis alkekengi*, bearing white flowers and globular orange fruits enclosed in an orange-red, papery calyx. **Chinese puzzle** a very intricate puzzle or problem. **Chinese water chestnut** see *water chestnut* 2. **Chinese white** zinc oxide as a white pigment.

Chink /chingk/ *n. sl. offens.* a Chinese person. □□ **Chinky** *adj.* [abbr.]

chink[1] /chingk/ *n.* **1** an unintended crack that admits light or allows an attack; a flaw. **2** a narrow opening; a slit. [16th c.: rel. to CHINE[2]]
■ **1** fissure, breach, split, rift, crack, crevice, gap, opening, cleft, cranny; see also FLAW[1] *n.* 1. **2** slit, aperture, gap, opening.

chink[2] /chingk/ *v. & n.* ● *v.* **1** *intr.* make a slight ringing sound, as of glasses or coins striking together. **2** *tr.* cause to make this sound. ● *n.* this sound. [imit.]

chinless /chínlis/ *adj. colloq.* weak or feeble in character. □ **chinless wonder** *Brit.* an ineffectual, esp. upper-class, person.

chino /cheénō/ *n.* (*pl.* **-os**) **1** a cotton twill fabric, usu. khaki-colored. **2** (in *pl.*) a garment, esp. trousers, made from this. [Amer. Sp., = toasted]

Chino- /chínō/ *comb. form* = SINO-.

chinoiserie /sheenwáazəree/ *n.* **1** the imitation of Chinese motifs and techniques in painting and in decorating furniture. **2** an object or objects in this style. [F]

Chinook /shənŏŏk, chə-/ *n.* **1 a** a N. American people native to the northwestern coast of the US. **b** a member of this people. **2** the language of this people and other nearby peoples. **3** (**chinook**) **a** a warm, dry wind that blows east of the

Rocky Mountains. **b** a warm, wet southerly wind west of the Rocky Mountains. □ **chinook salmon** a large salmon, *Oncorhynchus tshawytscha*, of the N. Pacific. □□ **Chinookan**, *adj.*

chintz /chints/ *n. & adj.* ● *n.* a printed, multicolored cotton fabric with a glazed finish. ● *adj.* made from or upholstered with this fabric. [earlier *chints* (pl.) f. Hindi *chīnt* f. Skr. *citra* variegated]

chintzy /chíntsee/ *adj.* (**chintzier, chintziest**) **1** like chintz. **2** gaudy; cheap. **3** characteristic of the decor associated with chintz soft furnishings. □□ **chintzily** *adv.* **chintziness** *n.*
■ **2** see GAUDY[1].

chionodoxa /kíənədóksə/ *n.* any liliaceous plant of the genus *Chionodoxa*, having early-blooming blue flowers. Also called *glory-of-the-snow.* [mod.L f. Gk *khiōn* snow + *doxa* glory]

chip /chip/ *n. & v.* ● *n.* **1** a small piece removed by or in the course of chopping, cutting, or breaking, esp. from hard material such as wood or stone. **2** the place where such a chip has been made. **3 a** = *potato chip.* **b** (usu. in *pl.*) a strip of potato, deep fried (*fish and chips*). **4** a counter used in some gambling games to represent money. **5** *Electronics* = MICROCHIP. **6** *Brit.* **a** a thin strip of wood, straw, etc., used for weaving hats, baskets, etc. **b** a basket made from these. **7** *Soccer*, etc., & *Golf* a short shot, kick, or pass with the ball describing an arc. ● *v.* (**chipped, chipping**) **1** *tr.* (often foll. by *off, away*) cut or break (a piece) from a hard material. **2** *intr.* (foll. by *at, away at*) cut pieces off (a hard material) to alter its shape, break it up, etc. **3** *intr.* (of stone, china, etc.) be susceptible to being chipped; be apt to break at the edge (*will chip easily*). **4** *tr.* (also *absol.*) *Soccer*, etc., & *Golf* strike or kick (the ball) with a chip (cf. sense 7 of *n.*). **5** *tr.* (usu. as **chipped** *adj.*) cut into chips. □ **chip in** *colloq.* **1** interrupt or contribute abruptly to a conversation (*chipped in with a reminiscence*). **2** contribute (money or resources). **a chip off the old block** a child who resembles a parent, esp. in character. **a chip on one's shoulder** *colloq.* a disposition or inclination to feel resentful or aggrieved. **chip shot** = sense 7 of *n.* **have had one's chips** *Brit. colloq.* be unable to avoid defeat, punishment, etc. **in the chips** *sl.* moneyed; affluent. **when the chips are down** *colloq.* in times of discouragement or disappointment. [ME f. OE *cipp*, *cyp* beam]
■ *n.* **1** fragment, piece, shard, sherd, splinter, flake, sliver. **2** nick. **3 b** (*chips*) French fried potatoes, French fries. **4** counter, marker, token, *Cards* check. ● *v.* **1** cut, break, snap. **2** chisel, whittle; (*chip away at*) hew. □ **chip in 1** interrupt, break in, intrude, interfere, intercede, interpose, cut in, butt in, chime in. **2** contribute, help out, *colloq.* shell out, *sl.* fork out *or* up.

chipboard /chípbawrd/ *n.* a rigid sheet or panel made from compressed wood chips and resin.

chipmunk /chípmungk/ *n.* any ground squirrel of the genus *Tamias* or *Eutamias*, having alternate light and dark stripes running down the body. [Algonquian]

chipolata /chípəláatə/ *n. Brit.* a small, thin sausage. [F f. It. *cipollata* a dish of onions f. *cipolla* onion]

Chippendale /chípəndayl/ *adj.* **1** (of furniture) designed or made by the English cabinetmaker Thomas Chippendale (d. 1779). **2** in the ornately elegant style of Chippendale's furniture.

chipper /chípər/ *adj. colloq.* **1** cheerful. **2** smartly dressed. [perh. f. No. of Engl. dial. *kipper* lively]
■ **1** see SPRIGHTLY.

Chippewa /chípəwaw, -wə, -waa, -way/ *n.* = OJIBWA.

chippie var. of CHIPPY[2].

chipping /chíping/ *n. Brit.* **1** a small fragment of stone, wood, etc. **2** (in *pl.*) these used as a surface for roads, roofs, etc.

chippy[1] /chípee/ *adj.* (**chippier, chippiest**) marked by belligerence or aggression, esp. in the play of ice hockey.

chippy[2] /chípee/ *n.* (also **chippie**) (*pl.* **-ies**) **1** *derog.* a promiscuous female; a prostitute. **2** *Brit. colloq.* a fish-and-chip store.

chiral /kírəl/ *adj. Chem.* (of a crystal, etc.) not superimposable on its mirror image. □□ **chirality** /-rálitee/ *n.* [Gk *kheir* hand]

chiro- /kírō/ (also **cheiro-**) *comb. form* of the hand. [Gk *kheir* hand]

chirography /kirógrəfee/ *n.* handwriting; calligraphy.
■ see WRITING 2.

chiromancy /kírəmansee/ *n.* palmistry.

chiropody /kirópədee/ *n.* = PODIATRY. □□ **chiropodist** *n.* [CHIRO- + Gk *pous podos* foot]

chiropractic /kírəpráktik/ *n.* the diagnosis and manipulative treatment of mechanical disorders of the joints, esp. of the spinal column. □□ **chiropractor** *n.* [CHIRO- + Gk *praktikos*: see PRACTICAL]

chiropteran /kíróptərən/ *n.* any member of the order Chiroptera, with membraned limbs serving as wings including bats and flying foxes. □□ **chiropterous** *adj.* [CHIRO- + Gk *pteron* wing]

chirp /chərp/ *v. & n.* ● *v.* **1** *intr.* (usu. of small birds, grasshoppers, etc.) utter a short, sharp, high-pitched note. **2** *tr. & intr.* (esp. of a child) speak or utter in a lively or jolly way. ● *n.* a chirping sound. □□ **chirper** *n.* [ME, earlier *chirk, chirt*: imit.]
■ *v.* **1** tweet, sing, twitter, chirrup, warble, trill, cheep, chirr, pipe. ● *n.* tweet, peep, twitter, chirrup, warble, trill, cheep, chirr.

chirpy /chə́rpee/ *adj. colloq.* (**chirpier, chirpiest**) cheerful; lively. □□ **chirpily** *adv.* **chirpiness** *n.*
■ see LIVELY 1.

chirr /chər/ *v. & n.* (also **churr**) ● *v.intr.* (esp. of insects) make a prolonged low trilling sound. ● *n.* this sound. [imit.]
■ *v.* see CHIRP *v.* ● *n.* see CHIRP *n.*

chirrup /chírəp/ *v. & n.* ● *v.intr.* (**chirruped, chirruping**) (esp. of small birds) chirp, esp. repeatedly; twitter. ● *n.* a chirruping sound. □□ **chirrupy** *adj.* [trilled form of CHIRP]
■ *v.* see CHIRP *v.* ● *n.* see CHIRP *n.*

chisel /chízəl/ *n. & v.* ● *n.* a hand tool with a squared, beveled blade for shaping wood, stone, or metal. ● *v.* **1** *tr.* (**chiseled, chiseling**; esp. *Brit.* **chiselled, chiselling**) cut or shape with a chisel. **2** *tr.* (as **chiseled** *adj.*) (of facial features) clear-cut; fine. **3** *tr. & intr. sl.* cheat; swindle. □□ **chiseler** *n.* [ME f. ONF ult. f. LL *cisorium* f. L *caedere caes-* cut]
■ *v.* **1** carve, cut, sculpt, sculpture, shape, fashion, model; incise, engrave, inscribe, *archaic* grave; gouge, groove, dig, hollow out. **2** (**chiseled**) fine, distinct, distinctive, crisp, well-defined, clear-cut, marked, honed. **3** see CHEAT *v.* 1a.

chit[1] /chit/ *n.* **1** *derog.* or *joc.* a young, small, or frail girl or woman (esp. *a chit of a girl*). **2** a young child. [ME, = whelp, cub, kitten, perh. = dial. *chit* sprout]
■ **1** see LASS.

chit[2] /chit/ *n.* **1** a note of requisition; a note of a sum owed, esp. for food or drink. **2** esp. *Brit.* a note or memorandum. [earlier *chitty*: Anglo-Ind. f. Hindi *cițțhī* pass f. Skr. *citra* mark]

chital /cheet'l/ *n.* = AXIS[2]. [Hindi *cītal*]

chitchat /chítchat/ *n. & v. colloq.* ● *n.* light conversation; gossip. ● *v.intr.* (**-chatted, -chatting**) talk informally; gossip. [redupl. of CHAT[1]]
■ *n.* see GOSSIP *n.* 1. ● *v.* see CHAT[1] *v.*

chitin /kít'n/ *n. Chem.* a polysaccharide forming the major constituent in the exoskeleton of arthropods and in the cell walls of fungi. □□ **chitinous** *adj.* [F *chitine* irreg. f. Gk *khitōn*: see CHITON]

chiton /kít'n, -ton/ *n.* **1** a long, woolen tunic worn by ancient Greeks. **2** any marine mollusk of the class Amphineura, having a shell of overlapping plates. [Gk *khitōn* tunic]

chitterlings /chítlin/ *n.* (also **chitlings, chitlins**) the small intestines of pigs, etc., esp. as cooked for food. [ME: orig. uncert.]

chivalrous /shívəlrəs/ *adj.* **1** (usu. of a male) gallant; hon-

---

/.../ **pronunciation**	● **part of speech**
□ **phrases, idioms, and compounds**	
□□ **derivatives**	■ **synonym section**
cross-references appear in SMALL CAPITALS or *italics*	

orable; courteous. **2** involving or showing chivalry. □□ **chivalrously** *adv.* [ME f. OF *chevalerous*: see CHEVALIER]

■ honorable, courtly, gracious, courteous, gallant, heroic, noble, chivalric, gentlemanly, decent, dignified, well-bred, well-mannered, *poet.* knightly.

chivalry /shĭvəlree/ *n.* **1** the medieval knightly system with its religious, moral, and social code. **2** the combination of qualities expected of an ideal knight, esp. courage, honor, courtesy, justice, and readiness to help the weak. **3** a man's courteous behavior, esp. toward women. **4** *archaic* knights, noblemen, and horsemen collectively. □□ **chivalric** *adj.* [ME f. OF *chevalerie*, etc., f. med.L *caballerius* for LL *caballarius* horseman: see CAVALIER]

■ **2** honor, courtliness, gallantry, nobility, knightliness, knight-errantry, graciousness, gentlemanliness, decency, dignity, virtuousness; bravery, courage. **3** see COURTESY.

chive /chīv/ *n.* a small alliaceous plant, *Allium schoenoprasum*, having purple-pink flowers and dense tufts of long tubular leaves, which are used as an herb. [ME f. OF *cive* f. L *cepa* onion]

chivvy /chĭvee/ *v.tr.* (**-ies, -ied**) (also **chivy, chevy** /chévee/) harass; nag; pursue. [*chevy* (n. & v.), prob. f. the ballad of *Chevy Chase*, a place on the Scottish border]

■ see HARASS 1.

chlamydia /kləmídeeə/ *n.* (*pl.* **chlamydiae** /-dee-ee/) any parasitic bacterium of the genus *Chlamydia*, some of which cause diseases such as trachoma, psittacosis, and nonspecific urethritis. [mod.L f. Gk *khlamus -udos* cloak]

chlamydomonas /klámidəmṓnəs/ *n.* any unicellular green freshwater alga of the genus *Chlamydomonas*. [mod.L (as CHLAMYDIA)]

chlor- var. of CHLORO-.

chloral /kláwrəl/ *n.* **1** a colorless liquid aldehyde used in making DDT. **2** (in full **chloral hydrate**) *Pharm.* a colorless crystalline solid made from chloral and used as a sedative. [F f. *chlore* chlorine + *alcool* alcohol]

chloramphenicol /kláwramfénikawl, -kol/ *n. Pharm.* an antibiotic prepared from *Streptomyces venezuelae* or produced synthetically and used esp. against typhoid fever. [CHLORO- + AMIDE + PHENO- + NITRO- + GLYCOL]

chlorate /kláwrayt/ *n. Chem.* any salt of chloric acid.

chlorella /kláwréllə/ *n.* any nonmotile, unicellular green alga of the genus *Chlorella*. [mod.L, dimin. of Gk *khlōros* green]

chloric acid /kláwrik/ *n. Chem.* a colorless liquid acid with strong oxidizing properties. [CHLORO- + -IC]

chloride /kláwrīd/ *n. Chem.* **1** any compound of chlorine with another element or group. **2** any bleaching agent containing chloride. [CHLORO- + -IDE]

chlorinate /kláwrinayt/ *v.tr.* **1** impregnate or treat with chlorine. **2** *Chem.* cause to react or combine with chlorine. □□ **chlorinator** *n.*

chlorination /kláwrináyshən/ *n.* **1** the treatment of water with chlorine to disinfect it. **2** *Chem.* a reaction in which chlorine is introduced into a compound.

chlorine /kláwreen/ *n. Chem.* a poisonous, greenish-yellow gaseous element of the halogen group occurring naturally in salt, seawater, rock salt, etc., and used for purifying water, bleaching, and the manufacture of many organic chemicals. ¶ Symb.: **Cl**. [Gk *khlōros* green + -INE⁴]

chlorite /kláwrīt/ *n. Chem.* any salt of chlorous acid. □□ **chloritic** /-rítik/ *adj.*

chloro- /kláwrō/ *comb. form* (also **chlor-** esp. before a vowel) **1** *Bot.* & *Mineral.* green. **2** *Chem.* chlorine. [Gk *khlōros* green: in sense 2 f. CHLORINE]

chlorofluorocarbon see CFC.

chloroform /kláwrəfawrm/ *n.* & *v.* ● *n.* a colorless, volatile, sweet-smelling liquid used as a solvent and formerly used as a general anesthetic. ¶ Chem. formula: $CHCl_3$. ● *v.tr.* render (a person) unconscious with this. [F *chloroforme* formed as CHLORO- + *formyle*: see FORMIC (ACID)]

Chloromycetin /kláwrōmīseetin/ *n. propr.* = CHLORAMPHENICOL. [CHLORO- + Gk *mukēs -ētos* fungus]

chlorophyll /kláwrəfil/ *n.* the green pigment found in most plants, responsible for light absorption to provide energy for photosynthesis. □□ **chlorophyllous** /-filəs/ *adj.* [F *chlorophylle* f. Gk *phullon* leaf: see CHLORO-]

chloroplast /kláwrōplast/ *n.* a plastid containing chlorophyll, found in plant cells undergoing photosynthesis. [G: (as CHLORO-, PLASTID)]

chlorosis /klərṓsis/ *n.* **1** *hist.* a severe form of anemia from iron deficiency esp. in young women, causing a greenish complexion (cf. GREENSICK). **2** *Bot.* a reduction or loss of the normal green coloration of plants. □□ **chlorotic** /-rótik/ *adj.* [CHLORO- + -OSIS]

chlorous acid /kláwrəs/ *n. Chem.* a pale yellow liquid acid with oxidizing properties. ¶ Chem. formula: $HClO_2$. [CHLORO- + -OUS]

chlorpromazine /klawrprómǝzeen/ *n. Pharm.* a drug used as a sedative and to control nausea and vomiting. [F (as CHLORO-, PROMETHAZINE)]

choc /chok/ *n.* & *adj. Brit. colloq.* chocolate. [abbr.]

chock /chok/ *n., v.,* & *adv.* ● *n.* a block or wedge of wood to check motion, esp. of a cask or a wheel. ● *v.tr.* **1** fit or make fast with chocks. **2** (usu. foll. by *up*) *Brit.* cram full. ● *adv.* as closely or tightly as possible. □ **chock-full** = CHOCKABLOCK (*chock-full of rubbish*). [prob. f. OF *çouche, çoche*, of unkn. orig.]

■ *n.* see WEDGE¹ *n.* 1.

chockablock /chókəblók/ *adj.* & *adv.* crammed close together; crammed full (*a street chockablock with cars*). [orig. Naut., with ref. to tackle with the two blocks run close together]

■ see FULL¹ *adj.* 1.

chocker /chókər/ *adj. Brit. sl.* fed up; disgusted. [CHOCKABLOCK]

chocolate /cháwkələt, cháwklət, chók-/ *n.* & *adj.* ● *n.* **1 a** a food preparation in the form of a paste or solid block made from roasted and ground cacao seeds, usually sweetened. **b** a candy made of or coated with this. **c** a drink made with chocolate. **2** a deep brown color. ● *adj.* **1** made from or of chocolate. **2** chocolate-colored. □□ **chocolaty** *adj.* (also **chocolatey**). [F *chocolat* or Sp. *chocolate* f. Aztec *chocolatl*]

Choctaw /chóktaw/ *n.* (*pl.* same or **Choctaws**) **1 a** a N. American people orig. from Alabama. **b** an individual of this people. **c** the language of this people. **2** (in skating) a step from one edge of a skate to the other edge of the other skate in the opposite direction. [native name]

choice /choys/ *n.* & *adj.* ● *n.* **1 a** the act or an instance of choosing. **b** a thing or person chosen (*not a good choice*). **2** a range from which to choose. **3** (usu. foll. by *of*) the élite; the best. **4** the power or opportunity to choose (*what choice have I?*). ● *adj.* of superior quality; carefully chosen. □□ **choicely** *adv.* **choiceness** *n.* [ME f. OF *chois* f. *choisir* CHOOSE]

■ *n.* **1** selection, election, preference, pick. **2** see SELECTION 3. **3** finest, pick, élite, flower, best, select, cream, crème de la crème. **4** option, discretion; possibility, opportunity, alternative. ● *adj.* special, fine, good, superior, prime, high-quality, excellent, outstanding, preeminent, best, prize, first-rate, first-class, exceptional, splendid, preferred, *colloq.* plum, plummy; dainty; selected, select, elect, handpicked, well-chosen, fit, appropriate, fitting, apposite, apt.

choir /kwīr/ *n.* **1** a regular group of singers, esp. taking part in church services. **2** the part of a cathedral or large church between the altar and the nave, used by the choir and clergy. **3** a company of singers, birds, angels, etc. (*a heavenly choir*). **4** *Mus.* a group of instruments of one family playing together. □ **choir loft** a church gallery in which the choir is situated. [ME f. OF *quer* f. L *chorus*: see CHORUS]

■ **1, 4** see ENSEMBLE 3.

choirboy /kwírboy/ *n.* a boy who sings in a church or cathedral choir.

■ see *singer* (SING).

choke¹ /chōk/ *v.* & *n.* ● *v.* **1** *tr.* hinder or impede the breathing of (a person or animal), esp. by constricting the windpipe or (of gas, smoke, etc.) by being unbreathable. **2** *intr.* suffer a hindrance or stoppage of breath. **3** *tr.* & *intr.* make or become speechless from emotion. **4** *tr.* retard the growth of or kill (esp. plants) by the deprivation of light, air, nourishment, etc. **5** *tr.* (often foll. by *back*) suppress (feelings) with difficulty. **6** *tr.* block or clog (a passage, tube, etc.). **7** *tr.* (as **choked** *adj.*) *Brit. colloq.* disgusted; disappointed. **8** *tr.* enrich the fuel mixture in (an internal combustion engine) by reducing the intake of air. ● *n.* **1** the valve in the carburetor of an internal combustion engine that controls the intake of air, esp. to enrich the fuel mixture. **2** *Electr.* an inductance coil used to smooth the variations of an alternating current or to alter its phase. □ **choke chain** (or **collar**) a chain looped around a dog's neck to exert control by pressure on its windpipe when the dog pulls. **choke down** swallow with difficulty. **choke up 1** become overly anxious or emotionally affected (*got all choked up over that sad movie*). **2** block (a channel, etc.). [ME f. OE *ācēocian* f. *cēoce, cēce* CHEEK]

■ *v.* **1** suffocate, asphyxiate, smother, stifle, strangle, throttle, garrotte. **2** gag, retch. **5** (*choke back*) hold *or* keep back, hold in (check), suppress, repress, stifle, swallow (back), restrain, withhold. **6** choke up, stop *or* clog *or* bung *or* block (up), fill (up), obstruct, congest, dam (up), constrict, stuff *or* silt (up), foul (up). □ **choke up 2** see CHOKE *v.* 6 above.

choke² /chōk/ *n.* the center part of an artichoke. [prob. confusion of the ending of *artichoke* with CHOKE¹]

chokeberry /chōkberee/ *n.* (*pl.* **-ies**) *Bot.* **1** any rosaceous shrub of the genus *Aronia*. **2** its scarlet berrylike fruit.

chokecherry /chōkcheree/ *n.* (*pl.* **-cherries**) an astringent N. American cherry, *Prunus virginiana*.

chokedamp /chōkdamp/ *n.* carbon dioxide in mines, wells, etc.

choker /chōkər/ *n.* **1** a close-fitting necklace or ornamental neckband. **2** a clerical or other high collar.

■ **1** see STRING *n.* 6.

choky¹ /chōkee/ *n.* (also **chokey**) (*pl.* **-ies** or **-eys**) *Brit. sl.* prison. [orig. Anglo-Ind., f. Hindi *caukī* shed]

choky² /chōkee/ *adj.* (**chokier, chokiest**) tending to choke or to cause choking.

cholangiography /kōlanjeeógrəfee/ *n. Med.* X-ray examination of the bile ducts, used to find the site and nature of any obstruction. [CHOLE- + Gk *aggeion* vessel + -GRAPHY]

chole- /kōlee/ *comb. form* (also **chol-** esp. before a vowel) *Med. & Chem.* bile. [Gk *kholē* gall, bile]

cholecalciferol /kōlikalsífərawl, -rol/ *n.* one of the D vitamins, produced by the action of sunlight on a cholesterol derivative widely distributed in the skin, a deficiency of which results in rickets in children and osteomalacia in adults. Also called *vitamin D₃*. [CHOLE- + CALCIFEROL]

cholecystography /kōlisistógrəfee/ *n. Med.* X-ray examination of the gallbladder, esp. used to detect the presence of any gallstones. [CHOLE- + CYSTO- + -GRAPHY]

choler /kólər/ *n.* **1** *hist.* one of the four humors, bile. **2** *poet.* or *archaic* anger; irascibility. [ME f. OF *colere* bile, anger f. L *cholera* f. Gk *kholera* diarrhea, in LL = bile, anger, f. Gk *kholē* bile]

■ **2** see ANGER *n.*

cholera /kólərə/ *n. Med.* an infectious and often fatal disease of the small intestine caused by the bacterium *Vibrio cholerae*, resulting in severe vomiting and diarrhea. □ **chicken** (or **fowl**) **cholera** an infectious disease of fowls. □□ **choleraic** /-ráyik/ *adj.* [ME f. L f. Gk *kholera*: see CHOLER]

choleric /kólərik, kəlérik/ *adj.* irascible; angry. □□ **cholerically** *adv.* [ME f. OF *cholerique* f. L *cholericus* f. Gk *kholerikos*: see CHOLER]

■ see CANTANKEROUS.

cholesterol /kəléstərawl, -rōl/ *n. Biochem.* a sterol found in most body tissues, including the blood, where high concentrations promote arteriosclerosis. [*cholesterin* f. Gk *kholē* bile + *stereos* stiff]

choli /chōlee/ *n.* (*pl.* **cholis**) a type of short-sleeved bodice worn by Hindu women. [Hindi *colī*]

choliambus /kōleeámbəs/ *n. Prosody* a line of iambic meter with the last foot being a spondee or trochee. □□ **choliambic** /-ámbik/ *adj.* [LL *choliambus* f. Gk *khōliambos* f. *khōlos* lame: see IAMBUS]

choline /kōleen/ *n. Biochem.* a basic nitrogenous organic compound occurring widely in living matter. [G *Cholin* f. Gk *kholē* bile]

chomp /chomp/ *v.tr.* = CHAMP¹. [imit.]

chondrite /kóndrīt/ *n.* a stony meteorite containing small mineral granules. [G *Chondrit* f. Gk *khondros* granule]

chondrocranium /kóndrōkráyneeəm/ *n. Anat.* the embryonic skull composed of cartilage and later replaced by bone. [Gk *khondros* grain, cartilage]

choo-choo /chōōchōō/ *n. colloq.* (esp. as a child's word) a railroad train or locomotive, esp. a steam engine. [imit.]

■ see TRAIN *n.* 1.

chook /chook/ *n.* (also **chookie**) *Austral. & NZ colloq.* **1** a chicken or fowl. **2** *sl.* an older woman. [E dial. *chuck* chicken]

choose /chōōz/ *v.* (*past* **chose** /chōz/; *past part.* **chosen** /chōzən/) **1** *tr.* select out of a greater number. **2** *intr.* (usu. foll. by *between, from*) take or select one or another. **3** *tr.* (usu. foll. by *to* + infin.) decide; be determined (*chose to stay behind*). **4** *tr.* (foll. by complement) select as (*was chosen king*). **5** *tr. Theol.* (esp. as **chosen** *adj.*) destine to be saved (*God's chosen people*). □ **cannot choose but** *archaic* must. **nothing** (or **little**) **to choose between them** they are equivalent. □□ **chooser** *n.* [OE *cēosan* f. Gmc]

■ **1** select, elect, pick (out), opt for, go for, settle *or* decide *or* fix *or* fasten upon *or* on, single out, pitch on *or* upon. **3** determine, opt, elect, resolve, make up one's mind, undertake; see also DECIDE 1. **5** elect, save. □ **cannot choose but** have to, be obliged *or* obligated to, be required to, can only, can but, cannot but; can't help.

choosy /chōōzee/ *adj.* (**choosier, choosiest**) *colloq.* fastidious. □□ **choosily** *adv.* **choosiness** *n.*

■ discriminating, discerning, fastidious, finicky, finical, particular, overparticular, fussy, demanding, exacting, difficult, hard to please, *colloq.* picky, persnickety.

chop¹ /chop/ *v. & n.* ● *v.tr.* (**chopped, chopping**) **1** (usu. foll. by *off, down*, etc.) cut or fell by a blow, usu. with an axe. **2** (often foll. by *up*) cut (esp. meat or vegetables) into small pieces. **3** strike (esp. a ball) with a short heavy edgewise blow. **4** *colloq.* dispense with; shorten or curtail. ● *n.* **1** a cutting blow, esp. with an axe. **2** a thick slice of meat (esp. pork or lamb) usu. including a rib. **3** a short, edgewise stroke or blow in tennis, karate, boxing, etc. **4** the broken motion of water, usu. owing to the action of the wind against the tide. **5** (prec. by *the*) *Brit. sl.* **a** a dismissal from employment. **b** the action of killing or being killed. □ **chop logic** argue pedantically; engage in choplogic. **chop shop** *colloq.* a garage in which stolen cars are dismantled so that the parts can be sold separately. [ME, var. of CHAP¹]

■ *v.* **1** cut, hack, hew, lop, crop, slice; fell; (*chop off*) sever. **2** (*chop up*) cut up, mince, dice; hash (up). **4** see ABOLISH, CURTAIL 1. ● *n.* **1** cut, blow, stroke; swing, *colloq.* swipe. □ **chop logic** see QUIBBLE *v.*

chop² /chop/ *n.* (usu. in *pl.*) the jaw of an animal, etc. [16th-c. var. (occurring earlier) of CHAP³, of unkn. orig.]

chop³ /chop/ *v.intr.* (**chopped, chopping**) □ **chop and change** *Brit.* vacillate; change direction frequently. [ME, perh. rel. to *chap* f. OE *cēapian* (as CHEAP)]

chop⁴ /chop/ *n. Brit. archaic* a trademark; a brand of goods. □ **not much chop** esp. *Austral. & NZ* no good. [orig. in India & China, f. Hindi *chāp* stamp]

chop-chop /chópchóp/ *adv. & int.* (pidgin English) quickly; quick. [f. Chin. dial. *k'wâi-k'wâi*]

■ see *on the double* (DOUBLE).

choplogic /chóplojik/ *n. & adj.* ● *n.* overly pedantic or complicated argument. ● *adj.* (also **choplogical**) engaging in or exhibiting such.

chopper /chópər/ *n.* **1 a** *Brit.* a short axe with a large blade.

/.../ **pronunciation**	● **part of speech**
□ **phrases, idioms, and compounds**	
□□ **derivatives**	■ **synonym section**
cross-references appear in SMALL CAPITALS or *italics*	

b a butcher's cleaver. **2** *colloq.* a helicopter. **3** a device for regularly interrupting an electric current or light beam. **4** *colloq.* a type of bicycle or motorcycle with high handlebars. **5** (in *pl.*) *sl.* teeth.

choppy /chópee/ *adj.* (**choppier, choppiest**) (of the sea, the weather, etc.) fairly rough. □□ **choppily** *adv.* **choppiness** *n.* [CHOP¹ + -Y¹]
■ see ROUGH *adj.* 5.

chopstick /chópstik/ *n.* each of a pair of small thin sticks of wood or ivory, etc., held both in one hand as eating utensils by the Chinese, Japanese, etc. [pidgin Engl. f. *chop* = quick + STICK¹ equivalent of Cantonese *k'wâi-tsze* nimble ones]

chop suey /chopsóo-ee/ *n.* (*pl.* **-eys**) a Chinese-style dish of meat stewed and fried with bean sprouts, bamboo shoots, onions, and served with rice. [Cantonese *shap sui* mixed bits]

choral /káwrəl/ *adj.* of, for, or sung by a choir or chorus. □□ **chorally** *adv.* [med.L *choralis* f. L *chorus*: see CHORUS]

chorale /kərál, -raál/ *n.* (also **choral**) **1** a stately and simple hymn tune; a harmonized version of this. **2** a choir or choral society. [G *Choral*(*gesang*) f. med.L *cantus choralis*]

chord¹ /kawrd/ *n. Mus.* a group of (usu. three or more) notes sounded together, as a basis of harmony. □□ **chordal** *adj.* [orig. *cord* f. ACCORD: later confused with CHORD²]

chord² /kawrd/ *n.* **1** *Math.* & *Aeron.*, etc., a straight line joining the ends of an arc, the wings of an airplane, etc. **2** *Anat.* = CORD. **3** *poet.* the string of a harp, etc. **4** *Engin.* one of the two principal members, usu. horizontal, of a truss. □ **strike a chord 1** recall something to a person's memory. **2** elicit sympathy. **touch the right chord** appeal skillfully to the emotions. □□ **chordal** *adj.* [16th-c. refashioning of CORD after L *chorda*]

chordate /káwrdayt/ *n.* & *adj.* ● *n.* any animal of the phylum Chordata, possessing a notochord at some stage during its development. ● *adj.* of or relating to the chordates. [mod.L *chordata* f. L *chorda* CHORD² after *Vertebrata*, etc.]

chore /chawr/ *n.* a tedious or routine task, esp. domestic. [orig. dial. & US form of CHAR²]
■ see TASK *n.*

chorea /kawre'ə/ *n. Med.* a disorder characterized by jerky involuntary movements affecting esp. the shoulders, hips, and face. □ **Huntington's chorea** chorea accompanied by a progressive dementia. **Sydenham's chorea** chorea esp. in children as one of the manifestations of rheumatic fever; also called ST. VITUS'S DANCE. [L f. Gk *khoreia* (as CHORUS)]

choreograph /káwreeəgraf/ *v.tr.* compose the choreography for (a ballet, etc.). □□ **choreographer** /-reeógrəfər/ *n.* [back-form. f. CHOREOGRAPHY]

choreography /káwreeógrəfee/ *n.* **1** the design or arrangement of a ballet or other staged dance. **2** the sequence of steps and movements in dance. **3** the written notation for this. □□ **choreographic** /-reeəgráfik/ *adj.* **choreographically** *adv.* [Gk *khoreia* dance + -GRAPHY]

choreology /káwreeólʒee/ *n.* the study and description of the movements of dancing. □□ **choreologist** *n.*

choriambus /káwreeámbəs/ *n.* (*pl.* **choriambi** /-bī/) *Prosody* a metrical foot consisting of two short (unstressed) syllables between two long (stressed) ones. □□ **choriambic** *adj.* [LL Gk *khoriambos* f. *khoreios* of the dance + IAMBUS]

choric /káwrik/ *adj.* of, like, or for a chorus in drama or recitation. [LL *choricus* f. Gk *khorikos* (as CHORUS)]

chorine /káwreen/ *adj.* a chorus girl. [CHORUS + -INE³]

chorion /káwreeən/ *n.* the outermost membrane surrounding an embryo of a reptile, bird, or mammal. □□ **chorionic** /-reeónik/ *adj.* [Gk *khorion*]

chorister /káwristər, kór-/ *n.* **1** a member of a choir, esp. a choirboy. **2** the leader of a church choir. [ME, ult. f. OF *cueriste* f. *quer* CHOIR]
■ see *singer* (SING).

chorography /kərógrəfee/ *n.* the systematic description of regions or districts. □□ **chorographer** *n.* **chorographic** /káwrəgráfik/ *adj.* [F *chorographie* or L f. Gk *khōrographia* f. *khōra* region]

choroid /káwroyd/ *adj.* & *n.* ● *adj.* like a chorion in shape or vascularity. ● *n.* (in full **choroid coat** or **membrane**) a layer of the eyeball between the retina and the sclera. [Gk *khoroeidēs* for *khorioeidēs*: see CHORION]

chorology /kərólʒee/ *n.* the study of the geographical distribution of animals and plants. □□ **chorological** /káwrəlójikəl/ *adj.* **chorologist** *n.* [Gk *khōra* region + -LOGY]

chortle /cháwrt'l/ *v.* & *n.* ● *v.intr. colloq.* chuckle gleefully. ● *n.* a gleeful chuckle. [portmanteau word coined by Lewis Carroll, prob. f. CHUCKLE + SNORT]
■ *v.* see CHUCKLE *v.* ● *n.* see CHUCKLE *n.*

chorus /káwrəs/ *n.* & *v.* ● *n.* (*pl.* **choruses**) **1** a group (esp. a large one) of singers; a choir. **2** a piece of music composed for a choir. **3** the refrain or the main part of a popular song, in which a chorus participates. **4** any simultaneous utterance by many persons, etc. (*a chorus of disapproval followed*). **5** a group of singers and dancers performing in concert in a musical comedy, opera, etc. **6** *Gk Antiq.* **a** in Greek tragedy, a group of performers who comment together in voice and movement on the main action. **b** an utterance of the chorus. **7** esp. in Elizabethan drama, a character who speaks the prologue and other linking parts of the play. **8** the part spoken by this character. ● *v.tr.* & *intr.* (of a group) speak or utter simultaneously. □ **chorus girl** a young woman who sings or dances in the chorus of a musical comedy, etc. **in chorus** (uttered) together; in unison. [L f. Gk *khoros*]
■ *n.* **1** see ENSEMBLE 3. **3** see REFRAIN².

chose *past* of CHOOSE.

chosen *past part.* of CHOOSE.

chough /chuf/ *n.* a European corvine bird of the genus *Pyrrhocorax*, with a glossy, blue-black plumage and red legs. [ME, prob. orig. imit.]

choux pastry /shoo/ *n.* (also **chou**) very light pastry enriched with eggs. [F, pl. of *chou* cabbage, rosette]

chow /chow/ *n.* **1** *sl.* food. **2** *offens.* a Chinese. **3** (in full **chow chow**) **a** a dog of a Chinese breed with long hair and bluish-black tongue. **b** this breed. [shortened f. CHOWCHOW]
■ **1** see FOOD 1.

chowchow /chówchow/ *n.* **1** a Chinese preserve of ginger, orange-peel, etc., in syrup. **2** a mixed vegetable pickle. [pidgin Engl.]

chowder /chówdər/ *n.* a rich soup or stew usu. containing fresh fish, clams, or corn with potatoes, onions, etc. [perh. F *chaudière* pot: see CAULDRON]

chow mein /chów máyn/ *n.* a Chinese-style dish of fried noodles with shredded meat or shrimp, etc., and vegetables. [Chin. *chao mian* fried flour]

Chr. *abbr.* Chronicles (Old Testament).

chrestomathy /krestómɔthee/ *n.* (*pl.* **-ies**) a selection of passages used esp. to help in learning a language. [F *chrestomathie* or Gk *khrēstomatheia* f. *khrēstos* useful + -*matheia* learning]

chrism /krízəm/ *n.* a consecrated oil or unguent used esp. for anointing in Roman Catholic, Anglican, and Orthodox Christian rites. [OE *crisma* f. eccl.L f. Gk *khrisma* anointing]

chrisom /krízəm/ *n.* **1** = CHRISM. **2** (in full **chrisom cloth**) *hist.* a white robe put on a child at baptism, and used as its shroud if it died within the month. [ME, as pop. pronunc. of CHRISM]

Christ /krīst/ *n.* & *int.* ● *n.* **1** the title, also now treated as a name, given to Jesus of Nazareth, believed by Christians to have fulfilled the Old Testament prophecies of a coming Messiah. **2** the Messiah as prophesied in the Old Testament. **3** an image or picture of Jesus. ● *int. sl.* expressing surprise, anger, etc. □□ **Christhood** *n.* **Christlike** *adj.* **Christly** *adj.* [OE *Crīst* f. L *Christus* f. Gk *khristos* anointed one f. *khriō* anoint: transl. of Heb. *māšîah* MESSIAH]
■ *n.* **1, 2** see LORD *n.* 4.

Christadelphian /krístədélfeeən/ *n.* & *adj.* ● *n.* a member of a Christian sect rejecting the doctrine of the Trinity and expecting a second coming of Christ on Earth. ● *adj.* of or adhering to this sect and its beliefs. [CHRIST + Gk *adelphos* brother]

christen /krísən/ *v.tr.* **1** give a Christian name to at baptism as a sign of admission to a Christian church. **2** give a name to anything, esp. formally or with a ceremony. **3** *colloq.* use for the first time. □□ **christener** *n.* **christening** *n.* [OE *crīstnian* make Christian]

■ **1** baptize. **2** see CALL *v.* 7.

Christendom /krísəndəm/ *n.* Christians worldwide, regarded as a collective body. [OE *cristendōm* f. *cristen* CHRISTIAN + -DOM]

Christian /kríschən/ *adj.* & *n.* ● *adj.* **1** of Christ's teachings or religion. **2** believing in or following the religion based on the teachings of Jesus Christ. **3** showing the qualities associated with Christ's teachings. **4** *colloq.* (of a person) kind; fair; decent. ● *n.* **1 a** a person who has received Christian baptism. **b** an adherent of Christ's teachings. **2** a person exhibiting Christian qualities. □ **Christian era** the era calculated from the traditional date of Christ's birth. **Christian name** a forename, esp. as given at baptism. **Christian Science** a Christian sect believing in the power of healing by prayer alone. **Christian Scientist** an adherent of Christian Science. □□ **Christianize** *v.tr.* & *intr.* **Christianization** *n.* **Christianly** *adv.* [*Christianus* f. *Christus* CHRIST]

Christianity /krischeeánitee/ *n.* **1** the Christian religion; its beliefs and practices. **2** being a Christian; Christian quality or character. **3** = CHRISTENDOM. [ME *cristianite* f. OF *crestienté* f. *crestien* CHRISTIAN]

christie /krístee/ *n.* (also **christy**) (*pl.* **-ies**) *Skiing* a sudden turn in which the skis are kept parallel, used for changing direction fast or stopping short. [abbr. of *Christiania* (now Oslo) in Norway]

Christmas /krísməs/ *n.* & *int.* ● *n.* (*pl.* **Christmases**) **1** (also **Christmas Day**) the annual festival of Christ's birth, celebrated on Dec. 25. **2** the season in which this occurs; the time immediately before and after Dec. 25. ● *int. sl.* expressing surprise, dismay, etc. □ **Christmas-box** *Brit.* a present or gratuity given at Christmas, esp. to tradesmen and employees. **Christmas cake** *Brit.* a rich fruit cake, usu. covered with marzipan and icing and eaten at Christmas. **Christmas card** a card sent with greetings at Christmas. **Christmas club** a savings account into which weekly deposits are made to defray the cost of Christmas gifts. **Christmas Eve** the day or the evening before Christmas Day. **Christmas pudding** *Brit.* a rich boiled pudding eaten at Christmas, made with flour, suet, dried fruit, etc. **Christmas rose** a white-flowered, winter-blooming evergreen, *Helleborus niger*. **Christmas tree** an evergreen or artificial tree set up with decorations at Christmas. □□ **Christmassy** *adj.* [OE *Cristes mæsse* (MASS²)]

Christo- /krístō/ *comb. form* Christ.

Christology /kristóləjee/ *n.* the branch of theology relating to Christ.

christy var. of CHRISTIE. [abbr.]

chroma /krṓmə/ *n.* purity or intensity of color. [Gk *khrōma* color]

chromate /krṓmayt/ *n. Chem.* a salt or ester of chromic acid.

chromatic /krōmátik/ *adj.* **1** of or produced by color; in (esp. bright) colors. **2** *Mus.* **a** of or having notes not belonging to a diatonic scale. **b** (of a scale) ascending or descending by semitones. □ **chromatic aberration** *Optics* the failure of different wavelengths of electromagnetic radiation to come to the same focus after refraction. **chromatic semitone** *Mus.* an interval between a note and its flat or sharp. □□ **chromatically** *adv.* **chromaticism** /-tisizəm/ *n.* [F *chromatique* or L *chromaticus* f. Gk *khrōmatikos* f. *khrōma* -atos color]

chromaticity /krṓmətísitee/ *n.* the quality of color regarded independently of brightness.

chromatid /krṓmətid/ *n.* either of two threadlike strands into which a chromosome divides longitudinally during cell division. [Gk *khrōma* -atos color + -ID²]

chromatin /krṓmətin/ *n.* the material in a cell nucleus that stains with basic dyes and consists of protein, RNA, and DNA, of which eukaryotic chromosomes are composed. [G: see CHROMATID]

chromato- /krṓmətō/ *comb. form* (also **chromo-** /krṓmō/) color (*chromatopsia*). [Gk *khrōma* -atos color]

chromatography /krṓmətógrəfee/ *n. Chem.* the separation of the components of a mixture by slow passage through or over a material which adsorbs them differently. □□ **chromatograph** /-mátəgraf/ *n.* **chromatographic** *adj.* [G *Chromatographie* (as CHROMATO-, -GRAPHY)]

chromatopsia /krṓmətópseeə/ *n. Med.* abnormally colored vision. [CHROMATO- + Gk *-opsia* seeing]

chrome /krōm/ *n.* **1** chromium, esp. as plating. **2** (in full **chrome yellow**) a yellow pigment obtained from lead chromate. □ **chrome leather** leather tanned with chromium salts. **chrome-nickel** (of stainless steel) containing chromium and nickel. **chrome steel** a hard, fine-grained steel containing much chromium and used for tools, etc. [F, = chromium, f. Gk *khrōma* color]

chrome-plate /krōm-pláyt/ *n.* & *v.* ● *n.* an electrolytically deposited protective coating of chromium. ● *v.tr.* **1** coat with this. **2** (as **chrome-plated** *adj.*) pretentiously decorative.

chromic /krṓmik/ *adj. Chem.* of or containing trivalent chromium. □ **chromic acid** an acid that exists only in solution or in the form of chromate salts.

chromite /krṓmīt/ *n.* **1** *Mineral.* a black mineral of chromium and iron oxides, which is the principal ore of chromium. **2** *Chem.* a salt of bivalent chromium.

chromium /krṓmeeəm/ *n. Chem.* a hard, white metallic transition element, occurring naturally as chromite and used as a shiny decorative electroplated coating. ¶ Symb.: **Cr**. □ **chromium steel** = *chrome steel*. [mod.L f. F CHROME]

chromo /krṓmō/ *n.* (*pl.* **-os**) *Austral. sl.* a prostitute. [abbr. of CHROMOLITHOGRAPH, with ref. to her makeup]

chromo-¹ /krṓmō/ *comb. form Chem.* chromium.

chromo-² *comb. form* var. of CHROMATO-.

chromolithograph /krṓmōlíthəgraf/ *n.* & *v.* ● *n.* a colored picture printed by lithography. ● *v.tr.* print or produce by this process. □□ **chromolithographer** /-lithógrəfər/ *n.* **chromolithographic** *adj.* **chromolithography** /-lithógrəfee/ *n.*

chromosome /krṓməsōm/ *n. Biochem.* one of the threadlike structures, usu. found in the cell nucleus, that carry the genetic information in the form of genes. □ **chromosome map** a plan showing the relative positions of genes along the length of a chromosome. □□ **chromosomal** *adj.* [G *Chromosom* (as CHROMO-², -SOME³)]

chromosphere /krṓməsfeer/ *n.* a gaseous layer of the sun's atmosphere between the photosphere and the corona. □□ **chromospheric** /-sféerik, -sfér-/ *adj.* [CHROMO-² + SPHERE]

Chron. *abbr.* Chronicles (Old Testament).

chronic /krónik/ *adj.* **1** persisting for a long time (usu. of an illness or a personal or social problem). **2** having a chronic complaint. **3** *colloq. disp.* habitual; inveterate (*a chronic liar*). **4** *Brit. colloq.* very bad; intense; severe. □□ **chronically** *adv.*

chronicity /kronísitee/ *n.* [F *chronique* f. L *chronicus* (in LL of disease) f. Gk *khronikos* f. *khronos* time]

■ **1** long-lasting, long-standing, lingering, inveterate, persistent, continuing, lasting, long-lived, long-established, deep-rooted, perennial, nagging. **3** inveterate, habitual, persistent, dyed-in-the-wool, confirmed, hardened, incorrigible, out-and-out, unalterable, intractable, obdurate.

chronicle /krónikəl/ *n.* & *v.* ● *n.* **1** a register of events in order of their occurrence. **2** a narrative; a full account. **3** (**Chronicles**) the name of two of the historical books of the Old Testament or Hebrew bible. ● *v.tr.* record (events) in the order of their occurrence. □□ **chronicler** *n.* [ME f. AF *cronicle* ult. f. L *chronica* f. Gk *khronika* annals: see CHRONIC]

■ *n.* **1, 2** record, history, report, register, annals, chronology, diary, journal, account, narrative, description, commentary. ● *v.* record, register, list, enter, document, put *or* set down, write down, enroll; tell, describe, recount, narrate, report, relate, retail.

/.../ **pronunciation**   ● **part of speech**
□ **phrases, idioms, and compounds**
□□ **derivatives**   ■ **synonym section**
cross-references appear in SMALL CAPITALS or *italics*

chrono- /krŏnō/ *comb. form* time. [Gk *khronos* time]

chronograph /krónəgraf, krŏnə-/ *n.* **1** an instrument for recording time with extreme accuracy. **2** a stopwatch. □□ **chronographic** *adj.*

chronological /krónəlójikəl/ *adj.* **1** (of a number of events) arranged or regarded in the order of their occurrence. **2** of or relating to chronology. □□ **chronologically** *adv.*

chronology /krənóləjee/ *n.* (*pl.* **-ies**) **1** the study of historical records to establish the dates of past events. **2 a** the arrangement of events, dates, etc., in the order of their occurrence. **b** a table or document displaying this. □□ **chronologist** *n.* **chronologize** *v.tr.* [mod.L *chronologia* (as CHRONO-, -LOGY)]

■ **2 a** see SEQUENCE *n.* **b** account, record, calendar, almanac, journal, log, register, document, list.

chronometer /krənómitər/ *n.* a time-measuring instrument, esp. one keeping accurate time at all temperatures and used in navigation.

■ see WATCH *n.* 1.

chronometry /krənómitree/ *n.* the science of accurate time measurement. □□ **chronometric** /krónəmétrik/ *adj.* **chronometrical** *adj.* **chronometrically** *adv.*

chrysalis /krísəlis/ *n.* (also **chrysalid**) (*pl.* **chrysalides** /krisálideez/ or **chrysalises**) **1 a** a quiescent pupa of a butterfly or moth. **b** the hard outer case enclosing it. **2** a preparatory or transitional state. [L f. Gk *khrusallis -idos* f. *khrusos* gold]

chrysanth /krisánth/ *n. colloq.* any of the autumn-blooming cultivated varieties of chrysanthemum. [abbr.]

chrysanthemum /krisánthəməm/ *n.* any composite plant of the genus *Chrysanthemum*, having brightly colored flowers. [L f. Gk *khrusanthemon* f. *khrusos* gold + *anthemon* flower]

chryselephantine /kríselifántin, -tin/ *adj.* (of ancient Greek sculpture) overlaid with gold and ivory. [Gk *khruselephantinos* f. *khrusos* gold + *elephas* ivory]

chrysoberyl /krísəbéril/ *n.* a yellowish-green gem consisting of a beryllium salt. [L *chrysoberyllus* f. Gk *khrusos* gold + *bērullos* beryl]

chrysolite /krísəlīt/ *n.* a precious stone, a yellowish-green or brownish variety of olivine. [ME f. OF *crisolite* f. med.L *crisolitus* f. L *chrysolithus* f. Gk *khrusolithos* f. *khrusos* gold + *lithos* stone]

chrysoprase /krísəprayz/ *n.* **1** an apple-green variety of chalcedony containing nickel and used as a gem. **2** (in the New Testament) prob. a golden-green variety of beryl. [ME f. OF *crisopace* f. L *chrysopassus* var. of L *chrysoprasus* f. Gk *khrusoprasos* f. *khrusos* gold + *prason* leek]

chthonic /thónik/ (also **chthonian** /thóneeən/) *adj.* of, relating to, or inhabiting the underworld. [Gk *khthōn* earth]

chub /chub/ *n.* a thick-bodied, coarse-fleshed river fish, *Leuciscus cephalus*. [15th c.: orig. unkn.]

chubby /chúbee/ *adj.* (**chubbier, chubbiest**) plump and rounded (esp. of a person or a part of the body). □□ **chubbily** *adv.* **chubbiness** *n.* [CHUB]

■ stumpy, stubby, chunky, tubby, plump, dumpy, rotund, esp. *Brit. colloq.* pudgy; thickset, heavyset, heavy, overweight, fat.

chuck¹ /chuk/ *v. & n.* ● *v.tr.* **1** *colloq.* fling or throw carelessly or with indifference. **2** *colloq.* give up; reject; abandon; jilt (*chucked my job; chucked her boyfriend*). **3** touch playfully, esp. under the chin. ● *n.* a playful touch under the chin. □ **the chuck** *Brit. sl.* dismissal (*he got the chuck*). **chuck it** *sl.* stop; desist. **chuck off** *Austral. & NZ sl.* sneer; scoff. **chuck out** *colloq.* **1** expel (a person) from a gathering, etc. **2** get rid of; discard. [16th c., perh. f. F *chuquer, choquer* to knock]

■ *v.* **1** see THROW *v.* 1, 2. **2** see DROP *v.* 4. □ **chuck out 1** see *cast out.* **2** see *throw away* 1.

chuck² /chuk/ *n. & v.* ● *n.* **1** a cut of beef between the neck and the ribs. **2** a device for holding a workpiece in a lathe or a tool in a drill. ● *v.tr.* fix (wood, a tool, etc.) to a chuck. □ **chuck wagon** a wagon for storing food and preparing meals on a ranch, etc. [var. of CHOCK]

chuckle /chúkəl/ *v. & n.* ● *v.intr.* laugh quietly or inwardly.

● *n.* a quiet or suppressed laugh. □□ **chuckler** *n.* [*chuck* cluck]

■ *v.* laugh, chortle, giggle, titter, tehee, snigger, snicker. ● *n.* titter, tehee, laugh, chortle, giggle, snigger, snicker.

chucklehead /chúkəlhed/ *n. colloq.* a stupid person. □□ **chuckleheaded** *adj.* [*chuckle* clumsy, prob. rel. to CHUCK²]

■ see FOOL¹ *n.* 1.

chuddar var. of CHADOR.

chuff /chuf/ *v.intr.* (of a steam engine, etc.) work with a regular sharp puffing sound. [imit.]

chuffed /chuft/ *adj. Brit. sl.* delighted. [dial. *chuff* pleased]

chug /chug/ *v. & n.* ● *v.intr.* (**chugged, chugging**) **1** emit a regular muffled explosive sound, as of an engine running slowly. **2** move with this sound. ● *n.* a chugging sound. [imit.]

chukar /chukaár/ *n.* a red-legged partridge, *Alectoris chukar*, native to India. [Hindi *cakor*]

chukker /chúkər/ *n.* (also **chukka**) each of the periods of play into which a game of polo is divided. □ **chukka boot** an ankle-high leather boot as worn for polo. [Hindi *cakkar* f. Skr. *cakra* wheel]

chum¹ /chum/ *n. & v.* ● *n. colloq.* (esp. among schoolchildren) a close friend. ● *v.intr.* (often foll. by *with*) *Brit.* share rooms. □ **chum up** (often foll. by *with*) become a close friend (of). □□ **chummy** *adj.* (**chummier, chummiest**). **chummily** *adv.* **chumminess** *n.* [17th c.: prob. short for *chamber-fellow*]

■ *n.* friend, comrade, mate, playmate, (boon) companion, crony, confidant(e), intimate, second self, familiar, *colloq.* pal, sidekick, buddy, amigo, *Austral. & NZ colloq.* cobber, fellow, colleague. □ **chum up** (*chum up with*) ally (oneself) with, be friendly with, go with, associate with, team up with, *colloq.* pal up with. □□ **chummy** friendly, intimate, close, attached, matey, on good terms, *colloq.* pally, thick, solid.

chum² /chum/ *n. & v.* ● *n.* **1** refuse from fish used as bait. **2** chopped fish used as bait. ● *v.* **1** *intr.* fish using chum. **2** *tr.* bait (a fishing place) using chum. [19th c.: orig. unkn.]

chump /chump/ *n.* **1** *colloq.* a foolish person. **2** *Brit.* the thick end, esp. of a loin of lamb or mutton (*chump chop*). **3** a short thick block of wood. **4** *Brit. sl.* the head. □ **off one's chump** *Brit. sl.* crazy. [18th c.: blend of CHUNK and LUMP¹]

■ **1** see FOOL¹ *n.* 1.

chunder /chúndər/ *v.intr. & n. Austral. sl.* vomit. [20th c.: orig. unkn.]

chunk /chungk/ *n.* **1** a thick, solid slice or piece of something firm or hard. **2** a substantial amount or piece. [prob. var. of CHUCK²]

■ see PIECE *n.* 1a.

chunky /chúngkee/ *adj.* (**chunkier, chunkiest**) **1** containing or consisting of chunks. **2** short and thick; small and sturdy. **3** (of clothes) made of a thick material. □□ **chunkiness** *n.*

■ **1** see LUMPY 1. **2** see STOCKY. **3** see BULKY.

Chunnel /chúnəl/ *n. colloq.* a tunnel under the English Channel linking England and France. [portmanteau word f. *Channel tunnel*]

chunter /chúntər/ *v.intr. Brit. colloq.* mutter; grumble. [prob. imit.]

church /chərch/ *n. & v.* ● *n.* **1** a building for public (usu. Christian) worship. **2** a meeting for public worship in such a building (*go to church; met after church*). **3** (**Church**) the body of all Christians. **4** (**Church**) the clergy or clerical profession (*went into the Church*). **5** (**Church**) an organized Christian group or society of any time, country, or distinct principles of worship (*the Baptist Church; Church of England*). **6** institutionalized religion as a political or social force (*church and state*). ● *v.tr.* bring to church for a service of thanksgiving. □ **Church of England** the English Church, recognized by the government and having the sovereign as its head. **church school** a private school supported by a church or parish. [OE *cirice, circe,* etc. f. med. Gk *kurikon* f. Gk *kuriakon (dōma)* Lord's (house) f. *kurios* Lord: cf. KIRK]

■ *n.* **1** see TEMPLE[1]. **4** see MINISTRY 2, 3. **5** see DENOMINATION 1.

churchgoer /chə́rchgōər/ *n.* a person who goes to church, esp. regularly. □□ **churchgoing** *n.* & *adj.*

churchman /chə́rchmən/ *n.* (*pl.* **-men**) **1** a member of the clergy or of a church. **2** a supporter of the church.
■ **1** see CLERGYMAN.

churchwarden /chə́rchwáwrd'n/ *n.* **1** *Anglican Ch.* either of two elected lay representatives of a parish, assisting with routine administration. **2** *Brit.* a long-stemmed clay pipe.

churchwoman /chə́rchwŏŏmən/ *n.* (*pl.* **-women**) **1** a woman member of the clergy or of a church. **2** a woman supporter of the Church.

churchy /chə́rchee/ *adj.* **1** obtrusively or intolerantly devoted to the Church or opposed to religious dissent. **2** like a church. □□ **churchiness** *n.*

churchyard /chə́rchyaard/ *n.* the enclosed ground around a church, esp. as used for burials.
■ see GRAVEYARD.

churinga /chərínggə/ *n.* (*pl.* same or **churingas**) a sacred object, esp. an amulet, among the Australian Aboriginals. [Aboriginal]

churl /chərl/ *n.* **1** an ill-bred person. **2** *archaic* a peasant; a person of low birth. **3** *archaic* a surly or mean person. [OE *ceorl* f. a WG root, = man]
■ **1** see SLOB. **2** see PEASANT.

churlish /chə́rlish/ *adj.* surly; mean. □□ **churlishly** *adv.* **churlishness** *n.* [OE *cierlisc, ceorlisc* f. *ceorl* CHURL]
■ see MEAN[2] 5.

churn /chərn/ *n.* & *v.* ● *n.* **1** a machine for making butter by agitating milk or cream. **2** *Brit.* a large milk can. ● *v.* **1** *tr.* agitate (milk or cream) in a churn. **2** *tr.* produce (butter) in this way. **3** *tr.* (usu. foll. by *up*) cause distress to; upset; agitate. **4** *intr.* (of a liquid) seethe; foam violently (*the churning sea*). **5** *tr.* agitate or move (liquid) vigorously, causing it to foam. □ **churn out** produce routinely or mechanically, esp. in large quantities. [OE *cyrin* f. Gmc]
■ *n.* **2** see AGITATOR 2. ● *v.* **1** see STIR[1] *v.* 1. **3** see DISTURB 1. **4** see SWIRL *v.* □ **churn out** see *run off* 2.

churr var. of CHIRR.

chute[1] /shŏŏt/ *n.* **1** a sloping channel or slide, with or without water, for conveying things to a lower level. **2** a slide into a swimming pool. **3** a cataract or cascade of water; a steep descent in a riverbed producing a swift current. [F *chute* fall (of water, etc.), f. OF *cheoite* fem. past part. of *cheoir* fall f. L *cadere*; in some senses = SHOOT]
■ **1** slide, shaft, channel, ramp, runway, trough, conduit, race. **2** slide, flume. **3** waterfall, rapid.

chute[2] /shŏŏt/ *n. colloq.* parachute. □□ **chutist** *n.* [abbr.]

chutney /chútnee/ *n.* (*pl.* **-eys**) a pungent orig. Indian condiment made of fruits or vegetables, vinegar, spices, sugar, etc. [Hindi *caṭnī*]

chutzpah /khŏŏtspə/ *n.* (also **chutzpa**) *sl.* shameless audacity; gall. [Yiddish]
■ see NERVE *n.* 2b.

chyack var. of CHIACK.

chyle /kīl/ *n.* a milky fluid consisting of lymph and absorbed food materials from the intestine after digestion. □□ **chylous** *adj.* [LL *chylus* f. Gk *khulos* juice]

chyme /kīm/ *n.* the acidic, semisolid, and partly digested food produced by the action of gastric secretion. □□ **chymous** *adj.* [LL *chymus* f. Gk *khumos* juice]

CI *abbr.* Channel Islands.

Ci *abbr.* curie(s).

CIA *abbr.* Central Intelligence Agency.

ciao /chow/ *int. colloq.* **1** good-bye. **2** hello. [It.]
■ **1** see GOOD-BYE *int.* **2** see HELLO *int.*

ciborium /sibáwreeəm/ *n.* (*pl.* **ciboria** /-reeə/) **1** a vessel with an arched cover used to hold the Eucharist. **2** *Archit.* **a** a canopy. **b** a shrine with a canopy. □□ **ciborium** [med.L f. Gk *kibōrion* seed vessel of the water lily, a cup made from it]

cicada /sikáydə, -ka'adə/ *n.* (also **cicala** /sika'alə/) (*pl.* **cicadas** or **cicadae** /-dee/) any transparent-winged large insect of the family Cicadidae, the males of which make a loud, rhythmic, chirping sound. [L *cicada*, It. f. L *cicala*, It. *cigala*]

cicatrix /síkətriks, sikáy-/ *n.* (also **cicatrice** /síkətris/) (*pl.* **cicatrices** /-tríseez/) **1** any mark left by a healed wound; a scar. **2** *Bot.* **a** a mark on a stem, etc., left when a leaf or other part becomes detached. **b** a scar on the bark of a tree. □□ **cicatricial** /-tríshəl/ *adj.* [ME f. OF *cicatrice* or L *cicatrix -icis*]

cicatrize /síkətrīz/ *v.* **1** *tr.* heal (a wound) by scar formation. **2** *intr.* (of a wound) heal by scar formation. □□ **cicatrization** *n.* [F *cicatriser*: see CICATRIX]

cicely /sísəlee/ *n.* (*pl.* **-ies**) any of various umbelliferous plants, esp. sweet cicely (see SWEET). [app. f. L *seselis* f. Gk, assim. to the woman's Christian name]

cicerone /chícherōnee, sísə-/ *n.* (*pl.* **ciceroni** *pronunc.* same) a guide who gives information about antiquities, places of interest, etc., to sightseers. [It.: see CICERONIAN]
■ see GUIDE *n.* 1–3.

Ciceronian /sísərōneeən/ *adj.* (of language) eloquent, classical, or rhythmical, in the style of Cicero. [L *Ciceronianus* f. *Cicero -onis* Roman statesman and orator d. 43 BC]

cichlid /síklid/ *n.* any tropical freshwater fish of the family Cichlidae, esp. the kinds kept in aquariums. [mod.L *Cichlidae* f. Gk *kikhlē* a kind of fish]

CID *abbr.* (in the UK) Criminal Investigation Department.

-cide /sīd/ *suffix* forming nouns meaning: **1** a person or substance that kills (*regicide*; *insecticide*). **2** the killing of (*infanticide*; *suicide*). [F f. L *-cida* (sense 1), *-cidium* (sense 2), *caedere* kill]

cider /sídər/ *n.* **1** *US* a usu. unfermented drink made from crushed apples. **2** *Brit.* (also **cyder**) an alcoholic drink made from fermented apple juice. □ **cider press** a press for crushing apples to make cider. [ME f. OF *sidre*, ult. f. Heb. *šēkār* strong drink]

ci-devant /seedəvón/ *adj.* & *adv.* that has been (with person's earlier name or status); former or formerly. [F, = heretofore]
■ *adj.* see FORMER[1] 2. ● *adv.* see FORMERLY.

c.i.f. *abbr.* cost, insurance, freight (as being included in a price).

cig /sig/ *n. colloq.* cigarette; cigar. [abbr.]
■ see CIGARETTE.

cigar /siga'ar/ *n.* a cylinder of tobacco rolled in tobacco leaves for smoking. [F *cigare* or Sp. *cigarro*]

cigarette /sígərét/ *n.* (also **cigaret**) **1** a thin cylinder of finely cut tobacco rolled in paper for smoking. **2** a similar cylinder containing a narcotic or medicated substance. □ **cigarette butt** the unsmoked remainder of a cigarette. [F, dimin. of *cigare* CIGAR]
■ **1** *colloq.* cig, ciggy, smoke, *sl.* fag, burn, coffin nail, cancer stick, *Brit. sl.* gasper. **2** *sl.* joint, reefer, spliff, bomb.

cigarillo /sígərílō/ *n.* (*pl.* **-os**) a small cigar. [Sp., dimin. of *cigarro* CIGAR]

ciggy /sígee/ *n.* (*pl.* **-ies**) *colloq.* cigarette. [abbr.]
■ see CIGARETTE.

cilice /sílis/ *n.* **1** haircloth. **2** a garment of this. [F f. L *cilicium* f. Gk *kilikion* f. *Kilikia* Cilicia in Asia Minor]

cilium /síleeəm/ *n.* (*pl.* **cilia** /-leeə/) **1** a short, minute, hairlike vibrating structure on the surface of some cells, causing currents in the surrounding fluid. **2** an eyelash. □□ **ciliary** *adj.* **ciliate** /-ayt, -ət/ *adj.* **ciliated** *adj.* **ciliation** *n.* [L, = eyelash]

cimbalom var. of CYMBALOM.

C. in C. *abbr.* commander in chief.

cinch /sinch/ *n.* & *v.* ● *n.* **1** *colloq.* **a** a sure thing; a certainty. **b** an easy task. **2** a firm hold. **3** a girth for a saddle or pack. ● *v.tr.* **1** a tighten as with a cinch (*cinched at the waist with a belt*). **b** secure a grip on. **2** *sl.* make certain of. **3** put a cinch (sense 3) on. [Sp. *cincha*]
■ *n.* **1 a** see CERTAINTY 1b. **b** see PUSHOVER 1. **3** see GIRTH *n.* 2.

/.../ **pronunciation**	● **part of speech**
□ **phrases, idioms, and compounds**	
□□ **derivatives**	■ **synonym section**
cross-references appear in SMALL CAPITALS or *italics*	

cinchona /singkốnə/ *n.* **1 a** any evergreen tree or shrub of the genus *Cinchona,* native to S. America, with fragrant flowers and yielding cinchona bark. **b** the bark of this tree, containing quinine. **2** any drug from this bark formerly used as a tonic and to stimulate the appetite. □□ **cinchonic** /-kónik/ *adj.* **cinchonine** /síngkəneen/ *n.* [mod.L f. Countess of Chinchón d. 1641, introducer of drug into Spain]

cincture /síngkchər/ *n.* **1** *literary* a girdle, belt, or border. **2** *Archit.* a ring at either end of a column shaft. [L *cinctura* f. *cingere cinct-* gird]
  ■ **1** see BELT *n.* 1.

cinder /síndər/ *n.* **a** the residue of coal or wood, etc., that has stopped giving off flames but still has combustible matter in it. **b** slag. **c** (in *pl.*) ashes. □ **burned to a cinder** made useless by burning. **cinder block** a concrete building block, usu. made from cinders mixed with sand and cement. □□ **cindery** *adj.* [OE *sinder,* assim. to the unconnected F *cendre* and L *cinis* ashes]

Cinderella /síndəréllə/ *n.* **1** a person or thing of unrecognized or disregarded merit or beauty. **2** a neglected or despised member of a group. [the name of a girl in a fairy tale]

cine- /síne/ *comb. form* pertaining to film or movies (*cinephotography*). [abbr.]

cineaste /síneeast/ *n.* (also **cineast**) **1** a person who makes films, esp. professionally. **2** a movie lover. [F *cinéaste* (as CINE-): cf. ENTHUSIAST]

cinema /sínəmə/ *n.* **1 a** films collectively. **b** the production of films as an art or industry; cinematography. **2** *Brit.* a theater where motion pictures are shown. [F *cinéma:* see CINEMATOGRAPH]
  ■ **1 a** see PICTURE *n.* 3.

cinematheque /sínəmətek/ *n.* **1** a film library or archive. **2** a small movie theater. [F]

cinematic /sínəmátik/ *adj.* **1** having the qualities characteristic of the cinema. **2** of or relating to motion pictures. □□ **cinematically** *adv.*

cinematograph /sínəmátəgraf/ (also **kinematograph** /kín-/) *n.* **1** *Brit.* an apparatus for showing movies. **2** a movie camera. [F *cinématographe* f. Gk *kinēma -atos* movement f. *kineō* move]
  ■ **1** projector.

cinematography /sínəmətógrəfee/ *n.* the art of making motion pictures. □□ **cinematographer** *n.* **cinematographic** /-mátəgráfik/ *adj.* **cinematographically** *adv.*
  ■ □□ **cinematographer** see *photographer* (PHOTOGRAPH).

cinema verité /seénemaá véreetáy/ *n. Cinematog.* **1** the art or process of making realistic (esp. documentary) films that avoid artificiality and artistic effect. **2** such films collectively. [F, = cinema truth]

cineraria /sínəráireeə/ *n.* any of several varieties of the composite plant, *Cineraria cruentus,* having bright flowers and ash-colored down on its leaves. [mod.L, fem. of L *cinerarius* f. *cinis -eris* ashes, from the ash-colored down on the leaves]

cinerarium /sínəráireeəm/ *n.* (*pl.* **cineraria** /-eeə/) a place where a cinerary urn is deposited. [LL, neut. of *cinerarius:* see CINERARIA]

cinerary /sínəreree/ *adj.* of ashes. □ **cinerary urn** an urn for holding the ashes after cremation. [L *cinerarius:* see CINERARIA]

cinereous /sineéreeəs/ *adj.* (esp. of a bird or plumage) ash-gray. [L *cinereus* f. *cinis -eris* ashes]

Cingalese /síngəleéz/ *adj.* & *n.* (*pl.* same) *archaic* Sinhalese. [F *cing(h)alais:* see SINHALESE]

cingulum /síngyələm/ *n.* (*pl.* **cingula** /-lə/) *Anat.* a girdle, belt, or analogous structure, esp. a ridge surrounding the base of the crown of a tooth. [L, = belt]
  ■ see RING¹ *n.* 2.

cinnabar /sínəbaar/ *n.* **1** a bright red mineral form of mercuric sulfide from which mercury is obtained. **2** vermilion. **3** a moth (*Callimorpha jacobaeae*) with reddish marked wings. [ME f. L *cinnabaris* f. Gk *kinnabari,* of Oriental orig.]

cinnamon /sínəmən/ *n.* **1** an aromatic spice from the peeled, dried, and rolled bark of a SE Asian tree. **2** any tree of the genus *Cinnamomum,* esp. *C. zeylanicum* yielding the spice.

3 yellowish-brown. [ME f. OF *cinnamome* f. L *cinnamomum* f. Gk *kinnamōmon,* and L *cinnamon* f. Gk *kinnamon,* f. Semitic (cf. Heb. *ḳinnāmōn*)]

cinque /singk, sangk/ *n.* the five on dice, playing cards, etc. [ME f. OF *cinc, cink,* f. L *quinque* five]

cinquecento /chíngkwichéntō/ *n.* the style of Italian art and literature of the 16th c., with a reversion to classical forms. □□ **cinquecentist** *n.* [It., = 500, used with ref. to the years 1500–99]

cinquefoil /síngkfoyl/ *n.* **1** any plant of the genus *Potentilla,* with compound leaves of five leaflets. **2** *Archit.* a five-cusped ornament in a circle or arch. [ME f. L *quinquefolium* f. *quinque* five + *folium* leaf]

Cinque Ports /síngk páwrts/ *n.pl.* (in the UK) a group of ports (orig. five only) on the SE coast of England with ancient privileges. [ME f. OF *cink porz,* L *quinque portus* five ports]

cion var. of SCION 1.

cipher /sífər/ *n.* & *v.* (*Brit.* **cipher** or **cypher**) ● *n.* **1 a** a secret or disguised way of writing. **b** a thing written in this way. **c** the key to it. **2** the arithmetical symbol (0) denoting no amount but used to occupy a vacant place in decimal, etc., numeration (as in 12.05). **3** a person or thing of no importance. **4** the interlaced initials of a person or company, etc.; a monogram. **5** any Arabic numeral. **6** continuous sounding of an organ pipe, caused by a mechanical defect. ● *v.* **1** *tr.* put into secret writing; encipher. **2 a** *tr.* (usu. foll. by *out*) work out by arithmetic; calculate. **b** *intr. archaic* do arithmetic. [ME, f. OF *cif(f)re,* ult. f. Arab *ṣifr* ZERO]
  ■ *n.* **1 a** see CODE *n.* 2. **2** see ZERO *n.* 1. **3** see NOBODY *n.* **4** see SIGN *n.* 2. **5** see FIGURE *n.* 6a.

cipolin /sípəlin/ *n.* an Italian white and green marble. [F *cipolin* or It. *cipollino* f. *cipolla* onion]

cir. *abbr.* (also **circ.**) **1** circle. **2** circuit. **3** circular. **4** circulation. **5** circumference.

circa /sórkə/ *prep.* (preceding a date) about. [L]
  ■ see AROUND *prep.* 4b.

circadian /sərkáydeeən/ *adj. Physiol.* occurring or recurring about once per day. [irreg. f. L *circa* about + *dies* day]
  ■ see DAILY *adj.* 1.

Circe /sórsee/ *n.* a dangerously attractive enchantress. [L f. Gk *Kirkē,* an enchantress in Gk mythol.]

circinate /sórsinayt/ *adj. Bot.* & *Zool.* rolled up with the apex in the center, e.g., of young fronds of ferns. [L *circinatus* past part. of *circinare* make round f. *circinus* pair of compasses]

circle /sórkəl/ *n.* & *v.* ● *n.* **1 a** a round plane figure whose circumference is everywhere equidistant from its center. **b** the line enclosing a circle. **2** a roundish enclosure or structure. **3** a ring. **4** a curved upper tier of seats in a theater, etc. (*dress circle*). **5** a circular route. **6** *Archaeol.* a group of (usu. large embedded) stones arranged in a circle. **7** persons grouped around a center of interest. **8** a set or class or restricted group (*literary circles; not done in the best circles*). **9** a period or cycle (*the circle of the year*). **10** (in full **vicious circle**) **a** an unbroken sequence of reciprocal cause and effect. **b** the fallacy of proving a proposition from another which depends on the first for its own proof. ● *v.* **1** *intr.* (often foll. by *around, about*) move in a circle. **2** *tr.* **a** revolve around. **b** form a circle around. □ **circle back** move in a wide loop toward the starting point. **come full circle** return to the starting point. **go around in circles** make no progress despite effort. **great** (or **small**) **circle** a circle on the surface of a sphere whose plane passes (or does not pass) through the sphere's center. **run around in circles** *colloq.* be fussily busy with little result. □□ **circler** *n.* [ME f. OF *cercle* f. L *circulus* dimin. of *circus* ring]
  ■ *n.* **1** disk, round. **3** ring, hoop, band, loop, coil; esp. *Math.* & *Biol.* annulus. **8** set, coterie, clique, class, sphere, division, group, camp, faction, *Austral. sl.* push; society, company, crowd. **9** see CYCLE *n.* 1a. ● *v.* **1** see REVOLVE 1, 2. **2** go around, tour, circumnavigate, *formal* circumambulate; encircle, surround, enclose, circumscribe, ring, hoop, girth, clasp, enlace, environ, orb, fillet, wreathe, fringe, *literary* gird; shut in, hem in.

□ **go around in circles** get nowhere, take two steps forward and one step back, spin one's wheels. **run around in circles** see FUSS v. 1c.

circlet /sə́rklit/ n. **1** a small circle. **2** a circular band, esp. of gold or jeweled, etc., as an ornament.

■ see RING¹ n. 2.

circs /sərks/ n.pl. Brit. colloq. circumstances. [abbr.]

circuit /sə́rkit/ n. **1 a** a line or course enclosing an area; the distance around; the circumference. **b** the area enclosed. **2** Electr. **a** the path of a current. **b** the apparatus through which a current passes. **3 a** the journey of a judge in a particular district to hold courts. **b** this district. **c** the lawyers following a circuit. **4** a chain of theaters, etc., under a single management. **5** Brit. an automobile racing track. **6 a** a sequence of sporting events (the US tennis circuit). **b** a sequence of athletic exercises. **7** a roundabout journey. **8 a** a group of local Methodist churches forming a minor administrative unit. **b** the journey of an itinerant minister within this. □ **circuit board** Electronics a board of nonconductive material on which integrated circuits, printed circuits, etc., are mounted or etched. **circuit breaker** an automatic device for stopping the flow of current in an electrical circuit. [ME f. OF, f. L circuitus f. CIRCUM- + ire it- go]

■ **1 a** round, tour, ambit, circle, orbit, course, lap, revolution; compass, circumference, perimeter, periphery, girth, border, boundary, edge, limit, ambit, margin, outline, confine(s), bound, pale. **3, 8b** see ROUND n. 3. **6 a** sequence, series. **b** see SEQUENCE n. **7** see JOURNEY n.

circuitous /sərkyo͞o-itəs/ adj. **1** indirect (and usu. long). **2** going a long way around. □□ **circuitously** adv. **circuitousness** n. [med.L circuitosus f. circuitus CIRCUIT]

■ see INDIRECT 1, 2.

circuitry /sə́rkitree/ n. (pl. -ies) **1** a system of electric circuits. **2** the equipment forming this.

circular /sə́rkyələr/ adj. & n. ● adj. **1 a** having the form of a circle. **b** moving or taking place along a circle; indirect; circuitous (circular route). **2** Logic (of reasoning) depending on a vicious circle. **3** (of a letter or advertisement, etc.) printed for distribution to a large number of people. ● n. a circular letter, leaflet, etc. □ **circular saw** a power saw with a rapidly rotating toothed disk. □□ **circularity** /-láritee/ n. **circularly** adv. [ME f. AF circuler, OF circulier, cerclier f. LL circularis f. L circulus CIRCLE]

■ adj. **1 a** round, disk-shaped, disklike, discoid; ring-shaped, ringlike, annular. **b** roundabout, indirect, circuitous, tortuous, twisting, twisted, anfractuous; periphrastic, circumlocutory; devious. **2** illogical, inconsistent, redundant, fallacious, irrational, sophistic, sophistical.

circularize /sə́rkyələrīz/ v.tr. **1** distribute circulars to. **2** seek opinions of (people) by means of a questionnaire. □□ **circularization** n.

circulate /sə́rkyəlayt/ v. **1** intr. go around from one place or person, etc., to the next and so on; be in circulation. **2** tr. **a** cause to go around; put into circulation. **b** give currency to (a report, etc.). **c** circularize. **3** intr. be actively sociable at a party, gathering, etc. □ **circulating library** a library with books available for borrowing; a lending library. **circulating medium** notes or gold, etc., used in exchange. □□ **circulative** adj. **circulator** n. [L circulare circulat- f. circulus CIRCLE]

■ **1** move or go about or around, orbit, flow, course, run, circle. **2 a, b** spread, distribute, disseminate, issue, publish, air, announce, proclaim, make known, noise abroad, bruit about, report, broadcast, reveal, divulge, advertise, publicize, promulgate, put about, bring or put out, pass out or around. **3** go around, mix, mingle, move around, socialize, fraternize.

circulation /sə́rkyəláyshən/ n. **1 a** movement to and fro, or from and back to a starting point, esp. of a fluid in a confined area or circuit. **b** the movement of blood from and to the heart. **c** a similar movement of sap, etc. **2 a** the transmission or distribution (of news or information or books, etc.). **b** the number of copies sold, esp. of journals and newspapers.

3 a currency, coin, etc. **b** the movement or exchange of this in a country, etc. □ **in** (or **out of**) **circulation** participating (or not participating) in activities, etc. [F circulation or L circulatio f. circulare CIRCULATE]

■ **1** circuit, course, orbit, flow, motion. **2 a** spreading, dissemination, transmission, passage, distribution, diffusion, publication, advertisement, announcement, issuance, pronouncement, proclamation, promulgation, broadcast, broadcasting. **3 a** currency, coin, specie; change, cash, silver.

circulatory /sə́rkyələtawree/ adj. of or relating to the circulation of blood or sap.

circum- /sə́rkəm/ comb. form round; about; around; used: **1** adverbially (circumambient; circumfuse). **2** prepositionally (circumlunar; circumocular). [from or after L circum prep. = round, about]

circum. abbr. circumference.

circumambient /sə́rkəmámbeeənt/ adj. (esp. of air or another fluid) surrounding. □□ **circumambience** /-beeəns/ n. **circumambiency** n.

■ see surrounding (SURROUND).

circumambulate /sə́rkəmámbyəlayt/ v.tr. & intr. formal walk around or about. □□ **circumambulation** /-láyshən/ n. **circumambulatory** /-lətáwree/ adj. [CIRCUM- + ambulate f. L ambulare walk]

circumcircle /sə́rkəmsərkəl/ n. Geom. a circle touching all the vertices of a triangle or polygon.

circumcise /sə́rkəmsiz/ v.tr. **1** cut off the foreskin, as a Jewish or Muslim rite or a surgical operation. **2** cut off the clitoris (and sometimes the labia), usu. as a religious rite. **3** Bibl. purify (the heart, etc.). [ME f. OF f. L circumcidere circumcis- (as CIRCUM-, caedere cut)]

circumcision /sə́rkəmsízhən/ n. **1** the act or rite of circumcising or being circumcised. **2** (**Circumcision**) Eccl. the feast of the Circumcision of Christ, Jan. 1. [ME f. OF circoncision f. LL circumcisio -onis (as CIRCUMCISE)]

circumference /sərkúmfərəns/ n. **1** the enclosing boundary, esp. of a circle or other figure enclosed by a curve. **2** the distance around. □□ **circumferential** /-fərénshəl/ adj. **circumferentially** adv. [ME f. OF circonference f. L circumferentia (as CIRCUM-, ferre bear)]

■ **1** see PERIMETER.

circumflex /sə́rkəmfleks/ n. & adj. ● n. (in full **circumflex accent**) a mark (ˆ) placed over a vowel in some languages to indicate a contraction, length, or a special quality. ● adj. Anat. curved, bending around something else (circumflex nerve). [L circumflexus (as CIRCUM-, flectere flex- bend), transl. of Gk perispōmenos drawn around]

circumfluent /sərkúmflo͞oənt/ adj. flowing around, surrounding. □□ **circumfluence** n. [L circumfluere (as CIRCUM-, fluere flow)]

circumfuse /sə́rkəmfyo͞oz/ v.tr. pour around or about. [CIRCUM- + L fundere fus- pour]

circumjacent /sə́rkəmjáysənt/ adj. situated around. [L circumjacēre (as CIRCUM-, jaceō lie)]

■ see surrounding (SURROUND).

circumlocution /sə́rkəmlōkyo͞oshən/ n. **1 a** a roundabout expression. **b** evasive talk. **2** the use of many words where fewer would do; verbosity. □□ **circumlocutional** adj. **circumlocutionary** adj. **circumlocutory** /-lókyətáwree/ adj. [ME f. F circumlocution or L circumlocutio (as CIRCUM-, LOCUTION), transl. of Gk PERIPHRASIS]

■ **1 a** periphrasis. **b** see EVASION 2. **2** see TAUTOLOGY 1.

circumlunar /sə́rkəmlo͞onər/ adj. moving or situated around the moon.

circumnavigate /sə́rkəmnávigayt/ v.tr. sail around (esp. the world). □□ **circumnavigation** /-gáyshən/ n. **circumnavigator** n. [L circumnavigare (as CIRCUM-, NAVIGATE)]

/. . ./ **pronunciation**	● **part of speech**
□ **phrases, idioms, and compounds**	
□□ **derivatives**	■ **synonym section**
cross-references appear in SMALL CAPITALS or italics	

251

■ see CIRCLE *v.* 2.

circumpolar /sə́rkəmpṓlər/ *adj.* **1** *Geog.* around or near one of the earth's poles. **2** *Astron.* (of a star or motion, etc.) above the horizon at all times in a given latitude.

circumscribe /sə́rkəmskrīb/ *v.tr.* **1** (of a line, etc.) enclose or outline. **2** lay down the limits of; confine; restrict. **3** *Geom.* draw (a figure) around another, touching it at points but not cutting it (cf. INSCRIBE). □□ **circumscribable** *adj.* **circumscriber** *n.* **circumscription** /-skrípshən/ *n.* [L *circumscribere* (as CIRCUM-, *scribere script-* write)]
■ **1** see DEFINE 4. **2** see RESTRICT.

circumsolar /sə́rkəmsṓlər/ *adj.* moving or situated around or near the sun.

circumspect /sə́rkəmspekt/ *adj.* wary; cautious; taking everything into account. □□ **circumspection** /-spékshən/ *n.* **circumspectly** *adv.* [ME f. L *circumspicere circumspect-* (as CIRCUM-, *specere spect-* look)]
■ see CAUTIOUS.

circumstance /sə́rkəmstans/ *n.* **1 a** a fact, occurrence, or condition, esp. (in *pl.*) the time, place, manner, cause, occasion, etc., or surroundings of an act or event. **b** (in *pl.*) the external conditions that affect or might affect an action. **2** (often foll. by *that* + clause) an incident, occurrence, or fact, as needing consideration (*the circumstance that he left early*). **3** (in *pl.*) one's state of financial or material welfare (*in reduced circumstances*). **4** ceremony; fuss (*pomp and circumstance*). **5** full detail in a narrative (*told it with much circumstance*). □ **in** (or **under**) **the** (or **these**) **circumstances** the state of affairs being what it is. **in** (or **under**) **no circumstances** not at all; never. □□ **circumstanced** *adj.* [ME f. OF *circonstance* or L *circumstantia* (as CIRCUM-, *stantia* f. *sto* stand)]
■ **1** situation, condition(s), state (of affairs); fact; event, incident, episode, occurrence, affair, happening, occasion. **2** see INCIDENT *n.* 1a. **3** (*circumstances*) status, station, resources, income, finances. **4** see CEREMONY 2, 3. **5** see *elaboration* (ELABORATE). □ **in** (or **under**) **no circumstances** see NEVER 1b, 2.

circumstantial /sə́rkəmstánshəl/ *adj.* **1** given in full detail (*a circumstantial account*). **2** (of evidence, a legal case, etc.) tending to establish a conclusion by inference from known facts hard to explain otherwise. **3 a** depending on circumstances. **b** adventitious; incidental. □□ **circumstantiality** /-sheeálitee/ *n.* **circumstantially** *adv.* [L *circumstantia*: see CIRCUMSTANCE]
■ **1** detailed, particular, precise, explicit, specific. **2** indirect, presumptive, deduced, presumed, presumable, implicative, implied, inferred, inferential. **3 b** accidental, incidental, indirect, unimportant, adventitious, provisional, secondary, unessential, nonessential, fortuitous, chance, extraneous.

circumterrestrial /sə́rkəmtəréstreeəl/ *adj.* moving or situated around the earth.

circumvallate /sə́rkəmválayt/ *v.tr.* surround with or as with a rampart. [L *circumvallare circumvallat-* (as CIRCUM-, *vallare* f. *vallum* rampart)]

circumvent /sə́rkəmvént/ *v.tr.* **1 a** evade (a difficulty); find a way around. **b** baffle; outwit. **2** entrap (an enemy) by surrounding. □□ **circumvention** /-vénshən/ *n.* [L *circumvenire circumvent-* (as CIRCUM-, *venire* come)]
■ **1 a** see EVADE 1, 2. **b** see FOIL¹ *v.*

circumvolution /sə́rkəmvəlṓōshən/ *n.* **1** rotation. **2** the winding of one thing around another. **3** a sinuous movement. [ME f. L *circumvolvere circumvolut-* (as CIRCUM-, *volvere* roll)]

circus /sə́rkəs/ *n.* (*pl.* **circuses**) **1** a traveling show of performing animals, acrobats, clowns, etc. **2** *colloq.* **a** a scene of lively action; a disturbance. **b** a group of people in a common activity, esp. sports. **3** *Brit.* an open space in a town or city, where several streets converge (*Piccadilly Circus*). **4** a circular hollow surrounded by hills. **5** *Rom. Antiq.* **a** a rounded or oval arena with tiers of seats, for equestrian and other sports and games. **b** a performance given there (*bread and circuses*). [L, = ring]
■ **5 a** see RING¹ *n.* 6a.

ciré /siráy/ *n. & adj.* ● *n.* a fabric with a smooth shiny surface obtained esp. by waxing and heating. ● *adj.* having such a surface. [F, = waxed]

cire perdue /seér perdŏō, -dyŏō/ *n.* a method of bronze casting using a clay core and a wax coating placed in a mold: the wax is melted in the mold and bronze poured into the space left, producing a hollow bronze figure when the core is discarded. [F, = lost wax]

cirque /sərk/ *n.* **1** *Geol.* a deep, bowl-shaped hollow at the head of a valley or on a mountainside. **2** *poet.* **a** a ring. **b** an amphitheater or arena. [F f. L CIRCUS]

cirrhosis /sirṓsis/ *n.* a chronic disease of the liver marked by the degeneration of cells and the thickening of surrounding tissues, as a result of alcoholism, hepatitis, etc. □□ **cirrhotic** /sirótik/ *adj.* [mod.L f. Gk *kirrhos* tawny]

cirriped /síriped/ *n.* (also **cirripede** /síripeed/) any marine crustacean of the class Cirripedia, having a valved shell and usu. sessile when adult, e.g., a barnacle. [mod.L *Cirripedia* f. L *cirrus* curl (from the form of the legs) + *pes pedis* foot]

cirro- /sírō/ *comb. form* cirrus (cloud).

cirrus /sírəs/ *n.* (*pl.* **cirri** /-rī/) **1** *Meteorol.* a form of white wispy cloud, esp. at high altitude. **2** *Bot.* a tendril. **3** *Zool.* a long, slender appendage or filament. □□ **cirrose** *adj.* **cirrous** *adj.* [L, = curl]

cis- /sis/ *prefix* (opp. TRANS- or ULTRA-). **1** on this side of; on the side nearer to the speaker or writer (*cisatlantic*). **2** *Rom. Antiq.* on the Roman side of (*cisalpine*). **3** (of time) closer to the present (*cis-Elizabethan*). **4** *Chem.* (of an isomer) having two atoms or groups on the same side of a given plane in the molecule. [L *cis* on this side of]

cisalpine /sisálpīn/ *adj.* on the southern side of the Alps.

cisatlantic /sísətlántik/ *adj.* on this side of the Atlantic.

cisco /siskō/ *n.* (*pl.* **-oes**) any of various freshwater whitefish of the genus *Coregonus*, native to N. America. [19th c.: orig. unkn.]

cislunar /sislṓōnər/ *adj.* between the earth and the moon.

cispontine /sispóntin/ *adj.* on the north side of the Thames River in London. [CIS- (orig. the better-known side) + L *pons pont-* bridge]

cissy esp. *Brit.* var. of SISSY.

cist¹ /sist, kist/ *n.* (also **kist** /kist/) *Archaeol.* a coffin or burial chamber made from stone or a hollowed tree. [Welsh, = CHEST]

cist² /sist/ *n.* *Gk Antiq.* a box used for sacred utensils. [L *cista* f. Gk *kistē* box]

Cistercian /sistə́rshən/ *n. & adj.* ● *n.* a monk or nun of an order founded in 1098 as a stricter branch of the Benedictines. ● *adj.* of the Cistercians. [F *cistercien* f. L *Cistercium* Cîteaux near Dijon in France, where the order was founded]

cistern /sístərn/ *n.* **1** a tank or container for storing water, etc. **2** an underground reservoir for rainwater. [ME f. OF *cisterne* f. L *cisterna* (as CIST²)]

cistus /sístəs/ *n.* any shrub of the genus *Cistus*, with large white or red flowers. Also called *rock rose*. [mod.L f. Gk *kistos*]

cit. *abbr.* **1** citation. **2** cited. **3** citizen.

citadel /sítəd'l, -del/ *n.* **1** a fortress, usu. on high ground protecting or dominating a city. **2** a meeting hall of the Salvation Army. [F *citadelle* or It. *citadella*, ult. f. L *civitas -tatis* city]
■ **1** see STRONGHOLD 1.

citation /sītáyshən/ *n.* **1** the citing of a book or other source; a passage cited. **2** a mention in an official dispatch. **3** a note accompanying an award, describing the reasons for it.
■ **1** see QUOTATION 2. **2** see MENTION *n.* 1.

cite /sīt/ *v.tr.* **1** adduce as an instance. **2** quote (a passage, book, or author) in support of an argument, etc. **3** mention in an official dispatch. **4** summon to appear in a court of law. □□ **citable** *adj.* [ME f. F f. L *citare* f. *ciēre* set moving]
■ **1, 2** see QUOTE *v.* 1. **3** see MENTION *v.* 1, 2. **4** subpoena.

citified /sítifīd/ *adj.* (also **cityfied**) usu. *derog.* citylike or urban in appearance or behavior.

citizen /sítizən/ *n.* **1** a member of a nation or commonwealth, either native or naturalized (*American citizen*). **2** (usu. foll. by *of*) **a** an inhabitant of a city. **b** a freeman of a city. **3** a civilian. □ **citizen of the world** a person who is at home anywhere; a cosmopolitan. **citizen's arrest** an arrest by an ordinary person without a warrant, allowable in certain cases. **citizens band** a system of local intercommunication by individuals on special radio frequencies. □□ **citizenhood** *n.* **citizenry** *n.* **citizenship** *n.* [ME f. AF *citesein*, OF *citeain* ult. f. L *civitas -tatis* city: cf. DENIZEN]

■ **1** voter; native, resident, inhabitant, dweller, *poet.* denizen; subject. **2 a** city dweller, town dweller, townsman, townswoman, *Brit.* burgess.

citole /sitól/ *n.* a small cittern. [ME f. OF: rel. to CITTERN with dimin. suffix]

citric /sítrik/ *adj.* derived from citrus fruit. □ **citric acid** a sharp-tasting, water-soluble organic acid found in the juice of lemons and other sour fruits. □□ **citrate** *n.* [F *citrique* f. L *citrus* citron]

citrin /sítrin/ *n.* a group of substances occurring mainly in citrus fruits and black currants, and formerly thought to be a vitamin. Also called BIOFLAVONOID.

citrine /sítreen, sitreen/ *adj. & n.* ● *adj.* lemon-colored. ● *n.* a transparent yellow variety of quartz. Also called *false topaz.* [ME f. OF *citrin* (as CITRUS)]

citron /sítron/ *n.* **1** a shrubby tree, *Citrus medica*, bearing large lemonlike fruits with thick fragrant peel. **2** this fruit. [F f. L CITRUS, after *limon* lemon]

citronella /sítrənélə/ *n.* **1** any fragrant grass of the genus *Cymbopogon*, native to S. Asia. **2** the scented oil from these, used in insect repellent, and in perfume and soap manufacture. [mod.L, formed as CITRON + dimin. suffix]

citrus /sítrəs/ *n.* **1** any tree of the genus *Citrus*, including citron, lemon, lime, orange, and grapefruit. **2** (in full **citrus fruit**) a fruit from such a tree. □□ **citrous** *adj.* [L, = citron tree or thuja]

cittern /sítərn/ *n. hist.* a wire-stringed, lutelike instrument usu. played with a plectrum. [L *cithara*, Gk *kithara* a kind of harp, assim. to GITTERN]

city /sítee/ *n.* (*pl.* -**ies**) **1 a** a large town. **b** *US* a state-chartered municipal corporation occupying a definite area. **c** *Brit.* (strictly) a town created a city by charter and containing a cathedral. **2** (**the City**) **a** the major center of a region. **b** the part of London governed by the Lord Mayor and the Corporation. **c** the business part of this. **d** *Brit.* commercial circles; high finance. □ **City Company** (in the UK) a corporation descended from an ancient trade guild. **city desk** a department of a newspaper dealing with local news. **city editor** the editor dealing with local news. **city father** (usu. in *pl.*) a person concerned with or experienced in the administration of a city. **city hall** municipal offices or officers. **city manager** (in some US cities) an official directing the administration of a city. **city page** *Brit.* the part of a newspaper or magazine dealing with the financial and business news. **city slicker** usu. *derog.* **1** a smart and sophisticated city dweller. **2** a plausible rogue as found in cities. **city-state** esp. *hist.* a city that with its surrounding territory forms an independent state. □□ **cityward** *adj. & adv.* **citywards** *adv.* [ME f. OF *cité* f. L *civitas -tatis* f. *civis* citizen]

■ **1 a** metropolis, municipality, borough, town; conurbation, megalopolis, urban area, *colloq.* burg.
□ **city slicker 1** *colloq.* slicker, *derog.* townee. **2** *colloq.* slicker.

cityfied var. of CITIFIED.

cityscape /síteeskayp/ *n.* **1** a view of a city (actual or depicted). **2** city scenery.
■ see VIEW *n.* 2a, b.

civet /sívit/ *n.* **1** (in full **civet cat**) any catlike animal of the mongoose family, esp. *Civetticus civetta* of Central Africa, having well-developed anal scent glands. **2** a strong musky perfume obtained from the secretions of these scent glands. [F *civette* f. It. *zibetto* f. med.L *zibethum* f. Arab. *azzabād* f. *al* the + *zabād* this perfume]

civic /sívik/ *adj.* **1** of a city; municipal. **2** or proper to citizens (*civic virtues*). **3** of citizenship; civil. □ **civic center 1** *Brit.* the area where municipal offices and other public buildings are situated; the buildings themselves. **2 a** municipal building with space for conventions, sports events, etc.,

and other public facilities, often publicly supported. □□ **civically** *adv.* [F *civique* or L *civicus* f. *civis* citizen]
■ **1** see MUNICIPAL. **2** see PUBLIC *adj.* 1.

civics /síviks/ *n.pl.* (usu. treated as *sing.*) the study of the rights and duties of citizenship.

civil /sívəl/ *adj.* **1** of or belonging to citizens. **2** of ordinary citizens and their concerns, as distinct from military or naval or ecclesiastical matters. **3** polite; obliging; not rude. **4** *Law* relating to civil law (see below), not criminal or political matters (*civil court; civil lawyer*). **5** (of the length of a day, year, etc.) fixed by custom or law, not natural or astronomical. **6** occurring within a community or among fellow citizens; internal (*civil unrest*). □ **civil aviation** nonmilitary, esp. commercial aviation. **civil defense** the organization and training of civilians for the protection of lives and property during and after attacks in wartime, natural disasters, emergencies, etc. **civil disobedience** the refusal to comply with certain laws or to pay taxes, etc., as a peaceful form of political protest. **civil engineer** an engineer who designs or maintains roads, bridges, dams, etc. **civil engineering** this work. **civil law 1** law concerning private rights (opp. *criminal law*). **2** *hist.* Roman or nonecclesiastical law. **civil libertarian** an advocate of increased civil liberty. **civil liberty** (often in *pl.*) freedom of action and speech subject to the law. **civil list** (in the UK) an annual allowance voted by Parliament for the royal family's household expenses. **civil marriage** a marriage solemnized as a civil contract without religious ceremony. **civil rights** the rights of citizens to political and social freedom and equality. **civil servant** a member of the civil service. **civil service** the permanent professional branches of governmental administration, excluding military and judicial branches and elected politicians. **civil war** a war between citizens of the same country. **civil year** see YEAR 2. □□ **civilly** *adv.* [ME f. OF f. L *civilis* f. *civis* citizen]

■ **2** civilian, nonmilitary; lay, laic, laical, nonclerical, secular. **3** polite, courteous, respectful, well-mannered, proper, civilized, cordial, genial, formal, courtly, gallant, chivalrous, urbane, polished, refined, gracious, obliging, *Brit.* decent. **6** internal, domestic; public. □ **civil servant** civil-service employee *or* worker, public servant, (government *or* state) official, officeholder, government worker.

civilian /sívilyən/ *n. & adj.* ● *n.* a person not in the armed services or the police force. ● *adj.* of or for civilians.

civilianize /sívilyəniz/ *v.tr.* make civilian in character or function. □□ **civilianization** *n.*

civility /sívilitee/ *n.* (*pl.* -**ies**) **1** politeness. **2** an act of politeness. [ME f. OF *civilité* f. L *civilitas -tatis* (as CIVIL)]
■ **1** courtesy, politeness, respect, comity, urbanity, amiability, consideration, courteousness, cordiality, propriety, tact, diplomacy, politesse, protocol. **2** courtesy, politeness.

civilization /sívilǝzáyshǝn/ *n.* **1** an advanced stage or system of social development. **2** those peoples of the world regarded as having this. **3** a people or nation (esp. of the past) regarded as an expression of social evolution (*ancient civilizations; the Inca civilization*). **4** making or becoming civilized.
■ **1** culture, refinement, cultivation, enlightenment, edification, sophistication, polish. **3** see PEOPLE *n.* 1a, NATION.

civilize /sívilíz/ *v.tr.* **1** bring out of a barbarous or primitive stage of society. **2** enlighten; refine and educate. □□ **civilizable** *adj.* **civilizer** *n.* [F *civiliser* (as CIVIL)]
■ **2** enlighten, refine, polish, edify, educate, acculturate, broaden, elevate.

civvies /síveez/ *n.pl. sl.* civilian clothes. [abbr.]

Civvy Street /sívee/ *n. Brit. sl.* civilian life. [abbr.]

CJ *abbr.* Chief Justice.

/.../ **pronunciation**   ● **part of speech**
□ **phrases, idioms, and compounds**
□□ **derivatives**   ■ **synonym section**
cross-references appear in SMALL CAPITALS or *italics*

Cl *symb. Chem.* the element chlorine.

cl *abbr.* **1** centiliter(s). **2** class.

clack /klak/ *v. & n.* ● *v.intr.* **1** make a sharp sound as of boards struck together. **2** chatter, esp. loudly. ● *n.* **1** a clacking sound. **2** clacking talk. □□ **clacker** *n.* [ME, = to chatter, prob. f. ON *klaka*, of imit. orig.]
■ *v.* **2** see CHATTER *v.* 1. ● *n.* **2** see PRATTLE *n.*

clad¹ /klad/ *adj.* **1** clothed. **2** provided with cladding. [past part. of CLOTHE]

clad² /klad/ *v.tr.* (**cladding**; *past* and *past part.* **cladded** or **clad**) provide with cladding. [app. f. CLAD¹]

cladding /kláding/ *n.* a covering or coating on a structure or material, etc.
■ see FACING.

clade /klayd/ *n. Biol.* a group of organisms evolved from a common ancestor. [Gk *klados* branch]

cladistics /klədístiks/ *n.pl.* (usu. treated as *sing.*) *Biol.* a method of classification of animals and plants on the basis of shared characteristics, which are assumed to indicate common ancestry. □□ **cladism** /kládizəm/ *n.* [as CLADE + -IST + -ICS]

cladode /kladōd/ *n.* a flattened, leaflike stem. [Gk *kladōdēs* many-shooted f. *klados* shoot]

claim /klaym/ *v. & n.* ● *v.tr.* **1 a** (often foll. by *that* + clause) demand as one's due or property. **b** (usu. *absol.*) submit a request for payment under an insurance policy. **2 a** represent oneself as having or achieving (*claim victory*; *claim accuracy*). **b** (foll. by *to* + infin.) profess (*claimed to be the owner*). **c** assert; contend (*claim that one knows*). **3** have an achievement or a consequence (*could then claim five wins*; *the fire claimed many victims*). **4** (of a thing) deserve (one's attention, etc.). ● *n.* **1 a** a demand or request for something considered one's due (*lay claim to*; *put in a claim*). **b** an application for compensation under the terms of an insurance policy. **2** (foll. by *to, on*) a right or title to a thing (*his only claim to fame*; *have many claims on my time*). **3** a contention or assertion. **4** a thing claimed. **5** a statement of the novel features in a patent. **6** *Mining* a piece of land allotted or taken. □ **claims adjuster** an insurance agent who assesses the amount of compensation arising from a loss. □□ **claimable** *adj.* **claimer** *n.* [ME f. OF *claime* f. *clamer* call out f. L *clamare*]
■ *v.* **1 a** demand, seek, ask *or* call (for), exact, insist on *or* upon. **2** profess, declare, assert, allege, state, put *or* set forth, affirm, contend, maintain. **4** see DESERVE 1. ● *n.* **1** demand, request, requisition, petition, application. **2** (*claim to*) right to, title to; (*claim on*) call on, demand on. **3** see ASSERTION 1, 2.

claimant /kláymənt/ *n.* a person making a claim, esp. in a lawsuit or for a government benefit.

clairaudience /klairáwrdeeəns/ *n.* the supposed faculty of perceiving, as if by hearing, what is inaudible. □□ **clairaudient** /-deeənt/ *adj. & n.* [F *clair* CLEAR, + AUDIENCE, after CLAIRVOYANCE]

clairvoyance /klairvóyəns/ *n.* **1** the supposed faculty of perceiving things or events in the future or beyond normal sensory contact. **2** exceptional insight. [F *clairvoyance* f. *clair* CLEAR + *voir* voy- see]

clairvoyant /klairvóyənt/ *n. & adj.* ● *n.* a person having clairvoyance. ● *adj.* having clairvoyance. □□ **clairvoyantly** *adv.*
■ *n.* see PSYCHIC *n.* ● *adj.* see PSYCHIC *adj.* 1a.

clam /klam/ *n. & v.* ● *n.* **1** any bivalve mollusk, esp. the edible N. American hard or round clam (*Mercenaria mercenaria*) or the soft or long clam (*Mya arenaria*). **2** *colloq.* a shy or withdrawn person. ● *v.intr.* (**clammed, clamming**) **1** dig for clams. **2** (foll. by *up*) *colloq.* refuse to talk. [16th c.: app. f. *clam* a clamp]

clamant /kláymənt/ *adj. literary* noisy; insistent; urgent. □□ **clamantly** *adv.* [L *clamare clamant-* cry out]

clambake /klámbayk/ *n.* a picnic at the seashore typically featuring clams, lobsters, and ears of corn steamed over hot stones beneath a layer of seaweed.

clamber /klámbər/ *v. & n.* ● *v.intr.* climb with hands and feet, esp. with difficulty or laboriously. ● *n.* a difficult climb. [ME, prob. f. *clamb*, obs. past tense of CLIMB]
■ *v.* see SCRAMBLE *v.* 1.

clammy /klámee/ *adj.* (**clammier, clammiest**) **1** unpleasantly damp and sticky or slimy. **2** (of weather) cold and damp. □□ **clammily** *adv.* **clamminess** *n.* [ME f. *clam* to daub]
■ **1** moist, damp, sticky, gummy, pasty, viscous, slimy. **2** moist, damp, wet.

clamor /klámər/ *n. & v.* (*Brit.* **clamour**) ● *n.* **1** loud or vehement shouting or noise. **2** a protest or complaint; an appeal or demand. ● *v.* **1** *intr.* make a clamor. **2** *tr.* utter with a clamor. □□ **clamorous** *adj.* **clamorously** *adv.* **clamorousness** *n.* [ME f. OF f. L *clamor -oris* f. *clamare* cry out]
■ *n.* **1** see NOISE *n.* 1, 2. **2** see OUTCRY.

clamp¹ /klamp/ *n. & v.* ● *n.* a device, esp. a brace or band of iron, etc., for strengthening other materials or holding things together. ● *v.tr.* **1** strengthen or fasten with a clamp. **2** place or hold firmly. **3** immobilize (an illegally parked car) by fixing a clamp to one of its wheels. □ **clamp down 1** (often foll. by *on*) be rigid in enforcing a rule, etc. **2** (foll. by *on*) try to suppress. [ME prob. f. MDu., MLG *klamp(e)*]
■ *n.* clasp, vice, brace, clip, fastener. ● *v.* **1** fasten (together), clip (together), bracket, make fast, clasp. **2** grip, grasp, clutch, clasp, hold. □ **clamp down 2** see SUPPRESS 1.

clamp² /klamp/ *n. Brit.* **1** a heap of potatoes or other root vegetables stored under straw or earth. **2** a pile of bricks for burning. **3** a pile of turf or peat or garden rubbish, etc. [16th c.: prob. f. Du. *klamp* heap (in sense 2 related to CLUMP)]

clampdown /klámpdown/ *n.* severe restriction or suppression.
■ see *suppression* (SUPPRESS).

clan /klan/ *n.* **1** a group of people with a common ancestor, esp. in the Scottish Highlands. **2** a large family as a social group. **3** a group with a strong common interest. **4 a** a genus, species, or class. **b** a family or group of animals, e.g., elephants. [ME f. Gael. *clann* f. L *planta* sprout]
■ **1** tribe, family, sib, dynasty, line, house. **3** fraternity, brotherhood, party, set, clique, coterie, circle, crowd, group, fellowship, society, faction; band, ring, gang. **4 a** genus, species, class; see also KIND¹ 2.

clandestine /klandéstin/ *adj.* surreptitious; secret. □□ **clandestinely** *adv.* **clandestinity** /-tínitee/ *n.* [F *clandestin* or L *clandestinus* f. *clam* secretly]
■ see SECRET *adj.* 3.

clang /klang/ *n. & v.* ● *n.* a loud, resonant, metallic sound as of a bell or hammer, etc. ● *v.* **1** *intr.* make a clang. **2** *tr.* cause to clang. [imit.: infl. by L *clangere* resound]
■ *n.* see CLASH *n.* 1a. ● *v.* see CLASH *v.* 1.

clanger /klángər/ *n. Brit. sl.* a mistake or blunder. □ **drop a clanger** commit a conspicuous indiscretion.

clangor /klánggər/ *n.* (*Brit.* **clangour**) **1** a prolonged or repeated clanging noise. **2** an uproar or commotion. □□ **clangorous** *adj.* **clangorously** *adv.* [L *clangor* noise of trumpets, etc.]
■ see NOISE *n.* 1, 2.

clank /klangk/ *n. & v.* ● *n.* a sound as of heavy pieces of metal meeting or a chain rattling. ● *v.* **1** *intr.* make a clanking sound. **2** *tr.* cause to clank. □□ **clankingly** *adv.* [imit.: cf. CLANG, CLINK¹, Du. *klank*]
■ *n.* see JANGLE *n.* 1. ● *v.* see JANGLE *v.* 1.

clannish /klánish/ *adj.* usu. *derog.* **1** (of a family or group) tending to hold together. **2** of or like a clan. □□ **clannishly** *adv.* **clannishness** *n.*
■ **1** see EXCLUSIVE *adj.* 3, 4. **2** see SECTARIAN *adj.* 1.

clanship /klánship/ *n.* **1** a patriarchal system of clans. **2** loyalty to one's clan.

clansman /klánzmən/ *n.* (*pl.* **-men**; *fem.* **clanswoman**, *pl.* **-women**) a member or fellow member of a clan.

clap¹ /klap/ *v. & n.* ● *v.* (**clapped, clapping**) **1 a** *intr.* strike the palms of one's hands together as a signal or repeatedly as applause. **b** *tr.* strike (the hands) together in this way. **2** *tr.* **a** *Brit.* applaud or show one's approval of (esp. a person) in this way. **b** slap with the palm of the hand as a sign of approval or encouragement. **3** *tr.* (of a bird) flap (its wings) audibly. **4** *tr.* put or place quickly or with determination (*clapped him in prison; clap a tax on whiskey*). ● *n.* **1** the act of clapping, esp. as applause. **2** an explosive sound, esp. of thunder. **3** a slap; a pat. □ **clap eyes on** *colloq.* see. **clap on the back** = *slap on the back*. **clapped-out** *Brit. sl.* worn out (esp. of machinery, etc.); exhausted. [OE *clappian* throb, beat, of imit. orig.]

■ *v.* **1 a** applaud, cheer. **2 a** applaud, cheer, give a person a round of applause, *colloq.* give a person a (big) hand. **b** slap, strike, pat. **3** beat, flutter, flap, thrash. **4** put, place, slap, fling, toss, cast, *colloq.* stick; impose, lay, apply. ● *n.* **2** crack, slap, report, crash, bang, snap. **3** see SLAP *n.*, PAT¹ *n.* 1, 2.

clap² /klap/ *n. coarse sl.* venereal disease, esp. gonorrhea. [OF *clapoir* venereal bubo]

clapboard /klábərd, klápbawrd/ *n. & v.* ● *n.* **1** each of a series of horizontal boards with edges overlapping to keep out the rain, etc., used as a siding esp. of houses. **2** = CLAPPERBOARD. ● *v.tr.* fit or supply with clapboards (in sense 1 of *n.*). [Anglicized f. LG *klappholt* cask stave]

clapper /klápər/ *n.* the tongue or striker of a bell. □ **like the clappers** *Brit. sl.* very fast or hard.

■ tongue, striker.

clapperboard /klápərbawrd/ *n. Cinematog.* a device of hinged boards struck together to synchronize the starting of picture and sound machinery in filming.

claptrap /kláptrap/ *n.* **1** insincere or pretentious talk; nonsense. **2** language used or feelings expressed only to gain applause. [CLAP¹ + TRAP¹]

■ **1** see NONSENSE 1. **2** see MOUTH *n.* 4.

claque /klak/ *n.* a group of people hired to applaud in a theater, etc. [F f. *claquer* to clap]

■ see CROWD *n.* 3.

claqueur /klakŏr/ *n.* a member of a claque. [F (as CLAQUE)]

clarabella /klárəbélə/ *n.* an organ stop of flute quality. [fem. forms of L *clarus* clear and *bellus* pretty]

clarence /klárəns/ *n. hist.* a four-wheeled closed carriage with seats for four inside and two on the box. [Duke of *Clarence*, afterward William IV]

claret /klárət/ *n. & adj.* ● *n.* **1** red wine, esp. from Bordeaux. **2** a deep purplish-red. **3** *archaic sl.* blood. ● *adj.* claret-colored. [ME f. OF (*vin*) *claret* f. med.L *claratum* (*vinum*) f. L *clarus* clear]

clarify /klárifī/ *v.* (**-ies, -ied**) **1** *tr. & intr.* make or become clearer. **2** *tr.* **a** free (liquid, butter, etc.) from impurities. **b** make transparent. **c** purify. □□ **clarification** *n.* **clarifier** *n.* [ME f. OF *clarifier* f. L *clarus* clear]

■ **1** elucidate, make clear, simplify, make plain, clear up, explain, shed *or* throw light (up)on, illuminate, explicate. **2 a** clear, purify, clean. **c** see PURIFY.

clarinet /klárinét/ *n.* **1 a** a woodwind instrument with a single-reed mouthpiece, a cylindrical tube with a flared end, holes, and keys. **b** its player. **2** an organ stop with a quality resembling a clarinet. □□ **clarinetist** *n.* (also **clarinettist**). [F *clarinette*, dimin. of *clarine* a kind of bell]

clarion /kláreeən/ *n. & adj.* ● *n.* **1** a clear, rousing sound. **2** *hist.* a shrill, narrow-tubed war trumpet. **3** an organ stop with the quality of a clarion. ● *adj.* clear and loud. [ME f. med.L *clario -onis* f. L *clarus* clear]

■ *adj.* see CLEAR *adj.* 6a.

clarity /kláritee/ *n.* the state or quality of being clear, esp. of sound or expression. [ME f. L *claritas* f. *clarus* clear]

■ clearness, lucidity, limpidity, pellucidity, definition, definiteness, distinctness; comprehensibility, intelligibility.

clarkia /kláarkeeə/ *n.* any plant of the genus *Clarkia*, with showy white, pink, or purple flowers. [mod.L f. W. *Clark*, US explorer d. 1838]

clary /kláiree/ *n.* (*pl.* **-ies**) any of various aromatic herbs of the genus *Salvia*. [ME f. obs. F *clarie* repr. med.L *sclarea*]

clash /klash/ *n. & v.* ● *n.* **1 a** a loud, jarring sound as of metal objects being struck together. **b** a collision, esp. with force. **2 a** a conflict or disagreement. **b** a discord of colors, etc. ● *v.* **1** *intr.* make a clashing sound. **b** *tr.* cause to

clash. **2** *intr.* collide; coincide awkwardly. **3** *intr.* (often foll. by *with*) **a** come into conflict or be at variance. **b** (of colors) be discordant. □□ **clasher** *n.* [imit.: cf. *clack, clang, crack, crash*]

■ *n.* **1 a** crash, clang, clank, clangor. **b** collision, smash. **2 a** (hostile) encounter, conflict, engagement, fight, battle, disagreement, difference, argument, dispute, altercation, quarrel, squabble. ● *v.* **1** crash, clang, clank, smash, bang, boom. **3 a** come into conflict, disagree, differ, argue, dispute, quarrel, squabble, feud, wrangle, cross swords. **b** disharmonize, jar, be at odds *or* out of keeping; (*clash with*) *colloq.* swear at.

clasp /klasp/ *n. & v.* ● *n.* **1 a** a device with interlocking parts for fastening. **b** a buckle or brooch. **c** a metal fastening on a book cover. **2 a** an embrace; a person's reach. **b** a grasp or handshake. **3** a bar of silver on a medal ribbon with the name of the battle, etc., at which the wearer was present. ● *v.* **1** *tr.* fasten with or as with a clasp. **2** *tr.* **a** grasp; hold closely. **b** embrace, encircle. **3** *intr.* fasten a clasp. □ **clasp hands** shake hands with fervor or affection. **clasp one's hands** interlace one's fingers. **clasp knife** a folding knife, usu. with a catch holding the blade when open. □□ **clasper** *n.* [ME: orig. unkn.]

■ *n.* **1** fastener, fastening, hook, catch, clip, pin, brooch, buckle. **2** embrace, hug, hold, grasp, grip; handshake; reach. ● *v.* **1** fasten, secure, close, hold, hook, clip, pin, clamp. **2** hold, embrace, take hold of, hug, enclose, encircle, envelop; grab, grasp, seize, clutch, grip.

clasper /kláspər/ *n.* (in *pl.*) the appendages of some male fish and insects used to hold the female in copulation.

class /klas/ *n. & v.* ● *n.* **1** any set of persons or things grouped together, or graded or differentiated from others esp. by quality (*first class; economy class*). **2 a** a division or order of society (*upper class; professional classes*). **b** a caste system; a system of social classes. **c** (**the classes**) *archaic* the rich or educated. **3** *colloq.* distinction or high quality in appearance, behavior, etc.; stylishness. **4 a** a group of students taught together. **b** the occasion when they meet. **c** their course of instruction. **5** all the college or school students of the same standing or graduating in a given year (*the class of 1990*). **6** (in conscripted armies) all the recruits born in a given year (*the 1950 class*). **7** *Brit.* a division of candidates according to merit in an examination. **8** *Biol.* a grouping of organisms, the next major rank below a division or phylum. ● *v.tr.* assign to a class or category. □ **class-conscious** aware of and reacting to social divisions or one's place in a system of social class. **class-consciousness** this awareness. **class war** conflict between social classes. **in a class of** (or **on**) **its** (or **one's**) **own** unequaled. **no class** *colloq.* a lack of quality or distinction, esp. in behavior. [L *classis* assembly]

■ *n.* **1** category, division, classification, group, genre, league, realm, domain; kind, sort, type. **2 a** rank, grade, level, order, stratum; caste, lineage, birth, pedigree, stock, extraction, descent. **b** caste system, social ladder, hierarchy; caste, *often derog.* casteism. **3** excellence, merit, refinement, elegance, stylishness, prestige, importance, taste, discernment, distinction, bearing, presence, savoir faire, savoir vivre, breeding. **4a, c** *Brit.* year, grade; form. **6** recruits, conscripts. ● *v.* classify, group, arrange, assort, type, categorize, rank, grade, rate, order. □ **in a class of** (or **on**) **its** (or **one's**) **own** see UNPARALLELED.

classic /klásik/ *adj. & n.* ● *adj.* **1 a** of the first class; of acknowledged excellence. **b** remarkably typical; outstandingly important (*a classic case*). **c** having enduring worth; timeless. **2 a** of ancient Greek and Latin literature, art, or culture. **b** (of style in art, music, etc.) simple, harmonious,

---

well-proportioned; in accordance with established forms (cf. ROMANTIC). **3** having literary or historic associations (*classic ground*). **4** (of clothes) made in a simple elegant style not much affected by changes in fashion. ● *n.* **1** a classic writer, artist, work, or example. **2 a** an ancient Greek or Latin writer. **b** (in *pl.*) the study of ancient Greek and Latin literature and history. **c** *archaic* a scholar of ancient Greek and Latin. **3** a follower of classic models (cf. ROMANTIC). **4** a garment in classic style. **5** (in *pl.*) *Brit.* the classic races. □ **classic races** (in the UK) the five main flat races in British horse racing, namely the Two Thousand and the One Thousand Guineas, the Derby, the Oaks, and the St. Leger. [F *classique* or L *classicus* f. *classis* class]
■ *adj.* **1 a** outstanding, first-rate, superior, excellent, noteworthy, notable, exemplary. **b** typical, standard, leading, outstanding, prototypic(al), definitive, model, ideal, archetypal, paradigmatic; see also IMPORTANT 1, 2. **c** legendary, immortal, enduring, deathless, ageless, timeless, undying, venerable, time-honored, vintage. **2b, 4** see SIMPLE *adj.* 2. ● *n.* **1** paragon, epitome, outstanding example, exemplar, model, paradigm, prototype; masterpiece, masterwork.

classical /klásikəl/ *adj.* **1 a** of ancient Greek or Latin literature or art. **b** (of language) having the form used by the ancient standard authors (*classical Latin*; *classical Hebrew*). **c** based on the study of ancient Greek and Latin (*a classical education*). **d** learned in classical studies. **2 a** (of music) serious or conventional; following traditional principles and intended to be of permanent rather than ephemeral value (cf. POPULAR, LIGHT). **b** of the period *c.*1750–1800 (cf. ROMANTIC). **3 a** in or following the restrained style of classical antiquity (cf. ROMANTIC). **b** (of a form or period of art, etc.) representing an exemplary standard; having a long-established worth. **4** *Physics* relating to the concepts that preceded relativity and quantum theory. □□ **classicalism** *n.* **classicalist** *n.* **classicality** /-kálitee/ *n.* **classically** *adv.* [L *classicus* (as CLASSIC)]
■ **1 a** Greek, Latin, Roman. **3 b** standard, model, exemplary, traditional, established, influential, authoritative, serious, weighty.

classicism /klásisizəm/ *n.* **1** the following of a classic style. **2 a** classical scholarship. **b** the advocacy of a classical education. **3** an ancient Greek or Latin idiom. □□ **classicist** *n.*

classicize /klásisīz/ *v.* **1** *tr.* make classic. **2** *intr.* imitate a classical style.

classified /klásifīd/ *adj.* **1** arranged in classes or categories. **2** (of information, etc.) designated as officially secret. **3** *Brit.* (of a road) assigned to a category according to its importance. **4** (of newspaper advertisements) arranged in columns according to various categories.
■ **2** see CONFIDENTIAL 1.

classify /klásifī/ *v.tr.* (**-ies**, **-ied**) **1 a** arrange in classes or categories. **b** assign (a thing) to a class or category. **2** designate as officially secret or not for general disclosure. □□ **classifiable** *adj.* **classification** *n.* **classificatory** /klásifikətáwree, kləsifi-, klásifikáytəree/ *adj.* **classifier** *n.* [backform. f. *classification* f. F (as CLASS)]
■ **1** see ORGANIZE 1.

classless /kláslis/ *adj.* making or showing no distinction of classes (*classless society*; *classless accent*). □□ **classlessness** *n.*
■ see DEMOCRATIC 2.

classmate /klásmayt/ *n.* a fellow member of a class, esp. at school.

classroom /klásrōm, -rŏŏm/ *n.* a room in which a class of students is taught, esp. in a school.

classy /klásee/ *adj.* (**classier**, **classiest**) *colloq.* superior; stylish. □□ **classily** *adv.* **classiness** *n.*
■ see STYLISH 1.

clastic /klástik/ *adj.* *Geol.* composed of broken pieces of older rocks. □ **clastic rocks** conglomerates, sandstones, etc. [F *clastique* f. Gk *klastos* broken in pieces]

clathrate /kláthrayt/ *n.* *Chem.* a solid in which one component is enclosed in the structure of another. [L *clathratus* f. *clathri* lattice bars f. Gk *klēthra*]

clatter /klátər/ *n.* & *v.* ● *n.* **1** a rattling sound as of many hard objects struck together. **2** noisy talk. ● *v.* **1** *intr.* **a** make a clatter. **b** fall or move, etc., with a clatter. **2** *tr.* cause (plates, etc.) to clatter. [OE, of imit. orig.]
■ *n.* **1** see RATTLE *n.* 1. ● *v.* see RATTLE *v.* 1a.

claudication /kláwdikáyshən/ *n.* *Med.* a cramping pain, esp. in the leg, caused by arterial obstruction; limping. [L *claudicare* limp f. *claudus* lame]
■ see LIMP¹ *n.*

clause /klawz/ *n.* **1** *Gram.* a distinct part of a sentence, including a subject and predicate. **2** a single statement in a treaty, law, bill, or contract. □□ **clausal** *adj.* [ME f. OF f. L *clausula* conclusion f. *claudere claus-* shut]
■ **1** see PHRASE *n.* 1. **2** see *stipulation* (STIPULATE¹).

claustral /kláwstrəl/ *adj.* **1** of or associated with the cloister; monastic. **2** narrow-minded. [ME f. LL *claustralis* f. *claustrum* CLOISTER]

claustrophobia /kláwstrəfóbeeə/ *n.* an abnormal fear of confined places. □□ **claustrophobe** /-rəfōb/ *n.* [mod.L f. L *claustrum*: see CLOISTER]

claustrophobic /kláwstrəfóbik/ *adj.* **1** suffering from claustrophobia. **2** inducing claustrophobia. □□ **claustrophobically** *adv.*

clavate /kláyvayt/ *adj.* *Bot.* club-shaped. [mod.L *clavatus* f. L *clava* club]

clave¹ /klayv/ *n.* *Mus.* a hardwood stick used in pairs to make a hollow sound when struck together. [Amer. Sp. f. Sp., = keystone, f. L *clavis* key]

clave² *past* of CLEAVE².

clavicembalo /klávichémbəlō/ *n.* (*pl.* **-os**) a harpsichord. [It.]

clavichord /klávikawrd/ *n.* a small keyboard instrument with a very soft tone. [ME f. med.L *clavichordium* f. L *clavis* key, *chorda* string: see CHORD²]

clavicle /klávikəl/ *n.* the collarbone. □□ **clavicular** /kləvíkyələr/ *adj.* [L *clavicula* dimin. of *clavis* key (from its shape)]

clavier /kləveer, kláyveeər, kláyveeər/ *n.* *Mus.* **1** any keyboard instrument. **2** its keyboard. [F *clavier* or G *Klavier* f. med.L *claviarius*, orig. = key-bearer, f. L *clavis* key]

claviform /klávifawrm/ *adj.* club-shaped. [L *clava* club]

claw /klaw/ *n.* & *v.* ● *n.* **1 a** a pointed horny nail on an animal's or bird's foot. **b** a foot armed with claws. **2** the pincers of a shellfish. **3** a device for grappling, holding, etc. ● *v.* **1 a** *tr.* & *intr.* scratch, maul, or pull (a person or thing) with claws. **b** *intr.* (often foll. by *at*) grasp, clutch, or scrabble at as with claws. **2** *tr.* & *intr.* *Sc.* scratch gently. **3** *intr.* *Naut.* beat to windward. □ **claw back** regain laboriously or gradually. **claw hammer** a hammer with one side of the head forked for extracting nails. □□ **clawed** *adj.* (also in *comb.*). **clawer** *n.* **clawless** *adj.* [OE *clawu*, *clawian*]
■ *n.* **1** talon, nail. **3** vice. ● *v.* **1 a** scratch, tear, scrape, rake, slash. **b** grapple, grab, grasp, clutch, scrabble.

clay /klay/ *n.* **1** a stiff, sticky earth, used for making bricks, pottery, ceramics, etc. **2** *poet.* the substance of the human body. **3** (in full **clay pipe**) a tobacco pipe made of clay. □ **clay pigeon** a breakable disk thrown up from a trap as a target for shooting. □□ **clayey** *adj.* **clayish** *adj.* **claylike** *adj.* [OE *clǣg* f. WG]
■ **1** see EARTH *n.* 2b.

claymore /kláymawr/ *n.* **1** *hist.* **a** a Scottish two-edged broadsword. **b** a broadsword, often with a single edge, having a hilt with a basketwork design. **2** a type of antipersonnel mine. [Gael. *claidheamh mór* great sword]

claypan /kláypan/ **1** hardpan consisting mostly of clay. **2** *Austral.* a natural hollow in clay soil, retaining water after rain.

-cle /kəl/ *suffix* forming (orig. diminutive) nouns (*article*; *particle*). [as -CULE]

clean /kleen/ *adj.*, *adv.*, *v.*, & *n.* ● *adj.* **1** (often foll. by *of*) free from dirt or contaminating matter; unsoiled. **2** clear; unused or unpolluted; preserving what is regarded as the original state (*clean air*; *clean page*). **3** free from obscenity or indecency. **4** attentive to personal hygiene and cleanliness. **b** (of animals) house-trained. **5** complete; clear-cut; unobstructed; even. **6 a** (of a ship, aircraft, or car) streamlined; smooth. **b** well-formed; slender and shapely (*clean-limbed*; *the car has clean lines*). **7** adroit; skillful (*clean fielding*). **8** (of a nuclear weapon) producing relatively little fallout. **9 a** free from ceremonial defilement or from disease. **b** (of food) not prohibited. **10 a** free from any record of a crime, offense, etc. (*a clean driving record*). **b** *colloq.* (of an alcoholic or drug addict) not possessing or using alcohol or drugs. **c** *sl.* not carrying a weapon or incriminating material; free from suspicion. **11** (of a taste, smell, etc.) sharp; fresh; distinctive. **12** (of lumber) free from knots. ● *adv.* **1** completely; outright; simply (*cut clean through; clean forgot*). **2** in a clean manner. ● *v.* **1** *tr.* (also foll. by *of*) & *intr.* make or become clean. **2** *tr.* eat all the food on (one's plate). **3** *tr.* *Cookery* remove the innards of (fish or fowl). **4** *intr.* make oneself clean. ● *n.* esp. *Brit.* the act or process of cleaning or being cleaned (*give it a clean*). □ **clean bill of health** see BILL[1]. **clean break** a quick and final separation. **clean-cut 1** sharply outlined. **2** neatly groomed. **clean hands** freedom from guilt. **clean-living** of upright character. **clean out 1** clean or clear thoroughly. **2** *sl.* empty or deprive (esp. of money). **clean-shaven** without beard, whiskers, mustache. **clean slate** freedom from commitments or imputations; the removal of these from one's record. **clean up 1 a** clear (a mess) away. **b** (also *absol.*) make (things) neat. **c** make (oneself) clean. **2** restore order or morality to. **3** *sl.* acquire as gain or profit. **b** make a gain or profit. **come clean** *colloq.* own up; confess everything. **make a clean breast of** see BREAST. **make a clean sweep of** see SWEEP. □□ **cleanable** *adj.* **cleanish** *adj.* **cleanness** *n.* [OE *clǣne* (adj. & adv.), *clēne* (adv.), f. WG]

■ *adj.* **1** pure, undefiled, unsullied, unmixed, unadulterated, uncontaminated, unpolluted, uninfected, unsoiled, untainted, unstained, unspoiled, unspoilt, sanitary, disinfected; antiseptic, decontaminated, purified, sterile; cleanly, (freshly) laundered, washed, scrubbed, *usu. formal* cleansed; spotless, immaculate, clear. **2, 3** see PURE 3, 4. **4 a** hygienic, cleanly. **5** complete, clean-cut, neat, simple, definite, clear-cut, unobstructed, uncomplicated, smooth, even, straight, trim, tidy. **6 a** see STREAMLINE *v.* 3a. **b** see SLENDER 1, SHAPELY. **7** see SKILLFUL. **9 a** undefiled, uninfected, uncontaminated. **b** halal, kosher. **10 a** innocent, inoffensive, respectable; see also BLAMELESS. **c** unarmed, weaponless. ● *adv.* **1** completely, outright, entirely, thoroughly, fully, totally, wholly, altogether, quite, utterly, simply, absolutely. ● *v.* **1** wash, sponge, mop, scrub, scour, sweep, brush, wipe, clean down *or* out, dust, vacuum, launder, esp. *Brit.* hoover, wash up, *usu. formal* cleanse, *literary* lave; tidy, neaten, do up, straighten up *or* out. **4** wash, (have *or* take a) shower, have *or* take a bath, clean oneself up, bathe, wash up, *Brit.* bath. □ **clean-cut 1** see CLEAR *adj.* 6c. **clean-living** see UPRIGHT *adj.* 3. **clean hands** a clear conscience. **clean out 2** see DEFRAUD. **clean up 1 a, b** see *clear up* 1. **c** clean, wash, (have *or* take a) shower, have *or* take a bath, bathe, wash up, *Brit.* bath. **come clean** confess, acknowledge *or* admit guilt, make a clean breast of it, own up, *sl.* sing.

cleaner /klē'nər/ *n.* **1** a person employed to clean the interior of a building. **2** (*usu. in pl.*) a commercial establishment for cleaning clothes. **3** a device or substance for cleaning. □ **take to the cleaners** *sl.* **1** defraud or rob (a person) of all his or her money. **2** criticize severely.

■ **1** see SERVANT 1. **3** see DETERGENT *n.*

cleanly[1] /klēn'lee/ *adv.* **1** in a clean way. **2** efficiently; without difficulty. [OE *clǣnlīce*: see CLEAN, -LY[2]]

■ **1** clean. **2** see EASILY 1.

cleanly[2] /klén'lee/ *adj.* (**cleanlier, cleanliest**) habitually clean; with clean habits. □□ **cleanlily** *adv.* **cleanliness** *n.* [OE *clǣnlic*: see CLEAN, -LY[1]]

■ □□ **cleanliness** see PURITY 1.

cleanse /klenz/ *v.tr.* **1** *usu. formal* make clean. **2** (often foll. by *of*) purify from sin or guilt. **3** *archaic* cure (a leper, etc.). □ **cleansing cream** cream for removing unwanted matter from the face, hands, etc. **cleansing department** *Brit.* a local service of refuse collection, etc. [OE *clǣnsian* (see CLEAN)]

■ **1** wash, scour, scrub; see also CLEAN *v.* 1. **2** purify, depurate, purge.

cleanser /klénzər/ *n.* **1** one that cleanses. **2** an agent, as a lotion or an abrasive powder, used for cleansing.

cleanskin /klēn'skin/ *n.* *Austral.* **1** an unbranded animal. **2** *sl.* a person free from blame, without a police record, etc.

cleanup /klēn'up/ *n.* **1** an act of cleaning up. **2** *sl.* a huge profit. **3** *Baseball* the fourth position in the batting order.

■ see PROFIT *n.* 2.

clear /kleer/ *adj., adv.,* & *v.* ● *adj.* **1** free from dirt or contamination. **2** (of weather, the sky, etc.) not dull or cloudy. **3 a** transparent. **b** lustrous; shining; free from obscurity. **c** (of the complexion) fresh and unblemished. **4** (of soup) not containing solid ingredients. **5** (of a fire) burning with little smoke. **6 a** distinct; easily perceived by the senses. **b** unambiguous; easily understood (*make a thing clear; make oneself clear*). **c** manifest; not confused nor doubtful (*clear evidence*). **7** that discerns or is able to discern readily and accurately (*clear thinking; clear-sighted*). **8** (usu. foll. by *about, on,* or *that* + clause) confident; convinced; certain. **9** (of a conscience) free from guilt. **10** (of a road, etc.) unobstructed; open. **11 a** net; without deduction (*a clear $1,000*). **b** complete (*three clear days*). **12** (often foll. by *of*) free; unhampered; unencumbered by debt, commitments, etc. **13** (foll. by *of*) not obstructed by. ● *adv.* **1** clearly (*speak loud and clear*). **2** completely (*he got clear away*). **3** apart; out of contact (*keep clear; stand clear of the doors*). **4** (foll. by *to*) all the way. ● *v.* **1** *tr.* & *intr.* make or become clear. **2 a** *tr.* (often foll. by *of*) free from prohibition or obstruction. **b** *tr.* & *intr.* make or become empty or unobstructed. **c** *tr.* free (land) for cultivation or building by cutting down trees, etc. **d** *tr.* cause people to leave (a room, etc.). **3** *tr.* (often foll. by *of*) show or declare (a person) to be innocent (*cleared them of complicity*). **4** *tr.* approve (a person) for special duty, access to information, etc. **5** *tr.* pass over or by safely or without touching, esp. by jumping. **6** *tr.* make (an amount of money) as a net gain or to balance expenses. **7** *tr.* pass (a check) through a clearinghouse. **8** *tr.* pass through (a customs office, etc.). **9** *tr.* remove (an obstruction, an unwanted object, etc.) (*clear them out of the way*). **10** *tr.* (also *absol.*) *Sports* send (the ball, puck, etc.) out of one's defensive zone. **11** *intr.* (often foll. by *away, up*) (of physical phenomena) disappear; gradually diminish (*mist cleared by lunchtime; my cold has cleared up*). **12** *tr.* (often foll. by *off*) discharge (a debt). □ **clear the air 1** make the air less sultry. **2** disperse an atmosphere of suspicion, tension, etc. **clear away 1** remove completely. **2** remove the remains of a meal from the table. **clear-cut 1** sharply defined. **2** obvious. **clear the decks** prepare for action, esp. fighting. **clear off 1** get rid of. **2** *colloq.* go away. **clear out 1** empty. **2** remove. **3** *colloq.* go away. **clear one's throat** cough slightly to make one's voice clear. **clear up 1** tidy up. **2** solve (a mystery, etc.); remove (a difficulty, etc.). **3** (of weather) become fine. **clear the way 1** remove obstacles. **2** stand aside. **clear a thing with** get approval or authorization for a thing from (a person). **in clear** not in cipher or code. **in the clear** free from suspicion or difficulty. **out of a clear (blue) sky** as a complete surprise. □□ **clearable** *adj.* **clearer** *n.* **clearly** *adv.* **clearness** *n.* [ME f. OF *cler* f. L *clarus*]

■ *adj.* **1** see CLEAN *adj.* 1. **2** unclouded, cloudless, sunny, fair, sunlit, fine. **3 a** transparent, limpid, crystalline; translucent, uncloudy, unclouded, pellucid. **b** bright, lustrous, shining, shiny, sparkling. **c** bright, fresh, unblemished, unscarred. **6 a** distinct, sharp, well-defined, definite, vivid; legible, readable; pure, unwavering, clarion. **b** understandable, intelligible, perspicuous, lucid, comprehensible, apprehensible, discernible, plain, obvious, patent, unambiguous, unequivocal, explicit, definite, unmistakable,

---

/.../ **pronunciation**	● **part of speech**
□ **phrases, idioms, and compounds**	
□□ **derivatives**	■ **synonym section**
cross-references appear in SMALL CAPITALS or *italics*	

indisputable, undisputed, unquestionable, incontrovertible. **c** manifest, distinct, evident, unclouded, unconfused, explicit, plain, definite, clear-cut, palpable. **7** acute, sensitive, perspicacious, discerning, keen; see also PERCEPTIVE. **8** certain, sure, convinced, confident, positive, determined, definite, assured. **9** pure, guiltless, blameless, faultless; not guilty; see also INNOCENT *adj.* 2. **10** open, unencumbered, free, unblocked, unobstructed, unimpeded, direct. **11 a** unencumbered, free, net. **b** complete, entire, whole; uninterrupted. **12** see UNIMPEDED. **13** disengaged, disentangled, unentangled, free, freed, rid, quit, loose, released. ● *adv.* **1** distinctly, clearly, audibly. **2** completely, utterly, entirely, clean(ly), wholly, totally. **3** see APART 3a. ● *v.* **1** (*tr.*) clarify, clean, purify, purge, *usu. formal* cleanse. **2 b** open (up), free; unblock, unclog, unstop. **d** vacate, evacuate. **3** exonerate, absolve, acquit; excuse, forgive. **5** leap *or* jump over, vault, hurdle. **9** remove, eliminate, take (away); clear away, cut away *or* down, dislodge. **11** see DISAPPEAR 1, DIMINISH 1. **12** settle, discharge, pay, square. □ **clear away 1** see REMOVE *v.* 2a. **clear-cut** see CLEAR *adj.* 6c above. **clear off 1** see *get rid of* (RID). **2** see LEAVE¹ *v.* 1b, 3, 4. **clear out 1** see EMPTY *v.* 1. **2** see REMOVE *v.* 2a. **3** see *go away* (GO¹). **clear up 1** tidy (up), neaten (up), put *or* set in order, clear. **2** explain, elucidate, explicate, clarify, make plain *or* clear, disambiguate; settle, remove, eliminate. **3** become fair *or* fine *or* cloudless *or* sunny. **in the clear** innocent, not guilty; exonerated, forgiven, absolved; unburdened, disburdened, unencumbered, free. **out of a clear (blue) sky** see *suddenly* (SUDDEN). □□ **clearly** distinctly, audibly, understandably, clear; evidently, plainly, apparently, manifestly, obviously, certainly, definitely, positively, unequivocally, unquestionably, incontestably, without doubt, undoubtedly, indubitably, demonstrably.

clearance /kleerəns/ *n.* **1** the removal of obstructions, etc., esp. removal of buildings, persons, etc., so as to clear land. **2** clear space allowed for the passing of two objects or two parts in machinery, etc. **3** special authorization or permission (esp. for an aircraft to take off or land, or for access to information, etc.). **4 a** the clearing of a person, body, etc., by customs. **b** a certificate showing this. **5** the clearing of checks. **6** making clear. □ **clearance sale** a sale to get rid of superfluous stock.
■ **2** margin, leeway, space, gap, hole, interval, separation, room, allowance. **3** approval, endorsement, authorization, license, leave, permission, consent.

clearcole /kleerkōl/ *n. & v.* ● *n.* a mixture of size and whiting or white lead, used as a primer for distemper. ● *v.tr.* paint with clearcole. [F *claire colle* clear glue]

clearing /kleering/ *n.* **1** in senses of CLEAR *v.* **2** an area in a forest cleared for cultivation.
■ **2** see FIELD *n.* 1.

clearinghouse /kleeringhows/ *n.* **1** a bankers' establishment where checks and bills from member banks are exchanged, so that only the balances need be paid in cash. **2** an agency for collecting and distributing information, etc.

clearstory var. of CLERESTORY.

clearway /kleerway/ *n. Brit.* a main road (other than a freeway) on which vehicles are not normally permitted to stop.

cleat /kleet/ *n.* **1** a piece of metal, wood, etc., bolted on for fastening ropes to, or to strengthen woodwork, etc. **2** a projecting piece on a spar, gangway, athletic shoe, etc., to give footing or prevent slipping. **3** a wedge. [OE: cf. CLOT]

cleavage /kleevij/ *n.* **1** the hollow between a woman's breasts, esp. as exposed by a low-cut garment. **2** a division or splitting. **3** the splitting of rocks, crystals, etc., in a preferred direction.
■ **2, 3** see SPLIT *n.* 2.

cleave¹ /kleev/ *v.* (*past* **cleaved** or **cleft** /kleft/ or **clove** /klōv/; *past part.* **cleaved** or **cleft** or **cloven** /klōvən/) *literary* **1 a** *tr.* chop or break apart, split, esp. along the grain or the line of cleavage. **b** *intr.* come apart in this way. **2** *tr.* make

one's way through (air or water). □□ **cleavable** *adj.* [OE *cléofan* f. Gmc]
■ **1 a** split, divide, cut, cut or chop or hew in two, bisect, halve, separate, slit, *archaic or poet.* rive, *literary* cut or chop or hew asunder. **b** see *come apart*.

cleave² /kleev/ *v.intr.* (*past* **cleaved** or **clove** /klōv/ or **clave** /klayv/) (foll. by *to*) *literary* stick fast; adhere. [OE *cleofian, clifian* f. WG: cf. CLAY]

cleaver /kleevər/ *n.* **1** a tool for cleaving, esp. a heavy chopping tool used by butchers. **2** a person who cleaves.

cleavers /kleevərz/ *n.* (also **clivers** /klívərz/) (treated as *sing.* or *pl.*) a plant, *Galium aparine*, having hooked bristles on its stem that catch on clothes, etc. Also called GOOSE-GRASS. [OE *clife*, formed as CLEAVE²]

clef /klef/ *n. Mus.* any of several symbols placed at the beginning of a staff, indicating the pitch of the notes written on it. [F f. L *clavis* key]

cleft¹ /kleft/ *adj.* split; partly divided. □ **cleft lip, palate** a congenital split in the lip or the roof of the mouth. **in a cleft stick** *Brit.* in a difficult position, esp. one allowing neither retreat nor advance. [past part. of CLEAVE¹]

cleft² /kleft/ *n.* a split or fissure; a space or division made by cleaving. [OE (rel. to CLEAVE¹): assim. to CLEFT¹]
■ see SPLIT *n.* 2.

cleistogamic /klístəgámik/ *adj. Bot.* (of a flower) permanently closed and self-fertilizing. [Gk *kleistos* closed + *gamos* marriage]

clematis /klémətis, kləmátis/ *n.* any erect or climbing plant of the genus *Clematis*, bearing white, pink, or purple flowers and feathery seeds, e.g., old man's beard. [L f. Gk *klēmatis* f. *klēma* vine branch]

clement /klémənt/ *adj.* **1** mild (*clement weather*). **2** merciful. □□ **clemency** /-mənsee/ *n.* [ME f. L *clemens -entis*]
■ **1** see MILD 3. **2** see MERCIFUL.

clementine /kléməntin, -teen/ *n.* a small citrus fruit, thought to be a hybrid between a tangerine and sweet orange. [F *clémentine*]

clench /klench/ *v. & n.* ● *v.tr.* **1** close (the teeth or fingers) tightly. **2** grasp firmly. **3** = CLINCH *v.* 4. ● *n.* **1** a clenching action. **2** a clenched state. [OE f. Gmc: cf. CLING]

clepsydra /klépsidrə/ *n.* an ancient time-measuring device worked by a flow of water. [L f. Gk *klepsudra* f. *kleptō* steal + *hudōr* water]
■ water clock.

clerestory /kleerstawree/ *n.* (also **clearstory**) (*pl.* **-ies**) **1** an upper row of windows in a cathedral or large church, above the level of the aisle roofs. **2** a raised section of the roof of a railroad car, with windows or ventilators. [ME f. CLEAR + STORY]

clergy /klárjee/ *n.* (*pl.* **-ies**) (usu. treated as *pl.*) **1** (usu. prec. by *the*) the body of all persons ordained for religious duties. **2** a number of such persons (*ten clergy were present*). [ME, partly f. OF *clergé* f. eccl.L *clericatus*, partly f. OF *clergie* f. *clerc* CLERK]
■ **1** see MINISTRY 2.

clergyman /klárjeemən/ *n.* (*pl.* **-men**; *fem.* **clergywoman**, *pl.* **-women**) a member of the clergy.
■ ecclesiastic, churchman, cleric, divine, man of the cloth, man of God, holy man, priest, minister, chaplain, father, pastor, parson, rector, vicar, dean, bishop, canon, presbyter, deacon, *archaic* clerk, *colloq.* reverend, *formal* clerk in holy orders, *Mil. sl.* sky pilot, *orig. Naut. sl.* holy Joe.

cleric /klérik/ *n.* a member of the clergy. [(orig. adj.) f. eccl.L f. Gk *klērikos* f. *klēros* lot, heritage, as in Acts 1:17]
■ see CLERGYMAN.

clerical /klérikəl/ *adj.* **1** of the clergy or clergymen. **2** of or done by a clerk or clerks. □ **clerical collar** a stiff upright white collar fastening at the back, as worn by the clergy in some churches. **clerical error** an error made in copying or writing out. □□ **clericalism** *n.* **clericalist** *n.* **clerically** *adv.* [eccl.L *clericalis* (as CLERIC)]
■ **1** ecclesiastical, churchly, pastoral, sacerdotal, priestly, hieratic, ministerial, episcopal. **2** white-collar, office, secretarial, stenographic.

clerihew /klérihyōō/ *n.* a short comic or nonsensical verse, usu. in two rhyming couplets with lines of unequal length and referring to a famous person. [E. *Clerihew* Bentley, Engl. writer d. 1956, its inventor]

clerk /klərk/ *n. & v.* ● *n.* **1** a person employed in an office, bank, etc., to keep records, accounts, etc. **2** a secretary, agent, or record keeper of a municipality (*town clerk*), court, etc. **3** a lay officer of a church (*parish clerk*), college chapel, etc. **4** *Brit.* a senior official in Parliament. **5** a person who works at the sales counter of a store, at a hotel desk, etc. **6** *archaic* a clergyman. ● *v.intr.* work as a clerk. □ **clerk in holy orders** *Brit. formal* a clergyman. **clerk of the works** (or **of works**) the official supervisor of a construction project, etc. □□ **clerkdom** *n.* **clerkess** *n. Sc.* **clerkish** *adj.* **clerkly** *adj.* **clerkship** *n.* [OE *cleric, clerc,* & OF *clerc,* f. eccl.L *clericus* CLERIC]
■ *n.* **1** see BOOKKEEPER. **2** see SCRIBE *n.* **1.** **6** see CLERGYMAN.

clever /klévər/ *adj.* (**cleverer, cleverest**) **1 a** skillful; talented; quick to understand and learn. **b** showing good sense or wisdom; wise. **2** adroit; dextrous. **3** (of the doer or the thing done) ingenious; cunning. □ **clever Dick** *Brit. colloq.* a person who is or purports to be smart or knowing. **not too clever** *Austral. colloq.* unwell; indisposed. □□ **cleverly** *adv.* **cleverness** *n.* [ME, = adroit: perh. rel. to CLEAVE[2], with sense 'apt to seize']
■ **1 a** skilled, talented, skillful, gifted, quick-witted, intelligent, brainy, smart, perceptive, discerning, sharp, sharp-witted, adept, able. **b** sensible, wise, sage. **2** deft, adroit, nimble-fingered, handy, agile, skillful, skilled; see also DEXTEROUS. **3** ingenious, original, resourceful, inventive, creative, imaginative; shrewd, cunning, guileful, canny, artful, crafty, sly, wily, foxy.

clevis /klévis/ *n.* **1** a U-shaped piece of metal at the end of a beam for attaching tackle, etc. **2** a connection in which a bolt holds one part that fits between the forked ends of another. [16th c.: rel. to CLEAVE[1]]

clew /klōō/ *n. & v.* ● *n.* **1** *Naut.* **a** a lower or after corner of a sail. **b** a set of small cords suspending a hammock. **2** *archaic* **a** a ball of thread or yarn, esp. with reference to the legend of Theseus and the labyrinth. **b** *Brit.* = CLUE. ● *v.tr. Naut.* **1** (foll. by *up*) draw the lower ends of (a sail) to the upper yard or the mast ready for furling. **2** (foll. by *down*) let down (a sail) by the clews in unfurling. [OE *cliwen, cleowen*]

clianthus /kleeánthəs/ *n.* any leguminous plant of the genus *Clianthus*, native to Australia and New Zealand, bearing drooping clusters of red pealike flowers. [mod.L, app. f. Gk *klei-, kleos* glory + *anthos* flower]

cliché /kleesháy/ *n.* (also **cliche**) **1** a hackneyed phrase or opinion. **2** *Brit.* a metal casting of a stereotype or electrotype. [F f. *clicher* to stereotype]
■ **1** stereotype, bromide, trite saying, old saw *or* maxim, truism, platitude, commonplace, banality.

clichéd /kleesháyd/ *adj.* hackneyed; full of clichés.

click /klik/ *n. & v.* ● *n.* **1** a slight, sharp sound, as of a switch being operated. **2** a sharp nonvocal suction, used as a speech sound in some languages. **3** a catch in machinery acting with a slight, sharp sound. **4** (of a horse) an action causing a hind foot to touch the shoe of a forefoot. ● *v.* **1** *intr.* make a click. **b** *tr.* cause (one's tongue, heels, etc.) to click. **2** *intr. colloq.* **a** become clear or understandable (often prec. by *it* as subject: *when I saw them it all clicked*). **b** be successful; secure one's object. **c** (foll. by *with*) become friendly, esp. with a person of the opposite sex. **d** come to an agreement. □ **click beetle** any of a family of beetles (Elateridae) that make a click in recovering from being overturned. □□ **clicker** *n.* [imit.: cf. Du. *klikken*, F *cliquer*]
■ *n.* **1** see SNAP *n.* **1.** ● *v.* **1 a** see SNAP *v.* 2, 3. **2 b** see ACHIEVE 3.

client /klíənt/ *n.* **1** a person using the services of a lawyer, architect, social worker, or other professional person. **2** a customer. **3** *Rom.Hist.* a plebeian under the protection of a patrician. **4** *archaic* a dependent or hanger-on. □□ **clientship** *n.* [ME f. L *cliens -entis* f. *cluere* hear, obey]

■ **1** patron; patient. **2** customer, shopper; patron. **4** see *hanger-on* (HANGER[1]).

clientele /klíəntél, kleéon-/ *n.* **1** clients collectively. **2** customers, esp. of a store or restaurant. **3** the patrons of a theater, etc. [L *clientela* clientship & F *clientèle*]
■ **1** clients, patrons, customers. **2** clients, patrons, customers; custom, business, trade, patronage, following. **3** patrons; public, audience.

cliff /klif/ *n.* a steep rock face, as at the edge of the sea. □ **cliffhanger** a story, etc., with a strong element of suspense; a suspenseful ending to an episode of a serial. **cliff-hanging** full of suspense. □□ **clifflike** *adj.* **cliffy** *adj.* [OE *clif* f. Gmc]
■ precipice, bluff, escarpment, scarp, rock face, scar, *Geog.* cuesta, crag.

climacteric /klimáktərik, klímaktérik/ *n. & adj.* ● *n.* **1** *Med.* the period of life when fertility and sexual activity are in decline. **2** a supposed critical period in life (esp. occurring at intervals of seven years). ● *adj.* **1** *Med.* occurring at the climacteric. **2** constituting a crisis; critical. [F *climatérique* or L *climactericus* f. Gk *klimaktērikos* f. *klimaktēr* critical period f. *klimax -akos* ladder]
■ **1** menopause, male menopause.

climactic /klimáktik/ *adj.* of or forming a climax. □□ **climactically** *adv.* [CLIMAX + -IC, perh. after SYNTACTIC or CLIMACTERIC]

climate /klímit/ *n.* **1** the prevailing weather conditions of an area. **2** a region with particular weather conditions. **3** the prevailing trend of opinion or public feeling. □□ **climatic** /-mátik/ *adj.* **climatical** *adj.* **climatically** *adv.* [ME f. OF *climat* or LL *clima climat-* f. Gk *klima* f. *klinō* slope]
■ **1** weather, *literary* clime. **3** consensus; atmosphere, ambience, air; feeling, mood, aura, milieu, feel.

climatology /klímətólajee/ *n.* the scientific study of climate. □□ **climatological** /-təlójikəl/ *adj.* **climatologist** *n.*

climax /klímaks/ *n. & v.* ● *n.* **1** the event or point of greatest intensity or interest; a culmination or apex. **2** a sexual orgasm. **3** *Rhet.* **a** a series arranged in order of increasing importance, etc. **b** the last term in such a series. **4** *Ecol.* a state of equilibrium reached by a plant community. ● *v.tr. & intr. colloq.* bring or come to a climax. [LL f. Gk *klimax -akos* ladder, climax]
■ *n.* **1** culmination, height, acme, apex, summit, zenith, apogee, peak, high point, maximum, supreme moment. ● *v.* (*intr.*) culminate, peak, come to a head.

climb /klim/ *v. & n.* ● *v.* **1** *tr. & intr.* (often foll. by *up*) ascend, mount, go or come up, esp. by using one's hands. **2** *intr.* (of a plant) grow up a wall, tree, trellis, etc., by clinging with tendrils or by twining. **3** *intr.* make progress from one's own efforts, esp. in social rank, intellectual or moral strength, etc. **4** *intr.* (of an aircraft, the sun, etc.) go upward. **5** *intr.* slope upward. ● *n.* **1** an ascent by climbing. **2 a** a place, esp. a hill, climbed or to be climbed. **b** a recognized route up a mountain, etc. □ **climb down 1** descend with the help of one's hands. **2** withdraw from a stance taken up in argument, negotiation, etc. **climb-down** *n.* such a withdrawal. **climbing iron** a set of spikes attachable to a boot, etc., for climbing trees or ice slopes. □□ **climbable** *adj.* [OE *climban* f. WG, rel. to CLEAVE[2]]
■ *v.* **1** mount, ascend, go up, scale, shin (up), clamber up, *colloq.* shinny (up). **2** creep, trail, twine; grow. **3** see PROGRESS *v.* 1. **4** rise, ascend, go up, esp. *archaic &* *poet.* arise. □ **climb down 1** descend, go *or* come down, move down, get down. **2** retreat, withdraw, back away *or* off, give up, backpedal; (*climb down from*) abandon, renounce. **climb-down** withdrawal, pullback, retraction.

climber /klímər/ *n.* **1** a mountaineer. **2** a climbing plant. **3** a person with strong social, etc., aspirations.

/.../ **pronunciation**	● **part of speech**
□ **phrases, idioms, and compounds**	
□□ **derivatives**	■ **synonym section**
cross-references appear in SMALL CAPITALS or *italics*	

clime /klīm/ *n. literary* **1** a region. **2** a climate. [LL *clima*: see CLIMATE]
  ■ **2** see CLIMATE 1.
clinch /klinch/ *v. & n.* ● *v.* **1** *tr.* confirm or settle (an argument, bargain, etc.) conclusively. **2** *intr. Boxing & Wrestling* (of participants) become too closely engaged. **3** *intr. colloq.* embrace. **4** *tr.* secure (a nail or rivet) by driving the point sideways when through. **5** *tr. Naut.* fasten (a rope) with a particular half hitch. ● *n.* **1 a** a clinching action. **b** a clinched state. **2** *colloq.* an (esp. amorous) embrace. **3** *Boxing & Wrestling* an action or state in which participants become too closely engaged. [16th-c. var. of CLENCH]
  ■ *v.* **1** secure, settle, confirm, determine, conclude, dispose of, complete, wind up, finalize, *colloq.* sew up. **3** see EMBRACE *v.* 1. ● *n.* **2** hug, clasp, embrace, cuddle, squeeze.
clincher /klinchər/ *n. colloq.* a remark or argument that settles a matter conclusively.
  ■ finishing touch *or* stroke, punch line, *coup de grâce*, final *or* crowning blow, *sl.* pay off.
clincher-built var. of CLINKER-BUILT.
cline /klīn/ *n. Biol.* the graded sequence of differences within a species, etc. □□ **clinal** *adj.* [Gk *klinō* to slope]
cling /kling/ *v. & n.* ● *v.intr.* (*past* and *past part.* **clung** /klung/) **1** (foll. by *to*) adhere, stick, or hold on (by means of stickiness, suction, grasping, or embracing). **2** (foll. by *to*) remain persistently or stubbornly faithful (to a friend, habit, idea, etc.). **3** maintain one's grasp; keep hold; resist separation. ● *n.* = CLINGSTONE. □ **cling together** remain in one body or in contact. □□ **clinger** *n.* **clingingly** *adv.* [OE *clingan* f. Gmc: cf. CLENCH]
  ■ *v.* **1** adhere; see also STICK² 4. **2** (*cling to*) favor, be *or* remain devoted *or* attached to, embrace, hang on to, retain, keep, cherish. □ **cling together** stick *or* stay together, embrace, hug, clasp one another, clutch one another, hold (fast) to one another, grasp one another, *literary* cleave to one another.
clingstone /klingstōn/ *n.* a variety of peach or nectarine in which the flesh adheres to the stone (cf. FREESTONE 2).
clingy /klingee/ *adj.* (**clingier, clingiest**) liable to cling. □□ **clinginess** *n.*
clinic /klinik/ *n.* **1** a private or specialized hospital. **2** a place or occasion for giving specialist medical treatment or advice (*eye clinic; fertility clinic*). **3** a gathering at a hospital bedside for the teaching of medicine or surgery. **4** a conference or short course on a particular subject (*golf clinic*). □□ **clinician** /klinishən/ *n.* [F *clinique* f. Gk *klinikē* (*tekhnē*) clinical, lit. bedside (art)]
  ■ **1** see INFIRMARY 1.
clinical /klinikəl/ *adj.* **1** *Med.* **a** of or for the treatment of patients. **b** taught or learned at the hospital bedside. **2** dispassionate; coldly detached. □ **clinical death** death judged by observation of a person's condition. **clinical medicine** medicine dealing with the observation and treatment of patients. **clinical thermometer** a thermometer with a small range, for measuring body temperature. □□ **clinically** *adv.* [L *clinicus* f. Gk *klinikos* f. *klinē* bed]
  ■ **2** see COLD *adj.* 4.
clink¹ /klingk/ *n. & v.* ● *n.* a sharp ringing sound. ● *v.* **1** *intr.* make a clink. **2** *tr.* cause (glasses, etc.) to clink. [ME, prob. f. MDu. *klinken*; cf. CLANG, CLANK]
  ■ *n.* see JINGLE *n.* 1. ● *v.* see JINGLE *v.*
clink² /klingk/ *n.* (often prec. by *in*) *sl.* prison. [16th c.: orig. unkn.]
  ■ see PRISON *n.* 1.
clinker¹ /klingkər/ *n.* **1** a mass of slag or lava. **2** a stony residue from burned coal. [earlier *clincard*, etc., f. obs. Du. *klinkaerd* f. *klinken* CLINK¹]
clinker² /klingkər/ *n.* **1** *sl.* a mistake or blunder. **2** *Brit. sl.* something excellent or outstanding. [CLINK¹ + -ER¹]
  ■ **1** see BLUNDER *n.*
clinker-built /klingkərbilt/ *adj.* (also **clincher-built** /klinchərbilt/) (of a boat) having external planks overlapping downward and secured with clinched copper nails. [*clink* No. of Engl. var. of CLINCH + -ER¹]

clinkstone /klingkstōn/ *n.* a kind of feldspar that rings like iron when struck.
clinometer /klinómitər/ *n. Surveying* an instrument for measuring slopes. [Gk *klinō* to slope + -METER]
cliometrics /klīəmétriks/ *n.pl.* (usu. treated as *sing.*) a method of historical research making much use of statistical information and methods. [*Clio*, Muse of history + METRIC + -ICS]
clip¹ /klip/ *n. & v.* ● *n.* **1** a device for holding things together or for attachment to an object as a marker, esp. a paper clip or a device worked by a spring. **2** a piece of jewelry fastened by a clip. **3** a set of attached cartridges for a firearm. ● *v.tr.* (**clipped, clipping**) **1** fix with a clip. **2** grip tightly. **3** surround closely. □ **clip-on** attached by a clip. [OE *clyppan* embrace f. WG]
  ■ *n.* **1** clasp, fastener. ● *v.* **1** clasp, fasten, fix, attach, hold; staple. **2** grip, grasp, clutch, clasp, hold. **3** see CIRCLE *v.* 2.
clip² /klip/ *v. & n.* ● *v.tr.* (**clipped, clipping**) **1** cut with shears or scissors, esp. cut short or trim (hair, wool, etc.). **2** trim or remove the hair or wool of (a person or animal). **3** *colloq.* hit smartly. **4 a** curtail; diminish; cut short. **b** omit (a letter, etc.) from a word; omit letters or syllables of (words pronounced). **5** *Brit.* remove a small piece of (a ticket) to show that it has been used. **6** cut (an extract) from a newspaper, etc. **7** *sl.* swindle; rob. **8** pare the edge of (a coin). ● *n.* **1** an act of clipping, esp. shearing or haircutting. **2** *colloq.* a smart blow, esp. with the hand. **3** a short sequence from a motion picture. **4** the quantity of wool clipped from a sheep, flock, etc. **5** *colloq.* speed, esp. rapid. □ **clip joint** *sl.* a club, etc., charging exorbitant prices. **clip a person's wings** prevent a person from pursuing ambitions or acting effectively. □□ **clippable** *adj.* [ME f. ON *klippa*, prob. imit.]
  ■ *v.* **1** trim (off), lop (off), cut (off), cut short, crop, chop, snip. **2** shear, fleece. **3** strike, hit, punch, smack, box, cuff, clout, *colloq.* sock, thwack, whack; *sl.* wallop. **4** shorten, reduce, abbreviate, diminish, curtail, cut (short), truncate. **7** cheat, overcharge, *sl.* rook, bilk; see also SWINDLE *v.* ● *n.* **1** cut, trim, haircutting, shearing. **2** blow, cuff, punch, hit, strike, smack, box, clout, *colloq.* whack, sock, *sl.* wallop. **3** segment, section, part, portion, extract, cutting, excerpt, bit, snippet, scrap, fragment. **5** pace, rate, speed. □ **clip a person's wings** see THWART *v.*
clipboard /klipbawrd/ *n.* a small board with a spring clip for holding papers, etc., and providing support for writing.
clip-clop /klipklóp/ *n. & v.* ● *n.* a sound such as the beat of a horse's hooves. ● *v.intr.* (**-clopped, -clopping**) make such a sound. [imit.]
clipper /klipər/ *n.* **1** (usu. in *pl.*) any of various instruments for clipping hair, fingernails, hedges, etc. **2** a fast sailing ship, esp. one with raking bows and masts. **3** a fast horse.
clippie /klipee/ *n. Brit. colloq.* a female bus conductor.
clipping /kliping/ *n.* a piece clipped or cut from something, esp. from a newspaper.
  ■ see EXTRACT *n.*
clique /kleek/ *n.* a small exclusive group of people. □□ **cliquey** *adj.* (**cliquier, cliquiest**). **cliquish** *adj.* **cliquishness** *n.* **cliquism** *n.* [F f. *cliquer* CLICK]
  ■ set, coterie, crowd, circle, group, *Austral.* push.
clitic /klitik/ *n.* (often *attrib.*) an enclitic or proclitic.
clitoris /klítoris, klī-/ *n.* a small erectile part of the female genitals at the upper end of the vulva. □□ **clitoral** *adj.* [mod.L f. Gk *kleitoris*]
clivers var. of CLEAVERS.
cloaca /klō-áykə/ *n.* (*pl.* **cloacae** /-áysee/) **1** the genital and excretory cavity at the end of the intestinal canal in birds, reptiles, etc. **2** a sewer. □□ **cloacal** *adj.* [L, = sewer]
  ■ **2** see DRAIN *n.* 1a.
cloak /klōk/ *n. & v.* ● *n.* **1** an outdoor overgarment, usu. sleeveless, hanging loosely from the shoulders. **2** a covering (*cloak of snow*). **3** *Brit.* (in *pl.*) = CLOAKROOM. ● *v.tr.* **1** cover with a cloak. **2** conceal; disguise. □ **cloak-and-dagger** involving intrigue and espionage. **under the cloak of** using as a pretext or for concealment. [ME f. OF *cloke*, dial. var.

of *cloche* bell, cloak (from its bell shape) f. med.L *clocca* bell: see CLOCK[1]]

■ *n.* **1** mantle, cape, robe, wrap, poncho, overcoat. **2** mantle, covering, cover, screen, shroud, veil. ● *v.* **1** see DRESS *v.* 1. **2** conceal, hide, mask, screen, veil, shroud, cover up; disguise.

cloakroom /klókrŏŏm, -rŏŏm/ *n.* **1** a room where outdoor clothes or luggage may be left by visitors, clients, etc. **2** *Brit. euphem.* a toilet.

clobber[1] /klóbər/ *v.tr. sl.* **1** hit repeatedly; beat up. **2** defeat. **3** criticize severely. [20th c.: orig. unkn.]

■ **1** see HIT *v.* 1a. **2** see SLAUGHTER *v.* 3.

clobber[2] /klóbər/ *n. Brit. sl.* clothing or personal belongings. [19th c.: orig. unkn.]

cloche /klōsh/ *n.* **1** a small translucent cover for protecting or forcing outdoor plants. **2** (in full **cloche hat**) a woman's close-fitting, bell-shaped hat. [F, = bell, f. med.L *clocca*: see CLOCK[1]]

clock[1] /klok/ *n. & v.* ● *n.* **1** an instrument for measuring time, driven mechanically or electrically and indicating hours, minutes, etc., by hands on a dial or by displayed figures. **2 a** any measuring device resembling a clock. **b** *colloq.* a speedometer, taximeter, or stopwatch. **3** time taken as an element in competitive sports, etc. (*ran against the clock*). **4** *Brit. sl.* a person's face. **5** *Brit.* a downy seed head, esp. that of a dandelion. ● *v.tr.* **1** *colloq.* **a** (often foll. by *up*) attain or register (a stated time, distance, or speed, esp. in a race). **b** time (a race) with a stopwatch. **2** *sl.* hit, esp. on the head. □ **around the clock** all day and (usu.) night. **clock golf** a game in which a golf ball is putted into a hole from successive points in a circle. **clock in** (or **on**) register one's arrival at work, esp. by means of an automatic recording clock. **clock off** (or **out**) register one's departure similarly. **clock radio** a combined radio and alarm clock. **clock-watcher** one who works while watching the time closely so as not to exceed minimum working hours. [ME f. MDu., MLG *klocke* f. med.L *clocca* bell, perh. f. Celt.]

■ *n.* **1** see WATCH *n.* 1. □ **clock in** see REPORT *v.* 4. **clock off** see *knock off* 2a.

clock[2] /klok/ *n.* an ornamental pattern on the side of a stocking or sock near the ankle. [16th c.: orig. unkn.]

clockwise /klókwīz/ *adj. & adv.* in a curve corresponding in direction to the movement of the hands of a clock.

clockwork /klókwərk/ *n.* **1** a mechanism like that of a mechanical clock, with a spring and gears. **2** (*attrib.*) **a** driven by clockwork. **b** regular; mechanical. □ **like clockwork** smoothly; regularly; automatically.

■ **1** see WORK *n.* 8.

clod /klod/ *n.* **1** a lump of earth, clay, etc. **2** *sl.* a silly or foolish person. **3** meat cut from the neck of an ox. □□ **cloddy** *adj.* [ME: var. of CLOT]

■ **1** lump, mass, wad, hunk, chunk, piece. **2** idiot, fool, dolt, blockhead, simpleton, nincompoop, dunce, oaf, ass, clown, ninny, bumpkin, clodhopper, *archaic* clodpoll, *colloq.* imbecile, *Brit. colloq.* clot, *sl.* jerk, dope.

cloddish /klódish/ *adj.* loutish; foolish; clumsy. □□ **cloddishly** *adv.* **cloddishness** *n.*

clodhopper /klódhopər/ *n.* **1** (usu. in *pl.*) *colloq.* a large heavy shoe. **2** = CLOD 2.

clodhopping /klódhoping/ *adj.* = CLODDISH.

clodpoll /klódpol/ *n. sl.* = CLOD 2.

clog /klawg, klog/ *n. & v.* ● *n.* **1** a shoe with a thick wooden sole. **2** *archaic* an encumbrance or impediment. **3** a block of wood to impede an animal's movement. ● *v.* (**clogged, clogging**) **1** (often foll. by *up*) **a** *tr.* obstruct, esp. by accumulation of glutinous matter. **b** *intr.* become obstructed. **2** *tr.* impede; hamper. **3** *tr. & intr.* (often foll. by *up*) fill with glutinous or choking matter. □ **clog dance** a dance performed in clogs. [ME: orig. unkn.]

■ *n.* **2** see IMPEDIMENT. ● *v.* **1** obstruct, choke (up), block, congest, jam. **2** see IMPEDE.

cloggy /klawgee, klógee/ *adj.* (**cloggier, cloggiest**) **1** lumpy; knotty. **2** sticky.

cloisonné /klóyzənáy, klwaá-/ *n. & adj.* ● *n.* **1** an enamel finish produced by forming areas of different colors sepa-

rated by strips of wire placed edgeways on a metal backing. **2** this process. ● *adj.* (of enamel) made by this process. [F f. *cloison* compartment]

cloister /klóystər/ *n. & v.* ● *n.* **1** a covered walk, often with a wall on one side and a colonnade open to a quadrangle on the other, esp. in a convent, monastery, college, or cathedral. **2** monastic life or seclusion. **3** a convent or monastery. ● *v.tr.* seclude or shut up usu. in a convent or monastery. □□ **cloistral** *adj.* [ME f. OF *cloistre* f. L *claustrum, clostrum* lock, enclosed place f. *claudere claus-* CLOSE[2]]

■ *n.* **3** see MONASTERY. ● *v.* see ISOLATE 1.

cloistered /klóystərd/ *adj.* **1** secluded; sheltered. **2** monastic.

■ **1** see SECLUDE 2.

clomp var. of CLUMP *v.* 2.

clone /klōn/ *n. & v.* ● *n.* **1 a** a group of organisms produced asexually from one stock or ancestor. **b** one such organism. **2** a person or thing regarded as identical with another. ● *v.tr.* propagate as a clone. □□ **clonal** *adj.* [Gk *klōn* twig, slip]

■ *n.* **1b, 2** see DUPLICATE *n.* 1. ● *v.* see IMITATE 3.

clonk /klongk, klawngk/ *n. & v.* ● *n.* an abrupt heavy sound of impact. ● *v.* **1** *intr.* make such a sound. **2** *tr. colloq.* hit. [imit.]

■ *n.* see THUD *n.* ● *v.* **1** see THUD *v.* **2** see HIT *v.* 1a.

clonus /klōnəs/ *n. Physiol.* a spasm with alternate muscular contractions and relaxations. □□ **clonic** *adj.* [Gk *klonos* turmoil]

clop /klop/ *n. & v.* ● *n.* the sound made by a horse's hooves. ● *v.intr.* (**clopped, clopping**) make this sound. [imit.]

cloque /klōkáy/ *n.* (also **cloqué**) a fabric with an irregularly raised surface. [F, = blistered]

close[1] /klōs/ *adj., adv., & n.* ● *adj.* **1** (often foll. by *to*) situated at only a short distance or interval. **2 a** having a strong or immediate relation or connection (*close friend*; *close relative*). **b** in intimate friendship or association (*were very close*). **c** corresponding almost exactly (*close resemblance*). **d** fitting tightly (*close cap*). **e** (of hair, etc.) short; near the surface. **3** in or almost in contact (*close combat*; *close proximity*). **4** dense; compact; with no or only slight intervals (*close texture*; *close writing*; *close formation*; *close thicket*). **5** in which competitors are almost equal (*close contest*; *close election*). **6** leaving no gaps or weaknesses; rigorous (*close reasoning*). **7** concentrated; searching (*close examination*; *close attention*). **8** (of air, etc.) stuffy or humid. **9 a** closed; shut. **b** shut up; under secure confinement. **10** limited or restricted to certain persons, etc. (*close corporation*; *close scholarship*). **11 a** hidden; secret; covered. **b** secretive. **12** (of a danger, etc.) directly threatening; narrowly avoided (*that was close*). **13** niggardly. **14** (of a vowel) pronounced with a relatively narrow opening of the mouth. **15** narrow; confined; contracted. **16** under prohibition. ● *adv.* **1** (often foll. by *by, to*) at only a short distance or interval (*they live close by*; *close to the church*). **2** closely; in a close manner (*shut close*). ● *n.* **1** an enclosed space. **2** *Brit.* a street closed at one end. **3** *Brit.* the precinct of a cathedral. **4** *Brit.* a school playing field or playground. **5** *Sc.* an entry from the street to a common stairway or to a court at the back. □ **at close quarters** very close together. **close-fitting** (of a garment) fitting close to the body. **close-grained** without gaps between fibers, etc. **close harmony** harmony in which the notes of the chord are close together. **close-hauled** (of a ship) with the sails hauled aft to sail close to the wind. **close-knit** tightly bound or interlocked; closely united in friendship. **close score** *Mus.* a score with more than one part on the same staff. **close-set** separated only by a small interval or intervals. **close shave** *colloq.* a narrow escape. **close to the wind** see SAIL. **close-up 1** a photograph, etc., taken at close range and showing the subject on a large scale. **2** an intimate description. **go close** (of a racehorse) win or almost win. □□ **closely** *adv.* **closeness**

/.../ **pronunciation**	● **part of speech**
□ **phrases, idioms, and compounds**	
□□ **derivatives**	■ **synonym section**
cross-references appear in SMALL CAPITALS or *italics*	

n. **closish** *adj.* [ME f. OF *clos* f. L *clausum* enclosure & *clausus* past part. of *claudere* shut]

■ *adj.* **1** adjacent, near. **2 a, b** intimate, devoted, familiar, inseparable, close-knit, solid, fast; attached, friendly, *colloq.* thick, thick as thieves, pally. **d** see TIGHT *adj.* 1, 2a. **4** dense, compact, tight, cramped, compressed. **5** nearly equal *or* even, neck and neck, tight. **6** see METICULOUS. **7** careful, assiduous, precise, detailed, concentrated, strict, rigorous, minute, searching, attentive, alert, intent, intense, thorough, painstaking. **8** stuffy, humid, musty, stale, fusty, oppressive, airless, unventilated, stifling, suffocating. **9 b** shut up, secure, fast. **11 a** private, secret, guarded, closely guarded, confidential; secluded, concealed, shut up *or* away, hidden, covered, *archaic* privy. **b** secretive, reticent, taciturn, reserved, closemouthed, tight-lipped, silent. **13** stingy, mean, miserly, niggardly, tight-fisted, close-fisted, parsimonious, penurious, penny-pinching, scrooge-like, skinflinty, near, mingy. **15** see NARROW *adj.*1b. ● *adv.* **1** near, in the neighborhood (of), not far (from *or* off), adjacent (to); alongside; at hand, nearby, close by; (*close to* or *on*) nearly, almost, practically, approximately, approaching, *archaic or dial.* nigh unto *or* on. **2** see *tightly* (TIGHT). □ **at close quarters** close, near, cheek by jowl. **close-fitting** tight-fitting, tight, skin-tight, snug. **close-knit** see CLOSE *adj.* 2a, b above.

close[2] / klōz/ *v. & n.* ● *v.* **1 a** *tr.* shut (a lid, box, door, room, house, etc.). **b** *intr.* become shut (*the door closed slowly*). **c** *tr.* block up. **2 a** *tr. & intr.* bring or come to an end. **b** *intr.* finish speaking (*closed with an expression of thanks*). **c** *tr.* settle (a bargain, etc.). **3 a** *intr.* end the day's business. **b** *tr.* end the day's business at (a store, office, etc.). **4** *tr. & intr.* bring or come closer or into contact (*close ranks*). **5** *tr.* make (an electric circuit, etc.) continuous. **6** *intr.* (foll. by *with*) express agreement (with an offer, terms, or the person offering them). **7** *intr.* (often foll. by *with*) come within striking distance; grapple. **8** *intr.* (foll. by *on*) (of a hand, box, etc.) grasp or entrap. ● *n.* **1** a conclusion; an end. **2** *Mus.* a cadence. □ **close down 1** (of a store, factory, etc.) discontinue business, esp. permanently. **2** *Brit.* (of a broadcasting station) end transmissions, esp. until the next day. **close one's eyes 1** (foll. by *to*) pay no attention. **2** die. **close in 1** enclose. **2** come nearer. **3** (of days) get successively shorter with the approach of the winter solstice. **close off** prevent access to by blocking or sealing the entrance. **close out** discontinue; terminate; dispose of (a business). **close up 1** (often foll. by *to*) move closer. **2** shut, esp. temporarily. **3** block up. **4** (of an aperture) grow smaller. **5** coalesce. **closing time** the time at which a bar, store, etc., ends business. □□ **closable** *adj.* **closer** *n.* [ME f. OF *clos-* stem of *clore* f. L *claudere* shut]

■ *v.* **1 a** shut, close up, seal; close off, lock, padlock, secure, fasten. **b** shut, be shut. **2 a** conclude, end, finish, bring to a close *or* an end, terminate, climax; complete, wind up; come to a close *or* an end. **b** end, conclude, terminate, finish. **c** conclude, sign, seal, make, settle, clinch, agree, arrange, work out, establish. **3 a** shut, *Brit.* put up the shutters. **b** shut. ● *n.* **1** end, termination, conclusion, finish, completion; culmination. □ **close down 1** shut down, go out of business, shut up shop, cease operations, close (up), wind up, *Brit.* put up the shutters. **close one's eyes 1** (*close one's eyes to*) ignore, overlook, disregard. **close in 1** see ENCLOSE 1, 6. **2** see APPROACH *v.* 1, 2. **close off** seal, make inaccessible, shut (off), obstruct, block. **close out** see TERMINATE. **close up 1** see APPROACH *v.* 1, 2. **2** close, shut (up), lock up. **3** see CLOG *v.* **5** see COMBINE *v.* 3.

closed / klōzd/ *adj.* **1** not giving access; shut. **2** (of a store, etc.) having ceased business temporarily. **3** (of a society, system, etc.) self-contained; not communicating with others. **4** (of a sport, etc.) restricted to specified competitors, etc. □ **closed book** see BOOK. **closed-captioned** (of a television program) broadcast with captions visible only to

viewers with a decoding device attached to their television set. **closed-circuit** (of television) transmitted by wires to a restricted set of receivers. **closed-end** having a predetermined extent (cf. *open-ended*). **closed season** the season when something, esp. the killing of game, etc., is illegal. **closed shop 1** a place of work, etc., where all employees must belong to an agreed trade union. **2** this system. **closed syllable** a syllable ending in a consonant.

■ **3** self-contained, withdrawn, uncommunicative, aloof, distant.

closefisted /klōsfistid/ *adj.* niggardly.

■ see CLOSE[1] *adj.* 13.

closemouthed /klōsmówthd/ *adj.* reticent.

■ see *reticent* (RETICENCE).

closet / klózit/ *n. & v.* ● *n.* **1** a small or private room. **2** a cupboard or recess. **3** *Brit.* = *water closet.* **4** (*attrib.*) secret; covert (*closet homosexual*). ● *v.tr.* (**closeted, closeting**) shut away, esp. in a place of work, etc., where all employees must belong to an agreed trade union. □ **closet drama** a play to be read rather than acted. **come out of the closet** stop hiding something about oneself, esp. one's homosexuality. [ME f. OF, dimin. of *clos*: see CLOSE[1]]

■ *n.* **1** see CABINET 3. **2** see WARDROBE 1. **4** see STEALTHY.
□ **come out of the closet** come out.

closure / klōzhər/ *n. & v.* ● *n.* **1** the act or process of closing. **2** a closed condition. **3** something that closes or seals, e.g., a cap or tie. [ME f. OF f. LL *clausura* f. *claudere* claus-CLOSE[2]]

clot / klot/ *n. & v.* ● *n.* **1 a** a thick mass of coagulated liquid, esp. of blood exposed to air. **b** a mass of material stuck together. **2** *Brit. colloq.* a silly or foolish person. ● *v.tr. & intr.* (**clotted, clotting**) form into clots. □ **clotted cream** esp. *Brit.* thick cream obtained by slow scalding. [OE *clot(t)* f. WG: cf. CLEAT]

■ *n.* **1** see LUMP[1] *n.* 1, 2. ● *v.* see COAGULATE.

cloth / klawth, kloth/ *n.* (*pl.* **cloths** /kloths, klothz/) **1** woven or felted material. **2** a piece of this. **3** a piece of cloth for a particular purpose; a tablecloth, dishcloth, etc. **4** woolen woven fabric as used for clothes. **5 a** a profession or status, esp. of the clergy, as shown by clothes (*respect due to his cloth*). **b** (prec. by *the*) the clergy. □ **cloth book** a children's book made out of cloth. **cloth-cap** relating to or associated with the working class. **cloth-eared** *colloq.* somewhat deaf. **cloth of gold** (or **silver**) tissue of gold (or silver) threads interwoven with silk or wool. [OE *clāth*, of unkn. orig.]

■ **1** fabric, material, textile. **5 b** (*the cloth*) the clergy, the (religious) ministry, the priesthood.

clothe / klōth/ *v.tr.* (*past* and *past part.* **clothed** or *formal* **clad**) **1** put clothes on; provide with clothes. **2** cover as with clothes or a cloth. **3** (foll. by *with*) endue (with qualities, etc.). [OE: rel. to CLOTH]

■ **1** dress, garb, outfit, fit out *or* up, accoutre, esp. *Brit.* kit out *or* up, *archaic* apparel, *formal* attire. **2** cover, garb, robe, sheathe, *formal* attire. **3** endow, endue, invest, caparison, provide, supply, furnish.

clothes / klōz, klōthz/ *n.pl.* **1** garments worn to cover the body and limbs. **2** bedclothes. □ **clothes moth** any moth of the family Tineidae, with a larva destructive to wool, fur, etc. **clothes-peg** *Brit.* = CLOTHESPIN. [OE *clāthas* pl. of *clāth* CLOTH]

■ **1** clothing, wear, dress, garments, wardrobe, vestment(s), *archaic* raiment, *colloq.* togs, gear, *formal* attire, apparel, *sl.* threads, duds, *Brit. sl.* clobber.

clotheshorse / klōzhawrs, klōthz-/ *n.* **1** a frame for airing washed clothes. **2** *colloq.* an affectedly fashionable person.

clothesline /klōzhawrs, klōthz-/ *n.* a rope or wire, etc., on which washed clothes are hung to dry.

clothespin / klōzpin, klōthz-/ *n.* a clip or forked device for securing clothes to a clothesline.

clothier / klōtheeər/ *n.* a seller of clothes. [ME *clother* f. CLOTH]

■ see TAILOR *n.*

clothing / klōthing/ *n.* clothes collectively.

cloture / klōchər/ *n. & v.* ● *n.* the legislative procedure for ending debate and taking a vote. ● *v.tr.* apply cloture. [F *clôture* f. OF CLOSURE]

clou /kloo/ n. **1** the point of greatest interest; the chief attraction. **2** the central idea. [F, = nail]

cloud /klowd/ n. & v. ● n. **1** a visible mass of condensed watery vapor floating in the atmosphere high above the general level of the ground. **2** a mass of smoke or dust. **3** (foll. by of) a great number of insects, birds, etc., moving together. **4 a** a state of gloom, trouble, or suspicion. **b** a frowning or depressed look (a cloud on his brow). **5** a local dimness or a vague patch of color in or on a liquid or a transparent body. **6** an unsubstantial or fleeting thing. **7** obscurity. ● v. **1** tr. cover or darken with clouds or gloom or trouble. **2** intr. (often foll. by over, up) become overcast or gloomy. **3** tr. make unclear. **4** tr. variegate with vague patches of color. □ **cloud-castle** Brit. a daydream. **cloud chamber** a device containing vapor for tracking the paths of charged particles, X rays, and gamma rays. **clouded leopard** a mottled arboreal S. Asian feline, Neofelis nebulosa. **cloud-hopping** movement of an aircraft from cloud to cloud esp. for concealment. **in the clouds 1** unreal; imaginary; mystical. **2** (of a person) abstracted; inattentive. **on cloud nine** (or Brit. **seven**) colloq. extremely happy. **under a cloud** out of favor, discredited; under suspicion. **with one's head in the clouds** daydreaming; unrealistic. □□ **cloudless** adj. **cloudlessly** adv. **cloudlet** n. [OE clūd mass of rock or earth, prob. rel. to CLOD]

■ n. **1, 2** see VAPOR n. **1**. **3** see SWARM[1] n. **1–3**. ● v. **1** see SHADE v. **1**, **2**. **2** see FOG[1] v. **1a**, **3** see MUDDY v. □ **in the clouds** see ABSENTMINDED. **on cloud nine** see HAPPY **1**. □□ **cloudless** see CLEAR adj. **2**.

cloudberry /klówdberee/ n. (pl. **-ies**) a small mountain bramble, Rubus chamaemorus, with a white flower and an orange-colored fruit.

cloudburst /klówdbərst/ n. a sudden violent rainstorm.

■ see STORM n. **1**.

cloud-cuckoo-land /klowdkookooland, -kookoo-/ n. a fanciful or ideal place. [transl. of Gk Nephelokokkugia f. nephelē cloud + kokkux cuckoo (in Aristophanes' Birds)]

cloudland /klówdland/ a Utopia or fairyland.

■ see UTOPIA.

cloudscape /klówdskayp/ n. **1** a picturesque grouping of clouds. **2** a picture or view of clouds. [CLOUD n., after landscape]

cloudy /klówdee/ adj. (**cloudier, cloudiest**) **1 a** (of the sky) covered with clouds; overcast. **b** (of weather) characterized by clouds. **2** not transparent; unclear. □□ **cloudily** adv. **cloudiness** n.

■ **1** see DULL adj. **3**. **2** see OPAQUE adj. **1, 2**.

clough /kluf/ n. dial. a steep valley usu. with a torrent bed; a ravine. [OE clōh f. Gmc]

■ see RAVINE.

clout /klowt/ n. & v. ● n. **1** a heavy blow. **2** colloq. influence; power of effective action esp. in politics or business. **3** dial. a piece of cloth or clothing (cast not a clout). **4** Archery hist. a piece of canvas on a frame, used as a mark. **5** a nail with a large, flat head. **6** a patch. ● v.tr. **1** hit hard. **2** mend with a patch. [OE clūt, rel. to CLEAT, CLOT]

■ n. **1** see BLOW[2] **1**. **2** see INFLUENCE n. ● v. **1** see HIT v. **1a**.

clove[1] /klōv/ n. **1 a** a dried flower bud of a tropical plant, Eugenia aromatica, used as a pungent aromatic spice. **b** this plant. **2** (in full **clove gillyflower** or **clove pink**) a clove-scented pink, Dianthus caryophyllus, the original of the carnation and other double pinks. [ME f. OF clou (de girofle) nail (of gillyflower), from its shape, GILLYFLOWER being orig. the name of the spice; later applied to the similarly scented pink]

clove[2] /klōv/ n. any of the small bulbs making up a compound bulb of garlic, shallot, etc. [OE clufu, rel. to CLEAVE[1]]

clove[3] past of CLEAVE[1].

clove hitch n. a knot by which a rope is secured by passing it twice around a spar or rope that it crosses at right angles. [old past part. of CLEAVE[1], as showing parallel separate lines]

cloven /klóv'n/ adj. split; partly divided. □ **cloven hoof** (or **foot**) the divided hoof of ruminant quadrupeds (e.g., oxen, sheep, goats); also ascribed to the god Pan, and so to the Devil. **show the cloven hoof** reveal one's evil nature. □□ **cloven-footed** /-footid/ adj. **cloven-hoofed** /-hooft/ adj. [past part. of CLEAVE[1]]

clover /klóvər/ n. any leguminous fodder plant of the genus Trifolium, having dense flower heads and leaves each consisting of usu. three leaflets. □ **in clover** in ease and luxury. [OE clāfre f. Gmc]

■ □ **in clover** see OPULENT **1**.

cloverleaf /klóvərleef/ n. a junction of roads intersecting at different levels with connecting sections forming the pattern of a four-leaf clover.

clown /klown/ n. & v. ● n. **1** a comic entertainer, esp. in a pantomime or circus, usu. with traditional costume and makeup. **2** a silly, foolish, or playful person. **3** archaic a rustic. ● v. **1** intr. (often foll. by about, around) behave like a clown; act foolishly or playfully. **2** tr. perform (a part, an action, etc.) like a clown. □□ **clownery** n. **clownish** adj. **clownishly** adv. **clownishness** n. [16th c.: perh. of LG orig.]

■ n. **1** jester, fool, zany, comic, comedian, comedienne, funny man or woman, merry andrew. **2** buffoon, clod, clodhopper, fool, colloq. lummox, sl. jerk. **3** boor, rustic, yahoo, oaf, lout, bumpkin, provincial, peasant, yokel, colloq. hick, colloq. often derog. hillbilly. ● v. **1** (clown around or about) fool (around or about), play or act the fool, horse around or about, mess around or about, engage in high jinks, cut up, colloq. cut (up) didoes.

cloy /kloy/ v.tr. (usu. foll. by with) satiate or sicken with an excess of sweetness, richness, etc. □□ **cloyingly** adv. [ME f. obs. acloy f. AF acloyer, OF encloyer f. Rmc: cf. ENCLAVE]

■ see SATE **2**.

cloze /klōz/ n. the exercise of supplying a word that has been omitted from a passage as a test of readability or comprehension (usu. attrib.: cloze test). [CLOSURE]

CLU abbr. chartered life underwriter.

club /klub/ n. & v. ● n. **1** a heavy stick with a thick end, used as a weapon, etc. **2** a stick used in a game, esp. a stick with a head used in golf. **3 a** a playing card of a suit denoted by a black trefoil. **b** (in pl.) this suit. **4** an association of persons united by a common interest, usu. meeting periodically for a shared activity (tennis club; yacht club). **5 a** an organization or premises offering members social amenities, meals, and temporary residence, etc. **b** a nightclub. **6** an organization offering subscribers certain benefits (book club). **7** a group of persons, nations, etc., having something in common. **8** = CLUBHOUSE. **9** a structure or organ, esp. in a plant, with a knob at the end. ● v. (**clubbed, clubbing**) **1** tr. beat with or as with a club. **2** intr. (foll. by together, with) combine for joint action, esp. making up a sum of money for a purpose. **3** tr. contribute (money, etc.) to a common stock. □ **club sandwich** a sandwich with two layers of filling between three slices of toast or bread. **club soda** = SODA n. **2**. **in the club** Brit. sl. pregnant. □□ **clubber** n. [ME f. ON klubba assim. form of klumba club, rel. to CLUMP]

■ n. **1** cudgel, bat, blackjack, bludgeon, billy, truncheon, lathi, Austral. & NZ waddy, Brit. colloq. cosh, hist. mace. **4** association, society, organization, fraternity, sorority, fellowship, brotherhood, sisterhood, federation, union, guild, lodge. **5 b** nightclub, cabaret, colloq. nightspot. **7** alliance, league, order, consortium, company, federation. ● v. **1** beat, cudgel, bludgeon, bat, belabor, baste, thrash, trounce, colloq. lambaste. **2** (club together) band or join or league (together), team (up), join forces, combine, associate, confederate, cooperate. **3** pool.

clubbable /klúbəbəl/ adj. sociable; fit for membership of a club. □□ **clubbability** /-bílitee/ n. **clubbableness** n.

clubby /klúbee/ adj. (**clubbier, clubbiest**) sociable; friendly.

/. . ./ **pronunciation**	● **part of speech**
□ **phrases, idioms, and compounds**	
□□ **derivatives**	■ **synonym section**
cross-references appear in SMALL CAPITALS or italics	

■ see FRIENDLY *adj.* 2.

clubfoot /klúbfŏŏt/ *n.* a congenitally deformed foot. □□ **club-footed** *adj.*

clubhouse /klúbhows/ *n.* the premises used by a club.

clubman /klúbmən, -man/ *n.* (*pl.* **-men**; *fem.* **-woman**, *pl.* **-women**) a member of one or more social clubs.

clubmoss /klúbmaws, -mos/ *n.* any pteridophyte of the family Lycopodiaceae, bearing upright spikes of spore cases.

clubroot /klúbrŏŏt/ *n.* a disease of cabbages, etc., with swelling at the base of the stem.

cluck /kluk/ *n. & v.* ● *n.* **1** a guttural cry like that of a hen. **2** *sl.* a silly or foolish person (*dumb cluck*). ● *v.intr.* emit a cluck or clucks. [imit.]

clue /klŏŏ/ *n. & v.* ● *n.* **1** a fact or idea that serves as a guide, or suggests a line of inquiry, in a problem or investigation. **2** a piece of evidence, etc., in the detection of a crime. **3** a verbal formula serving as a hint as to what is to be inserted in a crossword. **4 a** the thread of a story. **b** a train of thought. ● *v.tr.* (**clues, clued, clueing** or **cluing**) provide a clue to. □ **clue in** (or *Brit.* **up**) *sl.* inform. **not have a clue** *colloq.* be ignorant or incompetent. [var. of CLEW]

■ *n.* **1, 2** hint, indication, pointer, lead, trace, intimation, suggestion; inkling, idea; key, answer, indicator. **4 a** see THREAD *n.* 3. □ **clue in** see INFORM 1. **not have a clue** see IGNORANT 1a, INCOMPETENT *adj.*

clueless /klŏŏlis/ *adj. colloq.* ignorant; stupid. □□ **cluelessly** *adv.* **cluelessness** *n.*

clump /klump/ *n. & v.* ● *n.* **1** (foll. by *of*) a cluster of plants, esp. trees or shrubs. **2** an agglutinated mass of blood cells, etc. **3** a thick extra sole on a boot or shoe. ● *v.* **1 a** *intr.* form a clump. **b** *tr.* heap or plant together. **2** *intr.* (also **clomp** /klomp/) walk with heavy tread. **3** *tr. colloq.* hit. □□ **clumpy** *adj.* (**clumpier, clumpiest**). [MLG *klumpe*, MDu. *klompe*: see CLUB]

■ *n.* **1** bunch, cluster; thicket. **2** lump, mass, clot, clod, glob, *sl.* gob. ● *v.* **1 b** lump, mass, clot, heap, collect, gather, bunch, pile. **3** see HIT *v.* 1a.

clumsy /klúmzee/ *adj.* (**clumsier, clumsiest**) **1** awkward in movement or shape; ungainly. **2** difficult to handle or use. **3** tactless. □□ **clumsily** *adv.* **clumsiness** *n.* [obs. *clumse* be numb with cold (prob. f. Scand.)]

■ **1** awkward, ungainly, ungraceful, gawky, maladroit, unhandy, unskillful, inept, bungling, bumbling, cloddish, uncoordinated, lubberly, oafish, gauche, *colloq.* butterfingered, ham-fisted, ham-handed, *Brit. colloq.* cack-handed. **2** see UNWIELDY. **3** see TACTLESS.

clung *past and past part.* of CLING.

clunk /klungk/ *n. & v.* ● *n.* a dull sound as of thick pieces of metal meeting. ● *v.intr.* make such a sound. [imit.]

■ *n.* see THUD *n.* ● *v.* see THUD *v.*

cluster /klústər/ *n. & v.* ● *n.* **1** a close group or bunch of similar things growing together. **2** a close group or swarm of people, animals, faint stars, gems, etc. **3** a group of successive consonants or vowels. ● *v.* **1** *tr.* bring into a cluster or clusters. **2** *intr.* be or come into a cluster or clusters. **3** *intr.* (foll. by *around*) gather; congregate. □ **cluster bomb** an antipersonnel bomb spraying pellets on impact. **cluster pine** a Mediterranean pine *Pinus pinaster* with clustered cones: also called PINASTER. [OE *clyster*: cf. CLOT]

■ *n.* **1, 2** collection, bunch, clutch, tuft, bundle, knot; group, swarm, body, band, company, gathering, crowd, assembly, congregation, throng, flock, assemblage. ● *v.* **2, 3** collect, gather, bunch, group, band, congregate, assemble, accumulate, mass, aggregate; crowd, throng.

clustered /klústərd/ *adj.* **1** growing in or brought into a cluster. **2** *Archit.* (of pillars, columns, or shafts) several close together, or disposed around or half detached from a pier.

clutch[1] /kluch/ *v. & n.* ● *v.* **1** *tr.* seize eagerly; grip tightly. **2** *intr.* (foll. by *at*) snatch suddenly. ● *n.* **1 a** a tight grasp. **b** (foll. by *at*) grasping. **2** (in *pl.*) grasping hands, esp. as representing a cruel or relentless grasp or control. **3 a** (in a motor vehicle) a device for connecting and disconnecting the engine to the transmission. **b** the pedal operating this. **c** an arrangement for connecting or disconnecting working parts of a machine. **4** a critical situation in a game, etc. (*always comes through in the clutch*). □ **clutch bag** a slim, flat handbag without handles. [ME *clucche, clicche* f. OE *clyccan* crook, clench, f. Gmc]

■ *v.* **1** seize, snatch, grab, grasp, take *or* lay hold of; hold, grip. **2** snatch, grab, grasp, pluck. ● *n.* **1 a** grasp, hold, grip, clasp, embrace, lock. **2** (*clutches*) grasp, hold, *literary* thralldom; embrace; domination, dominance, influence, control, power, possession.

clutch[2] /kluch/ *n.* **1** a set of eggs for hatching. **2** a brood of chickens. [18th c.: prob. S.Engl. var. of *cletch* f. *cleck* to hatch f. ON *klekja*, assoc. with CLUTCH[1]]

clutter /klútər/ *n. & v.* ● *n.* **1** a crowded and untidy collection of things. **2** an untidy state. ● *v.tr.* (often foll. by *up*, *with*) crowd untidily; fill with clutter. [partly var. of *clotter* coagulate, partly assoc. with CLUSTER, CLATTER]

■ *n.* **1** mess, litter, jumble, mishmash, olla podrida, olio, confusion, hash, gallimaufry, hodgepodge, muddle, farrago, medley. **2** confusion, tangle; see also CHAOS 1a. ● *v.* mess up, litter, strew.

Clydesdale /klídzdayl/ *n.* **1 a** a horse of a heavy powerful breed, used as draft horses. **b** this breed. **2** a kind of small terrier. [orig. bred near the *Clyde* river in Scotland: see DALE]

clypeus /klípeeəs/ *n.* (*pl.* **clypei** /-pee-ī/) the hard protective area of an insect's head. □□ **clypeal** *adj.* **clypeate** *adj.* [L, = round shield]

clyster /klístər/ *n. & v. archaic* ● *n.* an enema. ● *v.tr.* treat with an enema. [ME f. OF *clystere* or f. L f. Gk *klustēr* syringe f. *kluzō* wash out]

Cm *symb. Chem.* the element curium.

cm *abbr.* centimeter(s).

Cmdr. *abbr.* commander.

Cmdre. *abbr.* commodore.

CMG *abbr.* (in the UK) Companion (of the Order) of St. Michael and St. George.

cnr. *abbr.* corner.

CNS *abbr.* central nervous system.

CO *abbr.* **1** Colorado (in official postal use). **2** commanding officer. **3** conscientious objector. **4** carbon monoxide.

Co *symb. Chem.* the element cobalt.

Co. *abbr.* **1** company. **2** county. □ **and Co.** /kō/ *Brit. colloq.* and the rest of them; and similar things.

c/o *abbr.* care of.

co- /kō/ *prefix* **1** added to: **a** nouns, with the sense 'joint, mutual, common' (*coauthor; coequality*). **b** adjectives and adverbs, with the sense 'jointly, mutually' (*cobelligerent; coequal; coequally*). **c** verbs, with the sense 'together with another or others' (*cooperate; coauthor*). **2** *Math.* **a** of the complement of an angle (*cosine*). **b** the complement of (*colatitude; coset*). [orig. a form of COM-]

coach /kōch/ *n. & v.* ● *n.* **1** a passenger bus, usu. comfortably equipped for longer journeys. **2** a railroad car. **3** a horse-drawn carriage, usu. closed, esp. a stagecoach. **4 a** an instructor or trainer in sport. **b** a private tutor. **5** economy-class seating in an aircraft. **6** *Austral.* a docile cow or bullock used as a decoy to attract wild cattle. ● *v.* **1** *tr.* **a** train or teach (a pupil, sports team, etc.) as a coach. **b** give hints to; prime with facts. **2** *intr.* travel by stagecoach (*in the old coaching days*). □ **coach-built** *Brit.* (of automobile bodies) individually built by craftsmen. **coach house** an outbuilding for carriages. **coach station** *Brit.* a stopping place for a number of tour buses, usu. with buildings and amenities. [F *coche* f. Magyar *kocsi* (adj.) f. Kocs in Hungary]

■ *n.* **1** bus, motor coach, *formal* omnibus, *Brit. hist.* charabanc. **4** tutor, trainer, instructor, *colloq.* crammer; see also TEACHER. ● *v.* **1** tutor, train, instruct, guide, direct, drill, prepare, prompt, school, exercise, *colloq.* cram.

coachman /kōchmən/ *n.* (*pl.* **-men**) the driver of a horse-drawn carriage.

coachwood /kōchwŏŏd/ *n. Austral.* any tree, esp. *Ceratopetalum apetalum*, with close-grained wood suitable for cabinetmaking.

coachwork /kōchwərk/ *n.* the bodywork of a road or rail vehicle.

coadjutor /kō-ájətər, kő̄əjŏŏ-/ *n.* an assistant, esp. an assistant bishop. [ME f. OF *coadjuteur* f. LL *coadjutor* (as CO-, *adjutor* f. *adjuvare -jut-* help)]

■ see AIDE.

coagulant /kō-ágyələnt/ *n.* a substance that produces coagulation.

coagulate /kō-ágyəlayt/ *v.tr.* & *intr.* **1** change from a fluid to a solid or semisolid state. **2** clot; curdle. **3** set; solidify. □□ **coagulable** *adj.* **coagulative** /-láytiv, -lətiv/ *adj.* **coagulator** *n.* [ME f. L *coagulare* f. *coagulum* rennet]

■ congeal, gel, clot, curdle, *colloq.* jell; set, solidify.

coagulation /kō̄-agyəláyshən/ *n.* the process by which a liquid changes to a semisolid mass. [as COAGULATE]

coagulum /kō-ágyələm/ *n.* (*pl.* **coagula** /-lə/ or **coagulums**) a mass of coagulated matter. [L: see COAGULATE]

coal /kōl/ *n.* & *v.* ● *n.* **1 a** a hard black or blackish rock, mainly carbonized plant matter, found in underground seams and used as a fuel and in the manufacture of gas, tar, etc. **b** *Brit.* a piece of this for burning. **2** a red-hot piece of coal, wood, etc., in a fire. ● *v.* **1** *intr.* take in a supply of coal. **2** *tr.* put coal into (an engine, fire, etc.). □ **coal bed** a stratum of coal. **coal-black** completely black. **coal-fired** heated or driven by coal. **coal gas** mixed gases extracted from coal and used for lighting and heating. **coal measures** a series of rocks formed by seams of coal with intervening strata. **coal mine** a mine in which coal is dug. **coal miner** a worker in a coal mine. **coal oil** petroleum or kerosene. **coal scuttle** a container for coal to supply a domestic fire. **coal seam** a stratum of coal suitable for mining. **coals to Newcastle** something brought or sent to a place where it is already plentiful. **coal tar** a thick, black, oily liquid distilled from coal and used as a source of benzene. **haul** (or **call**) **over the coals** reprimand. □□ **coaly** *adj.* [OE *col* f. Gmc]

coaler /kṓlər/ *n.* a ship, etc., transporting coal.

coalesce /kṓəlés/ *v.intr.* **1** come together and form one whole. **2** combine in a coalition. □□ **coalescence** *n.* **coalescent** *adj.* [L *coalescere* (as CO-, *alescere alit-* grow f. *alere* nourish)]

■ see MERGE.

coalface /kṓlfays/ *n.* an exposed surface of coal in a mine.

coalfield /kṓlfeeld/ *n.* an extensive area with strata containing coal.

coalfish /kṓlfish/ *n.* = SAITHE.

coalhole /kṓlhōl/ *n.* **1** a hole, as from a sidewalk, leading to a coal bin. **2** *Brit.* (as **coal-hole**) a compartment for storing coal.

coalition /kṓəlíshən/ *n.* **1** *Polit.* a temporary alliance for combined action, esp. of distinct parties forming a government, or of nations. **2** fusion into one whole. □□ **coalitionist** *n.* [med.L *coalitio* (as COALESCE)]

■ **1** see ALLIANCE 1.

coalman /kṓlmən/ *n.* (*pl.* **-men**) a person who carries or delivers coal.

Coalsack /kṓlsak/ *n. Astron.* a black patch in the Milky Way, esp. the one near the Southern Cross.

coaming /kṓming/ *n.* a raised border around the hatches, etc., of a ship to keep out water. [17th c.: orig. unkn.]

coarse /kawrs/ *adj.* **1 a** rough or loose in texture or grain; made of large particles. **b** (of a person's features) rough or large. **2** lacking refinement or delicacy; crude; obscene (*coarse humor*). **3** rude; uncivil. **4** inferior; common. □ **coarse fish** *Brit.* any freshwater fish other than salmon and trout. □□ **coarsely** *adv.* **coarseness** *n.* **coarsish** *adj.* [ME: orig. unkn.]

■ **1 a** rough, uneven, scratchy, prickly, bristly; crude, rough-hewn, unfinished, unrefined. **b** rough, thickset, rough-hewn, heavy, large, crude. **2** boorish, loutish, crude, unpolished, rough, uncouth, unrefined; rude, indecent, improper, indelicate, obscene, lewd, vulgar, gross, smutty, dirty, filthy, foul, offensive, lascivious, ribald, bawdy; foulmouthed. **3** ill-mannered, impolite, uncivil; see also RUDE 1. **4** inferior, common, low-quality, second-rate, shoddy, tawdry, trashy.

coarsen /káwrsən/ *v.tr.* & *intr.* make or become coarse.

coast /kōst/ *n.* & *v.* ● *n.* **1 a** the border of the land near the sea; the seashore. **b** (**the Coast**) the Pacific coast of the US. **2 a** a rīn, usu. downhill, on a bicycle without pedaling or in a motor vehicle without using the engine. **b** a toboggan slide or slope. ● *v.intr.* **1** ride or move, usu. downhill, without use of power; freewheel. **2** make progress without much effort. **3** slide down a hill on a toboggan or other sled. **4 a** sail along the coast. **b** trade between ports on the same coast. □ **the coast is clear** there is no danger of being observed or caught. **coast-to-coast** across an island or continent. □□ **coastal** *adj.* [ME f. OF *coste, costeier* f. L *costa* rib, flank, side]

■ *n.* **1 a** seaside, seashore, shore, beach, littoral, coastline, seaboard, *rhet. or poet.* strand. ● *v.* **1** glide, skim, slide, sail; freewheel. **2** freewheel.

coaster /kṓstər/ *n.* **1** a ship that travels along the coast from port to port. **2** a small tray or mat for a bottle or glass.

Coast Guard /kṓst gaard/ *n.* the U.S. military service that protects coastal waters, aids shipping and pleasure craft, and enforces maritime laws.

coastline /kṓstlin/ *n.* the line of the seashore, esp. with regard to its shape (*a rugged coastline*).

coastwise /kṓstwiz/ *adj.* & *adv.* along, following, or connected with the coast.

coat /kōt/ *n.* & *v.* ● *n.* **1** an outer garment with sleeves and often extending below the hips; an overcoat or jacket. **2 a** an animal's fur, hair, etc. **b** *Physiol.* a structure, esp. a membrane, enclosing or lining an organ. **c** a skin, rind, or husk. **d** a layer of a bulb, etc. **3 a** a layer or covering. **b** a covering of paint, etc., laid on a surface at one time. ● *v.tr.* **1** (usu. foll. by *with, in*) **a** apply a coat of paint, etc., to; provide with a layer or covering. **b** (as **coated** *adj.*) covered with. **2** (of paint, etc.) form a covering to. □ **coat armor** coats of arms. **coat hanger** see HANGER[1]. **coat of arms** the heraldic bearings or shield of a person, family, or corporation. **coat of mail** a jacket of mail armor (see MAIL[2]). □□ **coated** *adj.* (also in *comb.*). [ME f. OF *cote* f. Rmc f. Frank., of unkn. orig.]

■ *n.* **1** overcoat, topcoat, coatee, esp. *Brit.* greatcoat; jacket, anorak, parka. **2 c** see SKIN *n.* 4. **3** coating, layer, covering, film. ● *v.* **1 a** cover, paint, spread. **b** (coated) see SPREAD *v.* 4a.

coatdress /kṓtdres/ *n.* a woman's tailored dress resembling a coat.

coati /kō-aátee/ *n.* (*pl.* **coatis**) any raccoonlike, flesh-eating mammal of the genus *Nasua*, with a long, flexible snout and a long, usu. ringed tail. [Tupi f. *cua* belt + *tim* nose]

coatimundi /kō̄-aateemúndee/ *n.* (*pl.* **coatimundis**) = COATI. [as COATI + Tupi *mondi* solitary]

coating /kṓting/ *n.* **1** a thin layer or covering of paint, etc. **2** material for making coats.

coattail /kṓttayl/ *n.* **1** the back flap of a man's jacket or coat. **2** (in *pl.*) **a** the back skirts of a dress coat, cutaway, etc. **b** *Polit.* (of a party candidate) popularity such as to attract votes for other party candidates.

coauthor /kō̄-áwthər/ *n.* & *v.* ● *n.* a joint author. ● *v.tr.* be a joint author of.

coax /kōks/ *v.tr.* **1** (usu. foll. by *into*, or *to* + infin.) persuade (a person) gradually or by flattery. **2** (foll. by *out of*) obtain (a thing from a person) by coaxing. **3** manipulate (a thing) carefully or slowly. □□ **coaxer** *n.* **coaxingly** *adv.* [16th c.: f. 'make a *cokes* of' f. obs. *cokes* simpleton, of unkn. orig.]

■ **1, 2** persuade, wheedle, cajole, beguile, charm, inveigle, manipulate, *colloq.* jolly.

coaxial /kō-ákseeəl/ *adj.* **1** having a common axis. **2** *Electr.* (of a cable or line) transmitting by means of two concentric conductors separated by an insulator. □□ **coaxially** *adv.*

cob[1] /kob/ *n.* **1** = *corn cob* (see CORN[2]). **2** a sturdy riding or driving horse with short legs. **3** a male swan. **4** *Brit.* a roundish lump, loaf of bread, etc. [ME: orig. unkn.]

cob[2] /kob/ *n. Brit.* a material for walls, made from compressed

/.../ **pronunciation**	● **part of speech**
□ **phrases, idioms, and compounds**	
□□ **derivatives**	■ **synonym section**
cross-references appear in SMALL CAPITALS or *italics*	

earth, clay, or chalk reinforced with straw. [17th c.: orig. unkn.]

cobalt /kṓbawlt/ *n. Chem.* a silvery-white, magnetic metallic element occurring naturally as a mineral in combination with sulfur and arsenic, and used in many alloys. ¶ Symb.: **Co.** □ **cobalt blue 1** a pigment containing a cobalt salt. **2** the deep-blue color of this. □□ **cobaltic** /kōbáwltik/ *adj.* **cobaltous** /kōbáwltəs/ *adj.* [G *Kobalt*, etc., prob. = KOBOLD in mines]

cobber /kóbər/ *n. Austral. & NZ colloq.* a companion or friend. [19th c.: perh. rel. to E dial. *cob* take a liking to]

cobble[1] /kóbəl/ *n. & v.* ● *n.* **1** (in full **cobblestone**) a small rounded stone of a size used for paving. **2** (in *pl.*) *Brit.* coal in lumps of this size. ● *v.tr.* pave with cobbles. [ME *cobel(-ston)*, f. COB[1]]

cobble[2] /kóbəl/ *v.tr.* **1** mend or patch up (esp. shoes). **2** (often foll. by *together*) join or assemble roughly. [back-form. f. COBBLER]

cobbler /kóblər/ *n.* **1** a person who mends shoes, esp. professionally. **2** an iced drink of wine, etc., sugar, and lemon (*sherry cobbler*). **3** a fruit pie with a rich, thick biscuit crust usu. only on the top. **4** (in *pl.*) *Brit. sl.* nonsense. **5** *Austral. & NZ sl.* the last sheep to be shorn. [ME, of unkn. orig.: sense 4 f. rhyming sl. *cobbler's awls* = *balls*: sense 5 with pun on LAST[3]]

cobelligerent /kṓbilíjərənt/ *n. & adj.* ● *n.* any of two or more nations engaged in war as allies. ● *adj.* of or as a cobelligerent. □□ **cobelligerence** /-rəns/ *n.* **cobelligerency** *n.*

coble /kṓbəl/ *n.* a flat-bottomed fishing boat in Scotland and NE England. [OE, perh. f. Celt.]

COBOL /kṓbawl/ *n. Computing* a programming language designed for use in commerce. [*common business oriented language*]

cobra /kṓbrə/ *n.* any venomous snake of the genus *Naja*, native to Africa and Asia, with a neck dilated like a hood when excited. [Port. f. L *colubra* snake]

cobweb /kóbweb/ *n.* **1 a** a fine network of threads spun by a spider from a liquid secreted by it, used to trap insects, etc., **b** the thread of this. **2** anything compared with a cobweb, esp. in flimsiness of texture. **3** a trap or insidious entanglement. **4** (in *pl.*) a state of languishing; fustiness. □□ **cobwebbed** *adj.* **cobwebby** *adj.* [ME *cop(pe)web* f. obs. *coppe* spider]

■ **1** spiderweb.

coca /kṓkə/ *n.* **1** a S. American shrub, *Erythroxylum coca.* **2** its dried leaves, chewed as a stimulant. [Sp. f. Quechua *cuca*]

Coca-Cola /kṓkəkṓlə/ *n. propr.* a carbonated soft drink flavored with extract of cola nuts.

cocaine /kōkáyn/ *n.* a drug derived from coca or prepared synthetically, used as a local anesthetic and as a stimulant. [COCA + -INE[4]]

coccidiosis /kóksideeṓsis/ *n.* a disease of birds and mammals caused by any of various parasitic protozoa, esp. of the genus *Eimeria*, affecting the intestine. [*coccidium* (mod.L f. Gk *kokkis* dimin. of *kokkos* berry) + -OSIS]

coccus /kókəs/ *n.* (*pl.* **cocci** /kóksī, kókī/) any spherical or roughly spherical bacterium. □□ **coccal** *adj.* **coccoid** *adj.* [mod.L f. Gk *kokkos* berry]

coccyx /kóksiks/ *n.* (*pl.* **coccyges** /-sijeez/ or **coccyxes**) the small triangular bone at the base of the spinal column in humans and some apes. □□ **coccygeal** /koksíjeeəl/ *adj.* [L f. Gk *kokkux -ugos* cuckoo (from being shaped like its bill)]

Cochin /kṓchin/ *n.* (in full **Cochin China**) **1** a fowl of an Asian breed with feathery legs. **2** this breed. [*Cochin China* in Vietnam]

cochineal /kóchineel/ *n.* **1** a scarlet dye used esp. for coloring food. **2** the dried bodies of the female of the Mexican insect, *Dactylopius coccus*, yielding this. [F *cochenille* or Sp. *cochinilla* f. L *coccinus* scarlet f. Gk *kokkos* berry]

cochlea /kókleeə/ *n.* (*pl.* **cochleas** or **cochleae** /-lee-ee/) the spiral cavity of the internal ear. □□ **cochlear** *adj.* [L, = snail shell, f. Gk *kokhlias*]

■ □□ **cochlear** see SPIRAL *adj.*

cock[1] /kok/ *n. & v.* ● *n.* **1** a male bird, esp. of a domestic fowl. **2** *coarse sl.* the penis. **3** *Brit. sl.* (usu. **old cock** as a form of address) a friend; a fellow. **4** *Brit. sl.* nonsense. ¶ In senses 2, 4 usually considered a taboo word. **5 a** a firing lever in a gun which can be raised to be released by the trigger. **b** the cocked position of this (*at full cock*). **6** a tap or valve controlling flow. ● *v.tr.* **1** raise or make upright or erect. **2** turn or move (the eye or ear) attentively or knowingly. **3** set aslant, or turn up the brim of (a hat). **4** raise the cock of (a gun). □ **at half cock** only partly ready. **cock-a-doodle-doo** a cock's crow. **cock-and-bull story** an absurd or incredible account. **cocked hat** a brimless triangular hat pointed at the front, back, and top. **cock-of-the-rock** a S. American bird, *Rupicola rupicola*, having a crest and bright orange plumage. **cock of the walk** a dominant or arrogant person. **cock of the wood** (or **woods**) **1** a capercaillie. **2** a pileated woodpecker. **cock a snook** = *thumb one's nose* (see THUMB). **cock up** *Brit. sl.* bungle; make a mess of. **cock-up** *n. Brit. sl.* a muddle or mistake. **knock into a cocked hat** defeat utterly. [OE *cocc* and OF *coq* prob. f. med.L *coccus*]

■ *n.* **6** see TAP[1] *n.* 1. □ **cock-and-bull story** see YARN *n.* 2.

cock[2] /kok/ *n. & v.* ● *n.* a small pile of hay, straw, etc., with vertical sides and a rounded top. ● *v.tr.* pile into cocks. [ME, perh. of Scand. orig.]

■ *n.* see STACK *n.* 1.

cockade /kokáyd/ *n.* a rosette, etc., worn in a hat as a badge of office or party, or as part of a livery. □□ **cockaded** *adj.* [F *cocarde* orig. in *bonnet à la coquarde*, f. fem. of obs. *coquard* saucy f. *coq* COCK[1]]

cock-a-hoop /kókəhoōp/ *adj. & adv.* esp. *Brit.* ● *adj.* exultant; crowing boastfully. ● *adv.* exultantly. [16th c.: orig. in phr. *set cock a hoop* denoting some action preliminary to hard drinking]

cock-a-leekie /kókəleékee/ *n.* (also **cocky-leeky** /kókee-/) a soup traditionally made in Scotland with boiled chicken and leeks. [COCK[1] + LEEK]

cockalorum /kókəláwrəm/ *n. colloq.* a self-important little person. [18th c.: arbitr. f. COCK[1]]

cockatiel /kókəteel/ *n.* (also **cockateel**) *Austral.* a small, delicately colored crested parrot, *Nymphicus hollandicus*. [Du. *kaketielje*]

cockatoo /kókətoō/ *n.* **1** any of several parrots of the family Cacatuinae, having powerful beaks and erectile crests. **2** *Austral. & NZ colloq.* a small farmer. [Du. *kaketoe* f. Malay *kakatua*, assim. to COCK[1]]

cockatrice /kókətris, -tris/ *n.* **1** = BASILISK 1. **2** *Heraldry* a fabulous animal, a cock with a serpent's tail. [ME f. OF *cocatris* f. L *calcare* tread, track, rendering Gk *ikhneumōn* tracker: see ICHNEUMON]

cockboat /kókbōt/ *n.* a small boat, esp. one used as a ship's tender. [obs. *cock* small boat (f. OF *coque*) + BOAT]

cockchafer /kókchayfər/ *n.* a large nocturnal beetle, *Melolontha melolontha*, which feeds on leaves and whose larva feeds on roots of crops, etc. [perh. f. COCK[1] as expressing size or vigor + CHAFER]

cockcrow /kókkrō/ *n.* dawn.

■ see DAWN *n.* 1.

cocker /kókər/ *n.* (in full **cocker spaniel**) **1** a small spaniel of a breed with a silky coat. **2** this breed. [as COCK[1], from use in hunting woodcocks, etc.]

cockerel /kókrəl/ *n.* a young cock. [ME: dimin. of COCK[1]]

cockeyed /kókíd/ *adj. colloq.* **1** crooked; askew; not level. **2** (of a scheme, etc.) absurd; not practical. **3** drunk. **4** squinting. [19th c.: app. f. COCK[1] + EYE]

■ **1** see LOPSIDED. **2** see STUPID *adj.* 2. **3** see DRUNK *adj.* 1.

cockfight /kókfīt/ *n.* a fight between cocks as sport. □□ **cockfighting** *n.*

cockle[1] /kókəl/ *n.* **1 a** an edible mollusk of the genus *Cardium*, having a chubby, ribbed bivalve shell. **b** (in full **cockleshell**) its shell. **2** (in full **cockleshell**) a small shallow boat. □ **warm the cockles of one's heart** make one contented; be satisfying. [ME f. OF *coquille* shell ult. f. Gk *kogkhulion* f. *kogkhē* CONCH]

cockle[2] /kókəl/ *n.* **1** any of various plants, esp. the pink-flowered corn cockle, *Agrostemma githago*, growing with grain, esp. wheat. **2** a disease of wheat that turns the grains black. [OE *coccul*, perh. ult. f. LL COCCUS]

cockle[3] /kókəl/ *v. & n.* ● *v.* **1** *intr.* pucker; wrinkle. **2** *tr.* cause to cockle. ● *n.* a pucker or wrinkle in paper, glass, etc. [F *coquiller* blister (bread in cooking) f. *coquille*: see COCKLE[1]]

cockney /kóknee/ *n. & adj.* ● *n.* (*pl.* **-eys**) **1 a** a native of East London, esp. one born within hearing of Bow Bells (of the Bow church in London's East End district). **b** the dialect or accent typical of this area. **2** *Austral.* a young snapper fish, *Chrysophrys auratus*. ● *adj.* of or characteristic of cockneys or their dialect or accent. □□ **cockneyism** *n.* [ME *cokeney* cock's egg, later derog. for 'townsman']

cockpit /kókpit/ *n.* **1 a** a compartment for the pilot (or the pilot and crew) of an aircraft or spacecraft. **b** a similar compartment for the driver in a racing car. **c** a space for the helmsman in some small yachts. **2** an arena of war or other conflict. **3** a place where cockfights are held. [orig. in sense 3, f. COCK[1] + PIT[1]]

cockroach /kókrōch/ *n.* any of various flat brown insects, esp. *Blatta orientalis*, infesting kitchens, bathrooms, etc. [Sp. *cucaracha*, assim. to COCK[1], ROACH[1]]

cockscomb /kókskōm/ *n.* **1** the crest or comb of a cock. **2** a garden plant, *Celosia cristata*, with a terminal broad plume of usu. crimson or reddish-purple flowers.

cocksfoot /kóksfŏŏt/ *n. Brit.* any pasture grass of the genus *Dactylis*, with broad leaves and green or purplish spikes.

cockshy /kókshī/ *n.* (*pl.* **-shies**) *Brit.* **1 a** a target for throwing at with sticks, stones, etc. **b** a throw at this. **2** an object of ridicule or criticism.

cocksure /kókshŏŏr/ *adj.* **1** presumptuously or arrogantly confident. **2** (foll. by *of*, *about*) absolutely sure. □□ **cocksurely** *adv.* **cocksureness** *n.* [*cock* = God + SURE]
■ **1** see CONFIDENT 1.

cocktail /kóktayl/ *n.* **1** a usu. alcoholic drink made by mixing various spirits, fruit juices, etc. **2** a dish of mixed ingredients (*fruit cocktail*; *shellfish cocktail*). **3** any hybrid mixture. □ **cocktail dress** a usu. short evening dress suitable for wearing at a cocktail party. **cocktail party** a social gathering, usu. in the early evening, at which cocktails and hors d'oeuvres, etc. are served. [orig. unkn.: cf. earlier sense 'docked horse' f. COCK[1]: the connection is unclear]

cocky[1] /kókee/ *adj.* (**cockier, cockiest**) **1** conceited; arrogant. **2** saucy; impudent. □□ **cockily** *adv.* **cockiness** *n.* [COCK[1] + -Y[1]]
■ **1** overconfident, arrogant, haughty, conceited, self-important, egotistical, proud, vain, prideful, cocksure. **2** saucy, cheeky, brash; see also IMPUDENT 1, 2.

cocky[2] /kókee/ *n.* (*pl.* **-ies**) *Austral. & NZ colloq.* = COCKATOO 2. [abbr.]

cocky-leeky var. of COCK-A-LEEKIE.

coco /kókō/ *n.* (*pl.* **cocos**) a tall tropical palm tree, *Cocos nucifera*, bearing coconuts. [Port. & Sp. *coco* grimace: the base of the shell resembles a face]

cocoa /kókō/ *n.* **1** a powder made from crushed cacao seeds, often with other ingredients. **2** a hot drink made from this. □ **cocoa bean** a cacao seed. **cocoa butter** a fatty substance obtained from cocoa beans and used for candy, cosmetics, etc. [alt. of CACAO]

coco-de-mer /kókōdəmáir/ *n.* a tall palm tree, *Lodoicea maldivica*, of the Seychelles. [F]

coconut /kókənut/ *n.* (also **cocoanut**) **1 a** a large ovate brown seed of the coco, with a hard shell and edible white fleshy lining enclosing a milky juice. **b** = COCO. **c** the edible white fleshy lining of a coconut. **2** *sl.* the human head. □ **coconut matting** a matting made of fiber from coconut husks. **coconut oil** a solid oil obtained from the lining of the coconut, and used in soap, candles, ointment, etc. **double coconut** a very large nut of the coco-de-mer. [COCO + NUT]
■ **2** see HEAD *n.* 1.

cocoon /kəkŏŏn/ *n. & v.* ● *n.* **1 a** a silky case spun by many insect larvae for protection as pupae. **b** a similar structure made by other animals. **2** a protective covering, esp. to prevent corrosion of metal equipment. ● *v.* **1** *tr. & intr.* wrap in or form a cocoon. **2** *tr.* spray with a protective coating. [F *cocon* f. mod. Prov. *coucoun* dimin. of *coca* shell]

cocotte /kəkót, kawkáwt/ *n.* **1 a** a small fireproof dish for cooking and serving an individual portion of food. **b** a deep cooking pot with a tight-fitting lid and handles. **2** *archaic* a fashionable prostitute. [F]
■ **2** see PROSTITUTE *n.* 1a.

COD *abbr.* **1 a** cash on delivery. **b** collect on delivery. **2** Concise Oxford Dictionary.

cod[1] /kod/ *n.* (*pl.* same) any large marine fish of the family Gadidae, used as food, esp. *Gadus morhua*. □ **cod-liver oil** an oil pressed from the fresh liver of cod, which is rich in vitamins D and A. [ME: orig. unkn.]

cod[2] /kod/ *n. & v. Brit. sl.* ● *n.* **1** a parody. **2** a hoax. **3** (*attrib.*) = MOCK *adj.* ● *v.* (**codded, codding**) **1 a** *intr.* perform a hoax. **b** *tr.* play a trick on; fool. **2** *tr.* parody. [19th c.: orig. unkn.]

cod[3] /kod/ *n. Brit. sl.* nonsense. [abbr. of CODSWALLOP]

coda /kódə/ *n.* **1** *Mus.* the concluding passage of a piece or movement, usu. forming an addition to the basic structure. **2** *Ballet* the concluding section of a dance. **3** a concluding event or series of events. [It. f. L *cauda* tail]

coddle /kód'l/ *v.tr.* **1 a** treat as an invalid; protect attentively. **b** *Brit.* (foll. by *up*) strengthen by feeding. **2** cook (an egg) in water below boiling point. □□ **coddler** *n.* [prob. dial. var. of *caudle* invalids' gruel]
■ **1 a** pamper, baby, cosset, mollycoddle, indulge, humor, spoil.

code /kōd/ *n. & v.* ● *n.* **1** a system of words, letters, figures, or symbols, used to represent others for secrecy or brevity. **2** a system of prearranged signals, esp. used to ensure secrecy in transmitting messages. **3** *Computing* a piece of program text. **4 a** a systematic collection of statutes, a body of laws so arranged as to avoid inconsistency and overlapping. **b** a set of rules on any subject. **5 a** the prevailing morality of a society or class (*code of honor*). **b** a person's standard of moral behavior. ● *v.tr.* put (a message, program, etc.) into code. □ **code name** (or **number**) a word or symbol (or number) used for secrecy or convenience instead of the usual name. □□ **coder** *n.* [ME f. OF f. L CODEX]
■ *n.* **2** cipher. **4** law(s), regulation(s), rule(s), constitution. **5** system, practice(s), convention(s), standard(s), criteria, principle(s), rule(s), maxim(s), custom(s), pattern(s), structure, tradition(s), protocol.
● *v.* encode, encipher, encrypt.

codebook /kódbŏŏk/ *n.* a list of symbols, etc., used in a code.

codeine /kódeen/ *n.* an alkaloid derived from morphine and used to relieve pain. [Gk *kōdeia* poppyhead + -INE[4]]

codependency /kódipéndənsee/ *n.* addiction to a supportive role in a relationship. □□ **codependent** /-dənt/ *adj. & n.* [CO- + DEPENDENCY]

codetermination /kóditərmináyshən/ *n.* cooperation between management and workers in decision making. [CO- + DETERMINATION, after G *Mitbestimmung*]

codex /kódeks/ *n.* (*pl.* **codices** /kódiseez, kód-/) **1** an ancient manuscript text in book form. **2** a collection of pharmaceutical descriptions of drugs, etc. [L, = block of wood, tablet, book]

codfish /kódfish/ *n.* = COD[1].

codger /kójər/ *n.* (usu. in **old codger**) *colloq.* a person, esp. an old or strange one. [perh. var. of *cadger*: see CADGE]

codices *pl.* of CODEX.

codicil /kódisil/ *n.* an addition explaining, modifying, or revoking a will or part of one. □□ **codicillary** /kódisíləree/ *adj.* [L *codicillus*, dimin. of CODEX]
■ see SUPPLEMENT *n.* 1, 2.

codicology /kódikóləjee/ *n.* the study of manuscripts.

/. . ./ **pronunciation**	● **part of speech**
□ **phrases, idioms, and compounds**	
□□ **derivatives**	■ **synonym section**
cross-references appear in SMALL CAPITALS or *italics*	

□□ **codicological** /-kəlójikəl/ *adj.* **codicologically** *adv.* [F *codicologie* f. L *codex codicis*: see CODEX]

codify /kódifí, kŏd-/ *v.tr.* (**-ies, -ied**) arrange (laws, etc.) systematically into a code. □□ **codification** /-fikáyshən/ *n.* **codifier** *n.*
■ see ORGANIZE 1.

codling[1] /kódling/ *n. Brit.* (also **codlin**) **1** any of several varieties of cooking apple, having a long tapering shape. **2** a small moth, *Carpocapsa pomonella*, the larva of which feeds on apples. [ME f. AF *quer de lion* lion heart]

codling[2] /kódling/ *n.* a small codfish.

codomain /kódōmayn/ *n. Math.* a set that includes all the possible expressions of a given function. [CO- 2 + DOMAIN]

codon /kódon/ *n. Biochem.* a sequence of three nucleotides, forming a unit of genetic code in a DNA or RNA molecule. [CODE + -ON]

codpiece /kódpees/ *n. hist.* an appendage like a small bag or flap at the front of a man's breeches. [ME, f. *cod* scrotum + PIECE]

codriver /kódrívər/ *n.* a person who shares the driving of a vehicle with another, esp. in a race, rally, etc.

codswallop /kódzwoləp/ *n.* esp. *Brit. sl.* nonsense. [20th c.: orig. unkn.]

coed /kó-ed, -éd/ *n. & adj. colloq.* ● *n.* **1** a coeducational system or institution. **2** a female student at a coeducational institution. ● *adj.* coeducational. [abbr.]
■ *n.* **2** see MISS[2].

coeducation /kóejŏŏkáyshən/ *n.* the education of pupils of both sexes together. □□ **coeducational** *adj.*

coefficient /kŏifíshənt/ *n.* **1** *Math.* a quantity placed before and multiplying an algebraic expression (e.g., 4 in $4x^y$). **2** *Physics* a multiplier or factor that measures some property (*coefficient of expansion*). [mod.L *coefficiens* (as CO-, EFFICIENT)]

coelacanth /seéləkanth/ *n.* a large bony marine fish, *Latimeria chalumnae*, formerly thought to be extinct, having a trilobed tail fin and fleshy pectoral fins. [mod.L *Coelacanthus* f. Gk *koilos* hollow + *akantha* spine]

-coele *comb. form* var. of -CELE.

coelenterate /seeléntərayt, -tərit/ *n.* any marine animal of the phylum Coelenterata with a simple tube-shaped or cup-shaped body, e.g., jellyfish, corals, and sea anemones. [mod.L *Coelenterata* f. Gk *koilos* hollow + *enteron* intestine]

coeliac esp. *Brit.* var. of CELIAC.

coelom /seéləm/ *n.* (also **celom**) (*pl.* **-oms** or **-omata** /-lŏmətə/) *Zool.* the principal body cavity in animals, between the intestinal canal and the body wall. □□ **coelomate** *adj. & n.* [Gk *koilōma* cavity]

coelostat /seéləstat/ *n. Astron.* an instrument with a rotating mirror that continuously reflects the light from the same area of sky allowing the path of a celestial body to be monitored. [L *caelum* sky + -STAT]

coenobite esp. *Brit.* var. of CENOBITE.

coenzyme /kō-énzim/ *n. Biochem.* a nonproteinaceous compound that assists in the action of an enzyme.

coequal /kō-eékwəl/ *adj. & n. archaic* or *literary* ● *adj.* equal with one another. ● *n.* an equal. □□ **coequality** /kŏ-eekwólitee/ *n.* **coequally** *adv.* [ME f. L or eccl.L *coaequalis* (as CO-, EQUAL)]

coerce /kō-árs/ *v.tr.* (often foll. by *into*) persuade or restrain (an unwilling person) by force (*coerced you into signing*). □□ **coercible** *adj.* [ME f. L *coercēre* restrain (as CO-, *arcēre* restrain)]
■ see FORCE[1] *v.* 1.

coercion /kō-órzhən, -shən/ *n.* **1** the act or process of coercing. **2** government by force. □□ **coercive** /-siv/ *adj.* **coercively** *adv.* **coerciveness** *n.* [OF *cohercion, -tion* f. L *coer(c)tio, coercitio -onis* (as COERCE)]
■ **1** see FORCE[1] *n.* 1.

Coeur d'Alene /kárd'lán/ *n.* **1 a** a N. American people native to northern Idaho. **b** a member of this people. **2** the language of this people.

coeval /kō-eévəl/ *adj. & n.* ● *adj.* **1** having the same age or date of origin. **2** living or existing at the same epoch. **3** having the same duration. ● *n.* a coeval person, a contempo-

rary. □□ **coevality** /-válitee/ *n.* **coevally** *adv.* [LL *coaevus* (as CO-, L *aevum* age)]
■ *adj.* **1, 2** see CONTEMPORARY *adj.* 1.

coexist /kóigzíst/ *v.intr.* (often foll. by *with*) **1** exist together (in time or place). **2** (esp. of nations) exist in mutual tolerance though professing different ideologies, etc. □□ **coexistence** *n.* **coexistent** *adj.* [LL *coexistere* (as CO-, □□ EXIST)]
■ □□ **coexistent** see CONTEMPORARY *adj.* 1.

coextensive /kóiksténsiv/ *adj.* extending over the same space or time.
■ see IDENTICAL 1.

C. of E. *abbr.* Church of England.

coffee /káwfee, kófee/ *n.* **1 a** a drink made from the roasted and ground beanlike seeds of a tropical shrub. **b** a cup of this. **2 a** any shrub of the genus *Coffea*, yielding berries containing one or more seeds. **b** these seeds raw, or roasted and ground. **3** a pale brown color, as of coffee mixed with milk. □ **coffee bar** a bar or café serving coffee and light refreshments from a counter. **coffee bean** the beanlike seeds of the coffee shrub. **coffee break** a short rest from work during which refreshments are usually taken. **coffee cake** a type of cake or sweetened bread, often served with coffee. **coffee cup** a cup for serving coffee. **coffee mill** a small machine for grinding roasted coffee beans. **coffee shop** a small informal restaurant, esp. in a hotel or department store. **coffee table** a small low table. **coffee-table book** a large, lavishly illustrated book. [ult. f. Turk. *kahveh* f. Arab. *kahwa*, the drink]
■ □ **coffee shop** see CAFÉ 1.

coffeehouse /káwfeehows, kóf-/ *n.* a place serving coffee and other refreshments, and often providing informal entertainment.

coffer /káwfər, kóf-/ *n.* **1** a box, esp. a large strongbox for valuables. **2** (in *pl.*) a treasury or store of funds. **3** a sunken panel in a ceiling, etc. □□ **coffered** *adj.* [ME f. OF *coffre* f. L *cophinus* f. Gk *kophinos* basket]
■ **1** see SAFE *n.* 1. **2** (*coffers*) see TREASURY 1.

cofferdam /káwfərdam, kóf-/ *n.* a watertight enclosure pumped dry to permit work below the waterline on building bridges, etc., or for repairing a ship.

coffin /káwfin, kóf-/ *n. & v.* ● *n.* **1** a long, narrow, usu. wooden box in which a corpse is buried or cremated. **2** the part of a horse's hoof below the coronet. ● *v.tr.* (**coffined, coffining**) put in a coffin. □ **coffin bone** a bone in a horse's hoof. **coffin joint** the joint at the top of a horse's hoof. **coffin nail** *sl.* a cigarette. [ME f. OF *cof(f)in* little basket, etc. f. L *cophinus*: see COFFER]
■ *n.* **1** casket; sarcophagus. □ **coffin-nail** see CIGARETTE.

coffle /káwfəl, kóf-/ *n.* a line of animals, slaves, etc., fastened together. [Arab. *kāfila* caravan]

cog /kawg, kog/ *n.* **1** each of a series of projections on the edge of a wheel or bar transferring motion by engaging with another series. **2** an unimportant member of an organization, etc. □ **cog railway** a railway with a cogged third rail designed to mesh with a cogwheel on a locomotive to prevent slippage on steep slopes. □□ **cogged** *adj.* [ME: prob. of Scand. orig.]
■ **1** tooth, gear tooth, sprocket. **2** underling, pawn, subordinate, nonentity, zero, cipher, nothing, nobody.

cogent /kójənt/ *adj.* (of arguments, reasons, etc.) convincing; compelling. □□ **cogency** /-jənsee/ *n.* **cogently** *adv.* [L *cogere* compel (as CO-, *agere act-* drive)]
■ see PERSUASIVE. □□ **cogency** see FORCE[1] *n.* 4.

cogitable /kójitəbəl/ *adj.* able to be grasped by the mind; conceivable. [L *cogitabilis* (as COGITATE)]

cogitate /kójitayt/ *v.tr. & intr.* ponder; meditate. □□ **cogitation** /-táyshən/ *n.* **cogitative** *adj.* **cogitator** *n.* [L *cogitare* think (as CO-, AGITATE)]
■ see PONDER. □□ **cogitative** see THOUGHTFUL 1.

cogito /kógitō, kójitō/ *n. Philos.* the principle establishing the existence of a being from the fact of its thinking or awareness. [L, = I think, in Fr. philosopher Descartes's formula (1641) *cogito, ergo sum* I think, therefore I exist]

cognac /káwnyak, kón-/ *n.* a high-quality brandy, properly that distilled in Cognac in W. France.

cognate /kógnayt/ *adj. & n.* ● *adj.* **1** related to or descended from a common ancestor (cf. AGNATE). **2** *Philol.* (of a word) having the same linguistic family or derivation (as another); representing the same original word or root (e.g., English *father*, German *Vater*, Latin *pater*). ● *n.* **1** a relative. **2** a cognate word. □ **cognate object** *Gram.* an object that is related in origin and sense to the verb governing it (as in *live a good life*). □□ **cognately** *adv.* **cognateness** *n.* [L *cognatus* (as CO-, *natus* born)]
  ■ *adj.* **1** see LIKE¹ *adj.* 1a.

cognition /kogníshən/ *n.* **1** *Philos.* knowing, perceiving, or conceiving as an act or faculty distinct from emotion and volition. **2** a result of this; a perception, sensation, notion, or intuition. □□ **cognitional** *adj.* **cognitive** /kógnitiv/ *adj.* [L *cognitio* (as CO-, *gnoscere gnit-* apprehend)]
  ■ **1** see KNOWLEDGE 1a.

cognizable /kógnizəbəl, kón-, kogní-/ *adj.* **1** perceptible; recognizable; clearly identifiable. **2** within the jurisdiction of a court. □□ **cognizably** *adv.* [COGNIZANCE + -ABLE]
  ■ **1** see SENSIBLE 3a.

cognizance /kógnizəns/ *n.* **1** knowledge or awareness; perception; notice. **2** the sphere of one's observation or concern. **3** *Law* the right of a court to deal with a matter. **4** *Heraldry* a distinctive device or mark. □ **have cognizance of** know, esp. officially. **take cognizance of** attend to; take account of. [ME f. OF *conoisance* ult. f. L *cognoscent-* f. *cognitio*: see COGNITION]
  ■ **1** knowledge, awareness, perception, notice, consciousness, mindfulness. **2** sphere, scope, province, domain. **3** see JURISDICTION 2. **4** see DEVICE 3.

cognizant /kógnizənt/ *adj.* (foll. by *of*) having knowledge or being aware of.
  ■ see AWARE 1.

cognomen /kognṓmen/ *n.* **1** a nickname. **2** an ancient Roman's personal name or epithet, as in Marcus Tullius *Cicero*, Publius Cornelius Scipio *Africanus*. [L]

cognoscente /kónyəshéntee, kógnə-/ *n.* (*pl.* **cognoscenti** *pronunc.* same) (usu. in *pl.*) a connoisseur. [obs. It.]

cogwheel /kóghweel, -weel/ *n.* a wheel with cogs.

cohabit /kōhábit/ *v.intr.* (**cohabited, cohabiting**) live together, esp. as husband and wife without being married to one another. □□ **cohabitant** *n.* **cohabitation** *n.* **cohabitee** /-tée/ *n.* **cohabiter** *n.* [L *cohabitare* (as CO-, *habitare* dwell)]

cohere /kōheer/ *v.intr.* **1** (of parts or a whole) stick together; remain united. **2** (of reasoning, etc.) be logical or consistent. [L *cohaerēre cohaes-* (as CO-, *haerēre* stick)]
  ■ **1** see STICK² *v.* 4. **2** hold, hang together, be logical.

coherent /kōheerənt, -hér-/ *adj.* **1** (of a person) able to speak intelligibly and articulately. **2** (of speech, an argument, etc.) logical and consistent; easily followed. **3** cohering; sticking together. **4** *Physics* (of waves) having a constant phase relationship. □□ **coherence** /-rəns/ *n.* **coherency** *n.* **coherently** *adv.* [L *cohaerēre cohaerent-* (as COHERE)]
  ■ **1, 2** consistent, orderly, organized, well-organized, logical, rational, reasonable, sensible, well-ordered; understandable, comprehensible, intelligible, articulate, lucid, clear. □□ **coherence** see UNITY 1.

cohesion /kōheézhən/ *n.* **1 a** the act or condition of sticking together. **b** a tendency to cohere. **2** *Chem.* the force with which molecules cohere. □□ **cohesive** /-heesiv/ *adj.* **cohesively** /-heesivlee/ *adv.* **cohesiveness** /-heesivnis/ *n.* [L *cohaes-* (see COHERE) after *adhesion*]

coho /kṓhō/ *n.* (also **cohoe**) (*pl.* same or **-os** or **-oes**) a silver salmon, *Oncorhynchus kisutch*, of the N. Pacific. [19th c.: orig. unkn.]

cohort /kṓhawrt/ *n.* **1** an ancient Roman military unit, equal to one-tenth of a legion. **2** a band of warriors. **3 a** persons banded or grouped together, esp. in a common cause. **b** a group of persons with a common statistical characteristic. **4** a companion or colleague. [ME f. F *cohorte* or L *cohors cohort-* enclosure, company]
  ■ **2** troop, squad, squadron, platoon, brigade, unit, cadre, wing, detachment, contingent. **3 a** company, band, group, faction, set, body, corps. **4** companion,

confederate, accomplice, associate, fellow, comrade, friend, confrère.

coif /koyf/ *n. hist.* **1** a close-fitting cap, esp. as worn by nuns under a veil. **2** a protective metal skullcap worn under armor. **3** = COIFFURE. [ME f. OF *coife* f. LL *cofia* helmet]

coiffeur /kwaafőr/ *n.* (*fem.* **coiffeuse** /-főz/) a hairdresser. [F]

coiffure /kwaafyṓr/ *n. & v.* ● *n.* (also **coif**) the way hair is arranged; a hairstyle. ● *v.* to provide a coiffure. [F]

coign /koyn/ *n.* □ **coign of vantage** a favorable position for observation or action. [earlier spelling of COIN in the sense 'cornerstone']

coil¹ /koyl/ *n. & v.* ● *n.* **1** anything arranged in a joined sequence of concentric circles. **2** a length of rope, a spring, etc., arranged in this way. **3** a single turn of something coiled, e.g., a snake. **4** a lock of hair twisted and coiled. **5** an intrauterine contraceptive device in the form of a coil. **6** *Electr.* a device consisting of a coiled wire for converting low voltage to high voltage, esp. for transmission to the spark plugs of an internal combustion engine. **7** a piece of wire, piping, etc., wound in circles or spirals. **8** a roll of postage stamps. ● *v.* **1** *tr.* arrange in a series of concentric loops or rings. **2** *tr. & intr.* twist or be twisted into a circular or spiral shape. **3** *intr.* move sinuously. [OF *coillir* f. L *colligere* COLLECT¹]
  ■ *n.* **1–3** circle, loop, twist, turn, *Naut.* fake; winding, whorl, spiral, helix. ● *v.* **1, 2** wind, twist, snake, wrap, spiral, *Naut.* fake, *literary* enwrap. **3** see WIND² *v.* 1.

coil² /koyl/ *n.* □ **this mortal coil** the difficulties of earthly life (with ref. to Shakesp. *Hamlet* III. i. 67). [16th c.: orig. unkn.]

coin /koyn/ *n. & v.* ● *n.* **1** a piece of flat, usu. round metal stamped and issued by authority as money. **2** (*collect.*) metal money. ● *v.tr.* **1** make (coins) by stamping. **2** make (metal) into coins. **3** invent or devise (esp. a new word or phrase). □ **coin box** *Brit.* **1** a telephone operated by inserting coins. **2** the receptacle for these. **coin money** make much money quickly. **coin-op** a self-serve laundry, etc., with automatic machines operated by inserting coins. **to coin a phrase** *iron.* introducing a banal remark or cliché. [ME f. OF, = stamping die, f. L *cuneus* wedge]
  ■ *n.* **2** specie; change, cash, silver. ● *v.* **1** mint, stamp. **3** invent, devise, make up, create, conceive, originate, start, fabricate, concoct, think *or* dream up. □ **coin money** earn *or* make money, become wealthy, enrich oneself, *colloq.* rake it in.

coinage /kóynij/ *n.* **1** the act or process of coining. **2 a** coins collectively. **b** a system or type of coins in use (*decimal coinage*; *bronze coinage*). **3** an invention, esp. of a new word or phrase. [ME f. OF *coigniage*]
  ■ **3** see NEOLOGISM.

coincide /kṓinsíd/ *v.intr.* **1** occur at or during the same time. **2** occupy the same portion of space. **3** (often foll. by *with*) be in agreement; have the same view. [med.L *coincidere* (as CO-, INCIDENT)]
  ■ **1, 2** fall *or* come *or* go together, co-occur, synchronize. **3** agree, (be in) accord, *colloq.* jibe; correspond, match, tally.

coincidence /kō-ínsidəns/ *n.* **1 a** occurring or being together. **b** an instance of this. **2** a remarkable concurrence of events or circumstances without apparent causal connection. **3** *Physics* the presence of ionizing particles, etc., in two or more detectors simultaneously, or of two or more signals simultaneously in a circuit. [med.L *coincidentia* (as COINCIDE)]
  ■ **1** co-occurrence, simultaneity, correspondence, concurrence, contemporaneity, synchronism, synchrony, coextension, coevality, coinstantaneity, concomitance, congruence. **2** chance occurrence, fluke, chance, accident, luck, fortuity, happenstance.

/.../ **pronunciation**	● **part of speech**
□ **phrases, idioms, and compounds**	
□□ **derivatives**	■ **synonym section**
cross-references appear in SMALL CAPITALS or *italics*	

coincident /kō-ínsídənt/ adj. **1** occurring together in space or time. **2** (foll. by *with*) in agreement; harmonious. □□ **coincidently** adv.

coincidental /kō-ínsídént'l/ adj. **1** in the nature of or resulting from a coincidence. **2** happening or existing at the same time. □□ **coincidentally** adv.

■ **1** chance, fortuitous, accidental, unexpected, unpredicted, unpredictable, unforeseen. **2** see SIMULTANEOUS.

coiner /kóynər/ n. **1** a person who coins money, esp. *Brit.* the maker of counterfeit coin. **2** a person who invents or devises something (esp. a new word or phrase).

Cointreau /kwáantrō/ n. propr. a colorless orange-flavored liqueur. [F]

coir /kóyər/ n. fiber from the outer husk of the coconut, used for ropes, matting, etc. [Malayalam *kāyar* cord f. *kāyaru* be twisted]

coition /kō-íshən/ n. Med. = COITUS. [L *coitio* f. *coire coit-* go together]

coitus /kṓ-itəs, kō-ée-/ n. Med. sexual intercourse. □ **coitus interruptus** /íntərúptəs/ sexual intercourse in which the penis is withdrawn before ejaculation. □□ **coital** adj. [L (as COITION)]

■ see *sexual intercourse*.

Coke /kōk/ n. propr. Coca-Cola. [abbr.]

coke[1] /kōk/ n. & v. ● n. **1** a solid substance left after the gases have been extracted from coal. **2** a residue left after the incomplete combustion of gasoline, etc. ● v.tr. convert (coal) into coke. [prob. f. N.Engl. dial. *colk* core, of unkn. orig.]

coke[2] /kōk/ n. sl. cocaine. [abbr.]

Col. abbr. **1** colonel. **2** Colossians (New Testament).

col /kol/ n. **1** a depression in the summit line of a chain of mountains, generally affording a pass from one slope to another. **2** Meteorol. a low-pressure region between anticyclones. [F, = neck, f. L *collum*]

■ **1** see PASS[2]. **2** depression, low-pressure area, cyclone.

col. abbr. column.

col- /kol/ prefix assim. form of COM- before *l*.

COLA /kṓlə/ abbr. **1** cost-of-living adjustment. **2** cost-of-living allowance.

cola /kṓlə/ n. (also **kola**) **1** any small tree of the genus *Cola*, native to W. Africa, bearing seeds containing caffeine. **2** a carbonated drink usu. flavored with these seeds. □ **cola nut** a seed of the tree. [W.Afr.]

■ **2** see POP[1] n. 2.

colander /kúləndər, kól-/ n. a perforated vessel used to strain off liquid in cookery. [ME, ult. f. L *colare* strain]

■ see SCREEN n. 11.

colatitude /kōlátitōōd, -tyōōd/ n. Astron. the complement of the latitude, the difference between it and 90°.

colchicine /kólchiseen, kól-, kólkee-/ n. a yellow alkaloid obtained from colchicum, used in the treatment of gout.

colchicum /kólchikəm, kólkee-/ n. **1** any liliaceous plant of the genus *Colchicum*, esp. meadow saffron. **2** its dried corm or seed. Also called *autumn crocus*. [L f. Gk *kolkhikon* of Kolkhis, a region east of the Black Sea]

cold /kōld/ adj., n., & adv. ● adj. **1** of or at a low or relatively low temperature, esp. when compared with the human body. **2** not heated; cooled after being heated. **3** (of a person) feeling cold. **4** lacking ardor, friendliness, or affection; undemonstrative; apathetic. **5** depressing; dispiriting; uninteresting (*cold facts*). **6 a** dead. **b** colloq. unconscious. **7** colloq. at one's mercy (*had me cold*). **8** sexually frigid. **9** (of soil) slow to absorb heat. **10** (of a scent in hunting) having become weak. **11** (in children's games) far from finding or guessing what is sought. **12** without preparation or rehearsal. ● n. **1 a** the prevalence of a low temperature, esp. in the atmosphere. **b** cold weather; a cold environment (*went out into the cold*). **2** an infection in which the mucous membrane of the nose and throat becomes inflamed, causing running at the nose, sneezing, sore throat, etc. ● adv. completely; entirely (*was stopped cold mid-sentence*). □ **catch a cold 1** become infected with a cold. **2** esp. *Brit.* encounter trouble or difficulties. **cold call** sell goods or services by making unsolicited calls on prospective customers by telephone or in person. **cold cathode** a cathode that emits electrons without being heated. **cold chisel** a chisel suitable for cutting metal. **cold comfort** poor or inadequate consolation. **cold cream** ointment for cleansing and softening the skin. **cold cuts** slices of cold cooked meats. **cold feet** colloq. loss of nerve or confidence. **cold frame** an unheated frame with a glass top for growing small plants. **cold front** the forward edge of an advancing mass of cold air. **cold fusion** hypothetical nuclear fusion at room temperature esp. as a possible energy source. **cold shoulder** a show of intentional unfriendliness. **cold-shoulder** v.tr. be deliberately unfriendly to. **cold sore** inflammation and blisters in and around the mouth, caused by a virus infection. **cold storage 1** storage in a refrigerator or other cold place for preservation. **2** a state in which something (esp. an idea) is put aside temporarily. **cold sweat** a state of sweating induced by fear or illness. **cold turkey** sl. **1** a series of blunt statements or behavior. **2** abrupt withdrawal from addictive drugs; the symptoms of this. **cold war** a state of hostility between nations without actual fighting. **cold wave 1** a temporary spell of cold weather over a wide area. **2** a kind of permanent wave for the hair using chemicals and without heat. **in cold blood** without feeling or passion; deliberately; ruthlessly. **out in the cold** ignored; neglected. **throw** (or **pour**) **cold water on** be discouraging or depreciatory about. □□ **coldish** adj. **coldly** adv. **coldness** n. [OE *cald* f. Gmc, rel. to L *gelu* frost]

■ adj. **1** chilly, frosty, icy, freezing, frigid, ice-cold, stone-cold, bitter, raw, keen, biting, gelid, wintry, glacial, polar, hyperborean, chill, Siberian, colloq. nippy, arctic. **2** chilled, cooled; unheated. **3** freezing, frozen, stone-cold. **4** indifferent, apathetic, chilly, cool, icy, dispassionate, unsympathetic, aloof, unresponsive, clinical, spiritless, frigid, unfriendly, uncordial, lukewarm; cold-blooded, insensitive, uncaring, unemotional, undemonstrative, reserved, unmoved, callous, remote, distant, standoffish, unapproachable, stonyhearted, emotionless, unfeeling, cold-hearted. **5** depressing, cheerless, gloomy, dispiriting, deadening, disheartening, bleak, dismal, discouraging; uninteresting. **6 a** see DEAD adj. 1. **b** see DEAD adj. 4. **7** at one's mercy, vulnerable, colloq. over a barrel. **8** see FRIGID 2. **10** weak, faint, stale, old, dead. **11** off the track, far away, distant, remote. **12** see UNPREPARED. ● n. **1** coldness, frigidity, iciness. **2** common cold, sniffle(s), Med. coryza, , sl. bug. ● adv. completely, thoroughly, entirely, absolutely, unhesitatingly, promptly, immediately, unreservedly, abruptly. □ **cold-shoulder** rebuff, snub, ostracize, put down, reject, exclude, shun, cut (dead), give the cold shoulder to, send to Coventry, colloq. freeze out.

cold-blooded /kṓldblúdid/ adj. **1** having a body temperature varying with that of the environment (e.g., of fish); poikilothermic. **2 a** callous; deliberately cruel. **b** without excitement or sensibility, dispassionate. □□ **cold-bloodedly** adv. **cold-bloodedness** n.

■ **2 a** callous, cruel, brutal, savage, inhuman, barbarous, vicious, barbaric, merciless, pitiless, ruthless; thick-skinned, insensitive, heartless, uncaring, stony, steely, stony-hearted, cold-hearted, unsympathetic. **b** indifferent, unresponsive, dispassionate, unemotional, cool, unimpassioned.

cold-hearted /kṓldháartid/ adj. lacking affection or warmth; unfriendly. □□ **cold-heartedly** adv. **cold-heartedness** n.

■ unfriendly, insensitive, unsympathetic, indifferent, unfeeling, uncaring, callous, thick-skinned, cold, cool, frigid, cold-blooded, hard-hearted, heartless, unkind, thoughtless, unthoughtful, uncharitable, ruthless, pitiless, unmerciful, cruel, merciless.

cole /kōl/ n. (usu. in comb.) **1** cabbage. **2** = RAPE[2]. [ME f. ON *kál* f. L *caulis* stem, cabbage]

coleopteron /kóleeóptərən/ n. any insect of the order Coleoptera, with front wings modified into sheaths to protect the hinder wings, e.g., a beetle or weevil. □□ **coleopteran**

adj. **coleopterist** *n.* **coleopterous** *adj.* [mod.L *Coleoptera* f. Gk *koleopteros* f. *koleon* sheath + *pteron* wing]

coleoptile /kóleeóptil/ *n. Bot.* a sheath protecting a young shoot tip in grasses. [Gk *koleon* sheath + *ptilon* feather]

coleseed /kṓlseed/ *n.* = COLE 2.

coleslaw /kṓlslaw/ *n.* a dressed salad of sliced raw cabbage, carrot, onion, etc. [Du. *koolsla*: see COLE, SLAW]

coleus /kṓleeəs/ *n.* any plant of the genus *Coleus*, having variegated colored leaves. [mod.L f. Gk *koleon* sheath]

colic /kólik/ *n.* a severe spasmodic abdominal pain. ▭▭ **colicky** *adj.* [ME f. F *colique* f. LL *colicus*: see COLON[2]]

▪ see GRIPE *n.* 1.

coliseum /kóliseeəm/ *n.* (also **colosseum**) a large stadium or amphitheater (see COLOSSEUM).

colitis /kólítis/ *n.* inflammation of the lining of the colon.

coll. *abbr.* **1** collect. **2** collection. **3** collateral. **4** college.

collaborate /kəlábərayt/ *v.intr.* (often foll. by *with*) **1** work jointly, esp. in a literary or artistic production. **2** cooperate traitorously with an enemy. ▭▭ **collaboration** /-ráyshən/ *n.* **collaborationist** *n.* & *adj.* **collaborative** /-ráytiv, -rətiv/ *adj.* **collaborator** *n.* [L *collaborare collaborat-* (as COM-, *laborare* work)]

▪ **1** cooperate, join (forces), work together, team up.

collage /kəláazh/ *n.* **1** a form of art in which various materials (e.g., photographs, pieces of paper, matchsticks) are arranged and glued to a backing. **2** a work of art done in this way. **3** a collection of unrelated things. ▭▭ **collagist** *n.* [F, = gluing]

collagen /kóləjən/ *n.* a protein found in animal connective tissue, yielding gelatin on boiling. [F *collagène* f. Gk *kolla* glue + *-gène* = -GEN]

collapse /kəláps/ *n.* & *v.* ● *n.* **1** the tumbling down or falling in of a structure; folding up; giving way. **2** a sudden failure of a plan, undertaking, etc. **3** a physical or mental breakdown. ● *v.* **1 a** *intr.* undergo or experience a collapse. **b** *tr.* cause to collapse. **2** *intr. colloq.* lie or sit down and relax, esp. after prolonged effort (*collapsed into a chair*). **3 a** *intr.* (of furniture, etc.) be foldable into a small space. **b** *tr.* fold (furniture, etc.) in this way. ▭▭ **collapsible** *adj.* **collapsibility** /-səbílitee/ *n.* [L *collapsus* past part. of *collabi* (as COM-, *labi* slip)]

▪ *n.* **1** cave-in, breakdown, disintegration, subsidence; see also RUIN *n.* 2a. **2** failure, downfall, ruin; disintegration, dissolution, bankruptcy. **3** (mental *or* nervous) breakdown, prostration, *colloq.* crack-up. ● *v.* **1 a** fall (down *or* in *or* apart), crumple, cave in, deflate, crumble, tumble down, break down; fail, (come to an) end, fall through, peter out, disintegrate, dissolve, fall flat, founder, break up *or* down, disappear, evaporate, go up in smoke, go bankrupt, go under, go to the wall; pass out, faint, drop, keel over, *literary* swoon; have a (mental *or* nervous) breakdown, go to pieces, *colloq.* crack up.

collar /kólər/ *n.* & *v.* ● *n.* **1** the part of a shirt, dress, coat, etc., that goes around the neck, either upright or turned over. **2** a band of linen, lace, etc., completing the upper part of a costume. **3** a band of leather or other material put around an animal's (esp. a dog's) neck. **4** a restraining or connecting band, ring, or pipe in machinery. **5** a colored marking resembling a collar around the neck of a bird or animal. **6** *Brit.* a piece of meat rolled up and tied. ● *v.tr.* **1** seize (a person) by the collar or neck. **2** capture; apprehend. **3** *colloq.* accost. **4** *sl.* take, esp. illicitly. ▭▭ **collared** *adj.* (also in *comb.*). **collarless** *adj.* [ME f. AF *coler*, OF *colier*, f. L *collare* f. *collum* neck]

▪ *v.* **2** see CAPTURE *v.* 1.

collarbone /kólərbōn/ *n.* either of two bones joining the breastbone and the shoulder blades; the clavicle.

collate /kəláyt, kólayt, kṓ-/ *v.tr.* **1** analyze and compare (texts, statements, etc.) to identify points of agreement and difference. **2 a** arrange (pages) in proper sequence. **b** *Bibliog.* verify the order of (sheets) by their signatures. **3** assemble (information) from different sources. **4** (often foll. by *to*) *Eccl.* appoint (a clergyman) to a benefice. ▭▭ **collator** *n.* [L *collat-* past part. stem of *conferre* compare]

▪ **1** see SEPARATE *v.* 6a. **3** see COMPILE 1.

collateral /kəlátərəl/ *n.* & *adj.* ● *n.* **1** security pledged as a guarantee for repayment of a loan. **2** a person having the same descent as another but by a different line. ● *adj.* **1** descended from the same stock but by a different line. **2** side by side; parallel. **3 a** additional but subordinate. **b** contributory. **c** connected but aside from the main subject, course, etc. ▭▭ **collaterality** /-rálitee/ *n.* **collaterally** *adv.* [ME f. med.L *collateralis* (as COM-, LATERAL)]

▪ *n.* **1** see SECURITY 4. **3** see EXTRA *adj.*

collation /kəláyshən, ko-/ *n.* **1** the act or an instance of collating. **2** *RC Ch.* a light meal allowed during a fast. **3** a light informal meal. [ME f. OF f. L *collatio -onis* (see COLLATE): sense 2 f. Cassian's *Collationes Patrum* (= *Lives of the Fathers*) read by Benedictines and followed by a light meal]

▪ **2, 3** see MEAL[1].

colleague /kóleeg/ *n.* a fellow official or worker, esp. in a profession or business. [F *collègue* f. L *collega* (as COM-, *legare* depute)]

▪ teammate, fellow worker, coworker; associate, comrade, ally, confrère.

collect[1] /kəlékt/ *v.*, *adj.*, & *adv.* ● *v.* **1** *tr.* & *intr.* bring or come together; assemble; accumulate. **2** *tr.* systematically seek and acquire (books, stamps, etc.), esp. as a continuing hobby. **3 a** *tr.* obtain (taxes, contributions, etc.) from a number of people. **b** *intr. colloq.* receive money. **4** *tr.* call for; fetch (*went to collect the laundry*). **5 a** *refl.* regain control of oneself esp. after a shock. **b** *tr.* concentrate (one's energies, thoughts, etc.). **c** *tr.* (as **collected** *adj.*) calm and cool; not perturbed nor distracted. **6** *tr.* infer; gather; conclude. ● *adj.* & *adv.* to be paid for by the receiver (of a telephone call, parcel, etc.). ▭▭ **collectable** *adj.* **collectedly** *adv.* [F *collecter* or med.L *collectare* f. L *collectus* past part. of *colligere* (as COM-, *legere* pick)]

▪ *v.* **1** gather (together), get *or* bring *or* come together, amass, accumulate, assemble, compile, pile up, heap up, rack up; convene, congregate, converge, rally, meet. **3 b** see RECEIVE 1, 2. **4** see FETCH[1] *v.* 1. **5 a** see COMPOSE 4a. **b** summon (up), concentrate, draw (up), muster, gather (up). **c** (**collected**) calm, serene, controlled, cool, sedate, composed, nonchalant, poised, unruffled, unperturbed, undistracted, at ease, comfortable, tranquil, unexcited; imperturbable; confident.

collect[2] /kólekt, -ikt/ *n.* a short prayer of the Anglican and Roman Catholic churches, esp. one assigned to a particular day or season. [ME f. OF *collecte* f. L *collecta* fem. past part. of *colligere*: see COLLECT[1]]

collectible /kəléktibəl/ *adj.* & *n.* ● *adj.* worth collecting. ● *n.* an item sought by collectors.

collection /kəlékshən/ *n.* **1** the act or process of collecting or being collected. **2** a group of things collected together (e.g., works of art, literary items, or specimens), esp. systematically. **3** (foll. by *of*) an accumulation; a mass or pile (*a collection of dust*). **4 a** the collecting of money, esp. in church or for a charitable cause. **b** the amount collected. **5** the regular removal of mail, esp. from a public mailbox, for dispatch. **6** (in *pl.*) *Brit.* college examinations held at the end of a term, esp. at Oxford University. [ME f. OF f. L *collectio -onis* (as COLLECT[1])]

▪ **1** accumulation, amassment, aggregation. **2** accumulation, hoard, store, assemblage; anthology. **3** see MASS[1] *n.* 1, 2. **4a** contribution(s), alms.

collective /kəléktiv/ *adj.* & *n.* ● *adj.* **1** formed by or constituting a collection. **2** taken as a whole; aggregate (*our collective opinion*). **3** of or from several or many individuals; common. ● *n.* **1 a** = *collective farm.* **b** any cooperative enterprise. **c** its members. **2** = *collective noun.* ▭ **collective bargaining** negotiation of wages, etc., by an organized

---

/.../ **pronunciation**	● **part of speech**
▭ **phrases, idioms, and compounds**	
▭▭ **derivatives**	▪ **synonym section**
cross-references appear in SMALL CAPITALS or *italics*	

body of employees. **collective farm** a jointly operated esp. government-owned amalgamation of several small farms. **collective noun** *Gram.* a noun that is grammatically singular and denotes a collection or number of individuals (e.g., *assembly*, *family*, *troop*). **collective ownership** ownership of land, means of production, etc., by all for the benefit of all. **collective unconscious** *Psychol.* (in Jungian theory) the part of the unconscious mind derived from ancestral memory and experience common to all mankind, as distinct from the personal unconscious. □□ **collectively** *adv.* **collectiveness** *n.* **collectivity** /kólektívitee/ *n.* [F *collectif* or L *collectivus* (as COLLECT[1])]

■ *adj.* **2** see JOINT *adj.* **3** see COMMON *adj.* 2.

collectivism /kəléktivizəm/ *n.* the theory and practice of the collective ownership of land and the means of production. □□ **collectivist** *n.* **collectivistic** /-vístik/ *adj.*

collectivize /kəléktiviz/ *v.tr.* organize on the basis of collective ownership. □□ **collectivization** *n.*

collector /kəléktər/ *n.* **1** a person who collects, esp. things of interest as a hobby. **2** a person who collects money, etc., due (*tax collector*; *ticket collector*). **3** *Electronics* the region in a transistor that absorbs carriers of a charge. □ **collector's item** (or **piece**) a valuable object, esp. one of interest to collectors. [ME f. AF *collectour* f. med.L *collector* (as COLLECT[1])]

■ **1** gatherer, accumulator, hoarder.

colleen /koleén/ *n. Ir.* a girl. [Ir. *cailín*, dimin. of *caile* countrywoman]

college /kólij/ *n.* **1** an establishment for further or higher education, sometimes part of a university. **2** an establishment for specialized professional education (*business college*; *college of music*; *naval college*). **3** *Brit.* the buildings or premises of a college (*lived in college*). **4** the students and teachers in a college. **5** *Brit.* a public school. **6** an organized body of persons with shared functions and privileges (*electoral college*). □ **College of Arms** (in the UK) a corporation recording lineage and granting arms. **college pudding** *Brit.* a small baked or steamed suet pudding with dried fruit. □□ **collegial** /kəleéjəl/ *adj.* [ME f. OF *college* or L *collegium* f. *collega* (as COLLEAGUE)]

■ **1–5** see INSTITUTE *n.* 1.

collegian /kəleéjən/ *n.* a member of a college. [med.L *collegianus* (as COLLEGE)]

collegiate /kəleéjət/ *adj.* constituted as or belonging to a college; corporate. □ **collegiate church 1** a church endowed for a chapter of canons but without a bishop's see. **2** esp. *US* & *Sc.* a church or group of churches established under a joint pastorate. □□ **collegiately** *adv.* [LL *collegiatus* (as COLLEGE)]

collenchyma /koléngkimə/ *n. Bot.* a tissue of cells with thick cellulose cell walls, strengthening young stems, etc. [Gk *kolla* glue + *egkhuma* infusion]

Colles' fracture /kólis/ *n.* a fracture of the lower end of the radius with a backward displacement of the hand. [A. *Colles*, Ir. surgeon d. 1843]

collet /kólit/ *n.* **1** a flange or socket for setting a gem in jewelry. **2** *Engin.* a segmented band or sleeve put around a shaft or spindle and tightened to grip it. **3** *Horol.* a small collar to which the inner end of a balance spring is attached. [F, dimin. of COL]

collide /kəlíd/ *v.intr.* (often foll. by *with*) **1** come into abrupt or violent impact. **2** be in conflict. [L *collidere collis-* (as COM-, *laedere* strike, damage)]

■ **1** crash, strike *or* dash together; (*collide with*) crash into, smash into, run into, bump into, smack into. **2** see CONFLICT *v.* 1.

collie /kólee/ *n.* **1** a sheepdog orig. of a Scottish breed, with a long pointed nose and usu. dense, long hair. **2** this breed. [perh. f. *coll* COAL (as being orig. black)]

collier /kólyər/ *n.* **1** a coal miner. **2** a coal-carrying ship. [ME, f. COAL + -IER]

colliery /kólyəree/ *n.* (*pl.* **-ies**) a coal mine and its associated buildings.

■ see MINE[2] *n.* 1.

colligate /kóligayt/ *v.tr.* bring into connection (esp. isolated

facts by a generalization). □□ **colligation** /-gáyshən/ *n.* [L *colligare colligat-* (as COM-, *ligare* bind)]

collimate /kólimayt/ *v.tr.* **1** adjust the line of sight of (a telescope, etc.). **2** make (telescopes or rays) accurately parallel. □□ **collimation** /-máyshən/ *n.* [L *collimare*, erron. for *collineare* align (as COM-, *linea* line)]

collimator /kólimaytər/ *n.* **1** a device for producing a parallel beam of rays or radiation. **2** a small fixed telescope used for adjusting the line of sight of an astronomical telescope, etc.

collinear /kəlíneeər/ *adj. Geom.* (of points) lying in the same straight line. □□ **collinearity** /-neeáiritee/ *n.* **collinearly** *adv.*

collins /kólinz/ *n.* (also **Collins**) an iced drink made of gin or whiskey, etc., with soda water, lemon or lime juice, and sugar. [20th c.: orig. unkn.]

collision /kəlízhən/ *n.* **1** a violent impact of a moving body, esp. a vehicle or ship, with another or with a fixed object. **2** the clashing of opposed interests or considerations. **3** *Physics* the action of particles striking or coming together. □ **collision course** a course or action that is bound to cause a collision or conflict. □□ **collisional** *adj.* [ME f. LL *collisio* (as COLLIDE)]

■ **1** smash, crash, *colloq.* smashup, pileup, crack-up. **2** clash, conflict, difference; see also STRUGGLE *n.* 2.

collocate /kóləkayt/ *v.tr.* **1** place together or side by side. **2** arrange; set in a particular place. **3** (often foll. by *with*) *Linguistics* juxtapose (a word, etc.) with another. □□ **collocation** /-káyshən/ *n.* [L *collocare collocat-* (as COM-, *locare* to place)]

■ □□ **collocation** see PHRASE *n.* 1.

collocutor /kóləkyōōtər, kōlókyətər/ *n.* a person who takes part in a conversation. [LL f. *colloqui* (as COM-, *loqui locut-* talk)]

collodion /kəlōdeeən/ *n.* a syrupy solution of cellulose nitrate in a mixture of alcohol and ether, used in photography and surgery. [Gk *kollōdēs* gluelike f. *kolla* glue]

collogue /kəlōg/ *v.intr.* (**collogues, collogued, colloguing**) (foll. by *with*) talk confidentially. [prob. alt. of obs. *colleague* conspire, by assoc. with L *colloqui* converse]

colloid /kóloyd/ *n.* **1** *Chem.* **a** a substance consisting of ultramicroscopic particles. **b** a mixture of such a substance uniformly dispersed through a second substance esp. to form a viscous solution. **2** *Med.* a substance of a homogeneous gelatinous consistency. □□ **colloidal** /kəlóyd'l/ *adj.* [Gk *kolla* glue + -OID]

collop /kóləp/ *n.* a slice, esp. of meat or bacon; an escalope. [ME, = fried bacon and eggs, of Scand. orig.]

■ see SLICE *n.* 1.

colloquial /kəlṓkweeəl/ *adj.* belonging to or proper to ordinary or familiar conversation, not formal or literary. □□ **colloquially** *adv.* [L *colloquium* COLLOQUY]

■ see VERNACULAR *adj.*

colloquialism /kəlṓkweeəlizəm/ *n.* **1** a colloquial word or phrase. **2** the use of colloquialisms.

colloquium /kəlṓkweeəm/ *n.* (*pl.* **colloquiums** or **colloquia** /-kweeə/) an academic conference or seminar. [L: see COLLOQUY]

■ see CONFERENCE 2.

colloquy /kóləkwee/ *n.* (*pl.* **-quies**) **1** the act of conversing. **2** a conversation. **3** *Eccl.* a gathering for discussion of theological questions. [L *colloquium* (as COM-, *loqui* speak)]

■ **1, 2** see CONVERSATION 1. **3** see CONFERENCE 1.

collotype /kólətip/ *n. Printing* **1** a thin sheet of gelatin exposed to light, treated with reagents, and used to make high quality prints by lithography. **2** a print made by this process. [Gk *kolla* glue + TYPE]

collude /kəlṓd/ *v.intr.* come to an understanding or conspire together, esp. for a fraudulent purpose. □□ **colluder** *n.* [L *colludere collus-* (as COM-, *ludere lus-* play)]

■ see PLOT *v.* 2.

collusion /kəlṓzhən/ *n.* **1** a secret understanding, esp. for a fraudulent purpose. **2** *Law* such an understanding between ostensible opponents in a lawsuit. □□ **collusive** /-lṓsiv/ *adj.* **collusively** *adv.* [ME f. OF *collusion* or L *collusio* (as COLLUDE)]

■ **1** see INTRIGUE *n*. 1.

collyrium /kəléereeəm/ *n*. (*pl.* **collyria** /-reeə/ or **collyriums**) a medicated eyewash. [L f. Gk *kollurion* poultice f. *kollura* coarse bread roll]

■ see WASH *n*. 7, 10.

collywobbles /kóleewobəlz/ *n.pl. colloq.* **1** a rumbling or pain in the stomach. **2** a feeling of strong apprehension. [fanciful, f. COLIC + WOBBLE]

Colo. *abbr.* Colorado.

colobus /kóləbəs/ *n.* any leaf-eating monkey of the genus *Colobus*, native to Africa, having shortened thumbs. [mod.L f. Gk *kolobos* docked]

colocynth /kóləsinth/ *n.* (also **coloquintida** /kóləkwíntidə/) **1 a** a plant of the gourd family, *Citrullus colocynthis*, bearing a pulpy fruit. **b** this fruit. **2** a bitter purgative drug obtained from the fruit. [L *colocynthis* f. Gk *kolokunthis*]

cologne /kəlṓn/ *n.* (in full **cologne water**) eau de cologne or a similar scented toilet water. [abbr.]

colon[1] /kṓlən/ *n.* a punctuation mark (:), used esp. to introduce a quotation or a list of items or to separate clauses when the second expands or illustrates the first; also between numbers in a statement of proportion (as in 10:1) and in Biblical references (as in Exodus 3:2). [L f. Gk *kōlon* limb, clause]

colon[2] /kṓlən/ *n. Anat.* the lower and greater part of the large intestine, from the cecum to the rectum. □□ **colonic** /kəlónik/ *adj.* [ME, ult. f. Gk *kolon*]

colonel /kə́rnəl/ *n.* **1** an army, air force, or marine officer, immediately below a brigadier general in rank. **2** = *lieutenant colonel.* □ **Colonel Blimp** see BLIMP *n.* 1. □□ **colonelcy** *n.* (*pl.* **-ies**). [obs. F *coronel* f. It. *colonnello* f. *colonna* COLUMN]

colonial /kəlṓneeəl/ *adj. & n.* ● *adj.* **1** of, relating to, or characteristic of a colony or colonies. **2** (esp. of architecture or furniture) built or designed in, or in a style characteristic of, the period of the British colonies in America before independence. ● *n.* **1** a native or inhabitant of a colony. **2** a house built in colonial style. □ **colonial goose** *Austral. & NZ* a boned and stuffed roast leg of mutton. □□ **colonially** *adv.*

colonialism /kəlṓneeəlizəm/ *n.* **1** a policy of acquiring or maintaining colonies. **2** *derog.* this policy regarded as the esp. economic exploitation of weak or backward peoples by a larger power. □□ **colonialist** *n.*

■ **2** neocolonialism, *usu. derog.* imperialism.

colonist /kólənist/ *n.* a settler in or inhabitant of a colony.

■ see SETTLER.

colonize /kólənīz/ *v.* **1** *tr.* **a** establish a colony or colonies in (a country or area). **b** settle as colonists. **2** *intr.* establish or join a colony. **3** *tr. Polit.* plant voters in (a district) for party purposes. **4** *tr. Biol.* (of plants and animals) become established (in an area). □□ **colonization** *n.* **colonizer** *n.*

■ **1, 2** see SETTLE[1] 12.

colonnade /kólənáyd/ *n.* a row of columns, esp. supporting an entablature or roof. □□ **colonnaded** *adj.* [F f. *colonne* COLUMN]

■ see PORTICO.

colony /kólənee/ *n.* (*pl.* **-ies**) **1 a** a group of settlers in a new country (whether or not already inhabited) fully or partly subject to the mother country. **b** the settlement or its territory. **2 a** people of one nationality or race or occupation in a city, esp. if living more or less in isolation or in a special quarter. **b** a separate or segregated group (*nudist colony*). **3** *Biol.* a collection of animals, plants, etc., connected, in contact, or living close together. [ME f. L *colonia* f. *colonus* farmer f. *colere* cultivate]

■ **1** see SETTLEMENT 2.

colophon /kóləfon, -fən/ *n.* **1** a publisher's device or imprint, esp. on the title page. **2** a tailpiece in a manuscript or book, often ornamental, giving the writer's or printer's name, the date, etc. [LL f. Gk *kolophōn* summit, finishing touch]

■ **1** see STAMP *n.* 2, 4.

colophony /kəlófonee/ *n.* = ROSIN. [L *colophonia* (resin) from Colophon in Asia Minor]

coloquintida var. of COLOCYNTH.

color /kúlər/ *n. & v.* ● *n.* (*Brit.* **colour**) **1 a** the sensation produced on the eye by rays of light when resolved as by a prism, selective reflection, etc., into different wavelengths. **b** perception of color; a system of colors. **2** one, or any mixture, of the constituents into which light can be separated as in a spectrum or rainbow, sometimes including (loosely) black and white. **3** a coloring substance, esp. paint. **4** the use of all colors, not only black and white, as in photography and television. **5 a** pigmentation of the skin, esp. when dark. **b** this as a ground for prejudice or discrimination. **6** ruddiness of complexion (*a healthy color*). **7** (in *pl.*) appearance or aspect (*see things in their true colors*). **8** (in *pl.*) **a** *Brit.* a colored ribbon or uniform, etc., worn to signify membership of a school, club, team, etc. **b** the flag of a regiment or ship. **c** a national flag. **9** quality, mood, or variety in music, literature, speech, etc.; distinctive character or timbre. **10** a show of reason; a pretext (*lend color to; under color of*). ● *v.* **1** *tr.* apply color to, esp. by painting or dyeing or with colored pens or pencils. **2** *tr.* influence (*an attitude colored by experience*). **3** *tr.* misrepresent, exaggerate, esp. with spurious detail (*a highly colored account*). **b** disguise. **4** *intr.* take on color; blush. □ **color-blind 1** unable to distinguish certain colors. **2** ignoring racial prejudice. **color-blindness** the condition of being color-blind. **color code** use of colors as a standard means of identification. **color-code** *v.tr.* identify by means of a color code. **color scheme** an arrangement or planned combination of colors esp. in interior design. **color sergeant** the senior sergeant of an infantry company. **queen's** (or **king's** or **regimental**) **color** a flag carried by a regiment. **show one's true colors** reveal one's true character or intentions. **under false colors** falsely; deceitfully. **with flying colors** see FLYING. [ME f. OF *color, colorer* f. L *color, colorare*]

■ *n.* **2** hue, tint, shade, tone, tinge, tincture. **3** pigmentation, pigment, dye, paint. **5 a** coloration, coloring. **6** bloom, flush, blush, redness, ruddiness, rosiness, glow. **7** (*colors*) appearance, aspect, identity, light. **8** (*colors*) **b** flag, ensign, standard, pennant, banner. **9** see CHARACTER *n.* 1. ● *v.* **1** tint, dye, stain, paint, tincture, tinge; pigment. **2** affect, bias; see also INFLUENCE *v.* **3 a** misrepresent, exaggerate, distort, falsify, taint, warp, twist, skew, slant, pervert. **b** mask, disguise, conceal. **4** blush, redden, flush, become red-faced.

colorable /kúlərəbəl/ *adj.* **1** specious; plausible. **2** counterfeit. □□ **colorably** *adv.*

Colorado potato beetle /kólərádō, -raádō/ *n.* a yellow and black striped beetle, *Leptinotarsa decemlineata*, the larva of which is highly destructive to the potato plant. [the state of *Colorado*]

colorant /kúlərənt/ *n.* a coloring substance.

■ see TINT *n.* 3.

coloration /kúləráyshən/ *n.* **1** coloring; a scheme or method of applying color. **2** the natural (esp. variegated) color of living things or animals. [F *coloration* or LL *coloratio* f. *colorare* COLOR]

coloratura /kúlərətōŏrə, -tyōŏr-/ *n.* **1** elaborate ornamentation of a vocal melody. **2** a singer (esp. a soprano) skilled in coloratura singing. [It. f. L *colorare* COLOR]

colored /kúlərd/ *adj. & n.* ● *adj.* **1** having color(s). **2** (also **Colored**) **a** often *offens.* wholly or partly of nonwhite descent. **b** *S.Afr.* of mixed white and nonwhite descent. ● *n.* (also **Colored**) **1** a colored person. **2** *S.Afr.* a person of mixed descent speaking Afrikaans or English as the mother tongue.

■ **2** see *adj.* BLACK *adj.* 3.

colorfast /kúlərfast/ *adj.* dyed in colors that will not fade nor be washed out. □□ **colorfastness** *n.*

colorful /kúlərfŏŏl/ *adj.* **1** having much or varied color; bright. **2** full of interest; vivid; lively. □□ **colorfully** *adv.* **colorfulness** *n.*

/.../ **pronunciation**	● **part of speech**
□ **phrases, idioms, and compounds**	
□□ **derivatives**	■ **synonym section**
cross-references appear in SMALL CAPITALS or *italics*	

■ **1** see VIVID 1. **2** see DRAMATIC 4.

colorific /kúlərífik/ *adj.* **1** producing color. **2** highly colored. [F *colorifique* or mod.L *colorificus* (as COLOR)]

colorimeter /kúlərímitər/ *n.* an instrument for measuring the intensity of color. □□ **colorimetric** /-métrik/ *adj.* **colorimetry** *n.* [L *color* COLOR + -METER]

coloring /kúləring/ *n.* **1** the process of or skill in using color(s). **2** the style in which a thing is colored, or in which an artist uses color. **3** facial complexion.

colorist /kúlərist/ *n.* a person who uses color, esp. in art.

colorize /kúləriz/ *v.tr.* (**colorized, colorizing**) add color to (orig. black-and-white movie film) using computer technology.

colorless /kúlərlis/ *adj.* **1** without color. **2** lacking character or interest. **3** dull or pale in hue. **4** neutral; impartial; indifferent. □□ **colorlessly** *adv.*

■ **1, 3** pale, pallid, blanched, white; wan, washed out, ashen, sallow, waxen, sickly; dull. **2** dull, drab, uninteresting, vacuous, vapid, lifeless, boring, tedious, spiritless, dry, dryasdust, dreary, characterless, insipid, bland, lackluster, uninspiring, uninspired. **4** see INDIFFERENT 4.

colossal /kəlósəl/ *adj.* **1** of immense size; huge, gigantic. **2** *colloq.* remarkable; splendid. **3** *Archit.* (of an order) having more than one story of columns. **4** *Sculpture* (of a statue) about twice life size. □□ **colossally** *adv.* [F f. *colosse* COLOSSUS]

■ **1** huge, vast, enormous, gigantic, giant, mammoth, massive, gargantuan, immense, monumental, titanic, elephantine, *colloq.* jumbo; Herculean. **2** spectacular, remarkable, splendid, stupendous, wonderful, awe-inspiring, staggering, extraordinary, incredible, overwhelming, unbelievable, *colloq.* fantastic.

Colosseum /kóləseéəm/ *n.* **1** an ancient Roman amphitheater, built in the first century AD. **2** (**colosseum**) = COLISEUM. [med.L, neut. of *colosseus* gigantic (as COLOSSUS)]

colossus /kəlósəs/ *n.* (*pl.* **colossi** /-sī/ or **colossuses**) **1** a statue much bigger than life size. **2** a gigantic person, animal, building, etc. **3** an imperial power personified. [L f. Gk *kolossos*]

■ **1** see STATUE. **2** see GIANT *n.* 1.

colostomy /kəlóstəmee/ *n.* (*pl.* **-ies**) *Surgery* an operation on the colon to make an opening in the abdominal wall to provide an artificial anus. [as COLON² + Gk *stoma* mouth]

colostrum /kəlóstrəm/ *n.* the first secretion from the mammary glands occurring after giving birth. [L]

colotomy /kəlótəmee/ *n.* (*pl.* **-ies**) *Surgery* an incision in the colon. [as COLON² + -TOMY]

colour *Brit.* var. of COLOR.

colposcopy /kolpóskəpee/ *n.* examination of the vagina and the neck of the womb. □□ **colposcope** /kólpəskōp/ *n.* [Gk *kolpos* womb + -SCOPY]

colt /kōlt/ *n.* a young, uncastrated male horse, usu. less than four years old. □□ **colthood** *n.* **coltish** *adj.* **coltishly** *adv.* **coltishness** *n.* [OE, = young ass or camel]

colter /kōltər/ *n.* esp. (*Brit.* **coulter**) a vertical cutting blade fixed in front of a plowshare. [OE f. L *culter*]

coltsfoot /kōltsfŏŏt/ *n.* (*pl.* **coltsfoots**) a wild composite plant, *Tussilago farfara*, with large leaves and yellow flowers.

colubrine /kóləbrin, kólyə-/ *adj.* **1** snakelike. **2** of the subfamily Colubrinae of nonpoisonous snakes. [L *colubrinus* f. *coluber* snake]

Columbine /kóləmbin/ *n.* the partner of Harlequin in pantomime. [F *Colombine* f. It. *Colombina* f. *colombino* dovelike]

columbine /kóləmbin/ *n.* any plant of the genus *Aquilegia*, esp. *A. vulgaris*, having purple-blue flowers. Also called AQUILEGIA. [ME f. OF *columbine* f. med.L *columbina herba* dovelike plant f. L *columba* dove (from the supposed resemblance of the flower to a cluster of 5 doves)]

columbite /kəlúmbīt/ *n. Chem.* an ore of iron and niobium found in America. [*Columbia*, a poetic name for America, + -ITE¹]

columbium /kəlúmbiəm/ *n. Chem.* = NIOBIUM.

column /kóləm/ *n.* **1** *Archit.* an upright cylindrical pillar often slightly tapering and usu. supporting an entablature or arch,

or standing alone as a monument. **2** a structure or part shaped like a column. **3** a vertical cylindrical mass of liquid or vapor. **4 a** a vertical division of a page, chart, etc., containing a sequence of figures or words. **b** the figures or words themselves. **5** a part of a newspaper regularly devoted to a particular subject (*gossip column*). **6 a** *Mil.* an arrangement of troops in successive lines, with a narrow front. **b** *Naut.* a similar arrangement of ships. □ **column inch** a quantity of print (esp. newsprint) occupying a one-inch length of a column. **dodge the column** *Brit. colloq.* shirk one's duty; avoid work. □□ **columnar** /kəlúmnər/ *adj.* **columned** *adj.* [ME f. OF *columpne* & L *columna* pillar]

■ **1–3** see PILLAR 1. **5** see EDITORIAL.

columnist /kóləmnist, -mist/ *n.* a journalist contributing regularly to a newspaper.

■ see JOURNALIST.

colure /kəlŏŏr/ *n. Astron.* either of two great circles intersecting at right angles at the celestial poles and passing through the ecliptic at either the equinoxes or the solstices. [ME f. LL *colurus* f. Gk *kolouros* truncated]

colza /kólzə, kŏl-/ *n.* = RAPE². [F *kolza(t)* f. LG *kōlsāt* (as COLE, SEED)]

COM *abbr.* computer output on microfilm or microfiche.

com- /kom, kəm, kum/ *prefix* (also **co-, col-, con-, cor-**) with; together; jointly; altogether. ¶ *com-* is used before *b, m, p,* and occas. before vowels and *f; co-* esp. before vowels, *h,* and *gn; col-* before *l, cor-* before *r,* and *con-* before other consonants. [L *com-, cum* with]

coma¹ /kōmə/ *n.* (*pl.* **comas**) a prolonged deep unconsciousness, caused esp. by severe injury or excessive use of drugs. [med.L f. Gk *kōma* deep sleep]

■ see STUPOR.

coma² /kōmə/ *n.* (*pl.* **comae** /-mee/) **1** *Astron.* a cloud of gas and dust surrounding the nucleus of a comet. **2** *Bot.* a tuft of silky hairs at the end of some seeds. [L f. Gk *komē* hair of head]

Comanche /kəmánchee/ *n.* **1 a** a N. American people native to the western plains. **b** a member of this people. **2** the language of this people.

comatose /kōmətōs, kóm-/ *adj.* **1** in a coma. **2** drowsy; sleepy; lethargic.

■ **1** see UNCONSCIOUS *adj.* **2** see *lethargic* (LETHARGY).

comb /kōm/ *n.* & *v.* ● *n.* **1** a toothed strip of rigid material for tidying and arranging the hair, or for keeping it in place. **2** a part of a machine having a similar design or purpose. **3 a** the red, fleshy crest of a fowl, esp. a cock. **b** an analogous growth in other birds. **4** a honeycomb. ● *v.tr.* **1** arrange or tidy (the hair) by drawing a comb through. **2** curry (a horse). **3** dress (wool or flax) with a comb. **4** search (a place) thoroughly. □ **comb out 1** tidy and arrange (hair) with a comb. **2** remove with a comb. **3** search or attack systematically. **4** search out and get rid of (anything unwanted). □□ **combed** *adj.* [OE *camb* f. Gmc]

■ *v.* **4** see SEARCH *v.* 1, 3.

combat *n.* & *v.* ● *n.* /kómbat, kúm-/ **1** a fight; an armed encounter or conflict; fighting; battle. **2** a struggle, contest, or dispute. ● *v.* /kəmbát, kómbat/ (**combated, combating**) **1** *intr.* engage in combat. **2** *tr.* engage in combat with. **3** *tr.* oppose; strive against. □ **combat fatigue** a mental disorder caused by stress in wartime combat. **single combat** a duel. [F *combat* f. *combattre* f. LL (as COM-, L *batuere* fight)]

■ *n.* **1** fight, encounter, engagement, duel, conflict, skirmish; action, fighting, battle. **2** struggle, contest, strife, controversy, dispute, quarrel, disagreement, altercation, confrontation. ● *v.* **1** fight, (do) battle, engage, war, clash, contend, duel, wrestle, come to blows, spar, grapple, *hist.* joust. **3** fight, struggle or strive against, oppose, defy, withstand; challenge, enter the lists against. □ **combat fatigue** shell shock.

combatant /kəmbat'nt, kómbət'nt/ *n.* & *adj.* ● *n.* a person engaged in fighting. ● *adj.* **1** fighting. **2** for fighting.

■ *n.* see CHAMPION *n.* 2b. ● *adj.* **1** see MILITANT *adj.* 2.

combative /kəmbátiv/ *adj.* ready or eager to fight; pugnacious. □□ **combatively** *adv.* **combativeness** *n.*

■ see PUGNACIOUS.

combe var. of COOMB.

comber[1] /kṓmər/ *n.* **1** a person or thing that combs, esp. a machine for combing cotton or wool very fine. **2** a long curling wave; a breaker.

■ **2** see WAVE *n.* 1, 2.

comber[2] /kṓmər/ *n. Brit.* a fish of the perch family, *Serranus cabrilla.* [18th c.: orig. unkn.]

combination /kómbináyshən/ *n.* **1** the act or an instance of combining; the process of being combined. **2** a combined state (*in combination with*). **3** a combined set of things or people. **4** a sequence of numbers or letters used to open a combination lock. **5** *Brit.* a motorcycle with sidecar attached. **6** (in *pl.*) a single undergarment for the body and legs. **7** a group of things chosen from a larger number without regard to their arrangement. **8 a** united action. **b** *Chess* a coordinated and effective sequence of moves. **9** *Chem.* a union of substances in a compound with new properties. □ **combination lock** a lock that can be opened only by a specific sequence of movements. □□ **combinative** /kómbináytiv, kəmbĭnə-/ *adj.* **combinational** *adj.* **combinatory** /kəmbĭnətawree/ *adj.* [obs. F *combination* or LL *combinatio* (as COMBINE)]

■ **1** union, conjunction, mixture, mix, grouping, amalgamation, compound; blend. **2** conjunction, tandem; see also ASSOCIATION 2. **3** set, array; association, alliance, coalition, union, federation, confederation, combine, syndicate, consortium, trust, bloc, cartel, party, society, organization, league; see also MIXTURE 2.

combinatorial /kómbinətáwreeəl, kəmbĭnə-/ *adj. Math.* relating to combinations of items.

combine *v. & n.* ● *v.* /kəmbĭn/ **1** *tr. & intr.* join together; unite for a common purpose. **2** *tr.* possess (qualities usually distinct) together (*combines charm and authority*). **3 a** *intr.* coalesce in one substance. **b** *tr.* cause to do this. **c** *intr.* form a chemical compound. **4** *intr.* cooperate. **5** /kómbĭn/ *tr.* harvest (crops, etc.) by means of a combine harvester. ● *n.* /kómbĭn/ a combination of esp. commercial interests to control prices, etc. □ **combine harvester** /kómbĭn/ a mobile machine that reaps and threshes in one operation. **combining form** *Gram.* a linguistic element used in combination with another element to form a word (e.g., *Anglo-* = English, *bio-* = life, *-graphy* writing). ¶ In this dictionary, *combining form* is used of an element that contributes to the particular sense of words (as with both elements of *biography*), as distinct from a prefix or suffix that adjusts the sense of or determines the function of words (as with *un-*, *-able*, and *-ation*). □□ **combinable** /kəmbĭnəbəl/ *adj.* [ME f. OF *combiner* or LL *combinare* (as COM-, L *bini* two)]

■ *v.* **1** unite, unify, join, connect, relate, link, conjoin, integrate, merge, pool; band, ally, join forces. **2** see FUSE[1] *v.* **3** come together; blend, fuse, synthesize, bind, bond, unite, coalesce, join, mingle, amalgamate, mix, merge, integrate, meld, bind, bond, *literary* commingle; compound, bring *or* put together, conflate. **4** see COOPERATE.

combing /kṓming/ *n.* (in *pl.*) hairs combed off. □ **combing wool** long-stapled wool, suitable for combing and making into worsted.

combo /kómbō/ *n.* (*pl.* **-os**) *sl.* a small jazz or dance band. [abbr. of COMBINATION + -o]

■ see BAND[2] *n.* 2.

combust /kəmbúst/ *v.tr.* subject to combustion. [obs. *combust* (adj.) f. L *combustus* past part. (as COMBUSTION)]

combustible /kəmbústibəl/ *adj. & n.* ● *adj.* **1** capable of or used for burning. **2** excitable; easily irritated. ● *n.* a combustible substance. □□ **combustibility** /-bílitee/ *n.* [F *combustible* or med.L *combustibilis* (as COMBUSTION)]

■ *adj.* **1** see FLAMMABLE.

combustion /kəmbúschən/ *n.* **1** burning; consumption by fire. **2** *Chem.* the development of light and heat from the chemical combination of a substance with oxygen. □□ **combustive** /-bústiv/ *adj.* [ME f. F *combustion* or LL *combustio* f. L *comburere combust-* burn up]

Comdr. *abbr.* commander.

come /kum/ *v. & n.* ● *v.intr.* (*past* **came** /kaym/; *past part.* **come**) **1** move, be brought toward, or reach a place thought of as near or familiar to the speaker or hearer (*come and see me*; *shall we come to your house?*; *the books have come*). **2** reach or be brought to a specified situation or result (*you'll come to no harm*; *have come to believe it*; *has come to be used wrongly*; *came into prominence*). **3** reach or extend to a specified point (*the road comes within a mile of us*). **4** traverse or accomplish (with compl.: *have come a long way*). **5** occur; happen; become present instead of future (*how did you come to break your leg?*). **6** take or occupy a specified position in space or time (*it comes on the third page*; *Clinton came after Bush*; *it does not come within the scope of the inquiry*). **7** become perceptible or known (*the church came into sight*; *the news comes as a surprise*; *it will come to me*). **8** be available (*the dress comes in three sizes*; *this model comes with optional features*). **9** become (with compl.: *the handle has come loose*). **10** (foll. by *of*) **a** be descended from (*comes of a rich family*). **b** be the result of (*that comes of complaining*). **11** *colloq.* play the part of; behave like (with compl.: *don't come the bully with me*). **12** *sl.* have a sexual orgasm. **13** (in *subj.*) *colloq.* when a specified time is reached (*come next month*). **14** (as *int.*) expressing caution or reserve (*come now, it cannot be that bad*). ● *n. sl.* semen ejaculated at a sexual orgasm. □ **as . . . as they come** typically or supremely so (*is as tough as they come*). **come about 1** happen; take place. **2** *Naut.* tack. **come across 1 a** be effective or understood. **b** appear or sound in a specified way (*you came across very well*; *the ideas came across clearly*). **2** (foll. by *with*) *sl.* hand over what is wanted. **3** meet or find by chance (*came across an old jacket*). **come again** *colloq.* **1** make a further effort. **2** (as *imper.*) what did you say? **come along 1** make progress; move forward. **2** (as *imper.*) hurry up. **come and go 1** pass to and fro; be transitory. **2** pay brief visits. **come apart** fall or break into pieces; disintegrate. **come around 1** pay an informal visit. **2** recover consciousness. **3** be converted to another person's opinion. **4** (of a date or regular occurrence) recur; be imminent again. **come at 1** reach; discover; get access to. **2** attack (*came at me with a knife*). **come-at-able** /kumátəbəl/ *adj.* reachable; accessible. **come away 1** become detached or broken off (*came away in my hands*). **2** (foll. by *with*) be left with a feeling, impression, etc. (*came away with many misgivings*). **come back 1** return. **2** recur to one's memory. **3** become fashionable or popular again. **4** reply; retort. **come before** be dealt with by (a judge, etc.). **come between 1** interfere with the relationship of. **2** separate; prevent contact between. **come by 1** pass; go past. **2** call on a visit (*why not come by tomorrow?*). **3** acquire; obtain; attain (*came by a new bicycle*). **come clean** see CLEAN. **come down 1** come to a place or position regarded as lower. **2** lose position or wealth (*has come down in the world*). **3** be handed down by tradition or inheritance. **4** be reduced; show a downward trend (*prices are coming down*). **5** (foll. by *against, in favor of, on the side of*) reach a decision or recommendation (*the report came down against change*). **6** (foll. by *to*) signify or betoken basically; be dependent on (a factor) (*it comes down to who is willing to go*). **7** (foll. by *on*) criticize harshly; rebuke; punish. **8** (foll. by *with*) begin to suffer from (a disease). **come for 1** come to collect or receive. **2** attack (*came for me with a hammer*). **come forward 1** advance. **2** offer oneself for a task, post, etc. **come-hither** *attrib.adj. colloq.* (of a look or manner) enticing; flirtatious. **come in 1** enter a house or room. **2 a** take a specified position in a race, etc. (*came in third*). **b** *colloq.* win. **3** become fashionable or seasonable. **4 a** have a useful role or function. **b** (with compl.) prove to be (*came in very handy*). **c** have a part to play (*where do I come in?*). **5** be received (*more news has just come in*). **6** begin speaking, esp. in radio transmission. **7** be elected; come to power. **8** *Cricket* begin an in-

---

/. . ./ **pronunciation**	● **part of speech**
□ **phrases, idioms, and compounds**	
□□ **derivatives**	■ **synonym section**
cross-references appear in SMALL CAPITALS or *italics*	

nings. **9** (foll. by *for*) receive; be the object of (usu. something unwelcome) (*came in for much criticism*). **10** (foll. by *on*) join (an enterprise, etc.). **11** (of a tide) turn to high tide. **12** (of a train, ship, or aircraft) approach its destination. **come into 1** see senses 2, 7 of *v.* **2** receive, esp. as heir. **come near** see NEAR. **come of age** see AGE. **come off 1** *colloq.* (of an action) succeed; be accomplished. **2** (with compl.) fare; turn out (*came off badly; came off the winner*). **3** *Brit. coarse sl.* have a sexual orgasm. **4** be detached or detachable (from). **5** fall (from). **6** be reduced or subtracted from (*$5 came off the price*). **come off it** (as *imper.*) *colloq.* an expression of disbelief or refusal to accept another's opinion, behavior, etc. **come on 1** continue to come. **2 a** advance, esp. to attack. **b** (foll. by *to*) make sexual advances. **3** make progress; thrive (*is really coming on*). **4** (foll. by *to* + infin.) *Brit.* begin (*it came on to rain*). **5** appear on the stage, field of play, etc. **6** be heard or seen on television, on the telephone, etc. **7** arise to be discussed. **8** (as *imper.*) expressing encouragement. **9** = *come upon.* **come-on** *n. sl.* a lure or enticement. **come out 1 a** emerge; become known (*it came out that he had left*). **b** end; turn out. **2** appear or be published (*comes out every Saturday*). **3 a** declare oneself; make a decision (*came out in favor of joining*). **b** openly declare that one is a homosexual. **4** *Brit.* go on strike. **5 a** be satisfactorily visible in a photograph, etc., or present in a specified way (*the dog didn't come out; he came out badly*). **b** (of a photograph) be produced satisfactorily in a specified way (*only three have come out; they all came out well*). **6** attain a specified result in an examination, etc. **7** (of a stain, etc.) be removed. **8** make one's début on stage or in society. **9** (foll. by *in*) be covered with (*came out in spots*). **10** (of a problem) be solved. **11** (foll. by *with*) declare openly; disclose. **come over 1** come from some distance or nearer to the speaker (*came over from Paris; come over here a moment*). **2** change sides or one's opinion. **3 a** (of a feeling, etc.) overtake or affect (a person). **b** *Brit. colloq.* feel suddenly (*came over faint*). **4** esp. *Brit.* = *come across* 1 b. **5** affect or influence (*I don't know what came over me*). **come through 1** be successful; survive. **2** be received by telephone. **3** survive or overcome (a difficulty) (*came through the ordeal*). **come to 1** recover consciousness. **2** *Naut.* bring a vessel to a stop. **3** reach in total; amount to. **4** *refl.* **a** recover consciousness. **b** *Brit.* stop being foolish. **5** have as a destiny; reach (*what is the world coming to?*). **6** be a question of (*when it comes to wine, he is an expert*). **come to hand** *Brit.* become available; be recovered. **come to light** see LIGHT[1]. **come to nothing** have no useful result in the end; fail. **come to pass** happen; occur. **come to rest** cease moving. **come to one's senses** see SENSE. **come to that** *colloq.* in fact; if that is the case. **come under 1** be classified as or among. **2** be subject to (influence or authority). **come up 1** come to a place or position regarded as higher. **2** attain wealth or position (*come up in the world*). **3** (of an issue, problem, etc.) arise; present itself; be mentioned or discussed. **4** (often foll. by *to*) **a** approach a person, esp. to talk. **b** (foll. by *to, on*) approach or draw near to a specified time, event, etc. (*is coming up to eight o'clock*). **5** (foll. by *to*) match (a standard, etc.). **6** (foll. by *with*) produce (an idea, etc.). esp. in response to a challenge. **7** (of a plant, etc.) spring up out of the ground. **8** become brighter (e.g., with polishing); shine more brightly. **come up against** be faced with or opposed by. **come upon 1** meet or find by chance. **2** attack by surprise. **come what may** no matter what happens. **have it coming to one** *colloq.* be about to get one's deserts. **how come?** *colloq.* **1** why is that? **2** how did that happen? **if it comes to that** in that case. **to come** future; in the future (*the year to come; many problems were still to come*). [OE *cuman* f. Gmc]

▪ *v.* **1** approach, advance, (draw) near, move closer, *archaic or dial.* draw nigh; arrive, appear, make *or* put in an appearance, turn *or* show up, *colloq.* blow in. **3** extend, reach, stretch *or* spread (out), range, go. **5** see CHANCE *v.* 2. **9** see BECOME 1. **10 a** see SPRING *v.* 3. **b** see SPRING *v.* 4. **11** see ACT *v.* 5a. **12** climax. □ **come about 1** occur, happen, take place, *disp.* transpire, *poet.* befall. **2** *Naut.* tack, go about. **come across 1** be

communicated *or* understandable, penetrate, sink in; go over, be received, esp. *Brit.* come over; sound, appear. **2** see DELIVER 5. **3** find, discover, encounter, run across *or* into, happen *or* chance upon, hit *or* light upon, stumble (up)on. **come again 1** see PERSEVERE. **come along 1** do, progress, move along, *literary* fare; see also *get on* 1. **2** see HURRY *v.* 1. **come apart** disintegrate, crumble, fall apart *or* to pieces, separate, break (apart *or* up). **come around 1** see VISIT *v.* 1. **2** see *come to* 1 below. **3** see *change one's mind.* **4** see RECUR. **come at 1** see REACH *v.* 4. **2** attack, assault, charge, rush (at), fly at, descend (up)on, make for, *colloq.* go for. **come-at-able** see ACCESSIBLE 1. **come away 1** see DETACH 1, BREAK[1] *v.* 1a. **2** go, go away *or* off, leave, depart. **come back 1** see RETURN *v.* 1. **4** reply, answer, respond, retort, rejoin, return. **come between 1** see INTERFERE 2. **2** see SEPARATE *v.* 1. **come by 1** pass (by), go past, move *or* proceed past. **2** see CALL *v.* 4. **3** acquire, obtain, get, procure; secure, find, take *or* get possession of, get *or* lay hold of, get *or* lay *or* put (one's) hands on; win, earn, attain. **come down 1** see DESCEND 1. **4** see FALL *v.* 8. **5** resolve, rule; see also DECIDE 1. **6** see DEPEND 1. **7** (*come down on*) punish, pounce on *or* upon, rebuke, criticize, revile, reprimand, bear down on. **8** (*come down with*) succumb to, contract, catch, be afflicted with, get, *archaic* be stricken with. **come for 2** see ATTACK *v.* 1. **come forward 1** see ADVANCE *v.* 1, 2. **come-hither** see *flirtatious* (FLIRT). **come in 1** enter, go in *or* into. **2 a** finish, end up, come, arrive. **b** win, succeed, *colloq.* finish (in the money). **4 b** be, prove (to be), turn out (to be). **9** see INCUR. **12** arrive. **come into 2** see RECEIVE 1, 2. **come off 1** succeed; occur, happen, be accomplished, come to pass, take place. **2** turn out, emerge, result as, end up; see also FARE *v.* 1. **4** see DETACH 1. **5** see FALL *v.* 1a. **come off it** see *go on!* **come on 3** see ADVANCE *v.* 1, 2, BOOM[2] *v.* **5** see ENTER 1c. **6** appear. **7** see ARISE 3. **come-on** lure, attraction, enticement, inducement, temptation, bait. **come out 1 a** be revealed, become public *or* known *or* common knowledge, get about *or* around, get *or* leak out, emerge. **b** end, conclude, terminate, finish, turn out. **2** appear, be published *or* issued *or* produced *or* distributed, be shown, be in print, première. **3 a** see DECIDE 1. **b** come out of the closet. **7** go, vanish, disappear. **11** see DISCLOSE 1. **come over 1** see JOURNEY *v.*, COME *v.* 1 above. **2** change over, change, convert, switch, shift. **3 a** see OVERTAKE 2, AFFECT[1] 2. **come through 1** succeed, be successful, not fail *or* disappoint; survive, get well *or* better. **3** recover from, recuperate from. **come to 1** regain *or* recover consciousness, awake(n), revive, wake up, come around. **3** amount to, add up to, total, aggregate, (be) equal (to), mount up to, tot up to, make. **4 a** see *come to* 1 above. **5** see BECOME 1. **6** regard, concern, relate to, be a question of, involve, be relevant to, be involved. **come to nothing** see FAIL *v.* 1, 2a. **come to pass** see HAPPEN *v.* 1. **come to rest** see STOP *v.* 3. **come to that** see *in fact* 1 (FACT). **come under 2** see SUBJECT *adj.* 1. **come up 1** rise, esp. *archaic & poet.* arise. **2** see PROSPER. **3** arise, surface, present itself, be brought up, be broached, crop up. **4** see APPROACH *v.* 1, 2. **6** see *think up.* **7** appear, sprout, spring up, shoot up, grow. **come up against** face, experience, meet (with), contend with, be faced with, come into contact with, wrestle with. **come upon 1** see STUMBLE *v.* 4. **how come?** why? **if it comes to that** in that case. **to come** see FORTHCOMING 1.

comeback /kúmbak/ *n.* **1** a return to a previous (esp. successful) state. **2** *sl.* a retaliation or retort. **3** *Austral.* a sheep bred from crossbred and purebred parents for both wool and meat.

▪ **1** see REVIVAL 1, 3. **2** see RETORT *n.* 1, 3.

comedian /kəméedeeən/ *n.* **1** a humorous entertainer on stage, television, etc. **2** an actor in comedy. [F *comédien* f. *comédie* COMEDY]

■ **1** comic, comedienne, humorist, wit, wag, funny man *or* woman, jokesmith.

comedienne /kəmeédee-én/ *n.* a female comedian. [F fem. (as COMEDIAN)]

comedist /kómidist/ *n.* a writer of comedies.

comedo /kómidō/ *n.* (*pl.* **comedones** /-dōneez/) *Med.* a blackhead. [L, = glutton f. *comedere* eat up]

■ see SPOT *n.* 1c.

comedown /kúmdown/ *n.* **1** a loss of status; decline or degradation. **2** a disappointment.

comedy /kómidee/ *n.* (*pl.* **-ies**) **1 a** a play, film, etc., of an amusing or satirical character, usu. with a happy ending. **b** the dramatic genre consisting of works of this kind (*she excels in comedy*) (cf. TRAGEDY). **2** an amusing or farcical incident or series of incidents in everyday life. **3** humor, esp. in a work of art, etc. □ **comedy of manners** see MANNER. □□ **comedic** /kəmeédik/ *adj.* [ME f. OF *comedie* f. L *comoedia* f. Gk *kōmōidia* f. *kōmōidos* comic poet f. *kōmos* revel]

■ **3** see HUMOR *n.* 1.

comely /kúmlee/ *adj.* (**comelier, comeliest**) pleasant to look at. □□ **comeliness** /kúmleenis/ *n.* [ME *cumelich, cumli* prob. f. *becumelich* f. BECOME]

■ good-looking, pretty, lovely, fair, beautiful, handsome, attractive, appealing, wholesome, winsome.

comer /kúmər/ *n.* **1** a person who comes, esp. as an applicant, participant, etc. (*offered the job to the first comer*). **2** *colloq.* a person likely to be a success. □ **all comers** any applicants (with reference to a position, or esp. a challenge to a champion, that is unrestricted in entry).

comestible /kəméstibəl/ *n.* (usu. in *pl.*) *formal* or *joc.* food. [ME f. F f. med.L *comestibilis* f. L *comedere comest-* eat up]

■ see FOOD 1.

comet /kómit/ *n.* a hazy object usu. with a nucleus of ice and dust surrounded by gas and with a tail pointing away from the sun, moving in an eccentric orbit around the sun. □□ **cometary** *adj.* [ME f. OF *comete* f. L *cometa* f. Gk *komētes* long-haired (star)]

■ see STAR *n.* 1.

comeuppance /kumúpəns/ *n.* *colloq.* one's deserved fate or punishment (*got his comeuppance*). [COME + UP + -ANCE]

■ see DESERT³ 1b.

comfit /kúmfit/ *n.* *archaic* a sweet consisting of a nut, seed, etc., coated in sugar. [ME f. OF *confit* f. L *confectum* past part. of *conficere* prepare: see CONFECTION]

■ see SWEET *n.* 1.

comfort /kúmfərt/ *n.* & *v.* ● *n.* **1** consolation; relief in affliction. **2 a** a state of physical well-being; being comfortable (*live in comfort*). **b** (usu. in *pl.*) things that make life easy or pleasant (*has all the comforts*). **3** a cause of satisfaction (*a comfort to me that you are here*). **4** a person who consoles or helps one (*he's a comfort to her in her old age*). ● *v.tr.* **1** soothe in grief; console. **2** make comfortable (*comforted by the warmth of the fire*). □ **comfort station** *euphem.* a public lavatory. [ME f. OF *confort(er)* f. LL *confortare* strengthen (as COM-, L *fortis* strong)]

■ *n.* **1** consolation, solace, relief, cheer, help, support. **2 a** ease, luxury, security, abundance, plenty, opulence. **3** pleasure, delight, joy, treat, blessing. **4** see HELP *n.* 2. ● *v.* **1** console, solace, soothe, assuage, reassure, relieve, hearten, cheer, gladden.

comfortable /kúmftəbəl, -fərtəbəl/ *adj.* **1 a** such as to avoid hardship or trouble and give comfort or ease (*a comfortable pair of shoes*). **b** (of a person) relaxing to be with; congenial. **2** free from discomfort; at ease (*I'm quite comfortable, thank you*). **3** *colloq.* having an adequate standard of living; free from financial worry. **4 a** having an easy conscience (*did not feel comfortable about refusing him*). **b** *colloq.* complacent; placidly self-satisfied. **5** with a wide margin (*a comfortable win*). □□ **comfortableness** *n.* **comfortably** *adv.* [ME f. AF *confortable* (as COMFORT)]

■ **1** congenial, amiable, pleasant, agreeable, relaxing; see also SNUG *adj.* 1a, b. **2** at ease, easy; relaxed, untroubled, undisturbed. **3** see *well off* 1 (WELL¹).

4 a see RIGHT *adj.* 1. **b** self-satisfied, complacent, smug. **5** easy, secure; see also *assured* (ASSURE 5a).

comforter /kúmfərtər/ *n.* **1** a person who comforts. **2** a warm quilt. **3** *Brit.* a baby's pacifier. **4** *archaic* a woolen scarf. [ME f. AF *confortour*, OF *-ëor* (as COMFORT)]

■ **2** see COVER *n.* 1f.

comfortless /kúmfərtlis/ *adj.* **1** dreary, cheerless. **2** without comfort.

comfrey /kúmfree/ *n.* (*pl.* **-eys**) any of various plants of the genus *Symphytum*, esp. *S. officinale* having large, hairy leaves and clusters of usu. white or purple bell-shaped flowers. [ME f. AF *cumfrie*, ult. f. L *conferva* (as COM-, *fervēre* boil)]

comfy /kúmfee/ *adj.* (**comfier, comfiest**) *colloq.* comfortable. □□ **comfily** *adv.* **comfiness** *n.* [abbr.]

comic /kómik/ *adj.* & *n.* ● *adj.* **1** (often *attrib.*) of, or in the style of, comedy (*a comic actor; comic opera*). **2** causing or meant to cause laughter; funny (*comic to see his struggles*). ● *n.* **1** a professional comedian. **2** (*pl.*) section or page of a newspaper featuring several comic strips. □ **comic book** a magazine in the form of comic strips. **comic opera 1** an opera with much spoken dialogue, usu. with humorous treatment. **2** this genre of opera. **comic strip** a horizontal series of drawings in a comic book, newspaper, etc., telling a story. [L *comicus* f. Gk *kōmikos* f. *kōmos* revel]

■ *adj.* **2** funny, amusing, droll, comical, comedic, humorous, hilarious, sidesplitting, mirthful, jocose, jocular, witty, waggish. ● *n.* **1** see COMEDIAN. □ **comic opera** buffa.

comical /kómikəl/ *adj.* funny; causing laughter. □□ **comicality** /-kálitee/ *n.* **comically** *adv.* [COMIC]

coming /kúming/ *adj.* & *n.* ● *attrib.adj.* **1** approaching; next (*in the coming week; this coming Sunday*). **2** of potential importance (*a coming man*). ● *n.* **1** arrival; approach.

Comintern /kómintərn/ *n.* the Third International (see INTERNATIONAL *n.* 2), a communist organization (1919–43). [Russ. *Komintern* f. Russ. forms of *communist, international*]

comitadji /kómitǎjee/ *n.* (also **komitadji, komitaji**) a member of an irregular band of soldiers in the Balkans. [Turk. *komitaci*, lit. 'member of a (revolutionary) committee']

comity /kómitee/ *n.* (*pl.* **-ies**) **1** courtesy; civility; considerate behavior toward others. **2 a** an association of nations, etc., for mutual benefit. **b** (in full **comity of nations**) the mutual recognition by nations of the laws and customs of others. [L *comitas* f. *comis* courteous]

■ **1** see CIVILITY 1.

comm. *abbr.* **1** commerce. **2** commercial. **3** commissioner. **4** commission. **5** committee. **6** common. **7** commonwealth. **8** community.

comma /kómə/ *n.* **1** a punctuation mark (,) indicating a pause between parts of a sentence, or dividing items in a list, string of figures, etc. **2** *Mus.* a definite minute interval or difference of pitch. □ **comma bacillus** a comma-shaped bacillus causing cholera. [L f. Gk *komma* clause]

command /kəmánd/ *v.* & *n.* ● *v.tr.* **1** (also *absol.*; often foll. by *to* + infin., or *that* + clause) give formal order or instructions to (*commands us to obey; commands that it be done*). **2** (also *absol.*) have authority or control over. **3 a** (often *refl.*) restrain; master. **b** gain the use of; have at one's disposal or within reach (skill, resources, etc.) (*commands an extensive knowledge of history; commands a salary of $40,000*). **4** deserve and get (sympathy, respect, etc.). **5** *Mil.* dominate (a strategic position) from a superior height; look down over. ● *n.* **1** an authoritative order; an instruction. **2** mastery; control; possession (*a good command of languages; has command of the resources*). **3** the exercise or tenure of authority, esp. naval or military (*has command of this ship*). **4** *Mil.* **a** a body of troops, etc. (*Artillery Command*). **b** a district under a commander (*Western Command*). **5** *Computing* **a** an instruction causing a computer to perform one of its basic functions. **b**

/. . ./ **pronunciation**	● **part of speech**
□ **phrases, idioms, and compounds**	
□□ **derivatives**	■ **synonym section**
cross-references appear in SMALL CAPITALS or *italics*	

a signal initiating such an operation. □ **at command** ready to be used at will. **at** (or **by**) **a person's command** in pursuance of a person's bidding. **command module** the control compartment in a spacecraft. **command performance** a theatrical or film performance given at the request of a head of state or sovereign. **command post** the headquarters of a military unit. **in command of** commanding; having under control. **under command of** commanded by. [ME f. AF *comaunder*, OF *comander* f. LL *commandare* COMMEND]

■ *v.* **1** order, direct, enjoin, charge, request, require, demand, instruct, *archaic or literary* bid; say, prescribe, decree. **2, 5** control, dominate, wield authority *or* influence over, hold sway over; lead, rule, govern, have under one's thumb; head (up); look down on *or* over. **3 b** have, enjoy, possess; muster, draw (up)on, summon. **4** attract, earn; exact, compel, demand.
● *n.* **1** order, direction, instruction, mandate, charge, bidding, *literary* behest. **2** mastery, control, (thorough) grasp *or* knowledge, possession. **3** control, authority, power, sovereignty, dominion, regulation, direction, management, government, supervision, oversight, leadership, charge, sway, stewardship, jurisdiction. □ **at command** see *at will* 1 (WILL²). **in command of** (*be in command*) see *call the shots*.

commandant /kómandánt, -daánt/ *n.* a commanding officer, esp. of a particular force, military academy, etc. □□ **commandantship** *n.* [F *commandant*, or It. or Sp. *commandante* (as COMMAND)]
■ see LEADER 1.

commandeer /kómandeér/ *v.tr.* **1** seize (men or goods) for military purposes. **2** take possession of without authority. [S.Afr. Du. *kommanderen* f. F *commander* COMMAND]
■ see SEIZE 2.

commander /kamándar/ *n.* **1** a person who commands, esp. a naval officer next in rank below captain. **2** an officer in charge of a London police district. **3** (in full **knight commander**) a member of a higher class in some orders of knighthood. **4** a large wooden mallet. □ **commander in chief** the supreme commander, esp. of a nation's forces. □□ **commandership** *n.* [ME f. OF *comandere, -eör* f. Rmc (as COMMAND)]
■ **1, 2** see MASTER *n.* 1.

commanding /kamánding/ *adj.* **1** dignified; exalted; impressive. **2** (of a hill or other high point) giving a wide view. **3** (of an advantage, a position, etc.) controlling; superior (*has a commanding lead*). □□ **commandingly** *adv.*
■ **1** see MAGNIFICENT 1. **2** see *panoramic* (PANORAMA). **3** see DOMINANT *adj.*

commandment /kamándmant/ *n.* a divine command. □ **the Ten Commandments** the divine rules of conduct given by God to Moses on Mount Sinai, according to Exod. 20:1–17. [ME f. OF *comandement* (as COMMAND)]
■ see ORDER *n.* 2.

commando /kamándō/ *n.* (*pl.* **-os**) *Mil.* **1 a** a unit of amphibious shock troops. **b** a member of such a unit. **2 a** a party of men called out for military service. **b** a body of troops. **3** (*attrib.*) of or concerning a commando (*a commando operation*). [Port. f. *commandar* COMMAND]

comme ci, comme ça /kum seé kum saá/ *adv.* & *adj.* so-so; middling or middlingly. [F, = like this, like that]
■ see *so-so adj.* (SO¹).

commedia dell'arte /kumáydeea delaártay/ *n.* an improvised kind of popular comedy in Italian theaters in the 16th–18th c., based on stock characters. [It., = comedy of art]

comme il faut /kúm eel fő/ *adj.* & *adv.* ● *predic.adj.* (esp. of behavior, etiquette, etc.) proper; correct. ● *adv.* properly; correctly. [F, = as is necessary]
■ *adj.* see PROPER *adj.* 2.

commemorate /kamémarayt/ *v.tr.* **1** celebrate in speech or writing. **2 a** preserve in memory by some celebration. **b** (of a stone, plaque, etc.) be a memorial of. □□ **commemorative** /-ráytiv, -rativ/ *adj.* **commemorator** *n.* [L *commemorare* (as COM-, *memorare* relate f. *memor* mindful)]
■ **1** see CELEBRATE 1. **2** memorialize, remember,

celebrate, observe; reverence, revere, honor, venerate, pay tribute *or* homage to, salute, solemnize, sanctify, hallow; immortalize.

commemoration /kamémaráyshan/ *n.* **1** an act of commemorating. **2** a service or part of a service in memory of a person, an event, etc. [ME f. F *commemoration* or L *commemoratio* (as COMMEMORATE)]

commence /kaméns/ *v.tr.* & *intr. formal* begin. [ME f. OF *com(m)encier* f. Rmc (as COM-, L *initiare* INITIATE)]
■ begin, enter upon, start, open, initiate, launch, inaugurate, embark on *or* upon.

commencement /kaménsmant/ *n. formal* **1** a beginning. **2** a ceremony of degree conferment. [ME f. OF (as COMMENCE)]

commend /kaménd/ *v.tr.* **1** (often foll. by *to*) entrust; commit (*commends his soul to God*). **2** praise (*commends her singing voice*). **3** recommend (*method commends itself*). □ **commend me to** *archaic* remember me kindly to. **highly commended** (of a competitor, etc.) just missing the top places. [ME f. L *commendare* (as COM-, *mendare* = *mandare* entrust: see MANDATE)]
■ **1** see TRUST *v.* 4. **2** see PRAISE *v.* 1. **3** see RECOMMEND 1b, SUGGEST 1.

commendable /kaméndabal/ *adj.* praiseworthy. □□ **commendably** *adv.* [ME f. OF f. L *commendabilis* (as COMMEND)]
■ see PRAISEWORTHY.

commendation /kómendáyshan/ *n.* **1** an act of commending or recommending (esp. a person to another's favor). **2** praise. [ME f. OF f. L *commendatio* (as COMMEND)]
■ **1** see *recommendation* (RECOMMEND). **2** see PRAISE *n.*

commendatory /kaméndatawree/ *adj.* commending; recommending. [LL *commendatorius* (as COMMEND)]
■ see COMPLIMENTARY 1.

commensal /kaménsal/ *adj.* & *n.* ● *adj.* **1** *Biol.* of, relating to, or exhibiting commensalism. **2** (of a person) eating at the same table as another. ● *n.* **1** *Biol.* a commensal organism. **2** one who eats at the same table as another. □□ **commensality** /kómansálitee/ *n.* [ME f. F *commensal* or med.L *commensalis* (in sense 2) (as COM-, *mensa* table)]

commensalism /kaménsalizam/ *n. Biol.* an association between two organisms in which one benefits and the other derives no benefit or harm.

commensurable /kaménsarabal, -shara-/ *adj.* **1** (often foll. by *with, to*) measurable by the same standard. **2** (foll. by *to*) proportionate to. **3** *Math.* (of numbers) in a ratio equal to the ratio of integers. □□ **commensurability** *n.* **commensurably** *adv.* [LL *commensurabilis* (as COM-, MEASURE)]

commensurate /kaménsarat, -sharat/ *adj.* **1** (usu. foll. by *with*) having the same size, duration, etc.; coextensive. **2** (often foll. by *to, with*) proportionate. □□ **commensurately** *adv.* [LL *commensuratus* (as COM-, MEASURE)]
■ **1** see EQUAL *adj.* 1, 3, 4. **2** see PROPORTIONAL *adj.*

comment /kóment/ *n.* & *v.* ● *n.* **1 a** a remark, esp. critical; an opinion (*passed a comment on her hat*). **b** commenting; criticism (*his behavior aroused much comment; an hour of news and comment*). **2 a** an explanatory note (e.g., on a written text). **b** written criticism or explanation (e.g., of a text). **3** (of a play, book, etc.) a critical illustration; a parable (*his art is a comment on society*). ● *v.intr.* **1** (often foll. by *on, upon,* or *that* + clause) make (esp. critical) remarks (*commented on her choice of friends*). **2** (often foll. by *on, upon*) write explanatory notes. □ **no comment** *colloq.* I decline to answer your question. □□ **commenter** *n.* [ME f. L *commentum* contrivance (in LL also = interpretation), neut. past part. of *comminisci* devise, or F *commenter* (v.)]
■ *n.* **1** opinion, remark, view, observation, reaction; animadversion, criticism. **2 a** remark, reference, note, annotation, exposition, explanation, elucidation, clarification, footnote. **3** statement, judgment; see also CRITICISM 2. ● *v.* **1** remark, observe, opine, say; (*comment on* or *about*) discuss, talk about, remark on. **2** (*comment on* or *upon*) annotate.

commentary /kómantee/ *n.* (*pl.* **-ies**) **1** a set of explanatory or critical notes on a text, etc. **2** a descriptive spoken account (esp. on radio or television) of an event or a performance as it happens. [L *commentarius, -ium* adj. used as noun (as COMMENT)]

■ **1** see EXPLANATION 1. **2** see DESCRIPTION 1b.

commentate /kómǝntayt/ *v.intr. disp.* act as a commentator. [back-form. f. COMMENTATOR]

commentator /kómǝntaytǝr/ *n.* **1** a person who provides a commentary on an event, etc. **2** the writer of a commentary. **3** a person who writes or speaks on current events. [L f. *commentari* frequent. of *comminisci* devise]

■ **1, 3** see JOURNALIST.

commerce /kómǝrs/ *n.* **1** financial transactions, esp. the buying and selling of merchandise, on a large scale. **2** social intercourse (*the daily commerce of gossip and opinion*). **3** *archaic* sexual intercourse. [F *commerce* or L *commercium* (as COM-, *mercium* f. *merx mercis* merchandise)]

■ **1** business, marketing; see also TRADE *n.* 1a, b. **2** see INTERCOURSE. **3** see *sexual intercourse.*

commercial /kǝmǝ́rshǝl/ *adj. & n.* ● *adj.* **1** of, engaged in, or concerned with, commerce. **2** having profit as a primary aim rather than artistic, etc., value; philistine. **3** (of chemicals) supplied in bulk more or less unpurified. ● *n.* a television or radio advertisement. □ **commercial art** art used in advertising, selling, etc. **commercial broadcasting** television or radio broadcasting in which programs are financed by advertisements. **commercial traveler** *Brit.* a firm's traveling salesman or saleswoman who visits stores to get orders. **commercial vehicle** a vehicle used for carrying goods or fare-paying passengers. □□ **commercialism** *n.* **commerciality** /-sheeálitee/ *n.* **commercially** *adv.*

■ *adj.* **1** see ECONOMIC 1. **2** see PHILISTINE *adj.* ● *n.* **1** see ADVERTISEMENT 1.

commercialize /kǝmǝ́rshǝlīz/ *v.tr.* **1** exploit or spoil for the purpose of gaining profit. **2** make commercial. □□ **commercialization** *n.*

commère /kómair/ *n. Brit.* a female compère. [F, fem. of COMPÈRE]

commie /kómee/ *n. sl. derog.* (also **Commie**) a Communist. [abbr.]

commination /kómináyshǝn/ *n.* **1** the threatening of divine vengeance. **2 a** the recital of divine threats against sinners in the Anglican liturgy for Ash Wednesday. **b** the service that includes this. [ME f. L *comminatio* f. *comminari* threaten]

■ **1** see THREAT 1a.

comminatory /kǝmínǝtawree, kóminǝ-/ *adj.* threatening; denunciatory. [med.L *comminatorius* (as COMMINATION)]

■ see *threatening* (THREATEN).

commingle /kǝmínggǝl/ *v.tr. & intr. literary* mingle together.

comminute /kómǝnoot, -nyoot/ *v.tr.* **1** reduce to small fragments. **2** divide (property) into small portions. □ **comminuted fracture** a fracture producing multiple bone splinters. □□ **comminution** /-nooshǝn, -nyoo-/ *n.* [L *comminuere comminut-* (as COM-, *minuere* lessen)]

■ **1** see PULVERIZE 1, 2.

commis /kómee/ *n. Brit.* (*pl.* **commis** /kómeé, komeéz/) a junior waiter or chef. [orig. = deputy, clerk, f. F, past part. of *commettre* entrust (as COMMIT)]

commiserate /kǝmízǝrayt/ *v.* **1** *intr.* (usu. foll. by *with*) express or feel pity. **2** *tr. archaic* express or feel pity for (*commiserate you on your loss*). □□ **commiseration** /-ráyshǝn/ *n.* **commiserative** /-ráytiv/ *adj.* **commiserator** *n.* [L *commiserari* (as COM-, *miserari* pity f. *miser* wretched)]

■ see SYMPATHIZE 1.

commissar /kómisaar/ *n. hist.* **1** an official of the former Soviet Communist party responsible for political education and organization. **2** the head of a government department in the former USSR before 1946. [Russ. *komissar* f. F *commissaire* (as COMMISSARY)]

commissariat /kómisáireeǝt/ *n.* **1** esp. *Mil.* **a** a department for the supply of food, etc. **b** the food supplied. **2** *hist.* a government department of the former USSR before 1946. [F *commissariat* & med.L *commissariatus* (as COMMISSARY)]

commissary /kómiseree/ *n.* (*pl.* **-ies**) **1** *Mil.* **a** a store for the supply of food, etc., to soldiers. **b** an officer responsible

for the supply of food, etc., to soldiers. **2 a** a restaurant in a movie studio, etc. **b** the food supplied. **3** a deputy or delegate. **4** a representative or deputy of a bishop. □□ **commissarial** *adj.* **commissaryship** *n.* [ME f. med.L *commissarius* person in charge (as COMMIT)]

commission /kǝmíshǝn/ *n. & v.* ● *n.* **1 a** the authority to perform a task or certain duties. **b** a person or group entrusted esp. by a government with such authority (*set up a commission to look into it*). **c** an instruction, command, or duty given to such a group or person (*their commission was to simplify the procedure; my commission was to find him*). **2** an order for something, esp. a work of art, to be produced specially. **3** *Mil.* **a** a warrant conferring the rank of officer in the army, navy, marines, or air force. **b** the rank so conferred. **4 a** the authority to act as agent for a company, etc., in trade. **b** a percentage paid to the agent from the profits of goods, etc., sold, or business obtained (*his wages are low, but he gets 20 percent commission*). **c** the pay of a commissioned agent. **5** the act of committing (a crime, sin, etc.). **6** the office or department of a commissioner. ● *v.tr.* **1** authorize or empower by a commission. **2 a** give (an artist, etc.) a commission for a piece of work. **b** order (a work) to be written (*commissioned a new concerto*). **3** *Naut.* **a** give (an officer) the command of a ship. **b** prepare (a ship) for active service. **4** bring (a machine, equipment, etc.) into operation. □ **commission agent** *Brit.* a bookmaker. **in commission** (of a warship, etc.) manned, armed, and ready for service. **out of commission** (esp. of a ship) not in service; not in working order. [ME f. OF f. L *commissio -onis* (as COMMIT)]

■ *n.* **1 b** see COMMITTEE. **2** see ORDER *n.* 6. **4 b** see CUT *n.* 9. **6** see OFFICE 2, 3, 7. ● *v.* **1** see AUTHORIZE 2. **2** see ORDER *v.* 3. □ **out of commission** see *out of order* 1 (ORDER).

commissionaire /kǝmíshǝnáir/ *n.* esp. *Brit.* a uniformed door attendant at a theater, etc. [F (as COMMISSIONER)]

commissioner /kǝmíshǝnǝr/ *n.* **1** a person appointed by a commission to perform a specific task, e.g., a municipal police commissioner, etc. **2** a person appointed as a member of a government commission (*Civil Service Commissioner*). **3** a representative of the supreme authority in a district, department, etc. [ME f. med.L *commissionarius* (as COMMISSION)]

■ see OFFICER *n.* 1, 3, 4.

commissure /kómishoor/ *n.* **1** a junction, joint, or seam. **2** *Anat.* **a** the joint between two bones. **b** a band of nerve tissue connecting the hemispheres of the brain, the two sides of the spinal cord, etc. **c** the line where the upper and lower lips, or eyelids, meet. **3** *Bot.* any of several joints, etc., between different parts of a plant. □□ **commissural** /-míshǝrǝl/ *adj.* [ME f. L *commissura* junction (as COMMIT)]

commit /kǝmít/ *v.tr.* (**committed, committing**) **1** (usu. foll. by *to*) entrust or consign for: **a** safe keeping (*I commit him to your care*). **b** treatment, usu. destruction (*committed the book to the flames*). **c** official custody as a criminal or as insane (*you could be committed for such behavior*). **2** perpetrate, do (esp. a crime, sin, or blunder). **3** pledge, involve, or bind (esp. oneself) to a certain course or policy (*does not like committing herself; committed by the vow he had made*). **4** (as **committed** *adj.*) (often foll. by *to*) **a** morally dedicated or politically aligned (*a committed Christian; committed to the cause; a committed socialist*). **b** obliged (to take certain action) (*felt committed to staying there*). **5** *Polit.* refer (a bill, etc.) to a committee. □ **commit to memory** memorize. **commit to prison** consign officially to custody, esp. on remand. □□ **committable** *adj.* **committer** *n.* [ME f. L *committere* join, entrust (as COM-, *mittere miss-* send)]

■ **1 a** entrust, consign, transfer, assign, delegate, hand over, deliver, give; allot, pledge, allocate. **c** sentence, confine, shut up, intern, put away, imprison, commit to prison, incarcerate, send up, *Brit.* send down. **2** do, perform, carry out; see also PERPETRATE. **3** (*commit oneself*) pledge, promise, covenant, agree, assure, swear, give one's word, vow, engage, undertake, guarantee, bind oneself. **4 a** (**committed**) see DEVOTED. **5** see REFER 3. □ **commit to prison** see COMMIT 1c above.

commitment /kəmítmənt/ *n.* **1** an engagement or (esp. financial) obligation that restricts freedom of action. **2** the process or an instance of committing oneself; a pledge or undertaking. **3** dedication, application.
▪ **1** see BOND *n.* 2b. **2** see UNDERTAKING 2. **3** see APPLICATION 4.

committal /kəmít'l/ *n.* **1** the act of committing a person to an institution, esp. prison or a mental hospital. **2** the burial of a dead body.

committee /kəmítee/ *n.* **1 a** a body of persons appointed for a specific function by, and usu. out of, a larger body. **b** such a body appointed by a legislature, etc. to consider the details of proposed legislation. **2** /kómítee/ *Law* a person entrusted with the charge of another person or another person's property. □ **select committee** a small committee appointed by a legislative body, etc., for a special purpose. **standing committee** a committee that is permanent during the existence of the appointing body. [COMMIT + -EE]
▪ **1** council, board, cabinet, panel, body, commission, working party.

commix /kəmíks/ *v.tr. & intr. archaic* or *poet.* mix. □□ **commixture** *n.* [ME: back-form. f. *commixt* past part. f. L *commixtus* (as COM-, MIXED)]

commo /kómō/ *n.* (also **Commo**) (*pl.* **-os**) chiefly *Austral. & NZ sl.* a Communist. [abbr.]

commode /kəmṓd/ *n.* **1** a chest of drawers. **2 a** = TOILET 1. **b** (also **night commode**) a bedside table with a cupboard containing a chamber pot. **3** = CHIFFONIER. [F, adj. (as noun) f. L *commodus* convenient (as COM-, *modus* measure)]
▪ **1** see *chest of drawers.* **2** see *chamber pot.*

commodious /kəmṓdeeəs/ *adj.* **1** roomy and comfortable. **2** *archaic* convenient. □□ **commodiously** *adv.* **commodiousness** *n.* [F *commodieux* or f. med.L *commodiosus* f. L *commodus* (as COMMODE)]
▪ **1** see ROOMY. **2** see CONVENIENT 1.

commodity /kəmóditee/ *n.* (*pl.* **-ies**) **1** *Commerce* an article or raw material that can be bought and sold, esp. a product as opposed to a service. **2** a useful thing. [ME f. OF *commodité* or f. L *commoditas* (as COMMODE)]
▪ **1** see PRODUCT 1. **2** see THING 2, 3.

commodore /kómədawr/ *n.* **1** a naval officer above a captain and below a rear admiral. **2** the commander of a squadron or other division of a fleet. **3** the president of a yacht club. **4** the senior captain of a shipping line. [prob. f. Du. *komandeur* f. F *commandeur* COMMANDER]

common /kómən/ *adj. & n.* ● *adj.* (**commoner, commonest**) **1 a** occurring often (*a common mistake*). **b** occurring too frequently; overused; trite. **c** ordinary; of ordinary qualities; without special rank or position (*no common mind; common soldier; the common people*). **2 a** shared by, coming from, or done by, more than one (*common knowledge; by common consent; our common benefit*). **b** belonging to, open to, or affecting, the whole community or the public (*common land*). **3** *derog.* low-class; vulgar; inferior (*a common little man*). **4** of the most familiar type (*common cold; common nightshade*). **5** *Math.* belonging to two or more quantities (*common denominator; common factor*). **6** *Gram.* (of gender) referring to individuals of either sex (e.g., *teacher*). **7** *Prosody* (of a syllable) that may be either short or long. **8** *Mus.* having two or four beats, esp. four quarter notes, in a bar. **9** *Law* (of a crime) of lesser importance (cf. GRAND, PETTY). ● *n.* **1** a piece of open public land, esp. in a village or town. **2** *Eccl.* a service used for each of a group of occasions. **3** (in full **right of common**) *Law* a person's right over another's land, e.g., for pasturage. □ **common carrier** a person or firm undertaking to transport any goods or person in a specified category. **common chord** *Mus.* any note with its major or minor third and perfect fifth. **common crier** see CRIER.

common denominator see DENOMINATOR. **Common Era** the Christian era. **common fraction** a fraction expressed by numerator and denominator, not decimally. **common ground** a point or argument accepted by both sides in a dispute. **common jury** a jury with members of no particular social standing (cf. *special jury*). **common law** law derived from custom and judicial precedent rather than statutes (cf. *case law* (see CASE[1]), *statute law*). **common-law husband** (or **wife**) a partner in a marriage recognized by common law, esp. after a period of cohabitation. **Common Market** the European Economic Community. **common measure** (or **meter**) a hymn stanza of four lines with 8, 6, 8, and 6 syllables. **common noun** (or **name**) *Gram.* a name denoting a class of objects or a concept as opposed to a particular individual (e.g., *boy, chocolate, beauty*). **common or garden** *Brit. colloq.* ordinary. **Common Prayer** the Church of England liturgy orig. set forth in the *Book of Common Prayer* of Edward VI (1549). **common room** esp. *Brit.* **1** a room in some colleges, schools, etc., which members may use for relaxation or work. **2** the members who use this. **common salt** see SALT. **common sense** sound practical sense, esp. in everyday matters. **common soldier** see SOLDIER. **common stock** *US* ordinary shares of stock in a corporation (cf. *preferred stock*). **common weal** public welfare. **common year** see YEAR 2. **in common 1** in joint use; shared. **2** of joint interest (*have little in common*). **in common with** in the same way as. **least** (or **lowest**) **common denominator, multiple** see DENOMINATOR, MULTIPLE. □□ **commonly** *adv.* **commonness** *n.* [ME f. OF *comun* f. L *communis*]
▪ *adj.* **1 a** frequent, usual, familiar, customary, prevalent. **b** trite, stale, hackneyed, worn-out, banal, tired, overused, clichéd, stereotypic(al). **c** ordinary, everyday, commonplace, prosaic, run-of-the-mill, general, normal, standard, conventional, regular, routine, stock, average, mediocre, middling, plain, simple, workaday, undistinguished, unexceptional, *colloq.* common or garden. **2** public, general, community, communal, collective, nonprivate; well-known; universal, joint, shared, *colloq. disp.* mutual. **3** low-class, inferior, low-grade, mean, cheap, vulgar, base, ordinary, plain, simple, plebeian, bourgeois, proletarian, vulgar, unrefined. **4** familiar, commonplace, plain, simple, *colloq.* common or garden; see also FAMILIAR 1.
□ **common or garden** see ORDINARY *adj.* **common sense** see GUMPTION 2. **in common with** (just) like, in the same way as.

commonable /kómənəbəl/ *adj.* **1** (of an animal) that may be pastured on common land. **2** (of land) that may be held in common. [obs. *common* to exercise right of common + -ABLE]

commonage /kómənij/ *n.* **1** = *right of common* (see COMMON *n.* 3). **2 a** land held in common. **b** the state of being held in common. **3** the common people; commonalty.

commonality /kómənálitee/ *n.* (*pl.* **-ies**) **1** the sharing of an attribute. **2** a common occurrence. **3** = COMMONALTY. [var. of COMMONALTY]

commonalty /kómənəltee/ *n.* (*pl.* **-ies**) **1** the common people. **2** the general body (esp. of mankind). **3** a corporate body. [ME f. OF *comunalté* f. med.L *communalitas -tatis* (as COMMON)]
▪ **1** see PEOPLE *n.* 2.

commoner /kómənər/ *n.* **1** one of the common people, as opposed to the aristocracy. **2** a person who has the right of common. **3** a student at a British university who does not have a scholarship. [ME f. med.L *communarius* f. *communa* (as COMMUNE[1])]
▪ **1** see PLEBEIAN *n.*

commonplace /kómənplays/ *adj. & n.* ● *adj.* lacking originality; trite. ● *n.* **1 a** an everyday saying; a platitude (*uttered a commonplace about the weather*). **b** an ordinary topic of conversation. **2** anything usual or trite. **3** a notable passage in a book, etc., copied into a commonplace book. □ **commonplace book** a book into which notable extracts from other works are copied for personal use. □□ **commonplaceness**

n. [transl. of L *locus communis* = Gk *koinos topos* general theme]

■ *adj.* see BANAL. ● *n.* **1 a** see TRUISM.

commons /kómənz/ *n.pl.* **1** *US* a dining hall at a university, etc. **2** *New Eng.* a central public park or ground in a town, etc. **3** (**the Commons**) = *House of Commons*. **4 a** the common people. **b** (prec. by *the*) the common people regarded as a part of a political, esp. British, system. □ **short commons** *Brit.* insufficient food. [ME pl. of COMMON]

commonsensical /kómənsénsikəl/ *adj.* possessing or marked by common sense. [*common sense* (see COMMON)]

■ see SENSIBLE 1, 3.

commonweal /kómənweel/ *n. archaic* **1** = *common weal*. **2** = COMMONWEALTH.

commonwealth /kómənwelth/ *n.* **1 a** an independent state or community, esp. a democratic republic. **b** such a community or organization of shared interests in a nonpolitical field (*the commonwealth of learning*). **2** (**the Commonwealth**) **a** (in full **the British Commonwealth of Nations**) an international association consisting of the UK together with nations that were previously part of the British Empire. **b** the republican period of government in Britain 1649–60. **c** a part of the title of Puerto Rico and some of the states of the US. **d** the title of the federated Australian states. □ **Commonwealth Day** a day each year commemorating the British Commonwealth (formerly called *Empire Day*). [COMMON + WEALTH]

commotion /kəmṓshən/ *n.* **1 a** a confused and noisy disturbance or outburst. **b** loud and confusing noise. **2** a civil insurrection. [ME f. OF *commotion* or L *commotio* (as COM-, MOTION)]

■ **1** see NOISE 1, 2. **2** see DISORDER *n.* 2.

communal /kəmyṓnəl, kómyə-/ *adj.* **1** relating to or benefiting a community; for common use (*communal baths*). **2** of a commune, esp. the Paris Commune. □□ **communality** /-nálitee/ *n.* **communally** *adv.* [F f. LL *communalis* (as COMMUNE[1])]

■ **1** see COMMON *adj.* 2.

communalism /kəmyṓnəlizəm, kómyənə-/ *n.* **1** a principle of political organization based on federated communes. **2** the principle of communal ownership, etc. □□ **communalist** *n.* **communalistic** *adj.*

communalize /kəmyṓnəliz, kómyənə-/ *v.tr.* make communal. □□ **communalization** *n.*

communard /kómyənaard/ *n.* **1** a member of a commune. **2** (also **Communard**) *hist.* a supporter of the Paris Commune. [F (as COMMUNE[1])]

commune[1] /kómyōōn/ *n.* **1 a** a group of people, not necessarily related, sharing living accommodation, goods, etc., esp. as a political act. **b** a communal settlement esp. for the pursuit of shared interests. **2 a** the smallest French territorial division for administrative purposes. **b** a similar division elsewhere. **3** (**the Commune**) the communalistic government in Paris in 1871. [F f. med.L *communia* neut. pl. of L *communis* common]

commune[2] /kəmyṓōn/ *v.intr.* **1** (usu. foll. by *with*) **a** speak confidentially and intimately (*communed together about their loss*; *communed with his heart*). **b** feel in close touch (with nature, etc.) (*communed with the hills*). **2** receive Holy Communion. [ME f. OF *comuner* share f. *comun* COMMON]

■ **1** communicate.

communicable /kəmyṓōnikəbəl/ *adj.* **1** (esp. of a disease) able to be passed on. **2** *archaic* communicative. □□ **communicability** *n.* **communicably** *adv.* [ME f. OF *communicable* or LL *communicabilis* (as COMMUNICATE)]

■ **1** see INFECTIOUS 2, 3.

communicant /kəmyṓōnikənt/ *n.* **1** a person who receives Holy Communion, esp. regularly. **2** a person who imparts information. [L *communicare communicant-* (as COMMON)]

communicate /kəmyṓōnikayt/ *v.* **1** *tr.* **a** transmit or pass on by speaking or writing (*communicated his ideas*). **b** transmit (heat, motion, etc.). **c** pass on (an infectious illness). **d** impart (feelings, etc.) nonverbally (*communicated his affection*). **2** *intr.* (often foll. by *with*) be in communication; succeed in conveying information, evoking understanding, etc. (*she*

communicates well). **3** *intr.* (often foll. by *with*) share a feeling or understanding; relate socially. **4** *intr.* (often foll. by *with*) (of a room, etc.) have a common door (*my room communicates with yours*). **5 a** *tr.* administer Holy Communion to. **b** *intr.* receive Holy Communion. □□ **communicator** *n.* **communicatory** /-nikətáwree/ *adj.* [L *communicare communicat-* (as COMMON)]

■ **1 a** make known, impart, confer, transmit, transfer, hand on *or* down, share, pass on *or* along, get *or* put across, make understandable, send on, spread; tell, divulge, disclose, reveal, announce, promulgate, proffer, tender, offer, convey, present. **2** be in communication, converse, talk, correspond, associate, be in contact *or* touch; get through, make oneself understood. **3** be of one mind, be in tune, relate, be in rapport, be en rapport, *colloq.* be on the same wavelength.

communication /kəmyṓōnikáyshən/ *n.* **1 a** the act of imparting, esp. news. **b** an instance of this. **c** the information, etc., communicated. **2** a means of connecting different places, such as a door, passage, road, or railroad. **3** social intercourse (*it was difficult to maintain communication in the uproar*). **4** (in *pl.*) the science and practice of transmitting information esp. by electronic or mechanical means. **5** (in *pl.*) *Mil.* the means of transport between a base and the front. □ **communication cord** *Brit.* a cord or chain in a railroad car that may be pulled to stop the train in an emergency. **communication** (or **communications**) **satellite** an artificial satellite used to relay telephone circuits or broadcast programs. **communication theory** the study of the principles and methods by which information is conveyed.

■ **1** see INFORMATION 1, 3. **4** (*communications*) see TRANSMISSION 1.

communicative /kəmyṓōnikáytiv, -kətiv/ *adj.* **1** open; talkative; informative. **2** ready to communicate. □□ **communicatively** *adv.* [LL *communicativus* (as COMMUNICATE)]

■ **1** see TALKATIVE. **2** see RESPONSIVE.

communion /kəmyṓōnyən/ *n.* **1** a sharing, esp. of thoughts, etc.; fellowship (*their minds were in communion*). **2** participation; a sharing in common (*communion of interests*). **3** (**Communion, Holy Communion**) **a** the Eucharist. **b** participation in the Communion service. **c** (*attrib.*) of or used in the Communion service (*Communion table*; *Communion cloth*; *Communion rail*). **4** fellowship, esp. between branches of the Catholic Church. **5** a body or group within the Christian faith (*the Methodist communion*). □ **communion of saints** fellowship between Christians living and dead. [ME f. OF *communion* or L *communio* f. *communis* common]

communiqué /kəmyṓōnikáy/ *n.* an official communication, esp. a news report. [F, = communicated]

■ see BULLETIN 1.

communism /kómyənizəm/ *n.* **1** a political theory derived from Marx, advocating class war and leading to a society in which all property is publicly owned and each person is paid and works according to his or her needs and abilities. **2** (usu. **Communism**) **a** the communistic form of society established in the former USSR and elsewhere. **b** any movement or political doctrine advocating communism. **3** = COMMUNALISM. [F *communisme* f. *commun* COMMON]

communist /kómyənist/ *n. & adj.* ● *n.* **1** a person advocating or practicing communism. **2** (**Communist**) a member of a Communist party. ● *adj.* of or relating to communism (*a communist play*). □□ **communistic** /-nístik/ *adj.* [COMMUNISM]

■ *n.* **1** see left-winger (LEFT[1]). ● *adj.* see LEFT[1] *adj.* 3.

communitarian /kəmyṓōnitáireeən/ *n. & adj.* ● *n.* a member of a communistic community. ● *adj.* of or relating to

---

/. . ./ **pronunciation**	● **part of speech**
□ **phrases, idioms, and compounds**	
□□ **derivatives**	■ **synonym section**
cross-references appear in SMALL CAPITALS or *italics*	

such a community. [COMMUNITY + -ARIAN after *unitarian*, etc.]

community /kəmyóōnitee/ *n.* (*pl.* **-ies**) **1 a** all the people living in a specific locality. **b** a specific locality, including its inhabitants. **2** a body of people having a religion, a profession, etc., in common (*the immigrant community*). **3** fellowship of interests, etc.; similarity (*community of intellect*). **4** a monastic, socialistic, etc., body practicing common ownership. **5** joint ownership or liability (*community of goods*). **6** (prec. by *the*) the public. **7** a body of nations unified by common interests. **8** *Ecol.* a group of animals or plants living or growing together in the same area. □ **community center** a place providing social, etc., facilities for a neighborhood. **community charge** *hist.* (in the UK) a local tax levied on every adult in a community. **community college** a nonresidential junior college offering college courses to a local community or region. **community home** *Brit.* a center for housing young offenders and other juveniles in need of custodial care. **community service** unpaid work performed in service to the community, esp. as part of a criminal sentence. **community singing** singing by a large crowd or group, esp. of old popular songs or hymns. **community spirit** a feeling of belonging to a community, expressed in mutual support, etc. [ME f. OF *comuneté* f. L *communitas -tatis* (as COMMON)]

■ **1 b** see DISTRICT *n.* **2** see BROTHERHOOD 2. **6** see PUBLIC *n.* 1.

communize /kómyənīz/ *v.tr.* **1** make (land, etc.) common property. **2** make (a person, etc.) communistic. □□ **communization** *n.* [L *communis* COMMON]

commutable /kəmyóōtəbəl/ *adj.* **1** convertible into money; exchangeable. **2** *Law* (of a punishment) able to be commuted. **3** within commuting distance. □□ **commutability** *n.* [L *commutabilis* (as COMMUTE)]

commutate /kómyətayt/ *v.tr. Electr.* **1** regulate the direction of (an alternating current), esp. to make it a direct current. **2** reverse the direction (of an electric current). [L *commutare commutat-* (as COMMUTE)]

commutation /kómyətáyshən/ *n.* **1** the act or process of commuting or being commuted (in legal and exchange senses). **2** *Electr.* the act or process of commutating or being commutated. **3** *Math.* the reversal of the order of two quantities. □ **commutation ticket** a pass for travel on a public transportation line, purchased for a specified time or number of trips. [F *commutation* or L *commutatio* (as COMMUTE)]

commutative /kómyóōtətiv/ *adj.* **1** relating to or involving substitution. **2** *Math.* unchanged in result by the interchange of the order of quantities. [F *commutatif* or med.L *commutativus* (as COMMUTE)]

commutator /kómyətaytər/ *n.* **1** *Electr.* a device for reversing electric current. **2** an attachment connected with the armature of a dynamo which directs and makes continuous the current produced.

commute /kəmyóōt/ *v.* **1** *intr.* travel to and from one's daily work, usu. in a city, esp. by car or train. **2** *Law* (usu. foll. by *to*) change (a judicial sentence, etc.) to another less severe. **3** *tr.* (often foll. by *into, for*) **a** change (one kind of payment) for another. **b** make a payment, etc., to change (an obligation, etc.) for another. **4** *tr.* **a** exchange; interchange (two things). **b** change (to another thing). **5** *tr. Electr.* commutate. **6** *intr. Math.* have a commutative relation. **7** *intr.* buy and use a season ticket. [L *commutare commutat-* (as COM-, *mutare* change)]

■ **1** see TRAVEL *v.* 1. **2** see REPRIEVE *v.* 3, 4 see TRANSPOSE.

commuter /kəmyóōtər/ *n.* a person who travels some distance to work, esp. in a city, usu. by car or train.

comose /kǒmōs/ *adj. Bot.* (of seeds, etc.) having hairs; downy. [L *comosus* (as COMA²)]

■ see HAIRY 1.

comp /komp/ *n. & v. colloq.* ● *n.* **1** compensation. **2** a complimentary item or service. **3** *Brit.* a competition. **4** *Printing* a compositor. **5** *Mus.* an accompaniment. ● *v.* **1** *Mus.* **a** *tr.* accompany. **2** *intr.* play an accompaniment. **2** *Printing* **a** *intr.* work as a compositor. **b** *tr.* work as a compositor on. [abbr.]

comp. *abbr.* **1** companion. **2** comparative. **3** compensation. **4** compilation. **5** compiled. **6** compiler. **7** complete. **8** composite. **9** composition. **10** compositor. **11** comprehensive.

compact¹ *adj., v., & n.* ● *adj.* /kəmpákt, kóm-/ **1** closely or neatly packed together. **2** (of a piece of equipment, a room, etc.) well-fitted and practical though small. **3** (of style, etc.) condensed; brief. **4** (esp. of the human body) small but well-proportioned. **5** (foll. by *of*) composed or made up of. ● *v.tr.* /kəmpákt/ **1** join or press firmly together. **2** condense. **3** (usu. foll. by *of*) compose; make up. ● *n.* /kómpakt/ **1** a small, flat, usu. decorated, case for face powder, a mirror, etc. **2** an object formed by compacting powder. **3** a medium-sized automobile. □ **compact disc** /kómpakt/ a disc on which information or sound is recorded digitally and reproduced by reflection of laser light. □□ **compaction** /-pákshən/ *n.* **compactly** *adv.* **compactness** *n.* **compactor** *n.* [ME f. L *compingere compact-* (as COM-, *pangere* fasten)]

■ *adj.* **1** packed, compacted, closely knit, condensed, consolidated, compressed; dense, solid, firm, tight, thick. **3** condensed, terse, laconic, close, pithy, succinct, concise, brief, compendious, epigrammatic, aphoristic. ● *v.* **1, 2** compress, condense, squash (together), squeeze or push *or* press together.

compact² /kómpakt/ *n.* an agreement or contract between two or more parties. [L *compactum* f. *compacisci compact-* (as COM-, *pacisci* covenant): cf. PACT]

compages /kəmpáyjeez/ *n.* (*pl.* same) **1** a framework; a complex structure. **2** something resembling a compages in complexity, etc. [L *compages* (as COM-, *pages* f. *pangere* fasten)]

companion¹ /kəmpányən/ *n. & v.* ● *n.* **1 a** (often foll. by *in, of*) a person who accompanies, associates with, or shares with, another (*a companion in adversity; they were close companions*). **b** a person, esp. an unmarried or widowed woman, employed to live with and assist another. **2** a handbook or reference book on a particular subject (*A Companion to North Wales*). **3** a thing that matches another (*the companion of this bookend is over there*). **4** (**Companion**) a member of the lowest grade of some orders of knighthood (*Companion of the Bath*). **5** *Astron.* a star, etc., that accompanies another. **6** esp. *Brit.* equipment or a piece of equipment that combines several uses. ● *v.* **1** *tr.* accompany. **2** *intr. literary* (often foll. by *with*) be a companion. □ **companion in arms** esp. *Brit.* comrade in arms; a fellow soldier. [ME f. OF *compaignon* ult. f. L *panis* bread]

■ *n.* **1 a** fellow, associate, comrade, colleague, confrère, brother, mate, *colloq.* pal, chum, buddy. **2** vade mecum, manual, handbook, guide, reference book, *formal* enchiridion. **3** complement, counterpart, match, fellow. ● *v.* see ACCOMPANY 1.

companion² /kəmpányən/ *n. Naut.* **1** a raised frame on a quarterdeck used for lighting the cabins, etc., below. **2** = COMPANIONWAY. □ **companion hatch** a wooden covering over a companionway. **companion hatchway** an opening in a deck leading to a cabin. **companion ladder** a ladder from a deck to a cabin. [obs. Du. *kompanje* quarterdeck f. OF *compagne* f. It. (*camera della*) *compagna* pantry, prob. ult. rel. to COMPANION¹]

companionable /kəmpányənəbəl/ *adj.* agreeable as a companion; sociable. □□ **companionableness** *n.* **companionably** *adv.*

■ see SOCIABLE *adj.*

companionate /kəmpányənit/ *adj.* **1** well-suited; (of clothes) matching. **2** of or like a companion.

companionship /kəmpányənship/ *n.* good fellowship; friendship.

■ fellowship, friendship, camaraderie, comradeship, company, society, amity, fraternity, *Austral.* mateship.

companionway /kəmpányənway/ *n. Naut.* a staircase to a ship's cabin.

company /kúmpənee/ *n. & v.* ● *n.* (*pl.* **-ies**) **1 a** a number of people assembled; a crowd; an audience (*addressed the company*). **b** guests or a guest (*am expecting company*). **2** a state of being a companion or fellow; companionship, esp. of a specific kind (*enjoys low company; do not care for his com-*

pany). **3 a** a commercial business. **b** (usu. **Co.**) the partner or partners not named in the title of a firm (*Smith and Co.*). **4** a troupe of actors or entertainers. **5** *Mil.* a subdivision of an infantry battalion usu. commanded by a major or a captain. ● *v.* (**-ies, -ied**) **1** *tr. archaic* accompany. **2** *intr. literary* (often foll. by *with*) be a companion. □ **be in good company** discover that one's companions, or better people, have done the same as oneself. **company officer** a captain or a lower commissioned officer. **good** (or **bad**) **company 1** a pleasant (or dull) companion. **2** a suitable (or unsuitable) associate or group of friends. **in company** not alone. **in company with** together with. **keep company** (often foll. by *with*) associate habitually. **keep** (*archaic* **bear**) **a person company** accompany a person; be sociable. **part company** (often foll. by *with*) cease to associate. **ship's company** the entire crew. [ME f. AF *compainie*, OF *compai(g)nie* f. Rmc (as COMPANION¹)]
■ *n.* **1 a** assemblage, party, audience, band, group, circle, assembly, gathering, convention, body, crowd, throng; troop, followers, following, retinue, entourage, suite, train. **b** guest(s), visitor(s), caller(s). **2** companionship, society, fellowship; attendance, presence. **3 a** firm, business, house, concern, institution, establishment, enterprise; partnership, corporation. **4** troupe, cast, ensemble, players, actors and actresses, performers. ● *v.* see ACCOMPANY 1.

comparable /kómpərəbəl/ *adj.* **1** (often foll. by *with*) able to be compared. **2** (often foll. by *to*) fit to be compared; worth comparing. ¶ Use with *to* and *with* corresponds to the senses at *compare*; *to* is more common. □□ **comparability** *n.* **comparableness** *n.* **comparably** *adv.* [ME f. OF f. L *comparabilis* (as COMPARE)]

comparative /kəmpárətiv/ *adj. & n.* ● *adj.* **1** perceptible by comparison; relative (*in comparative comfort*). **2** estimated by comparison (*the comparative merits of the two ideas*). **3** of or involving comparison (esp. of sciences, etc.). **4** *Gram.* (of an adjective or adverb) expressing a higher degree of a quality, but not the highest possible (e.g., *braver, more fiercely*) (cf. POSITIVE, SUPERLATIVE). ● *n. Gram.* **1** the comparative expression or form of an adjective or adverb. **2** a word in the comparative. □□ **comparatively** *adv.* [ME f. L *comparativus* (as COMPARE)]

comparator /kəmpárətər/ *n. Engin.* a device for comparing a product, an output, etc., with a standard, esp. an electronic circuit comparing two signals.

compare /kəmpáir/ *v. & n.* ● *v.* **1** *tr.* (usu. foll. by *to*) express similarities in; liken (*compared the landscape to a painting*). **2** *tr.* (often foll. by *to*, *with*) estimate the similarity or dissimilarity of; assess the relation between (*compared radio with television; that lacks quality compared to this*). ¶ In current use *to* and *with* are generally interchangeable, but *with* often implies a greater element of formal analysis, as in *compared my account with yours*. **3** *intr.* (often foll. by *with*) bear comparison (*compares favorably with the rest*). **4** *intr.* (often foll. by *with*) be equal or equivalent to. **5** *tr. Gram.* form the comparative and superlative degrees of (an adjective or an adverb). ● *n. literary* comparison (*beyond compare; without compare; has no compare*). □ **compare notes** exchange ideas or opinions. [ME f. OF *comparer* f. L *comparare* (as COM-, *parare* f. *par* equal)]
■ *v.* **1** liken, associate, make (an) analogy of *or* between, analogize. **2** contrast, weigh up, juxtapose, set side by side, relate, correlate. **3, 4** (*compare with*) resemble, be *or* look like, be on a par with, be in the same class with, correspond, match, parallel, approach, approximate (to), bear *or* merit comparison with; rival, compete with *or* against, be a match for. ● *n.* see COMPARISON 3, MATCH¹ *n.* 2a, b.

comparison /kəmpárisən/ *n.* **1** the act or an instance of comparing. **2** a simile or semantic illustration. **3** capacity for being likened; similarity (*there's no comparison*). **4** (in full **degrees of comparison**) *Gram.* the positive, comparative, and superlative forms of adjectives and adverbs. □ **bear** (or **stand**) **comparison** (often foll. by *with*) be able to be compared favorably. **beyond comparison 1** totally different in

quality. **2** greatly superior; excellent. **in comparison with** compared to. [ME f. OF *comparesoun* f. L *comparatio -onis* (as COMPARE)]
■ **1** contrasting, contrast, juxtaposing, juxtaposition, balance, weighing, likening. **3** match, similarity, resemblance, likeness, comparability, relation, relationship, commensurability, kinship, point of agreement *or* correspondence, *literary* compare. □ **bear** (or **stand**) **comparison** see COMPARE *v.* 3, 4. **beyond comparison 1** see *poles apart* (POLE²). **2** see *peerless* (PEER²). **in comparison with** compared to *or* with, beside, in contrast with, against, over against.

compartment /kəmpáartmənt/ *n. & v.* ● *n.* **1** a space within a larger space, separated from the rest by partitions, e.g., in a railroad car, wallet, desk, etc. **2** *Naut.* a watertight division of a ship. **3** an area of activity, etc., kept apart from others in a person's mind. ● *v.tr.* put into compartments. □□ **compartmentation** /-mentáyshən/ *n.* [F *compartiment* f. It. *compartimento* f. LL *compartiri* (as COM-, *partiri* share)]
■ *n.* **1** division, section, partition, part, space, chamber, bay, alcove, cell, pigeonhole, locker, cubbyhole, cubby, niche, cubicle, slot. **3** see AREA 4. ● *v.* compartmentalize, separate; see also DIVIDE *v.* 1, 3a.

compartmental /kómpaartmént'l/ *adj.* consisting of or relating to compartments or a compartment. □□ **compartmentally** *adv.*

compartmentalize /kómpaartmént'liz, kómpaart-/ *v.tr.* divide into compartments or categories. □□ **compartmentalization** *n.*
■ see DIVIDE *v.* 1, 3a.

compass /kúmpəs, kóm-/ *n. & v.* ● *n.* **1** (in full **magnetic compass**) an instrument showing the direction of magnetic north and bearings from it. **2** (often *pl.*) an instrument for taking measurements and describing circles, with two arms connected at one end by a movable joint. **3** a circumference or boundary. **4** area, extent; scope (e.g., of knowledge or experience) (*beyond my compass*). **5** the range of tones of a voice or a musical instrument. ● *v.tr. literary* **1** hem in. **2** grasp mentally. **3** contrive; accomplish. **4** go around. □ **compass card** a circular rotating card showing the 32 principal bearings, forming the indicator of a magnetic compass. **compass rose** a circle of the principal directions marked on a chart. **compass saw** a saw with a narrow blade, for cutting curves. **compass window** a bay window with a semicircular curve. □□ **compassable** *adj.* [ME f. OF *compas* ult. f. L *passus* PACE¹]
■ *n.* **3** see BOUNDARY. **4** see SCOPE¹.

compassion /kəmpáshən/ *n.* pity inclining one to help or be merciful. □□ **compassionless** *adj.* [ME f. OF f. eccl.L *compassio -onis* f. *compati* (as COM-, *pati* pass- suffer)]
■ see PITY *n.* 1.

compassionate /kəmpáshənət/ *adj.* sympathetic; pitying. □ **compassionate leave** *Brit.* leave granted on grounds of bereavement, etc. □□ **compassionately** *adv.* [obs. F *compassioné* f. *compassioner* feel pity (as COMPASSION)]
■ see SYMPATHETIC *adj.* 1.

compatible /kəmpátəbəl/ *adj.* **1** (often foll. by *with*) **a** able to coexist; well-suited; mutually tolerant (*a compatible couple*). **b** consistent (*their views are not compatible with their actions*). **2** (of equipment, machinery, etc.) capable of being used in combination. □□ **compatibility** *n.* **compatibly** *adv.* [F f. med.L *compatibilis* (as COMPASSION)]
■ **1 a** well-matched, well-suited. **b** see CONSISTENT 1.

compatriot /kəmpáytreeət, -ot/ *n.* a fellow countryman. □□ **compatriotic** /-reeótik/ *adj.* [F *compatriote* f. LL *compatriota* (as COM-, *patriota* PATRIOT)]

compeer /kómpeer, -péer/ *n.* **1** an equal; a peer. **2** a comrade. [ME f. OF *comper* (as COM-, PEER²)]
■ **1** see PEER² *n.* 2. **2** see FRIEND *n.* 1.

/.../ **pronunciation**	● **part of speech**
□ **phrases, idioms, and compounds**	
□□ **derivatives**	■ **synonym section**
cross-references appear in SMALL CAPITALS or *italics*	

compel /kəmpél/ *v.tr.* (**compelled, compelling**) **1** (usu. foll. by *to* + infin.) force, constrain (*compelled them to admit it*). **2** bring about (an action) by force (*compel submission*). **3** (as **compelling** *adj.*) rousing strong interest, attention, conviction, or admiration. **4** *archaic* drive forcibly. □□ **compellable** *adj.* **compellingly** *adv.* [ME f. L *compellere compuls-* (as COM-, *pellere* drive)]
■ **1, 2, 4** see FORCE¹ *v.* 1. **3** (**compelling**) see INTERESTING.

compendious /kəmpéndeeəs/ *adj.* (esp. of a book, etc.) comprehensive but fairly brief. □□ **compendiously** *adv.* **compendiousness** *n.* [ME f. OF *compendieux* f. L *compendiosus* brief (as COMPENDIUM)]
■ see CONCISE.

compendium /kəmpéndeeəm/ *n.* (*pl.* **compendiums** or **compendia** /-deeə/) **1** esp. *Brit.* a usu. one-volume handbook or encyclopedia. **2 a** a summary or abstract of a larger work. **b** an abridgment. **3 a** a collection of games in a box. **b** any collection or mixture. **4** a package of writing paper, envelopes, etc. [L, = what is weighed together, f. *compendere* (as COM-, *pendere* weigh)]
■ **2 a** see SUMMARY *n.* **b** see ABRIDGMENT 1a.

compensate /kómpənsayt/ *v.* **1** *tr.* (often foll. by *for*) recompense (a person) (*compensated him for his loss*). **2** *intr.* (usu. foll. by *for* a thing, *Brit.* *to* a person) make amends (*compensated for the insult*; *will compensate to her in full*). **3** *tr.* counterbalance. **4** *tr. Mech.* provide (a pendulum, etc.) with extra or less weight, etc., to neutralize the effects of temperature, etc. **5** *intr. Psychol.* offset a disability or frustration by development in another direction. □□ **compensative** /kəmpénsətiv, kómpənsáytiv/ *adj.* **compensator** *n.* **compensatory** /-pénsətáwree/ *adj.* [L *compensare* (as COM-, *pensare* frequent. of *pendere pens-* weigh)]
■ **1** recompense, make restitution *or* reparation to, repay, indemnify, repay, reimburse, requite. **2** atone, make amends; (*compensate for*) expiate, offset, make up for, make good, make restitution *or* reparation for, redress. **3** counterbalance, balance, counterpoise, equalize, neutralize, even (up), offset. □□ **compensative, compensatory** restitutive, restitutory, expiatory, reparative, reparatory, compensational, *formal* piacular.

compensation /kómpensáyshən/ *n.* **1 a** the act of compensating. **b** the process of being compensated. **2** something, esp. money, given as a recompense. **3** *Psychol.* **a** an act of compensating. **b** the result of compensating. **4** a salary or wages. □ **compensation pendulum** *Physics* a pendulum designed to neutralize the effects of temperature variation. □□ **compensational** *adj.* [ME f. OF f. L *compensatio* (as COMPENSATE)]
■ **1, 2** see RESTITUTION 2. **4** see SALARY *n.*

compère /kómpair/ *n.* & *v. Brit.* ● *n.* a person who introduces and links the performers in a variety show, etc.; a master of ceremonies. ● *v.* **1** *tr.* act as a compère to. **2** *intr.* act as compère. [F, = godfather f. Rmc (as COM-, L *pater* father)]

compete /kəmpeét/ *v.intr.* **1** (often foll. by *with*, *against* a person, *for* a thing) strive for superiority or supremacy (*competed with his brother*; *compete against the Russians*; *compete for the victory*). **2** (often foll. by *in*) take part (in a contest, etc.) (*competed in the hurdles*). [L *competere competit-*, in late sense 'strive after or contend for (something)' (as COM-, *petere* seek)]
■ **1** contend, vie, struggle, strive; fight, battle, fence, *hist.* joust.

competence /kómpit'ns/ *n.* (also **competency** /kómpitənsee/) **1** (often foll. by *for*, or *to* + infin.) ability; the state of being competent. **2** an income large enough to live on, usu. unearned. **3** *Law* the legal capacity (of a court, a magistrate, etc.) to deal with a matter.
■ **1** see proficiency (PROFICIENT).

competent /kómpit'nt/ *adj.* **1 a** (usu. foll. by *to* + infin. or *for*) properly qualified or skilled (*not competent to drive*); adequately capable; satisfactory. **2** *Law* (of a judge, court, or witness) legally qualified or qualifying. □□ **competently** *adv.* [ME f. OF *competent* or L *competent-* (as COMPETE)]

■ **1 a** qualified, skilled, fit, capable; adequate, suitable, sufficient, satisfactory, acceptable, all right, *colloq.* OK.

competition /kómpətíshən/ *n.* **1** (often foll. by *for*) competing, esp. in an examination, in trade, etc. **2** an event or contest in which people compete. **3 a** the people competing against a person. **b** the opposition they represent. [LL *competitio* rivalry (as COMPETITIVE)]
■ **1** contention, striving, struggle; see also RIVALRY. **2** contest, match, meet, game, tournament, event, championship. **3** see COMPETITOR.

competitive /kəmpétitiv/ *adj.* **1** involving, offered for, or by competition (*competitive contest*). **2** (of prices, etc.) low enough to compare well with those of rival traders. **3** (of a person) having a strong urge to win; keen to compete. □□ **competitively** *adv.* **competitiveness** *n.* [*competit-*, past part. stem of L *competere* COMPETE]

competitor /kəmpétitər/ *n.* a person who competes; a rival, esp. in business or commerce. [F *compétiteur* or L *competitor* (as COMPETE)]
■ rival, opponent, adversary, antagonist; contestant, contender; (*competitors*) competition, opposition.

compilation /kómpiláyshən/ *n.* **1 a** the act of compiling. **b** the process of being compiled. **2** something compiled, esp. a book, etc., composed of separate articles, stories, etc. [ME f. OF f. L *compilatio -onis* (as COMPILE)]

compile /kəmpíl/ *v.tr.* **1 a** collect (material) into a list, volume, etc. **b** make up (a volume, etc.) from such material. **2** accumulate (a large number of) (*compiled a score of 160*). **3** *Computing* produce (a machine-coded form of a high-level program). [ME f. OF *compiler* or its apparent source, L *compilare* plunder, plagiarize]
■ **1** collect, put together, gather, accumulate, assemble, amass, collate, organize, order, systematize; anthologize, compose. **2** see AMASS.

compiler /kəmpílər/ *n.* **1** *Computing* a program for translating a high-level programming language into machine code. **2** a person who compiles.
■ **2** see EDITOR 3.

complacency /kəmpláysənsee/ *n.* (also **complacence**) **1** smug self-satisfaction. **2** tranquil pleasure. [med.L *complacentia* f. L *complacēre* (as COM-, *placēre* please)]

complacent /kəmpláysənt/ *adj.* **1** smugly self-satisfied. **2** calmly content. ¶ Often confused with *complaisant*. □□ **complacently** *adv.* [L *complacēre*: see COMPLACENCY]
■ **1** see SMUG.

complain /kəmpláyn/ *v.intr.* **1** (often foll. by *about*, *at*, or *that* + clause) express dissatisfaction (*complained at the state of the room*; *is always complaining*). **2** (foll. by *of*) **a** announce that one is suffering from an ailment (*complained of a headache*). **b** state a grievance concerning (*complained of the delay*). **3** make a mournful sound; groan, creak under a strain. □□ **complainer** *n.* **complainingly** *adv.* [ME f. OF *complaindre* (stem *complaign-*) f. med.L *complangere* bewail (as COM-, *plangere planct-* lament)]
■ **1, 2b** grumble, moan, groan, wail, carp, whimper, cry, squawk, kick, *colloq.* gripe, grouch, grouse, bitch, crab, *sl.* bellyache, beef. **3** see GROAN *v.* 1.

complainant /kəmpláynənt/ *n. Law* a plaintiff in certain lawsuits.

complaint /kəmpláynt/ *n.* **1** an act of complaining. **2** a grievance. **3** an ailment or illness. **4** *Law* the plaintiff's case in a civil action. [ME f. OF *complainte* f. *complaint* past part. of *complaindre*: see COMPLAIN]
■ **1** moan (and groan). **2** grumble, grievance, squawk, *colloq.* gripe, grouse, *sl.* beef(s). **3** see AILMENT.

complaisant /kəmpláysənt/ *adj.* **1** politely deferential. **2** willing to please; acquiescent. ¶ Often confused with *complacent*. □□ **complaisance** /-səns/ *n.* [F f. *complaire* (stem *complais-*) acquiesce to please, f. L *complacēre*: see COMPLACENCY]
■ **1** see PASSIVE 2. **2** see ACCOMMODATING.

compleat *archaic* var. of COMPLETE.

complement *n.* & *v.* ● *n.* /kómplimənt/ **1 a** something that completes. **b** one of a pair, or one of two things that go together. **2** (often **full complement**) the full number needed to man a ship, fill a conveyance, etc. **3** *Gram.* a word or phrase added to a verb to complete the predicate of a sentence. **4** *Biochem.* a group of proteins in the blood capable of lysing bacteria, etc. **5** *Math.* any element not belonging to a specified set or class. **6** *Geom.* the amount by which an angle is less than 90° (cf. SUPPLEMENT). ● *v.tr.* /kómpliment/ **1** complete. **2** form a complement to (*the scarf complements her dress*). □□ **complemental** /-mént'l/ *adj.* [ME f. L *complementum* (as COMPLETE)]

■ *v.* **1 a** completion, finishing touch, consummation. **b** companion, twin, fellow. **2** crew, team, company, band, outfit; quota, allowance, quorum. ● *v.* **1** complete, perfect, round out *or* off, set off, top off. **2** supplement, add to; see also ENHANCE.

complementarity /kómplimentáritee/ *n.* (*pl.* **-ies**) **1** a complementary relationship or situation. **2** *Physics* the concept that a single model may not be adequate to explain atomic systems in different experimental conditions.

complementary /kómplimént∂ree/ *adj.* **1** completing; forming a complement. **2** (of two or more things) complementing each other. □ **complementary angle** either of two angles making up 90°. **complementary color** a color that combined with a given color makes white or black. **complementary medicine** alternative medicine. □□ **complementarily** /-táir∂lee/ *adv.* **complementariness** *n.*

■ **1** see COORDINATE *adj.* 1. **2** see HARMONIOUS 2.

complete /k∂mpleét/ *adj.* & *v.* ● *adj.* **1** having all its parts; entire (*the set is complete*). **2** finished (*my task is complete*). **3** of the maximum extent or degree (*a complete surprise*; *a complete stranger*). **4** (also **compleat** after Walton's *Compleat Angler*) *joc.* accomplished (*the complete horseman*). ● *v.tr.* **1** finish. **2 a** make whole or perfect. **b** make up the amount of (*completes the quota*). **3** fill in the answers to (a questionnaire, etc.). **4** (usu. *absol.*) *Law* conclude a sale of property. □ **complete with** having (as an important accessory) (*comes complete with instructions*). □□ **completely** *adv.* **completeness** *n.* **completion** /-pleéshʒn/ *n.* [ME f. OF *complet* or L *completus* past part. of *complēre* fill up]

■ *adj.* **1** entire, whole, intact, uncut, unbroken, undivided, unabridged, full, undiminished, unabated, unreduced. **2** finished, ended, concluded, over, done, accomplished, terminated; settled, executed, performed. **3** entire, total, thorough, absolute, utter, unqualified, unmixed, unalloyed, pure, unmitigated, rank, *colloq.* blithering. **4** accomplished, perfect, consummate, exemplary, ideal, model, superior, superlative, superb, faultless, flawless. ● *v.* **1** conclude, finish (off), end, bring to an end, wrap up; accomplish, achieve, do; finalize. **2** round out, round off, perfect; crown, culminate; see also *make up* 2. **3** fill in *or* out, answer, make out. □□ **completely** entirely, fully, quite, wholly, totally, altogether, *in toto*, thoroughly, perfectly, exactly, precisely, from the word go, in full; lock, stock, and barrel; hook, line, and sinker; with all one's heart, root and branch, unqualifiedly, unconditionally, utterly, absolutely, unreservedly, clearly, expressly, explicitly, unambiguously, unequivocally, truly, categorically, flatly. **completion** conclusion, end, close, termination, culmination, finish; fulfillment, realization, accomplishment; finalization, windup, finishing off, completing.

complex *n.* & *adj.* ● *n.* /kómpleks/ **1** a building, a series of rooms, a network, etc. made up of related parts (*the arts complex*). **2** *Psychol.* a related group of usu. repressed feelings or thoughts which cause abnormal behavior or mental states (see *inferiority complex* (see OEDIPUS COMPLEX)). **3** (in general use) a preoccupation or obsession (*has a complex about punctuality*). **4** *Chem.* a compound in which molecules or ions form coordinate bonds to a metal atom or ion. ● *adj.* /k∂mpléks, kómpleks/ **1** consisting of related parts; composite. **2** complicated (*a complex problem*). **3** *Math.* containing real and imaginary parts (cf. IMAGINARY). □ **complex sentence** a sentence containing a subordinate clause or clauses. □□ **complexity** /-pléksitee/ *n.* (*pl.* **-ies**). **complexly**

adv. [F *complexe* or L *complexus* past part. of *complectere* embrace, assoc. with *complexus* plaited]

■ *n.* **3** see OBSESSION. ● *adj.* **2** see COMPLICATE 2.

□□ **complexity** complication, convolution; intricacy, involvement, complicatedness; inscrutability.

complexion /k∂mplékshʒn/ *n.* **1** the natural color, texture, and appearance, of the skin, esp. of the face. **2** an aspect; a character (*puts a different complexion on the matter*). □□ **complexioned** *adj.* (also in *comb.*) [ME f. OF f. L *complexio -onis* (as COMPLEX): orig. = combination of supposed qualities determining the nature of a body]

■ **2** see CHARACTER *n.* 1.

complexionless /k∂mplékshʒnlis/ *adj.* pale-skinned.

compliance /kʒmplíʒns/ *n.* **1** the act or an instance of complying; obedience to a request, command, etc. **2** *Mech.* **a** the capacity to yield under an applied force. **b** the degree of such yielding. **3** unworthy acquiescence. □ **in compliance with** according to (a wish, command, etc.).

■ **1** see OBEDIENCE.

compliant /kʒmplíʒnt/ *adj.* disposed to comply; yielding; obedient. □□ **compliantly** *adv.*

■ see OBEDIENT.

complicate /kómplikayt/ *v.tr.* & *intr.* **1** (often foll. by *with*) make or become difficult, confused, intricate, or complex. **2** (as **complicated** *adj.*) complex; intricate. □□ **complicatedly** *adv.* **complicatedness** *n.* [L *complicare complicat-* (as COM-, *plicare* fold)]

■ **1** make complicated *or* complex, make involved *or* intricate, make a mess *or* muddle of; tangle, entangle, mix up, confuse, confound, muddle. **2** (**complicated**) involved, intricate, complex, elaborate; ornate, Byzantine, tangled, knotty, confused, labyrinthine.

complication /kómplikáyshn/ *n.* **1 a** an involved or confused condition or state. **b** a complicating circumstance; a difficulty. **2** *Med.* a secondary disease or condition aggravating a previous one. [F *complication* or LL *complicatio* (as COMPLICATE)]

■ **1 a** complexity, involvement, intricacy, convolution; see also SUBTLETY 1. **b** difficulty, problem, predicament, obstacle, obstruction, snag, drawback, *disp.* dilemma.

complicity /kʒmplísitee/ *n.* partnership in a crime or wrongdoing. [*complice* (see ACCOMPLICE) + -ITY]

compliment *n.* & *v.* ● *n.* /kómplimʒnt/ **1 a** a spoken or written expression of praise. **b** an act or circumstance implying praise (*their success was a compliment to their efforts*). **2** (in *pl.*) **a** formal greetings, esp. as a written accompaniment to a gift, etc. (*with the compliments of the management*). **b** praise (*my compliments to the cook*). ● *v.tr.* /kómpliment/ **1** (often foll. by *on*) congratulate; praise (*complimented him on his roses*). **2** (often foll. by *with*) present as a mark of courtesy (*complimented her with his attention*). □ **compliments of the season** greetings appropriate to the time of year, esp. Christmas. **pay a compliment to** praise. **return the compliment 1** give a compliment in return for another. **2** retaliate or recompense in kind. [F *complimenter* f. It. *complimento* ult. f. L (as COMPLEMENT)]

■ *n.* **1** commendation, bouquet, tribute, honor. **2** (*compliments*) **a** respects, regards, good *or* best wishes, felicitations, salutations, greetings. ● *v.* **1, 2** congratulate, praise, felicitate, pay homage *or* tribute to, commend, slap on the back, laud, honor; flatter. □ **pay a compliment to** see PRAISE *v.* 1. **return the compliment 2** see RETALIATE 1.

complimentary /kómpliméntʒree/ *adj.* **1** expressing a compliment; praising. **2** (of a ticket for a play, etc.) given free of charge, esp. as a mark of favor. □□ **complimentarily** *adv.*

■ **1** laudatory, laudative, congratulatory, commendatory, approving, encomiastic, panegyrical, eulogistic, flattering. **2** gratis, on the house; see also FREE *adj.* 7.

/.../ **pronunciation**	● **part of speech**
□ **phrases, idioms, and compounds**	
□□ **derivatives**	■ **synonym section**
cross-references appear in SMALL CAPITALS or *italics*	

compline /kómplin, -plin/ (also **complin**) *n. Eccl.* **1** the last of the canonical hours of prayer. **2** the service taking place during this. [ME f. OF *complie*, fem. past part. of obs. *complir* complete, ult. f. L *complēre* fill up]

comply /kəmplí/ *v.intr.* (**-ies, -ied**) (often foll. by *with*) act in accordance (with a wish, command, etc.) (*complied with her expectation*; *had no choice but to comply*). [It. *complire* f. Cat. *complir*, Sp. *cumplir* f. L *complēre* fill up]
■ agree, obey, conform, consent, acquiesce, concur, submit, yield, accede.

compo /kómpō/ *n. & adj.* ● *n.* (*pl.* **-os**) a composition of plaster, etc., e.g., stucco. ● *adj.* = COMPOSITE. □ **compo rations** *Brit.* a large pack of food designed to last for several days. [abbr.]

component /kəmpốnənt/ *n. & adj.* ● *n.* **1** a part of a larger whole, esp. part of a motor vehicle. **2** *Math.* one of two or more vectors equivalent to a given vector. ● *adj.* being part of a larger whole (*assembled the component parts*). □□ **componential** /kómpənénshəl/ *adj.* [L *componere* component- (as COM-, *ponere* put)]
■ *n.* **1** see PART *n.* 3.

comport /kəmpáwrt/ *v.refl. literary* conduct oneself; behave. □ **comport with** suit; befit. □□ **comportment** *n.* [L *comportare* (as COM-, *portare* carry)]
■ see BEHAVE 1a. □□ **comportment** see BEHAVIOR 1a.

compos var. of COMPOS MENTIS.

compose /kəmpốz/ *v.* **1 a** *tr.* construct or create (a work of art, esp. literature or music). **b** *intr.* compose music (*gave up composing in 1917*). **2** *tr.* constitute; make up (*six tribes which composed the German nation*). ¶ Preferred to *comprise* in this sense. **3** *tr.* put together to form a whole, esp. artistically; order; arrange (*composed the group for the photographer*). **4** *tr.* **a** (often *refl.*) calm; settle (*compose your expression*; *composed himself to wait*). **b** (as **composed** *adj.*) calm; settled. **5** *tr.* settle (a dispute, etc.). **6** *tr. Printing* set up (type) to form words and blocks of words. **b** set up (a manuscript, etc.) in type. □ **composed of** made up of; consisting of (*a flock composed of sheep and goats*). □□ **composedly** /-zidlee/ *adv.* [F *composer*, f. L *componere* (as COM-, *ponere* put)]
■ **1 a** write, create, imagine, think up, originate, frame, formulate, make (up), devise, construct, *disp.* author; set to music, arrange. **2** constitute, form, make (up), be the constituents *or* ingredients *or* components *or* elements of. **3** see ARRANGE 1. **4 a** settle; (*compose oneself*) calm (down), quiet *or Brit.* quieten (down), pacify, control oneself, get control of *or* over oneself. **b** (**composed**) see collected (COLLECT[1] *v.* 5c). **5** see SETTLE[1] 5–7, 8b. □ **composed of** consisting of *or* in, comprising, formed *or* made (up) of, constituted of.

composer /kəmpốzər/ *n.* a person who composes (esp. music).

composite /kəmpózit/ *adj., n., & v.* ● *adj.* **1** made up of various parts; blended. **2** (esp. of a synthetic building material) made up of recognizable constituents. **3** *Archit.* of the fifth classical order of architecture, consisting of elements of the Ionic and Corinthian orders. **4** *Bot.* of the plant family Compositae. ● *n.* **1** a thing made up of several parts or elements. **2** a synthetic building material. **3** a reconstructed picture of a person (esp. one sought by the police) made by combining images of separate facial features (cf. IDENTI-KIT). **4** *Bot.* any plant of the family Compositae, having a head of many small flowers forming one bloom, e.g., the daisy or the dandelion. **5** *Polit.* a resolution composed of two or more related resolutions. ● *v.tr. Polit.* amalgamate (two or more similar resolutions). □ **composite school** *Can.* a comprehensive school (see COMPREHENSIVE *n.*). □□ **compositely** *adv.* **compositeness** *n.* [F f. L *compositus* past part. of *componere* (as COM-, *ponere posit-* put)]
■ *adj.* **1** compound, multiform, multifaceted. ● *n.* **1** see COMPOUND[1] *n.* 1.

composition /kómpəzíshən/ *n.* **1 a** the act of putting together; formation or construction. **b** something so composed; a mixture. **c** the constitution of such a mixture; the nature of its ingredients (*the composition is two parts oil to one part vinegar*). **2 a** a literary or musical work. **b** the act or art of producing such a work. **c** an essay, esp. written by a schoolchild. **d** an artistic arrangement (of parts of a picture, subjects for a photograph, etc.). **3** mental constitution; character (*jealousy is not in his composition*). **4** (often *attrib.*) a compound artificial substance, esp. one serving the purpose of a natural one. **5** *Printing* the setting-up of type. **6** *Gram.* the formation of words into a compound word. **7** *Law* **a** a compromise, esp. a legal agreement to pay a sum in lieu of a larger sum, or other obligation (*made a composition with his creditors*). **b** a sum paid in this way. **8** *Math.* the combination of functions in a series. □□ **compositional** *adj.* **compositionally** *adv.* [ME f. OF, f. L *compositio -onis* (as COMPOSITE)]
■ **1a, c, 2d** formation, construction, combination, makeup, structure, form, assembly, setup, organization, layout, arrangement, configuration, shaping; balance, harmony, proportion, placement, placing. **1 b** combination, aggregate, mixture, compound, mix, formulation, composite, amalgam, alloy, mélange, medley. **2 a** see WORK *n.* 5. **b** creation, production, making, generation; writing; see also FORMATION 1, 2. **c** essay, article, paper, story. **3** see CHARACTER *n.* 1.

compositor /kəmpózitər/ *n. Printing* a person who sets up type for printing. [ME f. AF *compositour* f. L *compositor* (as COMPOSITE)]
■ typesetter.

compos mentis /kómpəs méntis/ *adj.* (also **compos**) having control of one's mind; sane. [L]
■ see SANE 1.

compossible /kəmpósibəl/ *adj. formal* (often foll. by *with*) able to coexist. [OF f. med.L *compossibilis* (as COM-, POSSIBLE)]

compost /kómpōst/ *n. & v.* ● *n.* **1 a** mixed manure, esp. of organic origin. **b** a loam soil or other medium with added compost, used for growing plants. **2** a mixture of ingredients (*a rich compost of lies and innuendo*). ● *v.tr.* **1** treat (soil) with compost. **2** make (manure, vegetable matter, etc.) into compost. □ **compost heap** (or **pile**) a layered structure of garden refuse, soil, etc., which decays to become compost. [ME f. OF *composte* f. L *compos(i)tum* (as COMPOSITE)]
■ *v.* **1** see FERTILIZE 1.

composure /kəmpốzhər/ *n.* a tranquil manner; calmness. [COMPOSE + -URE]
■ see CALM *n.* 1.

compote /kómpōt/ *n.* fruit preserved or cooked in syrup. [F f. OF *composte* (as COMPOSITE)]

compound[1] *n., adj., & v.* ● *n.* /kómpownd/ **1** a mixture of two or more things, qualities, etc. **2** (also **compound word**) a word made up of two or more existing words. **3** *Chem.* a substance formed from two or more elements chemically united in fixed proportions. ● *adj.* /kómpownd/ **1 a** made up of several ingredients. **b** consisting of several parts. **2** combined; collective. **3** *Zool.* consisting of individual organisms. **4** *Biol.* consisting of several or many parts. ● *v.* /kəmpównd/ **1** *tr.* mix or combine (ingredients, ideas, motives, etc.) (*grief compounded with fear*). **2** *tr.* increase or complicate (difficulties, etc.) (*anxiety compounded by discomfort*). **3** *tr.* make up or concoct (a composite whole). **4** *tr.* (also *absol.*) settle (a debt, dispute, etc.) by concession or special arrangement. **5** *tr. Law* a condone (a liability or offense) in exchange for money, etc. **b** forbear from prosecuting (a felony) from private motives. **6** *intr.* (usu. foll. by *with, for*) *Law* come to terms with a person, for forgoing a claim, etc., for an offense. **7** *tr.* combine (words or elements) into a word. □ **compound eye** an eye consisting of numerous visual units, as found in insects and crustaceans. **compound fracture** a fracture complicated by a skin wound. **compound interest** interest payable on capital and its accumulated interest (cf. *simple interest*). **compound interval** *Mus.* an interval exceeding one octave. **compound leaf** a leaf consisting of several or many leaflets. **compound sentence** a sentence with more than one main, independent clause. **compound time** *Mus.* music having more than one group of simple-time units in each bar. □□ **compoundable**

/-pówndəbəl/ *adj.* [ME *compoun(e)* f. OF *compondre* f. L *componere* (as COM-, *ponere* put: *-d* as in *expound*)]

■ *n.* **1** composite, blend, synthesis, combination, consolidation, mixture, amalgam, alloy, mix. ● *adj.* **1** composite, multiform, multifaceted. **2** combined; collective; see also JOINT *adj.* ● *v.* **1, 7** put together, mix, blend, merge, unite, fuse; see also COMBINE *v.* 3. **2** aggravate, intensify, exacerbate, heighten, augment, add to, worsen, increase, enhance, multiply, complicate. **3** concoct, compose, formulate; see also MAKE *v.* 1.

compound[2] /kómpownd/ *n.* **1** a large open enclosure for housing workers, etc., esp. miners in S. Africa. **2** an enclosure, esp. in India, China, etc., in which a factory or a house stands (cf. KAMPONG). **3** a large enclosed space in a prison or prison camp. **4** = POUND[3]. [Port. *campon* or Du. *kampong* f. Malay]

comprador /kómprədáwr/ *n.* (also **compradore**) **1** *hist.* a Chinese business agent of a foreign company. **2** an agent of a foreign power. [Port. *comprador* buyer f. LL *comparator* f. L *comparare* purchase]

comprehend /kómprihénd/ *v.tr.* **1** grasp mentally; understand (a person or a thing). **2** include; take in. [ME f. OF *comprehender* or L *comprehendere comprehens-* (as COM-, *prehendere* grasp)]

■ **1** understand, see, grasp, conceive, take in, apprehend, realize, fathom, perceive, discern, appreciate; see also DIGEST *v.* 2. **2** include, take in, comprise, assimilate, absorb.

comprehensible /kómprihénsibəl/ *adj.* **1** that can be understood; intelligible. **2** that can be included or contained. □□ **comprehensibility** /-bílitee/ *n.* **comprehensibly** *adv.* [F *compréhensible* or L *comprehensibilis* (as COMPREHEND)]

■ **1** see INTELLIGIBLE.

comprehension /kómprihénshən/ *n.* **1 a** the act or capability of understanding, esp. writing or speech. **b** *Brit.* an extract from a text set as an examination, with questions designed to test understanding of it. **2** inclusion. **3** *Eccl. hist.* the inclusion of Nonconformists in the Anglican Church. [F *compréhension* or L *comprehensio* (as COMPREHENSIBLE)]

■ **1 a** see UNDERSTANDING *n.* 1.

comprehensive /kómprihénsiv/ *adj.* & *n.* ● *adj.* **1** complete; including all or nearly all elements, aspects, etc. (*a comprehensive grasp of the subject*). **2** of or relating to understanding (*the comprehensive faculty*). **3** (of motor-vehicle insurance) providing complete protection. ● *n.* (in full **comprehensive school**) *Brit.* a secondary school catering to children of all abilities from a given area. □□ **comprehensively** *adv.* **comprehensiveness** *n.* [F *compréhensif -ive* or LL *comprehensivus* (as COMPREHENSIBLE)]

■ *adj.* **1** (all-)inclusive, (all-)encompassing, thorough, extensive, full, exhaustive, complete, sweeping, all-embracing, wide, broad, encyclopedic. **2** cognitive; see also MENTAL *adj.* 1, 2.

compress *v.* & *n.* ● *v.tr.* /kəmprés/ **1** squeeze together. **2** bring into a smaller space or shorter extent. ● *n.* /kómpres/ a pad of cotton, etc., pressed on to part of the body to relieve inflammation, stop bleeding, etc. □ **compressed air** air at more than atmospheric pressure. □□ **compressible** /kəmprésəbəl/ *adj.* **compressibility** *n.* **compressive** /kəmprésiv/ *adj.* [ME f. OF *compresser* or LL *compressare* frequent. of L *comprimere compress-* (as COM-, *premere* press)]

■ *v.* **1** see SQUEEZE *v.* 1. **2** see CONTRACT *v.* 1.

compression /kəmpréshən/ *n.* **1** the act of compressing or being compressed. **2** the reduction in volume (causing an increase in pressure) of the fuel mixture in an internal combustion engine before ignition. [F f. L *compressio* (as COMPRESS)]

■ **1** see PRESSURE *n.* 1a, b.

compressor /kəmprésər/ *n.* an instrument or device for compressing, esp. a machine used for increasing the pressure of air or other gases.

comprise /kəmpríz/ *v.tr.* **1** include; comprehend. **2** consist of; be composed of (*the book comprises 350 pages*). **3** *disp.* make up, compose (*the essays comprise his total work*).

□□ **comprisable** *adj.* [ME f. F, fem. past part. of *comprendre* COMPREHEND]

■ **1** see INCLUDE 1.

compromise /kómprəmīz/ *n.* & *v.* ● *n.* **1** the settlement of a dispute by mutual concession (*reached a compromise by bargaining*). **2** (often foll. by *between*) an intermediate state between conflicting opinions, actions, etc., reached by mutual concession or modification (*a compromise between ideals and material necessity*). ● *v.* **1 a** *intr.* settle a dispute by mutual concession (*compromised over the terms*). **b** *tr. archaic* settle (a dispute) by mutual concession. **2** *tr.* bring into disrepute or danger esp. by indiscretion or folly. □□ **compromiser** *n.* **compromisingly** *adv.* [ME f. OF *compromis* f. LL *compromissum* neut. past part. of *compromittere* (as COM-, *promittere* PROMISE)]

■ *n.* see ACCOMMODATION 2b. ● *v.* **1** see *come to terms* (TERM).

compte rendu /káwnt rondý/ *n.* (*pl.* **comptes rendus** *pronunc.* same) a report; a review; a statement. [F]

comptroller /kəntrólər/ *n.* a controller (used in the title of some financial officers) (*comptroller and auditor general*). [var. of CONTROLLER, by erron. assoc. with COUNT[1], L *computus*]

compulsion /kəmpúlshən/ *n.* **1** a constraint; an obligation. **2** *Psychol.* an irresistible urge to a form of behavior, esp. against one's conscious wishes. □ **under compulsion** because one is compelled. [ME f. F f. LL *compulsio -onis* (as COMPEL)]

■ **1** see OBLIGATION 1, 3. **2** see URGE *n.* 1.

compulsive /kəmpúlsiv/ *adj.* **1** compelling. **2** resulting or acting from, or as if from, compulsion (*a compulsive gambler*). **3** *Psychol.* resulting or acting from compulsion against one's conscious wishes. **4** irresistible (*compulsive viewing*). □□ **compulsively** *adv.* **compulsiveness** *n.* [med.L *compulsivus* (as COMPEL)]

■ **1** compelling, coercive, urgent, overwhelming; compulsory, obligatory, required; see also FORCEFUL 2. **2** obsessive, unshakable; see also INCORRIGIBLE 2. **4** irresistible, compelling, gripping; see also FORCEFUL 2.

compulsory /kəmpúlsəree/ *adj.* **1** required by law or a rule (*it is compulsory to keep dogs on leashes*). **2** essential; necessary. □□ **compulsorily** *adv.* **compulsoriness** *n.* [med.L *compulsorius* (as COMPEL)]

■ **1** see MANDATORY *adj.* **2** see NECESSARY *adj.* 1.

compunction /kəmpúngkshən/ *n.* (usu. with *neg.*) **1** the pricking of the conscience. **2** a slight regret; a scruple (*without compunction*; *have no compunction in refusing her*). □□ **compunctious** /-shəs/ *adj.* **compunctiously** /-shəslee/ *adv.* [ME f. OF *componction* f. eccl.L *compunctio -onis* f. L *compungere compunct-* (as COM-, *pungere* prick)]

■ **1** remorse, contrition, regret, uneasiness of mind, pang *or* pricking of conscience, self-reproach. **2** regret, second thought(s), misgiving, qualm; see also SCRUPLE *n.*

compurgation /kómpərgáyshən/ *n.* *Law hist.* an acquittal from a charge or accusation obtained by the oaths of witnesses. □□ **compurgatory** /kəmpárgətáwree/ *adj.* [med.L *compurgatio* f. L *compurgare* (as COM-, *purgare* purify)]

compurgator /kómpərgaytər/ *n.* *Law hist.* a witness who swore to the innocence or good character of an accused person.

compute /kəmpyōot/ *v.* **1** *tr.* (often foll. by *that* + clause) reckon or calculate (a number, an amount, etc.). **2** *intr.* make a reckoning, esp. using a computer. □□ **computability** /-təbílitee/ *n.* **computable** *adj.* **computation** /kómpyōotáyshən/ *n.* **computational** *adj.* [F *computer* or L *computare* (as COM-, *putare* reckon)]

■ **1** calculate, reckon, figure (out), work out,

/.../ **pronunciation**	● **part of speech**
□ **phrases, idioms, and compounds**	
□□ **derivatives**	■ **synonym section**
cross-references appear in SMALL CAPITALS or *italics*	

determine, ascertain, estimate. □□ **computation** see CALCULATION 1.

computer /kəmpyṓotər/ *n.* **1** a usu. electronic device for storing and processing data (usu. in binary form), according to instructions given to it in a variable program. **2** a person who computes or makes calculations. □ **computer-literate** able to use computers; familiar with the operation of computers. **computer science** the study of the principles and use of computers. **computer virus** a hidden code within a computer program intended to corrupt a system or destroy data stored in it.

computerize /kəmpyṓotərīz/ *v.tr.* **1** equip with a computer; install a computer in. **2** store, perform, or produce by computer. □□ **computerization** *n.*

comrade /kómrad, -rid/ *n.* **1** (also **comrade in arms**) **a** (usu. of males) a coworker, friend, or companion. **b** fellow soldier, etc. **2** *Polit.* a fellow socialist or communist (often as a form of address). □□ **comradely** *adj.* **comradeship** *n.* [earlier *cama- camerade* f. F *camerade, camarade* (orig. fem.) f. Sp. *camarada* roommate (as CHAMBER)]
■ **1 a** colleague, associate, friend, companion, crony, mate, confrère, *colloq.* pal, chum, buddy, *Austral. & NZ colloq.* cobber. **2** brother, sister, tovarish.

con[1] /kon/ *n. & v. sl.* ● *n.* a confidence trick. ● *v.tr.* (**conned, conning**) swindle; deceive (*conned him into thinking he had won*). □ **con man** = *confidence man.* [abbr.]
■ *n.* see SWINDLE *n.* 1, 3. ● *v.* see SWINDLE *v.*

con[2] /kon/ *n., prep., & adv.* ● *n.* (usu. in *pl.*) a reason against. ● *prep. & adv.* against (cf. PRO[2]). [L *contra* against]

con[3] /kon/ *n. sl.* a convict. [abbr.]
■ see CONVICT *n.*

con[4] *Brit.* var. of CONN.

con[5] /kon/ *v.tr.* (**conned, conning**) *archaic* (often foll. by *over*) study; learn by heart (*conned his part well*). [ME *cunn-, con*, forms of CAN[1]]
■ see STUDY *v.* 2.

con- /kon, kən/ *prefix* assim. form of COM- before *c, d, f, g, j, n, q, s, t, v,* and sometimes before vowels.

con amore /kón amáwree, káwn aamáwray/ *adv.* **1** with devotion or zeal. **2** *Mus.* tenderly. [It., = with love]

conation /kōnáyshən/ *n. Philos. & Psychol.* **1** the desire to perform an action. **2** voluntary action; volition. □□ **conative** /kónətiv, kṓ-/ *adj.* [L *conatio* f. *conari* try]

con brio /kón brée-ō, káwn/ *adv. Mus.* with vigor. [It.]

concatenate /konkát'nayt/ *v. & adj.* ● *v.tr.* link together (a chain of events, things, etc.). ● *adj.* joined; linked. □□ **concatenation** /-náyshən/ *n.* [LL *concatenare* (as COM-, *catenare* f. *catena* chain)]
■ *v.* see LINK[1] *v.* 1. □□ **concatenation** see CHAIN *n.* 3.

concave /kónkáyv/ *adj.* having an outline or surface curved like the interior of a circle or sphere (cf. CONVEX). □□ **concavely** *adv.* **concavity** /-kávitee/ *n.* [L *concavus* (as COM-, *cavus* hollow), or through F *concave*]
■ see HOLLOW *adj.* 1.

conceal /kənseél/ *v.tr.* **1** (often foll. by *from*) keep secret (*concealed her motive from him*). **2** not allow to be seen; hide (*concealed the letter in her pocket*). □□ **concealer** *n.* **concealment** *n.* [ME f. OF *conceler* f. L *concelare* (as COM-, *celare* hide)]
■ **1** keep secret *or* hidden, keep quiet about, disguise; see also HIDE[1] *v.* 3. **2** hide, secrete, bury, squirrel away, cover (up), disguise, camouflage.

concede /kənseéd/ *v.tr.* **1 a** (often foll. by *that* + clause) admit (a defeat, etc.) to be true (*conceded that his work was inadequate*). **b** admit defeat in. **2** (often foll. by *to*) grant, yield, or surrender (a right, a privilege, points or a start in a game, etc.). **3** *Sports* allow an opponent to score (a run, goal, etc.) or to win (a match), etc. □□ **conceder** *n.* [F *concéder* or L *concedere concess-* (as COM-, *cedere* yield)]
■ **1 a** admit, allow, grant, acknowledge, confess, own (up to), accept. **b** see *give up* 1. **2** grant, yield, surrender, cede, give up, submit, resign, relinquish, abandon, waive.

conceit /kənseét/ *n.* **1** personal vanity; pride. **2** *literary* **a** a far-fetched comparison, esp. as a stylistic affectation; a con-

voluted or unlikely metaphor. **b** a fanciful notion. [ME f. CONCEIVE after *deceit, deceive,* etc.]
■ **1** vanity, pride, egotism, self-admiration, self-love, narcissism, arrogance, *literary* vainglory. **2 a** elaborate figure (of speech), trope, affectation; mixed metaphor. **b** see FANCY *n.* 2.

conceited /kənseétid/ *adj.* vain; proud. □□ **conceitedly** *adv.* **conceitedness** *n.*
■ vain, egotistical, self-centered, egocentric, self-admiring, narcissistic, prideful, proud, arrogant, self-important, self-satisfied, smug, complacent, snobbish, *colloq.* stuck-up, snotty, *literary* vainglorious, *Brit. sl.* toffee-nosed.

conceivable /kənseévəbəl/ *adj.* capable of being grasped or imagined; understandable. □□ **conceivability** /-bílitee/ *n.* **conceivably** *adv.*
■ see PLAUSIBLE 1.

conceive /kənseév/ *v.* **1** *intr.* become pregnant. **2** *tr.* become pregnant with (a child). **3** *tr.* (often foll. by *that* + clause) **a** imagine; fancy; think (*can't conceive that he could be guilty*). **b** (usu. in *passive*) formulate; express (a belief, a plan, etc.). □ **conceive of** form in the mind; imagine. [ME f. OF *conceiv-* stressed stem of *concevoir* f. L *concipere concept-* (as COM-, *capere* take)]
■ **3 a** conceive of, think (up), imagine, fancy, speculate (on), perceive, see, understand, realize, comprehend, envision, envisage, conjure up, dream up, hypothesize, postulate, posit, suggest, suppose. **b** see EXPRESS[1] 1, 2. □ **conceive of** see CONCEIVE 3a above.

concelebrate /konsélibrayt/ *v.intr. RC Ch.* **1** (of two or more priests) celebrate the mass together. **2** (esp. of a newly ordained priest) celebrate the mass with the ordaining bishop. □□ **concelebrant** /-brənt/ *n.* **concelebration** /-bráyshən/ *n.* [L *concelebrare* (as COM-, *celebrare* CELEBRATE)]

concenter /kənséntər/ *v.tr. & intr.* (*Brit.* **concentre**) bring or come to a common center. [F *concentrer:* see CONCENTRATE]

concentrate /kónsəntrayt/ *v. & n.* ● *v.* **1** *intr.* (often foll. by *on, upon*) focus all one's attention or mental ability. **2** *tr.* bring together (troops, power, attention, etc.) to one point; focus. **3** *tr.* increase the strength of (a liquid, etc.) by removing water or any other diluting agent. **4** *tr.* (as **concentrated** *adj.*) of hate, etc.) intense; strong. ● *n.* **1** a concentrated substance. **2** a concentrated form of esp. food. □□ **concentratedly** *adv.* **concentrative** /-tráytiv, -séntrə-/ *adj.* **concentrator** *n.* [after *concentre* f. F *concentrer* (as CON- + CENTER)]
■ *v.* **1** focus; think, focus one's thoughts *or* attention, apply oneself. **2** focus, direct, center, concentre, centralize, consolidate; gather, collect, congregate, draw *or* bring together, crowd, cluster, group. **3** condense, reduce, distill, intensify, refine, strengthen. **4** (**concentrated**) see INTENSE 1, 3. ● *n.* **1** see ESSENCE 2a.

concentration /kónsəntráyshən/ *n.* **1 a** the act or power of concentrating (*needs to develop concentration*). **b** an instance of this (*interrupted my concentration*). **2** something concentrated (*a concentration of resources*). **3** something brought together; a gathering. **4** the weight of substance in a given weight or volume of material. □ **concentration camp** a camp for the detention of political prisoners, internees, etc., esp. in Nazi Germany.
■ **1** see THOUGHT[1] 3a. **2** see POCKET *n.* 4.

concentric /kənséntrik/ *adj.* (often foll. by *with*) (esp. of circles) having a common center (cf. ECCENTRIC). □□ **concentrically** *adv.* **concentricity** /kónsentrísitee/ *n.* [ME f. OF *concentrique* or med.L *concentricus* (as COM-, *centricus* as CENTER)]

concept /kónsept/ *n.* **1** a general notion; an abstract idea (*the concept of evolution*). **2** *colloq.* an idea or invention to help sell or publicize a commodity (*a new concept in swimwear*). **3** *Philos.* an idea or mental picture of a group or class of objects formed by combining all their aspects. [LL *conceptus* f. *concept-:* see CONCEIVE]
■ **1, 2** see IDEA 1, 2a, b.

conception /kənsépshən/ *n.* **1 a** the act or an instance of conceiving; the process of being conceived. **b** the faculty of conceiving in the mind; apprehension; imagination. **2** an idea or plan, esp. as being new or daring (*the whole conception showed originality*). □ **no conception of** an inability to imagine. □□ **conceptional** *adj.* [ME f. OF f. L *conceptio -onis* (as CONCEPT)]
■ **1** birth, beginning, genesis, inception, emergence, start, inauguration, initiation, launch, origin, origination, formation, formulation, introduction, *formal* commencement; understanding, apprehension, knowledge, appreciation, imagination, comprehension. **2** design, scheme, proposal, outline; see also IDEA 1, 2a, b, PLAN *n.* 1a.

conceptive /kənséptiv/ *adj.* **1** conceiving mentally. **2** of conception. [L *conceptivus* (as CONCEPTION)]

conceptual /kənsépchooəl/ *adj.* of mental conceptions or concepts. □□ **conceptually** *adv.* [med.L *conceptualis* (*conceptus* as CONCEPT)]
■ see ABSTRACT *adj.* 1a.

conceptualism /kənsépchooəlizəm/ *n. Philos.* the theory that universals exist, but only as concepts in the mind. □□ **conceptualist** *n.*

conceptualize /kənsépchooəlīz/ *v.tr.* form a concept or idea of. □□ **conceptualization** *n.*
■ see IMAGINE 1.

concern /kənsə́rn/ *v. & n.* ● *v.tr.* **1 a** be relevant or important to (*this concerns you*). **b** relate to; be about. **2** (usu. *refl.*; often foll. by *with, in, about,* or *to* + infin.) interest or involve oneself (*don't concern yourself with my problems*). **3** worry; cause anxiety to (*it concerns me that he is always late*). ● *n.* **1 a** anxiety; worry (*felt a deep concern*). **b** solicitous regard; care; consideration. **2 a** a matter of interest or importance to one (*no concern of mine*). **b** (usu. in *pl.*) affairs; private business (*meddling in my concerns*). **3** a business; a firm (*quite a prosperous concern*). **4** *colloq.* a complicated or awkward thing (*have lost the whole concern*). □ **have a concern in** have an interest or share in. **have no concern with** have nothing to do with. **to whom it may concern** to those who have a proper interest in the matter (as an address to the reader of a testimonial, reference, etc.). [F *concerner* or LL *concernere* (as COM-, *cernere* sift, discern)]
■ *v.* **1** be relevant to, affect, have (a) bearing *or* (an) influence on, involve, touch; interest, be of importance *or* interest to. **b** refer *or* relate to, have relation *or* reference to, be about, pertain *or* appertain to, be pertinent *or* relevant to, regard, apply to, be connected *or* involved with, bear on, be germane to, involve, touch (on). **2** see BOTHER *v.* 2. **3** worry, trouble, disturb, bother, perturb, unsettle, upset, distress. ● *n.* **1 a** anxiety, worry, solicitude, apprehension, distress, apprehensiveness, uneasiness, disquiet, disquietude. **b** interest, regard, consideration, care, thought, awareness, attention. **2 a** business, affair, problem, matter, issue; responsibility, duty, charge, task, *colloq.* thing, *sl.* bag. **b** affairs, matters, business, concerns, things. **3** business, firm, company, house, establishment, enterprise, organization.

concerned /kənsə́rnd/ *adj.* **1** involved; interested (*the people concerned; concerned with proving his innocence*). **2** (often foll. by *that, about, at, for,* or *to* + infin.) troubled; anxious (*concerned about her; concerned to hear that*). □ **as** (or **so**) **far as I am concerned** as regards my interests. **be concerned** (often foll. by *in*) take part. **I am not concerned** it is not my business. □□ **concernedly** /-sə́rnidlee/ *adv.* **concernedness** /-sə́rnidnis/ *n.*
■ **1** involved, responsible, interested. **2** troubled, vexed, anxious, worried, distressed, uneasy, perturbed, bothered, upset, disturbed. □ **as** (or **so**) **far as I am concerned** as for me, for myself. **be concerned** see *take part* (PART).

concerning /kənsə́rning/ *prep.* about; regarding.
■ about; regarding, relative *or* relating to, referring to, with *or* in reference to, as regards, in *or* with regard to, with an eye to, with respect to, respecting, apropos (of), as to *or* for, in the matter of, on the subject of, anent, esp. *Law & Commerce* re.

concernment /kənsə́rnmənt/ *n. formal* **1** an affair or business. **2** importance. **3** (often foll. by *with*) a state of being concerned; anxiety.

concert *n. & v.* ● *n.* /kónsərt/ **1 a** a musical performance of usu. several separate compositions. **b** a comedy, etc., performance in a large hall. **2** agreement, accordance, harmony. **3** a combination of voices or sounds. ● *v.tr.* /kənsə́rt/ arrange (by mutual agreement or coordination). □ **concert grand** the largest size of grand piano, used for concerts. **concert overture** *Mus.* a piece like an overture but intended for independent performance. **concert performance** *Mus.* a performance (of an opera, etc.) without scenery, costumes, or action. **concert pitch 1** *Mus.* the pitch internationally agreed in 1960 whereby the A above middle C = 440 Hz. **2** a state of unusual readiness, efficiency, and keenness (for action, etc.). **in concert 1** (often foll. by *with*) acting jointly and accordantly. **2** (*predic.*) (of a musician) in a performance. [F *concert* (n.), *concerter* (v.) f. It. *concertare* harmonize]
■ *n.* **1** see PERFORMANCE 2. **2** see ACCORD *n.* 1.

concerted /kənsə́rtid/ *adj.* **1** combined together; jointly arranged or planned (*a concerted effort*). **2** *Mus.* arranged in parts for voices or instruments.
■ **1** see UNITED 2a.

concertgoer /kónsərtgōər/ *n.* a person who often goes to concerts. □□ **concertgoing** *adj.*

concertina /kónsərteenə/ *n. & v.* ● *n.* a musical instrument held in the hands and stretched and squeezed like bellows, having reeds and a set of buttons at each end to control the valves. ● *v.tr. & intr.* (**concertinas, concertinaed** /-nəd/, **concertinaing**) compress or collapse in folds like those of a concertina (*the car concertinaed into the bridge*). □ **concertina wire** coiled barbed wire placed on top of walls, etc., for security. [CONCERT + -INA]
■ *v.* crush, squash, telescope.

concertino /kóncherteenō/ *n.* (*pl.* **-os**) *Mus.* **1** a simple or short concerto. **2** a solo instrument or solo instruments playing in a concerto. [It., dimin. of CONCERTO]

concertmaster /kónsərtmástər/ *n.* the leading first-violin player in some orchestras.
■ see LEADER 7.

concerto /kəncháirtō/ *n.* (*pl.* **concerti** /-tee or **-os**/) *Mus.* a composition for a solo instrument or instruments accompanied by an orchestra. □ **concerto grosso** /grōsō/ (*pl.* **concerti grossi** /-see/ or **concerto grossos**) a composition for a group of solo instruments accompanied by an orchestra. [It. (see CONCERT): *grosso* big]

concession /kənséshən/ *n.* **1 a** the act or an instance of conceding (*made the concession that we were right*). **b** a thing conceded. **2** a reduction in price for a certain category of person. **3 a** the right to use land or other property, granted esp. by a government or local authority, esp. for a specific use. **b** the right, given by a company, to sell goods, esp. in a particular territory. **c** the land or property used or given. □□ **concessionary** *adj.* (also **concessional**). [F *concession* f. L *concessio* (as CONCEDE)]
■ **1** see ADMISSION 1. **3 a, b** see PRIVILEGE *n.* 1a.

concessionaire /kənséshənáir/ *n.* (also **concessioner**) the holder of a concession or grant, esp. for the use of land or trading rights. [F *concessionnaire* (as CONCESSION)]

concessive /kənsésiv/ *adj.* **1** of or tending to concession. **2** *Gram.* **a** (of a preposition or conjunction) introducing a phrase or clause which might be expected to preclude the action of the main clause, but does not (e.g., *in spite of, although*). **b** (of a phrase or clause) introduced by a concessive preposition or conjunction. [LL *concessivus* (as CONCEDE)]

conch /kongk, konch/ *n.* (*pl.* **conchs** /kongks/ or **conches**

/.../ **pronunciation**	● **part of speech**
□ **phrases, idioms, and compounds**	
□□ **derivatives**	■ **synonym section**
cross-references appear in SMALL CAPITALS or *italics*	

/kónchiz/) **1 a** a thick, heavy spiral shell, occasionally bearing long projections, of various marine gastropod mollusks of the family Strombidae. **b** any of these gastropods. **2** *Archit.* the domed roof of a semicircular apse. **3** = CONCHA. [L *concha* shell f. Gk *kogkhē*]

concha /kónkə/ *n.* (*pl.* **conchae** /-kee/) *Anat.* any part resembling a shell, esp. the depression in the external ear leading to its central cavity. [L: see CONCH]

conchie /kónchee/ *n.* (also **conchy**) (*pl.* **-ies**) *Brit. sl. derog.* a conscientious objector. [abbr.]

conchoidal /kongkóyd'l/ *adj. Mineral.* (of a solid fracture, etc.) resembling the surface of a bivalve shell.

conchology /kongkóləjee/ *n. Zool.* the scientific study of shells. □□ **conchological** /-kəlójikəl/ *adj.* **conchologist** *n.* [Gk *kogkhē* shell + -LOGY]

conchy var. of CONCHIE.

concierge /konseeáirzh, káwnsyáirzh/ *n.* **1** a hotel worker who arranges tours, transportation, etc., for guests. **2** (esp. in France) a doorkeeper or porter for an apartment building, etc. [F, prob. ult. f. L *conservus* fellow slave]
■ **2** see PORTER[2].

conciliar /kənsíleeər/ *adj.* of or concerning a council, esp. an ecclesiastical council. [med.L *consiliarius* counselor]

conciliate /kənsíleeayt/ *v.tr.* **1** make calm and amenable; pacify. **2** gain (esteem or goodwill). **3** *archaic* reconcile; make compatible. □□ **conciliative** /-síleeətiv, -áytiv/ *adj.* **conciliator** *n.* **conciliatory** /-síleeətáwree/ *adj.* **conciliatoriness** *n.* [L *conciliare* combine, gain (*concilium* COUNCIL)]
■ **1** see DISARM 6. □□ **conciliator** see *mediator* (MEDIATE).

conciliation /kənsílee-áyshən/ *n.* the use of conciliating measures; reconcilement. [L *conciliatio* (as CONCILIATE)]
■ see *reconciliation* (RECONCILE).

concinnity /kənsínitee/ *n.* elegance or neatness of literary style. □□ **concinnous** *adj.* [L *concinnitas* f. *concinnus* well-adjusted]

concise /kənsís/ *adj.* (of speech, writing, style, or a person) brief but comprehensive in expression. □□ **concisely** *adv.* **conciseness** *n.* [F *concis* or L *concisus* past part. of *concidere* (as COM-, *caedere* cut)]
■ brief, terse, laconic, compact, direct, succinct, epigrammatic, cogent, pithy, compendious, summary, trenchant, compressed, condensed, short; shortened, abridged, curtailed, abbreviated.

concision /kənsízhən/ *n.* (esp. of literary style) conciseness. [ME f. L *concisio* (as CONCISE)]
■ see BREVITY.

conclave /kónklayv, kóng-/ *n.* **1** a private meeting. **2** *RC Ch.* **a** the assembly of cardinals for the election of a pope. **b** the meeting place for a conclave. [ME f. OF f. L *conclave* lockable room (as COM-, *clavis* key)]
■ **1** see MEETING 2, 5.

conclude /kənklōōd/ *v.* **1** *tr. & intr.* bring or come to an end. **2** *tr.* (often foll. by *from*, or *that* + clause) infer (from given premises) (*what did you conclude?*; *concluded from the evidence that he had been mistaken*). **3** *tr.* settle; arrange (a treaty, etc.). **4** *intr.* decide. [ME f. L *concludere* (as COM-, *claudere* shut)]
■ **1** see END *v.* 1. **2** see INFER 1. **3, 4** see SETTLE[1] 5–7, 8b.

conclusion /kənklōōzhən/ *n.* **1** a final result; a termination. **2** a judgment reached by reasoning. **3** the summing-up of an argument, article, book, etc. **4** a settling; an arrangement (*the conclusion of peace*). **5** *Logic* a proposition that is reached from given premises; the third and last part of a syllogism. □ **in conclusion** lastly; to conclude. **try conclusions with** engage in a trial of skill, etc., with. [ME f. OF *conclusion* or L *conclusio* (as CONCLUDE)]
■ **1** see RESULT *n.* 1. **2** see THINKING *n.* 1.

conclusive /kənklōōsiv/ *adj.* decisive; convincing. □□ **conclusively** *adv.* **conclusiveness** *n.* [LL *conclusivus* (as CONCLUSION)]
■ see UNQUESTIONABLE.

concoct /kənkókt/ *v.tr.* **1** make by mixing ingredients (*concocted a stew*). **2** invent (a story, a lie, etc.). □□ **concoction** /-kókshən/ *n.* **concoctor** *n.* [L *concoquere concoct-* (as COM-, *coquere* cook)]
■ **2** see INVENT 1.

concomitance /kənkómit'ns/ *n.* (also **concomitancy**) **1** coexistence. **2** *Theol.* the doctrine of the coexistence of the body and blood of Christ both in the bread and in the wine of the Eucharist. [med.L *concomitantia* (as CONCOMITANT)]
■ **1** see COINCIDENCE 1.

concomitant /kənkómit'nt/ *adj. & n.* ● *adj.* going together; associated (*concomitant circumstances*). ● *n.* an accompanying thing. □□ **concomitantly** *adv.* [LL *concomitari* (as COM-, *comitari* f. L *comes -mitis* companion)]
■ *adj.* see ATTENDANT *adj.* 1.

concord /kónkawrd, kóng-/ *n.* **1** agreement or harmony between people or things. **2** a treaty. **3** *Mus.* a chord that is pleasing or satisfactory in itself. **4** *Gram.* agreement between words in gender, number, etc. [ME f. OF *concorde* f. L *concordia* f. *concors* of one mind (as COM-, *cors* f. *cor cordis* heart)]
■ **1** see AGREEMENT 1, 2. **2** see PACT.

concordance /kənkáwrd'ns/ *n.* **1** agreement. **2** a book containing an alphabetical list of the important words used in a book or by an author, usu. with citations of the passages concerned. [ME f. OF f. med.L *concordantia* (as CONCORDANT)]
■ **1** see AGREEMENT 1, 2. **2** see INDEX *n.* 1.

concordant /kənkáwrd'nt/ *adj.* **1** (often foll. by *with*) agreeing; harmonious. **2** *Mus.* in harmony. □□ **concordantly** *adv.* [ME f. OF f. L *concordare* f. *concors* (as CONCORD)]
■ **1** see HARMONIOUS 2.

concordat /kənkáwrdat/ *n.* an agreement, esp. between the Roman Catholic Church and a nation. [F *concordat* or L *concordatum* neut. past part. of *concordare* (as CONCORDANCE)]
■ see AGREEMENT 3.

concourse /kónkawrs/ *n.* **1** a crowd. **2** a coming together; a gathering (*a concourse of ideas*). **3** an open central area in a large public building, a railroad station, etc. [ME f. OF *concours* f. L *concursus* (as CONCUR)]

concrescence /kənkrésəns/ *n. Biol.* coalescence; growing together. □□ **concrescent** /-sənt/ *adj.* [CON-, after *excrescence*, etc.]

concrete /kónkreet, kóng-, konkreét, kong-/ *adj., n., & v.* ● *adj.* **1 a** existing in a material form; real. **b** specific; definite (*concrete evidence*; *a concrete proposal*). **2** *Gram.* (of a noun) denoting a material object as opposed to an abstract quality, state, or action. ● *n.* (often *attrib.*) a composition of gravel, sand, cement, and water, used for building. ● *v.* **1** *tr.* **a** cover with concrete. **b** embed in concrete. **2** /konkreét, kong-/ **a** *tr. & intr.* form into a mass; solidify. **b** *tr.* make concrete instead of abstract. □ **concrete mixer** = *cement mixer.* **concrete music** = MUSIQUE CONCRÈTE. **concrete poetry** poetry using unusual typographical layout to enhance the effect on the page. **in the concrete** esp. *Brit.* in reality or in practice. □□ **concretely** *adv.* **concreteness** *n.* [F *concret* or L *concretus* past part. of *concrescere* (as COM-, *crescere cret-* GROW)]
■ *adj.* **1** real, actual, literal, realistic, authentic, valid, genuine, bona fide, reliable; specific, particular, definite, definitive, clear-cut, material, physical, tangible, substantial. ● *v.* **2 a** see SOLIDIFY. **b** see EMBODY 1, 3.

concretion /kənkreéshən/ *n.* **1 a** a hard, solid concreted mass. **b** the forming of this by coalescence. **2** *Med.* a stony mass formed within the body. **3** *Geol.* a small, round mass of rock particles embedded in limestone or clay. □□ **concretionary** *adj.* [F f. L *concretio* (as CONCRETE)]
■ **1 a** see MASS *n.* 1, 2.

concretize /kónkritīz/ *v.tr.* make concrete instead of abstract. □□ **concretization** *n.*
■ see EMBODY 1, 3.

concubinage /konkyōōbinij/ *n.* **1** the cohabitation of a man and woman not married to each other. **2** the state of being or having a concubine. [ME f. F (as CONCUBINE)]

concubine /kóngkyəbīn/ *n.* **1** a woman who lives with a man as his wife. **2** (among polygamous peoples) a secondary wife. □□ **concubinary** /kənkyōōbineree/ *adj.* [ME f. OF f. L *concubina* (as COM-, *cubina* f. *cubare* lie)]
■ see WOMAN 3.

concupiscence /konkyōōpisəns/ *n. formal* sexual desire. □□ **concupiscent** /-sənt/ *adj.* [ME f. OF f. LL *concupiscentia* f. L *concupiscere* begin to desire (as COM-, inceptive f. *cupere* desire)]
■ see DESIRE *n.* 2.

concur /kənkər/ *v.intr.* (**concurred, concurring**) **1** happen together; coincide. **2** (often foll. by *with*) **a** agree in opinion. **b** express agreement. **3** combine together for a cause; act in combination. [L *concurrere* (as COM-, *currere* run)]
■ **1** see AGREE 3a. **2** see AGREE 1.

concurrent /kənkərənt, -kúr-/ *adj.* **1** (often foll. by *with*) **a** existing or in operation at the same time (*served two concurrent sentences*). **b** existing or acting together. **2** *Geom.* (of three or more lines) meeting at or tending toward one point. **3** agreeing; harmonious. □□ **concurrence** /-rəns/ *n.* **concurrently** *adv.*
■ **1** see SIMULTANEOUS.

concuss /kənkús/ *v.tr.* **1** subject to concussion. **2** shake violently. **3** *archaic* intimidate. [L *concutere concuss-* (as COM-, *cutere = quatere* shake)]

concussion /kənkúshən/ *n.* **1** *Med.* temporary unconsciousness or incapacity due to injury to the head. **2** violent shaking; shock. [L *concussio* (as CONCUSS)]

condemn /kəndém/ *v.tr.* **1** express utter disapproval of; censure (*was condemned for her irresponsible behavior*). **2 a** find guilty; convict. **b** (usu. foll. by *to*) sentence to (a punishment, esp. death). **c** bring about the conviction of (*his looks condemn him*). **3** pronounce (a building, etc.) unfit for use or habitation. **4** (usu. foll. by *to*) doom or assign (to something unwelcome or painful) (*condemned to spending hours at the kitchen sink*). **5 a** declare (smuggled goods, property, etc.) to be forfeited. **b** pronounce incurable. □□ **condemnable** /-démnəbəl/ *adj.* **condemnation** /kóndemnáyshən/ *n.* **condemnatory** /-démnətáwree/ *adj.* [ME f. OF *condem(p)ner* f. L *condemnare* (as COM-, *damnare* DAMN)]
■ **1** censure, blame, criticize, remonstrate with *or* against, denounce, disparage, reproach, rebuke, reprove, scold, reprimand, upbraid. **2 a** convict, find guilty. **b** sentence. **4** doom, damn, destine, fate, ordain, foreordain; consign, assign.

condensate /kəndénsayt, kóndən-/ *n.* a substance produced by condensation.

condensation /kóndensáyshən/ *n.* **1** the act of condensing. **2** any condensed material (esp. water on a cold surface). **3** an abridgment. **4** *Chem.* the combination of molecules with the elimination of water or other small molecules. □ **condensation trail** = *vapor trail.* [LL *condensatio* (as CONDENSE)]
■ **3** see ABRIDGMENT 1a.

condense /kəndéns/ *v.* **1** *tr.* make denser or more concentrated. **2** *tr.* express in fewer words; make concise. **3** *tr. & intr.* reduce or be reduced from a gas or solid to a liquid. □ **condensed milk** milk thickened by evaporation and sweetened. □□ **condensable** *adj.* [F *condenser* or L *condensare* (as COM-, *densus* thick)]
■ **1, 3** see CONCENTRATE *v.* 3. **2** see ABRIDGE 1.

condenser /kəndénsər/ *n.* **1** an apparatus or vessel for condensing vapor. **2** *Electr.* = CAPACITOR. **3** a lens or system of lenses for concentrating light. **4** a person or thing that condenses.

condescend /kóndisénd/ *v.intr.* **1** (usu. foll. by *to* + infin.) be gracious enough (to do a thing) esp. while showing one's sense of dignity or superiority (*condescended to attend the meeting*). **2** (foll. by *to*) behave as if one is on equal terms with (an inferior), usu. while maintaining an attitude of superiority. **3** (as **condescending** *adj.*) patronizing; kind to inferiors. □□ **condescendingly** *adv.* [ME f. OF *condescendre* f. eccl.L *condescendere* (as COM-, DESCEND)]
■ **1** stoop, deign, vouchsafe, lower *or* humble *or* demean oneself, come down off one's high horse. **3** (**condescending**) patronizing, belittling, disdainful, contemptuous, pompous, overbearing, high-handed, imperious, snobbish, haughty, supercilious, *colloq.* snooty, snotty, *Brit. sl.* toffee-nosed.

condescension /kóndisénshən/ *n.* **1** a patronizing manner.

2 affability toward inferiors. [obs. F f. eccl.L *condescensio* (as CONDESCEND)]

condign /kəndín/ *adj.* (of a punishment, etc.) severe and well-deserved. □□ **condignly** *adv.* [ME f. OF *condigne* f. L *condignus* (as COM-, *dignus* worthy)]
■ see JUST *adj.* 2.

condiment /kóndimənt/ *n.* a seasoning or relish for food. [ME f. L *condimentum* f. *condire* pickle]
■ see SPICE *n.* 1.

condition /kəndíshən/ *n. & v.* ● *n.* **1** a stipulation; something upon the fulfillment of which something else depends. **2 a** the state of being or fitness of a person or thing (*arrived in bad condition; not in a condition to be used*). **b** an ailment or abnormality (*a heart condition*). **3** (in *pl.*) circumstances, esp. those affecting the functioning or existence of something (*working conditions are good*). **4** *archaic* social rank (*all sorts and conditions of men*). **5** *Gram.* a clause expressing a condition. **6** a requirement that a student must pass an examination, etc., within a stated time to receive credit for a course. **b** the grade indicating this. ● *v.tr.* **1 a** bring into a good or desired state or condition. **b** make fit (esp. dogs or horses). **2** teach or accustom to adopt certain habits, etc. (*conditioned by society*). **3** govern; determine (*his behavior was conditioned by his drunkenness*). **4 a** impose conditions on. **b** be essential to (*the two things condition each other*). **5** test the condition of (textiles, etc.). **6** subject (a student) to a condition. □ **conditioned reflex** a reflex response to a nonnatural stimulus, established by training. **in** (or **out of**) **condition** in good (or bad) condition. **in no condition to** certainly not fit to. **on condition that** with the stipulation that. [ME f. OF *condicion* (n.), *condicionner* (v.) or med.L *condicionare* f. L *condicio -onis* f. *condicere* (as COM-, *dicere* say)]
■ *n.* **1** stipulation, proviso, demand, requirement, term, qualification, contingency, requisite, prerequisite. **2 a** state, circumstance, shape; working order; fitness, form, fettle, health. **3** (*conditions*) circumstances; environment, surroundings. **4** see RANK¹ *n.* 1a. ● *v.* **1** a ready, get *or* make ready, prepare, equip, outfit, fit (out *or* up), adapt, modify. **2** train, educate, teach; brainwash; influence, mold; accustom, inure, adapt, acclimatize, acclimate; (*conditioned to*) used to. **3** see DETERMINE 3. **4 b** demand, cry out for, necessitate, need, want, call for, require. □ **in condition** fit, in good shape. **out of condition** unfit, out of shape. **on condition that** see PROVIDED *conj.*

conditional /kəndíshənəl/ *adj. & n.* ● *adj.* **1** (often foll. by *on*) dependent; not absolute; containing a condition or stipulation (*a conditional offer*). **2** *Gram.* (of a clause, mood, etc.) expressing a condition. ● *n. Gram.* **1** a conditional clause, etc. **2** the conditional mood. □□ **conditionality** /-nálitee/ *n.* **conditionally** *adv.* [ME f. OF *condicionel* or f. LL *condicionalis* (as CONDITION)]
■ *adj.* **1** see PROVISIONAL *adj.*

conditioner /kəndíshənər/ *n.* an agent that brings something into good condition, esp. a substance applied to the hair.

condo /kóndō/ *n.* (*pl.* **-os**) *colloq.* a condominium. [abbr.]

condolatory /kəndṓlətawree/ *adj.* expressing condolence. [CONDOLE, after *consolatory*, etc.]

condole /kəndṓl/ *v.intr.* (foll. by *with*) express sympathy with a person over a loss, grief, etc. ¶ Often confused with *console.* [LL *condolēre* (as COM-, *dolēre* suffer)]
■ see SYMPATHIZE 1.

condolence /kəndṓləns/ *n.* (often in *pl.*) an expression of sympathy (*sent my condolences*).
■ see PITY *n.* 1.

condom /kóndom/ *n.* a rubber sheath worn on the penis during sexual intercourse as a contraceptive or to prevent infection. [18th c.: orig. unkn.]

/. . ./ **pronunciation**	● **part of speech**
□ **phrases, idioms, and compounds**	
□□ **derivatives**	■ **synonym section**
cross-references appear in SMALL CAPITALS or *italics*	

condominium /kóndəmíneeəm/ *n.* **1** a building or complex containing apartments that are individually owned. **2** the joint control of a nation's affairs by other nations. [mod.L (as COM-, *dominium* DOMINION)]

condone /kəndṓn/ *v.tr.* **1** forgive or overlook (an offense or wrongdoing). **2** approve or sanction, usu. reluctantly. **3** (of an action) atone for (an offense); make up for. □□ **condonation** /kóndənáyshən/ *n.* **condoner** *n.* [L *condonare* (as COM-, *donare* give)]

condor /kóndawr/ *n.* **1** (in full **Andean condor**) a large vulture, *Vultur gryphus*, of S. America, having black plumage with a white neck ruff and a fleshy wattle on the forehead. **2** (in full **California condor**) a small vulture, *Gymnogyps californianus*, of California. [Sp. f. Quechua *cuntur*]

condottiere /kóndətyáiree, -tyáiray/ *n.* (*pl.* **condottieri** /-tyáiree/) *hist.* a leader or a member of a troop of mercenaries in Italy, etc. [It. f. *condotto* troop under contract (*condotta*) (as CONDUCT)]

conduce /kəndṓos, -dyṓos/ *v.intr.* (foll. by *to*) (usu. of an event or attribute) lead or contribute to (a result). [L *conducere* conduct- (as COM-, *ducere duct-* lead)]

conducive /kəndṓosiv, -dyṓo-/ *adj.* (often foll. by *to*) contributing or helping (toward something) (*not a conducive atmosphere for negotiation; good health is conducive to happiness*).
■ see INSTRUMENTAL *adj.*

conduct *n. & v.* ● *n.* /kóndukt/ **1** behavior (esp. in its moral aspect). **2** the action or manner of directing or managing (business, war, etc.). **3** *Art* mode of treatment; execution. **4** leading; guidance. ● *v.* /kəndúkt/ **1** *tr.* lead or guide (a person or persons). **2** *tr.* direct or manage (business, etc.). **3** *tr.* (also *absol.*) be the conductor of (an orchestra, choir, etc.). **4** *tr.* transmit (heat, electricity, etc.) by conduction; serve as a channel for. **5** *refl.* behave (*conducted himself appropriately*). □ **conducted tour** a tour led by a guide on a fixed itinerary. **conduct sheet** *Brit.* a record of a person's offenses and punishments. □□ **conductible** /kəndúktibəl/ *adj.* **conductibility** *n.* [ME f. L *conductus* (as COM-, *ducere duct-* lead): (v.) f. OF *conduite* past part. of *conduire*]
■ *n.* **1** behavior, actions, demeanor, manners, deportment, attitude, *literary* comportment.
2, 4 guidance, direction, management, supervision, leadership, administration, government, running, handling, control, command, regulation, operation.
● *v.* **1** guide, escort, show, usher; see also LEAD[1] *v.* 1.
2 direct, supervise, manage, carry on, run, control, administer, regulate, operate. **4** channel, carry, transmit, convey; direct. **5** (*conduct oneself*) act, demean oneself, deport oneself, acquit oneself, *literary* comport oneself; see also BEHAVE 1a.

conductance /kəndúktəns/ *n. Physics* the power of a specified material to conduct electricity.

conduction /kəndúkshən/ *n.* **1 a** the transmission of heat through a substance from a region of higher temperature to a region of lower temperature. **b** the transmission of electricity through a substance by the application of an electric field. **2** the transmission of impulses along nerves. **3** the conducting of liquid through a pipe, etc. [F *conduction* or L *conductio* (as CONDUCT)]

conductive /kəndúktiv/ *adj.* having the property of conducting (esp. heat, electricity, etc.). □□ **conductively** *adv.*

conductivity /kónduktívitee/ *n.* the conducting power of a specified material.

conductor /kəndúktər/ *n.* **1** a person who directs the performance of an orchestra or choir, etc. **2** (*fem.* **conductress** /-tris/) **a** an official in charge of a train. **b** a person who collects fares in a bus, etc. **3** *Physics* **a** a thing that conducts or transmits heat or electricity, esp. regarded in terms of its capacity to do this (*a poor conductor*). **b** = *lightning rod.* **4** a guide or leader. **5** a manager or director. □□ **conductorship** *n.* [ME f. F *conducteur* f. L *conductor* (as CONDUCT)]
■ **1** maestro, director, leader. **2 b** *Brit.* guard. **4** see GUIDE *n.* 1–3. **5** see LEADER 1.

conductus /kəndúktəs/ *n.* (*pl.* **conducti** /-tī/) a musical composition of the 12th–13th c., with Latin text. [med.L: see CONDUIT]

conduit /kóndōoit, -dyōoit, -dit/ *n.* **1** a channel or pipe for conveying liquids. **2 a** a tube or trough for protecting insulated electric wires. **b** a length or stretch of this. [ME f. OF *conduit* f. med.L *conductus* CONDUCT *n.*]
■ **1** see CHANNEL[1] *n.* 5a, 6.

condyle /kóndīl, -d'l/ *n. Anat.* a rounded process at the end of some bones, forming an articulation with another bone. □□ **condylar** *adj.* **condyloid** *adj.* [F f. L *condylus* f. Gk *kondulos* knuckle]

cone /kōn/ *n. & v.* ● *n.* **1** a solid figure with a circular (or other curved) plane base, tapering to a point. **2** a thing of a similar shape, solid or hollow, e.g., as used to mark off areas of roads. **3** the dry fruit of a conifer. **4** a cone-shaped wafer for holding ice cream. **5** any of the minute cone-shaped structures in the retina. **6** a conical mountain esp. of volcanic origin. **7** (in full **cone shell**) any marine gastropod mollusk of the family Conidae. **8** *Pottery* a ceramic pyramid, melting at a known temperature, used to indicate the temperature of a kiln. ● *v.tr.* **1** shape like a cone. **2** (foll. by *off*) *Brit.* mark off (a road, etc.) with cones. [F *cône* f. L *conus* f. Gk *kōnos*]

Conestoga /kónəstṓgə/ *n.* **1** a N. American people native to the northeastern US. **2** a member of this people.

coney /kṓnee/ *n.* (also **cony**) (*pl.* **-eys** or **-ies**) **1 a** a rabbit. **b** its fur. **2** *Bibl.* a hyrax. [ME *cunin(g)* f. AF *coning*, OF *conin*, f. L *cuniculus*]

confab /kónfab/ *n. & v. colloq.* ● *n.* = confabulation (see CONFABULATE). ● *v.intr.* (**confabbed, confabbing**) = CONFABULATE. [abbr.]

confabulate /kənfábyələyt/ *v.intr.* **1** converse; chat. **2** *Psychol.* fabricate imaginary experiences as compensation for the loss of memory. □□ **confabulation** /-láyshən/ *n.* **confabulatory** /-lətáwree/ *adj.* [L *confabulari* (as COM-, *fabulari* f. *fabula* tale)]
■ **1** see CHAT[1] *v.* □□ **confabulation** see CHAT[1] *n.* 2.

confect /kənfékt/ *v.tr. literary* make by putting together ingredients. [L *conficere confect-* put together (as COM-, *facere* make)]

confection /kənfékshən/ *n.* **1** a dish or delicacy made with sweet ingredients. **2** mixing; compounding. **3** a fashionable or elaborate article of women's dress. □□ **confectionary** *adj.* (in sense 1). [ME f. OF f. L *confectio -onis* (as CONFECT)]
■ **1** see CANDY *n.*

confectioner /kənfékshənər/ *n.* a maker or retailer of confectionery. □ **confectioners' sugar** very fine powdered sugar used in making icings, candy, etc.

confectionery /kənfékshəneree/ *n.* candy and other confections.
■ see CANDY *n.*

confederacy /kənfédərəsee/ *n.* (*pl.* **-ies**) **1** a league or alliance, esp. of confederate nations. **2** a league for an unlawful or evil purpose; a conspiracy. **3** the condition or fact of being confederate; alliance; conspiracy. **4** (**the Confederacy**) = *Confererate States of America.* [ME, AF, OF *confederacie* (as CONFEDERATE)]
■ **1, 2** see LEAGUE[1] *n.* 1, 3.

confederate *adj., n., & v.* ● *adj.* /kənfédərət/ esp. *Polit.* allied; joined by an agreement or treaty. ● *n.* /kənfédərət/ **1** an ally, esp. (in a bad sense) an accomplice. **2** (**Confederate**) a supporter of the Confederate States of America. ● *v.* /kənfédərayt/ (often foll. by *with*) **1** *tr.* bring (a person, state, or oneself) into alliance. **2** *intr.* come into alliance. □ **Confederate States of America** the eleven Southern states that seceded from the US in 1860–61. [LL *confoederatus* (as COM-, FEDERATE)]
■ *n.* **1** see ACCOMPLICE. ● *v.* see ASSOCIATE *v.* 1.

confederation /kənfédəráyshən/ *n.* **1** a union or alliance of nations, etc. **2** the act or an instance of confederating; the state of being confederated. [F *confédération* (as CONFEDERATE)]
■ **1** see ALLIANCE 1.

confer /kənfər/ *v.* (**conferred, conferring**) **1** *tr.* (often foll. by *on, upon*) grant or bestow (a title, degree, favor, etc.). **2** *intr.* (often foll. by *with*) converse; consult. □□ **conferrable** *adj.* [L *conferre* (as COM-, *ferre* bring)]

■ **1** give, grant, present, award, bestow. **2** converse, consult, talk, take counsel, communicate, parley, negotiate, have a (little) talk, (have a) chat, confabulate.

conferee /kónfərée/ n. **1** a person on whom something is conferred. **2** a participant in a conference.

conference /kónfərəns, -frəns/ n. **1** consultation; discussion. **2** a meeting for discussion, esp. a regular one held by an association or organization. **3** an annual assembly of the Methodist Church. **4** an association in commerce, sport, etc. **5** the linking of several telephones, computer terminals, etc., so that each user may communicate with the others simultaneously. □ **conference call** a telephone call in which three or more people are connected. **in conference** engaged in discussion. □□ **conferential** /kónfərénshəl/ adj. [F conférence or med.L conferentia (as CONFER)]

■ **1** consultation, talk, colloquy, bull session; see also DISCUSSION 1. **2** meeting, convention, symposium, congress, seminar, forum, colloquium. **4** see ASSOCIATION 1.

conferment /kənfə́rmənt/ n. **1** the conferring of a degree, honor, etc. **2** an instance of this.

conferral /kənfə́rəl/ n. esp. US = CONFERMENT.

confess /kənfés/ v. **1 a** tr. (also absol.) acknowledge or admit (a fault, wrongdoing, etc.). **b** intr. (foll. by to) admit to (confessed to having lied). **2** tr. admit reluctantly (confessed it would be difficult). **3 a** tr. (also absol.) declare (one's sins) to a priest. **b** tr. (of a priest) hear the confession of. **c** refl. declare one's sins to a priest. [ME f. OF confesser f. Rmc f. L confessus past part. of confitēri (as COM-, fatēri declare, avow)]

■ **1 a** acknowledge, admit, own (up to), declare, confirm, concede, affirm, testify, avow, make a clean breast of; disclose, reveal, divulge, formal aver. **b** see come clean (CLEAN).

confessant /kənfésənt/ n. a person who confesses to a priest.

confessedly /kənfésidlee/ adv. by one's own or general admission.

confession /kənféshən/ n. **1 a** confessing or acknowledgment of a fault, wrongdoing, a sin to a priest, etc. **b** an instance of this. **c** a thing confessed. **2** (in full **confession of faith**) **a** a declaration of one's religious beliefs. **b** a statement of one's principles. □□ **confessionary** adj. [ME f. OF f. L confessio -onis (as CONFESS)]

■ **1** see ADMISSION 1. **2** see PROFESSION 3.

confessional /kənféshənəl/ n. & adj. • n. an enclosed stall in a church in which a priest hears confessions. • adj. **1** of or relating to confession. **2** denominational. [F f. It. confessionale f. med.L, neut. of confessionalis (as CONFESSION)]

confessor /kənfésər/ n. **1** a person who makes a confession. **2** a priest who hears confessions and gives spiritual counsel. **3** a person who avows a religion in the face of its suppression, but does not suffer martyrdom. [ME f. AF confessur, OF -our, f. eccl.L confessor (as CONFESS)]

■ **2** see PRIEST.

confetti /kənfétee/ n. small bits of colored paper thrown during celebrations, etc. [It., = sweetmeats f. L (as COMFIT)]

confidant /kónfidánt, -daánt/ n. (fem. **confidante** pronunc. same) a person trusted with knowledge of one's private affairs. [18th-c. for earlier CONFIDENT n., prob. to represent the pronunc. of F confidente (as CONFIDE)]

■ see INTIMATE[1] n.

confide /kənfíd/ v. **1** tr. (usu. foll. by to) tell (a secret, etc.) in confidence. **2** tr. (foll. by to) entrust (an object of care, a task, etc.) to. **3** intr. (foll. by in) **a** have trust or confidence in. **b** talk confidentially to. □□ **confidingly** adv. [L confidere (as COM-, fidere trust)]

■ **1** see IMPART 1. **2** see TRUST v. 4. **3 a** see TRUST v. 1.

confidence /kónfidəns/ n. **1** firm trust (have confidence in his ability). **2 a** a feeling of reliance or certainty. **b** a sense of self-reliance; boldness. **3 a** something told confidentially. **b** the telling of private matters with mutual trust. □ **confidence game** (Brit. **trick**) a swindle in which the victim is persuaded to trust the swindler in some way. **confidence man** a man who robs by means of a confidence game. **in confidence** as a secret. **in a person's confidence** trusted

with a person's secrets. **take into one's confidence** confide in. [ME f. L confidentia (as CONFIDE)]

■ **1** trust, faith, belief. **2 a** reliance; conviction, certitude; see also CERTAINTY 2. **b** assurance, self-confidence, boldness, courage, nerve, self-assurance, self-reliance, poise, aplomb, coolness. **3 a** secret, private or confidential matter or affair. □ **confidence game** see SWINDLE n. 1, 3. **confidence man** see FRAUD 3. **in confidence** in secrecy, secretly, in privacy, privately, confidentially, intimately, on the quiet, colloq. on the q.t.

confident /kónfid'nt/ adj. & n. • adj. **1** feeling or showing confidence; self-assured; bold (spoke with a confident air). **2** (often foll. by of, or that + clause) assured; trusting (confident of your support; confident that she will come). • n. archaic = CONFIDANT. □□ **confidently** adv. [F f. It. confidente (as CONFIDE)]

■ adj. **1** self-confident, self-assured, self-possessed, reliant, self-reliant, dauntless, bold, cool, cocksure, fearless, courageous. **2** secure, sure, certain, assured, positive, convinced, trusting, satisfied.

confidential /kónfidénshəl/ adj. **1** spoken or written in confidence. **2** entrusted with secrets (a confidential secretary). **3** confiding. □□ **confidentiality** /-sheeálitee/ n. **confidentially** adv.

■ **1** private, secret, classified, top secret, colloq. hush-hush. **3** see INTIMATE[1] adj. 1.

configuration /kənfígyəráyshən/ n. **1 a** an arrangement of parts or elements in a particular form or figure. **b** the form, shape, or figure resulting from such an arrangement. **2** Astron. & Astrol. the relative position of planets, etc. **3** Psychol. = GESTALT. **4** Physics the distribution of electrons among the energy levels of an atom, or of nucleons among the energy levels of a nucleus, as specified by quantum numbers. **5** Chem. the fixed three-dimensional relationship of the atoms in a molecule. **6** Computing **a** the interrelating or interconnecting of a computer system or elements of it so that it will accommodate a particular specification. **b** an instance of this. □□ **configurational** adj. **configure** v.tr. (in senses 1, 2, 6). [LL configuratio f. L configurare (as COM-, figurare fashion)]

■ **1** see FORM n. 1a.

confine v. & n. • v.tr. /kənfín/ (often foll. by in, to, within) **1** keep or restrict (within certain limits, etc.). **2** hold captive; imprison. • n. /kónfin/ (usu. in pl.) a limit or boundary (within the confines of the town). □ **be confined** be in childbirth. [(v.) f. F confiner, (n.) ME f. F confins (pl.), f. L confinia (as COM-, finia neut. pl. f. finis end, limit)]

■ v. **1** see RESTRICT. **2** see IMPRISON 2. • n. see BOUND[2] n. 1.

confinement /kənfínmənt/ n. **1** the act or an instance of confining; the state of being confined. **2** the time of a woman's giving birth.

■ **1** see CAPTIVITY. **2** see LABOR n. 3.

confirm /kənfə́rm/ v.tr. **1** provide support for the truth or correctness of; make definitely valid (confirmed my suspicions; confirmed his arrival time). **2** ratify (a treaty, possession, title, etc.); make formally valid. **3** (foll. by in) encourage (a person) in (an opinion, etc.). **4** establish more firmly (power, possession, etc.). **5** administer the religious rite of confirmation to. □□ **confirmative** adj. **confirmatory** adj. [ME f. OF confermer f. L confirmare (as COM-, FIRM[1])]

■ **1, 2** strengthen, encourage, fortify, support, reinforce, uphold, back up, corroborate, substantiate, buttress, prove; ratify, sanction, authorize, endorse, sustain, approve, validate, verify, recognize; authenticate, accredit. **3** see SUPPORT v. 4, 6. **4** establish, settle, affirm, ensure, clinch, substantiate, guarantee, bind, seal.

/.../ **pronunciation**   • **part of speech**
□ **phrases, idioms, and compounds**
□□ **derivatives**   ■ **synonym section**
cross-references appear in SMALL CAPITALS or italics

confirmand /kónfərmand/ n. Eccl. a person who is to be or has just been confirmed.

confirmation /kónfərmáyshən/ n. **1 a** the act or an instance of confirming; the state of being confirmed. **b** an instance of this. **2 a** a religious rite confirming a baptized person, esp. at the age of discretion, as a member of the Christian Church. **b** a ceremony of confirming persons of about this age in the Jewish faith. [ME f. OF f. L confirmatio -onis (as CONFIRM)]
■ **1** see ENDORSEMENT 1.

confirmed /kənfərmd/ adj. firmly settled in some habit or condition (confirmed in her ways; a confirmed bachelor).
■ see HABITUAL 3.

confiscate /kónfiskayt/ v.tr. **1** take or seize by authority. **2** appropriate to the public treasury (by way of a penalty). □□ **confiscable** /kənfískəbəl/ adj. **confiscation** /-káyshən/ n. **confiscator** n. **confiscatory** /kənfískətáwree/ adj. [L confiscare (as COM-, fiscare f. fiscus treasury)]
■ **1, 2** appropriate, seize, impound, expropriate, take (away), commandeer, Law sequester, sequestrate.

conflagration /kónfləgráyshən/ n. a great and destructive fire. [L conflagratio f. conflagrare (as COM-, flagrare blaze)]
■ fire, holocaust, inferno.

conflate /kənfláyt/ v.tr. blend or fuse together (esp. two variant texts into one). □□ **conflation** /-fláyshən/ n. [L conflare (as COM-, flare blow)]

conflict n. & v. ● n. /kónflikt/ **1 a** a state of opposition or hostilities. **b** a fight or struggle. **2** (often foll. by of) **a** the clashing of opposed principles, etc. **b** an instance of this. **3** Psychol. **a** the opposition of incompatible wishes or needs in a person. **b** an instance of this. **c** the distress resulting from this. ● v.intr. /kənflíkt/ **1** clash; be incompatible. **2** (often foll. by with) struggle or contend. **3** (as **conflicting** adj.) contradictory. □ **in conflict** conflicting. □□ **confliction** /-flíkshən/ n. **conflictual** /kənflíkchōōəl/ adj. [ME f. L confligere conflict- (as COM-, fligere strike)]
■ n. **1 a** battle, combat, war; dispute, controversy, contention, disagreement. **b** fight, engagement, struggle, fray, fracas, affray, donnybrook; dispute, argument, wrangle, altercation, feud, quarrel, squabble, tiff, colloq. row, spat, set-to. **2** antagonism, opposition, disagreement, variance, discord; clash, dispute; see also disagreement (DISAGREE). ● v. **1** clash, disagree, differ, be incompatible or at odds or at variance, be in opposition. **2** see STRUGGLE v. 3. **3** (conflicting) see CONTRADICTORY. □ **in conflict** see CONTRADICTORY.

confluence /kónflōōəns/ n. **1** a place where two rivers meet. **2 a** a coming together. **b** a crowd of people. [L confluere (as COM-, fluere flow)]
■ **1, 2a** see MEETING 1.

confluent /kónflōōənt/ adj. & n. ● adj. flowing together; uniting. ● n. a stream joining another.

conflux /kónfluks/ n. = CONFLUENCE. [LL confluxus (as CONFLUENCE)]

conform /kənfáwrm/ v. **1** intr. comply with rules or general custom. **2** intr. & tr. (often foll. by to) be or make accordant or suitable. **3** tr. (often foll. by to) form according to a pattern; make similar. **4** intr. (foll. by to, with) comply with; be in accordance with. □□ **conformer** n. [ME f. OF conformer f. L conformare (as COM-, FORM)]
■ **1** fit (in), harmonize. **2** accord, agree, concur, coincide, correspond, harmonize, square, tally, fit in, be consistent, be in accord or in accordance; match, fit. **4** (conform to or with) comply with, follow, observe, obey, respect, abide by, adapt or adjust to.

conformable /kənfáwrməbəl/ adj. **1** (often foll. by to) similar. **2** (often foll. by with) consistent. **3** (often foll. by to) adapted. **4** tractable; submissive. **5** Geol. (of strata in contact) lying in the same direction. □□ **conformability** n. **conformably** adv. [med.L conformabilis (as CONFORM)]
■ **4** see OBEDIENT.

conformal /kənfáwrməl/ adj. (of a map) showing any small area in its correct shape. □□ **conformally** adv. [LL conformalis (as CONFORM)]

conformance /kənfáwrməns/ n. (often foll. by to, with) = CONFORMITY 1, 2.

conformation /kónfawrmáyshən/ n. **1** the way in which a thing is formed; shape; structure. **2** (often foll. by to) adjustment in form or character; adaptation. **3** Chem. any spatial arrangement of atoms in a molecule from the rotation of part of the molecule about a single bond. [L conformatio (as CONFORM)]
■ **1** see FORM n. 1a. **2** see ACCOMMODATION 2a.

conformist /kənfáwrmist/ n. & adj. ● n. **1** a person who conforms to an established practice; a conventional person. **2** Brit. a person who conforms to the practices of the Church of England. ● adj. (of a person) conforming to established practices; conventional. □□ **conformism** n.
■ n. **1** see SQUARE n. 6. ● adj. see CONSERVATIVE adj. 1a.

conformity /kənfáwrmitee/ n. **1** (often foll. by to, with) action or behavior in accordance with established practice; compliance. **2** (often foll. by to, with) correspondence in form or manner; likeness; agreement. **3** Brit. compliance with the practices of the Church of England. [ME f. OF conformité or LL conformitas (as CONFORM)]
■ **1** see OBEDIENCE. **2** see ACCORD n. 1.

confound /kənfównd/ v. & int. ● v.tr. **1** throw into perplexity or confusion. **2** mix up; confuse (in one's mind). **3** archaic defeat; overthrow. ● int. expressing annoyance (confound you!). [ME f. AF conf(o)undre, OF confondre f. L confundere mix up (as COM-, fundere fus- pour)]
■ **1** see PERPLEX 1. **2** see CONFUSE 2.

confounded /kənfówndid/ adj. colloq. damned (a confounded nuisance!). □□ **confoundedly** adv.

confraternity /kónfrətérnitee/ n. (pl. **-ies**) a brotherhood, esp. religious or charitable. [ME f. OF confraternité f. med.L confraternitas (as COM-, FRATERNITY)]

confrere /kónfrair/ n. (also **confrère**) a fellow member of a profession, scientific body, etc. [ME f. OF f. med.L confrater (as COM-, frater brother)]
■ see COLLEAGUE.

confront /kənfrúnt/ v.tr. **1 a** face in hostility or defiance. **b** face up to and deal with (a problem, difficulty, etc.). **2** (of a difficulty, etc.) present itself to (countless obstacles confronted us). **3** (foll. by with) **a** bring (a person) face to face with (a circumstance), esp. by way of accusation (confronted them with the evidence). **b** set (a thing) face to face with (another) for comparison. **4** meet or stand facing. □□ **confrontation** /kónfruntáyshən/ n. **confrontational** /kónfruntáyshənəl/ adj. [F confronter f. med.L confrontare (as COM-, frontare f. frons frontis face)]
■ **1** see FACE v. 3a, b.

Confucian /kənfyōōshən/ adj. & n. ● adj. of or relating to Confucius, Chinese philosopher d. 479 BC, or his philosophy. ● n. a follower of Confucius. □□ **Confucianism** n. **Confucianist** n. [Confucius, Latinization of Kongfuze Kong the master]

confusable /kənfyōōzəbəl/ adj. that is able or liable to be confused. □□ **confusability** /-bílitee/ n.

confuse /kənfyōōz/ v.tr. **1 a** disconcert; perplex; bewilder. **b** embarrass. **2** mix up in the mind; mistake (one for another). **3** make indistinct (that point confuses the issue). **4** (as **confused** adj.) **a** mentally decrepit. **b** puzzled; perplexed. **5** (often as **confused** adj.) make muddled or disorganized; throw into disorder (a confused jumble of clothes). □□ **confusedly** /kənfyōōzidlee/ adv. **confusing** adj. **confusingly** adv. [19th-c. back-form. f. confused (14th c.) f. OF confus f. L confusus: see CONFOUND]
■ **1 a** disconcert, perplex, puzzle, bewilder, mystify, baffle, bemuse, befuddle, discomfit, confound, fluster, upset, disorient, colloq. flummox, rattle, throw, joc. discombobulate. **b** abash, shame, embarrass. **2** confuse, muddle (up), mistake, get the wrong way around. **3** disorder, confound, throw into disarray, muddle, mix up, snarl (up), ensnarl, tangle (up), entangle; blur. **4** (**confused**) a muddleheaded, decrepit; see also SENILE adj. **b** bewildered, perplexed, puzzled, nonplussed, baffled, befuddled, bemused, mixed up, dazed, flustered, colloq. flummoxed, stumped, Austral. & NZ

colloq. bushed. **5** (**confused**) mixed up, jumbled, disordered, disorganized, disorderly, muddled, messy, topsy-turvy, chaotic, higgledy-piggledy.

confusion /kənfyōōzhən/ *n.* **1 a** the act of confusing (*the confusion of fact and fiction*). **b** an instance of this; a misunderstanding (*confusions arise from a lack of communication*). **2 a** the result of confusing; a confused state; embarrassment; disorder (*thrown into confusion by his words*; *trampled in the confusion of battle*). **b** (foll. by *of*) a disorderly jumble (*a confusion of ideas*). **3 a** civil commotion (*confusion broke out at the announcement*). **b** an instance of this. [ME f. OF *confusion* or L *confusio* (as CONFUSE)]
- **1 a** confounding, muddling, jumbling, blurring. **b** misconception, mix-up; see also MISUNDERSTANDING 1. **2 a** disorder, disarray, disarrangement, chaos, tumult, commotion, turmoil, pandemonium, bedlam; embarrassment, discomfiture, mortification, abashment, chagrin. **b** mix-up, mess, jumble, muddle, *colloq.* shambles; assortment, mixture, potpourri, gallimaufry, hodgepodge. **3** see UPROAR.

confute /kənfyōōt/ *v.tr.* **1** prove (a person) to be in error. **2** prove (an argument) to be false. □□ **confutation** /kónfyootáyshən/ *n.* [L *confutare* restrain]
- see DISPROVE.

Cong. *abbr.* **1** Congress. **2** Congressional. **3** Congregational.

conga /kónggə/ *n.* & *v.* ● *n.* **1 a** Latin American dance of African origin, usu. with several persons in a single line, one behind the other. **2** (also **conga drum**) a tall, narrow, low-toned drum beaten with the hands. ● *v.intr.* (**congas, congaed** /-gəd/, **congaing** /-gəing/) perform the conga. [Amer. Sp. f. Sp. *conga* (fem.) of the Congo]

congé /kónzhay, kawnzháy/ *n.* an unceremonious dismissal; leavetaking. [F: earlier *congee*, ME f. OF *congié* f. L *commeatus* leave of absence f. *commeare* go and come (as COM-, *meare* go): now usu. treated as mod. F]
- see *dismissal* (DISMISS).

congeal /kənjeél/ *v.tr.* & *intr.* **1** make or become semisolid by cooling. **2** (of blood, etc.) coagulate. □□ **congealable** *adj.* **congealment** *n.* [ME f. OF *congeler* f. L *congelare* (as COM-, *gelare* f. *gelu* frost)]
- see COAGULATE.

congelation /kónjiláyshən/ *n.* **1** the process of congealing. **2** a congealed state. **3** a congealed substance. [ME f. OF *congelation* or L *congelatio* (as CONGEAL)]

congener /kónjənər/ *n.* a thing or person of the same kind or category as another, esp. animals or plants of a specified genus (*the goldfinch is a congener of the canary*). [L (as CON-, GENUS)]

congeneric /kónjinérik/ *adj.* **1** of the same genus, kind, or race. **2** allied in nature or origin; akin. □□ **congenerous** /kənjénərəs/ *adj.*

congenial /kənjeényəl/ *adj.* **1** (often foll. by *with, to*) (of a person, character, etc.) pleasant because akin to oneself in temperament or interests. **2** (often foll. by *to*) suited or agreeable. □□ **congeniality** /-jeéneeálitee/ *n.* **congenially** *adv.* [CON- + GENIAL[1]]
- **1** see LIKABLE.

congenital /kənjénitəl/ *adj.* **1** (esp. of a disease, defect, etc.) existing from birth. **2** that is (or as if) such from birth (*a congenital liar*). □□ **congenitally** *adv.* [L *congenitus* (as COM-, *genitus* past part. of *gigno* beget)]
- **1** see INBORN. **2** see INHERENT 1.

conger /kónggər/ *n.* (in full **conger eel**) any large marine eel of the family Congridae. [ME f. OF *congre* f. L *conger, congrus*, f. Gk *goggros*]

congeries /kənjeéreez, kónjə-/ *n.* (*pl.* same) a disorderly collection; a mass or heap. [L, formed as CONGEST]
- see HEAP *n.* 1.

congest /kənjést/ *v.tr.* (esp. as **congested** *adj.*) affect with congestion; obstruct, block (*congested streets*; *congested lungs*). □□ **congestive** *adj.* [L *congerere congest-* (as COM-, *gerere* bring)]
- see BLOCK *v.* 1a; (**congested**) snarled up, obstructed, (over)crowded; blocked (up), stuffed (up).

congestion /kənjés-chən/ *n.* abnormal accumulation,

crowding, or obstruction, esp. of traffic, etc. or of blood or mucus in a part of the body. [F f. L *congestio -onis* (as CONGEST)]

conglomerate *adj., n.,* & *v.* ● *adj.* /kənglómərət/ **1** gathered into a rounded mass. **2** *Geol.* (of rock) made up of small stones held together (cf. AGGLOMERATE). ● *n.* /kənglómərət/ **1** a number of things or parts forming a heterogeneous mass. **2** a group or corporation formed by the merging of separate and diverse firms. **3** *Geol.* conglomerate rock. ● *v.tr.* & *intr.* /kənglómərayt/ collect into a coherent mass. □□ **conglomeration** /-ráyshən/ *n.* [L *conglomeratus* past part. of *conglomerare* (as COM-, *glomerare* f. *glomus -eris* ball)]
- *n.* **2** see ORGANIZATION 2.

Congolese /kónggəleéz/ *adj.* & *n.* ● *adj.* of or relating to the Republic of the Congo in Central Africa, or the region surrounding the Congo River. ● *n.* a native of either of these regions. [F *congolais*]

congou /kónggōō, -gō/ *n.* a variety of black China tea. [Chin. dial. *kung hu tē* tea labored for]

congrats /kəngráts/ *n.pl.* & *int. colloq.* congratulations. [abbr.]

congratulate /kəngráchəlayt, -gráj-, kəng-/ *v.tr.* & *refl.* (often foll. by *on, upon*) **1** *tr.* express pleasure at the happiness or good fortune or excellence of (a person) (*congratulated them on their success*). **2** *refl.* think oneself fortunate or clever. □□ **congratulant** *adj.* & *n.* **congratulator** *n.* **congratulatory** /-lətáwree/ *adj.* [L *congratulari* (as COM-, *gratulari* show joy f. *gratus* pleasing)]
- **1** see COMPLIMENT *v.* **2** pat oneself on the back.

congratulation /kəngráchəláyshən -gráj-, kəng-/ *n.* **1** congratulating. **2** (also as *int.*; usu. in *pl.*) an expression of this (*congratulations on winning!*). [L *congratulatio* (as CONGRATULATE)]
- **2** (*congratulations*) felicitations, well done, good for you, *colloq.* nice going, good show; many happy returns.

congregant /kónggrigənt/ *n.* a member of a congregation. [L *congregare* (as CONGREGATE)]

congregate /kónggrigayt/ *v.intr.* & *tr.* collect or gather into a crowd or mass. [ME f. L *congregare* (as COM-, *gregare* f. *grex gregis* flock)]
- see GATHER *v.* 1.

congregation /kónggrigáyshən/ *n.* **1** the process of congregating; collection into a crowd or mass. **2** a crowd or mass gathered together. **3 a** a body assembled for religious worship. **b** a body of persons regularly attending a particular church, etc. **c** *RC Ch.* a body of persons obeying a common religious rule. **d** *RC Ch.* any of several permanent committees of the Roman Catholic College of Cardinals. **4** (**Congregation**) *Brit.* (in some universities) a general assembly of resident senior members. [ME f. OF *congregation* or L *congregatio* (as CONGREGATE)]
- **2, 3a** see ASSEMBLY 1, 2a.

congregational /kónggrigáyshənəl/ *adj.* **1** of a congregation. **2** (**Congregational**) of or adhering to Congregationalism.

Congregationalism /kónggrigáyshənəlizəm/ *n.* a system of ecclesiastical organization whereby individual churches are largely self-governing. □□ **Congregationalist** *n.* **Congregationalize** *v.tr.*

congress /kónggris/ *n.* **1** a formal meeting of delegates for discussion. **2** (**Congress**) a national legislative body, esp. that of the US. **3** a society or organization. **4** coming together; meeting. **Congressional Medal of Honor** = *Medal of Honor.* □□ **congressional** /kəngréshən'l/ *adj.* [L *congressus* f. *congredi* (as COM-, *gradi* walk)]
- **1** see CONFERENCE 2. **2** see PARLIAMENT 2.

congressman /kónggrismən/ *n.* (*pl.* **-men**; *fem.* **congresswoman**, *pl.* **-women**) a member of the US Congress, esp. of the US House of Representatives.

/.../ **pronunciation**	● **part of speech**
□ **phrases, idioms, and compounds**	
□□ **derivatives**	■ **synonym section**
cross-references appear in SMALL CAPITALS or *italics*	

■ see REPRESENTATIVE *n.* 4.

congruence /kónggrŏŏəns, kəngrŏŏ-/ *n.* (also **congruency** /-ənsee/) **1** agreement; consistency. **2** *Geom.* the state of being congruent. [ME f. L *congruentia* (as CONGRUENT)]

■ **1** see ACCORD *n.* 2. **2** see COINCIDENCE 1.

congruent /kónggrŏŏənt, kəngrŏŏ-/ *adj.* **1** (often foll. by *with*) suitable; agreeing. **2** *Geom.* (of figures) coinciding exactly when superimposed. □□ **congruently** *adv.* [ME f. L *congruere* agree]

■ **2** see PARALLEL *adj.* 2.

congruous /kónggrŏŏəs/ *adj.* (often foll. by *with*) suitable; agreeing; fitting. □□ **congruity** /-grŏŏitee/ *n.* **congruously** *adv.* [L *congruus* (as CONGRUENT)]

■ □□ **congruity** see HARMONY 3.

conic /kónik/ *adj. & n.* ● *adj.* of a cone. ● *n.* **1** a conic section. **2** (in *pl.*) the study of conic sections. □ **conic section** a figure formed by the intersection of a cone and a plane. [mod.L *conicus* f. Gk *kōnikos* (as CONE)]

conical /kónikəl/ *adj.* cone-shaped. □□ **conically** *adv.*

conidium /kənídeeəm/ *n.* (*pl.* **conidia** /-deeə/) a spore produced asexually by various fungi. [mod.L dimin. f. Gk *konis* dust]

conifer /kónifər, kŏ́-/ *n.* any evergreen tree of a group usu. bearing cones, including pines, yews, cedars, and redwoods. □□ **coniferous** /kənífərəs/ *adj.* [L (as CONE, -FEROUS)]

coniform /kŏ́nifawrm/ *adj.* cone-shaped. [L *conus* cone + -FORM]

coniine /kŏ́nee-een/ *n.* a poisonous alkaloid found in hemlock that paralyzes the nerves. [L *conium* f. Gk *kōneion* hemlock]

conj. *abbr.* conjunction.

conjectural /kənjékchərəl/ *adj.* based on, involving, or given to conjecture. □□ **conjecturally** *adv.* [F f. L *conjecturalis* (as CONJECTURE)]

■ see SPECULATIVE 1.

conjecture /kənjékchər/ *n. & v.* ● *n.* **1 a** the formation of an opinion on incomplete information; guessing. **b** an opinion or conclusion reached in this way. **2 a** (in textual criticism) the guessing of a reading not in the text. **b** a proposed reading. ● *v.* **1** *tr. & intr.* guess. **2** *tr.* (in textual criticism) propose or (a reading). □□ **conjecturable** *adj.* [ME f. OF *conjecture* or L *conjectura* f. *conjicere* (as COM-, *jacere* throw)]

■ *n.* **1** see GUESS *n.* ● *v.* **1** see GUESS *v.* 2.

conjoin /kənjóyn/ *v.tr. & intr.* join; combine. [ME f. OF *conjoign-* pres. stem of *conjoindre* f. L *conjungere* (as COM-, *jungere* *junct-* join)]

■ see COMBINE *v.* 1.

conjoint /kənjóynt/ *adj.* associated, conjoined. □□ **conjointly** *adv.* [ME f. OF, past part. (as CONJOIN)]

conjugal /kónjəgəl/ *adj.* of marriage or the relation between husband and wife. □ **conjugal rights** those rights (esp. to sexual relations) regarded as exercisable in law by each partner in a marriage. □□ **conjugality** /-gálitee/ *n.* **conjugally** *adv.* [L *conjugalis* f. *conjux* consort (as COM-, *-jux* *-jugis* f. root of *jungere* join)]

■ see *matrimonial* (MATRIMONY).

conjugate *v., adj., & n.* ● *v.* /kónjəgayt/ **1** *tr. Gram.* give the different forms of (a verb). **2** *intr.* **a** unite sexually. **b** (of gametes) become fused. **3** *intr. Chem.* (of protein) combine with nonprotein. ● *adj.* /kónjəgət, -gayt/ **1** joined together, esp. as a pair. **2** *Gram.* derived from the same root. **3** *Biol.* fused. **4** *Chem.* (of an acid or base) related by loss or gain of an electron. **5** *Math.* joined in a reciprocal relation, esp. having the same real parts, and equal magnitudes but opposite signs of imaginary parts. ● *n.* /kónjəgət, -gayt/ a conjugate word or thing. □□ **conjugately** *adv.* [L *conjugare* yoke together (as COM-, *jugare* f. *jugum* yoke)]

conjugation /kónjəgáyshən/ *n.* **1** *Gram.* a system of verbal inflection. **2 a** the act or an instance of conjugating. **b** an instance of this. **3** *Biol.* the fusion of two gametes in reproduction. □□ **conjugational** *adj.* [L *conjugatio* (as CONJUGATE)]

conjunct /kənjúngkt/ *adj.* joined together; combined; associated. [ME f. L *conjunctus* (as CONJOIN)]

conjunction /kənjúngkshən/ *n.* **1 a** the action of joining; the condition of being joined. **b** an instance of this. **2** *Gram.* a word used to connect clauses or sentences or words in the same clause (e.g., *and, but, if*). **3 a** a combination (of events or circumstances). **b** a number of associated persons or things. **4** *Astron. & Astrol.* the alignment of two bodies in the solar system so that they have the same longitude as seen from the earth. □ **in conjunction with** together with. □□ **conjunctional** *adj.* [ME f. OF *conjonction* f. L *conjunctio -onis* (as CONJUNCT)]

■ **1** see JUNCTION 2, 3. **3 a** see COMBINATION 3.

conjunctiva /kónjungktívə, kənjúngktivə/ *n.* (*pl.* **conjunctivas** or **conjunctivae** /-vee/) *Anat.* the mucous membrane that covers the front of the eye and lines the inside of the eyelids. □□ **conjunctival** *adj.* [med.L (*membrana*) *conjunctiva* (as CONJUNCTIVE)]

conjunctive /kənjúngktiv/ *adj. & n.* ● *adj.* **1** serving to join; connective. **2** *Gram.* of the nature of a conjunction. ● *n. Gram.* a conjunctive word. □□ **conjunctively** *adv.* [LL *conjunctivus* (as CONJOIN)]

conjunctivitis /kənjúngktivítis/ *n.* inflammation of the conjunctiva.

conjuncture /kənjúngkchər/ *n.* a combination of events; a state of affairs. [obs. F f. It. *congiuntura* (as CONJOIN)]

conjuration /kónjəráyshən/ *n.* an incantation; a magic spell. [ME f. OF f. L *conjuratio -onis* (as CONJURE)]

■ see MUMBO JUMBO 1.

conjure /kónjər/ *v.* **1** *tr.* call upon (a spirit) to appear. **2** *tr.* (usu. foll. by *out of, away, to*, etc.) cause to appear or disappear as if by magic (*conjured a rabbit out of a hat*; *conjured them to a desert island*; *his pain was conjured away*). **3** *intr.* esp. *Brit.* perform tricks that are seemingly magical, esp. by rapid movements of the hands. **4** *intr.* perform marvels. **5** *tr.* /kənjŏor/ (often foll. by *to* + infin.) appeal solemnly to (a person). □ **conjure up** **1** bring into existence or cause to appear as if by magic. **2** cause to appear to the eye or mind; evoke. [ME f. OF *conjurer* plot, exorcise f. L *conjurare* band together by oath (as COM-, *jurare* swear)]

■ □ **conjure up 2** see EVOKE 2.

conjurer /kónjərər, kún-/ *n.* (also **conjuror**) **1** a person who conjures. **2** *Brit.* = MAGICIAN 2. [CONJURE + -ER[1] & AF *conjurour* (OF *-eor*) f. med.L *conjurator* (as CONJURE)]

conk[1] /kongk/ *v.intr.* (usu. foll. by *out*) *colloq.* **1** (of a machine, etc.) break down. **2** (of a person) become exhausted and give up; faint; die. [20th c.: orig. unkn.]

■ **1** see BREAK[1] *v.* 1b. **2** see DIE[1] 1.

conk[2] /kongk/ *v.tr. sl.* hit on the head, etc. [19th c.: perh. = CONCH]

■ see HIT *v.* 1a.

conker /kóngkər/ *n. Brit.* **1** the hard fruit of a horse chestnut. **2** (in *pl.*) *Brit.* a children's game played with conkers on strings, one hit against another to try to break it. [dial. *conker* snail shell (orig. used in the game), assoc. with CONQUER]

con moto /kón mṓtō, káwn/ *adv. Mus.* with movement. [It., = with movement]

Conn. *abbr.* Connecticut.

conn /kon/ *n. & v. Naut.* ● *v.tr.* direct the steering of (a ship). ● *n.* **1** the act of conning. **2** the responsibility or station of one who conns. [app. weakened form of obs. *cond, condie,* F *conduire* f. L *conducere* CONDUCT]

■ *v.* see NAVIGATE 1, 5.

connate /kónayt/ *adj.* **1** existing in a person or thing from birth; innate. **2** formed at the same time. **3** allied; congenial. **4** *Bot.* (of organs) congenitally united so as to form one part. **5** *Geol.* (of water) trapped in sedimentary rock during its deposition. [LL *connatus* past part. of *connasci* (as COM-, *nasci* be born)]

■ **1** see INBORN.

connatural /kənáchərəl/ *adj.* **1** (often foll. by *to*) innate; belonging naturally. **2** of like nature. □□ **connaturally** *adv.* [LL *connaturalis* (as COM-, NATURAL)]

connect /kənékt/ *v.* **1 a** *tr.* (often foll. by *to, with*) join (one thing with another) (*connected the hose to the faucet*). **b** *tr.* join (two things) (*a track connected the two villages*). **c** *intr.* be joined or joinable (*the two parts do not connect*). **2** *tr.* (often foll. by *with*) associate mentally or practically (*did not connect* *the two ideas*; *never connected her with the theater*). **3** *intr.* (foll. by *with*) (of a train, etc.) be synchronized at its destination with another train, etc., so that passengers can transfer (*the train connects with the boat*). **4** *tr.* put into communication by telephone. **5 a** *tr.* (usu. in *passive*; foll. by *with*) unite or associate with others in relationships, etc. (*am connected with the royal family*). **b** *intr.* form a logical sequence; be meaningful. **6** *intr. colloq.* hit or strike effectively. □ **connecting rod** the rod between the piston and the crankshaft, etc., in an internal combustion engine or between the wheels of a locomotive. □□ **connectable** *adj.* **connector** *n.* [L *connectere connex-* (as COM-, *nectere* bind)]

■ **1 a, b** join *or* link *or* tie (together); fasten, bind, attach, couple, put together, secure, fit together, fix, affix, stick together; pin, hook, staple, tack, glue, cement, fuse, seal, strap, bolt, lash. **c** join, fit together. **2, 5a** associate, affiliate, link, relate, league, tie (in), make a connection between. **5 b** follow, make sense; see also *add up* 3.

connected /kənéktid/ *adj.* **1** joined in sequence. **2** (of ideas, etc.) coherent. **3** related or associated. □ **well-connected** associated, esp. by birth, with persons of good social position. □□ **connectedly** *adv.* **connectedness** *n.*

connection /kənékshən/ *n.* (also *Brit.* **connexion**) **1 a** the act of connecting; the state of being connected. **b** an instance of this. **2** the point at which two things are connected (*broke at the connection*). **3 a** a thing or person that connects; a link; a relationship or association (*a radio formed the only connection with the outside world*; *cannot see the connection between the two ideas*). **b** a telephone link (*got a bad connection*). **4** arrangement or opportunity for catching a connecting train, etc.; the train, etc., itself (*missed the connection*). **5** *Electr.* **a** the linking up of an electric current by contact. **b** a device for effecting this. **6** (often in *pl.*) a relative or associate, esp. one with influence (*has connections in the State Department*; *heard it through a business connection*). **7** a relation of ideas; a context (*in this connection I have to disagree*). **8** *sl.* **a** a transaction involving illegal drugs. **b** a supplier of narcotics. **9** a religious body, esp. Methodist. □ **in connection with** with reference to. **in this** (or **that**) **connection** with reference to this (or that). □□ **connectional** *adj.* [L *connexio* (as CONNECT): spelling *-ct-* after CONNECT]

■ **1** linking, linkage, union, join, bond, link; tie, relationship, association, relevance, appropriateness. **2** see JOINT *n.* 1. **3 a** see LINK¹ *n.* 2a, b. **6** (*connections*) contacts, friends (at court); influence, pull, *colloq.* clout, *sl.* drag; relatives, relations, family, kin, kith and kin. **7** see CONTEXT.

connective /kənéktiv/ *adj. & n.* ● *adj.* serving or tending to connect. ● *n.* something that connects. □ **connective tissue** *Anat.* a fibrous tissue that supports, binds, or separates more specialized tissue.

conning tower /kóning/ *n.* **1** the superstructure of a submarine from which steering, firing, etc., are directed on or near the surface, and which contains the periscope. **2** the armored pilothouse of a warship. [CON⁴ + -ING¹]

conniption /kənípshən/ *n.* a fit of anger, agonized distress, or hysteria. [orig. unknown]

connivance /kəníivəns/ *n.* **1** (often foll. by *at, in*) conniving (*connivance in the crime*). **2** tacit permission (*done with his connivance*). [F *connivence* or L *conniventia* (as CONNIVE)]

■ **1** see CONSPIRACY 2.

connive /kəníiv/ *v.intr.* **1** (foll. by *at*) disregard or tacitly consent to (a wrongdoing). **2** (usu. foll. by *with*) conspire. □□ **conniver** *n.* [F *conniver* or L *connivēre* shut the eyes (to)]

■ **1** see ABET. **2** see SCHEME *v.* 1.

connoisseur /kónəsőr/ *n.* (often foll. by *of, in*) an expert judge in matters of taste (*a connoisseur of fine wine*). □□ **connoisseurship** *n.* [F, obs. spelling of *connaisseur* f. pres. stem of *connaître* know + *-eur* -OR¹: cf. *reconnoiter*]

■ see EXPERT *n.*

connotation /kónətáyshən/ *n.* **1** that which is implied by a word, etc., in addition to its literal or primary meaning (*a letter with sinister connotations*). **2** the act of connoting or implying.

■ see IMPLICATION.

connote /kənőt/ *v.tr.* **1** (of a word, etc.) imply in addition to the literal or primary meaning. **2** (of a fact) imply as a consequence or condition. **3** mean; signify. □□ **connotative** /kónətaytiv, kənőtətiv/ *adj.* [med.L *connotare* mark in addition (as COM-, *notare* f. *nota* mark)]

■ **1, 2** see IMPLY 3. **3** see MEAN¹ 4, 6.

connubial /kənőőbeeəl, kənyőő-/ *adj.* of or relating to marriage or the relationship of husband and wife. □□ **connubiality** /-beeálitee/ *n.* **connubially** *adv.* [L *connubialis* f. *connubium* (*nubium* f. *nubere* marry)]

■ see *matrimonial* (MATRIMONY).

conoid /kónoyd/ *adj. & n.* ● *adj.* (also **conoidal** /-nóyd'l/) cone-shaped. ● *n.* a cone-shaped object.

conquer /kóngkər/ *v.tr.* **1 a** overcome and control (an enemy or territory) by military force. **b** *absol.* be victorious. **2** overcome (a habit, emotion, disability, etc.) by effort (*conquered his fear*). **3** climb (a mountain) successfully. □□ **conquerable** *adj.* [ME f. OF *conquerre* f. Rmc f. L *conquirere* (as COM-, *quaerere* seek, get)]

■ **1 a** overcome, beat, defeat, subdue, crush, subjugate, *literary* vanquish; capture, seize, win, gain, acquire, obtain; occupy, annex. **2** overcome, triumph *or* prevail over, beat, surmount, master, win out (over); *sl.* kick.

conqueror /kóngkərər/ *n.* **1** a person who conquers. **2** *Brit.* = CONKER. [ME f. AF *conquerour* (OF *-eor*) f. *conquerre* (as CONQUER)]

■ **1** see VICTOR.

conquest /kóngkwest/ *n.* **1** the act or an instance of conquering; the state of being conquered. **2 a** a conquered territory. **b** something won. **3** a person whose affection or favor has been won. **4** (**the Conquest** or **Norman Conquest**) the conquest of England by William ("the Conqueror") of Normandy in 1066. □ **make a conquest of** win the affections of. [ME f. OF *conquest(e)* f. Rmc (as CONQUER)]

■ **1** subjugation, domination, subjection; (*conquest of*) mastery *or* control of, triumph over; see also DEFEAT *n.* **2 b** see TROPHY 1. □ **make a conquest of** see CAPTIVATE.

conquistador /konkwístədawr, kongkeéstə-/ *n.* (*pl.* **conquistadores** /-dáwrez/ or **conquistadors**) a conqueror, esp. one of the Spanish conquerors of Mexico and Peru in the 16th c. [Sp.]

Cons. *abbr.* Conservative.

consanguineous /kónsanggwíneeəs/ *adj.* descended from the same ancestor; akin. □□ **consanguinity** *n.* [L *consanguineus* (as COM-, *sanguis -inis* blood)]

■ see KIN *adj.*

conscience /kónshəns/ *n.* **1** a moral sense of right and wrong esp. as felt by a person and affecting behavior (*my conscience won't allow me to do that*). **2** an inner feeling as to the goodness or otherwise of one's behavior (*my conscience is clear*; *has a guilty conscience*). □ **case of conscience** a matter in which one's conscience has to decide a conflict of principles. **conscience clause** a clause in a law, ensuring respect for the consciences of those affected. **conscience money** a sum paid to relieve one's conscience, esp. about a payment previously evaded. **conscience-stricken** (or **-struck**) made uneasy by a bad conscience. **for conscience** (or **conscience's**) **sake** to satisfy one's conscience. **freedom of conscience** a system allowing all citizens a free choice of religion. **in all conscience** *colloq.* by any reasonable standard; by all that is fair. **on one's conscience** causing one feelings of guilt. **prisoner of conscience** a person imprisoned by a government for holding political or religious views it does not tolerate. □□ **conscienceless** *adj.* [ME f. OF f. L *conscientia* f. *conscire* be privy to (as COM-, *scire* know)]

■ **1, 2** morality, morals, judgment, fairness, sense of right

---

/.../ **pronunciation**	● **part of speech**
□ **phrases, idioms, and compounds**	
□□ **derivatives**	■ **synonym section**
cross-references appear in SMALL CAPITALS or *italics*	

and wrong, ethics, honor, standards, principles, scruples. □ **conscience-stricken** (or **-struck**) see BAD *adj.* 6. **in all conscience** in all fairness, reasonably.

conscientious /kónshee-énshəs/ *adj.* (of a person or conduct) governed by a sense of duty; diligent and scrupulous. □ **conscientious objector** a person who for reasons of conscience objects to conforming to a requirement, esp. that of military service. □□ **conscientiously** *adv.* **conscientiousness** *n.* [F *consciencieux* f. med.L *conscientiosus* (as CONSCIENCE)]

■ principled, fair, moral, ethical, strict, righteous, rightminded, upstanding, upright, honorable, just, responsible, high-minded, incorruptible; careful, exacting, scrupulous, meticulous, punctilious, painstaking, diligent, particular, rigorous, thorough; prudent, sensible, attentive, serious.

conscious /kónshəs/ *adj.* & *n.* ● *adj.* **1** awake and aware of one's surroundings and identity. **2** (usu. foll. by *of*, or *that* + clause) aware; knowing (*conscious of his inferiority*). **3** (of actions, emotions, etc.) realized or recognized by the doer; intentional (*made a conscious effort not to laugh*). **4** (in comb.) aware of; concerned with (*appearance-conscious*). ● *n.* (prec. by *the*) the conscious mind. □□ **consciously** *adv.* [L *conscius* knowing with others or in oneself f. *conscire* (as COM-, *scire* know)]

■ *adj.* **1** aware, alert; see also AWAKE *adj.* 1b. **2** see AWARE 1. **3** deliberate, intentional, purposive, purposeful, willful, studied.

consciousness /kónshəsnis/ *n.* **1** the state of being conscious (*lost consciousness during the fight*). **2 a** awareness; perception (*had no consciousness of being ridiculed*). **b** (in comb.) awareness of (*class consciousness*). **3** the totality of a person's thoughts and feelings, or of a class of these (*moral consciousness*). □ **consciousness-raising** the activity of increasing esp. social or political sensitivity or awareness.

■ **2** see PERCEPTION. **3** see SPIRIT *n.* 1.

conscribe /kənskríb/ *v.tr.* = CONSCRIPT *v.* [L *conscribere* (as CONSCRIPTION)]

conscript *v.* & *n.* ● *v.tr.* /kənskrípt/ enlist by conscription. ● *n.* /kónskript/ a person enlisted by conscription. [(v.) back-form. f. CONSCRIPTION: (n.) f. F *conscrit* f. L *conscriptus* (as CONSCRIPTION)]

■ *v.* see ENLIST 1. ● *n.* see RECRUIT *n.* 1, 2.

conscription /kənskrípshən/ *n.* compulsory enlistment for government service, esp. military service. [F f. LL *conscriptio* levying of troops f. L *conscribere conscript-* enroll (as COM-, *scribere* write)]

■ draft, impressment, call-up, *Brit. hist.* national service, *US hist.* selective service.

consecrate /kónsikrayt/ *v.tr.* **1** make or declare sacred; dedicate formally to a religious or divine purpose. **2** (in Christian belief) make (bread and wine) into the body and blood of Christ. **3** (foll. by *to*) devote (one's life, etc.) to (a purpose). **4** ordain (esp. a bishop) to a sacred office. □□ **consecration** /-kráyshən/ *n.* **consecrator** *n.* **consecratory** /-krətáwree/ *adj.* [ME f. L *consecrare* (as COM-, *secrare* = *sacrare* dedicate f. *sacer* sacred)]

■ **1** see SANCTIFY 1. **3** see DEVOTE.

consecution /kónsikyōōshən/ *n.* **1** logical sequence (in argument or reasoning). **2** sequence; succession (of events, etc.). [L *consecutio* f. *consequi consecut-* overtake (as COM-, *sequi* pursue)]

consecutive /kənsékyətiv/ *adj.* **1 a** following continuously. **b** in unbroken or logical order. **2** *Gram.* expressing consequence. □ **consecutive intervals** *Mus.* intervals of the same kind (esp. fifths or octaves), occurring in succession between two voices or parts in harmony. □□ **consecutively** *adv.* **consecutiveness** *n.* [F *consécutif -ive* f. med.L *consecutivus* (as CONSECUTION)]

■ **1** see SUCCESSIVE.

consensual /kənséshōōəl/ *adj.* of or by consent or consensus. □□ **consensually** *adv.* [L *consensus* (see CONSENSUS) + -AL]

consensus /kənsénsəs/ *n.* (often foll. by *of*) **1 a** general agreement (of opinion, testimony, etc.). **b** an instance of

this. **2** (*attrib.*) majority view; collective opinion (*consensus politics*). [L, = agreement (as CONSENT)]

■ **1** see AGREEMENT 1, 2.

consent /kənsént/ *v.* & *n.* ● *v.intr.* (often foll. by *to*) express willingness; give permission; agree. ● *n.* voluntary agreement; permission; compliance. □ **age of consent** the age at which consent to sexual intercourse is valid in law. **consenting adult** an adult who consents to something, esp. a sexual act. [ME f. OF *consentir* f. L *consentire* (as COM-, *sentire sens-* feel)]

■ *v.* agree, comply, concur, accede, acquiesce, concede, yield, submit, cede, conform, give in; (*consent to*) permit, allow, agree to, give in to, approve, authorize. ● *n.* approval, assent, permission, sanction, authorization, imprimatur, seal of approval, go-ahead, *colloq.* OK, okay; agreement, acceptance, acquiescence, compliance, approval, concurrence.

consentient /kənsénshənt/ *adj.* **1** agreeing; united in opinion. **2** concurrent. **3** (often foll. by *to*) consenting. [L *consentient-* (as CONSENT)]

consequence /kónsikwens, -kwəns/ *n.* **1** the result or effect of an action or condition. **2 a** importance (*it is of no consequence*). **b** social distinction (*persons of consequence*). **3** (in *pl.*) a game in which a narrative is made up by the players, each ignorant of what has already been contributed. □ **in consequence** as a result. **take the consequences** accept the results of one's choice or action. [ME f. OF f. L *consequentia* (as CONSEQUENT)]

■ **1** see RESULT *n.* 1. **2** see IMPORTANCE 2, 3. □ **in consequence** see ACCORDINGLY 2.

consequent /kónsikwənt/ *adj.* & *n.* ● *adj.* **1** (often foll. by *on, upon*) following as a result or consequence. **2** logically consistent. ● *n.* **1** a thing that follows another. **2** *Logic* the second part of a conditional proposition, dependent on the antecedent. [ME f. OF f. L *consequi* (as CONSECUTION)]

■ *adj.* **1** see ATTENDANT *adj.* 1. **2** see NATURAL *adj.* 8.

consequential /kónsikwénshəl/ *adj.* **1** following as a result or consequence. **2** resulting indirectly (*consequential damage*). **3 a** significant. **b** (of a person) self-important. □□ **consequentiality** /-sheeálitee/ *n.* **consequentially** *adv.* [L *consequentia*]

consequently /kónsikwentlee/ *adv.* & *conj.* as a result; therefore.

■ so, therefore, as a result *or* consequence, in consequence, accordingly, ergo, hence, *formal* thus.

conservancy /kənsárvənsee/ *n.* (*pl.* **-ies**) **1** a body concerned with the preservation of natural resources (*Nature Conservancy*). **2** conservation; official preservation (of forests, etc.). **3** *Brit.* a commission, etc., controlling a port, river, etc. (*Thames Conservancy*). [18th-c. alt. of obs. *conservacy* f. AF *conservacie* f. AL *conservatia* f. L *conservatio* (as CONSERVE)]

conservation /kónsərváyshən/ *n.* preservation, esp. of the natural environment. □ **conservation area** an area containing a noteworthy environment and specially protected by law against undesirable changes. **conservation of energy** (or **mass** or **momentum**, etc.) *Physics* the principle that the total quantity of energy, etc., of any system not subject to external action remains constant. □□ **conservational** *adj.* [ME f. OF *conservation* or L *conservatio* (as CONSERVE)]

■ preservation, protection, safekeeping, maintenance, upkeep, management, safeguarding; husbandry, environmentalism, greenness.

conservationist /kónsərváyshənist/ *n.* a supporter or advocate of environmental conservation.

■ environmentalist, ecologist, preservationist; see also NATURALIST.

conservative /kənsárvətiv/ *adj.* & *n.* ● *adj.* **1 a** averse to rapid change. **b** (of views, taste, etc.) moderate; avoiding extremes (*conservative in her dress*). **2** (of an estimate, etc.) purposely low; moderate; cautious. **3** (**Conservative**) of or characteristic of Conservatives or the Conservative party. **4** tending to conserve. ● *n.* **1** a conservative person. **2** (**Conservative**) a supporter or member of the Conservative party. □ **Conservative Judaism** Judaism allowing only minor changes in traditional ritual, etc. **Conservative party 1** a British political party promoting free enterprise and private ownership. **2** a similar party elsewhere. **conservative surgery** surgery that seeks to preserve tissues as far as possible. □□ **conservatism** n. **conservatively** adv. **conservativeness** n. [ME f. LL *conservativus* (as CONSERVE)]

■ adj. **1 a** unprogressive, orthodox, traditional, conformist, hidebound, conventional, fundamentalist, true-blue, dyed-in-the-wool, inveterate. **b** cautious, careful, prudent, moderate, traditional, temperate, middle-of-the-road, sober, stable. **2** low, moderate; cautious, tentative, hesitant. **3** Tory. ● n. **1** reactionary, fundamentalist; moderate, middle-of-the-roader. **2** Tory.

conservatoire /kənsɔ́rvətwaár/ n. a (usu. European) school of music or other arts. [F f. It. *conservatorio* (as CONSERVATORY)]

■ conservatory, *Austral.* conservatorium.

conservator /kənsɔ́rvətər, kónsərvaytər/ n. a person who preserves something; an official custodian (of a museum, etc.). [ME f. AF *conservatour*, OF *-ateur* f. L *conservator -oris* (as CONSERVE)]

conservatorium /kənsɔ́rvətáwreeəm/ n. *Austral.* = CONSERVATOIRE.

conservatory /kənsɔ́rvətawree/ n. (pl. **-ies**) **1** a greenhouse for tender plants, esp. one attached to and communicating with a house. **2** = CONSERVATOIRE. [LL *conservatorium* (as CONSERVE): sense 2 through It. *conservatorio*]

■ **1** see HOTHOUSE n. 1.

conserve /kənsɔ́rv/ v. & n. ● v.tr. **1** store up; keep from harm or damage, esp. for later use. **2** *Physics* maintain a quantity of (heat, etc.). **3** preserve (food, esp. fruit), usu. with sugar. ● n. /also kónsərv/ **1** fruit, etc., preserved in sugar. **2** fresh fruit jam. [ME f. OF *conserver* f. L *conservare* (as COM-, *servare* keep)]

■ v. **1** keep, preserve, hold on to, store up, save, spare, reserve; maintain, keep up, take care of. **3** see PRESERVE v. 4a. ● n. **2** see PRESERVE n. 1.

consider /kənsídər/ v.tr. (often *absol.*) **1** contemplate mentally, esp. in order to reach a conclusion. **2** examine the merits of (a course of action, a candidate, claim, etc.). **3** give attention to. **4** reckon with; take into account. **5** (foll. by *that* + clause) have the opinion. **6** (foll. by compl.) believe; regard as (*consider it to be genuine*; *consider it settled*). **7** (as **considered** adj.) formed after careful thought (*a considered opinion*). □ **all things considered** taking everything into account. [ME f. OF *considerer* f. L *considerare* examine]

■ **1** think about *or* over, deliberate (over *or* about), contemplate, ponder, mull over, cogitate on, meditate (on *or* upon *or* over *or* about), reflect (on *or* upon *or* about), ruminate (on *or* over *or* about), chew over, study, examine. **2** see DELIBERATE v. 2. **3** see HEED v. 4 heed, mark, take into account *or* consideration, reckon with, bear in mind, think of *or* about, note, observe, make allowance for; respect, have regard for. **5** see RECKON 4a. **6** regard, look upon; judge, take to be, think, believe, gauge, rate, estimate, reckon, *formal* deem.

considerable /kənsídərəbəl/ adj. **1** enough in amount or extent to need consideration. **2** much; a lot of (*considerable pain*). **3** notable; important. □□ **considerably** adv.

■ **1, 2** sizable, substantial, large, big, great, no little, appreciable, respectable, noticeable, largish, biggish, goodly, decent, fair, *colloq.* tidy; much, a lot of. **3** important, worthy, of consequence, of distinction, distinguished, illustrious, noteworthy, notable, remarkable, estimable, influential, respectable.

considerate /kənsídərət/ adj. **1** thoughtful toward other people; careful not to cause hurt or inconvenience. **2** *archaic* careful. □□ **considerately** adv.

■ **1** thoughtful, kind, kindly, kindhearted, good-hearted, helpful, friendly, neighborly, gracious, obliging, accommodating, charitable, generous, unselfish; sympathetic, compassionate, sensitive, attentive, solicitous, *Psychol.* empathetic, empathic.

consideration /kənsídəráyshən/ n. **1** the act of considering; careful thought. **2** thoughtfulness for others; being considerate. **3** a fact or a thing taken into account in deciding or judging something. **4** compensation; a payment or reward. **5** *Law* (in a contractual agreement) anything given or promised or forborne by one party in exchange for the promise or undertaking of another. **6** *archaic* importance or consequence. □ **in consideration of** in return for; on account of. **take into consideration** include as a factor, reason, etc.; make allowance for. **under consideration** being considered. [ME f. OF f. L *consideratio -onis* (as CONSIDER)]

■ **1** thought, deliberation, reflection, contemplation, rumination, cogitation; study, examination. **2** thoughtfulness, regard, concern, attentiveness, solicitude, compassion, kindness, kindliness, kindheartedness, considerateness, respect, care, concern, *Psychol.* empathy. **3** see POINT n. 11. **4** reward, compensation, remuneration, fee, payment, recompense, emolument, tip, gratuity, *pourboire*, baksheesh, honorarium. **6** see IMPORTANCE 2.

considering /kənsídəring/ prep. **1** in view of; taking into consideration (*considering their youth*; *considering that it was snowing*). **2** (without compl.) *colloq.* all in all; taking everything into account (*not so bad, considering*).

■ **1** in view of, in (the) light of, bearing in mind, making allowance for, taking into consideration *or* account, looking at, inasmuch as, insomuch as. **2** all things *or* everything considered; see also *on the whole* (WHOLE).

consign /kənsín/ v.tr. (often foll. by *to*) **1** hand over; deliver to a person's possession or trust. **2** assign; commit decisively or permanently (*consigned it to the trash can*; *consigned to years of misery*). **3** transmit or send (goods), usu. by a public carrier. □□ **consignee** /kónsineé/ n. **consignor** n. [ME f. F *consigner* or L *consignare* mark with a seal (as COM-, SIGN)]

■ **1** see ENTRUST 1. **2** dispatch, dismiss, relegate; see also DOWNGRADE v. 1. **3** see SEND 1a.

consignment /kənsínmənt/ n. **1** the act or an instance of consigning; the process of being consigned. **2** a batch of goods consigned. **3** an agreement to pay a supplier of goods after the goods are sold.

■ **2** see CARGO 1b, 2b.

consist /kənsíst/ v.intr. **1** (foll. by *of*) be composed; have specified ingredients or elements. **2** (foll. by *in, of*) have its essential features as specified (*its beauty consists in the use of color*). **3** (usu. foll. by *with*) harmonize; be consistent. [L *consistere* exist (as COM-, *sistere* stop)]

■ **1** (*consist of*) contain, comprise, be composed of, include, have in it.

consistency /kənsístənsee/ n. (also **consistence**) (pl. **-ies** or **-es**) **1** the degree of density, firmness, or viscosity, esp. of thick liquids. **2** the state of being consistent; conformity with other or earlier attitudes, practice, etc. **3** the state or quality of holding or sticking together and retaining shape. [F *consistence* or LL *consistentia* (as CONSIST)]

■ **1** texture, viscosity, density, firmness, compactness. **2** see UNIFORMITY.

consistent /kənsístənt/ adj. (usu. foll. by *with*) **1** compatible or in harmony; not contradictory. **2** (of a person) constant to the same principles of thought or action. □□ **consistently** adv. [L *consistere* (as CONSIST)]

■ **1** in agreement, in harmony, in keeping, harmonious, in concordance, in conformance *or* conformity, accordant, compatible, in accord *or* accordance, consonant, consequent. **2** dependable, regular, constant, predictable, undeviating, steady, steadfast, unchanging, unswerving. □□ **consistently** steadily, constantly, regularly, often, frequently; reliably, dependably, uniformly, unswervingly, devotedly, firmly, resolutely, faithfully, unfailingly, undeviatingly.

/.../ **pronunciation**	● **part of speech**
□ **phrases, idioms, and compounds**	
□□ **derivatives**	■ **synonym section**
cross-references appear in SMALL CAPITALS or *italics*	

consistory /kənsístəree/ *n.* (*pl.* **-ies**) **1** *RC Ch.* the council of cardinals (with or without the pope). **2** (in full **consistory court**) (in the Church of England) a court presided over by a bishop, for the administration of ecclesiastical law in a diocese. **3** (in other churches) a local administrative body. □□ **consistorial** /kónsistáwreeəl/ *adj.* [ME f. AF *consistorie*, OF *-oire* f. LL *consistorium* (as CONSIST)]
■ **1** see SOCIETY 8.

consociation /kənsōsheeáyshən, kənsōsee-/ *n.* **1** close association, esp. of churches or religious communities. **2** *Ecol.* a closely related subgroup of plants having one dominant species. [L *consociatio, -onis* f. *consociare* (as COM-, *socius* fellow)]
■ **1** see SOCIETY 8.

consolation /kónsəláyshən/ *n.* **1** the act or an instance of consoling; the state of being consoled. **2** a consoling thing, person, or circumstance. □ **consolation prize** a prize given to a competitor who just fails to win a main prize. □□ **consolatory** /kənsōlətawree, -sól-/ *adj.* [ME f. OF, f. L *consolatio -onis* (as CONSOLE[1])]
■ see COMFORT *n.* 1.

console[1] /kənsōl/ *v.tr.* comfort, esp. in grief or disappointment. ¶ Often confused with *condole*. □□ **consolable** *adj.* **consoler** *n.* **consolingly** *adv.* [F *consoler* f. L *consolari*]
■ comfort, soothe, calm, assuage, solace, cheer (up), reassure, relieve, hearten, cheer, gladden.

console[2] /kónsōl/ *n.* **1** a panel or unit accommodating a set of switches, controls, etc. **2** a cabinet for television or radio equipment, etc. **3** *Mus.* a cabinet with the keyboards, stops, pedals, etc., of an organ. **4** an ornamented bracket supporting a shelf, etc. □ **console table** a table supported by a bracket against a wall. [F, perh. f. *consolider* (as CONSOLIDATE)]

consolidate /kənsólidayt/ *v.* **1** *tr. & intr.* make or become strong or solid. **2** *tr.* reinforce or strengthen (one's position, power, etc.). **3** *tr.* combine (territories, companies, debts, etc.) into one whole. □ **consolidated fund** (or **annuities**) *Brit.* a Bank of England fund into which tax revenue is paid and from which payments no dependent on annual votes in Parliament are made. □□ **consolidation** /-dáyshən/ *n.* **consolidator** *n.* **consolidatory** *adj.* [L *consolidare* (as COM-, *solidare* f. *solidus* solid)]
■ **1, 2** see STRENGTHEN. **3** see AMALGAMATE.

consols /kónsolz/ *n.pl.* British government securities without redemption date and with fixed annual interest. [abbr. of *consolidated annuities*]

consommé /kónsəmáy/ *n.* a clear soup made with meat stock. [F, past part. of *consommer* f. L *consummare* (as CONSUMMATE)]
■ see BROTH.

consonance /kónsənəns/ *n.* **1** agreement; harmony. **2** *Prosody* a recurrence of similar-sounding consonants. **3** *Mus.* a harmonious combination of notes; a harmonious interval. [ME f. OF *consonance* or L *consonantia* (as CONSONANT)]
■ **1** see HARMONY 3.

consonant /kónsənənt/ *n. & adj.* ● *n.* **1** a speech sound in which the breath is at least partly obstructed, and which to form a syllable must be combined with a vowel. **2** a letter or letters representing this. ● *adj.* (foll. by *with, to*) **1** consistent; in agreement or harmony. **2** similar in sound. **3** *Mus.* making a concord. □□ **consonantal** /-nánt'l/ *adj.* **consonantly** *adv.* [ME f. F f. L *consonare* (as COM-, *sonare* sound f. *sonus*)]
■ *adj.* **1** see CONSISTENT 1.

con sordino /kón sawrdéenō, káwn/ *adv. Mus.* with the use of a mute. [It.]

consort[1] *n. & v.* ● *n.* /kónsawrt/ **1** a wife or husband, esp. of royalty (*prince consort*). **2** a companion or associate. **3** a ship sailing with another. ● *v.* /kənsórt/ **1** *intr.* (usu. foll. by *with, together*) **a** keep company; associate. **b** harmonize. **2** *tr.* class or bring together. [ME f. F f. L *consors* sharer, comrade (as COM-, *sors sortis* lot, destiny)]
■ *n.* **1** see MATE[1] *n.* 3b. ● *v.* **1 a** see ASSOCIATE *v.* 5.

consort[2] /kónsawrt/ *n. Mus.* a group of players or instruments, esp. playing early music (*recorder consort*). [earlier form of CONCERT]

consortium /kənsáwrsheeəm, -teeəm/ *n.* (*pl.* **consortia** /-sheeə, -teeə/ or **consortiums**) **1** an association, esp. of several business companies. **2** *Law* the right of association with a husband or wife (*loss of consortium*). [L, = partnership (as CONSORT[1])]
■ **1** see ASSOCIATION 1.

conspecific /kónspisifik/ *adj. Biol.* of the same species.

conspectus /kənspéktəs/ *n.* **1** a general or comprehensive survey. **2** a summary or synopsis. [L f. *conspicere conspect-* (as COM-, *spicere* look at)]
■ **2** see SYNOPSIS 1, 2.

conspicuous /kənspíkyŏŏəs/ *adj.* **1** clearly visible; striking to the eye; attracting notice. **2** remarkable of its kind (*conspicuous extravagance*). □□ **conspicuously** *adv.* **conspicuousness** *n.* [L *conspicuus* (as CONSPECTUS)]
■ **1** obvious, unmistakable, prominent, outstanding, noticeable, impressive, vivid, obtrusive; striking, loud, blatant; evident, apparent, clear-cut, unquestionable, incontestable, incontrovertible. **2** notable, noteworthy, exceptional, outstanding, eminent, unusual, marked, extraordinary, remarkable, distinguished, impressive, awesome, awe-inspiring, glorious.

conspiracy /kənspírəsee/ *n.* (*pl.* **-ies**) **1** a secret plan to commit a crime or do harm, often for political ends; a plot. **2** the act of conspiring. □ **conspiracy of silence** an agreement to say nothing. [ME f. AF *conspiracie*, alt. form of OF *conspiration* f. L *conspiratio -onis* (as CONSPIRE)]
■ **1** plot, scheme, stratagem, cabal, intrigue, machination. **2** collusion, connivance, intrigue, foul play, dirty work *or* tricks.

conspirator /kənspírətər/ *n.* a person who takes part in a conspiracy. □□ **conspiratorial** /-táwreeəl/ *adj.* **conspiratorially** *adv.* [ME f. AF *conspiratour*, OF *-teur* (as CONSPIRE)]
■ see ACCOMPLICE.

conspire /kənspír/ *v.intr.* **1** combine secretly to plan and prepare an unlawful or harmful act. **2** (often foll. by *against*, or *to* + infin.) (of events or circumstances) seem to be working together, esp. disadvantageously. [ME f. OF *conspirer* f. L *conspirare* agree, plot (as COM-, *spirare* breathe)]
■ **1** see PLOT *v.* 2.

constable /kónstəbəl, kún-/ *n.* **1** esp. *Brit.* **a** a policeman or policewoman. **b** (also **police constable**) a police officer of the lowest rank. **2** the governor of a royal castle. **3** *hist.* the principal officer in a royal household. [ME f. OF *conestable* f. LL *comes stabuli* count of the stable]

constabulary /kənstábyəleree/ *n. & adj.* ● *n.* **1** (*pl.* **-ies**) an organized body of police; a police force. **2** armed police organized as a military unit. ● *attrib.adj.* of or concerning the police force. [med.L *constabularius* (as CONSTABLE)]
■ *n.* **1** see POLICE *n.*

constancy /kónstənsee/ *n.* **1** the quality of being unchanging and dependable; faithfulness. **2** firmness; endurance. [L *constantia* (as CONSTANT)]
■ **1** see LOYALTY. **2** see DETERMINATION 1.

constant /kónstənt/ *adj. & n.* ● *adj.* **1** continuous (*needs constant attention*). **2** occurring frequently (*receive constant complaints*). **3** (often foll. by *to*) unchanging; faithful; dependable. ● *n.* **1** anything that does not vary. **2** *Math.* a component of a relationship between variables that does not change its value. **3** *Physics* **a** a number expressing a relation, property, etc., and remaining the same in all circumstances. **b** such a number that remains the same for a substance in the same conditions. □□ **constantly** *adv.* [ME f. OF f. L *constare* (as COM-, *stare* stand)]
■ *adj.* **1** continuous, continual; incessant, unceasing, ceaseless, perpetual, persistent, uninterrupted, steady, regular, invariable, unremitting, unvarying, relentless, unrelenting, unending, endless, never-ending, nonstop, perennial, eternal, everlasting, *rhet.* sempiternal. **2** frequent, numerous; see also MANY *adj.* **3** unchanging, invariable, unvarying, fixed, uniform, unalterable, inalterable, immutable, changeless; resolute, immovable, steadfast, firm, dependable, unshakable, determined, unswerving, undeviating, persevering,

unwearying, unwearied, untiring, indefatigable, tireless, unflagging, unwavering, unfailing, unfaltering, persistent; loyal, true, tried and true, devoted, staunch, faithful, *archaic* trusty.

constantan /kónstəntan/ *n.* an alloy of copper and nickel used in electrical equipment. [CONSTANT + -AN]

constellate /kónstəlayt/ *v.tr.* **1** form into (or as if into) a constellation. **2** adorn as with stars.

constellation /kónstəláyshən/ *n.* **1** a group of fixed stars whose outline is traditionally regarded as forming a particular figure. **2** a group of associated persons, ideas, etc. [ME f. OF f. LL *constellatio -onis* (as COM-, *stella* star)]

consternate /kónstərnayt/ *v.tr.* (usu. in *passive*) dismay; fill with anxiety. [L *consternare* (as COM-, *sternere* throw down)]

consternation /kónstərnáyshən/ *n.* anxiety or dismay causing mental confusion. [F *consternation* or L *consternatio* (as CONSTERNATE)]

■ see DISMAY *n.* 1.

constipate /kónstipayt/ *v.tr.* (esp. as **constipated** *adj.*) affect with constipation. [L *constipare* (as COM-, *stipare* press)]

constipation /kónstipáyshən/ *n.* **1** a condition with hardened feces and difficulty in emptying the bowels. **2** a restricted state. [ME f. OF *constipation* or LL *constipatio* (as CONSTIPATE)]

constituency /kənstíchōōənsee/ *n.* (*pl.* **-ies**) **1** a body of voters in a specified area who elect a representative member to a legislative body. **2** the area represented in this way. **3** a body of customers, supporters, etc.

constituent /kənstíchōōənt/ *adj.* & *n.* ● *adj.* **1** composing or helping to make up a whole. **2** able to make or change a (political, etc.) constitution (*constituent assembly*). **3** appointing or electing. ● *n.* **1** a member of a constituency (esp. political). **2** a component part. **3** *Law* a person who appoints another as agent. [L *constituent-* partly through F *-ant* (as CONSTITUTE)]

■ *n.* 2 see INGREDIENT.

constitute /kónstitōōt, tyōōt/ *v.tr.* **1** be the components or essence of; make up; form. **2** be equivalent or tantamount to (*this constitutes an official warning*). **b** formally establish (*does not constitute a precedent*). **3** give legal or constitutional form to; establish by law. □□ **constitutor** *n.* [L *constituere* (as COM-, *statuere* set up)]

■ **1** see FORM *v.* 3. **2 a** see MAKE *v.* 5. **b** see ESTABLISH 1.

constitution /kónstitōōshən, -tyōō-/ *n.* **1** the act or method of constituting; the composition (of something). **2 a** the body of fundamental laws, principles, or established precedents according to which a nation, state, or other organization is acknowledged to be governed. **b** a (usu. written) record of this. **c** (**Constitution**) the US Constitution. **3** a person's physical state as regards vitality, health, strength, etc. **4** a person's mental or psychological makeup. **5** *hist.* a decree or ordinance. [ME f. OF *constitution* or L *constitutio* (as CONSTITUTE)]

■ **1** see STRUCTURE *n.* 2. **2, 5** see LAW 1a, b. **3** see HEALTH 2. **4** see MAKEUP 5.

constitutional /kónstitōōshənəl, -tyōō-/ *adj.* & *n.* ● *adj.* **1** of, consistent with, authorized by, or limited by a political constitution (*constitutional duties of office*). **2** inherent in, stemming from, or affecting the physical or mental constitution. ● *n.* a walk taken regularly to maintain or restore good health. □□ **constitutionality** /-nálitee/ *n.* **constitutionalize** *v.tr.* **constitutionally** *adv.*

■ *adj.* **1** see LEGITIMATE *adj.* 1, 2. **2** see INHERENT 1. ● *n.* see WALK *n.* 2b.

constitutionalism /kónstitōōshənəlizəm, -tyōō-/ *n.* **1** a constitutional system of government. **2** the adherence to or advocacy of such a system. □□ **constitutionalist** *n.*

constitutive /kónstitōōtiv, -tyōō-/ *adj.* **1** able to form or appoint. **2** component. **3** essential. □□ **constitutively** *adv.* [LL *constitutivus* (as CONSTITUTE)]

constrain /kənstráyn/ *v.tr.* **1** compel; urge irresistibly or by necessity. **2 a** confine forcibly; imprison. **b** restrict severely as regards action, behavior, etc. **3** bring about by compulsion. **4** (as **constrained** *adj.*) forced; embarrassed (*a constrained voice; a constrained manner*). □□ **constrainedly**

/-nidlee/ *adv.* [ME f. OF *constraindre* f. L *constringere* (as COM-, *stringere strict-* tie)]

■ **1, 3** see FORCE[1] *v.* 1. **2** see BOUND[2] *v.* **4** (**constrained**) see STRAINED 1.

constraint /kənstráynt/ *n.* **1** the act or result of constraining or being constrained; restriction of liberty. **2** something that constrains; a limitation on motion or action. **3** the restraint of natural feelings or their expression; a constrained manner. [ME f. OF *constreinte*, fem. past part. (as CONSTRAIN)]

constrict /kənstríkt/ *v.tr.* **1** make narrow or tight; compress. **2** *Biol.* cause (organic tissue) to contract. □□ **constriction** /-stríkshən/ *n.* **constrictive** *adj.* [L (as CONSTRAIN)]

■ **1** see CONTRACT *v.* 1.

constrictor /kənstríktər/ *n.* **1** any snake (esp. a boa) that kills by coiling around its prey and compressing it. **2** *Anat.* any muscle that compresses or contracts an organ or part of the body. [mod.L (as CONSTRICT)]

construct *v.* & *n.* ● *v.tr.* /kənstrúkt/ **1** make by fitting parts together; build; form (something physical or abstract). **2** *Geom.* draw or delineate, esp. accurately to given conditions (*construct a triangle*). ● *n.* /kónstrukt/ **1** a thing constructed, esp. by the mind. **2** *Linguistics* a group of words forming a phrase. □□ **constructor** *n.* [L *construere construct-* (as COM-, *struere* pile, build)]

■ *v.* **1** build, erect, make, put together, frame, set up, put up, assemble; fabricate, devise, create, forge, invent, formulate, compose, form, shape, fashion. ● *n.* **1** see INVENTION 1.

construction /kənstrúkshən/ *n.* **1** the act or a mode of constructing. **2** a thing constructed. **3** an interpretation or explanation (*they put a generous construction on his act*). **4** *Gram.* an arrangement of words according to syntactical rules. □□ **constructional** *adj.* **constructionally** *adv.* [ME f. OF f. L *constructio -onis* (as CONSTRUCT)]

■ **1, 2** see STRUCTURE *n.* 1a, b, 2. **3** see RENDITION 1.

constructionism /kənstrúkshənizəm/ *n.* **1** *Law* interpretation of a law or constitution in a particular way (*strict constructionism*). **2** = CONSTRUCTIVISM. □□ **constructionist** *n.*

constructive /kənstrúktiv/ *adj.* **1 a** of construction; tending to construct. **b** tending to form a basis for ideas (*constructive criticism*). **2** helpful; positive (*a constructive approach*). **3** derived by inference; not expressed (*constructive permission*). **4** belonging to the structure of a building. □□ **constructively** *adv.* **constructiveness** *n.* [LL *constructivus* (as CONSTRUCT)]

■ **2** helpful, useful, practicable, practical, productive, beneficial, positive. **3** virtual, inferential, implicit, inferred, derived, deduced. **4** structural.

constructivism /kənstrúktivizəm/ *n.* *Art* a Russian movement in which assorted (usu. mechanical or industrial) objects are combined into nonrepresentational and mobile structural forms. □□ **constructivist** *n.* [Russ. *konstruktivizm* (as CONSTRUCT)]

construe /kənstrōō/ *v.tr.* (**construes, construed, construing**) **1** interpret (words or actions) (*their decision can be construed in many ways*). **2** (often foll. by *with*) combine (words) grammatically (*"rely" is construed with "on"*). **3** analyze the syntax of (a sentence). **4** translate word for word. □□ **construable** *adj.* **construal** *n.* [ME f. L *construere* CONSTRUCT]

■ **1** see INTERPRET 4.

consubstantial /kónsəbstánshəl/ *adj.* *Theol.* of the same substance (esp. of the three persons of the Trinity). □□ **consubstantiality** /-sheeálitee/ *n.* [ME f. eccl.L *consubstantialis*, transl. Gk *homoousios* (as COM-, SUBSTANTIAL)]

consubstantiation /kónsəbstánsheeáyshən/ *n.* *Theol.* the doctrine of the real substantial presence of the body and blood of Christ in and with the bread and wine in the Eucharist. [mod.L *consubstantiatio*, after *transubstantiatio* TRANSUBSTANTIATION]

consuetude /kónswitōōd, -tyōōd/ *n.* a custom, esp. one hav-

/.../ **pronunciation**	● **part of speech**
□ **phrases, idioms, and compounds**	
□□ **derivatives**	■ **synonym section**
cross-references appear in SMALL CAPITALS or *italics*	

ing legal force in Scotland. □□ **consuetudinary** /kónswi-tóōd'neree, -tyóōd-/ *adj.* [ME f. OF *consuetude* or L *consuetudo -dinis* f. *consuetus* accustomed]

consul /kónsəl/ *n.* **1** an official appointed by a government to live in a foreign city and protect the government's citizens and interests there. **2** *hist.* either of two annually elected chief magistrates in ancient Rome. **3** any of the three chief magistrates of the French republic (1799–1804). □□ **consular** *adj.* **consulship** *n.* [ME f. L, rel. to *consulere* take counsel]
■ **1** see MINISTER *n.* 2, 3.

consulate /kónsələt/ *n.* **1** the building officially used by a consul. **2** the office, position, or period of office of consul. **3** *hist.* government by consuls. **4** *hist.* the period of office of a consul. **5** *hist.* (**Consulate**) the government of France by three consuls (1799–1804). [ME f. L *consulatus* (as CONSUL)]

consult /kənsúlt/ *v. & n.* **1** *tr.* seek information or advice from (a person, book, watch, etc.). **2** *intr.* (often foll. by *with*) refer to a person for advice, an opinion, etc. **3** *tr.* seek permission or approval from (a person) for a proposed action. **4** *tr.* take into account; consider (feelings, interests, etc.). ● *n.* /kónsult/ = CONSULTATION 1, 2. □□ **consultative** /-súltətiv/ *adj.* [F *consulter* f. L *consultare* frequent. of *consulere consult-* take counsel]
■ **1, 2** refer to, look in *or* at; confer (with), discuss (with), deliberate (with), talk over (with), inquire (of), seek advice (from), ask (of), question, take counsel (with). **4** see CONSIDER 4.

consultancy /kənsúlt'nsee/ *n.* (*pl.* **-ies**) the professional practice or position of a consultant.

consultant /kənsúlt'nt/ *n.* **1** a person providing professional advice, etc., esp. for a fee. **2** *Brit.* a senior specialist in a branch of medicine responsible for patients in a hospital. [prob. F (as CONSULT)]
■ **1** expert, counselor; see also ADVISER.

consultation /kónsəltáyshən/ *n.* **1** a meeting arranged to consult (esp. with a consultant). **2** the act or an instance of consulting. **3** a conference. [ME f. OF *consultation* or L *consultatio* (as CONSULTANT)]
■ **1, 2** see TALK *n.* 1. **3** see CONFERENCE 1.

consulting /kənsúlting/ *attrib.adj.* giving professional advice to others working in the same field or subject (*consulting physician*).

consumable /kənsóōməbəl/ *adj. & n.* ● *adj.* that can be consumed; intended for consumption. ● *n.* (usu. in *pl.*) a commodity that is eventually used up, worn out, or eaten.

consume /kənsóōm/ *v.tr.* **1** eat or drink. **2** completely destroy; reduce to nothing or to tiny particles (*fire consumed the building*). **3** (often as **consumed** *adj.*) possess or entirely take up (foll. by *with*: *consumed with rage*). **4** use up (time, energy, etc.). □□ **consumingly** *adv.* [ME f. L *consumere* (as COM-, *sumere sumpt-* take up): partly through F *consumer*]
■ **1** devour, eat (up), gulp (down), swallow, put away, gobble (up); drink (up); digest. **2** destroy, ruin, (lay) waste, demolish, devastate, wreck, ravage, gut, raze, *sl.* total. **3** overcome, overwhelm, possess, eat up, devour; (**consumed**) preoccupied, obsessed, absorbed. **4** use up, exhaust, occupy, absorb, deplete, drain, expend; waste, squander, fritter away, dissipate, lose, throw away, lavish, *sl.* blow.

consumer /kənsóōmər/ *n.* **1** a person who consumes, esp. one who uses a product. **2** a purchaser of goods or services. □ **consumer goods** goods put to use by consumers, not used in producing other goods (opp. *capital goods* (see CAPITAL¹)). **consumer research** investigation of purchasers' needs and opinions. **consumer society** a society in which the marketing of goods and services is an important social and economic activity.
■ **1** see USER 1. **2** see BUYER.

consumerism /kənsóōmərizəm/ *n.* the protection or promotion of consumers' interests in relation to the producer. □□ **consumerist** *adj. & n.*

consummate *v. & adj.* ● *v.tr.* /kónsəmayt/ **1** complete; make perfect. **2** complete (a marriage) by sexual inter-

course. ● *adj.* /kənsúmit, kónsəmit/ complete; perfect; fully skilled (*a consummate general*). □□ **consummately** *adv.* **consummative** /kónsəmáy-/ *adj.* **consummator** *n.* [L *consummare* (as COM-, *summare* complete f. *summus* utmost)]
■ *v.* **1** see FINISH *v.* 1a. ● *adj.* see COMPLETE *adj.* 4.

consummation /kónsəmáyshən/ *n.* **1** completion, esp. of a marriage by sexual intercourse. **2** a desired end or goal; perfection. [ME f. OF *consommation* or L *consummatio* (as CONSUMMATE)]
■ **1** completion, accomplishment, fulfillment, finish, end, realization, attainment, achievement, success. **2** acme, perfection, peak, culmination, finishing touch, conclusion, grand finale, climax.

consumption /kənsúmpshən/ *n.* **1** the act or an instance of consuming; the process of being consumed. **2** any disease causing wasting of tissues, esp. pulmonary tuberculosis. **3** an amount consumed. **4** the purchase and use of goods, etc. [ME f. OF *consomption* f. L *consumptio* (as CONSUME)]
■ **1, 4** see USE *n.* 1.

consumptive /kənsúmptiv/ *adj. & n.* ● *adj.* **1** of or tending to consumption. **2** tending to or affected with pulmonary tuberculosis. ● *n.* a consumptive patient. □□ **consumptively** *adv.* [med.L *consumptivus* (as CONSUMPTION)]
■ *adj.* **2** tuberculate, tuberculous, tubercular, phthisic(al); see also EMACIATE. ● *n.* tubercular.

cont. *abbr.* **1** contents. **2** continued.

contact *n. & v.* ● *n.* /kóntakt/ **1** the state or condition of touching, meeting, or communicating. **2** a person who is or may be communicated with for information, supplies, assistance, etc. **3** *Electr.* **a** a connection for the passage of a current. **b** a device for providing this. **4** a person likely to carry a contagious disease through being associated with an infected person. **5** (usu. in *pl.*) *colloq.* a contact lens. ● *v.tr.* /kóntakt, kəntákt/ **1** get into communication with (a person). **2** begin correspondence or personal dealings with. □ **contact lens** a small lens placed directly on the eyeball to correct the vision. **contact print** a photographic print made by placing a negative directly on sensitized paper, etc., and illuminating it. **contact sport** a sport in which participants necessarily come into bodily contact with one another. □□ **contactable** *adj.* [L *contactus* f. *contingere* (as COM-, *tangere* touch)]
■ *n.* **1** conjunction, connection, touch, communication, meeting, association. **2** acquaintance, friend; see also CONNECTION 6. ● *v.* **1, 2** get in touch with, communicate with, reach, get hold of, speak to *or* with, write to.

contagion /kəntáyjən/ *n.* **1 a** the communication of disease from one person to another by bodily contact. **b** a contagious disease. **2** a contagious or harmful influence. **3** moral corruption, esp. when tending to be widespread. [ME f. L *contagio* (as COM-, *tangere* touch)]
■ **1 b** see DISEASE 3. **2, 3** see POISON *n.* 2.

contagious /kəntáyjəs/ *adj.* **1 a** (of a person) likely to transmit disease by contact. **b** (of a disease) transmitted in this way. **2** (of emotions, reactions, etc.) likely to affect others (*contagious enthusiasm*). □ **contagious abortion** brucellosis of cattle. □□ **contagiously** *adv.* **contagiousness** *n.* [ME f. LL *contagiosus* (as CONTAGION)]
■ **1b, 2** see INFECTIOUS 2, 3.

contain /kəntáyn/ *v.tr.* **1** hold or be capable of holding within itself; include; comprise. **2** (of measures) consist of or be equal to (*a gallon contains eight pints*). **3** prevent (an enemy, difficulty, etc.) from moving or extending. **4** control or restrain (oneself, one's feelings, etc.). **5** (of a number) be divisible by (a factor) without a remainder. □□ **containable** *adj.* [ME f. OF *contenir* f. L *continēre content-* (as COM-, *tenēre* hold)]
■ **1** hold, have in it, comprise, lodge; bear, carry; see also INCLUDE 1. **2** consist of, equal; hold. **3, 4** restrain, control, restrict, confine, repress, hold back *or* in, curb, bridle, keep under control, suppress, check, stifle.

container /kəntáynər/ *n.* **1** a vessel, box, etc., for holding particular things. **2** a large boxlike receptacle of standard

design for the transport of goods, esp. one readily transferable from one form of transport to another (also *attrib.*: *container ship*).
- see RECEPTACLE.

containerize /kəntáynəriz/ *v.tr.* **1** pack in or transport by container. **2** adapt to transport by container. □□ **containerization** *n.*
- **1** see PACKAGE *v.*

containment /kəntáynmənt/ *n.* the action or policy of preventing the expansion of a hostile country or influence.

contaminate /kəntáminayt/ *v.tr.* **1** pollute, esp. with radioactivity. **2** infect; corrupt. □□ **contaminant** /-minənt/ *n.* **contamination** /-náyshən/ *n.* **contaminator** *n.* [L *contaminare* (as COM-, *tamen-* rel. to *tangere* touch)]
- **1** defile, pollute, dirty, poison, foul, spoil, grime, *poet.* befoul, sully; debase, adulterate, vitiate. **2** stain, corrupt, soil, taint, infect.

contango /kəntánggō/ *n.* (*pl.* **-os**) *Brit. Stock Exch.* **1** the postponement of the transfer of stock from one account day to the next. **2** a percentage paid by the buyer for such a postponement. [19th c.: prob. an arbitrary formation]

conte /koNt/ *n.* **1** a short story (as a form of literary composition). **2** a medieval narrative tale. [F]

contemn /kəntém/ *v.tr. literary* despise; treat with disregard. □□ **contemner** /-témər, -témnər/ *n.* [ME f. OF *contemner* or L *contemnere* (as COM-, *temnere tempt-* despise)]
- see DESPISE.

contemplate /kóntəmplayt/ *v.* **1** *tr.* survey with the eyes or in the mind. **2** *tr.* regard (an event) as possible. **3** *tr.* intend; have as one's purpose (*we contemplate leaving tomorrow*). **4** *intr.* meditate. □□ **contemplation** /-pláyshən/ *n.* **contemplator** *n.* [L *contemplari* (as COM-, *templum* place for observations)]
- **1** look at *or* (up)on, gaze at *or* (up)on, view, survey, observe, regard, eye, scan, *literary* behold; ruminate on *or* over, ponder on *or* over, deliberate over, meditate *or* reflect on, think about *or* over, mull over, cogitate over, turn over in one's mind, brood on *or* over, chew on *or* over, consider, *literary* muse on *or* over. **2** see ENVISAGE 2. **3** plan, think of *or* about, consider, entertain the idea *or* notion of; see also INTEND 1, 2. **4** see MEDITATE 1.

contemplative /kəntémplətiv, kóntəmpláy-/ *adj.* & *n.*
- *adj.* of or given to (esp. religious) contemplation; meditative.
- *n.* a person whose life is devoted to religious contemplation. □□ **contemplatively** *adv.* [ME f. OF *contemplatif -ive*, or L *contemplativus* (as CONTEMPLATE)]
- *adj.* see MEDITATIVE.

contemporaneous /kəntémpəráyneeəs/ *adj.* (usu. foll. by *with*) **1** existing or occurring at the same time. **2** of the same period. □□ **contemporaneity** /-pəranáyitee, -neé-/ *n.* **contemporaneously** *adv.* **contemporaneousness** *n.* [L *contemporaneus* (as COM-, *temporaneus* f. *tempus -oris* time)]
- see SIMULTANEOUS. □□ **contemporaneity** see COINCIDENCE 1.

contemporary /kəntémpəreree/ *adj.* & *n.* ● *adj.* **1** living or occurring at the same time. **2** approximately equal in age. **3** following modern ideas or fashion in style or design. ● *n.* (*pl.* **-ies**) **1** a person or thing living or existing at the same time as another. **2** a person of roughly the same age as another. □□ **contemporarily** /-rérilee/ *adv.* **contemporariness** *n.* **contemporarize** /-tém-/ *v.tr.* [med.L *contemporarius* (as CONTEMPORANEOUS)]
- *adj.* **1** contemporaneous, coeval, coexistent, concurrent, synchronous, synchronic. **3** modern, current, present-day, new, up-to-date, stylish, fashionable, modish, à la mode, latest, in, novel, *colloq.* with it, *colloq. often derog.* trendy, *derog.* newfangled.
- *n.* **1** peer, compeer, coeval.

contempt /kəntémpt/ *n.* **1** a feeling that a person or a thing is beneath consideration or worthless, or deserving scorn or extreme reproach. **2** the condition of being held in contempt. **3** (in full **contempt of court**) disobedience to or disrespect for a court of law and its officers. □ **beneath contempt** utterly despicable. **hold in contempt** despise. [ME f. L *contemptus* (as CONTEMN)]

- **1** scorn, disdain, disgust; loathing, abhorrence, hatred, odium, hate. **2** contumely. □ **beneath contempt** see DESPICABLE.

contemptible /kəntémptibəl/ *adj.* deserving contempt; despicable. □□ **contemptibility** /-bilitee/ *n.* **contemptibly** *adv.* [ME f. OF or LL *contemptibilis* (as CONTEMN)]
- despicable, unworthy, shabby, shameful, scurvy, cheap, low, mean, base, measly, fiddling, misbegotten, miserable, wretched, paltry, petty, pitiable, pitiful, picayune, *colloq.* nasty, pipsqueak, snotty, pathetic, *sl.* putrid; loathsome, detestable; currish, vile, ignominious.

contemptuous /kəntémpchōōəs/ *adj.* (often foll. by *of*) showing contempt; scornful; insolent. □□ **contemptuously** *adv.* [med.L *contemptuosus* f. L *contemptus* (as CONTEMPT)]
- scornful, disdainful, sneering, derisive, insulting, contumelious, insolent.

contend /kənténd/ *v.* **1** *intr.* (usu. foll. by *with*) strive; fight. **2** *intr.* compete (*fatigue contended with our desire to finish the project*). **3** *tr.* (usu. foll. by *that* + clause) assert; maintain. □□ **contender** *n.* [OF *contendre* or L *contendere* (as COM-, *tendere tent-* stretch, strive)]
- **1, 2** see STRIVE 2. **3** see MAINTAIN 3.

content[1] /kəntént/ *adj.*, *v.*, & *n.* ● *predic.adj.* **1** satisfied; adequately happy; in agreement. **2** (foll. by *to* + infin.) willing. ● *v.tr.* make content; satisfy. ● *n.* a contented state; satisfaction. □ **to one's heart's content** to the full extent of one's desires. [ME f. OF f. L *contentus* satisfied, past part. of *continēre* (as CONTAIN)]
- *adj.* **1** pleased, satisfied, happy, delighted, contented, gratified, glad, cheerful; comfortable, fulfilled; in agreement. **2** see WILLING *adj.* ● *v.* satisfy, please, gratify, soothe, cheer, gladden, delight. ● *n.* pleasure, satisfaction, gratification, happiness, contentment, contentedness, felicity, delight.

content[2] /kóntent/ *n.* **1** (usu. in *pl.*) what is contained in something, esp. in a vessel, book, or house. **2** the amount of a constituent contained (*low sodium content*). **3** the substance or material dealt with (in a speech, work of art, etc.) as distinct from its form or style; significance. **4** the capacity or volume of a thing. [ME f. med.L *contentum* (as CONTAIN)]
- **1** (*contents*) components, constituents; load. **3** substance, subject matter, material, theme, topic, thesis, text; see also SIGNIFICANCE 2. **4** capacity, volume, size.

contented /kənténtid/ *adj.* (often foll. by *with*, or *to* + infin.) **1** happy; satisfied. **2** (foll. by *with*) willing to be content (*was contented with the outcome*). □□ **contentedly** *adv.* **contentedness** *n.*

contention /kənténshən/ *n.* **1** a dispute or argument; rivalry. **2** a point contended for in an argument (*it is my contention that you are wrong*). □ **in contention** competing, esp. with a good chance of success. [ME f. OF *contention* or L *contentio* (as CONTEND)]
- **1** see RIVALRY. **2** see ARGUMENT 2.

contentious /kənténshəs/ *adj.* **1** argumentative; quarrelsome. **2** likely to cause an argument; disputed; controversial. □□ **contentiously** *adv.* **contentiousness** *n.* [ME f. OF *contentieux* f. L *contentiosus* (as CONTENTION)]
- **1** see ARGUMENTATIVE. **2** see CONTROVERSIAL 1.

contentment /kənténtmənt/ *n.* a satisfied state; tranquil happiness.
- ease, comfort, tranquillity, serenity, peace, peacefulness; see also JOY *n.* 1.

conterminous /kəntə́rminəs/ *adj.* (often foll. by *with*) **1** having a common boundary. **2** coextensive; coterminous. □□ **conterminously** *adv.* [L *conterminus* (as COM-, *terminus* boundary)]

/.../ pronunciation	● part of speech
□ phrases, idioms, and compounds	
□□ derivatives	■ synonym section
cross-references appear in SMALL CAPITALS or *italics*	

contessa /kontésə/ *n.* an Italian countess. [It. f. LL *comitissa*: see COUNTESS]

contest *n.* & *v.* ● *n.* /kóntest/ **1** a process of contending; a competition. **2** a dispute; a controversy. ● *v.tr.* /kəntést, kóntest/ **1** challenge or dispute (a decision, etc.). **2** debate (a point, statement, etc.). **3** contend or compete for (a prize, parliamentary seat, etc.); compete in (an election). □□ **contestable** /kəntéstəbəl/ *adj.* **contester** /kəntéstər/ *n.* [L *contestari* (as COM-, *testis* witness)]
■ *n.* **1** competition, match, tournament, championship, meet, game. **2** controversy, dispute, debate, altercation, argument, *archaic* velitation; conflict, struggle, fight, battle, war; strife, contention. ● *v.* **1** argue against, dispute, challenge, (call into) question, oppose, counter, object to, *Law* litigate, *disp.* refute. **2** debate. **3** contend for, compete in *or* for.

contestant /kəntéstənt/ *n.* a person who takes part in a contest or competition.
■ contender, competitor, entrant, player, participant; opponent, rival, adversary.

contestation /kóntestáyshən/ *n.* **1** a disputation. **2** an assertion contended for. [L *contestatio* partly through F (as CONTEST)]

context /kóntekst/ *n.* **1** the parts of something written or spoken that immediately precede and follow a word or passage and clarify its meaning. **2** the circumstances relevant to something under consideration (*must be seen in context*). □ **out of context** without the surrounding words or circumstances and so not fully understandable. □□ **contextual** /kəntéks-chōōəl/ *adj.* **contextualize** /kəntéks-chōōəlīz/ *v.tr.* **contextualization** *n.* **contextually** *adv.* [ME f. L *contextus* (as COM-, *texere* text- weave)]
■ structure, framework, environment, situation, circumstance(s); surround, surroundings, frame (of reference), setting, background, connection.

contiguity /kóntigyōōitee/ *n.* **1** being contiguous; proximity; contact. **2** *Psychol.* the proximity of ideas or impressions in place or time, as a principle of association.
■ **1** see PROXIMITY.

contiguous /kəntígyōōəs/ *adj.* (usu. foll. by *with, to*) touching, esp. along a line or border; in contact. □□ **contiguously** *adv.* [L *contiguus* (as COM-, *tangere* touch)]
■ see NEAR *adj.* 1.

continent[1] /kóntinənt/ *n.* **1** any of the main continuous expanses of land (Europe, Asia, Africa, N. and S. America, Australia, Antarctica). **2** (**the Continent**) *Brit.* the mainland of Europe as distinct from the British Isles. **3** continuous land; a mainland. [L *terra continens* (see CONTAIN) continuous land]

continent[2] /kóntinənt/ *adj.* **1** able to control movements of the bowels and bladder. **2** exercising self-restraint, esp. sexually. □□ **continence** /-nəns/ *n.* **continently** *adv.* [ME f. L (as CONTAIN)]
■ **2** see TEMPERATE 4. □□ **continence** see *celibacy* (CELIBATE).

continental /kóntinént'l/ *adj.* & *n.* ● *adj.* **1** of or characteristic of a continent. **2** (**Continental**) *Brit.* of, relating to, or characteristic of mainland Europe. ● *n.* an inhabitant of mainland Europe. □ **continental breakfast** a light breakfast of coffee, rolls, etc. **continental climate** a climate having wide variations of temperature. **continental drift** *Geol.* the hypothesis that the continents are moving slowly over the surface of the earth on a deep-lying plastic substratum. **continental quilt** *Brit.* a duvet. **continental shelf** an area of relatively shallow seabed between the shore of a continent and the deeper ocean. □□ **continentally** *adv.*

contingency /kəntínjənsee/ *n.* (*pl.* **-ies**) **1** a future event or circumstance regarded as likely to occur, or as influencing present action. **2** something dependent on another uncertain event or occurrence. **3** uncertainty of occurrence. **4 a** one thing incident to another. **b** an incidental or unanticipated expense, etc. □ **contingency fund** a fund to cover incidental or unforeseen expenses. [earlier *contingence* f. LL *contingentia* (as CONTINGENT)]
■ **1** see EVENTUALITY. **2** see CONDITION *n.* 1.

contingent /kəntínjənt/ *adj.* & *n.* ● *adj.* **1** (usu. foll. by *on, upon*) conditional; dependent (on an uncertain event or circumstance). **2** associated. **3** (usu. foll. by *to*) incidental. **4 a** that may or may not occur. **b** fortuitous; occurring by chance. **5** true only under existing or specified conditions. ● *n.* a body (esp. of troops, ships, etc.) forming part of a larger group. □□ **contingently** *adv.* [L *contingere* (as COM-, *tangere* touch)]
■ *adj.* **1** see PROVISIONAL. ● *n.* see COHORT 2.

continual /kəntínyōōəl/ *adj.* constantly or frequently recurring; always happening. □□ **continually** *adv.* [ME f. OF *continuel* f. *continuer* (as CONTINUE)]
■ constant, incessant, perpetual, nonstop, persistent, uninterrupted, regular, steady, unbroken, unceasing, ceaseless, eternal, unremitting, interminable, endless, unending, continuous.

continuance /kəntínyōōəns/ *n.* **1** a state of continuing in existence or operation. **2** the duration of an event or action. **3** *Law* a postponement or adjournment. [ME f. OF (as CONTINUE)]

continuant /kəntínyōōənt/ *n.* & *adj.* *Phonet.* ● *n.* a speech sound in which the vocal tract is only partly closed, allowing the breath to pass through and the sound to be prolonged (as with *f, r, s, v*). ● *adj.* of or relating to such a sound. [F *continuant* and L *continuare* (as CONTINUE)]

continuation /kəntínyōō-áyshən/ *n.* **1** the act or an instance of continuing; the process of being continued. **2** a part that continues something else. **3** *Brit. Stock Exch.* the carrying over of an account to the next settling day. [ME f. OF f. L *continuatio -onis* (as CONTINUE)]
■ **1** see MAINTENANCE 1. **2** see SUPPLEMENT *n.* 1.

continuative /kəntínyōō-áytiv, -ətiv/ *adj.* tending or serving to continue. [LL *continuativus* (as CONTINUATION)]

continue /kəntínyōō/ *v.* (**continues, continued, continuing**) **1** *tr.* (often foll. by verbal noun, or *to* + infin.) persist in, maintain, not stop (an action, etc.). **2 a** *tr.* (also *absol.*) resume or prolong (a narrative, journey, etc.). **b** *intr.* recommence after a pause (*the concert will continue shortly*). **3** *tr.* be a sequel to. **4** *intr.* **a** remain in existence or unchanged. **b** (with compl.) remain in a specified state (*the weather continued fine*). **5** *tr.* *Law* postpone or adjourn (proceedings). □□ **continuable** *adj.* **continuer** *n.* [ME f. OF *continuer* f. L *continuare* make or be CONTINUOUS]
■ **1** carry on (with), proceed with, keep (up *or* on *or* at), go on (with), pursue, persist (in *or* with), persevere in; maintain, prolong, sustain. **2** resume, pick up, take up, carry on (with); prolong. **4 a** endure, last, go on, persist, be prolonged, remain, extend.

continuity /kóntinōōitee, -nyōō-/ *n.* (*pl.* **-ies**) **1 a** the state of being continuous. **b** an unbroken succession. **c** a logical sequence. **2** the detailed and self-consistent scenario of a film or broadcast. **3** the linking of broadcast items. □ **continuity girl** (or **man**) the person responsible for agreement of detail between different sessions of filming. [F *continuité* f. L *continuitas -tatis* (as CONTINUOUS)]
■ **1** see UNITY 2.

continuo /kəntínyōō-ō/ *n.* (*pl.* **-os**) *Mus.* an accompaniment providing a bass line and harmonies which are indicated by figures, usu. played on a keyboard instrument. [*basso continuo* (It., = continuous bass)]

continuous /kəntínyōōəs/ *adj.* **1** unbroken; uninterrupted; connected throughout in space or time. **2** *Gram.* = PROGRESSIVE. □ **continuous creation** the creation of the universe or the matter in it regarded as a continuous process. □□ **continuously** *adv.* **continuousness** *n.* [L *continuus* uninterrupted f. *continēre* (as COM-, *tenēre* hold)]
■ **1** connected, unbroken, uninterrupted; incessant, persistent, perpetual, nonstop, unceasing, ceaseless, constant, unremitting, interminable, endless, unending, continual.

continuum /kəntínyōōəm/ *n.* (*pl.* **continua** /-yōōə/ or **continuums**) anything seen as having a continuous, not discrete, structure (*space-time continuum*). [L, neut. of *continuus*: see CONTINUOUS]

contort /kəntáwrt/ v.tr. twist or force out of normal shape. [L *contorquēre contort-* (as COM-, *torquēre* twist)]
■ see TWIST v. 1a, b.

contortion /kəntáwrshən/ n. **1** the act or process of twisting. **2** a twisted state, esp. of the face or body. [L *contortio* (as CONTORT)]
■ see WARP n.

contortionist /kəntáwrshənist/ n. an entertainer who adopts contorted postures.

contour /kóntoŏr/ n. & v. ● n. **1** an outline, esp. representing or bounding the shape or form of something. **2** the outline of a natural feature, e.g., a coast or mountain mass. **3** a line separating differently colored parts of a design. ● v.tr. **1** mark with contour lines. **2** carry (a road or railroad) around the side of a hill. □ **contour line** a line on a map joining points of equal altitude. **contour map** a map marked with contour lines. **contour plowing** plowing along lines of constant altitude to minimize soil erosion. [F f. It. *contorno* f. *contornare* draw in outline (as COM-, *tornare* turn)]
■ n. **1, 2** see OUTLINE n. 4. ● v. **1** see LINE¹ v. 1.

contra /kóntrə/ n. (pl. **contras**) a member of a counterrevolutionary guerrilla force in Nicaragua. [abbr. of Sp. *contrarevolucionario* counterrevolutionary]

contra- /kóntrə/ comb. form **1** against; opposite (*contradict*). **2** Mus. (of instruments, organ stops, etc.) pitched an octave below (*contrabassoon*). [L *contra* against]

contraband /kóntrəband/ n. & adj. ● n. **1** goods that have been smuggled, or imported or exported illegally. **2** prohibited trade; smuggling. **3** (in full **contraband of war**) goods forbidden to be supplied by neutrals to belligerents. ● adj. **1** forbidden to be imported or exported (at all or without payment of duty). **2** concerning traffic in contraband (*contraband trade*). □□ **contrabandist** n. [Sp. *contrabanda* f. It. (as CONTRA-, *bando* proclamation)]

contrabass /kóntrəbays/ n. Mus. = *double bass*. [It. (*basso BASS*¹)]

contraception /kóntrəsépshən/ n. the intentional prevention of pregnancy; the use of contraceptives. [CONTRA- + CONCEPTION]
■ birth control.

contraceptive /kóntrəséptiv/ adj. & n. ● adj. preventing pregnancy. ● n. a contraceptive device or drug.

contract n. & v. ● n. /kóntrakt/ **1** a written or spoken agreement between two or more parties, intended to be enforceable by law. **2** a document recording this. **3** marriage regarded as a binding commitment. **4** Bridge, etc., an undertaking to win the number of tricks bid. ● v. /kəntrákt, kóntrakt/ **1** tr. & intr. make or become smaller. **2 a** intr. (usu. foll. by *with*) make a contract. **b** intr. (usu. foll. by *for*, or *to* + infin.) enter formally into a business or legal arrangement. **c** tr. (often foll. by *out*) arrange (work) to be done by contract. **3** tr. catch or develop (a disease). **4** tr. form or develop (a friendship, habit, etc.). **5** tr. enter into (marriage). **6** tr. incur (a debt, etc.). **7** tr. shorten (a word) by combination or elision. **8** tr. draw (one's muscles, brow, etc.) together. □ **contract bridge** the most common form of bridge, in which only tricks bid and won count toward the game. **contract in** (or **out**) (also *refl.*) Brit. choose to be involved in (or withdraw or remain out of) a scheme or commitment. □□ **contractive** /kəntráktiv/ adj. [earlier as adj., = contracted: OF, f. L *contractus* (as COM-, *trahere tract-* draw)]
■ n. **1** agreement, understanding, deal, bargain, arrangement, pact, compact. **2** agreement, Law memorandum. ● v. **1** diminish, reduce, shrink, draw together, narrow, constrict, compress, condense. **2 b** engage, agree, promise, covenant, undertake. **3** catch, acquire, get, come down with, develop, become infected with, Brit. go down with. **4** form, forge; see also DEVELOP 1. **8** wrinkle, knit, crease, corrugate, pucker.

contractable /kəntráktəbəl/ adj. (of a disease) that can be contracted.

contractible /kəntráktibəl/ adj. that can be shrunk or drawn together.

contractile /kəntrákt'l, til/ adj. capable of or producing contraction. □□ **contractility** /kóntraktílitee/ n.
■ see ELASTIC adj. 1, 2.

contraction /kəntrákshən/ n. **1** the act of contracting. **2** Med. (usu. in pl.) shortening of the uterine muscles during childbirth. **3** shrinking; diminution. **4 a** a shortening of a word by combination or elision. **b** a contracted word or group of words. [F f. L *contractio -onis* (as CONTRACT)]
■ **2** see LABOR n. 3. **4** see ABBREVIATION.

contractor /kəntráktər/ n. a person who undertakes a contract, esp. to provide materials, conduct building operations, etc. [LL (as CONTRACT)]

contractual /kəntrákchōōəl/ adj. of or in the nature of a contract. □□ **contractually** adv.

contradict /kóntrədíkt/ v.tr. **1** deny or express the opposite of (a statement). **2** deny or express the opposite of a statement made by (a person). **3** be in opposition to or in conflict with (*new evidence contradicted our theory*). □□ **contradictor** n. [L *contradicere contradict-* (as CONTRA-, *dicere* say)]
■ **1** counter, dispute, controvert, rebut, deny, reject, *disp.* refute. **2** rebut, argue against, oppose, *archaic or literary* gainsay.

contradiction /kóntrədíkshən/ n. **1 a** statement of the opposite; denial. **b** an instance of this. **2** inconsistency. □ **contradiction in terms** a self-contradictory statement or group of words. [ME f. OF f. L *contradictio -onis* (as CONTRADICT)]

contradictory /kóntrədíktəree/ adj. **1** expressing a denial or opposite statement. **2** (of statements, etc.) mutually opposed or inconsistent. **3** (of a person) inclined to contradict. **4** Logic (of two propositions) so related that one and only one must be true. □□ **contradictorily** adv. **contradictoriness** n. [ME f. LL *contradictorius* (as CONTRADICT)]
■ **2** inconsistent, opposed, conflicting, incompatible, discrepant.

contradistinction /kóntrədistíngkshən/ n. a distinction made by contrasting.

contradistinguish /kóntrədistínggwish/ v.tr. (usu. foll. by *from*) distinguish two things by contrasting them.
■ see DIFFERENTIATE 2.

contraflow /kóntrəflō/ n. Brit. a flow (esp. of road traffic) alongside, and in a direction opposite to, an established or usual flow, esp. as a temporary or emergency arrangement.

contrail /kóntrayl/ n. a condensation trail, esp. from an aircraft. [abbr.]

contraindicate /kóntraíndikayt/ v.tr. Med. act as an indication against (the use of a particular substance or treatment). □□ **contraindication** /-káyshən/ n.

contralto /kəntráltō/ n. (pl. **-os**) **1 a** the lowest female singing voice. **b** a singer with this voice. **2** a part written for contralto. [It. (as CONTRA-, ALTO)]

contraposition /kóntrəpəzíshən/ n. **1** opposition or contrast. **2** Logic conversion of a proposition from *all A is B* to *all not-B is not-A*. □□ **contrapositive** /-pózitiv/ adj. & n. [LL *contrapositio* (as CONTRA-, *ponere posit-* place)]

contraption /kəntrápshən/ n. often *derog.* or *joc.* a machine or device, esp. a strange or cumbersome one. [19th c.: perh. f. CONTRIVE, INVENTION: assoc. with TRAP¹]
■ machine, contrivance, device, gadget, implement, mechanism, apparatus, doodad, toy, *colloq.* widget, hickey, *sl.* gizmo, jigger.

contrapuntal /kóntrəpúnt'l/ adj. Mus. of or in counterpoint. □□ **contrapuntally** adv. **contrapuntist** n. [It. *contrappunto* counterpoint]

contrariety /kóntrərí-itee/ n. **1** opposition in nature, quality, or action. **2** disagreement; inconsistency. [ME f. OF *contrarieté* f. LL *contrarietas -tatis* (as CONTRARY)]
■ **2** see DISCREPANCY.

/. . ./ **pronunciation** ● **part of speech**
□ **phrases, idioms, and compounds**
□□ **derivatives** ■ **synonym section**
cross-references appear in SMALL CAPITALS or *italics*

contrariwise /kəntráireewiz/ adv. **1** on the other hand. **2** in the opposite way. **3** perversely. [ME f. CONTRARY + -WISE]
■ **2** see VICE VERSA.

contrary /kóntreree/ adj., n., & adv. ● adj. **1** (usu. foll. by to) opposed in nature or tendency. **2** /kəntráiree/ colloq. perverse; self-willed. **3** (of a wind) unfavorable; impeding. **4** mutually opposed. **5** opposite in position or direction. ● n. (pl. -ies) (prec. by the) the opposite. ● adv. (foll. by to) in opposition or contrast (contrary to expectations it rained). □ **on the contrary** intensifying a denial of what has just been implied or stated. **to the contrary** to the opposite effect (can find no indication to the contrary). □□ **contrarily** /-trérilee/ adv. **contrariness** /-tréreenis/ n. [ME f. AF contrarie, OF contraire, f. L contrarius f. contra against]
■ adj. **1** antipathetic; opposite, opposing, opposed, different, contradictory, conflicting, antagonistic. **2** antagonistic, perverse, contrarious, hostile, unfriendly, inimical, cross-grained, intractable, awkward, difficult, refractory, stubborn, contumacious, self-willed, argumentative, unaccommodating, uncooperative, antipathetic, archaic froward. **3** adverse, unfavorable, impeding. ● n. opposite, reverse, converse, antithesis.

contrast n. & v. ● n. /kóntrast/ **1 a** a juxtaposition or comparison showing striking differences. **b** a difference so revealed. **2** (often foll. by to) a thing or person having qualities noticeably different from another. **3 a** the degree of difference between tones in a television picture or a photograph. **b** the change of apparent brightness or color of an object caused by the juxtaposition of other objects. ● v. /kəntrást, kóntrast/ (often foll. by with) **1** tr. distinguish or set together so as to reveal a contrast. **2** intr. have or show a contrast. □□ **contrastingly** /-trást-/ adv. **contrastive** /-trástiv/ adj. [F contraste, contraster, f. It. contrasto f. med.L contrastare (as CONTRA-, stare stand)]
■ n. **1** comparison, juxtaposition; difference, distinction, disparity, dissimilarity. ● v. **1** juxtapose, oppose, compare, distinguish, differentiate, discriminate, set or place against or together. **2** conflict, differ, diverge.

contrasty /kontrástee, kón-/ adj. (of photographic negatives or prints or of a television picture) showing a high degree of contrast.

contrasuggestible /kóntrəsəgéstibəl, -səjés-/ adj. Psychol. tending to respond to a suggestion by believing or doing the contrary.

contrate wheel /kóntrayt/ n. = crown wheel. [med.L & Rmc contrata: see COUNTRY]

contravene /kóntrəveén/ v.tr. **1** infringe (a law or code of conduct). **2** (of things) conflict with. □□ **contravener** n. [LL contravenire (as CONTRA-, venire vent- come)]
■ **1** see INFRINGE 1.

contravention /kóntrəvénshən/ n. **1** infringement. **2** an instance of this. □ **in contravention of** infringing; violating (a law, etc.). [F f. med.L contraventio (as CONTRAVENE)]

contretemps /kóntrətóN/ n. **1** an awkward or unfortunate occurrence. **2** an unexpected mishap. [F]
■ see MISFORTUNE 2.

■ **contribute** /kəntríbyōot/ v. (often foll. by to) **1** tr. give (money, an idea, help, etc.) toward a common purpose (contributed $5 to the fund). **2** intr. help to bring about a result, etc. (contributed to their downfall). **3** tr. (also absol.) supply (an article, etc.) for publication with others in a journal, etc. □□ **contributive** adj. [L contribuere contribut- (as COM-, tribuere bestow)]
■ **1** give, donate, bestow, grant, present, provide, supply. **2** (contribute to) add to, promote, advance, help, aid, support, forward, have a hand in, play a part or role in.

contribution /kóntribyōoshən/ n. **1** the act of contributing. **2** something contributed, esp. money. **3** an article, etc., contributed to a publication. [ME f. OF contribution or LL contributio (as CONTRIBUTE)]
■ **1** see DONATION 1. **2** see DONATION 2.

contributor /kəntríbyətər/ n. a person who contributes (esp. an article or literary work).

contributory /kəntríbyətawree/ adj. **1** that contributes. **2** operated by means of contributions (contributory pension plan).

□ **contributory negligence** Law negligence on the part of the injured party through failure to take precautions against an accident. [med.L contributorius (as CONTRIBUTE)]
■ adj. **1** see INSTRUMENTAL adj.

contrite /kəntrít, kóntrit/ adj. **1** completely penitent. **2** feeling remorse or penitence; affected by guilt. **3** (of an action) showing a contrite spirit. □□ **contritely** adv. **contriteness** n. [ME f. OF contrit f. L contritus bruised (as COM-, terere trit- rub)]
■ **1, 2** see REMORSEFUL.

contrition /kəntríshən/ n. the state of being contrite; thorough penitence. [ME f. OF f. LL contritio -onis (as CONTRITE)]
■ see penitence (PENITENT).

contrivance /kəntrívəns/ n. **1** something contrived, esp. a mechanical device or a plan. **2** an act of contriving, esp. deceitfully. **3** inventive capacity.
■ **1** see DEVICE 1a. **2** see SUBTERFUGE 1.

contrive /kəntrív/ v.tr. **1** devise; plan or make resourcefully or with skill. **2** (often foll. by to + infin.) manage (contrived to make matters worse). □□ **contrivable** adj. **contriver** n. [ME f. OF controver find, imagine f. med.L contropare compare]
■ **1** see DEVISE v. 1. **2** see MANAGE v. 2, 3, 5a.

contrived /kəntrívd/ adj. planned so carefully as to seem unnatural; artificial; forced (the plot seemed contrived).
■ see ARTIFICIAL 3.

control /kəntrṓl/ n. & v. ● n. **1** the power of directing; command (under the control of). **2** the power of restraining, esp. self-restraint. **3** a means of restraint; a check. **4** (usu. in pl.) a means of regulating prices, etc. **5** (usu. in pl.) switches and other devices by which a machine, esp. an aircraft or vehicle, is controlled (also attrib.: control panel; control room). **6 a** a place where something is controlled or verified. **b** a person or group that controls something. **7** (also attrib.: control group) a standard of comparison for checking the results of a survey or experiment. ● v.tr. (**controlled, controlling**) **1** have control or command of; dominate. **2** exert control over; regulate. **3** hold in check; restrain (told him to control himself). **4** serve as control to. **5** check; verify. □ **controlling interest** a means of determining the policy of a business, etc., esp. by ownership of a majority of the stock. **control rod** a rod of neutron-absorbing material used to vary the output power of a nuclear reactor. **control tower** a tall building at an airport, etc., from which air traffic is controlled. **in control** (often foll. by of) directing an activity. **out of control** no longer subject to containment, restraint, or guidance. **under control** being controlled; in order. □□ **controllable** adj. **controllability** n. **controllably** adv. [ME f. AF contreroller keep a copy of a roll of accounts, f. med.L contrarotulare (as CONTRA-, rotulus ROLL n.): (n.) perh. f. F contrôle]
■ n. **1** command, direction, power, authority, leadership, management, guidance, supervision, oversight, charge; sway, rule, jurisdiction. **2** restraint, self-restraint, mastery, command, dominance, domination. **3** check, curb. **5** knob, button, dial, handle, lever, switch; device, mechanism. ● v. **1, 2** command, dominate, direct, steer, pilot, hold sway over, rule, exercise power or authority over, govern, manage, lead, conduct, be in control of, guide, oversee, supervise, regulate. **3** check, hold back or in check, restrain, curb, repress, contain, manage; suppress, put down, master, subdue.

controller /kəntrṓlər/ n. **1** a person or thing that controls. **2** a person in charge of expenditure, esp. a steward or comptroller. □□ **controllership** n. [ME counterroller f. AF contrerollour (as CONTROL)]

controversial /kóntrəvérshəl/ adj. **1** causing or subject to controversy. **2** of controversy. **3** given to controversy. □□ **controversialism** n. **controversialist** n. **controversially** adv. [LL controversialis (as CONTROVERSY)]
■ **1** debatable, contentious, disputable, questionable, litigious, moot, doubtful, unsettled. **2** polemic(al). **3** disputatious, argumentative, provocative, litigious, factious.

controversy /kóntrəvərsee/ *n.* (*pl.* **-ies**) a prolonged argument or dispute, esp. when conducted publicly. [ME f. L *controversia* (as CONTROVERT)]

■ dispute, debate, contention, disagreement, argument, wrangling, confrontation, questioning; quarrel.

controvert /kóntrəvért/ *v.tr.* **1** dispute; deny. **2** argue about; discuss. □□ **controvertible** *adj.* [orig. past part.; f. F *controvers(e)* f. L *controversus* (as CONTRA-, *vertere vers-* turn)]

■ **1** see DENY 1.

contumacious /kóntoomáyshəs, -tyoo-/ *adj.* insubordinate, stubbornly or willfully disobedient, esp. to a court order. □□ **contumaciously** *adv.* [L *contumax*, perh. rel. to *tumēre* swell]

■ see INSUBORDINATE.

contumacy /kóntooməsee, -tyoo-/ *n.* stubborn refusal to obey or comply. [L *contumacia* f. *contumax*: see CONTUMACIOUS]

■ see REBELLION.

contumelious /kóntoomeéleeəs, -tyoo-/ *adj.* reproachful, insulting, or insolent. □□ **contumeliously** *adv.* [ME f. OF *contumelieus* f. L *contumeliosus* (as CONTUMELY)]

■ see INSOLENT.

contumely /kóntoomələe, -toomlee, -too, -tyoo/ *n.* **1** insolent or reproachful language or treatment. **2** disgrace. [ME f. OF *contumelie* f. L *contumelia* (as COM-, *tumēre* swell)]

■ **1** see DERISION. **2** see DISGRACE *n.*

contuse /kəntooz, -tyooz/ *v.tr.* injure without breaking the skin; bruise. □□ **contusion** /-zhən/ *n.* [L *contundere contus-* (as COM-, *tundere* thump)]

■ see BRUISE *v.* 1. □□ **contusion** see BRUISE *n.*

conundrum /kənúndrəm/ *n.* **1** a riddle, esp. one with a pun in its answer. **2** a hard or puzzling question. [16th c.: orig. unkn.]

■ **1** see RIDDLE[1] *n.*

conurbation /kónərbáyshən/ *n.* an extended urban area, esp. one consisting of several towns and merging suburbs. [CON- + L *urbs urbis* city + -ATION]

■ see CITY 1a.

conure /kónyər/ *n.* any medium-sized parrot of the genus *Pyrrhura*, with mainly green plumage and a long gradated tail. [mod.L *conurus* f. Gk *kōnos* cone + *oura* tail]

convalesce /kónvəlés/ *v.intr.* recover one's health after illness or medical treatment. [ME f. L *convalescere* (as COM-, *valēre* be well)]

■ recover, improve, get better, recuperate.

convalescent /kónvəlésənt/ *adj. & n.* ● *adj.* **1** recovering from an illness. **2** of or for persons in convalescence. /-səns/ ● *n.* a convalescent person. □□ **convalescence** /-səns/ *n.*

■ *adj.* **1** see *on the mend* (MEND). ● *n.* see INVALID[1] *n.* 1.

convection /kənvékshən/ *n.* **1** transference of heat in a gas or liquid by upward movement of the heated and less dense medium. **2** *Meteorol.* the transfer of heat by the upward flow of hot air or downward flow of cold air. □ **convection current** circulation that results from convection. □□ **convectional** *adj.* **convective** *adj.* [LL *convectio* f. L *convehere convect-* (as COM-, *vehere vect-* carry)]

convector /kənvéktər/ *n.* a heating appliance that circulates warm air by convection.

convenance /kónvənaáns/ *n.* (usu. in *pl.*) conventional propriety. [F f. *convenir* be fitting (as CONVENE)]

convene /kənveén/ *v.* **1** *tr.* summon or arrange (a meeting, etc.). **2** *intr.* assemble. **3** *tr.* summon (a person) before a tribunal. □□ **convenable** *adj.* **convener** *n.* **convenor** *n.* [ME f. L *convenire convent-* assemble, agree, fit (as COM-, *venire* come)]

■ **1** see SUMMON 3. **2** see ASSEMBLE 1.

convenience /kənveényəns/ *n. & v.* ● *n.* **1** the quality of being convenient; suitability. **2** freedom from difficulty or trouble; material advantage (*for convenience*). **3** an advantage (*a great convenience*). **4** a useful thing, esp. an installation or piece of equipment. **5** *Brit.* a bathroom or toilet, esp. a public one. ● *v.tr.* afford convenience to; suit; accommodate. □ **at one's convenience** at a time or place that suits one. **at one's earliest convenience** as soon as one

can. **convenience food** food, esp. complete meals, sold in convenient form and requiring very little preparation. **convenience store** a store that stocks basic groceries, etc., usu. having extended opening hours. **make a convenience of** take advantage of (a person) insensitively. [ME f. L *convenientia* (as CONVENE)]

■ *v.* **2** see ADVANTAGE *n.* 1, 3. □ **at one's convenience** see *at leisure* 2 (LEISURE).

convenient /kənveényənt/ *adj.* **1** (often foll. by *for, to*) **a** serving one's comfort or interests; easily accessible. **b** suitable. **c** free of trouble or difficulty. **2** available or occurring at a suitable time or place (*will try to find a convenient moment*). **3** well situated for some purpose (*convenient for shopping*). □□ **conveniently** *adv.* [ME (as CONVENE)]

■ **1** suitable, useful, helpful, handy, serviceable, expedient, advantageous, *archaic* commodious; trouble-free; see also CONVENIENT 3 below. **2** opportune, well-timed. **3** accessible, well placed *or* situated, nearby, within (easy) reach, at one's fingertips, close at hand, handy, available, (at the) ready.

convent /kónvent, -vənt/ *n.* **1** a religious community, esp. of nuns, under vows. **2** the premises occupied by this. **3** (in full **convent school**) a school attached to and run by a convent. [ME f. AF *covent*, OF *convent* f. L *conventus* assembly (as CONVENE)]

conventicle /kənvéntikəl/ *n.* esp. *hist.* **1** a secret or unlawful religious meeting, esp. of dissenters. **2** a building used for this. [ME f. L *conventiculum* (place of) assembly, dimin. of *conventus* (as CONVENE)]

convention /kənvénshən/ *n.* **1 a** general agreement, esp. agreement on social behavior, etc., by implicit consent of the majority. **b** a custom or customary practice, esp. an artificial or formal one. **2 a** a formal assembly or conference for a common purpose. **b** an assembly of the delegates of a political party to select candidates for office. **c** *Brit. hist.* a meeting of Parliament without a summons from the sovereign. **3 a** a formal agreement. **b** an agreement between nations, esp. one less formal than a treaty. **4** *Cards* an accepted method of play (in leading, bidding, etc.) used to convey information to a partner. **5** the act of convening. [ME f. OF f. L *conventio -onis* (as CONVENE)]

■ **1 b** practice, custom, tradition, usage, formality, rule. **2 a** assembly, meeting, gathering, congregation, congress, conference, symposium, council, conclave, diet, synod, seminar.

conventional /kənvénshənəl/ *adj.* **1** depending on or according to convention. **2** (of a person) attentive to social conventions. **3** usual; of agreed significance. **4** not spontaneous nor sincere nor original. **5** (of weapons or power) nonnuclear. **6** *Art* following tradition rather than nature. □□ **conventionalism** *n.* **conventionalist** *n.* **conventionality** /-shənálitee/ *n.* **conventionalize** *v.tr.* **conventionally** *adv.* [F *conventionnel* or LL *conventionalis* (as CONVENTION)]

■ **1** traditional, orthodox, established, accustomed, received, agreed. **2** formal, conservative, conformist, petty-bourgeois, old-fashioned, respectable, ordinary, stodgy, stuffy, *colloq.* straight, uptight, *sl.* square. **3** usual, normal, regular, standard, customary, habitual, ordinary, everyday, common, commonplace. **4** insincere, unoriginal, unspontaneous, formal, formulaic, formulistic, stock, hackneyed, *colloq.* old hat. **6** classical, traditional.

conventioneer /kənvénshəneér/ *n.* a person attending a convention.

conventual /kənvénchooəl/ *adj. & n.* ● *adj.* **1** of or belonging to a convent. **2** of the less strict branch of the Franciscans, living in large convents. ● *n.* **1** a member of a convent.

/.../ **pronunciation**	● **part of speech**
□ **phrases, idioms, and compounds**	
□□ **derivatives**	■ **synonym section**
cross-references appear in SMALL CAPITALS or *italics*	

2 a conventual Franciscan. [ME f. med.L *conventualis* (as CONVENT)]

converge /kənvə́rj/ *v.intr.* **1** come together as if to meet or join. **2** (of lines) tend to meet at a point. **3** (foll. by *on, upon*) approach from different directions. **4** *Math.* (of a series) approximate in the sum of its terms toward a definite limit. [LL *convergere* (as COM-, *vergere* incline)]
  ■ **1** come *or* go together, meet, join, unite, merge, coincide.

convergent /kənvə́rjənt/ *adj.* **1** converging. **2** *Biol.* (of unrelated organisms) having the tendency to become similar while adapting to the same environment. **3** *Psychol.* (of thought) tending to reach only the most rational result. □□ **convergence** /-jəns/ *n.* **convergency** *n.*

conversant /kənvə́rsənt, kónvərs-/ *adj.* (foll. by *with*) well experienced or acquainted with a subject, person, etc. □□ **conversance** /-vérsəns/ *n.* **conversancy** *n.* [ME f. OF, pres. part. of *converser* CONVERSE[1]]
  ■ see FAMILIAR *adj.* 2.

conversation /kónvərsáyshən/ *n.* **1** the informal exchange of ideas by spoken words. **2** an instance of this. □ **conversation piece 1** a small genre painting of a group of figures. **2** a thing that serves as a topic of conversation because of its unusualness, etc. **conversation stopper** *colloq.* an unexpected remark, esp. one that cannot readily be answered. [ME f. OF f. L *conversatio -onis* (as CONVERSE[1])]
  ■ discussion, gossip, chattering, chatter, *archaic* converse, *colloq.* nattering, confab, chitchat, *literary* discourse; talk, chat, dialogue, colloquy, parley, bull session, powwow, *sl.* chin-wag.

conversational /kónvərsáyshənəl/ *adj.* **1** of or in conversation. **2** fond of or good at conversation. **3** colloquial. □□ **conversationally** *adv.*

conversationalist /kónvərsáyshənəlist/ *n.* one who is good at or fond of conversing.
  ■ talker, chatterer, deipnosophist.

conversazione /kónvərsaatseeṓnee, káwnveraatsyáwne/ *n.* (*pl.* **conversaziones** or **conversazioni** /-tseeṓnee, tsy-áwnee/) a social gathering held by a learned or art society. [It. f. L (as CONVERSATION)]

converse[1] *v. & n.* ● *v.intr.* /kənvə́rs/ (often foll. by *with*) engage in conversation (*conversed with him about various subjects*). ● *n.* /kónvərs/ *archaic* conversation. □□ **converser** /kənvə́rsər/ *n.* [ME f. OF *converser* f. L *conversari* keep company (with), frequent. of *convertere* (CONVERT)]
  ■ *v.* discuss, talk, speak, chat, parley, discourse, gossip, chatter, *colloq.* natter, chitchat, *Austral. & NZ colloq.* yabber, *sl.* chin-wag.

converse[2] *adj. & n.* ● *adj.* /kənvə́rs, kónvərs/ opposite; contrary; reversed. ● *n.* /kónvərs/ **1** something that is opposite or contrary. **2** a statement formed from another statement by the transposition of certain words, e.g., *some philosophers are men* from *some men are philosophers*. **3** *Math.* a theorem whose hypothesis and conclusion are the conclusion and hypothesis of another. □□ **conversely** *adv.* [L *conversus*, past part. of *convertere* (CONVERT)]

conversion /kənvə́rzhən, -shən/ *n.* **1** the act or an instance of converting or the process of being converted, esp. in belief or religion. **2 a** an adaptation of a building for new purposes. **b** a converted building. **3** transposition; inversion. **4** *Theol.* the turning of sinners to God. **5** the transformation of fertile into fissile material in a nuclear reactor. **6** *Football* the scoring of an extra point or points after scoring a touchdown. **7** *Psychol.* the change of an unconscious conflict into a physical disorder or disease. [ME f. OF f. L *conversio -onis* (as CONVERT)]
  ■ **2 a** see *alteration* (ALTER). **3** see TRANSFORMATION.

convert *v. & n.* ● *v.* /kənvə́rt/ **1** *tr.* (usu. foll. by *into*) change in form, character, or function. **2** *tr.* cause (a person) to change beliefs, opinion, party, etc. **3** *tr.* change (money, stocks, units in which a quantity is expressed, etc.) into others of a different kind. **4** *tr.* make structural alterations in (a building) to serve a new purpose. **5** *tr.* (also *absol.*) *Football* score an extra point or points after a touchdown. **6** *intr.* be converted or convertible (*the sofa converts into a bed*). **7** *tr.*

Logic interchange the terms of (a proposition). ● *n.* /kónvərt/ (often foll. by *to*) a person who has been converted to a different belief, opinion, etc. □ **convert to one's own use** wrongfully make use of (another's property). [ME f. OF *convertir* ult. f. L *convertere* *convers-* turn about (as COM-, *vertere* turn)]
  ■ *v.* **1, 4** change, modify, alter, transform, transmute, mutate, transfigure, remodel, remake, metamorphose, *joc.* transmogrify. **2** proselytize, proselyte. **6** change, turn; metamorphose. ● *n.* proselyte, neophyte.

converter /kənvə́rtər/ *n.* (also **convertor**) **1** a person or thing that converts. **2** *Electr.* **a** an electrical apparatus for the interconversion of alternating current and direct current. **b** *Electronics* an apparatus for converting a signal from one frequency to another. **3** a reaction vessel used in making steel. □ **converter reactor** a nuclear reactor that converts fertile material into fissile material.

convertible /kənvə́rtibəl/ *adj. & n.* ● *adj.* **1** that may be converted. **2** (of currency, etc.) that may be converted into other forms, esp. into gold or US dollars. **3** (of a car) having a folding or detachable roof. **4** (of terms) synonymous. ● *n.* a car with a folding or detachable roof. □□ **convertibility** *n.* **convertibly** *adv.* [OF f. L *convertibilis* (as CONVERT)]
  ■ *adj.* **1** see CHANGEABLE 2. **2** see LIQUID *adj.* 5.

convex /kónveks, kənvéks/ *adj.* having an outline or surface curved like the exterior of a circle or sphere (cf. CONCAVE). □□ **convexity** /-véksitee/ *n.* **convexly** *adv.* [L *convexus* vaulted, arched]

convey /kənváy/ *v.tr.* **1** transport or carry (goods, passengers, etc.). **2** communicate (an idea, meaning, etc.). **3** *Law* transfer the title to (property). **4** transmit (sound, smell, etc.). □□ **conveyable** *adj.* [ME f. OF *conveier* f. med.L *conviare* (as COM-, L *via* way)]
  ■ **1** see TRANSPORT *v.* 1. **2** see COMMUNICATE 1a. **4** see TRANSMIT 1a.

conveyance /kənváyəns/ *n.* **1 a** the act or process of carrying. **b** the communication (of ideas, etc.). **c** transmission. **2** a means of transport; a vehicle. **3** *Law* **a** the transfer of property from one owner to another. **b** a document effecting this. □□ **conveyancer** *n.* (in sense 3). **conveyancing** *n.* (in sense 3).
  ■ **1** see TRANSMISSION 1. **2** vehicle.

conveyor /kənváyər/ *n.* (also **conveyer**) a person or thing that conveys. □ **conveyor belt** an endless moving belt for conveying articles or materials, esp. in a factory or at a supermarket checkout.
  ■ see CARRIER 1, 2.

convict *v. & n.* ● *v.tr.* /kənvíkt/ **1** (often foll. by *of*) prove to be guilty (of a crime, etc.). **2** declare guilty by the verdict of a jury or the decision of a judge. ● *n.* /kónvikt/ **1** a person found guilty of a criminal offense. **2** a person serving a prison sentence. [ME f. L *convincere* *convict-* (as COM-, *vincere* conquer): noun f. obs. *convict* convicted]
  ■ *v.* **1** find *or* prove guilty. ● *n.* **2** prisoner, captive, *sl.* jailbird, con, lifer, yardbird, esp. *Brit.* (old) lag.

conviction /kənvíkshən/ *n.* **1 a** the act or process of proving or finding guilty. **b** an instance of this (*has two previous convictions*). **2 a** the action or resulting state of being convinced. **b** a firm belief or opinion. **c** an act of convincing. [L *convictio* (as CONVICT)]
  ■ **2 a** certainty, sureness, positiveness, confidence, assurance, certitude. **b** (firm) belief, opinion, view, persuasion, position.

convince /kənvíns/ *v.tr.* **1** (often foll. by *of*, or *that* + clause) persuade (a person) to believe or realize. **2** (as **convinced** *adj.*) firmly persuaded (*a convinced pacifist*). □□ **convincer** *n.* **convincible** *adj.* [L (as CONVICT)]
  ■ **1** win over, persuade, bring around, sway. **2** (**convinced**) see CERTAIN *adj.* 1a.

convincing /kənvínsing/ *adj.* **1** able to or such as to convince. **2** leaving no margin of doubt; substantial (*a convincing victory*). □□ **convincingly** *adv.*

convivial /kənvíveeəl/ *adj.* **1** fond of good company; sociable and lively. **2** festive (*a convivial atmosphere*). □□ **conviviality**

/-veeálitee/ *n.* **convivially** *adv.* [L *convivialis* f. *convivium* feast (as COM-, *vivere* live)]
■ **1** see SOCIABLE.

convocation /kónvəkáyshən/ *n.* **1** the act of calling together. **2** a large formal gathering of people, esp.: **a** *US* a formal ceremony at a university, as for giving awards. **b** *Brit.* a provincial synod of the Anglican clergy of Canterbury or York. **c** *Brit.* a legislative or deliberative assembly of a university. □□ **convocational** *adj.* [ME f. L *convocatio* (as CONVOKE)]
■ **2** see ASSEMBLY 1, 2*a*.

convoke /kənvók/ *v.tr. formal* call (people) together to a meeting, etc.; summon to assemble. [L *convocare convocat-* (as COM-, *vocare* call)]
■ see SUMMON 3.

convoluted /kónvəlóotid/ *adj.* **1** coiled; twisted. **2** complex; intricate. □□ **convolutedly** *adv.* [past part. of *convolute* f. L *convolutus* (as COM-, *volvere volut-* roll)]
■ **1** see TORTUOUS 1. **2** see INTRICATE.

convolution /kónvəlóoshən/ *n.* **1** coiling; twisting. **2** a coil or twist. **3** complexity. **4** a sinuous fold in the surface of the brain. □□ **convolutional** *adj.* [med.L *convolutio* (as CONVOLUTED)]
■ **2** see TWIST *n.* 4. **3** see *complexity* (COMPLEX).

convolve /kənvólv/ *v.tr. & intr.* (esp. as **convolved** *adj.*) roll together; coil up. [L *convolvere* (as CONVOLUTED)]

convolvulus /kənvólvyələs/ *n.* any twining plant of the genus *Convolvulus*, with trumpet-shaped flowers, e.g., bindweed. [L]

convoy /kónvoy/ *n. & v.* ● *n.* **1** a group of ships traveling together or under escort. **2** a supply of provisions, etc., under escort. **3** a group of vehicles traveling on land together or under escort. **4** the act of traveling or moving in a group or under escort. ● *v.tr.* **1** (of a warship) escort (a merchant or passenger vessel). **2** escort, esp. with armed force. [OF *convoyer* var. of *conveier* CONVEY]
■ *n.* **1** see FLEET[1]. ● *v.* see ESCORT *v.*

convulsant /kənvúlsənt/ *adj. & n. Pharm.* ● *adj.* producing convulsions. ● *n.* a drug that may produce convulsions. [F f. *convulser* (as CONVULSE)]

convulse /kənvúls/ *v.tr.* **1** (usu. in *passive*) affect with convulsions. **2** cause to laugh uncontrollably. **3** shake violently; agitate; disturb. [L *convellere convuls-* (as COM-, *vellere* pull)]

convulsion /kənvúlshən/ *n.* **1** (usu. in *pl.*) violent irregular motion of a limb or limbs or the body caused by involuntary contraction of muscles, esp. as a disorder of infants. **2** a violent natural disturbance, esp. an earthquake. **3** violent social or political agitation. **4** (in *pl.*) uncontrollable laughter. □□ **convulsionary** *adj.* [F *convulsion* or L *convulsio* (as CONVULSE)]
■ **1** see FIT[2] 1. **3** see AGITATION 1.

convulsive /kənvúlsiv/ *adj.* **1** characterized by or affected with convulsions. **2** producing convulsions. □□ **convulsively** *adv.*
■ **1** see SPASMODIC 1.

cony var. of CONEY.

coo /kōo/ *n., v., & int.* ● *n.* a soft murmuring sound like that of a dove or pigeon. ● *v.* (**coos, cooed**) **1** *intr.* make the sound of a coo. **2** *intr. & tr.* talk or say in a soft or amorous voice. ● *int. Brit. sl.* expressing surprise or incredulity. □□ **cooingly** *adv.* [imit.]

cooee /kōo-ee/ *n., int., & v. Brit. colloq.* ● *n. & int.* a sound used to attract attention, esp. at a distance. ● *v.intr.* (**cooees, cooeed, cooeeing**) make this sound. □ **within cooee** (or **a cooee**) **of** *Austral. & NZ colloq.* very near to. [imit. of a signal used by Australian Aboriginals and copied by settlers]

cook /kŏok/ *v. & n.* ● *v.* **1** *tr.* prepare (food) by heating it. **2** *intr.* (of food) undergo cooking. **3** *tr. colloq.* falsify (accounts, etc.); alter to produce a desired result. **4** *tr. sl.* ruin; spoil. **5** *tr.* (esp. as **cooked** *adj.*) *Brit. sl.* fatigue; exhaust. **6** *tr. & intr. colloq.* do or proceed successfully. **7** *intr.* (as be **cooking**) *colloq.* be happening or about to happen (*went to find out what was cooking*). ● *n.* a person who cooks, esp. professionally or in a specified way (*a good cook*). □ **cook a person's goose** ruin a person's chances. **cook up** *colloq.*

invent or concoct (a story, excuse, etc.). □□ **cookable** *adj. & n.* [OE *cōc* f. pop.L *cocus* for L *coquus*]
■ **1** see PREPARE 2. **3** see FALSIFY 1. □ **cook up** see INVENT 2.

cookbook /kŏokbŏok/ *n.* a book containing recipes and other information about cooking.

cooker /kŏokər/ *n.* **1 a** a container or device for cooking food. **b** *Brit.* an appliance powered by gas, electricity, etc., for cooking food. **2** *Brit.* a fruit, etc., (esp. an apple) that is more suitable for cooking than for eating raw.
■ **1** stove, cooking stove, range.

cookery /kŏokəree/ *n.* (*pl.* **-ies**) the art or practice of cooking. □ **cookery book** *Brit.* a cookbook.

cookhouse /kŏok-hows/ *n.* **1** a camp kitchen. **2** an outdoor kitchen in warm countries. **3** a ship's galley.
■ see KITCHEN.

cookie /kŏokee/ *n.* (also **cooky**) (*pl.* **cookies**) a small sweet cake. □ **cookie-cutter** made or done to an unchanging pattern; unvarying. **that's the way the cookie crumbles** *colloq.* that is how things turn out; that is the unalterable state of affairs. [Du. *koekje* dimin. of *koek* cake]

cooking /kŏoking/ *n.* **1** the art or process by which food is cooked. **2** (*attrib.*) suitable for or used in cooking (*cooking apple*; *cooking utensils*).

cookout /kŏokowt/ *n.* a gathering with an open-air cooked meal; a barbecue.
■ see PICNIC *n.* 2.

cookshop /kŏokshop/ *n.* an establishment where prepared food is served or sold; a restaurant.

cookware /kŏokwair/ *n.* utensils for cooking, esp. dishes, pans, etc.

cool /kōol/ *adj., n., & v.* ● *adj.* **1** of or at a fairly low temperature, fairly cold (*a cool day*; *a cool bath*). **2** suggesting or achieving coolness (*cool colors*; *cool clothes*). **3 a** (of a person) calm; unexcited. **b** (of an act) done without emotion. **4** lacking zeal or enthusiasm. **5** unfriendly; lacking cordiality (*got a cool reception*). **6** (of jazz playing) restrained; relaxed. **7** calmly audacious (*a cool customer*). **8** (prec. by *a*) *colloq.* at least; not less than (*cost me a cool thousand*). **9** *sl.* excellent; marvelous; suave; stylish. ● *n.* **1** coolness. **2** cool air; a cool place. **3** *sl.* calmness; composure (*keep one's cool*; *lose one's cool*). ● *v.* (often foll. by *down*, *off*) **1** *tr. & intr.* make or become cool. **2** *intr.* (of anger, emotions, etc.) lessen; become calmer. □ **cool one's heels** see HEEL[1]. **cooling-off period** an interval to allow for a change of mind before commitment to action. **cooling tower** a tall structure for cooling hot water before reuse, esp. in industry. **cool it** *sl.* relax, calm down. □□ **coolish** *adj.* **coolly** /kōol-lee/ *adv.* **coolness** *n.* [OE *cōl*, *cōlian*, f. Gmc: cf. COLD]
■ *adj.* **1** chilly, cold, fresh, chill; chilled; unheated. **3 a** calm, serene, collected, levelheaded, quiet, unexcited, unemotional, undisturbed, unexcitable, unruffled, coolheaded, relaxed, controlled, under control, self-possessed, self-controlled, unperturbed, phlegmatic, composed, imperturbable, *colloq.* unflappable.
b dispassionate, cold, cold-blooded, emotionless, deliberate, coldhearted, calculated, willful, premeditated, purposeful, purposive. **4** unenthusiastic, uninvolved, uninterested, unconcerned, apathetic.
5 unfriendly, lukewarm, unsympathetic, uncordial, unsociable, unapproachable, standoffish, forbidding, unwelcoming, cold, coldhearted, cold-blooded; distant, remote, aloof, detached, removed. **7** bold, audacious, brazen, overconfident, presumptuous, shameless, unabashed, impertinent, impudent, insolent. **9** see SUPERB, WORLDLY 2. ● *n.* **1** coolness, chill, chilliness. **3** calmness, control, self-control, composure, sangfroid, aplomb, poise, sedateness. ● *v.* **1** (*tr.*) chill, refrigerate,

---

/. . ./ **pronunciation**	● **part of speech**
□ **phrases, idioms, and compounds**	
□□ **derivatives**	■ **synonym section**
cross-references appear in SMALL CAPITALS or *italics*	

ice. **2** diminish, reduce, lessen, abate, moderate. □ **cool it** see RELAX 4.

coolabah /koólǝbaa/ n. (also **coolibah** /-libaa/) *Austral.* any of various gum trees, esp. *Eucalyptus microtheca*. [Aboriginal]

coolant /koólǝnt/ n. **1** a cooling agent, esp. fluid, to remove heat from an engine, nuclear reactor, etc. **2** a fluid used to lessen the friction of a cutting tool. [COOL + -ANT after *lubricant*]

cooler /koólǝr/ n. **1** a vessel in which a thing is cooled. **2 a** a refrigerated room. **b** an insulated container for keeping foods, etc., cold. **3** a long drink, esp. a spritzer. **4** *sl.* prison or a prison cell.
■ **4** see PRISON n. 1.

coolheaded /koólhédid/ adj. not easily excited.
■ see CALM adj. 2, COOL adj. 3a.

coolibah var. of COOLABAH.

coolie /koólee/ n. offens. (also **cooly**) (pl. **-ies**) an unskilled native laborer in Asian countries. □ **coolie hat** a broad conical hat as worn by coolies. [perh. f. *Kulī*, an aboriginal tribe of Gujarat, India]

coomb /koóm/ n. (also **combe**) *Brit.* **1** a valley or hollow on the side of a hill. **2** a short valley running up from the coast. [OE *cumb*: cf. CWM]

coon /koón/ n. **1** a raccoon. **2** *sl. offens.* a black person. [abbr.]

cooncan /koónkan/ n. a simple card game like rummy (orig. Mexican). [Sp. *con quién* with whom?]

coonskin /koónskin/ n. **1** the skin of a raccoon. **2** a cap, etc., made of this.

coop /koóp/ n. & v. ● n. **1** a cage placed over sitting or fattening fowls. **2** building for keeping chickens, etc. **3** a small place of confinement, esp. a prison. **4** *Brit.* a basket used in catching fish. ● v.tr. **1** put or keep (a fowl) in a coop. **2** (often foll. by *up*, *in*) confine (a person) in a small space. [ME *cupe* basket f. MDu., MLG *kūpe*, ult. f. L *cupa* cask]
■ n. **1, 2** see CAGE n. **3** see JAIL n. 1. ● v. see *shut up* 2.

co-op /kó-op/ n. colloq. **1** a cooperative business or enterprise. **2** = COOPERATIVE 4. [abbr.]

cooper /koópǝr/ n. & v. ● n. a maker or repairer of casks, barrels, etc. ● v.tr. make or repair (a cask). [ME f. MDu., MLG *kūper* f. *kūpe* COOP]

cooperage /koópǝrij/ n. **1** the work or establishment of a cooper. **2** money payable for a cooper's work.

cooperate /kō-ópǝrayt/ v.intr. (also **co-operate**) **1** (often foll. by *with*) work or act together; assist. **2** (of things) concur in producing an effect. □□ **cooperant** /-rǝnt/ adj. **cooperator** n. [eccl.L *cooperari* (as CO-, *operari* f. *opus operis* work)]
■ **1** collaborate, work together, join, unite, interact, team up, join forces, act jointly *or* in concert, coordinate (one's efforts); participate, contribute, lend a hand, help, assist.

cooperation /kō-ópǝráyshǝn/ n. (also **co-operation**) **1** working together to the same end; assistance. **2** *Econ.* the formation and operation of cooperatives. [ME f. L *cooperatio* (as COOPERATE): partly through F *coopération*]
■ **1** collaboration, teamwork, interaction, coordination; support, help, aid, assistance, patronage, backing, advocacy, favor, helping hand, friendship, blessing, sponsorship, auspices, backup.

cooperative /kō-ópǝrǝtiv, -óprǝ-/ adj. & n. (also **co-operative**) ● adj. **1** of or affording cooperation. **2** willing to cooperate. **3** *Econ.* (of a farm, shop, or other business) owned and run jointly by its members, with profits shared among them. **4** (of an apartment building) with individual units owned by their occupiers. ● n. a cooperative farm or society or business. □□ **cooperatively** adv. **cooperativeness** n. [LL *cooperativus* (as COOPERATE)]

co-opt /kō-ópt, kó-opt/ v.tr. appoint to membership of a body by invitation of the existing members. □□ **co-optation** /-optáyshǝn/ n. **co-option** /-ópshǝn/ n. **co-optive** adj. [L *cooptare* (as CO-, *optare* choose)]

coordinate v., adj., & n. (also **co-ordinate**) ● v. /kō-áwrd'nayt/ **1** tr. bring (various parts, movements, etc.) into

a proper or required relation to ensure harmony or effective operation, etc. **2** intr. work or act together effectively. **3** tr. make coordinate; organize; classify. ● adj. /kō-áwrd'nǝt/ **1** equal in rank or importance. **2** in which the parts are coordinated; involving coordination. **3** *Gram.* (of parts of a compound sentence) equal in status (cf. SUBORDINATE). **4** *Chem.* denoting a type of covalent bond in which one atom provides both the shared electrons. ● n. /kō-áwrd'nǝt/ **1** *Math.* each of a system of magnitudes used to fix the position of a point, line, or plane. **2** a person or thing equal in rank or importance. **3** (in pl.) matching items of clothing. □□ **coordinately** adv. **coordination** /-d'náyshǝn/ n. **coordinative** adj. **coordinator** n. [CO- + L *ordinare ordinat-* f. *ordo -inis* order]
■ v. **1** harmonize, correlate, synchronize, integrate; see also UNIFY. **2** pull together, work together; see also COOPERATE. **3** organize, classify, order, arrange, systemize, systematize, codify, categorize, group, match (up), rate, rank, grade. ● adj. **1** equivalent, parallel, corresponding, complementary, equal, *archaic* correspondent. **2** coordinating, coordinative, coordinated. □□ **coordination** see HARMONY 3, COOPERATION, ORGANIZATION 1.

coot /koót/ n. **1** any black aquatic bird of the genus *Fulica*, esp. *F. atra* with the upper mandible extended backward to form a white plate on the forehead. **2** colloq. a stupid person. [ME, prob. f. LG]

cootie /koótee/ n. sl. a body louse. [perh. f. Malay *kutu* a biting parasite]

cop[1] /kop/ n. & v. sl. ● n. **1** a policeman. **2** *Brit.* a capture or arrest (*it's a fair cop*). ● v.tr. (**copped**, **copping**) **1** catch or arrest (an offender). **2** *Brit.* receive; suffer. **3** take; seize. □ **cop it** *Brit.* **1** get into trouble; be punished. **2** be killed. **cop out 1** withdraw; give up an attempt. **2** go back on a promise. **3** escape. **cop-out 1** a cowardly or feeble evasion. **2** an escape; a way of escape. **cop a plea** sl. = *plea-bargain.* **cop-shop** *Brit.* a police station. **not much** (or **no**) **cop** *Brit.* of little or no value or use. [perh. f. obs. *cap* arrest f. OF *caper* seize f. L *capere*: (n.) cf. COPPER[2]]
■ n. **1** see *police officer.* ● v. **1** see ARREST v. 1a.

cop[2] /kop/ n. (in spinning) a conical ball of thread wound on a spindle. [OE *cop* summit]

copacetic /kópǝsétik/ adj. sl. excellent; in good order. [20th c.: orig. unkn.]
■ see FABULOUS 2.

copaiba /kǝpíbǝ, -páy-/ n. an aromatic oil or resin from any plant of the genus *Copaifera*, used in medicine and perfumery. [Sp. & Port. f. Guarani *cupauba*]

copal /kópǝl/ n. a resin from any of various tropical trees, used for varnish. [Sp. f. Aztec *copalli* incense]

copartner /kópáartnǝr/ n. a partner or associate, esp. when sharing equally. □□ **copartnership** n.

cope[1] /kōp/ v.intr. **1** (foll. by *with*) deal effectively or contend successfully with a person or task. **2** manage successfully; deal with a situation or problem (*found they could no longer cope*). [ME f. OF *coper*, *colper* f. *cop*, *colp* blow f. med.L *colpus* f. L *colaphus* f. Gk *kolaphos* blow with the fist]
■ **1** (*cope with*) withstand, contend with, handle, dispose of; see also DEAL[1] v. 1a. **2** manage, get along *or* by, make do, survive, subsist, come *or* pull through, scrape by *or* along, muddle through, colloq. make out.

cope[2] /kōp/ n. & v. ● n. **1** *Eccl.* a long, cloaklike vestment worn by a priest or bishop in ceremonies and processions. **2** esp. poet. a covering compared with a cope. ● v.tr. cover with a cope or coping. [ME ult. f. LL *cappa* CAP, CAPE[1]]

copeck var. of KOPECK.

copepod /kópǝpod/ n. any small aquatic crustacean of the class Copepoda, many of which form the minute components of plankton. [Gk *kōpē* oar-handle + *pous podos* foot]

Copernican system /kǝpérnikǝn/ n. (also **Copernican theory**) *Astron.* the theory that the planets (including the earth) move around the sun (cf. *Ptolemaic system*). [*Copernicus* latinized f. M. *Kopernik*, Polish astronomer d. 1543]

copestone /kópstōn/ n. **1** a stone used in a coping. **2** a finishing touch. [COPE[2] + STONE]

copiable /kópeeəbəl/ adj. that can or may be copied.

copier /kópeeər/ n. a machine or person that copies (esp. documents).
■ see SCRIBE n. 1.

copilot /kópílət/ n. a second pilot in an aircraft.

coping /kóping/ n. the top (usu. sloping) course of masonry in a wall or parapet.

coping saw /kóping/ n. a D-shaped saw for cutting curves in wood. [cope cut wood f. OF coper: see COPE¹]

copingstone /kópingstōn/ n. esp. Brit. = COPESTONE.

copious /kópeeəs/ adj. **1** abundant; plentiful. **2** producing much. **3** providing much information. **4** profuse in speech. □□ **copiously** adv. **copiousness** n. [ME f. OF copieux or f. L copiosus f. copia plenty]
■ **1** see ABUNDANT 1. **2** see PROFUSE 2.

copita /kəpéetə/ n. **1** a tulip-shaped sherry glass. **2** a glass of sherry. [Sp., dimin. of copa cup]

coplanar /kópláynər/ adj. Geom. in the same plane. □□ **coplanarity** /-plənáiritee/ n.

copolymer /kópólimər/ n. Chem. a polymer with units of more than one kind. □□ **copolymerize** v.tr. & intr.

copper¹ /kópər/ n., adj., & v. ● n. **1** Chem. a malleable, red-brown metallic element of the transition series occurring naturally, esp. in cuprous oxide and malachite, and used esp. for electrical cables and apparatus. ¶ Symb.: Cu. **2** a bronze coin. **3** Brit. a large metal vessel for boiling, esp. laundry. ● adj. made of or colored like copper. ● v.tr. cover (a ship's bottom, a pan, etc.) with copper. □ **copper beech** a variety of beech with copper-colored leaves. **copper belt** a copper-mining area of Central Africa. **copper bit** a soldering tool pointed with copper. **copper-bottomed 1** having a bottom sheathed with copper (esp. of a ship or pan). **2** Brit. genuine or reliable (esp. financially). **copper pyrites** a double sulfide of copper and iron: also called CHALCOPYRITE. **copper sulfate** a blue crystalline solid used in electroplating, textile dyeing, etc. **copper vitriol** copper sulfate. [OE copor, coper, ult. f. L cyprium aes Cyprus metal]

copper² /kópər/ n. sl. a policeman. [COP¹ + -ER¹]
■ see police officer.

copperas /kópərəs/ n. green iron-sulfate crystals. [ME coperose f. OF couperose f. med.L cup(e)rosa: perh. orig. aqua cuprosa copper water]

copperhead /kópərhed/ n. **1** a venomous viper, Agkistrodon contortrix, native to N. America. **2** a venomous cobra, Denisonia superba, native to Australia.

copperplate /kópərplayt/ n. & adj. ● n. **1 a** a polished copper plate for engraving or etching. **b** a print made from this. **2** an ornate style of handwriting resembling that orig. used in engravings. ● adj. of or in copperplate writing.

coppersmith /kópərsmith/ n. a person who works in copper.

coppery /kópəree/ adj. of or like copper, esp. in color.

coppice /kópis/ n. & v. ● n. an area of undergrowth and small trees, grown for periodic cutting. ● v.tr. cut back (young trees) periodically to stimulate growth of shoots. □□ **coppiced** adj. [OF copeïz ult. f. med.L colpus blow: see COPE¹]
■ n. grove, wood, stand, thicket, brake, Brit. spinney.

copra /kóprə/ n. the dried kernels of the coconut. [Port. f. Malayalam koppara coconut]

coprecipitation /kóprisípitáyshən/ n. Chem. the simultaneous precipitation of more than one compound from a solution.

copro- /kóprō/ comb. form dung; feces. [Gk kopros dung]

coproduction /kóprədúkshən/ n. a production of a play, broadcast, etc., jointly by more than one company.

coprolite /kóprəlīt/ n. Archaeol. fossil dung or a piece of it.

coprophagous /koprófəgəs/ adj. Zool. dung-eating. [COPRO-]

coprophilia /kóprəfíleeə/ n. an abnormal interest in feces and defecation.

coprosma /kəprózmə/ n. any small evergreen plant of the genus Coprosma, native to Australasia. [mod.L f. Gk kopros dung + osmē smell]

copse /kops/ n. **1** = COPPICE. **2** (in general use) a small forest. □□ **copsy** adj. [shortened f. COPPICE]

copsewood /kópswōod/ n. undergrowth.

Copt /kopt/ n. **1** a native Egyptian in the Hellenistic and Roman periods. **2** a native Christian of the independent Egyptian Church. [F Copte or mod.L Coptus f. Arab. al-ḳibṭ, al-ḳubṭ Copts f. Coptic Gyptios f. Gk Aiguptios Egyptian]

copter /kóptər/ n. a helicopter. [shortening f. helicopter]

Coptic /kóptik/ n. & adj. ● n. the language of the Copts, now used only in the Coptic Church. ● adj. of or relating to the Copts.

copula /kópyələ/ n. (pl. **copulas** or **copulae** /-lee/) Logic & Gram. a connecting word, esp. a part of the verb be connecting a subject and predicate. □□ **copular** adj. [L (as CO-, apere fasten)]

copulate /kópyəlayt/ v.intr. (often foll. by with) have sexual intercourse. □□ **copulatory** /-latáwree/ adj. [L copulare fasten together (as COPULA)]
■ see MATE¹ v. 1b.

copulation /kópyəláyshən/ n. **1** sexual union. **2** a grammatical or logical connection. [ME f. OF f. L copulatio (as COPULATE)]
■ **1** see SEX n. 5.

copulative /kópyəlaytiv, -lətiv/ adj. **1** serving to connect. **2** Gram. **a** (of a word) that connects words or clauses linked in sense (cf. DISJUNCTIVE). **b** connecting a subject and predicate. **3** relating to sexual union. □□ **copulatively** adv. [ME f. OF copulatif -ive or LL copulativus (as COPULATE)]

copy /kópee/ n. & v. ● n. (pl. **-ies**) **1** a thing made to imitate or be identical to another. **2** a single specimen of a publication or issue (ordered twenty copies). **3 a** a matter to be printed. **b** material for a newspaper or magazine article (scandals make good copy). **c** the text of an advertisement. **4 a** a model to be copied. **b** a page written after a model (of penmanship). ● v. (**-ies, -ied**) **1** tr. **a** make a copy of. **b** (often foll. by out) transcribe. **2** intr. make a copy, esp. clandestinely. **3** tr. (foll. by to) send a copy of (a letter) to a third party. **4** tr. do the same as; imitate. □ **copy editor** a person who edits copy for printing. **copy-typist** a person who makes typewritten transcripts of documents. [ME f. OF copie, copier, ult. f. L copia abundance (in med.L = transcript)]
■ n. **1** reproduction, replica, facsimile, likeness, imitation, duplication, duplicate, transcript, replication; carbon (copy), photocopy, print. **2** example, sample, specimen; number, issue. **3** text, writing, material. ● v. **1** reproduce, duplicate, replicate, transcribe; see also IMITATE 3. **4** mimic, impersonate, emulate, ape, echo; see also IMITATE 1, 2. □ **copy editor** copyreader, Brit. subeditor.

copybook /kópeebōok/ n. **1** a book containing models of handwriting for learners to imitate. **2** (attrib.) **a** tritely conventional. **b** accurate, exemplary.

copycat /kópeekat/ n. colloq. a person who copies another, esp. closely.
■ see MIMIC n.

copydesk /kópeedesk/ n. the desk at which copy is edited for printing.

copyedit /kópee-édit/ v.tr. edit (copy) for printing.
■ copyread.

copyhold /kópeehōld/ n. Brit. hist. **1** tenure of land based on manorial records. **2** land held in this way. □□ **copyholder** n.

copyist /kópee-ist/ n. **1** a person who makes (esp. written) copies. **2** an imitator. [earlier copist f. F copiste or med.L copista (as COPY)]
■ **1** see SCRIBE n. 1.

copyreader /kópeereedər/ n. a person who reads and edits copy for a newspaper or book. □□ **copyread** v.tr.

copyright /kópeerit/ n., adj., & v. ● n. the exclusive legal right granted for a specified period to an author, designer, etc., or another appointed person, to print, publish, per-

---

/.../ pronunciation	● part of speech
□ phrases, idioms, and compounds	
□□ derivatives	■ synonym section
cross-references appear in SMALL CAPITALS or italics	

form, film, or record original literary, artistic, or musical material. ● *adj.* (of such material) protected by copyright. ● *v.tr.* secure copyright for (material). □ **copyright library** *Brit.* a library entitled to a free copy of each book published in the UK.

copywriter /kópeerîtər/ *n.* a person who writes or prepares copy (esp. of advertising material) for publication. □□ **copywriting** *n.*

coq au vin /kōk ō ván/ *n.* a casserole of chicken pieces cooked in wine. [F]

coquetry /kṓkitree, kōkétree/ *n.* (*pl.* **-ies**) **1** coquettish behavior. **2** a coquettish act. **3** trifling with serious matters. [F *coquetterie* f. *coqueter* (as COQUETTE)]

coquette /kōkét/ *n.* **1** a woman who flirts. **2** any crested hummingbird of the genus *Lophornis.* □□ **coquettish** *adj.* **coquettishly** *adv.* **coquettishness** *n.* [F, fem. of *coquet* wanton, dimin. of *coq* cock]

▪ **1** see FLIRT *n.* 1.

coquina /kōkéenə/ *n.* a soft limestone of broken shells, used in roadmaking. [Sp., = cockle]

coquito /kōkéetō/ *n.* (*pl.* **-os**) a palm tree, *Jubaea chilensis,* native to Chile, yielding honey from its sap, and fiber. [Sp., dimin. of *coco* coconut]

Cor. *abbr.* **1** Corinthians (New Testament). **2** coroner.

cor /kawr/ *int. Brit. sl.* expressing surprise, alarm, exasperation, etc. □ **cor blimey** see BLIMEY. [corrupt. of *God*]

cor- /kər/ *prefix* assim. form of COM- before *r.*

coracle /káwrəkəl, kór-/ *n. Brit.* a small boat of wickerwork covered with watertight material, used on Welsh and Irish lakes and rivers. [Welsh *corwgl* (*corwg* = Ir. *currach* boat: cf. CURRACH)]

coracoid /káwrəkoyd, kór-/ *n.* (in full **coracoid process**) a short projection from the shoulder blade in vertebrates. [mod.L *coracoides* f. Gk *korakoeidēs* ravenlike f. *korax -akos* raven]

coral /káwrəl, kór-/ *n. & adj.* ● *n.* **1 a** a hard red, pink, or white calcareous substance secreted by various marine polyps for support and habitation. **b** any of these usu. colonial organisms. **2** the unimpregnated roe of a lobster or scallop. ● *adj.* **1** like coral, esp. in color. **2** made of coral. □ **coral island** (or **reef**) one formed by the growth of coral. **coral snake** any of various brightly colored poisonous snakes, esp. *Micrurus fulvius,* native to the southeastern US. [ME f. OF f. L *corallum* f. Gk *korallion,* prob. of Semitic orig.]

coralline /káwrəlin, -līn, kór-/ *n. & adj.* ● *n.* **1** any seaweed of the genus *Corallina* having a calcareous jointed stem. **2** (in general use) the name of various plantlike compound organisms. ● *adj.* **1** coral red. **2** of or like coral. [F *corallin* & It. *corallina* f. LL *corallinus* (as CORAL)]

corallite /káwrəlit, kór-/ *n.* **1** the coral skeleton of a marine polyp. **2** fossil coral. [L *corallum* CORAL]

coralloid /káwrəloyd, kór-/ *adj. & n.* ● *adj.* like or akin to coral. ● *n.* a coralloid organism.

coram populo /káwrəm pópyəlō/ *adv.* in public. [L, = in the presence of the people]

cor anglais /káwr ONGláy/ *n.* (*pl.* **cors anglais** *pronunc.* same) esp. *Brit.* = *English horn.*

corbel /káwrbəl, -bel/ *n. & v. Archit.* ● *n.* **1** a projection of stone, timber, etc., jutting out from a wall to support a weight. **2** a short timber laid longitudinally under a beam to help support it. ● *v.tr. & intr.* (**corbeled, corbeling;** esp. *Brit.* **corbelled, corbelling**) (foll. by *out, off*) support or project on corbels. □ **corbel steps** = CORBIESTEPS. **corbel table** a projecting course resting on corbels. [ME f. OF, dimin. of *corp:* see CORBIE]

▪ *n.* **1** see BRACKET *n.* 1.

corbie /káwrbee/ *n. Sc.* **1** a raven. **2** a carrion crow. [ME f. OF *corb, corp* f. L *corvus* crow]

corbiesteps /káwrbeesteps/ *n.* the steplike projections on the sloping sides of a gable.

cord /kawrd/ *n. & v.* ● *n.* **1 a** long, thin, flexible material made from several twisted strands. **b** a piece of this. **2** *Anat.* a structure in the body resembling a cord (*spinal cord*). **3 a** ribbed fabric, esp. corduroy. **b** (in *pl.*) corduroy trousers. **c** a cordlike rib on fabric. **4** an electric flex. **5** a measure of

cut wood (usu. 128 cu.ft., 3.6 cubic meters). **6 a** moral or emotional tie (*cords of affection; fourfold cord of evidence*). ● *v.tr.* **1** fasten or bind with cord. **2** (as **corded** *adj.*) **a** (of cloth) ribbed. **b** provided with cords. **c** (of muscles) standing out like taut cords. □□ **cordlike** *adj.* [ME f. OF *corde* f. L *chorda* f. Gk *khordē* gut, string of musical instrument]

▪ *n.* **1** line, twine, rope, *Brit.* flex; see also STRING *n.* 1, 2.

cordage /káwrdij/ *n.* cords or ropes, esp. in the rigging of a ship. [ME f. F (as CORD)]

cordate /káwrdayt/ *adj.* heart-shaped. [mod.L *cordatus* f. L *cor cordis* heart]

cordelier /káwrd'leer/ *n.* a Franciscan friar of the strict rule (wearing a knotted cord around the waist). [ME f. OF f. *cordele* dimin. of *corde* CORD]

cordial /káwrjəl/ *adj. & n.* ● *adj.* **1** heartfelt; sincere. **2** warm; friendly. ● *n.* **1 a** a liqueur. **b** *Brit.* a fruit-flavored drink. □□ **cordiality** /-jeeálitee/ *n.* **cordially** *adv.* [ME f. med.L *cordialis* f. L *cor cordis* heart]

▪ *adj.* **1** see SINCERE. **2** friendly, warm, affable, amiable, kindly, genial, gracious, welcoming, open-armed, pleasant, good-natured, nice, courteous, polite.

cordillera /káwrd'lyáirə, kawrdílərə/ *n.* a system or group of usu. parallel mountain ranges together with intervening plateaus, etc., esp. of the Andes and in Central America and Mexico. [Sp. f. *cordilla* dimin. of *cuerda* CORD]

cordite /káwrdit/ *n.* a smokeless explosive made from cellulose nitrate and nitroglycerine. [CORD (from its appearance) + -ITE¹]

cordless /káwrdlis/ *adj.* (of an electrical appliance, telephone, etc.) working from an internal source of energy, etc. (esp. a battery), and without a connection to an electrical supply or central unit.

cordon /káwrd'n/ *n. & v.* ● *n.* **1** a line or circle of police, soldiers, guards, etc., esp. preventing access to or from an area. **2 a** an ornamental cord or braid. **b** the ribbon of a knightly order. **3** a fruit tree trained to grow as a single stem. **4** *Archit.* a stringcourse. ● *v.tr.* (often foll. by *off*) enclose or separate with a cordon of police, etc. [It. *cordone* augmentative of *corda* CORD, & F *cordon* (as CORD)]

▪ *n.* **2a** see BRAID *n.* 1. ● *v.* see *lay siege to* (SIEGE).

cordon bleu /káwrdawn blö/ *adj. & n. Cookery* ● *adj.* of the highest class. ● *n.* a cook of this class. [F, = blue ribbon]

cordon sanitaire /kawrdáwn sáneetáir/ *n.* **1** a guarded line between infected and uninfected districts. **2** any measure designed to prevent communication or the spread of undesirable influences.

cordovan /káwrdəvən/ *n.* a kind of soft leather. [Sp. *cordovan* of Cordova (*Córdoba*) where it was orig. made]

corduroy /káwrdəroy/ *n.* **1** a thick cotton fabric with velvety ribs. **2** (in *pl.*) corduroy trousers. □ **corduroy road** a road made of tree trunks laid across a swamp. [18th c.: prob. f. CORD ribbed fabric + obs. *duroy* coarse woolen fabric]

cordwainer /káwrdwaynər/ *n. Brit. archaic* a shoemaker (usu. in names of guilds, etc.). [obs. *cordwain* CORDOVAN]

cordwood /káwrdwŏod/ *n.* wood that is or can easily be measured in cords.

CORE /kawr/ *abbr.* Congress of Racial Equality.

core /kawr/ *n. & v.* ● *n.* **1** the horny central part of various fruits, containing the seeds. **2 a** the central or most important part of anything (also *attrib.: core curriculum*). **b** the central part, of different character from the surroundings. **3** the central region of the earth. **4** the central part of a nuclear reactor, containing the fissile material. **5** a magnetic structural unit in a computer, storing one bit of data (see BIT⁴). **6** the inner strand of an electric cable, rope, etc. **7** a piece of soft iron forming the center of an electromagnet or an induction coil. **8** an internal mold filling a space to be left hollow in a casting. **9** the central part cut out (esp. of rock, etc., in boring). **10** *Archaeol.* a piece of flint from which flakes or blades have been removed. ● *v.tr.* remove the core from. □ **core memory** *Computing* the memory of a computer consisting of many cores. □□ **corer** *n.* [ME: orig. unkn.]

▪ *n.* **1** center, heart, middle, inside(s), kernel, pit, stone, pip(s). **2 a** essence, marrow, heart, pith, quintessence, substance, crux, nub; basics, fundamentals, *sl.* nitty-gritty. ● *v.* seed, stone, pip, pit.

corelation esp. *Brit.* var. of CORRELATION.

coreligionist /kŏrilíjənist/ *n.* an adherent of the same religion.

corella /kərélə/ *n. Austral.* either of two small white cockatoos, *Cacatua tenuirostris* or *C. sanguinea.* [app. Latinized f. Aboriginal *ca-rall*]

coreopsis /káwreeópsis/ *n.* any composite plant of the genus *Coreopsis,* having rayed usu. yellow flowers. [mod.L f. Gk *koris* bug + *opsis* appearance, with ref. to the shape of the seed]

corespondent /kŏ-rispóndənt/ *n.* a person cited in a divorce case as having committed adultery with the respondent.

corf /kawrf/ *n.* (*pl.* **corves** /kawrvz/) *Brit.* **1** a basket in which fish are kept alive in the water. **2** a small wagon, formerly a large basket, used in mining. [MDu., MLG *korf,* OHG *chorp, korb* f. L *corbis* basket]

corgi /káwrgee/ *n.* (*pl.* **corgis**) (in full **Welsh corgi**) **1** a dog of a short-legged breed with foxlike head. **2** this breed. [Welsh f. *cor* dwarf + *ci* dog]

coriaceous /káwree-áyshəs/ *adj.* like leather; leathery. [LL *coriaceus* f. *corium* leather]

coriander /káwreeándər/ *n.* **1** a plant, *Coriandrum sativum,* with leaves used for flavoring and small, round, aromatic fruits. **2** (also **coriander seed**) the dried fruit used for flavoring curries, etc. [ME f. OF *coriandre* f. L *coriandrum* f. Gk *koriannon*]

Corinthian /kərintheeən/ *adj.* & *n.* ● *adj.* **1** of ancient Corinth in southern Greece. **2** *Archit.* of an order characterized by ornate decoration and flared capitals with rows of acanthus leaves, used esp. by the Romans. **3** *archaic* profligate. ● *n.* a native of Corinth. [L *Corinthius* f. Gk *Korinthios* + -AN]

Coriolis effect /káwreeŏlis/ *n.* a hypothetical force used to explain rotating systems, such that the movement of air or water over the surface of the rotating earth is directed clockwise in the northern hemisphere and counterclockwise in the southern hemisphere. [G. G. *Coriolis,* Fr. scientist d. 1843]

corium /káwreeəm/ *n. Anat.* the dermis. [L, = skin]

cork /kawrk/ *n.* & *v.* ● *n.* **1** the buoyant light-brown bark of the cork oak. **2** a bottle stopper of cork or other material. **3** a float of cork used in fishing, etc. **4** *Bot.* a protective layer of dead cells immediately below the bark of woody plants. **5** (*attrib.*) made of cork. ● *v.tr.* (often foll. by *up*) **1** stop or confine. **2** restrain (feelings, etc.). **3** blacken with burned cork. □ **cork oak** a S. European oak, *Quercus suber.* **cork-tipped** *Brit.* (of a cigarette) having a filter of corklike material. □□ **corklike** *adj.* [ME f. Du. & LG *kork* f. Sp. *alcorque* cork sole, perh. f. Arab.]

■ *n.* **2** see STOPPER *n.* ● *v.* **1** see PLUG *v.* 1.

corkage /káwrkij/ *n.* a charge made by a restaurant or hotel for serving wine, etc., when brought in by customers.

corked /kawrkt/ *adj.* **1** stopped with a cork. **2** (of wine) spoiled by a decayed cork. **3** blackened with burned cork.

corker /káwrkər/ *n. sl.* an excellent or astonishing person or thing.

corking /káwrking/ *adj. sl.* strikingly large or splendid.

corkscrew /káwrkskroō/ *n.* & *v.* ● *n.* **1** a spirally twisted steel device for extracting corks from bottles. **2** (often *attrib.*) a thing with a spiral shape. ● *v.tr.* & *intr.* move spirally; twist.

■ *n.* **2** see SPIRAL *n.*

corkwood /káwrkwood/ *n.* **1** any shrub of the genus *Duboisia,* yielding a light porous wood. **2** this wood.

corky /káwrkee/ *adj.* (**corkier, corkiest**) **1** corklike. **2** (of wine) corked.

corm /kawrm/ *n. Bot.* an underground swollen stem base of some plants, e.g., crocus. [mod.L *cormus* f. Gk *kormos* trunk with boughs lopped off]

cormorant /káwrmərənt, -mərant/ *n.* any diving sea bird of the family Phalacrocoracidae, esp. *Phalacrocorax carbo* having lustrous black plumage. [ME f. OF *cormaran* f. med.L *corvus marinus* sea raven: for ending -*ant* cf. *peasant, tyrant*]

corn[1] /kawrn/ *n.* & *v.* ● *n.* **1 a** a tall-growing orig. N. American cereal plant, *Zea mays,* cultivated in many varieties, bearing kernels on a long ear (cob). **b** the cobs or kernels of this plant. **2** *Brit.* **a** any cereal before or after harvesting, esp. the chief crop of a region. **b** a grain or seed of a cereal plant. **2** *colloq.* something corny or trite. ● *v.tr.* (as **corned** *adj.*) sprinkled or preserved with salt or brine (*corned beef*). □ **corn bread** bread made with cornmeal. **corn cockle** see COCKLE[2]. **corn dolly** a symbolic or decorative figure made of plaited straw, corn husks, etc. **corn flour** *Brit.* = CORNSTARCH. **corn marigold** a daisylike, yellow-flowered plant, *Chrysanthemum segetum.* **corn on the cob** corn cooked and eaten from the cob. **corn salad** a plant, *Valerianella locusta,* used in salad. **corn whiskey** whiskey distilled from corn. [OE f. Gmc: rel. to L *granum* grain]

■ *n.* **2** see *sentimentality* (SENTIMENTAL). ● *v.* (**corned**) see SALT *adj.*

corn[2] /kawrn/ *n.* a small area of horny usu. tender skin esp. on the toes, extending into subcutaneous tissue. [ME f. AF f. L *cornu* horn]

■ see LUMP[1] *n.* 3.

cornball /kórnbawl/ *n.* & *adj.* ● *n.* an unsophisticated or mawkishly sentimental person. ● *adj.* = CORNY *adj.* 1.

cornbrash /káwrnbrash/ *n. Geol. Brit.* an earthy limestone layer of the Jurassic period. [CORN[1] + BRASH[2]]

corncob /káwrnkaab/ *n.* the cylindrical center of the corn ear to which rows of grains (kernels) are attached. □ **corncob pipe** a tobacco pipe made from a corncob.

corncrake /káwrnkrayk/ *n.* a rail, *Crex crex,* inhabiting grassland and nesting on the ground.

cornea /káwrneeə/ *n.* the transparent circular part of the front of the eyeball. □□ **corneal** *adj.* [med.L *cornea tela* horny tissue, f. L *corneus* horny f. *cornu* horn]

cornel /káwrnəl, -nel/ *n.* any plant of the genus *Cornus,* esp. a dwarf kind, *C. suecica.* [ME f. L *cornus*]

cornelian var. of CARNELIAN.

corneous /káwrneeəs/ *adj.* hornlike; horny. [L *corneus* f. *cornu* horn]

corner /káwrnər/ *n.* & *v.* ● *n.* **1** a place where converging sides or edges meet. **2** a projecting angle, esp. where two streets meet. **3** the internal space or recess formed by the meeting of two sides, esp. of a room. **4** a difficult position, esp. one from which there is no escape (*driven into a corner*). **5** a secluded or remote place. **6** a region or quarter, esp. a remote one (*from the four corners of the earth*). **7** the action or result of buying or controlling the whole available stock of a commodity, thereby dominating the market. **8** *Boxing & Wrestling* **a** an angle of the ring, esp. one where a contestant rests between rounds. **b** a contestant's supporters offering assistance at the corner between rounds. **9** *Soccer* a free kick or hit from a corner of the field after the ball has been kicked over the goal line by a defending player. ● *v.* **1** *tr.* force (a person or animal) into a difficult or inescapable position. **2** *tr.* **a** establish a corner in (a commodity). **b** dominate (dealers or the market) in this way. **3** *intr.* (esp. of or in a vehicle) go around a corner. □ **corner shop** a small local store, esp. at a street corner. **just around the corner** *colloq.* very near; imminent. [ME f. AF ult. f. L *cornu* horn]

■ *n.* **1, 2** see ANGLE[1] *n.* 2. **3** see NOOK. **4** see HOLE *n.* 5. **6** see PART *n.* 11. ● *v.* **1** see TRAP[1] *v.* 1, 2. **2** see MONOPOLIZE. **3** see TURN *v.* 3b.

cornerstone /káwrnərstōn/ *n.* **1 a** a stone in a projecting angle of a wall. **b** a foundation stone. **2** an indispensable part or basis of something.

■ **2** see KEYSTONE.

cornerwise /káwrnərwiz/ *adv.* diagonally.

cornet[1] *n.* **1** /kawrnét/ *Mus.* **a** a brass instrument resembling a trumpet but shorter and wider. **b** its player. **c** an organ stop with the quality of a cornet. **d** a cornetto. **2** /káwrnit,

---

/.../ **pronunciation**	● **part of speech**
□ **phrases, idioms, and compounds**	
□□ **derivatives**	■ **synonym section**
cross-references appear in SMALL CAPITALS or *italics*	

kawrnét/ *Brit.* an ice-cream cone. ▫▫ **cornetist** or **cornet-tist** *n.* [ME f. OF ult. f. L *cornu* horn]

cornet[2] /káwrnit/ *n. Brit. hist.* the fifth commissioned officer in a cavalry troop, who carried the colors. ▫▫ **cornetcy** *n.* (*pl.* -ies). [earlier sense 'pennon, standard' f. F *cornette* dimin. of *corne* ult. f. L *cornua* horns]

cornett /kawrnét/ *n. Mus.* = CORNETTO. [var. of CORNET[1]]

cornetto /kawrnétō/ *n.* (*pl.* **cornetti** /-tee/) *Mus.* an old woodwind instrument like a flageolet. [It., dimin. of *corno* horn (as CORNET[1])]

cornfield /káwrnfeeld/ *n.* a field in which corn is being grown.

cornflake /káwrnflayk/ *n.* **1** (in *pl.*) a breakfast cereal of toasted flakes made from cornmeal. **2** a flake of this cereal.

cornflower /káwrnflowr/ *n.* any plant of the genus *Centaurea* growing among corn, esp. *C. cyanus*, with deep-blue flowers.

cornice /káwrnis/ *n.* **1** *Archit.* **a** an ornamental molding around the wall of a room just below the ceiling. **b** a horizontal molded projection crowning a building or structure, esp. the uppermost member of the entablature of an order, surmounting the frieze. **2** *Mountaineering* an overhanging mass of hardened snow at the edge of a precipice. ▫▫ **corniced** *adj.* [F *corniche*, etc., f. It. *cornice*, perh. f. L *cornix -icis* crow]

corniche /káwrnish, kawrneésh/ *n.* (in full **corniche road**) **1** a road cut into the edge of a cliff, etc. **2** a coastal road with wide views. [F: see CORNICE]

Cornish /káwrnish/ *adj. & n.* ● *adj.* of or relating to Cornwall in SW England. ● *n.* the ancient Celtic language of Cornwall. ▫ **Cornish cream** clotted cream. **Cornish pasty** seasoned meat and vegetables baked in a pastry envelope.

cornmeal /káwrnmeel/ *n.* meal ground from corn.

cornrow /kórnrō/ *n. & v.* ● *n.* any of usu. several narrow plaits of hair braided close to the scalp. ● *v.tr.* plait (hair) in cornrows.

cornstarch /káwrnstaarch/ *n.* fine-ground flour made from corn.

cornstone /káwrnstōn/ *n. Brit. Geol.* a mottled red and green limestone usu. formed under arid conditions, esp. in the Devonian period.

cornucopia /káwrnəkṓpeeə, -nyə-/ *n.* **1 a** a symbol of plenty consisting of a goat's horn overflowing with flowers, fruit, etc. **b** an ornamental vessel shaped like this. **2** an abundant supply. ▫▫ **cornucopian** *adj.* [LL f. L *cornu copiae* horn of plenty]

■ **2** see ABUNDANCE 1.

corny /káwrnee/ *adj.* (**cornier, corniest**) **1** *colloq.* **a** trite. **b** feebly humorous. **c** sentimental. **d** old-fashioned; out of date. **2** of or abounding in corn. ▫▫ **cornily** *adv.* **corniness** *n.* [CORN[1] + -Y[1]: sense 1 f. sense 'rustic']

■ **1 a** see BANAL. **c** see SENTIMENTAL. **d** see *out-of-date* (DATE).

corolla /kərólə, -rṓ-/ *n. Bot.* a whorl or whorls of petals forming the inner envelope of a flower. [L, dimin. of *corona* crown]

corollary /káwrəleree, kór-/ *n. & adj.* ● *n.* (*pl.* -ies) **1 a** a proposition that follows from (and is often appended to) one already proved. **b** an immediate deduction. **2** (often foll. by *of*) a natural consequence or result. ● *adj.* **1** supplementary; associated. **2** (often foll. by *to*) forming a corollary. [ME f. L *corollarium* money paid for a garland; gratuity: neut. adj. f. COROLLA]

corona[1] /kərṓnə/ *n.* (*pl.* **coronas** or **coronae** /-nee/) **1 a** a small circle of light around the sun or moon. **b** the rarefied gaseous envelope of the sun, seen as an irregularly shaped area of light around the moon's disk during a total solar eclipse. **2** a circular chandelier hung from a roof. **3** *Anat.* a crown or crownlike structure. **4** *Bot.* a crownlike outgrowth from the inner side of a corolla. **5** *Archit.* a broad vertical face of a cornice, usu. of considerable projection. **6** *Electr.* the glow around a conductor at high potential. [L, = crown]

■ **1** see HALO *n.* 1, 3.

corona[2] /kərṓnə/ *n.* a long cigar with straight sides. [Sp. *La Corona* the crown]

coronach /káwrənək, -nəkh/ *n. Sc. & Ir.* a funeral song or dirge. [Ir. *coranach*, Gael. *corranach* f. *comh-* together + *rànach* outcry]

coronagraph /kərṓnəgraf/ *n.* an instrument for observing the sun's corona, esp. other than during a solar eclipse.

coronal[1] /kərṓnəl, káwrən'l, kór-/ *adj.* **1** *Astron. & Bot.* of a corona. **2** *Anat.* of the crown of the head. ▫ **coronal bone** the frontal bone of the skull. **coronal plane** an imaginary plane dividing the body into dorsal and ventral parts. **coronal suture** a transverse suture of the skull separating the frontal bone from the parietal bones. [F *coronal* or L *coronalis* (as CORONA[1])]

coronal[2] /káwrən'l, kór-/ *n.* **1** a circlet (esp. of gold or gems) for the head. **2** a wreath or garland. [ME, app. f. AF f. *corone* CROWN]

coronary /káwrəneree, kór-/ *adj. & n.* ● *adj. Anat.* resembling or encircling like a crown. ● *n.* (*pl.* -ies) **1** = *coronary thrombosis.* **2** a heart attack. ▫ **coronary artery** an artery supplying blood to the heart. **coronary care unit** a hospital unit providing specialized care for patients with serious heart conditions. **coronary thrombosis** *Med.* a blockage of the blood flow caused by a blood clot in a coronary artery. [L *coronarius* f. *corona* crown]

coronation /káwrənáyshən, kór-/ *n.* the ceremony of crowning a sovereign or a sovereign's consort. [ME f. OF f. med.L *coronatio -onis* f. *coronare* to crown f. CORONA[1]]

■ see *inauguration* (INAUGURATE).

coroner /káwrənər, kór-/ *n.* an officer of a county, district, or municipality, holding inquests on deaths thought to be violent or accidental, and *Brit.* inquiries in cases of treasure trove. ▫▫ **coronership** *n.* [ME f. AF *cor(o)uner* f. *coro(u)ne* CROWN]

coronet /káwrənit, -nét, kór-/ *n.* **1** a small crown (esp. as worn, or used as a heraldic device, by a peer or peeress). **2** a circlet of precious materials, esp. as a woman's headdress or part of one. **3** a garland for the head. **4** the lowest part of a horse's pastern. **5** a ring of bone at the base of a deer's antler. ▫▫ **coroneted** *adj.* [OF *coronet(t)e* dimin. of *corone* CROWN]

■ **1, 2** see CROWN *n.* 1.

corozo /kərṓzō/ *n.* (*pl.* -os) *Bot.* any of various palm trees native to S. America. ▫ **corozo nut** a seed of one species of palm, *Phytelephas macrocarpa*, which when hardened forms vegetable ivory: also called *ivory nut*. [Sp.]

Corp. *abbr.* **1** corporal. **2** corporation.

corpora *pl.* of CORPUS.

corporal[1] /káwrpərəl, káwrprəl/ *n.* **1** a noncommissioned army, air force, or marine officer ranking next below sergeant. **2** (in full **ship's corporal**) *Brit.* an officer under the master-at-arms, attending to police matters. **3** a freshwater fallfish, *Semotilus corporalis*. [obs. F, var. of *caporal* f. It. *caporale* prob. f. L *corporalis* (as CORPORAL[2]), confused with It. *capo* head]

corporal[2] /káwrpərəl, káwrprəl/ *adj.* of or relating to the human body (cf. CORPOREAL). ▫ **corporal punishment** punishment inflicted on the body, esp. by beating. ▫▫ **corporally** *adv.* [ME f. OF f. L *corporalis* f. *corpus -oris* body]

■ bodily, physical.

corporal[3] /káwrpərəl, káwrprəl/ *n.* a cloth on which the vessels containing the consecrated elements are placed during the celebration of the Eucharist. [OE f. OF *corporal* or med.L *corporale pallium* body cloth (as CORPORAL[2])]

corporality /káwrpərálitee/ *n.* (*pl.* -ies) **1** material existence. **2** a body. [ME f. LL *corporalitas* (as CORPORAL[2])]

corporate /káwrpərət, káwrprit/ *adj.* **1** forming a corporation (*corporate body; body corporate*). **2** forming one body of many individuals. **3** of or belonging to a corporation or group (*corporate responsibility*). **4** corporative. ▫ **corporate raider** a person who mounts an unwelcome takeover bid by buying up a company's shares on the stock market. ▫▫ **corporately** *adv.* **corporatism** *n.* [L *corporare corporat-* form into a body (*corpus -oris*)]

corporation /káwrpəráyshən/ *n.* **1** a group of people autho-

rized to act as an individual and recognized in law as a single entity, esp. in business. **2** (in the UK) the municipal authorities of a borough, town, or city. **3** *joc.* a protruding stomach. [LL *corporatio* (as CORPORATE)]
■ **1** see COMPANY *n.* 3a. **3** see PAUNCH *n.*

corporative /káwrpərətiv, -ráytiv/ *adj.* **1** of a corporation. **2** governed by or organized in corporations, esp. of employers and employed. □□ **corporativism** *n.*

corporeal /kawrpáwreeəl/ *adj.* **1** bodily, physical, material, esp. as distinct from spiritual (cf. CORPORAL²). **2** *Law* consisting of material objects. □□ **corporeality** /-reeálitee/ *n.* **corporeally** *adv.* [LL *corporealis* f. L *corporeus* f. *corpus -oris* body]
■ **1** see PHYSICAL *adj.* 2.

corporeity /káwrpəreéitee, -ráy-/ *n.* **1** the quality of being or having a material body. **2** bodily substance. [F *corporéité* or med.L *corporeitas* f. L *corporeus* (as CORPOREAL)]

corposant /káwrpəzant/ *n.* = ST. ELMO´S FIRE. [OSp., Port., It. *corpo santo* holy body]

corps /kawr/ *n.* (*pl.* **corps** /kawrz/) **1** *Mil.* **a** a body of troops with special duties (*intelligence corps*; *Marine Corps*). **b** a main subdivision of an army in the field, consisting of two or more divisions. **2** a body of people engaged in a special activity (*diplomatic corps*; *press corps*). [F (as CORPSE)]
■ **1 a** troop(s), cadre, unit, detachment, cohort, division, battalion, brigade, platoon, squad, squadron.

corps de ballet /káwr də baláy/ *n.* the company of ensemble dancers in a ballet. [F]

corps d'élite / kárwdayleét/ *n.* a select group. [F]

corps diplomatique /káwrdípləmateéek/ *n.* a diplomatic corps. [F]

corpse /kawrps/ *n.* a dead (usu. human) body. □ **corpse candle 1** a lambent flame seen in a churchyard or over a grave, regarded as an omen of death. **2** a lighted candle placed beside a corpse before burial. [ME *corps*, var. spelling of *cors* (CORSE), f. OF *cors* f. L *corpus* body]
■ body, remains, cadaver, *archaic* corse, *sl.* stiff; carcass.

corpulent /káwrpyələnt/ *adj.* bulky in body; fat. □□ **corpulence** /-ləns/ *n.* **corpulency** *n.* [ME f. L *corpulentus* f. *corpus* body]
■ see FAT *adj.* 1. □□ **corpulence** see FAT *n.* 3.

corpus /káwrpəs/ *n.* (*pl.* **corpora** /káwrpərə/ or **corpuses**) **1** a body or collection of writings, texts, spoken material, etc. **2** *Anat.* a structure of a special character in the animal body. [ME f. L, = body]

Corpus Christi /káwrpəs krístee/ *n.* a feast commemorating the Eucharist, observed on the Thursday after Trinity Sunday. [ME f. L, = Body of Christ]

corpuscle /káwrpusəl/ *n.* a minute body or cell in an organism, esp. (in *pl.*) the red or white cells in the blood of vertebrates. □□ **corpuscular** /kawrpúskyələr/ *adj.* [L *corpusculum* (as CORPUS)]

corpus delicti /káwrpəs dilíktī/ *n. Law* the facts and circumstances constituting a breach of a law. [L, = body of offense]

corpus luteum /káwrpəs loőteeəm/ *n.* (*pl.* **corpora lutea** /loőteeə/) *Anat.* a body developed in the ovary after discharge of the ovum, remaining in existence only if pregnancy has begun. [mod.L f. CORPUS + *luteus, -um* yellow]

corr. *abbr.* **1** correction. **2** correspondence.

corral /kərál/ *n. & v.* ● *n.* **1** a pen for cattle, horses, etc. **2** an enclosure for capturing wild animals. **3** *hist.* a defensive enclosure of wagons in an encampment. ● *v.tr.* (**corralled, corralling**) **1** put or keep in a corral. **2** form (wagons) into a corral. **3** *colloq.* gather in; acquire. [Sp. & OPort. (as KRAAL)]
■ *n.* **1, 2** see PEN² *n.* 1. ● *v.* **1** see PEN² *v.* 2.

corrasion /kəráyzhən/ *n. Geol.* erosion of the earth's surface by rock material being carried over it by water, ice, etc. [L *corradere corras-* scrape together (as COM-, *radere* scrape)]

correct /kərékt/ *adj. & v.* ● *adj.* **1** true; right; accurate. **2** (of conduct, manners, etc.) proper; right. **3** in accordance with good standards of taste, etc. ● *v.tr.* **1** set right; amend (an error, omission, etc., or the person responsible for it). **2** mark the errors in (written or printed work, etc.). **3** substi-

tute the right thing for (the wrong one). **4 a** admonish or rebuke (a person). **b** punish (a person or fault). **5** counteract (a harmful quality). **6** adjust (an instrument, etc.) to function accurately or accord with a standard. □□ **correctly** *adv.* **correctness** *n.* [ME (adj. through F) f. L *corrigere correct-* (as COM-, *regere* guide)]
■ *adj.* **1** accurate, right, precise, exact, factual, valid, true, proper, suitable, appropriate. **2, 3** proper, decorous, decent, appropriate, (socially) acceptable, suitable, fit, right, *comme il faut*, meet, fitting, befitting, apt; faultless, perfect, unimpeachable; in order, de rigueur, *colloq.* done; conventional, set, established, standard, normal, orthodox, approved, usual, natural, customary, traditional. ● *v.* **1** right, set *or* put right, amend, redress, rectify, remedy, repair, fix, cure. **2** mark, grade; revise, edit. **4 a** scold, admonish, rebuke, reprimand, berate, reprove, castigate, chastise, *archaic or literary* chide; censure, blame. **b** chastise, chasten, discipline, castigate; see also PUNISH 1. **5** reverse, offset, counteract, counterbalance, neutralize, nullify, make up for, annul, cancel. **6** see ADJUST 1.

correction /kərékshən/ *n.* **1 a** the act or process of correcting. **b** an instance of this. **2** a thing substituted for what is wrong. **3** a program of incarceration, parole, probation, etc., for dealing with convicted offenders. **4** *archaic* punishment. □□ **correctional** *adj.* [ME f. OF f. L *correctio -onis* (as CORRECT)]
■ **1** emendation, rectification, redress, reparation, amendment; improvement. **4** castigation, chastisement; see also PUNISHMENT 1, 2.

correctitude /kəréktitōod, -tyōod/ *n.* correctness, esp. conscious correctness of conduct. [19th c., f. CORRECT + RECTITUDE]

corrective /kəréktiv/ *adj. & n.* ● *adj.* serving or tending to correct or counteract something undesired or harmful. ● *n.* a corrective measure or thing. □□ **correctively** *adv.* [F *correctif -ive* or LL *correctivus* (as CORRECT)]
■ *adj.* see THERAPEUTIC 1. ● *n.* see ANTIDOTE 2.

corrector /kəréktər/ *n.* a person who corrects or points out faults. [ME f. AF *correctour* f. L *corrector* (as CORRECT)]

correlate /káwrəlayt, kór-/ *v. & n.* ● *v.* **1** *intr.* (foll. by *with, to*) have a mutual relation. **2** *tr.* (usu. foll. by *with*) bring into a mutual relation. ● *n.* each of two related or complementary things (esp. so related that one implies the other). [back-form. f. CORRELATION, CORRELATIVE]
■ *v.* see RELATE 3.

correlation /káwrəláyshən, kór-/ *n.* (also esp. *Brit.* **corelation** /kŏ-ree-/) **1** a mutual relation between two or more things. **2 a** interdependence of variable quantities. **b** a quantity measuring the extent of this. **3** the act of correlating. □□ **correlational** *adj.* [med.L *correlatio* (as CORRELATIVE)]
■ **1, 3** see PARALLEL *n.* 2.

correlative /kərélətiv/ *adj. & n.* ● *adj.* **1** (often foll. by *with, to*) having a mutual relation. **2** *Gram.* (of words) corresponding to each other and regularly used together (as *neither* and *nor*). ● *n.* a correlative word or thing. □□ **correlatively** *adv.* **correlativity** /-tívitee/ *n.* [med.L *correlativus* (as COM-, RELATIVE)]
■ *adj.* **1** see RECIPROCAL *adj.* 4.

correspond /káwrispónd, kór-/ *v.intr.* **1 a** (usu. foll. by *to*) be analogous or similar. **b** (usu. foll. by *to*) agree in amount, position, etc. **c** (usu. foll. by *with, to*) be in harmony or agreement. **2** (usu. foll. by *with*) communicate by interchange of letters. □ **corresponding member** an honorary member of a learned society, etc., with no voice in the society's affairs. □□ **correspondingly** *adv.* [F *correspondre* f. med.L *correspondere* (as COM-, RESPOND)]
■ **1** be alike *or* similar *or* analogous; agree, conform, tally, comply, accord, harmonize, be congruous, coincide;

/. . ./ **pronunciation**	● **part of speech**
□ **phrases, idioms, and compounds**	
□□ **derivatives**	■ **synonym section**
cross-references appear in SMALL CAPITALS or *italics*	

(*correspond to*) match. **2** write (letters), communicate, exchange letters.

correspondence /káwrispóndəns, kór-/ *n.* **1** (usu. foll. by *with, to, between*) agreement, similarity, or harmony. **2 a** communication by letters. **b** letters sent or received. □ **correspondence school** (or **college**) a college conducting correspondence courses. **correspondence column** *Brit.* the part of a newspaper, etc., that contains letters from readers. **correspondence course** a course of study conducted by mail. [ME f. OF f. med.L *correspondentia* (as CORRESPOND)]
■ **1** see ACCORD *n.* 1. **2** see LETTER *n.* 2a.

correspondent /káwrispóndənt, -kór-/ *n.* & *adj.* ● *n.* **1** a person who writes letters to a person or a newspaper, esp. regularly. **2** a person employed to contribute material for publication in a periodical or for broadcasting (*our business correspondent*; *NBC's Moscow correspondent*). **3** a person or firm having regular business relations with another, esp. in another country. ● *adj.* (often foll. by *to, with*) *archaic* corresponding. □□ **correspondently** *adv.* [ME f. OF *correspondant* or med.L (as CORRESPOND)]
■ *n.* **2** journalist, reporter, newspaperman, pressman, newsman, newsperson, *colloq.* stringer.

corrida /kawreedə, -thaa/ *n.* **1 a** bullfight. **2** bullfighting. [Sp. *corrida de toros* running of bulls]

corridor /káwridər, -dor, kór-/ *n.* **1** a passage from which doors lead into rooms (orig. an outside passage connecting parts of a building, now usu. a main passage in a large building). **2** *Brit.* a passage in a railroad car from which doors lead into compartments. **3** a strip of the territory of one nation passing through that of another, esp. securing access to the sea. **4** a route to which aircraft are restricted, esp. over a foreign country. □ **corridors of power** places where covert influence is said to be exerted in government. [F f. It. *corridore* corridor for *corridojo* running-place f. *correre* run, by confusion with *corridore* runner]
■ **1** hallway, passage, passageway, hall.

corrie /káwree, kór-/ *n. Sc.* a circular hollow on a mountainside; a cirque. [Gael. *coire* cauldron]

corrigendum /káwrijéndəm, kór-/ *n.* (*pl.* **corrigenda** /-də/) a thing to be corrected, esp. an error in a printed book. [L, neut. gerundive of *corrigere*: see CORRECT]

corrigible /káwrijibəl, kór-/ *adj.* **1** capable of being corrected. **2** (of a person) submissive; open to correction. □□ **corrigibly** *adv.* [ME f. F f. med.L *corrigibilis* (as CORRECT)]

corroborate /kəróbərayt/ *v.tr.* confirm or give support to (a statement or belief, or the person holding it), esp. in relation to witnesses in a court of law. □□ **corroboration** /-ráyshən/ *n.* **corroborative** /-rətiv, -ráytiv/ *adj.* **corroborator** *n.* **corroboratory** /-rətáwree/ *adj.* [L *corroborare* strengthen (as COM-, *roborare* f. *robur -oris* strength)]
■ see SUBSTANTIATE.

corroboree /kəróbəree/ *n.* **1** a festive or warlike dance-drama with song of Australian Aboriginals. **2** a noisy party. [Aboriginal dial.]

corrode /kəród/ *v.* **1 a** *tr.* wear away, esp. by chemical action. **b** *intr.* be worn away; decay. **2** *tr.* destroy gradually (*optimism corroded by recent misfortunes*). □□ **corrodible** *adj.* [ME f. L *corrodere corros-* (as COM-, *rodere* gnaw)]
■ **1** see WEAR[1] *v.* 5.

corrosion /kərózhən/ *n.* **1** the process of corroding, esp. of a rusting metal. **2 a** damage caused by corroding. **b** a corroded area.

corrosive /kərósiv/ *adj.* & *n.* ● *adj.* tending to corrode or consume. ● *n.* a corrosive substance. □ **corrosive sublimate** mercuric chloride, a strong acid poison, used as a fungicide, antiseptic, etc. □□ **corrosively** *adv.* **corrosiveness** *n.* [ME f. OF *corosif -ive* (as CORRODE)]
■ *adj.* see CAUSTIC *adj.* 1, INCISIVE 3.

corrugate /káwrəgayt, kór-/ *v.* **1** *tr.* (esp. as **corrugated** *adj.*) form into alternate ridges and grooves, esp. to strengthen (*corrugated iron*; *corrugated cardboard*). **2** *tr.* & *intr.* contract into wrinkles or folds. □□ **corrugation** /-gáyshən/ *n.* [L *corrugare* (as COM-, *rugare* f. *ruga* wrinkle)]
■ see WRINKLE *v.* 1.

corrugator /káwrəgaytər, kór-/ *n. Anat.* either of two muscles that contract the brow in frowning. [mod.L (as CORRUGATE)]

corrupt /kərúpt/ *adj.* & *v.* ● *adj.* **1** morally depraved; wicked. **2** influenced by or using bribery or fraudulent activity. **3** (of a text, language, etc.) harmed (esp. made suspect or unreliable) by errors or alterations. **4** rotten. ● *v.* **1** *tr.* & *intr.* make or become corrupt or depraved. **2** *tr.* affect or harm by errors or alterations. **3** *tr.* infect; taint. □ **corrupt practices** fraudulent activity, esp. at elections. □□ **corrupter** *n.* **corruptible** *adj.* **corruptibility** *n.* **corruptive** *adj.* **corruptly** *adv.* **corruptness** *n.* [ME f. OF *corrupt* or L *corruptus* past part. of *corrumpere corrupt-* (as COM-, *rumpere* break)]
■ *adj.* **1** debased, depraved, perverted, evil, wicked, degraded, corrupted; see also DEGENERATE *adj.* **2** dishonest, untrustworthy, dishonorable, underhand(ed), venal, *colloq.* crooked, *sl.* bent. **3** harmed, debased, corrupted; unreliable. ● *v.* **1** debase, pervert, subvert, degrade, deprave, warp; bribe, suborn, buy (off). **3** infect, contaminate, pollute, taint, defile, spoil, poison, adulterate.

corruption /kərúpshən/ *n.* **1** moral deterioration, esp. widespread. **2** use of corrupt practices, esp. bribery or fraud. **3 a** irregular alteration (of a text, language, etc.) from its original state. **b** an irregularly altered form of a word. **4** decomposition, esp. of a corpse or other organic matter. [ME f. OF *corruption* or L *corruptio* (as CORRUPT)]
■ **1** see SIN[1] *n.* 1. **2** see GRAFT[2] *n.* 1. **3** see MISUSE *n.* 4 see ROT *n.* 1.

corsage /kawrsáazh/ *n.* **1** a small bouquet worn by a woman. **2** the bodice of a woman's dress. [ME f. OF f. *cors* body: see CORPSE]
■ **1** buttonhole, boutonnière.

corsair /káwrsair/ *n.* **1** a pirate ship. **2** a pirate. **3** *hist.* a privateer, esp. of the Barbary Coast. [F *corsaire* f. med.L *cursarius* f. *cursus* inroad f. *currere* run]
■ **2, 3** see PIRATE *n.* 1a.

corse /kawrs/ *n. archaic* a corpse. [var. of CORPSE]

corselet /káwrsəlét/ *n.* **1** (also **corselette**) a woman's foundation garment combining girdle and brassiere. **2** (also **corslet** /káwrslit/) *hist.* a piece of armor covering the trunk. [OF *corselet*, dimin. formed as CORSET]

corselette var. of CORSELET. [propr.]

corset /káwrsit/ *n.* & *v.* ● *n.* **1** a closely fitting undergarment worn by women to support the abdomen. **2** a similar garment worn by men and women because of injury, weakness, or deformity. ● *v.tr.* **1** provide with a corset. **2** control closely. □□ **corseted** *adj.* **corsetry** *n.* [ME f. OF, dimin. of *cors* body: see CORPSE]

corsetiere /káwrsityáir/ *n.* a woman who makes or fits corsets. [F, fem. of *corsetier* (as CORSET, -IER)]

Corsican /káwrsikən/ *adj.* & *n.* ● *adj.* of or relating to Corsica, an island in the Mediterranean under French rule. ● *n.* **1** a native of Corsica. **2** the Italian dialect of Corsica.

corslet var. of CORSELET.

cortege /kawrtéyzh/ *n.* (also **cortège**) **1** a procession, esp. for a funeral. **2** a train of attendants. [F]
■ **1** see PROCESSION 1. **2** see TRAIN *n.* 4.

Cortes /kawrtéz, -tés/ *n.* the legislative assembly of Spain and formerly of Portugal. [Sp. & Port., pl. of *corte* COURT]

cortex /káwrteks/ *n.* (*pl.* **cortices** /-tiseez/ or **cortexes**) **1** *Anat.* the outer part of an organ, esp. of the brain (**cerebral cortex**) or kidneys (**renal cortex**). **2** *Bot.* **a** an outer layer of tissue immediately below the epidermis. **b** bark. □□ **cortical** /káwrtikəl/ *adj.* [L *cortex, -icis* bark]

Corti /káwrtee/ *n.* □ **organ of Corti** *Anat.* a structure in the inner ear of mammals, responsible for converting sound signals into nerve impulses. [A. *Corti*, It. anatomist d. 1876]

corticate /káwrtikayt/ *adj.* (also **corticated**) **1** having bark or rind. **2** barklike. [L *corticatus* (as CORTEX)]

corticotrophic hormone /káwrtikōtróffik, -tróf-/ *adj.* (also **corticotropic**) = ADRENOCORTICOTROPHIC HORMONE.

corticotrophin /káwrtikōtróffin/ *n.* (also **corticotropin**) = ADRENOCORTICOTROPHIN.

cortisone /káwrtisōn, -zōn/ *n. Biochem.* a steroid hormone produced by the adrenal cortex or synthetically, used medicinally esp. against inflammation and allergy. [Chem. name 17-hydroxy-11-dehydro*corti*coster*one*]

corundum /kərúndəm/ *n. Mineral.* extremely hard crystallized alumina, used esp. as an abrasive, and varieties of which, e.g., ruby and sapphire, are used for gemstones. [Tamil *kurundam* f. Skr. *kuruvinda* ruby]

coruscate /káwrəskayt, kór-/ *v.intr.* **1** give off flashing light; sparkle. **2** be showy or brilliant. □□ **coruscation** / káyshən/ *n.* [L *coruscare* glitter]
■ **1** see SPARKLE *v.* 1a.

corvée /kawrváy/ *n.* **1** *hist.* a day's work of unpaid labor due to a lord from a vassal. **2** labor exacted in lieu of paying taxes. **3** an onerous task. [ME f. OF ult. f. L *corrogare* ask for, collect (as COM-, *rogare* ask)]

corves *pl.* of CORF.

corvette /kawrvét/ *n. Naut.* **1** a small naval escort vessel. **2** *hist.* a flush-decked warship with one tier of guns. [F f. MDu. *korf* kind of ship + dimin. -ETTE]

corvine /káwrvīn, -vin/ *adj.* of or akin to the raven or crow. [L *corvinus* f. *corvus* raven]

corybantic /káwribántik, kór-/ *adj.* wild; frenzied. [*Corybantes* priests of Cybele performing wild dances (L f. Gk *Korubantes*)]

corymb /káwrimb, -im, kór-/ *n. Bot.* a flat-topped cluster of flowers with the flower stalks proportionally longer lower down the stem. □□ **corymbose** *adj.* [F *corymbe* or L *corymbus* f. Gk *korumbos* cluster]

coryphée /káwrifay, kór-/ *n.* a leading dancer in a corps de ballet. [F f. Gk *koruphaios* leader of a chorus f. *koruphē* head]

coryza /kərízə/ *n.* **1** a catarrhal inflammation of the mucous membrane in the nose; a cold in the head. **2** any disease with this as a symptom. [L f. Gk *koruza* running at the nose]
■ see COLD *n.* 2.

cos¹ /kaws, kos/ *n.* a variety of lettuce with crisp narrow leaves forming a long, upright head. [L f. Gk *Kōs*, island in the Aegean, where it originated]
■ romaine.

cos² /kos, koz/ *abbr.* cosine.

cos³ /kawz, koz/ *conj. & adv.* (also **'cos**) *colloq.* because. [abbr.]

Cosa Nostra /kósə nóstrə/ *n.* a US criminal organization resembling and related to the Mafia. [It., = our affair]
■ see UNDERWORLD 1.

cosec /kósek/ *abbr.* cosecant.

cosecant /kóseékant, -kənt/ *n. Math.* the ratio of the hypotenuse (in a right triangle) to the side opposite an acute angle; the reciprocal of sine. [mod.L *cosecans* and F *cosécant* (as CO-, SECANT)]

coseismal /kōsízməl/ *adj. & n.* ● *adj.* of or relating to points of simultaneous arrival of an earthquake wave. ● *n.* a straight line or a curve connecting these points. [CO- + *seismal* (see SEISMIC)]

coset /kóset/ *n. Math.* a set composed of all the products obtained by multiplying on the right or on the left each element of a subgroup in turn by one particular element of the group containing the subgroup. [CO- + SET²]

cosh¹ /kosh/ *n. & v. Brit. colloq.* ● *n.* a heavy blunt weapon. ● *v.tr.* hit with a cosh. [19th c.: orig. unkn.]

cosh² /kosh, kosáych/ *abbr. Math.* hyperbolic cosine.

cosign /kósīn/ *v.tr.* sign (a promissory note) jointly with another person. □□ **cosigner** *n.*

cosignatory /kōsígnətáwree/ *n. & adj.* ● *n.* (*pl.* -**ies**) a person or nation signing (a treaty, etc.) jointly with others. ● *adj.* signing jointly.

cosine /kósīn/ *n. Math.* the ratio of the side adjacent to an acute angle (in a right triangle) to the hypotenuse. [mod.L *cosinus* (as CO-, SINE)]

cosmetic /kozmétik/ *adj. & n.* ● *adj.* **1** intended to adorn or beautify the body, esp. the face. **2** intended to improve only appearances; superficially improving or beneficial (*a cosmetic change*). **3** (of surgery or a prosthetic device) imitating, restoring, or enhancing the normal appearance. ● *n.* a cosmetic preparation, esp. for the face. □□ **cosmetically**

adv. [F *cosmétique* f. Gk *kosmētikos* f. *kosmeō* adorn f. *kosmos* order, adornment]
■ *adj.* **2** see SUPERFICIAL 3.

cosmetology /kozmətóləjee/ *n.* the art and technique of treating the skin, nails, and hair with cosmetic preparations. □□ **cosmetologist** *n.* [f. F *cosmétologie*]

cosmic /kózmik/ *adj.* **1** of the universe or cosmos, esp. as distinct from the earth. **2** of or for space travel. □ **cosmic dust** small particles of matter distributed throughout space. **cosmic rays** (or **radiation**) radiations from space, etc., that reach the earth from all directions, usu. with high energy and penetrative power. □□ **cosmical** *adj.* **cosmically** *adv.*
■ **1** see UNIVERSAL *adj.*

cosmogony /kozmógənee/ *n.* (*pl.* -**ies**) **1** the origin of the universe. **2** a theory about this. □□ **cosmogonic** /-məgónik/ *adj.* **cosmogonical** *adj.* **cosmogonist** /-móg-/ *n.* [Gk *kosmogonia* f. *kosmos* world + -*gonia* -begetting]

cosmography /kozmógrəfee/ *n.* (*pl.* -**ies**) a description or mapping of general features of the universe. □□ **cosmographer** *n.* **cosmographic** /-məgráfik/ *adj.* **cosmographical** *adj.* [ME f. F *cosmographie* or f. LL f. Gk *kosmographia* (as COSMOS¹, -GRAPHY)]

cosmology /kozmóləjee/ *n.* the science or theory of the universe. □□ **cosmological** /-məlójikəl/ *adj.* **cosmologist** *n.* [F *cosmologie* or mod.L *cosmologia* (as COSMOS¹, -LOGY)]

cosmonaut /kózmənawt/ *n.* a Russian astronaut. [Russ. *kosmonavt*, as COSMOS¹, after *astronaut*]

cosmopolis /kozmópəlis/ *n.* a cosmopolitan city. [Gk *kosmos* world + *polis* city]

cosmopolitan /kozməpólit'n/ *adj. & n.* ● *adj.* **1 a** of or from or knowing many parts of the world. **b** consisting of people from many or all parts. **2** free from national limitations or prejudices. **3** *Ecol.* (of a plant, animal, etc.) widely distributed. ● *n.* **1** a cosmopolitan person. **2** *Ecol.* a widely distributed animal or plant. □□ **cosmopolitanism** *n.* **cosmopolitanize** *v.tr. & intr.* [COSMOPOLITE + -AN]
■ *adj.* **1** see INTERNATIONAL *adj.* **2** see WORLDLY 2.

cosmopolite /kozmópəlit/ *n. & adj.* ● *n.* **1** a cosmopolitan person. **2** *Ecol.* = COSMOPOLITAN *n.* 2. ● *adj.* free from national attachments or prejudices. [F f. Gk *kosmopolitēs* f. *kosmos* world + *politēs* citizen]

cosmos¹ /kózmōs, -məs, -mos/ *n.* **1** the universe, esp. as a well-ordered whole. **2 a** an ordered system of ideas, etc. **b** a sum total of experience. [Gk *kosmos*]
■ **1** see UNIVERSE 1a.

cosmos² /kózməs, -mos, -mōs/ *n.* any composite plant of the genus *Cosmos*, bearing single dahlialike blossoms of various colors. [mod.L f. Gk *kosmos* in sense 'ornament']

Cossack /kósak/ *n. & adj.* ● *n.* **1** a member of a people of southern Imperial Russia, orig. famous for their military skill. **2** a member of a Cossack military unit. ● *adj.* of, relating to, or characteristic of the Cossacks. [F *cosaque* f. Russ. *kazak* f. Turki *quzzāq* nomad, adventurer]

cosset /kósit/ *v.tr.* pamper. [dial. *cosset* = pet lamb, prob. f. AF *coscet, cozet* f. OE *cotsǣta* cottager (as COT², SIT)]
■ see PAMPER.

cossie / kózee/ *n.* (also **cozzie**) chiefly *Austral. sl.* a swimming costume. [abbr.]

cost /kawst/ *v. & n.* ● *v.* (*past* and *past part.* **cost**) **1** be obtainable for (a sum of money); have as a price (*what does it cost?*; *it cost me $50*). **2** *tr.* involve as a loss or sacrifice (*it cost them much effort*; *it cost him his life*). **3** *tr.* (*past* and *past part.* **costed**) fix or estimate the cost or price of. **4** *colloq.* **a** *tr.* be costly to (*it'll cost you*). **b** *intr.* be costly. ● *n.* **1** what a thing costs; the price paid or to be paid. **2** a loss or sacrifice; an expenditure of time, effort, etc. **3** (in *pl.*) legal expenses, esp. those allowed in favor of the winning party or against the losing party in a suit. □ **at all costs** (or **at any**

/.../ **pronunciation**	● **part of speech**
□ **phrases, idioms, and compounds**	
□□ **derivatives**	■ **synonym section**
cross-references appear in SMALL CAPITALS or *italics*	

cost) no matter what the cost or risk may be. **at cost** at the initial cost; at cost price. **at the cost of** at the expense of losing or sacrificing. **cost accountant** an accountant who records costs and (esp. overhead) expenses in a business concern. **cost-benefit** assessing the relation between the cost of an operation and the value of the resulting benefits (*cost-benefit analysis*). **cost a person dear** (or **dearly**) involve a person in a high cost or a heavy penalty. **cost-effective** effective or productive in relation to its cost. **cost of living** the level of prices esp. of the basic necessities of life. **cost-plus** calculated as the basic cost plus a profit factor. **cost-push** *Econ.* factors other than demand that cause inflation. **to a person's cost** at a person's expense; with loss or disadvantage to a person. [ME f. OF *coster*, *couster*, *coust* ult. f. L *constare* stand firm, stand at a price (as COM-, *stare* stand)]
■ *v.* **1** sell for, get, fetch, bring in; *colloq.* set a person back. **2** see INVOLVE 2. ● *n.* **1** price, payment, charge, expense, expenditure, rate, tariff; outlay. **2** see LOSS 1. □ **at all costs** see *by all means* 3 (MEANS).

costal /kóst'l, káwst'l/ *adj.* of the ribs. [F f. mod.L *costalis* f. L *costa* rib]

costar /kóstaar/ *n. & v.* ● *n.* a movie or stage star appearing with another or others of equal importance. ● *v.* (**-starred**, **-starring**) **1** *intr.* take part as a costar. **2** *tr.* (of a production) include as a costar.

costard /kóstərd/ *n. Brit.* **1** a large ribbed variety of apple. **2** *archaic joc.* the head. [ME f. AF f. *coste* rib f. L *costa*]

costate /kóstayt, káw-/ *adj.* ribbed; having ribs or ridges. [L *costatus* f. *costa* rib]

coster /kóstər/ *n. Brit.* = COSTERMONGER. [abbr.]

costermonger /kóstərmunggər, -monggər/ *n. Brit.* a person who sells fruit, vegetables, etc., in the street from a barrow. [COSTARD + MONGER]

costive /kóstiv/ *adj.* **1** constipated. **2** niggardly. □□ **costively** *adv.* **costiveness** *n.* [ME f. OF *costivé* f. L *constipatus*: see CONSTIPATE]

costly /káwstlee/ *adj.* (**costlier**, **costliest**) **1** costing much; expensive. **2** of great value. □□ **costliness** *n.*
■ **1** see EXPENSIVE 1. **2** see PRECIOUS *adj.* 1.

costmary /káwstmairee/ *n.* (*pl.* **-ies**) an aromatic composite plant, *Balsamita major*, formerly used in medicine and for flavoring beer, etc. [OE *cost* f. L *costum* f. Gk *kostos* f. Arab. *ḳusṭ* an aromatic plant + (*St.*) *Mary* (with whom it was associated in medieval times)]

costume /kóstōōm, -tyōō-/ *n. & v.* ● *n.* **1** a style or fashion of dress, esp. that of a particular place, time, or class. **2** a set of clothes. **3** clothing for a particular activity (*dancing costume*). **4** an actor's clothes for a part. **5** a woman's matching jacket and skirt. ● *v.tr.* provide with a costume. □ **costume jewelry** artificial jewelry worn to adorn clothes. **costume play** (or **piece** or **drama**) a play or television drama in which the actors wear historical costume. [F f. It. f. L *consuetudo* CUSTOM]
■ *n.* **1, 2** dress, clothing, clothes, garb, garments, outfit, vestment, livery, uniform, esp. *Brit.* kit, *archaic* raiment, *colloq.* togs, *formal* attire, apparel, *sl.* threads. **5** suit. ● *v.* see DRESS *v.* 1a.

costumer /kóstōōmər, -tyōō-/ *n.* (also esp. *Brit.* **costumier** /kostōōmeeər, -tyōō-/) a person who makes or deals in costumes, esp. for theatrical use. [F *costumier* (as COSTUME)]
■ see TAILOR *n.*

cosy esp. *Brit.* var. of COZY.

cot[1] /kot/ *n.* **1** a small folding bed. **2** a hospital bed. **3** *Brit.* a small bed with high sides, esp. for a baby or very young child; crib. **4** *Ind.* a light bedstead. **5** *Naut.* a kind of swinging bed hung from deck beams, formerly used by officers. [Anglo-Ind., f. Hindi *khāṭ* bedstead, hammock]

cot[2] /kot/ *n. & v.* ● *n.* **1** a small shelter; a cote. **2** *poet.* a cottage. ● *v.tr.* (**cotted**, **cotting**) put (sheep) in a cot. [OE f. Gmc, rel. to COTE]

cot[3] /kot/ *abbr. Math.* cotangent.

cotangent /kótánjənt/ *n. Math.* the ratio of the side adjacent to an acute angle (in a right triangle) to the opposite side.

cote /kōt/ *n.* a shelter, esp. for animals or birds; a shed or stall (*sheepcote*). [OE f. Gmc, rel. to COT[2]]
■ see STALL[1] *n.* 2.

coterie /kótəree/ *n.* **1** an exclusive group of people sharing interests. **2** a select circle in society. [F, orig. = association of tenants, ult. f. MLG *kote* COTE]
■ see GROUP *n.* 3.

coterminous /kōtárminəs/ *adj.* (often foll. by *with*) having the same boundaries or extent (in space, time, or meaning). [CO- + TERMINUS + -OUS]
■ coextensive, conterminous.

coth /koth/ *abbr. Math.* hyperbolic cotangent.

cotidal line /kōtíd'l/ *n.* a line on a map connecting points at which tidal levels (as high tide or low tide) occur simultaneously.

cotillion /kətílyən/ *n.* **1** any of various French dances with elaborate steps, figures, and ceremonial. **2 a** a ballroom dance resembling a quadrille. **b** a formal ball. [F *cotillon* petticoat, dimin. of *cotte* f. OF *cote* COAT]

cotoneaster /kətōneeástər/ *n.* any rosaceous shrub of the genus *Cotoneaster*, bearing usu. bright red berries. [mod.L f. L *cotoneum* QUINCE + -ASTER]

cotta /kótə/ *n. Eccl.* a short surplice. [It., formed as COAT]

cottage /kótij/ *n.* **1** a small, simple house, esp. in the country. **2** a dwelling forming part of a farm establishment, used by a worker. □ **cottage cheese** soft white cheese made from curds of skimmed milk without pressing. **cottage industry** a business activity partly or wholly carried on at home. **cottage pie** *Brit.* a dish of ground meat topped with browned mashed potato. □□ **cottagey** *adj.* [ME f. AF, formed as COT[2], COTE]
■ **1** hut, cabin, bungalow, lodge, chalet, shanty, *poet.* cot.

cottager /kótijər/ *n.* a person who lives in a cottage.

cottar /kótər/ *n.* (also **cotter**) *Sc. & hist.* a farm laborer or tenant occupying a cottage in return for labor as required. [COT[2] + -ER[1] (Sc. -*ar*)]

cotter /kótər/ *n.* **1** a bolt or wedge for securing parts of machinery, etc. **2** (in full **cotter pin**) a split pin that opens after passing through a hole. [17th c. (rel. to earlier *cotterel*): orig. unkn.]

cotton /kót'n/ *n. & v.* ● *n.* **1** a soft, white fibrous substance covering the seeds of certain plants. **2 a** (in full **cotton plant**) such a plant, esp. any of the genus *Gossypium*. **b** cotton plants cultivated as a crop for the fiber or the seeds. **3** (*attrib.*) made of cotton. ● *v.intr.* (foll. by *to*) be attracted by (a person). □ **cotton cake** compressed cotton seed used as food for cattle. **cotton candy** a fluffy mass of spun sugar, usu. served on a stick. **cotton gin** a machine for separating cotton from its seeds. **cotton grass** any grasslike plant of the genus *Eriophorum*, with long, white silky hairs. **cotton-picking** *sl.* unpleasant; wretched. **cotton to** (or **on to**) *colloq.* **1** begin to be fond of or agreeable to. **2** begin to understand. **cotton waste** refuse yarn used to clean machinery, etc. **cotton wool 1** esp. *Brit.* fluffy wadding of a kind orig. made from raw cotton. **2** raw cotton. □□ **cottony** *adj.* [ME f. OF *coton* f. Arab. *ḳuṭn*]
■ □ **cotton to** (or **on to**) **2** see REALIZE 2.

cottonmouth /kót'nmowth/ *n.* a venomous pit viper, *Agkistrodon piscivorus*, of swampy areas of the southeastern US, related to the coppermouth. Also called **water moccasin**. [f. the whitish lining of its mouth]

cottontail /kót'ntayl/ *n.* any rabbit of the genus *Sylvilagus*, native to America, having a mainly white fluffy tail.

cottonwood /kót'nwŏŏd/ *n.* **1** any of several poplars, native to N. America, having seeds covered in white cottony hairs. **2** any of several trees native to Australia, esp. a downy-leaved tree, *Bedfordia arborescens*.

cotyledon /kót'leéd'n/ *n.* **1** an embryonic leaf in seed-bearing plants. **2** any succulent plant of the genus *Umbilicus*, e.g., pennywort. □□ **cotyledonary** *adj.* **cotyledonous** *adj.* [L, = pennywort, f. Gk *kotulēdōn* cup-shaped cavity f. *kotulē* cup]

coucal /kŏŏkəl/ *n.* any ground-nesting bird of the genus *Centropus*, related to the cuckoos. [F, perh. f. *coucou* cuckoo + *alouette* lark]

couch[1] /kowch/ *n. & v.* ● *n.* **1** an upholstered piece of furniture for several people; a sofa. **2** a long padded seat with a headrest at one end, esp. one on which a psychiatrist's or doctor's patient reclines during examination. ● *v.* **1** *tr.* (foll. by *in*) express in words of a specified kind (*couched in simple language*). **2** *tr.* lay on or as on a couch. **3** *intr.* **a** (of an animal) lie, esp. in its lair. **b** lie in ambush. **4** *tr.* lower (a spear, etc.) to the position for attack. **5** *tr. Med.* treat (a cataract) by displacing the lens of the eye. □ **couch potato** *sl.* a person who likes lazing at home, esp. watching television. [ME f. OF *couche, coucher* f. L *collocare* (as COM-, *locare* place)]

■ *n.* **1** sofa, settee, divan, love seat, studio couch, settle, chaise longue; tête-à-tête, canapé, chesterfield, davenport. ● *v.* **1** phrase, embed, frame, formulate, style; see also EXPRESS[1] 1, 2. □ **couch potato** see LOAFER.

couch[2] /kowch, kŏŏch/ *n.* (in full **couch grass**) any of several grasses of the genus *Agropyron*, esp. *A. repens*, having long, creeping roots. [var. of QUITCH]

couchant /kówchənt/ *adj.* (placed after noun) *Heraldry* (of an animal) lying with the body resting on the legs and the head raised. [F, pres. part. of *coucher*: see COUCH[1]]

couchette /kŏŏshét/ *n.* **1** a railroad car with seats convertible into sleeping berths. **2** a berth in this. [F, = little bed, dimin. of *couche* COUCH[1]]

coudé /kŏŏdáy/ *adj. & n.* ● *adj.* of or relating to a telescope in which rays are bent to a focus off the axis. ● *n.* such a telescope. [F, past part. of *couder* bend at right angles f. *coude* elbow formed as CUBIT]

Couéism /kŏŏáyizəm/ *n.* a system of usu. optimistic autosuggestion as psychotherapy. [E. *Coué*, Fr. psychologist d. 1926]

cougar /kŏŏgər/ *n.* a puma. [F, repr. Guarani *guaçu ara*]

cough /kawf, kof/ *v. & n.* ● *v.intr.* **1** expel air from the lungs with a sudden, sharp sound produced by abrupt opening of the glottis, to remove an obstruction or congestion. **2** (of an engine, gun, etc.) make a similar sound. ● *n.* **1** an act of coughing. **2** a condition of the respiratory organs causing coughing. **3** a tendency to cough. □ **cough drop** a medicated lozenge to relieve a cough. **cough medicine** (or **syrup**) a medicated liquid to relieve a cough. **cough out 1** eject by coughing. **2** say with a cough. **cough up 1** = *cough out*. **2** *sl.* bring out or give (money or information) reluctantly. **3** *sl.* confess. □□ **cougher** *n.* [ME *coghe, cowhe*, rel. to MDu. *kuchen*, MHG *kūchen*, of imit. orig.]

■ □ **cough up 2** see PAY[1] *v.* 2.

could *past of* CAN[1].

couldn't /kŏŏd'nt/ *contr.* could not.

coulee /kŏŏlee/ *n. Geol.* **1** a solidified lava flow. **2** a deep ravine. [F, fem. past part. of *couler* flow, f. L *colare* strain, filter]

■ **2** see CANYON.

coulisse /kŏŏlees/ *n.* **1** (usu. in *pl.*) *Theatr.* a piece of side scenery or a space between two of these; the wings. **2** a place of informal discussion or negotiation. [F f. *coulis* sliding: see PORTCULLIS]

couloir /kŏŏlwaár/ *n.* a steep, narrow gully on a mountainside. [F f. *couler* glide: see COULEE]

■ see PASS[2].

coulomb /kŏŏlom/ *n. Electr.* the SI unit of electric charge, equal to the quantity of electricity conveyed in one second by a current of one ampere. ¶ Symb.: **C**. [C. A. de *Coulomb*, Fr. physicist d. 1806]

coulometry /kŏŏlómitree/ *n. Chem.* a method of chemical analysis by measurement of the number of coulombs used in electrolysis. □□ **coulometric** /kŏŏləmétrik/ *adj.*

coulter *Brit.* var. of COLTER.

coumarin /kŏŏmərin/ *n.* an aromatic substance found in many plants and formerly used for flavoring food. [F *coumarine* f. Tupi *cumarú* tonka bean]

coumarone /kŏŏmərōn/ *n.* an organic liquid obtained from coal tar by synthesis and used in paints and varnishes. □ **coumarone resin** a thermoplastic resin formed by polymerization of coumarone. [COUMARIN + -ONE]

council /kównsəl/ *n.* **1 a** an advisory, deliberative, or administrative body of people formally constituted and meeting regularly. **b** a meeting of such a body. **2 a** the elected local legislative body of a town, city, or county. **3** a body of persons chosen as advisers. **4** an ecclesiastical assembly (*ecumenical council*). □ **council of war 1** an assembly of officers called in a special emergency. **2** any meeting held to plan a response to an emergency. [ME f. AF *cuncile* f. L *concilium* convocation, assembly f. *calare* summon: cf. COUNSEL]

■ **1 a** board, ministry, directors, cabinet, panel, committee, body, directorate, *hist.* Directory. **b** assembly, meeting, conclave, conference, convention, congress, congregation, gathering, convocation.

councillor /kównsələr, -slər/ *n.* an elected member of a council, esp. a local one. □□ **councillorship** *n.* [ME, alt. of COUNSELOR: assim. to COUNCIL]

councilman /kównsəlmən/ *n.* (*pl.* **-men**; *fem.* **councilwoman**, *pl.* **-women**) a member of a council.

counsel /kównsəl/ *n. & v.* ● *n.* **1** advice, esp. formally given. **2** consultation, esp. to seek or give advice. **3** (*pl.* same) an attorney or other legal adviser; a body of these advising in a case. **4** a plan of action. ● *v.tr.* **1** (often foll. by *to* + infin.) advise (a person). **2 a** give advice to (a person) on social or personal problems, esp. professionally. **b** assist or guide (a person) in resolving personal difficulties. **3** (often foll. by *that*) recommend (a course of action). □ **counsel of despair** action to be taken when all else fails. **counsel of perfection 1** advice that is ideal but not feasible. **2** advice guiding toward moral perfection. **keep one's own counsel** not confide in others. **queen's** (or **king's**) **counsel** *Brit.* a counsel to the Crown, taking precedence over other barristers. **take counsel** (usu. foll. by *with*) consult. [ME f. OF *c(o)unseil, conseiller* f. L *consilium* consultation, advice]

■ *n.* **1** advice, judgment, direction, opinion, guidance, instruction, recommendation, exhortation. **2** consultation, deliberation; see also DISCUSSION 1. **3** adviser, guide, counselor, lawyer, attorney, counselor-at-law, *Brit.* barrister. ● *v.* **1** direct, instruct; see also ADVISE 1, 2. **3** recommend, urge, exhort, advocate; see also SUGGEST 1. ■ **take counsel** see CONSULT 1, 2.

counseling /kównsəling, -sling/ *n.* **1** the act or process of giving counsel. **2** the process of assisting and guiding clients, esp. by a trained person on a professional basis, to resolve esp. personal, social, or psychological problems and difficulties (cf. COUNSEL *v.* 2b).

counselor /kównsələr, -slər/ *n.* **1** a person who gives counsel; an adviser. **2** a person trained to give guidance on personal, social, or psychological problems (*marriage counselor; guidance counselor*). **3** a senior officer in the diplomatic service. **4** (also **counselor-at-law**) a lawyer, esp. one who gives advice in law.[ME f. OF *conseiller* (f. L *consiliarius*), *conseillour, -eur* (f. L *consiliator*): see COUNSEL]

■ **4** adviser, counsel, attorney, lawyer, *Brit.* barrister.

count[1] /kownt/ *v. & n.* ● *v.* **1** *tr.* determine the total number or amount of, esp. by assigning successive numbers (*count the stations*). **2** *intr.* repeat numbers in ascending order; conduct a reckoning. **3 a** *tr.* (often foll. by *in*) include in one's reckoning or plan (*you can count me in; fifteen people, counting the guide*). **b** *intr.* be included in a reckoning or plan. **4** *tr.* consider (a thing or a person) to be (lucky, etc.) (*count no man happy until he is dead*). **5** *intr.* (often foll. by *for*) have value; matter (*his opinion counts for a great deal*). ● *n.* **1 a** the act of counting; a reckoning (*after a count of fifty*). **b** the sum total of a reckoning (*blood count; pollen count*). **2** *Law* each charge in an indictment (*guilty on ten counts*). **3** a count of up to ten seconds by a referee when a boxer is knocked down. **4** *Polit.* the act of counting the votes after a general or local election. **5** one of several points under discussion. **6** the measure of the fineness of a yarn expressed as the weight of a given length or the length of a given weight. **7**

/.../ **pronunciation**	● **part of speech**
□ **phrases, idioms, and compounds**	
□□ **derivatives**	■ **synonym section**
cross-references appear in SMALL CAPITALS or *italics*

Physics the number of ionizing particles detected by a counter. □ **count against** be reckoned to the disadvantage of. **count one's blessings** be grateful for what one has. **count one's chickens** be overoptimistic or hasty in anticipating good fortune. **count the cost** consider the risks before taking action; calculate the damage resulting from an action. **count the days** (or **hours**, etc.) be impatient. **count down** recite numbers backward to zero, esp. as part of a rocket-launching procedure. **count noun** a countable noun (see COUNTABLE 2). **count on** (or **upon**) depend on; rely on; expect confidently. **count out 1** count while taking from a stock. **2** complete a count of ten seconds over (a fallen boxer, etc.), indicating defeat. **3** (in children's games) select (a player) for dismissal or a special role by use of a counting rhyme, etc. **4** *colloq.* exclude from a plan or reckoning (*I'm too tired, count me out*). **5** *Brit. Polit.* procure the adjournment of (the House of Commons) when fewer than 40 members are present. **count up** find the sum of. **down for the count 1** *Boxing* defeated by being unable to rise within ten seconds. **2 a** defeated or demoralized. **b** sound asleep. **keep count** take note of how many there have been, etc. **lose count** fail to take note of the number, etc. **not counting** excluding from the reckoning. **take the count** *Boxing* be defeated. [ME f. OF *co(u)nter, co(u)nte* f. LL *computus, computare* COMPUTE]

■ *v.* **1** count up *or* off, enumerate, number, calculate, add up, total, reckon, compute, tally, figure (out), quantify. **3 a** include, consider. **4** see CONSIDER 6. **5** see MATTER *v.* □ **count on** (or **upon**) rely on *or* upon, depend on *or* upon, be sure of, trust, bank on, be confident of, *colloq.* reckon on, figure on *or* upon. **count out 4** see EXCLUDE 3. **count up** see COUNT[1] *v.* 1 above. **down for the count 2 a** defeated, demoralized; see also *dejected* (DEJECT). **b** sound asleep, sleeping like a baby; see also *dead to the world.*

count [2] /kownt/ *n.* a noble of continental Europe corresponding in rank to a British earl. □ **count palatine** *hist.* a high official of the Holy Roman Empire with royal authority within his domain. □□ **countship** *n.* [OF *conte* f. L *comes comitis* companion]

countable /kówntəbəl/ *adj.* **1** that can be counted. **2** *Gram.* (of a noun) that can form a plural or be used with the indefinite article (e.g., *book, kindness*).

countdown /kówntdown/ *n.* **1 a** the act of counting down, esp. at the launching of a rocket, etc. **b** the procedures carried out during this time. **2** the final moments before any significant event.

countenance /kówntinəns/ *n. & v.* ● *n.* **1 a** the face. **b** facial expression. **2** composure. **3** moral support. ● *v.tr.* **1** give approval to (an act, etc.) (*cannot countenance this breach of the rules*). **2** (often foll. by *in*) encourage (a person or a practice). □ **change countenance** alter one's expression as an effect of emotion. **keep one's countenance** maintain composure, esp. by refraining from laughter. **keep a person in countenance** support or encourage a person. **lose countenance** become embarrassed. **out of countenance** disconcerted. [ME f. AF *c(o)untenance*, OF *contenance* bearing f. *contenir*: see CONTAIN]

■ *n.* **1 a** see FACE *n.* 1. **b** see EXPRESSION 4. ● *v.* **1** see APPROVE. **2** see SUPPORT *v.* 11.

counter [1] /kównter/ *n.* **1 a** a long, flat-topped fixture in a store, bank, etc., across which business is conducted with customers. **b** a similar structure used for serving food, etc., in a cafeteria or bar. **2 a** a small disk used for keeping the score, etc., esp. in board games. **b** a token representing a coin. **c** something used in bargaining; a pawn (*a counter in the struggle for power*). **3** an apparatus used for counting. **4** *Physics* an apparatus used for counting individual ionizing particles, etc. **5** a person or thing that counts. □ **over the counter a** (of stock) sold through a broker directly, not on an exchange **b** by ordinary retail purchase. **under the counter** (esp. of the sale of scarce goods) surreptitiously, esp. illegally. [AF *count(e)our*, OF *conteo(i)r*, f. med.L *computatorium* (as COMPUTE)]

■ **1** table, bar; desk. **2 a, b** token, disk, chip, piece,

marker, check. □ **under the counter** see *on the sly* (SLY), *illegally* (ILLEGAL).

counter [2] /kównter/ *v., adv., adj., & n.* ● *v.* **1** *tr.* **a** oppose; contradict (*countered our proposal with their own*). **b** meet by a countermove. **2** *intr.* **a** make a countermove. **b** make an opposing statement ("*I shall!*" *he countered*). **3** *intr. Boxing* give a return blow while parrying. ● *adv.* **1** in the opposite direction (*ran counter to the fox*). **2** contrary (*her action was counter to my wishes*). ● *adj.* **1** opposed; opposite. **2** duplicate; serving as a check. ● *n.* **1** a parry; a countermove. **2** something opposite or opposed. □ **act** (or **go**) **counter to** disobey (instructions, etc.). **go** (or **run** or *Brit.* **hunt**) **counter** run or ride against the direction taken by a quarry. **run counter to** act contrary to. [ME f. OF *countre* f. L *contra* against: see COUNTER-]

counter [3] /kównter/ *n.* **1** the part of a horse's breast between the shoulders and under the neck. **2** the curved part of the stern of a ship. **3** *Printing* a part of a printing type, etc., that is completely enclosed by an outline (e.g., the loop of P). [17th c.: orig. unkn.]

counter [4] /kównter/ *n.* the back part of a shoe or a boot around the heel. [abbr. of *counterfort* buttress]

counter- /kównter/ *comb. form* denoting: **1** retaliation, opposition, or rivalry (*counterthreat; countercheck*). **2** opposite direction (*countercurrent*). **3** correspondence, duplication, or substitution (*counterpart; countersign*). [from or after AF *countre-*, OF *contre* f. L *contra* against]

counteract /kównterákt/ *v.tr.* **1** hinder or oppose by contrary action. **2** neutralize. □□ **counteraction** /-ákshən/ *n.* **counteractive** *adj.*

■ **1** see HINDER[1], OPPOSE 1–3. **2** counterbalance, neutralize, correct, annul, nullify, cancel, mitigate.

counterattack *n. & v.* ● *n.* /kównterətak/ an attack in reply to an attack by an enemy or opponent. ● *v.tr. & intr.* /kównterətak/ attack in reply.

■ *v.* see OPPOSE 1–3.

counterattraction /kównterətrákshən/ *n.* **1** a rival attraction. **2** the attraction of a contrary tendency.

counterbalance *n. & v.* ● *n.* /kównterbaləns/ **1** a weight balancing another. **2** an argument, force, etc., balancing another. ● *v.tr.* /kównterbaləns/act as a counterbalance to.

■ *n.* **2** see OFFSET *n.* ● *v.* see BALANCE *v.* 1, 2.

counterblast /kównterblast/ *n.* (often foll. by *to*) an energetic or violent verbal or written reply to an argument, etc.

counterchange /kówntercháynj/ *v.* **1** *tr.* change (places or parts); interchange. **2** *tr. literary* checker, esp. with contrasting colors, etc. **3** *intr.* change places or parts. [F *contrechanger* (as COUNTER-, CHANGE)]

countercharge *n. & v.* ● *n.* /kówntercharj/ a charge or accusation in return for one received. ● *v.tr.* /kówntercharj/make a countercharge against.

■ *n.* see *recrimination* (RECRIMINATE).

countercheck *n. & v.* ● *n.* /kówntercheck/ **1 a** a restraint that opposes something. **b** a restraint that operates against another. **2** a second check, esp. for security or accuracy. **3** *archaic* a retort. ● *v.tr.* /kównterchék/ make a countercheck on.

counterclaim *n. & v.* ● *n.* /kównterklaym/ **1** a claim made against another claim. **2** *Law* a claim made by a defendant in a suit against the plaintiff. ● *v.tr. & intr.* /kównterkláym/ make a counterclaim (for).

counterclockwise /kównterklókwiz/ *adv. & adj.* ● *adv.* in a curve opposite in direction to the movement of the hands of a clock. ● *adj.* moving counterclockwise.

counterculture /kównterkulcher/ *n.* a way of life, etc., opposed to that usually considered normal.

counterespionage /kównterréspeeənaazh, -nij/ *n.* action taken to frustrate enemy spying.

counterfeit /kównterfit/ *adj., n., & v.* ● *adj.* **1** (of a coin, writing, etc.) made in imitation; not genuine; forged. **2** (of a claimant, etc.) pretended. ● *n.* a forgery; an imitation. ● *v.tr.* **1 a** imitate fraudulently (a coin, handwriting, etc.); forge. **b** make an imitation of. **2** simulate (feelings, etc.) (*counterfeited interest*). **3** resemble closely. □□ **counterfeiter** *n.* [ME f. OF *countrefet, -fait*, past part. of *contrefaire* f. Rmc]

■ *adj.* **1** forged, fake, fraudulent, imitation, bogus, spurious, sham, *colloq.* phony. **2** make-believe, sham, pretended, feigned, insincere, fake, faked, false, artificial, meretricious, pseudo, factitious, fictitious, synthetic, unreal, simulated, *colloq.* pretend. ● *n.* fake, imitation, forgery, reproduction, *colloq.* phony. ● *v.* **1** forge, falsify; copy, reproduce, imitate. **2** feign, pretend, simulate, put on, fake, make a pretense of, dissemble, sham, affect. □ **counterfeiter** forger, *Brit.* coiner.

counterintelligence /kównterintélijens/ *n.* = COUNTERESPIONAGE.

counterirritant /kównterírit'nt/ *n.* **1** *Med.* something used to produce surface irritation of the skin, thereby counteracting more painful symptoms. **2** anything resembling a counterirritant in its effects. □□ **counterirritation** /-iritáyshen/ *n.*

countermand *v.* & *n.* ● *v.tr.* /kówntermánd/ **1** *Mil.* **a** revoke (an order or command). **b** recall (forces, etc.) by a contrary order. **2** cancel an order for (goods, etc.). ● *n.* /kówntermand/ an order revoking a previous one. [ME f. OF *contremander* f. med.L *contramandare* (as CONTRA-, *mandare* order)]

■ *v.* **1a, 2** see CANCEL *v.* 1a.

countermarch *v.* & *n.* ● *v.intr.* & *tr.* /kówntermaárch/ esp. *Mil.* march or cause to march in the opposite direction, e.g., with the front marchers turning and marching back through the ranks. ● *n.* /kówntermaarch/ an act of countermarching.

countermeasure /kówntermezher/ *n.* an action taken to counteract a danger, threat, etc.

■ see PREVENTIVE *n.*

countermine *n.* & *v.* ● *n.* /kówntermin/ **1** *Mil.* **a** a mine dug to intercept another dug by an enemy. **b** a submarine mine sunk to explode an enemy's mines. **2** a counterplot. ● *v.tr.* /kówntermín/ make a countermine against.

countermove *n.* & *v.* ● *n.* /kówntermoov/ a move or action in opposition to another. ● *v.intr.* /kówntermoov/ make a countermove. □□ **countermovement** *n.*

counteroffensive /kównterefénsiv/ *n.* **1** *Mil.* an attack made from a defensive position in order to effect an escape. **2** any attack made from a defensive position.

counterpane /kównterpayn/ *n.* a bedspread. [alt. (with assim. to *pane* in obs. sense 'cloth') f. obs. *counterpoint* f. OF *contrepointe* alt. f. cou(*l*)*tepointe* f. med.L *culcita puncta* quilted mattress]

counterpart /kównterpaart/ *n.* **1 a** a person or thing extremely like another. **b** a person or thing forming a natural complement or equivalent to another. **2** *Law* one of two copies of a legal document. □ **counterpart funds** funds, etc., in a local currency equivalent to goods, etc., received from abroad.

■ **1** see MATCH[1] *n.* 2c.

counterplot *n.* & *v.* ● *n.* /kównterplot/ a plot intended to defeat another plot. ● *v.* /kównterplót/ (**-plotted, -plotting**) **1** *intr.* make a counterplot. **2** *tr.* make a counterplot against.

counterpoint /kównterpoynt/ *n.* & *v.* ● *n.* **1** *Mus.* **a** the art or technique of setting, writing, or playing a melody or melodies in conjunction with another, according to fixed rules. **b** a melody played in conjunction with another. **2** a contrasting argument, plot, idea, or literary theme, etc., used to set off the main element. ● *v.tr.* **1** *Mus.* add counterpoint to. **2** set (an argument, plot, etc.) in contrast to (a main element). □ **strict counterpoint** an academic exercise in writing counterpoint, not necessarily intended as a composition. [OF *contrepoint* f. med.L *contrapunctum* pricked or marked opposite, i.e., to the original melody (as CONTRA-, *pungere punct-* prick)]

■ *n.* **1** polyphony.

counterpoise *n.* & *v.* ● *n.* /kównterpoyz/ **1** a force, etc., equivalent to another on the opposite side. **2** a state of equilibrium. **3** a counterbalancing weight. ● *v.tr.* /kównterpóyz/ **1** counterbalance. **2** compensate. **3** bring into or

keep in equilibrium. [ME f. OF *contrepeis*, *-pois*, *contrepeser* (as COUNTER-, *peis, pois* f. L *pensum* weight: cf. POISE[1])]

■ *v.* **1** see BALANCE *v.* 2.

counterproductive /kównterprodúktiv/ *adj.* having the opposite of the desired effect.

■ see PREJUDICIAL.

counterreformation /kówntereréformáyshen/ *n.* **1** (**Counter-Reformation**) *hist.* the reform of the Roman Catholic Church in the 16th and 17th centuries that took place in response to the Protestant Reformation. **2** a reformation running counter to another.

counterrevolution /kówntererévelooshen/ *n.* a revolution opposing a former one or reversing its results. □□ **counterrevolutionary** *adj.* & *n.* (*pl.* **-ies**).

counterscarp /kównterskaarp/ *n.* *Mil.* the outer wall or slope of a ditch in a fortification. [F *contrescarpe* f. It. *contrascarpa* (as CONTRA-, SCARP)]

countershaft /kówntershaft/ *n.* an intermediate shaft driven by a main shaft and transmitting motion to a particular machine, etc.

countersign /kówntersin/ *v.* & *n.* ● *v.tr.* **1** add a signature to (a document already signed by another). **2** ratify. ● *n.* **1** a watchword or password spoken to a person on guard. **2** a mark used for identification, etc. □□ **countersignature** /-signecher/ *n.* [F *contresigner* (v.), *contresigne* (n.) f. It. *contrasegno* (as COUNTER-, SIGN)]

■ *v.* **1** see SIGN *v.* 1. **2** see ENDORSE 2. ● *n.* **1** see PASSWORD.

countersink /kówntersingk/ *v.tr.* (*past* and *past part.* **-sunk**) **1** enlarge and bevel (the rim of a hole) so that a screw or bolt can be inserted flush with the surface. **2** sink (a screw, etc.) in such a hole.

counterstroke /kównterstrōk/ *n.* a blow given in return for another.

countertenor /kówntertener/ *n.* *Mus.* **1 a** the highest adult male singing voice, above tenor. **b** a singer with this voice. **2** a part written for countertenor. [ME f. F *contre-teneur* f. obs. It. *contratenore* (as CONTRA-, TENOR)]

countertop /kówntertop/ *n.* a horizontal, flat work surface, as in a kitchen.

countervail /kówntervayl/ *v.* **1** *tr.* counterbalance. **2** *tr.* & *intr.* (often foll. by *against*) oppose forcefully and usu. successfully. □ **countervailing duty** a tax put on imports to offset a subsidy in the exporting country or a tax on similar goods not from abroad. [ME f. AF *contrevaloir* f. L *contra valēre* be of worth against]

■ **1** see BALANCE *v.* 2. **2** see RESIST *v.* 1, 2.

counterweight /kównterwayt/ *n.* a counterbalancing weight.

countess /kówntis/ *n.* **1** the wife or widow of a count or an earl. **2** a woman holding the rank of count or earl. [ME f. OF *contesse*, *cuntesse*, f. LL *comitissa* fem. of *comes* COUNT[2]]

■ see PEER[2] *n.* 1.

countinghouse /kówntinghows/ *n.* where accounts are kept.

countless /kówntlis/ *adj.* too many to be counted.

countrified /kúntrifid/ *adj.* (also **countryfied**) often *derog.* rural or rustic, esp. of manners, appearance, etc. [past part. of *countrify* f. COUNTRY]

■ see RUSTIC *adj.* 2.

country /kúntree/ *n.* (*pl.* **-ies**) **1 a** the territory of a nation with its own government; a nation. **b** a territory possessing its own language, people, culture, etc. **2** (often *attrib.*) rural districts as opposed to towns and cities or the capital (*a cottage in the country; a country town*). **3** the land of a person's birth or citizenship; a fatherland. **4 a** a territory, esp. an area of interest or knowledge. **b** a region associated with a particular person, esp. a writer (*Faulkner country*). **5** a national population, esp. as voters (*the country won't stand for it*). □ **across country** not keeping to roads. **country and west-**

ern rural or cowboy music originating in the US, and usu. accompanied by a guitar, etc. **country club** a golfing and social club, often in a rural setting. **country cousin** often *derog.* a person with a countrified appearance or manners. **country dance** a traditional sort of dance, esp. English, with couples facing each other in long lines. **country gentleman** a gentleman with landed property. **country music** = *country and western.* **go** (or **appeal**) **to the country** *Brit.* test public opinion by dissolving Parliament and holding a general election. [ME f. OF *cuntree,* f. med.L *contrata* (*terra*) (land) lying opposite (CONTRA)]

■ **1** nation, state, power; territory, *formal esp. Law* realm. **2** countryside, rural area, provinces, hinterlands, esp. *Austral.* outback, *literary* champaign, *sl.* sticks. **3** (native) land, homeland, fatherland, motherland, mother country. **4 a** see TERRITORY 1, 7, SPHERE *n.* 4a. **b** territory, land, terrain. **5** see POPULATION 1a.
□ **country cousin** see RUSTIC *n.*

countryfied var. of COUNTRIFIED.

countryman /kúntreemən/ *n.* (*pl.* **-men**; *fem.* **countrywoman,** *pl.* **-women**) **1** a person living in a rural area. **2 a** a person of one's own country or district. **b** (often in *comb.*) a person from a specified country or district (*north-countryman*).
■ **1** see RUSTIC *n.*

countryside /kúntreesíd/ *n.* **1 a** a rural area. **b** rural areas in general. **2** the inhabitants of a rural area.
■ **1** see COUNTRY 2.

countrywide /kúntreewíd/ *adj.* extending throughout a nation.

county /kówntee/ *n.* & *adj.* ● *n.* (*pl.* **-ies**) **1** *US* a political and administrative division of a state. **2** any of the territorial divisions of some countries, forming the chief unit of local administration. □ **county court** a judicial court for civil and criminal cases. **county seat** the administrative capital of a county. [ME f. AF *counté,* OF *conté, cunté,* f. L *comitatus* (as COUNT²)]

coup /koo/ *n.* (*pl.* **coups** /kooz/) **1** a notable or successful stroke or move. **2** = COUP D´ÉTAT. [F f. med.L *colpus* blow: see COPE¹]
■ **1** see TRIUMPH *n.* 1b.

coup de grâce /koo də graás/ *n.* a finishing stroke, esp. to kill a wounded animal or person. [F, lit. stroke of grace]
■ see KILL¹ *n.* 1.

coup de main /koo də mán/ *n.* a sudden vigorous attack. [F, lit. stroke of the hand]

coup d'état /koo daytaá/ *n.* a violent or illegal seizure of power. [F, lit. stroke of the state]
■ see REVOLT *n.*

coupe¹ /koop/ *n.* **1** a shallow glass or dish used for serving fruit, ice-cream, etc. **2** fruit, ice-cream, etc., served in this. [F, = goblet]

coupe² /koop/ *n.* (also **coupé** /koopáy/) **1** a two-door car with a hard top. **2** *hist.* a four-wheeled enclosed carriage for two passengers and a driver. [F, past part. of *couper* cut (formed as COUP)]

couple /kúpəl/ *n.* & *v.* ● *n.* **1** (usu. foll. by *of*; often as *sing.*) **a** two (*a couple of girls*). **b** about two (*a couple of hours*). **2** (often as *sing.*) **a** a married or engaged pair. **b** a pair of partners in a dance, a game, etc. **c** a pair of rafters. **3** (*pl.* **couple**) a pair of hunting dogs (*six couple of hounds*). **4** (in *pl.*) a pair of joined collars used for holding hounds together. **5** *Mech.* a pair of equal and parallel forces acting in opposite directions, and tending to cause rotation about an axis perpendicular to the plane containing them. ● *v.* **1** *tr.* fasten or link together; connect (esp. railroad car). **2** *tr.* (often foll. by *together, with*) associate in thought or speech (*papers coupled their names; couple our congratulations with our best wishes*). **3** *intr.* copulate. **4** *tr. Physics* connect (oscillators) with a coupling. [ME f. OF *cople, cuple, copler, cupler* f. L *copulare,* L COPULA]

■ *n.* **1 a** two; pair, brace, yoke. **b** (*a couple of*) a few, a handful (of), two or three; see also SEVERAL *adj.* **2** pair, duo, twosome. ● *v.* **1** join, connect, link, fasten, yoke,

lock, combine, unite. **2** see ASSOCIATE *v.* 1. **3** see *make love* (LOVE).

coupler /kúplər/ *n.* **1** *Mus.* **a** a device in an organ for connecting two manuals, or a manual with pedals, so that they both sound when only one is played. **b** (also **octave coupler**) a similar device for connecting notes with their octaves above or below. **2** anything that connects two things, esp. a transformer used for connecting electric circuits.
■ **2** see TERMINAL *n.* 4.

couplet /kúplit/ *n. Prosody* two successive lines of verse, usu. rhyming and of the same length. [F dimin. of *couple,* formed as COUPLE]

coupling /kúpling/ *n.* **1 a** a link connecting railroad car, etc. **b** a device for connecting parts of machinery. **2** *Physics* a connection between two systems, causing one to oscillate when the other does so. **3** *Mus.* **a** the arrangement of items on a phonograph record. **b** each such item. **4** (an act of) sexual intercourse.
■ **1** see JUNCTION 3. **4** see SEX *n.* 5.

coupon /kóopon, kyóo-/ *n.* **1** a form, etc., in a newspaper, magazine, etc., that may be filled in and sent as an application for a purchase, information, etc., or that may be redeemed for a discount on a product or service. **2** *Brit.* an entry form for a soccer pool or other competition. **3** a voucher given with a retail purchase, a certain number of which entitle the holder to a discount, etc. **4 a** a detachable ticket entitling the holder to a ration of food, clothes, etc., esp. in wartime. **b** a similar ticket entitling the holder to payment, goods, a discount, services, etc. [F, = piece cut off f. *couper* cut: see COUPE²]

courage /kərij, kúr-/ *n.* the ability to disregard fear; bravery. □ **courage of one's convictions** the courage to act on one's beliefs. **lose courage** become less brave. **pluck up** (or **take**) **courage** muster one's courage. **take one's courage in both hands** nerve oneself to a venture. [ME f. OF *corage,* f. L *cor* heart]
■ courageousness, bravery, valor, boldness, intrepidity, gallantry, dauntlessness, daring, fearlessness, heroism, nerve, pluck, *colloq.* grit, guts, spunk, sand, *sl.* moxie, *Brit. sl.* bottle,

courageous /kəráyjəs/ *adj.* brave; fearless. □□ **courageously** *adv.* **courageousness** *n.* [ME f. AF *corageous,* OF *corageus* (as COURAGE)]
■ brave, valiant, valorous, bold, intrepid, unafraid, gallant, dauntless, undaunted, daring, fearless, heroic, plucky, audacious, stalwart, *archaic or joc.* doughty, *colloq.* spunky, gutsy.

courante /kooraant/ *n.* **1** *hist.* a running or gliding dance. **2** *Mus.* the music used for this, esp. as a movement of a suite. [F, fem. pres. part. (as noun) of *courir* run f. L *currere*]

courgette /koorzhét/ *n. Brit.* = ZUCCHINI. [F, dimin. of *courge* gourd]

courier /kóoreeər, kár-, kúr-/ *n.* **1** a person employed, usu. by a travel company, to guide and assist a group of tourists. **2** a special messenger. [ME f. obs. F, f. It. *corriere,* & f. OF *coreor,* both f. L *currere* run]
■ **2** see MESSENGER.

course /kawrs/ *n.* & *v.* ● *n.* **1** a continuous onward movement or progression. **2 a** a line along which a person or thing moves; a direction taken (*has changed course; the course of the winding river*). **b** a correct or intended direction or line of movement. **c** the direction taken by a ship or aircraft. **3 a** the ground on which a race (or other sport involving extensive linear movement) takes place. **b** a series of fences, hurdles, or other obstacles to be crossed in a race, etc. **4 a** a series of lectures, lessons, etc., in a particular subject. **b** a book for such a course (*A Modern French Course*). **5** any of the successive parts of a meal. **6** *Med.* a sequence of medical treatment, etc. (*prescribed a course of antibiotics*). **7** a line of conduct (*disappointed by the course he took*). **8** *Archit.* a continuous horizontal layer of brick, stone, etc., in a building. **9** a channel in which water flows. **10** the pursuit of game (esp. hares) with hounds, esp. greyhounds, by sight rather than scent. **11** *Naut.* a sail on a square-rigged ship (*fore* course; *main course*). ● v. **1** *intr.* (esp. of liquid) run, esp. fast (*blood coursed through his veins*). **2** *tr.* (also *absol.*) **a** use (hounds) to hunt. **b** pursue (hares, etc.) in hunting. □ **the course of nature** ordinary events or procedure. **in the course of** during. **in the course of time** as time goes by; eventually. **a matter of course** the natural or expected thing. **of course** naturally; as is or was to be expected; admittedly. **on** (or **off**) **course** following (or deviating from) the desired direction or goal. **run** (or **take**) **its course** (esp. of an illness) complete its natural development. □□ **courser** n. (in sense 2 of v.). [ME f. OF *cours* f. L *cursus* f. *currere* curs- run]

■ n. **2** path, way, orbit, route, run, track, ambit, line, circuit, passage; direction, tack. **4** a class, seminar. **9** see CHANNEL[1] n. 5a, 6. ● v. **1** see RUN v. 11a, 13. □ **in the course of time** see *eventually* (EVENTUAL). **of course** naturally, certainly, positively, obviously, definitely, assuredly, by all means; undoubtedly, indubitably, without (a) doubt, no doubt, absolutely, that goes without saying, *colloq.* (for) sure, you bet, *sl.* you bet your boots *or* bottom dollar; admittedly, needless to say, it goes without saying (that), to be sure.

courser[1] /káwrsər/ n. *poet.* a swift horse. [ME f. OF *corsier* f. Rmc]

courser[2] /káwrsər/ n. any fast-running ploverlike bird of the genus *Cursorius*, native to Africa and Asia, having long legs and a slender bill. [LL *cursorius* adapted for running]

court /kawrt/ n. & v. ● n. **1** (in full **court of law**) **a** a judge or assembly of judges or other persons acting as a tribunal in civil and criminal cases. **b** = COURTROOM. **2 a** an enclosed quadrangular area for games, which may be open or covered (*tennis court*; *squash court*). **b** an area marked out for lawn tennis, etc. (*hit the ball out of court*). **3 a** a small enclosed street in a town, having a yard surrounded by houses, and adjoining a larger street. **b** *Brit.* = COURTYARD. **c** the name of a large house, block of apartments, street, etc. (*Grosvenor Court*). **d** (at Cambridge University) a college quadrangle. **e** a subdivision of a building, usu. a large hall extending to the ceiling with galleries and staircases. **4 a** the establishment, retinue, and courtiers of a sovereign. **b** a sovereign and his or her councilors, constituting a ruling power. **c** a sovereign's residence. **d** an assembly held by a sovereign; a state reception. **5** attention paid to a person whose favor, love, or interest is sought (*paid court to her*). **6 a** the qualified members of a company or a corporation. **c** a meeting of a court. ● v.tr. **1 a** try to win the affection or favor of (a person). **b** pay amorous attention to (*courting couples*). **2** seek to win (applause, fame, etc.). **3** invite (misfortune) by one's actions (*you are courting disaster*). □ **court card** *Brit.* = *face card*. **court circular** *Brit.* a daily report of royal court affairs, published in some newspapers. **court dress** formal dress worn at a royal court. **court of record** a court whose proceedings are recorded and available as evidence of fact. **court reporter** a stenographer who makes a verbatim record and transcription of the proceedings in a court of law. **Court of St. James's** the British sovereign's court. **court order** a direction issued by a court or a judge, usu. requiring a person to do or not do something. **court tennis** the original form of tennis played on an indoor court. **go to court** take legal action. **in court** appearing as a party or an advocate in a court of law. **out of court 1** (of a plaintiff) not entitled to be heard. **2** (of a settlement) arranged before a hearing or judgment can take place. **3** not worthy of consideration (*that suggestion is out of court*). [ME f. AF *curt*, OF *cort*, ult. f. L *cohors, -hortis* yard, retinue: (v.) after OIt. *corteare*, OF *courtoyer*]

■ n. **1** see TRIBUNAL 2. **4 a** see TRAIN n. 4. ● v. **1 a** see CULTIVATE 3b. **b** woo, pay suit *or* court to, seek the hand of, press one's suit with, set one's cap at, go after, chase, pursue, *archaic* make love to.

court bouillon /ko͞or bo͞olyón, -yáwN, káwr-; *Fr.* ko͞orbo͞oyón/ n. (*pl.* **courts bouillons** /ko͞or bo͞olyónz, -yawnz; *Fr.* ko͞or bo͞oyón/) stock usu. made from wine, veg-

etables, etc., often used in fish dishes. [F f. *court* short + BOUILLON]

courteous /kárteeəs/ adj. polite, kind, or considerate in manner; well-mannered. □□ **courteously** adv. **courteousness** n. [ME f. OF *corteis, curteis* f. Rmc (as COURT): assim. to words in -OUS]

■ polite, well-mannered, well-behaved, chivalrous, gentlemanly, ladylike, well-bred, polished, urbane, civilized, respectful, civil, courtly, proper, decorous, tactful, considerate, diplomatic, *joc.* couth.

courtesan /káwrtizán/ n. *literary* **1** a prostitute, esp. one with wealthy or upper-class clients. **2** the mistress of a wealthy man. [F *courtisane* f. It. *cortigiana*, fem. of *cortigiano* courtier f. *corte* COURT]

■ **1** see PROSTITUTE n. 1a.

courtesy /kártisee/ n. (*pl.* **-ies**) **1** courteous behavior; good manners. **2** a courteous act. **3** *archaic* = CURTSY. □ **by courtesy** by favor, not by right. **by courtesy of** with the formal permission of (a person, etc.). **courtesy light** a light in a car that is switched on by opening a door. [ME f. OF *curtesie, co(u)rtesie* f. *curteis*, etc., COURTEOUS]

■ **1** politeness, courtliness, politesse, chivalry, courteousness, respect, respectfulness, good manners, formality, civility.

courthouse /káwrthows/ n. **1** a building in which a judicial court is held. **2** a building containing the administrative offices of a county.

courtier /káwrteeər/ n. a person who attends or frequents a sovereign's court. [ME f. AF *courte(i)our*, f. OF f. *cortoyer* be present at court]

courtly /káwrtlee/ adj. (**courtlier, courtliest**) **1** polished or refined in manners. **2** obsequious. **3** punctilious. □ **courtly love** the conventional medieval tradition of knightly love for a lady, and the etiquette used in its (esp. literary) expression. □□ **courtliness** n. [COURT]

■ **1, 3** see *polished* (POLISH v. 2). **2** see SMOOTH adj. 9.

court-martial /káwrt maarshəl/ n. & v. ● n. (*pl.* **courts-martial**) a judicial court for trying members of the armed services. ● v.tr. try by a court-martial.

courtroom /káwrtro͞om, -ro͝om/ n. the place or room in which a court of law meets.

■ see BAR[1] n. 5d.

courtship /káwrtship/ n. **1 a** a courting with a view to marriage. **b** the courting behavior of male animals, birds, etc. **c** a period of courting. **2** an attempt, often protracted, to gain advantage by flattery, attention, etc.

courtyard /káwrtyaard/ n. an area enclosed by walls or buildings, often opening off a street.

■ see AREA 5.

couscous /ko͞osko͞os/ n. a N. African dish of semolina steamed over broth, often with meat or fruit added. [F f. Arab. *kuskus* f. *kaskasa* to pound]

cousin /kúzən/ n. **1** (also **first cousin, cousin-german**) the child of one's uncle or aunt. **2** (usu. in *pl.*) applied to the people of kindred races or nations (*our British cousins*). **3** *hist.* a title formerly used by a sovereign in addressing another sovereign or a noble of his or her own country. □ **second cousin** a child of one's parent's first cousin. □□ **cousinhood** n. **cousinly** adj. **cousinship** n. [ME f. OF *cosin, cusin*, f. L *consobrinus* mother's sister's child]

couth /ko͞oth/ adj. *joc.* cultured; well-mannered. [back-form. as antonym of UNCOUTH]

couture /ko͞oto͞or, -týr/ n. the design and manufacture of fashionable clothes; = HAUTE COUTURE. [F, = sewing, dressmaking]

couturier /ko͞oto͞oree-ay, -eeər/ n. (*fem.* **couturière** /-reeáir/) a fashion designer or dressmaker. [F]

■ see DRESSMAKER.

couvade /ko͞ováad/ n. a custom by which a father appears to

/.../ **pronunciation**	● **part of speech**
□ **phrases, idioms, and compounds**	
□□ **derivatives**	■ **synonym section**
cross-references appear in SMALL CAPITALS or *italics*	

undergo labor and childbirth when his child is being born. [F f. *couver* hatch f. L *cubare* lie down]

couvert /kōōváir/ *n.* = COVER *n.* 6. [F]

covalency /kōváylənsee/ *n. Chem.* **1** the linking of atoms by a covalent bond. **2** the number of pairs of electrons an atom can share with another.

covalent /kōváylənt/ *adj. Chem.* of, relating to, or characterized by covalency. □ **covalent bond** *Chem.* a bond formed by sharing of electrons usu. in pairs by two atoms in a molecule. □□ **covalence** *n.* **covalently** *adv.* [CO- + *valent*, after *trivalent*, etc.]

cove[1] /kōv/ *n. & v.* ● *n.* **1** a small, esp. sheltered, bay or creek. **2** a sheltered recess. **3** *Archit.* a concave arch or arched molding, esp. one formed at the junction of a wall with a ceiling. ● *v.tr. Archit.* **1** provide (a room, ceiling, etc.) with a cove. **2** slope (the sides of a fireplace) inward. [OE *cofa* chamber f. Gmc]
■ *n.* **1** see CREEK 1.

cove[2] /kōv/ *n. Brit. sl. archaic* a fellow; a chap. [16th-c. cant: orig. unkn.]

coven /kúvən/ *n.* an assembly of witches. [var. of *covent*; see CONVENT]

covenant /kúvənənt/ *n. & v.* ● *n.* **1** an agreement; a contract. **2** *Law* a contract drawn up under a seal, esp. undertaking to make regular payments to a charity. **b** a clause of a covenant. **3** (**Covenant**) *Bibl.* the agreement between God and the Israelites (see *Ark of the Covenant*). ● *v.tr. & intr.* agree, esp. by legal covenant. □ **land of the Covenant** Canaan. □□ **covenantal** /-nánt'l/ *adj.* **covenantor** *n.* [ME f. OF, pres. part. of *co(n)venir*, formed as CONVENE]
■ *n.* **1, 2** see AGREEMENT 3. ● *v.* see UNDERTAKE 2.

covenanted /kúvənəntid/ *adj.* bound by a covenant.

covenanter /kúvənəntər, -nantər/ *n.* **1** a person who covenants. **2** (**Covenanter**) *hist.* an adherent of the National Covenant of the Solemn League and Covenant in 17th-c. Scotland, in support of Presbyterianism.

cover /kúvər/ *v. & n.* ● *v.tr.* **1 a** (often foll. by *with*) protect or conceal by means of a cloth, lid, etc. **b** prevent the perception or discovery of; conceal (*to cover my embarrassment*). **2 a** extend over; occupy the whole surface of (*covered in dirt; covered with writing*). **b** (often foll. by *with*) strew thickly or thoroughly (*covered the floor with straw*). **c** lie over; be a covering to (*the blanket scarcely covered him*). **3 a** protect; clothe. **b** (as **covered** *adj.*) wearing a hat; having a roof. **4** include; comprise; deal with (*the talk covered recent discoveries*). **5** travel (a specified distance) (*covered sixty miles*). **6** *Journalism* **a** report (events, a meeting, etc.). **b** investigate as a reporter. **7** be enough to defray (expenses, a bill, etc.) (*$20 should cover it*). **8** a *refl.* take precautionary measures so as to protect oneself (*had covered myself by saying I might be late*). **b** (*absol.*; foll. by *for*) deputize or stand in for (a colleague, etc.) (*will you cover for me?*). **9** *Mil.* **a** aim a gun, etc., at. **b** (of a fortress, guns, etc.) command (a territory). **c** stand behind (a person in the front rank). **d** protect (an exposed person, etc.) by being able to return fire. **10** (also *absol.*) (in some card games) play a card higher than (one already played to the same trick). **11** (of a stallion, a bull, etc.) copulate with. ● *n.* **1** something that covers or protects, esp.: **a** a lid. **b** the binding of a book. **c** either board of this. **d** an envelope or the wrapping of a mailed package (*under separate cover*). **e** the outer case of a pneumatic tire. **f** (in *pl.*) bedclothes. **2** a hiding place; a shelter. **3** woods or undergrowth sheltering game or covering the ground (see COVERT). **4 a** a pretense; a screen (*under cover of humility*). **b** a spy's pretended identity or activity, intended as concealment. **c** *Mil.* a supporting force protecting an advance party from attack. **5** a place setting at table, esp. in a restaurant. □ **break cover** (of an animal, esp. game, or a hunted person) leave a place of shelter, esp. vegetation. **cover charge** an extra charge levied per head in a restaurant, nightclub, etc. **cover crop** a crop grown for the protection and enrichment of the soil. **cover girl** a female model whose picture appears on magazine covers, etc. **cover in** provide with a roof, etc. **covering** (or **cover**) **letter** (or **note**) an explanatory letter sent with an enclosure. **cover note** *Brit.* a temporary certificate of cur-

rent insurance. **cover story** a news story in a magazine, that is illustrated or advertised on the front cover. **cover one's tracks** conceal evidence of what one has done. **cover up 1** completely cover or conceal. **2** conceal (circumstances, etc., esp. illicitly) (also *absol.*: *refused to cover up for them*). **cover-up** *n.* an act of concealing circumstances, esp. illicitly. **from cover to cover** from beginning to end of a book, etc. **take cover** use a natural or prepared shelter against an attack. □□ **coverable** *adj.* **coverer** *n.* [ME f. OF *covrir, cuvrir* f. L *cooperire* (as CO-, *operire opert-* cover)]
■ *v.* **1 a** conceal, hide, bury, mask, shroud, obscure; enclose, envelop, wrap, swaddle. **b** see HIDE[1] *v.* 3. **2 a** overlie, spread *or* extend over, overspread, lie on, coat, blanket. **b** see STREW. **3 a** protect, shelter, shield, screen; dress (up), clothe, garb, robe, sheathe, *formal* attire. **4** include, comprehend, take in, deal with, comprise, contain, embody, incorporate, account for, take into account. **5** traverse, complete, pass *or* travel over, travel, cross. **7** pay *or* compensate for, defray, be enough *or* sufficient for; counter, offset, counterbalance, make up for. **8 b** deputize, act, take over responsibility, stand *or* sit in, substitute, take over, run things, hold the fort. **9 b** guard, defend, command. ● *n.* **1 a** lid, top, cap, covering. **b** binding, boards, wrapper, dust jacket, jacket. **f** (*covers*) blankets, bedclothes, bedding, covering(s), (bed) linen, quilt, eiderdown, duvet, comfort(er). **2** shelter, hiding place, hideout, retreat, refuge, *colloq.* hidey-hole; blind, *Brit.* hide; protection, concealment. **4 a** cloak, screen, disguise, pretense, front, camouflage, smokescreen, cover-up, mask, covering. □ **cover up 1** see CONCEAL 2. **2** see HIDE[1] *v.* 3. **cover-up** see PRETENSE 2b.

coverage /kúvərij/ *n.* **1** an area or an amount covered. **2** *Journalism* the amount of press, etc., publicity received by a particular story, person, etc. **3** a risk covered by an insurance policy. **4** an area reached by a particular broadcasting station or advertising medium.

coverall /kúvərawl/ *n. & adj.* ● *n.* **1** something that covers entirely. **2** (usu. in *pl.*) a full-length protective outer garment often zipped up the front. ● *attrib.adj.* covering entirely (*a coverall term*).

covering /kúvəring/ *n.* something that covers, esp. a bedspread, blanket, etc., or clothing.

coverlet /kúvərlit/ *n.* a bedspread. [ME f. AF *covrelet, -lit* f. OF *covrir* cover + *lit* bed]
■ see SPREAD *n.* 10.

covert /kōvərt, kú-/ *adj. & n.* ● *adj.* secret or disguised (*a covert glance; covert operations*). ● *n.* **1** a shelter, esp. a thicket hiding game. **2** a feather covering the base of a bird's flight feather. □□ **covertly** *adv.* **covertness** *n.* [ME f. OF *covert* past part. of *covrir* COVER]
■ *adj.* see SECRET *adj.* 4. ● *n.* **1** see THICKET.

coverture /kúvərchər/ *n.* **1** covering; shelter. **2** *Law hist.* the position of a married woman, considered to be under her husband's protection. [ME f. OF (as COVERT)]

covet /kúvit/ *v.tr.* desire greatly (esp. something belonging to another person) (*coveted her friend's earrings*). □□ **covetable** *adj.* [ME f. OF *cu-, coveitier* f. Rmc]
■ see DESIRE *v.* 1.

covetous /kúvitəs/ *adj.* (usu. foll. by *of*) **1** greatly desirous (esp. of another person's property). **2** grasping; avaricious. □□ **covetously** *adv.* **covetousness** *n.* [ME f. OF *coveitous* f. Gallo-Roman]
■ **1** see HUNGRY 3a. **2** see *avaricious* (AVARICE).

covey /kúvee/ *n.* (*pl.* **-eys**) **1** a brood of partridges. **2** a small party or group of people or things. [ME f. OF *covee* f. Rmc f. L *cubare* lie]
■ **1** see FLIGHT[1] *n.* 3a. **2** see GROUP *n.* 1.

covin /kúvin/ *n.* **1** *Law* a conspiracy to commit a crime, etc., against a third party. **2** *archaic* fraud; deception. [ME f. OF *covin(e)* f. med.L *convenium -ia* f. *convenire*: see CONVENE]

coving *n.* = COVE[1] *n.* 3.

cow[1] /kow/ *n.* **1** a fully grown female of any bovine animal, esp. of the genus *Bos*, used as a source of milk and beef. **2** the female of other large animals, esp. the elephant, whale,

and seal. **3** *sl. derog.* **a** a woman, esp. a coarse or unpleasant one. **b** *Austral.* & *NZ* an unpleasant person, thing, situation, etc. □ **cow parsley** a tall hedgerow plant, *Anthriscus sylvestris*, having lacelike umbels of flowers resembling Queen Anne's lace. **cow tree** a tree, *Brosimum galactodendron*, native to S. America, yielding a milklike juice which is used as a substitute for cow's milk. **till the cows come home** *colloq.* an indefinitely long time. [OE *cū* f. Gmc, rel. to L *bos*, Gk *bous*]
■ **3 a** see BAG *n.* 5. □ **till the cows come home** see EVER 1.

cow² /kow/ *v.tr.* (usu. in *passive*) intimidate or dispirit (*cowed by ill-treatment*). [prob. f. ON *kúga* oppress]
■ see INTIMIDATE.

cowage var. of COWHAGE.

coward /kówərd/ *n. & adj.* ● *n.* a person who is easily frightened or intimidated by danger or pain. ● *adj. poet.* easily frightened. [ME f. OF *cuard, couard* ult. f. L *cauda* tail]
■ *n.* poltroon, craven, baby, mouse, milksop, *archaic* scaramouch, *colloq.* sissy, yellowbelly.

cowardice /kówərdis/ *n.* a lack of bravery. [ME f. OF *couardise* (as COWARD)]
■ cowardliness, chickenheartedness, faintheartedness, timidity, timorousness, pusillanimity.

cowardly /kówərdlee/ *adj. & adv.* ● *adj.* **1** of or like a coward; lacking courage. **2** (of an action) done against one who cannot retaliate. ● *adv. archaic* like a coward; with cowardice. □□ **cowardliness** *n.*
■ *adj.* **1** timid, fainthearted, timorous, chickenhearted, chicken-livered, lily-livered, craven, fearful, frightened, afraid, scared, dastardly, pusillanimous, *colloq.* yellow, yellow-bellied, chicken.

cowbane /kówbayn/ *n.* = *water hemlock*.

cowbell /kówbel/ *n.* **1** a bell worn around a cow's neck for easy location of the animal. **2** a similar bell used as a percussion instrument.

cowberry /kówberee/ *n.* (*pl.* **-ies**) **1** an evergreen shrub, *Vaccinium vitis-idaea*, bearing dark-red berries. **2** the berry of this plant.

cowboy /kówboy/ *n.* **1** (*fem.* **cowgirl**) a person who herds and tends cattle, esp. in the western US. **2** this as a conventional figure in American folklore, esp. in films. **3** *colloq.* an unscrupulous or reckless person in business, esp. an unqualified one.

cowcatcher /kówkachər/ *n.* a peaked metal frame at the front of a locomotive for pushing aside obstacles on the line.

cower /kowr/ *v.intr.* **1** crouch or shrink back, esp. in fear; cringe. **2** stand or squat in a bent position. [ME f. MLG *kūren* lie in wait, of unkn. orig.]
■ **1** see CRINGE *v.* 1.

cowfish /kówfish/ *n.* **1** any of several plant-eating marine mammals, e.g., the manatee. **2** a marine fish, *Lactoria diaphana*, covered in hard bony plates and having hornlike spines over the eyes and on other parts of the body.

cowhage /kówij/ *n.* (also **cowage**) a climbing plant, *Mucuna pruritum*, having hairy pods which cause stinging and itching. [Hindi *kawāñch*]

cowhand /kówhand/ *n.* = COWBOY *n.* 1.

cowherd /kówhərd/ *n.* a person who tends cattle.

cowhide /kówhīd/ *n.* **1 a** a cow's hide. **b** leather made from this. **2** a leather whip made from cowhide.

cowhouse /kówhows/ *n.* esp. *Brit.* a shed or shelter for cows.

cowl /kowl/ *n.* **1 a** the hood of a monk's habit. **b** a loose hood. **c** a monk's hooded habit. **2** the hood-shaped covering of a chimney or ventilating shaft. **3** the removable cover of a vehicle or aircraft engine. □□ **cowled** *adj.* (in sense 1). [OE *cugele, cūle* f. eccl.L *cuculla* f. L *cucullus* hood of a cloak]

cowlick /kówlik/ *n.* a projecting lock of hair.

cowling /kówling/ *n.* = COWL 3.

cowman /kówmən/ *n.* (*pl.* **-men**) **1** = COWHERD. **2** a cattle owner.

coworker /kō-wŕkər/ *n.* a person who works in collaboration with another.
■ see COLLEAGUE.

cowpat /kówpat/ *n.* a flat, round piece of cow dung.

cowpea /kówpee/ *n.* **1** a plant of the pea family, *Vigna unguiculata*, grown esp. in the southern US for forage and green manure. **2** its edible seed. (Also called **black-eyed pea**).

cowpoke /kówpōk/ *n.* = COWBOY 1.

cowpox /kówpoks/ *n.* a disease of cows, of which the virus was formerly used in vaccination against smallpox.

cowpuncher /kówpunchər/ *n.* = COWBOY 1.

cowrie /kówree/ *n.* (also **cowry**) (*pl.* **-ies**) **1** any gastropod mollusk of the family Cypraeidae, having a smooth, glossy, and usu. brightly colored shell. **2** its shell, esp. used as money in parts of Africa and S. Asia. [Urdu & Hindi *kauṛī*]

cowshed /kówshed/ *n.* **1** a shed for cattle that are not at pasture. **2** a milking shed.
■ see STALL¹ *n.* 2.

cowslip /kówslip/ *n.* **1** a primula, *Primula veris*, with fragrant yellow flowers and growing in pastures. **2** a marsh marigold. [OE *cūslyppe* f. *cū* COW¹ + *slyppe* slimy substance, i.e., cow dung]

cox /koks/ *n. & v.* ● *n.* a coxswain, esp. of a racing boat. ● *v.* **1** *intr.* act as a cox (*coxed for Harvard*). **2** *tr.* act as cox for (*coxed the winning boat*). [abbr.]

coxa /kóksə/ *n.* (*pl.* **coxae** /-see/) **1** *Anat.* the hipbone or hip joint. **2** *Zool.* the first segment of an insect's leg. □□ **coxal** *adj.* [L]

coxcomb /kókskōm/ *n.* an ostentatiously conceited man; a dandy. □□ **coxcombry** /-kōmree, -kəmree/ *n.* (*pl.* **-ies**). [= *cock's comb* (see COCK¹), orig. (a cap worn by) a jester]
■ see DANDY *n.*

coxswain /kóksən, -swayn/ *n. & v.* ● *n.* a person who steers and directs the crew, esp. in a rowing boat. ● *v.* **1** *intr.* act as a coxswain. **2** *tr.* act as a coxswain of. □□ **coxswainship** *n.* [ME f. *cock* (see COCKBOAT) + SWAIN: cf. BOATSWAIN]

coy /koy/ *adj.* (**coyer, coyest**) **1** archly or affectedly shy. **2** irritatingly reticent (*always coy about her age*). **3** (esp. of a girl) modest or shy. □□ **coyly** *adv.* **coyness** *n.* [ME f. OF *coi, quei* f. L *quietus* QUIET]
■ **2** reticent, reluctant, evasive. **3** shy, modest, diffident, demure, timid, bashful, self-conscious, sheepish, timorous, unassuming, unpretentious, reserved, self-effacing, retiring.

coyote /kīyṓtee, kīyṓt/ *n.* (*pl.* same or **coyotes**) a wolflike wild dog, *Canis latrans*, native to N. America. [Mex. Sp. f. Aztec *coyotl*]

coypu /kóypōō/ *n.* (*pl.* **coypus**) = NUTRIA 1. [Araucan]

coz /kuz/ *n. archaic* cousin. [abbr.]

cozen /kúzən/ *v. literary* **1** *tr.* (often foll. by *of, out of*) cheat; defraud. **2** *tr.* (often foll. by *into*) beguile; persuade. **3** *intr.* act deceitfully. □□ **cozenage** *n.* [16th-c. cant, perh. rel. to COUSIN]
■ see CHEAT *v.* 1a.

cozy /kṓzee/ *adj., n., & v.* (esp. *Brit.* **cosy**) ● *adj.* (**cozier, coziest**) **1** comfortable and warm; snug. **2** *derog.* complacent; self-serving. **3** warm and friendly. ● *n.* (*pl.* **-ies**) **1** a cover to keep something hot, esp. a teapot or a boiled egg. **2** *Brit.* a canopied corner seat for two. ● *v.tr.* (**-ies, -ied**) (often foll. by *along*) *colloq.* reassure, esp. deceptively. □ **cozy up to** *colloq.* **1** ingratiate oneself with. **2** snuggle up to. □□ **cozily** *adv.* **cosiness** *n.* [18th c. f. Sc., of unkn. orig.]
■ *adj.* **1** comfortable, snug, warm, restful, secure, relaxing, *colloq.* comfy. **2** complacent, self-serving; see also SMUG. **3** see WARM *adj.* 3a. □ **cozy up to 1** see INGRATIATE.

cozzie var. of COSSIE.

cp. *abbr.* compare.

c.p. *abbr.* candlepower.

CPA *abbr.* certified public accountant.

cpd. *abbr.* compound.

CPI *abbr.* consumer price index.

/. . ./ **pronunciation**	● **part of speech**
□ **phrases, idioms, and compounds**	
□□ **derivatives**	■ **synonym section**
cross-references appear in SMALL CAPITALS or *italics*	

Cpl. *abbr.* corporal.

CPR *abbr.* cardiopulmonary resuscitation.

cps *abbr.* (also **c.p.s.**) **1** *Computing* characters per second. **2** cycles per second.

Cpt. *abbr.* captain.

CPU *abbr. Computing* central processing unit.

Cr *symb. Chem.* the element chromium.

crab[1] /krab/ *n.* **1 a** any of numerous ten-footed crustaceans having the first pair of legs modified as pincers. **b** the flesh of a crab, esp. *Cancer pagurus,* as food. **2** (**the Crab**) the zodiacal sign or constellation Cancer. **3** (in full **crab louse**) (often in *pl.*) a parasitic louse, *Phthirus pubis,* infesting hairy parts of the body and causing extreme irritation. **4** a machine for hoisting heavy weights. □ **catch a crab** *Rowing* effect a faulty stroke in which the oar is jammed under water or misses the water altogether. □□ **crablike** *adj.* [OE *crabba,* rel. to ON *krafla* scratch]

crab[2] /krab/ *n.* **1** (in full **crab apple**) a small sour, applelike fruit. **2** (in full **crab tree** or **crab apple tree**) any of several trees bearing this fruit. **3** a sour person. [ME, perh. alt. (after CRAB[1] or CRABBED) of earlier *scrab,* prob. of Scand. orig.]

crab[3] /krab/ *v.* (**crabbed, crabbing**) *colloq.* **1** *tr.* & *intr.* criticize adversely or captiously; grumble. **2** *tr.* act so as to spoil (*the mistake crabbed his chances*). [orig. of hawks fighting, f. MLG *krabben*]

crabbed /krábid/ *adj.* **1** irritable or morose. **2** (of handwriting) ill-formed and hard to decipher. **3** perverse or cross-grained. **4** difficult to understand. □□ **crabbedly** *adv.* **crabbedness** *n.* [ME f. CRAB[1], assoc. with CRAB[2]]

■ **1** see IRRITABLE 1.

crabby /krábee/ *adj.* (**crabbier, crabbiest**) = CRABBED 1,3. □□ **crabbily** *adv.* **crabbiness** *n.*

crabgrass /krábgras/ *n.* a creeping grass infesting lawns.

crabwise /krábwīz/ *adv.* & *attrib.adj.* (of movement) sideways or backward like a crab.

■ see SIDEWAYS *adv.*

crack /krak/ *n., v.,* & *adj.* ● *n.* **1 a** a sudden sharp or explosive noise (*the crack of a whip; a rifle crack*). **b** (in a voice) a sudden harshness or change in pitch. **2** a sharp blow (*a crack on the head*). **3 a** a narrow opening formed by a break (*entered through a crack in the wall*). **b** a partial fracture, with the parts still joined (*the teacup has a crack in it*). **c** a chink (*looked through the crack formed by the door; a crack of light*). **4** *colloq.* a mischievous or malicious remark or aside (*a nasty crack about my age*). **5** *colloq.* an attempt (*I'll have a crack at it*). **6** the exact moment (*at the crack of noon; the crack of dawn*). **7** *sl.* a potent hard crystalline form of cocaine broken into small pieces and inhaled or smoked for its stimulating effect. ● *v.* **1** *tr.* & *intr.* break without a complete separation of the parts (*cracked the window; the cup cracked on hitting the floor*). **2** *intr.* & *tr.* make or cause to make a sudden sharp or explosive sound. **3** *intr.* & *tr.* break or cause to break with a sudden, sharp sound. **4** *intr.* & *tr.* give way or cause to give way (under torture, etc.); yield. **5** *intr.* (of the voice, esp. of an adolescent boy or a person under strain) become dissonant; break. **6** *tr. colloq.* find a solution to (a problem, code, etc.). **7** *tr.* say (a joke, etc.) in a jocular way. **8** *tr. colloq.* hit sharply or hard (*cracked her head on the ceiling*). **9** *tr. Chem.* decompose (heavy oils) by heat and pressure with or without a catalyst to produce lighter hydrocarbons (such as gasoline). **10** *tr.* break (wheat) into coarse pieces. ● *attrib.adj. colloq.* excellent; first-rate (*a crack regiment; a crack shot*). □ **crack a bottle** open a bottle, esp. of wine, and drink it. **crack down on** *colloq.* take severe measures against. **crack of doom** a peal of thunder announcing the Day of Judgment. **crack up** *colloq.* **1** collapse under strain. **2** laugh. **3** repute (*not all it's cracked up to be*). **crack-up** *n. colloq.* **1** a mental breakdown. **2** a car crash. **get cracking** *colloq.* begin promptly and vigorously. **have a crack at** *colloq.* attempt. [OE *cracian* resound]

■ *n.* **1 a** snap, report, bang, clap, shot, slap. **2** see KNOCK *n.* 3. **3** break, fracture, crevice, rift, rupture, breach, slit, gap, cleft, check; split, fissure, flaw; chink; (*cracks*) craquelure. **4** see GIBE *n.* **5** see ATTEMPT *n.* **6** moment, instant, time, second. ● *v.* **1** break, fracture, rupture;

fissure, split; craze. **2** snap. **4** see *give way* 1 (WAY). **6** see SOLVE. **8** see HIT *v.* 1a. □ **crack up 1** see COLLAPSE *v.* **2** see LAUGH *v.* 1. **3** (*cracked up*) reputed, supposed, suggested, rumored, reported, intimated, whispered, said. **crack-up 1** see BREAKDOWN 1b. **2** see COLLISION 1. **get cracking** see *get a move on* 2 (MOVE). **have a crack at** see TRY *v.* 1, 2.

crackbrain /krákbrayn/ *n.* a crackpot. □□ **crackbrained** *adj.*

■ **crackbrained** see CRAZY 1.

crackdown /krákdown/ *n. colloq.* severe measures (esp. against lawbreakers, etc.).

■ see *suppression* (SUPPRESS).

cracked /krakt/ *adj.* **1** having cracks. **2** (*predic.*) *sl.* crazy. □ **cracked wheat** wheat that has been crushed into small pieces.

■ **1** see BROKEN 1. **2** see CRAZY 1.

cracker /krákər/ *n.* **1** a thin, dry biscuit often eaten with cheese. **2** a firework exploding with a sharp noise. **3** (usu. in *pl.*) an instrument for cracking (*nutcrackers*). **4** a paper cylinder both ends of which are pulled at Christmas, etc., making a sharp noise and releasing a small toy, etc. **5** *Brit. sl.* a notable or attractive person. **6** *offens.* = *poor white.* □ **cracker-barrel** (of philosophy, etc.) homespun; unsophisticated.

crackerjack /krákərjak/ *adj.* & *n. sl.* ● *adj.* exceptionally fine or expert. ● *n.* an exceptionally fine thing or person.

■ *adj.* see EXPERT *adj.* 1. ● *n.* see MASTER *n.* 5.

crackers /krákərz/ *predic.adj. sl.* crazy.

■ see CRAZY 1.

cracking /kráking/ *adj.* & *adv. Brit. sl.* ● *adj.* **1** outstanding; very good (*a cracking performance*). **2** (*attrib.*) fast and exciting (*a cracking speed*). ● *adv.* outstandingly (*a cracking good time*).

crackle /krákəl/ *v.* & *n.* ● *v.intr.* make a repeated slight cracking sound (*radio crackled; fire was crackling*). ● *n.* **1** such a sound. **2 a** paintwork, china, or glass decorated with a pattern of minute surface cracks. **b** the smooth surface of such paintwork, etc. □□ **crackly** *adj.* [CRACK + -LE[4]]

■ *n.* **1** see RATTLE *n.* 1.

crackling /krákling/ *n.* **1** the crisp skin of roast pork. **2** *Brit. joc.* or *offens.* attractive women regarded collectively as objects of sexual desire.

cracknel /kráknəl/ *n.* a light, crisp biscuit. [ME f. F *craquelin* f. MDu. *krākelinc* f. *krāken* CRACK]

crackpot /krákpot/ *n.* & *adj. sl.* ● *n.* an eccentric or impractical person. ● *adj.* mad; unworkable (*a crackpot scheme*).

■ *n.* see WEIRDO. ● *adj.* see IMPRACTICAL 1.

cracksman /kráksmən/ *n.* (*pl.* **-men**) *sl.* a burglar, esp. a safecracker.

■ see BURGLAR.

cracky /krákee/ *adj.* covered with cracks. □□ **crackiness** *n.*

-cracy /krəsee/ *comb. form* denoting a particular form of government, rule, or influence (*aristocracy; bureaucracy*). [from or after F *-cratie* f. med.L *-cratia* f. Gk *-kratia* f. *kratos* strength, power]

cradle /kráyd'l/ *n.* & *v.* ● *n.* **1 a** a child's bed, esp. one mounted on rockers. **b** a place in which a thing begins, esp. a civilization, etc., or is nurtured in its infancy (*cradle of choral singing; cradle of democracy*). **2** a framework resembling a cradle, esp.: **a** that on which a ship, a boat, etc., rests during construction or repairs. **b** that on which a worker is suspended to work on a ceiling, a ship, the vertical side of a building, etc. **c** the part of a telephone on which the receiver rests when not in use. ● *v.tr.* **1** contain or shelter as if in a cradle (*cradled his head in her arms*). **2** place in a cradle. □ **cradle-robber** (or **-snatcher**) *sl.* a person amorously attached to a much younger person. **from the cradle** from infancy. **from the cradle to the grave** from infancy till death (esp. of government welfare). [OE *cradol,* perh. rel. to OHG *kratto* basket]

■ *n.* **1 a** bed, crib, cot. **b** see ORIGIN 1. ● *v.* **1** see HOLD[1] *v.* 1a, c.

cradlesong /kráyd'lsong/ *n.* a lullaby.

cradling /kráydling/ *n. Archit.* a wooden or iron framework, esp. one used as a structural support in a ceiling.

craft /kraft/ *n. & v.* ● *n.* **1** skill, esp. in practical arts. **2 a** (esp. in *comb.*) a trade or an art (*statecraft; handicraft; priestcraft; the craft of pottery*). **b** the members of a craft. **3** (*pl.* **craft**) **a** a boat or vessel. **b** an aircraft or spacecraft. **4** cunning or deceit. **5** (**the Craft**) the brotherhood of Freemasons. ● *v.tr.* make in a skillful way (*crafted a poem; a well-crafted piece of work*). □ **craft guild** *hist.* a guild of workers of the same trade. [OE *cræft*]

■ *n.* **1** skill, ability, artisanship, craftsmanship, workmanship, ingenuity, skillfulness, art, talent, dexterity, cleverness, mastery, expertness, expertise, flair, genius, technique, know-how. **2 a** trade, art, occupation, calling, vocation, métier, profession. **3** vessel, ship, boat; aircraft, airplane, *colloq.* plane; spaceship, spacecraft, rocket. **4** deceit, guile, cunning, art, fraud, trickery, wiliness, foxiness, artfulness, craftiness, duplicity. ● *v.* make, fashion, fabricate.

craftsman /kráftsmən/ *n.* (*pl.* **-men**; *fem.* **craftswoman**, *pl.* **-women**) **1** a skilled worker; an artisan. **2** a person who practices a handicraft. □□ **craftsmanship** *n.* [ME, orig. *craft's man*]

■ **1** see TRADESMAN. □□ **craftsmanship** see WORKMANSHIP.

crafty /kráftee/ *adj.* (**craftier, craftiest**) cunning; artful; wily. □□ **craftily** *adv.* **craftiness** *n.* [OE *cræftig*]

■ artful, cunning, clever, shrewd, foxy, canny, wily, sly, scheming, calculating, designing, plotting, tricky, sneaky, deceitful, dodgy, guileful, insidious, double-dealing, two-faced, duplicitous, treacherous, *colloq.* shifty.

crag[1] /krag/ *n.* a steep or rugged rock. [ME, of Celt. orig.]

■ cliff, bluff, tor, rock, scarp, precipice, *Geol.* escarpment; (*crags*) palisades.

crag[2] /krag/ *n. Geol.* rock consisting of a shelly sand. [18th c.: perh. f. CRAG[1]]

craggy /krágee/ *adj.* (**craggier, craggiest**) **1** (esp. of a person's face) rugged; rough-textured. **2** (of a landscape) having crags. □□ **craggily** *adv.* **cragginess** *n.*

cragsman /krágzmən/ *n.* (*pl.* **-men**) a skilled climber of crags.

crake /krayk/ *n.* **1** any rail (see RAIL[3]), esp. a corncrake. **2** the cry of a corncrake. [ME f. ON *kráka* (imit.): cf. CROAK]

cram /kram/ *v.* (**crammed, cramming**) **1** *tr.* **a** fill to bursting; stuff (*the room was crammed*). **b** (foll. by *in, into*) force (a thing) into (*cram the sandwiches into the bag*). **2** *tr. & intr.* prepare for an examination by intensive study. **3** *tr.* (often foll. by *with*) feed (poultry, etc.) to excess. **4** *tr. & intr. colloq.* eat greedily. □ **cram-full** as full as possible. **cram in** push in to bursting point (*crammed in another five minutes' work*). [OE *crammian* f. Gmc]

■ **1** pack, stuff, overstuff, overcrowd, jam, fill (to bursting); force, shove. **2** study, burn the midnight oil, grind (away), *Brit. colloq.* swot, *literary* lucubrate. □ **cram-full** see *jam-packed.*

crambo /krámbō/ *n.* a game in which a player gives a word or line of verse to which each of the others must find a rhyme. [earlier *crambe*, app. allusive f. L *crambe repetita* cabbage served up again]

cramp /kramp/ *n. & v.* ● *n.* **1 a** a painful involuntary contraction of a muscle or muscles from the cold, exertion, etc. **b** = *writer's cramp* (see WRITER). **2** (also **cramp iron**) a metal bar with bent ends for holding masonry, etc., together. **3** a portable tool for holding two planks, etc., together; a clamp. **4** a restraint. ● *v.tr.* **1** affect with cramp. **2** confine narrowly. **3** restrict (energies, etc.). **4** (as **cramped** *adj.*) **a** (of handwriting) small and difficult to read. **b** (of a room, etc.) uncomfortably crowded; lacking space. **5** fasten with a cramp. □ **cramp a person's style** prevent a person from acting freely or naturally. **cramp up** confine narrowly. [ME f. OF *crampe* f. MDu., MLG *krampe*, OHG *krampfo* f. adj. meaning 'bent': cf. CRIMP]

■ *n.* **1 a** see GRIPE *n.* 1. **4** see RESTRAINT 2. ● *v.* **2** see BOX[1] *v.* 2. **3** see INHIBIT 1. **4 b** (**cramped**) tight, crowded, incommodious, uncomfortable, close.

crampon /krámpən/ *n.* (also **crampoon** /-poon/) (usu. in *pl.*) **1** an iron plate with spikes fixed to a boot for walking on ice, climbing, etc. **2** a metal hook for lifting timber, rock, etc.; a grappling iron. [ME f. F (as CRAMP)]

cranage /kráynij/ *n.* **1** the use of a crane or cranes. **2** the money paid for this.

cranberry /kránberee/ *n.* (*pl.* **-ies**) **1** any evergreen shrub of the genus *Vaccinium*, esp. *V. macrocarpon* of America and *V. oxycoccos* of Europe, yielding small, red, acid berries. **2 a** berry from this used for a sauce and in cooking. [17th c.: named by Amer. colonists f. G *Kranbeere*, LG *kranebere* crane berry]

crane /krayn/ *n. & v.* ● *n.* **1** a machine for moving heavy objects, usu. by suspending them from a projecting arm or beam. **2** any tall wading bird of the family Gruidae, with long legs, long neck, and straight bill. **3** a moving platform supporting a television camera or movie camera. ● *v.tr.* **1** (also *absol.*) stretch out (one's neck) in order to see something. **2** *tr.* move (an object) by a crane. □ **crane fly** (*pl.* **flies**) any fly of the family Tipulidae, having two wings and long legs: also called *daddy longlegs*. [OE *cran*, rel. to L *grus*, Gk *geranos*]

■ *n.* **1** see HOIST *n.* ● *v.* **1** see STRAIN[1] *v.* 1.

cranesbill /kráynzbil/ *n.* any of various plants of the genus *Geranium*, having beaked fruits.

cranial /kráyneeəl/ *adj.* of or relating to the skull. □ **cranial index** the ratio of the width and length of a skull. [CRANIUM + -AL]

craniate /kráyneeət, -ayt/ *adj. & n.* ● *adj.* having a skull. ● *n.* a craniate animal. [mod.L *craniatus* f. CRANIUM]

cranio- /kráyneeō/ *comb. form* cranium.

craniology /kráyneeóləjee/ *n.* the scientific study of the shape and size of the human skull. □□ **craniological** /-nee-əlójikəl/ *adj.* **craniologist** *n.*

craniometry /kráyneeómitree/ *n.* the scientific measurement of skulls. □□ **craniometric** /-neeəmétrik/ *adj.*

craniotomy /kráyneeótəmee/ *n.* (*pl.* **-ies**) **1** surgical removal of a portion of the skull. **2** surgical perforation of the skull of a dead fetus to ease delivery.

cranium /kráyneeəm/ *n.* (*pl.* **craniums** or **crania** /-neeə/) **1** the skull. **2** the part of the skeleton that encloses the brain. [ME f. med.L f. Gk *kranion* skull]

■ see HEAD *n.* 1.

crank[1] /krangk/ *n. & v.* ● *n.* **1** part of an axle or shaft bent at right angles for interconverting reciprocal and circular motion. **2** an elbow-shaped connection in bell hanging. ● *v.tr.* **1** cause to move by means of a crank. **2 a** bend into a crank shape. **b** furnish or fasten with a crank. □ **crank up 1** start (a car engine) by turning a crank. **2** *sl.* increase (speed, etc.) by intensive effort. [OE *cranc*, app. f. *crincan*, rel. to *cringan* fall in battle, orig. 'curl up']

crank[2] /krangk/ *n.* **1 a** an eccentric person, esp. one obsessed by a particular theory (*health-food crank*). **b** a bad-tempered person. **2** *literary* a fanciful turn of speech (*quips and cranks*). [back-form. f. CRANKY]

■ **1 a** eccentric, character, oddity, *sl.* nut, nutcase, *Brit. sl.* nutter; monomaniac, zealot, fanatic, freak.

crank[3] /krangk/ *adj. Naut.* liable to capsize. [perh. f. *crank* weak, shaky, or CRANK[1]]

crankcase /krángk-kays/ *n.* a case enclosing a crankshaft.

crankpin /krángkpin/ *n.* a pin by which a connecting rod is attached to a crank.

crankshaft /krángkshaft/ *n.* a shaft driven by a crank (see CRANK[1] *n.* 1).

cranky /krángkee/ *adj.* (**crankier, crankiest**) **1** ill-tempered or crotchety. **2** working badly; shaky. **3** *colloq.* eccentric, esp. obsessed with a particular theory (*cranky ideas about*

/.../ **pronunciation**	● **part of speech**
□ **phrases, idioms, and compounds**	
□□ **derivatives**	■ **synonym section**
cross-references appear in SMALL CAPITALS or *italics*	

women). □□ **crankily** *adv.* **crankiness** *n.* [perh. f. obs. *crank* rogue feigning sickness]

■ **1** ill-tempered, crotchety, testy, grouchy, crabby, short-tempered, surly, irascible, waspish, churlish, gruff, curmudgeonly, cantankerous, choleric, bilious, snappish, petulant, peevish, contentious, querulous, irritable, splenetic. **2** see SHAKY. **3** eccentric, odd, weird, strange, queer, peculiar, quirky, obsessed, obsessive, capricious, whimsical. □□ **crankily** see BADLY 1. **crankiness** see *eccentricity* (ECCENTRIC), *ill humor*.

crannog /kránəg/ *n.* an ancient lake-dwelling in Scotland or Ireland. [Ir. f. *crann* tree, beam]

cranny /kránee/ *n.* (*pl.* **-ies**) a chink; a crevice; a crack. □□ **crannied** /-need/ *adj.* [ME f. OF *crané* past part. of *craner* f. *cran* f. pop.L *crena* notch]

■ chink, crevice, crack, fissure, fracture, break, furrow, split, cleft.

crap[1] /krap/ *n.* & *v. coarse sl.* ● *n.* **1** (often as *int.*) nonsense; rubbish (*he talks crap*). **2** feces. ● *v.intr.* (**crapped, crapping**) defecate. ¶ Usually considered a taboo word. □ **crap out 1** be unsuccessful. **2** withdraw from a game, etc. [earlier senses 'chaff, refuse from fat-boiling': ME f. Du. *krappe*]

■ *n.* **1** see NONSENSE.

crap[2] /krap/ *n.* a losing throw of 2, 3, or 12 in craps. □ **crap game** a game of craps. [formed as CRAPS]

crape /krayp/ *n.* **1** crepe, usu. of black silk or imitation silk, formerly used for mourning clothes. **2** a band of this formerly worn around a person's hat, etc., as a sign of mourning. □ **crape fern** a NZ fern, *Leptopteris superba*, with tall dark-green fronds. □□ **crapy** *adj.* [earlier *crispe, crespe* f. F *crespe* CREPE]

crappy /krápee/ *adj.* (**crappier, crappiest**) *coarse sl.* **1** rubbishy; cheap. **2** disgusting.

■ **1** see SHODDY *adj.* 1.

craps /kraps/ *n.pl.* a gambling game played with dice. □ **shoot craps** play craps. [19th c.: perh. f. *crab* lowest throw at dice]

crapshoot /krápshoot/ *n. sl.* a venture marked by uncertainty and risk.

crapulent /krápyələnt/ *adj.* **1** given to indulging in alcohol. **2** resulting from drunkenness. **3 a** drunk. **b** suffering from the effects of drunkenness. □□ **crapulence** /-ləns/ *n.* **crapulous** *adj.* [LL *crapulentus* very drunk f. L *crapula* inebriation f. Gk *kraipalē* drunken headache]

■ **1** see EPICUREAN *adj.* **3** see DRUNK *adj.* 1.

craquelure /kráklŏŏr, kraklŏŏr/ *n.* a network of fine cracks in a painting or its varnish. [F]

crash[1] /krash/ *v., n., & adv.* ● *v.* **1** *intr.* & *tr.* make or cause to make a loud smashing noise (*the cymbals crashed; crashed the plates together*). **2** *tr.* & *intr.* throw, drive, move, or fall with a loud smashing noise. **3** *intr.* & *tr.* **a** collide or cause (a vehicle) to collide violently with another vehicle, obstacle, etc.; overturn at high speed. **b** fall or cause (an aircraft) to fall violently on to the land or the sea (*crashed the plane; the pilot crashed into the sea*). **4** *intr.* (usu. foll. by *into*) collide violently (*crashed into the window*). **5** *intr.* undergo financial ruin. **6** *tr. colloq.* enter without permission (*crashed the cocktail party*). **7** *intr. colloq.* be heavily defeated (*crashed to a 4–0 defeat*). **8** *intr. Computing* (of a machine or system) fail suddenly. **9** *tr. Brit. colloq.* pass (a red traffic light, etc.). **10** *intr.* (often foll. by *out*) *sl.* sleep for a night, esp. in an improvised setting. ● *n.* **1 a** a loud and sudden smashing noise (*a thunder crash; the crash of dishes*). **b** a breakage (esp. of china, pottery, glass, etc.). **2 a** a violent collision, esp. of one vehicle with another or with an object. **b** the violent fall of an aircraft on to the land or sea. **3** ruin, esp. financial. **4** *Computing* a sudden failure which puts a system out of action. **5** (*attrib.*) done rapidly or urgently (*a crash course in first aid*). ● *adv.* with a crash (*the window went crash*). □ **crash-dive 1** *intr.* **a** (of a submarine or its pilot) dive hastily and steeply in an emergency. **b** (of an aircraft or pilot) dive and crash. **2** *tr.* cause to crash-dive. **crash dive** such a dive. **crash helmet** a helmet worn esp. by a motorcyclist to protect the head in a crash. **crash-land 1** *intr.* (of an aircraft or airman) land hurriedly with a crash, usu. without

lowering the undercarriage. **2** *tr.* cause (an aircraft) to crash-land. **crash landing** a hurried landing with a crash. **crash pad** *sl.* a place to sleep, esp. in an emergency. [ME: imit.]

■ *v.* **1** bang, boom, smash, clash, clang, clank. **3 a** smash (into); collide, bang together; (*crash into*) drive *or* run into. **4** see COLLIDE 1. **5** see FAIL *v.* 7b. **6** gatecrash, invade, intrude *or* break into. ● *n.* **1 a** bang, smash, clash, explosion, blast, clangor; see also BOOM[1] *n.* **2 a** see COLLISION 1. **3** ruin, disaster, collapse, failure.

crash[2] /krash/ *n.* a coarse plain linen, cotton, etc., fabric. [Russ. *krashenina* colored linen]

crashing /kráshing/ *adj. colloq.* overwhelming (*a crashing bore*).

crasis /kráysis/ *n.* (*pl.* **crases** /-seez/) the contraction of two adjacent vowels in ancient Greek into one long vowel or diphthong. [Gk *krasis* mixture]

crass /kras/ *adj.* **1** grossly stupid (*a crass idea*). **2** gross (*crass stupidity*). **3** *literary* thick or gross. □□ **crassitude** *n.* **crassly** *adv.* **crassness** *n.* [L *crassus* solid, thick]

■ see GROSS *adj.* 2.

-crat /krat/ *comb. form* a member or supporter of a particular form of government or rule (*autocrat; democrat*). [from or after F *-crate*: see -CRACY]

crate /krayt/ *n.* & *v.* ● *n.* **1** a large wickerwork basket or slatted wooden case, etc., for packing esp. fragile goods for transportation. **2** *sl.* an old airplane or other vehicle. ● *v.tr.* pack in a crate. □□ **crateful** *n.* (*pl.* **-fuls**). [ME, perh. f. Du. *krat* basket, etc.]

■ *n.* **1** see BOX[1] *n.* 1, 2a. ● *v.* see BOX[1] *v.* 1.

crater /kráytər/ *n.* & *v.* ● *n.* **1** the mouth of a volcano. **2** a bowl-shaped cavity, esp. that made by the explosion of a shell or bomb. **3** *Astron.* a hollow with a raised rim on the surface of a planet or moon, caused by the impact of a meteorite. ● *v.tr.* form a crater in. □□ **craterous** *adj.* [L f. Gk *kratēr* mixing bowl: see CRASIS]

■ **1–3** see HOLLOW *n.* 1.

-cratic /krátik/ *comb. form* (also **-cratical**) denoting a particular kind of government or rule (*autocratic; democratic*). □□ **-cratically** *comb. form (adv.)* [from or after F *-cratique*: see -CRACY]

cravat /krəvát/ *n.* **1** a scarf worn by men inside an open-necked shirt. **2** *hist.* a necktie. □□ **cravatted** *adj.* [F *cravate* f. G *Krawat, Kroat* f. Serbo-Croatian *Hrvat* Croat]

■ see TIE *n.* 2.

crave /krayv/ *v.* **1** *tr.* **a** long for (*craved affection*). **b** beg for (*craves a blessing*). **2** *intr.* (foll. by *for*) long for; beg for (*craved for comfort*). □□ **craver** *n.* [OE *crafian*, rel. to ON *krefja*]

■ **1a, 2** see LONG[2] *v.* **1 b** see BEG 2.

craven /kráyvən/ *adj.* & *n.* ● *adj.* (of a person, behavior, etc.) cowardly; abject. ● *n.* a cowardly person. □□ **cravenly** *adv.* **cravenness** *n.* [ME *cravand*, etc., perh. f. OF *cravanté* defeated, past part. of *cravanter* ult. f. L *crepare* burst; assim. to -EN[3]]

■ *adj.* see COWARDLY *adj.* ● *n.* see COWARD *n.*

craving /kráyving/ *n.* (usu. foll. by *for*) a strong desire or longing.

■ see LONGING *n.*

craw /kraw/ *n. Zool.* the crop of a bird or insect. □ **stick in one's craw** be unacceptable. [ME, rel. to MDu. *crāghe*, MLG *krage*, MHG *krage* neck, throat]

crawfish /kráwfish/ *n.* & *v.* ● *n.* = CRAYFISH. ● *v.intr.* retreat; back out. [var. of CRAYFISH]

crawl /krawl/ *v.* & *n.* ● *v.intr.* **1** move slowly, esp. on hands and knees. **2** (of an insect, snake, etc.) move slowly with the body close to the ground, etc. **3** walk or move slowly (*the train crawled into the station*). **4** (often foll. by *to*) *colloq.* behave obsequiously or ingratiatingly in the hope of advantage. **5** (often foll. by *with*) be covered or filled with crawling or moving things, or with people, etc., compared to this. **6** (esp. of the skin) feel a creepy sensation. **7** swim with a crawl stroke. ● *n.* **1** an act of crawling. **2** a slow rate of movement. **3** a high-speed swimming stroke with alternate overarm movements and rapid straight-legged kicks. **4** *Brit.* **a** (usu. in *comb.*) *colloq.* a leisurely journey between places of interest (*church crawl*). **b** = *pub-crawl*. □□ **crawlingly** *adv.* **crawly** *adj.* (in senses 5, 6 of *v.*). [ME: orig. unkn.: cf. Sw. *kravla*, Da. *kravle*]

■ *v.* **2** creep, worm, wriggle, squirm, slither, *colloq.* wiggle. **3** inch, creep; see also EDGE *v.* 1. **4** grovel, toady, fawn, cower, *colloq.* creep, suck up; (*crawl to*) *archaic* lackey; see also CRINGE *v.* 2. **5** (*crawl with*) see TEEM[1] 2.

crawler /kráwlər/ *n.* **1** (usu. in *pl.*) a baby's overall for crawling in. **2** anything that crawls, esp. an insect. **3** *sl.* a person who behaves obsequiously in the hope of advantage.

cray /kray/ *n. Austral. & NZ* = CRAYFISH.

crayfish /kráyfish/ *n.* (also **crawdad** or **crawfish**) (*pl.* same) **1** a small, lobsterlike freshwater crustacean. **2** a large marine spiny lobster. [ME f. OF *crevice*, *crevis*, ult. f. OHG *krebiz* CRAB[1]: assim. to FISH[1]]

crayon /kráyon/ *n. & v.* ● *n.* **1** a stick or pencil of colored chalk, wax, etc., used for drawing. **2** a drawing made with this. ● *v.tr.* draw with crayons. [F f. *craie* f. L *creta* chalk]

craze /krayz/ *v. & n.* ● *v.* **1** *tr.* (usu. as **crazed** *adj.*) make insane (*crazed with grief*). **2 a** *tr.* produce fine surface cracks on (pottery glaze, etc.). **b** *intr.* develop such cracks. ● *n.* **1 a** a usu. temporary enthusiasm (*a craze for hula hoops*). **b** the object of this. **2** an insane fancy or condition. [ME, orig. = break, shatter, perh. f. ON]

■ *v.* **1** (crazed) see MAD *adj.* 1. ● *n.* **1 a** fashion, trend, enthusiasm, mania, obsession. **b** rage, fad, thing; last word, dernier cri.

crazy /kráyzee/ *adj.* (**crazier, craziest**) **1** *colloq.* (of a person, an action, etc.) insane or mad; foolish. **2** *colloq.* (usu. foll. by *about*) extremely enthusiastic. **3** *sl.* exciting; unrestrained. **4** (*attrib.*) (of paving, a quilt, etc.) made of irregular pieces fitted together. **5** *archaic* (of a ship, building, etc.) unsound; shaky. □ **crazy bone** the funny bone. **like crazy** *colloq.* = *like mad* (see MAD). □□ **crazily** *adv.* **craziness** *n.*

■ **1** mad, insane, demented, deranged, unbalanced, unhinged, lunatic, *non compos mentis, non compos,* certifiable, touched, out of one's mind *or* head, crazed, *colloq.* mental, dotty, crackbrained, out to lunch, *sl.* bananas, off one's head *or* rocker *or* trolley, cuckoo, cracked, dippy, daffy, nuts, bonkers, batty, bats, loony, screwy, gaga, goofy, nutty (as a fruit cake), loco, up the creek, *sl.* flaky, kooky, balmy, crackers, *Brit. sl.* barmy, potty, off one's chump; silly, absurd, foolish, nonsensical, inane, ridiculous, preposterous, laughable, risible, ludicrous, asinine, stupid, imbecile, *colloq.* imbecilic, idiotic, moronic, cretinous, esp. *Brit. colloq.* daft, *sl.* crackpot, screwball; impractical, impracticable, unworkable, unsound, pointless, imprudent, rash, reckless, harebrained, ill-considered; (*be crazy*) have a screw loose, be as mad as a hatter *or* March hare, have bats in the belfry; (*go crazy*) *sl.* go ape. **2** enthusiastic, avid, zealous, keen, excited; infatuated, obsessed, wild, mad, *colloq.* dotty, mental, *sl.* nuts, nutty. **3** see WILD *adj.* 4. □□ **crazily** see MADLY 1.

creak /kreek/ *n. & v.* ● *n.* a harsh scraping or squeaking sound. ● *v.intr.* **1** make a creak. **2 a** move with a creaking noise. **b** move stiffly and awkwardly. **c** show weakness or frailty under strain. □□ **creakingly** *adv.* [ME, imit.: cf. CRAKE, CROAK]

creaky /kréekee/ *adj.* (**creakier, creakiest**) **1** liable to creak. **2 a** stiff or frail (*creaky joints*). **b** (of a practice, institution, etc.) decrepit; dilapidated; outmoded. □□ **creakily** *adv.* **creakiness** *n.*

■ **2 b** see DECREPIT 2.

cream /kreem/ *n., v., & adj.* ● *n.* **1 a** the fatty content of milk which gathers at the top and can be made into butter by churning. **b** this eaten (often whipped) with a dessert, as a cake filling, etc. (*strawberries and cream; cream cake*). **2** the part of a liquid that gathers at the top. **3** (usu. prec. by *the*) the best or choicest part of something, esp.: **a** the point of an anecdote. **b** an elite group of people (*the cream of the crop*). **4** a creamlike preparation, esp. a cosmetic (*hand cream*). **5** a very pale yellow or off-white color. **6 a** a dish like or made with cream. **b** a soup or sauce containing milk or cream. **c**

a full-bodied, mellow, sweet sherry. **d** a chocolate-covered usu. fruit-flavored fondant confection. ● *v.* **1** *tr.* (usu. foll. by *off*) **a** take the cream from (milk). **b** take the best or a specified part from (*creamed off the brightest pupils*). **2** *tr.* work (butter, etc.) to a creamy consistency. **3** *tr.* treat (the skin, etc.) with cosmetic cream. **4** *tr.* add cream to (coffee, etc.). **5** *intr.* (of milk or any other liquid) form a cream or scum. **6** *tr. colloq.* defeat soundly or by a wide margin (esp. in a sporting contest). ● *adj.* pale yellow; off-white. □ **cream bun** (or **cake**) *Brit.* a bun or cake filled or topped with cream. **cream cheese** a soft, rich cheese made from unskimmed milk and cream. **cream-colored** pale yellowish white. **cream of tartar** purified and crystallized potassium hydrogen tartrate, used in medicine, baking powder, etc. **cream puff 1** a cake made of puff pastry filled with custard or whipped cream. **2** *colloq.* an ineffectual or effeminate person. **cream soda** a carbonated vanilla-flavored soft drink. **cream tea** *Brit.* afternoon tea with scones, jam, and cream. [ME f. OF *cre(s)me* f. LL *cramum* (perh. f. Gaulish) & eccl.L *chrisma* CHRISM]

■ *n.* **3** see BEST *n.* 1, 2. **4** see LOTION. ● *v.* **1** (*cream off*) skim off. **2** see PRESS[1] *v.* 2b. **6** see BEAT *v.* 3a. □ **cream puff 2** see DRIP *n.* 2.

creamer /kréemər/ *n.* **1** a flat dish used for skimming the cream off milk. **2** a machine used for separating cream from milk. **3** a small pitcher for cream.

creamery /kréeməree/ *n.* (*pl.* -ies) **1** a factory producing butter and cheese. **2** a store where milk, cream, etc., are sold; a dairy. [CREAM, after F *crémerie*]

creamy /kréemee/ *adj.* (**creamier, creamiest**) **1** like cream in consistency or color. **2** rich in cream. □□ **creamily** *adv.* **creaminess** *n.*

■ **1** see WHITE *adj.* 1. **2** see RICH 6.

crease[1] /krees/ *n. & v.* ● *n.* **1 a** a line in paper, etc., caused by folding. **b** a fold or wrinkle. **2** an area near the goal in ice hockey or lacrosse into which the puck or the ball must precede the players. **3** *Cricket* a line marking the position of the bowler or batsman (see *bowling crease*). ● *v.* **1** *tr.* make creases in (material). **2** *intr.* become creased (*linen creases badly*). **3** *tr. & intr. Brit. sl.* (often foll. by *up*) make or become incapable through laughter. [earlier *creast* = CREST ridge in material]

■ *n.* **1** see FOLD[1] *n.* ● *v.* **1** see FOLD[1] *v.* 1.

crease[2] var. of KRIS.

create /kree-áyt/ *v.* **1** *tr.* **a** (of natural or historical forces) bring into existence; cause (*poverty creates resentment*). **b** (of a person or persons) make or cause (*create a diversion; create a good impression*). **2** *tr.* originate (*an actor creates a part*). **3** *tr.* invest (a person) with a rank (*created him a lord*). **4** *intr. Brit. sl.* make a fuss; grumble. □□ **creatable** *adj.* [ME f. L *creare*]

■ **1** make, cause, produce, form, bring into being, originate, conceive, generate, invent, imagine, think up, frame, forge, fashion, fabricate, manufacture, develop, design, contrive, devise, produce, dream up, initiate; engender, give rise to, spawn, *literary* beget.

creatine /kréeəteen, -tin/ *n.* a product of protein metabolism found in the muscles of vertebrates. [Gk *kreas* meat + -INE[4]]

creation /kree-áyshən/ *n.* **1 a** the act of creating. **b** an instance of this. **2 a** (usu. **the Creation**) the creating of the universe regarded as an act of God. **b** (usu. **Creation**) everything so created; the universe. **3** a product of human intelligence, esp. of imaginative thought or artistic ability. **4 a** the act of investing with a title or rank. **b** an instance of this. [ME f. OF f. L *creatio -onis* (as CREATE)]

■ **1 a** generation, making; beginning, origin, start, inception, genesis, *rhet.* birth; see also FORMATION 1, 2. **2 b** the world, the universe, the cosmos. **3** see INVENTION 1, 2.

/. . ./ **pronunciation**	● **part of speech**
□ **phrases, idioms, and compounds**	
□□ **derivatives**	■ **synonym section**
cross-references appear in SMALL CAPITALS or *italics*	

creationism /krée-áyshənizəm/ n. Theol. a theory attributing all matter, biological species, etc., to separate acts of creation, rather than to evolution. □□ **creationist** n.

creative /kree-áytiv/ adj. **1** inventive and imaginative. **2** creating or able to create. □□ **creatively** adv. **creativeness** n. **creativity** /-aytívitee, -ətív-/ n.
■ **1** imaginative, inventive, originative, artistic, original, ingenious, resourceful. **2** see PRODUCTIVE 2 b.

creator /kree-áytər/ n. **1** a person who creates. **2** (as **the Creator**) God. [ME f. OF creat(o)ur f. L creator -oris (as CREATE)]
■ **1** originator, author, initiator, founder, father, inventor, architect, designer, framer, maker, prime mover. **2** (**the Creator**) God, the Supreme Being, the Deity.

creature /kréechər/ n. **1 a** an animal, as distinct from a human being. **b** any living being (we are all God's creatures). **2** a person of a specified kind (poor creature). **3** a person owing status to and obsequiously subservient to another. **4** anything created; a creation. □ **creature comforts** material comforts such as good food, warmth, etc. **creature of habit** a person set in an unvarying routine. □□ **creaturely** adj. [ME f. OF f. LL creatura (as CREATE)]
■ **1** animal, beast; being, organism, entity, living thing. **2** see PERSON. □ **creature comforts** luxuries, material comforts.

crèche /kresh/ n. **1** a representation of a Nativity scene. **2** Brit. a day nursery for babies and young children. [OF creche f. Gmc: rel. to CRIB]

credal see CREED.

credence /kréed'ns/ n. **1** belief. **2** (in full **credence table**) a small table, shelf, or niche which holds the elements of the Eucharist before they are consecrated. □ **give credence to** believe. **letter of credence** a letter of introduction, esp. of an ambassador. [ME f. OF f. med.L credentia f. credere believe]
■ **1** see BELIEF 1.

credential /kridénshəl/ n. (usu. in pl.) **1** evidence of a person's achievements or trustworthiness, usu. in the form of certificates, references, etc. **2** a letter or letters of introduction. [med.L credentialis (as CREDENCE)]
■ **1** see WARRANT n. 2.

credenza /kridénzə/ n. a sideboard or cupboard. [It. f. med.L (as CREDENCE)]

credibility /krédibílitee/ n. **1** the condition of being credible or believable. **2** reputation; status. □ **credibility gap** an apparent difference between what is said and what is true.

credible /krédibəl/ adj. **1** (of a person or statement) believable or worthy of belief. **2** (of a threat, etc.) convincing. □□ **credibly** adv. [ME f. L credibilis f. credere believe]
■ see PLAUSIBLE 1.

credit /krédit/ n. & v. ● n. **1** (usu. of a person) a source of honor, pride, etc. (is a credit to the school). **2** the acknowledgment of merit (must give her credit for consistency). **3** a good reputation (his credit stands high). **4 a** belief or trust (I place credit in that). **b** something believable or trustworthy (that statement has credit). **5 a** a person's financial standing; the sum of money at a person's disposal in a bank, etc. **b** the power to obtain goods, etc., before payment (based on the trust that payment will be made). **6** (usu. in pl.) an acknowledgment of a contributor's services to a film, television program, etc. **7** Brit. a grade above a pass in an examination. **8** a reputation for solvency and honesty in business. **9 a** (in bookkeeping) the acknowledgment of being paid by an entry on the credit side of an account. **b** the sum entered. **c** the credit side of an account. **10** a certification indicating that a student has completed a course. ● v.tr. **1** believe (cannot credit it). **2** (usu. foll. by to, with) **a** enter on the credit side of an account (credited $20 to him; credited him with $20). **b** ascribe a good quality or achievement to (the goal was credited to Barnes; he was credited with the improved sales). □ **credit account** Brit. = charge account. **credit card** a card from a bank, etc., authorizing the obtaining of goods on credit. **credit rating** an estimate of a person's suitability to receive commercial credit. **credit title** a person's name appearing at the beginning or end of a

movie or broadcast, etc., as an acknowledgment. **credit transfer** a transfer from one person's bank account to another's. **credit a person with** ascribe (a good quality) to a person. **credit union** a cooperative association that makes low-interest loans to its members. **do credit to** (or **do a person credit**) enhance the reputation of. **get credit for** be given credit for. **give a person credit for 1** enter (a sum) to a person's credit. **2** ascribe (a good quality) to a person. **give credit to** believe. **letter of credit** a letter from a banker authorizing a person to draw money up to a specified amount, usu. from another bank. **on credit** with an arrangement to pay later. **to one's credit** in one's praise, commendation, or defense (to his credit, he refused the offer). [F crédit f. It. credito or L creditum f. credere credit- believe, trust]
■ n. **2** praise, commendation, tribute, recognition, acknowledgment, acclaim. **3** honor, esteem, merit, reputation, standing, stature, position, status, name, repute. **4 a** belief, faith, trust, credence; confidence. **b** believability, credibility, conceivability, plausibility; reliability, trustworthiness, honesty, probity, dependability. **6** (credits) end credits, acknowledgments, titles, credit titles. ● v. **1** give credit to, believe, trust, accept, put or place one's faith or confidence in, have faith or confidence in, rely on, depend on or upon. **2 b** accredit, ascribe, attribute, assign. □ **give credit to** see CREDIT v. 1 above.

creditable /kréditəbəl/ adj. (often foll. by to) bringing credit or honor. □□ **creditability** n. **creditably** adv.
■ see MERITORIOUS.

creditor /kréditər/ n. **1** a person to whom a debt is owing. **2** a person or company that gives credit for money or goods (cf. DEBTOR). [ME f. AF creditour (OF -eur) f. L creditor -oris (as CREDIT)]

creditworthy /kréditwərthee/ adj. considered suitable to receive commercial credit. □□ **creditworthiness** n.
■ see SOLVENT adj.

credo /kréeydō, kráy-/ n. (pl. **-os**) **1** (**Credo**) a statement of belief; a creed, esp. the Apostles' or Nicene Creed beginning in Latin with credo. **2** a musical setting of the Nicene Creed. [ME f. L, = I believe]
■ **1** see CREED.

credulous /kréjələs/ adj. **1** too ready to believe; gullible. **2** (of behavior) showing such gullibility. □□ **credulity** /kridōōlitee, -dyōō-/ n. **credulously** adv. **credulousness** n. [L credulus f. credere believe]
■ see GULLIBLE.

Cree /kree/ n. & adj. ● n. (pl. same or **Crees**) **1 a** a N. American people of E. and central Canada. **b** a member of this people. **2** the language of this people. ● adj. of or relating to the Crees or their language. [Canadian F Cris (earlier Cristinaux) f. Algonquian]

creed /kreed/ n. **1** a set of principles or opinions, esp. as a philosophy of life (his creed is moderation in everything). **2 a** (often **the Creed**) = Apostles' Creed (see APOSTLE). **b** a brief formal summary of Christian doctrine (cf. NICENE CREED, ATHANASIAN CREED). **c** the Creed as part of the Mass. □□ **creedal** /kréed'l/ adj. **credal** adj. [OE crēda f. L CREDO]
■ **1** dogma, doctrine, Credo, teaching, principles, belief, set of beliefs, philosophy, maxim.

Creek /kreek/ n. **1 a** a confederacy of N. American peoples that formerly occupied much of Alabama and Georgia. **b** a member of these peoples. **2** the language used by these peoples.

creek /kreek, krik/ n. **1** US Regional a stream. **2** Brit. **a** a small bay or harbor on a seacoast. **b** a narrow inlet on a seacoast or in a riverbank. □ **up shit creek** coarse sl. = up the creek. **up the creek** sl. in difficulties or trouble. [ME crike f. ON kriki nook (or partly f. OF crique f. ON), & ME crēke f. MDu. krēke (or f. crike by lengthening): ult. orig. unkn.]
■ **1** stream, streamlet, brook, rivulet, rill, runnel, run, Sc. burn. **2** inlet, bay, cove, harbor. □ **up the creek** see in trouble 1 (TROUBLE).

creel /kreel/ *n.* **1** a large wicker basket for fish. **2** an angler's fishing basket. [ME, orig. Sc.: ult. orig. unkn.]

creep /kreep/ *v.* & *n.* ● *v.intr.* (*past* and *past part.* **crept** /krept/) **1** move with the body prone and close to the ground; crawl. **2** (often foll. by *in, out, up,* etc.) come, go, or move slowly and stealthily or timidly (*crept out without being seen*). **3** enter slowly (into a person's affections, life, awareness, etc.) (*a feeling crept over her; crept into her heart*). **4** *colloq.* act abjectly or obsequiously in the hope of advancement. **5** (of a plant) grow along the ground or up a wall by means of tendrils, etc. **6** (as **creeping** *adj.*) developing slowly and steadily (*creeping inflation*). **7** (of the flesh) feel as if insects, etc., were creeping over it, as a result of fear, horror, etc. **8** (of metals, etc.) undergo deformation. ● *n.* **1 a** the act of creeping. **b** an instance of this. **2** (in *pl.*; prec. by *the*) *colloq.* a nervous feeling of revulsion or fear (*gives me the creeps*). **3** *sl.* an unpleasant person. **4** the gradual downward movement of disintegrated rock due to gravitational forces, etc. **5** (of metals, etc.) a gradual change of shape under stress. **6** a low arch under a railroad embankment, road, etc. □ **creeping Jenny** (or **Jennie**) any of various creeping plants, esp. moneywort. **creeping Jesus** *Brit. sl.* an abject or hypocritical person. **creep up on** approach (a person) stealthily or unnoticed. [OE *crēopan* f. Gmc]
   ■ *v.* **1** crawl, slither, inch, squirm, wriggle, *colloq.* wiggle; (*creep by*) drag. **2** steal, sneak; slink, skulk, tiptoe, pussyfoot, sidle. **3** make its way. **4** see CRAWL *v.* 4. ● *n.* **2** (*the creeps*) see JITTER *n.* **3** see WRETCH 2.

creeper /kréepər/ *n.* **1** *Bot.* any climbing or creeping plant. **2** any bird that climbs, esp. a tree creeper. **3** *sl.* a soft-soled shoe.
   ■ **1** see RUNNER 2b.

creepy /kréepee/ *adj.* (**creepier, creepiest**) **1** *colloq.* having or producing a creeping of the flesh (*I feel creepy; a creepy movie*). **2** given to creeping. □□ **creepily** *adv.* **creepiness** *n.* [CREEP]
   ■ **1** see SCARY.

creepy-crawly /kréepeekráwlee/ *n.* & *adj. colloq.* ● *n.* (*pl.* **-ies**) an insect, worm, etc. ● *adj.* creeping and crawling.
   ■ *n.* see BUG *n.* 1.

creese var. of KRIS.

cremate /kréemayt, krimáyt/ *v.tr.* consume (a corpse, etc.) by fire. □□ **cremation** /krimáyshən/ *n.* **cremator** *n.* [L *cremare* burn]
   ■ □□ **cremation** see FUNERAL *n.*

crematorium /kréemətáwreeəm/ *n.* (*pl.* **crematoriums** or **crematoria** /-reeə/) a place for cremating corpses in a furnace. [mod.L (as CREMATE, -ORY)]

crematory /kréemətawree, krém-/ *adj.* & *n.* ● *adj.* of or relating to cremation. ● *n.* (*pl.* **-ies**) = CREMATORIUM.

crème /krem/ *n.* **1** = CREAM *n.* 6a. **2** a name for various creamy liqueurs (*crème de cassis*). □ **crème brûlée** /brōōláy/ a pudding of cream or custard topped with caramelized sugar. **crème caramel** a custard coated with caramel. **crème de la crème** /də laa krém/ the best part; the elite. **crème de menthe** /də maánt, ménth, mínt/ a peppermint-flavored liqueur. [F, = cream]
   ■ □ **crème de la crème** see BEST *n.* 1, 2.

crenate /kréenayt/ *adj. Bot.* & *Zool.* having a notched edge or rounded teeth. □□ **crenated** *adj.* **crenation** /krináyshən/ *n.* **crenature** /krénətyoor, krée-/ *n.* [mod.L *crenatus* f. pop.L *crena* notch]
   ■ see *notched* (NOTCH).

crenel /krénəl/ *n.* (also **crenelle** /krinél/) an indentation or gap in the parapet of a tower, castle, etc., orig. for shooting through, etc. [ME f. OF *crenel,* ult. f. pop.L *crena* notch]

crenellate /krénəlayt/ *v.tr.* provide (a tower, etc.) with battlements or loopholes. □□ **crenellation** /-láyshən/ *n.* [F *créneler* (as CRENEL)]

Creole /krée-ōl/ *n.* & *adj.* ● *n.* **1 a** a descendant of European (esp. Spanish) settlers in the W. Indies or Central or S. America. **b** a white descendant of French settlers, esp. in Louisiana. **c** a person of mixed European and black descent. **2** a mother tongue formed from the contact of a European language (esp. English, French, or Portuguese) with an-

other (esp. African) language. ● *adj.* **1** of or relating to a Creole or Creoles. **2** (usu. **creole**) of Creole origin or production (*creole cooking*). [F *créole, criole* f. Sp. *criollo,* prob. f. Port. *crioulo* home-born slave f. *criar* breed f. L *creare* CREATE]

creolize /krée-əliz/ *v.tr.* form a Creole from (another language). □□ **creolization** *n.*

creosote /krée-əsōt/ *n.* & *v.* ● *n.* **1** (in full **creosote oil**) a dark-brown oil distilled from coal tar, used as a wood preservative. **2** a colorless oily fluid distilled from wood tar, used as an antiseptic. ● *v.tr.* treat with creosote. [G *Kreosot* f. Gk *kreas* flesh + *sōtēr* preserver, with ref. to its antiseptic properties]

crepe /krayp/ *n.* (also **crêpe**) **1** a fine, often gauzelike fabric with a wrinkled surface. **2** a thin pancake, usu. with a savory or sweet filling. **3** (also **crepe rubber**) a very hard-wearing wrinkled sheet rubber used for the soles of shoes, etc. □ **crepe** (or **crêpe**) **de chine** (or **Chine**) /də sheén/ a fine silk crepe. **crêpe paper** thin crinkled paper. **crêpe suzette** (or **Suzette**) /sōōzét/ a small dessert pancake flamed in alcohol at the table. □□ **crepey** *adj.* **crepy** *adj.* [F f. OF *crespe* curled f. L *crispus*]

crepitate /krépitayt/ *v.intr.* **1** make a crackling sound. **2** *Zool.* (of a beetle) eject pungent fluid with a sharp report. □□ **crepitant** *adj.* [L *crepitare* frequent. of *crepare* creak]

crepitation /krépitáyshən/ *n.* **1** *Med.* = CREPITUS. **2** the action or sound of crackling or rattling.

crepitus /krépitəs/ *n. Med.* **1** a grating noise from the ends of a fractured bone rubbing together. **2** a similar sound heard from the chest in pneumonia, etc. [L f. *crepare* rattle]

crept *past* and *past part.* of CREEP.

crepuscular /kripúskyələr/ *adj.* **1 a** of twilight. **b** dim. **2** *Zool.* appearing or active in twilight. [L *crepusculum* twilight]
   ■ **1 a** see TWILIGHT 6. **b** see DIM *adj.* 1a.

Cres. *abbr.* Crescent.

cresc. *abbr.* (also **cres.**) *Mus.* = CRESCENDO.

crescendo /krishéndō/ *n., adv., adj.,* & *v.* ● *n.* (*pl.* **-os**) *Mus.* a passage gradually increasing in loudness. **2** a progress toward a climax (*a crescendo of emotions*). **b** *disp.* a climax (*reached a crescendo then died away*). ● *adv.* & *adj.* with a gradual increase in loudness. ● *v.intr.* (**-oes, -oed**) increase gradually in loudness or intensity. [It., part. of *crescere* grow (as CRESCENT)]
   ■ *n.* **2** see HEAD *n.* 21.

crescent /krésənt/ *n.* & *adj.* ● *n.* **1** the curved sickle shape of the waxing or waning moon. **2** anything of this shape, esp. *Brit.* a street forming an arc. **3 a** the crescent-shaped emblem of Islam or Turkey. **b** (**the Crescent**) the world or power of Islam. ● *adj.* **1** *poet.* increasing. **2** crescent-shaped. □□ **crescentic** /kriséntik/ *adj.* [ME f. AF *cressaunt,* OF *creissant,* f. L *crescere* grow]
   ■ *n.* **2** arc, lunette, *Geom.* lune, *Math.* meniscus. ● *adj.* **1** increasing, growing. **2** crescentic, *Math.* meniscoid.

cresol /krée-sawl/ *n.* any of three isomeric phenols present in creosote and used as disinfectants. □□ **cresyl** /krée-sil/ *adj.* [CREOSOTE + -OL²]

cress /kres/ *n.* any of various cruciferous plants usu. with pungent edible leaves, e.g., watercress. [OE *cresse* f. WG]

cresset /krésit/ *n. hist.* a metal container filled with fuel, lighted and usu. mounted on a pole for illumination. [ME f. OF *cresset, craisset,* f. *craisse* = *graisse* GREASE]

crest /krest/ *n.* & *v.* ● *n.* **1 a** a comb or tuft of feathers, fur, etc., on a bird's or animal's head. **b** something resembling this, esp. a plume of feathers on a helmet. **c** the top of a helmet. **2** the top of something, esp. of a mountain, wave, roof, etc. **3** *Heraldry* **a** a device above the shield and helmet of a coat of arms. **b** such a device reproduced on writing paper or on a seal, signifying a family. **4 a** a line along the top of the neck of some animals. **b** the hair grow-

---

/.../ **pronunciation**	● **part of speech**
□ **phrases, idioms, and compounds**	
□□ **derivatives**	■ **synonym section**
cross-references appear in SMALL CAPITALS or *italics*	

ing from this; a mane. **5** *Anat.* a ridge along the surface of a bone. ● *v.* **1** *tr.* reach the crest of (a hill, wave, etc.). **2** *tr.* **a** provide with a crest. **b** serve as a crest to. **3** *intr.* (of a wave) form into a crest. □ **on the crest of a wave** at the most favorable moment in one's progress. □□ **crested** *adj.* (also in *comb.*). **crestless** *adj.* [ME f. OF *creste* f. L *crista* tuft]

■ *n.* **2** top, summit, pinnacle, peak, head, ridge. **3** seal, device, figure, badge, emblem, insignia, symbol, design. ● *v.* **2 a** top, crown, surmount, cap. **3** level out *or* off.

crestfallen /krést fawlən/ *adj.* **1** dejected; dispirited. **2** with a fallen or drooping crest.
■ **1** see *dejected* (DEJECT).

cretaceous /kritáyshəs/ *adj.* & *n.* ● *adj.* **1** of the nature of chalk. **2** (**Cretaceous**) *Geol.* of or relating to the last period of the Mesozoic era, with evidence of the first flowering plants, the extinction of dinosaurs, and extensive deposits of chalk. ¶ Cf. Appendix VII. ● *n. Geol.* this era or system. [L *cretaceus* f. *creta* chalk]

Cretan /kréetən/ *n.* & *adj.* ● *n.* a native of Crete, an island SE of the Greek mainland. ● *adj.* of or relating to Crete or the Cretans. [L *Cretanus* f. *Creta* f. Gk *Krētē* Crete]

cretic /kréetik/ *n. Prosody* a foot containing one short or unstressed syllable between two long or stressed ones. [L *Creticus* f. Gk *Krētikos* (as CRETAN)]

cretin /kréetin/ *n.* **1** a person who is deformed and mentally retarded as the result of a thyroid deficiency. **2** *colloq.* a stupid person. □□ **cretinism** *n.* **cretinize** *v.tr.* **cretinous** *adj.* [F *crétin* f. Swiss F. *creitin, crestin* f. L *Christianus* CHRISTIAN]
■ □□ **cretinism** see *stupidity* (STUPID).

cretonne /kretón, kréeton/ *n.* (often *attrib.*) a heavy cotton fabric with a usu. floral pattern printed on one or both sides, used for upholstery. [F f. *Creton* in Normandy]

crevasse /krəvás/ *n.* **1** a deep open crack, esp. in a glacier. **2** a breach in a river levee. [F f. OF *crevace*: see CREVICE]
■ gorge, chasm, abyss, ravine, fissure, crack, furrow.

crevice /krévis/ *n.* a narrow opening or fissure, esp. in a rock or building, etc. [ME f. OF *crevace* f. *crever* burst f. L *crepare*]
■ crack, fissure, chink, cleft, cranny, groove, furrow, break, split, rift.

crew[1] /kroo/ *n.* & *v.* ● *n.* (often treated as *pl.*) **1 a** a body of people manning a ship, aircraft, train, etc. **b** such a body as distinguished from the captain or officers. **c** a body of people working together; a team. **2** *colloq.* a company of people; a gang (*a motley crew*). ● *v.* **1** *tr.* supply or act as a crew or member of a crew for. **2** *intr.* act as a crew or member of a crew. □ **crew cut** a very short haircut orig. for men and boys. **crew neck** a close-fitting round neckline, esp. on a sweater. [ME f. OF *creüe* increase, fem. past part. of *croistre* grow f. L *crescere*]
■ *n.* group, company, band, troupe, party, gang, team, corps, body.

crew[2] esp. *Brit. past* of CROW[2].

crewel /krooəl/ *n.* a thin worsted yarn used for tapestry and embroidery. [ME *crule*, etc., of unkn. orig.]

crewelwork /krooəlwərk/ *n.* a design worked in crewel on linen or other fabric.

crewman /kroomən/ *n.* (*pl.* -**men**) a member of a crew.

crib /krib/ *n.* & *v.* ● *n.* **1 a** a child's bed with barred or latticed sides. **2** a barred container or rack for animal fodder. **3** *colloq.* **a** a translation of a text for the (esp. surreptitious) use of students. **b** plagiarized work, etc. **4** a small house or cottage. **5** a framework lining the shaft of a mine. **6** *colloq.* **a** cribbage. **b** a set of cards given to the dealer at cribbage by all the players. **7** heavy crossed timbers used in foundations in loose soil, etc. **8** *sl.* a brothel. **9** *Austral.* & *NZ* a light meal; food. ● *v.tr.* (also *absol.*) (**cribbed, cribbing**) **1** *colloq.* copy (another person's work) unfairly or without acknowledgment. **2** confine in a small space. **3** *colloq.* pilfer; steal. **4** *Brit. colloq.* grumble. □ **crib biting** a horse's habit of biting the manger while noisily breathing in and swallowing. **crib death** = *sudden infant death syndrome*. □□ **cribber** *n.* [OE *crib(b)*]
■ *n.* **1 a** cradle, bed, cot. **3 a** translation, gloss,

interpretation, *sl.* trot. **4** see CABIN *n.* 1. **7** cribwork. **8** see BROTHEL. ● *v.* **1** copy, plagiarize. **2** see RESTRICT. **3** see STEAL *v.* 1.

cribbage /kríbij/ *n.* a card game for two, three, or four players, in which the dealer may score from the cards in the crib (see CRIB *n.* 6b). □ **cribbage board** a board with pegs and holes used for scoring at cribbage. [17th c.: orig. unkn.]

cribo /kríbō, kríbō/ *n.* (*pl.* -**os**) a large harmless snake, *Drymarchon corais*, of tropical America. Also called *gopher snake* (see GOPHER[1]). [19th c.: orig. unkn.]

cribriform /kríbrifawrm/ *adj. Anat.* & *Bot.* having numerous small holes. [L *cribrum* sieve + -FORM]

cribwork /kríbwərk/ *n.* = CRIB *n.* 7.

crick /krik/ *n.* & *v.* ● *n.* a sudden painful stiffness in the neck or the back, etc. ● *v.tr.* produce a crick in (the neck, etc.). [ME: orig. unkn.]

cricket[1] /kríkit/ *n.* & *v.* ● *n.* a game played on a grass field with two teams of 11 players taking turns to bowl at a wicket defended by a batting player of the other team. ● *v.intr.* play cricket. □ **not cricket** *Brit. colloq.* underhand or unfair behavior. □□ **cricketer** *n.* [16th c.: orig. uncert.]

cricket[2] /kríkit/ *n.* any of various grasshopperlike insects of the order Orthoptera, the males of which produce a characteristic chirping sound. [ME f. OF *criquet* f. *criquer* creak, etc. (imit.)]

cricoid /kríkoyd/ *adj.* & *n.* ● *adj.* ring-shaped. ● *n.* (in full **cricoid cartilage**) *Anat.* the ring-shaped cartilage of the larynx. [mod.L *cricoides* f. Gk *krikoeidēs* f. *krikos* ring]

cri de coeur /kree də kőr/ *n.* (*pl.* **cris de coeur** *pronunc.* same) a passionate appeal, complaint, or protest. [F, = cry from the heart]

cried *past* and *past part.* of CRY.

crier /kríər/ *n.* (also **cryer**) **1** a person who cries. **2** an officer who makes public announcements in a court of justice. □ **town** (or **common**) **crier** *hist.* an officer employed by a town council, etc., to make public announcements in the streets or marketplace. [ME f. AF *criour*, OF *criere* f. *crier* CRY]

crikey /kríkee/ *int. Brit. sl.* an expression of astonishment. [euphem. for CHRIST]

crim /krim/ *n.* & *adj. Austral. sl.* = CRIMINAL. [abbr.]

crime /krim/ *n.* **1 a** an offense punishable by law. **b** illegal acts as a whole (*resorted to crime*). **2** an evil act (*a crime against humanity*). **3** *colloq.* a shameful act (*a crime to tease them*). □ **crime of passion** a crime, esp. murder, committed in a fit of sexual jealousy. **crime wave** a sudden increase in crime. [ME f. OF f. L *crimen -minis* judgment, offense]
■ *n.* **1 a** offense, violation, misdeed, wrong, misdemeanor; felony. **b** lawlessness. **2** see EVIL *n.* 1.

criminal /kríminəl/ *n.* & *adj.* ● *n.* a person who has committed a crime or crimes. ● *adj.* **1** of, involving, or concerning crime (*criminal records*). **2** having committed (and usu. been convicted of) a crime. **3** *Law* relating to or expert in criminal law rather than civil or political matters (*criminal code*; *criminal lawyer*). **4** *colloq.* scandalous; deplorable. □ **criminal law** law concerned with punishment of offenders (opp. *civil law*). **criminal libel** see LIBEL. □□ **criminality** *n.* /-nálitee/ **criminally** *adv.* [ME f. LL *criminalis* (as CRIME)]
■ *n.* felon, lawbreaker, outlaw, culprit, offender, malefactor, wrongdoer, racketeer, *colloq.* crook, *Brit. colloq.* villain; villain, miscreant, scoundrel, knave, blackguard; *colloq.* bad guy, black hat, baddie; see also THUG. ● *adj.* **2** illegal, unlawful, illicit, lawless, dishonest, *colloq.* crooked. **4** scandalous, deplorable, disgraceful, reprehensible, *colloq.* awful; wicked, evil, bad, wrong, corrupt, vile, immoral, amoral, sinful, villainous, iniquitous, flagitious.

criminalistic /kríminəlístik/ *adj.* relating to criminals or their habits.

criminalistics /kríminəlístiks/ *n.pl.* forensic science. □ **criminalist** /kríminəlist/ one who practices this science, esp. for a law enforcement agency.

criminology /kríminóləjee/ *n.* the scientific study of crime.

□□ **criminological** /-nəlójikəl/ *adj.* **criminologist** *n.* [L *crimen -minis* CRIME + -OLOGY]

crimp /krimp/ *v. & n.* ● *v.tr.* **1** compress into small folds or ridges; frill. **2** make narrow wrinkles or flutings in; corrugate. **3** make waves in (the hair) with a hot iron. ● *n.* a crimped thing or form. □ **put a crimp in** *sl.* thwart; interfere with. □□ **crimper** *n.* **crimpy** *adj.* **crimpily** *adv.* **crimpiness** *n.* [ME, prob. ult. f. OHG *krimphan*]
■ *v.* **1, 2** see WRINKLE *v.* 1. ● *n.* see FOLD[1] *n.*

crimson /krimzən/ *adj., n., & v.* ● *adj.* of a rich, deep red inclining to purple. ● *n.* this color. ● *v.tr. & intr.* make or become crimson. [ME *cremesin, crimesin*, ult. f. Arab. *ḳirmizī* KERMES]
■ *adj.* see RED *adj.* 1. ● *v.* see FLUSH[1] *v.* 1a.

cringe /krinj/ *v. & n.* ● *v.intr.* **1** shrink back in fear or apprehension; cower. **2** (often foll. by *to*) behave obsequiously. ● *n.* the act or an instance of cringing. □□ **cringer** *n.* [ME *crenge, crenche*, OE *cringan, crincan*: see CRANK[1]]
■ *v.* **1** cower, wince, flinch, quail, recoil, blench, tremble, quiver, shrink back, *colloq.* quake *or* shake in one's boots *or* shoes. **2** defer, kowtow, grovel, fawn, *Austral. & NZ* smoodge, *colloq.* bootlick, crawl, suck up; (*cringe to*) archaic lackey. ● *n.* embarrassment.

cringle /kríŋgəl/ *n. Naut.* an eye of rope containing a thimble for another rope to pass through. [LG *kringel* dimin. of *kring* ring f. root of CRANK[1]]

crinkle /kríŋkəl/ *n. & v.* ● *n.* a wrinkle or crease in paper, cloth, etc. ● *v.* **1** *intr.* form crinkles. **2** *tr.* form crinkles in. □ **crinkle-cut** (of vegetables) cut with wavy edges. □□ **crinkly** *adj.* [ME f. OE *crincan*: see CRANK[1]]
■ *n.* see WRINKLE *n.* 1, 2. ● *v.* see WRINKLE *v.* 2.

crinoid /krínoyd/ *n. & adj.* ● *n.* any echinoderm of the class Crinoidea, usu. sedentary with feathery arms, e.g., sea lilies and feather stars. ● *adj.* lily-shaped. □□ **crinoidal** /-nóyd'l/ *adj.* [Gk *krinoeidēs* f. *krinon* lily]

crinoline /krínəlin/ *n.* **1** a stiffened or hooped petticoat formerly worn to make a long skirt stand out. **2** a stiff fabric of horsehair, etc., used for linings, hats, etc. [F f. L *crinis* hair + *linum* thread]

cripple /krípəl/ *n. & v.* ● *n.* usu. *offens.* a person or animal who is permanently lame. ● *v.tr.* **1** make a cripple of; lame. **2** disable; impair. **3** weaken or damage (an institution, enterprise, etc.) seriously (*crippled by the loss of funding*). □□ **crippledom** *n.* **cripplehood** *n.* **crippler** *n.* [OE *crypel*, rel. to CREEP]
■ *n.* invalid, paralytic, paraplegic. ● *v.* disable, lame; incapacitate, handicap, maim; impair, damage, weaken, debilitate, emasculate.

cris var. of KRIS.

crisis /krísis/ *n.* (*pl.* **crises** /-seez/) **1 a** a decisive moment. **b** a time of danger or great difficulty. **2** the turning point, esp. of a disease. [L f. Gk *krisis* decision f. *krinō* decide]
■ **1 b** disaster, emergency, calamity, catastrophe, danger. **2** turning point, critical time *or* moment.

crisp /krisp/ *adj., n., & v.* ● *adj.* **1** hard but brittle. **2 a** (of air) bracing. **b** (of a style or manner) lively; brisk and decisive. **c** (of features, etc.) neat and clear-cut. **d** (of paper) stiff and crackling. **e** (of hair) closely curling. ● *n.* **1** (in full **potato crisp**) *Brit.* = **potato chip**. **2** a thing overdone in roasting, etc. (*burned to a crisp*). ● *v.tr. & intr.* **1** make or become crisp. **2** curl in short, stiff folds or waves. □□ **crisply** *adv.* **crispness** *n.* [OE f. L *crispus* curled]
■ *adj.* **1** brittle, crunchy, friable, breakable, crumbly, frangible. **2 a** see *bracing* (BRACE *v.* 3). **b** see LIVELY 1, 2, EMPHATIC. **c** see *chiseled* (CHISEL *v.* 2). **e** curly, crispy, crinkly, frizzy, frizzled.

crispate /kríspayt/ *adj.* **1** crisped. **2** *Bot. & Zool.* having a wavy margin. [L *crispare* curl]

crispbread /kríspbred/ *n.* **1** a thin, crisp cracker of crushed rye, etc. **2** these collectively (*a box of crispbread*).

crisper /kríspər/ *n.* a compartment in a refrigerator for storing fruit and vegetables.

crispy /kríspee/ *adj.* (**crispier, crispiest**) **1** crisp; brittle. **2** curly. **3** brisk. □□ **crispiness** *n.*

crisscross /krískráws, -krós/ *n., adj., adv., & v.* ● *n.* **1** a pattern of crossing lines. **2** the crossing of lines or currents, etc. ● *adj.* crossing; in cross lines (*crisscross marking*). ● *adv.* crosswise; at cross purposes. ● *v.* **1** *intr.* **a** intersect repeatedly. **b** move crosswise. **2** *tr.* mark or make with a crisscross pattern. [15th c., f. *Christ's cross*: later treated as redupl. of CROSS]
■ *n.* **1** see NETWORK *n.* 2. ● *v.* **1** see TRAVERSE *v.* 1.

crista /krístə/ *n.* (*pl.* **cristae** /-tee/) **1** *Anat. & Zool.* a ridge or crest. **2** *Anat.* an infold of the inner membrane of a mitochondrion. □□ **cristate** *adj.* [L]

cristobalite /kristóbəlit/ *n. Mineral.* a principal form of silica, occurring as opal. [G *Cristobalit* f. Cerro San *Cristóbal* in Mexico]

criterion /krīteéreeən/ *n.* (*pl.* **criteria** /-reeə/ or **criterions**) a principle or standard that a thing is judged by. □□ **criterial** *adj.* [Gk *kritērion* means of judging (cf. CRITIC)]
■ see STANDARD *n.* 1, 8.

critic /krítik/ *n.* **1** a person who censures. **2** a person who reviews or judges the merits of literary, artistic, or musical works, etc., esp. regularly or professionally. **3** a person engaged in textual criticism. [L *criticus* f. Gk *kritikos* f. *kritēs* judge f. *krinō* judge, decide]
■ **1** see ASSAILANT. **2** see JUDGE *n.* 3b.

critical /krítikəl/ *adj.* **1 a** making or involving adverse or censorious comments or judgments. **b** expressing or involving criticism. **2** skillful at or engaged in criticism. **3** providing textual criticism (*a critical edition of Frost*). **4 a** of or at a crisis; involving risk or suspense (*in a critical condition*; *a critical operation*). **b** decisive; crucial (*of critical importance*; *at the critical moment*). **5 a** *Math. & Physics* marking transition from one state, etc., to another (*critical angle*). **b** *Physics* (of a nuclear reactor) maintaining a self-sustaining chain reaction. □ **critical apparatus** = APPARATUS 4. **critical list** a list of those critically ill, esp. in a hospital. **critical mass** *Physics* the amount of fissile material needed to maintain a nuclear chain reaction. **critical path** the sequence of stages determining the minimum time needed for an operation. **critical temperature** *Chem.* the temperature above which a gas cannot be liquefied. □□ **criticality** /-kálitee/ *n.* (in sense 5). **critically** *adv.* **criticalness** *n.* [L *criticus*: see CRITIC]
■ **1** censorious, disparaging, depreciatory, deprecatory, deprecative, deprecating, judgmental; adverse. **4 a** risky, uncertain, perilous, dangerous, touch and go, ticklish, sensitive, touchy, *archaic or joc.* parlous; grave, severe, serious. **b** crucial, important, essential, basic, key, decisive, pivotal, vital, momentous, climacteric.

criticaster /krítikástər/ *n.* a minor or inferior critic.

criticism /krítisizəm/ *n.* **1 a** finding fault; censure. **b** a statement or remark expressing this. **2 a** the work of a critic. **b** an article, essay, etc., expressing or containing an analytical evaluation of something. □ **the higher criticism** criticism dealing with the origin and character, etc., of texts, esp. of Biblical writings. **the lower criticism** textual criticism of the Bible. [CRITIC or L *criticus* + -ISM]
■ **1 a** censure, faultfinding, disapproval, condemnation, disparagement. **2 a** judgment, evaluation, appraisal, analysis, assessment, estimation, valuation. **b** critique, review, commentary.

criticize /krítisīz/ *v.tr.* (also *absol.*) **1** find fault with; censure. **2** discuss critically. □□ **criticizable** *adj.* **criticizer** *n.*
■ **1** censure, find fault (with), carp (at), cavil (at), condemn, attack, cut up, denounce, impugn, *colloq.* pan, lambaste, put down, *Brit. colloq.* slate, *sl.* knock. **2** judge, evaluate, assess, appraise; discuss, analyze, critique.

critique /kriteék/ *n. & v.* ● *n.* a critical essay or analysis; an instance or the process of formal criticism. ● *v.tr.* (*cri-*

/. . ./ **pronunciation**	● **part of speech**
□ **phrases, idioms, and compounds**	
□□ **derivatives**	■ **synonym section**
cross-references appear in SMALL CAPITALS or *italics*	

333

tiques, **critiqued, critiquing**) discuss critically. [F f. Gk *kritikē tekhnē* critical art]

■ *n.* see ANALYSIS 1. ● *v.* see ANALYZE 3.

critter /krítər/ *n.* **1** *dial.* or *joc.* a creature. **2** *derog.* a person. [var. of CREATURE]

croak /krōk/ *n. & v.* ● *n.* **1** a deep, hoarse sound as of a frog or a raven. **2** a sound resembling this. ● *v.* **1 a** *intr.* utter a croak. **b** *tr.* utter with a croak or in a dismal manner. **2** *sl.* **a** *intr.* die. **b** *tr.* kill. [ME: imit.]

■ *v.* **1** see RASP *v.* 2. **2 a** see DIE¹ 1.

croaker /krōkər/ *n.* **1** an animal that croaks. **2** a prophet of evil.

croaky /krōkee/ *adj.* (**croakier, croakiest**) (of a voice) croaking; hoarse. □□ **croakily** *adv.* **croakiness** *n.*

Croat /krō-at/ *n. & adj.* ● *n.* **1 a** a native of Croatia in the former Yugoslavia. **b** a person of Croatian descent. **2** the Slavonic dialect of the Croats (cf. SERBO-CROAT). ● *adj.* of or relating to the Croats or their dialect. [mod.L *Croatae* f. Serbo-Croatian *Hrvat*]

Croatian /krō-áyshən/ *n. & adj.* = CROAT.

croc /krok/ *n. colloq.* a crocodile. [abbr.]

croceate /krōseeayt/ *adj.* saffron-colored. [L *croceus* f. CROCUS]

crochet /krōsháy/ *n. & v.* ● *n.* **1** a handicraft in which yarn is made up into a patterned fabric by means of a hooked needle. **2** work made in this way. ● *v.* (**crocheted** /-sháyd/; **crocheting** /-sháying/) **1** *tr.* make by crocheting. **2** *intr.* do crochet. □□ **crocheter** *n.* [F, dimin. of *croc* hook]

crocidolite /krōsídəlīt/ *n.* a fibrous blue or green silicate of iron and sodium; blue asbestos. [Gk *krokis -idos* nap of cloth]

crock¹ /krok/ *n.* **1** an earthenware pot or jar. **2** a broken piece of earthenware. [OE *croc(ca)*]

■ **1** see JAR¹ 1.

crock² /krok/ *n. colloq.* nonsense; exaggeration (*his explanation is just a crock*). [perhaps for *crock of shit*; CROCK¹]

crock³ /krok/ *n. & v. Brit. colloq.* ● *n.* **1** an inefficient, broken-down, or worn-out person. **2** a worn-out vehicle, ship, etc. ● *v.* **1** *intr.* (foll. by *up*) break down, collapse. **2** *tr.* (often foll. by *up*) disable; cause to collapse. [orig. Sc., perh. f. Flem.]

crockery /krókəree/ *n.* earthenware or china dishes, plates, etc. [obs. *crocker* potter: see CROCK²]

■ see POTTERY.

crocket /krókit/ *n. Archit.* a small carved ornament (usu. a bud or curled leaf) on the inclined side of a pinnacle, etc. [ME f. var. of OF *crochet*: see CROCHET]

crocodile /krókədīl/ *n.* **1 a** any large tropical amphibious reptile of the order Crocodilia, with thick scaly skin, long tail, and long jaws. **b** leather from its skin, used to make bags, shoes, etc. **2** *Brit. colloq.* a line of schoolchildren, etc., walking in pairs. ● **crocodile tears** insincere grief (from the belief that crocodiles wept while devouring or alluring their prey). □□ **crocodilian** /-díleeən/ *adj.* [ME f. OF *cocodrille* f. med.L *cocodrillus* f. L *crocodilus* f. Gk *krokodilos* f. *krokē* pebble + *drilos* worm]

crocus /krōkəs/ *n.* (*pl.* **crocuses**) any dwarf plant of the genus *Crocus*, growing from a corm and having brilliant usu. yellow or purple flowers. [ME, = saffron, f. L f. Gk *krokos* crocus, of Semitic orig.]

Croesus /kreesəs/ *n.* a person of great wealth. [name of a king of Lydia (6th c. BC)]

croft /krawft, kroft/ *n. & v. Brit.* ● *n.* **1** an enclosed piece of (usu. arable) land. **2** a small rented farm in Scotland or N. of England. ● *v.intr.* farm a croft; live as a crofter. [OE: orig. unkn.]

crofter /kráwftər, króf-/ *n. Brit.* a person who rents a small piece of land, esp. a joint tenant of a divided farm in parts of Scotland.

croissant /krwaasáaN, krəsánt/ *n.* a crescent-shaped roll made of rich yeast pastry. [F, formed as CRESCENT]

Cro-Magnon /krōmágnən, -mányən/ *adj. Anthropol.* of a tall, broad-faced European race of late Paleolithic times. [name of a hill in the Dordogne, France, where remains were found in 1868]

cromlech /krómlekh, -lek/ *n.* **1** a dolmen; a megalithic tomb. **2** a circle of upright prehistoric stones. [Welsh f. *crom* fem. of *crwm* bent + *llech* flat stone]

crone /krōn/ *n.* **1** a withered old woman. **2** an old ewe. [ME, ult. f. ONF *carogne* CARRION]

■ **1** see HAG¹ 1.

cronk /krongk, krawngk/ *adj. Austral. colloq.* **1** unsound; liable to collapse. **2 a** fraudulent. **b** (of a horse) dishonestly run; unfit. [19th c.: cf. CRANK³]

crony /krōnee/ *n.* (*pl.* **-ies**) a close friend or companion. [17th-c. *chrony*, university sl. f. Gk *khronios* long-standing f. *khronos* time]

■ see FRIEND *n.* 1.

crook /krook/ *n., v., & adj.* ● *n.* **1** the hooked staff of a shepherd or bishop. **2 a** a bend, curve, or hook. **b** anything hooked or curved. **3** *colloq.* **a** a rogue; a swindler. **b** a professional criminal. ● *v.tr. & intr.* bend; curve. ● *adj.* **1** *Brit.* crooked. **2** *Austral. & NZ colloq.* **a** unsatisfactory; out of order; (of a person) unwell or injured. **b** unpleasant. **c** dishonest; unscrupulous. **d** bad-tempered; irritable; angry. □ **crook-backed** hunchbacked. **go crook** (usu. foll. by *at*, *on*) *Austral. & NZ colloq.* lose one's temper; become angry. □□ **crookery** *n.* [ME f. ON *krókr* hook]

■ *n.* **1** see STAFF¹ *n.* 1a, b. **2** see BEND¹ *n.* **3** see CRIMINAL *n.* ● *v.* see BEND¹ *v.* 1.

crookback /krookbak/ *n.* a hunchback. □□ **crookbacked** *adj.*

crooked /krookid/ *adj.* (**crookeder, crookedest**) **1 a** not straight or level; bent; curved; twisted. **b** deformed; bent with age. **2** *colloq.* not straightforward; dishonest. **3** /krookt/ *Austral. & NZ sl.* = CROOK *adj.* 2. **4** (foll. by *on*) *Austral. sl.* hostile to. □□ **crookedly** *adv.* **crookedness** *n.* [ME f. CROOK, prob. after ON *krókóttr*]

■ **1** bent, bowed, curved, askew, awry, deformed, distorted, contorted, lopsided, twisted, misshapen, disfigured, warped, gnarled. **2** criminal, dishonest, *sl.* bent; illegal, unlawful, illicit, wrong; perverse. **4** see HOSTILE 2.

croon /kroon/ *v. & n.* ● *v.tr. & intr.* hum or sing in a low subdued voice, esp. in a sentimental manner. ● *n.* such singing. □□ **crooner** *n.* [ME (orig. Sc. & N.Engl.) f. MDu. & MLG *krōnen* groan, lament]

■ *v.* see SING *v.* 1.

crop /krop/ *n. & v.* ● *n.* **1 a** the produce of cultivated plants, esp. cereals. **b** the season's total yield of this (*a good crop*). **2** a group or an amount produced or appearing at one time (*this year's crop of students*). **3** (in full **hunting crop**) the stock or handle of a whip. **4** a style of hair cut very short. **b** the cropping of hair. **5** *Zool.* **a** the pouch in a bird's gullet where food is prepared for digestion. **b** a similar organ in other animals. **6** the entire tanned hide of an animal. **7** a piece cut off or out of something. ● *v.* (**cropped, cropping**) **1** *tr.* **a** cut off. **b** (of animals) bite off (the tops of plants). **2** *tr.* cut (hair, cloth, edges of a book, etc.) short. **3** *tr.* gather or reap (produce). **4** *tr.* (foll. by *with*) sow or plant (land) with a crop. **5** *intr.* (of land) bear a crop. □ **crop circle** a circular depression in a standing crop, often only visible from the air. **crop-dusting** the sprinkling of powdered insecticide or fertilizer on crops, esp. from the air. **crop-eared** having the ears (esp. of animals) or hair cut short. **crop out** *Geol.* appear at the surface. **crop up** **1** (of a subject, circumstance, etc.) appear or come to one's notice unexpectedly. **2** *Geol.* appear at the surface. [OE *crop(p)*]

■ *n.* **1** see HARVEST *n.* 2. **3** see WHIP *n.* ● *v.* **1, 2** see CUT *v.* 3a. □ **crop up** **1** see ARISE 3.

cropper /krópər/ *n.* a crop-producing plant of specified quality (*a good cropper*; *a heavy cropper*). ■ **come a cropper** *sl.* **1** fall heavily. **2** fail badly.

croquet /krōkáy/ *n. & v.* ● *n.* **1** a game played on a lawn, with wooden balls which are driven through a series of hoops with mallets. **2** the act of croqueting a ball. ● *v.tr.* (**croqueted** /-káyd/; **croqueting** /-káying/) drive away (one's opponent's ball in croquet) by placing one's own against it and striking one's own. [perh. dial. form of F CROCHET hook]

croquette /krōkét/ *n.* a fried, breaded roll or ball of mashed potato or ground meat, etc. [F f. *croquer* crunch]

crore /krawr/ *n. Ind.* **1** ten million. **2** one hundred lakhs (of rupees, units of measurement, persons, etc.). [Hindi *k(a)rōr*, ult. f. Skr. *koṭi* apex]

crosier /krṓzhər/ *n.* (also **crozier**) **1** a hooked staff carried by a bishop as a symbol of pastoral office. **2** a crook. [orig. = bearer of a crook, f. OF *crocier* & OF *croisier* f. *crois* CROSS]

cross /kraws, kros/ *n., v., & adj.* ● *n.* **1** an upright post with a transverse bar, as used in antiquity for crucifixion. **2 a** (**the Cross**) in Christianity, the cross on which Christ was crucified. **b** a representation of this as an emblem of Christianity. **c** = *sign of the cross.* **3** a staff surmounted by a cross and borne before an archbishop or in a religious procession. **4 a** a thing or mark shaped like a cross, esp. a figure made by two short intersecting lines (+ or x). **b** a monument in the form of a cross, esp. one in the center of a town or on a tomb. **5** a cross-shaped decoration indicating rank in some orders of knighthood or awarded for personal valor. **6 a** an intermixture of animal breeds or plant varieties. **b** an animal or plant resulting from this. **7** (foll. by *between*) a mixture or compromise of two things. **8 a** a crosswise movement, e.g., of an actor on stage. **b** *Soccer*, etc., a pass of the ball across the direction of play. **c** *Boxing* a blow with a crosswise movement of the fist. **9** a trial or affliction; something to be endured (*bear one's crosses*). ● *v.* **1** *tr.* (often foll. by *over*; also *absol.*) go across or to the other side of (a road, river, sea, etc.). **2 a** *intr.* intersect or be across one another (*the roads cross near the bridge*). **b** *tr.* cause to do this; place crosswise (*cross one's legs*). **3** *tr.* **a** draw a line or lines across. **b** *Brit.* mark (a check) with two parallel lines, and often an annotation, to indicate that it must be paid into a named bank account. **4** *tr.* (foll. by *off, out, through*) cancel or obliterate or remove from a list with lines drawn across. **5** *tr.* (often *refl.*) make the sign of the cross on or over. **6** *intr.* **a** pass in opposite or different directions. **b** (of letters between two correspondents) each be dispatched before receipt of the other. **c** (of telephone lines) become wrongly interconnected so that intrusive calls can be heard. **7** *tr.* **a** cause to interbreed. **b** cross-fertilize (plants). **8** *tr.* thwart or frustrate (*crossed in love*). **9** *tr. sl.* cheat. ● *adj.* **1** (often foll. by *with*) peevish; angry. **2** (usu. *attrib.*) transverse; reaching from side to side. **3** (usu. *attrib.*) intersecting. **4** (usu. *attrib.*) contrary; opposed; reciprocal. □ **at cross purposes** misunderstanding or conflicting with one another. **cross-dress** wear clothing typically worn by members of the opposite sex. **cross one's fingers** (or **keep one's fingers crossed**) **1** put one finger across another as a sign of hoping for good luck. **2** trust in good luck. **cross the floor** *Brit.* join the opposing side in a debating assembly. **cross one's heart** make a solemn pledge, esp. by crossing one's front. **cross one's mind** (of a thought, etc.) occur to one, esp. transiently. **cross a person's palm** (usu. foll. by *with*) **1** pay a person for a favor. **2** bribe. **cross the path of 1** meet with (a person). **2** thwart. **cross swords** (often foll. by *with*) encounter in opposition; have an argument or dispute. **cross wires** (or **get one's wires crossed**) **1** become wrongly connected by telephone. **2** have a misunderstanding. **on the cross** *Brit.* **1** diagonally. **2** *sl.* fraudulently; dishonestly. □□ **crossly** *adv.* **crossness** *n.* [OE *cros* f. ON *kross* f. OIr. *cros* f. L *crux cruc-*]

■ *n.* **1, 2b** crucifix, rood. **6 b** hybrid, crossbreed, mongrel. **7** mixture, blend, combination. **9** see TRIAL 3. ● *v.* **1** cross over, go across, pass over, span, traverse. **2 a** intersect; meet, join. **4** (*cross off* or *out*) obliterate, strike out, erase, cancel, rub out, delete, wipe out. **7** interbreed, cross breed, cross-fertilize, cross-pollinate. **8** see FRUSTRATE *v.* 2. ● *adj.* **1** irritated, annoyed, piqued, in a huff *or* mood, *Brit. colloq.* shirty; peevish, irritable, testy, snappish, irascible, crotchety, choleric, splenetic, grouchy, huffish, huffy, pettish, grumpy, touchy, moody, fractious, vexed, curmudgeonly, petulant, waspish, querulous, cantankerous, crusty, short-tempered, cranky, *colloq.* on a short fuse. □ **cross one's fingers 2** hope *or* pray for the best, touch wood, keep one's fingers crossed, knock (on) wood. **cross**

one's heart see SWEAR *v.* 1a, 2 **cross one's mind** see OCCUR 2. **cross the path of 1** see MEET[1] *v.* 1. **cross swords** see CLASH *v.* 3a.

cross- /kraws, kros/ *comb. form* **1** denoting movement or position across something (*cross-channel*; *cross-country*). **2** denoting interaction (*crossbreed*; *cross-cultural*; *cross-fertilize*). **3 a** passing from side to side; transverse (*crossbar*; *crosscurrent*). **b** having a transverse part (*crossbow*). **4** describing the form or figure of a cross (*crossroads*).

crossbar /kráwsbaar, krós-/ *n.* a horizontal bar, esp. held on a pivot or between two upright bars, etc., e.g., of a bicycle or of a football goal.

cross-bedding /kráwsbeding, krós-/ *n. Geol.* lines of stratification crossing the main rock strata.

crossbill /kráwsbil, krós-/ *n.* any stout finch of the genus *Loxia*, having a bill with crossed mandibles for opening pine cones.

crossbones /kráwsbōnz, krós-/ *n.* a representation of two crossed leg or arm bones (see SKULL).

crossbow /kráwsbō, krós-/ *n.* esp. *hist.* a bow fixed across a wooden stock, with a groove for an arrow and a mechanism for drawing and releasing the string. □□ **crossbowman** *n.* (*pl.* **-men**).

crossbreed *n. & v.* ● *n.* /kráwsbreed, krós-/ **1** a breed of animals or plants produced by crossing. **2** an individual animal or plant of a crossbreed. ● *v.tr.* /kráwsbreed, krós-/ (*past* and *past part.* **-bred**) produce by crossing.

■ *n.* see HYBRID *n.* 1.

cross-check *v. & n.* ● *v.tr.* /kráws-chék, krós-/ check by a second or alternative method, or by several methods. ● *n.* /kráws-chek, krós-/ an instance of cross-checking.

cross-country /kráwskúntree, krós-/ *adj. & adv.* **1** across fields or open country. **2** not keeping to main or direct roads.

crosscut *adj. & n.* ● *adj.* /kráwskút, krós-/ cut across the main grain or axis. ● *n.* /kráwskut, krós-/ a diagonal cut, path, etc. □ **crosscut saw** a saw for cutting across the grain of wood.

cross-dating /kráwsdáyting, krós-/ *n. Archaeol.* dating by correlation with another site or level.

crosse /kraws, kros/ *n.* a stick with a triangular net at the end for conveying the ball in lacrosse. [F f. OF *croce, croc* hook]

cross-examine /kráwsigzámin, krós-/ *v.tr.* examine (esp. a witness in a court of law) to check or extend testimony already given. □□ **cross-examination** /-náyshən/ *n.* **cross-examiner** *n.*

cross-eyed /kráwsíd, krós-/ *adj.* (as a disorder) having one or both eyes turned permanently inward toward the nose.

cross-fade /kráwsfáyd, krós-/ *v.intr. Radio*, etc., fade in one sound as another is faded out.

cross-fertilize /kráwsfért'līz, krós-/ *v.tr.* **1** fertilize (an animal or plant) from one of a different species. **2** help by the interchange of ideas, etc. □□ **cross-fertilization** *n.*

crossfire /kráwsfīr, krós-/ *n.* (also **cross fire**) **1** firing in two crossing directions simultaneously. **2 a** attack or criticism from several sources at once. **b** a lively or combative exchange of views, etc.

cross-grain /kráwsgrayn, krós-/ *n.* a grain in lumber, running across the regular grain.

cross-grained /kráwsgráynd, krós-/ *adj.* **1** (of lumber) having a cross-grain. **2** perverse; intractable.

■ **2** see PERVERSE 2.

crosshair /kráws-hair, krós-/ *n.* a fine wire at the focus of an optical instrument, gun, sight, etc.

crosshatch /kráws-hách, krós-/ *v.tr.* shade with intersecting sets of parallel lines.

crosshead /kráws-hed, krós-/ *n.* **1** a bar between the piston

---

/.../ **pronunciation**	● **part of speech**
□ **phrases, idioms, and compounds**	
□□ **derivatives**	■ **synonym section**
cross-references appear in SMALL CAPITALS or *italics*	

rod and connecting rod in a steam engine. **2** = CROSSHEAD-ING.

crossheading /kráws-heding, krós-/ *n.* a heading to a paragraph printed across a column in the body of an article in a newspaper, etc.

crossing /kráwsing, krós-/ *n.* **1** a place where things (esp. roads) cross. **2** a place at which one may cross a street, etc. (*pedestrian crossing*). **3** a journey across water (*had a smooth crossing*). **4** the intersection of a church nave and transepts. **5** *Biol.* mating. □ **crossing over** *Biol.* an exchange of genes between homologous chromosomes (cf. RECOMBINATION).
■ **1** see JUNCTION 2. **3** see PASSAGE[1] 1, 4.

cross-legged /kráwslégid, -légd, krós-/ *adj.* with one leg crossed over the other.

cross-link /kráwslingk, krós-/ *n.* (also **cross-linkage**) *Chem.* a bond between chains of atoms in a polymer, etc.

cross-match /kráwsmách, krós-/ *v.tr. Med.* test the compatibility of (a donor's and a recipient's blood). □□ **cross-matching** *n.* **crossmatch** *n.*

crossover /kráwsōvər, krós-/ *n. & adj.* ● *n.* a point or place of crossing from one side to the other. ● *adj.* having a crossover.

crosspatch /kráwspach, krós-/ *n. colloq.* a bad-tempered person. [CROSS *adj.* 1 + obs. *patch* fool, clown]

crosspiece /kráwspees, krós-/ *n.* a transverse beam or other component of a structure, etc.

cross-pollinate /kráwspólinayt, krós-/ *v.tr.* pollinate (a plant) from another. □□ **cross-pollination** /-náyshən/ *n.*

cross-question /kráwskwés-chən, krós-/ *n.* = CROSS-EXAMINE.

cross-refer /kráwsrifér, krós-/ *v.intr.* (**-referred, -referring**) refer from one part of a book, article, etc., to another.

cross-reference /kráwsréfərəns, krós-/ *n. & v.* ● *n.* a reference from one part of a book, article, etc., to another.
● *v.tr.* provide with cross-references.

crossroad /kráwsrōd, krós-/ *n.* **1** (usu. in *pl.*) an intersection of two or more roads. **2** a road that crosses a main road or joins two main roads. □ **at the crossroads** at a critical point in one's life.

crossruff /kráwsrúf, krós-/ *n. & v. Bridge*, etc. ● *n.* the alternate trumping of partners' leads. ● *v.intr.* play in this way.

cross section /kráws-sékshən, krós-/ *n.* **1 a** a cutting of a solid at right angles to an axis. **b** a plane surface produced in this way. **c** a representation of this. **2** a representative sample, esp. of people. **3** *Physics* a quantity expressing the probability of interaction between particles. □□ **cross-sectional** *adj.*
■ **2** see SAMPLE *n.* 1.

cross-stitch /kráws-stich, krós-/ *n. & v.* ● *n.* **1** a stitch formed of two stitches crossing each other. **2** needlework done using this stitch. ● *v.intr. & v.tr.* work in cross-stitch.

crosstalk /kráws-tawk, krós-/ *n.* (also **cross talk**) **1** unwanted transfer of signals between communication channels. **2** *Brit.* witty talk; repartee.

crosstrees /kráws-treéz, krós-/ *n.pl. Naut.* a pair of horizontal timbers at the top of a lower mast, supporting the topmast.

cross-voting /kráwsvóting, krós-/ *n.* voting for a party not one's own, or for more than one party.

crosswalk /kráwswawk, krós-/ *n.* a pedestrian crossing.

crossways /kráwswayz, krós-/ *adv.* = CROSSWISE.

crosswind /kráwswind, krós-/ *n.* a wind blowing across one's direction of travel.

crosswise /kráwswīz, krós-/ *adj. & adv.* **1** in the form of a cross; intersecting. **2** transverse or transversely.

crossword /kráwswərd, krós-/ *n.* (also **crossword puzzle**) a puzzle of a grid of squares and blanks into which words crossing vertically and horizontally have to be filled from clues.

crotch /kroch/ *n.* a place where something forks, esp. the legs of the human body or a garment (cf. CRUTCH). [perh. = ME & OF *croc*(*he*) hook, formed as CROOK]

crotchet /króchit/ *n.* **1** a whimsical fancy. **2** a small hook. **3**

Brit. = *quarter note.* [ME f. OF *crochet* dimin. of *croc* hook (see CROTCH)]
■ **1** see FANCY *n.* 2.

crotchety /króchitee/ *adj.* peevish; irritable. □□ **crotchetiness** *n.* [CROTCHET + -Y[1]]
■ see CROSS *adj.* 1, IRRITABLE 1.

croton /krṓt'n/ *n.* **1** any of various small tropical trees or shrubs of the genus *Croton*, producing a capsulelike fruit. **2** any small tree or shrub of the genus *Codiaeum*, esp. *C. variegatum*, with colored ornamental leaves. □ **croton oil** a powerful purgative obtained from the fruit of *Croton tiglium*. [mod.L f. Gk *krotōn* sheep tick, croton (from the shape of its seeds)]

crouch /krowch/ *v. & n.* ● *v.intr.* lower the body with the limbs close to the chest, esp. for concealment, or (of an animal) before pouncing; be in this position. ● *n.* an act of crouching; a crouching position. [ME, perh. f. OF *crochir* be bent f. *croc* hook: cf. CROOK]
■ *v.* bend (down), squat (down); scrunch down, stoop.
● *n.* squat, bend; see also STOOP[1] *n.* 1.

croup[1] /krōōp/ *n.* an inflammation of the larynx and trachea in children, with a hard cough and difficulty in breathing. □□ **croupy** *adj.* [*croup* to croak (imit.)]

croup[2] /krōōp/ *n.* the rump or hindquarters esp. of a horse. [ME f. OF *croupe*, rel. to CROP]
■ see TAIL[1] *n.* 1.

croupier /krōōpeeər, -eeay/ *n.* **1** the person in charge of a gaming table, raking in and paying out money, etc. **2** the assistant chairperson at a public dinner, seated at the foot of the table. [F, orig. = rider on the croup: see CROUP[2]]

crouton /krōṓton/ *n.* a small piece of fried or toasted bread served with soup or used as a garnish. [F f. *croûte* CRUST]

Crow /krō/ *n.* **1 a** a N. American people native to eastern Montana. **b** a member of this people. **2** the language of this people.

crow[1] /krō/ *n.* **1** any large, black bird of the genus *Corvus*, having a powerful black beak. **2** any similar bird of the family Corvidae, e.g., the raven, rook, and jackdaw. **3** *sl. derog.* a woman, esp. an old or ugly one. □ **as the crow flies** in a straight line. **crow's-foot** (*pl.* **-feet**) **1** (usu. in *pl.*) a wrinkle at the outer corner of a person's eye. **2** *Mil.* a caltrop. **crow's nest** a barrel or platform fixed at the masthead of a sailing vessel as a shelter for a lookout. **eat crow** submit to humiliation. [OE *crāwe* ult. f. WG]
■ □ **as the crow flies** see STRAIGHT *adv.* 1. **crow's-foot 1** see WRINKLE *n.* 1.

crow[2] /krō/ *v. & n.* ● *v.intr.* **1** (*past* **crowed** or esp. *Brit.* **crew** /krōō/) (of a cock) utter its characteristic loud cry. **2** (of a baby) utter happy cries. **3** (usu. foll. by *over*) express unrestrained gleeful satisfaction. ● *n.* **1** the cry of a cock. **2** a happy cry of a baby. [OE *crāwan*, of imit. orig.]
■ *v.* **3** see GLOAT *v.*

crowbar /krṓbaar/ *n.* an iron bar with a flattened end, used as a lever.

crowberry /krṓberee/ *n.* (*pl.* **-ies**) **1 a** a heathlike evergreen shrub *Empetrum nigrum*, bearing black berries. **b** the flavorless edible berry of this plant. **2** a cranberry.

crowd /krowd/ *n. & v.* ● *n.* **1** a large number of people gathered together, usu. without orderly arrangement. **2** a mass of spectators; an audience. **3** *colloq.* a particular company or set of people (*met the crowd from the sales department*). **4** (prec. by *the*) the mass or multitude of people (*go along with the crowd*). **5** a large number (of things). **6** actors representing a crowd. ● *v.* **1 a** *intr.* come together in a crowd. **b** *tr.* cause to do this. **c** *intr.* force one's way. **2** *tr.* **a** (foll. by *into*) force or compress into a confined space. **b** (often foll. by *with*; usu. in *passive*) fill or make abundant with (*was crowded with tourists*). **3** *tr.* **a** (of a number of people) come aggressively close to. **b** *colloq.* harass or pressure (a person). □ **crowd out** exclude by crowding. □□ **crowdedness** *n.* [OE *crūdan* press, drive]
■ *n.* **1** throng, multitude, horde, host, swarm, mass, press, flood, mob, flock, pack. **3** company, set, circle, lot, gang, bunch, group, coterie, clique, claque, faction. **5** see MASS[1] *n.* 3. ● *v.* **1 a** throng, swarm, herd, pour,

pile, press, cluster, gather, get together, flood, flock, assemble, congregate, collect. **2 a** compress, squeeze, pack, jam, stuff, cram, push, press, drive, shove, thrust, force, load. **b** filled, crowded, jammed, crammed.

3 b see HARASS 1.

crowfoot /krṓfŏŏt/ *n.* (*pl.* **crowfoots** for 1 & 2, **crowfeet** for 3 & 4) **1** any of various plants of the genus *Ranunculus*, esp. buttercup, often characterized by divided leaves that resemble a crow's foot. **2** any of various other plants whose leaves, etc., bear a similar resemblance. **3** *Mil.* a caltrop. **4** a three-legged antislip support for a motion-picture camera's tripod.

crown /krown/ *n. & v.* ● *n.* **1** a monarch's ornamental and usu. jeweled headdress. **2** (**the Crown**) **a** the monarch, esp. as head of state. **b** the power or authority residing in the monarchy. **3 a** a wreath of leaves or flowers, etc., worn on the head, esp. as an emblem of victory. **b** an award or distinction gained by a victory or achievement, esp. in sport. **4** a crown-shaped thing, esp. a device or ornament. **5** the top part of a thing, esp. of the head or a hat. **6 a** the highest or central part of an arched or curved thing (*crown of the road*). **b** a thing that completes or forms the summit. **7** the part of a plant just above and below the ground. **8** the upper part of a cut gem above the girdle. **9 a** the part of a tooth projecting from the gum. **b** an artificial replacement or covering for this. **10 a** a former British coin equal to five shillings (25 pence). **b** any of several foreign coins with a name meaning 'crown,' esp. the krona or krone. **11** a former size of paper, 504 x 384 mm. ● *v.tr.* **1** put a crown on (a person or a person's head). **2** invest (a person) with a royal crown or authority. **3** be a crown to; encircle or rest on the top of. **4 a** (often as **crowning** *adj.*) be or cause to be the consummation, reward, or finishing touch to (*the crowning glory*). **b** bring (efforts) to a happy issue. **5** fit a crown to (a tooth). **6** *sl.* hit on the head. □ **crown colony** (also **Crown Colony**) a British colony controlled by the Crown. **crown court** a court of criminal jurisdiction in England and Wales. **crown glass** glass made without lead or iron and orig. in a circular sheet; used formerly in windows, now as optical glass of low refractive index. **crown imperial** a tall fritillary, *Fritillaria imperialis*, with a flower cluster at the top of the stalk. **crown jewels** the regalia and other jewelry worn by the sovereign on certain state occasions. **crown of thorns** any starfish of the genus *Acanthaster* feeding on coral. **crown prince** a male heir to a sovereign throne. **crown princess 1** the wife of a crown prince. **2** a female heir to a sovereign throne. **crown roast** a roast of rib pieces of pork or lamb arranged like a crown. **crown wheel** a wheel with teeth set at right angles to its plane, esp. in the gears of motor vehicles. [ME f. AF *corune*, OF *corone* f. L *corona*]

■ *n.* **1** coronet, diadem, circlet, tiara. **2 a** monarch, ruler, sovereign, potentate; king, queen; His *or* Her Majesty, His *or* Her Highness. **b** monarchy, government, *formal esp. Law* realm. ● *v.* **2** enthrone. **3** see ENCIRCLE 1, TOP[1] *v.* 1. **4** cap, top, surmount, culminate, climax, consummate, fulfill, reward. **6** see BRAIN *v.* 2.

crowsteps /krṓsteps/ *n.* = CORBIESTEPS.

crozier var. of CROSIER.

CRT *abbr.* cathode-ray tube.

cru /krṓṓ/ *n.* **1** a French vineyard or wine-producing region. **2** the grade of wine produced from it. [F f. *crû* grown]

cruces *pl.* of CRUX.

crucial /krṓṓshǝl/ *adj.* **1** decisive; critical. **2** *colloq. disp.* very important. **3** *sl.* excellent. □□ **cruciality** /-sheeálitee/ *n.* (*pl.* -ies). **crucially** *adv.* [F f. L *crux crucis* cross]

■ **1** critical, decisive, pivotal, vital, momentous, essential, major; key. **3** see EXCELLENT.

crucian /krṓṓshǝn/ *n.* a yellow cyprinoid fish, *Carassius carassius*, allied to the goldfish. [LG *karusse*, etc.]

cruciate /krṓṓsheeayt/ *adj. Zool.* cross-shaped. [mod.L *cruciatus* f. L (as CRUCIBLE)]

crucible /krṓṓsibǝl/ *n.* **1** a melting pot for metals, etc. **2** a severe test or trial. [ME f. med.L *crucibulum* night lamp, crucible, f. L *crux crucis* cross]

crucifer /krṓṓsifǝr/ *n.* **1** one who carries a cross in an ecclesiastical procession. **2** a cruciferous plant.

cruciferous /krṓṓsifǝrǝs/ *adj. Bot.* of the family Cruciferae, having flowers with four petals arranged in a cross. [LL *crucifer* (as CRUCIAL, -FEROUS)]

crucifix /krṓṓsifiks/ *n.* a model or image of a cross with a figure of Christ on it. [ME f. OF f. eccl.L *crucifixus* f. L *cruci fixus* fixed to a cross]

■ cross, rood.

crucifixion /krṓṓsifíkshǝn/ *n.* **1 a** crucifying or being crucified. **b** an instance of this. **2** (**Crucifixion**) **a** the crucifixion of Christ. **b** a representation of this. [eccl.L *crucifixio* (as CRUCIFIX)]

cruciform /krṓṓsifawrm/ *adj.* cross-shaped (esp. of a church with transepts). [L *crux crucis* cross + -FORM]

crucify /krṓṓsifī/ *v.tr.* (**-ies, -ied**) **1** put to death by fastening to a cross. **2 a** cause extreme pain to. **b** persecute; torment. **c** *sl.* defeat thoroughly in an argument, match, etc. □□ **crucifier** *n.* [ME f. OF *crucifier* f. LL *crucifigere* (as CRUCIFIX)]

■ **2** see TORMENT *v.* 1.

cruck /kruk/ *n. Brit. hist.* either of a pair of curved timbers extending to the ground in the framework of a type of medieval house roof. [var. of CROOK]

crud /krud/ *n. sl.* **1 a** a deposit of unwanted impurities, grease, etc. **b** something disgusting or undesirable **c** a corrosive deposit in a nuclear reactor. **2** an unpleasant person. **3** nonsense. □□ **cruddy** *adj.* (**cruddier, cruddiest**). [var. of CURD]

■ **1** see FILTH 1. □□ **cruddy** see FILTHY *adj.* 1.

crude /krṓṓd/ *adj. & n.* ● *adj.* **1 a** in the natural or raw state; not refined. **b** rough; unpolished; lacking finish. **2 a** (of an action or statement or manners) rude; blunt. **b** offensive; indecent (*a crude gesture*). **3 a** *Statistics* (of numerical totals) not adjusted or corrected. **b** rough (*a crude estimate*). ● *n.* natural mineral oil. □□ **crudely** *adv.* **crudeness** *n.* **crudity** *n.* [ME f. L *crudus* raw, rough]

■ *adj.* **1 a** unrefined, raw, natural, original, unprocessed. **b** rough, unpolished, unfinished, rudimentary, immature, undeveloped, primitive, unrefined. **2 a** blunt, rough, coarse, rude, brusque, unsophisticated, indelicate, unrefined, uncouth, crass, gross, rustic, uncivil, impolite. **b** obscene, rude, indecent, offensive, vulgar, tasteless. **3** see ROUGH *adj.* 11a.

crudités /krṓṓditáy/ *n.pl.* an hors-d'oeuvre of mixed raw vegetables, often served with a sauce into which they are dipped. [F]

cruel /krṓṓǝl/ *adj.* ● *adj.* (**crueler, cruelest**) **1** indifferent to or gratified by another's suffering. **2** causing pain or suffering, esp. deliberately. □□ **cruelly** *adv.* **cruelness** *n.* [ME f. OF f. L *crudelis*, rel. to *crudus* (as CRUDE)]

■ merciless, pitiless, hard-hearted, harsh, stonyhearted, heartless, unsparing, callous, sadistic, beastly, cold-blooded, ruthless, vicious, unkind, hard; ferocious, inhuman, barbaric, barbarous, brutal, brute, savage, fiendish.

cruelty /krṓṓǝltee/ *n.* (*pl.* -ies) **1** a cruel act or attitude; indifference to another's suffering. **2** a succession of cruel acts; a continued cruel attitude (*suffered much cruelty*). **3** *Law* physical or mental harm inflicted (whether or not intentional), esp. as a ground for divorce. □ **cruelty-free** (of cosmetics, etc.) produced without involving any cruelty to animals in the development or manufacturing process. [OF *crualté* ult. f. L *crudelitas*]

cruet /krṓṓit/ *n.* **1** a small container for oil or vinegar for use at the table. **2** (in full **cruet-stand**) a stand holding cruets. **3** *Eccl.* a small container for the wine and water in the celebration of the Eucharist. [ME through AF f. OF *crue* pot f. OS *krūka*: rel. to CROCK[2]]

cruise /krṓṓz/ *v. & n.* ● *v.* **1** *intr.* make a journey by sea

---

/. . . / **pronunciation**	● **part of speech**
□ **phrases, idioms, and compounds**	
□□ **derivatives**	■ **synonym section**
cross-references appear in SMALL CAPITALS or *italics*	

calling at a series of ports usu. according to a predetermined plan, esp. for pleasure. **2** *intr.* sail about without a precise destination. **3** *intr.* **a** (of a motor vehicle or aircraft) travel at a moderate or economical speed. **b** (of a vehicle or its driver) travel at random, esp. slowly. **4** *intr.* achieve an objective, win a race, etc., with ease. **5** *intr.* & *tr. sl.* walk or drive about (the streets, etc.) in search of a sexual (esp. homosexual) partner. ● *n.* a cruising voyage, esp. as a vacation. □ **cruise control** a device on a motor vehicle that automatically maintains a constant speed and relieves the operator of the need to depress the accelerator. **cruise missile** one able to fly at a low altitude and guide itself by reference to the features of the region it traverses. **cruising speed** a comfortable and economical speed for a motor vehicle, below its maximum speed. [prob. f. Du. *kruisen* f. *kruis* CROSS]

■ *v.* **1** sail, coast, travel, journey, voyage. ● *n.* sail, voyage, journey, boat trip.

cruiser /króŏzər/ *n.* **1** a warship of high speed and medium armament. **2** = *cabin cruiser.* **3** a police patrol car. [Du. *kruiser* (as CRUISE)]

cruiserweight /króŏzərwayt/ *n.* a weight class in professional boxing between light heavyweight and heavyweight.

cruller /krúlər/ *n.* a small cake made of a rich dough twisted or curled and fried in fat. [prob. f. Du. *krullen* curl]

crumb /krum/ *n.* & *v.* ● *n.* **1 a** a small fragment, esp. of bread. **b** a small particle (*a crumb of comfort*). **2** the soft inner part of a loaf of bread. **3** *sl.* an objectionable person. ● *v.tr.* **1** cover with breadcrumbs. **2** break into crumbs. [OE *cruma*]

■ *n.* **1** fragment, morsel, bite, scrap, particle, shred, snippet, sliver, bit, speck, *colloq.* atom. **3** see WRETCH 2.

crumble /krúmbəl/ *v.* & *n.* ● *v.* **1** *tr.* & *intr.* break or fall into crumbs or fragments. **2** *intr.* (of power, a reputation, etc.) gradually disintegrate. ● *n.* **1** a crumbly or crumbled substance. **2** *Brit.* a mixture of flour and fat, rubbed to the texture of breadcrumbs and cooked as a topping for fruit, etc. (*apple crumble*; *vegetable crumble*). [ME f. OE, formed as CRUMB]

■ *v.* **1** disintegrate, fragment, break apart, break up, shiver, come to pieces. **2** see COLLAPSE *v.*

crumbly /krúmblee/ *adj.* (**crumblier, crumbliest**) consisting of, or apt to fall into, crumbs or fragments. □□ **crumbliness** *n.*

crumbs /krumz/ *int. Brit. sl.* expressing dismay or surprise. [euphem. for *Christ*]

crumby /krúmee/ *adj.* (**crumbier, crumbiest**) **1** like or covered in crumbs. **2** = CRUMMY.

crumhorn var. of KRUMMHORN.

crummy /krúmee/ *adj.* (**crummier, crummiest**) *colloq.* dirty; squalid; inferior; worthless. □□ **crummily** *adv.* **crumminess** *n.* [var. of CRUMBY]

■ see INFERIOR *adj.* 1.

crump /krump/ *n.* & *v. Mil. sl.* ● *n.* the sound of a bursting bomb or shell. ● *v.intr.* make this sound. [imit.]

crumpet /krúmpit/ *n.* **1** a soft, flat cake of a yeast mixture cooked on a griddle and eaten toasted and buttered. **2** *Brit. joc.* or *offens.* **a** a sexually attractive person, esp. a woman. **b** women regarded collectively, esp. as objects of sexual desire. [17th c.: orig. uncert.]

crumple /krúmpəl/ *v.* & *n.* ● *v.* **1** *tr.* & *intr.* (often foll. by *up*) a crush or become crushed into creases. **b** ruffle; wrinkle. **2** *intr.* (often foll. by *up*) collapse; give way. ● *n.* a crease or wrinkle. □ **crumple zone** a part of a motor vehicle, esp. the extreme front and rear, designed to crumple easily in a crash and absorb impact. □□ **crumply** *adj.* [obs. *crump* (v. & adj.) (make or become) curved]

■ *v.* **1** wrinkle, crease, rumple, ruffle, crinkle, crush, mangle. **2** see COLLAPSE *v.* ● *n.* see WRINKLE *n.* 1, 2.

crunch /krunch/ *v.* & *n.* ● *v.* **1** *tr.* **a** crush noisily with the teeth. **b** grind (gravel, dry snow, etc.) under foot, wheels, etc. **2** *intr.* (often foll. by *up, through*) make a crunching sound in walking, moving, etc. ● *n.* **1** crunching; a crunching sound. **2** *colloq.* a decisive event or moment. [earlier *cra(u)nch*, assim. to *munch*]

■ *v.* **1 a** chew, bite, crush, grind, munch, champ, chomp,

scrunch. ● *n.* **2** moment of truth, decision time, crisis, critical moment, showdown, crux, juncture.

crunchy /krúnchee/ *adj.* (**crunchier, crunchiest**) that can be or has been crunched or crushed into small pieces; hard and crispy. □□ **crunchily** *adv.* **crunchiness** *n.*

■ see CRISP *adj.* 1.

crupper /krúpər/ *n.* **1** a strap buckled to the back of a saddle and looped under the horse's tail to hold the harness back. **2** the hindquarters of a horse. [ME f. OF *cropiere* (cf. CROUP²)]

crural /króŏrəl/ *adj. Anat.* of the leg. [F *crural* or L *cruralis* f. *crus cruris* leg]

crusade /króŏsáyd/ *n.* & *v.* ● *n.* **1 a** any of several medieval military expeditions made by Europeans to recover the Holy Land from the Muslims. **b** a war instigated by the Roman Catholic Church for alleged religious ends. **2** a vigorous campaign in favor of a cause. ● *v.intr.* engage in a crusade. □□ **crusader** *n.* [earlier *croisade* (F f. *croix* cross) or *crusado* (Sp. f. *cruz* cross)]

■ *n.* **1 b** campaign, expedition, holy war; jihad. **2** see CAMPAIGN *n.* 1. ● *v.* campaign, war, battle; lobby, fight.

cruse /króŏz/ *n. archaic* an earthenware pot or jar. [OE *crūse,* of unkn. orig.]

crush /krush/ *v.* & *n.* ● *v.tr.* **1** compress with force or violence, so as to break, bruise, etc. **2** reduce to powder by pressure. **3** crease or crumple by rough handling. **4** defeat or subdue completely (*crushed by my reply*). ● *n.* **1** an act of crushing. **2** a crowded mass of people. **3** a drink made from the juice of crushed fruit. **4** *colloq.* **a** (usu. foll. by *on*) a (usu. passing) infatuation. **b** the object of an infatuation (*who's the latest crush?*). □□ **crushable** *adj.* **crusher** *n.* **crushingly** *adv.* [ME f. AF *crussir, corussier,* OF *croissir, cruissir,* gnash (teeth), crack, f. Rmc]

■ *v.* **1** break, smash, crunch, shiver, splinter; squash, pulp, mash, mangle, squeeze, compress, press. **2** pulverize, pound; see also GRIND *v.* 1a. **3** crumple, wrinkle, crease, crinkle, rumple. **4** overcome, defeat, conquer, beat, thrash, *literary* vanquish; subdue, put down, quash, quell, overwhelm, squelch, suppress, repress; mortify, depress, devastate. ● *n.* **2** press, crowd, jam, throng. **4 a** (*have a crush on*) see LOVE *v.* 1. **b** see PASSION 3b.

crust /krust/ *n.* & *v.* ● *n.* **1 a** the hard outer part of a loaf of bread. **b** a piece of this with some soft bread attached. **c** a hard, dry scrap of bread. **d** esp. *Austral. sl.* a livelihood (*what do you do for a crust?*). **2** the pastry covering of a pie. **3** a hard casing of a softer thing, e.g., a harder layer over soft snow. **4** *Geol.* the outer portion of the earth. **5 a** a coating or deposit on the surface of anything. **b** a hard, dry formation on the skin; a scab. **6** a deposit of tartar formed in bottles of old wine. **7 a** *sl.* impudence (*you have a lot of crust!*). **b** a superficial hardness of manner. ● *v.tr.* & *intr.* **1** cover or become covered with a crust. **2** form into a crust. □□ **crustal** *adj.* (in sense 4 of *n.*). [ME f. OF *crouste* f. L *crusta* rind, shell]

■ *n.* **1** see HEEL¹ *n.* 5. **3–5** see SKIN *n.* 4. **7 a** see GALL¹ 1.

crustacean /krustáyshən/ *n.* & *adj.* ● *n.* any arthropod of the class Crustacea, having a hard shell and usu. aquatic, e.g., the crab, lobster, and shrimp. ● *adj.* of or relating to crustaceans. □□ **crustaceology** /-sheeólэjee/ *n.* **crustaceous** /-shəs/ *adj.* [mod.L *crustaceus* f. *crusta:* see CRUST]

crusted /krústid/ *adj.* **1 a** having a crust. **b** (of wine) having deposited a crust. **2** antiquated; venerable (*crusted prejudice*).

crusty /krústee/ *adj.* (**crustier, crustiest**) **1** having a crisp crust (*a crusty loaf*). **2** irritable; curt. **3** hard; crustlike. □□ **crustily** *adv.* **crustiness** *n.*

■ **2** see IRRITABLE 1.

crutch /kruch/ *n.* **1** a support for a lame person, usu. with a crosspiece at the top fitting under the armpit (*pair of crutches*). **2** any support or prop. **3** the crotch of the human body or garment. [OE *cryc(c)* f. Gmc]

crux /kruks/ *n.* (*pl.* **cruxes** or **cruces** /króŏseez/) **1** the decisive point at issue. **2** a difficult matter; a puzzle. [L, = cross]

■ **1** see NUB 1.

cruzado /krōōzáadō/ n. (pl. **-os**) the chief monetary unit of Brazil from 1986 to 1994. [Port. *cruzado, crusado,* = marked with the cross]

cruzeiro /krōōzáirō/ n. (pl. **-os**) the monetary unit of Brazil before 1986 and (as **cruzeiro real**) since July 1994. [Port., = large cross]

cry /krī/ v. & n. ● v. (**cries, cried**) **1** intr. (often foll. by *out*) make a loud or shrill sound, esp. to express pain, grief, etc., or to appeal for help. **2 a** intr. shed tears; weep. **b** tr. shed (tears). **3** tr. (often foll. by *out*) say or exclaim loudly or excitedly. **4** intr. (of an animal, esp. a bird) make a loud call. **5** tr. (of a hawker, etc.) proclaim (wares, etc.) in the street. ● n. (pl. **cries**) **1** a loud inarticulate utterance of grief, pain, fear, joy, etc. **2** a loud excited utterance of words. **3** an urgent appeal or entreaty. **4** a spell of weeping. **5** a public demand; a strong movement of opinion. **b** a watchword or rallying call. **6** the natural utterance of an animal, esp. of hounds on the scent. **7** the street call of a hawker, etc. □ **cry down** disparage; belittle. **cry one's eyes** (or **heart**) **out** weep bitterly. **cry from the heart** a passionate appeal or protest. **cry off** *colloq.* withdraw from a promise or undertaking. **cry out for** demand as a self-evident requirement or solution. **cry over spilled milk** see MILK. **cry up** praise; extol. **cry wolf** see WOLF. **a far cry 1** a long way. **2** a very different thing. **for crying out loud** *colloq.* an exclamation of surprise or annoyance. **in full cry** (of hounds) in keen pursuit. [ME f. OF *crier, cri* f. L *quiritare* wail]

■ v. **1** see SHOUT v. **2 a** weep, sob, wail, keen, bawl, shed tears, whimper, snivel, mewl, *colloq.* turn on the waterworks, *literary* pule. ● n. **1, 2** scream, shriek, wail, howl, yowl, screech, yelp, whoop, yell, shout. **3** see APPEAL n. 1. **5 b** war cry, battle cry, rallying cry; slogan, watchword. **6** call, sound, note. □ **cry down** see DISPARAGE 1. **cry out for** demand, need, call *or* ask for, beg *or* plead for. **cry up** see PRAISE v. 1. **a far cry 1** a long way, quite a distance, remote, distant, faraway, far-off. **2** (*a far cry from*) not (at all), not quite *or* exactly, very different from, anything but.

crybaby /kríbaybee/ n. a person, esp. a child, who sheds tears frequently.

cryer var. of CRIER.

crying /krí-ing/ attrib.adj. (of an injustice or other evil) flagrant; demanding redress (*a crying need*; *a crying shame*).

cryo- /krío/ comb. form (extreme) cold. [Gk *kruos* frost]

cryobiology /krīōbíóləjee/ n. the biology of organisms below their normal temperatures. □□ **cryobiological** /-bīəlójikəl/ adj. **cryobiologist** n.

cryogen /kríəjən/ n. a freezing mixture; a substance used to produce very low temperatures.

cryogenics /kríəjéniks/ n. the branch of physics dealing with the production and effects of very low temperatures. □□ **cryogenic** adj.

cryolite /kríəlīt/ n. Mineral. a lustrous mineral of sodium aluminum fluoride, used in the manufacture of aluminum.

cryopump /kríōpump/ n. a vacuum pump using liquefied gases.

cryostat /kríəstat/ n. an apparatus for maintaining a very low temperature.

cryosurgery /kríōsárjəree/ n. surgery using the local application of intense cold for anesthesia or therapy.

crypt /kript/ n. an underground room or vault, esp. one beneath a church, used usu. as a burial place. [ME f. L *crypta* f. Gk *kruptē* f. *kruptos* hidden]

■ tomb, vault, mausoleum, sepulcher, grave, catacomb; cellar, basement.

cryptanalysis /kríptənálisis/ n. the art or process of deciphering cryptograms by analysis. □□ **cryptanalyst** /-tánəl-ist/ n. **cryptanalytic** /-tanəlítik/ adj. **cryptanalytical** adj. [CRYPTO- + ANALYSIS]

cryptic /kríptik/ adj. **1 a** obscure in meaning. **b** (of a crossword clue, etc.) indirect; indicating the solution in a way that is not obvious. **c** secret; mysterious; enigmatic. **2** Zool. (of coloration, etc.) serving for concealment. □□ **cryptically** adv. [LL *crypticus* f. Gk *kruptikos* (as CRYPTO-)]

■ **1 a** obscure, unclear, nebulous, vague, inscrutable, recondite, puzzling. **c** secret, occult, mystical, hidden, esoteric, mystic, cabalistic; mysterious, arcane, enigmatic.

crypto /kríptō/ n. (pl. **-os**) colloq. a person having a secret allegiance to a political creed, etc., esp. communism. [as CRYPTO-]

crypto- /kríptō/ comb. form concealed; secret (*crypto-communist*). [Gk *kruptos* hidden]

cryptocrystalline /kríptōkrístəlin, -līn/ adj having a crystalline structure visible only when magnified.

cryptogam /kríptəgám/ n. a plant that has no true flowers or seeds, e.g., ferns, mosses, algae, and fungi. □□ **cryptogamic** adj. **cryptogamous** /-tógəməs/ adj. [F *cryptogame* f. mod.L *cryptogamae* (*plantae*) formed as CRYPTO- + Gk *gamos* marriage]

cryptogram /kríptəgram/ n. a text written in code.

cryptography /kriptógrəfee/ n. the art of writing or solving codes and ciphers. □□ **cryptographer** n. **cryptographic** /-təgráfik/ adj. **cryptographically** adv.

■ □□ **cryptographic** see SECRET adj. 1.

cryptomeria /kríptəme'ereeə/ n. a tall evergreen tree, *Cryptomeria japonica*, native to China and Japan, with long, curved, spirally arranged leaves and short cones. Also called *Japanese cedar*. [CRYPTO- + Gk *meros* part (because the seeds are enclosed by scales)]

crystal /kríst'l/ n. & adj. ● n. **1 a** a clear transparent mineral, esp. rock crystal. **b** a piece of this. **2** (in full **crystal glass**) a highly transparent glass; flint glass. **b** articles made of this. **3** the glass over a watch face. **4** *Electronics* a crystalline piece of semiconductor. **5** *Chem.* **a** an aggregation of molecules with a definite internal structure and the external form of a solid enclosed by symmetrically arranged plane faces. **b** a solid whose constituent particles are symmetrically arranged. ● adj. (usu. *attrib.*) made of, like, or clear as crystal. □ **crystal ball** a glass globe used in crystal gazing. **crystal class** *Crystallog.* any of 32 categories of crystals classified according to their symmetry. **crystal clear** unclouded; transparent. **crystal gazing** the process of concentrating one's gaze on a crystal ball supposedly in order to obtain a picture of future events, etc. **crystal lattice** *Crystallog.* the regular repeating pattern of atoms, ions, or molecules in a crystalline substance. **crystal set** a simple early form of radio receiving apparatus with a crystal touching a metal wire as the rectifier. **crystal system** *Crystallog.* any of seven possible unique combinations of unit cells, crystal lattices, and symmetry elements of a crystal class. [OE f. OF *cristal* f. L *crystallum* f. Gk *krustallos* ice, crystal]

■ n. **1 b** see GRAIN n. 3. □ **crystal clear** see PLAIN¹ adj. 1, 2. **crystal gazing** see PROPHECY 2.

crystalline /kríst'lin, -līn/ adj. **1** of, like, or clear as crystal. **2** *Chem. & Mineral.* having the structure and form of a crystal. □ **crystalline lens** a transparent lens enclosed in a membranous capsule behind the iris of the eye. □□ **crystallinity** /-línitee/ n. [ME f. OF *cristallin* f. L *crystallinus* f. Gk *krustallinos* (as CRYSTAL)]

■ **1** see CLEAR adj. 3a.

crystallite /kríst'līt/ n. **1** a small crystal. **2** an individual perfect crystal or grain in a metal, etc. **3** *Bot.* a region of cellulose, etc., with a crystallike structure.

crystallize /kríst'līz/ v. **1** tr. & intr. form or cause to form crystals. **2** (often foll. by *out*) **a** intr. (of ideas or plans) become definite. **b** tr. make definite. **3** tr. & intr. coat or impregnate or become coated or impregnated with sugar (*crystallized fruit*). □□ **crystallizable** adj. **crystallization** n.

■ **2** see FORM v. 2. □□ **crystallization** see FORMATION 1, 2.

crystallography /kríst'lógrəfee/ n. the science of crystal

/. . . / **pronunciation**	● **part of speech**
□ **phrases, idioms, and compounds**	
□□ **derivatives**	■ **synonym section**
cross-references appear in SMALL CAPITALS or *italics*	

form and structure. □□ **crystallographer** *n.* **crystallographic** /-ləgráfik/ *adj.*

crystalloid /kríst'loyd/ *adj. & n.* ● *adj.* **1** crystallike. **2** having a crystalline structure. ● *n.* a substance that in solution is able to pass through a semipermeable membrane (cf. COLLOID).

Cs *symb. Chem.* the element cesium.

c/s *abbr.* cycles per second.

csardas var. of CZARDAS.

C-section *abbr.* of *cesarean section.*

CSF *abbr.* cerebrospinal fluid.

CST *abbr.* central standard time.

CT *abbr.* Connecticut (in official postal use).

ct. *abbr.* **1** carat. **2** cent.

ctenoid /téenoyd, tén-/ *adj. Zool.* (of fish scales) characterized by tiny toothlike processes (cf. PLACOID). [Gk *kteis ktenos* comb]

ctenophore /téenəfawr, tén-/ *n.* any marine animal of the phylum Ctenophora, having a jellyfishlike body bearing rows of cilia, e.g., sea gooseberries. [mod.L *ctenophorus* (as CTENOID)]

ctn. *abbr.* **1** carton. **2** cotangent.

Cu *symb. Chem.* the element copper.

cu. *abbr.* cubic.

cub /kub/ *n. & v.* ● *n.* **1** the young of a fox, bear, lion, etc. **2** an ill-mannered young man. **3** (**Cub**) (in full **Cub Scout**) a member of the junior branch of the Boy Scouts. **4** (in full **cub reporter**) *colloq.* a young or inexperienced newspaper reporter. **5** an apprentice. ● *v.tr.* (**cubbed, cubbing**) (also *absol.*) give birth to (cubs). □□ **cubhood** *n.* [16th c.: orig. unkn.]

■ **2** see PUP *n.* 3.

Cuban /kyōōbən/ *adj. & n.* ● *adj.* of or relating to Cuba, an island republic in the Caribbean, or its people. ● *n.* a native or national of Cuba. □ **Cuban heel** a moderately high straight heel of a woman's shoe.

cubby /kúbee/ *n.* (*pl.* **-ies**) (in full **cubbyhole**) **1** a very small room. **2** a snug or confined space. **3** a boxlike compartment for storage, etc. [dial. *cub* stall, pen, of LG orig.]

■ **2** see SANCTUM 2, COMPARTMENT *n.* 1.

cube /kyōōb/ *n. & v.* ● *n.* **1** a solid contained by six equal squares. **2** a cube-shaped block. **3** *Math.* the product of a number multiplied by its square. ● *v.tr.* **1** find the cube of (a number). **2** cut (food for cooking, etc.) into small cubes. **3** tenderize (meat) by scoring it in a criss-cross pattern. □ **cube root** the number which produces a given number when cubed. **cube steak** a thin slice of steak that has been cubed. □□ **cuber** *n.* [F *cube* or L *cubus* f. Gk *kubos*]

■ *n.* **2** see BLOCK *n.* 1. ● *v.* **2** see cut up 1.

cubeb /kyōōbeb/ *n.* **1** a climbing plant, *Piper cubeba*, bearing pungent berries. **2** this berry crushed for use in medicated cigarettes. [ME f. OF *cubebe, quibibe* ult. f. Arab. *kobāba, kubāba*]

cubic /kyōōbik/ *adj.* **1** cube-shaped. **2** of three dimensions. **3** involving the cube (and no higher power) of a number (*cubic equation*). **4** *Crystallog.* having three equal axes at right angles. □ **cubic content** the volume of a solid expressed in cubic units. **cubic foot**, etc., the volume of a cube whose edge is one foot, etc. [F *cubique* or L *cubicus* f. Gk *kubikos* (as CUBE)]

■ **2** solid, three-dimensional.

cubical /kyōōbikəl/ *adj.* cube-shaped. □□ **cubically** *adv.*

cubicle /kyōōbikəl/ *n.* **1** a small partitioned space, screened for privacy. **2** a small, separate sleeping compartment. [L *cubiculum* f. *cubare* lie down]

■ **1** see BOOTH 2.

cubiform /kyōōbifawrm/ *adj.* cube-shaped.

cubism /kyōōbizəm/ *n.* a style and movement in art, esp. painting, in which objects are represented as an assemblage of geometrical forms. □□ **cubist** *n. & adj.* [F *cubisme* (as CUBE)]

cubit /kyōōbit/ *n.* an ancient measure of length, approximately equal to the length of a forearm. [ME f. L *cubitum* elbow, cubit]

cubital /kyōōbit'l/ *adj.* **1** *Anat.* of the forearm. **2** *Zool.* of the corresponding part in animals. [ME f. L *cubitalis* (as CUBIT)]

cuboid /kyōōboyd/ *adj. & n.* ● *adj.* cube-shaped; like a cube. ● *n.* **1** *Geom.* a rectangular parallelepiped. **2** (in full **cuboid bone**) *Anat.* the outer bone of the tarsus. □□ **cuboidal** /-bóyd'l/ *adj.* [mod.L *cuboides* f. Gk *kuboeidēs* (as CUBE)]

cucking stool /kúkingstōōl/ *n. hist.* a chair on which disorderly offenders were ducked in water, publicly mocked, etc., as a punishment. [ME f. obs. *cuck* defecate]

cuckold /kúkōld/ *n. & v.* ● *n.* the husband of an adulteress. ● *v.tr.* make a cuckold of. □□ **cuckoldry** *n.* [ME *cukeweld, cokewold*, f. OF *cucu* cuckoo]

cuckoo /kōōkōō/ *n. & adj.* ● *n.* any bird of the family Culidae, esp. *Cuculus canorus*, having a characteristic cry, and depositing its eggs in the nests of small birds. ● *predic.adj. sl.* crazy; foolish. □ **cuckoo clock** a clock that strikes the hour with a sound like a cuckoo's call, usu. with the emergence on each note of a mechanical cuckoo. **cuckoo in the nest** an unwelcome intruder. **cuckoo spit** froth exuded by larvae of insects of the family Cercopidae on leaves, stems, etc. [ME f. OF *cucu*, imit.]

■ *adj.* see CRAZY 1.

cuckooflower /kōōkōōflówər/ *n.* **1** a meadow plant, *Cardamine pratensis*, with pale lilac flowers. **2** = ragged robin.

cuckoopint /kōōkōōpint/ *n.* a wild arum, *Arum maculatum*, with arrow-shaped leaves and scarlet berries: also called *lords-and-ladies*.

cucumber /kyōōkumbər/ *n.* **1** a long, green, fleshy fruit, used in salads. **2** the climbing plant, *Cucumis sativus*, yielding this fruit. [ME f. OF *co(u)combre* f. L *cucumer*]

cucurbit /kyōōkə́rbit/ *n.* = GOURD. □□ **cucurbitaceous** /-táyshəs/ *adj.* [L *cucurbita*]

cud /kud/ *n.* half-digested food returned from the first stomach of ruminants to the mouth for further chewing. [OE *cwidu, cudu* what is chewed, corresp. to OHG *kuti, quiti* glue]

cuddle /kúd'l/ *v. & n.* ● *v.* **1** *tr.* hug; embrace; fondle. **2** *intr.* nestle together; lie close and snug; kiss and fondle amorously. ● *n.* a prolonged and fond hug. □□ **cuddlesome** *adj.* [16th c.: perh. f. dial. *couth* snug]

■ *v.* **1** see CARESS *v.* **2** nestle together, embrace, snuggle up, bill and coo; pet, *Austral. & NZ* smoodge, *archaic* make love, *colloq.* neck, make out, smooch. ● *n.* see CARESS *n.*

cuddly /kúdlee/ *adj.* (**cuddlier, cuddliest**) tempting to cuddle; given to cuddling.

cuddy /kúdee/ *n.* (*pl.* **-ies**) *Sc.* **1** a donkey. **2** a stupid person. [perh. a pet-form of the name *Cuthbert*]

cudgel /kújəl/ *n. & v.* ● *n.* a short, thick stick used as a weapon. ● *v.tr.* beat with a cudgel. □ **cudgel one's brains** think hard about a problem. **take up the cudgels** (often foll. by *for*) make a vigorous defense. [OE *cycgel*, of unkn. orig.]

■ *n.* see CLUB *n.* 1. ● *v.* see CLUB *v.* 1. □ **cudgel one's brains** see WONDER *v.* 3.

cudweed /kúdweed/ *n.* any wild composite plant of the genus *Gnaphalium*, with scales and round flower heads, formerly given to cattle that had lost their cud.

cue[1] /kyōō/ *n. & v.* ● *n.* **1 a** the last words of an actor's speech serving as a signal to another actor to enter or speak. **b** a similar signal to a singer or player, etc. **2 a** a stimulus to perception, etc. **b** a signal for action. **c** a hint on how to behave in particular circumstances. **3** a facility for or an instance of cueing audio equipment (see sense 2 of *v.*). ● *v.tr.* (**cues, cued, cuing** or **cueing**) **1** give a cue to. **2** put (a piece of audio equipment, esp. a record player or tape recorder) in readiness to play a particular part of the recorded material. □ **cue bid** *Bridge* an artificial bid to show a particular card, etc., in the bidder's hand. **cue card** *colloq.* a card or board displaying a television script to a speaker as an aid to memory. **cue in 1** insert a cue for. **2** give information to. **on cue** at the correct moment. **take one's cue from** follow the example or advice of. [16th c.: orig. unkn.]

■ *n.* **1, 2** prompt, hint, reminder, signal, sign. ● *v.* **1** signal, prompt, remind. □ **take one's cue from** see FOLLOW 5.

cue[2] /kyoo/ *n. & v. Billiards*, etc. ● *n.* a long, straight, tapering rod for striking the ball. ● *v.* (**cues, cued, cuing** or **cueing**) **1** *tr.* strike (a ball) with a cue. **2** *intr.* use a cue. □ **cue ball** the ball that is to be struck with the cue. □□ **cueist** *n.* [var. of QUEUE]

cuesta /kwéstə/ *n. Geog.* a gentle slope, esp. one ending in a steep drop. [Sp., = slope, f. L *costa:* see COAST]
■ see CLIFF.

cuff[1] /kuf/ *n.* **1 a** the end part of a sleeve. **b** a separate band of linen worn around the wrist so as to appear under the sleeve. **c** the part of a glove covering the wrist. **2** a turned-up hem on pants. **3** (in *pl.*) *colloq.* handcuffs. □ **cuff link** a device of two joined studs, etc., to fasten the sides of a cuff together. **off-the-cuff** *colloq.* without preparation; extempore. □□ **cuffed** *adj.* (also in *comb.*). [ME: orig. unkn.]
■ □ **off the cuff** see EXTEMPORANEOUS.

cuff[2] /kuf/ *v. & n.* ● *v.tr.* strike with an open hand. ● *n.* such a blow. [16th c.: perh. imit.]
■ *v.* see HIT *v.* 1a. ● *n.* see BLOW[2] 1.

Cufic var. of KUFIC.

cui bono /kweé bónō/ who stands, or stood, to gain? (with the implication that this person is responsible). [L, = to whom (is it) a benefit?]

cuirass /kwirás/ *n.* **1** *hist.* a piece of armor consisting of breastplate and backplate fastened together. **2** a device for artificial respiration. [ME f. OF *cuirace*, ult. f. LL *coriaceus* f. *corium* leather]

cuirassier /kwírəseér/ *n. hist.* a cavalry soldier wearing a cuirass. [F (as CUIRASS)]

cuish var. of CUISSE.

cuisine /kwizeén/ *n.* a style or method of cooking, esp. of a particular country or establishment. [F f. L *coquina* f. *coquere* to cook]

cuisse /kwis/ *n.* (also **cuish** /kwish/) (usu. in *pl.*) *hist.* thigh armor. [ME, f. OF *cuisseaux* pl. of *cuissel* f. LL *coxale* f. *coxa* hip]

cul-de-sac /kúldəsak, kool-/ *n.* (*pl.* **culs-de-sac** *pronunc.* same) **1** a street or passage closed at one end. **2** a route or course leading nowhere; a position from which one cannot escape. **3** *Anat.* = DIVERTICULUM. [F, = sack bottom]

-cule /kyool/ *suffix* forming (orig. diminutive) nouns (*molecule*). [F *-cule* or L *-culus*]

culinary /kyóoləneree, kúl-/ *adj.* of or for cooking or the kitchen. □□ **culinarily** *adv.* [L *culinarius* f. *culina* kitchen]

cull /kul/ *v. & n.* ● *v.tr.* **1** select, choose, or gather from a large quantity or amount (*knowledge culled from books*). **2** pick or gather (flowers, fruit, etc.). **3** select (animals) according to quality, esp. poor surplus specimens for killing. ● *n.* **1** an act of culling. **2** an animal or animals culled. □□ **culler** *n.* [ME f. OF *coillier*, etc., ult. f. L *colligere* COLLECT[1]]
■ *v.* see PICK[1] *v.* 1.

cullet /kúlit/ *n.* recycled waste or broken glass used in glassmaking. [var. of COLLET]

culm[1] /kulm/ *n.* **1** coal dust, esp. of anthracite. **2** *Geol.* strata under coal measures, esp. in SW England. [ME, prob. rel. to COAL]

culm[2] /kulm/ *n. Bot.* the stem of a plant, esp. of grasses. □□ **culmiferous** /-mífərəs/ *adj.* [L *culmus* stalk]

culminant /kúlminənt/ *adj.* **1** at or forming the top. **2** *Astron.* on the meridian. [as CULMINATE + -ANT]

culminate /kúlminayt/ *v.* **1** *intr.* (usu. foll. by *in*) reach its highest or final point (*the antagonism culminated in war*). **2** *tr.* bring to its highest or final point. **3** *intr. Astron.* be on the meridian. □□ **culmination** /-náyshən/ *n.* [LL *culminare culminat-* f. *culmen* summit]
■ **1, 2** see FINISH *v.* 2a.

culottes /koolóts, kyoo-/ *n.pl.* women's (usu. short) trousers cut to resemble a skirt. [F, = knee-breeches]

culpable /kúlpəbəl/ *adj.* deserving blame. □□ **culpability** *n.* **culpably** *adv.* [ME f. OF *coupable* f. L *culpabilis* f. *culpare* f. *culpa* blame]
■ see GUILTY 1, 4.

culprit /kúlprit/ *n.* a person accused of or guilty of an offense. [17th c.: orig. in the formula *Culprit, how will you be tried?*, said by the clerk of the Crown to a prisoner pleading 'not guilty': perh. abbr. of AF *Culpable: prest d'averrer*, etc. (You are) guilty: (I am) ready to prove, etc.]
■ offender, criminal, malefactor, wrongdoer.

cult /kult/ *n.* **1** a system of religious worship esp. as expressed in ritual. **2 a** devotion or homage to a person or thing (*the cult of aestheticism*). **b** a popular fashion esp. followed by a specific section of society. **3** (*attrib.*) denoting a person or thing popularized in this way (*cult film; cult figure*). □□ **cultic** *adj.* **cultism** *n.* **cultist** *n.* [F *culte* or L *cultus* worship f. *colere cult-* inhabit, till, worship]
■ □□ **cultist** see SECTARIAN *n.* 1.

cultivar /kúltivaar/ *n. Bot.* a plant variety produced by cultivation. [CULTIVATE + VARIETY]

cultivate /kúltivayt/ *v.tr.* **1 a** prepare and use (soil, etc.) for crops or gardening. **b** break up (the ground) with a cultivator. **2 a** raise or produce (crops). **b** culture (bacteria, etc.). **3 a** (often as **cultivated** *adj.*) apply oneself to improving or developing (the mind, manners, etc.). **b** pay attention to or nurture (a person or a person's friendship); ingratiate oneself with (a person). □□ **cultivable** *adj.* **cultivatable** *adj.* **cultivation** *n.* [med.L *cultivare* f. *cultiva (terra)* arable (land) (as CULT)]
■ **1 a** till, plow, farm, work. **2 a** grow, raise, tend, produce. **3 a** (**cultivated**) sophisticated, cultured, educated, refined, elegant, soigné, civilized, polished, aristocratic, urbane, suave, cosmopolitan. **b** develop, nurture, work on, pay attention to, promote, further, encourage, foster, advance; woo, court, make advances to; ingratiate oneself with, pay court to, curry favor with, shine up to, *sl.* suck up to, butter up. □□ **cultivation** see CULTURE *n.* 1b, *farming* (FARM).

cultivator /kúltivaytər/ *n.* **1** a mechanical implement for breaking up the ground and uprooting weeds. **2** a person or thing that cultivates.

cultural /kúlchərəl/ *adj.* of or relating to the cultivation of the mind or manners, esp. through artistic or intellectual activity. □□ **culturally** *adv.*

culture /kúlchər/ *n. & v.* ● *n.* **1 a** the arts and other manifestations of human intellectual achievement regarded collectively (*a city lacking in culture*). **b** a refined understanding of this; intellectual development (*a person of culture*). **2** the customs, civilization, and achievements of a particular time or people (*studied Chinese culture*). **3** improvement by mental or physical training. **4 a** the cultivation of plants; the rearing of bees, silkworms, etc. **b** the cultivation of the soil. **5** a quantity of microorganisms and the nutrient material supporting their growth. ● *v.tr.* maintain (bacteria, etc.) in conditions suitable for growth. □ **culture shock** the feeling of disorientation experienced by a person suddenly subjected to an unfamiliar culture or way of life. **culture vulture** *colloq.* a person eager to acquire culture. [ME f. F *culture* or L *cultura* (as CULT): (v.) f. obs. F *culturer* or med.L *culturare*]
■ *n.* **1 b** cultivation, refinement, sophistication, urbanity, suavity, elegance, (good) breeding, background, erudition, education, enlightenment, learning, taste, discrimination, savoir faire, savoir vivre, discernment. **2** civilization, mores, customs, lifestyle, way of life, (sense of) culture. **4** see BREEDING 1, *farming* (FARM).

cultured /kúlchərd/ *adj.* having refined taste and manners and a good education. □ **cultured pearl** a pearl formed by an oyster after the insertion of a foreign body into its shell.

cultus /kúltəs/ *n.* a system of religious worship; a cult. [L: see CULT]

culverin /kúlvərin/ *n. hist.* **1** a long cannon. **2** a small firearm. [ME f. OF *coulevrine* f. *couleuvre* snake ult. f. L *colubra*]

/. . ./ **pronunciation**	● **part of speech**
□ **phrases, idioms, and compounds**	
□□ **derivatives**	■ **synonym section**
cross-references appear in SMALL CAPITALS or *italics*	

culvert /kúlvərt/ *n.* an underground channel carrying water across a road, etc. [18th c.: orig. unkn.]
■ see DRAIN *n.* 1a.

cum /kum/ *prep.* (usu. in *comb.*) with; combined with; also used as (*a bedroom-cum-study*). [L]

cum. *abbr.* cumulative.

cumber /kúmbər/ *v. & n.* ● *v.tr. literary* hamper; hinder; inconvenience. ● *n.* a hindrance, obstruction, or burden. [ME, prob. f. ENCUMBER]
■ *v.* see OVERLOAD *v.*

cumbersome /kúmbərsəm/ *adj.* inconvenient in size, weight, or shape; unwieldy. □□ **cumbersomely** *adv.* **cumbersomeness** *n.* [ME f. CUMBER + -SOME¹]
■ see UNWIELDY.

Cumbrian /kúmbreeən/ *adj. & n.* ● *adj.* **1** of Cumberland. **2 a** of the ancient British kingdom of Cumbria. **b** of the modern county of Cumbria. ● *n.* a native of Cumberland or of ancient or modern Cumbria. [med.L *Cumbria* f. Welsh *Cymry* Welshmen + -AN]

cumbrous /kúmbrəs/ *adj.* = CUMBERSOME. □□ **cumbrously** *adv.* **cumbrousness** *n.* [CUMBER + -OUS]

cum grano salis /kúm gráanō sáalis/ *adv.* with a grain of salt (see *take with a grain of salt* (see SALT)). [L]

cumin /kúmin, koŏ-, kyoŏ-/ *n.* **1** an umbelliferous plant, *Cuminum cyminum*, bearing aromatic seeds. **2** these seeds used as flavoring, esp. ground and used in curry powder. [ME f. OF *cumin, comin* f. L *cuminum* f. Gk *kuminon*, prob. of Semitic orig.]

cummerbund /kúmərbund/ *n.* a waist sash. [Hind. & Pers. *kamar-band* loin band]

cumquat var. of KUMQUAT.

cumulate *v. & adj.* ● *v.tr. & intr.* /kyoŏmyəlayt/ accumulate; amass; combine. ● *adj.* /kyoŏmyələt/ heaped up, massed. □□ **cumulation** /-láyshən/ *n.* [L *cumulare* f. *cumulus* heap]
■ *v.* see ACCUMULATE 1.

cumulative /kyoŏmyələtiv, -láytiv/ *adj.* **1 a** increasing or increased in amount, force, etc., by successive additions (*cumulative evidence*). **b** formed by successive additions (*learning is a cumulative process*). **2** *Stock Exch.* (of shares) entitling holders to arrears of interest before any other distribution is made. □ **cumulative error** an error that increases with the size of the sample revealing it. **cumulative voting** a system in which each voter has as many votes as there are candidates and may give all to one candidate. □□ **cumulatively** *adv.* **cumulativeness** *n.*

cumulo- /kyoŏmyəlō/ *comb. form* cumulus (cloud).

cumulus /kyoŏmyələs/ *n.* (*pl.* **cumuli** /-lī/) a cloud formation consisting of rounded masses heaped on each other above a horizontal base. □□ **cumulous** *adj.* [L, = heap]

cuneate /kyoŏneeət, -ayt/ *adj.* wedge-shaped. [L *cuneus* wedge]

cuneiform /kyoŏnéeəfawrm, kyoŏneeə-, kyoŏni-/ *adj. & n.* ● *adj.* **1** wedge-shaped. **2** of, relating to, or using the wedge-shaped writing impressed usu. in clay in ancient Babylonian, etc., inscriptions. ● *n.* cuneiform writing. [F *cunéiforme* or mod.L *cuneiformis* f. L *cuneus* wedge]

cunnilingus /kúnilínggəs/ *n.* (also **cunnilinctus** /-língktəs/) oral stimulation of the female genitals. [L f. *cunnus* vulva + *lingere* lick]

cunning /kúning/ *adj. & n.* ● *adj.* (**cunninger, cunningest**) **1 a** skilled in ingenuity or deceit. **b** selfishly clever or crafty. **2** ingenious (*a cunning device*). **3** attractive; quaint. ● *n.* **1** craftiness; skill in deceit. **2** skill; ingenuity. □□ **cunningly** *adv.* **cunningness** *n.* [ME f. ON *kunnandi* knowing f. *kunna* know: cf. CAN¹]
■ *adj.* **1** see CRAFTY. **2** see INGENIOUS. ● *n.* **1** see CRAFT *n.* 4. **2** see INGENUITY.

cunt /kunt/ *n. coarse sl.* **1** the female genitals. **2** *offens.* an unpleasant or stupid person. ¶ A highly taboo word. [ME f. Gmc]

cup /kup/ *n. & v.* ● *n.* **1** a small bowl-shaped container, usu. with a handle for drinking from. **2 a** its contents (*a cup of tea*). **b** = CUPFUL. **3** a cup-shaped thing, esp. the calyx of a flower or the socket of a bone. **4** flavored wine, cider, etc.,

usu. chilled. **5** an ornamental cup-shaped trophy as a prize for victory or prowess, esp. in a sports contest. **6** one's fate or fortune (*a bitter cup*). **7** either of the two cup-shaped parts of a brassiere. **8** the chalice used or the wine taken at the Eucharist. **9** *Golf* the hole on a putting green or the metal container in it. ● *v.tr.* (**cupped, cupping**) **1** form (esp. one's hands) into the shape of a cup. **2** take or hold as in a cup. **3** *hist.* bleed (a person) by using a glass in which a partial vacuum is formed by heating. □ **cup lichen** a lichen, *Cladonia pyxidata*, with cup-shaped processes arising from the thallus. **one's cup of tea** *colloq.* what interests or suits one. **in one's cups** while drunk; drunk. [OE *cuppe* f. med.L *cuppa* cup, prob. differentiated from L *cupa* tub]
■ *n.* **1** see MUG¹ *n.* 1. **5** see TROPHY 1. □ **in one's cups** see DRUNK *adj.* 1.

cupbearer /kúpbairər/ *n.* a person who serves wine, esp. an officer of a royal or noble household.
■ see WAITER.

cupboard /kúbərd/ *n.* a recess or piece of furniture with a door and (usu.) shelves, in which things are stored. □ **cupboard love** a display of affection meant to secure some gain. [ME f. CUP + BOARD]
■ see CABINET 1a.

cupcake /kúpkayk/ *n.* a small cake baked in a cup-shaped metal, foil, or paper container and often iced.

cupel /kyoŏpəl/ *n. & v.* ● *n.* a small, flat, porous vessel used in assaying gold or silver in the presence of lead. ● *v.tr.* assay or refine in a cupel. □□ **cupellation** /-pəláyshən/ *n.* [F *coupelle* f. LL *cupella* dimin. of *cupa*: see CUP]

cupful /kúpfoŏl/ *n.* (*pl.* **-fuls**) **1** the amount held by a cup, esp. a half-pint (8-ounce) measure in cookery. **2** a cup full of a substance (*drank a cupful of water*). ¶ A **cupful** is a measure, and so *three cupfuls* is a quantity regarded in terms of a cup; *three cups full* denotes the actual cups, as in *three cups full of water*. Sense 2 is an intermediate use.

Cupid /kyoŏpid/ *n.* **1** (in Roman mythology) the Roman god of love represented as a naked winged boy with a bow and arrows. **2** (also **cupid**) a representation of Cupid. □ **Cupid's bow** the upper lip, etc., shaped like the double-curved bow carried by Cupid. [ME f. L *Cupido* f. *cupere* desire]

cupidity /kyoŏpíditee/ *n.* greed for gain; avarice. [ME f. OF *cupidité* or L *cupiditas* f. *cupidus* desirous]
■ see AVARICE.

cupola /kyoŏpələ/ *n.* **1 a** a rounded dome forming a roof or ceiling. **b** a small rounded dome adorning a roof. **2 a** revolving dome protecting mounted guns on a warship or in a fort. **3** (in full **cupola furnace**) a furnace for melting metals. □□ **cupolaed** /-ləd/ *adj.* [It. f. LL *cupula* dimin. of *cupa* cask]

cuppa /kúpə/ *n.* (also **cupper** /kúpə/) *Brit. colloq.* **1** a cup of. **2** a cup of tea. [corruption]

cuprammonium /kyoŏprəmóneeəm/ *n.* a complex ion of divalent copper and ammonia, solutions of which dissolve cellulose. [LL *cuprum* + AMMONIUM]

cupreous /koŏpreeəs, kyoŏ-/ *adj.* of or like copper. [LL *cupreus* f. *cuprum* copper]

cupric /koŏprik, kyoŏ-/ *adj.* of copper, esp. divalent copper. □□ **cupriferous** /-prífərəs/ *adj.* [LL *cuprum* copper]

cupro- /koŏprō, kyoŏ-/ *comb. form* copper (*cupronickel*).

cupronickel /koŏprōníkəl, kyoŏ-/ *n.* an alloy of copper and nickel, esp. in the proportions 3:1 as used in 'silver' coins.

cuprous /koŏprəs, kyoŏ-/ *adj.* of copper, esp. monovalent copper. [LL *cuprum* copper]

cupule /kyoŏpyoŏl/ *n. Bot. & Zool.* a cup-shaped organ, receptacle, etc. [LL *cupula* CUPOLA]

cur /kər/ *n.* **1** a worthless or snappy dog. **2** *colloq.* a contemptible person. [ME, prob. orig. in *cur-dog*, perh. f. ON *kurr* grumbling]
■ **1** see MONGREL *n.* **2** see WRETCH 2.

cur. *abbr.* **1** currency. **2** current.

curable /kyoŏrəbəl/ *adj.* that can be cured. □□ **curability** *n.* [CURE]
■ see BENIGN 4.

curaçao /kyoŏrəsō, -sów/ *n.* (also **curaçoa** /-sóə/) (*pl.* **-os** or **curaçoas**) a liqueur of spirits flavored with the peel of bitter oranges. [F *Curaçao*, name of the Caribbean island producing these oranges]

curacy /kyŏŏrəsee/ *n.* (*pl.* **-ies**) a curate's office or the tenure of it.

curare /kyŏŏraaree, kŏŏ-/ *n.* a resinous bitter substance prepared from S. American plants of the genera *Strychnos* and *Chondodendron*, paralyzing the motor nerves, used by native peoples to poison arrows and blowpipe darts, and formerly used as a muscle relaxant in surgery. [Carib]

curassow /kyŏŏrəsō, kŏŏr-/ *n.* any game bird of the family Cracidae, found in Central and S. America. [Anglicized f. CURAÇAO]

curate /kyŏŏrət/ *n.* **1** a member of the clergy engaged as assistant to a parish priest. **2** *archaic* an ecclesiastical pastor. □ **curate's egg** esp. *Brit.* a thing that is partly good and partly bad. [ME f. med.L *curatus* f. L *cura* CURE]
■ see MINISTER *n.* 1.

curative /kyŏŏrətiv/ *adj. & n.* ● *adj.* tending or able to cure (esp. disease). ● *n.* a curative medicine or agent. [F *curatif -ive* f. med.L *curativus* f. L *curare* CURE]
■ *adj.* see THERAPEUTIC 1.

curator /kyŏŏráytər, kyŏŏrə-/ *n.* a keeper or custodian of a museum or other collection. □□ **curatorial** /kyŏŏrətáwreeəl/ *adj.* **curatorship** *n.* [ME f. AF *curatour* (OF *-eur*) or L *curator* (as CURATIVE)]

curb /kərb/ *n. & v.* ● *n.* **1** a check or restraint. **2** a rim of concrete, stone, etc., along the side of a paved road. **3** a strap, etc., fastened to the bit and passing under a horse's lower jaw, used as a check. **4** an enclosing border or edging such as the frame around the top of a well or a fender around a hearth. ● *v.tr.* **1** restrain. **2** put a curb on (a horse). □ **curb roof** a roof of which each face has two slopes, as a gambrel or mansard roof. [ME f. OF *courber* f. L *curvare* bend, CURVE]
■ *n.* **1** restraint, control; see also CHECK¹ *n.* 2c. ● *v.* **1** check, bridle, control, contain, repress, subdue, suppress; see also RESTRAIN 1.

curbside /kárbsīd/ *n.* the side of a paved road or roadbed bordered by a curb.

curbstone /kárbstōn/ *n.* each of a series of stones forming a curb, as along a street.

curcuma /kárkyəmə/ *n.* **1** the spice turmeric. **2** any tuberous plant of the genus *Curcuma*, yielding this and other commercial substances. [med.L or mod.L f. Arab. *kurkum* saffron f. Skr. *kuṅkama*ᵐ]

curd /kərd/ *n.* **1** (often in *pl.*) a coagulated substance formed by the action of acids on milk, which may be made into cheese or eaten as food. **2** a fatty substance found between flakes of boiled salmon flesh. **3** the edible head of a cauliflower. □ **curds and whey** the result of acidulating milk. **curd soap** a white soap made of tallow and soda. □□ **curdy** *adj.* [ME: orig. unkn.]

curdle /kərd'l/ *v.tr. & intr.* make into or become curds, (of milk) turn sour; congeal. □ **make one's blood curdle** fill one with horror. □□ **curdler** *n.* [frequent. form of CURD (as verb)]
■ see TURN *v.* 10, COAGULATE.

cure /kyŏŏr/ *v. & n.* ● *v.* **1** *tr.* (often foll. by *of*) restore (a person or animal) to health (*was cured of pleurisy*). **2** *tr.* eliminate (a disease, evil, etc.). **3** *tr.* preserve (meat, fruit, tobacco, or skins) by salting, drying, etc. **4** *tr.* **a** vulcanize (rubber). **b** harden (concrete or plastic). **5** *intr.* effect a cure. **6** *intr.* undergo a process of curing. ● *n.* **1** restoration to health. **2** a thing that effects a cure. **3** a course of medical or healing treatment. **4 a** the office or function of a curate. **b** a parish or other sphere of spiritual ministration. **5 a** the process of curing rubber or plastic. **b** (with qualifying adj.) the degree of this. □ **cure-all** a panacea; a universal remedy. □□ **curer** *n.* [ME f. OF *curer* f. L *curare* take care of f. *cura* care]
■ *v.* **1** heal, restore to health, make better. **2** see ELIMINATE 1a. **3** preserve; smoke, pickle, dry, salt, corn, marinate. ● *n.* **1** restoration, healing. **2, 3** course of treatment, therapy, remedy, medication, medicament,

medicine, drug, prescription; cure-all. □ **cure-all** panacea, universal remedy, *Brit.* heal-all.

curé /kyŏŏráy, kyŏŏray/ *n.* a parish priest in France, etc. [F f. med.L *curatus*: see CURATE]
■ see MINISTER *n.* 1.

curettage /kyŏŏritaazh/ *n.* the use of or an operation involving the use of a curette. [F (as CURETTE)]

curette /kyŏŏrét/ *n. & v.* ● *n.* a surgeon's small scraping instrument. ● *v.tr. & intr.* clean or scrape with a curette. [F, f. *curer* cleanse (as CURE)]

curfew /kárfyōō/ *n.* **1 a** a regulation restricting or forbidding the public circulation of people, esp. requiring people to remain indoors between specified hours, usu. at night. **b** the hour designated as the beginning of such a restriction. **c** a daily signal indicating this. **2** *hist.* **a** a medieval regulation requiring people to extinguish fires at a fixed hour in the evening. **b** the hour for this. **c** the bell announcing it. **3** the ringing of a bell at a fixed evening hour. [ME f. AF *coverfu*, OF *cuevrefeu* f. the stem of *couvrir* COVER + *feu* fire]

curia /kyŏŏreeə/ *n.* (also **Curia**) (*pl.* **curiae**) the papal court; the government departments of the Vatican. □□ **Curial** *adj.* [L: orig. a division of an ancient Roman tribe, the senate house at Rome, a feudal court of justice]

curie /kyŏŏree/ *n.* **1** a unit of radioactivity, corresponding to 3.7×10^{10} disintegrations per second. ¶ Abbr.: **Ci. 2** a quantity of radioactive substance having this activity. [P. *Curie*, Fr. scientist d. 1906]

curio /kyŏŏreeō/ *n.* (*pl.* **-os**) a rare or unusual object or person. [19th-c. abbr. of CURIOSITY]
■ see RARITY 2.

curiosa /kyŏŏreeōsə/ *n.pl.* **1** curiosities. **2** erotic or pornographic books. [neut. pl. of L *curiosus*: see CURIOUS]

curiosity /kyŏŏreeósitee/ *n.* (*pl.* **-ies**) **1** an eager desire to know; inquisitiveness. **2** strangeness. **3** a strange, rare, or interesting object. [ME f. OF *curiouseté* f. L *curiositas -tatis* (as CURIOUS)]
■ **1** inquisitiveness, interest, *colloq.* nosiness. **2** strangeness, peculiarity, unusualness, uncommonness, weirdness; see also ODDITY 3. **3** curio, oddity, rarity, conversation piece, *objet d'art*; knickknack, bauble, trinket, gewgaw, bibelot.

curious /kyŏŏreeəs/ *adj.* **1** eager to learn; inquisitive. **2** strange; surprising; odd. **3** *euphem.* (of books, etc.) erotic; pornographic. □□ **curiously** *adv.* **curiousness** *n.* [ME f. OF *curios* f. L *curiosus* careful f. *cura* care]
■ **1** inquisitive, interested, inquiring, prying, investigative, *colloq.* nosy, snoopy. **2** odd, peculiar, eccentric, strange, outré, queer, unusual, outrageous, offbeat, weird, bizarre, unconventional, freakish, exotic, surprising, singular, out of the ordinary, extraordinary, erratic, quaint, outlandish, aberrant, abnormal, irregular, deviant, *colloq.* kinky. **3** see EROTIC.

curium /kyŏŏreeəm/ *n.* an artificially made transuranic radioactive metallic element, first produced by bombarding plutonium with helium ions. ¶ Symb.: **Cm**. [M. *Curie* d. 1934 and P. *Curie* d. 1906, Fr. scientists]

curl /kərl/ *v. & n.* ● *v.* **1** *tr. & intr.* (often foll. by *up*) bend or coil into a spiral; form or cause to form curls. **2** *intr.* move in a spiral form (*smoke curling upward*). **3 a** *intr.* (of the upper lip) be raised slightly on one side as an expression of contempt or disapproval. **b** *tr.* cause (the lip) to do this. **4** *intr.* play curling. ● *n.* **1** a lock of curled hair. **2** anything spiral or curved inward. **3 a** a curling movement or act. **b** the state of being curled. **4** a disease of plants in which the leaves are curled up. □ **curl up 1** lie or sit with the knees drawn up. **2** *colloq.* writhe with embarrassment, horror, or amusement. **make a person's hair curl** *colloq.* shock or horrify a person. [ME; earliest form *crolled*, *crulled* f. obs. adj. *crolle*, *crulle* curly f. MDu. *krul*]

■ *v.* **1, 2** see WIND² *v.* 4. ● *n.* **1** see LOCK² 1a. **2** see SPIRAL *n.* □ **curl up 1** see NESTLE. **2** cringe, shrink; collapse into giggles *or* hysterics.

curler /kə́rlər/ *n.* **1** a pin or roller, etc., for curling the hair. **2** a player in the game of curling.

curlew /kə́rlo͞o, -lyo͞o/ *n.* any wading bird of the genus *Numenius*, esp. *N. arquatus*, possessing a usu. long, slender, down-curved bill. [ME f. OF *courlieu, courlis* orig. imit., but assim. to *courliu* courier f. *courre* run + *lieu* place]

curlicue /kə́rlikyo͞o/ *n.* a decorative curl or twist. [CURLY + CUE² (= pigtail) or Q¹]
■ see KINK *n.* 1.

curling /kə́rling/ *n.* **1** in senses of CURL *v.* **2** a game played on ice, esp. in Canada and Scotland, in which large, round, flat stones are slid across the surface toward a mark. □ **curling iron** a heated device for shaping the hair into curls.

curly /kə́rlee/ *adj.* (**curlier, curliest**) **1** having or arranged in curls. **2** moving in curves. □ **curly kale** see KALE. □□ **curliness** *n.*
■ **1** see KINKY 3.

curmudgeon /kərmújən/ *n.* a bad-tempered person. □□ **curmudgeonly** *adj.* [16th c.: orig. unkn.]
■ □□ **curmudgeonly** see IRRITABLE 1.

currach /kúrəkh, kúrə/ *n.* (also **curragh**) *Ir.* a coracle. [Ir.: cf. CORACLE]

currajong var. of KURRAJONG.

currant /kə́rənt, kúr-/ *n.* **1** a dried fruit of a small seedless variety of grape grown esp. in California and in the Levant and much used in cookery. **2 a** any of various shrubs of the genus *Ribes* producing red, white, or black berries. **b** a berry of these shrubs. □ **flowering currant** an ornamental species of currant native to N. America. [ME *raysons of coraunce* f. AF, = grapes of Corinth (the orig. source)]

currawong /kúrəwawng, -wong/ *n. Austral.* any crowlike songbird of the genus *Strepera*, possessing a resonant call. [Aboriginal]

currency /kə́rənsee, kúr-/ *n.* (*pl.* **-ies**) **1 a** the money in general use in a country. **b** any other commodity used as a medium of exchange. **2** the condition of being current; prevalence (e.g., of words or ideas). **3** the time during which something is current.
■ **1** see MONEY 1.

current /kə́rənt, kúr-/ *adj. & n.* ● *adj.* **1** belonging to the present time; happening now (*current events; the current week*). **2** (of money, opinion, a rumor, a word, etc.) in general circulation or use. ● *n.* **1** a body of water, air, etc., moving in a definite direction, esp. through a stiller surrounding body. **2 a** an ordered movement of electrically charged particles. **b** a quantity representing the intensity of such movement. **3** (usu. foll. by *of*) a general tendency or course (of events, opinions, etc.). □ **current account** *Brit.* a bank account from which money may be drawn without notice. **pass current** *Brit.* be generally accepted as true or genuine. □□ **currentness** *n.* [ME f. OF *corant* f. L *currere* run]
■ *adj.* **1** contemporary, ongoing, present, contemporaneous, latest, up-to-date. **2** prevalent, prevailing, common, popular, accepted, known, widespread, reported, in circulation, going around, bruited about, widely known, in the air, present-day.
● *n.* **1** stream, flow, undercurrent, tide. **3** course, progress, tendency, tenor, drift, trend, inclination, stream, direction, tide, mainstream.

currently /kə́rəntlee, kúr-/ *adv.* at the present time; now.

curricle /kúrikəl/ *n. hist.* a light, open two-wheeled carriage drawn by two horses abreast. [L *curriculum*: see CURRICULUM]

curriculum /kəríkyələm/ *n.* (*pl.* **curricula** /-lə/ or **curriculums**) **1** the subjects that are studied or prescribed for study in a school (*not part of the school curriculum*). **2** any program of activities. □□ **curricular** *adj.* [L, = course, racechariot, f. *currere* run]
■ see PROGRAM *n.* 4.

curriculum vitae /kəríkyələm vítee, veetī/ *n.* (*pl.* **curricula**

vitae) a brief account of one's education, qualifications, and previous occupations. [L, = course of life]
■ see RÉSUMÉ 2.

currier /kə́reeər, kúr-/ *n.* a person who dresses and colors tanned leather. [ME f. OF *corier,* f. L *coriarius* f. *corium* leather]

currish /kə́rish, kúr-/ *adj.* **1** like a cur; snappish. **2** ignoble. □□ **currishly** *adv.* **currishness** *n.*
■ see CONTEMPTIBLE.

curry¹ /kə́ree, kúree/ *n. & v.* ● *n.* (*pl.* **-ies**) a dish of meat, vegetables, etc., cooked in a sauce of hot-tasting spices, usu. served with rice. ● *v.tr.* (**-ies, -ied**) prepare or flavor with a sauce of hot-tasting spices (*curried eggs*). □ **curry powder** a preparation of turmeric and other spices for making curry. [Tamil]

curry² /kə́ree, kúree/ *v.tr.* (**-ies, -ied**) **1** groom (a horse) with a currycomb. **2** treat (tanned leather) to improve its properties. **3** thrash. □ **curry favor** ingratiate oneself. [ME f. OF *correier* ult. f. Gmc]
■ **1** see GROOM *v.* 1. □ **curry favor** see INGRATIATE.

currycomb /kə́reekōm, kúree-/ *n. & v.* ● *n.* a handheld metal serrated device for grooming horses. ● *v.tr.* use a currycomb.

curse /kərs/ *n. & v.* ● *n.* **1** a solemn utterance intended to invoke a supernatural power to inflict destruction or punishment on a person or thing. **2** the evil supposedly resulting from a curse. **3** a violent exclamation of anger; a profane oath. **4** a thing that causes evil or harm. **5** (prec. by *the*) *colloq.* menstruation. **6** a sentence of excommunication. ● *v.* **1** *tr.* **a** utter a curse against. **b** (in *imper.*) may God curse. **2** *tr.* (usu. in *passive*; foll. by *with*) afflict with (*cursed with blindness*). **3** *intr.* utter expletive curses; swear. **4** *tr.* excommunicate. □□ **curser** *n.* [OE *curs, cursian,* of unkn. orig.]
■ *n.* **1** malediction, imprecation, denunciation, execration, anathema, *archaic* ban. **2** *archaic or joc.* plague. **3** profanity, oath, expletive, blasphemy, obscenity, dirty word, swearword, damn, curse word, *colloq.* cuss, cussword. **4** evil, bane, misfortune, affliction, torment, scourge, blight, cross to bear. ● *v.* **1 a** damn, execrate, denounce, anathematize, *colloq.* cuss; swear at, blaspheme at. **b** damn, confound, *colloq.* drat, *euphem.* bless, *sl.* blow. **2** afflict with, burden, saddle, weigh down, handicap. **3** swear.

cursed /kə́rsid, kərst/ *adj.* damnable; abominable. □□ **cursedly** *adv.* **cursedness** *n.*
■ see DAMNABLE.

cursive /kə́rsiv/ *adj. & n.* ● *adj.* (of writing) done with joined characters. ● *n.* cursive writing (cf. PRINT *v.* 4, UNCIAL). □□ **cursively** *adv.* [med.L (*scriptura*) *cursiva* f. L *currere* cursrun]

cursor /kə́rsər/ *n.* **1** *Computing* a movable indicator on a monitor screen identifying a particular position in the display, esp. the position that the program will operate on with the next keystroke. **2** *Math.,* etc., a transparent slide engraved with a hairline and forming part of a slide rule. [L, = runner (as CURSIVE)]

cursorial /kərsáwreeəl/ *adj. Anat.* having limbs adapted for running. [as CURSOR + -IAL]

cursory /kə́rsəree/ *adj.* hasty, hurried (*a cursory glance*). □□ **cursorily** *adv.* **cursoriness** *n.* [L *cursorius* of a runner (as CURSOR)]
■ superficial, hasty, hurried, passing, quick, slapdash, perfunctory, rapid, summary.

curst *archaic* var. of CURSED.

curt /kərt/ *adj.* noticeably or rudely brief. □□ **curtly** *adv.* **curtness** *n.* [L *curtus* cut short, abridged]
■ abrupt, short, terse, brief, laconic, concise; blunt, gruff, harsh, brusque, unceremonious, snappish, crusty, rude.

curtail /kərtáyl/ *v.tr.* cut short; reduce; terminate esp. prematurely (*curtailed his visit to Italy*). **2** (foll. by *of*) *archaic* deprive of. □□ **curtailment** *n.* [obs. *curtal* horse with docked tail f. F *courtault* f. *court* short f. L *curtus*: assim. to *tail*]
■ **1** shorten, abbreviate, cut short, abridge; diminish, reduce, cut, cut back, cut down, *Brit. colloq.* chop; terminate. **2** see DIVEST 2.

curtain /kértən/ *n.* & *v.* ● *n.* **1** a piece of cloth, etc., hung up as a screen, usu. moveable sideways or upward, esp. at a window or between the stage and auditorium of a theater. **2** *Theatr.* **a** the rise or fall of the stage curtain at the beginning or end of an act or scene. **b** = *curtain call.* **3** a partition or cover. **4** (in *pl.*) *sl.* the end. ● *v.tr.* **1** furnish or cover with a curtain or curtains. **2** (foll. by *off*) shut off with a curtain or curtains. ▫ **curtain call** *Theatr.* an audience's summons to actor(s) to take a bow after the fall of the curtain. **curtain lecture** a wife's private reproof to her husband, orig. behind bed curtains. **curtain-raiser 1** *Theatr.* a piece prefaced to the main performance. **2** a preliminary event. **curtain wall 1** *Fortification* the plain wall of a fortified place, connecting two towers, etc. **2** *Archit.* a piece of plain wall not supporting a roof. [ME f. OF *cortine* f. LL *cortina* transl. Gk *aulaia* f. *aulē* court]

curtana /kərtáynə, -táanə/ *n. Brit.* an unpointed sword borne before English sovereigns at their coronation, as an emblem of mercy. [ME f. AL *curtana* (*spatha* sword) f. AF *curtain*, OF *cortain* name of Roland's similar sword f. *cort* short (as CURT)]

curtilage /kért'lij/ *n.* an area attached to a house and forming one enclosure with it. [ME f. AF *curtilage*, OF *co(u)rtillage* f. *co(u)rtil* small court f. *cort* COURT]

curtsy /kártsee/ *n.* & *v.* (also **curtsey**) ● *n.* (*pl.* **-ies** or **-eys**) a woman's or girl's formal greeting or salutation made by bending the knees and lowering the body. ● *v.intr.* (**-ies**, **-ied** or **-eys**, **-eyed**) make a curtsy. [var. of COURTESY]

curule /kyốorōōl/ *adj. Rom.Hist.* designating or relating to the authority exercised by the senior Roman magistrates, chiefly the consul and praetor, who were entitled to use the *sella curulis* ('curule seat' or seat of office). [L *curulis* f. *currus* chariot (in which the chief magistrate was conveyed to the seat of office)]

curvaceous /kərváyshəs/ *adj. colloq.* (esp. of a woman) having a shapely curved figure.
■ see SHAPELY.

curvature /kárvəchər/ *n.* **1** the act or state of curving. **2** a curved form. **3** *Geom.* **a** the deviation of a curve from a straight line, or of a curved surface from a plane. **b** the quantity expressing this. [OF f. L *curvatura* (as CURVE)]
■ **1, 2** see BEND¹ *n.*

curve /kərv/ *n.* & *v.* ● *n.* **1** a line or surface having along its length a regular deviation from being straight or flat, as exemplified by the surface of a sphere or lens. **2** a curved form or thing. **3** a curved line on a graph. **4** *Baseball* a ball caused to deviate by the pitcher's spin. ● *v.tr.* & *intr.* bend or shape so as to form a curve. ▫▫ **curved** *adj.* [orig. as adj. (in *curve line*) f. L *curvus* bent: (v.) f. L *curvare*]
■ *n.* **1–3** see BEND¹ *n.* ● *v.* see BEND¹ *v.* 1.

curveball /kárvbawl/ *n.* = CURVE *n.* 4.

curvet /kərvét/ *n.* & *v.* ● *n.* a horse's leap with the forelegs raised together and the hind legs raised with a spring before the forelegs reach the ground. ● *v.intr.* (**curvetted, curvetting** or **curveted, curveting**) (of a horse or rider) make a curvet. [It. *corvetta* dimin. of *corva* CURVE]
■ *n.* see CAPER¹ *n.* 1. ● *v.* see LEAP *v.* 1.

curvi- /kárvee/ *comb. form* curved. [L *curvus* curved]

curvifoliate /kárvifōleeət, -ayt/ *adj. Bot.* with the leaves bent back.

curviform /kárvifawrm/ *adj.* having a curved shape.

curvilinear /kárvilíneeər/ *adj.* contained by or consisting of curved lines. ▫▫ **curvilinearly** *adv.* [CURVI- after *rectilinear*]
■ see ROUND *adj.* 1.

curvirostral /kárviróstrəl/ *adj.* with a curved beak.

curvy /kárvee/ *adj.* (**curvier, curviest**) **1** having many curves. **2** (of a woman's figure) shapely. ▫▫ **curviness** *n.*
■ **1** see SERPENTINE *adj.* 2. **2** *colloq.* curvaceous; see also SHAPELY.

cuscus¹ /kúskəs/ *n.* the aromatic fibrous root of an E. Indian grass, *Vetiveria zizanoides*, used for making fans, etc. [Pers. ḵaškaš]

cuscus² /kúskəs/ *n.* any of several nocturnal, usu. arboreal, marsupial mammals of the genus *Phalanger*, native to New Guinea and N. Australia. [native name]

cusec /kyốosek/ *n.* a unit of flow (esp. of water) equal to one cubic foot per second. [abbr.]

cush /kŏosh/ *n.* esp. *Billiards colloq.* a cushion. [abbr.]

cush-cush /kŏoshkŏosh/ *n.* a yam, *Dioscorea trifida*, native to S. America. [native name]

cushion /kŏoshən/ *n.* & *v.* ● *n.* **1** a bag of cloth, etc., stuffed with a mass of soft material, used as a soft support for sitting or leaning on, etc. **2** a means of protection against shock. **3** the elastic lining of the sides of a billiard table, from which the ball rebounds. **4** a body of air supporting a hovercraft, etc. **5** the frog of a horse's hoof. ● *v.tr.* **1** provide or protect with a cushion or cushions. **2** provide with a defense; protect. **3** mitigate the adverse effects of (*cushioned the blow*). **4** quietly suppress. **5** place or bounce (the ball) against the cushion in billiards. ▫▫ **cushiony** *adj.* [ME f. OF *co(i)ssin, cu(i)ssin* f. Gallo-Roman f. L *culcita* mattress, cushion]
■ *n.* **1** pillow, bolster, pad. **2** see DEFENSE 2a, b. ● *v.* **2** see PROTECT. **3** soften, absorb, buffer, damp, lessen. **4** see SUPPRESS 2.

Cushitic /kŏoshítik/ *n.* & *adj.* ● *n.* a group of E. African languages of the Hamitic type. ● *adj.* of this group. [*Cush* an ancient country in the Nile valley + -ITE¹ + -IC]

cushy /kŏoshee/ *adj.* (**cushier, cushiest**) *colloq.* **1** (of a job, etc.) easy and pleasant. **2** (of a seat, surroundings, etc.) soft; comfortable. ▫▫ **cushiness** *n.* [Anglo-Ind. f. Hind. ḵhūsh pleasant]
■ **1** see EASY *adj.* 1.

cusp /kusp/ *n.* **1** an apex or peak. **2** the horn of a crescent moon, etc. **3** *Astrol.* the initial point of a house. **4** *Archit.* a projecting point between small arcs in Gothic tracery. **5** *Geom.* the point at which two arcs meet from the same direction terminating with a common tangent. **6** *Bot.* a pointed end, esp. of a leaf. **7** a cone-shaped prominence on the surface of a tooth esp. a molar or premolar. **8** a pocket or fold in a valve of the heart. ▫▫ **cuspate** /kúspayt/ *adj.* **cusped** *adj.* **cuspidal** /kúspid'l/ *adj.* [L *cuspis, -idis* point, apex]
■ **1** see ANGLE¹ *n.* 2.

cuspidor /kúspidawr/ *n.* a spittoon. [Port., = spitter f. *cuspir* spit f. L *conspuere*]

cuss /kus/ *n.* & *v. colloq.* ● *n.* **1** a curse. **2** usu. *derog.* a person; a creature. ● *v.tr.* & *intr.* curse. [var. of CURSE]
■ *n.* **1** see CURSE *n.* 1. ● *v.* see CURSE *v.* 1a.

cussed /kúsid/ *adj. colloq.* awkward and stubborn. ▫▫ **cussedly** *adv.* **cussedness** *n.* [var. of CURSED]

cussword /kúswərd/ *n.* a swearword.
■ see CURSE *n.* 3.

custard /kústərd/ *n.* **1** a dish made with milk and eggs, usu. sweetened. **2** a sweet sauce made with milk and flavored cornstarch. ▫ **custard apple** a W. Indian fruit, *Annona reticulata*, with a custardlike pulp. **custard pie** a pie containing custard, commonly thrown in slapstick comedy. **custard-pie** *adj.* denoting slapstick comedy. [ME, earlier *crusta(r)de* f. AF f. OF *crouste* CRUST]

custodian /kustódeeən/ *n.* a guardian or keeper, esp. of a public building, etc. ▫▫ **custodianship** *n.* [CUSTODY + -AN, after *guardian*]
■ see GUARD *n.* 2. ▫▫ **custodianship** see CARE *n.* 4a.

custody /kústədee/ *n.* **1** guardianship; protective care. **2** imprisonment. ▫ **take into custody** arrest. ▫▫ **custodial** /kustódeeəl/ *adj.* [L *custodia* f. *custos -odis* guardian]
■ **1** care, custodianship, safekeeping, protection, charge, guardianship, keeping. **2** imprisonment, detention, incarceration, confinement. ▫ **take into custody** see ARREST *v.* 1a.

custom /kústəm/ *n.* **1 a** the usual way of behaving or acting (*a slave to custom*). **b** a particular established way of behaving (*our customs seem strange to foreigners*). **2** *Law* established usage having the force of law. **3** esp. *Brit.* business patronage;

/.../ **pronunciation**	● **part of speech**
▫ **phrases, idioms, and compounds**	
▫▫ **derivatives**	■ **synonym section**
cross-references appear in SMALL CAPITALS or *italics*	

regular dealings or customers (*lost a lot of custom*). **4** (in *pl.*; also treated as *sing.*) **a** a duty levied on certain imported and exported goods. **b** the official department that administers this. **c** the area at a port, frontier, etc., where customs officials deal with incoming goods, baggage, etc. □ **custom-built** (or **-made**, etc.) made to a customer's order. **customs union** a group of nations with an agreed common tariff, and usu. free trade with each other. [ME and OF *custume* ult. f. L *consuetudo -dinis*: see CONSUETUDE]

■ **1 a** practice, habit, usage, fashion, tradition, routine, convention, form, formality; *formal or joc.* wont. **b** (*customs*) ways, way of life, traditions, conventions, mores. **4** (*customs*) **a** toll, duty, impost, tax, excise, levy, dues, tariff. □ **custom-built** (or **-made**, etc.) built specially *or* especially *or* expressly *or* exclusively *or* particularly *or* to order, customized.

customary /kústəmeree/ *adj. & n.* ● *adj.* **1** usual; in accordance with custom. **2** *Law* in accordance with custom. ● *n.* (*pl.* **-ies**) *Law* a book, etc., listing the customs and established practices of a community. □□ **customarily** *adv.* **customariness** *n.* [med.L *custumarius* f. *custuma* f. AF *custume* (as CUSTOM)]

■ *adj.* **1** usual, normal, conventional, routine, everyday, common, commonplace, ordinary, traditional; accustomed, habitual, regular, wonted.

customer /kústəmər/ *n.* **1** a person who buys goods or services from a store or business. **2** a person one has to deal with (*an awkward customer*). [ME f. AF *custumer* (as CUSTOMARY), or f. CUSTOM + -ER¹]

■ **1** client, patron, buyer, purchaser; consumer. **2** fellow, character, person, soul, individual, being, *colloq.* chap.

customhouse /kústəmhows/ *n.* (also **customshouse**) the office at a port or international border, etc., at which customs duties are levied.

customize /kústəmīz/ *v.tr.* make to order or modify according to individual requirements.

cut /kut/ *v. & n.* ● *v.* (**cutting**; *past* and *past part.* **cut**) **1** *tr.* (also *absol.*) penetrate or wound with a sharp-edged instrument (*cut his finger*; *the knife won't cut*). **2** *tr. & intr.* (often foll. by *into*) divide or be divided with a knife, etc. (*cut the bread*; *cut the cloth into yard lengths*). **3** *tr.* **a** trim or reduce the length of (hair, a hedge, etc.) by cutting. **b** detach all or the significant part of (flowers, grain, etc.) by cutting. **c** reduce the length of (a book, movie, etc.). **4** *tr.* (foll. by *loose*, *open*, etc.) make loose, open, etc. by cutting. **5** *tr.* (esp. as **cutting** *adj.*) cause sharp physical or mental pain to (*a cutting remark*; *a cutting wind*; *was cut to the quick*). **6** *tr.* (often foll. by *down*) **a** reduce (wages, prices, time, etc.). **b** reduce or cease (services, etc.). **7** *tr.* **a** shape or fashion (a coat, gem, key, record, etc.) by cutting. **b** make (a path, tunnel, etc.) by removing material. **8** *tr.* perform; execute; make (*cut a caper*; *cut a sorry figure*; *cut a deal*). **9** *tr.* (also *absol.*) cross; intersect (*the line cuts the circle at two points*; *the two lines cut*). **10** *intr.* (foll. by *across*, *through*, etc.) pass or traverse, esp. in a hurry or as a shorter way (*cut across the grass*). **11** *tr.* **a** ignore or refuse to recognize (a person). **b** renounce (a connection). **12** *tr.* deliberately fail to attend (a class, etc.). **13** *Cards* **a** *tr.* divide (a deck) into two parts. **b** *intr.* select a dealer, etc., by dividing the deck. **14** *Cinematog.* **a** *tr.* edit (a movie or tape). **b** *intr.* (often in *imper.*) stop filming or recording. **c** *intr.* (foll. by *to*) go quickly to (another shot). **15** *tr.* switch off (an engine, etc.). **16** *tr.* **a** hit (a ball) with a chopping motion. **b** *Golf* slice (the ball). **17** *tr.* dilute; adulterate. **18** *tr.* (as **cut** *adj.*) *Brit. sl.* drunk. **19** *intr. Cricket* cut (of the ball) turn sharply on pitching. **20** *intr. sl.* run. **21** *tr.* castrate. ● *n.* **1** an act of cutting. **2** a division or wound made by cutting. **3** a stroke with a knife, sword, whip, etc. **4** a reduction (in prices, wages, etc.). **5** an excision of part of a play, movie, book, etc. **6** a wounding remark or act. **7** the way or style in which a garment, the hair, etc., is cut. **8** a piece of meat, etc., cut from a carcass. **9** *colloq.* commission; a share of profits. **10** *Tennis*, etc., a stroke made by cutting. **11** ignoring of or refusal to recognize a person. **12 a** an engraved block for printing. **b** a woodcut or other print.

13 a railroad cutting. **14** a new channel made for a river. □ **a cut above** *colloq.* noticeably superior to. **be cut out** (foll. by *for*, or *to* + infin.) be suited (*was not cut out to be a teacher*). **cut across 1** transcend or take no account of (normal limitations, etc.) (*their concern cuts across normal rivalries*). **2** see sense 10 of *v.* **cut-and-dried** (or **dry**) **1** completely decided; prearranged; inflexible. **2** (of opinions, etc.) ready-made; lacking freshness. **cut and run** *sl.* run away. **cut and thrust 1** a lively interchange of argument, etc. **2** the use of both the edge and the point of a sword. **cut back 1** reduce (expenditure, etc.). **2** prune (a tree, etc.). **3** *Cinematog.* repeat part of a previous scene for dramatic effect. **cut both ways 1** serve both sides of an argument, etc. **2** (of an action) have both good and bad effects. **cut a corner** go across and not around it. **cut corners** do a task, etc., perfunctorily or incompletely, esp. to save time. **cut dead** *Brit.* completely refuse to recognize (a person). **cut down 1 a** bring or throw down by cutting. **b** kill by means of a sword or disease. **2** see sense 6 of *v.* **3** reduce the length of (*cut down the pants to make shorts*). **4** (often foll. by *on*) reduce one's consumption (*tried to cut down on chocolate*). **cut a person down to size** *colloq.* ruthlessly expose the limitations of a person's importance, ability, etc. **cut one's eyeteeth** (or **teeth**) attain worldly wisdom. **cut glass** glass with patterns and designs cut on it. **cut in 1** interrupt. **2** pull in too closely in front of another vehicle (esp. having overtaken it). **3** give a share of profits, etc., to (a person). **4** connect (a source of electricity). **5** join in a card game by taking the place of a player who cuts out. **6** interrupt a dancing couple to take over from one partner. **cut-in** *Cinematog.* insert another image, as a still photo, caption, etc., into motion picture footage. **cut into 1** make a cut in (*they cut into the cake*). **2** interfere with and reduce (*traveling cuts into my free time*). **cut it fine** see FINE¹. **cut it out** (usu. in *imper.*) *sl.* stop doing that (esp. quarreling). **cut the knot** *Brit.* solve a problem in an irregular but efficient way. **cut loose 1** begin to act freely. **2** see sense 4 of *v.* **cut one's losses** (or **a loss**) abandon an unprofitable enterprise before losses become too great. **cut the mustard** *sl.* reach the required standard. **cut no ice** *sl.* **1** have no influence or importance. **2** achieve little or nothing. **cut off 1** remove (an appendage) by cutting. **2 a** (often in *passive*) bring to an abrupt end or (esp. early) death. **b** intercept; interrupt; prevent from continuing (*cut off supplies*; *cut off the gas*). **c** disconnect (a person engaged in a telephone conversation) (*was suddenly cut off*). **3 a** prevent from traveling or venturing out (*was cut off by the snow*). **b** (as **cut off** *adj.*) isolated; remote (*felt cut off in the country*). **4 a** disinherit (*was cut off without a penny*). **b** sever a relationship (*was cut off from the children*). **cut out 1** remove from the inside by cutting. **2** make by cutting from a larger whole. **3** omit; leave out. **4** *colloq.* stop doing or using (something) (*managed to cut out chocolate*; *let's cut out the arguing*). **5** cease or cause to cease functioning (*the engine cut out*). **6** outdo or supplant (a rival). **7** detach (an animal) from the herd. **8** *Cards* be excluded from a card game as a result of cutting the deck. **9** *colloq.* prepare; plan (*has his work cut out*). **cut rate** selling or sold at a reduced price. **cut short 1** interrupt; terminate prematurely (*cut short his visit*). **2** make shorter or more concise. **cut one's teeth on** acquire initial practice or experience from (something). **cut a tooth** have it appear through the gum. **cut up 1** cut into pieces. **2** destroy utterly. **4** criticize severely. **5** behave in a comical or unruly manner. **cut up rough** *Brit. sl.* show anger or resentment. **have one's work cut out** see WORK. [ME *cutte*, *kitte*, *kette*, perh. f. OE *cyttan* (unrecorded)]

■ *v.* **1** gash, slash; see also SLIT *v.* **2** slice, carve. **3 a** trim, snip, lop, clip, crop, shorten, shear, chop off; mow; dock. **c** abbreviate, shorten, crop, condense, abridge, edit, cut back, reduce, cut down, curtail. **5** cut up, hurt, wound, pain, upset, grieve, distress, slight, insult, offend, affront; (**cutting**) sarcastic, sardonic, bitter, scornful, sneering, acid, scathing, acerb, acerbic, wounding, stern, harsh, caustic, mordant, acrimonious, contemptuous; malicious, invidious, vicious, venomous; severe, biting, cold, icy, frigid, freezing, raw, piercing, penetrating, *literary* chill. **6** reduce, cut back (on), cut down (on), slash, diminish, decrease, retrench (on), curtail; discount, mark down; lessen, lower. **7 a** see SHAPE *v.* 1. **b** dig, burrow, gouge (out), scoop (out), hollow out; tunnel. **8** make, present, exhibit, display; perform, execute, do; conclude, settle, agree. **9** cross (over), intersect, meet; see also JOIN *v.* 8. **10** pass, go, make one's way; take a short cut. **11 a** see IGNORE 1. **12** avoid, fail to attend, *colloq.* skip, *literary* eschew. **15** turn *or* switch off. **17** dilute, thin, water (down), weaken; degrade, adulterate. **20** see RUN *v.* 1, 3. ● *n.* **2** gash, slash, incision, nick, wound. **3** stroke, *colloq.* swipe. **4** reduction, cutback, curtailment, decrease. **5** deletion, excision, omission. **6** affront, insult, offense, slight, snub, dig, slap in the face, *colloq.* jibe. **7** see STYLE *n.* 1, 6. **9** share, portion, percentage, dividend, commission. **12** engraving, plate, artwork, picture, illustration, plate, drawing, woodcut, linocut, print, halftone. □ **a cut above** better than, superior to. **be cut out** be suited *or* fit(ted) *or* equipped. **cut across 1** see TRANSCEND. **2** see CUT *v.* 10 above. **cut and dried** (or **dry**) **1** clear-cut, settled, arranged, decided; predetermined, prearranged, inflexible. **2** ready-made, automatic; stale, unoriginal, trite, hackneyed, old; dull, boring, manufactured, unchanging, unchanged. **cut and run** see RUN *v.* 2. **cut back 1** see CUT *v.* 6 above. **2** see PRUNE² 1. **cut down 1 a** fell, chop *or* hew down. **b** kill, cut off; murder, assassinate; see also KILL¹ *v.* 1a. **2** see CUT *v.* 6 above. **cut in 1** interrupt, butt in. **cut it out** see *pack it in* (PACK¹). **cut the mustard** see *make it* 2. **cut off 1** chop *or* lop *or* hack off, *literary* cleave; see also SEVER 1. **2 a** see *cut down* 1b above. **b** intercept, interrupt, discontinue, cease; end, stop, terminate, break off. **3 b** (*adj.*) see ISOLATED 1. **4 a** disinherit, disown, reject. **b** separate, sever, split, estrange. **cut out 1** extract, excise, remove, take out. **3** leave out, delete, remove, excise, strike *or* cross out, edit out, omit, cut, kill, *Printing* dele. **4, 5** stop, cease, quit, *literary* desist (from). **6** see OUTDO. **9** plan, prepare, ready, organize; destine. **cut rate** marked down, reduced (in price), esp. *Brit.* bargain-priced, on offer. **cut short 1** see INTERRUPT 1, 3. **2** abbreviate, shorten, crop, condense, abridge, edit, trim, cut, cut back *or* down, reduce; curtail. **cut up 1** chop (up), dice, cube, mince, cut, divide (up), carve (up). **2** see DEVASTATE 1. **3** see CRITICIZE 1. **5** misbehave.

cutaneous /kyŏŏtáyneeəs/ *adj.* of the skin. [mod.L *cutaneus* f. L *cutis* skin]

cutaway /kútəway/ *adj.* **1** (of a diagram, etc.) with some parts left out to reveal the interior. **2** (of a coat) with the front below the waist cut away.

cutback /kútbak/ *n.* an instance or the act of cutting back, esp. a reduction in expenditure.
■ see DECREASE *n.*.

cutch var. of COUCH².

cute /kyŏŏt/ *adj. colloq.* **1 a** attractive; quaint. **b** affectedly attractive. **2** clever; ingenious. □□ **cutely** *adv.* **cuteness** *n.* [shortening of ACUTE]
■ **1 a** pretty, attractive, adorable, dainty, lovely, beautiful; quaint, cunning. **2** clever, shrewd, ingenious, adroit, crafty, cunning.

cuticle /kyŏŏtikəl/ *n.* **1 a** the dead skin at the base of a fingernail or toenail. **b** the epidermis or other superficial skin. **2** *Bot.* a thin surface film on plants. □□ **cuticular** /-tikyələr/ *adj.* [L *cuticula*, dimin. of *cutis* skin]

cutie /kyŏŏtee/ *n. sl.* an attractive young woman.

cutis /kyŏŏtis/ *n. Anat.* the true skin or dermis, underlying the epidermis. [L, = skin]

cutlass /kútləs/ *n.* a short sword with a slightly curved blade, esp. of the type formerly used by sailors. [F *coutelas* ult. f. L *cultellus*: see CUTLER]
■ see KNIFE *n.* 1b.

cutler /kútlər/ *n.* a person who makes or deals in knives and

similar utensils. [ME f. AF *cotillere*, OF *coutelier* f. *coutel* f. L *cutellus* dimin. of *culter* COLTER]

cutlery /kútləree/ *n.* knives, forks, and spoons for use at table. [OF & F *coutel(l)erie* (as CUTLER)]
■ flatware.

cutlet /kútlit/ *n.* **1** a small piece of veal, etc., for frying. **2** a flat cake of ground meat or nuts and breadcrumbs, etc. [F *côtelette*, OF *costelet* dimin. of *coste* rib f. L *costa*]

cutline /kútlīn/ *n.* **1** a caption to an illustration. **2** the line in squash above which a served ball must strike the wall.

cutoff /kútawf/ *n.* **1** the point at which something is cut off. **2** a device for stopping a flow. **3** a shortcut. **4** (in *pl.*) shorts made from jeans, etc., whose legs have been cut off.

cutout /kútowt/ *n.* **1** a figure cut out of paper, etc. **2** a device for automatic disconnection, the release of exhaust gases, etc. □ **cutout box** = *fuse box* (see FUSE¹).

cutpurse /kútpərs/ *n. archaic* a pickpocket; a thief.
■ see THIEF.

cutter /kútər/ *n.* **1** a tailor, etc., who takes measurements and cuts cloth. **2** *Naut.* **a** a small, fast sailing ship. **b** a small boat carried by a large ship. **3** *Cricket* a ball turning sharply on pitching. **4** a light horse-drawn sleigh.

cutthroat /kútthrōt/ *n. & adj.* ● *n.* **1** a murderer. **2** *Brit.* (in full **cutthroat razor**) a straight-edge razor. **3** a species of trout, *Salmo clarki*, with a red mark under the jaw. ● *adj.* **1** (of competition) ruthless and intense. **2** (of a person) murderous. **3** (of a card game) three-handed.
■ *n.* **1** murderer, pirate, killer, gunman, assassin, *colloq.* hatchet man, *sl.* hit man, gunslinger, gunsel. ● *adj.* **1** intense, merciless, ruthless, unmerciful, unprincipled, relentless, pitiless, brutal, cold-blooded, coldhearted. **2** murderous, homicidal, lethal, deadly, barbaric, fierce, cruel, barbarous, savage, inhuman, brutal, violent, ferocious, bloodthirsty, sanguinary, bloody, feral, vicious.

cutting /kúting/ *n. & adj.* ● *n.* **1** a piece cut from a plant for propagation. **2** an excavated channel through high ground for a railroad or road. ● *adj.* see CUT *v.* 5. □ **cutting edge** the forefront; the vanguard. □□ **cuttingly** *adv.*
■ *n.* **1** scion, slip; clipping.

cuttle /kútʹl/ *n.* **1** = CUTTLEFISH. **2** = CUTTLEBONE.

cuttlebone /kútʹlbōn/ *n.* the internal shell of the cuttlefish crushed and used for polishing teeth, etc., or as a supplement to the diet of a cage bird. [OE *cudele*, ME *codel*, rel. to *cod* bag, with ref. to its ink-bag]

cuttlefish /kútʹlfish/ *n.* any marine cephalopod mollusk of the genera *Sepia* and *Sepiola*, having ten arms and ejecting a black fluid when threatened or pursued.

cutty /kútee/ *adj. & n. Sc. & No. of Engl.* ● *adj.* cut short; abnormally short. ● *n.* (*pl.* **-ies**) a short tobacco pipe. □ **cutty stool** *hist.* a stool of repentance.

cutup /kútup/ *n.* a person who clowns around; prankster.

cutwater /kútwawtər, -woter/ *n.* **1** the forward edge of a ship's prow. **2** a wedge-shaped projection from a pier or bridge.

cutworm /kútwərm/ *n.* any of various caterpillars that eat through the stems of young plants level with the ground.

cuvée /kyŏŏváy/ *n.* a blend or batch of wine. [F, = vatful f. *cuve* cask f. L *cupa*]

cuvette /kŏŏvét, kyŏŏ-/ *n.* a shallow vessel for liquid. [F, dimin. of *cuve* cask f. L *cupa*]

c.v. *abbr.* curriculum vitae.

cwm /kŏŏm/ *n.* **1** (in Wales) = COOMB. **2** *Geog.* a cirque. [Welsh]

cwo *abbr.* **1** chief warrant officer. **2** cash with order.

cwt. *abbr.* hundredweight.

-cy /see/ *suffix* (see also -ACY, -ANCY, -CRACY, -ENCY, -MANCY). **1** denoting state or condition (*bankruptcy*; *idiocy*). **2** denot-

---

/.../ pronunciation	● part of speech
□ phrases, idioms, and compounds	
□□ derivatives	■ synonym section
cross-references appear in SMALL CAPITALS or *italics*	

ing rank or status (*captaincy*). [from or after L *-cia, -tia*, Gk *-k(e)ia, -t(e)ia*]

cyan /sían/ *adj. & n.* ● *adj.* of a greenish-blue. ● *n.* a greenish-blue color. [Gk *kuan(e)os* dark blue]

cyanamide /siánəmid, mid/ *n. Chem.* a colorless crystalline amide of cyanogen; any salt of this, esp. the calcium one which is used as a fertilizer. ¶ Chem. formula: CH_2N_2. [CYANOGEN + AMIDE]

cyanic acid /siánik/ *n.* an unstable, colorless, pungent acid gas. ¶ Chem. formula: HCNO. [CYANOGEN]

cyanide /síənīd/ *n.* any of the highly poisonous salts or esters of hydrocyanic acid, esp. the potassium salt used in the extraction of gold and silver. [CYANOGEN + -IDE]

cyanobacterium /síənŏbakte'ereeəm, siánō-/ *n.* any prokaryotic organism of the division Cyanobacteria, found in many environments and capable of photosynthesizing. Also called *blue-green alga* (see BLUE[1]). [CYANOGEN + BACTERIUM]

cyanocobalamin /síənŏkōbáləmin, siánō-/ *n.* a vitamin of the B complex, found in foods of animal origin such as liver, fish, and eggs, a deficiency of which can cause pernicious anemia. Also called *vitamin B_{12}*. [CYANOGEN + *cobalamin* f. COBALT + VITAMIN]

cyanogen /siánəjən/ *n. Chem.* a colorless, highly poisonous gas intermediate in the preparation of many fertilizers. ¶ Chem. formula: C_2N_2. [F *cyanogène* f. Gk *kuanos* dark-blue mineral, as being a constituent of Prussian blue]

cyanosis /síənósis/ *n. Med.* a bluish discoloration of the skin due to the presence of oxygen-deficient blood. □□ **cyanotic** /-nótik/ *adj.* [mod.L f. Gk *kuanōsis* blueness (as CYANOGEN)]

cybernation /síbərnáyshən/ *n.* control by machines. □□ **cybernate** *v.tr.* [f. CYBERNETICS + -ATION]

cybernetics /síbərnétiks/ *n.pl.* (usu. treated as *sing.*) the science of communications and automatic control systems in both machines and living things. □□ **cybernetic** *adj.* **cybernetician** /-nítishən/ *n.* **cyberneticist** /-tisist/ *n.* [Gk *kubernētēs* steersman]

cyborg /síbawrg/ *n.* (in science fiction) a human being whose biological functions are bionically enhanced. [*cybernetic organism*]

cycad /síkad/ *n. Bot.* any of the palmlike plants of the order Cycadales (including fossil forms) inhabiting tropical and subtropical regions and often growing to a great height. [mod.L *cycas, cycad-* f. supposed Gk *kukas*, scribal error for *koikas*, pl. of *koix* Egyptian palm]

Cycladic /síkládik, see-/ *adj.* of the Cyclades, a group of islands east of the Greek mainland, esp. of the Bronze Age civilization that flourished there. [*Cyclades*, L f. Gk *Kuklades* f. *kuklos* circle (of islands)]

cyclamate /síkləmayt, sík-/ *n.* any of various salts or esters of sulfamic acid formerly used as artificial sweetening agents. [Chem. name *cyclohexylsulfamate*]

cyclamen /síkləmən, sík-/ *n.* 1 any plant of the genus *Cyclamen*, originating in Europe, having pink, red, or white flowers with reflexed petals, often grown in pots. 2 the shade of color of the red or pink cyclamen flower. [med.L f. Gk *kuklaminos*, perh. f. *kuklos* circle, with ref. to its bulbous roots]

cycle /síkəl/ *n. & v.* ● *n.* 1 a a recurrent round or period (of events, phenomena, etc.). b the time needed for one such round or period. 2 a *Physics*, etc., a recurrent series of operations or states. b *Electr.* = HERTZ. 3 a series of songs, poems, etc., usu. on a single theme. 4 a bicycle, tricycle, or similar machine. ● *v.intr.* 1 ride a bicycle, etc. 2 move in cycles. [ME f. OF, or f. LL *cyclus* f. Gk *kuklos* circle]
 ■ *n.* 1 a round, rotation, circle, course; series, sequence, run, succession, pattern. 4 bicycle, *colloq.* bike, *Brit. colloq.* push-bike; unicycle, tricycle. ● *v.* 2 recur, return, rotate, circle.

cyclic /síklik, sík-/ *adj.* 1 a recurring in cycles. b belonging to a chronological cycle. 2 *Chem.* with constituent atoms forming a ring. 3 of a cycle of songs, etc. 4 *Bot.* (of a flower) with its parts arranged in whorls. 5 *Math.* of a circle or cycle. [F *cyclique* or L *cyclicus* f. Gk *kuklikos* (as CYCLE)]
 ■ 1 see PERIODIC.

cyclical /síklikəl, sík-/ *adj.* = CYCLIC 1. □□ **cyclically** *adv.*

cyclist /síklist/ *n.* a rider of a bicycle.

cyclo- /síklō/ *comb. form* circle, cycle, or cyclic (*cyclometer; cyclorama*). [Gk *kuklos* circle]

cycloalkane /síklō-álkayn/ *n. Chem.* a saturated cyclic hydrocarbon.

cyclograph /síkləgraf/ *n.* an instrument for tracing circular arcs.

cyclohexane /síklōhéksayn/ *n. Chem.* a colorless liquid cycloalkane used as a solvent and paint remover. ¶ Chem. formula: C_6H_{12}.

cycloid /síkloyd/ *n. Math.* a curve traced by a point on a circle when the circle is rolled along a straight line. □□ **cycloidal** /-klóyd'l/ *adj.* [Gk *kukloeidēs* (as CYCLE, -OID)]

cyclometer /síklómitər/ *n.* 1 an instrument for measuring circular arcs. 2 an instrument for measuring the distance traversed by a bicycle, etc.

cyclone /síklōn/ *n.* 1 a system of winds rotating inward to an area of low barometric pressure; a depression. 2 a violent hurricane of limited diameter. □□ **cyclonic** /-klónik/ *adj.* **cyclonically** *adv.* [prob. repr. Gk *kuklōma* wheel, coil of a snake]
 ■ 1 see DEPRESSION 3. 2 see HURRICANE 1, 2.

cycloparaffin /síklōpárəfin/ *n. Chem.* = CYCLOALKANE.

cyclopean /síkləpee'ən, -klŏpeeən/ *adj.* (also **Cyclopean**) 1 (of ancient masonry) made with massive irregular blocks. 2 of or resembling a Cyclops.

cyclopedia /síkləpee'deeə/ *n.* (also esp. *Brit.* **cyclopaedia**) an encyclopedia. □□ **cyclopedic** *adj.* [shortening of ENCYCLOPEDIA]

cyclopropane /síklōprŏpayn/ *n. Chem.* a colorless, gaseous cycloalkane used as a general anesthetic. ¶ Chem. formula: C_3H_6.

Cyclops /síklops/ *n.* 1 (*pl.* **Cyclopes** /síklŏpeez/) (in Greek mythology) a member of a race of one-eyed giants. 2 (**cyclops**) (*pl.* **cyclops** or **cyclopes**) *Zool.* a crustacean of the genus *Cyclops*, with a single central eye. [L f. Gk *Kuklōps* f. *kuklos* circle + *ōps* eye]

cyclorama /síklərámə, -raámə/ *n.* a circular panorama, curved wall, or cloth at the rear of a stage, esp. one used to represent the sky. □□ **cycloramic** /-rámik/ *adj.*

cyclostome /síkləstōm/ *n.* any fishlike, jawless vertebrate of the subclass Cyclostomata, having a large sucking mouth, e.g., a lamprey. □□ **cyclostomate** /-klóstəmayt, -mət/ *adj.* [CYCLO- + Gk *stoma* mouth]

cyclostyle /síkləstīl/ *n. & v.* ● *n.* an apparatus for printing copies of writing from a stencil. ● *v.tr.* print or reproduce with this.

cyclothymia /síkləthímeeə/ *n. Psychol.* a disorder characterized by the occurrence of marked swings of mood from cheerfulness to misery. □□ **cyclothymic** *adj.* [CYCLO- + Gk *thumos* temper]

cyclotron /síklətron/ *n. Physics* an apparatus in which charged atomic and subatomic particles are accelerated by an alternating electric field while following an outward spiral or circular path in a magnetic field.

cyder *Brit.* var. of CIDER.

cygnet /sígnit/ *n.* a young swan. [ME f. AF *cignet* dimin. of OF *cigne* swan f. med.L *cycnus* f. Gk *kuknos*]

cyl. *abbr.* cylinder.

cylinder /sílindər/ *n.* 1 a a uniform solid or hollow body with straight sides and a circular section. b a thing of this shape, e.g., a container for liquefied gas. 2 a cylinder-shaped part of various machines, esp. a piston chamber in an engine. 3 *Printing* a metal roller. □ **cylinder seal** *Antiq.* a small barrel-shaped object of stone or baked clay bearing a cuneiform inscription, esp. for use as a seal. □□ **cylindrical** /silíndrikəl/ *adj.* **cylindrically** *adv.* [L *cylindrus* f. Gk *kulindros* f. *kulindō* roll]
 ■ 1 see ROLL *n.* 5a. 3 see ROLLER 1a.

cyma /símə/ *n.* 1 *Archit.* an ogee molding of a cornice. 2 = CYME. [mod.L f. Gk *kuma* wave, wavy molding]

cymbal /símbəl/ *n.* a musical instrument consisting of a concave brass or bronze plate, struck with another or with a stick, etc., to make a ringing sound. □□ **cymbalist** *n.* [ME f. L *cymbalum* f. Gk *kumbalon* f. *kumbē* cup]

cymbalom /símbələm/ *n.* (also **cimbalom**) a dulcimer. [Magyar f. It. *cembalo*]

cymbidium /simbídeeəm/ *n.* any tropical orchid of the genus *Cymbidium*, with a recess in the flower lip. [mod.L f. Gk *kumbē* cup]

cymbiform /símbifawrm/ *adj. Anat. & Bot.* boat-shaped. [L *cymba* f. Gk *kumbē* boat + -FORM]

cyme /sīm/ *n. Bot.* an inflorescence in which the primary axis bears a single terminal flower that develops first, the system being continued by the axes of secondary and higher orders each with a flower (cf. RACEME). □□ **cymose** *adj.* [F, var. of *cime* summit, ult. f. Gk *kuma* wave]

Cymric /kímrik, sím-/ *adj.* Welsh. [Welsh *Cymru* Wales]

cynic /sínik/ *n. & adj.* ● *n.* **1** a person who has little faith in human sincerity and goodness. **2** (**Cynic**) one of a school of ancient Greek philosophers founded by Antisthenes, marked by ostentatious contempt for ease and pleasure. ● *adj.* **1** (**Cynic**) of the Cynics. **2** = CYNICAL. □□ **cynicism** /-nisizəm/ *n.* [L *cynicus* f. Gk *kunikos* f. *kuōn kunos* dog, nickname for a Cynic]
■ *n.* **1** see SKEPTIC *n.* 1.

cynical /sínikəl/ *adj.* **1** of or characteristic of a cynic; incredulous of human goodness. **2** (of behavior, etc.) disregarding normal standards. **3** sneering; mocking. □□ **cynically** *adv.*
■ **1** see SKEPTICAL. **3** see SARDONIC 1.

cynocephalus /sínōséfələs/ *n.* **1** a fabled dog-headed man. **2** any flying lemur of the genus *Cynocephalus*, native to SE Asia. [Gk *kunokephalos* f. *kuōn kunos* dog + *kephalē* head]

cynosure /sínəshŏŏr, sín-/ *n.* **1** a center of attraction or admiration. **2** a guiding star. [F *cynosure* or L *cynosura* f. Gk *kunosoura* dog's tail, Ursa Minor f. *kuōn kunos* dog + *oura* tail]
■ **1** see FOCUS *n.* 3.

cypher var. of CIPHER.

cy pres /seé práy/ *adv. & adj. Law* as near as possible to the testator's or donor's intentions when these cannot be precisely followed. [AF, = *si près* so near]

cypress /síprəs/ *n.* **1** any coniferous tree of the genus *Cupressus* or *Chamaecyparis*, with hard wood and dark foliage. **2** this, or branches from it, as a symbol of mourning. [ME f. OF *cipres* f. LL *cypressus* f. Gk *kuparissos*]

Cyprian /sípreeən/ *n. & adj.* = CYPRIOT. [L *Cyprius* of Cyprus]

cyprinoid /síprinoyd/ *adj. & n.* ● *adj.* of or like a carp. ● *n.* a carp or related fish. [L *cyprinus* f. Gk *kuprinos* carp]

Cypriot /sípreeət/ *n. & adj.* (also **Cypriote** /-ōt/) ● *n.* a native or national of Cyprus. ● *adj.* of Cyprus. [Gk *Kupriōtes* f. *Kupros* Cyprus in E. Mediterranean]

cypripedium /sípripeédeeəm/ *n.* any orchid of the genus *Cypripedium*, esp. the lady's slipper. [mod.L f. Gk *Kupris* Aphrodite + *pedilon* slipper]

cypsela /sípsilə/ *n.* (*pl.* **cypselae** /-lee/) *Bot.* a dry single-seeded fruit formed from a double ovary of which only one develops into a seed, characteristic of the daisy family Compositae. [mod.L f. Gk *kupselē* hollow vessel]

Cyrillic /sirílik/ *adj. & n.* ● *adj.* denoting the alphabet used by the Slavonic peoples of the Orthodox Church; now used esp. for Russian and Bulgarian. ● *n.* this alphabet. [St. *Cyril* d. 869, its reputed inventor]

cyst /sist/ *n.* **1** *Med.* a sac containing morbid matter, a parasitic larva, etc. **2** *Biol.* **a** a hollow organ, bladder, etc., in an animal or plant, containing a liquid secretion. **b** a cell or

cavity enclosing reproductive bodies, an embryo, parasite, microorganism, etc. [LL *cystis* f. Gk *kustis* bladder]
■ **1** see LUMP[1] *n.* 3.

cysteine /sístee-een, -tee-in/ *n. Biochem.* a sulfur-containing amino acid, essential in the human diet and a constituent of many enzymes. [*cystine* (rel to CYST)+ *-eine* (var. of -INE⁴)]

cystic /sístik/ *adj.* **1** of the urinary bladder. **2** of the gallbladder. **3** of the nature of a cyst. □ **cystic fibrosis** *Med.* a hereditary disease affecting the exocrine glands and usu. resulting in respiratory infections. [F *cystique* or mod.L *cysticus* (as CYST)]

cystitis /sistítis/ *n.* an inflammation of the urinary bladder, often caused by infection, and usu. accompanied by frequent painful urination.

cysto- /sístō/ *comb. form* the urinary bladder (*cystoscope*; *cystotomy*). [Gk *kustē, kustis* bladder]

cystoscope /sístəskōp/ *n.* an instrument inserted in the urethra for examining the urinary bladder. □□ **cystoscopic** /-skópik/ *adj.* **cystoscopy** /sistóskəpee/ *n.*

cystotomy /sistótəmee/ *n.* (*pl.* **-ies**) a surgical incision into the urinary bladder.

-cyte /sīt/ *comb. form Biol.* a mature cell (*leukocyte*) (cf. -BLAST). [Gk *kutos* vessel]

cytidine /sítideen/ *n.* a nucleoside obtained from RNA by hydrolysis. [G *Cytidin* (as -CYTE)]

cyto- /sítō/ *comb. form Biol.* cells or a cell. [as -CYTE]

cytochrome /sítəkrōm/ *n. Biochem.* a compound consisting of a protein linked to a heme, which is involved in electron transfer reactions.

cytogenetics /sítōjinétiks/ *n.* the study of inheritance in relation to the structure and function of cells. □□ **cytogenetic** *adj.* **cytogenetical** *adj.* **cytogenetically** *adv.* **cytogeneticist** /-nétisist/ *n.*

cytology /sítóləjee/ *n.* the study of cells. □□ **cytological** /sítəlójikəl/ *adj.* **cytologically** *adv.* **cytologist** *n.*

cytoplasm /sítəplazəm/ *n.* the protoplasmic content of a cell apart from its nucleus. □□ **cytoplasmic** /-plázmik/ *adj.*

cytosine /sítəseen/ *n.* one of the principal component bases of the nucleotides and the nucleic acids DNA and RNA, derived from pyrimidine.

cytotoxic /sítətóksik/ *adj.* toxic to cells.

czar /zaar/ *n.* (also **tsar**) **1** *hist.* the title of the former emperor of Russia. **2** a person with great authority. □□ **czardom** *n.* **czarism** *n.* **czarist** *n.* [Russ. *tsar'*, ult. f. L *Caesar*]

czardas /chaárdaash/ *n.* (also **csardas**) (*pl.* same) a Hungarian dance with a slow start and a quick, wild finish. [Magyar *csárdás* f. *csárda* inn]

czarevich /zaárivich/ *n.* (also **tsarevich**) *hist.* the eldest son of an emperor of Russia. [Russ. *tsarevich* son of a czar]

czarina /zaareénə/ *n.* (also **tsarina**) *hist.* the title of the former empress of Russia. [It. & Sp. *(c)zarina* f. G *Czarin*, *Zarin*, fem. of *Czar*, *Zar*]

Czech /chek/ *n. & adj.* ● *n.* **1** a native or national of the Czech Republic, Bohemia, or (*hist.*) Czechoslovakia. **2** the West Slavonic language of the Czech people. ● *adj.* of or relating to the Czechs or their language. [Pol. spelling of Bohemian *čech*]

Czechoslovak /chékəslóvak, -vaak/ *n. & adj.* (also **Czechoslovakian** /-sləvaákeeən/) ● *n.* a native or national of Czechoslovakia, a former nation in central Europe including Bohemia, Moravia, and Slovakia. ● *adj.* of or relating to Czechoslovaks or the former nation of Czechoslovakia. [CZECH + SLOVAK]

/.../ **pronunciation** ● **part of speech**
□ **phrases, idioms, and compounds**
□□ **derivatives** ■ **synonym section**
cross-references appear in SMALL CAPITALS or *italics*

Dd

D¹ /dee/ *n.* (also **d**) (*pl.* **Ds** or **D's**) **1** the fourth letter of the alphabet. **2** *Mus.* the second note of the diatonic scale of C major. **3** (as a Roman numeral) 500. **4** = DEE. **5** the fourth highest class or category (of academic marks, etc.).

D² *symb. Chem.* the element deuterium.

D³ *abbr.* (also **D.**) **1** Democrat. **2** dimension (*3-D*).

d. *abbr.* **1** died. **2** departs. **3** delete. **4** daughter. **5** *Brit.* (predecimal) penny. **6** depth. **7** deci-. [sense 5 f. L *denarius* silver coin]

'd *v. colloq.* (usu. after pronouns) had; would (*I'd*; *he'd*). [abbr.]

DA *abbr.* **1** district attorney. **2** *sl.* = *duck's ass* (see DUCK¹).

D/A *abbr. Computing* digital to analog.

da *abbr.* deca-.

dab¹ /dab/ *v. & n.* ● *v.* (**dabbed, dabbing**) **1** *tr.* press (a surface) briefly with a cloth, sponge, etc., without rubbing, esp. in cleaning or to apply a substance. **2** *tr.* press (a sponge, etc.) lightly on a surface. **3** *tr.* (foll. by *on*) apply (a substance) by dabbing a surface. **4** *intr.* (usu. foll. by *at*) aim a feeble blow; tap. **5** *tr.* strike lightly; tap. ● *n.* **1** a brief application of a cloth, sponge, etc., to a surface without rubbing. **2** a small amount of something applied in this way (*a dab of paint*). **3** a light blow or tap. **4** (in *pl.*) *Brit. sl.* fingerprints. □□ **dabber** *n.* [ME, imit.]

■ *v.* **3** daub, touch; see also APPLY 4a. **5** see TAP² *v.* 1, 2. ● *n.* **1** daub, application, touch, administration, rubbing in, putting on. **2** touch, drop, trace, bit, mite, hint, suggestion, pinch, dash, spot, tinge, *colloq.* smidgen. **3** poke, pat, tap, touch; see also TAP² *v.*

dab² /dab/ *n.* any flatfish of the genus *Limanda*. [15th c.: orig. unkn.]

dab³ /dab/ *adj.* esp. *Brit. colloq.* □ **dab hand** (usu. foll. by *at*) a person especially skilled (in) (*a dab hand at cooking*). [17th c.: orig. unkn.]

dabble /dábbəl/ *v.* **1** *intr.* (usu. foll. by *in, at*) take a casual or superficial interest or part (in a subject or activity). **2** *intr.* move the feet, hands, etc., about in (usu. a small amount of) liquid. **3** *tr.* wet partly or intermittently; moisten; stain; splash. □□ **dabbler** *n.* [16th c.: f. Du. *dabbelen* or DAB¹]

■ **1** tinker, trifle, potter, dally; experiment. **3** moisten, dampen; splash, spatter, sprinkle, bespatter, besprinkle, bedabble, stain. □□ **dabbler** see DILETTANTE *n.*

dabchick /dábchik/ *n.* = *little grebe* (see GREBE). [16th c., in earlier forms *dap-, dop-*: perh. rel. to OE *dūfedoppa*, DEEP, DIP]

da capo /daa káapō/ *adv. Mus.* repeat from the beginning. [It.]

dace /days/ *n.* (*pl.* same) any small freshwater fish, esp. of the genus *Leuciscus*, related to the carp. [OF *dars*: see DART]

dacha /daachə/ *n.* a country house or cottage in Russia. [Russ., = gift]

dachshund /daaks-hoŏnt, daaksənt/ *n.* **1** a dog of a short-legged, long-bodied breed. **2** this breed. [G, = badger dog]

dacoit /dəkóyt/ *n.* (in India or Burma) a member of a band of armed robbers. [Hindi *ḍakait* f. *ḍākā* gang-robbery]

Dacron /dáykron/ *n. propr.* a synthetic polyester fiber used in textiles.

dactyl /dáktil/ *n.* a metrical foot (‾ ⌣ ⌣) consisting of one long (or stressed) syllable followed by two short (or unstressed).

[ME f. L *dactylus* f. Gk *daktulos* finger, the three bones corresponding to the three syllables]

dactylic /daktílik/ *adj. & n.* ● *adj.* of or using dactyls. ● *n.* (usu. in *pl.*) dactylic verse. [L *dactylicus* f. Gk *daktulikos* (as DACTYL)]

dad /dad/ *n. colloq.* father. [perh. imit. of a child's *da, da* (cf. DADDY)]

■ see FATHER *n.* 1a.

Dada /daadaa/ *n.* an early 20th-c. international movement in art, literature, music, and film, repudiating and mocking artistic and social conventions. □□ **Dadaism** /daadəizəm/ *n.* **Dadaist** *n. & adj.* **Dadaistic** *adj.* [F (the title of an early 20th-c. review) f. *dada* hobby-horse]

daddy /dádee/ *n.* (*pl.* **-ies**) *colloq.* **1** father. **2** (usu. foll. by *of*) the oldest or supreme example (*had a daddy of a headache*). □ **daddy longlegs 1** a harvestman. **2** *Brit.* a crane fly. [DAD + -Y³]

■ **1** see FATHER *n.* 1a.

dado /dáydō/ *n.* (*pl.* **-os**) **1** the lower part of the wall of a room when visually distinct from the upper part. **2** the plinth of a column. **3** the cube of a pedestal between the base and the cornice. [It., = DIE²]

daemon var. of DEMON¹ 5.

daemonic var. of DEMONIC.

daff /daf/ *n. colloq.* = DAFFODIL. [abbr.]

daffodil /dáfədil/ *n.* **1 a** a bulbous plant, *Narcissus pseudonarcissus*, with a yellow trumpet-shaped crown. **b** any of various other large-flowered plants of the genus *Narcissus*. **c** a flower of any of these plants. **2** a pale-yellow color. [earlier *affodill*, as ASPHODEL]

daffy /dáfee/ *adj.* (**daffier, daffiest**) *sl.* = DAFT. □□ **daffily** *adv.* **daffiness** *n.* [*daff* simpleton + -Y²]

daft /daft/ *adj. colloq.* **1** silly; foolish; crazy. **2** (foll. by *about*) fond of; infatuated with. □□ **daftly** *adv.* **daftness** *n.* [ME *dafte* = OE *gedæfte* mild, meek, f. Gmc]

■ **1** foolish, silly, giddy, senseless, absurd, ridiculous, stupid, nonsensical, fatuous, imbecile, imbecilic, idiotic, cretinous, boneheaded, fatheaded, dim-witted, witless, asinine, weak-minded, simpleminded, brainless, feebleminded, featherbrained, harebrained, slow-witted, addlebrained, *colloq.* dumb, dopey, moronic, cockeyed, halfwitted, dumb, esp. *Brit. colloq.* gormless, *sl.* daffy; see also CRAZY 1. **2** (*daft about*) fond of, mad about, infatuated with, besotted by or with, *colloq.* nuts about, sweet on, crazy about.

dag¹ /dag/ *n. & v. Austral. & NZ* ● *n.* (usu. in *pl.*) a lock of wool clotted with dung on the hinder parts of a sheep. ● *v.tr.* (**dagged, dagging**) remove dags from (a sheep). □ **rattle one's dags** *sl.* hurry up. □□ **dagger** *n.* [orig. Engl. dial.]

dag² /dag/ *n. Austral. & NZ sl.* an eccentric or noteworthy person; a character (*he's a bit of a dag*). [orig. Engl. dial., = a dare, challenge]

dagga /dágə/ *n. S.Afr.* **1** hemp used as a narcotic. **2** any plant of the genus *Leontis* used similarly. [Afrik. f. Hottentot *dachab*]

dagger /dágər/ *n.* **1** a short stabbing weapon with a pointed and edged blade. **2** *Printing* = OBELUS. □ **at daggers drawn** in bitter enmity. **look daggers at** glare angrily or venomously at. [ME, perh. f. obs. *dag* pierce, infl. by OF *dague* long dagger]

■ **1** knife, short sword, stiletto, dirk, kris, *hist.* skean, *literary* poniard, *poet.* blade. □ **look daggers at** see GLARE[1] *v.* 1.

dago /dáygō/ *n.* (*pl.* **-os** or **-oes**) *sl. offens.* a person of Italian, Spanish, or Portuguese ancestry. [Sp. *Diego* = James]

daguerreotype /dəgérətīp/ *n.* **1** a photograph taken by an early photographic process employing an iodine-sensitized silvered plate and mercury vapor. **2** this process. [L. *Daguerre*, Fr. inventor d. 1851]

dah /daa/ *n.* Telegraphy (in the Morse system) = DASH (cf. DIT). [imit.]

dahlia /dályə, daál-, dáyl-/ *n.* any composite garden plant of the genus *Dahlia*, of Mexican origin, cultivated for its many-colored single or double flowers. [A. *Dahl*, Sw. botanist d. 1789]

Dáil /doyl/ *n.* (in full **Dáil Éireann** /áirən/) the lower house of parliament in the Republic of Ireland. [Ir., = assembly (of Ireland)]

daily /dáylee/ *adj., adv.,* & *n.* ● *adj.* **1** done, produced, or occurring every day or every weekday. **2** constant; regular. ● *adv.* **1** every day; from day to day. **2** constantly. ● *n.* (*pl.* **-ies**) *colloq.* **1** a daily newspaper. **2** *Brit.* a cleaning woman or domestic help working daily. □ **daily bread** necessary food; a livelihood. **daily dozen** *colloq.* regular exercises, esp. on rising. [ME f. DAY + -LY[1], -LY[2]]

■ *adj.* **1** diurnal, everyday, quotidian, *Physiol.* circadian. **2** constant, continual, everyday, routine, regular, common, commonplace. ● *adv.* **1** every day, day after day. **2** constantly, always, habitually, routinely, regularly, continually, continuously. □ **daily bread** see SUSTENANCE 2.

daimon /dímōn/ *n.* = DEMON[1] 5. □□ **daimonic** /-mónik/ *adj.* [Gk, = deity]

dainty /dáyntee/ *adj.* & *n.* ● *adj.* (**daintier, daintiest**) **1** delicately pretty. **2** delicate of build or in movement. **3** (of food) choice. **4** fastidious; having delicate taste and sensibility. ● *n.* (*pl.* **-ies**) a choice morsel; a delicacy. □□ **daintily** *adv.* **daintiness** *n.* [AF *dainté*, OF *daintié, deintié* f. L *dignitas -tatis* f. *dignus* worthy]

■ *adj.* **1, 2** delicate, graceful, fine, elegant, exquisite, neat. **3** delicious, tasty, appetizing, palatable, toothsome, *literary* delectable; see also CHOICE *adj.* **4** fastidious, sensitive, squeamish, finicky, finical, overnice, overrefined, genteel, mincing. ● *n.* delicacy, sweetmeat, treat, tidbit, *bonne bouche*, morsel.

daiquiri /dákəree, dí-/ *n.* (*pl.* **daiquiris**) a cocktail of rum, lime juice, etc. [*Daiquiri* in Cuba]

dairy /dáiree/ *n.* (*pl.* **-ies**) **1** a building or room for the storage, processing, and distribution of milk and its products. **2** a store where milk and milk products are sold. **3** (*attrib.*) **a** of, containing, or concerning milk and its products (and sometimes eggs). **b** used for dairy products (*dairy cow*). [ME *deierie* f. *deie* maidservant f. OE *dǣge* kneader of dough]

dairying /dáireeing/ *n.* the business of producing, storing, and distributing milk and its products.

dairymaid /dáireemayd/ *n.* a woman employed in a dairy.

dairyman /dáireemən/ *n.* (*pl.* **-men**) **1** a person dealing in dairy products. **2** a person employed in a dairy.

dais /dáyis, dí-/ *n.* a low platform, usu. at the upper end of a hall and used to support a table, lectern, etc. [ME f. OF *deis* f. L *discus* disk, dish, in med.L = table]

daisy /dáyzee/ *n.* (*pl.* **-ies**) **1 a** a small composite plant, *Bellis perennis*, bearing flowers each with a yellow disk and white rays. **b** any other plant with daisylike flowers, esp. the larger oxeye daisy, the Michaelmas daisy, or the Shasta daisy. **2** *sl.* a first-rate specimen of anything. □ **daisy chain** a string of daisies threaded together. **daisy wheel** a disk of spokes extending radially from a central hub, each terminating in a printing character, used as a printer in word processors and typewriters. **pushing up the daisies** *sl.* dead and buried. [OE *dǣges ēage* day's eye, the flower opening in the morning]

Dak. *abbr.* Dakota.

Dakota /dəkṓtə/ *n.* **1 a** a N. American people native to the northern Mississippi valley. **b** a member of this people. **2** the language of this people. Also called **Lakota** or **Sioux**. □□ **Dakotan** *adj.*

dal /daal/ *n.* (also **dhal**) **1** a kind of split pulse, a common foodstuff in India. **2** a dish made with this. [Hindi]

Dalai lama /daálī laámə/ *n.* the spiritual head of Tibetan Buddhism, formerly also the chief ruler of Tibet (see LAMA). [Mongolian *dalai* ocean; see LAMA]

dale /dayl/ *n.* a valley, esp. in a broad one. [OE *dæl* f. Gmc]
■ see VALLEY *n.*

dalesman /dáylzmən/ *n.* (*pl.* **-men**) an inhabitant of the dales in Northern England.

dalliance /dáleeəns, -yəns/ *n.* **1** a leisurely or frivolous passing of time. **2** the act or an instance of lighthearted flirting. [DALLY + -ANCE]
■ **1** see SPORT *n.* 3. **2** see ROMANCE *n.* 2c.

dally /dálee/ *v.intr.* (**-ies, -ied**) **1** delay; waste time, esp. frivolously. **2** (often foll. by *with*) play about; flirt; treat frivolously (*dallied with her affections*). □ **dally away** waste or fritter (one's time, life, etc.). [ME f. OF *dalier* chat]
■ **1** see DELAY *v.* 3. **2** see FLIRT *v.* 1.

Dalmatian /dalmáyshən/ *n.* **1** a dog of a large, white, short-haired breed with dark spots. **2** this breed. [*Dalmatia* in Croatia]

dalmatic /dalmátik/ *n.* a wide-sleeved, long, loose vestment open at the sides, worn by deacons and bishops, and by a monarch at his or her coronation. [ME f. OF *dalmatique* or LL *dalmatica* (*vestis* robe) of Dalmatia]

dal segno /daal sáynyō/ *adv. Mus.* repeat from the point marked by a sign. [It., = from the sign]

daltonism /dáwltənizəm/ *n.* color blindness, esp. a congenital inability to distinguish between red and green. [F *daltonisme* f. J. *Dalton*, Engl. chemist d. 1844, who suffered from it]

dam[1] /dam/ *n.* & *v.* ● *n.* **1** a barrier constructed to hold back water and raise its level, forming a reservoir or preventing flooding. **2** a barrier constructed in a stream by a beaver. **3** anything functioning as a dam does. **4** a causeway. ● *v.tr.* (**dammed, damming**) **1** furnish or confine with a dam. **2** (often foll. by *up*) block up; hold back; obstruct. [ME f. MLG, MDu.]
■ *v.* see PLUG *v.* 1.

dam[2] /dam/ *n.* the female parent of an animal, esp. a four-footed one. [ME: var. of DAME]

damage /dámij/ *n.* & *v.* ● *n.* **1** harm or injury impairing the value or usefulness of something, or the health or normal function of a person. **2** (in *pl.*) *Law* a sum of money claimed or awarded in compensation for a loss or an injury. **3** the loss of what is desirable. **4** (prec. by *the*) *sl.* cost (*what's the damage?*). ● *v.tr.* **1** inflict damage on. **2** (esp. as **damaging** *adj.*) detract from the reputation of (*a most damaging admission*). □□ **damagingly** *adv.* [ME f. OF *damage* (n.), *damagier* (v.), f. *dam(me)* loss f. L *damnum* loss, damage]
■ *n.* **1** harm, injury, hurt, impairment, mutilation, destruction, devastation. **3** (*damages*) compensation, reparation, indemnity. **4** expense, price, cost; bill.
● *v.* **1** harm, hurt, injure, impair, mar, deface. **2** spoil, impair; see also DETRACT.

damascene /dáməseén/ *v., n.,* & *adj.* ● *v.tr.* decorate (metal, esp. iron or steel) by etching or inlaying, esp. with gold or silver, or with a watered pattern produced in welding. ● *n.* a design or article produced in this way. ● *adj.* of, relating to, or produced by this process. [*Damascene* of Damascus, f. L *Damascenus* f. Gk *Damaskēnos*]

damask /dáməsk/ *n., adj.,* & *v.* ● *n.* **1 a** a figured woven fabric (esp. silk or linen) with a pattern visible on both sides. **b** twilled table linen with woven designs shown by the reflection of light. **2** a tablecloth made of this material. **3** *hist.*

/ . . . / **pronunciation**   ● **part of speech**
□ **phrases, idioms, and compounds**
□□ **derivatives**   ■ **synonym section**
cross-references appear in SMALL CAPITALS or *italics*

steel with a watered pattern produced in welding. ● adj. **1** made of or resembling damask. **2** colored like a damask rose, velvety pink or vivid red. ● v.tr. **1** weave with figured designs. **2** = DAMASCENE v. **3** ornament. □ **damask rose** an old sweet-scented variety of rose, with very soft velvety petals, used to make attar. [ME, ult. f. L *Damascus*]

dame /daym/ n. **1** (**Dame**) **a** (in the UK) the title given to a woman with the rank of Knight Commander or holder of the Grand Cross in the Orders of Chivalry. **b** a woman holding this title. **2** *Brit.* a comic middle-aged woman in modern pantomime, usu. played by a man. **3** *archaic* a mature woman. **4** *sl.* a woman. □ **dame school** *hist.* a primary school kept by an elderly woman. [ME f. OF f. L *domina* mistress]
■ **4** see WOMAN 1.

damfool /dámfóol/ n. & adj. *colloq.* ● n. a foolish or stupid person. ● adj. (also **damfoolish** /dámfóolish/) foolish; stupid. [DAMN + FOOL[1]]

dammar /dámər/ n. **1** any E. Asian tree, esp. one of the genus *Agathis* or *Shorea*, yielding a resin used in making varnish. **2** this resin. [Malay *damar*]

dammit /dámit/ int. damn it.

damn /dam/ v., n., adj., & adv. ● v.tr. **1** (often *absol.* or as *int.* of anger or annoyance, = *may God damn*) curse (a person or thing). **2** doom to hell; cause the damnation of. **3** condemn; censure (*a review damning the performance*). **4 a** (often as **damning** adj.) (of a circumstance, piece of evidence, etc.) show or prove to be guilty; bring condemnation upon (*evidence against them was damning*). **b** be the ruin of. ● n. **1** an uttered curse. **2** *sl.* a negligible amount (*not worth a damn*). ● adj. & adv. *colloq.* = DAMNED. □ **damn all** *Brit. sl.* nothing at all. **damn well** *colloq.* (as an emphatic) simply (*damn well do as I say*). **damn with faint praise** commend so unenthusiastically as to imply disapproval. **I'll be damned if** *colloq.* I certainly do not, will not, etc. **not give a damn** see GIVE. **well I'll be damned** *colloq.* exclamation of surprise, dismay, etc. □□ **damningly** adv. [ME f. OF *damner* f. L *damnare* inflict loss on f. *damnum* loss]
■ v. **1** see CURSE v. 1. **2** doom, condemn, sentence. **3** condemn, criticize, find fault with, censure, berate, castigate, upbraid, attack, blast, reprimand, reprove, remonstrate, denounce. **4 b** see RUIN v. 1a. ● n. **1** see CURSE n. 1. **2** jot, tittle, *sl.* hoot, two hoots (in hell). □ **damn well** well enough, *Brit. colloq.* jolly well. **well I'll be damned** well I never, *colloq.* you don't say, *sl.* well I'll be blowed.

damnable /dámnəbəl/ adj. hateful; annoying. □□ **damnably** adv. [ME f. OF *damnable* (as DAMN)]
■ hateful, terrible, horrible, horrid, atrocious, abominable, dreadful, hideous, execrable, accursed, cursed, detestable, abhorrent, despicable, loathsome, wicked, sinful, offensive, heinous, pernicious, infernal, malicious, malevolent, outrageous, foul, rotten, base, vile, odious, *colloq.* awful, damned; see also IRKSOME.

damnation /damnáyshən/ n. & int. ● n. condemnation to eternal punishment, esp. in hell. ● int. expressing anger or annoyance. [ME f. OF *damnation* (as DAMN)]
■ n. see PERDITION.

damnatory /dámnətawree/ adj. conveying or causing censure or damnation. [L *damnatorius* (as DAMN)]

damned /damd/ adj. & adv. *colloq.* ● adj. damnable; infernal; unwelcome. ● adv. extremely (*damned hot; damned lovely*). □ **damned well** (as an emphatic) simply (*you've damned well got to*). **do one's damnedest** do one's utmost.
■ adj. see INFERNAL 1. ● adv. see *extremely* (EXTREME).

damnify /dámnifī/ v.tr. (**-ies**, **-ied**) *Law* cause injury to. □□ **damnification** /-fikáyshən/ n. [OF *damnifier*, etc., f. LL *damnificare* injure (as DAMN)]

damp /damp/ adj., n., & v. ● adj. slightly wet; moist. ● n. **1** diffused moisture in the air, on a surface, or in a solid, esp. as a cause of inconvenience or danger. **2** dejection; discouragement. **3** = FIREDAMP. ● v.tr. **1** make damp; moisten. **2** (often foll. by *down*) **a** take the force or vigor out of (*damp one's enthusiasm*). **b** make flaccid or spiritless. **c** make (a fire) burn less strongly by reducing the flow of air to it. **3** reduce

or stop the vibration of (esp. the strings of a musical instrument). **4** quiet. □ **damp off** (of a plant) die from a fungus attack in damp conditions. **damp squib** *Brit.* an unsuccessful attempt to impress, etc. □□ **damply** adv. **dampness** n. [ME f. MLG, = vapor, cf., OHG *dampf* steam f. WG]
■ adj. moist, wettish; humid, dank, steamy, clammy, muggy. ● n. **1** moistness, moisture, dampness, clamminess, humidity, wetness. **2** see DEPRESSION 1b. ● v. **1** see DAMPEN 1. **2 a, b** see DAMPEN 2. **4** quiet (down), calm (down), still. □□ **dampness** see DAMP n. 1 above.

dampen /dámpən/ v. **1** v.tr. & intr. make or become damp. **2** tr. make less forceful or vigorous; stifle; choke. □□ **dampener** n.
■ **1** damp, moisten, bedew; see also WET v. **2** stifle, deaden, choke, damp, damp down, check, chill, cool, restrain, retard, lessen, diminish, reduce, suppress, abate, moderate, allay, subdue, temper, dull, discourage.

damper /dámpər/ n. **1** a person or thing that discourages, or tempers enthusiasm. **2** a device that reduces shock or noise. **3** a metal plate in a flue to control the draft, and so the rate of combustion. **4** *Mus.* a pad silencing a piano string except when removed by means of a pedal or by the note's being struck. **5** esp. *Austral.* & *NZ* unleavened bread or cake of flour and water baked in wood ashes. □ **put a damper on** take the enjoyment out of.
■ **1** see SPOILSPORT.

damsel /dámzəl/ n. *archaic* or *literary* a young unmarried woman. [ME f. OF *dam(e)isele* ult. f. L *domina* mistress]
■ see MAID 2.

damselfish /dámzəlfish/ n. a small, brightly colored fish, *Chromis chromis*, found in or near coral reefs.

damselfly /dámzəlflī/ n. (*pl.* **-flies**) any of various insects of the order Odonata, like a dragonfly but with its wings folded over the body when resting.

damson /dámzən, -sən/ n. & adj. ● n. **1** (in full **damson plum**) **a** a small, dark-purple, plumlike fruit. **b** the small deciduous tree, *Prunus institia*, bearing this. **2** a dark-purple color. ● adj. damson-colored. [ME *damacene, -scene, -sene* f. L *damascenum* (*prunum* plum) of *Damascus*: see DAMASCENE]

Dan. abbr. Daniel (Old Testament).

dan[1] /daan, dan/ n. **1** any of twelve degrees of advanced proficiency in judo. **2** a person who has achieved any of these. [Jap.]

dan[2] /dan/ n. (in full **dan buoy**) a small buoy used as a marker in deep-sea fishing, or to mark the limits of an area cleared by minesweepers. [17th c.: orig. unkn.]

dance /dans/ v. & n. ● v. **1** intr. move about rhythmically alone or with a partner or in a set, usu. in fixed steps or sequences to music, for pleasure or as entertainment. **2** intr. move in a lively way; skip or jump about. **3** tr. **a** perform (a specified dance or form of dancing). **b** perform (a specified role) in a ballet, etc. **4** intr. move up and down (on water, in the field of vision, etc.). **5** tr. move (esp. a child) up and down; dandle. ● n. **1 a** a piece of dancing; a sequence of steps in dancing. **b** a special form of this. **2** a single round or turn of a dance. **3** a social gathering for dancing; a ball. **4** a piece of music for dancing to or in a dance rhythm. **5** a dancing or lively motion. □ **dance attendance on** follow or wait on (a person) obsequiously. **dance of death** a medieval dance in which a personified Death is represented as leading all to the grave. **dance to a person's tune** accede obsequiously to a person's demands and wishes. **lead a person a dance** (or **merry dance**) *Brit.* cause a person much trouble in following a course one has instigated. □□ **danceable** adj. [ME f. OF *dance, danse* (n.), *dancer, danser* (v.), f. Rmc, of unkn. orig.]
■ v. **1** *colloq.* bop, *sl.* boogie, hoof it. **2** gambol, caper, skip, leap, romp, jump about, frolic, *sl.* cavort. **4** see WAG[1] v. ● n. **3** ball, social, dancing party, tea dance, thé dansant, promenade, *colloq.* hop, prom, rave-up.

dancehall /dáns-hawl/ n. a public hall for dancing.

dancer /dánsər/ *n.* **1** a person who performs a dance. **2** a person whose profession is dancing.

d. and c. *n.* dilatation (of the cervix) and curettage (of the uterus), performed after a miscarriage or for the removal of cysts, tumors, etc.

dandelion /dánd′líən/ *n.* a composite plant, *Taraxacum officinale*, with jagged leaves and a large, bright-yellow flower on a hollow stalk, followed by a globular head of seeds with downy tufts. [F *dent-de-lion* transl. med.L *dens leonis* lion's tooth]

dander /dándər/ *n. colloq.* temper; anger; indignation. □ **get one's dander up** lose one's temper; become angry. [19th c.: orig. uncert.]

dandify /dándifí/ *v.tr.* (**-ies, -ied**) cause to resemble a dandy.

dandle /dánd′l/ *v.tr.* **1** dance (a child) on one's knees or in one's arms. **2** pamper; pet. [16th c.: orig. unkn.]
■ **2** see BABY *v.*

dandruff /dándruf/ *n.* **1** dead skin in small scales among the hair. **2** the condition of having this. [16th c.: *-ruff* perh. rel. to ME *rove* scurfiness f. ON *hrufa* or MLG, MDu. *rōve*]

dandy /dándee/ *n. & adj.* ● *n.* (*pl.* **-ies**) **1** a man unduly devoted to style, smartness, and fashion in dress and appearance. **2** *colloq.* an excellent thing. ● *adj.* (**dandier, dandiest**) *colloq.* very good of its kind; splendid; first-rate. □ **dandy brush** a brush for grooming a horse. **dandy roll** (or **roller**) a device for solidifying, and impressing a watermark in, paper during manufacture. □□ **dandyish** *adj.* **dandyism** *n.* [18th c.: perh. orig. = *Andrew*, in *Jack-a-dandy*]
■ *n.* **1** fop, coxcomb, beau, *Brit.* blood, *archaic* gallant, *colloq.* swell, clotheshorse, *sl.* dude, *Brit. sl.* toff. ● *adj.* see SPLENDID 3.

Dane /dayn/ *n.* **1** a native or national of Denmark. **2** *hist.* a Viking invader of England in the 9th–11th c. □ **Great Dane 1** a dog of a very large, short-haired breed. **2** this breed. [ME f. ON *Danir* (pl.), LL *Dani*]

danegeld /dáyngeld/ *n. hist.* (also **Danegeld**) **1** (in medieval England) an annual tax to raise funds for protection against Danish invaders. **2** appeasement by bribery. [OE (as DANE + ON *gjald* payment)]

Danelaw /dáynlaw/ *n. hist.* the part of N. & E. England occupied or administered by Danes in the 9th–11th c. [OE *Dena lagu* Danes' law]

danger /dáynjər/ *n.* **1** liability or exposure to harm. **2** a thing that causes or is likely to cause harm. **3** the status of a railroad signal directing a halt or caution. □ **danger list** *Brit.* = *critical list.* **in danger of** likely to incur or to suffer from. [earlier sense 'jurisdiction, power': ME f. OF *dangier* ult. f. L *dominus* lord]
■ **1, 2** peril, risk, threat, jeopardy, endangerment, hazard; (*in danger*) in jeopardy, at risk, under threat. □ **in danger of** likely to, liable to.

dangerous /dáynjərəs/ *adj.* involving or causing danger. □□ **dangerously** *adv.* **dangerousness** *n.* [ME f. AF *dangerous, daungerous*, OF *dangereus* (as DANGER)]
■ risky, perilous, treacherous, hazardous, unsafe, precarious, chancy; threatening, menacing, harmful. □□ **dangerously** perilously, hazardously, unsafely, precariously, recklessly; ominously, alarmingly.

dangle /dánggəl/ *v.* **1** *intr.* be loosely suspended, so as to be able to sway to and fro. **2** *tr.* hold or carry loosely suspended. **3** *tr.* hold out (a hope, temptation, etc.) enticingly. □□ **dangler** *n.* [16th c. (imit.): cf. Sw. *dangla*, Da. *dangle*]
■ **1** hang down, droop, swing, *archaic poet.* depend; see also HANG *v.* 10. **3** hold out, flaunt, brandish, wave, flourish.

Danish /dáynish/ *adj. & n.* ● *adj.* of or relating to Denmark or the Danes. ● *n.* **1** the Danish language. **2** (prec. by *the*; treated as *pl.*) the Danish people. □ **Danish blue** a soft, salty white cheese with blue veins. **Danish pastry** a cake of sweetened yeast pastry topped with icing, fruit, nuts, etc. [ME f. AF *danes*, OF *daneis* f. med.L *Danensis* (as DANE)]

dank /dangk/ *adj.* disagreeably damp and cold. □□ **dankly** *adv.* **dankness** *n.* [ME prob. f. Scand.: cf. Sw. *dank* marshy spot]
■ see DAMP *adj.*

danse macabre /dóns məkaábrə/ *n.* = *dance of death.* [F (as DANCE, MACABRE)]

danseur /donsőr/ *n.* (*fem.* **danseuse** /-sőz/) a ballet dancer. [F, = dancer]

Dantean /dánteeən, dánteéən/ *adj. & n.* ● *adj.* **1** of Dante. **2** in the style of or reminiscent of Dante's writings. ● *n.* a student or imitator of Dante. □□ **Dantesque** /-tésk/ *adj.* [*Dante* Alighieri, It. poet d. 1321]

dap /dap/ *v.* (**dapped, dapping**) **1** *intr.* fish by letting the bait bob on the water **2** *tr. & intr.* dip lightly. **3** *tr. & intr.* bounce on the ground. [cf. DAB¹]

daphne /dáfnee/ *n.* any flowering shrub of the genus *Daphne*, e.g., the spurge laurel or mezereon. [ME, = laurel, f. Gk *daphnē*]

daphnia /dáfneeə/ *n.* any freshwater branchiopod crustacean of the genus *Daphnia*, enclosed in a transparent carapace and with long antennae and prominent eyes. Also called *freshwater flea.* [mod.L f. *Daphne* name of a nymph in Gk mythol., f. DAPHNE]

dapper /dápər/ *adj.* **1** neat and precise, esp. in dress or movement. **2** sprightly. □□ **dapperly** *adv.* **dapperness** *n.* [ME f. MLG, MDu. *dapper* strong, stout]
■ **1** neat, spruce, smart, trim, well-dressed, well turned out, stylish, fashionable, elegant, chic, dressy, dressed to the nines, dressed to kill, swanky, *colloq.* nifty, swell, classy, sharp, ritzy, swank, *sl.* snazzy, spiffy. **2** see SPRIGHTLY.

dapple /dápəl/ *v. & n.* ● *v.* **1** *tr.* mark with spots or rounded patches of color or shade. **2** *intr.* become marked in this way. ● *n.* **1** a dappled effect. **2** a dappled animal, esp. a horse. □ **dapple gray 1** (of an animal's coat) gray or white with darker spots. **2** a horse of this color. [ME *dappled, dappeld*, (adj.), of unkn. orig.]
■ *v.* **1** spot, dot, mottle, speckle, stipple. ● *n.* **2** piebald, skewbald, dapple gray, pinto. □ **dapple gray 1** spotted, mottled, speckled, flecked, dappled, brindled; pied, piebald, skewbald, pinto. **2** see DAPPLE *n.* 2 above.

D.A.R. *abbr.* Daughters of the American Revolution.

darbies /daárbeez/ *n.pl. Brit. sl.* handcuffs. [allusive use of *Father Darby's bands*, some rigid form of agreement for debtors (16th c.)]

Darby and Joan /daárbee ənd jőn/ *n. Brit.* a devoted old married couple. [18th c.: perh. f. a poem of 1735 in the *Gentleman's Magazine*]

dare /dair/ *v. & n.* ● *v.tr.* (*3rd sing. present* usu. **dare** before an expressed or implied infinitive without *to*) **1** (foll. by infin. with or without *to*) venture (to); have the courage or impudence (to) (*dare he do it?*; *if they dare to come*; *how dare you?*; *I dare not speak*; *I do not dare to jump*). **2** (usu. foll. by *to* + infin.) defy or challenge (a person) (*I dare you to own up*). **3** *literary* attempt; take the risk of (*dare all things*; *dared their anger*). ● *n.* **1** an act of daring. **2** a challenge, esp. to prove courage. □ **I daresay 1** (often foll. by *that* + clause) it is probable. **2** probably; I grant that much (*I daresay, but you are still wrong*). □□ **darer** *n.* [OE *durran* with Gmc cognates: cf. Skr. *dhṛṣh*, Gk *tharseō* be bold]
■ *v.* **1** venture, risk, hazard, make bold, be so bold as. **2** challenge, defy. **3** see ATTEMPT *v.* ● *n.* **2** challenge, provocation, taunt.

daredevil /dáirdevəl/ *n. & adj.* ● *n.* a recklessly daring person. ● *adj.* recklessly daring. □□ **daredevilry** *n.* **daredeviltry** *n.*
■ *n.* adventurer, adventuress, swashbuckler, hero, heroine, soldier of fortune. ● *adj.* reckless, rash, death-defying, impulsive, daring, impetuous, incautious, wild, foolhardy, madcap, devil-may-care; audacious, bold, brave, fearless, gallant, courageous, intrepid.

daring /dáiring/ *n. & adj.* ● *n.* adventurous courage. ● *adj.* adventurous; bold; prepared to take risks. □□ **daringly** *adv.*

■ *n.* courage, boldness, bravery, valor, intrepidity, fearlessness, pluck, spirit, mettle, nerve, adventurousness, *colloq.* guts, grit, spunk, *literary joc.* derring-do. ● *adj.* bold, adventurous, audacious, courageous, brave, valorous, intrepid, fearless, unafraid, plucky, mettlesome, venturesome, *archaic or joc.* doughty, *colloq.* gutsy, nervy; rash, reckless.

Darjeeling /daarjéeling/ *n.* a high-quality tea from Darjeeling in NE India.

dark /daark/ *adj. & n.* ● *adj.* **1** with little or no light. **2** of a deep or somber color. **3** (of a person) with deep brown or black hair, complexion, or skin. **4** gloomy; depressing; dismal (*dark thoughts*). **5** evil; sinister (*dark deeds*). **6** sullen; angry (*a dark mood*). **7** remote; secret; mysterious; little-known (*the dark and distant past*; *keep it dark*). **8** ignorant; unenlightened. ● *n.* **1** absence of light. **2** nightfall (*don't go out after dark*). **3** a lack of knowledge. **4** a dark area or color, esp. in painting (*the skilled use of lights and darks*). □ **the Dark Ages** (or **Age**) **1** the period of European history preceding the Middle Ages, esp. the 5th–10th c. **2** any period of supposed unenlightenment. **dark chocolate** chocolate without added milk. **the Dark Continent** a name for Africa, esp. when little known to Europeans. **dark glasses** eyeglasses with dark-tinted lenses. **dark horse** a little-known person who is unexpectedly successful or prominent. **dark star** an invisible star known to exist from reception of physical data other than light. **in the dark** lacking information. □□ **darkish** *adj.* **darkly** *adv.* **darkness** *n.* **darksome** *poet. adj.* [OE *deorc* prob. f. Gmc]

■ *adj.* **1** unlit, unlighted, unilluminated, poorly-lit, sunless, *poet.* darkling; dim, murky, gloomy, dusky, shady, shadowy, *formal* subfusc, *literary* tenebrous; black, pitch-dark, pitch-black, jet-black, *literary* stygian. **2** deep; inky, sooty, dreary, dull, drab, somber. **3** brunette; black, swarthy, dark-complexioned, brown, *archaic* swart; (sun)tanned. **4** gloomy, depressing, dismal, bleak, cheerless, mournful, pessimistic, somber, doleful, joyless, grim, sad, melancholy, sorrowful. **5** evil, wicked, vile, base, foul, iniquitous, nefarious, black-hearted, villainous, sinister, satanic, devilish, hellish. **6** see SULLEN *adj.* 1. **7** mysterious, deep, remote, hidden, concealed, secret, incomprehensible, impenetrable, unfathomable, abstruse, little-known, recondite, arcane, obscure, occult, mystic, mystical, cryptic, enigmatic, puzzling. **8** unenlightened, benighted; see also IGNORANT 1a. ● *n.* **1** darkness, blackness, gloominess, murk, murkiness; see also GLOOM *n.* 1. **2** night, nighttime, nightfall; dusk, twilight, sunset, sundown, evening, *archaic or poet.* eventide, *poet.* gloaming, vesper. **3** darkness, obscurity; see also IGNORANCE. □ **in the dark** see IGNORANT 1a. □□ **darkness** see DARK *n.* 1 above.

darken /daarkən/ *v.* **1** *tr.* make dark or darker. **2** *intr.* become dark or darker. □ **never darken a person's door** keep away permanently. □□ **darkener** *n.*

■ **1** see SHADE *v.* 3. **2** see DIM *v.* 1.

darkie var. of DARKY.

darkling /daarkling/ *adj. & adv. poet.* in the dark; in the night.
■ *adj.* see *sunless* (SUN).

darkroom /daarkroom, -room/ *n.* a room for photographic work, with normal light excluded.

darky /daarkee/ *n.* (also **darkie**) (*pl.* **-ies**) *sl. offens.* a black person.

darling /daarling/ *n. & adj.* ● *n.* **1** a beloved or lovable person or thing. **2** a favorite. **3** *colloq.* a pretty or endearing person or thing. ● *adj.* **1** beloved; lovable. **2** favorite. **3** *colloq.* charming or pretty. [OE *deorling* (as DEAR, -LING[1])]
■ *n.* **1** sweetheart, beloved, love, dear, dearest, truelove, *archaic* leman. **2** pet, favorite, apple of one's eye, *colloq.* golden boy *or* girl. ● *adj.* **1** beloved, loved, cherished, adored, dear, precious, treasured. **2** see FAVORITE *adj.* **3** pleasing, fetching, attractive, adorable, enchanting, lovely, alluring, engaging, bewitching, charming.

darn[1] /daarn/ *v. & n.* ● *v.tr.* **1** mend (esp. knitted material, or a hole in it) by interweaving yarn across the hole with a

needle. **2** embroider with a large running stitch. ● *n.* a darned area in material. □ **darning needle 1** a long needle with a large eye, used in darning. **2** a dragonfly. [16th c.: perh. f. obs. *dern* hide]
■ *v.* **1** see PATCH *v.* 1, 2.

darn[2] /daarn/ *v.tr., int., adj.,* & *adv. colloq.* = DAMN (in imprecatory senses). [corrupt. of DAMN]

darned /daarnd/ *adj. & adv. colloq.* = DAMNED.
■ see *extremely* (EXTREME).

darnel /daarnəl/ *n.* any of several grasses of the genus *Lolium*, growing as weeds among cereal crops. [ME: cf. Walloon *darnelle*]

darner /daarnər/ *n.* a person or thing that darns, esp. a darning needle.

darning /daarning/ *n.* **1** the action of a person who darns. **2** things to be darned.

dart /daart/ *n. & v.* ● *n.* **1** a small pointed missile used as a weapon or in a game. **2** (in *pl.*; usu. treated as *sing.*) an indoor game in which light feathered darts are thrown at a circular target to score points. **3** a sudden rapid movement. **4** *Zool.* a dartlike structure, such as an insect's sting or the calcareous projections of a snail (used during copulation). **5** a tapering tuck stitched in a garment. ● *v.* **1** *intr.* (often foll. by *out, in, past,* etc.) move or go suddenly or rapidly (*darted into the store*). **2** *tr.* throw (a missile). **3** *tr.* direct suddenly (a glance, etc.). [ME f. OF *darz, dars,* f. Frank.]
■ *n.* **1** see BOLT[1] *n.* 5. **3** see DASH *n.* 1. ● *v.* **1** see DASH *v.* 1.

dartboard /daartbawrd/ *n.* a circular board marked with numbered segments, used as a target in darts.

darter /daartər/ *n.* **1** any large waterbird of the genus *Anhinga,* having a narrow head and long, thin neck. **2** any of various small, quick-moving freshwater fish of the family Percidae, native to N. America.

Dartmoor pony /daartmoor, -mawr/ *n.* **1** a small pony of a shaggy-coated breed. **2** this breed. [*Dartmoor* in SW England]

Darwinian /daarwíneeən/ *adj. & n.* ● *adj.* of or relating to Darwin's theory of the evolution of species by the action of natural selection. ● *n.* an adherent of this theory. □□ **Darwinism** /daarwinizəm/ *n.* **Darwinist** *n.* [C. *Darwin,* Engl. naturalist d. 1882]

dash /dash/ *v. & n.* ● *v.* **1** *intr.* rush hastily or forcefully (*dashed up the stairs*). **2** *tr.* strike or fling with great force, esp. so as to shatter (*dashed it to the ground; the cup was dashed from my hand*). **3** *tr.* frustrate; daunt; dispirit (*dashed their hopes*). **4** *tr. colloq.* (esp. **dash it** or **dash it all**) = DAMN *v.* 1. ● *n.* **1** a rush or onset; a sudden advance (*made a dash for shelter*). **2** a horizontal stroke in writing or printing to mark a pause or break in sense or to represent omitted letters or words. **3** impetuous vigor or the capacity for this. **4** showy appearance or behavior. **5** a sprinting race. **6** the longer signal of the two used in Morse code (cf. DOT[1] *n.* 3). **7** a slight admixture, esp. of a liquid. **8** = DASHBOARD. □ **cut a dash** *Brit.* make a brilliant show. **dash down** (or **off**) write or finish hurriedly. [ME, prob. imit.]
■ *v.* **1** rush, run, dart, spring, bolt, bound, race, sprint; hasten, fly, hurry, speed. **2** strike; hurl, toss, throw, fling, cast, pitch, *colloq.* chuck. **3** frustrate, daunt, dispirit, destroy, ruin, spoil. ● *n.* **1** dart, bolt, rush, run; spurt, bound, sprint. **3** vigor, energy, vivacity, impetuosity; élan, flair, liveliness, style, panache, spirit, brio, verve, zest; ardor, fervor. **4** see OSTENTATION. **7** bit, pinch, soupçon, hint, suggestion, touch, trace, sprinkling, tinge, taste, drop, splash, piece, *colloq.* smidgen, tad. □ **dash down** (or **off**) scribble, rush off.

dashboard /dáshbawrd/ *n.* **1** the surface below the windshield inside a motor vehicle or aircraft, containing instruments and controls. **2** *hist.* a board of wood or leather in front of a carriage, to keep out mud.

dashiki /daasheékee/ *n.* a loose, brightly colored shirt worn orig. by men in Africa. [W. Afr.]

dashing /dáshing/ *adj.* **1** spirited; lively. **2** stylish. □□ **dashingly** *adv.* **dashingness** *n.*
■ **1** spirited, impetuous, energetic, vigorous, dynamic,

animated, bouncy, *colloq.* peppy; see also LIVELY 1.
2 fashionable, stylish, chic, à la mode, modish,
smart, elegant, dapper, esp. *colloq.* swish.

dashpot /dáshpot/ *n.* a device for damping shock or vibration.

dassie /dásee, daás-/ *n. S.Afr.* **1** the Cape hyrax *Procavia
capensis.* Also called *rock rabbit* (see ROCK¹). **2** a small coastal
fish *Diplodus sargus* with rows of black stripes. [Afrik. f. Du.
dasje dimin. of *das* badger]

dastardly /dástərdlee/ *adj.* cowardly; despicable. □□ **das-
tardliness** *n.* [*dastard* base coward, prob. f. *dazed* past part.
+ -ARD, or obs. *dasart* dullard, DOTARD]

■ see COWARDLY.

dasyure /dáseeyŏŏr/ *n.* any small, flesh-eating marsupial of
the genus *Dasyurus.* [F f. mod.L *dasyurus* f. Gk *dasus* rough
+ *oura* tail]

DAT *abbr.* digital audiotape.

data /dáytə, dátə, daá-/ *n.pl.* (also treated as *sing.*, as in *that
is all the data we have,* although the singular form is strictly
datum) **1** known facts or things used as a basis for inference
or reckoning. **2** quantities or characters operated on by a
computer, etc. □ **data bank 1** a store or source of data. **2**
= DATABASE. **data capture** the action or process of entering
data into a computer. **data processing** a series of operations on data, esp. by a computer, to retrieve or classify,
etc., information. **data processor** a machine, esp. a computer, that carries out data processing. **data protection** legal control over access to data stored in computers. [pl. of
DATUM]

■ **1** facts, information, statistics, figures, details,
observations, material(s), evidence; text.

database /dáytəbays, dátə-/ *n.* a structured set of data held
in a computer, esp. one that is accessible or that can be
arranged in various ways.

datable /dáytəbəl/ *adj.* (often foll. by *to*) capable of being
dated (to a particular time).

date¹ /dayt/ *n. & v.* ● *n.* **1** a day of the month, esp. specified
by a number. **2** a particular day or year, esp. when a given
event occurred. **3** statement (usu. giving the day, month,
and year) in a document or inscription, etc., of the time of
composition or publication. **4** the period to which a work
of art, etc., belongs. **5** the time when an event happens or
is to happen. **6** *colloq.* **a** an engagement or appointment, esp.
with a person of the opposite sex. **b** a person with whom
one has a social engagement. ● *v.* **1** *tr.* mark with a date. **2**
tr. **a** assign a date to (an object, event, etc.). **b** (foll. by *to*)
assign to a particular time, period, etc. **3** *intr.* (often foll. by
from, back to, etc.) have its origins at a particular time. **4** *intr.*
be recognizable as from a past or particular period; become
evidently out of date (*a design that does not date*). **5** *tr.* indicate or expose as being out of date (*that hat really dates you*).
6 *colloq.* **a** *tr.* make an arrangement with (a person) to meet
socially. **b** *intr.* meet socially by agreement (*they are now
dating regularly*). □ **date rape** sexual assault involving two
people who have met socially. **date stamp 1** an adjustable rubber stamp, etc., used to record a date. **2** the impression made by this. **date-stamp** *v.tr.* mark with a date
stamp. **out of date** (*attrib.* **out-of-date**) old-fashioned; obsolete. **to date** until now. **up to date** (*attrib.* **up-to-date**)
meeting or according to the latest requirements, knowledge,
or fashion; modern. [ME f. OF f. med.L *data,* fem. past
part. of *dare* give: from the L formula used in dating letters,
data (epistola) (letter) given or delivered (at a particular time
or place)]

■ *n.* **4** time, year, season, period, day, age, era, epoch,
stage, phase. **5** *Brit.* time, fixture. **6 a** appointment,
meeting, engagement, rendezvous, assignation, *archaic*
tryst. **b** escort, companion, friend; boyfriend, girlfriend,
sweetheart, *colloq.* girl. ● *v.* **3** (*date from* or *back to*)
belong to, come from. **4** show one's or its age; go out
of fashion. **6** escort; have a relationship (with), *colloq.*
go steady (with); be together; see also *go out* 4 (GO¹).
□ **date rape** acquaintence rape. **out of date** outdated,
old-fashioned, behind the times, old, ancient, archaic,
antiquated, dated, passé, outmoded, outworn,

obsolete, fossil, obsolescent, anachronistic, anachronic,
behindhand, *colloq.* old hat, fossilized, antediluvian,
medieval, prehistoric, corny. **up to date** modern,
latest, current, contemporary, à la mode, fashionable,
colloq. often derog. trendy.

date² /dayt/ *n.* **1** a dark, oval, single-stoned fruit. **2** (in full
date palm) the tall tree *Phoenix dactylifera,* native to W.
Asia and N. Africa, bearing this fruit. [ME f. OF f. L *dactylus*
f. Gk *daktulos* finger, from the shape of its leaf]

dated /dáytid/ *adj.* **1** showing or having a date (*a dated letter*).
2 old-fashioned; out-of-date.

dateless /dáytlis/ *adj.* **1** having no date. **2** of immemorial age.
3 not likely to become out of date.

dateline /dáytlīn/ *n.* **1** (also **date line**; in full **international
date line**) the line from north to south partly along the
180th meridian, to the east of which the date is a day earlier
than it is to the west. **2** a line at the head of a dispatch or
special article in a newspaper showing the date and place of
writing.

dative /dáytiv/ *n. & adj. Gram.* ● *n.* the case of nouns and
pronouns (and words in grammatical agreement with them)
indicating an indirect object or recipient. ● *adj.* of or in the
dative. □□ **datival** /daytívəl/ *adj.* **datively** *adv.* [ME f. L
(*casus*) *dativus* f. *dare dat-* give]

datum /dáytəm, dátəm, daátəm/ *n.* (*pl.* **data:** see DATA as
main entry) **1** a piece of information. **2** a thing known or
granted; an assumption or premise from which inferences
may be drawn (see *sense-datum*). **3** a fixed starting point of
a scale, etc. (*datum-line*). [L, = thing given, neut. past part.
of *dare* give]

datura /dətŏŏrə, -tyŏŏrə/ *n.* any poisonous plant of the genus
Datura, e.g., the thorn apple. [mod.L f. Hindi *dhatura*]

daub /dawb/ *v. & n.* ● *v.tr.* **1** spread (paint, plaster, or some
other thick substance) crudely or roughly on a surface. **2**
coat or smear (a surface) with paint, etc. **3 a** (also *absol.*)
paint crudely or unskillfully. **b** lay (colors) on crudely and
clumsily. ● *n.* **1** paint or other substance daubed on a surface. **2** plaster, clay, etc., for coating a surface, esp. mixed
with straw and applied to laths or wattles to form a wall. **3**
a crude painting. [ME f. OF *dauber* f. L *dealbare* whitewash
f. *albus* white]

■ *v.* see SMEAR *v.* 1.

daube /dōb/ *n.* a stew of braised meat (usu. beef) with wine,
etc. [F]

daughter /dáwtər/ *n.* **1** a girl or woman in relation to either
or both of her parents. **2** a female descendant. **3** (foll. by
of) a female member of a family, nation, etc. **4** (foll. by *of*)
a woman who is regarded as the spiritual descendant of, or
as spiritually attached to, a person or thing. **5** a product or
attribute personified as a daughter in relation to its source
(*Fortune and its daughter Confidence*). **6** *Physics* a nuclide
formed by the radioactive decay of another. **7** *Biol.* a cell,
etc., formed by the division, etc., of another. □ **daughter-
in-law** (*pl.* **daughters-in-law**) the wife of one's son.
□□ **daughterhood** *n.* **daughterly** *adj.* [OE *dohtor* f. Gmc]

■ **1** see CHILD 2.

daunt /dawnt/ *v.tr.* discourage; intimidate. □□ **daunting** *adj.*
dauntingly *adv.* [ME f. AF *daunter,* OF *danter, donter* f. L
domitare frequent. of *domare* tame]

■ intimidate, discourage, put off, dishearten, dispirit,
unnerve, shake, upset, disconcert, discomfit, awe,
overawe, appall, alarm, threaten, frighten, terrify, scare.

dauntless /dáwntlis/ *adj.* intrepid; persevering. □□ **dauntlessly** *adv.* **dauntlessness** *n.*

■ fearless, undaunted, unafraid, unflinching, stalwart,
brave, courageous, bold, audacious, intrepid, valorous,
daring, gallant, heroic, venturesome, plucky,
stouthearted, valiant, persevering.

dauphin /dáwfin, dōfáN/ *n. hist.* the eldest son of the king of

/.../ **pronunciation**	● **part of speech**
□ **phrases, idioms, and compounds**	
□□ **derivatives**	■ **synonym section**
cross-references appear in SMALL CAPITALS or *italics*	

France. [ME f. F, ult. f. L *delphinus* DOLPHIN, as a family name]

davenport /dávənpawrt/ *n.* **1** a large, heavily upholstered sofa. **2** esp. *Brit.* an ornamental writing desk with drawers and a sloping surface for writing. [19th c.: from the name *Davenport*]

davit /dávit, dáyvit/ *n.* a small crane on board a ship, esp. one of a pair for suspending or lowering a lifeboat. [AF & OF *daviot* dimin. of *Davi* David]

Davy /dáyvee/ *n.* (*pl.* **-ies**) (in full **Davy lamp**) a miner's safety lamp with the flame enclosed by wire gauze to prevent an explosion of gas. [Sir H. *Davy*, Engl. chemist d. 1829, who invented it]

Davy Jones /jṓnz/ *n. sl.* **1** (in full **Davy Jones's locker**) the bottom of the sea, esp. regarded as the grave of those drowned at sea. **2** the evil spirit of the sea. [18th c.: orig. unkn.]

daw /daw/ *n.* = JACKDAW. [ME: cf. OHG *tāha*]

dawdle /dáwd'l/ *v. & n.* ● *v.* **1** *intr.* **a** walk slowly and idly. **b** delay; waste time. **2** *tr.* (foll. by *away*) waste (time). ● *n.* an act or instance of dawdling. □□ **dawdler** *n.* [perh. rel. to dial. *daddle, doddle* idle, dally]

▪ *v.* **1** linger, loiter, straggle, delay, procrastinate, dally, lounge, laze, idle, lag, lie about, waste time, *colloq.* dillydally, shilly-shally.

dawn /dawn/ *n. & v.* ● *n.* **1** the first light of day; daybreak. **2** the beginning or incipient appearance of something. ● *v.intr.* **1** (of a day) begin; grow light. **2** begin to appear or develop. **3** (often foll. by *on*, *upon*) begin to become evident or understood (by a person). □ **dawn chorus** the singing of many birds at the break of day. [orig. as verb: back-form. f. *dawning*, ME f. earlier *dawing* after Scand. (as DAY)]

▪ *n.* **1** daybreak, sunrise, break of day, crack of dawn, first light, dawning, cockcrow, sunup, *poet.* aurora. **2** dawning, beginning, start, awakening, inception, genesis, onset, origin, appearance, arrival, advent, emergence, inauguration, rise, *formal* commencement, *rhet.* birth. ● *v.* **1** break; brighten, lighten. **2** begin, originate, arise, appear, emerge, start, arrive, develop, unfold, *formal* commence. **3** (*dawn on* or *upon*) occur to, come to a person's mind, become apparent *or* evident to.

dawning /dáwning/ *n.* **1** daybreak. **2** the first beginning of something.

▪ **1** see DAWN *n.* 1. **2** see DAWN *n.* 2.

day /day/ *n.* **1** the time between sunrise and sunset. **2 a** a period of 24 hours as a unit of time, esp. from midnight to midnight, corresponding to a complete revolution of the earth on its axis. **b** a corresponding period on other planets (*Martian day*). **3** daylight (*clear as day*). **4** the time in a day during which work is normally done (*an eight-hour day*). **5 a** (also *pl.*) a period of the past or present (*the modern day*; *the old days*). **b** (prec. by *the*) the present time (*the issues of the day*). **6** the lifetime of a person or thing, esp. regarded as useful or productive (*have had my day*; *in my day things were different*). **7** a point of time (*will do it one day*). **8 a** the date of a specific festival. **b** a day associated with a particular event or purpose (*graduation day*; *payday*; *Christmas Day*). **9** a particular date; a date agreed on. **10** a day's endeavor, or the period of an endeavor, esp. as bringing success (*win the day*). □ **all in a** (or **the**) **day's work** part of normal routine. **at the end of the day** in the final reckoning, when all is said and done. **call it a day** end a period of activity, esp. resting content that enough has been done. **day after day** without respite. **day and night** all the time. **day boy** (or **girl**) *Brit.* a boy or girl who goes daily from home to school, esp. a school that also has boarders. **day by day** gradually. **day care** the supervision and care of young children, the elderly, the disabled, etc., during the day. **day in, day out** routinely; constantly. **day laborer** an unskilled laborer hired by the day. **day nursery** a nursery where children are looked after during the working day. **day off** a day's vacation from work. **Day of Judgment** = *Judgment Day*. **day of reckoning** see RECKONING. **day of rest** the Sabbath. **day out** a trip or excursion for a day. **day school** a school, esp.

private, for pupils living at home. **day-to-day** mundane; routine. **day-trip** a trip or excursion completed in one day. **day-tripper** *Brit.* a person who goes on a day-trip. **from day one** *colloq.* originally. **not one's day** a day of successive misfortunes for a person. **on one's day** at one's peak of capability. **one of these days** before very long. **one of those days** a day when things go badly. **some day** at some point in the future. **that will be the day** *colloq.* that will never happen. **this day and age** the present time or period. □□ **dayless** *adj.* [OE *dæg* f. Gmc]

▪ **3** daytime, daylight, broad daylight, light of day. **5 a** age, period, era, epoch; date. **b** see PRESENT[1] *n.*, NOW *adv.* 1, 4. **6** time, lifetime; hour, prime, heyday. □ **at the end of the day** see *ultimately* (ULTIMATE). **day after day** see *all the time* 2 (TIME). **day and night** see *all the time* 2 (TIME). **day by day** see *gradually* (GRADUAL). **day in, day out** see *all the time* 2 (TIME). **day out** outing, trip, jaunt, excursion. **day-to-day** see ROUTINE *adj.* 1. **from day one** see *originally* (ORIGINAL). **one of these days** see SOON 1. **this day and age** see PRESENT[1] *n.*, NOW *adv.* 1, 4.

Dayak /díak/ *n.* (also **Dyak**) an aboriginal of Borneo or Sarawak. [Malay *dayak* up-country]

daybook /dáybook/ *n.* an account book in which a day's transactions are entered, for later transfer to a ledger.

▪ journal, ledger.

daybreak /dáybrayk/ *n.* the first appearance of light in the morning.

▪ see DAWN *n.* 1.

daydream /dáydreem/ *n. & v.* ● *n.* a pleasant fantasy or reverie. ● *v.intr.* indulge in this. □□ **daydreamer** *n.*

▪ *n.* reverie, fantasy, fancy, dream, musing, castle(s) in the air *or* in Spain, pipedream. ● *v.* fantasize, dream; (*daydream about*) imagine, fancy, envisage, envision. □□ **daydreamer** see DREAMER.

Day-Glo /dáyglṓ/ *n. & adj.* ● *n. propr.* a brand of fluorescent paint or other coloring. ● *adj.* colored with or like this. [DAY + GLOW]

daylight /dáylīt/ *n.* **1** the light of day. **2** dawn (*before daylight*). **3 a** openness; publicity. **b** open knowledge. **4** a visible gap or interval, e.g., between boats in a race. **5** (usu. in *pl.*) *sl.* one's life or consciousness (orig. the internal organs), esp. as representing vulnerability to fear, attack, etc. (*scared the daylights out of me*; *beat the living daylights out of them*). □ **daylight robbery** *Brit. colloq.* a blatantly excessive charge. **daylight saving** the achieving of longer evening daylight, esp. in summer, by setting the time an hour ahead of the standard time. **see daylight** begin to understand what was previously obscure.

▪ **1** sunlight, sun, sunshine, light. **2** see DAWN *n.* 1. □ **see daylight** see *catch on* 2.

daylily /dáylilee/ *n.* any plant of the genus *Hemerocallis*, whose flowers last only a day.

daylong /dáylawng, -long/ *adj.* lasting for a day.

dayroom /dáyroom/ *n.* a room, esp. a communal room for leisure in an institution, used during the day.

dayside /dáysīd/ *n.* **1** staff, esp. of a newspaper, who work during the day. **2** *Astron.* the side of a planet that faces the sun.

daytime /dáytīm/ *n.* the part of the day when there is natural light.

▪ see DAY 3.

daywork /dáywərk/ *n.* work paid for according to the time taken.

daze /dayz/ *v. & n.* ● *v.tr.* stupefy; bewilder. ● *n.* a state of confusion or bewilderment (*in a daze*). □□ **dazedly** /-zidlee/ *adv.* [ME *dased* past part., f. ON *dasathr* weary]

▪ *v.* stun, stupefy, blind, dazzle, bedazzle; shock, stagger, startle, take aback, astonish, astound, amaze, surprise, overcome, overpower, dumbfound, benumb, paralyze, *colloq.* bowl over, floor, flabbergast, *sl.* knock out; befuddle, confuse, bemuse, bewilder, puzzle, mystify, baffle, perplex, nonplus. ● *n.* (*in a daze*) stupefied, in a trance, bewildered, confused, bemused, baffled, puzzled, mystified; perplexed, disoriented, dizzy, dazzled, bedazzled, overcome, overpowered, nonplussed, befuddled, flustered; startled, surprised, shocked, stunned, astonished, astounded, amazed, staggered, *colloq.* flabbergasted, bowled over, floored.

dazzle /dázəl/ *v. & n.* ● *v.* **1** *tr.* blind temporarily or confuse the sight of by an excess of light. **2** *tr.* impress or overpower (a person) with knowledge, ability, or any brilliant display or prospect. **3** *intr. archaic* (of eyes) be dazzled. ● *n.* bright confusing light. □□ **dazzlement** *n.* **dazzler** *n.* **dazzling** *adj.* **dazzlingly** *adv.* [ME, f. DAZE + -LE⁴]

■ *v.* **1** blind, stun, stupefy, bedazzle, overpower. **2** impress, bewitch, enchant, charm, beguile, intrigue, captivate, fascinate, spellbind, entrance, hypnotize, mesmerize; overpower. □□ **dazzling** bright, brilliant, resplendent, radiant, splendid, magnificent, glorious, sparkling, scintillating, *colloq. or joc.* splendiferous; overwhelming, overpowering, stupefying, dizzying, *colloq.* stunning, mind-boggling; gorgeous.

dB *abbr.* decibel(s).

DBE *abbr.* (in the UK) Dame Commander of the Order of the British Empire.

DBMS *abbr. Computing* database management system.

DBS *abbr.* **1** direct broadcast satellite. **2** direct broadcasting by satellite.

DC *abbr.* **1** (also **d.c.**) direct current. **2** District of Columbia. **3** da capo.

DCL *abbr.* doctor of civil law.

DD *abbr.* doctor of divinity.

D day /déeday/ *n.* (also **D Day**) **1** the day (June 6, 1944) on which Allied forces invaded N. France. **2** the day on which an important operation is to begin or a change to take effect. [*D* for *day* + DAY]

D.D.S *abbr.* **1** doctor of dental science. **2** doctor of dental surgery.

DDT *abbr.* dichlorodiphenyltrichloroethane, a colorless chlorinated hydrocarbon used as an insecticide.

DE *abbr.* Delaware (in official postal use).

de- /dee, di/ *prefix* **1** forming verbs and their derivatives: **a** down; away (*descend*; *deduct*). **b** completely (*declare*; *denude*; *deride*). **2** added to verbs and their derivatives to form verbs and nouns implying removal or reversal (*decentralize*; *de-ice*; *demoralization*). [from or after L *de* (adv. & prep.) = off, from: sense 2 through OF *des-* f. L *dis-*]

deacon /déekən/ *n. & v.* ● *n.* **1** (in Episcopal churches) a minister of the third order, below bishop and priest. **2** (in various, esp. Protestant, churches) a lay officer attending to a congregation's secular affairs. **3** (in the early Christian church) an appointed minister of charity. ● *v.tr.* appoint or ordain as a deacon. □□ **deaconate** *n.* **deaconship** *n.* [OE *diacon* f. eccl.L *diaconus* f. Gk *diakonos* servant]

deaconess /déekənés, déekənis/ *n.* a woman in the early Christian church and in some modern churches with functions analogous to a deacon's. [DEACON, after LL *diaconissa*]

deactivate /deeáktivayt/ *v.tr.* make inactive or less reactive. □□ **deactivation** /-váyshən/ *n.* **deactivator** *n.*

■ see STOP *v.* 1a.

dead /ded/ *adj., adv., & n.* ● *adj.* **1** no longer alive. **2** *colloq.* extremely tired or unwell. **3** benumbed; affected by loss of sensation (*my fingers are dead*). **4** (foll. by *to*) unappreciative or unconscious of; insensitive to. **5** no longer effective or in use; obsolete; extinct. **6** (of a match, of coal, etc.) no longer burning; extinguished. **7** inanimate. **8 a** lacking force or vigor; dull; lusterless; muffled. **b** (of sound) not resonant. **c** (of sparkling wine, etc.) no longer effervescent. **9 a** quiet; lacking activity (*the dead season*). **b** motionless; idle. **10 a** (of a microphone, telephone, etc.) not transmitting any sound, esp. because of a fault. **b** (of a circuit, conductor, etc.) carrying or transmitting no current; not connected to a source of electricity (*a dead battery*). **11** (of the ball in a game) out of play. **12** abrupt; complete; exact; unqualified; unrelieved (*come to a dead stop*; *a dead faint*; *a dead calm*; *in dead silence*; *a dead certainty*). **13** without spiritual life. ● *adv.* **1** absolutely; exactly; completely (*dead on target*; *dead level*; *dead tired*). **2** *colloq.* very; extremely (*dead good*; *dead easy*). ● *n.* (prec. by *the*) **1** (treated as *pl.*) those who have died. **2** a

time of silence or inactivity (*the dead of night*). □ **dead-and-alive** *Brit.* (of a place, person, activity, etc.) dull; monotonous; lacking interest. **dead as the dodo** see DODO. **dead as a doornail** see DOORNAIL. **dead beat** *colloq.* exhausted. **dead center 1** the exact center. **2** the position of a crank, etc., in line with the connecting rod and not exerting torque. **dead duck** *sl.* **1** an unsuccessful or useless person or thing. **2** a person who is beyond help; one who is doomed. **dead end 1** a closed end of a road, passage, etc. **2** (often with hyphen) *attrib.*) a situation offering no prospects of progress or advancement. **dead from the neck up** *colloq.* stupid. **dead hand** an oppressive persisting influence, esp. posthumous control; mortmain. **dead heat 1** a race in which two or more competitors finish exactly level. **2** the result of such a race. **dead in the water** unable to move or to function. **dead language** a language no longer commonly spoken, e.g., Latin. **dead letter 1** a law or practice no longer observed or recognized. **2** a letter that is undeliverable and unreturnable, esp. one with an incorrect address. **dead-letter office** the post office department that handles dead letters. **dead lift** the exertion of one's utmost strength to lift something. **dead loss** *Brit.* **1** *colloq.* a useless person or thing. **2** a complete loss. **dead-man's fingers 1** a kind of orchis, *Orchis mascula.* **2** any soft coral of the genus *Alcyonium,* with spongy lobes. **3** the fingerlike divisions of a lobster's or crab's gills. **dead man's handle** (or **pedal,** etc.) a control on an electric train, allowing power to be connected only as long as the operator presses on it. **dead march** a funeral march. **dead-nettle** any plant of the genus *Lamium,* having nettlelike leaves but without stinging hairs. **dead-on** exactly right. **dead reckoning** *Naut.* calculation of a ship's position from the log, compass, etc., when observations are impossible. **dead ringer** see RINGER. **dead shot** one who is extremely accurate. **dead soldiers** *colloq.* bottles (esp. of beer, liquor, etc.) after the contents have been drunk. **dead time** *Physics* the period after the recording of a pulse, etc., when the detector is unable to record another. **dead to the world** *colloq.* fast asleep; unconscious. **dead weight** DEADWEIGHT. **wouldn't be seen dead in** (or **with,** etc.) *colloq.* shall have nothing to do with; shall refuse to wear, etc. □□ **deadness** *n.* [OE *dēad* f. Gmc, rel. to DIE¹]

■ *adj.* **1** defunct, extinct, gone, departed, late, lifeless, no more, *formal* deceased, *Brit. sl.* gone for a burton. **2** tired (out), exhausted, worn out, fatigued, spent, in a state of collapse, beaten, *colloq.* all in, done in, dead beat, bushed, pooped, fagged (out), *sl.* beat, *Brit. sl.* knackered, cooked. **3** insensate, insensible, numb, paralyzed, benumbed, unfeeling, deadened, senseless, sensationless; without feeling. **4** insensible, unconscious, out; insensitive, indifferent, unconcerned, uninterested; hardened, impervious, inured. **5** extinct, obsolete, perished, past, outmoded, disused, expired. **6** out, smothered, extinguished. **7** lifeless, inert, inorganic; see also INANIMATE 1, 2. **8 a** dull, lusterless, flat, neutral, vapid, empty, bland, colorless, gray, beige, dun; boring, tedious, tiresome, monotonous, prosaic, uninteresting, run-of-the-mill, ordinary, commonplace, dry, insipid, two-dimensional, lifeless, stiff, rigid. **b** dull, muffled, deadened, anechoic, unresounding, nonresonant. **9 a** see INACTIVE 1, 2. **b** stagnant, motionless, still, standing, static, inert, unmoving, inactive, idle, quiet, calm. **12** complete, entire, total, full, absolute, downright, thorough, through and through, utter, all-out, out-and-out, unqualified, unrelieved, unbroken, categorical, outright; profound, deep; sudden, abrupt; exact, precise. ● *adv.* **1** completely, entirely, absolutely, totally, utterly, categorically, thoroughly, unconditionally, unqualifiedly; abruptly, suddenly; directly, exactly, precisely. **2** see VERY *adv.* ● *n.* **2** depth(s), extreme, midst, middle. □ **dead beat** see DEAD *adj.* 2 above.

dead duck a see DISASTER 2b. **dead from the neck up** see STUPID *adj.* 1, 5. **dead heat** tie, stalemate, draw, deadlock. **dead in the water** stuck, stymied, at an impasse. **dead-on** see RIGHT *adj.* 2. **dead to the world** (fast) asleep, unconscious, out, out for the count, *colloq.* (out) cold.

deadbeat /dédbeet/ *n. & adj.* ● *n.* **1** *colloq.* a penniless person. **2** *sl.* a person constantly in debt. ● *adj.* Physics (of an instrument) without recoil.

deadbolt /dédbōlt/ *n.* a bolt engaged by turning a knob or key, rather than by spring action.

deaden /déd'n/ *v.* **1** *tr. & intr.* deprive of or lose vitality, force, brightness, sound, feeling, etc. **2** *tr.* (foll. by *to*) make insensitive. □□ **deadener** *n.*

■ **1** weaken, tire (out), weary, lessen, diminish, reduce, decrease; drain, tax, exhaust, sap, debilitate, enfeeble, fatigue, wear out, dull, subdue, devitalize, take it out of, strain, break, crush, depress, dispirit, *Brit. sl.* knacker; moderate, soothe, mitigate, assuage, alleviate, cushion, soften, blunt, dull, dampen; grow tired, languish, falter, fail, dwindle, fade, deteriorate, waste away, degenerate, decline, abate, peter out, die, taper (off), ease (up), subside, slump, fall off, wane, ebb, sink, lag, *colloq.* let up. **2** numb, benumb, paralyze, anesthetize, desensitize, dull.

deadeye /dédī/ *n.* **1** *Naut.* a circular wooden block with a groove around the circumference to take a lanyard, used singly or in pairs to tighten a shroud. **2** *colloq.* an expert marksman.

deadfall /dédfawl/ *n.* a trap in which a raised weight is made to fall on and kill esp. large game.

deadhead /dédhed/ *n. & v.* ● *n.* **1** a useless or unenterprising person. **2** a passenger or member of an audience who has made use of a free ticket. **3** *Brit.* a faded flower head. ● *v.* **1** *intr.* (of a commercial driver, etc.) complete a trip without paying passengers or freight. **2** *tr.* remove faded flower heads from (a plant).

deadlight /dédlit/ *n. Naut.* **1** a shutter inside a porthole. **2** a skylight that cannot be opened.

deadline /dédlin/ *n.* **1** a time limit for the completion of an activity, etc. **2** *hist.* a line beyond which prisoners were not allowed to go.

deadlock /dédlok/ *n. & v.* ● *n.* **1** a situation, esp. one involving opposing parties, in which no progress can be made. **2** a type of lock requiring a key to open or close it. ● *v.tr. & intr.* bring or come to a standstill.

■ *n.* **1** standstill, impasse, stalemate, draw, standoff. ● *v.* bring *or* come to a standstill *or* impasse, stall, stop, halt.

deadly /dédlee/ *adj. & adv.* ● *adj.* (**deadlier**, **deadliest**) **1 a** causing or able to cause fatal injury or serious damage. **b** poisonous (*deadly snake*). **2** intense; extreme (*deadly dullness*). **3** (of an aim, etc.) extremely accurate or effective. **4** deathlike (*deadly pale*; *deadly faintness*; *deadly gloom*). **5** *colloq.* dreary; dull. **6** implacable. ● *adv.* **1** like death; as if dead (*deadly faint*). **2** extremely; intensely (*deadly serious*). □ **deadly nightshade** = BELLADONNA. **deadly sin** a sin regarded as leading to damnation, esp. pride, covetousness, lust, gluttony, envy, anger, and sloth. □□ **deadliness** *n.* [OE *dēadlic, dēadlīce* (as DEAD, -LY¹)]

■ *adj.* **1** lethal, fatal; dangerous, poisonous, toxic; baleful, harmful, noxious, *literary* nocuous. **2** see INTENSE 1, 3. **3** exact, precise, accurate, true, unerring, unfailing. **4** deathly, deathlike; pale, pallid, ghostly, cadaverous, ghastly, wan, livid, ashen. **5** boring, excruciating, dull, tiresome, tedious, dreary, humdrum, lackluster, wearying, wearisome. **6** see MORTAL *adj.* 5. ● *adv.* **2** see *extremely* (EXTREME).

deadpan /dédpán/ *adj. & adv.* with a face or manner totally lacking expression or emotion.

■ *adj.* see WOODEN 3a.

deadweight /dédwáyt/ *n.* (also **dead weight**) **1 a** an inert mass. **b** a heavy weight or burden. **2** a debt not covered by assets. **3** the total weight carried on a ship.

■ **1 b** see ENCUMBRANCE 1.

deadwood /dédwŏŏd/ *n.* **1** dead trees or branches. **2** *colloq.* one or more useless people or things. **3** *Bowling* knocked-down pins that remain on the alley.

deaerate /dee-áirayt/ *v.tr.* remove air from. □□ **de-aeration** /-ráyshən/ *n.*

deaf /def/ *adj.* **1** wholly or partly without hearing (*deaf in one ear*). **2** (foll. by *to*) refusing to listen or comply. **3** insensitive to harmony, rhythm, etc. (*tone-deaf*). □ **deaf-aid** *Brit.* a hearing aid. **deaf-and-dumb alphabet** (or **language**, etc.) *offens.* = *sign language* **deaf as a post** completely deaf. **deaf-mute** a deaf and dumb person. **fall on deaf ears** be ignored. **turn a deaf ear** (usu. foll. by *to*) be unresponsive. □□ **deafly** *adv.* **deafness** *n.* [OE *dēaf* f. Gmc]

■ **1** hard of hearing, stone-deaf. **2** unheedful, heedless, insensible, insensitive, impervious, indifferent, oblivious, unresponsive, unmoved, unconcerned, unyielding. □ **fall on deaf ears** fall on stony ground. **turn a deaf ear** see IGNORE 2.

deafen /défən/ *v.tr.* **1** (often as **deafening** *adj.*) overpower with sound. **2** deprive of hearing by noise, esp. temporarily. □□ **deafeningly** *adv.*

deal¹ /deel/ *v. & n.* ● *v.* (*past* and *past part.* **dealt** /delt/) **1** *intr.* **a** (foll. by *with*) take measures concerning (a problem, person, etc.), esp. in order to put something right. **b** (foll. by *with*) do business with; associate with. **c** (foll. by *with*) discuss or treat (a subject). **d** (often foll. by *by*) behave in a specified way toward a person (*dealt honorably by them*). **2** *intr.* (foll. by *in*) to sell or be concerned with commercially (*deals in insurance*). **3** *tr.* (often foll. by *out*) distribute or apportion to several people, etc. **4** *tr.* (also *absol.*) distribute (cards) to players for a game or round. **5** *tr.* cause to be received; administer (*deal a heavy blow*). **6** *tr.* assign as a share or deserts to a person (*life dealt them much happiness*). **7** *tr.* (foll. by *in*) *colloq.* include (a person) in an activity (*you can deal me in*). ● *n.* **1** (usu. **a good** or **great deal**) *colloq.* **a** a large amount (*a good deal of trouble*). **b** to a considerable extent (*is a great deal better*). **2** *colloq.* a business arrangement; a transaction. **3** a specified form of treatment given or received (*gave them a bad deal*; *got a fair deal*). **4 a** the distribution of cards by dealing. **b** a player's turn to do this (*it's my deal*). **c** the round of play following this. **d** a set of hands dealt to players. □ **it's a deal** *colloq.* expressing assent to an agreement. [OE *dǣl, dǣlan*, f. Gmc]

■ *v.* **1 a** (*deal with*) treat, handle, take care of, attend to, see to, reckon with, grapple with, act on. **b** see ASSOCIATE *v.* 5. **c** (*deal with*) see TREAT *v.* **d** behave, act, conduct oneself, deport oneself, *literary* comport oneself. **2** (*deal in*) buy and sell, handle, stock, do business in, trade in, traffic in. **3, 4** distribute, dole out, give *or* hand out, parcel out, allot, apportion, *literary* mete out; administer, dispense. **6** see ASSIGN *v.* 1a. ● *n.* **1** (**a good** or **great deal**) see LOT *n.* 1. **2** transaction, arrangement, negotiation, agreement, contract, bargain, understanding. **3** see TREATMENT 1.

deal² /deel/ *n.* **1** fir or pine timber, esp. sawn into boards of a standard size. **2 a** a board of this timber. **b** such boards collectively. [ME f. MLG, MDu. *dele* plank f. Gmc]

dealer /déelər/ *n.* **1** a person or business dealing in (esp. retail) goods (*contact your dealer*; *car dealer*; *a dealer in plumbing supplies*). **2** the player dealing at cards. **3** a person who sells illegal drugs. □□ **dealership** *n.* (in sense 1).

■ **1, 3** trader, businessman, businesswoman, merchant, tradesman, retailer, shopkeeper, vendor, merchandiser, storekeeper; wholesaler, distributor, supplier, jobber, *Brit.* stockist; broker, agent, salesman; trafficker.

dealings /déelingz/ *n.pl.* contacts or transactions, esp. in business. □ **have dealings with** associate with.

■ business, commerce, exchange, trade, traffic, transactions, negotiations; relations, relationships, affairs, contacts. □ **have dealings with** see ASSOCIATE *v.* 5.

dealt *past* and *past part.* of DEAL¹.

dean¹ /deen/ *n.* **1 a** a college or university official, esp. one with disciplinary and advisory functions. **b** the head of a university faculty or department or of a medical school. **2 a** the head of the chapter of a cathedral or collegiate church. **b** (usu. **rural dean**) *Brit.* a member of the clergy exercising supervision over a group of parochial clergy within a division of an archdeaconry. **3** = DOYEN. [ME f. AF *deen*, OF *deien*, f. LL *decanus* f. *decem* ten; orig. = chief of a group of ten]

dean² *Brit.* var. of DENE¹.

deanery /deˈenəree/ *n.* (*pl.* **-ies**) **1** a dean's house or office. **2** *Brit.* the group of parishes presided over by a rural dean.

dear /deer/ *adj., n., adv., & int.* ● *adj.* **1 a** beloved or much esteemed. **b** as a merely polite or ironic form (*my dear man*). **2** used as a formula of address, esp. at the beginning of letters (*Dear Sir*). **3** (often foll. by *to*) precious; much cherished. **4** (usu. in *superl.*) earnest; deeply felt (*my dearest wish*). **5 a** high-priced relative to its value. **b** having high prices. **c** (of money) available as a loan only at a high rate of interest. ● *n.* (esp. as a form of address) dear person. ● *adv.* at a high price or great cost (*buy cheap and sell dear; will pay dear*). ● *int.* expressing surprise, dismay, pity, etc. (*dear me!; oh dear!; dear, dear!*). □ **Dear John** *colloq.* a letter terminating a personal relationship. **for dear life** see LIFE. □□ **dearly** *adv.* (esp. in sense 3 of *adj.*). **dearness** *n.* [OE *dēore* f. Gmc]

■ *adj.* **1 a** beloved, loved, adored, darling, favored, esteemed, admired, venerated, honored. **3** precious, cherished, prized, valued, treasured. **4** see EARNEST *adj.* **5 a** expensive, costly, high-priced, highly priced, exorbitant, *colloq.* pricey, steep. ● *n.* dearest, darling, sweetheart, beloved, love, truelove, sweet, precious, pet, honey, *colloq.* sweetie, sweetie pie, treasure, *sl.* baby. ● *adv.* dearly; at great cost *or* expense, at a high *or* excessive price; (*cost dear*) cost an arm and a leg, cost a pretty penny, *Brit. colloq.* cost a packet. □□ **dearly** greatly, very much, indeed, sincerely; affectionately, fondly, lovingly, tenderly; expensively, dear, at great cost *or* expense, at a high *or* excessive price, punitively.

dearie /deˈeree/ *n.* (esp. as a form of address) usu. *joc.* or *iron.* my dear. □ **dearie me!** *int.* expressing surprise, dismay, etc.

dearth /dərth/ *n.* scarcity or lack, esp. of food. [ME, formed as DEAR]

■ scarcity, want, need, lack, deficiency, sparseness, sparsity, scantiness, insufficiency, inadequacy, shortage, paucity, exiguity, poverty, exiguousness; absence.

deasil /deˈsəl, deˈezəl/ *adv. Sc.* in the direction of the sun's apparent course (considered as lucky); clockwise. [Gael. *de-iseil*]

death /deth/ *n.* **1** the final cessation of vital functions in an organism; the ending of life. **2** the event that terminates life. **3 a** the fact or process of being killed or killing (*stone to death; fight to the death*). **b** the fact or state of being dead (*eyes closed in death; their deaths caused rioting*). **4 a** the destruction or permanent cessation of something (*was the death of our hopes*). **b** *colloq.* something terrible or appalling. **5** (usu. **Death**) a personification of death, esp. as a destructive power, usu. represented by a skeleton. **6** a lack of religious faith or spiritual life. □ **as sure as death** quite certain. **at death's door** close to death. **be in at the death 1** be present when an animal is killed, esp. in hunting. **2** witness the (esp. sudden) ending of an enterprise, etc. **be the death of 1** cause the death of. **2** be very harmful to. **catch one's death** *colloq.* catch a serious chill, etc. **death adder** any of various venomous snakes of the genus *Acanthopis*, esp. *A. antarcticus* of Australia. **death cap** (or **cup**) a poisonous mushroom, *Amanita phalloides*. **death cell** a prison cell for a person condemned to death. **death certificate** an official statement of the cause and date and place of a person's death. **death knell 1** the tolling of a bell to mark a person's death. **2** an event that heralds the end or destruction of something. **death mask** a cast taken of a dead person's face. **death penalty** punishment by being put to death. **death rate** the number of deaths per thousand of population per year. **death rattle** a gurgling sound sometimes heard in a dying person's throat. **death row** a prison block or section for prisoners sentenced to death. **death's-head** a human skull as an emblem of mortality. **death's-head moth** (or

hawkmoth) a large, dark hawkmoth, *Acherontia atropos*, with skull-like markings on the back of the thorax. **death squad** an armed paramilitary group, esp. in Central America, formed to kill political enemies, etc. **death tax** a tax on property payable on the owner's death. **death toll** the number of people killed in an accident, battle, etc. **death trap** *colloq.* a dangerous or unhealthy building, vehicle, etc. **death warrant 1** an order for the execution of a condemned person. **2** anything that causes the end of an established practice, etc. **death wish** *Psychol.* a desire (usu. unconscious) for the death of oneself or another. **do to death 1** kill. **2** overdo. **fate worse than death** *colloq.* a disastrous misfortune or experience. **like death warmed over** *sl.* very tired or ill. **put to death** kill or cause to be killed. **to death** to the utmost; extremely (*bored to death; worked to death*). □□ **deathless** *adj.* **deathlessness** *n.* **deathlike** *adj.* [OE *dēath* f. Gmc: rel. to DIE¹]

■ **1** demise, dying, end, exit, quietus, expiry, expiration, *euphem.* passing (away), *formal esp. Law* decease. **4 a** end, termination, cessation, expiration, expiry, finish; extinction, destruction, extermination, annihilation, eradication, obliteration, extirpation, liquidation; ruin, downfall, undoing. □ **as sure as death** see CERTAIN *adj.* **1a. catch one's death** catch a cold *or* chill, get pneumonia. **do to death 1** see KILL¹ *v.* 1. **2** see OVERDO 1. **put to death** see KILL¹ *v.* 1. **to death** see *extremely* (EXTREME). □□ **deathless** eternal, everlasting, immortal, undying, imperishable, permanent, unending, timeless, never-ending.

deathbed /déthbed/ *n.* a bed as the place where a person is dying or has died.

deathblow /déthblō/ *n.* **1** a blow or other action that causes death. **2** an event or circumstance that abruptly ends an activity, enterprise, etc.

■ see KILL¹ *n.* 1.

deathly /déthlee/ *adj. & adv.* ● *adj.* (**deathlier, deathliest**) suggestive of death (*deathly silence*). ● *adv.* in a deathly way (*deathly pale*).

■ *adj.* see DEADLY *adj.* 4.

deathwatch /déthwawch/ *n.* **1** (in full **deathwatch** beetle) a small beetle, *Xestobium rufovillosum*, which makes a sound like a watch ticking, once supposed to portend death, and whose larva bores in old wood. **2** a vigil kept beside a dead or dying individual. **3** a guard set over a person due for execution.

deb /deb/ *n. colloq.* a debutante. [abbr.]

debacle /daybaákəl, -bákel, də-/ *n.* (also **débâcle**) **1 a** an utter defeat or failure. **b** a sudden collapse or downfall. **2** a confused rush or rout; a stampede. **3 a** a breakup of ice in a river, with resultant flooding. **b** a sudden rush of water carrying along blocks of stone and other debris. [F f. *débâcler* unbar]

■ **1** see RUIN *n.* 2a. **3** see FLOOD *n.* 1.

debag /deebág/ *v.tr.* (**debagged, debagging**) *Brit. sl.* remove the pants of (a person), esp. as a joke.

debar /deebaár/ *v.tr.* (**debarred, debarring**) (foll. by *from*) exclude from admission or from a right; prohibit from an action (*was debarred from entering*). □□ **debarment** *n.* [ME f. F *débarrer*, OF *desbarrer* (as DE-, BAR¹)]

■ see BAN *v.*

debark¹ /dibaárk/ *v.tr. & intr.* land from a ship. □□ **debarkation** /-káyshən/ *n.* [F *débarquer* (as DE-, BARK³)]

■ see LAND *v.* 1, 3.

debark² /deébaárk/ *v.tr.* remove the bark from (a tree).

debase /dibáys/ *v.tr.* **1** lower in quality, value, or character. **2** depreciate (coin) by alloying, etc. □□ **debasement** *n.* **debaser** *n.* [DE- + obs. *base* for ABASE]

■ **1** lower, degrade, devalue, depreciate, depress, demote, deprecate, belittle, diminish, reduce, disparage.

debatable /dibáytəbəl/ *adj.* **1** questionable; subject to dispute. **2** capable of being debated. □□ **debatably** *adv.* [OF *debatable* or AL *debatabilis* (as DEBATE)]

■ **1** controversial, arguable, questionable, doubtful, dubious, problematic, problematical, disputable, open *or* subject to dispute *or* doubt *or* question, in dispute *or* doubt *or* question, moot, polemic, polemical; unsure, uncertain, unsettled, undecided.

debate /dibáyt/ *v. & n.* ● *v.* **1** *tr.* (also *absol.*) discuss or dispute about (an issue, proposal, etc.) esp. formally in a legislative assembly, public meeting, etc. **2 a** *tr.* consider; ponder (a matter). **b** *intr.* consider different sides of a question. ● *n.* **1** a formal discussion on a particular matter, esp. in a legislative assembly, etc. **2** debating; discussion (*open to debate*). □ **debating point** an inessential matter used to gain advantage in a debate. □□ **debater** *n.* [ME f. OF *debatre, debat* f. Rmc (as DE-, BATTLE)]

■ *v.* **1** argue *or* wrangle *or* dispute about, contest; discuss, moot, question. **2 a** deliberate, consider, reflect on, mull over, ponder (over), weigh, ruminate (over), meditate (on *or* over), think over *or* about, think through. ● *n.* **1** discussion, argument, dispute, altercation, polemic. **2** discussion, argumentation, argument, dispute, contention.

debauch /dibáwch/ *v. & n.* ● *v.tr.* **1** corrupt morally. **2** make intemperate or sensually indulgent. **3** deprave or debase (taste or judgment). **4** (as **debauched** *adj.*) dissolute. **5** seduce (a woman). ● *n.* **1** a bout of sensual indulgence. **2** debauchery. □□ **debaucher** *n.* [F *débauche(r),* OF *desbaucher,* of unkn. orig.]

■ *v.* **1** see DEMORALIZE 2. **4** (**debauched**) see DISSOLUTE. **5** see SEDUCE 1. ● *n.* **1** see ORGY 1.

debauchee /díbawchee, -shee, déb-/ *n.* a person addicted to excessive sensual indulgence. [F *débauché* past part.: see DE-BAUCH]

■ see *sensualist* (SENSUAL).

debauchery /dibáwchəree/ *n.* excessive sensual indulgence.

■ see DISSIPATION 1.

debenture /dibénchər/ *n.* **1** (in full **debenture bond**) a fixed-interest bond of a company or corporation, backed by general credit rather than specified assets. **2** *Brit.* an acknowledgment of indebtedness, esp. a bond of a company or corporation acknowledging a debt and providing for payment of interest at fixed intervals. [ME f. L *debentur* are owing f. *debēre* owe: assim. to -URE]

debilitate /dibílitayt/ *v.tr.* enfeeble; enervate. □□ **debilitatingly** *adv.* **debilitation** /-táyshən/ *n.* **debilitative** *adj.* [L *debilitare* (as DEBILITY)]

■ see ENERVATE *v.*

debility /dibílitee/ *n.* feebleness, esp. of health. [ME f. OF *debilité* f. L *debilitas -tatis* f. *debilis* weak]

■ see *infirmity* (INFIRM).

debit /débit/ *n. & v.* ● *n.* **1** an entry in an account recording a sum owed. **2** the sum recorded. **3** the total of such sums. **4** the debit side of an account. ● *v.tr.* (**debited, debiting**) **1** (foll. by *against, to*) enter (an amount) on the debit side of an account (*debited $500 against me*). **2** (foll. by *with*) enter (a person) on the debit side of an account (*debited me with $500*). [F *débit* f. L *debitum* DEBT]

■ *n.* see CHARGE *n.* 1b. ● *v.* bill, charge, invoice.

debonair /débənáir/ *adj.* **1** carefree; cheerful; self-assured. **2** having pleasant manners. □□ **debonairly** *adv.* [ME f. OF *debonaire = de bon aire* of good disposition]

■ **1** carefree, insouciant, gay, nonchalant, lighthearted, dashing, charming, cheerful, buoyant, jaunty, sprightly; smooth, unruffled; see also *self-assured* (SELF-ASSURANCE). **2** suave, elegant, urbane, refined, genteel, well-bred, courteous, civil, mannerly, gracious, polite, affable, obliging, pleasant.

debouch /dibówch, -bōosh/ *v.intr.* **1** (of troops or a stream) issue from a ravine, wood, etc., into open ground. **2** (often foll. by *into*) (of a river, road, etc.) merge into a larger body or area. □□ **debouchment** *n.* [F *déboucher* (as DE-, *bouche* mouth)]

debrief /deebreef/ *v.tr. colloq.* interrogate (a person, e.g., a

diplomat or pilot) about a completed mission or undertaking. □□ **debriefing** *n.*

debris /dəbree, day-, débree/ *n.* **1** scattered fragments, esp. of something wrecked or destroyed. **2** *Geol.* an accumulation of loose material, e.g., from rocks or plants. [F *débris* f. obs. *débriser* break down (as DE-, *briser* break)]

■ **1** see WRECKAGE 1, 2, WASTE *n.* 2.

debt /det/ *n.* **1** something that is owed, esp. money. **2** a state of obligation to pay something owed (*in debt; out of debt; get into debt*). □ **debt collector** a person who is employed to collect debts for creditors. **debt of honor** a debt not legally recoverable, esp. a sum lost in gambling. **in a person's debt** under an obligation to a person. [ME *det(te)* f. OF *dette* (later *debte*) ult. f. L *debitum* past part. of *debēre* owe]

■ **2** obligation; due, indebtedness, liability, responsibility, accountability, encumbrance; (*in debt*) under obligation, owing, accountable, beholden, indebted; in arrears, straitened, in dire straits, in (financial) difficulty *or* difficulties, insolvent, in the red, *colloq.* in hock.

debtor /détər/ *n.* a person who owes a debt, esp. money. [ME f. OF *det(t)or, -our* f. L *debitor* (as DEBT)]

debug /deebúg/ *v.tr.* (**debugged, debugging**) **1** *colloq.* trace and remove concealed listening devices from (a room, etc.). **2** *colloq.* identify and remove defects from (a machine, computer program, etc.). **3** remove bugs from.

debunk /deebúngk/ *v.tr. colloq.* **1** show the good reputation or aspirations of (a person, institution, etc.) to be spurious. **2** expose the falseness of (a claim, etc.). □□ **debunker** *n.*

■ see EXPLODE 4.

debus /deebús/ *v.tr. & intr.* (**debused, debusing** or **debussed, debussing**) esp. *Mil.* unload (personnel or stores) or alight from a motor vehicle.

debut /daybyōō, dáybyōō/ *n. & v.* ● *n.* (also **début**) **1** the first public appearance of a performer on stage, etc., or the opening performance of a show, etc. **2** the first appearance of a débutante in society. ● *v.* **1** *intr.* make a debut. **2** *tr.* introduce, esp. a performance, etc. [F f. *débuter* lead off]

■ *n.* **1** premiere, first night, opening (night). **2** appearance, coming out, introduction, initiation, inauguration, launch, launching.

debutante /débyətaant, dáybyōō-/ *n.* a (usu. wealthy) young woman making her social debut. [F, fem. part. of *débuter*: see DEBUT]

Dec. *abbr.* December.

dec. *abbr.* **1** deceased. **2** declared.

deca- /déka/ *comb. form* (also **dec-** before a vowel) **1** having ten. **2** tenfold. **3** ten, esp. of a metric unit (*decagram; decaliter*). [Gk *deka* ten]

decade /dékayd/ *n.* **1** a period of ten years. **2** a set, series, or group of ten. □□ **decadal** /dékəd'l/ *adj.* [ME f. F *décade* f. LL *decas -adis* f. Gk f. *deka* ten]

decadence /dékəd'ns/ *n.* **1** moral or cultural deterioration, esp. after a peak or culmination of achievement. **2** decadent behavior; a state of decadence. [F *décadence* f. med.L *decadentia* f. *decadere* DECAY]

■ **1** see DECAY *n.* 2.

decadent /dékədənt/ *adj. & n.* ● *adj.* **1 a** in a state of moral or cultural deterioration; showing or characterized by decadence. **b** of a period of decadence. **2** self-indulgent. ● *n.* a decadent person. □□ **decadently** *adv.* [F *décadent* (as DECADENCE)]

■ *adj.* **1 a** debased, degenerating, degenerative; corrupt, degenerate, immoral, debauched, dissipated; see also DISSOLUTE. **2** see SELF-INDULGENT. ● *n.* see DEGENERATE *n.*

decaffeinate /deekáfinayt/ *v.tr.* **1** remove the caffeine from. **2** reduce the quantity of caffeine in (usu. coffee).

decagon /dékəgon/ *n.* a plane figure with ten sides and angles. □□ **decagonal** /dikágənəl/ *adj.* [med.L *decagonum* f. Gk *dekagōnon* (as DECA-, -GON)]

decagynous /dikájinəs/ *adj. Bot.* having ten pistils. [mod.L *decagynus* (as DECA-, Gk *gūne* woman)]

decahedron /dékəheedrən/ *n.* a solid figure with ten faces. □□ **decahedral** *adj.* [DECA- + -HEDRON after POLYHEDRON]

decal /deékal/ n. = DECALCOMANIA 2. [abbr.]

decalcify /deekálsifī/ v.tr. (**-ies, -ied**) remove lime or calcareous matter from (a bone, tooth, etc.). □□ **decalcification** /-fikáyshən/ n. **decalcifier** n.

decalcomania /deekálkəmáyneeə/ n. **1** a process of transferring designs from specially prepared paper to the surface of glass, porcelain, etc. **2** a picture or design made by this process. [F *décalcomanie* f. *décalquer* transfer]

decaliter /dékəleetər/ n. a metric unit of capacity, equal to 10 liters.

Decalogue /dékəlawg, -log/ n. the Ten Commandments. [ME f. F *décalogue* or eccl.L *decalogus* f. Gk *dekalogos* (after *hoi deka logoi* the Ten Commandments)]

decameter /dékəmeetər/ n. a metric unit of length, equal to 10 meters.

decamp /dikámp/ v.intr. **1** break up or leave a camp. **2** depart suddenly; abscond. □□ **decampment** n. [F *décamper* (as DE-, CAMP[1])]
■ v. **1** see LEAVE[1] v. 1b, 3, 4.

decanal /dékənəl, dikáy-/ adj. **1** of a dean or deanery. **2** of the south side of a choir, the side on which the dean sits (cf. CANTORIAL). [med.L *decanalis* f. LL *decanus* DEAN[1]]

decandrous /dikándrəs/ adj. Bot. having ten stamens. [DECA- + Gk *andr-* man (= male organ)]

decani /dikáyni/ adj. Mus. to be sung by the decanal side in antiphonal singing (cf. CANTORIS). [L, genit. of *decanus* DEAN[1]]

decant /dikánt/ v.tr. **1** gradually pour off (liquid, esp. wine or a solution) from one container to another, esp. without disturbing the sediment. **2** empty out; move as if by pouring. [med.L *decanthare* (as DE-, L *canthus* f. Gk *kanthos* canthus, used of the lip of a beaker)]

decanter /dikántər/ n. a stoppered glass container into which wine or brandy, etc., is decanted.
■ see JUG n. 1, 2.

decapitate /dikápitayt/ v.tr. **1** behead (esp. as a form of capital punishment). **2** cut the head or end from. □□ **decapitation** /-táyshən/ n. **decapitator** n. [LL *decapitare* (as DE-, *caput -itis* head)]
■ see BEHEAD.

decapod /dékəpod/ n. **1** any crustacean of the chiefly marine order Decapoda, characterized by five pairs of walking legs, e.g., shrimps, crabs, and lobsters. **2** any of various mollusks of the class Cephalopoda, having ten tentacles, e.g., squids and cuttlefish. □□ **decapodan** /dikápəd'n/ adj. [F *décapode* f. Gk *deka* ten + *pous podos* foot]

decarbonize /deekáarbəniz/ v.tr. remove carbon or carbonaceous deposits from (an internal combustion engine, etc.). □□ **decarbonization** n.

decastyle /dékəstil/ n. & adj. Archit. ● n. a ten-columned portico. ● adj. having ten columns. [Gk *dekastulos* f. *deka* ten + *stulos* column]

decasyllable /dékəsiləbəl/ n. a metrical line of ten syllables. □□ **decasyllabic** /-silábik/ adj. & n.

decathlon /dikáthlən, -lon/ n. an athletic contest in which each competitor takes part in ten events. □□ **decathlete** /-leet/ n. [DECA- + Gk *athlon* contest]

decay /dikáy/ v. & n. ● v. **1 a** intr. rot; decompose. **b** tr. cause to rot or decompose. **2** intr. & tr. decline or cause to decline in quality, power, wealth, energy, beauty, etc. **3** intr. Physics **a** (usu. foll. by *to*) (of a substance, etc.,) undergo change by radioactivity. **b** undergo a gradual decrease in magnitude of a physical quantity. ● n. **1** a rotten or ruinous state; a process of wasting away. **2** decline in health, quality, etc. **3** Physics **a** change into another substance, etc. by radioactivity. **b** a decrease in the magnitude of a physical quantity, esp. the intensity of radiation or amplitude of oscillation. **4** decayed tissue. □□ **decayable** adj. [ME f. OF *decair* f. Rmc (as DE-, L *cadere* fall)]
■ v. **1 a** rot, decompose, molder, putrefy, spoil; turn, go bad, go off. **2** decline, degenerate, waste away, atrophy, weaken, wither, disintegrate, crumble, wane, ebb, dwindle, diminish, decrease; see also DETERIORATE.
● n. **1** rot, decomposition, mold, putrefaction, mortification. **2** decline, deterioration, decadence,

degeneration, dilapidation, disintegration, collapse, wasting, atrophy; downfall.

decease /disées/ n. & v. formal esp. Law ● n. death. ● v.intr. die. [ME f. OF *deces* f. L *decessus* f. *decedere* (as DE-, *cedere cess-* go)]
■ n. see DEATH 1. ● v. see DIE[1] 1.

deceased /diséest/ adj. & n. formal ● adj. dead. ● n. (usu. prec. by *the*) a person who has died, esp. recently.
■ adj. see DEAD adj. 1.

decedent /diséed'nt/ n. Law a deceased person. [L *decedere* die: see DECEASE]

deceit /diséet/ n. **1** the act or process of deceiving or misleading, esp. by concealing the truth. **2** a dishonest trick or stratagem. **3** willingness to deceive. [ME f. OF f. past part. of *deceveir* f. L *decipere* deceive (as DE-, *capere* take)]
■ **1** deception, deceitfulness, fraud, fraudulence, cheating, trickery, chicanery, chicane, dissimulation, dishonesty, misrepresentation, double-dealing, dirty business *or* dealing, duplicity, hypocrisy, treachery, underhandedness, subterfuge, hocus-pocus, guile, craft, slyness, craftiness, cunning, knavery, flimflam, archaic covin, colloq. monkey business, Brit. colloq. gammon, sl. hanky-panky, funny business. **2** trick, subterfuge, stratagem, fraud, cheat, ruse, maneuver, artifice, wile, hoax, swindle, double cross, pretense, imposture, sham, contrivance, shift, confidence game, blind, colloq. ploy, put-on, formal subreption, sl. con, con trick, scam.

deceitful /diséetfŏŏl/ adj. **1** (of a person) using deceit, esp. habitually. **2** (of an act, practice, etc.) intended to deceive. □□ **deceitfully** adv. **deceitfulness** n.
■ dishonest, underhand(ed), untrustworthy, misleading, crooked, insincere, false, fraudulent, counterfeit, disingenuous, lying, mendacious, untruthful; wily, crafty, sly, cunning, scheming, guileful, artful, sneaky, double-dealing, two-faced, hypocritical, duplicitous. □□ **deceitfulness** see DECEIT 1.

deceive /diséev/ v. **1** tr. make (a person) believe what is false; mislead purposely. **2** tr. be unfaithful to, esp. sexually. **3** intr. use deceit. **4** tr. archaic disappoint (esp. hopes). □ **be deceived** be mistaken or deluded. **deceive oneself** persist in a mistaken belief. □□ **deceivable** adj. **deceiver** n. [ME f. OF *deceivre* or *deceiv-* stressed stem of *deceveir* (as DECEIT)]
■ **1** mislead, delude, fool, hoax, trick, cheat, swindle, betray, double-cross, lead on, take in, lead up *or* down the garden path, lead astray, pull the wool over a person's eyes, archaic wilder, colloq. bamboozle, take for a ride, two-time, literary cozen, sl. con. **2** be unfaithful to, cuckold, colloq. cheat on. **3** see DISSIMULATE. **4** see DISAPPOINT 2. □ **be deceived** (deceived) see MISTAKEN.

decelerate /deesélərayt/ v. **1** intr. & tr. begin or cause to begin to reduce speed. **2** tr. make slower (decelerated motion). □□ **deceleration** /-ráyshən/ n. **decelerator** n. **decelerometer** /-rómitər/ n. [DE-, after ACCELERATE]
■ see SLOW v. 1, BRAKE[1] v. 2.

December /disémbər/ n. the twelfth month of the year. [ME f. OF *decembre* f. L *December* f. *decem* ten: orig. the tenth month of the Roman year]

decency /déesənsee/ n. (pl. **-ies**) **1** correct and tasteful standards of behavior as generally accepted. **2** conformity with current standards of behavior or propriety. **3** avoidance of obscenity. **4** (in pl.) the requirements of correct behavior. [L *decentia* f. *decēre* be fitting]
■ **1, 2** see PROPRIETY 1.

decennial /diséneeəl/ adj. **1** lasting ten years. **2** recurring every ten years. □□ **decennially** adv. [L *decennis* of ten years f. *decem* ten + *annus* year]

decent /déesənt/ adj. **1 a** conforming with current standards

---

/.../	**pronunciation**	●	**part of speech**
□	**phrases, idioms, and compounds**		
□□	**derivatives**	■	**synonym section**
cross-references appear in SMALL CAPITALS or *italics*			

of behavior or propriety. **b** avoiding obscenity. **2** respectable. **3** acceptable; passable; good enough. **4** kind; obliging; generous (*was decent enough to apologize*). □□ **decently** adv. [F *décent* or L *decēre* be fitting]

■ **1 a** proper, seemly, fitting, becoming, suitable, appropriate, right, correct, acceptable. **b** clean, inoffensive. **2** respectable, proper, well-bred, well brought up, well-mannered, mannerly, nice, clean, presentable, acceptable, seemly, decorous, dignified; chaste, pure, virtuous, modest. **3** adequate, acceptable, passable, satisfactory, fair, competent, mediocre, middling, fair to middling, moderate, respectable, ordinary, so-so, indifferent, not outstanding, unimpressive, average, neither here nor there, all right, comme ci, comme ça, reasonable, tolerable, good enough, *colloq.* OK, not bad. **4** courteous, proper, right, fair, honest, honorable, friendly, considerate, gracious, nice, thoughtful, obliging, kind, generous, accommodating. □□ **decently** see PROPERLY 4.

decentralize /deeséntrəliz/ v.tr. **1** transfer (powers, etc.) from a central to a local authority. **2** reorganize (a centralized institution, organization, etc.) on the basis of greater local autonomy. □□ **decentralist** /-list/ n. & adj. **decentralization** n.

deception /disépshən/ n. **1** the act or an instance of deceiving; the process of being deceived. **2** a thing that deceives; a trick or sham. [ME f. OF or LL *deceptio* f. *decipere* (as DECEIT)]

■ **1** see DECEIT 1. **2** see DECEIT 2.

deceptive /diséptiv/ adj. apt to deceive; easily mistaken for something else or as having a different quality. □□ **deceptively** adv. **deceptiveness** n. [OF *deceptif -ive* or LL *deceptivus* (as DECEPTION)]

■ misleading, false, illusory, deceiving, unreliable; fraudulent, deceitful, dishonest, untruthful, fake, false, *colloq.* shifty; tricky, dodgy, evasive, elusive, slippery.

decerebrate /deeséribrayt/ adj. having had the cerebrum removed.

deci- /désee/ comb. form one-tenth, esp. of a unit in the metric system (*deciliter*; *decimeter*). [L *decimus* tenth]

decibel /désibel/ n. a unit (one-tenth of a bel) used in the comparison of two power levels relating to electrical signals or sound intensities, one of the pair usually being taken as a standard. ¶ Abbr.: **dB**.

decide /disíd/ v. **1 a** intr. (often foll. by *on, about*) come to a resolution as a result of consideration. **b** tr. (usu. foll. by *to* + infin., or *that* + clause) have or reach as one's resolution about something (*decided to stay*; *decided that we should leave*). **2** tr. **a** Brit. cause (a person) to reach a resolution (*was unsure about going but the weather decided me*). **b** resolve or settle (a question, dispute, etc.). **3** intr. (usu. foll. by *between, for, against, in favor of*, or *that* + clause) give a judgment concerning a matter. □□ **decidable** adj. [ME f. F *décider* or f. L *decidere* (as DE-, *cædere* cut)]

■ **1** take or reach or come to a decision or conclusion, make up one's mind, determine, resolve; conclude; (*decide on*) fix or fasten or settle on, choose, select, pick (out), elect, opt for, commit oneself to. **2 b** resolve, arbitrate, judge, adjudicate; see also SETTLE¹ 5–7, 8b.

decided /disídid/ adj. (usu. attrib.) **1** definite; unquestionable (*a decided difference*). **2** (of a person, esp. as a characteristic) having clear opinions, resolute, not vacillating. □□ **decidedness** n.

■ **1** definite, pronounced, marked, unmistakable, unambiguous, unequivocal, certain, sure, absolute, obvious, clear, evident, unquestionable, unquestioned, indisputable, undisputed, undeniable, irrefutable, incontestable, unqualified, unconditional, incontrovertible, solid, real. **2** fixed, firm, resolute, determined, adamant, unhesitating, decisive, definite, unfaltering, assertive, asseverative, unswerving, uncompromising, unwavering.

decidedly /disídidlee/ adv. undoubtedly; undeniably.

■ see TRULY 2.

decider /disídər/ n. **1** a game, race, etc., to decide between

competitors finishing equal in a previous contest. **2** any person or thing that decides.

deciduous /disijooəs/ adj. **1** (of a tree) shedding its leaves annually. **2** (of leaves, horns, teeth, etc.) shed periodically. **3** (of an ant, etc.) shedding its wings after copulation. **4** fleeting; transitory. □□ **deciduousness** n. [L *deciduus* f. *decidere* f. *cadere* fall]

decigram /désigram/ n. (also Brit. **decigramme**) a metric unit of mass, equal to 0.1 gram.

decile /désil, -il/ n. Statistics any of the nine values of a random variable which divide a frequency distribution into ten groups, each containing one-tenth of the total population. [F *décile*, ult. f. L *decem* ten]

deciliter /désileetər/ n. a metric unit of capacity, equal to 0.1 liter.

decimal /désiməl/ adj. & n. ● adj. **1** (of a system of numbers, weights, measures, etc.) based on the number ten, in which the smaller units are related to the principal units as powers of ten (units, tens, hundreds, thousands, etc.). **2** of tenths or ten; reckoning or proceeding by tens. ● n. a decimal fraction. □ **decimal fraction** a fraction whose denominator is a power of ten, esp. when expressed positionally by units to the right of a decimal point. **decimal point** a period or dot placed before a numerator in a decimal fraction. **decimal scale** a scale with successive places denoting units, tens, hundreds, etc. **decimal system** a numerical system based on units of ten. □□ **decimally** adv. [mod.L *decimalis* f. L *decimus* tenth]

decimalize /désiməliz/ v.tr. **1** express as a decimal. **2** convert to a decimal system (esp. of coinage). □□ **decimalization** n.

decimate /désimayt/ v.tr. **1** disp. destroy a large proportion of. ¶ Now the usual sense, although often deplored as an inappropriate use. **2** orig. Mil. kill or remove one in every ten of. □□ **decimation** /-máyshən/ n. **decimator** n. [L *decimare* take the tenth man f. *decimus* tenth]

■ **1** see MASSACRE v. 2.

decimeter /désimeetər/ n. a metric unit of length, equal to 0.1 meter.

decipher /disífər/ v.tr. **1** convert (a text written in cipher) into an intelligible script or language. **2** determine the meaning of (anything obscure or unclear). □□ **decipherable** adj. **decipherment** n.

■ **1** decode, decrypt. **2** decode, unravel, unscramble, disentangle, translate, work out, explain, solve, figure out, interpret, make out; understand.

decision /disizhən/ n. **1** the act or process of deciding. **2** a conclusion or resolution reached, esp. as to future action, after consideration (*have made my decision*). **3** (often foll. by *of*) **a** the settlement of a question. **b** a formal judgment. **4** a tendency to decide firmly; resoluteness. [ME f. OF *decision* or L *decisio* (as DECIDE)]

■ **1** settlement, determination, resolution, arbitration. **2, 3** judgment, conclusion, resolution; verdict, sentence, ruling, finding, decree, settlement. **4** determination, firmness, decidedness, resolve, resolution, resoluteness, decisiveness, conclusiveness, steadfastness, purpose, purposefulness.

decisive /disísiv/ adj. **1** that decides an issue; conclusive. **2** (of a person, esp. as a characteristic) able to decide quickly and effectively. □□ **decisively** adv. **decisiveness** n. [F *décisif -ive* f. med.L *decisivus* (as DECIDE)]

■ **1** see ULTIMATE adj. 1, 2. **2** see FIRM¹ adj. 2a.

deck /dek/ n. & v. ● n. **1 a** a platform in a ship covering all or part of the hull's area at any level and serving as a floor. **b** the accommodation on a particular deck of a ship. **2** anything compared to a ship's deck, e.g., the floor or compartment of a bus. **3** a component, usu. a flat horizontal surface, that carries a particular recording medium (such as a disk or tape) in sound-reproduction equipment. **4 a** a pack of cards. **b** sl. a packet of narcotics. **5** sl. the ground. **6 a** any floor or platform, esp. the floor of a pier or a platform for sunbathing. **b** a platformlike structure, usu. made of lumber and unroofed, attached to a house, etc. ● v.tr. **1** (often foll. by *out*) decorate; adorn. **2** furnish with or cover as a deck.

□ **below deck** (or **decks**) in or into the space below the main deck. **deck chair** a folding chair of wood and canvas, of a kind used on deck on passenger ships. **deck tennis** a game in which a quoit of rope, rubber, etc., is tossed to and fro over a net. **on deck 1** in the open air on a ship's main deck. **2** ready for action, work, etc. [ME, = covering f. MDu. *dec* roof, cloak]
■ *n.* **1a, 2** story, level, floor. **4 a** pack, set, stack. ● *v.* **1** see DECORATE 1, 3.

-decker /dékər/ *comb. form* having a specified number of decks or layers (*double-decker*).

deckhand /dékhand/ *n.* a person employed in cleaning and odd jobs on a ship's deck.

deckle /dékəl/ *n.* a device in a papermaking machine for limiting the size of the sheet. □ **deckle edge** the rough uncut edge formed by a deckle. **deckle-edged** having a deckle edge. [G *Deckel* dimin. of *Decke* cover]

declaim /dikláym/ *v.* **1** *intr.* & *tr.* speak or utter rhetorically or affectedly. **2** *intr.* practice oratory or recitation. **3** *intr.* (foll. by *against*) protest forcefully. **4** *intr.* deliver an impassioned (rather than reasoned) speech. □□ **declaimer** *n.* [ME f. F *déclamer* or f. L *declamare* (as DE-, CLAIM)]
■ **1, 3, 4** see RANT *v.* 2, 3.

declamation /dékləmáyshən/ *n.* **1** the act or art of declaiming. **2** a rhetorical exercise or set speech. **3** an impassioned speech; a harangue. □□ **declamatory** /diklámətawree/ *adj.* [F *déclamation* or L *declamatio* (as DECLAIM)]
■ **1** see ORATORY. **2** see ORATION. **3** see HARANGUE *n.*

declarant /diklárənt/ *n.* a person who makes a legal declaration. [F *déclarant* part. of *déclarer* (as DECLARE)]

declaration /dékləráyshən/ *n.* **1** the act or process of declaring. **2 a** a formal, emphatic, or deliberate statement or announcement. **b** a statement asserting or protecting a legal right. **3** a written public announcement of intentions, terms of an agreement, etc. **4** *Cricket* an act of declaring an innings closed. **5** *Cards* **a** the naming of trumps. **b** an announcement of a combination held. **6** *Law* **a** a plaintiff's statement of claim. **b** an affirmation made instead of taking an oath. [ME f. L *declaratio* (as DECLARE)]
■ **1, 2a** statement, assertion, attestation, deposition, asseveration, affirmation, avowal, announcement, proclamation, pronouncement, profession. **2 b** proclamation, announcement, pronouncement, promulgation. **3** edict, manifesto, notice.

declare /dikláir/ *v.* **1** *tr.* announce openly or formally (*declare war*; *declare a dividend*). **2** *tr.* pronounce (a person or thing) to be something (*declared him to be an impostor*; *declared it invalid*). **3** *tr.* (usu. foll. by *that* + clause) assert emphatically; state explicitly. **4** *tr.* acknowledge possession of (dutiable goods, income, etc.). **5** *tr.* (as **declared** *adj.*) who admits to be such (*a declared atheist*). **6** *tr.* (also *absol.*) *Cricket* close (an innings) voluntarily before all the wickets have fallen. **7** *tr. Cards* **a** (also *absol.*) name (the trump suit). **b** announce that one holds (certain combinations of cards, etc.). **8** *tr.* (of things) make evident; prove (*your actions declare your honesty*). **9** *intr.* (foll. by *for*, *against*) take the side of one party or another. □ **declare oneself** reveal one's intentions or identity. **well, I declare** (or **I do declare**) an exclamation of incredulity, surprise, or vexation. □□ **declarable** *adj.* **declarative** /-klárətiv/ *adj.* **declaratively** *adv.* **declaratory** /-klárətawree/ *adj.* **declaredly** /-ridlee/ *adv.* **declarer** *n.* [ME f. L *declarare* (as DE-, *clarare* f. *clarus* clear)]
■ **1, 2** announce, make known, pronounce, decree, rule, proclaim, herald, promulgate, publish, broadcast, trumpet (forth). **3** assert, affirm, state, asseverate, avow, profess, protest, swear, claim, proclaim, say, *archaic or rhet.* avouch, *formal* aver; confirm, certify. **5** (**declared**) avowed, professed, proclaimed, *archaic or rhet.* avouched. **8** see PROVE 1. **9** (*declare for*) see SIDE *v.*; (*declare against*) see OPPOSE 1–3. □ **declare oneself** see DECLARE 3 above. **well, I declare** (or **I do declare**) see *well I'll be damned* (DAMN). □□ **declarative**, **declaratory** see ASSERTIVE 1.

déclassé /dayklasáy/ *adj.* (*fem.* **déclassée**) that has fallen in social status. [F]

declassify /deeklásifī/ *v.tr.* (**-ies**, **-ied**) declare (information, etc.) to be no longer secret. □□ **declassification** /-fikáyshən/ *n.*

declension /diklénshən/ *n.* **1** *Gram.* **a** the variation of the form of a noun, pronoun, or adjective, by which its grammatical case, number, and gender are identified. **b** the class in which a noun, etc., is put according to the exact form of this variation. **2** deterioration; declining. □□ **declensional** *adj.* [OF *declinaison* f. *decliner* DECLINE after L *declinatio*: assim. to ASCENSION, etc.]

declination /déklináyshən/ *n.* **1** a downward bend or turn. **2** *Astron.* the angular distance of a star, etc., north or south of the celestial equator. **3** *Physics* the angular deviation of a compass needle from true north. **4** a formal refusal. □□ **declinational** *adj.* [ME f. L *declinatio* (as DECLINE)]

decline /diklín/ *v.* & *n.* ● *v.* **1** *intr.* deteriorate; lose strength or vigor; decrease. **2 a** *tr.* reply with formal courtesy that one will not accept (an invitation, honor, etc.). **b** *tr.* refuse, esp. formally and courteously (*declined to be made use of*; *declined doing anything*). **c** *tr.* turn away from (a challenge, battle, discussion, etc.). **d** *intr.* give or send a refusal. **3** *intr.* slope downward. **4** *intr.* bend down; droop. **5** *tr. Gram.* state the forms of (a noun, pronoun, or adjective) corresponding to cases, number, and gender. **6** *intr.* (of a day, life, etc.) draw to a close. **7** *intr.* decrease in price, etc. **8** *tr.* bend down. ● *n.* **1** gradual loss of vigor or excellence (*on the decline*). **2** decay; deterioration. **3** setting; the last part of the course (of the sun, of life, etc.). **4** a fall in price. **5** *archaic* tuberculosis or a similar wasting disease. □ **declining years** old age. **on the decline** in a declining state. □□ **declinable** *adj.* **decliner** *n.* [ME f. OF *decliner* f. L *declinare* (as DE-, *clinare* bend)]
■ *v.* **1, 7** deteriorate, degenerate, worsen; go down, drop, diminish, lessen, decrease, dip, sink, wane, flag, peter out, trail *or* tail off, fall *or* taper off, subside, ebb, abate, dwindle, shrink, fade. **2** refuse, turn down, say no to. **3** slope *or* slant (downward), descend, drop *or* fall off, dip, sink. **4** see DROOP *v.* 1. **6** see STOP *v.* 2. ● *n.* **1, 4** diminution, decrease, lessening, ebb, downturn, falloff, reduction, abatement, slump, descent, fall, slide, drop. **2** decay, degeneration, deterioration, weakening, debility, worsening. □ **declining years** see AGE *n.* 3. **on the decline** on the wane, in decline, waning, in eclipse, declining, falling, slipping, falling off, out of favor, losing ground, going downhill, on the downgrade, *colloq.* on the skids.

declivity /diklívitee/ *n.* (*pl.* **-ies**) a downward slope, esp. a piece of sloping ground. □□ **declivitous** *adj.* [L *declivitas* f. *declivis* (as DE-, *clivus* slope)]
■ see SLOPE *n.* 1–3.

declutch /deeklúch/ *v.intr.* disengage the clutch of a motor vehicle.

deco /dékō/ *n.* (also **Deco**) (usu. *attrib.*) = *art deco*. [F *décoratif* DECORATIVE]

decoct /dikókt/ *v.tr.* extract the essence from by decoction. [ME f. L *decoquere* boil down]

decoction /dikókshən/ *n.* **1** a process of boiling down so as to extract some essence. **2** the extracted liquor resulting from this. [ME f. OF *decoction* or LL *decoctio* (as DE-, L *coquere coct-* boil)]
■ **2** see EXTRACT *n.* 2.

decode /deekṓd/ *v.tr.* convert (a coded message) into intelligible language. □□ **decodable** *adj.*
■ see DECIPHER 1, 2.

decoder /deekṓdər/ *n.* **1** a person or thing that decodes. **2** an electronic device for analyzing signals and feeding separate amplifier channels.

decollate /dikólayt/ *v.tr. formal* **1** behead. **2** truncate. □□ **de-**

/.../ **pronunciation**	● **part of speech**
□ **phrases, idioms, and compounds**	
□□ **derivatives**	■ **synonym section**
cross-references appear in SMALL CAPITALS or *italics*	

collation /deékəláyshən/ *n.* [L *decollare decollat-* (as DE-, *collum* neck)]
■ **1** see BEHEAD.

décolletage /dáykawltaázh/ *n.* a low neckline of a woman's dress, etc. [F (as DE-, *collet* collar of a dress)]

décolleté /daykawltáy/ *adj.* & *n.* ● *adj.* **1** (of a dress, etc.) having a low neckline. **2** (of a woman) wearing a dress with a low neckline. ● *n.* a low neckline. [F (as DÉCOLLETAGE)]

decolonize /deekólənīz/ *v.tr.* (of a nation) withdraw from (a colony), leaving it independent. □□ **decolonization** *n.*

decolorize /deekúlərīz/ *v.* **1** *tr.* remove the color from. **2** *intr.* lose color. □□ **decolorization** *n.*

decommission /deékəmíshən/ *v.tr.* **1** close down (a nuclear reactor, etc.). **2** take (a ship) out of service.

decompose /deékəmpóz/ *v.* **1** *intr.* decay; rot. **2** *tr.* separate (a substance, light, etc.) into its elements or simpler constituents. **3** *intr.* disintegrate; break up. □□ **decomposition** /deékompəzíshən/ *n.* [F *décomposer* (as DE-, COMPOSE)]
■ **1** rot, disintegrate, decay, molder, putrefy, break down; spoil, go off *or* bad. **2** separate, break up *or* down, take apart, dissect, anatomize, atomize, resolve, analyze. **3** break up *or* down, fall *or* come apart; see also DISINTEGRATE. □□ **decomposition** see DECAY *n.* 1.

decompress /deékəmprés/ *v.tr.* subject to decompression; relieve or reduce the compression on.

decompression /deékəmpréshən/ *n.* **1** release from compression. **2** a gradual reduction of air pressure on a person who has been subjected to high pressure (esp. underwater). □ **decompression chamber** an enclosed space for subjecting a person to decompression. **decompression sickness** = AEROEMBOLISM.

decompressor /deékəmprésər/ *n.* a device for reducing pressure in the engine of a motor vehicle.

decongestant /deékənjéstənt/ *adj.* & *n.* ● *adj.* that relieves (esp. nasal) congestion. ● *n.* a medicinal agent that relieves nasal congestion.

deconsecrate /deekónsikrayt/ *v.tr.* transfer (esp. a building) from sacred to secular use. □□ **deconsecration** /-kráyshən/ *n.*

deconstruct /deékənstrúkt/ *v.tr.* subject to deconstruction. □□ **deconstructive** *adj.* [back-form. f. DECONSTRUCTION]

deconstruction /deékənstrúkshən/ *n.* a method of critical analysis of philosophical and literary language. □□ **deconstructionism** *n.* **deconstructionist** *adj.* & *n.* [F *déconstruction* (as DE-, CONSTRUCTION)]

decontaminate /deékəntáminayt/ *v.tr.* remove contamination from (an area, person, clothes, etc.). □□ **decontamination** /-náyshən/ *n.*
■ see DISINFECT.

decontrol /deékəntról/ *v.* & *n.* ● *v.tr.* (**decontrolled, decontrolling**) release (a commodity, etc.) from controls or restrictions, esp. those imposed by the government. ● *n.* the act of decontrolling.
■ *v.* deregulate, derestrict. ● *n.* see LAISSEZ-FAIRE.

decor /daykáwr, dáykawr/ *n.* (also **décor**) **1** the furnishing and decoration of a room, etc. **2** the decoration and scenery of a stage. [F f. *décorer* (as DECORATE)]

decorate /dékərayt/ *v.tr.* **1** provide with adornments. **2** provide (a room or building) with new paint, wallpaper, etc. **3** serve as an adornment to. **4** confer an award or distinction on. □ **decorated** (or **Decorated**) **style** *Archit.* the second stage of English Gothic (14th c.), with increasing use of decoration and geometrical tracery. [L *decorare decorat-* f. *decus -oris* beauty]
■ **1, 3** bedeck, deck (out), trim, dress (up), spruce *or* smarten up, beautify, caparison, *Brit. colloq.* tart up; adorn, ornament, garnish, embroider; see also EMBELLISH 1. **2** paint, wallpaper, paper, redecorate, furbish, refurbish, renovate, fix up.

decoration /dékəráyshən/ *n.* **1** the process or art of decorating. **2** a thing that decorates or serves as an ornament. **3** a medal, etc., conferred and worn as an honor. **4** (in *pl.*) flags, etc., put up on an occasion of public celebration. □ **Decoration Day** = *Memorial Day.* [F *décoration* or LL *decoratio* (as DECORATE)]

■ **2** garnish, trim, trimming, adornment, embellishment, ornament, ornamentation, garnishment. **3** medal, laurel, award, badge, colors, order, ribbon, *Brit.* garter.

decorative /dékərətiv, dékrə-, -əray-/ *adj.* serving to decorate. □□ **decoratively** *adv.* **decorativeness** *n.* [F *décoratif* (as DECORATE)]
■ see FANCY *adj.* 1.

decorator /dékəraytər/ *n.* a person who decorates, esp. one who paints or papers houses professionally.

decorous /dékərəs/ *adj.* **1** respecting good taste or propriety. **2** dignified and decent. □□ **decorously** *adv.* **decorousness** *n.* [L *decorus* seemly]
■ becoming, dignified, decent, correct, proper, mannerly, seemly, refined, elegant, polite, well-behaved, well-mannered, well-bred, genteel, demure, polished, gentlemanly, ladylike, *joc.* couth. □□ **decorousness** see DECORUM 1–3.

decorticate /deekáwrtikayt/ *v.tr.* **1** remove the bark, rind, or husk from. **2** remove the outside layer from (the kidney, brain, etc.). [L *decorticare decorticat-* (as DE-, *cortex -icis* bark)]
■ **1** see PEEL[1] *v.* 1, 2.

decortication /deékawrtikáyshən/ *n.* **1** the removal of the outside layer from an organ (e.g., the kidney) or structure. **2** an operation removing the blood clot and scar tissue formed after bleeding in the chest cavity.

decorum /dikáwrəm/ *n.* **1 a** seemliness; propriety. **b** behavior required by politeness or decency. **2** a particular requirement of this kind. **3** etiquette. [L, neut. of *decorus* seemly]
■ **1** seemliness, propriety, correctness, protocol, punctilio, form, formality, conformity. **2** civility, courtesy, politeness, formality. **3** etiquette, politesse, good form, propriety, mannerliness, politeness, dignity, gentility, good manners, convenances, respectability, courtliness, deportment.

decoupage /dáykoōpaázh/ *n.* (also **découpage**) the decoration of surfaces with paper cutouts. [F, = the action of cutting out]

decouple /deekúpəl/ *v.tr.* **1** *Electr.* make the interaction between (oscillators, etc.) so weak that there is little transfer of energy between them. **2** separate; disengage; dissociate.

decoy *n.* & *v.* ● *n.* /deékoy, dikóy/ **1 a** a person or thing used to lure an animal or person into a trap or danger. **b** a bait or enticement. **2** a pond with narrow, netted arms into which wild duck may be tempted in order to catch them. ● *v.tr.* /dikóy/ (often foll. by *into, out of*) allure or entice, esp. by means of a decoy. [17th c.: perh. f. Du. *de kooi* the decoy f. *de* THE + *kooi* f. L *cavea* cage]
■ *n.* **1** bait, lure, trap, attraction, enticement, inducement; stool pigeon, shill, stool, *Brit. sl.* nark. ● *v.* lure, entice, allure, attract, induce, coax, seduce, bait, trick, inveigle, persuade, draw (in).

decrease *v.* & *n.* ● *v.tr.* & *intr.* /dikreés/ make or become smaller or fewer. ● *n.* /deékrees/ **1** the act or an instance of decreasing. **2** the amount by which a thing decreases. □□ **decreasingly** *adv.* [ME f. OF *de(s)creiss-*, pres. stem of *de(s)creistre* ult. f. L *decrescere* (as DE-, *crescere cret-* grow)]
■ *v.* diminish, decline, lessen, go down, drop (off *or* away), fall, abate, fall off, shrink, contract, dwindle, ebb, subside, wane, taper off, trail *or* tail off, slacken, let up, ease (off *or* up); bring down, reduce, shorten, lower, de-escalate, curtail, cut (down *or* back), step down, mark down, slash, roll back, *colloq.* knock down. ● *n.* diminution, reduction, decline, lessening, lowering, abatement, decrement, dwindling, ebb, subsidence, wane, de-escalation, slackening, easing (off *or* up), curtailment, cut, cut-back, drop, fall, falloff, tail off, slash, rollback.

decree /dikreé/ *n.* & *v.* ● *n.* **1** an official order issued by a legal authority. **2** a judgment or decision of certain courts of law, esp. in matrimonial cases. ● *v.tr.* (**decrees, decreeing**) ordain by decree. □ **decree absolute** a final order for divorce, enabling either party to remarry. **decree nisi** /nísi/ a provisional order for divorce, made absolute unless cause to the contrary is shown within a fixed

period. [ME f. OF *decré* f. L *decretum* neut. past part. of *decernere* decide (as DE-, *cernere* sift)]
■ *n.* **1** order, mandate, directive, ordinance, edict, law, statute, regulation, enactment, act, ruling, dictum, dictate, injunction, sanction, proclamation, announcement, promulgation, determination, rescript, prescription, firman, decretal. **2** see JUDGMENT 4. ● *v.* order, command, direct, rule, mandate, ordain, dictate, charge, enjoin, proclaim, pronounce, prescribe, decide, determine, adjudge.

decrement /dékrimənt/ *n.* **1** *Physics* the ratio of the amplitudes in successive cycles of a damped oscillation. **2** the amount lost by diminution or waste. **3** the act of decreasing. [L *decrementum* (as DECREASE)]
■ **2, 3** see DECREASE *n.*

decrepit /dikrépit/ *adj.* **1** weakened or worn out by age and infirmity. **2** worn out by long use; dilapidated. □□ **decrepitude** *n.* [ME f. L *decrepitus* (as DE-, *crepitus* past part. of *crepare* creak)]
■ **1** aged, old, elderly, ancient, superannuated, senescent, senile, feeble, enfeebled, weak, weakened, frail, infirm, wasted, worn out, unfit, debilitated, enervated, disabled, incapacitated, bedridden, doddering, broken-down, timeworn; out of shape, in bad shape, *sl.* gaga. **2** dilapidated, crumbling, decayed, decaying, withered, wasted, antiquated, tumbledown, broken-down, rickety, unstable, shaky, ramshackle, derelict, creaking, creaky, run-down, *Brit. sl.* clapped out. □□ **decrepitude** feebleness, weakness, frailness, frailty, infirmity, debilitation, enervation, incapacity, incapacitation, old age, superannuation, senescence, senility, dotage; dilapidation, deterioration, decay, ruin.

decrepitate /dikrépitayt/ *v.* **1** *tr.* roast or calcine (a mineral or salt) until it stops crackling. **2** *intr.* crackle under heat. □□ **decrepitation** /-táyshən/ *n.* [prob. mod.L *decrepitare* f. DE- + L *crepitare* crackle]

decrescendo /deékrishéndō, dáy-/ *adv., adj., & n.* (*pl.* **-os**) = DIMINUENDO. [It., part. of *decrescere* DECREASE]

decrescent /dikrésənt/ *adj.* (usu. of the moon) waning; decreasing. [L *decrescere*: see DECREASE]

decretal /dikreét'l/ *n.* **1** a papal decree. **2** (in *pl.*) a collection of these, forming part of canon law. [ME f. med.L *decretale* f. LL (*epistola*) *decretalis* (letter) of decree f. L *decernere*: see DECREE]

decriminalize /deekríminəlīz/ *v.tr.* cease to treat (an action, etc.) as criminal. □□ **decriminalization** *n.*

decry /dikrí/ *v.tr.* (**-ies, -ied**) disparage; belittle. □□ **decrial** *n.* **decrier** *n.* [after F *décrier*: cf. *cry down*]
■ see DISPARAGE 1.

decrypt /deekrípt/ *v.tr.* decipher (a cryptogram), with or without knowledge of its key. □□ **decryption** /-krípshən/ *n.* [DE- + CRYPTOGRAM]

decumbent /dikúmbənt/ *adj.* *Bot. & Zool.* (of a plant, shoot, or bristles) lying along the ground or a surface. [L *decumbere* *decumbent-* lie down]

decurve /deekárv/ *v.tr. & intr.* *Zool. & Bot.* (esp. as **decurved** *adj.*) curve or bend down (*a decurved bill*). □□ **decurvature** *n.*

decussate /deekúsayt/ *adj. & v.* ● *adj.* **1** X-shaped. **2** *Bot.* with pairs of opposite leaves, etc., each at right angles to the pair below. ● *v.tr. & intr.* **1** arrange or be arranged in a decussate form. **2** intersect. □□ **decussation** /-sáyshən/ *n.* [L *decussatus* past part. of *decussare* divide in a cross shape f. *decussis* the numeral ten or the shape X f. *decem* ten]

dedans /dədóN/ *n.* **1** (in court tennis) the open gallery at the end of the service side of a court. **2** the spectators watching a match. [F, = inside]

dedicate /dédikayt/ *v.tr.* **1** (foll. by *to*) devote (esp. oneself) to a special task or purpose. **2** (foll. by *to*) address (a book, piece of music, etc.) as a compliment to a friend, patron, etc. **3** (often foll. by *to*) devote (a building, etc.) to a deity or a sacred person or purpose. **4** (as **dedicated** *adj.*) **a** (of a person) devoted to an aim or vocation; having single-minded loyalty or integrity. **b** (of equipment, esp. a computer) designed for a specific purpose. □□ **dedicatee**

/-kaytée/ *n.* **dedicative** *adj.* **dedicator** *n.* **dedicatory** /-kətáwree/ *adj.* [L *dedicare* (DE-, *dicare* declare, dedicate)]
■ **1** devote, consecrate, give (up *or* over), offer (up), surrender, commit, pledge, assign. **2** inscribe; address, assign. **4 a** (**dedicated**) see DEVOTED.

dedication /dédikáyshən/ *n.* **1** the act or an instance of dedicating; the quality or process of being dedicated. **2** the words with which a book, etc., is dedicated. **3** a dedicatory inscription. [ME f. OF *dedicacion* or L *dedicatio* (as DEDICATE)]
■ **1** devotion, commitment, allegiance, adherence, faithfulness, fidelity, loyalty, devotedness, wholeheartedness, single-mindedness, fixedness, fealty; consecration, sanctification, hallowing. **2** inscription, address; message.

deduce /didoos, -dyoos/ *v.tr.* **1** (often foll. by *from*) infer; draw as a logical conclusion. **2** *archaic* trace the course or derivation of. □□ **deducible** *adj.* [L *deducere* (as DE-, *ducere* *duct-* lead)]
■ **1** conclude, infer, draw the conclusion, understand, gather, assume, presume, derive, work out, divine, glean, take it, suppose, surmise, *Brit. sl.* suss (out).

deduct /didúkt/ *v.tr.* (often foll. by *from*) subtract, take away, withhold (an amount, portion, etc.). [L (as DEDUCE)]
■ subtract, take away *or* out *or* off, take, remove, withdraw, withhold, knock off.

deductible /didúktibəl/ *adj. & n.* ● *adj.* that may be deducted, esp. from tax to be paid or taxable income. ● *n.* part of an insurance claim to be paid by the insured, esp. by prior agreement.

deduction /didúkshən/ *n.* **1 a** the act of deducting. **b** an amount deducted. **2 a** the inferring of particular instances from a general law (cf. INDUCTION). **b** a conclusion deduced. [ME f. OF *deduction* or L *deductio* (as DEDUCE)]
■ **1 a** subtraction, withdrawal, removal, abstraction. **2 b** conclusion, inference, supposition, assumption, finding, reasoning, result; surmise, divination, guess, conjecture.

deductive /didúktiv/ *adj.* of or reasoning by deduction. □□ **deductively** *adv.* [med.L *deductivus* (as DEDUCE)]
■ see LOGICAL 1.

dee /dee/ *n.* **1** the letter D. **2 a** a thing shaped like this. **b** *Physics* either of two hollow semicircular electrodes in a cyclotron. [the name of the letter]

deed /deed/ *n. & v.* ● *n.* **1** a thing done intentionally or consciously. **2** a brave, skillful, or conspicuous act. **3** actual fact or performance (*kind in word and deed; in deed and not in name*). **4** *Law* a written or printed document often used for a legal transfer of ownership and bearing the disposer's signature. ● *v.tr.* convey or transfer by legal deed. □ **deedbox** *Brit.* a strongbox. **deed poll** (*pl.* **deeds poll**) a deed made and executed by one party only, esp. to change one's name (the paper being polled or cut even, not indented). [OE *dēd* f. Gmc: cf. DO¹]
■ *n.* **1** see ACT *n.* 1. **2** exploit, feat, achievement, accomplishment, attainment. **4** title deed, document, instrument, contract, agreement.

deejay /deéjáy/ *n. sl.* a disk jockey. [abbr. DJ]

deem /deem/ *v.tr. formal* regard; consider; judge (*deem it my duty; was deemed sufficient*). [OE *dēman* f. Gmc, rel. to DOOM]
■ see CONSIDER 6.

de-emphasize /dee-émfəsiz/ *v.tr.* **1** remove emphasis from. **2** reduce emphasis on.
■ see MINIMIZE 2.

deemster /deémstər/ *n.* a judge of the Isle of Man. [DEEM + -STER]

deep /deep/ *adj., n., & adv.* ● *adj.* **1 a** extending far down from the top (*deep hole; deep water*). **b** extending far in from

---

/.../ pronunciation	● part of speech
□ phrases, idioms, and compounds	
□□ **derivatives**	■ synonym section
cross-references appear in SMALL CAPITALS or *italics*	

the surface or edge (*deep wound*; *deep plunge*; *deep shelf*; *deep border*). **2** (*predic.*) **a** extending to or lying at a specified depth (*water 6 feet deep*; *ankle-deep in mud*). **b** in a specified number of ranks one behind another (*soldiers drawn up six deep*). **3** situated far down or back or in (*hands deep in his pockets*). **4** coming or brought from far down or in (*deep breath*; *deep sigh*). **5** low-pitched; full-toned; not shrill (*deep voice*; *deep note*; *deep bell*). **6** intense; vivid; extreme (*deep disgrace*; *deep sleep*; *deep color*; *deep secret*). **7** heartfelt; absorbing (*deep affection*; *deep feelings*; *deep interest*). **8** (*predic.*) fully absorbed or overwhelmed (*deep in a book*; *deep in debt*). **9** profound; penetrating; not superficial; difficult to understand (*deep thinker*; *deep thought*; *deep insight*; *deep learning*). **10** *Cricket* distant from the batsman (*deep mid-off*). **11** *Football, Soccer, etc.* distant from the front line of one's team. **12** *sl.* cunning or secretive (*a deep one*). ● *n.* **1** (prec. by *the*) *poet.* the sea. **2** a deep part of the sea. **3** an abyss, pit, or cavity. **4** (prec. by *the*) *Cricket* the position of a fielder distant from the batsman. **5** a deep state (*deep of the night*). **6** *poet.* a mysterious region of thought or feeling. ● *adv.* deeply; far down or in (*dig deep*; *read deep into the night*). □ **deep breathing** breathing with long breaths, esp. as a form of exercise. **deep-drawn** (of metal, etc.) shaped by forcing through a die when cold. **deep freeze 1** a refrigerator in which food can be quickly frozen and kept for long periods at a very low temperature. **2** a suspension of activity. **deep-freeze** *v.tr.* freeze or store (food) in a deep freeze. **deep-fry** (**-fries, -fried**) fry (food) in an amount of fat or oil sufficient to cover it. **deep kiss** a kiss with contact between tongues. **deep-laid** (of a scheme) secret and elaborate. **deep mourning** mourning expressed by wearing only black clothes. **deep-rooted** (esp. of convictions) firmly established. **deep sea** the deeper parts of the ocean. **deep-seated** (of emotion, disease, etc.) firmly established; profound. **Deep South** the region of the SE US, usu. including South Carolina, Georgia, Alabama, Mississippi, and Louisiana. **deep space** the regions of outer space beyond the solar system. **deep therapy** curative treatment with short-wave X rays of high penetrating power. **go off the deep end** *colloq.* give way to anger or emotion. **in deep water** (or **waters**) in trouble or difficulty. **jump** (or **be thrown**) **in at the deep end** face a difficult problem, undertaking, etc., with little experience of it. □□ **deeply** *adv.* **deepness** *n.* [OE *dēop* (adj.), *dīope, dēope* (adv.), f. Gmc: rel. to DIP]

■ *adj.* **1** extensive, bottomless, abyssal, unfathomed, unfathomable, profound; yawning, chasmic. **3** far *or* deep *or* way down, far *or* way back. **5** low, low-pitched, resonant, booming, resounding, sonorous, rumbling. **6** rich, dark, strong; see also INTENSE 1, 3; VIVID 1. **7** profound, intense, sincere, serious, heartfelt, deep-seated, earnest, ardent, fervent, poignant, deep-rooted; see also ABSORBING. **8** rapt, absorbed, engrossed, occupied, preoccupied, intent, intense, involved, engaged, immersed, lost, overwhelmed, steeped. **9** profound, weighty, serious, heavy, arcane, recondite, abstruse, esoteric; obscure, unfathomable, inscrutable, incomprehensible, difficult, beyond *or* past comprehension; impenetrable, mysterious, mystic, mystical, occult; wise, learned, sage, sagacious, astute, perspicacious, discerning, acute, intense, penetrating, knowledgeable, knowing. **12** secretive, devious, cunning, shrewd, crafty, canny, clever, knowing, scheming, artful, designing. ● *n.* **1** (*the deep*) the ocean, the sea, the waters, the high seas, *archaic or poet.* the main, *poet.* the wave(s), *Brit. sl.* the briny (deep). **3** see ABYSS 1. **5** dead, middle. ● *adv.* see *deeply* below, *profoundly* (PROFOUND). □ **deep freeze 2** see PAUSE *n.* **deep kiss** French kiss. **deep-rooted, deep-seated** see INGRAINED 1, DEEP *adj.* 7 above. **go off the deep end** see RAGE *v.* □□ **deeply** deep, (far) downward *or* inward, way down, deep down; profoundly, intensely, strongly, powerfully, very (much), really, acutely, keenly, gravely, greatly, to a great extent, extremely, thoroughly, completely, entirely, seriously, severely,

irrevocably, unreservedly; passionately, heavily, emotionally. **deepness** see DEPTH 1, 4.

deepen /deepən/ *v.tr. & intr.* make or become deep or deeper.
■ dig out, scoop (out); intensify, increase, grow, concentrate, strengthen, expand, magnify, extend.

deepening / deepəning/ *n.* the act or process of making deeper, esp. the implementation of measures (such as economic and monetary union) to deepen and strengthen the ties among EC countries.

deer /deer/ *n.* (*pl.* same) any four-hoofed grazing animal of the family Cervidae, the males of which usu. have deciduous branching antlers. □ **deer lick** a spring or damp spot impregnated with salt, etc., where deer come to lick. [OE *dēor* animal, deer]

deerfly /deerflī/ *n.* any bloodsucking fly of the genus *Chrysops*.

deerhound /deerhownd/ *n.* a large, rough-haired greyhound.

deerskin /deerskin/ *n. & adj.* ● *n.* leather from a deer's skin. ● *adj.* made from a deer's skin.

deerstalker /deerstawkər/ *n.* **1** a soft cloth cap with peaks in front and behind and earflaps often joined at the top. **2** a person who stalks deer.

de-escalate /dee-éskəlayt/ *v.tr.* reduce the level or intensity of. □□ **de-escalation** /-láyshən/ *n.*
■ see DECREASE *v.*

deface /difáys/ *v.tr.* **1** spoil the appearance of; disfigure. **2** make illegible. □□ **defaceable** *adj.* **defacement** *n.* **defacer** *n.* [ME f. F *défacer* f. OF *desfacier* (as DE-, FACE)]
■ **1** mar, disfigure, spoil, ruin, deform, blemish, damage, mutilate, harm, impair, injure, destroy.

de facto /di fáktō, day/ *adv., adj., & n.* ● *adv.* in fact, whether by right or not. ● *adj.* that exists or is such in fact (*a de facto ruler*). ● *n.* (in full **de facto wife** or **husband**) a person living with another as if married. [L]
■ *adv.* see REALLY 1.

defalcate /deefálkayt, -fáwl-/ *v.intr. formal* misappropriate property in one's charge, esp. money. □□ **defalcator** *n.* [med.L *defalcare* lop (as DE-, L *falx -cis* sickle)]

defalcation /deefalkáyshən, -fawl-/ *n.* **1** *Law* **a** a misappropriation of money. **b** an amount misappropriated. **2** *formal* a shortcoming. **3** *formal* defection. [ME f. med.L *defalcatio* (as DEFALCATE)]

defame /difáym/ *v.tr.* attack the good reputation of; speak ill of. □□ **defamation** /défəmáyshən/ *n.* **defamatory** /difám-ətawree/ *adj.* **defamer** *n.* [ME f. OF *diffamer*, etc. f. L *diffamare* spread evil report (as DIS-, *fama* report)]

defat /deefát/ *v.tr.* (**defatted, defatting**) remove fat or fats from.

default /difáwlt/ *n. & v.* ● *n.* **1** failure to fulfill an obligation, esp. to appear, pay, or act in some way. **2** lack; absence. **3** a preselected option adopted by a computer program when no alternative is specified by the user or programmer. ● *v.* **1** *intr.* fail to fulfill an obligation, esp. to pay money or to appear in a court of law. **2** *tr.* declare (a party) in default and give judgment against that party. □ **go by default 1** be ignored because of absence. **2** be absent. **in default of** because of the absence of. **judgment by default** judgment given for the plaintiff on the defendant's failure to plead. **win by default** win because an opponent fails to be present. [ME f. OF *defaut(e)* f. *defaillir* fail f. Rmc (as DE-, L *fallere* deceive): cf. FAIL]
■ *n.* **1** failure, fault, defect, neglect, negligence, dereliction, lapse, oversight, nonperformance, nonfulfillment, delinquency, inaction; nonpayment. **2** see LACK *n.* ● *v.* **1** fail, lapse, fall short, come (up) short; (*default on*) neglect.

defaulter /difáwltər/ *n.* a person who defaults, esp. *Brit.* a soldier guilty of a military offense.

defeasance /difeezəns/ *n.* the act or process of rendering null and void. [ME f. OF *defesance* f. *de(s)faire* undo (as DE-, *faire* make f. L *facere*)]

defeasible /difeezibəl/ *adj.* **1** capable of annulment. **2** liable to forfeiture. □□ **defeasibility** *n.* **defeasibly** *adv.* [AF (as DEFEASANCE)]

defeat /difeet/ *v. & n.* ● *v.tr.* **1** overcome in a battle or other

contest. **2** frustrate; baffle. **3** reject (a motion, etc.) by voting. **4** *Law* annul. ● *n.* the act or process of defeating or being defeated. [ME f. OF *deffait, desfait* past part. of *desfaire* f. med.L *disfacere* (as DIS-, L *facere* do)]
■ *v.* **1** overcome, conquer, be victorious over, get the better *or* best of, subdue, overwhelm, overpower, prevail over, triumph over, surpass, bring down, worst, thrash, rout, repulse, overthrow, trounce, whip, crush, destroy, do in, best, *literary* vanquish, *sl.* whop; see also BEAT *v.* 3a. **2** thwart, frustrate, baffle, disappoint, check, balk, stop, terminate, end, finish, destroy; see also FOIL[1] *v.* **3** see *throw out* 6. **4** see CANCEL *v.* 4. ● *n.* conquest, overthrow, beating, repulse, trouncing, rout, *literary* vanquishment; frustration, end.

defeatism /diféetizəm/ *n.* **1** an excessive readiness to accept defeat. **2** conduct conducive to this. □□ **defeatist** *n.* & *adj.* [F *défaitisme* f. *défaite* DEFEAT]
■ see *desperation* (DESPERATE).

defecate /défikayt/ *v.intr.* discharge feces from the body. □□ **defecation** /-káyshən/ *n.* [earlier as adj., = purified, f. L *defaecare* (as DE-, *faex faecis* dregs)]
■ move the bowels, excrete, void, evacuate the bowels, have a (bowel) movement, open the bowels, relieve oneself, *Brit.* pass a motion, *colloq.* mess. □□ **defecation** see *bowel movement* 1.

defect *n.* & *v.* ● *n.* /déefekt, difékt/ **1** lack of something essential or required; imperfection. **2** a shortcoming or failing. **3** a blemish. **4** the amount by which a thing falls short. ● *v.intr.* /difékt/ abandon one's country or cause in favor of another. □□ **defector** *n.* [L *defectus* f. *deficere* desert, fail (as DE-, *facere* do)]
■ *n.* **1, 2** imperfection, deficiency, inadequacy, insufficiency, shortcoming, shortfall, failure, failing, weakness, frailty, weak point, irregularity. **3** blemish, imperfection, irregularity, flaw, fault, mark, stain, mistake, error. ● *v.* desert, change sides *or* loyalties, turn traitor, go over. □□ **defector** deserter, turncoat, traitor, renegade, rat.

defection /difékshən/ *n.* **1** the abandonment of one's country or cause. **2** ceasing in allegiance to a leader, party, religion, or duty. [L *defectio* (as DEFECT)]
■ see SECESSION.

defective /diféktiv/ *adj.* & *n.* ● *adj.* **1** having a defect or defects; incomplete; imperfect; faulty. **2** often *offens.* mentally subnormal. **3** (usu. foll. by *in*) lacking; deficient. **4** *Gram.* not having all the usual inflections. ● *n.* often *offens.* a mentally defective person. □□ **defectively** *adv.* **defectiveness** *n.* [ME f. OF *defectif -ive* or LL *defectivus* (as DEFECT)]
■ *adj.* **1** imperfect, faulty, flawed, deficient, incomplete, broken, out of order, impaired, marred, *sl.* on the blink, on the fritz. **2** retarded, simple, feebleminded, simpleminded, (mentally) deficient *or* incompetent, backward, subnormal, slow, *Brit.* ESN, educationally subnormal. **3** see DEFICIENT 1. □□ **defectiveness** see *inadequacy* (INADEQUATE).

defence *Brit.* var. of DEFENSE.

defend /difénd/ *v.tr.* (also *absol.*) **1** (often foll. by *against, from*) resist an attack made on; protect (a person or thing) from harm or danger. **2** support or uphold by argument; speak or write in favor of. **3** conduct the case for (a defendant in a lawsuit). □□ **defendable** *adj.* **defender** *n.* [ME f. OF *defendre* f. L *defendere*: cf. OFFEND]
■ **1** fortify, arm, secure; protect, watch over, guard, safeguard, keep (safe), shelter, shield, screen, preserve; fight for. **2, 3** plead for, speak *or* stand up for, stick up for, support, uphold, stand by, champion, back, stand with *or* behind *or* beside, argue for *or* in favor of, hold a brief for.

defendant /diféndənt, -ant/ *n.* a person, etc., sued or accused in a court of law. [ME f. OF, part. of *defendre*: see DEFEND]
■ see LITIGANT *n.*

defenestration /deéfenistráyshən/ *n. formal* or *joc.* the action of throwing (esp. a person) out of a window. □□ **defenestrate** /deefénistrayt/ *v.tr.* [mod.L *defenestratio* (as DE-, L *fenestra* window)]

defense /diféns/ *n.* (*Brit.* **defence**) **1** the act of defending from or resisting attack. **2 a** a means of resisting attack. **b** a thing that protects. **c** the military resources of a country. **3** (in *pl.*) fortifications. **4 a** justification; vindication. **b** a speech or piece of writing used to this end. **5 a** the defendant's case in a lawsuit. **b** the counsel for the defendant. **6** /déefens/ **a** the action or role of defending one's goal, etc., against attack. **b** the players on a team who perform this role. □ **defense mechanism 1** the body's reaction against disease organisms. **2** a usu. unconscious mental process to avoid conscious conflict or anxiety. □□ **defenseless** *adj.* **defenselessly** *adv.* **defenselessness** *n.* [ME f. OF *defens(e)* f. LL *defensum, -a,* past part. of *defendere*: see DEFEND]
■ **2 a, b** shelter, cover, guard, safeguard, shield; see also PROTECTION 1b, c. **3** (*defenses*) fortifications, armor, barricades, screen, bulwark(s), ramparts. **4 a** excuse, apology, reason, apologia, explanation; justification, vindication, argument, plea, advocacy, support. □□ **defenseless** unprotected, exposed, vulnerable, unguarded; helpless, weak, powerless, impotent. **defenselessness** susceptibility, vulnerability, insecurity, exposure; helplessness, weakness, frailty, impotence.

defensible /difénsibəl/ *adj.* **1** justifiable; supportable by argument. **2** that can be easily defended militarily. □□ **defensibility** *n.* **defensibly** *adv.* [ME f. LL *defensibilis* (as DEFEND)]
■ **1** see TENABLE.

defensive /difénsiv/ *adj.* **1** done or intended for defense or to defend. **2** (of a person or attitude) concerned to challenge criticism. □ **on the defensive 1** expecting criticism. **2** in an attitude or position of defense. □□ **defensively** *adv.* **defensiveness** *n.* [ME f. F *défensif -ive* f. med.L *defensivus* (as DEFEND)]
■ **1** see PROTECTIVE *adj.* 1.

defer[1] /difər/ *v.tr.* (**deferred, deferring**) **1** put off to a later time; postpone. **2** postpone the conscription of (a person). □ **deferred payment** payment by installments. □□ **deferment** *n.* **deferrable** *adj.* **deferral** *n.* [ME, orig. the same as DIFFER]
■ **1** put off, postpone, delay, shelve, stay, lay *or* put aside, table, carry *or* hold over, remit, shunt, put over. □□ **deferment, deferral** see *postponement* (POSTPONE), STAY[1] *n.* 2.

defer[2] /difər/ *v.intr.* (**deferred, deferring**) (foll. by *to*) yield or make concessions in opinion or action. □□ **deferrer** *n.* [ME f. F *déférer* f. L *deferre* (as DE-, *ferre* bring)]
■ give in, give ground *or* way, yield, submit, bow, capitulate, accede, acquiesce; comply, agree.

deference /défərəns, défrəns/ *n.* **1** courteous regard; respect. **2** compliance with the advice or wishes of another (*pay deference to*). □ **in deference to** out of respect for. [F *déférence* (as DEFER[2])]
■ **1** respect, regard, politeness, civility, courtesy, consideration, esteem. **2** obeisance, submission, acquiescence, obedience, compliance.

deferential /défərénshəl/ *adj.* showing deference; respectful. □□ **deferentially** *adv.* [DEFERENCE, after PRUDENTIAL, etc.]
■ see RESPECTFUL.

defiance /difíəns/ *n.* **1** open disobedience; bold resistance. **2** a challenge to fight or maintain a cause, assertion, etc. □ **in defiance of** disregarding; in conflict with. [ME f. OF (as DEFY)]
■ **1** see RESISTANCE 1. **2** see CHALLENGE *n.* 1.

defiant /difíənt/ *adj.* **1** showing defiance. **2** openly disobedient. □□ **defiantly** *adv.*
■ **1** challenging, bold, brazen, daring, self-willed, stubborn, unyielding, headstrong, recalcitrant, pugnacious, belligerent, antagonistic; see also

/.../ **pronunciation**	● **part of speech**

□ **phrases, idioms, and compounds**
□□ **derivatives** ■ **synonym section**
cross-references appear in SMALL CAPITALS or *italics*

AUDACIOUS 2. **2** rebellious, disobedient, recalcitrant, obstinate, refractory, insubordinate, mutinous, unruly, contumacious.

defibrillation /deéfibriláyshən/ *n. Med.* the stopping of the fibrillation of the heart. □□ **defibrillator** /deefíbrilaytər/ *n.*

deficiency /difíshənsee/ *n.* (*pl.* **-ies**) **1** the state or condition of being deficient. **2** (usu. foll. by *of*) a lack or shortage. **3** a thing lacking. **4** the amount by which a thing, esp. revenue, falls short. □ **deficiency disease** a disease caused by the lack of some essential or important element in the diet.
■ **1, 2** see ABSENCE 3. **3** see DEFECT *n.* 1, 2; OMISSION *n.* 2. **4** see DEFICIT.

deficient /difíshənt/ *adj.* **1** (usu. foll. by *in*) incomplete; not having enough of a specified quality or ingredient. **2** insufficient in quantity, force, etc. **3** (in full **mentally deficient**) incapable of adequate social or intellectual behavior through imperfect mental development. □□ **deficiently** *adv.* [L *deficiens* part. of *deficere* (as DEFECT)]
■ **1** wanting, lacking, short, defective; see also INCOMPLETE. **2** faulty, impaired, flawed, inadequate, insufficient, imperfect, incomplete, defective, inferior, unsatisfactory; sparse, sketchy, skimpy, scarce. **3** see DEFECTIVE *adj.* 2.

deficit /défisit/ *n.* **1** the amount by which a thing (esp. a sum of money) is too small. **2** an excess of liabilities over assets in a given period, esp. a financial year (opp. SURPLUS). □ **deficit financing** financing of (esp. government) spending by borrowing. **deficit spending** spending, esp. by a government, financed by borrowing. [F *déficit* f. L *deficit* 3rd sing. pres. of *deficere* (as DEFECT)]
■ **1** shortfall, shortage, default, loss, deficiency.

defier /difíər/ *n.* a person who defies.

defilade /défiláyd, -laád/ *v. & n.* ● *v.tr.* secure (a fortification) against enfilading fire. ● *n.* this precaution or arrangement. [DEFILE² + -ADE¹]

defile¹ /difíl/ *v.tr.* **1** make dirty; pollute; befoul. **2** corrupt. **3** desecrate; profane. **4** deprive (esp. a woman) of virginity. **5** make ceremonially unclean. □□ **defilement** *n.* **defiler** *n.* [ME *defoul* f. OF *defouler* trample down, outrage (as DE-, *fouler* tread, trample) altered after obs. *befile* f. OE *befylan* (BE-, *fūl* FOUL)]
■ **1** see FOUL *v.* 1. **2** see POISON *v.* 3, 5. **3, 5** see DESECRATE. **4** see DISHONOR *v.* 4.

defile² /difíl/ *n. & v.* ● *n.* /also deéfil/ **1** a narrow way through which troops can only march in file. **2** a gorge. ● *v.intr.* march in file. [F *défiler* and *défilé* past part. (as DE-, FILE²)]
■ *n.* **1, 2** see GORGE *n.* 2.

define /difín/ *v.tr.* **1** give the exact meaning of (a word, etc.). **2** describe or explain the scope of (*define one's position*). **3** make clear, esp. in outline (*well-defined image*). **4** mark out the boundary or limits of. **5** (of properties) make up the total character of. □□ **definable** *adj.* **definer** *n.* [ME f. OF *definer* ult. f. L *definire* (as DE-, *finire* finish, f. *finis* end)]
■ **1** give the meaning of, explain. **2, 3** describe, explain, spell out, detail, delineate, expand on, expatiate on *or* upon; characterize, state, name; see also CLARIFY 1. **4** demarcate, mark off *or* out, delimit, fix, circumscribe, specify, identify, delineate, describe, decide on, determine, establish.

definite /définit/ *adj.* **1** having exact and discernible limits. **2** clear and distinct; not vague. ¶ See the note at *definitive*. □ **definite article** see ARTICLE. **definite integral** see INTEGRAL. □□ **definiteness** *n.* [L *definitus* past part. of *definire* (as DEFINE)]
■ **1** specific, particular, exact, pronounced, explicit, express, precise, certain; firm. **2** clear, plain, well-defined, unambiguous, unequivocal, distinct, clear-cut, obvious, evident.

definitely /définitlee/ *adv. & int.* ● *adv.* **1** in a definite manner. **2** certainly; without doubt (*they were definitely there*). ● *int. colloq.* yes, certainly.
■ *adv.* **1** see *expressly* (EXPRESS²). **2** positively, absolutely, surely, to be sure, assuredly, certainly, indubitably, undoubtedly, without doubt, categorically,

unequivocally, unquestionably, decidedly, plainly, clearly, obviously, patently. ● *int.* see ABSOLUTELY 6.

definition /définíshən/ *n.* **1 a** the act or process of defining. **b** a statement of the meaning of a word or the nature of a thing. **2 a** the degree of distinctness in outline of an object or image (esp. of an image produced by a lens or shown in a photograph or on a motion picture or television screen). **b** making or being distinct in outline. [ME f. OF f. L *definitio* (as DEFINE)]
■ **1** description, explanation, explication, clarification; statement *or* outline (of meaning). **2** delineation, delimitation, demarcation; acutance, acuteness, resolution, distinctness, clarity, sharpness, focus, precision.

definitive /difínitiv/ *adj.* **1** (of an answer, treaty, verdict, etc.) decisive; unconditional; final. ¶ Often confused in this sense with *definite*, which does not have connotations of authority and conclusiveness: *a definite no* is a firm refusal, whereas *a definitive no* is an authoritative judgment or decision that something is not the case. **2** (of an edition of a book, etc.) most authoritative. **3** *Philately* (of a series of stamps) for permanent use, not commemorative, etc. □□ **definitively** *adv.* [ME f. OF *definitif* *-ive* f. L *definitivus* (as DEFINE)]
■ **1** clarifying, unambiguous, categorical, absolute, unqualified; see also FINAL *adj.* 2. **2** consummate, authoritative, reliable, dependable, complete; see also AUTHORITATIVE 1, 3.

deflagrate /déflagrayt/ *v.tr. & intr.* burn away with sudden flame. □□ **deflagration** /-gráyshən/ *n.* **deflagrator** *n.* [L *deflagrare* (as DE-, *flagrare* blaze)]

deflate /difláyt/ *v.* **1 a** *tr.* let air or gas out of (a tire, balloon, etc.). **b** *intr.* be emptied of air or gas. **2 a** *tr.* cause to lose confidence or conceit. **b** *intr.* lose confidence. **3** *Econ.* & *tr.* subject (a currency or economy) to deflation. **b** *intr.* pursue a policy of deflation. **4** *tr.* reduce the importance of, depreciate. □□ **deflator** *n.* [DE- + INFLATE]
■ **2 a** see MORTIFY 1.

deflation /difláyshən/ *n.* **1** the act or process of deflating or being deflated. **2** *Econ.* reduction of the amount of money in circulation to increase its value as a measure against inflation. **3** *Geol.* the removal of particles of rock, etc., by the wind. □□ **deflationary** *adj.* **deflationist** *n.*

deflect /diflékt/ *v.* **1** *tr. & intr.* bend or turn aside from a straight course or intended purpose. **2** (often foll. by *from*) **a** *tr.* cause to deviate. **b** *intr.* deviate. [L *deflectere* (as DE-, *flectere flex-* bend)]
■ avert, turn away *or* aside, divert, sidetrack, *Physics* scatter, refract; fend off; deviate, swerve, veer, bend, swing away, turn off.

deflection /diflékshən/ *n.* (also *Brit.* **deflexion**) **1** the act or process of deflecting or being deflected. **2** a lateral bend or turn; a deviation. **3** *Physics* the displacement of a pointer on an instrument from its zero position. [LL *deflexio* (as DEFLECT)]
■ **1, 2** see SHIFT *n.* 1a.

deflector /difléktər/ *n.* a thing that deflects, esp. a device for deflecting a flow of air, etc.

defloration /deéflawráyshən/ *n.* deflowering. [ME f. OF or f. LL *defloratio* (as DEFLOWER)]
■ see RAPE¹ *n.* 1.

deflower /diflówr/ *v.tr.* **1** deprive (esp. a woman) of virginity. **2** ravage; spoil. **3** strip of flowers. [ME f. OF *deflourer*, *des-*, ult. f. LL *deflorare* (as DE-, L *flos floris* flower)]
■ **1** see DISHONOR *v.* 4.

defocus /deefókəs/ *v.tr. & intr.* (**defocused, defocusing** or **defocussed, defocussing**) put or go out of focus.

defoliate /deefóleeayt/ *v.tr.* remove leaves from, esp. as a military tactic. □□ **defoliant** *n. & adj.* **defoliation** /-áyshən/ *n.* **defoliator** *n.* [LL *defoliare* f. *folium* leaf]
■ see BARE *v.* 1.

deforest /deefáwrist, -fór-/ *v.tr.* clear of forests or trees. □□ **deforestation** *n.*

deform /difáwrm/ *v.* **1** *tr.* make ugly; deface. **2** *tr.* put out of shape; misshape. **3** *intr.* undergo deformation; be deformed.

□□ **deformable** *adj.* [ME f. OF *deformer*, etc., f. med.L *difformare* ult. f. L *deformare* (as DE-, *formare* f. *forma* shape)]
■ **1** see DEFACE. **2** see DISTORT 1a.

deformation /deéfawrmáyshən/ *n.* **1** disfigurement. **2** *Physics* **a** (often foll. by *of*) change in shape. **b** a quantity representing the amount of this change. **3** a perverted form of a word (e.g., *dang* for *damn*). □□ **deformational** *adj.* [ME f. OF *deformation* or L *deformatio* (as DEFORM)]
■ **1** see BLEMISH *n.*, WARP *n.* 1.

deformed /difáwrmd/ *adj.* (of a person or limb) misshapen.
■ misshapen, malformed, distorted, twisted, grotesque, gnarled, crooked, contorted, awry, warped, bent; disfigured.

deformity /difáwrmitee/ *n.* (*pl.* **-ies**) **1** the state of being deformed; ugliness; disfigurement. **2** a malformation, esp. of body or limb. **3** a moral defect; depravity. [ME f. OF *deformité*, etc., f. L *deformitas -tatis* f. *deformis* (as DE-, *forma* shape)]
■ **2** see ABNORMALITY 2.

defraud /difráwd/ *v.tr.* (often foll. by *of*) cheat by fraud. □□ **defrauder** *n.* [ME f. OF *defrauder* or L *defraudare* (as DE-, FRAUD)]
■ cheat, swindle, trick, beguile, dupe, delude, fool, fleece, take in, deceive, humbug, hoodwink, flimflam, rook, *colloq.* do, put one over on, pull a fast one on, rip off, pull the wool over a person's eyes, *literary* cozen, *sl.* take for a ride, bilk, clean out, take to the cleaners, gyp, con; (*defraud of*) do a person out of. □□ **defrauder** see FRAUD 3.

defray /difráy/ *v.tr.* provide money to pay (a cost or expense). □□ **defrayable** *adj.* **defrayal** *n.* **defrayment** *n.* [F *défrayer* (as DE-, obs. *frai(t)* cost, f. med.L *fredum, -us* fine for breach of the peace)]
■ pay, settle, meet, discharge, liquidate, clear, cover, reimburse; (*defray the cost*) pick up the bill, foot the bill, *colloq.* pick up the tab *or* check. □□ **defrayment** see PAY¹ *n.*

defrock /deefrók/ *v.tr.* deprive (a person, esp. a priest) of ecclesiastical status. [F *défroquer* (as DE-, FROCK)]

defrost /difráwst, -fróst/ *v.* **1** *tr.* **a** free (the interior of a refrigerator) of excess frost, usu. by turning it off for a period. **b** remove frost or ice from (esp. the windshield of a motor vehicle). **2** *tr.* unfreeze (frozen food). **3** *intr.* become unfrozen. □□ **defroster** *n.*
■ **1a, 2, 3** see THAW *v.* 1, 5.

deft /deft/ *adj.* neatly skillful or dexterous; adroit. □□ **deftly** *adv.* **deftness** *n.* [ME, var. of DAFT in obs. sense 'meek']
■ see DEXTEROUS.

defunct /difúngkt/ *adj.* **1** no longer existing. **2** no longer used or in fashion. **3** dead or extinct. □□ **defunctness** *n.* [L *defunctus* dead, past part. of *defungi* (as DE-, *fungi* perform)]
■ **1, 2** inoperative, inapplicable, unused, unusable, invalid, expired, obsolete, passé, nonexistent, outmoded, out. **3** see DEAD *adj.* 1.

defuse /deefyo͞oz/ *v.tr.* **1** remove the fuse from (an explosive device). **2** reduce the tension or potential danger in (a crisis, difficulty, etc.).
■ **2** see MODERATE *v.* 1.

defy /difí/ *v.tr.* (**-ies, -ied**) **1** resist openly; refuse to obey. **2** (of a thing) present insuperable obstacles to (*defies solution*). **3** (foll. by *to* + infin.) challenge (a person) to do or prove something. **4** *archaic* challenge to combat. [ME f. OF *defier* f. Rmc (as DIS-, L *fidus* faithful)]
■ **1** resist; disobey, flout, go against, thumb one's nose at, *sl.* cock a snook at. **2** frustrate, thwart, baffle, confound; resist, withstand. **3** challenge, dare, invite, summon.

deg. *abbr.* degree.

dégagé /daygaazháy/ *adj.* (*fem.* **dégagée**) easy; unconstrained. [F, past part. of *dégager* set free]
■ see EASY *adj.* 3.

degas /deegás/ *v.tr.* (**degassed, degassing**) remove unwanted gas from.

degauss /deegóws/ *v.tr.* neutralize the magnetism in (a

thing) by encircling it with a current-carrying conductor. □□ **degausser** *n.* [DE + GAUSS]

degenerate *adj., n.,* & *v.* ● *adj.* /dijénərət/ **1** having lost the qualities that are normal and desirable or proper to its kind; fallen from former excellence. **2** *Biol.* having changed to a lower type. ● *n.* /dijénərət/ a degenerate person or animal. ● *v.intr.* /dijénərayt/ become degenerate. □□ **degeneracy** *n.* **degenerately** *adv.* [L *degeneratus* past part. of *degenerare* (as DE-, *genus -eris* race)]
■ *adj.* **1** debased, degraded, corrupt, corrupted, vitiated, decadent, depraved, reprobate, dissolute; ignoble, base, low, inferior, vile. ● *n.* reprobate, debauchee, wastrel, profligate, rake, roué; pervert, deviate, deviant. ● *v.* decline, deteriorate, decay, worsen, degrade; backslide, regress, retrogress, go to rack and ruin, *colloq.* go to pot, *sl.* go to the dogs.

degeneration /dijénəráyshən/ *n.* **1 a** the process of becoming degenerate. **b** the state of being degenerate. **2** *Med.* morbid deterioration of tissue or change in its structure. [ME f. F *dégénération* or f. LL *degeneratio* (as DEGENERATE)]
■ **1** see DECAY *n.* 2.

degenerative /dijénərətiv/ *adj.* **1** of or tending to degeneration. **2** (of disease) characterized by progressive often irreversible deterioration.

degrade /digráyd/ *v.* **1** *tr.* reduce to a lower rank, esp. as a punishment. **2** *tr.* bring into dishonor or contempt. **3** *tr. Chem.* reduce to a simpler molecular structure. **4** *tr. Physics* reduce (energy) to a less convertible form. **5** *tr. Geol.* wear down (rocks, etc.) by disintegration. **6** *intr.* degenerate. **7** *intr. Chem.* disintegrate. □□ **degradable** *adj.* **degradation** /dégrədáyshən/ *n.* **degradative** /-dáytiv/ *adj.* **degrader** *n.* [ME f. OF *degrader* f. eccl.L *degradare* (as DE-, L *gradus* step)]
■ **1** see DOWNGRADE *v.* 1. **2** reduce, lower, debase, abase, demean, dishonor, disgrace, humble, shame; humiliate, mortify, belittle, deprecate, depreciate, cheapen. **5** see ERODE. **6** see DEGENERATE *v.* □□ **degradation** degeneracy, degeneration, deterioration, corruptness, corruption, vitiation, baseness, depravity, *formal* turpitude; disrepute, discredit, shame, humiliation, ignominy, dishonor, disgrace, abasement, debasement.

degrading /digráyding/ *adj.* humiliating; causing a loss of self-respect. □□ **degradingly** *adv.*
■ demeaning, humiliating, shameful, debasing, lowering, ignominious, inglorious, unedifying; menial.

degrease /deegrees/ *v.tr.* remove unwanted grease or fat from.

degree /digrée/ *n.* **1** a stage in an ascending or descending scale, series, or process. **2** a stage in intensity or amount (*to a high degree; in some degree*). **3** relative condition (*each is good in its degree*). **4** *Math.* a unit of measurement of angles, one-ninetieth of a right angle or the angle subtended by one-three-hundred-and-sixtieth of the circumference of a circle. ¶ Symb.: ° (as in *45°*). **5** *Physics* a unit in a scale of temperature, hardness, etc. ¶ Abbr.: **deg.** (or omitted in the Kelvin scale of temperature). **6** *Med.* an extent of burns on a scale characterized by the destruction of the skin. **7** an academic rank conferred by a college or university after examination or after completion of a course, or conferred as an honor on a distinguished person. **8** a grade of crime or criminality (*murder in the first degree*). **9** a step in direct genealogical descent. **10** social or official rank. **11** *Math.* the highest power of unknowns or variables in an equation, etc. (*equation of the third degree*). **12** a masonic rank. **13** a thing placed like a step in a series; a tier or row. **14** *Mus.* the classification of a note by its position in the scale. □ **by degrees** a little at a time; gradually. **degree-day** a unit of measurement equal to one degree of variation between a standard temperature and the mean temperature on a given day. **degree of free-**

dom 1 *Physics* the independent direction in which motion can occur. **2** *Chem.* the number of independent factors required to specify a system at equilibrium. **3** *Statistics* the number of independent values or quantities that can be assigned to a statistical distribution. **degrees of comparison** see COMPARISON. **forbidden (or prohibited) degrees** a number of degrees of descent too few to allow marriage between two related persons. **to a degree** *colloq.* considerably. □□ **degreeless** *adj.* [ME f. OF *degré* f. Rmc (as DE-, L *gradus* step)]

■ **1** see STAGE *n.* 1. **2** measure, magnitude, extent, limit; amount, intensity. **10** grade, level, class, caste, rank, order, standing, status, station, position, situation, condition, *archaic or literary* estate. □ **by degrees** gradually, little by little, bit by bit, step by step, inch by inch, piecemeal, inchmeal, slowly. **to a degree** substantially, considerably, quite, decidedly, to a considerable extent.

degressive /digréssiv/ *adj.* **1** (of taxation) at successively lower rates on low amounts. **2** reducing in amount. [L *degredi* (as DE-, *gradi* walk)]

de haut en bas /də ŏt en báa/ *adv.* in a condescending or superior manner. [F, = from above to below]

dehisce /dihíss/ *v.intr.* gape or burst open (esp. of a pod or seed vessel or of a cut or wound). □□ **dehiscence** *n.* **dehiscent** *adj.* [L *dehiscere* (as DE-, *hiscere* incept. of *hiare* gape)]

dehorn /deeháwrn/ *v.tr.* remove the horns from (an animal).

dehumanize /deehyōōmənīz/ *v.tr.* **1** deprive of human characteristics. **2** make impersonal or machinelike. □□ **dehumanization** *n.*

dehumidify /deehyōōmidifī/ *v.tr.* (**-ies, -ied**) reduce the degree of humidity of; remove moisture from (a gas, esp. air). □□ **dehumidification** /-fikáyshən/ *n.* **dehumidifier** *n.*

dehydrate /deehīdráyt/ *v.* **1** *tr.* **a** remove water from (esp. foods for preservation and storage in bulk). **b** make dry, esp. make (the body) deficient in water. **c** render lifeless or uninteresting. **2** *intr.* lose water. □□ **dehydration** /-dráyshən/ *n.* **dehydrator** *n.*

■ **1a, b, 2** see DRY *v.*

dehydrogenate /deehīdrójinayt/ *v.tr. Chem.* remove a hydrogen atom or atoms from (a compound). □□ **dehydrogenation** /-náyshən/ *n.*

deice /deeíss/ *v.tr.* **1** remove ice from. **2** prevent the formation of ice on.

■ **1** see THAW *v.* 1, 5.

deicer /deeíssər/ *n.* a device or substance for deicing, esp. a windshield or an aircraft.

deicide /dée-isīd, dáy-/ *n.* **1** the killer of a god. **2** the killing of a god. [eccl.L *deicida* f. L *deus* god + -CIDE]

deictic /díktik/ *adj. & n. Philol. & Gram.* ● *adj.* pointing; demonstrative. ● *n.* a deictic word. [Gk *deiktikos* f. *deiktos* capable of proof f. *deiknumi* show]

deify /dée-ifī, dáyee-/ *v.tr.* (**-ies, -ied**) **1** make a god of. **2** regard or worship as a god. □□ **deification** /-fikáyshən/ *n.* [ME f. OF *deifier* f. eccl.L *deificare* f. *deus* god]

■ see IDOLIZE.

deign /dayn/ *v.* **1** *intr.* (foll. by *to* + infin.) think fit; condescend. **2** *tr.* (usu. with *neg.*) *archaic* condescend to give (an answer, etc.). [ME f. OF *degnier, deigner, daigner* f. L *dignare, -ari* deem worthy f. *dignus* worthy]

■ condescend, stoop, lower oneself, think fit, *formal* vouchsafe.

Dei gratia /dáyee gráatee・ə, deéī, gráasheeə/ *adv.* by the grace of God. [L]

deinstitutionalize /deeínstitōōshənəlīz, -tyōō-/ *v.tr.* (usu. as **deinstitutionalized** *adj.*) remove from an institution or from the effects of institutional life. □□ **deinstitutionalization** *n.*

deionize /deeíənīz/ *v.tr.* remove the ions or ionic constituents from (water, air, etc.). □□ **deionization** /-izáyshən/ *n.* **deionizer** *n.*

deipnosophist /dīpnósəfist/ *n.* a person skilled in dining and table talk. [Gk *deipnosophistēs* (in pl. as title of a work by Athenaeus (3rd c.) describing long discussions at a banquet) f. *deipnon* dinner + *sophistēs* wise man: see SOPHIST]

■ see CONVERSATIONALIST.

deism /deéizəm, dáy-/ *n.* belief in the existence of a supreme being arising from reason rather than revelation (cf. THEISM). □□ **deist** *n.* **deistic** *adj.* **deistical** *adj.* [L *deus* god + -ISM]

deity /deéitee, dáy-/ *n.* (*pl.* **-ies**) **1** a god or goddess. **2** divine status, quality, or nature. **3** (**the Deity**) the Creator, God. [ME f. OF *deité* f. eccl.L *deitas -tatis* transl. Gk *theotēs* f. *theos* god]

■ **1** goddess, supreme being, creator, divinity; see also GOD *n.* 1. **3** the Creator, God, the Supreme Being.

déjà vu /dáyzhaa vōō/ *n.* **1** *Psychol.* an illusory feeling of having already experienced a present situation. **2** something tediously familiar. [F, = already seen]

deject /dijékt/ *v.tr.* (usu. as **dejected** *adj.*) make sad or dispirited; depress. □□ **dejectedly** *adv.* [ME f. L *dejicere* (DE-, *jacēre* throw)]

■ (**dejected**) downcast, downhearted, depressed, dispirited, discouraged, despondent, down, low, chapfallen, crestfallen; melancholy, sad, unhappy, gloomy, glum, miserable, blue, low-spirited, in low spirits, forlorn, woebegone, disconsolate, sorrowful, morose, heartbroken, heavyhearted, in the doldrums, *colloq.* down in the dumps, down in the mouth. □□ **dejectedly** see *sadly* (SAD).

dejection /dijékshən/ *n.* a dejected state; low spirits. [ME f. L *dejectio* (as DEJECT)]

■ see DEPRESSION 1b.

de jure /dee jōōree, day jōōray/ *adj. & adv.* ● *adj.* rightful. ● *adv.* rightfully; by right. [L]

■ *adj.* see LEGITIMATE *adj.* 1, 2.

dekko /dékō/ *n.* (*pl.* **-os**) *Brit. sl.* a look or glance (*took a quick dekko*). [Hindi *dekho*, imper. of *dekhnā* look]

Del. *abbr.* Delaware.

Delaware /déləwair/ *n.* **1 a** a N. American people native to the northeastern US. **b** a member of this people. **2** the language of this people. Also called **Lenape** or **Lenni Lenape**.

delate /dilávt/ *v.tr. archaic* **1** inform against; impeach (a person). **2** report (an offense). □□ **delation** /-láyshən/ *n.* **delator** *n.* [L *delat-* (as DE-, *lat-* past part. stem of *ferre* carry)]

delay /diláy/ *v. & n.* ● *v.* **1** *tr.* postpone; defer. **2** *tr.* make late (*was delayed by the traffic lights*). **3** *intr.* loiter; be late (*don't delay!*). ● *n.* **1** the act or an instance of delaying; the process of being delayed. **2** time lost by inaction or the inability to proceed. **3** a hindrance. □ **delayed-action** (*attrib.*) (esp. of a bomb, camera, etc.) operating some time after being primed or set. **delay line** *Electr.* a device producing a desired delay in the transmission of a signal. □□ **delayer** *n.* [ME f. OF *delayer* (v.), *delai* (n.), prob. f. *des-* DIS- + *laier* leave: see RELAY]

■ *v.* **1** postpone, put off *or* aside, defer, break off, suspend, shelve, hold off *or* up (on), cut off *or* short, put on hold, hold in abeyance, table, pigeonhole, *colloq.* put on the back burner, put on ice. **2** hold up *or* back, detain, retard, keep, set back, slow (up *or* down), impede, hinder, bog down. **3** loiter, procrastinate, temporize, hesitate, drag (along), drag one's feet *or* heels, wait, lag (behind), dawdle, hang back *or* about, stall, linger, dither, dally, mark time, shilly-shally, potter, *archaic or literary* tarry, *colloq.* dillydally. ● *n.* **1, 2** postponement, deferral, deferment, holdup, setback, hitch, snag, lull, interlude, hiatus, interruption, gap, interval, lacuna, stop, stoppage, wait, waiting, suspension. **3** see HINDRANCE.

dele /deélee/ *v. & n. Printing* ● *v.tr.* (**deled, deleing**) delete or mark for deletion (a letter, word, etc., struck out of a text). ● *n.* a sign marking something to be deleted; a deletion. [L, imper. of *delēre*: see DELETE]

delectable /diléktəbəl/ *adj.* esp. *literary* delightful; pleasant. □□ **delectability** /-bílitee/ *n.* **delectably** *adv.* [ME f. OF f. L *delectabilis* f. *delectare* DELIGHT]

■ see PLEASANT.

delectation /deélektáyshən/ *n. literary* pleasure; enjoyment (*sang for his delectation*). [ME f. OF (as DELECTABLE)]

■ delight, enjoyment, amusement, entertainment, diversion, pleasure, satisfaction.

delegacy /déligəsee/ n. (pl. **-ies**) **1** a system of delegating. **2 a** an appointment as a delegate. **b** a body of delegates; a delegation.

delegate n. & v. ● n. /déligət/ **1** an elected representative sent to a conference. **2** a member of a committee. **3** a member of a deputation. ● v.tr. /déligayt/ **1** (often foll. by to) commit (authority, power, etc.) to an agent or deputy. **b** entrust (a task) to another person. **2** send or authorize (a person) as a representative; depute. □□ **delegable** /-gəbəl/ adj. [ME f. L delegatus (as DE-, legare depute)]

■ n. **1, 3** envoy, agent, representative, ambassador, plenipotentiary, minister, emissary, commissioner, (papal) nuncio, spokesperson, spokesman, spokeswoman, go-between, archaic legate. **2** committee member. ● v. **1** assign, give, hand over or on, pass over or on, depute, transfer, entrust. **2** depute, commission, appoint, designate, assign, name, nominate, accredit, authorize, empower, mandate.

delegation /déligáyshən/ n. **1** a body of delegates; a deputation. **2** the act or process of delegating or being delegated. [L delegatio (as DELEGATE)]

■ **1** see MISSION 3.

delete /dileét/ v.tr. remove or obliterate (written or printed matter), esp. by striking out. □□ **deletion** /-leéshən/ n. [L delēre delet- efface]

■ erase, cancel, rub out or off, cross out or off, remove, blot out, expunge, efface, eliminate, obliterate, wipe out, eradicate, strike out, cut or edit (out), blue-pencil, Printing dele.

deleterious /délitéereeəs/ adj. harmful (to the mind or body). □□ **deleteriously** adv. [med.L deleterius f. Gk dēlētērios noxious]

■ see HARMFUL.

delft /delft/ n. (also **delftware** /délftwair/) glazed, usu. blue and white, earthenware, made in Delft in Holland.

deli /délee/ n. (pl. **delis**) colloq. a delicatessen. [abbr.]

deliberate adj. & v. ● adj. /dilíbərət/ **1 a** intentional (a deliberate foul). **b** fully considered; not impulsive (made a deliberate choice). **2** slow in deciding; cautious (a ponderous and deliberate mind). **3** (of movement, etc.) leisurely and unhurried. ● v. /dilíbərayt/ **1** intr. think carefully; take counsel (the jury deliberated for an hour). **2** tr. consider; discuss carefully (deliberated the question). □□ **deliberately** /dilíbərətlee/ adv. **deliberateness** n. **deliberator** n. [L deliberatus past part. of deliberare (as DE-, librare weigh f. libra balance)]

■ adj. **1 a** intentional, planned, studied, willful, intended, premeditated, calculated, conscious, purposeful, preconceived, considered. **1b, 2** confident, considered, calm, dispassionate, composed; careful, prudent, cautious, painstaking, considered, considerate, thoughtful, well-thought-out, thorough, methodical, systematic, fastidious, orderly, punctilious. **3** slow, methodical, careful, unhurried, paced, measured, regular, even, steady, sure, unhesitating, unfaltering, leisurely. ● v. **1** ponder, take counsel, think, meditate, reflect, cogitate, ruminate. **2** consider, discuss, think about or over, weigh, debate, meditate on or over, reflect on or over, cogitate on or over, ruminate on or over, study. □□ **deliberately** intentionally, on purpose, purposely, willfully, consciously, wittingly, calculatedly, calculatingly, knowingly, pointedly, of one's (own) free will, with one's eyes (wide) open.

deliberation /dilíbəráyshən/ n. **1** careful consideration. **2 a** the discussion of reasons for and against. **b** a debate or discussion. **3 a** caution and care. **b** (of action or behavior) purposefulness; deliberateness. **c** (of movement) slowness or ponderousness. [ME f. OF f. L deliberatio -onis (as DELIBERATE)]

■ **1** see CONSIDERATION 1. **2** see DISCUSSION 2.

deliberative /dilíbərətiv, -ráytiv/ adj. of, or appointed for the purpose of, deliberation or debate (a deliberative assembly). □□ **deliberatively** adv. **deliberativeness** n. [F délibératif -ive or L deliberativus (as DELIBERATE)]

delicacy /délikəsee/ n. (pl. **-ies**) **1** (esp. in craftsmanship or artistic or natural beauty) fineness or intricacy of structure or texture; gracefulness. **2** susceptibility to injury or disease; weakness. **3** the quality of requiring discretion or sensitivity (a situation of some delicacy). **4** a choice or expensive food. **5 a** consideration for the feelings of others. **b** avoidance of immodesty or vulgarity. **6** (esp. in a person, a sense, or an instrument) accuracy of perception; sensitiveness. [ME f. DELICATE + -ACY]

■ **1** fineness, delicateness, grace, gracefulness, exquisiteness, daintiness; see also BEAUTY 1. **2** fragility, frailty, frailness, weakness, infirmity, feebleness, delicateness, tenderness. **3** sensitivity, sensitiveness, delicateness, difficulty, ticklishness, nicety, trickiness, awkwardness. **4** luxury, sweetmeat, dainty, tidbit, treat, morsel, archaic comfit. **5** consideration, tactfulness, tact, considerateness, thoughtfulness, discretion, discernment, sensitivity, sensibility, delicateness, finesse, artfulness, care. **6** sensitivity, sensitiveness; see also ACCURACY.

delicate /délikət/ adj. **1 a** fine in texture or structure; soft, slender, or slight. **b** of exquisite quality or workmanship. **c** (of color) subtle or subdued; not bright. **d** subtle; hard to appreciate. **2 a** (of a person) easily injured; susceptible to illness. **b** (of a thing) easily spoiled or damaged. **3 a** requiring careful handling; tricky (a delicate situation). **b** (of an instrument) highly sensitive. **4** deft (a delicate touch). **5** (of a person) avoiding the immodest or offensive. **6** (esp. of actions) considerate. **7** (of food) dainty; suitable for an invalid. □ **in a delicate condition** archaic pregnant. □□ **delicately** adv. **delicateness** n. [ME f. OF delicat or L delicatus, of unkn. orig.]

■ **1 a** fine, exquisite, dainty, graceful, slender, slight, airy, elegant, subtle, soft. **c** subtle, subdued, muted, soft, faint, pale, light, pastel. **d** see SUBTLE 2. **2 a** feeble, weak, sickly, frail, debilitated, weakened, unhealthy. **b** fragile, breakable, frail, tender, frangible, dainty, flimsy. **3 a** ticklish, sensitive, tricky, difficult, touchy, awkward, colloq. sticky, sl. hairy. **5, 6** tactful, considerate, thoughtful, discreet, sensitive, discriminating, discerning, proper. □ **in a delicate condition** see PREGNANT 1. □□ **delicateness** see DELICACY 1–3, 5–6.

delicatessen /délikətésən/ n. **1** a store selling cooked meats, cheeses, and unusual or foreign prepared foods. **2** (often attrib.) such foods collectively (a delicatessen counter). [G Delikatessen or Du. delicatessen f. F délicatesse f. délicat (as DELICATE)]

Delicious /dilíshəs/ n. a red or yellow variety of apple cultivated orig. in the US.

delicious /dilíshəs/ adj. **1** highly delightful and enjoyable to the taste or sense of smell. **2** (of a joke, etc.) very witty. □□ **deliciously** adv. **deliciousness** n. [ME f. OF f. LL deliciosus f. L deliciae delight]

■ **1** luscious, ambrosial, savory, mouthwatering, toothsome, choice, flavorful, tasty, appetizing, palatable, colloq. scrumptious, yummy, esp. Brit. colloq. scrummy, literary delectable.

delict /dilíkt/ n. archaic a violation of the law; an offense. [L delictum neut. past part. of delinquere offend (as DE-, linquere leave)]

delight /dilít/ v. & n. ● v. **1** tr. (often foll. by with, or that + clause, or to + infin.) please greatly (the gift delighted them; was delighted with the result; was delighted that you won; would be delighted to help). **2** intr. (often foll. by in, or to + infin.) take great pleasure; be highly pleased (he delighted in her success; they delight to humor him). ● n. **1** great pleasure. **2** something giving pleasure (her singing is a delight). □□ **de-**

/.../ pronunciation	● part of speech
□ phrases, idioms, and compounds	
□□ derivatives	■ synonym section
cross-references appear in SMALL CAPITALS or italics	

lighted *adj.* **delightedly** *adv.* [ME f. OF *delitier, delit,* f. L *delectare* frequent. of *delicere*: alt. after *light,* etc.]
▪ *v.* **1** please, gratify, satisfy, gladden, cheer, tickle, amuse, entertain, divert, excite, thrill, captivate, entrance, fascinate. **2** (*delight in*) relish, revel in, glory in, love, adore, enjoy, appreciate, like, savor, *colloq.* get a kick from *or* out of. ● *n.* **1** pleasure, gratification, joy, satisfaction, enjoyment, *literary* delectation; bliss, ecstasy, rapture. ▫▫ **delighted** pleased, happy, charmed, thrilled, enchanted, *colloq.* tickled pink *or* to death.

delightful /dilítfŏŏl/ *adj.* causing great delight; pleasant; charming. ▫▫ **delightfully** *adv.* **delightfulness** *n.*
▪ pleasing, agreeable, pleasurable, enjoyable, joyful, pleasant, lovely, amusing, entertaining, diverting, thrilling; attractive, congenial, winning, winsome, charming, engaging; captivating, ravishing, fascinating, entrancing, enchanting.

Delilah /dilílə/ *n.* a seductive and wily temptress. [*Delilah,* betrayer of Samson (Judges 16)]

delimit /dilímit/ *v.tr.* **1** determine the limits of. **2** fix the territorial boundary of. ▫▫ **delimitation** /-táyshən/ *n.* [F *délimiter* f. L *delimitare* (as DE-, *limitare* f. *limes -itis* boundary)]
▪ **1** see RESTRICT.

delimitate /dilímitayt/ *v.tr.* = DELIMIT.

delineate /dilíneeayt/ *v.tr.* portray by drawing, etc., or in words (*delineated her character*). ▫▫ **delineation** /-áyshən/ *n.* **delineator** *n.* [L *delineare delineat-* (as DE-, *lineare* f. *linea* line)]

delinquency /dilíngkwənsee/ *n.* (*pl.* -ies) **1 a** a crime, usu. not of a serious kind; a misdeed. **b** minor crime in general, esp. that of young people (*juvenile delinquency*). **2** wickedness (*moral delinquency; an act of delinquency*). **3** neglect of one's duty. [eccl. L *delinquentia* f. L *delinquens* part. of *delinquere* (as DELICT)]
▪ **1 a** see MISDEED. **b** see *misbehavior* (MISBEHAVE). **3** see DEFAULT *n.* 1.

delinquent /dilíngkwənt/ *n.* & *adj.* ● *n.* an offender (*juvenile delinquent*). ● *adj.* **1** guilty of a minor crime or a misdeed. **2** failing in one's duty. **3** in arrears. ▫▫ **delinquently** *adv.*
▪ *n.* malefactor, (young *or* youthful) offender, wrongdoer, lawbreaker, criminal, miscreant; hooligan, ruffian. ● *adj.* **2** neglectful, negligent, derelict, remiss, failing. **3** in arrears, overdue, past due, late, unpaid, behindhand.

deliquesce /délikwés/ *v.intr.* **1** become liquid; melt. **2** *Chem.* dissolve in water absorbed from the air. ▫▫ **deliquescence** *n.* **deliquescent** *adj.* [L *deliquescere* (as DE-, *liquescere* incept. of *liquēre* be liquid)]
▪ **1** see MELT *v.* 1, 2, 4.

delirious /dilíreeəs/ *adj.* **1** affected with delirium; temporarily or apparently mad; raving. **2** wildly excited; ecstatic. **3** (of behavior) betraying delirium or ecstasy. ▫▫ **deliriously** *adv.*
▪ **1** wild, hysterical, distracted, incoherent, rambling, irrational, raving, ranting, frenzied, frantic, crazed, disturbed, demented, deranged, unhinged; mad, *colloq.* crazy. **2** wild, excited, thrilled; see also ECSTATIC *adj.* 1, 2.

delirium /dilíreeəm/ *n.* **1** an acutely disordered state of mind involving incoherent speech, hallucinations, and frenzied excitement, occurring in metabolic disorders, intoxication, fever, etc. **2** great excitement; ecstasy. ▫ **delirium tremens** /tréemənz, -menz/ a psychosis of chronic alcoholism involving tremors and hallucinations. [L f. *delirare* be deranged (as DE-, *lira* ridge between furrows)]

deliver /dilívər/ *v.tr.* **1 a** distribute (letters, packages, ordered goods, etc.) to the addressee or the purchaser. **b** (often foll. by *to*) hand over (*delivered the boy safely to his teacher*). **2** (often foll. by *from*) save, rescue, or set free (*delivered him from his enemies*). **3 a** give birth to (*delivered a girl*). **b** (in *passive*; often foll. by *of*) give birth (*was delivered of a child*). **c** assist at the birth of (*delivered six babies that week*). **d** assist in giving birth (*delivered the patient successfully*). **4 a** (often *refl.*) utter or recite (an opinion, a speech, etc.) (*delivered himself of the observation; delivered the sermon well*). **b** (of a

judge) pronounce (a judgment). **5** (often foll. by *up, over*) abandon; resign; hand over (*delivered his soul up to God*). **6** present or render (an account). **7** launch or aim (a blow, a ball, or an attack). **8** *Law* hand over formally (esp. a sealed deed to a grantee). **9** *colloq.* = deliver the goods. **10** cause (voters, etc.) to support a candidate. ▫ **deliver the goods** *colloq.* carry out one's part of an agreement. ▫▫ **deliverable** *adj.* **deliverer** *n.* [ME f. OF *delivrer* f. Gallo-Roman (as DE-, LIBERATE)]
▪ **1 a** carry, bring, convey, distribute, give *or* hand out, take, cart, transport; purvey. **2** set free, liberate, extricate, release, save, rescue, emancipate, redeem, disencumber, disburden, *hist.* enfranchise, manumit. **3 a** bring forth, bear, give birth to, bring into the world, have; drop. **4 a** give, present, utter, recite, read, broadcast, give out; set forth, communicate, publish, hand over, hand out. **b** set forth, make known, express, promulgate, pronounce, hand down. **5** hand over, give, surrender, cede, yield, make over, relinquish, give up *or* over, commit, transfer, turn over, resign, abandon. **7** give, administer, inflict, deal, direct, aim, send, launch, impart, throw; cast, hurl, shoot, discharge, fire.
▫ **deliver the goods** perform, do one's bit, fulfill one's side of the bargain.

deliverance /dilívərəns/ *n.* **1 a** the act or an instance of rescuing; the process of being rescued. **b** a rescue. **2** a formally expressed opinion. [ME f. OF *delivrance* (as DELIVER)]
▪ **1** liberation, release, delivery, emancipation, relief, rescue; salvation.

delivery /dilívəree/ *n.* (*pl.* -ies) **1 a** the delivering of letters, etc. **b** a regular distribution of letters, etc. (*two deliveries a day*). **c** something delivered. **2 a** the process of childbirth. **b** an act of this. **3** deliverance. **4 a** an act of throwing, esp. of a cricket ball. **b** the style of such an act (*a good delivery*). **5** the act of giving or surrendering (*delivery of the town to the enemy*). **6 a** the uttering of a speech, etc. **b** the manner or style of such a delivery (*a measured delivery*). **7** *Law* **a** the formal handing over of property. **b** the transfer of a deed to a grantee or a third party. ▫ **take delivery of** receive (something purchased). [ME f. AF *delivree* fem. past part. of *delivrer* (as DELIVER)]
▪ **1 a** distribution, conveyance, transportation, transport. **2** childbirth, *formal* parturition. **3** see DELIVERANCE 1. **4** see THROW *n.* 1. **5** donation, presentation, bestowal; see also SURRENDER *n.* 6 **b** presentation, performance, execution; utterance, enunciation, articulation, pronunciation, expression. ▫ **take delivery of** see RECEIVE 1, 2.

dell /del/ *n.* a small usu. wooded hollow or valley. [OE f. Gmc]
▪ see VALLEY.

Della Cruscan /délə krúskən/ *adj.* & *n.* ● *adj.* **1** of or relating to the Academy della Crusca in Florence, concerned with the purity of Italian. **2** of or concerning a late 18th–c. school of English poets with an artificial style. ● *n.* a member of the Academy della Crusca or the late 18th–c. school of English poets. [It. (*Accademia*) *della Crusca* (Academy) of the bran (with ref. to sifting)]

delocalize /deelṓkəliz/ *v.tr.* **1 a** detach or remove (a thing) from its place. **b** not limit to a particular location. **2** (as **delocalized** *adj.*) *Chem.* (of electrons) shared among more than two atoms in a molecule. ▫▫ **delocalization** *n.*

delouse /deelóws/ *v.tr.* rid (a person or animal) of lice.

Delphic /délfik/ *adj.* (also **Delphian** /-feeən/) **1** (of an utterance, prophecy, etc.) obscure, ambiguous, or enigmatic. **2** of or concerning the ancient Greek oracle at Delphi.

delphinium /delfíneeəm/ *n.* any ranunculaceous garden plant of the genus *Delphinium*, with tall spikes of usu. blue flowers. [mod.L f. Gk *delphinion* larkspur f. *delphin* dolphin]

delphinoid /délfinoyd/ *adj.* & *n.* ● *adj.* **1** of the family that includes dolphins, porpoises, grampuses, etc. **2** dolphinlike. ● *n.* **1** a member of the delphinoid family of aquatic mammals. **2** a dolphinlike animal. [Gk *delphinoeidēs* f. *delphin* dolphin]

delta /déltə/ *n.* **1** a triangular tract of deposited earth, alluvium, etc., at the mouth of a river, formed by its diverging outlets. **2 a** the fourth letter of the Greek alphabet (Δ, δ). **b** a fourth-class mark given for a piece of work or in an examination. **3** *Astron.* the fourth star in a constellation. **4** *Math.* an increment of a variable. □ **delta connection** *Electr.* a triangular arrangement of three-phase windings with circuit wire from each angle. **delta rays** *Physics* rays of low penetrative power consisting of slow electrons ejected from an atom by the impact of ionizing radiation. **delta rhythm** (or **wave**) low-frequency electrical activity of the brain during sleep. **delta wing** the triangular swept-back wing of an aircraft. □□ **deltaic** /deltáyik/ *adj.* [ME f. Gk f. Phoen. *daleth*]

deltiology /délteeólǝjee/ *n.* the collecting and study of postcards. □□ **deltiologist** *n.* [Gk *deltion* dimin. of *deltos* writing-tablet + -LOGY]

deltoid /déltoyd/ *adj. & n.* ● *adj.* triangular; like a river delta. ● *n.* (in full **deltoid muscle**) a thick triangular muscle covering the shoulder joint and used for raising the arm away from the body. [F *deltoïde* or mod.L *deltoides* f. Gk *deltoeidēs* (as DELTA, -OID)]

delude /dilóōd/ *v.tr.* deceive or mislead (*deluded by false optimism*). □□ **deluder** *n.* [ME f. L *deludere* mock (as DE-, *ludere lus-* play)]
  ■ see DECEIVE 1.

deluge /délyōōj, -yoozh/ *n. & v.* ● *n.* **1** a great flood. **2** (**the Deluge**) the biblical Flood (Gen. 6–8). **3** a great outpouring (of words, paper, etc.). **4** a heavy fall of rain. ● *v.tr.* **1** flood. **2** inundate with a great number or amount (*deluged with complaints*). [ME f. OF f. L *diluvium*, rel. to *lavare* wash]
  ■ *n.* **1** see FLOOD *n.* 1. **3** see FLOOD *n.* 2b. **4** see DOWNPOUR. ● *v.* **1** see FLOOD *v.* 1. **2** see DROWN.

delusion /dilóōzhǝn/ *n.* **1** a false belief or impression. **2** *Psychol.* this as a symptom or form of mental disorder. □ **delusions of grandeur** a false idea of oneself as being important, noble, famous, etc. □□ **delusional** *adj.* [ME f. LL *delusio* (as DELUDE)]
  ■ **1** misapprehension, false *or* mistaken impression, illusion, mistake, error, misconception, misbelief, hallucination, misjudgment.

delusive /dilóōsiv/ *adj.* **1** deceptive or unreal. **2** disappointing. □□ **delusively** *adv.* **delusiveness** *n.*
  ■ **1** see NONEXISTENT.

delusory /dilóōsǝree, -zǝ-/ *adj.* = DELUSIVE. [LL *delusorius* (as DELUSION)]

deluster /deelústǝr/ *v.tr.* (*Brit.* **delustre**) remove the luster from (a textile).

deluxe /dǝ lúks, lóōks/ *adj.* **1** luxurious or sumptuous. **2** of a superior kind. [F, = of luxury]
  ■ see LUXURIOUS 1.

delve /delv/ *v.* **1** *intr.* (often foll. by *in, into*) **a** search energetically (*delved into his pocket*). **b** make a laborious search in documents, etc.; research (*delved into his family history*). **2** *tr. & intr. poet.* dig. □□ **delver** *n.* [OE *delfan* f. WG]
  ■ **1** see ROOT² *v.* 2a. **2** see TILL³.

Dem. *abbr.* Democrat.

demagnetize /deemágnitiz/ *v.tr.* remove the magnetic properties of. □□ **demagnetization** /-tizáyshǝn/ *n.* **demagnetizer** *n.*

demagogue /démǝgog, -gawg/ *n.* (also **-gog**) **1** a political agitator appealing to the basest instincts of a mob. **2** *hist.* a leader of the people, esp. in ancient times. □□ **demagogic** /-gójik, -gógik, -gō-/ *adj.* **demagoguery** /-gógǝree, -gáwg-/ *n.* **demagogy** /-gójee, -gáw-/ *n.* [Gk *dēmagōgos* f. *dēmos* the people + *agōgos* leading]
  ■ **1** see AGITATOR 1.

demand /dimánd/ *n. & v.* ● *n.* **1** an insistent and peremptory request, made as of right. **2** *Econ.* the desire of purchasers or consumers for a commodity (*no demand for solid tires these days*). **3** an urgent claim (*care of her mother makes demands on her*). ● *v.tr.* **1** (often foll. by *of, from,* or *to* + infin., or *that* + clause) ask for (something) insistently and urgently, as of right (*demanded to know; demanded five dollars from him; demanded that his wife be present*). **2** require or need (*a task demanding skill*). **3** insist on being told (*demanded the truth*).

4 (as **demanding** *adj.*) making demands; requiring skill, effort, etc. (*a demanding but worthwhile job*). □ **demand feeding** the practice of feeding a baby when it cries for food rather than at set times. **demand note 1** a written request for payment. **2** a bill payable at sight. **demand pull** *Econ.* available money as a factor causing economic inflation. **in demand** sought after. **on demand** as soon as a demand is made (*a check payable on demand*). □□ **demandable** *adj.* **demander** *n.* **demandingly** *adv.* [ME f. OF *demande* (n.), *demander* (v.) f. L *demandare* entrust (as DE-, *mandare* order: see MANDATE)]
  ■ *n.* **1** request, order, command, insistence, call, bidding, requisition, *archaic* hest, *archaic or literary* bid, *literary* behest. **2** want, need, requirement, call, desire, market. **3** see CLAIM *n.* 1. ● *v.* **1** require, order, call for, *archaic or literary* bid; insist (on), command, ask (for), request; requisition. **2** require, call for, need, want, necessitate, cry out for. **4** (**demanding**) insistent, clamorous, nagging, persistent; difficult, hard, exigent, tough, exacting, trying, taxing. □ **in demand** sought after, wanted, needed, coveted, popular, desired, desirable. **on demand** on call, on request, on presentation, when requested *or* required; at once, immediately, without delay.

demantoid /dimántoyd/ *n.* a lustrous green garnet. [G]

demarcation /deéemaarkáyshǝn/ *n.* **1** the act of marking a boundary or limits. **2** the trade-union practice of strictly assigning specific jobs to different unions. □ **demarcation dispute** an interunion dispute about who does a particular job. □□ **demarcate** /dimáarkayt, deémaar-/ *v.tr.* **demarcator** *n.* [Sp. *demarcación* f. *demarcar* mark the bounds of (as DE-, MARK¹)]
  ■ **1** see DEFINITION 2.

démarche /daymáarsh/ *n.* a political step or initiative. [F f. *démarcher* take steps (as DE-, MARCH¹)]

dematerialize /deémǝteéreeǝliz/ *v.tr. & intr.* make or become nonmaterial or spiritual (esp. of psychic phenomena, etc.). □□ **dematerialization** *n.*
  ■ □□ **dematerialization** see *evaporation* (EVAPORATE).

deme /deem/ *n.* **1 a** a political division of Attica in ancient Greece. **b** an administrative division in modern Greece. **2** *Biol.* a local population of closely related plants or animals. [Gk *dēmos* the people]

demean¹ /dimeén/ *v.tr.* (usu. *refl.*) lower the dignity of (*would not demean myself to take it*). [DE- + MEAN², after *debase*]
  ■ see LOWER² 4.

demean² /dimeén/ *v.refl.* (with *adv.*) behave (*demeaned himself well*). [ME f. OF *demener* f. Rmc (as DE-, L *minare* drive animals f. *minari* threaten)]
  ■ (*demean oneself*) see BEHAVE 1a.

demeanor /dimeénǝr/ *n.* (*Brit.* **demeanour**) outward behavior or bearing. [DEMEAN², prob. after obs. *havour* behavior]
  ■ see BEARING 1.

dement /dimént/ *n. archaic* a demented person. [orig. adj. f. F *dément* or L *demens* (as DEMENTED)]

demented /diméntid/ *adj.* mad; crazy. □□ **dementedly** *adv.* **dementedness** *n.* [past part. of *dement* verb f. OF *dementer* or f. LL *dementare* f. *demens* out of one's mind (as DE-, *mens mentis* mind)]
  ■ see MAD *adj.* 1.

démenti /daymóntee/ *n.* an official denial of a rumor, etc. [F f. *démentir* accuse of lying]

dementia /diménshǝ/ *n. Med.* a chronic or persistent disorder of the mental processes marked by memory disorders, personality changes, impaired reasoning, etc., due to brain disease or injury. □ **dementia praecox** /preékoks/ schizophrenia. [L f. *demens* (as DEMENTED)]

/.../ **pronunciation**	● **part of speech**
□ **phrases, idioms, and compounds**	
□□ **derivatives**	■ **synonym section**
cross-references appear in SMALL CAPITALS or *italics*	

demerara /déməráirə/ *n.* light-brown cane sugar coming orig. and chiefly from Demerara. [*Demerara* in Guyana]

demerit /dimérit/ *n.* **1** a quality or action deserving blame; a fault. **2** a mark given to an offender. □□ **demeritorious** /-táwreeəs/ *adj.* [ME f. OF *de(s)merite* or L *demeritum* neut. past part. of *demerēri* deserve]
■ 2 see STIGMA 1.

demersal /dimə́rsəl/ *adj.* (of a fish, etc.) being or living near the sea bottom (cf. PELAGIC). [L *demersus* past part. of *demergere* (as DE-, *mergere* plunge)]

demesne /dimáyn, -meén/ *n.* **1** a a sovereign's or nation's territory; a domain. **b** land attached to a mansion, etc. **c** landed property; an estate. **2** (usu. foll. by *of*) a region or sphere. **3** *Law hist.* possession (of real property) as one's own. □ **held in demesne** (of an estate) occupied by the owner, not by tenants. [ME f. AF, OF *demeine* (later AF *demesne*) belonging to a lord f. L *dominicus* (as DOMINICAL)]

demi- /démee/ *prefix* **1** half; half-size. **2** partially or imperfectly such (*demigod*). [ME f. F f. med.L *dimedius* half, for L *dimidius*]

demigod /démeegod/ *n.* (*fem.* **-goddess** /-godis/) **1 a** a partly divine being. **b** the offspring of a god or goddess and a mortal. **2** *colloq.* a person of compelling beauty, powers, or personality.
■ 1 see GOD *n.* 1a.

demijohn /démeejon/ *n.* a bulbous, narrow-necked bottle holding from 3 to 10 gallons and usu. in a wicker cover. [prob. corrupt. of F *dame-jeanne* Lady Jane, assim. to DEMI- + the name *John*]

demilitarize /deemílitəriz/ *v.tr.* remove a military organization or forces from (a frontier, a zone, etc.). □□ **demilitarization** *n.*

demimondaine /démeemondayn/ *n.* a woman of a demimonde.

demimonde /démeemond, -máwND/ *n.* **1 a** *hist.* a class of women in 19th-c. France considered to be of doubtful social standing and morality. **b** a similar class of women in any society. **2** any group considered to be on the fringes of respectable society. [F, = half-world]

demineralize /deemínərəliz/ *v.tr.* remove salts from (sea water, etc.). □□ **demineralization** *n.*

demi-pension /dəmeepáwNsyawN/ *n.* hotel accommodations with bed, breakfast, and one main meal per day. [F (as DEMI-, PENSION²)]

demirep /démeerep/ *n.* *archaic* a woman of doubtful sexual reputation. [abbr. of *demi-reputable*]

demise /dimíz/ *n.* & *v.* ● *n.* **1** death (*left a will on her demise*; *the demise of the agreement*). **2** *Law* conveyance or transfer (of property, a title, etc.) by demising. ● *v.tr. Law* **1** convey or grant (an estate) by will or lease. **2** transmit (a title, etc.) by death. [AF use of past part. of OF *de(s)mettre* DISMISS, in refl. abdicate]
■ *n.* 1 see DEATH 1. ● *v.* 1 see LEASE *v.*, make over 1.

demisemiquaver /démeesémeekwayvər/ *n.* *Mus.* esp. *Brit.* = thirty-second note.

demist /deemíst/ *v.tr. Brit.* defrost (a windscreen, etc.). □□ **demister** *n.*

demit /dimít/ *v.tr.* (**demitted, demitting**) (often *absol.*) resign or abdicate (an office, etc.). □□ **demission** /-míshən/ *n.* [F *démettre* f. L *demittere* (as DE-, *mittere* miss- send)]

demitasse /démeetas, -taas/ *n.* **1** a small coffee cup. **2** its contents. [F, = half-cup]

demiurge /démeeərj/ *n.* **1** (in the philosophy of Plato) the creator of the universe. **2** (in Gnosticism, etc.) a heavenly being subordinate to the Supreme Being. □□ **demiurgic** *adj.* [eccl.L f. Gk *dēmiourgos* craftsman f. *dēmios* public f. *dēmos* people + *-ergos* working]

demo /démō/ *n.* (*pl.* **-os**) *colloq.* = DEMONSTRATION 2, 3. [abbr.]

demob /deemób/ *v.* & *n. Brit. colloq.* ● *v.tr.* (**demobbed, demobbing**) demobilize. ● *n.* demobilization. [abbr.]

demobilize /deemṓbiliz/ *v.tr.* disband (troops, ships, etc.). □□ **demobilization** *n.* [F *démobiliser* (as DE-, MOBILIZE)]
■ see DISBAND.

democracy /dimókrəsee/ *n.* (*pl.* **-ies**) **1 a** a system of gov-

ernment by the whole population, usu. through elected representatives. **b** a nation so governed. **c** any organization governed on democratic principles. **2** a classless and tolerant form of society. **3 a** the principles of the Democratic party. **b** its members. [F *démocratie* f. LL *democratia* f. Gk *dēmokratia* f. *dēmos* the people + -CRACY]

democrat /démkrat/ *n.* **1** an advocate of democracy. **2** (**Democrat**) a member of the Democratic party. □□ **democratism** /dimókrətizəm/ *n.* [F *démocrate* (as DEMOCRACY), after *aristocrate*]

democratic /démkrátik/ *adj.* **1** of, like, practicing, advocating, or constituting democracy or a democracy. **2** favoring social equality. □ **democratic centralism** an organizational system in which policy is decided centrally and is binding on all members. **Democratic party** one of the two main US political parties, considered to support social reform and strong federal powers. (cf. *Republican party*). □□ **democratically** *adv.* [F *démocratique* f. med.L *democraticus* f. Gk *dēmokratikos* f. *dēmokratia* DEMOCRACY]
■ 1 representative, popular; elected. 2 egalitarian, classless.

democratize /dimókrətiz/ *v.tr.* make (a nation, institution, etc.) democratic. □□ **democratization** *n.*

démodé /dáymōdáy/ *adj.* out of fashion. [F, past part. of *démoder* (as DE-, *mode* fashion)]
■ see OUT *adv.* 16.

demodulate /deemójəlayt/ *v.tr. Physics* extract (a modulating signal) from its carrier. □□ **demodulation** /-láyshən/ *n.* **demodulator** *n.*

demography /dimógrəfee/ *n.* the study of the statistics of births, deaths, disease, etc., as illustrating the conditions of life in communities. □□ **demographer** *n.* **demographic** /démgráfik/ *adj.* **demographical** *adj.* **demographically** *adv.* [Gk *dēmos* the people + -GRAPHY]

demoiselle /démwazél/ *n.* **1** *Zool.* a small crane, *Anthropoides virgo*, native to Asia and N. Africa. **2 a** a damselfly. **b** a damselfish. **3** *archaic* a young woman. [F, = DAMSEL]

demolish /dimólish/ *v.tr.* **1 a** pull down (a building). **b** completely destroy or break. **2** overthrow (an institution). **3** refute (an argument, theory, etc.). **4** *joc.* eat up completely and quickly. □□ **demolisher** *n.* **demolition** /déməlíshən/ *n.* **demolitionist** *n.* [F *démolir* f. L *demoliri* (as DE-, *moliri* molit- construct f. *moles* mass)]
■ 1 a tear *or* pull down, knock down, dismantle, reduce to ruin(s), pull to pieces, raze, topple, destroy, level. **b** see DESTROY 1. 2 bring to an end, make an end of, put an end to; see also OVERTHROW *v.* 3 refute, disprove, dispose of; destroy, overturn, crush, defeat, suppress, squelch, quash. 4 see DEVOUR 1.

demon¹ /deémən/ *n.* **1 a** an evil spirit or devil, esp. one thought to possess a person. **b** the personification of evil passion. **2** a malignant supernatural being; the Devil. **3** (often *attrib.*) a forceful, fierce, or skillful performer (*a demon on the tennis court*; *a demon player*). **4** a cruel or destructive person. **5** (also **daemon**) **a** an inner or attendant spirit; a genius (*the demon of creativity*). **b** a supernatural being in ancient Greece. □ **a demon for work** *colloq.* a person who works strenuously. [ME f. med.L *demon* f. L *daemon* f. Gk *daimōn* deity]
■ 1 a devil, evil spirit, fiend, cacodemon; monster, ghoul, ogre, beast, hellhound. 2 see DEVIL *n.* 1, 2. 3 expert, master, maestro, wizard, adept, genius, talent, old hand, professional, virtuoso, esp. *Brit. colloq.* dab hand, *sl.* ace; (*attrib.*) see *first-rate adj.*

demon² / deémən/ *n. Austral. sl.* a police officer. [app. f. Van Diemen's Land, early name for Tasmania, after DEMON¹]

demonetize /deemónitiz, -mún-/ *v.tr.* withdraw (a coin, etc.) from use as money. □□ **demonetization** *n.* [F *démonétiser* (as DE-, L *moneta* MONEY)]

demoniac /dimṓneeak/ *adj.* & *n.* ● *adj.* **1** fiercely energetic or frenzied. **2 a** supposedly possessed by an evil spirit. **b** of or concerning such possession. **3** of or like demons. ● *n.* a person possessed by an evil spirit. □□ **demoniacal** /deémənníəkəl/ *adj.* **demoniacally** *adv.* [ME f. OF *demon-*

iaque f. eccl.L *daemoniacus* f. *daemonium* f. Gk *daimonion* dimin. of *daimōn*: see DEMON¹]

demonic /dimónik/ *adj.* (also **daemonic**) **1** = DEMONIAC. having or seeming to have supernatural genius or power. [LL *daemonicus* f. Gk *daimonikos* (as DEMON¹)]
■ **2** clairvoyant, telepathic, psychic, divinatory; witchlike.

demonism /deémənizəm/ *n.* belief in the power of demons.

demonize /deémənīz/ *v.tr.* **1** make into or like a demon. **2** represent as a demon.

demonolatry /deémənólətree/ *n.* the worship of demons.

demonology /deémənólejee/ *n.* the study of demons, etc. □□ **demonologist** *n.*

demonstrable /dimónstrəbəl/ *adj.* capable of being shown or logically proved. □□ **demonstrability** *n.* **demonstrably** *adv.* [ME f. L *demonstrabilis* (as DEMONSTRATE)]
■ provable, confirmable, attestable, verifiable; evident, self-evident, obvious, undeniable, apparent, manifest, indisputable, unquestionable, positive, certain, conclusive.

demonstrate /démənstrayt/ *v.* **1** *tr.* show evidence of (feelings, etc.). **2** *tr.* describe and explain (a scientific proposition, machine, etc.) by experiment, practical use, etc. **3** *tr.* **a** logically prove the truth of. **b** be proof of the existence of. **4** *intr.* take part in or organize a public demonstration. **5** *intr.* act as a demonstrator. [L *demonstrare* (as DE-, *monstrare* show)]
■ **1, 3** show, make evident, establish, evince, evidence, exhibit, manifest; see also PROVE 1. **2** display, describe, present, report, illustrate; see also EXPLAIN 1. **4** march, parade, rally, protest.

demonstration /démənstráyshən/ *n.* **1** (foll. by *of*) **a** the outward showing of feeling, etc. **b** an instance of this. **2** a public meeting, march, etc., for a political or moral purpose. **3 a** the exhibiting or explaining of specimens or experiments as a method of esp. scientific teaching. **b** an instance of this. **4** proof provided by logic, argument, etc. **5** *Mil.* a show of military force. □□ **demonstrational** *adj.* [ME f. OF *demonstration* or L *demonstratio* (as DEMONSTRATE)]
■ **1** show, manifestation, exhibition, display. **2** march, parade, protest, rally, sit-in, *colloq.* demo. **3** presentation, display, show, explanation, description, exposition, *colloq.* demo. **4** proof, evidence, testimony, indication, confirmation, verification, substantiation.

demonstrative /dimónstrətiv/ *adj. & n.* ● *adj.* **1** given to or marked by an open expression of feeling, esp. of affection (*a very demonstrative person*). **2** (usu. foll. by *of*) logically conclusive; giving proof (*the work is demonstrative of their skill*). **3 a** serving to point out or exhibit. **b** involving esp. scientific demonstration (*demonstrative technique*). **4** *Gram.* (of an adjective or pronoun) indicating the person or thing referred to (e.g., *this, that, those*). ● *n. Gram.* a demonstrative adjective or pronoun. □□ **demonstratively** *adv.* **demonstrativeness** *n.* [ME f. OF *demonstratif -ive* f. L *demonstrativus* (as DEMONSTRATION)]
■ *adj.* **1** open, expressive, unrestrained, unconstrained, unreserved, expansive, effusive, emotional; affectionate. **2** illustrative, indicative, representative, probative, evidential; conclusive.

demonstrator /démənstraytər/ *n.* **1** a person who takes part in a political demonstration, etc. **2** a person who demonstrates, esp. machines, equipment, etc., to prospective customers. **3** a person who teaches by demonstration, esp. in a laboratory, etc. [L (as DEMONSTRATE)]
■ **1** protestor, activist, agitator.

demoralize /dimáwrəlīz, -mór-/ *v.tr.* **1** destroy (a person's) morale; make hopeless. **2** *archaic* corrupt (a person's) morals. □□ **demoralization** *n.* **demoralizing** *adj.* **demoralizingly** *adv.* [F *démoraliser* (as DE-, MORAL)]
■ **1** dispirit, daunt, dishearten, discourage, demotivate, defeat; devitalize, depress, subdue, crush. **2** corrupt, pervert, deprave, vitiate, debase, debauch.

demote /dimót/ *v.tr.* reduce to a lower rank or class. □□ **demotion** /-móshən/ *n.* [DE- + PROMOTE]
■ see DOWNGRADE *v.* 1.

demotic /dimótik/ *n. & adj.* ● *n.* **1** the popular colloquial form of a language. **2** a popular simplified form of ancient Egyptian writing (cf. HIERATIC). ● *adj.* **1** (esp. of language) popular, colloquial, or vulgar. **2** of or concerning the ancient Egyptian or modern Greek demotic. [Gk *dēmotikos* f. *dēmotēs* one of the people (*dēmos*)]

demotivate /deémótivayt/ *v.tr.* (also *absol.*) cause to lose motivation; discourage. □□ **demotivation** /-váyshən/ *n.*

demount /deémównt/ *v.tr.* **1** take (apparatus, a gun, etc.) from its mounting. **2** dismantle for later reassembly. □□ **demountable** *adj. & n.* [F *démonter*: cf. DISMOUNT]

demulcent /dimúlsənt/ *adj. & n.* ● *adj.* soothing. ● *n.* an agent that forms a protective film soothing irritation or inflammation in the mouth. [L *demulcēre* (as DE-, *mulcēre* soothe)]

demur /dimár/ *v. & n.* ● *v.intr.* (**demurred, demurring**) **1** (often foll. by *to, at*) raise scruples or objections. **2** *Law* put in a demurrer. ● *n.* (also **demurral** /dimárəl/) (usu. in *neg.*) **1** an objection (*agreed without demur*). **2** the act or process of objecting. □□ **demurrant** /dimárənt/ *n.* (in sense 2 of *v.*). [ME f. OF *demeure* (n.), *demeurer* (v.) f. Rmc (as DE-, L *morari* delay)]
■ *v.* **1** see PROTEST *v.* 1. ● *n.* **1** see OBJECTION.

demure /dimyoŏr/ *adj.* (**demurer, demurest**) **1** composed, quiet, and reserved; modest. **2** affectedly shy and quiet; coy. **3** decorous (*a demure high collar*). □□ **demurely** *adv.* **demureness** *n.* [ME, perh. f. AF *demuré* f. OF *demoré* past part. of *demorer* remain, stay (as DEMUR): infl. by OF *meür* f. L *maturus* ripe]
■ **1** see MODEST 1, 2. **2** see COY 3, *prudish* (PRUDE). **3** see DECOROUS, SEEMLY.

demurrable /dimárəbəl/ *adj.* esp. *Law* open to objection.

demurrage /dimárij, -múr-/ *n.* **1 a** a rate or amount payable to a shipowner by a charterer for failure to load or discharge a ship within the time agreed. **b** a similar charge on railroad trucks or goods. **2** such a detention or delay. [OF *demo(u)rage* f. *demorer* (as DEMUR)]

demurrer /dimárər, -múr-/ *n. Law* an objection raised or exception taken. [AF (infin. as noun), = DEMUR]

demy /dimí/ *n. Printing* a size of paper, 564 x 444 mm. [ME, var. of DEMI-]

demystify /deémístifī/ *v.tr.* (**-ies, -ied**) **1** clarify (obscure beliefs or subjects, etc.). **2** reduce or remove the irrationality in (a person). □□ **demystification** /-fikáyshən/ *n.*

demythologize /deémithóləjīz/ *v.tr.* **1** remove mythical elements from (a legend, famous person's life, etc.). **2** reinterpret what some consider to be the mythological elements in (the Bible).

den /den/ *n.* **1** a wild animal's lair. **2** a place of crime or vice (*den of iniquity; opium den*). **3** a small private room for pursuing a hobby, etc. [OE *denn* f. Gmc, rel. to DEAN²]
■ **1** see LAIR *n.* 1a. **3** see SANCTUM 2.

denarius /dináireeəs/ *n.* (*pl.* **denarii** /-ree-ī/) an ancient Roman silver coin. [L, = (coin) of ten asses (as DENARY: see AS²)]

denary /dénəree, deé-/ *adj.* of ten; decimal. □ **denary scale** = *decimal scale.* [L *denarius* containing ten (*deni* by tens)]

denationalize /deénáshənəliz/ *v.tr.* **1** transfer (a nationalized industry or institution, etc.) from public to private ownership. **2 a** deprive (a nation) of its status or characteristics as a nation. **b** deprive (a person) of nationality or national characteristics. □□ **denationalization** *n.* [F *dénationaliser* (as DE-, NATIONAL)]

denaturalize /deénáchərəliz/ *v.tr.* **1** change the nature or properties of; make unnatural. **2** deprive of the rights of citizenship. **3** = DENATURE *v.* 1. □□ **denaturalization** *n.*

denature /deénáychər/ *v.tr.* **1** change the properties of (a protein, etc.) by heat, acidity, etc. **2** make (alcohol) unfit for drinking, esp. by the addition of another substance. □□ **de-**

/.../	**pronunciation**	●	**part of speech**
□	**phrases, idioms, and compounds**		
□□	**derivatives**	■	**synonym section**
	cross-references appear in SMALL CAPITALS or *italics*		

naturant *n.* **denaturation** /deénaychəráyshən/ *n.* [F *dén-aturer* (as DE-, NATURE)]

dendrite /déndrīt/ *n.* **1 a** a stone or mineral with natural treelike or mosslike markings. **b** such marks on stones or minerals. **2** *Chem.* a crystal with branching treelike growth. **3** *Zool.* & *Anat.* a branching process of a nerve cell conducting signals to a cell body. [F f. Gk *dendritēs* (adj.) f. *dendron* tree]

dendritic /dendrítik/ *adj.* **1** of or like a dendrite. **2** treelike in shape or markings. □□ **dendritically** *adv.*

dendrochronology /déndrōkrənóləjee/ *n.* **1** a system of dating using the characteristic patterns of annual growth rings of trees to assign dates to timber. **2** the study of these growth rings. □□ **dendrochronological** /-krónəlójikəl/ *adj.* **dendrochronologist** *n.* [Gk *dendron* tree + CHRONOLOGY]

dendroid /déndroyd/ *adj.* tree-shaped. [Gk *dendrōdēs* treelike + -OID]

dendrology /dendróləjee/ *n.* the scientific study of trees. □□ **dendrological** /-drəlójikəl/ *adj.* **dendrologist** *n.* [Gk *dendron* tree + -LOGY]

dene[1] /deen/ *n.* (also **dean**) *Brit.* **1** a narrow wooded valley. **2** a vale (esp. as the ending of place-names). [OE *denu*, rel. to DEN]

dene[2] /deen/ *n. Brit.* a bare sandy tract, or a low sand hill, by the sea. [orig. unkn.: cf. DUNE]

dengue /dénggay, -gee/ *n.* an infectious viral disease of the tropics causing a fever and acute pains in the joints. [W. Ind. Sp., f. Swahili *denga, dinga*, with assim. to Sp. *dengue* fastidiousness, with ref. to the stiffness of the patient's neck and shoulders]

deniable /diníəbəl/ *adj.* that may be denied. □□ **deniability** *n.*

denial /diníəl/ *n.* **1** the act or an instance of denying. **2** a refusal of a request or wish. **3** a statement that a thing is not true; a rejection (*denial of the accusation*). **4** a disavowal of a person as one's leader, etc. **5** = SELF-DENIAL.
 ▪ **1** contradiction, negation, repudiation, refutation, disavowal, disclaimer, disaffirmation. **2** refusal, rejection, rebuff. **3** rejection, repudiation, démenti; renunciation, retraction, recantation, negation, withdrawal.

denier /dényər, dənyáy, dəneér/ *n.* a unit of weight by which the fineness of silk, rayon, or nylon yarn is measured. [orig. the name of a small coin: ME f. OF f. L *denarius*]

denigrate /dénigrayt/ *v.tr.* defame or disparage the reputation of (a person); blacken. □□ **denigration** /-gráyshən/ *n.* **denigrator** *n.* **denigratory** /-grətáwree/ *adj.* [L *denigrare* (as DE-, *nigrare* f. *niger* black)]
 ▪ see VILIFY.

denim /dénim/ *n.* **1** (often *attrib.*) a usu. blue, hard-wearing, cotton twill fabric used for jeans, overalls, etc., (*a denim skirt*). **2** (in *pl.*) *colloq.* jeans, overalls, etc., made of this. [for *serge de Nim* f. *Nîmes* in S. France]

denitrify /deenítrifī/ *v.tr.* (**-ies**, **-ied**) remove the nitrates or nitrites from (soil, etc.). □□ **denitrification** /-fikáyshən/ *n.*

denizen /dénizən/ *n.* **1** a foreigner admitted to certain rights in his or her adopted country. **2** a naturalized foreign word, animal, or plant. **3** (usu. foll. by *of*) *poet.* an inhabitant or occupant. □□ **denizenship** *n.* [ME f. AF *deinzein* f. OF *deinz* within f. L *de* from + *intus* within + -*ein* f. L -*aneus*: see -ANEOUS]
 ▪ **1** see ALIEN *n.* 1. **3** inhabitant, dweller, occupant, frequenter, resident.

denominate /dinóminayt/ *v.tr.* **1** give a name to. **2** call or describe (a person or thing) as. [L *denominare* (as DE-, NOMINATE)]
 ▪ see CALL *v.* 7.

denomination /dinóminávshən/ *n.* **1** a church or religious sect. **2** a class of units within a range or sequence of numbers, weights, money, etc. (*money of small denominations*). **3 a** a name or designation, esp. a characteristic or class name. **b** a class or kind having a specific name. **4** the rank of a playing card within a suit, or of a suit relative to others. □ **denominational education** education according to the principles of a church or sect. □□ **denominational** *adj.* [ME f. OF *denomination* or L *denominatio* (as DENOMINATE)]
 ▪ **1** sect, persuasion, school, church, order. **2** unit, size, value; see also CLASS *n.* 1. **3 a** designation, name, identification, style, title, tag, term, *formal* appellation. **b** sort, kind, type, nature, variety; grade, class, genus, species, order, classification.

denominative /dinóminávtiv, -nətiv/ *adj.* serving as or giving a name. [LL *denominativus* (as DENOMINATION)]

denominator /dinóminaytər/ *n. Math.* the number below the line in a vulgar fraction; a divisor. □ **common denominator 1** a common multiple of the denominators of several fractions. **2** a common feature of members of a group. **least** (or **lowest**) **common denominator** the lowest common multiple as above. [F *dénominateur* or med.L *denominator* (as DE-, NOMINATE)]

de nos jours /də nō zhŏōr/ *adj.* (placed after noun) of the present time. [F, = of our days]
 ▪ latter-day, contemporary, modern.

denote /dinṓt/ *v.tr.* **1** be a sign of; indicate (*the arrow denotes direction*). **2** (usu. foll. by *that* + clause) mean; convey. **3** stand as a name for; signify. □□ **denotation** /deénōtáyshən/ *n.* **denotative** /deénōtáytiv, dinṓtətiv/ *adj.* [F *dénoter* or f. L *denotare* (as DE-, *notare* mark f. *nota* NOTE)]
 ▪ **1** specify, signify, mark; see also INDICATE 2. **2** mean, convey. **3** name, symbolize, represent, betoken, signify.

denouement /daynōōmón/ *n.* (also **dénouement**) **1** the final unraveling of a plot or complicated situation. **2** the final scene in a play, novel, etc., in which the plot is resolved. [F *dénouement* f. *dénouer* unknot (as DE-, L *nodare* f. *nodus* knot)]

denounce /dinówns/ *v.tr.* **1** accuse publicly; condemn (*denounced him as a traitor*). **2** inform against (*denounced her to the police*). **3** give notice of the termination of (an armistice, treaty, etc.). □□ **denouncement** *n.* **denouncer** *n.* [ME f. OF *denoncier* f. L *denuntiare* (as DE-, *nuntiare* make known f. *nuntius* messenger)]
 ▪ **1** accuse, brand, stigmatize, charge, blame, incriminate, implicate, complain about; criticize, condemn, decry, denunciate, attack, assail, censure, impugn, declaim *or* rail (against), vituperate, revile, vilify, inveigh against; (hold up to) shame, pillory, (heap) scorn (upon), cast a slur on. **2** betray, report, reveal, *archaic* delate; see also INFORM 2.
 □□ **denouncement** see ACCUSATION.

de nouveau /də nōōvṓ/ *adv.* starting again; anew. [F]

de novo /dee nṓvō, day/ *adv.* starting again; anew. [L]

dense /dens/ *adj.* **1** closely compacted in substance; thick (*dense fog*). **2** crowded together (*the population is less dense on the outskirts*). **3** *colloq.* stupid. □□ **densely** *adv.* **denseness** *n.* [F *dense* or L *densus*]
 ▪ **1** compact, thick, compressed, condensed, close, solid, heavy, impenetrable. **2** crowded, packed, tight, congested, teeming, populous, jammed, crammed. **3** slow, slow-witted, thickheaded, dull, thick-witted, obtuse, *colloq.* thick, dim, dim-witted, dumb; see also STUPID *adj.* 1, 5.

densitometer /dénsitómitər/ *n.* an instrument for measuring the photographic density of an image on a film or photographic print.

density /dénsitee/ *n.* (*pl.* **-ies**) **1** the degree of compactness of a substance. **2** *Physics* degree of consistency measured by the quantity of mass per unit volume. **3** the opacity of a photographic image. **4** a crowded state. **5** stupidity. [F *densité* or L *densitas* (as DENSE)]
 ▪ **1** see BODY *n.* 8.

dent /dent/ *n.* & *v.* ● *n.* **1** a slight mark or hollow in a surface made by, or as if by, a blow with a hammer, etc. **2** a noticeable effect (*lunch made a dent in our funds*). ● *v.tr.* **1** mark with a dent. **2** have (esp. an adverse) effect on (*the news dented our hopes*). [ME, prob. f INDENT[1]]
 ▪ *n.* **1** see IMPRESSION 4. ● *v.* **1** see MARK[1] *v.* 1a.

dent. *abbr.* **1** dental. **2** dentist. **3** dentistry.

dental /dént'l/ *adj.* **1** of the teeth; of or relating to dentistry. **2** *Phonet.* (of a consonant) produced with the tip of the tongue against the upper front teeth (as *th*) or the ridge of the teeth (as *n, s, t*). □ **dental floss** a thread of floss, silk, etc., used to clean between the teeth. **dental hygienist** a person who is trained and licensed to clean and examine teeth, and who usu. works with or for a dentist. **dental technician** a person who makes and repairs artificial teeth. □□ **dentalize** *v.tr.* [LL *dentalis* f. L *dens dentis* tooth]

dentalium /dentáyleeəm/ *n.* (*pl.* **dentalia** /-leeə/) **1** any marine mollusk of the genus *Dentalium*, having a conical foot protruding from a tusklike shell. **2** this shell used as an ornament or as a form of currency. [mod.L f. LL *dentalis*: see DENTAL]

dentate /déntayt/ *adj. Bot. & Zool.* toothed; with toothlike notches; serrated. [L *dentatus* f. *dens dentis* tooth]
■ see *notched* (NOTCH).

denticle /déntikəl/ *n. Zool.* a small tooth or toothlike projection, scale, etc. □□ **denticulate** /dentíkyōōlət/ *adj.* [ME f. L *denticulus* dimin. of *dens dentis* tooth]

dentifrice /déntifris/ *n.* a paste or powder for cleaning the teeth. [F f. L *dentifricium* f. *dens dentis* tooth + *fricare* rub]

dentil /déntil/ *n. Archit.* each of a series of small rectangular blocks as a decoration under the molding of a cornice in classical architecture. [obs. F *dentille* dimin. of *dent* tooth f. L *dens dentis*]

dentilingual /déntilínggwəl/ *adj. Phonet.* formed by the teeth and the tongue.

dentin /dént'n/ *n.* (also **dentine** /-teen/) a hard, dense, bony tissue forming the bulk of a tooth. □□ **dentinal** /déntinəl/, denteé-/ *adj.* [L *dens dentis* tooth + -INE⁴]

dentist /déntist/ *n.* a person who is qualified to treat the diseases and conditions that affect the mouth, jaws, teeth, and their supporting tissues, esp. the repair and extraction of teeth and the insertion of artificial ones. □□ **dentistry** *n.* [F *dentiste* f. *dent* tooth]

dentition /dentíshən/ *n.* **1** the type, number, and arrangement of teeth in a species, etc. **2** the cutting of teeth; teething. [L *dentitio* f. *dentire* to teethe]

denture /dénchər/ *n.* a removable artificial replacement for one or more teeth carried on a removable plate or frame. [F f. *dent* tooth]

denuclearize /deenōōkleeəriz, -nyōō-/ *v.tr.* remove nuclear armaments from (a country, etc.). □□ **denuclearization** *n.*

denude /dinōōd, -nyōōd/ *v.tr.* **1** make naked or bare. **2** (foll. by *of*) **a** strip of clothing, a covering, etc. **b** deprive of a possession or attribute. **3** *Geol.* lay (rock or a formation, etc.) bare by removing what lies above. □□ **denudation** /deenōōdáyshən, -nyōō-, dényōō-/ *n.* **denudative** /-dətiv/ *adj.* [L *denudare* (as DE-, *nudus* naked)]
■ **1** see BARE *v.* 1.

denumerable /dinōōmərəbəl, -nyōō-/ *adj. Math.* countable by correspondence with the infinite set of integers. □□ **denumerability** *n.* **denumerably** *adv.* [LL *denumerare* (as DE-, *numerare* NUMBER)]

denunciation /dinúnsee-áyshən, -shee-/ *n.* **1** the act of denouncing (a person, policy, etc.); public condemnation. **2** an instance of this. □□ **denunciate** /-seeayt/ *v.tr.* **denunciative** /-seeətiv, -seeáytiv/ *adj.* **denunciator** *n.* **denunciatory** /-seeətawree/ *adj.* [F *dénonciation* or L *denunciatio* (as DENOUNCE)]
■ see ACCUSATION.

deny /diní/ *v.tr.* (**-ies, -ied**) **1** declare untrue or nonexistent (*denied the charge*; *denied that it is so*; *denied having lied*). **2** repudiate or disclaim (*denied his faith*; *denied her signature*). **3** (often foll. by *to*) refuse (a person or thing, or something to a person) (*this was denied to me*; *denied him the satisfaction*). **4** refuse access to (a person sought) (*denied him his son*). □ **deny oneself** be abstinent. □□ **denier** *n.* [ME f. OF *denier* f. L *denegare* (as DE-, *negare* say no)]
■ **1** contradict, controvert, disaffirm, disclaim, dispute, challenge, *archaic or literary* gainsay; negate, rebut, confute, *disp.* refute. **2** disavow, repudiate, renounce, disown, forswear, disclaim. **3** reject, refuse, withhold, forbid, turn down, decline, disallow; recall, revoke, recant.

deoch an doris /dáw<u>kh</u> ən dáwris, dók ən dóris/ *n.* (also

doch-an-dorris) *Sc. & Ir.* a drink taken at parting; a stirrup cup. [Gael. *deoch an doruis* drink at the door]

deodar /deéədaar/ *n.* the Himalayan cedar *Cedrus deodara*, the tallest of the cedar family, with drooping branches bearing large, barrel-shaped cones. [Hindi *dē' odār* f. Skr. *devadāru* divine tree]

deodorant /deeōdərənt/ *n.* (often *attrib.*) a substance sprayed or rubbed on to the body or sprayed into the air to remove or conceal unpleasant smells (*a roll-on deodorant*; *has a deodorant effect*). [as DEODORIZE + -ANT]

deodorize /deeōdəriz/ *v.tr.* remove or destroy the (usu. unpleasant) smell of. □□ **deodorization** *n.* **deodorizer** *n.* [DE- + L *odor* smell]
■ see FRESHEN 1.

Deo gratias /dáyō graátee-aas, graásheeəs/ *int.* thanks be to God. [L, = (we give) thanks to God]

deontic /deeóntik/ *adj. Philos.* of or relating to duty and obligation as ethical concepts. [Gk *deont-* part. stem of *dei* it is right]

deontology /deeontóləjee/ *n. Philos.* the study of duty. □□ **deontological** /-təlójikəl/ *adj.* **deontologist** *n.*

Deo volente /dáyō vəléntay/ *adv.* God willing; if nothing prevents it. [L]

deoxygenate /deeóksijənayt/ *v.tr.* remove oxygen, esp. free oxygen, from. □□ **deoxygenation** /-náyshən/ *n.*

deoxyribonucleic acid /deéokseeríbōnōōkleéik, -kláyik, -nyōō-/ *n.* see DNA. [DE- + OXYGEN + RIBONUCLEIC (ACID)]

dep. *abbr.* **1** departs. **2** deputy.

depart /dipaárt/ *v.* **1** *intr.* **a** (usu. foll. by *from*) go away; leave (*the train departs from this platform*). **b** (usu. foll. by *for*) start; set out (*flights depart for New York every hour*). **2** *intr.* (usu. foll. by *from*) diverge; deviate (*departs from standard practice*). **3 a** *intr.* leave by death; die. **b** *tr. formal* or *literary* leave by death (*departed this life*). [ME f. OF *departir* ult. f. L *dispertire* divide]
■ **1** go, go away *or* out *or* off, leave, walk off, exit, set out *or* forth *or* off, start; take one's leave, check out, retire, retreat, withdraw. **2** deviate, diverge, turn (aside *or* away), differ, vary, break away, stray, veer; (*depart from*) leave, abandon. **3 a** see DIE¹ 1.

departed /dipaártid/ *adj. & n.* ● *adj.* bygone (*departed greatness*). ● *n.* (prec. by *the*) *euphem.* a particular dead person or dead people (*we are here to mourn the departed*).

department /dipaártmənt/ *n.* **1** a separate part of a complex whole, esp.: **a** a branch of municipal or federal administration (*State Department*; *Department of Africulture*). **b** a branch of study and its administration at a university, school, etc. (*the physics department*). **c** a specialized section of a large store (*hardware department*). **2** *colloq.* an area of special expertise. **3** an administrative district in France and other countries. □ **department store** a large retail establishment stocking many varieties of goods in different departments. [F *département* (as DEPART)]
■ **1 a** division, subdivision, branch, office, bureau, section, segment, unit, part. **2** responsibility, concern, worry, sphere, jurisdiction, domain, control, area *or* sphere of influence *or* activity, *colloq.* thing, *joc.* bailiwick.

departmental /deépaartmént'l/ *adj.* of or belonging to a department. □ **departmental store** *Brit.* = *department store*. □□ **departmentalism** *n.* **departmentalize** *v.tr.* **departmentalization** *n.* **departmentally** *adv.*

departure /dipaárchər/ *n.* **1** the act or an instance of departing. **2** (often foll. by *from*) a deviation (from the truth, a standard, etc.). **3** (often *attrib.*) the starting of a train, an aircraft, etc. (*the departure was late*; *departure lounge*). **4** a new course of action or thought (*driving a car is rather a departure for him*). **5** *Naut.* the amount of a ship's change of longitude. [OF *departeüre* (as DEPART)]

/.../ **pronunciation**	● **part of speech**
□ **phrases, idioms, and compounds**	
□□ **derivatives**	■ **synonym section**
cross-references appear in SMALL CAPITALS or *italics*	

■ **1** see EXIT *n.* 2a. **2** see DIVERSION 1. **3** see TAKEOFF 1.

depasture /deepáschər/ *v.* **1 a** *tr.* (of cattle) graze upon. **b** *intr.* graze. **c** *tr.* put (cattle) to graze. **2** *tr.* (of land) provide pasturage for (cattle). □□ **depasturage** *n.*

depend /dipénd/ *v.intr.* **1** (often foll. by *on, upon*) be controlled or determined by (*success depends on hard work; it depends on whether they agree; it depends how you tackle the problem*). **2** (foll. by *on, upon*) **a** be unable to do without (*depends on her mother*). **b** rely on (*I'm depending on you to come*). **3** (foll. by *on, upon*) be grammatically dependent on. **4** (often foll. by *from*) *archaic poet.* hang down. □ **depend upon it!** you may be sure! **it** (or **it all** or **that**) **depends** expressing uncertainty or qualification in answering a question (*Will they come? It depends*). [ME f. OF *dependre* ult. f. L *dependēre* (as DE-, *pendēre* hang)]

■ **1** (*depend on* or *upon*) be contingent *or* dependent *or* conditional on, turn on, hinge on, pivot on, hang on, be subject to, rest on, be influenced *or* determined *or* conditioned *or* controlled by. **2 b** (*depend on* or *upon*) trust (in), rely on, count on, reckon on, bank on, put one's faith *or* trust in. **4** hang down, be suspended.

dependable /dipéndəbəl/ *adj.* reliable. □□ **dependability** *n.* **dependableness** *n.* **dependably** *adv.*

■ see RELIABLE.

dependant *Brit.* var. of DEPENDENT *n.*.

dependence /dipéndəns/ *n.* **1** the state of being dependent, esp. on financial or other support. **2** reliance; trust; confidence (*shows great dependence on his judgment*). [F *dépendance* (as DEPEND)]

■ **2** see TRUST *n.* 1, 5.

dependency /dipéndənsee/ *n.* (*pl.* **-ies**) **1** a country or province controlled by another. **2** anything subordinate or dependent.

■ **1** see PROVINCE 1.

dependent /dipéndənt/ *adj. & n.* ● *adj.* **1** (usu. foll. by *on*) depending, conditional, or subordinate. **2** unable to do without (esp. a drug). **3** maintained at another's cost. **4** *Math.* (of a variable) having a value determined by that of another variable. **5** *Gram.* (of a clause, phrase, or word) subordinate to a sentence or word. ● *n.* **1** a person who relies on another, esp. for financial support. **2** a servant. □□ **dependently** *adv.* [F *dépendant* pres. part. of *dépendre* (as DEPEND)]

■ *n.* **1** see WARD *n.* 3.

depersonalization /deepə́rsənəlizáyshən/ *n.* esp. *Psychol.* the loss of one's sense of identity.

depersonalize /deepə́rsənəlīz/ *v.tr.* **1** make impersonal. **2** deprive of personality.

depict /dipíkt/ *v.tr.* **1** represent in a drawing or painting, etc. **2** portray in words; describe (*the play depicts him as vain and petty*). □□ **depicter** *n.* **depiction** /-píkshən/ *n.* **depictive** *adj.* **depictor** *n.* [L *depingere depict-* (as DE-, *pingere* paint)]

■ **2** see CHARACTERIZE 1, 2.

depilate /dépilayt/ *v.tr.* remove the hair from. □□ **depilation** /-láyshən/ *n.* [L *depilare* (as DE-, *pilare* f. *pilus* hair)]

depilatory /dipílətawree/ *adj. & n.* ● *adj.* that removes unwanted hair. ● *n.* (*pl.* **-ies**) a depilatory substance.

deplane /deepláyn/ *v.* **1** *intr.* disembark from an airplane. **2** *tr.* remove from an airplane.

deplete /dipleét/ *v.tr.* (esp. in *passive*) **1** reduce in numbers or quantity (*depleted forces*). **2** empty out; exhaust (*their energies were depleted*). □□ **depletion** /-pleéshən/ *n.* [L *deplēre* (as DE-, *plēre plet-* fill)]

■ **1** see DIMINISH 1. **2** see CONSUME 4.

deplorable /dipláwrəbəl/ *adj.* **1** exceedingly bad (*a deplorable meal*). **2** that can be deplored. □□ **deplorably** *adv.*

■ **1** bad, execrable, *colloq.* terrible, dreadful, abominable, appalling; see also AWFUL 1a, b. **2** shameful, disgraceful, scandalous, reprehensible, lamentable, regrettable.

deplore /dipláwr/ *v.tr.* **1** grieve over; regret. **2** be scandalized by; find exceedingly bad. □□ **deploringly** *adv.* [F *déplorer* or It. *deplorare* f. L *deplorare* (as DE-, *plorare* bewail)]

■ **1** see MOURN. **2** see DISAPPROVE.

deploy /diplóy/ *v.* **1** *Mil.* **a** *tr.* cause (troops) to spread out

from a column into a line. **b** *intr.* (of troops) spread out in this way. **2** *tr.* bring (arguments, forces, etc.) into effective action. □□ **deployment** *n.* [F *déployer* f. L *displicare* (as DIS-, *plicare* fold) & LL *deplicare* explain]

■ **1** see *draw up* 2.

deplume /deeploˉom/ *v.tr.* **1** strip of feathers; pluck. **2** deprive of honors, etc. [ME f. F *déplumer* or f. med.L *deplumare* (as DE-, L *pluma* feather)]

depolarize /deepólərīz/ *v.tr. Physics* reduce or remove the polarization of. □□ **depolarization** *n.*

depoliticize /deépəlítisīz/ *v.tr.* **1** make (a person, an organization, etc.) nonpolitical. **2** remove from political activity or influence. □□ **depoliticization** *n.*

depolymerize /deepólimərīz/ *v.tr. & intr. Chem.* break down into monomers or other smaller units. □□ **depolymerization** *n.*

deponent /dipónənt/ *adj. & n.* ● *adj. Gram.* (of a verb, esp. in Latin or Greek) passive or middle in form but active in meaning. ● *n.* **1** *Gram.* a deponent verb. **2** *Law* **a** a person making a deposition under oath. **b** a witness giving written testimony for use in court, etc. [L *deponere* (as DE-, *ponere posit-* place): adj. from the notion that the verb had laid aside the passive sense]

depopulate /deepópyəlayt/ *v.* **1** *tr.* reduce the population of. **2** *intr.* decline in population. □□ **depopulation** /-láyshən/ *n.* [L *depopulari* (as DE-, *populari* lay waste f. *populus* people)]

■ **1** see DESOLATE *v.* 1.

deport /dipáwrt/ *v.tr.* **1 a** remove (an immigrant or foreigner) forcibly to another country; banish. **b** exile (a native) to another country. **2** *refl.* conduct (oneself) or behave (in a specified manner) (*deported himself well*). □□ **deportable** *adj.* **deportation** /-táyshən/ *n.* [OF *deporter* and (sense 1) F *déporter* (as DE-, L *portare* carry)]

■ **1** see BANISH 1. **2** (*deport oneself*) see ACT *v.* 1.

deportee /deépawrteé/ *n.* a person who has been or is being deported.

■ see EXILE *n.* 3.

deportment /dipáwrtmənt/ *n.* bearing, demeanor, or manners, esp. of a cultivated kind. [F *déportement* (as DEPORT)]

■ see CONDUCT *n.* 1.

depose /dipóz/ *v.* **1** *tr.* remove from office, esp. dethrone. **2** *intr. Law* (usu. foll. by *to*, or *that* + clause) bear witness, esp. on oath in court. [ME f. OF *deposer* after L *deponere*: see DEPONENT, POSE¹]

■ **1** see OVERTHROW *v.* **2** see ATTEST 1, 3.

deposit /dipózit/ *n. & v.* ● *n.* **1 a** a sum of money placed in an account in a bank. **b** anything stored or entrusted for safekeeping, usu. in a bank. **2 a** a sum payable as a first installment on a time-payment purchase, or as a pledge for a contract. **b** a returnable sum payable on the short-term rental of a car, boat, etc. **3 a** a natural layer of sand, rock, coal, etc. **b** a layer of precipitated matter on a surface, e.g., on the inside of a kettle. ● *v.tr.* (**deposited, depositing**) **1 a** put or lay down in a (usu. specified) place (*deposited the book on the floor*). **b** (of water, wind, etc.) leave (matter, etc.) lying in a displaced position. **2 a** store or entrust for keeping. **b** pay (a sum of money) into a bank account, esp. a deposit account. **3** pay (a sum) as a first installment or as a pledge for a contract. □ **deposit account** *Brit.* a savings account. [L *depositum* (n.), med.L *depositare* f. L *deponere deposit-* (as DEPONENT)]

■ *n.* **2 a** down payment, part *or* partial payment, advance payment; see also EARNEST² 1. **3** sediment, accumulation, deposition, alluvium, *Chem.* precipitate. ● *v.* **1 a** place, leave, set *or* lay (down); see also PUT¹ *v.* 1. **2** entrust, leave, lodge, consign, keep, place, put; store, save, set *or* put aside, bank, lay *or* put away, pay in, stow, *colloq.* stash (away).

depositary /dipóziteree/ *n.* (*pl.* **-ies**) a person to whom something is entrusted; a trustee. [LL *depositarius* (as DEPOSIT)]

deposition /dépəzíshən/ *n.* **1** the act or an instance of deposing, esp. a monarch; dethronement. **2** *Law* **a** the process of giving sworn evidence; allegation. **b** an instance of this. **c** evidence given under oath; a testimony. **3** the act or an

instance of depositing. **4** (**the Deposition**) **a** the taking down of the body of Christ from the Cross. **b** a representation of this. [ME f. OF f. L *depositio -onis* f. *deponere*: see DEPOSIT]
■ **1** see REMOVAL 3a. **2** see ALLEGATION, TESTIMONY 1, 2.

depositor /dipózitər/ *n.* a person who deposits money, property, etc.

depository /dipózitawree/ *n.* (*pl.* **-ies**) **1 a** a storehouse for furniture, etc. **b** a store (of wisdom, knowledge, etc.) (*the book is a depository of wit*). **2** = DEPOSITARY. [LL *depositorium* (as DEPOSIT)]
■ **1 a** see STOREHOUSE. **b** see MINE² *n.* 2.

depot /deépō, dépō/ *n.* **1** a storehouse. **2** *Mil.* **a** a storehouse for equipment, etc. **b** *Brit.* the headquarters of a regiment. **3 a** a building for the servicing, parking, etc., of esp. buses, trains, or goods vehicles. **b** a railroad or bus station. [F *dépôt*, OF *depost* f. L (as DEPOSIT)]
■ **1** see WAREHOUSE *n.* **2 b** see BASE¹ *n.* 3.

deprave /dipráyv/ *v.tr.* pervert or corrupt, esp. morally. □□ **depravation** /déprəváyshən/ *n.* **depraved** *adj.* [ME f. OF *depraver* or L *depravare* (as DE-, *pravare* f. *pravus* crooked)]
■ see CORRUPT *v.* 1.

depravity /diprávitee/ *n.* (*pl.* **-ies**) **1 a** moral corruption; wickedness. **b** an instance of this; a wicked act. **2** *Theol.* the innate corruptness of human nature. [DE- + obs. *pravity* f. L *pravitas* (as DEPRAVE)]
■ **1** see VICE¹ 1, 2.

deprecate /déprikayt/ *v.tr.* **1** express disapproval of or a wish against; deplore (*deprecate hasty action*). ¶ Often confused with *depreciate*. **2** plead earnestly against. **3** *archaic* pray against. □□ **deprecatingly** *adv.* **deprecation** /-káyshən/ *n.* **deprecative** /-kaytiv, -kətiv/ *adj.* **deprecator** *n.* **deprecatory** /-kətawree/ *adj.* [L *deprecari* (as DE-, *precari* pray)]
■ **1** see DISAPPROVE. **2** see IMPEACH 3.

depreciate /dipreésheeaayt/ *v.* **1** *tr.* & *intr.* diminish in value (*the car has depreciated*). **2** *tr.* disparage; belittle (*they are always depreciating his taste*). **3** *tr.* reduce the purchasing power of (money). □□ **depreciatingly** *adv.* **depreciatory** /-sheeətawree/ *adj.* [LL *depretiare* (as DE-, *pretiare* f. *pretium* price)]
■ **1** devalue, lessen, reduce, bring down, lower, depress, cheapen, mark down; go down, decrease, diminish. **2** disparage, deride, decry, underrate, undervalue, underestimate, minimize, belittle, slight, deprecate, discredit, denigrate, run down, play down, talk down, *formal* derogate.

depreciation /dipreésheeáyshən/ *n.* **1** the amount of wear and tear (of a property, etc.) for which a reduction may be made in a valuation, an estimate, or a balance sheet. **2** *Econ.* a decrease in the value of a currency. **3** the act or an instance of depreciating; belittlement.
■ **2** see SLUMP *n.* **3** see MOCKERY 1a; *humiliation* (HUMILIATE).

depredation /dépridáyshən/ *n.* (usu. in *pl.*) **1** despoiling, ravaging, or plundering. **2** an instance or instances of this. [F *déprédation* f. LL *depraedatio* (as DE-, *praedatio -onis* f. L *praedari* plunder)]
■ plunder, plundering, pillage, pillaging, despoliation, despoiling, ravaging, sacking, laying waste, devastation, destruction; ransacking, robbery, looting; ravages.

depredator /dépridaytər/ *n.* a despoiler or pillager. □□ **depredatory** /dépridáytəree, dipréedətawree/ *adj.* [LL *depraedator* (as DEPREDATION)]

depress /diprés/ *v.tr.* **1** push or pull down; lower (*depressed the lever*). **2** make dispirited or dejected. **3** *Econ.* reduce the activity of (esp. trade). **4** (as **depressed** *adj.*) **a** dispirited or miserable. **b** *Psychol.* suffering from depression. □ **depressed area** an area suffering from economic depression. □□ **depressible** *adj.* **depressing** *adj.* **depressingly** *adv.* [ME f. OF *depresser* f. LL *depressare* (as DE-, *pressare* frequent. of *premere* press)]
■ **1** press (down), push *or* pull down (on), push, pull, lower. **2** deject, dispirit, oppress, sadden, grieve, cast down, bring down, dishearten, discourage, dampen,

cast a gloom *or* pall over, burden, weigh down. **3** weaken, dull, sap; depreciate; lower, bring down, reduce. **4 a** (**depressed**) see MISERABLE 1.
□□ **depressing** see OPPRESSIVE 1, 2; SAD 2.

depressant /diprésənt/ *adj.* & *n.* ● *adj.* **1** that depresses. **2** *Med.* sedative. ● *n.* **1** *Med.* an agent, esp. a drug, that sedates. **2** an influence that depresses.
■ *n.* **1** see SEDATIVE *n.*

depression /dipréshən/ *n.* **1 a** *Psychol.* a state of extreme dejection or morbidly excessive melancholy; a mood of hopelessness and feelings of inadequacy, often with physical symptoms. **b** a reduction in vitality, vigor, or spirits. **2 a** a long period of financial and industrial decline; a slump. **b** (**the Depression**) the depression of 1929–34. **3** *Meteorol.* a lowering of atmospheric pressure, esp. the center of a region of minimum pressure or the system of winds around it. **4** a sunken place or hollow on a surface. **5 a** a lowering or sinking (often foll. by *of*: *depression of freezing point*). **b** pressing down. **6** *Astron.* & *Geog.* the angular distance of an object below the horizon or a horizontal plane. [ME f. OF or L *depressio* (as DE-, *premere* press- press)]
■ **1 b** dejection, despair, gloom, downheartedness, sadness, melancholy, discouragement, despondency, gloominess, glumness, the blues, unhappiness; see also MELANCHOLY *n.* **2 a** recession, slump, (economic) decline, downturn. **3** low-pressure area, cyclone, col. **4** indentation, dent, dimple, impression, pit, hollow, recess, cavity, concavity, dip.

depressive /diprésiv/ *adj.* & *n.* ● *adj.* **1** tending to depress. **2** *Psychol.* involving or characterized by depression. ● *n.* *Psychol.* a person suffering or with a tendency to suffer from depression. [F *dépressif -ive* or med.L *depressivus* (as DE-PRESSION)]

depressor /diprésər/ *n.* **1** *Anat.* **a** (in full **depressor muscle**) a muscle that causes the lowering of some part of the body. **b** a nerve that lowers blood pressure. **2** *Surgery* an instrument for pressing down an organ, etc. [L (as DEPRESSION)]

depressurize /deepréshəriz/ *v.tr.* cause an appreciable drop in the pressure of the gas inside (a container), esp. to the ambient level. □□ **depressurization** *n.*

deprivation /dépriváyshən/ *n.* **1** (usu. foll. by *of*) the act or an instance of depriving; the state of being deprived (*deprivation of liberty*; *suffered many deprivations*). **2 a** a deposition from esp. an ecclesiastical office. **b** an instance of this. [med.L *deprivatio* (as DEPRIVE)]
■ **1** see PRIVATION 1.

deprive /diprív/ *v.tr.* **1** (usu. foll. by *of*) strip, dispossess; debar from enjoying (*illness deprived him of success*). **2** (as **deprived** *adj.*) **a** (of a child, etc.) suffering from the effects of a poor or loveless home. **b** (of an area) with inadequate housing, facilities, employment, etc. **3** *archaic* depose (esp. a clergyman) from office. □□ **deprivable** *adj.* **deprival** *n.* [ME f. OF *depriver* f. med.L *deprivare* (as DE-, L *privare* deprive)]
■ **1** deny, refuse; strip, dispossess, debar; mulct; see also DIVEST 2. **2** (**deprived**) needy, in want, in need, impoverished, badly off, destitute, poor, poverty-stricken, underprivileged, disadvantaged.

de profundis /dáy prōfoōndis/ *adv.* & *n.* ● *adv.* from the depths (of sorrow, etc.). ● *n.* a cry from the depths. [opening L words of Ps. 130]

Dept. *abbr.* Department.

depth /depth/ *n.* **1 a** deepness (*the depth is not great at the edge*). **b** the measurement from the top down, from the surface inward, or from the front to the back (*depth of the drawer is 12 inches*). **2** difficulty; abstruseness. **3 a** sagacity; wisdom. **b** intensity of emotion, etc. (*the poem has little depth*). **4** an intensity of color, darkness, etc. **5** (in *pl.*) **a** deep water, a

---

deep place; an abyss. **b** a low, depressed state. **c** the lowest or inmost part (*the depths of the country*). **6** the middle (*in the depth of winter*). □ **depth charge** (or **bomb**) a bomb capable of exploding under water, esp. for dropping on a submerged submarine, etc. **depth psychology** psychoanalysis to reveal hidden motives, etc. **in depth** comprehensively, thoroughly, or profoundly. **in-depth** *adj.* thorough; done in depth. **out of one's depth 1** in water over one's head. **2** engaged in a task or on a subject too difficult for one. [ME (as DEEP, -TH²)]

■ **1** deepness, profundity, profoundness; see also MEASUREMENT 2. **2** difficulty, profundity, profoundness, abstruseness, obscurity, reconditeness, complexity, intricacy. **3 a** profundity, wisdom, sagacity, sageness, understanding, perception, astuteness, perspicacity, perspicaciousness, insight, intuition, acumen, penetration. **b** see INTENSITY 1. **4** intensity, strength, deepness; vividness, brilliance, brilliancy, brightness, richness. **5 a, c** (*depths*) deep(s), abyss, chasm, bowels of the earth, (bottomless) pit, nethermost reaches *or* regions, nadir. **6** see MIDDLE *n.* 1. □ **in depth** thoroughly, comprehensively, in detail, profoundly, deeply, extensively, intensively, concentratedly, probingly. **in-depth** see THOROUGH 1.

depthless /dépthlis/ *adj.* **1** extremely deep; fathomless. **2** shallow; superficial.

depurate /dépyərayt/ *v.tr.* & *intr.* make or become free from impurities. □□ **depuration** /-ráyshən/ *n.* **depurative** *adj.* & *n.* **depurator** *n.* [med.L *depurare* (as DE-, *purus* pure)]

deputation /dépyŏŏtáyshən/ *n.* a group of people appointed to represent others, usu. for a specific purpose; a delegation. [ME f. LL *deputatio* (as DEPUTE)]

■ see MISSION 3.

depute *v.* & *n.* ● *v.tr.* /dipyŏŏt/ (often foll. by *to*) **1** appoint as a deputy. **2** delegate (a task, authority, etc.) (*deputed the leadership to her*). ● *n.* /dépyŏŏt/ *Sc.* a deputy. [ME f. OF *député* past part. of *deputer* f. L *deputare* regard as, allot (as DE-, *putare* think)]

■ *v.* **2** see DELEGATE *v.* 1.

deputize /dépyətiz/ *v.intr.* (usu. foll. by *for*) act as a deputy or understudy.

■ see COVER *v.* 8b.

deputy /dépyətee/ *n.* (*pl.* **-ies**) **1** a person appointed or delegated to act for another or others (also *attrib.*: *deputy sheriff*). **2** *Polit.* a parliamentary representative in certain countries, e.g., France. □ **by deputy** by proxy. □□ **deputyship** *n.* [ME var. of DEPUTE *n.*]

■ **1** substitute, replacement, surrogate, stand-in, reserve, proxy; agent, operative, representative, go-between, intermediary, spokesperson, spokesman, spokeswoman, delegate, ambassador, minister, emissary, envoy, (papal) nuncio, alternate, *archaic* legate, *Austral. colloq.* offsider.

deracinate /di-rásinayt/ *v.tr. literary* **1** tear up by the roots. **2** obliterate; expunge. □□ **deracination** /-náyshən/ *n.* [F *déraciner* (as DE-, *racine* f. LL *radicina* dimin. of *radix* root)]

■ **2** see ABOLISH.

derail /diráyl/ *v.tr.* (usu. in *passive*) cause (a train, etc.) to leave the rails. □□ **derailment** *n.* [F *dérailler* (as DE-, RAIL¹)]

derailleur /dəráylər/ *n.* a gear-shifting mechanism on a bicycle that moves the chain from one sprocket wheel to another. [F]

derange /diráynj/ *v.tr.* **1** throw into confusion; disorganize; cause to act irregularly. **2** (esp. as **deranged** *adj.*) make insane (*deranged by the tragic events*). **3** disturb; interrupt. □□ **derangement** *n.* [F *déranger* (as DE-, *rang* RANK¹)]

■ **1** see UPSET *v.* 3. **2** (**deranged**) mad, insane, demented, lunatic, unhinged, unbalanced, berserk, crazy, crazed, psychotic, irrational, non compos (mentis), out of one's mind *or* senses, of unsound mind, mad as a hatter *or* March hare, off the rails, *colloq.* touched, mental, crackbrained, not all there, dotty, *sl.* out of one's head *or* skull, cracked, bats, cuckoo, bonkers, dippy, batty, screwy, loony, nuts,

nutty, off one's rocker *or Brit.* chump, (plumb) loco, *Brit. sl.* potty, barmy.

deration /dee-ráshən/ *v.tr.* free (food, etc.) from rationing.

derby /dárbee/ *n.* (*pl.* **-ies**) **1** any of several horse races that are run annually, esp. for three-year olds (*Kentucky Derby*). **2** a sporting contest, etc., esp. one open to all comers. **3** a bowler hat. □ **Derby Day** the day on which the Kentucky Derby is run. [the 12th Earl of *Derby* d. 1834, founder in 1780 of a horse race at Epsom Downs, England]

deregister /dee-réjistər/ *v.tr.* remove from a register. □□ **deregistration** /-stráyshən/ *n.*

deregulate /dee-régyəlayt/ *v.tr.* remove regulations or restrictions from. □□ **deregulation** /-láyshən/ *n.*

■ decontrol, derestrict.

derelict /dérilikt/ *adj.* & *n.* ● *adj.* **1** abandoned; ownerless (esp. of a ship at sea or an empty decrepit property). **2** (esp. of property) ruined; dilapidated. **3** negligent (of duty, etc.). ● *n.* **1** a social outcast; a person without a home, a job, or property. **2** abandoned property, esp. a ship. [L *derelictus* past part. of *derelinquere* (as DE-, *relinquere* leave)]

■ *adj.* **1** deserted, abandoned, forsaken, ownerless, neglected. **2** ruined, dilapidated, run-down, tumbledown. **3** negligent, remiss, neglectful, delinquent, dilatory, careless, heedless, lax, slack, irresponsible, slipshod, slovenly, sloppy. ● *n.* **1** vagrant, tramp, outcast, pariah, loafer, wastrel, good-for-nothing, ne'er-do-well, malingerer, vagabond, slacker, down-and-out, hobo, *sl.* bum.

dereliction /dérilíkshən/ *n.* **1** (usu. foll. by *of*) **a** neglect; failure to carry out one's obligations (*dereliction of duty*). **b** an instance of this. **2** the act or an instance of abandoning; the process of being abandoned. **3 a** the retreat of the sea exposing new land. **b** the land so exposed. [L *derelictio* (as DERELICT)]

■ **1** see NEGLECT *n.* 1.

derequisition /dee-rékwizíshən/ *v.tr.* return (requisitioned property) to its former owner.

derestrict /dee-ristríkt/ *v.tr.* **1** remove restrictions from. **2** remove speed restrictions from (a road, area, etc.). □□ **derestriction** /-tríkshən/ *n.*

deride /diríd/ *v.tr.* laugh scornfully at; mock. □□ **derider** *n.* **deridingly** *adv.* [L *deridēre* (as DE-, *ridēre ris-* laugh)]

■ mock (at), ridicule, scoff at, jeer at, laugh at, make fun *or* sport of, tease, taunt, twit, poke fun at, make a laughingstock of, sneer at, scorn, flout at, disdain, pooh-pooh, belittle, diminish, disparage, rally, *archaic* hold *or* have in derision, *sl.* knock.

de rigueur /də rigőr/ *predic.adj.* required by custom or etiquette (*evening dress is de rigueur*). [F, = of strictness]

■ see CORRECT *adj.* 2, 3.

derision /diríҳhən/ *n.* ridicule; mockery (*bring into derision*). □ **hold** (or **have**) **in derision** *archaic* mock at. □□ **derisible** /diríҲibəl/ *adj.* [ME f. OF f. LL *derisio -onis* (as DERIDE)]

■ ridicule, mockery, raillery, sarcasm, contempt, scorn, contumely, disrespect, *Austral. or dial.* mullock. □ **hold** (or **have**) **in derision** see DERIDE.

derisive /diríҳiv/ *adj.* scoffing; ironical; scornful (*derisive cheers*). □□ **derisively** *adv.* **derisiveness** *n.*

■ mocking, scoffing, scornful, derisive, disdainful, contemptuous, taunting, insulting, contumelious, jeering; sardonic, sarcastic, ironic, ironical.

derisory /diríҳəree, zə-/ *adj.* **1** = DERISIVE. **2** so small or unimportant as to be ridiculous (*derisory offer*; *derisory costs*). [LL *derisorius* (as DERISION)]

derivation /dérivááyshən/ *n.* **1** the act or an instance of deriving or obtaining from a source; the process of being derived. **2 a** the formation of a word from another word or from a root. **b** a derivative. **c** the tracing of the origin of a word. **d** a statement or account of this. **3** extraction; descent. **4** *Math.* a sequence of statements showing that a formula, theorem, etc., is a consequence of previously accepted statements. □□ **derivational** *adj.* [F *dérivation* or L *derivatio* (as DERIVE)]

■ **2c, d, 3** origin, descent, extraction, source, beginning, foundation, ancestry, genealogy; etymology, root.

derivative /dirívətiv/ adj. & n. ● adj. derived from another source; not original (his music is derivative and uninteresting). ● n. **1** something derived from another source, esp.: **a** a word derived from another or from a root (e.g., quickly from quick). **b** Chem. a chemical compound that is derived from another. **2** Math. a quantity measuring the rate of change of another. □□ **derivatively** adv. [F dérivatif -ive f. L derivativus (as DERIVE)]
■ adj. derived, borrowed, unoriginal, secondhand, copied, imitative, plagiarized, plagiaristic. ● n. **1** derivation, development; spin-off, by-product, offshoot.

derive /dirív/ v. **1** tr. (usu. foll. by from) get, obtain, or form (derived satisfaction from work). **2** intr. (foll. by from) arise from, originate in, be descended or obtained from (happiness derives from many things). **3** tr. gather or deduce (derived the information from the clues). **4** tr. **a** trace the descent of (a person). **b** show the origin of (a thing). **5** tr. (usu. foll. by from) show or state the origin or formation of (a word, etc.) (derived the word from Latin). **6** tr. Math. obtain (a function) by differentiation. □□ **derivable** adj. [ME f. OF deriver or f. L derivare (as DE-, rivus stream)]
■ **1** draw, extract, get, obtain, acquire, procure, receive, secure, gain, collect, harvest, glean, cull. **2** (derive from) arise from or out of, originate in or with or from, emerge from or out of, come (forth) from or out of, arrive from, issue from, proceed from, develop from, spring from, flow from, emanate from, stem from, be traceable to. **3** elicit, educe, infer, gather; see also DEDUCE.

derma var. of DERMIS.

dermatitis /dàrmətítis/ n. inflammation of the skin. [Gk derma -atos skin + -ITIS]

dermatoglyphics /dàrmətōglífiks/ n. the science or study of skin markings or patterns, esp. of the fingers, hands, and feet. □□ **dermatoglyphic** adj. **dermatoglyphically** adv. [as DERMATITIS + Gk gluphē carving: see GLYPH]

dermatology /dàrmətóləjee/ n. the study of the diagnosis and treatment of skin disorders. □□ **dermatological** /-təlójikəl/ adj. **dermatologist** n. [as DERMATITIS + -LOGY]

dermis /dármis/ n. (also **derma** /dármə/) **1** (in general use) the skin. **2** Anat. the true skin, the thick layer of living tissue below the epidermis. □□ **dermal** adj. **dermic** adj. [mod.L, after EPIDERMIS]

dernier cri /dáirnyay kreé/ n. the very latest fashion. [F, = last cry]

derogate /dérəgayt/ v.intr. (foll. by from) formal **1** take away a part from; detract from (a merit, a right, etc.). **b** disparage. **2** deviate from (correct behavior, etc.). □□ **derogative** /dirógətiv/ adj. [L derogare (as DE-, rogare ask)]
■ **1 a** (derogate from) see DETRACT.

derogation /dérəgáyshən/ n. **1** (foll. by of) a lessening or impairment of (a law, authority, position, dignity, etc.). **2** deterioration; debasement. [ME f. F dérogation or L derogatio (as DEROGATE)]
■ **1** see IMPAIRMENT (IMPAIR).

derogatory /dirógətawree/ adj. (often foll. by to) involving disparagement or discredit; insulting; depreciatory (made a derogatory remark; derogatory to my position). □□ **derogatorily** adv. [LL derogatorius (as DEROGATE)]
■ depreciatory, depreciative, disparaging, uncomplimentary, offensive, insulting, abasing, debasing, denigrating, belittling, demeaning.

derrick /dérik/ n. **1** a kind of crane for moving or lifting heavy weights, having a movable pivoted arm. **2** the framework over an oil well or similar excavation, holding the drilling machinery. [obs. senses hangman, gallows, f. the name of a London hangman c.1600]

derriere /déreeáir/ n. colloq. euphem. (also **derrière**) the buttocks. [F, = behind]
■ buttocks, seat, posterior, rump, colloq. backside, behind, bottom, rear, sl. butt, fanny, can, keister.

derring-do /déringdóo/ n. literary joc. heroic courage or action. [ME, = daring to do, misinterpreted by Spenser and by Scott]

■ see DARING n.

derringer /dérinjər/ n. a small large-bore pistol. [H. Deringer, Amer. inventor d. 1868]

derris /déris/ n. **1** any woody, tropical climbing leguminous plant of the genus Derris, bearing leathery pods. **2** an insecticide made from the powdered root of some kinds of derris. [mod.L f. Gk, = leather covering (with ref. to its pod)]

dervish /dárvish/ n. a member of any of several Muslim fraternities vowed to poverty and austerity. □ **whirling** (or **dancing** or **howling**) **dervish** a dervish performing a wild dance, or howling, as a religious observance. [Turk. derviş f. Pers. darvēsh poor, a mendicant]

desalinate /deesálinayt/ v.tr. remove salt from (esp. sea water). □□ **desalination** /-náyshən/ n.

desalt /dessáwlt/ v.tr. = DESALINATE.

desaparecido /désaapaarəseédō/ n. a person who has 'disappeared' in a totalitarian state, esp. in South America. [Sp., lit. 'disappeared']

descale /deeskáyl/ v.tr. remove the scale from.
■ see PEEL¹ v. 1, 2.

descant n. & v. ● n. /déskant/ **1** Mus. an independent treble melody sung. sung or played above a basic melody, esp. of a hymn tune. **2** poet. a melody; a song. ● v.intr. /diskánt/ **1** (foll. by on, upon) talk lengthily and prosily, esp. in praise of. **2** Mus. sing or play a descant. □ **descant recorder** the most common size of recorder, with a range of two octaves. [ME f. OF deschant f. med.L discantus (as DIS-, cantus song, CHANT)]

descend /disénd/ v. **1** tr. & intr. go or come down (a hill, stairs, etc.). **2** intr. (of a thing) sink; fall (rain descended heavily). **3** intr. slope downward; lie along a descending slope (fields descended to the beach). **4** intr. (usu. foll. by on) **a** make a sudden attack. **b** make an unexpected and usu. unwelcome visit (hope they don't descend on us during the weekend). **5** intr. (usu. foll. by from, to) (of property, qualities, rights, etc.) be passed by inheritance (the house descends from my grandmother; the property descended to me). **6** intr. **a** sink in rank, quality, etc. **b** (foll. by to) degrade oneself morally to (an unworthy act) (descend to violence). **7** intr. Mus. (of sound) become lower in pitch. **8** intr. (usu. foll. by to) proceed (in discourse or writing): **a** in time (to a subsequent event, etc.). **b** from the general (to the particular) (now let's descend to details). **9** tr. go along (a river, etc.) to the sea, etc. **10** intr. Printing (of a letter) have its tail below the line. □ **be descended from** have as an ancestor. □□ **descendent** adj. [ME f. OF descendre f. L descendere (as DE-, scandere climb)]
■ **1** come or go down, move down, climb down, get down (off or from). **2** see SINK v. 1, FALL v. 1. **3** go down, decline, incline (downward), slope down, slant down, dip, drop, fall, plunge. **4 a** (descend on) attack, assault, invade, pounce on or upon, swoop down on or upon. **6 b** sink, stoop, lower or abase or debase or humble or degrade oneself.

descendant /diséndənt/ n. (often foll. by of) a person or thing descended from another (a descendant of John Adams). [F, part. of descendre (as DESCEND)]
■ heir, scion; offshoot; (descendants) offspring, progeny, Law issue.

descender /diséndər/ n. Printing a part of a letter that extends below the line.

descendible /diséndibəl/ adj. **1** (of a slope, etc.) that may be descended. **2** Law capable of descending by inheritance. [OF descendable (as DESCEND)]

descent /disént/ n. **1 a** the act of descending. **b** an instance of this. **c** a downward movement. **2 a** a way or path, etc., by which one may descend. **b** a downward slope. **3 a** being descended; lineage; family origin (traces his descent from Sitting Bull). **b** the transmission of qualities, property, privileges, etc., by inheritance. **4 a** a decline; a fall. **b** a lowering (of pitch, temperature, etc.). **5** a sudden violent attack. [ME f. OF *descente* f. *descendre* DESCEND]

■ **1** see DROP *n.* 2a, b. **2** see SLOPE *n.* 1–3. **3** see LINEAGE. **4** see DECLINE *n.* 1, 4; DECREASE *n.* **5** see SWOOP *n.*

descramble /deeskrámbəl/ *v.tr.* **1** convert or restore (a signal) to intelligible form. **2** counteract the effects of (a scrambling device). **3** recover an original signal from (a scrambled signal). □□ **descrambler** *n.*

describe /diskríb/ *v.tr.* **1 a** state the characteristics, appearance, etc., of, in spoken or written form (*described the landscape*). **b** (foll. by *as*) assert to be; call (*described him as a habitual liar*). **2 a** mark out or draw (esp. a geometrical figure) (*described a triangle*). **b** move in (a specified way, esp. a curve) (*described a parabola through the air*). □□ **describable** *adj.* **describer** *n.* [L *describere* (as DE-, *scribere script-* write)]

■ **1 a** tell (of), recount, relate, give an account of, narrate, recite, report, chronicle, retail; detail. **b** characterize, portray, paint, depict, identify, label, style. **2 a** mark out, outline, draw; see also TRACE¹ *v.* 3.

description /diskrípshən/ *n.* **1 a** the act or an instance of describing; the process of being described. **b** a spoken or written representation (of a person, object, or event). **2** a sort, kind, or class (*no food of any description*). □ **answers** (or **fits**) **the description** has the qualities specified. [ME f. OF f. L *descriptio -onis* (as DESCRIBE)]

■ **1 a** see *narration* (NARRATE). **b** account, narrative, story, report, representation, statement, definition; explanation, commentary; portrayal, characterization, depiction, (thumbnail) sketch, portrait; chronicle, history, record, narration; memoir. **2** sort, kind, nature, character, type, variety, brand, breed, species, category, genus, genre, class, *colloq. disp.* ilk; stripe, kidney.

descriptive /diskríptiv/ *adj.* **1** serving or seeking to describe (*a descriptive writer*). **2** describing or classifying without expressing feelings or judging (*a purely descriptive account*). **3** *Linguistics* describing a language without comparing, endorsing, or condemning particular usage, vocabulary, etc. **4** *Gram.* (of an adjective) describing the noun, rather than its relation, position, etc., e.g., *blue* as distinct from *few*. □□ **descriptively** *adv.* **descriptiveness** *n.* [LL *descriptivus* (as DESCRIBE)]

■ **1** see GRAPHIC *adj.* 1.

descriptor /diskríptər/ *n. Linguistics* a word or expression, etc., used to describe or identify. [L, = describer (as DESCRIBE)]

descry /diskrí/ *v.tr.* (**-ies, -ied**) *literary* catch sight of; discern (*described him in the crowd*); *descries no glimmer of light in her situation*). [ME (earlier senses 'proclaim, DECRY') f. OF *descrier*: prob. confused with var. of obs. *descrive* f. OF *descrivre* DESCRIBE]

■ see SIGHT *v.* 1–3.

desecrate /désikrayt/ *v.tr.* **1** violate (a sacred place or thing) with violence, profanity, etc. **2** deprive (a church, a sacred object, etc.) of sanctity; deconsecrate. □□ **desecration** /-kráyshən/ *n.* **desecrator** *n.* [DE- + CONSECRATE]

■ **1** profane, violate, defile, blaspheme (against), dishonor, degrade, debase, contaminate, pollute, corrupt, vitiate, *poet.* befoul.

deseed /deeseéd/ *v.tr.* remove the seeds from (a plant, vegetable, etc.).

desegregate /deeségrigayt/ *v.tr.* abolish racial segregation in (schools, etc.) or of (people, etc.). □□ **desegregation** /-gáyshən/ *n.*

■ see INTEGRATE *v.*

deselect /deeesilékt/ *v.tr.* **1** dismiss (esp. a trainee); discharge; reject. **2** *Polit.* decline to select or retain as a constituency candidate in an election. □□ **deselection** /-lékshən/ *n.*

desensitize /deesénsitiz/ *v.tr.* reduce or destroy the sensitiveness of (photographic materials, an allergic person, etc.). □□ **desensitization** *n.* **desensitizer** *n.*

■ see DEADEN 2.

desert¹ /dizórt/ *v.* **1** *tr.* abandon; give up; leave (*deserted the sinking ship*). **2** *tr.* forsake or abandon (a cause or a person, people, etc., having claims on one) (*deserted his wife and children*). **3** *tr.* fail (*his presence of mind deserted him*). **4** *intr. Mil.*

run away (esp. from military service). **5** *tr.* (as **deserted** *adj.*) empty; abandoned (*a deserted house*). □□ **deserter** *n.* (in sense 4 of *v.*). **desertion** /-zórshən/ *n.* [F *déserter* f. LL *desertare* f. L *desertus* (as DESERT²)]

■ **1** forsake, leave, abandon, give up. **2** forsake, leave, abandon, give up; jilt, throw over; maroon, strand, run *or* walk out on, leave in the lurch, leave high and dry, turn one's back on, *colloq.* dump, *sl.* ditch. **4** abscond, quit, run away, defect, *colloq.* go AWOL. **5** (**deserted**) abandoned, desolate, forsaken, neglected, uninhabited, unpeopled, vacant, vacated, unfrequented, unvisited, unoccupied, empty; godforsaken, isolated, solitary, lonely; friendless, stranded, rejected, left in the lurch. □□ **deserter** runaway, fugitive, escapee, escaper, absconder, defector, renegade; traitor, turncoat, rat.

desert² /dézərt/ *n. & adj.* ● *n.* a dry, barren, often sand-covered area of land, characteristically desolate, waterless, and without vegetation; an uninteresting or barren subject, period, etc. (*a cultural desert*). ● *adj.* **1** uninhabited; desolate. **2** uncultivated; barren. □ **Desert boot** *propr.* a suede, etc., boot reaching to or extending just above the ankle. **desert island** a remote (usu. tropical) island presumed to be uninhabited. **desert rat 1** any of various small rodents of arid regions. **2** desert dweller (esp. in US West), esp. a prospector. **3** a soldier (esp. *Brit.*) in the N. African desert campaign of 1941–42. [ME f. OF f. L *desertus*, eccl.L *desertum* (n.), past part. of *deserere* leave, forsake]

■ *n.* waste, wilderness, wasteland, dust bowl; badlands, barrens, wilds; emptiness, void. ● *adj.* barren, desolate, uninhabited, unpeopled, lonely, deserted; arid, bare, vacant, empty, wild, uncultivated.

desert³ /dizórt/ *n.* **1** (in *pl.*) **a** acts or qualities deserving reward or punishment. **b** such reward or punishment (*has gotten his just deserts*). **2** the fact of being worthy of reward or punishment; deservingness. [ME f. OF f. *deservir* DESERVE]

■ **1 b** (*deserts*) payment, recompense, requital, compensation, due, right, reward; retribution, justice, punishment, *colloq.* comeuppance.

desertification /dizórtifikáyshən/ *n.* the process of making or becoming a desert.

deserve /dizórv/ *v.tr.* **1** (often foll. by *to* + infin.) show conduct or qualities worthy of (reward, punishment, etc.) (*deserves to be imprisoned*; *deserves a prize*). **2** (as **deserved** *adj.*) rightfully merited or earned (*a deserved win*). □ **deserve well** (or **ill**) **of** esp. *Brit.* be worthy of good (or bad) treatment at the hands of (*deserves well of the electorate*). □□ **deservedly** /-vidlee/ *adv.* **deservedness** *n.* **deserver** *n.* [ME f. OF *deservir* f. L *deservire* (as DE-, *servire* serve)]

■ **1** merit, earn, be entitled to, be worthy of, rate, warrant, justify. **2** (**deserved**) merited, well-earned, earned, well-deserved, just, rightful, fitting, fit, proper, fair, meet, warranted, condign.

deserving /dizórving/ *adj.* meritorious. □ **deserving of** showing conduct or qualities worthy of (praise, blame, help, etc.). □□ **deservingly** *adv.* **deservingness** *n.*

■ meritorious, worthy, commendable, laudable, praiseworthy, creditable, estimable.

desex /deeséks/ *v.tr.* **1** castrate or spay (an animal). **2** deprive of sexual qualities or attractions.

■ **1** see NEUTER *v.*

desexualize /deesékshoóəliz/ *v.tr.* deprive of sexual character or of the distinctive qualities of a sex.

■ desex, unsex.

deshabille var. of DISHABILLE.

desiccant /désikənt/ *n. Chem.* a hygroscopic substance used as a drying agent.

desiccate /désikayt/ *v.tr.* remove the moisture from, dry (esp. food for preservation) (*desiccated coconut*). □□ **desiccation** /-káyshən/ *n.* **desiccative** *adj.* [L *desiccare* (as DE-, *siccus* dry)]

■ dry, dehydrate.

desiccator /désikaytər/ *n.* **1** an apparatus for desiccating. **2** *Chem.* an apparatus containing a drying agent to remove moisture from specimens.

desiderate /disídərayt/ *v.tr. archaic* feel to be missing; regret the absence of; wish to have. [L *desiderare* (as DE-, *siderare* as in CONSIDER)]

desiderative /disídərətiv, -ráytiv/ *adj.* & *n.* ● *adj.* **1** *Gram.* (of a verb, conjugation, etc.) formed from another verb, etc., and denoting a desire to perform the action of that verb, etc. **2** desiring. ● *n. Gram.* a desiderative verb, conjugation, etc. [LL *desiderativus* (as DESIDERATE)]

desideratum /disídəráytəm, -ráatəm/ *n.* (*pl.* **desiderata** /-tə/) something lacking but needed or desired. [L neut. past part.: see DESIDERATE]

■ see *requirement* (REQUIRE).

design /dizín/ *n.* & *v.* ● *n.* **1 a** a preliminary plan or sketch for the making or production of a building, machine, garment, etc. **b** the art of producing these. **2** a scheme of lines or shapes forming a pattern or decoration. **3** a plan, purpose, or intention. **4 a** the general arrangement or layout of a product. **b** an established version of a product (*one of our most popular designs*). ● *v.* **1** *tr.* produce a design for (a building, machine, picture, garment, etc.). **2** *tr.* intend, plan, or purpose (*the remark was designed to offend*; *a course designed for beginners*; *designed an attack*). **3** *absol.* be a designer. □ **argument from design** *Theol.* the argument that God's existence is provable by the evidence of design in the universe. **by design** on purpose. **have designs on** plan to harm or appropriate. [F *désigner* appoint or obs. F *desseing* ult. f. L *designare* DESIGNATE]

■ *n.* **1** a plan, scheme, conception, study, project, proposal; blueprint, draft, sketch, model, pattern, chart, diagram, layout, map, drawing, prototype. **2, 4** form, shape, configuration, pattern, style, motif, format, layout, makeup, delineation, arrangement, organization, composition, structure, construction. **3** plan, aim, purpose, intention, objective, object, goal, point, target, intent. ● *v.* **1** plan, invent, contrive, create, devise, originate, visualize, envisage, envision; sketch out, pattern, set up, delineate, lay out, draw up, think of *or* up, conceive (of), outline, work *or* map *or* block out; develop, organize, frame, shape, mold, form, forge, make, construct, fashion, sketch, draft, draw. **2** mean, plan, hope, aim, purpose, destine; (*designed for*) see INTEND 4a. □ **by design** see *on purpose* (PURPOSE).

designate *v.* & *adj.* ● *v.tr.* /dézignayt/ **1** (often foll. by *as*) appoint to an office or function (*designated him as postmaster general*; *designated her own successor*). **2** specify or particularize (*receives guests at designated times*). **3** (often foll. by *as*) describe as; entitle; style. **4** serve as the name or distinctive mark of (*English uses French words to designate ballet steps*). ● *adj.* /dézignət/ (placed after noun) appointed to an office but not yet installed (*bishop designate*). **designated driver** one member of a group who abstains from alcohol in order to drive the others safely. **designated hitter** *Baseball* a batter in the lineup who hits for the pitcher. ¶ Abbr.: **DH**. □□ **designator** *n.* [L *designare*, past part. *designatus* (as DE-, *signare* f. *signum* mark)]

■ *v.* **1** appoint, nominate, name, identify, select, pick, choose, elect, assign, delegate, depute. **2** indicate, specify, pinpoint, particularize, delineate, point out, identify, state, set forth, write *or* put down, name. **3** call, name, style, term, label, christen, dub, nickname, describe as, *archaic* entitle. **4** mean, stand for, symbolize, denote, represent, indicate, name, distinguish.

designation /dézignáyshən/ *n.* **1** a name, description, or title. **2** the act or process of designating. [ME f. OF *designation* or L *designatio* (as DESIGNATE)]

■ **1** see DENOMINATION 3a. **2** see APPOINTMENT 2c.

designedly /dizínidlee/ *adv.* by design; on purpose.

designer /dizínər/ *n.* **1** a person who makes artistic designs or plans for construction, e.g., for clothing, machines, theater sets; a draftsman. **2** (*attrib.*) (of clothing, etc.) bearing the name or label of a famous designer; prestigious. □ **designer drug** a synthetic analog, not itself illegal, of an illegal drug.

■ **1** creator, originator, architect, artificer, author,

deviser, inventor; (interior) decorator, artist; draftsman. **2** (*attrib.*) high-class, top quality; see also STYLISH.

designing /dizíning/ *adj.* crafty, artful, or scheming. □□ **designingly** *adv.*

■ scheming, conniving, calculating, wily, tricky, cunning, sly, underhand, underhanded, crafty, artful, shrewd, Machiavellian, guileful, deceitful, double-dealing, devious, treacherous, unscrupulous.

desirable /dizírəbəl/ *adj.* **1** worth having or wishing for (*it is desirable that nobody should smoke*). **2** arousing sexual desire; very attractive. □□ **desirability** *n.* **desirableness** *n.* **desirably** *adv.* [ME f. OF (as DESIRE)]

■ **1** sought-after, wanted, coveted, longed-for, looked-for, desired; profitable, worthwhile, beneficial, advantageous, valuable, worthy, estimable, commendable. **2** seductive, alluring, fetching, attractive, captivating, winning, winsome; sexy.

desire /dizír/ *n.* & *v.* ● *n.* **1 a** an unsatisfied longing or craving. **b** an expression of this; a request (*expressed a desire to rest*). **2** lust. **3** something desired (*achieved her heart's desire*). ● *v.tr.* **1** (often foll. by *to* + infin., or *that* + clause) long for; crave. **2** request (*desires a cup of coffee*). **3** *archaic* pray, entreat, or command (*desire him to wait*). [ME f. OF *desir* f. *desirer* f. L *desiderare* DESIDERATE]

■ *n.* **1** a longing, craving, yearning, hankering, hunger, thirst, appetite, *colloq.* yen. **b** wish, request, urge, requirement, requisition, demand. **2** passion, lust, libido, lustfulness, lecherousness, lechery, lasciviousness, salaciousness, prurience, *formal* concupiscence. **3** desideratum, whim; see also WISH *n.* ● *v.* **1** crave, want, fancy, covet, wish for, hope for, long *or* yearn for, pine *or* sigh for, hanker after, have an eye *or* taste for, hunger *or* thirst for *or* after, die for, have one's heart set on, *archaic* desiderate, *colloq.* have a yen for, *sl.* have the hots for. **2** ask for, request, order, demand, solicit, importune, summon, require.

desirous /dizírəs/ *predic.adj.* **1** (usu. foll. by *of*) ambitious; desiring (*desirous of stardom*; *desirous of doing well*). **2** (usu. foll. by *to* + infin., or *that* + clause) wishful; hoping (*desirous to do the right thing*). [ME f. AF *desirous*, OF *desireus* f. Rmc (as DESIRE)]

■ **1** see INTENT *adj.* 1a. **2** wishful, longing, yearning, hopeful, hoping, anxious, concerned.

desist /dizíst/ *v.intr.* (often foll. by *from*) *literary* abstain; cease (*please desist from interrupting*; *when requested, he desisted*). [OF *desister* f. L *desistere* (as DE-, *sistere* stop, redupl. f. *stare* stand)]

■ see CEASE *v.*

desk /desk/ *n.* **1** a piece of furniture or a portable box with a flat or sloped surface for writing on, and often drawers. **2** a counter in a hotel, bank, etc., which separates the customer from the assistant. **3** a section of a newspaper office, etc., dealing with a specified topic (*the sports desk*; *the features desk*). **4** *Mus.* a music stand in an orchestra regarded as a unit of two players. [ME f. med.L *desca* f. L DISCUS disk]

■ **1** writing desk, escritoire. **2** counter, table, bar. **3** see BUREAU 2.

deskbound /déskbownd/ *adj.* obliged to remain working at a desk.

desktop /désktop/ *n.* **1 a** the working surface of a desk. **b** the working area for manipulating windows, icons, etc., in some computer software environments. **2** (*attrib.*) (esp. of a microcomputer) suitable for use at an ordinary desk. □ **desktop publishing** the production of printed matter with a desktop computer and printer.

desman /désmən/ *n.* (*pl.* **desmans**) any aquatic flesh-eating shrewlike mammal of two species, one originating in Russia

/.../ pronunciation	● part of speech
□ phrases, idioms, and compounds	
□□ derivatives	■ synonym section
cross-references appear in SMALL CAPITALS or *italics*	

(*Desmana moschata*) and one in the Pyrenees (*Galemys pyr-enaicus*). [F & G f. Sw. *desman-råtta* muskrat]

desolate *adj. & v.* ● *adj.* /désələt/ **1** left alone; solitary. **2** (of a building or place) uninhabited; ruined; neglected; barren; dreary; empty (*a desolate beach*). **3** forlorn; wretched; miserable (*was left desolate and weeping*). ● *v.tr.* /désəlayt/ **1** depopulate or devastate; lay waste to. **2** (esp. as **desolated** *adj.*) make wretched or forlorn (*desolated by grief; inconsolable and desolated*). □□ **desolately** /-lətlee/ *adv.* **desolateness** *n.* **desolator** *n.* [ME f. L *desolatus* past part. of *desolare* (as DE-, *solare* f. *solus* alone)]

▪ *adj.* **1** solitary, lonely, isolated, deserted, alone, abandoned, neglected. **2** ruined, neglected, desert, uninhabited, empty, unfrequented, bare, barren, bleak, dreary, remote. **3** wretched, dreary, forsaken, friendless, wretched, joyless, cheerless, comfortless, miserable, unhappy, down, disconsolate, sad, melancholy, sorrowful, forlorn, mournful, woebegone, gloomy, brokenhearted, heavyhearted, inconsolable, dejected, downcast, downhearted, dispirited, low-spirited, depressed, melancholy, spiritless, despondent, distressed, discouraged, hopeless, dismal. ● *v.* **1** depopulate; destroy, devastate, ruin, lay waste, ravage, demolish, obliterate, annihilate, raze, gut, *literary* despoil. **2** dismay, dishearten, depress, daunt, devastate, dispirit, sadden, deject, discourage; (**desolated**) see WRETCHED 1.

desolation /désəláyshən/ *n.* **1 a** the act of desolating. **b** the process of being desolated. **2** loneliness, grief, or wretchedness, esp. caused by desertion. **3** a neglected, ruined, barren, or empty state. [ME f. LL *desolatio* (as DESOLATE)]

▪ **2** grief, sorrow, dreariness, despair, gloom, distress, melancholy, sadness, misery, anguish, wretchedness, dolefulness, unhappiness, *archaic or literary* woe, *literary* dolor; loneliness. **3** desolateness, destruction, ruin, devastation, waste, spoliation, despoliation, depredation, extirpation, barrenness, havoc, chaos.

desorb /disáwrb, -záwrb/ *v.* **1** *tr.* cause the release of (an adsorbed substance) from a surface. **2** *intr.* (of an adsorbed substance) become released. □□ **desorbent** *adj. & n.* **desorption** *n.* [DE-, after ADSORB]

despair /dispáir/ *n. & v.* ● *n.* the complete loss or absence of hope. ● *v.intr.* **1** (often foll. by *of*) lose or be without hope (*despaired of ever seeing her again*). **2** (foll. by *of*) lose hope about (*his life is despaired of*). □ **be the despair of** be the cause of despair by badness or unapproachable excellence (*he's the despair of his parents*). □□ **despairingly** *adv.* [ME f. OF *desespeir, desperer* f. L *desperare* (as DE-, *sperare* hope)]

▪ *n.* hopelessness, desperation, discouragement, disheartenment, despondency, despondence, dejection, depression, gloom, gloominess, misery, melancholy, wretchedness, distress, miserableness, anguish, *archaic* despond. ● *v.* **1** give up or lose hope, despond.

despatch var. of DISPATCH.

desperado /déspəraadō/ *n.* (*pl.* **-oes** or **-os**) a desperate or reckless person, esp. a criminal. [after DESPERATE (obs. n.) & words in -ADO]

▪ see CRIMINAL *n.*

desperate /déspərət, -prit/ *adj.* **1** reckless from despair; violent and lawless. **2 a** extremely dangerous or serious (*a desperate situation*). **b** staking all on a small chance (*a desperate remedy*). **3** very bad (*a desperate night; desperate poverty*). **4** (usu. foll. by *for*) needing or desiring very much (*desperate for recognition*). □□ **desperately** *adv.* **desperateness** *n.* **desperation** /-ráyshən/ *n.* [ME f. L *desperatus* past part. of *desperare* (as DE-, *sperare* hope)]

▪ **1** reckless, foolhardy, rash, impetuous, frantic, frenzied, panic-stricken; careless, hasty, devil-may-care, wild, mad, frenetic, furious; at one's wit's end, forlorn, despairing, despondent, wretched, at the end of one's tether. **2 a** urgent, pressing, compelling, serious, grave, acute, critical, crucial, great; precarious, perilous, life-threatening, hazardous, dangerous, hopeless, beyond hope or help. **3** see TERRIBLE 1. **4** anxious, craving,

hungry, thirsty, needful, desirous, covetous, eager, longing, yearning, wishing, hoping, aching, pining. □□ **desperately** see *extremely* (EXTREME), AWFULLY 2.

desperation desperateness, recklessness, impetuosity, rashness, foolhardiness, imprudence, heedlessness; despair, anguish, despondency, depression, dejection, discouragement, defeatism, pessimism, hopelessness, distress, misery, melancholy, wretchedness, gloom, sorrow.

despicable /déspikəbəl, dispík-/ *adj.* vile; contemptible, esp. morally. □□ **despicably** *adv.* [LL *despicabilis* f. *despicari* (as DE-, *specere* look at)]

▪ contemptible, below or beneath contempt, mean, detestable, base, low, scurvy, vile, sordid, wretched, miserable, ignoble, ignominious, shabby; shameful, shameless, reprehensible.

despise /dispíz/ *v.tr.* look down on as inferior, worthless, or contemptible. □□ **despiser** *n.* [ME f. *despis-* pres. stem of OF *despire* f. L *despicere* (as DE-, *specere* look at)]

▪ disdain, disesteem, scorn, look down on or upon, look down one's nose at, be contemptuous of, sneer at, spurn, *literary* contemn; hate, loathe, detest, abhor.

despite /dispít/ *prep. & n.* ● *prep.* in spite of. ● *n.* archaic or literary **1** outrage; injury. **2** malice; hatred (*died of mere despite*). □ **despite** (or **in despite**) **of** archaic in spite of. □□ **despiteful** *adj.* [ME f. OF *despit* f. L *despectus* noun f. *despicere* (as DESPISE)]

▪ *prep.* in spite of, notwithstanding, undeterred by, regardless of, in defiance of, without considering, without thought or consideration or regard for, ignoring, archaic despite of. ● *n.* **2** see ANIMOSITY.

despoil /dispóyl/ *v.tr. literary* (often foll. by *of*) plunder; rob; deprive (*despoiled the roof of its lead*). □□ **despoiler** *n.* **despoilment** *n.* **despoliation** /dispŏleeáyshən/ *n.* [ME f. OF *despoill(i)er* f. L *despoliare* (as DE-, *spoliare* SPOIL)]

▪ see PILLAGE *v.*

despond /dispónd/ *v. & n.* ● *v.intr.* lose heart or hope; be dejected. ● *n.* archaic despondency. [L *despondēre* give up, abandon (as DE-, *spondēre* promise)]

despondent /dispóndənt/ *adj.* in low spirits; dejected. □□ **despondence** /-dəns/ *n.* **despondency** *n.* **despondently** *adv.*

▪ dejected, sad, sorrowful, unhappy, melancholy, blue, depressed, down, downcast, downhearted, low, morose, miserable, disheartened, discouraged, dispirited, low-spirited, *colloq.* down in the dumps, down in the mouth, down on one's luck.

despot /déspət/ *n.* **1** an absolute ruler. **2** a tyrant or oppressor. □□ **despotic** /-spótik/ *adj.* **despotically** *adv.* [F *despote* f. med.L *despota* f. Gk *despotēs* master, lord]

▪ **1** absolute ruler or monarch, dictator, autocrat, overlord. **2** dictator, oppressor, autocrat, tyrant, bully. □□ **despotic** dictatorial, tyrannical, oppressive, authoritarian, imperious, domineering, totalitarian, absolute, autocratic, arbitrary.

despotism /déspətizəm/ *n.* **1 a** a rule by a despot. **b** a country ruled by a despot. **2** absolute power or control; tyranny.

▪ autocracy, monocracy, autarchy, totalitarianism, absolutism, dictatorship, tyranny, oppression, suppression, repression.

desquamate /déskwəmayt/ *v.intr. Med.* (esp. of the skin) come off in scales (as in some diseases). □□ **desquamation** /-máyshən/ *n.* **desquamative** /diskwáamətiv/ *adj.* **desquamatory** /diskwáamətawree/ *adj.* [L *desquamare* (as DE-, *squama* scale)]

des res /dez réz/ *n. Brit. sl.* a desirable residence. [abbr.]

dessert /dizárt/ *n.* **1** the sweet course of a meal, served at or near the end. **2** *Brit.* a course of fruit, nuts, etc., served after a meal. □ **dessert wine** usu. sweet wine drunk with or following dessert. [F, past part. of *desservir* clear the table (as DIS-, *servir* SERVE)]

▪ **1** sweet, *Brit.* pudding, *Brit. colloq.* afters.

dessertspoon /dizártspōōn/ *n.* **1** a spoon used for dessert, smaller than a tablespoon and larger than a teaspoon. **2** the amount held by this. □□ **dessertspoonful** *n.* (*pl.* **-fuls**).

destabilize /deestáybilīz/ *v.tr.* **1** render unstable. **2** subvert (esp. a foreign government). □□ **destabilization** *n.*

destination /déstináyshən/ *n.* a place to which a person or thing is going. [OF *destination* or L *destinatio* (as DESTINE)]
■ journey's end, terminus, stop, stopping place; goal, end, objective, target.

destine /déstin/ *v.tr.* (often foll. by *to*, *for*, or *to* + infin.) set apart; appoint; preordain; intend (*destined him for the navy*). □ **be destined to** be fated or preordained to (*was destined to become a great surgeon*). [ME f. F *destiner* f. L *destinare* (as DE-, *stanare* (unrecorded) settle f. *stare* stand)]
■ fate, predetermine, predestine, ordain, foreordain, preordain; doom; design, intend, mean, devote, assign, appoint, designate, purpose, mark, earmark, set aside or apart. □ **be destined to** (*destined*) meant, intended, designed, foreordained, preordained, predestined, fated, doomed; sure, bound, certain.

destiny /déstinee/ *n.* (*pl.* **-ies**) **1 a** the predetermined course of events; fate. **b** this regarded as a power. **2** what is destined to happen to a particular person, etc. (*it was their destiny to be rejected*). [ME f. OF *destinée* f. Rmc, past part. of *destinare*: see DESTINE]
■ **1** fate, fortune. **2** fate, doom, fortune, lot, portion, kismet, *Hinduism & Buddhism* karma.

destitute /déstitoot, -tyoot/ *adj.* **1** without food, shelter, etc.; completely impoverished. **2** (usu. foll. by *of*) lacking (*destitute of friends*). □□ **destitution** /-toshən, -tyoo-/ *n.* [ME f. L *destitutus* past part. of *destituere* forsake (as DE-, *statuere* place)]
■ **1** in want, impoverished, poverty-stricken, poor, indigent, down-and-out, needy, badly off, penniless, penurious, impecunious, insolvent, hard up, bankrupt, on skid row or road, *colloq.* broke, on one's uppers, strapped (for cash). **2** (*destitute of*) bereft of, deficient in, deprived of, devoid of, lacking (in), wanting (in), in need of, needful of, without, hard up for.

destrier /déstreeər/ *n. hist.* a war-horse. [ME f. AF *destrer*, OF *destrier* ult. f. L DEXTER[1] right (as the knight's horse was led by the squire with the right hand)]

destroy /distróy/ *v.tr.* **1** pull or break down; demolish (*destroyed the bridge*). **2** end the existence of (*the accident destroyed her confidence*). **3** kill (esp. a sick or savage animal). **4** make useless; spoil utterly. **5** ruin financially, professionally, or in reputation. **6** defeat (*destroyed the enemy*). [ME f. OF *destruire* ult. f. L *destruere* (as DE-, *struere struct-* build)]
■ **1** demolish, tear or pull down, raze, wipe out, ravage, wreck, smash, ruin, break up or down, *Astronaut.* destruct; annihilate, crush, eradicate, extirpate, exterminate, devastate, lay waste, vandalize, *colloq.* trash. **2** ruin, do away with, end, dash, make an end of, bring to an end, bring or put an end to, terminate, finish, kill. **3** kill, put away, put to sleep, exterminate, finish off. **4** negate, overturn, overthrow, ruin, spoil, undermine, weaken, enfeeble, devitalize, exhaust, disable, cripple; demolish, disprove, refute, confute, contradict. **5** see RUIN *v.* 1a, DISGRACE *v.* **6** see DEFEAT *v.* 1.

destroyer /distróyər/ *n.* **1** a person or thing that destroys. **2** *Naut.* a fast warship with guns and torpedoes used to protect other ships.

destruct /distrúkt/ *v. & n.* esp. *Astronaut.* ● *v.* **1** *tr.* destroy (one's own rocket, etc.) deliberately, esp. for safety reasons. **2** *intr.* be destroyed in this way. ● *n.* an act of destructing. [L *destruere* (as DESTROY) or as back-form. f. DESTRUCTION]

destructible /distrúktibəl/ *adj.* able to be destroyed. □□ **destructibility** /-bílitee/ *n.* [F *destructible* or LL *destructibilis* (as DESTROY)]

destruction /distrúkshən/ *n.* **1** the act or an instance of destroying; the process of being destroyed. **2** a cause of ruin; something that destroys (*greed was their destruction*). [ME f. OF f. L *destructio -onis* (as DESTROY)]
■ **1** demolition, ruin, ruining, ruination, breaking up or down, devastation, tearing or knocking down, laying waste, wiping out; rack and ruin; slaughter, annihilation, killing, eradication, murder,

extermination, holocaust, liquidation, massacre, extinction, genocide, slaying; termination, breakup, breakdown, collapse. **2** undoing, end, ruination, downfall; see also RUIN *n.* 2a.

destructive /distrúktiv/ *adj.* **1** (often foll. by *to*, *of*) destroying or tending to destroy (*destructive of her peace of mind*; *is destructive to organisms*; *a destructive child*). **2** negative in attitude or criticism; refuting without suggesting, helping, amending, etc. (opp. CONSTRUCTIVE) (*has only destructive criticism to offer*). □□ **destructively** *adv.* **destructiveness** *n.* [ME f. OF *destructif -ive* f. LL *destructivus* (as DESTROY)]
■ **1** harmful, injurious, pernicious, dangerous, hurtful, toxic, poisonous, virulent, noxious, bad, malignant, baleful, unwholesome, damaging, detrimental, deleterious, devastating, baneful. **2** negative, adverse, opposed, contrary, contradictory, antithetical, conflicting, unfavorable, condemnatory, derogatory, disparaging, disapproving, critical.

destructor /distrúktər/ *n. Brit.* a refuse-burning furnace.

desuetude /déswitood, -tyood/ *n.* a state of disuse (*the custom fell into desuetude*). [F *désuétude* or L *desuetudo* (as DE-, *suescere suet-* be accustomed)]

desultory /désəltáwree, déz-/ *adj.* **1** going constantly from one subject to another, esp. in a halfhearted way. **2** disconnected; unmethodical; superficial. □□ **desultorily** *adv.* **desultoriness** *n.* [L *desultorius* superficial f. *desultor* vaulter f. *desult-* (as DE-, *salt-* past part. stem of *salire* leap)]
■ shifting, unsteady, irregular, wavering, inconstant, fitful, spasmodic, unmethodical, disconnected, unsystematic, disorderly, disordered, unorganized, disorganized, inconsistent, random, haphazard, chaotic, erratic; see also SUPERFICIAL 2.

detach /ditách/ *v.tr.* **1** (often foll. by *from*) unfasten or disengage and remove (*detached the buttons*; *detached himself from the group*). **2** *Mil.* send (a ship, regiment, officer, messenger, etc.) on a separate mission. **3** (as **detached** *adj.*) **a** impartial; unemotional (*a detached viewpoint*). **b** (esp. of a house) not joined to another or others; separate. □□ **detachable** *adj.* **detachedly** /ditáchidlee/ *adv.* [F *détacher* (as DE-, ATTACH)]
■ **1** separate, uncouple, decouple, part, disjoin, disengage, disunite, disconnect, disentangle, free, unfasten, undo, cut off, remove. **3** (**detached**) **a** disinterested, aloof, uninvolved, unemotional, dispassionate, equanimous, dégagé, nonchalant, indifferent, impersonal, impartial, neutral, objective, unbiased, unprejudiced. **b** disconnected, unattached, separated, separate, free, freestanding, isolated, disentangled, unfastened, removed, cut off, divided, disjoined.

detachment /ditáchmənt/ *n.* **1 a** a state of aloofness from or indifference to other people, one's surroundings, public opinion, etc. **b** disinterested independence of judgment. **2 a** the act or process of detaching or being detached. **b** an instance of this. **3** *Mil.* a separate group or unit of an army, etc., used for a specific purpose. [F *détachement* (as DETACH)]
■ **1 a** aloofness, unconcern, indifference, coolness, nonchalance, inattention, insouciance; see also DISTANCE *n.* 4. **b** see *objectivity* (OBJECTIVE). **2** separation, disconnection, disengagement, dissociation, dissassociation, segregation. **3** see SQUAD.

detail /ditáyl, deétayl/ *n. & v.* ● *n.* **1 a** a small or subordinate particular; an item. **b** such a particular, considered (ironically) to be unimportant (*the truth of the statement is just a detail*). **2 a** small items or particulars (esp. in an artistic work) regarded collectively (*has an eye for detail*). **b** the treatment of them (*the detail was insufficient and unconvincing*). **3** (often in *pl.*) a number of particulars; an aggregate of small items (*filled in the details on the form*). **4 a** a minor

/.../ **pronunciation**	● **part of speech**
□ **phrases, idioms, and compounds**	
□□ **derivatives**	■ **synonym section**
cross-references appear in SMALL CAPITALS or *italics*	

decoration on a building, in a picture, etc. **b** a small part of a picture, etc., shown alone. **5** *Mil.* **a** the distribution of orders for the day. **b** a small detachment of soldiers, etc., for special duty. ● *v.tr.* **1** give particulars of (*detailed the plans*). **2** relate circumstantially (*detailed the anecdote*). **3** *Mil.* assign for special duty. **4** (as **detailed** *adj.*) **a** (of a picture, story, etc.) having many details. **b** itemized (*a detailed list*). □ **go into detail** give all the items or particulars. **in detail** item by item, minutely. [F *détail, détailler* (as DE-, *tailler* cut, formed as TAIL²)]

■ *n.* **1** particular, element, factor, point, fact, technicality, component, item, feature; aspect, respect, count; (*details*) minutiae, niceties, fine points, specifics, technicalities. **5 b** detachment, party, group, unit; see also SQUAD. ● *v.* **1, 2** specify, spell out, itemize, delineate, catalog, list, tabulate, enumerate, particularize, recount, cite, relate; describe, outline. **3** assign, appoint, charge, delegate, name, specify, send. **4** (**detailed**) itemized, exhaustive, comprehensive, thorough, full, complete, inclusive, particularized, precise, exact, blow-by-blow, circumstantial; intricate, complex, complicated, elaborate, ornate. □ **in detail** minutely, specifically, particularly, thoroughly, in depth, item by item, point by point, exhaustively, comprehensively, inside out, perfectly.

detain /dɪtáyn/ *v.tr.* **1** keep in confinement or under restraint. **2** keep waiting; delay. □□ **detainment** *n.* [ME f. OF *detenir* ult. f. L *detinēre detent-* (as DE-, *tenēre* hold)]

■ **1** see IMPRISON 2. **2** see DELAY *v.* 2.

detainee /dèetaynée/ *n.* a person detained in custody, esp. for political reasons.

■ see PRISONER.

detainer /dɪtáynər/ *n.* *Law* **1** the wrongful detaining of goods taken from the owner for distraint, etc. **2** the detention of a person in prison, etc. [AF *detener* f. OF *detenir* (as DETAIN)]

detect /dɪtékt/ *v.tr.* **1 a** (often foll. by *in*) reveal the guilt of; discover (*detected him in his crime*). **b** discover (a crime). **2** discover or perceive the existence or presence of (*detected a smell of burning; do I detect a note of sarcasm?*). **3** *Physics* use an instrument to observe (a signal, radiation, etc.). □□ **detectable** *adj.* **detectably** *adv.* [L *detegere detect-* (as DE-, *tegere* cover)]

■ **2** uncover, find (out), discover, locate, learn of, ascertain, determine, dig up, unearth; perceive, note, notice, identify, spot, observe, sense, read, scent, smell (out), sniff (out), discern, feel, catch, find.

detection /dɪtékshən/ *n.* **1 a** the act or an instance of detecting; the process of being detected. **b** an instance of this. **2** the work of a detective. **3** *Physics* the extraction of a desired signal; a demodulation. [LL *detectio* (as DETECT)]

■ **1** see IDENTIFICATION 1a, DISCOVERY 1.

detective /dɪtéktiv/ *n.* & *adj.* ● *n.* (often *attrib.*) a person, esp. a member of a police force, employed to investigate crime. ● *adj.* serving to detect. □ **private detective** a usu. freelance detective carrying out investigations for a private employer. [DETECT]

■ *n.* (private) investigator, private detective, policeman, operative, esp. *Brit.* constable, *colloq.* eye, private eye, sleuthhound, sleuth, snoop, snooper, tec, G-man, *sl.* dick, cop, copper, gumshoe, peeper, shamus. □ **private detective** see DETECTIVE *n.* above.

detector /dɪtéktər/ *n.* **1** a person or thing that detects. **2** *Physics* a device for the detection or demodulation of signals.

detent /dɪtént/ *n.* **1** a catch by the removal of which machinery is allowed to move. **2** (in a clock, etc.) a catch that regulates striking. [F *détente* f. OF *destente* f. *destendre* slacken (as DE-, L *tendere*)]

détente /daytóNt/ *n.* an easing of strained relations, esp. between nations. [F, = relaxation]

■ see *reconciliation* (RECONCILE).

detention /dɪténshən/ *n.* **1** detaining or being detained. **2 a** being kept in school after hours as a punishment. **b** an instance of this. **3** custody; confinement. [F *détention* or LL *detentio* (as DETAIN)]

■ **3** custody, confinement, imprisonment, captivity, internment, incarceration, restraint, *archaic* durance.

deter /dɪtór/ *v.tr.* (**deterred, deterring**) **1** (often foll. by *from*) discourage or prevent (a person) through fear or dislike of the consequences. **2** discourage, check, or prevent (a thing, process, etc.). □□ **determent** *n.* [L *deterrēre* (as DE-, *terrēre* frighten)]

■ dissuade, discourage, inhibit, intimidate, daunt, frighten off or away, scare off; prevent, stop, obstruct, check, hinder, impede.

detergent /dɪtórjənt/ *n.* & *adj.* ● *n.* a cleansing agent, esp. a synthetic substance (usu. other than soap) used with water as a means of removing dirt, etc. ● *adj.* cleansing, esp. in the manner of a detergent. [L *detergēre* (as DE-, *tergēre* terswipe)]

■ *n.* cleaner, cleanser, soap (powder or flakes), liquid soap; surfactant, surface-active agent. ● *adj.* cleaning, cleansing, washing, purifying.

deteriorate /dɪtéereeərayt/ *v.tr.* & *intr.* make or become bad or worse (*food deteriorates in hot weather; his condition deteriorated after the operation*). □□ **deterioration** /-ráyshən/ *n.* **deteriorative** *adj.* [LL *deteriorare deteriorat-* f. L *deterior* worse]

■ worsen, get worse, decline, degenerate, degrade, spoil, depreciate, slip, slide, *colloq.* go to pot, go downhill, *sl.* go to the dogs; decay, disintegrate, fall apart, crumble.

determinant /dɪtórminənt/ *adj.* & *n.* ● *adj.* serving to determine or define. ● *n.* **1** a determining factor, element, word, etc. **2** *Math.* a quantity obtained by the addition of products of the elements of a square matrix according to a given rule. [L *determinare* (as DETERMINE)]

■ *n.* **1** see FACTOR *n.* 1.

determinate /dɪtórminət/ *adj.* **1** limited in time, space, or character. **2** of definite scope or nature. □□ **determinacy** /-nəsee/ *n.* **determinately** *adv.* **determinateness** *n.* [ME f. L *determinatus* past part. (as DETERMINE)]

■ fixed, definite, exact, precise, distinct, determined, predetermined, ascertained, identified; limited.

determination /dɪtórmináyshən/ *n.* **1** firmness of purpose; resoluteness. **2** the process of deciding, determining, or calculating. **3 a** the conclusion of a dispute by the decision of an arbitrator. **b** the decision reached. **4** *Law* the cessation of an estate or interest. **5** *Law* a judicial decision or sentence. **6** *archaic* a tendency to move in a fixed direction. [ME (in sense 4) f. OF f. L *determinatio -onis* (as DETERMINE)]

■ **1** resoluteness, resolution, firmness, resolve, steadfastness, tenacity, perseverance, fortitude, doggedness, persistence, constancy, single-mindedness, will, willpower, determinedness, *colloq.* grit, guts. **2** fixing, settling, determining, calculating, deciding, decision making, ascertainment. **3** settlement, resolution, decision, solution, arbitration, judgment, verdict, outcome, result, upshot, conclusion, end, termination.

determinative /dɪtórmənáytiv, -nətiv/ *adj.* & *n.* ● *adj.* serving to define, qualify, or direct. ● *n.* a determinative thing or circumstance. □□ **determinatively** *adv.* [F *déterminatif -ive* (as DETERMINE)]

determine /dɪtórmin/ *v.* **1** *tr.* find out or establish precisely (*have to determine the extent of the problem*). **2** *tr.* decide or settle (*determined who should go*). **3** *tr.* be a decisive factor in regard to (*demand determines supply*). **4** *intr.* & *tr.* make or cause (a person) to make a decision (*we determined to go at once; what determined you to do it?*). **5** *tr.* & *intr.* esp. *Law* bring or come to an end. **6** *tr.* *Geom.* fix or define the position of. □ **be determined** be resolved (*was determined not to give up*). □□ **determinable** *adj.* [ME f. OF *determiner* f. L *determinare* (as DE-, *terminus* end)]

■ **1** ascertain, decide, find out, discover, learn, detect. **2, 4** settle (on or upon), fix on or upon, choose, select, resolve; make up one's mind; see also DECIDE 1. **3** affect, influence, act on, shape, condition, govern, regulate, dictate. **5** conclude, terminate; see also END *v.* 1.

determined /dɪtórmind/ *adj.* **1** showing determination; res-

olute; unflinching. **2** fixed in scope or character; settled; determinate. □□ **determinedly** *adv.* **determinedness** *n.*
■ **1** decided, resolute, resolved, purposeful, dogged, strong-willed, strong-minded, single-minded, tenacious, intent, firm, unflinching, unwavering, fixed, constant, persistent, persevering, steady, unfaltering, unhesitating, unyielding, stubborn, obstinate, adamant. **2** see DETERMINATE.

determiner /ditɔ́rminər/ *n.* **1** a person or thing that determines. **2** *Gram.* any of a class of words (e.g., *a, the, every*) that determine the kind of reference a noun or noun substitute has.

determinism /ditɔ́rminizəm/ *n. Philos.* the doctrine that all events, including human action, are determined by causes regarded as external to the will. □□ **determinist** *n.* **deterministic** / *adj.* **deterministically** /-nístikəlee/ *adv.*

deterrent /ditɔ́rənt, -túr-/ *adj. & n.* ● *adj.* that deters. ● *n.* a deterrent thing or factor, esp. a nuclear weapon regarded as deterring an enemy from attack. □□ **deterrence** /-rəns/ *n.*
■ *n.* hindrance, impediment, discouragement, disincentive, dissuasion, check, hitch, obstacle, obstruction, stumbling block; catch, snag, rub, fly in the ointment, bar, drawback.

detest /ditést/ *v.tr.* hate; loathe. □□ **detester** *n.* [L *detestari* (as DE-, *testari* call to witness f. *testis* witness)]
■ despise, loathe, hate, abhor, execrate, abominate, be nauseated by, *literary* contemn.

detestable /ditéstəbəl/ *adj.* intensely disliked; hateful. □□ **detestably** *adv.*
■ see HATEFUL.

detestation /déetestáyshən/ *n.* **1** intense dislike; hatred. **2** a detested person or thing. [ME f. OF f. L *detestatio -onis* (as DETEST)]
■ **1** see DISLIKE *n.* 1.

dethrone /deethrốn/ *v.tr.* **1** remove from the throne; depose. **2** remove from a position of authority or influence. □□ **dethronement** *n.*
■ **1** see OVERTHROW *v.* 1–3. **2** see DOWNGRADE *v.* 1.

detonate /dét'nayt/ *v.intr. & tr.* explode with a loud noise. □□ **detonative** *adj.* [L *detonare detonat-* (as DE-, *tonare* thunder)]
■ see EXPLODE 1.

detonation /dét'náyshən/ *n.* **1 a** the act or process of detonating. **b** a loud explosion. **2** the premature combustion of fuel in an internal combustion engine, causing it to knock. [F *détonation* f. *détoner* (as DETONATE)]
■ **1** see EXPLOSION 1, 2.

detonator /dét'naytər/ *n.* **1** a device for detonating an explosive. **2** a fog signal that detonates, e.g., as used on railroads.

detour /déetoor, ditóor/ *n. & v.* ● *n.* **1** a divergence from a direct or intended route; a roundabout course. **2** an alternative route, when a road is temporarily closed to traffic. ● *v.intr. & tr.* make or cause to make a detour. [F *détour* change of direction f. *détourner* turn away (as DE-, TURN)]
■ *n.* diversion, deviation, circuitous route *or* way, roundabout way, bypass. ● *v.* deviate (from), turn away (from), divert (from); see also BYPASS *v.*

detoxicate /deetóksikayt/ *v.tr.* = DETOXIFY. □□ **detoxication** /-káyshən/ *n.* [DE- + L *toxicum* poison, after *intoxicate*]

detoxify /deetóksifī/ *v.tr.* remove the poison from. □□ **detoxification** /-fikáyshən/ *n.* [DE- + L *toxicum* poison]

detract /ditrákt/ *v.tr.* (usu. foll. by *from*) take away (a part of something); reduce; diminish (*self-interest detracted nothing from their achievement*). □□ **detraction** /-trákshən/ *n.* **detractive** *adj.* **detractor** *n.* [L *detrahere detract-* (as DE-, *trahere* draw)]
■ (*detract from*) diminish, reduce, take (away) from, subtract from, lessen, depreciate, disparage.

detrain /deetráyn/ *v.intr. & tr.* alight or cause to alight from a train. □□ **detrainment** *n.*
■ see DISEMBARK.

detribalize /deetríbəliz/ *v.tr.* **1** make (a person) no longer a member of a tribe. **2** destroy the tribal habits of. □□ **detribalization** *n.*

detriment /détrimənt/ *n.* **1** harm; damage. **2** something caus-

ing this. [ME f. OF *detriment* or L *detrimentum* (as DE-, *terere trit-* rub, wear)]
■ disadvantage, drawback; damage, harm, ill, impairment, injury, hurt, loss.

detrimental /détrimént'l/ *adj.* harmful; causing loss. □□ **detrimentally** *adv.*
■ disadvantageous, harmful, injurious, hurtful, damaging, deleterious, destructive, prejudicial, adverse, unfavorable, inimical, pernicious.

detrition /ditríshən/ *n.* wearing away by friction. [med.L *detritio* (as DETRIMENT)]

detritus /ditrítəs/ *n.* **1** matter produced by erosion, such as gravel, sand, silt, rock debris, etc. **2** debris of any kind; rubbish; waste. □□ **detrital** /ditrít'l/ *adj.* [after F *détritus* f. L *detritus* (n.) = wearing down (as DETRIMENT)]
■ **2** see JUNK[1] *n.* 1, 2.

de trop /də trṓ/ *predic.adj.* not wanted; unwelcome; in the way. [F, = excessive]
■ see NEEDLESS.

detumescence /déetōōmésəns, -tyōō-/ *n.* subsidence from a swollen state. [L *detumescere* (as DE-, *tumescere* swell)]

deuce[1] /dōōs, dyōōs/ *n.* **1** the two on dice or playing cards. **2** (in tennis) the score of 40 all, at which two consecutive points are needed to win. [OF *deus* f. L *duo* (accus. *duos*) two]

deuce[2] /dōōs, dyōōs/ *n.* misfortune; the Devil, used esp. *colloq.* as an exclamation of surprise or annoyance (*who the deuce are you?*). □ **a** (or **the**) **deuce of a** very bad or remarkable (*a deuce of a problem; a deuce of a fellow*). **the deuce to pay** trouble to be expected. [LG *duus*, formed as DEUCE[1], two aces at dice being the worst throw]
■ see DEVIL *n.* 1, 2; (**the deuce**) see *the devil* (DEVIL *n.* 7).

deuced /dōōsid, dyōō-, dōōst, dyōōst/ *adj. & adv. Brit. archaic* damned; confounded (*a deuced liar*). □□ **deucedly** /dōōsidlee, dyōō-/ *adv.*

deus ex machina /dáyəs eks maákinə, mák-/ *n.* an unexpected power or event saving a seemingly hopeless situation, esp. in a play or novel. [mod.L transl. of Gk *theos ek mēkhanēs*, = god from the machinery (by which in the Greek theater the gods were suspended above the stage)]

Deut. *abbr.* Deuteronomy (Old Testament).

deuteragonist /dōōtərágənist, dyōō-/ *n.* the person second in importance to the protagonist in a drama. [Gk *deuteragōnistēs* (as DEUTERO-, *agōnistēs* actor)]

deuterate /dōōtərayt, dyōō-/ *v.tr.* replace the usual isotope of hydrogen in (a substance) by deuterium. □□ **deuteration** /-ráyshən/ *n.*

deuterium /dōōteéreeəm, dyōō-/ *n. Chem.* a stable isotope of hydrogen with a mass about double that of the usual isotope. [mod.L, formed as DEUTERO- + -IUM]

deutero- /dōōtərō, dyōō-/ *comb. form* second. [Gk *deuteros* second]

Deutero-Isaiah /dōōtərō-īzáyə, -zíə, dyōō-/ *n.* the supposed later author of Isaiah 40–55.

deuteron /dōōtəron, dyōō-/ *n. Physics* the nucleus of a deuterium atom, consisting of a proton and a neutron. [DEUTERIUM + -ON]

deutsche mark /dóychmaark/ *n.* (also **Deutschemark** /dóychə maark/) the chief monetary unit of Germany. [G, = German mark (see MARK[2])]

deutzia /dōōtseeə, dyōōt-, dóyt-/ *n.* any ornamental shrub of the genus *Deutzia*, with usu. white flowers. [J. *Deutz* 18th-c. Du. patron of botany]

devalue /deevályōō/ *v.tr.* (**devalues, devalued, devaluing**) **1** reduce the value of. **2** *Econ.* reduce the value of (a currency) in relation to other currencies or to gold (opp. REVALUE). □□ **devaluation** *n.*
■ see DEBASE.

Devanagari /dáyvənaágəree/ *n.* the alphabet used for San-

/.../ **pronunciation**	● **part of speech**
□ **phrases, idioms, and compounds**	
□□ **derivatives**	■ **synonym section**
cross-references appear in SMALL CAPITALS or *italics*	

skrit, Hindi, and other languages of India. [Skr., = divine town script]

devastate /dévəstayt/ v.tr. **1** lay waste; cause great destruction to. **2** (often in *passive*) overwhelm with shock or grief; upset deeply. □□ **devastation** /-táyshən/ n. **devastator** n. [L *devastare devastat-* (as DE-, *vastare* lay waste)]

■ **1** lay waste, ravage, destroy, waste, sack, raze, ruin, desolate, spoil, wreck, demolish, level, flatten, gut, obliterate. **2** disconcert, discomfit, take aback, shatter, overwhelm; see also SHOCK[1] v. 1.

devastating /dévəstayting/ adj. **1** crushingly effective; overwhelming. **2** colloq. **a** incisive; savage (*devastating accuracy, devastating wit*). **b** extremely impressive or attractive (*she wore a devastating black silk dress*). □□ **devastatingly** adv.

■ **1** overpowering, powerful, potent, awesome; see also OVERWHELMING. **2 a** keen, incisive, mordant, penetrating, trenchant, telling; brilliant, coruscating; sardonic, sarcastic, bitter, acid, satirical, virulent, savage, vitriolic. **b** spectacular, marvelous, splendid; ravishing, captivating, enthralling, bewitching, spellbinding, colloq. terrific; see also STUNNING.

develop /divéləp/ v. (**developed, developing**) **1** tr. & intr. **a** make or become bigger or fuller or more elaborate or systematic (*the new town developed rapidly*). **b** bring or come to an active or visible state or to maturity (*developed a plan of action*). **2 a** tr. begin to exhibit or suffer from (*developed a rattle*). **b** intr. come into existence; originate; emerge (*a fault developed in the engine*). **3** tr. **a** construct new buildings on (land). **b** convert (land) to a new purpose so as to use its resources more fully. **4** tr. treat (photographic film, etc.) to make the latent image visible. **5** tr. Mus. elaborate (a theme) by modification of the melody, harmony, rhythm, etc. **6** tr. Chess bring (a piece) into position for effective use. □ **developing country** a poor or undeveloped country that is becoming more advanced economically and socially. □□ **developer** n. [F *développer* f. Rmc (as DIS-, orig. of second element unknown)]

■ **1** bring out or forth, advance, expand (on or upon), broaden, enlarge (on or upon), amplify, evolve, expatiate (on or upon), elaborate (on or upon), reveal, lay open, expose, unfold, disclose, bare, (cause to) grow, realize the potential (of); cultivate, improve, promote, exploit, strengthen; mature, ripen, age; flower, blossom, bloom. **2 a** exhibit, display, show, demonstrate, manifest; come down with; see also CONTRACT v. 3. **b** emerge, arise, appear, come out, come to light, evolve, originate, begin, happen, occur, come about, formal commence; come forth, result. □ **developing country** underdeveloped country, third world country. □□ **developer** builder, construction company.

developable /divéləpəbəl/ adj. that can be developed. □ **developable surface** Geom. a surface that can be flattened into a plane without overlap or separation, e.g., a cylinder.

development /divéləpmənt/ n. **1** the act or an instance of developing; the process of being developed. **2 a** a stage of growth or advancement. **b** a thing that has developed, esp. an event or circumstance (*the latest developments*). **3** a full-grown state. **4** the process of developing a photograph. **5** a developed area of land. **6** Mus. the elaboration of a theme or themes, esp. in the middle section of a sonata movement. **7** Chess the developing of pieces from their original position.

■ **1** evolution, growth, evolvement, maturation, unfolding, increase, expansion, enlargement, increment; advance, advancement, progress; improvement; building, construction (work). **2 b** occurrence, happening, event, incident, circumstance, situation, condition, phenomenon.

developmental /divéləpmént'l/ adj. **1** incidental to growth (*developmental diseases*). **2** evolutionary. □□ **developmentally** adv.

deviant /déeveeənt/ adj. & n. ● adj. that deviates from the normal, esp. with reference to sexual practices. ● n. a deviant person or thing. □□ **deviance** /-veeəns/ n. **deviancy** n. [ME (as DEVIATE)]

■ adj. deviating, divergent, different, strange, uncommon, unusual, odd, peculiar, curious, eccentric, idiosyncratic, queer, quirky, weird, bizarre, offbeat, singular, freaky, freakish; perverse, aberrant, abnormal, unnatural, degenerate, depraved, colloq. kinky, esp. Brit. sl. bent. ● n. see ECCENTRIC n.

deviate v. & n. ● v.intr. /déeveeayt/ (often foll. by from) turn aside or diverge (from a course of action, rule, truth, etc.); digress. ● n. /déeveeət/ a deviant, a sexual pervert. □□ **deviator** n. **deviatory** /-veeətáwree/ adj. [LL *deviare deviat-* (as DE-, via way)]

■ v. turn aside or away, swerve, veer, wander, stray, drift, digress, diverge; divert. ● n. pervert, deviant, degenerate, debauchee.

deviation /déeveeáyshən/ n. **1 a** deviating; digressing. **b** an instance of this. **2** Polit. a departure from accepted (esp. Communist) party doctrine. **3** Statistics the amount by which a single measurement differs from the mean. **4** Naut. the deflection of a ship's compass needle caused by iron in the ship, etc. □ **standard deviation** Statistics a quantity calculated to indicate the extent of deviation for a group as a whole. □□ **deviational** adj. **deviationism** n. **deviationist** n. [F *déviation* f. med.L *deviatio -onis* (as DEVIATE)]

■ **1** see digression (DIGRESS).

device /divís/ n. **1 a** a thing made or adapted for a particular purpose, esp. a mechanical contrivance. **b** an explosive contrivance; a bomb. **2** a plan, scheme, or trick. **3 a** an emblematic or heraldic design. **b** a drawing or design. **4** archaic make, look (*things of rare device*). □ **leave a person to his** or **her own devices** leave a person to do as he or she wishes. [ME f. OF *devis* ult. f. L (as DIVIDE)]

■ **1 a** contrivance, mechanism, machine, machinery, implement, utensil, apparatus, instrument, appliance, tool, gadget, colloq. widget, doodad, thingamajig, thingummy, thingy, hickey, derog. or joc. contraption, sl. jigger, gizmo. **b** see BOMB n. 1. **2** stratagem, trick, artifice, ruse, plot, gambit, strategy, maneuver, machination, plan, colloq. ploy; see also SCHEME n. 2. **3** emblem, figure, Heraldry charge, cognizance, (heraldic) bearing; insignia, hallmark, badge, signet, coat of arms, seal, crest; design, drawing, symbol, colophon, logotype, monogram, colloq. logo. **4** look, make, appearance, aspect.

devil /dévəl/ n. & v. ● n. **1** (usu. **the Devil**) (in Christian and Jewish belief) the supreme spirit of evil; Satan. **2 a** an evil spirit; a demon; a superhuman malignant being. **b** a personified evil force or attribute. **3 a** a wicked or cruel person. **b** a mischievously energetic, clever, or self-willed person. **4** colloq. a person; a fellow (*lucky devil*). **5** fighting spirit; mischievousness (*the devil is in him tonight*). **6** colloq. something difficult or awkward (*this door is a devil to open*). **7** (**the devil** or **the Devil**) colloq. used as an exclamation of surprise or annoyance (*who the devil are you?*). **8** a literary hack exploited by an employer. **9** Brit. a junior legal counsel. **10** = Tasmanian devil. **11** applied to various instruments and machines, esp. when used for destructive work. ● v. (**deviled, deviling; devilled, devilling**) **1** tr. cook (food) with hot seasoning. **2** intr. act as a devil for an author or barrister. **3** tr. harass; worry. □ **between the devil and the deep blue sea** in a dilemma. **devil-may-care** cheerful and reckless. **a devil of** colloq. considerable, difficult, or remarkable (*a devil of a time*). **devil ray** any cartilaginous fish of the family Mobulidae, esp. the manta. **devil's advocate** a person who tests a proposition by arguing against it. **devil's-bit** any of various plants whose roots look bitten off, esp. a kind of scabious (*Succisa pratensis*). **devil's darning needle** a dragonfly or damselfly. **devil's dozen** esp. Brit. a baker's dozen; thirteen. **devils-on-horseback** Brit. a savory dish of prune or plum wrapped in slices of bacon. **devil's own** colloq. very difficult or unusual (*the devil's own job*). **devil take the hindmost** a motto of selfish competition. **the devil to pay** trouble to be expected. **go to the devil 1** be damned. **2** (in imper.) depart at once. **like the devil** with great energy. **play the devil with** cause severe damage to. **printer's devil** hist. an errand boy in a printing office.

speak (or **talk**) **of the devil** said when a person appears just after being mentioned. **the very devil** (*predic.*) *colloq.* a great difficulty or nuisance. [OE *dēofol* f. LL *diabolus* f. Gk *diabolos* accuser, slanderer f. *dia* across + *ballō* to throw]
■ *n.* **1, 2** Satan, Lucifer, Mephistopheles, Beelzebub, Abaddon, Belial, Prince of Darkness, Tempter, deuce, archenemy, evil one, *colloq.* Old Nick; fiend, spirit of evil, evil spirit, demon, cacodemon, bogey, bugaboo, gremlin, *archaic* bugbear. **3 a** brute, fiend, demon, beast, ogre, monster, rogue, scoundrel, knave, villain, ghoul, hellhound, barbarian. **b** imp, fox, mischief-maker, gamin, trickster, (little) monkey, *archaic or joc.* rapscallion, *colloq.* scamp, slyboots, *joc.* rogue, *often joc.* rascal. **4** fellow, person, chap, wretch, *colloq.* guy, beggar, *Brit. colloq.* blighter, *sl.* geezer, bastard, *Brit. sl.* bloke. **5** see MISCHIEF 1–3. **6** see PROBLEM 1, 2, BITCH *n.* 3. **7** (**the devil**) in heaven's name, in the world, in God's name, in the name of God, *colloq.* on earth, the dickens, the deuce. ● *v.* **3** see WORRY *v.* 2. □ **devil-may-care** see RECKLESS. **a devil of** see CONSIDERABLE 1, 2, DIFFICULT 1, REMARKABLE 1. **devil's own** fiendish, *colloq.* beastly; see also DIFFICULT 1, UNUSUAL 2. **go to the devil 2** see *beat it.* **like the devil** rapidly, very fast, at a gallop, *colloq.* like thunder, like a house on fire, like a bat out of hell, like greased lightning, like the wind, *literary* apace, *Brit. sl.* like the clappers; see also *vigorously* (VIGOROUS).

devilfish /dévəlfish/ *n.* (*pl.* same or **-fishes**) **1** = *devil ray.* **2** any of various fish, esp. the stonefish. **3** *hist.* an octopus.

devilish /dévəlish/ *adj.* & *adv.* ● *adj.* **1** of or like a devil; wicked. **2** mischievous. ● *adv. colloq.* very; extremely. □□ **devilishly** *adv.* **devilishness** *n.*
■ *adj.* **1** diabolical, diabolic, wicked, evil, satanic, Mephistophelian, fiendish, demonic, demoniacal, demoniac, infernal, hellish, villainous, sinister, iniquitous, sinful, flagitious, heinous, malign, malevolent, malignant, cruel. **2** impish, prankish, naughty; see also MISCHIEVOUS 1, 2. ● *adv.* see VERY *adv.*

devilment /dévəlmənt/ *n.* mischief; wild spirits.
■ see MISCHIEF 1–3.

devilry /dévilree/ *n.* (also **deviltry** /-tree/) (*pl.* **-ies**) **1 a** wickedness; reckless mischief. **b** an instance of this. **2 a** black magic. **b** the Devil and his works. [OF *diablerie*: *-try* wrongly after *harlotry*, etc.]
■ **1 a** devilishness, wickedness, evil, fiendishness, cruelty, malice, malevolence, viciousness, perversity, iniquity, hellishness, villainy; mischief, diablerie, mischievousness, roguery, naughtiness, roguishness, knavery, knavishness, *often joc.* rascality.

devious /déeveeəs/ *adj.* **1** (of a person, etc.) not straightforward; underhand. **2** winding; circuitous. **3** erring; straying. □□ **deviously** *adv.* **deviousness** *n.* [L *devius* f. DE- + *via* way]
■ **1** deceitful, underhanded, underhand, insincere, deceptive, misleading, sneaky, furtive, surreptitious, secretive, double-dealing, treacherous, dishonest, smooth, slick, cunning, slippery, scheming, plotting, designing, foxy, vulpine, wily, sly, crafty, tricky, *colloq.* shifty. **2** winding, indirect, roundabout, zigzag, evasive, circuitous, crooked, rambling, serpentine, tortuous, sinuous, anfractuous.

devise /divíz/ *v.* & *n.* ● *v.tr.* **1** plan or invent by careful thought. **2** *Law* leave (real estate) by the terms of a will (cf. BEQUEATH). ● *n.* **1** the act or an instance of devising. **2** *Law* a devising clause in a will. □□ **devisable** *adj.* **devisee** /-zeé/ *n.* (in sense 2 of *v.*). **deviser** *n.* **devisor** *n.* (in sense 2 of *v.*). [ME f. OF *deviser* ult. f. L *dividere divis-* DIVIDE: (n.) f. OF *devise* f. med.L *divisa* fem. past part. of *dividere*]
■ *v.* **1** concoct, make up, conceive, scheme, contrive, dream up, design, draft, frame, form, formulate, plan, work out, think up, originate, invent, create, *colloq.* cook up. **2** bequeath, will, convey, hand down, give, assign, dispose of, transfer, bestow.

devitalize /deevít'līz/ *v.tr.* take away strength and vigor from. □□ **devitalization** *n.*
■ see ENERVATE *v.*

devitrify /deevítrifī/ *v.tr.* (**-ies**, **-ied**) deprive of vitreous qualities; make (glass or vitreous rock) opaque and crystalline. □□ **devitrification** /-fikáyshən/ *n.*

devoid /divóyd/ *predic.adj.* (foll. by *of*) quite lacking or free from (*a book devoid of all interest*). [ME, past part. of obs. *devoid* f. OF *devoidier* (as DE-, VOID)]

devoir /dəvwaár, dévwaar/ *n. archaic* **1** duty; one's best (*do one's devoir*). **2** (in *pl.*) courteous or formal attentions; respects (*pay one's devoirs to*). [ME f. AF *dever* = OF *deveir* f. L *debēre* owe]

devolute /déevəlōōt/ *v.tr.* transfer by devolution. [as DE-VOLVE]

devolution /deevəlōōshən/ *n.* **1** the delegation of power, esp. by central government to local or regional administration. **2 a** descent or passing on through a series of stages. **b** descent by natural or due succession from one to another of property or qualities. **3** the lapse of an unexercised right to an ultimate owner. **4** *Biol.* degeneration. □□ **devolutionary** *adj.* **devolutionist** *n.* [LL *devolutio* (as DEVOLVE)]

devolve /divólv/ *v.* **1** (foll. by *on, upon,* etc.) **a** *tr.* pass (work or duties) to (a deputy, etc.). **b** *intr.* (of work or duties) pass to (a deputy, etc.). **2** *intr.* (foll. by *on, to, upon*) *Law* (of property, etc.) descend or fall by succession to. □□ **devolvement** *n.* [ME f. L *devolvere devolut-* (as DE-, *volvere* roll)]

Devonian /divôneeən/ *adj.* & *n.* ● *adj.* **1** of or relating to Devon in SW England. **2** *Geol.* of or relating to the fourth period of the Paleozoic era with evidence of the first amphibians and tree forests. ¶ Cf. Appendix VII. ● *n.* **1** this period or system. **2** a native of Devon. [med.L *Devonia* Devonshire]

devote /divốt/ *v.tr.* & *refl.* **1** (foll. by *to*) apply or give over (resources, etc., or oneself) to (a particular activity or purpose or person) (*devoted their time to reading; devoted himself to his guests*). **2** *archaic* doom to destruction. □□ **devotement** *n.* [L *devovēre devot-* (as DE-, *vovēre* vow)]
■ **1** apply, appropriate, assign, allot, commit, give up, allocate, set aside *or* apart, put aside, dedicate, consecrate; pledge.

devoted /divốtid/ *adj.* very loving or loyal (*a devoted husband*). □□ **devotedly** *adv.* **devotedness** *n.*
■ faithful, true, dedicated, committed, devout, loyal, loving, doting, staunch, tender, steadfast, constant; ardent, caring, fond, earnest, zealous, enthusiastic.

devotee /dévətée, -táy/ *n.* **1** (usu. foll. by *of*) a zealous enthusiast or supporter. **2** a zealously pious or fanatical person.
■ **1** fan, aficionado, adherent, votary, enthusiast, energumen, addict; hound, *colloq.* buff, *sl.* nut, freak, fiend. **2** fanatic, zealot, visionary, cultist, dévot, dévote, energumen.

devotion /divốshən/ *n.* **1** (usu. foll. by *to*) enthusiastic attachment or loyalty (to a person or cause); great love. **2 a** religious worship. **b** (in *pl.*) prayers. **c** devoutness; religious fervor. □□ **devotional** *adj.* [ME f. OF *devotion* or L *devotio* (as DEVOTE)]
■ **1** zeal, ardor, fervor, ardency, intensity, fanaticism, eagerness, enthusiasm, earnestness, readiness, willingness; love, passion, infatuation, fondness, affection, attachment, adherence, loyalty, allegiance; dedication, devotedness. **2 a** worship, prayer(s), praying, observance(s); ritual. **c** devotedness, devoutness, fervor, reverence, religiousness, piety, religiosity, pietism, godliness, holiness, spirituality, saintliness.

devour /divówr/ *v.tr.* **1** eat hungrily or greedily. **2** (of fire, etc.) engulf; destroy. **3** take in greedily with the eyes or ears (*devoured book after book*). **4** absorb the attention of (de-

---

/.../ **pronunciation**	● **part of speech**
□ **phrases, idioms, and compounds**	
□□ **derivatives**	■ **synonym section**
cross-references appear in SMALL CAPITALS or *italics*	

voured by anxiety). □□ **devourer** *n.* **devouringly** *adv.* [ME
f. OF *devorer* f. L *devorare* (as DE-, *vorare* swallow)]
■ **1** wolf (down), gulp (down), bolt, swallow (up), gorge,
gobble (up), gormandize, *colloq.* kill. **2** consume,
destroy, wipe out, ravage, annihilate, demolish, ruin,
wreak havoc (up)on, devastate, obliterate, eradicate;
engulf, swamp, overcome, overwhelm. **3** absorb, be
absorbed by; engulf, consume, drink in, eat up,
swallow up, take in. **4** consumed, absorbed, obsessed.
devout /divówt/ *adj.* **1** earnestly religious. **2** earnestly sincere
(*devout hope*). □□ **devoutly** *adv.* **devoutness** *n.* [ME f. OF
devot f. L *devotus* past part. (as DEVOTE)]
■ **1** devoted, pious, religious, reverent, faithful,
dedicated, staunch, churchgoing, *archaic* worshipful;
holy, godly, saintly, pure; devotional, reverential. **2**
earnest, sincere, genuine, hearty, heartfelt, devoted,
ardent, zealous, true.
DEW *abbr.* distant early warning.
dew /dōō, dyōō/ *n. & v.* ● *n.* **1** atmospheric vapor condensing
in small drops on cool surfaces at night. **2** beaded or glistening moisture resembling this, e.g., tears. **3** freshness; refreshing quality. ● *v.tr.* wet with or as with dew. □ **dew
point** the temperature at which dew forms. [OE *dēaw* f.
Gmc]
■ *v.* bedew, damp, dampen, moisten; see also WET v.
dewan /diwaán/ *n.* the prime minister or finance minister of
an E. Indian state. [Arab. & Pers. *diwān* fiscal register]
dewar /dōōər, dyōōər/ *n. Physics* (also **Dewar**) a double-
walled flask with a vacuum between the walls to reduce the
transfer of heat. [Sir James *Dewar*, Brit. physicist d. 1923]
dewberry /dōōberee, dyōō-/ *n.* (*pl.* **-ies**) **1** a bluish fruit like
the blackberry. **2** the shrub, *Rubus caesius,* bearing this.
dewclaw /dōōklaw, dyōō-/ *n.* **1** a rudimentary inner toe
found on some dogs. **2** a false hoof on a deer, etc.
dewdrop /dōōdrop, dyōō-/ *n.* a drop of dew.
Dewey system /dōō-ee, dyōō-ee/ *n.* a decimal system of library classification. [M. *Dewey,* Amer. librarian d. 1931, its
deviser]
dewfall /dōōfawl, dyōō-/ *n.* **1** the time when dew begins to
form. **2** the formation of dew.
dewlap /dōōlap, dyōō-/ *n.* **1** a loose fold of skin hanging from
the throat of cattle, dogs, etc. **2** similar loose skin around
the throat of an elderly person. [ME f. DEW + LAP¹, perh.
after ON (unrecorded) *döggleppr*]
dewy /dōō-ee, dyōō-ee/ *adj.* (**dewier, dewiest**) **1 a** wet with
dew. **b** moist as if with dew. **2** of or like dew. □ **dewy-eyed**
innocently trusting; naively sentimental. □□ **dewily** *adv.*
dewiness *n.* [OE *dēawig* (as DEW, -Y¹)]
■ **1** see MOIST 1a.
dexter¹ /dékstər/ *adj. Heraldry* on or of the right-hand
side (the observer's left) of a shield, etc. [L, = on the right]
dexter² /dékstər/ *n.* (also **Dexter**) **1** an animal of a small
hardy breed of Irish cattle. **2** this breed. [19th c.: perh. f.
the name of a breeder]
dexterity /dekstéritee/ *n.* **1** skill in handling. **2** manual or
mental adroitness. **3** right-handedness; using the right hand.
[F *dextérité* f. L *dexteritas* (as DEXTER¹)]
■ **1** touch, nimbleness, adroitness, deftness, facility,
knack, skill, proficiency; sleight of hand. **2** adroitness,
cleverness, ingenuity, ingeniousness, tact, astuteness,
keenness, sharpness, shrewdness, canniness, artfulness.
dexterous /dékstrəs, -stərəs/ *adj.* (also **dextrous,** -strəs)
having or showing dexterity. □□ **dexterously** *adv.* **dexterousness** *n.* [L DEXTER¹ + -OUS]
■ deft, lithe, nimble, supple, agile, quick, skillful, slick;
clever, ingenious, astute, keen, sharp, shrewd, canny,
artful, crafty.
dextral /dékstrəl/ *adj. & n.* ● *adj.* **1** (of a person) right-
handed. **2** of or on the right. **3** *Zool.* (of a spiral shell) with
whorls rising to the right and coiling in an anticlockwise
direction. **4** *Zool.* (of a flatfish) with the right side uppermost. ● *n.* a right-handed person. □□ **dextrality** /-trálitee/
n. **dextrally** *adv.* [med.L *dextralis* f. L *dextra* right hand]
dextran /dékstran, -strən/ *n. Chem. & Pharm.* **1** an amorphous gum formed by the fermentation of sucrose, etc. **2** a

degraded form of this used as a substitute for blood plasma.
[G (as DEXTRO- + -*an* as in Chem. names)]
dextrin /dékstrin/ *n. Chem.* a soluble gummy substance obtained from starch and used as an adhesive. [F *dextrine* f. L
dextra: see DEXTRO-, -IN]
dextro- /dékstrō/ *comb. form* on or to the right (*dextrorotatory;
dextrose*). [L *dexter, dextra* on or to the right]
dextrorotatory /dékstrō-rŏtǝtawree/ *adj. Chem.* having the
property of rotating the plane of a polarized light ray to the
right (cf. LEVOROTATORY). □□ **dextrorotation** /-táyshǝn/ *n.*
dextrorse /dékstrawrs/ *adj.* rising toward the right, esp. of a
spiral stem. [L *dextrorsus* (as DEXTRO-)]
dextrose /dékstrōs/ *n. Chem.* the dextrorotatory form of glucose. [formed as DEXTRO- + -OSE²]
dextrous var. of DEXTEROUS.
DF *abbr.* **1** Defender of the Faith. **2** direction finder. [in sense
1 f. L *Defensor Fidei*]
DFC *abbr.* Distinguished Flying Cross.
DG *abbr.* **1** *Dei gratia* (by the grace of God). **2** *Deo gratias*
(thanks be to God). **3** director general.
DH *abbr. Baseball* designated hitter.
dhal var. of DAL.
dharma /daármə/ *n. Ind.* **1** social custom; the right behavior.
2 the Buddhist truth. **3** the Hindu social or moral law. [Skr.,
= decree, custom]
dhoti /dótee/ *n.* (*pl.* **dhotis**) the loincloth worn by male Hindus. [Hindi *dhotī*]
dhow /dow/ *n.* a lateen-rigged ship used esp. on the Arabian
Sea. [19th c.: orig. unkn.]
dhurra var. of DURRA.
DI *abbr. Mil* drill instructor.
di-¹ /dī/ *comb. form* **1** twice, two-, double. **2** *Chem.* containing
two atoms, molecules, or groups of a specified kind (*dichro-
mate; dioxide*). [Gk f. *dis* twice]
di-² /dī, dee/ *prefix* form of DIS- occurring before *l, m, n, r, s*
(foll. by a consonant), *v,* usu. *g,* and sometimes *j.* [L var. of
dis-]
di-³ /dī/ *prefix* form of DIA- before a vowel.
dia. *abbr.* diameter.
dia- /díə/ *prefix* (also **di-** before a vowel) **1** through (*diaphanous*). **2** apart (*diacritical*). **3** across (*diameter*). [Gk f. *dia*
through]
diabetes /díəbeétis, -teez/ *n.* **1** any disorder of the metabolism with excessive thirst and the production of large
amounts of urine. **2** (in full **diabetes mellitus**) the commonest form of diabetes in which sugar and starch are not
properly absorbed from the blood, with thirst, emaciation,
and excessive excretion of urine with glucose. □ **diabetes
insipidus** a rare metabolic disorder due to a pituitary deficiency, with excessive urination and thirst. [orig. = siphon:
L f. Gk f. *diabainō* go through]
diabetic /díəbétik/ *adj. & n.* ● *adj.* **1** of or relating to or
having diabetes. **2** for use by diabetics. ● *n.* a person suffering from diabetes.
diablerie /dee-aáblǝree, -áblǝ-/ *n.* **1** the devil's work; sorcery.
2 wild recklessness. **3** the realm of devils; demon lore. [F f.
diable f. L *diabolus* DEVIL]
■ **2** see DEVILRY.
diabolic /díəbólik/ *adj.* (also **diabolical** /-bólikəl/) **1** of the
Devil. **2** devilish; inhumanly cruel or wicked. **3** fiendishly
clever or cunning or annoying. **4** *colloq.* disgracefully bad or
defective; outrageous, atrocious. □□ **diabolically** *adv.* [ME
f. OF *diabolique* or LL *diabolicus* f. L *diabolus* (as DEVIL)]
■ **1** devilish, satanic, Mephistophelian, demonic,
demoniacal, demoniac, fiendish, hellish, infernal.
2 devilish, cruel, wicked, iniquitous, evil, fiendish,
appalling, dreadful, inhuman, atrocious, execrable,
abominable, awful, terrible, damnable, accursed,
horrid, horrible, hideous, monstrous, odious, vile, base,
corrupt, foul, depraved, flagitious, heinous, malicious,
malevolent, malign, sinister, sinful, impious, bad,
literary maleficent. **4** see DISGRACEFUL.
diabolism /díábəlizəm/ *n.* **1 a** belief in or worship of the
Devil. **b** sorcery. **2** devilish conduct or character. □□ **diab-
olist** *n.* [Gk *diabolos* DEVIL]

■ **1 b** see *sorcery* (SORCERER).

diabolize /díábəliz/ *v.tr.* make into or represent as a devil.

diabolo /deeábəlō/ *n.* (*pl.* **-os**) **1** a game in which a two-headed top is thrown up and caught with a string stretched between two sticks. **2** the top itself. [It., = DEVIL: formerly called *devil on two sticks*]

diachronic /díəkrónik/ *adj. Linguistics,* etc., concerned with the historical development of a subject (esp. a language) (opp. SYNCHRONIC). □□ **diachronically** *adv.* **diachronism** /díákrənizəm/ *n.* **diachronistic** /díákrənístik/ *adj.* **diachronous** /díákrənəs/ *adj.* **diachrony** /díákrənee/ *n.* [F *diachronique* (as DIA-, CHRONIC)]

diaconal /díákənəl/ *adj.* of a deacon. [eccl.L *diaconalis* f. *diaconus* DEACON]

diaconate /díákənayt, -nət/ *n.* **1 a** the office of deacon. **b** a person's time as deacon. **2** a body of deacons. [eccl.L *diaconatus* (as DIACONAL)]

diacritic /díəkrítik/ *n. & adj.* ● *n.* a sign (e.g., an accent, diaeresis, cedilla) used to indicate different sounds or values of a letter. ● *adj.* = DIACRITICAL. [Gk *diakritikos* (as DIA-, CRITIC)]

diacritical /díəkrítikəl/ *adj. & n.* ● *adj.* distinguishing; distinctive. ● *n.* (in full **diacritical mark** or **sign**) = DIACRITIC.

diadelphous /díədélfəs/ *adj. Bot.* with the stamens united in two bundles (cf. MONADELPHOUS, POLYADELPHOUS). [DI-[1] + Gk *adelphos* brother]

diadem /díədem/ *n. & v.* ● *n.* **1** a crown or headband worn as a sign of sovereignty. **2** a wreath of leaves or flowers worn around the head. **3** sovereignty. **4** a crowning distinction or glory. ● *v.tr.* (esp. as **diademed** *adj.*) adorn with or as with a diadem. [ME f. OF *diademe* f. L *diadema* f. Gk *diadēma* (as DIA-, *deō* bind)]

■ *n.* **1** see CROWN *n.* 1. **2** see GARLAND *n.* 1.

diaeresis /dī-érəsis/ *n.* (also **dieresis**) (*pl.* **-ses** /-seez/) **1** a mark (as in *naïve*) over a vowel to indicate that it is sounded separately. **2** *Prosody* a break where a foot ends at the end of a word. [L f. Gk, = separation]

diag. *abbr.* **1** diagonal. **2** diagram.

diagenesis /díəjénisis/ *n. Geol.* the transformation occurring during the conversion of sedimentation to sedimentary rock.

diagnose /díəgnōs, -nōz/ *v.tr.* make a diagnosis of (a disease, a mechanical fault, etc.) from its symptoms. □□ **diagnosable** *adj.*

■ identify, name, determine, recognize, distinguish, pinpoint, interpret; analyze.

diagnosis /díəgnósis/ *n.* (*pl.* **diagnoses** /-seez/) **1 a** the identification of a disease by means of a patient's symptoms. **b** an instance or formal statement of this. **2 a** the identification of the cause of a mechanical fault, etc. **b** an instance of this. **3 a** the distinctive characterization in precise terms of a genus, species, etc. **b** an instance of this. [mod.L f. Gk (as DIA-, *gignōskō* recognize)]

■ **1, 2** see *interpretation* (INTERPRET).

diagnostic /díəgnóstik/ *adj. & n.* ● *adj.* of or assisting diagnosis. ● *n.* a symptom. □□ **diagnostically** *adv.* **diagnostician** /-nostíshən/ *n.* [Gk *diagnōstikos* (as DIAGNOSIS)]

diagnostics /díəgnóstiks/ *n.* **1** (treated as *pl.*) *Computing* programs and other mechanisms used to detect and identify faults in hardware or software. **2** (treated as *sing.*) the science or study of diagnosing disease.

diagonal /díágənəl/ *adj. & n.* ● *adj.* **1** crossing a straight-sided figure from corner to corner. **2** slanting; oblique. ● *n.* a straight line joining two nonadjacent corners. □□ **diagonally** *adv.* [L *diagonalis* f. Gk *diagōnios* (as DIA-, *gōnia* angle)]

■ *adj.* see OBLIQUE *adj.* 1.

diagram /díəgram/ *n. & v.* ● *n.* **1** a drawing showing the general scheme or outline of an object and its parts. **2** a graphic representation of the course or results of an action or process. **3** *Geom.* a figure made of lines used in proving a theorem, etc. ● *v.tr.* (**diagramed, diagraming** or **diagrammed, diagramming**) represent by means of a diagram. □□ **diagrammatic** /-grəmátik/ *adj.* **diagrammatically** *adv.* [L *diagramma* f. Gk (as DIA-, -GRAM)]

■ *n.* **1, 2** see PLAN *n.* 2.

diagrid /díəgrid/ *n. Archit.* a supporting structure of diagonally intersecting ribs of metal, etc. [DIAGONAL + GRID]

diakinesis /díəkinéesis, -ki-/ *n.* (*pl.* **diakineses** /-seez/) *Biol.* a stage during the prophase of meiosis when the separation of homologous chromosomes is complete and crossing over has occurred. [mod.L f. G *Diakinese* (as DIA-, Gk *kinēsis* motion)]

dial /díəl/ *n. & v.* ● *n.* **1** the face of a clock or watch, marked to show the hours, etc. **2** a similar flat plate marked with a scale for measuring weight, volume, pressure, consumption, etc., indicated by a pointer. **3** a movable disk on a telephone, with finger holes and numbers for making a connection. **4 a** a plate or disk, etc., on a radio or television set for selecting wavelength or channel. **b** a similar selecting device on other equipment, e.g., a washing machine. **5** *Brit. sl.* a person's face. ● *v.* **1** *tr.* (also *absol.*) select (a telephone number) by means of a dial or set of buttons (*dialed 911*). **2** *tr.* measure, indicate, or regulate by means of a dial. □ **dial tone** a sound indicating that a caller may start to dial. □□ **dialer** *n.* [ME, = sundial, f. med.L *diale* clock dial ult. f. L *dies* day]

■ *n.* **1, 2** see INDICATOR 2, 3. **4** see CONTROL *n.* 5. ● *v.* **1** see CALL *v.* 2.

dialect /díəlekt/ *n.* **1** a form of speech peculiar to a particular region. **2** a subordinate variety of a language with nonstandard vocabulary, pronunciation, or grammar. □□ **dialectal** /-lékt'l/ *adj.* **dialectology** /-tóləjee/ *n.* **dialectologist** /-tóləjist/ *n.* [F *dialecte* or L *dialectus* f. Gk *dialektos* discourse f. *dialegomai* converse]

■ **1** speech (pattern), phraseology, idiom, accent, pronunciation, patois, brogue, vernacular. **2** jargon, cant, slang, argot, language, tongue, *colloq.* lingo.

dialectic /díəléktik/ *n. & adj.* ● *n.* **1** (often in *pl.*) **a** the art of investigating the truth of opinions; the testing of truth by discussion. **b** logical disputation. **2** *Philos.* **a** inquiry into metaphysical contradictions and their solutions, esp. in the thought of Kant and Hegel. **b** the existence or action of opposing social forces, etc. ● *adj.* **1** of or relating to logical disputation. **2** fond of or skilled in logical disputation. [ME f. OF *dialectique* or L *dialectica* f. Gk *dialektikē* (*tekhnē*) (art) of debate (as DIALECT)]

■ *n.* **1** (*dialectics*) see LOGIC.

dialectical /díəléktikəl/ *adj.* of dialectic or dialectics. □ **dialectical materialism** the Marxist theory that political and historical events are due to a conflict of social forces caused by man's material needs. □□ **dialectically** *adv.*

dialectician /díəlektíshən/ *n.* a person skilled in dialectic. [F *dialecticien* f. L *dialecticus*]

dialectics /díəléktiks/ *n.* (treated as *sing.* or *pl.*) = DIALECTIC *n.*

dialogic /díəlójik/ *adj.* of or in dialogue. [LL *dialogicus* f. Gk *dialogikos* (as DIALOGUE)]

dialogist /díáləjist/ *n.* a speaker in or writer of dialogue. [LL *dialogista* f. Gk *dialogistēs* (as DIALOGUE)]

dialogue /díəlawg, -log/ *n.* (also **dialog**) **1 a** conversation. **b** conversation in written form; this as a form of composition. **2 a** a discussion, esp. one between representatives of two political groups. **b** a conversation; a talk (*long dialogues between the two main characters*). [ME f. OF *dialoge* f. L *dialogus* f. Gk *dialogos* f. *dialegomai* converse]

■ **1 a** see CONVERSATION. **2 a** duologue, conversation, discussion, meeting, conference, colloquy, communication, *colloq.* huddle. **b** conversation, parley, talk, chat, conference, colloquy, confabulation, bull session, *colloq.* confab, *sl.* rap (session), chin-wag.

dialyse *Brit.* var. of DIALYZE.

dialysis /díálisis/ *n.* (*pl.* **dialyses** /-seez/) **1** *Chem.* the separation of particles in a liquid by differences in their ability to pass through a membrane into another liquid. **2** *Med.* the

---

/. . ./ **pronunciation**	● **part of speech**
□ **phrases, idioms, and compounds**	
□□ **derivatives**	■ **synonym section**
cross-references appear in SMALL CAPITALS or *italics*	

clinical purification of blood by this technique. □□ **dialytic** /dīəlítik/ *adj.* [L f. Gk *dialusis* (as DIA-, *luō* set free)]

dialyze /dīəlīz/ *v.tr.* (*Brit.* **dialyse**) separate by means of dialysis.

diam. *abbr.* diameter.

diamagnetic /dīəmagnétik/ *adj.* & *n.* ● *adj.* tending to become magnetized in a direction at right angles to the applied magnetic field. ● *n.* a diamagnetic body or substance. □□ **diamagnetically** *adv.* **diamagnetism** /-mágnitizəm/ *n.*

diamanté /deeəmoNtáy/ *adj.* & *n.* ● *adj.* decorated with powdered crystal or another sparkling substance. ● *n.* fabric or costume jewelry so decorated. [F, past part. of *diamanter* set with diamonds f. *diamant* DIAMOND]

diamantine /dīəmántin, -teen/ *adj.* esp. *Brit.* of or like diamonds. [F *diamantin* f. *diamant* DIAMOND]

diameter /dīámitər/ *n.* **1 a** a straight line passing from side to side through the center of a body or figure, esp. a circle or sphere. **b** the length of this line. **2** a transverse measurement; width; thickness. **3** a unit of linear measurement of magnifying power (*a lens magnifying 2000 diameters*). □□ **diametral** *adj.* [ME f. OF *diametre* f. L *diametros* Gk *dia-metros* (*grammē*) (line) measuring across f. *metron* measure] ▪ **1, 2** see WIDTH 1.

diametrical /dīəmétrikəl/ *adj.* (also **diametric**) **1** of or along a diameter. **2** (of opposition, difference, etc.) complete, like that between opposite ends of a diameter. □□ **diametrically** *adv.* [Gk *diametrikos* (as DIAMETER)]

diamond /dīmənd, dīə-/ *n., adj., & v.* ● *n.* **1** a precious stone of pure carbon crystallized in octahedrons, etc., the hardest naturally occurring substance. **2** a figure shaped like the cross section of a diamond; a rhombus. **3 a** a playing card of a suit denoted by a red rhombus. **b** (in *pl.*) this suit. **4** a glittering particle or point (of frost, etc.). **5** a tool with a small diamond for cutting glass. **6** *Baseball* **a** the space delimited by the bases. **b** the entire field. ● *adj.* **1** made of or set with diamonds or a diamond. **2** rhombus-shaped. ● *v.tr.* adorn with or as with diamonds. □ **diamond jubilee** the 60th (or 75th) anniversary of an event, esp. a sovereign's accession. **diamond wedding** (or **anniversary**) a 60th (or 75th) wedding anniversary. □□ **diamondiferous** /-difərəs/ *adj.* [ME f. OF *diamant* f. med.L *diamas diamant-* var. of L *adamas* ADAMANT f. Gk]

diamondback /dīməndbak, dīə-/ *n.* **1** an edible freshwater terrapin, *Malaclemys terrapin*, native to N. America, with diamond-shaped markings on its shell. **2** any rattlesnake of the genus *Crotalus*, native to N. America, with diamond-shaped markings.

diamondiferous /dīmandífərəs/ *adj. Mining* diamond-yielding. [F *diamantifère* f. *diamant* DIAMOND]

diandrous /dīándrəs/ *adj.* having two stamens. [DI-¹ + Gk *anēr andr-* man]

dianthus /dīánthəs/ *n.* any flowering plant of the genus *Dianthus*, e.g., a carnation or pink. [Gk *Dios* of Zeus + *anthos* flower]

diapason /dīəpáyzən, -sən/ *n. Mus.* **1** the compass of a voice or musical instrument. **2** a fixed standard of musical pitch. **3** (in full **open** or **stopped diapason**) either of two main organ stops extending through the organ's whole compass. **4 a** a combination of notes or parts in a harmonious whole. **b** a melodious succession of notes, esp. a grand swelling burst of harmony. **5** an entire compass, range, or scope. [ME in sense 'octave' f. L *diapason* f. Gk *dia pasōn* (*khordōn*) through all (notes)]

diapause /dīəpawz/ *n.* a period of retarded or suspended development in some insects.

diaper /dípər, dīəpər/ *n.* & *v.* ● *n.* **1** a piece of toweling or other absorbent material wrapped around a baby to retain urine and feces. **2 a** a linen or cotton fabric with a small diamond pattern. **b** this pattern. **3** a similar ornamental design of diamonds, etc., for panels, walls, etc. ● *v.tr.* decorate with a diaper pattern. □ **diaper rash** inflammation of a baby's skin, caused by prolonged contact with a damp diaper. [ME f. OF *diapre* f. med.L *diasprum* f. med.Gk *diaspros* (adj.) (as DIA-, *aspros* white)]

diaphanous /dīáfənəs/ *adj.* (of fabric, etc.) light and delicate,

and almost transparent. □□ **diaphanously** *adv.* [med.L *diaphanus* f. Gk *diaphanes* (as DIA-, *phainō* show)] ▪ see FILMY 1.

diaphoresis /dīəfəreéesis/ *n.* (*pl.* **diaphoreses**) *Med.* sweating, esp. artificially induced. [LL f. Gk f. *diaphoreō* carry through]

diaphoretic /dīəfərétik/ *adj.* & *n.* ● *adj.* inducing perspiration. ● *n.* an agent inducing perspiration. [LL *diaphoreticus* f. Gk *diaphorētikos* (formed as DIAPHORESIS)]

diaphragm /dīəfram/ *n.* **1** a muscular partition separating the thorax from the abdomen in mammals. **2** a partition in animal and plant tissues. **3** a disk pierced by one or more holes in optical and acoustic systems, etc. **4** a device for varying the effective aperture of the lens in a camera, etc. **5** a thin contraceptive cap fitting over the cervix. **6** a thin sheet of material used as a partition, etc. □ **diaphragm pump** a pump using a flexible diaphragm in place of a piston. □□ **diaphragmatic** /-fragmátik/ *adj.* [ME f. LL *diaphragma* f. Gk (as DIA-, *phragma -atos* f. *phrassō* fence in)]

diapositive /dīəpózitiv/ *n.* a positive photographic slide or transparency.

diarchy /dīaarkee/ *n.* (also **dyarchy**) (*pl.* **-ies**) **1** government by two independent authorities (esp. in India 1921–37). **2** an instance of this. □□ **diarchal** /dīaarkəl/ *adj.* **diarchic** *adj.* [DI-¹ + Gk *-arkhia* rule, after *monarchy*]

diarist /dīərist/ *n.* a person who keeps a diary. □□ **diaristic** *adj.*

diarize /dīərīz/ *v.* **1** *intr.* keep a diary. **2** *tr.* enter in a diary.

diarrhea /dīəreéə/ *n.* a condition of excessively frequent and loose bowel movements. □□ **diarrheal** *adj.* **diarrheic** *adj.* [ME f. LL f. Gk *diarrhoia* (as DIA-, *rheō* flow)] ▪ loose bowels, *Brit.* runny motions or tummy, *sl.* the trots or runs.

diary /dīəree/ *n.* (*pl.* **-ies**) **1** a daily record of events or thoughts. **2** a book for this or for noting future engagements, usu. printed and with a calendar and other information. [L *diarium* f. *dies* day] ▪ **1** journal, chronicle, memoirs, log, record, annal(s). **2** appointment book, datebook, calendar, engagement book.

diascope /dīəskōp/ *n.* an optical projector giving images of transparent objects.

Diaspora /dīáspərə/ *n.* **1** (prec. by *the*) **a** the dispersion of the Jews among the Gentiles mainly in the 8th–6th c. BC. **b** Jews dispersed in this way. **2** (also **diaspora**) **a** any group of people similarly dispersed. **b** their dispersion. [Gk f. *diaspeirō* (as DIA-, *speirō* scatter)]

diastase /dīəstays, -stayz/ *n. Biochem.* = AMYLASE. □□ **diastasic** /-stáysik, -zik/ *adj.* **diastatic** /-státik/ *adj.* [F f. Gk *diastasis* separation (as DIA-, *stasis* placing)]

diastole /dīástəlee/ *n. Physiol.* the period between two contractions of the heart when the heart muscle relaxes and allows the chambers to fill with blood (cf. SYSTOLE). □□ **diastolic** /dīəstólik/ *adj.* [LL f. Gk *diastellō* (as DIA-, *stellō* place)]

diathermancy /dīəthərmənsee/ *n.* the quality of transmitting radiant heat. □□ **diathermic** *adj.* **diathermous** *adj.* [F *diathermansie* f. Gk *dia* through + *thermansis* heating: assim. to -ANCY]

diathermy /dīəthərmee/ *n.* the application of high-frequency electric currents to produce heat in the deeper tissues of the body. [G *Diathermie* f. Gk *dia* through + *thermon* heat]

diathesis /dīáthisis/ *n. Med.* a constitutional predisposition to a certain state, esp. a diseased one. [mod.L f. Gk f. *diatithēmi* arrange]

diatom /dīətom/ *n.* a microscopic unicellular alga with a siliceous cell wall, found as plankton and forming fossil deposits. □□ **diatomaceous** /-máyshəs/ *adj.* [mod.L *Diatoma* (genus-name) f. Gk *diatomos* (as DIA-, *temnō* cut)]

diatomic /dīətómik/ *adj.* consisting of two atoms. [DI-¹ + ATOM]

diatomite /dīátəmīt/ *n.* a deposit composed of the siliceous skeletons of diatoms.

diatonic /dīətónik/ *adj. Mus.* **1** (of a scale, interval, etc.) involving only notes proper to the prevailing key without chromatic alteration. **2** (of a melody or harmony) constructed from such a scale. [F *diatonique* or LL *diatonicus* f. Gk *diatonikos* at intervals of a tone (as DIA-, TONIC)]

diatribe /díətrīb/ *n.* a forceful verbal attack; a piece of bitter criticism. [F f. L *diatriba* f. Gk *diatribē* spending of time, discourse f. *diatribō* (as DIA-, *tribō* rub)]
■ see HARANGUE *n.*

diazepam /diázipam/ *n.* a tranquilizing muscle-relaxant drug with anticonvulsant properties used to relieve anxiety, tension, etc. [benzo*diaze*pine + *am*]

diazo /diázō, -áyzō/ *n.* (in full **diazotype**) a copying or coloring process using a diazo compound decomposed by light. □ **diazo compound** *Chem.* a chemical compound containing two usu. multiply bonded nitrogen atoms, often highly colored and used as dyes. [DI-¹ + AZO-]

dib /dib/ *v.intr.* (**dibbed, dibbing**) = DAP. [var. of DAB¹]

dibasic /dībáysik/ *adj.* *Chem.* having two replaceable protons. [DI-¹ + BASE¹ 6]

dibber /díbər/ *n.* = DIBBLE.

dibble /díbəl/ *n. & v.* ● *n.* a hand tool for making holes in the ground for seeds or young plants. ● *v.* **1** *tr.* sow or plant with a dibble. **2** *tr.* prepare (soil) with a dibble. **3** *intr.* use a dibble. [ME: perh. rel. to DIB]

dibs /dibz/ *n.pl.* *sl.* **1** money. **2** rights; claim (*I have dibs on the last slice of pizza*). [earlier sense 'pebbles for game,' also *dib-stones*, perh. f. DIB]

dice /dīs/ *n. & v.* ● *n.pl.* **1 a** small cubes with faces bearing 1–6 spots used in games of chance. **b** (treated as *sing.*) one of these cubes (see DIE²). **2** a game played with one or more such cubes. **3** food cut into small cubes for cooking. ● *v.* **1 a** *intr.* play dice. **b** *intr.* take great risks; gamble (*dicing with death*). **c** *tr.* (foll. by *away*) gamble away. **2** *tr.* cut (food) into small cubes. **3** *tr.* *Austral. sl.* reject; leave alone. **4** *tr.* mark with squares. □ **no dice** *sl.* no success or prospect of it. □□ **dicer** *n.* (in sense 1 of *v.*). [pl. of DIE²]
■ *v.* **2** see CHOP¹ *v.* 2.

dicey /dísee/ *adj.* (**dicier, diciest**) *sl.* risky; unreliable. [DICE + -Y¹]
■ risky, tricky, chancy, dangerous, difficult, ticklish, unpredictable, uncertain, unsure, doubtful, *colloq.* iffy, *sl.* hairy; see also UNRELIABLE.

dichotomy /dīkótəmee/ *n.* (*pl.* **-ies**) **1 a** a division into two, esp. a sharply defined one. **b** the result of such a division. **2** binary classification. **3** *Bot. & Zool.* repeated bifurcation. □□ **dichotomic** /-kətómik/ *adj.* **dichotomize** *v.* **dichotomous** *adj.* [mod.L *dichotomia* f. Gk *dikhotomia* f. *dikho-* apart + -TOMY]
■ **1** see SPLIT *n.* 3.

dichroic /díkrŏik/ *adj.* (esp. of doubly refracting crystals) showing two colors. □□ **dichroism** *n.* [Gk *dikhroos* (as DI-¹, *khrōs* color)]

dichromatic /díkrōmátik/ *adj.* **1** two-colored. **2 a** (of animal species) having individuals that show different colorations. **b** having vision sensitive to only two of the three primary colors. □□ **dichromatism** /díkrōmətizəm/ *n.* [DI-¹ + Gk *khrōmatikos* f. *khrōma -atos* color]

dick¹ /dik/ *n.* **1** *coarse sl.* the penis. ¶ In sense 1 usually considered a taboo word. **2** *Brit. colloq.* (in certain set phrases) fellow; person (*clever dick*). [pet form of the name *Richard*]

dick² /dik/ *n.* *sl.* a detective. [perh. abbr.]
■ see DETECTIVE *n.*

dick³ /dik/ *n.* *Brit.* □ **take one's dick** (often foll. by *that* + clause) *sl.* swear; affirm. [abbr. of *declaration*]

dickens /díkinz/ *n.* (usu. prec. by *how, what, why,* etc., *the*) *colloq.* (esp. in exclamations) deuce; the Devil (*what the dickens are you doing here?*). [16th c.: prob. a use of the surname *Dickens*]
■ see *the devil* (DEVIL *n.* 7).

Dickensian /dikénzeeən/ *adj. & n.* ● *adj.* **1** of or relating to Charles Dickens, Engl. novelist d. 1870, or his work. **2** resembling or reminiscent of the situations, poor social conditions, or comically repulsive characters described in Dickens's work. ● *n.* an admirer or student of Dickens or his work. □□ **Dickensianly** *adv.*

dicker /díkər/ *v. & n.* ● *v.* **1 a** *intr.* bargain; haggle. **b** *tr.* barter;

exchange. **2** *intr.* dither; hesitate. ● *n.* a deal; a barter. □□ **dickerer** *n.* [perh. f. *dicker* set of ten (hides), as a unit of trade]
■ *v.* **1** bargain, deal, haggle, negotiate, trade, barter, exchange. **2** see HESITATE 1. ● *n.* bargain, deal, haggle, barter; transaction, contract.

dickey¹ /díkee/ *n.* (also **dicky**) (*pl.* **-eys** or **-ies**) *colloq.* **1** a false shirtfront. **2** (in full **dickeybird**) a child's word for a little bird. **3** *Brit.* a driver's seat in a carriage. **4** *Brit.* an extra folding seat at the back of a vehicle; rumble seat. [some senses f. *Dicky* (as DICK¹)]

dickey² /díkee/ *adj.* (**dickier, dickiest**) *sl.* unsound; likely to collapse or fail. [19th c.: perh. f. 'as queer as Dick's hatband']

dickhead /dík-hed/ *n.* *coarse sl.* a stupid or obnoxious person.

dicot /díkot/ *n.* = DICOTYLEDON. [abbr.]

dicotyledon /díkot'leéd'n/ *n.* any flowering plant having two cotyledons. □□ **dicotyledonous** *adj.* [mod.L *dicotyledones* (as DI-¹, COTYLEDON)]

dicrotic /díkrótik/ *adj.* (of the pulse) having a double beat. [Gk *dikrotos*]

dict. *abbr.* **1** dictionary. **2** dictation.

dicta *pl.* of DICTUM.

Dictaphone /díktəfōn/ *n. propr.* a machine for recording and playing back dictated words. [DICTATE + PHONE]

dictate *v. & n.* ● *v.* /díktayt, diktáyt/ **1** *tr.* say or read aloud (words to be written down or recorded). **2 a** *tr.* prescribe or lay down authoritatively (terms, things to be done). **b** *intr.* lay down the law; give orders. ● *n.* /díktayt/ (usu. in *pl.*) an authoritative instruction (*dictates of conscience*). [L *dictare dictat-* frequent. of *dicere dict-* say]
■ *v.* **2** say, prescribe, ordain, decree, demand, command, order, pronounce; lay down the law, give orders. ● *n.* decree, demand, command, order, direction, instruction, charge, pronouncement, edict, fiat, mandate, caveat, injunction, requirement, bidding, *literary* behest.

dictation /diktáyshən/ *n.* **1 a** the saying of words to be written down or recorded. **b** an instance of this, esp. as a school exercise. **c** the material that is dictated. **2 a** authoritative prescription. **b** an instance of this. **c** a command. □ **dictation speed** a slow rate of speech suitable for dictation.

dictator /díktaytər, diktáy-/ *n.* **1** a ruler with (often usurped) unrestricted authority. **2** a person with supreme authority in any sphere. **3** a domineering person. **4** a person who dictates for transcription. **5** *Rom.Hist.* a chief magistrate with absolute power, appointed in an emergency. [ME f. L (as DICTATE)]
■ **1, 2** autocrat, absolute ruler *or* monarch, despot, overlord, tyrant, führer, czar, Big Brother. **3** tyrant, despot, bully, slave driver.

dictatorial /díktətáwreeəl/ *adj.* **1** of or like a dictator. **2** imperious; overbearing. □□ **dictatorially** *adv.* [L *dictatorius* (as DICTATOR)]
■ **1** absolute, arbitrary, totalitarian, authoritarian, autocratic, all-powerful, omnipotent, unlimited. **2** despotic, tyrannical, authoritarian, ironhanded, domineering, imperious, overbearing, high-handed, lordly, *colloq.* bossy.

dictatorship /díktáytərship/ *n.* **1** a nation ruled by a dictator. **2 a** the position, rule, or period of rule of a dictator. **b** rule by a dictator. **3** absolute authority in any sphere.
■ see DESPOTISM.

diction /díkshən/ *n.* **1** the manner of enunciation in speaking or singing. **2** the choice of words or phrases in speech or writing. [F *diction* or L *dictio* f. *dicere dict-* say]
■ **1** articulation, pronunciation, enunciation, delivery, elocution, oratory, presentation, speech, intonation,

---

/. . ./ **pronunciation**	● **part of speech**
□ **phrases, idioms, and compounds**	
□□ **derivatives**	■ **synonym section**
cross-references appear in SMALL CAPITALS or *italics*	

inflection. **2** language, wording, style, expression, usage, terminology, vocabulary, phraseology, phrasing, rhetoric, oratory, presentation.

dictionary /díkshəneree/ *n.* (*pl.* **-ies**) **1** a book that lists (usu. in alphabetical order) and explains the words of a language or gives equivalent words in another language. **2** a reference book on any subject, the items of which are arranged in alphabetical order (*dictionary of architecture*). [med.L *dictionarium* (*manuale* manual) & *dictionarius* (*liber* book) f. L *dictio* (as DICTION)]
■ **1** lexicon, glossary, wordbook, thesaurus, wordfinder. **2** encyclopedia, cyclopedia, reference (book), compendium, thesaurus.

dictum /díktəm/ *n.* (*pl.* **dicta** /-tə/ or **dictums**) **1** a formal utterance or pronouncement. **2** a saying or maxim. **3** *Law* = OBITER DICTUM. [L, = neut. past part. of *dicere* say]
■ **1** see DECREE *n.* 1. **2** see MAXIM.

dicty /díktee/ *adj. sl.* **1** conceited; snobbish. **2** elegant; stylish. [20th c.: orig. unkn.]

did past of DO[1].

didactic /dīdáktik/ *adj.* **1** meant to instruct. **2** (of a person) tediously pedantic. □□ **didactically** *adv.* **didacticism** /-ti-sizəm/ *n.* [Gk *didaktikos* f. *didaskō* teach]
■ **1** see INSTRUCTIVE. **2** see *pedantic* (PEDANT).

diddikai /dídiki/ *n. sl.* a gypsy; an itinerant tinker. [Romany]

diddle /díd'l/ *v. colloq.* **1** *tr.* cheat; swindle. **2** *intr.* waste time. □□ **diddler** *n.* [prob. back-form. f. Jeremy *Diddler* in Kenney's 'Raising the Wind' (1803)]
■ **1** see CHEAT *v.* 1a.

diddly /dídlee/ *n.* (also **diddly squat**) *sl.* the slightest amount (*he hasn't done diddly to help us out.*)

diddums /dídəmz/ *int. Brit.* expressing commiseration, esp. to a child. [= *did 'em*, i.e., did they (tease you, etc.)?]

didgeridoo /díjəreedoō/ *n.* (also **didjeridoo**) an Australian Aboriginal musical wind instrument of long tubular shape. [imit.]

didn't /díd'nt/ *contr.* did not.

dido /dídō/ *n.* (*pl.* **-oes** or **-os**) *colloq.* an antic; a caper; a prank. □ **cut** (or **cut up**) **didoes** play pranks. [19th c.: orig. unkn.]

didst /didst/ *archaic 2nd sing. past* of DO[1].

didymium /didímeeəm/ *n.* a mixture of prasodymium and neodymium, orig. regarded as an element. [mod.L f. Gk *didumos* twin (from being closely associated with lanthanum)]

die[1] /dī/ *v.* (**dies, died, dying** /dí-ing/) **1** *intr.* (often foll. by *of*) (of a person, animal, or plant) cease to live; expire, lose vital force (*died of hunger*). **2** *intr.* **a** come to an end; cease to exist; fade away (*the project died within six months*). **b** cease to function; break down (*the engine died*). **c** (of a flame) go out. **3** *intr.* (foll. by *on*) die or cease to function while in the presence or charge of (a person). **4** *intr.* (usu. foll. by *of, from, with*) be exhausted or tormented (*nearly died of boredom*; *was dying from the heat*). **5** *tr.* suffer (a specified death) (*died a natural death*). □ **be dying** (foll. by *for*, or *to* + infin.) wish for longingly or intently (*was dying for a drink*; *am dying to see you*). **die away** become weaker or fainter to the point of extinction. **die back** (of a plant) decay from the tip toward the root. **die down** become less loud or strong. **die hard** die reluctantly; not without a struggle (*old habits die hard*). **die-hard** *adj.* stubborn; strongly devoted. **die off** die one after another until few or none are left. **die out** become extinct; cease to exist. **never say die** keep up courage, not give in. [ME, prob. f. ON *deyja* f. Gmc]
■ **1** lose one's life, lay down one's life, perish, expire, suffer death, breathe one's last, be no more, close one's eyes, go (off), drop, drop dead, exit, fall, (go to) meet one's Maker, quit the scene, go to the happy hunting grounds, go to one's final *or* last resting place, pass through the Pearly Gates, go the way of all flesh, *archaic or colloq.* give up the ghost, *colloq.* turn up one's toes, pop off, cash in one's chips *or* checks, conk out, *euphem.* pass away *or* on *or* over, *formal esp. Law* decease, *formal or literary* depart (this life), *sl.* go west, bite the dust, go to glory, kick the bucket, croak,

Austral. & NZ sl. go bung, *Brit. sl.* snuff it, go for a burton. **2 a** come to an end, expire, end, stop, cease; die away, die out *or* down, dwindle, lessen, diminish, decrease, ebb, decline, wane, subside, wither (away), wilt, dissolve, peter out, fail, weaken, deteriorate, disintegrate, degenerate, fade (away), sink, vanish, disappear. **b** break down, fail. **c** see *go out* 3 (GO[1]). **4** see SUFFER 1a. □ **be dying** long, pine, yearn, hanker, hunger, ache; (*be dying for*) want, desire, crave. **die away** see DIE[1] 2a above. **die down** see DIE[1] 2a above. **die out** become extinct, perish. **never say die** (keep a) stiff upper lip, don't give in *or* up, be brave, *colloq.* chin up.

die[2] /dī/ *n.* **1** *sing.* of DICE *n.* 1a. ¶ *Dice* is now standard in general use in this sense. **2** (*pl.* **dies**) **a** an engraved device for stamping a design on coins, medals, etc. **b** a device for stamping, cutting, or molding material into a particular shape. **3** (*pl.* **dice** /dīs/) *Archit.* the cubical part of a pedestal between the base and the cornice; a dado or plinth. □ **as straight** (or **true**) **as a die 1** quite straight. **2** entirely honest or loyal. **die cast** cast (hot metal) in a die or mold. **die casting** the process or product of casting from metal molds. **the die is cast** an irrevocable step has been taken. **die stamping** embossing paper, etc., with a die. [ME f. OF *de* f. L *datum* neut. past part. of *dare* give, play]

diehard /díhaard/ *n.* a conservative or stubborn person.
■ see REACTIONARY *adj.*.

dieldrin /deéldrin/ *n.* a crystalline insecticide produced by the oxidation of aldrin. [O. *Diels*, Ger. chemist d. 1954 + AL-DRIN]

dielectric /dí-iléktrik/ *adj. & n. Electr.* ● *adj.* insulating. ● *n.* an insulating medium or substance. □ **dielectric constant** permittivity. □□ **dielectrically** *adv.* [DI-[3] + ELECTRIC = through which electricity is transmitted (without conduction)]

diene /dí-een/ *n. Chem.* any organic compound possessing two double bonds between carbon atoms. [DI-[1] + -ENE]

dieresis var. of DIAERESIS.

diesel /deézəl/ *n.* **1** (in full **diesel engine**) an internal combustion engine in which the heat produced by the compression of air in the cylinder ignites the fuel. **2** a vehicle driven by a diesel engine. **3** fuel for a diesel engine. □ **diesel-electric** *n.* a vehicle driven by the electric current produced by a diesel-engined generator. ● *adj.* of or powered by this means. **diesel oil** a heavy petroleum fraction used as fuel in diesel engines. □□ **dieselize** *v.tr.* [R. *Diesel*, Ger. engineer d. 1913]

diesinker /dísingkər/ *n.* an engraver of dies.

Dies Irae /deé-ays eéray/ *n.* a Latin hymn sung in a mass for the dead. [L (its first words), = day of wrath]

dies non /dí-eez nón, deé-ays nón/ *n. Law* **1** a day on which no legal business can be done. **2** a day that does not count for legal purposes. [L, short for *dies non juridicus* nonjudicial day]

diet[1] /díət/ *n. & v.* ● *n.* **1** the kinds of food that a person or animal habitually eats. **2** a special course of food to which a person is restricted, esp. for medical reasons or to control weight. **3** a regular occupation or series of activities to which one is restricted or which form one's main concern, usu. for a purpose (*a diet of light reading and fresh air*). ● *v.* (**dieted, dieting**) **1** *intr.* restrict oneself to small amounts or special kinds of food, esp. to control one's weight. **2** *tr.* restrict (a person or animal) to a special diet. □□ **dieter** *n.* [ME f. OF *diete* (n.), *dieter* (v.) f. L *diaeta* f. Gk *diaita* a way of life]
■ *n.* **1** (food) intake, consumption; fare, food, nourishment, nutriment, sustenance, subsistence, victuals, *formal* aliment. **2** dietary, regime, *Med.* regimen. **3** see SYSTEM 4a. ● *v.* **1** fast, abstain, starve (oneself); be on a diet, *Brit.* slim.

diet[2] /díət/ *n.* **1** a legislative assembly in certain countries. **2** *hist.* a national or international conference, esp. of a federal government or confederation. **3** *Sc. Law* a meeting or session of a court. [ME f. med.L *dieta* day's work, wages, etc.]

■ **1** council, congress, parliament, senate, legislature, house, chamber, assembly. **2** see CONFERENCE 2.

dietary /díəteree/ *adj.* & *n.* ● *adj.* of or relating to a diet. ● *n.* (*pl.* **-ies**) a regulated or restricted diet. [ME f. med.L *dietarium* (as DIET¹)]

dietetic /díətétik/ *adj.* of or relating to diet. □□ **dietetically** *adv.* [L *dieteticus* f. Gk *diaitētikos* (as DIET¹)]

dietetics /díətétiks/ *n.pl.* (usu. treated as *sing.*) the scientific study of diet and nutrition.

diethyl ether /dī-éthəl/ *n. Chem.* = ETHER 1.

dietitian /díətíshən/ *n.* (also **dietician**) an expert in dietetics.

dif- /dif/ *prefix* assim. form of DIS- before *f.* [L var. of DIS-]

differ /dífər/ *v.intr.* **1** (often foll. by *from*) be unlike or distinguishable. **2** (often foll. by *with*) disagree; be at variance (with a person). [ME f. OF *differer* f. L *differre*, differ, DEFER¹, (as DIS-, *ferre* bear, tend)]

■ **1** diverge, deviate, be separate *or* distinct, be dissimilar *or* different, contrast; depart. **2** disagree, conflict, be at variance *or* odds, take issue, part company, fall out, quarrel, argue.

difference /dífrəns/ *n.* & *v.* ● *n.* **1** the state or condition of being different or unlike. **2** a point in which things differ; a distinction. **3** a degree of unlikeness. **4 a** the quantity by which amounts differ; a deficit (*will have to make up the difference*). **b** the remainder left after subtraction. **5 a** a disagreement, quarrel, or dispute. **b** the grounds of disagreement (*put aside their differences*). **6** a notable change (*the difference in his behavior is remarkable*). **7** *Heraldry* an alteration in a coat of arms distinguishing members of a family. ● *v.tr. Heraldry* alter (a coat of arms) to distinguish members of a family. □ **make a** (or **all the**, etc.) **difference** (often foll. by *to*) have a significant effect or influence (on a person, situation, etc.). **make no difference** (often foll. by *to*) have no effect (on a person, situation, etc.). **with a difference** having a new or unusual feature. [ME f. OF f. L *differentia* (as DIFFERENT)]

■ *n.* **1** dissimilarity, discrepancy, unlikeness, disagreement, inconsistency, diversity, variation, imbalance, inequality, dissimilitude, incongruity, contrast, contrariety. **2** distinction, contradistinction, contrast, dissimilarity, disparity. **4 a** see DEFICIT. **b** rest, remainder, leftovers, balance, excess, surplus, residue, residuum. **5** dispute, argument, disagreement, conflict; see also QUARREL¹ *n.* **1**. **6** change, alteration, metamorphosis, reformation, transformation, conversion, adjustment, modification.

different /dífrənt/ *adj.* **1** (often foll. by *from, to, than*) unlike; distinguishable in nature, form, or quality (from another). ¶ *Different from* is generally regarded as the most acceptable collocation; *to* is common in less formal use; *than* is established in use, esp. when followed by a clause, e.g., *I am a different person than I was a year ago*. **2** distinct; separate; not the same one (as another). **3** *colloq.* unusual (*wanted to do something different*). **4** of various kinds; assorted; several; miscellaneous (*available in different colors*). □□ **differently** *adv.* **differentness** *n.* [ME f. OF *different* f. L *different-* (as DIFFER)]

■ **1, 2** unlike, unalike, dissimilar, conflicting; distinct, opposite, separate, contrary, discrete, contrastive, contrasting, disparate, divergent, diverse, distinguishable; another. **3** unique, unusual, peculiar, odd, offbeat, singular, particular, distinctive, personalized, individual, alternative, unorthodox, extraordinary, special, remarkable, bizarre, rare, weird, strange, unconventional, original, out of the ordinary, exceptional, *colloq.* way-out, *sl.* wacky; new, novel, unheard-of, original. **4** assorted, miscellaneous, multifarious, numerous, abundant, sundry, various, varied, many, several, *archaic or literary* divers, *literary* manifold.

differentia /dífərénsheeə/ *n.* (*pl.* **differentiae** /-shee-ee/) a distinguishing mark, esp. between species within a genus. [L: see DIFFERENCE]

differential /dífərénshəl/ *adj.* & *n.* ● *adj.* **1 a** of, exhibiting, or depending on a difference. **b** varying according to cir-

cumstances. **2** *Math.* relating to infinitesimal differences. **3** constituting a specific difference; distinctive; relating to specific differences (*differential diagnosis*). **4** *Physics* & *Mech.* concerning the difference of two or more motions, pressures, etc. ● *n.* **1** a difference between individuals or examples of the same kind. **2** *Brit.* a difference in wage or salary between industries or categories of employees in the same industry. **3** a difference between rates of interest, etc. **4** *Math.* **a** an infinitesimal difference between successive values of a variable. **b** a function expressing this as a rate of change with respect to another variable. **5** (in full **differential gear**) a gear allowing a vehicle's driven wheels to revolve at different speeds in cornering. □ **differential calculus** *Math.* a method of calculating rates of change, maximum or minimum values, etc. (cf. INTEGRAL). **differential coefficient** *Math.* = DERIVATIVE. **differential equation** *Math.* an equation involving differentials among its quantities. □□ **differentially** *adv.* [med. & mod.L *differentialis* (as DIFFERENCE)]

differentiate /dífərénsheeayt/ *v.* **1** *tr.* constitute a difference between or in. **2** *tr.* & (often foll. by *between*) *intr.* find differences (between); discriminate. **3** *tr.* & *intr.* make or become different in the process of growth or development (species, word forms, etc.). **4** *tr. Math.* transform (a function) into its derivative. □□ **differentiation** /-sheeáyshən/ *n.* **differentiator** *n.* [med.L *differentiare differentiat-* (as DIFFERENCE)]

■ **2** distinguish, discriminate, contradistinguish, separate, contrast, set off *or* apart, tell apart. **3** modify, specialize, change, alter, transform, transmute, convert, adapt, adjust, develop.

difficult /dífikult, -kəlt/ *adj.* **1 a** needing much effort or skill. **b** troublesome; perplexing. **2** (of a person): **a** not easy to please or satisfy. **b** uncooperative; troublesome. **3** characterized by hardships or problems (*a difficult period in his life*). □□ **difficultly** *adv.* **difficultness** *n.* [ME, back-form. f. DIFFICULTY]

■ **1 a** hard, arduous, toilsome, strenuous, tough, laborious, burdensome, onerous, demanding. **b** puzzling, perplexing, troublesome, baffling, complex, thorny, intricate, knotty, problematical, problematic, ticklish, scabrous, sensitive, delicate, awkward, tricky, *colloq.* sticky; profound, abstruse, obscure, recondite. **2** intractable, recalcitrant, obstructive, uncooperative, stubborn, unmanageable, obstinate, contrary, unaccommodating, refractory, unyielding, uncompromising, troublesome, awkward, *archaic* froward, esp. *Brit. colloq.* bloody-minded, *sl.* feisty; naughty, ill-behaved; fussy, particular, demanding. **3** troubled, troubling, tough, burdensome, onerous, demanding, trying, hard, grim, unfavorable, straitening.

difficulty /dífikultee, -kəl-/ *n.* (*pl.* **-ies**) **1** the state or condition of being difficult. **2 a** a difficult thing; a problem or hindrance. **b** (often in *pl.*) a cause of distress or hardship (*in financial difficulties*; *there was someone in difficulties in the water*). □ **make difficulties** be intransigent or unaccommodating. **with difficulty** not easily. [ME f. L *difficultas* (as DIS-, *facultas* FACULTY)]

■ **1** strain, hardship; hardness, toughness, arduousness, laboriousness, formidableness, painfulness; awkwardness, delicacy, trickiness, complexity, thorniness, knottiness, ticklishness. **2 a** hardship, obstacle, problem, hindrance, pitfall, predicament, tribulation, snag, *disp.* dilemma. **b** (*difficulties*) embarrassment, plight, problems, predicament, mess, (dire) strait(s), trouble, scrape, *colloq.* hot water, jam, pickle, fix. □ **make difficulties** cause *or* stir up trouble,

---

/.../ **pronunciation**	● **part of speech**
□ **phrases, idioms, and compounds**	
□□ **derivatives**	■ **synonym section**
cross-references appear in SMALL CAPITALS or *italics*	

stir things up, put *or* set a cat among the pigeons, throw a wrench in the works.

diffident /dífidənt/ *adj.* **1** shy; lacking self-confidence. **2** excessively modest and reticent. □□ **diffidence** /-dəns/ *n.* **diffidently** *adv.* [L *diffidere* (as DIS-, *fidere* trust)]
■ see SHY[1] *adj.* 1.

diffract /difrákt/ *v.tr. Physics* (of the edge of an opaque body, a narrow slit, etc.) break up (a beam of light) into a series of dark or light bands or colored spectra, or (a beam of radiation or particles) into a series of alternately high and low intensities. □□ **diffraction** /-frákshən/ *n.* **diffractive** *adj.* **diffractively** *adv.* [L *diffringere diffract-* (as DIS-, *frangere* break)]

diffractometer /difraktómitər/ *n.* an instrument for measuring diffraction, esp. in crystallographic work.

diffuse *adj.* & *v.* ● *adj.* /difyoo͞os/ **1** (of light, inflammation, etc.) spread out; diffused; not concentrated. **2** (of prose, speech, etc.) not concise; long-winded; verbose. ● *v.tr.* & *intr.* /difyoo͞oz/ **1** disperse or be dispersed from a center. **2** spread or be spread widely; reach a large area. **3** *Physics* (esp. of fluids) intermingle by diffusion. □□ **diffusely** /difyoo͞oslee/ *adv.* **diffuseness** /difyoo͞osnis/ *n.* **diffusible** /difyoo͞ozibəl/ *adj.* **diffusive** /difyoo͞osiv/ *adj.* [ME f. F *diffus* or L *diffusus* extensive (as DIS-, *fusus* past part. of *fundere* pour)]
■ *adj.* **1** spread out, diffused, scattered, dispersed, widespread; light. **2** wordy, verbose, prolix, long-winded, loquacious, discursive, digressive, rambling, circumlocutory, circumlocutionary, circumlocutional, meandering, roundabout, circuitous, periphrastic, diffusive. ● *v.* **1, 2** spread, circulate, distribute, dispense, disperse, dispel, scatter, broadcast, sow, disseminate, dissipate; spread out.

diffuser /difyoo͞ozər/ *n.* (also **diffusor**) **1** a person or thing that diffuses, esp. a device for diffusing light. **2** *Engin.* a duct for broadening an airflow and reducing its speed.

diffusion /difyoo͞ozhən/ *n.* **1** the act or an instance of diffusing; the process of being diffused. **2** *Physics & Chem.* the interpenetration of substances by the natural movement of their particles. **3** *Anthropol.* the spread of elements of culture, etc., to another region or people. □□ **diffusionist** *n.* [ME f. L *diffusio* (as DIFFUSE)]
■ **1** see RADIATION. **3** see CIRCULATION 2a.

dig /dig/ *v.* & *n.* ● *v.* (**digging**; *past* and *past part.* **dug** /dug/) **1** *intr.* break up and remove or turn over soil, ground, etc., with a tool, one's hands, (of an animal) claws, etc. **2** *tr.* **a** break up and displace (the ground, etc.) in this way. **b** (foll. by *up*) break up the soil of (fallow land). **3** *tr.* make (a hole, grave, tunnel, etc.) by digging. **4** *tr.* (often foll. by *up, out*) **a** obtain or remove by digging. **b** find or discover after searching. **5** *tr.* (also *absol.*) excavate (an archaeological site). **6** *tr. sl.* like, appreciate, or understand. **7** *tr.* & *intr.* (foll. by *in, into*) thrust or poke into or down into. **8** *intr.* make one's way by digging (*dug through the mountainside*). **9** *intr.* (usu. foll. by *into*) investigate or study closely; probe. ● *n.* **1** a piece of digging. **2** a thrust or poke (*a dig in the ribs*). **3** *colloq.* (often foll. by *at*) a pointed or critical remark. **4** an archaeological excavation. **5** (in *pl.*) *colloq.* living quarters. □ **dig one's feet** (or **heels** or **toes**) **in** be obstinate. **dig in** *colloq.* begin eating. **dig oneself in 1** prepare a defensive trench or pit. **2** establish one's position. [ME *digge*, of uncert. orig.: cf. OE *dīc* ditch]
■ *v.* **1** see EXCAVATE 1, BURROW *v.* 1, 2. **2 b** (*dig up*) break up, work; see also PLOW *v.* 1. **3** gouge (out), scoop (out), hollow out, spoon out, cut, dig out, excavate; make. **4** (*dig out* or *up*) unearth, disinter, disentomb, exhume, bring up, find, obtain, extract, ferret out, discover, bring to light, expose, dredge up, extricate, come up with, *Brit.* winkle out. **6** appreciate, enjoy, like, understand, go for, *colloq.* be into; see also LIKE[2] *v.* 1. **7** thrust, stab, jab, plunge, force, prod, nudge, poke. **9** (*dig into*) probe (into), delve into, go deeply into, inquire into, investigate, explore, look into, research, study. ● *n.* **2** thrust, poke, jab, stab, nudge, elbow. **3** insult, insinuation, gibe, slur, affront, taunt, jeer, slap

in the face, *colloq.* crack. **5** (*digs*) see ACCOMMODATION 1. □ **dig in** help oneself, set to, *colloq.* dive in, tuck in.

digamma /dīgámə/ *n.* the sixth letter (F, Ϝ) of the early Greek alphabet (prob. pronounced w), later disused. [L f. Gk (as DI-[1], GAMMA)]

digastric /dīgástrik/ *adj.* & *n. Anat.* ● *adj.* (of a muscle) having two wide parts with a tendon between. ● *n.* the muscle that opens the jaw. [mod.L *digastricus* (as DI-[1], Gk *gastēr* belly)]

digest *v.* & *n.* ● *v.tr.* /dijést, dī-/ **1** assimilate (food) in the stomach and bowels. **2** understand and assimilate mentally. **3** *Chem.* treat (a substance) with heat, enzymes, or a solvent in order to decompose it, extract the essence, etc. **4 a** reduce to a systematic or convenient form; classify; summarize. **b** think over; arrange in the mind. **5** bear without resistance; tolerate; endure. ● *n.* /díjest/ **1 a** a methodical summary, esp. of a body of laws. **b** (**the Digest**) the compendium of Roman law compiled in the reign of Justinian (6th c. AD). **2 a** a compendium or summary of information; a résumé. **b** a regular or occasional synopsis of current literature or news. □□ **digester** *n.* **digestible** *adj.* **digestibility** *n.* [ME f. L *digerere digest-* distribute, dissolve, digest (as DI-[2], *gerere* carry)]
■ *v.* **2** assimilate, take in, swallow; comprehend, grasp, get hold of, get, understand. **4 a** abbreviate, cut, condense, abridge, compress, epitomize, summarize, reduce, shorten; systematize; classify. **b** consider, study, ponder, meditate on *or* over, reflect on, think over. **5** bear, stand, endure, survive, accept, tolerate, swallow, stomach, *literary* brook. ● *n.* **2 a** condensation, abridgment, précis, résumé, compendium, summary, abbreviation. **b** abstract, synopsis, conspectus, survey, outline; see also SUMMARY *n.* □□ **digestible** palatable, easy to understand; see also INTELLIGIBLE, BEARABLE.

digestion /dijés-chən, dī-/ *n.* **1** the process of digesting. **2** the capacity to digest food (*has a weak digestion*). **3** digesting a substance by means of heat, enzymes, or a solvent. [ME f. OF f. L *digestio -onis* (as DIGEST)]

digestive /dijéstiv, dī-/ *adj.* & *n.* ● *adj.* **1** of or relating to digestion. **2** aiding or promoting digestion. ● *n.* **1** a substance that aids digestion. **2** (in full **digestive biscuit**) *Brit.* a usu. round semisweet wholewheat cookie. □□ **digestively** *adv.* [ME f. OF *digestif -ive* or L *digestivus* (as DIGEST)]

digger /dígər/ *n.* **1** a person or machine that digs, esp. a mechanical excavator. **2** a miner, esp. a gold digger. **3** *colloq.* an Australian or New Zealander, esp. a private soldier. **4** *Austral. & NZ colloq.* (as a form of address) mate; fellow.

diggings /dígingz/ *n.pl.* **1 a** a mine or goldfield. **b** material dug out of a mine, etc. **2** *Brit. colloq.* lodgings; accommodation.

dight /dīt/ *adj. archaic* clothed; arrayed. [past part. of *dight* (v.) f. OE *dihtan* f. L *dictare* DICTATE]

digit /díjit/ *n.* **1** any numeral from 0 to 9, esp. when forming part of a number. **2** *Anat. & Zool.* a finger, thumb, or toe. [ME f. L *digitus*]
■ **1** see FIGURE *n.* 6a.

digital /díjit'l/ *adj.* **1** of or using a digit or digits. **2** (of a clock, watch, etc.) that gives a reading by means of displayed digits instead of hands. **3** (of a computer) operating on data represented as a series of usu. binary digits or in similar discrete form. **4 a** (of a recording) with sound information represented in digits for more reliable transmission. **b** (of a recording medium) using this process. □ **digital audio tape** magnetic tape on which sound is recorded digitally. **digital to analog converter** *Computing* a device for converting digital values to analog form. □□ **digitalize** *v.tr.* **digitally** *adv.* [L *digitalis* (as DIGIT)]

digitalin /díjitálin/ *n.* the pharmacologically active constituent(s) of the foxglove. [DIGITALIS + -IN]

digitalis /díjitális/ *n.* a drug prepared from the dried leaves of foxgloves and containing substances that stimulate the heart muscle. [mod.L, genus name of foxglove after G *Fingerhut* thimble: see DIGITAL]

digitate /díjitayt/ *adj.* **1** *Zool.* having separate fingers or toes.

2 *Bot.* having deep radiating divisions. □□ **digitately** *adv.* **digitation** /-táyshən/ *n.* [L *digitatus* (as DIGIT)]

digitigrade /díjitigrayd/ *adj. & n. Zool.* ● *adj.* (of an animal) walking on its toes and not touching the ground with its heels, e.g., dogs, cats, and rodents. ● *n.* a digitigrade animal (cf. PLANTIGRADE). [F f. L *digitus* + *-gradus* -walking]

digitize /díjitīz/ *v.tr.* convert (data, etc.) into digital form, esp. for processing by a computer. □□ **digitization** *n.*

dignified /dígnifīd/ *adj.* having or expressing dignity; noble or stately in appearance or manner. □□ **dignifiedly** *adv.*
■ stately, noble, majestic, formal, solemn, serious, sober, grave, distinguished, honorable, distingué, elegant, august, sedate, reserved; regal, courtly, lordly, lofty, exalted, grand.

dignify /dígnifī/ *v.tr.* (**-ies, -ied**) **1** give dignity or distinction to. **2** ennoble; make worthy or illustrious. **3** give the form or appearance of dignity to (*dignified the house with the name of mansion*). [obs. F *dignifier* f. OF *dignefier* f. LL *dignificare* f. *dignus* worthy]
■ distinguish, ennoble, elevate, raise, exalt, glorify, upraise, lift, uplift, enhance, improve, better, upgrade.

dignitary /dígniteree/ *n.* (*pl.* **-ies**) a person holding high rank or office. [DIGNITY + -ARY[1], after PROPRIETARY]
■ personage, official, notable, worthy, magnate, VIP, power, big name, *Austral.* joss, *colloq.* bigwig, higher-up, big shot, hot stuff, hotshot, *sl.* big cheese, big gun, big chief, big daddy, fat cat, Mr. Big, big wheel; celebrity, lion, luminary.

dignity /dígnitee/ *n.* (*pl.* **-ies**) **1** a composed and serious manner or style. **2** the state of being worthy of honor or respect. **3** worthiness; excellence (*the dignity of work*). **4** a high or honorable rank or position. **5** high regard or estimation. **6** self-respect. □ **beneath one's dignity** not considered worthy enough for one to do. **stand on one's dignity** insist (esp. by one's manner) on being treated with due respect. [ME f. OF *digneté, dignité* f. L *dignitas -tatis* f. *dignus* worthy]
■ **1** stateliness, formality, nobility, majesty, gravity, seriousness, gravitas, solemnity, courtliness, grandeur, grandness; hauteur, loftiness; composure, control. **3** worth, worthiness, nobility, nobleness, excellence, honor, honorableness, respectability, respectableness, importance, greatness, glory. **4** standing, station, status, rank, honor, level, position. **6** self-respect, self-regard, amour propre, self-confidence, self-esteem, pride.

digraph /dígraf/ *n.* a group of two letters representing one sound, as in *ph* and *ey*. □□ **digraphic** /-gráfik/ *adj.*

digress /dīgrés/ *v.intr.* depart from the main subject temporarily in speech or writing. □□ **digresser** *n.* **digression** *n.* /-gréshən/ **digressive** *adj.* **digressively** *adv.* **digressiveness** *n.* [L *digredi digress-* (as DI-[2], *gradi* walk)]
■ get off the point, go off the track, go off at a tangent, get sidetracked, ramble, drift, wander, stray, diverge, deviate. □□ **digression** aside, departure, excursus, deviation, detour, obiter dictum, parenthesis, apostrophe.

digs see DIG *n.* 5.

dihedral /díhéedrəl/ *adj. & n.* ● *adj.* having or contained by two plane faces. ● *n.* = *dihedral angle*. □ **dihedral angle** an angle formed by two plane surfaces, esp. by an aircraft wing with the horizontal. [*dihedron* f. DI-[1] + -HEDRON]

dihydric /díhídrik/ *adj. Chem.* containing two hydroxyl groups. [DI-[1] + *hydric* containing hydrogen]

dik-dik /díkdik/ *n.* any dwarf antelope of the genus *Madoqua*, native to Africa. [name in E. Africa and in Afrik.]

dike[1] /dīk/ *n. & v.* (also **dyke**) ● *n.* **1** a long wall or embankment built to prevent flooding, esp. from the sea. **2 a** a ditch or artificial watercourse. **b** *Brit.* a natural watercourse. **3 a** a low wall, esp. of turf. **b** a causeway. **4** a barrier or obstacle; a defense. **5** *Geol.* an intrusion of igneous rock across sedimentary strata. **6** esp. *Austral. sl.* a toilet. ● *v.tr.* provide or defend with a dike or dikes. [ME f. ON *dík* or MLG *dík* dam, MDu. *dijc* ditch, dam: cf. DITCH]
■ **4** see PROTECTION 1b.

dike[2] var. of DYKE[2].

diktat /diktát/ *n.* a categorical statement or decree, esp. terms imposed after a war by a victor. [G, = DICTATE]

dilapidate /dilápidayt/ *v.intr. & tr.* fall or cause to fall into disrepair or ruin. [L *dilapidare* demolish, squander (as DI-[2], *lapis lapid-* stone)]

dilapidated /dilápidaytid/ *adj.* in a state of disrepair or ruin, esp. as a result of age or neglect.
■ ruined, broken-down, in ruins, gone to rack and ruin, wrecked, destroyed, falling apart, decrepit, derelict, battered, tumbledown, run-down, ramshackle, crumbling, decayed, decaying, rickety, shaky, *colloq.* beat-up.

dilapidation /dilápidáyshən/ *n.* **1 a** the process of dilapidating. **b** a state of disrepair. **2** (in *pl.*) repairs required at the end of a tenancy or lease. **3** *Eccl.* a sum charged against an incumbent for wear and tear during a tenancy. [ME f. LL *dilapidatio* (as DILAPIDATE)]
■ **1 b** see DISREPAIR.

dilatation /dílətáyshən, dī-/ *n.* **1** the widening or expansion of a hollow organ or cavity. **2** the process of dilating. □ **dilatation and curettage** an operation in which the cervix is expanded and the womb lining scraped off with a curette.

dilate /dīláyt, dílayt/ *v.* **1** *tr. & intr.* make or become wider or larger (esp. of an opening in the body) (*dilated pupils*). **2** *intr.* (often foll. by *on, upon*) speak or write at length. □□ **dilatable** *adj.* **dilation** /-láyshən/ *n.* [ME f. OF *dilater* f. L *dilatare* spread out (as DI-[2], *latus* wide)]
■ see EXPAND 1.

dilator /dīláytər, dílay-/ *n.* **1** *Anat.* a muscle that dilates an organ. **2** *Surgery* an instrument for dilating a tube or cavity in the body.

dilatory /dílətawree/ *adj.* given to or causing delay. □□ **dilatorily** *adv.* **dilatoriness** *n.* [LL *dilatorius* (as DI-[2], *dilat-* past part. stem of *differre* DEFER[1])]
■ see TARDY 1.

dildo /díldō/ *n.* (*pl.* **-os** or **-oes**) an object shaped like an erect penis and used, esp. by women, for sexual stimulation. [17th c.: orig. unkn.]

dilemma /dilémə/ *n.* **1** a situation in which a choice has to be made between two equally undesirable alternatives. **2** a state of indecision between two alternatives. **3** *disp.* a difficult situation. **4** an argument forcing an opponent to choose either of two unfavorable alternatives. [L f. Gk (as DI-[1], *lēmma* premise)]
■ **1** double bind, *colloq.* catch-22. **3** predicament, quandary, impasse, deadlock, stalemate; plight, difficulty, stymie, bind, *colloq.* fix, jam, spot, pickle, squeeze.

dilettante /dílitaánt/ *n. & adj.* ● *n.* (*pl.* **dilettantes** or **dilettanti** /-tee/) **1** a person who studies a subject or area of knowledge superficially. **2** a person who enjoys the arts. ● *adj.* trifling; not thorough; amateurish. □□ **dilettantish** *adj.* **dilettantism** *n.* [It. f. pres. part. of *dilettare* delight f. L *delectare*]
■ *n.* **1** dabbler, trifler, amateur, tinkerer. **2** see AESTHETE.
● *adj.* see SUPERFICIAL 1, 4, AMATEUR *adj.*

diligence[1] /dílijəns/ *n.* **1** careful and persistent application or effort. **2** (as a characteristic) industriousness. [ME f. OF f. L *diligentia* (as DILIGENT)]
■ see APPLICATION 4.

diligence[2] /dílijəns, déeleezhóns/ *n. hist.* a public stagecoach, esp. in France. [F, for *carrosse de diligence* coach of speed]

diligent /dílijənt/ *adj.* **1** careful and steady in application to one's work or duties. **2** showing care and effort. □□ **diligently** *adv.* [ME f. OF f. L *diligens* assiduous, part. of *diligere* love, take delight in (as DI-[2], *legere* choose)]
■ industrious, assiduous, attentive, conscientious, hardworking, sedulous, intent, steady, steadfast,

---

/. . ./ **pronunciation**	● **part of speech**
□ **phrases, idioms, and compounds**	
□□ **derivatives**	■ **synonym section**
cross-references appear in SMALL CAPITALS or *italics*	

focused, concentrated, earnest, constant; painstaking, careful, thorough, scrupulous, meticulous, punctilious.

dill[1] /dil/ *n.* **1** an umbelliferous herb, *Anethum graveolens*, with yellow flowers and aromatic seeds. **2** the leaves or seeds of this plant used for flavoring and medicinal purposes. □ **dill pickle** pickled cucumber, etc., flavored with dill. [OE *dile*]

dill[2] /dil/ *n. Austral. sl.* **1** a fool or simpleton. **2** the victim of a trickster. [app. back-form. f. DILLY[2]]

dilly[1] /dílee/ *n.* (*pl.* **-ies**) *sl.* a remarkable or excellent person or thing. [*dilly* (adj.) f. DELIGHTFUL or DELICIOUS]

dilly[2] /dílee/ *adj. Austral. sl.* **1** odd or eccentric. **2** foolish; stupid; mad. [perh. f. DAFT, SILLY]

dilly-bag /díleebag/ *n. Austral.* a small bag or basket. [Aboriginal *dilly* + BAG]

dillydally /díleedálee/ *v.intr.* (**-ies**, **-ied**) *colloq.* **1** dawdle; loiter. **2** vacillate. [redupl. of DALLY]
■ **1** see DELAY *v.* 3.

diluent /dílyōōənt/ *adj. & n. Chem. & Biochem.* ● *adj.* that serves to dilute. ● *n.* a diluting agent. [L *diluere* diluent- DILUTE]

dilute /dilōōt, dī-/ *v. & adj.* ● *v.tr.* **1** reduce the strength of (a fluid) by adding water or another solvent. **2** weaken or reduce the strength or forcefulness of, esp. by adding something. ● *adj.* /also dí-/ **1** (esp. of a fluid) diluted; weakened. **2** (of a color) washed out; low in saturation. **3** *Chem.* **a** (of a solution) having relatively low concentration of solute. **b** (of a substance) in solution (*dilute sulfuric acid*). □□ **diluter** *n.* **dilution** /-lōōshən/ *n.* [L *diluere* dilut- (as DI-[2], *luere* wash)]
■ *v.* water (down), thin (down *or* out), weaken, deplete, reduce, lessen, diminish, decrease, impoverish, *colloq.* split. ● *adj.* **1** weak, weakened, watered down, diluted, thinned out. **2** washed out, faded, bleached.

diluvial /dilōōveeəl/ *adj.* **1** of a flood, esp. of the Flood in Genesis. **2** *Geol.* of the Glacial Drift formation (see DRIFT *n.* 8). [LL *diluvialis* f. *diluvium* DELUGE]

diluvium /dilōōveeəm/ *n.* (*pl.* **diluvia** /-veeə/ *or* **diluviums**) *Geol.* = DRIFT *n.* 8. [L: see DILUVIAL]

dim /dim/ *adj. & v.* ● *adj.* (**dimmer, dimmest**) **1 a** only faintly luminous or visible; not bright. **b** obscure; ill-defined. **2** not clearly perceived or remembered. **3** *colloq.* stupid; slow to understand. **4** (of the eyes) not seeing clearly. ● *v.* (**dimmed, dimming**) **1** *tr. & intr.* make or become dim or less bright. **2** *tr.* switch (headlights) to low beam. □ **dim-witted** *colloq.* stupid; unintelligent. **take a dim view of** *colloq.* **1** disapprove of. **2** feel gloomy about. □□ **dimly** *adv.* **dimmish** *adj.* **dimness** *n.* [OE *dim, dimm*, of unkn. orig.]
■ *adj.* **1 a** faint, weak, weakened, pale, imperceptible, indiscernible, indistinguishable; dark, shadowy, murky, gloomy, somber, dusky, crepuscular, *literary* tenebrous. **b** obscure, obscured, vague, fuzzy, indistinct, ill-defined, undefined, foggy, clouded, cloudy, nebulous, blurred, blurry, unclear, dull, hazy, misty. **3** obtuse, doltish, dull, dull-witted, foolish, slow-witted, *colloq.* thick, dense, dim-witted, dumb; see also STUPID *adj.* 1, 5. ● *v.* **1** obscure, dull, becloud, cloud; darken, shroud, shade; weaken. □ **dim-witted** see STUPID *adj.* 1, 5. **take a dim view of 1** object to, resent, take exception to, mind; see also DISAPPROVE.

dim. *abbr.* diminuendo.

dime /dim/ *n. US & Can.* **1** a ten-cent coin. **2** *colloq.* a small amount of money. □ **a dime a dozen** very cheap or commonplace. **dime novel** a cheap popular novel. **dime store** = five-and-dime. **turn on a dime** *colloq.* make a sharp turn in a vehicle. [ME (orig. = tithe) f. OF *disme* f. L *decima pars* tenth part]

dimension /diménshən, dī-/ *n. & v.* ● *n.* **1** a measurable extent of any kind, as length, breadth, depth, area, and volume. **2** (in *pl.*) size; scope; extent. **3** an aspect or facet of a situation, problem, etc. **4** *Algebra* one of a number of unknown or variable quantities contained as factors in a product (x^3, x^2y, xyz, are all of three dimensions). **5** *Physics* the product of mass, length, time, etc., raised to the appropriate power, in a derived physical quantity. ● *v.tr.* (usu. as **dimensioned** *adj.*) mark the dimensions on (a diagram, etc.). □□ **dimensional** *adj.* (also in *comb.*). **dimensionless** *adj.*

[ME f. OF f. L *dimensio -onis* (as DI-[2], *metiri mensus* measure)]
■ *n.* **1** see MEASUREMENT 2.

dimer /dímər/ *n. Chem.* a compound consisting of two identical molecules linked together (cf. MONOMER). □□ **dimeric** /-mérik/ *adj.* [DI-[1] + *-mer* after POLYMER]

dimerous /dímərəs/ *adj.* (of a plant) having two parts in a whorl, etc. [mod.L *dimerus* f. Gk *dimerēs* bipartite]

dimeter /dímitər/ *n. Prosody* a line of verse consisting of two metrical feet. [LL *dimetrus* f. Gk *dimetros* (as DI-[1], METER)]

diminish /dimínish/ *v.* **1** *tr. & intr.* make or become smaller or less. **2** *tr.* lessen the reputation or influence of (a person). □ **law of diminishing returns** *Econ.* the fact that the increase of expenditure, investment, taxation, etc., beyond a certain point ceases to produce a proportionate yield. □□ **diminishable** *adj.* [ME, blending of earlier *minish* f. OF *menusier* (formed as MINCE) and *diminue* f. OF *diminuer* f. L *diminuere diminut-* break up small]
■ **1** decrease, decline, abate, shrink, contract; lessen, reduce, lower, curtail, compress, condense, pare (down), scale down; wane, fade, dwindle, ebb (away), die out *or* away, peter out, recede, subside; slacken, let up, wind down, slow (down), ease (off). **2** belittle, disparage, degrade, downgrade, discredit, detract from, vitiate, debase, deprecate, demean, depreciate, devalue, cheapen, *colloq.* put down, *formal* derogate.

diminished /dimínisht/ *adj.* **1** reduced; made smaller or less. **2** *Mus.* (of an interval, usu. a seventh or fifth) less by a semitone than the corresponding minor or perfect interval. □ **diminished responsibility** *Law* the limitation of criminal responsibility on the ground of mental weakness or abnormality.
■ **1** see SMALL *adj.* 3–5.

diminuendo /dimínyōō-éndō/ *adv. & n. Mus.* ● *adv.* with a gradual decrease in loudness. ● *n.* (*pl.* **-os**) a passage to be played in this way. [It., part. of *diminuire* DIMINISH]

diminution /dímínōōshən, -nyōō-/ *n.* **1 a** the act or an instance of diminishing. **b** the amount by which something diminishes. **2** *Mus.* the repetition of a passage in notes shorter than those originally used. [ME f. OF f. L *diminutio -onis* (as DIMINISH)]
■ **1** see DECREASE *n.*

diminutive /dimínyətiv/ *adj. & n.* ● *adj.* **1** remarkably small; tiny. **2** *Gram.* (of a word or suffix) implying smallness, either actual or imputed in token of affection, scorn, etc. (e.g., *-let*, *-kins*). ● *n. Gram.* a diminutive word or suffix. □□ **diminutival** /-tívəl/ *adj.* **diminutiveness** *n.* [ME f. OF *diminutif, -ive* f. LL *diminutivus* (as DIMINISH)]
■ *adj.* **1** small, tiny, little, miniature, petite, minute, minuscule, mini-, compact, undersized, pocket, pocket-sized, lilliputian, midget, esp. *Sc.* wee, *colloq.* teeny.

dimissory /dímísəree/ *adj.* **1** ordering or permitting to depart. **2** *Eccl.* granting permission for a candidate to be ordained outside the bishop's own see (*dimissory letters*). [ME f. LL *dimissorius* f. *dimittere dimiss-* send away (as DI-[2], *mittere* send)]

dimity /dímitee/ *n.* (*pl.* **-ies**) a cotton fabric woven with stripes or checks. [ME f. It. *dimito* or med.L *dimitum* f. Gk *dimitos* (as DI-[1], *mitos* warp-thread)]

dimmer /dímər/ *n.* **1** a device for varying the brightness of an electric light. **2 a** (in *pl.*) small parking lights on a motor vehicle. **b** headlights on low beam.

dimorphic /dímáwrfik/ *adj.* (also **dimorphous** /dímáwrfəs/) *Biol., Chem., & Mineral.* exhibiting, or occurring in, two distinct forms. □□ **dimorphism** *n.* [Gk *dimorphos* (as DI-[1], *morphē* form)]

dimple /dímpəl/ *n. & v.* ● *n.* a small hollow or dent in the flesh, esp. in the cheeks or chin. ● *v.* **1** *intr.* produce or show dimples. **2** *tr.* produce dimples in (a cheek, etc.). □□ **dimply** *adj.* [ME prob. f. OE *dympel* (unrecorded) f. a Gmc root *dump-*, perh. a nasalized form rel. to DEEP]
■ *n.* hollow, depression, dent, indentation.

dim sum /dim súm/ *n.* (also **dim sim** /sim/) **1** a meal or course of savory Cantonese-style snacks. **2** (usu. **dim sim**)

Austral. a dish of Cantonese origin, consisting of steamed or fried meat cooked in thin dough. [Cantonese *dim-sām*, lit. 'dot of the heart']

dimwit /dímwit/ *n. colloq.* a stupid person.
■ see FOOL¹ *n.*

DIN /din/ *n.* any of a series of technical standards originating in Germany and used internationally, esp. to designate electrical connections, film speeds, and paper sizes. [G, f. Deutsche *I*ndustrie-*N*orm]

din /din/ *n. & v.* ● *n.* a prolonged loud and distracting noise.
● *v.* (**dinned, dinning**) **1** *tr.* (foll. by *into*) instill (something to be learned) by constant repetition. **2** *intr.* make a din. [OE *dyne, dynn, dynian* f. Gmc]
■ *n.* noise, clamor, uproar, shouting, screaming, yelling, babel, clangor, clatter, commotion, racket, hullabaloo, hubbub, brouhaha, charivari, hurly-burly, *colloq.* row.
● *v.* **1** instill, drum, hammer, inculcate; implant, engrain.

dinar /dináar, deénaar/ *n.* **1** the chief monetary unit of Yugoslavia. **2** the chief monetary unit of certain countries of the Middle East and N. Africa. [Arab. & Pers. *dīnār* f. Gk *dēnarion* f. L *denarius*: see DENIER]

dine /dīn/ *v.* **1** *intr.* eat dinner. **2** *tr.* give dinner to. □ **dine out 1** dine away from home. **2** (foll. by *on*) *Brit.* be invited to dinner, etc., on account of one's ability to relate an interesting event, story, etc. □ **dining car** a railroad car equipped as a restaurant. **dining room** a room in which meals are eaten. [ME f. OF *diner, disner,* ult. f. DIS- + LL *jejunare* f. *jejunus* fasting]
■ **1** have dinner, eat, banquet, feast, *archaic* sup, *colloq.* feed.

diner /dínər/ *n.* **1** a person who dines, esp. in a restaurant. **2** a railroad dining car. **3** a small restaurant. **4** a small dining room.
■ **3** see CAFÉ 1.

dinette /dinét/ *n.* **1** a small room or part of a room used for eating meals. **2** (in full **dinette set**) table and chairs designed for such a room.

ding¹ /ding/ *v. & n.* ● *v.intr.* make a ringing sound. ● *n.* a ringing sound, as of a bell. [imit.: infl. by DIN]

ding² /ding/ *v. & n.* ● *v.tr.* cause surface damage; dent. ● *n.* nick; minor surface damage; dent. [ME *dingen*]

ding-a-ling /díngəling/ *n.* a foolish, flighty, or eccentric person.

ding an sich /díng an zíkh/ *n. Philos.* a thing in itself. [G]

dingbat /díngbat/ *n. sl.* **1** a stupid or eccentric person. **2** (in *pl.*) *Austral. & NZ* **a** madness. **b** discomfort; unease (*gives me the dingbats*). [19th c.: perh. f. *ding* to beat + BAT¹]
■ **1** see SILLY *n.*

dingdong /díngdawng, -dong/ *n., adj., & adv.* ● *n.* **1** the sound of alternate chimes, as of two bells. **2** *colloq.* an intense argument or fight. **3** *colloq.* a riotous party. ● *adj.* (of a contest, etc.) evenly matched and intensely waged; thoroughgoing. ● *adv.* with vigor and energy (*hammer away at it dingdong*). [16th c.: imit.]
■ *n.* **1** see CHIME¹ *n.* 1b.

dinge /dinj/ *n.* the condition of dinginess.

dinghy /díngee/ *n.* (*pl.* **-ies**) **1** a small boat carried by a ship. **2** a small pleasure boat. **3** a small inflatable rubber boat (esp. for emergency use). [orig. a row boat used in India f. Hindi *ḍiṅgī, ḍeṅgī*]
■ **1, 2** see TENDER³.

dingle /díngəl/ *n.* a deep, wooded valley or dell. [ME: orig. unkn.]
■ see VALLEY.

dingo /díngō/ *n.* (*pl.* **-oes**) **1** a wild or half-domesticated Australian dog, *Canis dingo.* **2** *Austral. sl.* a coward or scoundrel. [Aboriginal]

dingy /dínjee/ *adj.* (**dingier, dingiest**) dirty-looking; drab; dull-colored. □□ **dingily** *adv.* **dinginess** *n.* [perh. ult. f. OE *dynge* DUNG]
■ dark, dull, gloomy, dim, lackluster, faded, discolored, dusky, drab, dreary, dismal, cheerless, depressing, shadowy, gray-brown, *literary* tenebrous; grimy, dirty, soiled.

dinkum /díngkəm/ *adj. & n. Austral. & NZ colloq.* ● *adj.* genuine, right. ● *n.* work, toil. □ **dinkum oil** the honest truth. [19th c.: orig. unkn.]

dinky /díngkee/ *adj.* (**dinkier, dinkiest**) *colloq.* **1** trifling; insignificant. **2** *Brit.* (esp. of a thing) neat and attractive; small; dainty. [Sc. *dink* neat, trim, of unkn. orig.]

dinner /dínər/ *n.* **1** the main meal of the day, taken either at midday or in the evening. **2** a formal evening meal, often in honor of a person or event. □ **dinner dance** a formal dinner followed by dancing. **dinner jacket** a man's, usu. black, formal jacket for evening wear. **dinner service** a set of usu. matching dishes, etc., for serving a meal. [ME f. OF *diner, disner*: see DINE]
■ **1** see MEAL¹. **2** see BANQUET *n.*

dinnerware /dínərwair/ *n.* tableware, usu. including plates, glassware, and cutlery.

dinosaur /dínəsawr/ *n.* **1** an extinct reptile of the Mesozoic era, often of enormous size. **2** a large, unwieldy system or organization, esp. one not adapting to new conditions. □□ **dinosaurian** *adj. & n.* [mod.L *dinosaurus* f. Gk *deinos* terrible + *sauros* lizard]

dinothere /dínətheer/ *n.* any elephantlike animal of the extinct genus *Deinotherium,* having downward-curving tusks. [mod.L *dinotherium* f. Gk *deinos* terrible + *thērion* wild beast]

dint /dint/ *n. & v.* ● *n.* **1** a dent. **2** *archaic* a blow or stroke. ● *v.tr.* mark with dints. □ **by dint of** by force or means of. [ME f. OE *dynt,* and partly f. cogn. ON *dyntr*: ult. orig. unkn.]

diocesan /dīósisən/ *adj. & n.* ● *adj.* of or concerning a diocese. ● *n.* the bishop of a diocese. [ME f. F *diocésain* f. LL *diocesanus* (as DIOCESE)]

diocese /díəsis, -sees, -seez/ *n.* a district under the pastoral care of a bishop. [ME f. OF *diocise* f. LL *diocesis* f. L *dioecesis* f. Gk *dioikēsis* administration (as DI-³, *oikeō* inhabit)]

diode /díōd/ *n. Electronics* **1** a semiconductor allowing the flow of current in one direction only and having two terminals. **2** a thermionic valve having two electrodes. [DI-¹ + ELECTRODE]

dioecious /dī-eéshəs/ *adj.* **1** *Bot.* having male and female organs on separate plants. **2** *Zool.* having the two sexes in separate individuals (cf. MONOECIOUS). [DI-¹ + Gk *-oikos* -housed]

diol /díawl, -ol/ *n. Chem.* any alcohol containing two hydroxyl groups in each molecule. [DI-¹ + -OL¹]

Dionysiac /dīəníseeak/ *adj.* (also **Dionysian** /-níshən, -nízhən, -níseeən/) **1** wildly sensual; unrestrained. **2** (in Greek mythology) of or relating to Dionysus, the Greek god of wine, or his worship. [LL *Dionysiacus* f. L *Dionysus* f. Gk *Dionusos*]

Diophantine equation /díəfántin, -tin/ *n. Math.* an equation with integral coefficients for which integral solutions are required. [*Diophantus* of Alexandria, mathematician of uncert. date]

diopter /dióptər/ *n.* (*Brit.* **dioptre**) *Optics* a unit of refractive power of a lens, equal to the reciprocal of its focal length in meters. [F *dioptre* f. L *dioptra* f. Gk *dioptra*: see DIOPTRIC]

dioptric /dióptrik/ *adj. Optics* **1** serving as a medium for sight; assisting sight by refraction (*dioptric glass; dioptric lens*). **2** of refraction; refractive. [Gk *dioptrikos* f. *dioptra* a kind of theodolite]

dioptrics /dióptriks/ *n. Optics* the part of optics dealing with refraction.

diorama /díərámə, -ráamə/ *n.* **1** a scenic painting in which changes in color and direction of illumination simulate a sunrise, etc. **2** a small representation of a scene with three-dimensional figures, viewed through a window, etc. **3** a small-scale model or movie set, etc. □□ **dioramic** /-rámik/ *adj.* [DI-³ + Gk *horama -atos* f. *horaō* see]

diorite /díərit/ *n.* a coarse-grained, plutonic igneous rock

---

/. . ./ **pronunciation**	● **part of speech**
□ **phrases, idioms, and compounds**	
□□ **derivatives**	■ **synonym section**
cross-references appear in SMALL CAPITALS or *italics*	

containing quartz. □□ **dioritic** /-rítik/ *adj.* [F f. Gk *diorizō* distinguish]

dioxane /díóksayn/ *n.* (also **dioxan** /-óksən/) *Chem.* a colorless toxic liquid used as a solvent. ¶ *Chem.* formula: $C_4H_8O_2$.

dioxide /díóksīd/ *n. Chem.* an oxide containing two atoms of oxygen which are not linked together (*carbon dioxide*).

DIP /dip/ *n. Computing* a form of integrated circuit consisting of a small plastic or ceramic slab with two parallel rows of pins. □ **DIP switch** an arrangement of switches on a printer for selecting a printing mode. [abbr. of *dual in-line package*]

dip. *abbr.* diploma.

dip /dip/ *v. & n.* ● *v.* (**dipped**, **dipping**) **1** *tr.* put or let down briefly into liquid, etc.; immerse. **2** *intr.* **a** go below a surface or level (*the sun dipped below the horizon*). **b** (of a level of income, activity, etc.) decline slightly, esp. briefly (*profits dipped in May*). **3** *intr.* extend downward; take or have a downward slope (*the road dips after the curve*). **4** *intr.* go under water and emerge quickly. **5** *intr.* (foll. by *into*) **a** read briefly from (a book, etc.). **b** take a cursory interest in (a subject). **6** (foll. by *into*) **a** *intr.* put a hand, ladle, etc., into a container to take something out. **b** *tr.* put (a hand, etc.) into a container to do this. **c** *intr.* spend from or make use of one's resources (*dipped into our savings*). **7** *tr. & intr.* lower or be lowered, esp. in salute. **8** *tr. Brit.* lower the beam of (a vehicle's headlights). **9** *tr.* color (a fabric) by immersing it in dye. **10** *tr.* wash (esp. sheep) by immersion in a vermin-killing liquid. **11** *tr.* make (a candle) by immersing a wick briefly in hot tallow. **12** *tr.* baptize by immersion. **13** *tr.* (often foll. by *up, out of*) remove or scoop up (liquid, grain, etc., or something from liquid). ● *n.* **1** an act of dipping or being dipped. **2** a liquid into which something is dipped. **3** a brief swim in the ocean, lake, etc. **4** a brief downward slope, followed by an upward one, in a road, etc. **5** a sauce or dressing into which food is dipped before eating. **6** a depression in the skyline. **7** *Astron. & Surveying* the apparent depression of the horizon from the line of observation, due to the curvature of the earth. **8** *Physics* the angle made with the horizontal at any point by the earth's magnetic field. **9** *Geol.* the angle a stratum makes with the horizon. **10** *sl.* a pickpocket. **11** a quantity dipped up. **12** a candle made by dipping. [OE *dyppan* f. Gmc: rel. to DEEP]

■ *v.* **1** immerse, plunge, duck, dunk, douse, bathe, submerge. **2 b** decline, drop, go down, fall, descend, sag, sink, subside, slump. **5** (*dip into*) **a** skim (through), scan, look over, run one's eyes over, flick *or* thumb *or* leaf *or* flip through, peruse. **b** dabble in, trifle with, play at, trifle *or* toy *or* tinker *or* flirt with. **7** let *or* put down, lower, drop; be let *or* put down, be lowered *or* dropped. ● *n.* **1** lowering, fall, depression, drop, slump, decline; immersion. **3** swim, plunge, bathe, duck. **4** see SLOPE *n.* 1–3.

dipeptide /dípéptīd/ *n. Biochem.* a peptide formed by the combination of two amino acids.

diphtheria /difthéereeə, dip-/ *n.* an acute infectious bacterial disease with inflammation of a mucous membrane esp. of the throat, resulting in the formation of a false membrane causing difficulty in breathing and swallowing. □□ **diphtherial** *adj.* **diphtheric** /-thérik/ *adj.* **diphtheritic** /-thərítik/ *adj.* **diphtheroid** /dífthəroyd, díp-/ *adj.* [mod.L f. F *diphthérie,* earlier *diphthérite* f. Gk *diphthera* skin, hide]

diphthong /dífthawng, -thong, díp-/ *n.* **1** a speech sound in one syllable in which the articulation begins as for one vowel and moves as for another (as in *coin, loud,* and *side*). **2 a** a digraph representing the sound of a diphthong or single vowel (as in *feat*). **b** a compound vowel character; a ligature (as *æ*). □□ **diphthongal** /-tháwnggəl, -thóng-/ *adj.* [F *diphtongue* f. LL *diphthongus* f. Gk *diphthoggos* (as DI-¹, *phthoggos* voice)]

diphthongize /dífthawngīz, -thong-, díp-/ *v.tr.* pronounce as a diphthong. □□ **diphthongization** *n.*

diplo- /díplō/ *comb. form* double. [Gk *diplous* double]

diplococcus /díplōkókəs/ *n.* (*pl.* **diplococci** /-sī, -kī/) *Biol.* any coccus that occurs mainly in pairs.

diplodocus /díplódəkəs, dī-/ *n.* a giant plant-eating dinosaur of the order Sauropoda, with a long neck and tail. [DIPLO- + Gk *dokos* wooden beam]

diploid /díployd/ *adj. & n. Biol.* ● *adj.* (of an organism or cell) having two complete sets of chromosomes per cell. ● *n.* a diploid cell or organism. [G (as DIPLO-, -OID)]

diploidy /díploydee/ *n. Biol.* the condition of being diploid.

diploma /diplṓmə/ *n.* (*pl.* **diplomas**) **1** a certificate of qualification awarded by a college, etc. **2** a document conferring an honor or privilege. **3** (*pl.* also **diplomata** /-mətə/) a state paper; an official document; a charter. □□ **diplomaed** /-məd/ *adj.* [L f. Gk *diplṓma -atos* folded paper f. *diploō* to fold f. *diplous* double]

diplomacy /diplṓməsee/ *n.* **1 a** the management of international relations. **b** adroitness in personal relations; tact. [F *diplomatie* f. *diplomatique* DIPLOMATIC after *aristocratic*]

■ **1** international relations, foreign affairs, statecraft, statesmanship, negotiation. **2** tact, tactfulness, adroitness, discretion, delicacy, discernment.

diplomat /dípləmat/ *n.* **1** an official representing a country abroad; a member of a diplomatic service. **2** a tactful person. [F *diplomate,* back-form. f. *diplomatique:* see DIPLOMATIC]

■ **1** see AMBASSADOR. **2** see PEACEMAKER.

diplomate /dípləmayt/ *n.* a person who holds a diploma, esp. in medicine.

diplomatic /dípləmátik/ *adj.* **1 a** of or involved in diplomacy. **b** skilled in diplomacy. **2** tactful; adroit in personal relations. **3** (of an edition, etc.) exactly reproducing the original. □ **diplomatic corps** the body of diplomats representing other countries at a seat of government. **diplomatic immunity** the exemption of diplomatic staff abroad from arrest, taxation, etc. **diplomatic pouch** a container in which official mail, etc., is dispatched to or from an embassy, not usu. subject to customs inspection. **diplomatic service** the branch of public service concerned with the representation of a country abroad. □□ **diplomatically** *adv.* [mod.L *diplomaticus* and F *diplomatique* f. L DIPLOMA]

■ **2** tactful, discreet, prudent, wise, sensitive, politic, courteous, polite, discerning, perceptive, perspicacious, thoughtful.

diplomatist /diplṓmətist/ *n.* esp. *Brit.* = DIPLOMAT.

diplont /díplont/ *n. Biol.* an animal or plant which has a diploid number of chromosomes in its somatic cells. [DIPLO- + Gk *ont-* stem of *ōn* being]

diplotene /díplōteen/ *n. Biol.* a stage during the prophase of meiosis where paired chromosomes begin to separate. [DIPLO- + Gk *tainia* band]

dipolar /dípṓlər/ *adj.* having two poles, as in a magnet.

dipole /dípōl/ *n.* **1** *Physics* two equal and oppositely charged or magnetized poles separated by a distance. **2** *Chem.* a molecule in which a concentration of positive charges is separated from a concentration of negative charges. **3** an aerial consisting of a horizontal metal rod with a connecting wire at its center.

dipper /dípər/ *n.* **1** a diving bird, *Cinclus cinclus.* Also called *water ouzel.* **2** a ladle. **3** *colloq.* an Anabaptist or Baptist. □ **Big Dipper** see BIG. **Little Dipper** see LITTLE.

■ **2** see SCOOP *n.* 1b.

dippy /dípee/ *adj.* (**dippier, dippiest**) *sl.* crazy; silly. [20th c.: orig. uncert.]

■ see INANE 1.

dipso /dípsō/ *n.* (*pl.* **-os**) *colloq.* a dipsomaniac. [abbr.]

dipsomania /dípsəmáyneeə/ *n.* an abnormal craving for alcohol. □□ **dipsomaniac** /-máyneeak/ *n.* [Gk *dipso-* f. *dipsa* thirst + -MANIA]

■ see *drunkenness* (DRUNKEN).

dipstick /dípstik/ *n.* a graduated rod for measuring the depth of a liquid, esp. in a vehicle's engine.

dipteral /díptərəl/ *adj. Archit.* having a double peristyle. [L *dipteros* f. Gk (as DI-¹, *pteron* wing)]

dipteran /díptərən/ *n. & adj.* ● *n.* a dipterous insect. ● *adj.* = DIPTEROUS 1. [mod.L *diptera* f. Gk *diptera* neut. pl. of *dipterous* two-winged (as DI-², *pteron* wing)]

dipterous /díptərəs/ *adj.* **1** (of an insect) of the order Diptera, having two membranous wings, e.g., the fly, gnat, or mosquito. **2** *Bot.* having two winglike appendages. [mod.L *dipterus* f. Gk *dipteros*: see DIPTERAN]

diptych /díptik/ *n.* **1 a** a painting, esp. an altarpiece, on two hinged, usu. wooden panels which may be closed like a book. **2** an ancient writing tablet consisting of two hinged leaves with waxed inner sides. [LL *diptycha* f. Gk *diptukha* (as DI-¹, *ptukhē* fold)]

dire /dīr/ *adj.* **1 a** calamitous; dreadful (*in dire straits*). **b** ominous (*dire warnings*). **2** urgent (*in dire need*). □□ **direly** *adv.* **direness** *n.* [L *dirus*]

  ■ **1 a** see *calamitous* (CALAMITY). **b** see FEARFUL 2, 3.
  2 see SORE *adj.* 4.

direct /dirékt, dī-/ *adj., adv., & v.* ● *adj.* **1** extending or moving in a straight line or by the shortest route; not crooked or circuitous. **2 a** straightforward; going straight to the point. **b** frank; not ambiguous. **3** without intermediaries or the intervention of other factors (*direct rule*; *the direct result*; *made a direct approach*). **4** (of descent) lineal; not collateral. **5** exact; complete; greatest possible (esp. where contrast is implied) (*the direct opposite*). **6** *Mus.* (of an interval or chord) not inverted. **7** *Astron.* (of planetary, etc., motion) proceeding from East to West; not retrograde. ● *adv.* **1** in a direct way or manner; without an intermediary or intervening factor (*dealt with them direct*). **2** frankly; without evasion. **3** by a direct route (*send it direct to Chicago*). ● *v.tr.* **1** control; guide; govern the movements of. **2** (foll. by *to* + infin., or *that* + clause) give a formal order or command to. **3** (foll. by *to*) **a** address or give indications for the delivery of (a letter, etc.). **b** tell or show (a person) the way to a destination. **4** (foll. by *at, to, toward*) **a** point, aim, or cause (a blow or missile) to move in a certain direction. **b** point or address (one's attention, a remark, etc.). **5** guide as an adviser, as a principle, etc. (*I do as duty directs me*). **6 a** (also *absol.*) supervise the performing, staging, etc., of (a movie, play, etc.). **b** supervise the performance of (an actor, etc.). **7** (also *absol.*) guide the performance of (a group of musicians), esp. as a participant. □ **direct access** the facility of retrieving data immediately from any part of a computer file. **direct action** action such as a strike or sabotage directly affecting the community and meant to reinforce demands on a government, employer, etc. **direct address** *Computing* an address (see ADDRESS *n.* 1c) which specifies the location of data to be used in an operation. **direct current** (¶ Abbr.: **DC, d.c.**) an electric current flowing in one direction only. **direct debit** an arrangement for the regular debiting of a bank account at the request of the payee. **direct method** a system of teaching a foreign language using only that language and without the study of formal grammar. **direct object** *Gram.* the primary object of the action of a transitive verb. **direct proportion** a relation between quantities whose ratio is constant. **direct speech** (or **oration**) words actually spoken, not reported in the third person. **direct tax** a tax levied on the person who ultimately bears the burden of it, esp. on income. □□ **directness** *n.* [ME f. L *directus* past part. of *dirigere direct-* (as DI-², *regere* put straight)]

  ■ *adj.* **1** straight, unswerving, shortest, undeviating, through. **2** honest, open, uninhibited, unreserved, forthright, sincere, unequivocal; tactless; unmitigated, outright, categorical, plain, clear, unambiguous, unmistakable, to the point, unqualified, unequivocal, point-blank, explicit, express; see also BLUNT *adj.* 2. **3** uninterrupted, without interference, unobstructed; straight. **4** unbroken, lineal. **5** exact, complete; polar, diametrical. ● *v.* **1** control, manage, handle, conduct, pilot, steer, guide, look after, be at the helm, run, administer, govern, regulate, operate, superintend, supervise, command, head up, mastermind, rule. **2** rule, command, order, require, instruct, charge, dictate, enjoin, appoint, ordain, *literary* bid. **3 a** send, address, dispatch, deliver mail, esp. *Brit.* post. **b** guide, lead, show *or* point (the way), give directions; usher, escort. **4** aim, focus, level, point, target, train, turn; address. **5** advise, counsel, instruct, *literary* bid; see also COMMAND *v.* 1.

direction /dirékshən, dī-/ *n.* **1** the act or process of directing;

supervision. **2** (usu. in *pl.*) an order or instruction, esp. each of a set guiding use of equipment, etc. **3 a** the course or line along which a person or thing moves or looks, or which must be taken to reach a destination (*sailed in an easterly direction*). **b** (in *pl.*) guidance on how to reach a destination. **c** the point to or from which a person or thing moves or looks. **4** the tendency or scope of a theme, subject, or inquiry. □ **direction finder** a device for determining the source of radio waves, esp. as an aid in navigation. □□ **directionless** *adj.* [ME f. F *direction* or L *directio* (as DIRECT)]

  ■ **1** guidance, managing, management, administration, government, supervision, operation, running, leadership, directorship, directorate, control, captaincy, handling, regulation, rule, charge. **2** (*directions*) instruction(s), information, guidelines, guide, order. **3 a** bearing, route, avenue; see also COURSE *n.* 2, WAY *n.* 1, 2.

directional /dirékshənəl, dī-/ *adj.* **1** of or indicating direction. **2** *Electronics* **a** concerned with the transmission of radio or sound waves in a particular direction. **b** (of equipment) designed to receive radio or sound waves most effectively from a particular direction or directions and not others. □□ **directionality** /-álitee/ *n.* **directionally** *adv.*

directive /diréktiv, dī-/ *n. & adj.* ● *n.* a general instruction from one in authority. ● *adj.* serving to direct. [ME f. med.L *directivus* (as DIRECT)]

  ■ *n.* see INSTRUCTION 1.

directly /diréktlee, dī-/ *adv. & conj.* ● *adv.* **1 a** at once; without delay. **b** presently; shortly. **2** exactly; immediately (*directly opposite*; *directly after lunch*). **3** in a direct manner. ● *conj. Brit. colloq.* as soon as (*will tell you directly they come*).

  ■ *adv.* **1 a** immediately, at once, straightaway, right away, quickly, promptly, without delay, instantly, speedily, momentarily. **b** soon, later (on), presently, in a (little) while, shortly, *archaic or literary* anon. **2** exactly, precisely, just, immediately; completely, entirely; diametrically. **3** straight, in a beeline, unswervingly, undeviatingly; frankly, straightforwardly, openly, plainly, bluntly, unreservedly, forthrightly; tactlessly. ● *conj.* as soon as, when; see also IMMEDIATELY *conj.*

Directoire /dírektwaár/ *adj. Needlework & Art* in imitation of styles prevalent during the French Directory. [F (as DIRECTORY)]

director /diréktər, dī-/ *n.* **1** a person who directs or controls something. **2** a member of the managing board of a commercial company. **3** a person who directs a movie, play, etc., esp. professionally. **4** a person acting as spiritual adviser. **5** = CONDUCTOR 1. □ **director general** the chief executive of a large (esp. public) organization. □□ **directorial** /-táwreeəl/ *adj.* **directorship** *n.* (esp. in sense 2). [AF *directour* f. LL *director* governor (as DIRECT)]

  ■ **1** guide, leader, controller; steersman, helmsman, pilot, skipper, commander, commandant, captain; impresario. **2** executive, administrator, official, principal, governor, head, chief, manager, superintendent, supervisor, overseer, kingpin, *colloq.* top dog, *Brit. colloq.* gaffer, *sl.* big cheese, honcho, Mr. Big; see also BOSS¹ *n.* **5** maestro, concert-master, conductor, leader.

directorate /diréktərət, dī-/ *n.* **1** a board of directors. **2** the office of director.

  ■ **1** see COUNCIL 1a.

directory /diréktəree, dī-/ *n.* (*pl.* **-ies**) **1** a book listing alphabetically or thematically a particular group of individuals (e.g., telephone subscribers) or organizations with various details. **2 a** (**Directory**) *hist.* the revolutionary executive of five persons in power in France 1795–99. **b** a body of di-

┌───┐
│ /.../ **pronunciation**   ● **part of speech** │
│ □ **phrases, idioms, and compounds**   │
│ □□ **derivatives**   ■ **synonym section** │
│ **cross-references** appear in SMALL CAPITALS or *italics* │
└───┘

rectors. **3** a book of rules, esp. for the order of private or public worship. [LL *directorium* (as DIRECT)]
■ **1** see INDEX *n.* 1. **2 b** see COUNCIL 1a.

directress /diréktriss, di-/ *n.* (also **directrice** /-tre͞es/) a woman director. [DIRECTOR, F *directrice* (as DIRECTRIX)]

directrix /diréktriks, di-/ *n.* (*pl.* **directrixes** or **directrices** /-tris͞eez/) *Geom.* a fixed line used in describing a curve or surface. [med.L f. LL *director*: see DIRECTOR, -TRIX]

direful /dírfoͤol/ *adj. literary* terrible; dreadful. □□ **direfully** *adv.* [DIRE + -FUL]

dirge /dərj/ *n.* **1** a lament for the dead, esp. forming part of a funeral service. **2** any mournful song or lament. □□ **dirgeful** *adj.* [ME f. L *dirige* (imper.) direct, the first word in the Latin antiphon (from Ps. 5:8) in the matins part of the Office for the Dead]
■ see LAMENT *n.* 2.

dirham /dirám, dírəm/ *n.* the principal monetary unit of Morocco and the United Arab Emirates. [Arab. f. L DRACHMA]

dirigible /dírijibəl, diríj-/ *adj. & n.* ● *adj.* capable of being guided. ● *n.* a dirigible balloon or airship. [L *dirigere* arrange, direct: see DIRECT]

diriment /dírəmənt/ *adj. Law* nullifying. □ **diriment impediment** a factor (e.g., the existence of a prior marriage) rendering a marriage null and void from the beginning. [L *dirimere* f. *dir-* = DIS- + *emere* take]

dirk /dərk/ *n.* a long dagger, esp. as formerly worn by Scottish Highlanders. [17th-c. *durk*, of unkn. orig.]
■ see DAGGER.

dirndl /dərnd'l/ *n.* **1** a woman's dress styled in imitation of Alpine peasant costume, with close-fitting bodice, tight waistband, and full skirt. **2** a full skirt of this kind. [G dial., dimin. of *Dirne* girl]

dirt /dərt/ *n.* **1** unclean matter that soils. **2 a** earth; soil. **b** earth; cinders, etc., used to make a surface for a road, etc. (usu. *attrib.*: *dirt track*; *dirt road*). **3 a** foul or malicious words or talk. **b** scurrilous information; scandal; gossip; the lowdown. **4** excrement. **5** a dirty condition. **6** a person or thing considered worthless. □ **dirt bike** a motorcycle designed for use on unpaved roads and tracks, esp. in scrambling. **dirt cheap** *colloq.* extremely cheap. **dirt poor** extremely poor; lacking basic necessities. **dirt track** a course made of rolled cinders, soil, etc., for motorcycle racing or flat racing. **do a person dirt** *sl.* harm or injure a person's reputation maliciously. **eat dirt 1** suffer insults, etc., without retaliating. **2** make a humiliating confession. **treat like dirt** treat (a person) contemptuously; abuse. [ME f. ON *drit* excrement]
■ **1** slime, mud, mire, grime, slime, scum, sludge, dust, soot, filth, *colloq.* muck, *Brit. colloq.* gunge, esp. *US sl.* grunge. **2 a** soil, earth, loam, ground, clay, sod, mold. **3** indecency, obscenity, smut, pornography, foulness, corruption, filth, vileness; gossip, scandal, rumor, inside information, *colloq.* lowdown, dope, scuttlebutt. **4** excrement, ordure, manure; see also DUNG *n.*, *bowel movement* 2. **6** waste, refuse, trash, garbage, rubbish, junk, dross, sweepings, leavings; *colloq.* scum. □ **do a person dirt** see BLACKEN 2, *run down* 6. **treat like dirt** see ABUSE *v.* 3.

dirty /dɔ́rtee/ *adj., adv., & v.* ● *adj.* (**dirtier, dirtiest**) **1** soiled; unclean. **2** causing one to become dirty (*a dirty job*). **3** sordid; lewd; morally illicit or questionable (*dirty joke*). **4** unpleasant; nasty. **5** dishonest; dishonorable; unfair (*dirty play*). **6** (of weather) rough; stormy. **7** (of a color) not pure nor clear; dingy. **8** *colloq.* (of a nuclear weapon) producing considerable radioactive fallout. ● *adv. Brit. sl.* (with adjectives expressing magnitude) very (*a dirty great diamond*). ● *v.tr. & intr.* (**-ies, -ied**) make or become dirty. □ **dirty dog** *colloq.* a scoundrel; a despicable person. **the dirty end of the stick** *colloq.* the difficult or unpleasant part of an undertaking, situation, etc. **dirty linen** (or **laundry** or **wash**) *colloq.* intimate secrets, esp. of a scandalous nature. **dirty look** *colloq.* a look of disapproval, anger, or disgust. **dirty trick 1** a dishonorable and deceitful act. **2** (in *pl.*) underhand political activity, esp. to discredit an opponent. **dirty weekend** *Brit. colloq.* a weekend spent clandestinely with a lover. **dirty word 1** an offensive or indecent word.

2 a word for something which is disapproved of (*profit is a dirty word*). **dirty work 1** unpleasant tasks. **2** dishonorable or illegal activity, esp. done clandestinely. **do the dirty on** esp. *Brit. colloq.* play a mean trick on. □□ **dirtily** *adv.* **dirtiness** *n.*
■ *adj.* **1** foul, unclean, muddy, grubby, soiled, begrimed, sooty, black, grimy, filthy, mucky, polluted, squalid, sullied, messy, stained, unwashed, scummy, muddied, Augean, impure, insanitary, unsanitary, bedraggled, *colloq.* crummy, *Brit. colloq.* gungy, poet. befouled, *sl.* grotty, grungy. **3** sordid, smutty, indecent, obscene, crude, rude, coarse, ribald, prurient, risqué, salacious, lewd, lascivious, pornographic, licentious, blue, scabrous, off color. **4** unpleasant, nasty, horrible; bitter, malicious, malevolent, resentful, angry, furious, *literary* wrathful; sordid, base, mean, despicable, contemptible, scurvy, low, low-down, ignominious, vile. **5** unfair, unscrupulous, unsporting, dishonest, mean, rotten, underhanded, underhand, unsportsmanlike, dishonorable, ignoble, deceitful, corrupt, treacherous, perfidious, villainous, disloyal. **6** rough, bad, foul, nasty, stormy, squally, rainy, windy, blowy. ● *v.* stain, soil, begrime, besmirch, pollute, muddy, smear, defile, blacken, tarnish, drabble, foul, muck, *poet.* sully, befoul. □ **dirty dog** see SCOUNDREL. **dirty word 1** see EXPLETIVE *n.* 1.

dis /dis/ *v.tr. sl.* var. of DISS.

dis- /dis/ *prefix* forming nouns, adjectives, and verbs: **1** expressing negation (*dishonest*). **2** indicating reversal or absence of an action or state (*disengage*; *disbelieve*). **3** indicating removal of a thing or quality (*dismember*; *disable*). **4** indicating separation (*distinguish*; *dispose*). **5** indicating completeness or intensification of the action (*disembowel*; *disgruntled*). **6** indicating expulsion from (*disbar*). [L *dis-*, sometimes through OF *des-*]

disability /dísəbílitee/ *n.* (*pl.* **-ies**) **1** physical incapacity, either congenital or caused by injury, disease, etc. **2** a lack of some asset, quality, or attribute, that prevents one's doing something. **3** a legal disqualification.
■ **1** handicap, impairment, defect, infirmity, disablement. **2** inability, incapacity, unfitness, inadequacy, impotence, powerlessness, helplessness.

disable /disáybəl/ *v.tr.* **1** render unable to function; deprive of an ability. **2** (often as **disabled** *adj.*) deprive of or reduce the power to walk or do other normal activities, esp. by crippling. □□ **disablement** *n.*
■ **2** see CRIPPLE *v.*; (**disabled**) handicapped, incapacitated, crippled, lame; game, *archaic* halt; invalid.

disabuse /dísəbyo͞oz/ *v.tr.* **1** (foll. by *of*) free from a mistaken idea. **2** disillusion; undeceive.
■ see DISILLUSION *v.*

disaccord /dísəkáwrd/ *n. & v.* ● *n.* disagreement; disharmony. ● *v.intr.* (usu. foll. by *with*) disagree; be at odds. [ME f. F *désaccorder* (as ACCORD)]
■ *n.* see *disagreement* (DISAGREE).

disadvantage /dísədvántij/ *n. & v.* ● *n.* **1** an unfavorable circumstance or condition. **2** damage to one's interest or reputation. ● *v.tr.* cause disadvantage to. □ **at a disadvantage** in an unfavorable position or aspect. [ME f. OF *desavantage*: see ADVANTAGE]
■ *n.* **1** setback, drawback, liability, handicap, defect, flaw, shortcoming, weakness, weak spot, fault; problem. **2** detriment, harm, loss, hurt, disservice; see also INJURY 3.

disadvantaged /dísədvántijd/ *adj.* placed in unfavorable circumstances (esp. of a person lacking the normal social opportunities).
■ see *deprived* (DEPRIVE 2).

disadvantageous /dísádvəntáyjəs, dísad-/ *adj.* **1** involving disadvantage or discredit. **2** derogatory. □□ **disadvantageously** *adv.*
■ **1** see DETRIMENTAL.

disaffected /dísəféktid/ *adj.* **1** disloyal, esp. to one's superiors. **2** estranged; no longer friendly; discontented. □□ **dis-**

affectedly *adv.* [past part. of *disaffect* (v.), orig. = dislike, disorder (as DIS-, AFFECT²)]

disaffection /dísəfékshən/ *n.* **1** disloyalty. **2** political discontent.

disaffiliate /dísəfíleeayt/ *v.* **1** *tr.* end the affiliation of. **2** *intr.* end one's affiliation. **3** *tr.* & *intr.* detach. □□ **disaffiliation** /-leeáyshən/ *n.*

disaffirm /dísəfərm/ *v.tr. Law* **1** reverse (a previous decision). **2** repudiate (a settlement). □□ **disaffirmation** /-máyshən/ *n.*

■ see REVERSE *v.* 2, 5.

disafforest /dísəfáwrist, -fór-/ *v.tr. Brit.* **1** clear of forests or trees. **2** reduce from the legal status of forest to that of ordinary land. □□ **disafforestation** *n.* [ME f. AL *disafforestare* (as DIS-, AFFOREST)]

disagree /dísəgreé/ *v.intr.* (**-agrees, -agreed, -agreeing**) (often foll. by *with*) **1** hold a different opinion. **2** quarrel. **3** (of factors or circumstances) not correspond. **4** have an adverse effect upon (a person's health, digestion, etc.). □□ **disagreement** *n.* [ME f. OF *desagreer* (as DIS-, AGREE)]

■ **1** dissent, diverge; see DIFFER 2. **2** dispute, quarrel, argue, contend, contest, bicker, fight, fall out, squabble, wrangle, debate. □□ **disagreement** difference, discrepancy, disparity, discord, discordance, discordancy, dissimilarity, disaccord, diversity, incongruity, nonconformity, incompatibility; dissent, opposition, conflict, strife, controversy, contention, dissension; quarrel, argument, dispute, altercation, debate, clash, *archaic* velitation, *sl.* rhubarb.

disagreeable /dísəgreéəbəl/ *adj.* **1** unpleasant; not to one's liking. **2** quarrelsome; rude or bad-tempered. □□ **disagreeableness** *n.* **disagreeably** *adv.* [ME f. OF *desagreable* (as DIS-, AGREEABLE)]

■ **1** unpleasant, offensive, distasteful, disgusting, repugnant, obnoxious, repellent, repulsive, objectionable, revolting, odious, noxious, unsavory, unpalatable, nauseating, nauseous, nasty, sickening, repellent. **2** quarrelsome, bad-tempered, ill-tempered, disobliging, uncooperative, unfriendly, uncivil, abrupt, blunt, curt, brusque, short, uncourtly, impolite, bad-mannered, ill-mannered, discourteous, rude, testy, splenetic, cross, ill-humored, peevish, morose, sulky, sullen, *colloq.* grouchy.

disallow /dísəlów/ *v.tr.* refuse to allow or accept as valid; prohibit. □□ **disallowance** *n.* [ME f. OF *desalouer* (as DIS-, ALLOW)]

■ see PROHIBIT 1.

disambiguate /dísambígyoo-ayt/ *v.tr.* remove ambiguity from. □□ **disambiguation** /-áyshən/ *n.*

disamenity /dísəménitee/ *n.* (*pl.* **-ies**) an unpleasant feature (of a place, etc.); a disadvantage.

disappear /dísəpeér/ *v.intr.* **1** cease to be visible; pass from sight. **2** cease to exist or be in circulation or use (*rotary telephones had all but disappeared*). □□ **disappearance** *n.*

■ **1** vanish, evaporate, vaporize, fade (away *or* out), evanesce. **2** die (out *or* off), become extinct, cease (to exist), perish (without a trace).

disappoint /dísəpóynt/ *v.tr.* **1** (also *absol.*) fail to fulfill a desire or expectation of (a person). **2** frustrate (hopes, etc.); cause the failure of (a plan, etc.). □ **be disappointed** (foll. by *with, at, in,* or *to* + infin., or *that* + clause) fail to have one's expectation, etc., fulfilled in some regard (*was disappointed in you; disappointed at the result; am disappointed to be last*). □□ **disappointed** *adj.* **disappointedly** *adv.* **disappointing** *adj.* **disappointingly** *adv.* [ME f. F *désappointer* (as DIS-, APPOINT)]

■ **1** let down, fail, dissatisfy, disenchant, disillusion. **2** foil, thwart, balk, defeat; see also FRUSTRATE *v.* 2. □ **be disappointed** see *disappointed* below. □□ **disappointed** frustrated, dissatisfied, disenchanted, disillusioned, discouraged, disheartened, discontent(ed), *colloq.* choked; saddened, unhappy, dejected, downcast. **disappointing** discouraging, dissatisfying, unsatisfactory, unsatisfying, disconcerting; poor,

second-rate, bad, sorry, inadequate, insufficient, inferior, *colloq.* pathetic.

disappointment /dísəpóyntmənt/ *n.* **1** an event, thing, or person that disappoints. **2** a feeling of distress, vexation, etc., resulting from this (*I cannot hide my disappointment*).

■ **1** setback, letdown, comedown, failure, defeat, blow, calamity, disaster, anticlimax, nonevent, *colloq.* washout. **2** frustration, dissatisfaction, vexation, discouragement, disenchantment, distress, regret, mortification, chagrin.

disapprobation /dísáprəbáyshən/ *n.* strong (esp. moral) disapproval.

■ see *disapproval* (DISAPPROVE).

disapprove /dísəproov/ *v.* **1** *intr.* (usu. foll. by *of*) have or express an unfavorable opinion. **2** *tr.* be displeased with. □□ **disapproval** *n.* **disapprover** *n.* **disapproving** *adj.* **disapprovingly** *adv.*

■ **1** (*disapprove of*) condemn, criticize, disfavor, censure, object to, decry, denounce, put *or* run down, deplore, deprecate, belittle, look down on, look down one's nose at, frown on *or* upon, *sl.* knock; see also CRITICIZE 1. □□ **disapproval** disapprobation, condemnation, censure, criticism, reproof, reproach, objection, exception, disfavor, displeasure, dissatisfaction. **disapproving** see CRITICAL 1.

disarm /disaárm/ *v.* **1** *tr.* **a** take weapons away from (a person, nation, etc.) (often foll. by *of*: *were disarmed of their rifles*). **b** *Fencing*, etc., deprive of a weapon. **2** *tr.* deprive (a ship, etc.) of its means of defense. **3** *intr.* (of a nation, etc.) disband or reduce its armed forces. **4** *tr.* remove the fuse from (a bomb, etc.). **5** *tr.* deprive of the power to injure. **6** *tr.* pacify or allay the hostility or suspicions of; mollify; placate. □□ **disarmer** *n.* **disarming** *adj.* (esp. in sense 6). **disarmingly** *adv.* [ME f. OF *desarmer* (as DIS-, ARM²)]

■ **4, 5** deactivate, defuse, incapacitate, put out of action. **6** win over, put *or* set at ease, mollify, appease, placate, pacify, reconcile, conciliate, propitiate, charm. □□ **disarming** conciliatory; charming; see also *enchanting* (ENCHANT).

disarmament /disaármamant/ *n.* the reduction by a nation of its military forces and weapons.

disarrange /dísəráynj/ *v.tr.* bring into disorder. □□ **disarrangement** *n.*

■ see DISORDER *v.*

disarray /dísəráy/ *n.* & *v.* ● *n.* (often prec. by *in, into*) disorder; confusion (esp. among people). ● *v.tr.* throw into disorder.

■ *n.* see DISORDER *n.* 1. ● *v.* see DISORDER *v.*

disarticulate /dísaartíkyəlayt/ *v.tr.* & *intr.* separate at the joints. □□ **disarticulation** /-láyshən/ *n.*

disassemble /dísəsémbəl/ *v.tr.* take (a machine, etc.) to pieces. □□ **disassembly** *n.*

■ see SEPARATE *v.* 1.

disassociate /dísəsósheeayt, -seeayt/ *v.tr.* & *intr.* = DISSOCIATE. □□ **disassociation** /-áyshən/ *n.*

disaster /dizástər/ *n.* **1** a great or sudden misfortune. **2 a** complete failure. **b** a person or enterprise ending in failure. □□ **disastrous** *adj.* **disastrously** *adv.* [orig. 'unfavorable aspect of a star,' f. F *désastre* or It. *disastro* (as DIS-, *astro* f. L *astrum* star)]

■ **1** catastrophe, calamity, cataclysm, tragedy, misfortune, accident, mishap, act of God, trouble, reverse. **2 a** debacle, collapse, downfall, breakdown, failure, *colloq.* washout. **b** failure, *colloq.* dead loss, *sl.* dead duck, esp. *Brit.* no-hoper. □□ **disastrous** calamitous, catastrophic, cataclysmic, tragic, destructive, ruinous, devastating, appalling, harrowing, terrible, dire, horrendous, horrible, horrifying, dreadful, *colloq.* awful; unlucky, unfortunate, detrimental, grievous, harmful.

/ . . . / **pronunciation**   ● **part of speech**
□ **phrases, idioms, and compounds**
□□ **derivatives**   ■ **synonym section**
cross-references appear in SMALL CAPITALS or *italics*

disavow /dísəvów/ v.tr. disclaim knowledge of, responsibility for, or belief in. □□ **disavowal** n. [ME f. OF desavouer (as DIS-, AVOW)]

■ see DENY 2.

disband /disbánd/ v. **1** intr. (of an organized group, etc.) cease to work or act together; disperse. **2** tr. cause (such a group) to disband. □□ **disbandment** n. [obs. F desbander (as DIS-, BAND¹ n. 6)]

■ disperse, scatter, break up, dissolve, retire; demobilize, disarm, unarm.

disbar /disbáar/ v.tr. (**disbarred, disbarring**) deprive (an attorney) of the right to practice; expel from the bar. □□ **disbarment** n.

disbelieve /dísbileev/ v. **1** tr. be unable or unwilling to believe (a person or statement). **2** intr. have no faith. □□ **disbelief** /-leef/ n. **disbeliever** n. **disbelievingly** adv.

■ **1** see DISTRUST v.

disbound /disbównd/ adj. (of a pamphlet, etc.) removed from a bound volume.

disbud /disbúd/ v.tr. (**disbudded, disbudding**) remove (esp. superfluous) buds from.

disburden /disbárd'n/ v.tr. **1** (often foll. by of) relieve (a person, one's mind, etc.) of a burden. **2** get rid of; discharge (a duty, anxiety, etc.).

■ (disburden of) see RELIEVE v. 6.

disburse /disbárs/ v. **1** tr. expend (money). **2** tr. defray (a cost). **3** intr. pay money. □□ **disbursal** n. **disbursement** n. **disburser** n. [OF desbourser (as DIS-, BOURSE)]

■ **1** see SPEND 1. **2** see DEFRAY.

disc var. of DISK.

discalced /diskálst/ adj. (of a friar or a nun) barefoot or wearing only sandals. [var. of discalceated (after F déchaux) f. L discalceatus (as DIS-, calceatus f. calceus shoe)]

discard v. & n. ● v.tr. /diskáard/ **1** reject or get rid of as unwanted or superfluous. **2** (also absol.) Cards remove or put aside (a card) from one's hand. ● n. /dískaard/ (often in pl.) a discarded item, esp. a card in a card game. □□ **discardable** adj. [DIS- + CARD¹]

■ v. **1** get rid of, dispense with, reject, dispose of, throw away or out, toss out or away, abandon, jettison, scrap, dump, colloq. trash, sl. ditch. ● n. reject, castoff; (discards) scraps, leavings, leftovers.

discarnate /diskáarnət, -nayt/ adj. having no physical body; separated from the flesh. [DIS-, L caro carnis flesh]

discern /disárn/ v.tr. **1** perceive clearly with the mind or the senses. **2** make out by thought or by gazing, listening, etc. □□ **discerner** n. **discernible** adj. **discernibly** adv. [ME f. OF discerner f. L (as DIS-, cernere cret- separate)]

■ **1** see PERCEIVE. **2** see make out 1, 2. □□ **discernible** perceptible, visible, seeable, perceivable, apparent, clear, observable, plain, detectable, conspicuous, noticeable, distinguishable, recognizable, identifiable, distinct, real, tangible, actual, palpable.

discerning /disárning/ adj. having or showing good judgment or insight. □□ **discerningly** adv.

■ see JUDICIOUS.

discernment /disárnmənt/ n. good judgment or insight.

■ see DISCRIMINATION 2, 3.

discerptible /disárptibəl/ adj. literary able to be plucked apart; divisible. □□ **discerptibility** n. [L discerpere discerpt- (as DIS-, carpere pluck)]

discerption /disárpshən/ n. archaic **1 a** pulling apart; severance. **b** an instance of this. **2** a severed piece. [LL discerptio (as DISCERPTIBLE)]

discharge v. & n. ● v. /dischaárj/ **1** tr. **a** let go, or release, esp. from a duty, commitment, or period of confinement. **b** relieve (a bankrupt) of residual liability. **2** tr. dismiss from office, employment, army commission, etc. **3** tr. **a** fire (a gun, etc.). **b** (of a gun, etc.) fire (a bullet, etc.). **4 a** tr. (also absol.) pour out or cause to pour out (pus, liquid, etc.) (the wound was discharging). **b** tr. throw; eject (discharged a stone at the gopher). **c** tr. utter (abuse, etc.). **d** intr. (foll. by into) (of a river, etc.) flow into (esp. the sea). **5** tr. **a** carry out; perform (a duty or obligation). **b** relieve oneself of (a financial commitment) (discharged his debt). **6** tr. Law cancel (an

order of court). **7** tr. Physics release an electrical charge from. **8** tr. **a** relieve (a ship, etc.) of its cargo. **b** unload (a cargo) from a ship. ● n. /díschaarj, dischaárj/ **1** the act or an instance of discharging; the process of being discharged. **2** a dismissal, esp. from the armed services. **3 a** a release, exemption, acquittal, etc. **b** a written certificate of release, etc. **4** an act of firing a gun, etc. **5 a** an emission (of pus, liquid, etc.). **b** the liquid or matter so discharged. **6** (usu. foll. by of) **a** the payment (of a debt). **b** the performance (of a duty, etc.). **7** Physics **a** the release of a quantity of electric charge from an object. **b** a flow of electricity through the air or other gas, esp. when accompanied by the emission of light. **c** the conversion of chemical energy in a cell into electrical energy. **8** the unloading (of a ship or a cargo). □□ **dischargeable** adj. **discharger** n. (in sense 7 of v.). [ME f. OF descharger (as DIS-, CHARGE)]

■ v. **1 a** let out, dismiss, let go, send away; liberate, (set) free; see also RELEASE v. 1. **b** relieve, acquit, let off, absolve; see also EXCUSE v. 4. **2** expel, oust, cashier, eject, give a person notice, give a person the brush-off, colloq. sack, give a person the boot or sack sl. fire, kick out; see also DISMISS 2. **3** shoot, fire (off); set or let off, detonate, explode. **4 a** emit, send out or forth, pour out or forth, exude; ooze, leak. **b** see THROW v. 1, 2. **5 a** carry out, perform, fulfill, accomplish, do, execute. **b** pay, settle, liquidate, clear, honor, meet, square. **8 b** unload, offload, empty. ● n. **2** expulsion, dismissal, ejection, ouster. **3 a** acquittal, exoneration; see also exemption (EXEMPT), RELEASE n. 1. **4** shooting, firing; salvo, fusillade, volley; detonation, explosion, burst. **5** emission, release, excretion, seepage, exudate, exudation; ooze, pus, suppuration, secretion, Physiol. matter. **6 a** payment, settlement, clearance. **b** performance, fulfillment, accomplishment, execution, observance. **8** unloading, offloading, emptying.

disciple /disípəl/ n. **1** a follower or pupil of a leader, teacher, philosophy, etc. (a disciple of Zen Buddhism). **2** any early believer in Christ, esp. one of the twelve Apostles. □□ **discipleship** n. **discipular** /disípyoolər/ adj. [OE discipul f. L discipulus f. discere learn]

■ **1** apprentice, pupil, student, proselyte, learner, chela; follower, adherent, devotee, votary.

disciplinarian /dísiplináireeən/ n. a person who upholds or practices firm discipline (a strict disciplinarian).

■ (hard) taskmaster, taskmistress, martinet, slave driver, drill sergeant; tyrant, despot, dictator, authoritarian.

disciplinary /dísiplinéree/ adj. of, promoting, or enforcing discipline. [med.L disciplinarius (as DISCIPLINE)]

■ regulatory; correctional, punitive, penal.

discipline /dísiplin/ n. & v. ● n. **1 a** control or order exercised over people or animals, esp. children, prisoners, military personnel, church members, etc. **b** the system of rules used to maintain this control. **c** the behavior of groups subjected to such rules (poor discipline in the ranks). **2 a** mental, moral, or physical training. **b** adversity as used to bring about such training (left the course because he couldn't take the discipline). **3** a branch of instruction or learning (philosophy is a hard discipline). **4** punishment. **5** Eccl. mortification by physical self-punishment, esp. scourging. ● v.tr. **1** punish; chastise. **2** bring under control by training in obedience; drill. □□ **disciplinable** adj. **disciplinal** /dísiplin'l, dísiplín'l/ adj. [ME f. OF discipliner or LL & med.L disciplinare, disciplina f. discipulus DISCIPLE]

■ n. **1 a** order, direction, rule, regulation, government, authority, control, subjection, restriction, restraint, routine. **b** see CODE 4, 5. **c** behavior, conduct, attitude. **2 a** training, drilling, exercise, practice, drill, inculcation, indoctrination, instruction, schooling, esp. Med. regimen. **3** subject, course, branch of knowledge, area, field, specialty. **4** chastisement, castigation, archaic correction; see also PUNISHMENT 1, 2. ● v. **1** punish, chastise, correct, penalize, reprove, criticize, reprimand, rebuke; see also CASTIGATE. **2** train, break in, condition, drill, exercise, instruct, coach, teach, tutor, school, indoctrinate, inculcate; check, curb, restrain, bridle, control, govern, direct, run, supervise, manage, regulate, hold *or* keep in check, ride herd on.

disclaim /diskláym/ *v.tr.* **1** deny or disown (*disclaim all responsibility*). **2** (often *absol.*) *Law* renounce a legal claim to (property, etc.). [ME f. AF *desclaim*- stressed stem of *desclamer* (as DIS-, CLAIM)]
■ see DENY 1, 2.

disclaimer /diskláymər/ *n.* a renunciation or disavowal, esp. of responsibility. [ME f. AF (= DISCLAIM as noun)]
■ see DENIAL 1.

disclose /disklṓz/ *v.tr.* **1** make known; reveal (*disclosed the truth*). **2** remove the cover from; expose to view. □□ **discloser** *n.* [ME f. OF *desclos*- stem of *desclore* f. Gallo-Roman (as DIS-, CLOSE²)]
■ **1** reveal, make known, impart, divulge, release, report, tell, blurt out, blab, leak, let slip, betray. **2** bare, reveal, expose, uncover, show, unveil.

disclosure /disklṓzhər/ *n.* **1** the act or an instance of disclosing; the process of being disclosed. **2** something disclosed; a revelation. [DISCLOSE + -URE after *closure*]
■ see REVELATION 2.

disco /dískṓ/ *n.* & *v. colloq.* • *n.* (*pl.* **-os**) = DISCOTHEQUE. • *v.intr.* (**-oes**, **-oed**) **1** attend a discotheque. **2** dance to disco music (*discoed the night away*). □ **disco music** popular dance music characterized by a heavy bass rhythm. [abbr.]

discobolus /diskóbələs/ *n.* (*pl.* **discoboli** /-lī/) **1** a discus thrower in ancient Greece. **2** a statue of a discobolus. [L f. Gk *diskobolos* f. *diskos* DISCUS + *-bolos* -throwing f. *ballō* to throw]

discography /diskógrəfee/ *n.* (*pl.* **-ies**) **1** a descriptive catalog of recordings, esp. of a particular performer or composer. **2** the study of recordings. □□ **discographer** *n.* [DISC + -GRAPHY after *biography*]

discoid /dískoyd/ *adj.* disk-shaped. [Gk *diskoeidēs* (as DISCUS, -OID)]

discolor /diskúlər/ *v.tr.* & *intr.* (*Brit.* **discolour**) spoil or cause to spoil the color of; stain; tarnish. □□ **discoloration** *n.* [ME f. OF *descolorer* or med.L *discolorare* (as DIS-, COLOR)]
■ see STAIN *v.* 1.

discombobulate /dískəmbóbyəlayt/ *v.tr. joc.* disturb; disconcert. [prob. based on *discompose* or *discomfit*]
■ see DISTURB 1.

discomfit /diskúmfit/ *v.tr.* **1 a** disconcert or baffle. **b** thwart. **2** *archaic* defeat in battle. □□ **discomfiture** *n.* [ME f. *discomfit* f. OF past part. of *desconfire* f. Rmc (as DIS-, L *conficere* put together: see CONFECTION)]
■ **1 a** embarrass, abash, disconcert, disturb, make uneasy *or* uncomfortable, discompose, fluster, ruffle, perturb, upset, worry, unsettle, unnerve, *colloq.* rattle, faze, *joc.* discombobulate; baffle, confuse, confound. **b** frustrate, foil, check, defeat, outdo, outwit, overcome, *colloq.* trump; see also THWART *v.*

discomfort /diskúmfərt/ *n.* & *v.* • *n.* **1 a** lack of ease; slight pain (*tight collar caused discomfort*). **b** mental uneasiness (*his presence caused her discomfort*). **2** a lack of comfort. • *v.tr.* make uneasy. [ME f. OF *desconfort(er)* (as DIS-, COMFORT)]
■ *n.* **1 a** pain, soreness, irritation; bother, inconvenience. **b** uneasiness, difficulty, trouble, care, worry, distress, vexation. • *v.* see DISCOMFIT 1a.

discommode /dískəmṓd/ *v.tr.* inconvenience (a person, etc.). □□ **discommodious** *adj.* [obs. F *discommoder* var. of *incommoder* (as DIS-, INCOMMODE)]
■ see INCONVENIENCE *v.*

discompose /dískəmpṓz/ *v.tr.* disturb the composure of; agitate; disturb. □□ **discomposure** /-pṓzhər/ *n.*
■ see UPSET *v.* 2.

disconcert /dískənsə́rt/ *v.tr.* **1** (often as **disconcerted** *adj.*) disturb the composure of; agitate; fluster (*disconcerted by his expression*). **2** spoil or upset (plans, etc.). □□ **disconcertedly** *adv.* **disconcerting** *adj.* **disconcertingly** *adv.* **disconcertion** /-sə́rshən/ *n.* **disconcertment** *n.* [obs. F *desconcerter* (as DIS-, CONCERT)]
■ **1** see AGITATE. **2** see UPSET *v.* 3. □□ **disconcerting** awkward, upsetting, unnerving, unsettling, disturbing,

Brit. off-putting; confusing, bewildering, perplexing, baffling, puzzling.

disconfirm /dískənfə́rm/ *v.tr. formal* disprove or tend to disprove (a hypothesis, etc.). □□ **disconfirmation** /-konfərmáyshən/ *n.*
■ disprove, invalidate.

disconformity /dískənfáwrmitee/ *n.* (*pl.* **-ies**) **1 a** lack of conformity. **b** an instance of this. **2** *Geol.* a difference of plane between two parallel, approximately horizontal sets of strata.

disconnect /dískənékt/ *v.tr.* **1** (often foll. by *from*) break the connection of (things, ideas, etc.). **2** put (an electrical device) out of action by disconnecting the parts, esp. by pulling out the plug.
■ **1** separate, disjoin, disunite, uncouple, decouple, detach, unhook, undo, disengage, unhitch, cut *or* break off, cut *or* pull apart, part, divide, sever. **2** turn off, switch off, shut off, stop, deactivate.

disconnected /dískənéktid/ *adj.* **1** not connected; detached; separated. **2** (of speech, writing, argument, etc.) incoherent and illogical. □□ **disconnectedly** *adv.* **disconnectedness** *n.*
■ **1** separate, apart, detached, unattached; split, separated. **2** unconnected, incoherent, irrational, confused, illogical, garbled, disjointed, rambling, mixed-up, unintelligible, uncoordinated, random.

disconnection /dískənékshən/ *n.* (also *Brit.* **disconnexion**) the act or an instance of disconnecting; the state of being disconnected.
■ see DETACHMENT 2.

disconsolate /diskónsələt/ *adj.* **1** forlorn or inconsolable. **2** unhappy or disappointed. □□ **disconsolately** *adv.* **disconsolateness** *n.* **disconsolation** /-láyshən/ *n.* [ME f. med.L *disconsolatus* (as DIS-, *consolatus* past part. of L *consolari* console)]
■ see WOEBEGONE.

discontent /dískəntént/ *n., adj.,* & *v.* • *n.* lack of contentment; restlessness, dissatisfaction. • *adj.* dissatisfied (*was discontent with his lot*). • *v.tr.* (esp. as **discontented** *adj.*) make dissatisfied. □□ **discontentedly** *adv.* **discontentedness** *n.* **discontentment** *n.*
■ *n.* displeasure, unhappiness, dissatisfaction, discontentedness, discontentment, uneasiness, restlessness; malaise. • *adj.* see *discontented* below. • *v.* (**discontented**) displeased, dissatisfied, discontent, annoyed, vexed, irritated, piqued, disgruntled, exasperated, fed up, *sl.* browned off, *Brit. sl.* cheesed off.

discontinue /dískəntínyōō/ *v.* (**-continues**, **-continued**, **-continuing**) **1** *intr.* & *tr.* cease or cause to cease to exist or be made (*a discontinued line*). **2** *tr.* give up; cease from (*discontinued his visits*). **3** *tr.* cease taking or paying (a newspaper, a subscription, etc.). □□ **discontinuance** *n.* **discontinuation** *n.* [ME f. OF *discontinuer* f. med.L *discontinuare* (as DIS-, CONTINUE)]
■ **1** stop, put an end to; interrupt; see also STOP *v.* 1c.

discontinuous /dískəntínyōōəs/ *adj.* lacking continuity in space or time; intermittent. □□ **discontinuity** /-kontinōō-itee, -nyōō-/ *n.* **discontinuously** *adv.* [med.L *discontinuus* (as DIS-, CONTINUOUS)]
■ see INTERMITTENT.

discord *n.* & *v.* • *n.* /dískawrd/ **1** disagreement; strife. **2** harsh clashing noise; clangor. **3** *Mus.* **a** a lack of harmony between notes sounding together. **b** an unpleasing or unfinished chord needing to be completed by another. **c** any interval except unison, an octave, a perfect fifth and fourth, a major and minor third and sixth, and their octaves. **d** a single note dissonant with another. • *v.intr.* /diskáwrd/ **1** (usu. foll. by *with*) **a** disagree or quarrel. **b** be different or incon-

---

/.../ pronunciation	• part of speech
□ phrases, idioms, and compounds	
□□ derivatives	■ synonym section
cross-references appear in SMALL CAPITALS or *italics*	

sistent. **2** jar; clash; be dissonant. [ME f. OF *descord*, (n.), *descorder* (v.) f. L *discordare* f. *discors* discordant (as DIS-, *cor cord*- heart)]

■ *n.* **1** strife, dissension, disagreement, conflict, disharmony, contention, disunity, discordance, division, incompatibility. **2** see NOISE *n.* 1, 2. ● *v.* **1 a** see DISAGREE. **b** see DIFFER 1. **2** grate, jangle, jar, clash, disharmonize.

discordant /diskáwrd'nt/ *adj.* (usu. foll. by *to, from, with*) **1** disagreeing; at variance. **2** (of sounds) not in harmony; dissonant. □□ **discordance** /-d'ns/ *n.* **discordancy** *n.* **discordantly** *adv.* [ME f. OF, part. of *discorder*: see DISCORD]

■ **1** contrary, disagreeing, divergent, opposite, opposed, adverse, contradictory, incompatible, differing, different, conflicting, at odds, incongruous, inconsonant, in conflict, in disagreement, at variance. **2** inharmonious, unharmonious, dissonant, jarring, cacophonous, unmelodious, unmusical, harsh, strident, jangling, grating.

discotheque /dískəték/ *n.* **1** a club, etc., for dancing to recorded popular music. **2 a** the professional lighting and sound equipment used at a discotheque. **b** a business that provides this. **3** a party with dancing to popular music, esp. using such equipment. [F, = record library]

discount *n. & v.* ● *n.* /dískownt/ **1** a deduction from a bill or amount due given esp. in consideration of prompt or advance payment or to a special class of buyers. **2** a deduction from the amount of a bill of exchange, etc., by a person who gives value for it before it is due. **3** the act or an instance of discounting. ● *v.tr.* /diskównt/ **1** disregard as being unreliable or unimportant (*discounted his story*). **2** reduce the effect of (an event, etc.) by previous action. **3** detract from; lessen; deduct (esp. an amount from a bill, etc.). **4** give or get the present worth of (a bill not yet due). □ **at a discount 1** below the nominal or usual price (cf. PREMIUM). **2** not in demand; depreciated. **discount house 1** = discount store. **2** *Brit.* a firm that discounts bills. **discount rate** the minimum lending rate. **discount store** a store, etc., that sells goods at less than the normal retail price. □□ **discountable** *adj.* **discounter** *n.* [obs. F *descompte, -conte, descompter* or It. *(di)scontare* (as DIS-, COUNT¹)]

■ *n.* **1, 2** reduction, markdown, deduction; rebate, allowance. ● *v.* **1** disregard, omit, pass *or* gloss *or* gloze over, overlook, pay no attention to, dismiss, ignore. **3** reduce, mark down, deduct, lower, knock down; diminish, lessen, minimize, detract from, take away from.

discountenance /diskówntinəns/ *v.tr.* **1** (esp. in *passive*) disconcert (*was discountenanced by his abruptness*). **2** refuse to countenance; show disapproval of.

■ **1** see DISCOMFIT 1a. **2** see FROWN *v.* 2.

discourage /diskérij, -kúr-/ *v.tr.* **1** deprive of courage, confidence, or energy. **2** (usu. foll. by *from*) dissuade (*discouraged her from going*). **3** inhibit or seek to prevent (an action, etc.) by showing disapproval; oppose (*smoking is discouraged*). □□ **discouragement** *n.* **discouragingly** *adv.* [ME f. OF *descouragier* (as DIS-, COURAGE)]

■ **1** dispirit, dishearten, depress, daunt, unman, dismay, unnerve; see also DEMORALIZE 1. **2** deter, dissuade; (*discourage from*) put off, advise against, talk out of, divert from. **3** disapprove of, inhibit, hinder, slow, suppress; see also OPPOSE 1–3.

discourse *n. & v.* ● *n.* /dískawrs/ **1** *literary* **a** conversation; talk. **b** a dissertation or treatise on an academic subject. **c** a lecture or sermon. **2** *Linguistics* a connected series of utterances; a text. ● *v.* /diskórs/ **1** *intr.* talk; converse. **2** *intr.* (usu. foll. by *of, on, upon*) speak or write learnedly or at length (on a subject). **3** *tr. archaic* give forth (music, etc.). [ME f. L *discursus* (as DIS-, COURSE): (v.) partly after F *discourir*]

■ *n.* **1 a** see CONVERSATION. **b, c** see LECTURE *n.* 1. ● *v.* **1** see CONVERSE *v.* **2** see LECTURE *v.* 1.

discourteous /diskórteeəs/ *adj.* impolite, rude. □□ **discourteously** *adv.* **discourteousness** *n.*

■ uncivil, impolite, rude, unmannerly, ill-mannered, bad-mannered, disrespectful, boorish, abrupt, curt, brusque, short, blunt, ungentlemanly, unladylike, insolent, impertinent, ungracious.

discourtesy /diskórtəsee/ *n.* (*pl.* **-ies**) **1** bad manners; rudeness. **2** an impolite act or remark.

■ **1** see INCIVILITY *n.* 1, 2. **2** see INSULT *n.* 1.

discover /diskúvər/ *v.tr.* **1** (often foll. by *that* + clause) **a** find out or become aware of, whether by research or searching or by chance (*discovered a new entrance; discovered that they had been overpaid*). **b** be the first to find or find out (*who discovered America?*). **c** devise or pioneer (*discover new techniques*). **2** give (check) in a game of chess by removing one's own obstructing piece. **3** (in show business) find and promote as a new singer, actor, etc. **4** *archaic* **a** make known. **b** exhibit; manifest. **c** disclose; betray. **d** catch sight of; espy. □□ **discoverable** *adj.* **discoverer** *n.* [ME f. OF *descovrir* f. LL *discooperire* (as DIS-, COVER)]

■ **1 a, b** find (out), locate, unearth, become aware of, uncover, bring to light, turn *or* dig up, track down, come *or* chance *or* stumble upon, root *or* ferret out; determine, detect, discern, ascertain, identify; realize, notice, perceive, learn, *sl.* dope out. **c** originate, conceive (of), devise, contrive, invent, make up, design, pioneer. **4 d** see, spot, catch sight *or* a glimpse of, lay eyes on, view, encounter, meet (with), *literary* espy, descry, behold. □□ **discoverer** explorer, voyager; see also PIONEER *n.* 2.

discovery /diskúvəree/ *n.* (*pl.* **-ies**) **1 a** the act or process of discovering or being discovered. **b** an instance of this (*the discovery of a new planet*). **2** a person or thing discovered. **3** *Law* the compulsory disclosure, by a party to an action, of facts or documents on which the other party wishes to rely. [DISCOVER after *recover, recovery*]

■ **1** finding, uncovering, unearthing, determining; exploration, disclosure, detection, identification, revelation; realization, recognition, perception. **2** find, catch, revelation; see also INVENTION 2.

discredit /diskrédit/ *n. & v.* ● *n.* **1** harm to reputation (*brought discredit on the enterprise*). **2** a person or thing causing this (*he is a discredit to his family*). **3** lack of credibility; doubt; disbelief (*throws discredit on her story*). **4** the loss of commercial credit. ● *v.tr.* **1** harm the good reputation of. **2** cause to be disbelieved. **3** refuse to believe.

■ *n.* **1** dishonor, degradation, disfavor, disrepute, ill repute, disgrace, ignominy, infamy, stigma, shame, scandal, obloquy, opprobrium, odium, humiliation, defamation; damage, harm, blot, brand, tarnish, blemish, taint. **3** doubt, suspicion, skepticism, dubiousness, doubtfulness, incredulity, distrust, mistrust, disbelief. ● *v.* **1** disparage, defame, dishonor, disgrace, degrade, bring into disfavor *or* disrepute, bring down, deprecate, demean, lower, devalue, depreciate, devaluate, belittle, diminish, reduce; slander, vilify, calumniate, sully, soil, mark, smear, blacken, taint, tarnish, besmirch, smirch, stigmatize, asperse, malign, libel, slur. **2** detract from, *colloq.* debunk; see also EXPLODE 4. **3** disbelieve, deny, dispute, doubt, question, raise doubts about, distrust, mistrust, give no credit *or* credence to; reject; mock, ridicule.

discreditable /diskréditəbəl/ *adj.* bringing discredit; shameful. □□ **discreditably** *adv.*

■ see SHAMEFUL.

discreet /diskreét/ *adj.* (**discreeter, discreetest**) **1 a** circumspect in speech or action, esp. to avoid social disgrace or embarrassment. **b** tactful; trustworthy. **2** unobtrusive (*a discreet touch of rouge*). □□ **discreetly** *adv.* **discreetness** *n.* [ME f. OF *discret -ete* f. L *discretus* separate (as DIS-, *cretus* past part. of *cernere* sift), with LL sense f. its derivative *discretio* discernment]

■ **1** careful, cautious, prudent, circumspect, wary, chary, heedful, guarded; judicious, tactful, diplomatic, considerate, trustworthy, thoughtful. **2** see UNOBTRUSIVE.

discrepancy /diskrépənsee/ n. (pl. **-ies**) **1** difference; failure to correspond; inconsistency. **2** an instance of this. □□ **discrepant** adj. [L discrepare be discordant (as DIS-, crepare creak)]

■ difference, disparity, dissimilarity, deviation, divergence, disagreement, incongruity, incompatibility, inconsistency, variance, conflict, discordance, discordancy, opposition, disaccord, contrariety, contradiction, contradictoriness, irreconcilability; gap, lacuna.

discrete /diskreét/ adj. individually distinct; separate; discontinuous. □□ **discretely** adv. **discreteness** n. [ME f. L discretus: see DISCREET]

■ separate, individual, disconnected, distinct, unattached, discontinuous; see also DISTINCT 1a.

discretion /diskréshən/ n. **1** being discreet; discreet behavior (treats confidences with discretion). **2** prudence; self-preservation. **3** the freedom to act and think as one wishes, usu. within legal limits (it is within his discretion to leave). **4** Law a court's freedom to decide a sentence, etc. □ **at discretion** as one pleases. **at the discretion of** to be settled or disposed of according to the judgment or choice of. **discretion is the better part of valor** reckless courage is often self-defeating. **use one's discretion** act according to one's own judgment. **years** (or **age**) **of discretion** the esp. legal age at which a person is able to manage his or her own affairs. □□ **discretionary** adj. [ME f. OF f. L discretio -onis (as DISCREET)]

■ **1** tact, diplomacy, discernment, tactfulness, delicacy, sound judgment, sagacity, common sense, good sense, wisdom, discrimination. **2** care, circumspection, carefulness; see also prudence (PRUDENT). **3** choice, option, judgment, preference, disposition, volition, formal pleasure; wish, will, liking, inclination.

discriminate /diskríminayt/ v. **1** intr. (often foll. by between) make or see a distinction; differentiate (cannot discriminate between right and wrong). **2** intr. make a distinction, esp. unjustly and on the basis of race, color, or sex. **3** intr. (foll. by against) select for unfavorable treatment. **4** tr. (usu. foll. by from) make or see or constitute a difference in or between (many things discriminate one person from another). **5** intr. (esp. as **discriminating** adj.) observe distinctions carefully; have good judgment. **6** tr. mark as distinctive; be a distinguishing feature of. □□ **discriminately** /-nətlee/ adv. **discriminative** /-nətiv/ adj. **discriminator** n. **discriminatory** /-nətáwree/ adj. [L discriminare f. discrimen -minis distinction f. discernere DISCERN]

■ **1** distinguish, separate, differentiate, discern, draw a distinction, tell the difference. **3** (discriminate against) disfavor, show favor or prejudice or bias against, be intolerant toward. **4** distinguish, differentiate, separate, mark out, set aside or apart, segregate. **5** be thoughtful, have discernment, be discerning, show diplomacy; (**discriminating**) see DISCRIMINATING.

discriminating /diskríminayting/ adj. **1** able to discern, esp. distinctions. **2** having good taste. □□ **discriminatingly** adv.

■ discerning, discriminative, perceptive, thoughtful, critical, keen, selective, particular, refined, cultivated.

discrimination /diskrímináyshən/ n. **1** unfavorable treatment based on prejudice, esp. regarding race, color, age, or sex. **2** good taste or judgment in artistic matters, etc. **3** the power of discriminating or observing differences. **4** a distinction made with the mind or in action.

■ **1** bigotry, prejudice, bias, intolerance, favoritism, one-sidedness, unfairness, inequity. **2, 3** (good) taste, perception, perceptiveness, discernment, refinement, acumen, insight, penetration, keenness, (good) judgment, sensitivity; connoisseurship, aestheticism.

discursive /diskársiv/ adj. **1** rambling or digressive. **2** Philos. proceeding by argument or reasoning (opp. INTUITIVE). □□ **discursively** adv. **discursiveness** n. [med.L discursivus f. L discurrere discurs- (as DIS-, currere run)]

■ **1** extensive, long, lengthy, prolix; wandering, digressive, rambling, circuitous, roundabout, diffuse, long-winded, verbose, wordy, colloq. windy.

discus /dískəs/ n. (pl. **discuses**) **1** a heavy, thick-centered disk thrown in ancient Greek games. **2** a similar disk thrown in modern field events. [L f. Gk diskos]

discuss /diskús/ v.tr. **1** hold a conversation about (discussed their vacations). **2** examine by argument, esp. written; debate. □□ **discussable** adj. **discussant** n. **discusser** n. **discussible** adj. [ME f. L discutere discuss- disperse (as DIS-, quatere shake)]

■ **1** converse about, talk over or of or about, chat about, deliberate (over), review, examine, consult on, bat around, colloq. kick around. **2** argue, thrash out; see also DEBATE v.

discussion /diskúshən/ n. **1** a conversation, esp. on specific subjects; a debate (had a discussion about what they should do). **2** an examination by argument, written or spoken. [ME f. OF f. LL discussio -onis (as DISCUSS)]

■ **1** conversation, talk, chat, dialogue, colloquy, exchange, confabulation, conference, parley, powwow, bull session, sl. skull session; debate, argument. **2** deliberation, examination, scrutiny, analysis, review.

disdain /disdáyn/ n. & v. ● n. scorn; contempt. ● v.tr. **1** regard with disdain. **2** think oneself superior to; reject (disdained his offer; disdained to enter; disdained answering). [ME f. OF desdeign(ier) ult. f. L dedignari (as DE-, dignari f. dignus worthy)]

■ n. see CONTEMPT 1. ● v. see DESPISE.

disdainful /disdáynfŏŏl/ adj. showing disdain or contempt. □□ **disdainfully** adv. **disdainfulness** n.

■ contemptuous, scornful, contumelious, derisive, sneering, superior, supercilious, pompous, arrogant, haughty, snobbish, snobby, lordly, regal, colloq. hoity-toity, high-and-mighty, uppity, highfalutin, stuck-up, snotty; jeering, mocking, insulting.

disease /dizeéz/ n. **1** an unhealthy condition of the body (or a part of it) or the mind; illness; sickness. **2** a corresponding physical condition of plants. **3** a particular kind of disease with special symptoms or location. [ME f. OF desaise]

■ **1** sickness, affliction, ailment, malady, illness, infection, complaint, disorder, condition, affection. **2** blight, infestation, archaic murrain. **3** cancer, virus, plague; contagion, infection.

diseased /dizeézd/ adj. **1** affected with disease. **2** abnormal; disordered. [ME, past part. of disease (v.) f. OF desaisier (as DISEASE)]

■ **1** unhealthy, unwell, ill, sick, ailing, unsound, infirm, infected, contaminated, afflicted. **2** abnormal; unwholesome, morbid; see also ILL adj. 2.

diseconomy /dísikónəmee/ n. Econ. the absence or reverse of economy, esp. the increase of costs in a large-scale operation.

disembark /dísimbaárk/ v.tr. & intr. put or go ashore or land from a ship or an aircraft. □□ **disembarkation** n. [F désembarquer (as DIS-, EMBARK)]

■ land, alight, go or put ashore, get or step off, get or step out, leave; debark, detrain, deplane.

disembarrass /dísimbárəs/ v.tr. **1** (usu. foll. by of) relieve (of a load, etc.). **2** free from embarrassment. □□ **disembarrassment** n.

disembody /dísimbódee/ v.tr. (**-ies**, **-ied**) **1** (esp. as **disembodied** adj.) separate or free (esp. the soul) from the body or a concrete form (disembodied spirit). **2** archaic disband (troops). □□ **disembodiment** n.

■ **1** (**disembodied**) bodiless, incorporeal, discarnate; intangible, immaterial, insubstantial, unsubstantial, unreal; spiritual, ghostly, spectral, wraithlike.

disembogue /dísimbṓg/ v.tr. & intr. (**disembogues, disembogued, disemboguing**) (of a river, etc.) pour forth (waters) at the mouth. [Sp. desembocar (as DIS-, en in, boca mouth)]

/.../ **pronunciation**	● **part of speech**
□ **phrases, idioms, and compounds**	
□□ **derivatives**	■ **synonym section**
cross-references appear in SMALL CAPITALS or italics	

disembowel /dísimbówəl/ v.tr. (**-emboweled, -emboweling**; esp. Brit. **-embowelled, -embowelling**) remove the bowels or entrails of. □□ **disembowelment** n.
■ draw, gut.

disembroil /dísimbróyl/ v.tr. extricate from confusion or entanglement.

disenchant /dísinchánt/ v.tr. free from enchantment; disillusion. □□ **disenchantingly** adv. **disenchantment** n. [F désenchanter (as DIS-, ENCHANT)]
■ see DISILLUSION v.

disencumber /dísinkúmbər/ v.tr. free from encumbrance.
■ (disencumber of) see RELIEVE 6.

disendow /dísindów/ v.tr. strip (esp. a church) of endowments. □□ **disendowment** n.

disenfranchise var. of DISFRANCHISE.

disengage /dísingáyj/ v. & n. ● v. **1 a** tr. detach, free, loosen, or separate (parts, etc.) (disengaged the clutch). **b** refl. detach oneself; get loose (disengaged ourselves from their company). **2** tr. Mil. remove (troops) from a battle or a battle area. **3** intr. become detached. **4** intr. Fencing pass the point of one's sword to the other side of one's opponent's. **5** intr. (as **disengaged** adj.) **a** unoccupied; free; vacant. **b** uncommitted, esp. politically. ● n. Fencing a disengaging movement.
■ v. **1** loose, loosen, unloose, detach, unfasten, release, disconnect, disjoin, undo, disunite, unjoint, uncouple, extricate, unbuckle, unhitch, unclasp, unlatch, unbolt, unlock, unleash, unfetter, unchain, unlace, unhook, unbind, untie; (set) free, liberate, disentangle; divide, separate, part; throw off, shake (off), cut loose, get rid of; (disengage oneself) get out, get away, break away. **3** come off or away, separate, part, divide. **5** (**disengaged**) **a** unoccupied, vacant; see also FREE adj. 8b. **b** see NEUTRAL adj. 1, 2.

disengagement /dísingáyjmənt/ n. **1 a** the act of disengaging. **b** an instance of this. **2** freedom from ties; detachment. **3** the dissolution of an engagement to marry. **4** ease of manner or behavior. **5** Fencing = DISENGAGE.

disentail /dísintáyl/ v.tr. Law free (property) from entail; break the entail of.

disentangle /dísintánggəl/ v. **1** tr. **a** unravel; untwist. **b** free from complications; extricate (disentangled her from the difficulty). **2** intr. become disentangled. □□ **disentanglement** n.
■ see STRAIGHTEN, EXTRICATE.

disenthrall /dísinthráwl/ v.tr. (also **disenthral**) literary free from enthrallment. □□ **disenthrallment** n.

disentitle /dísintít'l/ v.tr. (usu. foll. by to) deprive of any rightful claim.

disentomb /dísintóŏm/ v.tr. literary **1** remove from a tomb; disinter. **2** unearth. □□ **disentombment** /-tŏŏm-mənt/ n.

disequilibrium /díseekwilíbreeəm/ n. a lack or loss of equilibrium; instability.

disestablish /dísistáblish/ v.tr. **1** deprive (a church) of government support. **2** depose from an official position. **3** terminate the establishment of. □□ **disestablishment** n.

disesteem /dísisteém/ v. & n. ● v.tr. have a low opinion of; despise. ● n. low esteem or regard.

diseuse /deezőz/ n. (masc. **diseur** /deezőr/) a female entertainer who performs monologues. [F, = talker f. dire dis-say]

disfavor /disfáyvər/ n. & v. (Brit. **disfavour**) ● n. **1** disapproval or dislike. **2** the state of being disliked (fell into disfavor). ● v.tr. regard or treat with disfavor.
■ n. **1** disapproval, dislike, displeasure, disapprobation, dissatisfaction. **2** low esteem or regard, disesteem, discredit, dishonor, disgrace, disrepute; see also DISCREDIT n. 1. ● v. dislike, discountenance, frown on or upon; see also DISAPPROVE.

disfigure /disfígyər/ v.tr. spoil the beauty of; deform; deface. □□ **disfigurement** n. [ME f. OF desfigurer f. Rmc (as DIS-, FIGURE)]
■ mar, damage, scar, deface, mutilate, injure, impair, deform, distort, spoil, ruin.

disforest /disfáwrist, -fór-/ v.tr. Brit. = DISAFFOREST. □□ **disforestation** n.

disfranchise /disfránchīz/ v.tr. (also **disenfranchise** /disfinránchīz/) **1 a** deprive (a person) of the right to vote. **b** deprive (a place) of the right to send a representative to parliament. **2** deprive (a person) of rights as a citizen or of a franchise held. □□ **disfranchisement** n.

disfrock /disfrók/ v.tr. unfrock.

disgorge /disgáwrj/ v.tr. **1** eject from the throat or stomach. **2** pour forth; discharge (contents, ill-gotten gains, etc.). □□ **disgorgement** n. [ME f. OF desgorger (as DIS-, GORGE)]
■ **1** see REGURGITATE 1.

disgrace /disgráys/ n. & v. ● n. **1** the loss of reputation; shame; ignominy (brought disgrace on his family). **2** a dishonorable, inefficient, or shameful person, thing, state of affairs, etc. (the bus service is a disgrace). ● v.tr. **1** bring shame or discredit on; be a disgrace to. **2** degrade from a position of honor; dismiss from favor. □ **in disgrace** having lost respect or reputation; out of favor. [F disgrâce, disgracier f. It. disgrazia, disgraziare (as DIS-, GRACE)]
■ n. **1** ignominy, shame, humiliation, embarrassment, degradation, debasement, dishonor, discredit, disfavor, disrepute, vitiation, infamy, stigma, scandal, vilification, disesteem, contempt, odium, obloquy, opprobrium. ● v. **1** shame, humiliate, embarrass, mortify; degrade, debase, dishonor, discredit, disfavor, vitiate, defame, disparage, scandalize, stain, taint, stigmatize, sully, besmirch, smirch, tarnish, smear, asperse, calumniate, vilify, blacken, drag through the mud, slur. □ **in disgrace** out of favor, sl. in the doghouse; see also UNPOPULAR.

disgraceful /disgráysfŏŏl/ adj. shameful; dishonorable; degrading. □□ **disgracefully** adv.
■ shameful, humiliating, embarrassing, dishonorable, disreputable, infamous, ignominious, degrading, debased, base, vile, corrupt, bad, wrong, evil, low, mean, despicable, contemptible, awful, terrible, shameless, outrageous, shocking, scandalous, improper, unseemly, unworthy, objectionable.

disgruntled /disgrúnt'ld/ adj. discontented; moody; sulky. □□ **disgruntlement** n. [DIS- + gruntle obs. frequent. of GRUNT]
■ discontented, displeased, unhappy, dissatisfied, irritated, vexed, cross, exasperated, annoyed, disappointed, put out, malcontent, discontent(ed), testy, peevish, grumpy, moody, sullen, sulky, crotchety, fractious, out of temper, in a bad temper, crabby, ill-humored, bad-tempered, ill-tempered, cranky, colloq. fed up, peeved, grouchy, sl. browned off, Brit. sl. cheesed off.

disguise /disgíz/ v. & n. ● v.tr. **1** (often foll. by as) alter the appearance, sound, smell, etc., of, so as to conceal the identity; make unrecognizable (disguised herself as a police officer; disguised the taste by adding sugar). **2** misrepresent or cover up (disguised the truth; disguised their intentions). ● n. **1 a** a costume, false beard, makeup, etc., used to alter the appearance so as to conceal or deceive. **b** any action, manner, etc., used for deception. **2 a** the act or practice of disguising; the concealment of reality. **b** an instance of this. □ **in disguise 1** wearing a concealing costume, etc. **2** appearing to be the opposite (a blessing in disguise). □□ **disguisement** n. [ME f. OF desguis(i)er (as DIS-, GUISE)]
■ v. **1** camouflage, cover up, conceal, hide, mask. **2** misrepresent, falsify, counterfeit, distort, twist, fake. ● n. **1** guise, false identity, camouflage, appearance, semblance, form; outfit, costume. **2 a** pretense, deception, dissimulation, semblance, concealment; see also DECEIT 1. **b** cover-up, façade, front, bluff, pretense; see also MASQUERADE n. 1.

disgust /disgúst/ n. & v. ● n. (usu. foll. by at, for) **1** strong aversion; repugnance; profound indignation. **2** strong distaste for (some item of) food, drink, medicine, etc.; nausea. ● v.tr. cause disgust in (their behavior disgusts me; was disgusted to find a slug). □ **in disgust** as a result of disgust (left in disgust). □□ **disgustedly** adv. [OF degoust, desgouster, or It. disgusto, disgustare (as DIS-, GUSTO)]
■ n. **1** loathing, contempt, hatred, abhorrence,

repugnance, aversion, odium, animus, animosity, enmity, antagonism, antipathy, dislike; outrage, indignation. **2** revulsion, nausea, sickness, repugnance, distaste, aversion. ● *v.* sicken, offend, nauseate, repel, revolt, put off, appall, *sl.* gross out; outrage.

disgustful /disgústfŏŏl/ *adj.* **1** disgusting; repulsive. **2** (of curiosity, etc.) caused by disgust.

disgusting /disgústing/ *adj.* arousing aversion or indignation (*disgusting behavior*). □□ **disgustingly** *adv.* **disgustingness** *n.*

■ nauseating, sickening, offensive, repulsive, disgustful, revolting, repugnant, repellent, objectionable, distasteful, obnoxious, loathsome, gross, vile, foul, nasty, horrible, *Brit.* off-putting, *Brit. colloq.* sick-making; unappetizing, unsavory; outrageous.

dish /dish/ *n. & v.* ● *n.* **1 a** a shallow, usu. flat-bottomed container for cooking or serving food, made of glass, ceramics, metal, etc. **b** the food served in a dish (*all the dishes were delicious*). **c** a particular kind of food (*a meat dish*). **2** (in *pl.*) dirty plates, cutlery, cooking pots, etc. after a meal. **3 a** a dish-shaped receptacle, object, or cavity. **b** = satellite dish. **4** *sl.* a sexually attractive person. ● *v.tr.* **1** put (food) into a dish ready for serving. **2** *colloq.* a outmaneuver. **b** *Brit.* destroy (one's hopes, chances, etc.). **3** make concave or dish-shaped. □ **dish antenna** an antenna with a concave, dish-shaped reflector designed to receive radio, microwave, etc., signals. **dish out** *sl.* distribute, esp. carelessly or indiscriminately. **dish up 1** serve or prepare to serve (food). **2** *colloq.* seek to present (facts, argument, etc.) attractively. □□ **dishful** *n.* (*pl.* **-fuls**). **dishlike** *adj.* [OE *disc* plate, bowl (with Gmc and ON cognates) f. L *discus* DISK]

■ *n.* **1 a** see PLATE *n.* 1a. **b** see PLATE *n.* 1b.

dishabille /disəbeél, -beé/ *n.* (also **deshabille** /dezəbeél, -beé/) a state of being only partly or carelessly clothed. [F, = undressed]

disharmony /dis-haármənee/ *n.* a lack of harmony; discord. □□ **disharmonious** /-mōneeəs/ *adj.* **disharmoniously** *adv.* **disharmonize** /-nīz/ *v.tr.*

■ see DISCORD *n.* 1.

dishcloth /dishklawth, -kloth/ *n.* a usu. open-weave cloth for washing dishes. □ **dishcloth gourd** a loofah.

dishearten /dis-haárt'n/ *v.tr.* cause to lose courage or confidence; make despondent. □□ **dishearteningly** *adv.* **disheartenment** *n.*

■ see DISCOURAGE 1.

disheveled /dishévəld/ *adj.* (esp. *Brit.* **dishevelled**) (of the hair, a person, etc.) untidy; ruffled; disordered. □□ **dishevel** *v.tr.* (**disheveled, disheveling**; esp. *Brit.* **dishevelled, dishevelling**). **dishevelment** *n.* [ME *dischevelee* f. OF *deschevelé* past part. (as DIS-, *chevel* hair f. L *capillus*)]

■ see UNTIDY.

dishonest /disónist/ *adj.* (of a person, act, or statement) fraudulent or insincere. □□ **dishonestly** *adv.* [ME f. OF *deshoneste* (as DIS-, HONEST)]

■ untrustworthy, underhanded, underhand, shady, dishonorable, fraudulent, deceptive, unfair, double-dealing, thievish, knavish, cheating, deceitful, lying, untruthful, mendacious, treacherous, perfidious, corrupt, unscrupulous, unprincipled, *colloq.* crooked, esp. *Brit. sl.* bent; insincere, two-faced, hypocritical.

dishonesty /disónistee/ *n.* (*pl.* **-ies**) **1 a** a lack of honesty. **b** deceitfulness; fraud. **2** a dishonest or fraudulent act. [ME f. OF *deshon(n)esté* (as DISHONEST)]

dishonor /disónər/ *n. & v.* (*Brit.* **dishonour**) ● *n.* **1** a state of shame or disgrace; discredit. **2** something that causes dishonor (*a dishonor to her profession*). ● *v.tr.* **1** treat without honor or respect. **2** disgrace (*dishonored his name*). **3** refuse to accept or pay (a check or a bill of exchange). **4** *archaic* violate the chastity of; rape. [ME f. OF *deshonor, deshonorer* f. med.L *dishonorare* (as DIS-, HONOR)]

■ *n.* **1** discredit, disesteem, disrespect, ignominy, disgrace, shame, disrepute, indignity, loss of face. **2** disgrace, slight, insult, offense, affront, embarrassment. ● *v.* **1** insult, abuse, affront, slight, offend, injure. **2** degrade, discredit, shame, debase, humiliate, mortify,

abase; see also DISGRACE *v.* 1. **4** defile, violate, ravish, rape, deflower, sexually assault, *euphem.* assault.

dishonorable /disónərəbəl/ *adj.* (*Brit.* **dishonourable**) **1** causing disgrace; ignominious. **2** unprincipled. □□ **dishonorableness** *n.* **dishonorably** *adv.*

■ **1** disgraceful, degrading, inglorious, ignominious, shameful, discreditable, humiliating. **2** unprincipled, shameless, corrupt, unscrupulous, untrustworthy, treacherous, traitorous, perfidious, disloyal, unfaithful, faithless, dishonest, hypocritical, two-faced, duplicitous, disreputable, base, despicable; improper, unseemly, unbecoming, unworthy, objectionable, reprehensible, flagrant, bad, evil, vile, low, mean, contemptible, below *or* beneath contempt, foul, heinous, dirty, filthy.

dishpan /dishpan/ *n.* a large, deep, usu. circular pan for washing dishes.

dishrag /dishrag/ *n.* = DISHCLOTH.

dishwasher /dishwoshər, -wawshər/ *n.* **1** a machine for automatically washing dishes. **2** a person employed to wash dishes. □ **dull as dishwater** extremely dull; boring.

dishwater /dishwawtər, -woter/ *n.* water in which dishes are being or have been washed.

dishy /dishee/ *adj.* (**dishier, dishiest**) *Brit. colloq.* sexually attractive. [DISH *n.* 4 + -Y¹]

disillusion /disilōōzhən/ *n. & v.* ● *n.* freedom from illusions; disenchantment. ● *v.tr.* rid of illusions; disenchant. □□ **disillusionize** *v.tr.* **disillusionment** *n.*

■ *n.* disillusionment, disenchantment, disappointment, *literary* disenthrallment. ● *v.* disabuse, disappoint, disenchant, *literary* disenthrall; enlighten, set straight, undeceive, put right.

disincentive /disinséntiv/ *n. & adj.* ● *n.* **1** something that tends to discourage a particular action, etc. **2** *Econ.* a source of discouragement to productivity or progress. ● *adj.* tending to discourage.

■ *n.* **1** see DETERRENT.

disinclination /disinklináyshən/ *n.* (usu. foll. by *for*, or *to* + infin.) the absence of willingness; a reluctance (*a disinclination for work; disinclination to go*).

■ see *reluctance* (RELUCTANT).

disincline /disinklín/ *v.tr.* (usu. foll. by *to* + infin. or *for*) **1** make unwilling or reluctant. **2** (as **disinclined** *adj.*) unwilling; averse.

■ **2** (**disinclined**) unwilling, reluctant, hesitant, loath, opposed, averse.

disincorporate /disinkáwrpərayt/ *v.tr.* dissolve (a corporate body).

disinfect /disinfékt/ *v.tr.* cleanse (a wound, a room, clothes, etc.) of infection, esp. with a disinfectant. □□ **disinfection** /-fékshən/ *n.* [F *désinfecter* (as DIS-, INFECT)]

■ clean, purify, purge, sanitize, fumigate, decontaminate, sterilize, *usu. formal* cleanse.

disinfectant /disinféktənt/ *n. & adj.* ● *n.* a usu. commercially produced chemical liquid that destroys germs, etc. ● *adj.* causing disinfection.

■ *n.* germicide, antiseptic, sterilizer, bactericide, sanitizer, fumigant, purifier, cleaner, cleanser.

disinfest /disinfést/ *v.tr.* rid (a person, a building, etc.) of vermin, infesting insects. etc. □□ **disinfestation** /-stáyshən/ *n.*

disinflation /disinfláyshən/ *n. Econ.* a policy designed to counteract inflation without causing deflation. □□ **disinflationary** *adj.*

disinformation /disinfərmáyshən/ *n.* false information, intended to mislead.

■ see LIE² *n.*

disingenuous /disinjényōōəs/ *adj.* having secret motives;

/.../ **pronunciation**	● **part of speech**
□ **phrases, idioms, and compounds**	
□□ **derivatives**	■ **synonym section**
cross-references appear in SMALL CAPITALS or *italics*	

dishonest; insincere. □□ **disingenuously** *adv.* **disingenuousness** *n.*

■ insincere, false, dishonest, tricky, devious, deceitful, underhanded, underhand, guileful, double-dealing, two-faced, duplicitous, hypocritical, calculating, designing, *colloq.* shifty.

disinherit /dísinhérit/ *v.tr.* reject as one's heir; deprive of the right of inheritance. □□ **disinheritance** *n.* [ME f. DIS- + INHERIT in obs. sense 'make heir']
■ disown, cut off, reject.

disintegrate /disíntigrayt/ *v.* **1** *tr.* & *intr.* **a** separate into component parts or fragments. **b** lose or cause to lose cohesion. **2** *intr. colloq.* deteriorate mentally or physically; decay. **3** *intr.* & *tr. Physics* undergo or cause to undergo disintegration. □□ **disintegrator** *n.*
■ **1** break up *or* apart, shatter, come *or* fall apart, come *or* go *or* fall to pieces, crumble, fragment, fall to bits. **2** break down, collapse, go to pieces, have a (nervous) breakdown, *colloq.* crack up. **3** decompose, rot, decay, molder.

disintegration /disíntigráyshən/ *n.* **1** the act or an instance of disintegrating. **2** *Physics* any process in which a nucleus emits a particle or particles or divides into smaller nuclei.
■ **1** see DECAY *n.* 2.

disinter /dísintér/ *v.tr.* (**disinterred, disinterring**) **1** remove (esp. a corpse) from the ground; unearth; exhume. **2** find after a protracted search (*disinterred the letter from the back of the drawer*). □□ **disinterment** *n.* [F *désenterrer* (as DIS-, INTER)]
■ see DIG *v.* 4.

disinterest /dísíntrist, -íntərist/ *n.* **1** impartiality. **2** *disp.* lack of interest; unconcern.
■ **1** see *objectivity* (OBJECTIVE). **2** see INDIFFERENCE 1.

disinterested /dísíntristid, -íntəri-/ *adj.* **1** not influenced by one's own advantage; impartial. **2** *disp.* uninterested. □□ **disinterestedly** *adv.* **disinterestedness** *n.* [past part. of *disinterest* (v.) divest of interest]
■ **1** unbiased, impartial, unprejudiced, objective, fair, neutral, open-minded, equitable, just, dispassionate, detached, evenhanded, impersonal, uninvolved. **2** see INDIFFERENT 4.

disinvest /dísinvést/ *v.intr.* (foll. by *from*, or *absol.*) reduce or dispose of one's investment (in a place, company, etc.). □□ **disinvestment** *n.*

disjecta membra /disjéktə mémbrə/ *n.pl.* scattered remains; fragments, esp. of written work. [L, alt. of *disjecti membra poetae* (Horace) limbs of a dismembered poet]

disjoin /disjóyn/ *v.tr.* separate or disunite; part. [ME f. OF *desjoindre* f. L *disjungere* (as DIS-, *jungere junct-* join)]

disjoint /disjóynt/ *v.* & *adj.* ● *v.tr.* **1** take apart at the joints. **2** (as **disjointed** *adj.*) (esp. of conversation) incoherent; desultory. **3** disturb the working or connection of; dislocate. ● *adj.* (of two or more sets) having no elements in common. □□ **disjointedly** *adv.* **disjointedness** *n.* [ME f. obs. *disjoint* (adj.) f. past part. of OF *desjoindre* (as DISJOIN)]
■ *v.* **1** disjoin, separate, take apart *or* to bits, disconnect, divide, split (up). **2** (**disjointed**) loose, incoherent, confused, aimless, directionless, rambling, muddled, jumbled, mixed up, fitful, discontinuous, disorganized, unorganized, disorderly, disordered, desultory, disconnected, unmethodical, inconsistent, unsystematic.

disjunction /disjúngkshən/ *n.* **1** the process of disjoining; separation. **2** an instance of this. [ME f. OF *disjunction* or L *disjunctio* (as DISJOIN)]
■ see SEPARATION.

disjunctive /disjúngktiv/ *adj.* & *n.* ● *adj.* **1** involving separation; disjoining. **2** *Gram.* (esp. of a conjunction) expressing a choice between two words, etc., e.g., *or* in *asked if he were going or staying* (cf. COPULATIVE). **3** *Logic* (of a proposition) expressing alternatives. ● *n.* **1** *Gram.* a disjunctive conjunction or other word. **2** *Logic* a disjunctive proposition. □□ **disjunctively** *adv.* [ME f. L *disjunctivus* (as DISJOIN)]

disk /disk/ *n.* (also **disc**) **1 a** a flat thin circular object. **b** a

round, flat or apparently flat surface (*the sun's disk*). **c** a mark of this shape. **2** a layer of cartilage between vertebrae. **3 a** a phonograph record. **b** = *compact disc.* **4 a** (in full **magnetic disk**) a computer storage device consisting of several flat, circular, magnetically coated plates formed into a rotatable disk. **b** (in full **optical disc** or **disk**) a smooth nonmagnetic disk with large storage capacity for data recorded and read by laser. **5** *Brit.* a device with a pointer or rotating disk indicating time of arrival or latest permitted time of departure, for display in a parked motor vehicle. □ **disk** (often **disc**) **brake** a brake employing the friction of pads against a disk. **disk drive** *Computing* a mechanism for rotating a disk and reading or writing data from or to it. **disk harrow** a harrow with cutting edges consisting of a row of concave disks set at an oblique angle. **disk** (also **disc**) **jockey** the presenter of a selection of phonograph records, compact discs, etc., of popular music, esp. in a broadcast. [F *disque* or L *discus*: see DISCUS]
■ **1 a** see COUNTER[1] 2a, b. **c** circle, ring, round. **3** see RECORD *n.* 3a.

diskette /diskét/ *n. Computing* = *floppy disk.*

dislike /dislík/ *v.* & *n.* ● *v.tr.* have an aversion or objection to; not like. ● *n.* **1** a feeling of repugnance or not liking. **2** an object of dislike. □□ **dislikable** *adj.* (also **dislikeable**).
■ *v.* **1** be averse to, mind, have no time *or* use for, turn from, disfavor, be put *or* turned off by, disrelish, *archaic* mislike; loathe, scorn, despise, disesteem, detest, abominate, execrate, *colloq.* hate, *literary* contemn. ● *n.* **1** aversion, displeasure, distaste, disfavor, disesteem, disrelish, disinclination, *archaic* mislike; loathing, hate, hatred, animus, animosity, antipathy, detestation, contempt, execration, ill will; disgust, repugnance; hostility, antagonism. **2** see AVERSION 2.

dislocate /díslōkayt, disló-/ *v.tr.* **1** disturb the normal connection of (esp. a joint in the body). **2** disrupt; put out of order. **3** displace. [prob. back-form. f. DISLOCATION]
■ **1** see DISJOINT *v.* 1. **2, 3** see DISRUPT 1, DISPLACE.

dislocation /díslōkáyshən/ *n.* **1** the act or result of dislocating. **2** *Crystallog.* the displacement of part of a crystal lattice structure. [ME f. OF *dislocation* or med.L *dislocatio* f. *dislocare* (as DIS-, *locare* place)]

dislodge /dislój/ *v.tr.* remove from an established or fixed position (*was dislodged from his directorship*). □□ **dislodgment** *n.* (also **dislodgement**). [ME f. OF *dislog(i)er* (as DIS-, LODGE)]
■ see EXPEL 2, 3.

disloyal /dislóyəl/ *adj.* (often foll. by *to*) **1** not loyal; unfaithful. **2** untrue to one's allegiance; treacherous to one's government, etc. □□ **disloyalist** *n.* **disloyally** *adv.* **disloyalty** *n.* [ME f. OF *desloial* (as DIS-, LOYAL)]
■ unfaithful, faithless, untrue, false, untrustworthy; treasonable, treasonous, treacherous, traitorous, unpatriotic, subversive, perfidious, deceitful; renegade, apostate, heretical, *literary* recreant.

dismal /dízməl/ *adj.* **1** causing or showing gloom; miserable. **2** dreary or somber (*dismal brown walls*). **3** *colloq.* feeble or inept (*a dismal performance*). □ **the dismals** *Brit. colloq.* melancholy. **the dismal science** esp. *Brit. joc.* economics. □□ **dismally** *adv.* **dismalness** *n.* [orig. noun = unlucky days: ME f. AF *dis mal* f. med.L *dies mali* two days in each month held to be unpropitious]
■ **1, 2** depressing, gloomy, cheerless, melancholy, somber, dreary, sad, bleak, funereal, solemn, dark, grim; lugubrious, mournful, forlorn, miserable, morose, wretched, woebegone, woeful, black, blue, joyless, doleful, unhappy, pessimistic, *literary or joc.* dolorous. **3** see FEEBLE 2.

dismantle /dismánt'l/ *v.tr.* **1** take to pieces; pull down. **2** deprive of defenses or equipment. **3** (often foll. by *of*) strip of covering or protection. □□ **dismantlement** *n.* **dismantler** *n.* [OF *desmanteler* (as DIS-, MANTLE)]
■ **1** see DEMOLISH 1a.

dismast /dismást/ *v.tr.* deprive (a ship) of masts; break down the mast or masts of.

dismay /dismáy/ *v.* & *n.* ● *v.tr.* fill with consternation or anxiety; discourage or depress; reduce to despair. ● *n.* **1** consternation or anxiety. **2** depression or despair. [ME f. OF *desmaiier* (unrecorded) ult. f. a Gmc root = deprive of power (as DIS-, MAY)]

■ *v.* alarm, frighten, scare, terrify, appall, panic, horrify, petrify, startle, shock, take aback, intimidate, disconcert, unnerve, unsettle, discompose, upset, discourage, depress. ● *n.* **1** consternation, alarm, anxiety, agitation, terror, panic, horror, shock, fright, fear, trepidation, apprehension, dread, awe. **2** see DEPRESSION 1b, DESPAIR *n.*

dismember /dismémbər/ *v.tr.* **1** tear or cut the limbs from. **2** partition or divide up (an empire, country, etc.). □□ **dismemberment** *n.* [ME f. OF *desmembrer* f. Rmc (as DIS-, L *membrum* limb)]

■ **1** see MUTILATE 1. **2** see PARTITION *v.* 1.

dismiss /dismís/ *v.* **1 a** *tr.* send away; cause to leave one's presence; disperse; disband (an assembly or army). **b** *intr.* (of an assembly, etc.) disperse; break ranks. **2** *tr.* discharge from employment, office, etc., esp. dishonorably. **3** *tr.* put out of one's thoughts; cease to feel or discuss (*dismissed him from memory*). **4** *tr.* treat (a subject) summarily (*dismissed his application*). **5** *tr. Law* refuse further hearing to (a case); send out of court. **6** *tr. Cricket* put (a batsman or a side) out (*was dismissed for 75 runs*). **7** *intr.* (in *imper.*) *Mil.* a word of command at the end of drilling. □□ **dismissal** *n.* **dismissible** *adj.* **dismission** *n.* [ME, orig. as past part. after OF *desmis* f. med.L *dismissus* (as DIS-, L *mittere* miss- send)]

■ **1** disperse, disband; release, send away, discharge, let go; break ranks. **2** discharge, oust, release, give notice, let go, lay off, throw out, remove, send a person about his *or* her business, *Brit.* give a person his *or* her cards, boot (out), esp. *Mil.* cashier, *Mil.* drum out, *colloq.* send packing, kick out, sack, give a person the sack *or* boot, give a person his *or* her walking papers, give a person his *or* her marching orders, esp. *Brit. colloq.* turn off, *sl.* fire, give a person the (old) heave-ho, *Brit. sl.* give a person the chop. **4** reject, set aside, repudiate; spurn, discount, disregard, lay aside, wave aside, put out of one's mind, think no more of, write off, have *or* be done with, scorn, discard, ignore, shrug off, brush aside, laugh off, *Austral. & NZ sl.* wipe; belittle, pooh-pooh. □□ **dismissal** dismission, discharge, expulsion, notice, *colloq.* marching orders, walking papers, the sack, the boot, *sl.* the (old) heave-ho, *Brit. sl.* chop; discharge, release, disbandment, dispersal; congé.

dismissive /dismísiv/ *adj.* tending to dismiss from consideration; disdainful. □□ **dismissively** *adv.* **dismissiveness** *n.*

■ see DISDAINFUL.

dismount *v. & n.* ● *v.* /dismównt/ **1 a** *intr.* alight from a horse, bicycle, etc. **b** *tr.* (usu. in *passive*) throw from a horse; unseat. **2** *tr.* remove (a thing) from its mounting (esp. a gun from its carriage). ● *n.* /dismównt, dís-/ the act of dismounting.

■ **1 a** see *get down* 1.

disobedient /dísəbeédeeənt/ *adj.* disobeying; rebellious; rule-breaking. □□ **disobedience** /-deeəns/ *n.* **disobediently** *adv.* [ME f. OF *desobedient* (as DIS-, OBEDIENT)]

■ insubordinate, unruly, rebellious, naughty, mischievous, bad, ill-behaved, badly behaved, obstreperous, unmanageable, refractory, fractious, ungovernable, unsubmissive, wayward, noncompliant, intractable, defiant, delinquent, contrary, perverse, willful, headstrong, stubborn, recalcitrant, obdurate, obstinate, contumacious, cross-grained, opposed, mutinous.

disobey /dísəbáy/ *v.tr.* (also *absol.*) fail or refuse to obey; disregard (orders); break (rules) (*disobeyed his mother; how dare you disobey!*). □□ **disobeyer** *n.* [ME f. OF *desobeir* f. Rmc (as DIS-, OBEY)]

■ defy, break, contravene, flout, disregard, ignore, resist, oppose, violate, transgress, overstep, go counter to, fly in the face of, infringe, thumb one's nose at, snap one's

fingers at, *Brit. sl.* cock a snook at; mutiny, rebel, revolt.

disoblige /dísəblíj/ *v.tr.* **1** refuse to consider the convenience or wishes of. **2** (as **disobliging** *adj.*) uncooperative. [F *désobliger* f. Rmc (as DIS-, OBLIGE)]

disorder /disáwrdər/ *n. & v.* ● *n.* **1** a lack of order; confusion. **2** a riot; a commotion. **3** *Med.* a usu. minor ailment or disease. ● *v.tr.* **1** throw into confusion; disarrange. **2** *Med.* put out of good health; upset. [ME, alt. after ORDER *v.* of earlier *disordain* f. OF *desordener* (as DIS-, ORDAIN)]

■ *n.* **1** disarray, confusion, chaos, disorderliness, disorganization, untidiness; derangement, mess, muddle, jumble, tangle, clutter, *colloq.* shambles. **2** tumult, riot, disturbance, pandemonium, upheaval, ferment, fuss, unrest, uproar, hubbub, hullabaloo, commotion, clamor, turbulence, turmoil, bedlam, free-for-all, brouhaha, fracas, melee, affray, fray, scuffle, brawl, breach of the peace, battle royal, donnybrook, *colloq.* rumpus, esp. *Brit. colloq.* kerfuffle; *archaic* distemper. **3** ailment, illness, sickness, affliction, malady, affection, complaint, disease. ● *v.* **1** upset, disarrange, muddle, confuse, confound, unsettle, disorganize, discompose, shake up, disturb, mix (up), befuddle, jumble, scramble, tangle.

disorderly /disáwrdərlee/ *adj.* **1** untidy; confused. **2** irregular; unruly; riotous. **3** *Law* contrary to public order or morality. □ **disorderly house** *Law* a brothel. □□ **disorderliness** *n.*

■ **1** confused, chaotic, scrambled, muddled, disordered, irregular, untidy, messy, messed-up, disarranged, disorganized, unorganized, jumbled, cluttered, haphazard, in disarray, back to front, pell-mell, helter-skelter, topsy-turvy, higgledy-piggledy. **2** unruly, uncontrolled, riotous, undisciplined, ungoverned, disobedient, mutinous, rebellious, lawless, obstreperous, refractory, turbulent, violent, tumultuous, unrestrained, boisterous, noisy, rowdy, wild, unmanageable, ungovernable, uncontrollable, intractable; irregular. □ **disorderly house** see BROTHEL.

disorganize /disáwrgəníz/ *v.tr.* **1** destroy the system or order of; throw into confusion. **2** (as **disorganized** *adj.*) lacking organization or system. □□ **disorganization** *n.* [F *désorganiser* (as DIS-, ORGANIZE)]

■ **1** see JUMBLE *v.* 1.

disorient /disáwreeənt/ *v.tr.* **1** confuse (a person) as to his or her whereabouts or bearings. **2** (often as **disoriented** *adj.*) confuse (a person) (*disoriented by his unexpected behavior*). [F *désorienter* (as DIS-, ORIENT *v.*)]

■ (**disoriented**) confused, bewildered, lost, adrift, disoriented.

disorientate /disáwriəntayt/ *v.tr.* = DISORIENT. □□ **disorientation** /-táyshən/ *n.*

disown /disṓn/ *v.tr.* **1** refuse to recognize; repudiate; disclaim. **2** renounce one's connection with or allegiance to. □□ **disowner** *n.*

■ see REPUDIATE 1a.

disparage /dispárij/ *v.tr.* **1** speak slightingly of; depreciate. **2** bring discredit on. □□ **disparagement** *n.* **disparagingly** *adv.* [ME f. OF *desparagier* marry unequally (as DIS-, *parage* equality of rank ult. f. L *par* equal)]

■ **1** belittle, diminish, depreciate, cheapen, run down, talk down, decry, demean, criticize, speak ill of, traduce, denigrate, deprecate, backbite, underrate, undervalue, downgrade, reduce, minimize, *formal* derogate. **2** slander, libel, discredit, dishonor, defame, malign, vilify, insult, stab in the back, bad-mouth.

disparate /dispərət, dispár-/ *adj. & n.* ● *adj.* essentially different in kind; without comparison or relation. ● *n.* (in *pl.*) things so unlike that there is no basis for their comparison.

/.../ **pronunciation**	● **part of speech**
□ **phrases, idioms, and compounds**	
□□ **derivatives**	■ **synonym section**
cross-references appear in SMALL CAPITALS or *italics*	

□□ **disparately** adv. **disparateness** n. [L disparatus separated (as DIS-, paratus past part. of parare prepare), infl. in sense by L dispar unequal]
■ adj. see DIVERGENT.

disparity /dispáritee/ n. (pl. **-ies**) **1** inequality; difference; incongruity. **2** an instance of this. [F disparité f. LL disparitas -tatis (as DIS-, PARITY[1])]
■ difference, discrepancy, gap, inequality, unevenness, imbalance, dissimilarity, contrast, imparity, inconsistency, incongruity.

dispassionate /dispásh∂n∂t/ adj. free from passion; calm; impartial. □□ **dispassionately** adv. **dispassionateness** n.
■ cool, calm, composed, self-possessed, unemotional, unexcited, unexcitable, levelheaded, sober, self-controlled, even-tempered, unruffled, unmoved, tranquil, equable, equanimous, placid, peaceful, serene, colloq. unflappable; fair, impartial, neutral, disinterested, detached, equitable, evenhanded, unbiased, just, objective, unprejudiced, open-minded.

dispatch /dispách/ v. & n. (also **despatch**) ● v.tr. **1** send off to a destination or for a purpose (dispatched her with the message; dispatched the letter yesterday). **2** perform (business, a task, etc.) promptly; finish off. **3** kill; execute (dispatched him with the revolver). **4** colloq. eat (food, a meal, etc.) quickly. ● n. **1** the act or an instance of sending (a messenger, letter, etc.). **2** the act or an instance of killing; execution. **3** /also díspach/ **a** an official written message on state or esp. military affairs. **b** a report sent in by a newspaper's correspondent, usu. from a foreign country. **4** promptness; efficiency (done with dispatch). □ **dispatch** a container for esp. official government or military documents or dispatches; attaché case. □□ **dispatcher** n. [It. dispacciare or Sp. despachar expedite (as DIS-, It. impacciare and Sp. empachar hinder, of uncert. orig.)]
■ v. **1** send off or away or out, send on one's way; send, mail, transmit, forward, ship, express, remit, convey, esp. Brit. freight, post. **2** hasten or hurry or speed through, get done, accomplish, get through, conclude, finish off, complete, execute, do, colloq. knock off. **3** murder, dispose of, eliminate, put to death, execute, assassinate, liquidate, put an end to, put away (for good), colloq. polish off, do away with, literary or joc. slay, sl. finish (off), do in, bump off, knock off, zap, take for a ride, hit, rub out, ice, waste; see also KILL[1] v. 1a. **4** see GULP v. 1. ● n. **1** see TRANSMISSION 1. **2** execution, killing, murder, disposal, assassination. **3 b** communiqué, report, bulletin, story, news (item), communication, message, piece; document, instruction, joc. missive. **4** haste, speed, promptness, quickness, efficiency, expedition, expeditiousness, alacrity, swiftness, rapidity, archaic or literary celerity.

dispel /dispél/ v.tr. (**dispelled**, **dispelling**) dissipate; disperse; scatter (the dawn dispelled their fears). □□ **dispeller** n. [L dispellere (as DIS-, pellere drive)]
■ see DISSIPATE 1a.

dispensable /dispéns∂b∂l/ adj. **1** able to be done without; unnecessary. **2** (of a law, etc.) able to be relaxed in special cases. □□ **dispensability** n. [med.L dispensabilis (as DISPENSE)]
■ **1** disposable, nonessential, unessential, inessential, unnecessary, unneeded, expendable, superfluous, needless, useless, incidental.

dispensary /dispéns∂ree/ n. (pl. **-ies**) **1** a place where medicines, etc., are dispensed. **2** a public or charitable institution for medical advice and the dispensing of medicines. [med.L dispensarius (as DISPENSE)]
■ **1** see PHARMACY 2. **2** see INFIRMARY 1.

dispensation /díspensáysh∂n/ n. **1 a** the act or an instance of dispensing or distributing. **b** (foll. by with) the state of doing without (a thing). **c** something distributed. **2** (usu. foll. by from) **a** exemption from a penalty or duty; an instance of this. **b** permission to be exempted from a religious observance; an instance of this. **3** a religious or political system obtaining in a nation, etc. (the Christian dispensation). **4 a** the ordering or management of the world by providence.

b a specific example of such ordering (of a community, a person, etc.). □□ **dispensational** adj. [ME f. OF dispensation or L dispensatio (as DISPENSE)]
■ **1 a** see ADMINISTRATION 6. **c** see SHARE n. 1. **2 a** see exemption (EXEMPT).

dispense /dispéns/ v. **1** tr. distribute; deal out. **2** tr. administer (a sacrament, justice, etc.). **3** tr. make up and give out (medicine, etc.) according to a doctor's prescription. **4** tr. (usu. foll. by from) grant a dispensation to (a person) from an obligation, esp. a religious observance. **5** intr. (foll. by with) **a** do without; render needless. **b** give exemption from (a rule). [ME f. OF despenser f. L dispensare frequent. of dispendĕre weigh or pay out (as DIS-, pendĕre pens- weigh)]
■ **1** distribute, give out, hand or pass out, supply, provide, give away, deal out, dole out, parcel out, share (out), issue, apportion, allocate, allot, assign, literary mete out, sl. dish out. **2** administer, discharge, apply, implement, enforce, carry out, execute, conduct, direct, operate, superintend, supervise. **4** (dispense from) see EXEMPT v. **5 a** (dispense with) manage or do without, forgo, give up, relinquish, waive, forswear, abstain from, renounce, reject, literary eschew; do away with, get rid of, eliminate, dispose of, abolish, remove, cancel, ignore, render or make unnecessary or superfluous.

dispenser /dispéns∂r/ n. **1** a person or thing that dispenses something, e.g., medicine, good advice. **2** an automatic machine that dispenses an item or a specific amount of something (e.g., cash).

dispersant /dispérs∂nt/ n. Chem. an agent used to disperse small particles in a medium.

disperse /dispérs/ v. **1** intr. & tr. go, send, drive, or distribute in different directions or over a wide area. **2 a** intr. (of people at a meeting, etc.) leave and go their various ways. **b** tr. cause to do this. **3** tr. send to or station at separate points. **4** tr. put in circulation; disseminate. **5** tr. Chem. distribute (small particles) uniformly in a medium. **6** tr. Physics divide (white light) into its colored constituents. □□ **dispersable** adj. **dispersal** n. **disperser** n. **dispersible** adj. **dispersive** adj. [ME f. L dispergere dispers- (as DIS-, spargere scatter)]
■ **1** spread, scatter, broadcast, distribute; diffuse, dissipate, dispel, break up, spread out. **2 a** disband, scatter, break up, leave, go (away). **b** dismiss, rout, send off or away, disband, scatter. **4** disseminate, broadcast, send; see also CIRCULATE 2a, b.

dispersion /dispérzh∂n, -sh∂n/ n. **1** the act or an instance of dispersing; the process of being dispersed. **2** Chem. a mixture of one substance dispersed in another. **3** Physics the separation of white light into colors or of any radiation according to wavelength. **4** Statistics the extent to which values of a variable differ from the mean. **5** (**the Dispersion**) the Jews dispersed among the Gentiles after the Captivity in Babylon. [ME f. LL dispersio (as DISPERSE), transl. Gk diaspora: see DIASPORA]
■ **1** see SPREAD n. 1.

dispirit /dispírit/ v.tr. **1** (esp. as **dispiriting** adj.) make despondent; discourage. **2** (as **dispirited** adj.) dejected; discouraged. □□ **dispiritedly** adv. **dispiritedness** n. **dispiritingly** adv.
■ **1** see DEMORALIZE 1. **2** (**dispirited**) see MISERABLE 1.

displace /displáys/ v.tr. **1** shift from its accustomed place. **2** remove from office. **3** take the place of; oust. □ **displaced person** a person who is forced to leave his or her home country because of war, persecution, etc.; a refugee.
■ **1** move, transfer, shift, relocate, resettle, dislocate; disturb, unsettle. **2** expel, unseat, eject, evict, exile, banish, throw out, boot out, depose, remove, oust, discharge, esp. Mil. cashier, colloq. kick out, sack, sl. fire; see also DISMISS 2. **3** take the place of, oust, supplant, replace, supersede, succeed, take over from. □ **displaced person** see REFUGEE.

displacement /displáysm∂nt/ n. **1 a** the act or an instance of displacing; the process of being displaced. **b** an instance of this. **2** Physics the amount of a fluid displaced by a solid floating or immersed in it (a ship with a displacement of

11,000 *tons*). **3** *Psychol.* **a** the substitution of one idea or impulse for another. **b** the unconscious transfer of strong unacceptable emotions from one object to another. **4** the amount by which a thing is shifted from its place.

display /displáy/ *v. & n.* ● *v.tr.* **1** expose to view; exhibit; show. **2** show ostentatiously. **3** allow to appear; reveal; betray (*displayed his ignorance*). ● *n.* **1** the act or an instance of displaying. **2** an exhibition or show. **3** ostentation; flashiness. **4** the distinct behavior of some birds and fish, esp. used to attract a mate. **5 a** the presentation of signals or data on a visual display unit, etc. **b** the information so presented. **6** *Printing* the arrangement and choice of type in order to attract attention. □□ **displayer** *n.* [ME f. OF *despleier* f. L *displicare* (as DIS-, *plicare* fold): cf. DEPLOY]
■ *v.* **1** show, exhibit, air, put *or* set forth, present; advertise, publicize. **2** show off, flaunt, boast about, parade, flourish, *colloq.* flash, *literary* vaunt. **3** betray, reveal, unveil, disclose, uncover, make visible, expose, evince, manifest, demonstrate. ● *n.* **1** show, demonstration, exposition, manifestation, revelation. **2** show, exhibition, exhibit, demonstration, presentation, array, panoply, spectacle, parade. **3** ostentation, showiness, flashiness, ceremony, pageantry, pageant, splendor, magnificence, grandeur, pomp, éclat, élan, dash.

displease /displeéz/ *v.tr.* make indignant or angry; offend; annoy. □ **be displeased** (often foll. by *at, with*) be indignant or dissatisfied; disapprove. □□ **displeasing** *adj.* **displeasingly** *adv.* [ME f. OF *desplaisir* (as DIS-, L *placēre* please)]
■ offend, put out, dissatisfy, ruffle, upset, exasperate, worry, trouble, vex, annoy, irritate, pique, nettle, chafe, anger, infuriate, frustrate, *colloq.* miff, peeve, get a person's goat, rile, *sl.* bug; see also IRK. □ **be displeased** (*be displeased at* or *with*) see DISAPPROVE.

displeasure /displézhər/ *n. & v.* ● *n.* disapproval; anger; dissatisfaction. ● *v.tr. archaic* cause displeasure to; annoy. [ME f. OF (as DISPLEASE): assim. to PLEASURE]
■ *n.* dissatisfaction, disapproval, disfavor, discontentment, distaste, dislike; annoyance, anger, irritation, vexation, chagrin, indignation, resentment, dudgeon, exasperation, *literary* ire. ● *v.* see IRK.

disport /dispáwrt/ *v. & n.* ● *v.intr. & refl.* frolic; gambol; enjoy oneself (*disported on the beach*; *disported themselves in the ocean*). ● *n. archaic* relaxation. **2** a pastime. [ME f. AF & OF *desporter* (as DIS-, *porter* carry f. L *portare*)]
■ *v.* see PLAY *v.* 1.

disposable /dispṓzəbəl/ *adj. & n.* ● *adj.* **1** intended to be used once and then thrown away (*disposable diapers*). **2** that can be got rid of, made over, or used. **3** (esp. of financial assets) at the owner's disposal. ● *n.* a thing designed to be thrown away after one use. □ **disposable income** income after taxes, etc., available for spending. □□ **disposability** *n.*
■ *adj.* **1** discardable, throwaway, nonreturnable, biodegradable; paper, plastic. **2, 3** usable, obtainable, available, liquid, spendable.

disposal /dispṓzəl/ *n.* (usu. foll. by *of*) **1** the act or an instance of disposing of something. **2** the arrangement, disposition, or placing of something. **3** control or management (of a person, business, etc.). **4** (esp. as **waste disposal**) the disposing of rubbish. □ **at one's disposal 1** available for one's use. **2** subject to one's orders or decisions.
■ **2** see DISPOSITION 2b. **3** see DISPOSITION 4b.

dispose /dispṓz/ *v.* **1** *tr.* (usu. foll. by *to*, or *to* + infin.) **a** make willing; incline (*disposed him to the idea*; *was disposed to release them*). **b** give a tendency to (*the wheel was disposed to buckle*). **2** *tr.* place suitably or in order (*disposed the pictures in sequence*). **3** *tr.* (as **disposed** *adj.*) have a specified mental inclination (usu. in *comb.*: *ill-disposed*). **4** *intr.* determine the course of events (*man proposes, God disposes*). □ **dispose of 1 a** deal with. **b** get rid of. **c** finish. **d** kill. **e** distribute; dispense; bestow. **2** sell. **3** prove (a claim, an argument, an opponent, etc.) to be incorrect. **4** consume (food). □□ **disposer** *n.* [ME f. OF *disposer* (as DIS-, POSE¹) after L *disponere disposit-*]
■ **1** incline, influence, persuade, induce, bend, tempt,

move, motivate, lead, prompt, urge; (*be disposed*) be inclined *or disp.* liable *or* apt, tend, lean, be prone *or* subject *or* given, be willing. **2** place, arrange, adjust, order, array, organize, set up, situate, group, distribute, put. □ **dispose of 1 a, c** deal with, settle, sort out, take care of, attend to, see to, handle, decide, determine, conclude, finish (with), complete. **b** throw away *or* out, discard, get rid of, dump, do away with, jettison, scrap, junk, *colloq.* trash. **d** see KILL¹ *v.* 1a. **e** distribute, give out, deal out, give (away), dispense, apportion, parcel out, allot, part with, transfer, make over, bestow. **2** see SELL *v.* 1. **3** see DISPROVE. **4** consume, devour, eat (up), put away, gobble (up), *joc.* demolish.

disposition /díspəzíshən/ *n.* **1 a** (often foll. by *to*) a natural tendency; an inclination (*a disposition to overeat*). **b** a person's temperament or attitude, esp. as displayed in dealings with others. (*a happy disposition*). **2 a** a setting in order; arranging. **b** the relative position of parts; an arrangement. **3** (usu. in *pl.*) **a** *Mil.* the stationing of troops ready for attack or defense. **b** preparations; plans. **4 a** a bestowal by deed or will. **b** control; the power of disposing. **5** ordinance; dispensation. [ME f. OF f. L *dispositio* (as DIS-, *ponere posit-* place)]
■ **1 a** inclination, tendency; predisposition, susceptibility, partiality, predilection, leaning, preference, proclivity, penchant, bent, propensity. **b** character, temper, attitude, temperament, nature, personality, bent, frame of mind, humor, makeup, spirit. **2 b** arrangement, organization, placement, disposal, grouping. **4 a** bestowal, transfer, transference, dispensation, disposal, assignment, settlement, determination, distribution. **b** determination, choice, disposal, power, command, control, management, discretion, decision, regulation, dispensation.

dispossess /díspəzés/ *v.tr.* **1** dislodge; oust (a person). **2** (usu. foll. by *of*) deprive. □□ **dispossession** /-zéshən/ *n.* [OF *despossesser* (as DIS-, POSSESS)]
■ **1** evict, expel, oust, eject, turn *or* drive out, dislodge, throw *or* push out, kick out, boot out. **2** deny, disallow; see also DIVEST 2.

dispraise /dispráyz/ *v. & n.* ● *v.tr.* express disapproval or censure of. ● *n.* disapproval; censure. [ME f. OF *despreisier* ult. f. LL *depretiare* DEPRECIATE]

disproof /disprṓof/ *n.* **1** something that disproves. **2 a** refutation. **b** an instance of this.

disproportion /dísprəpáwrshən/ *n.* **1** a lack of proportion. **2** an instance of this. □□ **disproportional** *adj.* **disproportionally** *adv.*
■ inequality, unevenness, disparity, imbalance, asymmetry, irregularity, lopsidedness, dissimilarity, inconsistency, incongruity.

disproportionate /dísprəpáwrshənət/ *adj.* **1** lacking proportion. **2** relatively too large or small, long or short, etc. □□ **disproportionately** *adv.* **disproportionateness** *n.*
■ unbalanced, out of proportion, asymmetrical, irregular, lopsided; inconsistent, incommensurate, incongruous; unfair, unequal, uneven.

disprove /disprṓov/ *v.tr.* prove false; refute. □□ **disprovable** *adj.* **disproval** *n.* [ME f. OF *desprover* (as DIS-, PROVE)]
■ refute, confute, invalidate, contradict, negate, rebut, discredit, controvert, puncture, demolish, destroy, disconfirm, shoot down.

disputable /dispyóotəbəl/ *adj.* open to question; uncertain. □□ **disputably** *adv.* [F or f. L *disputabilis* (as DISPUTE)]
■ debatable, moot, doubtful, in doubt, uncertain, dubious, questionable, open to question, undecided, unsettled, unsure, controversial, arguable, unresolved, in the balance, (up) in the air.

disputation /díspyətáyshən/ *n.* **1 a** a disputing; debating. **b** an

---

/.../ **pronunciation**	● **part of speech**
□ **phrases, idioms, and compounds**	
□□ **derivatives**	■ **synonym section**
cross-references appear in SMALL CAPITALS or *italics*	

argument; a controversy. **2** a formal debate. [ME f. F *disputation* or L *disputatio* (as DISPUTE)]
■ **1 b** see CONTROVERSY.

disputatious /díspyətáyshəs/ *adj.* fond of or inclined to argument. □□ **disputatiously** *adv.* **disputatiousness** *n.*
■ see ARGUMENTATIVE 1.

dispute /dispyŏot/ *v. & n.* ● *v.* **1** *intr.* (usu. foll. by *with*, *against*) **a** debate; argue (*was disputing with them about the meaning of life*). **b** quarrel. **2** *tr.* discuss, esp. heatedly (*disputed whether it was true*). **3** *tr.* question the truth or correctness or validity of (a statement, alleged fact, etc.) (*I dispute that number*). **4** *tr.* contend for; strive to win (*disputed the crown; disputed the title*). **5** *tr.* resist (a landing, advance, etc.). ● *n.* **1** a controversy; a debate. **2** a quarrel. **3** a disagreement between management and employees, esp. one leading to industrial action. **4** *archaic* a fight or altercation; a struggle. □ **beyond** (or **past** or **without**) **dispute 1** certainly; indisputably. **2** certain; indisputable. **in dispute 1** being argued about. **2** (of a workforce) involved in industrial action. □□ **disputant** /-spyŏot'nt/ *n.* **disputer** *n.* [ME f. OF *desputer* f. L *disputare* estimate (as DIS-, *putare* reckon)]
■ *v.* **1** see ARGUE 1. **2** argue about, debate, quarrel about, wrangle over; see also DISCUSS. **3** argue with *or* against, question, challenge, impugn, deny, oppose, fight (against), object to, take exception to, disagree with, contest, quarrel with, doubt, raise doubts about, dissent from, *archaic or literary* gainsay. **4** see AIM *v.* 1, 4. ● *n.* **1, 2** argument, debate, disagreement, difference (of opinion), controversy, polemic, conflict, quarrel, wrangle, discussion, *archaic* velitation. **4** conflict, disturbance, fight, altercation, disagreement, brawl, donnybrook, feud, fracas, *colloq.* row, rumpus; strife, discord; tiff, spat, *archaic* velitation. □ **beyond** (or **past** or **without**) **dispute 1** see *undoubtedly* (UNDOUBTED). **2** see UNDISPUTED. **in dispute 1** see UNCERTAIN 1.

disqualification /diskwólifikáyshən/ *n.* **1** the act or an instance of disqualifying; the state of being disqualified. **2** something that disqualifies.

disqualify /diskwólifī/ *v.tr.* (**-ies, -ied**) **1** (often foll. by *from*) debar from a competition or pronounce ineligible as a winner because of an infringement of the rules, etc. (*disqualified from the race for taking drugs*). **2** (often foll. by *for, from*) make or pronounce ineligible or unsuitable (*his age disqualifies him for the job; a criminal record disqualified him from applying*). **3** (often foll. by *from*) incapacitate legally; pronounce unqualified (*disqualified from practicing as a doctor*).
■ declare ineligible *or* unqualified, turn down *or* away, reject, exclude, bar, debar, rule out, outlaw.

disquiet /diskwíət/ *v. & n.* ● *v.tr.* deprive of peace; worry. ● *n.* anxiety; unrest. □□ **disquieting** *adj.* **disquietingly** *adv.*
■ *v.* see PERTURB 1. ● *n.* see ANXIETY 1, 2.

disquietude /diskwíətōod, -tyōod/ *n.* a state of uneasiness; anxiety.
■ see CONCERN *n.* 1a.

disquisition /diskwizíshən/ *n.* a long or elaborate treatise or discourse on a subject. □□ **disquisitional** *adj.* [F f. L *disquisitio* (as DIS-, *quaerere quaesit-* seek)]
■ see LECTURE *n.* 1.

disrate /disráyt/ *v.tr. Naut.* reduce (a sailor) to a lower rating or rank.

disregard /dísrigaárd/ *v. & n.* ● *v.tr.* **1** pay no attention to; ignore. **2** treat as of no importance. **3** *archaic* neglect contemptuously; slight; snub. ● *n.* (often foll. by *of, for*) indifference; neglect. □□ **disregardful** *adj.* **disregardfully** *adv.*
■ *v.* **1** ignore, overlook, pay no heed *or* attention to, take no notice *or* account of, dismiss from one's mind *or* thoughts, turn a blind eye to *or* deaf ear to, brush aside, pass over, wink *or* blink at, let go, gloss over, bury. **2** make light of, underrate, underestimate, undervalue, minimize, dismiss, brush off, write off, shrug off, trivialize. **3** snub, slight, turn up one's nose at, disparage, despise, disdain, scorn, (give the) cold shoulder (to), cut, *literary* contemn; give the go-by. ● *n.* indifference, inattention, nonobservance, neglect,

heedlessness, *formal* pretermission; disrespect, contempt, disdain, low regard, disesteem.

disrelish /disrélish/ *n. & v.* ● *n.* dislike; distaste. ● *v.tr.* regard with dislike or distaste.
■ *n.* see DISTASTE.

disremember /dísrimémbər/ *v.tr. & intr. dial.* fail to remember; forget.

disrepair /dísripáir/ *n.* poor condition due to neglect (*in disrepair; in a state of disrepair*).
■ decay, ruin, collapse, dilapidation, deterioration, ruination.

disreputable /disrépyətəbəl/ *adj.* **1** of bad reputation; discreditable. **2** not respectable in appearance; dirty; untidy. □□ **disreputableness** *n.* **disreputably** *adv.*
■ **1** low, base, abject, unworthy, discreditable, dishonorable, disgraceful, reprehensible, shameful, despicable, ugly, ignominious, bad, raffish, misbegotten, vile, louche, questionable, dubious, shady, seamy. **2** disheveled, unkempt, slovenly, untidy, shabby, disordered, messy, dirty, bedraggled, scruffy, seedy, threadbare, tattered, down at heel, raddled, sloppy, *sl.* grotty.

disrepute /dísripyŏot/ *n.* a lack of good reputation or respectability; discredit (esp. *fall into disrepute*).

disrespect /dísrispékt/ *n.* a lack of respect; discourtesy. □□ **disrespectful** *adj.* **disrespectfully** *adv.*
■ rudeness, impoliteness, discourtesy, incivility, unmannerliness, indecorum; irreverence, impudence, insolence, cheek; see also *impertinence* (IMPERTINENT). □□ **disrespectful** impolite, rude, discourteous, uncivil, unmannerly, ill-mannered, bad-mannered, irreverent, impudent, insolent, indecorous, pert, saucy, forward, cheeky, *colloq.* fresh; see also IMPERTINENT 1.

disrobe /disrōb/ *v.tr. & refl.* (also *absol.*) **1** divest (oneself or another) of a robe or a garment; undress. **2** divest (oneself or another) of office, authority, etc.
■ **1** undress, bare oneself; see also STRIP[1] *v.* 1, 2.

disrupt /disrúpt/ *v.tr.* **1** interrupt the flow or continuity of (a meeting, speech, etc.); bring disorder to. **2** separate forcibly; shatter. □□ **disrupter** *n.* (also **disruptor**). **disruption** /-rúpshən/ *n.* **disruptive** *adj.* **disruptively** *adv.* **disruptiveness** *n.* [L *disrumpere disrupt-* (as DIS-, *rumpere* break)]
■ **1** disorder, upset, disorganize, disturb, unsettle, shake up, disconcert, agitate; interrupt, break in on, break into, interfere with, butt in on, cut in on, intrude on. **2** see SEVER 2, SHATTER 1, 2. □□ **disruptive** see UNRULY.

diss /dis/ *v.tr. sl.* put down (a person) verbally; bad-mouth. [shortened f. DISRESPECT]

dissatisfy /disátisfī/ *v.tr.* (**-ies, -ied**) (often as **dissatisfied** *adj.*) make discontented; fail to satisfy (*dissatisfied with the accommodation; dissatisfied to find him gone*). □□ **dissatisfaction** /-fákshən/ *n.* **dissatisfactory** /-fáktəree/ *adj.* **dissatisfiedly** *adv.*
■ see DISPLEASE; (**dissatisfied**) discontent(ed), displeased, unsatisfied, discontent, disgruntled, unhappy, frustrated. □□ **dissatisfaction** discontent, discontentment, unhappiness, displeasure, nonfulfillment, disappointment, frustration, discomfort, uneasiness, disquiet, malaise; annoyance, irritation.

dissect /disékt, dī-/ *v.tr.* **1** cut into pieces. **2** cut up (a plant or animal) to examine its parts, structure, etc., or (a corpse) for a post mortem. **3** analyze; criticize or examine in detail. □□ **dissection** /-sékshən/ *n.* **dissector** *n.* [L *dissecare dissect-* (as DIS-, *secare* cut)]
■ see ANALYZE 1, 2b, 3.

dissemble /disémbəl/ *v.* **1** *intr.* conceal one's motives; talk or act hypocritically. **2** *tr.* **a** disguise or conceal (a feeling, intention, act, etc.). **b** simulate (*dissembled grief in public*). □□ **dissemblance** *n.* **dissembler** *n.* **dissemblingly** *adv.* [ME, alt. after *semblance* of obs. *dissimule* f. OF *dissimuler* f. L *dissimulare* (as DIS-, SIMULATE)]
■ see DISSIMULATE.

disseminate /diséminayt/ *v.tr.* scatter about; spread (esp. ideas) widely. □ **disseminated sclerosis** = SCLEROSIS 2.

□□ **dissemination** /-náyshən/ *n.* **disseminator** *n.* [L *disseminare* (as DIS-, *semen -inis* seed)]
■ see SPREAD *v.* 3.

dissension /disénshən/ *n.* disagreement giving rise to discord. [ME f. OF f. L *dissensio* (as DIS-, *sentire sens-* feel)]
■ disagreement, dissent, discord, contention, strife, conflict, discordance, friction, opposition, disaccord, discordancy.

dissent /disént/ *v. & n.* ● *v.intr.* (often foll. by *from*) **1** think differently; disagree; express disagreement. **2** differ in religious opinion, esp. from the doctrine of an established or orthodox church. ● *n.* **1 a** a difference of opinion. **b** an expression of this. **2** the refusal to accept the doctrines of an established or orthodox church; nonconformity. □□ **dissenting** *adj.* **dissentingly** *adv.* [ME f. L *dissentire* (as DIS-, *sentire* feel)]
■ *v.* **1** see DIFFER 2. ● *n.* **1** see DISSENSION.

dissenter /diséntər/ *n.* **1** a person who dissents. **2** (**Dissenter**) *Brit.* a member of a nonestablished church; a Nonconformist.
■ **1** see NONCONFORMIST.

dissentient /disénshənt/ *adj. & n.* ● *adj.* disagreeing with a majority or official view. ● *n.* a person who dissents. [L *dissentire* (as DIS-, *sentire* feel)]

dissertation /dísərtáyshən/ *n.* a detailed discourse on a subject, esp. one submitted in partial fulfillment of the requirements of a degree or diploma. □□ **dissertational** *adj.* [L *dissertatio* f. *dissertare* discuss, frequent. of *disserere dissert-* examine (as DIS-, *serere* join)]
■ see ESSAY *n.* 1.

disservice /dis-sə́rvis/ *n.* an ill turn; an injury, esp. done when trying to help. □□ **disserve** *v.tr. archaic.*
■ injury, wrong, unkindness, bad turn, disfavor, injustice; harm, damage. □□ **disserve** see HARM *v.*

dissever /disévər/ *v.tr. & intr.* sever; divide into parts. □□ **disseverance** *n.* **disseverment** *n.* [ME f. AF *dis(c)everer*, OF *dessevrer* f. LL *disseparare* (as DIS-, SEPARATE)]
■ see SEVER 1.

dissidence /dísid'ns/ *n.* disagreement; dissent. [F *dissidence* or L *dissidentia* (as DISSIDENT)]

dissident /dísid'nt/ *adj. & n.* ● *adj.* disagreeing, esp. with an established government, system, etc. ● *n.* a dissident person. [F or f. L *dissidēre* disagree (as DIS-, *sedēre* sit)]
■ *adj.* disagreeing, nonconformist, dissenting, dissentient, discordant, conflicting, heterodox, unorthodox; see also REBELLIOUS 1. ● *n.* dissenter, nonconformist, dissentient, protester, heretic, rebel, apostate, recusant; revolutionary, insurgent.

dissimilar /disímilər/ *adj.* (often foll. by *to*) unlike; not similar. □□ **dissimilarity** /-láritee/ *n.* (*pl.* -ies). **dissimilarly** *adv.*
■ different, unlike, unalike, distinct, separate, contrasting, diverse, unrelated, differing. □□ **dissimilarity** difference, dissimilitude, unlikeness, disparity, distinction, contrast; discrepancy.

dissimilate /disímilayt/ *v.* (often foll. by *to*) *Phonet.* **1** *tr.* change (a sound or sounds in a word) to another when the word originally had the same sound repeated, as in *cinnamon*, orig. *cinnamom*. **2** *intr.* (of a sound) be changed in this way. □□ **dissimilation** /-láyshən/ *n.* **dissimilatory** /-lətáwree/ *adj.* [L *dissimilis* (as DIS-, *similis* like), after *assimilate*]

dissimilitude /dísimílitōod, tyōod/ *n.* unlikeness; dissimilarity. [L *dissimilitudo* (as DISSIMILATE)]

dissimulate /disímyəlayt/ *v.tr. & intr.* dissemble. □□ **dissimulation** /-láyshən/ *n.* **dissimulator** *n.* [L *dissimulare* (as DIS-, SIMULATE)]
■ dissemble, feign, disguise, camouflage, cover up, conceal, misrepresent, fake, counterfeit; pretend, deceive. □□ **dissimulation** deception, misrepresentation, dissembling, deceit, hypocrisy, pretense, duplicity, double-dealing.

dissipate /dísipayt/ *v.* **1 a** *tr.* cause (a cloud, vapor, fear, darkness, etc.) to disappear or disperse. **b** *intr.* disperse; scatter; disappear. **2** *intr. & tr.* break up; bring or come to nothing. **3** *tr.* squander or fritter away (money, energy, etc.).

4 *intr.* (as **dissipated** *adj.*) given to dissipation; dissolute. □□ **dissipater** *n.* **dissipative** *adj.* **dissipator** *n.* [L *dissipare dissipat-* (as DIS-, *sipare* (unrecorded) throw)]
■ **1 a** scatter, disperse, spread, dispel, break up, dissolve; shed. **b** scatter, spread out, disperse, be dispelled, diffuse, break up, move apart, separate; evaporate, vanish, disappear, vaporize, clear, go, dissolve, lift. **3** squander, waste, fritter away, throw away, burn up, use up, exhaust, run *or* go through. **4** (**dissipated**) see DISSOLUTE.

dissipation /dísipáyshən/ *n.* **1** intemperate, dissolute, or debauched living. **2** (usu. foll. by *of*) wasteful expenditure (*dissipation of resources*). **3** scattering, dispersion, or disintegration. **4** a frivolous amusement. [F *dissipation* or L *dissipatio* (as DISSIPATE)]
■ **1** intemperance, dissoluteness, dissolution, abandon, abandonment, self-indulgence, self-gratification, overindulgence, hedonism, *dolce vita*, excess(es), wantonness, debauchery, carousing, rakishness, voluptuousness, sensualism, sybaritism. **2** waste, wastefulness, profligacy, recklessness, extravagance, prodigality. **3** disappearance, dispersion, dispersal, diffusion, scattering, vanishing, disintegration, evaporation. **4** distraction, amusement; see also DIVERSION 3.

dissociate /disṓsheeayt, -seeayt/ *v.* **1** *tr. & intr.* (usu. foll. by *from*) disconnect or become disconnected; separate (*dissociated her from their guilt*). **2** *tr. Chem.* decompose, esp. reversibly. **3** *tr. Psychol.* cause (a person's mind) to develop more than one center of consciousness. □ **dissociated personality** *Psychol.* the pathological coexistence of two or more distinct personalities in the same person. **dissociate oneself from 1** declare oneself unconnected with. **2** decline to support or agree with (a proposal, etc.). □□ **dissociative** /-sheeətiv, -seeətiv/ *adj.* [L *dissociare* (as DIS-, *socius* companion)]
■ **1** separate, cut off, sever, disassociate, disjoin, disconnect, abstract, disengage, detach, isolate, distance, break off *or* away, divorce, set apart, segregate.

dissociation /disṓseeáyshən, -shee-/ *n.* **1** the act or an instance of dissociating. **2** *Psychol.* the state of suffering from dissociated personality.
■ **1** see SEPARATION.

dissoluble /disólyəbəl/ *adj.* able to be disintegrated, loosened, or disconnected; soluble. □□ **dissolubility** *n.* **dissolubly** *adv.* [F *dissoluble* or L *dissolubilis* (as DIS-, SOLUBLE)]

dissolute /dísəlōōt/ *adj.* lax in morals; licentious. □□ **dissolutely** *adv.* **dissoluteness** *n.* [ME f. L *dissolutus* past part. of *dissolvere* DISSOLVE]
■ dissipated, debauched, abandoned, corrupt, degenerate, rakish, profligate, wanton, intemperate, incontinent, loose, lax, licentious, overindulgent, self-indulgent, hedonistic, amoral, libidinous, unrestrained, depraved; see also IMMORAL 3.

dissolution /dísəlōōshən/ *n.* **1** disintegration; decomposition. **2** (usu. foll. by *of*) the undoing or relaxing of a bond, esp.: **a** a marriage. **b** a partnership. **c** an alliance. **3** the dismissal or dispersal of an assembly, esp. of a parliament at the end of its term. **4** death. **5** bringing or coming to an end; fading away; disappearance. **6** dissipation; debauchery. [ME f. OF *dissolution* or L *dissolutio* (as DISSOLVE)]
■ **1** disintegration, separation, breakup, breakdown, collapse, discontinuation; decomposition, decay, destruction, ruin. **2** annulment, nullification, rescission, cancellation, rescindment, repeal, repudiation, abrogation, reversal, revocation, disavowal, retraction; divorce. **3** dismissal, dispersal, adjournment, dissolving, disbandment. **4** see DEATH 4a. **5** ending, end,

---

/.../ **pronunciation**	● **part of speech**
□ **phrases, idioms, and compounds**	
□□ **derivatives**	■ **synonym section**
cross-references appear in SMALL CAPITALS or *italics*	

termination, conclusion, finish; recess, cessation; see also DISSIPATION 3. **6** see DISSIPATION 1.

dissolve /dizólv/ *v. & n.* ● *v.* **1** *tr. & intr.* make or become liquid, esp. by immersion or dispersion in a liquid. **2** *intr. & tr.* disappear or cause to disappear gradually. **3 a** *tr.* dismiss or disperse (an assembly, esp. parliament). **b** *intr.* (of an assembly) be dissolved (cf. DISSOLUTION 3). **4** *tr.* annul or put an end to (a partnership, marriage, etc.). **5** *intr.* (of a person) become enfeebled or emotionally overcome (*completely dissolved when he saw her*; *dissolved into tears*). **6** *intr.* (often foll. by *into*) *Cinematog.* change gradually (from one picture into another). ● *n. Cinematog.* the act or process of dissolving a picture. □□ **dissolvable** *adj.* [ME f. L *dissolvere dissolut-* (as DIS-, *solvere* loosen)]

■ *v.* **1** melt, liquefy, disperse, disintegrate, diffuse, decompose, deliquesce. **2** vanish, disappear, fade (away), diminish, decline, peter out; see also ERODE. **3 a** break up, disperse, dismiss, adjourn, disband, wind up, recess; terminate, finish, conclude. **b** adjourn, break up, disperse, disband, recess. **4** see CANCEL *v.* 4. **5** be overcome, collapse, break down; (*dissolve into*) break (down) into, melt into. **6** see MERGE.

dissolvent /dizólvənt/ *adj. & n.* ● *adj.* tending to dissolve or dissipate. ● *n.* a dissolvent substance. [L *dissolvere* (as DISSOLVE)]

dissonant /dísənənt/ *adj.* **1** *Mus.* harsh-toned; inharmonious. **2** incongruous; clashing. □□ **dissonance** /-nəns/ *n.* **dissonantly** *adv.* [ME f. OF *dissonant* or L *dissonare* (as DIS-, *sonare* sound)]

■ see INCONGRUOUS.

dissuade /diswáyd/ *v.tr.* (often foll. by *from*) discourage (a person); persuade against (*dissuaded her from continuing*; *was dissuaded from his belief*). □□ **dissuader** *n.* **dissuasion** /-swáyzhən/ *n.* **dissuasive** *adj.* [L *dissuadēre* (as DIS-, *suadēre suas-* persuade)]

■ see DISCOURAGE 2.

dissyllable var. of DISYLLABLE.

dissymmetry /dis-símitree/ *n.* (*pl.* **-ies**) **1 a** lack of symmetry. **b** an instance of this. **2** symmetry as of mirror images or the left and right hands (esp. of crystals with two corresponding forms). □□ **dissymmetrical** /dís-simétrikəl/ *adj.*

distaff /dístaf/ *n.* **1 a** a cleft stick holding wool or flax wound for spinning by hand. **b** the corresponding part of a spinning wheel. **2** *archaic* women's work. □ **distaff side** the female branch of a family. [OE *distæf* (as STAFF[1]), the first element being app. rel. to LG *diesse*, MLG *dise(ne)* bunch of flax]

distal /díst'l/ *adj. Anat.* situated away from the center of the body or point of attachment; terminal. □□ **distally** *adv.* [DISTANT + -AL]

distance /dístəns/ *n. & v.* ● *n.* **1** the condition of being far off; remoteness. **2 a** a space or interval between two things. **b** the length of this (*a distance of twenty miles*). **3** a distant point or place (*came from a distance*). **4** the avoidance of familiarity; aloofness; reserve (*there was a certain distance between them*). **5** a remoter field of vision (*saw him in the distance*). **6** an interval of time (*can't remember what happened at this distance*). **7 a** the full length of a race, etc. **b** *Brit. Racing* a length of 240 yards from the winning post on a racecourse. **c** *Boxing* the scheduled length of a fight. ● *v.tr.* (often *refl.*) **1** place far off (*distanced herself from them*; *distanced the painful memory*). **2** leave far behind in a race or competition. □ **at a distance** far off. **distance post** *Racing* a post at the distance on a racecourse, used to disqualify runners who have not reached it by the end of the race. **distance runner** an athlete who competes in long- or middle-distance races. **go the distance 1** *Boxing* complete a fight without being knocked out. **2** complete, esp. a hard task; endure an ordeal. **keep one's distance** maintain one's reserve. **middle distance** the part of a landscape or painting between the foreground and the furthest part. **within walking distance** near enough to reach by walking. [ME f. OF *distance*, *destance* f. L *distantia* f. *distare* stand apart (as DI-[2], *stare* stand)]

■ *n.* **2** space, gap, interval, mileage, footage, stretch. **4** aloofness, detachment, reserve, coolness, guardedness,

reticence, remoteness; haughtiness, hauteur, stiffness, rigidity, coldness, standoffishness. ● *v.* **1** separate, detach, dissociate, disassociate, set apart. □ **at a distance** see DISTANT 1a. **go the distance 2** get there, make it, bring it off; see also ENDURE 3. **within walking distance** see NEARBY *adv.*

distant /dístənt/ *adj.* **1 a** far away in space or time. **b** (usu. *predic.*; often foll. by *from*) at a specified distance (*three miles distant from them*). **2** remote or far apart in position, time, resemblance, etc. (*a distant prospect*; *a distant relation*; *a distant likeness*). **3** not intimate; reserved; cool (*a distant nod*). **4** remote; abstracted (*a distant stare*). **5** faint; vague (*he was a distant memory to her*). □ **distant early warning** a radar system for the early detection of a missile attack. **distant signal** *Railroads* a railroad signal preceding a home signal to give warning. □□ **distantly** *adv.* [ME f. OF *distant* or L *distant-* part. stem of *distare*: see DISTANCE]

■ **1 a** far, far-off, remote, faraway, far-removed, outlying, far-flung. **b** away, off. **3** aloof, detached, reserved, cool, cold, haughty, standoffish, unapproachable, inaccessible, withdrawn, reticent, ceremonious, formal, stiff, rigid, frigid, unfriendly. **4** remote, abstracted, distracted, absent, faraway, detached, distrait. **5** see VAGUE 1.

distaste /distáyst/ *n.* (usu. foll. by *for*) dislike; repugnance; aversion, esp. slight (*a distaste for prunes*; *a distaste for polite company*). □□ **distasteful** *adj.* **distastefully** *adv.* **distastefulness** *n.*

■ dislike, disfavor, antipathy, aversion, disrelish, disinclination; dissatisfaction, displeasure, discontent(ment). □□ **distasteful** nasty, disagreeable, off-putting, unpalatable, obnoxious, objectionable, offensive, unpleasing, unpleasant, displeasing; disgusting, revolting, nauseating, nauseous, *Brit. colloq.* sick-making.

dist. atty. *abbr.* district attorney.

distemper[1] /distémpər/ *n. & v.* ● *n.* **1** a kind of paint using glue or size instead of an oil base, for use on walls or for scene painting. **2** a method of mural and poster painting using this. ● *v.tr.* paint (walls, etc.) with distemper. [earlier as verb, f. OF *destremper* or LL *distemperare* soak, macerate: see DISTEMPER[2]]

distemper[2] /distémpər/ *n.* **1** a disease of some animals, esp. dogs, causing fever, coughing, and catarrh. **2** *archaic* political disorder. [earlier as verb, = upset, derange: ME f. LL *distemperare* (as DIS-, *temperare* mingle correctly)]

distend /disténd/ *v.tr. & intr.* swell out by pressure from within (*distended stomach*). □□ **distensible** /-sténsibəl/ *adj.* **distensibility** /-sténsibílitee/ *n.* **distension** /-sténshən/ *n.* [ME f. L *distendere* (as DIS-, *tendere tens-* stretch)]

■ see SWELL *v.* 3, INFLATE 1, 2.

distich /dístik/ *n. Prosody* a pair of verse lines; a couplet. [L *distichon* f. Gk *distikhon* (as DI-[1], *stikhos* line)]

distichous /dístikəs/ *adj. Bot.* arranged in two opposite vertical rows. [L *distichus* (as DISTICH)]

distill /distíl/ *v.* (*Brit.* **distil**) (**distilled, distilling**) **1** *tr. Chem.* purify (a liquid) by vaporizing it with heat, then condensing it with cold and collecting the result. **2** *tr. a Chem.* extract the essence of (a plant, etc.) usu. by heating it in a solvent. **b** extract the essential meaning or implications of (an idea, etc.). **3** *tr.* make (whiskey, essence, etc.) by distilling raw materials. **4** *tr.* (foll. by *off*, *out*) *Chem.* drive (the volatile constituent) off or out by heat. **5** *tr. & intr.* come as or give forth in drops; exude. **6** *intr.* undergo distillation. □□ **distillatory** *adj.* [ME f. L *distillare* f. *destillare* (as DE-, *stilla* drop)]

■ **2 b** see EXTRACT *v.* 8.

distillate /dístilit, -áyt/ *n.* a product of distillation.

■ see EXTRACT *n.* 2.

distillation /dístiláyshən/ *n.* **1** the process of distilling or being distilled (in various senses). **2** something distilled.

■ **1** see REFINEMENT 1. **2** see EXTRACT *n.* 2.

distiller /dístilər/ *n.* a person who distills, esp. a manufacturer of alcoholic liquor.

416

distillery /distíləree/ n. (pl. -ies) a place where alcoholic liquor is distilled.

distinct /distíngkt/ adj. **1** (often foll. by from) **a** not identical; separate; individual. **b** different in kind or quality; unlike. **2 a** clearly perceptible; plain. **b** clearly understandable; definite. **3** unmistakable, decided (had a distinct impression of being watched). □□ **distinctly** adv. **distinctness** n. [ME f. L distinctus past part. of distinguere DISTINGUISH]
■ **1 a** separate, discrete, different, distinguishable, individual, sui generis, unique, special, singular. **b** dissimilar, different, unlike, unalike, contrastive, contrasting. **2** clear, perceptible, plain, vivid, sharp, definite, well-defined, marked, noticeable, recognizable, obvious, precise, exact; understandable, manifest, evident, apparent, explicit, unambiguous, patent, clear-cut, palpable, unequivocal, lucid, pellucid, limpid, transparent. **3** unmistakable, decided; see also DEFINITE 2.

distinction /distíngkshən/ n. **1 a** the act or an instance of discriminating or distinguishing. **b** an instance of this. **c** the difference made by distinguishing. **2 a** something that differentiates, e.g., a mark, name, or title. **b** the fact of being different. **3** special consideration or honor. **4** distinguished character; excellence; eminence (a film of distinction; shows distinction in his bearing). **5** a grade in an examination denoting great excellence (passed with distinction). □ **distinction without a difference** a merely nominal or artificial distinction. [ME f. OF f. L distinctio -onis (as DISTINGUISH)]
■ **1 a** differentiation, discrimination, separation, division. **c** see CONTRAST n. **2 b** distinctiveness, distinctness, difference, differentness; uniqueness, individuality. **3** see HONOR n. 1, PRESTIGE. **4** honor, credit, prominence, eminence, preeminence, superiority, greatness, excellence, quality, merit, worth, value, prestige, note, importance, significance, consequence, renown, fame, repute, reputation, celebrity, glory, account.

distinctive /distíngktiv/ adj. distinguishing; characteristic. □□ **distinctively** adv. **distinctiveness** n.
■ distinguishing, characteristic, unique, singular, distinct, individual, personal, typical, idiosyncratic, peculiar.

distingué /dístanggáy, deestaNGáy/ adj. (fem. **distinguée** pronunc. same) having a distinguished air, features, manner, etc. [F, past part. of distinguer: see DISTINGUISH]
■ see DISTINGUISHED 2.

distinguish /distínggwish/ v. **1** tr. (often foll. by from) **a** see or point out the difference of; draw distinctions between (cannot distinguish one from the other). **b** constitute such a difference (the mole distinguishes him from his twin). **c** draw distinctions between; differentiate. **2** tr. be a mark or property of; characterize (distinguished by her greed). **3** tr. discover by listening, looking, etc. (could distinguish two voices). **4** tr. (usu. refl.; often foll. by by) make prominent or noteworthy (distinguished himself by winning first prize). **5** tr. (often foll. by into) divide; classify. **6** intr. (foll. by between) make or point out a difference between. □□ **distinguishable** adj. [F distinguer or L distinguere (as DIS-, stinguere stinct- extinguish): cf. EXTINGUISH]
■ **1** differentiate, tell apart, separate; set apart, single out. **2** characterize, individualize, individuate, particularize, mark (out), identify, indicate; define, designate, denote. **3** sense, make out, perceive, discern, pick out, recognize, identify, detect, notice, literary descry; see, literary espy; hear. **4** (distinguish oneself) see stand out 1. **5** classify, categorize, grade, group, separate, segregate; see also DIVIDE v. 3c. **6** differentiate, discriminate, draw a distinction, tell the difference, judge, decide, tell who's who or what's what.

distinguished /distínggwisht/ adj. **1** (often foll. by for, by) of high standing; eminent; famous. **2** = DISTINGUÉ. □ **Distinguished Flying Cross** a US military decoration for heroism or extraordinary achievement in aerial flight. **Distinguished Service Cross** a US Army decoration for extraordinary heroism in combat. **Distinguished Service Medal** a US military decoration for exceptionally meritorious service in a duty of great responsibility.

■ **1** celebrated, famous, illustrious, noted, renowned, notable, noteworthy, preeminent, eminent, prominent, honored, respected, honorable. **2** dignified, noble, grand, stately, distingué, royal, regal, aristocratic.

distort /distáwrt/ v.tr. **1 a** put out of shape; make crooked or unshapely. **b** distort the appearance of, esp. by curved mirrors, etc. **2** misrepresent (motives, facts, statements, etc.). □□ **distortedly** adv. **distortedness** n. [L distorquēre distort- (as DIS-, torquēre twist)]
■ **1 a** twist, warp, deform, misshape, contort, gnarl, bend, disfigure; alter, change. **2** misrepresent, twist, warp, slant, tamper with, color, torture, pervert, falsify, misstate, bend.

distortion /distáwrshən/ n. **1** the act or an instance of distorting; the process of being distorted. **2** Electronics a change in the form of a signal during transmission, etc., usu. with some impairment of quality. □□ **distortional** adj. **distortionless** adj. [L distortio (as DISTORT)]
■ see TWIST n. 6c, GLOSS² n. 2.

distr. abbr. **1** distribution. **2** distributor. **3** district.

distract /distrákt/ v.tr. **1** (often foll. by from) draw away the attention of (a person, the mind, etc.). **2** bewilder; perplex. **3** (as **distracted** adj.) troubled or distraught (distracted by grief; distracted with worry). **4** amuse, esp. in order to take the attention from pain or worry. □□ **distractedly** adv. [ME f. L distrahere distract- (as DIS-, trahere draw)]
■ **1** divert, deflect, sidetrack, turn aside, draw away; (be distracted) lose concentration, daydream, be miles away, be in a world of one's own, be preoccupied. **2** bewilder, confuse, confound, perplex, puzzle, discompose, befuddle, mystify, disconcert, fluster, rattle, bemuse, daze. **3** (distracted) see DISTRAUGHT. **4** divert, amuse, entertain, occupy, interest.

distraction /distrákshən/ n. **1 a** the act of distracting, esp. the mind. **b** something that distracts; an interruption. **2** a relaxation from work; an amusement. **3** a lack of concentration. **4** confusion; perplexity. **5** frenzy; madness. □ **to distraction** almost to a state of madness. [ME f. OF distraction or L distractio (as DISTRACT)]
■ **1 b** see interruption (INTERRUPT). **2** diversion, entertainment, amusement, pastime, recreation, divertissement; relaxation, break, colloq. breather. **3** see absentmindedness (ABSENTMINDED). **4** confusion, perplexity, bewilderment, befuddlement, puzzlement, mystification, bemusement; disorder, disturbance, upset, confusion, agitation, discomposure. **5** see madness (MAD), FRENZY n. 1.

distrain /distráyn/ v.intr. Law (usu. foll. by upon) impose distraint (on a person, goods, etc.). □□ **distrainee** /-neé/ n. **distrainer** n. **distrainment** n. **distrainor** n. [ME f. OF destreindre f. L distringere (as DIS-, stringere strict- draw tight)]

distraint /distráynt/ n. Law the seizure of chattels to make a person pay rent, etc., or meet an obligation, or to obtain satisfaction by their sale. [DISTRAIN, after constraint]

distrait /distráy/ adj. (fem. **distraite** /-stráyt/) not paying attention; absentminded; distraught. [ME f. OF destrait past part. of destraire (as DISTRACT)]
■ see ABSENTMINDED.

distraught /distráwt/ adj. distracted with worry, fear, etc.; extremely agitated. [ME, alt. of obs. distract (adj.) (as DISTRACT), after straught obs. past part. of STRETCH]
■ distracted, agitated, troubled, disturbed, beside oneself, upset, perturbed, worked up, excited, frantic, at one's wit's end, overwrought, frenetic, nervous, frenzied, feverish, wild, hysterical, delirious, irrational; mad, insane, berserk.

distress /distrés/ n. & v. ● n. **1** severe pain, sorrow, anguish, etc. **2** the lack of money or comforts. **3** Law = DISTRAINT. **4** breathlessness; exhaustion. ● v.tr. **1** subject to distress; ex-

/.../ **pronunciation** ● **part of speech**
□ **phrases, idioms, and compounds**
□□ **derivatives** ■ **synonym section**
cross-references appear in SMALL CAPITALS or italics

417

haust; afflict. **2** cause anxiety to; make unhappy; vex. □ **distress signal** a signal from a ship, aircraft, etc., in danger. **in distress 1** suffering or in danger. **2** (of a ship, aircraft, etc.) in danger or damaged. □□ **distressful** adj. **distressingly** adv. [ME f. OF destresse, etc., AF destresser, OF -ecier f. Gallo-Roman (as DISTRAIN)]

■ n. **1** anguish, anxiety, affliction, angst, grief, misery, torment, ache, pain, suffering, agony, torture, woefulness, wretchedness, archaic or literary woe; unhappiness, sorrow, sadness, depression, heartache, desolation. **2** misfortune, difficulty, trouble, hardship, adversity, straits. **4** see EXHAUSTION n. 2. ● v. bother, disturb, perturb, upset, trouble, worry, harrow, harry, vex, harass, plague, oppress, grieve, torment, torture, afflict; see also TIRE[1] 1. □ **in distress** in jeopardy, in danger, in trouble; see also in pain (PAIN).

distressed /distrést/ adj. **1** suffering from distress. **2** impoverished (in distressed circumstances). **3** (of furniture, leather, etc.) having simulated marks of age and wear. □ **distressed area 1** a region needful of food, shelter, government aid, etc., due to the devastation of flood, earthquake, hurricane, etc. **2** Brit. = depressed area (see DEPRESS)

■ **1** see WORRY v. 4. **2** see STRAITEN v. 2.

distributary /distríbyəteree/ n. (pl. **-ies**) a branch of a river or glacier that does not return to the main stream after leaving it (as in a delta).

distribute /distríbyoot/ v.tr. **1** give shares of; deal out. **2** spread about; scatter (distributed the seeds evenly over the garden). **3** divide into parts; arrange; classify. **4** Printing separate (type that has been set up) and return the characters to their separate boxes. **5** Logic use (a term) to include every individual of the class to which it refers. □□ **distributable** adj. [ME f. L distribuere distribut- (as DIS-, tribuere assign)]

■ **1** deal or dole out, parcel out, give (out), dispense, apportion, allot, share (out), partition, divide up, assign, issue, pass out, pass around, hand out, deliver, convey, literary mete out, sl. dish out. **2** disperse, scatter, strew, spread (about), diffuse, disseminate. **3** sort, classify, class, categorize, assort, arrange, group, file, order; see also DIVIDE v. 3c.

distribution /distribyóoshən/ n. **1** the act or an instance of distributing; the process of being distributed. **2** Econ. **a** the dispersal of goods, etc., among consumers, brought about by commerce. **b** the extent to which different groups, classes, or individuals share in the total production or wealth of a community. **3** Statistics the way in which a characteristic is spread over members of a class. □□ **distributional** adj. [ME f. OF distribution or L distributio (as DISTRIBUTE)]

■ **1, 2a** apportionment, allotment, allocation, assignment, sharing; issuance, dissemination, giving (out), dispersal, dispensation; deployment. **3** arrangement, disposition, grouping, ordering.

distributive /distríbyətiv/ adj. & n. ● adj. **1** of, concerned with, or produced by distribution. **2** Logic & Gram. (of a pronoun, etc.) referring to each individual of a class, not to the class collectively (e.g., each, either). ● n. Gram. a distributive word. □□ **distributively** adv. [ME f. F distributif -ive or LL distributivus (as DISTRIBUTE)]

distributor /distríbyətər/ n. **1** a person or thing that distributes. **2** an agent who supplies goods. **3** Electr. a device in an internal combustion engine for passing current to each spark plug in turn.

■ **2** see DEALER.

district /distrikt/ n. & v. ● n. **1 a** (often attrib.) a territory marked off for special administrative purposes. **b** Brit. an administrative division of a county or region. **2** an area which has common characteristics; a region (the wine-growing district). ● v.tr. divide into districts. □ **district attorney** the prosecuting officer of a district. **district court 1** (in several US states) the court of general jurisdiction. **2** the federal trial court in each federal judicial district. **district heating** a supply of heat or hot water from one source to a district or a group of buildings. [F f. med.L districtus (territory of) jurisdiction (as DISTRAIN)]

■ n. territory, region, locality, area, locale; section, sector,

part, precinct, department, province, community, quarter, neighborhood, ward.

distrust /distrúst/ n. & v. ● n. a lack of trust; doubt; suspicion. ● v.tr. have no trust or confidence in; doubt. □□ **distruster** n. **distrustful** adj. **distrustfully** adv.

■ n. mistrust, doubt, doubtfulness, uncertainty, misgiving(s), skepticism, suspicion, disbelief, incredulity, incredulousness. ● v. mistrust, doubt, question, be skeptical of, suspect, be suspicious or wary of, discredit, disbelieve, take with a pinch or grain of salt. □□ **distrustful** distrusting, untrusting, mistrustful, incredulous, doubting, suspicious, skeptical, doubtful, dubious, cynical, disbelieving, unbelieving, questioning.

disturb /distɔ́rb/ v.tr. **1** break the rest, calm, or quiet of; interrupt. **2 a** agitate; worry (your story disturbs me). **b** irritate. **3** move from a settled position; disarrange (the papers had been disturbed). **4** (as **disturbed** adj.) Psychol. emotionally or mentally unstable or abnormal. □□ **disturber** n. **disturbing** adj. **disturbingly** adv. [ME f. OF desto(u)rber f. L disturbare (as DIS-, turbare f. turba tumult)]

■ **1** agitate, stir or churn (up), shake (up), unsettle, upset, ruffle; interrupt, disrupt, intrude on, interfere with; inconvenience, discommode, put out. **2 a** agitate, worry, trouble, disconcert, discomfit, perturb, ruffle, fluster, upset, put off, bother, concern, put out, unsettle, distress, alarm, shake (up). **b** annoy, irritate, irk, bother, pester, plague, hector, harry, harass, provoke, pique, get on a person's nerves, colloq. hassle, peeve, get under a person's skin, get in a person's hair, drive a person crazy or up the wall, sl. drive a person nuts or bats or batty or bananas, bug. **3** disorder, upset, disarrange, confuse, change, move. **4** (**disturbed**) unstable, psychoneurotic, neurotic, unbalanced, maladjusted. □□ **disturbing** upsetting, off-putting, perturbing, troubling, unsettling, worrying, disconcerting, disquieting, alarming, distressing.

disturbance /distɔ́rbəns/ n. **1** the act or an instance of disturbing; the process of being disturbed. **2** a tumult; an uproar. **3** agitation; worry. **4** an interruption. **5** Law interference with rights or property; molestation. [ME f. OF desto(u)rbance (as DISTURB)]

■ **1, 4** disruption, upset, disorder, disorganization, disarrangement, disarray, confusion; upheaval, interruption, intrusion, interference; turmoil, turbulence, trouble, agitation. **2** commotion, disorder, upset, outburst, tumult, hubbub, hullabaloo, hurlyburly, uproar, brouhaha, brawl, melee, breach of the peace, donnybrook, fray, affray, fracas, ruckus, colloq. row, rumpus. **3** see ANXIETY 1, 2.

disulfide /dīsúlfīd/ n. (esp. Brit. **disulphide**) Chem. a binary chemical containing two atoms of sulfur in each molecule.

disunion /disyóonyən/ n. a lack of union; separation; dissension. □□ **disunite** /dísyóonít/ v.tr. & intr. **disunity** n.

■ see DIVISION n. 3.

disuse n. & v. ● n. /disyóos/ **1** lack of use or practice; discontinuance. **2** a disused state. ● v.tr. /disyóoz/ (esp. as **disused** adj.) cease to use. □ **fall into disuse** cease to be used. [ME f. OF desuser (as DIS-, USE)]

■ v. (**disused**) neglected, unused; see also ABANDONED 1b.

disutility /dísyootílitee/ n. (pl. **-ies**) **1** harmfulness; injuriousness. **2** a factor tending to nullify the utility of something; a drawback.

disyllable /dísiləbəl, di-/ n. (also **dissyllable**) Prosody a word or metrical foot of two syllables. □□ **disyllabic** /-lábik/ adj. [F disyllabe f. L disyllabus f. Gk disullabos (as DI-[1], SYLLABLE)]

dit /dit/ n. Telegraphy (in the Morse system) = DOT (cf. DAH). [imit.]

ditch /dich/ n. & v. ● n. **1** a long, narrow excavated channel esp. for drainage or to mark a boundary. **2** a watercourse, stream, etc. ● v. **1** intr. make or repair ditches. **2** tr. provide with ditches; drain. **3** tr. sl. leave in the lurch; abandon. **4** tr. colloq. **a** bring (an aircraft) down on water in an emergency. **b** drive (a vehicle) into a ditch. **5** intr. colloq. (of an aircraft) make a forced landing on water. **6** tr. sl. defeat;

frustrate. **7** *tr.* derail (a train). □ **last ditch** see LAST. □□ **ditcher** *n.* [OE *dīc*, of unkn. orig.: cf. DIKE¹]

■ *n.* see CHANNEL¹ 5a, 6. ● *v.* **3** see DESERT¹ 2.

ditchwater /díchwawtər/ *n.* stagnant water in a ditch. **dull as ditchwater** = *dull as dishwater* (see DISHWATER).

ditheism /dítheeizəm/ *n. Theol.* **1** a belief in two gods; dualism. **2** a belief in equal independent ruling principles of good and evil. □□ **ditheist** *n.*

dither /díthər/ *v. & n.* ● *v.intr.* **1** hesitate; be indecisive. **2** *dial.* tremble; quiver. ● *n. colloq.* **1** a state of agitation or apprehension. **2** a state of hesitation; indecisiveness. □ **in a dither** *colloq.* in a state of extreme agitation or vacillation. □□ **ditherer** *n.* **dithery** *adj.* [var. of *didder*, DODDER¹]

■ *v.* **1** see HESITATE 1. **2** see FLUTTER *v.* 7. ● *n.* **1** see SWEAT *n.* 3.

dithyramb /díthiram, -ramb/ *n.* **1 a** a wild choral hymn in ancient Greece, esp. to Dionysus. **b** a bacchanalian song. **2** any passionate or inflated poem, speech, etc. □□ **dithyrambic** /-rámbik/ *adj.* [L *dithyrambus* f. Gk *dithurambos*, of unkn. orig.]

ditsy /dítsee/ *adj.* (also **ditzy**; **ditsier** or **ditzier**, **ditsiest** or **ditziest**) *colloq.* silly; foolishly giddy; scatterbrained. [perh. f. DOTTY and DIZZY]

dittany /dít'nee/ *n.* (*pl.* **-ies**) any herb of the genus *Dictamnus*, formerly used medicinally. [ME f. OF *dita(i)n* f. med.L *dictamus* f. L *dictamnus* f. Gk *diktamnon* perh. f. *Diktē*, a mountain in Crete]

ditto /dítō/ *n. & v.* ● *n.* (*pl.* **-os**) **1** (in accounts, inventories, lists, etc.) the aforesaid; the same. ¶ Often represented by " under the word or sum to be repeated. **2** *colloq.* (replacing a word or phrase to avoid repetition) the same (*came in late last night and ditto the night before*). **3** a similar thing; a duplicate. ● *v.tr.* (**-oes**, **-oed**) repeat (another's action or words). □ **ditto marks** apostrophes, inverted commas, etc., representing 'ditto.' **say ditto to** esp. *Brit. colloq.* agree with; endorse. [It. dial. f. *dicere* past part. of *dicere* say]

dittography /ditógrəfee/ *n.* (*pl.* **-ies**) **1** a copyist's mistaken repetition of a letter, word, or phrase. **2** an example of this. □□ **dittographic** /dítəgráfik/ *adj.* [Gk *dittos* double + -GRAPHY]

ditty /dítee/ *n.* (*pl.* **-ies**) a short simple song. [ME f. OF *dité* composition f. L *dictatum* neut. past part. of *dictare* DICTATE]

■ see SONG.

ditty bag /díteebag/ *n.* (also **ditty box** /-boks/) a sailor's or fisherman's receptacle for odds and ends. [19th c.: orig. unkn.]

ditz /dits/ *n. sl.* a ditsy person.

diuresis /díəreesis/ *n. Med.* an increased excretion of urine. [mod.L f. Gk (as DI-³, *ourēsis* urination)]

diuretic /díərétik/ *adj. & n.* ● *adj.* causing increased output of urine. ● *n.* a diuretic drug. [ME f. OF *diuretique* or LL *diureticus* f. Gk *diourētikos* f. *dioureō* urinate]

diurnal /dī-ə́rnəl/ *adj.* **1** of or during the day; not nocturnal. **2** daily; of each day. **3** *Astron.* occupying one day. **4** *Zool.* (of animals) active in the daytime. **5** *Bot.* (of plants) open only during the day. □□ **diurnally** *adv.* [ME f. LL *diurnalis* f. L *diurnus* f. *dies* day]

■ **1, 2** daily, daytime, *Physiol.* circadian; day-to-day, regular, everyday, quotidian.

div. *abbr.* division.

diva /déevə/ *n.* (*pl.* **divas** or **dive** /-vay/) a great or famous woman singer; a prima donna. [It. f. L, = goddess]

■ see STAR *n.* 8a.

divagate /dívəgayt, div-/ *v.intr. literary* stray; digress. □□ **divagation** /-gáyshən/ *n.* [L *divagari* (as DI-², *vagari* wander)]

■ see STRAY *v.* 1.

divalent /dívávlənt/ *adj. Chem.* **1** having a valence of two; bivalent. **2** having two valencies. □□ **divalence** *n.* [DI-¹ + *valent-* part. stem (as VALENCE)]

divan /diván, dī-/ *n.* **1 a** a long, low, padded seat set against a wall; a backless sofa. **b** a bed consisting of a base and mattress, usu. with no board at either end. **2** a Middle Eastern state legislative body, council chamber, or court of justice. **3** *archaic* **a** a tobacco shop. **b** a smoking room attached

to such a shop. [F *divan* or It. *divano* f. Turk. *dīvān* f. Arab. *dīwān* f. Pers. *dīvān* anthology, register, court, bench]

■ **1 a** see COUCH¹ *n.*

divaricate /dívárikayt, dee-/ *v.intr.* diverge; branch; separate widely. □□ **divaricate** /-kət/ *adj.* **divarication** /-káyshən/ *n.* [L *divaricare* (as DI-², *varicus* straddling)]

dive /dīv/ *v. & n.* ● *v.* (**dived** or **dove** /dōv/) **1** *intr.* plunge head first into water, esp. as a sport. **2** *intr.* **a** *Aeron.* (of an aircraft) plunge steeply downward at speed. **b** *Naut.* (of a submarine) submerge. **c** (of a person) plunge downward. **3** *intr.* (foll. by *into*) *colloq.* **a** put one's hand into (a pocket, handbag, vessel, etc.) quickly and deeply. **b** occupy oneself suddenly and enthusiastically with (a subject, meal, etc.). **4** *tr.* (foll. by *into*) plunge (a hand, etc.) into. ● *n.* **1** an act of diving; a plunge. **2 a** the submerging of a submarine. **b** the steep descent of an aircraft. **3** a sudden darting movement. **4** *colloq.* a disreputable nightclub, drinking establishment, etc. **5** *Boxing sl.* a pretended knockout (*took a dive in the second round*). □ **dive-bomb** bomb (a target) while diving in an aircraft. **dive-bomber** an aircraft designed to dive-bomb. **dive in** *colloq.* help oneself (to food). **diving bell** an open-bottomed box or bell, supplied with air, in which a person can descend into deep water. **diving board** an elevated board used for diving from. **diving suit** a watertight suit usu. with a helmet and an air supply, worn for working under water. [OE *dūfan* (v.intr.) dive, sink, and *dȳfan* (v.tr.) immerse, f. Gmc: rel. to DEEP, DIP]

■ *v.* **1, 2** plunge, nosedive, jump, leap, duck (down), descend, dip, swoop, plummet; submerge, go under, sink. **3 b** plunge; launch oneself; immerse oneself, involve oneself, bury oneself. ● *n.* **1, 2** plunge, nosedive; descent. **3** see DASH *n.* 1. **4** bar, saloon, club, nightclub, drinking establishment, nightspot, *colloq.* honky-tonk, *sl.* joint. □ **dive in** help oneself, set to, *colloq.* tuck in, dig in.

diver /dívər/ *n.* **1** a person who dives. **2 a** a person who wears a diving suit to work under water for long periods. **b** a pearl diver, etc. **3** any of various diving birds, esp. large waterbirds of the family Gaviidae.

diverge /dívə́rj/ *v.* **1** *intr.* **a** proceed in a different direction or in different directions from a point (*diverging rays; the path diverges here*). **b** take a different course or different courses (*their interests diverged*). **2** *intr.* **a** (often foll. by *from*) depart from a set course (*diverged from the track; diverged from his parents' wishes*). **b** differ markedly (*they diverged as to the best course*). **3** *tr.* cause to diverge; deflect. **4** *intr. Math.* (of a series) increase indefinitely as more of its terms are added. [med.L *divergere* (as DI-², L *vergere* incline)]

■ **1 a** divide, subdivide, fork, branch (off *or* out), ramify, split, separate, radiate (out), spread (apart *or* out), divaricate. **b** see PART *v.* 1, 3;2. **2 a** deviate, turn aside *or* away, wander, digress, stray, depart, drift, *literary* divagate; (*diverge from*) go off, get off, turn off.

divergent /dívə́rjənt/ *adj.* **1** diverging. **2** *Psychol.* (of thought) tending to reach a variety of possible solutions when analyzing a problem. **3** *Math.* (of a series) increasing indefinitely as more of its terms are added; not convergent. □□ **divergence** /-jəns/ *n.* **divergency** *n.* **divergently** *adv.*

■ **1** differing, different, diverse, dissimilar, disparate, separate, diverging, disagreeing, conflicting, discrepant.

divers /dívərz/ *adj. archaic* or *literary* more than one; sundry; several. [ME f. OF f. L *diversus* DIVERSE (as DI-², *versus* past part. of *vertere* turn)]

■ various, several, sundry; miscellaneous, varied, assorted.

diverse /dívə́rs, di-/ *adj.* unlike in nature or qualities; varied. □□ **diversely** *adv.* [ME (as DIVERS)]

■ varied, diversified, divergent, heterogeneous, multiform, various, varying, mixed, miscellaneous,

---

/.../ **pronunciation**	● **part of speech**
□ **phrases, idioms, and compounds**	
□□ **derivatives**	■ **synonym section**
cross-references appear in SMALL CAPITALS or *italics*	

assorted, *archaic or literary* divers; distinctive, different, distinct, separate, discrete, dissimilar, differing.

diversify /divə́rsifī, dī-/ *v.* (**-ies, -ied**) **1** *tr.* make diverse; vary; modify. **2** *tr. Commerce* **a** spread (investment) over several enterprises or products, esp. to reduce the risk of loss. **b** introduce a spread of investment in (an enterprise, etc.). **3** *intr.* (often foll. by *into*) esp. *Commerce* (of a firm, etc.) expand the range of products handled. □□ **diversification** /-fikáyshən/ *n.* [ME f. OF *diversifier* f. med.L *diversificare* (as DIVERS)]
▪ **1** vary, variegate, change, mix, modify. **3** expand, extend, spread out, branch out.

diversion /divə́rzhən, dī-/ *n.* **1** the act of diverting; deviation. **b** an instance of this. **2 a** the diverting of attention deliberately. **b** a stratagem for this purpose (*created a diversion to secure their escape*). **3** a recreation or pastime. **4** *Brit.* = detour *n.* 2. □□ **diversional** *adj.* **diversionary** *adj.* [LL *diversio* (as DIVERT)]
▪ **1** deviation, redirection, deflection, digression, departure; modification, change. **2 b** distraction, interruption, interlude. **3** amusement, distraction, entertainment, pastime, recreation, divertissement, game; relaxation.

diversionist /divə́rzhənist, dī-/ *n.* **1** a person who engages in disruptive or subversive activities. **2** *Polit.* (esp. used by Communists) a conspirator against the government; a saboteur.

diversity /divə́rsitee, dī-/ *n.* (*pl.* **-ies**) **1** being diverse; variety. **2** a different kind; a variety. [ME f. OF *diversité* f. L *diversitas -tatis* (as DIVERS)]
▪ **1** variety, diverseness, variation, heterogeneity, multiplicity, multifariousness, variegation, multiformity; difference, disparity, divergence, contrast, differentiation; distinctiveness, individuality.

divert /divə́rt, dī-/ *v.tr.* **1** (often foll. by *from, to*) **a** turn aside; deflect. **b** draw the attention of; distract. **2** (often as **diverting** *adj.*) entertain; amuse. □□ **divertingly** *adv.* [ME f. F *divertir* f. L *divertere* (as DI-², *vertere* turn)]
▪ **1 a** switch, rechannel, redirect, deflect, siphon (off), set aside, turn away, turn aside, avert, reroute, sidetrack, *Brit.* hive off; change, alter, shift. **2** entertain, amuse, distract, interest, beguile, engage, occupy, absorb.

diverticular /dívertíkyələr/ *adj. Med.* of or relating to a diverticulum. □ **diverticular disease** a condition with abdominal pain as a result of muscle spasms in the presence of diverticula.

diverticulitis /dívertíkyəlítis/ *n. Med.* inflammation of a diverticulum.

diverticulum /dívertíkyələm/ *n.* (*pl.* **diverticula** /-lə/) *Anat.* a blind tube forming at weak points in a cavity or passage esp. of the alimentary tract. □□ **diverticulosis** /-lṓsis/ *n.* [med.L, var. of L *deverticulum* byway f. *devertere* (as DE-, *vertere* turn)]

divertimento /divə́rtiméntō, diváir-/ *n.* (*pl.* **divertimenti** /-tee/ or **-os**) *Mus.* a light and entertaining composition, often in the form of a suite for chamber orchestra. [It., = diversion]

divertissement /divə́rtismənt, deeaváirteesmón/ *n.* **1** a diversion; an entertainment. **2** a short ballet, etc., between acts or longer pieces. [F, f. *divertiss-* stem of *divertir* DIVERT]
▪ **1** see AMUSEMENT 1.

Dives /díveez/ *n.* a rich man. [L, in Vulgate transl. of Luke 16]

divest /divést, dī-/ *v.tr.* **1** (usu. foll. by *of*; often *refl.*) unclothe; strip (*divested himself of his jacket*). **2** deprive; dispossess; free; rid (*cannot divest herself of the idea*). □□ **divestiture** *n.* **divestment** *n.* **divesture** *n.* [earlier *devest* f. OF *desvestir*, etc. (as DIS-, L *vestire* f. *vestis* garment)]
▪ **1** (*divest oneself of*) take *or* put off, remove, *literary* doff. **2** deprive, dispossess, strip, rid, rob, relieve, free, disencumber, *literary* despoil.

divide /divíd/ *v.* & *n.* ● *v.* **1** *tr.* & *intr.* (often foll. by *in, into*) separate or be separated into parts; break up; split (*the river divides into two; the road divides; divided them into three*

groups). **2** *tr.* & *intr.* (often foll. by *out*) distribute; deal; share (*divide it out between them*). **3** *tr.* **a** cut off; separate; part (*divide the sheep from the goats*). **b** mark out into parts (*a ruler divided into inches*). **c** specify different kinds of, classify (*people can be divided into two types*). **4** *tr.* cause to disagree; set at variance (*religion divided them*). **5** *Math.* **a** *tr.* find how many times (a number) contains another (*divide 20 by 4*). **b** *intr.* (of a number) be contained in (a number) without a remainder (*4 divides into 20*). **c** *intr.* be susceptible of division (*10 divides by 2 and 5*). **d** *tr.* find how many times (a number) is contained in another (*divide 4 into 20*). **6** *intr. Math.* do division (*can divide well*). **7** *Parl.* **a** *intr.* (of a legislative assembly, etc.) part into two groups for voting (*the House divided*). **b** *tr.* so divide (a parliament, etc.) for voting. ● *n.* **1** a dividing or boundary line (*the divide between rich and poor*). **2** a watershed. □ **divided against itself** formed into factions. **divided highway** a highway with a median strip separating the two opposing flows of traffic. **the Great Divide 1** a vast continental divide or watershed between two drainage systems, esp. the Rocky Mountains of N. America. **2** the boundary between life and death. [ME f. L *dividere divis-* (as DI-², *vid-* separate)]
▪ *v.* **1, 3a** separate, split (up), break up, cut up, partition, segregate, subdivide, cut off, *literary* cleave; disconnect, disjoin, detach, sever, part, *archaic or literary* sunder; branch (out), ramify. **2** distribute, share (out), measure out, parcel out, partition, dole (out), deal (out), allocate, allot, apportion, dispense, give (out), *literary* mete out. **3 c** categorize, classify, sort, assort, grade, group, order, rank, organize, arrange. **4** separate, split, cause to disagree, part, alienate, disunite, set at odds, sow dissension among, pit *or* set against one another, set at variance, estrange. ● *n.* **1** see BOUNDARY.

dividend /dívidend/ *n.* **1 a** a sum of money to be divided among a number of persons, esp. that paid by a company to shareholders. **b** a similar sum payable to winners in a betting pool, to members of a cooperative, or to creditors of an insolvent estate. **c** an individual's share of a dividend. **2** *Math.* a number to be divided by a divisor. **3** a benefit from any action (*their long training paid dividends*). □ **dividend yield** a dividend expressed as a percentage of a current share price. [AF *dividende* f. L *dividendum* (as DIVIDE)]
▪ **1** see CUT *n.* 9.

divider /divídər/ *n.* **1** a screen, piece of furniture, etc., dividing a room into two parts. **2** (in *pl.*) a measuring compass, esp. with a screw for setting small intervals.
▪ **1** see PARTITION *n.* 2.

divi-divi /díveedivee/ *n.* (*pl.* **divi-divis**) **1** a small tree, *Caesalpinia coriaria*, native to tropical Africa, bearing curved pods. **2** this pod used as a source of tannin. [Carib]

divination /dívináyshən/ *n.* **1** supposed insight into the future or the unknown gained by supernatural means. **2 a** a skillful and accurate forecast. **b** a good guess. □□ **divinatory** /-vínətáwree/ *adj.* [ME f. OF *divination* or L *divinatio* (as DIVINE)]
▪ **1** see PROPHECY 2.

divine /divín/ *adj., v.,* & *n.* ● *adj.* (**diviner, divinest**) **1 a** of, from, or like God or a god. **b** devoted to God; sacred (*divine service*). **2 a** more than humanly excellent, gifted, or beautiful. **b** *colloq.* excellent; delightful. ● *v.* **1** *tr.* discover by guessing, intuition, inspiration, or magic. **2** *tr.* foresee; predict; conjecture. **3** *intr.* practice divination. **4** *intr.* dowse. ● *n.* **1** a cleric, usu. an expert in theology. **2** (**the Divine**) providence or God. □ **divine office** see OFFICE. **divine right of kings** the doctrine that kings derive their sovereignty and authority from God, not from their subjects. **divining rod** = *dowsing rod* (see DOWSE¹). □□ **divinely** *adv.* **divineness** *n.* **diviner** *n.* **divinize** /díviniz/ *v.tr.* [ME f. OF *devin -ine* f. L *divinus* f. *divus* godlike]
▪ *adj.* **1 a** godlike, godly, holy; heavenly, celestial. **b** sacred, sanctified, hallowed, consecrated, religious, spiritual. **2 a** superhuman, supernatural, saintly, preeminent, superior, supreme, exalted, transcendent, extraordinary. **b** marvelous, splendid, delightful, superlative, admirable, wonderful, perfect, excellent,

beautiful, *colloq.* great, superb, glorious, super, terrific, smashing, fantastic, magic, brilliant, fabulous, A1, ripsnorting, *colloq. or joc.* splendiferous, *sl.* ace, awesome, bad. ● *v.* **1, 2** intuit, imagine, conjecture, guess, assume, presume, infer, suppose, hypothesize, surmise, suspect, theorize; determine, discover; predict, speculate, foretell, have foreknowledge of, foresee. ● *n.* **1** holy man, priest, clergyman, cleric, ecclesiastic, minister, pastor, reverend, churchman, churchwoman; theologian. **2** (**the Divine**) see *the Creator* (CREATOR 2).

divinity /divínitee/ *n.* (*pl.* **-ies**) **1** the state or quality of being divine. **2 a** a god; a divine being. **b** (as **the Divinity**) God. **3** the study of religion; theology. [ME f. OF *divinité* f. L *divinitas -tatis* (as DIVINE)]
■ **1** see SANCTITY 1. **2 a** see GOD *n.* 1a.

divisible /divízibəl/ *adj.* **1** capable of being divided, physically or mentally. **2** (foll. by *by*) *Math.* containing (a number) a number of times without a remainder (*15 is divisible by 3 and 5*). □□ **divisibility** /-bílitee/ *n.* [F *divisible* or LL *divisibilis* (as DIVIDE)]
■ **1** see SEPARABLE.

division /divízhən/ *n.* **1** the act or an instance of dividing; the process of being divided. **2** *Math.* the process of dividing one number by another (see also *long division* (see LONG¹), *short division*). **3** disagreement or discord (*division of opinion*). **4** *Parl.* the separation of members of a legislative body into two sets for counting votes for and against. **5 a** one of two or more parts into which a thing is divided. **b** the point at which a thing is divided. **6** a major unit of administration or organization, esp.: **a** a group of army brigades or regiments. **b** *Sports* a grouping of teams within a league. **7 a** a district defined for administrative purposes. **b** *Brit.* a part of a county or borough returning a Member of Parliament. **8 a** *Bot.* a major taxonomic grouping. **b** *Zool.* a subsidiary category between major levels of classification. **9** *Logic* a classification of kinds, parts, or senses. □ **division of labor** the improvement of efficiency by giving different parts of a manufacturing process, etc., to different people. **division sign** the sign (÷) indicating that one quantity is to be divided by another. □□ **divisional** *adj.* **divisionally** *adv.* **divisionary** *adj.* [ME f. OF *divisiun* f. L *divisio -onis* (as DIVIDE)]
■ **1** dividing, splitting, separation, segmentation, segmenting; compartmentation, compartmentalization; split, partition. **3** discord, disagreement, conflict, argument, strife, disunity, disunion, dissension, disharmony, discordance, incompatibility. **5 a** section, compartment, segment, sector, unit; partition; part, space, chamber, cell. **b** boundary (line), border, borderline, frontier, margin, line, dividing line. **6** branch, department, sector, section, unit, group, arm. **7 a** see DISTRICT.

divisive /divísiv/ *adj.* tending to divide, esp. in opinion; causing disagreement. □□ **divisively** *adv.* **divisiveness** *n.* [LL *divisivus* (as DIVIDE)]
■ see SCHISMATIC *adj.*

divisor /divízər/ *n. Math.* **1** a number by which another is to be divided. **2** a number that divides another without a remainder. [ME f. F *diviseur* or L *divisor* (as DIVIDE)]

divorce /diváwrs/ *n.* & *v.* ● *n.* **1 a** the legal dissolution of a marriage. **b** a legal decree of this. **2** a severance or separation (*a divorce between thought and feeling*). ● *v.* **1 a** *tr.* (usu. as **divorced** *adj.*) (often foll. by *from*) legally dissolve the marriage of (*a divorced couple; he wants to get divorced from her*). **b** *intr.* separate by divorce (*they divorced last year*). **c** *tr.* end one's marriage with (*divorced him for neglect*). **2** *tr.* (often foll. by *from*) detach; separate (*divorced from reality*). **3** *tr. archaic* dissolve (a union). □□ **divorcement** *n.* [ME f. OF *divorce* (n.), *divorcer* (v.) f. LL *divortiare* f. L *divortium* f. *divortere* (as DI-², *vertere* turn)]
■ *n.* **1 a** separation, breakup, split, split-up; severance; see also DISSOLUTION 2. **2** see SEPARATION. ● *v.* **2** separate, cut off, break off, divide, split (off), part, sever, detach, dissociate, disassociate.

divorcé /divawrsáy/ *n.* a divorced man.

divorcée /divawrsáy/ *n.* a divorced woman.

divot /dívət/ *n.* **1** a piece of turf cut out by a golf club in making a stroke. **2** esp. *Sc.* a piece of turf; a sod. [16th c.: orig. unkn.]

divulge /divúlj, dī-/ *v.tr.* disclose; reveal (a secret, etc.). □□ **divulgation** /-vulgáyshən/ *n.* **divulgement** *n.* **divulgence** *n.* [L *divulgare* (as DI-², *vulgare* publish f. *vulgus* common people)]
■ see DISCLOSE 1.

divvy /dívee/ *n.* & *v. colloq.* ● *n.* (*pl.* **-ies**) **1** a distribution. **2** *Brit.* a dividend; a share, esp. of profits earned by a cooperative. ● *v.tr.* (**-ies, -ied**) (often foll. by *up*) share out; divide. [abbr. of DIVIDEND]
■ *v.* see PARCEL *v.* 1.

Diwali /deewaalee/ *n.* a Hindu festival with illuminations, held between September and November. [Hind. *dīwalī* f. Skr. *dīpāvalī* row of lights f. *dīpa* lamp]

Dixie /díksee/ *n.* the southern states of the US. [19th c.: orig. uncert.]

dixie /díksee/ *n.* a large iron cooking pot used by campers, etc. [Hind. *degchī* cooking pot f. Pers. *degcha* dimin. of *deg* pot]

Dixieland /díkseeland/ *n.* **1** = DIXIE. **2** a kind of jazz with a strong, two-beat rhythm and collective improvisation. [DIXIE]

dizzy /dízee/ *adj.* & *v.* ● *adj.* (**dizzier, dizziest**) **1 a** giddy; unsteady. **b** lacking mental stability; confused. **2** causing giddiness (*dizzy heights; dizzy speed*). ● *v.tr.* **1** make dizzy. **2** bewilder. □□ **dizzily** *adv.* **dizziness** *n.* [OE *dysig* f. WG]
■ *adj.* **1 a** giddy, unsteady, vertiginous, light-headed, light (in the head), faint, dazed, *colloq.* woozy. **b** confused, silly, giddy, empty-headed, muddled, befuddled, flighty, absentminded, simpleminded, light-headed, wrongheaded, featherheaded, featherbrained, harebrained, birdbrained, scatterbrained; see also *in a daze* (DAZE *n.*). ● *v.* **2** see BEWILDER, DISORDER *v.*

DJ *abbr.* **1** disk jockey. **2** district judge.

djellaba /jəlaábə/ *n.* (also **djellabah, jellaba**) a loose, hooded, usu. woolen cloak worn or as worn by Arab men. [Arab. *jallaba, jallābīya*]

djibba (also **djibbah**) var. of JIBBA.

DL *abbr. Sports* disabled list.

dl *abbr.* deciliter(s).

D-layer /deélayər/ *n.* the lowest layer of the ionosphere able to reflect low-frequency radio waves. [*D* (arbitrary)]

D.Litt. *abbr.* Doctor of Letters. [L *Doctor Litterarum*]

DM *abbr.* (also **D-mark**) deutsche mark.

dm *abbr.* decimeter(s).

D.M.D. *abbr.* doctor of dental medicine. [L *Dentariae Medicinae Doctor* or *Doctor Medicinae Dentalis*]

D.Mus. *abbr.* Doctor of Music.

DMZ *abbr.* demilitarized zone.

DNA *abbr.* deoxyribonucleic acid, the self-replicating material present in nearly all living organisms, esp. as a constituent of chromosomes, which is the carrier of genetic information. □ **DNA fingerprinting** the identification of an individual by analysis of DNA structure from body tissue, hair, blood, etc., esp. as used for forensic purposes.

D-notice /deénōtis/ *n. Brit.* a government notice to news editors not to publish items on specified subjects, for reasons of security. [defense + NOTICE]

do¹ /dōo/ *v.* & *n.* ● *v.* (*3rd sing. present* **does** /duz/; *past* **did** /did/; *past part.* **done** /dun/) **1** *tr.* perform; carry out; achieve; complete (work, etc.) (*did his homework; there's a lot to do; he can do anything*). **2** *tr.* produce; make (*she was doing a painting; I did a translation; decided to do a casserole*). **b** provide (*do you do lunches?*). **3** *tr.* bestow; grant; have a specified effect on (*a walk would do you good; do me a favor*). **4** *intr.* act; behave; proceed (*do as I do; she would do well to*

/.../ **pronunciation**	● **part of speech**
□ **phrases, idioms, and compounds**	
□□ **derivatives**	■ **synonym section**
cross-references appear in SMALL CAPITALS or *italics*	

accept the offer). **5** *tr.* work at; study; be occupied with (*what does your father do?*; *we're doing Chaucer next term*). **6 a** *intr.* be suitable or acceptable; suffice (*this dress won't do for a wedding*; *a sandwich will do until we get home*; *that will never do*). **b** *tr.* satisfy; be suitable for (*that hotel will do me nicely*). **7** *tr.* deal with; put in order (*the garden needs doing*; *the barber will do you next*; *I must do my hair before we go*). **8** *intr.* **a** fare; get on (*the patients were doing excellently*; *he did badly in the test*). **b** perform; work (*could do better*). **9** *tr.* solve; work out (*we did the puzzle*). **b** (prec. by *can* or *be able to*) be competent at (*can you do cartwheels?*; *I never could do algebra*). **10** *tr.* **a** traverse (a certain distance) (*we did fifty miles today*). **b** travel at a specified speed (*he overtook us doing about eighty*). **11** *tr. colloq.* **a** act or behave like (*did a Houdini*). **b** *esp. Brit.* play the part of (*she was asked to do hostess*). **12** *intr.* **a** *colloq.* finish (*have you done annoying me?*; *I'm done in the bathroom*). **b** (as **done** *adj.*) be over (*the day is done*). **13** *tr.* produce or give a performance of (*the school does many plays and concerts*; *we've never done* Pygmalion). **14** *tr.* cook, esp. to the right degree (*do it in the oven*; *the potatoes aren't done yet*). **15** *intr.* be in progress (*what's doing?*). **16** *tr. colloq.* visit; see the sights of (*we did all the art galleries*). **17** *tr. colloq.* **a** (often as **done** *adj.*; often foll. by *in*) exhaust; tire out (*the climb has completely done me in*). **b** beat up; defeat; kill. **c** ruin (*now you've done it*). **18** *tr.* (foll. by *into*) translate or transform (*the book was done into French*). **19** *tr. esp. Brit. colloq.* (with qualifying adverb) provide food, etc., for in a specified way (*they do one very well here*). **20** *tr. sl.* **a** rob (*they did a liquor store downtown*). **b** *Brit.* swindle (*I was done at the market*). **21** *tr. Brit. sl.* prosecute; convict (*they were done for shoplifting*). **22** *tr. sl.* undergo (a specified term of imprisonment) (*he did two years for fraud*). **23** *tr. coarse sl.* have sexual intercourse with. **24** *tr. sl.* take (a drug). ● *v.aux.* **1 a** (except with *be, can, may, ought, shall, will*) in questions and negative statements (*do you understand?*; *I don't smoke*). **b** (except with *can, may, ought, shall, will*) in negative commands (*don't be silly*; *do not come tomorrow*). **2** *ellipt.* or in place of verb or verb and object (*you know her better than I do*; *I wanted to go and I did so*; *tell me, do!*). **3** forming emphatic present and past tenses (*I do want to*; *do tell me*; *they did go but she was out*). **4** in inversion for emphasis (*rarely does it happen*; *did she but know it*). ● *n.* (*pl.* **dos** or **do's**) **1** *colloq.* an elaborate event, party, or operation. **2** *Brit. sl.* a swindle or hoax. □ **be done with** see DONE. **do about** see ABOUT *prep.* 1d. **do away with** *colloq.* **1** abolish. **2** kill. **do battle** enter into combat. **do one's best** see BEST. **do one's bit** see BIT. **do by** treat or deal with in a specified way (*do as you would be done by*). **do credit to** see CREDIT. **do down** *colloq.* **1** cheat; swindle. **2** get the better of; overcome. **do for 1** be satisfactory or sufficient for. **2** *colloq.* (esp. as **done for** *adj.*) destroy; ruin; kill (*he knew he was done for*). **3** *esp. Brit. colloq.* act as housekeeper for. **do one's head** (or **nut**) *Brit. sl.* be extremely angry or agitated. **do the honors** see HONOR. **do in 1** *sl.* **a** kill. **b** ruin; do injury to. **2** *colloq.* exhaust; tire out. **do-it-yourself** *adj.* (of work, esp. building, painting, decorating, etc.) done or to be done by an amateur at home. ● *n.* such work. **do justice to** see JUSTICE. **do nothing for** (or **to**) *colloq.* detract from the appearance or quality of (*such behavior does nothing for our reputation*). **do or die** persist regardless of danger. **do out** *Brit. colloq.* clean or redecorate (a room). **do a person out of** *colloq.* unjustly deprive a person of; swindle out of (*he was done out of his pension*). **do over 1** *sl.* attack; beat up. **2** *colloq.* redecorate, refurbish. **3** *colloq.* do again. **do proud** see PROUD. **dos and don'ts** rules of behavior. **do something for** (or **to**) *colloq.* enhance the appearance or quality of (*that carpet does something for the room*). **do to** (*archaic* **unto**) = **do by**. **do to death** see DEATH. **do the trick** see TRICK. **do up 1** fasten; secure. **2** *colloq.* **a** refurbish; renovate. **b** adorn; dress up. **3** *Brit. sl.* ruin; get the better of. **b** beat up. **do well for oneself** prosper. **do well out of** profit by. **do with** (prec. by *could*) would be glad to have; would profit by (*I could do with a rest*; *you could do with a wash*). **do without** manage without; forgo (also *absol.*: *we shall just have to do without*). **have nothing to do with 1** have no connection or dealings with (*our problem has*

nothing to do with the latest news; *after the disagreement he had nothing to do with his father*). **2** be no business or concern of (*the decision has nothing to do with her*). **have to do** (or **something to do**) **with** be connected with (*his limp has to do with a car accident*). [OE *dōn* f. Gmc: rel. to Skr *dádhāmi* put, Gk *tithemi* place, L *facere* do]

■ *v.* **1** see EFFECT *v.* 1, 2. **2 a** see MAKE *v.* 1. **b** see PROVIDE 1. **4** see ACT *v.* 1. **5** see STUDY *v.* 1, 3. **6** see SERVE *v.* 5a–c. **7** see *see about* 1 (SEE¹). **8 a** see FARE *v.* 1. **10** see MAKE *v.* 15. **13** see PERFORM 2. **17 b** see ATTACK *v.* 1. ● *n.* **1** see PARTY *n.* 1.

do² /dō/ *n.* (also **doh**) *Mus.* **1** (in tonic sol-fa) the first and eighth notes of a major scale. **2** the note C in the fixed-do system. [18th c.: f. It. *do*]

do. *abbr.* ditto.

DOA *abbr.* dead on arrival (at a hospital, etc.).

doable /dōˊəbəl/ *adj.* that can be done.

■ see PRACTICABLE.

DOB *abbr.* date of birth.

dobbin /dóbin/ *n.* a draft horse; a farm horse. [pet form of the name *Robert*]

■ farm horse, draft horse, jade, *colloq.* nag.

Doberman /dóˊbərmən/ *n.* (in full **Doberman pinscher** /pínshər/) **1** a large dog of a German breed with a smooth coat. **2** this breed. [L. *Dobermann*, 19th-c. Ger. dog breeder + G *Pinscher* terrier]

doc /dok/ *n. colloq.* doctor. [abbr.]

■ see DOCTOR *n.* 1.

docent /dóˊsənt/ *n.* **1** a teacher or lecturer in a college or university. **2** a person who serves as a well-informed guide, as in a museum. [f. G *Dozent*, f. L *docere* to teach]

docile /dósəl/ *adj.* **1** submissive, easily managed. **2** *archaic* teachable. □□ **docilely** *adv.* **docility** /-sílitee/ *n.* [ME f. L *docilis* f. *docēre* teach]

■ **1** see SUBMISSIVE.

dock¹ /dok/ *n. & v.* ● *n.* **1** an artificially enclosed body of water for the loading, unloading, and repair of ships. **2** (in *pl.*) a range of docks with wharves and offices; a dockyard. **3** a ship's berth, a wharf. **4** = dry dock. **5** *Theatr.* = scene dock. ● *v.* **1** *tr. & intr.* bring or come into a dock. **2 a** *tr.* join (spacecraft) together in space. **b** *intr.* (of spacecraft) be joined. **3** *tr.* provide with a dock or docks. □ **in dock** *Brit. colloq.* in the hospital or (of a vehicle) awaiting repairs. [MDu. *docke*, of unkn. orig.]

■ *n.* **2, 3** pier, wharf, jetty, quay; (*docks*) harbor, dockyard. ● *v.* **1** (drop) anchor, berth, tie up, moor, land, put in.

dock² /dok/ *n.* the enclosure in a criminal court for the accused. □ **in the dock** on trial. [16th c.: prob. orig. cant = Flem. *dok* cage, of unkn. orig.]

dock³ /dok/ *n.* any weed of the genus *Rumex*, with broad leaves. [OE *docce*]

dock⁴ /dok/ *v. & n.* ● *v.tr.* **1 a** cut short (an animal's tail). **b** cut short the tail of (an animal). **2 a** (often foll. by *from*) deduct (a part) from wages, supplies, etc. **b** reduce (wages, etc.) in this way. ● *n.* **1** the solid, bony part of an animal's tail. **2** the crupper of a saddle or harness. □ **dock-tailed** having a docked tail. [ME, of uncert. orig.]

dockage /dókij/ *n.* **1** the charge made for using docks. **2** dock accommodation. **3** the berthing of vessels in docks.

docker /dókər/ *n.* a person employed to load and unload ships.

■ stevedore, longshoreman.

docket /dókit/ *n. & v.* ● *n.* **1** a list of causes for trial or persons having causes pending. **2** a list of things to be done. **3** *Brit.* **a** a document or label listing goods delivered or the contents of a package, or recording payment of customs dues, etc. **b** a voucher; an order form. ● *v.tr.* label with a docket. [15th c.: orig. unkn.]

dockhand /dókhand/ *n.* a person employed to load and unload ships; a longshoreman.

dockland /dóklənd/ *n.* a district near docks. [DOCK¹]

dockside /dóksīd/ *n.* the area adjacent to a dock (*boats tethered at dockside*).

dockyard /dókyaard/ *n.* an area with docks and equipment for building and repairing ships, esp. for naval use.

doctor /dóktər/ *n. & v.* ● *n.* **1 a** a qualified practitioner of medicine; a physician. **b** a qualified dentist or veterinary surgeon. **2** a person who holds a doctorate (*Doctor of Civil Law*). **3** *colloq.* a person who carries out repairs. **4** *archaic* a teacher or learned man. **5** *sl.* a cook on board a ship or in a camp. **6** (in full **doctor-blade**) *Printing* esp. *Brit.* a blade for removing surplus ink, etc. **7** an artificial fishing fly. ● *v. colloq.* **1 a** *tr.* treat medically. **b** *intr.* (esp. as **doctoring** *n.*) practice as a physician. **2** *tr. Brit.* castrate or spay. **3** *tr.* patch up (machinery, etc.); mend. **4** *tr.* adulterate. **5** *tr.* tamper with; falsify. **6** *tr.* confer a degree of doctor on. □ **Doctor of the Church** any of several early ecclesiastics of noted learning. **Doctor of Philosophy** a doctorate in any faculty except law, medicine, or sometimes theology. **go for the doctor** *Austral. sl.* **1** make an all-out effort. **2** bet all one has. **(just) what the doctor ordered** *colloq.* something beneficial or desirable. □□ **doctorhood** *n.* **doctorial** /-táwreeəl/ *adj.* **doctorly** *adj.* **doctorship** *n.* [ME f. OF *doctour* f. L *doctor* f. *docēre doct-* teach]

■ *n.* **1 a** physician, medical practitioner, MD, general practitioner, GP, *colloq.* medic, medico, doc, *sl.* sawbones. **3** repairman, technician, engineer, fixer. **4** see TEACHER. ● *v.* **1** treat, attend, medicate; cure, heal; practice (medicine). **3** mend, repair, patch (up), fix. **4** adulterate, dilute, water (down), cut; spike, drug, poison, contaminate, pollute. **5** falsify, tamper with, meddle with, interfere with, tinker with, disguise, change, modify, alter.

doctoral /dóktərəl/ *adj.* of or for a degree of doctor.

doctorate /dóktərət/ *n.* the highest university degree in any faculty, often honorary.

doctrinaire /dóktrináir/ *adj. & n.* ● *adj.* seeking to apply a theory or doctrine in all circumstances without regard to practical considerations; theoretical and impractical. ● *n.* a doctrinaire person; a pedantic theorist. □□ **doctrinairism** *n.* **doctrinarian** *n.* [F f. *doctrine* DOCTRINE + *-aire* -ARY[1]]

■ *adj.* see *pedantic* (PEDANT).

doctrinal /dóktrinəl/ *adj.* of or inculcating a doctrine or doctrines. □□ **doctrinally** *adv.* [LL *doctrinalis* (as DOCTRINE)]

■ see ORTHODOX.

doctrine /dóktrin/ *n.* **1** what is taught; a body of instruction. **2 a** a principle of religious or political, etc., belief. **b** a set of such principles; dogma. □□ **doctrinism** *n.* **doctrinist** *n.* [ME f. OF f. L *doctrina* teaching (as DOCTOR)]

■ **1** teaching, body of instruction. **2** principle, precept, tenet, belief, opinion, idea, concept, theory, proposition, thesis, conviction, postulate; credo, dogma, article of faith, canon, creed.

docudrama /dókyōōdraamə, -dramə/ *n.* a dramatized television movie based on real events. [DOCUMENTARY + DRAMA]

document *n. & v.* ● *n.* /dókyəmənt/ a piece of written or printed matter that provides a record or evidence of events, an agreement, ownership, identification, etc. ● *v.tr.* /dókyəment/ **1** prove by or provide with documents or evidence. **2** record in a document. □□ **documental** /-mént'l/ *adj.* [ME f. OF f. L *documentum* proof f. *docēre* teach]

■ *n.* paper, certificate, instrument, report, chronicle, record. ● *v.* record, chronicle, particularize, detail, describe; verify, validate, certify, authenticate, corroborate, substantiate.

documentalist /dókyəmént'list/ *n.* a person engaged in documentation.

documentary /dókyəméntəree/ *adj. & n.* ● *adj.* **1** consisting of documents (*documentary evidence*). **2** providing a factual record or report. ● *n.* (*pl.* **-ies**) a documentary film, etc. □□ **documentarily** *adv.*

documentation /dókyəmentáyshən/ *n.* **1** the accumulation, classification, and dissemination of information. **2** the material collected or disseminated. **3** the collection of documents relating to a process or event, esp. the written specification and instructions accompanying a computer program.

■ **2** see MATERIAL *n.* 5.

DOD *abbr.* Department of Defense.

dodder[1] /dódər/ *v.intr.* tremble or totter, esp. from age. □□ **dodderer** *n.* **doddering** *adj.* [17th c.: var. of obs. dial. *dadder*]

■ see TOTTER *v.* □□ **doddering** feeble, weak, infirm, frail; doddery, shambling, faltering, shaky, unsteady, trembly; see also AGED 2.

dodder[2] /dódər/ *n.* any climbing parasitic plant of the genus *Cuscuta*, with slender, leafless, threadlike stems. [ME f. Gmc]

doddered /dódərd/ *adj.* (of a tree, esp. an oak) having lost its top or branches. [prob. f. obs. *dod* poll, lop]

doddery /dódəree/ *adj.* tending to tremble or totter, esp. from age. □□ **dodderiness** *n.* [DODDER[1] + -Y[1]]

■ see *doddering* (DODDER[1]).

doddle /dód'l/ *n. Brit. colloq.* an easy task. [perh. f. *doddle* = TODDLE]

dodeca- /dódekə/ *comb. form* twelve. [Gk *dōdeka* twelve]

dodecagon /dōdékəgon/ *n.* a plane figure with twelve sides.

dodecahedron /dódekəheedrən/ *n.* a solid figure with twelve faces. □□ **dodecahedral** *adj.*

dodecaphonic /dódekəfónik/ *adj. Mus.* = *twelve-tone*.

dodge /doj/ *v. & n.* ● *v.* **1** *intr.* (often foll. by *about, behind, around*) move quickly to one side or quickly change position, to elude a pursuer, blow, etc. (*dodged behind the chair*). **2** *tr.* **a** evade by cunning or trickery (*dodged paying the fare*). **b** elude (a pursuer, opponent, blow, etc.) by a sideward movement, etc. **3** *tr. Austral. sl.* acquire dishonestly. **4** *intr.* (of a bell in change ringing) move one place contrary to the normal sequence. ● *n.* **1** a quick movement to avoid or evade something. **2** a clever trick or expedient. **3** the dodging of a bell in change ringing. [16th c.: orig. unkn.]

■ *v.* **1** dart, shift, move aside, sidestep, duck, bob, weave, swerve, veer. **2 a** evade, sidestep, *colloq.* duck. **b** avoid, elude, evade, escape from, sidestep; duck. ● *n.* **2** trick, expedient, subterfuge, scheme, ruse, device, stratagem, plan, plot, machination, deception, prevarication, contrivance, evasion, *colloq.* ploy, *Austral. colloq.* lurk, *sl.* racket.

dodgem /dójəm/ *n.* (also **Dodgem**) = *bumper cars*.

dodger /dójər/ *n.* **1** a person who dodges, esp. an artful or elusive person. **2** a screen on a ship's bridge, etc., as protection from spray, etc. **3** a small handbill. **4** (in full **corn-dodger**) **a** esp. *southern US* a small, hard cornmeal cake. **b** esp. *S. Atlantic US* a boiled cornmeal dumpling. **5** esp. *Austral. sl.* a sandwich; bread; food.

dodgy /dójee/ *adj.* (**dodgier, dodgiest**) **1** *colloq.* awkward; unreliable; tricky. **2** *Brit.* cunning; artful.

■ **1** tricky, dangerous, perilous, risky, chancy, difficult, ticklish, sensitive, delicate, touchy, awkward, *colloq.* iffy, *sl.* hairy, dicey; uncertain, doubtful, dubious, unreliable, unsound, rickety, dickey.

dodo /dódō/ *n.* (*pl.* **-oes** or **-os**) **1** any large flightless bird of the extinct family Raphidae, formerly native to Mauritius. **2** an old-fashioned, stupid, or inactive person. □ **as dead as the** (or **a**) **dodo 1** completely or unmistakably dead. **2** entirely obsolete. [Port. *doudo* simpleton]

■ **2** see *stick-in-the-mud* (STICK[2]), SILLY *n.*

DOE *abbr.* Department of Energy.

doe /dō/ *n.* a female fallow deer, reindeer, hare, or rabbit. [OE *dā*]

doer /dōōər/ *n.* **1** a person who does something. **2** one who acts rather than merely talking or thinking. **3** (in full **hard doer**) *Austral.* an eccentric or amusing person.

does *3rd sing. present of* DO[1].

doeskin /dóskin/ *n.* **1 a** the skin of a doe fallow deer. **b** leather made from this. **2** a fine cloth resembling it.

doesn't /dúzənt/ *contr.* does not.

doest /dóõist/ *archaic 2nd sing. present of* DO[1].

/.../ **pronunciation**	● **part of speech**
□ **phrases, idioms, and compounds**	
□□ **derivatives**	■ **synonym section**
cross-references appear in SMALL CAPITALS or *italics*	

doeth /dōُoith/ *archaic* = DOTH.

doff /dawf, dof/ *v.tr. literary* take off (one's hat, clothing). [ME, = *do off*]
■ see *take off* 1a.

dog /dawg, dog/ *n. & v.* ● *n.* **1** any four-legged, flesh-eating animal of the genus *Canis*, of many breeds domesticated and wild, kept as pets or for work or sport. **2** the male of the dog, or of the fox (also **dog fox**) or wolf (also **dog wolf**). **3 a** *colloq.* a despicable person. **b** *colloq.* a person or fellow of a specified kind (*a lucky dog*). **c** *Austral. sl.* an informer; a traitor. **d** *sl.* a horse that is difficult to handle. **e** *sl. derog.* an unattractive or slovenly woman. **4** a mechanical device for gripping. **5** *sl.* something poor; a failure. **6** = FIREDOG. **7** (in *pl.*; prec. by *the*) *Brit. colloq.* greyhound racing. ● *v.tr.* (**dogged, dogging**) **1** follow closely and persistently; pursue; track. **2** *Mech.* grip with a dog. □ **die like a dog** die miserably or shamefully. **dog biscuit** a hard, thick biscuit for feeding dogs. **dog clutch** *Mech.* a device for coupling two shafts in the transmission of power, one member having teeth which engage with slots in another. **dog collar 1** a collar for a dog. **2 a** *colloq.* a clerical collar. **b** a straight high collar. **dog days** the hottest period of the year (reckoned in antiquity from the heliacal rising of the Dog Star). **dog-eared** (of a book, etc.) with the corners worn or battered with use. **dog-eat-dog** *colloq.* ruthlessly competitive. **dog-end** *Brit. sl.* a cigarette-end. **dog in the manger** a person who prevents others from using something, although that person has no use for it. **dog paddle** an elementary swimming stroke like that of a dog. **dog-paddle** *v.intr.* swim using this stroke. **dog rose** a wild rose, *Rosa canina*: also called *brier rose*. **dog's breakfast** (or **dinner**) *Brit. & Can. colloq.* a mess. **dog's disease** *Austral. sl.* influenza. **dog's life** a life of misery or harassment. **dogs of war** *poet.* the havoc accompanying war. **Dog Star** the chief star of the constellation Canis Major or Minor, esp. Sirius. **dog tag 1** a usu. metal plate attached to a dog's collar, giving owner's address, etc. **2** an identification tag, esp. as worn by a member of the military. **dog-tired** tired out. **go to the dogs** *sl.* deteriorate, be ruined. **hair of the dog** further alcoholic drink to cure hangover from that drink. **like a dog's dinner** *Brit. colloq.* smartly or flashily (dressed, arranged, etc.). **not a dog's chance** no chance at all. **put on the dog** *colloq.* behave pretentiously. □□ **doglike** *adj.* [OE *docga*, of unkn. orig.]
■ *n.* **3 a** see VILLAIN 1, 3. **d** see JADE² 1. **e** see BAG *n.* 5.
● *v.* **1** see PURSUE 1.

dogberry /dáwgberee, dóg-/ *n.* (*pl.* **-ies**) the fruit of the dogwood.

dogcart /dáwgkaart, dóg-/ *n.* a two-wheeled driving cart with cross seats back to back.

dogcatcher /dáwgkachər, dóg-/ *n.* an official who rounds up and impounds stray dogs in a community.

doge /dōj/ *n. hist.* the chief magistrate of Venice or Genoa. [F f. It. f. Venetian *doze* f. L *dux ducis* leader]

dogfight /dáwgfīt, dóg-/ *n.* **1** a close combat between fighter aircraft. **2** uproar; a fight like that between dogs.

dogfish /dáwgfish, dóg-/ *n.* (*pl.* same or **dogfishes**) any of various small sharks, esp. of the families Scyliorhinidae or Squalidae.

dogged /dáwgid, dóg-/ *adj.* tenacious; grimly persistent. □□ **doggedly** *adv.* **doggedness** *n.* [ME f. DOG + -ED¹]

dogger¹ /dáwgər, dóg-/ *n.* a two-masted, bluff-bowed Dutch fishing boat. [ME f. MDu., = fishing boat]

dogger² /dáwgər, dóg-/ *n. Geol.* a large spherical concretion occurring in sedimentary rock. [dial., = kind of ironstone, perh. f. DOG]

doggerel /dáwgərəl, dóg-/ *n.* poor or trivial verse. [ME, app. f. DOG: cf. -REL]

doggie var. of DOGGY *n.*

doggish /dáwgish, dóg-/ *adj.* **1** of or like a dog. **2** currish; malicious; snappish. □□ **doggishly** *adv.* **doggishness** *n.*

doggo /dáwgō, dógō/ *adv.* □ **lie doggo** *Brit. sl.* lie motionless or hidden, making no sign. [prob. f. DOG: cf. -O]

doggone /dáwg-gon, dóg-/ *adj., adv., & int. sl.* ● *adj. & adv.*

damned. ● *int.* expressing annoyance. [prob. f. *dog on it* = *God damn it*]

doggy /dáwgee, dógée/ *adj. & n.* ● *adj.* **1** of or like a dog. **2** devoted to dogs. ● *n.* (also **doggie**) (*pl.* **-ies**) a little dog; a pet name for a dog. □ **doggy** (usu. **doggie**) **bag** a bag given to a customer in a restaurant or to a guest at a party, etc., for putting leftovers in to take home. □□ **dogginess** *n.*

doghouse /dáwghows, dóg-/ *n.* a dog's shelter. □ **in the doghouse** *sl.* in disgrace or disfavor.

dogie /dṓgee/ *n.* a motherless or neglected calf. [19th c.: orig. unkn.]

dogleg /dáwgleg, dóg-/ *n., adj., & v.* ● *n.* something with a sharp, abrupt bend, as a road. ● *adj.* (also **dog-legged**) bent like a dog's hind leg. ● *v.intr.* proceed around a dogleg or on a dogleg course. □ **dogleg hole** *Golf* a hole at which a player cannot aim directly at the green from the tee.

dogma /dáwgmə, dóg-/ *n.* **1 a** a principle, tenet, or system of these, esp. as laid down by the authority of a church. **b** such principles collectively. **2** an arrogant declaration of opinion. [L f. Gk *dogma -matos* opinion f. *dokeō* seem]
■ **1** see PRINCIPLE 1, CODE *n.* 4.

dogmatic /dawgmátik, dóg-/ *adj.* **1 a** (of a person) given to asserting or imposing personal opinions; arrogant. **b** intolerantly authoritative. **2 a** of or in the nature of dogma; doctrinal. **b** based on a priori principles, not on induction. □□ **dogmatically** *adv.* [LL *dogmaticus* f. Gk *dogmatikos* (as DOGMA)]
■ **1** arbitrary, categorical, dictatorial, pontifical, imperious, peremptory, overbearing, authoritarian, autocratic, uncompromising, high-handed, self-assertive, emphatic, insistent, assertive, arrogant, domineering, obdurate, stubborn, intolerant, opinionated, pushful, *colloq.* pushy.

dogmatics /dawgmátiks, dóg-/ *n.* **1** the study of religious dogmas; dogmatic theology. **2** a system of dogma. [DOGMATIC]

dogmatism /dáwgmətizəm, dóg-/ *n.* a tendency to be dogmatic. □□ **dogmatist** *n.* [F *dogmatisme* f. med.L *dogmatismus* (as DOGMA)]
■ see *intolerance* (INTOLERANT).

dogmatize /dáwgmətīz, dóg-/ *v.* **1** *intr.* make positive unsupported assertions; speak dogmatically. **2** *tr.* express (a principle, etc.) as a dogma. [F *dogmatiser* or f. LL *dogmatizare* f. Gk (as DOGMA)]

do-gooder /dōُogōُodər/ *n.* a well-meaning but unrealistic philanthropist or reformer. □□ **do-good** /dōُogōُod/ *adj. & n.* **do-goodery** *n.* **do-goodism** *n.*

dogsbody /dáwgzbodee, dógz-/ *n.* (*pl.* **-ies**) **1** *colloq.* a drudge. **2** *Naut. sl.* a junior officer.
■ **1** see SLAVE *n.* 2.

dogshore /dáwgshawr, dóg-/ *n.* a temporary wooden support for a ship just before launching.

dogskin /dáwgskin, dóg-/ *n.* leather made of or imitating dog's skin, used for gloves.

dogtooth /dáwgtoōُth, dóg-/ *n.* **1** a small pointed ornament or molding esp. in Norman and Early English architecture. **2** *Brit.* a houndstooth check. □ **dogtooth violet** any liliaceous plant of the genus *Erythronium*, esp. *E. dens-canis* with speckled leaves, purple flowers, and a toothed perianth.

dogtrot /dáwgtrot, dóg-/ *n.* a gentle easy trot.
■ see JOG *n.* 2.

dogwatch /dáwgwoch, dóg-/ *n. Naut.* either of two short watches (4–6 or 6–8 p.m.).

dogwood /dáwgwōُod, dóg-/ *n.* **1** any of various shrubs of the genus *Cornus*, esp. the wild cornel with dark red branches, greenish-white flowers, and purple berries, found in woods and hedgerows. **2** any of various similar trees. **3** the wood of the dogwood.

doh var. of DO².

DOI *abbr.* (in the US) Department of the Interior.

doily /dóylee/ *n.* (also **doyley**) (*pl.* **-ies** or **-eys**) a small ornamental mat of paper, lace, etc., on a plate for cakes, etc. [orig. the name of a fabric: f. *Doiley*, the name of a draper]

doing /dōُoing/ *n.* **1 a** (usu. in *pl.*) an action; the performance of a deed (*famous for his doings*; *it was my doing*). **b** activity;

effort (*it takes a lot of doing*). **2** *colloq.* a scolding; a beating. **3** (in *pl.*) *sl.* things needed; adjuncts; things whose names are not known (*have we got all the doings?*).

■ **1 a** see ACTION *n.* 4.

doit /doyt/ *n. archaic* a very small amount of money. [MLG *doyt*, MDu. *duit*, of unkn. orig.]

dojo /dṓjō/ *n.* (*pl.* **-os**) **1** a room or hall in which judo and other martial arts are practiced. **2** a mat on which judo, etc., is practiced. [Jap.]

dol. *abbr.* dollar(s).

Dolby /dṓlbee/ *n. propr.* an electronic noise-reduction system used esp. in tape recording to reduce hiss. [R. M. *Dolby*, US inventor]

dolce far niente /dṓlchay faár nyéntay/ *n.* pleasant idleness. [It., = sweet doing nothing]

dolce vita /dṓlchay veéta/ *n.* a life of pleasure and luxury. [It., = sweet life]

■ see DISSIPATION 1.

doldrums /dṓldrəmz/ *n.pl.* (usu. prec. by *the*) **1** low spirits; a feeling of boredom or depression. **2** a period of inactivity or state of stagnation. **3** an equatorial ocean region of calms, sudden storms, and light unpredictable winds. [prob. after *dull* and *tantrum*]

■ **1** see GLOOM *n.* 2.

dole[1] /dōl/ *n. & v.* ● *n.* **1** (usu. prec. by *the*) *Brit. colloq.* benefit claimable by the unemployed from the government. **2** a charitable distribution. **b** a charitable (esp. sparing, niggardly) gift of food, clothes, or money. **3** *archaic* one's lot or destiny. ● *v.tr.* (usu. foll. by *out*) deal out sparingly. □ **dole bludger** *Austral. sl.* one who allegedly prefers the dole to work. **on the dole** *colloq.* receiving welfare, etc., payments from the government. [OE *dāl* f. Gmc]

■ *n.* **2 a** distribution, apportionment, allocation, dispensation. **b** portion, allotment, share, quota, lot, allowance, parcel; donation, gift, gratuity, handout, *hist.* alms. **3** see LOT *n.* 4. ● *v.* give (out), deal (out), distribute, hand out, share (out), dispense, allot, allocate, apportion, *literary* mete out, *sl.* dish out.

dole[2] /dōl/ *n. poet.* grief; woe; lamentation. [ME f. OF *do(e)l*, etc., f. pop.L *dolus* f. L *dolēre* grieve]

doleful /dṓlfŏŏl/ *adj.* **1** mournful; sad. **2** dreary; dismal. □□ **dolefully** *adv.* **dolefulness** *n.* [ME f. DOLE[2] + -FUL]

■ **1** sad, sorrowful, melancholy, gloomy, mournful, depressed, disconsolate, blue, down, distressed, dejected, downhearted, forlorn, unhappy, lugubrious, wretched, miserable, woebegone, woeful, *colloq.* down in the mouth, (down) in the dumps, *literary or joc.* dolorous; distressing, funereal, depressing, grievous, harrowing. **2** dreary, cheerless, joyless, somber, gloomy; see also DISMAL 1, 2.

dolerite /dṓlərīt/ *n.* a coarse basaltic rock. [F *dolérite* f. Gk *doleros* deceptive (because it is difficult to distinguish from diorite)]

dolichocephalic /dṓlikōsifálik/ *adj.* (also **dolichocephalous** /-séfələs/) having a long or narrow head. [Gk *dolikhos* long + -CEPHALIC, -CEPHALOUS]

dolina /dəleéna/ *n.* (also **doline** /dəleén/) *Geol.* an extensive depression or basin. [Russ. *dolina* valley]

doll /dol/ *n. & v.* ● *n.* **1** a small model of a human figure, esp. a baby or a child, as a child's toy. **2 a** *colloq.* a pretty but silly young woman. **b** *sl.* a young woman, esp. an attractive one. **3** a ventriloquist's dummy. ● *v.tr. & intr.* (foll. by *up*; often *refl.*) dress up smartly. □ **doll's house** esp. *Brit.* = DOLLHOUSE. [pet form of the name *Dorothy*]

dollar /dólər/ *n.* **1** the chief monetary unit in the US, Canada, and Australia. **2** the chief monetary unit of certain countries in the Pacific, West Indies, SE Asia, Africa, and S. America. □ **dollar diplomacy** diplomatic activity aimed at advancing a country's international influence by furthering its financial and commercial interests abroad. **dollar gap** the excess of a country's import trade with the dollar area over the corresponding export trade. **dollar sign** the sign $, used to indicate currency in dollars. [LG *daler* f. G *Taler*, short for *Joachimstaler*, a coin from the silver mine of *Joachimstal*, now *Jáchymov* in the Czech Republic]

dollarspot /dólərspot/ *n.* **1** a fungal disease of lawns, etc. **2** a discolored patch caused by this.

dollhouse /dólhows/ *n.* **1** a miniature toy house for dolls. **2** a very small house.

dollop /dóləp/ *n. & v.* ● *n.* a shapeless lump of food, etc. ● *v.tr.* (usu. foll. by *out*) serve out in large, shapeless quantities. [perh. f. Scand.]

■ *n.* see HELPING.

dolly /dólee/ *n., v., & adj.* ● *n.* (*pl.* **-ies**) **1** a child's name for a doll. **2** a movable platform for a movie camera. **3** *Cricket colloq.* an easy catch or hit. **4** a stick for stirring in clothes washing. **5** = *corn dolly* (see CORN[1]). **6** *colloq.* = *dolly bird*. ● *v.* (**-ies, -ied**) **1** *tr.* (foll. by *up*) dress up smartly. **2** *intr.* (foll. by *in*, *up*) move a cine-camera in or up to a subject, or out from it. ● *adj.* (**dollier, dolliest**) **1** *Brit. colloq.* (esp. of a girl) attractive, stylish. **2** *Cricket colloq.* easily hit or caught. □ **dolly bird** *Brit. colloq.* an attractive and stylish young woman. **dolly mixture** *Brit.* any of a mixture of small variously shaped and colored candies.

Dolly Varden /dólee vaárd'n/ *n.* **1** a woman's large hat with one side drooping and with a floral trimming. **2** a brightly spotted char, *Salvelinus malma*, of western N. America. [a character in Dickens's *Barnaby Rudge*]

dolma /dōlmə/ *n.* (*pl.* **dolmas** or **dolmades** /-maáthez/) a SE European delicacy of spiced rice or meat, etc., wrapped in vine or cabbage leaves. [Turk. f. *dolmak* fill, be filled: *dolmades* f. mod.Gk]

dolman /dōlmən/ *n.* **1** a long Turkish robe open in front. **2** a hussar's jacket worn with the sleeves hanging loose. **3** a woman's mantle with capelike or dolman sleeves. □ **dolman sleeve** a loose sleeve cut in one piece with the body of the coat, etc. [ult. f. Turk. *dolama*]

dolmen /dōlmən/ *n.* a megalithic tomb with a large, flat stone laid on upright ones. [F, perh. f. Cornish *tolmēn* hole of stone]

dolomite /dṓləmīt, dól-/ *n.* a mineral or rock of calcium magnesium carbonate. □□ **dolomitic** /-mítik/ *adj.* [F f. D. de *Dolomieu*, Fr. geologist d. 1801]

dolor /dṓlər/ *n.* (*Brit.* **dolour**) *literary* sorrow; distress. [ME f. OF f. L *dolor -oris* pain, grief]

■ see SORROW *n.* 1.

dolorous /dṓlərəs/ *adj. literary or joc.* **1** distressing; painful; doleful; dismal. **2** distressed; sad. □□ **dolorously** *adv.* [ME f. OF *doleros* f. LL *dolorosus* (as DOLOR)]

■ see DISMAL 1, 2.

dolphin /dólfin/ *n.* **1** any of various porpoiselike sea mammals of the family Delphinidae having a slender, beaklike snout. **2** (in general use) = DORADO 1. **3** a pile or buoy for mooring. **4** a structure for protecting the pier of a bridge. **5** a curved fish in heraldry, sculpture, etc. [ME, also *delphin* f. L *delphinus* f. Gk *delphis -inos*]

dolphinarium /dólfináireeəm/ *n.* (*pl.* **dolphinariums**) an aquarium for dolphins, esp. one open to the public.

dolt /dōlt/ *n.* a stupid person. □□ **doltish** *adj.* **doltishly** *adv.* **doltishness** *n.* [app. related to *dol*, *dold*, obs. var. of DULL]

■ fool, ass, blockhead, dunce, dullard, ignoramus, numskull, nincompoop, ninny, simpleton, dunderhead, *colloq.* moron, imbecile, idiot, fathead, donkey, nitwit, dimwit, chump, dummy, halfwit, birdbrain, pinhead, chucklehead, knucklehead, *Brit.* muggins, *colloq.* lamebrain, *Brit. colloq.* clot, *sl.* jerk, dope, dumbbell, bonehead, goon, clod, clodhopper, dingbat, *Austral. sl.* alec, *Austral. & NZ sl. derog.* drongo, esp. *Brit. sl.* twit.

Dom /dom/ *n.* **1** a title prefixed to the names of some Roman Catholic dignitaries, and Benedictine and Carthusian monks. **2** the Portuguese equivalent of Don (see DON[1]). [L *dominus* master: sense 2 through Port.]

-dom /dəm/ *suffix* forming nouns denoting: **1** state or condition (*freedom*). **2** rank or status (*earldom*). **3** domain (*king-*

/.../ **pronunciation**	● **part of speech**
□ **phrases, idioms, and compounds**	
□□ **derivatives**	■ **synonym section**
cross-references appear in SMALL CAPITALS or *italics*	

dom). **4** a class of people (or the attitudes, etc., associated with them) regarded collectively (*officialdom*). [OE *-dōm*, orig. = DOOM]

domain /dōmáyn/ *n.* **1** an area under one rule; a realm. **2** an estate or lands under one control. **3** a sphere of control or influence. **4** *Math.* the set of possible values of an independent variable. **5** *Physics* a discrete region of magnetism in ferromagnetic material. □□ **domanial** /-máyneeəl/ *adj.* [ME f. F *domaine*, OF *demeine* DEMESNE, assoc. with L *dominus* lord]
  ■ **1** realm, dominion, territory, property, land(s), province, kingdom, empire. **3** province, territory, field, area, department, sphere, discipline, specialty, specialization, concern, *formal esp. Law* realm, *joc.* bailiwick.

domaine /dōmáyn/ *n.* a vineyard. [F: see DOMAIN]

dome /dōm/ *n. & v.* ● *n.* **1 a** a rounded vault as a roof, with a circular, elliptical, or polygonal base; a large cupola. **b** the revolving, openable hemispherical roof of an observatory. **2 a** a natural vault or canopy (of the sky, trees, etc.). **b** the rounded summit of a hill, etc. **3** *Geol.* a dome-shaped structure. **4** *sl.* the head. **5** *poet.* a stately building. ● *v.tr.* (usu. as **domed** *adj.*) cover with or shape as a dome. □□ **domelike** *adj.* [F *dôme* f. It. *duomo* cathedral, dome f. L *domus* house]
  ■ **4** see HEAD *n.* 1.

Domesday /dōōmzday/ *n.* (in full **Domesday Book**) a record of the lands of England made in 1086 by order of William I. [ME var. of doomsday, as being a book of final authority]

domestic /dəméstik/ *adj. & n.* ● *adj.* **1** of the home, household, or family affairs. **2 a** of one's own country, not foreign or international. **b** homegrown or homemade. **3** (of an animal) kept by or living with humans. **4** fond of home life. ● *n.* a household servant. □ **domestic science** the study of household management. □□ **domestically** *adv.* [F *domestique* f. L *domesticus* f. *domus* home]
  ■ *adj.* **1** home, private, family, familial; residential, household. **2 a** home, native, indigenous, internal; homegrown. **3** tame, domesticated, housebroken, trained, *Brit.* house-trained. **4** home-loving.
  ● *n.* servant, (hired) help, housekeeper, cleaner; majordomo, steward.

domesticate /dəméstikayt/ *v.tr.* **1** tame (an animal) to live with humans. **2** accustom to home life and management. **3** naturalize (a plant or animal). □□ **domesticable** /-kəbəl/ *adj.* **domestication** /-káyshən/ *n.* [med.L *domesticare* (as DOMESTIC)]
  ■ **1** see TAME *v.* 1.

domesticity /dōməstísitee/ *n.* **1** the state of being domestic. **2** domestic or home life.

domicile /dómisil, -sil, dŏ-/ *n. & v.* (also **domicil** /-sil/) ● *n.* **1** a dwelling place; one's home. **2** *Law* **a** a place of permanent residence. **b** the fact of residing. **3** the place at which a bill of exchange is made payable. ● *v.tr.* **1** (usu. as **domiciled** *adj.*) (usu. foll. by *at, in*) establish or settle in a place. **2** (usu. foll. by *at*) make (a bill of exchange) payable at a certain place. [ME f. OF f. L *domicilium* f. *domus* home]
  ■ *n.* **1** residence, abode, home, house, habitation, (living) quarters, housing, rooms, accommodation(s), lodging(s), *colloq.* pad, digs, *Brit. colloq.* diggings, *formal* dwelling place). ● *v.* **1** house, locate, lodge, settle, establish, situate; (**domiciled**) see RESIDENT *adj.* 1.

domiciliary /dómisílee-eree/ *adj.* of a dwelling place (esp. of a doctor's, official's, etc., visit to a person's home). [F *domiciliaire* f. med.L *domiciliarius* (as DOMICILE)]

dominance /dóminəns/ *n.* **1** the state of being dominant. **2** control, authority.
  ■ see POWER *n.* 3a, 5.

dominant /dóminənt/ *adj. & n.* ● *adj.* **1** dominating; prevailing; most influential. **2** (of a high place) prominent; overlooking others. **3 a** (of an allele) expressed even when inherited from only one parent. **b** (of an inherited characteristic) appearing in an individual even when its allelic counterpart is also inherited (cf. RECESSIVE). ● *n. Mus.*

the fifth note of the diatonic scale of any key. □□ **dominantly** *adv.* [F f. L *dominari* (as DOMINATE)]
  ■ *adj.* **1** dominating, commanding, authoritative, controlling, governing, ruling, leading, influential, assertive, supreme, superior, ascendant; predominant, chief, main, principal, primary, prevailing, outstanding, preeminent, paramount.

dominate /dóminayt/ *v.* **1** *tr. &* (foll. by *over*) *intr.* have a commanding influence on; exercise control over (*fear dominated them for years*; *dominates over his friends*). **2** *intr.* (of a person, sound, feature of a scene, etc.) be the most influential or conspicuous. **3** *tr. &* (foll. by *over*) *intr.* (of a building, etc.) have a commanding position over; overlook. □□ **dominator** *n.* [L *dominari dominat-* f. *dominus* lord]
  ■ **1** command, control, govern, rule, direct, lead, reign over, exercise command *or* authority *or* control *or* rule over, have under one's thumb; have the whip *or* upper hand (over), be in control, rule the roost *or* roast, call the shots *or* tune, be in the driver's seat, pull the strings, be in the saddle, wear the trousers, be at the wheel, *colloq.* run the show. **2** predominate, preponderate, stand out, stick out. **3** overlook, look (out) over, tower over *or* above, rise above, overshadow.

domination /dómináyshən/ *n.* **1 a** command; control. **b** oppression; tyranny. **2** the act or an instance of dominating; the process of being dominated. **3** (in *pl.*) angelic beings of the fourth order of the celestial hierarchy. [ME f. OF f. L *dominatio -onis* (as DOMINATE)]
  ■ **1 a** authority, control, rule, power, command, influence, sway, supremacy, ascendancy, hegemony, preeminence, mastery. **b** oppression, subjection, repression, suppression, subordination, enslavement; enthrallment; dictatorship, despotism, tyranny.

domineer /dóminéer/ *v.intr.* (often as **domineering** *adj.*) behave in an arrogant and overbearing way. □□ **domineeringly** *adv.* [Du. *domineren* f. F *dominer*]
  ■ throw one's weight about; dominate over, tyrannize over; (**domineering**) overbearing, imperious, officious, arrogant, autocratic, authoritarian, high-handed, high and mighty, masterful, arbitrary, peremptory, dictatorial, despotic, tyrannical, oppressive, strict, hard, harsh, tough, *colloq.* bossy, pushy.

dominical /dəmínikəl/ *adj.* **1** of the Lord's day, of Sunday. **2** of the Lord (Jesus Christ). □ **dominical letter** the one of the seven letters A–G indicating the dates of Sundays in a year. [F *dominical* or L *dominicalis* f. L *dominicus* f. *dominus* lord]

Dominican /dəmínikən/ *adj. & n.* ● *adj.* **1** of or relating to St. Dominic or the order of preaching friars which he founded in 1215–16. **2** of or relating to either of the two orders of female religious founded on Dominican principles. ● *n.* a Dominican friar, nun, or sister (see also *Black Friar*). [med.L *Dominicanus* f. *Dominicus* L name of *Domingo* de Guzmán (St. Dominic)]

dominie /dóminee/ *n. Sc.* a schoolmaster. [later spelling of *domine* sir, voc. of L *dominus*]

dominion /dəmínyən/ *n.* **1** sovereignty; control. **2** the territory of a sovereign or government; a domain. **3** *hist.* the title of each of the self-governing territories of the British Commonwealth. [ME f. OF f. med.L *dominio -onis* f. L *dominium* f. *dominus* lord]
  ■ **1** rule, authority, control, dominance, domination, grasp, mastery, grip, command, jurisdiction, power, sovereignty, sway, ascendancy, preeminence, primacy, supremacy, hegemony. **2** domain, territory, region, area, country, kingdom, *formal esp. Law* realm.

domino /dóminō/ *n.* (*pl.* **-oes** or **-os**) **1 a** any of 28 small oblong pieces marked with 0–6 dots in each half. **b** (in *pl.*, usu. treated as *sing.*) a game played with these. **2 a** a loose cloak with a mask for the upper part of the face, worn at masquerades. □ **domino theory** the theory that a political event, etc., in one country will cause similar events in neighboring countries, like a row of falling dominoes. [F, prob. f. L *dominus* lord, but unexplained]

don[1] /don/ *n.* **1** a university teacher, esp. a senior member of a college at Oxford or Cambridge. **2** (**Don**) **a** a Spanish title prefixed to a forename. **b** a Spanish gentleman; a Spaniard. [Sp. f. L *dominus* lord]

■ **1** see TEACHER.

don[2] /don/ *v.tr.* (**donned, donning**) put on (clothing). [= *do on*]

■ see *put on* 1 (PUT[1]).

dona /dŏnə/ *n.* (also **donah**) *Brit. sl.* a woman; a sweetheart. [Sp. *doña* or Port. *dona* f. L (as DONNA)]

donate /dŏnayt, dōnáyt/ *v.tr.* give or contribute (money, etc.), esp. voluntarily to a fund or institution. □□ **donator** *n.* [back-form. f. DONATION]

■ give, provide, supply, present, contribute, subscribe (to *or* for), pledge, award, bestow, confer, grant, will, bequeath, *formal* vouchsafe.

donation /dōnáyshən/ *n.* **1** the act or an instance of donating. **2** something, esp. an amount of money, donated. [ME f. OF f. L *donatio -onis* f. *donare* give f. *donum* gift]

■ **1** giving, contribution, bestowal, allotment. **2** gift, contribution, present, dole, grant, offer, award, offering, bequest, *hist.* alms.

donative /dŏnətiv, dón-/ *n.* & *adj.* ● *n.* a gift or donation, esp. one given formally or officially as a largesse. ● *adj.* **1** given as a donation or bounty. **2** *hist.* (of a benefice) given directly, not presentative. [ME f. L *donativum* gift, largesse f. *donare*: see DONATION]

done /dun/ *past part.* of DO[1]. ● *adj.* **1** *colloq.* socially acceptable (*the done thing; it isn't done*). **2** (often with *in, up*) *colloq.* tired out. **3** (esp. as *int.* in reply to an offer, etc.) accepted. □ **be done with** be finished with. **done for** *colloq.* in serious trouble. **have done** have ceased or finished. **have done with** be rid of; have finished dealing with.

■ **1** see CORRECT *adj.* 2, 3.

donee /dōneé/ *n.* the recipient of a gift. [DONOR + -EE]

dong[1] /dawng, dong/ *v.* & *n.* ● *v.* **1** *intr.* make the deep sound of a large bell. **2** *tr. Austral.* & *NZ colloq.* hit; punch. ● *n.* **1** the deep sound of a large bell. **2** *Austral.* & *NZ colloq.* a heavy blow. [imit.]

dong[2] /dawng, dong/ *n.* the chief monetary unit of Vietnam. [Vietnamese]

donga /dóngɡə, dáwng-/ *n. S.Afr.* & *Austral.* **1** a dry watercourse. **2** a ravine caused by erosion. [Zulu]

dongle /dáwngɡəl, dóng-/ *n. Computing sl.* a security attachment required by a computer to enable protected software to be used. [arbitrary form.]

donjon /dónjən, dún-/ *n.* the great tower or innermost keep of a castle. [archaic spelling of DUNGEON]

■ see DUNGEON *n.* 2.

Don Juan /don waán, hwaán, jŏŏən/ *n.* a seducer of women; a libertine. [name of a legendary Sp. nobleman celebrated in fiction, e.g., by Byron]

■ see LIBERTINE *n.* 1.

donkey /dóngkee, dúng-, dáwng-/ *n.* (*pl.* **-eys**) **1** a domestic ass. **2** *colloq.* a stupid or foolish person. □ **donkey engine** a small auxiliary engine. **donkey jacket** *Brit.* a thick weatherproof jacket worn by workers and as a fashion garment. **donkey's years** *colloq.* a very long time. [earlier with pronunc. as *monkey*: perh. f. DUN[1], or the Christian name *Duncan*]

■ **2** see DOLT.

donkeywork /dónkeewərk, dúng-, dáwng-/ *n.* the laborious part of a job; drudgery.

donna /dónə/ *n.* **1** an Italian lady. **2** (**Donna**) the title of such a lady. [It. f. L *domina* mistress fem. of *dominus*: cf. DON[1]]

donnée /dónáy, daw-/ *n.* **1** the subject or theme of a story, etc. **2** a basic fact or assumption. [F, fem. or masc. past part. of *donner* give]

■ **2** see GIVEN *n.*

donnish /dónish/ *adj.* like or resembling a college don, esp. in supposed pedantry. □□ **donnishly** *adv.* **donnishness** *n.*

■ see *pedantic* (PEDANT).

donnybrook /dóneebrŏŏk/ *n.* (also **Donnybrook**) an uproar; a free fight. [*Donnybrook* near Dublin, Ireland, formerly site of annual fair]

donor /dŏnər/ *n.* **1** a person who gives or donates something (e.g., to a charity). **2** one who provides blood for a transfusion, semen for insemination, or an organ or tissue for transplantation. **3** *Chem.* an atom or molecule that provides a pair of electrons in forming a coordinate bond. **4** *Physics* an impurity atom in a semiconductor which contributes a conducting electron to the material. □ **donor card** an official card authorizing use of organs for transplant, carried by the donor. [ME f. AF *donour*, OF *doneur* f. L *donator -oris* f. *donare* give]

■ **1** giver, provider, supplier, benefactor, contributor, supporter, backer, patron.

don't /dōnt/ *contr.* do not. ● *n.* a prohibition (*dos and don'ts*).

donut var. of DOUGHNUT.

doodad /dŏŏdad/ *n.* **1** a fancy article; a trivial ornament. **2** a gadget or thingamajig. [20th c.: orig. unkn.]

■ **1** see TRIFLE *n.* 1. **2** see THING 2, 3.

doodle /dŏŏd'l/ *v.* & *n.* ● *v.intr.* scribble or draw, esp. absentmindedly. ● *n.* a scrawl or drawing made. □□ **doodler** *n.* [orig. = foolish person; cf. LG *dudelkopf*]

doodlebug /dŏŏd'lbug/ *n.* **1** any of various insects, esp. the larva of an ant lion. **2** an unscientific device for locating minerals. **3** *colloq.* a robot bomb.

doohickey /dŏŏhikee/ *n.* (*pl.* **-eys** *or* **-ies**) *US colloq.* a small object, esp. mechanical. [DOODAD + HICKEY]

■ see GADGET.

doom /dŏŏm/ *n.* & *v.* ● *n.* **1 a** a grim fate or destiny. **b** death or ruin. **2 a** a condemnation; a judgment or sentence. **b** the Last Judgment (*the crack of doom*). **3** *hist.* a statute, law, or decree. ● *v.tr.* **1** (usu. foll. by *to*) condemn or destine (*a city doomed to destruction*). **2** (esp. as **doomed** *adj.*) consign to misfortune or destruction. □ **doom palm** var. of DOUM palm. [OE *dōm* statute, judgment f. Gmc: rel. to DO[1]]

■ *n.* **1** fate, destiny, fortune, lot, kismet; downfall, destruction, death, ruin, extinction, annihilation, end, termination, terminus. **2 a** see SENTENCE *n.* ● *v.* **1** see DESTINE. **2** (**doomed**) fated, cursed, condemned, damned; accursed, bedeviled, ill-fated, luckless, bewitched, *archaic* star-crossed; see also INAUSPICIOUS 1.

doomsday /dŏŏmzday/ *n.* the day of the Last Judgment. □ **till doomsday** for ever (cf. DOMESDAY). [OE *dōmes dæg*: see DOOM]

■ □ **till doomsday** see EVER 1.

doomwatch /dŏŏmwoch/ *n.* organized vigilance or observation to avert danger, esp. from environmental pollution. □□ **doomwatcher** *n.*

door /dawr/ *n.* **1 a** a hinged, sliding, or revolving barrier for closing and opening an entrance to a building, room, cupboard, etc. **b** this as representing a house, etc. (*lives two doors away*). **2 a** an entrance or exit; a doorway. **b** a means of access or approach. □ **close the door to** exclude the opportunity for. **door prize** a prize awarded usu. by lottery at a dance, party, charity event, etc. **door-to-door** (of selling, etc.) done at each house in turn. **lay** (*or* **lie**) **at the door of** impute (or be imputable) to. **leave the door open** ensure that an option remains available. **next door** in or to the next house or room. **next door to 1** in the next house to. **2** nearly, almost, near to. **open the door to** create an opportunity for. **out of doors** in or into the open air. □□ **doored** *adj.* (also in *comb.*). [OE *duru, dor* f. Gmc]

■ **1a, 2** see ENTRY 3a.

doorbell /dáwrbel/ *n.* a bell in a house, etc., rung by visitors outside to signal their arrival.

doorcase /dáwrkays/ *n.* the outermost part of a doorframe.

doorframe /dáwrfraym/ *n.* the framework of a doorway.

doorkeeper /dáwrkeepər/ *n.* = DOORMAN 1.

/.../ pronunciation	● part of speech
□ **phrases, idioms, and compounds**	
□□ **derivatives**	■ **synonym section**
cross-references appear in SMALL CAPITALS *or italics*	

doorknob /dáwrnob/ *n.* a knob for turning to release the latch of a door.

doorman /dáwrman, -mən/ *n.* (*pl.* **-men**) **1** a person on duty at the door to a large building. **2** *Brit.* a janitor or porter.

doormat /dáwrmat/ *n.* **1** a mat at an entrance for wiping mud, etc., from the shoes. **2** a feebly submissive person.
■ **2** see DRIP *n.* 2.

doornail /dáwrnayl/ *n.* a nail with which doors were studded for strength or ornament. □ **dead as a doornail** completely or unmistakably dead.

doorplate /dáwrplayt/ *n.* a plate on the door of a house or room bearing the name of the occupant.

doorpost /dáwrpōst/ *n.* each of the uprights of a doorframe, on one of which the door is hung.

doorstep /dáwrstep/ *n. & v.* ● *n.* **1** a step leading up to the outer door of a house, etc. **2** *Brit. sl.* a thick slice of bread. ● *v.intr.* (**-stepped, -stepping**) go from door to door selling, canvassing, etc. □ **on one's** (or **the**) **doorstep** very close.
■ *n.* **1** see THRESHOLD 1.

doorstop /dáwrstop/ *n.* a device for keeping a door open or to prevent it from striking a wall, etc., when opened.

doorway /dáwrway/ *n.* an opening filled by a door.
■ see THRESHOLD 1.

dooryard /dáwryaard/ *n.* a yard or garden near the door of a house.

doozy /dóōzee/ *n.* (*pl.* **doozies**) (also **doozie**) *colloq.* one that is outstanding of its kind (*a mistake that was a doozy*). [orig. unknown]

dopa /dópə/ *n. Pharm.* a crystalline amino acid derivative used in the treatment of Parkinson's disease. [G f. *Dioxyphenylalanine*, former name of the compound]

dopant /dópənt/ *n. Electronics* a substance used in doping a semiconductor.

dope /dōp/ *n. & v.* ● *n.* **1** a varnish applied to the cloth surface of airplane parts to strengthen them, keep them airtight, etc. **2** a thick liquid used as a lubricant, etc. **3** a substance added to gasoline, etc., to increase its effectiveness. **4 a** *sl.* a narcotic; a stupefying drug. **b** a drug, etc., given to a horse or greyhound, or taken by an athlete, to affect performance. **5** *sl.* a stupid person. **6** *sl.* **a** information about a subject, esp. if not generally known. **b** misleading information. ● *v.* **1** *tr.* administer dope to; drug. **2** *tr. Electronics* add an impurity to (a semiconductor) to produce a desired electrical characteristic. **3** *tr.* smear; daub; apply dope to. **4** *intr.* take addictive drugs. □ **dope out** *sl.* discover. □□ **doper** *n.* [Du. *doop* sauce f. *doopen* to dip]
■ *n.* **4** a narcotic, drug, opiate, hallucinogen, psychedelic, *sl.* upper, downer. **5** see DOLT. **6 a** information, data, facts, news, details, story, message, *colloq.* info, lowdown, score, *literary* tidings, *sl.* poop. ● *v.* **3** see SMEAR *v.* 1. □ **dope out** see DISCOVER 1a, b.

dopey /dópee/ *adj.* (also **dopy**) (**dopier, dopiest**) *colloq.* **1 a** half asleep. **b** stupefied by or as if by a drug. **2** stupid; silly. □□ **dopily** *adv.* **dopiness** *n.*
■ **1 b** see GROGGY. **2** see STUPID *adj.* 1, 5.

doppelgänger /dópəlgangər/ *n.* an apparition or double of a living person. [G, = double-goer]
■ see DOUBLE *n.*, GHOST *n.* 1.

Doppler effect /dóplər/ *n.* (also **Doppler shift**) *Physics* an increase (or decrease) in the frequency of sound, light, or other waves as the source and observer move toward (or away) from each other. [C. J. *Doppler*, Austrian physicist d. 1853]

Doppler radar /dóplər/ *n.* a radar system using the Doppler effect to determine velocity and location, as of storm clouds, etc.

dopy var. of DOPEY.

dorado /dəraádō/ *n.* (*pl.* **-os**) **1** a blue and silver marine fish, *Coryphaena hippurus*, showing brilliant colors when dying out of water. **2** a brightly colored freshwater fish, *Salminus maxillosus*, native to S. America. [Sp. f. LL *deauratus* gilt f. *aurum* gold]

Dorian /dáwreeən/ *n. & adj.* ● *n.* (in *pl.*) a Greek-speaking people thought to have entered Greece from the north

*c.*1100 BC and settled in parts of Central and S. Greece. ● *adj.* of or relating to the Dorians or to Doris in Central Greece. □ **Dorian mode** *Mus.* the mode represented by the natural diatonic scale D–D. [L *Dorius* f. Gk *Dōrios* f. *Dōros*, the mythical ancestor]

Doric /dáwrik, dór-/ *adj. & n.* ● *adj.* **1** (of a dialect) broad; rustic. **2** *Archit.* of the oldest, sturdiest, and simplest of the Greek orders. ● *n.* **1** rustic English or esp. Scots. **2** *Archit.* the Doric order. **3** the dialect of the Dorians in ancient Greece. [L *Doricus* f. Gk *Dōrikos* (as DORIAN)]

dork /dawrk/ *n. sl.* a dull, slow-witted, or oafish person. □□ **dorky** *adj.*

dorm /dawrm/ *n. colloq.* dormitory. [abbr.]

dormant /dáwrmənt/ *adj.* **1** lying inactive as in sleep; sleeping. **2 a** (of a volcano, etc.) temporarily inactive. **b** (of potential faculties, etc.) in abeyance. **3** (of plants) alive but not actively growing. **4** *Heraldry* (of a beast) lying with its head on its paws. □□ **dormancy** *n.* [ME f. OF, pres. part. of *dormir* f. L *dormire* sleep]
■ **1** asleep, sleeping, resting, at rest, quiet, inactive, still, inert, unmoving, motionless, stationary, immobile, quiescent, comatose, torpid, hibernating, slumberous, *poet. rhet.* slumbering. **2 b** latent, potential, hidden, concealed, undisclosed, unrevealed, unexpressed; see also ABEYANCE.

dormer /dáwrmər/ *n.* (in full **dormer window**) a projecting upright window in a sloping roof. [OF *dormĕor* (as DORMANT)]

dormitory /dáwrmitáwree/ *n.* (*pl.* **-ies**) **1** a sleeping room with several beds, esp. in a school or institution. **2** (in full **dormitory town**, etc.) esp. *Brit.* a small town or suburb from which people travel to work in a city, etc. **3** a university or college hall of residence or hostel. [ME f. L *dormitorium* f. *dormire* *dormit-* sleep]

dormouse /dáwrmows/ *n.* (*pl.* **dormice**) any small, mouselike hibernating rodent of the family Gliridae, having a long, bushy tail. [ME: orig. unkn., but assoc. with F *dormir*, L *dormire*: see DORMANT]

doronicum /dərónikəm/ *n.* = *leopard's-bane* (see LEOPARD). [mod.L (Linnaeus) ult. f. Arab. *darānaj*]

dorp /dawrp/ *n. S.Afr.* a village or small township. [Du. (as THORP)]

dorsal /dáwrsəl/ *adj. Anat., Zool., & Bot.* **1** of, on, or near the back (cf. VENTRAL). **2** ridge-shaped. □□ **dorsally** *adv.* [F *dorsal* or LL *dorsalis* f. L *dorsum* back]

dory[1] /dáwree/ *n.* (*pl.* **-ies**) any of various marine fish having a compressed body and flat head, esp. the John Dory, used as food. [ME f. F *dorée* fem. past part. of *dorer* gild (as DORADO)]

dory[2] /dáwree/ *n.* (*pl.* **-ies**) a flat-bottomed fishing boat with high bow and flaring sides. [Miskito *dóri* dugout]

DOS /dos, daws/ *n. Computing* a software operating system for personal computers. [abbr. of *disk operating system*]

dos-à-dos /dóʒaadō/ *adj. & n.* ● *adj.* (of two books) bound together with a shared central board and facing in opposite directions. ● *n.* (*pl.* same) a seat, carriage, etc., in which the occupants sit back to back (cf. DO-SI-DO). [F, = back to back]

dosage /dósij/ *n.* **1** the giving of medicine in doses. **2** the size of a dose.

dose /dōs/ *n. & v.* ● *n.* **1** an amount of a medicine or drug for taking or taken at one time. **2** a quantity of something administered or allocated (e.g., work, praise, punishment, etc.). **3** the amount of ionizing radiation received by a person or thing. **4** *sl.* a venereal infection. ● *v.tr.* **1** treat (a person or animal) with doses of medicine. **2** give a dose or doses to. **3** adulterate or blend (esp. wine with spirit). □ **like a dose of salts** *Brit. colloq.* very fast and efficiently. [F f. LL *dosis* f. Gk *dosis* gift f. *didōmi* give]
■ *n.* **2** portion, quantity, amount, measure, allotment.
● *v.* **1** see TREAT *v.* 3.

do-si-do /dósee dō/ *n.* (*pl.* **-os**) a figure in which two dancers pass around each other back to back and return to their original positions. [corrupt. of DOS-À-DOS]

dosimeter /dōsímitər/ *n.* a device used to measure an absorbed dose of ionizing radiation. □□ **dosimetric** /-métrik/ *adj.* **dosimetry** *n.*

doss /dos/ *v. & n. Brit. sl.* ● *v.intr.* (often foll. by *down*) sleep, esp. roughly or in a cheap rooming house, motel, etc. ● *n.* a bed, esp. in a cheap rooming house, motel, etc. □ **dosshouse** a cheap rooming house, motel, etc., esp. for vagrants. [prob. = *doss* ornamental covering for a seat back, etc., f. OF *dos* ult. f. L *dorsum* back]

dossal /dósəl/ *n.* a hanging cloth behind an altar or around a chancel. [med.L *dossale* t. LL *dorsalis* DORSAL]

dosser /dósər/ *n. Brit. sl.* **1** a person who dosses. **2** = *dosshouse.*

dossier /dósee-ay, dáw-/ *n.* a set of documents, esp. a collection of information about a person, event, or subject. [F, so called from the label on the back, f. *dos* back f. L *dorsum*] ■ file, papers, document.

dost /dust/ *archaic 2nd sing. present* of DO¹.

DOT *abbr.* Department of Transportation.

dot¹ /dot/ *n. & v.* ● *n.* **1 a** a small spot, speck, or mark. **b** such a mark written or printed as part of an *i* or *j*, as a diacritical mark, as one of a series of marks to signify omission, or as a full stop. **c** a decimal point. **2** *Mus.* a dot used to denote the lengthening of a note or rest, or to indicate staccato. **3** the shorter signal of the two used in Morse code (cf. DASH *n.* 6). **4** a tiny or apparently tiny object (*a dot on the horizon*). ● *v.tr.* (**dotted, dotting**) **1 a** mark with a dot or dots. **b** place a dot over (a letter). **2** *Mus.* mark (a note or rest) to show that the time value is increased by half. **3** (often foll. by *about*) scatter like dots. **4** partly cover as with dots (*an ocean dotted with ships*). **5** *Brit. sl.* hit (*dotted him one in the eye*). □ **dot the i's and cross the t's** *colloq.* **1** be minutely accurate; emphasize details. **2** add the final touches to a task, exercise, etc. **dot matrix printer** *Computing* a printer with characters formed from dots printed by configurations of the tips of small wires. **dotted line** a line of dots on a document, esp. to show a place left for a signature. **on the dot** exactly on time. **the year dot** *Brit. colloq.* far in the past. □□ **dotter** *n.* [OE *dott* head of a boil, perh. infl. by Du. *dot* knot]

■ *n.* **1** spot, speck, mark; decimal point, full stop, period. **4** spot, speck, point, mark, fleck. ● *v.* **1a, 4** spot, fleck, speckle, stipple. **5** see HIT *v.* 1a. □ **dot the i's and cross the t's 1** be pedantic *or* fussy *or* meticulous *or* precise *or* accurate *or* exact *or* fastidious *or* scrupulous *or* punctilious *or* finicky *or* perfectionist, *colloq.* be persnickety. **on the dot** on time, promptly, punctually.

dot² /dot/ *n.* a woman's dowry. [F f. L *dos dotis*]

dotage /dótij/ *n.* feeble-minded senility (*in his dotage*). ● see *decrepitude* (DECREPIT).

dotard /dótərd/ *n.* a person who is feeble-minded, esp. from senility. [ME f. DOTE + -ARD]

dote /dōt/ *v.intr.* **1** (foll. by *on, upon*) be foolishly or excessively fond of. **2** be silly or feeble-minded, esp. from old age. □□ **doter** *n.* **dotingly** *adv.* [ME, corresp. to MDu. *doten* be silly]

■ **1** (*dote on* or *upon*) be fond of, be infatuated with, love, idolize, hold dear, adore, make much of; coddle, pamper, spoil, indulge.

doth /duth/ *archaic 3rd sing. present* of DO¹.

dotterel /dótərəl/ *n.* a small migrant plover, *Eudromias morinellus*. [ME f. DOTE + -REL, named from the ease with which it is caught, taken to indicate stupidity]

dottle /dót'l/ *n.* a remnant of unburned tobacco in a pipe. [DOT¹ + -LE¹]

dotty /dótee/ *adj.* (**dottier, dottiest**) *colloq.* **1** feeble-minded, silly. **2** eccentric. **3** absurd. **4** (foll. by *about, on*) infatuated with; obsessed by. □□ **dottily** *adv.* **dottiness** *n.* [earlier = unsteady: f. DOT¹ + -Y¹]

■ **1–3** see CRAZY 1. **4** see CRAZY 2.

douane /doō-aán/ *n.* a foreign customhouse. [F f. It. *do(g)ana* f. Turk. *duwan*, Arab. *dīwān*: cf. DIVAN]

Douay Bible /doō-ay, doō-áy/ *n.* (also **Douay Version**) an English translation of the Bible formerly used in the Roman Catholic Church, completed at Douai in France early in the seventeenth century.

double /dúbəl/ *adj., adv., n., & v.* ● *adj.* **1 a** consisting of two usu. equal parts or things; twofold. **b** consisting of two identical parts. **2** twice as much or many (*double the amount*; *double the number*; *double thickness*). **3** having twice the usual size, quantity, strength, etc. (*double whiskey*). **4** designed for two people (*double bed*). **5 a** having some part double. **b** (of a flower) having more than one circle of petals. **c** (of a domino) having the same number of pips on each half. **6** having two different roles or interpretations, esp. implying confusion or deceit (*double meaning*; *leads a double life*). **7** *Mus.* lower in pitch by an octave (*double bassoon*). ● *adv.* **1** at or to twice the amount, etc. (*counts double*). **2** two together (*sleep double*). ● *n.* **1 a** a double quantity or thing; twice as much or many. **b** *colloq.* a double measure of liquor. **2 a** a counterpart of a person or thing; a person who looks exactly like another. **b** an understudy. **c** a wraith. **3** (in *pl.*) *Sports* (esp. tennis) a game between two pairs of players. **4** *Sports* a pair of victories over the same team, a pair of championships at the same game, etc. **5** a system of betting in which the winnings and stake from the first bet are transferred to a second. **6** *Bridge* the doubling of an opponent's bid. **7** *Darts* a hit on the narrow ring enclosed by the two outer circles of a dartboard, scoring double. **8** a sharp turn, esp. of the tracks of a hunted animal, or the course of a river. ● *v.* **1** *tr. & intr.* make or become twice as much or many; increase twofold; multiply by two. **2** *tr.* amount to twice as much as. **3 a** *tr.* fold or bend (paper, cloth, etc.) over on itself. **b** *intr.* become folded. **4 a** *tr.* (of an actor) play (two parts) in the same piece. **b** *intr.* (often foll. by *for*) be understudy, etc. **5** *intr.* (usu. foll. by *as*) play a twofold role. **6** *intr.* turn sharply in flight or pursuit; take a tortuous course. **7** *tr. Naut.* sail around (a headland). **8** *tr. Bridge* make a call increasing the value of the points to be won or lost on (an opponent's bid). **9** *Mus.* **a** *intr.* (often foll. by *on*) play two or more musical instruments (*the clarinettist doubles on tenor sax*). **b** *tr.* add the same note in a higher or lower octave to (a note). **10** *tr.* clench (a fist). **11** *intr.* move at twice the usual speed; run. **12** *Billiards* **a** *intr.* rebound. **b** *tr.* cause to rebound. □ **double acrostic** SEE ACROSTIC. **double agent** one who spies simultaneously for two rival countries, etc. **double axe** an axe with two blades. **double back** take a new direction opposite to the previous one. **double-barreled 1** (of a gun) having two barrels. **2** twofold; having a dual purpose. **double bass 1** the largest and lowest-pitched instrument of the violin family. **2** (also **double bassist**) its player. **double bill** a program with two principal items. **double bind** a dilemma. **double-blind** *adj.* (of a test or experiment) in which neither the tester nor the subject has knowledge of identities, etc., that might lead to bias. ● *n.* such a test or experiment. **double boiler** a saucepan with a detachable upper compartment heated by boiling water in the lower one. **double bond** *Chem.* a pair of bonds between two atoms in a molecule. **double-book** accept two reservations simultaneously for (the same seat, room, etc.). **double-breasted** (of a coat, etc.) having two fronts overlapping across the body. **double-check** verify twice or in two ways. **double chin** a chin with a fold of loose flesh below it. **double-chinned** having a double chin. **double concerto** a concerto for two solo instruments. **double cream 1** a soft French cheese. **2** *Brit.* thick cream with a high fat content. **double-cross** deceive or betray (a person one is supposedly helping). **double cross** *n.* an act of double-crossing. **double-crosser** a person who double-crosses. **double dagger** *Printing* a sign (‡) used to introduce a reference. **double-dealer** a deceiver. **double-dealing** *n.* deceit, esp. in business. ● *adj.* deceitful; practicing deceit. **double-decker 1** esp. *Brit.* a bus having an upper and lower deck. **2** *colloq.*

anything consisting of two layers. **double decomposition** *Chem.* a chemical reaction involving exchange of radicals between two reactants: also called METATHESIS. **double density** *Computing* designating a storage device, esp. a disk, having twice the basic capacity. **double dummy** *Bridge* play with two hands exposed, allowing every card to be located. **double Dutch 1** a synchronized jump-rope game using two outstretched ropes swung in opposite directions. **2** *Brit. colloq.* incomprehensible talk. **double eagle 1** a figure of a two-headed eagle. **2** *Golf* a score of three strokes under par at any hole. **3** *hist.* a coin worth twenty dollars. **double-edged 1** having two functions or (often contradictory) applications. **2** (of a knife, etc.) having two cutting edges. **double entry** a system of bookkeeping in which each transaction is entered as a debit in one account and a credit in another. **double exposure** *Photog.* the accidental or deliberate repeated exposure of a plate, film, etc. **double-faced 1** insincere. **2** (of a fabric or material) finished on both sides so that either may be used as the right side. **double fault** (in tennis) two consecutive faults in serving. **double feature** a movie program with two full-length films. **double figures** the numbers from 10 to 99. **double first** *Brit.* **1** first-class honors in two subjects or examinations at a university. **2** a person achieving this. **double glazing 1** a window consisting of two layers of glass with a space between them, designed to reduce loss of heat and exclude noise. **2** the provision of this. **Double Gloucester** a kind of hard cheese orig. made in Gloucestershire, England. **double helix** a pair of parallel helices with a common axis, esp. in the structure of the DNA molecule. **double indemnity** a clause in a life-insurance policy providing double payment to the beneficiary if the insured person dies accidentally. **double-jointed** having joints that allow unusual bending of the fingers, limbs, etc. **double knit** (of fabric) knit of two joined layers for extra thickness. **double-lock** lock by a double turn of the key. **double negative** *Gram.* a negative statement containing two negative elements (e.g., *didn't say nothing*). ¶ Considered ungrammatical in standard English. **double or nothing** (or esp. *Brit.* **quits**) a gamble to decide whether a player's loss or debt be doubled or canceled. **double-park** park (a vehicle) alongside one that is already parked at the roadside. **double play** *Baseball* putting out two runners. **double pneumonia** pneumonia affecting both lungs. **double-quick** very quick or quickly. **double refraction** *Optics* refraction forming two separate rays from a single incident ray. **double rhyme** a rhyme including two syllables, as in *station*, *nation*. **double salt** *Chem.* a salt composed of two simple salts and having different crystal properties from either. **double standard 1** a rule or principle applied more strictly to some people than to others (or to oneself). **2** bimetallism. **double star** two stars actually or apparently very close together. **double-stopping** *Mus.* the sounding of two strings at once on a violin, etc. **double take** a delayed reaction to a situation, etc., immediately after one's first reaction. **double-talk** verbal expression that is (usu. deliberately) ambiguous or misleading. **double time 1** payment of an employee at twice the normal rate. **2** *Mil.* the regulation running pace. **double-tonguing** rapid articulation in playing a wind instrument. **double up 1 a** bend or curl up. **b** cause to do this, esp. by a blow. **2** be overcome with pain or laughter. **3** share or assign to a room, quarters, etc., with another or others. **4** fold or become folded. **5** use winnings from a bet as stake for another. **on** (or *Brit.* **at**) **the double** running; hurrying. □□ **doubler** *n.* **doubly** *adv.* [ME f. OF *doble, duble* (n.), *dobler, dubler* (v.) f. L *duplus* DUPLE]

■ *adj.* **1** paired, coupled, duplicate(d), doubled; twofold. **2** twice. **6** dual, twofold, ambiguous; deceitful, dishonest, treacherous, traitorous, insincere, hypocritical, double-dealing, false. ● *n.* **2 a, b** twin, duplicate, copy, replica, facsimile, clone, counterpart, doppelgänger, look-alike, *colloq.* spitting image; stand-in, understudy, reserve. ● *v.* **3 a** bend, fold, double up. **11** see RUN *v.* 1, 3. □ **double bind** dilemma, *colloq.* catch-22. **double-cross** defraud, swindle, hoodwink, trick, deceive, mislead, play false with, *colloq.* two-time;

see also BETRAY 2, CHEAT *v.* 1a. (*n.*) see *betrayal* (BETRAY). **double-crosser** see *swindler* (SWINDLE). **double-dealer** see *swindler* (SWINDLE). **double-dealing** (*n.*) see DECEIT 1. (*adj.*) see DECEITFUL. **double Dutch 1** see GIBBERISH. **double-faced 1** see INSINCERE. **double-quick** see IMMEDIATELY *adv.* 1, *on the double* below. **double-talk** see AMBIGUITY 1a. **double up 1** see STOOP¹ *v.* 1. **2** see FLINCH¹ *v.*, LAUGH *v.* 1. **on the double** quickly, briskly, chop-chop, on the run, at a run, double-quick, at full speed *or* tilt, *colloq.* PDQ; immediately, at once, without delay; see also *instantaneously* (INSTANTANEOUS).

double entendre /dúbəl aantaándrə, doooblaan taándrə/ *n.* **1** a word or phrase open to two interpretations, one usu. risqué or indecent. **2** humor using such words or phrases. [obs. F, = double understanding]

■ see AMBIGUITY 1b.

doubleganger /dúbəlgangər/ *n.* = DOPPELGÄNGER.

doubleheader /dúbəlhedər/ *n.* **1** a train pulled by two locomotives coupled together. **2 a** two games (esp. baseball), etc., in succession between the same opponents. **b** two games (esp. basketball), etc., in succession between different opponents. **3** *Austral. colloq.* a coin with a head on both sides.

doublet /dúblit/ *n.* **1** either of a pair of similar things, esp. either of two words of the same derivation but different sense (e.g., *fashion* and *faction*, *cloak* and *clock*). **2** *hist.* a man's short, close-fitting jacket, with or without sleeves. **3** a historical or biblical account occurring twice in differing contexts, usu. traceable to different sources. **4** (in *pl.*) the same number on two dice thrown at once. **5** a pair of associated lines close together in a spectrum. **6** a combination of two simple lenses. [ME f. OF f. *double*: see DOUBLE]

doublethink /dúbəlthingk/ *n.* the mental capacity to accept contrary opinions or beliefs at the same time, esp. as a result of political indoctrination.

doubloon /dubloon/ *n.* **1** *hist.* a Spanish gold coin. **2** (in *pl.*) *sl.* money. [F *doublon* or Sp. *doblón* (as DOUBLE)]

doublure /dəbloor, doo-/ *n.* an ornamental lining, usu. leather, inside a book cover. [F, = lining (*doubler* to line)]

doubt /dowt/ *n. & v.* ● *n.* **1** a feeling of uncertainty; an undecided state of mind (*be in no doubt about; have no doubt that*). **2** (often foll. by *of, about*) an inclination to disbelieve (*have one's doubts about*). **3** an uncertain state of things. **4** a lack of full proof or clear indication (*benefit of the doubt*). ● *v.* **1** *tr.* (often foll. by *whether, if, that* + clause; also foll. (after *neg.* or *interrog.*) by *but, but that*) feel uncertain or undecided about (*I doubt that you are right; I do not doubt but that you are wrong*). **2** *tr.* hesitate to believe or trust. **3** *intr.* (often foll. by *of*) feel uncertain or undecided; have doubts (*never doubted of success*). **4** *tr.* call in question. **5** *tr. dial.* rather think; suspect or fear that (*I doubt we are late*). □ **beyond doubt** certainly. **doubting Thomas** an incredulous or skeptical person (after John 20:24–29). **in doubt** uncertain; open to question. **no doubt** certainly; probably; admittedly. **without doubt** (or **a doubt**) certainly. □□ **doubtable** *adj.* **doubter** *n.* **doubtingly** *adv.* [ME *doute* f. OF *doute* (n.), *douter* (v.) f. L *dubitare* hesitate; mod. spelling after L]

■ *n.* **1** uncertainty, hesitation, misgiving, reservation(s), qualm(s), anxiety, worry, apprehension, disquiet, fear; indecision, indecisiveness, incertitude, irresolution; dubiousness, *literary* dubitation, dubiety. **2** distrust, mistrust, suspicion, incredulity, skepticism, doubtfulness, lack of faith *or* conviction. ● *v.* **2** disbelieve, discredit, mistrust, distrust, have misgivings about, question, suspect. **3** hesitate, be uncertain, entertain doubts, have reservations. **5** see SUSPECT *v.* 3. □ **beyond doubt** see *undoubtedly* (UNDOUBTED). **doubting Thomas** see NONBELIEVER. **in doubt** see UNCERTAIN 1. **no doubt** see *undoubtedly* (UNDOUBTED), *probably* (PROBABLE). **without doubt** see *undoubtedly* (UNDOUBTED).

doubtful /dówtfool/ *adj.* **1** feeling doubt or misgivings; unsure or guarded in one's opinion. **2** causing doubt; ambig-

uous; uncertain in meaning, etc. **3** unreliable (*a doubtful ally*). □□ **doubtfully** *adv.* **doubtfulness** *n.*
■ **1** skeptical, unconvinced, distrustful, mistrustful, suspicious, uncertain, unsure, undecided, hesitant, indecisive, *literary* dubitative. **2** in doubt, dubious, questionable, open to question, problematic, debatable, disputable, uncertain; unpredictable, indeterminate, unsettled, unresolved, conjectural; indefinite, unclear, obscure, vague, anybody's guess, up in the air. **3** see UNRELIABLE.

doubtless /dówtlis/ *adv.* (often qualifying a sentence) **1** certainly; no doubt. **2** probably. □□ **doubtlessly** *adv.*
■ **1** certainly, doubtlessly, undoubtedly, no doubt, indubitably, indisputably, unquestionably, surely, for certain, naturally, without (a) doubt, beyond *or* without (a shadow of) a doubt, truly, positively, absolutely, *colloq.* for sure. **2** probably, most *or* very likely, in all probability *or* likelihood, presumably.

douce /doos/ *adj. Sc.* sober; gentle; sedate. [ME f. OF *dous douce* f. L *dulcis* sweet]

douche /doosh/ *n. & v.* ● *n.* **1** a jet of liquid applied to a body part or cavity for cleansing or medicinal purposes. **2** a device for producing such a jet. ● *v.* **1** *tr.* treat with a douche. **2** *intr.* use a douche. [F f. It. *doccia* pipe f. *docciare* pour by drops ult. f. L *ductus*: see DUCT]

dough /dō/ *n.* **1** a thick mixture of flour, etc., and liquid (usu. water), for baking into bread, pastry, etc. **2** *sl.* money. [OE *dāg* f. Gmc]
■ **2** see MONEY 1.

doughboy /dóboy/ *n.* **1** *colloq.* a United States infantryman, esp. in World War I. **2** a boiled dumpling.
■ **2** see SOLDIER *n.*

doughnut /dónut/ *n.* (also **donut**) **1** a small fried cake of sweetened dough, usu. in the shape of a ball or ring. **2** a ring-shaped object, esp. *Physics* a vacuum chamber for acceleration of particles in a betatron or synchrotron.

doughty /dówtee/ *adj.* (**doughtier, doughtiest**) *archaic* or *joc.* valiant; stouthearted. □□ **doughtily** *adv.* **doughtiness** *n.* [OE *dohtig* var. of *dyhtig* f. Gmc]
■ see STOUT *adj.* 3.

doughy /dóee/ *adj.* (**doughier, doughiest**) **1** having the form or consistency of dough. **2** pale and sickly in color. □□ **doughiness** *n.*

Douglas fir /dúglas/ *n.* (also **Douglas pine** or **spruce**) any large conifer of the genus *Pseudotsuga*, of Western N. America. [D. *Douglas*, Sc. botanist d. 1834]

doum /dōōm, dowm/ *n.* (in full **doum palm**; also **doom palm**) a palm tree, *Hyphaene thebaica*, with edible fruit. [Arab. *dawm, dūm*]

dour /dōōr, dowr/ *adj.* severe, stern, or sullenly obstinate in manner or appearance. □□ **dourly** *adv.* **dourness** *n.* [ME (orig. Sc.), prob. f. Gael. *dúr* dull, obstinate, perh. f. L *durus* hard]
■ sullen, sour, unfriendly, forbidding, hard, tough, austere, severe, hardy, inflexible, obstinate, stubborn, unyielding, uncompromising, strict, rigid, obdurate, stern, harsh, *colloq.* hard-nosed; gloomy, morose, grim.

douroucouli /dōōrəkōōlee/ *n.* (*pl.* **douroucoulis**) any nocturnal monkey of the genus *Aotus*, native to S. America, having large staring eyes. [Indian name]

douse /dows/ *v.tr.* (also **dowse**) **1 a** throw water over. **b** plunge into water. **2** extinguish (a light). **3** *Naut.* **a** lower (a sail). **b** close (a porthole). [16th c.: perh. rel. to MDu., LG *dossen* strike]
■ **1** see SOAK *v.* 1. **2** see QUENCH 2.

dove[1] /duv/ *n.* **1** any bird of the family Columbidae, with short legs, small head, and large breast. **2** a gentle or innocent person. **3** *Polit.* an advocate of peace or peaceful policies (cf. HAWK[1]). **4** (**Dove**) *Relig.* a representation of the Holy Spirit (John 1:32). **5** a soft gray color. □□ **dovelike** *adj.* [ME f. ON *dúfa* f. Gmc]

dove[2] *past* and *past part.* of DIVE.

dovecote /dúvkōt, -kot/ *n.* (also **dovecot**) a shelter with nesting holes for domesticated pigeons.

dovetail /dúvtayl/ *n. & v.* ● *n.* **1** a joint formed by a mortise

with a tenon shaped like a dove's spread tail or a reversed wedge. **2** such a tenon. ● *v.* **1** *tr.* join together by means of a dovetail. **2** *tr. & intr.* (often foll. by *into, with*) fit readily together; combine neatly or compactly.
■ *v.* **2** see COMBINE *v.* 1, FIT[1] *v.* 1c.

dowager /dówəjər/ *n.* **1** a widow with a title or property derived from her late husband (*Queen dowager; dowager duchess*). **2** *colloq.* a dignified elderly woman. [OF *douag(i)ere* f. *douage* (as DOWER)]

dowdy /dówdee/ *adj. & n.* ● *adj.* (**dowdier, dowdiest**) **1** (of clothes) unattractively dull; unfashionable. **2** (of a person, esp. a woman) dressed in dowdy clothes. ● *n.* (*pl.* **-ies**) a dowdy woman. □□ **dowdily** *adv.* **dowdiness** *n.* [ME *dowd* slut, of unkn. orig.]
■ *adj.* **1** drab, dull, shabby, tatty, unseemly, unbecoming, *colloq.* tacky; old-fashioned, unfashionable. **2** frowzy, frumpy, frumpish. ● *n.* frump.

dowel /dówəl/ *n. & v.* ● *n.* a headless peg of wood, metal, or plastic for holding together components of a structure. ● *v.tr.* (**doweled, doweling;** esp. *Brit.* **dowelled, dowelling**) fasten with a dowel or dowels. [ME f. MLG *dovel*: cf. THOLE[1]]
■ *n.* see PEG *n.*

doweling /dówəling/ *n.* round rods for cutting into dowels.

dower /dowər/ *n. & v.* ● *n.* **1** a widow's share for life of her husband's estate. **2** *archaic* a dowry. **3** *archaic* a natural gift or talent. ● *v.tr.* **1** *archaic* give a dowry to. **2** (foll. by *with*) endow with talent, etc. □ **dower house** *Brit.* a smaller house near a big one, forming part of a widow's dower. □□ **dowerless** *adj.* [ME f. OF *douaire* f. med.L *dotarium* f. L *dos dotis*]

Dow-Jones average /dowjōnz/ *n.* (also **Dow-Jones index**) a figure based on the average price of selected stocks, indicating the relative price of shares on the New York Stock Exchange. [C. H. *Dow* d. 1902 & E. D. *Jones* d. 1920, Amer. economists]

down[1] /down/ *adv., prep., adj., v., & n.* ● *adv.* (*superl.* **downmost**) **1** into or toward a lower place, esp. to the ground (*fall down; knelt down*). **2** in a lower place or position (*blinds were down*). **3** to or in a place regarded as lower, esp.: **a** southward. **b** *Brit.* away from a major city or a university. **4 a** in or into a low or weaker position, mood, or condition (*hit a man when he's down; many down with colds*). **b** in a position of lagging or loss (*our team was three goals down; $5 down on the transaction*). **c** (of a computer system) out of action or unavailable for use (esp. temporarily). **5** from an earlier to a later time (*customs handed down; down to 1600*). **6** to a finer or thinner consistency or a smaller amount or size (*grind down; water down; boil down*). **7** cheaper; lower in price or value (*bread is down; stocks are down*). **8** into a more settled state (*calm down*). **9** in writing; in or into recorded or listed form (*copy it down; I got it down on tape; you are down to speak next*). **10** (of part of a larger whole) paid; dealt with (*$5 down, $20 to pay; three down, six to go*). **11** *Naut.* **a** with the current or wind. **b** (of a ship's helm) with the rudder to windward. **12** inclusively of the lower limit in a series (*read down to the third paragraph*). **13** (as *int.*) lie down, put (something) down, etc. **14** (of a crossword clue or answer) read vertically (*cannot do five down*). **15** downstairs, esp. after rising (*is not down yet*). **16** swallowed (*could not get the pill down*). **17** *Football* (of the ball) no longer in play. ● *prep.* **1** downward along, through, or into. **2** from top to bottom of. **3** along (*walk down the road; cut down the middle*). **4** at or in a lower part of (*situated down the river*). ● *adj.* (*superl.* **downmost**) **1** directed downward. **2** *Brit.* of travel away from a capital or center (*the down train; the down platform*). **3** *colloq.* unhappy; depressed. ● *v.tr. colloq.* **1** knock or bring down. **2** swallow (a drink). ● *n.* **1** an act of putting down (as an opponent in wrestling). **2** a reverse of fortune (*ups and downs*). **3** *colloq.* a period of depression. **4**

/ ... / pronunciation	● part of speech
□ phrases, idioms, and compounds	
□□ derivatives	■ synonym section
cross-references appear in SMALL CAPITALS or *italics*	

Football **a** one of a series of plays (up to four) in which the offensive team must advance the ball 10 yards in order to keep the ball. **b** the declaring of the ball as no longer in play. □ **be** (or **have a**) **down on** *colloq.* disapprove of; show animosity toward. **be down to 1** be attributable to. **2** be the responsibility of. **3** have used up everything except (*down to their last can of rations*). **down-and-out** *adj.* **1** penniless; destitute. **2** *Boxing* unable to resume the fight. ● *n.* a destitute person. **down-at-the-heels** (also **down-at-heel**, **down-at-the-heel**) shabby; slovenly. **down in the mouth** *colloq.* looking unhappy. **down-market** *adj. & adv. colloq.* toward or relating to the cheaper or less affluent sector of the market. **down on one's luck** *colloq.* **1** temporarily unfortunate. **2** dispirited by misfortune. **down payment** a partial payment made at the time of purchase. **down-to-earth** practical; realistic. **down to the ground** *colloq.* completely. **down tools** *Brit. colloq.* cease work, esp. to go on strike. **down under** *colloq.* (also **Down Under**) in the antipodes, esp. Australia. **down with** *int.* expressing strong disapproval or rejection of a specified person or thing. [OE *dūn(e)* f. *adūne* off the hill]

■ *adv.* **1** see DOWNWARD *adv.* 7 cheaper, lower, reduced. ● *adj.* **3** see MISERABLE 1. ● *v.* **1** see *knock down* 1. **2** see SWALLOW[1] *v.* 1. ● *n.* **2** nadir, low point; (*downs*) bad times, hard times; misfortunes. **3** see DEPRESSION 1b. □ **be down to 1, 2** be up to; see also *attributable* (ATTRIBUTE). **down-and-out** *adj.* **1** indigent, poverty-stricken, poor, penniless, destitute, impoverished, *colloq.* on the skids, on skid row *or* road, *sl.* on the bum, *Brit. sl.* skint; see also BROKE. ● *n.* derelict, beggar, outcast, tramp, vagrant, vagabond; see also BUM[2] *n.* **down-at-the-heels** see SHABBY 1, 2. **down in the mouth** see UNHAPPY 1. **down-market** see CHEAP *adj.* 1, 2, INFERIOR *adj.* 1. **down on one's luck** see UNFORTUNATE *adj.* 1. **down-to-earth** see PRACTICAL *adj.* 3. **down to the ground** see *completely* (COMPLETE).

down[2] /down/ *n.* **1 a** the first covering of young birds. **b** a bird's under-plumage, used in cushions, etc. **c** a layer of fine, soft feathers. **2** fine, soft hair esp. on the face. **3** short, soft hairs on some leaves, fruit, seeds, etc. **4** a fluffy substance, e.g., thistledown. [ME f. ON *dúnn*]

■ **1, 4** see FLUFF *n.* 1.

down[3] /down/ *n.* **1** an area of open rolling land. **2** (in *pl.*; usu. prec. by *the*) **a** undulating chalk and limestone uplands esp. in S. England, with few trees and used mainly for pasture. **b** (**Downs**) a part of the sea (opposite the North Downs) off E. Kent, England. □□ **downy** *adj.* [OE *dūn* perh. f. OCelt.]

■ **1** see PLAIN *n.*

downbeat /dównbeet/ *n. & adj.* ● *n. Mus.* an accented beat, usu. the first of the bar. ● *adj.* **1** pessimistic; gloomy. **2** relaxed.

■ *n.* see RHYTHM 1, 2.

downcast /dównkast/ *adj. & n.* ● *adj.* **1** (of eyes) looking downward. **2** (of a person) dejected. ● *n.* a shaft dug in a mine for extra ventilation.

■ *adj.* **2** see *dejected* (DEJECT).

downcomer /dównkumər/ *n.* a pipe for downward transport of water or gas.

downdraft /dówndraft/ *n.* a downward draft, esp. one down a chimney into a room.

downer /dównər/ *n. sl.* **1** a depressant or tranquilizing drug, esp. a barbiturate. **2** a depressing person or experience; a failure. **3** = DOWNTURN.

■ **1** see TRANQUILIZER.

downfall /dównfawl/ *n.* **1 a** a fall from prosperity or power. **b** the cause of this. **2** a sudden heavy fall of rain, etc.

■ **1** fall, collapse; ruin, undoing, debacle, degradation, defeat, overthrow, breakdown.

downfold /dównfōld/ *n. Geol.* a syncline.

downgrade *v. & n. & v.tr.* ● *v.tr.* /dówngráyd/ **1** make lower in rank or status. **2** speak disparagingly of. ● *n.* /dówngrayd/ **1** a descending slope of a road or railroad. **2** a deterioration. □ **on the downgrade** in decline.

■ *v.* **1** demote, dethrone, humble, lower, reduce,

displace, depose, dispossess, *Naut.* disrate, *colloq.* bring *or* take down a peg (or two), bust. **2** belittle, minimize, play down, decry, denigrate, run down, downplay; see also DISPARAGE 1. ● *n.* **1** descent, decline, declination, (downward) slope, gradient. **2** see DECLINE *n.* 2. □ **on the downgrade** see *on the decline* (DECLINE).

downhearted /dównháartid/ *adj.* dejected; in low spirits. □□ **downheartedly** *adv.* **downheartedness** *n.*

■ discouraged, depressed, low-spirited, dispirited, miserable, blue, downcast, dejected *colloq.* down in the mouth; see also SAD 1.

downhill *adv., adj., & n.* ● *adv.* /dównhíl/ in a descending direction, esp. toward the bottom of an incline. ● *adj.* /dównhil/ **1** sloping down; descending. **2** declining; deteriorating. ● *n.* /dównhil/ **1** *Skiing* a downhill race. **2** a downward slope. **3** a decline. □ **go downhill** *colloq.* decline; deteriorate (in health, state of repair, moral state, etc.).

■ □ **go downhill** see DETERIORATE.

downland /dównlənd/ *n.* = DOWN[3].

download /dównlōd/ *v.tr. Computing* transfer (data) from one storage device or system to another (esp. smaller remote one).

downmost /dównmōst/ *adj. & adv.* the furthest down.

downpipe /dównpīp/ *n. Brit.* = DOWNSPOUT.

downplay /dównpláy/ *v.tr.* play down; minimize the importance of.

■ see MINIMIZE 2.

downpour /dównpawr/ *n.* a heavy fall of rain.

■ rainstorm, deluge, inundation, downfall, cloudburst, thunderstorm, torrent, thundershower.

downright /dównrīt/ *adj. & adv.* ● *adj.* **1** plain; definite; straightforward; blunt. **2** utter; complete (*a downright lie*; *downright nonsense*). ● *adv.* thoroughly; completely; positively (*downright rude*). □□ **downrightness** *n.*

■ *adj.* **1** direct, straightforward, plain, frank, open, candid, plainspoken, explicit, blunt, brash, bluff, outspoken, unreserved, unabashed, unrestrained, unconstrained, bold. **2** utter, unambiguous, out-and-out, outright, absolute; see also COMPLETE *adj.* 3. ● *adv.* completely, totally, thoroughly, certainly, (most) assuredly, positively, definitely, absolutely, unconditionally, unequivocally; very, extremely, unqualifiedly, uncompromisingly, unmitigatedly, utterly, unquestionably, undoubtedly, indubitably; see also *profoundly* (PROFOUND).

downscale /dównskáyl/ *v. & adj.* ● *v.tr.* reduce or restrict in size, scale, or extent. ● *adj.* at the lower end of a scale, esp. a social scale; inferior.

downshift /dównshift/ *v.intr. & tr.* shift (an automotive vehicle) into a lower gear.

downside /dównsīd/ *n.* a downward movement of share prices, etc.

downsize /dównsīz/ *v.tr.* (**downsized, downsizing**) **1** reduce in size; make smaller. **2** cut back on the number of employees in (a company).

downspout /dównspowt/ *n.* a pipe to carry rainwater from a roof to a drain or to ground level.

■ see SPOUT *n.* 1a.

Down's syndrome /downz/ *n. Med.* (also **Down syndrome**) a congenital disorder due to a chromosome defect, characterized by mental retardation and physical abnormalities (cf. MONGOLISM). [J. L. H. *Down*, Engl. physician d. 1896]

downstage /dównstayj/ *n., adj., & adv. Theatr.* ● *n.* the frontmost portion of the stage. ● *adj. & adv.* at or to the front of the stage.

downstairs *adv., adj., & n.* ● *adv.* /dównstáirz/ **1** down a flight of stairs. **2** to or on a lower floor. ● *adj.* /dównstairz/ (also **downstair**) situated downstairs. ● *n.* /dównstáirz/ the lower floor.

■ *adv.* see BELOW *adv.* 2a.

downstate /dównstáyt/ *adj., n., & adv.* ● *adj.* of or in a southern part of a state, esp. a part remote from large cities esp. the southern. ● *n.* a downstate area. ● *adv.* in a downstate area.

downstream /dównstreém/ adv. & adj. ● adv. in the direction of the flow of a stream, etc. ● adj. moving downstream.

downstroke /dównstrōk/ n. a stroke made or written downward.

downthrow /dównthrō/ n. Geol. a downward dislocation of strata.

downtime /dówntim/ n. time during which a machine, esp. a computer, is out of action or unavailable for use.

downtown /dówntówn/ adj., n., & adv. ● adj. of or in the lower or more central part, or the business part, of a town or city. ● n. a downtown area. ● adv. in or into a downtown area.

downtrodden /dówntród'n/ adj. oppressed; badly treated; kept under.
■ subjugated, oppressed, burdened, afflicted, exploited, overwhelmed, cowed, overcome, beaten, abused, mistreated, maltreated, tyrannized.

downturn /dówntərn/ n. a decline, esp. in economic or business activity.
■ see DECLINE n. 1, 4.

downward /dównwərd/ adv. & adj. ● adv. (also **downwards**) toward what is lower, inferior, less important, or later. ● adj. moving, extending, pointing, or leading downward. ▫▫ **downwardly** adv.
■ adv. down, below, lower, downwardly.
● adj. declining, descending.

downwarp /dównwawrp/ n. Geol. a broad surface depression; a syncline.

downwind /dównwínd/ adj. & adv. in the direction in which the wind is blowing.

downy /dównee/ adj. (**downier, downiest**) **1 a** of, like, or covered with down. **b** soft and fluffy. **2** Brit. sl. aware; knowing. ▫▫ **downily** adv. **downiness** n.
■ **1** see SOFT adj. 2.

dowry /dówree/ n. (pl. **-ies**) **1** property or money brought by a bride to her husband. **2** a talent; a natural gift. [ME f. AF dowarie, OF douaire DOWER]
■ **1** dot; archaic dower. **2** see ENDOWMENT 2.

dowse[1] /dowz/ v.intr. search for underground water or minerals by holding a Y-shaped stick or rod which supposedly dips abruptly when over the right spot. ▫ **dowsing** (or **divining**) **rod** such a stick or rod. ▫▫ **dowser** n. [17th c.: orig. unkn.]

dowse[2] var. of DOUSE.

doxology /doksólajee/ n. (pl. **-ies**) a liturgical formula of praise to God. ▫▫ **doxological** /-səlójikəl/ adj. [med.L doxologia f. Gk doxologia f. doxa glory + -LOGY]

doxy /dóksee/ n. (also **doxie**) (pl. **-ies**) literary **1** a lover or mistress. **2** a prostitute. [16th-c. cant: orig. unkn.]
■ **1** see MISTRESS 5. **2** see TART[2] n.

doyen /dóyén, dóyən, dwaáyən/ n. (fem. **doyenne** /dóyén, dwaayén/) the senior member of a body of colleagues, esp. the senior ambassador at a court. [F (as DEAN[1])]
■ see LEADER 1.

doyley var. of DOILY.

doz. abbr. dozen.

doze /dōz/ v. & n. ● v.intr. sleep lightly; be half asleep. ● n. a short, light sleep. ▫ **doze off** fall lightly asleep. ▫▫ **dozer** n. [17th c.: cf. Da. d se make drowsy]
■ v. (take or have a) nap, catnap, drowse, sleep, colloq. snooze, have forty winks, grab some shut-eye, Brit. sl. kip, poet. rhet. slumber. ● n. nap, catnap, siesta, sleep, esp. Brit. lie-down, colloq. snooze, forty winks, shut-eye, Brit. sl. kip. ▫ **doze off** fall asleep, colloq. drop or nod off; see also NOD v. 2.

dozen /dúzən/ n. **1** (prec. by a or a number) (pl. **dozen**) twelve, regarded collectively (a dozen eggs; two dozen packages; ordered three dozen). **2** a set or group of twelve (packed in dozens). **3** colloq. about twelve, a fairly large indefinite number. **4** (in pl.; usu. foll. by of) colloq. very many (made dozens of mistakes). **5** (**the dozens**) a game or ritualized exchange of verbal insults. ▫ **by the dozen** in large quantities. **talk nineteen to the dozen** Brit. talk incessantly. ▫▫ **dozenth** adj. & n. [ME f. OF dozeine, ult. f. L duodecim twelve]
■ **4** (dozens) see SCORE n. 3.

dozer /dózər/ n. colloq. = BULLDOZER. [abbr.]

dozy /dózee/ adj. (**dozier, doziest**) **1** drowsy; tending to doze. **2** Brit. colloq. stupid or lazy. ▫▫ **dozily** adv. **doziness** n.
■ **1** see SLEEPY 1.

DP abbr. **1** data processing. **2** displaced person.
■ **2** see OUTCAST n.

D.Ph. abbr. Doctor of Philosophy.

DPP abbr. deferred payment plan.

DPT abbr (vaccination against) diphtheria, pertussis, and tetanus.

Dr. abbr. **1** Doctor. **2** Drive. **3** debtor.

dr. abbr. **1** dram(s). **2** drachma(s).

drab[1] /drab/ adj. & n. ● adj. (**drabber, drabbest**) **1** dull; uninteresting. **2** of a dull brownish color. ● n. **1** drab color. **2** monotony. ▫▫ **drably** adv. **drabness** n. [prob. f. obs. drap cloth f. OF f. LL drappus, perh. of Celt. orig.]
■ adj. **1** dull, colorless, dreary, dingy, lackluster, lusterless, dismal, cheerless, gray, somber; see also BORING. ● n. **2** see TEDIUM 1.

drab[2] /drab/ see DRIBS AND DRABS.

drab[3] /drab/ n. **1** a slut; a slattern. **2** a prostitute. [perh. rel. to LG drabbe mire, Du. drab dregs]

drabble /drábəl/ v.intr. & tr. become or make dirty and wet with water or mud. [ME f. LG drabbelen paddle in water or mire: cf. DRAB[3]]

drachm /dram/ n. Brit. var. of DRAM 2. [ME dragme f. OF dragme or LL dragma f. L drachma f. Gk drakhmē Attic weight and coin]

drachma /drákmə/ n. (pl. **drachmas** or **drachmai** /-mi/ or **drachmae** /-mee/) **1** the chief monetary unit of Greece. **2** a silver coin of ancient Greece. [L f. Gk drakhmē]

drack /drak/ adj. Austral. sl. **1** (esp. of a woman) unattractive. **2** dismal; dull. [20th c.: orig. unkn.]

dracone /drákōn/ n. a large flexible container for liquids, towed on the surface of the sea. [L draco -onis (as DRAGON)]

draconian /drəkṓneeən, dray-/ adj. (also **draconic** /-kónik/) very harsh or severe (esp. of laws and their application). [Drakōn, 7th-c. BC Athenian legislator]
■ see HARSH 2.

draff /draf/ n. **1** dregs; lees. **2** refuse. [ME, perh. repr. OE dræf (unrecorded)]

draft /draft/ n. & v. ● n. **1 a** a preliminary written version of a speech, document, etc. **b** a rough preliminary outline of a scheme. **c** a sketch of work to be carried out. **2 a** a written order for payment of money by a bank. **b** the drawing of money by means of this. **3** (foll. by on) a demand made on a person's confidence, friendship, etc. **4 a** a party detached from a larger group for a special duty or purpose. **b** the selection of this. **5** compulsory military service. **6** a reinforcement. **7** a current of air in a confined space (e.g., a room or chimney). **8** pulling; traction. **9** Naut. the depth of water needed to float a ship. **10** the drawing of liquor from a cask, etc. **11 a** a single act of drinking. **b** the amount drunk in this. **c** a dose of liquid medicine. **12 a** the drawing in of a fishing net. **b** the fish taken at one drawing.▫ **draft beer** beer drawn from a cask, not bottled. **draft horse** a horse used for pulling heavy loads, esp. a cart or plow. **feel the draft** Brit. colloq. suffer from adverse (usu. financial) conditions. ● v.tr. **1** prepare a draft of (a document, scheme, etc.). **2** select for a special duty or purpose. **3** conscript for military service. ▫ **draft board** a board of civilians that selects and classifies persons for compulsory US military service. ▫▫ **draftee** /-tee/ n. **drafter** n. [phonetic spelling of DRAFT]
■ n. **1** plan, sketch, drawing, outline, blueprint, diagram. **2 a** bill of exchange, check, money order, postal order; letter of credit. **3** claim, demand. **4 a** division, unit; see also SQUAD. **5** military service, conscription, call-up,

---

/.../ pronunciation	● part of speech
▫ phrases, idioms, and compounds	
▫▫ derivatives	■ synonym section
cross-references appear in SMALL CAPITALS or italics	

Brit. hist. national service, *US hist.* selective service. **7** breeze, breath (of air), (light) wind, current (of air), puff (of air *or* wind). **11** drink, swallow, sip, gulp, potation, *colloq.* swig, *joc.* libation; nip, tot, dram, *colloq.* tipple; dose, portion, measure, quantity. ● *v.* **1** sketch (out), delineate, outline, design, plan, frame, block out, draw (up). **2** see APPOINT 1. **3** recruit, call up, conscript, induct.

draftsman /dráftsmən/ *n.* (*pl.* **-men**) **1** a person who makes drawings, plans, or sketches. **2** a person who drafts documents. □□ **draftsmanship** *n.*

drafty/dráftee/ *adj. Brit.* **draughty** (**-ier, -iest**) (of a room, etc.) letting in sharp currents of air. □□ **draftily** *adv.* **draftiness** *n.*

■ see BREEZY 1.

drag /drag/ *v. & n.* ● *v.* (**dragged, dragging**) **1** *tr.* pull along with effort or difficulty. **2 a** *tr.* allow (one's feet, tail, etc.) to trail along the ground. **b** *intr.* trail along the ground. **c** *intr.* (of time, etc.) go or pass heavily or slowly or tediously. **3 a** *intr.* (usu. foll. by *for*) use a grapnel or drag (to find a drowned person or lost object). **b** *tr.* search the bottom of (a river, etc.) with grapnels, nets, or drags. **4** *tr.* (often foll. by *to*) *colloq.* take (a person to a place, etc., esp. against his or her will). **5** *intr.* (foll. by *on, at*) draw on (a cigarette, etc.). **6** *intr.* (often foll. by *on*) continue at tedious length. ● *n.* **1 a** an obstruction to progress. **b** *Aeron.* the longitudinal retarding force exerted by air. **c** slow motion; impeded progress. **d** an iron shoe for retarding a horse-drawn vehicle downhill. **2** *colloq.* a boring or dreary person, duty, performance, etc. **3 a** a strong-smelling lure drawn before hounds as a substitute for a fox. **b** a hunt using this. **4** an apparatus for dredging or recovering drowned persons, etc. from under water. **5** = DRAGNET. **6** *sl.* a draw on a cigarette, etc. **7** *sl.* **a** women's clothes worn by men. **b** a party at which these are worn. **c** clothes in general. **8** an act of dragging. **9** *sl.* in full **drag race** an acceleration race between cars usu. for a short distance. **10** *sl.* influence; pull. **11** *sl.* a street or road (*the main drag*). **12** *hist.* a private vehicle like a stagecoach, drawn by four horses. □ **drag anchor** (of a ship) move from a moored position when the anchor fails to hold. **drag-anchor** *n.* = *sea anchor.* **drag one's feet** (or **heels**) be deliberately slow or reluctant to act. **drag in** introduce (a subject) irrelevantly. **drag out** protract. **drag queen** *sl.* a male transvestite. **drag race** a race between two or more vehicles to determine which accelerates the fastest. **drag strip** a straight stretch of road on which drag races are held. **drag through the mud** see MUD. **drag up** *colloq.* **1** deliberately mention (an unwelcome subject). **2** esp. *Brit.* rear (a child) roughly and without proper training. [ME f. OE *dragan* or ON *draga* DRAW]

■ *v.* **1** pull (along), haul, tow, tug, trail, lug. **6** go on, last, continue, be prolonged, be extended, be drawn out. ● *n.* **2** bore, nuisance, annoyance, pest, irritant, *colloq.* pain (in the neck), headache, bind, hassle, *disp.* aggravation; see also BOTHER *n.* 1. **8** pull, draw, tug. **10** see INFLUENCE *n.* **11** street, road, thoroughfare. □ **drag one's feet** (or **heels**) delay, procrastinate, hang back, stall, go slow, hold back. **drag in** drag up, bring up. **drag out** see *string out*. **drag through the mud** see SMEAR *v.* 3.

dragée /drazháy/ *n.* **1** a sugar-coated almond, etc. **2** a small silver ball for decorating a cake. **3** a chocolate-coated candy. [F: see DREDGE²]

draggle /drágəl/ *v.* **1** *tr.* make dirty or wet or limp by trailing. **2** *intr.* hang trailing. **3** *intr.* lag; straggle in the rear. □ **draggle-tailed** (of a woman) with untidily trailing skirts. [DRAG + -LE⁴]

■ **3** see LAG¹ *v.*

draggy /drágee/ *adj.* (**draggier, draggiest**) *colloq.* **1** tedious. **2** unpleasant.

draghound /drághownd/ *n.* a hound used to hunt with a drag.

dragline /dráglin/ *n.* an excavator with a bucket pulled in by a wire rope.

dragnet /drágnet/ *n* **1** a net drawn through a river or across

ground to trap fish or game. **2** a systematic hunt for criminals, etc.

dragoman /drágəmən/ *n.* (*pl.* **dragomans** or **dragomen**) an interpreter or guide, esp. in countries speaking Arabic, Turkish, or Persian. [F f. It. *dragomano* f. med.Gk *dragomanos* f. Arab. *tarjumān* f. *tarjama* interpret, f. Aram. *targēm* f. Assyr. *targumânu* interpreter]

dragon /drágən/ *n.* **1** a mythical monster like a reptile, usu. with wings and claws and able to breathe out fire. **2** a fierce person, esp. a woman. **3** (in full **flying dragon**) a lizard, *Draco volans,* with a long tail and membranous winglike structures. Also called *flying lizard.* □ **dragon's blood** a red gum that exudes from the fruit of some palms and the dragon tree. **dragon's teeth** *Mil. colloq.* obstacles resembling teeth pointed upward, used esp. against tanks. **dragon tree** a tree, *Dracaena draco,* native to the Canary Islands. [ME f. OF f. L *draco -onis* f. Gk *drakōn* serpent]

■ **1** see MONSTER 1. **2** see SHREW.

dragonet /drágənit/ *n.* any marine spiny fish of the family Callionymidae, the males of which are brightly colored. [ME f. F, dimin. of DRAGON]

dragonfish /drágənfish/ *n.* (*pl.* same or **-fishes**) any marine deepwater fish of the family Stomiatidae, having a long, slender body and a barbel on the chin with luminous tissue, serving to attract prey.

dragonfly /drágənfli/ *n.* (*pl.* **-ies**) any of various insects of the order Odonata, having a long, slender body and two pairs of large transparent wings usu. spread while resting.

dragonnade /drágənáyd/ *n. & v.* ● *n.* a persecution by use of troops, esp. (in *pl.*) of French Protestants under Louis XIV by quartering dragoons on them. ● *v.tr.* subject to a dragonnade. [F f. *dragon*: see DRAGOON]

dragoon /drəgo͞on/ *n. & v.* ● *n.* **1** a cavalryman (orig. a mounted infantryman armed with a carbine). **2** a rough, fierce fellow. **3** a variety of pigeon. ● *v.tr.* **1** (foll. by *into*) coerce into doing something, esp. by use of strong force. **2** persecute, esp. with troops. [orig. = carbine (thought of as breathing fire) f. F *dragon* DRAGON]

dragster /drágstər/ *n.* a car built or modified to take part in drag races.

drail /drayl/ *n.* a fishhook and line weighted with lead for dragging below the surface of the water. [app. var. of TRAIL]

drain /drayn/ *v. & n.* ● *v.* **1** *tr.* draw off liquid from, esp.: **a** make (land, etc.) dry by providing an outflow for moisture. **b** (of a river) carry off the superfluous water of (a district). **c** remove purulent matter from (an abscess). **2** *tr.* (foll. by *off, away*) draw off (liquid) esp. by a pipe. **3** *intr.* (foll. by *away, off, through*) flow or trickle away. **4** *intr.* (of a wet cloth, a vessel, etc.) become dry as liquid flows away (*put it there to drain*). **5** *tr.* (often foll. by *of*) exhaust or deprive (a person or thing) of strength, resources, property, etc. **6** *tr.* **a** drink (liquid) to the dregs. **b** empty (a vessel) by drinking the contents. ● *n.* **1 a** a channel, conduit, or pipe carrying off liquid, esp. an artificial conduit for water or sewage. **b** a tube for drawing off the discharge from an abscess, etc. **2** a constant outflow, withdrawal, or expenditure (*a great drain on my resources*). □ **down the drain** *colloq.* lost; wasted. **laugh like a drain** *Brit.* laugh copiously; guffaw. [OE *drē(a)hnian* f. Gmc]

■ *v.* **2** (*drain off* or *away*) draw off, tap, extract, remove, take away, withdraw, pump off *or* out. **3** seep, trickle (away), drip, flow from *or* out of, disappear, ebb, leach (away). **4** dry, dry off, get *or* become dry. **5** sap, exhaust, deplete, bleed (white); weaken, debilitate, impair, cripple; see also DEPRIVE 1. **6 a** drink up *or* down, swallow, finish, *literary* quaff. ● *n.* **1 a** ditch, channel, trench, culvert, conduit, pipe, drainpipe, gutter, outlet, watercourse; sewer, cloaca, soil pipe. **2** depletion, reduction, sap, strain, drag; outflow, withdrawal, expenditure, disbursement. □ **down the drain** wasted, gone, thrown away, lost, *Brit. sl.* up the spout.

drainage /dráynij/ *n.* **1** the process or means of draining (*the land has poor drainage*). **2** a system of drains, artificial or natural. **3** what is drained off, esp. sewage.

drainboard /dráynbawrd/ n. a sloping usu. grooved surface beside a sink, on which washed dishes, etc., are left to drain.

drainer /dráynər/ n. **1** a device for draining; anything on which things are put to drain, e.g., a drainboard. **2** a person who drains.

drainpipe /dráynpīp/ n. **1** a pipe for carrying off water, sewage, etc., from a building. **2** (attrib.) Brit. (of pants, etc.) very narrow. **3** (in pl.) Brit. (also **drainpipe trousers**) very narrow pants.

drake /drayk/ n. a male duck. [ME prob. f. Gmc]

dram /dram/ n. **1** a small drink of liquor. **2** a weight or measure formerly used by apothecaries, equivalent to 60 grains or one eighth of an ounce, or (in full **fluid dram**) 60 minims, one eighth of a fluid ounce. [ME f. OF drame or med.L drama, dragma: cf. DRAM]
■ **1** see DRINK n. 2b.

drama /dráomə, draáomə/ n. **1** a play for acting on stage or for broadcasting. **2** (often prec. by the) the art of writing and presenting plays. **3** an exciting or emotional event, set of circumstances, etc. **4** dramatic quality (the drama of the situation). [LL f. Gk drama -atos f. draō do]
■ **1** play, stage play, (stage) show, (theatrical) piece, (stage) production. **2** dramaturgy, stagecraft, dramatics, theater art(s), acting, theater, dramatic art(s), the stage. **3** event, colloq. (big) thing; theatricals; see also FUSS n. 1, 2a. **4** theatricalism, theatricality, histrionics, dramatics, staginess, theatrics.

dramatic /drəmátik/ adj. **1** of drama or the study of drama. **2** (of an event, circumstance, etc.) sudden and exciting or unexpected. **3** vividly striking. **4** (of a gesture, etc.) theatrical; overdone; absurd. □ **dramatic irony** = tragic irony. □□ **dramatically** adv. [LL dramaticus f. Gk dramatikos (as DRAMA)]
■ **1** theatrical, dramaturgical, dramaturgic, thespian, histrionic, stage. **2, 3** vivid, sensational, startling, breathtaking, striking, noticeable, extraordinary, impressive, marked, shocking, graphic, effective, radical, drastic, serious; see also EXCITING, SUDDEN adj. **4** flamboyant, melodramatic, colorful, showy, stirring, spectacular; large, big; theatrical, absurd, histrionic, exaggerated, overdone.

dramatics /drəmátiks/ n.pl. (often treated as sing.) **1** the production and performance of plays. **2** exaggerated or showy behavior.
■ **1** see THEATER 2a. **2** see DRAMA 4.

dramatis personae /drámətis pərsṓnee, draáomətis pərsṓnī/ n.pl. (often treated as sing.) **1** the characters in a play. **2** a list of these. [L, = persons of the drama]

dramatist /drámətist, draáomə-/ n. a writer of dramas.
■ playwright, dramaturge, screenwriter, scriptwriter, scenarist.

dramatize /drámətīz, draáomə-/ v. **1 a** tr. adapt (a novel, etc.) to form a stage play. **b** intr. admit of such adaptation. **2** tr. make a drama or dramatic scene of. **3** tr. (also absol.) express or react to in a dramatic way. □□ **dramatization** n.
■ **3** exaggerate, overplay, overstate, overdo, overpitch, colloq. make a (big) thing (out) of, make a song and dance about; put it on, make a mountain out of a molehill, colloq. lay it on (thick), lay it on with a trowel, pile it on, go it strong, sl. ham (it) up.

dramaturge /drámətərj, draáomə-/ n. (also **dramaturg**) **1** a specialist in theatrical production. **2** a dramatist. [F f. Gk dramatourgos (as DRAMA, -ergos worker)]
■ **2** see PLAYWRIGHT.

dramaturgy /drámətərjee, draáomə-/ n. **1** the art of theatrical production; the theory of dramatics. **2** the application of this. □□ **dramaturgic** adj. **dramaturgical** adj.
■ see DRAMA 2.

Drambuie /drambóōee/ n. propr. a Scotch whiskey liqueur. [Gael. dram buidheach satisfying drink]

drank past of DRINK.

drape /drayp/ v. & n. ● v.tr. **1** hang, cover loosely, or adorn with cloth, etc. **2** arrange (clothes or hangings) carefully in folds. ● n. **1** (often in pl.) a curtain or drapery. **2** a piece of

drapery. **3** the way in which a garment or fabric hangs. [ME f. OF draper f. drap f. LL drappus cloth]
■ v. **1** hang, festoon, swathe, deck, array, bedeck, adorn, ornament, decorate. ● n. **1** drapery, curtain.

draper /dráypər/ n. Brit. a retailer of textile fabrics. [ME f. AF, OF drapier (as DRAPE)]

drapery /dráypəree/ n. (pl. **-ies**) **1** clothing or hangings arranged in folds. **2** (often in pl.) a curtain or hanging. **3** Brit. cloth; textile fabrics. **4** Brit. the trade of a draper. **5** the arrangement of clothing in sculpture or painting. [ME f. OF draperie f. drap cloth]
■ **2** drapes, curtains; hanging, valance, tapestry, portiere, Theatr. drop, lambrequin, hist. arras.

drastic /drástik/ adj. having a strong or far-reaching effect; severe. □□ **drastically** adv. [Gk drastikos f. draō do]
■ serious, violent, severe, extreme, strong, powerful, all-embracing, sweeping, thorough, exhaustive, potent, fierce, forceful, vigorous, rigorous, harsh, radical, desperate, dire, literary or archaic puissant.

drat /drat/ v. & int. colloq. ● v.tr. (**dratted, dratting** (usu. as an exclam.)) curse; confound (drat the thing!). ● int. expressing anger or annoyance. □□ **dratted** adj. [for 'od (= God) rot]

draught /draft/ n. & v. ● n. **1** (in pl.; usu. treated as sing.) Brit. = checkers (see CHECKER²). **2** Brit. = DRAFT. ● v.tr. Brit. = DRAFT. [ME draht, perh. f. ON drahtr, dráttr f. Gmc, rel. to DRAW]

draughtboard /dráftbawrd/ n. Brit. a checkerboard, as used in checkers (Brit. draughts).

draughtsman /dráftsmən/ n. (pl. **-men**) **1** Brit. = DRAFTSMAN. **2** /dráftsman/ Brit. a piece in the game of draughts.

draughty Brit. var. of DRAFTY.

Dravidian /drəvídeeən/ n. & adj. ● n. **1** a member of a dark-skinned aboriginal people of S. India and Sri Lanka (including the Tamils and Kanarese). **2** any of the group of languages spoken by this people. ● adj. of or relating to this people or group of languages. [Skr. Dravida, a province of S. India]

draw /draw/ v. & n. ● v. (past **drew** /droo/; past part. **drawn** /drawn/) **1** tr. pull or cause to move toward or after one. **2** tr. pull (a thing) up, over, or across. **3** tr. pull (curtains, etc.) open or shut. **4** tr. take (a person) aside, esp. to talk to. **5** tr. attract; bring to oneself or to something; take in (drew a deep breath; I felt drawn to her; drew my attention to the matter; draw him into conversation; the match drew large crowds). **6** intr. (foll. by at, on) suck smoke from (a cigarette, pipe, etc.). **7** tr. **a** (also absol.) take out; remove (e.g., a tooth, a gun from a holster, etc.). **b** select by taking out (e.g., a card from a pack). **8** tr. obtain or take from a source (draw a salary; draw inspiration). **9** tr. trace (a line, mark, furrow, or figure). **10 a** tr. produce (a picture) by tracing lines and marks. **b** tr. represent (a thing) by this means. **c** absol. make a drawing. **11** tr. (also absol.) finish (a contest or game) with neither side winning. **12** intr. make one's or its way; proceed; move; come (drew near the bridge; draw to a close; the second horse drew even; drew ahead of the field; the time draws near). **13** tr. infer; deduce (a conclusion). **14** tr. **a** elicit; evoke. **b** bring about; entail (draw criticism). **c** induce (a person) to reveal facts, feelings, or talent (refused to be drawn). **d** (foll. by to + infin.) induce (a person) to do something. **e** Cards cause to be played (drew all the trumps). **15** tr. haul up (water) from a well. **16** tr. bring out (liquid from a vessel or blood from a wound). **17** tr. extract a liquid essence from. **18** intr. (of a chimney or pipe) promote or allow a draft. **19** intr. (of tea) infuse. **20 a** tr. obtain by lot (drew the winner). **b** absol. draw lots. **21** intr. (foll. by on) make a demand on a person, a person's skill, memory, imagination, etc. **22** tr. write out (a bill, check, or draft) (drew a check on the bank). **23** tr. frame (a document) in due form; compose. **24** tr. formulate or

perceive (a comparison or distinction). **25** *tr.* (of a ship) require (a specified depth of water) to float in. **26** *tr.* disembowel (*hang, draw, and quarter; draw the fowl before cooking it*). **27** *tr.* *Hunting* search (cover) for game. **28** *tr.* drag (a badger or fox) from a hole. **29** *tr.* **a** protract; stretch; elongate (*long-drawn agony*). **b** make (wire) by pulling a piece of metal through successively smaller holes. **30** *tr.* **a** *Golf* drive (the ball) to the left (or, of a left-handed player, the right) esp. purposely. **b** *Bowls* cause (a bowl) to travel in a curve to the desired point. **31** *intr.* (of a sail) swell tightly in the wind. ● *n.* **1** an act of drawing. **2 a** a person or thing that draws custom, attention, etc. **b** the power to attract attention. **3** the drawing of lots, esp. a raffle. **4** a drawn game. **5** a suck on a cigarette, etc. **6** the act of removing a gun from its holster in order to shoot (*quick on the draw*). **7** strain; pull. **8** the movable part of a drawbridge. □ **draw back** withdraw from an undertaking. **draw a bead on** see BEAD. **draw bit** = *draw rein*. **draw a blank** see BLANK. **draw bridle** = *draw rein*. **draw a person's fire** attract hostility, criticism, etc., away from a more important target. **draw in 1 a** (of successive days) become shorter because of the changing seasons. **b** (of a day) approach its end. **c** (of successive evenings or nights) start earlier because of the changing seasons. **2** persuade to join; entice. **3** (of a train, etc.) arrive at a station. **draw in one's horns** become less assertive or ambitious; draw back. **draw the line at** set a limit (of tolerance, etc.) at. **draw lots** see LOT. **draw off 1** withdraw (troops). **2** drain off (a liquid), esp. without disturbing sediment. **draw on 1** approach; come near. **2** lead to; bring about. **3** allure. **4** put (gloves, boots, etc.) on. **draw out 1** prolong. **2** elicit. **3** induce to talk. **4** (of successive days) become longer because of the changing seasons. **5** (of a train, etc.) leave a station, etc. **6** write out in proper form. **7** lead out, detach, or array (troops). **draw rein** see REIN. **draw one's sword against** attack. **draw up 1** compose or draft (a document, etc.). **2** bring or come into regular order. **3** come to a halt. **4** make (oneself) stiffly erect. **5** (foll. by *with, to*) gain on or overtake. **draw-well** *Brit.* a deep well with a rope and a bucket. **quick on the draw** quick to act or react. [OE *dragan* f. Gmc]
■ *v.* **1** pull, tug, tow, drag, haul, lug. **5** attract, allure, lure; bring out *or* forth, elicit, pull. **6** take in, inhale, breathe (in), inspire, pull, suck in. **7 a** pull *or* take out, bring out, extract, remove; unsheathe. **b** choose, pick, select, take. **8** draw out, withdraw, take (out); receive, get, acquire, obtain, secure, procure. **9** see TRACE¹ *v.* 3. **10** sketch, paint; depict, portray, represent, outline, delineate, design, *archaic* limn. **12** see PROCEED *v.* 1. **13** (*draw the conclusion*) see INFER 1. **14 a** see ELICIT. **15** draw off, haul up. **16** draw off *or* out, bring out. **21** (*draw on*) employ, use, make use of, exploit, have resort *or* recourse to, resort to, fall back on, rely *or* depend on. **23** see *draw up* 1 below. **24** see PERCEIVE 2. **29** see *draw out* 1 below. ● *n.* **1** pull, tug, drag. **2 b** magnetism, attraction, lure, enticement, *colloq.* pull. **4** tie, stalemate, dead heat, deadlock. □ **draw back** retreat, recoil, shrink back, draw off, draw *or* pull in one's horns; see WITHDRAW 5. **draw in 1 a** shorten, get shorter. **2** see LURE *v.* **3** arrive, pull in, come in. **draw off 1** see WITHDRAW 3. **2** tap, pour, decant. **draw on 1** come close *or* near, near, approach, advance, *archaic or dial.* draw nigh. **3** see ATTRACT 2. **draw out 1** extend, drag out, prolong, protract, lengthen, stretch, spin out. **2** see ELICIT. **4** lengthen, get longer. **5** leave, pull out, depart, go, set off, get away. **draw one's sword against** see ATTACK *v.* 1. **draw up 1** draft, compose, prepare, put down (in writing), frame, compile, put together, formulate, devise, contrive, draw. **2** arrange, deploy, position, order, rank, marshal. **3** halt, stop, pull up *or* over, come to a halt *or* stop.

drawback /dráwbak/ *n.* **1** a thing that impairs satisfaction; a disadvantage. **2** (foll. by *from*) a deduction. **3** an amount of excise or import duty paid back or remitted on goods exported. □ **drawback lock** a lock with a spring bolt that can be drawn back by an inside knob.

■ **1** disadvantage, hindrance, stumbling block, obstacle, impediment, hurdle, obstruction, snag, problem, difficulty, hitch, catch, handicap, flaw, defect, *colloq.* fly in the ointment.

drawbridge /dráwbrij/ *n.* a bridge, esp. over water, hinged at one end so that it may be raised to prevent passage or to allow ships, etc., to pass.

drawee /drawée/ *n.* the person on whom a draft or bill is drawn.

drawer *n.* **1** /dráwər/ a person or thing that draws, esp. a person who draws a check, etc. **2** /drawr/ a boxlike storage compartment without a lid, sliding in and out of a frame, table, etc. (*chest of drawers*). **3** (in *pl.*) /drawrz/ an undergarment worn next to the body below the waist. □□ **drawerful** *n.* (*pl.* **-fuls**).

drawing /dráwing/ *n.* **1 a** the art of representing by line. **b** delineation without color or with a single color. **c** the art of representing with pencils, pens, crayons, etc., rather than paint. **2** a picture produced in this way. □ **back to the drawing board** *colloq.* back to begin afresh (after earlier failure). **drawing board** a board for spreading drawing paper on. **drawing paper** stout paper for drawing pictures, etc., on. **drawing pin** *Brit.* a thumbtack. **out of drawing** incorrectly depicted.
■ **2** picture, depiction, representation, sketch, plan, outline, design, composition, monochrome, cartoon.

drawing room /dráwingroom, -room/ *n.* **1** a room for comfortable sitting or entertaining in a private house. **2** (*attrib.*) restrained; observing social proprieties (*drawing room conversation*). **3** a private compartment in a train. **4** *Brit. hist.* a levee, a formal reception esp. at court. [earlier *withdrawing room*, because orig. used for women to withdraw to after dinner]
■ **1** see PARLOR.

drawl /drawl/ *v.* & *n.* ● *v.* **1** *intr.* speak with drawn-out vowel sounds. **2** *tr.* utter in this way. ● *n.* a drawling utterance or way of speaking. □□ **drawler** *n.* [16th c.: prob. orig. cant, f. LG, Du. *dralen* delay, linger]

drawn /drawn/ *past part.* of DRAW. ● *adj.* **1** looking strained from fear, anxiety, or pain. **2** (of butter) melted. **3** (of a position in chess, etc.) that will result in a draw if both players make the best moves available.
■ **1** haggard, worn out, tired, fatigued, strained, pinched, tense, exhausted.

drawnwork /dráwnwərk/ *n.* ornamental work on linen, etc., done by drawing out threads, usu. with additional needlework.

drawsheet /dráwsheet/ *n.* a sheet that can be taken from under a patient without remaking the bed.

drawstring /dráwstring/ *n.* a string that can be pulled to tighten the mouth of a bag, the waist of a garment, etc.

dray¹ /dray/ *n.* a low cart without sides for heavy loads, esp. beer barrels. **2** *Austral.* & *NZ* a two-wheeled cart. □ **dray horse** a large, powerful horse. [ME f. OE *drӕge* dragnet, *dragan* DRAW]

dray² var. of DREY.

drayman /dráymən/ *n.* (*pl.* **-men**) a brewer's driver.

dread /dred/ *v.*, *n.*, & *adj.* ● *v.tr.* **1** (foll. by *that*, or *to* + infin.) fear greatly. **2** shrink from; look forward to with great apprehension. **3** be in great fear of. ● *n.* **1** great fear; apprehension; awe. **2** an object of fear or awe. ● *adj.* **1** dreaded. **2** *archaic* awe-inspiring; revered. [OE *ādrēdan, ondrēdan*]
■ *v.* **2, 3** fear, be afraid of, be in fear of, apprehend, flinch from, shrink *or* recoil from, cringe *or* quail *or* blench *or* wince at, view with horror *or* alarm. ● *n.* **1** fear, fright, fearfulness, trepidation, apprehension, apprehensiveness, awe, uneasiness, alarm, nervousness, qualm(s), queasiness, misgiving(s), dismay, worry, anxiety, consternation, concern, distress, perturbation, disquiet, aversion, horror, terror, panic. **2** see TERROR 1. ● *adj.* **1** feared, dreaded, dreadful, terrifying, terrible. **2** see AWESOME 1.

dreadful /drédfool/ *adj.* & *adv.* ● *adj.* **1** terrible; inspiring fear or awe. **2** *colloq.* troublesome; disagreeable; very bad.

● *adv. colloq.* dreadfully; very. ▫▫ **dreadfully** *adv.* **dreadfulness** *n.*

■ *adj.* **1** grievous, dire, horrible, horrendous, horrifying, horrid, monstrous, fearful, feared, frightful, dread, dreaded, frightening, shocking, alarming, appalling, fearsome, hideous, ghastly, atrocious, *poet.* awful. **2** bad, disagreeable, *colloq.* lousy, terrible, *sl.* rotten; see also AWFUL 1a, b, TROUBLESOME. ▫▫ **dreadfully** see AWFULLY.

dreadlocks /drédloks/ *n.pl.* **1** a Rastafarian hairstyle in which the hair is twisted into tight braids or ringlets hanging down on all sides. **2** hair dressed in this way.

dreadnought /drédnawt/ *n.* **1** (usu. **Dreadnought**) *Brit. hist.* a type of battleship greatly superior in armament to all its predecessors (from the name of the first, launched in 1906). **2** *archaic* a fearless person. **3** *archaic* **a** a thick coat for stormy weather. **b** the cloth used for such coats.

dream /dreem/ *n. & v.* ● *n.* **1** **a** a series of pictures or events in the mind of a sleeping person. **b** the act or time of seeing this. **c** (in full **waking dream**) a similar experience of one awake. **2** a daydream or fantasy. **3** an ideal, aspiration, or ambition, esp. of a nation. **4** a beautiful or ideal person or thing. **5** a state of mind without proper perception of reality (*goes about in a dream*). ● *v.* (*past* and *past part.* **dreamed** or **dreamt** /dremt/) **1** *intr.* experience a dream. **2** *tr.* imagine in or as if in a dream. **3** (usu. with *neg.*) **a** *intr.* (foll. by *of*) contemplate the possibility of; have any conception or intention of (*would not dream of upsetting them*). **b** *tr.* (often foll. by *that* + clause) think of as a possibility (*never dreamed that he would come*). **4** *tr.* (foll. by *away*) spend (time) unprofitably. **5** *intr.* be inactive or unpractical. **6** *intr.* fall into a reverie. □ **dream up** imagine; invent. **like a dream** *colloq.* easily; effortlessly. ▫▫ **dreamful** *adj.* **dreamless** *adj.* **dreamlike** *adj.* [ME f. OE *drēam* joy, music]

■ *n.* **2** reverie, daydream, delusion, fantasy, hallucination, illusion, mirage, pipe dream, (flight of) fancy, castles in the air. **3** ideal, ambition, vision; see also ASPIRATION. **5** cloud, daydream, different world, another world; cloudland, cloud-cuckoo-land, dreamland. ● *v.* **1, 2** imagine, fancy, conjure up, hallucinate. **3 a** (*dream of*) think of, contemplate, entertain the thought of. **4** (*dream away*) see FRITTER[1]. □ **dream up** see *think up*. **like a dream** easily, effortlessly, without difficulty, without a hitch *or* hiccup, like a dream come true, like a charm; wonderfully, perfectly, successfully. ▫▫ **dreamlike** unreal, fantastic, unbelievable, phantasmagorical, phantasmagoric, hallucinatory, surreal, illusional, delusive, delusory, illusory, illusive, insubstantial, unsubstantial, dreamy, imaginary, chimerical, fanciful, visionary.

dreamboat /dréembōt/ *n. colloq.* **1** a very attractive or ideal person, esp. of the opposite sex. **2** a very desirable or ideal thing.

■ **1** see BEAUTY 3.

dreamer /dréemər/ *n.* **1** a person who dreams. **2** a romantic or unpractical person.

■ **2** fantasist, fantasizer, visionary, idealist, romantic, idealizer, Utopian; daydreamer, escapist.

dreamland /dréemland/ *n.* an ideal or imaginary land.

■ see FAIRYLAND.

dreamtime /dréemtim/ *n. Austral.* the alcheringa.

dreamy /dréemee/ *adj.* (**dreamier, dreamiest**) **1** given to daydreaming; fanciful; unpractical. **2** dreamlike; vague; misty. **3** *colloq.* delightful; marvelous. **4** *poet.* full of dreams. ▫▫ **dreamily** *adv.* **dreaminess** *n.*

■ **1** absentminded, absent, faraway, abstracted, pensive, thoughtful; daydreaming, musing, occupied; sleepy, drowsy, lazy; see also *idealistic* (IDEALISM). **2** dreamlike, vague, indefinite, indistinct, undefined, intangible, misty, shadowy, faint. **3** see DELIGHTFUL.

drear /dreer/ *adj. poet.* = DREARY. [abbr.]

dreary /dréeree/ *adj.* (**drearier, dreariest**) dismal; dull; gloomy. ▫▫ **drearily** *adv.* **dreariness** *n.* [OE *drēorig* f. *drēor* gore: rel. to *drēosan* to drop f. Gmc]

■ dismal, joyless, cheerless, gloomy, bleak, somber,

doleful, depressing, melancholy, miserable, *poet.* drear; boring, lifeless, colorless, drab, dull, arid, dry, uninteresting, dead, monotonous, prosaic, tedious, tiresome, tiring, wearisome, wearying, humdrum, ordinary, vapid, run-of-the-mill, unstimulating, unexciting, banal, pedestrian, uninspired.

dreck /drek/ *n. sl.* (also **drek**) rubbish, trash. [Yiddish *drek* f. G *Dreck* filth, dregs]

dredge[1] /drej/ *v. & n.* ● *v.* **1** *tr.* **a** (often foll. by *up*) bring up (lost or hidden material) as if with a dredge (*don't dredge all that up again*). **b** (often foll. by *away, up, out*) bring up or clear (mud, etc.) from a river, harbor, etc. with a dredge. **2** *tr.* clean (a harbor, river, etc.) with a dredge. **3** *intr.* use a dredge. ● *n.* an apparatus used to scoop up oysters, specimens, etc., or to clear mud, etc., from a riverbed or seabed. [15th-c. Sc. *dreg*, perh. rel. to MDu. *dregghe*]

■ *v.* **1 b** see WASH *v.* 10a.

dredge[2] /drej/ *v.tr.* **1** sprinkle with flour, sugar, etc. **2** (often foll. by *over*) sprinkle (flour, sugar, etc.) on. [obs. *dredge* sweetmeat f. OF *dragie, dragee*, perh. f. L *tragemata* f. Gk *tragēmata* spices]

■ powder, dust, flour.

dredger[1] /dréjər/ *n.* **1** a machine used for dredging rivers, etc.; a dredge. **2** a boat containing this.

dredger[2] /dréjər/ *n.* a container with a perforated lid used for sprinkling flour, sugar, etc.

dree /dree/ *v.tr.* (**drees, dreed, dreeing**) *Sc.* or *archaic* endure. □ **dree one's weird** submit to one's destiny. [OE *drēogan* f. Gmc]

dreg /dreg/ *n.* **1** (usu. in *pl.*) **a** a sediment; grounds, lees, etc. **b** a worthless part; refuse (*the dregs of humanity*). **2** a small remnant (*not a dreg*). □ **drain** (or **drink**) **to the dregs** consume leaving nothing (*drained life to the dregs*). ▫▫ **dreggy** *adj. colloq.* [ME prob. f. ON *dreggjar*]

■ **1** (*dregs*) **a** sediment, grounds, lees, deposit, draff, residue, solids, remains; precipitate. **b** outcasts, pariahs, losers; riffraff, scum. **2** see BIT[1] 1.

drench /drench/ *v. & n.* ● *v.tr.* **1 a** wet thoroughly (*was drenched by the rain*). **b** saturate; soak (in liquid). **2** force (an animal) to take medicine. **3** *archaic* cause to drink. ● *n.* **1** a soaking; a downpour. **2** medicine administered to an animal. **3** *archaic* a medicinal or poisonous draft. [OE *drencan, drenc* f. Gmc: rel. to DRINK]

■ *v.* **1** soak, saturate, wet, inundate, immerse, drown.

Dresden china /drézdən/ *n.* (also **Dresden porcelain**) **1** delicate and elaborate chinaware orig. made at Dresden in Germany, now made at nearby Meissen. **2** (*attrib.*) delicately pretty.

dress /dres/ *v. & n.* ● *v.* **1 a** *tr.* clothe; array (*dressed in rags; dressed her quickly*). **b** *intr.* wear clothes of a specified kind or in a specified way (*dresses well*). **2** *intr.* **a** put on clothes. **b** put on formal or evening clothes, esp. for dinner. **3** *tr.* esp. *Brit.* decorate or adorn. **4** *tr. Med.* **a** treat (a wound) with ointment, etc. **b** apply a dressing to (a wound). **5** *tr.* trim, comb, brush, or smooth (the hair). **6** *tr.* **a** clean and prepare (poultry, a crab, etc.) for cooking or eating. **b** add a dressing to (a salad, etc.). **7** *tr.* apply manure, etc., to a field, garden, etc. **8** *tr.* finish the surface of (fabric, building stone, etc.). **9** *tr.* groom (a horse). **10** *tr.* curry (leather, etc.). **11** *Mil.* **a** *tr.* correct the alignment of (troops, etc.). **b** *intr.* (of troops) come into alignment. **12** *tr.* make (an artificial fly) for use in fishing. ● *n.* **1** a one-piece woman's garment consisting of a bodice and skirt. **2** clothing, esp. a whole outfit, etc. (*fussy about his dress; wore the dress of a Cherokee*). **3** formal or ceremonial costume (*evening dress; morning dress*). **4** an external covering; the outward form (*birds in their winter dress*). □ **dress circle** the first gallery in a theater, in which evening dress was formerly required. **dress coat** a man's swallow-tailed evening coat; a tailcoat. **dress code** a set of

─────────────────────────

/.../ **pronunciation** ● **part of speech**

□ **phrases, idioms, and compounds**

▫▫ **derivatives** ■ **synonym section**

cross-references appear in SMALL CAPITALS or *italics*

rules, usu. written, describing acceptable dress, as at a school, restaurant, etc. **dress down** *colloq.* **1** reprimand or scold. **2** dress casually, esp. for an informal affair. **dress length** a piece of material sufficient to make a dress. **dress out** attire conspicuously. **dress parade 1** *Mil.* a military parade in full dress uniform. **2** a display of clothes worn by models. **dress rehearsal** the final rehearsal of a play, etc., wearing costume. **dress shield** a piece of waterproof material fastened in the armpit of a dress to protect it from perspiration. **dress shirt** a man's usu. starched white shirt worn with evening dress. **dress up 1** dress (oneself or another) elaborately for a special occasion. **2** dress in fancy dress. **3** disguise (unwelcome facts) by embellishment. [ME f. OF *dresser* ult. f. L *directus* DIRECT]

■ *v.* **1 a** clothe, robe, outfit, fit out, garb, accoutre, array, deck out, bedeck, rig out, *archaic* apparel, *formal* attire, *poet.* bedizen. **2** get dressed, dress oneself; dress up, robe. **4** treat, medicate, *colloq.* doctor; bandage, swathe, bind (up). **6** clean; prepare, make ready. **9** see GROOM *v.* 1. ● *n.* **1** frock, gown. **2** outfit, costume, garb, garments, clothing, clothes, vestments, robes, *archaic* raiment, *colloq.* getup, gear, *formal* attire, apparel. □ **dress down 1** reprimand, scold, berate, rebuke, reprove, upbraid, haul (*or* call) over the coals, *colloq.* tell off, tear a strip off a person, chew out; see also CASTIGATE. **dress up 1** dress, put on one's best bib and tucker, *colloq.* put on one's glad rags, *joc.* put on one's (Sunday) best. **2** put on a costume, disguise oneself, masquerade, camouflage oneself, put on fancy dress. **3** see EMBELLISH 2, MASK *v.* 2.

dressage /drisaázh, dre-/ *n.* the training of a horse in obedience and deportment, esp. for competition. [F f. *dresser* to train]

dresser[1] /drésər/ *n.* **1** a kitchen sideboard with shelves above for displaying plates, etc. **2** a dressing table or chest of drawers. [ME f. OF *dresseur* f. *dresser* prepare: cf. med.L *directorium*]

■ **2** see BUREAU 1.

dresser[2] /drésər/ *n.* **1** a person who assists actors to dress, takes care of their costumes, etc. **2** *Med.* a surgeon's assistant in operations. **3** a person who dresses elegantly or in a specified way (*a snappy dresser*).

dressing /drésing/ *n.* **1** in senses of DRESS *v.* **2 a** an accompaniment to salads, usu. a mixture of oil with other ingredients; a sauce or seasoning (*French dressing*). **b** stuffing, esp. for poultry. **3 a** a bandage for a wound. **b** ointment, etc., used to dress a wound. **4** size or stiffening used to finish fabrics. **5** compost, manure, etc., spread over land (*a top dressing of peat*). □ **dressing case** a case containing toiletries, etc. **dressing-down** *colloq.* a scolding; a severe reprimand. **dressing gown** esp. *Brit.* = ROBE *n.* 2. **dressing room 1** a room for changing clothes, etc., in a theater, sports facility, etc. **2** a small room attached to a bedroom, containing clothes. **dressing station** esp. *Mil.* a place for giving emergency treatment to wounded people. **dressing table** a table with a mirror, drawers, etc., used while applying makeup, etc.

■ **3 b** see SALVE *n.* 1.

dressmaker /drésmaykər/ *n.* a person who makes clothes professionally. □□ **dressmaking** *n.*

■ seamstress, tailor, couturier, couturière, modiste, clothier, outfitter, garment maker, costumier.

dressy /drésee/ *adj.* (**dressier, dressiest**) **1 a** fond of smart clothes. **b** overdressed. **c** (of clothes) stylish or elaborate. **2** overelaborate (*the design is rather dressy*). □□ **dressiness** *n.*

■ **1 b** formal, overdressed, dressed-up, over-the-top. **c** elegant, smart, stylish, fancy, chic, elaborate, fashionable, *colloq.* classy, ritzy, swish. **2** overelaborate, *colloq.* over-the-top.

drew *past* of DRAW.

drey /dray/ *n. Brit.* (also **dray**) a squirrel's nest. [17th c.: orig. unkn.]

dribble /dríbəl/ *v.* & *n.* ● *v.* **1** *intr.* allow saliva to flow from the mouth. **2** *intr.* & *tr.* flow or allow to flow in drops or a trickling stream. **3** *tr.* (also *absol.*) **a** *Basketball* bounce (the

ball) repeatedly, esp. to retain control of it. **b** esp. *Soccer & Hockey* move (the ball, puck, etc.) forward with slight touches of the feet, the stick, etc. ● *n.* **1** the act or an instance of dribbling. **2** a small trickling stream. □□ **dribbler** *n.* **dribbly** *adj.* [frequent. of obs. *drib*, var. of DRIP]

■ *v.* **1** see SLAVER[2] *v.* **2** see TRICKLE *v.* ● *n.* **1** see SLAVER[2] *n.* **1**. **2** see TRICKLE *n.*

driblet /dríblit/ *n.* **1 a** a small quantity. **b** a petty sum. **2** a thin stream; a dribble. [*drib* (see DRIBBLE) + -LET]

dribs and drabs /dríbz ənd drábz/ *n.pl. colloq.* small scattered amounts (*did the work in dribs and drabs*). [as DRIBBLE + *drab* redupl.]

dried *past* and *past part.* of DRY.

drier[1] *compar.* of DRY.

drier[2] /dríər/ *n.* (also **dryer**) **1** a machine for drying the hair, laundry, etc. **2** a substance mixed with oil paint or ink to promote drying.

driest *superl.* of DRY.

drift /drift/ *n.* & *v.* ● *n.* **1 a** a slow movement or variation. **b** such movement caused by a slow current. **2** the intention, meaning, scope, etc. of what is said, etc. (*didn't understand his drift*). **3** a large mass of snow, sand, etc., accumulated by the wind. **4** esp. *derog.* a state of inaction. **5 a** *Naut.* a ship's deviation from its course, due to currents. **b** *Aeron.* an aircraft's deviation due to side winds. **c** a projectile's deviation due to its rotation. **d** a controlled slide of a racing car, etc. **6** *Mining* a horizontal passage following a mineral vein. **7** a large mass of esp. flowering plants (*a drift of bluebells*). **8** *Geol.* **a** material deposited by the wind, a current of water, etc. **b** (**Drift**) Pleistocene ice detritus, e.g., boulder clay. **9** the movement of cattle, esp. a gathering on an appointed day to determine ownership, etc. **10** a tool for enlarging or shaping a hole in metal. ● *v.* **1** *intr.* be carried by or as if by a current of air or water. **2** *intr.* move or progress passively, casually, or aimlessly (*drifted into teaching*). **3 a** *tr.* & *intr.* pile or be piled by the wind into drifts. **b** *tr.* cover (a field, a road, etc.) with drifts. **4** *tr.* form or enlarge (a hole) with a drift. **5** *tr.* (of a current) carry. □ **drift ice** ice driven or deposited by water. **drift net** a large net for herrings, etc., allowed to drift with the tide. □□ **driftage** *n.* [ME f. ON & MDu., MHG *trift* movement of cattle: rel. to DRIVE]

■ *n.* **1** see CURRENT *n.* **2** trend, tendency, direction, course, current, bias, inclination, flow, sweep, bent; intention, meaning, purport, essence, gist, purpose, import, aim, object; tenor, tone, spirit, color. **3** accumulation, pile, heap, mass, bank, mound. **5** see TURN *n.* 2. **7** mass, host, bank, carpet. ● *v.* **1, 2** coast, float, waft, bob; wander, roam, meander, stray, rove, ramble, *sl.* mosey.

drifter /dríftər/ *n.* **1** an aimless or purposeless person. **2** a boat used for drift-net fishing.

■ **1** rambler, wanderer, itinerant, nomad, ranger, rover, vagrant, tramp, vagabond, hobo, *colloq.* knight of the road, dropout, *sl.* bum.

driftwood /dríftwŏod/ *n.* wood, etc., driven or deposited by water.

drill[1] /dril/ *n.* & *v.* ● *n.* **1** a pointed, esp. revolving, steel tool or machine used for boring cylindrical holes, sinking wells, etc. **2 a** esp. *Mil.* instruction or training in military exercises. **b** rigorous discipline or methodical instruction, esp. when learning or performing tasks. **c** routine procedure to be followed in an emergency (*fire drill*). **d** a routine or exercise (*drills in irregular verb patterns*). **3** *colloq.* a recognized procedure (*I expect you know the drill*). **4** any of various mollusks, esp. *Urosalpinx cinera*, that bore into the shells of young oysters. ● *v.* **1** *tr.* (also *absol.*) **a** (of a person or a tool) make a hole with a drill through or into (wood, metal, etc.). **b** make (a hole) with a drill. **2** *tr.* & *intr.* esp. *Mil.* subject to or undergo discipline by drill. **3** *tr.* impart (knowledge, etc.) by a strict method. **4** *tr. sl.* shoot with a gun (*drilled him full of holes*). □ **drill press** a drilling machine with a vertical bit that is lowered into the item being drilled. **drill rig** a structure with equipment for drilling an oil well. **drill sergeant 1** *Mil.* a noncommissioned officer who trains soldiers, esp. new recruits. **2** a strict disciplinarian. □□ **driller** *n.* [earlier as verb, f. MDu. *drillen* bore, of unkn. orig.]

■ *n.* **1** auger, (brace and) bit, gimlet, bradawl. **2** training, instruction, repetition, exercise, practice, rehearsal; discipline. **3** procedure, pattern, form, formula, practice, method, approach, strategy, routine, custom. ● *v.* **1 a** penetrate, pierce, cut a hole in, perforate. **b** bore. **2** train, discipline, exercise, teach, instruct, school, tutor, coach, indoctrinate. **3** drive, bang, knock, force.

drill[2] /dril/ *n. & v.* ● *n.* **1** a machine used for making furrows, sowing, and covering seed. **2** a small furrow for sowing seed in. **3** a ridge with such furrows on top. **4** a row of plants so sown. ● *v.tr.* **1** sow (seed) with a drill. **2** plant (the ground) in drills. [perh. f. obs. *drill* rill (17th c., of unkn. orig.)]

drill[3] /dril/ *n.* a W. African baboon, *Papio leucophaeus*, related to the mandrill. [prob. a native name: cf. MANDRILL]

drill[4] /dril/ *n.* a coarse twilled cotton or linen fabric. [earlier *drilling* f. G *Drillich* f. L *trilix -licis* f. *tri-* three + *licium* thread]

drillmaster /drílmastər/ *n.* **1** *Mil.* one who instructs or leads others (often recruits) in military drill. **2** a rigorous, exacting, or severe instructor.

drily var. of DRYLY.

drink /dringk/ *v. & n.* ● *v.* (*past* **drank** /drangk/; *past part.* **drunk** /drungk/) **1 a** *tr.* swallow (a liquid). **b** *tr.* swallow the liquid contents of (a vessel). **c** *intr.* swallow liquid; take drafts (*drank from the stream*). **2** *intr.* take alcohol, esp. to excess (*I have heard that she drinks*). **3** *tr.* (of a plant, porous material, etc.) absorb (moisture). **4** *refl.* bring (oneself, etc.) to a specified condition by drinking (*drank himself into a stupor*). **5** *tr.* (usu. foll. by *away*) spend (wages, etc.) on drink (*drank away the money*). **6** *tr.* wish (a person's good health, luck, etc.) by drinking (*drank his health*). ● *n.* **1 a** a liquid for drinking (*milk is a high-cholesterol drink*). **b** a draft or specified amount of this (*had a drink of milk*). **2 a** alcoholic liquor (*got the drink for Christmas*). **b** a portion, glass, etc., of this (*have a drink*). **c** excessive indulgence in alcohol (*drink is his vice*). **3** (as **the drink**) *colloq.* the sea. □ **drink deep** take a large draft or drafts. **drink driver** *Brit.* = *drunk driver.* **drink driving** *Brit.* = *drunk driving.* **drink in** listen to closely or eagerly (*drank in his every word*). **drinking song** a song sung while drinking, usu. concerning drink. **drinking-up time** *Brit.* a short period legally allowed for finishing drinks bought before closing time in a public house. **drinking water** water for drinking. **drink off** *Brit.* drink the whole (contents) of at once. **drink to** toast; wish success to. **drink a person under the table** remain sober longer than one's drinking companion. **drink up** drink the whole of; empty. **in drink** drunk. **strong drink** alcohol, esp. liquor. □□ **drinkable** *adj.* **drinker** *n.* [OE *drincan* (v.), *drinc(a)* (n.) f. Gmc]

■ *v.* **1** sip, gulp, swallow, lap (up), *literary* quaff, *sl.* knock back; swill, guzzle, *colloq.* swig; imbibe, *colloq.* wet one's whistle. **2** tipple, nip, indulge, carouse, imbibe, fuddle, sot, *archaic or literary* tope, *colloq.* booze, have a few, drown one's sorrows, *colloq.* go on a pub crawl, *sl.* hit the bottle, go on a binge *or* bender, binge, knock it back, lush. ● *n.* **1** a potation, liquid refreshment, beverage; liquid. **b** draft, sip, taste, gulp, swallow, slug, *colloq.* swig. **2 a** alcohol, strong drink, (hard) liquor, esp. *Brit.* spirits, *colloq.* booze, the bottle, firewater, hooch, esp. *Brit. colloq.* plonk, *sl.* rotgut, lush, red-eye, juice; hard stuff, gargle, *Brit. sl.* bevvy, wallop. **b** tot, nip, draft, jigger, glass, dram, *colloq.* snort, tipple, *Brit. colloq.* pint, *sl.* snifter; eye-opener, nightcap, stirrup cup, *Brit. colloq.* sundowner. **3** (**the drink**) the sea, the ocean, *archaic or poet.* the main, *joc.* the pond, *poet.* the deep, *sl.* Davy Jones's locker, *Brit. sl.* the briny. □ **drink to** toast, salute, celebrate. **in drink** see DRUNK *adj.* 1. **strong drink** hard liquor, drink, esp. *Brit.* spirit(s), *colloq.* firewater, *sl.* hard stuff.

drip /drip/ *v. & n.* ● *v.* (**dripped, dripping**) **1** *intr. & tr.* fall or let fall in drops. **2** *intr.* (often foll. by *with*) be so wet as to shed drops (*dripped with sweat*). ● *n.* **1 a** the act or an instance of dripping (*the steady drip of rain*). **b** a drop of liquid (*a drip of paint*). **c** a sound of dripping. **2** *colloq.* a stupid, dull, or ineffective person. **3** (*Med.* **drip-feed**) the drip-by-drip intravenous administration of a solution of salt, sugar, etc. **4** *Archit.* a projection, esp. from a windowsill, keeping the rain off the walls. □ **drip-dry** *v.* (**-dries, -dried**) **1** *intr.* (of fabric, etc.) dry crease-free when hung up to drip. **2** *tr.* leave (a garment, etc.) hanging up to dry. ● *adj.* able to be drip-dried. **drip-mat** *Brit.* a small mat under a glass; a coaster. **dripping wet** very wet. [MDa. *drippe* f. Gmc (cf. DROP)]

■ *v.* **1** see TRICKLE *v.* **2** be soaked, be sopping, be saturated, be wet through, be drenched, be sodden, be streaming, be wringing *or* dripping wet. ● *n.* **1** dribble, trickle, drop, dripping. **2** milksop, bore, weed, *colloq.* wimp, drag, cream puff, *sl.* dud. □ **dripping wet** soaked, sopping, saturated, wet through, drenched, sodden, streaming, wringing wet.

dripping /dríping/ *n.* (usu. *pl.*) **1** fat melted from roasted meat and used for cooking or as a spread. **2** water, grease, etc., dripping from anything.

drippy /drípee/ *adj.* (**drippier, drippiest**) **1** tending to drip. **2** *sl.* (of a person) ineffectual; sloppily sentimental. □□ **drippily** *adv.* **drippiness** *n.*

■ **2** see SENTIMENTAL.

dripstone /drípstōn/ *n.* **1** *Archit.* a stone, etc., projection that deflects rain, etc., from walls. **2** calcium carbonate in the form of stalagmites and stalactites.

drive /drīv/ *v. & n.* ● *v.* (*past* **drove** /drōv/; *past part.* **driven** /drívən/) **1** *tr.* (usu. foll. by *away, back, in, out, to,* etc.) urge in some direction, esp. forcibly (*drove back the wolves*). **2** *tr.* **a** (usu. foll. by *to* + infin., or *to* + verbal noun) compel or constrain forcibly (*was driven to complain; drove her to stealing*). **b** (often foll. by *to*) force into a specified state (*drove him mad; driven to despair*). **c** (often *refl.*) urge to overwork (*drives himself too hard*). **3 a** *tr.* (also *absol.*) operate and direct the course of (a vehicle, a locomotive, etc.) (*drove a sports car; drives well*). **b** *tr. & intr.* convey or be conveyed in a vehicle (*drove them to the station; drove to the station in a bus*) (cf. RIDE). **c** *tr.* (also *absol.*) be licensed or competent to drive (a vehicle) (*does he drive?*). **d** *tr.* (also *absol.*) urge and direct the course of (an animal drawing a vehicle or plow). **4** *tr.* (of wind, water, etc.) carry along, propel, send, or cause to go in some direction (*pure as the driven snow*). **5** *tr.* **a** (often foll. by *into*) force (a stake, nail, etc.) into place by blows (*drove the nail home*). **b** *Mining* bore (a tunnel, horizontal cavity, etc.). **6** *tr.* effect or conclude forcibly (*drove a hard bargain; drove her point home*). **7** *tr.* (of steam or other power) set or keep (machinery) going. **8** *intr.* (usu. foll. by *at*) work hard; dash, rush, or hasten. **9** *tr.* *Baseball & Tennis* hit (the ball) hard from a freely swung bat or racket. **10** *tr.* (often *absol.*) *Golf* strike (a ball) with a driver from the tee. **11** *tr.* chase or frighten (game, wild beasts, an enemy in warfare, etc.) from a large area to a smaller, to kill or capture; corner. **12** *tr. Brit.* hold a drift in (a forest, etc.) (see DRIFT *n.* 9). ● *n.* **1** an act of driving in a motor vehicle; a journey or excursion in such a vehicle (*went for a pleasant drive; lives an hour's drive from us*). **2 a** the capacity for achievement; motivation and energy (*lacks the drive needed to succeed*). **b** *Psychol.* an inner urge to attain a goal or satisfy a need (*unconscious emotional drives*). **3 a** a usu. landscaped street or road. **b** *Brit.* a usu. private road through a garden or park to a house; a driveway. **4** *Golf, Cricket, & Tennis* a driving stroke of the club, etc. **5** an organized effort to achieve a usu. charitable purpose (*a famine-relief drive*). **6 a** the transmission of power to machinery, the wheels of a motor vehicle, etc. (*belt drive; front-wheel drive*). **b** the position of a steering wheel in a motor vehicle (*left-hand drive*). **c** *Computing* = *disk drive.* **7** *Brit.* an organized competition, for many players, of whist, bingo, etc. **8** an act of driving

/.../ pronunciation	● part of speech
□ phrases, idioms, and compounds	
□□ **derivatives**	■ **synonym section**
cross-references appear in SMALL CAPITALS or *italics*	

game or an enemy. **9** *Austral.* & *NZ* a line of partly cut trees on a hillside felled when the top one topples on the others. □ **drive at** seek, intend, or mean (*what is he driving at?*). **drive-by** (of a crime, etc.) carried out from a moving vehicle. **drive-in** *attrib.adj.* (of a bank, movie theater, etc.) able to be used while sitting in one's car. ● *n.* such a bank, movie theater, etc. **drive-on** (of a ship) on to which motor vehicles may be driven. **drive out** take the place of; oust; exorcize; cast out (evil spirits, etc.). **driving licence** *Brit.* = *driver's license* (see DRIVER). **driving rain** an excessive windblown downpour. **driving range** *Golf* an area for practicing drives. **driving test** an official test of a motorist's competence that must be passed to obtain a driver's license. **driving wheel 1** the large wheel of a locomotive. **2** a wheel communicating motive power in machinery. **let drive** aim a blow or missile. □□ **drivable** *adj.* [OE *drīfan* f. Gmc]
■ *v.* **1** force, urge, push, propel, thrust, press, prod, send; herd, shepherd. **2 a** push, compel, constrain, coerce, impel, force, pressure, make, press, move, motivate, actuate, pressurize; spur, goad, incite. **3 a** operate, conduct, maneuver, manipulate, handle, steer, control; pilot. **b** convey, take, bring, give a person a lift; ride, travel, motor, go, move, proceed, journey, tour, *sl.* tool along. **5** a force, plunge, thrust, sink, push, send, ram. **7** see ACTIVATE. **8** see LABOR *v.* 1, 2, DASH *v.* 1. ● *n.* **1** ride, trip, outing, journey, run, tour, excursion, *colloq.* spin. **2 a** energy, motivation, effort, impetus, vigor, vim, push, enterprise, industry, initiative, ambition, ambitiousness, determination, persistence, urgency, zeal, enthusiasm, keenness, aggressiveness, aggression, *colloq.* get-up-and-go, spunk, pep, zip, go. **b** see URGE *n.* **3** driveway, approach, road, street, avenue, boulevard, lane, route, way. **5** campaign, effort, appeal, crusade. □ **drive at** hint (at), suggest, imply, intimate, allude *or* refer to, intend, mean, have in mind, indicate, *colloq.* get at; seek. **drive out** see LAY¹ *v.* 6b, *cast out.*

drivel /drívəl/ *n.* & *v.* ● *n.* silly nonsense; twaddle. ● *v.* (**driveled, driveling;** esp. *Brit.* **drivelled, drivelling**) **1** *intr.* run at the mouth or nose; dribble. **2** *intr.* talk childishly or idiotically. **3** *tr.* (foll. by *away*) fritter; squander away. □□ **driveler** *n.* (esp. *Brit.* **driveller**). [OE *dreflian* (v.)]
■ *n.* gibberish, rubbish, (stuff and) nonsense, twaddle, garbage, balderdash, blarney, bunkum, slaver, claptrap, pap, fandango, flummery, *colloq.* hogwash, piffle, tripe, malarkey, flapdoodle, esp. *Brit.* tosh, *sl.* hooey, tommyrot, hot air, bosh, baloney, jive, eyewash, bull, bilge, poppycock, rhubarb, rot, bunk, guff, kibosh, *Brit. sl.* codswallop, cock, flannel. ● *v.* **1** dribble, drool, slobber, slaver. **2** prate, prattle, gibber, jabber, burble, gabble, chatter, blather, *colloq.* gab, natter, *Brit. colloq.* waffle; see also BABBLE *v.* 1a, b. **3** (*drivel away*) see FRITTER¹.

driven *past part.* of DRIVE.

driver /drívər/ *n.* **1** (often in *comb.*) a person who drives a vehicle (*bus driver*). **2** *Golf* a club with a flat face and wooden head, used for driving from the tee. **3** *Electr.* a device or part of a circuit providing power for output. **4** *Mech.* a wheel, etc., receiving power directly and transmitting motion to other parts. □ **driver's license** a license permitting a person to drive a motor vehicle. **in the driver's seat** in charge. □□ **driverless** *adj.*
■ **1** see OPERATOR 1.

driveshaft /drívshaft/ *n.* a rotating shaft that transmits power to machinery.

drivetrain /drívtrayn/ *n.* the components in an automotive vehicle that connect the transmission with the driving wheels.

driveway /drívway/ *n.* a usu. private road from a public street, etc., to a house, garage, etc.

drizzle /drízəl/ *n.* & *v.* ● *n.* very fine rain. ● *v.intr.* (esp. of rain) fall in very fine drops (*it's drizzling again*). □□ **drizzly** *adj.* [prob. f. ME *drēse*, OE *drēosan* fall]
■ *n.* mizzle; rain, rainfall, precipitation. ● *v.* mizzle, spit; rain.

drogue /drōg/ *n.* **1** *Naut.* **a** a buoy at the end of a harpoon

line. **b** a sea anchor. **2** *Aeron.* a truncated cone of fabric used as a brake, a target for gunnery, a wind sock, etc. [18th c.: orig. unkn.]

droit /droyt/ *n. Law* a right or due. [ME f. OF f. L *directum* (n.) f. *directus* DIRECT]

droit de seigneur /drwaá də senyŏr/ *n. hist.* the alleged right of a feudal lord to have sexual intercourse with a vassal's bride on her wedding night. [F, = lord's right]

droll /drōl/ *adj.* & *n.* ● *adj.* **1** quaintly amusing. **2** strange; odd; surprising. ● *n. archaic* **1** a jester; an entertainer. **2** a quaintly amusing person. □□ **drollery** *n.* (*pl.* **-ies**). **drolly** *adv.* **drollness** *n.* [F *drôle*, perh. f. MDu. *drolle* little man]
■ *adj.* **1** see COMIC *adj.* ● *n.* see JOKER 1.

-drome /drōm/ *comb. form* forming nouns denoting: **1** a place for running, racing, or other forms of movement (*aerodrome*; *hippodrome*). **2** a thing that runs or proceeds in a certain way (*palindrome*; *syndrome*). [Gk *dromos* course, running]

dromedary /drómideree, drúm-/ *n.* (*pl.* **-ies**) a one-humped camel, *Camelus dromedarius*, bred for riding and racing. Also called *Arabian camel*. [ME f. OF *dromedaire* or LL *dromedarius* ult. f. Gk *dromas -ados* runner]

dromond /drómənd, drúm-/ *n. hist.* a large medieval ship used for war or commerce. [ME f. OF *dromon*(t) f. LL *dromo -onis* f. late Gk *dromōn* light vessel]

drone /drōn/ *n.* & *v.* ● *n.* **1** a nonworking male of certain bees, as the honeybee, whose sole function is to mate with fertile females. **2** an idler. **3** a deep humming sound. **4** a monotonous speech or speaker. **5 a** a pipe, esp. of a bagpipe, sounding a continuous note of fixed low pitch. **b** the note emitted by this. **6** a remote-controlled pilotless aircraft or missile. ● *v.* **1** *intr.* make a deep humming sound. **2** *intr.* & *tr.* speak or utter monotonously. **3 a** *intr.* be idle. **b** *tr.* (often foll. by *away*) idle away (one's time, etc.). [OE *drān, drǣn* prob. f. WG]
■ *n.* **2** see IDLER. **3, 4** see HUM¹ *n.* 1. ● *v.* **1** see HUM¹ *v.* 1. **2** see MURMUR *v.* 1, 2.

drongo /drónggō/ *n.* (*pl.* **-os**) **1** any black bird of the family Dicruridae, native to India, Africa, and Australia, having a long, forked tail. **2** *Austral.* & *NZ sl. derog.* a simpleton. [Malagasy]

droob /drōōb/ *n. Austral. sl.* a hopeless-looking ineffectual person. [perh. f. DROOP]

drool /drōōl/ *v.* & *n.* ● *v.intr.* **1** drivel; slobber. **2** (often foll. by *over*) show much pleasure or infatuation. ● *n.* slobbering; driveling. [contr. of *drivel*]
■ *v.* **1** see SLAVER² *v.* ● *n.* see SLAVER² *n* 1.

droop /drōōp/ *v.* & *n.* ● *v.* **1** *intr.* & *tr.* hang or allow to hang down; languish, decline, or sag, esp. from weariness. **2** *intr.* **a** (of the eyes) look downward. **b** *poet.* (of the sun) sink. **3** *intr.* lose heart; be dejected; flag. ● *n.* **1** a drooping attitude. **2** a loss of spirit or enthusiasm. □ **droop-snoot** *Brit. colloq.* ● *adj.* (of an aircraft) having an adjustable nose or leading-edge flap. ● *n.* such an aircraft. [ME f. ON *drúpa* hang the head f. Gmc: cf. DROP]
■ *v.* **1** sag, hang (down), wilt, dangle; languish, weaken, flag, wilt, decline, wither, be limp, slump, sag. **2 b** sink, go down, droop, set.

droopy /drōōpee/ *adj.* (**droopier, droopiest**) **1** drooping. **2** dejected; gloomy. □□ **droopily** *adv.* **droopiness** *n.*

drop /drop/ *n.* & *v.* ● *n.* **1 a** a small, round or pear-shaped portion of liquid that hangs or falls or adheres to a surface (*drops of dew*; *tears fell in large drops*). **b** a very small amount of usu. drinkable liquid (*just a drop left in the glass*). **c** a glass, etc., of alcoholic liquor (*take a drop with us*). **2 a** an abrupt fall or slope. **b** the amount of this (*a drop of fifteen feet*). **c** an act of falling or dropping (*had a nasty drop*). **d** a reduction in prices, temperature, etc. **e** a deterioration or worsening (*a drop in status*). **3** something resembling a drop, esp.: **a** a pendant or earring. **b** a crystal ornament on a chandelier, etc. **c** (often in *comb.*) a candy or lozenge (*lemon drop*; *cough drop*). **4** something that drops or is dropped, esp.: **a** *Theatr.* a painted curtain or scenery let down on to the stage. **b** a platform or trapdoor on a gallows, the opening of which causes the victim to fall. **5** *Med.* **a** the smallest separable quantity of a liquid. **b** (in *pl.*) liquid medicine to be measured in drops (*eye drops*). **6** a minute quantity (*not a drop of pity*). **7** *sl.* **a** a hiding place for stolen or illicit goods. **b** a secret place where documents, etc., may be left or passed on in espionage. **8** *sl.* a bribe. **9** a box for letters, etc. ● *v.* (**dropped, dropping**) **1** *intr.* & *tr.* fall or let fall in drops (*tears dropped on to the book*; *dropped the soup down her shirt*). **2** *intr.* & *tr.* fall or allow to fall; relinquish; let go (*dropped the box*; *the egg dropped from my hand*). **3 a** *intr.* & *tr.* sink or cause to sink or fall to the ground from exhaustion, a blow, a wound, etc. **b** *intr.* die. **4 a** *intr.* & *tr.* cease or cause to cease; lapse or let lapse; abandon (*the connection dropped*; *dropped the friendship*; *drop everything and come at once!*). **b** *tr. colloq.* cease to associate with. **5** *tr.* set down (a passenger, etc.) (*drop me at the station*). **6** *tr.* & *intr.* utter or be uttered casually (*dropped a hint*; *the remark dropped into the conversation*). **7** *tr.* send casually (*drop me a postcard*). **8 a** *intr.* & *tr.* fall or allow to fall in direction, amount, condition, degree, pitch, etc. (*his voice dropped*; *the wind dropped*; *we dropped the price by $20*; *the road dropped southward*). **b** *intr.* (of a person) jump down lightly; let oneself fall. **c** *tr.* remove (clothes, esp. trousers) rapidly, allowing them to fall to the ground. **9** *tr. colloq.* lose (money, esp. in gambling). **10** *tr.* **a** omit (*drop this article*). **b** omit (a letter, esp. 'h,' a syllable, etc.) in speech. **11** *tr.* (as **dropped** *adj.*) in a lower position than usual (*dropped handlebars*; *dropped waist*). **12** *tr.* give birth to (esp. a lamb, a kitten, etc.). **13 a** *intr.* (of a card) be played in the same trick as a higher card. **b** *tr.* play or cause (a card) to be played in this way. **14** *tr. Sports* lose (a game, a point, a contest, a match, etc.). **15** *tr. Aeron.* deliver (supplies, etc.) by parachute. **16** *tr. Football* **a** send (a ball) by a dropkick. **b** score points by a dropkick. **17** *tr. colloq.* dismiss or exclude (*was dropped from the team*). □ **at the drop of a hat** given the slightest excuse. **drop anchor** anchor ship. **drop asleep** fall gently asleep. **drop away** decrease or depart gradually. **drop back** (or **behind** or **to the rear**) fall back; get left behind. **drop back into** use. *Brit.* return to (a habit, etc.). **drop a brick** *Brit. colloq.* make an indiscreet or embarrassing remark. **drop curtain** *Theatr.* a painted curtain or scenery (cf. sense 4 of *n.*). **drop a curtsy** *Brit.* make a curtsy. **drop dead!** *sl.* an exclamation of intense scorn. **drop down** descend a hill, etc. **drop-forging** a method of forcing white-hot metal through an open-ended die by a heavy weight. **drop hammer** a heavy weight raised mechanically and allowed to drop, as used in drop-forging and pile-driving. **drop in** (or **by**) *colloq.* call casually as a visitor. **a drop in the ocean** (or **a bucket**) a very small amount, esp. compared with what is needed or expected. **drop into** *colloq.* **1** call casually at (a place). **2** *esp. Brit.* fall into (a habit, etc.). **drop it!** *sl.* stop that! **drop-leaf** (of a table, etc.) having a hinged flap. **drop off 1** decline gradually. **2** *colloq.* fall asleep. **3** = sense 5 of *v.* **drop on** reprimand or punish. **drop out** *colloq.* cease to participate, esp. in a race, a course of study, or in conventional society. **drop shot** (in tennis) a shot dropping abruptly over the net. **drop a stitch** let a stitch fall off the end of a knitting needle. **drop to** *Brit. sl.* become aware of. **have the drop on** *colloq.* have the advantage over. **have had a drop too much** *colloq.* be slightly drunk. **ready to drop** extremely tired. □□ **droplet** *n.* [OE *dropa*, *drop(p)ian* ult. f. Gmc: cf. DRIP, DROOP]

■ *n.* **1 a** globule, bead, drip, droplet, tear. **b** bit, spot, dot, taste, dram, sip, nip, pinch, dash, dab, *colloq.* smidgen. **2 a, b** descent, fall; decline, slope, falloff, drop-off, declivity. **d** see DECREASE *n.* **e** see DECLINE *n.* 2. **6** see TRACE¹ 1b. **8** see BRIBE *n.* ● *v.* **1** drip, trickle, dribble, fall. **2** release, let go (of), relinquish; fall. **3 a** fall (down), collapse, sink (down), go down. **b** see DIE¹ 1. **4** desert, forsake, give up, abandon, leave, quit, throw over, jilt, discard, get rid of, leave in the lurch, reject, repudiate, renounce, *colloq.* chuck, dump, *sl.* ditch; relinquish, shed, cast off, let go; discontinue, lapse, stop, cease, end, terminate. **5** drop off, set down, let off or out, leave. **8 a** fall, descend, sink, go down, drop away or down or off, dive, plunge, plummet, decline, collapse, decrease, fall off, diminish, slacken, slack or taper off, subside, lessen, wane, ebb, let up,

ease (off or up); put or bring down, lower. **9** see WASTE *v.* 1. **10** omit, leave out, exclude, eliminate, delete. **14** lose, concede, let slip. **17** dismiss, let go, discharge, oust, *colloq.* sack, give a person the sack, *sl.* fire; see also DISMISS 2, OMIT 1. □ **drop asleep** see NOD *v.* 2. **drop away** see DECREASE *v.* **drop dead!** *colloq.* shut up, *sl.* (go) take a running jump, get lost. **drop in** (or **by**) visit, call in or around, pay a visit, pop in or by, come by, stop in or by. **drop off 1** see DIMINISH 1. **2** see NOD *v.* 2. **drop on** see CASTIGATE. **drop out** see WITHDRAW 5. **have the drop on** have an advantage over, have the edge on or over, have something on or over, have the jump on, *sl.* have the goods on.

drophead /dróphed/ *n. Brit.* **1** a convertible automobile. **2** the adjustable roof of such an automobile.

dropkick /drópkik/ *n. Football* a kick made by dropping the ball and kicking it on the bounce.

dropout /drópowt/ *n. colloq.* a person who has dropped out, esp. from school.

dropper /drópər/ *n.* **1** a device for administering liquid, esp. medicine, in drops. **2** *Austral., NZ, & S.Afr.* a light vertical stave in a fence.

droppings /drópingz/ *n.pl.* **1** the dung of animals or birds. **2** something that falls or has fallen in drops, e.g., wax from candles.

■ **1** see DUNG *n.*

dropsy /drópsee/ *n.* (*pl.* **-ies**) **1** = EDEMA. **2** *sl.* a tip or bribe. □□ **dropsical** /-sikəl/ *adj.* (in sense 1). [ME f. *idrop(e)sie* f. OF *idropesie* ult. f. L *hydropisis* f. Gk *hudrōps* dropsy (as HYDRO-)]

dropwort /drópwərt, -wawrt/ *n.* a plant, *Filipendula vulgaris*, with tuberous root fibers.

droshky /dróshkee/ *n.* (*pl.* **-ies**) a Russian low, four-wheeled open carriage. [Russ. *drozhki* dimin. of *drogi* wagon f. *droga* shaft]

drosophila /drəsófilə/ *n.* any fruit fly of the genus *Drosophila*, used extensively in genetic research. [mod.L f. Gk *drosos* dew, moisture + *philos* loving]

dross /draws, dros/ *n.* **1** rubbish. **2 a** the scum separated from metals in melting. **b** foreign matter mixed with anything; impurities. □□ **drossy** *adj.* [OE *drōs*: cf. MLG *drōsem*, OHG *truosana*]

■ **1** see RUBBISH *n.* 1.

drought /drowt/ *n.* **1** the continuous absence of rain; dry weather. **2** the prolonged lack of something. **3** *archaic* a lack of moisture; thirst; dryness. □□ **droughty** *adj.* [OE *drūgath* f. *drȳge* DRY]

drouth /drowth/ *n. poet.* var. of DROUGHT.

drove¹ *past* of DRIVE.

drove² /drōv/ *n.* **1 a** a large number (of people, etc.) moving together; a crowd; a multitude; a shoal. **b** (in *pl.*) *colloq.* a great number (*people arrived in droves*). **2** a herd or flock being driven or moving together. □ **drove road** an ancient cattle track. [OE *drāf* f. *drīfan* DRIVE]

■ see THRONG *n.*

drover /drōvər/ *n.* a person who drives herds to market; a cattle dealer. □□ **drove** *v.tr.* **droving** *n.*

drown /drown/ *v.* **1** *tr.* & *intr.* kill or be killed by submersion in liquid. **2** *tr.* submerge; flood; drench (*drowned the fields in six feet of water*). **3** *tr.* (often foll. by *in*) deaden (grief, etc.) with drink (*drowned his sorrows in drink*). **4** *tr.* (often foll. by *out*) make (a sound) inaudible by means of a louder sound. □ **drowned valley** a valley partly or wholly submerged by a change in land levels. **drown out** drive out by flood. **like a drowned rat** *colloq.* extremely wet and bedraggled. [ME (orig. north.) *drun(e)*, *droun(e)*, perh. f. OE *drūnian* (unrecorded), rel. to DRINK]

■ **2** flood, inundate, swamp, deluge, drench, immerse, submerge, engulf; overwhelm, overcome, overpower.

/. . ./ **pronunciation**	● **part of speech**
□ **phrases, idioms, and compounds**	
□□ **derivatives**	■ **synonym section**
cross-references appear in SMALL CAPITALS or *italics*	

drowse /drowz/ v. & n. ● v. **1** intr. be dull and sleepy or half asleep. **2** tr. **a** (often foll. by away) pass (the time) in drowsing. **b** make drowsy. **3** intr. archaic be sluggish. ● n. a condition of sleepiness. [back-form. f. DROWSY]

■ v. **1** see SLEEP v.

drowsy /drówzee/ adj. (**drowsier, drowsiest**) **1** half asleep; dozing. **2** soporific; lulling. **3** sluggish. □□ **drowsily** adv. **drowsiness** n. [prob. rel. to OE drúsian be languid or slow, drēosan fall: cf. DREARY]

■ **1, 3** sleepy, heavy-lidded, half asleep, dozy, dozing, groggy, somnolent, yawning; torpid, sluggish, tired, weary, listless, lethargic, lazy.

drub /drub/ v.tr. (**drubbed, drubbing**) **1** thump; belabor. **2** beat in a fight. **3** (usu. foll. by into, out of) beat (an idea, attitude, etc.) into or out of a person. □□ **drubbing** n. [ult. f. Arab. ḍaraba beat]

■ **1** see BEAT v. 1. **2** see OVERCOME v. 1.

drudge /druj/ n. & v. ● n. a servile worker, esp. at menial tasks; a hack. ● v.intr. (often foll. by at) work slavishly (at menial, hard, or dull work). □□ **drudgery** /drújəree/ n. [15th c.: perh. rel. to DRAG]

■ n. hack, plodder, toiler; see also MENIAL n. 1. ● v. see SLAVE v. 1, LABOR v. 1, 2. □□ **drudgery** toil, labor, (hack)work, donkeywork, slog, slogging, archaic moil, colloq. grind, sweat, literary travail.

drug /drug/ n. & v. ● n. **1** a medicinal substance. **2** a narcotic, hallucinogen, or stimulant, esp. one causing addiction. ● v. (**drugged, drugging**) **1** tr. add a drug to (food or drink). **2** tr. **a** administer a drug to. **b** stupefy with a drug. **3** intr. take drugs as an addict. □ **drug addict** a person who is addicted to a narcotic drug. **drug on the market** a commodity that is plentiful but no longer in demand. [ME drogges, drouges f. OF drogue, of unkn. orig.]

■ n. **1** medicine, medicament, pharmaceutical, remedy, cure, treatment. **2** opiate, narcotic, stimulant, hallucinogen, psychedelic, sl. dope, downer, upper. ● v. **2 a** dose, medicate, treat. **b** anesthetize, dope, narcotize, knock out, sedate, stupefy, numb, benumb, dull; poison. □ **drug addict** see ADDICT n. 1.

drugget /drúgit/ n. **1** a coarse woven fabric used as a floor or table covering. **2** such a covering. [F droguet, of unkn. orig.]

druggie /drúgee/ n. & adj. colloq. ● n. (also **druggy**) (pl. **-ies**) a drug addict. ● adj. of or associated with narcotic drugs.

druggist /drúgist/ n. a pharmacist. [F droguiste (as DRUG)]

■ pharmacist, Brit. dispensing chemist, chemist, archaic apothecary.

drugpusher /drúgpŏŏshər/ n. a person who sells esp. addictive drugs illegally.

drugstore /drúgstawr/ n. a pharmacy also selling miscellaneous drugs, cosmetics, and often light refreshments.

■ see PHARMACY 2.

Druid /drŏŏid/ n. (fem. **Druidess**) **1** an ancient Celtic priest, magician, or soothsayer of Gaul, Britain, or Ireland. **2** a member of a Welsh, etc., Druidic order, esp. the Gorsedd. □□ **Druidism** n. **Druidic** /-ídik/ adj. **Druidical** /-ídikəl/ adj. [F druide or L pl. druidae, -des, Gk druidai f. Gaulish druides]

drum[1] /drum/ n. & v. ● n. **1 a** a percussion instrument or toy made of a hollow cylinder or hemisphere covered at one or both ends with stretched skin or parchment and sounded by striking (bass drum; kettledrum). **b** (often in pl.) a drummer or a percussion section (the drums are playing too loud). **c** a sound made by or resembling that of a drum. **2** something resembling a drum in shape, esp.: **a** a cylindrical container or receptacle for oil, dried fruit, etc. **b** a cylinder or barrel in machinery on which something is wound, etc. **c** Archit. the solid part of a Corinthian or composite capital. **d** Archit. a stone block forming a section of a shaft. **3** Zool. & Anat. the membrane of the middle ear; the eardrum. **4** Brit. sl. **a** a house. **b** a nightclub. **c** a brothel. **5** (in full **drumfish**) any marine fish of the family Sciaenidae, having a swim bladder that produces a drumming sound. **6** hist. an evening or afternoon tea party. **7** Austral. sl. a piece of reliable information, esp. a racing tip. ● v. (**drummed,**

drumming) **1** intr. & tr. play on a drum. **2** tr. & intr. beat, tap, or thump (knuckles, feet, etc.) continuously (on something) (drummed on the table; drummed his feet; drumming at the window). **3** intr. (of a bird or an insect) make a loud, hollow noise with quivering wings. **4** tr. Austral. sl. provide with reliable information. □ **drum brake** a brake in which shoes on a vehicle press against the drum on a wheel. **drum into** drive (a lesson) into (a person) by persistence. **drum machine** an electronic device that imitates the sound of percussion instruments. **drum major 1** the leader of a marching band. **2** archaic an NCO commanding the drummers of a regiment. **drum majorette** a female member of a baton-twirling parading group. **drum out** Mil. cashier (a soldier) by the beat of a drum; dismiss with ignominy. **drum up** summon, gather, or call up (needs to drum up more support). [obs. drombslade, drombyllsclad, f. LG trommelslag drumbeat f. trommel drum + slag beat]

■ n. **1 c** see PATTER[1] n. **2 b** see ROLLER 1a. ● v. **2** see TAP[2] v. 1, 2.

drum[2] /drum/ n. (also **drumlin** /drúmlin/) Geol. a long, oval mound of boulder clay molded by glacial action. □□ **drumlinoid** n. [Gael. & Ir. druim ridge: -lin perh. for -LING[1]]

drumbeat /drúmbeet/ n. the sound of a drum or drums being beaten.

drumfire /drúmfir/ n. **1** Mil. heavy continuous rapid artillery fire, usu. heralding an infantry attack. **2** a barrage of criticism, etc.

drumfish /drúmfish/ n. see DRUM n. 5.

drumhead /drúmhed/ n. **1** the skin or membrane of a drum. **2** an eardrum. **3** the circular top of a capstan. **4** (attrib.) improvised (drumhead court-martial).

drumlin var. of DRUM[2].

drummer /drúmər/ n. **1** a person who plays a drum or drums. **2** colloq. a commercial traveler. **3** Brit. sl. a thief.

■ **2** see SELLER.

drumstick /drúmstik/ n. **1** a stick used for beating a drum. **2** the lower joint of the leg of a cooked chicken, turkey, etc.

drunk /drungk/ adj. & n. ● adj. **1** rendered incapable by alcohol (blind drunk; dead drunk; drunk as a skunk). **2** (often foll. by with) overcome or elated with joy, success, power, etc. ● n. **1** a habitually drunk person. **2** sl. a drinking bout; a period of drunkenness. □ **drunk driver** a person who drives a vehicle with an excess of alcohol in the blood. **drunk driving** the act or an instance of this. [past part. of DRINK]

■ adj. **1** drunken, intoxicated, inebriated, besotted, mellow, tipsy, sotted, crapulent, crapulous, in one's cups, pixilated, soaked, roaring drunk, the worse for drink, colloq. soused, under the influence, under the weather, high (as a kite), tight, boozy, well-oiled, cockeyed, sozzled, woozy, lit (up), stewed, happy, jolly, elevated, shot, out (cold), under the table, tanked (up), esp. Brit. colloq. tiddly, well away, Brit. colloq. merry, joc. the worse for wear, sl. pie-eyed, blind, fried, loaded, paralytic, stoned, pickled, squiffed, out of it, sloshed, plastered, screwed, stinko, zonked, smashed, blotto, shicker, shickered, half-seas over, cut, esp. Brit. sl. squiffy, Brit. sl. (feeling) queer. **2** overcome, inspired, exhilarated, excited, exuberant, invigorated, inspirited, animated, ecstatic; elated, flushed, feverish, inflamed, imbued, aflame, fervent, fervid, delirious. ● n. **1** drunkard, drinker, tippler, sot, winebibber; dipsomaniac, alcoholic, problem or serious or hard drinker, guzzler, archaic bibber, archaic or literary toper, colloq. soak, souse, swiller, boozer, dipso, barfly, sponge, sl. wino, lush, juicer. **2** see BENDER.

drunkard /drúngkərd/ n. a person who is drunk, esp. habitually.

■ see DRUNK n. 1.

drunken /drúngkən/ adj. (usu. attrib.) **1** = DRUNK. **2** caused by or exhibiting drunkenness (a drunken brawl). **3** fond of drinking; often drunk. □□ **drunkenly** adv. **drunkenness** n.

■ **1** see DRUNK adj. 1. **3** bibulous, crapulent, crapulous. □□ **drunkenness** intoxication, insobriety, intemperance, bibulousness, inebriety, crapulence, tipsiness; dipsomania, alcoholism.

drupe /drōōp/ n. any fleshy or pulpy fruit enclosing a stone containing one or a few seeds, e.g., an olive, plum, or peach. □□ **drupaceous** /-páyshəs/ adj. [L drupa f. Gk druppa olive]

drupelet /drōōplit/ n. a small drupe usu. in an aggregate fruit, e.g., a blackberry or raspberry.

druse /drōōz/ n. **1** a crust of crystals lining a rock cavity. **2** a cavity lined with this. [F f. G, = weathered ore]

druthers /drúthərz/ n.pl. colloq. preference; choice (if I had my druthers, I'd stay at home. [alt. of would rather]

Druze /drōōz/ n. (often attrib.) (also **Druse**) a member of a political or religious sect linked with Islam and living near Mt. Lebanon (Druze militia). [F f. Arab. durūz (pl.), prob. f. their founder al-Darazī (11th c.)]

dry /drī/ adj., v., & n. ● adj. (**drier** /drīər/; **driest** /drī-ist/) **1** free from moisture, not wet, esp.: **a** with any moisture having evaporated, drained, or been wiped away (the clothes are not dry yet). **b** (of the eyes) free from tears. **c** (of a climate, etc.) with insufficient rainfall; not rainy (a dry spell); (of land, etc.) receiving little rain. **d** (of a river, well, etc.) dried up; not yielding water. **e** (of a liquid) having disappeared by evaporation, etc. **f** not connected with or for use without moisture (dry shampoo). **g** (of a shave) with an electric razor. **2** (of wine, etc.) not sweet (dry sherry). **3 a** meager, plain, or bare (dry facts). **b** uninteresting; dull (dry as dust). **4** (of a sense of humor, a joke, etc.) subtle, ironic, and quietly expressed; not obvious. **5** (of a country, of legislation, etc.) prohibiting the sale of alcoholic drink. **6** (of toast, bread, etc.) without butter, margarine, etc. **7** (of provisions, groceries, etc.) solid; not liquid (dry goods). **8** impassive; unsympathetic; hard; cold. **9** (of a cow, etc.) not yielding milk. **10** colloq. thirsty or thirst-making (feel dry; this is dry work). **11** Polit. Brit. colloq. of or being a political 'dry'. ● v. (**dries**, **dried**) **1** tr. & intr. make or become dry by wiping, evaporation, draining, etc. **2** tr. (usu. as **dried** adj.) preserve (food, etc.) by removing the moisture (dried egg; dried fruit; dried flowers). **3** intr. (often foll. by up) Theatr. colloq. forget one's lines. **4** tr. & intr. (often foll. by off) cease or cause (a cow, etc.) to cease yielding milk. ● n. (pl. **dries**) **1** the process or an instance of drying. **2** Brit. sl. a politician, esp. a Conservative, who advocates individual responsibility, free trade, and economic stringency, and opposes high government spending. **3 a** (prec. by the) esp. Austral. colloq. the dry season. **b** Austral. a desert area; waterless country. **4** a prohibitionist. **5** esp. Brit. **a** dry ginger ale. **b** dry wine, sherry, etc. □ **dry battery** Electr. an electric battery consisting of dry cells. **dry cell** Electr. a cell in which the electrolyte is absorbed in a solid and cannot be spilled. **dry-clean** clean (clothes, etc.) with organic solvents without using water. **dry cleaner** an individual or a firm that specializes in dry cleaning. **dry cough** a cough not producing phlegm. **dry-cure** cure (meat, etc.) without pickling in liquid. **dry dock** an enclosure for the building or repairing of ships, from which water can be pumped out. **dry-fly** adj. (of fishing) with an artificial fly floating on the surface. ● v.intr. (**-flies**, **-flied**) fish by such a method. **dry goods** fabric, thread, clothing, etc., esp. as distinct from hardware, groceries, etc. **dry ice** solid carbon dioxide. **dry land** land as opposed to the sea, a river, etc. **dry measure** a measure of capacity for dry goods. **dry milk** dehydrated milk. **dry nurse** a nurse for young children, not required to breast-feed. **dry out 1** become fully dry. **2** (of a drug addict, alcoholic, etc.) undergo treatment to cure addiction. **dry plate** Photog. a photographic plate with sensitized film hard and dry for convenience of keeping, developing at leisure, etc. **dry rot 1** a decayed state of wood when not ventilated, caused by certain fungi. **2** these fungi. **dry run** colloq. a rehearsal. **dry-salt** = dry-cure. **dry-shod** without wetting the shoes. **dry up 1** make utterly dry. **2** Brit. dry dishes. **3** (of moisture) disappear utterly. **4** (of a well, etc.) cease to yield water. **5** colloq. (esp. in imper.) cease talking. **go dry** enact legislation for the prohibition of alcohol. □□ **dryish** adj. **dryness** n. [OE dryge, drygan, rel. to MLG dröge, MDu. dröghe, f. Gmc] ■ adj. **1** waterless, moistureless, dehydrated,

desiccated. **c** arid, parched, waterless, literary sear; barren, bare. **3 a** unadorned, unembellished, meager; see also PLAIN[1] adj. 3, BARE adj. 4. **b** dreary, boring, tiresome, wearisome, wearying, tiring, dull, uninteresting, monotonous, prosaic, commonplace, stale, uninspired; see also TEDIOUS. **4** subtle, ironic, droll, wry, cynical, biting, sarcastic, cutting, keen. **8** see COLD adj. 4. ● v. **1** dehydrate, desiccate, parch, dry up; dry out or off, drain; wither, shrivel, shrink, wilt. □ **dry run** see REHEARSAL 2. **dry up 5** see HUSH int..

dryad /dríad, dríəd/ n. Mythol. a nymph inhabiting a tree; a wood nymph. [ME f. OF dryade f. L f. Gk druas -ados f. drus tree]

dryer var. of DRIER[2].

dryly /drílee/ adv. (also **drily**) **1** (said) in a dry manner; humorously. **2** in a dry way or condition.

drypoint /drípoynt/ n. **1** a needle for engraving on a bare copper plate without acid. **2** an engraving produced with this.

drysalter /drísawltər/ n. Brit. a dealer in dyes, gums, drugs, oils, pickles, canned meats, etc.

drystone /dríston/ adj. esp. Brit. (of a wall, etc.) built without mortar.

drywall /dríwawl/ n. = PLASTERBOARD.

DS abbr. **1** dal segno. **2** disseminated sclerosis.

DSC abbr. Distinguished Service Cross.

D.Sc. abbr. Doctor of Science.

DSM abbr. Distinguished Service Medal.

DST abbr. daylight saving(s) time.

DT abbr. (also **DT's** /deeteez/) delirium tremens.

DTP abbr. desktop publishing.

dual /dōōəl, dyōōəl/ adj., n., & v. ● adj. **1** of two; twofold. **2** divided in two; double (dual ownership). **3** Gram. (in some languages) denoting two persons or things (additional to singular and plural). ● n. (also **dual number**) Gram. a dual form of a noun, verb, etc. ● v.tr. Brit. convert (a road) into a divided highway. □ **dual carriageway** Brit. a divided highway. **dual control** (of a vehicle or an aircraft) having two sets of controls, one of which is used by the instructor. **dual in-line package** Computing see DIP. **dual-purpose** (of a vehicle) usable for passengers or goods. □□ **duality** /-álitee/ n. **dualize** v.tr. **dually** adv. [L dualis f. duo two] ■ adj. **1** see DOUBLE adj. 6.

dualism /dōōəlizəm, dyōō-/ n. **1** being twofold; duality. **2** Philos. the theory that in any domain of reality there are two independent underlying principles, e.g., mind and matter, form and content (cf. IDEALISM, MATERIALISM). **3** Theol. **a** the theory that the forces of good and evil are equally balanced in the universe. **b** the theory of the dual (human and divine) personality of Christ. □□ **dualist** n. **dualistic** adj. **dualistically** adv.

dub[1] /dub/ v.tr. (**dubbed**, **dubbing**) **1** make (a person) a knight by touching his shoulders with a sword. **2** give (a person) a name, nickname, or title (dubbed him a crank). **3** Brit. dress (an artificial fishing fly). **4** smear (leather) with grease. [OE f. AF duber, aduber, OF adober equip with armor, repair, of unkn. orig.] ■ **2** see NAME v. 1.

dub[2] /dub/ v.tr. (**dubbed**, **dubbing**) **1** provide (a movie, etc.) with an alternative soundtrack, esp. in a different language. **2** add (sound effects or music) to a movie or a broadcast. **3** combine (soundtracks) into one. **4** transfer or make a copy of (a soundtrack). [abbr. of DOUBLE]

dub[3] /dub/ n. sl. an inexperienced or unskillful person. [perh. f. DUB[1] in sense 'beat flat']

dub[4] /dub/ v.intr. (**dubbed**, **dubbing**) Brit. sl. (foll. by in, up) pay up; contribute money. [19th c.: orig. uncert.]

dubbin /dúbin/ n. & v. ● n. (also **dubbing** /dúbing/) prepared grease for softening and waterproofing leather. ● v.tr.

/. . ./ **pronunciation**	● **part of speech**
□ **phrases, idioms, and compounds**	
□□ **derivatives**	■ **synonym section**
cross-references appear in SMALL CAPITALS or italics	

(**dubbined, dubbining**) apply dubbin to (boots, etc.). [see DUB¹ 4]

dubbing /dúbing/ n. an alternative soundtrack to a movie, etc.

dubiety /doōbíətee, dyoō-/ n. (pl. **-ies**) literary **1** a feeling of doubt. **2** a doubtful matter. [LL dubietas f. dubium doubt]
∎ **1** see DOUBT n. 2.

dubious /doōbeeəs, dyoō-/ adj. **1** hesitating or doubting (dubious about going). **2** of questionable value or truth (a dubious claim). **3** unreliable; suspicious (dubious company). **4** of doubtful result (a dubious undertaking). □□ **dubiously** adv. **dubiousness** n. [L dubiosus f. dubium doubt]
∎ **1** see SKEPTICAL. **2** see DEBATABLE. **3** see UNRELIABLE, SHADY 3. **4** see SPECULATIVE 2.

dubitation /doōbitáyshən, dyoō-/ n. literary doubt; hesitation. [ME f. OF dubitation or L dubitatio f. dubitare DOUBT]

dubitative /doōbitaytiv, dyoō-/ adj. literary of, expressing, or inclined to doubt or hesitation. □□ **dubitatively** adv. [F dubitatif -ive or LL dubitativus (as DUBITATION)]

Dubonnet /doōbənáy, dyoō-/ n. propr. **1** a sweet French aperitif. **2** a glass of this. [name of a family of French wine merchants]

ducal /doōkəl, dyoō-/ adj. of, like, or bearing the title of a duke. [F f. duc DUKE]

ducat /dúkət/ n. **1** hist. a gold coin, formerly current in most European countries. **2 a** a coin. **b** (in pl.) money. **3** a ticket to a performance. [ME f. It. ducato or med.L ducatus DUCHY]

Duce /doōchay/ n. a leader, esp. (**Il Duce**) the title assumed by Mussolini (d. 1945). [It., = leader]

duchess /dúchis/ n. (as a title usu. **Duchess**) **1** a duke's wife or widow. **2** a woman holding the rank of duke in her own right. [ME f. OF duchesse f. med.L ducissa (as DUKE)]
∎ see PEER² n. 1.

duchesse /doōshés, dúchis/ n. **1** a soft heavy kind of satin. **2** a dressing table with a pivoting mirror. □ **duchesse lace** a kind of Brussels bobbin lace. **duchesse potatoes** mashed potatoes mixed with egg, baked or fried, and served as small cakes. **duchesse set** a cover or a set of covers for a dressing table. [F, = DUCHESS]

duchy /dúchee/ n. (pl. **-ies**) **1** the territory of a duke or duchess; a dukedom. **2** (often as **the Duchy**) the royal dukedom of Cornwall or Lancaster, each with certain estates, revenues, and jurisdiction of its own. [ME f. OF duché(e) f. med.L ducatus f. L dux ducis leader]
∎ **1** see REALM 1.

duck¹ /duk/ n. (pl. same or **ducks**) **1 a** any of various swimming birds of the family Anatidae, esp. the domesticated form of the mallard or wild duck. **b** the female of this (opp. DRAKE). **c** the flesh of a duck as food. **2** Cricket (in full **duck-egg**) a batsman's score of zero. **3** (also **ducks**) Brit. colloq. (esp. as a form of address) dear; darling. □ **duck hawk 1** Brit. a marsh harrier. **2** US a peregrine. **ducks and drakes** a game of making a flat stone skim along the surface of water. **duck's ass** coarse sl. a haircut with the hair on the back of the head shaped like a duck's tail (usu. abbr. as **DA**). **duck soup** sl. an easy task. **like a duck to water** adapting very readily. **like water off a duck's back** colloq. (of remonstrances, etc.) producing no effect. **play ducks and drakes with** colloq. squander. [OE duce, dúce; rel. to DUCK²]

duck² /duk/ v. & n. ● v. **1** intr. & tr. plunge, dive, or dip under water and emerge (ducked him in the pond). **2** intr. & tr. bend (the head or the body) quickly to avoid a blow or being seen, or as a bow or curtsy; bob (ducked out of sight; ducked her head under the beam). **3** tr. & intr. colloq. avoid or dodge; withdraw (from) (ducked out of the engagement; ducked the meeting). **4** intr. Bridge lose a trick deliberately by playing a low card. ● n. **1** a quick dip or swim. **2** a quick lowering of the head, etc. □ **ducking stool** hist. a chair fastened to the end of a pole, which could be plunged into a pond, used formerly for ducking public offenders, etc. □□ **ducker** n. [OE dūcan (unrecorded) f. Gmc]
∎ v. **1** dunk, push under, submerge, immerse, dip; plunge (in), dive. **2** bob, dodge, dip, dive, stoop, bow, bend, crouch. **3** avoid, sidestep, evade, dodge, elude, shun, steer clear of, shy away from, shirk, withdraw (from). ● n. **1** swim, plunge, bathe, dip.

duck³ /duk/ n. **1** a strong, untwilled linen or cotton fabric used for small sails and the outer clothing of sailors. **2** (in pl.) pants made of this (white ducks). [MDu. doek, of unkn. orig.]

duck⁴ /duk/ n. colloq. an amphibious landing craft. [DUKW, its official designation]

duckbill /dúkbil/ n. (also **duck-billed platypus**) = PLATYPUS.

duckboard /dúkbawrd/ n. (usu. in pl.) a path of wooden slats placed over muddy ground or in a trench.

duckling /dúkling/ n. **1** a young duck. **2** its flesh as food.

duckweed /dúkweed/ n. any of various aquatic plants, esp. of the genus Lemna, growing on the surface of still water.

ducky /dúkee/ n. & adj. esp. Brit. colloq. ● n. (pl. **-ies**) darling; dear. ● adj. sweet; pretty; splendid.

duct /dukt/ n. & v. ● n. **1** a channel or tube for conveying fluid, cable, etc. **2 a** a tube in the body conveying secretions such as tears, etc. **b** Bot. a tube formed by cells that have lost their intervening end walls, holding air, water, etc. ● v.tr. convey through a duct. [L ductus leading, aqueduct f. ducere duct- lead]
∎ n. **1** see PIPE n. 1.

ductile /dúktəl, -til/ adj. **1** (of a metal) capable of being drawn into wire; pliable, not brittle. **2** (of a substance) easily molded. **3** (of a person) docile, gullible. □□ **ductility** /-tíli-tee/ n. [ME f. OF ductile or L ductilis f. ducere duct- lead]
∎ **2** see PLASTIC adj. 1a. **3** see ADAPTABLE 2.

ducting /dúkting/ n. **1** a system of ducts. **2** material in the form of a duct or ducts.

ductless /dúktlis/ adj. lacking or not using a duct or ducts. □ **ductless gland** a gland secreting directly into the bloodstream: also called endocrine gland.

ductwork /dúktwərk/ n. a series of interlinked ducts, as for a ventilation system.

dud /dud/ n. & adj. sl. ● n. **1** a futile or ineffectual person or thing (a dud at the job). **2** a counterfeit article. **3** a shell, etc., that fails to explode. **4** (in pl.) clothes. ● adj. **1** useless, worthless; unsatisfactory or futile. **2** counterfeit. [ME: orig. unkn.]
∎ n. **1** failure, colloq. washout, sl. flop. **2** fake, counterfeit, sham; forgery, imitation. **4** (duds) see CLOTHES.
● adj. **1** worthless, valueless, broken, unusable, useless, inoperative, nonfunctioning, malfunctioning, unsatisfactory, colloq. bust, busted, Austral. & NZ colloq. crook, sl. kaput, Austral. & NZ sl. bung, Brit. sl. up the spout. **2** see COUNTERFEIT adj. 1.

dude /doōd, dyoōd/ n. sl. **1** a fastidious aesthetic person, usu. male; a dandy. **2** a vacationer on a ranch in the western US, esp. when unused to ranch life. **3** a fellow; a guy. □ **dude ranch** a cattle ranch converted to a vacation resort for tourists, etc. **dude up** colloq. dress up; dress in one's best or showiest clothing. □□ **dudish** adj. [19th c.: prob. f. G dial. dude fool]
∎ **1** dandy, fop, fancy dresser, popinjay, man about town, coxcomb, colloq. swell, hist. macaroni, Brit. sl. toff.
3 see FELLOW 1.

dudgeon /dújən/ n. a feeling of offense; resentment. □ **in high dudgeon** very angry or angrily. [16th c.: orig. unkn.]
∎ see DISPLEASURE n.

due /doō, dyoō/ adj., n., & adv. ● adj. **1** (predic.) owing or payable as a debt or an obligation (our thanks are due to him; $500 was due on the 15th). **2** (often foll. by to) merited; appropriate; fitting (her due reward; received the applause due to a hero). **3** rightful; proper; adequate (after due consideration). **4** (predic.; foll. by to) to be ascribed to (a cause, an agent, etc.) (the discovery was due to Edison). **5** (predic.) intended to arrive at a certain time (a train is due at 7:30). **6** (foll. by to + infin.) under an obligation or agreement to do something (due to speak tonight). ● n. **1** a person's right; what is owed to a person (a fair hearing is my due). **2** (in pl.) **a** what one owes (pays his dues). **b** a legally demandable toll or fee (harbor dues; university dues). ● adv. (of a point of the compass) exactly, directly (went due east; a due north wind). □ **due process** a course of legal proceedings in accordance with a state's or nation's legal system, such that individual rights are protected. **due to** *disp.* because of; owing to (*was late due to an accident*) (cf. sense 4 of *adj.*). **fall** (or **become**) **due** (of a bill, etc.) be immediately payable. **in due course 1** at about the appropriate time. **2** in the natural order. [ME f. OF *deü* ult. f. L *debitus* past part. of *debēre* owe]

■ *adj.* **1** payable, owed, owing, unpaid, outstanding, in arrears. **2, 3** fitting, right, rightful, correct, proper, appropriate, apropos, apposite, suitable, apt, meet; deserved, well-earned, merited, just, justified; necessary, needed, adequate, sufficient, enough, satisfactory, ample. **4** (*due to*) owing to, *Brit.* down to. **5** expected, *disp.* anticipated. ● *n.* **1** see PREROGATIVE. **2 b** (*dues*) (membership) fee, charge(s), toll. ● *adv.* directly, exactly, precisely, straight. □ **due to** because of, owing to, on account of, by reason of, thanks to, through, as a result of, resulting from, by virtue of, in consequence of. **in due course 1** see PRESENTLY 1.

duel /dóōəl, dyóōəl/ *n. & v.* ● *n.* **1** *hist.* a contest with deadly weapons between two people, in the presence of two seconds, to settle a point of honor. **2** any contest between two people, parties, causes, animals, etc. (*a duel of wits*). ● *v.intr.* fight a duel or duels. □□ **dueler** *n.*. **duelist** *n.*. [It. *duello* or L *duellum* (archaic form of *bellum* war), in med.L = single combat]

■ *n.* **2** see BATTLE *n.* 2. ● *v.* see COMBAT *v.* 1.

duende /dōō-énday/ *n.* **1** an evil spirit. **2** inspiration. [Sp.]

■ **2** see INSPIRATION 1a.

duenna /dōō-énə, dyōō-/ *n.* an older woman acting as a governess and companion in charge of girls, esp. in a Spanish family; a chaperon. [Sp. *dueña* f. L *domina* mistress]

■ chaperon, companion, attendant; see also ESCORT *n.* 1.

duet /dōō-ét, dyōō-/ *n.* **1** *Mus.* **a** a performance by two voices, instrumentalists, etc. **b** a composition for two performers. **2** a dialogue. □□ **duettist** *n.* [G *Duett* or It. *duetto* dimin. of *duo* duet f. L *duo* two]

duff[1] /duf/ *n.* a boiled pudding. [North of Engl. form of DOUGH]

duff[2] /duf/ *adj. Brit. sl.* **1** worthless; counterfeit. **2** useless; broken. [perh. = DUFF[1]]

duff[3] /duf/ *v.tr. sl.* **1** *Brit. Golf* mishit (a shot, a ball); bungle. **2** *Austral.* steal and alter brands on (cattle). □ **duff up** *Brit. sl.* beat; thrash. [perh. back-form. f. DUFFER]

duffel /dúfəl/ *n.* (also **duffle**) **1** a coarse woolen cloth with a thick nap. **2** a sportsman's or camper's equipment. □ **duffel bag** a cylindrical canvas, etc., bag closed by a drawstring and carried over the shoulder. **duffle** (or **duffel**) **coat** a hooded overcoat of heavy esp. woolen fabric, usu. fastened with toggles. [*Duffel* in Belgium]

duffer /dúfər/ *n. sl.* **1** an inefficient, useless, or stupid person. **2** *Austral.* a person who duffs cattle. **3** *Austral.* an unproductive mine. [perh. f. Sc. *doofart* stupid person f. *douf* spiritless]

■ **1** incompetent, blunderer, bungler, oaf, *colloq.* lummox; see also CLOD 2.

dug[1] past and past part. of DIG.

dug[2] /dug/ *n.* **1** the udder, breast, teat, or nipple of a female animal. **2** *derog.* the breast of a woman. [16th c.: orig. unkn.]

dugong /dóōgawng, -gong/ *n.* (*pl.* same or **dugongs**) a marine mammal, *Dugong dugon*, of Asian seas and coasts. Also called *sea cow.* [ult. f. Malay *dūyong*]

dugout /dúgowt/ *n.* **1 a** a roofed shelter esp. for troops in trenches. **b** an underground air-raid or nuclear shelter. **c** *Baseball* a roofed seating area for players, facing the field. **2** a canoe made from a hollowed tree trunk. **3** *Brit. sl.* a retired officer, etc., recalled to service.

duiker /díkər/ *n.* **1** any African antelope of the genus *Cephalophus*, usu. having a crest of long hair between its horns. **2** *S.Afr.* the long-tailed cormorant, *Phalacrocorax africanus*. [Du. *duiker* diver: in sense 1, from plunging through bushes when pursued]

duke /dōōk, dyōōk/ *n.* (as a title usu. **Duke**) **1 a** a person holding the highest hereditary title of the nobility. **b** a sovereign prince ruling a duchy or small state. **2** (usu. in *pl.*) *sl.* the hand; the fist (*put up your dukes!*). **3** *Bot.* a kind of cherry, neither very sweet nor very sour. □ **royal duke** *Brit.*

a duke who is also a royal prince. [ME f. OF *duc* f. L *dux ducis* leader]

■ **1 a** see PEER[2] *n.* 1.

dukedom /dóōkdəm, dyóōk-/ *n.* **1** a territory ruled by a duke. **2** the rank of duke.

dulcet /dúlsit/ *adj.* (esp. of sound) sweet and soothing. [ME, earlier *doucet* f. OF dimin. of *doux* f. L *dulcis* sweet]

■ see SWEET *adj.* 3.

dulcify /dúlsifī/ *v.tr.* (**-ies, -ied**) *literary* **1** make gentle. **2** sweeten. □□ **dulcification** /-fikáyshən/ *n.* [L *dulcificare* f. *dulcis* sweet]

dulcimer /dúlsimər/ *n.* a musical instrument with strings of graduated length stretched over a sounding board or box, played by being struck with hammers. [OF *doulcemer*, said to repr. L *dulce* sweet, *melos* song]

dulcitone /dúlsitōn/ *n. Mus.* a keyboard instrument with steel tuning forks which are struck by hammers. [L *dulcis* sweet + TONE]

dulia /dōōlíə, dyōō-/ *n. RC Ch.* the reverence accorded to saints and angels. [med.L f. Gk *douleia* servitude f. *doulos* slave]

dull /dul/ *adj. & v.* ● *adj.* **1** slow to understand; stupid. **2** tedious; boring. **3** (of the weather) overcast; gloomy. **4 a** (esp. of a knife edge, etc.) blunt. **b** (of color, light, sound, or taste) not bright, shining, vivid, or keen. **5** (of a pain, etc.) usu. prolonged and indistinct; not acute (*a dull ache*). **6 a** (of a person, an animal, trade, etc.) sluggish, slow-moving, or stagnant. **b** (of a person) listless; depressed (*he's a dull fellow since the accident*). **7** (of the ears, eyes, etc.) without keen perception. ● *v.tr. & intr.* make or become dull. □ **dull the edge of** make less sensitive, interesting, effective, amusing, etc.; blunt. **dull-witted** = DULL *adj.* 1. □□ **dullish** *adj.* **dullness** *n.* (also **dulness**). **dully** *adv.* [ME f. MLG, MDu. *dul*, corresp. to OE *dol* stupid]

■ *adj.* **1** dull-witted, slow-witted, unintelligent, bovine, cloddish, backward, slow, obtuse, doltish, *colloq.* thick, dense, dim, dim-witted, *colloq.* dumb; see also STUPID *adj.* 1, 5. **2** boring, tiresome, monotonous, uninspired, uninspiring, unoriginal, uninteresting, humdrum; see also TEDIOUS. **3** overcast, dismal, dreary, depressing, somber, gray, dark, murky, gloomy, cloudy, clouded, sunless. **4 a** blunted; obtuse; see also BLUNT *adj.* 1. **b** hazy, blurry, opaque; drab, dingy, lackluster, lusterless, gray, somber; muffled. **5** numbing, numb, muted. **6** stagnant, slow-moving, sluggish, slow; lifeless, indifferent, unresponsive, inactive, torpid, depressed, down; see also LISTLESS. **7** insensitive, numb, insensible, imperceptive, unresponsive. ● *v.* allay, assuage, relieve, mitigate, lessen, reduce; dim, tarnish, obscure, blur, cloud, becloud, *poet.* bedim; stupefy, narcotize, numb, benumb, desensitize, deaden, blunt, obtund. □ **dull the edge of** see DAMPEN 2, BLUNT *v.*

dullard /dúlərd/ *n.* a stupid person.

■ see DOLT.

dulse /duls/ *n.* an edible seaweed, *Rhodymenia palmata*, with red wedge-shaped fronds. [Ir. & Gael. *duileasg*]

duly /dóōlee, dyóō-/ *adv.* **1** in due time or manner. **2** rightly; properly; fitly.

■ **1** punctually, on time; see also *promptly* (PROMPT). **2** properly, fittingly, fitly, deservedly, appropriately, suitably, befittingly, rightly, correctly, accordingly.

duma /dóōmə/ *n. hist.* a Russian council of state, esp. the elected body existing between 1905 and 1917. [Russ.: orig. an elective municipal council]

dumb /dum/ *adj.* **1 a** (of a person) unable to speak, usu. because of a congenital defect or deafness. **b** (of an animal) naturally unable to speak (*our dumb friends*). **2** silenced by surprise, shyness, etc. (*struck dumb by this revelation*). **3** taciturn or reticent, esp. insultingly (*dumb insolence*). **4** (of an

---

/. . ./ **pronunciation**   ● **part of speech**

□ **phrases, idioms, and compounds**

□□ **derivatives**   ■ **synonym section**

cross-references appear in SMALL CAPITALS or *italics*

action, etc.) performed without speech. **5** (often in *comb.*) giving no sound; without voice or some other property normally belonging to things of the name (*a dumb piano*). **6** *colloq.* stupid; ignorant. **7** (usu. of a class, population, etc.) having no voice in government; inarticulate (*the dumb masses*). **8** (of a computer terminal, etc.) able only to transmit data to or receive data from a computer; not programmable (opp. INTELLIGENT. □ **dumb animals** animals, esp. as objects of pity. **dumb blonde** a pretty but stupid blonde woman. **dumb cluck** *sl.* a stupid person. **dumb-iron** *Brit.* the curved sidepiece of a motor-vehicle chassis, joining it to the front springs. **dumb piano** *Mus.* a silent or dummy keyboard. **dumb show 1** significant gestures or mime, used when words are inappropriate. **2** a part of a play in early drama, acted in mime. □□ **dumbly** /dúmlee/ *adv.* **dumbness** /dúmnis/ *n.* [OE: orig. unkn.: sense 6 f. G *dumm*]

■ **1, 2** mute, speechless, voiceless, wordless; silent, quiet, *colloq.* mum; inarticulate. **3** see TACITURN. **4** silent, unspeaking, mute, speechless, voiceless, wordless; mimed. **6** dull, *colloq.* thick, dense, dim; see also STUPID *adj.* 1, 5. **dumb blonde** see MISS², FOOL *n.* 1. **dumb cluck** see FOOL¹ *n.* 1.

dumbbell /dúmbel/ *n.* **1** a short bar with a weight at each end, used for exercise, muscle-building, etc. **2** *sl.* a stupid person.

■ **2** see MISS², FOOL *n.* 1.

dumbfound /dúmfównd/ *v.tr.* (also **dumfound**; esp. as **dumbfounded** *adj.*) strike dumb; confound; nonplus. [DUMB, CONFOUND]

■ strike dumb, make speechless, amaze, shock, surprise, startle, take aback, astonish, astound, bewilder, stagger, stun, nonplus, confuse, bewilder, confound, *colloq.* flabbergast, floor, bowl over, *sl.* knock out; (*be dumbfounded*) be at a loss for words, be speechless, be thunderstruck, be dumbstruck, *colloq.* be flabbergasted.

dumbhead /dúmhed/ *n.* *sl.* a stupid person.

dumbo /dúmbō/ *n.* (*pl.* **-os**) *sl.* a stupid person; a fool. [DUMB + -o]

dumbstruck /dúmstruk/ *adj.* greatly shocked or surprised and so lost for words.

■ see SPEECHLESS 1.

dumbwaiter /dúmwaytər/ *n.* **1** a small elevator for carrying food, plates, etc., between floors. **2** a movable table, esp. with revolving shelves, used in a dining room.

dumdum /dúmdum/ *n.* (in full **dumdum bullet**) a kind of soft-nosed bullet that expands on impact and inflicts a severe wound. [*Dum-Dum* in India, where it was first produced]

dummy /dúmee/ *n., adj., & v.* ● *n.* (*pl.* **-ies**) **1** a model of a human being, esp.: **a** a ventriloquist's doll. **b** a figure used to model clothes in a store window, etc. **c** a target used for firearms practice. **2** (often *attrib.*) **a** a counterfeit object used to replace or resemble a real or normal one. **b** a prototype, esp. in publishing. **3** *colloq.* a stupid person. **4** a person taking no significant part; a figurehead. **5** *Brit.* a baby's pacifier. **6** an imaginary fourth player at whist, whose hand is turned up and played by a partner. **7** *Bridge* **a** the partner of the declarer, whose cards are exposed after the first lead. **b** this player's hand. **8** *Mil.* a blank round of ammunition. **9** *colloq.* a dumb person. ● *adj.* sham; counterfeit. □ **dummy run 1** a practice attack, etc.; a trial run. **2** a rehearsal. **dummy up** *sl.* keep quiet; give no information. [DUMB + -Y²]

■ *n.* **1 b** mannequin, model, figure. **2 a** copy, reproduction, likeness, imitation, mock-up, simulation; counterfeit, colloq. phony. **3** fool, idiot, dunce, blockhead, ninny, ass, dolt, numskull, simpleton, *colloq.* dimwit; see also FOOL¹ *n.* 1. **4** see FIGUREHEAD. ● *adj.* see SHAM *adj.* □ **dummy up** keep quiet, lie low, keep one's lips sealed, *colloq.* keep mum, play one's cards close to one's chest.

dump /dump/ *n. & v.* ● *n.* **1 a** a place for depositing trash, garbage, etc. **b** a heap of trash, garbage, etc. **2** *colloq.* an unpleasant or dreary place. **3** *Mil.* a temporary store of ammunition, provisions, etc. **4** an accumulated pile of ore, earth, etc. **5** *Computing* **a** a printout of stored data. **b** the

process or result of dumping data. ● *v.tr.* **1** put down firmly or clumsily (*dumped the shopping on the table*). **2** deposit or dispose of (rubbish, etc.). **3** *colloq.* abandon; desert. **4** *Mil.* leave (ammunition, etc.) in a dump. **5** *Econ.* send (goods unsalable at a high price in the home market) to a foreign market for sale at a low price, to keep up the price at home, and to capture a new market. **6** *Computing* **a** copy (stored data) to a different location. **b** reproduce the contents of (a store) externally. □ **dump on** *sl.* criticize or abuse; get the better of. **dump truck** a truck with a body that tilts or opens at the back for unloading. □□ **dumping** *n.* [ME perh. f. Norse; cf. Da. *dumpe*, Norw. *dumpa* fall suddenly]

■ *n.* **1 a** garbage dump, *Brit.* rubbish dump, (rubbish) tip. **b** see HEAP *n.* 1, REFUSE². **2** see HOLE *n.* 4a. ● *v.* **1** put down, unload, offload, drop, deposit, throw *or* fling down. **2** get rid of, throw away, scrap, discard, jettison, dispose of, toss out *or* away, junk, *colloq.* chuck (out), bin, unload, *colloq.* trash, *sl.* ditch. **3** see DESERT¹ 1, 2. □ **dump on** see CRITICIZE 1, DEFEAT *v.* 1.

dumper /dúmpər/ *n.* **1** a person or thing that dumps. **2** *Austral. & NZ* a large wave that breaks and hurls the swimmer or surfer on to the beach.

dumpling /dúmpling/ *n.* **1 a** a small ball of usu. shortening, flour, and water, boiled in stew or water, and eaten. **b** a dessert consisting of apple or other fruit enclosed in dough and baked. **2** a small fat person. [app. dimin., of *dump* small round object, but recorded much earlier]

dumps /dumps/ *n.pl.* *colloq.* depression; melancholy (*in the dumps*). [prob. f. LG or Du., fig. use of MDu. *domp* exhalation, haze, mist: rel. to DAMP]

■ (*in the dumps*) see DESPONDENT.

Dumpster /dúmpstər/ *n. propr.* a large trash receptacle designed to be hoisted and emptied into a truck.

dumpy /dúmpee/ *adj.* (**dumpier, dumpiest**) short and stout. □□ **dumpily** *adv.* **dumpiness** *n.* [*dump* (cf. DUMPLING) + -Y¹]

■ stocky, squat, chunky, chubby, heavy, tubby, stout, plump, portly, fat, thickset, *colloq.* pudgy.

dun¹ /dun/ *adj. & n.* ● *adj.* **1** dull grayish brown. **2** *poet.* dark; dusky. ● *n.* **1** a dun color. **2** a dun horse. **3** (in full **dun fly**) a dark fishing fly. [OE *dun, dunn*]

dun² /dun/ *n. & v.* ● *n.* **1** a debt collector; an importunate creditor. **2** a demand for payment. ● *v.tr.* (**dunned, dunning**) importune for payment of a debt; pester. [abbr. f. obs. *dunkirk* privateer, f. *Dunkirk* in France]

■ *v.* press, importune, solicit; plague, nag, harass; see also PESTER.

dunce /duns/ *n.* a person slow at learning; a dullard. □ **dunce** (or **dunce's**) **cap** a paper cone formerly put on the head of a dunce at school as a mark of disgrace. [John *Duns* Scotus, scholastic theologian d. 1308, whose followers were ridiculed by 16th-c. humanists and reformers as enemies of learning]

■ see FOOL¹ *n.* 1.

dunderhead /dúndərhed/ *n.* a stupid person. □□ **dunderheaded** *adj.* [17th c.: perh. rel. to dial. *dunner* resounding noise]

■ see DOLT.

dune /doon, dyoon/ *n.* a mound or ridge of loose sand, etc., formed by the wind, esp. beside the sea or in a desert. □ **dune buggy** a low, wide-wheeled motor vehicle for driving on sand. [F f. MDu. *dūne*: cf. DOWN³]

■ see MOUND *n.* 3.

dung /dung/ *n. & v.* ● *n.* the excrement of animals; manure. ● *v.tr.* apply dung to; manure (land). □ **dung beetle** any of a family of beetles whose larvae develop in dung. **dung fly** any of various flies feeding on dung. [OE, rel. to OHG *tunga*, Icel. *dyngja*, of unkn. orig.]

■ *n.* manure, muck, droppings, guano, excrement, feces.

dungaree /dúnggəree/ *n.* **1** (in *pl.*) **a** overalls, etc., usu. made of blue denim, worn esp. by workers. **b** blue jeans. **2** a coarse E. Indian calico. [Hindi *dungrī*]

dungeon /dúnjən/ *n. & v.* ● *n.* **1** a strong underground cell for prisoners. **2** *archaic* a donjon. ● *v.tr. archaic* (usu. foll.

by *up*) imprison in a dungeon. [orig. = *donjon*: ME f. OF *donjon* ult. f. L *dominus* lord]

■ *n.* **1** cell, prison, oubliette. **2** donjon, keep, tower, fortress, stronghold, fastness. ● *v.* see IMPRISON.

dunghill /dúnghil/ *n.* a heap of dung or refuse, esp. in a farmyard.

dunk /dungk/ *v.tr.* **1** dip (a doughnut, etc.) into milk, coffee, etc. before eating. **2** immerse; dip (*was dunked in the river*). **dunk shot** *Basketball* a shot made by a player jumping up and thrusting the ball down through the basket. [Pennsylvanian G *dunke* to dip f. G *tunken*]

■ see DIP *v.* 1.

dunlin /dúnlin/ *n.* a long-billed sandpiper, *Calidris alpina*. [prob. f. DUN¹ + -LING¹]

dunnage /dúnij/ *n. Naut.* **1** mats, brushwood, etc., stowed under or among cargo to prevent wetting or chafing. **2** *colloq.* miscellaneous baggage. [AL *dennagium*, of unkn. orig.]

dunno /dənó/ *colloq.* (I) do not know. [corrupt.]

dunnock /dúnək/ *n. Brit.* the hedge sparrow. [app. f. DUN¹ + -OCK, from its brown and gray plumage]

dunny /dúnee/ *n.* (*pl.* **-ies**) **1** *Sc.* an underground passage or cellar, esp. in an apartment building. **2** esp. *Austral. & NZ sl.* an outhouse; privy. [20th c.: orig. uncert.]

duo /dōo-ō, dyōo-ō/ *n.* (*pl.* **-os**) **1** a pair of actors, entertainers, singers, etc. (*a comedy duo*). **2** *Mus.* a duet. [It. f. L, = two]

■ see PAIR *n.* 1.

duodecimal /dōo-ōdésiməl, dyōo-/ *adj. & n.* ● *adj.* relating to or using a system of numerical notation that has 12 as a base. ● *n.* **1** the duodecimal system. **2** duodecimal notation. □□ **duodecimally** *adv.* [L *duodecimus* twelfth f. *duodecim* twelve]

duodecimo /dōo-ōdésimō, dyōo-/ *n.* (*pl.* **-os**) *Printing* **1** a book size in which each leaf is one-twelfth of the size of the printing sheet. **2** a book of this size. [L (*in*) *duodecimo* in a twelfth (as DUODECIMAL)]

duodenary /dōoədénəree, -deénə-, dyōo-/ *adj.* proceeding by twelves or in sets of twelve. [L *duodenarius* f. *duodeni* distrib. of *duodecim* twelve]

duodenum /dōoədeénəm, dyōo-, dōo-ód'nəm, dyōo-/ *n. Anat.* the first part of the small intestine immediately below the stomach. □□ **duodenal** *adj.* **duodenitis** /-nítis/ *n.* [ME f. med.L f. *duodeni* (see DUODENARY) from its length of about 12 fingers' breadth]

duologue /dōoəlawg, -log, dyōo-/ *n.* **1** a conversation between two people. **2** a play or part of a play for two actors. [irreg. f. L *duo* or Gk *duo* two, after *monologue*]

■ **1** see CONVERSATION.

duomo /dwōmō/ *n.* (*pl.* **-os**) an Italian cathedral. [It., = DOME]

duopoly /dōo-ópəlee, dyōo-/ *n.* (*pl.* **-ies**) *Econ.* the possession of trade in a commodity, etc., by only two sellers. [Gk *duo* two + *pōleō* sell, after *monopoly*]

duotone /dōoətōn, dyōo-/ *n. & adj. Printing* ● *n.* **1** a halftone illustration in two colors from the same original with different screen angles. **2** the process of making a duotone. ● *adj.* in two colors. [L *duo* two + TONE]

dupe /dōop, dyōop/ *n. & v.* ● *n.* a victim of deception. ● *v.tr.* make a fool of; cheat; gull. □□ **dupable** *adj.* **duper** *n.* **dupery** *n.* [F f. dial. F *dupe* hoopoe, from the bird's supposedly stupid appearance]

■ *n.* fool, gull, victim, pigeon, cat's-paw, pawn, tool, puppet, *colloq.* stooge, *sl.* fall guy, sucker, sap, mark, patsy, *Brit. sl.* mug. ● *v.* deceive, fool, outwit, trick, take in, defraud, humbug, hoax, swindle, hoodwink, flimflam, rook, gull, delude, mislead, make a fool of, *colloq.* bamboozle, rip off, put one over on, pull a fast one on, *literary* cozen, *sl.* con, bilk, snow, do a snow job on; see also CHEAT *v.* 1a.

dupion /dōopeeən, dyōo-/ *n.* **1** a rough silk fabric woven from the threads of double cocoons. **2** an imitation of this with other fibers. [F *doupion* f. It. *doppione* f. *doppio* double]

duple /dōopəl, dyōo-/ *adj.* of two parts. □ **duple ratio** *Math.* a ratio of 2 to 1. **duple time** *Mus.* that with two beats to the bar. [L *duplus* f. *duo* two]

duplex /dōopleks, dyōo-/ *n. & adj.* ● *n.* **1** an apartment on two levels. **2** a house subdivided for two families. ● *adj.* **1** having two elements; twofold. **2 a** (of an apartment) two-story. **b** (of a house) for two families. **3** *Computing* (of a circuit) allowing the transmission of signals in both directions simultaneously (opp. SIMPLEX). □ **half duplex** *Computing* (of a circuit) allowing the transmission of signals in both directions but not simultaneously. [L *duplex duplicis* f. *duo* two + *plic-* fold]

duplicate *adj., n., & v.* ● *adj.* /dōoplikət, dyōo-/ **1** exactly like something already existing; copied (esp. in large numbers). **2 a** having two corresponding parts. **b** existing in two examples; paired. **c** twice as large or many; doubled. ● *n.* /dōoplikət, dyōo-/ **1 a** one of two identical things, esp. a copy of an original. **b** one of two or more specimens of a thing exactly or almost identical. **2** *Law* a second copy of a letter or document. **3** (in full **duplicate bridge** or **whist**) a form of bridge or whist in which the same hands are played successively by different players. **4** *archaic* a pawnbroker's ticket. ● *v.tr.* /dōoplikayt, dyōo-/ **1** multiply by two; double. **2 a** make or be an exact copy of. **b** make or supply copies of (*duplicated the leaflet for distribution*). **3** repeat (an action, etc.), esp. unnecessarily. □ **duplicate ratio** *Math.* the proportion of the squares of two numbers. **in duplicate** consisting of two exact copies. □□ **duplicable** /dōoplikəbəl, dyōo-/ *adj.* **duplication** /-káyshən/ *n.* [L *duplicatus* past part. of *duplicare* (as DUPLEX)]

■ *adj.* **1** identical, twin, matching; copied. ● *n.* **1** (exact *or* carbon) copy, double, clone, (perfect) match, lookalike, twin, reproduction, replica, facsimile, replication; photocopy, machine copy, *propr.* Xerox. ● *v.* **2** match, replicate, imitate, reproduce; copy, photocopy, *propr.* Xerox. **3** see REPEAT *v.* 1, REPRODUCE 1, 2.

duplicator /dōoplikaytər, dyōo-/ *n.* **1** a machine for making copies of a document, leaflet, etc. **2** a person or thing that duplicates.

duplicity /dōoplísitee, dyōo-/ *n.* **1** double-dealing; deceitfulness. **2** *archaic* doubleness. □□ **duplicitous** *adj.* [ME f. OF *duplicité* or LL *duplicitas* (as DUPLEX)]

■ **1** see DECEIT 1.

durable /dōorəbəl, dyōor-/ *adj. & n.* ● *adj.* **1** capable of lasting; hard-wearing. **2** (of goods) not for immediate consumption; able to be kept. ● *n.* (in *pl.*) durable goods. □□ **durability** *n.* **durableness** *n.* **durably** *adv.* [ME f. OF f. L *durabilis* f. *durare* endure f. *durus* hard]

■ *adj.* **1** hard-wearing, wear-resistant, heavy-duty, sturdy, tough, stout, strong, firm, sound, dependable, reliable, substantial. **2** enduring, long-lasting.

duralumin /dōorályəmin, dyōor-/ *n.* a light, hard alloy of aluminum with copper, etc. [perh. f. *Düren* in the Rhineland or L *durus* hard + ALUMINUM]

dura mater /dōorə máytər, maá-, dyōorə/ *n. Anat.* the tough outermost membrane enveloping the brain and spinal cord (see MENINX). [med.L = hard mother, transl. Arab. *al-'umm al-jāfiya* ('mother' in Arab. indicating the relationship of things)]

duramen /dōoráymen, dyōor-/ *n.* = HEARTWOOD. [L f. *durare* harden]

durance /dōorəns, dyōor-/ *n. archaic* imprisonment (*in durance vile*). [ME f. F f. *durer* last f. L *durare*: see DURABLE]

■ see CAPTIVITY.

duration /dōoráyshən, dyōor-/ *n.* **1** the length of time for which something continues. **2** a specified length of time (*after the duration of a minute*). □ **for the duration 1** until the end of something obstructing normal activities, as a war. **2** for a very long time. □□ **durational** *adj.* [ME f. OF f. med.L *duratio -onis* (as DURANCE)]

■ see TIME *n.* 4, 6.

/.../ **pronunciation**	● **part of speech**
□ **phrases, idioms, and compounds**	
□□ **derivatives**	■ **synonym section**
cross-references appear in SMALL CAPITALS or *italics*	

durative /dŏŏrətiv, dyŏŏr-/ *adj. Gram.* denoting continuing action.

durbar /dɔ́rbaar/ *n. hist.* **1** the court of an E. Indian ruler. **2** a public levee of an E. Indian prince or an Anglo-Indian governor or viceroy. [Urdu f. Pers. *darbār* court]

duress /dŏŏrés, dyŏŏ-/ *n.* **1** compulsion, esp. imprisonment, threats, or violence, illegally used to force a person to act against his or her will (*under duress*). **2** forcible restraint or imprisonment. [ME f. OF *duresse* f. L *duritia* f. *durus* hard]
■ **1** coercion, threat, pressure, constraint, compulsion, force. **2** confinement, incarceration, captivity, restraint, *archaic* durance; see also *imprisonment* (IMPRISON).

durian /dŏŏreeən/ *n.* **1** a large tree, *Durio zibethinus*, native to SE Asia, bearing oval spiny fruits containing a creamy pulp with a fetid smell and an agreeable taste. **2** this fruit. [Malay *durian* f. *dūrī* thorn]

during /dŏŏring, dyŏŏr-/ *prep.* **1** throughout the course or duration of (*read during the meal*). **2** at some point in the duration of (*came in during the evening*). [ME f. OF *durant* ult. f. L *durare* last, continue]
■ **1** see THROUGHOUT *prep.*

durmast /dɔ́rmast, -maast/ *n.* an oak tree, *Quercus petraea*, having sessile flowers. [*dur-* (perh. erron. for DUN¹) + MAST²]

durn *dial.* var. of DARN².

durned *dial.* var. of DARNED.

durra /dŏŏrə/ *n.* (also **dhurra**) a kind of sorghum, *Sorghum vulgare*, native to Asia, Africa, and the US. [Arab. *dura*, *durra*]

durst /dərst/ *archaic past* of DARE.

durum /dŏŏrəm, dyŏŏ-/ *n.* a kind of wheat, *Triticum turgidum*, having hard seeds and yielding a flour used in the manufacture of spaghetti, etc. [L, neut. of *durus* hard]

dusk /dusk/ *n., adj., & v.* ● *n.* **1** the darker stage of twilight. **2** shade; gloom. ● *adj. poet.* shadowy; dim; dark-colored. ● *v.tr. & intr. poet.* make or become shadowy or dim. [ME *dosk, dusk* f. OE *dox* dark, swarthy, *doxian* darken in color]
■ *n.* **1** twilight, sundown, nightfall, evening, sunset, *archaic or poet.* eventide. **2** see GLOOM 1. ● *adj.* see SHADOWY 1, 2, DARK *adj.* 1. ● *v.* see DIM *v.*

dusky /dúskee/ *adj.* (**duskier, duskiest**) **1** shadowy; dim. **2** dark-colored, darkish. □□ **duskily** *adv.* **duskiness** *n.*
■ **1** shadowy, shady, dim, dark, dull, unilluminated, unlit, murky, gloomy, obscure, black, fuliginous, umber, *formal* subfusc, *poet.* dun. **2** dark, black, fuscous, umber; swarthy, dark-complexioned, *archaic* swart.

dust /dust/ *n. & v.* ● *n.* **1 a** finely powdered earth, dirt, etc., lying on the ground or on surfaces, and blown about by the wind. **b** fine powder of any material (*pollen dust; gold dust*). **c** a cloud of dust. **2** a dead person's remains (*honored dust*). **3** confusion or turmoil (*raised quite a dust*). **4** *archaic or poet.* the mortal human body (*we are all dust*). **5** the ground; the earth (*kissed the dust*). ● *v.* **1** *tr.* (also *absol.*) clear (furniture, etc.) of dust, etc., by wiping, brushing, etc. **2** *tr.* **a** sprinkle (esp. a cake) with powder, dust, sugar, etc. **b** sprinkle or strew (sugar, powder, etc.). **3** *tr.* make dusty. **4** *intr. archaic* (of a bird) take a dust-bath. □ **dust and ashes** something very disappointing. **dust-bath** a bird's rolling in dust to freshen its feathers. **dust bowl** an area denuded of vegetation by drought or erosion and reduced to desert. **dust devil** a whirlwind visible as a column of dust. **dust down** *Brit.* **1** dust the clothes of (a person). **2** *colloq.* reprimand. **3** = *dust off.* **dusting powder 1** talcum powder. **2** any dusting or drying powder. **dust jacket** a usu. decorated paper cover used to protect a book from dirt, etc. **dust off 1** remove the dust from (an object on which it has long been allowed to settle). **2** use and enjoy again after a long period of neglect. **dust shot** the smallest size of shot. **dust storm** a storm with clouds of dust carried in the air. **dust wrapper** esp. *Brit.* = *dust jacket.* **in the dust 1** humiliated. **2** dead. **when the dust settles** when things quiet down. □□ **dustless** *adj.* [OE *dūst*: cf. LG *dunst* vapor]
■ *n.* **1 a** see DIRT 1. ● *v.* **1** see CLEAN *v.* 1. **2** powder, dredge, flour.

dustbin /dústbin/ *n. Brit.* a garbage can, esp. one kept outside.

dustcart /dústkaart/ *n. Brit.* a garbage truck.

dustcover /dústkuvər/ *n.* **1** a cloth put over furniture to protect it from dust. **2** = *dust jacket.*

duster /dústər/ *n.* **1 a** a cloth for dusting furniture, etc. **b** a person or contrivance that dusts. **2** a woman's light, loose, full-length coat.

dustman /dústmən/ *n.* (*pl.* **-men**) *Brit.* **1** a person employed to clear household refuse; garbage collector. **2** the sandman.

dustpan /dústpan/ *n.* a small pan into which dust, etc., is brushed from the floor.

dustup /dústup/ *n. colloq.* a fight.

dusty /dústee/ *adj.* (**dustier, dustiest**) **1** full of, covered with, or resembling dust. **2** dry as dust; uninteresting. **3** (of a color) dull or muted. □ **dusty answer** *Brit.* a curt rejection of a request. **dusty miller 1** any of various plants, esp. *Artemisia stelleriana*, having white down on the leaves and flowers. **2** an artificial fishing fly. **not so dusty** *Brit. sl.* fairly good. □□ **dustily** *adv.* **dustiness** *n.* [OE *dústig* (as DUST)]

Dutch /duch/ *adj. & n.* ● *adj.* **1** of, relating to, or associated with the Netherlands. **2** *sl.* German. **3** *S.Afr.* of Dutch descent. **4** *archaic* of Germany including the Netherlands. ● *n.* **1 a** the language of the Netherlands. **b** *S.Afr.* usu. *derog.* Afrikaans. **2** (prec. by *the*; treated as *pl.*) **a** the people of the Netherlands. **b** *S.Afr.* Afrikaans speakers. **3** *archaic* the language of Germany including the Netherlands. □ **beat the Dutch** *colloq.* do something remarkable. **Dutch auction** see AUCTION. **Dutch bargain** a bargain concluded by drinking together. **Dutch barn** *Brit.* a barn roof over hay, etc., set on poles and having no walls. **Dutch cap 1** a contraceptive diaphragm. **2** a woman's lace cap with triangular flaps on each side. **Dutch courage** false courage gained from alcohol. **Dutch doll** a jointed wooden doll. **Dutch door** a door divided into two parts horizontally allowing one part to be shut and the other open. **Dutch elm disease** a disease affecting elms caused by the fungus *Ceratocystis ulmi*, first found in the Netherlands. **Dutch hoe** a hoe pushed forward by the user. **Dutch interior** a painting of Dutch domestic life, esp. by P. de Hooch (d. 1683). **Dutch metal** a copper-zinc alloy imitating gold leaf. **Dutch oven 1** a metal box the open side of which is turned toward a fire. **2** a covered cooking pot for braising, etc. **Dutch treat** a party, outing, etc. to which each person makes a contribution. **Dutch uncle** a person giving advice with benevolent firmness. **Dutch wife** a framework of cane, etc., or a bolster, used for resting the legs in bed. **go Dutch** share expenses equally. [MDu. *dutsch*, etc., Hollandish, Netherlandish, German, OHG *diutisc* national]

dutch /duch/ *n. Brit. sl.* a wife (esp. *old dutch*). [abbr. of *duchess* (also in this sense)]

Dutchman /dúchmən/ *n.* (*pl.* **-men**; *fem.* **Dutchwoman**, *pl.* **-women**) **1 a** a native or national of the Netherlands. **b** a person of Dutch descent. **2** a Dutch ship. **3** *sl.* a German. □ **Dutchman's-breeches** a plant, *Dicentra cucullaria*, with white flowers and finely divided leaves. **Flying Dutchman 1** a ghostly ship. **2** its captain. **I'm a Dutchman** *Brit.* expression of disbelief or refusal.

duteous /dŏŏteeəs, dyŏŏ-/ *adj. literary* (of a person or conduct) dutiful; obedient. □□ **duteously** *adv.* **duteousness** *n.* [DUTY + -OUS: cf. *beauteous*]
■ see DUTIFUL.

dutiable /dŏŏteeəbəl, dyŏŏ-/ *adj.* liable to customs or other duties.

dutiful /dŏŏtifŏŏl, dyŏŏ-/ *adj.* doing or observant of one's duty; obedient. □□ **dutifully** *adv.* **dutifulness** *n.*
■ obedient, responsible, diligent, attentive, punctilious, respectful, pious, polite, considerate, deferential, submissive, acquiescent, compliant, filial, faithful, conscientious, reliable, *literary* duteous.

duty /dŏŏtee, dyŏŏ-/ *n.* (*pl.* **-ies**) **1 a** a moral or legal obligation; a responsibility (*her duty to report it*). **b** the binding force of what is right (*strong sense of duty*). **c** what is required of one (*do one's duty*). **2** payment to the public revenue, esp.: **a** that levied on the import, export, manufacture, or sale of goods (*customs duty*). **b** that levied on the transfer of property, licenses, the legal recognition of documents, etc. (*death duty*; *probate duty*). **3** a job or function (*his duties as caretaker*). **4** the behavior due to a superior; deference, respect. **5** the measure of an engine's effectiveness in units of work done per unit of fuel. **6** *Eccl.* the performance of church services. □ **do duty for** serve as or pass for (something else). **duty-bound** obliged by duty. **duty-free** (of goods) on which duty is not leviable. **duty-free shop** a store at an airport, etc., at which duty-free goods can be bought. **duty officer** the officer currently on duty. **duty-paid** (of goods) on which duty has been paid. **duty visit** a visit paid from obligation, not from pleasure. **on** (or **off**) **duty** engaged (or not engaged) in one's work. [AF *deweté, dueté* (as DUE)]

■ **1 a** see OBLIGATION 2. **b** see MORALITY 1, 2, 6, RESPONSIBILITY 1a. **c** office, work, assignment, job, occupation, charge; part, bit, stint. **2** tax, excise, tariff, impost, levy, customs. **3** job, function, role, task, chore. **4** respect, deference, loyalty, fealty, fidelity, faithfulness, allegiance. □ **do duty for** pass for, serve as, act as. **duty-bound** (*be duty-bound*) see SUPPOSE 7a, MUST[1] *v.* **off duty** off, free, on leave, on holiday, unoccupied, unengaged.

duumvir /doo-úmvər, dyoo-/ *n. Rom.Hist.* one of two coequal magistrates or officials. □□ **duumvirate** /-virət/ *n.* [L f. *duum virum* of the two men]

duvet /doováy/ *n.* a thick, soft quilt with a detachable cover, used instead of an upper sheet and blankets. [F]

■ see SPREAD *n.* 10.

dux /duks/ *n. Sc., Austral., NZ, & S.Afr.* the top pupil in a class or in a school. [L, = leader]

DV *abbr.* Deo volente.

D.V.M. *abbr.* doctor of veterinary medicine.

dwarf /dwawrf/ *n. & v.* ● *n.* (*pl.* **dwarfs** or **dwarves** /dwawrvz/) **1 a** *Offens.* a person of abnormally small stature, esp. one with a normal-sized head and body but short limbs. **b** an animal or plant much below the ordinary size for the species. **2** a small mythological being with supernatural powers. **3** (in full **dwarf star**) a small usu. dense star. **4** (*attrib.*) **a** of a kind very small in size (*dwarf bean*). **b** puny; stunted. ● *v.tr.* **1** stunt in growth. **2** cause (something similar or comparable) to seem small or insignificant (*efforts dwarfed by their rivals' achievements*). □□ **dwarfish** *adj.* [OE *dweorg* f. Gmc]

■ *n.* **4 b** see PUNY 1, 2. ● *v.* **1** see STUNT[1] 2. **2** overshadow, dominate; diminish, minimize, lessen, make small, dim.

dwarfism /dwáwrfizəm/ *n.* the condition of being a dwarf.

dweeb /dweeb/ *n. sl.* a studious or tedious person. [orig. unkn.]

■ *colloq.* grind *Brit. colloq.* swot; see also FOOL[1] *n.* 1.

dwell /dwel/ *v. & n.* ● *v.intr.* (*past* and *past part.* **dwelled** or **dwelt**) **1** *literary* (usu. foll. by *in, at, near, on,* etc.) live; reside (*dwelt in the forest*). **2** (of a horse) be slow in raising its feet; pause before taking a fence. ● *n.* a slight, regular pause in the motion of a machine. □ **dwell on** (or **upon**) **1** spend time on; linger over; write, brood, or speak at length on (a specified subject) (*always dwells on his grievances*). **2** prolong (a note, a syllable, etc.). □□ **dweller** *n.* [OE *dwellan* lead astray, later 'continue in a place,' f. Gmc]

■ *v.* **1** reside, live, lodge, stay, remain, rest, be domiciled, *archaic* abide. □ **dwell on** (or **upon**) **1** harp on, emphasize, stress, belabor, focus on, linger over, brood on *or* over, elaborate (on), talk about, *colloq.* go on about.

dwelling /dwéling/ *n.* (also **dwelling place**) *formal* a house; a residence; an abode. □ **dwelling house** a house used as a residence, not as an office, etc.

■ habitation, house, domicile, lodging, quarters, home, residence, homestead; see also ABODE[1].

DWI *abbr.* **1** driving while intoxicated. **2** Dutch West Indies.

dwindle /dwínd'l/ *v.intr.* **1** become gradually smaller; shrink; waste away. **2** lose importance; decline; degenerate. [*dwine* fade away f. OE *dwīnan*, ON *dvina*]

■ **1** diminish, decrease, shrink, lessen, wane, fade,

contract, condense, reduce, peter out, waste away, die out *or* down *or* away, ebb, decline, subside, taper off, shrivel (up *or* away). **2** see DEGENERATE *v.*

dwt. *abbr. hist.* pennyweight.

d.w.t. *abbr.* deadweight ton(s); deadweight tonnage.

Dy *symb. Chem.* the element dysprosium.

dyad /díad/ *n. Math.* an operator which is a combination of two vectors. □□ **dyadic** /-ádik/ *adj.* [LL *dyas dyad-* f. Gk *duas duados* f. *duo* two]

Dyak /díak/ *n.* var. of DAYAK.

dyarchy var. of DIARCHY.

dybbuk /díbook, deebook/ *n.* (*pl.* **dybbukim** /dibookim, deebookeém/ or **dybbuks**) a malevolent spirit in Jewish folklore. [Heb. *dibbūḳ* f. *dāḇaḳ* cling]

dye /dí/ *n. & v.* ● *n.* **1 a** a substance used to change the color of hair, fabric, wood, etc. **b** a color produced by this. **2** (in full **dyestuff**) a substance yielding a dye, esp. for coloring materials in solution. ● *v.tr.* (**dyeing**) **1** impregnate with dye. **2** make (a thing) a specified color with dye (*dyed it yellow*). □ **dyed-in-the-wool 1** out and out; unchangeable; inveterate. **2** (of a fabric) made of yarn dyed in its raw state. □□ **dyeable** *adj.* [OE *deag, deagian*]

■ *n.* see COLOR *n.* 3. ● *v.* see COLOR *v.* 1.

dyeline /dílin/ *n.* a print made by the diazo process.

dyer /díər/ *n.* a person who dyes cloth, etc. □ **dyer's broom** (or **greenweed** or **oak,** etc.) names of plants yielding dyes.

dying /dí-ing/ *adj.* about to die, mortally ill; connected with, or at the time of, death (*his dying words*). □ **dying oath** an oath made at, or with the solemnity proper to, death. **to one's dying day** for the rest of one's life. [pres. part. of DIE[1]]

■ at death's door, on one's deathbed, with one foot in the grave, on one's last legs, *in extremis*, moribund; last, final. □ **to one's dying day** see ALWAYS 4.

dyke[1] var. of DIKE[1].

dyke[2] /dík/ *n.* (also **dike**) *sl.* a lesbian. [20th c.: orig. unkn.]

■ see HOMOSEXUAL *n.*

dyn *abbr.* dyne(s).

dynamic /dínámik/ *adj. & n.* ● *adj.* (also **dynamical**) **1** energetic; active; potent. **2** *Physics* **a** concerning motive force (opp. STATIC). **b** concerning force in actual operation. **3** of or concerning dynamics. **4** *Mus.* relating to the volume of sound. **5** *Philos.* relating to dynamism. **6** (as **dynamical**) *Theol.* (of inspiration) endowing with divine power, not impelling mechanically. ● *n.* **1** an energizing or motive force. **2** *Mus.* = DYNAMICS 3. □ **dynamic equilibrium** see EQUILIBRIUM. **dynamic viscosity** see VISCOSITY. □□ **dynamically** *adv.* [F *dynamique* f. Gk *dunamikos* f. *dunamis* power]

■ *adj.* **1** vigorous, active, forceful, potent, powerful, highpowered, lively, spry, vital, electric, spirited, zealous, eager; see also ENERGETIC 1, 2. ● *n.* **1** see ENERGY 1.

dynamics /dínámiks/ *n.pl.* **1** (usu. treated as *sing.*) **a** *Mech.* the branch of mechanics concerned with the motion of bodies under the action of forces (cf. STATICS). **b** the branch of any science in which forces or changes are considered (*aerodynamics; population dynamics*). **2** the motive forces, physical or moral, affecting behavior and change in any sphere. **3** *Mus.* the varying degree of volume of sound in musical performance. □□ **dynamicist** /-məsist/ *n.* (in sense 1).

dynamism /dínəmizəm/ *n.* **1** energizing or dynamic action or power. **2** *Philos.* the theory that phenomena of matter or mind are due to the action of forces (rather than to motion or matter). □□ **dynamist** *n.* [Gk *dunamis* power + -ISM]

■ **1** vigor, vitality, liveliness, spirit, vim, spiritedness, forcefulness, power, drive, initiative, enterprise, *colloq.* get-up-and-go, pep, zip, push, go; see also ENERGY 1.

dynamite /dínəmit/ *n. & v.* ● *n.* **1** a high explosive consisting of nitroglycerine mixed with an absorbent. **2** a potentially dangerous person, thing, or situation. **3** *sl.* a narcotic, esp.

/.../ **pronunciation**	● **part of speech**	
□ **phrases, idioms, and compounds**		
□□ **derivatives**	■ **synonym section**	
cross-references appear in SMALL CAPITALS or *italics*		

heroin. ● *v.tr.* charge or shatter with dynamite. □□ **dynamiter** *n.* [formed as DYNAMISM + -ITE¹]

■ *n.* **1** see EXPLOSIVE *n.* ● *v.* see BLAST *v.* 1.

dynamo /dínəmō/ *n.* (*pl.* **-os**) **1** a machine converting mechanical into electrical energy, esp. by rotating coils of copper wire in a magnetic field. **2** *colloq.* an energetic person. [abbr. of *dynamoelectric machine* f. Gk *dunamis* power, force]

dynamometer /dínəmómitər/ *n.* an instrument measuring energy expended. [F *dynamomètre* f. Gk *dunamis* power, force]

dynast /dínast, -nəst/ *n.* **1** a ruler. **2** a member of a dynasty. [L f. Gk *dunastēs* f. *dunamai* be able]

dynasty /dínəstee/ *n.* (*pl.* **-ies**) **1** a line of hereditary rulers. **2** a succession of leaders in any field. □□ **dynastic** /-nástik/ *adj.* **dynastically** *adv.* [F *dynastie* or LL *dynastia* f. Gk *dunasteia* lordship (as DYNAST)]

■ **1** line, ancestry, family, house.

dynatron /dínətron/ *n.* *Electronics* a thermionic valve, used to generate continuous oscillations. [Gk *dunamis* power + -TRON]

dyne /dīn/ *n.* *Physics* a unit of force that, acting on a mass of one gram, increases its velocity by one centimeter per second every second along the direction that it acts. ¶ Abbr.: **dyn.** [F f. Gk *dunamis* force, power]

dys- /dis/ *comb. form* esp. *Med.* bad; difficult. [Gk *dus-* bad]

dysentery /dísənteree/ *n.* a disease with inflammation of the intestines, causing severe diarrhea with blood and mucus. □□ **dysenteric** *adj.* [OF *dissenterie* or L *dysenteria* f. Gk *dusenteria* (as DYS-, *enteria* f. *entera* bowels)]

dysfunction /dísfúngkshən/ *n.* an abnormality or impairment of function. □□ **dysfunctional** *adj.*

dysgraphia /disgráfeeə/ *n.* an inability to write coherently. □□ **dysgraphic** *adj.* [DYS- + Gk *graphia* writing]

dyslexia /dislékseeə/ *n.* an abnormal difficulty in reading and spelling, caused by a condition of the brain. □□ **dyslexic** *adj.* & *n.* **dyslectic** /-léktik/ *adj.* & *n.* [G *Dyslexie* (as DYS-, Gk *lexis* speech)]

dysmenorrhea /dísmenəreeə/ *n.* painful or difficult menstruation.

dyspepsia /dispépseeə/ *n.* indigestion. [L *dyspepsia* f. Gk *duspepsia* (as DYS-, *peptos* cooked, digested)]

■ see INDIGESTION.

dyspeptic /dispéptik/ *adj.* & *n.* ● *adj.* of or relating to dyspepsia or the resulting depression. ● *n.* a person suffering from dyspepsia.

■ *adj.* see TOUCHY 1.

dysphasia /disfáyzhə, -zheeə/ *n.* *Med.* lack of coordination in speech, owing to brain damage. □□ **dysphasic** /-zik, -sik/ *adj.* [Gk *dusphatos* hard to utter (as DYS-, PHATIC)]

dysphoria /disfáwreeə/ *n.* a state of unease or mental discomfort. □□ **dysphoric** /-fáwrik/ *adj.* [Gk *dusphoria* f. *dusphoros* hard to bear (as DYS-, *pherō* bear)]

dysplasia /displáyzhə, -zheeə/ *n.* *Med.* abnormal growth of tissues, etc. □□ **dysplastic** /-plástik/ *adj.* [mod.L, formed as DYS- + Gk *plasis* formation]

dyspnea /dispneeə/ *n.* (*Brit.* **dyspnoea**) *Med.* difficult or labored breathing. □□ **dyspneic** *adj.* [L f. Gk *duspnoia* (as DYS-, *pneō* breathe)]

dysprosium /disprózeeəm/ *n.* *Chem.* a naturally occurring soft metallic element of the lanthanide series, used as a component in certain magnetic alloys. ¶ Symb.: **Dy.** [mod.L f. Gk *dusprositos* hard to get at + -IUM]

dystocia /distóshə/ *n.* *Med.* difficult or prolonged childbirth. [DYS- + Gk *tokos* childbirth]

dystrophy /dístrəfee/ *n.* defective nutrition. □ **muscular dystrophy** a hereditary progressive weakening and wasting of the muscles. □□ **dystrophic** /distrófik, -trố-/ *adj.* [mod.L *dystrophia* formed as DYS- + Gk *-trophia* nourishment]

dysuria /disyŏŏreeə/ *n.* painful or difficult urination. [LL f. Gk *dusouria* (as DYS-, *ouron* urine)]

dz. *abbr.* dozen.

dzho /zō, dzō, zhō/ *n.* (also **dzo, zho**) (*pl.* same or **-os**) a hybrid of a cow and a yak. [Tibetan *ṃdso*]

E¹ /ee/ *n.* (also **e**) (*pl.* **Es** or **E's**) **1** the fifth letter of the alphabet. **2** *Mus.* the third note of the diatonic scale of C major.

E² *abbr.* (also **E.**) **1** east; eastern. **2** English. **3** energy. **4** see E-NUMBER.

e *symb.* **1** *Math.* the base of natural logarithms, equal to approx. 2.71828. **2** used on packaging (in conjunction with specification of weight, size, etc.) to indicate compliance with EEC regulations.

e- /ee, e/ *prefix* form of EX-¹ 1 before some consonants.

ea. *abbr.* each.

each /eech/ *adj. & pron.* ● *adj.* every one of two or more persons or things, regarded separately (*each person; five in each class*). ● *pron.* each person or thing (*each of us; have two books each; cost a penny each*). □ **each and every** every single. **each other** one another (used as a compound reciprocal pron.: *they hate each other; they wore each other's hats*). **each way** *Brit.* (of a bet) backing a horse, etc., for both a win and a place. [OE *ǣlc* f. WG (as AYE², ALIKE)]

eager /éegər/ *adj.* **1 a** full of keen desire; enthusiastic. **b** (of passions, etc.) keen; impatient. **2** keen; impatient; strongly desirous (*eager to learn; eager for news*). □ **eager beaver** *colloq.* a very or excessively diligent person. □□ **eagerly** *adv.* **eagerness** *n.* [ME f. AF *egre*, OF *aigre* keen, ult. f. L *acer acris*]

■ **1** avid, zealous, ardent, earnest, keen, enthusiastic, hot, hungry, fervent, fervid, passionate, spirited, energetic, energized, animated, excited, stimulated, impatient. **2** keen, desirous, yearning, desiring, craving, longing, itchy, impatient, anxious, itching, dying. □ **eager beaver** fanatic, zealot, workaholic, *colloq.* buff, freak, maniac, *sl.* fiend, nut. □□ **eagerness** avidity, zeal, earnestness, keenness, enthusiasm, fervor, hunger, vehemence, animation, vitality, appetite, zest, relish, spirit, spiritedness, gusto, verve, dash, élan, vim, vigor, energy, *colloq.* get-up-and-go, zip, go; desire, longing, yearning, craving.

eagle /éegəl/ *n.* **1 a** any of various large birds of prey of the family Accipitridae, with keen vision and powerful flight. **b** a figure of an eagle, esp. as a symbol of the US, or formerly as a Roman or French ensign. **2** *Golf* a score of two strokes under par at any hole. **3** *US* a gold coin worth ten dollars. □ **eagle eye** keen sight, watchfulness. **eagle-eyed** keen-sighted, watchful. **Eagle Scout** the highest rank a Boy Scout can attain. **eagle owl** any large owl of the genus *Bubo*, with long ear tufts. [ME f. AF *egle*, OF *aigle* f. L *aquila*]

■ □ **eagle-eyed** sharp-eyed, sharp-sighted, keen-eyed, keen-sighted, lynx-eyed, hawkeyed, lyncean; perceptive, perspicacious, discerning, sharp, watchful, vigilant, Argus-eyed; see also ALERT *adj.* 1.

eaglet /éeglit/ *n.* a young eagle.

eagre /éegər, áygər/ *n.* esp. *Brit.* = BORE³. [17th c.: orig. unkn.]

-ean /éeən/ *suffix* var. of -AN.

ear¹ /eer/ *n.* **1 a** the organ of hearing and balance in humans and other vertebrates, esp. the external part of this. **b** an organ sensitive to sound in other animals. **2** the faculty for discriminating sounds (*an ear for music*). **3** an ear-shaped thing, esp. the handle of a jug. **4** listening; attention. □ **all ears** listening attentively. **bring about one's ears** bring down upon oneself. **ear drops** medicinal drops for the ear. **ear-piercing** loud and shrill. **ear trumpet** a trumpet-shaped device formerly used as a hearing aid. **give ear to** listen to. **have a person's ear** receive a favorable hearing. **have** (or **keep**) **an ear to the ground** be alert to rumors or the trend of opinion. **in one ear and out the other** heard but disregarded or quickly forgotten. **out on one's ear** dismissed ignominiously. **up to one's ears** (often foll. by *in*) *colloq.* deeply involved or occupied. □□ **eared** *adj.* (also in *comb.*). **earless** *adj.* [OE *ēare* f. Gmc: rel. to L *auris*, Gk *oụs*]

■ **2** sensitivity, appreciation, taste, discrimination. **4** attention, heed, notice, regard, consideration. □ **all ears** intent, heedful; see also OBSERVANT *adj.* 1a. **ear-piercing** see SHRILL *adj.* **give ear to** see HEED *v.* **have** (or **keep**) **an ear to the ground** watch out, be on the alert, keep one's eyes open *or* peeled *or* skinned. **out on one's ear** (*be out on one's ear*) see GO¹ *v.* 13a. **up to one's ears** see ENGAGED 2a.

ear² /eer/ *n.* the seed-bearing head of a cereal plant. [OE *ēar* f. Gmc]

earache /éerayk/ *n.* a (usu. prolonged) pain in the ear.

earbash /éerbash/ *v.tr.* esp. *Austral. sl.* talk inordinately to; harangue. □□ **earbasher** *n.* **earbashing** *n.*

eardrop /éerdrop/ *n.* a hanging earring.

eardrum /éerdrum/ *n.* the membrane of the middle ear (= *tympanic membrane*).

earful /éerfŏŏl/ *n.* (*pl.* **-fuls**) *colloq.* **1** a copious or prolonged amount of talking. **2** a strong reprimand.

earl /url/ *n.* a British nobleman ranking between a marquess and a viscount (cf. COUNT²). □ **earl palatine** *hist.* an earl having royal authority within his country or domain. □□ **earldom** *n.* [OE *eorl*, of unkn. orig.]

■ see PEER² *n.* 1.

earlobe /éerlōb/ *n.* the lower soft pendulous external part of the ear.

early /úrlee/ *adj., adv., & n.* ● *adj. & adv.* (**earlier, earliest**) **1** before the due, usual, or expected time (*was early for my appointment; the train arrived early*). **2 a** not far on in the day or night, or in time (*early evening; at the earliest opportunity*). **b** prompt (*early payment appreciated; at your earliest convenience*). **3 a** not far on in a period, development, or process of evolution; being the first stage (*Early English architecture; the early Christians; early spring*). **b** of the distant past (*early man*). **c** not far on in a sequence or serial order (*the early chapters; appears early on the list*). **4 a** of childhood, esp. the preschool years (*early learning*). **b** (of a piece of writing, music, etc.) immature; youthful (*an early work*). **5** forward in flowering, ripening, etc. (*early peaches*). ● *n.* (*pl.* **-ies**) (usu. in *pl.*) an early fruit or vegetable, esp. potatoes. □ **at the earliest** (often placed after a specified time) not before (*will arrive on Monday at the earliest*). **early bird** *colloq.* one who arrives, gets up, etc., early. **early closing** *Brit.* the shutting of business premises on the afternoon of one particular day

/.../ **pronunciation**	● **part of speech**
□ **phrases, idioms, and compounds**	
□□ **derivatives**	■ **synonym section**
cross-references appear in SMALL CAPITALS or *italics*	

451

of the week. **early days** *Brit.* early in time for something to happen, etc. **early grave** an untimely or premature death. **early hours** the very early morning, usu. before dawn. **early** (or **earlier**) **on** at an early (or earlier) stage. **early warning** advance warning of an imminent (esp. nuclear) attack. □□ **earliness** *n.* [orig. as adv., f. OE *ǣrlīce, ārlīce* (*ǣr* ERE)]

■ *adj. & adv.* **1** beforehand, ahead (of time), in advance, before, prematurely; in good time, *literary* betimes. **2 a** at cockcrow, at (the crack *or* break of) dawn, at daybreak; first, soonest. **b** see PROMPT *adj.* 1b. **3 a** initially, originally, at *or* near the start, at *or* near the beginning; first, initial, original. **b** primeval, primitive, primordial, ancient, old, prehistoric, antediluvian; antique, antiquated. **4 b** see IMMATURE 1. **5** untimely; premature, precocious, forward.

earmark /ˈeermaark/ *n. & v.* ● *n.* **1** an identifying mark. **2** an owner's mark on the ear of an animal. ● *v.tr.* **1** set aside (money, etc.) for a special purpose. **2** mark (sheep, etc.) with such a mark.

■ *n.* **1** see HALLMARK *n.* 2. ● *v.* **1** see ASSIGN *v.* 1a. **2** see LABEL *v.* 1.

earmuff /ˈeermuf/ *n.* a wrap or cover for the ears, protecting them from cold, noise, etc.

earn /ərn/ *v.tr.* **1** (also *absol.*) **a** (of a person) obtain (income) in the form of money in return for labor or services (*earn a weekly wage; happy to be earning at last*). **b** (of capital invested) bring in as interest or profit. **2 a** deserve; be entitled to; obtain as the reward for hard work or merit (*have earned a vacation; earned our admiration; earn one's keep*). **b** incur (a reproach, reputation, etc.). □ **earned income** income derived from wages, etc. (opp. *unearned income*). [OE *earnian* f. WG, rel. to Gmc roots assoc. with reaping]

■ **1** make, gross, net, clear, receive, get, collect, reap, bring in, take home, draw, *colloq.* pull down, *sl.* knock down; realize, amass; yield. **2 a** merit, deserve, be worthy of, be entitled to, win, warrant, rate, qualify for, have a claim *or* right to. **b** see INCUR.

earner /ˈərnər/ *n.* **1** a person or thing that earns (often in *comb.: wage earner*). **2** *Brit. sl.* a lucrative job or enterprise.

earnest[1] /ˈərnist/ *adj. & n.* ● *adj.* ardently or intensely serious; zealous; not trifling or joking. ● *n.* seriousness. □ **in** (or **in real**) **earnest** serious(ly), not joking(ly); with determination. □□ **earnestly** *adv.* **earnestness** *n.* [OE *eornust, eornost* (with Gmc cognates): cf. ON *ern* vigorous]

■ *adj.* serious, solemn, grave, sober, intense, steady, resolute, resolved, firm, determined, assiduous, diligent, industrious, hardworking, sincere, dedicated, committed, devoted, thoughtful, conscientious; zealous, ardent, eager, keen, fervent, fervid, enthusiastic, passionate. ● *n.* see FERVOR 1, SOLEMNITY 1. □ **in earnest** serious, sincere, earnest, determined; earnestly, sincerely, seriously, determinedly, fervently, fervidly, passionately, enthusiastically, eagerly, ardently, zealously.

earnest[2] /ˈərnist/ *n.* **1** money paid as an installment, esp. to confirm a contract, etc. **2** a token or foretaste (*in earnest of what is to come*). [ME *ernes,* prob. var. of *erles, arles* prob. f. med.L *arrhula* (unrecorded) f. *arr(h)a* pledge]

■ **1** deposit, down payment, handsel, guarantee, security, pledge. **2** token, foretaste; anticipation.

earnings /ˈərningz/ *n.pl.* money earned. □ **earnings-related** (of benefit, a pension, etc.) calculated on the basis of past or present income.

■ wages, salary, income, pay, stipend, emolument; proceeds, return, revenue, yield, takings, take.

earphone /ˈeerfōn/ *n.* a device applied to the ear to aid hearing or receive radio or telephone communications.

earpiece /ˈeerpees/ *n.* the part of a telephone, etc., applied to the ear during use.

earplug /ˈeerplug/ *n.* a piece of wax, etc., placed in the ear to protect against cold air, water, or noise.

earring /ˈeering/ *n.* a piece of jewelry worn in or on (esp. the lobe of) the ear.

earshot /ˈeershot/ *n.* the distance over which something can be heard (esp. *within* or *out of earshot*).

■ hearing, reach, range, call.

earsplitting /ˈeersplitiŋ/ *adj.* excessively loud.

■ see SHRILL *adj.*, LOUD *adj.* 1.

earth /ərth/ *n. & v.* ● *n.* **1 a** (also **Earth**) one of the planets of the solar system orbiting about the sun between Venus and Mars; the planet on which we live. **b** land and sea, as distinct from sky. **2 a** dry land; the ground (*fell to earth*). **b** soil; clay; mold. **c** bodily matter (*earth to earth*). **3** *Relig.* the present abode of mankind, as distinct from heaven or hell; the world. **4** *Brit. Electr.* = GROUND[1] *n.* 11. **5** the hole of a badger, fox, etc. **6** (prec. by *the*) *colloq.* a huge amount; everything (*cost the earth; want the earth*). ● *v.* **1** *tr.* (foll. by *up*) cover (the roots and lower stems of plants) with heaped-up earth. **2 a** *tr.* drive (a fox) to its earth. **b** *intr.* (of a fox, etc.) run to its earth. **3** *tr. Brit. Electr.* = GROUND[1] *v.* 5. □ **come back** (or **down**) **to earth** return to realities. **earth mother 1** *Mythol.* a spirit or deity symbolizing the earth. **2** a sensual and maternal woman. **earth sciences** the sciences concerned with the earth or part of it, or its atmosphere (e.g., geology, oceanography, meteorology). **earth-shattering** *colloq.* having a traumatic or devastating effect. **earth-shatteringly** *colloq.* devastatingly; remarkably. **earth tremor** see TREMOR *n.* 3. **gone to earth** in hiding. **on earth** *colloq.* **1** existing anywhere (*the happiest man on earth; looked nothing on earth*). **2** as an intensifier (*what on earth?*). □□ **earthward** *adj. & adv.* **earthwards** *adv.* [OE *eorthe* f. Gmc]

■ *n.* **1 a** globe, mother earth, planet, world. **2 b** soil, dirt, loam, sod, clay, ground, mold. **6** see PILE[1] *n.* 3a. □ **earth-shattering** see OVERWHELMING. **gone to earth** in hiding, gone underground, gone to ground, hiding out, lying low, *colloq.* holed up, *Brit. sl.* lying doggo. **on earth 2** see DEVIL *n.* 7.

earthbound /ˈərthbownd/ *adj.* **1** attached to the earth or earthly things. **2** moving toward the earth.

■ **1** see TERRESTRIAL *adj.* 1, 2.

earthen /ˈərthən/ *adj.* **1** made of earth. **2** made of baked clay.

earthenware /ˈərthənwair/ *n. & adj.* ● *n.* pottery, vessels, etc., made of clay fired to a porous state, which can be made impervious to liquids by the use of a glaze (cf. PORCELAIN). ● *adj.* made of fired clay. [EARTHEN + WARE[1]]

■ *n.* see POTTERY.

earthling /ˈərthliŋ/ *n.* an inhabitant of the earth, esp. as regarded in fiction by outsiders.

■ terrestrial, tellurian, mortal, human.

earthly /ˈərthlee/ *adj.* **1 a** of the earth; terrestrial. **b** of human life on earth; worldly, material; carnal. **2** (usu. with *neg.*) *colloq.* remotely possible or conceivable (*is no earthly use; there wasn't an earthly reason*). □ **not an earthly** *colloq.* no chance whatever. □□ **earthliness** *n.*

■ **1 a** terrestrial, terrene, telluric. **b** physical, material, worldly, nonspiritual, sensual, carnal, fleshly, corporeal, base, natural, human, temporal, sublunary, secular, profane, mortal. **2** conceivable, imaginable, feasible, possible. □ **not an earthly** no chance, no hope, *colloq.* not a hope in hell, not a hope, *Austral. & NZ colloq.* not a Buckley's.

earthmover /ˈərthmoovər/ *n.* a tractorlike vehicle, as a bulldozer, for pushing and hauling large amounts of earth at excavation sites.

earthnut /ˈərthnut/ *n.* any of various plants, or its edible roundish tuber, esp.: **1** an umbelliferous woodland plant, *Conopodium majus.* **2** the peanut.

earthquake /ˈərthkwayk/ *n.* **1** a convulsion of the superficial parts of the earth due to the release of accumulated stress as a result of faults in strata or volcanic action. **2** a social, etc., disturbance.

■ **1** quake, tremor.

earthshine /ˈərthshīn/ *n. Astron.* **1** the unilluminated portion of a crescent moon shining faintly because of sunlight reflected from the earth on to the moon. **2** illumination on the moon's surface caused by this.

earthstar /ˈərthstaar/ *n.* any woodland fungus of the genus

Geastrum, esp. *G. triplex,* with a spherical spore-containing fruit body surrounded by a fleshy star-shaped structure.

earthwork /ˈərthwərk/ *n.* **1** an artificial bank of earth in fortification or road building, etc. **2** the process of excavating soil in civil engineering work.
■ **1** see RAMPART *n.* 1a.

earthworm /ˈərthwərm/ *n.* any of various annelid worms, esp. of the genus *Lumbricus* or *Allolobophora,* living and burrowing in the ground.

earthy /ˈərthee/ *adj.* (**earthier, earthiest**) **1** of or like earth or soil. **2** somewhat coarse or crude; unrefined (*earthy humor*). □□ **earthily** *adv.* **earthiness** *n.*
■ **2** unrefined, coarse, vulgar, rough, dirty, indecent, obscene, ribald, bawdy, rude, shameless, wanton, uninhibited; see also CRUDE *adj.* 2a.

earwax /ˈeerwaks/ *n.* a yellow waxy secretion produced by the ear, = CERUMEN.

earwig /ˈeerwig/ *n. & v.* ● *n.* **1** any small elongate insect of the order Dermaptera, with a pair of terminal appendages in the shape of forceps. **2** a small centipede. ● *v.tr.* (**earwigged, earwigging**) *archaic* influence (a person) by secret communication. [OE *ēarwicga* f. *ēare* EAR + *wicga* earwig, prob. rel. to *wiggle*: once thought to enter the head through the ear]

ease /eez/ *n. & v.* ● *n.* **1** absence of difficulty; facility; effortlessness (*did it with ease*). **2 a** freedom or relief from pain, anxiety, or trouble. **b** freedom from embarrassment or awkwardness. **c** freedom or relief from constraint or formality. **d** freedom from poverty. ● *v.* **1** *tr.* **a** relieve from pain or anxiety, etc. (often foll. by *of: eased my mind; eased me of the burden*). **b** make easy or easier; help; facilitate. **2** *intr.* (often foll. by *off, up*) **a** become less painful or burdensome. **b** relax; begin to take it easy. **c** slow down; moderate one's behavior, habits, etc. **3** *tr. joc.* rob or extract money, etc., from (*let me ease you of your loose change*). **4** *intr. Meteorol.* become less severe (*the wind will ease tonight*). **5 a** *tr.* relax; slacken; make a less tight fit. **b** *tr. & intr.* (foll. by *through, into,* etc.) move or be moved carefully into place (*eased it into the hole*). **6** *intr.* (often foll. by *off*) *Stock Exch.* (of shares, etc.) descend in price or value. □ **at ease 1** free from anxiety or constraint. **2** *Mil.* **a** in a relaxed attitude, with the feet apart. **b** the order to stand in this way. **at one's ease** free from embarrassment, awkwardness, or undue formality. **ease away** (or **down** or **off**) *Naut.* slacken (a rope, sail, etc.). □□ **easer** *n.* [ME f. AF *ese,* OF *eise,* ult. f. L *adjacens* ADJACENT]
■ *n.* **1** easiness, simplicity, facility, effortlessness. **2 a** comfort, repose, relief, well-being, relaxation, leisure, rest, contentment, calmness, tranquillity, serenity, peacefulness, peace, peace and quiet. **b, c** naturalness, informality, unaffectedness, ingenuousness, casualness, artlessness, insouciance, nonchalance, aplomb, savoir faire. **d** affluence, wealth, prosperity, luxury, opulence, abundance, plenty. ● *v.* **1 a** relieve, comfort, relax, calm, tranquilize, quiet, still, pacify, soothe, disburden, *Brit.* quieten; mitigate, reduce, allay, alleviate, assuage, mollify, appease, palliate. **b** facilitate, expedite, simplify, smooth, further, clear, assist, aid, advance, forward, help. **2 a** lessen, diminish, abate, decrease. **b** see RELAX 1c. **c** calm down, relax, slacken off, remit, *colloq.* let up; see also SLOW *v.* 2. **4** drop, calm, remit, slacken, moderate; see also WANE *v.* **5 b** maneuver, manipulate, inch, guide, steer, slip. **6** see DROP *v.* 8a. □ **at ease 1** see TRANQUIL, EASY *adj.* 2a, 3. **at one's ease** see COMFORTABLE *adj.* 2, EASY *adj.* 3.

easel /ˈeezəl/ *n.* **1** a standing frame, usu. of wood, for supporting an artist's work, a blackboard, etc. **2** an artist's work collectively. [Du. *ezel* = G *Esel* ASS¹]

easement /ˈeezmənt/ *n. Law* a right of way or a similar right over another's land. [ME f. OF *aisement*]

easily /ˈeezilee/ *adv.* **1** without difficulty. **2** by far (*easily the best*). **3** very probably (*it could easily snow*).
■ **1** effortlessly, readily, simply, smoothly, comfortably, cleanly; without difficulty, hands down, without even trying, with one's eyes closed, with one's hands tied

behind one's back; without a hitch, like a charm *or* dream, like a bird. **2** by far, without doubt *or* question, beyond doubt, indisputably, indubitably, undoubtedly, doubtlessly, doubtless, unquestionably, clearly, far and away, definitely, conclusively, certainly, surely, undeniably, obviously, patently. **3** probably, most *or* very likely, well, almost certainly.

east /eest/ *n., adj., & adv.* ● *n.* **1 a** the point of the horizon where the sun rises at the equinoxes (cardinal point 90° to the right of north). **b** the compass point corresponding to this. **c** the direction in which this lies. **2** (usu. **the East**) **a** the regions or countries lying to the east of Europe. **b** the formerly Communist nations of eastern Europe. **3** the eastern part of a country, town, etc. **4** (**East**) *Bridge* a player occupying the position designated "east." ● *adj.* **1** toward, at, near, or facing east. **2** coming from the east (*east wind*). ● *adv.* **1** toward, at, or near the east. **2** (foll. by *of*) further east than. □ **East End** the part of London east of the city as far as the River Lea. **East Indiaman** *hist.* a large ship engaged in trade with the East Indies. **East Indies** the islands, etc., east of India, esp. the Malay archipelago. **east-north-east** (or **-southeast**) the direction or compass point midway between east and northeast (or southeast). **to the east** (often foll. by *of*) in an easterly direction. [OE *ēast-* f. Gmc]
■ *n.* **2 a** (**the East**) the Orient.

eastbound /ˈeestbownd/ *adj.* traveling or leading eastward.

Easter /ˈeestər/ *n.* **1** (also **Easter Sunday** or **Day**) the festival (held on a variable Sunday in March or April) commemorating Christ's resurrection. **2** the season in which this occurs, esp. the weekend from Good Friday to Easter Monday. □ **Easter egg 1** an egg that is dyed and often decorated as part of the Easter celebration. **2** an artificial usu. chocolate egg given at Easter, esp. to children. **Easter week** the week beginning on Easter Sunday. [OE *ēastre* app. f. *Ēostre,* a goddess associated with spring, f. Gmc]

easterly /ˈeestərlee/ *adj., adv., & n.* ● *adj. & adv.* **1** in an eastern position or direction. **2** (of a wind) blowing from the east. ● *n.* (*pl.* **-ies**) a wind blowing from the east.

eastern /ˈeestərn/ *adj.* **1** of or in the east; inhabiting the east. **2** lying or directed toward the east. **3** (**Eastern**) of or in the Far, Middle, or Near East. □ **Eastern Church** the Orthodox Church. **eastern hemisphere** (also **Eastern Hemisphere**) the half of the earth containing Europe, Asia, and Africa. **Eastern time** standard time used in the eastern US and eastern Canada or in eastern Australia. □□ **easternmost** *adj.* [OE *ēasterne* (as EAST, -ERN)]
■ **3** (**Eastern**) orient, oriental.

Easterner /ˈeestərnər/ *n.* a native or inhabitant of the east; esp. in the US.

Eastertide /ˈeestərtīd/ *n.* the period following Easter.
■ see SPRING *n.* 5a.

easting /ˈeesting/ *n. Naut.,* etc., the distance traveled or the angle of longitude measured eastward from either a defined north–south grid line or a meridian.

eastward /ˈeestwərd/ *adj., adv., & n.* ● *adj. & adv.* (also **eastwards**) toward the east. ● *n.* an eastward direction or region. □□ **eastwardly** *adj. & adv.*

easy /ˈeezee/ *adj., adv., & int.* (**easier, easiest**) ● *adj.* **1** not difficult; achieved without great effort. **2 a** free from pain, discomfort, anxiety, etc. **b** comfortably off; affluent (*easy circumstances*). **3** free from embarrassment, awkwardness, constraint, or pressure; relaxed and pleasant (*an easy manner*). **4 a** not strict; tolerant. **b** compliant; obliging; easily persuaded (*an easy touch*). **5** *Stock Exch.* (of goods, money on loan, etc.) not much in demand. ● *adv.* with ease; in an effortless or relaxed manner. ● *int.* go carefully; move gently. □ **easy as pie** see PIE¹. **easy chair** a large comfortable chair, usu. an armchair. **easy come easy go** *colloq.* what is easily obtained is soon lost or spent. **easy does it**

colloq. go carefully. **easy money** money obtained without effort (esp. of dubious legality). **easy of access** easily entered or approached. **easy on the eye** (or **ear**, etc.) *colloq.* pleasant to look at (or listen to, etc.). **easy-peasy** *Brit. sl.* very simple. **easy street** *colloq.* a situation of ease or affluence. **easy terms** payment by installments. **go easy** (foll. by *with, on*) be sparing or cautious. **I'm easy** *colloq.* I have no preference. **of easy virtue** (of a woman) sexually promiscuous. **stand easy!** *Brit. Mil.* permission to a squad standing at ease to relax their attitude further. **take it easy 1** proceed gently or carefully. **2** relax; avoid overwork. □□ **easiness** *n.* [ME f. AF *aisé,* OF *aisié* past part. of *aisier* EASE]

■ *adj.* **1** simple, effortless, straightforward, elementary, rudimentary, basic, uncomplicated, undemanding, foolproof, plain, clear, *colloq.* soft, cushy; easy as pie, child's play, easy as can be, *colloq.* as easy as 1, 2, 3. **2 a** carefree, easygoing, relaxed, untroubled, quiet, serene, restful, relaxing, tranquil, peaceful, undisturbed, unoppressive, gentle, mild, calm, comfortable, cozy, unhurried, leisurely, *colloq.* cushy. **3** relaxed, unstrained, gentle, moderate, unhurried, leisurely, even, steady, flowing, undemanding, comfortable; affable, unconstrained, friendly, pleasant, amiable, amicable, agreeable, outgoing, informal, unstudied, dégagé, unceremonious, down-to-earth, unreserved, relaxing, natural, easygoing, approachable. **4 a** tolerant, indulgent, lenient, flexible, undemanding. **b** tractable, pliant, compliant, obliging, submissive, acquiescent, amenable, accommodating, soft, suggestible, credulous, trusting, weak. ● *adv.* effortlessly; calmly, unexcitedly, temperately, peacefully, tranquilly, serenely, nonchalantly, casually. □ **I'm easy** I don't mind, it's all the same to me, whatever you like. **of easy virtue** see PROMISCUOUS 1a. **take it easy 1** go easy, be careful, take care, look out. **2** see RELAX 4.

easygoing /ēēzeegṓing/ *adj.* **1** placid and tolerant; relaxed in manner; accepting things as they are. **2** (of a horse) having an easy gait.

■ **1** relaxed, casual, mellow, carefree, undemanding, placid, even-tempered, forbearing, lenient, live-and-let-live, tolerant, permissive, *colloq.* laid-back; see also EASY *adj.* 3.

eat /eet/ *v.* (*past* **ate** /ayt/, esp. *Brit.* /et/; *past part.* **eaten** /ēet'n/) **1 a** *tr.* take into the mouth, chew, and swallow (food). **b** *intr.* consume food; take a meal. **c** *tr.* devour (*eaten by a lion*). **2** *intr.* (foll. by (*away*) *at, into*) **a** destroy gradually, esp. by corrosion, erosion, disease, etc. **b** begin to consume or diminish (resources, etc.). **3** *tr. colloq.* trouble; vex (*what's eating you?*). □ **eat dirt** see DIRT. **eat one's hat** *colloq.* admit one's surprise in being wrong (only as a proposition unlikely to be fulfilled: *said he would eat his hat*). **eat one's heart out** suffer from excessive longing or envy. **eat humble pie** see HUMBLE. **eat out** have a meal away from home, esp. in a restaurant. **eat out of a person's hand** be entirely submissive to a person. **eat salt with** see SALT. **eat up 1** (also *absol.*) eat or consume completely. **2** use or deal with rapidly or wastefully (*eats up time; eats up the miles*). **3** encroach upon or annex (*eating up the neighboring countries*). **4** absorb; preoccupy (*eaten up with pride*). **eat one's words** admit that one was wrong. [OE *etan* f. Gmc]

■ **1 a** consume, devour, take, have, ingest, munch, nibble, put away, eat up, gobble, guzzle, gormandize, *Brit.* tiffin, *colloq.* dispatch, partake of, tuck into, *joc.* demolish, *literary* manduct, *sl.* nosh, pig out, *sl. archaic* walk into. **b** have a meal, dine, have a bite, *Brit.* tiffin, *archaic* sup, *colloq.* feed, *sl.* nosh. **2 a** see ERODE. **3** see TROUBLE *v.* 1, 3. □ **eat out of a person's hand** be under a person's thumb *or* control, be wrapped *or* twisted around a person's little finger, be in the palm of a person's hand, be at a person's beck and call. **eat up 4** see CONSUME 3.

eatable /ēetabəl/ *adj. & n.* ● *adj.* that is in a condition to be eaten (cf. EDIBLE). ● *n.* (usu. in *pl.*) food.

■ *adj.* see EDIBLE *adj.* ● *n.* see FOOD 1.

eater /ēetər/ *n.* **1** a person who eats (*a big eater*). **2** *Brit.* an eating apple, etc.

eatery /ēetəree/ *n.* (*pl.* **-ies**) *colloq.* a restaurant, esp. a diner, luncheonette, etc.

■ see CAFÉ 1.

eating /ēeting/ *adj.* **1** suitable for eating (*eating apple*). **2** used for eating (*eating room*). □ **eating disorder** a neurotic condition, such as anorexia nervosa or bulimia, in which a person does not eat normally.

eats /eets/ *n.pl. colloq.* food.

■ see FOOD 1.

eau de cologne /ṓdəkəlṓn/ *n.* an alcohol-based perfume of a kind made orig. at Cologne. [F, lit. 'water of Cologne']

■ see PERFUME *n.* 2.

eau-de-vie /ṓdəvēe/ *n.* spirits, esp. brandy. [F, lit. 'water of life']

eaves /eevz/ *n.pl.* the underside of a projecting roof. [orig. sing., f. OE *efes*: prob. rel. to OVER]

eavesdrop /ēevzdrop/ *v.intr.* (**-dropped, -dropping**) listen secretly to a private conversation. □□ **eavesdropper** *n.* [*eavesdropper* orig. 'one who listens under walls' prob. f. ON *upsardropi* (cf. OE *yfæsdrypæ*): *eavesdrop* by back-form.]

■ listen in, spy, pry, *colloq.* snoop; tap, *sl.* bug.

ebb /eb/ *n. & v.* ● *n.* **1** the movement of the tide out to sea (also *attrib.*: *ebb tide*). **2** the process of draining away of floodwater, etc. **3** the process of declining or diminishing; the state of being in decline. ● *v.intr.* (often foll. by *away*) **1** (of tidewater) flow out to sea; recede; drain away. **2** decline; run low (*his life was ebbing away*). □ **at a low ebb** in a poor condition or state of decline. **ebb and flow** a continuing process of decline and upturn in circumstances. **on the ebb** in decline. [OE *ebba, ebbian*]

■ *n.* **3** decline, decay, decrease, diminution, wane, drop, slackening (off), dwindling, lessening, deterioration, degeneration. ● *v.* **1** recede, flow back, subside, go out, go down, drain away, fall back *or* away, retreat, retrocede, retire. **2** decline, flag, decay, wane, diminish, decrease, lessen, drop, slacken, fade (away), drain away, dwindle, peter out, waste away, deteriorate, fall off *or* away, die out *or* down *or* away, run low. □ **at a low ebb** see *on the decline* (DECLINE). **on the ebb** see *on the decline* (DECLINE).

ebonite /ébənīt/ *n.* = VULCANITE. [EBONY + -ITE[1]]

ebony /ébənee/ *n. & adj.* ● *n.* (*pl.* **-ies**) **1** a heavy, hard, dark wood used for furniture. **2** any of various trees of the genus *Diospyros* producing this. ● *adj.* **1** made of ebony. **2** black like ebony. [earlier *hebeny* f. (*h)eben(e) = ebon,* perh. after *ivory*]

■ *adj.* **2** see BLACK *adj.* 1.

ebullient /ibúlyənt, ibṓl-/ *adj.* **1** exuberant; high-spirited. **2** *Chem.* boiling. □□ **ebullience** /-yəns/ *n.* **ebulliency** *n.* **ebulliently** *adv.* [L *ebullire ebullient-* bubble out (as E-, *bullire* boil)]

■ **1** high-spirited, buoyant, exuberant, enthusiastic, zestful, effervescent, excited, effusive, exhilarated, elated, animated, ecstatic, rapturous, rapt.

EC *abbr.* **1** European Community. **2** executive committee.

ecad /ēekad/ *n. Ecol.* an organism modified by its environment. [Gk *oikos* house + -AD[1]]

écarté /aykaartáy/ *n.* **1** a card game for two persons in which cards from a player's hand may be exchanged for others from the pack. **2** a position in classical ballet with one arm and leg extended. [F, past part. of *écarter* discard]

ecce homo /ékay hṓmō, éksee/ *n. Art* one of the subjects of the Passion cycle: in Renaissance painting typically a depiction of Christ wearing the crown of thorns. [L, = 'behold the man,' the words of Pilate to the Jews after the crowning with thorns (John 19:5)]

eccentric /ikséntrik, ek-/ *adj. & n.* ● *adj.* **1** odd or capricious in behavior or appearance; whimsical. **2 a** not placed or not having its axis, etc., placed centrally. **b** (often foll. by *to*) (of a circle) not concentric (to another). **c** (of an orbit) not circular. ● *n.* **1** an eccentric person. **2** *Mech.* an eccentric contrivance for changing rotatory into backward-and-forward motion, e.g., the cam used in an internal combustion engine. □□ **eccentrically** adv. **eccentricity** /éksentrísitee/ n. (pl. **-ies**). [LL eccentricus f. Gk ekkentros f. ek out of + kentros CENTER]

■ adj. **1** unconventional, unusual, odd, peculiar, strange, curious, bizarre, outlandish, queer, quaint, far-out, quirky, offbeat, kinky, uncommon, abnormal, idiosyncratic, unorthodox, whimsical, capricious, out of the ordinary, irregular, atypical, errant, aberrant, exceptional, individual, singular, unique, colloq. weird, cranky, oddball. ● n. **1** original, individualist, nonconformist, crank, colloq. character, odd fish, freak, oddball, weirdo, weirdie, Austral. & NZ sl. dag, Brit. sl. oner. □□ **eccentricity** unconventionality, strangeness, oddness, bizarreness, bizarrerie, nonconformity, individuality, individualism, singularity, uniqueness, distinctiveness, capriciousness, weirdness; idiosyncrasy, quirk, peculiarity, whim, mannerism, crotchet, aberration, anomaly, oddity, curiosity, caprice.

eccl. abbr. **1** ecclesiastic. **2** ecclesiastical.

Eccles. abbr. Ecclesiastes (Old Testament).

ecclesial /iklee'zeeəl/ adj. of or relating to a church. [Gk ekklesia assembly, church f. ekklētos summoned out f. ek out + kaleō call]

ecclesiastic /iklee'zeeástik/ n. & adj. ● n. a priest or clergyman. ● adj. = ECCLESIASTICAL. □□ **ecclesiasticism** /-ti-sizəm/ n. [F ecclésiastique or LL ecclesiasticus f. Gk ekklēsiastikos f. ekklēsia assembly, church: see ECCLESIAL]

■ n. see CLERGYMAN.

ecclesiastical /iklee'zeeástikəl/ adj. of the church or the clergy. □□ **ecclesiastically** adv.

■ see CLERICAL 1.

ecclesiology /iklee'zeeóləjee/ n. **1** the study of churches, esp. church building and decoration. **2** theology as applied to the nature and structure of the Christian Church. □□ **ecclesiological** /-zeeəlójikəl/ adj. **ecclesiologist** n. [Gk ekklēsia assembly, church (see ECCLESIAL) + -LOGY]

Ecclus. abbr. Ecclesiasticus (Apocrypha).

eccrine /ékrin, -rin, -reen/ adj. (of a gland, e.g., a sweat gland) secreting without loss of cell material. [Gk ek out of + krinō sift]

ecdysis /ékdisis/ n. the action of casting off skin or shedding an exoskeleton, etc. [mod.L f. Gk ekdusis f. ekduō put off]

ECG abbr. electrocardiogram.

echelon /éshəlon/ n. & v. ● n. **1** a level or rank in an organization, in society, etc.; those occupying it (often in pl.: the upper echelons). **2** Mil. a formation of troops, ships, aircraft, etc., in parallel rows with the end of each row projecting further than the one in front (in echelon). ● v.tr. arrange in an echelon. [F échelon f. échelle ladder f. L scala]

■ n. **1** see GRADE n. 1a, CATEGORY.

echeveria /échəvəree'ə/ n. any succulent plant of the genus Echeveria, native to Central and S. America. [M. Echeveri, 19th-c. Mex. botanical illustrator]

echidna /ikídnə/ n. any of several egg-laying, pouch-bearing mammals native to Australia and New Guinea, with a covering of spines, and having a long snout and long claws. Also called spiny anteater. [mod.L f. Gk ekhidna viper]

echinoderm /ikínədərm/ n. any marine invertebrate of the phylum Echinodermata, usu. having a spiny skin, e.g., starfish and sea urchins. [ECHINUS + Gk derma -atos skin]

echinoid /ikínoyd/ n. a sea urchin.

echinus /ikínəs/ n. **1** any sea urchin of the genus Echinus, including the common European edible urchin, E. esculentus. **2** Archit. a rounded molding below an abacus on a Doric or Ionic capital. [ME f. L f. Gk ekhinos hedgehog, sea urchin]

echo /ékō/ n. & v. ● n. (pl. **-oes** or **-os**) **1 a** the repetition of a sound by the reflection of sound waves. **b** the secondary sound produced. **2** a reflected radio or radar beam. **3** a close imitation or repetition of something already done. **4** a person who slavishly repeats the words or opinions of another. **5** (often in pl.) circumstances or events reminiscent of or remotely connected with earlier ones. **6** Bridge, etc., a conventional mode of play to show the number of cards held in

the suit led, etc. ● v. (**-oes, -oed**) **1** intr. **a** (of a place) resound with an echo. **b** (of a sound) be repeated; resound. **2** tr. repeat (a sound) by an echo. **3** tr. **a** repeat (another's words). **b** imitate the words, opinions, or actions of (a person). □ **echo chamber** an enclosure with sound-reflecting walls. **echo sounder** sounding apparatus for determining the depth of the sea beneath a ship by measuring the time taken for an echo to be received. **echo-sounding** the use of an echo sounder. **echo verse** a verse form in which a line repeats the last syllables of the previous line. □□ **echoer** n. **echoless** adj. [ME f. OF or L f. Gk ēkhō, rel. to ēkhē a sound]

■ n. **1** reverberation, repercussion, repetition, iteration, reiteration. **3** imitation, copy, replica, replication, repetition, duplication, reproduction; reflection, mirror image. ● v. **1 a** resound, reverberate, ring. **3** imitate, ape, parrot, mimic, copy, duplicate, reproduce, simulate, repeat, emulate, mirror, reflect.

echocardiogram /ékōka'árdeeəgram/ n. Med. a record produced by echocardiography.

echocardiography /ékōka'árdeeógrəfee/ n. Med. the use of ultrasound waves to investigate the action of the heart. □□ **echocardiograph** /-deeəgraf/ n. **echocardiographer** n.

echoencephalogram /ékōenséfəlōgram/ n. Med. a record produced by echoencephalography.

echoencephalography /ékōenséfəlógrəfee/ n. Med. the use of ultrasound waves to investigate intracranial structures.

echogram /ékōgram/ n. a record made by an echo sounder.

echograph /ékōgraf/ n. a device for automatically recording echograms.

echoic /ekóik/ adj. Phonet. (of a word) imitating the sound it represents; onomatopoeic. □□ **echoically** adv.

echoism /ékōizəm/ n. = ONOMATOPOEIA.

echolalia /ékōláyleeə/ n. **1** the meaningless repetition of another person's spoken words. **2** the repetition of speech by a child learning to talk. [mod.L f. Gk ēkhō echo + lalia talk]

echolocation /ékōlōkáyshən/ n. the location of objects by reflected sound.

echovirus /ékōvírəs/ n. (also **ECHO virus**) any of a group of enteroviruses sometimes causing mild meningitis, encephalitis, etc. [f. enteric cytopathogenic human orphan (because not originally assignable to any known disease) + VIRUS]

echt /ekht/ adj. authentic; genuine; typical. [G]

éclair /aykláir/ n. a small, elongated light pastry filled with whipped cream or custard and iced with chocolate or coffee icing. [F, lit. lightning, flash]

éclaircissement /aykláirseesmóN/ n. archaic an enlightening explanation of something hitherto inexplicable (e.g., conduct, etc.). [F f. éclaircir clear up]

eclampsia /iklámpseeə/ n. a condition involving convulsions leading to coma, occurring esp. in pregnant women. □□ **eclamptic** adj. [mod.L f. F éclampsie f. Gk eklampsis sudden development f. eklampō shine forth]

éclat /ayklaá/ n. **1** brilliant display; dazzling effect. **2** social distinction; conspicuous success; universal approbation (with great éclat). [F f. éclater burst out]

■ **1** see PANACHE. **2** see RENOWN.

eclectic /ikléktik/ adj. & n. ● adj. **1** deriving ideas, tastes, style, etc., from various sources. **2** Philos. & Art selecting one's beliefs, etc., from various sources; attached to no particular school of philosophy. ● n. **1** an eclectic person. **2** a person who subscribes to an eclectic school of thought. □□ **eclectically** adv. **eclecticism** /-tisizəm/ n. [Gk eklektikos f. eklegō pick out]

■ adj. **1** see CATHOLIC adj. 2.

eclipse /iklíps/ n. & v. ● n. **1** the obscuring of the reflected light from one celestial body by the passage of another be-

---

/.../ **pronunciation**	● **part of speech**
□ **phrases, idioms, and compounds**	
□□ **derivatives**	■ **synonym section**
cross-references appear in SMALL CAPITALS or italics	

tween it and the eye or between it and its source of illumination. **2 a** a deprivation of light or the period of this. **b** obscuration or concealment; a period of this. **3** a rapid or sudden loss of importance or prominence, esp. in relation to another or a newly arrived person or thing. • *v.tr.* **1** (of a celestial body) obscure the light from or to (another). **2** intercept (light, esp. of a lighthouse). **3** deprive of prominence or importance; outshine; surpass. □ **in eclipse 1** surpassed; in decline. **2** (of a bird) having lost its courting plumage. □□ **eclipser** *n.* [ME f. OF f. L f. Gk *ekleipsis* f. *ekleipō* fail to appear, be eclipsed f. *leipō* leave]

■ *n.* **2** darkening, shading, dimming, concealment, covering, hiding, blocking, blockage, occultation, obscuring, obscuration. **3** downturn, slump, deterioration; see also PLUNGE *n.* • *v.* **1** conceal, hide, blot out, obscure, block, veil, shroud, cover. **3** overshadow, obscure, surpass, top, outshine. □ **in eclipse 1** see *on the decline* (DECLINE).

ecliptic /iklíptik/ *n. & adj.* • *n.* the sun's apparent path among the stars during the year. • *adj.* of an eclipse or the ecliptic. [ME f. L f. Gk *ekleiptikos* (as ECLIPSE)]

eclogue /éklawg, -log/ *n.* a short poem, esp. a pastoral dialogue. [L *ecloga* f. Gk *eklogē* selection f. *eklegō* pick out]

■ pastoral, idyll.

eclosion /iklózhən/ *n.* the emergence of an insect from a pupa case or of a larva from an egg. [F *éclosion* f. *éclore* hatch (as EX-¹, L *claudere* to close)]

eco- /ékō, eékō/ *comb. form* ecology, ecological.

ecoclimate /ékōklimit, eékō-/ *n.* climate considered as an ecological factor.

ecol. *abbr.* **1** ecological. **2** ecologist. **3** ecology.

ecology /ikóləjee/ *n.* **1** the branch of biology dealing with the relations of organisms to one another and to their physical surroundings. **2** (in full **human ecology**) the study of the interaction of people with their environment. □□ **ecological** /ékəlójikəl, eékə-/ *adj.* **ecologically** *adv.* **ecologist** *n.* [G *Ökologie* f. Gk *oikos* house]

■ □□ **ecologist** see CONSERVATIONIST, NATURALIST.

econ. *abbr.* **1** economics. **2** economy.

econometrics /ikónəmétriks/ *n.pl.* (usu. treated as *sing.*) a branch of economics concerned with the application of mathematical economics to economic data by the use of statistics. □□ **econometric** *adj.* **econometrical** *adj.* **econometrician** /-mətríshən/ *n.* **econometrist** *n.* [ECONOMY + METRIC]

economic /ékənómik, eékə-/ *adj.* **1** of or relating to economics. **2** maintained for profit; on a business footing. **3** adequate to repay or recoup expenditure with some profit (*not economic to run buses on Sunday*; *an economic rent*). **4** practical; considered or studied with regard to human needs (*economic geography*). [ME f. OF *economique* or L *oeconomicus* f. Gk *oikonomikos* (as ECONOMY)]

■ **1** financial, fiscal, pecuniary, monetary, budgetary; commercial, mercantile, *attrib.* trade. **3** profitable, cost-effective, moneymaking, remunerative, productive. **4** see PRACTICAL *adj.* 1, 2.

economical /ékənómikəl, eékə-/ *adj.* sparing in the use of resources; avoiding waste. □□ **economically** *adv.*

■ cost-effective, money saving; cheap, inexpensive, reasonable, economic; provident, thrifty, sparing, prudent, conservative, frugal, careful.

economics /ékənómiks, eékə-/ *n.pl.* (often treated as *sing.*) **1 a** the science of the production and distribution of wealth. **b** the application of this to a particular subject (*the economics of publishing*). **2** the condition of a country, etc., as regards material prosperity.

■ **1b, 2** see FINANCE *n.* 1.

economist /ikónəmist/ *n.* **1** an expert in or student of economics. **2** a person who manages financial or economic matters. [Gk *oikonomos* (as ECONOMY) + -IST]

economize /ikónəmīz/ *v.intr.* **1** be economical; make economies; reduce expenditure. **2** (foll. by *on*) use sparingly; spend less on. □□ **economization** *n.* **economizer** *n.*

■ **1** tighten one's belt, cut costs, scrimp (and save), pinch

pennies. **2** save, cut back, retrench, skimp, scrimp, spend less.

economy /ikónəmee/ *n.* (*pl.* **-ies**) **1 a** the wealth and resources of a community, esp. in terms of the production and consumption of goods and services. **b** a particular kind of this (*a capitalist economy*). **c** the administration or condition of an economy. **2 a** the careful management of (esp. financial) resources; frugality. **b** (often in *pl.*) an instance of this (*made many economies*). **3** sparing or careful use (*economy of language*). **4** (also **economy class**) the cheapest class of air travel. **5** (*attrib.*) (also **economy-size**) (of goods) consisting of a large quantity for a proportionally lower cost. [F *économie* or L *oeconomia* f. Gk *oikonomia* household management f. *oikos* house + *nemō* manage]

■ **2 a** thrift, husbandry, thriftiness, frugality, conservation, conservatism, restraint, control. **b** saving, cutback, reduction, cut. **3** brevity, briefness, succinctness, sparingness, terseness, curtness, conciseness, concision, compactness, restraint.

ecosphere /ékōsfeer, eékə-/ *n.* the region of space including planets where conditions are such that living things can exist.

ecosystem /ékōsistəm, eékō-/ *n.* a biological community of interacting organisms and their physical environment.

■ see ENVIRONMENT 3.

ecru /ékrōō, áykrōō/ *n.* the color of unbleached linen; light fawn. [F *écru* unbleached]

ecstasize /ékstəsīz/ *v.tr. & intr.* throw or go into ecstasies.

ecstasy /ékstəsee/ *n.* (*pl.* **-ies**) **1** an overwhelming feeling of joy or rapture. **2** *Psychol.* an emotional or religious frenzy or trancelike state. **3** *sl.* methylene dioxymethamphetamine, a powerful stimulant and hallucinatory drug (see MDA). [ME f. OF *extasie* f. LL *extasis* f. Gk *ekstasis* standing outside oneself f. *ek* out + *histēmi* to place]

■ **1** delight, joy, rapture, bliss, transport, exaltation, thrill, elation, excitement, nympholepsy, happiness, gladness, pleasure, enjoyment, gratification; heaven on earth.

ecstatic /ikstátik, ek-/ *adj. & n.* • *adj.* **1** in a state of ecstasy. **2** very enthusiastic or excited (*was ecstatic about her new job*). **3** producing ecstasy; sublime (*an ecstatic embrace*). • *n.* a person subject to (usu. religious) ecstasy. □□ **ecstatically** *adv.* [F *extatique* f. Gk *ekstatikos* (as ECSTASY)]

■ *adj.* **1, 2** exhilarated, thrilled, exultant, euphoric, rapturous, enraptured, nympholeptic, enchanted, transported, excited, elated, delighted, joyful, gleeful, overjoyed, happy, glad, beside oneself, cock-a-hoop, delirious, over the moon, in seventh heaven, *colloq.* on cloud nine *or* seven. **3** blissful, sublime, heavenly, rhapsodic, delightful, orgasmic; see also EXQUISITE *adj.*

ECT *abbr.* electroconvulsive therapy.

ecto- /éktō/ *comb. form* outside. [Gk *ekto-* stem of *ektos* outside]

ectoblast /éktōblast/ *n.* = ECTODERM. □□ **ectoblastic** *adj.*

ectoderm /éktōdərm/ *n. Biol.* the outermost layer of an animal embryo in early development. □□ **ectodermal** *adj.*

ectogenesis /éktōjénisis/ *n. Biol.* the production of structures outside the organism. □□ **ectogenetic** /-jinétik/ *adj.* **ectogenic** /-jénik/ *adj.* **ectogenous** /ektójinəs/ *adj.* [mod.L (as ECTO-, GENESIS)]

ectomorph /éktəmawrf/ *n.* a person with a lean body build. (cf. ENDOMORPH, MESOMORPH). □□ **ectomorphic** *adj.* **ectomorphy** *n.* [ECTO- + Gk *morphē* form]

-ectomy /éktəmee/ *comb. form* denoting a surgical operation in which a part of the body is removed (*appendectomy*). [Gk *ektomē* excision f. *ek* out + *temnō* cut]

ectopic /ektópik/ *adj. Med.* in an abnormal place or position. □ **ectopic pregnancy** a pregnancy occurring outside the uterus. [mod.L *ectopia* f. Gk *ektopos* out of place]

ectoplasm /éktəplazəm/ *n.* **1** the dense outer layer of the cytoplasm (cf. ENDOPLASM). **2** the supposed viscous substance exuding from the body of a spiritualistic medium during a trance. □□ **ectoplasmic** *adj.*

ectozoon /éktzō-on/ *n. Biol.* a parasite that lives on the outside of its host.

ECU *abbr.* (also **ecu** /ékyōō/) European currency unit.

ecumenical /ékyōōménikəl/ *adj.* **1** of or representing the whole Christian world. **2** seeking or promoting worldwide Christian unity. □□ **ecumenically** *adv.* [LL *oecumenicus* f. Gk *oikoumenikos* of the inhabited earth (*oikoumenē*)]
■ see BROAD *adj.* 8.

ecumenicalism /ékyōōménikəlizəm/ *n.* (also **ecumenism** /ékyəminizəm, ikyōōmənizəm/) the principle or aim of the unity of Christians worldwide.

eczema /éksimə, égzi-, igzée-/ *n.* inflammation of the skin, with itching and discharge from blisters. □□ **eczematous** /igzémətəs, egzém-, -zée-/ *adj.* [mod.L f. Gk *ekzema -atos* f. *ek* out + *zeō* boil]

ed. *abbr.* **1** edited by. **2** edition. **3** editor. **4** educated; education.

-ed[1] /əd, id/ *suffix* forming adjectives: **1** from nouns, meaning 'having, wearing, affected by, etc.' (*talented*; *trousered*; *diseased*). **2** from phrases of adjective and noun (*good-humored*; *three-cornered*). [OE *-ede*]

-ed[2] /əd, id/ *suffix* forming: **1** the past tense and past participle of weak verbs (*needed*; *risked*). **2** participial adjectives (*escaped prisoner*; *a pained look*). [OE *-ed, -ad, -od*]

edacious /idáyshəs/ *adj. literary* or *joc.* **1** greedy. **2** of eating. □□ **edacity** *n.* /idásitee/ [L *edax -acis* f. *edere* eat]

Edam /ée dəm, ée dam/ *n.* a round Dutch cheese, usu. pale yellow with a red rind. [*Edam* in Holland]

edaphic /idáfik/ *adj.* **1** *Bot.* of the soil. **2** *Ecol.* produced or influenced by the soil. [G *edaphisch* f. Gk *edaphos* floor]

Edda /édə/ *n.* **1** (also *Elder Edda*, *Poetic Edda*) a collection of medieval Icelandic poems on Norse legends. **2** (also *Younger Edda*, *Prose Edda*) a 13th-c. miscellaneous handbook to Icelandic poetry. [perh. a name in a Norse poem or f. ON *óthr* poetry]
■ **1** see LEGEND 1a–c.

eddo /édō/ *n.* (*pl.* **-oes**) = TARO. [Afr. word]

eddy /édee/ *n. & v.* ● *n.* (*pl.* **-ies**) **1** a circular movement of water causing a small whirlpool. **2** a movement of wind, fog, or smoke resembling this. ● *v.tr. & intr.* (**-ies, -ied**) whirl around in eddies. □ **eddy current** *Electr.* a localized current induced in a conductor by a varying magnetic field. [prob. OE *ed-* again, back, perh. of Scand. orig.]
■ *n.* swirl, whirl, vortex, whirlpool; whirlwind, dust devil; waterspout, twister. ● *v.* swirl, whirl, turn, spin.

edelweiss /áyd'lvīs/ *n.* an Alpine plant, *Leontopodium alpinum*, with woolly white bracts around the flower heads, growing in rocky places. [G f. *edel* noble + *weiss* white]

edema /idée mə/ *n.* (*Brit.* **oedema**) a condition characterized by an excess of watery fluid collecting in the cavities or tissues of the body. Also called DROPSY. □□ **edematose** /idémətōs, idée-/ *adj.* **edematous** *adj.* [LL f. GK *oidēma -atos* f. *oideō* swell]

Eden /ée dən/ *n.* (also **Garden of Eden**) a place or state of great happiness; paradise (with reference to the abode of Adam and Eve in the biblical account of the Creation). [ME f. LL f. Gk *Ēdēn* f. Heb. *῾ēden*, orig. = delight]
■ see HEAVEN 2.

edentate /idéntayt/ *adj. & n.* ● *adj.* having no or few teeth. ● *n.* any mammal, esp. of the order Edentata, having no or few teeth, e.g., an anteater or sloth. [L *edentatus* (as E-, *dens dentis* tooth)]

edge /ej/ *n. & v.* ● *n.* **1** a boundary line or margin of an area or surface. **2** a narrow surface of a thin object. **3** the meeting line of two surfaces of a solid. **4 a** the sharpened side of the blade of a cutting instrument or weapon. **b** the sharpness of this (*the knife has lost its edge*). **5** the area close to a steep drop (*along the edge of the cliff*). **6** anything compared to an edge, esp. the crest of a ridge. **7 a** effectiveness, force; incisiveness. **b** keenness; excitement (esp. as an element in an otherwise routine situation). **8** an advantage; superiority. ● *v.* **1** *tr. & intr.* (often foll. by *in, into, out*, etc.) move gradually or furtively toward an objective (*edged it into the corner*; *they all edged toward the door*). **2** *tr.* **a** provide with an edge or border. **b** form a border to. **c** trim the edge of. **3** *tr.* sharpen (a knife, tool, etc.). □ **have the edge on** (or **over**) have a slight advantage over. **on edge 1** tense and restless or irritable. **2** eager; excited. **on the edge of** almost involved in or affected by. **set a person's teeth on edge** (of a taste or sound) cause an unpleasant nervous sensation. **take the edge off** dull; weaken; make less effective or intense. □□ **edgeless** *adj.* **edger** *n.* [OE *ecg* f. Gmc]
■ *n.* **1** brink, verge, border, side, rim, lip, brim; fringe, margin, boundary, bound, limit, perimeter, periphery, *archaic* bourn. **4 b** acuteness, sharpness, keenness. **7 a** urgency, force, effectiveness; incisiveness, harshness, sharpness, acrimony, pungency. **b** see ANIMATION. **8** advantage, head start, superiority, lead, upper hand. ● *v.* **1** inch, move, sidle, crawl, creep, steal, worm, work one's way. **2 b** see BORDER *v.* 1, 2. **c** see TRIM *v.* 1b. □ **on edge 1** on tenterhooks, tense, nervous, touchy, sensitive, prickly, irascible, crabbed, crabby, peevish, apprehensive, edgy, anxious, ill at ease, restive, restless, fidgety, like a cat on a hot tin roof, *colloq.* uptight; (*be on edge*) have one's heart in one's mouth; see also IRRITABLE 1. **2** see EAGER 1. **take the edge off** tarnish, dim, cloud, becloud; see also MITIGATE.

edgewise /éjwiz/ *adv.* (also esp. *Brit.* **edgeways** /-wayz/) **1** with the edge uppermost or toward the viewer. **2** edge to edge. □ **get a word in edgewise** contribute to a conversation when the dominant speaker pauses briefly.
■ **1** see SIDEWAYS *adv.*

edging /éjing/ *n.* **1** something forming an edge or border, e.g., a fringe or lace. **2** the process of making an edge.
■ **1** see BORDER *n.* 3.

edgy /éjee/ *adj.* (**edgier, edgiest**) **1** irritable; nervously anxious. **2** disjointed (*edgy rhythms*). □□ **edgily** *adv.* **edginess** *n.*
■ **1** see ANXIOUS 1, TESTY.

edh /eth/ *n.* (also **eth** /eth/) the name of an Old English and Icelandic letter, = th. [Icel.]

edible /édibəl/ *adj. & n.* ● *adj.* fit or suitable to be eaten (cf. EATABLE). ● *n.* (in *pl.*) food. □□ **edibility** *n.* [LL *edibilis* f. *edere* eat]
■ *adj.* esculent, palatable, good *or* fit to eat, wholesome, *formal or joc.* comestible.

edict /ée dikt/ *n.* an order proclaimed by authority. □□ **edictal** /eedíkt'l/ *adj.* [ME f. L *edictum* f. *edicere* proclaim]
■ see LAW 1a.

edifice /édifis/ *n.* **1** a building, esp. a large imposing one. **2** a complex organizational or conceptual structure. [ME f. OF f. L *aedificium* f. *aedis* dwelling + *-ficium* f. *facere* make]
■ **1** see BUILDING.

edify /édifī/ *v.tr.* (**-ies, -ied**) (of a circumstance, experience, etc.) instruct and improve morally or intellectually. □□ **edification** /-fikáyshən/ *n.* **edifying** *adj.* **edifyingly** *adv.* [ME f. OF *edifier* f. L *aedificare* (as EDIFICE)]
■ see EDUCATE 1, 2. □□ **edification** enlightenment, improvement, guidance, education, information, tuition, teaching, schooling, instruction. **edifying** see INFORMATIVE.

edit /édit/ *v. & n.* ● *v.tr.* **1 a** assemble, prepare, modify, or condense (written material, esp. the work of another or others) for publication. **b** prepare an edition of (an author's work). **2** be in overall charge of the content and arrangement of (a newspaper, journal, etc.). **3** take extracts from and collate (movies, tape recordings, etc.) to form a unified sequence. **4 a** prepare (data) for processing by a computer. **b** alter (a text entered in a word processor, etc.). **5 a** reword to correct, or to alter the emphasis. **b** (foll. by *out*) remove (part) from a text, etc. ● *n.* **1 a** a piece of editing. **b** an edited item. **2 a** facility for editing. [F *éditer* (as EDITION); partly a back-form. f. EDITOR]
■ *v.* **1** redact, copyedit, copyread, *Brit.* subedit; prepare, compile, assemble, select, arrange, organize, order, reorganize, reorder; modify, alter, adapt, change,

---

/.../ **pronunciation**	● **part of speech**
□ **phrases, idioms, and compounds**	
□□ **derivatives**	■ **synonym section**
cross-references appear in SMALL CAPITALS *or italics*	

revise, style, restyle; cut, condense, compress, shorten, crop, reduce. **5 a** rewrite, rephrase, reword, restyle, correct, emend; bowdlerize, expurgate, clean up. **b** (*edit out*) blue-pencil, cut (out), delete, censor, erase.

edition /idíshən/ *n.* **1 a** one of the particular forms in which a literary work, etc., is published (*paperback edition; pocket edition*). **b** a copy of a book in a particular form (*a first edition*). **2** a whole number of copies of a book, newspaper, etc., issued at one time. **3** a particular version or instance of a broadcast, esp. of a regular program or feature. **4** a person or thing similar to or resembling another (*a miniature edition of her mother*). [F *édition* f. L *editio -onis* f. *edere edit-* put out (as E-, *dare* give)]

■ **1, 2** number, issue, copy; printing, print run; version.

editio princeps /idísheeō prínseps, edíteō príngkeps/ *n.* (*pl.* **editiones principes** /idísheeṓneez prínsipeez/) the first printed edition of a book, text, etc. [L]

editor /éditər/ *n.* **1** a person who edits material for publication or broadcasting. **2** a person who directs the preparation of a newspaper or periodical, or a particular section of one (*sports editor*). **3** a person who selects or commissions material for publication. **4** a person who edits film, sound track, etc. **5** a computer program for modifying data. □□ **editorship** *n.* [LL, = producer (of games), publisher (as EDIT)]

■ **1** writer, columnist, journalist, rewrite man *or* woman, rewriter, copy editor, copyreader, redactor, reviser, *Brit.* subeditor. **2** editorial writer, *Brit.* leader-writer. **3** commissioner, compiler, collector, selector; publisher.

editorial /éditáwreeəl/ *adj. & n.* ● *adj.* **1** of or concerned with editing or editors. **2** written or approved by an editor. ● *n.* a newspaper article written by or on behalf of an editor, esp. one giving an opinion on a topical issue. □□ **editorialist** *n.* **editorialize** *v.intr.* **editorially** *adv.*

■ *n.* essay, article, column, leading article, *Brit.* leader.

-edly /idlee/ *suffix* forming adverbs from verbs, meaning 'in a manner characterized by performance of or undergoing of the verbal action' (*allegedly; disgustedly; hurriedly*).

EDP *abbr.* electronic data processing.

EDT *abbr.* eastern daylight time.

educate /éjəkayt/ *v.tr.* (also *absol.*) **1** give intellectual, moral, and social instruction to (a pupil, esp. a child), esp. as a formal and prolonged process. **2** provide education for. **3** (often foll. by *in*, or *to* + *infin.*) train or instruct for a particular purpose. **4** advise; give information to. □□ **educable** /-kəbəl/ *adj.* **educability** /-kəbilitee/ *n.* **educatable** *adj.* **educative** *adj.* **educator** *n.* [L *educare educat-*, rel. to *educere* EDUCE]

■ **1, 2** teach, train, instruct, edify, tutor, school, form, inform, enlighten, cultivate, develop, civilize. **3** train, instruct, coach, drill, prepare, ready. **4** see INFORM 1.

educated /éjəkaytid/ *adj.* **1** having had an education, esp. to a higher level than average. **2** resulting from a (good) education (*an educated accent*). **3** based on experience or study (*an educated guess*).

■ **1** erudite, well-read, lettered, literary, scholarly, learned, well-informed, knowledgeable; cultivated, cultured, enlightened. **2** refined, polished, cultivated, civilized, cultured, *colloq.* posh.

education /éjəkáyshən/ *n.* **1 a** the act or process of educating or being educated; systematic instruction. **b** the knowledge gained from this. **2** a particular kind of or stage in education (*further education; a classical education*). **3 a** development of character or mental powers. **b** a stage in or aspect of this (*travel will be an education for you*). □□ **educational** *adj.* **educationalist** *n.* **educationally** *adv.* **educationist** *n.* [F *éducation* or L *educatio* (as EDUCATE)]

■ **1 a** teaching, schooling, training, instruction, tuition, tutelage, edification, tutoring, cultivation, drilling; learning. **b** lore, knowledge, information, erudition. □□ **educational** academic, scholastic, instructional, *archaic or derog.* pedagogical; informative, instructive, enlightening, edifying, eye-opening, revelatory, educative.

educe /idóos, idyóos/ *v.tr.* **1** bring out or develop from latent or potential existence; elicit. **2** infer; elicit a principle, num-

ber, etc., from data. □□ **educible** *adj.* **eduction** /idúkshen/ *n.* **eductive** /idúktiv/ *adj.* [ME f. L *educere educt-* lead out (as E-, *ducere* lead)]

■ **1** see DERIVE 1. **2** see DERIVE 3.

Edwardian /edwáwrdeeən, -waár-/ *adj. & n.* ● *adj.* of, characteristic of, or associated with the reign of King Edward VII of England (1901–10). ● *n.* a person belonging to this period.

-ee /ee/ *suffix* forming nouns denoting: **1** the person affected by the verbal action (*addressee; employee; lessee*). **2** a person concerned with or described as (*absentee; refugee*), **3** an object of smaller size (*bootee*). [from or after AF past part. in *-é* f. L *-atus*]

EEC *abbr.* European Economic Community.

EEG *abbr.* electroencephalogram.

eel /eel/ *n.* **1** any of various snakelike fish, with slender body and poorly developed fins. **2** a slippery or evasive person or thing. □□ **eellike** *adj.* **eely** *adj.* [OE *ǣl* f. Gmc]

eelgrass /éelgras/ *n.* **1** any marine plant of the genus *Zostera*, with long ribbonlike leaves. **2** any submerged freshwater plant of the genus *Vallisneria*.

eelpout /éelpowt/ *n.* **1** any fish of the family Zoarcidae, with slender body and dorsal and anal fins meeting to fuse with the tail. Also called POUT². **2** = BURBOT. [OE *ǣleputa* (as EEL, POUT²)]

eelworm /éelwərm/ *n.* any of various small nematode worms infesting plant roots.

e'en¹ /een/ *archaic or poet.* var. of EVEN¹.

e'en² /een/ *Sc.* var. of EVEN².

-een /een/ *suffix Ir.* forming diminutive nouns (*colleen*). [Ir. *-ín* dimin. suffix]

EEOC *abbr.* Equal Employment Opportunity Commission.

e'er /air/ *poet.* var. of EVER.

-eer /eer/ *suffix* forming: **1** nouns meaning 'person concerned with or engaged in' (*auctioneer; mountaineer; profiteer*). **2** verbs meaning 'be concerned with' (*electioneer*). [from or after F *-ier* f. L *-arius*: cf. -IER, -ARY¹]

eerie /éeree/ *adj.* (**eerier, eeriest**) gloomy and strange; weird, frightening (*an eerie silence*). □□ **eerily** *adv.* **eeriness** *n.* [orig. No. of Engl. and Sc. *eri*, of obscure orig.: cf. OE *earg* cowardly]

■ frightening, weird, strange, uncanny, ghostly, spectral, dreadful, unearthly, mysterious, frightful, eldritch, *colloq.* scary, creepy, spooky.

ef- /if, ef/ *prefix* assim. form of EX-¹ 1 before *f*.

efface /ifáys/ *v.* **1** *tr.* rub or wipe out (a mark, etc.). **2** *tr.* (in abstract senses) obliterate; wipe out (*effaced it from his memory*). **3** *tr.* utterly surpass; eclipse (*success has effaced all previous attempts*). **4** *refl.* treat or regard oneself as unimportant (*self-effacing*). □□ **effacement** *n.* [F *effacer* (as EX-¹, FACE)]

■ **1** see ERASE 1. **2** see ERASE 2.

effect /ifékt/ *n. & v.* ● *n.* **1** the result or consequence of an action, etc.; the significance or implication of this. **2** efficacy (*had little effect*). **3** an impression produced on a spectator, hearer, etc. (*lights had a pretty effect; my words had no effect*). **4** (in *pl.*) property; luggage. **5** (in *pl.*) the lighting, sound, etc., used to accompany a play, movie, broadcast, etc. **6** *Physics* a physical phenomenon, usually named after its discoverer (*Doppler effect*). **7** the state of being operative. ● *v.tr.* **1** bring about; accomplish. **2** cause to exist or occur. □ **bring** (or **carry**) **into effect** accomplish. **for effect** to create an impression. **give effect to** make operative. **in effect** for practical purposes; in reality. **take effect** become operative. **to the effect that** the general substance or gist being. **to that effect** having that result or implication. [ME f. OF *effect* or L *effectus* (as EX-¹, *facere* make)]

■ *n.* **1** result, consequence, outcome, conclusion, upshot; significance, meaning, signification, purport, sense, essence, drift, implication, import, tenor, purpose, intent, intention, object, objective. **2** effectiveness, efficacy, force, power, potency, influence, impression, impact, power, *colloq.* punch. **4** (*effects*) belongings, (personal) property, possessions, stuff, things, paraphernalia, chattels, goods, *colloq.* gear; baggage, luggage, bags, cases. ● *v.* bring *or* carry into effect, bring about, cause, make happen *or* take place, effectuate, achieve, accomplish, succeed in, secure, obtain, make, execute, carry out, produce, create. □ **bring into effect** see ACCOMPLISH. **in effect** effectively, virtually, for (all) practical purposes, more or less; actually, in (point of) fact, really, in reality, essentially, basically, at bottom, truly, to all intents and purposes, at the end of the day, whichever way you look at it, *disp.* in actual fact, *literary* in truth. **take effect** become operative *or* operational, come into operation, come into force, begin to operate, start to operate.

effective /iféktiv/ *adj. & n.* ● *adj.* **1** having a definite or desired effect. **2** powerful in effect; impressive. **3 a** actual; existing in fact rather than officially or theoretically (*took effective control in their absence*). **b** actually usable; realizable; equivalent in its effect (*effective money; effective demand*). **4** coming into operation (*effective as of May 1*). **5** (of manpower) fit for work or service. ● *n.* a soldier available for service. □□ **effectively** *adv.* **effectiveness** *n.* [ME f. L *effectivus* (as EFFECT)]
■ *adj.* **1** effectual, efficacious, productive; capable, useful, serviceable, competent, operative, able, functional, efficient. **2** impressive, outstanding, striking, powerful. **3** real, actual, true; realizable, usable. **4** operative, operational, in operation, functioning.

effector /iféktər/ *adj. & n. Biol.* ● *adj.* acting in response to a stimulus. ● *n.* an effector organ.

effectual /ifékchōōəl/ *adj.* **1** capable of producing the required result or effect; answering its purpose. **2** valid. □□ **effectuality** /-chōōálitee/ *n.* **effectually** *adv.* **effectualness** *n.* [ME f. med.L *effectualis* (as EFFECT)]
■ **1** effective, efficacious, efficient, functional, productive, useful, influential, powerful, adequate. **2** in force, valid, legal, lawful, binding, sound.

effectuate /ifékchōō-ayt/ *v.tr.* cause to happen; accomplish. □□ **effectuation** *n.* [med.L *effectuare* (as EFFECT)]
■ bring about, effect, cause, make happen, carry out, implement, accomplish, do, execute, realize, achieve.

effeminate /iféminət/ *adj.* (of a man) feminine in appearance or manner; unmasculine. □□ **effeminacy** *n.* **effeminately** *adv.* [ME f. L *effeminatus* past part. of *effeminare* (as EX-¹, *femina* woman)]
■ unmanly, womanish, womanly, unmasculine, feminine, emasculate, epicene, effete, milky; affected, *colloq.* camp, campy, sissy, *sl.* limp-wristed, *sl. offens.* faggy, *Brit. sl. derog.* poofy, nancy.

effendi /eféndee/ *n.* (*pl.* **effendis**) **1** a man of education or standing in eastern Mediterranean or Arab countries. **2** a former title of respect or courtesy in Turkey. [f. Turk. *efendi* f. mod. Gk *afentēs* f. Gk *authentēs* lord, master: see AUTHENTIC]

efferent /éfərənt/ *adj. Physiol.* conducting outward (*efferent nerves; efferent vessels*) (opp. AFFERENT). □□ **efference** /-rəns/ *n.* [L *efferre* (as EX-¹, *ferre* carry)]

effervesce /éfərvés/ *v.intr.* **1** give off bubbles of gas; bubble. **2** (of a person) be lively or energetic. □□ **effervescence** *n.* **effervescency** *n.* **effervescent** *adj.* [L *effervescere* (as EX-¹, *fervēre* be hot)]
■ **1** see FIZZ *v.* 2. □□ **effervescent** bubbling, fizzy, carbonated, sparkling, fizzing, gassy; foaming, foamy, frothing, frothy, bubbly; high-spirited, sparkly, sparkling, vivacious, ebullient, lively, exuberant, buoyant, animated, lively, exhilarated, excited, enthusiastic, irrepressible; see also ENERGETIC 1, 2.

effete /iféet/ *adj.* **1 a** feeble and incapable. **b** effeminate. **2** worn out; exhausted of its essential quality or vitality. □□ **effeteness** *n.* [L *effetus* worn out by bearing young (as EX-¹, FETUS)]
■ see WEAK 2.

efficacious /éfikáyshəs/ *adj.* (of a thing) producing or sure to produce the desired effect. □□ **efficaciously** *adv.* **efficaciousness** *n.* **efficacy** /éfikəsee/ *n.* [L *efficax* (as EFFICIENT)]

■ effective, effectual, productive, competent, successful, efficient, useful, serviceable.

efficiency /ifíshənsee/ *n.* (*pl.* **-ies**) **1** the state or quality of being efficient. **2** *Mech. & Physics* the ratio of useful work performed to the total energy expended or heat taken in. □ **efficiency bar** a point on a salary scale requiring evidence of efficiency for further promotion. [L *efficientia* (as EFFICIENT)]
■ **1** effectiveness, efficacy, efficaciousness, competence, productiveness, capability, proficiency.

efficient /ifíshənt/ *adj.* **1** productive with minimum waste or effort. **2** (of a person) capable; acting effectively. □ **efficient cause** *Philos.* an agent that brings a thing into being or initiates a change. □□ **efficiently** *adv.* [ME f. L *efficere* (as EX-¹, *facere* make, accomplish)]
■ **1** economic, thrifty; effective, efficacious, effectual, productive. **2** competent, proficient; see also CAPABLE 1.

effigy /éfijee/ *n.* (*pl.* **-ies**) a sculpture or model of a person. □ **in effigy** in the form of a (usu. crude) representation of a person. [L *effigies* f. *effingere* to fashion]
■ see IMAGE *n.* 1.

effleurage /éflŏráazh/ *n. & v.* ● *n.* a form of massage involving a circular inward stroking movement made with the palm of the hand, used esp. during childbirth. ● *v.intr.* massage with a circular stroking movement. [F f. *effleurer* to skim]

effloresce /éflərés/ *v.intr.* **1** burst out into flower. **2** *Chem.* **a** (of a substance) turn to a fine powder on exposure to air. **b** (of salts) come to the surface and crystallize on it. **c** (of a surface) become covered with salt particles. □□ **efflorescence** *n.* **efflorescent** *adj.* [L *efflorescere* (as EX-¹, *florēre* to bloom f. *flos floris* flower)]
■ **1** see FLOWER *v.* 1.

effluence /éflŏōəns/ *n.* **1** a flowing out (of light, electricity, etc.). **2** that which flows out. [F *effluence* or med.L *effluentia* f. L *effluere efflux-* flow out (as EX-¹, *fluere* flow)]
■ see STREAM *n.*

effluent /éflŏōənt/ *adj. & n.* ● *adj.* flowing forth or out. ● *n.* **1** sewage or industrial waste discharged into a river, the sea, etc. **2** a stream or lake flowing from a larger body of water.

effluvium /iflŏōveeəm/ *n.* (*pl.* **effluvia** /-veeə/) an unpleasant or noxious odor or exhaled substance affecting the lungs or the sense of smell, etc. [L (as EFFLUENT)]
■ see SMELL *n.* 3.

efflux /éfluks/ *n.* = EFFLUENCE. □□ **effluxion** /eflúkshən/ *n.* [med.L *effluxus* (as EFFLUENT)]

effort /éfərt/ *n.* **1** strenuous physical or mental exertion. **2** a vigorous or determined attempt. **3** *Mech.* a force exerted. **4** *colloq.* the result of an attempt; something accomplished (*not bad for a first effort*). □□ **effortful** *adj.* [F f. OF *esforcier* ult. f. L *fortis* strong]
■ **1** exertion, energy, striving, struggle, strain, labor, pains, toil, trouble, work, *colloq.* elbow grease. **2** endeavor, try, venture, *formal* essay; see also ATTEMPT *n.* **4** achievement, feat, deed, attainment, exploit; see also ACCOMPLISHMENT 3.

effortless /éfərtlis/ *adj.* **1** seemingly without effort; natural; easy. **2** requiring no effort (*effortless contemplation*). □□ **effortlessly** *adv.* **effortlessness** *n.*
■ simple, painless, smooth, trouble-free, uncomplicated; see also EASY *adj.* 1.

effrontery /ifrúntəree/ *n.* (*pl.* **-ies**) **1** shameless insolence; impudent audacity (esp. *have the effrontery to*). **2** an instance of this. [F *effronterie* f. *effronté* ult. f. LL *effrons -ontis* shameless (as EX-¹, *frons* forehead)]
■ **1** insolence, impertinence, impudence, audacity, presumption, presumptuousness, brazenness, boldness, temerity, brashness, arrogance, front, face, cheek,

---

/.../ **pronunciation**	● **part of speech**
□ **phrases, idioms, and compounds**	
□□ **derivatives**	■ **synonym section**
cross-references appear in SMALL CAPITALS or *italics*	

colloq. brass, nerve, lip, mouth, esp. *Austral. & NZ*
colloq. hide, *sl.* gall, chutzpah, *Brit. sl.* side.

effulgent /ifúljənt/ *adj. literary* radiant; shining brilliantly. □□ **effulgence** /-jəns/ *n.* **effulgently** *adv.* [L *effulgēre* shine forth (as EX-¹, *fulgēre* shine)]
■ see RADIANT *adj.* 1.

effuse *adj. & v.* ● *adj.* /ifyóōs/ *Bot.* (of an inflorescence, etc.) spreading loosely. ● *v.tr.* /ifyōōz/ **1** pour forth (liquid, light, etc.). **2** give out (ideas, etc.). [ME f. L *effusus* past part. of *effundere effus-* pour out (as EX-¹, *fundere* pour)]

effusion /ifyōōzhən/ *n.* **1** a copious outpouring. **2** usu. *derog.* an unrestrained flow of speech or writing. [ME f. OF *effusion* or L *effusio* (as EFFUSE)]
■ see OUTPOURING.

effusive /ifyóōsiv/ *adj.* **1** gushing; demonstrative; exuberant (*effusive praise*). **2** *Geol.* (of igneous rock) poured out when molten and later solidified; volcanic. □□ **effusively** *adv.* **effusiveness** *n.*
■ **1** demonstrative, gushing, enthusiastic, overenthusiastic, expansive, emotional, exuberant, rhapsodic, ebullient, lavish, voluble, profuse, *disp.* fulsome.

EFL *abbr.* English as a foreign language.

eft /eft/ *n.* a newt. [OE *efeta*, of unkn. orig.]

EFTA /éftə/ *n.* European Free Trade Association. [abbr.]

EFTPOS /éftpoz/ *abbr.* electronic funds transfer at point of sale.

e.g. *abbr.* for example. [L *exempli gratia*]
■ see *for example* (EXAMPLE).

egad /eegád, igád/ *int. archaic* or *joc.* by God. [prob. orig. *a* ah + GOD]

egalitarian /igálitáireeən/ *adj. & n.* ● *adj.* **1** of or relating to the principle of equal rights and opportunities for all (*an egalitarian society*). **2** advocating this principle. ● *n.* a person who advocates or supports egalitarian principles. □□ **egalitarianism** *n.* [F *égalitaire* f. *égal* EQUAL]
■ *adj.* **1** democratic, classless.

egg¹ /eg/ *n.* **1 a** the spheroidal reproductive body produced by females of animals such as birds, reptiles, fish, etc., enclosed in a protective layer and capable of developing into a new individual. **b** the egg of the domestic hen, used for food. **2** *Biol.* the female reproductive cell in animals and plants. **3** *colloq.* a person or thing qualified in some way (*a tough egg*). **4** anything resembling or imitating an egg, esp. in shape or appearance. □ **as sure as eggs is** (or **are**) **eggs** *Brit. colloq.* without any doubt. **egg-flip** *Brit.* = EGGNOG. **eggs** (or **egg**) **and bacon** *Brit.* = *butter-and-eggs*. **egg timer** a device for timing the cooking of an egg. **egg tooth** a projection of an embryo bird or reptile used for breaking out of the shell. **egg white** the white of an egg. **have** (or **put**) **all one's eggs in one basket** *colloq.* risk everything on a single venture. **with egg on one's face** *colloq.* made to look foolish. □□ **eggless** *adj.* **eggy** *adj.* (**eggier**, **eggiest**). [ME f. ON, rel. to OE *ǣg*]
■ **2** see SEED *n.* 1a. □ **egg white** albumen, glair.

egg² /eg/ *v.tr.* (foll. by *on*) urge (*egged us on to it*; *egged them on to do it*). [ME f. ON *eggja* = EDGE]
■ see MOTIVATE.

eggbeater /égbeetər/ *n.* **1** a device for beating eggs. **2** *sl.* a helicopter.

eggcup /égkup/ *n.* a cup for holding a boiled egg.

egger /égər/ *n.* (also **eggar**) any of various large moths of the family Lasiocampidae, esp. *Lasiocampa quercus*, with an egg-shaped cocoon; tent caterpillar. [prob. f. EGG¹ + -ER¹]

egghead /éghed/ *n. colloq.* an intellectual; an expert.
■ see INTELLECTUAL *n.*

eggnog /égnog/ *n.* a drink made from a mixture of eggs, cream, and flavorings, often with alcohol.

eggplant /égplant/ *n.* **1** a tropical plant, *Solanum melongena*, having erect or spreading branches bearing purple or white egg-shaped fruit. **2** this fruit eaten as a vegetable. **3** the dark purple color of this fruit.

eggshell /égshel/ *n. & adj.* ● *n.* **1** the shell of an egg. **2** anything very fragile. **3** a pale yellowish-white color. ● *adj.* **1**

(of china) thin and fragile. **2** (of paint) with a slight gloss finish.

eglantine /égləntīn, -teen/ *n.* sweetbrier. [ME f. F *églantine* f. OF *aiglent* ult. f. L *acus* needle]

ego /éegō/ *n.* (*pl.* **-os**) **1** *Metaphysics* a conscious thinking subject. **2** *Psychol.* the part of the mind that reacts to reality and has a sense of individuality. **3** self-esteem. □ **ego ideal 1** *Psychol.* the part of the mind developed from the ego by an awareness of social standards. **2** (in general use) idealization of oneself. **ego trip** *colloq.* activity, etc., devoted entirely to one's own interests or feelings. [L, = I]

egocentric /éegōséntrik, égō-/ *adj.* **1** centered in the ego. **2** self-centered; egoistic. □□ **egocentrically** *adv.* **egocentricity** /-trísitee/ *n.* [EGO + -CENTRIC after *geocentric*, etc.]
■ **2** see *egoistic, egoistical* (EGOISM).

egoism /éegōizəm, égō-/ *n.* **1** an ethical theory that treats self-interest as the foundation of morality. **2** systematic self-ishness. **3** self-opinionatedness. **4** = EGOTISM. □□ **egoist** *n.* **egoistic** *adj.* **egoistical** *adj.* [F *égoïsme* ult. f. mod.L *egoismus* (as EGO)]
■ **2** self-centeredness, self-absorption, self-love, self-interest, self-indulgence, selfishness, egocentricity, egomania; see also EGOTISM 2, INTEREST *n.* 7. **3** see *intolerance* (INTOLERANT). □□ **egoistic, egoistical** self-centered, egocentric, narcissistic, self-seeking, self-absorbed, egomaniacal, selfish, self-serving, self-indulgent, self-important, self-opinionated, self-aggrandizing; see also *egotistic, egotistical* (EGOTISM).

egomania /éegōmáyneeə, égō-/ *n.* morbid egotism. □□ **egomaniac** *n.* **egomaniacal** /-məníəkəl/ *adj.*

egotism /éegətizəm, égə-/ *n.* **1** excessive use of 'I' and 'me.' **2** the practice of talking about oneself. **3** an exaggerated opinion of oneself. **4** selfishness. □□ **egotist** *n.* **egotistic** *adj.* **egotistical** *adj.* **egotistically** *adv.* **egotize** *v.intr.* [EGO + -ISM with intrusive -*t*-]
■ **2** self-obsession, self-absorption, self-love, self-centeredness, egocentricity, egomania. **3** see VANITY 1. **4** see INTEREST *n.* 7. □□ **egotistic, egotistical** conceited, proud, overweening, arrogant, boastful, boasting, *colloq.* swell(ed)-headed, swollen-headed; vain, self-worshiping, self-admiring, self-important, egocentric, selfish, egomaniacal, *literary* vainglorious; see also *egoistic, egoistical* (EGOISM).

egregious /igréejəs/ *adj.* **1** outstandingly bad; shocking (*egregious folly*; *an egregious ass*). **2** *archaic* or *joc.* remarkable. □□ **egregiously** *adv.* **egregiousness** *n.* [L *egregius* illustrious, lit. 'standing out from the flock' f. *grex gregis* flock]
■ **1** see TERRIBLE 1.

egress /éegres/ *n.* **1 a** a going out. **b** the right of going out. **2** an exit; a way out. **3** *Astron.* the end of an eclipse or transit. □□ **egression** /-gréshən/ *n.* (in senses 1, 2). [L *egressus* f. *egredi egress-* (as E-, *gradi* to step)]
■ **2** exit, way out, door, gate.

egret /éegrit/ *n.* any of various herons of the genus *Egretta* or *Bulbulcus*, usu. having long white feathers in the breeding season. [ME, var. of AIGRETTE]

Egyptian /ijípshən/ *adj. & n.* ● *adj.* **1** of or relating to Egypt in NE Africa. **2** of or for Egyptian antiquities (e.g., in a museum) (*Egyptian room*). ● *n.* **1** a native of ancient or modern Egypt; a national of the Arab Republic of Egypt. **2** the Hamitic language used in ancient Egypt until the 3rd c. AD. □□ **Egyptianize** *v.tr.* **Egyptianization** *n.*

Egyptology /éejiptóləjee/ *n.* the study of the language, history, and culture of ancient Egypt. □□ **Egyptologist** *n.*

eh /ay/ *int. colloq.* **1** expressing inquiry or surprise. **2** inviting assent. **3** asking for something to be repeated or explained. [ME *ey*, instinctive exclam.]

-eian /eeən/ *suffix* corresp. to *-ey* (or *-y*) + *-an* (*Bodleian*; *Rugbeian*).

eider /ídər/ *n.* **1** (in full **eider duck**) any of various large northern ducks, esp. of the genus *Somateria*. **2** = EIDERDOWN 1. [Icel. *aethr*]

eiderdown /ídərdown/ *n.* **1** small, soft feathers from the breast of the eider duck. **2** a quilt stuffed with down (orig.

from the eider) or some other soft material, esp. as the upper layer of bedclothes. ■ **2** see SPREAD *n.* 10.

eidetic /īdétik/ *adj. & n.* ● *adj. Psychol.* (of a mental image) having unusual vividness and detail, as if actually visible. ● *n.* a person able to see eidetic images. □□ **eidetically** *adv.* [G *eidetisch* f. Gk *eidētikos* f. *eidos* form]

eidolon /īdṓlən/ *n.* (*pl.* **eidolons** or **eidola** /-lə/) **1** a specter; a phantom. **2** an idealized figure. [Gk *eidōlon*: see IDOL] ■ **1** see VISION *n.* 2.

eigen- /ī́gən/ *comb. form Math. & Physics* proper; characteristic. [G *eigen* OWN]

eigenfrequency /ī́gənfreekwənsee/ *n.* (*pl.* **-ies**) *Math. & Physics* one of the natural resonant frequencies of a system.

eigenfunction /ī́gənfungkshən/ *n. Math. & Physics* that function which under a given operation generates some multiple of itself.

eigenvalue /ī́gənvalyōō/ *n. Math. & Physics* that value by which an eigenfunction of an operation is multiplied after the eigenfunction has been subjected to that operation.

eight /ayt/ *n. & adj.* ● *n.* **1** one more than seven, or two less than ten; the product of two units and four units. **2** a symbol for this (8, viii, VIII). **3** a figure resembling the form of 8. **4** a size, etc., denoted by eight. **5** an eight-oared rowing boat or its crew. **6** the time of eight o'clock (*is it eight yet?*). **7** a card with eight pips. ● *adj.* that amount to eight. □ **have one over the eight** *Brit. sl.* get slightly drunk. [OE *ehta, eahta*]

eighteen /áyteen/ *n. & adj.* ● *n.* **1** one more than seventeen, or eight more than ten; the product of two units and nine units. **2** a symbol for this (18, xviii, XVIII). **3** a size, etc., denoted by eighteen. **4** a set or team of eighteen individuals. ● *adj.* that amount to eighteen. □ **eighteen-wheeler** a large tractor-trailer with eighteen wheels. □□ **eighteenth** *adj. & n.* [OE *ehtatēne, eaht-*] ■ *n.* **4** see SIDE 5a.

eighteenmo /áyteenmō/ *n.* = OCTODECIMO.

eightfold /áytfōld/ *adj. & adv.* **1** eight times as much or as many. **2** consisting of eight parts. **3** amounting to eight.

eighth /ayt-th, ayth/ *n. & adj.* ● *n.* **1** the position in a sequence corresponding to the number 8 in the sequence 1–8. **2** something occupying this position. **3** one of eight equal parts of a thing. ● *adj.* that is the eighth. □ **eighth note** *Mus.* a note having the time value of an eighth of a whole note and represented by a large dot with a hooked stem. Also called esp. *Brit.* **quaver.** □□ **eighthly** *adv.*

eightsome /áytsəm/ *n.* **1** (in full **eightsome reel**) a lively Scottish reel for eight dancers. **2** the music for this.

eighty /áytee/ *n. & adj.* ● *n.* (*pl.* **-ies**) **1** the product of eight and ten. **2** a symbol for this (80, lxxx, LXXX). **3** (in *pl.*) the numbers from 80 to 89, esp. the years of a century or of a person's life. ● *adj.* that amount to eighty. □ **eighty-first, -second**, etc., the ordinal numbers between eightieth and ninetieth. **eighty-one, -two**, etc., the cardinal numbers between eighty and ninety. □□ **eightieth** *adj. & n.* **eightyfold** *adj. & adv.* [OE *-eahtatig* (as EIGHT, -TY²)]

einkorn /ī́nkawrn/ *n.* a kind of wheat (*Triticum monococcum*). [G f. *ein* one + *Korn* seed]

einsteinium /īnstíneeəm/ *n. Chem.* a transuranic radioactive metallic element produced artificially from plutonium. ¶ Symb.: Es. [A. *Einstein*, Ger.-Amer. physicist d. 1955]

eirenic var. of IRENIC.

eisteddfod /īstéthvod, aystéth-/ *n.* (*pl.* **eisteddfods** or **eisteddfodau** /-dī/) a congress of Welsh bards; a national or local festival for musical competitions, etc. □□ **eisteddfodic** /-vódik/ *adj.* [Welsh, lit. = session, f. *eistedd* sit]

either /eéthər, íthər/ *adj., pron., adv., & conj.* ● *adj. & pron.* **1** one or the other of two (*either of you can go; you may have either book*). **2** each of two (*houses on either side of the road; either will do*). ● *adv. & conj.* **1** as one possibility (*is either black or white*). **2** as one choice or alternative; which way you will (*either come in or go out*). **3** (with *neg.* or *interrog.*) **a** any more than the other (*I didn't like it either; if you do not go, I shall not either*). **b** moreover (*there is no time to lose, either*). □ **either-or** *n.* an unavoidable choice between alternatives.

● *adj.* involving such a choice. **either way** in either case or event. [OE *ǣgther* f. Gmc]

ejaculate *v. & n.* ● *v.tr.* /ijákyəlayt/ (also *absol.*) **1** utter suddenly (words esp. of prayer or other emotion). **2** eject (fluid, etc., esp. semen) from the body. ● *n.* /ijákyələt/ semen that has been ejaculated from the body. □□ **ejaculation** /-láyshən/ *n.* **ejaculator** *n.* **ejaculatory** /ijákyələtáwree/ *adj.* [L *ejaculari* to dart (as E-, *jaculum* javelin)] ■ *v.* **1** see EXCLAIM.

eject /ijékt/ *v.tr.* **1 a** send or drive out precipitately or by force, esp. from a building or other property; compel to leave. **b** dismiss from employment or office. **2 a** cause (the pilot, etc.) to be propelled from an aircraft or spacecraft in an emergency. **b** (*absol.*) (of the pilot, etc.) be ejected in this way (*they both ejected at 1,000 feet*). **3** cause to be removed or drop out (e.g., a spent cartridge from a gun). **4** dispossess (a tenant, etc.) by legal process. **5** dart forth; emit. □□ **ejective** *adj.* **ejectment** *n.* [L *ejicere eject-* (as E-, *jacere* throw)] ■ **1 a** force *or* drive out, cast out, fling out, expel, oust, remove, get rid of, evict, throw out, boot out, *colloq.* kick out, *Brit. colloq.* turf out, *sl.* bounce. **b** discharge, dismiss, cashier, drum out, lay off, *colloq.* fire, sack, boot out, *sl.* give the sack *or* boot *or* axe, give a person his *or* her marching orders *or* walking papers, send packing. **5** emit, throw up *or* out, spew (forth), discharge, spout, disgorge, vomit (up *or* forth), send out *or* forth, dart forth; ooze, exude, extravasate.

ejection /ijékshən/ *n.* the act or an instance of ejecting; the process of being ejected. □ **ejection seat** a device for the automatic ejection of the pilot, etc., of an aircraft or spacecraft in an emergency. ■ expulsion, disgorgement, discharge, emission; banishment, deportation, ejectment, ouster, removal, eviction; dismissal, discharge, congé, cashiering, layoff, *colloq.* firing, sacking, *sl.* the sack, the boot, the axe, the (old) heave-ho, the bounce.

ejector /ijéktər/ *n.* a device for ejecting. □ **ejector seat** = ejection seat.

eke /eek/ *v.tr.* □ **eke out 1** (foll. by *with, by*) supplement; make the best use of (defective means, etc.). **2** contrive to make (a livelihood) or support (an existence). [OE *ēacan*, rel. to L *augēre* increase]

EKG *abbr.* electrocardiogram. [L, ult. f. Gk *elektron* + *kardio* + *gram*]

-el var. of -LE².

elaborate *adj. & v.* ● *adj.* /ilábərət/ **1** carefully or minutely worked out. **2** highly developed or complicated. ● *v.* /ilábərayt/ **1 a** *tr.* work out or explain in detail. **b** *tr.* make more intricate or ornate. **c** *intr.* (often foll. by *on*) go into details (*I need not elaborate*). **2** *tr.* produce by labor. **3** *tr.* (of a natural agency) produce (a substance, etc.) from its elements or sources. □□ **elaborately** *adv.* **elaborateness** *n.* **elaboration** /-ráyshən/ *n.* **elaborative** *adj.* **elaborator** *n.* [L *elaboratus* past part. of *elaborare* (as E-, *labor* work)] ■ *adj.* **1** detailed, painstaking, meticulous, punctilious, comprehensive, thorough, complete, exhaustive, intricate, involved, minute, precise, exact. **2** complicated, complex, convoluted, ornate, fancy, Byzantine, extravagant, showy, baroque, rococo, highly ornamented, florid, busy, fussy. ● *v.* **1** work out, enlarge, expand (upon *or* on), amplify, flesh out, enhance, develop; go into detail, expatiate; see also EMBELLISH. □□ **elaboration** enlargement, development, amplification, expansion, enhancement, embellishment, garnishment, refinement, adornment.

élan /aylón, aylón/ *n.* vivacity; dash. [F f. *élancer* launch] ■ see VERVE.

eland /eélənd/ *n.* any antelope of the genus *Taurotragus*, na-

/.../	**pronunciation**	● **part of speech**
	□ **phrases, idioms, and compounds**	
	□□ **derivatives**	■ **synonym section**
	cross-references appear in SMALL CAPITALS or *italics*	

461

tive to Africa, having spirally twisted horns, esp. the largest of living antelopes *T. derbianus*. [Du.,= elk]

elapse /iláps/ *v.intr.* (of time) pass by. [L *elabor elaps-* slip away]

■ pass (by), go (by), slip by *or* away, pass away, slide by, glide by.

elasmobranch /ilázməbrangk/ *n. Zool.* any cartilaginous fish of the subclass Chondrichthyes, e.g., sharks, skates, rays. [mod.L *elasmobranchii* f. Gk *elasmos* beaten metal + *bragkhia* gills]

elasmosaurus /ilázməsáwrəs/ *n.* a large extinct marine reptile with paddlelike limbs and tough crocodilelike skin. [mod.L f. Gk *elasmos* beaten metal + *sauros* lizard]

elastic /ilástik/ *adj. & n.* ● *adj.* **1** able to resume its normal bulk or shape spontaneously after contraction, dilatation, or distortion. **2** springy. **3** (of a person or feelings) buoyant. **4** flexible; adaptable (*elastic conscience*). **5** *Econ.* (of demand) variable according to price. **6** *Physics* (of a collision) involving no decrease of kinetic energy. ● *n.* **1** elastic cord or fabric, usu. woven with strips of rubber. **2** (in full **elastic band**) = *rubber band* (see RUBBER¹). □□ **elastically** *adv.* **elasticity** /ílastísitee, eelas-/ *n.* **elasticize** /ilástisiz/ *v.tr.* [mod.L *elasticus* f. Gk *elastikos* propulsive f. *elaunō* drive]

■ *adj.* **1, 2** flexible, stretchable, stretchy, bendable, pliable, springy, plastic, extensile, extensible, extendable, expansible, expandable, contractile, resilient, bouncy, compressible, *colloq.* bendy. **3** see BUOYANT 2. **4** adjustable, adaptable, accommodating, flexible, variable. □□ **elasticity** flexibility, resilience, rubberiness, plasticity, ductility, springiness, stretchability, stretchiness, suppleness, pliancy, give; adaptability, tolerance.

elasticated /ilástikaytid/ *adj.* (of a fabric) made elastic by weaving with rubber thread.

elastomer /ilástəmər/ *n.* a natural or synthetic rubber or rubberlike plastic. □□ **elastomeric** /-mérik/ *adj.* [ELASTIC, after *isomer*]

elate /iláyt/ *v. & adj.* ● *v.tr.* **1** (esp. as **elated** *adj.*) inspirit; stimulate. **2** make proud. ● *adj. archaic* in high spirits; exultant; proud. □□ **elatedly** *adv.* **elatedness** *n.* **elation** /-láyshən/ *n.* [ME f. L *efferre elat-* raise]

■ *v.* **1** see INTOXICATE 2; (**elated**) exhilarated, uplifted, inspirited, stimulated, elevated, gleeful, joyful, jubilant, joyous, exultant, ecstatic, blissful, happy, delighted, euphoric, overjoyed, excited, thrilled, transported, pleased as Punch, delirious, over the moon, in seventh heaven, in raptures, *colloq.* tickled to death, on top of the world, tickled pink, on cloud nine, *Brit. sl.* chuffed. □□ **elation** see JOY *n.* 1.

elater /élətər/ *n.* a click beetle. [mod.L f. Gk *elatēr* driver f. *elaunō* drive]

E layer /éelayər/ *n.* a layer of the ionosphere able to reflect medium-frequency radio waves. [*E* (arbitrary) + LAYER]

elbow /élbō/ *n. & v.* ● *n.* **1 a** the joint between the forearm and the upper arm. **b** the part of the sleeve of a garment covering the elbow. **2** an elbow-shaped bend or corner; a short piece of piping bent through a right angle. ● *v.tr.* (foll. by *in, out, aside*, etc.) **1** thrust or jostle (a person or oneself). **2** make (one's way) by thrusting or jostling. **3** nudge or poke with the elbow. □ **at one's elbow** close at hand. **elbow grease** *colloq.* vigorous polishing; hard work. **give a person the elbow** *colloq.* send a person away; dismiss or reject a person. **out at the elbows 1** (of a coat) worn out. **2** (of a person) ragged; poor. [OE *elboga, elnboga*, f. Gmc (as ELL, BOW¹)]

■ *v.* **1, 2** see HUSTLE *v.* 1. **3** see DIG *v.* 7.

elbowroom /élbōrōōm/ *n.* plenty of room to move or work in.

eld /eld/ *n. archaic* or *poet.* **1** old age. **2** olden time. [OE (*i*)*eldu* f. Gmc: cf. OLD]

elder¹ /éldər/ *adj. & n.* ● *attrib.adj.* (of two indicated persons, esp. when related) senior; of a greater age (*my elder brother*). ● *n.* (often prec. by *the*) **1** the older or more senior of two indicated (esp. related) persons (*which is the elder?*; *is my elder by ten years*). **2** (in *pl.*) **a** persons of greater age or sen-

iority (*respect your elders*). **b** persons venerable because of age. **3** a person advanced in life. **4** *hist.* a member of a senate or governing body. **5** an official in the early Christian, Presbyterian, or Mormon churches. □ **elder hand** *Cards* the first player. **elder statesman** an influential experienced person, esp. a politician, of advanced age. □□ **eldership** *n.* [OE *eldra*, rel. to OLD]

■ *attrib.adj.* older, senior; venerable, veteran. ● *n.* **2** (*elders*) superiors, seniors; patriarchs, matriarchs, elder statesmen, doyens, deans.

elder² /éldər/ *n.* any shrub or tree of the genus *Sambucus*, with white flowers and usu. blue-black or red berries. [OE *ellærn*]

elderberry /éldərberee/ *n.* (*pl.* **-ies**) the berry of the elder, esp. common elder (*Sambucus nigra*) used for making jelly, wine, etc.

elderly /éldərlee/ *adj. & n.* ● *adj.* **1** somewhat old. **2** (of a person) past middle age. ● *n.* (*collect.*) (prec. by *the*) elderly people. □□ **elderliness** *n.*

■ *adj.* **2** old, past middle age, oldish, advanced in years, of advanced age, gray, aging, aged, venerable, hoary, ancient, long in the tooth, senescent; decrepit, superannuated, infirm; senile; *colloq.* over the hill, past it. ● *n.* (**the elderly**) the retired, the old, senior citizens, oldsters, golden-agers, *Brit.* pensioners, OAPs, old-age pensioners, *colloq.* old-timers, (old) geezers, (old) fogies *or* fogeys.

eldest /éldist/ *adj. & n.* ● *adj.* first-born or oldest surviving (member of a family, son, daughter, etc.). ● *n.* (often prec. by *the*) the eldest of three or more indicated (*who is the eldest?*). □ **eldest hand** *Cards* the first player. [OE (as ELDER¹)]

El Dorado /éldəráadō/ *n.* (*pl.* **-os**) **1** any imaginary country or city abounding in gold. **2** a place of great abundance. [Sp. *el dorado* the gilded]

eldritch /éldrich/ *adj. Sc.* **1** weird. **2** hideous. [16th c.: perh. f. OE *elfrīce* (unrecorded) 'fairy realm']

elec. *abbr.* **1** electric. **2** electrical. **3** electricity.

elecampane /élikampáyn/ *n.* **1** a sunflowerlike plant, *Inula helenium*, with bitter aromatic leaves and roots, used in herbal medicine and cookery. **2** an esp. candied confection flavored with this. [corrupt. of med.L *enula* (for L *inula* f. Gk *helenion*) *campana* (prob. = of the fields)]

elect /ilékt/ *v. & adj.* ● *v.tr.* **1** (usu. foll. by *to* + infin.) choose (*the principles they elected to follow*). **2** choose (a person) by vote (*elected a new chairman*). **3** *Theol.* (of God) choose (persons) in preference to others for salvation. ● *adj.* **1** chosen. **2** select; choice. **3** *Theol.* chosen by God. **4** (after a noun designating office) chosen but not yet in office (*president elect*). [ME f. L *electus* past part. of *eligere elect-* (as E-, *legere* pick)]

■ *v.* **1, 2** select, pick, determine, designate; see also CHOOSE 1, 3, VOTE *v.* 1. ● *adj.* **1** chosen, elected, selected. **2** see CHOICE *adj.*

election /ilékshən/ *n.* **1** the process of electing or being elected, esp. of members of a political body. **2** the act or an instance of electing. [ME f. OF f. L *electio -onis* (as ELECT)]

■ **1** selection, choice, nomination, designation, appointment. **2** poll, vote, referendum, plebiscite.

electioneer /ilékshəneér/ *v. & n.* ● *v.intr.* take part in an election campaign. ● *n.* a person who electioneers.

■ *v.* canvass, campaign, stump, *Brit.* stand.

elective /iléktiv/ *adj. & n.* ● *adj.* **1 a** (of an office or its holder) filled or appointed by election. **b** (of authority) derived from election. **2** (of a body) having the power to elect. **3** having a tendency to act on or be concerned with some things rather than others (*elective affinity*). **4** (of a course of study) chosen by the student; optional. **5** (of a surgical operation, etc.) optional; not urgently necessary. ● *n.* an elective course of study. □□ **electively** *adv.* [F *électif -ive* f. LL *electivus* (as ELECT)]

■ *adj.* **4, 5** see OPTIONAL.

elector /iléktər/ *n.* **1** a person who has the right of voting. **2** (also **Elector**) *hist.* a German prince entitled to take part in the election of the emperor. **3** a member of the electoral college. □□ **electorship** n. [ME f. F *électeur* f. L *elector* (as ELECT)]

electoral /iléktərəl/ adj. relating to or ranking as electors. □ **electoral college 1** a body of persons representing each of the states of the US, who cast votes for the election of the president and vice president. **2** a body of electors. □□ **electorally** adv.

electorate /iléktərət/ n. **1** a body of electors. **2** *Austral.* & *NZ* an area represented by one member of parliament. **3** *hist.* the office or territories of a German elector.

Electra complex /iléktrə/ n. *Psychol.* a daughter's subconscious sexual attraction to her father and hostility toward her mother, corresponding to the Oedipus complex in a son. [*Electra* in Gk tragedy, who caused her mother to be murdered for having murdered Electra's father]

electret /iléktrit/ n. *Physics* a permanently polarized piece of dielectric material, analogous to a permanent magnet. [ELECTRICITY + MAGNET]

electric /iléktrik/ adj. & n. • adj. **1** of, worked by, or charged with electricity; producing or capable of generating electricity. **2** causing or charged with sudden and dramatic excitement (*the news had an electric effect; the atmosphere was electric*). • n. **1** an electric light, vehicle, etc. **2** (in *pl.*) electrical equipment. □ **electric blanket** a blanket that can be heated electrically by an internal element. **electric blue** a steely or brilliant light blue. **electric chair** an electrified chair used for capital punishment. **electric eel** an eellike freshwater fish, *Electrophorus electricus*, native to S. America, that kills its prey by electric shock. **electric eye** *colloq.* a photoelectric cell operating a relay when the beam of light illuminating it is obscured. **electric fence** a fence charged with electricity, often consisting of one strand. **electric field** a region of electrical influence. **electric fire** *Brit.* a usu. portable electric heater. **electric guitar** a guitar with a built-in electrical sound pickup rather than a soundbox. **electric organ 1** *Biol.* the organ in some fishes giving an electric shock. **2** *Mus.* an electrically operated organ. **electric ray** any of several rays that can give an electric shock (see RAY²). **electric razor** (or **shaver**) an electrical device for shaving, with oscillating blades behind a metal guard. **electric shock** the effect of a sudden discharge of electricity on a person or animal, usually with stimulation of the nerves and contraction of the muscles. **electric storm** a violent disturbance of the electrical condition of the atmosphere. □□ **electrically** adv. [mod.L *electricus* f. L *electrum* f. Gk *ēlektron* amber, the rubbing of which causes electrostatic phenomena]
■ adj. **2** charged, alive, electrical, buzzing, astir, tense, energized, stimulating, exciting, thrilling, electrifying, moving, stirring, dynamic.

electrical /iléktrikəl/ adj. **1** of or concerned with or of the nature of electricity. **2** operating by electricity. **3** suddenly or dramatically exciting (*the effect was electrical*). □ **electrical tape** an adhesive tape used to cover exposed electrical wires, etc.

electrician /iléktríshən, eélek-/ n. a person who installs or maintains electrical equipment, esp. professionally.

electricity /iléktrísitee, eélek-/ n. **1** a form of energy resulting from the existence of charged particles (electrons, protons, etc.), either statically as an accumulation of charge or dynamically as a current. **2** the branch of physics dealing with electricity. **3** a supply of electric current for heating, lighting, etc. **4** a state of heightened emotion; excitement; tension.
■ **4** excitement, verve, energy, tension, tenseness, fervency, intensity, ardor.

electrify /iléktrifī/ v.tr. (**-ies, -ied**) **1** charge (a body) with electricity. **2** convert (machinery or the place or system employing it) to the use of electric power. **3** cause dramatic or sudden excitement in. □□ **electrification** /-fikáyshən/ n. **electrifier** n.
■ **3** excite, galvanize, animate, move, rouse, stir, stimulate, vitalize, fire, thrill, arouse, charge, energize.

electro /iléktrō/ n. & v. • n. (*pl.* **-os**) **1** = ELECTROTYPE n. **2** = ELECTROPLATE n. • v.tr. (**-oes, -oed**) *colloq.* **1** = ELECTROTYPE v. **2** = ELECTROPLATE v. [abbr.]

electro- /iléktrō/ comb. form Electr. of, relating to, or caused by electricity (*electrocute; electromagnet*). [Gk *ēlektron* amber: see ELECTRIC]

electrobiology /iléktrōbíóləjee/ n. the study of the electrical phenomena of living things.

electrocardiogram /iléktrōkaárdeeəgram/ n. a record of the heartbeat traced by an electrocardiograph. [G *Elektrocardiogramm* (as ELECTRO-, CARDIO-, -GRAM)]

electrocardiograph /iléktrōkaárdeeəgraf/ n. an instrument recording the electric currents generated by a person's heartbeat. □□ **electrocardiographic** adj. **electrocardiography** /-deeógrəfee/ n.

electrochemical /iléktrōkémikəl/ adj. involving electricity as applied to or occurring in chemistry. □□ **electrochemist** n. **electrochemistry** n.

electroconvulsive /iléktrōkənvúlsiv/ adj. (of a therapy) employing the use of the convulsive response to the application of electric shocks.

electrocute /iléktrəkyōōt/ v.tr. **1** kill by electricity (as a form of capital punishment). **2** cause death of by electric shock. □□ **electrocution** /-kyoóshən/ n. [ELECTRO-, after EXECUTE]

electrode /iléktrōd/ n. a conductor through which electricity enters or leaves an electrolyte, gas, vacuum, etc. [ELECTRIC + Gk *hodos* way]

electrodialysis /iléktrōdíálisis/ n. dialysis in which electrodes are placed on either side of a semipermeable membrane, as used in obtaining pure water from salt water.

electrodynamics /iléktrōdínámiks/ n.pl. (usu. treated as *sing.*) the branch of mechanics concerned with electric current applied to motive forces. □□ **electrodynamic** adj.

electroencephalogram /iléktrōinséfələgram/ n. a record of the brain's activity traced by an electroencephalograph. [G *Elektrenkephalogramm* (as ELECTRO-, ENCEPHALO-, -GRAM)]

electroencephalograph /iléktrōinséfələgraf/ n. an instrument recording the electrical activity of the brain. □□ **electroencephalography** /-lógrəfee/ n.

electroluminescence /iléktrōlōōminésəns/ n. *Chem.* luminescence produced electrically, esp. by the application of a voltage. □□ **electroluminescent** /-sənt/ adj.

electrolysis /iléktrólisis, eélek-/ n. **1** *Chem.* the decomposition of a substance by the application of an electric current. **2** *Med.* this process applied to the destruction of tumors, hair roots, etc. □□ **electrolytic** /iléktrōlítik/ adj. **electrolytical** adj. **electrolytically** adv. [ELECTRO- + -LYSIS]

electrolyte /iléktrəlīt/ n. **1** a substance that conducts electricity when molten or in solution, esp. in an electric cell or battery. **2** a solution of this. [ELECTRO- + Gk *lutos* released f. *luō* loosen]

electrolyze /iléktrəlīz/ v.tr. (*Brit.* **-yse**) subject to or treat by electrolysis. □□ **electrolyzer** n. [ELECTROLYSIS after *analyze*]

electromagnet /iléktrōmágnit/ n. a soft metal core made into a magnet by the passage of electric current through a coil surrounding it.

electromagnetic /iléktrōmagnétik/ adj. having both an electrical and a magnetic character or properties. □ **electromagnetic radiation** a kind of radiation including visible light, radio waves, gamma rays, X rays, etc., in which electric and magnetic fields vary simultaneously. **electromagnetic spectrum** the range of wavelengths over which electromagnetic radiation extends. **electromagnetic units** a system of units derived primarily from the magnetic properties of electric currents. □□ **electromagnetically** adv.

electromagnetism /iléktrōmágnitizəm/ n. **1** the magnetic forces produced by electricity. **2** the study of this.

electromechanical /iléktrōmikánikəl/ adj. relating to the application of electricity to mechanical processes, devices, etc.

electrometer /ilektrómitər, eélek-/ n. an instrument for measuring electrical potential without drawing any current

---

/.../ **pronunciation**	● **part of speech**
□ **phrases, idioms, and compounds**	
□□ **derivatives**	■ **synonym section**
cross-references appear in SMALL CAPITALS or *italics*	

from the circuit. □□ **electrometric** /-métrik/ *adj.* **electrometry** *n.*

electromotive /iléktrōmṓtiv/ *adj.* producing or tending to produce an electric current. □ **electromotive force** a force set up in an electric circuit by a difference in potential.

electron /iléktron/ *n.* a stable elementary particle with a charge of negative electricity, found in all atoms and acting as the primary carrier of electricity in solids. □ **electron beam** a stream of electrons in a gas or vacuum. **electron diffraction** the diffraction of a beam of electrons by atoms or molecules, used for determining crystal structures, etc. **electron gun** a device for producing a narrow stream of electrons from a heated cathode. **electron lens** a device for focusing a stream of electrons by means of electric or magnetic fields. **electron microscope** a microscope with high magnification and resolution, employing electron beams in place of light and using electron lenses. **electron pair** an electron and a positron. **electron spin resonance** a spectroscopic method of locating electrons within the molecules of a paramagnetic substance. ¶ Abbr.: **ESR**. [ELECTRIC + -ON]

electronegative /iléktrōnégətiv/ *adj.* **1** electrically negative. **2** *Chem.* (of an element) tending to acquire electrons.

electronic /ilektrónik, eélek-/ *adj.* **1 a** produced by or involving the flow of electrons. **b** of or relating to electrons or electronics. **2** (of a device) using electronic components. **3 a** (of music) produced by electronic means, and usu. recorded on tape. **b** (of a musical instrument) producing sounds by electronic means. □ **electronic flash** a device that produces a flash of light from a gas-discharge tube, used in high-speed photography. **electronic mail** messages distributed by electronic means, esp. from one computer system to one or more recipients: also called E-MAIL. **electronic publishing** the publication of books, etc., in machine-readable form rather than on paper. □□ **electronically** *adv.*

electronics /ilektróniks, eélek-/ *n.pl.* (usu. treated as *sing.*) **1** a branch of physics and technology concerned with the behavior and movement of electrons in a vacuum, gas, semiconductor, etc. **2** the circuits used in this.

electronvolt /iléktronvōlt/ *n.* a unit of energy equal to the work done on an electron in accelerating it through a potential difference of one volt. ¶ Abbr.: **eV**.

electrophilic /iléktrōfílik/ *adj. Chem.* having an affinity for electrons. □□ **electrophile** /iléktrōfīl/ *n.*

electrophoresis /iléktrōfəreésis/ *n. Physics & Chem.* the movement of colloidal particles in a fluid under the influence of an electric field. □□ **electrophoretic** /-fərétik/ *adj.* [ELECTRO- + Gk *phorēsis* being carried]

electrophorus /iléktrófərəs, eélek-/ *n.* a device for repeatedly generating static electricity by induction. [mod.L f. ELECTRO- + Gk *-phoros* bearing]

electroplate /iléktrəplayt/ *v. & n.* ● *v.tr.* coat (a utensil, etc.) by electrolytic deposition with chromium, silver, etc. ● *n.* electroplated articles. □□ **electroplater** *n.*

electropositive /iléktrōpózitiv/ *adj.* **1** electrically positive. **2** *Chem.* (of an element) tending to lose electrons.

electroscope /iléktrəskōp/ *n.* an instrument for detecting and measuring electricity, esp. as an indication of the ionization of air by radioactivity. □□ **electroscopic** /-skópik/ *adj.*

electroshock /iléktrōshok/ *attrib.adj.* (of medical treatment) by means of electric shocks.

electrostatic /iléktrōstátik/ *adj.* of electricity at rest. □ **electrostatic units** a system of units based primarily on the forces between electric charges. [ELECTRO- + STATIC after *hydrostatic*]

electrostatics /iléktrōstátiks/ *n.pl.* (treated as *sing.*) the study of electricity at rest.

electrotechnology /iléktrōteknóləjee/ *n.* the science of the application of electricity in technology. □□ **electrotechnic** /-téknik/ *adj.* **electrotechnical** *adj.* **electrotechnics** *n.*

electrotherapy /iléktrōthérəpee/ *n.* the treatment of diseases by the use of electricity. □□ **electrotherapeutic**

/-pyōótik/ *adj.* **electrotherapeutical** *adj.* **electrotherapist** *n.*

electrothermal /iléktrōthə́rməl/ *adj.* relating to heat electrically derived.

electrotype /iléktrōtīp/ *v. & n.* ● *v.tr.* copy by the electrolytic deposition of copper on a mold, esp. for printing. ● *n.* a copy so formed. □□ **electrotyper** *n.*

electrovalent /iléktrōváylənt/ *adj. Chem.* linking ions by a bond resulting from electrostatic attraction. □□ **electrovalence** /-ləns/ *n.* **electrovalency** *n.* [ELECTRO- + -*valent* after *trivalent*, etc.]

electrum /iléktrəm/ *n.* **1** an alloy of silver and gold used in ancient times. **2** native argentiferous gold ore. [ME f. L f. Gk *ēlektron* amber, electrum]

electuary /ilékchōóeree/ *n.* (*pl.* **-ies**) medicinal powder, etc., mixed with honey or other sweet substance. [ME f. LL *electuarium*, prob. f. Gk *ekleikton* f. *ekleikhō* lick up]

eleemosynary /éləmósineree, -móz-, éleeə-/ *adj.* **1** of or dependent on alms. **2** charitable. **3** gratuitous. [med.L *eleemosynarius* f. LL *eleemosyna*: see ALMS]
■ **2** see CHARITABLE 1.

elegant /éligənt/ *adj.* **1** graceful in appearance or manner. **2** tasteful; refined. **3** (of a mode of life, etc.) of refined luxury. **4** ingeniously simple and pleasing. **5** excellent. □□ **elegance** /-gəns/ *n.* **elegantly** *adv.* [F *élégant* or L *elegant-*, rel. to *eligere*: see ELECT]
■ **1, 2** tasteful, exquisite, handsome, graceful, superior, fine, select, refined; delicate, discerning, dignified, genteel, sophisticated, cultivated, polished, urbane, suave, soigné, well-groomed, debonair, well-bred. **3** luxurious, sumptuous, grand, opulent, plush, swanky, smart, high-class, *colloq.* ritzy, swank. **4** apt, clever, ingenious, neat. **5** see EXCELLENT. □□ **elegance** refinement, grace, tastefulness, good taste, gentility, polish, culture, propriety, dignity; luxury, grandeur, luxuriousness, opulence, sumptuousness, exquisiteness, plushness, splendor, beauty, handsomeness, smartness, swankiness, *colloq.* ritziness.

elegiac /élijíək, ileéjeeak/ *adj. & n.* ● *adj.* **1** (of a meter) used for elegies. **2** mournful. ● *n.* (in *pl.*) verses in an elegiac meter. □ **elegiac couplet** a pair of lines consisting of a dactylic hexameter and a pentameter, esp. in Greek and Latin verse. □□ **elegiacally** *adv.* [F *élégiaque* or f. LL *elegiacus* f. Gk *elegeiakos*: see ELEGY]

elegize /élijīz/ *v.* **1** *intr.* (often foll. by *upon*) write an elegy. **2** *intr.* write in a mournful strain. **3** *tr.* write an elegy upon. □□ **elegist** *n.*

elegy /élijee/ *n.* (*pl.* **-ies**) **1** a song of lament, esp. for the dead (sometimes vaguely used of other poems). **2** a poem in elegiac meter. [F *élégie* or L *elegia* f. Gk *elegeia* f. *elegos* mournful poem]
■ **1** see LAMENT *n.* 2.

elem. *abbr.* elementary.

element /élimənt/ *n.* **1** a component part or group; a contributing factor or thing. **2** *Chem. & Physics* any of the hundred or so substances that cannot be resolved by chemical means into simpler substances. **3 a** any of the four substances (earth, water, air, and fire) in ancient and medieval philosophy. **b** any of these as a being's natural abode or environment. **c** a person's appropriate or preferred sphere of operation. **4** *Electr.* a resistance wire that heats up in an electric heater, cooker, etc.; an electrode. **5** (in *pl.*) atmospheric agencies, esp. wind and storm. **6** (in *pl.*) the rudiments of learning or of a branch of knowledge. **7** (in *pl.*) the bread and wine of the Eucharist. **8** *Math. & Logic* an entity that is a single member of a set. □ **in** (or **out of**) **one's element** in (or out of) one's accustomed or preferred surroundings. **reduced to its elements** analyzed. [ME f. OF f. L *elementum*]
■ **1** component, constituent, ingredient, part, unit, piece, segment, feature, detail, particular; factor; sector, group. **3 c** environment, surroundings, atmosphere, situation, locale, territory, sphere, habitat, medium, domain. **5** (*elements*) (adverse *or* unfavorable) weather; outdoors. **6** (*elements*) rudiments, basics, fundamentals,

foundations, essentials, principles. □ **reduced to its elements** (*reduce to its elements*) see ANALYZE 1, 2.

elemental /élimént'l/ *adj. & n.* ● *adj.* **1** of the four elements. **2** of the powers of nature (*elemental worship*). **3** comparable to a force of nature (*elemental grandeur*; *elemental tumult*). **4** uncompounded (*elemental oxygen*). **5** essential. ● *n.* an entity or force thought to be physically manifested by occult means. □□ **elementalism** *n.* (in senses 1, 2). [med.L *elementalis* (as ELEMENT)]

■ *adj.* **2, 3** primal, original, primordial, primitive. **5** basic, fundamental, key, main; see also INTRINSIC.

elementary /éliméntəree, -tree/ *adj.* **1 a** dealing with or arising from the simplest facts of a subject; rudimentary; introductory. **b** simple. **2** *Chem.* not decomposable. □ **elementary particle** *Physics* any of several subatomic particles supposedly not decomposable into simpler ones. **elementary school** a school in which elementary subjects are taught to young children. □□ **elementarily** /-tárəlee/ *adv.* **elementariness** *n.* [ME f. L *elementarius* (as ELEMENT)]

■ **1 a** rudimentary, basic, fundamental, primary, introductory, initial, beginning, elemental. **b** simple, straightforward, uncomplicated, clear, understandable, plain; see also EASY *adj.* 1. □ **elementary school** primary school, grade school, *Brit.* first school.

elenchus /iléngkəs/ *n.* (*pl.* **elenchi** /-kī/) *Logic* logical refutation. □ **Socratic elenchus** an attempted refutation of an opponent's position by short question and answer. □□ **elenctic** *adj.* [L f. Gk *elegkhos*]

elephant /élifənt/ *n.* (*pl.* same or **elephants**) **1** the largest living land animal, of which two species survive, the larger African (*Loxodonta africana*) and the smaller Indian (*Elephas maximus*), both with a trunk and long curved ivory tusks. **2** *Brit.* a size of paper (23 x 28 in). □ **elephant grass** any of various tall African grasses, esp. *Pennisetum purpureum*. **elephant seal** any large seal of the genus *Mirounga*, the male of which has a proboscis: also called *sea elephant*. **elephant shrew** any small insect-eating mammal of the family Macroscelididae, native to Africa, having a long snout and long hind limbs. □□ **elephantoid** /-fantóyd/ *adj.* [ME *olifaunt*, etc., f. OF *oli-*, *elefant* ult. f. L *elephantus*, *elephans* f. Gk *elephas -antos* ivory, elephant]

elephantiasis /élifəntíəsis/ *n.* gross enlargement of the body, esp. the limbs, due to lymphatic obstruction, esp. by a nematode parasite. [L f. Gk (as ELEPHANT)]

elephantine /élifánteen, -tīn, éləfən-/ *adj.* **1** of elephants. **2 a** huge. **b** clumsy; unwieldy (*elephantine movements*; *elephantine humor*). [L *elephantinus* f. Gk *elephantinos* (as ELEPHANT)]

■ **2 a** see HUGE 1. **b** see PONDEROUS 1.

Eleusinian /élyōōsíneeən/ *adj.* of or relating to Eleusis near Athens. □ **Eleusinian mysteries** *Gk Hist.* the annual celebrations held at ancient Eleusis in honor of Demeter. [L *Eleusinius* f. Gk *Eleusinios*]

elev. *abbr.* elevation.

elevate /élivayt/ *v.tr.* **1** bring to a higher position. **2** *Eccl.* hold up (the Host or the chalice) for adoration. **3** raise; lift (one's eyes, etc.). **4** raise the axis of (a gun). **5** raise (a railroad, etc.) above ground level. **6** exalt in rank, etc. **7** (usu. as **elevated** *adj.*) **a** raise the spirits of; elate. **b** raise morally or intellectually (*elevated style*). **8** (as **elevated** *adj.*) *colloq.* slightly drunk. □□ **elevatory** *adj.* [L *elevare* raise (as E-, *levis* light)]

■ **3** raise, upraise, uplift, lift (up). **6** see EXALT 1. **7 a** (**elevated**) elated, cheerful, happy, exhilarated, animated, joyful, glad. **b** see CIVILIZE; (**elevated**) uplifted, noble, lofty, high, grand, exalted, dignified, eminent, preeminent, ennobled, notable, illustrious, distinguished, imposing, impressive, sublime. **8** (**elevated**) see JOLLY¹ *adj.* 3.

elevation /éliv, áyshən/ *n.* **1 a** the process of elevating or being elevated. **b** the angle with the horizontal, esp. of a gun or of the direction of a heavenly body. **c** the height above a given level, esp. sea level. **d** a raised area; a swelling on the skin. **2** loftiness; grandeur; dignity. **3 a** a drawing or diagram made by projection on a vertical plane (cf. PLAN). **b** a flat drawing of the front, side, or back of a house, etc. **4** *Ballet*

a the capacity of a dancer to attain height in springing movements. **b** the action of tightening the muscles and uplifting the body. □□ **elevational** *adj.* (in sense 2). [ME f. OF *elevation* or L *elevatio*: see ELEVATE]

■ **1 a** advancement, promotion, advance; exaltation; uplifting, raising. **c** altitude, height. **d** hill, height, rise, hillock, prominence; swelling, lump, wen. **2** grandeur, nobleness, loftiness, exaltation, sublimity, distinction, dignity, refinement, cultivation.

elevator /élivaytər/ *n.* **1** a hoisting machine. **2** *Aeron.* the movable part of a tailplane for changing the pitch of an aircraft. **3 a** a platform or compartment housed in a shaft for raising and lowering persons or things to different floors of a building or different levels of a mine, etc. **b** a place for lifting and storing quantities of grain. **4** that which elevates, esp. a muscle that raises a limb. [mod.L (as ELEVATE)]

eleven /ilévən/ *n. & adj.* ● *n.* **1** one more than ten; the sum of six units and five units. **2** a symbol for this (11, xi, XI). **3** a size, etc., denoted by eleven. **4** a set or team of eleven individuals. **5** the time of eleven o'clock (*is it eleven yet?*). ● *adj.* that amount to eleven. [OE *endleofon* f. Gmc]

elevenfold /ilévənfōld/ *adj. & adv.* **1** eleven times as much or as many. **2** consisting of eleven parts.

elevenses /ilévənziz/ *n.* (usu. in *pl.*) *Brit. colloq.* light refreshment, usu. with tea or coffee, taken about 11 a.m.

eleventh /ilévənth/ *n. & adj.* ● *n.* **1** the position in a sequence corresponding to the number 11 in the sequence 1–11. **2** something occupying this position. **3** one of eleven equal parts of a thing. **4** *Mus.* **a** an interval or chord spanning an octave and a third in the diatonic scale. **b** a note separated from another by this interval. ● *adj.* that is the eleventh. □ **the eleventh hour** the last possible moment.

elevon /élivon/ *n. Aeron.* the movable part of the trailing edge of a delta wing. [ELEVATOR + AILERON]

elf /elf/ *n.* (*pl.* **elves** /elvz/) **1** a mythological being, esp. one that is small and mischievous. **2** a sprite or little creature. □□ **elfish** *adj.* **elvish** *adj.* [OE f. Gmc]

■ sprite, fairy, puck, *literary* fay; see also GOBLIN.

elfin /élfin/ *adj. & n.* ● *adj.* of elves; elflike; tiny; dainty. ● *n.* archaic a dwarf; a child. [ELF, perh. infl. by ME *elvene* genit. pl. of *elf*, and by *Elphin* in Arthurian romance]

■ *adj.* elvish, elfish, elflike, impish, puckish; frolicsome, sprightly, playful, mischievous; small, diminutive, tiny, little, dainty, lilliputian, esp. *Sc. or colloq.* wee.

elflock /élflok/ *n.* (usu. in *pl.*) a tangled mass of hair.

elicit /ilísit/ *v.tr.* **1** draw out; evoke (an admission, response, etc.). **2** draw forth (what is latent). □□ **elicitation** *n.* **elicitor** *n.* [L *elicere elicit-* (as E-, *lacere* entice)]

■ **1** draw out *or* forth, call forth, evoke, bring out *or* forth, bring to light, extract, get, wring, wrest, wrench.

elide /ilíd/ *v.tr.* omit (a vowel or syllable) by elision. [L *elidere elis-* crush out (as E-, *laedere* knock)]

eligible /élijibəl/ *adj.* **1** (often foll. by *for*) fit or entitled to be chosen (*eligible for a rebate*). **2** desirable or suitable, esp. as a partner in marriage. □□ **eligibility** *n.* **eligibly** *adv.* [F *éligible* f. LL *eligibilis* (as ELECT)]

■ **1** fit, worthy, entitled, qualified, suitable, appropriate, fitting. **2** desirable, suitable, available, free.

eliminate /ilíminayt/ *v.tr.* **1 a** remove; get rid of. **b** kill; murder. **2** exclude from consideration; ignore as irrelevant. **3** exclude from further participation in a competition, etc., on defeat. **4** *Physiol.* discharge (waste matter). **5** *Chem.* remove (a simpler substance) from a compound. **6** *Algebra* remove (a quantity) by combining equations. □□ **eliminable** /-nəbəl/ *adj.* **elimination** /-náyshən/ *n.* **eliminator** *n.* **eliminatory** /-nətáwree/ *adj.* [L *eliminare* (as E-, *limen liminis* threshold)]

■ **1 a** remove, get rid of, dispose of, take out *or* away, erase, eradicate, expel, stamp out, expunge, obliterate;

/.../ **pronunciation**	● **part of speech**
□ **phrases, idioms, and compounds**	
□□ **derivatives**	■ **synonym section**
cross-references appear in SMALL CAPITALS or *italics*	

strike (out), cross out *or* off, cut (out), excise, delete, edit (out). **b** kill, murder, assassinate, terminate, exterminate, dispose of, liquidate, finish off, annihilate, destroy, *colloq.* polish off, *literary or joc.* slay, *sl.* bump off, rub out, take for a ride, bury, ice, waste. **2** exclude, rule out, drop, leave out, omit. **3** exclude, knock out; defeat, trounce.

elision /ilízhən/ *n.* **1** the omission of a vowel or syllable in pronouncing (as in *I'm, let's, e'en*). **2** the omission of a passage in a book, etc. [LL *elisio* (as ELIDE)]

elite /ayleét, əleét/ *adj. & n.* ● *n.* **1** (prec. by *the*) the best or choice part of a larger body or group. **2** a select group or class. **3** a size of letter in typewriting (12 per inch). ● *adj.* of or belonging to an elite; exclusive. [F f. past part. of *élire* f. Rmc: rel. to ELECT]

   ▪ *n.* **1** best, crème de la crème; see also CHOICE *n.* 3. **2** cream, gentry, aristocracy, aristocrats, elect, upper classes, nobility, privileged classes, four hundred, *colloq.* upper crust, beautiful people, esp. *iron.* superior persons. ● *adj.* aristocratic, elect, upper-class, privileged, blue-blooded, noble, exclusive, choice, best, top.

elitism /ayleétizəm, əleet-/ *n.* **1** advocacy of or reliance on leadership or dominance by a select group. **2** a sense of belonging to an elite. □□ **elitist** *n. & adj.*

elixir /iliksər/ *n.* **1** *Alchemy* **a** a preparation supposedly able to change metals into gold. **b** (in full **elixir of life**) a preparation supposedly able to prolong life indefinitely. **c** a supposed remedy for all ills. **2** *Pharm.* an aromatic solution used as a medicine or flavoring. **3** the quintessence or kernel of a thing. [ME f. med.L f. Arab. *al-iksīr* f. *al* the + *iksīr* prob. f. Gk *xērion* powder for drying wounds f. *xēros* dry]

   ▪ **1 c** panacea, cure-all, wonder drug, miracle drug, sovereign remedy. **3** pith, core, kernel, heart, essence, quintessence, principle, extract, base, basis, soul, PHILOS. quiddity.

Elizabethan /ilízəbeéthən/ *adj. & n.* ● *adj.* of the time of England's Queen Elizabeth I (1558–1603) or of Queen Elizabeth II (1952–). ● *n.* a person, esp. a writer, of the time of Queen Elizabeth I or II.

elk /elk/ *n.* (*pl.* same or **elks**) **1** a large deer, *Aces alces*, of N. Europe and Asia, with palmate antlers and a growth of skin hanging from the neck; a moose. **2** a wapiti. [ME, prob. repr. OE *elh, eolh*]

elkhound /élkhownd/ *n.* (in full **Norwegian elkhound**) a large Scandinavian hunting dog with a shaggy coat.

ell /el/ *n. hist.* a former measure of length, about 45 inches. [OE *eln*, rel. to L *ulna*: see ULNA]

ellipse /ilíps/ *n.* a regular oval, traced by a point moving in a plane so that the sum of its distances from two other points is constant, or resulting when a cone is cut by a plane that does not intersect the base and makes a smaller angle with the base than the side of the cone makes (cf. HYPERBOLA). [F f. L *ellipsus* f. Gk *elleipsis* f. *elleipō* come short f. *en* in + *leipō* leave]

ellipsis /ilípsis/ *n.* (*pl.* **ellipses** /-seez/) **1** the omission from a sentence of words needed to complete the construction or sense. **2** the omission of a sentence at the end of a paragraph. **3** a set of three dots, etc., indicating an omission.

ellipsoid /ilípsoyd/ *n.* a solid of which all the plane sections normal to one axis are circles and all the other plane sections are ellipses. □□ **ellipsoidal** /-sóyd'l/ *adj.*

   ▪ □□ **ellipsoidal** see OVAL *adj.*

elliptic /ilíptik/ *adj.* (also **elliptical**) of, relating to, or having the form of an ellipse or ellipsis. □□ **elliptically** *adv.* **ellipticity** /éliptísitee/ *n.* [Gk *elleiptikos* defective f. *elleipō* (as ELLIPSE)]

elm /elm/ *n.* **1** any tree of the genus *Ulmus*, esp. *U. procera* with rough serrated leaves. **2** (in full **elmwood**) the wood of the elm. □□ **elmy** *adj.* [OE, rel. to L *ulmus*]

elocution /éləkyóoshən/ *n.* **1** the art of clear and expressive speech, esp. of distinct pronunciation and articulation. **2** a particular style of speaking. □□ **elocutionary** *adj.* **elocutionist** *n.* [L *elocutio* f. *eloqui elocut-* speak out (as E-, *loqui* speak)]

   ▪ see SPEECH 3.

elongate /iláwnggayt, -long-/ *v. & adj.* ● *v.* **1** *tr.* lengthen; prolong. **2** *intr. Bot.* be of slender or tapering form. ● *adj. Bot. & Zool.* long in proportion to width. [LL *elongare* (as E-, L *longus* long)]

   ▪ *v.* **1** see LENGTHEN.

elongation /ilawnggáyshən, ilong-, eélawng-, eélong-/ *n.* **1** the act or an instance of lengthening; the process of being lengthened. **2** a part of a line, etc., formed by lengthening. **3** *Mech.* the amount of extension under stress. **4** *Astron.* the angular separation of a planet from the sun or of a satellite from a planet. [ME f. LL *elongatio* (as ELONGATE)]

elope /ilṓp/ *v.intr.* **1** run away to marry secretly, esp. without parental consent. **2** run away with a lover. □□ **elopement** *n.* **eloper** *n.* [AF *aloper* perh. f. a ME form *alope*, rel. to LEAP]

eloquence /éləkwəns/ *n.* **1** fluent and effective use of language. **2** rhetoric. [ME f. OF f. L *eloquentia* f. *eloqui* speak out (as E-, *loqui* speak)]

   ▪ see RHETORIC 1.

eloquent /éləkwənt/ *adj.* **1** possessing or showing eloquence. **2** (often foll. by *of*) clearly expressive or indicative. □□ **eloquently** *adv.* [ME f. OF f. L *eloqui* (as ELOQUENCE)]

   ▪ **1** articulate, silver-tongued, fluent, well-spoken, effective, persuasive, impressive, convincing, cogent, incisive; smooth, oratorical, rhetorical. **2** expressive, suggestive, indicative.

else /els/ *adv.* **1** (prec. by indef. or interrog. pron.) besides; in addition (*someone else; nowhere else; who else*). **2** instead; other; different (*what else could I say?; he did not love her, but someone else*). **3** otherwise; if not (*run, (or) else you will be late*). [OE *elles*, rel. to L *alius*, Gk *allos*]

elsewhere /éls-hwair, -wáir/ *adv.* in or to some other place. [OE *elles hwǣr* (as ELSE, WHERE)]

   ▪ somewhere else, to another place, abroad; in another place, absent, away.

eluant /élyōoənt/ *n.* (also **eluent**) *Chem.* a fluid used for elution. [L *eluere* wash out (as E-, *luere lut-* wash)]

eluate /élyōo-it, -ayt/ *n. Chem.* a solution or gas stream obtained by elution. [formed as ELUENT]

elucidate /ilṓosidáyt/ *v.tr.* throw light on; explain. □□ **elucidation** /-dáyshən/ *n.* **elucidative** *adj.* **elucidator** *n.* **elucidatory** *adj.* [LL *elucidare* (as E-, LUCID)]

   ▪ see EXPLAIN 1.

elude /ilṓod/ *v.tr.* **1** escape adroitly from (a danger, difficulty, pursuer, etc.); dodge. **2** avoid compliance with (a law, request, etc.) or fulfillment of (an obligation). **3** (of a fact, solution, etc.) escape from or baffle (a person's memory or understanding). □□ **elusion** /ilṓozhən/ *n.* **elusory** /-lṓosəree/ *adj.* [L *eludere elus-* (as E-, *ludere* play)]

   ▪ **1** evade, escape, avoid, dodge, slip away from, give the slip, shake off. **2** avoid, *colloq.* duck (out of); see also SIDESTEP *v.* **3** evade, escape; baffle, puzzle, confuse, bewilder, confound; frustrate, stump, thwart; see also FLOOR *v.* 3.

eluent var. of ELUANT.

elusive /ilṓosiv/ *adj.* **1** difficult to find or catch; tending to elude. **2** difficult to remember or recall. **3** (of an answer, etc.) avoiding the point raised; seeking to elude. □□ **elusively** *adv.* **elusiveness** *n.*

   ▪ **1** evasive, elusory, slippery, fugitive; indefinable, intangible, impalpable. **3** evasive, equivocal, indirect.

elute /ilṓot/ *v.tr. Chem.* remove (an adsorbed substance) by washing. □□ **elution** /-lṓoshən/ *n.* [L *eluere* (as ELUENT)]

elutriate /ilṓotreeayt/ *v.tr. Chem.* separate (lighter and heavier particles in a mixture) by suspension in an upward flow of liquid or gas. □□ **elutriation** /-áyshən/ *n.* [L *elutriare elutriat-* (as E-, *lutriare* wash)]

elver /élvər/ *n.* a young eel. [var. of *eel-fare* (see FARE) = a brood of young eels]

elves *pl.* of ELF.

elvish see ELF.

Elysium /ilízeeəm, ilízh-/ *n.* **1** (also **Elysian fields**) (in Greek mythology) the abode of the blessed after death. **2** a place or state of ideal happiness. □□ **elysian** or **Elysian** *adj.* [L f. Gk *Elusion* (*pedion* plain)]

elytron /élitron/ *n.* (*pl.* **elytra** /-trə/) the outer hard, usu. brightly colored wing case of a coleopterous insect. [Gk *elutron* sheath]

em /em/ *n.* *Printing* **1** a unit for measuring the amount of printed matter in a line, usually equal to the nominal width of capital M. **2** a unit of measurement equal to 12 points. □ **em rule** (or **dash**) a long dash used in punctuation. [name of the letter *M*]

em- /ɪm, em/ *prefix* assim. form of EN-¹, EN-² before *b*, *p*.

'em /əm/ *pron.* *colloq.* them (*let 'em all come*). [orig. a form of ME *hem*, dative and accus. 3rd pers. pl. pron.: now regarded as an abbr. of THEM]

emaciate /imáysheeayt/ *v.tr.* (esp. as **emaciated** *adj.*) make abnormally thin or feeble. □□ **emaciation** /-áyshən/ *n.* [L *emaciare emaciat-* (as E-, *macies* leanness)]
■ waste away, shrink, enfeeble, get thin; (**emaciated**) atrophied, shriveled, wizened, shrunken, haggard, gaunt, drawn, pinched, bony, skeletal, cadaverous, withered, wasted, consumptive, scrawny, skinny, thin, spare, undernourished, underfed, starved, half-starved, anorexic, anorectic, *Med.* phthisic.

E-mail /éemayl/ *n.* (also **e-mail**) = *electronic mail*.

emanate /émənayt/ *v.* **1** *intr.* (usu. foll. by *from*) (of an idea, rumor, etc.) issue; originate (from a source). **2** *intr.* (usu. foll. by *from*) (of gas, light, etc.) proceed; issue. **3** *tr.* emit; send forth. [L *emanare* flow out]
■ **1** see ORIGINATE 2. **2** issue, come (out), emerge, proceed, flow, ooze, exude; radiate, disperse. **3** radiate, give off *or* out, send out *or* forth, disseminate, discharge, put out, emit; ooze, exude.

emanation /émənáyshən/ *n.* **1** the act or process of emanating. **2** something that emanates from a source (esp. of virtues, qualities, etc.). **3** *Chem.* a radioactive gas formed by radioactive decay. □□ **emanative** *adj.* [LL *emanatio* (as EMANATE)]
■ **1** see OUTPOURING. **2** see AURA 1.

emancipate /imánsipayt/ *v.tr.* **1** free from restraint, esp. legal, social, or political. **2** (usu. as **emancipated** *adj.*) cause to be less inhibited by moral or social convention. **3** free from slavery. □□ **emancipation** /-páyshən/ *n.* **emancipator** *n.* **emancipatory** *adj.* [L *emancipare* transfer property (as E-, *manus* hand + *capere* take)]
■ **1, 3** release, liberate, deliver, loose, let loose, free, let go, set free; unfetter, unchain, unshackle, *hist.* enfranchise, manumit, *literary* disenthrall. **2** (**emancipated**) liberated, liberalized; uninhibited, free and easy, free.

emasculate *v.* & *adj.* ● *v.tr.* /imáskyəlayt/ **1** deprive of force or vigor; make feeble or ineffective. **2** castrate. ● *adj.* /imáskyələt/ **1** deprived of force or vigor. **2** castrated. **3** effeminate. □□ **emasculation** /-láyshən/ *n.* **emasculator** *n.* **emasculatory** /-lətáwree/ *adj.* [L *emasculatus* past part. of *emasculare* (as E-, *masculus* dimin. of *mas* male)]
■ *v.* **1** see WEAKEN 1. **2** see NEUTER *v.*

embalm /embáam, im-/ *v.tr.* **1** preserve (a corpse) from decay orig. with spices, now by means of arterial injection. **2** preserve from oblivion. **3** endue with balmy fragrance. □□ **embalmer** *n.* **embalmment** *n.* [ME f. OF *embaumer* (as EN-¹, BALM)]

embank /embángk, im-/ *v.tr.* shut in or confine (a river, etc.) with an artificial bank.

embankment /embángkmənt, im-/ *n.* an earth or stone bank for keeping back water, or for carrying a road or railroad.
■ see WALL *n.* 1.

embargo /embaárgō/ *n.* & *v.* ● *n.* (*pl.* **-oes**) **1** an order of a government forbidding foreign ships to enter, or any ships to leave, its ports. **2** an official suspension of commerce or other activity (*be under an embargo*). **3** an impediment. ● *v.tr.* (**-oes, -oed**) **1** place (ships, trade, etc.) under embargo. **2** seize (a ship, goods) for government service. [Sp. f. *embargar* arrest f. Rmc (as IN-², BAR¹)]
■ *n.* **1–3** restraint, block, blockage, bar, ban, stoppage, proscription, prohibition, interdiction, check, restriction, barrier; hindrance, impediment. ● *v.* **1**

restrain, block, bar, ban, stop, cease, proscribe, prohibit, interdict, prevent, restrict, hold back.

embark /embáark, im-/ *v.* **1** *tr.* & *intr.* (often foll. by *for*) put or go on board a ship or aircraft (to a destination). **2** *intr.* (foll. by *on*, *upon*) engage in an activity or undertaking. □□ **embarkation** *n.* (in sense 1). [F *embarquer* (as IN-², BARK³)]
■ **1** board, go aboard, get on; emplane. **2** (*embark on*) begin, enter (upon), undertake, initiate, launch on, start, go into, set about, take up *or* on, assume, tackle, *formal* commence.

embarras de choix /ónbaráa də shwaá/ *n.* (also **embarras de richesse(s)** /reeshés/) more choices than one needs or can deal with. [F, = embarrassment of choice, riches]

embarrass /embárəs, im-/ *v.tr.* **1 a** cause (a person) to feel awkward or self-conscious or ashamed. **b** (as **embarrassed** *adj.*) having or expressing a feeling of awkwardness or self-consciousness. **2** (as **embarrassed** *adj.*) encumbered with debts. **3** encumber; impede. **4** complicate (a question, etc.). **5** perplex. □□ **embarrassedly** *adv.* **embarrassing** *adj.* **embarrassingly** *adv.* **embarrassment** *n.* [F *embarrasser* (orig. = hamper) f. Sp. *embarazar* f. It. *imbarrare* bar in (as IN-², BAR¹)]
■ **1 b** (**embarrassed**) ashamed, self-conscious, uncomfortable, red-faced, shamefaced. □□ **embarrassing** awkward, uncomfortable, humiliating. **embarrassment** awkwardness, discomposure, discomfort, self-consciousness, mortification, chagrin; excess, superfluity, superabundance, surplus, profusion, *embarras de richesses*.

embassy /émbəsee/ *n.* (*pl.* **-ies**) **1 a** the residence or offices of an ambassador. **b** the ambassador and staff attached to an embassy. **2** a deputation or mission to a foreign country. [earlier *ambassy* f. OF *ambassée*, etc., f. med.L *ambasciata* f. Rmc (as AMBASSADOR)]

embattle /embát'l, im-/ *v.tr.* **1 a** set (an army, etc.) in battle array. **b** fortify against attack. **2** provide (a building or wall) with battlements. **3** (as **embattled** *adj.*) **a** prepared or arrayed for battle. **b** involved in a conflict or difficult undertaking. **c** *Heraldry* like battlements in form. [ME f. OF *embataillier* (as EN-¹, BATTLE): see BATTLEMENT]

embay /embáy, im-/ *v.tr.* **1** enclose in or as in a bay; shut in. **2** form (a coast) into bays. □□ **embayment** *n.*

embed /embéd, im-/ *v.tr.* (also **imbed**) (**-bedded, -bedding**) **1** (esp. as **embedded** *adj.*) fix firmly in a surrounding mass (*embedded in concrete*). **2** (of a mass) surround so as to fix firmly. **3** place in or as in a bed. □□ **embedment** *n.*
■ **1, 2** see IMPLANT *v.* 1.

embellish /embélish, im-/ *v.tr.* **1** beautify; adorn. **2** add interest to (a narrative) with fictitious additions. □□ **embellisher** *n.* **embellishment** *n.* [ME f. OF *embellir* (as EN-¹, *bel* handsome f. L *bellus*)]
■ **1** beautify, adorn, dress (up), trick out *or* up, enhance, elaborate, enrich, embroider, gild, garnish, decorate, ornament, deck (out), bedeck, trim, caparison, *colloq.* titivate. **2** elaborate, embroider, exaggerate, enhance, dress up. □□ **embellishment** decoration, ornamentation, elaboration, adornment, embroidery, garnishment, gilding, enrichment, beautification; exaggeration; ornament, enhancement, frill, trimming, extra, garnish.

ember¹ /émbər/ *n.* **1** (usu. in *pl.*) a small piece of glowing coal or wood in a dying fire. **2** an almost extinct residue of a past activity, feeling, etc. [OE *ǣmyrge* f. Gmc]
■ **2** remains, remnant, residue; see also VESTIGE 1.

ember² /émbər/ *n.* (in full **ember-goose**) = *great northern diver*. [Norw. *emmer*]

ember day /émbər/ *n.pl.* any of the days in the quarterly

/.../ **pronunciation**	● **part of speech**
□ **phrases, idioms, and compounds**	
□□ **derivatives**	■ **synonym section**
cross-references appear in SMALL CAPITALS or *italics*	

three-day periods traditionally reserved for fasting and prayer in the Christian Church, now associated with ordinations. [OE *ymbren* (n.), perh. f. *ymbryne* period f. *ymb* about + *ryne* course]

embezzle /embézəl, im-/ *v.tr.* (also *absol.*) divert (money, etc.) fraudulently to one's own use. □□ **embezzlement** *n.* **embezzler** *n.* [AF *embesiler* (as EN-¹, OF *besillier* maltreat, ravage, of unkn. orig.)]

■ misappropriate, peculate, misapply, misuse, make off *or* away with, *formal* defalcate; *colloq.* have one's hand in the till.

embitter /embítər, im-/ *v.tr.* **1** arouse bitter feelings in (a person). **2** make more bitter or painful. **3** render (a person or feelings) hostile. □□ **embitterment** *n.*

■ **1** sour, poison, envenom, aggrieve, pain, dispirit, make bitter; make angry *or* resentful *or* rancorous. **3** see EXASPERATE 1.

emblazon /embláyzən, im-/ *v.tr.* **1 a** portray conspicuously, as on a heraldic shield. **b** adorn (a shield) with heraldic devices. **2** adorn brightly and conspicuously. **3** celebrate, extol. □□ **emblazonment** *n.*

■ **1, 2** see ILLUMINATE 3.

emblem /émbləm/ *n.* **1** a symbol or representation typifying or identifying an institution, quality, etc. **2** (foll. by *of*) (of a person) the type (*the very emblem of courage*). **3** a heraldic device or symbolic object as a distinctive badge. □□ **emblematic** /-mátik/ *adj.* **emblematical** *adj.* **emblematically** *adv.* [ME f. L *emblema* f. Gk *emblēma -matos* insertion f. *emballō* throw in (as EN-¹, *ballō* throw)]

■ **1, 3** badge, symbol, representation, device, seal, crest, token, sign; trademark, logotype, *colloq.* logo. **2** see TYPE *n.* 2. □□ **emblematic, emblematical** symbolical, representational; see also REPRESENTATIVE *adj.* 4.

emblematize /imblémətiz/ *v.tr.* **1** serve as an emblem of. **2** represent by an emblem.

emblements /émblimənts/ *n.pl.* *Law* crops normally harvested annually, regarded as personal property. [ME f. OF *emblaement* f. *emblaier* (as EN-¹, *blé* grain)]

embody /embódee, im-/ *v.tr.* (**-ies, -ied**) **1** give a concrete or discernible form to (an idea, concept, etc.). **2** (of a thing or person) be an expression of (an idea, etc.). **3** express tangibly (*courage embodied in heroic actions*). **4** form into a body. **5** include; comprise. **6** provide (a spirit) with bodily form. □□ **embodiment** *n.*

■ **1, 3** concretize, realize, materialize, reify, actualize, incarnate, body forth; manifest, express, personify, demonstrate, epitomize. **2** typify, represent; see also EXEMPLIFY. **5** incorporate, comprise; see also INCLUDE 1. □□ **embodiment** incarnation, realization, concretization, manifestation, expression, personification, epitome, materialization, actualization, reification, substantiation; incorporation, inclusion.

embolden /embóldən, im-/ *v.tr.* (often foll. by *to* + infin.) make bold; encourage.

■ see ENCOURAGE 1.

embolism /émbəlizəm/ *n.* an obstruction of any artery by a clot of blood, air bubble, etc. [ME, = 'intercalation' f. LL *embolismus* f. Gk *embolismos* f. *emballō* (as EMBLEM)]

■ see STROKE *n.* 2.

embolus /émbələs/ *n.* (*pl.* **emboli** /-lī/) an object causing an embolism. [L, = piston, f. Gk *embolos* peg, stopper]

embonpoint /ónbawNpwáN/ *n.* plumpness (of a person). [F *en bon point* in good condition]

■ see *fatness* (FAT).

embosom /embŏŏzəm, im-/ *v.tr.* *literary* **1** embrace. **2** enclose; surround.

emboss /embós, im-/ *v.tr.* **1** carve or mold in relief. **2** form figures, etc., so that they stand out on (a surface). **3** make protuberant. □□ **embosser** *n.* **embossment** *n.* [ME, f. OF (as EN-¹, BOSS²)]

■ **2** chase.

embouchure /ómbŏŏshŏŏr/ *n.* **1** *Mus.* **a** the mode of applying the mouth to the mouthpiece of a brass or wind instrument. **b** the mouthpiece of some instruments. **2** the mouth

of a river. **3** the opening of a valley. [F f. *s'emboucher* discharge itself by the mouth (as EN-¹, *bouche* mouth)]

■ **2, 3** see MOUTH *n.* 3.

embowel /embówəl, im-/ *v.tr.* (**emboweled, emboweling**; esp. *Brit.* **embowelled, embowelling**) *archaic* = DISEMBOWEL. [OF *emboweler* f. *esboueler* (as EX-¹, BOWEL)]

embower /embówr, im-/ *v.tr.* *literary* enclose as in a bower.

embrace /embráys, im-/ *v. & n.* ● *v.tr.* **1 a** hold (a person) closely in the arms, esp. as a sign of affection. **b** (*absol.*, of two people) hold each other closely. **2** clasp; enclose. **3** accept eagerly (an offer, opportunity, etc.). **4** adopt (a course of action, doctrine, cause, etc.). **5** include; comprise. **6** take in with the eye or mind. ● *n.* an act of embracing; holding in the arms. □□ **embraceable** *adj.* **embracement** *n.* **embracer** *n.* [ME f. OF *embracer*, ult. f. L *in-* IN-¹ + *bracchium* arm]

■ *v.* **1** hug, clasp, grasp, hold, enfold, cuddle, enclasp, *archaic* clip, *colloq.* clinch, *literary* embosom, *poet.* fold. **2** see CLASP *v.* 2, ENCLOSE 1, 6. **3** see ACCEPT 2. **4** adopt, espouse, support, welcome, advocate. **5** include, comprise, embody, incorporate, comprehend, encompass. **6** see COMPREHEND 1. ● *n.* hug, squeeze, cuddle, clasp, *colloq.* clinch.

embranchment /embránchmənt, im-/ *n.* a branching out (of the arm of a river, etc.). [F *embranchement* BRANCH (as EN-¹, BRANCH)]

embrasure /embráyzhər, im-/ *n.* **1** the beveling of a wall at the sides of a door or window; splaying. **2** a small opening in a parapet of a fortified building, splayed on the inside. □□ **embrasured** *adj.* [F f. *embraser* splay, of unkn. orig.]

embrittle /embrít'l, im-/ *v.tr.* make brittle. □□ **embrittlement** *n.*

embrocation /émbrōkáyshən/ *n.* a liquid used for rubbing on the body to relieve muscular pain, etc. [F *embrocation* or med.L *embrocatio* ult. f. Gk *embrokhē* lotion]

■ see LOTION.

embroider /embróydər, im-/ *v.tr.* **1** (also *absol.*) **a** decorate (cloth, etc.) with needlework. **b** create (a design) in this way. **2** add interest to (a narrative) with fictitious additions. □□ **embroiderer** *n.* [ME f. AF *enbrouder* (as EN-¹, OF *brouder, broisder* f. Gmc)]

■ **1** see ORNAMENT *v.* **2** see EMBELLISH 2.

embroidery /embróydəree, im-/ *n.* (*pl.* **-ies**) **1** the art of embroidering. **2** embroidered work; a piece of this. **3** unnecessary or extravagant ornament. [ME f. AF *enbrouderie* (as EMBROIDER)]

■ **3** see ORNAMENT *n.* 1, 2.

embroil /embróyl, im-/ *v.tr.* **1** (often foll. by *with*) involve (a person) in conflict or difficulties. **2** bring (affairs) into a state of confusion. □□ **embroilment** *n.* [F *embrouiller* (as EN-¹, BROIL²)]

■ **1** see ENTANGLE 3. **2** see ENTANGLE 4.

embryo /émbreeō/ *n.* (*pl.* **-os**) **1 a** an unborn or unhatched offspring. **b** a human offspring in the first eight weeks from conception. **2** a rudimentary plant contained in a seed. **3** a thing in a rudimentary stage. **4** (*attrib.*) undeveloped; immature. □ **in embryo** undeveloped. □□ **embryoid** /-breeoyd/ *adj.* **embryonal** /émbreeənəl, émbreeōnəl/ *adj.* **embryonic** /émbreeónik/ *adj.* **embryonically** *adv.* [LL *embryo -onis* f. Gk *embruon* fetus (as EN-², *bruō* swell, grow)]

■ **3** see GERM 3.

embryo- /émbreeō/ *comb. form* embryo.

embryogenesis /émbreeōjénisis/ *n.* the formation of an embryo.

embryology /émbreeóləjee/ *n.* the study of embryos. □□ **embryologic** /-breeəlójik/ *adj.* **embryological** *adj.* **embryologically** *adv.* **embryologist** *n.*

embus /embús, im-/ *v.* (**embused, embusing** or **embussed, embussing**) *Mil.* **1** *tr.* put (men or equipment) into a motor vehicle. **2** *intr.* board a motor vehicle.

emcee /émsée/ *n. & v. colloq.* ● *n.* a master of ceremonies. ● *v.tr. & intr.* (**emcees, emceed**) act as a master of ceremonies. [the letters *MC*]

■ *n.* see MODERATOR 2. ● *v.* see PRESENT² *v.* 3b.

-eme /eem/ *suffix Linguistics* forming nouns denoting units of structure, etc. (*grapheme*; *morpheme*). [F *-ème* unit f. Gk *-ēma*]

emend /iménd/ *v.tr.* edit (a text, etc.) to remove errors and corruptions. □□ **emendation** /eémendáyshən/ *n.* **emendator** *n.* **emendatory** *adj.* [ME f. L *emendare* (as E-, *menda* fault)]
  ■ see REVISE *v.* 1.

emerald /émərəld, émrəld/ *n.* **1** a bright-green precious stone, a variety of beryl. **2** (also **emerald green**) the color of this. □ **Emerald Isle** *literary* Ireland. □□ **emeraldine** /-dīn, -dín/ *adj.* [ME f. OF *emeraude, esm-*, ult. f. Gk *smaragdos*]

emerge /imárj/ *v.intr.* (often foll. by *from*) **1** come up or out into view, esp. when formerly concealed. **2** come up out of a liquid. **3** (of facts, circumstances, etc.) come to light; become known, esp. as a result of inquiry, etc. **4** become recognized or prominent (*emerged as a leading contender*). **5** (of a question, difficulty, etc.) become apparent. **6** survive (an ordeal, etc.) with a specified result (*emerged unscathed*). □□ **emergence** *n.* [L *emergere emers-* (as E-, *mergere* dip)]
  ■ **1** appear, come out, come forth, come up, rise; arise, surface, come into view, be revealed. **3, 5** be revealed, come to light, turn out, become known, become apparent, transpire. **6** see SURVIVE 1. □□ **emergence** emersion, surfacing; materialization, manifestation; see also APPEARANCE 1.

emergency /imárjensee/ *n.* (*pl.* **-ies**) **1** a sudden state of danger, conflict, etc., requiring immediate action. **2 a** a medical condition requiring immediate treatment. **b** a patient with such a condition. **3** (*attrib.*) characterized by or for use in an emergency. □ **emergency medical technician** a person trained and licensed to provide basic medical assistance in emergencies. ¶ Abbr.: **EMT.** **emergency room** the part of a hospital that treats those requiring immediate medical attention. **state of emergency** a condition of danger or disaster affecting a country, esp. with normal constitutional procedures suspended. [med.L *emergentia* (as EMERGE)]
  ■ **1** crisis, exigency, danger, predicament, difficulty.

emergent /imárjent/ *adj.* **1** becoming apparent; emerging. **2** (of a nation) newly formed or made independent.

emeritus /imérités/ *adj.* **1** retired and retaining one's title as an honor (*emeritus professor*; *professor emeritus*). **2** honorably discharged from service. [L, past part. of *emerēri* (as E-, *merēri* earn)]
  ■ see OUTGOING *adj.* 2, 3.

emersion /imárzhən, -shən/ *n.* **1** the act or an instance of emerging. **2** *Astron.* the reappearance of a celestial body after its eclipse or occultation. [LL *emersio* (as EMERGE)]

emery /éməree/ *n.* **1** a coarse rock of corundum and magnetite or hematite used for polishing metal or other hard materials. **2** (*attrib.*) covered with emery. □ **emery board** a strip of thin wood or board coated with emery or another abrasive, used as a nail file. **emery cloth** cloth or paper covered with emery, used for polishing or cleaning metals, etc. [F *émeri(l)* f. It. *smeriglio* ult. f. Gk *smuris, smēris* polishing powder]

emetic /imétik/ *adj.* & *n.* ● *adj.* that causes vomiting. ● *n.* an emetic medicine. [Gk *emetikos* f. *emeō* vomit]
  ■ *adj.* see NAUSEOUS 2, 3.

EMF *abbr.* electromotive force.

-emia /eémeeə/ *comb. form* (also **-hemia** /heémeeə/, esp. *Brit.* **-aemia, -haemia** /heémeeə/) forming nouns denoting that a substance is (esp. excessively) present in the blood (*bacteremia*; *pyemia*). [mod.L f. GK *-aimia* f. *haima* blood]

emigrant /émigrənt/ *n.* & *adj.* ● *n.* a person who emigrates. ● *adj.* emigrating.
  ■ *n.* émigré, expatriate, settler, displaced person, DP, refugee, exile.

emigrate /émigrayt/ *v.* **1** *intr.* leave one's own country to settle in another. **2** *tr.* assist (a person) to emigrate. □□ **emigration** /-gráyshən/ *n.* **emigratory** /-grətáwree/ *adj.* [L *emigrare emigrat-* (as E-, *migrare* depart)]
  ■ **1** migrate, move, relocate, resettle; (*emigrate from*) leave, quit, depart.

émigré /émigray/ *n.* (also **emigré**) an emigrant, esp. a political exile. [F, past part. of *émigrer* EMIGRATE]
  ■ see EXILE *n.* 3.

eminence /éminəns/ *n.* **1** distinction; recognized superiority. **2** a piece of rising ground. **3** (**Eminence**) a title used in addressing or referring to a cardinal (*Your Eminence*; *His Eminence*). **4** an important person. [L *eminentia* (as EMINENT)]
  ■ **1** see DISTINCTION *n.* 4. **2** see RISE *n.* 2. **4** see WORTHY *n.* 2.

éminence grise /áymeenóns greéz/ *n.* (*pl.* **éminences grises** *pronunc.* same) **1** a person who exercises power or influence without holding office. **2** a confidential agent. [F, = gray cardinal (see EMINENCE): orig. applied to Cardinal Richelieu's private secretary, Père Joseph d. 1638]

eminent /éminənt/ *adj.* **1** distinguished; notable. **2** (of qualities) remarkable in degree. □ **eminent domain** sovereign control over all property in a government jurisdiction, with the right of expropriation. □□ **eminently** *adv.* [ME f. L *eminēre eminent-* jut]
  ■ **1** distinguished, esteemed, exalted, respected, revered, honored, notable, noteworthy, important, noted, outstanding, prominent, preeminent, conspicuous, superior, great, illustrious, famous, renowned, well-known, celebrated. **2** remarkable, conspicuous, outstanding, marked, singular. □□ **eminently** very, exceedingly, extremely, exceptionally, remarkably, singularly, signally.

emir /emeér/ *n.* **1** a title of various Muslim rulers. **2** *archaic* a male descendant of Muhammad. [F *émir* f. Arab. *'amīr*: cf. AMIR]

emirate /imeérit, -ayt, aymeér-, émərit/ *n.* the rank, domain, or reign of an emir.

emissary /émiseree/ *n.* (*pl.* **-ies**) a person sent on a special mission (usu. diplomatic, formerly usu. odious or underhand). [L *emissarius* scout, spy (as EMIT)]
  ■ see ENVOY¹.

emission /imíshən/ *n.* **1** (often foll. by *of*) the process or an act of emitting. **2** a thing emitted. [L *emissio* (as EMIT)]
  ■ **2** see DISCHARGE *n.* 5.

emissive /imísiv/ *adj.* having the power to radiate light, heat, etc. □□ **emissivity** /eémisívitee/ *n.*

emit /imít/ *v.tr.* (**emitted, emitting**) **1 a** send out (heat, light, vapor, etc.). **b** discharge from the body. **2** utter (a cry, etc.). [L *emittere emiss-* (as E-, *mittere* send)]
  ■ **1** discharge, eject, expel, emanate, send out *or* forth, pour out *or* forth, give off *or* out, vent, radiate; exude, ooze. **2** see VOICE *v.*

emitter /imítər/ *n.* that which emits, esp. a region in a transistor producing carriers of current.

Emmentaler /éməntaalər/ *n.* (also **Emmenthaler** or **Emmental** or **Emmenthal**) a kind of hard Swiss cheese with many holes in it, similar to Gruyère. [G *Emmentaler* f. *Emmental* in Switzerland]

emmer /émər/ *n.* a kind of wheat, *Triticum dicoccum*, grown mainly for fodder. [G dial.]

emmet /émit/ *n. archaic or dial.* an ant. [OE *ǣmete*: see ANT]

Emmy /émee/ *n.* (*pl.* **-ies**) one of the statuettes awarded annually to outstanding television programs and performers. [perh. f. *Immy* = *image orthicon tube*]

emollient /imólyənt/ *adj.* & *n.* ● *adj.* that softens or soothes the skin. ● *n.* an emollient agent. □□ **emollience** /-yəns/ *n.* [L *emollire* (as E-, *mollis* soft)]
  ■ *adj.* see *soothing* (SOOTHE). ● *n.* see OINTMENT.

emolument /imólyəmənt/ *n.* a salary, fee, or profit from employment or office. [ME f. OF *emolument* or L *emolumentum*, orig. prob. 'payment for grain-grinding,' f. *emolere* (as E-, *molere* grind)]
  ■ see SALARY *n.*

/. . ./ **pronunciation**	● **part of speech**
□ **phrases, idioms, and compounds**	
□□ **derivatives**	■ **synonym section**
cross-references appear in SMALL CAPITALS or *italics*	

emote /imṓt/ *v.intr. colloq.* show excessive emotion. □□ **emoter** *n.* [back-form. f. EMOTION]

emotion /imṓshən/ *n.* a strong mental or instinctive feeling such as love or fear. [earlier = agitation, disturbance of the mind, f. F *émotion* f. *émouvoir* excite]
■ feeling, passion, sentiment, sensation.

emotional /imṓshənəl/ *adj.* **1** of or relating to the emotions. **2** (of a person) liable to excessive emotion. **3** expressing or based on emotion (*an emotional appeal*). **4** likely to excite emotion (*an emotional issue*). □□ **emotionalism** *n.* **emotionalist** *n.* **emotionality** /-álitee/ *n.* **emotionalize** *v.tr.* **emotionally** *adv.*
■ **2** excitable, highly strung, high-strung, temperamental, volatile, hotheaded, demonstrative, irrational, hysterical, sentimental. **3** passionate, impassioned, ardent, enthusiastic, heated, zealous, heartfelt, excited, fervent, fervid. **4** sensitive, moving, poignant, stirring, emotive, affective, touching.

emotive /imṓtiv/ *adj.* **1** of or characterized by emotion. **2** tending to excite emotion. **3** arousing feeling; not purely descriptive. □□ **emotively** *adv.* **emotiveness** *n.* **emotivity** /éemōtívitee/ *n.* [L *emovēre emot-* (as E-, *movēre* move)]
■ see MOVING 2.

empanel /empánəl, im-/ esp. *Brit.* var. of IMPANEL.

empathize /émpəthīz/ *v. Psychol.* **1** *intr.* (usu. foll. by *with*) exercise empathy. **2** *tr.* treat with empathy.
■ (*empathize with*) see IDENTIFY 5.

empathy /émpəthee/ *n. Psychol.* the power of identifying oneself mentally with (and so fully comprehending) a person or object of contemplation. □□ **empathetic** /-thétik/ *adj.* **empathetically** *adv.* **empathic** /empáthik/ *adj.* **empathically** *adv.* **empathist** *n.* [transl. G *Einfühlung* f. *ein* in + *Fühlung* feeling, after Gk *empatheia*: see SYMPATHY]
■ see FEELING *n.* 3.

empennage /empénij/ *n. Aeron.* an arrangement of stabilizing surfaces at the tail of an aircraft. [F f. *empenner* to feather (an arrow)]

emperor /émpərər/ *n.* **1** the sovereign of an empire. **2** a sovereign of higher rank than a king. □ **emperor moth** a large moth, *Saturnia pavonia*, of the silk-moth family, with eye-spots on all four wings. **emperor penguin** the largest known penguin, *Aptenodytes forsteri*, of the Antarctic. □□ **emperorship** *n.* [ME f. OF *emperere, empereor* f. L *imperator -oris* f. *imperare* command]
■ see SOVEREIGN *n.* 1.

emphasis /émfəsis/ *n.* (*pl.* **emphases** /-seez/) **1** special importance or prominence attached to a thing, fact, idea, etc. (*emphasis on economy*). **2** stress laid on a word or words to indicate special meaning or importance. **3** vigor or intensity of expression, feeling, action, etc. **4** prominence, sharpness of contour. [L f. Gk f. *emphainō* exhibit (as EN-², *phainō* show)]
■ **1** importance, stress, significance, prominence, attention, weight, gravity, force, preeminence, priority. **3** force, vigor; see also INTENSITY 1.

emphasize /émfəsīz/ *v.tr.* **1** bring (a thing, fact, etc.) into special prominence. **2** lay stress on (a word in speaking).
■ **1** stress, accentuate, accent, underscore, point up, underline, call *or* draw attention to, highlight, play up, spotlight, feature.

emphatic /emfátik/ *adj.* **1** (of language, tone, or gesture) forcibly expressive. **2** of words: **a** bearing the stress. **b** used to give emphasis. **3** expressing oneself with emphasis. **4** (of an action or process) forcible; significant. □□ **emphatically** *adv.* [LL *emphaticus* f. Gk *emphatikos* (as EMPHASIS)]
■ **1, 3** expressive, demonstrative, pronounced, strong, clear, definite; firm, uncompromising, determined, decided, resolute, dogged; earnest, unequivocal, unambiguous, distinct, categorical, explicit, insistent, affirmative, positive, sure, certain, unmistakable, specific, definitive, direct; forceful, vigorous, energetic, assertive, intense.

emphysema /émfiseémə, -zeémə/ *n.* **1** enlargement of the air sacs of the lungs causing breathlessness. **2** a swelling caused by the presence of air in the connective tissues of the body. [LL f. Gk *emphusēma* f. *emphusaō* puff up]

empire /émpīr/ *n.* **1** an extensive group of lands or countries under a single supreme authority, esp. an emperor. **2 a** supreme dominion. **b** (often foll. by *over*) *archaic* absolute control. **3** a large commercial organization, etc., owned or directed by one person or group. **4** (**the Empire**) *hist.* **a** the British Empire. **b** the Holy Roman Empire. **5** a type or period of government in which the sovereign is called emperor. **6** (**Empire**) (*attrib.*) **a** denoting a style of furniture or dress fashionable during the first (1804–14) or second (1852–70) French Empire. **b** *Brit.* denoting produce from the Commonwealth. □ **empire-builder** a person who deliberately acquires extra territory, authority, etc., esp. unnecessarily. **Empire Day** *hist.* the former name of Commonwealth Day, orig. May 24. [ME f. OF f. L *imperium* rel. to *imperare*: see EMPEROR]
■ **1** see DOMAIN 1.

empiric /empírik, im-/ *adj. & n.* ● *adj.* = EMPIRICAL. ● *n.* *archaic* **1** a person relying solely on experiment. **2** a quack doctor. □□ **empiricism** /-sizəm/ *n.* **empiricist** *n.* [L *empiricus* f. Gk *empeirikos* f. *empeiria* experience f. *empeiros* skilled]

empirical /empírikəl, im-/ *adj.* **1** based or acting on observation or experiment, not on theory. **2** *Philos.* regarding sense-data as valid information. **3** deriving knowledge from experience alone. □ **empirical formula** *Chem.* a formula showing the constituents of a compound but not their configuration. □□ **empirically** *adv.*
■ **1** empiric, experiential, observational, practical, observed, pragmatic, experimental.

emplacement /empláysmənt, im-/ *n.* **1** the act or an instance of putting in position. **2** a platform or defended position where a gun is placed for firing. **3** situation; position. [F (as EN-¹, PLACE)]
■ **1, 3** see *placement* (PLACE).

emplane var. of ENPLANE.

employ /emplóy, im-/ *v. & n.* ● *v.tr.* **1** use the services of (a person) in return for payment; keep (a person) in one's service. **2** (often foll. by *for, in, on*) use (a thing, time, energy, etc.) esp. to good effect. **3** (often foll. by *in*) keep (a person) occupied. ● *n.* the state of being employed, esp. for wages. □ **in the employ of** employed by. □□ **employable** *adj.* **employability** *n.* **employer** *n.* [ME f. OF *employer* ult. f. L *implicari* be involved f. *implicare* enfold: see IMPLICATE]
■ *v.* **1** hire, engage, enlist, recruit, enroll, sign (up), take on, contract; keep, retain. **2** use, make use of, utilize, apply. **3** occupy, engage, involve, engross.
□□ **employer** proprietor, owner, patron, manager, director, chief, head, *colloq.* boss, old man, *Brit. colloq.* gaffer, *Brit. sl.* governor, guv; company, firm, corporation, business, establishment, organization.

employee /emplóyee, -ployée/ *n.* (also **employe**) a person employed for wages or salary, esp. at a nonexecutive level.
■ worker, staffer, member of the staff, wage earner; hand; (*employees*) staff, workforce.

employment /emplóymənt, im-/ *n.* **1** the act of employing or the state of being employed. **2** a person's regular trade or profession. □ **employment agency** a business that finds employers or employees for those seeking them.
■ **1** hire, hiring, engagement, enlistment; use, utilization, application, operation, implementation. **2** occupation, job, trade, work, business, profession, vocation, métier, skill, craft.

emporium /empáwreeəm/ *n.* (*pl.* **-ums** or **emporia** /-reeə/) **1** a large retail store selling a wide variety of goods. **2** a center of commerce; a market. [L f. Gk *emporion* f. *emporos* merchant]

empower /empówər, im-/ *v.tr.* (foll. by *to* + infin.) **1** authorize, license. **2** give power to; make able. □□ **empowerment** *n.*
■ **1** see AUTHORIZE.

empress /émpris/ *n.* **1** the wife or widow of an emperor. **2** a woman emperor. [ME f. OF *emperesse* fem. of *emperere* EMPEROR]
■ see SOVEREIGN *n.* 1.

empty /émptee/ *adj., v.,* & *n.* ● *adj.* (**emptier, emptiest**) **1** containing nothing. **2** (of a space, place, house, etc.) unoccupied; uninhabited; deserted; unfurnished. **3** (of a transport vehicle, etc.) without a load, passengers, etc. **4 a** meaningless; hollow; insincere (*empty threats; an empty gesture*). **b** without substance or purpose (*an empty existence*). **c** (of a person) lacking sense or knowledge; vacant; foolish. **5** *colloq.* hungry. **6** (foll. by *of*) devoid; lacking. ● *v.* (**-ies, -ied**) **1** *tr.* **a** make empty; remove the contents of. **b** (foll. by *of*) deprive of certain contents (*emptied the room of its chairs*). **c** remove (contents) from a container, etc. **2** *tr.* (often foll. by *into*) transfer (the contents of a container). **3** *intr.* become empty. **4** *intr.* (usu. foll. by *into*) (of a river) discharge itself (into the sea, etc.). ● *n.* (*pl.* **-ies**) *colloq.* a container (esp. a bottle) lacking empty of its contents. □ **empty-handed 1** bringing or taking nothing. **2** having achieved or obtained nothing. **empty-headed** foolish; lacking common sense. **empty nester** either of a couple whose children have grown up and left home. **on an empty stomach** see STOMACH. □□ **emptily** *adv.* **emptiness** *n.* [OE *æmtig, æmetig* f. *æmetta* leisure]

■ *adj.* **1** void, unfilled, hollow, bare, barren, vacant, blank; clean, new, unused, clear; emptied, drained, spent, exhausted. **2** vacant, unoccupied, untenanted, uninhabited, deserted, unpeopled; desolate, wild, waste, bare, barren, forsaken; unfurnished. **4 a** trivial, shallow, insincere, hypocritical, hollow, cheap, worthless, valueless, meaningless, insignificant, insubstantial, vain, idle. **b** see PURPOSELESS. **c** vacant, blank; vacuous, fatuous, stupid, foolish, inane. **6** (*empty of*) devoid of, lacking (in), wanting, in want of, deficient in, destitute of, without, *archaic or joc.* sans. ● *v.* **1 a, b** clear (out), vacate, evacuate; drain, exhaust; void; see also DIVEST 2. **c** take out *or* away, put out, cast *or* throw out, eject, remove; dump, pour out, **2** see TRANSFER *v.* 1a. **4** discharge, unload. □ **empty-headed** see FOOLISH. □□ **emptiness** voidness, hollowness, vacantness, vacancy, vacuity, blankness, bareness, barrenness, desertedness; senselessness, meaninglessness, pointlessness, aimlessness, purposelessness, futility, uselessness, worthlessness, hollowness; vacuousness, expressionlessness, emotionlessness.

empurple /empúrpəl, im-/ *v.tr.* **1** make purple or red. **2** make angry.

empyema /émpī-éemə/ *n.* a collection of pus in a cavity, esp. in the pleura. [LL f. Gk *empuēma* f. *empueō* suppurate (as EN-², *puon* pus)]

empyrean /émpəreéən, empíreeən/ *n.* & *adj.* ● *n.* **1** the highest heaven, as the sphere of fire in ancient cosmology or as the abode of God in early Christianity. **2** the visible heavens. ● *adj.* of the empyrean. □□ **empyreal** /empíreeəl, émpīreeəl/ *adj.* [med.L *empyreus* f. Gk *empurios* (as EN-², *pur* fire)]

■ *n.* **2** see SKY *n.* 1. ● *adj.* see CELESTIAL 1.

EMS *abbr.* European Monetary System.

EMT *abbr.* emergency medical technician.

emu /éemyōō/ *n.* a large flightless bird, *Dromaius novaehollandiae*, native to Australia, and capable of running at high speed. [earlier *emia, eme* f. Port. *ema*]

e.m.u. *abbr.* electromagnetic unit(s).

emulate /émyəlayt/ *v.tr.* **1** try to equal or excel. **2** imitate zealously. **3** rival. □□ **emulation** /-láyshən/ *n.* **emulative** *adj.* **emulator** *n.* [L *aemulari* (as EMULOUS)]

■ see IMITATE 1, 2.

emulous /émyələs/ *adj.* **1** (usu. foll. by *of*) seeking to emulate. **2** actuated by a spirit of rivalry. □□ **emulously** *adv.* [ME f. L *aemulus* rival]

emulsifier /imúlsifīər/ *n.* **1** any substance that stabilizes an emulsion, esp. a food additive used to stabilize processed foods. **2** an apparatus used for producing an emulsion.

emulsify /imúlsifī/ *v.tr.* (**-ies, -ied**) convert into an emulsion. □□ **emulsifiable** *adj.* **emulsification** /-fikáyshən/ *n.*

emulsion /imúlshən/ *n.* **1** a fine dispersion of one liquid in another, esp. as paint, medicine, etc. **2** a mixture of a silver compound suspended in gelatin, etc., for coating plates or films. □ **emulsion paint** a water-thinned paint containing a nonvolatile substance, e.g., synthetic resin, as its binding medium. □□ **emulsionize** *v.tr.* **emulsive** /-siv/ *adj.* [F *émulsion* or mod.L *emulsio* f. *emulgēre* (as E-, *mulgēre muls-* to milk)]

■ **1** see SOLUTION 2.

en /en/ *n. Printing* a unit of measurement equal to half an em. □ **en rule** (or **dash**) a short dash used in punctuation. [name of the letter *N*]

en-¹ /en, in/ *prefix* (also **em-** before *b, p*) forming verbs, = IN-¹: **1** from nouns, meaning 'put into or on' (*engulf; entrust; embed*). **2** from nouns or adjectives, meaning 'bring into the condition of' (*enslave*); often with the suffix *-en* (*enlighten*). **3** from verbs: **a** in the sense 'in, into, on' (*enfold*). **b** as an intensive (*entangle*). [from or after F *en-* f. L *in-*]

en-² /en, in/ *prefix* (also **em-** before *b, p*) in, inside (*energy; enthusiasm*). [Gk]

-en¹ /ən/ *suffix* forming verbs: **1** from adjectives, usu. meaning 'make or become so or more so' (*deepen; fasten; moisten*). **2** from nouns (*happen; strengthen*). [OE *-nian* f. Gmc]

-en² /ən/ *suffix* (also **-n**) forming adjectives from nouns, meaning: **1** made or consisting of (often with extended and figurative senses) (*wooden*). **2** resembling; of the nature of (*golden; silvern*). [OE f. Gmc]

-en³ /ən/ *suffix* (also **-n**) forming past participles of strong verbs: **1** as a regular inflection (*spoken; sworn*). **2** with restricted sense (*drunken*). [OE f. Gmc]

-en⁴ /ən/ *suffix* forming the plural of a few nouns (*children; brethren; oxen*). [ME reduction of OE *-an*]

-en⁵ /ən/ *suffix* forming diminutives of nouns (*chicken; maiden*). [OE f. Gmc]

-en⁶ /ən/ *suffix* **1** forming feminine nouns (*vixen*). **2** forming abstract nouns (*burden*). [OE f. Gmc]

enable /enáybəl/ *v.tr.* **1** (foll. by *to* + infin.) give (a person, etc.) the means or authority to do something. **2** make possible. **3** esp. *Computing* make (a device) operational; switch on. □ **enabling act** a statute empowering a person or body to take certain action. **2** a statute legalizing something otherwise unlawful. □□ **enabler** *n.*

■ **1** qualify, authorize, entitle, permit, allow, sanction, approve, empower, license; capacitate, facilitate, help, aid, assist. **3** see *turn on* 1 (TURN).

enact /enákt, in-/ *v.tr.* **1 a** (often foll. by *that* + clause) ordain; decree. **b** make (a bill, etc.) law. **2** play (a part or scene on stage or in life). □□ **enactable** *adj.* **enaction** /-akshən/ *n.* **enactive** *adj.* **enactor** *n.* **enactory** *adj.*

■ **1 a** ordain, decree, rule, command, order, authorize. **b** pass, ratify; see also APPROVE. **2** act (out), represent, play, portray, depict, perform, appear as.

enactment /enáktmənt, in-/ *n.* **1** a law enacted. **2** the process of enacting.

■ **1** see LAW 1a. **2** see PASSAGE¹ *n.* 7.

enamel /inámǝl/ *n.* & *v.* ● *n.* **1** a glasslike opaque or semi-transparent coating on metallic or other hard surfaces for ornament or as a preservative lining. **2 a** a smooth, hard coating. **b** a cosmetic simulating this. **3** the hard, glossy natural coating over the crown of a tooth. **4** painting done in enamel. **5** *poet.* a smooth, bright surface coloring, verdure, etc. ● *v.tr.* (**enameled, enameling;** esp. *Brit.* **enamelled, enamelling**) **1** inlay or encrust (a metal, etc.) with enamel. **2** portray (figures, etc.) with enamel. **3** *archaic* adorn with varied colors. □ **enamel paint** a paint that dries to give a smooth, hard coat. □□ **enameler** *n.* **enamelwork** *n.* [ME f. AF *enameler, enamailler* (as EN-¹, OF *esmail* f. Gmc)]

■ *n.* **1, 2** see GLAZE *n.*

enamelware /inámǝlwair/ *n.* enameled kitchenware.

enamor /inámǝr/ *v.tr.* (*Brit.* **enamour**) (usu. in *passive*; foll. by *of*) **1** inspire with love or liking. **2** charm; delight. [ME f. OF *enamourer* f. *amourer* (as EN-¹, AMOUR)]

/. . ./ **pronunciation**	● **part of speech**
□ **phrases, idioms, and compounds**	
□□ **derivatives**	■ **synonym section**
cross-references appear in SMALL CAPITALS or *italics*	

■ see CAPTIVATE.

enanthema /énantheémə/ *n. Med.* an eruption occurring on a mucus-secreting surface such as the inside of the mouth. [mod.L f. Gk *enanthēma* eruption (as EN-¹, EXANTHEMA)]

enantiomer /enánteeəmər/ *n. Chem.* a molecule with a mirror image. □□ **enantiomeric** /-mérik/ *adj.* [Gk *enantios* opposite+ -MER]

enantiomorph /enánteeəmawrf/ *n.* a mirror image; a form (esp. of a crystal structure, etc.) related to another as an object is to its mirror image. □□ **enantiomorphic** *adj.* **enantiomorphism** *n.* **enantiomorphous** *adj.* [G f. Gk *enantios* opposite + *morphē* form]

enarthrosis /énaarthrōsis/ *n.* (*pl.* **enarthroses** /-seez/) *Anat.* a ball-and-socket joint. [Gk f. *enarthros* jointed (as EN-², *arthron* joint)]

en bloc /ON bláwk/ *adv.* in a block; all at the same time; wholesale. [F]

en brosse /ON bráws/ *adj.* (of hair) cut short and bristly. [F]

encaenia /enseéneeə/ *n.* **1** (at Oxford University, England) an annual celebration in memory of founders and benefactors. **2** a dedication festival. [L f. Gk *egkainia* (as EN-², *kainos* new)]

encage /enkáyj/ *v.tr.* confine in or as in a cage.

encamp /enkámp/ *v.tr. & intr.* **1** settle in a military camp. **2** lodge in the open in tents.
■ see CAMP¹ *v.* 1.

encampment /enkámpmənt, in-/ *n.* **1** a place where troops, etc., are encamped. **2** the process of setting up a camp.
■ see CAMP¹ *n.* 1a, 2.

encapsulate /enkápsəlayt, -syōō-, in-/ *v.tr.* **1** enclose in or as in a capsule. **2** summarize; express the essential features of. **3** isolate. □□ **encapsulation** /-láyshən/ *n.* [EN-¹ + L *capsula* CAPSULE]
■ **2** see *sum up* 1 (SUM).

encase /enkáys, in-/ *v.tr.* (also **incase**) **1** put into a case. **2** surround as with a case. □□ **encasement** *n.*
■ see CASE² *v.* 1.

encash /enkásh, in-/ *v.tr. Brit.* **1** convert (bills, etc.) into cash. **2** receive in the form of cash; realize. □□ **encashable** *adj.* **encashment** *n.*

encaustic /enkáwstik, in-/ *adj. & n.* ● *adj.* **1** (in painting, ceramics, etc.) using pigments mixed with hot wax, which are burned in as an inlay. **2** (of bricks and tiles) inlaid with differently colored clays burned in. ● *n.* **1** the art of encaustic painting. **2** a painting done with this technique. [L *encausticus* f. Gk *egkaustikos* (as EN-², CAUSTIC)]

-ence /əns/ *suffix* forming nouns expressing: **1** a quality or state or an instance of one (*patience*; *an impertinence*). **2** an action (*reference*; *reminiscence*). [from or after F *-ence* f. L *-entia*, *-antia* (cf. -ANCE) f. pres. part. stem *-ent-*, *-ant-*]

enceinte /ensáynt, aansánt, ONsÁNt/ *n. & adj.* ● *n.* an enclosure, esp. in fortification. ● *adj. archaic* pregnant. [F, ult. f. L *cingere cinct-* gird: see CINCTURE]
■ *adj.* see *be expecting* (EXPECT).

encephalic /énsifálik/ *adj.* of or relating to the brain. [Gk *egkephalos* brain (as EN-², *kephalē* head)]

encephalitis /énséfalítis/ *n.* inflammation of the brain. □ **encephalitis lethargica** /lithaárjikə/ an infectious encephalitis caused by a virus, with headache and drowsiness leading to coma; sleepy sickness. □□ **encephalitic** /-lítik/ *adj.*

encephalo- /énséfəlō/ *comb. form* brain. [Gk *egkephalos* brain]

encephalogram /énséfələgram/ *n.* an X-ray photograph of the brain.

encephalograph /énséfələgraf/ *n.* an instrument for recording the electrical activity of the brain.

encephalon /énséfəlon/ *n. Anat.* the brain.

encephalopathy /énséfólópəthee/ *n.* disease of the brain.

enchain /encháyn, in-/ *v.tr.* **1** chain up; fetter. **2** hold fast (the attention, emotions, etc.). □□ **enchainment** *n.* [ME f. F *enchaîner* ult. f. L *catena* chain]
■ **1** see ENSLAVE.

enchant /enchánt, in-/ *v.tr.* **1** charm; delight. **2** bewitch. □□ **enchantedly** *adv.* **enchanting** *adj.* **enchantingly** *adv.*

enchantment *n.* [ME f. F *enchanter* f. L *incantare* (as IN-², *canere cant-* sing)]
■ **1** charm, fascinate, delight, beguile, captivate, enthrall, enrapture, attract, allure, entrance, spellbind. **2** bewitch, cast a spell on, spellbind, hypnotize, mesmerize, voodoo, bedevil, charm, hoodoo, hex, *Brit.* magic, *archaic* witch, *poet.* glamour. □□ **enchanting** charming, fascinating, captivating, intriguing, enthralling, alluring, delightful, hypnotic, attractive, appealing, winsome, ravishing, seductive; beguiling, bewitching, entrancing, spellbinding, *archaic* witching. **enchantment** witchcraft, sorcery, magic, wizardry, thaumaturgy; charm, beguilement, allure, fascination, attraction; conjuration; spell, charm, hex, *colloq.* jinx.

enchanter /enchántər, in-/ *n.* (*fem.* **enchantress**) a person who enchants, esp. by supposed use of magic. □ **enchanter's nightshade** a small plant, *Circaea lutetiana*, with white flowers.
■ see MAGICIAN 1, *charmer* (CHARM).

enchase /encháys, in-/ *v.tr.* **1** (foll. by *in*) place (a jewel) in a setting. **2** (foll. by *with*) set (gold, etc.) with gems. **3** inlay with gold, etc. **4** adorn with figures in relief. **5** engrave. [ME f. F *enchâsser* (as EN-¹, CHASE²)]
■ **5** see SCRIBE *v.*

enchilada /énchiláadə/ *n.* a tortilla with chili sauce and usu. a filling, esp. meat. [Amer. Sp., fem. past part. of *enchilar* season with chili]

enchiridion /énkirídeeən/ *n.* (*pl.* **enchiridia** /-deeə/ or **enchiridions**) *formal* a handbook. [LL f. Gk *egkheiridion* (as EN-², *kheir* hand, *-idion* dimin. suffix)]
■ see MANUAL *n.*

encipher /ensífər, in-/ *v.tr.* **1** write (a message, etc.) in cipher. **2** convert into coded form using a cipher. □□ **encipherment** *n.*
■ code, encode, encrypt.

encircle /ensúrkəl, in-/ *v.tr.* **1** (usu. foll. by *with*) surround; encompass. **2** form a circle around. □□ **encirclement** *n.*
■ **1** surround, circle, enclose, ring, encompass, *literary* gird; confine, hem *or* hold in. **2** see CIRCLE *v.* 2.

encl. *abbr.* **1** enclosed. **2** enclosure.

en clair /ON kláir/ *adj. & adv.* (of a telegram, official message, etc.) in ordinary language (not in code or cipher). [F, lit. 'in clear']

enclasp /enklásp, in-/ *v.tr.* hold in a clasp or embrace.

enclave /énklayv, ón-/ *n.* **1** a portion of territory of one country surrounded by territory of another or others, as viewed by the surrounding territory (cf. EXCLAVE). **2** a group of people who are culturally, intellectually, or socially distinct from those surrounding them. [F f. *enclaver* ult. f. L *clavis* key]

enclitic /enklítik/ *adj. & n. Gram.* ● *adj.* (of a word) pronounced with so little emphasis that it forms part of the preceding word. ● *n.* such a word, e.g., *not* in *cannot*. □□ **enclitically** *adv.* [LL *encliticus* f. Gk *egklitikos* (as EN-², *klinō* lean)]

enclose /enklōz, in-/ *v.tr.* (also **inclose**) **1** (often foll. by *with*, *in*) **a** surround with a wall, fence, etc. **b** shut in on all sides. **2** fence in (common land) so as to make it private property. **3** put in a receptacle (esp. in an envelope together with a letter). **4** (usu. as **enclosed** *adj.*) seclude (a religious community) from the outside world. **5** esp. *Math.* bound on all sides; contain. **6** hem in on all sides. [ME f. OF *enclos* past part. of *enclore* ult. f. L *includere* (as INCLUDE)]
■ **1, 6** surround, pen, encircle, encompass, bound, envelop, hedge in, ring, circle, wall in, immure, fence in *or* off, corral; lock, confine, shut in, close *or* hem in. **3** insert, include.

enclosure /enklōzhər, in-/ *n.* (also **inclosure**) **1** the act of enclosing, esp. of common land. **2** *Brit.* an enclosed space or area, esp. for a special class of persons at a sporting event. **3** a thing enclosed with a letter. **4** an enclosing fence, etc. [AF & OF (as ENCLOSE)]
■ **4** fence, wall, rail, railing, barrier, hedge, barricade, boundary.

encode /enkōd, in-/ *v.tr.* put (a message, etc.) into code or cipher. □□ **encoder** *n.*

■ code, encipher, encrypt.

encomiast /enkṓmeeast/ n. **1** the composer of an encomium. **2** a flatterer. □□ **encomiastic** /-ástik/ adj. [Gk egkōmiastēs (as ENCOMIUM)]

encomium /enkṓmeeəm/ n. (pl. **encomiums** or **encomia** /-meeə/) a formal or high-flown expression of praise. [L f. Gk egkōmion (as EN-², kōmos revelry)]
■ see EULOGY.

encompass /enkúmpəs, in-/ v.tr. **1** surround or form a circle about, esp. to protect or attack. **2** contain. □□ **encompassment** n.
■ **1** see CIRCLE v. 2. **2** see INCLUDE 1.

encore /óngkawr/ n., v., & int. ● n. **1** a call by an audience or spectators for the repetition of an item, or for a further item. **2** such an item. ● v.tr. **1** call for the repetition of (an item). **2** call back (a performer) for this. ● int. /also -kór/ again; once more. [F, = again]

encounter /enkówntər, in-/ v. & n. ● v.tr. **1** meet by chance or unexpectedly. **2** meet as an adversary. **3** meet with; experience (problems, opposition, etc.). ● n. **1** a meeting by chance. **2** a meeting in conflict. **3** participation in an encounter group. □ **encounter group** a group of persons seeking psychological benefit through close contact with one another. [ME f. OF encontrer, encontre ult. f. L contra against]
■ v. **1** meet, come upon, run into or across, happen upon, chance upon, stumble upon, colloq. bump into. **2** come into conflict with, contend with, assail, cross swords with, grapple with, engage, do battle with, confront, clash with, hist. joust with. **3** face, experience, meet with, contend with, be faced with, come into contact with, wrestle with. ● n. **2** confrontation, brush, quarrel, disagreement, dispute, altercation, Nengagement, action, fight, clash, conflict, skirmish, contest, competition, duel, struggle, run-in, tussle, to-do, wrangle, colloq. dustup, scrap, set-to.

encourage /enkárij, -kúr-, in-/ v.tr. **1** give courage, confidence, or hope to. **2** (foll. by to + infin.) urge; advise. **3** stimulate by help, reward, etc. **4** promote or assist (an enterprise, opinion, etc.). □□ **encouragement** n. **encourager** n. **encouraging** adj. **encouragingly** adv. [ME f. F encourager (as EN-¹, COURAGE)]
■ **1** hearten, embolden, reassure, buoy (up), stimulate, animate, support, inspirit, inspire, cheer (up), colloq. pep up. **2** spur (on), incite, egg on; see also URGE v. 2, ADVISE. **4** promote, advance, aid, support, help, assist, abet, foster, forward, colloq. boost, give a shot in the arm. □□ **encouragement** reassurance, stimulation, support, promotion, inspiration; exhortation; incitement; stimulus, help, aid, support, colloq. pep talk, boost, shot in the arm.

encroach /enkrṓch, in-/ v.intr. **1** (foll. by on, upon) intrude, esp. on another's territory or rights. **2** advance gradually beyond due limits. □□ **encroacher** n. **encroachment** n. [ME f. OF encrochier (as EN-¹, crochier f. croc hook: see CROOK)]
■ **1** intrude, trespass, make inroads; (encroach on or upon) invade, infringe. **2** invade, penetrate, infiltrate, permeate; enter, advance.

encrust /enkrúst, in-/ v. (also **incrust**) **1** tr. cover with a crust. **2** tr. overlay with an ornamental crust of precious material. **3** intr. form a crust. □□ **encrustment** n. [F incruster f. L incrustare (as IN-², crustare f. crusta CRUST)]
■ **3** see CAKE v. 2.

encrustation var. of INCRUSTATION.

encrypt /enkrípt, in-/ v.tr. **1** convert (data) into code, esp. to prevent unauthorized access. **2** conceal by this means. □□ **encryption** /-krípshən/ n. [EN-¹ + Gk kruptos hidden]
■ code, encode, encipher.

encumber /enkúmbər, in-/ v.tr. **1** be a burden to. **2** hamper; impede. **3** burden (a person or estate) with debts, esp. mortgages. **4** fill or block (a place), esp. with lumber. □□ **encumberment** n. [ME f. OF encombrer block up f. Rmc]
■ **1** burden, weigh down, load (up or down), overload, overburden, strain, oppress, saddle, tax, overtax.

2 hamper, impede, hinder, handicap, inconvenience, trammel, retard, slow (down), literary cumber.

encumbrance /enkúmbrəns, in-/ n. **1** a burden. **2** an impediment. **3** a mortgage or other charge on property. **4** an annoyance. □ **without encumbrance** having no children. [ME f. OF encombrance (as ENCUMBER)]
■ **1** weight, burden, onus, cross (to bear), load, albatross, millstone, encumberment, cumber. **2** handicap, impediment, hindrance, obstacle, obstruction, liability, disadvantage. **4** colloq. drag, bind; see also NUISANCE. □ **without encumbrance** childless, Law without issue, issueless.

ency. abbr. (also **encyc.**) encyclopedia.

-ency /ənsee/ suffix forming nouns denoting a quality (efficiency; fluency) or state (presidency) but not action (cf. -ENCE). [L -entia (cf. -ANCY)]

encyclical /ensíklikəl/ n. & adj. ● n. a papal letter sent to all bishops of the Roman Catholic Church. ● adj. (of a letter) for wide circulation. [LL encyclicus f. Gk egkuklios (as EN-², kuklos circle)]

encyclopedia /ensíkləpeédeeə/ n. (also **encyclopaedia**) a book, often in several volumes, giving information on many subjects, or on many aspects of one subject, usu. arranged alphabetically. [mod.L f. spurious Gk egkuklopaideia for egkuklios paideia all-around education: cf. ENCYCLICAL]

encyclopedic /ensíkləpeédik/ adj. (also **encyclopaedic**) (of knowledge or information) comprehensive.
■ comprehensive, inclusive, broad, extensive, universal, thorough, exhaustive, wide-ranging, complete.

encyclopedism /ensíkləpeédizəm/ n. (also **encyclopaedism**) encyclopedic learning.

encyclopedist /ensíkləpeédist/ n. (also **encyclopaedist**) a person who writes, edits, or contributes to an encyclopedia.

encyst /ensíst, in-/ v.tr. & intr. Biol. enclose or become enclosed in a cyst. □□ **encystation** /-táyshən/ n. **encystment** n.

end /end/ n. & v. ● n. **1 a** the extreme limit; the point beyond which a thing does not continue. **b** an extremity of a line, or of the greatest dimension of an object. **c** the furthest point (to the ends of the earth). **2** the surface bounding a thing at either extremity; an extreme part (a piece of wood with a nail in one end). **3 a** a conclusion; finish (no end to his misery). **b** the latter or final part. **c** death; destruction; downfall (met an untimely end). **d** result; outcome. **e** an ultimate state or condition. **4 a** a thing one seeks to attain; a purpose (will do anything to achieve her ends; to what end?). **b** the object for which a thing exists. **5** a remnant; a piece left over (a board end). **6** (prec. by the) colloq. the limit of endurability. **7** the half of a sports field or court occupied by one team or player. **8** the part or share with which a person is concerned (no problem at my end). **9** Football a player at the extremity of the offensive or defensive line. ● v. **1** tr. & intr. bring or come to an end. **2** tr. put an end to; destroy. **3** intr. (foll. by in) have as its result (will end in tears). **4** intr. (foll. by by) do or achieve eventually (ended by marrying an heiress). □ **at an end** exhausted or completed. **at the end of one's tether** see TETHER. **come to a bad end** meet with ruin or disgrace. **come to an end 1** be completed or finished. **2** become exhausted. **end around** n. Football an offensive play in which an end carries the ball around the opposite end. ● adj. Computing involving the transfer of a digit from one end of a register to the other. **end it all** (or **end it**) colloq. commit suicide. **end of the road** the point at which a hope or endeavor has to be abandoned. **end of the world** the cessation of mortal life. **end on** with the end facing one, or with the end adjoining the end of the next object. **end point 1** the final stage of a process, esp. the point at which an effect is observed in titration, dilution, etc. **2** var. of END-POINT. **end product** the final product of manufacture, ra-

dioactive decay, etc. **end result** final outcome. **end run 1** *Football* an attempt by the ballcarrier to run around the offensive end. **2** an evasive tactic, esp. in war or politics. **endstopped** (of verse) having a pause at the end of each line. **end to end** with the end of each of a series adjoining the end of the next. **end up** reach a specified state, action, or place eventually (*ended up a drunk*; *ended up making a fortune*). **end user** the person, customer, etc., who is the ultimate user of a product. **end zone** *Football* the area at each end of a football field where points are scored. **in the end** finally; after all. **keep one's end up** do one's part despite difficulties. **make an end of** put a stop to. **make ends** (or **both ends**) **meet** live within one's income. **no end** *colloq.* to a great extent; very much. **no end of** *colloq.* much or many of. **on end 1** upright (*hair stood on end*). **2** continuously (*for three weeks on end*). **put an end to 1** stop (an activity, etc.). **2** abolish; destroy. □□ **ender** *n.* [OE *ende, endian,* f. Gmc]
■ *n.* **1** extremity, extreme, extent, bounds, tip, endpoint, limit, terminus. **3 a, b** termination, conclusion, cessation, finish, completion; close, finale, ending, windup, denouement. **c** destruction, expiration, expiry, ruin, extermination, annihilation; see DEATH 4a. **d** consequence, result, outcome, effect, upshot. **4** aim, purpose, intention, intent, objective, object, goal, aspiration; point, reason, raison d'être; destination. **5** see REMNANT. **6** (*the end*) the worst, the last straw, the final blow, *colloq.* the limit, too much. ● *v.* **1** terminate, conclude, bring to an end, stop, halt, cease, wind up *or* down, discontinue, break off, cut off, close, finish; come to an end, die (out), expire, peter out, vanish. **2** put an end to, put a stopper on, get rid of, annihilate, terminate, extinguish; destroy, ruin. **3** see RESULT *v.* 2. **4** end up, culminate, finish (up) by. □ **end it all** commit suicide, suicide, take one's own life. **end product** result, outcome, product. **end run 2** see SUBTERFUGE 1. **end up** finish up, turn out, end. **in the end** see *finally* (FINAL). **make an end of** see STOP *v.* 1a, c. **make ends meet** see MANAGE *v.* 2, 3, 5a. **no end** see HIGHLY 1. **no end of** see ENDLESS 3. **on end 1** upright, erect, standing. **2** continuously, uninterruptedly, unceasingly, incessantly, running, consecutively, without a break, *colloq.* without letup. **put an end to 1** see STOP *v.* 1. **2** see ABOLISH.

-end /end, ənd/ *suffix* forming nouns in the sense 'person or thing to be treated in a specified way' (*dividend*; *reverend*). [L gerundive ending *-endus*]

endanger /endáynjər, in-/ *v.tr.* place in danger. □ **endangered species** a species in danger of extinction. □□ **endangerment** *n.*
■ imperil, jeopardize, put in jeopardy, threaten, expose (to danger); risk, put at risk, hazard; chance, venture.

endear /endeér, in-/ *v.tr.* (usu. foll. by *to*) make dear to or beloved by.

endearing /endeéring, in-/ *adj.* inspiring affection. □□ **endearingly** *adv.*
■ attractive, engaging, likable, appealing, pleasing, winsome, captivating, winning, lovable.

endearment /endeérmənt, in-/ *n.* **1** an expression of affection. **2** liking; affection.

endeavor /endévər, in-/ *v. & n.* (*Brit.* **endeavour**) ● *v.* **1** *tr.* (foll. by *to* + infin.) try earnestly. **2** *intr.* (foll. by *after*) *archaic* strive. ● *n.* (often foll. by *at,* or *to* + infin.) effort directed toward a goal; an earnest attempt. [ME f. *put oneself in* DEVOIR]
■ *v.* **1** try, attempt, strive, make an effort, struggle, do one's best, *formal* essay; exert oneself, *colloq.* take a stab at, have a go *or* crack *or* whack *or* shot at; aim, aspire. ● *n.* effort, pains, attempt, try, striving, struggle, venture, enterprise, *formal* essay.

endemic /endémik/ *adj. & n.* ● *adj.* regularly or only found among a particular people or in a certain region. ● *n.* an endemic disease or plant. □□ **endemically** *adv.* **endemicity** /éndimísitee/ *n.* **endemism** *n.* [F *endémique* or mod.L *endemicus* f. Gk *endēmos* native (as EN-[2], *dēmos* the people)]
■ *adj.* native, indigenous, local.

endermic /endərmik/ *adj.* acting on or through the skin. □□ **endermically** *adv.* [EN-[2] + Gk *derma* skin]

endgame /éndgaym/ the final stage of a game (esp. chess), when few pieces remain.

ending /énding/ *n.* **1** an end or final part, esp. of a story. **2** an inflected final part of a word. [OE (as END, -ING[1])]
■ **1** see END *n.* 3a, b. **2** termination, suffix.

endive /éndīv, óndeev/ *n.* **1** a curly-leaved plant, *Cichorium endivia,* used in salads. **2** a chicory crown. [ME f. OF f. LL *endivia* ult. f. Gk *entubon*]

endless /éndlis/ *adj.* **1** infinite; without end; eternal. **2** continual; incessant (*tired of their endless complaints*). **3** *colloq.* innumerable. **4** (of a belt, chain, etc.) having the ends joined for continuous action over wheels, etc. □ **endless screw** *Brit.* a short length of screw revolving to turn a cogwheel. □□ **endlessly** *adv.* **endlessness** *n.* [OE *endelēas* (as END, -LESS)]
■ **1** infinite, immeasurable, illimitable, limitless, measureless, unlimited, boundless, unbounded, unending; eternal, perpetual, ceaseless, without end, everlasting, perennial. **2** continual, incessant, ceaseless, unceasing, unending, constant, never-ending, perpetual, everlasting, interminable, nonstop, continuous, uninterrupted, unremitting, relentless, persistent. **3** innumerable, countless, numerous, numberless, uncounted, untold, infinite, *literary* myriad. □□ **endlessly** ceaselessly, incessantly, constantly, eternally, perpetually, everlastingly, continually, continuously, interminably, relentlessly. **endlessness** ceaselessness, unendingness, everlastingness, eternity, perpetuity.

endmost /éndmōst/ *adj.* nearest the end.
■ see EXTREME *adj.* 3.

endnote /éndnōt/ *n.* a note printed at the end of a book or section of a book.

endo- /éndō/ *comb. form* internal. [Gk *endon* within]

endocarditis /éndōkaardítis/ *n.* inflammation of the endocardium. □□ **endocarditic** /-dítik/ *adj.*

endocardium /éndōkaárdeeəm/ *n.* the lining membrane of the heart. [ENDO- + Gk *kardia* heart]

endocarp /éndōkaarp/ *n.* the innermost layer of the pericarp. □□ **endocarpic** *adj.* [ENDO- + PERICARP]

endocrine /éndōkrin, -kreen, -krīn/ *adj.* (of a gland) secreting directly into the blood; ductless. [ENDO- + Gk *krinō* sift]

endocrinology /éndōkrinóləjee/ *n.* the study of the structure and physiology of endocrine glands. □□ **endocrinological** /-nəlójikəl/ *adj.* **endocrinologist** *n.*

endoderm /éndōdərm/ *n.* *Biol.* the innermost layer of an animal embryo in early development. □□ **endodermal** *adj.* **endodermic** *adj.* [ENDO- + Gk *derma* skin]

endogamy /endógəmee/ *n.* **1** *Anthropol.* marrying within the same tribe. **2** *Bot.* pollination from the same plant. □□ **endogamous** *adj.* [ENDO- + Gk *gamos* marriage]

endogenous /endójinəs/ *adj.* growing or originating from within. □□ **endogenesis** /éndəjénisis/ *n.* **endogeny** /endójinee/ *n.*

endolymph /éndōlimf/ *n.* the fluid in the membranous labyrinth of the ear.

endometrium /éndōmeétreeəm/ *n.* *Anat.* the membrane lining the uterus. □□ **endometritis** /éndōmitrítis/ *n.* [ENDO- + Gk *mētra* womb]

endomorph /éndōmawrf/ *n.* **1** a person with a soft, round body build and a high proportion of fat tissue (cf. ECTOMORPH, MESOMORPH). **2** *Mineral.* a mineral enclosed within another. □□ **endomorphic** *adj.* **endomorphy** *n.* [ENDO- + Gk *morphē* form]

endoparasite /éndōpárəsīt/ *n.* a parasite that lives on the inside of its host.

endoplasm /éndōplazəm/ *n.* the inner fluid layer of the cytoplasm.

endoplasmic reticulum /éndōplázmik/ *n.* *Biol.* a system of membranes within the cytoplasm of a eukaryotic cell forming a link between the cell and nuclear membranes and usu. having ribosomes attached to its surface.

endorphin /endáwrfin/ *n.* Biochem. any of a group of peptide neurotransmitters occurring naturally in the brain and having pain-relieving properties. [F *endorphine* f. *endogène* endogenous + MORPHINE]

endorse /endáwrs, in-/ *v.tr.* (also **indorse**) **1 a** confirm (a statement or opinion). **b** declare one's approval of. **2** sign or write on the back of (a document), esp. the back of (a bill, check, etc.) as the payee or to specify another as payee. **3** write (an explanation or comment) on the back of a document. □□ **endorsable** *adj.* **endorsee** /éndorseé/ *n.* **endorser** *n.* [med.L *indorsare* (as IN-², L *dorsum* back)]
■ **1 a** confirm, ratify, sustain, support, back (up), second, subscribe to. **b** approve, sanction, authorize, advocate, countenance, agree to, assent to, rubber-stamp, put one's stamp *or* seal (of approval) on, set one's seal (of approval) to, give the go-ahead *or* thumbs up to, give one's imprimatur *or* blessing to, *colloq.* OK, okay, give the green light to. **2** ratify, countersign.

endorsement /endáwrsmənt, in-/ *n.* (also **indorsement**) **1** the act or an instance of endorsing. **2** something with which a document, etc., is endorsed, esp. a signature.
■ **1** approval, sanction, authorization, confirmation, ratification, support, backing, consent, agreement, approbation, go-ahead, seal *or* stamp of approval, imprimatur, rubber stamp, thumbs up, blessing, *colloq.* OK, okay, green light. **2** countersignature, rubber stamp.

endoscope /éndəskōp/ *n.* Surgery an instrument for viewing the internal parts of the body. □□ **endoscopic** /-skópik/ *adj.* **endoscopically** *adv.* **endoscopist** /endóskəpist/ *n.* **endoscopy** /endóskəpee/ *n.*

endoskeleton /éndōskélitən/ *n.* an internal skeleton, as found in vertebrates.

endosperm /éndəspərm/ *n.* albumen enclosed with the germ in seeds.

endospore /éndəspawr/ *n.* **1** a spore formed by certain bacteria. **2** the inner coat of a spore.

endothelium /éndōtheéleeəm/ *n.* Anat. a layer of cells lining the blood vessels, heart, and lymphatic vessels. [ENDO- + Gk *thēlē* teat]

endothermic /éndōthə́rmik/ *adj.* occurring or formed with the absorption of heat.

endow /endów, in-/ *v.tr.* **1** bequeath or give a permanent income to (a person, institution, etc.). **2** (esp. as **endowed** *adj.*) (usu. foll. by *with*) provide (a person) with talent, ability, etc. □□ **endower** *n.* [ME f. AF *endouer* (as EN-¹, OF *douer* f. L *dotare* f. *dos dotis* DOWER)]
■ **1** see AWARD *v.* **2** see BLESS 5.

endowment /endówmənt, in-/ *n.* **1** the act or an instance of endowing. **2** assets, esp. property or income, with which a person or body is endowed. **3** (usu. in *pl.*) skill, talent, etc., with which a person is endowed. **4** (*attrib.*) denoting forms of life insurance involving payment by the insurer of a fixed sum on a specified date, or on the death of the insured person if earlier.
■ **1** presentation, bestowal, giving, award, allocation, apportionment, allotment, settlement; bequeathal. **2** grant, (financial) aid, award, funding, funds, subsidy, subvention, allowance, allotment, contribution, donation, gift, present; bequest, inheritance, dowry. **3** (*endowments*) talent(s), gift(s), abilities, aptitude(s), powers, capabilities, capacities, qualifications, strengths, qualities.

endpaper /éndpaypər/ *n.* a usu. blank leaf of paper at the beginning and end of a book, fixed to the inside of the cover.

endplay /éndplay/ *n.* Bridge a method of play in the last few tricks to force an opponent to make a disadvantageous lead.

endpoint /éndpoynt/ *n.* (also **end point**) Math. a point or value that marks the end of a ray or one of the ends of a line segment or interval.

endue /endoo, -dyoo, in-/ *v.tr.* (also **indue**) (foll. by *with*) invest or provide (a person) with qualities, powers, etc. [earlier = induct, put on clothes: ME f. OF *enduire* f. L *inducere* lead in, assoc. in sense with L *induere* put on (clothes)]
■ see CLOTHE 3.

endurance /endoorəns, -dyoor-, in-/ *n.* **1** the power or habit of enduring (*beyond endurance*). **2** the ability to withstand prolonged strain (*endurance test*). **3** the act of enduring. **4** ability to last; enduring quality. [OF f. *endurer*: see ENDURE]
■ **1** see BEARING 3. **2** stamina, resilience, stay, staying power, robustness, hardiness; perseverance, persistence, resolution, fortitude, tenacity, patience, tolerance, *colloq.* grit. **3** survival, duration, persistence. **4** lasting *or* enduring quality, durability, longevity.

endure /endoor, -dyoor, in-/ *v.* **1** *tr.* undergo (a difficulty, hardship, etc.). **2** *tr.* **a** tolerate (a person) (*cannot endure him*). **b** (esp. with *neg.*; foll. by *to* + infin.) bear. **3** *intr.* (often as **enduring** *adj.*) remain in existence; last. **4** *tr.* submit to. □□ **endurable** *adj.* **enduringly** *adv.* [ME f. OF *endurer* f. L *indurare* harden (as IN-², *durus* hard)]
■ **1** undergo, face, brave, go through with, survive, stand, bear, tolerate, abide, take, support, withstand, weather, suffer, stomach, hold out (against), last through, cope with, hold up *or* bear up *or* stand up under, *colloq.* stick *or* sweat out, *literary* brook. **2** bear, stand, put up with, submit to, abide, tolerate, support, stomach, cope with, handle, face, *literary* brook. **3** remain, last, stay, persist, carry on, linger, survive, live (on), continue, be left, hold, *archaic* abide; (**enduring**) lasting, continuing, persisting, persistent, durable, abiding, long-standing, permanent; steady. **4** submit to, bow to; see also ENDURE 1 above.

enduro /endoorō, -dyoorō, in-/ *n.* (*pl.* **-os**) a long-distance race for motor vehicles, designed to test endurance.

endways /éndwayz/ *adv.* **1** with its end uppermost or foremost or turned toward the viewer. **2** end to end.

endwise /éndwīz/ *adv.* = ENDWAYS.

ENE *abbr.* east-northeast.

-ene /een/ *suffix* **1** forming names of inhabitants of places (*Nazarene*). **2** *Chem.* forming names of unsaturated hydrocarbons containing a double bond (*benzene*; *ethylene*). [from or after Gk *-ēnos*]

enema /énimə/ *n.* (*pl.* **enemas** or **enemata** /inémətə/) **1** the injection of liquid or gas into the rectum, esp. to expel its contents. **2** a fluid or syringe used for this. [LL f. Gk *enema* f. *eniēmi* inject (as EN-², *hiēmi* send)]

enemy /énəmee/ *n.* (*pl.* **-ies**) **1** a person or group actively opposing or hostile to another, or to a cause, etc. **2 a** a hostile nation or army, esp. in war. **b** a member of this. **c** a hostile ship or aircraft. **3** (usu. foll. by *of*, *to*) an adversary or opponent. **4** a thing that harms or injures. **5** (*attrib.*) of or belonging to an enemy (*destroyed by enemy action*). [ME f. OF *enemi* f. L *inimicus* (as IN-¹, *amicus* friend)]
■ **1-3** opponent, antagonist, rival, opposition, other side, adversary, esp. *poet. or formal* foe. **4** foe, opponent, hostile *or* harmful influence.

energetic /énərjétik/ *adj.* **1** strenuously active. **2** forcible; vigorous. **3** powerfully operative. □□ **energetically** *adv.* [Gk *energētikos* f. *energeō* (as EN-², *ergon* work)]
■ **1, 2** lively, active, vigorous, dynamic, alive, animated, spirited, untiring, tireless, indefatigable, sprightly, brisk, racy, vibrant, spry, zesty, zestful, zealous, enthusiastic, eager, go-ahead, enterprising, ambitious, *colloq.* peppy, full of pep, full of get-up-and-go, zippy, zingy, full of beans. **3** vital, invigorating, life-giving, vitalizing, energizing, powerful, high-powered.

energetics /énərjétiks/ *n.pl.* the science of energy.

energize /énərjīz/ *v.tr.* **1** infuse energy into (a person or work). **2** provide energy for the operation of (a device). □□ **energizer** *n.*
■ stimulate, enliven, animate, liven up, invigorate, vitalize, vivify, inspire, inspirit, rouse, stir, arouse, awaken, waken, rally, excite, *colloq.* enthuse, pep up; activate, actuate, move, impel, drive, motivate,

---

/.../ **pronunciation**	● **part of speech**
□ **phrases, idioms, and compounds**	
□□ **derivatives**	■ **synonym section**
cross-references appear in SMALL CAPITALS or *italics*	

galvanize, spark, electrify, switch *or* turn on, fire (up), kick-start.

energy /énərjee/ *n.* (*pl.* **-ies**) **1** force; vigor; capacity for activity. **2** (in *pl.*) individual powers in use (*devote your energies to this*). **3** *Physics* the capacity of matter or radiation to do work. **4** the means of doing work by utilizing matter or radiation. [F *énergie* or LL *energia* f. Gk *energeia* f. *ergon* work]
■ **1** force, power, strength, might, forcefulness, *archaic* puissance; vigor, drive, dynamism, push, élan, dash, bounce, brio, zip, go, vim, vim and vigor, *colloq.* get-up-and-go, pep, zing, *sl.* zap; vitality, liveliness, vivacity, animation, vivaciousness, spirit, spiritedness, exuberance, zest, gusto, enthusiasm, verve, zeal, *sl.* oomph, pizzazz. **2** (*energies*) see POWER *n.* 2.

enervate *v. & adj.* ● *v.tr.* /énərvayt/ deprive of vigor or vitality. ● *adj.* /inə́rvət/ enervated. □□ **enervation** /-váyshən/ *n.* [L *enervatus* past part. of *enervare* (as E-, *nervus* sinew)]
■ *v.* weaken, tire (out), weary, drain, tax, exhaust, sap, debilitate, enfeeble, fatigue, wear out, dull, subdue, devitalize, take it out of, strain, break, crush, depress, dispirit. ● *adj.* see TIRED 1.

en famille /ón fameéy/ *adv.* **1** in or with one's family. **2** at home. [F, = in family]

enfant terrible /aaNfaaN tereéblə/ *n.* a person who causes embarrassment by indiscreet or unruly behavior. [F, = terrible child]

enfeeble /enfeébəl, in-/ *v.tr.* make feeble. □□ **enfeeblement** *n.* [ME f. OF *enfeblir* (as EN-¹, FEEBLE)]
■ see WEAKEN 1.

en fête /oN fét/ *adv. & predic.adj.* holding or ready for a holiday or celebration. [F, = in festival]

enfetter /enfétər, in-/ *v.tr. literary* **1** bind in or as in fetters. **2** (foll. by *to*) enslave.
■ **1** fetter, bind, tie up, shackle, manacle.

enfilade /énfiláyd, -láad/ *n. & v.* ● *n.* gunfire directed along a line from end to end. ● *v.tr.* direct an enfilade at (troops, a road, etc.). [F f. *enfiler* (as EN-¹, *fil* thread)]

enfold /enfóld, in-/ *v.tr.* (also **infold**) **1** (usu. foll. by *in*, *with*) wrap up; envelop. **2** clasp; embrace.
■ **1** see WRAP *v.* 1. **2** see EMBRACE *v.* 1.

enforce /enfáwrs, in-/ *v.tr.* **1** compel observance of (a law, etc.). **2** (foll. by *on*, *upon*) impose (an action, conduct, one's will). **3** persist in (a demand or argument). □□ **enforceable** *adj.* **enforceability** *n.* **enforcedly** /-sidlee/ *adv.* **enforcer** *n.* [ME f. OF *enforcir*, *-ier* ult. f. L *fortis* strong]
■ **1** insist upon *or* on, impose, implement, put into effect, apply, administer, bring to bear, prosecute, carry out, discharge, maintain, uphold, support, reinforce.
2 inflict, force; see also IMPOSE 1, 2, 4. **3** persist in, persevere with, keep to, be staunch *or* steadfast in, adhere *or* stick to, force, press, lay stress upon *or* on.

enforcement /enfáwrsmənt, in-/ *n.* the act or an instance of enforcing. [ME f. OF, as ENFORCE + -MENT]
■ see IMPOSITION 1.

enfranchise /enfránchīz, in-/ *v.tr.* **1** give (a person) the right to vote. **2** give (a town, city, etc.) municipal or parliamentary rights. **3** *hist.* free (a slave, villein, etc.). □□ **enfranchisement** *n.* [OF *enfranchir* (as EN-¹, *franc franche* FRANK)]
■ **3** see FREE *v.* 1.

ENG *abbr.* electronic news gathering.

engage /en-gáyj, in-/ *v.* **1** *tr.* employ or hire (a person). **2** *tr.* **a** (usu. in *passive*) employ busily; occupy (*are you engaged tomorrow?*). **b** hold fast (a person's attention). **3** *tr.* (usu. in *passive*) bind by a promise, esp. of marriage. **4** *tr.* (usu. foll. by *to* + infin.) bind by a contract. **5** *tr.* arrange beforehand to occupy (a room, seat, etc.). **6** (usu. foll. by *with*) *Mech.* **a** *tr.* interlock (parts of a gear, etc.); cause (a part) to interlock. **b** *intr.* (of a part, gear, etc.) interlock. **7 a** *intr.* (usu. foll. by *with*) (of troops, etc.) come into battle. **b** *tr.* bring (troops) into battle. **c** *tr.* come into battle with (an enemy, etc.). **8** *intr.* take part (*engage in politics*). **9** *intr.* (foll. by *that* + clause or *to* + infin.) pledge oneself. **10** *tr.* (usu. as **engaged** *adj.*) *Archit.* attach (a column) to a wall. **11** *tr.* (of fencers, etc.) interlock (weapons). □□ **engager** *n.* [F *engager*, rel. to GAGE¹]

■ **1** employ, hire, recruit, take on, appoint, sign up *or* on, put under contract, retain, enlist, *hist.* indenture. **2 a** occupy, keep busy, absorb, involve, preoccupy, take up, tie up. **b** attract, hold, capture, absorb, catch, draw; involve, interest, intrigue, engross, rivet, fascinate. **3** betroth, *literary* affiance. **4** contract, put under contract, commit, bind. **5** book, reserve, save, set *or* put aside, earmark, secure, bespeak, take, rent, hire. **7 a, c** join in battle *or* combat (with), battle *or* struggle *or* war (against), contend (with), wage war (against), take up arms (against), clash (with), skirmish; meet (with), fight (against); encounter. **8** (*engage in*) participate *or* take part in, be *or* become *or* get involved in, join *or* partake in, be *or* become associated with, enter into. **9** pledge, agree, undertake, promise, commit oneself, guarantee, contract, covenant.

engagé /oN-gazháy/ *adj.* (of a writer, etc.) morally committed. [F, past part. of *engager*: see ENGAGE]

engaged /en-gáyjd, in-/ *adj.* **1** under a promise to marry. **2 a** occupied; busy. **b** reserved; booked. **3** *Brit.* (of a telephone line) unavailable because already in use. □ **engaged signal** (or **tone**) *Brit.* = *busy signal.*
■ **1** betrothed, pledged, *archaic* promised, plighted, *literary* affianced; spoken for. **2 a** busy, occupied, tied up, wrapped up, employed, involved, absorbed, preoccupied. **b** reserved, booked, occupied, taken, spoken for.

engagement /en-gáyjmənt, in-/ *n.* **1** the act or state of engaging or being engaged. **2** an appointment with another person. **3** a betrothal. **4** an encounter between hostile forces. **5** a moral commitment. **6** a period of paid employment; a job. □ **engagement ring** a ring given by a man to a woman when they promise to marry. [F f. *engager*: see ENGAGE]
■ **1** employment, hire, recruitment, appointment, enlistment. **2** appointment, meeting, rendezvous, arrangement, commitment, assignation, *archaic* tryst, *colloq.* date. **4** fight, battle, war, conflict, struggle, clash, fray, encounter, meeting, skirmish. **5** agreement, commitment, obligation, bond, promise, pledge, guarantee, covenant, contract, undertaking. **6** job, position, post, commission, booking; employment, work; *colloq.* spot, gig.

engaging /en-gáyjing, in-/ *adj.* attractive; charming. □□ **engagingly** *adv.* **engagingness** *n.*
■ attractive, charming, pleasant, genial, sociable, delightful, prepossessing, enchanting, endearing, winsome, appealing, winning, agreeable, pleasing, likable.

engender /enjéndər, in-/ *v.tr.* **1** give rise to; bring about (a feeling, etc.). **2** *archaic* beget. [ME f. OF *engendrer* f. L *ingenerare* (as IN-², *generare* GENERATE)]
■ see CREATE 1.

engine /énjin/ *n.* **1** a mechanical contrivance consisting of several parts working together, esp. as a source of power. **2 a** a railroad locomotive. **b** = *fire engine.* **c** = *steam engine.* **3** *archaic* a machine or instrument, esp. a contrivance used in warfare. □ **engine driver** *Brit.* = ENGINEER *n.* 4. **engine room** a room containing engines (esp. in a ship). □□ **engined** *adj.* (also in *comb.*). **engineless** *adj.* [OF *engin* f. L *ingenium* talent, device: cf. INGENIOUS]
■ **1** motor, machine, mechanism, appliance, apparatus, contrivance, device, *often derog. or joc.* contraption.

engineer /énjineér/ *n. & v.* ● *n.* **1** a person qualified in a branch of engineering, esp. as a professional. **2** = *civil engineer.* **3** a person who makes or is in charge of engines. **4** the operator or supervisor of an engine, esp. a railroad locomotive. **5** a person who designs and constructs military works; a soldier trained for this purpose. **6** (foll. by *of*) a skillful or artful contriver. ● *v.* **1** *tr.* arrange, contrive, or bring about, esp. artfully. **2** *intr.* act as an engineer. **3** *tr.* construct or manage as an engineer. □□ **engineership** *n.* [ME f. OF *enginneor* f. med.L *ingeniator -oris* f. *ingeniare* (as ENGINE)]
■ **4** driver, motorman, *Brit.* engine driver. **6** designer,

inventor, conceiver, originator, author, creator, contriver, architect, planner, mastermind, *colloq.* brain(s). ● *v.* **1** arrange, plan, organize, orchestrate, contrive, mastermind, manage, maneuver, plot, rig, scheme, devise, design, concoct, create, bring about *or* off, set up, work out, develop, achieve, effect, settle, accomplish, put over, *colloq.* wangle, swing, fix, work it, finagle.

engineering /énjinéering/ *n.* the application of science to the design, building, and use of machines, constructions, etc. □ **engineering science** engineering as a field of study.

enginery /énjinree/ *n.* engines and machinery generally.

engird /en-górd, in-/ *v.tr.* surround with or as with a girdle.
■ see ENCIRCLE 1.

engirdle /en-górdəl, in-/ *v.tr.* engird.

English /íngglish/ *adj.* & *n.* ● *adj.* of or relating to England or its people or language. ● *n.* **1** the language of England, now used in many varieties in the British Isles, the United States, and most Commonwealth or ex-Commonwealth countries, and often internationally. **2** (prec. by *the*; treated as *pl.*) the people of England. **3** *Billiards* a spinning motion given to the cue ball by striking it off center. □ **English bond** *Building* a bond of brickwork arranged in alternate courses of stretchers and headers. **English horn** *Mus.* **1** an alto woodwind instrument of the oboe family. **2** its player. **3** an organ stop with the quality of an English horn. **English muffin** a flat round bread-dough muffin, usu. baked on a griddle, served sliced and toasted. **the Queen's** (or **King's**) **English** the English language as correctly written or spoken in Britain. □□ **Englishness** *n.* [OE *englisc, ænglisc* (as ANGLE, -ISH¹)]
■ □ **English horn** cor anglais.

Englishman /íngglishmən/ *n.* (*pl.* **-men**) a person who is English by birth or descent.

Englishwoman /ínglishwŏomən/ *n.* (*pl.* **-women**) a woman who is English by birth or descent.

engorge /en-gáwrj, in-/ *v.tr.* **1** (in *passive*) **a** be crammed. **b** *Med.* be congested with blood. **2** devour greedily. □□ **engorgement** *n.* [F *engorger* (as EN-¹, GORGE)]
■ **2** see DEVOUR 1.

engr. *abbr.* **1** engineer. **2** engraved. **3** engraver. **4** engraving.

engraft /en-gráft, in-/ *v.tr.* (also **ingraft**) **1** *Bot.* (usu. foll. by *into, upon*) insert (a scion of one tree into another). **2** (usu. foll. by *in*) implant (principles, etc.) in a person's mind. **3** (usu. foll. by *into*) incorporate permanently. □□ **engraftment** *n.*

engrail /en-gráyl, in-/ *v.tr.* (usu. as **engrailed** *adj.*) esp. *Heraldry* indent the edge of; give a serrated appearance to. [ME f. OF *engresler* (as EN-¹, *gresle* hail)]

engrain /en-gráyn, in-/ *v.tr.* **1** implant (a habit, belief, or attitude) ineradicably in a person (see also INGRAINED). **2** cause (dye, etc.) to sink deeply into a thing. [ME f. OF *engrainer* dye in grain (*en graine*): see GRAIN]
■ **1** see INSTILL 1.

engrained /en-gráynd, in-/ *adj.* inveterate (see also INGRAINED).

engram /éngram/ *n.* a memory trace, a supposed permanent change in the brain accounting for the existence of memory. □□ **engrammatic** /-grəmátik/ *adj.* [G *Engramm* f. Gk *en* in + *gramma* letter of the alphabet]

engrave /en-gráyv, in-/ *v.tr.* **1** (often foll. by *on*) inscribe, cut, or carve (a text or design) on a hard surface. **2** (often foll. by *with*) inscribe or ornament (a surface) in this way. **3** cut (a design) as lines on a metal plate, block, etc., for printing. **4** (often foll. by *on*) impress deeply on a person's memory, etc. □□ **engraver** *n.* [EN-¹ + GRAVE³]
■ **1, 2** inscribe, cut, carve, chisel, incise, score, etch, *archaic* grave; chase, enchase. **4** impress, stamp, imprint, print, engrain, fix, set, lodge, record, embed.

engraving /en-gráyving, in-/ *n.* a print made from an engraved plate, block, or other surface.
■ print, impression, etching, drypoint, lithograph; woodcut, linocut, wood *or* steel engraving, anaglyph, block, cut.

engross /en-grós, in-/ *v.tr.* **1** absorb the attention of; occupy fully (*engrossed in studying*). **2** make a fair copy of a legal document. **3** reproduce (a document, etc.) in larger letters or larger format. **4** *archaic* monopolize (a conversation, etc.). □□ **engrossing** *adj.* (in sense 1). **engrossment** *n.* [ME f. AF *engrosser*: senses 2 and 3 f. *en* in + *grosse* large writing: senses 1 and 4 f. *en gros* wholesale]
■ **1** see OCCUPY 6.

engulf /en-gúlf, in-/ *v.tr.* (also **ingulf**) **1** flow over and swamp; overwhelm. **2** swallow or plunge into a gulf. □□ **engulfment** *n.*
■ **1** see DROWN 1. **2** see SWALLOW *v.* 6.

enhance /enháns, in-/ *v.tr.* heighten or intensify (qualities, powers, value, etc.); improve (something already of good quality). □□ **enhancement** *n.* **enhancer** *n.* [ME f. AF *enhauncer*, prob. alt. f. OF *enhaucier* ult. f. L *altus* high]
■ heighten, intensify, raise, increase, augment, add to, deepen, strengthen, reinforce, sharpen, develop, amplify, magnify, enlarge, expand, maximize, lift, swell, elevate, exalt, *colloq.* boost; improve, refine, better, polish, upgrade, enrich, *formal* ameliorate.

enharmonic /énhaarmónik/ *adj. Mus.* of or having intervals smaller than a semitone (esp. such intervals as that between G sharp and A flat, these notes being made the same in a scale of equal temperament). □□ **enharmonically** *adv.* [LL *enharmonicus* f. Gk *enarmonikos* (as EN-², *harmonia* HARMONY)]

enigma /inígmə/ *n.* **1** a puzzling thing or person. **2** a riddle or paradox. □□ **enigmatic** /énigmátik/ *adj.* **enigmatical** *adj.* **enigmatically** *adv.* **enigmatize** /inígmətīz/ *v.tr.* [L *aenigma* f. Gk *ainigma -matos* f. *ainissomai* speak allusively f. *ainos* fable]
■ **1** puzzle, mystery, riddle, problem. **2** riddle, conundrum, paradox, poser, puzzler, problem, *colloq.* teaser, brainteaser, *Brit. colloq.* brain-twister.
□□ **enigmatic** see *puzzling* (PUZZLE *v.* 3).

enjambment /enjámənt/ *n.* (also **enjambement**) *Prosody* the continuation of a sentence without a pause beyond the end of a line, couplet, or stanza. [F *enjambement* f. *enjamber* (as EN-¹, *jambe* leg)]

enjoin /enjóyn, in-/ *v.tr.* **1 a** (foll. by *to* + infin.) command or order (a person). **b** (foll. by *that* + clause) issue instructions. **2** (often foll. by *on*) impose or prescribe (an action or conduct). **3** (usu. foll. by *from*) *Law* prohibit (a person) by order. □□ **enjoinment** *n.* [ME f. OF *enjoindre* f. L *injungere* (as IN-², *jungere* join)]
■ **1 a** see COMMAND *v.* 1. **1b, 2** see ORDER *v.* 1, 2, 5, 6.

enjoy /enjóy, in-/ *v.tr.* **1** take delight or pleasure in. **2** have the use or benefit of. **3** experience (*enjoy poor health*). □ **enjoy oneself** experience pleasure. □□ **enjoyer** *n.* **enjoyment** *n.* [ME f. OF *enjoier* give joy to or *enjoïr* enjoy, ult. f. L *gaudēre* rejoice]
■ **1** (take) delight in, take pleasure in, like, derive pleasure *or* satisfaction from, be partial to, appreciate, have a taste *or* preference *or* passion for, admire, cherish, be fond of, be keen on, relish (in), savor, revel *or* glory in, take to, *colloq.* be into, get a kick from *or* out of, *sl.* dig, get a lift from *or* out of, get a buzz out of, get high on, get off on, get a bang from *or* out of; love, adore. **2** have the use *or* benefit of, benefit *or* profit from, take advantage of, use to advantage, use, utilize, make use of, have, possess, command, have at one's disposal. **3** experience, have, possess; suffer with *or* from. □ **enjoy oneself** have a good *or* great *or* super time, make merry, have fun, have the time of one's life, revel, indulge oneself, disport oneself, go wild *or* crazy *or* out of one's mind, *colloq.* have a whale of a time, paint the town red, live it up, *sl.* groove, have a ball. □□ **enjoyment** pleasure, delight, joy, gratification,

---

/.../ **pronunciation**	● **part of speech**
□ **phrases, idioms, and compounds**	
□□ **derivatives**	■ **synonym section**
cross-references appear in SMALL CAPITALS or *italics*	

satisfaction, relish, zest, recreation, entertainment, diversion, amusement, *literary* delectation; use, utilization, exercise, possession, benefit, advantage.

enjoyable /enjóyəbəl, in-/ *adj.* pleasant; giving enjoyment. □□ **enjoyability** *n.* **enjoyableness** *n.* **enjoyably** *adv.*
■ see PLEASANT.

enkephalin /enkéfəlin/ *n. Biochem.* either of two morphine-like peptides occurring naturally in the brain and thought to control levels of pain. [Gk *egkephalos* brain]

enkindle /enkíndəl, in-/ *v.tr. literary* **1 a** cause (flames) to flare up. **b** stimulate (feeling, passion, etc.). **2** inflame with passion.
■ **1b, 2** see INFLAME *v.* 1.

enlace /enláys, in-/ *v.tr.* **1** encircle tightly. **2** entwine. **3** enfold. □□ **enlacement** *n.* [ME f. OF *enlacier* ult. f. L *laqueus* noose]

enlarge /enláarj, in-/ *v.* **1** *tr. & intr.* make or become larger or wider. **2 a** *tr.* describe in greater detail. **b** *intr.* (usu. foll. by *upon*) expatiate. **3** *tr. Photog.* produce an enlargement of (a negative). [ME f. OF *enlarger* (as EN-¹, LARGE)]
■ **1, 3** make *or* become larger *or* greater *or* bigger *or* wider, magnify, elongate, add to, supplement; expand, increase, extend, develop, widen, broaden, lengthen, stretch, *colloq.* blow up. **2 a** detail, amplify, expound, embellish, embroider, refine, explain, flesh out. **b** expatiate, expand, go into detail, elaborate.

enlargement /enláarjmənt, in-/ *n.* **1** the act or an instance of enlarging; the state of being enlarged. **2** *Photog.* a print that is larger than the negative from which it is produced.
■ **1** see INCREASE *n.* 1, 2.

enlarger /enláarjər, in-/ *n. Photog.* an apparatus for enlarging or reducing negatives or positives.

enlighten /enlít'n, in-/ *v.tr.* **1 a** (often foll. by *on*) instruct or inform (a person) about a subject. **b** (as **enlightened** *adj.*) well-informed; knowledgeable. **2** (esp. as **enlightened** *adj.*) free from prejudice or superstition. **3** *rhet.* or *poet.* **a** shed light on (an object). **b** give spiritual insight to (a person). □□ **enlightener** *n.*
■ **1 a** instruct, inform, educate, teach, illuminate, edify, civilize, make aware, raise a person's consciousness, apprise, guide, direct, advise, counsel, school, train. **b** (**enlightened**) well-informed, informed, educated, aware, knowledgeable, literate, cultivated, civilized, sophisticated, *colloq.* in the know. **2** (**enlightened**) unprejudiced, sensible, rational, reasonable, commonsensical, sound, levelheaded, fair-minded, clearheaded, sane, broad-minded, open-minded, liberal, emancipated, liberated; commonsense. **3 a** see ILLUMINATE 1. **b** illuminate, make a person see the light, guide, teach.

enlightenment /enlít'nmənt, in-/ *n.* **1** the act or an instance of enlightening; the state of being enlightened. **2** (**the Enlightenment**) the 18th-c. philosophy emphasizing reason and individualism rather than tradition.
■ **1** see *illumination* (ILLUMINATE).

enlist /enlíst, in-/ *v.* **1** *intr. & tr.* enroll in the armed services. **2** *tr.* secure as a means of help or support. □ **enlisted man** a soldier or sailor below the rank of officer. □□ **enlister** *n.* **enlistment** *n.*
■ **1** join up, volunteer; enroll, sign up or on, register; recruit, call up, conscript, draft. **2** secure, obtain, get, procure, employ, rally, drum up, muster (up), mobilize, gather, organize; retain.

enliven /enlívən, in-/ *v.tr.* **1** give life or spirit to. **2** make cheerful; brighten (a picture or scene). □□ **enlivener** *n.* **enlivenment** *n.*
■ **1** invigorate, stimulate, energize, vivify, breathe life into, put (some) life into, bring to life, vitalize, quicken, liven up, shake up, stir (up); get going, kindle, fire (up), spark (off), galvanize, electrify, activate, motivate, rally, revitalize, refresh, revive, *colloq.* pep up, *literary* enkindle; inspirit, animate, inspire, (a)wake, (a)waken, wake up, arouse, rouse, excite. **2** make cheerful, cheer *or* brighten (up), liven up, (up)lift, warm, lift up.

en masse /oN más/ *adv.* **1** all together. **2** in a mass. [F]

enmesh /enmésh, in-/ *v.tr.* entangle in or as in a net. □□ **enmeshment** *n.*
■ see ENTANGLE 1, 2.

enmity /énmitee/ *n.* (*pl.* **-ies**) **1** the state of being an enemy. **2** a feeling of hostility. [ME f. OF *enemitié* f. Rmc (as ENEMY)]
■ **2** see HOSTILITY 1.

ennead /éneead/ *n.* a group of nine. [Gk *enneas enneados* f. *ennea* nine]

ennoble /enṓbəl, in-/ *v.tr.* **1** make (a person) a noble. **2** make noble; elevate. □□ **ennoblement** *n.* [F *ennoblir* (as EN-¹, NOBLE)]
■ **2** see LIFT *v.* 4a.

ennui /onweé/ *n.* mental weariness from lack of occupation or interest; boredom. [F f. L *in odio*: cf. ODIUM]
■ see BOREDOM.

enology /eenólǝjee/ *n.* (*Brit.* **oenology**) the study of wines. □□ **enological** /eénəlójikəl/ *adj.* **enologist** *n.* [GK *oinos* wine]

enormity /ináwrmitee/ *n.* (*pl.* **-ies**) **1** extreme wickedness. **2** an act of extreme wickedness. **3** a serious error. **4** *disp.* great size; enormousness. [ME f. F *énormité* f. L *enormitas -tatis* f. *enormis* (as ENORMOUS)]
■ **1** wickedness, evil, heinousness, viciousness, atrociousness, monstrousness, brutality, barbarity, savagery, cruelty, violence, horribleness, horridness, flagitiousness, outrageousness, inhumanity. **2** atrocity, horror, barbarity, evil, iniquity, infamy, crime, offense, villainy, outrage. **4** see SIZE *n.*

enormous /ináwrmǝs/ *adj.* very large; huge (*enormous animals*; *an enormous difference*). □□ **enormously** *adv.* **enormousness** *n.* [L *enormis* (as E-, *norma* pattern, standard)]
■ big, large, huge, immense, vast, massive, gigantic, mammoth, colossal, great, giant, *colloq.* whacking, thumping, socking, *sl.* humongous, whopping; gross, obese, gargantuan, monstrous, elephantine, monumental, monolithic, titanic, behemoth, leviathan, strapping, bulky, king-size, prodigious, *colloq.* hulking, jumbo; tremendous, stupendous, thundering, *sl.* walloping. □□ **enormousness** see SIZE *n.*

enosis /inṓsis, énōsees/ *n.* the political union of Cyprus and Greece, as an ideal or proposal. [mod. Gk *enōsis* f. *ena* one]

enough /inúf/ *adj.*, *n.*, *adv.*, & *int.* ● *adj.* as much or as many as required (*we have enough apples*; *we do not have enough sugar*; *earned enough money to buy a house*). ● *n.* an amount or quantity that is enough (*we have enough of everything now*; *enough is as good as a feast*). ● *adv.* **1** to the required degree; adequately (*are you warm enough?*). **2** fairly (*she sings well enough*). **3** very; quite (*you know well enough what I mean*; *oddly enough*). ● *int.* that is enough (in various senses, esp. to put an end to an action, thing said, etc.). □ **have had enough of** want no more of; be satiated with or tired of. [OE *genog* f. Gmc]
■ *adj.* sufficient, adequate, ample. ● *n.* plenty; ample supply, abundance, (one's) fill; sufficiency, adequacy. ● *adv.* **1, 2** adequately, sufficiently, reasonably, fairly, satisfactorily. **3** very, quite, perfectly, full, *archaic* right, *colloq.* jolly, damn(ed), darned, *sl.* plumb. ● *int.* stop, halt, no more, hold it, *colloq.* that's it.

en passant /óN pasóN/ *adv.* **1** by the way. **2** *Chess* used with reference to the permitted capture of an opponent's pawn that has just advanced two squares in its first move with a pawn that could have taken it if it had advanced only one square. [F, = in passing]
■ **1** see *in passing* (PASS¹).

enplane /enpláyn, in-/ *v.intr. & .tr.* (also **emplane** /em-, im-/) go or put on board an airplane.
■ see EMBARK 1.

enquire var. of INQUIRE.

enquiry var. of INQUIRY.

enrage /enráyj, in-/ *v.tr.* (often foll. by *at, by, with*) make furious. □□ **enragement** *n.* [F *enrager* (as EN-¹, RAGE)]
■ anger, infuriate, madden, incense, provoke, inflame, make a person's blood boil, get *or* put a person's back

up, make a person's hackles rise, raise a person's hackles, make a person see red, empurple, excite a person to (a) frenzy *or* rage, get on a person's nerves, *Brit.* get a person's blood up, *colloq.* get a person's dander up, drive crazy *or* mad *or* up the wall *or* around the bend, wind up, *sl.* burn up.

en rapport /ón rapáwr/ *adv.* (usu. foll. by *with*) in harmony or rapport. [F: see RAPPORT]
- see SYMPATHIZE 1.

enrapture /enrápchər, in-/ *v.tr.* give intense delight to.
- thrill, delight, electrify, transport, carry away, intoxicate; charm, enchant, bewitch, spellbind, enthrall, captivate, beguile, fascinate, rivet, transfix, mesmerize, entrance, hypnotize.

enrich /enrích, in-/ *v.tr.* **1** make rich or richer. **2** make richer in quality, flavor, nutritive value, etc. **3** add to the contents of (a collection, museum, or book). **4** increase the content of an isotope in (material), esp. enrich uranium with isotope U-235. □□ **enrichment** *n.* [ME f. OF *enrichir* (as EN-[1], RICH)]
- **1, 2** enhance, improve, upgrade, better, raise, increase, intensify, elevate, refine, add to, *formal* ameliorate. **3** add to, expand, enlarge, extend; revise, improve, elaborate, develop, lengthen. □□ **enrichment** enhancement, improvement, embellishment.

enrobe /enrṓb, in-/ *v.intr.* put on a robe, vestment, etc.
- see ROBE *v.* 2.

enroll /enrṓl, in-/ *v.* (also **enrol**) (**enrolled, enrolling**) **1** *intr.* enter one's name on a list, esp. as a commitment to membership. **2** *tr.* **a** write the name of (a person) on a list. **b** (usu. foll. by *in*) incorporate (a person) as a member of a society, etc. **3** *tr. hist.* enter (a deed, etc.) among the rolls of a court of justice. **4** *tr.* record. □□ **enrollee** /-lee/ *n.* **enroller** *n.* [ME f. OF *enroller* (as EN-[1], *rolle* ROLL)]
- **1** register, sign up *or* on, give one's name; enlist, join. **2** write *or* note *or* put down, register, sign up *or* on *or* in; list; enlist, recruit. **4** record, chronicle, set *or* put down, register, note, list, inscribe, catalog.

enrollment /enrṓlmənt, in-/ *n.* (also **enrolment**) **1** the act or an instance of enrolling; the state of being enrolled. **2** the number of persons enrolled, esp. at a school or college.
- **1** see *initiation* (INITIATE).

en route /ón rōōt/ *adv.* (usu. foll. by *to, for*) on the way. [F]
Ens. *abbr.* ensign.

ensconce /enskóns, in-/ *v.tr.* (usu. *refl.* or in *passive*) establish or settle comfortably, safely, or secretly.
- see ESTABLISH 1, 2.

ensemble /onsómbəl/ *n.* **1 a** a thing viewed as the sum of its parts. **b** the general effect of this. **2** a set of clothes worn together; an outfit. **3** a group of actors, dancers, musicians, etc., performing together, esp. subsidiary dancers in ballet, etc. **4** *Mus.* **a** a concerted passage for an ensemble. **b** the manner in which this is performed (*good ensemble*). **5** *Physics* a group of systems with the same constitution but possibly in different states. [F, ult. f. L *insimul* (as IN-[2], *simul* at the same time)]
- **1** composite, aggregate; collection, set, assemblage, agglomeration, conglomeration, body, group, grouping. **2** outfit, costume, suit, equipage, uniform, *colloq.* getup, rig, *poet.* array. **3** band, group, orchestra, chorus, choir, *sl.* combo; company, troupe, cast.

enshrine /enshrín, in-/ *v.tr.* **1** enclose in or as in a shrine. **2** serve as a shrine for. **3** preserve or cherish. □□ **enshrinement** *n.*
- **3** see REVERE.

enshroud /enshrówd, in-/ *v.tr. literary* **1** cover with or as with a shroud. **2** cover completely; hide from view.
- see ENVELOP 1.

ensign /énsin, -sīn/ *n.* **1 a** a banner or flag, esp. the military or naval flag of a nation. **b** *Brit.* a flag with the union in the corner. **2** a standard-bearer. **3 a** *hist.* the lowest commissioned infantry officer. **b** the lowest commissioned officer in the US Navy or US Coast Guard. □ **white ensign** *Brit.* the ensign of the Royal Navy and the Royal Yacht Squadron.

ensigncy *n.* [ME f. OF *enseigne* f. L *insignia*: see INSIGNIA]
- **1 a** see FLAG[1] *n.*

ensilage /énsilij/ *n. & v.* ● *n.* = SILAGE. ● *v.tr.* treat (fodder) by ensilage. [F (as ENSILE)]

ensile /ensíl, in-/ *v.tr.* **1** put (fodder) into a silo. **2** preserve (fodder) in a silo. [F *ensiler* f. Sp. *ensilar* (as EN-[1], SILO)]

enslave /ensláyv, in-/ *v.tr.* make (a person) a slave. □□ **enslavement** *n.* **enslaver** *n.*
- enthrall, bind, yoke, fetter, enchain, shackle, trammel, *literary* enfetter; subjugate, oppress, dominate, overpower, subject, put down, humiliate, reduce. □□ **enslavement** see SLAVERY 1.

ensnare /ensnáir, in-/ *v.tr.* catch in or as in a snare; entrap. □□ **ensnarement** *n.*
- see TRAP[1] *v.* 1.

ensue /ensṓo, in-/ *v.intr.* **1** happen afterward. **2** (often foll. by *from, on*) occur as a result. [ME f. OF *ensuivre* ult. f. L *sequi* follow]
- see RESULT *v.* 1.

en suite /ón swéet/ *adv.* forming a single unit (*bedroom with bathroom en suite*). [F, = in sequence]

ensure /enshṓor, in-/ *v.tr.* **1** (often foll. by *that* + clause) make certain. **2** (usu. foll. by *to, for*) secure (a thing for a person, etc.). **3** (usu. foll. by *against*) make safe. □□ **ensurer** *n.* [ME f. AF *enseürer* f. OF *aseürer* ASSURE]
- **1** make sure *or* certain, guarantee; see (to it), insure. **3** make safe, protect, guard, shelter, shield, safeguard, secure, insure.

enswathe /enswáyth, in-/ *v.tr.* bind or wrap in or as in a bandage. □□ **enswathement** *n.*
- swathe, bind, wrap, bandage.

ENT *abbr.* ear, nose, and throat.

-ent /ənt, ent/ *suffix* **1** forming adjectives denoting attribution of an action (*consequent*) or state (*existent*). **2** forming nouns denoting an agent (*coefficient*; *president*). [from or after F *-ent* or L *-ent-* pres. part. stem of verbs (cf. -ANT)]

entablature /entáblǝchər, in-/ *n. Archit.* the upper part of a classical building supported by columns or a colonnade, comprising architrave, frieze, and cornice. [It. *intavolatura* f. *intavolare* board up (as IN-[2], *tavola* table)]

entablement /entáybəlmənt, in-/ *n.* a platform supporting a statue, above the dado and base. [F, f. *entabler* (as EN-[1], TABLE)]

entail /entáyl, in-/ *v. & n.* ● *v.tr.* **1 a** necessitate or involve unavoidably (*the work entails much effort*). **b** give rise to; involve. **2** *Law* bequeath (property, etc.) so that it remains within a family. **3** (usu. foll. by *on*) bestow (a thing) inalienably. ● *n. Law* **1** an entailed estate. **2** the succession to such an estate. □□ **entailment** *n.* [ME, f. EN-[1] + AF *taile* TAIL[2]]
- *v.* **1** necessitate, involve, mean, require, call for, demand; presuppose, imply. **b** give rise to, occasion, lead to, cause, create.

entangle /entánggəl, in-/ *v.tr.* **1** cause to get caught in a snare or among obstacles. **2** cause to become tangled. **3** involve in difficulties or illicit activities. **4** make (a thing) tangled or intricate; complicate.
- **1, 2** tangle (up), mesh, enmesh, snarl, ensnarl, catch (up), entwine, intertwine, entrammel, trammel, ravel (up), snag, foul (up), knot (up), twist (up), intertwist, coil, entrap, trap, lock, jam. **3** involve, embroil, mix up, entwine, catch up, tangle (up), tie up, draw *or* drag in, ensnare, enmesh, snarl, ensnarl, implicate, associate. **4** make involved *or* intricate, confuse, throw into confusion *or* perplexity, blur, muddle, confound, befuddle, mix up, jumble (up); complicate, make complicated *or* complex, compound.

entanglement /entánggəlmənt, in-/ *n.* **1** the act or condition of entangling or being entangled. **2 a** a thing that entangles.

/.../ **pronunciation**	● **part of speech**
□ **phrases, idioms, and compounds**	
□□ **derivatives**	■ **synonym section**
cross-references appear in SMALL CAPITALS or *italics*	

b *Mil.* an extensive barrier erected to obstruct an enemy's movements (esp. one made of stakes and interlaced barbed wire). **3** a compromising (esp. amorous) relationship.
■ **1, 2a** see TANGLE *n.* 1. **3** see LIAISON 2.

entasis /éntəsis/ *n. Archit.* a slight convex curve in a column shaft to correct the visual illusion that straight sides give of curving inward. [mod.L f. Gk f. *enteinō* to stretch]

entellus /entéləs, in-/ *n.* = HANUMAN. [name of a Trojan in Virgil's *Aeneid*]

entente /aantaánt/ *n.* **1** = ENTENTE CORDIALE. **2** a group of nations in such a relation. [F, = understanding (as INTENT)]

entente cordiale /ontóNt kawrdyaál/ *n.* a friendly understanding between nations, esp. (often **Entente Cordiale**) that reached in 1904 between Britain and France. [F, = cordial understanding: see ENTENTE]

enter /éntər/ *v.* **1 a** *intr.* (often foll. by *into*) go or come in. **b** *tr.* go or come into. **c** *intr.* come on stage (as a direction: *enter Macbeth*). **2** *tr.* penetrate; go through; spread through (*a bullet entered his chest; a smell of toast entered the room*). **3** *tr.* (often foll. by *up*) write (a name, details, etc.) in a list, book, etc. **4 a** *intr.* register or announce oneself as a competitor (*entered the long jump*). **b** *tr.* become a competitor in (an event). **c** *tr.* record the name of (a person, etc.) as a competitor (*entered two horses for the Kentucky Derby*). **5** *tr.* **a** become a member of (a society, etc.). **b** enroll as a member or prospective member of a society, school, etc.; admit or obtain admission for. **6** *tr.* make known; present for consideration (*entered a protest*). **7** *tr.* put into an official record. **8** *intr.* (foll. by *into*) **a** engage in (conversation, relations, an undertaking, etc.). **b** subscribe to; bind oneself by (an agreement, etc.). **c** form part of (one's calculations, plans, etc.). **d** sympathize with (feelings, etc.). **9** *intr.* (foll. by *on, upon*) **a** begin; undertake; begin to deal with (a subject). **b** assume the functions of (an office). **c** assume possession of (property). **10** *intr.* (foll. by *up*) complete a series of entries in (account books, etc.). □□ **enterer** *n.* [ME f. OF *entrer* f. L *intrare*]

■ **1 a** go *or* come in, go *or* come into. **b** go *or* come into, pass into. **c** come *or* go on (stage), make an entrance. **2** penetrate, pierce, lance, spear, stab, stick (into), bore (into), go *or* pass through, go *or* pass into, puncture, perforate, riddle; spread *or* seep through(out), pervade, permeate, invade; infiltrate. **3** write *or* put *or* note (down), make a note of, set down, inscribe, take (down), jot down, record, register, list; log, document, chronicle, minute. **4** put in (for), put oneself forward (for), register (for). **5** enroll in, join, become a member of, sign up for; admit, let in, allow to enter, take *or* allow in. **6** make known, communicate, inform of; present, submit, tender, offer, proffer, lodge, file, prefer, put forward, advance, propose. **7** file, submit, register, record. **8** (*enter into*) **a** engage *or* participate *or* take part *or* partake in. **b** subscribe to, sign, be (a) party to, co-sign, countersign. **c** form part of, come into, play a part in, feature in. **9 a** (*enter on* or *upon*) begin, start, set about, undertake, *formal* commence; take up *or* on, go *or* launch into, embark on, pursue, investigate, analyze, discuss, tackle, proceed to, touch on. **b** take up, begin, start. **c** see ACQUIRE 2.

enteric /entérik/ *adj. & n.* ● *adj.* of the intestines. ● *n.* (in full **enteric fever**) typhoid. □□ **enteritis** /éntərítis/ *n.* [Gk *enterikos* (as ENTERO-)]

entero- /éntərō/ *comb. form* intestine. [Gk *enteron* intestine]

enterostomy /éntəróstəmee/ *n.* (*pl.* **-ies**) *Surgery* a surgical operation in which the small intestine is brought through the abdominal wall and opened, in order to bypass the stomach or the colon.

enterotomy /éntərótəmee/ *n.* (*pl.* **-ies**) *Surgery* the surgical cutting open of the intestine.

enterovirus /éntərōvírəs/ *n.* a virus infecting the intestines and sometimes spreading to other parts of the body, esp. the central nervous system.

enterprise /éntərprīz/ *n.* **1** an undertaking, esp. a bold or difficult one. **2** (as a personal attribute) readiness to engage in such undertakings (*has no enterprise*). **3** a business firm.

□ **enterprise zone** a depressed (usu. urban) area where government incentives such as tax concessions are available to encourage investment. □□ **enterpriser** *n.* [ME f. OF *entreprise* fem. past part. of *entreprendre* var. of *emprendre* ult. f. L *prendere, prehendere* take]

■ **1** undertaking, project, venture, adventure, initiative, speculation, plan, scheme, design, program, activity, endeavor, effort, operation, task, concern. **2** initiative, resourcefulness, adventurousness, assertiveness, boldness, daring, nerve, audacity, verve, courage, pluck, mettle, spirit, vigor, energy, zip, drive, dynamism, go, dash, push, ambition, determination, resolve, purposefulness, purpose, motivation, willpower, aggressiveness, zeal, enthusiasm, keenness, *colloq.* get-up-and-go, gumption, guts, grit, spunk, pep, vim, zing. **3** business, firm, company, practice, house, concern, establishment, institution, organization, *colloq.* outfit; corporation, partnership.

enterprising /éntərprizing/ *adj.* **1** ready to engage in enterprises. **2** resourceful; imaginative; energetic. □□ **enterprisingly** *adv.*

■ go-ahead, progressive, venturesome, forward-looking, adventurous, daring, courageous, bold, brave, plucky, mettlesome, audacious, clever, resourceful, ingenious, imaginative, inspired, inventive, innovative, original, creative, aspiring, ambitious, confident, fearless, intrepid, high-flying, goal-oriented, determined, persevering, resolved, resolute, purposeful, purposive, eager, keen, zealous, enthusiastic, spirited, vigorous, aggressive, assertive, energetic, indefatigable, tireless, *colloq.* pushy, go-getting, on the make, gutsy. □□ **enterprisingly** adventurously, resourcefully, imaginatively, energetically.

entertain /éntərtáyn/ *v.tr.* **1** amuse; occupy agreeably. **2 a** receive or treat as a guest. **b** (*absol.*) receive guests (*they entertain a great deal*). **3** give attention or consideration to (an idea, feeling, or proposal). [ME f. F *entretenir* ult. f. L *tenēre* hold]

■ **1** amuse, make laugh, tickle, cheer, delight, please, thrill, titillate, *colloq.* tickle pink *or* to death; beguile, divert, distract, absorb, engross, interest, engage, occupy. **2 a** receive, accommodate, treat, feed, regale. **b** have people over, have visitors *or* guests. **3** contemplate, consider, ponder, dwell on; harbor, experience; tolerate, allow; foster, encourage, nurse.

entertainer /éntərtáynər/ *n.* a person who entertains, esp. professionally on stage, etc.
■ see PLAYER 3.

entertaining /éntərtáyning/ *adj.* amusing; diverting.
■ amusing, funny, comic, humorous, comical, witty, hilarious, droll, *colloq.* hysterical; diverting, engaging, beguiling, absorbing, interesting, delightful, enjoyable, pleasant, fun, pleasing, pleasurable, charming, agreeable.

entertainment /éntərtáynmənt/ *n.* **1** the act or an instance of entertaining; the process of being entertained. **2** a public performance or show. **3** diversions or amusements for guests, etc. **4** amusement (*much to my entertainment*). **5** hospitality. □ **entertainment center** a piece of furniture, usu. with several shelves to accommodate a television, video cassette recorder, stereo system, etc.

■ **1** amusement, diversion, distraction, pleasure, play, sport, interest; divertissement, beguilement, fun, enjoyment, recreation, leisure, relaxation, R and R, rest and recreation, relief, *literary* delectation. **2, 3** performance, show, production, presentation, piece, extravaganza, spectacular, pageant, spectacle. **4** see AMUSEMENT 2.

enthalpy /énthəlpee, enthálpee/ *n. Physics* the total thermodynamic heat content of a system. [Gk *enthalpō* warm in (as EN-[1], *thalpō* to heat)]

enthrall /enthráwl, in-/ *v.tr.* (also **enthral, inthral, inthrall**) (**-thralled, -thralling**) **1** (often as **enthralling** *adj.*) captivate; please greatly. **2** enslave. □□ **enthrallment** *n.* [EN-[1] + THRALL]

■ **1** see CAPTIVATE; (**enthralling**) captivating, mesmerizing, spellbinding, hypnotizing, fascinating, gripping, absorbing, riveting, entrancing, enchanting, bewitching, intriguing, beguiling. **2** see ENSLAVE.

enthrone /enthrṓn, in-/ *v.tr.* **1** install (a king, bishop, etc.) on a throne, esp. ceremonially. **2** exalt. □□ **enthronement** *n.*

■ **1** see INSTALL 2.

enthuse /enthŏŏz, in-/ *v.intr.* & *tr. colloq.* be or make enthusiastic. [back-form. f. ENTHUSIASM]

■ see ENERGIZE.

enthusiasm /enthŏŏzeeazəm, in-/ *n.* **1** (often foll. by *for, about*) **a** a strong interest or admiration. **b** great eagerness. **2** an object of enthusiasm. **3** *archaic* extravagant religious emotion. [F *enthousiasme* or LL *enthusiasmus* f. Gk *enthousiasmos* f. *entheos* possessed by a god, inspired (as EN-², *theos* god)]

■ **1** interest, passion, fascination, infatuation, obsession, mania, fanaticism, rage, devotion, devotedness, admiration, liking, predilection, love; eagerness, keenness, appetite, relish, avidity, (burning) desire, fervor, earnestness, ardor, feeling, zeal, gusto, zest, excitement. **2** passion, craze, mania, fad, obsession, *colloq.* thing, *sl.* bag; interest, hobby, pastime.

enthusiast /enthŏŏzeeast, in-/ *n.* **1** (often foll. by *for*) a person who is full of enthusiasm. **2** a visionary; a self-deluded person. [F *enthousiaste* or eccl.L *enthousiastes* f. Gk (as ENTHUSIASM)]

■ **1** fan, devotee, aficionado, admirer, lover, *colloq.* buff; fanatic, zealot, energumen, addict, hound, faddist, hobbyist, *colloq.* freak, maniac, *sl.* fiend, nut, bug; champion.

enthusiastic /enthŏŏzeeástik, in-/ *adj.* having or showing enthusiasm. □□ **enthusiastically** *adv.* [Gk *enthousiastikos* (as ENTHUSIASM)]

■ eager, keen, obsessive, avid, fervent, compulsive, fervid, ardent, *literary* perfervid; vehement, animated, spirited, impassioned, enthused, fiery, exuberant, zestful, excited; hearty, vigorous; passionate, earnest, dedicated, committed, devoted, active, devout, zealous, mad, maniacal, rabid, fanatic, fanatical, wild, hotheaded, extreme.

enthymeme /énthimeem/ *n. Logic* a syllogism in which one premise is not explicitly stated. [L *enthymema* f. Gk *enthumēma* f. *enthumeomai* consider (as EN-², *thumos* mind)]

entice /entís, in-/ *v.tr.* (often foll. by *from, into,* or *to* + infin.) persuade by the offer of pleasure or reward. □□ **enticement** *n.* **enticer** *n.* **enticingly** *adv.* [ME f. OF *enticier* prob. f. Rmc]

■ lure, tempt, wile away, allure, attract, draw (on), decoy, seduce, charm, coax, persuade, prevail (up)on, induce, beguile, cajole, blandish, coax, wheedle, lead on, inveigle, *colloq.* sweet-talk, soft-soap. □□ **enticement** temptation, allurement, beguilement, seduction, cajolery, wheedling, blandishment, coaxing, persuasion, *colloq.* soft soap; lure, bait, decoy, trap, inducement, attraction, temptation, *colloq.* come-on. **enticingly** seductively, temptingly, persuasively, beguilingly.

entire /entír, in-/ *adj.* & *n.* ● *adj.* **1** whole; complete. **2** not broken or decayed. **3** unqualified; absolute (*an entire success*). **4** in one piece; continuous. **5** not castrated. **6** *Bot.* without indentation. **7** pure; unmixed. ● *n.* an uncastrated animal. [ME f. AF *enter,* OF *entier* f. L *integer* (as IN-², *tangere* touch)]

■ *adj.* **1** whole, complete, total, full, undivided; uncut, unabridged, undiminished, uncensored. **2** intact, whole, perfect, unbroken, undamaged, unharmed, inviolate, sound, unscathed, unblemished; in one piece, without a scratch. **3** see ABSOLUTE *adj.* 1. **4** continuous, full, whole, complete, total, uninterrupted, unbroken, unrelieved. **7** unmixed, unalloyed; see also PURE 1, 2.

entirely /entírlee, in-/ *adv.* **1** wholly; completely (*the stock is entirely exhausted*). **2** solely; exclusively (*did it entirely for my benefit*).

■ **1** completely, wholly, altogether, fully, perfectly, totally, utterly, thoroughly, absolutely, quite, a *or* one hundred per cent; lock, stock, and barrel; in every respect, in all respects, in every way, in toto, in full, in its entirety, every inch, to the nth degree, unreservedly, without exception *or* reservation, unqualifiedly, unequivocally; clear, clean; from head to toe *or* foot; (right) down to the ground; from A to Z, from beginning to end, from cover to cover, from start to finish; hook, line, and sinker; heart and soul, body and soul; root and branch; head over heels. **2** solely, exclusively, only, merely.

entirety /entíərtee, in-/ *n.* (*pl.* **-ies**) **1** completeness. **2** (usu. foll. by *of*) the sum total. □ **in its entirety** in its complete form; completely. [ME f. OF *entiereté* f. L *integritas -tatis* f. *integer*: see ENTIRE]

■ **1** completeness, totality, whole(ness), fullness; perfection, togetherness, unity, integrity. **2** whole, sum total, aggregate, *colloq.* the (whole *or* entire) lot, the whole shooting match, *sl.* the whole (kit and) caboodle. □ **in its entirety** see *in full* (FULL¹).

entitle /entítəl, in-/ *v.tr.* **1 a** (usu. foll. by *to*) give (a person, etc.) a just claim. **b** (foll. by *to* + infin.) give (a person, etc.) a right. **2 a** give (a book, etc.) the title of. **b** *archaic* give (a person) the title of (*entitled him sultan*). □□ **entitlement** *n.* [ME f. AF *entitler,* OF *entiteler* f. LL *intitulare* (as IN-², TITLE)]

■ **1 a** allow, permit; make eligible, qualify. **b** allow, permit, authorize, give leave *or* permission, empower, qualify, fit; license. **2 a** name, title, call. **b** see CALL *v.* 7.

entity /éntitee/ *n.* (*pl.* **-ies**) **1** a thing with distinct existence, as opposed to a quality or relation. **2** a thing's existence regarded distinctly; a thing's essential nature. □□ **entitative** /-títətiv/ *adj.* [F *entité* or med.L *entitas* f. LL *ens* being]

■ **1** thing, object, phenomenon, element, unit, quantity, being; organism, specimen, creature, individual, body. **2** life, being, existence; essence, quintessence, *Philos.* quiddity.

ento- /éntō/ *comb. form* within. [Gk *entos* within]

entomb /entŏŏm, in-/ *v.tr.* **1** place in or as in a tomb. **2** serve as a tomb for. □□ **entombment** *n.* [OF *entomber* (as EN-¹, TOMB)]

entomo- /éntəmō/ *comb. form* insect. [Gk *entomos* cut up (in neut. = INSECT) f. EN-² + *temnō* cut]

entomology /éntəmóləjee/ *n.* the study of the forms and behavior of insects. □□ **entomological** /-məlójikəl/ *adj.* **entomologist** *n.* [F *entomologie* or mod.L *entomologia* (as ENTOMO-, -LOGY)]

entomophagous /éntəmófəgəs/ *adj. Zool.* insect-eating.

entomophilous /éntəmófiləs/ *adj. Biol.* pollinated by insects.

entophyte /éntōfīt/ *n. Bot.* a plant growing inside a plant or animal.

entourage /óntŏŏráazh/ *n.* **1** people attending an important person. **2** surroundings. [F f. *entourer* surround]

■ **1** see RETINUE.

entr'acte /aantrákt, aán-/ *n.* an interval between two acts of a play. **2** a piece of music or a dance performed during this. [F f. *entre* between + *acte* act]

■ see INTERLUDE 1, 2.

entrails /éntraylz, -trəlz/ *n.pl.* **1** the bowels and intestines of a person or animal. **2** the innermost parts (*entrails of the earth*). [ME f. OF *entrailles* f. med.L *intralia* alt. f. L *interaneus* internal f. *inter* among]

■ see GUT *n.* 1, 2.

entrain¹ /entráyn, in-/ *v.intr.* & *tr.* go or put on board a train. □□ **entrainment** *n.*

entrain² /entráyn, in-/ *v.tr.* **1** (of a fluid) carry (particles, etc.) along in its flow. **2** drag along. □□ **entrainment** *n.* [F *entraîner* (as EN-¹, *traîner* drag, formed as TRAIN)]

/.../ **pronunciation**	● **part of speech**
□ **phrases, idioms, and compounds**	
□□ **derivatives**	■ **synonym section**
cross-references appear in SMALL CAPITALS or *italics*	

entrance[1] /éntrəns/ *n.* **1** the act or an instance of going or coming in. **2** a door, passage, etc., by which one enters. **3** right of admission. **4** the coming of an actor on stage. **5** *Mus.* = ENTRY 8. **6** (foll. by *into*, *upon*) entering into office, etc. **7** (in full **entrance fee**) a fee paid for admission to a society, club, exhibition, etc. [OF (as ENTER, -ANCE)]
■ **1, 4** going *or* coming in, going *or* coming on, coming, entry, arrival, appearance; ingress. **2** entry, entranceway, entryway, door, doorway, gate, way in, access, inlet, ingress; opening. **3** (right of) entry, access, admission, admittance, entrée, leave *or* permission to enter. **6** start, arrival, entry, inception, *formal* commencement. **7** see CHARGE *n.* 1a.

entrance[2] /entráns, in-/ *v.tr.* **1** enchant; delight. **2** put into a trance. **3** (often foll. by *with*) overwhelm with strong feeling. □□ **entrancement** *n.* **entrancing** *adj.* **entrancingly** *adv.*
■ **1** enchant, bewitch, spellbind, fascinate, transport, carry away, delight, enrapture, intoxicate, thrill, electrify, ravish, charm, attract, allure, beguile, mesmerize, hypnotize, stun, transfix, captivate, enthrall, take a person's breath away, overpower, hex, *archaic* witch, *colloq.* bowl over, send, *poet.* trance. **2** hypnotize, mesmerize, *poet.* trance. **3** see OVERWHELM 1.

entrant /éntrənt/ *n.* a person who enters (esp. an examination, profession, etc.). [F, part. of *entrer*: see ENTER]
■ see ENTRY 7a.

entrap /entráp, in-/ *v.tr.* (**entrapped, entrapping**) **1** catch in or as in a trap. **2** (often foll. by *into* + verbal noun) beguile or trick (a person). □□ **entrapper** *n.* [OF *entraper* (as EN-[1], TRAP[1])]
■ **1** see TRAP[1] *v.* 1. **2** see BEGUILE 3, SEDUCE 2.

entrapment /entrápmənt, in-/ *n.* **1** the act or an instance of entrapping; the process of being entrapped. **2** *Law* inducement to commit a crime, esp. by the authorities to secure a prosecution.

entreat /entreét, in-/ *v.tr.* **1 a** (foll. by *to* + infin. or *that* + clause) ask (a person) earnestly. **b** ask earnestly for (a thing). **2** *archaic* treat; act toward (a person). □□ **entreatingly** *adv.* [ME f. OF *entraiter* (as EN-[1], *traiter* TREAT)]
■ **1** see ASK 2.

entreaty /entreétee, in-/ *n.* (*pl.* **-ies**) an earnest request; a supplication. [ENTREAT, after TREATY]
■ see REQUEST *n.* 1, 2.

entrechat /óntrəsháa/ *n.* a leap in ballet, with one or more crossings of the legs while in the air. [F f. It. (*capriola*) *intrecciata* complicated (caper)]

entrecôte /óntrəkōt/ *n.* a boned steak cut off the sirloin. [F f. *entre* between + *côte* rib]

entrée /óntray/ *n.* (also **entree**) **1** *Cookery* **a** esp. *US* the main dish of a meal. **b** *Brit.* a dish served between the fish and meat courses. **2** the right or privilege of admission. [F, = ENTRY]
■ **2** see ADMISSION 2a.

entremets /óntrəmáy/ *n.* **1** a sweet dish. **2** any light dish served between two courses. [F f. *entre* between + *mets* dish]

entrench /entrénch, in-/ *v.* (also **intrench**) **1** *tr.* establish firmly (in a defensible position, in office, etc.). **2** *tr.* surround (a post, army, town, etc.) with a trench as a fortification. **3** *tr.* apply extra safeguards to (rights, etc., guaranteed by legislation). **4** *intr.* entrench oneself. **5** *intr.* (foll. by *upon*) encroach; trespass. □ **entrench oneself** adopt a well-defended position. □□ **entrenchment** *n.*
■ **1** fix, establish, root, embed, plant, set. **5** encroach, trespass, intrude, make inroads; (*entrench upon*) invade, infringe.

entre nous /óntrə nōō/ *adv.* **1** between you and me. **2** in private. [F, = between ourselves]

entrepôt /óntrəpō/ *n.* **1** a warehouse for temporary storage of goods in transit. **2** a commercial center for import and export, and for collection and distribution. [F f. *entre-* INTER- + *poser* place]

entrepreneur /óntrəprənŏōr/ *n.* **1** a person who undertakes an enterprise or business, with the chance of profit or loss.

2 a contractor acting as an intermediary. **3** the person in effective control of a commercial undertaking. **4** a person who organizes entertainments, esp. musical performances. □□ **entrepreneurial** *adj.* **entrepreneurialism** *n.* (also **entrepreneurism**). **entrepreneurially** *adv.* **entrepreneurship** *n.* [F f. *entreprendre* undertake: see ENTERPRISE]
■ **1** see ADVENTURER 2. **2** see INTERMEDIARY. **3** see EXECUTIVE *n.* 1.

entresol /óntrəsol/ *n.* a low story between the first and the ground floor; a mezzanine floor. [F f. *entre* between + *sol* ground]

entrism var. of ENTRYISM.

entropy /éntrəpee/ *n.* **1** *Physics* a measure of the unavailability of a system's thermal energy for conversion into mechanical work. **2** *Physics* a measure of the disorganization or degradation of the universe. **3** a measure of the rate of transfer of information in a message, etc. □□ **entropic** /-trópik/ *adj.* **entropically** *adv.* [G *Entropie* (as EN-[2], Gk *tropē* transformation)]

entrust /entrúst, in-/ *v.tr.* (also **intrust**) **1** (foll. by *to*) give responsibility for (a person or a thing) to a person in whom one has confidence. **2** (foll. by *with*) assign responsibility for a thing to (a person). □□ **entrustment** *n.*
■ **1** assign, delegate, depute, leave, consign, commit, give. **2** trust, charge, burden.

entry /éntree/ *n.* (*pl.* **-ies**) **1 a** the act or an instance of going or coming in. **b** the coming of an actor on stage. **c** ceremonial entrance. **2** liberty to go or come in. **3 a** a place of entrance; a door, gate, etc. **b** a lobby. **4** *Brit.* a passage between buildings. **5** the mouth of a river. **6 a** an item entered (in a diary, list, account book, etc.). **b** the recording of this. **7 a** a person or thing competing in a race, contest, etc. **b** a list of competitors. **8** the start or resumption of music for a particular instrument in an ensemble. **9** *Law* the act of taking possession. **10** *Bridge* **a** the transfer of the lead to one's partner's hand. **b** a card providing this. □ **entry form** an application form for a competition. [ME f. OF *entree* ult. f. L *intrare* ENTER]
■ **1** going *or* coming in, going *or* coming on, coming, entrance, arrival, appearance; ingress. **2** access, entrance, entrée, admittance, admission, leave *or* permission to enter. **3 a** entrance, entranceway, entryway, door, doorway, gate, way in, access, inlet, ingress. **b** see LOBBY *n.* 1. **6 a** record, item, note, point, **b** recording, registration, listing. **7 a** competitor, entrant, contestant, participant, player, candidate.

entryism /éntreeizəm/ *n.* (also **entrism**) infiltration into a political organization to change or subvert its policies or objectives. □□ **entrist** *n.* **entryist** *n.*

entwine /entwín, in-/ *v.* (also **intwine** /in-/) **1** *tr.* & *intr.* (foll. by *with*, *about*, *around*) twine together (a thing with or around another). **2** *tr.* (as **entwined** *adj.*) entangled. **3** *tr.* interweave. □□ **entwinement** *n.*
■ **1** interlace, braid, weave, intertwine, twine, plait, wreathe, twist, wind, splice, pleach, tie, knit, crisscross. **2** (**entwined**) entangled, tangled. **3** interweave, interlace, wreathe.

enucleate /inŏōkleeayt, inyŏō-/ *v.tr.* *Surgery* extract (a tumor, etc.). □□ **enucleation** /-áyshən/ *n.* [L *enucleare* (as E-, NUCLEUS)]

E-number /éenumbər/ *n.* the letter E followed by a code number, designating food additives according to EC directives.

enumerate /inŏōmərayt, inyŏō-/ *v.tr.* **1** specify (items); mention one by one. **2** count; establish the number of. □□ **enumerable** *adj.* **enumeration** /-ráyshən/ *n.* **enumerative** /-raytiv, -rətiv/ *adj.* [L *enumerare* (as E-, NUMBER)]
■ **1** specify, mention, name, identify, cite, list, itemize, catalog, recite, tick *or* check off, reel *or* rattle off, run through. **2** count (up), calculate, figure (up), compute, reckon (up), work out, tally, tot (up), total (up) add (up), sum, number, quantify. □□ **enumeration** see ACCOUNT *n.* 6.

enumerator /inŏōməraytər, inyŏō-/ *n.* **1** a person who enumerates. **2** a person employed in census taking.

enunciate /inúnseeayt/ *v.tr.* **1** pronounce (words) clearly. **2** express (a proposition or theory) in definite terms. **3** proclaim. ▫▫ **enunciation** /-áyshən/ *n.* **enunciative** /-seeətiv/ *adj.* **enunciator** *n.* [L *enuntiare* (as E-, *nuntiare* announce f. *nuntius* messenger)]

■ **1** pronounce, articulate, say, speak, utter, voice, deliver, vocalize, sound. **2** see EXPRESS[1] 1, 2. **3** proclaim, state, declare, assert, pronounce, affirm, *formal* aver; promulgate, announce, make public, communicate, make known, broadcast, advertise, publicize, publish, trumpet, herald, circulate. ▫▫ **enunciation** see SPEECH 3.

enure /inyŏŏr/ *v.intr. Law* take effect. [var. of INURE]

enuresis /ényŏŏreésis/ *n. Med.* involuntary urination, esp. while sleeping. ▫▫ **enuretic** /-rétik/ *adj. & n.* [mod.L f. Gk *enoureō* urinate in (as EN-[2], *ouron* urine)]

■ bed-wetting.

envelop /envéləp, in-/ *v.tr.* (**enveloped, enveloping**) **1** (often foll. by *in*) **a** wrap up or cover completely. **b** make obscure; conceal (*was enveloped in mystery*). **2** *Mil.* completely surround (an enemy). ▫▫ **envelopment** *n.* [ME f. OF *envoluper* (as EN-[1]; cf. DEVELOP)]

■ **1 a** wrap, enfold, clothe, cover, swathe, swaddle, bind, mantle, shroud, engulf, enclose, sheathe, cocoon, encase, *literary* enwrap, enshroud. **b** (make) obscure, conceal, hide, disguise, screen, shield, veil, mask, cloak, clothe, mantle, shroud, cover, surround, bury, *literary* enshroud.

envelope /énvələp, ón-/ *n.* **1** a folded paper container, usu. with a sealable flap, for a letter, etc. **2** a wrapper or covering. **3** the structure within a balloon or airship containing the gas. **4** the outer metal or glass housing of a vacuum tube, electric light, etc. **5** *Electr.* a curve joining the successive peaks of a modulated wave. **6** *Bot.* any enveloping structure, esp. the calyx or corolla (or both). **7** *Math.* a line or curve tangent to each line or curve of a given family. [F *enveloppe* (as ENVELOP)]

■ **1, 2** see WRAPPER 1, 2.

envenom /envénəm, in-/ *v.tr.* **1** put poison on or into; make poisonous. **2** infuse venom or bitterness into (feelings, words, or actions). [ME f. OF *envenimer* (as EN-[1], *venim* VENOM)]

■ see POISON *v.* 3.

enviable /énveeəbəl/ *adj.* (of a person or thing) exciting or likely to excite envy. ▫▫ **enviably** *adv.*

■ desirable, desired, sought-after, covetable, coveted.

envious /énveeəs/ *adj.* (often foll. by *of*) feeling or showing envy. ▫▫ **enviously** *adv.* [ME f. AF *envious*, OF *envieus* f. *envie* ENVY]

■ jealous, green-eyed, covetous, desirous, resentful, jaundiced, begrudging; green (with envy).

environ /envírən, vírn, in-/ *v.tr.* encircle; surround (esp. hostilely or protectively). [ME f. OF *environer* f. *environ* surroundings f. *en* in + *viron* circuit f. *virer* turn, VEER[1]]

environment /envírənmənt, -vírn-, in-/ *n.* **1** physical surroundings and conditions, esp. as affecting people's lives. **2** conditions or circumstances of living. **3** *Ecol.* external conditions affecting the growth of plants and animals. **4** a structure designed to be experienced from inside as a work of art. **5** *Computing* the overall structure within which a user, computer, or program operates. ▫ **environment-friendly** not harmful to the environment. ▫▫ **environmental** /-mentʼl/ *adj.* **environmentalist** *n.* **environmentally** *adv.*

■ **1, 2** surroundings, environs, ambience, conditions, atmosphere, climate, circumstances; habitat, quarters, medium, milieu, element, territory; sphere, setting, context, situation, background, backdrop. **3** conditions, climate, biosphere, ecosystem; habitat, environs; nature, countryside.

environmentalist /envírənméntəlist, -vírn-, in-/ *n.* **1** a person who is concerned with or advocates the protection of the environment. **2** a person who considers that environment has the primary influence on the development of a person or group. ▫▫ **environmentalism** *n.*

■ **1** ecologist, conservationist, Green, naturalist, nature lover.

environs /envírənz, -vírnz, in-/ *n.pl.* a surrounding district, esp. around an urban area.

■ see NEIGHBORHOOD.

envisage /envízij, in-/ *v.tr.* **1** have a mental picture of (a thing or conditions not yet existing). **2** contemplate or conceive, esp. as a possibility or desirable future event. **3** *archaic* **a** face (danger, facts, etc.). **b** look in the face of. ▫▫ **envisagement** *n.* [F *envisager* (as EN-[1], VISAGE)]

■ **1** visualize, imagine, picture, form a picture of, envision, see (in one's mind's eye), have (a) vision(s) of, fancy, conceive (of), dream *or* conjure up, concoct, create, devise, *colloq.* think up. **2** contemplate, conceive (of), picture, imagine, visualize, have (a) vision(s) of, see, foresee, predict, forecast, prophesy, anticipate, look forward to, dream of, fantasize about. **3** see FACE *v.* 3.

envision /envízhən, in-/ *v.tr.* envisage; visualize.

■ see ENVISAGE 1, 2.

envoy[1] /énvoy, ón-/ *n.* **1** a messenger or representative, esp. on a diplomatic mission. **2** (in full **envoy extraordinary**) a minister plenipotentiary, ranking below ambassador and above chargé d'affaires. ▫▫ **envoyship** *n.* [F *envoyé*, past part. of *envoyer* send f. *en voie* on the way f. L *via*]

■ **1** messenger, representative, emissary, agent, ambassador, minister, delegate, deputy, proxy, substitute, surrogate, factor, stand-in, spokeswoman, spokesman, spokesperson, attaché, diplomat, *RC Ch.* (papal) nuncio, *archaic* legate.

envoy[2] /énvoy, ón-/ *n.* (also **envoi**) **1** a short stanza concluding a ballade, etc. **2** *archaic* an author's concluding words. [ME f. OF *envoi* f. *envoyer* (as ENVOY[1])]

envy /énvee/ *n. & v.* ● *n.* (*pl.* **-ies**) **1** a feeling of discontented or resentful longing aroused by another's better fortune, etc. **2** the object or ground of this feeling (*their house is the envy of the neighborhood*). ● *v.tr.* (**-ies, -ied**) feel envy of (a person, circumstances, etc.) (*I envy you your position*). ▫▫ **envier** *n.* [ME f. OF *envie* f. L *invidia* f. *invidēre* envy (as IN-[1], *vidēre* see)]

■ *n.* **1** jealousy, enviousness, resentment, bitterness, indignation, animosity, antipathy; covetousness, desire, longing, craving, yearning, hankering. ● *v.* resent, begrudge, grudge; covet, desire, crave, long *or* yearn for, hanker after *or* for.

enweave var. of INWEAVE.

enwrap /enráp, in-/ *v.tr.* (also **inwrap**) (**-wrapped, -wrapping**) (often foll. by *in*) *literary* wrap or enfold.

■ see WRAP *v.* 1.

enwreathe /enreéth, in-/ *v.tr.* (also **inwreathe**) *literary* surround with or as with a wreath.

Enzed /énzéd/ *n. Austral. & NZ colloq.* a popular written form of: **1** New Zealand. **2** a New Zealander. ▫▫ **Enzedder** *n.* [pronunc. of NZ]

enzootic /énzō-ótik/ *adj. & n.* ● *adj.* regularly affecting animals in a particular district or at a particular season (cf. ENDEMIC, EPIZOOTIC). ● *n.* an enzootic disease. [Gk *en* in + *zōion* animal]

enzyme /énzīm/ *n. Biochem.* a protein acting as a catalyst in a specific biochemical reaction. ▫▫ **enzymatic** /-zīmátik/ *adj.* **enzymic** *adj.* **enzymology** /-zīmóləjee/ *n.* [G *Enzym* f. med. Gk *enzumos* leavened f. Gk *en* in + *zumē* leaven]

Eocene /eéəseen/ *adj. & n. Geol.* ● *adj.* of or relating to the second epoch of the Tertiary period with evidence of an abundance of mammals including horses, bats, and whales. ¶ Cf. Appendix VII. ● *n.* this epoch or system. [Gk *ēōs* dawn + *kainos* new]

eolian /ee-ṓlee-ən/ *adj.* (*Brit.* **aeolian**) wind-borne. [as AEOLIAN]

/.../ **pronunciation**	● **part of speech**
▫ **phrases, idioms, and compounds**	
▫▫ **derivatives**	■ **synonym section**
cross-references appear in SMALL CAPITALS or *italics*	

eolith /ée͞əlith/ *n. Archaeol.* any of various flint objects found in Tertiary strata and thought to be early artifacts. [Gk *ēos* dawn + *lithos* stone]

eolithic /ée͞əlíthik/ *adj. Archaeol.* of the period preceding the Paleolithic age, thought to include the earliest use of flint tools. [F *éolithique* (as EOLITH)]

e.o.m. *abbr.* (also **E.O.M.**) end of month.

eon /ée͞on/ *n.* (also **aeon**) **1** a very long or indefinite period. **2** an age of the universe. **3** a billion years. **4** an eternity. **5** *Philos.* (in Neoplatonism, Platonism, and Gnosticism) a power existing from eternity, an emanation or phase of the supreme deity.[eccl.L f. GK *aiōn* age]
■ **1** see AGE *n.* 2a.

eosin /ée͞əsin/ *n.* a red fluorescent dyestuff used esp. as a stain in optical microscopy. [Gk *ēos* dawn + -IN]

eosinophil /ée͞əsínəfil/ *n.* a white blood cell readily stained by eosin.

-eous /ee͞əs/ *suffix* forming adjectives meaning 'of the nature of' (*erroneous*; *gaseous*).

EP *abbr.* **1** European plan. **2** extended play.

Ep. *abbr.* Epistle.

ep- /ep, ip, eep/ *prefix* form of EPI- before a vowel or *h*.

EPA *abbr.* Environmental Protection Agency.

epact /ée͞pakt/ *n.* the number of days by which the solar year exceeds the lunar year. [F *épacte* f. LL *epactae* f. Gk *epaktai* (*hēmerai*) intercalated (days) f. *epagō* intercalate (as EPI-, *agō* bring)]

eparch /ée͞paark/ *n.* the chief bishop of an eparchy. [Gk *eparkhos* (as EPI-, *arkhos* ruler)]

eparchy /ée͞paarkee/ *n.* (*pl.* **-ies**) a province of the Orthodox Church. [Gk *eparkhia* (as EPARCH)]

epaulet /ée͞pəlét/ *n.* (also **epaulette**) an ornamental shoulder piece on a coat, dress, etc., esp. on a uniform. [F *épaulette* dimin. of *épaule* shoulder f. L *spatula*: see SPATULA]

épée /aypáy, épay/ *n.* a sharp-pointed dueling sword, used (with the end blunted) in fencing. □□ **épéeist** *n.* [F, = sword, f. OF *espee*: see SPAY]

epeirogeny /épírójənee/ *n.* (also **epeirogenesis** /epírōjénisis, ipí-/) *Geol.* the regional uplift of extensive areas of the earth's crust. □□ **epeirogenic** /-jénik/ *adj.* [Gk *epeiros* mainland + -*genesis*, -*geny*]

epenthesis /epénthisis/ *n.* (*pl.* **epentheses** /-seez/) the insertion of a letter or sound within a word, e.g., in the pronunciation of *elm* as "eləm." □□ **epenthetic** /épenthétik/ *adj.* [LL f. Gk f. *epentithēmi* insert (as EPI- + EN-² + *tithēmi* place)]

epergne /ipə́rn, aypérn/ *n.* an ornament (esp. in branched form) for the center of a dinner-table, holding flowers or fruit. [18th c.: perh. a corrupt. of F *épargne* saving, economy]

epexegesis /epéksijée͞sis/ *n.* (*pl.* **epexegeses** /-seez/) **1** the addition of words to clarify meaning (e.g., *to do* in *difficult to do*). **2** the words added. □□ **epexegetic** /-jétik/ *adj.* **epexegetical** *adj.* **epexegetically** *adv.* [Gk *epexēgēsis* (as EPI-, EXEGESIS)]

Eph. *abbr.* Ephesians (New Testament).

ephebe /éfeeb, ifée͞b/ *n. Gk Hist.* a young man of 18–20 undergoing military training. □□ **ephebic** /ifée͞bik/ *adj.* [L *ephebus* f. Gk *ephēbos* (as EPI-, *hēbē* early manhood)]

ephedra /ifédrə/ *n.* any evergreen shrub of the genus *Ephedra*, with trailing stems and scalelike leaves. [mod.L f. Gk *ephedra* sitting upon]

ephedrine /ifédrin, éfədreen/ *n.* an alkaloid drug found in some ephedras, causing constriction of the blood vessels and widening of the bronchial passages, used to relieve asthma, etc. [EPHEDRA + -INE⁴]

ephemera¹ /ifémərə/ *n.* (*pl.* **ephemera** or **ephemerae** /-ree/ or **ephemeras**) **1 a** an insect living only a day or a few days. **b** any insect of the order Ephemeroptera, e.g., the mayfly. **2** = EPHEMERON. [mod.L f. Gk *ephēmeros* lasting only a day (as EPI-, *hēmera* day)]

ephemera² *pl.* of EPHEMERON 1.

ephemeral /ifémərəl/ *adj.* **1** lasting or of use for only a short time; transitory. **2** lasting only a day. **3** (of an insect, flower, etc.) lasting a day or a few days. □□ **ephemerality** /-rálitee/

n. **ephemerally** *adv.* **ephemeralness** *n.* [Gk *ephēmeros*: see EPHEMERA]
■ *adj.* **1** see TRANSIENT *adj.* 1.

ephemeris /iféməris/ *n.* (*pl.* **ephemerides** /éfimérideez/) *Astron.* an astronomical almanac or table of the predicted positions of celestial bodies. [L f. Gk *ephēmeris* diary (as EPHEMERAL)]

ephemerist /ifémərist/ *n.* a collector of ephemera.

ephemeron /ifémərən/ *n.* **1** (*pl.* **ephemera** /-rə/) (usu. in *pl.*) **a** a thing (esp. a printed item) of short-lived interest or usefulness. **b** a short-lived thing. **2** (*pl.* **ephemerons**) = EPHEMERA¹ 1. [as EPHEMERA¹]

ephod /éfod, eéfod/ *n.* a Jewish priestly vestment. [ME f. Heb. 'ēpôd]

ephor /éfawr/ *n. Gk Hist.* any of five senior magistrates in ancient Sparta. □□ **ephorate** *n.* [Gk *ephoros* overseer (as EPI-, *horaō* see)]

epi- /épi-/ *prefix* (usu. **ep-** before a vowel or *h*) **1** upon (*epicycle*). **2** above (*epicotyl*). **3** in addition (*epiphenomenon*). [Gk *epi* (prep.)]

epiblast /épiblast/ *n. Biol.* the outermost layer of a gastrula, etc.; the ectoderm. [EPI- + -BLAST]

epic /épik/ *n. & adj.* ● *n.* **1** a long poem narrating the adventures or deeds of one or more heroic or legendary figures, e.g., the *Iliad*, *Paradise Lost*. **2** an imaginative work of any form, embodying a nation's conception of its history. **3** a book or motion picture based on an epic narrative or heroic in type or scale. **4** a subject fit for recital in an epic. ● *adj.* **1** of or like an epic. **2** grand; heroic. □□ **epical** *adj.* **epically** *adv.* [L *epicus* f. Gk *epikos* f. *epos* word, song]
■ *n.* **1–3** see LEGEND 1a–c. ● *adj.* see HEROIC *adj.* 2b.

epicarp /épikaarp/ *n. Bot.* the outermost layer of the pericarp. [EPI- + Gk *karpos* fruit]

epicedium /épisée͞deeəm/ *n.* (*pl.* **epicedia** /-deeə/) a funeral ode. □□ **epicedian** *adj.* [L f. Gk *epikēdeion* (as EPI-, *kēdos* care)]
■ see KEEN² *n.*

epicene /épiseen/ *adj. & n.* ● *adj.* **1** *Gram.* denoting either sex without change of gender. **2** of, for, or used by both sexes. **3** having characteristics of both sexes. **4** having no characteristics of either sex. **5** effete; effeminate. ● *n.* an epicene person. [ME f. LL *epicoenus* f. Gk *epikoinos* (as EPI-, *koinos* common)]
■ **3** see BISEXUAL *adj.* **4** see NEUTER 3.

epicenter /épisentər/ *n.* **1** *Geol.* the point at which an earthquake reaches the earth's surface. **2** the central point of a difficulty. □□ **epicentral** /-séntrəl/ *adj.* [Gk *epikentros* (adj.) (as EPI-, CENTER)]

epicontinental /épikóntinént'l/ *adj.* (of the sea) over the continental shelf.

epicotyl /épikót'l/ *n. Bot.* the region of an embryo or seedling stem above the cotyledon(s).

epicure /épikyo͞or/ *n.* a person with refined tastes, esp. in food and drink. □□ **epicurism** *n.* [med.L *epicurus* one preferring sensual enjoyment: see EPICUREAN]
■ gourmet, connoisseur, gastronome, *colloq.* foodie, *disp.* gourmand.

Epicurean /épikyo͞oreéən, -kyo͞oree-/ *n. & adj.* ● *n.* **1** a disciple or student of the Greek philosopher Epicurus (d. 270 BC), who taught that the highest good is personal happiness. **2** (**epicurean**) a person devoted to (esp. sensual) enjoyment. ● *adj.* **1** of or concerning Epicurus or his ideas. **2** (**epicurean**) characteristic of an epicurean. □□ **Epicureanism** *n.* [F *épicurien* or L *epicureus* f. Gk *epikoureios* f. *Epikouros* Epicurus]
■ *n.* **2** (**epicurean**) see SYBARITE *n.* ● *adj.* **2** (**epicurean**) pleasure-seeking, hedonistic, pleasure-orientated, voluptuous, voluptuary, sybarite, sybaritic(al), pampered, luxurious, sensual, carnal, orgiastic, libidinous, wild, bacchanalian, saturnalian, extravagant, immoderate, unrestrained, debauched, dissolute, dissipated, licentious, profligate, intemperate, overindulgent, crapulent, crapulous, gluttonous, greedy, self-indulgent, porcine, *colloq.* piggish.

epicycle /épisīkəl/ *n. Geom.* a small circle moving around the circumference of a larger one. □□ **epicyclic** /-síklik, -síklik/ *adj.* [ME f. OF or LL *epicyclus* f. Gk *epikuklos* (as EPI-, *kuklos* circle)]

epicycloid /épisíkloyd/ *n. Math.* a curve traced by a point on the circumference of a circle rolling on the exterior of another circle. □□ **epicycloidal** *adj.*

epideictic /épidíktik/ *adj.* meant for effect or display, esp. in speaking. [Gk *epideiktikos* (as EPI-, *deiknumi* show)]

epidemic /épidémik/ *n. & adj.* ● *n.* **1** a widespread occurrence of a disease in a community at a particular time. **2** such a disease. **3** (foll. by *of*) a wide prevalence of something usu. undesirable. ● *adj.* in the nature of an epidemic (cf. ENDEMIC). □□ **epidemically** *adv.* [F *épidémique* & *épidémie* f. LL *epidemia* f. Gk *epidēmia* prevalence of disease f. *epidēmios* (adj.) (as EPI-, *dēmos* the people)]

■ *n.* **1, 2** plague, pestilence, disease; outbreak, spread; scourge. **3** see *prevalence* (PREVALENT). ● *adj.* widespread, common, pandemic, rampant, rife, flourishing, mushrooming, nationwide, worldwide, international, universal, ubiquitous, general, prevalent; prevailing.

epidemiology /épideemeeólajee/ *n.* the study of the incidence and distribution of diseases, and of their control and prevention. □□ **epidemiological** /-meeəlójikəl/ *adj.* **epidemiologist** *n.*

epidermis /épidérmis/ *n.* **1** the outer cellular layer of the skin. **2** *Bot.* the outer layer of cells of leaves, stems, roots, etc. □□ **epidermal** *adj.* **epidermic** *adj.* **epidermoid** *adj.* [LL f. Gk (as EPI-, DERMIS)]

■ **1** skin, dermis.

epidiascope /épidíəskōp/ *n.* an optical projector capable of giving images of both opaque and transparent objects. [EPI- + DIA- + -SCOPE]

epididymis /épidídimis/ *n.* (*pl.* **epididymides** /-didími-deez/) *Anat.* a convoluted duct behind the testis, along which sperm passes to the vas deferens. [Gk *epididumis* (as EPI-, *didumoi* testicles)]

epidural /épidŏorəl, -dyŏor-/ *adj. & n.* ● *adj.* **1** *Anat.* on or around the dura mater. **2** (of an anesthetic) introduced into the space around the dura mater of the spinal cord. ● *n.* an epidural anesthetic, used esp. in childbirth to produce loss of sensation below the waist. [EPI- + DURA (MATER)]

epifauna /épifawnə/ *n.* animals living on the seabed, either attached to animals, plants, etc., or free-living. [Da. (as EPI-, FAUNA)]

epigastrium /épigástreeəm/ *n.* (*pl.* **epigastria** /-reeə/) *Anat.* the part of the abdomen immediately over the stomach. □□ **epigastric** *adj.* [LL f. Gk *epigastrion* (neut. adj.) (as EPI-, *gastēr* belly)]

epigeal /épijéeəl/ *adj. Bot.* **1** having one or more cotyledons above the ground. **2** growing above the ground. [Gk *epigeios* (as EPI-, *gē* earth)]

epigene /épijeen/ *adj. Geol.* produced on the surface of the earth. [F *épigène* f. Gk *epigenēs* (as EPI-, *genēs* born)]

epiglottis /épiglótis/ *n. Anat.* a flap of cartilage at the root of the tongue, which is depressed during swallowing to cover the windpipe. □□ **epiglottal** *adj.* **epiglottic** *adj.* [Gk *epiglōttis* (as EPI-, *glōtta* tongue)]

epigone /épigōn/ *n.* (*pl.* **epigones** or **epigoni** /ipígoni/) one of a later (and less distinguished) generation. [pl. f. F *épigones* f. L *epigoni* f. Gk *epigonoi* those born afterward (as EPI-, root of *gignomai* be born)]

epigram /épigram/ *n.* **1** a short poem with a witty ending. **2** a saying or maxim, esp a proverbial one. **3 a** a pointed remark or expression, esp. a witty one. **b** the use of concise witty remarks. □□ **epigrammatic** /-grəmátik/ *adj.* **epigrammatically** *adv.* **epigrammatist** /-grámətist/ *n.* **epigrammatize** /-grámətīz/ *v.tr. & intr.* [F *épigramme* or L *epigramma* f. Gk *epigramma -atos* (as EPI-, -GRAM)]

■ **2** (old) saying, proverb, aphorism, maxim, gnome, saw, adage, byword, catchphrase, catchword, motto, slogan, apothegm, *colloq.* (old) chestnut. **3 a** bon mot, quip, sally, mot, nice turn of phrase, atticism; witticism, pun, double entendre, paronomasia, equivoque, *colloq.* wisecrack. □□ **epigrammatic** pithy, terse, succinct,

piquant, pungent, trenchant, sententious, witty, pointed, proverbial, aphoristic, apothegmatic, *colloq.* snappy, punchy.

epigraph /épigraf/ *n.* an inscription on a statue or coin, at the head of a chapter, etc. [Gk *epigraphē* f. *epigraphō* (as EPI-, *graphō* write)]

epigraphy /ipígrəfee/ *n.* the study of (esp. ancient) inscriptions. □□ **epigraphic** /épigráfik/ *adj.* **epigraphical** *adj.* **epigraphically** *adv.* **epigraphist** /-pígrəfist/ *n.*

epilate /épilayt/ *v.tr.* remove hair from. □□ **epilation** /-láyshən/ *n.* [F *épiler* (cf. DEPILATE)]

epilepsy /épilepsee/ *n.* a nervous disorder with convulsions and often loss of consciousness. [F *épilepsie* or LL *epilepsia* f. Gk *epilēpsia* f. *epilambanō* attack (as EPI-, *lambanō* take)]

epileptic /épiléptik/ *adj. & n.* ● *adj.* of or relating to epilepsy. ● *n.* a person with epilepsy. [F *épileptique* f. LL *epilepticus* f. Gk *epilēptikos* (as EPILEPSY)]

epilimnion /épilímneeən/ *n.* (*pl.* **epilimnia** /-neeə/) the upper layer of water in a stratified lake. [EPI- + Gk *limnion* dimin. of *limnē* lake]

epilogist /ipílǝjist/ *n.* the writer or speaker of an epilogue.

epilogue /épilawg, -og/ *n.* (also **epilog**) **1 a** the concluding part of a literary work. **b** an appendix. **2** a speech or short poem addressed to the audience by an actor at the end of a play. **3** *Brit.* a short piece at the end of a day's broadcasting (cf. PROLOGUE). [ME f. F *épilogue* f. L *epilogus* f. Gk *epilogos* (as EPI-, *logos* speech)]

■ **1, 2** see SUPPLEMENT *n.* 1, 2.

epimer /épimər/ *n. Chem.* either of two isomers with different configurations of atoms about one of several asymmetric carbon atoms present. □□ **epimeric** /-mérik/ *adj.* **epimerism** *n.* [G (as EPI-, -MER)]

epimerize /épimərīz/ *v.tr. Chem.* convert (one epimer) into the other.

epinasty /épinastee/ *n. Bot.* a tendency in plant organs to grow more rapidly on the upper side. [EPI- + Gk *nastos* pressed]

epinephrine /épinéfrin/ *n.* (also **epinephrin**) **1** *Biochem.* a hormone secreted by the adrenal glands, affecting circulation and muscular action, and causing excitement and stimulation. **2** *Pharm.* the same substance obtained from animals or by synthesis, used as a stimulant. Also called *adrenaline.* [EPI- + *nephros* kidney]

epiphany /ipífənee/ *n.* (*pl.* **-ies**) **1** (**Epiphany**) **a** the manifestation of Christ to the Magi according to the biblical account. **b** the festival commemorating this on January 6. **2** any manifestation of a god or demigod. □□ **epiphanic** /épi-fánik/ *adj.* [ME f. Gk *epiphaneia* manifestation f. *epiphainō* reveal (as EPI-, *phainō* show): sense 1 through OF *epiphanie* and eccl.L *epiphania*]

epiphenomenon /épifinóminən/ *n.* (*pl.* **epiphenomena** /-nə/) **1** a secondary symptom, which may occur simultaneously with a disease, etc., but is not regarded as its cause or result. **2** *Psychol.* consciousness regarded as a by-product of brain activity. □□ **epiphenomenal** *adj.*

epiphysis /ipífisis/ *n.* (*pl.* **epiphyses** /-seez/) *Anat.* **1** the end part of a long bone, initially growing separately from the shaft. **2** = *pineal gland.* [mod.L f. Gk *epiphusis* (as EPI-, *phusis* growth)]

epiphyte /épifīt/ *n.* a plant growing but not parasitic on another, e.g., a moss. □□ **epiphytal** /-fit'l/ *adj.* **epiphytic** /-fí-tik/ *adj.* [EPI- + Gk *phuton* plant]

episcopacy /ipískəpəsee/ *n.* (*pl.* **-ies**) **1** government of a church by bishops. **2** (prec. by *the*) the bishops.

episcopal /ipískəpəl/ *adj.* **1** of a bishop or bishops. **2** (of a Church) constituted on the principle of government by bishops. □ **Episcopal Church** a Protestant Church in the US and Scotland, with elected bishops, and doctrine, forms of worship, etc., inherited from the Church of England.

/... / **pronunciation** ● **part of speech**
□ **phrases, idioms, and compounds**
□□ **derivatives** ■ **synonym section**
cross-references appear in SMALL CAPITALS or *italics*

□□ **episcopalism** *n.* **episcopally** *adv.* [ME f. F *épiscopal* or eccl.L *episcopalis* f. *episcopus* BISHOP]
■ **1** see CLERICAL 1.

episcopalian /ipískəpáyleeən/ *adj.* & *n.* ● *adj.* **1** of or advocating government of a church by bishops. **2** of or belonging to an episcopal church or (**Episcopalian**) the Episcopal Church. ● *n.* **1** an adherent of episcopacy. **2** (**Episcopalian**) a member of the Episcopal Church. □□ **episcopalianism** *n.*

episcopate /ipískəpət/ *n.* **1** the office or tenure of a bishop. **2** (prec. by *the*) the bishops collectively. [eccl.L *episcopatus* f. *episcopus* BISHOP]

episcope /épiskōp/ *n.* an optical projector giving images of opaque objects.

episematic /épisimátik/ *adj.* Zool. (of coloration, markings, etc.) serving to help recognition by animals of the same species. [EPI- + Gk *sēma sēmatos* sign]

episiotomy /ipeézeeótəmee/ *n.* (*pl.* **-ies**) a surgical cut made at the opening of the vagina during childbirth, to aid delivery. [Gk *epision* pubic region]

episode /épisōd/ *n.* **1** one event or a group of events as part of a sequence. **2** each of the parts of a serial story or broadcast. **3** an incident or set of incidents in a narrative. **4** an incident that is distinct but contributes to a whole (*a romantic episode in her life*). **5** Mus. a passage containing distinct material or introducing a new subject. **6** the part between two choric songs in Greek tragedy. [Gk *epeisodion* (as EPI- + *eisodos* entry f. *eis* into + *hodos* way)]
■ **1, 3, 4** event, incident, occurrence, happening, circumstance, occasion, experience, adventure, escapade, ordeal, trial, affair, matter. **2** installment, part, chapter.

episodic /épisódik/ *adj.* (also **episodical** /-sódikəl/) **1** in the nature of an episode. **2** sporadic; occurring at irregular intervals. □□ **episodically** *adv.*
■ **2** see OCCASIONAL 1.

epistaxis /épistáksis/ *n.* Med. a nosebleed. [mod.L f. Gk (as EPI-, *stazō* drip)]

epistemic /épisteémik, -stémik/ *adj.* Philos. relating to knowledge or to the degree of its validation. □□ **epistemically** *adv.* [Gk *epistēmē* knowledge]

epistemology /ipístimólǝjee/ *n.* the theory of knowledge, esp. with regard to its methods and validation. □□ **epistemological** /-mǝlójikǝl/ *adj.* **epistemologically** *adv.* **epistemologist** *n.*

epistle /ipísǝl/ *n.* **1** *formal or joc.* a letter, esp. a long one on a serious subject. **2** (**Epistle**) **a** any of the letters of the apostles in the New Testament. **b** an extract from an Epistle read in a church service. **3** a poem or other literary work in the form of a letter or series of letters. [ME f. OF f. L *epistola* f. Gk *epistolē* f. *epistellō* send news (as EPI-, *stellō* send)]
■ **1** see LETTER 2.

epistolary /ipístǝlǝree/ *adj.* **1** in the style or form of a letter or letters. **2** of, carried by, or suited to letters. [F *épistolaire* or L *epistolaris* (as EPISTLE)]

epistrophe /ipístrǝfee/ *n.* the repetition of a word at the end of successive clauses. [Gk (as EPI-, *strophē* turning)]

epistyle /épistīl/ *n.* Archit. = ARCHITRAVE. [F *épistyle* or L *epistylium* f. Gk *epistulion* (as EPI-, *stulos* pillar)]

epitaph /épitaf/ *n.* words written in memory of a person who has died, esp. as a tomb inscription. [ME f. OF *epitaphe* f. L *epitaphium* f. Gk *epitaphion* funeral oration (as EPI-, *taphos* tomb)]

epitaxy /épitaksee/ *n.* Crystallog. the growth of a thin layer on a single-crystal substrate that determines the lattice structure of the layer. □□ **epitaxial** /-tákseeǝl/ *adj.* [F *épitaxie* (as EPI-, Gk *taxis* arrangement)]

epithalamium /épithǝláymeeǝm/ *n.* (*pl.* **epithalamiums** or **epithalamia** /-meeǝ/) a song or poem celebrating a marriage. □□ **epithalamial** *adj.* **epithalamic** /-lámik/ *adj.* [L f. Gk *epithalamion* (as EPI-, *thalamos* bridal chamber)]

epithelium /épitheéleeǝm/ *n.* (*pl.* **epithelia** /-leeǝ/ or **epitheliums**) the tissue forming the outer layer of the body surface and lining many hollow structures. □□ **epithelial** *adj.* [mod.L f. EPI- + Gk *thēlē* teat]

epithet /épithet/ *n.* **1** an adjective or other descriptive word expressing a quality or attribute, esp. used with or as a name. **2** such a word as a term of abuse. □□ **epithetic** /-thétik/ *adj.* **epithetical** *adj.* **epithetically** *adv.* [F *épithète* or L *epitheton* f. Gk *epitheton* f. *epitithēmi* add (as EPI-, *tithēmi* place)]
■ **1** see TITLE *n.* 5. **2** see EXPLETIVE *n.* 1.

epitome /ipítǝmee/ *n.* **1** a person or thing embodying a quality, class, etc. **2** a thing representing another in miniature. **3** a summary of a written work; an abstract. □□ **epitomist** *n.* [L f. Gk *epitomē* f. *epitemnō* abridge (as EPI-, *temnō* cut)]
■ **1** embodiment, incarnation, personification, image, picture, essence, quintessence, model, paragon, ideal, beau ideal, standard, criterion, measure, yardstick, (typical) example, archetype, exemplar, prototype. **3** summary, abstract, résumé, précis, outline, synopsis, *aperçu*, abbreviation, conspectus, condensation, abridgment, digest, potted version, compendium, concise edition *or* version, cut edition *or* version, *RC Ch.* syllabus.

epitomize /ipítǝmīz/ *v.tr.* **1** be a perfect example of (a quality, etc.); typify. **2** make an epitome of (a work). □□ **epitomization** *n.*
■ **1** see EXEMPLIFY.

epizoon /épizō-on/ *n.* (*pl.* **epizoa** /-zōǝ/) an animal living on another animal. [mod.L (as EPI-, Gk *zōion* animal)]

epizootic /épizō-ótik/ *adj.* & *n.* ● *adj.* (of a disease) temporarily prevalent among animals (cf. ENZOOTIC). ● *n.* an outbreak of such a disease. [F *épizootique* f. *épizootie* (as EPIZOON)]

epoch /épǝk, eépok/ *n.* **1** a period of history or of a person's life marked by notable events. **2** the beginning of an era. **3** Geol. a division of a period, corresponding to a set of strata. □ **epoch-making** remarkable; historic; of major importance. □□ **epochal** *adj.* [mod.L *epocha* f. Gk *epokhē* stoppage]
■ **1** see ERA 1, 2.

epode /épōd/ *n.* **1** a form of lyric poem written in couplets each of a long line followed by a shorter one. **2** the third section of an ancient Greek choral ode or of one division of it. [F *épode* or L *epodos* f. Gk *epōidos* (as EPI-, ODE)]

eponym /épǝnim/ *n.* **1** a person (real or imaginary) after whom a discovery, invention, place, institution, etc., is named or thought to be named. **2** the name given. □□ **eponymous** /ipónimǝs/ *adj.* [Gk *epōnumos* (as EPI-, *-ōnumos* f. *onoma* name)]

epoxide /ipóksid/ *n.* Chem. a compound containing an oxygen atom bonded in a triangular arrangement to two carbon atoms. [EPI- + OXIDE]

epoxy /ipóksee/ *adj.* Chem. relating to or derived from an epoxide. □ **epoxy resin** a synthetic thermosetting resin containing epoxy groups. [EPI- + OXY-²]

epsilon /épsilon/ *n.* the fifth letter of the Greek alphabet (E, ε). [ME f. Gk, = bare E f. *psilos* bare]

Epsom salts /épsǝm/ *n.* a preparation of magnesium sulfate used as a purgative, etc. [*Epsom* in Surrey, England, where it was first found occurring naturally]

epyllion /epíleeǝn/ *n.* (*pl.* **epyllia** /-leeǝ/) a miniature epic poem. [Gk *epullion* dimin. of *epos* word, song]

equable /ékwǝbǝl/ *adj.* **1** even; not varying. **2** uniform and moderate (*an equable climate*). **3** (of a person) not easily disturbed or angered. □□ **equability** /-bílitee/ *n.* **equably** *adv.* [L *aequabilis* (as EQUATE)]
■ **1, 2** even, unvarying, stable, steady, regular, unchanging, constant, invariable, consistent, unvaried, uniform. **3** even-tempered, easygoing, imperturbable, unexcitable, serene, calm, placid, composed, equanimous, self-possessed, dispassionate, cool, levelheaded, collected, tranquil, peaceful, *colloq.* unflappable.

equal /eékwǝl/ *adj.*, *n.*, & *v.* ● *adj.* **1** (often foll. by *to*, *with*) the same in quantity, quality, size, degree, rank, level, etc. **2** evenly balanced (*an equal contest*). **3** having the same rights or status (*human beings are essentially equal*). **4** uniform in application or effect. ● *n.* a person or thing equal to another, esp. in rank, status, or characteristic quality (*their* *treatment of the subject has no equal*; *is the equal of any man*). ● *v.tr.* (**equaled, equaling**; esp. *Brit.* **equalled, equalling**) **1** be equal to in number, quality, etc. **2** achieve something that is equal to (an achievement) or to the achievement of (a person). □ **be equal to** have the ability or resources for. **equal opportunity** (often in *pl.*) the opportunity or right to be employed, paid, etc., without discrimination on grounds of sex, race, etc. **equal** (or **equals**) **sign** the symbol =. [ME f. L *aequalis* f. *aequus* even]

■ *adj.* **1, 3, 4** identical, mirror-image, the same, one and the same, interchangeable, level, fifty-fifty, on a par, *archaic or literary* coequal; similar, equivalent, commensurate; alike; like; (*equal to*) tantamount to. **2** (evenly) balanced, (evenly) matched, corresponding, symmetrical, *archaic* correspondent; equivalent, even, commensurate, comparable, proportionate, proportional; fifty-fifty, neck and neck, tied, nip and truck, *Brit.* level pegging, *colloq.* even-steven. ● *n.* peer, match, compeer, counterpart, equivalent, fellow. ● *v.* **1** see AMOUNT *v.* 1. **2** (be a) match (for), compete with, rival, challenge, compare with, touch, come *or* get near, come *or* get close to, parallel, be on a par with, be in the same league *or* class as *or* with; even, come up to, approach; hold a candle to, copy, imitate, repeat. □ **be equal to** be up to, be capable of, measure up to, be suited to, be qualified for, be fit(ted) for.

equalitarian /ikwólitáireeən/ *n.* = EGALITARIAN. □□ **equalitarianism** *n.* [EQUALITY, after *humanitarian*, etc.]

equality /ikwólitee/ *n.* the state of being equal. [ME f. OF *equalité* f. L *aequalitas -tatis* (as EQUAL)]

■ parity, sameness, identity, uniformity, equivalence, similarity, *archaic or literary* coequality; impartiality, fairness, justice; egalitarianism.

equalize /eekwəliz/ *v.* **1** *tr.* & *intr.* make or become equal. **2** *intr.* reach one's opponent's score in a game, after being behind. □□ **equalization** *n.*

■ **1** make equal, counterbalance, counterpoise, equilibrate, offset, compensate, regularize, standardize; even up, match (up), balance. **2** draw level, catch up, even up, draw even.

equalizer /eekwəlizər/ *n.* **1** an equalizing score or goal, etc., in a game. **2** *sl.* a weapon, esp. a gun. **3** *Electr.* a connection in a system that compensates for any undesirable frequency or phase response with the system.

equally /eekwəlee/ *adv.* **1** in an equal manner (*treated them all equally*). **2** to an equal degree (*is equally important*). ¶ In sense 2 construction with *as* (*equally as important*) is often found, but is *disp.*).

■ see ALIKE *adv.*

equanimity /eekwənímitee, ékwə-/ *n.* mental composure; evenness of temper, esp. in misfortune. □□ **equanimous** /ikwánimǝs/ *adj.* [L *aequanimitas* f. *aequanimis* f. *aequus* even + *animus* mind]

■ see TEMPER *n.* 4.

equate /ikwáyt/ *v.* **1** *tr.* (usu. foll. by *to, with*) regard as equal or equivalent. **2** *intr.* (foll. by *with*) **a** be equal or equivalent to. **b** agree or correspond. □□ **equatable** *adj.* [ME f. L *aequare aequat-* f. *aequus* equal]

■ **1** see IDENTIFY 4. **2** (*equate with*) see PARALLEL *v.* 1.

equation /ikwáyzhən/ *n.* **1** the process of equating or making equal; the state of being equal. **2** *Math.* a statement that two mathematical expressions are equal (indicated by the sign =). **3** *Chem.* a formula indicating a chemical reaction by means of symbols for the elements taking part. □□ **equational** *adj.* [ME f. OF *equation* or L *aequatio* (as EQUATE)]

equator /ikwáytər/ *n.* **1** an imaginary line around the earth or other body, equidistant from the poles. **2** *Astron.* = *celestial equator*. [ME f. OF *equateur* or med.L *aequator* (as EQUATION)]

equatorial /ékwətáwreeəl, eekwə-/ *adj.* of or near the equator. □ **equatorial telescope** a telescope attached to an axis perpendicular to the plane of the equator. □□ **equatorially** *adv.*

equerry /ékwəree/ *n.* (*pl.* **-ies**) **1** an officer of the British royal household attending members of the royal family. **2** *hist.* an

officer of a prince's or noble's household having charge over the horses. [earlier *esquiry* f. OF *esquierie* company of squires, prince's stables, f. OF *esquier* ESQUIRE: perh. assoc. with L *equus* horse]

■ **2** see GROOM *n.* 1.

equestrian /ikwéstreeən/ *adj.* & *n.* ● *adj.* **1** of or relating to horses and horseback riding. **2** on horseback. ● *n.* (*fem.* **equestrienne** /-tree-én/) a rider or performer on horseback. □□ **equestrianism** *n.* [L *equestris* f. *eques* horseman, knight, f. *equus* horse]

equi- /eekwee, ékwi/ *comb. form* equal. [L *aequi-* f. *aequus* equal]

equiangular /eekweeángyələr, ékwee-/ *adj.* having equal angles.

equidistant /eekwidístənt, ékwi-/ *adj.* at equal distances. □□ **equidistantly** *adv.*

equilateral /eekwilátərəl, ékwi-/ *adj.* having all its sides equal in length.

■ regular, equiangular.

equilibrate /ikwílibrayt, eekwilíbrayt/ *v.* **1** *tr.* cause (two things) to balance. **2** *intr.* be in equilibrium; balance. □□ **equilibration** *n.* **equilibrator** *n.* [LL *aequilibrare aequilibrat-* (as EQUI-, *libra* balance)]

equilibrist /ikwílibrist/ *n.* an acrobat, esp. on a high rope.

■ funambulist, tightrope walker, high-wire walker.

equilibrium /eekwilíbreeəm, ékwi-/ *n.* (*pl.* **equilibriums** or **equilibria** /-reeə/) **1** a state of physical balance. **2** a state of mental or emotional equanimity. **3** a state in which the energy in a system is evenly distributed and forces, influences, etc., balance each other. [L (as EQUI-, *libra* balance)]

■ **1, 3** see BALANCE *n.* 3.

equine /eekwin, ékwin/ *adj.* of or like a horse. [L *equinus* f. *equus* horse]

equinoctial /eekwinókshəl, ékwi-/ *adj.* & *n.* ● *adj.* **1** happening at or near the time of an equinox (*equinoctial gales*). **2** of or relating to equal day and night. **3** at or near the (terrestrial) equator. ● *n.* (in full **equinoctial line**) = *celestial equator*. □ **equinoctial point** the point at which the ecliptic cuts the celestial equator (twice each year at an equinox). **equinoctial year** see YEAR. [ME f. OF *equinoctial* or L *aequinoctialis* (as EQUINOX)]

equinox /eekwinoks, ékwi-/ *n.* **1** the time or date (twice each year) at which the sun crosses the celestial equator, when day and night are of equal length. **2** = *equinoctial point*. □ **autumnal equinox** about Sept. 22. **vernal** (or **spring**) **equinox** about March 20. [ME f. OF *equinoxe* or med.L *equinoxium* for L *aequinoctium* (as EQUI-, *nox noctis* night)]

equip /ikwíp/ *v.tr.* (**equipped, equipping**) supply with what is needed. □□ **equipper** *n.* [F *équiper*, prob. f. ON *skipa* to man (a ship) f. *skip* SHIP]

■ supply, furnish, provide, stock (up), outfit, fit (out *or* up), rig (out *or* up), fix up, accoutre, deck (out), caparison, kit (out *or* up), provision.

equipage /ékwipij/ *n.* **1 a** requisites for an undertaking. **b** an outfit for a special purpose. **2** a carriage and horses with attendants. [F *équipage* (as EQUIP)]

■ **1 a** see EQUIPMENT. **b** see ROBE *n.* 4.

equipment /ikwípmənt/ *n.* **1** the necessary articles, clothing, etc., for a purpose. **2** the process of equipping or being equipped. [F *équipement* (as EQUIP)]

■ **1** gear, apparatus, paraphernalia, kit, material, accoutrements, matériel, equipage, outfit, panoply, rig, rigging, gadgetry, tackle, tack, impedimenta, baggage, luggage, stuff.

equipoise /eekwipoyz, ékwi-/ *n.* & *v.* ● *n.* **1** equilibrium; a balanced state. **2** a counterbalancing thing. ● *v.tr.* counterbalance.

equipollent /eekwipólənt, ékwi-/ *adj.* & *n.* ● *adj.* **1** equal in power, force, etc. **2** practically equivalent. ● *n.* an equi-

---

/ . . . / **pronunciation**   ● **part of speech**

□ **phrases, idioms, and compounds**

□□ **derivatives**   ■ **synonym section**

cross-references appear in SMALL CAPITALS or *italics*

pollent thing. □□ **equipollence** *n.* **equipollency** *n.* [ME f. OF *equipolent* f. L *aequipollens -entis* of equal value (as EQUI-, *pollēre* be strong)]

equipotential /éekwipəténshəl, ékwi-/ *adj.* & *n.* *Physics* ● *adj.* (of a surface or line) having the potential of a force the same or constant at all its points. ● *n.* an equipotential line or surface.

equiprobable /éekwiprôbəbəl, ékwi-/ *adj.* *Logic* equally probable. □□ **equiprobability** *n.*

equitable /ékwitəbəl/ *adj.* **1** fair; just. **2** *Law* valid in equity as distinct from law. □□ **equitableness** *n.* **equitably** *adv.* [F *équitable* (as EQUITY)]

■ **1** fair, just, fair-minded, right, square, decent, good, correct, rightful, evenhanded, impartial, dispassionate, detached, objective, unbiased, neutral, uncolored, nonpartisan, disinterested, unprejudiced, nonprejudicial, unjaundiced, open-minded, unbigoted, reasonable, judicious, ethical, principled, moral, (right and) proper, upright, sound, respectable, regular, honest, clean, open, valid, honorable, righteous, scrupulous, conscientious, straight, straightforward, upstanding, right-minded, *colloq.* fair and square, upfront; (open and) aboveboard; *colloq.* on the level, on the up and up.

equitation /ékwitáyshən/ *n.* the art and practice of horsemanship and horseback riding. [F *équitation* or L *equitatio* f. *equitare* ride a horse f. *eques equitis* horseman f. *equus* horse]

equity /ékwitee/ *n.* (*pl.* **-ies**) **1** fairness. **2** the application of the principles of justice to correct or supplement the law. **3 a** the value of the shares issued by a company. **b** (in *pl.*) stocks and shares not bearing fixed interest. **4** the net value of a mortgaged property after the deduction of charges. **5** (**Equity**) = *Actors' Equity Association* (see ACTOR). [ME f. OF *equité* f. L *aequitas -tatis* f. *aequus* fair]

■ **1, 2** fairness, justice, rightfulness, justness, evenhandedness, equitableness, fair play, fairmindedness, objectivity, objectiveness, disinterest, dispassionateness, disinterestedness, neutrality, impartiality, open-mindedness, tolerance, judiciousness.

equivalent /ikwívələnt/ *adj.* & *n.* ● *adj.* **1** (often foll. by *to*) equal in value, amount, importance, etc. **2** corresponding. **3** (of words) having the same meaning. **4** having the same result. **5** /éekwəváylənt/ *Chem.* (of a substance) equal in combining or displacing capacity. ● *n.* **1** an equivalent thing, amount, word, etc. **2** (in full **equivalent weight**) *Chem.* the weight of a substance that can combine with or displace one gram of hydrogen or eight grams of oxygen. □□ **equivalence** /-ləns/ *n.* **equivalency** *n.* **equivalently** *adv.* [ME f. OF f. LL *aequivalēre* (as EQUI-, *valēre* be worth)]

■ *adj.* **1** equal, (virtually *or* nearly *or* (pretty) much) the same, one and the same, identical, interchangeable, comparable, analogous, similar, parallel, not unlike, *archaic or literary* coequal; like; alike, close, akin, along the same lines; commensurate, of a piece *or* kind, consistent, in keeping *or* line, tantamount. **2** see COORDINATE *adj.* 1. **3** see SYNONYMOUS 1. ● *n.* **1** match, counterpart, coordinate, twin; equal, peer, fellow, *archaic or literary* coequal; parallel, analog, replica, copy.

equivocal /ikwívəkəl/ *adj.* **1** of double or doubtful meaning; ambiguous. **2** of uncertain nature. **3** (of a person, character, etc.) questionable; suspect. □□ **equivocality** /-kálitee/ *n.* **equivocally** *adv.* **equivocalness** *n.* [LL *aequivocus* (as EQUI-, *vocare* call)]

■ **1, 2** equivocating, dubious, doubtful; ambiguous, vague, obscure, hazy, misty, foggy, muddy, murky, blurry, blurred, ill-defined, indistinct, obscure, fuzzy, unclear, indefinite, imprecise, inexact, undefined, unspecified, nonspecific, inexplicit, indistinct, indeterminate, uncertain, confused, confusing, mysterious, mystifying, enigmatic(al), cryptic, puzzling, oracular, Delphic, Delphian. **3** see SUSPECT *adj.* □□ **equivocality, equivocalness** see AMBIGUITY 1a. **equivocally** ambiguously; see also *vaguely* (VAGUE).

equivocate /ikwívəkayt/ *v.intr.* use ambiguity to conceal the truth. □□ **equivocacy** *n.* **equivocation** /-káyshən/ *n.* **equivocator** *n.* **equivocatory** *adj.* [ME f. LL *aequivocare* (as EQUIVOCAL)]

■ prevaricate, quibble, hedge, fence, tergiversate, double-talk, palter, be evasive, beat about the bush. □□ **equivocacy, equivocation** see AMBIGUITY 1a, b.

equivoque /ékwivōk, éekwi-/ *n.* (also **equivoke**) a pun or ambiguity. [ME in the sense 'equivocal' f. OF *equivoque* or LL *aequivocus* EQUIVOCAL]

■ see PUN[1] *n.*

ER *abbr.* **1** emergency room. **2** Queen Elizabeth. [L *Elizabetha Regina*.]

Er *symb. Chem.* the element erbium.

er /ər/ *int.* expressing hesitation or a pause in speech. [imit.]

-er[1] /ər/ *suffix* forming nouns from nouns, adjectives, and many verbs, denoting: **1** a person, animal, or thing that performs a specified action or activity (*cobbler*; *lover*; *executioner*; *poker*; *computer*; *eye-opener*). **2** a person or thing that has a specified attribute or form (*foreigner*; *four-wheeler*; *second-rater*). **3** a person concerned with a specified thing or subject (*hatter*; *geographer*). **4** a person belonging to a specified place or group (*villager*; *New Zealander*; *sixth-grader*). [orig. 'one who has to do with': OE *-ere* f. Gmc]

-er[2] /ər/ *suffix* forming the comparative of adjectives (*wider*; *hotter*) and adverbs (*faster*). [OE *-ra* (adj.), *-or* (adv.) f. Gmc]

-er[3] /ər/ *suffix* used in slang formations usu. distorting the root word (*rugger*; *soccer*). [prob. an extension of -ER[1]]

-er[4] /ər/ *suffix* forming iterative and frequentative verbs (*blunder*; *glimmer*; *twitter*). [OE *-erian*, *-rian* f. Gmc]

-er[5] /ər/ *suffix* **1** forming nouns and adjectives through OF or AF, corresponding to: **a** L *-aris* (*sampler*) (cf. -AR[1]). **b** L *-arius*, *-arium* (*butler*; *carpenter*; *danger*). **c** (through OF *-eüre*) L *-atura* or (through OF *-eör*) L *-atorium* (see COUNTER[1], FRITTER[2]). **2** = -OR.

-er[6] /ər/ *suffix* esp. *Law* forming nouns denoting verbal action or a document effecting this (*disclaimer*; *misnomer*). ¶ The same ending occurs in *dinner* and *supper*. [AF infin. ending of verbs]

ERA *abbr.* **1** *Baseball* earned run average. **2** Equal Rights Amendment.

era /éerə, érə/ *n.* **1** a system of chronology reckoning from a noteworthy event (*the Christian era*). **2** a large distinct period of time, esp. regarded historically (*the pre-Roman era*). **3** a date at which an era begins. **4** *Geol.* a major division of time. [LL *aera* number expressed in figures (pl. of *aes aeris* money, treated as fem. sing.)]

■ **1, 2** age, period, time(s), day(s), epoch; eon.

eradicate /irádikayt/ *v.tr.* root out; destroy completely; get rid of. □□ **eradicable** *adj.* **eradication** /-káyshən/ *n.* **eradicator** *n.* [ME f. L *eradicare* tear up by the roots (as E-, *radix -icis* root)]

■ see REMOVE *v.* 2b.

erase /iráys/ *v.tr.* **1** rub out; obliterate. **2** remove all traces of (*erased it from my memory*). **3** remove recorded material from (a magnetic tape or medium). □□ **erasable** *adj.* **erasure** *n.* [L *eradere eras-* (as E-, *radere* scrape)]

■ **1** rub or wipe out, wipe, efface, delete, blot out, obliterate, cancel, scratch out, cross *or* rule out, strike out *or* off, cut (out), expunge, censor, expurgate, *Printing* dele *colloq.* scrub. **2** remove, efface, obliterate, eradicate, eliminate, destroy, annihilate, do away with, get rid of.

eraser /iráysər/ *n.* a thing that erases, esp. a piece of rubber or plastic used for removing pencil and ink marks.

erbium /ə́rbeeəm/ *n.* *Chem.* a soft, silvery, metallic element of the lanthanide series, occurring mainly in apatite and xenotine. ¶ Symb.: **Er**. [mod.L f. *Ytterby* in Sweden]

ere /air/ *prep.* & *conj.* *poet.* or *archaic* before (of time) (*ere noon*; *ere they come*). [OE *ǣr* f. Gmc]

erect /irékt/ *adj.* & *v.* ● *adj.* **1** upright; vertical. **2** (of the penis, clitoris, or nipples) enlarged and rigid, esp. in sexual excitement. **3** (of hair) bristling, standing up from the skin. ● *v.tr.* **1** raise; set upright. **2** build. **3** establish (*erect a theory*).

□□ **erectable** *adj.* **erectly** *adv.* **erectness** *n.* **erector** *n.* [ME f. L *erigere erect-* set up (as E-, *regere* direct)]

■ *adj.* **1** (bolt) upright, vertical, standing (up), upstanding, straight, plumb, *joc.* perpendicular; on one's feet. **2** enlarged, rigid, swollen, tumescent, stiff, hard. **3** bristling, upright, (standing) on end. ● *v.* **1, 2** raise, set up, assemble, put together, fabricate, manufacture, frame, make, build, put up, construct; pitch. **3** establish, found, set up, put together, frame, formulate, institute, form, devise, create.

erectile /irékt'l, -tīl/ *adj.* that can be erected or become erect. □ **erectile tissue** *Physiol.* animal tissue that is capable of becoming rigid, esp. with sexual excitement. [F *érectile* (as ERECT)]

erection /irékshən/ *n.* **1** the act or an instance of erecting; the state of being erected. **2** a building or structure. **3** *Physiol.* an enlarged and erect state of erectile tissue, esp. of the penis. [F *érection* or L *erectio* (as ERECTILE)]

■ **1** see FABRICATION 1. **2** see BUILDING.

E region the part of the ionosphere that contains the E layer.

eremite /érimīt/ *n.* a hermit or recluse (esp. Christian). □□ **eremitic** /-mítik/ *adj.* **eremitical** *adj.* **eremitism** *n.* [ME f. OF, var. of *hermite, ermite* HERMIT]

■ see HERMIT.

erethism /érithizəm/ *n.* **1** an excessive sensitivity to stimulation of any part of the body, esp. the sexual organs. **2** a state of abnormal mental excitement or irritation. [F *éréthisme* f. Gk *erethismos* f. *erethizō* irritate]

erg[1] /ərg/ *n. Physics* a unit of work or energy, equal to the work done by a force of one dyne when its point of application moves one centimeter in the direction of action of the force. [Gk *ergon* work]

erg[2] /erg/ *n.* (*pl.* **ergs** or **areg** /aáreg/) an area of shifting sand dunes in the Sahara. [F f. Arab. *´irj*]

ergo /árgō, ér-/ *adv.* therefore. [L]

■ see THEREFORE.

ergocalciferol /árgōkalsífə-rōl, -rol/ *n.* = CALCIFEROL. [ERGOT + CALCIFEROL]

ergonomics /árgənómiks/ *n.* the study of the efficiency of persons in their working environment. □□ **ergonomic** *adj.* **ergonomist** /ergónəmist/ *n.* [Gk *ergon* work: cf. ECONOMICS]

ergosterol /ərgóstərawl, -rōl, -rol/ *n. Biochem.* a plant sterol that is converted to vitamin D_2 when irradiated with ultraviolet light. [ERGOT, after CHOLESTEROL]

ergot /árgət, -got/ *n.* **1** a disease of rye and other cereals caused by the fungus *Claviceps purpurea.* **2 a** this fungus. **b** the dried spore-containing structures of this, used as a medicine to aid childbirth. [F f. OF *argot* cock's spur, from the appearance produced]

ergotism /árgətizəm/ *n.* poisoning produced by eating food affected by ergot.

erica /érikə/ *n.* any shrub or heath of the genus *Erica*, with small leathery leaves and bell-like flowers. □□ **ericaceous** /-káyshəs/ *adj.* [L f. Gk *ereikē* heath]

erigeron /irígəron/ *n.* any hardy composite herb of the genus *Erigeron*, with daisylike flowers. [Gk *ērigerōn* f. *ēri* early + *gerōn* old man, because some species bear gray down]

Erin /érin/ *n. archaic* or *poet.* Ireland. [Ir.]

Erinys /erínis/ *n.* (*pl.* **Erinyes** /-nee-eez/) *Mythol.* a Fury. [Gk]

eristic /erístik/ *adj.* & *n.* ● *adj.* **1** of or characterized by disputation. **2** (of an argument or arguer) aiming at winning rather than at reaching the truth. ● *n.* **1** the practice of disputation. **2** an exponent of disputation. □□ **eristically** *adv.* [Gk *eristikos* f. *erizō* wrangle f. *eris* strife]

erk /ərk/ *n. Brit. sl.* **1** a naval rating. **2** an aircraftman. **3** a disliked person. [20th c.: orig. unkn.]

erlking /árl-king/ *n.* (in Germanic mythology) a bearded giant or goblin who lures little children to the land of death. [G *Erlkönig* alder-king, a mistransl. of Da. *ellerkonge* king of the elves]

ermine /ármin/ *n.* (*pl.* same or **ermines**) **1** the stoat, esp. when in its white winter fur. **2** its white fur, used as trimming for the robes of judges, peers, etc. **3** *Heraldry* a white fur marked with black spots. □□ **ermined** *adj.* [ME f. OF *(h)ermine* prob. f. med.L *(mus) Armenius* Armenian (mouse)]

ern var. of ERNE.

-ern /ərn/ *suffix* forming adjectives (*northern*). [OE *-erne* f. Gmc]

erne /ern/ *n.* (also **ern**) *poet.* a sea eagle. [OE *earn* f. Gmc]

erode /irṓd/ *v.* **1** *tr.* & *intr.* wear away; destroy or be destroyed gradually. **2** *tr. Med.* (of ulcers, etc.) destroy (tissue) little by little. □□ **erodible** *adj.* [F *éroder* or L *erodere eros-* (as E-, *rodere ros-* gnaw)]

■ **1** wear (away *or* down), eat away (at), gnaw away, consume, devour, corrode, grind down, abrade, rub down *or* away, whittle (away), pare (down *or* away), wash away; reduce, diminish, destroy.

erogenous /irójinəs/ *adj.* **1** (esp. of a part of the body) sensitive to sexual stimulation. **2** giving rise to sexual desire or excitement. [as EROTIC + -GENOUS]

■ **2** see EROTIC.

erosion /irṓzhən/ *n.* **1** *Geol.* the wearing away of the earth's surface by the action of water, wind, etc. **2** the act or an instance of eroding; the process of being eroded. □□ **erosional** *adj.* **erosive** *adj.* [F *érosion* f. L *erosio* (as ERODE)]

■ wearing (away *or* down), eating away, gnawing away, corrosion, corroding, grinding down, washing away, abrasion, abrading, fraying, wear (and tear), attrition, damage, weathering.

erotic /irótik/ *adj.* of or causing sexual love, esp. tending to arouse sexual desire or excitement. □□ **erotically** *adv.* [F *érotique* f. Gk *erōtikos* f. *erōs erōtos* sexual love]

■ sensual, suggestive, titillating, risqué, bawdy, ribald, seductive, voluptuous, lustful, sexy; amatory, sexual, venereal, amorous, anacreontic; erogenous, erotogenic, carnal, arousing, rousing, aphrodisiac, libidinous, lubricious, prurient, lascivious, lewd, salacious, obscene, indecent, pornographic, dirty, filthy, blue, *formal* concupiscent, *colloq.* or *joc.* naughty.

erotica /irótikə/ *n.pl.* erotic literature or art.

■ see PORNOGRAPHY *n.*

eroticism /irótisizəm/ *n.* **1** erotic nature or character. **2** use of or response to erotic images or stimulation.

erotism /érətizəm/ *n.* sexual desire or excitement; eroticism.

eroto- /irótō, irṓ-/ *comb. form* erotic; eroticism. [Gk *erōs erōtos* sexual love]

erotogenic /irótəjénik, irṓ-/ *adj.* = EROGENOUS.

erotology /érətóləjee/ *n.* the study of sexual love.

erotomania /irótəmáyneeə, irṓ-/ *n.* **1** excessive or morbid erotic desire. **2** a preoccupation with sexual passion. □□ **erotomaniac** /-neeak/ *n.*

err /ər, er/ *v.intr.* **1** be mistaken or incorrect. **2** do wrong; sin. □ **err on the right side** act so that the least harmful of possible errors is the most likely to occur. **err on the side of** act with a specified bias (*errs on the side of generosity*). [ME f. OF *errer* f. L *errare* stray: rel. to Goth. *airzei* error, *airzjan* lead astray]

■ **1** be wrong, be in error, be mistaken, be inaccurate, be incorrect, be in the wrong, go wrong, go astray, make a mistake, miscalculate, (make a) blunder, make a mess, make a faux pas, *colloq.* slip (up), drop a brick, *sl.* goof (up), *Brit. sl.* drop a clanger, boob. **2** do wrong, sin, misbehave, lapse, fall, *literary* or *archaic* trespass.

errand /érənd/ *n.* **1** a short journey, esp. on another's behalf, to take a message, collect goods, etc. **2** the object of such a journey. □ **errand of mercy** a journey to relieve suffering, etc. [OE *ǣrende* f. Gmc]

■ **1** see JOURNEY *n.* **2** object, assignment, charge, task, duty, commission; see also MISSION 1a.

errant /érənt/ *adj.* **1** erring; deviating from an accepted standard. **2** *literary* or *archaic* traveling in search of adventure

---

/.../ **pronunciation**	● **part of speech**
□ **phrases, idioms, and compounds**	
□□ **derivatives**	■ **synonym section**
cross-references appear in SMALL CAPITALS or *italics*	

(*knight errant*). □□ **errancy** /-ənsee/ *n.* (in sense 1). **errantry** *n.* (in sense 2). [ME: sense 1 formed as ERR: sense 2 f. OF *errer* ult. f. LL *itinerare* f. *iter* journey]
■ **1** see ECCENTRIC *adj.* 1. **2** see *traveling* (TRAVEL), VENTURESOME 1.

erratic /irátik/ *adj.* **1** inconsistently variable in conduct, opinions, etc.; unpredictable; eccentric. **2** uncertain in movement. □ **erratic block** *Geol.* a large rock carried from a distance by glacial action. □□ **erratically** *adv.* [ME f. OF *erratique* f. L *erraticus* (as ERR)]
■ **1** inconsistent, variable, irregular, unpredictable, random, haphazard, capricious, wayward, changeable, flighty, unreliable, unstable; peculiar, abnormal, wayward, odd, eccentric, outlandish, strange, unusual, unorthodox, extraordinary, queer, quaint, bizarre, weird, unconventional. **2** wandering, meandering, planetary, directionless, aimless, haphazard.

erratum /iráatəm, irát-/ *n.* (*pl.* **errata** /-tə/) an error in printing or writing, esp. (in *pl.*) a list of corrected errors attached to a book, etc. [L, neut. past part. (as ERR)]
■ see MISPRINT *n.*

erroneous /iróneəs/ *adj.* incorrect; arising from error. □□ **erroneously** *adv.* **erroneousness** *n.* [ME f. OF *erroneus* or L *erroneus* f. *erro -onis* vagabond (as ERR)]
■ incorrect, wrong, mistaken, false, unsound, invalid, untrue, faulty, misleading, flawed, fallacious, spurious, inaccurate, inexact, imprecise; amiss, awry, off course, *colloq.* off the mark, off (the) beam.

error /érər/ *n.* **1** a mistake. **2** the condition of being wrong in conduct or judgment (*led into error*). **3** a wrong opinion or judgment. **4** the amount by which something is incorrect or inaccurate in a calculation or measurement. □□ **errorless** *adj.* [ME f. OF *errour* f. L *error -oris* (as ERR)]
■ **1** mistake, inaccuracy, fault, flaw, solecism, slip, blunder, gaffe, foul-up, *colloq.* slipup, howler, *sl.* bloomer, booboo, fluff, boner, goof, *Brit. sl.* clanger, boob; erratum, misprint, *Printing* literal, *colloq.* typo. **2** sin, transgression, indiscretion, wrongdoing, misconduct, iniquity, evil, wickedness, flagitiousness; (*in error*) wrong, mistaken, incorrect, at fault; mistakenly, incorrectly, by mistake, erroneously.

ersatz /érzaats, -saats, erzáats, -sáats/ *adj.* & *n.* ● *adj.* substitute; imitation (esp. of inferior quality). ● *n.* an ersatz thing. [G, = replacement]
■ *adj.* see IMITATION *adj.*

Erse /ərs/ *adj.* & *n.* ● *adj.* Irish or Highland Gaelic. ● *n.* the Gaelic language. [early Sc. form of IRISH]

erst /ərst/ *adv. archaic* formerly; of old. [OE *ǣrest* superl. of *ǣr*: see ERE]

erstwhile /érst-hwil, -wil/ *adj.* & *adv.* ● *adj.* former; previous. ● *adv. archaic* = ERST.
■ *adj.* see FORMER[1] 2.

erubescent /éroŏbésənt/ *adj.* reddening; blushing. [L *erubescere* (as E-, *rubescere* f. *rubēre* be red)]

eructation /iruktáyshən, eéruk-/ *n.* the act or an instance of belching. [L *eructatio* f. *eructare* (as E-, *ructare* belch)]

erudite /éryədit, érə-/ *adj.* **1** (of a person) learned. **2** (of writing, etc.) showing great learning. □□ **eruditely** *adv.* **erudition** /-díshən/ *n.* [ME f. L *eruditus* past part. of *erudire* instruct, train (as E-, *rudis* untrained)]
■ see LEARNED 1.

erupt /irúpt/ *v.intr.* **1** break out suddenly or dramatically. **2** (of a volcano) become active and eject lava, etc. **3 a** (of a rash, boil, etc.) appear on the skin. **b** (of the skin) produce a rash, etc. **4** (of the teeth) break through the gums in normal development. □□ **eruption** /-rúpshən/ *n.* **eruptive** *adj.* [L *erumpere erupt-* (as E-, *rumpere* break)]
■ **2** spout, gush, explode, blow up, vomit, spit, *colloq.* throw up. **3** break out, come out, appear, flare up. □□ **eruption** outbreak, outburst, discharge, emission, bursting forth, expulsion, explosion, spouting, vomiting (up *or* forth), belching forth; rash.

-ery /əree/ *suffix* forming nouns denoting: **1** a class or kind (*greenery*; *machinery*). **2** employment; state or condition (*archery*; *dentistry*; *slavery*; *bravery*). **3** a place of work or

cultivation or breeding (*brewery*; *rookery*). **4** behavior (*mockery*). **5** often *derog.* all that has to do with (*knavery*; *popery*; *tomfoolery*). [ME, from or after F *-erie, -ere* ult. f. L *-ario-, -ator*]

erysipelas /érisípiləs/ *n. Med.* a streptococcal infection producing inflammation and a deep red color on the skin, esp. of the face and scalp. [ME f. L f. Gk *erusipelas*, perh. rel. to *eruthros* red + a root *pel-* skin]

erythema /éritheémə/ *n.* a superficial reddening of the skin, usu. in patches. □□ **erythemal** *adj.* **erythematic** /-thimátik/ *adj.* [mod.L f. Gk *eruthēma* f. *eruthainō* be red f. *eruthros* red]

erythro- /irithrō/ *comb. form* red. [Gk *eruthros* red]

erythroblast /iríthrəblast/ *n.* an immature erythrocyte. [G]

erythrocyte /iríthrəsit/ *n.* a red blood cell, which contains the pigment hemoglobin and transports oxygen and carbon dioxide to and from the tissues. □□ **erythrocytic** /-sítik/ *adj.*

erythroid /érithroyd/ *adj.* of or relating to erythrocytes.

Es *symb. Chem.* the element einsteinium.

-es[1] /iz/ *suffix* forming plurals of nouns ending in sibilant sounds (such words in -*e* dropping the *e*) (*kisses*; *cases*; *boxes*; *churches*). [var. of -S[1]]

-es[2] /iz, z/ *suffix* forming the 3rd person sing. present of verbs ending in sibilant sounds (such words in -*e* dropping the *e*) and ending in -*o* (but not -*oo*) (*goes*; *places*; *pushes*). [var. of -S[2]]

ESA *abbr.* European Space Agency.

escadrille /éskədríl/ *n.* a French squadron of airplanes. [F]

escalade /éskəláyd, -láad/ *n.* the scaling of fortified walls with ladders, as a military attack. [F f. Sp. *escalada, -ado* f. med.L *scalare* f. *scala* ladder]

escalate /éskəlayt/ *v.* **1** *intr.* & *tr.* increase or develop (usu. rapidly) by stages. **2** *tr.* cause (an action, activity, or process) to become more intense. □□ **escalation** /-láyshən/ *n.* [backform. f. ESCALATOR]
■ see INTENSIFY.

escalator /éskəlaytər/ *n.* a moving staircase consisting of a circulating belt forming steps. [f. the stem of *escalade* 'climb a wall by ladder' + -ATOR]

escallonia /éskəlṓneeə/ *n.* any evergreen shrub of the genus *Escallonia*, bearing rose-red flowers. [*Escallon*, 18th-c. Sp. traveler]

escallop /iskáləp/ *n.* **1** = SCALLOP 1, 2. **2** = ESCALOPE. **3** (in *pl.*) = SCALLOP 3. **4** *Heraldry* a scallop shell as a device. [formed as ESCALOPE]

escalope /éskəlóp/ *n.* a thin slice of meat without any bone, esp. from a leg of veal. [F (in OF = shell): see SCALLOP]
■ see SLICE *n.* 1.

escapade /éskəpáyd/ *n.* a piece of daring or reckless behavior. [F f. Prov. or Sp. *escapada* (as ESCAPE)]
■ see ADVENTURE *n.* 2.

escape /iskáyp/ *v.* & *n.* ● *v.* **1** *intr.* (often foll. by *from*) get free of the restriction or control of a place, person, etc. **2** *intr.* (of a gas, liquid, etc.) leak from a container or pipe, etc. **3** *intr.* succeed in avoiding danger, punishment, etc.; get off safely. **4** *tr.* get completely free of (a person, grasp, etc.). **5** *tr.* avoid or elude (a commitment, danger, etc.). **6** *tr.* elude the notice or memory of (*nothing escapes you*; *the name escaped me*). **7** *tr.* (of words, etc.) issue unawares from (a person, a person's lips). ● *n.* **1** the act or an instance of escaping; avoidance of danger, injury, etc. **2** the state of having escaped (*was a narrow escape*). **3** a means of escaping (often *attrib.*: *escape hatch*). **4** a leakage of gas, etc. **5** a temporary relief from reality or worry. **6** a garden plant running wild. □ **escape clause** *Law* a clause specifying the conditions under which a contracting party is free from an obligation. **escape velocity** the minimum velocity needed to escape from the gravitational field of a body. **escape wheel** a toothed wheel in the escapement of a watch or clock. □□ **escapable** *adj.* **escaper** *n.* [ME f. AF, ONF *escaper* ult. f. med.L (as EX-[1], *cappa* cloak)]
■ *v.* **1** get away, break out *or* free *or* loose, bolt, flee, fly, run away *or* off, decamp, abscond, steal *or* slip off, steal *or* slip away, take off, take to one's heels, take French leave, disappear, vanish, *Brit.* levant, *colloq.* clear out,

make oneself scarce, skedaddle, skip (it), scram, hightail (it), *Brit. colloq. sl.* blow, cut and run, cut, take a powder, vamoose, go on the lam, *Brit sl.* do a bunk, mizzle off. **2** leak, drain, issue, seep, discharge, emanate. **5** avoid, elude, evade, dodge. **6** elude, evade, baffle, stump, mystify, puzzle. ● *n.* **1** getaway, flight, departure, decampment, bolt, jailbreak, prison break, break, breakout. **4** leakage, leaking, seepage, seeping, drainage, draining, leak, discharge, outpouring, outflow, effluence, efflux, effluxion. **5** relief, distraction, diversion, recreation.

escapee /iskaypeé/ *n.* a person, esp. a prisoner, who has escaped.
■ see RUNAWAY 1.

escapement /iskáypmənt/ *n.* **1** the part of a clock or watch that connects and regulates the motive power. **2** the part of the mechanism in a piano that enables the hammer to fall back immediately after striking the string. **3** *archaic* a means of escape. [F *échappement* f. *échapper* ESCAPE]

escapism /iskáypizəm/ *n.* the tendency to seek distraction and relief from reality, esp. in the arts or through fantasy.
□□ **escapist** *n.* & *adj.*

escapology /éskəpóləjee/ *n.* the methods and techniques of escaping from confinement, esp. as a form of entertainment.
□□ **escapologist** *n.*

escargot /eskaargó/ *n.* an edible snail. [F]

escarpment /iskáarpmənt/ *n.* (also **escarp**) *Geol.* a long, steep slope at the edge of a plateau, etc. [F *escarpement* f. *escarpe* SCARP]
■ see CLIFF.

-esce /es/ *suffix* forming verbs, usu. initiating action (*effervesce*; *fluoresce*). [from or after L *-escere*]

-escent /ésənt/ *suffix* forming adjectives denoting the beginning of a state or action (*effervescent*; *fluorescent*). □□ **-escence** *suffix* forming nouns. [from or after F *-escent* or L *-escent-*, pres. part. stem of verbs in *-escere*]

eschatology /éskətóləjee/ *n.* the part of theology concerned with death and final destiny. □□ **eschatological** /-tǝlójikǝl/ *adj.* **eschatologist** *n.* [Gk *eskhatos* last + -LOGY]

escheat /ischeét/ *n.* & *v.* *hist.* ● *n.* **1** the reversion of property to the state, or (in feudal law) to a lord, on the owner's dying without legal heirs. **2** property affected by this. ● *v.* **1** *tr.* hand over (property) as an escheat. **2** *tr.* confiscate. **3** *intr.* revert by escheat. [ME f. OF *eschete*, ult. f. L *excidere* (as EX-¹, *cadere* fall)]

eschew /ischoó/ *v.tr.* *literary* avoid; abstain from. □□ **eschewal** *n.* [ME f. OF *eschiver*, ult. f. Gmc: rel. to SHY¹]
■ see AVOID 1.

eschscholtzia /eshóltseeə/ *n.* any yellow-flowering plant of the genus *Eschscholtzia*, esp. the Californian poppy (see POPPY). [J. F. von *Eschscholtz*, Ger. botanist d. 1831]

escort *n.* & *v.* ● *n.* /éskawrt/ **1** one or more persons, vehicles, ships, etc., accompanying a person, vehicle, etc., esp. for protection or security or as a mark of rank or status. **2** a person accompanying a person of the opposite sex socially. **3** a person or group acting as a guide or leader, esp. on a journey. ● *v.tr.* /iskáwrt/ act as an escort to. [F *escorte*, *escorter* f. It. *scorta* fem. past part. of *scorgere* conduct]
■ *n.* **1** guard, bodyguard, convoy, safe-conduct; protection; guardian, protector, chaperon, companion, cortège, retinue, entourage. **2** companion, boyfriend, partner, beau; *colloq.* date; gigolo. **3** guide, attendant, conductor, leader, cicerone. ● *v.* accompany, shepherd, squire, usher, conduct, attend; guard, convoy, protect, watch over.

escritoire /éskritwaár/ *n.* a writing desk with drawers, etc. [F f. L *scriptorium* writing room: see SCRIPTORIUM]

escrow /éskrō/ *n.* & *v.* *Law* ● *n.* **1** money, property, or a written bond, kept in the custody of a third party until a specified condition has been fulfilled. **2** the status of this (*in escrow*). ● *v.tr.* place in escrow. [AF *escrowe*, OF *escroe* scrap, scroll, f. med.L *scroda* f. Gmc]

escudo /eskoódō/ *n.* (*pl.* **-os**) the principal monetary unit of Portugal and Chile. [Sp. & Port. f. L *scutum* shield]

esculent /éskyələnt/ *adj.* & *n.* ● *adj.* fit to eat; edible. ● *n.* an edible substance. [L *esculentus* f. *esca* food]
■ *adj.* see EDIBLE *adj.*

escutcheon /iskúchən/ *n.* **1** a shield or emblem bearing a coat of arms. **2** the middle part of a ship's stern where the name is placed. **3** the protective plate around a keyhole or door handle. □□ **escutcheoned** *adj.* [AF & ONF *escuchon* ult. f. L *scutum* shield]
■ **1** see SYMBOL *n.*

Esd. *abbr.* Esdras (Apocrypha).

ESE *abbr.* east-southeast.

-ese /eez/ *suffix* forming adjectives and nouns denoting: **1** an inhabitant or language of a country or city (*Japanese*; *Milanese*; *Viennese*). ¶ Plural forms are the same. **2** often *derog.* character or style, esp. of language (*officialese*). [OF *-eis* ult. f. L *-ensis*]

esker /éskər/ *n.* *Geol.* a long ridge of postglacial gravel in river valleys. [Ir. *eiscir*]

Eskimo /éskimō/ *n.* & *adj.* ● *n.* (*pl.* same or **-os**) **1** a member of a people inhabiting N. Canada, Alaska, Greenland, and E. Siberia. **2** the language of this people. ● *adj.* of or relating to the Eskimos or their language. ¶ The term *Inuit* is preferred by the people themselves. [Da. f. F *Esquimaux* (pl.) f. Algonquian]

ESL *abbr.* English as a second language.

esophagus /isófəgəs, ee-/ *n.* (*Brit.* **oesophagus**) (*pl.* **esophagi** /-gī, -jī/) the part of the alimentary canal from the mouth to the stomach; the gullet. □□ **esophageal** /isófəjéeəl, eesəfájeeəl/ *adj.* [ME f. GK *oisophagos*]

esoteric /ésətérik/ *adj.* **1** intelligible only to those with special knowledge. **2** (of a belief, etc.) intended only for the initiated. □□ **esoterical** *adj.* **esoterically** *adv.* **esotericism** /-rəsizəm/ *n.* **esotericist** *n.* [Gk *esōterikos* f. *esōterō* compar. of *esō* within]
■ see OCCULT *adj.* 2.

ESP *abbr.* extrasensory perception.

espadrille /éspədríl/ *n.* a light canvas shoe with a plaited fiber sole. [F f. Prov. *espardillo* f. *espart* ESPARTO]

espalier /ispályər, -yay/ *n.* **1** a latticework along which the branches of a tree or shrub are trained to grow flat against a wall, etc. **2** a tree or shrub trained in this way. [F f. It. *spalliera* f. *spalla* shoulder]

esparto /espaártō/ *n.* (*pl.* **-os**) (in full **esparto grass**) a coarse grass, *Stipa tenacissima*, native to Spain and N. Africa, with tough, narrow leaves, used to make ropes, wickerwork, and good-quality paper. [Sp. f. L *spartum* f. Gk *sparton* rope]

especial /ispéshəl/ *adj.* **1** notable; exceptional. **2** attributed or belonging chiefly to one person or thing (*your especial charm*). [ME f. OF f. L *specialis* special]
■ **1** see SPECIAL *adj.* 1a. **2** see SPECIAL *adj.* 1b, 2.

especially /ispéshəlee, espésh-/ *adv.* chiefly; much more than in other cases.
■ chiefly, mainly, predominantly, primarily, principally, first, first and foremost, firstly, first of all, above all; particularly, specially, specifically, exceptionally, conspicuously, singularly, remarkably, extraordinarily, unusually, uncommonly, peculiarly, outstandingly, notably, strikingly, noticeably, markedly, signally; *abbr.* esp.

Esperanto /éspərántō, -raán-/ *n.* an artificial universal language devised in 1887, based on roots common to the chief European languages. □□ **Esperantist** *n.* [the pen name (f. L *sperare* hope) of its inventor, L. L. Zamenhof, Polish physician d. 1917]

espial /ispíəl/ *n.* **1** the act or an instance of catching sight of or of being seen. **2** *archaic* spying. [ME f. OF *espiaille* f. *espier*: see ESPY]

espionage /éspeeənaazh/ *n.* the practice of spying or of using

---

/.../ **pronunciation**	● **part of speech**
□ **phrases, idioms, and compounds**	
□□ **derivatives**	■ **synonym section**
cross-references appear in SMALL CAPITALS or *italics*	

spies, esp. by governments. [F *espionnage* f. *espionner* f. *espion* SPY]

■ see *spying* (SPY).

esplanade /ésplənáad, -náyd/ *n.* **1** a long, open level area for walking on, esp. beside the ocean. **2** a level space separating a fortress from a town. [F f. Sp. *esplanada* f. *esplanar* make level f. L *explanare* (as EX-¹, *planus* level)]

■ see PROMENADE *n.* 4a.

espousal /ispówzəl, -səl/ *n.* **1** (foll. by *of*) the espousing of a cause, etc. **2** *archaic* a marriage or betrothal. [ME f. OF *espousailles* f. L *sponsalia* neut. pl. of *sponsalis* (as ESPOUSE)]

■ **1** see *promotion* (PROMOTE).

espouse /ispówz/ *v.tr.* **1** adopt or support (a cause, doctrine, etc.). **2** *archaic* **a** (usu. of a man) marry. **b** (usu. foll. by *to*) give (a woman) in marriage. □□ **espouser** *n.* [ME f. OF *espouser* f. L *sponsare* f. *sponsus* past part. of *spondēre* betroth]

■ **1** see PROMOTE 2. **2 a** see WED 1.

espresso /isprésō/ *n.* (also **expresso** /ekspréssō/) (*pl.* **-os**) **1** strong, concentrated black coffee made under steam pressure. **2** a machine for making this. [It., = pressed out]

esprit /espreé/ *n.* sprightliness; wit. □ **esprit de corps** /də káwr/ a feeling of devotion to and pride in the group one belongs to. **esprit de l'escalier** /də leskalyáy/ an apt retort or clever remark that comes to mind after the chance to make it is gone. [F f. L *spiritus* SPIRIT (+ *corps* body, *escalier* stairs)]

■ see VERVE.

espy /ispí/ *v.tr.* (**-ies**, **-ied**) *literary* catch sight of; perceive. [ME f. OF *espier*: see SPY]

■ see PERCEIVE 1.

Esq. *abbr.* esquire.

-esque /esk/ *suffix* forming adjectives meaning 'in the style of' or 'resembling' (*romanesque*; *Schumannesque*; *statuesque*). [F f. It. *-esco* f. med.L *-iscus*]

Esquimau /éskimō/ *n.* (*pl.* **-aux** /-mōz/) = ESKIMO. [F]

esquire /éskwir, iskwír/ *n.* **1** (usu. as abbr. **Esq.**) **a** a title appended to a man's surname when no other form of address is used, esp. as a form of address for letters. **b** a title placed after the name of an attorney (male or female), esp. in correspondence. **2** *archaic* = SQUIRE. [ME f. OF *esquier* f. L *scutarius* shield-bearer f. *scutum* shield]

ESR *abbr. Physics* electron spin resonance.

-ess¹ /is/ *suffix* forming nouns denoting females (*actress*; *lioness*; *mayoress*). [from or after F *-esse* f. LL *-issa* f. Gk *-issa*]

-ess² /es/ *suffix* forming abstract nouns from adjectives (*duress*). [ME f. F *-esse* f. L *-itia*; cf. -ICE]

essay *n.* & *v.* ● *n.* /ésay/ **1** a composition, usu. short and in prose, on any subject. **2** (often foll. by *at*, *in*) *formal* an attempt. ● *v.tr.* /esáy/ *formal* attempt, try. □□ **essayist** *n.* [ME f. ASSAY, assim. to F *essayer* ult. f. LL *exagium* weighing f. *exigere* weigh: see EXACT]

■ *n.* **1** composition, article, paper, piece, theme; tract; thesis, dissertation. **2** attempt, try, effort, endeavor, venture; *colloq.* go, shot. ● *v.* attempt, try, undertake, tackle, test, go about, *colloq.* have a shot *or* go at, have *or* take a crack at, have *or* take a stab at, *sl.* have a whack *or* bash at.

essence /ésəns/ *n.* **1** the indispensable quality or element identifying a thing or determining its character; fundamental nature or inherent characteristics. **2 a** an extract obtained by distillation, etc., esp. a volatile oil. **b** a perfume or scent, esp. made from a plant or animal substance. **3** the constituent of a plant that determines its chemical properties. **4** an abstract entity; the reality underlying a phenomenon or all phenomena. □ **in essence** fundamentally. **of the essence** indispensable; vital. [ME f. OF f. L *essentia* f. *esse* be]

■ **1** quintessence, substance, core, heart, pith, kernel, marrow, soul, crux, cornerstone, *Philos.* quiddity; nature, spirit, being, *colloq.* bottom line. **2 a** extract, concentrate, distillate, distillation, quintessence, elixir, tincture, decoction, attar. **b** see PERFUME *n.* 2. **4** see NATURE 1, 7. □ **in essence** fundamentally, essentially, basically, at bottom, in the final analysis, *au fond.* **of the essence** indispensable, vital, essential, critical, crucial, requisite, important.

Essene /éseen, eséen/ *n.* a member of an ancient Jewish ascetic sect living communally. [L pl. *Esseni* f. Gk pl. *Essēnoi*]

essential /isénshəl/ *adj.* & *n.* ● *adj.* **1** absolutely necessary; indispensable. **2** fundamental; basic. **3** of or constituting the essence of a person or thing. **4** (of a disease) with no known external stimulus or cause; idiopathic. ● *n.* (esp. in *pl.*) a basic or indispensable element or thing. □ **essential element** any of various elements required by living organisms for normal growth. **essential oil** a volatile oil derived from a plant, etc., with its characteristic odor. □□ **essentiality** /-sheeálitee/ *n.* **essentially** *adv.* **essentialness** *n.* [ME f. LL *essentialis* (as ESSENCE)]

■ *adj.* **1** indispensable, imperative, vital, necessary, requisite, required, important, material. **2** fundamental, basic, primary, key, main, leading, chief, principal, elementary, quintessential, intrinsic, elemental. **3** see INTRINSIC. **4** idiopathic, spontaneous. ● *n.* see NECESSITY 1a.

EST *abbr.* **1** eastern standard time. **2** electroshock treatment.

est. *abbr.* **1** established. **2** estimate. **3** estimated.

-est¹ /ist/ *suffix* forming the superlative of adjectives (*widest*; *nicest*; *happiest*) and adverbs (*soonest*). [OE *-ost-*, *-ust-*, *-ast-*]

-est² /ist/ *suffix* (also **-st**) *archaic* forming the 2nd person sing. of verbs (*canst*; *findest*; *gavest*). [OE *-est*, *-ast*, *-st*]

establish /istáblish/ *v.tr.* **1** set up or consolidate (a business, system, etc.) on a permanent basis. **2** (foll. by *in*) settle (a person or oneself) in some capacity. **3** (esp. as **established** *adj.*) achieve permanent acceptance for (a custom, belief, practice, institution, etc.). **4** validate; place beyond dispute (a fact, etc.). □ **established church** a church recognized by the government as the national church. □□ **establisher** *n.* [ME f. OF *establir* (stem *establiss-*) f. L *stabilire* f. *stabilis* STABLE¹]

■ **1** set up, found, create, form, institute, start, begin, inaugurate, organize; constitute; decree, enact, introduce. **2** settle, secure, fix, entrench, install, ensconce. **3** (**established**) see STANDARD *adj.* 2–4. **4** validate, prove, verify, certify, confirm, corroborate, determine, authenticate, affirm, demonstrate, show, substantiate, support, back up.

establishment /istáblishmənt/ *n.* **1** the act or an instance of establishing; the process of being established. **2 a** a business organization or public institution. **b** a place of business. **c** a residence. **3 a** the staff or equipment of an organization. **b** a household. **4** any organized body permanently maintained for a purpose. **5** a church system organized by law. **6** (**the Establishment**) **a** the group in a society exercising authority or influence, and seen as resisting change. **b** any influential or controlling group (*the literary Establishment*).

■ **1** foundation, founding, formation, construction, institution, inauguration, setting up, creation, organization. **2 a** business, concern, firm, company, enterprise, institution, organization; office. **b** office, workplace, consulting room, business, premises, shop, store, market. **c** see RESIDENCE 2. **3 a** see STAFF¹ *n.* 2, APPARATUS. **b** household, family, ménage. **6 a** (**the Establishment**) the system, the government, the authorities, the administration, the power structure, the ruling class, the (established) order, the powers that be.

establishmentarian /istáblishməntáireeən/ *adj.* & *n.* ● *adj.* adhering to or advocating the principle of an established church. ● *n.* a person adhering to or advocating this. □□ **establishmentarianism** *n.*

estaminet /estaameenáy/ *n.* a small French café, etc., selling alcoholic drinks. [F f. Walloon *staminé* byre f. *stamo* a pole for tethering a cow, prob. f. G *Stamm* stem]

estate /istáyt/ *n.* **1** a property consisting of an extensive area of land usu. with a large house. **2** *Brit.* a housing development. **3** all of a person's assets and liabilities, esp. at death. **4** a property where rubber, tea, grapes, etc., are cultivated. **5** (in full **estate of the realm**) an order or class forming (or regarded as) a part of the body politic. **6** *archaic* or *literary* a state or position in life (*the estate of holy matrimony*; *poor man's estate*). □ **estate agent** *Brit.* **1** a real-estate agent. **2** the steward of an estate. **estate car** *Brit.* a station wagon.

estate tax a tax levied on the net value of property of a deceased person. [ME f. OF *estat* (as STATUS)]

■ **1** property, holding, domain, demesne, land, manor. **3** assets, liabilities, property, holding(s), capital, resources, wealth, fortune; belongings, possessions, chattels. **4** plantation, farm, holding. **5** see ORDER *n.* 4. **6** state, position, standing, (social) status, station, place, situation, stratum, level, rank.

esteem /istéem/ *v. & n.* ● *v.tr.* **1** (usu. in *passive*) have a high regard for; greatly respect; think favorably of. **2** *formal* consider; deem (*esteemed it an honor*). ● *n.* high regard; respect; favor (*held them in esteem*). [ME f. OF *estimer* f. L *aestimare* fix the price of]

■ *v.* **1** respect, value, treasure, prize, cherish, hold dear, appreciate, admire, look up to, regard highly, venerate, revere, reverence, honor, defer to; like, love, adore. **2** consider, view as, judge, regard as, hold, account, believe, think, reckon, *formal* deem. ● *n.* high regard, (high) opinion; respect, admiration; favor, approval, approbation.

ester /éstər/ *n. Chem.* any of a class of organic compounds produced by replacing the hydrogen of an acid by an alkyl, aryl, etc., radical, many of which occur naturally as oils and fats. □□ **esterify** /estérifī/ *v.tr.* (**-ies, -ied**). [G, prob. f. *Essig* vinegar + *Äther* ether]

Esth. *abbr.* Esther (Old Testament & Apocrypha).

esthete var. of AESTHETE.

esthetic var. of AESTHETIC.

estimable /éstiməbəl/ *adj.* worthy of esteem. □□ **estimably** *adv.* [F f. L *aestimabilis* (as ESTEEM)]

■ esteemed, respected, admired, valued, worthy, honored, excellent, good; respectable, admirable, valuable, creditable, meritorious, reputable, honorable, laudable, praiseworthy, commendable.

estimate *n. & v.* ● *n.* /éstimət/ **1** an approximate judgment, esp. of cost, value, size, etc. **2** a price specified as that likely to be charged for work to be undertaken. **3** opinion; judgment; estimation. ● *v.tr.* (also *absol.*) /éstimayt/ **1** form an estimate or opinion of. **2** (foll. by *that* + clause) make a rough calculation. **3** (often foll. by *at*) form an estimate; adjudge. **4** fix (a price, etc.) by estimate. □□ **estimative** *adj.* **estimator** *n.* [L *aestimare aestimat-* fix the price of]

■ *n.* **1, 2** reckoning, calculation, approximation, guess, conjecture, *colloq.* guestimate, ballpark figure; evaluation, assessment, appraisal. **3** estimation, belief, opinion, judgment, thinking, feeling, sentiment, sense, (point of) view, viewpoint. ● *v.* **1** consider, think, believe, guess, conjecture, judge. **2, 3** guess, calculate, reckon, work out, gauge; judge, determine; assess, appraise, value, evaluate, adjudge. **4** price, evaluate, value, rate, cost, assess.

estimation /éstimáyshən/ *n.* **1** the process or result of estimating. **2** judgment or opinion of worth (*in my estimation*). **3** *archaic* esteem (*hold in estimation*). [ME f. OF *estimation* or L *aestimatio* (as ESTIMATE)]

■ **1** estimate, guess, approximation. **2** judgment, opinion, (way of) thinking; see also VIEW *n.* 5. **3** esteem, regard, respect; see also ADMIRATION 2.

estival /éstəvəl, estívəl/ *adj.* (also **aestival**) *formal* belonging to or appearing in summer. [ME f. OF *estival* f. L *aestivalis* f. *aestivus* f. *aestus* heat]

estivate /éstəvayt/ *v.intr.* (also **aestivate**) **1** *Zool.* spend the summer or dry season in a state of torpor. **2** *formal* pass the summer. [L *aestivare aesticat-*]

estivation /éstiváyshən/ *n.* (also **aestivation**) **1** *Bot.* the arrangement of petals in a flower bud before it opens (cf. VERNATION). **2** *Zool.* spending the summer or dry season in a state of torpor.

Estonian /estóneeən/ *n. & adj* ● *n.* **1 a** a native of Estonia, a Baltic republic. **b** a person of Estonian descent. **2** the Finno-Ugric language of Estonia. ● *adj.* of or relating to Estonia or its people or language.

estop /estóp/ *v.tr.* (**estopped, estopping**) (foll. by *from*) *Law* bar or preclude, esp. by estoppel. □□ **estoppage** *n.* [ME f.

AF, OF *estoper* f. LL *stuppare* stop up f. L *stuppa* tow: cf. STOP, STUFF]

estoppel /estópəl/ *n. Law* the principle which precludes a person from asserting something contrary to what is implied by a previous action or statement of that person or by a previous pertinent judicial determination. [OF *estouppail* bung f. *estoper* (as ESTOP)]

estovers /estóvərz/ *n.pl. hist.* necessaries allowed by law to a tenant (esp. fuel, or wood for repairs). [AF *estover*, OF *estoveir* be necessary, f. L *est opus*]

estrange /istráynj/ *v.tr.* (usu. in *passive*; often foll. by *from*) cause (a person or group) to turn away in feeling or affection; alienate. □□ **estrangement** *n.* [ME f. AF *estraunger*, OF *estranger* f. L *extraneare* treat as a stranger f. *extraneus* stranger]

■ (*estranged*) alienated, divided, separated, driven apart, disassociated; see also ALIENATE.

estreat /estréet/ *n. & v. Brit. Law* ● *n.* **1** a copy of a court record of a fine, etc., for use in prosecution. **2** the enforcement of a fine or forfeiture of a recognizance. ● *v.tr.* enforce the forfeit of (a fine, etc., esp. surety for bail). [ME f. AF *estrete*, OF *estraite* f. *estraire* f. L *extrahere* EXTRACT]

estrogen /éstrəjən/ *n.* (*Brit.* **oestrogen** /ées-/) **1** any of various steroid hormones developing and maintaining female characteristics of the body. **2** this hormone produced artificially for use in oral contraceptives, etc. □□ **estrogenic** /-jénik/ *adj.* **estrogenically** /-jénikəlee/ *adv.* [ESTRUS + -GEN]

estrus /éstrəs/ *n.* (also **estrum**, *Brit.* **oestrus**, **oestrum** /ées-/) a recurring period of sexual receptivity in many female mammals; heat. □□ **estrous** *adj.* [GK *oistros* gadfly, frenzy]

estuary /és-chōōeree/ *n.* (*pl.* **-ies**) a wide tidal mouth of a river. □□ **estuarine** /-ərin, -əreen/ *adj.* [L *aestuarium* tidal channel f. *aestus* tide]

e.s.u. *abbr.* electrostatic unit(s).

esurient /isōōreeənt/ *adj. archaic* or *joc.* **1** hungry. **2** impecunious and greedy. □□ **esuriently** *adv.* [L *esurire* (v.) hunger f. *edere es-* eat]

■ see GREEDY 1.

ET *abbr.* extraterrestrial.

-et[1] /it/ *suffix* forming nouns (orig. diminutives) (*baronet*; *bullet*; *sonnet*). [OF *-et -ete*]

-et[2] /it/ *suffix* (also **-ete** /eet/) forming nouns usu. denoting persons (*comet*; *poet*; *athlete*). [Gk *-ētēs*]

ETA *abbr.* estimated time of arrival.

eta /áytə, éetə/ *n.* the seventh letter of the Greek alphabet (Η, η). [Gk]

et al. /et ál/ *abbr.* and others. [L *et alii, et alia,* etc.]

etalon /áyt'lon/ *n. Physics* a device consisting of two reflecting plates, for producing interfering light beams. [F *étalon* standard]

etc. *abbr.* = ET CETERA.

et cetera /et sétərə, sétrə/ *adv. & n.* (also **etcetera**) ● *adv.* **1 a** and the rest; and similar things or people. **b** or similar things or people. **2** and so on. ● *n.* (in *pl.*) the usual sundries or extras. [ME f. L]

etch /ech/ *v. & n.* ● *v.* **1 a** *tr.* reproduce (a picture, etc.) by engraving a design on a metal plate with acid (esp. to print copies). **b** *tr.* engrave (a plate) in this way. **2** *intr.* practice this craft. **3** *tr.* (foll. by *on, upon*) impress deeply (esp. on the mind). ● *n.* the action or process of etching. □□ **etcher** *n.* [Du. *etsen* f. G *ätzen* etch f. OHG *azzen* cause to eat or to be eaten f. Gmc]

■ *v.* **1 a** print, reproduce. **b** engrave, carve, incise, inscribe, cut, score, scratch, *archaic* grave. **3** impress, imprint, engrave, grave. ● *n.* engraving, etching; photogravure, gravure.

etchant /échənt/ *n.* a corrosive used in etching.

/.../ **pronunciation**	● **part of speech**
□ **phrases, idioms, and compounds**	
□□ **derivatives**	■ **synonym section**
cross-references appear in SMALL CAPITALS or *italics*	

etching /éching/ n. **1** a print made from an etched plate. **2** the art of producing these plates.
■ see ENGRAVING.

ETD abbr. estimated time of departure.

-ete suffix var. of -ET².

eternal /itə́rnəl/ adj. **1** existing always; without an end or (usu.) beginning in time. **2** essentially unchanging (eternal truths). **3** colloq. constant; seeming not to cease (your eternal nagging). □ **the Eternal** God. **Eternal City** Rome. **eternal triangle** a relationship of three people involving sexual rivalry. □□ **eternality** /-nálitee/ n. **eternalize** v.tr. **eternally** adv. **eternalness** n. **eternize** v.tr. [ME f. OF f. LL aeternalis f. L aeternus f. aevum age]
■ **1** everlasting, timeless, infinite, endless, limitless, immortal. **2** unchanging, unchangeable, immutable, unchanged, invariable, unvarying, unalterable, permanent, fixed, constant, everlasting, enduring, lasting. **3** constant, continuous, unending, endless, ceaseless, unceasing, incessant, perpetual, interminable, uninterrupted, nonstop, unremitting, persistent, relentless; continual, recurrent. □ **the Eternal** see LORD n. 4. □□ **eternally** see ALWAYS 4.

eternity /itə́rnitee/ n. (pl. **-ies**) **1** infinite or unending (esp. future) time. **2** Theol. endless life after death. **3** the state of being eternal. **4** colloq. (often prec. by an) a very long time. **5** (in pl.) eternal truths. [ME f. OF eternité f. L aeternitas -tatis f. aeternus: see ETERNAL]
■ **1, 3** infinity, endlessness, perpetuity, everlastingness, unendingness, boundlessness, timelessness. **2** see immortality (IMMORTAL). **4** see AGE n. 2a.

Etesian /iteézhən/ adj. □ **Etesian winds** NW winds blowing each summer in the E. Mediterranean. [L etesius f. Gk etēsios annual f. etos year]

eth var. of EDH.

-eth¹ var. of -TH¹.

-eth² /ith/ suffix (also **-th**) archaic forming the 3rd person sing. present of verbs (doeth; saith). [OE -eth, -ath, -th]

ethanal /éthənal/ n. = ACETALDEHYDE. [ETHANE + ALDEHYDE]

ethane /éthayn/ n. Chem. a gaseous hydrocarbon of the alkane series, occurring in natural gas. ¶ Chem. formula: C_2H_6. [ETHER + -ANE²]

ethanol /éthənawl, -nol/ n. Chem. = ALCOHOL 1. [ETHANE + ALCOHOL]

ethene /étheen/ n. Chem. = ETHYLENE. [ETHER + -ENE]

ether /éethər/ n. **1** Chem. **a** a colorless volatile organic liquid used as an anesthetic or solvent. Also called DIETHYL ETHER. ¶ Chem. formula: $C_2H_5OC_2H_5$. **b** any of a class of organic compounds with a similar structure to this, having an oxygen joined to two alkyl, etc., groups. **2** a clear sky; the upper regions of air beyond the clouds. **3** hist. **a** a medium formerly assumed to permeate space and fill the interstices between particles of matter. **b** a medium through which electromagnetic waves were formerly thought to be transmitted. □□ **etheric** /eethérik/ adj. [ME f. OF ether or L aether f. Gk aithēr f. root of aithō burn, shine]
■ **2, 3a** see SKY n.

ethereal /itheéreeəl/ adj. **1** light; airy. **2** highly delicate, esp. in appearance. **3** heavenly; celestial. **4** Chem. of or relating to ether. □□ **ethereality** /-reeálitee/ n. **ethereally** adv. [L aethereus, -ius f. Gk aitherios (as ETHER)]
■ **1, 2** see IMMATERIAL 2. **3** see CELESTIAL 1.

etherize /éethəriz/ v.tr. hist. treat or anesthetize with ether. □□ **etherization** n.

ethic /éthik/ n. & adj. ● n. a set of moral principles (the Quaker ethic). ● adj. = ETHICAL. [ME f. OF éthique or L ethicus f. Gk ēthikos (as ETHOS)]

ethical /éthikəl/ adj. **1** relating to morals, esp. as concerning human conduct. **2** morally correct; honorable. **3** (of a medicine or drug) not advertised to the general public, and usu. available only on a doctor's prescription. □ **ethical investment** investment in companies that meet ethical and moral criteria specified by the investor. □□ **ethicality** /-kálitee/ n. **ethically** adv.
■ **2** moral, correct, right, proper, just, righteous;

honorable, decent, upright, principled, fair, honest, good, virtuous, noble.

ethics /éthiks/ n.pl. (also treated as sing.) **1** the science of morals in human conduct. **2 a** moral principles; rules of conduct. **b** a set of these (medical ethics). □□ **ethicist** /éthisist/ n.
■ **2 a, b** see MORAL n. 2.

Ethiopian /éetheeṓpeeən/ n. & adj. ● n. **1 a** a native or national of Ethiopia in NE Africa. **b** a person of Ethiopian descent. **2** archaic a black person. ● adj. of or relating to Ethiopia. [Ethiopia f. L Aethiops f. Gk Aithiops f. aithō burn + ōps face]

Ethiopic /éetheeópik, -ṓpik/ n. & adj. ● n. the Christian liturgical language of Ethiopia. ● adj. of or in this language. [L aethiopicus f. Gk aithiopikos: see ETHIOPIAN]

ethmoid /éthmoyd/ adj. sievelike. □ **ethmoid bone** a square bone at the root of the nose, with many perforations through which the olfactory nerves pass to the nose. □□ **ethmoidal** /-móyd'l/ adj. [Gk ēthmoeidēs f. ēthmos sieve]

ethnic /éthnik/ adj. & n. ● adj. **1 a** (of a social group) having a common national or cultural tradition. **b** (of clothes, etc.) resembling those of a non-European exotic people. **2** denoting origin by birth or descent rather than nationality (ethnic Turks). **3** relating to race or culture (ethnic group; ethnic origins). **4** archaic pagan; heathen. ● n. **1** a member of an (esp. minority) ethnic group. **2** (in pl., usu. treated as sing.) = ETHNOLOGY. □ **ethnic cleansing** euphem. the practice of mass expulsion or killing of people from opposing ethnic or religious groups within a certain area. **ethnic minority** a (usu. identifiable) group differentiated from the main population of a community by racial origin or cultural background. □□ **ethnically** adv. **ethnicity** /-nísitee/ n. [ME f. eccl.L ethnicus f. Gk ethnikos heathen f. ethnos nation]
■ adj. **1 a** see RACIAL. **3** see NATIVE adj. 2, 5.

ethnical /éthnikəl/ adj. relating to ethnology.

ethno- /éthnō/ comb. form ethnic; ethnological. [Gk ethnos nation]

ethnoarchaeology /éthnō-aárkeeóləjee/ n. the study of a society's institutions based on examination of its material attributes. □□ **ethnoarchaeological** /-keeəlójikəl/ adj. **ethnoarchaeologist** n.

ethnocentric /éthnōséntrik/ adj. evaluating other races and cultures by criteria specific to one's own. □□ **ethnocentrically** adv. **ethnocentricity** /-trísitee/ n. **ethnocentrism** n.

ethnography /ethnógrəfee/ n. the scientific description of races and cultures of mankind. □□ **ethnographer** n. **ethnographic** /-nəgráfik/ adj. **ethnographical** adj.

ethnology /ethnóləjee/ n. the comparative scientific study of human peoples. □□ **ethnologic** /-nəlójik/ adj. **ethnological** adj. **ethnologist** n.

ethnomusicology /éthnōmyōōzikóləjee/ n. the study of the music of one or more (esp. non-European) cultures. □□ **ethnomusicologist** n.

ethogram /éethəgram/ n. Zool. a list of the kinds of behavior or activity observed in an animal. [Gk ētho- (see ETHOS) + -GRAM]

ethology /eethóləjee/ n. **1** the science of animal behavior. **2** the science of character formation in human behavior. □□ **ethological** /éethəlójikəl/ adj. **ethologist** n. [L ethologia f. Gk ēthologia (as ETHOS)]

ethos /éethos/ n. the characteristic spirit or attitudes of a community, people, or system, or of a literary work, etc. [mod.L f. Gk ēthos nature, disposition]

ethyl /éthil/ n. (attrib.) Chem. the univalent radical derived from ethane by removal of a hydrogen atom (ethyl alcohol). [G (as ETHER, -YL)]

ethylene /éthileen/ n. Chem. a gaseous hydrocarbon of the alkene series, occurring in natural gas and used in the manufacture of polyethylene. Also called ETHENE. ¶ Chem. formula: C_2H_4. □ **ethylene glycol** Chem. a colorless viscous hygroscopic liquid used as an antifreeze and in the manufacture of polyesters. ¶ Chem. formula: $C_2H_6O_2$. □□ **ethylenic** /-leénik, -lénik/ adj.

-etic /étik/ suffix forming adjectives and nouns (ascetic; emetic; genetic; synthetic). [Gk -ētikos or -ētikos: cf. -IC]

etiolate /éeteeəláyt/ *v.tr.* **1** make (a plant) pale by excluding light. **2** give a sickly hue to (a person). □□ **etiolation** /-láyshən/ *n.* [F *étioler* f. Norman F *étieuler* make into haulm f. *éteule* ult. f. L *stipula* straw]

etiology /éeteeóləjee/ *n.* (esp. *Brit.* **aetiology**) **1** the assignment of a cause or reason. **2** the philosophy of causation. **3** *Med.* the science of the causes of disease. □□ **etiologic** /-tee-əlójik/ *adj.* **etiological** /-teeəlójikəl/ *adj.* **etiologically** /-teeəlójikəlee/ *adv.* [LL *aetiologia* f. GK *aitologia* f. *aitia* cause]

etiquette /étikət, -kit/ *n.* **1** the conventional rules of social behavior. **2 a** the customary behavior of members of a profession toward each other. **b** the unwritten code governing this (*medical etiquette*). [F *étiquette* label, etiquette]
  ■ **1** rules, code (of behavior), form, convention, convenances, protocol, ceremony, formalities, custom(s), decorum, (good) manners, propriety, politesse, politeness, courtesy, civility, seemliness. **2** see FORM *n.* 7.

Eton collar /éet'n/ *n.* a broad stiff collar worn outside the coat collar, esp. of an Eton jacket.

Etonian /eetőneeən/ *n.* a past or present member of Eton College in S. England.

Eton jacket /éet'n/ *n.* a short jacket reaching only to the waist, as formerly worn by pupils of Eton College.

étrier /aytree-áy/ *n. Mountaineering* a short rope ladder with a few rungs of wood or metal. [F, = stirrup]

Etruscan /itrúskən/ *adj. & n.* ● *adj.* of ancient Etruria in Italy, esp. its pre-Roman civilization and physical remains. ● *n.* **1** a native of Etruria. **2** the language of Etruria. □□ **Etruscology** /-kóləjee/ *n.* [L *Etruscus*]

et seq. *abbr.* (also **et seqq.**) and the following (pages, etc.). [L *et sequentia*]

-ette /et/ *suffix* forming nouns meaning: **1** small (*kitchenette; cigarette*). **2** imitation or substitute (*leatherette; flannelette*). **3** often *offens.* female (*usherette; suffragette*). [from or after OF *-ette*, fem. of -ET[1]]

étude /áytŏod, -tyŏod/ *n.* a short musical composition or exercise, usu. for one instrument, designed to improve the technique of the player. [F, = study]

etui /etweé/ *n.* a small case for needles, etc. [F *étui* f. OF *estui* prison]

-etum /éetəm/ *suffix* forming nouns denoting a collection of trees or other plants (*arboretum; pinetum*). [L]

etym. *abbr.* **1** etymological. **2** etymology.

etymologize /étimóləjīz/ *v.* **1** *tr.* give or trace the etymology of. **2** *intr.* study etymology. [med.L *etymologizare* f. L *etymologia* (as ETYMOLOGY)]

etymology /étimóləjee/ *n.* (*pl.* **-ies**) **1 a** the historically verifiable sources of the formation of a word and the development of its meaning. **b** an account of these. **2** the branch of linguistic science concerned with etymologies. □□ **etymological** /-məlójikəl/ *adj.* **etymologically** *adv.* **etymologist** *n.* [OF *ethimologie* f. L *etymologia* f. Gk *etumologia* (as ETYMON, -LOGY)]
  ■ **1a** see DERIVATION.

etymon /étimən/ *n.* (*pl.* **etyma** /-mə/ or **etymons**) the word that gives rise to a derivative or a borrowed or later form. [L f. Gk *etumon* (neut. of *etumos* true), the literal sense or original form of a word]

EU *abbr.* European Union.

Eu *symb. Chem.* the element europium.

eu- /yŏo/ *comb. form* well; easily. [Gk]

eucalyptus /yŏokəlíptəs/ *n.* (also **eucalypt**) (*pl.* **eucalypti** /-tī/ or **eucalyptuses** or **eucalypts**) **1** any tree of the genus *Eucalyptus*, native to Australasia, cultivated for its wood and for the oil from its leaves. **2** (in full **eucalyptus oil**) this oil used as an antiseptic, etc. [mod.L f. EU- + Gk *kaluptos* covered f. *kaluptō* to cover, the unopened flower being protected by a cap]

eucaryote var. of EUKARYOTE.

eucharis /yŏokəris/ *n.* any bulbous plant of the genus *Eucharis*, native to S. America, with white umbellate flowers. [Gk *eukharis* pleasing (as EU-, *kharis* grace)]

Eucharist /yŏokərist/ *n.* **1** the Christian sacrament commemorating the Last Supper, in which bread and wine are con-

secrated and consumed. **2** the consecrated elements, esp. the bread (*receive the Eucharist*). □□ **Eucharistic** *adj.* **Eucharistical** *adj.* [ME f. OF *eucariste*, ult. f. eccl.Gk *eukharistia* thanksgiving f. Gk *eukharistos* grateful (as EU-, *kharizomai* offer willingly)]
  ■ **1** (Holy) Communion, Mass, Lord's Supper, (Blessed *or* Holy) Sacrament, *archaic* mystery.

euchre /yŏokər/ *n. & v.* ● *n.* a card game for two, three, or four players. ● *v.tr.* **1** (in euchre) gain the advantage over (another player) when that player fails to take three tricks. **2** deceive; outwit. **3** *Austral.* exhaust; ruin. [19th c.: orig. unkn.]
  ■ *v.* **2** see CHEAT *v.* 1a.

euclidean /yŏoklídeeən/ *adj.* (also **Euclidean**) of or relating to Euclid, 3rd-c. BC Alexandrian geometrician, esp. the system of geometry based on his principles. □ **euclidean space** space for which euclidean geometry is valid. [L *Euclideus* f. Gk *Eukleideios*]

eudemonic /yŏodimónik/ *adj.* (also **eudaemonic**) conducive to happiness. [Gk *eudaimonikos* (as EUDEMONISM)]

eudemonism /yŏodeémənizəm/ *n.* (also **eudaemonism**) a system of ethics that bases moral obligation on the likelihood of actions producing happiness. □□ **eudemonist** *n.* **eudemonistic** *adj.* [Gk *eudaimonismos* system of happiness f. *eudaimōn* happy (as EU-, *daimōn* guardian spirit)]

eudiometer /yŏodeeómitər/ *n. Chem.* a graduated glass tube in which gases may be chemically combined by an electric spark, used to measure changes in volume of gases during chemical reactions. □□ **eudiometric** /-deeəmétrik/ *adj.* **eudiometrical** *adj.* **eudiometry** *n.* [Gk *eudios* clear (weather): orig. used to measure the amount of oxygen, thought to be greater in clear air]

eugenics /yŏojéniks/ *n.pl.* (also treated as *sing.*) the science of improving the (esp. human) population by controlled breeding for desirable inherited characteristics. □□ **eugenic** *adj.* **eugenically** *adv.* **eugenicist** /yŏojénisist/ *n.* **eugenist** /yŏojinist/ *n.*

eukaryote /yŏokáreeōt/ *n.* (also **eucaryote**) *Biol.* an organism consisting of a cell or cells in which the genetic material is contained within a distinct nucleus (cf. PROKARYOTE). □□ **eukaryotic** /-reeótik/ *adj.* [EU- + KARYO- + -*ote* as in ZYGOTE]

eulogium /yŏolőjeeəm/ *n.* (*pl.* **eulogia** /-jeeə/ or **-ums**) = EULOGY. [med.L: see EULOGY]

eulogize /yŏoləjīz/ *v.tr.* praise in speech or writing. □□ **eulogist** /-jist/ *n.* **eulogistic** *adj.* **eulogistically** *adv.*
  ■ praise, extol, laud, applaud, compliment, sing the praises of, sound the praises of, acclaim, panegyrize. □□ **eulogistic** see COMPLIMENTARY 1.

eulogy /yŏoləjee/ *n.* (*pl.* **-ies**) **1 a** a speech or writing in praise of a person. **b** an expression of praise. **2** a funeral oration in praise of a person. [med.L *eulogium* f. (app. by confusion with L *elogium* epitaph) LL *eulogia* praise f. Gk]
  ■ praise, encomium, accolade, paean, panegyric, acclaim, acclamation, commendation, tribute, homage, plaudits; see also ORATION.

eunuch /yŏonək/ *n.* **1** a castrated man, esp. one formerly employed at an Oriental harem or court. **2** a person lacking effectiveness (*political eunuch*). [ME f. L *eunuchus* f. Gk *eunoukhos* lit. bedchamber attendant f. *eunē* bed + second element rel. to *ekhō* hold]

euonymus /yŏo-óniməs/ *n.* any tree of the genus *Euonymus*, e.g., the spindle tree. [L f. Gk *euōnumos* of lucky name (as EU-, *onoma* name)]

eupeptic /yŏopéptik/ *adj.* of or having good digestion. [Gk *eupeptos* (as EU-, *peptō* digest)]

euphemism /yŏofimizəm/ *n.* **1** a mild or vague expression substituted for one thought to be too harsh or direct (e.g., *pass over* for *die*). **2** the use of such expressions. □□ **euphe-**

/.../ pronunciation	● part of speech
□ phrases, idioms, and compounds	
□□ derivatives	■ synonym section
cross-references appear in SMALL CAPITALS or *italics*	

mist *n.* **euphemistic** *adj.* **euphemistically** *adv.* **euphemize** *v.tr.* & *intr.* [Gk *euphēmismos* f. *euphēmos* (as EU-, *phēmē* speaking)]

euphonious /yŏofōneeəs/ *adj.* **1** sounding pleasant; harmonious. **2** concerning euphony. □□ **euphoniously** *adv.*
  ■ **1** see MELODIOUS 2.

euphonium /yŏofōneeəm/ *n.* a brass wind instrument of the tuba family. [mod.L f. Gk *euphōnos* (as EUPHONY)]

euphony /yŏofənee/ *n.* (*pl.* **-ies**) **1 a** pleasantness of sound, esp. of a word or phrase; harmony. **b** a pleasant sound. **2** the tendency to make a phonetic change for ease of pronunciation. □□ **euphonic** /-fónik/ *adj.* **euphonize** *v.tr.* [F *euphonie* f. LL *euphonia* f. Gk *euphōnia* (as EU-, *phōnē* sound)]
  ■ **1 a** see MELODY 4. **2** haplology, *Gram.* metathesis, *Phonet.* assimilation.

euphorbia /yŏofáwrbeeə/ *n.* any plant of the genus *Euphorbia*, including spurges. [ME f. L *euphorbea* f. *Euphorbus*, 1st-c. Gk physician]

euphoria /yŏofáwreeə/ *n.* a feeling of well-being, esp. one based on overconfidence or overoptimism. □□ **euphoric** /-fáwrik, fór-/ *adj.* **euphorically** *adv.* [Gk f. *euphoros* well-bearing (as EU-, *pherō* bear)]
  ■ see RAPTURE.

euphoriant /yŏofáwreeənt/ *adj.* & *n.* ● *adj.* inducing euphoria. ● *n.* a euphoriant drug.

euphuism /yŏofōōizəm/ *n.* an affected or high-flown style of writing or speaking. □□ **euphuist** *n.* **euphuistic** *adj.* **euphuistically** *adv.* [Gk *euphuēs* well endowed by nature: orig. of writing imitating Lyly's *Euphues* (1578–80)]

Eurasian /yŏoráyzhən/ *adj.* & *n.* ● *adj.* **1** of mixed European and Asian parentage. **2** of Europe and Asia. ● *n.* a Eurasian person.

Euratom /yŏorátəm/ *n.* European Atomic Energy Community. [abbr.]

eureka /yŏoreekə/ *int.* & *n.* ● *int.* I have found it! (announcing a discovery, etc.). ● *n.* the exultant cry of 'eureka'. [Gk *heurēka* 1st pers. sing. perfect of *heuriskō* find: attributed to Archimedes]

eurhythmic var. of EURYTHMIC.

eurhythmics var. of EURYTHMICS.

euro /yŏorō/ *n.* (*pl.* **-os**) *Austral.* a large reddish kangaroo. [Aboriginal]

Euro- /yŏorō/ *comb. form* Europe; European. [abbr.]

Eurocommunism /yŏorōkómyənizəm/ *n.* a form of communism in Western European countries independent of the former Soviet Communist party. □□ **Eurocommunist** *adj.* & *n.*

Eurocrat /yŏorōkrat/ *n.* usu. *derog.* a bureaucrat in the administration of the European Community.

Eurodollar /yŏorōdolər/ *n.* a dollar held in a bank in Europe.

European /yŏorəpéeən/ *adj.* & *n.* ● *adj.* **1** of or in Europe. **2 a** descended from natives of Europe. **b** originating in or characteristic of Europe. **3 a** happening in or extending over Europe. **b** concerning Europe as a whole rather than its individual countries. **4** of or relating to the European Economic Community. ● *n.* **1 a** a native or inhabitant of Europe. **b** a person descended from natives of Europe. **c** a white person. **2** a person concerned with European matters. □ **European Community** (or **European Economic Community**) an economic and political association of certain European countries as a unit with internal free trade and common external tariffs. **European plan** a system of charging for a hotel room only without meals. **European Union** name used of the European Community from November 1993. □□ **Europeanism** *n.* **Europeanize** *v.tr.* & *intr.* **Europeanization** *n.* [F *européen* f. L *europaeus* f. L *Europa* f. Gk *Eurōpē* Europe]

europium /yŏorōpeeəm/ *n.* *Chem.* a soft, silvery metallic element of the lanthanide series, occurring naturally in small quantities. ¶ Symb.: **Eu.** [mod.L f. *Europe*]

Eurovision /yŏorōvizhən/ *n.* a network of European television production administered by the European Broadcasting Union.

eurythmic /yŏoríthmik/ *adj.* (also **eurhythmic**) of or in harmonious proportion (esp. of architecture). [*eurhythmy* harmony of proportions f. L *eur(h)ythmia* f. Gk *eurhuthmia* (as EU-, *rhuthmos* proportion, rhythm)]

eurythmics /yŏoríthmiks/ *n.pl.* (also treated as *sing.*) (also **eurhythmics**) harmony of bodily movement, esp. as developed with music and dance into a system of education.

Eustachian tube /yŏostáyshən, -keeən/ *n.* *Anat.* a tube leading from the pharynx to the cavity of the middle ear and equalizing the pressure on each side of the eardrum. [L *Eustachius* = B. *Eustachio*, It. anatomist d. 1574]

eustasy /yŏostəsee/ *n.* a change in sea level throughout the world caused by tectonic movements, melting of glaciers, etc. □□ **eustatic** /-státik/ *adj.* [back-form. f. G *eustatisch* (adj.) (as EU-, STATIC)]

eutectic /yŏotéktik/ *adj.* & *n.* *Chem.* ● *adj.* (of a mixture, alloy, etc.) having the lowest freezing point of any possible proportions of its constituents. ● *n.* a eutectic mixture. □ **eutectic point** (or **temperature**) the minimum freezing point for a eutectic mixture. [Gk *eutēktos* (as EU-, *tēkō* melt)]

euthanasia /yŏothənáyzhə/ *n.* **1** the bringing about of a gentle and easy death in the case of incurable and painful disease. **2** such a death. [Gk (as EU-, *thanatos* death)]

eutrophic /yŏotrófik, -trŏfik/ *adj.* (of a lake, etc.) rich in nutrients and therefore supporting a dense plant population, which kills animal life by depriving it of oxygen. □□ **eutrophicate** *v.tr.* **eutrophication** *n.* **eutrophy** /yŏotrəfee/ *n.* [*eutrophy* f. Gk *eutrophia* (as EU-, *trephō* nourish)]

eV *abbr.* electronvolt.

EVA *abbr. Astronaut.* extravehicular activity.

evacuate /ivákyŏo-ayt/ *v.tr.* **1 a** remove (people) from a place of danger to stay elsewhere for the duration of the danger. **b** empty or leave (a place) in this way. **2** make empty (a vessel of air, etc.). **3** (of troops) withdraw from (a place). **4** empty (the bowels or other bodily organ). **b** discharge (feces, etc.). □□ **evacuant** *n.* & *adj.* **evacuation** /-áyshən/ *n.* **evacuative** *adj.* & *n.* **evacuator** *n.* [L *evacuare* (as E-, *vacuus* empty)]
  ■ **1 a** remove, move, relocate, transfer. **b** empty, vacate, leave, quit, go away from, depart (from), withdraw *or* retire from, decamp from, move out of *or* from, pull out of *or* from, abandon, desert. **2** see EMPTY *v.* 1. **3** pull out from *or* of, withdraw from; see also EVACUATE 1b above. **4 a** empty, clear (out), drain, purge. **b** discharge, excrete, void.

evacuee /ivákyŏo-ée/ *n.* a person evacuated from a place of danger.

evade /iváyd/ *v.tr.* **1 a** escape from, avoid, esp. by guile or trickery. **b** avoid doing (one's duty, etc.). **c** avoid answering (a question) or yielding to (an argument). **2 a** fail to pay (tax due). **b** defeat the intention of (a law, etc.), esp. while complying with its letter. **3** (of a thing) elude or baffle (a person). □□ **evadable** *adj.* **evader** *n.* [F *évader* f. L *evadere* (as E-, *vadere vas-* go)]
  ■ **1, 2** escape (from), get away from, avoid, elude, dodge, get out of, sidestep, duck (out of), circumvent, shirk, shuffle out of, weasel out of; see also FENCE *v.* 7. **3** see ELUDE 3.

evaginate /ivájinayt/ *v.tr.* *Med.* & *Physiol.* turn (a tubular organ) inside out. □□ **evagination** /-náyshən/ *n.* [L *evaginare* (as E-, *vaginare* as VAGINA)]

evaluate /ivályŏo-ayt/ *v.tr.* **1** assess; appraise. **2 a** find or state the number or amount of. **b** find a numerical expression for. □□ **evaluation** /-áyshən/ *n.* **evaluative** *adj.* **evaluator** *n.* [back-form. f. *evaluation* f. F *évaluation* f. *évaluer* (as E-, VALUE)]
  ■ **1** assess, appraise, value. **2** estimate, gauge, calculate, figure, reckon, compute, judge; rate, rank; quantify. □□ **evaluation** appraisal, valuation, assessment; estimate, estimation, judgment, reckoning, figuring, calculation, computation, rating, ranking.

evanesce /évənés/ *v.intr.* **1** fade from sight; disappear. **2** become effaced. [L *evanescere* (as E-, *vanus* empty)]
  ■ see DISAPPEAR 1.

evanescent /évənésənt/ *adj.* (of an impression or appearance, etc.) quickly fading. □□ **evanescence** /-səns/ *n.* **evanescently** *adv.*

■ see FLEETING.

evangel /ivánjəl/ *n.* **1** *archaic* **a** the gospel. **b** any of the four Gospels. **2** a basic doctrine or set of principles. **3** = EVANGELIST. [ME f. OF *evangile* f. eccl.L *evangelium* f. Gk *euaggelion* good news (as EU-, ANGEL)]

evangelic /ēévanjélik, évən-/ *adj.* = EVANGELICAL.

evangelical /ēévanjélikəl, évən-/ *adj.* & *n.* ● *adj.* **1** of or according to the teaching of the gospel or the Christian religion. **2** of the Protestant school maintaining that the doctrine of salvation by faith in the Atonement is the essence of the gospel. ● *n.* a member of the evangelical school. □□ **evangelicalism** *n.* **evangelically** *adv.* [eccl.L *evangelicus* f. eccl.Gk *euaggelikos* (as EVANGEL)]

evangelism /ivánjəlizəm/ *n.* **1** the preaching or promulgation of the gospel. **2** evangelicalism.

evangelist /ivánjəlist/ *n.* **1** any of the writers of the four Gospels (Matthew, Mark, Luke, John). **2** a preacher of the gospel. **3** a lay person doing missionary work.
■ **2, 3** see MINISTER *n.* 1.

evangelistic /ivánjəlístik/ *adj.* **1** = EVANGELICAL. **2** of preachers of the gospel. **3** of the four evangelists.

evangelize /ivánjəliz/ *v.tr.* **1** (also *absol.*) preach the gospel to. **2** convert (a person) to Christianity. □□ **evangelization** *n.* **evangelizer** *n.* [ME f. eccl.L *evangelizare* f. Gk *euaggelizomai* (as EVANGEL)]

evaporate /ivápərayt/ *v.* **1** *intr.* turn from solid or liquid into vapor. **2** *intr.* & *tr.* lose or cause to lose moisture as vapor. **3** *intr.* & *tr.* disappear or cause to disappear (*our courage evaporated*). □ **evaporated milk** milk concentrated by partial evaporation. □□ **evaporable** *adj.* **evaporation** /-ráyshən/ *n.* **evaporative** /-vápərətiv, -raytiv/ *adj.* **evaporator** *n.* [L *evaporare* (as E-, *vaporare* as VAPOR)]
■ **1** vaporize; steam. **2** vaporize, boil off *or* away; dehydrate, desiccate. **3** disappear, vanish, evanesce, fade (away), melt away, dissolve; dispel, dissipate, disperse. □□ **evaporation** vaporization, drying (up *or* out), dehydration, desiccation, parching; disappearance, evanescence, dematerialization, dissolution, fading (away), melting (away); dispersion, dispelling, dissipation.

evasion /iváyzhən/ *n.* **1** the act or a means of evading. **2 a** subterfuge or a prevaricating excuse. **b** an evasive answer. [ME f. OF f. L *evasio -onis* (as EVADE)]
■ **1** escape, avoidance, shirking, dodging. **2** subterfuge, deceit, deception, chicanery, chicane, artifice, cunning, trickery, lying, sophistry; prevarication, dodging, fudging, evasiveness, quibbling, equivocation.

evasive /iváysiv/ *adj.* **1** seeking to evade something. **2** not direct in one's answers, etc. **3** enabling or effecting evasion (*evasive action*). **4** (of a person) tending to evasion; habitually practicing evasion. □□ **evasively** *adv.* **evasiveness** *n.*
■ **1, 3, 4** equivocal, ambiguous; devious, dissembling, cunning, tricky, deceitful, *colloq.* shifty, *often offens.* jesuitical. **2** indirect, oblique, equivocating, equivocal, ambiguous, *colloq.* cagey; devious, sophistical, casuistic, misleading.

eve /eev/ *n.* **1** the evening or day before a church festival or any date or event (*Christmas Eve; the eve of the funeral*). **2** the time just before anything (*the eve of the election*). **3** *archaic* evening. [ME, = EVEN²]
■ **1** evening *or* day *or* night before. **2** time *or* period before; *Eccl.* vigil.

evection /ivékshən/ *n.* *Astron.* a perturbation of the moon's motion caused by the sun's attraction. [L *evectio* (as E-, *vehere vect-* carry)]

even¹ /ēévən/ *adj.*, *adv.*, & *v.* ● *adj.* (**evener, evenest**) **1** level; flat and smooth. **2 a** uniform in quality; constant. **b** equal in number or amount or value, etc. **c** equally balanced. **3** (usu. foll. by *with*) in the same plane or line. **4** (of a person's temper, etc.) equable; calm. **5 a** (of a number such as 4, 6) divisible by two without a remainder. **b** bearing such a number (*no parking on even days*). **c** not involving fractions; exact (*in even dozens*). ● *adv.* **1** used to invite comparison of the stated assertion, negation, etc., with an implied one that is less strong or remarkable (*never even*

opened [let alone read] *the letter; does he even suspect* [not to say realize] *the danger?; ran even faster* [not just as fast as before]; *even if my watch is right we shall be late* [later if it is slow]). **2** used to introduce an extreme case (*even you must realize it; it might even cost $100*). **3** (sometimes foll. by *with* or *though*) in spite of; notwithstanding (*even with the delays, we arrived on time*). ● *v.* **1** *tr.* & *intr.* (often foll. by *up* or *out*) make or become even. **2** *tr.* (often foll. by *to*) *archaic* treat as equal or comparable. □ **even as** at the very moment that. **even break** *colloq.* an equal chance. **even chance** an equal chance of success or failure. **even money 1** betting odds offering the gambler the chance of winning the amount he or she staked. **2** equally likely to happen or not (*it's even money he'll fail to arrive*). **even now 1** now as well as before. **2** at this very moment. **even so 1** notwithstanding that; nevertheless. **2** quite so. **3** in that case as well as in others. **even-steven** (or **Steven**) *colloq.* even; equal; level. **get** (or **be**) **even with** have one's revenge on. **of even date** *Law* & *Commerce* of the same date. **on an even keel 1** (of a ship or aircraft) not listing. **2** (of a plan or person) untroubled. □□ **evenly** *adv.* **evenness** *n.* [OE *efen, efne*]
■ *adj.* **1** level, flat, smooth, plane, regular, uniform, flush, straight. **2 a** uniform, regular, steady, consistent; constant, unvaried, unvarying, unchanging, set, stable; measured, orderly, ordered, monotonous, unbroken, uninterrupted. **b** equal, balanced, the same, identical, level, fifty-fifty, *archaic or literary* coequal; drawn, on a par, tied, neck and neck, *Brit.* level pegging, *colloq.* even-steven. **3** level, uniform, coextensive, flush, parallel. **4** equable, calm, even-tempered, composed, placid, serene, peaceful, cool, tranquil, imperturbable, impassive, steady, temperate, equanimous, self-possessed, sober, staid, sedate. **5 c** exact, precise, round; rounded off *or* out *or* up *or* down. ● *adv.* **3** (*even with* or *though*) notwithstanding, despite, in spite of, disregarding. ● *v.* **1** smooth, flatten, level; align; equalize, balance (out). □ **even break** see CHANCE *n.* 4. **even so** notwithstanding (that), nevertheless, none the less, still, yet, all the same, in spite of that, despite that. **get even with** have one's revenge on, revenge oneself on, be revenged on, repay, settle accounts with, settle a *or* the score with; requite. **be even with** be square with, be quits with, be equal with. **on an even keel 1** balanced, stable, level. **2** see LEVEL *adj.* 4, STABLE¹ 2.

even² /ēévən/ *n.* *poet.* evening. [OE *æfen*]

evenhanded /ēévənhándid/ *adj.* impartial; fair. □□ **evenhandedly** *adv.* **evenhandedness** *n.*

evening /ēévning/ *n.* & *int.* ● *n.* **1** the end part of the day, esp. from about 6 p.m. to bedtime (*this evening; during the evening; evening meal*). **2** this time spent in a particular way (*had a lively evening*). **3** a time compared with this, esp. the last part of a person's life. ● *int.* = *good evening* (see GOOD *adj.* 14). □ **evening dress** formal dress for evening wear. **evening primrose** any plant of the genus *Oenothera* with pale yellow flowers that open in the evening. **evening star** a planet, esp. Venus, conspicuous in the west after sunset. [OE *æfnung,* rel. to EVEN²]
■ *n.* **1** nightfall, dusk, twilight, sunset, sundown, p.m., night, *archaic or poet.* eventide, *poet.* gloaming. **3** autumn, twilight, waning; see also AGE *n.* 3.

evensong /ēévənsawng, -song/ *n.* a service of evening prayer esp. in the Anglican Church. [EVEN² + SONG]

event /ivént/ *n.* **1** a thing that happens or takes place, esp. one of importance. **2 a** the fact of a thing's occurring. **b** a result or outcome. **3** an item in a sports program, or the program as a whole. **4** *Physics* a single occurrence of a process, e.g., the ionization of one atom. **5** something on the result of which money is staked. □ **event horizon** *Astron.* the gravitational boundary enclosing a black hole, from

---

/. . ./ **pronunciation** ● **part of speech**
□ **phrases, idioms, and compounds**
□□ **derivatives** ■ **synonym section**
cross-references appear in SMALL CAPITALS or *italics*

which no light escapes. **in any event** (or **at all events**) whatever happens. **in the event** as it turns (or turned) out. **in the event of** if (a specified thing) happens. **in the event that** *disp.* if it happens that. [L *eventus* f. *evenire* event- happen (as E-, *venire* come)]

■ **1** occurrence, happening, incident, episode, occasion, circumstance, affair, experience. **2** result, outcome, issue, consequence, conclusion, upshot, effect, end. **3** see HEAT *n.* 6, CONTEST *n.* 1. □ **in any event** (or **at all events**) whatever happens, come what may, in any case, at any rate, anyhow, anyway; regardless. **in the event** as it turns *or* turned out, as things turn *or* turned out, as it happens, when it happened, in reality *or* actuality.

eventful /ivéntfŏŏl/ *adj.* marked by noteworthy events. □□ **eventfully** *adv.* **eventfulness** *n.*

■ busy, full, active, lively, exciting, interesting; important, significant, signal, notable, noteworthy, momentous, memorable.

eventide /éevəntid/ *n. archaic* or *poet.* = EVENING. [OE *æfentíd* (as EVEN², TIDE)]

■ see EVENING *n.* 1.

eventing /ivénting/ *n. Brit.* participation in equestrian competitions, esp. dressage and show jumping. [EVENT 3 as in *three-day event*]

eventless /ivéntlis/ *adj.* without noteworthy or remarkable events. □□ **eventlessly** *adv.*

eventual /ivénchŏŏəl/ *adj.* occurring or existing in due course or at last; ultimate. □□ **eventually** *adv.* [as EVENT, after *actual*]

■ due, expected, consequent, resultant, resulting, unavoidable, inevitable, ineluctable, foreordained, preordained, predestined, likely, probable, *disp.* anticipated; ultimate, final, last, concluding, resulting. □□ **eventually** ultimately, finally, in the end *or* long run, at the end of the day, sooner or later, at last, when all is said and done, in the final analysis, in due course, in (the course of) time, after all.

eventuality /ivénchŏŏ-álitee/ *n.* (*pl.* **-ies**) a possible event or outcome.

■ possibility, likelihood, chance, probability; circumstance, contingency, event, occurrence, happening, case.

eventuate /ivénchŏŏ-ayt/ *v.intr. formal* **1** turn out in a specified way as the result. **2** (often foll. by *in*) result. □□ **eventuation** /-áyshən/ *n.* [as EVENT, after *actuate*]

■ see *turn out* 9 (TURN).

ever /évər/ *adv.* **1** at all times; always (*ever hopeful*; *ever after*). **2** at any time (*have you ever been to Paris?*; *nothing ever happens*; *as good as ever*). **3** as an emphatic word: **a** in any way; at all (*how ever did you do it?*; *when will they ever learn?*). **b** (prec. by *as*) in any manner possible (*be as quick as ever you can*). **4** (in *comb.*) constantly (*ever-present*; *ever-recurring*). **5** (foll. by *so, such*) esp. *Brit. colloq.* very; very much (*is ever so easy*; *was ever such a nice man*; *thanks ever so*). **6** (foll. by *compar.*) constantly; increasingly (*grew ever larger*). □ **did you ever?** *colloq.* did you ever hear or see the like? **ever since** throughout the period since. **for ever 1** for all future time. **2** *colloq.* for a long time (cf. FOREVER). [OE *æfre*]

■ **1** at all times, always, all the time, for ever, eternally, perpetually, endlessly, everlastingly, constantly, continuously, continually, for ever and a day, till the end of time, till doomsday, *colloq.* till the cows come home, till kingdom come; yet, still, even. **2** (at) any time, at all, at any point, at any period, on any occasion; by any chance. □ **for ever 1** see ALWAYS 4.

evergreen /évərgreen/ *adj. & n.* ● *adj.* **1** always green or fresh. **2** (of a plant) retaining green leaves throughout the year. ● *n.* an evergreen plant (cf. DECIDUOUS).

everlasting /évərlásting/ *adj. & n.* ● *adj.* **1** lasting for ever. **2** lasting for a long time, esp. so as to become unwelcome. **3** (of flowers) keeping their shape and color when dried. ● *n.* **1** eternity. **2** = IMMORTELLE. □□ **everlastingly** *adv.* **everlastingness** *n.*

■ *adj.* **1** eternal, perpetual, immortal, undying, deathless,

infinite, timeless. **2** never-ending, perpetual, eternal, constant, continual, continuous, permanent, unceasing, incessant, interminable, endless. ● *n.* **1** see ETERNITY.

evermore /évərmáwr/ *adv.* for ever; always.

■ see ALWAYS 1.

evert /ivárt/ *v.tr.* turn outward or inside out. □□ **eversion** /-várzhən/ *n.* [L *evertere* (as E-, *vertere* vers- turn)]

every /évree/ *adj.* **1** each single (*heard every word*; *watched her every move*). **2** each at a specified interval in a series (*take every third one*; *comes every four days*). **3** all possible; the utmost degree of (*there is every prospect of success*). □ **every bit as** *colloq.* (in comparisons) quite as (*every bit as good*). **every now and again** (or **now and then**) from time to time. **every one** each one (see also EVERYONE). **every other** each second in a series (*every other day*). **every so often** at intervals; occasionally. **every time** *colloq.* **1** without exception. **2** without hesitation. **every which way** *colloq.* **1** in all directions. **2** in a disorderly manner. [OE *æfre ælc* ever each]

everybody /évreebodee, -budee/ *pron.* every person.

■ see EVERYONE.

everyday /évreedáy/ *adj.* **1** occurring every day. **2** suitable for or used on ordinary days. **3** commonplace; usual. **4** mundane; mediocre; inferior.

■ **1** daily, day-to-day; quotidian, diurnal; *Physiol.* circadian. **2, 3** ordinary, common, usual, customary, familiar, regular, habitual, routine, commonplace, run-of-the-mill; unexceptional, conventional; accustomed. **4** prosaic, mundane, dull, unimaginative, unexciting, mediocre, inferior.

everyman /évreeman/ *n.* (also **Everyman**) the ordinary or typical human being; the "man in the street." [the principal character in a 15th-c. morality play]

■ see PEOPLE *n.* 2.

everyone /évreewun/ *pron.* every person; everybody.

■ everybody, all (and sundry), one and all, each and every one *or* person, the whole world, everybody under the sun, every man jack, *usu. derog.* every Tom, Dick, and Harry.

everything /évreething/ *pron.* **1** all things; all the things of a group or class. **2** *colloq.* a great deal (*gave me everything*). **3** an essential consideration (*speed is everything*). □ **have everything** *colloq.* possess all the desired attributes, etc.

■ **1** all things, all, the (whole *or* entire) lot, the entirety, *sl.* the whole (kit and) caboodle, the whole shooting match, everything but the kitchen sink, the whole shebang; the total, the aggregate. **2** see LOT *n.* 1. **3** see ESSENTIAL *adj.*

everywhere /évreehwair, -wair/ *adv.* **1** in every place. **2** *colloq.* in many places.

■ in each *or* every place, to each *or* every place, in all places, in every nook and cranny, high and low, far and wide, near and far; ubiquitously, universally, globally, all over.

evict /ivíkt/ *v.tr.* expel (a tenant) from a property by legal process. □□ **eviction** /-víkshən/ *n.* **evictor** *n.* [L *evincere evict-* (as E-, *vincere* conquer)]

■ expel, turn out (of house and home), oust, remove, eject, dispossess, put out, kick *or* throw *or* boot out, *colloq.* toss out, *Brit. colloq.* turf out. □□ **eviction** expulsion, removal, ejection, ouster, dispossession.

evidence /évidəns/ *n. & v.* ● *n.* **1** (often foll. by *for, of*) the available facts, circumstances, etc., supporting or otherwise a belief, proposition, etc., or indicating whether or not a thing is true or valid. **2** *Law* **a** information given personally or drawn from a document, etc., and tending to prove a fact or proposition. **b** statements or proofs admissible as testimony in a court of law. **3** clearness; obviousness. ● *v.tr.* be evidence of; attest. □ **call in evidence** *Law* summon (a person) as a witness. **in evidence** noticeable; conspicuous. **state's evidence** *Law* evidence for the prosecution given by a participant in or accomplice to the crime at issue. [ME f. OF f. L *evidentia* (as EVIDENT)]

■ *n.* **1** facts, circumstances, proof, grounds, data, documentation, support; indication, sign(s), hint, marks, traces, manifestation(s), suggestion(s), token(s), clue(s). **2** testimony, attestation, deposition, affidavit, averment, statement, assertion. **3** see CLARITY. ● *v.* attest, demonstrate, show, manifest, evince, display, signify, exhibit, reveal, denote, prove, testify, bear witness to, witness. □ **in evidence** see NOTICEABLE 1.

evident /évidənt/ *adj.* **1** plain or obvious (visually or intellectually); manifest. **2** seeming; apparent (*his evident anxiety*). [ME f. OF *evident* or L *evidēre evident-* (as E-, *vidēre* see)]
■ plain, obvious, clear, apparent, patent; manifest, perceptible, perceivable, discernible, noticeable, conspicuous; palpable, unmistakable, recognizable; express.

evidential /évidénshəl/ *adj.* of or providing evidence. □□ **evidentially** *adv.*
■ see DEMONSTRATIVE *adj.* 2.

evidentiary /évidénshəree, -shee-eree/ *adj.* = EVIDENTIAL.

evidently /évidəntlee, -déntlee/ *adv.* **1** as shown by evidence. **2** seemingly; as it appears (*was evidently unwilling to go*).
■ **1** clearly, obviously, plainly, manifestly, palpably, patently, indubitably, undoubtedly, doubtless(ly), without a doubt, indisputably, incontestably, incontrovertibly, undeniably, unquestionably, certainly. **2** seemingly, apparently, outwardly, it would seem (so), so it seems, as far as one can tell, to all appearances, ostensibly.

evil /ēevəl/ *adj.* & *n.* ● *adj.* **1** morally bad; wicked. **2** harmful or tending to harm, esp. intentionally or characteristically. **3** disagreeable or unpleasant (*has an evil temper*). **4** unlucky; causing misfortune (*evil days*). ● *n.* **1** an evil thing; an instance of something evil. **2** evil quality; wickedness; harm. □ **evil eye** a gaze or stare superstitiously believed to be able to cause material harm. **speak evil of** slander. **evil-minded** having evil intentions. □□ **evilly** *adv.* **evilness** *n.* [OE *yfel* f. Gmc]
■ *adj.* **1** bad, wicked, awful, wrong, immoral, sinful, nefarious, iniquitous, heinous, base, corrupt, vile, damnable, villainous, flagitious, foul, nasty, abominable, infamous, atrocious, horrible, horrid, ghastly, grisly, dreadful, depraved, vicious, malevolent, evil-minded, *colloq.* accursed. **2** harmful, hurtful, destructive, pernicious, injurious, mischievous, detrimental, ruinous, deleterious, disastrous, catastrophic, noxious, malignant, malign, poisonous, deadly, lethal, black-hearted, *literary* malefic; virulent, toxic; treacherous, traitorous, perfidious, insidious, unscrupulous, unprincipled, dishonest, knavish, dishonorable, crooked, criminal, felonious, sinister, *literary* maleficent. **3** disagreeable, unpleasant, bad, disgusting, repulsive, awful, nasty, foul, vile, offensive, noxious; putrid, mephitic. **4** unlucky, unfortunate, ominous, inauspicious, dire, unpropitious, infelicitous. ● *n.* **1** sin, vice, iniquity, crime. **2** wickedness, badness, evildoing, wrongdoing, iniquity, immorality, devilry, villainy, nefariousness, viciousness, vileness, heinousness, flagitiousness, foulness, baseness, corruption, degradation, depravity, degeneracy, *formal* turpitude; harm, hurt, injury, mischief, damage; ruin, calamity, misfortune, catastrophe, destruction, disaster; misery, suffering, pain, sorrow, agony, anguish, *archaic or literary* woe. □ **evil eye** see JINX *n.* **speak evil of** see DISCREDIT *v.* 1. **evil-minded** vicious, hateful, malicious, spiteful, malevolent, evil, wicked, bad.

evildoer /ēevəldoōər/ *n.* a person who does evil. □□ **evildoing** *n.*

evince /ivíns/ *v.tr.* **1** indicate or make evident. **2** show that one has (a quality). □□ **evincible** *adj.* **evincive** *adj.* [L *evincere*: see EVICT]
■ see DEMONSTRATE 1, 3.

eviscerate /ivísərayt/ *v.tr. formal* **1** disembowel. **2** empty or deprive of essential contents. □□ **evisceration** /-ráyshən/ *n.* [L *eviscerare eviscerat-* (as E-, VISCERA)]
■ see GUT *v.* 2.

evocative /ivókətiv/ *adj.* tending to evoke (esp. feelings or memories). □□ **evocatively** *adv.* **evocativeness** *n.*
■ see SUGGESTIVE 1.

evoke /ivók/ *v.tr.* **1** inspire or draw forth (memories, feelings, a response, etc.). **2** summon (a supposed spirit from the dead). □□ **evocation** /évəkáyshən, eévō-/ *n.* **evoker** *n.* [L *evocare* (as E-, *vocare* call)]
■ **1** see *call forth*. **2** summon (up), call up *or* forth, conjure (up), invoke, recall; wake, awake, waken, rouse, arouse, raise, reawaken.

evolute /évəloōt/ *n.* (in full **evolute curve**) *Math.* a curve which is the locus of the centers of curvature of another curve that is its involute. [L *evolutus* past part. (as EVOLVE)]

evolution /évəloōshən/ *n.* **1** gradual development, esp. from a simple to a more complex form. **2** a process by which species develop from earlier forms, as an explanation of their origins. **3** the appearance or presentation of events, etc., in due succession (*the evolution of the plot*). **4** a change in the disposition of troops or ships. **5** the giving off or evolving of gas, heat, etc. **6** an opening out. **7** the unfolding of a curve. **8** *Math.* the extraction of a root from any given power (cf. INVOLUTION). □□ **evolutional** *adj.* **evolutionally** *adv.* **evolutionary** *adj.* **evolutionarily** *adv.* [L *evolutio* unrolling (as EVOLVE)]
■ **1–3** development, growth, advance, progress, progression, evolvement, maturation; phylogeny, phylogenesis.

evolutionist /évəloōshənist/ *n.* a person who believes in evolution as explaining the origin of species. □□ **evolutionism** *n.* **evolutionistic** /-nístik/ *adj.*

evolve /ivólv/ *v.* **1** *intr.* & *tr.* develop gradually by a natural process. **2** *tr.* work out or devise (a theory, plan, etc.). **3** *intr.* & *tr.* unfold; open out. **4** *tr.* give off (gas, heat, etc.). □□ **evolvable** *adj.* **evolvement** *n.* [L *evolvere evolut-* (as E-, *volvere* roll)]
■ **1–3** see DEVELOP 1.

evzone /évzōn/ *n.* a member of a select Greek infantry regiment. [mod. Gk *euzōnos* f. Gk, = dressed for exercise (as EU-, *zōnē* belt)]

ewe /yoō/ *n.* a female sheep. □ **ewe lamb** one's most cherished possession (2 Sam. 12). **ewe-necked** (of a horse) having a thin concave neck. [OE *ēowu* f. Gmc]

ewer /yoōər/ *n.* a large pitcher or water jug with a wide mouth. [ME f. ONF *eviere*, OF *aiguiere*, ult. f. L *aquarius* of water f. *aqua* water]
■ see JUG *n.* 1, 2.

ex¹ /eks/ *prep.* **1** (of goods) sold from (*ex factory*). **2** (of stocks or shares) without; excluding. [L, = out of]

ex² /eks/ *n. colloq.* a former husband or wife. [absol. use of EX-¹ 2]

ex-¹ /eks/ *prefix* (also **e-** before some consonants, **ef-** before *f*) **1** forming verbs meaning: **a** out; forth (*exclude*; *exit*). **b** upward (*extol*). **c** thoroughly (*excruciate*). **d** bring into a state (*exasperate*). **e** remove or free from (*expatriate*; *exonerate*). **2** forming nouns from titles of office, status, etc., meaning 'formerly' (*ex-convict*; *ex-president*; *ex-wife*). [L f. *ex* out of]

ex-² /eks/ *prefix* out (*exodus*). [Gk f. *ex* out of]

exa- /éksə/ *comb. form* denoting a factor of 10^{18}. [perh. f. HEXA-]

exacerbate /igzásərbayt/ *v.tr.* **1** make (pain, anger, etc.) worse. **2** irritate (a person). □□ **exacerbation** /-báyshən/ *n.* [L *exacerbare* (as EX-¹, *acerbus* bitter)]
■ **1** see AGGRAVATE 1. **2** see AGGRAVATE 2.

exact /igzákt/ *adj.* & *v.* ● *adj.* **1** accurate; correct in all details (*an exact description*). **2 a** precise. **b** (of a person) tending to precision. ● *v.tr.* (often foll. by *from, of*) **1** demand and enforce payment of (money, fees, etc.) from a person. **2 a** demand; insist on. **b** (of circumstances) require urgently. □ **exact science** a science admitting of absolute or quantitative precision. □□ **exactable** *adj.* **exactitude** *n.* **exactness** *n.* **exactor** *n.* [L *exigere exact-* (as EX-¹, *agere* drive)]
■ *adj.* **1, 2a** accurate, correct, precise, faithful, true,

---

identical, literal, perfect. **2 b** careful, meticulous, strict, rigorous, fastidious, severe, scrupulous, thorough, painstaking, accurate, punctilious, rigid. ● *v.* demand, extort, enforce, insist on *or* upon, wrest, require; claim, compel, call for, requisition.

exacting /igzákting/ *adj.* **1** making great demands. **2** calling for much effort. □□ **exactingly** *adv.* **exactingness** *n.*
■ demanding, challenging, hard, tough, severe, rigid, stern, stringent, harsh, unsparing, merciless, rigorous; difficult, burdensome, taxing; oppressive, tyrannical.

exaction /igzákshən/ *n.* **1** the act or an instance of exacting; the process of being exacted. **2 a** an illegal or exorbitant demand; an extortion. **b** a sum or thing exacted. [ME f. L *exactio* (as EXACT)]
■ **2 a** see TRIBUTE 2. **b** see TOLL¹ 2.

exactly /igzáktlee/ *adv.* **1** accurately; precisely; in an exact manner (*worked it out exactly*). **2** in exact terms (*exactly when did it happen?*). **3** (said in reply) quite so; I quite agree. **4** just; in all respects. □ **not exactly** *colloq.* **1** by no means. **2** not precisely.
■ **1** accurately, precisely, perfectly, correctly, faultlessly, faithfully, scrupulously, strictly, literally, to the letter, literatim, word for word, verbatim, closely; methodically, systematically. **3** see ABSOLUTELY 6.
4 absolutely, undeniably, certainly, unequivocally, completely, in every respect, in all respects, particularly, specifically, explicitly, just, quite, expressly, precisely, truly, *Brit. colloq.* bang on.

exaggerate /igzájərayt/ *v.tr.* **1** (also *absol.*) give an impression of (a thing), esp. in speech or writing, that makes it seem larger or greater, etc., than it really is. **2** enlarge or alter beyond normal or due proportions (*spoke with exaggerated politeness*). □□ **exaggeratedly** *adv.* **exaggeratingly** *adv.* **exaggeration** /-ráyshən/ *n.* **exaggerative** *adj.* **exaggerator** *n.* [L *exaggerare* (as EX-¹, *aggerare* heap up f. *agger* heap)]
■ **1** overstate, magnify, inflate, overdraw, stretch, enlarge, overemphasize, overstress, overplay, overdo; *colloq.* lay it on thick, lay (it) on with a trowel, pile (it) on, *sl.* stick it on. **2** see AMPLIFY 2. □□ **exaggeration** overstatement, extravagance, overemphasis, hyperbole; magnification; excess; empty talk, bombast, puffery, *sl.* hot air, bull.

exalt /igzáwlt/ *v.tr.* **1** raise in rank or power, etc. **2** praise highly. **3** (usu. as **exalted** *adj.*) **a** make lofty or noble (*exalted aims; an exalted style*). **b** make rapturously excited. **4** (as **exalted** *adj.*) elevated in rank or character; eminent; celebrated. **5** stimulate (a faculty, etc.) to greater activity; intensify; heighten. □□ **exaltedly** *adv.* **exaltedness** *n.* **exalter** *n.* [ME f. L *exaltare* (as EX-¹, *altus* high)]
■ **1** elevate, raise (up *or* on high), lift (up *or* on high), upraise, uplift, upgrade, promote, advance, *colloq.* boost. **2** praise, honor, extol, glorify, idolize, dignify, ennoble, revere, reverence, venerate, pay homage *or* tribute to, celebrate; lionize. **3** (**exalted**) **a** lofty, noble, elevated, uplifting, grand, high-flown, exaggerated, overblown, inflated, heightened, superior. **b** elated, excited, exultant, ecstatic, jubilant, overjoyed, joyful, rapturous, transported, blissful, happy, joyous, in seventh heaven, uplifted; *Brit.* over the moon, *colloq.* on cloud nine. **4** (**exalted**) elevated, lofty, high, eminent, notable, noted, prominent, famous, famed, celebrated, distinguished, dignified, honored, prestigious, glorified, sublime, grand. **5** stimulate, excite, animate, rouse, arouse, fire, inspire, electrify, awaken, spur, stir (up), inspirit; intensify; heighten.

exaltation /égzawltáyshən/ *n.* **1** the act or an instance of exalting; the state of being exalted. **2** elation; rapturous emotion. [ME f. OF *exaltation* or LL *exaltatio* (as EXALT)]
■ **1** see GLORY *n.* 1, 3. **2** see JOY *n.* 1.

exam /igzám/ *n.* = EXAMINATION 3.

examination /igzámináyshən/ *n.* **1** the act or an instance of examining; the state of being examined. **2** a detailed inspection. **3** the testing of the proficiency or knowledge of students or other candidates for a qualification by oral or

written questions. **4** an instance of examining or being examined medically. **5** *Law* the formal questioning of the accused or of a witness in court. □□ **examinational** *adj.* [ME f. OF f. L *examinatio -onis* (as EXAMINE)]
■ **1, 2** investigation, study, analysis, inspection, inquiry, exploration, research, appraisal, assessment; scrutiny; probe, search, survey, checkup, check, checkout, *colloq.* going-over. **3** testing, quiz, exam, test, trial; viva voce, *colloq.* oral, *Brit. colloq.* viva. **4** checkup, check, *colloq.* going-over. **5** questioning, interrogation, inquisition, inquiry, catechism, cross-examination, *colloq.* third degree, grilling.

examine /igzámin/ *v.* **1** *tr.* inquire into the nature or condition, etc., of. **2** *tr.* look closely or analytically at. **3** *tr.* test the proficiency of, esp. by examination (see EXAMINATION 3). **4** *tr.* check the health of (a patient) by inspection or experiment. **5** *tr. Law* formally question (the accused or a witness) in court. **6** *intr.* (foll. by *into*) inquire. □□ **examinable** *adj.* **examinee** /-neé/ *n.* **examiner** *n.* [ME f. OF *examiner* f. L *examinare* weigh, test f. *examen* tongue of a balance, ult. f. *exigere* examine, weigh: see EXACT]
■ **1, 2** inquire into, investigate, look over *or* into, inspect, go over *or* through *or* into, scrutinize, analyze, research, study, peruse, scan, pore over, sift, probe, search, explore, survey, check up on, check, appraise, assess, weigh, vet, check out. **3** see TEST¹ *v.* 1. **5** interrogate, quiz, cross-examine, question, grill, pump, sound out. **6** see INQUIRE 1.

example /igzáampəl/ *n. & v.* ● *n.* **1** a thing characteristic of its kind or illustrating a general rule. **2** a person, thing, or piece of conduct, regarded in terms of its fitness to be imitated (*must set him an example; you are a bad example*). **3** a circumstance or treatment seen as a warning to others; a person so treated (*shall make an example of you*). **4** a problem or exercise designed to illustrate a rule. ● *v.tr.* (usu. in *passive*) serve as an example of. □ **for example** by way of illustration. [ME f. OF f. L *exemplum* (as EXEMPT)]
■ *n.* **1** instance, case, sample, specimen, illustration, exemplum. **2** model, standard, exemplar, prototype, archetype, pattern, benchmark, norm, criterion. **3** warning, admonition; see also LESSON 4. **4** illustration, application; problem; exercise. □ **for example** for instance, by way of illustration, by way of example, as an illustration, as an example, as a case in point, to illustrate, e.g.

exanimate /igzánimət/ *adj.* **1** dead; lifeless (esp. in appearance); inanimate. **2** lacking animation or courage. [L *exanimatus* past part. of *exanimare* deprive of life, f. EX-¹ + *anima* breath of life]

exanthema /éksanthéemə, égzan-/ *n. Med.* a skin rash accompanying any eruptive disease or fever. [LL f. Gk *exanthēma* eruption f. *exantheō* (as EX-², *anthos* blossom)]

exarch /éksaark/ *n.* in the Orthodox Church, a bishop lower in rank than a patriarch and having jurisdiction wider than the metropolitan of a diocese. □□ **exarchate** *n.* [eccl.L f. Gk *exarkhos* (as EX-², *arkhos* ruler)]

exasperate /igzáaspərayt/ *v.tr.* **1** (often as **exasperated** *adj.* or **exasperating** *adj.*) irritate intensely; infuriate; enrage. **2** make (a pain, ill feeling, etc.) worse. □□ **exasperatedly** *adv.* **exasperatingly** *adv.* **exasperation** /-ráyshən/ *n.* [L *exasperare exasperat-* (as EX-¹, *asper* rough)]
■ **1** irritate, irk, annoy, bother, harass, pique, gall, nettle, provoke, vex, pester, torment, plague, rub the wrong way, *colloq.* needle, peeve, get, get under a person's skin, *disp.* aggravate, *sl.* bug, get a person's goat; anger, infuriate, enrage, incense, madden, rile, drive mad; embitter; inflame, *colloq.* drive crazy, drive up the wall. **2** see AGGRAVATE 1. □□ **exasperation** see ANNOYANCE 1.

ex cathedra /éks kətheédrə/ *adj. & adv.* with full authority (esp. of a papal pronouncement, implying infallibility as doctrinally defined). [L, = from the (teacher's) chair]

excavate /ékskəvayt/ *v.tr.* **1 a** make (a hole or channel) by digging. **b** dig out material from (the ground). **2** reveal or extract by digging. **3** (also *absol.*) *Archaeol.* dig systematically into the ground to explore (a site). □□ **excavation**

/-váyshən/ *n.* **excavator** *n.* [L *excavare* (as EX-¹, *cavus* hollow)]

■ **1** dig (out *or* up), hollow *or* gouge (out), scoop out, burrow, cut (out). **2, 3** reveal, unearth, uncover, expose, lay bare, dig up, disinter, exhume; clear, dredge up. □□ **excavation** cavity, hole, pit, crater, ditch, trench, trough, burrow, hollow; shaft, tunnel; mine, quarry; *Archaeol.* dig.

exceed /iksee'd/ *v.tr.* **1** (often foll. by *by* an amount) be more or greater than (in number, extent, etc.). **2** go beyond or do more than is warranted by (a set limit, esp. of one's instructions or rights). **3** surpass; excel (a person or achievement). [ME f. OF *exceder* f. L *excedere* (as EX-¹, *cedere* cessgo)]

■ **1, 3** surpass, be superior to, beat, go beyond, better, outdistance, overtake, outstrip, outrank, outrun, outdo, outpace; excel, top, pass; outshine, outreach, transcend, overshadow, eclipse. **2** go beyond, overstep; overdo.

exceeding /iksee'ding/ *adj. & adv.* ● *adj.* **1** surpassing in amount or degree. **2** preeminent. ● *adv. archaic* = EXCEEDINGLY 2.

■ *adj.* great, huge, enormous, outstanding, extraordinary, excessive, exceptional, surpassing; see also PREEMINENT 2.

exceedingly /iksee'ding-lee/ *adv.* **1** very; to a great extent. **2** surpassingly; preeminently.

■ **1** very, extremely, exceptionally, extraordinarily, remarkably, incomparably, immeasurably; excessively, greatly, hugely, enormously. **2** see *preeminently* (PREEMINENT).

excel /iksél/ *v.* (**excelled, excelling**) (often foll. by *in, at*) **1** *tr.* be superior to. **2** *intr.* be preeminent or the most outstanding (*excels at games*). □ **excel oneself** *Brit.* surpass one's previous performance. [ME f. L *excellere* (as EX-¹, *celsus* lofty)]

■ **1** surpass, be superior to, beat, exceed, go beyond, outdo, outstrip, outrank, outpace, outshine, eclipse, top, *sl.* whip. **2** dominate, shine, stand out, be preeminent, be superior, be excellent, be outstanding.

excellence /éksələns/ *n.* **1** the state of excelling; surpassing merit or quality. **2** the activity, etc., in which a person excels. [ME f. OF *excellence* or L *excellentia* (as EXCEL)]

■ **1** superiority, merit, distinction, greatness, prominence, eminence, preeminence, supremacy; (high) quality, value, worth. **2** see SPECIALTY.

Excellency /éksələnsee/ *n.* (*pl.* **-ies**) (usu. prec. by *Your, His, Her, Their*) a title used in addressing or referring to certain high officials, e.g., ambassadors and governors, and (in some countries) senior church dignitaries. [ME f. L *excellentia* (as EXCEL)]

excellent /éksələnt/ *adj.* extremely good; preeminent. □□ **excellently** *adv.* [ME f. OF (as EXCEL)]

■ superb, splendid, great, marvelous, remarkable, sterling, exceptional, superior, supreme, superlative, prime, choice, select, *colloq.* smashing, super, terrific, fantastic, magic, brilliant, ripsnorting, *sl.* wicked, bad, cool; distinguished, noteworthy, notable, worthy, admirable; preeminent, outstanding, capital, first-class, first-rate, matchless, peerless, unequaled, nonpareil, *colloq.* tiptop, A1, champion, A-OK, esp. *Brit. colloq.* slap-up, top-hole, *Austral. sl.* bonzer; grouse; without equal.

excelsior /iksélseeər/ *int. & n.* ● *int.* higher; outstanding (esp. as a motto or trademark). ● *n.* soft wood shavings used for stuffing, packing, etc. [L, compar. of *excelsus* lofty]

except /iksépt/ *v., prep., & conj.* ● *v.tr.* (often as **excepted** *adj.* placed after object) exclude from a general statement, condition, etc. (*excepted him from the amnesty; present company excepted*). ● *prep.* (often foll. by *for* or *that*) not including; other than (*all failed except her; all here except for John; is all right except that it is too long*). ● *conj. archaic* unless (*except he be born again*). [ME f. L *excipere except-* (as EX-¹, *capere* take)]

■ *v.* exclude; omit, leave out, excuse. ● *prep.* not

including, not counting, other than, excepting, barring, bar, with the exception of, apart from, but for, saving, excluding, exclusive of; but for the fact that, *archaic or poet.* save (that); but.

excepting /iksépting/ *prep. & conj.* ● *prep.* = EXCEPT *prep.* ● *conj. archaic* = EXCEPT *conj.*

exception /iksépshən/ *n.* **1** the act or an instance of excepting; the state of being excepted (*made an exception in my case*). **2** a thing that has been or will be excepted. **3** an instance that does not follow a rule. □ **take exception** (often foll. by *to*) object; be resentful (about). **with the exception of** except; not including. [ME f. OF f. L *exceptio -onis* (as EXCEPT)]

■ **3** anomaly, irregularity, special case, departure; oddity, rarity, peculiarity, quirk. □ **take exception (to)** object (to), make an objection (to *or* against), raise an objection (to *or* against), raise objections (to *or* against), demur (to *or* at), find fault (with), take offense *or* umbrage (at), be offended (by); (call into) question, challenge, oppose, disagree (with).

exceptionable /iksépshənəbəl/ *adj.* open to objection. □□ **exceptionably** *adv.*

■ objectionable, unsatisfactory, criticizable; see also UNACCEPTABLE.

exceptional /iksépshənəl/ *adj.* **1** forming an exception. **2** unusual; not typical (*exceptional circumstances*). **3** unusually good; outstanding. □□ **exceptionality** /-nálitee/ *n.* **exceptionally** *adv.*

■ **1, 2** special, especial; unusual, out of the ordinary, untypical, atypical, uncommon, rare, extraordinary, singular, strange, irregular, aberrant, anomalous, odd, peculiar. **3** outstanding, gifted, talented, above average, excellent, superior, prodigious, extraordinary.

excerpt *n. & v.* ● *n.* /éksərpt/ a short extract from a book, motion picture, piece of music, etc. ● *v.tr.* /iksérpt/ (also *absol.*) **1** take an excerpt or excerpts from (a book, etc.). **2** take (an extract) from a book, etc. □□ **excerptible** *adj.* **excerption** /-sérpshən/ *n.* [L *excerpere excerpt-* (as EX-¹, *carpere* pluck)]

■ *n.* extract, passage, quotation, selection, citation, pericope. ● *v.* extract, select; quote, cite; take, cull.

excess /iksés, ékses/ *n. & adj.* ● *n.* **1** the state or an instance of exceeding. **2** the amount by which one quantity or number exceeds another. **3** exceeding of a proper or permitted limit. **4 a** the overstepping of the accepted limits of moderation, esp. intemperance in eating or drinking. **b** (in *pl.*) outrageous or immoderate behavior. **5** an extreme or improper degree or extent (*an excess of cruelty*). **6** part of an insurance claim to be paid by the insured, esp. by prior agreement. ● *attrib.adj.* /usu. ékses/ **1** that exceeds a limited or prescribed amount (*excess weight*). **2** required as extra payment (*excess postage*). □ **excess baggage 1** (or **luggage**) that exceeding a weight allowance and liable to an extra charge. **2** something unnecessary and burdensome. **in** (or **to**) **excess** exceeding the proper amount or degree. **in excess of** more than; exceeding. [ME f. OF *exces* f. L *excessus* (as EXCEED)]

■ *n.* **1** overabundance, overflow, superabundance, superfluity, redundancy; surplus, surfeit, plethora, glut, leftovers; overkill; supererogation. **2** balance, difference, discrepancy. **4 a** (*excesses*) debauchery, immoderation, profligacy, overindulgence, intemperance, dissipation, dissoluteness, extravagance. ● *attrib.adj.* **1** surplus, extra, superfluous, excessive, leftover, remaining, residual. **2** further, extra; see also SUPPLEMENTARY. □ **in excess of** more than, exceeding; see also OVER *prep.* 10.

excessive /iksésiv/ *adj.* **1** too much or too great. **2** more than

---

what is normal or necessary. □□ **excessively** *adv.* **excessiveness** *n.*

▪ immoderate, inordinate, disproportionate, exorbitant, superfluous, extravagant, excess, undue, enormous, extreme, overdone, unreasonable, unwarranted, unjustifiable, outrageous, unconscionable, *colloq.* over-the-top; fulsome, cloying, nauseating, disgusting.

exchange /ikscháynj/ *n. & v.* ● *n.* **1** the act or an instance of giving one thing and receiving another in its place. **2 a** the giving of money for its equivalent in the money of the same or another country. **b** the fee or percentage charged for this. **3** the central telephone office of a district, where connections are effected. **4** a place where merchants, bankers, etc., gather to transact business. **5 a** an office where certain information is given or a service provided, usu. involving two parties. **b** an employment office. **6** a system of settling debts between persons (esp. in different countries) without the use of money, by bills of exchange (see BILL[1]). **7 a** a short conversation, esp. a disagreement or quarrel. **b** a sequence of letters between correspondents. **8** *Chess* the capture of an important piece (esp. a rook) by one player at the loss of a minor piece to the opposing player. **9** (*attrib.*) forming part of an exchange, e.g., of personnel between institutions (*an exchange student*). ● *v.* **1** *tr.* (often foll. by *for*) give or receive (one thing) in place of another. **2** *tr.* give and receive as equivalents (e.g., things or people, blows, information, etc.); give one and receive another of. **3** *intr.* (often foll. by *with*) make an exchange. □ **exchange rate** the value of one currency in terms of another. **in exchange** (often foll. by *for*) as a thing exchanged (for). □□ **exchangeable** *adj.* **exchangeability** *n.* **exchanger** *n.* [ME f. OF *eschangier* f. Rmc (as EX-[1], CHANGE)]

▪ *n.* **1** trade, barter, traffic, truck, change, transfer, interchange, switch, swap; reciprocity, reciprocation; quid pro quo, tit for tat. **4** market, stock market, stock exchange, securities exchange, bourse, Wall Street, *Brit.* the Market, *colloq.* Big Board. **5** see BUREAU 2. **7a** conversation, altercation, argument, disagreement, dispute; see also QUARREL[1] *n.* 1. ● *v.* **1, 2** trade, barter, switch, change, interchange, reciprocate, swap.

exchequer /ikschékər/ *n.* **1** *Brit.* the former government department in charge of national revenue. ¶ Its functions now belong to the Treasury, although the name formally survives, esp. in the title *Chancellor of the Exchequer.* **2** a royal or national treasury. the money of a private individual or group. [ME f. AF *escheker,* OF *eschequier* f. med.L *scaccarium* chessboard (its orig. sense, with ref. to keeping accounts on a checkered cloth)]

▪ see TREASURY 2.

excise[1] /éksiz/ *n. & v.* ● *n.* **1 a** a duty or tax levied on goods and commodities produced or sold within the country of origin. **2** a tax levied on certain licenses. ● *v.tr.* **1** charge excise on (goods). **2** force (a person) to pay excise. [MDu. *excijs, accijs,* perh. f. Rmc: rel. to CENSUS]

▪ *n.* **1** see CUSTOM 4a.

excise[2] /iksíz/ *v.tr.* **1** remove (a passage of a book, etc.). **2** cut out (an organ, etc.) by surgery. □□ **excision** /iksízhən/ *n.* [L *excidere excis-* (as EX-[1], *caedere* cut)]

▪ **1** see cut out 3. **2** see cut out 1 .

exciseman /éksizman/ *n.* (*pl.* **-men**) *Brit. hist.* an officer responsible for collecting excise duty.

excitable /iksítəbəl/ *adj.* **1** (esp. of a person) easily excited. **2** (of an organism, tissue, etc.) responding to a stimulus, or susceptible to stimulation. □□ **excitability** *n.* **excitably** *adv.*

▪ **1** emotional, nervous, jumpy, restive, restless, fidgety, edgy, touchy, testy, high-strung, volatile, mercurial, quick-tempered, hot-blooded, feverish, hysterical, *colloq.* on a short fuse. **2** see SENSITIVE 3, 4, 6.

excitation /éksitáyshən/ *n.* **1 a** the act or an instance of exciting. **b** the state of being excited; excitement. **2** the action of an organism, tissue, etc., resulting from stimulation. **3** *Electr.* **a** the process of applying current to the winding of an electromagnet to produce a magnetic field. **b** the process of applying a signal voltage to the control electrode of an

electron tube or the base of a transistor. **4** *Physics* the process in which an atom, etc., acquires a higher energy state.

▪ **1 b** see *excitement* (EXCITE).

excite /iksít/ *v.tr.* **1 a** rouse the feelings or emotions of (a person). **b** bring into play; rouse up (feelings, faculties, etc.). **c** arouse sexually. **2** provoke; bring about (an action or active condition). **3** promote the activity of (an organism, tissue, etc.) by stimulus. **4** *Electr.* **a** cause (a current) to flow in the winding of an electromagnet. **b** supply a signal. **5** *Physics* **a** cause the emission of (a spectrum). **b** cause (a substance) to emit radiation. **c** put (an atom, etc.) into a state of higher energy. □□ **excitant** /éksit'nt, iksít'nt/ *adj. & n.* **excitative** /-tətiv/ *adj.* **excitatory** /-tətawree/ *adj.* **excitedly** *adv.* **excitedness** *n.* **excitement** *n.* **exciter** *n.* (esp. in senses 4, 5). [ME f. OF *exciter* or L *excitare* frequent. of *exciēre* (as EX-[1], *ciēre* set in motion)]

▪ **1 a, b** rouse, arouse, stir (up), awake, wake, awaken, waken, inspire, stimulate, rally, galvanize; foment, fire, inflame, kindle, ignite; rouse up, call forth; summon up, elicit; inspirit, electrify, animate, enliven, activate, motivate, invigorate, energize, *colloq.* enthuse. **c** arouse, thrill, titillate, *colloq.* turn on. **2** provoke, stir up, stimulate, inspire, call forth, prod; bring about, cause, incite, spur (on), instigate, generate, occasion, begin, start, initiate, effect, set in motion, spark (off).

□□ **excitedness, excitement** agitation, restlessness, jumpiness, nervousness, excitation, tension, unrest, disquiet, disquietude; perturbation, upset, action, ado, activity, ferment, furor, turmoil, tumult, to-do, stir, commotion, hubbub, brouhaha, fuss, hurly-burly, fireworks; animation, eagerness, enthusiasm, exhilaration, ebullience.

exciting /iksíting/ *adj.* arousing great interest or enthusiasm; stirring. □□ **excitingly** *adv.* **excitingness** *n.*

▪ rousing, stimulating, inspiring, stirring, moving; seductive, sensuous, voluptuous, ravishing, captivating, charming, tempting, enticing, alluring, provocative, titillating, sexy; intoxicating, heady, thrilling, exhilarating, stirring, electrifying, galvanizing, energizing, invigorating; overwhelming, overpowering, astounding, astonishing, amazing, *colloq.* mind-boggling, *sl.* mind-blowing.

exciton /eksíton, éksiton/ *n. Physics* a combination of an electron with a hole in a crystalline solid. [EXCITATION + -ON]

exclaim /ikskláym/ *v.* **1** *intr.* cry out suddenly, esp. in anger, surprise, pain, etc. **2** *tr.* (foll. by *that*) utter by exclaiming. [F *exclamer* or L *exclamare* (as EX-[1]; cf. CLAIM)]

▪ **1** call *or* cry (out), shout, yell, bawl, bellow, burst out, blurt out, *colloq.* holler. **2** call *or* cry (out), proclaim, declare, shout, yell, bawl, bellow, *colloq.* holler.

exclamation /éksklamáyshən/ *n.* **1** the act or an instance of exclaiming. **2** words exclaimed; a strong sudden cry. □ **exclamation point** (or esp. *Brit.* **mark**) a punctuation mark (!) indicating an exclamation. [ME f. OF *exclamation* or L *exclamatio* (as EXCLAIM)]

▪ call, cry, utterance, ejaculation, interjection, outcry, vociferation, shout, yell, bellow, *colloq.* holler.

exclamatory /iksklámətawree/ *adj.* of or serving as an exclamation.

exclave /éksklayv/ *n.* a portion of territory of one country completely surrounded by territory of another or others, as viewed by the home territory (cf. ENCLAVE). [EX-[1] + ENCLAVE]

exclosure /eksklṓzhər/ *n. Forestry* etc., an area from which unwanted animals are excluded. [EX-[1] + ENCLOSURE]

exclude /iksklṓōd/ *v.tr.* **1** shut or keep out (a person or thing) from a place, group, privilege, etc. **2** expel and shut out. **3** remove from consideration (*no theory can be excluded*). **4** prevent the occurrence of; make impossible (*excluded all doubt*). □ **excluded middle** *Logic* the principle that of two contradictory propositions one must be true. □□ **excludable** *adj.* **excluder** *n.* [ME f. L *excludere exclus-* (as EX-[1], *claudere* shut)]

▪ **1** shut *or* lock out, keep out *or* away, ban, bar, debar, prohibit, interdict, forbid, proscribe. **2** expel, shut out, eject, evict, oust, get rid of, remove, throw out, *sl.*

bounce. **3** leave out, eliminate, reject, omit, except, preclude, *colloq.* count out. **4** see STOP *v.* 1b.

exclusion /ikskloōzhən/ *n.* the act or an instance of excluding; the state of being excluded. □ **exclusion principle** *Physics* see PAULI EXCLUSION PRINCIPLE. **to the exclusion of** so as to exclude. □□ **exclusionary** *adj.* [L *exclusio* (as EX-CLUDE)]
■ ban, banning, bar, prohibition, interdiction, proscription, forbiddance, lockout; expulsion, ejection, eviction, ouster, removal, riddance; elimination, rejection, omission, exception, preclusion.

exclusionist /ikskloōzhənist/ *adj.* & *n.* ● *adj.* favoring exclusion, esp. from rights or privileges. ● *n.* a person favoring exclusion.

exclusive /ikskloōsiv/ *adj.* & *n.* ● *adj.* **1** excluding other things. **2** (*predic.*; foll. by *of*) not including; except for. **3** tending to exclude others, esp. socially; select. **4** catering for few or select customers; high-class. **5 a** (of a commodity) not obtainable elsewhere. **b** (of a newspaper article) not published elsewhere. **6** (*predic.*; foll. by *to*) restricted or limited to; existing or available only in. **7** (of terms, etc.) excluding all but what is specified. **8** employed or followed or held to the exclusion of all else (*my exclusive occupation; exclusive rights*). ● *n.* an article or story published by only one newspaper or periodical. □ **Exclusive Brethren** a more exclusive section of the Plymouth Brethren. □□ **exclusively** *adv.* **exclusiveness** *n.* **exclusivity** /ékskloosívitee/ *n.* [med.L *exclusivus* (as EXCLUDE)]
■ *adj.* **2** (*exclusive of*) not including, not counting, excluding, omitting, ignoring, apart from, leaving aside, barring; except for, excepting. **3, 4** select, choice, closed, restricted, restrictive, private, snobbish, *usu. derog.* clannish; chic, fashionable, elegant, stylish, upper-class, high-class, aristocratic, *colloq.* classy, *colloq. often derog.* trendy. **5, 6** unique, restricted, limited. **8** only, single, one, sole, unique, singular. ● *n.* scoop, special; *Brit. colloq.* one-off.

excogitate /ekskójitayt/ *v.tr.* think out; contrive. □□ **excogitation** /-táyshən/ *n.* [L *excogitare excogitat-* (as EX-[1], *cogitare* COGITATE)]

excommunicate *v., adj.,* & *n.* *Eccl.* ● *v.tr.* /ékskəmyoōnikayt/ officially exclude (a person) from participation in the sacraments, or from formal communion with the church. ● *adj.* /ékskəmyoōnikət/ excommunicated. ● *n.* /ékskəmyoōnikət/ an excommunicated person. □□ **excommunication** /-káyshən/ *n.* **excommunicative** /-kətiv, -kaytiv/ *adj.* **excommunicator** *n.* **excommunicatory** /-kətáwree/ *adj.* [L *excommunicare -atus* (as EX-[1], *communis* COMMON)]
■ *v.* unchurch, curse; see also BANISH 1.

ex-con /ékskón/ *n. colloq.* an ex-convict; a former inmate of a prison. [abbr.]

excoriate /ekskáwreeayt/ *v.tr.* **1 a** remove part of the skin of (a person, etc.) by abrasion. **b** strip or peel off (skin). **2** censure severely. □□ **excoriation** /-áyshən/ *n.* [L *excoriare excoriat-* (as EX-[1], *corium* hide)]
■ **1 a** see SKIN *v.* 1. **b** see PARE 1. **2** see BERATE.

excrement /ékskrimənt/ *n.* (in *sing.* or *pl.*) feces. □□ **excremental** /-ment'l/ *adj.* [F *excrément* or L *excrementum* (as EXCRETE)]

excrescence /ikskrésəns/ *n.* **1** an abnormal or morbid outgrowth on the body or a plant. **2** an ugly addition. □□ **excrescent** /-sənt/ *adj.* **excrescential** /ékskrisénshəl/ *adj.* [L *excrescentia* (as EX-[1], *crescere* grow)]
■ **1** see GROWTH 4.

excreta /ikskreétə/ *n.pl.* waste discharged from the body, esp. feces and urine. [L neut. pl.: see EXCRETE]
■ see FILTH 1.

excrete /ikskreét/ *v.tr.* (also *absol.*) (of an animal or plant) separate and expel (waste matter) as a result of metabolism. □□ **excreter** *n.* **excretion** /-kreéshən/ *n.* **excretive** *adj.* **excretory** /ékskrətáwree/ *adj.* [L *excernere excret-* (as EX-[1], *cernere* sift)]
■ see DEFECATE.

excruciate /ikskroōsheeayt/ *v.tr.* (esp. as **excruciating** *adj.*) torment acutely (a person's senses); torture mentally. □□ **ex-**cruciatingly** *adv.* **excruciation** /-sheeáyshən/ *n.* [L *excruciare excruciat-* (as EX-[1], *cruciare* torment f. *crux crucis* CROSS)]
■ (**excruciating**) tormenting, torturing, torturous, agonizing, painful, racking, intense, extreme, unbearable, unendurable, insufferable, severe, acute, harrowing, distressful, distressing.

exculpate /ékskulpayt, ikskúl-/ *v.tr. formal* **1** free from blame. **2** (foll. by *from*) clear (a person) of a charge. □□ **exculpation** /-páyshən/ *n.* **exculpatory** /-kúlpətáwree/ *adj.* [med.L *exculpare exculpat-* (as EX-[1], *culpa* blame)]
■ see VINDICATE 1.

excursion /ikskə́rzhən/ *n.* **1** a short journey or ramble for pleasure, with return to the starting point. **2** a digression. **3** *Astron.* a deviation from a regular path. **4** *archaic* a sortie (see ALARUM). □□ **excursional** *adj.* **excursionary** *adj.* **excursionist** *n.* [L *excursio* f. *excurrere excurs-* (as EX-[1], *currere* run)]
■ **1** journey, trip, tour, outing, expedition, voyage, cruise, junket, jaunt; detour, side trip; ramble, stroll, walk, hike, trek, drive, ride, sail. **2** digression, deviation, excursus, diversion.

excursive /ikskə́rsiv/ *adj.* digressive; diverse. □□ **excursively** *adv.* **excursiveness** *n.*

excursus /ikskə́rsəs/ *n.* **1** a detailed discussion of a special point in a book, usu. in an appendix. **2** a digression in a narrative. [L, verbal noun formed as EXCURSION]
■ **2** see *digression* (DIGRESS).

excuse *v.* & *n.* ● *v.tr.* /ikskyoōz/ **1** attempt to lessen the blame attaching to (a person, act, or fault). **2** (of a fact or circumstance) serve in mitigation of (a person or act). **3** obtain exemption for (a person or oneself). **4** (foll. by *from*) release (a person) from a duty, etc. (*excused from kitchen duties*). **5** overlook or forgive (a fault or offense). **6** (foll. by *for*) forgive (a person) for a fault. **7** not insist upon (what is due). **8** *refl.* apologize for leaving. ● *n.* /ikskyoōs/ **1** a reason put forward to mitigate or justify an offense, fault, etc. **2** an apology (*made my excuses*). **3** (foll. by *for*) a poor or inadequate example of. **4** the action of excusing; indulgence; pardon. □ **be excused** be allowed to leave a room, etc., e.g., to go to the bathroom. **excuse me** a polite apology for lack of ceremony, for an interruption, etc., or for disagreeing. □□ **excusable** /-kyoōzəbəl/ *adj.* **excusably** *adv.* **excusatory** /-kyoōzətáwree/ *adj.* [ME f. OF *escuser* f. L *excusare* (as EX-[1], *causa* CAUSE, accusation)]
■ *v.* **1** condone, justify, vindicate, defend, mitigate, extenuate, palliate, warrant, allow, permit, explain, rationalize; apologize for. **2** see *explain away.* **4** (*excuse from*) release from, let off, liberate from, free from *or* of, relieve of, exempt from, absolve of *or* from, *colloq.* let off the hook for. **5** overlook, forgive, pardon, disregard, ignore, wink at, pass over, be blind to, pay no attention *or* heed to, turn a blind eye to, turn a deaf ear to. **7** see WAIVE. **8** see LEAVE[1] 1b, 3, 4. ● *n.* **1, 2** reason, explanation, story, argument; apology, justification, defense, plea, vindication, rationalization; basis, ground(s), foundation, cause. **3** see APOLOGY 4. **4** forgiveness, remission, pardon, indulgence, reprieve, clearing, absolution, exoneration, acquittal, vindication, clearance, acquittance, *formal* exculpation.

ex-directory /éksdiréktəree, -dī-/ *adj. Brit.* not listed in a telephone directory, at the wish of the subscriber.

ex div. *abbr.* ex dividend.

ex dividend /eks dívidend/ *adj.* & *adv.* (of stocks or shares) exclusive of dividend; not including the previously announced dividend.

exeat /ékseeat/ *n.* **1** *Brit.* permission granted to a student by a college for temporary absence. **2** permission granted to a priest by a bishop to move to another diocese. [L, 3rd sing. pres. subjunctive of *exire* go out (as EX-[1], *ire* go)]

/.../ **pronunciation**	● **part of speech**
□ **phrases, idioms, and compounds**	
□□ **derivatives**	■ **synonym section**
cross-references appear in SMALL CAPITALS or *italics*	

exec /igzék/ *n.* an executive. [abbr.]

execrable /éksikrəbəl/ *adj.* abominable; detestable. □□ **execrably** *adv.* [ME f. OF f. L *execrabilis* (as EXECRATE)]
■ see ABOMINABLE 1.

execrate /éksikrayt/ *v.* **1** *tr.* express or feel abhorrence for. **2** *tr.* curse (a person or thing). **3** *intr.* utter curses. □□ **execration** /-kráyshən/ *n.* **execrative** *adj.* **execratory** /-krətáwree/ *adj.* [L *exsecrare* (as EX-¹, *sacrare* devote f. *sacer* sacred, accursed)]
■ **1** see ABHOR. **2, 3** see CURSE *v.* 1a.

executant /igzékyət'nt/ *n. formal* **1** a performer, esp. of music. **2** one who carries something into effect. [F *exécutant* pres. part. (as EXECUTE)]

execute /éksikyōōt/ *v.tr.* **1 a** carry out a sentence of death on (a condemned person). **b** kill as a political act. **2** carry into effect; perform (a plan, duty, command, operation, etc.). **3 a** carry out a design for (a product of art or skill). **b** perform (a musical composition, dance, etc.). **4** make (a legal instrument) valid by signing, sealing, etc. **5** put into effect (a judicial sentence, the terms of a will, etc.). □□ **executable** *adj.* [ME f. OF *executer* f. med.L *executare* f. L *exsequi exsecut-* (as EX-¹, *sequi* follow)]
■ **1 a** put to death, kill. **b** assassinate, kill, liquidate, murder, snuff out, *colloq.* remove, *sl.* bump off, wipe out, knock off, rub out, waste, ice. **2** effect, perform, fulfill, accomplish, do, carry out *or* through, discharge, dispatch, implement, engineer, cut, pull off, carry off, *colloq.* swing. **3 a** carry out, complete, finish, deliver. **b** perform, present, put on. **4** effect; sign, seal, validate, ratify, countersign. **5** see *carry out* (CARRY).

execution /éksikyōōshən/ *n.* **1** the carrying out of a sentence of death. **2** the act or an instance of carrying out or performing something. **3** technique or style of performance in the arts, esp. music. **4 a** seizure of the property or person of a debtor in default of payment. **b** a judicial writ enforcing a judgment. □□ **executionary** *adj.* [ME f. OF f. L *executio -onis* (as EXECUTE)]
■ **1** killing; assassination, murder, liquidation, removal. **2** carrying out, performance, accomplishment, doing, discharge, dispatch, implementation, prosecution, realization, enactment; completion, fulfillment, achievement, attainment, implementation. **3** technique, style, rendering, rendition, manner, touch, approach, delivery, production, skill, art, mastery. **4 a** see SEIZURE 1.

executioner /éksikyōōshənər/ *n.* an official who carries out a sentence of death.
■ hangman, headsman.

executive /igzékyətiv/ *n. & adj.* ● *n.* **1** a person or body with managerial or administrative responsibility in a business organization, etc.; a senior businessman. **2** a branch of a government or organization concerned with executing laws, agreements, etc., or with other administration or management. ● *adj.* **1** concerned with executing laws, agreements, etc., or with other administration or management. **2** relating to or having the function of executing. □ **executive council 1** a council with executive authority. **2** a council that advises the head of government. **executive officer 1** *Mil.* an officer second in command. **2** (in a corporation, organization, etc.) one with executive duties. **executive session** a usu. private meeting of a legislative body for executive business. □□ **executively** *adv.* [med.L *executivus* (as EXECUTE)]
■ *n.* **1** chairman (of the board), chairperson, chairwoman, director, managing director, chief, chief executive, president, manager, head, leader, principal, administrator, official; supervisor, superintendent, overseer, master, kingpin, *colloq.* top dog, boss, *sl.* top banana, (big) cheese, (head) honcho, Mr. Big. **2** administration, management, directorship, directorate, government, leadership. ● *adj.* administrative, managerial, supervisory, official, governing, governmental.

executor /igzékyətər/ *n.* (*fem.* **executrix** /-triks/, *pl.* **-trices** /-tríseez/ or **-trixes**) a person appointed by a testator to carry out the terms of his or her will. □ **literary executor** a person entrusted with a writer's papers, unpublished works, etc. □□ **executorial** /-táwreeəl/ *adj.* **executorship** *n.* **executory** *adj.* [ME f. AF *executor*, *-our* f. L *executor -oris* (as EXECUTE)]

exegesis /éksijeésis/ *n.* (*pl.* **exegeses** /-seez/) critical explanation of a text, esp. of Scripture. □□ **exegete** /éksijeet/ *n.* **exegetic** /-jétik/ *adj.* **exegetical** *adj.* **exegetist** /-jétist/ *n.* [Gk *exēgēsis* f. *exēgeomai* interpret (as EX-², *hēgeomai* lead)]
■ see GLOSS² *n.* 1, 3b.

exemplar /igzémplər, -plaar/ *n.* **1** a model or pattern. **2** a typical instance of a class of things. **3** a parallel instance. [ME f. OF *exemplaire* f. LL *exemplarium* (as EXAMPLE)]
■ **1** see EXAMPLE *n.* 2. **2** see EPITOME 1.

exemplary /igzémpləree/ *adj.* **1** fit to be imitated; outstandingly good. **2 a** serving as a warning. **b** *Law* (of damages) exceeding the amount needed for simple compensation. **3** illustrative; representative. □□ **exemplarily** *adv.* **exemplariness** *n.* [LL *exemplaris* (as EXAMPLE)]
■ **1** model; outstanding, excellent, meritorious, admirable, commendable, praiseworthy, noteworthy, superior. **2 a** cautionary, admonitory, warning, *literary* monitory. **3** illustrative, representative, typical, characteristic; archetypal; paradigmatic.

exemplify /igzémplifī/ *v.tr.* (**-ies, -ied**) **1** illustrate by example. **2** be an example of. **3** *Law* make an attested copy of (a document) under an official seal. □□ **exemplification** /-fikáyshən/ *n.* [ME f. med.L *exemplificare* (as EXAMPLE)]
■ **1, 2** illustrate, typify, represent, epitomize, instance, instantiate; embody, personify; demonstrate, display, show, exhibit, model, depict.

exemplum /igzémpləm/ *n.* (*pl.* **exempla** /-plə/) an example or model, esp. a moralizing or illustrative story. [L: see EXAMPLE]

exempt /igzémpt/ *adj., n., & v.* ● *adj.* **1** free from an obligation or liability, etc., imposed on others. **2** (foll. by *from*) not liable to. ● *n.* a person who is exempt, esp. from payment of tax. ● *v.tr.* (usu. foll. by *from*) free from an obligation, esp. one imposed on others. □□ **exemption** /-zémpshən/ *n.* [ME f. L *exemptus* past part. of *eximere exempt-* (as EX-¹, *emere* take)]
■ *adj.* **1** exempted, free, let off, excepted, excused, immune, *colloq.* off the hook. **2** (*exempt from*) exempted from, free from or of, liberated from, released from, excused from, relieved of, spared, let off, excepted from. ● *v.* spare, let off, *colloq.* let off the hook; (*exempt from*) free *or* release from, excuse *or* relieve from, absolve from *or* of. □□ **exemption** exception, immunity, freedom, release, impunity, dispensation, exclusion.

exequies /éksikweez/ *n.pl. formal* funeral rites. [ME f. OF f. L *exsequiae* (as EX-¹, *sequi* follow)]
■ see FUNERAL *n.*

exercise /éksərsīz/ *n. & v.* ● *n.* **1** activity requiring physical effort, done esp. as training or to sustain or improve health. **2** mental or spiritual activity, esp. as practice to develop a skill. **3** (often in *pl.*) a particular task or set of tasks devised as exercise, practice in a technique, etc. **4 a** the use or application of a mental faculty, right, etc. **b** practice of an ability, quality, etc. **5** (often in *pl.*) military drill or maneuvers. **6** (foll. by *in*) a process directed at or concerned with something specified (*was an exercise in public relations*). ● *v.* **1** *tr.* use or apply (a faculty, right, influence, restraint, etc.). **2** *tr.* perform (a function). **3 a** *intr.* take (esp. physical) exercise; do exercises. **b** *tr.* provide (an animal) with exercise. **c** *tr.* train (a person). **4** *tr.* **a** tax the powers of. **b** perplex; worry. □□ **exercisable** *adj.* **exerciser** *n.* [ME f. OF *exercice* f. L *exercitium* f. *exercere exercit-* keep at work (as EX-¹, *arcēre* restrain)]
■ *n.* **1** activity, movement, working out, warming up; training, drilling; see also PRACTICE *n.* 3. **2** see PRACTICE *n.* 3. **3** (*exercises*) workout, warm-up, practice, drill; callisthenics, aerobics, isometrics, gymnastics. **4** use, utilization, employment, application, practice, operation, performance. **5** see MANEUVER *n.* 2. ● *v.* **1** use, employ, apply, practice, bring to bear, put to *or*

into use, put to effect; exert, wield, execute. **2** see PERFORM 1. **3 a** work out, limber up, warm up, train, drill. **b** see WALK v. 4. **c** see TRAIN v. 1a. **4 b** perplex, worry, concern, distress, burden, try, trouble, perturb, disturb, agitate, make nervous, harry, harass, vex, *colloq.* drive crazy, drive up the wall.

exergue /eksórg/ n. **1** a small space usu. on the reverse of a coin or medal, below the principal device. **2** an inscription on this space. [F f. med.L *exergum* f. Gk *ex-* (as EX-²) + *ergon* work]

exert /igzórt/ v.tr. **1** exercise; bring to bear (a quality, force, influence, etc.). **2** refl. (often foll. by for, or to + infin.) use one's efforts or endeavors; strive. □□ **exertion** /-zórshən/ n. [L *exserere exsert-* put forth (as EX-¹, *serere* bind)]
■ **1** exercise, bring to bear, use, bring into play, utilize, put to use, put to work *or* effect, employ, wield, deploy, expend. **2** (*exert oneself*) try, make an effort, apply oneself, strive, do one's best, work, strain, struggle, toil, push (oneself), drive oneself, go all out, give one's all, cudgel one's brains, *colloq.* knock oneself out, beat one's brains out, do one's damnedest, bust a gut. □□ **exertion** effort, striving, strain, work, struggle, toil, drive, push, diligence, industry, action, assiduity, assiduousness, sedulousness, sedulity.

exeunt /ékseeənt, -ōont/ v.intr. (as a stage direction) (actors) leave the stage. □ **exeunt omnes** all leave the stage. [L, = they go out: 3rd pl. pres. of *exire* go out: see EXIT]

exfiltrate /éksfiltrayt/ v.tr. (also absol.) withdraw (troops, spies, etc.) surreptitiously, esp. from danger. □□ **exfiltration** /-tráyshən/ n.

exfoliate /eksfóleeayt/ v.intr. **1** (of bone, the skin, a mineral, etc.) come off in scales or layers. **2** (of a tree) throw off layers of bark. □□ **exfoliation** /-áyshən/ n. **exfoliative** adj. [LL *exfoliare exfoliat-* (as EX-¹, *folium* leaf)]
■ **1** see FLAKE¹ v.

ex gratia /eks gráysheeə/ adv. & adj. ● adv. as a favor rather than from an (esp. legal) obligation. ● adj. granted on this basis. [L, = from favor]

exhalation /éks-həláyshən/ n. **1 a** an expiration of air. **b** a puff of breath. **2** a mist; vapor. **3** an emanation or effluvium. [ME f. L *exhalatio* (as EXHALE)]
■ **1** expiration, exhaling, breath; breathing (out), respiration. **2, 3** mist, vapor, whiff, emission, gas, fume; emanation, effluvium.

exhale /eks-háyl/ v. **1** tr. (also absol.) breathe out (esp. air or smoke) from the lungs. **2** tr. & intr. give off or be given off in vapor. □□ **exhalable** adj. [ME f. OF *exhaler* f. L *exhalare* (as EX-¹, *halare* breathe)]
■ **1** breathe (out), blow *or* puff out, discharge, emit, give forth, eject, expel. **2** breathe (out), blow out, puff (out); evaporate; emanate, issue (forth), blow off; pass, discharge, emit, give forth, eject, expel.

exhaust /igzáwst/ v. & n. ● v.tr. **1** consume or use up the whole of. **2** (often as **exhausted** adj. or **exhausting** adj.) use up the strength or resources of (a person); tire out. **3** study or expound on (a subject) completely. **4** (often foll. by of) empty (a vessel, etc.) of its contents. **5** (often as **exhausted** adj.) drain of strength or resources; (of land) make barren. ● n. **1 a** waste gases, etc., expelled from an engine after combustion. **b** (also **exhaust pipe**) the pipe or system by which these are expelled. **c** the process of expulsion of these gases. **2 a** the production of an outward current of air by the creation of a partial vacuum. **b** an apparatus for this. □□ **exhauster** n. **exhaustible** adj. **exhaustibility** n. **exhaustibly** adv. [L *exhaurire exhaust-* (as EX-¹, *haurire* draw (water), drain)]
■ v. **1** consume, use (up), expend, finish, deplete, spend, run through, fritter away, squander, waste, *sl.* blow.
2 use up, sap, tire out, take it out of; (**exhausted**) (dead) tired, tired out, fatigued, weary, wearied, worn out, shattered, enervated, debilitated, drained, overtired, strained, taxed, weak, weakened, prostrate, fagged out, burned-out, spent, dog-tired, *colloq.* frazzled, all in, dead, knocked out, done in, pooped, *sl.* (dead) beat, *Brit. sl.* knackered; (**exhausting**) tiring,

fatiguing, wearying, enervating, wearing, debilitating; arduous, laborious, backbreaking, strenuous, hard, grueling, burdensome, onerous. **3** see RANSACK 2, AMPLIFY 2. **4** empty, drain, evacuate, void, clean *or* clear out. **5** (**exhausted**) spent, worn out, depleted, impoverished, poor, infertile, barren. ● n. **1 a** gases, fumes, emissions; waste.

exhaustion /igzáwschən/ n. **1** the action or process of draining or emptying something; the state of being depleted or emptied. **2** a total loss of strength or vitality. **3** the process of establishing a conclusion by eliminating alternatives. [LL *exhaustio* (as EXHAUST)]
■ **1** emptying, draining, evacuation, voiding, depletion. **2** tiredness, fatigue, enervation, debilitation, weariness, lassitude. **3** elimination, rejection, exclusion.

exhaustive /igzáwstiv/ adj. **1** thorough; comprehensive. **2** tending to exhaust a subject. □□ **exhaustively** adv. **exhaustiveness** n.
■ thorough, comprehensive, complete, all-inclusive, all-embracing, all-encompassing, encyclopedic, extensive, far-reaching, sweeping, full-scale, in-depth, maximal; thoroughgoing, definitive.

exhibit /igzíbit/ v. & n. ● v.tr. **1** show or reveal publicly (for amusement, in competition, etc.). **2 a** show; display. **b** manifest (a quality). **3** submit for consideration. ● n. **1** a thing or collection of things forming part or all of an exhibition. **2** a document or other item or object produced in a court of law as evidence. □□ **exhibitory** adj. [L *exhibēre exhibit-* (as EX-¹, *habēre* hold)]
■ v. **1, 2a** show, reveal, present, display, offer, demonstrate, betray, manifest, exemplify, evince, evidence, disclose, express. **2b** manifest, show, reveal, display, expose, betray, demonstrate, exemplify, evince, evidence, disclose, express. **3** see SUBMIT 2. ● n. **1** see DISPLAY 2. **2** see EVIDENCE 2.

exhibition /éksibíshən/ n. **1** a display (esp. public) of works of art, industrial products, etc. **2** the act or an instance of exhibiting; the state of being exhibited. **3** Brit. a scholarship, esp. from the funds of a school, college, etc. □ **make an exhibition of oneself** behave so as to appear ridiculous or foolish. [ME f. OF f. LL *exhibitio -onis* (as EXHIBIT)]
■ **1** exposition, fair, show, showing, display, presentation, exhibit, expo, demonstration, *colloq.* demo. **2** see DEMONSTRATION 3.

exhibitioner /éksibíshənər/ n. Brit. a student who has been awarded an exhibition.

exhibitionism /éksibíshənizəm/ n. **1** a tendency toward display or extravagant behavior. **2** Psychol. a mental condition characterized by the compulsion to display one's genitals indecently in public. □□ **exhibitionist** n. **exhibitionistic** adj. **exhibitionistically** adv.
■ **1** see OSTENTATION.

exhibitor /igzíbitər/ n. a person who provides an item or items for an exhibition.

exhilarate /igzílərayt/ v.tr. (often as **exhilarating** adj. or **exhilarated** adj.) affect with great liveliness or joy; raise the spirits of. □□ **exhilarant** adj. & n. **exhilaratingly** adv. **exhilaration** /-ráyshən/ n. **exhilarative** adj. [L *exhilarare* (as EX-¹, *hilaris* cheerful)]
■ (**exhilarating**) invigorating, bracing, stimulating, vivifying, enlivening, rejuvenating, refreshing, vitalizing, fortifying, restorative, tonic; cheering, uplifting, gladdening, elating, inspiriting, heartening, comforting, reassuring; (**exhilarated**) see ECSTATIC 1, 2.

exhort /igzáwrt/ v.tr. (often foll. by to + infin.) urge or advise strongly or earnestly. □□ **exhortative** /-tətiv/ adj. **exhortatory** /-tətawree/ adj. **exhorter** n. [ME f. OF *exhorter* or L *exhortari* (as EX-¹, *hortari* exhort)]
■ see URGE v. 2.

/.../ **pronunciation**	● **part of speech**
□ **phrases, idioms, and compounds**	
□□ **derivatives**	■ **synonym section**
cross-references appear in SMALL CAPITALS or *italics*	

exhortation /égzawrtáyshən/ n. **1** the act or an instance of exhorting; the state of being exhorted. **2** a formal or liturgical address. [ME f. OF *exhortation* or L *exhortatio* (as EX-HORT)]
■ **1** inducement, persuasion, influence; see also *encouragement* (ENCOURAGE). **2** see SERMON 1.

exhume /igzṓŏm, -zyṓŏm, eks-hyṓŏm/ v.tr. dig out; unearth (esp. a buried corpse). □□ **exhumation** n. [F *exhumer* f. med.L *exhumare* (as EX-¹, *humus* ground)]
■ see DIG v. 4.

ex hypothesi /éks hĩpóthəsee/ adv. according to the hypothesis proposed. [mod.L]

exigency /éksijənsee, igzíj-/ n. (pl. **-ies**) (also **exigence** /éksijəns/) **1** an urgent need or demand. **2** an emergency. [F *exigence* & LL *exigentia* (as EXIGENT)]
■ **1** see NEED n. 3, 4. **2** see EMERGENCY.

exigent /éksijənt/ adj. **1** requiring much; exacting. **2** urgent; pressing. [ME f. L *exigere* EXACT]
■ **1** see SEVERE 1, 5. **2** see URGENT 1.

exiguous /igzígyŏōəs, iksíg-/ adj. scanty; small. □□ **exiguity** /éksigyŏōitee/ n. **exiguously** adv. **exiguousness** n. [L *exiguus* scanty f. *exigere* weigh exactly: see EXACT]
■ see MEAGER 1.

exile /éksil, égzil/ n. & v. ● n. **1** expulsion, or the state of being expelled, from one's native land or (**internal exile**) native town, etc. **2** long absence abroad, esp. enforced. **3** a person expelled or long absent from his or her native country. **4** (**the Exile**) the captivity of the Jews in Babylon in the 6th c. BC. ● v.tr. (foll. by *from*) officially expel (a person) from his or her native country or town, etc. □□ **exilic** /-sílik, -zílik/ adj. (esp. in sense 4 of n.). [ME f. OF *exil, exiler* f. L *exilium* banishment]
■ n. **1** expulsion, expatriation, banishment, deportation, *hist.* transportation. **3** expatriate, émigré, emigrant, deportee, displaced person, DP; alien, outsider.
● v. expel, deport, expatriate, banish, oust, displace, eject, transport, drive *or* cast out, exclude, bar, ban; extradite.

exist /igzíst/ v.intr. **1** have a place as part of objective reality. **2 a** have being under specified conditions. **b** (foll. by *as*) exist in the form of. **3** (of circumstances, etc.) occur; be found. **4** live with no pleasure under adverse conditions (*felt he was merely existing*). **5** continue in being; maintain life (*can hardly exist on this salary*). **6** be alive; live. [prob. back-form. f. EXISTENCE; cf. LL *existere*]
■ **1, 2a** be, prevail, endure, continue, *archaic* abide; live, breathe. **2 b** see FORM v. 3. **3** occur, be found, be present; obtain, prevail. **4** see ENDURE 3. **5** survive, subsist, eke out a living *or* an existence, stay alive, *colloq.* get by. **6** see LIVE¹ 1–4.

existence /igzístəns/ n. **1** the fact or condition of being or existing. **2** continued being; the manner of one's existing or living, esp. under adverse conditions (*a wretched existence*). **3** an existing thing. **4** all that exists. [ME f. OF *existence* or LL *existentia* f. L *exsistere* (as EX-¹, *stare* stand)]
■ **1** fact, being, presence, actuality, essence; *Philos.* quiddity. **2** continuance, continuation, persistence, permanence, duration, endurance; see also LIFE 5. **3** being, entity, creature. **4** see WORLD 2a.

existent /igzístənt/ adj. existing; actual; current.

existential /égzisténshəl/ adj. **1** of or relating to existence. **2** *Logic* (of a proposition, etc.) affirming or implying the existence of a thing. **3** *Philos.* concerned with existence, esp. with human existence as viewed by existentialism. □□ **existentially** adv. [LL *existentialis* (as EXISTENCE)]

existentialism /égzisténshəlizəm/ n. a philosophical theory emphasizing the existence of the individual person as a free and responsible agent determining his or her own development. □□ **existentialist** n. [G *Existentialismus* (as EXISTENTIAL)]

exit /égzit, éksit/ n. & v. ● n. **1** a passage or door by which to leave a room, building, etc. **2 a** the act of going out. **b** the right to go out. **3** a place where vehicles can leave a highway or major road. **4** the departure of an actor from the stage. **5** death. ● v.intr. **1** go out of a room, building, etc.

2 (as a stage direction) (an actor) leaves the stage (*exit Macbeth*). **3** die. □ **exit permit** (or **visa**, etc.) authorization to leave a particular country. **exit poll** a survey usu. of voters leaving voting booths, used to predict an election's outcome, analyze voting patterns, etc. [L, 3rd sing. pres. of *exire* go out (as EX-¹, *ire* go): cf. L *exitus* going out]
■ n. **1** way out, egress, door, gate. **2 a** departure, leave-taking, withdrawal, leaving, retreat, retirement; flight, exodus, escape. **3** turnoff. **5** see DEATH 1. ● v. **1** go (out *or* away), (take one's) leave, depart, take *or* make one's departure, retire, (beat a) retreat, withdraw, walk out, escape, take to one's heels, take off, vanish, disappear, *colloq.* show a clean pair of heels, skedaddle, run, *sl.* beat it, take a powder, go on the lam. **3** see DIE¹ 1.

ex libris /eksleébris/ n. (pl. same) a usu. decorated bookplate or label bearing the owner's name, pasted into the front of a book. [L *ex libris* among the books of]

ex nihilo /eks níhilō, neé-/ adv. out of nothing (*creation ex nihilo*). [L]

exo- /éksō/ comb. form external. [Gk *exō* outside]

exobiology /éksōbiólŏjee/ n. the study of life outside the earth. □□ **exobiologist** n.

Exocet /éksəset/ n. propr. a short-range guided missile used esp. in sea warfare. [F *exocet* flying fish]

exocrine /éksəkrin, -kreen, -krin/ adj. (of a gland) secreting through a duct (cf. ENDOCRINE). [EXO- + Gk *krinō* sift]

Exod. abbr. Exodus (Old Testament).

exodus /éksədəs/ n. **1** a mass departure of people (esp. emigrants). **2** (**Exodus**) *Bibl.* **a** the departure of the Israelites from Egypt. **b** the book of the Old Testament relating this. [eccl.L f. Gk *exodos* (as EX-², *hodos* way)]
■ **1** see FLIGHT².

ex officio /eksəfísheeō/ adv. & adj. by virtue of one's office or status. [L]

exogamy /eksógəmee/ n. **1** *Anthropol.* marriage of a man outside his own tribe. **2** *Biol.* the fusion of reproductive cells from distantly related or unrelated individuals. □□ **exogamous** adj.

exogenous /eksójinəs/ adj. *Biol.* growing or originating from outside. □□ **exogenously** adv.

exon /ékson/ n. *Brit.* each of the four officers acting as commanders of the Yeomen of the Guard. [repr. F pronunc. of EXEMPT]

exonerate /igzónərayt/ v.tr. (often foll. by *from*) **1** free or declare free from blame, etc. **2** release from a duty, etc. □□ **exoneration** /-ráyshən/ n. **exonerative** adj. [L *exonerare exonerat-* (as EX-¹, *onus, oneris* burden)]
■ **1** see VINDICATE 1.

exophthalmos /éksofthálməs/ n. (also **exophthalmus, exophthalmia** /-meeə/) *Med.* abnormal protrusion of the eyeball. □□ **exophthalmic** adj. [mod.L f. Gk *exophthalmos* having prominent eyes (as EX-², *ophthalmos* eye)]

exor. abbr. executor.

exorbitant /igzáwrbit'nt/ adj. (of a price, demand, etc.) grossly excessive. □□ **exorbitance** /-təns/ n. **exorbitantly** adv. [LL *exorbitare* (as EX-¹, *orbita* ORBIT)]
■ excessive, outrageous, extortionate, unreasonable, unconscionable, extravagant, immoderate, extreme, inordinate, disproportionate, preposterous, unwarranted, unjustifiable, unjustified.

exorcize /éksawrsiz, -sər-/ v.tr. **1** expel (a supposed evil spirit) by invocation or by use of a holy name. **2** (often foll. by *of*) free (a person or place) of a supposed evil spirit. □□ **exorcism** /-sízəm/ n. **exorcist** n. **exorcization** /-sizáyshən/ n. [F *exorciser* or eccl.L *exorcizare* f. Gk *exorkizō* (as EX-², *horkos* oath)]

exordium /eksáwrdeeəm/ n. (pl. **exordiums** or **exordia** /-deeə/) the beginning or introductory part, esp. of a discourse or treatise. □□ **exordial** adj. **exordially** adv. [L f. *exordiri* (as EX-¹, *ordiri* begin)]
■ see PREFACE n.

exoskeleton /éksōskélit'n/ n. a rigid external covering for the body in certain animals, esp. arthropods, providing support and protection. □□ **exoskeletal** adj.

exosphere /éksōsfeer/ n. the layer of atmosphere furthest from the earth.

exothermic /éksōthármik/ adj. (also **exothermal** /-məl/) esp. *Chem.* occurring or formed with the evolution of heat. □□ **exothermally** adv. **exothermically** adv.

exotic /igzótik/ adj. & n. ● adj. **1** introduced from or originating in a foreign (esp. tropical) country (*exotic fruits*). **2** attractively or remarkably strange or unusual; bizarre. **3** (of a fuel, metal, etc.) of a kind newly brought into use. ● n. an exotic person or thing. □ **exotic dancer** a striptease dancer. □□ **exotically** adv. **exoticism** /-tisizəm/ n. [L *exoticus* f. Gk *exōtikos* f. *exō* outside]
■ adj. **1** foreign, alien, nonnative, imported. **2** strange, unusual, unique, singular; bizarre, extraordinary, remarkable, out of the ordinary, odd, peculiar, different, outlandish, *colloq.* weird, crazy. ● n. see WONDER n. 2.

exotica /igzótikə/ n.pl. remarkably strange or rare objects. [L, neut. pl. of *exoticus*: see EXOTIC]

expand /ikspánd/ v. **1** tr. & intr. increase in size or bulk or importance. **2** intr. (often foll. by *on*) give a fuller description or account. **3** intr. become more genial or effusive; discard one's reserve. **4** tr. set or write out in full (something condensed or abbreviated). **5** tr. & intr. spread out flat. □ **expanded metal** sheet metal slit and stretched into a mesh, used to reinforce concrete and other brittle materials. □□ **expandable** adj. **expander** n. **expansible** /ikspánsibəl/ adj. **expansibility** /-bílitee/ n. [ME f. L *expandere expans-* spread out (as EX-¹, *pandere* spread)]
■ **1** increase, enlarge, extend, stretch, inflate, distend, dilate; spread (out), open out, swell, amplify, magnify, broaden, widen, augment, heighten, develop. **2** (*expand on* or *upon*) enlarge on, develop, amplify, expatiate on or upon, elaborate (on), flesh out. **5** see SPREAD v. 1a.

expanse /ikspáns/ n. **1** a wide continuous area or extent of land, space, etc. **2** an amount of expansion. [mod.L *expansum* neut. past part. (as EXPAND)]
■ **1** area, space, stretch, extent, range, sweep, reach, spread.

expansile /ikspánsəl, -sīl/ adj. **1** of expansion. **2** capable of expansion.

expansion /ikspánshən/ n. **1** the act or an instance of expanding; the state of being expanded. **2** enlargement of the scale or scope of (esp. commercial) operations. **3** increase in the amount of a country's territory or area of control. **4** an increase in the volume of fuel, etc., on combustion in the cylinder of an engine. **5** the action of making or becoming greater in area, bulk, capacity, etc.; dilatation; the degree of this (*alternate expansion and contraction of the muscle*). □□ **expansionary** adj. **expansionism** n. **expansionist** n. **expansionistic** adj. (all in senses 2, 3). [LL *expansio* (as EXPAND)]
■ **1, 2** development, increase, augmentation, enlargement, extension, growth, flourishing, spread, *literary* burgeoning. **5** stretching; dilatation, dilation, distension; inflation, swelling.

expansive /ikspánsiv/ adj. **1** able or tending to expand. **2** extensive, wide-ranging. **3** (of a person, feelings, or speech) effusive; open. □□ **expansively** adv. **expansiveness** n. **expansivity** /-sívitee/ n.
■ **1** expansible, expandable, extensible, extendible, extendable; extending, expanding. **2** extensive; wide-ranging, broad, far-reaching, comprehensive, widespread. **3** effusive, open, free, easy, genial, amiable, friendly, warm, affable, sociable, outgoing, communicative, outspoken, extrovert, extroverted, talkative, loquacious, garrulous, frank, unreserved.

ex parte /eks paártee/ adj. & adv. *Law* in the interests of one side only or of an interested outside party. [L]

expat /ékspát/ n. & adj. *Brit. colloq.* = EXPATRIATE. [abbr.]

expatiate /ikspáysheeayt/ v.intr. (usu. foll. by *on*, *upon*) speak or write at length or in detail. □□ **expatiation** /-áyshən/ n. **expatiatory** /-sheeətáwree/ adj. [L *exspatiari* digress (as EX-¹, *spatium* SPACE)]
■ (*expatiate on*) see EXPLAIN 1.

expatriate adj., n., & v. ● adj. /ékspáytreeət/ **1** living abroad, esp. for a long period. **2** expelled from one's country; exiled. ● n. /ekspáytreeət/ an expatriate person. ● v.tr. /ekspáytreeayt/ **1** expel or remove (a person) from his or her native country. **2** refl. withdraw (oneself) from one's citizenship or allegiance. □□ **expatriation** /-áyshən/ n. [med.L *expatriare* (as EX-¹, *patria* native country)]
■ n. see EXILE n. 3. ● v. **1** see EXILE v.

expect /ikspékt/ v.tr. **1** (often foll. by *to* + infin., or *that* + clause) **a** regard as likely; assume as a future event or occurrence. **b** (often foll. by *of*) look for as appropriate or one's due (from a person) (*I expect cooperation*; *expect you to be here*; *expected better of you*). **2** colloq. (often foll. by *that* + clause) think; suppose (*I expect we'll be on time*). **3** be shortly to have (a baby) (*is expecting twins*). □ **be expecting** colloq. be pregnant. □□ **expectable** adj. [L *exspectare* (as EX-¹, *spectare* look, frequent. of *specere* see)]
■ **1 a** look forward or ahead to, envisage, contemplate, foresee, envision, disp. anticipate; await, watch or look for, wait for. **b** look for, want, require, need, demand, reckon on or upon, calculate or count on, calculate or count upon, hope for. **2** think, suppose, guess, assume, presume, imagine, believe, trust, surmise, conjecture; foresee. □ **be expecting** be pregnant, *archaic* be enceinte, *colloq.* be in a or the family way, *literary* be with child, *literary or Zool.* be gravid, *sl.* have a bun in the oven.

expectancy /ikspéktənsee/ n. (pl. **-ies**) **1** a state of expectation. **2** a prospect, esp. of future possession. **3** (foll. by *of*) a prospective chance. [L *exspectantia*, *exp-* (as EXPECT)]
■ **1** see EXPECTATION 1.

expectant /ikspéktənt/ adj. & n. ● adj. **1** (often foll. by *of*) expecting. **2** having the expectation of possession, status, etc. **3** (attrib.) expecting a baby (said of the mother or father). ● n. **1** one who expects. **2** a candidate for office, etc. □□ **expectantly** adv.
■ adj. **1** waiting, ready, eager, apprehensive, anxious, hopeful, watchful; (*expectant of*) expecting. **2** see HOPEFUL adj. 1. ● n. **2** see CANDIDATE 1, 3.

expectation /ékspektáyshən/ n. **1** the act or an instance of expecting or looking forward. **2** something expected or hoped for. **3** (foll. by *of*) the probability of an event. **4** (in pl.) one's prospects of inheritance. [L *expectatio* (as EXPECT)]
■ **1** expectancy, confidence, hopefulness, watchfulness, apprehension, apprehensiveness, suspense, disp. anticipation. **2** belief, assumption, presumption, surmise, supposition, conjecture, guess, hope; wish, desire, want, demand, requirement. **3** see PROBABILITY. **4** (*expectations*) see PROSPECT n. 1a.

expectorant /ikspéktərənt/ adj. & n. ● adj. causing the coughing out of phlegm, etc. ● n. an expectorant medicine.

expectorate /ikspéktərayt/ v.tr. (also absol.) cough or spit out (phlegm, etc.) from the chest or lungs. □□ **expectoration** /-ráyshən/ n. **expectorator** n. [L *expectorare expectorat-* (as EX-¹, *pectus -oris* breast)]
■ see SPIT¹ v. 2a.

expedient /ikspeédeeənt/ adj. & n. ● adj. **1** advantageous; advisable on practical rather than moral grounds. **2** suitable; appropriate. ● n. a means of attaining an end; a resource. □□ **expedience** /-əns/ n. **expediency** n. **expediently** adv. [ME f. L *expedire*: see EXPEDITE]
■ adj. **1** advantageous, beneficial, useful, practical, utilitarian, helpful, effective, desirable; advisable, recommended, prudent, politic, wise, propitious, opportune. **2** suitable, appropriate, fitting, fit, befitting, proper, apropos, right, correct, pertinent, applicable, practical, *archaic* meet. ● n. means, measure, contrivance, resort, recourse; resource, device.

expedite /ékspidīt/ v.tr. **1** assist the progress of; hasten (an

---

/. . ./ **pronunciation**	● **part of speech**
□ **phrases, idioms, and compounds**	
□□ **derivatives**	■ **synonym section**
cross-references appear in SMALL CAPITALS or *italics*	

action, process, etc.). **2** accomplish (business) quickly. □□ **expediter** n. [L *expedire expedit-* extricate, put in order (as EX-[1], *pes pedis* foot)]

■ **1** assist, enable, facilitate, ease, advance, promote, forward; hasten, rush, hurry, speed up, step up, accelerate. **2** dispatch, despatch; see also COMPLETE v. 1.

expedition /ékspidíshən/ n. **1** a journey or voyage for a particular purpose, esp. exploration, scientific research, or war. **2** the personnel or ships, etc., undertaking this. **3** promptness; speed. □□ **expeditionist** n. [ME f. OF f. L *expeditio -onis* (as EXPEDITE)]

■ **1** journey, voyage, exploration, (field) trip, tour, excursion; mission; quest. **2** see PARTY[1] n. 2. **3** promptness, speed, alacrity, dispatch, haste, rapidity, swiftness, quickness, *archaic or literary* celerity.

expeditionary /ékspidíshəneree/ adj. of or used in an expedition, esp. military.

expeditious /ékspidíshəs/ adj. **1** acting or done with speed and efficiency. **2** suited for speedy performance. □□ **expeditiously** adv. **expeditiousness** n. [EXPEDITION + -OUS]

■ ready, quick, rapid, swift, fast, brisk, speedy, efficient, *poet. or literary* fleet.

expel /ikspél/ v.tr. (**expelled, expelling**) (often foll. by *from*) **1** deprive (a person) of the membership of or involvement in (a school, society, etc.). **2** force out or eject (a thing from its container, etc.). **3** order or force to leave a building, etc. □□ **expellable** adj. **expellee** /-leé/ n. **expellent** adj. **expeller** n. [ME f. L *expellere expuls-* (as EX-[1], *pellere* drive)]

■ **1** deprive, proscribe, ban, bar, debar, dismiss, exclude, cashier, discharge, oust, *Mil.* drum out. **2, 3** throw or cast out, force or drive out, eject, push out, remove, dislodge, displace, evict, show the door, dismiss, *Brit. colloq.* turf out; banish, deport, exile, expatriate.

expend /ikspénd/ v.tr. spend or use up (money, time, etc.). [ME f. L *expendere expens-* (as EX-[1], *pendere* weigh)]

■ spend, use up, finish (off), consume, exhaust, dissipate, drain; pay out, disburse, use, employ, lay out, *colloq.* shell out, *sl.* dish or fork out.

expendable /ikspéndəbəl/ adj. **1** that may be sacrificed or dispensed with, esp. to achieve a purpose. **2 a** not regarded as worth preserving or saving. **b** unimportant; insignificant. **3** not normally reused. □□ **expendability** n. **expendably** adv.

■ **1, 2** dispensable, disposable, nonessential, inessential, unessential, unnecessary, replaceable; unimportant, insignificant; see DISPOSABLE adj. 1.

expenditure /ikspéndichər/ n. **1** the process or an instance of spending or using up. **2** a thing (esp. a sum of money) expended. [EXPEND, after obs. *expenditor* officer in charge of expenditure, f. med.L f. *expenditus* irreg. past part. of L *expendere*]

■ **2** outlay, disbursement, spending, expense, cost; outgoings; price, charge, fee.

expense /ikspéns/ n. **1** cost incurred; payment of money. **2** (usu. in *pl.*) **a** costs incurred in doing a particular job, etc. (*will pay your expenses*). **b** an amount paid to reimburse this (*offered me $40 per day expenses*). **3** a thing that is a cause of much expense (*the house is a real expense to run*). □ **at the expense of** so as to cause loss or damage or discredit to. **expense account** a list of an employee's expenses payable by the employer. [ME f. AF, alt. of OF *espense* f. LL *expensa* (money) spent, past part. of L *expendere* EXPEND]

■ **1** payment, outlay, disbursement; price, charge, fee, rate; expenditure, spending; cost(s); sacrifice. **2** costs, out-of-pocket expenses, outlays, outgoings; expenditure, spending. **3** see BURDEN n. 1, 2.

expensive /ikspénsiv/ adj. **1** costing much. **2** making a high charge. **3** causing much expense (*has expensive tastes*). □□ **expensively** adv. **expensiveness** n.

■ **1** costly, dear, high-priced, upmarket, overpriced; valuable, precious, priceless; see also EXTRAVAGANT 2. **3** see EXTRAVAGANT 1.

experience /ikspeéreeəns/ n. & v. ● n. **1** actual observation of or practical acquaintance with facts or events. **2** knowl-

edge or skill resulting from this. **3 a** an event regarded as affecting one (*an unpleasant experience*). **b** the fact or process of being so affected (*learned by experience*). ● v.tr. **1** have experience of; undergo. **2** feel or be affected by (an emotion, etc.). □□ **experienceable** adj. [ME f. OF f. L *experientia* f. *experiri expert-* try]

■ n. **1, 3b** observation, participation, contact, involvement, practice, exposure; acquaintance, familiarity, knowledge. **2** knowledge, common sense, wisdom, sagacity, know-how, savoir faire, savoir vivre, sophistication, skill, judgment, *sl.* savvy. **3 a** event, incident, happening, affair, episode, occurrence, circumstance, adventure, encounter; trial, test, ordeal. ● v. **1** undergo, live through, go through, suffer, endure, sustain, face, encounter, meet (with). **2** feel, sense, taste, sample, be familiar with, know.

experienced /ikspeéreeənst/ adj. **1** having had much experience. **2** skilled from experience (*an experienced driver*).

■ **1** mature, seasoned, sophisticated, battle-scarred, seasoned, veteran. **2** skilled, adept, skillful, accomplished, practiced, proficient, knowledgeable, knowing, wise, sage, sagacious, shrewd, (well-) informed, trained, (well-)versed, expert, master, masterly, qualified, prepared, professional; *colloq.* in the know, *au fait, sl.* savvy.

experiential /ikspeéree-énshəl/ adj. involving or based on experience. □ **experiential philosophy** a philosophy that treats all knowledge as based on experience. □□ **experientialism** n. **experientialist** n. **experientially** adv.

■ see EMPIRICAL.

experiment /ikspérimənt/ n. & v. ● n. **1** a procedure adopted on the chance of its succeeding, for testing a hypothesis, etc., or to demonstrate a known fact. **2** (foll. by *of*) a test or trial of. ● v.intr. (often foll. by *on, with*) make an experiment. □□ **experimentation** n. **experimenter** n. [ME f. OF *experiment* or L *experimentum* (as EXPERIENCE)]

■ n. procedure, policy; test, trial, investigation, inquiry, examination, experimentation, research. ● v. test, try, examine, investigate, research, probe.

experimental /ikspériméntʼl/ adj. **1** based on or making use of experiment (*experimental psychology*). **2 a** used in experiments. **b** serving or resulting from (esp. incomplete) experiment; tentative, provisional. **3** based on experience, not on authority or conjecture. □□ **experimentalism** n. **experimentalist** n. **experimentalize** v.intr. **experimentally** adv. [ME f. med.L *experimentalis* (as EXPERIMENT)]

■ **1, 3** empirical; experiential. **2 b** tentative, speculative, conjectural, hypothetical, theoretical; exploratory.

expert /ékspərt/ adj. & n. ● adj. **1** (often foll. by *at, in*) having special knowledge or skill in a subject. **2** involving or resulting from this (*expert evidence; an expert piece of work*). ● n. (often foll. by *at, in*) a person having special knowledge or skill. □□ **expertly** adv. **expertness** n. [ME f. OF f. L *expertus* past part. of *experiri*: see EXPERIENCE]

■ adj. **1** skillful, skilled, trained, knowledgeable, learned, experienced, practiced, qualified, adept, proficient, accomplished, adroit, dexterous, masterful, masterly, first-rate, excellent, superb, wonderful, superior, *colloq.* A 1, top-notch, champion, *sl.* crackerjack, esp. *Brit. sl.* wizard; virtuoso, *colloq.* crack; *au fait;* see also KNOWLEDGEABLE. **2** see *first-rate.* ● n. authority, professional, specialist, scholar, master, connoisseur, wizard, ace, *colloq.* whiz, maven, pro, esp. *Brit. colloq.* dab hand, boffin, *often iron.* pundit.

expertise /éksparteéz/ n. expert skill, knowledge, or judgment. [F (as EXPERT)]

■ expertness, skill, dexterity, adroitness, knowledge, know-how, mastery, judgment, *sl.* savvy.

expertize /ékspərtiz/ v. **1** intr. give an expert opinion. **2** tr. give an expert opinion concerning.

expiate /ékspeeayt/ v.tr. **1** pay the penalty for (wrongdoing). **2** make amends for. □□ **expiable** /-peeəbəl/ adj. **expiatory** /-peéətawree/ adj. **expiation** /-áyshən/ n. **expiator** n. [L *expiare expiat-* (as EX-[1], *pius* devout)]

■ **2** see COMPENSATE 2.

expiration /ékspəráyshən/ n. **1** breathing out. **2** the end of the validity or duration of something. [L *expiratio* (as EXPIRE)]

■ **1** exhalation, exhaling, breath, respiration, breathing (out). **2** expiry, finish, end, termination, conclusion, concluding, close, closing, discontinuation, discontinuance.

expire /ikspír/ v. **1** intr. (of a period of time, validity, etc.) come to an end. **2** intr. (of a document, authorization, etc.) cease to be valid; become void. **3** intr. (of a person) die. **4** tr. (usu. foll. by *from*; also *absol.*) exhale (air, etc.) from the lungs. □□ **expiratory** adj. (in sense 4). [ME f. OF *expirer* f. L *exspirare* (as EX-[1], *spirare* breathe)]

■ **1, 2** (come to an) end, cease, finish, terminate; run out, close. **3** breathe one's last, perish, pass away, *formal esp. Law* decease; see also DIE[1] 1. **4** exhale, breathe out, expel.

expiry /ikspíree/ n. **1** expiration. **2** death.

■ **1** see EXPIRATION 2. **2** see DEATH.

explain /ikspláyn/ v.tr. **1** make clear or intelligible with detailed information, etc. (also *absol.*: *let me explain*). **2** (foll. by *that* + clause) say by way of explanation. **3** account for (one's conduct, etc.). □ **explain away** minimize the significance of (a difficulty or mistake) by explanation. **explain oneself 1** make one's meaning clear. **2** give an account of one's motives or conduct. □□ **explainable** adj. **explainer** n. [L *explanare* (as EX-[1], *planus* flat, assim. to PLAIN[1])]

■ **1** make clear, define, explicate, detail, delineate, make plain, get across, clarify, spell out, simplify, interpret, elucidate, expound, describe, clear up, unravel, untangle. **2** see SAY v. 1b. **3** see *account for* 2b. □ **explain away** justify, account for, excuse, rationalize; extenuate, palliate; see also *account for* 2b.

explanation /éksplənáyshən/ n. **1** the act or an instance of explaining. **2** a statement or circumstance that explains something. **3** a declaration made with a view to mutual understanding or reconciliation. [ME f. L *explanatio* (as EXPLAIN)]

■ **1** interpretation, definition, explication, delineation, description, exposition, account; exegesis, commentary, criticism, analysis. **2** cause, motive, reason, key. **3** excuse, rationalization, justification, vindication.

explanatory /iksplánətawree/ adj. serving or intended to serve to explain. □□ **explanatorily** adv. [LL *explanatorius* (as EXPLAIN)]

■ elucidative, interpretive, interpretative, expository, exegetic, exegetical.

explant /eksplánt/ v. & n. Biol. ● v.tr. transfer (living cells, tissues, or organs) from animals or plants to a nutrient medium. ● n. a piece of explanted tissue, etc. □□ **explantation** n. [mod.L *explantare* (as EX-[1], *plantare* PLANT)]

expletive /éksplətiv/ n. & adj. ● n. **1** an oath, swearword, or other expression, used in an exclamation. **2** a word used to fill out a sentence, etc., esp. in verse. ● adj. serving to fill out (esp. a sentence, line of verse, etc.). [LL *expletivus* (as EX-[1], *plēre plet-* fill)]

■ n. **1** oath, swearword, curse, obscenity, epithet, dirty word, four-letter word, cussword. ● adj. wordy, verbose, prolix, tautological, pleonastic; redundant, unnecessary, superfluous.

explicable /éksplikəbəl, iksplík-/ adj. that can be explained.

explicate /éksplikayt/ v.tr. **1** develop the meaning or implication of (an idea, principle, etc.). **2** make clear; explain (esp. a literary text). □□ **explication** /-káyshən/ n. **explicative** /éksplikaytiv, iksplíkətiv/ adj. **explicator** n. **explicatory** /éksplikətawree, ikslík-/ adj. [L *explicare explicat-* unfold (as EX-[1], *plicare plicat-* or *plicit-* fold)]

■ see EXPLAIN 1.

explicit /iksplísit/ adj. **1** expressly stated, leaving nothing merely implied; stated in detail. **2** (of knowledge, a notion, etc.) definite; clear. **3** (of a person, book, etc.) expressing views unreservedly; outspoken. □□ **explicitly** adv. **explicitness** n. [F *explicite* or L *explicitus* (as EXPLICATE)]

■ **1** express, clear, plain, overt, manifest, definite,

positive, unmistakable, categorical, distinct, unambiguous, unequivocal; specific, well-defined, precise, exact. **2** see DEFINITE. **3** unreserved, open, outspoken, forthright, definite; unrestrained, candid, frank, direct, straightforward.

explode /iksplód/ v. **1 a** intr. (of gas, gunpowder, a bomb, a boiler, etc.) expand suddenly with a loud noise owing to a release of internal energy. **b** tr. cause (a bomb, etc.) to explode. **2** intr. give vent suddenly to emotion, esp. anger. **3** intr. (of a population, etc.) increase suddenly or rapidly. **4** tr. show (a theory, etc.) to be false or baseless. **5** tr. (as **exploded** adj.) (of a drawing, etc.) showing the components of a mechanism as if separated by an explosion but in the normal relative positions. □□ **exploder** n. [earliest in sense 4: L *explodere* hiss off the stage (as EX-[1], *plodere plos-* = *plaudere* clap)]

■ **1** blow up, fly apart, go off, erupt, burst; blast; set off, detonate. **2** lose one's temper, throw a tantrum, rant, rave, rage, storm, *colloq.* get into a tizzy, blow one's top, fly off the handle, go through *or* hit *or* raise the roof, hit the ceiling, lose one's cool, go up the wall, freak (out), blow one's stack, *sl.* flip (one's lid), blow *or* lose one's cool. **3** see GROW 1. **4** discredit, disprove, reject, repudiate, pick holes in, refute, belie, give the lie to, *colloq.* debunk.

exploit n. & v. ● n. /éksployt/ a bold or daring feat. ● v.tr. /iksplóyt/ **1** make use of (a resource, etc.); derive benefit from. **2** usu. *derog.* utilize or take advantage of (esp. a person) for one's own ends. □□ **exploitable** adj. **exploitation** n. **exploitative** /iksplóytətiv/ adj. **exploiter** n. **exploitive** adj. [ME f. OF *esploit, exploiter* ult. f. L *explicare*: see EXPLICATE]

■ n. feat, achievement, attainment, accomplishment, deed. ● v. use, take advantage of, utilize, turn to account, make capital out of, profit from; work; manipulate.

exploration /ékspləráyshən/ n. **1** an act or instance of exploring. **2** the process of exploring. □□ **explorational** adj.

■ examination, investigation, inquiry, study, analysis, review, scrutiny, inspection, survey, observation; search, probe; reconnaissance, expedition; research.

exploratory /ikspláwrətawree/ adj. **1** (of discussion, etc.) preliminary; serving to establish procedure, etc. **2** of or concerning exploration or investigation (*exploratory surgery*).

■ **1** see PRELIMINARY adj. **2** see EXPERIMENTAL 2b.

explore /ikspláwr/ v.tr. **1** travel extensively through (a country, etc.) in order to learn or discover about it. **2** inquire into; investigate thoroughly. **3** Surgery examine (a part of the body) in detail. □□ **explorative** /-rətiv/ adj. [F *explorer* f. L *explorare*]

■ **1** travel, tour, traverse; survey, reconnoiter. **2** inquire into, examine, look into, inspect, search, investigate, probe; research, study, analyze, review. **3** see INSPECT.

explorer /ikspláwrər/ n. a traveler into undiscovered or uninvestigated territory, esp. to get scientific information.

■ see PIONEER n. 2.

explosion /iksplózhən/ n. **1** the act or an instance of exploding. **2** a loud noise caused by something exploding. **3 a** a sudden outburst of noise. **b** a sudden outbreak of feeling, esp. anger. **4** a rapid or sudden increase, esp. of population. [L *explosio* scornful rejection (as EXPLODE)]

■ **1** burst, eruption. **2** blast, bang, report, boom, clap, crack, crash; detonation. **3 a** outburst, blast, crash. **b** outburst, outbreak, paroxysm, flare-up, eruption, burst, spasm, *colloq.* fit. **4** increase, expansion, mushrooming, blossoming, *literary* burgeoning.

explosive /iksplósiv/ adj. & n. ● adj. **1** able or tending to explode. **2** likely to cause a violent outburst, etc.;

(of a situation, etc.) dangerously tense. ● *n.* an explosive substance. □□ **explosively** *adv.* **explosiveness** *n.*
■ *adj.* **2** volatile, tense, fraught, (highly) charged, flammable, precarious, dangerous, perilous, hazardous, chancy, unstable, shaky, uncertain, unpredictable, critical, touch-and-go, sensitive, delicate, nasty, ugly, *colloq.* iffy, *sl.* dicey. ● *n.* dynamite, gelignite, gunpowder, TNT.

expo /ékspō/ *n.* (also **Expo**) (*pl.* **-os**) a large international exhibition. [abbr. of EXPOSITION 4]
■ see EXHIBITION 1.

exponent /ikspṓnənt/ *n.* & *adj.* ● *n.* **1** a person who favors or promotes an idea, etc. **2** a representative or practitioner of an activity, profession, etc. **3** a person who explains or interprets something. **4** an executant (of music, etc.). **5** a type or representative. **6** *Math.* a raised symbol or expression beside a numeral indicating how many times it is to be multiplied by itself (e.g., $2^3 = 2 \times 2 \times 2$). ● *adj.* that sets forth or interprets. [L *exponere* (as EX-[1], *ponere posit-* put)]
■ *n.* **1** see PROPONENT *n.*

exponential /ékspənénshəl/ *adj.* **1** *Math.* of or indicated by a mathematical exponent. **2** (of an increase, etc.) more and more rapid. □ **exponential function** *Math.* a function that increases as a quantity raised to a power determined by the variable on which the function depends. **exponential growth** *Biol.* a form of population growth in which the rate of growth is related to the number of individuals present. □□ **exponentially** *adv.* [F *exponentiel* (as EXPONENT)]

export *v.* & *n.* ● *v.tr.* /ikspáwrt, éks-/ send out (goods or services) esp. for sale in another country. ● *n.* /ékspawrt/ **1** the process of exporting. **2 a** an exported article or service. **b** (in *pl.*) an amount exported (*exports exceeded $50 billion*). **3** (*attrib.*) suitable for export, esp. of better quality. □□ **exportable** *adj.* **exportability** *n.* **exportation** *n.* **exporter** *n.* [L *exportare* (as EX-[1], *portare* carry)]

expose /ikspṓz/ *v.tr.* **1** leave uncovered or unprotected, esp. from the weather. **2** (foll. by *to*) **a** cause to be liable to or in danger of (*was exposed to great danger*). **b** lay open to the action or influence of; introduce to (*exposed to bad influences, exposed to Hemingway at a young age*). **3** (as **exposed** *adj.*) **a** (foll. by *to*) open to; unprotected from (*exposed to the east*). **b** vulnerable; risky. **4** *Photog.* subject (film) to light, esp. by operation of a camera. **5** reveal the identity or fact of (esp. a person or thing disapproved of or guilty of crime, etc.). **6** disclose; make public. **7** exhibit; display. **8** put up for sale. □ **expose oneself** display one's body, esp. the genitals, publicly and indecently. □□ **exposer** *n.* [ME f. OF *exposer* after L *exponere*: see EXPONENT, POSE[1]]
■ **2 a** see SUBJECT *v.* 1. **b** (*expose to*) introduce to, acquaint with, bring into contact with. **3** (**exposed**) **b** see VULNERABLE 1. **5** reveal, disclose, divulge, unveil, unmask, lay bare, uncover, let out, leak, betray, bring to light, make known, *archaic* discover. **6** make public, make known; see also DISCLOSE 1. **7** exhibit, display, show, reveal, bare, uncover. □ **expose oneself** see DISPLAY *v.* 2.

exposé /ekspōzáy/ *n.* (also **expose**) **1** an orderly statement of facts. **2** the act or an instance of revealing something discreditable. [F, past part. of *exposer* (as EXPOSE)]
■ **1** see RECORD *n.* 1, REPORT *n.* 1, 2. **2** see REVELATION.

exposition /ékspəzíshən/ *n.* **1** an explanatory statement or account. **2** an explanation or commentary; an interpretative article or treatise. **3** *Mus.* the part of a movement, esp. in sonata form, in which the principal themes are first presented. **4** a large public exhibition. **5** *archaic* exposure. □□ **expositional** *adj.* **expositive** /-pózitiv/ *adj.* [ME f. OF *exposition*, or L *expositio* (as EXPONENT)]
■ **1, 2** statement, account; explanation, description, commentary, interpretation, exegesis; explication, clarification; paper, theme, article, essay, thesis, dissertation, treatise, disquisition, study, critique. **4** exhibition, show, showing, exhibit, display, expo; presentation, demonstration. **5** see EXPOSURE 3.

expositor /ikspózitər/ *n.* an expounder or interpreter. □□ **expository** *adj.*

ex post facto /éks pōst fáktō/ *adj.* & *adv.* with retrospective action or force. [L *ex postfacto* in the light of subsequent events]

expostulate /ikspóschəlayt/ *v.intr.* (often foll. by *with* a person) make a protest; remonstrate earnestly. □□ **expostulation** /-láyshən/ *n.* **expostulatory** /-lətáwree/ *adj.* [L *expostulare expostulat-* (as EX-[1], *postulare* demand)]
■ see PROTEST *v.* 1.

exposure /ikspṓzhər/ *n.* **1** (foll. by *to*) the act or condition of exposing or being exposed (to air, cold, danger, etc.). **2** the condition of being exposed to the elements, esp. in severe conditions (*died from exposure*). **3** the revelation of an identity or fact, esp. when concealed or likely to find disapproval. **4** *Photog.* **a** the action of exposing film, etc., to the light. **b** the duration of this action. **c** the area of film, etc., affected by it. **5** an aspect or outlook (*has a fine southern exposure*). **6** experience, esp. of a specified kind of work. □ **exposure meter** *Photog.* a device for measuring the strength of the light to determine the correct duration of exposure. [EXPOSE after *enclosure*, etc.]
■ **3** revelation, disclosure, revealing, uncovering, disclosing, exposé, unmasking, unveiling, baring, laying open, leak, leaking, divulging; publication, publishing. **5** aspect, view, outlook, orientation, frontage; setting, location, direction. **6** familiarity, knowledge, acquaintance, experience, contact, conversancy.

expound /ikspównd/ *v.tr.* **1** set out in detail (a doctrine, etc.). **2** explain or interpret (esp. Scripture). □□ **expounder** *n.* [ME f. OF *espondre* (as EXPONENT)]
■ see EXPLAIN 1.

express[1] /iksprés/ *v.tr.* **1** represent or make known (thought, feelings, etc.) in words or by gestures, conduct, etc. **2** *refl.* say what one thinks or means. **3** esp. *Math.* represent by symbols. **4** squeeze out (liquid or air). □□ **expresser** *n.* **expressible** *adj.* [ME f. OF *expresser* f. Rmc (as EX-[1], PRESS[1])]
■ **1, 2** articulate, verbalize, utter, voice, state, put into words, enunciate, set forth, put forward, put *or* get across, communicate, *formal* put forth; phrase, word, put; say; show, indicate, demonstrate, manifest, exhibit, evince, evidence, reveal, expose, disclose, divulge, make known, intimate, denote, convey, betoken, signify; embody, depict. **3** symbolize, represent, signify, denote. **4** squeeze *or* press *or* wring *or* force out, extract, expel.

express[2] /iksprés/ *adj., adv., n., & v.* ● *adj.* **1** operating at high speed. **2** /also ékspres / **a** definitely stated, not merely implied. **b** *archaic* (of a likeness) exact. **3 a** done, made, or sent for a special purpose. **b** (of messages or goods) delivered by a special messenger or service. ● *adv.* **1** at high speed. **2** by express messenger or train. ● *n.* **1 a** an express train or messenger. **b** an express rifle. **2** a company undertaking the transport of packages, etc. ● *v.tr.* send by express messenger or delivery. □ **express train** a fast train, stopping at few intermediate stations. □□ **expressly** *adv.* (in senses 2 and 3a of *adj.*) [ME f. OF *expres* f. L *expressus* distinctly shown, past part. of *exprimere* (as EX-[1], *premere* press)]
■ *adj.* **1** speedy, quick, swift, fast, rapid, prompt, direct. **2** explicit, definite, clear, plain, unambiguous, direct, straightforward, outright, specific, categorical, unmistakable, well-defined, distinct, exact. **3 a** special, specific, particular; marked, customized. ● *adv.* **1** see *promptly* (PROMPT). □□ **expressly** definitely, categorically, distinctly, explicitly, directly, unambiguously, unequivocally, unmistakably, plainly, pointedly, clearly, positively; purposely, especially, purposefully, particularly, specifically, specially; on purpose.

expression /ikspréshən/ *n.* **1** the act or an instance of expressing. **2 a** a word or phrase expressed. **b** manner or means of expressing in language; wording; diction. **3** *Math.* a collection of symbols expressing a quantity. **4** a person's facial appearance or intonation of voice, esp. as indicating feeling. **5** depiction of feeling, movement, etc., in art. **6** conveying of feeling in the performance of a piece of music. □□ **expressional** *adj.* **expressionless** *adj.* **expression-**

lessly adv. **expressionlessness** n. [ME f. OF expression or L expressio f. exprimere: see EXPRESS[1]]

■ **1** verbalization, representation, declaration, utterance, assertion, asseveration, pronouncement, communication, announcement; voicing, airing; manifestation, sign, show, demonstration, indication, evidence, token, symbol. **2 a** word, term, phrase, idiom, turn of phrase, locution, saying. **b** wording, phrasing, phraseology, language, style, diction, usage, speech, delivery. **4** look, air, appearance, face, aspect, countenance, literary mien; intonation, tone, note. **6** tone, intonation, touch, shading; expressiveness, emotion, feeling, sensitivity, passion, spirit, depth, ardor, intensity, pathos.

expressionism /ikspréshənizəm/ n. a style of painting, music, drama, etc., in which an artist or writer seeks to express emotional experience rather than impressions of the external world. □□ **expressionist** n. & adj. **expressionistic** adj. **expressionistically** adv.

expressive /iksprésiv/ adj. **1** full of expression (an expressive look). **2** (foll. by of) serving to express (words expressive of contempt). □□ **expressively** adv. **expressiveness** n. **expressivity** /-sívitee/ n. [ME f. F expressif -ive or med.L expressivus (as EXPRESSION)]

■ **1** vivid, striking, loaded, forceful, moving, emotional, poignant, provocative, pointed, explicit, pithy, telling, eloquent, meaningful, significant, pregnant. **2** indicative, suggestive, revealing, denotative.

expresso var. of ESPRESSO.

expressway /iksprésway/ n. a divided highway for high-speed traffic.

■ see ROAD[1] 1.

expropriate /ekspṓpreeayt/ v.tr. **1** (esp. of the government) take away (property) from its owner. **2** (foll. by from) dispossess. □□ **expropriation** /-áyshən/ n. **expropriator** n. [med.L expropriare expropriat- (as EX-[1], proprium property: see PROPER)]

■ see APPROPRIATE v. 1.

expulsion /ikspúlshən/ n. the act or an instance of expelling; the process of being expelled. □□ **expulsive** /-púlsiv/ adj. [ME f. L expulsio (as EXPEL)]

■ ejection, expelling, sl. the bounce; removal, dismissal, discharge, ouster, colloq. the boot, the sack, sacking; eviction.

expunge /ikspúnj/ v.tr. (foll. by from) erase; remove (esp. a passage from a book or a name from a list). □□ **expunction** /ikspúngkshən/ n. **expunger** n. [L expungere expunct- (as EX-[1], pungere prick)]

■ see REMOVE v. 2b.

expurgate /ékspərgayt/ v.tr. **1** remove matter thought to be objectionable from (a book, etc.). **2** remove (such matter). □□ **expurgation** /-gáyshən/ n. **expurgator** n. **expurgatorial** /ikspórgətáwreeəl/ adj. **expurgatory** adj. [L expurgare expurgat- (as EX-[1], purgare cleanse)]

■ see EDIT v. 5.

exquisite /ékskwizit, ikskwízit/ adj. & n. ● adj. **1** extremely beautiful or delicate. **2** acute; keenly felt (exquisite pleasure). **3 a** keen; highly sensitive or discriminating (exquisite taste). **b** elaborately devised or accomplished; consummate; perfect. ● n. a person of refined (esp. affected) tastes. □□ **exquisitely** adv. **exquisiteness** n. [ME f. L exquirere exquisit- (as EX-[1], quaerere seek)]

■ adj. **1** beautiful, perfect, lovely, attractive, handsome; comely, good-looking, smart, chic, striking, elegant; delicate, fine, graceful, excellent, choice, well-crafted, well-made, well-executed, refined. **2** acute, sharp, keen, excruciating, agonizing, intense. **3** superb, superior, peerless, matchless, incomparable, unequaled, rare, consummate, outstanding, superlative, excellent, flawless, perfect, wonderful, splendid, marvelous; see also ACUTE adj. 1a. ● n. aesthete, connoisseur, art lover, lover of beauty, epicure, gourmet, dilettante.

exsanguinate /iksánggwinayt/ Med. v.tr. drain of blood.

□□ **exsanguination** /-náyshən/ n. [L exsanguinatus (as EX-[1], sanguis -inis blood)]

exsert /iksórt/ v.tr. Biol. put forth. [L exserere: see EXERT]

ex-service /éks-sə́rvis/ adj. Brit. **1** having formerly been a member of the armed forces. **2** relating to former servicemen and -women.

ex-serviceman /éks-sə́rvismən/ n. (pl. -men) a former member of the armed forces.

ex-servicewoman /éks-sə́rviswoomən/ n. (pl. -women) a former woman member of the armed forces.

ext. abbr. **1** exterior. **2** external.

extant /ékstənt, ekstánt/ adj. (esp. of a document, etc.) still existing; surviving. [L exstare exstant- (as EX-[1], stare stand)]

■ see ACTUAL 2.

extemporaneous /ikstémpəráyneeəs/ adj. spoken or done without preparation. □□ **extemporaneously** adv. **extemporaneousness** n.

■ impromptu, improvised, spontaneous, unrehearsed, extemporized, extempore, extemporary, unprepared, unstudied, unplanned, unpremeditated, unscripted, offhand, ad lib, colloq. off the cuff.

extemporary /ikstémpəreree/ adj. = EXTEMPORANEOUS. □□ **extemporarily** /-ráirəlee/ adv. **extemporariness** n.

extempore /ikstémpəree/ adj. & adv. **1** without preparation. **2** offhand. [L ex tempore on the spur of the moment, lit. out of the time f. tempus time]

■ see EXTEMPORANEOUS.

extemporize /ikstémpəriz/ v.tr. (also absol.) compose or produce (music, a speech, etc.) without preparation; improvise. □□ **extemporization** n.

■ see IMPROVISE 1.

extend /iksténd/ v. **1** tr. & intr. lengthen or make larger in space or time. **2 a** tr. stretch or lay out at full length. **b** tr. & intr. (often foll. by over) (cause to) stretch or span over a period of time. **3** intr. & tr. (foll. by to, over) reach or be or make continuous over a certain area. **4** intr. (foll. by to) have a certain scope (the permit does not extend to camping). **5** tr. offer or accord (an invitation, hospitality, kindness, etc.). **6** tr. (usu. refl. or in passive) tax the powers of (an athlete, horse, etc.) to the utmost. □ **extended family 1** a family group that includes relatives living in one household. **2** all the members of a family, including cousins, in-law, etc. **extended-play** (of a phonograph record) playing for longer than most singles, usu. at 45 r.p.m.; (of a videocassette recording) playing at the slowest recordable speed. □□ **extendable** adj. **extendability** n. **extendible** adj. **extendibility** n. **extensible** /-sténsibəl/ adj. **extensibility** n. [ME f. L extendere extens- or extent- stretch out (as EX-[1], tendere stretch)]

■ **1** lengthen, elongate, add to, increase, augment; widen, broaden, enlarge, stretch (out). **2 a** stretch or lay out, hold out, stretch forth, offer, proffer, give, tender, present; see also SPREAD v. 1a. **b** last, stretch, continue, go or carry on, drag on; perpetuate, drag out, prolong. **3** stretch or spread (out); reach, range; carry on, continue. **4** (extend to) see INCLUDE 1. **5** offer, bestow, accord, grant, impart, confer, advance. **6** see CHALLENGE v. 3a.

extender /iksténdər/ n. **1** a person or thing that extends. **2** a substance added to paint, ink, glue, etc., to dilute its color or increase its bulk.

extensile /iksténsəl, -sīl/ adj. capable of being stretched out or protruded.

■ see ELASTIC adj. 1.

extension /iksténshən/ n. **1** the act or an instance of extending; the process of being extended. **2** prolongation; enlargement. **3** a part enlarging or added on to a main structure or building. **4** an additional part of anything. **5 a** a subsidiary telephone on the same line as the main one. **b** its number.

/.../ **pronunciation**	● **part of speech**
□ **phrases, idioms, and compounds**	
□□ **derivatives**	■ **synonym section**
cross-references appear in SMALL CAPITALS or italics	

6 a an additional period of time, esp. extending allowance for a project, etc. **b** permission for the sale of alcoholic drinks until later than usual, granted to licensed premises on special occasions. **7** extramural instruction by a university or college (*extension course*). **8** extent; range. **9** *Logic* a group of things denoted by a term. □□ **extensional** *adj.* [ME f. LL *extensio* (as EXTEND)]

■ **1, 2** enlargement, expansion, increase, augmentation, development, amplification, broadening, widening, lengthening, stretching. **3** annex, wing, addition. **4** addition, appendage, adjunct, supplement. **6 a** see RESPITE *n.* 2. **8** extent, range, scope, magnitude, sweep, reach, extensiveness, capacity, span, compass, gauge, size, dimensions; breadth, width, height, length, spread, stretch, volume.

extensive /iksténsiv/ *adj.* **1** covering a large area in space or time. **2** having a wide scope; far-reaching; comprehensive (*an extensive knowledge of music*). **3** *Agriculture* involving cultivation from a large area, with a minimum of special resources (cf. INTENSIVE). □□ **extensively** *adv.* **extensiveness** *n.* [F *extensif -ive* or LL *extensivus* (as EXTENSION)]

■ **1** large, big, great, huge, substantial, considerable, sizable, immense, enormous, vast, gigantic, massive; spacious, voluminous, commodious, capacious. **2** wide, broad; far-reaching, far-ranging, wide-ranging, sweeping, widespread, far-flung; comprehensive, catholic, all-embracing; national, nationwide, international, intercontinental, cosmopolitan, worldwide, global, universal; cosmic.

extensometer /ékstensómitər/ *n.* **1** an instrument for measuring deformation of metal under stress. **2** an instrument using such deformation to record elastic strains in other materials. [L *extensus* (as EXTEND) + -METER]

extensor /iksténsər/ *n.* (in full **extensor muscle**) *Anat.* a muscle that extends or straightens out part of the body (cf. FLEXOR). [mod.L (as EXTEND)]

extent /ikstént/ *n.* **1** the space over which a thing extends. **2** the width or limits of application; scope (*to a great extent*; *to the full extent of their power*). [ME f. AF *extente* f. med.L *extenta* past part. of L *extendere*: see EXTEND]

■ **1** space, magnitude, dimensions, compass, size, range, scale, sweep, scope, amplitude; expanse, area, region, tract, territory. **2** limits, lengths; scope; see also RANGE *n.* 1a–c.

extenuate /ikstényoo-ayt/ *v.tr.* (often as **extenuating** *adj.*) lessen the seeming seriousness of (guilt or an offense) by reference to some mitigating factor. □□ **extenuatingly** *adv.* **extenuation** /-áyshən/ *n.* **extenuatory** /-yoootáwree/ *adj.* [L *extenuare extenuat-* (as EX-¹, *tenuis* thin)]

■ (**extenuating**) mitigating, tempering, palliating, qualifying, moderating, lessening.

exterior /ikstéereeər/ *adj. & n.* ● *adj.* **1 a** of or on the outer side (opp. INTERIOR). **b** (foll. by *to*) situated on the outside of (a building, etc.). **c** coming from outside. **2** *Cinematog.* outdoor. ● *n.* **1** the outward aspect or surface of a building, etc. **2** the outward or apparent behavior or demeanor of a person. **3** *Cinematog.* an outdoor scene. □ **exterior angle** the angle between the side of a rectilinear figure and the adjacent side extended outward. □□ **exteriority** /-ree-áwritee, -ree-ór-/ *n.* **exteriorize** *v.tr.* **exteriorly** *adv.* [L, compar. of *exterus* outside]

■ *adj.* **1 a** outer, outside, external, outward; surface, superficial. **c** outside, external, extrinsic, extraneous, foreign, alien, exotic. **2** see OUTDOOR. ● *n.* **1** aspect, surface, outside, front, face, façade; skin, shell, covering, coating. **2** see BEARING 1.

exterminate /ikstérminayt/ *v.tr.* **1** destroy utterly (esp. something living). **2** get rid of; eliminate (a pest, disease, etc.). □□ **extermination** /-náyshən/ *n.* **exterminatory** /-nətáwree/ *adj.* [L *exterminare exterminat-* (as EX-¹, *terminus* boundary)]

■ destroy, eradicate, extirpate, annihilate, eliminate, root out, get rid of, wipe out, obliterate, put an end to, terminate, liquidate, kill off, *sl.* rub out, waste.

external /ikstérnəl/ *adj. & n.* ● *adj.* **1 a** of or situated on the

outside or visible part (opp. INTERNAL). **b** coming or derived from the outside or an outside source. **2** relating to a country's foreign affairs. **3** outside the conscious subject (*the external world*). **4** (of medicine, etc.) for use on the outside of the body. **5** for or concerning students taking the examinations of a university without attending it. ● *n.* (in *pl.*) **1** the outward features or aspect. **2** external circumstances. **3** inessentials. □ **external evidence** evidence derived from a source independent of the thing discussed. □□ **externality** /-nálitee/ *n.* (*pl.* **-ies**). **externally** *adv.* [med.L f. L *externus* f. *exterus* outside]

■ *adj.* **1a, 3** outside, outward, exterior, visible, apparent, perceptible. **1 b** outside, exterior, extrinsic, extraneous, alien, foreign, exotic. **3** international, overseas, foreign. ● *n.* (**externals**) **1** see ASPECT 2b. **2** see ENVIRONMENT 1, 2. **3** see ACCESSORY *n.* 2.

externalize /ikstérnəlīz/ *v.tr.* give or attribute external existence to. □□ **externalization** *n.*

exteroceptive /ékstərōséptiv/ *adj. Biol.* relating to stimuli produced outside an organism. [irreg. f. L *externus* exterior + RECEPTIVE]

exterritorial /éksteritáwreeəl/ *adj.* = EXTRATERRITORIAL. □□ **exterritoriality** /-reeálitee/ *n.*

extinct /ikstíngkt/ *adj.* **1** (of a family, class, or species) that has died out. **2 a** (of fire, etc.) no longer burning. **b** (of a volcano) that no longer erupts. **3** (of life, hope, etc.) terminated; quenched. **4** (of an office, etc.) obsolete. **5** (of a title of nobility) having no qualified claimant. [ME f. L *exstinguere exstinct-* (as EX-¹, *stinguere* quench)]

■ **1** dead, departed, vanished; defunct, died out, gone. **2** inactive, dormant; extinguished, quenched, burned-out. **3** see DEAD *adj.* 1. **4** dated, outmoded, old-fashioned, antiquated, obsolete, archaic, out-of-date, ancient, passé, démodé, *colloq.* antediluvian, old hat.

extinction /ikstíngkshən/ *n.* **1** the act of making extinct; the state of being or process of becoming extinct. **2** the act of extinguishing; the state of being extinguished. **3** total destruction or annihilation. **4** the wiping out of a debt. **5** *Physics* a reduction in the intensity of radiation by absorption, scattering, etc. □□ **extinctive** *adj.* [L *extinctio* (as EXTINCT)]

■ **1, 3** see DESTRUCTION 1. **2** see *suppression* (SUPPRESS).

extinguish /ikstínggwish/ *v.tr.* **1** cause (a flame, light, etc.) to die out; put out. **2** make extinct; annihilate; destroy (*a program to extinguish disease*). **3** put an end to; terminate; obscure utterly (a feeling, quality, etc.). **4 a** abolish; wipe out (a debt). **b** *Law* render void. **5** *colloq.* reduce to silence (*the argument extinguished the opposition*). **6** *archaic* surpass by superior brilliance. □□ **extinguishable** *adj.* **extinguishment** *n.* [irreg. f. L *extinguere* (as EXTINCT): cf. *distinguish*]

■ **1** put *or* snuff *or* blow out, quench; turn off *or* out. **2, 3** annihilate, destroy, exterminate, kill (off), eliminate, end, finish, nullify, obliterate, terminate, eradicate, extirpate, remove, wipe *or* blot *or* root out, obscure, *colloq.* do away with. **4** see ABOLISH. **5** see SILENCE *v.* **6** obscure, eclipse, dim, outdo, put in the shade, overshadow, adumbrate, *colloq.* show up.

extinguisher /ikstínggwishər/ *n.* a person or thing that extinguishes, esp. = *fire extinguisher.*

extirpate /ékstərpayt/ *v.tr.* root out; destroy completely. □□ **extirpation** /-páyshən/ *n.* **extirpator** *n.* [L *exstirpare exstirpat-* (as EX-¹, *stirps* stem)]

■ see *root out* (ROOT¹).

extol /ikstṓl/ *v.tr.* (**extolled, extolling**) praise enthusiastically. □□ **extoller** *n.* **extolment** *n.* [L *extollere* (as EX-¹, *tollere* raise)]

■ praise, laud, applaud, commend, acclaim, celebrate, pay tribute *or* homage to, exalt, sing the praises of, make much of, glorify, honor, compliment.

extort /ikstáwrt/ *v.tr.* obtain by force, threats, persistent demands, etc. □□ **extorter** *n.* **extortive** *adj.* [L *extorquēre extort-* (as EX-¹, *torquēre* twist)]

■ obtain, exact, extract, force, wring, wrest.

extortion /ikstáwrshən/ *n.* **1** the act or an instance of extorting, esp. money. **2** illegal exaction. □□ **extortioner** *n.* **extortionist** *n.* [ME f. LL *extortio* (as EXTORT)]

■ see BLACKMAIL *n.* 2.

extortionate /ikstáwrshənət/ *adj.* **1** (of a price, etc.) exorbitant. **2** using or given to extortion (*extortionate methods*). □□ **extortionately** *adv.*

■ **1** see EXORBITANT. **2** see RAPACIOUS.

extra /ékstrə/ *adj., adv., & n.* ● *adj.* additional; more than is usual or necessary or expected. ● *adv.* **1** more than usually. **2** additionally (*was charged extra*). ● *n.* **1** an extra thing. **2** a thing for which an extra charge is made; such a charge. **3** a person engaged temporarily to fill out a scene in a motion picture or play, esp. as one of a crowd. **4** a special issue of a newspaper, etc. □ **extra time** *Sports Brit.* = OVERTIME 3. [prob. a shortening of EXTRAORDINARY]

■ *adj.* additional, added, further; accessory, supplementary, supplemental; adventitious; auxiliary, subsidiary, collateral. ● *adv.* **1** unusually, exceptionally, extraordinarily, uncommonly, unexpectedly, surprisingly, amazingly, remarkably, notably, strikingly, very, particularly, especially, extremely. **2** additionally, more, again, in addition. ● *n.* **1** see ADDITION 2. **2** supplement, markup, surcharge. **3** supernumerary, walk-on, *Theatr.* super. **4** special, *Brit.* one-off; exclusive.

extra- /ékstrə/ *comb. form* **1** outside; beyond (*extragalactic*). **2** beyond the scope of (*extracurricular*). [med.L f. L *extra* outside]

extracellular /ékstrəsélyələr/ *adj.* situated or taking place outside a cell or cells.

extract *v. & n.* ● *v.tr.* /ikstrákt/ **1** remove or take out, esp. by effort or force (anything firmly rooted). **2** obtain (money, an admission, etc.) with difficulty or against a person's will. **3** obtain (a natural resource) from the earth. **4** select or reproduce for quotation or performance (a passage of writing, music, etc.). **5** obtain (juice, etc.) by suction, pressure, distillation, etc. **6** derive (pleasure, etc.). **7** *Math.* find (the root of a number). **8** *archaic* deduce (a principle, etc.). ● *n.* /ékstrakt/ **1** a short passage taken from a book, piece of music, etc.; an excerpt. **2** a preparation containing the active principle of a substance in concentrated form (*malt extract*). □□ **extractable** *adj.* **extractability** *n.* [L *extrahere extract-* (as EX-¹, *trahere* draw)]

■ *v.* **1** remove, take *or* pluck out, draw *or* pull (out), withdraw, draw forth, extricate. **2** obtain, wrench, wring, wrest, extort, extricate; worm out, prize out, esp. *Brit.* winkle out, force out. **3** see MINE² *v.* 1, 2. **4** select, choose, glean, cull, abstract, quote, cite; reproduce, copy. **6** see DERIVE 1. **8** deduce, derive, glean, draw, distill, get, obtain. ● *n.* **1** passage, excerpt, quotation, citation, clipping, cutting, selection. **2** concentrate, essence, distillation, distillate, quintessence, decoction.

extraction /ikstrákshən/ *n.* **1** the act or an instance of extracting; the process of being extracted. **2** the removal of a tooth. **3** origin; lineage; descent (*of German extraction*). **4** something extracted; an extract. [ME f. F f. LL *extractio -onis* (as EXTRACT)]

■ **1** removal, extrication, uprooting, withdrawal. **2** removal, pulling. **3** origin, birth, lineage, ancestry, descent, derivation, blood, parentage, race, stock, pedigree. **4** extract, concentrate, distillate, essence, distillation, quintessence, concentration, decoction.

extractive /ikstráktiv/ *adj.* of or involving extraction, esp. extensive extracting of natural resources without provision for their renewal.

extractor /ikstráktər/ *n.* **1** a person or machine that extracts. **2** (*attrib.*) (of a device) that extracts bad air, etc., or ventilates a room (*extractor fan; extractor hood*).

extracurricular /ékstrəkəríkyələr/ *adj.* (of a subject of study) not included in the normal curriculum.

extraditable /ékstrədítəbəl/ *adj.* **1** liable to extradition. **2** (of a crime) warranting extradition.

extradite /ékstrədīt/ *v.tr.* hand over (a person accused or convicted of a crime) to the country, state, etc., in which the crime was committed.

■ see BANISH 1.

extradition /ékstrədíshən/ *n.* **1** the extraditing of a person accused or convicted of a crime. **2** *Psychol.* the localizing of a sensation at a distance from the center of sensation.

extrados /ékstrədos, -dōs, ekstráydos/ *n.* *Archit.* the upper or outer curve of an arch (opp. INTRADOS). [EXTRA- + *dos* back f. L *dorsum*]

extragalactic /ékstrəgəláktik/ *adj.* occurring or existing outside the galaxy.

extrajudicial /ékstrəjŏŏdíshəl/ *adj.* **1** not legally authorized. **2** (of a confession) not made in court. □□ **extrajudicially** *adv.*

extramarital /ékstrəmárit'l/ *adj.* (esp. of sexual relations) occurring outside marriage. □□ **extramaritally** *adv.*

extramundane /ékstrəmundáyn/ *adj.* outside or beyond the physical world.

■ see SUPERNATURAL *adj.*

extramural /ékstrəmyŏŏrəl/ *adj. & n.* ● *adj.* **1** taught or conducted off the premises of a university, college, or school. **2** additional to normal teaching or studies, esp. for nonresident students. **3** outside the walls or boundaries of a town or city. ● *n.* an extramural lesson, course, etc. □□ **extramurally** *adv.* [L *extra muros* outside the walls]

extraneous /ikstráyneeəs/ *adj.* **1** of external origin. **2** (often foll. by *to*) **a** separate from the object to which it is attached, etc. **b** external to; irrelevant or unrelated to. **c** inessential; superfluous. □□ **extraneously** *adv.* **extraneousness** *n.* [L *extraneus*]

■ **1** see EXTERNAL *adj.* 1b. **2 b** irrelevant, unrelated, inapposite, unconnected, impertinent, inapplicable, inapt, unapt, unfitting, inappropriate, remote, foreign, alien, strange, outlandish, external, extrinsic; out of place, beside *or* off the point, beside *or* off *or* wide of the mark, off the subject. **c** unessential, nonessential, inessential, peripheral, superfluous, unnecessary, unneeded, extra, added, additional, supernumerary, incidental, needless.

extraordinary /ikstráwrd'neree, ékstrəáwr-/ *adj.* **1** unusual or remarkable; out of the usual course. **2** unusually great (*an extraordinary talent*). **3** so exceptional as to provoke astonishment or admiration. **4 a** (of an official, etc.) additional; specially employed (*envoy extraordinary*). **b** (of a meeting) specially convened. □□ **extraordinarily** *adv.* **extraordinariness** *n.* [L *extraordinarius* f. *extra ordinem* outside the usual order]

■ **1, 2** unusual, remarkable, exceptional, uncommon, outstanding, rare, special, singular, signal, particular, abnormal, unprecedented, unparalleled, *disp.* unique; unheard-of, curious, peculiar, odd, bizarre, strange, queer. **3** amazing, surprising, astonishing, astounding, remarkable, notable, noteworthy, marvelous, fantastic, incredible, unbelievable, impressive, fabulous, miraculous, unparalleled, far-out, *colloq.* super, smashing, gorgeous, *sl.* unreal. **4** see SPECIAL *adj.* 2.

extrapolate /ikstrápəlayt/ *v.tr.* (also *absol.*) **1** *Math. & Philos.* **a** calculate approximately from known values, data, etc. (others which lie outside the range of those known). **b** calculate on the basis of (known facts) to estimate unknown facts, esp. extend (a curve) on a graph. **2** infer more widely from a limited range of known facts. □□ **extrapolation** /-láyshən/ *n.* **extrapolative** *adj.* **extrapolator** *n.* [EXTRA- + INTERPOLATE]

extrasensory /ékstrəsénsəree/ *adj.* regarded as derived by means other than the known senses, e.g., by telepathy, clairvoyance, etc. □ **extrasensory perception** a person's supposed faculty of perceiving by such means.

■ see PSYCHIC *adj.* 1b.

extraterrestrial /ékstrətəréstreeəl/ *adj. & n.* ● *adj.* **1** outside the earth or its atmosphere. **2** (in science fiction) from outer space. ● *n.* (in science fiction) a being from outer space.

/. . ./ **pronunciation**   ● **part of speech**
□ **phrases, idioms, and compounds**
□□ **derivatives**   ■ **synonym section**
cross-references appear in SMALL CAPITALS or *italics*

■ *adj.* see UNEARTHLY 3. ● *n.* alien, ET, martian.

extraterritorial /ékstrətéritáwreeəl/ *adj.* **1** situated or (of laws, etc.) valid outside a country's territory. **2** (of an ambassador, etc.) free from the jurisdiction of the territory of residence. □□ **extraterritoriality** /-reeálitee/ *n.* [L *extra territorium* outside the territory]

extravagance /ikstrávəgəns/ *n.* **1** excessive spending or use of resources; being extravagant. **2** an instance or item of this. **3** unrestrained or absurd behavior, speech, thought, or writing. □□ **extravagancy** *n.* (*pl.* **-ies**). [F (as EXTRAVAGANT)]

■ **1** overspending, excess, thriftlessness, improvidence, dissipation, wastefulness, waste, lavishness, squandering, profligacy, prodigality, recklessness. **2** see SPLURGE *n.* 2. **3** immoderation, immoderateness, excessiveness, outrageousness, unrestraint, superfluity, superfluousness, preposterousness, unreasonableness, irrationality, absurdity; capriciousness, whimsicality, flightiness.

extravagant /ikstrávəgənt/ *adj.* **1** spending (esp. money) excessively; immoderate or wasteful in use of resources. **2** exorbitant; costing much. **3** exceeding normal restraint or sense; unreasonable; absurd (*extravagant claims*). □□ **extravagantly** *adv.* [ME f. med.L *extravagari* (as EXTRA-, *vagari* wander)]

■ **1** lavish, improvident, spendthrift, immoderate, wasteful, profligate, prodigal, reckless. **2** exorbitant, expensive, costly, extortionate, unreasonable, overpriced; dear, *colloq.* steep. **3** unrestrained, wild, outrageous, immoderate; unreasonable, absurd, preposterous, ridiculous, fanciful, flamboyant, high-sounding, exaggerated; undeserved, unjustified, unjustifiable.

extravaganza /ikstrávəgánzə/ *n.* **1** a fanciful literary, musical, or dramatic composition. **2** a spectacular theatrical or television production, esp. of light entertainment. [It. *estravaganza* extravagance]

■ **1** see FANCY *n.* 2. **2** spectacular, spectacle, pageant, production, show.

extravasate /ikstrávəsayt/ *v.* **1** *tr.* force out (a fluid, esp. blood) from its proper vessel. **2** *intr.* (of blood, lava, etc.) flow out. □□ **extravasation** /-sáyshən/ *n.* [L *extra* outside + *vas* vessel]

■ **1** see EJECT 4. **2** see LEAK *v.* 1b.

extravehicular /ékstrəvihíkyələr/ *adj.* outside a vehicle, esp. a spacecraft.

extrema *pl.* of EXTREMUM.

extreme /ikstréem/ *adj.* & *n.* ● *adj.* **1** reaching a high or the highest degree; exceedingly great or intense; exceptional (*extreme old age*; *in extreme danger*). **2 a** severe; stringent; lacking restraint or moderation (*take extreme measures*; *an extreme reaction*). **b** (of a person, opinion, etc.) going to great lengths; advocating immoderate measures. **3** outermost; furthest from the center; situated at either end (*the extreme edge*). **4** *Polit.* on the far left or right of a party. **5** utmost; last. ● *n.* **1** (often in *pl.*) one or other of two things as remote or as different as possible. **2** a thing at either end of anything. **3** the highest degree of anything. **4** *Math.* the first or the last term of a ratio or series. **5** *Logic* the subject or predicate in a proposition; the major or the minor term in a syllogism. □ **extreme unction** the last rites in the Roman Catholic and Orthodox churches. **go to extremes** take an extreme course of action. **go to the other extreme** take a diametrically opposite course of action. **in the extreme** to an extreme degree. □□ **extremely** *adv.* **extremeness** *n.* [ME f. OF f. L *extremus* superl. of *exterus* outward]

■ *adj.* **1** unusual, uncommon, exceptional, extraordinary, abnormal, remarkable, outstanding; see also GREAT *adj.* 1a. **2 a** severe, acute, intense; stringent, rigid, stern, strict, harsh, draconian, stiff, uncompromising, drastic; immoderate, excessive; inordinate, extravagant, outrageous; beyond the pale, beyond the limits *or* bounds; unconventional, radical, outrageous, wild. **b** immoderate, unconventional, radical, outrageous, wild, far-out, bizarre, queer, offbeat, exotic, eccentric, outré,

colloq. weird, different, way-out, *sl.* kooky. **3** outermost, endmost, farthest, very, remotest. **5** utmost, uttermost, final, last, ultimate. ● *n.* **1, 3** limit, bounds, maximum; extremity, height, apex, apogee, peak, acme, zenith, pinnacle, summit; depth, nadir. □ **in the extreme** extremely, very, exceptionally, exceedingly, extraordinarily, unusually. □□ **extremely** very, exceedingly, not a little, exceptionally, extraordinarily, unusually, uncommonly, outrageously, *colloq.* damned, darned, *Brit. colloq.* hellishly; to the nth degree.

extremist /ikstréemist/ *n.* (also *attrib.*) a person who holds extreme or fanatical political or religious views and esp. resorts to or advocates extreme action. □□ **extremism** *n.*

■ radical, revolutionary, fanatic, zealot, militant, ultra(ist).

extremity /ikstrémitee/ *n.* (*pl.* **-ies**) **1** the extreme point; the very end. **2** (in *pl.*) the hands and feet. **3** a condition of extreme adversity or difficulty. **4** excessiveness; extremeness. [ME f. OF *extremité* or L *extremitas* (as EXTREME)]

■ **1** extreme; end, limit, edge, boundary, bound, margin, periphery; border, frontier; maximum. **2** (*extremities*) hands, feet; fingers, fingertips, toes; arms, legs, limbs. **3** see CALAMITY 2. **4** see EXCESS *n.* 1, 4a.

extremum /ikstréeməm/ *n.* (*pl.* **extrema** /-mə/) *Math.* the maximum or minimum value of a function. □□ **extremal** *adj.* [L, neut. of *extremus* EXTREME]

extricate /ékstrikayt/ *v.tr.* (often foll. by *from*) free or disentangle from a constraint or difficulty. □□ **extricable** *adj.* **extrication** /-káyshən/ *n.* [L *extricare extricat-* (as EX-[1], *tricae* perplexities)]

■ (set) free, disentangle, disengage, liberate, release, rescue, save, deliver.

extrinsic /ekstrínsik, -zik/ *adj.* **1** not inherent or intrinsic; not essential (opp. INTRINSIC). **2** (often foll. by *to*) extraneous; lying outside; not belonging (to). **3** originating or operating from without. □□ **extrinsically** *adv.* [LL *extrinsicus* outward f. L *extrinsecus* (adv.) f. *exter* outside + *secus* beside]

■ **1** see IRRELEVANT. **2, 3** extraneous, outside, external, exterior, outer, outward; unrelated, irrelevant.

extrovert /ékstrəvərt/ *n.* & *adj.* ● *n.* **1** *Psychol.* a person predominantly concerned with external things or objective considerations. **2** an outgoing or sociable person. ● *adj.* typical or characteristic of an extrovert. □□ **extroversion** /-vŕzhən/ *n.* **extroverted** *adj.* [*extro-* = EXTRA- (after *intro-*) + L *vertere* turn]

extrude /ikstrood/ *v.tr.* **1** (foll. by *from*) thrust or force out. **2** shape metal, plastics, etc., by forcing them through a die. □□ **extrusion** /-troozhən/ *n.* **extrusile** /-troosəl, -sil/ *adj.* **extrusive** /-troosiv/ *adj.* [L *extrudere extrus-* (as EX-[1], *trudere* thrust)]

exuberant /igzoobərənt/ *adj.* **1** lively, high-spirited. **2** (of a plant, etc.) prolific; growing copiously. **3** (of feelings, etc.) abounding; lavish; effusive. □□ **exuberance** /-rəns/ *n.* **exuberantly** *adv.* [F *exubérant* f. L *exuberare* (as EX-[1], *uberare* be fruitful f. *uber* fertile)]

■ **1** lively, high-spirited, buoyant, animated, spirited, spry, sprightly, vivacious, energetic, vigorous, ebullient, effervescent, cheerful, joyful, happy, glad, delighted, overjoyed, ecstatic, enthusiastic, zealous; in seventh heaven, *colloq.* on cloud nine. **2** see PROLIFIC 3. **3** see EFFUSIVE. □□ **exuberance** liveliness, buoyancy, animation, spirit, spiritedness, sprightliness, vitality, vivacity, cheerfulness, joy, joyfulness, ebullience, effervescence, exhilaration, enthusiasm, excitement, zeal, zest, energy, vigor; abundance, copiousness, superabundance, superfluity, excess, profusion, prodigality; lavishness, flamboyance.

exuberate /igzoobərayt/ *v.intr.* be exuberant.

exude /igzood, iksood/ *v.* **1** *tr.* & *intr.* (of a liquid, moisture, etc.) escape or cause to escape gradually; ooze out; give off. **2** *tr.* emit (a smell). **3** *tr.* display (an emotion, etc.) freely or abundantly (*exuded displeasure*). □□ **exudate** /éksyoodayt, éksə-/ *n.* **exudation** *n.* **exudative** *adj.* [L *exsudare* (as EX-[1], *sudare* sweat)]

■ **1, 2** see EMANATE 2, 3.

exult /igzúlt/ *v.intr.* (often foll. by *at, in, over,* or *to* + infin.) **1** be greatly joyful. **2** (often foll. by *over*) have a feeling of triumph (over a person). □□ **exultancy** /-tənsee/ *n.* **exultation** /égzultáyshən, éksul-/ *n.* **exultant** *adj.* **exultantly** *adv.* **exultingly** *adv.* [L *exsultare* (as EX-¹, *saltare* frequent. of *salire* salt- leap)]

■ **1** rejoice, revel, glory, triumph, delight, jump for joy; celebrate, make merry. □□ **exultant** delighted, jubilant, triumphant, overjoyed, elated, joyful, gleeful, glad, ecstatic, exuberant; in seventh heaven, *colloq.* on cloud nine, *Brit. colloq.* over the moon.

exurb /éksərb, égzərb/ *n.* a district outside a city or town, esp. a prosperous area beyond the suburbs. □□ **exurban** *adj.* **exurbanite** /eksórbənìt, égzór-/ *n.* [L *ex* out of + *urbs* city, or back-form. f. *exurban* (as EX-¹ + URBAN, after *suburban*)]

■ see MUNICIPALITY.

exurbia /eksórbeeə, egzór-/ *n.* the exurbs collectively; the region beyond the suburbs. [EX-¹, after *suburbia*]

exuviae /igzōōvee-ee/ *n.pl.* (also treated as *sing.*) an animal's cast skin or covering. □□ **exuvial** *adj.* [L, = animal's skins, spoils of the enemy, f. *exuere* divest oneself of]

exuviate /igzōōveeàyt/ *v.tr.* shed (a skin, etc.). □□ **exuviation** /-áyshən/ *n.*

ex voto /eks vótō/ *n.* (*pl.* **-os**) an offering made in pursuance of a vow. [L, = out of a vow]

-ey /ee/ *suffix* var. of -Y².

eyas /íəs/ *n.* a young hawk, esp. one taken from the nest for training in falconry. [orig. *nyas* f. F *niais* ult. f. L *nidus* nest: for loss of *n-* cf. ADDER]

eye /ī/ *n.* & *v.* ● *n.* **1 a** the organ of sight in humans and other animals. **b** the light-detecting organ in some invertebrates. **2** the eye characterized by the color of the iris (*has blue eyes*). **3** the region around the eye (*eyes red from crying*). **4** a glass or plastic ball serving as an artificial eye. **5** (in *sing.* or *pl.*) sight; the faculty of sight (*demonstrate the eye*; *need perfect eyes to be a pilot*). **6** a particular visual faculty or talent; visual appreciation; perspicacity (*a straight eye*; *cast an expert eye over*). **7 a** (in *sing.* or *pl.*) a look, gaze, or glance, esp. as indicating the disposition of the viewer (*a friendly eye*). **b** (**the eye**) a flirtatious or sexually provocative glance. **8** mental awareness; consciousness. **9** a person or animal, etc., that sees on behalf of another. **10 a** = *electric eye.* **b** = *private eye.* **11** a thing like an eye, esp.: **a** a spot on a peacock's tail. **b** the leaf bud of a potato. **12** the center of something circular, e.g., a flower or target. **13** the relatively calm region at the center of a storm or hurricane. **14** an aperture in an implement, esp. a needle, for the insertion of something, e.g., thread. **15** a ring or loop for a bolt or hook, etc., to pass through. ● *v.tr.* (**eyes, eyed, eyeing** or **eying**) watch or observe closely, esp. admiringly or with curiosity or suspicion. □ **all eyes 1** watching intently. **2** general attention (*all eyes were on us*). **before one's** (or **one's very**) **eyes** right in front of one. **do a person in the eye** esp. *Brit. colloq.* defraud or thwart a person. **eye bath** = EYECUP. **eye-catching** *colloq.* striking; attractive. **eye contact** looking directly into another person's eyes. **an eye for an eye** retaliation in kind (Exodus 21:24). **eye language** the process of communication by the expression of the eyes. **eye level** the level seen by the eyes looking horizontally (*put it at eye level*). **eye mask 1** a covering of soft material saturated with a lotion for refreshing the eyes. **2** a covering for the eyes. **eye-opener** *colloq.* **1** an enlightening experience; an unexpected revelation. **2** an alcoholic drink taken on waking up. **eye rhyme** a correspondence of words in spelling but not in pronunciation (e.g., *love* and *move*). **eyes front** (or **left** or **right**) *Mil.* a command to turn the head in the direction stated. **eye shadow** a colored cosmetic applied to the skin around the eyes. **3** a thing like an eye, esp. a spot on a peacock's tail (cf. EYELET *n.* 3). **eye worm** a nematode worm, *Loa loa*, parasitic on humans and other primates in Central and West Africa. **have one's eye on** wish or plan to procure. **have an eye for 1** be quick to notice. **2** be partial to. **have an eye to** have as one's objective; prudently consider. **have eyes for** be interested in; wish to acquire. **have an eye to** have as one's objective; prudently consider. **hit a**

person in the eye (or **between the eyes**) *colloq.* be very obvious or impressive. **keep an eye on 1** pay attention to. **2** look after; take care of. **keep an eye open** (or **out**) (often foll. by *for*) watch carefully. **keep one's eyes open** (or **peeled** or **skinned**) watch out; be on the alert. **lower one's eyes** look modestly or sheepishly down or away. **make eyes** (or **sheep's eyes**) (foll. by *at*) look amorously or flirtatiously at. **my eye** *sl.* nonsense. **one in the eye** (foll. by *for*) *Brit.* a disappointment or setback. **open a person's eyes** be enlightening or revealing to a person. **raise one's eyes** look upward. **see eye to eye** (often foll. by *with*) be in full agreement. **set eyes on** catch sight of. **take one's eyes off** (usu. in *neg.*) stop watching; stop paying attention to. **under the eye of** under the supervision or observation of. **up to the** (or **one's**) **eyes in 1** deeply engaged or involved in; inundated with (*up to the eyes in work*). **2** to the utmost limit (*mortgaged up to the eyes*). **with one's eyes open** deliberately; with full awareness. **with one's eyes shut** (or **closed**) **1** easily; with little effort. **2** without awareness; unobservant (*goes around with his eyes shut*). **with an eye to** with a view to; prudently considering. **with a friendly** (or **jealous**, etc.) **eye** with a feeling of friendship, jealousy, etc. **with one eye on** directing one's attention partly to. **with one eye shut** *colloq.* easily; with little effort (*could do this with one eye shut*). □□ **eyed** *adj.* (also in *comb.*). **eyeless** *adj.* [OE *ēage* f. Gmc]

■ *n.* **1** eyeball, *archaic or joc.* optic, *poet.* orb. **5** (eye)sight, vision, visual acuity. **6** discernment, perception, taste, judgment, discrimination, percipience, perspicacity, appreciation, sensitivity, comprehension. **7 a** gaze, glance, look, regard, stare. **b** ogle, leer, look, wink, sidelong glance, *colloq.* glad eye. **8** see UNDERSTANDING *n.* 1. **12** see MIDDLE *n.* 1. **13** see HEART 5a. **14, 15** slit, slot; see also APERTURE. see LOOP *n.* ● *v.* watch, observe, contemplate, study, look *or* gaze *or* peer at, look *or* gaze upon, regard, view, inspect, examine, scrutinize, *literary* behold. □ **all eyes** see ALERT *adj.* 1. **eye-catching** see ATTRACTIVE. **an eye for an eye** *lex talionis*, tit for tat, measure for measure; retaliation. **eye-opener** **1** discovery, revelation; see also SURPRISE *n.* 1. **have an eye for 1** see APPRECIATE 1a, c. **2** like, be fond of, be partial to, appreciate, have a liking *or* affection *or* fondness for. **have an eye to** concentrate *or* focus on, be concentrated *or* centered on, pinpoint; see also HEED *v.* **have eyes for** see DESIRE *v.* 1. **keep an eye on 1, 2** see WATCH *v.* 2a, 4; 2b. **keep an eye open** (or **out**) see WATCH *v.* 2a, 4; 2b. **keep one's eyes open** (or **peeled** or **skinned**) see *watch out.* **make eyes** (or **sheep's eyes**) see FLIRT *v.* 1. **my eye** see NONSENSE. **open a person's eyes** see EDUCATE 1, 2. **see eye to eye** see AGREE 1. **set eyes on** see *catch sight of* (SIGHT). **under the eye of** under the supervision *or* observation *or* scrutiny of. **up to the** (or **one's**) **eyes in 1** see DEEP *adj.* 8. **with one's eyes open** see *deliberately* (DELIBERATE). **with one's eyes shut** (or **closed**) **1** see EASILY 1. **2** see BLIND 2. **with an eye to** with a view to, with the aim *or* intention *or* purpose *or* plan *or* idea *or* notion of. **with one eye shut** see EASILY 1.

eyeball /íbawl/ *n.* & *v.* ● *n.* the ball of the eye within the lids and socket. ● *v. sl.* **1** *tr.* look or stare at. **2** *intr.* look or stare. □ **eyeball to eyeball** *colloq.* confronting closely. **to** (or **up to**) **the eyeballs** *colloq.* completely (permeated, soaked, etc.).

● *v.* see LOOK *v.* 1a, 2b.

eyeblack /íblak/ *n. Brit.* = MASCARA.

eyebolt /íbōlt/ *n.* a bolt or bar with an eye at the end for a hook, etc.

eyebright /íbrìt/ *n.* any plant of the genus *Euphrasia*, formerly used as a remedy for weak eyes.

/. . ./ **pronunciation**	● **part of speech**
□ **phrases, idioms, and compounds**	
□□ **derivatives**	■ **synonym section**
cross-references appear in SMALL CAPITALS or *italics*	

eyebrow /íbrow/ *n.* the line of hair growing on the ridge above the eye socket. □ **raise one's eyebrows** show surprise, disbelief, or mild disapproval.

eyecup /íkup/ *n.* a small glass or vessel for applying eyewash to the eye.

eyedropper /ídropər/ *n.* DROPPER *n.* 1.

eyeful /ífŏŏl/ *n.* (*pl.* **-fuls**) *colloq.* **1** a long, steady look. **2** a visually striking person or thing. **3** anything thrown or blown into the eye.

eyeglass /íglas/ *n.* **1 a** a lens for correcting or assisting defective sight. **b** (in *pl.*) a pair of these, usu. set into a frame that rests on the nose and has side pieces that curve over the ears. **2** an eyecup.

■ **1b** (*eyeglasses*) see SPECTACLES.

eyehole /íhŏl/ *n.* a hole to look through.

eyelash /ílash/ *n.* each of the hairs growing on the edges of the eyelids. □ **by an eyelash** by a very small margin.

eyelet /ílit/ *n.* & *v.* ● *n.* **1** a small hole in paper, leather, cloth, etc., for string or rope, etc., to pass through. **2** a metal ring reinforcement for this. **3** a small eye, esp. the ocellus on a butterfly's wing. **4** a form of decoration in embroidery. **5** a small hole for observation, shooting through, etc. ● *v.tr.* (**eyeleted, eyeleting; eyeletted, eyeletting**) provide with eyelets. [ME f. OF *oillet* dimin. of *oil* eye f. L *oculus*]

eyelid /ílid/ *n.* the upper or lower fold of skin closing to cover the eye.

eyeliner /ílinər/ *n.* a cosmetic applied as a line around the eye.

eyepiece /ípees/ *n.* the lens or lenses at the end of a microscope, telescope, etc., to which the eye is applied.

eyeshade /íshayd/ *n.* a device, esp. a visor, to protect the eyes, esp. from strong light.

eyeshot /íshot/ *n.* seeing distance (*out of eyeshot*).
■ see SIGHT *n.* 4.

eyesight /ísit/ *n.* the faculty or power of seeing.
■ see SIGHT *n.* 1a.

eyesore /ísawr/ *n.* a visually offensive or ugly thing, esp. a building.
■ see SIGHT *n.* 7.

eyespot /íspot/ *n.* **1 a** a light-sensitive area on the bodies of some invertebrate animals, e.g., flatworms, starfish, etc.; an ocellus. **b** *Bot.* an area of light-sensitive pigment found in some algae, etc. **2** any of several fungus diseases of plants characterized by yellowish oval spots on the leaves and stems.

eyestalk /ístawk/ *n.* *Zool.* a movable stalk carrying the eye, esp. in crabs, shrimps, etc.

eyestrain /ístrayn/ *n.* fatigue of the (internal or external) muscles of the eye.

eyetooth /ítŏŏth/ *n.* a canine tooth just under or next to the eye, esp. in the upper jaw.

eyewash /íwosh, íwawsh/ *n.* **1** lotion for the eye. **2** *sl.* nonsense; bunkum; pretentious or insincere talk.
■ **1** see WASH *n.* 7, 10. **2** see NONSENSE.

eyewear /íwair/ *n.* spectacles, goggles, or lenses for improving eyesight or protecting the eyes.

eyewitness /íwitnis/ *n.* a person who has personally seen a thing done or happen and can give evidence of it.
■ witness, observer, spectator, viewer, watcher; bystander, onlooker.

eyot *Brit.* var. of AIT.

eyra /áirə/ *n.* *Zool.* a red form of jaguarundi. [Tupi (*e*)*irara*]

eyrie var. of AERIE.

Ezek. *abbr.* Ezekiel (Old Testament).

F¹ /ef/ *n.* (also **f**) (*pl.* **Fs** or **F's**) **1** the sixth letter of the alphabet. **2** *Mus.* the fourth note of the diatonic scale of C major. **3** a grade indicating failure.

F² *abbr.* (also **F.**) **1** Fahrenheit. **2** farad(s). **3** female. **4** *Brit.* fine (pencil lead). **5** *Biol.* filial generation (as F₁ for the first filial generation, F₂ for the second, etc.).

F³ *symb. Chem.* the element fluorine.

f *abbr.* (also **f.**) **1** female. **2** feminine. **3** following page, etc. **4** *Mus.* forte. **5** folio. **6** focal length (cf. F-NUMBER). **7** femto-. **8** filly. **9** foreign. **10** frequency.

fa /faa/ *n.* (also **fah**) *Mus.* **1** (in tonic sol-fa) the fourth note of a major scale. **2** the note F in the fixed-do system. [ME *fa* f. L *famuli*: see GAMUT]

FAA *abbr.* Federal Aviation Administration.

fab /fab/ *adj. colloq.* fabulous; marvelous. [abbr.]
■ see FABULOUS 2.

Fabian /fáybeeən/ *n. & adj.* ● *n.* a member or supporter of the Fabian Society, an organization of socialists aiming at a gradual rather than revolutionary achievement of socialism; founded in England (1884). ● *adj.* **1** relating to or characteristic of the Fabians. **2** employing a cautiously persistent and dilatory strategy to wear out an enemy (*Fabian tactics*). □□ **Fabianism** *n.* **Fabianist** *n.* [L *Fabianus* f. the name of Q. *Fabius* Maximus Cunctator (= delayer), Roman general of the 3rd c. BC, noted for cautious strategies]

fable /fáybəl/ *n. & v.* ● *n.* **1 a** a story, esp. a supernatural one, not based on fact. **b** a tale, esp. with animals as characters, conveying a moral. **2** (*collect.*) myths and legendary tales (*in fable*). **3 a** a false statement; a lie. **b** a thing only supposed to exist. ● *v.* **1** *intr.* tell fictitious tales. **2** *tr.* describe fictitiously. **3** *tr.* (as **fabled** *adj.*) celebrated in fable; famous; legendary. □□ **fabler** /fáyblər/ *n.* [ME f. OF *fabler* f. L *fabulari* f. *fabula* discourse f. *fari* speak]
■ *n.* **1, 2** see MYTH 4. **3** see FABRICATION 3. ● *v.* **3** (**fabled**) see LEGENDARY 3.

fabliau /fábleeō/ *n.* (*pl.* **fabliaux** /-ōz/) a metrical tale in early French poetry, often coarsely humorous. [F f. OF dialect *fabliaux, -ax* pl. of *fablel* dimin. (as FABLE)]

fabric /fábrik/ *n.* **1 a** a woven material; a textile. **b** other material resembling woven cloth. **2** a structure or framework, esp. the walls, floor, and roof of a building. **3** (in abstract senses) the essential structure or essence of a thing (*the fabric of society*). [ME f. F *fabrique* f. L *fabrica* f. *faber* metal worker, etc.]
■ **1** material, cloth; textile. **2** see STRUCTURE *n.* 1b. **3** structure, constitution, construction, makeup, foundation, framework, organization; essence, core, heart.

fabricate /fábrikayt/ *v.tr.* **1** construct or manufacture, esp. from prepared components. **2** invent or concoct (a story, evidence, etc.). **3** forge (a document). □□ **fabricator** *n.* [L *fabricare fabricat-* (as FABRIC)]
■ **1** construct, manufacture, build, erect, frame, raise, put *or* set up, assemble, fashion, form, make, produce. **2** invent, concoct, create, originate, devise, make up, manufacture, hatch, *colloq.* think up, cook up. **3** forge, counterfeit, fake.

fabrication /fábrikáyshən/ *n.* **1** the action or process of manufacturing or constructing something. **2** the invention of a lie, forging of a document, etc. **3** an invention or falsehood; a forgery. [L *fabricatio* (as FABRICATE)]
■ **1** construction, manufacture, building, constructing, erection, framing, putting together, assembly, assemblage, fashioning, formation, forming, making, production. **2** invention, concoction, creation, origination, making up, manufacture, hatching, contrivance. **3** falsehood, lie, tale, fable, untruth, fiction, cock-and-bull story, fairy story, fairy tale, *colloq.* story; forgery, falsification, fake, sham.

fabulist /fábyəlist/ *n.* **1** a composer of fables. **2** a liar. [F *fabuliste* f. L *fabula*: see FABLE]

fabulous /fábyələs/ *adj.* **1** incredible; exaggerated; absurd (*fabulous wealth*). **2** *colloq.* marvelous (*looking fabulous*). **3 a** celebrated in fable. **b** legendary; mythical. □□ **fabulosity** /-lósitee/ *n.* **fabulously** *adv.* **fabulousness** *n.* [F *fabuleux* or L *fabulosus* (as FABLE)]
■ **1** incredible, unbelievable, inconceivable, astounding, astonishing, amazing, fantastic, extraordinary, phenomenal, exaggerated, absurd. **2** marvelous, wonderful, far-out, *colloq.* superb, terrific, great, super, smashing, keen, fab, magic, *sl.* hot, groovy, ace, cool, copacetic, neat. **3** fabled, mythic, mythical, legendary, celebrated, fictitious, fictional, imaginary, fanciful, *literary* storied; storybook, fairy-tale.

façade /fəsaád/ *n.* **1** the face of a building, esp. its principal front. **2** an outward appearance or front, esp. a deceptive one. [F (as FACE)]
■ see FACE *n.* 4e.

face /fays/ *n. & v.* ● *n.* **1** the front of the head from the forehead to the chin. **2 a** the expression of the facial features (*had a happy face*). **b** an expression of disgust; a grimace (*make a face*). **3** composure; coolness; effrontery. **4** the surface of a thing, esp. as regarded or approached, esp.: **a** the visible part of a celestial body. **b** a side of a mountain, etc. (*the north face*). **c** the (usu. vertical) surface of a coal seam, excavation, etc. **d** *Geom.* each surface of a solid. **e** the façade of a building. **f** the plate of a clock or watch bearing the digits, hands, etc. **5 a** the functional or working side of a tool, etc. **b** the distinctive side of a playing card. **c** the obverse of a coin. **6** = TYPEFACE. **7 a** the outward appearance or aspect (*the unacceptable face of capitalism*). **b** outward show; disguise; pretense (*put on a brave face*). **8** a person, esp. conveying some quality or association (*a face from the past; some young faces for a change*). **9** credibility or respect; good reputation; dignity (*lose face*). ● *v.* **1** *tr. & intr.* look or be positioned toward or in a certain direction (*face toward the window; facing the window; the room faces north*). **2** *tr.* be opposite (*facing page 20*). **3** *tr.* **a** meet resolutely or defiantly; confront (*face one's critics*). **b** not shrink from (*face the facts*). **4** *tr.* present itself to; confront (*the problem that faces us; faces us with a problem*). **5** *tr.* **a** cover the surface of (a thing) with a coating, extra layer, etc. **b** put a facing on (a garment). **6** *intr. & tr.* turn or cause to turn in a certain direction. □ **face**

/. . ./ pronunciation	● part of speech
□ phrases, idioms, and compounds	
□□ derivatives	■ synonym section
cross-references appear in SMALL CAPITALS or *italics*	

517

card *Cards* a king, queen, or jack. **face cloth 1** a cloth for washing one's face. **2** *Brit.* a smooth-surfaced woolen cloth. **face cream** a cosmetic cream applied to the face to improve the complexion. **face down** (or **downward**) with the face or surface turned toward the ground, floor, etc. **face a person down** overcome a person by a show of determination or by browbeating. **face facts** (or **the facts**) recognize the truth. **face flannel** *Brit.* = **face cloth** 1. **face-lift 1** (also **face-lifting**) cosmetic surgery to remove wrinkles, etc., by tightening the skin of the face. **2** a procedure to improve the appearance of a thing. **face the music** *colloq.* put up with or stand up to unpleasant consequences, esp. criticism. **face-pack** *Brit.* a preparation used to improve the complexion, spread over the face and removed when dry. **face powder** a cosmetic powder for reducing the shine on the face. **face-saving** preserving one's reputation, credibility, etc. **face to face** (often foll. by *with*) facing; confronting each other. **face up** (or **upward**) with the face or surface turned upward to view. **face up to** accept bravely; confront; stand up to. **face value 1** the nominal value as printed or stamped on money. **2** the superficial appearance or implication of a thing. **have the face** be shameless enough. **in one's** (or **the**) **face 1** straight against one; as one approaches. **2** confronting. **in the face of 1** despite. **2** confronted by. **let's face it** *colloq.* we must be honest and realistic about it. **on the face of it** as it would appear. **put a bold** (or **brave**) **face on it** accept difficulty, etc., cheerfully or with courage. **put one's face on** *colloq.* apply makeup to one's face. **put a good face on** make (a matter) look good. **put a new face on** alter the aspect of. **save face** preserve esteem; avoid humiliation. **save a person's face** enable a person to save face; forbear from humiliating a person. **show one's face** see SHOW. **set one's face against** oppose or resist with determination. **to a person's face** openly in a person's presence. □□ **faced** *adj.* (also in *comb.*). **facing** *adj.* (also in *comb.*). [ME f. OF ult. f. L *facies*]
■ *n.* **1** countenance, physiognomy, *Brit. colloq.* phiz, *literary* visage, *sl.* mug, pan. **2** expression, look, appearance, aspect, *literary* mien. **3** effrontery, boldness, daring, audacity, impudence, coolness, impertinence, presumption, brashness, cheek, *colloq.* brass, nerve, guts, gutsiness, *sl.* gall; composure; see also POISE[1] *n.* 1. **4 e** façade, exterior, front, outside; surface, cover, facing. **7** front, guise, appearance, aspect, look, exterior; mask, veneer, façade, camouflage, pretense, disguise, (false) impression, semblance, masquerade, show. **8** see FIGURE *n.* 2b. **9** credibility, respect, self-respect, dignity, standing, status, reputation, name, honor. ● *v.* **1** look out on *or* over *or* toward, give (out) on to, front *or* to *or* toward *or* upon, overlook. **2** see FRONT *v.* 1, 5a. **3** meet (with), encounter, confront, brave, deal *or* cope with, face up to; appear before; experience, come up against, go up against. **b** confront, brave, deal *or* cope with, face up to. **4** see CHALLENGE *v.* 3a. **5 a** cover, coat, overlay; finish, surface, veneer. **b** overlay; finish. **6** see TURN *v.* 3b. □ **face a person down** confront, intimidate, cow, subdue, overawe, browbeat. **face to face** facing (each other), vis-à-vis, tête-à-tête, à deux, *colloq.* eyeball-to-eyeball. **face up to** accept, admit, acknowledge, allow, confess; confront, stand up to, deal *or* cope with, brave, go up against; bite the bullet; see also FACE *v.* 3a, b above. **in the face of 1** despite, in spite of, notwithstanding. **on the face of it** to all appearances, to outward appearances, seemingly, apparently, as far as can be seen, superficially. **set one's face against** see OPPOSE 1–3. **to a person's face** openly, face to face, directly, brazenly, candidly, frankly.

faceless /fáyslis/ *adj.* **1** without identity; purposely not identifiable. **2** lacking character. **3** without a face. □□ **facelessly** *adv.* **facelessness** *n.*

facer /fáysər/ *n. colloq.* **1** *Brit.* a sudden difficulty or obstacle. **2** a blow in the face. **3** one that faces.

facet /fásit/ *n.* **1** a particular aspect of a thing. **2** one side of

a many-sided body, esp. a flat surface of a cut gem, a bone, etc. **3** one segment of a compound eye. □□ **faceted** *adj.* (also in *comb.*). [F *facette* dimin. (as FACE, -ETTE)]
■ **1** see ASPECT 1a. **2** see SIDE *n.* 1a.

facetiae /fəseeshee-ee/ *n.pl.* pleasantries; witticisms. [L, pl. of *facetia* jest f. *facetus* witty]

facetious /fəseeshəs/ *adj.* **1** characterized by flippancy or inappropriate humor. **2** (of a person) intending to be amusing, esp. inappropriately. □□ **facetiously** *adv.* **facetiousness** *n.* [F *facétieux* f. *facétie* f. L *facetia* jest]
■ **1** see FLIPPANT.

facia var. of FASCIA.

facial /fáyshəl/ *adj.* & *n.* ● *adj.* of or for the face. ● *n.* a beauty treatment for the face. □□ **facially** *adv.* [med.L *facialis* (as FACE)]

-facient /fáyshənt/ *comb. form* forming adjectives and nouns indicating an action or state produced (*abortifacient*). [from or after L *-faciens -entis* part. of *facere* make]

facies /fáyshee-eez, -sheez/ *n.* (*pl.* same) **1** *Med.* the appearance or facial expression of an individual. **2** *Geol.* the character of rock, etc., expressed by its composition, fossil content, etc. [L, = FACE]

facile /fásil/ *adj.* usu. *derog.* **1** easily achieved but of little value. **2** (of speech, writing, etc.) fluent; ready; glib. □□ **facilely** *adv.* **facileness** *n.* [F *facile* or L *facilis* f. *facere* do]
■ **2** see GLIB.

facilitate /fəsílitayt/ *v.tr.* make easy or less difficult or more easily achieved. □□ **facilitation** /-táyshən/ *n.* **facilitative** *adj.* **facilitator** *n.* [F *faciliter* f. It. *facilitare* f. *facile* easy f. L *facilis*]
■ ease, expedite, smooth, assist, aid, help, further, promote, advance.

facility /fəsílitee/ *n.* (*pl.* **-ies**) **1** ease; absence of difficulty. **2** fluency; dexterity; aptitude (*facility of expression*). **3** (esp. in *pl.*) an opportunity, the equipment, or the resources for doing something. **4** a plant, installation, or establishment. **5** *euphem.* (in *pl.*) a (public) toilet. [F *facilité* or L *facilitas* (as FACILE)]
■ **1, 2** ease, fluency, effortlessness, skill, skillfulness, deftness, dexterity, adroitness, ability, aptitude, expertise, expertness, proficiency, mastery, masterfulness, masterliness; efficiency, smoothness, quickness, alacrity, swiftness, speed, *archaic or literary* celerity. **3** (*facilities*) opportunity, potential, capacity; see also APPARATUS. **4** plant, installation, establishment, system, buildings, structure, complex. **5** (*facilities*) lavatory, toilet, powder room, men's room, ladies' room, rest room, privy, *Brit.* WC, water closet, convenience, the ladies, *Brit. colloq.* loo, the Gents, *sl.* john, *Brit sl.* bog.

facing /fáysing/ *n.* **1 a** a layer of material covering part of a garment, etc., for contrast or strength. **b** (in *pl.*) the cuffs, collar, etc., of a military jacket. **2** an outer layer covering the surface of a wall, etc.
■ **1 a** overlay. **2** façade, surface, front, cladding.

facsimile /faksímilee/ *n.* & *v.* ● *n.* **1** an exact copy, esp. of writing, printing, a picture, etc. (often *attrib.*: *facsimile edition*). **2 a** a production of an exact copy of a document, etc., by electronic scanning and transmission of the resulting data (see also FAX). **b** a copy produced in this way. ● *v.tr.* (**facsimiled, facsimileing**) make a facsimile of. □ **in facsimile** as an exact copy. [mod.L f. L *fac* imper. of *facere* make + *simile* neut. of *similis* like]
■ *n.* **1** copy, reproduction, carbon copy, duplicate, replica. **2** photocopy, duplicate, fax, *colloq.* dupe, *propr.* Xerox (copy), Photostat. ● *v.* see DUPLICATE *v.* 2.

fact /fakt/ *n.* **1** a thing that is known to have occurred, to exist, or to be true. **2** a datum of experience (often foll. by an explanatory clause or phrase: *the fact that fire burns*; *the fact of my having seen them*). **3** (usu. in *pl.*) an item of verified information; a piece of evidence. **4** truth; reality. **5** a thing assumed as the basis for argument or inference. □ **before** (or **after**) **the fact** before (or after) the committing of a crime. **a fact of life** something that must be accepted. **facts and figures** precise details. **fact sheet** a paper setting

out relevant information. **the facts of life** information about sexual functions and practices. **in** (or **in point of**) **fact 1** in reality; as a matter of fact. **2** (in summarizing) in short. [L *factum* f. *facere* do]
■ **1** occurrence, event, happening, incident, experience. **2, 4** truth, reality, actuality, certainty. **3** data, information, particular, detail, point, item, factor, inside information, *colloq.* lowdown, info, score, *sl.* poop. **5** see BASIS. □ **facts and figures** see PARTICULAR *n.* **in** (or **in point of**) **fact 1** in reality, as a matter of fact, actually, really, indeed, to be sure, truly, truthfully, factually, *literary* in truth. **2** see *in short* (SHORT).

faction[1] /fákshən/ *n.* **1** a small organized dissenting group within a larger one, esp. in politics. **2** a state of dissension within an organization. [F f. L *factio -onis* f. *facere* fact- do, make]
■ **1** group, cabal, cadre, camp, splinter group, circle, camarilla, clique, set, coterie, lobby, pressure group, junta, ring, *Brit.* ginger group. **2** dissension, disharmony, discord, disagreement, quarreling, infighting, contention, controversy, sedition, intrigue, strife, schism.

faction[2] /fákshən/ *n.* a book, movie, etc., using real events as a basis for a fictional narrative or dramatization. [blend of FACT and FICTION]

-faction /fákshən/ *comb. form* forming nouns of action from verbs in *-fy* (*petrifaction*; *satisfaction*). [from or after L *-factio -factionis* f. *-facere* do, make]

factional /fákshənəl/ *adj.* **1** of or characterized by faction. **2** belonging to a faction. □□ **factionalism** *n.* **factionalize** *v.tr.* & *intr.* **factionally** *adv.* [FACTION[1]]
■ see SECTARIAN *adj.* 1.

factious /fákshəs/ *adj.* of, characterized by, or inclined to faction. □□ **factiously** *adv.* **factiousness** *n.*
■ divisive, conflicting, discordant, contentious, disputatious, argumentative, quarrelsome, seditious, mutinous, refractory, rebellious; at odds, at loggerheads.

factitious /faktíshəs/ *adj.* **1** contrived; not genuine (*factitious value*). **2** artificial; not natural (*factitious joy*). □□ **factitiously** *adv.* **factitiousness** *n.* [L *facticius* f. *facere* fact- do, make]
■ contrived, manufactured, fabricated, engineered, unauthentic; artificial, insincere, unreal, fake, false, bogus, falsified, spurious, sham, simulated, imitation, counterfeit, synthetic, *colloq.* phony; mock.

factitive /fáktitiv/ *adj. Gram.* (of a verb) having a sense of regarding or designating, and taking a complement as well as an object (e.g., *appointed me captain*). [mod.L *factitivus*, irreg. f. L *factitare* frequent. of *facere* fact- do, make]

factoid /fáktoyd/ *n.* & *adj.* ● *n.* **1** an assumption or speculation that is reported and repeated so often that it becomes accepted as fact; a simulated or imagined fact. **2** a trivial fact or news item. ● *adj.* being or having the character of a factoid; containing factoids.

factor /fáktər/ *n.* & *v.* ● *n.* **1** a circumstance, fact, or influence contributing to a result. **2** *Math.* a whole number, etc., that when multiplied with another produces a given number or expression. **3** *Biol.* a gene, etc., determining hereditary character. **4** (foll. by identifying number) *Med.* any of several substances in the blood contributing to coagulation (*factor eight*). **5 a** a business agent; a merchant buying and selling on commission. **b** *Sc.* a land agent or steward. **c** an agent or a deputy. **6** an agent or company that buys a manufacturer's invoices and takes responsibility for collecting the payments due on them; a backer. ● *v.tr.* **1** *Math.* resolve into factors or components. **2** *tr.* sell (one's receivable debts) to a factor. □ **factor analysis** *Statistics* a process by which the relative importance of variables in the study of a sample is assessed by mathematical techniques. □□ **factorable** *adj.* [F *facteur* or L *factor* f. *facere* fact- do, make]
■ *n.* **1** circumstance, fact, ingredient, element, consideration, particular, aspect, influence, determinant, cause. **5 a** agent, representative,

middleman, intermediary, deputy, go-between. **6** banker, financier, backer, moneylender, lender.

factorage /fáktərij/ *n.* **1** commission or charges payable to a factor. **2** the business of a factor.

factorial /faktáwreeəl/ *n.* & *adj. Math.* ● *n.* **1** the product of a number and all the whole numbers below it (*four factorial* = $4 \times 3 \times 2 \times 1$). ¶ Symb.: ! (as in 4!). **2** the product of a series of factors in an arithmetical progression. ● *adj.* of a factor or factorial. □□ **factorially** *adv.*

factorize /fáktərīz/ *v. Math.* **1** *tr.* resolve into factors. **2** *intr.* be capable of resolution into factors. □□ **factorization** *n.*

factory /fáktəree/ *n.* (*pl.* **-ies**) **1** a building or buildings containing equipment for manufacturing machinery or goods. **2** (usu. *derog.*) a place producing mass quantities or a low quality of goods, etc. (*a degree factory*). **3** *hist.* a merchant company's foreign trading station. □ **factory farm** a farm employing factory farming. **factory farming** a system of rearing livestock using industrial or intensive methods. **factory ship** a fishing ship with facilities for immediate processing of the catch. [Port. *feitoria* and LL *factorium*]
■ **1** plant, mill, works, workshop.

factotum /faktótəm/ *n.* (*pl.* **factotums**) an employee who does all kinds of work. [med.L f. L *fac* imper. of *facere* do, make + *totum* neut. of *totus* whole]
■ see SERVANT.

factual /fákch〇〇əl/ *adj.* **1** based on or concerned with fact or facts. **2** actual; true. □□ **factuality** /-ch〇〇álitee/ *n.* **factually** *adv.* **factualness** *n.* [FACT, after *actual*]
■ real, true, actual, authentic, verifiable, genuine, realistic, true to life; faithful, bona fide, accurate, precise; objective, unbiased, unprejudiced, undistorted, unvarnished, straightforward.

factum /fáktəm/ *n.* (*pl.* **factums** or **facta** /-tə/) *Law* **1** an act or deed. **2** a statement of the facts. [F f. L: see FACT]

facture /fákchər/ *n.* the quality or manner of execution of an artwork, etc. [ME f. OF f. L *factura* f. *facere* fact- do, make]

facula /fákyələ/ *n.* (*pl.* **faculae** /-lee/) *Astron.* a bright spot or streak on the sun. □□ **facular** *adj.* **faculous** *adj.* [L, dimin. of *fax facis* torch]

facultative /fákəltaytiv/ *adj.* **1** *Law* enabling an act to take place. **2** that may occur. **3** *Biol.* not restricted to a particular function, mode of life, etc. **4** of a faculty. □□ **facultatively** *adv.* [F *facultatif -ive* (as FACULTY)]

faculty /fákəltee/ *n.* (*pl.* **-ies**) **1** an aptitude or ability for a particular activity. **2** an inherent mental or physical power. **3 a** the teaching staff of a university, college, or secondary school. **b** a department of a university, etc., teaching a specific branch of learning (*faculty of modern languages*). **c** *Brit.* a branch of art or science; those qualified to teach it. **4** the members of a particular profession, esp. medicine. **5** authorization; power conferred by an authority. [ME f. OF *faculté* f. L *facultas -tatis* f. *facilis* easy]
■ **1, 2** aptitude, ability, capacity, capability, skill, talent, flair, knack, gift, genius, cleverness; potential. **3 a** staff, personnel, members; *Brit.* dons. **b** division, department, school. **4** membership; associates, fellows, members. **5** authorization, power, sanction, license, prerogative, privilege, right, permission, liberty.

FAD *abbr.* flavin adenine dinucleotide.

fad /fad/ *n.* **1** a craze. **2** a peculiar notion or idiosyncrasy. □□ **faddish** *adj.* **faddishly** *adv.* **faddishness** *n.* **faddism** *n.* **faddist** *n.* [19th c. (orig. dial.): prob. f. *fidfad* f. FIDDLE-FADDLE]
■ **1** craze, mania, rage, fashion, trend, vogue. **2** see *eccentricity* (ECCENTRIC).

faddy /fádee/ *adj.* (**faddier**, **faddiest**) *Brit.* having arbitrary likes and dislikes, esp. about food. □□ **faddily** *adv.* **faddiness** *n.*

fade /fayd/ *v.* & *n.* ● *v.* **1** *intr.* & *tr.* lose or cause to lose

/.../ **pronunciation**	● **part of speech**
□ **phrases, idioms, and compounds**	
□□ **derivatives**	■ **synonym section**
cross-references appear in SMALL CAPITALS or *italics*	

color. **2** *intr.* lose freshness or strength; (of flowers, etc.) droop; wither. **3** *intr.* **a** (of color, light, etc.) disappear gradually; grow pale or dim. **b** (of sound) grow faint. **4** *intr.* (of a feeling, etc.) diminish. **5** *intr.* (foll. by *away, out*) (of a person, etc.) disappear or depart gradually. **6** *tr.* (foll. by *in, out*) *Cinematog. & Broadcasting* **a** cause (a picture) to come gradually in or out of view on a screen, or to merge into another shot. **b** make (the sound) more or less audible. **7** *intr.* (of a radio signal) vary irregularly in intensity. **8** *intr.* (of a brake) temporarily lose effectiveness. **9** *Golf* **a** *intr.* (of a ball) deviate from a straight course, esp. in a deliberate slice. **b** *tr.* cause (a ball) to fade. ● *n.* the action or an instance of fading. □ **fade away** *colloq.* languish; grow thin. **fade-in** *Cinematog. & Broadcasting* the action or an instance of fading in a picture or sound. **fade-out 1** *colloq.* disappearance; death. **2** *Cinematog. & Broadcasting* the action or an instance of fading out a picture or sound. □□ **fadeless** *adj.* **fader** *n.* (in sense 6 of *v.*). [ME f. OF *fader* f. *fade* dull, insipid prob. ult. f. L *fatuus* silly + *vapidus* VAPID]

■ *v.* **1, 3a** (grow) dim *or* pale, cloud (over); grow faint, blanch; discolor. **2, 3b** ebb, flag, fade away, wane, waste away, diminish, dwindle, decline, languish, deteriorate; die out *or* away, peter out *or* away; droop, wilt, wither, shrivel, perish. **4** see DIMINISH 1. **6 a** see MERGE. **9** see TURN *v.* 3b. ● *n.* see DECREASE *n.* □ **fade away** see FLAG[1] *v.* 1a, WASTE *v.* 4. **fade-out 1** see PASSING *n.*

fadge /faj/ *n. Austral. & NZ* **1** a limp package of wool. **2** a loosely packed wool bale. [16th-c. Engl. dial.: orig. uncert.]

faeces *Brit.* var. of FECES.

faerie /fáiree/ *n.* (also **faery**) *archaic* **1** Fairyland; the fairies, esp. as represented by Spenser (*the Faerie Queene*). **2** (*attrib.*) visionary; imagined. [var. of FAIRY]

Faeroese /fáirō-éez/ *adj. & n.* (also **Faroese**) ● *adj.* of or relating to the Faeroes, an island group in the N. Atlantic between Norway and Iceland. ● *n.* (*pl.* same) **1** a native of the Faeroes; a person of Faeroese descent. **2** the Norse language of this people.

faff /faf/ *v. & n. Brit. colloq.* ● *v.intr.* (often foll. by *about, around*) fuss; dither. ● *n.* a fuss. [imit.]

fag[1] /fag/ *n. & v.* ● *n.* **1** esp. *Brit. colloq.* a piece of drudgery; a wearisome or unwelcome task. **2** *sl.* a cigarette. **3** *Brit.* (at public schools) a junior pupil who runs errands for a senior. ● *v.* (**fagged, fagging**) **1** *colloq.* **a** *tr.* (often foll. by *out*) tire out; exhaust. **b** *intr. Brit.* toil. **2** *intr. Brit.* (in public schools) act as a fag. **3** *tr. Naut.* (often foll. by *out*) fray (the end of a rope, etc.). □ **fag end** *sl.* **1** an inferior or useless remnant. **2** *Brit.* a cigarette butt. [orig. unkn.: cf. FLAG[1]]

■ . **1 a** tire (out), exhaust, wear out, weary, fatigue, *colloq.* poop. □ **fag end 1** see REMNANT 2.

fag[2] /fag/ *n. sl.* often *offens.* a male homosexual. [abbr. of FAG-GOT]

faggot /fágət/ *n.* **1** *sl. derog.* **a** often *offens.* a male homosexual. **b** *Brit.* an unpleasant woman. **2** *Brit.* (usu. in *pl.*) a ball or roll of seasoned chopped liver, etc., baked or fried. **3** a bunch of herbs. □□ **faggoty** *adj.* [ME f. OF *fagot*, of uncert. orig.]

fagoting /fágəting/ *n.* (also **faggoting**) **1** embroidery in which threads are fastened together like a fagot. **2** the joining of materials in a similar manner.

fagot /fágət/ *n. & v.* (also **faggot**) **1** a bundle of sticks or twigs bound together as fuel. **2** a bundle of iron rods for heat treatment. ● *v.tr.* (**fagoted, fagoting**) **1** bind in or make into faggots. **2** join by fagoting (see FAGOTING).

fah var. of FA.

Fahr. *abbr.* Fahrenheit.

Fahrenheit /fárənhīt/ *adj.* of or measured on a scale of temperature on which water freezes at 32° and boils at 212° under standard conditions. [G. *Fahrenheit*, Ger. physicist d. 1736]

faience /fī-óns, fay-/ *n.* decorated and glazed earthenware and porcelain, e.g., delft or majolica. [F *faïence* f. *Faenza* in Italy]

fail /fayl/ *v. & n.* ● *v.* **1** *intr.* not succeed (*failed in persuading; failed to qualify; tried but failed*). **2 a** *tr. & intr.* be unsuc-

cessful in (an examination, test, interview, etc.); be rejected as a candidate. **b** *tr.* (of a commodity, etc.) not pass (a test of quality). **c** *tr.* reject (a candidate, etc.); adjudge or grade as unsuccessful. **3** *intr.* be unable to; neglect to; choose not to (*I fail to see the reason; he failed to appear*). **4** *tr.* disappoint; let down; not serve when needed. **5** *intr.* (of supplies, crops, etc.) be or become lacking or insufficient. **6** *intr.* become weaker; cease functioning; break down (*her health is failing; the engine has failed*). **7** *intr.* **a** (of an enterprise) collapse; come to nothing. **b** become bankrupt. ● *n.* a failure in an examination or test. □ **fail-safe** reverting to a safe condition in the event of a breakdown, etc. **without fail** for certain; whatever happens. [ME f. OF *faillir* (v.), *fail(l)e* (n.) ult. f. L *fallere* deceive]

■ *v.* **1, 2a** be unsuccessful (in); not succeed; come to grief; fall through, come to naught *or* nothing, founder, run aground, miscarry, abort, go wrong, misfire, meet with disaster, *colloq.* go up in smoke, *sl.* flop; *colloq.* flunk, go belly up; fall short, be (found) lacking *or* wanting, be deficient, be *or* prove inadequate. **2 c** see REJECT *v.* 1. **4** disappoint, let down, dissatisfy. **5** see *run out* 1. **6** weaken, decline, wane, diminish, deteriorate, dwindle, flag, ebb, sink, languish, disappear, fade *or* die (away); give out, peter out, stop. **7 a** see COLLAPSE *v.* **b** go bankrupt, crash, go out of business, go under, go into receivership, become insolvent, close up, close down, cease operation(s), *Brit.* go to the wall, *colloq.* fold (up), go broke, go bust. □ **without fail** see *for a certainty* (CERTAINTY).

failed /fayld/ *adj.* **1** unsuccessful; not good enough (*a failed actor*). **2** weak; deficient; broken down (*a failed crop; a failed battery*).

■ **1** see UNSUCCESSFUL.

failing /fáyling/ *n. & prep.* ● *n.* a fault or shortcoming; a weakness, esp. in character. ● *prep.* in default of; if not.

■ *n.* fault, shortcoming, weakness, flaw, defect, foible, weak point *or* spot, blind spot, imperfection. ● *prep.* in default of, in the absence of, without, *archaic or joc.* sans.

failure /fáylyər/ *n.* **1** lack of success; failing. **2** an unsuccessful person, thing, or attempt. **3** nonperformance; nonoccurrence. **4** breaking down or ceasing to function (*heart failure; engine failure*). **5** running short of supply, etc. **6** bankruptcy; collapse. [earlier *failer* f. AF, = OF *faillir* FAIL]

■ **1** see IMPERFECTION 2. **2** incompetent, *colloq.* lemon; also-ran, loser, nonentity, *colloq.* nonstarter, *sl.* flop, dud, dead duck; washout, lead balloon, *Brit. colloq.* damp squib, *Austral. colloq.* gutzer. **3** nonperformance, neglect, dereliction; default, remissness, failing, deficiency; nonoccurrence. **4** breakdown, collapse, decline, failing, decay, deterioration, loss. **5** see SLACK[1] *n.* 2. **6** bankruptcy, collapse, ruin, insolvency, crash, *colloq.* folding.

fain /fayn/ *adj. & adv. archaic* ● *predic.adj.* (foll. by *to* + infin.) **1** willing under the circumstances to. **2** left with no alternative but to. ● *adv.* gladly (esp. *would fain*). [OE *fægen* f. Gmc]

fainéant /fáyneeənt, faynáyoN/ *n. & adj.* ● *n.* an idle or ineffective person. ● *adj.* idle; inactive. □□ **fainéancy** /-ənsee/ *n.* [F f. *fait* does + *néant* nothing]

faint /faynt/ *adj., v., & n.* ● *adj.* **1** indistinct; pale; dim; quiet; not clearly perceived. **2** (of a person) weak or dizzy; inclined to faint. **3** slight; remote; inadequate (*a faint chance*). **4** feeble; halfhearted (*faint praise*). **5** timid (*a faint heart*). ● *v.intr.* **1** lose consciousness. **2** become faint. ● *n.* a sudden loss of consciousness; fainting. □ **faint-hearted** cowardly; timid. **faint-heartedly** in a faint-hearted manner. **faint-heartedness** cowardliness; timidity. **not have the faintest** *colloq.* have no idea. □□ **faintness** *n.* [ME f. OF, past part. of *faindre* FEIGN]

■ *adj.* **1** indistinct, pale, dim, feeble, weak, subdued, flickering, blurred, ill-defined, blurry, dull, vague, muzzy, hazy; faded; imperceptible, indiscernible, unclear; low, soft, quiet, slight, hushed, muffled, muted, stifled, inaudible. **2** weak, giddy, dizzy, light-headed, unsteady, *colloq.* woozy. **3** see REMOTE 4, INADEQUATE 1. **4** see FEEBLE 2. **5** see TIMID. ● *v.* **1** lose consciousness, pass out, black out, collapse, keel over, *literary* swoon. **2** see SUBSIDE 1. ● *n.* loss of consciousness, blackout, collapse, *Med.* syncope, *literary* swoon. □ **faint-hearted** cowardly, weak, feeble, timorous, afraid, frightened, scared, faint, lily-livered, chicken, chickenhearted, chicken-livered, *colloq.* yellow, yellow-bellied; timid, pusillanimous, shy, diffident. **not have the faintest** have no idea, *colloq.* not have a clue; (*I haven't the faintest*) see ask me another.

faintly /fáyntlee/ *adv.* **1** very slightly (*faintly amused*). **2** indistinctly; feebly.

fair[1] /fair/ *adj., adv., n.,* & *v.* ● *adj.* **1** just; unbiased; equitable; in accordance with the rules. **2** blond; light or pale in color or complexion. **3 a** of (only) moderate quality or amount; average. **b** considerable; satisfactory (*a fair chance of success*). **4** (of weather) fine and dry; (of the wind) favorable. **5** clean; clear; unblemished (*fair copy*). **6** beautiful; attractive. **7** *archaic* kind; gentle. **8 a** specious (*fair speeches*). **b** complimentary (*fair words*). **9** *Austral.* & *NZ* complete; unquestionable. **10** unobstructed; open. ● *adv.* **1** in a fair manner (*play fair*). **2** *Brit.* exactly; completely (*was hit fair on the jaw*). ● *n.* **1** a fair thing. **2** *archaic* a beautiful woman. ● *v.* **1** *tr.* make (the surface of a ship, aircraft, etc.) smooth and streamlined. **2** *intr. dial.* (often foll. by *off, up*) (of the weather) become fair. □ **fair and square** *adv.* & *adj.* **1** exactly. **2** straightforward; honest; aboveboard. **a fair deal** equitable treatment. **Fair Deal** a Democratic Party social program during the administration of Pres. Harry Truman. **fair dos** /dooz/ *Brit. colloq.* fair shares. **fair enough** *colloq.* that is reasonable or acceptable. **fair game** a thing or person one may legitimately pursue, exploit, etc. **fair-minded** just; impartial. **fair-mindedly** justly; impartially. **fair-mindedness** a sense of justice; impartiality. **fair play** reasonable treatment or behavior. **the fair sex** women. **fair's fair** *colloq.* all involved should act fairly. **fair-spoken** courteous. **fair-weather friend** a friend or ally who is unreliable in times of difficulty. **in a fair way to** likely to. □□ **fairish** *adj.* **fairness** *n.* [OE *fæger* f. Gmc]

■ *adj.* **1** just, equitable, unbiased, impartial, fair-minded, unprejudiced, objective, disinterested, evenhanded; square, fair and square, honest, straightforward, aboveboard, upright, proper, honorable, lawful, legitimate, trustworthy. **2** blond(e), fair-haired, flaxen-haired, towheaded, tow-colored; light, pale, light-complexioned, peaches and cream. **3 a** see MEDIOCRE 1. **b** considerable, satisfactory, adequate, respectable, pretty good, tolerable, passable, average, decent, reasonable, middling, mediocre, indifferent, *colloq.* OK, so-so, *comme ci, comme ça*, all right, not bad. **4** fine, dry, sunny, bright, clear, cloudless, pleasant, halcyon; favorable, benign. **5** clean, clear, unblemished, spotless, immaculate. **6** beautiful, attractive, pretty, lovely, comely, good-looking, handsome, *literary* pulchritudinous, *poet.* beauteous. **7** see GENTLE *adj.* 1. **8 a** see SPECIOUS. **b** civil, courteous, polite, gracious, complimentary, agreeable. **10** unobstructed, open, clear, free. ● *adv.* **1** see FAIRLY 1. □ **fair and square** (*adv.* & *adj.*) **1** see EXACTLY 1. **2** see HONEST 3. **fair-minded** see IMPARTIAL. **fair-mindedly** see FAIRLY 1. **fair-mindedness** see *objectivity* (OBJECTIVE). **fair play** see JUSTICE 1–3. **the fair sex** see WOMAN 2. **fair-spoken** see COURTEOUS.

fair[2] /fair/ *n.* **1** a gathering of stalls, amusements, etc., for public (usu. outdoor) entertainment. **2** a periodical gathering for the sale of goods, often with entertainments. **3** an exhibition of farm products, usu. held annually, with competitions, entertainments, etc. **4** an exhibition, esp. to promote particular products. [ME f. OF *feire* f. LL *feria* sing. f. L *feriae* holiday]

■ **1** fête, festival, carnival. **2** market, fête, bazaar, mart, kermis. **4** exhibition, exposition, show, exhibit.

fairground /fáirgrownd/ *n.* an outdoor area where a fair is held.

fairing[1] /fáiring/ *n.* **1** a streamlining structure added to a ship, aircraft, vehicle, etc. **2** the process of streamlining. [FAIR[1] *v.* 1 + -ING[1]]

fairing[2] /fáiring/ *n. Brit. archaic* a present bought at a fair.

Fair Isle /fáir íl/ *n.* (also *attrib.*) a piece of clothing knitted in a characteristic multicolored design. [*Fair Isle* in the Shetlands, where the design was first devised]

fairlead /fáirleed/ *n. Naut.* a device to guide rope, etc., e.g., to prevent cutting or chafing.

fairly /fáirlee/ *adv.* **1** in a fair manner; justly. **2** moderately; acceptably (*fairly good*). **3** to a noticeable degree (*fairly narrow*). **4** utterly; completely (*fairly beside himself*). **5** actually (*fairly jumped for joy*).

■ **1** justly, equitably, properly, honestly, impartially, objectively; fair. **2** moderately, acceptably, tolerably, passably, quite, rather, sufficiently, adequately, *colloq.* pretty. **3** see SOMEWHAT *adv.* **4** utterly, completely, absolutely, totally, positively. **5** actually, veritably, really, positively.

fairwater /fáirwawtər, -wotər/ *n.* a structure on a ship, etc., assisting its passage through water.

fairway /fáirway/ *n.* **1** a navigable channel; a regular course or track of a ship. **2** the part of a golf course between a tee and its green, kept free of rough grass.

fairy /fáiree/ *n.* & *adj.* ● *n.* (*pl.* **-ies**) **1** a small imaginary being with magical powers. **2** *sl. derog.* a male homosexual. ● *adj.* of fairies; fairylike; delicate; small. □ **fairy cake** *Brit.* a small individual frosted sponge cake. **fairy cycle** *Brit.* a small bicycle for a child. **fairy godmother** a benefactress. **fairy ring** a ring of mushrooms or darker grass caused by fungi. **fairy tale** (or **story**) **1** a tale about fairies or other fantastic creatures. **2** an incredible story; a fabrication. □□ **fairylike** *adj.* [ME f. OF *faerie* f. *fae* FAY]

■ *n.* **1** see IMP *n.* 2.

fairyland /fáireeland/ *n.* **1** the imaginary home of fairies. **2** an enchanted region.

■ dreamland, wonderland, never-never land, paradise, cloudland, cloud-cuckoo-land, Shangri-la.

fait accompli /fet aakawɴplee´, -komplee´/ *n.* a thing that has been done and is past arguing about or altering. [F]

faith /fayth/ *n.* **1** complete trust or confidence. **2** firm belief, esp. without logical proof. **3 a** a system of religious belief (*the Christian faith*). **b** belief in religious doctrines. **c** spiritual apprehension of divine truth apart from proof. **d** things believed or to be believed. **4** duty or commitment to fulfill a trust, promise, etc.; obligation; allegiance (*keep faith*). **5** (*attrib.*) concerned with a supposed ability to cure by faith rather than treatment (*faith healing*). □ **bad faith** intent to deceive. **good faith** honesty or sincerity of intention. **faith healer** one who uses religious faith and prayer to heal. [ME f. AF *fed* f. OF *feid* f. L *fides*]

■ **1, 2** belief, trust, confidence; certainty, conviction, certitude. **3 a** religion, creed, persuasion; teaching, doctrine, dogma; denomination, sect. **b, c** see BELIEF. **4** duty, commitment, obligation, promise; allegiance, faithfulness, loyalty, fidelity, devotion, consecration, dedication, fealty, obedience. □ **bad faith** see CANT[1] *n.* 1. **good faith** see *sincerity* (SINCERE).

faithful /fáythfool/ *adj.* **1** showing faith. **2** (often foll. by *to*) loyal; trustworthy; constant. **3** accurate; true to fact (*a faithful account*). **4** thorough in performing one's duty; conscientious. **5** (**the Faithful**) the believers in a religion, esp. Christianity or Islam. □□ **faithfulness** *n.*

■ **2** loyal, true, constant, devoted, dedicated; steadfast, staunch, *archaic* trusty; trustworthy, reliable, dependable; trusted. **3** accurate, close, exact, precise, perfect; literal; true, valid. **4** conscientious, dutiful, scrupulous, careful, meticulous, thorough, punctilious,

---

/. . ./ **pronunciation**	● **part of speech**
□ **phrases, idioms, and compounds**	
□□ **derivatives**	■ **synonym section**
cross-references appear in SMALL CAPITALS or *italics*	

finicky, finical, fastidious, rigorous, rigid, severe, particular.

faithfully /fáythfŏŏlee/ adv. in a faithful manner. □ **yours faithfully** a formula for ending a business or formal letter.
■ see *consistently* (CONSISTENT), EXACTLY 1.

faithless /fáythlis/ adj. **1** false; unreliable; disloyal. **2** without religious faith. □□ **faithlessly** adv. **faithlessness** n.
■ **1** false, insincere, hypocritical, untrustworthy, crooked, unscrupulous, *colloq.* shifty; unreliable; disloyal, unfaithful, inconstant, fickle, treacherous, traitorous, perfidious. **2** skeptical, doubting, unbelieving, disbelieving, agnostic, atheistic, atheistical, freethinking.

fajitas /faaheétəs, fə-/ n.pl. *Mexican Cookery* thin strips of fried or broiled meat, usu. seasoned with salsa. [Amer. Sp., pl. of *fajita* little sash, f. Sp. *faja* belt, sash, strip]

fake¹ /fayk/ n., adj., & v. ● n. **1** a thing or person that is not genuine. **2** a trick. **3** *Sport* a feint. ● adj. counterfeit; not genuine. ● v.tr. **1** make (a false thing) appear genuine; forge; counterfeit. **2** make a pretense of having (a feeling, illness, etc.). **3** *Sport* feint. **4** improvise (*I'm not exactly sure, but I can fake it.*) □□ **faker** n. **fakery** n. [obs. *feak, feague* thrash f. G *fegen* sweep, thrash]
■ n. **1** forgery, imitation, counterfeit; sham; faker, impostor, charlatan, fraud, mountebank, cheat, humbug, quack, pretender, *colloq.* phony. **2** see HOAX n. ● adj. counterfeit, forged, fraudulent; imitation, pinchbeck; false, bogus; sham, spurious, factitious, *colloq.* phony. ● v. **1** forge, counterfeit, fabricate, manufacture; doctor, tamper with, falsify, alter. **2** pretend, feign, make a pretense of, dissemble, sham, simulate, affect.

fake² /fayk/ n. & v. *Naut.* ● n. one loop of a coil of rope. ● v.tr. coil (rope). [ME: cf. Scottish *faik* fold]

fakir /fəkéer, fáykeer/ n. (also **faquir**) a Muslim or Hindu religious mendicant or ascetic. [Arab. *fakīr* needy man]

falafel /fəláafəl/ n. (also **felafel**) (in Near Eastern countries) a spicy dish of fried patties made from mashed chick peas or beans. [Arab. *falāfil*]

Falange /fálánj/ n. the Fascist movement in Spain, founded in 1933. □□ **Falangism** n. **Falangist** n. [Sp., = PHALANX]

falcate /fálkayt/ adj. *Anat.* curved like a sickle. [L *falcatus* f. *falx falcis* sickle]

falchion /fáwlchən/ n. *hist.* a broad curved sword with a convex edge. [ME *fauchoun* f. OF *fauchon* ult. f. L *falx falcis* sickle]

falciform /fálsifawrm/ adj. *Anat.* curved like a sickle. [L *falx falcis* sickle]

falcon /fálkən, fáwl-/ n. **1** any diurnal bird of prey of the family Falconidae, having long pointed wings, and sometimes trained to hunt small game for sport. **2** (in falconry) a female falcon (cf. TERCEL). [ME f. OF *faucon* f. LL *falco -onis*, perh. f. L *falx* scythe or f. Gmc]

falconer /fálkənər, fáwl-/ n. **1** a keeper and trainer of hawks. **2** a person who hunts with hawks. [ME f. AF *fauconer*, OF *fauconier* (as FALCON)]

falconet /fálkənit, fáwl-/ n. **1** *hist.* a light cannon. **2** *Zool.* a small falcon. [sense 1 f. It. *falconetto* dimin. of *falcone* FALCON: sense 2 f. FALCON + -ET¹]

falconry /fálkənree, fáwl-/ n. the breeding and training of hawks; the sport of hawking. [F *fauconnerie* (as FALCON)]

falderal /fáldəral/ n. (also **folderol** /fóldərol/) **1** a gewgaw or trifle. **2 a** a nonsensical refrain in a song. **b** nonsense. [perh. f. *falbala* trimming on a dress]

faldstool /fáwldstŏŏl/ n. **1** a bishop's backless folding chair. **2** a small movable desk for kneeling at prayer. [OE *fældestōl* f. med.L *faldistolium* f. WG (as FOLD¹, STOOL)]

fall /fawl/ v. & n. ● v.intr. (*past* **fell** /fel/; *past part.* **fallen** /fáwlən/) **1 a** go or come down freely; descend rapidly from a higher to a lower level (*fell from the top floor; rain was falling*). **b** drop or be dropped (*supplies fell by parachute; the curtain fell*). **2 a** (often foll. by *over* or *down*) cease to stand; come suddenly to the ground from loss of balance, etc. **b** collapse forward or downward, esp. of one's own volition (*fell into my arms*). **3** become detached and descend or dis-

appear. **4** take a downward direction: **a** (of hair, clothing, etc.) hang down. **b** (of ground, etc.) slope. **c** (foll. by *into*) (of a river, etc.) discharge into. **5 a** find a lower level; sink lower. **b** subside; abate. **6** (of a barometer, thermometer, etc.) show a lower reading. **7** occur; become apparent or present (*darkness fell*). **8** decline; diminish (*demand is falling; standards have fallen*). **9 a** (of the face) show dismay or disappointment. **b** (of the eyes or a glance) look downward. **10 a** lose power or status (*the government will fall*). **b** lose esteem, moral integrity, etc. **11** commit sin; yield to temptation. **12** take or have a particular direction or place (*his eye fell on me; the accent falls on the first syllable*). **13 a** find a place; be naturally divisible (*the subject falls into three parts*). **b** (foll. by *under, within*) be classed among. **14** occur at a specified time (*Easter falls early this year*). **15** come by chance or duty (*it fell to me to answer*). **16 a** pass into a specified condition (*fall into decay; fell ill*). **b** become (*fall asleep*). **17 a** (of a position, etc.) be overthrown or captured; succumb to attack. **b** be defeated; fail. **18** die (*fall in battle*). **19** (foll. by *on, upon*) **a** attack. **b** meet with. **c** embrace or embark on avidly. **20** (foll. by *to* + verbal noun) begin (*fell to wondering*). **21** (foll. by *to*) lapse; revert (*revenues fall to the state*). ● n. **1** the act or an instance of falling; a sudden rapid descent. **2** that which falls or has fallen, e.g., snow, rocks, etc. **3** the recorded amount of rainfall, etc. **4** a decline or diminution; depreciation in price, value, demand, etc. **5** overthrow; downfall (*the fall of Rome*). **6 a** a succumbing to temptation. **b** (**the Fall**) the biblical sin of Adam and its consequences, as described in Genesis. **7** (of material, land, light, etc.) a downward direction; a slope. **8** (also **Fall**) autumn. **9** (esp. in *pl.*) a waterfall, cataract, or cascade. **10** *Mus.* a cadence. **11 a** a wrestling bout; a throw in wrestling that keeps the opponent on the ground for a specified time. **b** a controlled act of falling, esp. as a stunt or in judo, etc. **12 a** the birth of young of certain animals. **b** the number of young born. **13** a rope of a hoisting tackle. □ **fall about** *Brit. colloq.* be helpless, esp. with laughter. **fall apart** (or **to pieces**) **1** break into pieces. **2** (of a situation, etc.) disintegrate; be reduced to chaos. **3** lose one's capacity to cope. **fall away 1** (of a surface) incline abruptly. **2** become few or thin; gradually vanish. **3** desert; revolt; abandon one's principles. **fall back** retreat. **fall back on** have recourse to in difficulty. **fall behind 1** be outstripped by one's competitors, etc.; lag. **2** be in arrears. **fall down** (often foll. by *on*) *colloq.* fail; perform poorly; fail to deliver (payment, etc.). **fall flat** fail to achieve expected success or evoke a desired response. **fall for** *colloq.* **1** be captivated or deceived by. **2** yield to the charms or merits of. **fall foul of** come into conflict with; quarrel with. **fall guy** *sl.* **1** an easy victim. **2** a scapegoat. **fall in 1 a** take one's place in military formation. **b** (as *int.*) the order to do this. **2** collapse inward. **falling star** a meteor. **fall in love** see LOVE. **fall into line 1** take one's place in the ranks. **2** conform or collaborate with others. **fall into place** begin to make sense or cohere. **fall in with 1** meet or become involved with by chance. **2** agree with; accede to; humor. **3** coincide with. **fall off 1** (of demand, etc.) decrease; deteriorate. **2** withdraw. **fall out 1** quarrel. **2** (of the hair, teeth, etc.) become detached. **3** *Mil.* come out of formation. **4** result; come to pass; occur. **fall out of** gradually discontinue (a habit, etc.). **fall over oneself** *colloq.* **1** be eager or competitive. **2** be awkward; stumble through haste, confusion, etc. **fall short 1** be or become deficient or inadequate. **2** (of a missile, etc.) not reach its target. **fall short of** fail to reach or obtain. **fall through** fail; come to nothing; miscarry. **fall to** begin an activity, e.g., eating or working. [OE *fallan, feallan* f. Gmc]
■ v. **1 a** descend, plummet, plunge, dive, nosedive; come down, cascade. **b** drop (down), come down. **2 a** tumble, topple (over *or* down), keel over; trip, stumble, overbalance. **b** collapse, slump, drop. **4 a** see HANG v. 10. **b** slope (away *or* down), fall away. **5 a** see SUBSIDE 4, SINK v. 1. **b** see SUBSIDE 1. **6** see DROP v. 8a. **7, 14** see OCCUR 1. **8** decline; come *or* go down, (become) lower, drop, sink; fall *or* drop off, decrease, diminish, dwindle, subside. **10 a** see *give way* 1 (WAY). **11** see

SIN[1] v. 1. **16** see BECOME 1. **17** be overthrown, be captured, be taken, be defeated *or* conquered, be lost, be destroyed; succumb, surrender, yield, give up *or* in, capitulate. **18** die, perish, be killed, *literary or joc.* be slain. **19** (*fall on* or *upon*) a attack, assault, assail, set upon. **b** see MEET[1] v. 1. **c** see EMBARK 2. **20** (*fall to*) see COMMENCE. **21** (*fall to*) see REVERT. ● *n.* **1** descent, drop, dive, nosedive, plunge, tumble. **2** covering, coating, layer. **4** decline, diminution, decrease, downturn, downswing, drop, drop off, lowering, sinking, abatement, slump, collapse; depreciation. **5** overthrow, downfall, capture, taking, seizure, defeat, conquest, ruin, destruction; surrender, capitulation, submission; decline, collapse, eclipse. **6 a** see SIN[1]. **7** slope, sloping, drop, descent; decline. **9** cataract, cascade; see also WATERFALL. □ **fall apart** (or **to pieces**)**1** break into pieces, disintegrate, break apart, fragment, shatter. **2** collapse, break up; see also DISINTEGRATE. **3** disintegrate, crumble, go to pieces, collapse, have a nervous breakdown. **fall away 1** see INCLINE v. 3, 4. **2** see DISAPPEAR. **3** see REVOLT v. 1a. **fall back** retreat, withdraw, draw back; retire. **fall back on** have recourse to, rely or depend on, rely *or* depend upon, return to, count on *or* upon, resort to, call on *or* upon, make use of, use, employ. **fall behind 1** lag, trail (behind), drop back *or* behind *or* to the rear. **2** be in arrears, be behind. **fall down** be found wanting *or* lacking, be unsuccessful, be *or* prove inadequate, be *or* prove disappointing; see also FAIL v. 1, 2a. **fall flat** collapse, fail, *sl.* flop, bomb, go down like a lead balloon. **fall for 1** be captivated *or* deceived by, be fooled *or* duped *or* taken in by, swallow, *sl.* be a sucker for, be a patsy for. **2** fall in love with, become infatuated with. **fall guy 1** see FOOL[1] n. 3. **2** see SCAPEGOAT n. **fall in 2** collapse (inward), sink inward; see also *cave in* 1a (CAVE). **fall into line 1** see *line up* 1 (LINE[1]). **2** see CONFORM 2. **fall into place** see *add up* 3. **fall in with 1** become associated *or* allied with, befriend, join, associate with. **2** agree with, go along with, concur with, support, accept; cooperate with; accede to; humor. **fall off 1** decrease, diminish, deteriorate; see also DECLINE v. 1, 7. **2** see WITHDRAW 5. **fall out 1** quarrel, disagree, differ, clash, squabble, wrangle, dispute, fight. **4** see RESULT v. 1. **fall out of** see DISCONTINUE. **fall over oneself 1** see RUSH v. 1. **2** see STUMBLE v. 1. **fall short 1** be *or* prove deficient, be *or* prove inadequate, be *or* prove insufficient, be *or* prove lacking, be *or* prove disappointing; disappoint, fail. **fall through** come to nothing *or* naught, miscarry, die, *colloq.* fizzle (out); see also FAIL v. 1, 2a. **fall to** begin, start, *formal* commence; get moving, *colloq.* get the show on the road, get cracking, get a move on, move it, *sl.* get a wiggle on.

fallacy /fálasee/ *n.* (*pl.* **-ies**) **1** a mistaken belief, esp. based on unsound argument. **2** faulty reasoning; misleading or unsound argument. **3** *Logic* a flaw that vitiates an argument. □□ **fallacious** /fəláyshəs/ *adj.* **fallaciously** *adv.* **fallaciousness** *n.* [L *fallacia* f. *fallax -acis* deceiving f. *fallere* deceive] ■ **1, 2** misconception, misjudgment, miscalculation, mistake, error; non sequitur, *Logic* paralogism. □□ **fallacious** see UNSOUND 3a.

fallback /fáwlbak/ *n.* **1** (also *attrib.*) an alternative resource, as in an emergency. **2** emergency, esp. *Brit.* (of wages) the minimum paid when no work is available.

fallen *past part.* of FALL v. ● *adj.* **1** (*attrib.*) having lost one's honor or reputation. **2** killed in war. □□ **fallenness** *n.* ■ **2** see *lost* (LOSE 14b).

fallfish /fáwlfish/ *n.* a N. American freshwater fish like the chub.

fallible /fálibəl/ *adj.* **1** capable of making mistakes. **2** liable to be erroneous. □□ **fallibility** *n.* **fallibly** *adv.* [med.L *fallibilis* f. L *fallere* deceive]

falloff /fáwlawf/ *n.* a decrease, deterioration, withdrawal, etc.

Fallopian tube /fəlṓpeeən/ *n. Anat.* either of two tubes in female mammals along which ova travel from the ovaries to the uterus. [*Fallopius*, Latinized name of G. *Fallopio*, It. anatomist d. 1562]

fallout /fáwlowt/ *n.* **1** radioactive debris caused by a nuclear explosion or accident. **2** the adverse side effects of a situation, etc. ■ **2** see UPSHOT.

fallow[1] /fálō/ *adj., n.,* & *v.* ● *adj.* **1 a** (of land) plowed and harrowed but left unsown for a year. **b** uncultivated. **2** (of an idea, etc.) potentially useful but not yet in use. **3** inactive. **4** (of a sow) not pregnant. ● *n.* fallow or uncultivated land. ● *v.tr.* break up (land) for sowing or to destroy weeds. □□ **fallowness** *n.* [ME f. OE *fealh* (n.), *fealgian* (v.)]

fallow[2] /fálō/ *adj.* of a pale brownish or reddish yellow. □ **fallow deer** any small deer of the genus *Dama*, having a white-spotted reddish brown coat in the summer. [OE *falu, fealu* f. Gmc]

false /fawls/ *adj.* & *adv.* ● *adj.* **1** not according with fact; wrong; incorrect (*a false idea*). **2 a** spurious; sham; artificial (*false gods; false teeth; false modesty*). **b** acting as such; appearing to be such, esp. deceptively (*a false lining*). **3** illusory; not actually so (*a false economy*). **4** improperly so called (*false acacia*). **5** deceptive. **6** (foll. by *to*) deceitful, treacherous, or unfaithful. **7** illegal (*false imprisonment*). ● *adv.* in a false manner (esp. *play false*). □ **false acacia** see ACACIA. **false alarm** an alarm given needlessly. **false colors** deceitful pretense. **false dawn** a transient light in the east before dawn. **false gharial** see GHARIAL. **false pretenses** misrepresentations made with intent to deceive (esp. *under false pretenses*). **false rib** = *floating rib*. **false start 1** an invalid or disallowed start in a race. **2** an unsuccessful attempt to begin something. **false step** a slip; a mistake. **false topaz** = CITRINE. □□ **falsely** *adv.* **falseness** *n.* **falsity** *n.* (*pl.* **-ies**). [OE *fals* and OF *fals, faus* f. L *falsus* past part. of *fallere* deceive]

■ *adj.* **1** untrue, inaccurate, inexact, imprecise, untruthful, unfactual, invalid, unsound, fictitious, spurious, unreal; wrong, incorrect, mistaken, fallacious, erroneous, faulty, flawed. **2 a** spurious, sham, artificial, feigned, affected, insincere, fake, faked, simulated, synthetic, pseudo, factitious, unnatural, bogus, ersatz, counterfeit, imitation, forged; mock; *colloq.* phony. **b** deceptive, misleading, untrue, untrustworthy, fraudulent, deceitful, deceiving, treacherous, *colloq.* phony. **3** see ILLUSORY. **5** see DECEPTIVE. **6** see DISLOYAL. **7** see ILLEGAL 1. □ **false colors** see DISGUISE *n.* 1. **false step** see SLIP[1] *n.* □□ **falseness, falsity** untruthfulness, falsehood, mendacity, mendaciousness, insincerity, dishonesty, spuriousness, speciousness, deceptiveness, deceit, deceitfulness, fraudulence; casuistry, sophistry; hypocrisy; treachery, perfidy.

falsehood /fáwls-hŏŏd/ *n.* **1** the state of being false, esp. untrue. **2** a false or untrue thing. **3 a** the act of lying. **b** a lie or lies. ■ **1** see *falseness, falsity* (FALSE). **2, 3b** untruth, fiction, fabrication, distortion; lie, fib, tale, story, fairy tale *or* story, *colloq.* cock-and-bull story.

falsetto /fawlsétō/ *n.* (*pl.* **-os**) **1** a method of voice production used by male singers, esp. tenors, to sing notes higher than their normal range. **2** a singer using this method. [It., dimin. of *falso* FALSE]

falsework /fáwlswərk/ *n.* a temporary framework or support used during building to form arches, etc.

falsies /fáwlseez/ *n.pl. colloq.* padded material to increase the apparent size of the breasts.

falsify /fáwlsifī/ *v.tr.* (**-ies, -ied**) **1** fraudulently alter or make false (a document, evidence, etc.). **2** misrepresent. **3** make wrong; pervert. **4** show to be false. **5** disappoint (a hope, fear, etc.). □□ **falsifiable** *adj.* **falsifiability** *n.* **falsification**

/. . ./ **pronunciation**	● **part of speech**
□ **phrases, idioms, and compounds**	
□□ **derivatives**	■ **synonym section**
cross-references appear in SMALL CAPITALS or *italics*	

n. [ME f. F *falsifier* or med.L *falsificare* f. L *falsificus* making false f. *falsus* false]

■ **1** alter, *colloq.* massage, cook. **2** distort, twist; see also MISREPRESENT. **3** see PERVERT *v.* 1–3. **4** see EXPOSE 5. **5** see FRUSTRATE *v.* 4.

falter /fáwltər/ *v.* **1** *intr.* stumble; stagger; go unsteadily. **2** *intr.* waver; lose courage. **3** *tr. & intr.* stammer; speak hesitatingly. □□ **falterer** *n.* **falteringly** *adv.* [ME: orig. uncert.]

■ **1** see HOBBLE *v.* 1. **2** see HESITATE 1, DOUBT *v.* 3. **3** see STAMMER *v.*

fame /faym/ *n.* **1** renown; the state of being famous. **2** reputation. **3** *archaic* public report; rumor. □ **ill fame** disrepute. [ME f. OF f. L *fama*]

■ **1, 2** renown, reputation, celebrity, stardom, name, illustriousness, (pre)eminence, prominence, repute; notoriety, notoriousness. **3** see RUMOR *n.* 1. □ **ill fame** see DISCREDIT *n.* 1.

famed /faymd/ *adj.* **1** (foll. by *for*) famous; much spoken of (*famed for its good food*). **2** *archaic* currently reported.

■ **1** see FAMOUS 1.

familial /fəmílyəl/ *adj.* of, occurring in, or characteristic of a family or its members. [F f. L *familia* FAMILY]

■ see DOMESTIC *adj.* 1.

familiar /fəmílyər/ *adj. & n.* ● *adj.* **1 a** (often foll. by *to*) well known; no longer novel. **b** common; usual; often encountered or experienced. **2** (foll. by *with*) knowing a thing well or in detail (*am familiar with all the problems*). **3** (often foll. by *with*) **a** well acquainted (with a person); in close friendship; intimate. **b** sexually intimate. **4** excessively informal; impertinent. **5** unceremonious; informal. **6** (of animals) tame. ● *n.* **1** a close friend or associate. **2** a person rendering certain services in a high-ranking household. **3** (in full **familiar spirit**) a demon, esp. in animal form, supposedly attending and obeying a witch, etc. □□ **familiarly** *adv.* [ME f. OF *familier* f. L *familiaris* (as FAMILY)]

■ *adj.* **1** commonplace, common, usual, customary, habitual, routine, everyday, ordinary, traditional; see also *well-known* 2 (WELL¹). **2** (*familiar with*) knowledgeable about *or* of *or* in, conversant *or* acquainted with, up on *or* in, (well-)versed in, (well-)informed about, *au fait* with, au courant with, *colloq.* in the know about; aware *or* conscious *or* cognizant of, no stranger to. **3** well acquainted, friendly, close, *colloq.* chummy; see also INTIMATE¹ *adj.* 1. **4** overfriendly, informal, free, unrestrained, free and easy, bold, forward, presumptuous, presuming, disrespectful, impudent, insolent, impertinent. **5** casual, unceremonious, unstructured, unofficial, relaxed, informal. ● *n.* **1** see ASSOCIATE *n.* 2, FRIEND *n.* 1. **3** see DEMON 1a.

familiarity /fəmíleeáritee, -yár-/ *n.* (*pl.* **-ies**) **1** the state of being well known (*the familiarity of the scene*). **2** (foll. by *with*) close acquaintance. **3** a close relationship. **4 a** sexual intimacy. **b** (in *pl.*) acts of physical intimacy. **5** familiar or informal behavior, esp. excessively so. [ME f. OF *familiarité* f. L *familiaritas -tatis* (as FAMILIAR)]

■ **2** (*familiarity with*) knowledge of, cognizance of, acquaintance with, conversance *or* conversancy with, experience of; awareness of. **3** see FRIENDSHIP 1. **5** informality, unceremoniousness; overfamiliarity, boldness, presumptuousness, presumption, impudence, insolence, impertinence, impropriety.

familiarize /fəmílyəriz/ *v.tr.* **1** (foll. by *with*) make (a person) conversant or well acquainted. **2** make (a thing) well known. □□ **familiarization** *n.* [F *familiariser* f. *familiaire* (as FAMILIAR)]

■ **1** (*familiarize with*) accustom to, make familiar *or* acquaint with, initiate in *or* into, inform about *or* on, enlighten about *or* as to, teach about, educate *or* instruct *or* tutor in. **2** see PUBLICIZE.

famille /famée/ *n.* a Chinese enameled porcelain with a predominant color: (**famille jaune** /zhōn/) yellow, (**famille noire** /nwaar/) black, (**famille rose** /rōz/) red, (**famille verte** /vairt/) green. [F, = family]

family /fámilee/ *n.* (*pl.* **-ies**) **1** a set of parents and children,

or of relations, living together or not. **2 a** the members of a household, esp. parents and their children. **b** a person's children. **c** (*attrib.*) serving the needs of families (*family butcher*). **3 a** all the descendants of a common ancestor; a house; a lineage. **b** a race or group of peoples from a common stock. **4** all the languages ultimately derived from a particular early language, regarded as a group. **5** a brotherhood of persons or nations united by political or religious ties. **6** a group of objects distinguished by common features. **7** *Math.* a group of curves, etc., obtained by varying one quantity. **8** *Biol.* a group of related genera of organisms within an order in taxonomic classification. □ **family man** a man having a wife and children, esp. one fond of family life. **family name** a surname. **family planning** birth control. **family practice** a medical specialty in which a physician provides general care for individuals and families. **family tree** a chart showing relationships and lines of descent. **in the** (or **a**) **family way** *colloq.* pregnant. [ME f. L *familia* household f. *famulus* servant]

■ **1** (kith and) kin, kinsmen, kindred, kinfolk, kinsfolk, next of kin, relatives, relations, folks, people, one's own flesh and blood, one's nearest and dearest, household, ménage. **2 a** household, ménage. **b** children, offspring, progeny, *Law* issue, *colloq.* brood, *sl.* kids. **3 a** ancestors, forebears, forefathers, progenitors; ancestry, parentage, descent, extraction, derivation, lineage, pedigree, genealogy, family tree, house, line, bloodline, dynasty; blood, stock, strain. **b** see LINE¹ *n.* 18, RACE². **4** group, set, division, subdivision, class, type, kind, order, species, genus. **5** see BROTHERHOOD 2. **6** see GROUP *n.* 1. □ **in the** (or **a**) **family way** see PREGNANT 1.

famine /fámin/ *n.* **1 a** extreme scarcity of food. **b** a shortage of something specified (*water famine*). **2** *archaic* hunger; starvation. [ME f. OF f. *faim* f. L *fames* hunger]

■ **1 b** shortage, scarcity, dearth, paucity, exiguity, lack. **2** see *starvation* (STARVE).

famish /fámish/ *v.tr. & intr.* (usu. in *passive*) **1** reduce or be reduced to extreme hunger. **2** *colloq.* (esp. as **famished** *adj.*) feel very hungry. [ME f. obs. *fame* f. OF *afamer* ult. f. L *fames* hunger]

■ **2** (**famished**) hungry, ravenous, empty, *colloq.* starving, starved.

famous /fáyməs/ *adj.* **1** (often foll. by *for*) celebrated; well known. **2** *colloq.* excellent. □□ **famousness** *n.* [ME f. AF, OF *fameus* f. L *famosus* f. *fama* fame]

■ **1** celebrated, well-known, renowned, famed, (pre)eminent, prominent, illustrious, noted, notable, acclaimed, venerable, distinguished; legendary. **2** see EXCELLENT.

famously /fáyməslee/ *adv.* **1** *colloq.* excellently (*got on famously*). **2** notably.

■ **1** excellently, (very) well, superbly, marvelously, splendidly, capitally, spectacularly, superlatively. **2** see *notably* (NOTABLE).

famulus /fámyələs/ *n.* (*pl.* **famuli** /-lī/) *hist.* an attendant to a magician or scholar. [L, = servant]

fan¹ /fan/ *n. & v.* ● *n.* **1** an apparatus, usu. with rotating blades, giving a current of air for ventilation, etc. **2** a device, usu. folding and forming a semicircle when spread out, for agitating the air to cool oneself. **3** anything spread out like a fan, e.g., a bird's tail or kind of ornamental vaulting (*fan tracery*). **4** a device for winnowing grain. **5** a fan-shaped deposit of alluvium, esp. where a stream begins to descend a gentler slope. **6** a small sail for keeping the head of a windmill toward the wind. ● *v.* (**fanned, fanning**) **1** *tr.* **a** blow a current of air on, with or as with a fan. **b** agitate (the air) with a fan. **2** *tr.* (of a breeze) blow gently on; cool. **3** *tr.* **a** winnow (grain). **b** winnow away (chaff). **4** *tr.* sweep away by or as by the wind from a fan. **5** *intr. & tr.* (usu. foll. by *out*) spread out in the shape of a fan. **6 a** *tr.* strike (a batter) out. **b** *intr.* strike out. □ **fan belt** a belt that drives a fan to cool the radiator in a motor vehicle. **fan dance** a dance in which the dancer is (apparently) nude and partly concealed by fans. **fan heater** an electric heater in which a fan drives air over an element. **fan-jet** = TURBOFAN. **fan palm** a palm tree with fan-shaped leaves. □□ **fanlike** *adj.* **fanner** *n.* [OE *fann* (in sense 4 of *n.*) f. L *vannus* winnowing fan]

fan² /fan/ *n.* a devotee of a particular activity, performer, etc. (*theater fan; football fan*). □ **fan club** an organized group of devotees. **fan mail** letters from fans. □□ **fandom** *n.* [abbr. of FANATIC]

■ devotee, admirer, enthusiast, lover, adherent, follower, supporter, aficionado, fanatic, zealot, *colloq.* buff, addict, freak, *sl.* fiend, bug, nut, groupie.

fanatic /fənátik/ *n. & adj.* ● *n.* a person filled with excessive and often misguided enthusiasm for something. ● *adj.* excessively enthusiastic. □□ **fanatical** *adj.* **fanatically** *adv.* **fanaticism** /-tisizəm/ *n.* **fanaticize** /-tisíz/ *v.intr. & tr.* [F *fanatique* or L *fanaticus* f. *fanum* temple (orig. in religious sense)]

■ *n.* extremist, maniac, zealot, *sl.* nut, *Austral. sl.* wowser. ● *adj.* see ENTHUSIASTIC. □□ **fanatical** fanatic, extreme, maniacal, mad, rabid, compulsive, monomaniacal, obsessive, frenzied, feverish, frantic, frenetic, zealous, excessive, immoderate, passionate. **fanaticism** extremism, hysteria, franticness, frenzy, zeal; monomania, obsessiveness, single-mindedness, mania, madness.

fancier /fánseeər/ *n.* a connoisseur or follower of some activity or thing (*dog fancier*).

fanciful /fánsifŏŏl/ *adj.* **1** existing only in the imagination or fancy. **2** indulging in fancies; whimsical; capricious. **3** fantastically designed, ornamented, etc.; odd looking. □□ **fancifully** *adv.* **fancifulness** *n.*

■ **1** extravagant, fantastic, chimerical, fabulous, unreal, illusory, visionary, imaginary; make-believe, fairy-tale. **2** capricious, impulsive, fickle; see also WHIMSICAL 1. **3** odd, curious, peculiar, bizarre, unusual, original; see also FANTASTIC 2, 3.

fancy /fánsee/ *n., adj., & v.* ● *n.* (*pl.* **-ies**) **1** an individual taste or inclination (*take a fancy to*). **2** a caprice or whim. **3** a thing favored, e.g., a horse to win a race. **4** an arbitrary supposition. **5 a** the faculty of using imagination or of inventing imagery. **b** a mental image. **6** delusion; unfounded belief. **7** (*prec. by the*) those who have a certain hobby; fanciers, esp. patrons of boxing. ● *adj.* (usu. *attrib.*) (**fancier**, **fanciest**) **1** ornamental; not plain. **2** capricious; whimsical; extravagant (*at a fancy price*). **3** based on imagination, not fact. **4 a** (of foods, etc.) above average quality. **b** of superior skill. **5** (of flowers, etc.) particolored. **6** (of an animal) bred for particular points of beauty, etc. ● *v.tr.* (**-ies**, **-ied**) **1** (foll. by *that* + clause) be inclined to suppose. **2** *colloq.* feel a desire for (*do you fancy a drink?*). **3** *colloq.* find sexually attractive. **4** *Brit. colloq.* have an unduly high opinion of (oneself, one's ability, etc.). **5** (in *imper.*) an exclamation of surprise (*fancy their doing that!*). **6 a** picture to oneself; conceive; imagine. **b** (as **fancied** *adj.*) having no basis in fact; imaginary. □ **catch** (or **take**) **the fancy of** please; appeal to. **fancy dress** fanciful costume, esp. for masquerading as a different person or as an animal, etc., at a party. **fancy-free** without (esp. emotional) commitments. **fancy goods** ornamental novelties, etc. **fancy man** *sl. derog.* **1** a woman's lover. **2** a pimp. **fancy woman** *sl. derog.* a mistress. □□ **fanciable** *adj.* (in sense 3 of *v.*). **fancily** *adv.* **fanciness** *n.* [contr. of FANTASY]

■ *n.* **1** taste, inclination, penchant, preference, partiality, predilection, liking, fondness, attraction. **2** caprice, whim, idea, whimsy, notion, vagary, quirk, crotchet, peculiarity, impulse. **3** see PREFERENCE 2. **4** see SUPPOSITION. **5 a** imagination, inventiveness, creativity, creativeness. **b** see IMAGE *n.* 8. **6** delusion, illusion, fantasy, make-believe, unreality, hallucination. ● *adj.* **1** ornamental, decorative, ornate, decorated, ornamented, elaborate, embellished, embroidered, fanciful, extravagant, rococo, baroque, Byzantine, intricate; gingerbread. **2** capricious, whimsical, fanciful, fantastic, far-fetched, visionary, grandiose, delusive, illusory, unrealistic; extravagant; high, exorbitant, inflated, outrageous. **3** see IMAGINARY. **4** deluxe, luxury,

luxurious, choice, select, superior, high-class, special; quality, prime; *colloq.* posh. ● *v.* **1** suppose, think, guess, conjecture, presume, surmise, assume, take it, infer, reckon, imagine, believe, suspect, understand. **2** see WANT *v.* 1a. **5** just imagine. **6 a** picture, imagine, visualize, envisage, envision, think *or* dream about. **b** (**fancied**) imaginary, unreal, fanciful, imagined, illusory, make-believe, fairy-tale. □ **catch** (or **take**) **the fancy of** see ATTRACT 2. **fancy-free** see FREE *adj.* 3d. **fancy goods** see BAUBLE. **fancy man 1** see SUITOR 1. **2** see PIMP *n.* **fancy woman** see MISTRESS 5.

fancywork /fánseewərk/ *n.* ornamental sewing, etc.
■ see *embellishment* (EMBELLISH).

fandango /fandánggō/ *n.* (*pl.* **-oes** or **-os**) **1 a** a lively Spanish dance for two. **b** the music for this. **2** nonsense; tomfoolery. [Sp.: orig. unkn.]

fane /fayn/ *n. poet.* = TEMPLE¹. [ME f. L *fanum*]

fanfare /fánfair/ *n.* **1** a short showy or ceremonious sounding of trumpets, bugles, etc. **2** an elaborate display; a burst of publicity. [F, imit.]
■ **1** flourish, fanfaronade, trumpet blast, blast, trumpet blare, blare. **2** fuss, commotion, stir, ado, to-do, ballyhoo, hullabaloo, hubbub, brouhaha.

fanfaronade /fánfarənáyd, -naád/ *n.* **1** arrogant talk; bravado. **2** a fanfare. [F *fanfaronnade* f. *fanfaron* braggart (as FANFARE)]

fang /fang/ *n.* **1** a canine tooth, esp. of a dog or wolf. **2** the tooth of a venomous snake, by which poison is injected. **3** the root of a tooth or its prong. **4** *colloq.* a person's tooth. □□ **fanged** *adj.* (also in *comb.*). **fangless** *adj.* [OE f. ON *fang* f. a Gmc root = to catch]

fanlight /fánlīt/ *n.* a small, orig. semicircular window over a door or another window.

fanny /fánee/ *n.* (*pl.* **-ies**) **1** *sl.* the buttocks. **2** *Brit. coarse sl.* the female genitals. ¶ Usually considered a taboo word in *Brit.* use. □ **fanny pack** a pouch for personal items, worn on a belt around the waist or hips. [20th c.: orig. unkn.]
■ **1** see BUTTOCK.

Fanny Adams /fánee ádəmz/ *n. Brit. sl.* **1** (also **sweet Fanny Adams**) nothing at all. ¶ Sometimes understood as a euphemism for *fuck all.* **2** *Naut.* **a** canned meat. **b** stew. [name of a murder victim *c.*1870]

fantail /fántayl/ *n.* **1** a pigeon with a broad, fan-shaped tail. **2** any flycatcher of the genus *Rhipidura*, with a fan-shaped tail. **3** a fan-shaped tail or end. **4** the fan of a windmill. **5** the projecting part of a boat's stern. □□ **fantailed** *adj.*

fan-tan /fántan/ *n.* **1** a Chinese gambling game in which players try to guess the remainder after the banker has divided a number of hidden objects into four groups. **2** a card game in which players build on sequences of sevens. [Chin., = repeated divisions]

fantasia /fantáyzhə, -zheeə, fántəzeéə/ *n.* a musical or other composition free in form and often in improvisatory style, or that is based on several familiar tunes. [It., = FANTASY]

fantasize /fántəsīz/ *v.* **1** *intr.* have a fantasy or fanciful vision. **2** *tr.* imagine; create a fantasy about. □□ **fantasist** *n.*
■ **1** dream, daydream, speculate, *literary* muse; build castles in the air *or* in Spain; hallucinate. **2** see IMAGINE 1.

fantast /fántast/ *n.* a visionary; a dreamer. [med.L f. Gk *phantastēs* boaster f. *phantazomai* make a show f. *phainō* show]

fantastic /fantástik/ *adj.* (also **fantastical**) **1** *colloq.* excellent; extraordinary. **2** extravagantly fanciful; capricious; eccentric. **3** grotesque or bizarre in design, etc. □□ **fantasticality** /-kálitee/ *n.* **fantastically** *adv.* [ME f. OF *fantastique* f. med.L *fantasticus* f. LL *phantasticus* f. Gk *phantastikos* (as FANTAST)]
■ **1** marvelous, spectacular, splendid, wonderful,

/. . . / **pronunciation**	● **part of speech**
□ **phrases, idioms, and compounds**	
□□ **derivatives**	■ **synonym section**
cross-references appear in SMALL CAPITALS or *italics*	

525

tremendous, overwhelming, *colloq.* great, fabulous, terrific; extraordinary; see also EXCELLENT. **2** extravagant, fanciful, imaginary, illusory, imagined, illusive, unreal, irrational, visionary; capricious, eccentric, extraordinary, unbelievable, incredible, preposterous, implausible, absurd, unlikely. **3** grotesque, eccentric, outlandish, fanciful, remarkable, strange, peculiar, odd, queer, bizarre, quaint, exotic, extravagant, *colloq.* weird.

fantasticate /fantástikayt/ *v.tr.* make fantastic. □□ **fantastication** /-káyshən/ *n.*

fantasy /fántəsee, -zee/ *n. & v.* ● *n.* (*pl.* **-ies**) **1** the faculty of inventing images, esp. extravagant or visionary ones. **2** a fanciful mental image; a daydream. **3** a whimsical speculation. **4** a fantastic invention or composition; a fantasia. **5** fabrication; pretense; make-believe (*his account was pure fantasy*). **6** a fiction genre that features supernatural, magical, or otherworldly elements. ● *v.tr.* (**-ies, -ied**) imagine in a visionary manner. [ME f. OF *fantasie* f. L *phantasia* appearance f. Gk (as FANTAST)]

▪ *n.* **1** imagination, fancy, creativity, inventiveness, originality. **2** vision, hallucination, mirage, illusion, delusion, chimera; daydream, dream, (flight of) fancy, pipedream. **3** see HOPE *n.* 1, 3. **5** invention, make-believe, fiction, fabrication, fable, concoction, pretense.

Fanti /fántee, faán-/ *n.* (also **Fante** (*pl.* same or **Fantis**) **1** a member of a people native to Ghana. **2** the language of this people. [native name]

FAO *abbr.* Food and Agriculture Organization (of the United Nations).

far /faar/ *adv. & adj.* (**farther, farthest** or **further, furthest**) ● *adv.* **1** at or to or by a great distance (*far away*; *far off*; *far out*). **2** a long way (off) in space or time (*are you traveling far?*; *we talked far into the night*). **3** to a great extent or degree; by much (*far better*; *far too early*). ● *adj.* **1** situated at or extending over a great distance in space or time; remote (*a far cry*; *a far country*). **2** more distant (*the far end of the hall*). **3** extreme (*far right militants*). □ **as far as 1** to the distance of (a place). **2** to the extent that (*travel as far as you like*). **by far 1** by a great amount. **2** (as an intensifier) without doubt. **far and away** by a very large amount. **far and near** everywhere. **far and wide** over a large area. **far be it from me** (foll. by *to* + infin.) I am reluctant to (esp. express criticism, etc.). **far cry** a long way. **the Far East** China, Japan, and other countries of E. Asia. **Far Eastern** of or in the Far East. **far-fetched** (of an explanation, etc.) strained; unconvincing. **far-flung 1** extending far; widely distributed. **2** remote; distant. **far from** very different from; tending to the opposite of (*the problem is far from being solved*). **far gone 1** advanced in time. **2** *colloq.* in an advanced state of illness, drunkenness, etc. **3** *colloq.* in a dilapidated state; beyond help. **far-off** remote. **far-out 1** distant. **2** avant-garde; unconventional. **far-reaching 1** widely applicable. **2** having important consequences or implications. **go far 1** achieve much. **2** contribute greatly. **3** be adequate. **go too far** go beyond the limits of what is reasonable, polite, etc. **how far** to what extent. **so far 1** to such an extent or distance; to this point. **2** until now. **so** (or **in so**) **far as** (or **that**) to the extent that. **so far so good** progress has been satisfactory up to now. □□ **farness** *n.* [OE *feorr*]

▪ *adv.* **1, 2** far away, far off, a good or great or long way (off or away); afar, far out, a good or great or long distance (off or away). **3** (very) much, considerably, decidedly, incomparably. ● *adj.* **1** remote or distant, faraway, far-off. **2** extreme, farthest, further; other, opposite. □ **by far** much, considerably, incomparably, immeasurably; far and away, easily, *Brit.* by a long chalk; definitely, undoubtedly, indubitably, without (a) doubt, unquestionably, beyond (the shadow of a) doubt. **far and away** see *undoubtedly* (UNDOUBTED). **far and near** see *far and wide*. **far and wide** near and far, far and near, far and near, extensively, widely, high and low; here, there, and everywhere; see also EVERYWHERE. **far-**

fetched strained, forced, unconvincing, unbelievable, incredible, improbable, implausible, unlikely, doubtful, dubious, questionable, unrealistic, fantastic, preposterous; difficult *or* hard to believe; *sl.* fishy. **far-flung 1** see EXTENSIVE 2. **2** see REMOTE 1. **far gone 2** see DRUNK *adj.* 1; seriously *or* acutely *or* dangerously *or* critically *or* terminally ill. **3** beyond *or* past help, deteriorated, worn out, dilapidated, near the end. **far-off** see REMOTE 1, 4. **far-out 1** see DISTANT 1a. **2** see AVANT-GARDE *adj.* **far-reaching 1** see EXTENSIVE 2. **2** see IMPORTANT 1. **go far 1** succeed, get ahead, rise in the world, make a name for oneself, become successful, set the world on fire, *colloq.* go places. **2** contribute, help, aid, play a part. **go too far** go overboard, go over the top, not know when to stop, go to extremes. **so far 1** to such an extent *or* distance, to a certain extent *or* limit *or* point. **2** until *or* till *or* up to now *or* then, until *or* till *or* up to the present, until *or* till *or* up to this *or* that point, to date, to this *or* that point in time, *formal* thus far; see also YET *adv.* 2.

farad /fárəd, -ad/ *n. Electr.* a unit of capacitance, such that one coulomb of charge causes a potential difference of one volt. ¶ Abbr.: F. [shortening of FARADAY]

faraday /fárəday/ *n.* (also **Faraday's constant**) *Electr.* the quantity of electric charge carried by one mole of electrons. ¶ Abbr.: F. □ **Faraday cage** *Electr.* a grounded metal screen used for shielding electrostatic influences. **Faraday effect** *Physics* the rotation of the plane of polarization of electromagnetic waves in certain substances in a magnetic field. [M. *Faraday*, Engl. physicist d. 1867]

faradic /fərádik/ *adj.* (also **faradaic** /fárədáyik/) *Electr.* inductive; induced. [see FARADAY]

farandole /fárəndōl/ *n.* **1** a lively Provençal dance. **2** the music for this. [F f. mod. Prov. *farandoulo*]

faraway /fáarəwáy/ *adj.* **1** remote; long past. **2** (of a look) dreamy. **3** (of a voice) sounding as if from a distance.

▪ **1** distant, far-off, far-flung; see also REMOTE 1, 2. **2** dreamy, detached, absent, absentminded, preoccupied, abstracted. **3** see FAINT *adj.* 1.

farce /faars/ *n.* **1 a** a broadly comic dramatic work based on ludicrously improbable events. **b** this branch of drama. **2** absurdly futile proceedings; pretense; mockery. [F, orig. = stuffing, f. OF *farsir* f. L *farcire* to stuff, used metaph. of interludes, etc.]

▪ **2** see MOCKERY 2.

farceur /faarsőr/ *n.* **1** a joker or wag. **2** an actor or writer of farces. [F f. *farcer* act farces]

farcical /fáarsikəl/ *adj.* **1** extremely ludicrous or futile. **2** of or like farce. □□ **farcicality** /-kálitee/ *n.* **farcically** *adv.*

▪ **1** ludicrous, futile, laughable, ridiculous, absurd, risible, funny, comical, humorous, droll, amusing, silly, foolish.

farcy /fáarsee/ *n.* glanders with inflammation of the lymph vessels. □ **farcy bud** (or **button**) a small lymphatic tumor as a result of farcy. [ME f. earlier & OF *farcin* f. LL *farciminum* f. *farcire* to stuff]

farded /fáardid/ *adj. archaic* (of a face, etc.) painted with cosmetics. [past part. of obs. *fard* f. OF *farder*]

fare /fair/ *n. & v.* ● *n.* **1 a** the price a passenger has to be conveyed by bus, train, etc. **b** a passenger paying to travel in a public vehicle. **2** a range of food provided by a restaurant, etc. ● *v.intr.* **1** progress; get on (*how did you fare?*). **2** happen; turn out. **3** journey; go; travel. □ [OE *fær*, *faru* journeying, *faran* (v.), f. Gmc]

▪ *n.* **1 a** see CHARGE *n.* 1a. **b** see PASSENGER. **2** food, meals, victuals, provisions, eatables, *formal* viands.

● *v.* **1** get on *or* along, manage, do, make one's way, survive, *colloq.* make out. **2** see *turn out* 9. **3** see TRAVEL *v.* 1.

farewell /fáirwél/ *int. & n.* ● *int.* good-bye; adieu. ● *n.* **1** leave-taking; departure (also *attrib.*: *a farewell kiss*). **2** parting good wishes. [ME f. imper. of FARE + WELL[1]]

▪ *int.* **1** good-bye, adieu, adios, Godspeed, God bless, vale, *au revoir*, *colloq.* toodle-oo, so long, ciao, bye, bye-bye, see you, see you later, *Brit. colloq.* ta ta. ● *n.* **1** leave-taking, departure, congé, parting, send-off, goodbye.

farina /fəreénə/ *n.* **1** the flour or meal of cereal, nuts, or starchy roots. **2** a powdery substance. **3** *Brit.* starch. □□ **farinaceous** /fárináyshəs/ *adj.* [L f. *far* corn]

farl /faarl/ *n. Sc.* a thin cake, orig. triangular, of oatmeal or flour. [obs. *fardel* quarter (as FOURTH, DEAL¹)]

farm /faarm/ *n. & v.* ● *n.* **1** an area of land and its buildings used under one management for growing crops, rearing animals, etc. **2** a place or establishment for breeding a particular type of animal, growing fruit, etc. (*trout farm*; *mink farm*). **3** = FARMHOUSE. **4** a place with many tanks for the storage of oil or oil products. ● *v.* **1 a** *tr.* use (land) for growing crops, rearing animals, etc. **b** *intr.* be a farmer; work on a farm. **2** *tr.* breed (fish, etc.) commercially. **3** *tr.* (often foll. by *out*) **a** delegate or subcontract (work) to others. **b** contract (the collection of taxes) to another for a fee. **c** arrange for (a person) to be looked after by another, with payment. **4** *tr.* lease the labor or services of (a person) for hire. **5** *tr.* contract to maintain and care for (a person, esp. a child) for a fixed sum. □ **farm hand** a worker on a farm. □□ **farmable** *adj.* **farming** *n.* [ME f. OF *ferme* f. med.L *firma* fixed payment f. L *firmus* FIRM¹: orig. applied only to leased land]
■ *n.* **1** farmstead, grange, *Austral. & NZ* station, *Brit.* small holding, croft, steading; see also SPREAD *n.* 12.
● *v.* **1 a** cultivate, work, till. **b** work the land. **3 a** subcontract, give; see also DELEGATE *v.* 1. **4** (*farm out*) see JOB¹ *v.* 1b. □□ **farming** agriculture, cultivation, husbandry; agribusiness.

farmer /faármər/ *n.* **1** a person who cultivates a farm. **2** a person to whom the collection of taxes is contracted for a fee. **3** a person who looks after children or performs other services for payment. [ME f. AF *fermer*, OF *fermier* f. med.L *firmarius, firmator* f. *firma* FIRM²]

farmhouse /faármhows/ *n.* a dwelling place (esp. the main one) attached to a farm.

farmland /faármland/ *n.* land used or suitable for farming.

farmstead /faármsted/ *n.* a farm and its buildings regarded as a unit.
■ see FARM *n.*

farmyard /faármyaard/ *n.* a yard or enclosure attached to a farmhouse or other farm buildings.

faro /fáirō/ *n.* a gambling card game in which bets are placed on the order of appearance of the cards. [F *pharaon* PHARAOH (said to have been the name of the king of hearts)]

Faroese var. of FAEROESE.

farouche /fərōōsh/ *adj.* **1** sullen; shy. **2** wild; fierce. [F f. OF *faroche, forache* f. med.L *forasticus* f. L *foras* out of doors]

farrago /fəraágō, -ráy-/ *n.* (*pl.* **-oes** or *Brit.* **-os**) a medley or hodgepodge. □□ **farraginous** /-rá'ajinəs/ *adj.* [L *farrago farraginis* mixed fodder f. *far* corn]
■ see MEDLEY *n.*

farrier /fáreeər/ *n.* **1** a smith who shoes horses. **2** *Brit.* a horse doctor. □□ **farriery** *n.* [OF *ferrier* f. L *ferrarius* f. *ferrum* iron, horseshoe]

farrow /fárō/ *n. & v.* ● *n.* **1** a litter of pigs. **2** the birth of a litter. ● *v.tr.* (also *absol.*) (of a sow) produce (pigs). [OE *fearh, færh* pig f. WG]

farruca /fərōōkə/ *n.* a type of flamenco dance. [Sp.]

farseeing /faárseéing/ *adj.* shrewd in judgment; prescient.
■ see SHREWD.

Farsi /faársee/ *n.* the modern Persian language. [Pers.: cf. PARSEE]

farsighted /faársítid/ *adj.* **1** having foresight; prudent. **2** able to see clearly only what is comparatively distant. □□ **farsightedly** *adv.* **farsightedness** *n.*
■ **1** foresighted, prescient, farseeing, provident; prudent, wise, sensible; imaginative; see also SHREWD. **2** longsighted, hypermetropic, presbyopic.

fart /faart/ *v. & n. coarse sl.* ● *v.intr.* **1** emit intestinal gas from the anus. **2** (foll. by *around*, esp. *Brit. about*) behave foolishly; waste time. ● *n.* **1** an emission of intestinal gas from the anus. **2** an unpleasant person. ¶ Usually considered a taboo word. [OE (recorded in *feorting* verbal noun) f. Gmc]

farther /faárthər/ *adv. & adj.* (also **further** /fúrthər/) ● *adv.* **1** to or at a more advanced point in space or time (*unsafe to proceed farther*). **2** at a greater distance (*nothing was farther from his thoughts*). ● *adj.* more distant or advanced (*on the farther side*). □□ **farthermost** *adj.*

farthest /faárthist/ *adj. & adv.* (also **furthest** /fúrthist/) ● *adj.* most distant. ● *adv.* to or at the greatest distance. □ **at the farthest** (or **at farthest**) at the greatest distance; at the latest; at most. [ME, superl. f. FARTHER]
■ *adj.* see ULTIMATE *adj.* 1, 2.

farthing /faárthing/ *n.* **1** (in the UK) a former coin and monetary unit worth a quarter of an old penny. **2** the least possible amount (*it doesn't matter a farthing*). [OE *fēorthing* f. *fēortha* fourth]

farthingale /faárthinggayl/ *n. hist.* a hooped petticoat or a stiff curved roll to extend a woman's skirt. [earlier *vardingale, verd-* f. F *verdugale* f. Sp. *verdugado* f. *verdugo* rod]

fasces /fáseez/ *n.pl.* **1** *Rom.Hist.* a bundle of rods with a projecting ax blade, carried by a lictor as a symbol of a magistrate's power. **2** *hist.* (in Fascist Italy) emblems of authority. [L, pl. of *fascis* bundle]

fascia /fáyshə/ *n.* **1** a stripe or band. **2** *Archit.* **a** a long flat surface between moldings on the architrave in classical architecture. **b** a flat surface, usu. of wood, covering the ends of rafters. **3** /fásheeə/ *Anat.* a thin sheath of fibrous connective tissue. **4** *Brit.* (also **facia**) **a** the instrument panel of a motor vehicle. **b** any similar panel for operating machinery. **5** *Brit.* the upper part of a storefront with the store's name, etc. □□ **fascial** *adj.* [L, = band, door frame, etc.]

fasciate /fásheeayt/ *adj.* (also **fasciated**) **1** *Bot.* (of contiguous parts) compressed or growing into one. **2** striped or banded. □□ **fasciation** /-áyshən/ *n.* [L *fasciatus* past part. of *fasciare* swathe (as FASCIA)]

fascicle /fásikəl/ *n.* **1** (also **fascicule** /-kyōōl/) a separately published installment of a book, usu. not complete in itself. **2** a bunch or bundle. **3** (also **fasciculus** /fásíkyələs/) *Anat.* a bundle of fibers. □□ **fascicled** *adj.* **fascicular** /fasíkyələr/ *adj.* **fasciculate** /-síkyōōlayt/ *adj.* **fasciculation** /-síkyōōláyshən/ *n.* [L *fasciculus* bundle, dimin. of *fascis*: see FASCES]

fascinate /fásinayt/ *v.tr.* **1** capture the interest of; attract irresistibly. **2** (esp. of a snake) paralyze (a victim) with fear. □□ **fascinated** *adj.* **fascinating** *adj.* **fascinatingly** *adv.* **fascination** /-náyshən/ *n.* **fascinator** *n.* [L *fascinare* f. *fascinum* spell]
■ **1** intrigue, beguile, absorb, engross, enthrall, captivate, spellbind, hold spellbound, cast a spell on *or* over, put *or* have under a spell, bewitch, enchant, charm, hypnotize, mesmerize, transfix, entrance; see also ENTICE. **2** see PARALYZE. □□ **fascination** enchantment, entrancement, attraction, attractiveness, draw, pull, magnetism, charm, allure, influence, sorcery, magic, witchcraft.

fascine /faseén/ *n.* a long fagot used for engineering purposes and (esp. in war) for lining trenches, filling ditches, etc. [F f. L *fascina* f. *fascis* bundle: see FASCES]

Fascism /fáshizəm/ *n.* **1** the totalitarian principles and organization of the extreme right-wing nationalist movement in Italy (1922–43). **2** (also **fascism**) **a** any similar nationalist and authoritarian movement. **b** *disp.* any system of extreme right-wing or authoritarian views. □□ **Fascist** *n. & adj.* (also **fascist**). **Fascistic** *adj.* (also **fascistic**). [It. *fascismo* f. *fascio* political group f. L *fascis* bundle: see FASCES]
■ **2b** see TYRANNY.

fashion /fáshən/ *n. & v.* ● *n.* **1** the current popular custom or style, esp. in dress or social conduct. **2** a manner or style of doing something (*in a peculiar fashion*). **3** (in *comb.*) in a specified manner (*in a peaceable fashion*). **4** fashionable so-

---

/. . ./ **pronunciation**	● **part of speech**
□ **phrases, idioms, and compounds**	
□□ **derivatives**	■ **synonym section**
cross-references appear in SMALL CAPITALS or *italics*	

ciety (*a woman of fashion*). ● *v.tr.* (often foll. by *into*) make into a particular or the required form. □ **after** (or **in**) **a fashion** as well as is practicable, though not satisfactorily. **in** (or **out of**) **fashion** fashionable (or not fashionable) at the time in question. □□ **fashioner** *n.* [ME f. AF *fasun*, OF *façon*, f. L *factio -onis* f. *facere* fact- do, make]

■ *n.* **1** custom, style, mode, vogue, trend, look, fad, mania, craze, rage; the latest thing, dernier cri. **2** manner, style, mode, way. ● *v.* make, model, style, shape, form, mold, forge, create, construct, work, manufacture. □ **in fashion** see FASHIONABLE. **out of fashion** see PASSÉ.

fashionable /fáshənəbəl/ *adj.* **1** following, suited to, or influenced by the current fashion. **2** characteristic of or favored by those who are leaders of social fashion. □□ **fashionableness** *n.* **fashionably** *adv.*

■ in fashion, chic, à la mode, modish, voguish, in vogue, in, *colloq.* with it, all the go, *colloq. often derog.* trendy; stylish.

fast[1] /fast/ *adj. & adv.* ● *adj.* **1** rapid; quick-moving. **2** capable of high speed (*a fast car*). **3** enabling or causing or intended for high speed (*a fast road; fast lane*). **4** (of a clock, etc.) showing a time ahead of the correct time. **5** (of a field, etc., in a sport) likely to make the ball bounce or run quickly. **6 a** (of a photographic film) needing only a short exposure. **b** (of a lens) having a large aperture. **7 a** firmly fixed or attached. **b** secure; firmly established (*a fast friendship*). **8** (of a color) not fading in light or when washed. **9** (of a person) immoral; dissipated. ● *adv.* **1** quickly; in quick succession. **2** firmly; fixedly; tightly; securely (*stand fast; eyes fast shut*). **3** soundly; completely (*fast asleep*). **4** close; immediately (*fast on their heels*). **5** in a dissipated manner; extravagantly; immorally. □ **fast breeder** (or **fast breeder reactor**) a reactor using fast neutrons to produce the same fissile material as it uses. **fast buck** see BUCK[2]. **fast food** food that can be prepared and served quickly and easily, esp. in a snack bar or restaurant. **fast neutron** a neutron with high kinetic energy, esp. not slowed by a moderator, etc. **fast reactor** a nuclear reactor using mainly fast neutrons. **fast-talk** *colloq.* persuade by rapid or deceitful talk. **fast track** a course or situation leading to rapid advancement or promotion, as in a career. **fast worker** *colloq.* a person who achieves quick results, esp. in love affairs. **pull a fast one** (often foll. by *on*) *colloq.* try to deceive or gain an unfair advantage. [OE *fæst* f. Gmc]

■ *adj.* **1, 2** rapid, quick-moving, quick, swift, speedy, brisk, *colloq.* zippy, nippy, *poet. or literary* fleet; hurried, hasty, high-speed, expeditious, express. **7 a** fixed, attached, fastened, secured, tied, bound, connected; firm, secure. **b** secure, firm, stable, solid, immovable, unshakable, settled; steadfast, staunch, unwavering, constant, lasting, close, loyal, devoted, faithful, permanent. **9** immoral, dissipated, loose, profligate, dissolute, unrestrained, wild, extravagant, intemperate, irresponsible, indecorous, licentious, wanton, rakish, self-indulgent, promiscuous, lecherous. ● *adv.* **1** quick, quickly, swiftly, rapidly, speedily, briskly, hastily, hurriedly, presto, with all speed *or* haste, expeditiously, posthaste, in a flash, in a wink, in a trice, in no time (at all), like a bat out of hell, *colloq.* before you can say Jack Robinson, like a shot, PDQ, lickety-split, *literary* apace. **2** soundly, firmly, fixedly, tightly, tight, securely, immovably, solidly, unshakably. **3** see *completely* (COMPLETE). **4** closely, close, immediately, near, right. **5** loosely, wildly, recklessly, irresponsibly, fecklessly, extravagantly, intemperately, sybaritically, self-indulgently, dissolutely, unrestrainedly, indecorously, rakishly, licentiously, promiscuously, immorally, wantonly, lecherously, lustfully. □ **pull a fast one** (*pull a fast one on*) see SWINDLE *v.*

fast[2] /fast/ *v. & n.* ● *v.intr.* abstain from all or some kinds of food or drink, esp. as a religious observance. ● *n.* an act or period of fasting. □□ **faster** *n.* [ON *fasta* f. Gmc (as FAST[1])]

■ *v.* abstain, go hungry, deny oneself, diet, starve (oneself). ● *n.* diet; hunger strike; sacrifice.

fastback /fástbak/ *n.* **1** an automobile with the rear sloping continuously down to the bumper. **2** such a back.

fasten /fásən/ *v.* **1** *tr.* make or become fixed or secure. **2** *tr.* (foll. by *in, up*) lock securely; shut in. **3** *tr.* **a** (foll. by *on, upon*) direct (a look, thoughts, etc.) fixedly or intently. **b** focus or direct the attention fixedly upon (*fastened him with her eyes*). **4** *tr.* (foll. by *on, upon*) fix (a designation or imputation, etc.). **5** *intr.* (foll. by *on, upon*) **a** take hold of. **b** single out. □□ **fastener** *n.* [OE *fæstnian* f. Gmc]

■ **1** fix, attach, bind, bond, stick, affix, anchor; tie, lock, hook (up); secure; join, connect, link, fuse, cement, clamp. **2** (*fasten in* or *up*) see LOCK *v.* **3** *tr.* fix, rivet, focus, concentrate, direct, aim, point. **5** (*fasten on* or *upon*) **a** see HOLD *v.* 1a, c. **b** see SINGLE *v.*

fastening /fásəning/ *n.* a device that fastens something; a fastener.

■ fastener, catch, clasp, clip, lock, tie.

fastidious /fastídeəs/ *adj.* **1** very careful in matters of choice or taste; fussy. **2** easily disgusted; squeamish. □□ **fastidiously** *adv.* **fastidiousness** *n.* [ME f. L *fastidiosus* f. *fastidium* loathing]

■ **1** fussy, meticulous, finicky, finical, nice, particular, difficult, critical, hypercritical, overprecise, punctilious, *colloq.* persnickety, picky, nitpicking. **2** see SQUEAMISH 1.

fastigiate /fastíjeeət/ *adj. Bot.* **1** having a conical or tapering outline. **2** having parallel upright branches. [L *fastigium* gable top]

fastness /fástnis/ *n.* **1** a stronghold or fortress. **2** the state of being secure. [OE *fæstnes* (as FAST[1])]

fat /fat/ *n., adj., & v.* ● *n.* **1** a natural oily or greasy substance occurring esp. in animal bodies. **2** the part of anything containing this. **3** excessive presence of fat in a person or animal; corpulence. **4** *Chem.* any of a group of natural esters of glycerol and various fatty acids existing as solids at room temperature. **5** overbundance or excess. ● *adj.* (**fatter, fattest**) **1** (of a person or animal) having excessive fat; corpulent. **2** (of an animal) made plump for slaughter; fatted. **3** containing much fat. **4** greasy; oily; unctuous. **5** (of land or resources) fertile; rich; yielding abundantly. **6 a** thick; substantial in content (*a fat book*). **b** substantial as an asset or opportunity (*a fat check; was given a fat part in the play*). **7 a** (of coal) bituminous. **b** (of clay, etc.) sticky. **8** *colloq. iron.* very little; not much (*a fat chance*). **9** *Baseball* (of a pitch) easy to hit. ● *v.tr. & intr.* (**fatted, fatting**) make or become fat. □ **fat cat** *sl.* **1** a wealthy person, esp. as a benefactor. **2** a highly paid executive or official. **fat city** a situation or condition of ease, prosperity, comfort, etc. (*since winning the lottery, she's living in fat city*). **the fat is in the fire** trouble is imminent. **kill the fatted calf** celebrate, esp. at a prodigal's return (Luke 15). **live off** (or **on**) **the fat of the land** have the best of everything. □□ **fatless** *adj.* **fatly** *adv.* **fatness** *n.* **fattish** *adj.* [OE *fæt* (adj.), *fættian* (v.) f. Gmc]

■ *n.* **3** corpulence, obesity, stoutness, heaviness, plumpness, rotundity, portliness, chubbiness, pudginess, tubbiness, fleshiness, paunchiness, flabbiness, esp. *Brit.* podginess. ● *adj.* **1** obese, stout, overweight, corpulent, portly, rotund, heavy, bulky, well-fed, plump, chubby, pudgy, roly-poly, tubby, fleshy, paunchy, pot-bellied, overfed, flabby, elephantine, broad in the beam, *Brit.* podgy, *colloq.* beefy, porky. **4** greasy, oily, unctuous, oleaginous, fatty, sebaceous, adipose, *formal or joc.* pinguid. **5** fertile, abundant, fruitful, profitable; rich. **6 a** see BULKY. **b** see SUBSTANTIAL 1. □ **fat cat 1** see TYCOON. **2** see DIGNITARY. **kill the fatted calf** see CELEBRATE 4. **live off** (or **on**) **the fat of the land** see PROSPER. □□ **fatness** obesity, stoutness, corpulence, embonpoint, portliness, plumpness, chubbiness, pudginess, *Brit.* podginess.

fatal /fáytəl/ *adj.* **1** causing or ending in death (*a fatal accident*). **2** (often foll. by *to*) destructive; ruinous; ending in disaster (*was fatal to their chances*; *made a fatal mistake*). **3** fateful; decisive. □□ **fatally** adv. **fatalness** n. [ME f. OF *fatal* or L *fatalis* (as FATE)]

■ **1** deadly, lethal, mortal, murderous, final, terminal; poisonous, toxic, baneful. **2** destructive, ruinous, fateful, calamitous, disastrous, catastrophic, devastating, cataclysmic, harmful, damaging, dreadful. **3** fateful, decisive, fated, destined, predestined, decreed, ordained, foreordained, preordained, predetermined, inevitable, unavoidable, necessary, essential, inescapable, ineluctable.

fatalism /fáyt'lizəm/ n. **1** the belief that all events are predetermined and therefore inevitable. **2** a submissive attitude to events as being inevitable. □□ **fatalist** n. **fatalistic** adj. **fatalistically** /-lístiklee/ adv.

fatality /fətálətee, fay-/ n. (*pl.* **-ies**) **1 a** an occurrence of death by accident or in war, etc. **b** a person killed in this way. **2** a fatal influence. **3** a predestined liability to disaster. **4** subjection to or the supremacy of fate. **5** a disastrous event; a calamity. [F *fatalité* or LL *fatalitas* f. L *fatalis* FATAL]

■ **1 a** death, casualty, killing. **b** see CASUALTY 1. **5** catastrophe, disaster, calamity, cataclysm.

fate /fayt/ n. & v. ● n. **1** a power regarded as predetermining events unalterably. **2 a** the future regarded as determined by such a power. **b** an individual's appointed lot. **c** the ultimate condition or end of a person or thing (*that sealed our fate*). **3** death; destruction. **4** (usu. **Fate**) a goddess of destiny, esp. one of three Greek or Scandinavian goddesses. ● v.tr. **1** (usu. in *passive*) preordain (*was fated to win*). **2** (as **fated** adj.) **a** doomed to destruction. **b** unavoidable; preordained; fateful. □ **fate worse than death** see DEATH. [ME f. It. *fato* & L *fatum* that which is spoken, f. *fari* speak]

■ n. **1** fortune, luck, chance, life, destiny, providence, a person's lot, kismet, *Buddhism & Hinduism* karma, *archaic* God's will, *colloq.* the way the cookie crumbles. **2** future, end, outcome; see also DESTINY. **3** death, destruction, doom, downfall, undoing, ruin, disaster, nemesis, end, finish. ● v. **1** preordain, foreordain, predestine, predetermine, destine, ordain, doom; (*be fated*) be sure or certain. **2** (**fated**) doomed, damned, cursed; fatal, fateful, unavoidable, inescapable, inevitable, ineluctable.

fateful /fáytfòōl/ adj. **1** important; decisive; having far-reaching consequences. **2** controlled as if by fate. **3** causing or likely to cause disaster. **4** prophetic. □□ **fatefully** adv. **fatefulness** n.

■ **1** important, significant, major, consequential, momentous, critical, crucial, weighty, portentous, earthshaking, decisive, pivotal. **3** disastrous, catastrophic, fatal, ruinous, cataclysmic, lethal, deadly, destructive. **4** see PROPHETIC.

fathead /fat-hed/ n. *colloq.* a stupid person. □□ **fatheaded** adj. **fatheadedness** n.

■ n. see DOLT. □ **fatheaded** see STUPID adj. 1, 5.

father /fáathər/ n. & v. ● n. **1 a** a man in relation to a child or children born from his fertilization of an ovum. **b** a man who has continuous care of a child, esp. by adoption. **2** any male animal in relation to its offspring. **3** (usu. in *pl.*) a progenitor or forefather. **4** an originator, designer, or early leader. **5** a person who deserves special respect (*the father of his country*). **6** (**Fathers** or **Fathers of the Church**) early Christian theologians whose writings are regarded as especially authoritative. **7** (also **Father**) **a** (often as a title or form of address) a priest, esp. of a religious order. **b** a religious leader. **8** (**the Father**) (in Christian belief) the first person of the Trinity. **9** (**Father**) a venerable person, esp. as a title in personifications (*Father Time*). **10** the oldest member or doyen. **11** (usu. in *pl.*) the leading men or elders in a city, etc. (*city fathers*). ● v.tr. **1** beget; be the father of. **2** behave as a father toward. **3** originate (a scheme, etc.). **4** appear as or admit that one is the father or originator of. **5** (foll. by *on*) assign the paternity of (a child, book, etc.) to a person. □ **father figure** an older man who is respected like a father; a trusted leader. **father-in-law** (*pl.* **fathers-in-law**) the father of one's husband or wife. **Father's Day** a

day (usu. the third Sunday in June) established for a special tribute to fathers. **Father Time** see TIME. □□ **fatherhood** n. **fatherless** adj. **fatherlessness** n. **fatherlike** adj. & adv. **fathership** n. [OE *fæder* with many Gmc cognates: rel. to L *pater*, Gk *patēr*]

■ n. **1 a** paterfamilias, *archaic* papa, *archaic poet.* sire, *colloq.* dad, daddy, old man, pa, pop, *Brit. sl.* governor, pater. **3** progenitor, forefather, forebear, ancestor, primogenitor. **4** originator, creator, founder, initiator, inventor, author, architect, designer, framer. **5** see LEADER 1. **7 a** priest, confessor, curé, abbé, minister, pastor, parson, chaplain, padre, *sl.* sky pilot. **8** see CREATOR 2. **10** see SAGE² n. 1. **11** (*fathers*) see ELDER n. ● v. **1** procreate, sire, *archaic* get, engender, *literary* beget. **3** originate, found, invent, establish, initiate, institute, create, frame, *disp.* author. □ **father figure** see SAGE² n. 1, LEADER 1.

fatherland /fáathərland/ n. one's native country.

■ native country, native land, motherland, homeland, birthplace; mother country, (old) country.

fatherly /fáathərlee/ adj. **1** like or characteristic of a father in affection, care, etc. (*fatherly concern*). **2** of or proper to a father. □□ **fatherliness** n.

■ **1** fatherlike, paternal, protective, kindly, kind, warm, friendly, affectionate, amiable, benevolent, well-meaning, benign, caring, sympathetic, indulgent, understanding. **2** paternal, fatherlike.

fathom /fáthəm/ n. & v. ● n. (*pl.* often **fathom** when prec. by a number) **1** a measure of six feet, esp. used in taking depth soundings. **2** *Brit.* a quantity of wood six feet square in cross section. ● v.tr. **1** grasp or comprehend (a problem or difficulty). **2** measure the depth of (water) with a sounding line. □□ **fathomable** adj. **fathomless** adj. [OE *fæthm* outstretched arms f. Gmc]

■ v. **1** grasp, comprehend, understand, penetrate, divine, determine, ascertain, work out, get to the bottom of, sound out. **2** measure, gauge, plumb, sound.

Fathometer /fəthómitər/ n. *propr.* a type of echo sounder.

fatigue /fəteeg/ n. & v. ● n. **1** extreme tiredness after exertion. **2** weakness in materials, esp. metal, caused by repeated variations of stress. **3** a reduction in the efficiency of a muscle, organ, etc., after prolonged activity. **4** an activity that causes fatigue. **5 a** a nonmilitary duty in the army, often as a punishment. **b** (in full **fatigue party**) a group of soldiers ordered to do fatigues. **c** (in *pl.*) work clothing worn by soldiers on fatigue duty. ● v.tr. (**fatigues**, **fatigued**, **fatiguing**) **1** cause fatigue in; tire; exhaust. **2** (as **fatigued** adj.) weary; listless. □□ **fatigable** /-gəbəl/ adj. **fatigability** n. **fatigueless** adj. [F *fatigue*, *fatiguer* f. L *fatigare* tire out]

■ n. **1** tiredness, weariness, exhaustion, lassitude, weakness, enervation, lethargy, languor, sluggishness, listlessness. **2, 3** see WEAKNESS 1. **4** see *exertion* (EXERT). ● v. **1** tire, weary, exhaust, weaken, drain, enervate, *colloq.* fag (out). **2** (**fatigued**) weary, wearied, tired, overtired, dead tired, weak, weakened, exhausted, listless, lethargic, languorous, sluggish, enervated, strained; dead, *colloq.* knocked out, all in, pooped, bushed, tuckered (out), esp. *Brit. colloq.* whacked, *sl.* beat, dead beat.

Fatimid /fátimid/ n. (also **Fatimite** /-mit/) **1** a descendant of Fatima, the daughter of Muhammad. **2** a member of a dynasty ruling in N. Africa in the 10th–12th c.

fatling /fátling/ n. a young fatted animal.

fatso /fátsō/ n. (*pl.* **-oes**) *sl. joc.* or *offens.* a fat person. [prob. f. FAT or the designation *Fats*]

fatstock /fátstok/ n. *Brit.* livestock fattened for slaughter.

fatten /fát'n/ v. **1** tr. & intr. (esp. with ref. to meat-producing animals) make or become fat. **2** tr. enrich (soil).

fatty /fátee/ adj. & n. ● adj. (**fattier**, **fattiest**) **1** like fat; oily;

/.../	**pronunciation**	●	**part of speech**
	□ **phrases, idioms, and compounds**		
	□□ **derivatives**	■	**synonym section**
	cross-references appear in SMALL CAPITALS or *italics*		

greasy. **2** consisting of or containing fat; adipose. **3** marked by abnormal deposition of fat, esp. in fatty degeneration. ● *n.* (*pl.* **-ies**) *colloq.* usu. *offens.* a fat person (esp. as a nickname). □ **fatty acid** *Chem.* any of a class of organic compounds consisting of a hydrocarbon chain and a terminal carboxyl group, esp. those occurring as constituents of lipids. **fatty oil** = *fixed oil.* □□ **fattily** *adv.* **fattiness** *n.*
■ *adj.* **1** see GREASY 1.

fatuous /fáchōōəs/ *adj.* vacantly silly; purposeless; idiotic. □□ **fatuity** /fətóōitee, -tyōō-/ *n.* (*pl.* **-ies**). **fatuously** *adv.* **fatuousness** *n.* [L *fatuus* foolish]
■ see SENSELESS 2, 3.

fatwa /fátwaa/ *n.* (in Islamic countries) an authoritative ruling on a religious matter. [Arab. *fatwa*]

faubourg /fôbŏŏrg/ *n.* a suburb, esp. of a French city or New Orleans. [F: cf. med.L *falsus burgus* not the city proper]

fauces /fáwseez/ *n.pl. Anat.* a cavity at the back of the mouth. □□ **faucial** /fáwshəl/ *adj.* [L, = throat]

faucet /fáwsit/ *n.* a device by which a flow of liquid from a pipe or vessel can be controlled. [ME f. OF *fausset* vent peg f. Prov. *falset* f. *falsar* to bore]
■ see TAP[1] *n.* 1.

fault /fawlt/ *n.* & *v.* ● *n.* **1** a defect or imperfection of character or of structure, appearance, etc. **2** a break or other defect in an electric circuit. **3** a transgression, offense, or thing wrongly done. **4 a** *Tennis*, etc., a service of the ball not in accordance with the rules. **b** (in show jumping) a penalty for an error. **5** responsibility for wrongdoing, error, etc. (*it will be your own fault*). **6** a defect regarded as the cause of something wrong (*the fault lies in the teaching methods*). **7** *Geol.* an extended break in the continuity of strata or a vein. ● *v.* **1** *tr.* find fault with; blame. **2** *tr.* declare to be faulty. **3** *tr. Geol.* break the continuity of (strata or a vein). **4** *intr.* commit a fault. **5** *intr. Geol.* show a fault. □ **at fault** guilty; to blame. **find fault** (often foll. by *with*) make an adverse criticism; complain. **to a fault** (usu. of a commendable quality, etc.) excessively (*generous to a fault*). [ME *faut(e)* f. OF ult. f. L *fallere* FAIL]
■ *n.* **1** defect, imperfection, blemish, flaw, deficiency, shortcoming, failing, weakness, frailty, foible, peccadillo. **2** see BREAK[1] *n.* 1a. **3** transgression, offense, sin, trespass, misdeed, misdemeanor, vice, indiscretion; mistake, error, lapse, failure, oversight, gaffe, blunder, gaucherie, faux pas, *colloq.* slipup, howler, *sl.* goof, boner, booboo, *Brit. sl.* clanger, boob. **5** blame, culpability, accountability, liability, answerability; see also RESPONSIBILITY 1a. **6** see REASON *n.* 1, 2. **7** see BREAK[1] *n.* 1a. ● *v.* **1** find fault with, blame, censure, criticize; call to account, hold a person responsible *or* accountable, hold a person to blame, lay at a person's door, accuse. **2** see CRITICIZE 1. **3** see BREAK[1] *v.* 1a. **4** *at fault* guilty, to blame, culpable, in the wrong, blamable, blameworthy; responsible, accountable, answerable, liable. **find fault** (*find fault with*) complain about, criticize, censure, take exception to, pick on, *sl.* knock; pick at, carp at, cavil at *or* about, pick apart, pick holes in. **to a fault** excessively, extremely, to an extreme, in the extreme, exceedingly, unduly, disproportionately, immoderately, irrationally, overly.

faultfinder /fáwltfindər/ *n.* a person given to continually finding fault.
■ nag, *colloq.* fusspot, nitpicker.

faultfinding /fáwltfinding/ *n.* & *adj.* ● *n.* continual criticism. ● *adj.* given to finding fault; carping.
■ *n.* criticism, censure, carping, caviling, captiousness, quibbling, fussiness, hairsplitting, pettifogging, *colloq.* nitpicking.

faultless /fáwltlis/ *adj.* without fault; free from defect or error. □□ **faultlessly** *adv.* **faultlessness** *n.*
■ flawless, immaculate; perfect, ideal, exemplary, irreproachable, unimpeachable, *Brit. colloq.* bang on, spot on.

faulty /fáwltee/ (**faultier, faultiest**) *adj.* having faults; imperfect; defective. □□ **faultily** *adv.* **faultiness** *n.*

■ flawed, unsound, imperfect; defective, impaired; out of order, malfunctioning, broken, bad; damaged; *sl.* on the blink, on the fritz.

faun /fawn/ *n.* a Roman rural deity with a human face and torso and a goat's horns, legs, and tail. [ME f. OF *faune* or L *Faunus*, a Roman god identified with Gk Pan]

fauna /fáwnə/ *n.* (*pl.* **faunas** or **faunae** /-nee/) **1** the animal life of a region or geological period (cf. FLORA). **2** a treatise on or list of this. □□ **faunal** *adj.* **faunist** *n.* **faunistic** /-nístik/ *adj.* [mod.L f. the name of a rural goddess, sister of Faunus: see FAUN]

faute de mieux /fōt də myŏ́/ *adv.* for want of a better alternative. [F]

fauteuil /fṓtil, fōtố-i/ *n.* an armchair with open sides and upholstered arms. [F f. OF *faudestuel*, *faldestoel* FALDSTOOL]

fauve /fōv/ *n.* a person who practices or favors fauvism.

fauvism /fṓvizəm/ *n.* a style of painting with vivid use of color. □□ **fauvist** *n.* [F *fauve* wild beast, applied to painters of the school of Matisse]

faux /fō/ *adj.* imitation; counterfeit (*faux emeralds*) [F, false]

faux pas /fō paá/ *n.* (*pl.* same, *pronunc.* /paaz/) **1** a tactless mistake; a blunder. **2** a social indiscretion. [F, = false step]
■ **1** see MISTAKE *n.* **2** see PECCADILLO.

fave /fayv/ *n.* & *adj. sl.* = FAVORITE. [abbr.]

favela /fəvélə/ *n.* a Brazilian shack, slum, or shanty town. [Port.]

favor /fáyvər/ *n.* & *v.* (*Brit.* **favour**) ● *n.* **1** an act of kindness beyond what is due or usual (*did it as a favor*). **2** esteem; liking; approval; goodwill; friendly regard (*gained their favor; look with favor on*). **3** partiality; too lenient or generous treatment. **4** aid; support (*under favor of night*). **5** a thing given or worn as a mark of favor or support, e.g., a badge or a knot of ribbons. **6** a small present or token given out, as at a party. **7** *archaic* leave; pardon (*by your favor*). **8** *Commerce archaic* a letter (*your favor of yesterday*). **9** *archaic* appearance; features. ● *v.tr.* **1** regard or treat with favor or partiality. **2** give support or approval to; promote; prefer. **a** be to the advantage of (a person). **b** facilitate (a process, etc.). **4** tend to confirm (an idea or theory). **5** (foll. by *with*) oblige (*favor me with a reply*). **6** (as **favored** *adj.*) having special advantages. **b** preferred; favorite. **7** *colloq.* resemble in features. **8** treat gingerly or gently. (*favored her injured wrist*). □ **in favor 1** meeting with approval. **2** (foll. by *of*) **a** in support of. **b** to the advantage of. **out of favor** lacking approval. □□ **favorer** *n.* [ME f. OF f. L *favor -oris* f. *favēre* show kindness to]
■ *n.* **1** kindness, courtesy, good *or* kind deed, good turn, gesture, *beau geste*. **2** esteem, regard, (good) opinion, consideration, grace; goodwill, approval, liking, approbation; (*in a person's favor*) in a person's good *or* bad books. **3** partiality, favoritism, preference, bias, prejudice; lenience, leniency. **4** see SHELTER *n.* 1, 3, SUPPORT *n.* **5** see DECORATION 3. **7** see PARDON *n.* ● *v.* **1, 2** have a liking *or* preference for, be partial to, like, side with, take the side of, take the part of; incline to *or* toward, go for, opt for, choose, adopt, go in for; support, back, approve, promote, endorse, champion, advocate, prefer, espouse, recommend. **3 a** see BENEFIT *v.* 1. **b** facilitate, help, benefit, aid, assist, expedite, promote, encourage, smile upon, advance, forward. **4** see SUPPORT *v.* 5. **5** see OBLIGE 3. **6** (**favored**) **a** advantaged, privileged, blessed, prosperous, wealthy, rich, affluent, well off. **b** preferred, chosen, choice, selected, popular, favorite, *often joc.* pet. **7** see RESEMBLE. □ **in favor 2** (*in favor of*) in support of, for, pro; on the side of, behind, in back of, at the back of; at a person's back. **out of favor** see UNPOPULAR.

favorable /fáyvərəbəl/ *adj.* (*Brit.* **favourable**) **1 a** well-disposed; propitious. **b** commendatory; approving. **2** giving consent (*a favorable answer*). **3** promising; auspicious; satisfactory (*a favorable aspect*). **4** (often foll. by *to*) helpful; suitable. □□ **favorableness** *n.* **favorably** *adv.* [ME f. OF *favorable* f. L *favorabilis* (as FAVOR)]
■ **1a, 3** well-disposed, propitious, promising, auspicious, fair, encouraging; satisfactory, advantageous, beneficial,

helpful, convenient, useful, suitable, appropriate. **1 b** commendatory, approving, laudatory, enthusiastic, eager, good, positive, encouraging, reassuring, sympathetic, promising, affirmative. **2** see WILLING *adj.* **4** see *advantageous* (ADVANTAGE). □□ **favorably** enthusiastically, positively, sympathetically, agreeably; genially, graciously, indulgently; advantageously, affirmatively.

favorite /fáyvərit, fáyvrit/ *adj. & n.* (*Brit.* **favourite**) ● *adj.* preferred to all others (*my favorite book*). ● *n.* **1** a particularly favored person. **2** *Sports* a competitor thought most likely to win. □ **favorite son 1** a person preferred as the presidential candidate by delegates from the candidate's home state. **2** a celebrity particularly popular in his hometown. [obs. F *favorit* f. It. *favorito* past part. of *favorire* favor]
■ *adj.* preferred, beloved, best-liked, most-liked, chosen, favored, *often joc.* pet. ● *n.* **1** darling, pet, apple of one's eye, ideal, preference, *Brit. colloq. usu. derog.* blue-eyed boy.

favoritism /fáyvəritizəm, fáyvri-/ *n.* (*Brit.* **favouritism**) the unfair favoring of one person or group at the expense of another.
■ partiality, bias, prepossession, prejudice, predisposition, partisanship, nepotism.

fawn[1] /fawn/ *n., adj., & v.* ● *n.* **1** a young deer in its first year. **2** a light yellowish brown. ● *adj.* fawn colored. ● *v.tr.* (also *absol.*) (of a deer) bring forth (young). □ **in fawn** (of a deer) pregnant. [ME f. OF *faon*, etc., ult. f. L *fetus* offspring: cf. FETUS]

fawn[2] /fawn/ *v.intr.* **1** (often foll. by *on*) (of a person) behave servilely; cringe. **2** (of an animal, esp. a dog) show extreme affection. □□ **fawner** *n.* **fawning** *adj.* **fawningly** *adv.* [OE *fagnian, fægnian* (as FAIN)]
■ **1** see CRINGE *v.* 2.

fax /faks/ *n. & v.* ● *n.* **1** facsimile transmission (see FACSIMILE *n.* 2). **2 a** a copy produced by this. **b** a machine for transmitting and receiving these. ● *v.tr.* transmit (a document) in this way. [abbr. of FACSIMILE]
■ *n.* see FACSIMILE *n.* 2. ● *v.* see TRANSMIT 1a.

fay /fay/ *n. literary* a fairy. [ME f. OF *fae, faie* f. L *fata* (pl.) the Fates]

faze /fayz/ *v.tr.* (often as **fazed** *adj.*) *colloq.* disconcert; perturb; disorient. [var. of *feeze* drive off, f. OE *fēsian*, of unkn. orig.]
■ see DISCOMFIT 1a.

FBA *abbr.* Fellow of the British Academy.
FBI *abbr.* Federal Bureau of Investigation.
FCC *abbr.* Federal Communications Commission.
fcp. *abbr.* foolscap.
FD *abbr.* **1** fire department. **2** Defender of the Faith. [L *Fidei Defensor*]
FDA *abbr.* Food and Drug Administration.
FDIC *abbr.* Federal Deposit Insurance Corporation.
Fe *symb. Chem.* the element iron.

fealty /féeəltee/ *n.* (*pl.* **-ies**) **1** *hist.* **a** a feudal tenant's or vassal's fidelity to a lord. **b** an acknowledgment of this. **2** allegiance. [ME f. OF *feaulté* f. L *fidelitas -tatis* f. *fidelis* faithful f. *fides* faith]

fear /feer/ *n. & v.* ● *n.* **1 a** an unpleasant emotion caused by exposure to danger, expectation of pain, etc. **b** a state of alarm (*be in fear*). **2** a cause of fear (*all fears removed*). **3** (often foll. by *of*) dread or fearful respect (for) (*had a fear of heights*). **4** anxiety for the safety of (*in fear of their lives*). **5** danger; likelihood (of something unwelcome) (*there is little fear of failure*). ● *v.* **1 a** *tr.* feel fear about or toward (a person or thing). **b** *intr.* feel fear. **2** *intr.* (foll. by *for*) feel anxiety or apprehension about (*feared for my life*). **3** *tr.* apprehend; have uneasy expectation of (*fear the worst*). **4** *tr.* (usu. foll. by *that* + clause) apprehend with fear or regret (*I fear that you are wrong*). **5** *tr.* **a** (foll. by *to* + infin.) hesitate. **b** (foll. by verbal noun) shrink from; be apprehensive about (*he feared meeting his ex-wife*). **6** *tr.* show reverence toward. □ **for fear of** (or **that**) to avoid the risk of (or that). **never fear** there is no danger of that. [OE f. Gmc]
■ *n.* **1 a** dread, terror, horror; panic, fright, timidity. **b**

alarm, dread, terror, horror, panic, fright, trepidation, apprehension, fearfulness, apprehensiveness, consternation, dismay. **2** horror, specter, nightmare, bogey, phobia, bugbear, bête noire, misgivings, forebodings. **3** dread, terror, horror; awe, respect, reverence, veneration. **4** anxiety, solicitude, angst, foreboding, distress, concern, apprehension, worry, uneasiness, unease. **5** see DANGER. ● *v.* **1 a** be afraid *or* scared *or* fearful *or* frightened of; dread, shrink from; tremble *or* shudder at. **b** be afraid *or* scared *or* fearful *or* frightened; quiver, tremble, shudder, quail, quake. **2** see WORRY *v.* 1. **3** expect, suspect, imagine, foresee, *disp.* anticipate. **5 a** see HESITATE 2. **b** see DREAD *v.* **6** respect, venerate, be *or* stand in awe of; see also REVERE.

fearful /féerfŏŏl/ *adj.* **1** (usu. foll. by *of*, or *that* + clause) afraid. **2** terrible; awful. **3** *colloq.* extremely unwelcome or unpleasant (*a fearful row*). □□ **fearfully** *adv.* **fearfulness** *n.*
■ **1** afraid, scared, frightened, terrified, alarmed, panic-stricken, terror-stricken, terror-struck, intimidated, jumpy, nervous, edgy, panicky, anxious, apprehensive; cowardly, pusillanimous, hesitant, timid, timorous, shy, diffident, *colloq.* yellow, jittery. **2, 3** terrible, awful, dire, dreadful, frightful, appalling, ghastly, atrocious, horrific, horrible, horrendous, hideous, gruesome, grisly, grim, unspeakable; terrifying, frightening, horrifying, fearsome, monstrous, loathsome, repugnant, repulsive, revolting, disgusting, nauseating, nauseous. □□ **fearfully** apprehensively, anxiously, edgily, nervously, hesitantly, timidly, timorously, shyly, diffidently; frightfully, awfully, terribly, very, extremely, exceedingly, tremendously.

fearless /féerlis/ *adj.* **1** courageous; brave. **2** (foll. by *of*) without fear. □□ **fearlessly** *adv.* **fearlessness** *n.*
■ **1** courageous, brave, bold, intrepid, valorous, dauntless, valiant, plucky, daring, audacious, heroic, venturesome, gallant, chivalrous. **2** (*fearless of*) see *heedless* (HEED).

fearsome /féersəm/ *adj.* **1** appalling or frightening, esp. in appearance. **2** timid; fearful. □□ **fearsomely** *adv.* **fearsomeness** *n.*
■ **1** appalling, frightening, terrifying, menacing, terrible, dreadful, awesome, formidable, frightful, daunting, intimidating.

feasibility /féezibílitee/ *n.* the state or degree of being feasible. □ **feasibility study** a study of the practicability of a proposed project.
■ practicability, workability, workableness, viability, practicality.

feasible /féezibəl/ *adj.* **1** practicable; possible; easily or conveniently done. **2** *disp.* likely; probable (*it is feasible that they will get the job*). □□ **feasibly** *adv.* [ME f. OF *faisable, -ible* f. *fais-* stem of *faire* f. L *facere* do, make]
■ **1** practicable, workable, doable, viable, practical, realizable, possible, achievable, attainable, realistic. **2** see LIKELY *adj.* 1.

feast /feest/ *n. & v.* ● *n.* **1** a large or sumptuous meal, esp. with entertainment. **2** a gratification to the senses or mind. **3 a** an annual religious celebration. **b** a day dedicated to a particular saint. ● *v.* **1** *intr.* partake of a feast; eat and drink sumptuously. **2** *tr.* a regale. **b** pass (time) in feasting. □ **feast day** a day on which a feast (esp. in sense 3) is held. **feast one's eyes on** take pleasure in beholding. □□ **feaster** *n.* [ME f. OF *feste, fester* f. L *festus* joyous]
■ *n.* **1** banquet, (lavish) dinner, *colloq.* spread, blowout. **2** treat, delight, pleasure; see also *gratification* (GRATIFY). **3** celebration, feast day, holy day, holiday, festival, fête; saint's day. ● *v.* **1** dine, wine and dine; gorge (oneself), gormandize, eat one's fill; wine, indulge,

---

/.../ **pronunciation**	● **part of speech**
□ **phrases, idioms, and compounds**	
□□ **derivatives**	■ **synonym section**
cross-references appear in SMALL CAPITALS or *italics*	

overindulge. **2 a** regale, entertain, feed; see also
BANQUET *v.* □ **feast day** see FEAST *n.* 3 above.

feat /feet/ *n.* a noteworthy act or achievement. [ME f. OF
fait, fet (as FACT)]

■ achievement, accomplishment, exploit, deed, act, tour
de force.

feather /féthǝr/ *n. & v.* ● *n.* **1** any of the appendages growing
from a bird's skin, with a horny hollow stem and fine
strands. **2** one or more of these as decoration, fletching on
an arrow, etc. **3** (*collect.*) **a** plumage. **b** game birds. ● *v.* **1**
tr. cover or line with feathers. **2** *tr. Rowing* turn (an oar) so
that it passes through the air edgewise. **3** *tr. Aeron. & Naut.*
a cause (the propeller blades) to rotate in such a way as to
lessen the air or water resistance. **b** vary the angle of incidence of (helicopter blades). **4** *intr.* float, move, or wave like
feathers. □ **feather bed** a bed with a mattress stuffed with
feathers. **a feather in one's cap** an achievement to one's
credit. **feather one's nest** enrich oneself. **in fine** (or **high**)
feather *colloq.* in good spirits. □□ **feathered** *adj.* (also in
comb.). **featherless** *adj.* **feathery** *adj.* **featheriness** *n.* [OE
fether, gefithrian, f. Gmc]

featherbed /féthǝrbed/ *v.tr.* (**-bedded, -bedding**) provide
with (esp. financial) advantages.

featherbedding /féthǝrbeding/ *n.* the employment of excess
staff, esp. due to union rules.

featherbrain /féthǝrbrayn/ *n.* (or **-head**) a silly or absentminded person.

featherbrained /féthǝrbraynd/ *adj.* (or **-headed**) silly; absent-minded.

featheredge /féthǝrej/ *n.* the thin edge of a wedge-shaped
board.

feathering /féthǝring/ *n.* **1** bird's plumage. **2** the feathers of
an arrow. **3** a featherlike structure in an animal's coat. **4**
Archit. cusps in tracery.

featherstitch /féthǝrstich/ *n.* ornamental zigzag sewing.

featherweight /féthǝrwayt/ *n.* **1 a** any of various weight
classes in certain sports intermediate between bantamweight and lightweight. **b** a boxer, weightlifter, etc., of this
weight. **2** a very light person or thing. **3** (usu. *attrib.*) a trifling or unimportant thing.

feature /féechǝr/ *n. & v.* ● *n.* **1** a distinctive or characteristic
part of a thing. **2** (usu. in *pl.*) (a distinctive part of) the face,
esp. with regard to shape and visual effect. **3 a** a distinctive
or regular article in a newspaper or magazine. **b** a special
attraction at an event, etc. **4 a** (in full **feature film**) a full-
length movie intended as the main at a showing. **b** (in full
feature program) a broadcast devoted to a particular
topic. ● *v.* **1** *tr.* make a special display or attraction of; give
special prominence to. **2** *tr. & intr.* have as or be an important actor, participant, or topic in a movie, broadcast, etc.
3 *intr.* be a feature. □□ **featured** *adj.* (also in *comb.*). **featureless** *adj.* [ME f. OF *feture, faiture* form f. L *factura* formation: see FACTURE]

■ *n.* **1** characteristic, attribute, trait, mark, hallmark,
earmark, property, character, quality, aspect, facet,
peculiarity, quirk, idiosyncrasy. **2** (*features*) face,
physiognomy, countenance, looks, *literary* visage,
sl. mug, kisser. **3 a** column, article, piece. **b** (main)
attraction, draw, special attraction, high point, best
or memorable part, *sl.* high spot. **4 a** see FILM *n.* 3a, b.
b see BROADCAST. ● *v.* **1** promote, publicize, advertise,
sl. hype; stress, emphasize, highlight, call attention to,
spotlight, put into the limelight. **2** (*intr.*) act, perform,
take a role *or* part, star; have a role *or* part, be involved.

Feb. *abbr.* February.

febrifuge /fébrifyōōj/ *n.* a medicine or treatment that reduces
fever; a cooling drink. □□ **febrifugal** /fibrífyǝgǝl, fébri-
fyōōgǝl/ *adj.* [F *fébrifuge* f. L *febris* fever + -FUGE]

febrile /fébral, fée-/ *adj.* of or relating to fever; feverish.
□□ **febrility** /fibrílitee/ *n.* [F *fébrile* or med.L *febrilis* f. L *febris*
fever]

■ see FEVERISH 1.

February /fébrōōeree, fébyōō-/ *n.* (*pl.* **-ies**) the second
month of the year. [ME f. OF *feverier* ult. f. L *februarius* f.
februa a purification feast held in this month]

feces /féeseez/ *n.pl.* (*Brit.* **faeces**) waste matter discharged
from the bowels. □□ **fecal** /féekǝl/ *adj.* [L, pl. of *faex* dregs]

■ see DUNG *n.*

feckless /féklis/ *adj.* **1** feeble; ineffective. **2** unthinking; irresponsible (*feckless gaiety*). □□ **fecklessly** *adv.* **feckless-
ness** *n.* [Sc. *feck* f. *effeck* var. of EFFECT]

■ **1** see FEEBLE 2. **2** see IRRESPONSIBLE 1.

feculent /fékyǝlǝnt/ *adj.* **1** murky; filthy. **2** containing sediments or dregs. □□ **feculence** *n.* [F *féculent* or L *faeculentus*
(as FECES)]

■ **1** see MUDDY *adj.* 2.

fecund /féekǝnd, fék-/ *adj.* **1** prolific; fertile. **2** fertilizing.
□□ **fecundity** /fikúnditee/ *n.* [ME f. F *fécond* or L *fecundus*]

■ **1** see PROLIFIC 1.

fecundate /féekǝndayt, fék-/ *v.tr.* **1** make fruitful. **2** = FER-
TILIZE 2. □□ **fecundation** /-dáyshǝn/ *n.* [L *fecundare* f. *fecundus* fruitful]

Fed /fed/ *n. sl.* **1** a federal agent or official, esp. a member of
the FBI. **2 a** the Federal Reserve System. **b** the Federal
Reserve Board. [abbr. of FEDERAL]

fed *past* and *past part.* of FEED. □ **fed up** (or **fed to death**)
(often foll. by *with*) discontented or bored, esp. from a surfeit of something (*am fed up with the rain*).

fedayeen /fédaayéen/ *n.pl.* Arab guerrillas operating esp.
against Israel. [colloq. Arab. *fidā'iyīn* pl. f. Arab. *fidā'ī* ad-
venturer]

federal /fédǝrǝl/ *adj.* **1** of a system of government in which
several states or provinces, etc., form a union but remain
independent in internal affairs. **2** relating to or affecting such
a federation (*federal laws*). **3** relating to or favoring centralized government. **4** (**Federal**) of or loyal to the Union army
and federal government in the US Civil War. **5** comprising
an association of largely independent units. □ **Federal Reserve System** a national system of reserve cash available to
banks. **Federal Reserve Board** the governing body of the
Federal Reserve System. □□ **federalism** *n.* **federalist** *n.*
federalize *v.tr.* **federalization** *n.* **federally** *adv.* [L *foedus
-eris* league, covenant]

■ **1, 2** see NATIONAL *adj.*

federate *v. & adj.* ● *v.tr. & intr.* /fédǝrayt/ organize or be
organized on a federal basis. ● *adj.* /fédǝrǝt/ having a federal organization. □□ **federative** /fédǝraytiv, -rǝtiv/ *adj.* [LL
foederare foederat- (as FEDERAL)]

■ *v.* see BAND² *v.*

federation /fédǝráyshǝn/ *n.* **1** a federal group of states. **2** a
federated society or group. **3** the act or an instance of fed-
erating. □□ **federationist** *n.* [F *fédération* f. LL *foederatio* (as
FEDERAL)]

■ **1** confederacy, confederation. **2** society, group,
association, league. **3** amalgamation, alliance, union,
unification.

fedora /fidáwrǝ/ *n.* a soft felt hat with a low crown creased
lengthways. [*Fédora,* drama by V. Sardou (1882)]

fee /fee/ *n. & v.* ● *n.* **1** a payment made to a professional
person or to a professional or public body in exchange for
advice or services. **2** money paid as part of a special transaction, for a privilege, admission to a society, etc. (*enrollment
fee*). **3** (in *pl.*) money regularly paid (esp. to a school) for
continuing services. **4** *Law* an inherited estate, unlimited
(**fee simple**) or limited (**fee tail**) as to the category of heir.
5 *hist.* a fief; a feudal benefice. ● *v.tr.* (**fee'd** or **feed**) **1**
pay a fee to. **2** engage for a fee. [ME f. AF, = OF *feu, fieu,*
etc. f. med.L *feodum, feudum,* perh. f. Frank.: cf. FEUD², FIEF]

■ *n.* **1** payment, wage, rate, stipend, salary,
compensation; honorarium; pay. **2** charge, price, cost,
bill, payment. ● *v.* **1** see PAY¹ *v.* 1. **2** see ENGAGE 1.

feeble /féebǝl/ *adj.* **1** weak; infirm. **2** lacking energy, force,
or effectiveness. **3** dim; indistinct. **4** deficient in character
or intelligence. □□ **feebleness** *n.* **feeblish** *adj.* **feebly** *adv.*
[ME f. AF & OF *feble, fieble, fleible* f. L *flebilis* lamentable f.
flère weep]

■ **1** weak, infirm, frail, puny, slight, decrepit, *Brit. sl.*
wonky; debilitated, enfeebled, exhausted, weakened,
effete; delicate, fragile, languid, spiritless, sickly, ailing.
2 weak, effete, half-baked, lame, flimsy, unconvincing,

poor, unsatisfactory, insufficient, inadequate; shoddy, thin, insubstantial, meager, paltry, insignificant; ineffectual, feckless, ineffective, impotent, impuissant, namby-pamby, wishy-washy, *Brit. colloq.* wet. **3** dim, indistinct, weak, obscure, imperceptible, faint, unclear. **4** see WEAK 3a, DEFECTIVE *adj.* 2.

feebleminded /féebəlmíndid/ *adj.* **1** unintelligent. **2** mentally deficient. □□ **feeblemindedly** *adv.* **feeblemindedness** *n.*

■ **1** unintelligent, stupid, simple, dull, dull-witted, witless, simpleminded, imbecile, slow, slow-witted, obtuse, softheaded, empty-headed, vacant, *colloq.* halfwitted, moronic, idiotic, cretinous, dim-witted, slow on the uptake, thick, esp. *Brit. colloq.* gormless, *colloq.* dumb, *sl.* boneheaded. **2** mentally defective, weak-minded, (mentally) deficient, retarded, halfwitted, softheaded, moronic, idiotic, imbecile, imbecilic, cretinous, simpleminded.

feed /feed/ *v. & n.* ● *v.* (*past* and *past part.* **fed** /fed/) **1** *tr.* **a** supply with food. **b** put food into the mouth of. **2** *tr.* **a** give as food, esp. to animals. **b** graze (cattle). **3** *tr.* serve as food for. **4** *intr.* (usu. foll. by *on*) (esp. of animals, or *colloq.* of people) take food; eat. **5** *tr.* nourish; make grow. **6 a** *tr.* maintain supply of raw material, fuel, etc., to (a fire, machine, etc.). **b** *tr.* (foll. by *into*) supply (material) to a machine, etc. **c** *tr.* supply or send (an electronic signal) for broadcast, etc. **d** *intr.* (often foll. by *into*) (of a river, etc.) flow into another body of water. **e** *tr.* insert further coins into (a meter) to continue its function, validity, etc. **7** *intr.* (foll. by *on*) **a** be nourished by. **b** derive benefit from. **8** *tr.* use (land) as pasture. **9** *tr. Theatr. sl.* supply (an actor, etc.) with cues. **10** *tr. Sports* send passes to (a player) in a basketball game, soccer or hockey match, etc. **11** *tr.* gratify (vanity, etc.). **12** *tr.* provide (advice, information, etc.) to. ● *n.* **1** an amount of food, esp. for animals or (*Brit.*) infants. **2** the act or an instance of feeding; the giving of food. **3** *colloq.* a meal. **4** pasturage; green crops. **5 a** a supply of raw material to a machine, etc. **b** the provision of this or a device for it. **c** an electronic signal fed to a television or radio station. **6** the charge of a gun. **7** *Theatr. sl.* an actor who supplies another with cues. □ **feed back** produce feedback. **feed bag** a bag containing fodder, hung on a horse's head. **feed the fishes 1** meet one's death by drowning. **2** be seasick. **feeding-bottle** *Brit.* a bottle with a nipple for feeding infants. **feed up 1** fatten. **2** satiate (cf. *fed up* (see FED)). □□ **feedable** *adj.* [OE *fēdan* f. Gmc]

■ *v.* **1 a** supply, provision, cater or provide for, victual; maintain, board. **4** graze, pasture; see also EAT *v.* 1b; (*feed on*) see EAT *v.* 1a. **5** make grow, nurture; sustain; see also NOURISH 1. **6 a** maintain, fuel; stoke. **7** (*feed on*) **a** be nourished by, subsist or survive or depend on. **b** benefit from, thrive on or upon. **11** see PANDER *v.* **12** see ADVISE 3. ● *n.* **1** food; fodder, provender, forage, silage. **3** see MEAL¹. **4** see PASTURE *n.* □ **feed up 2** see SATE 2.

feedback /féedbak/ *n.* **1** information about the result of an experiment, etc.; response. **2** *Electronics* **a** the return of a fraction of the output signal from one stage of a circuit, amplifier, etc., to the input of the same or a preceding stage. **b** a signal so returned. **3** *Biol.*, etc., the modification or control of a process or system by its results or effects, esp. by the difference between the desired and the actual result.

■ **1** see RESPONSE 1, INFORMATION 1.

feeder /féedər/ *n.* **1** a person or thing that feeds. **2** a person who eats in a specified manner. **3** *Brit.* a baby's bottle. **4** *Brit.* a bib for an infant. **5** a tributary stream. **6** a branch road, railroad line, etc., linking outlying districts with a main communication system. **7** *Electr.* a main conductor carrying electricity to a distribution point. **8** a hopper or feeding apparatus in a machine.

■ **5** see TRIBUTARY *n.*

feel /feel/ *v. & n.* ● *v.* (*past* and *past part.* **felt** /felt/) **1** *tr.* **a** examine or search by touch. **b** (*absol.*) have the sensation of touch (*was unable to feel*). **2** *tr.* perceive or ascertain by touch; have a sensation of (*could feel the warmth; felt that it*

was cold). **3** *tr.* **a** undergo; experience (*shall feel my anger*). **b** exhibit or be conscious of (an emotion, sensation, conviction, etc.). **4 a** *intr.* have a specified feeling or reaction (*felt strongly about it*). **b** *tr.* be emotionally affected by (*felt the rebuke deeply*). **5** *tr.* (usu. foll. by *that* + clause) have a vague or unreasoned impression (*I feel that I am right*). **6** *tr.* consider; think (*I feel it is useful to go*). **7** *intr.* seem; give an impression of being; be perceived as (*the air feels chilly*). **8** *intr.* be consciously; consider oneself (*I feel happy; do not feel well*). **9** *intr.* **a** (foll. by *with*) have sympathy with. **b** (foll. by *for*) have pity or compassion for. **10** *tr.* (often foll. by *up*) *sl.* fondle the breasts or genitals of. ● *n.* **1** the act or an instance of feeling; testing by touch. **2** the sensation characterizing a material, situation, etc. **3** the sense of touch. □ **feel free** (often foll. by *to* + infin.) not be reluctant or hesitant (*do feel free to criticize*). **feel like** have a wish for; be inclined toward. **feel one's oats** see OAT. **feel oneself** be fit or confident, etc. **feel out** investigate cautiously. **feel strange** see STRANGE. **feel up to** be ready to face or deal with. **feel one's way** proceed carefully; act cautiously. **get the feel of** become accustomed to using. **make one's influence** (or **presence, etc.**) **felt** assert one's influence; make others aware of one's presence, etc. [OE *fēlan* f. WG]

■ *v.* **1 a** touch, handle, manipulate, finger. **2** perceive, note; see also SENSE *v.* **3 a** undergo, experience, suffer, bear, endure, withstand, stand, tolerate, go through. **b** sense, be conscious of, be aware *or* sensible of, experience. **5, 6** sense, believe, think, perceive, judge, consider, know, discern, intuit, have a (funny) feeling, get *or* have the impression, *archaic* trow, *colloq.* have a hunch, feel in one's bones, *formal* deem; see also THINK *v.* 2. **7** seem, appear; give an impression of being, strike one as, have a *or* the feeling of being. **8** seem to be, be, consider oneself, regard *or* characterize oneself as. **9** (*feel with* or *for*) have sympathy with *or* for, sympathize *or* empathize with, commiserate with, be sorry for, pity, have compassion for. **10** see FONDLE. ● *n.* **2** texture, touch, sensation; feeling, air, atmosphere, climate, ambience, sense, note, tone, quality. □ **feel like** have a wish for, want, desire, crave, *colloq.* fancy; be inclined to *or* toward. **get the feel of** see ACCUSTOM.

feeler /féelər/ *n.* **1** an organ in certain animals for testing things by touch or for searching for food. **2** a tentative proposal or suggestion, esp. to elicit a response (*put out feelers*). **3** a person or thing that feels. □ **feeler gauge** a gauge equipped with blades for measuring narrow gaps, etc.

■ **1** antenna, tentacle, palp. **3** prober, tester; probe, sensor.

feeling /féeling/ *n. & adj.* ● *n.* **1 a** the capacity to feel; a sense of touch (*lost all feeling in his arm*). **b** a physical sensation. **2 a** (often foll. by *of*) a particular emotional reaction; an atmosphere (*a feeling of despair*). **b** (in *pl.*) emotional susceptibilities or sympathies (*hurt my feelings; had strong feelings about it*). **c** intense emotion (*said it with such feeling*). **3** a particular sensitivity (*had a feeling for literature*). **4 a** an opinion or notion, esp. a vague or irrational one (*my feelings on the subject; had a feeling she would be there*). **b** vague awareness (*had a feeling of safety*). **c** sentiment (*the general feeling was against it*). **5** readiness to feel sympathy or compassion. **6 a** the general emotional response produced by a work of art, piece of music, etc. **b** emotional commitment or sensibility in artistic execution (*played with feeling*). ● *adj.* **1** sensitive; sympathetic. **2** showing emotion or sensitivity. □□ **feeling-less** *adj.* **feelingly** *adv.*

■ *n.* **1** sense of touch, sensibility, sensitivity, sensation, sense; feel. **2 a** feel, mood, atmosphere, climate, sense, air, ambience; see also EMOTION. **b** (*feelings*) susceptibilities, sympathies, emotions, sensibilities.

/.../ **pronunciation**	● **part of speech**
□ **phrases, idioms, and compounds**	
□□ **derivatives**	■ **synonym section**
cross-references appear in SMALL CAPITALS or *italics*	

c ardor, warmth, passion, fervency, fervor, ardency, intensity, heat, sentiment, emotion, vehemence. **3** sensitivity, appreciation, sympathy, empathy, identification, compassion, tenderness, concern, regard, understanding. **4 a** opinion, view; notion, idea, intuition, instinct, inkling, suspicion, belief, hunch, sense; premonition, presentiment, sense of foreboding, impression, sensation. **b** awareness, consciousness; see also IMPRESSION 1. **c** see ATTITUDE 1. **5, 6b** see SENSITIVITY. **6 a** see IMPRESSION 1. ● *adj.* **1** sensitive, sympathetic, tenderhearted, compassionate; see also TENDER¹ 5. **2** see DEMONSTRATIVE *adj.* 1, DELICATE 5, 6.

feet *pl.* of FOOT.

feign /fayn/ *v.* **1** *tr.* simulate; pretend to be affected by (*feign madness*). **2** *tr. archaic* invent (an excuse, etc.). **3** *intr.* indulge in pretense. [ME f. *feign-* stem of OF *feindre* f. L *fingere* mold, contrive]
■ **1, 3** see DISSIMULATE.

feijoa /fayóə/ *n.* **1** any evergreen shrub or tree of the genus *Feijoa*, bearing edible guava-like fruit. **2** this fruit. [mod.L f. J. da Silva *Feijo*, 19th-c. Brazilian naturalist]

feint /faynt/ *n. & v.* ● *n.* **1** a sham attack or blow, etc., to divert attention or fool an opponent or enemy. **2** pretense. ● *v.intr.* make a feint. [F *feinte*, fem. past part. of *feindre* FEIGN]
■ *n.* **1** sham *or* mock attack, distraction, diversion; see also MANEUVER *n.* 1, 3. **2** pretense, bluff, ruse, subterfuge, deception, gambit, artifice, *colloq.* ploy. ● *v.* see ATTACK *v.* 6, MANEUVER *v.* 3.

feisty /fístee/ *adj.* (**feistier**, **feistiest**) *sl.* **1** aggressive; exuberant. **2** touchy. □□ **feistiness** *n.* [*feist* (= fist) small dog]

felafel var. of FALAFEL.

feldspar /féldspaar/ *n.* (also esp. *Brit.* **felspar** /félspaar/) *Mineral.* any of a group of aluminum silicates of potassium, sodium, or calcium, which are the most abundant minerals in the earth's crust. □□ **feldspathic** /-spáthik/ *adj.* **feldspathoid** /féldspəthoyd, félspə-/ *n.* [G *Feldspat*, -*spath* f. *Feld* FIELD + *Spat, Spath* SPAR³: *felspar* by false assoc. with G *Fels* rock]

felicitate /fəlísitayt/ *v.tr.* congratulate. □□ **felicitation** /-táyshən/ *n.* (usu. in *pl.*). [LL *felicitare* make happy f. L *felix -icis* happy]
■ see COMPLIMENT *v.*

felicitous /fəlísitəs/ *adj.* (of an expression, quotation, civilities, or a person making them) strikingly apt; pleasantly ingenious. □□ **felicitously** *adv.* **felicitousness** *n.*
■ see APPROPRIATE *adj.*

felicity /fəlísitee/ *n.* (*pl.* -**ies**) **1** intense happiness; being happy. **2** a cause of happiness. **3 a** a capacity for apt expression; appropriateness. **b** an appropriate or well-chosen phrase. **4** a fortunate trait. [ME f. OF *felicité* f. L *felicitas -tatis* f. *felix -icis* happy]
■ **1** see *happiness* (HAPPY). **3 a** see *fitness* (FIT¹).

feline /féelin/ *adj. & n.* ● *adj.* **1** of or relating to the cat family. **2** catlike, esp. in beauty or slyness. ● *n.* an animal of the cat family Felidae. □□ **felinity** /filínitee/ *n.* [L *felinus* f. *feles* cat]

fell¹ *past* of FALL *v.*

fell² /fel/ *v. & n.* ● *v.tr.* **1** cut down (esp. a tree). **2** strike or knock down (a person or animal). **3** stitch down (the edge of a seam) to lie flat. ● *n.* an amount of timber cut. □□ **feller** *n.* [OE *fellan* f. Gmc, rel. to FALL]
■ *v.* **1** cut down, hew (down). **2** cut *or* knock *or* strike down, floor, prostrate, *colloq.* flatten.

fell³ /fel/ *n. No. of Engl.* **1** a hill. **2** a stretch of hills or moorland. [ME f. ON *fjall, fell* hill]

fell⁴ /fel/ *adj. poet.* or *rhet.* **1** fierce; ruthless. **2** terrible; destructive. □ **at** (or **in**) **one fell swoop** in a single (orig. deadly) action. [ME f. OF *fel* f. Rmc FELON¹]

fell⁵ /fel/ *n.* an animal's hide or skin with its hair. [OE *fel, fell* f. Gmc]

fellah /félə/ *n.* (*pl.* **fellahin** /-ləhéen/) an Egyptian peasant. [Arab. *fallāḥ* husbandman f. *falaḥa* till the soil]

fellatio /filáysheeō, felaáteeō/ *n.* oral stimulation of the pe-

nis. □□ **fellate** /filáyt/ *v.tr.* **fellator** /filáytər/ *n.* [mod.L f. L *fellare* suck]

feller /félər/ *n.* = FELLOW 1, 2. [repr. an affected or sl. pronunc.]

felloe /félō/ *n.* (also **felly** /félee/) (*pl.* -**oes** or -**ies**) the outer circle (or a section of it) of a wheel, to which the spokes are fixed. [OE *felg*, of unkn. orig.]

fellow /félō/ *n.* **1** *colloq.* a man or boy (*poor fellow!*; *my dear fellow*). **2** *derog.* a person regarded with contempt. **3** (usu. in *pl.*) a person associated with another; a comrade (*were separated from their fellows*). **4** a counterpart or match; the other of a pair. **5** an equal; one of the same class. **6** a contemporary. **7 a** *Brit.* an incorporated senior member of a college. **b** a selected graduate receiving a stipend for a period of research. **c** a member of the governing body in some universities. **8** a member of a learned society. **9** (*attrib.*) belonging to the same class or activity (*fellow soldier*; *fellow citizen*). □ **fellow feeling** sympathy from common experience. **fellow traveler 1** a person who travels with another. **2** a sympathizer with, or a secret member of, the Communist Party. [OE *fēolaga* f. ON *félagi* f. *fé* cattle, property, money: see LAY¹]
■ **1** man, boy, gentleman, person, individual, *archaic* wight, *colloq.* guy, chap, *sl.* geezer, *Brit. sl.* bloke, *sl. often derog.* gink. **2** *sl.* bastard, jerk, son of a bitch, *sl. often derog.* gink; see also WRETCH 2. **3** associate, companion, colleague, ally; see also COMRADE. **4** counterpart, match, complement, mate, partner. **5** see EQUAL *n.* **6** contemporary, peer, compeer. **9** associate(d), affiliate(d), allied, related; co-, joint.

fellowship /félōship/ *n.* **1** companionship; friendliness. **2** participation; sharing; community of interest. **3** a body of associates; a company. **4** a brotherhood or fraternity. **5** a guild or corporation. **6** a financial grant to a scholar. **7** *Brit.* the status or emoluments of a fellow of a college or society.
■ **1** companionship, friendship, amity, comradeship, brotherhood, fraternization, association; friendliness, amicability, sociability, companionability, camaraderie, affability, kindliness, cordiality, congeniality, warmth, hospitality, familiarity, affinity, intimacy, togetherness. **2** see RAPPORT. **3–5** company, circle, community, order, organization, society, club, association, alliance, guild, corporation, league, union, sisterhood, brotherhood, fraternity, sorority, clan; see also ASSOCIATION 1.

felly var. of FELLOE.

felon¹ /félən/ *n. & adj.* ● *n.* a person who has committed a felony. ● *adj. archaic* cruel; wicked. □□ **felonry** *n.* [ME f. OF f. med.L *felo -onis*, of unkn. orig.]
■ *n.* criminal, outlaw, lawbreaker, offender, miscreant, malefactor, wrongdoer. ● *adj.* see WICKED 1, 2.

felon² /félən/ *n.* an inflamed sore on the finger near the nail. [ME, perh. as FELON¹: cf. med.L *felo, fello* in the same sense]

felonious /filṓneeəs/ *adj.* **1** criminal. **2** *Law adj.* of or involving felony. **b** who has committed felony. □□ **feloniously** *adv.*
■ **1, 2a** see ILLEGAL 2. **2 b** see MISCREANT *adj.*

felony /félənee/ *n.* (*pl.* -**ies**) a crime regarded by the law as grave, and usu. involving violence. [ME f. OF *felonie* (as FELON¹)]
■ see CRIME 1a.

felspar var. of FELDSPAR.

felt¹ /felt/ *n. & v.* ● *n.* **1** a kind of cloth made by rolling and pressing wool, etc., or by weaving and shrinking it. **2** a similar material made from other fibers. ● *v.* **1** *tr.* make into felt; mat together. **2** *tr.* cover with felt. **3** *intr.* become matted. □ **felt-tipped** (or **felt-tip**) **pen** a pen with a writing point made of felt or fiber. □□ **felty** *adj.* [OE f. WG]

felt² *past* and *past part.* of FEEL.

felucca /filúkə, -lǒǒkə/ *n.* a small Mediterranean coasting vessel with oars or lateen sails or both. [It. *felucca* f. obs. Sp. *faluca* f. Arab. *fulk*, perh. f. Gk *epholkion* sloop]

FEMA /féemə/ *abbr.* Federal Emergency Management Agency.

female /féemayl/ *adj. & n.* ● *adj.* **1** of the sex that can bear offspring or produce eggs. **2** (of plants or their parts) fruit-bearing; having a pistil and no stamens. **3** of or consisting

of women or female animals or female plants. **4** (of a screw, socket, etc.) manufactured hollow to receive a corresponding inserted part. ● *n.* a female person, animal, or plant. ◻ **female impersonator** a male performer impersonating a woman. ◻◻ **femaleness** *n.* [ME f. OF *femelle* (n.) f. L *femella* dimin. of *femina* a woman, assim. to *male*]
■ *n.* see WOMAN 1.

feme /fem/ *n. Law* a woman or wife. ◻ **feme covert** a married woman. **feme sole** a woman without a husband (esp. if divorced). [ME f. AF & OF f. L *femina* woman]

feminine /féminin/ *adj. & n.* ● *adj.* **1** of or characteristic of women. **2** having qualities associated with women. **3** womanly; effeminate. **4** *Gram.* of or denoting the gender proper to women's names. ● *n. Gram.* a feminine gender or word. ◻◻ **femininely** *adv.* **feminineness** *n.* **femininity** /-nínitee/ *n.* [ME f. OF *feminin -ine* or L *femininus* f. *femina* woman]
■ *adj.* **1** female, womanlike, womanly, ladylike, *archaic* feminal. **3** effeminate, unmanly, unmasculine, effete, *colloq.* sissy, sissified, *usu. derog.* womanish.

feminism /féminizm/ *n.* **1** the advocacy of women's rights on the ground of the equality of the sexes. **2** *Med.* the development of female characteristics in a male person. ◻◻ **feminist** *n.* (in sense 1). [L *femina* woman (in sense 1 after F *féminisme*)]

feminity /feminitee/ *n.* = *femininity* (see FEMININE). [ME f. OF *feminité* f. med.L *feminitas -tatis* f. L *femina* woman]

feminize /féminīz/ *v.tr. & intr.* make or become feminine or female. ◻◻ **feminization** *n.*

femme fatale /fém fətál, -taál, fay-/ *n.* (*pl.* **femmes fatales** *pronunc.* same) a seductively attractive woman. [F]
■ see SIREN 4a.

femto- /fémtō/ *comb. form* denoting a factor of 10^{-15} (*femtometer*). [Da. or Norw. *femten* fifteen]

femur /fee´mər/ *n.* (*pl.* **femurs** or **femora** /fémərə/) **1** *Anat.* the thigh bone, the thick bone between the hip and the knee. **2** the corresponding part of an insect. ◻◻ **femoral** /fémərəl/ *adj.* [L *femur femoris* thigh]

fen /fen/ *n.* a low marshy or flooded area of land. ◻◻ **fenny** *adj.* [OE *fenn* f. Gmc]
■ **1** see MARSH.

fence /fens/ *n. & v.* ● *n.* **1** a barrier or railing or other upright structure enclosing an area of ground, esp. to prevent or control access. **2** a large upright obstacle in steeplechasing or show jumping. **3** *sl.* a receiver of stolen goods. **4** a guard or guide in machinery. ● *v.* **1** *tr.* surround with or as with a fence. **2** *tr.* **a** (foll. by *in, off*) enclose or separate with or as with a fence. **b** (foll. by *up*) seal with or as with a fence. **3** *tr.* (foll. by *from, against*) screen; shield; protect. **4** *tr.* (foll. by *out*) exclude with or as with a fence; keep out. **5** *tr.* (also *absol.*) *sl.* deal in (stolen goods). **6** *intr.* practice the sport of fencing; use a sword. **7** *intr.* (foll. by *with*) evade answering (a person or question). **8** *intr.* (of a horse, etc.) leap fences. ◻ **sit on the fence** remain neutral or undecided in a dispute, etc. ◻◻ **fenceless** *adj.* **fencer** *n.* [ME f. DEFENSE]
■ *n.* **1** barrier, railing, palisade, enclosure, barricade; confine, wall, rampart. **2** see JUMP *n.* 4. **4** shield, guard, safeguard, screen, cover; guide. ● *v.* **1** surround, enclose, encircle, circumscribe, hedge, bound. **2 a** enclose, separate, coop (up *or* in), confine, hedge in. **b** (*fence up*) see *close off* (CLOSE²). **3** see SHIELD *v.* 4 (*fence out*) see *shut out* 1. **5** see DEAL¹ *v.* 2. **7** hedge; (*fence with*) parry, avoid, fend off, sidestep, dodge, evade; see also DUCK² *v.* 3. **8** see JUMP *v.* 1, 2. ◻ **sit on the fence** remain neutral *or* undecided *or* indecisive *or* uncommitted *or* uncertain *or* irresolute *or* impartial *or* unaligned *or* nonaligned *or* independent; vacillate.

fencing /fénsing/ *n.* **1** a set or extent of fences. **2** material for making fences. **3** the art or sport of swordplay.

fend /fend/ *v.* **1** *intr.* (foll. by *for*) look after (esp. oneself). **2** *tr.* (usu. foll. by *off*) keep away; ward off (an attack, etc.). [ME f. DEFEND]
■ **1** (*fend for oneself*) look after oneself, get along (on one's own), make do, shift for oneself, *colloq.* get by, take care of oneself. **2** (*fend off*) keep away, keep *or*

hold at bay, stave *or* ward *or* fight off, parry, resist, repel, deflect.

fender /féndər/ *n.* **1** a low frame bordering a fireplace to keep in falling coals, etc. **2** *Naut.* a piece of old timber, matting, etc., hung over a vessel's side to protect it against impact. **3 a** a thing used to keep something off, prevent a collision, etc. **b** a device or enclosure over or around the wheel of a motor vehicle, bicycle, etc.

fenestra /finéstrə/ *n.* (*pl.* **fenestrae** /-tree/) **1** *Anat.* a small hole or opening in a bone, etc., esp. one of two (**fenestra ovalis** /ōváylis/, **fenestra rotunda**) in the inner ear. **2** a perforation in a surgical instrument. **3** a hole made by surgical fenestration. [L, = window]

fenestrate /fénistrayt, finés-/ *adj. Bot. & Zool.* having small window-like perforations or transparent areas. [L *fenestratus* past part. of *fenestrare* f. *fenestra* window]

fenestrated /fénistraytid, finés-/ *adj.* **1** *Archit.* having windows. **2** perforated. **3** = FENESTRATE. **4** *Surgery* having fenestrae.

fenestration /fénistráyshən/ *n.* **1** *Archit.* the arrangement of windows in a building. **2** *Bot. & Zool.* being fenestrate. **3** a surgical operation in which a new opening is formed, esp. in the bony labyrinth of the inner ear, as a form of treatment in some cases of deafness.

Fenian /fee´neeən/ *n. & adj.* ● *n. hist.* a member of a 19th-c. league among the Irish in the US & Ireland for promoting revolution and overthrowing British government in Ireland. ● *adj.* of or relating to the Fenians. ◻◻ **Fenianism** *n.* [OIr. *féne* name of an ancient Irish people, confused with *fíann* guard of legendary kings]

fennec /fénik/ *n.* a small fox, *Vulpes zerda*, native to N. Africa, having large pointed ears. [Arab. *fanak*]

fennel /fénəl/ *n.* **1** a yellow-flowered fragrant umbelliferous plant, *Foeniculum vulgare*, with leaves or leaf stalks used in salads, soups, etc. **2** the seeds of this used as flavoring. [OE *finugl*, ends. & OF *fenoil* f. L *feniculum* f. *fenum* hay]

fenugreek /fényəgreek, fénə-/ *n.* **1** a leguminous plant, *Trigonella foenum-graecum*, having aromatic seeds. **2** these seeds used as flavoring, esp. ground and used in curry powder. [OE *fenogrecum*, superseded in ME f. OF *fenugrec* f. L *faenugraecum* (*fenum graecum* Greek hay), used by the Romans as fodder]

feoffment /féfmənt, feef-/ *n. hist.* a mode of conveying a freehold estate by a formal transfer of possession. ◻◻ **feoffee** /fefee, feefee/ *n.* **feoffor** *n.* [ME f. AF *feoffement*, rel. to FEE]

feral /fe´erəl, férəl/ *adj.* **1** (of an animal or plant) wild; untamed; uncultivated. **2 a** (of an animal) in a wild state after escape from captivity. **b** born in the wild of such an animal. **3** brutal. [L *ferus* wild]
■ **1, 2a** see WILD *adj.* 1. **3** see VICIOUS 1.

fer de lance /fáir də láns/ *n.* a large highly venomous snake, *Bothrops atrox*, native to Central and S. America. [F, = iron (head) of a lance]

ferial /fe´ereeəl, féreeəl/ *adj. Eccl.* **1** (of a day) ordinary; not appointed for a festival or fast. **2** (of a service, etc.) for use on a ferial day. [ME f. OF *ferial* or med.L *ferialis* f. L *feriae*: see FAIR²]

fermata /fermaátə/ *n.* (*pl.* **fermatas**) *Mus.* **1** an unspecified prolongation of a note or rest. **2** a sign ⌢ indicating this. [It.]

ferment *n. & v.* ● *n.* /fə́rment/ **1** agitation; excitement; tumult. **2 a** fermenting; fermentation. **b** a fermenting agent or leaven. ● *v.* /fərmént/ **1** *intr. & tr.* undergo or subject to fermentation. **2** *intr. & tr.* effervesce or cause to effervesce. **3** *tr.* excite; stir up; foment. ◻◻ **fermentable** *adj.* **fermenter** /-méntər/ *n.* [ME f. OF *ferment* or L *fermentum* f. L *fervēre* boil]
■ *n.* **1** see AGITATION 1. ● *v.* **1** leaven, brew; stir up; simmer, seethe. **2** effervesce, bubble, foam, froth; boil,

---

/. . ./ **pronunciation**   ● **part of speech**
◻ **phrases, idioms, and compounds**
◻◻ **derivatives**   ■ **synonym section**
cross-references appear in SMALL CAPITALS or *italics*

seethe. **3** excite, agitate, inflame, rouse; stir up, foment, incite, instigate, provoke.

fermentation /fə́rmentáyshən/ *n.* **1** the breakdown of a substance by microorganisms, such as yeasts and bacteria, usu. in the absence of oxygen, esp. of sugar to ethyl alcohol in making beers, wines, and spirits. **2** agitation; excitement. □□ **fermentative** /-méntətiv/ *adj.* [ME f. LL *fermentatio* (as FERMENT)]

fermi /fə́rmee, fér-/ *n.* (*pl.* **fermis**) a unit of length equal to 10⁻¹⁵ meter, formerly used in nuclear physics. [E. *Fermi*, Ital.-Amer. physicist d. 1954]

fermion /fə́rmeeon, fér-/ *n. Physics* any of several elementary particles with half-integral spin, e.g., nucleons (cf. BOSON). [as FERMI + -ON]

fermium /fə́rmeeəm, fér-/ *n. Chem.* a transuranic radioactive metallic element produced artificially. ¶ Symb.: **Fm**. [as FERMI + -IUM]

fern /fərn/ *n.* (*pl.* same or **ferns**) any flowerless plant of the order Filicales, reproducing by spores and usu. having feathery fronds. □□ **fernery** *n.* (*pl.* **-ies**). **fernless** *adj.* **ferny** *adj.* [OE *fearn* f. WG]

ferocious /fərṓshəs/ *adj.* fierce; savage; wildly cruel. □□ **ferociously** *adv.* **ferociousness** *n.* [L *ferox -ocis*]

■ fierce, savage, wild, feral, cruel, vicious, brutal, bestial, merciless, ruthless, pitiless, inhuman, barbaric, barbarous, violent, destructive, murderous, bloodthirsty, sanguinary, predatory, fiendish, diabolic, devilish, hellish, monstrous, *poet. or rhet.* fell.

ferocity /fərósitee/ *n.* (*pl.* **-ies**) a ferocious nature or act. [F *férocité* or L *ferocitas* (as FEROCIOUS)]

■ see VIOLENCE 1.

-ferous /fərəs/ *comb. form* (usu. **-iferous**) forming adjectives with the sense 'bearing,' 'having' (*auriferous*; *odoriferous*). □□ **-ferously** *suffix* forming adverbs. **-ferousness** *suffix* forming nouns. [from or after F *-fère* or L *-fer* producing f. *ferre* bear]

ferrate /férayt/ *n. Chem.* a salt of (the hypothetical) ferric acid. [L *ferrum* iron]

ferret /férit/ *n. & v.* ● *n.* **1** a small semidomesticated polecat, *Mustela putorius furo*, used in catching rabbits, rats, etc. **2** a person who searches assiduously. ● *v.* **1** *intr.* hunt with ferrets. **2** *intr.* rummage; search out. **3** *tr.* (often foll. by *about, away, out*, etc.) **a** clear out (holes or an area of ground) with ferrets. **b** take or drive away (rabbits, etc.) with ferrets. **4** *tr.* (foll. by *out*) search out (secrets, criminals, etc.). □□ **ferreter** *n.* **ferrety** *adj.* [ME f. OF *fu(i)ret* alt. f. *fu(i)ron* f. LL *furo -onis* f. L *fur* thief]

ferri- /féree/ *comb. form.* containing iron, esp. in ferric compounds. [L *ferrum* iron]

ferriage /féreeij/ *n.* **1** conveyance by ferry. **2** a charge for using a ferry.

ferric /férik/ *adj.* **1** of iron. **2** *Chem.* containing iron in a trivalent form (cf. FERROUS).

ferrimagnetism /férimágnitizəm/ *n. Physics* a form of ferromagnetism with nonparallel alignment of neighboring atoms or ions. □□ **ferrimagnetic** /-magnétik/ *adj.* [F *ferrimagnétisme* (as FERRI-, MAGNETISM)]

Ferris wheel /féris/ *n.* a carnival ride consisting of a tall revolving vertical wheel with passenger cars suspended on its outer edge. [G. W. G. *Ferris*, Amer. engineer d. 1896]

ferrite /férit/ *n. Chem.* **1** a magnetic subtance, a compound of ferric oxide and another metallic oxide. **2** an allotrope of pure iron occurring in low-carbon steel. □□ **ferritic** /ferítik/ *adj.* [L *ferrum* iron]

ferro- /férō/ *comb. form Chem.* **1** iron, esp. in ferrous compounds (*ferrocyanide*). **2** (of alloys) containing iron (*ferromanganese*). [L *ferrum* iron]

ferroconcrete /férōkónkreet/ *n. & adj.* ● *n.* concrete reinforced with steel. ● *adj.* made of reinforced concrete.

ferroelectric /férōiléktrik/ *adj. & n. Physics* ● *adj.* exhibiting permanent electric polarization that varies in strength with the applied electric field. ● *n.* a ferroelectric substance. □□ **ferroelectricity** /-trísitee/ *n.* [ELECTRIC after *ferromagnetic*]

ferromagnetism /férōmágnitizəm/ *n. Physics* a phenomenon in which there is a high susceptibility to magnetization, the strength of which varies with the applied magnetizing field, and which may persist after removal of the applied field. □□ **ferromagnetic** /-magnétik/ *adj.*

ferrous /férəs/ *adj.* **1** containing iron (*ferrous and nonferrous metals*). **2** *Chem.* containing iron in a divalent form (cf. FERRIC). [L *ferrum* iron]

ferruginous /fərṓōjinəs/ *adj.* **1** of or containing iron rust, or iron as a chemical constituent. **2** rust colored; reddish brown. [L *ferrugo -ginis* rust f. *ferrum* iron]

ferrule /férōōl/ *n.* **1** a ring or cap strengthening the end of a stick or tube. **2** a band strengthening or forming a joint. [earlier *verrel*, etc., f. OF *virelle*, *virol(e)*, f. L *viriola* dimin. of *viriae* bracelet: assim. to L *ferrum* iron]

ferry /féree/ *n. & v.* ● *n.* (*pl.* **-ies**) **1** a boat or aircraft, etc., for conveying passengers and goods, esp. across water and as a regular service. **2** the service itself or the place where it operates. ● *v.* (**-ies**, **-ied**) **1** *tr. & intr.* convey or go in a boat, etc., across water. **2** *intr.* (of a boat, etc.) pass to and fro across water. **3** *tr.* transport from one place to another, esp. as a regular service. □□ **ferryman** /-mən/ *n.* (*pl.* **-men**). [ME f. ON *ferja* f. Gmc]

■ *v.* **3** see SHIP v. 1, 4.

fertile /fə́rt'l/ *adj.* **1 a** (of soil) producing abundant vegetation or crops. **b** fruitful. **2 a** (of a seed, egg, etc.) capable of becoming a new individual. **b** (of animals and plants) able to conceive young or produce fruit. **3** (of the mind) inventive. **4** (of nuclear material) able to become fissile by the capture of neutrons. □ **Fertile Crescent** the fertile region extending in a crescent shape from the E. Mediterranean to the Persian Gulf. □□ **fertility** /-tílitee/ *n.* [ME f. F f. L *fertilis*]

■ **1** productive, fructuous; see also FRUITFUL 1. **2 b** fecund; productive, prolific. **3** inventive, fecund, generative, luxuriant, teeming, prolific, rich.

fertilization /fə́rt'lizáyshən/ *n.* **1** *Biol.* the fusion of male and female gametes during sexual reproduction to form a zygote. **2 a** the act or an instance of fertilizing. **b** the process of being fertilized.

fertilize /fə́rt'līz/ *v.tr.* **1** make (soil, etc.) fertile or productive. **2** cause (an egg, female animal, or plant) to develop a new individual by introducing male reproductive material. □□ **fertilizable** *adj.*

■ **1** manure, mulch, feed, nourish, enrich, dress, compost. **2** impregnate, inseminate, fecundate, fructify, pollinate.

fertilizer /fə́rt'lizər/ *n.* a chemical or natural substance added to soil to make it more fertile.

ferula /férələ, féryə-/ *n.* **1** any plant of the genus *Ferula*, esp. the giant fennel (*F. communis*), having a tall sticklike stem and thick roots. **2** = FERULE. [ME f. L, = giant fennel, rod]

ferule /férəl, -rōōl/ *n. & v.* ● *n.* a flat ruler with a widened end formerly used for beating children. ● *v.tr.* beat with a ferule. [ME (as FERULA)]

fervent /fə́rvənt/ *adj.* **1** ardent; impassioned; intense (*fervent admirer*; *fervent hatred*). **2** hot; glowing. □□ **fervency** *n.* **fervently** *adv.* [ME f. OF f. L *fervēre* boil]

■ **1** ardent, eager, earnest, enthusiastic, zealous, animated, intense, impassioned, passionate, emotional, fervid, fiery, hotheaded, fanatical, fanatic; ecstatic, rapturous, rapt, heartfelt. **2** hot, glowing, inflamed, burning, *poet.* fervid.

fervid /fə́rvid/ *adj.* **1** ardent; intense. **2** hot; glowing. □□ **fervidly** *adv.* [L *fervidus* (as FERVENT)]

■ **1** see *on fire* 2 (FIRE). **2** see INCANDESCENT.

fervor /fə́rvər/ *n.* (*Brit.* **fervour**) **1** vehemence; passion; zeal. **2** a glowing condition; intense heat. [ME f. OF f. L *fervor -oris* (as FERVENT)]

■ **1** vehemence, passion, zeal, fervency, ardor, eagerness, earnestness, enthusiasm, animation, glow, gusto, ebullience, spirit, verve, intensity, warmth. **2** see *incandescence* (INCANDESCENT).

fescue /féskyōō/ *n.* any grass of the genus *Festuca*, valuable for pasture and fodder. [ME *festu(e)* f. OF *festu* ult. f. L *festuca* stalk, straw]

fess /fes/ *n.* (also **fesse**) *Heraldry* a horizontal stripe across the middle of a shield. □ **fess point** a point at the center of a shield. **in fess** arranged horizontally. [ME f. OF f. L *fascia* band]

festal /fést'l/ *adj.* **1** joyous; merry. **2** engaging in holiday activities. **3** of a feast. □□ **festally** *adv.* [OF f. LL *festalis* (as FEAST)]

fester /féstər/ *v. & n.* ● *v.* **1** *tr.* & *intr.* make or become septic. **2** *intr.* cause continuing annoyance. **3** *intr.* rot; stagnate. ● *n.* a pus-filled sore. [ME f. OF *festrir*, f. OF *festre* f. L *fistula*: see FISTULA]

■ **1** suppurate, decompose; see also ROT *v.* 1a. **2** see RANKLE 1. **3** putrefy, necrose, mortify, rot, decay, decompose; stagnate.

festival /féstivəl/ *n. & adj.* ● *n.* **1** a day or period of celebration, religious or secular. **2** a concentrated series of concerts, plays, etc., held regularly in a town, etc. ● *attrib.adj.* of or concerning a festival. [earlier as adj.: ME f. OF f. med.L *festivalis* (as FESTIVE)]

■ *n.* **1** holiday, holy day, fête, *fête champêtre*, fiesta, feast, anniversary, entertainment, carnival, red-letter day, gala (day), event.

festive /féstiv/ *adj.* **1** of or characteristic of a festival. **2** joyous. **3** fond of feasting; jovial. □□ **festively** *adv.* **festiveness** *n.* [L *festivus* f. *festum* (as FEAST)]

■ **1** see GALA *adj.* 1. **2** see JOLLY[1] *adj.* 1, 2.

festivity /féstívitee/ *n.* (*pl.* **-ies**) **1** gaiety; rejoicing. **2 a** a festive celebration. **b** (in *pl.*) festive proceedings. [ME f. OF *festivité* or L *festivitas* (as FESTIVE)]

■ **1** gaiety, rejoicing, mirth, jubilation, conviviality, merriment, revelry, merrymaking, glee, jollity, jollification, felicity, joyfulness. **2** festival, party, fun and games, entertainment; see also *celebration* (CELEBRATE).

festoon /festoon/ *n. & v.* ● *n.* **1** a chain of flowers, leaves, ribbons, etc., hung in a curve as a decoration. **2** a carved or molded ornament representing this. ● *v.tr.* (often foll. by *with*) adorn with or form into festoons; decorate elaborately. □□ **festoonery** *n.* [F *feston* f. It. *festone* f. *festa* FEAST]

■ *n.* **1** see GARLAND *n.* 1. ● *v.* see GARLAND *v.*

Festschrift /féstshrift/ *n.* (also **festschrift**) (*pl.* **-schriften** or **-schrifts**) a collection of writings published in honor of a scholar. [G f. *Fest* celebration + *Schrift* writing]

feta /fétə/ *n.* a crumbly white ewe's milk or goat's milk cheese cured in brine, made esp. in Greece. [mod.Gk *pheta*]

fetch[1] /fech/ *v. & n.* ● *v.tr.* **1** go for and bring back (a person or thing) (*fetch a doctor*). **2** be sold for; realize (a price) (*fetched $10*). **3** cause (blood, tears, etc.) to flow. **4** draw (breath); heave (a sigh). **5** *colloq.* give (a blow, slap, etc.) (usu. with recipient stated: *fetched him a slap on the face*). **6** excite the emotions of; delight or irritate. **7** *Naut.* to arrive at; to reach, esp. by sailing. ● *n.* **1** an act of fetching. **2** a dodge or trick. **3** *Naut.* **a** the distance traveled by wind or waves across open water. **b** the distance a vessel must sail to reach open water. □ **fetch and carry** run backward and forward with things; be a servant. **fetch up** *colloq.* **1** arrive; come to rest. **2** *Brit.* vomit. □□ **fetcher** *n.* [OE *fecc(e)an* var. of *fetian*, prob. rel. to a Gmc root = grasp]

■ *v.* **1** go for *or* after, get, bring (back), retrieve, obtain; summon, call, bring *or* draw forth. **2** sell for, go for, bring in, yield, earn, make. ● *n.* **2** see DODGE *n.* **3** reach; stretch, extent; see also RANGE *n.* 1a–c.

fetch[2] /fech/ *n.* a person's wraith or double, doppelgänger. [18th c.: orig. unkn.]

fetching /féching/ *adj.* attractive. □□ **fetchingly** *adv.*

■ attractive, alluring, taking, winsome, winning, *colloq.* cute.

fête /fayt, fet/ *n. & v.* ● *n.* **1** a great entertainment; a festival. **2** *Brit.* an outdoor function with the sale of goods, amusements, etc., esp. to raise funds for charity. **3** a saint's day. ● *v.tr.* honor or entertain lavishly. [F *fête* (as FEAST)]

■ *n.* **1** entertainment, celebration, party, frolic, festivities, reception, levee, *colloq.* get-together, social, shindig, *sl.* bash, blast, do, wingding; festival, jamboree, carnival. ● *v.* honor, celebrate, lionize, make a fuss of *or* over,

kill the fatted calf for, roll *or* bring out the red carpet for; entertain.

fête champêtre /fáyt shoNpáytrə/ *n.* an outdoor entertainment; a rural festival. [F (as FÊTE, *champêtre* rural)]

fetid /fétid, féetid/ *adj.* (also **foetid**) stinking. □□ **fetidly** *adv.* **fetidness** *n.* [L *fetidus* f. *fetēre* stink]

■ see STINKING *adj.* 1.

fetish /fétish/ *n.* **1** *Psychol.* a thing abnormally stimulating or attracting sexual desire. **2 a** an inanimate object worshiped for its supposed inherent magical powers or as being inhabited by a spirit. **b** a thing evoking irrational devotion or respect. □□ **fetishism** *n.* **fetishist** *n.* **fetishistic** /-shístik/ *adj.* [F *fétiche* f. Port. *feitiço* charm: orig. adj. = made by art, f. L *factitius* FACTITIOUS]

■ **2 a** charm, amulet, talisman, totem, periapt. **b** obsession, mania, compulsion, fixation, *idée fixe*.

fetlock /fétlok/ *n.* part of the back of a horse's leg above the hoof where a tuft of hair grows. [ME *fetlak*, etc., rel. to G *Fessel* fetlock f. Gmc]

fetor /féetər/ *n.* a stench. [L (as FETID)]

fetter /fétər/ *n. & v.* ● *n.* **1 a** a shackle for holding a prisoner by the ankles. **b** any shackle or bond. **2** (in *pl.*) captivity. **3** a restraint or check. ● *v.tr.* **1** put into fetters. **2** restrict; restrain; impede. [OE *feter* f. Gmc]

■ *n.* **1, 3** see TETHER *n.* ● *v.* see CHAIN *v.*

fettle /fét'l/ *n. & v.* ● *n.* condition or trim (*in fine fettle*). ● *v.tr.* **1** trim or clean (the rough edge of a metal casting, pottery before firing, etc.). **2** line a hearth, furnace, etc., with loose sand or gravel. [earlier as verb, f. dial. *fettle* (n.) = girdle, f. OE *fetel* f. Gmc]

■ *n.* see CONDITION *n.* 2a.

fettuccine /fetəchéenee/ *n.* (also **fettuccini**) pasta in the form of long flat ribbons. [It, f. *fetta* ribbon, slice]

fetus /féetəs/ *n.* (*Brit.* **foetus**) an unborn or unhatched offspring of a mammal, esp. a human one more than eight weeks after conception. □□ **fetal** *adj.* **feticide** /-tisíd/ *n.* [ME f. L *fetus* offspring]

feud[1] /fyood/ *n. & v.* ● *n.* **1** prolonged mutual hostility, esp. between two families, tribes, etc., with murderous assaults in revenge for a previous injury (*a family feud*; *be at feud with*). **2** a prolonged or bitter quarrel or dispute. ● *v.intr.* conduct a feud. [ME *fede* f. OF *feide*, *fede* f. MDu., MLG *vēde* f. Gmc, rel. to FOE]

■ *n.* **1** vendetta, blood feud. **2** quarrel, dispute, disagreement, argument, squabble, falling out. ● *v.* quarrel, fall out, dispute, disagree, clash, conflict, fight, be at odds, be at daggers drawn, *colloq.* row.

feud[2] /fyood/ *n.* a piece of land held under the feudal system or in fee; a fief. [med.L *feudum*: see FEE]

feudal /fyood'l/ *adj.* **1** of, according to, or resembling the feudal system. **2** of a feud or fief. **3** outdated (*had a feudal attitude*). □ **feudal system** the social system in medieval Europe whereby a vassal held land from a superior in exchange for allegiance and service. □□ **feudalism** *n.* **feudalist** *n.* **feudalistic** *adj.* **feudalize** *v.tr.* **feudalization** *n.* **feudally** *adv.* [med.L *feudalis*, *feodalis* f. *feudum*, *feodum* FEE, perh. f. Gmc]

feudality /fyoodálitee/ *n.* (*pl.* **-ies**) **1** the feudal system or its principles. **2** a feudal holding; a fief. [F *féodalité* f. *féodal* (as FEUDAL)]

feudatory /fyoodətáwree/ *adj. & n.* ● *adj.* (often foll. by *to*) feudally subject; under overlordship. ● *n.* (*pl.* **-ies**) a feudal vassal. [med.L *feudatorius* f. *feudare* enfeoff (as FEUD[2])]

feudist /fyoodist/ *n.* a person who is conducting a feud.

feuilleton /fő-yətáwN/ *n.* **1** a part of a European newspaper, etc., devoted to fiction, criticism, light literature, etc. **2** an item printed in this. [F, = leaflet]

fever /féevər/ *n. & v.* ● *n.* **1 a** an abnormally high body temperature, often with delirium, etc. **b** a disease characterized by this (*scarlet fever*; *typhoid fever*). **2** nervous excite-

---

/.../ **pronunciation**	● **part of speech**
□ **phrases, idioms, and compounds**	
□□ **derivatives**	■ **synonym section**
cross-references appear in SMALL CAPITALS or *italics*	

ment; agitation. ● *v.tr.* (esp. as **fevered** *adj.*) affect with fever or excitement. □ **fever pitch** a state of extreme excitement. [OE *fēfor* & AF *fevre*, OF *fievre* f. L *febris*]

■ *n.* 2 see FRENZY *n.* 1. ● *v.* (**fevered**) see IMPASSIONED.

feverfew /féevərfyŏŏ/ *n.* an aromatic bushy European plant, *Chrysanthemum parthenium*, with feathery leaves and white daisy-like flowers, formerly used to reduce fever. [OE *feferfuge* f. L *febrifuga* (as FEBRIFUGE)]

feverish /féevərish/ *adj.* **1** having the symptoms of a fever. **2** excited; fitful; restless. **3** (of a place) infested by fever; feverous. □□ **feverishly** *adv.* **feverishness** *n.*

■ **1** flushed, hot; febrile, pyretic, *Med.* pyrexic. **2** excited, frenzied, frantic, frenetic; fitful, restless; ardent, fervent, passionate, burning, fiery, heated, hot, inflamed; flushed, hot-blooded.

feverous /féevərəs/ *adj.* **1** *Brit.* infested with or apt to cause fever. **2** feverish.

few /fyŏŏ/ *adj.* & *n.* ● *adj.* not many (*few doctors smoke*; *visitors are few*). ● *n.* (as *pl.*) **1** (prec. by *a*) some but not many (*a few words should be added*; *a few of his friends were there*). **2** a small number; not many (*many are called but few are chosen*). **3** (prec. by *the*) **a** the minority. **b** the elect. **4** (**the Few**) *Brit. colloq.* the RAF pilots who took part in the Battle of Britain. □ **every few** once in every small group of (*every few days*). **few and far between** scarce. **a good few** *Brit. colloq.* a fairly large number. **have a few** *colloq.* have several alcoholic drinks. **no fewer than** as many as (a specified number). **not a few** a considerable number. **some few** some but not at all many. □□ **fewness** *n.* [OE *fēawe, fēawa* f. Gmc]

■ *adj.* not many, hardly *or* scarcely any; infrequent, occasional. ● *n.* **1** (*a few*) some, not many, one or two; a handful, a scattering, a small number. **2** not many, (only) one or two, (only) a handful *or* a scattering *or* a small number. □ **few and far between** see SCARCE *adj.* 2.

fey /fay/ *adj.* **1 a** strange; otherworldly; elfin; whimsical. **b** clairvoyant. **2** *Sc.* **a** fated to die soon. **b** overexcited or elated, as formerly associated with the state of mind of a person about to die. □□ **feyly** *adv.* **feyness** *n.* [OE *fǣge* f. Gmc]

■ **1 a** see WHIMSICAL 2, 3.

fez /fez/ *n.* (*pl.* **fezzes**) a flat-topped conical red cap with a tassel, worn by men in some Muslim countries. □□ **fezzed** *adj.* [Turk., perh. f. *Fez* (now *Fès*) in Morocco]

ff *abbr. Mus.* fortissimo.

ff. *abbr.* **1** following pages, etc. **2** folios.

FHA *abbr.* Federal Housing Administration.

fiacre /fiaákər/ *n. hist.* a small four-wheeled carriage. [the Hôtel de St. *Fiacre*, Paris]

fiancé /féeonsáy, fónsay/ *n.* (*fem.* **fiancée** *pronunc.* same) a person to whom another is engaged to be married. [F, past part. of *fiancer* betroth f. OF *fiance* a promise, ult. f. L *fidere* to trust]

■ betrothed, wife to be, bride to be, husband to be, intended.

fianchetto /féeənchétō/ *n.* & *v. Chess* ● *n.* (*pl.* **-oes**) the development of a bishop to a long diagonal of the board. ● *v.tr.* (**-oes, -oed**) develop (a bishop) in this way. [It., dimin. of *fianco* FLANK]

fiasco /feeáskō/ *n.* (*pl.* **-os**) a ludicrous or humiliating failure or breakdown (orig. in a dramatic or musical performance); an ignominious result. [It., = bottle (with unexplained allusion): see FLASK]

■ failure, disaster, muddle, mess, botch, *sl.* flop.

fiat /féeət, -at, -aat, fíat, fíət/ *n.* **1** an authorization. **2** a decree or order. □ **fiat money** inconvertible paper money made legal tender by a government decree. [L, = let it be done]

fib /fib/ *n.* & *v.* ● *n.* a trivial or venial lie. ● *v.intr.* (**fibbed, fibbing**) tell a fib. □□ **fibber** *n.* **fibster** *n.* [perh. f. obs. *fible-fable* nonsense, redupl. of FABLE]

■ *n.* (little) white lie, tale, fairy story *or* tale, untruth, falsehood, fabrication, invention, story, fiction, lie. ● *v.* see LIE² *v.* 1a.

fiber /fíbər/ *n.* (*Brit.* **fibre**) **1** *Biol.* any of the threads or filaments forming animal or vegetable tissue and textile substances. **2** a piece of glass in the form of a thread. **3 a** a substance formed of fibers. **b** a substance that can be spun, woven, or felted. **4** the structure, grain, or character of something (*lacks moral fiber*). **5** dietary material that is resistant to the action of digestive enzymes; roughage. □ **fiber optics** optics employing thin glass fibers, usu. for the transmission of light, esp. modulated to carry signals. □□ **fibered** *adj.* (also in *comb.*). **fiberless** *adj.* **fibriform** /fíbrifawrm/ *adj.* [ME f. F f. L *fibra*]

■ **1** thread, filament, strand, fibril. **4** structure, texture, mold, cast, composition, constitution, makeup, grain, material, substance, fabric, character, essence, nature, quality.

fiberboard /fíbərbawrd/ *n.* a building material made of wood or other plant fibers compressed into boards.

fiberglass /fíbərglas/ *n.* & *v.* ● *n.* **1** a textile fabric made from woven glass fibers. **2** a plastic reinforced by glass fibers. ● *v.tr.* repair or reinforce with fiberglass.

Fibonacci series /feebənaáchee/ *n. Math.* a series of numbers in which each number (**Fibonacci number**) is the sum of the two preceding numbers, esp. 1, 1, 2, 3, 5, 8, etc. [L. *Fibonacci*, It. mathematician *fl.* 1200]

fibre *Brit.* var. of FIBER.

fibril /fíbril, fib-/ *n.* **1** a small fiber. **2** a subdivision of a fiber. □□ **fibrillar** *adj.* **fibrillary** *adj.* [mod.L *fibrilla* dimin. of L *fibra* fiber]

fibrillate /fíbrilayt, fí-/ *v.* **1** *intr.* **a** (of a fiber) split up into fibrils. **b** (of a muscle, esp. in the heart) undergo a quivering movement in fibrils. **2** *tr.* break (a fiber) into fibrils. □□ **fibrillation** /-láyshən/ *n.*

fibrin /fíbrin/ *n.* an insoluble protein formed during blood clotting from fibrinogen. □□ **fibrinoid** *adj.* [FIBER + -IN]

fibrinogen /fibrínəjən/ *n.* a soluble blood plasma protein that produces fibrin when acted upon by the enzyme thrombin.

fibro- /fíbrō/ *comb. form* fiber.

fibroid /fíbroyd/ *adj.* & *n.* ● *adj.* **1** of or characterized by fibrous tissue. **2** resembling or containing fibers. ● *n.* a benign tumor of muscular and fibrous tissues, one or more of which may develop in the wall of the uterus.

fibroin /fíbrōin/ *n.* a protein that is the chief constituent of silk. [FIBRO- + -IN]

fibroma /fíbrōmə/ *n.* (*pl.* **fibromas** or **fibromata** /-mətə/) a fibrous tumor. [mod.L f. L *fibra* fiber + -OMA]

fibrosis /fíbrōsis/ *n. Med.* a thickening and scarring of connective tissue, usu. as a result of injury or disease. □□ **fibrotic** /-brótik/ *adj.* [mod.L f. L *fibra* fiber + -OSIS]

fibrositis /fíbrəsítis/ *n.* an inflammation of fibrous connective tissue, usu. rheumatic and painful. □□ **fibrositic** /-sítik/ *adj.* [mod.L f. L *fibrosus* fibrous + -ITIS]

fibrous /fíbrəs/ *adj.* consisting of or like fibers. □□ **fibrously** *adv.* **fibrousness** *n.*

■ see STRINGY 2.

fibula /fíbyələ/ *n.* (*pl.* **fibulae** /-lee/ or **fibulas**) **1** *Anat.* the smaller and outer of the two bones between the knee and the ankle in terrestrial vertebrates. **2** *Antiq.* a brooch or clasp. □□ **fibular** *adj.* [L, perh. rel. to *figere* fix]

-fic /fik/ *suffix* (usu. as **-ific**) forming adjectives meaning 'producing,' 'making' (*prolific*; *pacific*). □□ **-fically** *suffix* forming adverbs. [from or after F *-fique* or L *-ficus* f. *facere* do, make]

FICA /fíkə/ *abbr.* Federal Insurance Contributions Act.

-fication /fikáyshən/ *suffix* (usu. as **-ification** /ifikáyshən/) forming nouns of action from verbs in *-fy* (*acidification*; *purification*; *simplification*). [from or after F *-fication* or L *-ficatio -onis* f. *-ficare*: see -FY]

fiche /feesh/ *n.* (*pl.* same or **fiches**) a microfiche. [F, = slip of paper]

fichu /físhōo, feeshŏŏ/ *n.* a woman's small triangular shawl of lace, etc., for the shoulders and neck. [F]

fickle /fíkəl/ *adj.* inconstant or changeable, esp. in loyalty. □□ **fickleness** *n.* **fickly** *adv.* [OE *ficol*: cf. *befician* deceive, *fǣcne* deceitful]

■ inconstant, unfaithful, faithless, disloyal, changeable, changeful, unsteady, unsteadfast, wavering, indecisive, uncertain, unsure, wishy-washy, vacillating, erratic, flighty, capricious, unpredictable, moody, whimsical, fitful, unstable, unreliable, *literary* mutable.

fictile /fíktəl, -tíl/ *adj.* **1** made of earth or clay by a potter. **2** of pottery. [L *fictilis* f. *fingere fict-* fashion]

fiction /fíkshən/ *n.* **1** an invented idea or statement or narrative; an imaginary thing. **2** literature, esp. novels, describing imaginary events and people. **3** a conventionally accepted falsehood (*legal fiction; polite fiction*). **4** the act or process of inventing imaginary things. □□ **fictional** *adj.* **fictionality** /-nálitee/ *n.* **fictionalize** *v.tr.* **fictionalization** *n.* **fictionally** *adv.* **fictionist** *n.* [ME f. OF f. L *fictio -onis* (as FICTILE)]

■ **1, 3** see INVENTION 3. **2** see WRITING 4. □□ **fictional** unreal, imaginary, invented, made-up, fanciful, mythical, fictitious.

fictitious /fiktíshəs/ *adj.* **1** imaginary; unreal. **2** counterfeit; not genuine. **3** (of a name or character) assumed. **4** of or in novels. □□ **fictitiously** *adv.* **fictitiousness** *n.* [L *ficticius* (as FICTILE)]

■ **1** imaginary, unreal, imagined, fictive, fanciful, fictional, fancied, nonexistent, made-up, invented, fabricated, mythical, apocryphal, untrue. **2** counterfeit, false, bogus, spurious, made-up, invented, *colloq.* phony; make-believe, imaginary. **3** false, adopted, improvised, *colloq.* phony; see also ASSUMED 1.

fictive /fíktiv/ *adj.* **1** creating or created by imagination. **2** not genuine. □□ **fictively** *adv.* **fictiveness** *n.* [F *fictif -ive* or med.L *fictivus* (as FICTILE)]

■ see FICTITIOUS.

fid /fid/ *n.* **1** *Brit.* a small thick piece or wedge or heap of anything. **2** *Naut.* **a** a square wooden or iron bar to support the topmast. **b** a conical wooden pin used in splicing. [17th c.: orig. unkn.]

fiddle /fíd'l/ *n. & v.* ● *n.* **1** a stringed instrument played with a bow, esp. a violin. **2** *Brit. colloq.* an instance of cheating or fraud. **3** *Naut.* a contrivance for stopping things from rolling or sliding off a table in bad weather. ● *v.* **1** *intr.* **a** (often foll. by *with*) play restlessly. **b** (often foll. by *about*) move aimlessly. **c** act idly or frivolously. **d** (usu. foll. by *with*) make minor adjustments; tinker (esp. in an attempt to make improvements). **2** *tr. Brit. sl.* **a** cheat; swindle. **b** falsify. **c** get by cheating. **3 a** *intr.* play the fiddle. **b** *tr.* play (a tune, etc.) on the fiddle. □ **as fit as a fiddle** in very good health. **face as long as a fiddle** a dismal face. **fiddle back** a fiddle-shaped back of a chair or front of a chasuble. **fiddle pattern** the pattern of spoons and forks with fiddle-shaped handles. **play second** (or **first**) **fiddle** take a subordinate (or leading) role. [OE *fithele* f. Gmc f. a Rmc root rel. to VIOL]

■ *n.* **1** violin, viola, viol, cello, *formal* violoncello, *hist.* kit. ● *v.* **1 a** (*fiddle with*) play with, twiddle; see also TOY *v.* 1. **b** see FIDGET *v.* 1. **c** fool *or* fuss *or* mess about *or* around, frivol, trifle, monkey (around *or* about), *Brit. colloq.* muck about *or* around. **d** see TINKER *v.* □ **play first fiddle** see *call the shots.*

fiddle-de-dee /fíd'ldeedeé/ *int. & n.* nonsense!

fiddle-faddle /fíd'lfad'l/ *n., v., int., & adj.* ● *n.* trivial matters. ● *v.intr.* fuss; trifle. ● *int.* nonsense! ● *adj.* (of a person or thing) petty; fussy. [redupl. of FIDDLE]

fiddlehead /fíd'lhed/ *n.* **1** a scroll-like carving at a ship's bows. **2** the coiled frond of some ferns eaten as a vegetable.

fiddler /fíd'lər/ *n.* **1** a fiddle player. **2** any small N. American crab of the genus *Uca*, the male having one of its claws enlarged and held in a position like a violinist's arm. **3** *Brit. sl.* a swindler; a cheat. [OE *fithelere* (as FIDDLE)]

fiddlestick /fíd'lstik/ *n.* **1** (in *pl.*; as *int.*) nonsense! **2** *colloq.* a bow for a fiddle.

■ **1** (*fiddlesticks!*) nonsense, rubbish, fiddle-de-dee, fiddle-faddle, balderdash, stuff and nonsense, moonshine, rot, *colloq.* hogwash, *sl.* bosh, poppycock, tommyrot, eyewash, baloney, bilgewater, humbug, bull, *Brit. sl.* codswallop.

fiddling /fídling/ *adj.* **1 a** petty; trivial. **b** contemptible; futile. **2** *Brit. colloq.* = FIDDLY. **3** that fiddles.

fiddly /fídlee/ *adj.* (**fiddlier, fiddliest**) esp. *Brit. colloq.* intricate, awkward, or tiresome to do or use.

fideism /féedayizəm, fídee-/ *n.* the doctrine that all or some knowledge depends on faith or revelation. □□ **fideist** *n.* **fideistic** *adj.* [L *fides* faith + -ISM]

fidelity /fidélitee/ *n.* **1** (often foll. by *to*) faithfulness; loyalty. **2** strict conformity to truth or fact. **3** exact correspondence to the original. **4** precision in reproduction of sound or video (*high fidelity*). [F *fidélité* or L *fidelitas* (as FEALTY)]

■ **1** see ATTACHMENT 2.

fidget /fíjit/ *v. & n.* ● *v.* (**fidgeted, fidgeting**) **1** *intr.* move or act restlessly or nervously, usu. while maintaining basically the same posture. **2** *intr.* be uneasy; worry. **3** *tr.* make (a person) uneasy or uncomfortable. ● *n.* **1** a person who fidgets. **2** (usu. in *pl.*) **a** bodily uneasiness seeking relief in spasmodic movements; such movements. **b** a restless mood. □□ **fidgety** *adj.* **fidgetiness** *n.* [obs. or dial. *fidge* to twitch]

■ *v.* **1** squirm, twitch, shuffle, wriggle, jig about, fiddle, fuss, *colloq.* have ants in one's pants, wiggle. **2** see FRET¹ *v.* 1a. ● *n.* **1** *colloq.* cat on a hot tin roof. **2 a** (*the fidgets*) see JITTER *n.* **b** restlessness, fidgetiness, uneasiness, nervousness, itchiness, *colloq.* jimjams, *sl.* the heebie-jeebies.

fiducial /fido͞oshəl, -dyo͞o-, fi-/ *adj. Surveying, Astron.,* etc., (of a line, point, etc.) assumed as a fixed basis of comparison; a standard reference. [LL *fiducialis* f. *fiducia* trust f. *fidere* to trust]

fiduciary /fido͞oshee-eree, -shəree, -dyo͞o-, fi-/ *adj. & n.* ● *adj.* **1 a** of a trust, trustee, or trusteeship. **b** held or given in trust. **2** (of a paper currency) depending for its value on public confidence or securities. ● *n.* (*pl.* **-ies**) a trustee. [L *fiduciarius* (as FIDUCIAL)]

fie /fi/ *int.* expressing disgust, shame, or a pretense of outraged propriety. [ME f. OF f. L *fi* exclam. of disgust at a stench]

fief /feef/ *n.* **1** a piece of land held under the feudal system or in fee. **2** a person's sphere of operation or control. [F (as FEE)]

fiefdom /féefdəm/ *n.* a fief.

field /feeld/ *n. & v.* ● *n.* **1** an area of open land, esp. one used for pasture or crops, often bounded by hedges, fences, etc. **2** an area rich in some natural product (*gas field; diamond field*). **3** a piece of land for a specified purpose, esp. **a** an area marked out for a game or sport (*football field*), or **b** an airfield. **4 a** the participants in a contest or sport. **b** all the competitors in a race or all except those specified. **5** *Cricket* **a** the side fielding. **b** a fielder. **6** an expanse of ice, snow, sea, sky, etc. **7 a** the ground on which a battle is fought; a battlefield (*left his rival in possession of the field*). **b** the scene of a campaign. **c** (*attrib.*) (of artillery, etc.) light and mobile for use on campaign. **d** a battle. **8** an area of operation or activity; a subject of study (*each supreme in his own field*). **9 a** the region in which a force is effective (*gravitational field; magnetic field*). **b** the force exerted in such an area. **10** a range of perception (*field of view; wide field of vision; filled the field of the telescope*). **11** *Math.* a system subject to two operations analogous to those for the multiplication and addition of real numbers. **12** (*attrib.*) **a** (of an animal or plant) found in the countryside; wild (*field mouse*). **b** carried out or working in the natural environment, not in a laboratory, etc. (*field test*). **13 a** the background of a picture, coin, flag, etc. **b** *Heraldry* the surface of an escutcheon or of one of its divisions. **14** *Computing* a part of a database record, representing an item of data. ● *v.* **1** *Baseball, Cricket,* etc. **a** *intr.* act as a fielder. **b** *tr.* catch (and return) (the ball). **2** *tr.* select (a team or individual) to play in a game. **3** *tr.* deal with (a succession of questions, etc.). □ **field**

/.../ **pronunciation**	● **part of speech**
□ **phrases, idioms, and compounds**	
□□ **derivatives**	■ **synonym section**
cross-references appear in SMALL CAPITALS or *italics*	

day 1 wide scope for action or success; a time occupied with exciting events (*when crowds form, pickpockets have a field day*). **2** *Mil.* an exercise, esp. in maneuvering; a review. **3** a day spent in exploration, scientific investigation, etc., in the natural environment. **4** an all-day sports or athletics meet, esp. at a school. **field events** athletic events other than races (e.g., shot-putting, jumping, discus throwing). **field glasses** binoculars for outdoor use. **field goal 1** *Football* a score of three points by a kick from the field. **2** *Basketball* a goal scored when the ball is in normal play. **field grade** any rank in the air force, army, or marines above captain and below general. **field hockey** a field game played between two teams with curved sticks and a small hard ball. **field hospital** a temporary hospital near a battlefield. **Field Marshal** *Brit.* an army officer of the highest rank. **field mouse 1** a small rodent, *Apodemus sylvaticus*, with beady eyes, prominent ears, and a long tail. **2** various similar rodents inhabiting fields. **field mushroom** the edible fungus *Agaricus campestris*. **field officer** an army officer of field grade or (*Brit.*) rank. **field of honor** the place where a duel or battle is fought. **field rank** *Brit.* = *field grade*. **hold the field** not be defeated; remain in battle. **in the field 1** campaigning. **2** working, etc., away from one's laboratory, headquarters, etc. **keep the field** continue a campaign. **play the field** *colloq.* avoid exclusive attachment to one person or activity, etc. **take the field 1** begin a battle. **2** (of a sports team) go on to a field to begin a game. [OE *feld* f. WG]
■ *n.* **1** pasture, meadow, grassland, clearing, acreage, common, *Austral. & NZ* paddock, *poet.* lea, *poet. or archaic* mead. **3** playing field, court, ground, gridiron; airfield. **4** participants, competitors, players, entrants, contestants, competition. **7 a, b** battlefield, battleground. **8** area, domain, realm, territory, sphere, line, province, subject, division, department, métier, discipline, specialization, specialty, esp. *Brit.* speciality, *joc.* bailiwick; forte, strength. ● *v.* **1 b** stop, catch, return, retrieve. **3** deal *or* cope with, handle, answer, reply to, respond *or* react to.

fielder /féeldər/ *n. Baseball* a member of the team that is fielding.

fieldfare /féeldfair/ *n.* a European thrush, *Turdus pilaris*, having gray plumage with a speckled breast. [ME *feldefare*, perh. as FIELD + FARE]

fieldsman /féeldzmən/ *n.* (*pl.* **-men**) *Cricket* = FIELDER.

fieldstone /féeldstōn/ *n.* stone used in its natural form.

fieldwork /féeldwərk/ *n.* **1** the practical work of a surveyor, collector of scientific data, sociologist, etc., conducted in the natural environment rather than a laboratory, office, etc. **2** a temporary fortification. □□ **fieldworker** *n.*

fiend /feend/ *n.* **1 a** an evil spirit; a demon. **b** (prec. by *the*) the Devil. **2 a** a very wicked or cruel person. **b** a person causing mischief or annoyance. **3** (with a qualifying word) *sl.* a devotee or addict (*a fitness fiend*). **4** something difficult or unpleasant. □□ **fiendish** *adj.* **fiendishly** *adv.* **fiendishness** *n.* **fiendlike** *adj.* [OE *feond* f. Gmc]
■ **1** see DEVIL *n.* 1, 2. **3** fan, enthusiast, devotee, aficionado, follower, fanatic, *colloq.* addict, maniac, buff, freak, *sl.* nut. □□ **fiendish** wicked, cruel, malignant, malevolent, malicious, evil, bad, blackhearted, satanic, devilish, Mephistophelian, demonic, demoniac(al), diabolic(al); hellish, infernal, savage, inhuman, ghoulish, monstrous.

fierce /feers/ *adj.* (**fiercer, fiercest**) **1** vehemently aggressive or frightening in temper or action; violent. **2** eager; intense; ardent. **3** unpleasantly strong or intense; uncontrolled (*fierce heat*). **4** (of a mechanism) not smooth or easy in action. □□ **fiercely** *adv.* **fierceness** *n.* [ME f. AF *fers*, OF *fiers fier* proud f. L *ferus* savage]
■ **1** ferocious, savage, wild, truculent, violent, brutish, feral, bestial, tigerish, brutal, barbaric, barbarous, inhuman, dangerous, aggressive, cruel, murderous, bloodthirsty, sanguinary, homicidal, *poet. or rhet.* fell. **2** eager, intense, ardent, fiery, vehement, furious. **3** intense, frenzied, stormy, turbulent, tempestuous, tumultuous, uncontrollable; uncontrolled, severe, keen,

dire, raging, wild, merciless, bitter, biting, *colloq.* awful, dreadful. □□ **fiercely** very, extremely, exceedingly, intensely, furiously, ferociously; vehemently, violently, savagely, viciously.

fieri facias /fírí fáysheeəs, -shəs, fíree/ *n. Law* a writ to a sheriff for executing a judgment. [L, = cause to be made or done]

fiery /fíree/ *adj.* (**fierier, fieriest**) **1 a** consisting of or flaming with fire. **b** (of an arrow, etc.) fire-bearing. **2** like fire in appearance; bright red. **3 a** hot as fire. **b** acting like fire; producing a burning sensation. **4 a** flashing; ardent (*fiery eyes*). **b** eager; pugnacious; spirited; irritable (*fiery temper*). **c** (of a horse) mettlesome. **5** (of gas, a mine, etc.) flammable; liable to explode. □ **fiery cross** a wooden cross charred or set on fire as a symbol. □□ **fierily** *adv.* **fieriness** *n.*
■ **1 a** flaming, burning, blazing; afire, on fire, in flames, ablaze. **2** glowing, red, incandescent, brilliant, luminous, glaring, gleaming, radiant; aglow, afire. **3 a** hot, red-hot, white-hot, overheated. **4 a** see ARDENT, BRIGHT *adj.* 1. **b** eager, pugnacious, spirited, passionate, excited, excitable, peppery, irascible, touchy, irritable, edgy, hotheaded, fierce.

fiesta /fee-éstə/ *n.* **1** a holiday or festivity. **2** a religious festival in Spanish-speaking countries. [Sp., = feast]
■ **1** see FESTIVAL *n.*

FIFA /féefə/ *abbr.* International Football Federation. [F *Fédération Internationale de Football Association*]

fi. fa. *abbr.* fieri facias.

fife /fif/ *n. & v.* ● *n.* **1** a kind of small shrill flute used with the drum in military music. **2** its player. ● *v.* **1** *intr.* play the fife. **2** *tr.* play (an air, etc.) on the fife. □□ **fifer** *n.* [G *Pfeife* PIPE, or F *fifre* f. Swiss G *Pfifre* piper]

fife rail /fif rayl/ *n. Naut.* a rail around the mainmast with belaying pins. [18th c.: orig. unkn.]

fifteen /fíftéen/ *n. & adj.* ● *n.* **1** one more than fourteen, or five more than ten; the product of three units and five units. **2** a symbol for this (15, xv, XV). **3** a size, etc., denoted by fifteen. **4** a team of fifteen players, esp. in rugby. **5** (**the Fifteen**) *hist.* the Jacobite rebellion of 1715. ● *adj.* that amount to fifteen. □□ **fifteenth** *adj. & n.* [OE *fíftēne* (as FIVE, -TEEN)]

fifth /fifth/ *n. & adj.* ● *n.* **1** the position in a sequence corresponding to that of the number 5 in the sequence 1–5. **2** something occupying this position. **3** the fifth person, etc., in a race or competition. **4** any of five equal parts of a thing. **5** *Mus.* **a** an interval or chord spanning five consecutive notes in the diatonic scale (e.g., C to G). **b** a note separated from another by this interval. **6 a** a fifth of a gallon of liquor. **b** a bottle containing this. **7** (**the Fifth**) the Fifth Amendment to the US Constitution. ● *adj.* that is the fifth. □ **fifth column** a group working for an enemy within a country at war, etc. (from General Mola's reference to such support in besieged Madrid in 1936). **fifth columnist** a member of a fifth column; a traitor or spy. **fifth generation** *Computing* a stage in computer design involving machines that make use of artificial intelligence. **fifth part** = sense 4 of *n.* **fifth wheel 1** an extra wheel of a carriage. **2** a superfluous person or thing. **3** a horizontal turntable over the front axle of a carriage as an extra support to prevent its tipping. **4** a round coupling device to connect a tractor and trailer. **take the Fifth** exercise the right guaranteed by the Fifth Amendment to the Constitution of refusing to answer questions in order to avoid incriminating oneself. □□ **fifthly** *adv.* [earlier and dial. *fift* f. OE *fífta* f. Gmc, assim. to FOURTH]

fifty /fíftee/ *n. & adj.* ● *n.* (*pl.* **-ies**) **1** the product of five and ten. **2** a symbol for this (50, l (letter), L). **3** (in *pl.*) the numbers from 50 to 59, esp. the years of a century or of a person's life. **4** a set of fifty persons or things. **5** a large indefinite number (*have fifty things to tell you*). **6** a fifty-dollar bill. ● *adj.* that amount to fifty. □ **fifty-fifty** *adj.* equal; with equal shares or chances (*on a fifty-fifty basis*). ● *adv.* equally; half and half (*go fifty-fifty*). **fifty-first, -second**, etc., the ordinal numbers between fiftieth and sixtieth. **fifty-one, -two**, etc., the cardinal numbers between fifty and sixty. □□ **fiftieth** *adj.* & *n.* **fiftyfold** *adj.* & *adv.* [OE *fīftig* (as FIVE, -TY²)]

fig¹ /fig/ *n.* **1 a** a soft pear-shaped fruit with many seeds, eaten fresh or dried. **b** (in full **fig tree**) any deciduous tree of the genus *Ficus*, esp. *F. carica*, having broad leaves and bearing figs. **2** a valueless thing (*don't care a fig for*). □ **fig leaf 1** a leaf of a fig tree. **2** a device for concealing something, esp. the genitals (Gen. 3:7). [ME f. OF *figue* f. Prov. *fig(u)a* ult. f. L *ficus*]

fig² /fig/ *n.* & *v.* ● *n.* **1** dress or equipment (*in full fig*). **2** condition or form (*in good fig*). ● *v.tr.* (**figged, figging**) **1** (foll. by *out*) dress up (a person). **2** (foll. by *out*, *up*) make (a horse) lively. [var. of obs. *feague* (v.) f. G *fegen*: see FAKE¹] ■ *v.* **1** (*fig out*) see PRIMP 2.

fig. *abbr.* figure.

fight /fīt/ *v.* & *n.* ● *v.* (*past* and *past part.* **fought** /fawt/) **1** *intr.* **a** (often foll. by *against*, *with*) contend or struggle in war, battle, single combat, etc. **b** (often foll. by *with*) argue; quarrel. **2** *tr.* contend with (an opponent) in this way. **3** *tr.* take part or engage in (a battle, war, duel, boxing match, etc.). **4** *tr.* contend about (an issue, an election); maintain (a lawsuit, cause, etc.) against an opponent. **5** *intr.* campaign or strive determinedly to achieve something. **6** *tr.* strive to overcome (disease, fire, fear, etc.). **7** *tr.* make (one's way) by fighting. **8** *tr.* cause (cocks or dogs) to fight. **9** *tr.* handle (troops, a ship, etc.) in battle. ● *n.* **1 a** a combat, esp. unpremeditated, between two or more persons, animals, or parties. **b** a boxing match. **c** a battle. **d** an argument. **2 a** conflict or struggle; a vigorous effort in the face of difficulty. **3** power or inclination to fight (*has no fight left; showed fight*). □ **fight back 1** counterattack. **2** suppress (one's feelings, tears, etc.). **fight down** suppress (one's feelings, tears, etc.). **fight for 1** fight on behalf of. **2** fight to secure (a thing). **fighting chair** a fixed chair on a boat for use when catching large fish. **fighting chance** an opportunity to succeed by great effort. **fighting fish** (in full **Siamese fighting fish**) a freshwater fish, *Betta splendens*, native to Thailand, the males of which sometimes kill each other during fights for territory. **fighting fit** fit enough to fight; at the peak of fitness. **fighting words** *colloq.* words likely to start a fight. **fight off** repel with effort. **fight out** (usu. **fight it out**) settle (a dispute, etc.) by fighting. **fight shy of** avoid; be unwilling to approach (a person, task, etc.). **put up a fight** (or **make a fight of it**) offer resistance. [OE *feohtan, feoht(e)*, f. WG] ■ *v.* **1 a** contend, struggle, battle, conflict, war, engage, clash, feud, combat, bear *or* take up arms, brawl, strive, cross swords, lock horns, close, come to *or* exchange blows, go to *or* wage war, grapple, wrestle, skirmish, tussle, scuffle, *hist.* joust. **b** argue, dispute, bicker, quarrel, have words, wrangle, squabble, tiff, fall out, disagree, altercate, *colloq.* row, spat. **2** contend with, encounter, engage; see also TACKLE *v.* 2, 4. **3** see ENGAGE 8. **4** argue about *or* against, dispute, question, challenge; contest; maintain, argue, put, plead, claim, protest, try to prove, assert. **5** campaign, strive, rise up, make *or* take a stand, struggle, take up arms. **6** oppose, defy, resist, rail *or* struggle against, make *or* take a stand against, withstand, confront. ● *n.* **1 a** (single) combat, brawl, donnybrook, fray, riot, affray, fracas, disturbance, broil, mêlée, tussle, scuffle, scrimmage, skirmish, brush, free-for-all, *colloq.* set-to, scrap, row, *Brit. colloq.* scrum, *sl.* rumble, *hist.* duel. **b** see BOUT 2a. **c** battle, conflict, clash, war, struggle; engagement, encounter. **d** argument, altercation, quarrel, feud, dispute, run-in, disagreement, difference (of opinion), squabble, misunderstanding, ruckus, *colloq.* row, spat. **3** power, pugnacity, militancy, belligerence, truculence, mettle, spirit, pluck, zeal, enthusiasm, zest, feistiness. □ **fight back 1** see RETALIATE 1. **2** see SUPPRESS 2. **fight down** see SUPPRESS 2. **fight off** see REPULSE *v.* 1. **fight shy of** keep away from, keep *or* remain aloof from, keep *or* remain aloof of; be wary *or* cautious *or* watchful of; be unwilling *or* reluctant *or* averse *or* loath *or* disinclined *or* not disposed to; see also AVOID. **make a fight of it** struggle, battle; see also FIGHT *v.* 1a above.

fighter /fītər/ *n.* **1** a person or animal that fights. **2** a fast military aircraft designed for attacking other aircraft. □ **fighter-bomber** an aircraft serving as both fighter and bomber. ■ **1** see BRUISER 2, SOLDIER *n.*

figment /fígmənt/ *n.* a thing invented or existing only in the imagination. [ME f. L *figmentum*, rel. to *fingere* fashion] ■ see ILLUSION 4.

figural /fígyərəl/ *adj.* **1** figurative. **2** relating to figures or shapes. **3** *Mus.* florid in style. [OF *figural* or LL *figuralis* f. *figura* FIGURE]

figuration /fígyəráyshən/ *n.* **1 a** the act of formation. **b** a mode of formation; a form. **c** a shape or outline. **2 a** ornamentation by designs. **b** *Mus.* ornamental patterns of scales, arpeggios, etc., often derived from an earlier motif. **3** allegorical representation. [ME f. F or f. L *figuratio* (as FIGURE)]

figurative /fígyərətiv/ *adj.* **1 a** metaphorical, not literal. **b** metaphorically so called. **2** characterized by or addicted to figures of speech. **3** of pictorial or sculptural representation. **4** emblematic; serving as a type. □□ **figuratively** *adv.* **figurativeness** *n.* [ME f. LL *figurativus* (as FIGURE)] ■ **1a, 2** see *metaphoric, metaphorical* (METAPHOR).

figure /fígyər/ *n.* & *v.* ● *n.* **1 a** the external form or shape of a thing. **b** bodily shape (*has a model's figure*). **2 a** a person as seen in outline but not identified (*saw a figure leaning against the door*). **b** a person as contemplated mentally (*a public figure*). **3** appearance as giving a certain impression (*cut a poor figure*). **4 a** a representation of the human form in drawing, sculpture, etc. **b** an image or likeness. **c** an emblem or type. **5** *Geom.* a two-dimensional space enclosed by a line or lines, or a three-dimensional space enclosed by a surface or surfaces; any of the classes of these, e.g., the triangle, the sphere. **6 a** a numerical symbol, esp. any of the ten in Arabic notation. **b** a number so expressed. **c** an amount of money; a value (*cannot put a figure on it*). **d** (in *pl.*) arithmetical calculations. **7** a diagram or illustrative drawing. **8** a decorative pattern as in a textile. **9 a** a division of a set dance. **b** (in skating) a prescribed pattern of movements from a stationary position. **10** *Mus.* a short succession of notes producing a single impression, a brief melodic or rhythmic formula out of which longer passages are developed. **11** (in full **figure of speech**) a recognized form of rhetorical expression giving variety, force, etc., esp. metaphor or hyperbole. **12** *Gram.* a permitted deviation from the usual rules of construction, e.g., ellipsis. **13** *Logic* the form of a syllogism, classified according to the position of the middle term. ● *v.* **1** *intr.* appear or be mentioned, esp. prominently. **2** *tr.* represent in a diagram or picture. **3** *tr.* imagine; picture mentally. **4 a** *tr.* embellish with a pattern (*figured satin*). **b** *tr. Mus.* embellish with figures. **c** *intr.* perform a figure in skating or dancing. **5** *tr.* mark with numbers (*figured bass*) or prices. **6 a** *tr.* calculate. **b** *intr.* do arithmetic. **7** *tr.* be a symbol of; represent typically. **8 a** *tr.* understand; ascertain; consider. **b** *intr. colloq.* be likely or understandable (*that figures*). □ **figured bass** *Mus.* = CONTINUO. **figure of fun** esp. *Brit.* a ridiculous person. **figure on** count on; expect. **figure out 1** work out by arithmetic or logic. **2** estimate. **3** understand. **figure skater** a person who practices figure skating. **figure skating** the sport of performing jumps and spins, etc., in a dancelike performance while ice skating, and also including skating in prescribed patterns from a stationary position. □□ **figureless** *adj.* [ME f. OF *figure* (n.), *figurer* (v.) f. L *figura, figurare*, rel. to *fingere* fashion] ■ *n.* **1** a form, shape; outline, silhouette; cut; cast; conformation. **b** shape, form, physique, build, body, outline. **2 a** form, person, individual, being. **b** person, personality, presence, force, character, individual. **3** see APPEARANCE 2. **4 a** representation, statue, effigy, sculpture, bust, mold, cast, image, icon. **b** image, likeness, representation, semblance. **c** emblem, symbol, device; design, pattern, motif; type. **6 a** number, numeral, cipher, digit; symbol, character, sign. **7** diagram, drawing, illustration, picture, sketch, plate. ● *v.* **1** appear, feature, have a place, take *or* play a part, take *or* play a role; be mentioned *or* included, be featured *or* conspicuous. **3** imagine, picture, think, reckon, consider, judge, believe; assume, presume, suppose; take. **6 a** calculate, figure out, compute, reckon, work out; count, total (up), tot (up), enumerate, tally, sum. □ **figure on** count on, rely *or* depend on, trust in, put faith in; expect, plan on *or* upon, take into consideration *or* account, consider, make allowance for. **figure out 1** calculate, reckon, compute, work out; see also SOLVE. **3** understand, decipher, interpret, translate, grasp, solve, fathom, see, perceive, *colloq.* get, make head or tail of, get the hang of, get the drift of, catch on (to), *Brit. colloq.* twig, esp. *Brit. sl.* suss (out).

figurehead /fígyərhed/ *n.* **1** a nominal leader or head without real power. **2** a carving, usu. a bust or a full-length figure, at a ship's prow.
■ **1** puppet, dummy, mouthpiece, front man, man of straw.

figurine /fígyəréen/ *n.* a statuette. [F f. It. *figurina* dimin. of *figura* FIGURE]
■ see STATUE.

figwort /fígwərt, -wawrt/ *n.* any aromatic green-flowered plant of the genus *Scrophularia*, once believed to be useful against scrofula.

filagree var. of FILIGREE.

filament /fíləmənt/ *n.* **1** a slender threadlike body or fiber (esp. in animal or vegetable structures). **2** a conducting wire or thread with a high melting point in an electric bulb or vacuum tube, heated or made incandescent by an electric current. **3** *Bot.* the part of the stamen that supports the anther. **4** *archaic* (of air, light, etc.) a notional train of particles following each other. □□ **filamentary** /-méntəree/ *adj.* **filamented** *adj.* **filamentous** /-méntəs/ *adj.* [F *filament* or mod.L *filamentum* f. LL *filare* spin f. L *filum* thread]
■ **1** see FIBER 1.

filaria /fíláireeə/ *n.* (*pl.* **filariae** /-ree-ee/) any threadlike parasitic nematode worm of the family Filariidae introduced into the blood by certain biting flies and mosquitoes. □□ **filarial** *adj.* [mod.L f. L *filum* thread]

filariasis /fíləríəsis/ *n.* a disease common in the tropics, caused by the presence of filarial worms in the lymph vessels.

filature /fíləchər/ *n.* an establishment for or the action of reeling silk from cocoons. [F f. It. *filatura* f. *filare* spin]

filbert /fílbərt/ *n.* **1** the cultivated hazel, *Corylus maxima*, bearing edible ovoid nuts. **2** this nut. [ME *philliberd*, etc., f. AF *philbert*, dial. F *noix de filbert*, a nut ripe about St. Philibert's day (Aug. 20)]

filch /filch/ *v.tr.* pilfer; steal. □□ **filcher** *n.* [16th-c. thieves' sl.: orig. unkn.]
■ see STEAL *v.* 1.

file[1] /fíl/ *n. & v.* ● *n.* **1** a folder, box, etc., for holding loose papers, esp. arranged for reference. **2** a set of papers kept in this. **3** *Computing* a collection of (usu. related) data stored under one name. **4** a series of issues of a newspaper, etc., in order. **5** a stiff pointed wire on which documents, etc., are impaled for keeping. ● *v.tr.* **1** place (papers) in a file or among (esp. public) records; classify or arrange (papers, etc.). **2** submit (a petition for divorce, an application for a patent, etc.) to the appropriate authority. **3** (of a reporter) send (a story, information, etc.) to a newspaper. □ **filing cabinet** a case with drawers for storing documents. □□ **filer** *n.* [F *fil* f. L *filum* thread]
■ *n.* **1** portfolio, folder, box, case. **2** document, dossier, papers. ● *v.* **1** classify, organize, systematize, categorize, alphabetize, chronologize, order, arrange, pigeonhole, interfile, put *or* place in order, record,

register, enter. **2** submit, send in, complete, fill out, *Brit.* fill in, enter.

file[2] /fíl/ *n. & v.* ● *n.* **1** a line of persons or things one behind another. **2** *Chess* a line of squares from player to player (cf. RANK[1]). ● *v.intr.* walk in a file. [F *file* f. LL *filare* spin or L *filum* thread]
■ *n.* **1** line, column, row, rank, esp. *Brit.* queue.
● *v.* walk, march, troop, parade.

file[3] /fíl/ *n. & v.* ● *n.* a tool with a roughened surface or surfaces, usu. of steel, for smoothing or shaping wood, fingernails, etc. ● *v.tr.* **1** smooth or shape with a file. **2** elaborate or improve (a thing, esp. a literary work). □ **file away** remove (roughness, etc.) with a file. □□ **filer** *n.* [OE *fíl* f. WG]

filefish /fílfish/ *n.* any fish of the family Ostracionidae, with sharp dorsal fins and usu. bright coloration.

filet /fílit/ *n.* **1** a kind of net or lace with a square mesh. **2** a fillet of meat. □ **filet mignon** /fíláy minyón/ a small tender piece of beef from the end of the tenderloin. [F, = thread]

filial /fíleeəl/ *adj.* **1** of or due from a son or daughter. **2** *Biol.* bearing the relation of offspring (cf. F² 5). □□ **filially** *adv.* [ME f. OF *filial* or LL *filialis* f. *filius* son, *filia* daughter]
■ **1** see DUTIFUL.

filiation /fíleeáyshən/ *n.* **1** being the child of one or two specified parents. **2** (often foll. by *from*) descent or transmission. **3** the formation of offshoots. **4** a branch of a society or language. **5** a genealogical relation or arrangement. [F f. LL *filiatio -onis* f. L *filius* son]

filibuster /fílibustər/ *n. & v.* ● *n.* **1 a** the obstruction of progress in a legislative assembly, esp. by prolonged speaking. **b** a person who engages in a filibuster. **2** esp. *hist.* a person engaging in unauthorized warfare against a foreign nation. ● *v.* **1** *intr.* act as a filibuster. **2** *tr.* act in this way against (a motion, etc.). □□ **filibusterer** *n.* [ult. f. Du. *vrijbuiter* FREEBOOTER, infl. by F *flibustier*, Sp. *filibustero*]

filigree /fíligree/ *n.* (also **filagree** /fílə-/) **1** ornamental work of gold or silver or copper as fine wire formed into delicate tracery; fine metal openwork. **2** anything delicate resembling this. □□ **filigreed** *adj.* [earlier *filigreen, filigrane* f. F *filigrane* f. It. *filigrana* f. L *filum* thread + *granum* seed]
■ **2** see LACE *n.* 1.

filing /fíling/ *n.* (usu. in *pl.*) a particle rubbed off by a file.

Filipino /fílipéenō/ *n. & adj.* ● *n.* (*pl.* **-os**; *fem.* **Filipina** /-nə/) a native or inhabitant of the Philippines, a group of islands in the SW Pacific. ● *adj.* of or relating to the Philippines or the Filipinos. [Sp., = Philippine]

fill /fil/ *v. & n.* ● *v.* **1** *tr. & intr.* (often foll. by *with*) make or become full. **2** *tr.* occupy completely; spread over or through; pervade. **3** *tr.* block up (a cavity or hole in a tooth) with cement, amalgam, gold, etc.; drill and put a filling into (a decayed tooth). **4** *tr.* make level or raise the level of (low-lying land). **5** *tr.* appoint a person to hold (a vacant post). **6** *tr.* hold (a position); discharge the duties of (an office). **7** *tr.* carry out or supply (an order, commission, etc.). **8** *tr.* occupy (vacant time). **9** *intr.* (of a sail) be distended by wind. **10** *tr.* (usu. as **filling** *adj.*) (esp. of food) satisfy; satiate. **11** *tr.* satisfy; fulfill (a need or requirement). **12** *tr. Poker*, etc., complete (a straight or flush, etc.) by drawing the necessary cards. **13** *tr.* stock abundantly. ● *n.* **1** (prec. by possessive) as much as one wants or can bear (*eat your fill*). **2** enough to fill something (*a fill of tobacco*). **3** earth, etc., used to fill a cavity. □ **fill the bill** be suitable or adequate. **filled gold** gold in the form of a thin coating applied to a baser metal by rolling. **fill in 1** add information to complete (*Brit.* a form, document, blank check, etc.). **2 a** complete (a drawing, etc.) within an outline. **b** fill (an outline) in this way. **3** fill (a hole, etc.) completely. **4** (often foll. by *for*) act as a substitute. **5** occupy oneself during (time between other activities). **6** *colloq.* inform (a person) more fully. **7** *Brit. sl.* thrash, beat. **fill out 1** enlarge to the required size. **2** become enlarged or plump. **3** add information to complete (a document, etc.). **fill up 1** make or become completely full. **2** *Brit.* fill in (a document, etc.). **3** fill the fuel tank of (a car, etc.). **4** provide what is needed to occupy vacant parts or places or deal with deficiencies in. **5** do away with (a pond, etc.) by filling. **fill-up** *n.* **1** a thing that fills something up. **2** an act of filling something up. [OE *fyllan* f. Gmc, rel. to FULL[1]]

■ *v.* **1** make full, fill up; esp. *Brit.* top up. **2** occupy, crowd (into), stuff, cram (into), pack (into), squeeze into; jam, load; pervade, abound in, overflow, be abundant *or* plentiful in. **3** block, stop (up), close, stuff, seal, plug, fill in. **6** hold, occupy, take over; discharge, carry out, do, execute. **9** distend, inflate, swell, stretch, blow up, expand. **10** satisfy, satiate, bloat, sate, gorge, stuff. **11** satisfy, meet, fulfill, answer. **13** supply, stock, furnish, fill up. □ **fill in 1** complete, answer, fill out, make out, *Brit.* fill up. **3** see FILL *v.* 3 above. **4** (*fill in for*) take the place of, take a person's place, stand in for; see also SUBSTITUTE *v.* 1. **5** see OCCUPY 2. **6** inform, tell, advise, let in on, bring up to date. **fill out 1** see PAD[1] *v.* 2. **2** swell, expand, grow; distend, stretch; fatten, increase. **3** see *fill in* 1 above. **fill up 1** see FILL *v.* 1 above. **2** see *fill in* 1 above.

filler /fílər/ *n.* **1** material or an object used to fill a cavity or increase bulk. **2** an item filling space in a newspaper, etc. **3** paper for filling a binder or notebook. **4** a person or thing that fills.

■ **2** see ITEM *n.* 3.

fillet /fílit/ *n.* & *v.* ● *n.* **1** (usu. /fíláy/) **a** a fleshy boneless piece of meat from near the loins or the ribs. **b** (in full **fillet steak**) the tenderloin. **c** a boned longitudinal section of a fish. **2 a** a headband, ribbon, string, or narrow band, for binding the hair or worn round the head. **b** a band or bandage. **3 a** a thin narrow strip of anything. **b** a raised rim or ridge on any surface. **4** *Archit.* **a** a narrow flat band separating two moldings. **b** a small band between the flutes of a column. **5** *Carpentry* an added triangular piece of wood to round off an interior angle. **6 a** a plain line impressed on the cover of a book. **b** a roller used to impress this. **7** *Heraldry* a horizontal division of a shield, a quarter of the depth of a chief. ● *v.tr.* (**filleted, filleting**) **1** (also /fíláy, fílay/) **a** remove bones from (fish or meat). **b** divide (fish or meat) into fillets. **2** bind or provide with a fillet or fillets. **3** encircle with an ornamental band. □□ **filleter** *n.* [ME f. OF *filet* f. Rmc dimin. of L *filum* thread]

■ *n.* **2 a** see BAND[1] *n.* 1. **3 a** see STRIP[2].

filling /fíling/ *n.* **1** any material that fills or is used to fill, esp.: **a** a piece of material used to fill a cavity in a tooth. **b** the edible substance between the bread in a sandwich or between the pastry crusts in a pie. **2** weft. □ **filling station** an establishment selling automotive fuel, etc., to motorists.

■ **1** a filler, stuffing, padding, wadding; contents.

fillip /fílip/ *n.* & *v.* ● *n.* **1** a stimulus or incentive. **2 a** a sudden release of a finger or thumb when it has been bent and checked by a thumb or finger. **b** a slight sharp stroke given in this way. ● *v.* (**filliped, fillipping**) **1** *tr.* stimulate (*fillip one's memory*). **2** *tr.* strike slightly and sharply. **3** *tr.* propel (a coin, marble, etc.) with a fillip. **4** *intr.* make a fillip. [imit.]

■ *n.* **1** see STIMULANT *n.* 2.

filly /fílee/ *n.* (*pl.* **-ies**) **1** a young female horse, usu. before it is four years old. **2** *colloq.* a girl or young woman. [ME, prob. f. ON *fylja* f. Gmc (as FOAL)]

■ **2** see GIRL 2.

film /film/ *n.* & *v.* ● *n.* **1** a thin coating or covering layer. **2** *Photog.* a strip or sheet of plastic or other flexible base coated with light-sensitive emulsion for exposure in a camera, either as individual visual representations or as a sequence, forming the illusion of movement when shown in rapid succession. **3 a** a representation of a story, episode, etc., on a film, with the illusion of movement; a movie. **b** a story represented in this way; a movie. **c** (in *pl.*) the movie industry. **4** a slight veil or haze, etc. **5** a dimness or morbid growth affecting the eyes. **6** a fine thread or filament. ● *v.* **1 a** *tr.* make a photographic film of (a scene, person, etc.). **b** *tr.* (also *absol.*) make a movie or television film of (a book, etc.). **c** *intr.* be (well or ill) suited for reproduction on film. **2** *tr.* & *intr.* cover or become covered with or as with a film. □ **film star** a celebrated actor or actress in films. [OE *filmen* membrane f. WG, rel. to FELL[5]]

■ *n.* **1** coating, layer, covering, sheet, overlay; skin, coat, membrane, integument, cover, pellicle. **3 a, b** picture, movie, moving picture, motion picture, *colloq.* pic, flick; videotape, video. **4** veil, haze, dusting, murkiness, blur, mist, haziness, mistiness, vapor, fog. ● *v.* **1** photograph, shoot, take. **2** (*film over*) become coated *or* covered *or* veiled *or* dimmed *or* glazed *or* blurred *or* bleary *or* misty *or* cloudy.

filmgoer /fílmgōər/ *n.* a person who frequents movie theaters.

filmic /fílmik/ *adj.* of or relating to movies or cinematography.

■ cinematic, pictorial, photographic.

filmmaker /fílmaykər/ *n.* a person who makes motion pictures.

filmography /filmógrəfee/ *n.* (*pl.* **-ies**) a list of movies by one director, etc., or on one subject. [FILM + -GRAPHY after *bibliography*]

filmset /fílmset/ *v.tr.* (**-setting**; *past* and *past part.* **-set**) *Printing* set (material for printing) by filmsetting. □□ **filmsetter** *n.*

filmsetting /fílmseting/ *n.* = PHOTOCOMPOSITION.

filmstrip /fílmstrip/ *n.* a series of transparencies in a strip for projection as still pictures.

filmy /fílmee/ *adj.* (**filmier, filmiest**) **1** thin and translucent. **2** covered with or as with a film. □□ **filmily** *adv.* **filminess** *n.*

■ **1** gauzy, thin, sheer, gossamer(-like), cobwebby, diaphanous, delicate, flimsy, light, insubstantial, transparent, translucent, see-through, peekaboo. **2** murky, blurry, cloudy, hazy, misty, bleary, blurred, dim, clouded, milky, pearly, opalescent.

filo /féelō/ *n.* (also **phyllo**) dough that can be stretched into very thin layers; pastry made from this dough. [mod.Gk *phullo* leaf]

fils /fees/ *n.* (added to a surname to distinguish a son from a father) the son; junior (cf. PÈRE). [F, = son]

filter /fíltər/ *n.* & *v.* ● *n.* **1** a porous device for removing impurities or solid particles from a liquid or gas passed through it. **2** = *filter tip.* **3** a screen or attachment for absorbing or modifying light, X rays, etc. **4** a device for suppressing electrical or sound waves of frequencies not required. **5** *Brit.* **a** an arrangement for filtering traffic. **b** a traffic light signaling this. ● *v.* **1** *tr.* & *intr.* pass or cause to pass through a filter. **2** *tr.* (foll. by *out*) remove (impurities, etc.) by means of a filter. **3** *intr.* (foll. by *through*, *into*, etc.) make way gradually. **4** *intr.* (foll. by *out*) leak or cause to leak. **5** *tr.* & *intr. Brit.* allow (traffic) or (of traffic) be allowed to pass to the left or right at a junction while traffic going straight ahead is halted (esp. at traffic lights). □ **filter bed** a tank or pond containing a layer of sand, etc., for filtering large quantities of liquid. **filter paper** porous paper for filtering. **filter tip 1** a filter attached to a cigarette for removing impurities from the inhaled smoke. **2** a cigarette with this. [F *filtre* f. med.L *filtrum* felt used as a filter, f. WG]

■ *n.* **1** strainer, sieve, riddle. ● *v.* **1** filtrate, pass *or* run through, strain, drain; percolate, leach; clarify, refine, purify, clean. **2** screen, sift, winnow; separate, weed out, exclude, eliminate.

filterable /fíltərəbəl/ *adj.* (also **filtrable** /fíltrəbəl/) **1** *Med.* (of a virus) able to pass through a filter that retains bacteria. **2** that can be filtered.

filth /filth/ *n.* **1** repugnant or extreme dirt; excrement; refuse. **2** vileness; corruption; obscenity. **3** foul or obscene language. [OE *fylth* (as FOUL, -TH[2])]

■ **1** dirt, slime, filthiness, *colloq.* muck, *Brit. colloq.* gunge, *sl.* crud, grunge; excrement, feces, excreta, night soil, manure, dung, droppings, ordure, guano; sewage, sullage, sludge; rubbish, garbage, refuse, offal, soil, trash. **2** vileness, corruption, baseness, foulness, rottenness, debasement, defilement; pollution, adulteration, perversion, degradation, sullying, besmirchment, putrescence, putrefaction; obscenity, vulgarity, indecency, grossness, pornography. **3** see DIRT 3.

filthy / fílthee/ *adj. & adv.* ● *adj.* (**filthier, filthiest**) **1** extremely or disgustingly dirty. **2** obscene. **3** *Brit. colloq.* (of weather) very unpleasant. **4** vile; disgraceful. ● *adv.* **1** filthily (*filthy dirty*). **2** *colloq.* extremely (*filthy rich*). □ **filthy lucre 1** dishonorable gain (Tit. 1:11). **2** *joc.* money. □□ **filthily** *adv.* **filthiness** *n.*

■ *adj.* **1** dirty, unclean, begrimed, soiled, stained, grimy, mucky, disgusting; scummy, slimy, sordid, squalid, shabby, *Brit. colloq.* gungy, *sl.* cruddy, grungy; putrid, fetid, maggotty, fly-blown, purulent, feculent, fecal. **2** obscene, indecent, immoral, gross, impure, smutty, coarse, bawdy, ribald, depraved, corrupt, dirty, lewd, lascivious, licentious, offensive, foul-mouthed, dirty-minded, filthy-minded, blue, pornographic, taboo. **4** see DISGRACEFUL, VILE 1.

filtrable var. of FILTERABLE.

filtrate / fíltrayt/ *v. & n.* ● *v.tr.* filter. ● *n.* filtered liquid. □□ **filtration** /-tráyshən/ *n.* [mod.L *filtrare* (as FILTER)]

■ *v.* see FILTER *v.* 1.

fimbriated / fímbreeaytid/ *adj.* (also **fimbriate**) **1** *Bot. & Zool.* fringed or bordered with hairs, etc. **2** *Heraldry* having a narrow border. [L *fimbriatus* f. *fimbriae* fringe]

fin[1] / fin/ *n. & v.* ● *n.* **1** an organ on various parts of the body of many aquatic vertebrates and some invertebrates, including fish and cetaceans, for propelling, steering, and balancing (*dorsal fin*; *anal fin*). **2** a small projecting surface or attachment on an aircraft, rocket, or automobile for ensuring aerodynamic stability. **3** an underwater swimmer's flipper. **4** a sharp lateral projection on the share or colter of a plow. **5** a finlike projection on any device, for improving heat transfer, etc. ● *v.* (**finned, finning**) **1** *tr.* provide with fins. **2** *intr.* swim under water. □□ **finless** *adj.* **finned** *adj.* (also in *comb.*). [OE *fin(n)*]

fin[2] / fin/ *n. sl.* a five-dollar bill. [f. Yiddish *finf* five]

finable see FINE[2].

finagle / fináygəl/ *v.intr. & tr. colloq.* act or obtain dishonestly or deviously. □□ **finagler** *n.* [dial. *fainaigue* cheat]

■ see CHEAT *v.* 1a.

final / fínəl/ *adj. & n.* ● *adj.* **1** situated at the end; coming last. **2** conclusive; decisive; unalterable; putting an end to doubt. **3** concerned with the purpose or end aimed at. ● *n.* **1** (also in *pl.*) the last or deciding heat or game in sports or in a competition. **2** the edition of a newspaper published latest in the day. **3** an examination at the end of an academic course. **4** *Mus.* the principal or tonic note in any mode. □ **final cause** *Philos.* the end toward which a thing naturally develops or at which an action aims. **final clause** *Gram.* a clause expressing purpose, introduced by *in order that*, *lest*, etc. **final solution** the Nazi policy (1941–45) of exterminating European Jews. □□ **finally** *adv.* [ME f. OF or f. L *finalis* f. *finis* end]

■ *adj.* **1** last, closing, concluding, finishing, terminating, ultimate. **2** conclusive, decisive, definitive, unalterable, unchangeable, immutable, irreversible, irrevocable; incontrovertible, irrefutable, indisputable; settled, fixed, absolute, certain, sure. □□ **finally** lastly; at (long) last, eventually, in the end, ultimately, at length; when all is said and done, in the long run, at the end of the day; conclusively, once (and) for all, decisively, irrevocably, completely, absolutely, definitively, definitely, for good, for ever, for all time.

finale / fináalee, -náalee/ *n.* **1 a** the last movement of an instrumental composition. **b** a piece of music closing an act in an opera. **2** the close of a drama, etc. **3** a conclusion. [It. (as FINAL)]

■ **2, 3** see END *n.* 3a, b.

finalism / fínəlizəm/ *n.* the doctrine that natural processes (e.g., evolution) are directed toward some goal. □□ **finalistic** *adj.*

finalist / fínəlist/ *n.* a competitor in the final of a competition, etc.

finality / fīnálitee, fə-/ *n.* (*pl.* **-ies**) **1** the quality or fact of being final. **2** the belief that something is final. **3** a final act, state, or utterance. **4** the principle of final cause viewed as operative in the universe. [F *finalité* f. LL *finalitas -tatis* (as FINAL)]

■ **1** conclusiveness, decisiveness, unalterability, unchangeability, immutability, irreversibility, irrevocableness, incontrovertibility, irrefutability, indisputability; certainty, certitude, sureness, fixedness.

finalize / fínəlīz/ *v.tr.* **1** put into final form. **2** complete; bring to an end. **3** approve the final form or details of. □□ **finalization** *n.*

■ **2** complete, conclude, settle, decide, wrap up, clinch, *colloq.* sew up.

finance / fináns, fī-, fínans/ *n. & v.* ● *n.* **1** the management of (esp. public) money. **2** monetary support for an enterprise. **3** (in *pl.*) the money resources of a government, company, or person. ● *v.tr.* provide capital for (a person or enterprise). □ **finance company** a company concerned mainly with making small, often short-term loans. [ME f. OF f. *finer* settle a debt f. *fin* end: see FINE[2]]

■ *n.* **1** (money) management, financial affairs, business, commerce, economics, resources. **2** see SUPPORT *n.* 1. **3** (*finances*) money, resources, capital, cash, funds, assets, holdings, wealth; *colloq.* wherewithal. ● *v.* fund, invest in, back, capitalize, underwrite, subsidize, pay for, *colloq.* bankroll, stake.

financial / fínánshəl, fī-/ *adj.* **1** of finance. **2** *Austral. & NZ sl.* possessing money. □ **financial year** *Brit.* = *fiscal year*. □□ **financially** *adv.*

■ **1** monetary, pecuniary, fiscal, economic.

financier / fínənseer, fənan-, fīnən-/ *n. & v.* ● *n.* a person engaged in large-scale finance. ● *v.intr. usu. derog.* conduct financial operations. [F (as FINANCE)]

■ *n.* capitalist, banker, backer, moneyman, *derog. or joc.* plutocrat, *sl.* angel.

finback / fínbak/ *n.* (or **fin whale**) a rorqual, *Balaenoptera physalus.*

finch / finch/ *n.* any small seed-eating passerine bird of the family Fringillidae (esp. one of the genus *Fringilla*), including crossbills, canaries, and chaffinches. [OE *finc* f. WG]

find / fīnd/ *v. & n.* ● *v.tr.* (*past* and *past part.* **found** / fownd/) **1 a** discover by chance or effort (*found a key*). **b** become aware of. **2 a** get possession of by chance (*found a treasure*). **b** obtain; receive (*idea found acceptance*). **c** succeed in obtaining (*cannot find the money*; *can't find time to read*). **d** summon up (*found courage to protest*). **e** *Brit. sl.* steal. **3 a** seek out and provide (*will find you a book*). **b** supply; furnish (*each finds his own equipment*). **4** ascertain by study or calculation or inquiry (*could not find the answer*). **5 a** perceive or experience (*find no sense in it*; *find difficulty in breathing*). **b** (often in *passive*) recognize or discover to be present (*the word is not found in Shakespeare*). **c** regard or discover from experience (*finds Canada too cold*; *you'll find it pays*). **6** *Law* (of a jury, judge, etc.) decide and declare (*found him guilty*; *found it murder*). **7** reach by a natural or normal process (*water finds its own level*). **8 a** (of a letter) reach (a person). **b** (of an address) be adequate to enable a letter, etc., to reach (a person). **9** *archaic* reach the conscience of. ● *n.* **1** a discovery of treasure, minerals, etc. **2** a thing or person discovered, esp. when of value. □ **all found** *Brit.* (of an employee's wages) with board and lodging provided free. **find against** *Law* decide against (a person); judge to be guilty. **find fault** see FAULT. **find favor** prove acceptable. **find one's feet 1** become able to walk. **2** develop one's independent ability. **find for** *Law* decide in favor of (a person); judge to be innocent. **find it in one's heart** (esp. with *neg.*; foll. by *to* + infin.) prevail upon oneself; be willing. **find oneself 1** discover that one is (*woke to find myself in the hospital*; *found herself agreeing*). **2** discover one's own talents, strengths, etc. **find out 1** discover or detect (a wrongdoer, etc.). **2** (often foll. by *about*) get information (*find out about vacationing abroad*). **3** discover (*find out where we are*). **4**

(often foll. by *about*) discover the truth, a fact, etc. (*he never found out*). **5** devise. **6** solve. **find one's way 1** (often foll. by *to*) manage to reach a place. **2** (often foll. by *into*) be brought or get. □□ **findable** *adj.* [OE *findan* f. Gmc]

■ *v.* **1a, 2a** discover, come across, happen on *or* upon, come on *or* upon, hit on *or* upon, chance on *or* upon, light on *or* upon, stumble on *or* upon; recover, get back, repossess, recoup, *disp.* locate. **2 b** see RECEIVE 1, 2. **c** secure, get, procure, acquire, win, gain; set aside, allot, assign, manage. **d** summon up, command, gather (up), muster (up). **3 b** see SUPPLY *v.* 1, 2. **4** ascertain, find out, discover, learn, calculate, determine, work out. **5 a** perceive, see, notice, note, mark, remark, discern, distinguish; experience. **b** see SPOT *v.* 1. **c** regard, consider, think, view, feel *or* discover to be. **6** judge, decide *or* determine to be, pronounce, declare, *formal* deem. **8** see REACH *v.* 4. ● *n.* **1, 2** discovery, catch; bargain. □ **find out 1** discover, detect, lay one's hand(s) on, track down, turn up, identify, determine, ascertain, put one's finger on, point to, *sl.* finger. **2** see LEARN 4. **3** discover, light on *or* upon, catch sight of, see, detect, learn, spot, locate, identify, become aware of, determine, ascertain, put one's finger on, point to, *literary* espy, descry. **4** *colloq.* catch on (to), *Brit. colloq.* twig; (*find out about*) esp. *Brit. sl.* suss. **5** see DEVISE *v.* 1. **6** see SOLVE.

finder /fíndər/ *n.* **1** a person who finds. **2** a small telescope attached to a large one to locate an object for observation. **3** the viewfinder of a camera. □ **finders keepers** *colloq.* whoever finds a thing is entitled to keep it.

fin de siècle /fán də syéklə/ *adj.* **1** characteristic of the end of the nineteenth century. **2** decadent. [F, = end of century]

finding /fíndiŋ/ *n.* **1** (often in *pl.*) a conclusion reached by an inquiry. **2** (in *pl.*) small parts or tools used by artisans.
■ **1** (*findings*) conclusion, judgment, verdict, decree, decision, pronouncement, declaration.

fine[1] /fīn/ *adj., n., adv., & v.* ● *adj.* **1** of high quality (*they sell fine fabrics*). **2 a** excellent; of notable merit (*a fine painting*). **b** good; satisfactory (*that will be fine*). **c** fortunate (*has been a fine thing for him*). **d** well conceived or expressed (*a fine saying*). **3 a** pure; refined. **b** (of gold or silver) containing a specified proportion of pure metal. **4** of handsome appearance or size; imposing; dignified (*fine buildings*). **5** in good health (*I'm fine, thank you*). **6** (of weather, etc.) bright and clear with sunshine; free from rain. **7 a** thin; sharp. **b** in small particles. **c** worked in slender thread. **d** (esp. of print) small. **e** (of a pen) narrow-pointed. **8** *Cricket* behind the wicket and near the line of flight of the ball. **9** tritely complimentary; euphemistic (*say fine things about a person*; *call things by fine names*). **10** ornate; showy; smart. **11** fastidious; dainty; pretending refinement; (of speech or writing) affectedly ornate. **12 a** capable of delicate perception or discrimination. **b** perceptible only with difficulty (*a fine distinction*). **13 a** delicate; subtle; exquisitely fashioned. **b** (of feelings) refined; elevated. **14** (of wine or other goods) of a high standard; conforming to a specified grade. ● *n.* **1** (in *pl.*) very small particles in mining, milling, etc. **2** *Brit.* fine weather (*in rain or fine*). ● *adv.* **1** finely. **2** *colloq.* very well (*suits me fine*). ● *v.* **1** (often foll. by *down*) **a** *tr.* make (beer or wine) clear. **b** *intr.* (of liquid) become clear. **2** *tr. & intr.* (often foll. by *away, down, off*) make or become finer, thinner, or less coarse; dwindle or taper; or cause to do so. □ **cut it fine** allow very little margin of time, etc. **fine arts** those appealing to the mind or to the sense of beauty, as poetry, music, and esp. painting, sculpture, and architecture. **fine-draw** sew together (two pieces of cloth, edges of a tear, parts of a garment) so that the join is imperceptible. **fine-drawn 1** extremely thin. **2** subtle. **fine print** detailed printed information, esp. in legal documents, instructions, etc. **fine-spun 1** delicate. **2** (of a theory, etc.) too subtle; unpractical. **fine-tooth** (also **-toothed**) **comb** a comb with narrow close-set teeth. **fine-tune** make small adjustments to (a mechanism, etc.) in order to obtain the best possible results. **fine up** *Austral. colloq.* (of the weather) become fine. **go over with a fine-tooth** (also **-toothed**) **comb** check or

search thoroughly. **not to put too fine a point on it** (as a parenthetic remark) to speak bluntly. □□ **finely** *adv.* **fineness** *n.* [ME f. OF *fin* ult. f. L *finire* finish]

■ *adj.* **1, 14** superior, supreme, first-class, first-rate, prime, choice, select, top-grade, high-grade, *colloq.* quality. **2 a** excellent, magnificent, marvelous, exquisite, splendid, admirable, super, brilliant, outstanding, exceptional, consummate, great, commendable, meritorious, good; enjoyable, entertaining, amusing, satisfying, interesting; (*of an artist or a performance*) masterly, virtuoso, accomplished, skillful. **b** good, satisfactory, pleasant, nice, *Sc.* braw, *colloq.* out of this world, great, OK, peachy, keen, *colloq.* swell, *sl.* cool, neat, *Brit. archaic sl.* ripping. **3 a** see PURE 1, 2. **4** handsome, attractive, striking, beautiful, pretty, lovely; fair, good-looking, comely, esp. *Sc. & No. of Engl.* bonny, *colloq.* cute; imposing, dignified, impressive. **5** in good health, well, all right, healthy, *colloq.* OK. **6** bright, clear, sunny, fair, cloudless, pleasant, dry, balmy, nice. **7 a** thin, diaphanous, gauzy, sheer, gossamer, flimsy, delicate; sharp, keen, keen-edged, razor-sharp, pointed. **b** powdery, powdered, pulverized, crushed, fine-grained; comminuted. **c** slender, thin, gossamer, filamentous, threadlike. **9** see *flattering* (FLATTER). **10** see ELEGANT 1–3. **11** see DAINTY *adj.* 4, FLOWERY. **12 b** subtle, refined, nice, hairsplitting, delicate, close. **13 a** delicate, subtle, exquisite, well-made, dainty, elegant. **b** see REFINED 1.

fine[2] /fīn/ *n. & v.* ● *n.* **1** a sum of money exacted as a penalty. **2** *hist.* a sum of money paid by an incoming tenant in return for the rent's being small. ● *v.tr.* punish by a fine (*fined him $5*). □ **in fine** to sum up; in short. □□ **finable** /fínəbəl/ *adj.* [ME f. OF *fin* f. med.L *finis* sum paid on settling a lawsuit f. L *finis* end]

■ *n.* **1** penalty, charge, fee, mulct, forfeit, forfeiture, *Law* amercement. ● *v.* penalize, charge, mulct, *Law* amerce.

finery[1] /fínəree/ *n.* showy dress or decoration. [FINE[1] + -ERY, after BRAVERY]

■ decoration(s), ornaments, trappings, trinkets, frippery, showy dress, best bib and tucker, *colloq.* glad rags, *joc.* Sunday best.

finery[2] /fínəree/ *n.* (*pl.* **-ies**) *hist.* a hearth where pig iron was converted into wrought iron. [F *finerie* f. *finer* refine, FINE[1]]

fines herbes /feen áirb, feenz/ *n.pl.* mixed herbs used in cooking. [F, = fine herbs]

finesse /finés/ *n. & v.* ● *n.* **1** refinement. **2** subtle or delicate manipulation. **3** artfulness, esp. in handling a difficulty tactfully. **4** *Cards* an attempt to win a trick with a card that is not the highest held. ● *v.* **1** *intr. & tr.* use or achieve by finesse. **2** *Cards* **a** *intr.* make a finesse. **b** *tr.* play (a card) by way of finesse. **3** *tr.* evade or trick by finesse. [F, rel. to FINE[1]]

■ *n.* **1** refinement, grace, tact, diplomacy, discretion, taste, polish, delicacy, elegance. **2** trick(s), artifice(s), manipulation(s), stratagem(s), wile(s), ruse(s), scheme(s), machination(s), intrigue(s), device(s), expedient(s), maneuver(s), deception(s), deceit(s). **3** artfulness, subtlety, cunning, craftiness, cleverness, shrewdness, skill; style, dash, élan, panache; skillfulness, adroitness, expertness, expertise, adeptness, proficiency, ability, facility. ● *v.* **1** see MANEUVER *v.* 3. **3** evade, trick, bluff, delude, deceive, fool, hoodwink, *colloq.* finagle, *sl.* con.

finger /fíŋgər/ *n. & v.* ● *n.* **1** any of the terminal projections of the hand (including or excluding the thumb). **2** the part of a glove, etc., intended to cover a finger. **3 a** a finger-like object (*chicken finger*). **b** a long narrow structure. **4** *colloq.* a measure of liquor in a glass, based on the breadth of a finger. **5** *sl.* **a** an informer. **b** *Brit.* a pickpocket. **c** *Brit.* a policeman.

/ . . . / **pronunciation**   ● **part of speech**
□ **phrases, idioms, and compounds**
□□ **derivatives**   ■ **synonym section**
cross-references appear in SMALL CAPITALS or *italics*

● *v.tr.* **1** touch, feel, or handle with the fingers. **2** *Mus.* **a** play (a passage) with fingers used in a particular way. **b** mark (music) with signs showing which fingers are to be used. **c** play upon (an instrument) with the fingers. **3** *sl.* indicate (a victim, or a criminal to the police). □ **all fingers and thumbs** *Brit.* clumsy. **finger bowl** a small bowl for rinsing the fingers at the table. **finger mark** a mark left on a surface by a finger. **finger paint** *n.* paint that can be applied with the fingers. ● *v.intr.* apply paint with the fingers. **finger plate** a plate fixed to a door above the handle to prevent finger marks. **finger post** a pointing signpost at a road junction. **get** (or **pull**) **one's finger out** *Brit. sl.* cease prevaricating and start to act. **have a finger in** (or **in the pie**) be (esp. officiously) concerned in (the matter). **lay a finger on** touch however slightly. **point the finger at** *colloq.* accuse; blame. **put one's finger on** locate or identify exactly. **put the finger on** *sl.* **1** inform against. **2** identify (an intended victim). **slip through one's fingers** escape. **twist** (or **wind** or **wrap**) **around one's finger** (or **little finger**) persuade (a person) without difficulty; dominate (a person) completely. **work one's fingers to the bone** see BONE. □□ **fingered** *adj.* (also in *comb.*). **fingerless** *adj.* [OE f. Gmc]
■ *n.* **1** digit. **5 a** see INFORMER 1. ● *v.* **1** touch, feel, handle; toy *or* play *or* fiddle with. **3** indicate, identify, point out, *sl.* put the finger on. □ **have a finger in** (or **in the pie**) be *or* become *or* get involved in, figure in, have a hand in, influence; interfere in, tamper *or* meddle *or* tinker *or* monkey with. **lay a finger on** (so much as) touch; strike, hit, punch. **point the finger at** see ACCUSE 2. **put one's finger on** locate, find, discover, unearth, lay *or* put one's hands on, track down, get hold of, come by, acquire; identify, indicate, point to, pin down, zero in on; recall, remember, recollect, bring *or* call to mind, think of. **put the finger on 1** inform on *or* against, tell on, tattle on, betray, bear witness against, *colloq.* peach on *or* against, *sl.* snitch on, squeal on, finger. **slip through one's fingers** escape, get away, vanish, disappear. **twist** (or **wind** or **wrap**) **around one's finger** (or **little finger**) persuade, control, dominate, have under control, manipulate, maneuver, wield power *or* authority over, have under a person's thumb, have the upper hand over, be master of, influence.

fingerboard /fínggərbawrd/ *n.* a flat strip at the top end of a stringed instrument, against which the strings are pressed to determine tones.

fingering[1] /fínggəring/ *n.* **1** a manner or technique of using the fingers, esp. to play an instrument. **2** an indication of this in a musical score.

fingering[2] /fínggəring/ *n.* fine wool for knitting. [earlier *fin-gram*, perh. f. F *fin grain*, as GROGRAM f. *gros grain*]

fingerling /fínggərling/ *n.* a young fish, esp. a small salmon or trout.

fingernail /fínggərnayl/ *n.* the nail at the tip of each finger.

fingerprint /fínggərprint/ *n. & v.* ● *n.* **1** an impression made on a surface by the fine ridges on the fingertips, esp. as used for identifying individuals. **2** a distinctive characteristic, spectrum, etc. ● *v.tr.* record the fingerprints of (a person).
■ *n.* **2** see MARK[1] *n.* 2a, 3, 4a.

fingerspelling /fínggər-spéling/ *n.* a form of sign language in which individual letters are formed by the fingers to spell out words.

fingertip /fínggərtip/ *n.* the tip of a finger. □ **have at one's fingertips** be thoroughly familiar with (a subject, etc.).

finial /fíneeəl/ *n. Archit.* **1** an ornament finishing off the apex of a roof, pediment, gable, tower corner, canopy, etc. **2** the topmost part of a pinnacle. [ME f. OF *fin* f. L *finis* end]

finical /fínikəl/ *adj.* = FINICKY. □□ **finicality** /-kálitee/ *n.* **finically** *adv.* **finicalness** *n.* [16th c.: prob. orig. university sl. f. FINE[1] + -ICAL]

finicking /fíniking/ *adj.* = FINICKY. [FINICAL + -ING[2]]

finicky /fínikee/ *adj.* **1** overly particular; fastidious. **2** needing much care or attention to detail. □□ **finickiness** *n.*
■ **1** overparticular, fastidious, particular, finical, finicking, overnice, fussy, nice, critical, hard to please, difficult,

meticulous, overprecise, precise, punctilious, overscrupulous, scrupulous, *colloq.* choosy, persnickety, nitpicking, picky. **2** fussy, elaborate, detailed, fine.

finis /fínis, feenée, fínis/ *n.* **1** (at the end of a book) the end. **2** the end of anything, esp. of life. [L]

finish /fínish/ *v. & n.* ● *v.* **1** *tr.* **a** (often foll. by *off*) bring to an end; come to the end of; complete. **b** (usu. foll. by *off*) *colloq.* kill; overcome completely. **c** (often foll. by *off*, *up*) consume or get through the whole or the remainder of (food or drink) (*finish your dinner*). **2** *intr.* **a** come to an end; cease. **b** reach the end, esp. of a race. **c** = *finish up.* **3** *tr.* **a** complete the manufacture of (cloth, woodwork, etc.) by surface treatment. **b** put the final touches to; make perfect or highly accomplished (*finished manners*). **c** prepare (a girl) for entry into fashionable society. ● *n.* **1 a** the end; the last stage. **b** the point at which a race, etc., ends. **c** the death of a fox in a hunt (*be in at the finish*). **2** a method, material, or texture used for surface treatment of wood, cloth, etc. (*mahogany finish*). **3** what serves to give completeness. **4** an accomplished or completed state. □ **fight to the finish** fight until one party is completely beaten. **finishing school** a private school where girls are prepared for entry into fashionable society. **finish off** provide with an ending. **finish up** (often foll. by *in*, *by*) end in something, end by doing something (*he finished up last in the race; the plan finished up in the wastebasket; finished up by apologizing*). **finish with** have no more to do with; complete one's use of or association with. [ME f. OF *fenir* f. L *finire* f. *finis* end]
■ *v.* **1 a** bring to an end, come to the end of, complete, accomplish, perfect, achieve, carry out, fulfill, consummate, clinch, wrap up. **b** kill, exterminate, finish off, annihilate, destroy, get rid of, dispose of, dispatch, put an end to, administer *or* deliver *or* give the *coup de grâce* to, *colloq.* polish off, *sl.* bump off, rub out, waste, ice. **c** consume, dispose of, finish off *or* up, eat *or* drink (up), use (up), devour, drain, polish off. **2 a** come to an end, end, stop, conclude, close, finish up, terminate, wind up; culminate. **3 b** put the final touches to, finish off; perfect, polish, put a finish on. ● *n.* **1 a** end, conclusion, termination, close, closing, completion, ending, finale, culmination, winding up, windup; death, killing, annihilation, extermination, downfall, destruction, defeat. **2** surface, polish; see also TEXTURE *n.* 1, 2. □ **finish up** see *wind up* 6 (WIND[2]). **finish with** have *or* be done with, *colloq.* be through with.

finisher /fínishər/ *n.* **1** a person who finishes something. **2** a worker or machine doing the last operation in a manufacturing process. **3** *colloq.* a discomfiting thing, a crushing blow, etc.

finite /fínit/ *adj.* **1** limited; bounded; not infinite. **2** *Gram.* (of a part of a verb) having a specific number and person. **3** not infinitely small. □□ **finitely** *adv.* **finiteness** *n.* **finitude** /fínitōod, -tyōod/ *n.* [L *finitus* past part. of *finire* FINISH]
■ **1** limited, bounded, restricted, delimited, numerable, countable.

finitism /fínitizəm/ *n.* belief in the finiteness of the world, God, etc. □□ **finitist** /-tist/ *n.*

fink /fingk/ *n. & v. sl.* ● *n.* **1** an unpleasant person. **2** an informer. **3** a strikebreaker. ● *v.intr.* (foll. by *on*) inform on. [20th c.: orig. unkn.]
■ *n.* **2** see SNEAK *n.* ● *v.* see INFORM 2.

Finn /fin/ *n.* a native or inhabitant of Finland; a person of Finnish descent. [OE *Finnas* pl.]

finnan /fínən/ *n.* (in full **finnan haddie** or **haddock**) a haddock cured with the smoke of green wood, turf, or peat. [*Findhorn* or *Findon* in Scotland]

Finnic /fínik/ *adj.* **1** of the group of peoples related to the Finns. **2** of the group of languages related to Finnish.

Finnish /fínish/ *adj. & n.* ● *adj.* of the Finns or their language. ● *n.* the language of the Finns.

Finno-Ugric /fínō-ōógrik, -yōógrik/ *adj. & n.* (also **Finno-Ugrian** /-ōógreeən, -yōógreeən/) ● *adj.* belonging to the group of Uralic languages including Finnish, Estonian, Lapp, and Magyar. ● *n.* this group.

finny /fínee/ *adj.* **1** having fins; like a fin. **2** *poet.* of or teeming with fish.

fino /feénō/ *n.* (*pl.* **-os**) a light-colored dry sherry. [Sp., = fine]

fiord var. of FJORD.

fioritura /fee-áwritŏŏrə/ *n.* (*pl.* **fioriture** /-tŏŏray/) *Mus.* the usu. improvised decoration of a melody. [It., = flowering f. *fiorire* to flower]

fipple /fípəl/ *n.* a plug at the mouth end of a wind instrument. □ **fipple flute** a flute played by blowing endwise, e.g., a recorder. [17th c.: orig. unkn.]

fir /fər/ *n.* **1** (in full **fir tree**) any evergreen coniferous tree, esp. of the genus *Abies*, with needles borne singly on the stems (cf. PINE¹). **2** the wood of the fir. □ **fir cone** *Brit.* the fruit of the fir. □□ **firry** *adj.* [ME, prob. f. ON *fyri-* f. Gmc]

fire /fīr/ *n.* & *v.* ● *n.* **1 a** the state or process of combustion, in which substances combine chemically with oxygen from the air and usu. give out bright light and heat. **b** the active principle operative in this. **c** flame or incandescence. **2** a conflagration; a destructive burning (*forest fire*). **3** burning fuel in a fireplace, furnace, etc. **4** firing of guns (*open fire*). **5 a** fervor; spirit; vivacity. **b** poetic inspiration; lively imagination. **c** vehement emotion. **6** burning heat; fever. **7** luminosity; glow (*St. Elmo's fire*). ● *v.* **1 a** *tr.* discharge (a gun, etc.). **b** *tr.* propel (a missile) from a gun, etc. **c** *tr.* propel (a ball) with force or high speed. **d** *intr.* (often foll. by *at*, *into*, *on*) fire a gun or missile. **e** *tr.* produce (a broadside, salute, etc.) by discharge of guns. **f** *intr.* (of a gun, etc.) be discharged. **2** *tr.* cause (explosive) to explode. **3** *tr.* deliver or utter in rapid succession (*fired insults at us*). **4** *tr. sl.* dismiss (an employee) from a job. **5** *tr.* **a** set fire to with the intention of destroying. **b** kindle (explosives). **6** *intr.* catch fire. **7** *intr.* (of an internal combustion engine, or a cylinder in one) undergo ignition of its fuel. **8** *tr.* supply (a furnace, engine, boiler, or power station) with fuel. **9** *tr.* **a** stimulate (the imagination or emotion). **b** fill (a person) with enthusiasm. **10** *tr.* bake or dry (pottery, bricks, etc.). **b** cure (tea or tobacco) by artificial heat. **11** *intr.* become heated or excited. **12** *tr.* cause to glow or redden. □ **catch fire** begin to burn. **fire alarm** a device for giving warning of fire. **fire and brimstone** the supposed torments of hell. **fire away** *colloq.* begin; go ahead. **fire balloon** a balloon made buoyant by the heat of a fire burning at its mouth. **fire blight** a disease of plants, esp. hops and fruit trees, causing a scorched appearance. **fire brigade** esp. *Brit.* = fire department. **fire company 1** = *fire department*. **2** a fire-insurance company. **fire control** a system of regulating the fire of a ship's or a fort's guns. **fire department** an organized body of firefighters trained and employed to extinguish fires. **fire door** a fire-resistant door to prevent the spread of fire. **fire drill 1** a rehearsal of the procedures to be used in case of fire. **2** a primitive device for kindling fire with a stick and wood. **fire-eater 1** a performer who appears to swallow fire. **2** a person fond of quarreling or fighting. **fire engine** a vehicle carrying equipment for fighting large fires. **fire escape** an emergency staircase or apparatus for escape from a building on fire. **fire extinguisher** an apparatus with a jet for discharging liquid chemicals, water, or foam to extinguish a fire. **fire hose** a hose used in extinguishing fires. **fire irons** tongs, poker, and shovel, for tending a domestic fire. **fire-lighter** *Brit.* a piece of flammable material to help start a fire. **fire opal** girasol. **fire power 1** the destructive capacity of guns, etc. **2** financial, intellectual, or emotional strength. **fire-practice** *Brit.* a fire drill. **fire-raiser** *Brit.* an arsonist. **fire-raising** *Brit.* arson. **fire screen 1** a screen to keep off the direct heat of a fire. **2** a protective screen or grid placed in front of a fireplace. **3** an ornamental screen for a fireplace. **fire ship** *hist.* a ship loaded with combustibles and set adrift to ignite an enemy's ships, etc. **fire station** the headquarters of a fire department. **fire storm 1** a high wind or storm following a very intense fire. **2** a sudden outburst, esp. of criticism, etc. **fire up 1** start up, as an engine. **2** show sudden anger. **fire-walking** the (often cer-

emonial) practice of walking barefoot over white-hot stones, wood ashes, etc. **fire wall** a wall, usu. constructed of fireproof material, intended to prevent the spread of fire. **fire warden** a person employed to prevent or extinguish fires. **go on fire** *Sc.* & *Ir.* catch fire. **go through fire and water** face all perils. **on fire 1** burning. **2** excited. **set fire to** (or **set on fire**) ignite; kindle; cause to burn. **set the world on fire** do something remarkable or sensational. **take fire** catch fire. **under fire 1** being shot at. **2** being rigorously criticized or questioned. □□ **fireless** *adj.* **firer** *n.* [OE *fȳr*, *fȳrian*, t. WG]

■ *n.* **1 c** flame, blaze; see also *incandescence* (INCANDESCENT). **2** conflagration, holocaust, inferno, blaze. **4** firing, gunfire, fusillade, volley, barrage, bombardment, salvo, cannonade, shelling, broadside, flak. **5** fervor, spirit, feeling, passion, ardor, ardency, fervency, intensity, vigor, energy, vivacity, animation, liveliness, verve, élan, éclat, dash, vitality, enthusiasm, fever, feverishness, *colloq.* vim, pep; inspiration, imagination. **6** heat, torridity, fieriness, fever, feverishness. **7** see *radiance* (RADIANT). ● *v.* **1 a** see DISCHARGE *v.* 3. **b** propel, launch; throw, catapult, hurl. **d** open fire, shoot, blaze away, *colloq.* blast. **2** detonate, set *or* let off. **4** dismiss, discharge, oust, give a person notice, boot out, show a person the door, ax, give a person the ax, give a person his *or* her marching orders, *Brit.* ask for (or get) one's cards, make *or* declare redundant, *colloq.* sack, give a person the sack, give a person the boot, give a person his *or* her walking papers, *sl.* bounce, give a person the bounce. **5 a** set fire to, set afire *or* alight, set on fire, ignite, put to the torch, burn, *sl.* torch. **b** see KINDLE 1. **9 a** see STIMULATE. **b** excite, motivate, animate, inspire, energize, inspirit, vitalize, vivify, rouse, stir, awaken, move. □ **catch fire** burn, kindle, ignite, take fire. **fire away** see BEGIN 5b, *go ahead* (GO¹). **fire up 2** see FLARE *v.* 3. **on fire 1** burning, blazing, flaming; afire, alight, aflame. **2** excited, enthusiastic, eager, ardent, passionate, fervent, fervid, fired up, aroused, stirred, stimulated, inspired, intense. **set fire to** (or **set on fire**) see FIRE *v.* 5a above.

firearm /fíraarm/ *n.* (usu. in *pl.*) a gun, esp. a pistol or rifle.
■ see REVOLVER.

fireback /fírbak/ *n.* **1 a** the back wall of a fireplace. **b** an iron sheet for this. **2** a SE Asian pheasant of the genus *Lophura*.

fireball /fírbawl/ *n.* **1** a large meteor. **2** a ball of flame, esp. from a nuclear explosion. **3** an energetic person. **4** ball lightning. **5** *Mil. hist.* a ball filled with combustibles.

firebomb /fírbom/ *n.* an incendiary bomb.
■ see BOMB *n.* 1.

firebox /fírboks/ *n.* **1** the fuel chamber of a steam engine or boiler. **2** an alarm box used to alert a fire department.

firebrand /fírbrand/ *n.* **1** a piece of burning wood. **2** a cause of trouble, esp. a person causing unrest.
■ **2** see AGITATOR 1.

firebreak /fírbrayk/ *n.* an obstacle to the spread of fire in a forest, etc., esp. an open space.

firebrick /fírbrik/ *n.* a fireproof brick used in a grate.

firebug /fírbug/ *n. colloq.* a pyromaniac.

fireclay /fírklay/ *n.* clay capable of withstanding high temperatures, often used to make firebricks.

firecracker /fírkrakər/ *n.* an explosive firework.

firecrest /fírkrest/ *n.* a European warbler, *Regulus ignicapillus*, with red and orange crown feathers, which may be erected.

firedamp /fírdamp/ *n.* a miners' name for methane, which is explosive when mixed in certain proportions with air.

firedog /fírdawg, -dog/ *n.* a metal support for burning wood or for a grate or fire irons.

firedrake /fírdrayk/ n. (in Germanic mythology) a fiery dragon.

firefly /fírfli/ n. (pl. **-flies**) any soft-bodied beetle of the family Lampyridae, emitting phosphorescent light, including glowworms.

firefighter /fírfitər/ n. a person whose task is to extinguish fires.

fireguard /fírgaard/ n. **1** a fire screen. **2** a fire-watcher. **3** a firebreak.

firehouse /fírhows/ n. a fire station.

firelight /fírlīt/ n. light from a fire in a fireplace. [OE fyr-leoht (as FIRE, LIGHT¹)]
■ see LIGHT¹ n. 2.

firelock /fírlok/ n. hist. a musket in which the priming was ignited by sparks.

fireman /fírmən/ n. (pl. **-men**) **1** a member of a fire department; a person employed to extinguish fires. **2** a person who tends a furnace or the fire of a steam engine or steamship.

fireplace /fírplays/ n. Archit. **1** a place for a domestic fire, esp. a grate or hearth at the base of a chimney. **2** a structure surrounding this. **3** the area in front of this.

fireplug /fírplug/ n. a hydrant for a fire hose.

fireproof /fírprōōf/ adj. & v. ● adj. able to resist fire or great heat. ● v.tr. make fireproof.
■ adj. see INCOMBUSTIBLE.

fireside /fírsīd/ n. **1** the area around a fireplace. **2** a person's home or home life. □ **fireside chat** an informal talk.

firestone /fírstōn/ n. stone that resists fire, used for furnaces, etc.

firetrap /fírtrap/ n. a building without proper provision for escape in case of fire.

firewater /fírwawtər/ n. colloq. strong alcoholic liquor.

firewood /fírwŏōd/ n. wood for use as fuel.

firework /fírwərk/ n. **1** a device containing combustible chemicals that cause explosions or spectacular effects. **2** (in pl.) **a** an outburst of passion, esp. anger. **b** a display of wit or brilliance.
■ **2 a** see excitement (EXCITE).

firing /fíring/ n. **1** the discharging of guns. **2** material for a fire; fuel. **3** the heating process that hardens clay into pottery, etc. □ **firing line 1** the front line in a battle. **2** the leading part in an activity, etc. **firing squad** a group detailed to shoot a condemned person.
■ **1** see FIRE n. 4.

firkin /fə́rkin/ n. **1** a small cask for liquids, butter, fish, etc. **2** Brit. (as a measure) half a kilderkin (1/4 barrel or 8 or 9 imperial gallons). [ME ferdekyn, prob. f. MDu. vierdekijn (unrecorded) dimin. of vierde fourth]

firm¹ /fərm/ adj., adv., & v. ● adj. **1 a** of solid or compact structure. **b** fixed; stable. **c** steady; not shaking. **2 a** resolute; determined. **b** not easily shaken (firm belief). **c** steadfast; constant (a firm friend). **3 a** (of an offer, etc.) not liable to cancellation after acceptance. **b** (of a decree, law, etc.) established; immutable. **4** Commerce (of prices or goods) maintaining their level or value. ● adv. firmly (stand firm; hold firm to). ● v. **1** tr. & intr. make or become firm, secure, compact, or solid. **2** tr. fix (plants) firmly in the soil. □□ **firmly** adv. **firmness** n. [ME f. OF ferme f. L firmus]
■ adj. **1 a** solid, compact, dense, compressed, rigid, stiff, hard, unyielding, inelastic, inflexible. **b** fixed, stable, fast, secure, tight, stationary, anchored, moored, unmovable, immovable. **c** steady, strong, sturdy, unwavering, unshakable. **2 a** resolute, determined, persistent, dogged, definite, positive, decisive, unflinching. **b** staunch, unshakn, unshakable, unwavering, immovable, inflexible, rigid, undeviating, unswerving, unchanging, unchangeable, obstinate, obdurate, stubborn, strict, unyielding, unbending, unalterable, inalterable. **c** constant, staunch; see also STEADFAST. **3 b** established, immutable; see also FINAL adj. 2. ● v. **1** secure, settle, establish, consolidate, solidify, determine, set up. □□ **firmly** solidly, strongly, securely, tightly, rigidly, fast, immovably; resolutely,

steadfastly, determinedly, staunchly, unwaveringly, decisively, unhesitatingly, constantly.

firm² /fərm/ n. **1 a** a business concern. **b** the partners in such a concern. **2** Brit. a group of persons working together, esp. of hospital doctors and assistants. [earlier = signature; style: Sp. & It. firma f. med.L, f. L firmare confirm f. firmus FIRM¹]
■ **1** company, organization, business, enterprise, concern, house, partnership, corporation, colloq. outfit.

firmament /fə́rməmənt/ n. literary the sky regarded as a vault or arch. □□ **firmamental** /-mént'l/ adj. [ME f. OF f. L firmamentum f. firmare (as FIRM²)]
■ sky, skies, heaven, vault (of heaven), empyrean, poet. welkin, esp. poet. heavens.

firmware /fə́rmwair/ n. Computing a permanent kind of software programmed into a read-only memory.

firry see FIR.

first /fərst/ adj., n., & adv. ● adj. **1 a** earliest in time or order. **b** coming next after a specified or implied time (shall take the first train; the first cuckoo). **2** foremost in position, rank, or importance (first mate). **3** Mus. performing the highest or chief of two or more parts for the same instrument or voice. **4** most willing or likely (should be the first to admit the problem). **5** basic or evident (first principles). ● n. **1** (prec. by the) the person or thing first mentioned or occurring. **2** the first occurrence of something notable. **3** Brit. **a** a place in the first class in an examination. **b** a person having this. **4** the first day of a month. **5** first gear. **6 a** first place in a race. **b** the winner of this. **7** (in pl.) goods of the best quality. **8** first base. ● adv. **1** before any other person or thing (first of all; first and foremost; first come first served). **2** before someone or something else (must get this done first). **3** for the first time (when did you first see her?). **4** in preference; sooner (will see him damned first). □ **at first** at the beginning. **at first hand** directly from the original source. **first aid** help given to an injured person until proper medical treatment is available. **first and last** taking one thing with another; on the whole. **first base** Baseball **1** the base touched first by a base runner. **2 a** the fielder stationed nearest first base. **b** the position nearest first base. **first blood** see BLOOD. **first-born** adj. eldest. ● n. the eldest child of a person. **first cause** the creator or source of the universe. **first class 1** a set of persons or things grouped together as the best. **2** the best accommodation in a train, ship, etc. **3** the class of mail given priority in handling. **4** Brit. **a** the highest division in an examination list. **b** a place in this. **first-class** adj. **1** belonging to or traveling by the first class. **2** of the best quality; very good. ● adv. by the first class (travels first-class). **first cousin** see COUSIN. **first day cover** an envelope with stamps postmarked on their first day of issue. **first-degree** Med. denoting burns that affect only the surface of the skin, causing reddening. **first finger** the finger next to the thumb. **first floor** see FLOOR. **first fruit** (usu. in pl.) **1** the first agricultural produce of a season, esp. as an offering. **2** the first results of work, etc. **3** hist. a payment to a superior by the new holder of an office. **first gear** see GEAR. **first intention** see INTENTION. **First Lady** the wife of the US President. **first lesson** the first of several passages from the Bible read at a service in a church of the Anglican Communion. **first lieutenant** an army or air force officer ranking below captain. **first light** the time when light first appears in the morning. **first mate** (on a merchant ship) the officer second in command to the master. **first name** a personal name other than a surname. **first night** the first public performance of a play, etc. **first-nighter** a habitual attender of first nights. **first off** colloq. at first; first of all. **first offender** a criminal against whom no previous conviction is recorded. **first officer** the mate on a merchant ship. **first or last** sooner or later. **first person** see PERSON. **first post** see POST³. **first-rate** adj. of the highest class; excellent. ● adv. colloq. **1** very well (feeling first-rate). **2** excellently. **first reading** the occasion when a bill is presented to a legislature to permit its introduction. **first refusal** see REFUSAL. **first school** Brit. a school for children from 5 to 9 years old. **first sergeant** the highest ranking noncommissioned officer in a company. **first-strike** denoting a first aggressive attack with nuclear weapons. **first thing** *colloq.* before anything else; very early in the morning (*shall do it first thing*). **the first thing** even the most elementary fact or principle (*does not know the first thing about it*). **first things first** the most important things before any others (*we must do first things first*). **first up** *Austral.* first of all; at the first attempt. **from the first** from the beginning. **from first to last** throughout. **get to first base** achieve the first step toward an objective. **in the first place** as the first consideration. **of the first water** see WATER. [OE *fyrst* f. Gmc]

■ *adj.* **1 a** earliest, oldest, original; initial, maiden, opening. **2** foremost, leading, principal, preeminent, primary, chief, head, premier, prime. **3** chief, head, lead, principal. **5** basic, fundamental, elementary, primary, cardinal, key, essential, evident. ● *n.* **6 a** first place, gold (medal); see also WIN *n.* **b** see WINNER 1. ● *adv.* **1** before, in front, earliest, foremost; firstly, in the first place, before all, before anything else, to begin *or* start with, from the start, *sl.* for starters. **2** before, beforehand, ahead, sooner. **4** see RATHER 1. □ **at first** at *or* in the beginning, initially, at the start *or* outset, *colloq.* first off; see also *in the first instance* (INSTANCE). **first-class 2** see EXCELLENT. **first light** see DAWN *n.* 1. **first off** see *at first* (FIRST) above. **first-rate** (*adj.*) first-class, excellent, high-grade, prime, superior, superb, great, remarkable, admirable, fine, exceptional, outstanding, extraordinary, unparalleled, matchless, unsurpassed, top, *colloq.* A1, top-notch, tiptop, *sl.* ace, esp. *Brit. sl.* wizard. **from the first** see *originally* (ORIGINAL). **from first to last** see THROUGHOUT *adv.* **in the first place** see FIRST *adv.* 1 above.

firsthand /fɔ́rst-hánd/ *attrib. adj. & adv.* from the original source; direct.

firstling /fɔ́rstling/ *n.* (usu. in *pl.*) **1** the first result of anything; first fruits. **2** the first offspring; the first born in a season.

firstly /fɔ́rstlee/ *adv.* (in enumerating topics, arguments, etc.) in the first place; first (cf. FIRST *adv.*).

■ see FIRST *adv.* 1.

firth /fɔrth/ *n.* (also **frith** /frith/) **1** a narrow inlet of the sea. **2** an estuary. [ME (orig. Sc.) f. ON *fjörthr* FIORD]

■ see GULF *n.* 1.

fisc /fisk/ *n. Rom.Hist.* the public treasury; the emperor's privy purse. [F *fisc* or L *fiscus* rush basket, purse, treasury]

fiscal /fískəl/ *adj. & n.* ● *adj.* of public revenue; of financial matters. ● *n.* a legal official in some countries. □ **fiscal year** a year as reckoned for taxing or accounting. □□ **fiscally** *adv.* [F *fiscal* or L *fiscalis* (as FISC)]

■ *adj.* financial, economic, budgetary, pecuniary, monetary.

fiscality /fiskálitee/ *n.* (*pl.* **-ies**) **1** (in *pl.*) fiscal matters. **2** excessive regard for these.

fish¹ /fish/ *n. & v.* ● *n.* (*pl.* same or **fishes**) **1** a vertebrate cold-blooded animal with gills and fins living wholly in water. **2** any animal living wholly in water, e.g., cuttlefish, shellfish, jellyfish. **3** the flesh of fish as food. **4** *colloq.* a person remarkable in some way (usu. unfavorable) (*an odd fish*). **5** (**the Fish** or **Fishes**) the zodiacal sign or constellation Pisces. **6** *Naut. sl.* a torpedo; a submarine. ● *v.* **1** *intr.* try to catch fish, esp. with a line or net. **2** *tr.* fish for (a certain kind of fish) or in (a certain stretch of water). **3** *intr.* (foll. by *for*) **a** search for in water or a concealed place. **b** seek by indirect means (*fishing for compliments*). **4** *tr.* (foll. by *up*, *out*, etc.) retrieve with careful or awkward searching. □ **drink like a fish** drink excessively. **fish bowl** a usu. round glass bowl for keeping pet fish in. **fish cake** a cake of shredded fish and mashed potato, usu. eaten pan fried. **fish duck** a merganser. **fish eagle 1** any large eagle of the genus *Haliaeetus*, with long broad wings, strong legs, and a strong tail. **2** any of several other eagles catching and feeding on fish. **fish-eye lens** a very wide-angle lens with a curved front. **fish farm** a place where fish are bred for food. **fish hawk** an osprey, *Pandion haliaeetus*. **fish knife** a knife for eating or serving fish. **fish ladder** (or **leap**) a series of steps or other arrangement incorporated in a dam to allow fish to

pass upstream. **fish meal** ground dried fish used as fertilizer or animal feed. **fish out of water** a person in an unsuitable or unwelcome environment or situation. **fish-slice** *Brit.* a flat utensil for lifting fish and fried foods during and after cooking. **fish stick** (or *Brit.* **finger**) a small oblong piece of fish in batter or breadcrumbs. **fish story** *colloq.* an exaggerated account. **other fish to fry** other matters to attend to. □□ **fishlike** *adj.* [OE *fisc, fiscian* f. Gmc]

■ *v.* **1–3** see ANGLE² *v.* 2. **4** (*fish up* or *out*) see DIG *v.* 4.

fish² /fish/ *n. & v.* ● *n.* **1 a** flat plate of iron, wood, etc., to strengthen a beam or joint. **2** *Naut.* a piece of wood used to strengthen a mast, etc. ● *v.tr.* **1** mend or strengthen (a spar, etc.) with a fish. **2** join (rails) with a fishplate. □ **fish-bolt** a bolt used to fasten fishplates and rails together. [orig. as verb: f. F *ficher* fix ult. f. L *figere*]

fisher /físhər/ *n.* **1** any animal that catches fish, esp. the marten, *Martes pennanti,* valued for its fur. **2** *archaic* a fisherman. [OE *fiscere* f. Gmc (as FISH¹)]

fisherman /físhərmən/ *n.* (*pl.* **-men**) **1** a person who catches fish as a livelihood or for recreation. **2** a fishing boat.

fishery /físhəree/ *n.* (*pl.* **-ies**) **1** a place where fish or other aquatic animals are caught or reared. **2** the occupation or industry of catching or rearing fish or other aquatic animals.

fishhook /físh-hŏŏk/ *n.* a barbed hook for catching fish.

fishing /físhing/ *n.* the activity of catching fish, esp. for food or as recreation. □ **fishing line** a long thread of nylon filament, silk, etc., with a baited hook, sinker, float, etc., used for catching fish. **fishing rod** a long tapering usu. jointed rod to which a fishing line is attached. **fishing story** *Brit.* = *fish story.*

fishmonger /físhmunggər, -mong-/ *n.* esp. *Brit.* a dealer in fish.

fishnet /físhnet/ *n.* (often *attrib.*) an open-meshed fabric (*fishnet stockings*).

fishplate /físhplayt/ *n.* **a** a flat piece of iron, etc., connecting railroad rails. **b** a flat piece of metal with ends like a fish's tail, used to position masonry.

fishpond /físhpond/ *n.* a pond or pool in which fish are kept.

fishtail /físhtayl/ *n. & v.* ● *n.* a device, etc., shaped like a fish's tail. ● *v.intr.* move the tail of a vehicle from side to side. □ **fishtail burner** a kind of burner producing a broadening jet of flame.

fishwife /físhwif/ *n.* (*pl.* **-wives**) **1** an ill-mannered or noisy woman. **2** a woman who sells fish.

■ **1** see SCOLD *n.*

fishy /físhee/ *adj.* (**fishier, fishiest**) **1 a** smelling or tasting like fish. **b** like that of a fish. **c** (of an eye) dull; vacant-looking. **d** consisting of fish (*a fishy repast*). **e** *joc.* or *poet.* abounding in fish. **2** *sl.* of dubious character; questionable; suspect. □□ **fishily** *adv.* **fishiness** *n.*

■ **1 b** piscine, fishlike. **c** see VACANT 2. **2** dubious, questionable, doubtful, suspect, suspicious, not kosher, shady, funny, odd, peculiar, strange, queer; improbable, implausible, unlikely, far-fetched.

fisk /fisk/ *n. Sc.* the national treasury; the exchequer. [var. of FISC]

fissile /físəl, -íl/ *adj.* **1** capable of undergoing nuclear fission. **2** cleavable; tending to split. □□ **fissility** /-sílitee/ *n.* [L *fissilis* (as FISSURE)]

■ **2** see SEPARABLE.

fission /físhən/ *n. & v.* ● *n.* **1** *Physics* the spontaneous or impact-induced splitting of a heavy atomic nucleus, accompanied by a release of energy. **2** *Biol.* the division of a cell, etc., into new cells, etc., as a mode of reproduction. ● *v.intr. & tr.* undergo or cause to undergo fission. □ **fission bomb** an atomic bomb. □□ **fissionable** *adj.* [L *fissio* (as FISSURE)]

■ *n.* **2** see SEPARATION.

fissiparous /fisípərəs/ *adj.* **1** *Biol.* reproducing by fission. **2**

/.../ pronunciation	● part of speech
□ phrases, idioms, and compounds	
□□ derivatives	■ synonym section
cross-references appear in SMALL CAPITALS or *italics*	

tending to split. □□ **fissiparity** /físipáritee/ *n.* **fissiparously** *adv.* **fissiparousness** *n.* [L *fissus* past part. (as FISSURE) after *viviparous*]

fissure /físhər/ *n. & v.* ● *n.* **1** an opening, usu. long and narrow, made esp. by cracking, splitting, or separation of parts. **2** *Bot. & Anat.* a narrow opening in an organ, etc., esp. a depression between convolutions of the brain. **3** a cleavage. ● *v.tr. & intr.* split or crack. [ME f. OF *fissure* or L *fissura* f. *findere fiss-* cleave]

■ *n.* **1, 3** see CRACK *n.* 2. ● *v.* see CRACK *v.* 1.

fist /fist/ *n. & v.* ● *n.* **1** a tightly closed hand. **2** *sl.* handwriting (*writes a good fist*; *I know his fist*). **3** *sl.* a hand (*give us your fist*). **4** = INDEX *n.* 9. ● *v.tr.* **1** close into a fist. **2** *Naut.* handle (a sail, an oar, etc.). □ **make a good** (or **poor,** etc.) **fist** (foll. by *at, of*) *colloq.* make a good (or poor, etc.) attempt at. □□ **fisted** *adj.* (also in *comb.*). **fistful** *n.* (*pl.* **-fuls**). [OE *fȳst* f. WG]

fistfight /fístfīt/ *n.* a fight with bare fists.

fistic /fístik/ *adj.* (also **fistical**) *joc.* pugilistic.

fisticuffs /fístikufs/ *n.pl.* fighting with the fists. [prob. obs. *fisty* adj. = FISTIC, + CUFF²]

■ boxing, pugilism, prizefighting.

fistula /físchələ/ *n.* (*pl.* **fistulas** or **fistulae** /-lee/) **1** an abnormal or surgically made passage between a hollow organ and the body surface or between two hollow organs. **2** a natural pipe or spout in whales, insects, etc. □□ **fistular** *adj.* **fistulous** *adj.* [L, = pipe, flute]

fit¹ /fit/ *adj., v., n., & adv.* ● *adj.* (**fitter, fittest**) **1 a** (usu. foll. by *for,* or *to* + infin.) well adapted or suited. **b** (foll. by *to* + infin.) qualified; competent; worthy. **c** (foll. by *for,* or *to* + infin.) in a suitable condition; ready. **d** (foll. by *for*) good enough (*a dinner fit for a king*). **e** (foll. by *to* + infin.) sufficiently exhausted, troubled, or angry (*fit to drop*). **2** in good health or athletic condition. **3** proper; becoming; right (*it is fit that*). ● *v.* (**fitted, fitting**) **1 a** *tr.* (also *absol.*) be of the right shape and size for (*the dress fits her*; *the key doesn't fit the lock*; *these shoes don't fit*). **b** *tr.* make, fix, or insert (a thing) so that it is of the right size or shape (*fitted shelves in the alcoves*). **c** *tr.* (often foll. by *in, into*) (of a component) be correctly positioned (*that piece fits here*). **d** *tr.* find room for (*can't fit another person on the bench*). **2** *tr.* (foll. by *for,* or *to* + infin.) **a** make suitable; adapt. **b** make competent (*fitted him to be a priest*). **3** *tr.* (usu. foll. by *with*) supply; furnish (*fitted the boat with a new rudder*). **4** *tr.* fix in place (*fit a lock on the door*). **5** *tr.* try on (a garment). **6** *tr.* be in harmony with; befit; become (*it fits the occasion*; *the punishment fits the crime*). ● *n.* the way in which a garment, component, etc., fits (*a bad fit*; *a tight fit*). ● *adv.* (foll. by *to* + infin.) *colloq.* in a suitable manner; appropriately (*was laughing fit to bust*). □ **fit the bill** = *fill the bill*. **fit in 1** (often foll. by *with*) be (esp. socially) compatible or accommodating (*doesn't fit in with the rest of the group*; *tried to fit in with their plans*). **2** find space or time for (an object, engagement, etc.) (*the dentist fitted me in at the last minute*). **fit on** *Brit.* try on (a garment). **fit out** (or **up**) (often foll. by *with*) equip. **fit-up** *Brit. Theatr. sl.* **1** a temporary stage, etc. **2** a traveling company. **see** (or **think**) **fit** (often foll. by *to* + infin.) decide or choose (a specified course of action). □□ **fitly** *adv.* **fitness** *n.* [ME: orig. unkn.]

■ *adj.* **1 a** (well) adapted *or* suited, suitable, appropriate, fitted; apt. **b** (*fit to*) qualified to, competent to, prepared to, ready to, able to, adequate to, capable of, worthy of *or* to. **c** see READY *adj.* 1, 2. **e** (*fit to*) ready to, sufficiently exhausted, troubled *or* angry to, disposed to, likely to, about to. **2** in good health *or* condition *or* shape *or* trim, in fine fettle; healthy, well, hale, vigorous, strong, sturdy, robust, strapping, ablebodied. **3** proper, becoming, right, correct, fitting, applicable, apropos, *archaic* meet. ● *v.* **1 c** go together, join, match, correspond, dovetail. **d** see ACCOMMODATE 1. **2 a** adapt, adjust, modify, change, alter, shape. **b** see TRAIN *v.* 1a. **3** supply, furnish, equip, provide, fit out *or* up, install, rig out, gear up. **6** befit, suit, become, be suited to, be suitable *or* appropriate for; answer, satisfy. □ **fit in 1** harmonize, find one's

place *or* niche, fit; (*fit in with*) see CONFORM 4. **fit out** (or **up**) see EQUIP. □□ **fitness** aptness, appropriateness, pertinence, seemliness, suitability, suitableness; competence, eligibility, adequacy, qualification; health, healthiness, good (physical) condition, vigor, wellbeing, good shape, fine fettle, tone; wholesomeness, salubriousness, salubrity.

fit² /fit/ *n.* **1** a sudden seizure of epilepsy, hysteria, apoplexy, fainting, or paralysis, with unconsciousness or convulsions. **2** a sudden brief attack of an illness or of symptoms (*fit of coughing*). **3** a sudden short bout or burst (*fit of energy*; *fit of giggles*). **4** *colloq.* an attack of strong feeling (*fit of rage*). **5** a capricious impulse; a mood (*when the fit was on him*). □ **by** (or **in**) **fits and starts** spasmodically. **give a person a fit** *colloq.* surprise or outrage him or her. **have a fit** *colloq.* be greatly surprised or outraged. **in fits** laughing uncontrollably. [ME, = position of danger, perh. = OE *fitt* conflict (?)]

■ **1** seizure, attack, convulsion, paroxysm, spasm; *Med.* ictus. **2** attack, assault, bout. **3** bout, burst, outburst, outbreak, paroxysm, spell, period. **4** see OUTBURST. □ **by** (or **in**) **fits and starts** spasmodically, sporadically, occasionally, fitfully, intermittently, erratically, haphazardly, off and on, now and then, irregularly. **give a person a fit** see SURPRISE *v.* 1, 2. **in fits** (*be in fits*) see KILL *v.* 3b.

fit³ /fit/ *n.* (also **fytte**) *archaic* a section of a poem. [OE *fitt*]

fitch /fich/ *n.* **1** a polecat. **2 a** the hair or fur of a polecat. **b** a brush made from this or similar hair. [MDu. *fisse*, etc.: cf. FITCHEW]

fitchew /fichoo/ *n.* a polecat. [14th c. f. OF *ficheau, fissel* dimin. of MDu. *fisse*]

fitful /fítfool/ *adj.* active or occurring spasmodically or intermittently. □□ **fitfully** *adv.* **fitfulness** *n.*

■ spasmodic, intermittent, sporadic, occasional, periodic, erratic, haphazard, irregular, capricious; varying, fluctuating, variable, uneven.

fitment /fítmənt/ *n.* (usu. in *pl.*) esp. *Brit.* a fixed item of furniture.

fitted /fítid/ *adj.* **1** made or shaped to fill a space or cover something closely or exactly (*a fitted sheet*). **2** esp. *Brit.* provided with appropriate equipment, fittings, etc. (*a fitted kitchen*). **3** esp. *Brit.* built-in; filling an alcove, etc. (*fitted cupboards*).

■ **1** custom-made, tailor-made, tailored, *Brit.* bespoke.

fitter /fítər/ *n.* **1** a person who supervises the cutting, fitting, altering, etc., of garments. **2** a mechanic who fits together and adjusts machinery.

fitting /fíting/ *n. & adj.* ● *n.* **1** the process or an instance of having a garment, etc., fitted (*needed several fittings*). **2 a** (in *pl.*) the fixtures and furnishings of a building. **b** a piece of apparatus or a detachable part of a machine, fixture, etc. ● *adj.* proper; becoming; right. □□ **fittingly** *adv.* **fittingness** *n.*

■ *n.* **2 a** (*fittings*) fixtures, fitments, attachments, pieces, parts, units, furniture, appointments, furnishings, equipment, trappings, accoutrements, paraphernalia, trimmings; accessories, extras, installations. ● *adj.* proper, becoming, right, fit, befitting, suitable, appropriate, seemly, apt, apropos, apposite, germane, relevant, *archaic* meet; *comme il faut*.

FitzGerald contraction /fitsjérəld/ *n.* (also **FitzGerald effect**) (in full **FitzGerald-Lorentz**) *Physics* the shortening of a moving body in the direction of its motion, esp. at speeds close to that of light. [G. F. *FitzGerald*, Ir. physicist d. 1901 and H. A. *Lorentz*, Du. physicist d. 1928]

five /fīv/ *n. & adj.* ● *n.* **1** one more than four or one half of ten; the sum of three units and two units. **2** a symbol for this (5, v, V). **3** a size, etc., denoted by five. **4** a set or team of five individuals. **5** the time of five o'clock (*is it five yet?*). **6** a card with five pips. **7** a five-dollar bill. ● *adj.* that amount to five. □ **bunch of fives** *Brit. sl.* a hand or fist. **fiveand-dime** (or **-ten**) a store with a variety of inexpensive household sundries, toiletries, etc., originally sold for five or ten cents. **five-finger exercise 1** an exercise on the piano involving all the fingers. **2** an easy task. **five o'clock**

shadow beard growth visible on a man's face in the latter part of the day. **five-star** of the highest class. **five-year plan 1** (esp. in China and the former USSR) a government plan for economic development over five years. **2** a similar plan in another country. [OE *fīf* f. Gmc]
■ **five-and-dime** (or **-ten**) dime store, dry goods store.

fivefold /fívfōld/ adj. & adv. **1** five times as much or as many. **2** consisting of five parts. **3** amounting to five.

fiver /fívər/ n. colloq. **1** a five-dollar bill. **2** Brit. a five-pound note.

fives /fīvz/ n. esp. Brit. a game in which a ball is hit with a gloved hand or a bat against the walls of a court with three walls (**Eton fives**) or four walls (**Rugby fives**). [pl. of FIVE used as sing.: significance unkn.]

fivestones /fívstōnz/ n. Brit. jacks played with five pieces of metal, etc., and usu. without a ball.

fix /fiks/ v. & n. ● v. **1** tr. make firm or stable; fasten; secure (*fixed a picture to the wall*). **2** tr. decide; settle; specify (a price, date, etc.). **3** tr. mend; repair. **4** tr. implant (an idea or memory) in the mind (*couldn't get the rules fixed in his head*). **5** tr. **a** (foll. by *on, upon*) direct steadily; set (one's eyes, gaze, attention, or affection). **b** attract and hold (a person's attention, eyes, etc.). **c** (foll. by *with*) single out with one's eyes, etc. **6** tr. place definitely or permanently; establish; station. **7** tr. determine the exact nature, position, etc., of; refer (a thing or person) to a definite place or time; identify, locate. **8 a** tr. make (eyes, features, etc.) rigid. **b** intr. (of eyes, features, etc.) become rigid. **9** tr. colloq. prepare (food or drink) (*fixed me a drink*). **10 a** tr. deprive of fluidity or volatility; congeal. **b** intr. lose fluidity or volatility; become congealed. **11** tr. colloq. punish; kill; silence; deal with; take revenge on (a person). **12** tr. colloq. **a** secure the support of (a person) fraudulently, esp. by bribery. **b** arrange the result of (a race, match, etc.) fraudulently (*the competition was fixed*). **13** sl. **a** tr. inject (a person, esp. oneself) with a narcotic. **b** intr. take an injection of a narcotic. **14** tr. make (a color, photographic image, or microscope specimen) fast or permanent. **15** tr. (of a plant or microorganism) assimilate (nitrogen or carbon dioxide) by forming a nongaseous compound. **16** tr. castrate or spay (an animal). **17** tr. arrest changes or development in (a language or literature). **18** tr. determine the incidence of (liability, etc.). **19** intr. archaic take up one's position. **20** (as **fixed** adj.) **a** permanently placed; stationary. **b** without moving; rigid; (of a gaze, etc.) steady or intent. **c** definite. **d** sl. dishonest; fraudulent. ● n. **1** colloq. a position hard to escape from; a dilemma or predicament. **2 a** the act of finding one's position by bearings or astronomical observations (*get a fix on that star*). **b** a position found in this way. **3** sl. a dose of a narcotic drug to which one is addicted. **4** sl. bribery. □ **be fixed** (usu. foll. by *for*) be disposed or affected (regarding) (*how is he fixed for money?*; *how are you fixed for Friday?*). **fixed capital** machinery, etc., that remains in the owner's use. **fixed-do** Mus. applied to a system of sight-singing in which C is called 'do,' D is called 're,' etc., irrespective of the key in which they occur (cf. *movable-do*). **fixed focus** a camera focus at a distance from a lens that is not adjustable. **fixed idea** = IDÉE FIXE. **fixed income** income deriving from a pension, investment at fixed interest, etc. **fixed odds** predetermined odds in racing, etc. (opp. *starting price*). **fixed oil** an oil of animal or plant origin used in varnishes, lubricants, illuminants, soaps, etc. **fixed point** a system of mathematical notation or calculation in which the decimal point is fixed in one place. **fixed star** Astron. a star so far from the earth as to appear motionless. **fix on** (or **upon**) choose; decide on. **fix up 1** arrange; organize; prepare. **2** accommodate. **3** (often foll. by *with*) provide (a person) with (*fixed me up with a job*). **4** restore; refurbish (*fixed up the old house*). □□ **fixable** adj. **fixedly** /fíksidlee/ adv. **fixedness** /fíksidnis/ n. [ME, partly f. obs. *fix* fixed f. OF *fix* or L *fixus* past part. of *figere* fix, fasten, partly f. med.L *fixare* f. *fixus*]
■ v. **1** make firm or stable; fasten, secure, affix, anchor, retain, attach, make fast, set. **2** decide, resolve, settle, specify, establish, set, agree on, organize, arrange, prearrange, cement, conclude, arrive at. **3** mend,

repair, fix up, patch up, remedy, rectify, correct, emend, adjust, regulate, put or set to rights, straighten out, colloq. doctor. **4** see IMPLANT v. 2. **5 a** (*fix on* or *upon*) direct at, fasten on or upon, focus on, rivet on, concentrate on. **b** attract, hold, rivet. **c** see SINGLE v. **6** place, establish, station, settle, install, situate, locate, position. **7** determine, specify, establish, identify, locate; assign, allocate, attribute, ascribe, specify, pin, attach, fasten. **9** see PREPARE 2. **10** congeal, harden, thicken, set, solidify, rigidify, stiffen, freeze; become congealed or hard. **11** punish, deal with, take care of, see to, colloq. settle a person's hash, sort out; retaliate against, wreak vengeance on, hit or strike or get back at, get even with, even the score with, make reprisals against, avenge oneself against, take revenge on, take retribution against, repay, pay back. **12 a** bribe, buy, colloq. grease the palm of. **b** arrange, rig; prearrange, predetermine, set up, contrive, Brit. sl. fiddle. **13 a** see INJECT 1. **16** see STERILIZE 2. **17** set, settle, freeze, stabilize, solidify. **18** see DETERMINE 1, 2, 4. **20** (**fixed**) **a** fastened, attached, anchored, set, secure, secured, firm; immovable, immobile, stationary, rooted, solid, immobilized, stuck. **b** rigid, unchangeable, unchanging, unfluctuating, unwavering, undeviating, unflinching, unblinking, steady; intent. **c** definite, settled, firm, secure, established, decided, prearranged, unalterable. **d** crooked, dishonest, put-up, esp. Brit. sl. bent. ● n. **1** dilemma, predicament, difficulty, corner, double bind, quandary, mess, bad situation, dire or desperate straits, colloq. pickle, catch-22, jam, hole, tight spot, tough spot, bind. **4** bribery, subornation. □ **fix on** (or **upon**) decide (on or upon), set, agree (on or upon), choose, select, settle (on), determine, finalize. **fix up 1** see ARRANGE 2, 3. **2** see ACCOMMODATE 1. **3** provide, furnish, supply, accommodate, set up; Brit. lay on.

fixate /fíksáyt/ v.tr. **1** direct one's gaze on. **2** Psychol. **a** (usu. in passive; often foll. by *on, upon*) cause (a person) to acquire an abnormal attachment to persons or things (*was fixated on his son*). **b** arrest (part of the libido) at an immature stage, causing such attachment. [L *fixus* (see FIX) + -ATE³]

fixation /fiksáyshən/ n. **1** the act or an instance of being fixated. **2** an obsession; concentration on a single idea. **3** fixing or being fixed. **4** the process of rendering solid; coagulation. **5** the process of assimilating a gas to form a solid compound. [ME f. med.L *fixatio* f. *fixare*: see FIX]
■ **1, 2** mania, obsession, compulsion, fixed idea, *idée fixe*, monomania, preoccupation, fetish, colloq. thing.

fixative /fíksətiv/ adj. & n. ● adj. tending to fix or secure. ● n. a substance used to fix colors, hair, microscope specimens, etc.

fixer /fíksər/ n. **1** a person or thing that fixes. **2** Photog. a substance used for fixing a photographic image, etc. **3** colloq. a person who makes arrangements, esp. of an illicit kind.

fixings /fíksingz/ n.pl. **1** apparatus or equipment. **2** the trimmings for a dish. **3** the trimmings of a dress, etc.

fixity /fíksitee/ n. **1** a fixed state. **2** stability; permanence. [obs. *fix* fixed: see FIX]

fixture /fíkschər/ n. **1 a** something fixed or fastened in position. **b** an attached appliance, apparatus, etc. (*an electrical fixture*). **c** (usu. predic.) colloq. a person or thing confined to or established in one place (*he seems to be a fixture*). **2** Brit. **a** a sporting event, esp. a match, race, etc. **b** the date agreed for this. **3** (in pl.) Law articles attached to a house or land and regarded as legally part of it. [alt. of obs. *fixure* f. LL *fixura* f. L *figere* fix- fix]
■ **1** appliance, fitting, fitment, appendage.

fizz /fiz/ v. & n. ● v.intr. **1** make a hissing or spluttering sound. **2** (of a drink) make bubbles; effervesce. ● n. **1** effervescence. **2** esp. *Brit. colloq.* a carbonated drink, esp. champagne. [imit.]

■ *v.* **1** hiss, sputter, sizzle, splutter, fizzle. **2** bubble, effervesce, sparkle, froth. ● *n.* **1** effervescence, sparkle, carbonation, bubbling, froth, fizziness.

fizzer /fízər/ *n.* **1** *Brit.* an excellent or first-rate thing. **2** *Cricket colloq.* a very fast ball, or one that deviates with unexpected speed. **3** *Austral. sl.* a disappointing failure or fiasco.

fizzle /fízəl/ *v. & n.* ● *v.intr.* make a feeble hissing or spluttering sound. ● *n.* such a sound. □ **fizzle out** end feebly (*the party fizzled out at 10 o'clock*). [formed as FIZZ + -LE⁴]

■ *v.* see FIZZ *v.* 1. □ **fizzle out** die (out *or* away), expire, peter out, come to nothing *or* naught, fail, fall through, miscarry, abort, come to grief, misfire, collapse, cave in.

fizzy /fízee/ *adj.* (**fizzier, fizziest**) effervescent; carbonated. □□ **fizzily** *adv.* **fizziness** *n.*

■ see *effervescent* (EFFERVESCE).

fjord /fyawrd/ *n.* (also **fiord**) a long narrow inlet of sea between high cliffs, as in Norway. [Norw. f. ON *fjorthr* f. Gmc: cf. FIRTH, FORD]

■ see GULF *n.* 1.

FL *abbr.* Florida (in official postal use).

fl. *abbr.* **1** floor. **2** floruit. **3** fluid.

Fla. *abbr.* Florida.

flab /flab/ *n. colloq.* fat; flabbiness. [imit., or back-form. f. FLABBY]

flabbergast /flábərgast/ *v.tr.* (esp. as **flabbergasted** *adj.*) *colloq.* overwhelm with astonishment; dumbfound. [18th c.: perh. f. FLABBY + AGHAST]

■ see ASTONISH.

flabby /flábee/ *adj.* (**flabbier, flabbiest**) **1** (of flesh, etc.) hanging down; limp; flaccid. **2** (of language or character) feeble. □□ **flabbily** *adv.* **flabbiness** *n.* [alt. of earlier *flappy* f. FLAP]

■ **1** limp, flaccid, loose, slack, floppy, sagging, drooping, baggy, pendulous, soft. **2** feeble, weak, spineless, impotent, ineffective, ineffectual.

flaccid /flásid, fláksid/ *adj.* **1 a** (of flesh, etc.) hanging loose or wrinkled; limp; flabby. **b** (of plant tissue) soft; less rigid. **2** relaxed; drooping. **3** lacking vigor; feeble. □□ **flaccidity** /-síditee/ *n.* **flaccidly** *adv.* [F *flaccide* or L *flaccidus* f. *flaccus* flabby]

■ **1a, 2** see FLABBY 1.

flack¹ /flak/ *n. & v. sl.* ● *n.* a publicity agent. ● *v.intr.* act as a publicity agent. [20th c.: orig. unkn.]

flack² var. of FLAK.

flag¹ /flag/ *n. & v.* ● *n.* **1 a** a piece of cloth, usu. oblong or square, attachable by one edge to a pole or rope and used as a country's emblem or as a standard, signal, etc. **b** a small toy, device, etc., resembling a flag. **2** *Brit.* an oblong strip of metal, etc., that can be raised or lowered to indicate whether a taxi is available or occupied. **3** *Naut.* a flag carried by a flagship as an emblem of an admiral's rank afloat. ● *v.* (**flagged, flagging**) **1** *intr.* **a** grow tired; lose vigor; lag (*his energy flagged after the first lap*). **b** hang down; droop; become limp. **2** *tr.* **a** place a flag on or over. **b** mark out with or as if with a flag or flags. **3** *tr.* (often foll. by *that*) **a** inform (a person) by flag signals. **b** communicate (information) by flagging. □ **black flag 1** a pirate's ensign. **2** *hist.* a flag hoisted outside a prison to announce an execution. **flag captain** the captain of a flagship. **flag day** *Brit.* a day on which money is raised for a charity by the sale of small paper flags, etc., in the street. **Flag Day** June 14, the anniversary of the adoption of the Stars and Stripes as the official US flag in 1777. **flag down** signal to (a vehicle or driver) to stop. **flag of convenience** a foreign flag under which a ship is registered, usu. to avoid financial charges, etc. **flag officer** *Naut.* an admiral, vice admiral, or rear admiral, or the commodore of a yacht club. **flag of truce** a white flag indicating a desire for a truce. **flag rank** *Naut.* the rank attained by flag officers. **flag station** (also **stop**) a station at which trains stop only if signaled. **flag-wagging** *Brit. sl.* **1** signaling with hand-held flags. **2** = *flag-waving*. **flag-waver** a populist agitator; a patriotic chauvinist. **flag-waving** pop-

ulist agitation; patriotic chauvinism. **keep the flag flying** continue the fight. **put the flag out** celebrate victory, success, etc. **show the flag 1** make an official visit to a foreign port, etc. **2** ensure that notice is taken of one's country, oneself, etc.; make a patriotic display. □□ **flagger** *n.* [16th c.: perh. f. obs. *flag* drooping]

■ *n.* **1 a** banner, ensign, standard, pennant, pennon, streamer, jack, gonfalon, *Eccl.* vexillum. ● *v.* **1 a** grow tired, tire, weaken, languish, falter, fail, dwindle, fade, deteriorate, waste away, degenerate, decline, diminish, decrease, lessen, abate, peter out, die, taper (off), ease (up), subside, slump, fall off, wane, ebb, sink, lag, *colloq.* let up. **b** hang down, droop, sag, dangle, swag. **2 b** mark (out), tag, label, tab, identify. **3** inform; communicate; see also SIGNAL *v.* 1, 2a. □ **flag down** hail, stop. **flag-waver** see AGITATOR 1. **flag-waving** activism, agitation, militancy, chauvinism, *Brit. sl.* flag-wagging.

flag² /flag/ *n. & v.* ● *n.* (also **flagstone**) **1** a flat usu. rectangular stone slab used for paving. **2** (in *pl.*) a pavement made of these. ● *v.tr.* (**flagged, flagging**) pave with flags. [ME, = sod: cf. Icel. *flag* spot from which a sod has been cut out, ON *flaga* slab of stone, and FLAKE¹]

flag³ /flag/ *n.* **1** any plant with a bladed leaf (esp. several of the genus *Iris*) growing on moist ground. **2** the long slender leaf of such a plant. [ME: cf. MDu. *flag*, Da. *flæg*]

flag⁴ /flag/ *n.* (in full **flag feather**) a quill feather of a bird's wing. [perh. rel. to obs. *fag* loose flap: cf. FLAG¹ *v.*]

flagellant /flájələnt, fləjélənt/ *n. & adj.* ● *n.* **1** a person who scourges himself or herself or others as a religious discipline. **2** a person who engages in flogging as a sexual stimulus. ● *adj.* of or concerning flagellation. [L *flagellare* to whip f. FLAGELLUM]

■ see FLOG 1a.

flagellate¹ /flájəlayt/ *v.tr.* scourge; flog (cf. FLAGELLANT). □□ **flagellation** /-láyshən/ *n.* **flagellator** *n.* **flagellatory** /-lətawree/ *adj.*

■ see FLOG 1a.

flagellate² /flájilit, -layt/ *adj. & n.* ● *adj.* having flagella (see FLAGELLUM). ● *n.* a protozoan having one or more flagella.

flagellum /fləjéləm/ *n.* (*pl.* **flagella** /-lə/) **1** *Biol.* a long lash-like appendage found principally on microscopic organisms. **2** *Bot.* a runner; a creeping shoot. □□ **flagellar** /-lər/ *adj.* **flagelliform** /-lifawrm/ *adj.* [L, = whip, dimin. of *flagrum* scourge]

flageolet¹ /flájəlét, -láy/ *n.* **1** a small flute blown at the end, like a recorder but with two thumb holes. **2** an organ stop having a similar sound. [F, dimin. of OF *flag(e)ol* f. Prov. *flajol*, of unkn. orig.]

flageolet² /flájōláy, -lét/ *n.* a kind of French kidney bean. [F]

flagitious /fləjíshəs/ *adj.* deeply criminal; utterly villainous. □□ **flagitiously** *adv.* **flagitiousness** *n.* [ME f. L *flagitiosus* f. *flagitium* shameful crime]

flagman /flágmən/ *n.* (*pl.* **-men**) a person who signals with or as with a flag, e.g., in highway construction.

flagon /flágən/ *n.* **1** a large bottle in which wine, cider, etc., are sold, usu. holding 1.13 liters. **2 a** a large vessel usu. with a handle, spout, and lid, to hold wine, etc. **b** *Eccl.* a similar vessel used for the Eucharist. [ME *flakon* f. OF *flacon* ult. f. LL *flasco -onis* FLASK]

■ **1, 2a** see JAR¹ 1.

flagpole /flágpōl/ *n.* a pole on which a flag may be hoisted.

■ staff, pole, flagstaff.

flagrant /fláygrənt/ *adj.* (of an offense or an offender) glaring; notorious; scandalous. □□ **flagrancy** /-grənsee/ *n.* **flagrantly** *adv.* [F *flagrant* or L *flagrant-* part. stem of *flagrare* blaze]

■ glaring, blatant, conspicuous, gross, obvious, out-and-out, utter, complete, brazen, rank, bold, barefaced, open, defiant, audacious; notorious, scandalous, infamous, arrant, outrageous, shocking, egregious, shameless, atrocious, monstrous, heinous, villainous, treacherous, nefarious, awful, reprehensible, contemptible.

flagship /flágship/ *n.* **1** a ship having an admiral on board. **2**

something that is held to be the best or most important of its kind; a leader.

flagstaff / flágstaf/ *n.* = FLAGPOLE.

flagstone / flágstōn/ *n.* = FLAG².

flail / flayl/ *n. & v.* ● *n.* a threshing tool consisting of a wooden staff with a short heavy stick swinging from it. ● *v.* **1** *tr.* beat or strike with or as if with a flail. **2** *intr.* wave or swing wildly or erratically (*went into the fight with arms flailing*). [OE prob. f. L FLAGELLUM]
■ *v.* **1** see LASH *v.* 1, 2. **2** see FLAP *v.* 1.

flair / flair/ *n.* **1** an instinct for selecting or performing what is excellent, useful, etc.; a talent (*has a flair for knowing what the public wants*; *has a flair for languages*). **2** talent or ability, esp. artistic or stylistic. [F *flairer* to smell ult. f. L *fragrare*: see FRAGRANT]
■ instinct; talent, ability, aptitude, feel, forte, knack, genius, brilliance, skill, mind, gift, faculty, propensity, bent, proclivity, facility, capacity, virtuosity, ingenuity; see also STYLE *n.* 5a, VERVE.

flak / flak/ *n.* (also **flack**) **1** antiaircraft fire. **2** adverse criticism; abuse. □ **flak jacket** a protective jacket reinforced with bulletproof material, worn by soldiers, etc. [abbr. of G *Fliegerabwehrkanone*, lit. aviator-defence-gun]
■ **2** criticism, censure, abuse, disapproval, disapprobation, condemnation, blame, complaints, brickbats.

flake¹ / flayk/ *n. & v.* ● *n.* **1 a** a small thin light piece of snow. **b** a similar piece of another material. **2** a thin broad piece of material peeled or split off. **3** *Archaeol.* a piece of hard stone chipped off and used as a tool. **4** a natural division of the flesh of some fish. **5** the dogfish or other shark as food. **6** *sl.* a crazy or eccentric person. ● *v.tr. & intr.* (often foll. by *away*, *off*) **1** take off or come away in flakes. **2** sprinkle with or fall in snowlike flakes. □ **flake out** *colloq.* **1** fall asleep or drop from exhaustion; faint. **2** act strangely. [ME: orig. unkn.: cf. ON *flakna* flake off]
■ *n.* **1 a** a snowflake. **b** piece, chip, bit, scrap, scale, particle, tuft, flock, fragment, shaving, sliver, lamina, squama. ● *v.* **1** scale (off), chip (off), *Med.* desquamate, exfoliate; see also PEEL¹ *v.* 1, 2. □ **flake out 1** collapse, go to sleep, fall asleep, *colloq.* drop off (to sleep); faint, pass out, black out, lose consciousness, *literary* swoon.

flake² / flayk/ *n.* a stage for drying fish, storing produce, etc. [ME, perh. f. ON *flaki*, *fleki* wicker shield]

flaky / fláykee/ *adj.* (**flakier, flakiest**) **1** of or like flakes; separating easily into flakes. **2** *sl.* crazy; eccentric. □ **flaky pastry** pastry consisting of thin light layers. □□ **flakily** *adv.* **flakiness** *n.*
■ **2** see CRAZY 1.

flambé / flaambáy/ *adj.* (of food) covered with alcohol and set alight briefly. [F, past part. of *flamber* singe (as FLAMBEAU)]

flambeau / flámbō/ *n.* (*pl.* **flambeaus** or **flambeaux** /-bōz/) **1** a flaming torch, esp. composed of several thick waxed wicks. **2** a branched candlestick. [F f. *flambe* f. L *flammula* dimin. of *flamma* flame]

flamboyant / flambóyənt/ *adj.* **1** ostentatious; showy. **2** floridly decorated. **3** gorgeously colored. **4** *Archit.* (of decoration) marked by wavy flamelike lines. □□ **flamboyance** /-əns/ *n.* **flamboyancy** *n.* **flamboyantly** *adv.* [F (in Archit. sense), pres. part. of *flamboyer* f. *flambe*: see FLAMBEAU]
■ **1** ostentatious, showy, extravagant, gaudy, flashy, dazzling, brilliant, splendid; high, wide, and handsome; dashing, rakish, swashbuckling. **2** florid, decorated, elaborate, ornamented, ornate, embellished, baroque, rococo.

flame / flaym/ *n. & v.* ● *n.* **1 a** ignited gas (*the fire burned with a steady flame*). **b** one portion of this (*the flame flickered and died*). **c** (usu. in *pl.*) visible combustion (*burst into flames*). **2 a** a bright light; brilliant coloring. **b** a brilliant orange-red color. **3 a** a strong passion, esp. love (*fan the flame*). **b** *colloq.* a boyfriend or girlfriend. ● *v.* **1** *intr. & tr.* (often foll. by *away*, *forth*, *out*, *up*) emit or cause to emit flames. **2** *intr.* (often foll. by *out*, *up*) **a** (of passion) break out. **b** (of a person) become angry. **3** *intr.* shine or glow like flame (*leaves*

flamed in the autumn sun). **4** *intr. poet.* move like flame. **5** *tr.* send (a signal) by means of flame. **6** *tr.* subject to the action of flame. □ **flame gun** a device for throwing flames to destroy weeds, etc. **flame out** (of a jet engine) lose power through imperfect combustion in the combustion chamber. **flame tree** any of various trees with brilliant red or yellow flowers. **go up in flames** be consumed by fire. □□ **flameless** *adj.* **flamelike** *adj.* **flamy** *adj.* [ME f. OF *flame*, *flam(m)er* f. L *flamma*]
■ *n.* **2** see *incandescence* (INCANDESCENT). **3 a** passion, fervor, ardor, zeal, enthusiasm, eagerness, feverishness. **b** boyfriend, girlfriend, lover, sweetheart, beau, *colloq.* heartthrob. ● *v.* **1** see BURN¹ *v.* 2. **2 a** burn, flare up; see also *break out* 2. **b** see FLARE *v.* 3. **3** see SHINE *v.* 1.

flamen / fláymən/ *n. Rom.Hist.* a priest serving a particular deity. [ME f. L]

flamenco / fləméngkō/ *n.* (*pl.* **-os**) **1** a style of music played (esp. on the guitar) and sung by Spanish gypsies. **2** a dance performed to this music. [Sp., = Flemish]

flameproof / fláymprŏŏf/ *adj.* (esp. of a fabric) treated so as to be nonflammable.

flamethrower / fláymthrōər/ *n.* a weapon for throwing a spray of flame.

flaming / fláyming/ *adj.* **1** emitting flames. **2** very hot (*flaming day*). **3** *colloq.* **a** passionate; intense (*a flaming argument*). **b** expressing annoyance, or as an intensifier (*that flaming idiot*). **4** bright colored (*flaming red hair*).
■ **1** see ABLAZE *adj.* 1. **2** see HOT *adj.* 1. **3 a** see INTENSE 1, 3. **b** blasted, *colloq.* damn(ed), blooming, *Brit. sl.* blinking. **4** see BRIGHT *adj.* 2.

flamingo / fləmínggō/ *n.* (*pl.* **-os** or **-oes**) any tall longnecked web-footed wading bird of the family Phoenicopteridae, with crooked bill and pink, scarlet, and black plumage. [Port. *flamengo* f. Prov. *flamenc* f. *flama* flame + *-enc* = -ING³]

flammable / fláməbəl/ *adj.* easily set on fire; inflammable. ¶ Often used because *inflammable* can be mistaken for a negative (the true negative being *nonflammable*). □□ **flammability** *n.* [L *flammare* f. *flamma* flame]
■ inflammable, combustible, ignitable.

flan / flan/ *n.* **1 a** an open pastry case with a savory or sweet filling. **b** a custard topped with caramel glaze. **2** a disk of metal from which a coin, etc., is made. [F (orig. = round cake) f. OF *flaon* f. med.L *flado* *-onis* f. Frank.]
■ **1** see TART¹ 1.

flange / flanj/ *n. & v. Engin.* ● *n.* a projecting flat rim, collar, or rib, used for strengthening or attachment. ● *v.tr.* provide with a flange. □□ **flangeless** *n.* [17th c.: perh. f. *flange* widen out f. OF *flangir*, rel. to FLANK]

flank / flangk/ *n. & v.* ● *n.* **1 a** the side of the body between the ribs and the hip. **b** the side of an animal carved as meat (*flank of beef*). **2** the side of a mountain, building, etc. **3** the right or left side of an army or other body of persons. ● *v.tr.* **1** (often in *passive*) be situated at both sides of (*a road flanked by mountains*). **2** *Mil.* **a** guard or strengthen on the flank. **b** menace the flank of. [ME f. OF *flanc* f. Frank.]
■ *n.* **1** side, loin. **2** see SIDE *n.* 1. ● *v.* **1** edge, border, line.

flanker / flángkər/ *n.* **1** *Mil.* a fortification guarding or menacing the flank. **2** anything that flanks another thing. **3a** *Football* an offensive back positioned outside the tackle and behind the line of scrimmage. **b** *Rugby* a flank forward. **4** *Brit. sl.* a trick; a swindle (*pulled a flanker*).

flannel / flánəl/ *n. & v.* ● *n.* **1 a** a kind of woven wool fabric, usu. with a slight nap. **b** (in *pl.*) flannel garments, esp. underwear or trousers. **2** *Brit.* = WASHCLOTH. **3** *Brit. sl.* nonsense; flattery. ● *v.* (**flanneled, flanneling**; *Brit.* **flannelled, flannelling**) *Brit.* **1** *sl.* **a** *tr.* flatter. **b** *intr.* use flattery.

/ . . . / pronunciation	● part of speech
□ phrases, idioms, and compounds	
□□ derivatives	■ synonym section
cross-references appear in SMALL CAPITALS or *italics*	

2 *tr.* wash or clean with a flannel. □□ **flannelly** *adj.* [perh. f. Welsh *gwlanen* f. *gwlān* wool]

flannelboard /flánəlbawrd/ *n.* a piece of flannel as a base for paper or cloth cutouts, used as a toy or a teaching aid.

flannelette /flánəlét/ *n.* a napped cotton fabric similar to flannel. [FLANNEL]

flannelmouth /flánəlmowth/ *n. sl.* a flatterer; a braggart.
■ see *flatterer* (FLATTER), BRAGGART *n.*

flap /flap/ *v. & n.* ● *v.* (**flapped, flapping**) **1 a** *tr.* move (wings, the arms, etc.) up and down when flying, or as if flying. **b** *intr.* (of wings, the arms, etc.) move up and down; beat. **2** *intr. colloq.* be agitated or panicky. **3** *intr.* (esp. of curtains, loose cloth, etc.) swing or sway about; flutter. **4** *tr.* (usu. foll. by *away, off*) strike (flies, etc.) with something broad; drive. **5** *intr. colloq.* (of ears) listen intently. ● *n.* **1** a piece of cloth, wood, paper, etc., hinged or attached by one side only and often used to cover a gap, e.g., a pocket cover, the folded part of an envelope, a table leaf. **2** one up-and-down motion of a wing, an arm, etc. **3** *colloq.* a state of agitation; panic (*don't get into a flap*). **4** a hinged or sliding section of a wing used to control lift and drag. **5** a light blow with something broad. **6** an open mushroom top. □□ **flappy** *adj.* [ME, prob. imit.]
■ *v.* **1** move, flap, flail, wave, wag, flutter, thrash, oscillate, vibrate, *colloq.* waggle; thresh, thrash about *or* around, beat. **3** see SWING *v.* 1, 2a, c. ● *n.* **1** fold, fly, lappet, lap. **2** beat, flutter, wave, wag, oscillation, *colloq.* waggle. **3** upset, to-do, commotion, fuss; (*in a flap*) in a panic *or* flurry, *colloq.* in a state *or* tizzy *or* sweat.

flapdoodle /flápdōōd'l/ *n. colloq.* nonsense. [19th c.: orig. unkn.]

flapjack /flápjak/ *n.* a pancake. [FLAP + JACK[1]]

flapper /flápər/ *n.* **1** a person or thing that flaps. **2** an instrument that is flapped to kill flies, scare birds, etc. **3** a person who panics easily or is easily agitated. **4** *sl.* (in the 1920s) a young unconventional or lively woman. **5** *Brit.* a young mallard or partridge.

flare /flair/ *v. & n.* ● *v.* **1** *intr. & tr.* widen or cause to widen, esp. toward the bottom (*flared trousers*). **2** *intr. & tr.* burn or cause to burn suddenly with a bright unsteady flame. **3** *intr.* burst into anger; burst forth. ● *n.* **1 a** a dazzling irregular flame or light, esp. in the open air. **b** a sudden outburst of flame. **2 a** a signal light used at sea. **b** a bright light used as a signal. **c** a flame dropped from an aircraft to illuminate a target, etc. **3** *Astron.* a sudden burst of radiation from a star. **4 a** a gradual widening, esp. of a skirt or trousers. **b** (in *pl.*) wide-bottomed trousers. **5** an outward bulge in a ship's sides. **6** *Photog.* unnecessary illumination on a lens caused by internal reflection, etc. □ **flare up 1** burst into a sudden blaze. **2** become suddenly angry or active. **flare-up** *n.* an outburst of flame, anger, activity, etc. [16th c.: orig. unkn.]
■ *v.* **1** widen, flare out, spread (out *or* outward), broaden, expand, increase, enlarge, bulge, swell. **2** blaze *or* flame (up), flare up, flash; see also BURN[1] *v.* 1, 2. **3** explode, erupt, lose one's temper, flare up, flash out *or* up, throw a tantrum, become incensed *or* angry, see red, get worked up, get hot under the collar, *colloq.* blow up, blow one's top, fly off the handle, lose one's cool. ● *n.* **1** flame, blaze, flash, light, glare, dazzle, incandescence, brilliance, luminosity. **2** beacon, light, signal, torch. **4 a** widening, broadening, spread, expansion, increase, enlargement, bulge, swelling. □ **flare up 1** blaze, flame, flash, burn, flare. **2** see FLARE *v.* 3 above. **flare-up** see OUTBURST.

flash /flash/ *v., n., & adj.* ● *v.* **1** *intr. & tr.* emit or reflect or cause to emit or reflect light briefly, suddenly, or intermittently; gleam or cause to gleam. **2** *intr.* break suddenly into flame; give out flame or sparks. **3** *tr.* send or reflect like a sudden flame or blaze (*his eyes flashed fire*). **4** *intr.* **a** burst suddenly into view or perception (*the explanation flashed upon me*). **b** move swiftly (*the train flashed through the station*). **5** *tr.* **a** send (news, etc.) by radio, telegraph, etc. (*flashed a message to her*). **b** signal to (a person) by shining lights or headlights briefly. **6** *tr. colloq.* show ostentatiously (*flashed her engagement ring*). **7** *intr.* (of water) rush along; rise and

flow. **8** *intr. sl.* indecently expose oneself. ● *n.* **1** a sudden bright light or flame, e.g., of lightning. **2** a very brief time; an instant (*all over in a flash*). **3 a** a brief, sudden burst of feeling (*a flash of hope*). **b** a sudden display (of wit, understanding, etc.). **4** = NEWS FLASH. **5** *Photog.* = FLASHLIGHT 2. **6 a** a rush of water, esp. down a weir to take a boat over shallows. **b** a contrivance for producing this. **7** *Brit. Mil.* a colored patch of cloth on a uniform, etc., as a distinguishing emblem. **8** vulgar display; ostentation. **9** a bright patch of color. **10** *Cinematog.* the momentary exposure of a scene. **11** excess plastic or metal oozing from a mold during molding. ● *adj. Brit. colloq.* **1** gaudy; showy; vulgar (*a flash car*). **2** sudden; happening quickly. **3** counterfeit (*flash notes*). **4** connected with thieves, the underworld, etc. □ **flash bulb** a bulb for a photographic flashlight. **flash burn** a burn caused by sudden intense radiation, esp. from a nuclear explosion. **flash card** a card containing a small amount of information, held up for pupils to see, as an aid to learning. **flash flood** a sudden local flood due to heavy rain, etc. **flashing point** = *flash point.* **flash in the pan** a promising start followed by failure (from the priming of old guns). **flash lamp** a portable flashing electric lamp. **flash over** *Electr.* make an electric circuit by sparking across a gap. **flash point 1** the temperature at which vapor from oil, etc., will ignite in air. **2** the point at which anger, indignation, etc., becomes uncontrollable. **hot flash** a sudden sensation of heat, esp. during menopause. [ME orig. with ref. to the rushing of water: cf. SPLASH]
■ *v.* **1, 3** scintillate, sparkle, dazzle, glitter, coruscate, twinkle, flicker, shimmer, glimmer; gleam, beam, shine, glare. **2** flare (up), blaze, flame (up), spark, burn. **4 b** rush, race, speed, dash, streak, tear, hurry, hasten, flick, fly, zoom, shoot, run, sprint, dart; *colloq.* whiz. **6** see FLAUNT. ● *n.* **1** flare, burst, blaze, dazzle, spark, sparkle, coruscation, fulguration, glitter, twinkle, twinkling, flicker, flickering, scintilla, scintillation, glint, shimmer, glimmer, gleam, light, flame. **2** moment, (split) second, instant, twinkle, twinkling (of an eye), trice, minute, two shakes (of a lamb's tail), *colloq.* jiffy; before you can say Jack Robinson. **3 a** burst, outbreak; see also OUTBURST. **b** (sudden *or* momentary) display, stroke, flicker, spark. **8** see OSTENTATION. ● *adj.* **1** gaudy, showy, ostentatious, vulgar, flashy, *colloq.* swish, *sl.* snazzy. **3** see COUNTERFEIT *adj.* 1.

flashback /fláshbak/ *n.* a scene in a movie, novel, etc., set in a time earlier than the main action.

flashboard /fláshbawrd/ *n.* a board used for increasing the depth of water behind a dam.

flashcube /fláshkyōōb/ *n. Photog.* a set of four flash bulbs arranged as a cube and operated in turn.

flasher /fláshər/ *n.* **1** *sl.* a person, esp. a man, who indecently exposes himself. **2 a** an automatic device for switching lights rapidly on and off. **b** a sign or signal using this. **3** a person or thing that flashes.

flashgun /fláshgun/ *n. Photog.* a device used to operate a photographic flashlight.

flashing /fláshing/ *n.* a usu. metallic strip used to prevent water penetration at the junction of a roof with a wall, etc. [dial. *flash* seal with lead sheets or obs. *flash* flashing]

flashlight /fláshlīt/ *n.* **1** a battery-operated portable light. **2 a** a light giving an intense flash, used for photographing by night, indoors, etc. **b** a picture so taken. **3** a flashing light used for signals and in lighthouses.

flashover /fláshōvər/ *n.* an instance of flashing over.

flashy /fláshee/ *adj.* (**flashier, flashiest**) showy; gaudy; cheaply attractive. □□ **flashily** *adv.* **flashiness** *n.*
■ showy, ostentatious, *colloq.* flash; gaudy, loud, garish, glaring; cheap, vulgar, meretricious, pretentious, tawdry, tasteless, tacky, *sl.* glitzy.

flask /flask/ *n.* **1** a narrow-necked bulbous bottle for wine, etc., or as used in chemistry. **2** = *hip flask* (see HIP[1]). **3** *Brit.* = *vacuum flask.* **4** *hist.* = *powder flask.* [F *flasque* & (prob.) It. *fiasco* f. med.L *flasca, flasco:* cf. FLAGON]
■ **1** see JAR 1.

flat[1] /flat/ *adj., adv., n., & v.* ● *adj.* (**flatter, flattest**) **1 a**

horizontally level (*a flat roof*). **b** even; smooth; unbroken; without projection or indentation (*a flat stomach*). **c** with a level surface and little depth; shallow (*a flat cap*; *a flat heel*). **2** unqualified; plain; downright (*a flat refusal*; *a flat denial*). **3 a** dull; lifeless; monotonous (*spoke in a flat tone*). **b** without energy; dejected. **4** (of a carbonated drink) having lost its effervescence; stale. **5** *Brit.* (of a battery, etc.) having exhausted its charge. **6** *Mus.* **a** below true or normal pitch (*the violins are flat*). **b** (of a key) having a flat or flats in the signature. **c** (as **B**, **E**, etc., **flat**) a half step lower than B, E, etc. **7** *Photog.* lacking contrast. **8 a** (of paint, etc.) not glossy; matte. **b** (of a tint) uniform. **9** (of a tire) punctured; deflated. **10** (of a market, prices, etc.) inactive; sluggish. **11** of or relating to flat racing. ● *adv.* **1** lying at full length; spread out, esp. on another surface (*lay flat on the floor*; *the ladder was flat against the wall*). **2** *colloq.* **a** completely; absolutely (*turned it down flat*; *flat broke*). **b** exactly (*in five minutes flat*). **3** *Mus.* below the true or normal pitch (*always sings flat*). ● *n.* **1** the flat part of anything; something flat (*the flat of the hand*). **2** level ground, esp. a plain or swamp. **3** *Mus.* **a** a note lowered a half step below natural pitch. **b** the sign (♭) indicating this. **4** (as **the flat**) *Brit.* **a** flat racing. **b** the flat racing season. **5** *Theatr.* a flat section of scenery mounted on a frame. **6** *colloq.* a flat tire. **7** a shallow planter box for starting seedlings. **8** *Brit. sl.* a foolish person. ● *v.tr.* (**flatted, flatting**) **1** make flat; flatten (esp. in technical use). **2** *Mus.* make (a note) flat. □ **fall flat** fail to live up to expectations; not win applause. **flat arch** *Archit.* an arch with a flat lower or inner curve. **flat foot** a foot with a less than normal arch. **flat-four** (of an engine) having four cylinders all horizontal, two on each side of the crankshaft. **flat out 1** at top speed. **2** without hesitation or delay. **3** using all one's strength, energy, or resources. **flat race** a horse race over level ground, as opposed to a steeplechase or hurdles. **flat racing** the racing of horses in flat races. **flat rate** a rate that is the same in all cases, not proportional. **flat spin 1** *Aeron.* a nearly horizontal spin. **2** *Brit. colloq.* a state of agitation or panic. **flat-top 1** *Aeron. sl.* an aircraft carrier. **2** *sl.* a man's short flat haircut. **that's flat** *colloq.* let there be no doubt about it. □□ **flatly** *adv.* **flatness** *n.* **flattish** *adj.* [ME f. ON *flatr* f. Gmc]

■ *adj.* **1 a** level, horizontal, plane. **b** even, smooth; unbroken, uninterrupted. **2** unqualified, unreserved, unconditional, absolute, categorical; plain, direct, unequivocal, unambiguous; downright, outright, irrevocable, definite, firm, certain, sure, peremptory, positive, out-and-out, complete, total. **3 a** dull, insipid, bland, lifeless, spiritless, lackluster, prosaic, uninteresting, unexciting, dry, jejune, boring, dead, monotonous; tired, stale, two-dimensional, unrealistic. **b** see LISTLESS. **4** noneffervescent, decarbonated, dead; stale, insipid, tasteless, flavorless, unpalatable. **8 a** matte, nongloss(y), dull. **9** punctured, deflated, blown out. **10** inactive, sluggish, slow, depressed, dull. ● *adv.* **1** spread out, prostrate, prone, supine, stretched out, recumbent, outstretched, lying (down), reclining, spread-eagled, outspread. **2 a** completely, absolutely, categorically, utterly, wholly, uncompromisingly, irrevocably, positively, definitely, directly, flatly. **b** exactly, precisely. ● *n.* **2** plain, lowland, tundra, steppe, savannah, heath; pampas; swamp, marsh, bog, fen; mudflat. □ **fall flat** disappoint; founder, *sl.* bomb; see also FAIL *v.* 1, 2a. **flat out 1** at top *or* maximum *or* full *or* breakneck speed, speedily, quickly, rapidly, swiftly, at full gallop, posthaste, hell-for-leather, like a bat out of hell, *colloq.* like (greased) lightning, like the wind, *literary* apace. **2** unhesitatingly, directly, at once, immediately, forthwith, without delay; plainly, openly, flatly, baldly. **flat rate** standard *or* fixed rate.

flat² /flat/ *n. & v.* ● *n.* esp. *Brit.* = APARTMENT 1. ● *v.intr.* (**flatted, flatting**) (often foll. by *with*) *Austral.* share a flat (apartment) with. □□ **flatlet** *n.* [alt. f. obs. *flet* floor, dwelling f. Gmc (as FLAT¹)]

flatboat /flátbōt/ *n.* (or **flat-bottomed boat**) a boat with a flat bottom for transport in shallow water.

flatcar /flátkaar/ *n.* a railroad car without raised sides or ends.

flatfish /flátfish/ *n.* any marine fish of various families having an asymmetric appearance with both eyes on one side of a flattened body, including sole, turbot, plaice, etc.

flatfoot /flátfŏŏt/ *n.* (*pl.* **-foots** or **-feet**) *sl.* a police officer. ■ see *police officer*.

flat-footed /flátfŏŏtid/ *adj.* **1** having flat feet. **2** *colloq.* downright; positive. **3** *colloq.* unprepared; off guard (*was caught flat-footed*). □□ **flat-footedly** *adv.* **flat-footedness** *n.*

flathead /fláthed/ *n.* any marine fish of the family Platycephalidae, having a flattened body with both eyes on the top side.

flatiron /flátīərn/ *n.* an iron heated externally and used for pressing clothes, etc.

flatmate /flátmayt/ *n. Brit.* a person in relation to one or more others living in the same flat.

flatten /flát'n/ *v.* **1** *tr. & intr.* make or become flat. **2** *tr. colloq.* **a** humiliate. **b** knock down. □ **flatten out** bring an aircraft parallel to the ground. □□ **flattener** *n.*

■ **1** level (off *or* out), even (off *or* out). **2 b** knock down *or* over, knock out, floor, fell; level, raze (to the ground), tear down, demolish.

flatter /flátər/ *v.tr.* **1** compliment unduly; overpraise, esp. for gain or advantage. **2** (usu. *refl.*; usu. foll. by *that* + clause) please, congratulate, or delude (oneself, etc.) (*I flatter myself that I can sing*). **3 a** (of a color, a style, etc.) make (a person) appear to the best advantage (*that blouse flatters you*). **b** (esp. of a portrait, a painter, etc.) represent too favorably. **4** gratify the vanity of; make (a person) feel honored. **5** inspire (a person) with hope, esp. unduly (*was flattered into thinking himself invulnerable*). **6** please or gratify (the ear, the eye, etc.). □ **flattering unction** a salve that one administers to one's own conscience or self-esteem (Shakesp. esp. *Hamlet* III. iv. 136). □□ **flatterer** *n.* **flattering** *adj.* **flatteringly** *adv.* [ME, perh. rel. to OF *flater* to smooth]

■ **1** compliment, overpraise, toady (to), truckle to, fawn (on *or* upon), court, curry favor with, *colloq.* butter up, soft-soap, suck up to, sweet-talk, *Brit. sl.* flannel. **2** see FOOL¹ *v.* 1, 3. **3 a** see SUIT *v.* 1. **b** show to advantage, compliment, favor. □□ **flatterer** toady, sycophant, fawner, backscratcher, truckler, lickspittle, *colloq.* sweet-talker, yes-man, bootlicker, *coarse sl.* brownnoser. **flattering** becoming, enhancing; complimentary, adulatory, laudatory, fulsome, fawning, ingratiating, unctuous, slimy, sugary, *colloq.* smarmy.

flattery /flátəree/ *n.* (*pl.* **-ies**) **1** exaggerated or insincere praise. **2** the act or an instance of flattering.

■ adulation, cajolery, blandishment, toadying, sycophancy, *colloq.* sweet talk, soft soap, bootlicking, *Brit. sl.* flannel.

flatulent /fláchələnt/ *adj.* **1 a** causing formation of gas in the alimentary canal. **b** caused by or suffering from this. **2** (of speech, etc.) inflated; pretentious. □□ **flatulence** *n.* **flatulency** *n.* **flatulently** *adv.* [F f. mod.L *flatulentus* (as FLATUS)]

■ **2** see POMPOUS 2.

flatus /fláytəs/ *n.* wind in or from the stomach or bowels. [L, = blowing f. *flare* blow]

■ see WIND¹ *n.* 4.

flatware /flátwair/ *n.* **1** forks, knives, spoons, etc.; cutlery. **2** plates, saucers, etc. (opp. HOLLOWWARE).

flatworm /flátwərm/ *n.* any worm of the phylum Platyhelminthes, having a flattened body and no body cavity or blood vessels, including turbellaria, flukes, etc.

flaunt /flawnt/ *v. & n.* ● *v.tr. & intr.* **1** (often *refl.*) display ostentatiously (oneself or one's belongings); show off; parade (*liked to flaunt his gold cuff links*; *flaunted themselves before the crowd*). ¶ Often confused with *flout*. **2** wave or cause to wave proudly (*flaunted the banner*). ● *n.* an act or in-

---

/.../ **pronunciation**   ● **part of speech**
□ **phrases, idioms, and compounds**
□□ **derivatives**   ■ **synonym section**
cross-references appear in SMALL CAPITALS or *italics*

stance of flaunting. □□ **flaunter** n. **flaunty** adj. [16th c.: orig. unkn.]

■ v. **1** display, show (off), parade, flourish, exhibit, sport, spotlight.

flautist /fláwtist, flów-/ n. a flute player. [It. *flautista* f. *flauto* FLUTE]

flavescent /fləvésənt/ adj. turning yellow; yellowish. [L *flavescere* f. *flavus* yellow]

flavin /fláyvin/ n. (also **flavine** /-veen/) **1** the chemical compound forming the nucleus of various natural yellow pigments. **2** a yellow dye obtained from dyer's oak. □ **flavin adenine dinucleotide** a coenzyme derived from riboflavin, important in various biochemical reactions. ¶ Abbr.: **FAD**. [L *flavus* yellow + -IN]

flavine /fláyveen/ n. *Pharm.* an antiseptic derived from acridine. [as FLAVIN + -INE⁴]

flavone /fláyvōn/ n. *Biochem.* any of a group of naturally occurring white or yellow pigments found in plants. [as FLAVINE + -ONE]

flavoprotein /fláyvōprōteen/ n. *Biochem.* any of a group of conjugated proteins containing flavin that are involved in oxidation reactions in cells. [FLAVINE + PROTEIN]

flavor /fláyvər/ n. & v. (*Brit.* **flavour**) ● n. **1** a distinctive mingled sensation of smell and taste (*has a cheesy flavor*). **2** an indefinable characteristic quality (*music with a romantic flavor*). **3** (usu. foll. by *of*) a slight admixture of a usu. undesirable quality (*the flavor of failure hangs over the enterprise*). **4** = FLAVORING. ● v.tr. give flavor to; season. □ **flavor of the month** (or **week**) a temporary trend or fashion. □□ **flavorful** adj. **flavorless** adj. **flavorsome** adj. [ME f. OF *flaor* perh. f. L *flatus* blowing & *foetor* stench: assim. to *savor*]

■ n. **1** taste, tastiness, savor, tang, piquancy, zest, sapor. **2** quality, character, spirit, nature, property, mark, stamp, style, taste, feel, feeling, sense, tinge, aroma, air, atmosphere, hint, suggestion, soupçon, touch. ● v. season, spice.

flavoring /fláyvəring/ n. a substance used to flavor food or drink.

flavorous /fláyvərəs/ adj. having a pleasant or pungent flavor.

■ see TASTY.

flaw¹ /flaw/ n. & v. ● n. **1** an imperfection; a blemish (*has a character without a flaw*). **2** a crack or similar fault (*the cup has a flaw*). **3** *Law* an invalidating defect in a legal matter. ● v.tr. & intr. crack; damage; spoil. □□ **flawed** adj. **flawless** adj. **flawlessly** adv. **flawlessness** n. [ME perh. f. ON *flaga* slab f. Gmc: cf. FLAKE¹, FLAG²]

■ n. **1** imperfection, fault, defect, error, mistake, blemish, blot, stain, taint, chink, (black) mark, disfigurement, failing, weakness, weak spot. **2** crack, break, chip, fracture; split, cleft, slit, cut, gash, rent, rift, tear, rip; puncture, hole, perforation. ● v. crack, damage, harm, spoil, ruin, mark, disfigure; discredit, stigmatize, hurt, taint, mar, blot. □□ **flawed** damaged, harmed; tainted, stained, tarnished; defective, imperfect, unsound, faulty; marred, weakened. **flawless** perfect, pristine, pure, uncorrupted, chaste, virgin, clean, immaculate, unsullied, unspoiled, unspoilt, unsoiled, spotless, untarnished, impeccable, unblemished, faultless; undamaged, intact, whole, unimpaired; unassailable, unimpeachable, unquestionable, irrefutable, undeniable, foolproof, sound, demonstrable.

flaw² /flaw/ n. a squall of wind; a short storm. [prob. f. MDu. *vlāghe*, MLG *vlāge*, perh. = stroke]

flax /flaks/ n. **1 a** a blue-flowered plant, *Linum usitatissimum*, cultivated for its textile fiber and its seeds (see LINSEED). **b** a plant resembling this. **2 a** dressed or undressed flax fibers. **b** *archaic* linen; cloth of flax. □ **flax lily** (*pl.* **-ies**) *NZ* any plant of the genus *Phormium*, yielding valuable fiber. [OE *flæx* f. WG]

flaxen /fláksən/ adj. **1** of flax. **2** (of hair) colored like dressed flax; pale yellow.

■ **2** see GOLDEN 2.

flaxseed /fláksseed/ n. linseed.

flay /flay/ v.tr. **1** strip the skin or hide off, esp. by beating. **2** criticize severely (*the play was flayed by the critics*). **3** peel off

(skin, bark, peel, etc.). **4** strip (a person) of wealth by extortion or exaction. □□ **flayer** n. [OE *flēan* f. Gmc]

■ **1** see FLOG 1a. **2** see LAMBASTE 2. **3** see PEEL¹ v. 1, 2.

F layer /éf layər/ n. the highest and most strongly ionized region of the ionosphere. [*F* (arbitrary) + LAYER]

flea /flee/ n. **1** a small wingless jumping insect of the order Siphonaptera, feeding on human and other blood. **2 a** (in full **flea beetle**) a small jumping beetle infesting hops, cabbages, etc. **b** (in full **water flea**) daphnia. □ **flea-bitten 1** bitten by or infested with fleas. **2** shabby. **flea circus** a show of performing fleas. **flea collar** an insecticidal collar for pets. **a flea in one's ear** a sharp reproof. **flea market** a market selling secondhand goods, etc. **flea-pit** *Brit.* a dingy dirty place, esp. a run-down movie theater. [OE *flēa*, *flēah* f. Gmc]

fleabag /fléebag/ n. *sl.* a shabby or unattractive place or thing.

fleabane /fléebayn/ n. any of various composite plants of the genus *Inula* or *Pulicaria*, supposed to drive away fleas.

fleabite /fléebīt/ n. **1** the bite of a flea. **2** a trivial injury or inconvenience.

fleawort /fléewawrt/ n. any of several plants supposed to drive away fleas.

flèche /flesh, flaysh/ n. a slender spire, often perforated with windows, esp. at the intersection of the nave and the transept of a church. [F, orig. = arrow]

fleck /flek/ n. & v. ● n. **1** a small patch of color or light (*eyes with green flecks*). **2** a small particle or speck, esp. of dust. **3** a spot on the skin; a freckle. ● v.tr. mark with flecks; dapple; variegate. [perh. f. ON *flekkr* (n.), *flekka* (v.), or MLG, MDu. *vlecke*, OHG *flec*, *fleccho*]

■ n. see SPOT n. 1a, b. ● v. see DOT¹ v. 4; (*flecked*) dappled, spotted, pied, speckled, sprinkled, dotted, marked, stippled, dusted, specked, spattered, freckled.

flection var. of FLEXION.

fled past and past part. of FLEE.

fledge /flej/ v. **1** intr. (of a bird) grow feathers. **2** tr. provide (an arrow) with feathers. **3** tr. bring up (a young bird) until it can fly. **4** tr. (as **fledged** adj.) **a** able to fly. **b** independent; mature. **5** tr. deck or provide with feathers or down. [obs. *fledge* (adj.) 'fit to fly,' f. OE *flycge* (recorded in *unfligge*) f. a Gmc root rel. to FLY¹]

fledgling /fléjling/ n. (also *Brit.* **fledgeling**) **1** a young bird. **2** an inexperienced person. [FLEDGE + -LING¹]

■ **2** see NOVICE.

flee /flee/ v. (*past* and *past part.* **fled** /fled/) **1** intr. (often foll. by *from*, *before*) **a** run away. **b** seek safety by fleeing. **2** tr. run away from; leave abruptly; shun (*fled the room; fled his attentions*). **3** intr. vanish; cease; pass away. □□ **fleer** /fléeər/ n. [OE *flēon* f. Gmc]

■ **1** run away *or* off, escape, get away, fly, take (to) flight, bolt, go (away), decamp, abscond, make off *or* away, make an exit, make (good) one's escape, make a (clean) getaway, beat a (hasty) retreat, take to one's heels, take off, turn tail, vanish, disappear, make a run for it, take to the hills *or* woods, *colloq.* show a clean pair of heels, make tracks, scoot, make oneself scarce, clear out, skedaddle, scram, skip, hightail it, *sl.* cut and run, beat it, take a powder, split, blow, skiddoo, vamoose, go on the lam, *Brit. sl.* scarper, do a bunk. **2** run away from, quit, *colloq.* skip, *sl.* blow; avoid, evade, shun, escape from, *literary* eschew. **3** see DISAPPEAR.

fleece /flees/ n. & v. ● n. **1 a** the woolly covering of a sheep or a similar animal. **b** the amount of wool sheared from a sheep at one time. **2** something resembling a fleece, esp.: **a** a woolly or rough head of hair. **b** a soft warm fabric with a pile, used for lining coats, etc. **c** a white cloud, a blanket of snow, etc. **3** *Heraldry* a representation of a fleece suspended from a ring. ● v.tr. **1** (often foll. by *of*) strip (a person) of money, valuables, etc.; swindle. **2** remove the fleece from (a sheep, etc.); shear. **3** cover as if with a fleece (*a sky fleeced with clouds*). □ **Golden Fleece** see GOLDEN. □□ **fleeceable** adj. **fleeced** adj. (also in *comb.*). [OE *flēos*, *flēs* f. WG]

■ v. **1** swindle, cheat, defraud, overcharge, plunder, milk, rob, rook, soak, flimflam, bleed, pluck, *colloq.* diddle, rip off, *sl.* bilk, skin, take, gyp, take to the cleaners, chisel. **2** shear, shave, crop, strip, clip.

fleecy /fleeˈsee/ *adj.* (**fleecier, fleeciest**) **1** of or like a fleece. **2** covered with a fleece. ▫▫ **fleecily** *adv.* **fleeciness** *n.*
■ *adj.* **1** see WOOLLY *adj.* 2.

fleer /fleer/ *v. & n.* ● *v.intr.* laugh impudently or mockingly; sneer; jeer. ● *n.* a mocking look or speech. [ME, prob. f. Scand.: cf. Norw. & Sw. dial. *flira* to grin]

fleet[1] /fleet/ *n.* **1 a** a number of warships under one commander. **b** (prec. by *the*) all the warships and merchant ships of a nation. **2** a number of ships, aircraft, buses, trucks, taxis, etc., operating together or owned by one proprietor. [OE *flēot* ship, shipping f. *flēotan* float, FLEET[5]]
■ **1 a** armada, flotilla, naval task force, squadron, convoy, *poet.* navy.

fleet[2] /fleet/ *adj.* swift; nimble. ▫▫ **fleetly** *adv.* **fleetness** *n.* [prob. f. ON *fljótr* f. Gmc: cf. FLEET[5]]
■ swift, nimble, rapid, fast, speedy, quick, expeditious, agile.

fleet[3] /fleet/ *n. Brit. dial.* a creek; an inlet. ▫ **Fleet Street 1** the London press. **2** British journalism or journalists. [OE *flēot* f. Gmc: cf. FLEET[5]]

fleet[4] /fleet/ *adj. & adv. Brit. dial.* ● *adj.* (of water) shallow. ● *adv.* at or to a small depth (*plow fleet*). [orig. uncert.: perh. f. OE *flēat* (unrecorded), rel. to FLEET[5]]

fleet[5] /fleet/ *v.intr. archaic* **1** glide away; vanish; be transitory. **2** (usu. foll. by *away*) (of time) pass rapidly; slip away. **3** move swiftly; fly. [OE *flēotan* float, swim f. Gmc]

fleeting /fleeting/ *adj.* transitory; brief. ▫▫ **fleetingly** *adv.* [FLEET[5] + -ING[2]]
■ transitory, fugitive, transient, temporary, passing, ephemeral, evanescent, momentary, short-lived, short, brief, *literary* fugacious.

Fleming /fleming/ *n.* **1** a native of medieval Flanders in the Low Countries. **2** a member of a Flemish-speaking people inhabiting N. and W. Belgium (see also WALLOON). [OE f. ON *Flǣmingi* & MDu. *Vlāming* f. root of *Vlaanderen* Flanders]

Flemish /flemish/ *adj. & n.* ● *adj.* of or relating to Flanders. ● *n.* the language of the Flemings. ▫ **Flemish bond** *Building* a bond in which each course of bricks consists of alternate headers and stretchers. [MDu. *Vlāmisch* (as FLEMING)]

flense /flens/ *v.tr.* (also **flench** /flench/, **flinch** /flinch/) **1** cut up (a whale or seal). **2** flay (a seal). [Da. *flense*: cf. Norw. *flinsa, flunsa* flay]

flesh /flesh/ *n. & v.* ● *n.* **1 a** the soft, esp. muscular, substance between the skin and bones of an animal or a human. **b** plumpness; fat (*has put on flesh*). **c** *archaic* meat, esp. excluding poultry, game, and offal. **2** the body as opposed to the mind or the soul, esp. considered as sinful. **3** the pulpy substance of a fruit or a plant. **4 a** the visible surface of the human body with ref. to its color or appearance. **b** (also **flesh color**) a yellowish pink color. **5** animal or human life. ● *v.tr.* **1** embody in flesh. **2** incite (a hound, etc.) by the taste of blood. **3** initiate, esp. by aggressive or violent means, esp.: **a** use (a sword, etc.) for the first time on flesh. **b** use (wit, the pen, etc.) for the first time. **c** inflame (a person) by the foretaste of success. ▫ **all flesh** all human and animal life. **flesh and blood** ● *n.* **1** the body or its substance. **2** humankind. **3** human nature, esp. as being fallible. ● *adj.* actually living, not imaginary or supernatural. **flesh fly** (*pl.* **flies**) any fly of the family Sarcophagidae that deposits eggs or larvae in dead flesh. **flesh out** make or become substantial. **flesh side** the side of a hide that adjoined the flesh. **flesh tints** flesh colors as rendered by a painter. **flesh wound** a wound not reaching a bone or a vital organ. **in the flesh** in bodily form; in person. **lose** (or **put on**) **flesh** grow thinner or fatter. **make a person's flesh creep** (or **crawl**) frighten or horrify a person, esp. with tales of the supernatural, etc. **one flesh** (of two people) intimately united, esp. by virtue of marriage (Gen. 2:24). **one's own flesh and blood** near relatives; descendants. **sins of the flesh** unchastity. **the way of all flesh** experience common to all humankind. ▫▫ **fleshless** *adj.* [OE *flǣsc* f. Gmc]
■ *n.* **1 a** muscle, tissue. **b** see FAT *n.* **2** body, corporeality;

flesh and blood. ▫ **flesh and blood** (*n.*) **2** humankind, mankind, humanity; people. (*adj.*) living, real, corporeal, physical, human. **flesh out** give *or* lend substance to, fill out, enlarge *or* expand on, develop, amplify, expatiate on, elaborate on. **in the flesh** bodily, in person, in propria persona, personally, really, physically, alive, living. **make a person's flesh creep** (or **crawl**) see FRIGHTEN 1. **one flesh** married, *archaic* espoused; see ATTACHED 2. **one's own flesh and blood** relatives, kin, kinfolk, family, stock, blood, kith and kin, relations.

flesher /fleshər/ *n. Sc.* a butcher.

fleshings /fleshingz/ *n.pl.* an actor's flesh-colored tights.

fleshly /fleshlee/ *adj.* (**fleshlier, fleshliest**) **1** (of desire, etc.) bodily; lascivious; sensual. **2** mortal; not divine. **3** worldly. ▫▫ **fleshliness** *n.* [OE *flǣsclic* (as FLESH)]
■ **1** see SENSUAL. **2** see MORTAL *adj.* 1. **3** see WORLDLY 1.

fleshpots /fleshpots/ *n.pl.* luxurious living (Exod. 16:3).

fleshy /fleshee/ *adj.* (**fleshier, fleshiest**) **1** plump; fat. **2** of flesh; without bone. **3** (of plant or fruit tissue) pulpy. **4** like flesh. ▫▫ **fleshiness** *n.*
■ **1** see FAT *adj.*

fletcher /flechər/ *n.* a maker or seller of arrows. [ME f. OF *flech(i)er* f. *fleche* arrow]

fleur-de-lis /flôrdəlee/ *n.* (also **fleur-de-lys**) (*pl.* **fleurs-** pronunc. same) **1** the iris flower. **2** *Heraldry* a lily composed of three petals bound together near their bases. **b** the former royal arms of France. [ME f. OF *flour de lys* flower of lily]

fleuret /flŏŏrét/ *n.* an ornament like a small flower. [F *fleurette* f. *fleur* flower]

fleuron /flôron, flŏŏr-/ *n.* a flower-shaped ornament on a building, a coin, a book, etc. [ME f. OF *floron* f. *flour* FLOWER]

fleury /flŏŏree, flôŏree/ *adj.* (also **flory** /flôree/) *Heraldry* decorated with fleurs-de-lis. [ME f. OF *flo(u)ré* (as FLEURON)]

flew *past* of FLY[1].

flews /flŏŏz/ *n.pl.* the hanging lips of a bloodhound, etc. [16th c.: orig. unkn.]

flex[1] /fleks/ *v.* **1** *tr. & intr.* bend (a joint, limb, etc.) or be bent. **2** *tr.* & *intr.* move (a muscle) or (of a muscle) be moved to bend a joint. **3** *tr. Geol.* bend (strata). **4** *tr. Archaeol.* place (a corpse) with the legs drawn up under the chin. [L *flectere flex-* bend]
■ **1** see BEND[1] *v.* 1. **2** move, exercise, tense, tighten, contract.

flex[2] /fleks/ *n. Brit.* a flexible insulated cable used for carrying electric current to an appliance. [abbr. of FLEXIBLE]

flexible /fléksibəl/ *adj.* **1** able to bend without breaking; pliable; pliant. **2** easily led; manageable; docile. **3** adaptable; versatile; variable (*works flexible hours*). ▫▫ **flexibility** *n.* **flexibly** *adv.* [ME f. OF *flexible* or L *flexibilis* (as FLEX[1])]
■ **1** pliable, pliant, elastic, resilient, supple, bendable, limber, lithe, stretchy, stretchable, springy, extensible, extensile, ductile, tensile, yielding, willowy, *archaic* flexile. **2** persuadable, persuasible; manageable, tractable, malleable, cooperative, amenable, modifiable, conformable; docile, compliant, obedient, submissive. **3** versatile; variable; see also ADAPTABLE 1.
▫▫ **flexibility** pliability, pliancy, elasticity, resilience, resiliency, suppleness, flexibleness, limberness, give, stretch, spring, springiness, ductility; manageability, compliance, tractability, tractableness, malleability, conformability, adjustability; docility, obedience, submissiveness, agreeability, conformity; adaptability, versatility.

flexile /fléksəl, -sīl/ *adj. archaic* **1** supple; mobile. **2** tractable; manageable. **3** versatile. ▫▫ **flexility** /-sílitee/ *n.* [L *flexilis* (as FLEX[1])]

flexion /flékshən/ *n.* (also **flection**) **1 a** the act of bending

---

/.../ pronunciation	● part of speech
▫ phrases, idioms, and compounds	
▫▫ derivatives	■ synonym section
cross-references appear in SMALL CAPITALS or *italics*	

or the condition of being bent, esp. of a limb or joint. **b** a bent part; a curve. **2** *Gram.* inflection. **3** *Math.* = FLEXURE. □□ **flexional** *adj.* (in sense 2). **flexionless** *adj.* (in sense 2). [L *flexio* (as FLEX¹)]

flexitime /fléksitim/ *n.* var. of FLEXTIME.

flexography /fleksógrəfee/ *n. Printing* a rotary letterpress technique using rubber or plastic plates and synthetic inks or dyes for printing on fabrics, plastics, etc., as well as on paper. □□ **flexographic** /-səgráfik/ *adj.* [L *flexus* a bending f. *flectere* bend + -GRAPHY]

flexor /fléksər/ *n.* (in full **flexor muscle**) a muscle that bends part of the body (cf. EXTENSOR). [mod.L (as FLEX¹)]

flextime /flékstim/ *n.* **1** a system of working a set number of hours with the starting and finishing times chosen within agreed limits by the employee. **2** the hours worked in this way. [FLEXIBLE + TIME]

flexuous /fléksho͞oəs/ *adj.* full of bends; winding. □□ **flexuosity** /-yo͞o-ósitee/ *n.* **flexuously** *adv.* [L *flexuosus* f. *flexus* bending formed as FLEX¹]

flexure /flékshər/ *n.* **1 a** the act of bending or the condition of being bent. **b** a bend, curve, or turn. **2** *Math.* the curving of a line, surface, or solid, esp. from a straight line, plane, etc. **3** *Geol.* the bending of strata under pressure. □□ **flexural** *adj.* [L *flexura* (as FLEX¹)]

flibbertigibbet /flíbərteejíbit/ *n.* a gossiping, frivolous, or restless person. [imit. of chatter]

flick /flik/ *n. & v.* ● *n.* **1 a** a light, sharp, quickly retracted blow with a whip, etc. **b** the sudden release of a bent finger or thumb, esp. to propel a small object. **2** a sudden movement or jerk. **3** a quick turn of the wrist in playing games, esp. in throwing or striking a ball. **4** a slight, sharp sound. **5** *colloq.* **a** a movie. **b** (in *pl.*; prec. by *the*) the movies. ● *v.* **1** *tr.* (often foll. by *away, off*) strike or move with a flick (*flicked the ash off his cigar; flicked away the dust*). **2** *tr.* give a flick with (a whip, towel, etc.). **3** *intr.* make a flicking movement or sound. □ **flick-knife** *Brit.* a switchblade knife. **flick through** = *flip through*. [ME, imit.]

■ *n.* **2, 3** see WHISK *n.* 1. **5 a** see FILM *n.* 3a, b. ● *v.* **1** flip, brush, sweep, toss.

flicker¹ /flíkər/ *v. & n.* ● *v.intr.* **1** (of light) shine unsteadily or fitfully. **2** (of a flame) burn unsteadily, alternately flaring and dying down. **3 a** (of a flag, a reptile's tongue, an eyelid, etc.) move or wave to and fro; quiver; vibrate. **b** (of the wind) blow lightly and unsteadily. **4** (of hope, etc.) increase and decrease unsteadily and intermittently. ● *n.* a flickering movement, light, thought, etc. □ **flicker out** die away after a final flicker. [OE *flicorian, flycerian*]

■ *v.* **1** glimmer, shimmer, blink, twinkle, sparkle. **2** waver, flare; see also BLINK *v.* 5. **3 a** flap, flutter; quiver, vibrate, shake, tremble, fluctuate, oscillate. ● *n.* glimmer, glimmering, twinkle, twinkling, sparkle, flare; (of recognition) hint, spark.

flicker² /flíkər/ *n.* any woodpecker of the genus *Colaptes*, a ground-feeder native to N. America. [imit. of its note]

flier /flíər/ *n.* (also **flyer**) *colloq.* **1** an airman or airwoman. **2** a thing that flies in a specified way (*a poor flier*). **3** a fast-moving animal or vehicle. **4** an ambitious or outstanding person. **5** (usu. **flyer**) a small handbill or circular. **6** a speculative investment. **7** a flying jump.

■ **5** see LEAFLET *n.*

flight¹ /flit/ *n. & v.* ● *n.* **1 a** the act or manner of flying through the air (*studied swallows' flight*). **b** the swift movement or passage of a projectile, etc., through the air (*the flight of an arrow*). **2 a** a journey made through the air or in space. **b** a timetabled journey made by an airline. **c** a military air unit of two or more aircraft. **3 a** a flock or large body of birds, insects, etc., esp. when migrating. **b** a migration. **4** (usu. foll. by *of*) a series, esp. of stairs between floors, or of hurdles across a race track (*lives up six flights*). **5** an extravagant soaring; a mental or verbal excursion or sally (of wit, etc.) (*a flight of fancy; a flight of ambition*). **6** the trajectory and pace of a ball in games. **7** the distance that a bird, aircraft, or missile can fly. **8** (usu. foll. by *of*) a volley (*a flight of arrows*). **9** the tail of a dart. **10** the pursuit of game by a hawk. **11** swift passage (of time). ● *v.tr.* **1** provide (an ar-

row) with feathers. **2** shoot (wildfowl, etc.) in flight. **3** *Brit.* vary the trajectory and pace of (a cricket ball, etc.). □ **flight attendant** an airline employee who attends to passengers' safety and comfort during flights. **flight bag** a small, zippered, shoulder bag carried by air travelers. **flight control** an internal or external system directing the movement of aircraft. **flight deck 1** the deck of an aircraft carrier used for takeoff and landing. **2** the forward compartment occupied by the pilot, navigator, etc., in an aircraft. **flight feather** a bird's wing or tail feather. **flight path** the planned course of an aircraft or spacecraft. **flight recorder** a device in an aircraft to record technical details during a flight, which may be used in the event of an accident to discover its cause. **flight-test** test (an aircraft, rocket, etc.) during flight. **in the first** (or **top**) **flight** taking a leading place. **take** (or **wing**) **one's flight** fly. [OE *flyht* f. WG: rel to FLY¹]

■ *n.* **1a, 5** flying, soaring; winging. **2 a** (air *or* space) journey, (air *or* space) voyage, (air *or* space) trip. **3 a** flock, swarm, cloud; covey (of grouse *or* partridge), bevy (of quail *or* larks), skein (of geese). **b** see MOVEMENT 1. **8** see VOLLEY *n.* 1. **9** tail, feather.

flight² /flit/ *n.* **1 a** the act or manner of fleeing. **b** a hasty retreat. **2** *Econ.* the selling of currency, investments, etc., in anticipation of a fall in value (*flight from the dollar*). □ **put to flight** cause to flee. **take** (or **take to**) **flight** flee. [OE f. Gmc: rel. to FLEE]

■ **1** retreat, escape, departure, exit, exodus, getaway, fleeing, bolting. □ **put to flight** chase (off *or* away), drive (off *or* away), disperse, send off *or* away, *colloq.* send packing, dismiss, rout, stampede. **take** (or **take to**) **flight** see FLEE 1.

flightless /flitlis/ *adj.* (of a bird, etc.) naturally unable to fly.

flighty /flitee/ *adj.* (**flightier, flightiest**) **1** frivolous; fickle; changeable. **2** slightly crazy. □□ **flightily** *adv.* **flightiness** *n.* [FLIGHT¹ + -Y¹]

■ **1** frivolous, fickle, inconstant, capricious, fanciful, changeable, variable, unstable, unsteady. **2** mad, silly, harebrained, reckless, irresponsible, *sl.* nutty, screwy, dippy, *colloq.* dotty, crazy.

flimflam /flímflam/ *n. & v.* ● *n.* **1** a trifle; nonsense; idle talk. **2** humbug; deception. ● *v.tr.* (**flimflammed, flimflamming**) cheat; deceive. □□ **flimflammer** *n.* **flimflammery** /-məree/ *n.* (*pl.* **-ies**). [imit. redupl.]

■ *n.* **2** see DECEIT 1. ● *v.* see CHEAT *v.* 1a.

flimsy /flímzee/ *adj. & n.* ● *adj.* (**flimsier, flimsiest**) **1** lightly or carelessly assembled; insubstantial; easily damaged (*a flimsy structure*). **2** (of an excuse, etc.) unconvincing (*a flimsy pretext*). **3** paltry; trivial; superficial (*a flimsy play*). **4** (of clothing) thin (*a flimsy blouse*). ● *n. Brit.* (*pl.* **-ies**) **1 a** very thin paper. **b** a document, esp. a copy, made on this. **2** a flimsy thing, esp. women's underwear. □□ **flimsily** *adv.* **flimsiness** *n.* [17th c.: prob. f. FLIMFLAM: cf. TIPSY]

■ **1** makeshift, jerry-built, rickety, ramshackle, dilapidated; insubstantial, slight, unsubstantial, fragile, weak, delicate, frail, feeble, frangible, breakable; gimcrack. **2** unconvincing, feeble, weak, lame, implausible, unbelievable, unsatisfactory, poor, inadequate, makeshift, insubstantial, unsubstantial. **3** see PALTRY, SUPERFICIAL 4. **4** thin, delicate, light, gossamer, sheer; gauzy, transparent, see-through, filmy, diaphanous.

flinch¹ /flinch/ *v. & n.* ● *v.intr.* **1** draw back in pain or expectation of a blow, etc.; wince. **2** (often foll. by *from*) give way; shrink; turn aside (*flinched from his duty*). ● *n.* an act or instance of flinching. □□ **flincher** *n.* **flinchingly** *adv.* [OF *flenchir, flainchir* f. WG]

■ *v.* **1** draw back, wince, cower, withdraw, cringe, recoil, start, quail, shrink, shy (away); dodge, duck.

flinch² var. of FLENSE.

flinders /flíndərz/ *n.pl.* fragments; splinters. [ME, prob. f. Scand.]

fling /fling/ *v. & n.* ● *v.* (*past* and *past part.* **flung** /flung/) **1** *tr.* throw or hurl (an object) forcefully. **2** *refl.* **a** (usu. foll. by *into*) rush headlong (into a person's arms, a train, etc.). **b** (usu. foll. by *into*) embark wholeheartedly (on an enterprise). **c** (usu. foll. by *on*) throw (oneself) on a person's mercy, etc. **3** *tr.* utter (words) forcefully. **4** *tr.* (usu. foll. by *out*) suddenly spread (the arms). **5** *tr.* (foll. by *on, off*) put on or take off (clothes) carelessly or rapidly. **6** *intr.* go angrily or violently; rush (*flung out of the room*). **7** *tr.* put or send suddenly or violently (*was flung into jail*). **8** *tr.* (foll. by *away*) discard or put aside thoughtlessly or rashly (*flung away their reputation*). **9** *intr.* (usu. foll. by *out*) (of a horse, etc.) kick and plunge. **10** *tr. archaic* send; emit (sound, light, smell). ● *n.* **1** an act or instance of flinging; a throw; a plunge. **2 a** a spell of indulgence or wild behavior (*he's had his fling*). **b** *colloq.* an attempt (*give it a fling*). **3** a brief or casual romance. **4** an impetuous, whirling Scottish dance, esp. the Highland fling. □ **make a fling at 1** make an attempt at. **2** jeer at. □□ **flinger** *n.* [ME, perh. f. ON]

■ *v.* **1** throw, hurl, toss, pitch, cast, heave, sling, *colloq.* lob, chuck. **4** see OPEN *v.* 6a. **6** see STORM *v.* 2. **7, 8** see THROW *v.* 1, 2. **6** *n.* **1** see THROW *n.* 1. **2 a** indulgence, debauch, spree, *sl.* binge. **b** gamble, risk, venture, attempt, try, *colloq.* go, shot, crack, whirl, *sl.* bash. □ **have a fling at 1** see TRY *v.* 1, 2. **2** see MOCK *v.* 1, 3.

flint /flint/ *n.* **1 a** a hard gray stone of nearly pure silica occurring naturally as nodules or bands in chalk. **b** a piece of this, esp. as flaked or shaped to form a primitive tool or weapon. **2** a piece of hard alloy of rare earth metals used to give an igniting spark in a cigarette lighter, etc. **3** a piece of flint used with steel to produce fire, esp. in a flintlock gun. **4** anything hard and unyielding. □ **flint corn** a variety of corn having hard translucent kernels. **flint glass** a pure lustrous kind of glass orig. made with flint. □□ **flinty** *adj.* (**flintier, flintiest**). **flintily** *adv.* **flintiness** *n.* [OE]

flintlock /flintlok/ *n. hist.* **1** an old type of gun fired by a spark from a flint. **2** the lock producing such a spark.

flip[1] /flip/ *v., n., & adj.* ● *v.* (**flipped, flipping**) **1** *tr.* **a** flick or toss (a coin, ball, etc.) with a quick movement so that it spins in the air. **b** remove (a small object) from a surface with a flick of the fingers. **2** *tr.* **a** strike or flick (a person's ear, cheek, etc.) lightly or smartly. **b** move (a fan, whip, etc.) with a sudden jerk. **3** *tr.* turn or turn over. **4** *intr.* **a** make a fillip or flicking noise with the fingers. **b** (foll. by *at*) strike smartly at. **5** *intr.* move about with sudden jerks. **6** *intr. sl.* (often foll. by *out*) become suddenly angry, excited, or enthusiastic. ● *n.* **1** a smart light blow; a flick. **2** a somersault, esp. while in the air. **3** an act of flipping over (*gave the stone a flip*). **4** *colloq.* **a** a short pleasure flight in an aircraft. **b** a quick tour, etc. ● *adj. colloq.* glib; flippant. □ **flip chart** a large pad erected on a stand and bound so that one page can be turned over at the top to reveal the next. **flip one's lid** *sl.* **1** lose self-control. **2** go crazy. **flip side** *colloq.* the less important side of something (orig. of a phonograph record). **flip through 1** turn over (cards, pages, etc.). **2 a** a turn over the pages, etc., of, by a rapid movement of the fingers. **b** look cursorily through (a book, etc.).

■ see BROWSE *v.* 1. [prob. f. FILLIP]

■ *v.* **1** toss, spin; flick. **3** see TURN *v.* 2. **6** become angry *or* furious, go berserk, go out of one's head, *colloq.* go mad, go crazy, go off the deep end, lose one's cool, freak (out), *sl.* flip one's lid, go ape. ● *n.* **1** see RAP[1] *n.* 1. ● *adj.* see FLIPPANT. □ **flip one's lid** see FLIP[1] *v.* 6 above.

flip[2] /flip/ *n.* **1** a drink of heated beer and liquor. **2** = *egg-flip.* [perh. f. FLIP[1] in the sense *whip up*]

flip-flop /flipflop/ *n. & v.* ● *n.* **1** a usu. rubber sandal with a thong between the big and second toe. **2** a backward somersault. **3** an electronic switching circuit changed from one stable state to another, or through an unstable state back to its stable state, by a triggering pulse. **4** an esp. sudden change of direction, attitude, policy, etc. ● *v.intr.* (**-flopped, -flopping**) **1** move with a sound or motion suggested by "flip-flop." **2** to change direction, attitude, policy, etc., esp. suddenly. [imit.]

flippant /flipant/ *adj.* lacking in seriousness; treating serious things lightly; disrespectful. □□ **flippancy** /-pansee/ *n.* **flippantly** *adv.* [FLIP[1] + -ANT]

■ frivolous, facetious, lighthearted, jocular, unserious;

disrespectful, impudent, impertinent, irreverent, saucy, discourteous, pert, insolent, brash, rude, brazen, cheeky, *colloq.* flip. □ **flippancy** frivolousness, frivolity, facetiousness, levity, lightheartedness, jocularity, unseriousness; disrespect, disrespectfulness, impudence, impertinence, irreverence, sauciness, discourtesy, brashness, pertness, insolence, rudeness, brazenness, cheek, cheekiness, *colloq.* lip, mouth.

flipper /flipar/ *n.* **1** a broadened limb of a tortoise, penguin, etc., used in swimming. **2** a flat rubber, etc., attachment worn on the foot for underwater swimming. **3** *sl.* a hand.

flipping /fliping/ *adj. & adv. Brit. sl.* expressing annoyance, or as an intensifier (*where's the flipping towel?*; *he flipping beat me*). [FLIP[1] + -ING[2]]

flirt /flart/ *v. & n.* ● *v.* **1** *intr.* (usu. foll. by *with*) behave in a frivolously amorous or sexually enticing manner. **2** *intr.* (usu. foll. by *with*) **a** superficially interest oneself (with an idea, etc.). **b** trifle (with danger, etc.) (*flirted with disgrace*). **3** *tr.* wave or move (a fan, a bird's tail, etc.) briskly. **4** *intr. & tr.* move or cause to move with a jerk. ● *n.* **1** a person who indulges in flirting. **2** a quick movement; a sudden jerk. □□ **flirtation** *n.* **flirtatious** *adj.* **flirtatiously** *adv.* **flirtatiousness** *n.* **flirty** *adj.* (**flirtier, flirtiest**). [imit.]

■ *v.* **1** play *or* act the coquette, philander, play the field, womanize, carry on, dally, tease, toy, *colloq.* gallivant; (*flirt with*) make eyes at, *Brit. colloq.* chat up. **2** (*flirt with*) trifle *or* play with, entertain, think about *or* of; see also TOY *v.* 1. ● *n.* **1** coquette, tease, *colloq.* vamp, minx; playboy, lady-killer, *sl.* wolf; see also *philanderer* (PHILANDER). □□ **flirtatious** coquettish, seductive, flirty, philandering, provocative, enticing, alluring, amorous, *colloq.* come-hither.

flit /flit/ *v. & n.* ● *v.intr.* (**flitted, flitting**) **1** move lightly, softly, or rapidly (*flitted from one room to another*). **2** fly lightly; make short flights (*flitted from branch to branch*). **3** *Brit. colloq.* leave one's house, etc., secretly to escape creditors or obligations. **4** esp. *Sc. & No. of Engl.* change one's home; move. ● *n.* **1** an act of flitting. **2** (also **moonlight flit**) a secret change of abode in order to escape creditors, etc. □□ **flitter** *n.* [ME f. ON *flytja*; rel. to FLEET[5]]

■ *v.* **1** move, go, fly, skip, hop, dart, flick, whisk, flash. **2** flitter, flutter, fly.

flitch /flich/ *n.* **1** a side of bacon. **2** a slab of timber from a tree trunk, usu. from the outside. **3** (in full **flitch plate**) a strengthening plate in a beam, etc. □ **flitch beam** a compound beam, esp. of an iron plate between two slabs of wood. [OE *flicce* f. Gmc]

flitter /flitar/ *v.intr.* flit about; flutter. [FLIT + -ER[4]]

■ see FLUTTER *v.* 3, 4.

flivver /flivar/ *n. Old-fash. sl.* a cheap, old car. [20th c.: orig. uncert.]

float /flōt/ *v. & n.* ● *v.* **1** *intr. & tr.* rest or move or cause (a buoyant object) to rest or move on the surface of a liquid without sinking. **b** get afloat or set (a stranded ship) afloat. **2** *intr.* move with a liquid or current of air; drift (*the clouds floated high up*). **3** *intr. colloq.* **a** move in a leisurely or casual way (*floated about humming quietly*). **b** (often foll. by *before*) hover before the eye or mind (*the prospect of lunch floated before them*). **4** *intr.* (often foll. by *in*) move or be suspended freely in a liquid or a gas. **5** *tr.* bring (a company, scheme, etc.) into being; launch. **6** offer (stock, shares, etc.) on the stock market. **6** *Commerce* **a** *intr.* (of currency) be allowed to have a fluctuating exchange rate. **b** *tr.* cause (currency) to float. **c** *intr.* (of an acceptance) be in circulation. **7** *tr.* (of water, etc.) support; bear along (a buoyant object). **8** *intr. & tr.* circulate or cause (a rumor or idea) to circulate. **9** *tr.* put forward as a proposal. **10** waft (a buoyant object) through the air. **11** *tr. archaic* cover with liquid; inundate. ● *n.* **1** a thing that floats, esp.: **a** a raft. **b** a cork or other

/. . ./ **pronunciation**	● **part of speech**
□ **phrases, idioms, and compounds**	
□□ **derivatives**	■ **synonym section**
cross-references appear in SMALL CAPITALS or *italics*	

buoyant object on a fishing line as an indicator of a fish biting. **c** a cork supporting the edge of a fishing net. **d** the hollow or inflated part or organ supporting a fish, etc., in the water; an air bladder. **e** a hollow structure fixed underneath an aircraft enabling it to float on water. **f** a floating device on the surface of water, fuel, etc., controlling the flow. **2** *Brit.* a small vehicle or cart, esp. one powered by electricity (*milk float*). **3** a platform mounted on a truck or trailer and carrying a display in a parade, etc. **4 a** an amount of money outstanding but not yet collected by a bank, etc., such as checks written but not yet collected on. **b** the time between the writing of a check, etc., and the actual collection of funds. **5** *Brit.* **a** a sum of money used at the beginning of a period of selling in a shop, etc., to provide change. **b** a small sum of money for minor expenditure; petty cash. **6** *Theatr. Brit.* (in *sing.* or *pl.*) footlights. **7** a tool used for smoothing plaster or concrete. □ **float glass** a kind of glass made by drawing the molten glass continuously onto a surface of molten metal for hardening. **float process** the process used to make float glass. □□ **floatable** *adj.* **floatability** /-təbilitee/ *n.* [OE *flot, flotian* float, OE *flota* ship, ON *flota, floti* rel. to FLEET⁵: in ME infl. by OF *floter*]

▪ *v.* **1 a** hover, bob, waft, hang, be suspended *or* poised. **2** bob, coast, drift; waft. **5 a** launch, establish, set up, organize, found, initiate, get going *or* moving. **8** see SPREAD *v.* 3. ▪ *n.* **1 a** raft, pontoon.

floatage var. of FLOTAGE.

floatation var. of FLOTATION.

floater /flṓtər/ *n.* **1** a person or thing that floats. **2 a** a floating voter. **b** one who votes fraudulently, esp. repeatedly. **3** *Brit. sl.* a mistake; a gaffe. **4** a person who frequently changes occupations or duties. **5** *Stock Exch.* a government stock certificate, etc., recognized as a security. **6** an insurance policy for movable valuables, such as jewelry, etc.

floating /flṓting/ *adj.* not settled in a definite place; fluctuating; variable (*the floating population*). □ **floating anchor** a sea anchor. **floating bridge 1** a bridge on pontoons, etc. **2** a ferry working on chains. **floating debt** a usu. short-term debt repayable on demand, or at a stated time. **floating dock** a floating structure usable as a dry dock. **floating kidney 1** an abnormal condition in which the kidneys are unusually movable. **2** such a kidney. **floating point** *Computing* a decimal, etc., point that does not occupy a fixed position in the numbers processed. **floating rib** any of the lower ribs, which are not attached to the breastbone. **floating voter** a voter without allegiance to any political party. □□ **floatingly** *adv.*

▪ see VARIABLE *adj.* 2.

floaty /flṓtee/ *adj.* (esp. of a woman's garment or a fabric) light and airy. [FLOAT]

floc /flok/ *n.* a flocculent mass of fine particles. [abbr. of FLOCCULUS]

flocculate /flókyəlayt/ *v.tr.* & *intr.* form into flocculent masses. □□ **flocculation** /-láyshən/ *n.*

floccule /flókyool/ *n.* a small portion of matter resembling a tuft of wool.

flocculent /flókyələnt/ *adj.* **1** like tufts of wool. **2** consisting of or showing tufts; downy. **3** *Chem.* (of precipitates) loosely massed. □□ **flocculence** /-ləns/ *n.* [L *floccus* FLOCK²]

flocculus /flókyələs/ *n.* (*pl.* **flocculi** /-lī/) **1** a floccule. **2** *Anat.* a small ovoid lobe on the underside of the cerebellum. **3** *Astron.* a small cloudy wisp on the sun's surface. [mod.L, dimin. of FLOCCUS]

floccus /flókəs/ *n.* (*pl.* **flocci** /flóksī/) a tuft of woolly hairs or filaments. [L, = FLOCK²]

flock¹ /flok/ *n.* & *v.* ▪ *n.* **1 a** a number of animals of one kind, esp. birds, feeding or traveling together. **b** a number of domestic animals, esp. sheep, goats, or geese, kept together. **2** a large crowd of people. **3 a** a Christian congregation or body of believers, esp. in relation to one minister. **b** a family of children, a number of pupils, etc. ▪ *v.intr.* **1** congregate; mass. **2** (usu. foll. by *to, in, out, together*) go together in a crowd; troop (*thousands flocked to the polls*). [OE *flocc*]

▪ *n.* **1** flight, gaggle, bevy, covey; pride, pack, troop,

school, swarm, horde, host; herd, drove, mob. **2** crowd, body, company, group, band, bunch, troop, set, collection, assembly, gathering, mass, mob, throng, gang, multitude, number, quantity, host, horde, swarm, drove. **3 b** see BROOD *n.* 2. ▪ *v.* **1** congregate, assemble, meet, collect, gather, mass, mob. **2** crowd, throng, herd, band together; pour, flood, swarm; troop.

flock² /flok/ *n.* **1 a** a lock or tuft of wool, cotton, etc. **2 a** (also in *pl.*; often *attrib.*) material for quilting and stuffing made of wool refuse or torn-up cloth (*a flock pillow*). **b** powdered wool or cloth. □ **flock paper** (or **wallpaper**) wallpaper sized and sprinkled with powdered wool to make a raised pattern. □□ **flocky** *adj.* [ME f. OF *floc* f. L *floccus*]

floe /flō/ *n.* a sheet of floating ice. [prob. f. Norw. *flo* f. ON *fló* layer]

flog /flawg, flog/ *v.* (**flogged, flogging**) **1** *tr.* **a** beat with a whip, stick, etc. (as a punishment or to urge on). **b** make work through violent effort (*flogged the engine*). **2** *sl.* sell or promote aggressively. **3** *tr.* (usu. foll. by *into, out of*) drive (a quality, knowledge, etc.) into or out of a person, esp. by physical punishment. **4** *intr.* & *refl. Brit. sl.* proceed by violent or painful effort. □ **flog** (also **beat**) **a dead horse** waste energy on something unalterable. **flog to death** *colloq.* talk about or promote at tedious length. □□ **flogger** *n.* [17th-c. cant: prob. imit. or f. L *flagellare* to whip]

▪ **1** beat, whip, lash, horsewhip, strap, flagellate, flay, scourge, thrash, thresh; chastise.

flood /flud/ *n.* & *v.* ▪ *n.* **1 a** an overflowing or influx of water beyond its normal confines, esp. over land; an inundation. **b** the water that overflows. **2 a** an outpouring of water; a torrent (*a flood of rain*). **b** something resembling a torrent (*a flood of tears; a flood of relief*). **c** an abundance or excess. **3** the inflow of the tide (also in *comb.*: *flood tide*). **4** *colloq.* a floodlight. **5** (**the Flood**) the flood described in Genesis. **6** *poet.* a river; a stream; a sea. ▪ *v.* **1** *tr.* **a** cover with or overflow in a flood (*rain flooded the cellar*). **b** overflow as if with a flood (*the market was flooded with foreign goods*). **2** *tr.* irrigate (*flooded the rice paddies*). **3** *tr.* deluge (a burning house, a mine, etc.) with water. **4** *intr.* (often foll. by *in, through*) arrive in great quantities (*complaints flooded in; fear flooded through them*). **5** *intr.* become inundated (*the bathroom flooded*). **6** *tr.* overfill (a carburetor) with fuel. **7** *intr.* experience a uterine hemorrhage. **8** *tr.* (of rain, etc.) fill (a river) to overflowing. □ **flood out** drive out (of one's home, etc.) with a flood. **flood tide** the periodical exceptional rise of the tide because of lunar or solar attraction. [OE *flōd* f. Gmc]

▪ *n.* **1** overflowing, inundation, deluge, overflow, debacle. **2 a** outpouring, torrent, cataract, stream, spate; freshet. **b** torrent, surge, outpouring, stream, rush, flow, deluge, overflowing, tide, tidal wave. **c** abundance, glut, surfeit, satiety, profusion, overabundance, superabundance, plethora, excess, surplus, superfluity. ▪ *v.* **1** cover, pour over *or* into *or* through(out); overflow, inundate, deluge, submerge, swamp, drown, engulf, fill. **2** irrigate, inundate, water. **4** sweep, flow, pour, surge, rush, crowd, swarm.

floodgate /flúdgayt/ *n.* **1** a gate opened or closed to admit or exclude water, esp. the lower gate of a lock. **2** (usu. in *pl.*) a last restraint holding back tears, rain, anger, etc.

floodlight /flúdlīt/ *n.* & *v.* ▪ *n.* **1** a large powerful light (usu. one of several) to illuminate a building, stadium, stage, etc. **2** the illumination so provided. ▪ *v.tr.* illuminate with floodlights.

floodplain /flúdplayn/ *n.* flat terrain alongside a river that is subject to inundation when the river floods.

floodwater /flúdwawtər, -wo-/ *n.* the water overflowing as the result of a flood.

floor /flawr/ *n.* & *v.* ▪ *n.* **1 a** the lower surface of a room. **b** the boards, etc., of which it is made. **2 a** the bottom of the sea, a cave, a cavity, etc. **b** any level area. **3** all the rooms, etc., on the same level of a building; a story (*lives on the first floor; walked up to the fourth floor*). **4 a** (in a legislative assembly) the part of the house in which members sit and from which they speak. **b** the right to speak next in debate (*gave him the floor*). **5** *Stock Exch.* the large central hall where trading takes place. **6** the minimum of prices, wages, etc. **7** *colloq.* the ground. ● *v.tr.* **1** furnish with a floor; pave. **2** bring to the ground; knock (a person) down. **3** *colloq.* confound; baffle (*was floored by the puzzle*). **4** *colloq.* get the better of; overcome. **5** serve as the floor of (*leopard skins floored the hall*). **6** cause a vehicle to accelerate rapidly. □ **floor lamp** a lamp with a base that rests on the floor. **floor leader** the organizational or strategical leader of a party in a legislative assembly. **floor manager 1** the stage manager of a television production. **2** a person who directs activities, etc., from the floor, as at a political convention. **floor plan** a diagram of the rooms, etc., on one floor of a building. **floor price** = *reserve price*. **floor show** an entertainment presented at a nightclub, etc. **from the floor** (of a speech, etc.) given by a member of the audience, not by those on the platform, etc. **take the floor 1** begin to dance on a dance floor, etc. **2** speak in a debate. □□ **floorless** *adj.* [OE *flōr* f. Gmc]

■ *n.* **1 b** flooring, boarding, planking, parquet. **2 a** see BOTTOM *n.* 4. **3** story, level; deck. **6** minimum, base, lower limit, bottom. **7** ground, earth, *sl.* deck. ● *v.* **1** see PAVE 1. **2** bring to the ground, knock down *or* over, bowl over, fell, bring down. **3** confound, baffle, stump, bewilder, dumbfound, confuse, perplex, puzzle, nonplus, disconcert. **4** overcome, beat, defeat, conquer, destroy, rout, overwhelm, crush, trounce, thrash, drub, best, worst, *sl.* whip. □ **take the floor 2** debate, speak; see also LECTURE *v.* 1.

floorboard /fláwrbawrd/ *n.* a long wooden board used for flooring.

floorcloth /fláwrklawth, -kloth/ *n.* **1** a cloth for washing the floor. **2** a heavy cloth or covering for a floor.

flooring /fláwring/ *n.* the boards, etc., of which a floor is made.

■ floor, parquet, planking.

floorwalker /fláwrwawkər/ *n.* a person employed in a retail store who assists customers and supervises other workers.

floozy /flōozee/ *n.* (also **floozie**) (*pl.* **-ies**) *colloq.* a girl or a woman, esp. a disreputable one. [20th c.: cf. FLOSSY and dial. *floosy* fluffy]

■ see TART² *n.*

flop /flop/ *v., n., & adv.* ● *v.intr.* (**flopped, flopping**) **1** sway about heavily or loosely (*hair flopped over his face*). **2** move in an ungainly way (*flopped along the beach in flippers*). **3** (often foll. by *down, on, into*) sit, kneel, lie, or fall awkwardly or suddenly (*flopped down on to the bench*). **4** *sl.* (esp. of a play, movie, book, etc.) fail; collapse (*flopped on Broadway*). **5** *sl.* sleep. **6** make a dull sound as of a soft body landing, or of a flat thing slapping water. ● *n.* **1 a** a flopping movement. **b** the sound made by it. **2** *sl.* a failure. **3** *sl.* a place to sleep, esp. cheaply. **4** a piece of cow dung. ● *adv.* with a flop. [var. of FLAP]

■ *v.* **1** dangle, hang (down), droop, drop, tumble down; swing, wave, flap. **2** pad, tramp; see also PLOD *v.* **3** collapse, drop *or* fall *or* tumble (down), topple, plop down, plump (down), flounce down. **4** fall flat, founder, *sl.* bomb; see also FAIL *v.* 1, 2a. ● *n.* **2** failure, fiasco, disaster, nonstarter, debacle, lead balloon, *Brit.* damp squib, *colloq.* lemon, bomb, *sl.* washout, dud, turkey.

flophouse /flop-hows/ *n.* a cheap hotel or rooming house.

floppy /flópee/ *adj. & n.* ● *adj.* (**floppier, floppiest**) tending to flop; not firm or rigid. ● *n.* (*pl.* **-ies**) (in full **floppy disk**) *Computing* a flexible removable magnetic disk for the storage of data. □□ **floppily** *adv.* **floppiness** *n.*

■ *adj.* see LIMP² 1.

flor. *abbr.* floruit.

flora /fláwrə/ *n.* (*pl.* **floras** or **florae** /-ree/) **1** the plants of a particular region, geological period, or environment. **2** a treatise on or list of these. [mod.L f. the name of the goddess of flowers f. L *flos floris* flower]

floral /fláwrəl/ *adj.* **1** of flowers. **2** decorated with or depicting

flowers. **3** of flora or floras. □□ **florally** *adv.* [L *floralis* or *flos floris* flower]

floreat /fláwreeat/ *v.intr.* may (he, she, or it) flourish. [L, 3rd sing. pres. subj. of *florēre* flourish]

Florentine /fláwrənteen, -tin, flór-/ *adj. & n.* ● *adj.* **1** of or relating to Florence in Italy. **2** (**florentine** /-teen/) (of a dish) served on a bed of spinach. ● *n.* a native or citizen of Florence. [F *Florentin -ine* or L *Florentinus* f. *Florentia* Florence]

florescence /flawrésəns/ *n.* the process, state, or time of flowering. [mod.L *florescentia* f. L *florescere* f. *florēre* bloom]

floret /fláwrit/ *n.* *Bot.* **1** each of the small flowers making up a composite flower head. **2** each of the flowering stems making up a head of cauliflower, broccoli, etc. **3** a small flower. [L *flos floris* flower]

floriate /fláwriayt/ *v.tr.* decorate with flower designs, etc.

floribunda /fláwribúndə/ *n.* a plant, esp. a rose, bearing dense clusters of flowers. [mod.L f. *floribundus* freely flowering f. L *flos floris* flower, infl. by L *abundus* copious]

floriculture /fláwrikulchər/ *n.* the cultivation of flowers. □□ **floricultural** *adj.* **floriculturist** *n.* [L *flos floris* flower + CULTURE, after *horticulture*]

florid /fláwrid, flór-/ *adj.* **1** ruddy; flushed (*a florid complexion*). **2** (of a book, a picture, music, architecture, etc.) elaborately ornate; ostentatious; showy. **3** adorned with or as with flowers; flowery. □□ **floridity** *n.* **floridly** *adv.* **floridness** *n.* [F *floride* or L *floridus* f. *flos floris* flower]

■ **1** see ROSY 1. **2** see ORNATE.

floriferous /flawrífərəs/ *adj.* (of a seed or plant) producing many flowers. [L *florifer* f. *flos floris* flower]

florilegium /fláwrileéjeeəm/ *n.* (*pl.* **florilegia** /-jeeə/ or **florilegiums**) an anthology. [mod.L f. L *flos floris* flower + *legere* gather, transl. of Gk *anthologion* ANTHOLOGY]

florin /fláwrin, flór-/ *n.* *hist.* **1 a** a British silver or alloy two-shilling coin of the 19th–20th c. **b** an English gold coin of the 14th c. **2** a foreign coin of gold or silver, esp. a Dutch guilder. [ME f. OF f. It. *fiorino* dimin. of *fiore* flower f. L *flos floris*, the orig. coin having a figure of a lily on it]

florist /fláwrist, flór-/ *n.* a person who deals in or grows flowers. □□ **floristry** *n.* [L *flos floris* flower + -IST]

floristic /flawrístik/ *adj.* relating to the study of the distribution of plants. □□ **floristically** *adv.* **floristics** *n.*

floruit /fláwrōoit, flór-/ *v. & n.* ● *v.intr.* (he or she) was alive and working; flourished (used of a person, esp. a painter, a writer, etc., whose exact dates are unknown). ● *n.* the period or date at which a person lived or worked. [L, = he or she flourished]

flory var. of FLEURY.

floscular /flóskyələr/ *adj.* (also **flosculous** /-kyōōləs/) having florets or composite flowers. [L *flosculus* dimin. of *flos* flower]

floss /flaws, flos/ *n. & v.* ● *n.* **1** the rough silk enveloping a silkworm's cocoon. **2** untwisted silk thread used in embroidery. **3** = *dental floss.* ● *v.tr.* (also *absol.*) clean (the teeth) with dental floss. [F (*soie*) *floche* floss(-silk) f. OF *flosche* down, nap of velvet]

flossy /fláwsee/ *adj.* (**flossier, flossiest**) **1** of or like floss. **2** *colloq.* fancy; showy.

flotage /flṓtij/ *n.* **1** the act or state of floating. **2 a** floating objects or masses; flotsam. **b** *Brit.* the right of appropriating flotsam. **3 a** ships, etc., afloat on a river. **b** the part of a ship above the water line. **4** buoyancy; floating power.

flotation /flṓtáyshən/ *n.* (also **floatation**) **1** the process of launching or financing a commercial enterprise. **2** the separation of the components of crushed ore, etc., by their different capacities to float. **3** the capacity to float. □ **center of flotation** the center of gravity in a floating body. [alt. of *floatation* f. FLOAT, after *rotation*, etc.]

/.../ **pronunciation**	● **part of speech**
□ **phrases, idioms, and compounds**	
□□ **derivatives**	■ **synonym section**
cross-references appear in SMALL CAPITALS or *italics*	

flotilla /flōtílə/ n. **1** a small fleet. **2** a fleet of boats or small ships. [Sp., dimin. of *flota* fleet, OF *flote* multitude]
■ see FLEET¹.

flotsam /flótsəm/ n. wreckage found floating. □ **flotsam and jetsam 1** odds and ends; rubbish. **2** vagrants, etc. [AF *floteson* f. *floter* FLOAT]

flounce¹ /flowns/ v. & n. ● v.intr. (often foll. by *away*, *off*, *out*) go or move with an agitated, violent, or impatient motion (*flounced out in a huff*). ● n. a flouncing movement. [16th c.: orig. unkn.: perh. imit., as *bounce*, *pounce*]
■ v. strut, march, storm, stamp, stomp, bounce; fling, *colloq.* sashay.

flounce² /flowns/ n. & v. ● n. a wide ornamental strip of material gathered and sewn to a skirt, dress, etc.; a frill. ● v.tr. trim with a flounce or flounces. [alt. of earlier *frounce* fold, pleat, f. OF *fronce* f. *froncir* wrinkle]
■ n. frill, valance, furbelow, peplum; ruffle.

flounder¹ /flówndər/ v. & n. ● v.intr. **1** struggle in mud, or as if in mud, or when wading. **2** perform a task badly or without knowledge; (as of one's depth. ● n. an act of floundering. □□ **flounderer** n. [imit.: perh. assoc. with *founder*, *blunder*]
■ v. struggle, grope, blunder, stumble, tumble, stagger, plunge about.

flounder² /flówndər/ n. **1** an edible flatfish, *Pleuronectes flesus*, native to European shores. **2** any of various flatfish native to N. American shores. [ME f. AF *floundre*, OF *flondre*, prob. of Scand. orig.]

flour /flowər/ n. & v. ● n. **1** a meal or powder obtained by grinding and usu. sifting grain, esp. wheat. **2** any fine powder. ● v.tr. **1** sprinkle with flour. **2** grind into flour. □□ **floury** adj. (**flourier**, **flouriest**). **flouriness** n. [ME, different. spelling of FLOWER in the sense 'finest part']

flourish /flérish, flúr-/ v. & n. ● v. **1** intr. **a** grow vigorously; thrive. **b** prosper; be successful. **c** be in one's prime. **d** be in good health. **e** (as **flourishing** adj.) successful; prosperous. **2** intr. (usu. foll. by *in*, *at*, *about*) spend one's life; be active (at a specified time) (*flourished in the Middle Ages*) (cf. FLORUIT). **3** tr. show ostentatiously (*flourished her checkbook*). **4** tr. wave (a weapon, one's limbs, etc.) vigorously. ● n. **1** an ostentatious gesture with a weapon, a hand, etc. (*removed his hat with a flourish*). **2** an ornamental curving decoration of handwriting. **3** a florid verbal expression; a rhetorical embellishment. **4** *Mus.* **a** a fanfare played by brass instruments. **b** an ornate musical passage. **c** an extemporized addition played esp. at the beginning or end of a composition. **5** *archaic* an instance of prosperity; a flourishing. □□ **flourisher** n. **flourishy** adj. [ME f. OF *florir* ult. f. L *florēre* f. *flos floris* flower]
■ v. **1 a, d** thrive, bloom, blossom, flower, *literary* burgeon. **b** prosper, boom, succeed, get ahead, do well, go up *or* rise in the world, *colloq.* go great guns, *literary* fare well; bear fruit. **c** mature, develop, ripen, mellow, come of age. **e** (**flourishing**) successful, prosperous, booming, thriving, prospering. **4** wave, wield, brandish, wag, swing, twirl, flaunt, shake, swish, flap, *literary* vaunt. ● n. **1** gesture, gesturing, wave; show, display. **2** curl, curlicue. **3** embellishment, decoration, ornament(ation), adornment, frill. **4 a** see FANFARE 1.

flout /flowt/ v. & n. ● v. **1** tr. express contempt for (the law, rules, etc.) by word or action; mock; insult (*flouted convention by shaving her head*). ¶ Often confused with *flaunt*. **2** intr. (often foll. by *at*) mock or scoff. ● n. a flouting speech or act. [perh. f. Du. *fluiten* whistle, hiss: cf. FLUTE]
■ v. **1** mock, deride, scorn, jeer, disdain, spurn, guy, ridicule, disparage, decry, denigrate, belittle, depreciate, degrade, abase, deprecate, blaspheme, denounce, fly in the face of, *colloq.* put down, *literary* contemn, misprize; insult, affront. **2** mock, scoff, jeer, sneer, gibe, fleer, blaspheme.

flow /flō/ v. & n. ● v.intr. **1** glide along as a stream (*the Thames flows through London*). **2 a** (of a liquid, esp. water) gush out; spring. **b** (of blood, liquid, etc.) be spilled. **3** (of blood, money, electric current, etc.) circulate. **4** (of people or things) come or go in large numbers or smoothly (*traffic flowed along the highway*). **5** (of talk, literary style, etc.) proceed easily and smoothly. **6** (of a garment, hair, etc.) hang easily or gracefully; undulate. **7** (often foll. by *from*) result from; be caused by (*his failure flows from his diffidence*). **8** (esp. of the tide) be in flood; run full. **9** (of wine) be poured out copiously. **10** (of a rock or metal) undergo a permanent change of shape under stress. **11** menstruate. **12** (foll. by *with*) *archaic* be plentifully supplied with (*land flowing with milk and honey*). ● n. **1 a** a flowing movement in a stream. **b** the manner in which a thing flows (*a sluggish flow*). **c** a flowing liquid (*couldn't stop the flow*). **d** a copious outpouring; a stream (*a continuous flow of complaints*). **e** a hardened mass that formerly flowed (*walked out onto the lava flow*). **2** the rise of a tide or a river (*ebb and flow*). **3** the gradual deformation of a rock or metal under stress. **4** menstruation. **5** *Sc.* a bog or morass. □ **flow chart** (or **diagram** or **sheet**) **1** a diagram of the movement or action of things or persons engaged in a complex activity. **2** a graphical representation of a computer program in relation to its sequence of functions (as distinct from the data it processes). [OE *flōwan* f. Gmc, rel. to FLOOD]
■ v. **1** glide, run, course, stream, trickle, go, move, proceed, progress; purl. **2 a** gush *or* rush (out), surge, well forth *or* out *or* up, stream (out), spout, spurt, squirt, spew (out), flood (out), cascade; spring, issue, originate, come, emanate; (*flow over* or *on to*) spread over *or* on to, overspread, cover. **3** see CIRCULATE 1. **7** see STEM¹ v. 1. **12** (*flow with*) see ABOUND 2. ● n. **1 a** movement, current, course, stream, drift. **c, d** rush, gush, surge, outpouring; flood, overflow, overflowing, deluge, tide; see also STREAM n. 2a.

flower /flowər/ n. & v. ● n. **1** the part of a plant from which the fruit or seed is developed. **2** the reproductive organ in a plant containing one or more pistils or stamens or both, and usu. a corolla and calyx. **3** a blossom, esp. on a stem and used in bunches for decoration. **4** a plant cultivated or noted for its flowers. **5** (in *pl.*) ornamental phrases (*flowers of speech*). **6** the finest time, group, example, etc.; the peak. ● v. **1** intr. (of a plant) produce flowers; bloom or blossom. **2** intr. reach a peak. **3** tr. cause or allow (a plant) to flower. **4** tr. decorate with worked flowers or a floral design. □ **flower girl 1** a girl who carries flowers at a wedding as an attendant to the bride. **2** *Brit.* a woman who sells flowers, esp. in the street. **flower head** = HEAD n. 4d. **the flower of** the best or best part of. **flower people** (esp. in the 1960s) hippies carrying or wearing flowers as symbols of peace and love. **flower power** (esp. in the 1960s) the ideas of the flower people regarded as an instrument in changing the world. **flowers of sulfur** *Chem.* a fine powder produced when sulfur evaporates and condenses. **in flower** with the flowers out. □□ **flowered** adj. (also in *comb.*). **flowerless** adj. **flowerlike** adj. [ME f. AF *flur*, OF *flour*, *flor*, f. L *flos floris*]
■ n. **3** blossom, bloom, efflorescence, floweret, floret. ● v. **1** bloom, blossom, come out, open, effloresce, unfold, *literary* burgeon. **2** see PEAK v. □ **the flower (of)** the cream *or* best *or* pick *or* élite *or* crème de la crème *or* finest *or* choicest (of).

flowerer /flowərər/ n. a plant that flowers at a specified time (*a late flowerer*).

floweret /flówərit/ n. a small flower.
■ see FLOWER n.

flowering /flowəring/ adj. (of a plant) capable of producing flowers.

flowerpot /flówərpot/ n. a pot in which a plant may be grown.

flowery /flówəree/ adj. **1** decorated with flowers or floral designs. **2** (of literary style, manner of speech, etc.) highly embellished; ornate. **3** full of flowers (*a flowery meadow*). □□ **floweriness** n.
■ **2** high-flown, florid, fancy, showy, grandiloquent, bombastic, inflated, pompous; ornate, elaborate(d), decorated, ornamented, overwrought, embellished, rococo, euphuistic, affected, artificial.

flowing /flóing/ adj. **1** (of literary style, etc.) fluent; easy. **2**

(of a line, a curve, or a contour) smoothly continuous; not abrupt. **3** (of hair, a garment, a sail, etc.) unconfined. □□ **flowingly** adv.

■ **1** see FLUENT 1a. **3** see LOOSE adj. 3–5.

flown past part. of FLY[1].

flowstone /flṓstōn/ n. rock deposited in a thin sheet by a flow of water.

fl. oz. abbr. fluid ounce(s).

FLQ abbr. Front de Libération du Québec.

flu /floo/ n. colloq. influenza. [abbr.]

■ see COLD n. 2.

flub /flub/ v. & n. colloq. ● v.tr. (**flubbed, flubbing**) botch; bungle. ● n. something badly or clumsily done. [20th c.: orig. unkn.]

■ v. see FUMBLE v. 2a, BOTCH v. 1, BUNGLE v. 2. ● n. see MISTAKE n.

fluctuate /flúkchoo-ayt/ v.intr. vary irregularly; be unstable; vacillate; rise and fall, move to and fro. □□ **fluctuation** /-áyshən/ n. [L fluctuare f. fluctus flow, wave f. fluere fluctflow]

■ vary, change, shift, alternate, seesaw, yo-yo, swing, vacillate, oscillate, waver, undulate. □□ **fluctuation** variation(s), change(s), alternation(s), swing(s), vacillation(s), wavering(s), oscillation(s), undulation(s), up(s) and down(s); instability, unsteadiness, inconstancy, variability.

flue /floo/ n. **1** a smoke duct in a chimney. **2** a channel for conveying heat, esp. a hot-air passage in a wall; a tube for heating water in some kinds of boiler. □ **flue-cure** (tobacco) by artificial heat from flues. **flue pipe** an organ pipe into which the air enters directly, not striking a reed. [16th c.: orig. unkn.]

■ see VENT[1] n. 8.

fluence /floōəns/ n. Brit. colloq. influence. □ **put the fluence on** apply hypnotic, etc., suggestion to (a person). [shortening of INFLUENCE]

fluency /floōənsee/ n. **1** a smooth, easy flow, esp. in speech or writing. **2** a ready command of words or of a specified foreign language.

■ flow, articulateness, eloquence, control, command, ease, effortlessness, facility, smoothness, polish, slickness, glibness, volubility, felicity.

fluent /floōənt/ adj. **1 a** (of speech or literary style) flowing naturally and readily. **b** having command of a foreign language (is fluent in German). **c** able to speak quickly and easily. **2** flowing easily or gracefully (the fluent line of her arabesque). **3** archaic liable to change; unsettled. □□ **fluently** adv. [L fluere flow]

■ **1 a** flowing, natural, facile, effortless, ready, smooth, polished. **c** articulate, eloquent, well-spoken, felicitous, voluble, glib, slick.

fluff /fluf/ n. & v. ● n. **1** soft, light, feathery material coming off blankets, etc. **2** soft fur or feathers. **3** sl. **a** a mistake in delivering theatrical lines, in playing music, etc. **b** a mistake in playing a game. ● v. **1** tr. & intr. (often foll. by up) shake into or become a soft mass. **2** tr. & intr. colloq. make a mistake in (a theatrical part, a game, playing music, a speech, etc.); blunder (fluffed his opening line). **3** tr. make into fluff. **4** tr. put a soft surface on (the flesh side of leather). □ **bit of fluff** esp. Brit. sl. offens. a woman regarded as an object of sexual desire. [prob. dial. alt. of flue fluff]

■ n. **1** down, fuzz, lint, dust. **3** mistake, error, slip; colloq. howler, blooper. ● v. **1** shake out or up, puff up; aerate. **2** ruin, make a mess of, spoil, bungle, botch, foul up, mess up, sl. screw up, Brit. sl. cock up; blunder.

fluffy /flúfee/ adj. (**fluffier, fluffiest**) **1** of or like fluff. **2** covered in fluff; downy. **3** nonintellectual; frivolous; superficial. □□ **fluffily** adv. **fluffiness** n.

■ **1** downy, soft, puffy, light, lightweight, airy, feathery, thin, insubstantial, gossamer. **2** downy, woolly, linty.

flugelhorn /floōgəlhawrn/ n. a valved brass wind instrument like a cornet but with a broader tone. [G Flügelhorn f. Flügel wing + Horn horn]

fluid /floōid/ n. & adj. ● n. **1** a substance, esp. a gas or liquid,

lacking definite shape and capable of flowing and yielding to the slightest pressure. **2** a fluid part or secretion. ● adj. **1** able to flow and alter shape freely. **2** constantly changing or fluctuating (the situation is fluid). **3** (of a clutch, coupling, etc.) in which liquid is used to transmit power. □ **fluid dram** see DRAM. **fluid ounce** see OUNCE[1]. □□ **fluidify** /-ídifī/ v.tr. (**-ies, -ied**). **fluidity** /-íditee/ n. **fluidly** adv. **fluidness** n. [F fluide or L fluidus f. fluere flow]

■ n. **1** liquid, solution, liquor; ichor; gas, vapor. ● adj. **1** liquid, flowing, runny, watery, aqueous. **2** changeable, variable, flexible, adjustable, unfixed, nonstatic, liquid, mercurial, mobile, unstable, shifting, uncertain, indefinite, unsettled, literary mutable.

fluidics /floōídiks/ n.pl. (usu. treated as sing.) the study and technique of using small interacting flows and fluid jets for functions usu. performed by electronic devices. □□ **fluidic** adj.

fluidize /floōidīz/ v.tr. cause (a finely divided solid) to acquire the characteristics of a fluid by the upward passage of a gas, etc. □□ **fluidization** /-dizáyshən/ n.

fluidram /floōidram/ n. a fluid dram.

fluke[1] /flook/ n. & v. ● n. **1** a lucky accident (won by a fluke). **2** a chance breeze. ● v.tr. achieve by a fluke (fluked that shot). [19th c.: perh. f. dial. fluke guess]

■ n. **1** stroke of (good) luck, lucky or successful stroke, (happy) accident, quirk or twist of fate, colloq. lucky or big break.

fluke[2] /flook/ n. **1** any parasitic flatworm of the class Digenea or Monogenea, including liver flukes and blood flukes. **2** a flatfish, esp. a flounder. [OE flōc]

fluke[3] /flook/ n. **1** Naut. a broad triangular plate on the arm of an anchor. **2** the barbed head of a lance, harpoon, etc. **3** Zool. either of the lobes of a whale's tail. [16th c.: perh. f. FLUKE[2]]

fluky /floōkee/ adj. (**flukier, flukiest**) of the nature of a fluke; obtained or occurring more by chance than skill. □□ **flukily** adv. **flukiness** n.

flume /floōm/ n. & v. ● n. **1 a** an artificial channel conveying water, etc., for industrial use. **b** a water slide into a swimming pool, etc. **2** a ravine with a stream. ● v. **1** intr. build flumes. **2** tr. convey down a flume. [ME f. OF flum, flun f. L flumen river f. fluere flow]

flummery /flúməree/ n. (pl. **-ies**) **1** empty compliments; trifles; nonsense. **2** any of various sweet dishes made with beaten eggs, sugar, etc. [Welsh llymru, of unkn. orig.]

■ **1** see NONSENSE.

flummox /flúməks/ v.tr. colloq. bewilder; confound; disconcert. [19th c.: prob. dial., imit.]

■ bewilder, confound, disconcert, confuse, baffle, perplex, throw into confusion, stump, puzzle, mystify, nonplus, fox.

flump /flump/ v. & n. ● v. (often foll. by down) **1** intr. fall or move heavily. **2** tr. set or throw down with a heavy thud. ● n. the action or sound of flumping. [imit.]

flung past and past part. of FLING.

flunk /flungk/ v. & n. colloq. ● v. **1** tr. **a** fail (an examination, etc.). **b** fail (an examination candidate). **2** intr. (often foll. by out) fail utterly; give up. ● n. an instance of flunking. □ **flunk out** be dismissed from school, etc., after failing an examination, course, etc. [cf. FUNK[1] and obs. flink be a coward]

■ v. see FAIL v. 1, 2a.

flunky /flúngkee/ n. (also **flunkey**) (pl. **-ies** or **-eys**) usu. derog. **1** a liveried servant. **2** a toady. **3** a person who does menial work. [18th c. (orig. Sc.): perh. f. FLANK with the sense 'sidesman, flanker']

■ **1** servant, lackey, footman, menial, subordinate, inferior, colloq. jackal, esp. Brit. colloq. dogsbody, derog. minion, usu. derog. hireling, underling, hist. retainer, sl.

/. . ./ **pronunciation**	● **part of speech**
□ **phrases, idioms, and compounds**	
□□ **derivatives**	■ **synonym section**
cross-references appear in SMALL CAPITALS or italics	

gofer; slave. **2** toady, hanger-on, sycophant, *colloq.* lickspittle, *derog.* lackey; see also *yes-man.*

fluoresce / floŏrés, flaw-/ *v.intr.* be or become fluorescent.

fluorescence / floŏrésəns, flaw-/ *n.* **1** the visible or invisible radiation produced from certain substances as a result of incident radiation of a shorter wavelength such as X rays, ultraviolet light, etc. **2** the property of absorbing light of short (invisible) wavelength and emitting light of longer (visible) wavelength. [FLUORSPAR (which fluoresces) after *opalescence*]

fluorescent / floŏrésənt, flaw-/ *adj.* (of a substance) having or showing fluorescence. □ **fluorescent lamp** (or **bulb**) a lamp or bulb radiating largely by fluorescence, esp. a tubular lamp in which phosphor on the inside surface of the tube is made to fluoresce by ultraviolet radiation from mercury vapor. **fluorescent screen** a screen coated with fluorescent material to show images from X rays, etc.

fluoridate / floŏridayt, fláw-/ *v.tr.* add traces of fluoride to (drinking water, etc.).

fluoridation / floŏridáyshən, fláw-/ *n.* (also **fluoridization**) the addition of traces of fluoride to drinking water in order to prevent or reduce tooth decay.

fluoride / floŏrid, fláw-/ *n.* any binary compound of fluorine.

fluorinate / floŏrinayt, fláw-/ *v.tr.* **1** = FLUORIDATE. **2** introduce fluorine into (a compound) (*fluorinated hydrocarbons*). □□ **fluorination** /-náyshən/ *n.*

fluorine / floŏreen, fláw-/ *n.* a poisonous pale yellow gaseous element of the halogen group occurring naturally in fluorite and cryolite, and the most reactive of all elements. ¶ Symb.: F. [F (as FLUORSPAR)]

fluorite / floŏrit, fláw-/ *n.* a mineral form of calcium fluoride. [It. (as FLUORSPAR)]

fluoro- / floŏrō, fláw-/ *comb. form* **1** fluorine (*fluorocarbon*). **2** fluorescence (*fluoroscope*). [FLUORINE, FLUORESCENCE]

fluorocarbon / floŏrōkáarbən, fláw-/ *n.* a compound formed by replacing one or more of the hydrogen atoms in a hydrocarbon with fluorine atoms.

fluoroscope / floŏrəskōp, fláw-/ *n.* an instrument with a fluorescent screen on which X-ray images may be viewed without taking and developing X-ray photographs.

fluorosis / floŏrósis, fláw-/ *n.* poisoning by fluorine or its compounds. [F *fluorose* (as FLUORO- 1)]

fluorspar / floŏrspaar, floŏr-/ *n.* = FLUORITE. [*fluor* a flow, any of the minerals used as fluxes, fluorspar, f. L *fluor* f. *fluere* flow + SPAR³]

flurry / flúree, flúree/ *n. & v.* ● *n.* (*pl.* -**ies**) **1** a gust or squall (esp. of snow). **2** a sudden burst of activity. **3** a commotion; excitement; nervous agitation (*a flurry of speculation; the flurry of the city*). ● *v.tr.* (-**ies**, -**ied**) confuse by haste or noise; agitate. [imit.: cf. obs. *flurr* ruffle, *hurry*]

■ *n.* **2** see STIR¹ *n.* 2. **3** commotion, to-do, fuss, upset, stir, disturbance, tumult, whirl, furor, flutter, fluster, *literary* pother; excitement, activity, agitation, ado, hustle, bustle, hurry. ● *v.* confuse, bewilder, agitate, put out, disturb, excite, fluster, disconcert, upset, perturb, unsettle, shake (up), *colloq.* rattle.

flush¹ / flush/ *v. & n.* ● *v.* **1** *intr.* **a** blush; redden (*he flushed with embarrassment*). **b** glow with a warm color (*sky flushed pink*). **2** *tr.* (usu. as **flushed** *adj.*) cause to glow, blush, or be elated (often foll. by *with*: *flushed with pride*). **3** *tr.* **a** cleanse (a drain, toilet, etc.) by a rushing flow of water. **b** (often foll. by *away, down*) dispose of (an object) in this way (*flushed away the cigarette*). **4** *intr.* rush out; spurt. **5** *tr.* flood (*the river flushed the meadow*). **6** *intr.* (of a plant) throw out fresh shoots. ● *n.* **1 a** a blush. **b** a glow of light or color. **2 a** a rush of water. **b** the cleansing of a drain, toilet, etc., by flushing. **3 a** a rush of emotion. **b** the elation produced by a victory, etc. (*the flush of triumph*). **4** sudden abundance. **5** freshness; vigor (*in the first flush of womanhood*). **6 a** (also **hot flush**) = *hot flash.* **b** a feverish temperature. **c** facial redness, esp. caused by fever, alcohol, etc. **7** a fresh growth of grass, etc. □□ **flusher** *n.* [ME, perh. = FLUSH⁴ infl. by *flash* and *blush*]

■ *v.* **1 a** blush, redden, crimson, burn, color (up); glow.
2 (**flushed**) glowing; elated, delighted, thrilled,

cheered. **3 a** rinse, flush out, wash (out *or* away), douse, hose down, flood, drench, clean out, *usu. formal* cleanse. **b** wash away, sluice away. **4** see SPURT *v.* 1a. **5** see FLOOD *v.* 1. ● *n.* **1** blush, redness, pinkness; glow, radiance, rosiness. **2 a** rush *or* gush *or* surge of water, stream, flow; flood, deluge, drenching, soaking, inundation. **3 b** elation, euphoria, thrill, excitement, delight, tingle. **5** see VIGOR 1.

flush² / flush/ *adj. & v.* ● *adj.* **1** (often foll. by *with*) in the same plane; level; even (*the sink is flush with the counter; typed the numbers flush with the margin*). **2** (usu. *predic.*) *colloq.* **a** having plenty of money. **b** (of money) abundant; plentiful. **3** full to overflowing; in flood. ● *v.tr.* **1** make (surfaces) level. **2** fill in (a joint) level with a surface. □□ **flushness** *n.* [prob. f. FLUSH¹]

■ *adj.* **1** in the same plane, level, even, square, true. **2 a** wealthy, rich, prosperous, affluent, moneyed, well-to-do, well off, *colloq.* well-heeled, on easy street, in the money, rolling (in money *or* it), *sl.* in the chips, loaded. **b** see PLENTIFUL. **3** full, brimming, brimful, overflowing, replete, in flood.

flush³ / flush/ *n.* a hand of cards all of one suit, esp. in poker. □ **royal flush** a straight flush in poker headed by an ace. **straight flush** a flush that is in numerical sequence. [OF *flus, flux* f. L *fluxus* FLUX]

flush⁴ / flush/ *v.* **1** *tr.* cause (esp. a game bird) to fly up. **2** *intr.* (of a bird) fly up and away. □ **flush out 1** reveal. **2** drive out. [ME, imit.: cf. *fly, rush*]

fluster / flústər/ *v. & n.* ● *v.* **1** *tr. & intr.* make or become nervous or confused; flurry (*was flustered by the noise; he flusters easily*). **2** *tr.* confuse with drink; half-intoxicate. **3** *intr.* bustle. ● *n.* a confused or agitated state. [ME: orig. unkn.: cf. Icel. *flaustr(a)* hurry, bustle]

■ *v.* **1** make nervous, flurry, agitate, stir up, discompose, discomfit, discomfort, disconcert, shake (up), upset, disquiet, discommode, bother, put out *or* off, disturb, perturb, flutter, *colloq.* throw (out), rattle, hassle, faze, *US joc.* discombobulate; confuse, baffle, confound, puzzle, perplex, befuddle, bewilder, distract, daze. ● *n.* agitation, upset, nervousness, discomfort, disquiet, bother, disturbance, commotion, perturbation, flurry, flutter, *colloq.* dither; confusion, bafflement, befuddlement, perplexity, bewilderment, distraction.

flute / floot/ *n. & v.* ● *n.* **1 a** a high-pitched woodwind instrument of metal or wood, having holes along it stopped by the fingers or keys, and held horizontally. **b** an organ stop having a similar sound. **c** any of various wind instruments resembling a flute. **d** a flute player. **2 a** *Archit.* an ornamental vertical groove in a column. **b** a trumpet-shaped frill on a dress, etc. **c** any similar cylindrical groove. **3** a tall narrow wineglass. ● *v.* **1** *intr.* play the flute. **2** *intr.* speak, sing, or whistle in a fluting way. **3** *tr.* make flutes or grooves in. **4** *tr.* play (a tune, etc.) on a flute. □□ **flutelike** *adj.* **fluting** *n.* **flutist** *n.* (cf. FLAUTIST). **fluty** *adj.* (in sense 1a of *n.*). [ME f. OF *flēute, flāute, flahute,* prob. f. Prov. *flāut*]

flutter / flútər/ *v. & n.* ● *v.* **1 a** *intr.* flap the wings in flying or trying to fly (*butterflies fluttered in the sunshine*). **b** *tr.* flap (the wings). **2** *intr.* fall with a quivering motion (*leaves fluttered to the ground*). **3** *intr. & tr.* move or cause to move irregularly or tremblingly (*the wind fluttered the flag*). **4** *intr.* go about restlessly; flit; hover. **5** *tr.* agitate; confuse. **6** *intr.* (of a pulse or heartbeat) beat feebly or irregularly. **7** *intr.* tremble with excitement or agitation. ● *n.* **1 a** the act of fluttering. **b** an instance of this. **2** a tremulous state of excitement; a sensation (*was in a flutter; caused a flutter with his behavior*). **3** *Brit. sl.* a small bet, esp. on a horse. **4** an abnormally rapid but regular heartbeat. **5** *Aeron.* an undesired oscillation in a part of an aircraft, etc., under stress. **6** *Mus.* a rapid movement of the tongue (as when rolling one's rs) in playing a wind instrument. **7** *Electronics* a rapid variation of pitch, esp. of recorded sound (cf. wow²). **8** a vibration. □ **flutter the dovecotes** esp. *Brit.* cause alarm among normally imperturbable people. □□ **flutterer** *n.* **fluttery** *adj.* [OE *floterian, flotorian,* frequent. form rel. to FLEET⁵]

■ *v.* **3** flap, flop, wave, oscillate. **4** flit, flicker, flitter; hover, dance about; fuss. **5** see AGITATE 1. **7** tremble, shake, quiver, jump, twitch, *dial.* dither. ● *n.* **1** fluttering, flapping, flopping, wave, waving, oscillation, oscillating, trembling, quiver, quivering. **2** flurry, stir, whirl, *literary* pother; see also SENSATION 2a. **8** see QUAVER *n.*

fluvial /flóŏveeəl/ *adj.* of, found in, or produced by a river or rivers. [ME f. L *fluvialis* f. *fluvius* river f. *fluere* flow]

fluviatile /flóŏveeətil/ *adj.* of, found, or produced by rivers. [F f. L *fluviatilis* f. *fluviatus* moistened f. *fluvius*]

fluvio- /flóŏveeō/ *comb. form* river (*fluviometer*). [L *fluvius* river f. *fluere* flow]

fluvioglacial /flóŏveeōgláyshəl/ *adj.* of or caused by streams from glacial ice, or the combined action of rivers and glaciers.

fluviometer /flóŏveeómitər/ *n.* an instrument for measuring the rise and fall of rivers.

flux /fluks/ *n. & v.* ● *n.* **1** a process of flowing or flowing out. **2** an issue or discharge. **3** continuous change (*in a state of flux*). **4** *Metallurgy* a substance mixed with a metal, etc., to promote fusion. **5** *Physics* **a** the rate of flow of any fluid across a given area. **b** the amount of fluid crossing an area in a given time. **6** *Physics* the amount of radiation or particles incident on an area in a given time. **7** *Electr.* the total electric or magnetic field passing through a surface. **8** *Med.* an abnormal discharge of blood or excrement from the body. ● *v.* **1** *tr. & intr.* make or become fluid. **2** *tr.* **a** fuse. **b** treat with a fusing flux. [ME f. OF *flux* or L *fluxus* f. *fluere* flux-flow]

■ *n.* **3** fluctuation, instability, unrest, swing, swinging, wavering, movement, motion, oscillation, mutation, modification; see also CHANGE *n.* 1.

fluxion /flúkshən/ *n.* **1** an act or instance of flux or flowing. **2** *Math.* the rate at which a variable quantity changes; a derivative. [F *fluxion* or L *fluxio* (as FLUX)]

fly[1] /flī/ *v. & n.* ● *v.* (**flies**; *past* **flew** /flōō/; *past part.* **flown** /flōn/) **1** *intr.* move through the air under control, esp. with wings. **2** (of an aircraft or its occupants): **a** *intr.* travel through the air or through space. **b** *tr.* traverse (a region or distance) (*flew the English Channel*). **3** *tr.* **a** control the flight of (esp. an aircraft). **b** transport in an aircraft. **4 a** *tr.* cause to fly or remain aloft. **b** *intr.* (of a flag, hair, etc.) wave or flutter. **5** *intr.* pass or rise quickly through the air or over an obstacle. **6** *intr.* go or move quickly; pass swiftly (*time flies*). **7** *intr.* **a** flee. **b** *colloq.* depart hastily. **8** *intr.* be driven or scattered; be forced off suddenly (*sent me flying; the door flew open*). **9** *intr.* (foll. by *at, upon*) **a** hasten or spring violently. **b** attack or criticize fiercely. **10** *tr.* flee from; escape in haste. **11** *intr. Baseball* hit a fly ball. ● *n.* (*pl.* **-ies**) **1** (*Brit.* usu. in *pl.*) **a** a flap on a garment, esp. trousers, to contain or cover a fastening. **b** this fastening. **2 a** a fabric cover pitched over a tent for extra protection from rain, etc. **b** a flap at the entrance of a tent. **3** (in *pl.*) the space over the proscenium in a theater. **4** the act or an instance of flying. **5** *Baseball* a batted ball hit high in the air. **6** (*pl.* usu. **flys**) *Brit. hist.* a one-horse hackney carriage. **7** a speed-regulating device in clockwork and machinery. □ **fly ball** = sense 5 of *n.*. **fly-by** (*pl.* **-bys**) **1** a flight past a position, esp. the approach of a spacecraft to a planet for observation. **2** = FLYOVER. **fly-by-night** *adj.* **1** unreliable. **2** short-lived. ● *n.* an unreliable person. **fly-half** *Rugby* a stand-off half. **fly high 1** pursue a high ambition. **2** excel; prosper. **fly in the face of** openly disregard or disobey; conflict roundly with (probability, the evidence, etc.). **fly into a rage** (or **temper**, etc.) become suddenly or violently angry. **fly off the handle** *colloq.* lose one's temper suddenly and unexpectedly. **fly-past** *Brit.* = FLYOVER. □□ **flyable** *adj.* [OE *flēogan* f. Gmc]

■ *v.* **1** take wing, take to the air, wing, soar. **3 a** see PILOT *v.* **b** see TRANSPORT *v.* 1. **4 b** see FLAP *v.* 1. **6** hurry, make haste, hasten, sprint, *colloq.* tear; rush (by), run (on), dash *or* race (by). **7** see FLEE 1. **10** see FLEE 2. ● *n.* **1** flap, fly front, zipper, esp. *Brit.* zip. **4** see FLIGHT[1] *n.* 1a, 5;2a. □ **fly-by-night** (*adj.*) **1** unreliable, untrustworthy, irresponsible; disreputable, shady,

dubious, questionable; dishonest, sharp, *colloq.* shifty, crooked. **2** temporary, short-lived, transitory, fugitive, ephemeral, transient, fleeting, passing, brief, impermanent. **fly high 2** see EXCEL 2. **fly in the face of** flout, defy, go against, scorn, oppose, go *or* run counter to, counter, counteract, countervail, countermine, contradict, contravene, thumb one's nose at, *sl.* cock a snook at, *literary* contemn. **fly into a rage** (or **temper**, etc.) see FLARE *v.* 3, *fly off the handle* below. **fly off the handle** fly into a rage *or* fury *or* temper *or* passion, lose one's temper, go berserk, explode, get worked up, *colloq.* have a fit *or* tantrum, go crazy, go mad, lose one's cool, blow one's top, hit *or* go through *or* raise the roof, blow one's stack, *sl.* blow a gasket, flip (one's lid).

fly[2] /flī/ *n.* (*pl.* **flies**) **1** any insect of the order Diptera with two usu. transparent wings. **2** any other winged insect, e.g., a firefly or mayfly. **3** a disease of plants or animals caused by flies. **4** a natural or artificial fly used as bait in fishing. □ **fly agaric** a poisonous fungus *Amanita Muscaria*, forming bright-red mushrooms with white flecks. **fly-fish** *v.intr.* fish with a fly. **fly in the ointment** a minor irritation that spoils enjoyment. **fly on the wall** an unnoticed observer. **fly-post** *Brit.* display (posters, etc.) rapidly in unauthorized places. **fly swatter** an implement for killing flies and other insects, usu. consisting of a flat mesh square attached to a handle. **fly-tip** *Brit.* illegally dump (waste). **fly-tipper** *Brit.* a person who engages in fly-tipping. **like flies** in large numbers (usu. of people dying in an epidemic, etc.). **no flies on** *colloq.* nothing to diminish (a person's) astuteness. [OE *flȳge, flēoge* f. WG]

■ □ **fly in the ointment** hitch, snag, impediment, obstacle, obstruction, problem, difficulty, drawback, detraction, rub, hindrance, bogey, bugaboo.

fly[3] /flī/ *adj. Brit. sl.* knowing; clever; alert. □□ **flyness** *n.* [19th c.: orig. unkn.]

flyaway /flīəway/ *adj.* (of hair, etc.) tending to fly out or up; streaming.

flyblow /flīblō/ *n.* flies' eggs contaminating food, esp. meat.

flyblown /flīblōn/ *adj.* tainted, esp. by flies.

flycatcher /flíkachər/ *n.* any bird of the families Tyrannidae and Muscicapidae, catching insects, esp. in short flights from a perch.

flyer var. of FLIER.

flying /flí-ing/ *adj. & n.* ● *adj.* **1** fluttering or waving in the air; hanging loose. **2** hasty; brief (*a flying visit*). **3** designed for rapid movement. **4** (of an animal) able to make very long leaps by using winglike membranes, etc. ● *n.* flight, esp. in an aircraft. □ **flying boat** a seaplane with a boatlike fuselage. **flying bomb** = robot bomb. **flying buttress** a buttress slanting from a separate column, usu. forming an arch with the wall it supports. **flying doctor** esp. *Austral.* a doctor (esp. in a large sparsely populated area) who visits distant patients by aircraft. **flying fish** any tropical fish of the family Exocoetidae, with winglike pectoral fins for gliding through the air. **flying fox** any of various fruit-eating bats esp. of the genus *Pteropus*, with a foxlike head. **flying lemur** either of two mammals of the genus *Cynocephalus* of S. Asia, with a lemur-like appearance and having a membrane between the fore and hind limbs for gliding from tree to tree. **flying lizard** any lizard of the genus *Draco*, having membranes on elongated ribs for gliding. **flying phalanger** any of various phalangers having a membrane between the fore and hind limbs for gliding. **flying saucer** any unidentified, esp. circular, flying object, popularly supposed to have come from space. **flying squirrel** any of various squirrels, esp. of the genera *Glaucomys Pteromys*, with skin joining the fore and hind limbs for gliding from tree to tree. **flying start 1** a start (of a race, etc.) in which the starting point is passed at

---

/.../ **pronunciation**	● **part of speech**
□ **phrases, idioms, and compounds**	
□□ **derivatives**	■ **synonym section**
cross-references appear in SMALL CAPITALS or *italics*	

full speed. **2** a vigorous start giving an initial advantage. **fly-ing wing** an aircraft with little or no fuselage and no tail assembly. **with flying colors** with distinction.
■ *n.* see FLIGHT¹ *n.* 1a, 5.

flyleaf /flílleef/ *n.* (*pl.* **-leaves**) a blank leaf at the beginning or end of a book.

flyover /flíovǝr/ *n.* **1** a ceremonial flight of aircraft past a person or a place. **2** *Brit.* a bridge carrying one road or railroad over another.

flypaper /flípaypǝr/ *n.* sticky treated paper for catching flies.

flysheet /flísheet/ *n.* **1** a tract or circular of two or four pages. **2** *Brit.* = FLY 2a.

flytrap /flítrap/ *n.* any of various plants that catch flies, esp. the Venus flytrap.

flyweight /flíwayt/ *n.* **1** a weight in certain sports intermediate between light flyweight and bantamweight. **2** a boxer, wrestler, etc., of this weight. □ **light flyweight 1** a weight in amateur boxing below flyweight. **2** an amateur boxer of this weight.

flywheel /flíhweel, -weel/ *n.* a heavy wheel on a revolving shaft used to regulate machinery or accumulate power.

FM *abbr.* **1** frequency modulation. **2** Field Marshal.

Fm *symb. Chem.* the element fermium.

fm. *abbr.* (also **fm**) fathom(s).

FNMA /fáneemáy/ *n.* Federal National Mortgage Association.

f-number /éf numbǝr/ *n.* (also **f-stop**) *Photog.* the ratio of the focal length to the effective diameter of a lens (e.g., *f*/5, indicating that the focal length is five times the diameter). [*f* (denoting focal length) + NUMBER]

FO *abbr.* **1** financial officer. **2** *hist.* (in the UK) Foreign Office.

foal /fōl/ *n. & v.* ● *n.* the young of a horse or related animal. ● *v.tr.* (of a mare, etc.) give birth to (a foal). □ **in** (or **with**) **foal** (of a mare, etc.) pregnant. [OE *fola* f. Gmc: cf. FILLY]

foam /fōm/ *n. & v.* ● *n.* **1** a mass of small bubbles formed on or in liquid by agitation, fermentation, etc. **2** a froth of saliva or sweat. **3** a substance resembling these, e.g., rubber or plastic in a cellular mass. **4** the sea. ● *v.intr.* **1** emit foam; froth. **2** run with foam. **3** (of a vessel) be filled and overflow with foam. □ **foam at the mouth** be very angry. **foam rubber** a light, spongy foam used for mattresses, pillows, cushions, etc. □□ **foamless** *adj.* **foamy** *adj.* (**foamier, foamiest**). [OE *fām* f. WG]
■ *n.* **1** froth, spume, lather; bubbles, suds; head, effervescence, carbonation, fizz. ● *v.* **1, 2** bubble, froth, spume, lather, suds. □ **foam at the mouth** see RAGE *v.*

fob¹ /fob/ *n. & v.* ● *n.* **1** (in full **fob chain**) a chain attached to a watch for carrying in a waistcoat or pocket. **2** a small pocket for carrying a watch. **3** a tab on a key ring. ● *v.tr.* (**fobbed, fobbing**) put in one's fob; pocket. [orig. cant, prob. f. G]

fob² /fob/ *v.tr.* (**fobbed, fobbing**) cheat; deceive. □ **fob off 1** (often foll. by *with* a thing) deceive into accepting something inferior. **2** (often foll. by *on to* a person) palm or pass off (an inferior thing). [16th c.: cf. obs. *fop* to dupe, G *foppen* to banter]

f.o.b. *abbr.* free on board.

focal /fōkǝl/ *adj.* of, at, or in terms of a focus. □ **focal distance** (or **length**) the distance between the center of a mirror or lens and its focus. **focal plane** the plane through the focus perpendicular to the axis of a mirror or lens. **focal point** = FOCUS *n.* 1. [mod.L *focalis* (as FOCUS)]

focalize /fōkǝlīz/ *v.tr.* = FOCUS *v.* □□ **focalization** /-lizáyshǝn/ *n.*

fo'c's'le var. of FORECASTLE.

focus /fōkǝs/ *n. & v.* ● *n.* (*pl.* **focuses** or **foci** /fōsī/) **1** *Physics* **a** the point at which rays or waves meet after reflection or refraction. **b** the point from which diverging rays or waves appear to proceed. Also called *focal point.* **2 a** *Optics* the point at which an object must be situated for an image of it given by a lens or mirror to be well defined (*bring into focus*). **b** the adjustment of the eye or a lens necessary to produce a clear image (*the binoculars were not in focus*). **c** a state of clear definition (*the photograph was out of focus*). **3** the center of interest or activity (*focus of attention*). **4** *Geom.*

one of the points from which the distances to any point of a given curve are connected by a linear relation. **5** *Med.* the principal site of an infection or other disease. **6** *Geol.* the place of origin of an earthquake. ● *v.* (**focused, focusing** or **focussed, focussing**) **1** *tr.* bring into focus. **2** *tr.* adjust the focus of (a lens, the eye, etc.). **3** *tr. & intr.* (often foll. by *on*) concentrate or be concentrated on. **4** *intr. & tr.* converge or make converge to a focus. □ **focus group** a group that meets to discuss a particular problem, issue, etc. □□ **focuser** *n.* [L, = hearth]
■ *n.* **2c** (*in focus*) clear, clear-cut, distinct, sharp, well- or sharply defined; (*out of focus*) unclear, indistinct, blurred, blurry, fuzzy. **3** center, focal point, heart, core, hub; cynosure. ● *v.* **3** concentrate, center, direct, bring to bear; be concentrated, be centered, be directed, be brought to bear; (*focus on*) zero in on, pinpoint. **4** converge, merge, meet; come *or* bring into focus.

fodder /fódǝr/ *n. & v.* ● *n.* dried hay or straw, etc., for cattle, horses, etc. ● *v.tr.* give fodder to. [OE *fōdor* f. Gmc, rel. to FOOD]
■ *n.* see FEED *n.* 1.

foe /fō/ *n.* an enemy or opponent. [OE *fāh* hostile, rel. to FEUD¹]
■ see ENEMY 1–3.

foehn /fön/ *n.* (also **föhn**) **1** a hot southerly wind on the northern slopes of the Alps. **2** a warm dry wind on the lee side of mountains. [G, ult. f. L *Favonius* mild west wind]

foetid var. of FETID.

foetus *Brit.* var. of FETUS.

fog¹ /fawg, fog/ *n. & v.* ● *n.* **1 a** a thick cloud of water droplets or smoke suspended in the atmosphere at or near the earth's surface restricting or obscuring visibility. **b** obscurity in the atmosphere caused by this. **2** *Photog.* cloudiness on a developed negative, etc., obscuring the image. **3** an uncertain or confused position or state. ● *v.* (**fogged, fogging**) **1** *tr.* **a** (often foll. by *up*) cover with fog or condensed vapor. **b** bewilder or confuse as if with a fog. **2** *intr.* (often foll. by *up*) become covered with fog or condensed vapor. **3** *tr. Photog.* make (a negative, etc.) obscure or cloudy. □ **fog bank** a mass of fog at sea or in the distance. **in a fog** puzzled; at a loss. [perh. back-form. f. FOGGY]
■ *n.* **1** mist, haze, vapor, cloud, smog, *colloq.* pea soup, *Brit. colloq.* pea-souper. **3** see DISTRACTION 4. ● *v.* **1a, 2** fog up, mist *or* over, cloud up *or* over. **1b** bewilder, confuse, obscure, cloud, becloud, muddle. □ **in a fog** see DAZE *n.*

fog² /fawg, fog/ *n. & v.* esp. *Brit.* ● *n.* **1** a second growth of grass after cutting; aftermath. **2** long grass left standing in winter. ● *v.tr.* (**fogged, fogging**) **1** leave (land) under fog. **2** feed (cattle) on fog. [ME: orig. unkn.]

fogbound /fáwgbownd, fóg-/ *adj.* unable to proceed because of fog.

fogbow /fáwgbō, fóg-/ *n.* a manifestation like a rainbow, produced by light on fog.

fogey var. of FOGY.

foggy /fáwgee, fógee/ *adj.* (**foggier, foggiest**) **1** (of the atmosphere) thick or obscure with fog. **2** of or like fog. **3** vague; confused; unclear. □ **not have the foggiest** *colloq.* have no idea at all. □□ **foggily** *adv.* **fogginess** *n.*
■ **1** see MISTY. **3** see VAGUE 1.

foghorn /fáwghawrn, fóg-/ *n.* **1** a deep-sounding instrument for warning ships in fog. **2** *colloq.* a loud penetrating voice.
■ **1** see SIREN 1.

fogy /fógee/ *n.* (also **fogey**) (*pl.* **-ies** or **-eys**) a dull old-fashioned person (esp. *old fogy*). □□ **fogydom** *n.* **fogyish** *adj.* [18th c.: rel. to sl. *fogram*, of unkn. orig.]
■ old fogy, conservative, *colloq.* fossil, stick-in-the-mud, *sl.* fuddy-duddy, back number, square.

föhn var. of FOEHN.

foible /fóybǝl/ *n.* **1** a minor weakness or idiosyncrasy. **2** *Fencing* the part of a sword blade from the middle to the point. [F, obs. form of *faible* (as FEEBLE)]
■ **1** weakness, imperfection, weak point, fault, frailty, shortcoming, flaw, defect, failing, blemish, infirmity;

idiosyncrasy, peculiarity, quirk, crotchet, eccentricity, kink.

foie gras /fwaa graá/ *n. colloq.* = pâté de foie gras.

foil[1] /foyl/ *v. & n.* ● *v.tr.* **1** frustrate; baffle; defeat. **2** *Hunting* a run over or cross (ground or a scent) to confuse the hounds. **b** (*absol.*) (of an animal) spoil the scent in this way. ● *n.* **1** *Hunting* the track of a hunted animal. **2** *archaic* a repulse or defeat. [ME, = trample down, perh. f. OF *fouler* to full cloth, trample, ult. f. L *fullo* FULLER[1]]
■ *v.* **1** frustrate, outwit, baffle, defeat, thwart, offset, balk, check, impede, hamper, discomfit, circumvent, *Brit.* put a spoke in a person's wheel.

foil[2] /foyl/ *n.* **1 a** metal hammered or rolled into a thin sheet (*tin foil*). **b** a sheet of this or another material attached to mirror glass as a reflector. **c** a leaf of foil placed under a precious stone, etc., to brighten or color it. **2** a person or thing that enhances the qualities of another by contrast. **3** *Archit.* a leaf-shaped curve formed by the cusping of an arch or circle. [ME f. OF f. L *folium* leaf, and f. OF *foille* f. L *folia* (pl.)]

foil[3] /foyl/ *n.* a light blunt-edged sword with a button on its point used in fencing. [16th c.: orig. unkn.]

foil[4] /foyl/ *n.* = HYDROFOIL. [abbr.]

foist /foyst/ *v.tr.* **1** (foll. by *on, upon*) impose (an unwelcome person or thing). **2** (foll. by *on, upon*) falsely fix the authorship of (a composition). **3** (foll. by *in, into*) introduce surreptitiously or unwarrantably. [orig. of palming a false die, f. Du. dial. *vuisten* take in the hand f. *vuist* FIST]
■ **1** impose, thrust, force, press, *often joc.* inflict; (*foist on* or *upon*) saddle *or* lumber a person with.

fol. *abbr.* folio.

folacin /fốləsin/ *n.* = FOLIC ACID. [*folic acid* + -IN]

fold[1] /fōld/ *v. & n.* ● *v.* **1** *tr.* **a** bend or close (a flexible thing) over upon itself. **b** (foll. by *back, over, down*) bend a part of (a flexible thing) in the manner specified (*fold down the flap*). **2** *intr.* become or be able to be folded. **3** (foll. by *away, up*) make compact by folding. **4** *intr. colloq.* **a** collapse; disintegrate. **b** (of an enterprise) fail; go bankrupt. **5** *tr. poet.* embrace (esp. *fold in the arms* or *to the breast*). **6** *tr.* (foll. by *about, around*) clasp (the arms); wrap; envelop. **7** *tr.* (foll. by *in*) mix (an ingredient with others) using a gentle cutting and turning motion. ● *n.* **1** the act or an instance of folding. **2** a line made by or for folding. **3** a folded part. **4** esp. *Brit.* a hollow among hills. **5** *Geol.* a curvature of strata. □ **fold one's arms** place one's arms across the chest, side by side or entwined. **fold one's hands** clasp them. **folding door** a door with jointed sections, folding on itself when opened. **folding money** *colloq.* paper money. □□ **foldable** *adj.* [OE *falden, fealden* f. Gmc]
■ *v.* **1** bend, double (over *or* up), crease, pleat, gather, crimp. **4 a** see GIVE WAY 3 (WAY). **b** fail, go out of business, go bankrupt, go under, go to the wall, close down, shut down, *colloq.* go broke, go bust. **5, 6** embrace, hug; clasp, gather, wrap, enfold, enclose, envelop, *literary* enwrap. ● *n.* **3** crease, pleat, gather, crimp.

fold[2] /fōld/ *n. & v.* ● *n.* **1** = SHEEPFOLD. **2** a body of believers or members of a church. ● *v.tr.* enclose (sheep) in a fold. [OE *fald*]

-fold /fōld/ *suffix* forming adjectives and adverbs from cardinal numbers, meaning: **1** in an amount multiplied by (*repaid tenfold*). **2** consisting of so many parts (*threefold blessing*). [OE *-fald, -feald*, rel. to FOLD[1]: orig. sense 'folded in so many layers']

foldaway /fốldəway/ *adj.* adapted or designed to be folded away.

folder /fốldər/ *n.* **1** a folding cover or holder for loose papers. **2** a folded leaflet.
■ **1** see FILE[1] *n.* 1. **2** see LEAFLET *n.*

folderol var. of FALDERAL.

foldout /fốldowt/ *n.* an oversize page in a book, etc., to be unfolded by the reader.

foliaceous /fốlee-áyshəs/ *adj.* **1** of or like leaves. **2** having organs like leaves. **3** laminated. [L *foliaceus* leafy f. *folium* leaf]

foliage /fốleeij/ *n.* **1** leaves; leafage. **2** a design in art resembling leaves. □ **foliage leaf** a leaf excluding petals and other modified leaves. [ME f. F *feuillage* f. *feuille* leaf f. OF *foille*: see FOIL[2]]

foliar /fốleeər/ *adj.* of or relating to leaves. □ **foliar feed** feed supplied to leaves of plants. [mod.L *foliaris* f. L *folium* leaf]

foliate *adj. & v.* ● *adj.* /fốleeət/ **1** leaflike. **2** having leaves. **3** (in *comb.*) having a specified number of leaflets (*trifoliate*). ● *v.* /fốleeayt/ **1** *intr.* split into laminae. **2** *tr.* decorate with foils. **3** *tr.* number leaves (not pages) of (a volume) consecutively. □□ **foliation** /-áyshən/ *n.* [L *foliatus* leaved f. *folium* leaf]

folic acid /fốlik, fól-/ *n.* a vitamin of the B complex, found in leafy green vegetables, liver, and kidney, a deficiency of which causes pernicious anemia. Also called FOLACIN or PTEROYLGLUTAMIC ACID. [L *folium* leaf (because found esp. in green leaves) + -IC]

folio /fốleeō/ *n. & adj.* ● *n.* (*pl.* **-os**) **1** a leaf of paper, etc., esp. one numbered only on the front. **2 a** a leaf number of a book. **b** a page number of a book. **3** a sheet of paper folded once making two leaves of a book. **4** a book made of such sheets. ● *adj.* (of a book) made of folios, of the largest size. □ **in folio** made of folios. [L, ablat. of *folium* leaf, = *on leaf* (as specified)]
■ *n.* **1, 3** page, leaf, sheet.

foliole /fốleeōl/ *n.* a division of a compound leaf; a leaflet. [F f. LL *foliolum* dimin. of L *folium* leaf]

folk /fōk/ *n.* (*pl.* **folk** or **folks**) **1** (treated as *pl.*) people in general or of a specified class (*few folks about*; *townsfolk*). **2** (in *pl.*) (usu. **folks**) one's parents or relatives. **3** (treated as *sing.*) a people. **4** (treated as *sing.*) *colloq.* traditional music, esp. a style featuring acoustic guitar. **5** (*attrib.*) of popular origin; traditional (*folk art*). □ **folk dance 1** a dance of traditional origin. **2** the music for such a dance. **folk etymology** a popular modifying of the form of a word or phrase to make it seem to be derived from a more familiar word (e.g., *woodchuck* from Algonquian *otchek*). **folk memory** recollection of the past persisting among a people. **folk music** = sense 4 of *n.* **folk singer** a singer of folk songs. **folk song** a song of popular or traditional origin or style. **folk tale** a popular or traditional story. [OE *folc* f. Gmc]
■ **1** people, society, the nation, the (general) public, the populace, the population, the citizenry. **2** (*folks*) parents; relatives; see also FAMILY 1. **3** people, tribe, (ethnic) group, clan, race.

folkish /fốkish/ *adj.* of the common people; traditional; unsophisticated.

folklore /fốklawr/ *n.* the traditional beliefs and stories of a people; the study of these. □□ **folkloric** *adj.* **folklorist** *n.* **folkloristic** *adj.*
■ see LORE[1].

folksy /fốksee/ *adj.* (**folksier, folksiest**) **1** friendly; sociable; informal. **2 a** having the characteristics of folk art, culture, etc. **b** ostensibly or artificially folkish. □□ **folksiness** *n.*
■ **1** see INFORMAL.

folkways /fốkwayz/ *n.pl.* the traditional behavior of a people.

folky /fốkee/ *adj.* (**folkier, folkiest**) **1** = FOLKSY 2. **2** = FOLKISH. □□ **folkiness** *n.*

follicle /fốlikəl/ *n.* **1** a small sac or vesicle. **2** a small sacshaped secretory gland or cavity. **3** *Bot.* a single-carpelled dry fruit opening on one side only to release its seeds. □□ **follicular** /fólíkyələr/ *adj.* **folliculate** /fólíkyələt, -layt/ *adj.* **folliculated** /-laytid/ *adj.* [L *folliculus* dimin. of *follis* bellows]

follow /fốlō/ *v.* **1** *tr.* or (foll. by *after*) *intr.* go or come after (a person or thing proceeding ahead). **2** *tr.* go along (a route, path, etc.). **3** *tr. & intr.* come after in order or time (*Clinton followed Bush*; *dessert followed*; *my reasons are as follows*). **4** *tr.* take as a guide or leader. **5** *tr.* conform to (*follow your ex-*

ample). **6** *tr.* practice (a trade or profession). **7** *tr.* undertake (a course of study, etc.). **8** *tr.* understand the meaning or tendency of (a speaker or argument). **9** *tr.* maintain awareness of the current state or progress of (events, etc., in a particular sphere). **10** *tr.* (foll. by *with*) provide with a sequel or successor. **11** *intr.* happen after something else; ensue. **12** *intr.* **a** be necessarily true as a result of something else. **b** (foll. by *from*) be a result of. **13** *tr.* strive after; aim at; pursue (*followed fame and fortune*). □ **follow-my-leader** (also **follow the leader**) a game in which players must do as the leader does. **follow one's nose** trust to instinct. **follow on 1** continue. **2** (of a cricket team) have to bat again immediately after the first innings. **follow-on** *n.* an instance of this. **follow out** carry out; adhere precisely to (instructions, etc.). **follow suit 1** *Cards* play a card of the suit led. **2** conform to another person's actions. **follow through 1** continue (an action, etc.) to its conclusion. **2** *Sports* continue the movement of a stroke after the ball has been struck. **follow-through** *n.* the action of following through. **follow up 1** (foll. by *with*) pursue; develop; supplement. **2** make further investigation of. **follow-up** *n.* a subsequent or continued action, measure, experience, etc. [OE *folgian* f. Gmc]

■ **1** go *or* come after, go *or* walk *or* tread *or* move behind; string *or* tag along (with), go along (with); go *or* come next. **2** trace, keep to, pursue, continue *or* proceed along. **3** come after, succeed, supersede, take the place of, replace, supplant. **5** conform to, adhere to, comply with, obey, be guided by, be modeled after *or* on, observe, heed, mind, go along with, reflect, mirror, echo, imitate, *literary* cleave to. **6** see PURSUE 2, 9. **7** see UNDERTAKE 1. **8** understand, fathom, comprehend, grasp, see, appreciate, take in, catch, keep up with, *colloq.* get, *sl.* dig. **9** keep up with, keep abreast of, take an interest in, be a fan *or* aficionado of, pursue, watch. **11** ensue, arise, develop; see also RESULT *v.* 1. **12 b** (*follow from*) be a result *or* consequence of, result *or* develop from, issue *or* flow from. **13** see AIM *v.* 1, 4. □ **follow through 1** persist *or* persevere with, continue, conclude, realize, consummate, pursue, carry out, see through, make good, fulfill, effect, discharge. **follow-through** see EXECUTION 2. **follow up 1** pursue, develop, supplement, reinforce, consolidate, support, buttress, bolster, augment. **2** pursue, investigate, check (out), check up, inquire about, make inquiries into *or* about, look into, track down. **follow-up** reinforcement, support, backup, consolidation.

follower /fólōər/ *n.* **1** an adherent or devotee. **2** a person or thing that follows.

■ **1** adherent, disciple, student, pupil, protégé(e); devotee, supporter, fan, aficionado, enthusiast, advocate, champion, *sl.* groupie, rooter.

following /fólōing/ *prep., n.,* & *adj.* ● *prep.* coming after in time; as a sequel to. ● *n.* a body of adherents or devotees. ● *adj.* that follows or comes after.

■ *prep.* see SUBSEQUENT. ● *n.* see RETINUE. ● *adj.* see ATTENDANT *adj.* 1.

folly /fólee/ *n.* (*pl.* **-ies**) **1** foolishness; lack of good sense. **2** a foolish act, behavior, idea, etc. **3** an ornamental building, usu. a tower or mock Gothic ruin. **4** (in *pl.*) *Theatr.* **a** a revue with glamorous female performers, esp. scantily clad. **b** the performers. [ME f. OF *folie* f. *fol* mad, FOOL¹]

■ **1** foolishness, nonsense, absurdity, silliness, preposterousness, absurdness, senselessness, fatuousness, fatuity, stupidity, asininity, inanity, idiocy, imbecility, lunacy, insanity, madness, craziness, eccentricity, weak-mindedness, feeblemindedness, simplemindedness, muddleheadedness, thickheadedness, obtuseness, brainlessness, *colloq.* dopiness, dumbness, esp. *Brit. colloq.* daftness, *sl.* nuttiness, kookiness. **2** absurdity, brainstorm, blunder, faux pas, gaffe, *sl.* goof.

foment /fōmént/ *v.tr.* **1** instigate or stir up (trouble, sedition, etc.). **2 a** bathe with warm or medicated liquid. **b** apply warmth to. □□ **fomenter** *n.* [ME f. F *fomenter* f. LL *fomentare* f. L *fomentum* poultice, lotion f. *fovère* heat, cherish]

■ **1** instigate, stir *or* whip up, provoke, incite, initiate, prompt, start, inspire, work up, inflame, fan the flames of, kindle, galvanize, rally, excite, stimulate, encourage, promote, foster, cultivate, sow the seed *or* seeds of.

fomentation /fṓmentáyshən/ *n.* **1** the act or an instance of fomenting. **2** materials prepared for application to a wound, etc. [ME f. OF or LL *fomentatio* (as FOMENT)]

fond /fond/ *adj.* **1** (foll. by *of*) having affection or a liking for. **2** affectionate; loving; doting. **3** (of beliefs, etc.) foolishly optimistic or credulous; naive. □□ **fondly** *adv.* **fondness** *n.* [ME f. obs. *fon* fool, be foolish]

■ **1** (*fond of*) partial to, having affection *or* a liking for, affectionate toward, attached to, having a taste for, predisposed to *or* toward, inclined to *or* toward. **2** tender, loving, doting, affectionate, warm, adoring, caring. **3** foolish, credulous; see also NAÏVE. □□ **fondly** affectionately, lovingly, tenderly, warmly, adoringly, caressingly; foolishly, credulously, naively.

fondant /fóndənt/ *n.* a soft creamy candy of flavored sugar. [F, pres. part. of *fondre* melt f. L *fundere* pour]

fondle /fónd'l/ *v.tr.* touch or stroke lovingly; caress. □□ **fondler** *n.* [back-form. f. *fondling* fondled person (as FOND, -LING¹)]

■ caress, stroke, pet, pat, touch, feel, cuddle.

fondue /fóndŌō, -dyŌō/ *n.* **1** a dish of flavored melted cheese. **2** a dish of small pieces of food cooked at the table by dipping in hot melted chocolate, cheese, etc. [F, fem. past part. of *fondre* melt f. L *fundere* pour]

font¹ /font/ *n.* **1** a receptacle in a church for baptismal water. **2** the reservoir for oil in a lamp. □□ **fontal** *adj.* (in sense 1). [OE *font, fant* f. OIr. *fant, font* f. L *fons fontis* fountain, baptismal water]

font² /font/ *Printing* a set of type of one face or size. [F *fonte* f. *fondre* FOUND³]

fontanel /fóntənél/ *n.* (esp. *Brit.* **fontanelle**) a membranous space in an infant's skull at the angles of the parietal bones. [F *fontanelle* f. mod.L *fontanella* f. OF *fontenelle* dimin. of *fontaine* fountain]

food /fŌōd/ *n.* **1** a nutritious substance, esp. solid in form, that can be taken into an animal or a plant to maintain life and growth. **2** ideas as a resource for or stimulus to mental work (*food for thought*). □ **food additive** a substance added to food to enhance its color, flavor, or presentation, or for any other nonnutritional purpose. **food chain** *Ecol.* a series of organisms each dependent on the next for food. **food poisoning** illness due to bacteria or other toxins in food. **food processor** a machine for chopping and mixing food materials. **food pyramid 1** an ecological model of the food chain, with green plants at the base and predators at the apex. **2** a dietary model of recommended foods, with carbohydrates at the base and fats and sugars at the apex. [OE *fōda* f. Gmc: cf. FEED]

■ **1** nourishment, nutriment, sustenance, *formal* aliment; foodstuffs, edibles, eatables, bread, victuals, provisions, *Brit.* commons, *colloq.* grub, eats, scoff, *Brit. colloq.* tuck, *formal* viands, *formal or joc.* comestibles, *sl.* chow. **2** ideas, stimuli; inspiration, stimulation.

foodie /fŌōdee/ *n.* (also **foody**) (*pl.* **-ies**) *colloq.* a person who is particular about food; a gourmet.

foodstuff /fŌōdstuf/ *n.* any substance suitable as food.

fool¹ /fŌōl/ *n., v.,* & *adj.* ● *n.* **1** a person who acts unwisely or imprudently; a stupid person. **2** *hist.* a jester; a clown. **3** a dupe. **4** (often foll. by *for*) a devotee or fan (*a fool for the ballet*). ● *v.* **1** *tr.* deceive so as to cause to appear foolish. **2** *tr.* (foll. by *into* + verbal noun, or *out of*) trick; cause to do something foolish. **3** *tr.* play tricks on; dupe. **4** *intr.* act in a joking, frivolous, or teasing way. **5** *intr.* (foll. by *around*) behave in a playful or silly way. ● *adj. colloq.* foolish; silly. □ **act** (or **play**) **the fool** behave in a silly way. **fool's errand** a fruitless venture. **fool's gold** iron pyrites. **fool's paradise** happiness founded on an illusion. **fool's parsley** a species of hemlock resembling parsley. **make a fool of** make (a person or oneself) look foolish; trick or deceive. **no** (or **nobody's**) **fool** a shrewd or prudent person. [ME f. OF *fol* f. L *follis* bellows, empty-headed person]

■ *n.* **1** simpleton, ninny, nincompoop, ass, jackass, dunce, dolt, halfwit, numskull, greenhorn, oaf, blockhead, featherbrain, booby, mooncalf, pigeon, retardate, *colloq.* pinhead, silly, loon, goose, idiot, dimwit, nitwit, birdbrain, imbecile, moron, chump, fathead, chucklehead, knucklehead, *sl.* bonehead, goon, clod, clodpoll, jerk, dumbbell, twerp, sap, dope, *Austral. sl.* alec, esp. *Brit. sl.* twit, buffer, nit, mug. **2** (court) jester, clown, comic, comedian, comedienne, entertainer, zany, buffoon, merry andrew, farceur, joker, Punch, Punchinello, pierrot, harlequin, *archaic* droll. **3** butt, dupe, gull, victim, cat's-paw, *colloq.* stooge, *sl.* mark, fall guy, pigeon, sucker, *Brit. sl.* mug. ● *v.* **1, 3** trick, deceive, take in, hoax, hoodwink, bluff, dupe, gull, humbug, make a fool of, pull the wool over a person's eyes, pull a person's leg, tease, *colloq.* have on, kid, bamboozle, pull a fast one on, *sl.* josh, do a snow job on, snow. **2** trick, gull, dupe, delude, mislead, *colloq.* kid, *literary* cozen, *sl.* con. **4** joke, jest, banter, tease, *colloq.* kid. **5** (*fool around* or *about*) play around *or* about, mess around *or* about, gambol, frolic, romp, *colloq.* footle (about), *sl.* cavort. □ **act** (or **play**) **the fool** see FOOL¹ *v.* 4, 5 above. **make a fool of** see FOOL¹ *v.* 1, 3 above.

fool² /fool/ *n.* esp. *Brit.* a dessert of usu. stewed fruit crushed and mixed with cream, custard, etc. [16th c.: perh. f. FOOL¹]

foolery /foolaree/ *n.* (*pl.* **-ies**) **1** foolish behavior. **2** a foolish act.

foolhardy /foolhaardee/ *adj.* (**foolhardier, foolhardiest**) rashly or foolishly bold; reckless. □□ **foolhardily** *adv.* **foolhardiness** *n.* [ME f. OF *folhardi* f. *fol* foolish + *hardi* bold]

■ rash, imprudent, impetuous, reckless, brash, venturesome, bold, daring, audacious, adventurous, daredevil, incautious, hotheaded, careless, heedless, devil-may-care, hasty, thoughtless, unthinking, irresponsible, wild, madcap, nervy, *colloq.* gutsy, *literary* temerarious.

foolish /foolish/ *adj.* (of a person, action, etc.) lacking good sense or judgment; unwise; □□ **foolishly** *adv.* **foolishness** *n.*

■ senseless, incautious, imprudent, impolitic, indiscreet, unwise, absurd, preposterous, ridiculous, ludicrous, injudicious, ill-considered, ill-advised, misguided, shortsighted, impetuous, headlong, rash, brash, reckless, heedless, unwary, foolhardy, nonsensical, stupid, asinine, inane, silly, fatuous, obtuse, scatterbrained, featherbrained, harebrained, demented, irrational, simpleminded, light-headed, muddleheaded, bemused, feebleminded, halfwitted, slow-witted, witless, brainless, empty-headed, blockheaded, *colloq.* dimwitted, dopey, crazy, mad, insane, crackbrained, birdbrained, confused, moronic, idiotic, imbecilic, thickheaded, dotty, dim, thick, *colloq.* dumb, esp. *Brit. colloq.* daft, *sl.* boneheaded, balmy, nuts, nutty, dippy, goofy, screwy, wacky, cuckoo, batty, loony, *Brit. sl.* barmy, potty.

foolproof /foolproof/ *adj.* (of a procedure, mechanism, etc.) so straightforward or simple as to be incapable of misuse or mistake.

■ safe, certain, sure, trustworthy, dependable, reliable, infallible, unfailing, guaranteed, *colloq.* surefire.

foolscap /foolskap/ *n. Brit.* a size of paper, about 330 x 200 (or 400) mm. [named from the former watermark representing a fool's cap]

foot /foot/ *n. & v.* ● *n.* (*pl.* **feet** /feet/) **1 a** the lower extremity of the leg below the ankle. **b** the part of a sock, etc., covering the foot. **2 a** the lower or lowest part of anything, e.g., a mountain, a page, stairs, etc. **b** the lower end of a table. **c** the end of a bed where the user's feet normally rest. **3** the base, often projecting, of anything extending vertically. **4** a step, pace, or tread; a manner of walking (*fleet of foot*). **5** (*pl.* **feet** or **foot**) a unit of linear measure equal to 12 inches (30.48 cm). **6** *Prosody* a group of syllables (one usu. stressed) constituting a metrical unit. **b** a similar unit of speech, etc. **7** *Brit. hist.* infantry (*a regiment of foot*). **8** *Zool.*

the locomotive or adhesive organ of invertebrates. **9** *Bot.* the part by which a petal is attached. **10** a device on a sewing machine for holding the material steady as it is sewn. **11** (*pl.* **foots**) dregs; oil refuse. **12** (usu. in *pl.*) footlights. ● *v.tr.* **1** (usu. as **foot it**) **a** traverse (esp. a long distance) by foot. **b** dance. **2** pay (a bill, esp. one considered large). □ **at a person's feet** as a person's disciple or subject. **feet of clay** a fundamental weakness in a person otherwise revered. **foot-and-mouth disease** a contagious viral disease of cattle, etc. **foot fault** (in tennis) incorrect placement of the feet while serving. **foot-pound** the amount of energy required to raise 1 lb. a distance of 1 foot. **foot-pound-second system** a system of measurement with these as basic units. **foot rot** a bacterial disease of the feet in sheep and cattle. **foot soldier** a soldier who fights on foot. **get one's feet wet** begin to participate. **have one's** (or **both**) **feet on the ground** be practical. **have a foot in the door** have a prospect of success. **have one foot in the grave** be near death or very old. **my foot!** *int.* expressing strong contradiction. **not put a foot wrong** make no mistakes. **off one's feet** so as to be unable to stand, or in a state compared with this (*was rushed off my feet*). **on foot** walking; not riding, etc. **on one's feet** standing or walking. **put one's best foot forward** make every effort; proceed with determination. **put one's feet up** *colloq.* take a rest. **put one's foot down** *colloq.* **1** be firmly insistent or repressive. **2** accelerate a motor vehicle. **put one's foot in it** *colloq.* commit a blunder or indiscretion. **set foot in** (or **on**) enter; go into. □□ **footed** *adj.* (also in *comb.*). **footless** *adj.* [OE *fōt* f. Gmc]

footage /footij/ *n.* **1** length or distance in feet. **2** an amount of film made for showing, broadcasting, etc.

■ **1** see DISTANCE *n.* 2.

football /footbawl/ *n. & v.* ● *n.* **1** any of several outdoor games between two teams played with a ball on a field with goals at each end. ¶ In N. America generally American football is referred to, elsewhere usu. soccer or rugby is meant. **2** a large inflated ball of a kind used in these. **3** a topical issue or problem that is the subject of continued argument or controversy. ● *v.intr.* play football. □ **football pool** a form of gambling on the results of football games, the winners receiving sums accumulated from entry money. □□ **footballer** *n.*

footboard /footbawrd/ *n.* **1** a board to support the feet or a foot. **2** an upright board at the foot of a bed.

footbrake /footbrayk/ *n.* a brake operated by the foot in a motor vehicle.

footbridge /footbrij/ *n.* a bridge for use by pedestrians.

footer¹ /footər/ *n.* (in *comb.*) a person or thing of so many feet in length or height (*six-footer*).

footer² /footər/ *n. Brit. colloq.* = FOOTBALL 1.

footfall /footfawl/ *n.* the sound of a footstep.

■ step, footstep, tread.

foothill /foot-hil/ *n.* (often in *pl.*) any of the low hills around the base of a mountain.

■ see HILL *n.* 1.

foothold /foot-hōld/ *n.* **1** a place, esp. in climbing, where a foot can be supported securely. **2** a secure initial position or advantage.

■ **1** footing, toehold. **2** see OPENING *n.* 2.

footing /footing/ *n.* **1** a foothold; a secure position (*lost his footing*). **2** the basis on which an enterprise is established or operates; the position or status of a person in relation to others (*on an equal footing*). **3** the foundation of a wall, usu. with a course of brickwork wider than the base of the wall.

■ **1** foothold, toehold. **2** foundation, basis, base; level, position, state, rank; terms.

footle /foot'l/ *v.intr.* (usu. foll. by *around, about*) *colloq.* behave foolishly or trivially. [19th c.: perh. f. dial. *footer* idle]

/. . ./ **pronunciation**	● **part of speech**
□ **phrases, idioms, and compounds**	
□□ **derivatives**	■ **synonym section**
cross-references appear in SMALL CAPITALS or *italics*	

footlights /fŏŏtlīts/ *n.pl.* a row of lights along the front of a stage at the level of the actors' feet.

footling /fŏŏtling/ *adj. colloq.* trivial; silly.

footlocker /fŏŏlokər/ *n.* a small trunk usu. kept at the foot of a soldier's or camper's bunk to hold items of clothing or equipment.

footloose /fŏŏtlōōs/ *adj.* free to go where or act as one pleases.

footman /fŏŏtmən/ *n.* (*pl.* **-men**) **1** a liveried servant attending at the door, at table, or on a carriage. **2** *hist.* an infantryman.

■ **1** see SERVANT 1.

footmark /fŏŏtmaark/ *n.* a footprint.

footnote /fŏŏtnōt/ *n. & v.* ● *n.* a note printed at the foot of a page. ● *v.tr.* supply with a footnote or footnotes.

■ *n.* see NOTE *n.* 2, 5.

footpad /fŏŏtpad/ *n. hist.* an unmounted highwayman.

■ see THIEF.

footpath /fŏŏtpath/ *n.* **1** a trail or path for pedestrians (in the woods, etc.). **2** *Brit.* a path for pedestrians; a pavement.

■ see PATH 1.

footplate /fŏŏtplayt/ *n.* esp. *Brit.* the platform in the cab of a locomotive for the crew.

footprint /fŏŏtprint/ *n.* **1** the impression left by a foot or shoe. **2** *Computing* the area of desk space, etc., occupied by a computer or other piece of hardware. **3** the ground area covered by a communications satellite or affected by noise, etc., from aircraft.

■ **1** see STEP *n.* 6.

footrace /fŏŏtrays/ *n.* a race run by people on foot.

footrest /fŏŏtrest/ *n.* a support for the feet or a foot.

footsie /fŏŏtsee/ *n. colloq.* amorous play with the feet. [joc. dimin. of FOOT]

footslog /fŏŏtslog/ *v. & n. Brit.* ● *v.intr.* (**-slogged, -slogging**) walk or march, esp. laboriously for a long distance. ● *n.* a laborious walk or march. □□ **footslogger** *n.*

footsore /fŏŏtsawr/ *adj.* having sore feet, esp. from walking.

footstalk /fŏŏtstawk/ *n.* **1** *Bot.* a stalk of a leaf or peduncle of a flower. **2** *Zool.* an attachment of a barnacle, etc.

footstep /fŏŏtstep/ *n.* **1** a step taken in walking. **2** the sound of this. □ **follow** (or **tread**) **in a person's footsteps** do as another person did before.

■ **1** step, tread, pace, stride. **2** footfall, step, tread.

□ **follow** (or **tread**) **in a person's footsteps** follow a person's example *or* way of life *or* tradition.

footstool /fŏŏtstōōl/ *n.* a stool for resting the feet on when sitting.

footway /fŏŏtway/ *n. Brit.* a path or way for pedestrians.

footwear /fŏŏtwair/ *n.* shoes, socks, etc.

footwork /fŏŏtwərk/ *n.* the use of the feet, esp. skillfully, in sports, dancing, etc.

fop /fop/ *n.* an affectedly elegant or fashionable man; a dandy. □□ **foppery** *n.* **foppish** *adj.* **foppishly** *adv.* **foppishness** *n.* [17th c.: perh. f. earlier *fop* fool]

■ see DANDY *n.*

for /fawr, fər/ *prep. & conj.* ● *prep.* **1** in the interest or to the benefit of; intended to go to (*these flowers are for you; wish to see it for myself; did it all for my country; silly for you to go*). **2** in defense, support, or favor of (*fight for one's rights*). **3** suitable or appropriate for (*a dance for beginners; not for me to say*). **4** in respect of or with reference to; regarding; so far as concerns (*usual for ties to be worn; don't care for him at all; ready for bed*). **5** representing or in place of (*here for my uncle*). **6** in exchange against (*swapped it for a bigger one*). **7 a** as the price of (*give me $5 for it*). **b** at the price of (*bought it for $5*). **c** to the amount of (*a bill for $100*). **8** as the penalty of (*fined them heavily for it*). **9** in requital of (*that's for upsetting my sister*). **10** as a reward for (*here's $5 for your trouble*). **11 a** with a view to; in the hope or quest of; in order to get (*go for a walk; run for a doctor; did it for the money*). **b** on account of (*could not speak for laughing*). **12** corresponding to (*word for word*). **13** to reach; in the direction of; toward (*left for Rome; ran for the end of the road*). **14** conducive or conducively to; in order to achieve (*take the pills for a sound night's sleep*). **15** starting at (a specified time) (*we set the meet-*

ing for eight). **16** through or over (a distance or period); during (*walked for miles; sang for two hours*). **17** in the character of; as being (*for the last time; know it for a lie; I for one refuse*). **18** because of; on account of (*could not see for tears*). **19** in spite of; notwithstanding (*for all we know; for all your fine words*). **20** considering or making due allowance in respect of (*good for a beginner*). **21** in order to be (*gone for a soldier*). ● *conj.* because; since; seeing that. □ **be for it** *Brit. colloq.* be in imminent danger of punishment or other trouble. **for ever** see EVER; (cf. FOREVER). **o** (or **oh**) **for** I wish I had. [OE, prob. a reduction of Gmc *fora* (unrecorded) BEFORE (of place and time)]

■ *prep.* **1** in the interest of, to the benefit of, for the sake of, on *or* in behalf of. **2** in defense *or* support *or* favor of, on the side of, pro, in the service of, as a service to, on *or* in behalf of. **3** suitable *or* appropriate for, suited to, fit *or* fitting for, proper for; for the treatment of, as a remedy for, against. **4** in respect of, regarding, in *or* with regard to, as regards, respecting, concerning, as far as (a person) is concerned, (so far) as concerns, with reference to. **5** instead of, in place of, representing, as a replacement for, on *or* in behalf of. **9, 10** in return *or* exchange for, in compensation *or* recompense *or* payment *or* repayment for, in requital of, as a reward for, as recompense for. **11 a** in search *or* quest *or* pursuit of, in the hope of, seeking, looking for *or* after, after, with a view *or* an eye to. **b** because of, on account of, by reason of, owing to. **13** in the direction of, to, toward, into; to go to, bound *or* destined for. **14** conducive *or* conducively to, for the purpose of, with the object of, in the interest of, for the sake of. **16** for the duration of, through, over, during, in the course of, throughout. **19** despite, in spite of, notwithstanding, allowing for. ● *conj.* because, since, as, inasmuch as, seeing that, owing to the fact that, *disp.* due to the fact that, *archaic* forasmuch as.

f.o.r. *abbr.* free on rail.

for- /fawr, fər/ *prefix* forming verbs and their derivatives meaning: **1** away; off; apart (*forget; forgive*). **2** prohibition (*forbid*). **3** abstention or neglect (*forgo; forsake*). **4** excess or intensity (*forlorn*). [OE *for-, fær-*]

forage /fáwrij, fór-/ *n. & v.* ● *n.* **1** food for horses and cattle. **2** the act or an instance of searching for food. ● *v.* **1** *intr.* go searching; rummage (esp. for food). **2** *tr.* obtain food from; plunder. **3** *tr.* **a** get by foraging. **b** supply with food. □ **forage cap** an infantry undress cap. □□ **forager** *n.* [ME f. OF *fourrage, fourrager*, rel. to FODDER]

■ *n.* **1** see FEED *n.* 1. ● *v.* **1** see LOOK *v.* 2a, 3a.

foramen /fəráymen/ *n.* (*pl.* **foramina** /-rámina/) *Anat.* an opening, hole, or passage, esp. in a bone. □□ **foraminate** /-rámmət/ *adj.* [L *foramen -minis* f. *forare* bore a hole]

foraminifer /fáwrəmínifər, fór-/ *n.* (also **foraminiferan** /-fərən/) any protozoan of the order Foraminifera, having a perforated shell through which pseudopodia emerge. □□ **foraminiferous** /-nífərəs/ *adj.*

foraminiferan var. of FORAMINIFER.

forasmuch as /fáwrəzmúch/ *conj. archaic* because; since. [= for as much]

foray /fáwray, fór-/ *n. & v.* ● *n.* **1** a sudden attack; a raid or incursion. **2** an attempt or venture, esp. into a field not one's own. ● *v.intr.* make or go on a foray. [ME, prob. earlier as verb: back-form. f. *forayer* f. OF *forrier* forager, rel. to FODDER]

■ *n.* see INROAD 2.

forbade (also **forbad**) past of FORBID.

forbear[1] /fawrbáir/ *v.intr. & tr.* (*past* **forbore** /-báwr/; *past part.* **forborne** /-báwrn/) (often foll. by *from*, or *to* + infin.) *literary* abstain or desist (from) (*could not forbear (from) speaking out; forbore to mention it*). [OE *forberan* (as FOR-, BEAR[1])]

■ (*forbear from*) see REFRAIN[1].

forbear[2] var. of FOREBEAR.

forbearance /fawrbáirəns/ *n.* patient self-control; tolerance.

■ see TOLERANCE 1.

forbearing /fawrbáiring/ adj. patient; long-suffering. □□ **forbearingly** adv.

■ patient, long-suffering, tolerant, forgiving, lenient, accommodating.

forbid /farbíd, fawr-/ v.tr. (**forbidding**; past **forbade** /-bád, -báyd/ or **forbad** /-bád/; past part. **forbidden** /-bíd'n/) **1** (foll. by to + infin.) order not (I forbid you to go). **2** refuse to allow (a thing, or a person to have a thing) (I forbid it; was forbidden any wine). **3** refuse a person entry to (the gardens are forbidden to children). □ **forbidden degrees** see DEGREE. **forbidden fruit** something desired or enjoyed all the more because not allowed. **God forbid!** may it not happen! □□ **forbiddance** /-dəns/ n. [OE forbēodan (as FOR-, BID)]

■ **1** (forbid to) direct or command or instruct or charge or tell or bid or require not to, prohibit or ban or debar from, hinder or stop or prevent from, preclude or exclude from, archaic or literary bid not to. **2** prohibit, ban, outlaw, interdict, disallow, proscribe, taboo; veto.

forbidding /forbíding, fawr-/ adj. uninviting; repellent; stern. □□ **forbiddingly** adv.

■ uninviting, repellent, repulsive, odious, abhorrent, offensive; stern, hostile, unfriendly, harsh, menacing, threatening, ominous, dangerous, nasty, ugly, unpleasant, Brit. off-putting.

forbore past of FORBEAR[1].

forborne past part. of FORBEAR[1].

forbye /fawrbí/ prep. & adv. archaic or Sc. ● prep. besides. ● adv. in addition.

force[1] /fawrs/ n. & v. ● n. **1** power; exerted strength or impetus; intense effort. **2** coercion or compulsion, esp. with the use or threat of violence. **3 a** military strength. **b** (in pl.) troops; fighting resources. **c** an organized body of people, esp. soldiers, police, or workers. **4** binding power; validity. **5** effect; precise significance (the force of their words). **6 a** mental or moral strength; influence; efficacy (force of habit). **b** vividness of effect (described with much force). **7** Physics **a** an influence tending to cause the motion of a body. **b** the intensity of this equal to the mass of the body and its acceleration. **8** a person or thing regarded as exerting influence (is a force for good). ● v. **1** tr. constrain (a person) by force or against his or her will. **2** tr. make a way through or into by force; break open by force. **3** tr. (usu. with prep. or adv.) drive or propel violently or against resistance (forced it into the hole; the wind forced them back). **4** tr. (foll. by on, upon) impose or press (on a person) (forced their views on us). **5** tr. **a** cause or produce by effort (forced a smile). **b** attain by strength or effort (forced an entry; must force a decision). **6** tr. strain or increase to the utmost; overstrain. **7** tr. artificially hasten the development or maturity of (a plant). **8** tr. seek or demand quick results from; accelerate the process of (force the pace). **9** intr. Cards make a play that compels another particular play. □ **by force of** by means of. **force the bidding** (at an auction) make bids to raise the price rapidly. **forced labor** compulsory labor, esp. under harsh conditions. **forced landing** the unavoidable landing of an aircraft in an emergency. **forced march** a long and vigorous march, esp. by troops. **force-feed** force (esp. a prisoner) to take food. **force field** (in science fiction) an invisible barrier of force. **force a person's hand** make a person act prematurely or unwillingly. **force the issue** render an immediate decision necessary. **force pump** a pump that forces water under pressure. **in force 1** valid; effective. **2** in great strength or numbers. **join forces** combine efforts. □□ **forceable** adj. **forcer** n. [ME f. OF force, forcer ult. f. L fortis strong]

■ n. **1** power, might, energy, strength, potency, vigor, intensity, violence, impact; effort, strain, exertion. **2** coercion, pressure, force majeure, constraint, duress, compulsion, colloq. arm-twisting. **3 b** (forces) troops, soldiers, armed forces; see also SERVICE[1] n. 8. **4** power, weight, persuasiveness, cogency, effectiveness, strength, validity. **5** effect, meaning, import; see also SIGNIFICANCE 1. **6 a** strength, influence, efficacy; see also STRENGTH 1. **b** see INTENSITY 2. **8** see INFLUENCE n.
● v. **1** make, oblige, require, compel, coerce, constrain,

impel, pressure, pressurize, press, dragoon, colloq. bulldoze, put the squeeze on, twist a person's arm. **2** pry or wrench open, break open or down, jimmy, Brit. jemmy. **3** push, drive, thrust, propel. **4** see THRUST v. 2. **5b** see WRENCH v. 3, insist on. **6** see STRETCH v. 6. **8** see HURRY v. 2, QUICKEN 1. □ **by force of** see by means of (MEANS). **in force 1** in effect, effective, in operation, operative, valid, binding, current. **join forces** see COOPERATE.

force[2] /fawrs/ n. No. of Engl. a waterfall. [ON fors]

forced /fawrst/ adj. **1** obtained or imposed by force (forced entry). **2** (of a gesture, etc.) produced or maintained with effort; affected; unnatural (a forced smile).

■ **2** artificial, unnatural, contrived, stilted, labored, strained, stiff, false, feigned, affected, mannered, self-conscious, colloq. phony.

forceful /fáwrsfool/ adj. **1** vigorous; powerful. **2** (of speech) compelling; impressive. □□ **forcefully** adv. **forcefulness** n.

■ **1** vigorous, energetic, dynamic, aggressive, potent, strong, mighty, powerful, weighty, effective, convincing, compelling. **2** compelling, effective, efficacious, cogent, impressive, telling, convincing, persuasive, strong, forcible, powerful, irresistible; pithy.

force majeure /fáwrs mazhőr/ n. **1** irresistible compulsion or coercion. **2** an unforeseeable course of events excusing a person from the fulfillment of a contract. [F, = superior strength]

forcemeat /fáwrsmeet/ n. meat, etc., chopped and seasoned for use as a stuffing or a garnish. [obs. force, farce stuff f. OF farsir: see FARCE]

forceps /fáwrseps/ n. (pl. same) **1** surgical pincers, used for grasping and holding. **2** Bot. & Zool. an organ or structure resembling forceps. □□ **forcipate** /-sipət/ adj. [L forceps forcipis]

forcible /fáwrsibəl/ adj. done by or involving force; forceful. □□ **forcibleness** n. **forcibly** adv. [ME f. AF & OF (as FORCE[1])]

■ drastic, coercive, severe, stringent, aggressive, violent; forced; see also FORCEFUL.

ford /fawrd/ n. & v. ● n. a shallow place where a river or stream may be crossed by wading or in a vehicle. ● v.tr. cross (water) at a ford. □□ **fordable** adj. **fordless** adj. [OE f. WG]

■ v. see WADE v. 5.

fore /fawr/ adj., n., int., & prep. ● adj. situated in front. ● n. the front part, esp. of a ship; the bow. ● int. Golf a warning to a person in the path of a ball. ● prep. archaic (in oaths) in the presence of (fore God). □ **come to the fore** take a leading part. **fore and aft** at bow and stern; all over the ship. **fore-and-aft** adj. (of a sail or rigging) set lengthwise, not on the yards. **to the fore** in front; conspicuous. [OE f. Gmc.: (adj. & n.) ME f. compounds with FORE-]

■ n. see FRONT n. 1.

fore- /fawr/ prefix forming: **1** verbs meaning: **a** in front (foreshorten). **b** beforehand; in advance (foreordain; forewarn). **2** nouns meaning: **a** situated in front of (forecourt). **b** the front part of (forehead). **c** of or near the bow of a ship (forecastle). **d** preceding (forerunner).

forearm[1] /fáwraarm/ n. **1** the part of the arm from the elbow to the wrist or the fingertips. **2** the corresponding part in a foreleg or wing.

forearm[2] /fawraárm/ v.tr. prepare or arm beforehand.

forebear /fáwrbair/ n. (also **forbear**) (usu. in pl.) an ancestor. [FORE + obs. bear, beer (as BE, -ER[1])]

■ see ANCESTOR 1.

forebode /fawrbőd/ v.tr. **1** betoken; be an advance warning of (an evil or unwelcome event). **2** have a presentiment of (usu. evil).

■ **1** see BODE. **2** see PREDICT.

/.../ **pronunciation**	● **part of speech**
□ **phrases, idioms, and compounds**	
□□ **derivatives**	■ **synonym section**
cross-references appear in SMALL CAPITALS or italics	

foreboding /fawrbṓding/ n. an expectation of trouble or evil; a presage or omen. □□ **forebodingly** adv.
■ premonition, presentiment, foreshadowing; omen, sign, portent, intimation, forewarning, presage, warning, foretoken, augury, prophecy, prediction, prognostication; apprehension, apprehensiveness, misgiving, dread, suspicion, anxiety, fear.

forecast /fáwrkast/ v. & n. ● v.tr. (past and past part. **-cast** or **-casted**) predict; estimate or calculate beforehand. ● n. a calculation or estimate of something future, esp. coming weather. □□ **forecaster** n.
■ v. predict, foretell, prophesy, prognosticate, foresee, augur, presage, disp. anticipate, formal vaticinate; estimate, calculate. ● n. calculation, estimate, prediction, prophecy, prognosis, prognostication, augury, anticipation, formal vaticination.

forecastle /fṓksəl/ n. (also **fo'c's'le**) Naut. 1 the forward part of a ship where the crew has quarters. 2 hist. a short raised deck at the bow.

foreclose /fawrklṓz/ v.tr. 1 (also absol.; foll. by on) stop (a mortgage) from being redeemable or (a mortgager) from redeeming, esp. as a result of defaults in payment. 2 exclude; prevent. 3 shut out; bar. □□ **foreclosure** /-klṓzhər/ n. [ME f. OF forclos past part. of forclore f. for- out f. L foras + CLOSE²]

forecourt /fáwrkawrt/ n. 1 an enclosed space in front of a building. 2 Tennis the part of the court between the service line and the net. 3 Brit. the part of a filling station where gasoline is supplied.

foredeck /fṓrdek, fáwr-/ n. the forward section of a ship's main deck.

foredoom /fawrdṓom/ v.tr. (often foll. by to) doom or condemn beforehand.

forefather /fáwrfaathər/ n. (usu. in pl.) 1 an ancestor. 2 a member of a past generation of a family or people.
■ see ANCESTOR 1.

forefinger /fáwrfinggər/ n. the finger next to the thumb.

forefoot /fáwrfoot/ n. (pl. **-feet**) 1 either of the front feet of a four-footed animal. 2 Naut. the foremost section of a ship's keel.

forefront /fáwrfrunt/ n. 1 the foremost part. 2 the leading position.
■ 2 see FRONT n. 6.

foregather var. of FORGATHER.

forego¹ /fawrgṓ/ v.tr. & intr. (**-goes**; past **-went** /-wént/; past part. **-gone** /-gón/) precede in place or time. □□ **foregoer** n. [OE foregān]

forego² var. of FORGO.

foregoing /fáwrgṓing/ adj. preceding; previously mentioned.
■ preceding, former, previous, precedent, antecedent, earlier, preliminary, prior, anterior; above, aforementioned, aforesaid.

foregone /fáwrgawn, -gón/ past part. of FOREGO¹.
● attrib.adj. previous; preceding; completed. □ **foregone conclusion** an easily foreseen or predictable result.
■ previous, preceding; see also ABOVE adj.

foreground /fáwrgrownd/ n. 1 the part of a view, esp. in a picture, that is nearest the viewer. 2 the most conspicuous position. [Du. voorgrond (as FORE-, GROUND¹)]

forehand /fáwrhand/ n. 1 Tennis, etc. a a stroke played with the palm of the hand facing the opponent. b (attrib.) (also **forehanded**) of or made with a forehand. 2 the part of a horse in front of the seated rider.

forehead /fáwrid, -hed, fór-/ n. the part of the face above the eyebrows. [OE forhēafod (as FORE-, HEAD)]

foreign /fáwrin, fór-/ adj. 1 of or from or situated in or characteristic of a country or a language other than one's own. 2 dealing with other countries (foreign service). 3 of another district, society, etc. 4 (often foll. by to) unfamiliar; strange; uncharacteristic (his behavior is foreign to me). 5 coming from outside (a foreign body lodged in my eye). □ **foreign aid** money, food, etc., given or lent by one country to another. **foreign exchange** 1 the currency of other countries. 2 dealings in these. **foreign legion** a body of foreign volunteers in an army (esp. the French army). **foreign minister** (or

secretary) (in some governments) a government minister in charge of his or her country's relations with other countries. **foreign office** (in some governments) a government department dealing with other countries. □□ **foreignness** n. [ME f. OF forein, forain ult. f. L foras, -is outside: for -g- cf. sovereign]
■ 1 alien, imported, nonnative; overseas, distant; tramontane. 2 external, international, overseas. 4 strange, outlandish, unfamiliar, peculiar, odd, uncharacteristic, curious, exotic, unknown, remote. 5 see EXTERNAL adj. 1b. □ **foreign minister** (or secretary) secretary of state, minister of the exterior. **foreign office** foreign ministry, ministry for foreign affairs; State Department, Brit. Foreign and Commonwealth Office.

foreigner /fáwrinər, fór-/ n. 1 a person born in or coming from a foreign country or place. 2 dial. a person not native to a place. 3 a a foreign ship. b an imported animal or article.
■ 1 alien, nonnative, immigrant, outsider, outlander, stranger. 2 nonnative, outsider, stranger, newcomer, new arrival.

forejudge /fáwrjúj/ v.tr. judge or determine before knowing the evidence.

foreknow /fáwrnṓ/ v.tr. (past **-knew** /-nṓo, -nyṓo/; past part. **-known** /-nṓn/) know beforehand; have prescience of. □□ **foreknowledge** /fórnólij/ n.

forelady /fáwrlaydee/ n. (pl. **-ies**) = FOREWOMAN.

foreland /fáwrland/ n. 1 a cape or promontory. 2 a piece of land in front of something.

foreleg /fáwrleg/ n. each of the front legs of a quadruped.

forelimb /fáwrlim/ n. any of the front limbs of an animal.

forelock /fáwrlok/ n. a lock of hair growing just above the forehead. □ **take time by the forelock** seize an opportunity.

foreman /fáwrmən/ n. (pl. **-men**) 1 a worker with supervisory responsibilities. 2 the member of a jury who presides over its deliberations and speaks on its behalf.
■ 1 superintendent, supervisor, overseer, manager, floor walker, straw boss, Brit. shopwalker, colloq. boss, super, Brit. colloq. gaffer, Austral. sl. pannikin boss.

foremast /fáwrmast, -məst/ n. the forward (lower) mast of a ship.

foremost /fáwrmōst/ adj. & adv. ● adj. 1 the chief or most notable. 2 the most advanced in position; the front. ● adv. before anything else in position; in the first place (first and foremost). [earlier formost, formest, superl. of OE forma first, assim. to FORE, MOST]
■ adj. chief, first, primary, prime, leading, preeminent, supreme, paramount, main, best, superior. ● adv. first, firstly, primarily, in the first place, before anything else.

forename /fáwrnaym/ n. a first name.

forenoon /fáwrnṓon/ n. the part of the day before noon.

forensic /fərénsik, -zik/ adj. 1 of or used in connection with courts of law (forensic science). 2 disp. of or involving forensic science (sent for forensic examination). □ **forensic medicine** the application of medical knowledge to legal problems. □□ **forensically** adv. [L forensis f. FORUM]
■ see LEGAL 1.

foreordain /fáwrawrdáyn/ v.tr. predestinate; ordain beforehand. □□ **foreordination** /-d'náyshən/ n.

forepaw /fáwrpaw/ n. either of the front paws of a quadruped.

forepeak /fáwrpeek/ n. Naut. the end of the forehold in the angle of the bows.

foreplay /fáwrplay/ n. stimulation preceding sexual intercourse.

forerun /fáwr-rún/ v.tr. (**-running**; past **-ran** /-rán/; past part. **-run**) 1 go before. 2 indicate the coming of; foreshadow.

forerunner /fáwr-runər/ n. 1 a predecessor. 2 an advance messenger.
■ 1 predecessor, precursor, foregoer, ancestor,

progenitor. **2** herald, harbinger, envoy; see also MESSENGER.

foresail /fáwrsayl, -səl/ *n. Naut.* the principal sail on a foremast (the lowest square sail, or the fore-and-aft bent on the mast, or the triangular before the mast).

foresee /fáwrseé/ *v.tr.* (*past* **-saw** /-sáw/; *past part.* **-seen** /-seén/) (often foll. by *that* + clause) see or be aware of beforehand. □□ **foreseeable** *adj.* **foreseeability** *n.* **foreseer** /-seéər/ *n.* [OE *foreséon* (as FORE- + SEE[1])]
■ presage, foretell, envisage, forecast, predict, prophesy, augur, envision.

foreshadow /fáwrshádō/ *v.tr.* be a warning or indication of (a future event).
■ presage, foretoken, portend, augur, indicate, bode.

foresheets /fáwrsheets/ *n.pl. Naut.* the inner part of the bows of a boat with gratings for the bowman to stand on.

foreshore /fáwrshawr/ *n.* the part of the shore between high- and low-water marks, or between the water and cultivated or developed land.

foreshorten /fáwrsháwrt'n/ *v.tr.* show or portray (an object) with the apparent shortening due to visual perspective.

foreshow /fáwrshṓ/ *v.tr.* (*past part.* **-shown** /-shṓn/) **1** foretell. **2** foreshadow; portend; prefigure.

foresight /fáwrsīt/ *n.* **1** regard or provision for the future. **2** the process of foreseeing. **3** the front sight of a gun. **4** *Surveying* a sight taken forward. □□ **foresighted** /-sítid/ *adj.* **foresightedly** *adv.* **foresightedness** *n.* [ME, prob. after ON *forsjá, forsjó* (as FORE-, SIGHT)]
■ **1** providence, farsightedness, longsightedness. **2** prevision, vision, foreknowledge, prescience.

foreskin /fáwrskin/ *n.* the fold of skin covering the end of the penis. Also called PREPUCE.

forest /fáwrist, fór-/ *n. & v.* ● *n.* **1 a** (often *attrib.*) a large area covered chiefly with trees and undergrowth. **b** the trees growing in it. **c** a large number or dense mass of vertical objects (*a forest of masts*). **2** a district formerly a forest but now cultivated. **3** *hist.* (in the UK) an area usu. owned by the sovereign and kept for hunting. ● *v.tr.* **1** plant with trees. **2** convert into a forest. □ **forest ranger** a government official who protects and preserves forests. [ME f. OF f. LL *forestis silva* wood outside the walls of a park f. L *foris* outside]
■ *n.* **1 a, b** see WOOD 2.

forestall /fáwrstáwl/ *v.tr.* **1** act in advance of in order to prevent. **2** anticipate (the action of another, or an event). **3** anticipate the action of. **4** deal with beforehand. **5** *hist.* buy up (goods) in order to profit by an enhanced price. □□ **forestaller** *n.* **forestallment** *n.* [ME in sense 5: cf. AL *forestallare* f. OE *foresteall* an ambush (as FORE-, STALL)]
■ **1** anticipate, prevent, obstruct, hinder, thwart, frustrate, avert, ward *or* stave *or* fend off, intercept, parry, stop, delay. **2, 3** see ANTICIPATE 4.

forestay /fáwrstay/ *n. Naut.* a stay from the head of the foremast to the ship's deck to support the foremast.

forester /fáwristər, fór-/ *n.* **1** a person in charge of a forest or skilled in forestry. **2** a person or animal living in a forest. [ME f. OF *forestier* (as FOREST)]

forestry /fáwristree, fór-/ *n.* **1** the science or management of forests. **2** wooded country; forests.

foretaste *n. & v.* ● *n.* /fáwrtayst/ partial enjoyment or suffering in advance; anticipation. ● *v.tr.* /fáwrtáyst/ taste beforehand; anticipate the experience of.
■ *n.* earnest, token; anticipation.

foretell /fáwrtél/ *v.tr.* (*past* and *past part.* **-told** /-tṓld/) **1** tell of (an event, etc.) before it takes place; predict; prophesy. **2** presage; be a precursor of. □□ **foreteller** *n.*
■ **1** see PROPHESY.

forethought /fáwrthawt/ *n.* **1** care or provision for the future. **2** previous thinking or devising. **3** deliberate intention.
■ **1** farsightedness, longsightedness; preparation, planning, organization. **2** premeditation, preplanning, planning.

foretoken *n. & v.* ● *n.* /fáwrtōkən/ a sign of something to come. ● *v.tr.* /fáwrtŏkən/ portend; indicate beforehand. [OE *foretācn* (as FORE-, TOKEN)]

■ *n.* see INDICATION 1b. ● *v.* see FORESHADOW.

foretold *past* and *past part.* of FORETELL.

foretop /fáwrtop/ *n. Naut.* a platform at the top of a foremast (see TOP[1] *n.* 9). □ **foretop-gallant mast** the mast above the fore-topmast. **foretop-gallant-sail** the sail above the fore-topsail.

fore-topmast /fawrtópmast, -məst/ *n. Naut.* the mast above the foremast.

fore-topsail /fawrtópsayl, -səl/ *n. Naut.* the sail above the foresail.

forever /fərévər, fawr-/ *adv.* continually; persistently (*is forever complaining*) (cf. *for ever*).
■ constantly, continually, continuously, always, all the time, unceasingly, persistently, perpetually.

forevermore /fərévərmáwr, fawr-/ *adv.* an emphatic form of FOREVER or *for ever* (see EVER).
■ see *permanently* (PERMANENT).

forewarn /fáwrwáwrn/ *v.tr.* warn beforehand. □□ **forewarner** *n.*

forewent *past* of FOREGO[1], FOREGO[2].

forewoman /fáwrwŏŏmən/ *n.* (*pl.* **-women**) **1** a female worker with supervisory responsibilities. **2** a woman who presides over a jury's deliberations and speaks on its behalf.

foreword /fáwrwərd/ *n.* introductory remarks at the beginning of a book, often by a person other than the author. [FORE- + WORD after G *Vorwort*]
■ preface, prologue, preamble, prolegomenon, proem, introduction.

foreyard /fáwryaard/ *n. Naut.* the lowest yard on a foremast.

forfeit /fáwrfit/ *n., adj., & v.* ● *n.* **1** a penalty for a breach of contract or neglect; a fine. **2 a** a trivial fine for a breach of rules in clubs, etc., or in a game. **b** (in *pl.*) a game in which forfeits are exacted. **3** something surrendered as a penalty. **4** the process of forfeiting. **5** *Law* property or a right or privilege lost as a legal penalty. ● *adj.* lost or surrendered as a penalty. ● *v.tr.* (**forfeited, forfeiting**) lose the right to, be deprived of, or have to pay as a penalty. □□ **forfeitable** *adj.* **forfeiter** *n.* **forfeiture** /-fichər/ *n.* [ME (= crime) f. OF *forfet, forfait past part.* of *forfaire* transgress (f. L *foris* outside) + *faire* f. L *facere* do]
■ *n.* **1** penalty, fine, fee, charge, damages, mulct, *Law* amercement. **4** forfeiture, sequestration, confiscation, surrender, relinquishment, *Law* amercement.
● *v.* lose, yield, give up *or* over, relinquish, concede, surrender, cede, deliver up, turn *or* make over, be stripped *or* deprived of, forgo.

forfend /fawrfénd/ *v.tr.* **1** protect by precautions. **2** *archaic* avert; keep off.

forgather /fáwrgáthər/ *v.intr.* (also **foregather**) assemble; meet together; associate. [16th-c. Sc. f. Du. *vergaderen*, assim. to FOR-, GATHER]
■ see ASSEMBLE 1.

forgave *past* of FORGIVE.

forge[1] /fawrj/ *v. & n.* ● *v.tr.* **1 a** write (a document or signature) in order to pass it off as written by another. **b** make (money, etc.) in fraudulent imitation. **2** fabricate; invent. **3** shape (esp. metal) by heating in a fire and hammering. ● *n.* **1** a blacksmith's workshop; a smithy. **2 a** a furnace or hearth for melting or refining metal. **b** a workshop containing this. □□ **forgeable** *adj.* **forger** *n.* [ME f. OF *forge* (n.), *forger* (v.) f. L *fabricare* FABRICATE]
■ *v.* **1** falsify, fake, fabricate. **2** see INVENT 1. **3** make, construct, fashion, fabricate, manufacture, shape, beat, hammer out.

forge[2] /fawrj/ *v.intr.* move forward gradually or steadily. □ **forge ahead 1** take the lead in a race. **2** move forward or make progress rapidly. [18th c.: perh. an aberrant pronunc. of FORCE[1]]

forgery /fáwrjəree/ *n.* (*pl.* **-ies**) **1** the act or an instance of

/.../ **pronunciation**	● **part of speech**
□ **phrases, idioms, and compounds**	
□□ **derivatives**	■ **synonym section**
cross-references appear in SMALL CAPITALS or *italics*	

forging, counterfeiting, or falsifying a document, etc. **2 a** forged or spurious thing, esp. a document or signature.

■ **1** falsification, fraud, counterfeiting. **2** counterfeit, fake, sham, fraud, imitation, simulation, reproduction, *colloq.* phony.

forget /fərgét/ *v.* (**forgetting**; *past* **forgot** /-gót/; *past part.* **forgotten** /-gót'n/ or esp. *US* **forgot**) **1** *tr.* & (often foll. by *about*) *intr.* lose the remembrance of; not remember (a person or thing). **2** *tr.* (foll. by clause or *to* + infin.) not remember; neglect (*forgot to come*; *forgot how to do it*). **3** *tr.* inadvertently omit to bring or mention or attend to. **4** *tr.* (also *absol.*) put out of mind; cease to think of (*forgive and forget*). □ **forget-me-not** any plant of the genus *Myosotis*, esp. *M. alpestris* with small yellow-eyed bright blue flowers. **forget oneself 1** neglect one's own interests. **2** act unbecomingly or unworthily. □□ **forgettable** *adj.* **forgetter** *n.* [OE *forgietan* f. WG (as FOR-, GET)]

■ **1** fail to remember *or* recall, fail to think of, lose, lose sight of, draw a blank on, disremember. **2** omit, neglect, fail (in), overlook. **3** leave (behind), come *or* go without; overlook, miss, fail to notice, pass over. **4** ignore, disregard; dismiss from one's mind *or* thoughts, put out of one's mind, consign to oblivion, drop, sink, overlook, brush aside, gloss over, kiss good-bye.

forgetful /fərgétfŏŏl/ *adj.* **1** apt to forget; absent-minded. **2** (often foll. by *of*) forgetting; neglectful. □□ **forgetfully** *adv.* **forgetfulness** *n.*

■ **1** absent-minded, distrait, thoughtless, inattentive, lax, dreamy, oblivious; amnesic; (*be forgetful*) be in dreamland, be (with one's head) in the clouds, be in cloudland *or* cloud-cuckoo-land. **2** neglectful, negligent, heedless, unheeding, unheedful, unmindful, unthinking, remiss, careless, thoughtless.

forgive /fərgív/ *v.tr.* (also *absol.* or with double object) (*past* **forgave**; *past part.* **forgiven**) **1** cease to feel angry or resentful toward; pardon (an offender or offense) (*forgive us our mistakes*). **2** remit or let off (a debt or debtor). □□ **forgivable** *adj.* **forgivably** *adv.* **forgiver** *n.* [OE *forgiefan* (as FOR-, GIVE)]

■ **1** pardon, excuse, allow, make allowance(s) for; overlook, condone, indulge, ignore, disregard, pay no attention to, pass over; clear, acquit, absolve, exonerate, vindicate, reprieve, let off, *formal* exculpate. **2** remit, cancel, waive, abolish, void, nullify, erase, delete; let off.

forgiveness /fərgívnis/ *n.* **1** the act of forgiving; the state of being forgiven. **2** readiness to forgive. [OE *forgiefenes* (as FORGIVE)]

■ **1** pardon, absolution, exoneration, reprieve, remission, acquittal, vindication, indulgence, allowance, *archaic* shrift, *formal* exculpation. **2** mercy, mercifulness, compassion, grace, leniency, clemency, indulgence, tolerance.

forgiving /fərgíving/ *adj.* inclined readily to forgive. □□ **forgivingly** *adv.*

■ tolerant, lenient, forbearing, charitable, merciful, compassionate, conciliatory, magnanimous, indulgent, understanding, humane, softhearted, clement, placable.

forgo /fáwrgṓ/ *v.tr.* (also **forego**) (**-goes**; *past* **-went** /-wént/; *past part.* **-gone** /-gáwn, -gón/) **1** abstain from; go without; relinquish. **2** omit or decline to take or use (a pleasure, advantage, etc.). [OE *forgān* (as FOR-, GO¹)]

■ abstain from, do *or* go without, give up, turn down, deny oneself, sacrifice, cede, waive, decline, yield, surrender, relinquish, renounce, forswear, abdicate, forfeit, abandon, *colloq.* pass up, *literary* eschew.

forgot *past* of FORGET.

forgotten *past part.* of FORGET.

forint /fáwrint/ *n.* the chief monetary unit of Hungary. [Magyar f. It. *fiorino*: see FLORIN]

fork /fawrk/ *n.* & *v.* ● *n.* **1** an instrument with two or more prongs used in eating or cooking. **2** a similar much larger instrument used for digging, lifting, etc. **3** any pronged device or component (*tuning fork*). **4** a forked support for a bicycle wheel. **5 a** a divergence of anything, e.g., a stick,

road, or a river, into two parts. **b** the place where this occurs. **c** either of the two parts (*take the left fork*). **6** a flash of forked lightning. **7** *Chess* a simultaneous attack on two pieces by one. ● *v.* **1** *intr.* form a fork or branch by separating into two parts. **2** *intr.* take one or other road, etc., at a fork (*fork left for Danbury*). **3** *tr.* dig or lift, etc., with a fork. **4** *tr.* *Chess* attack (two pieces) simultaneously with one. □ **fork lunch** (or **supper**, etc.) *Brit.* a light meal eaten with a fork at a buffet, etc. **fork out** (or **over** or **up**) *sl.* hand over or pay, usu. reluctantly. [OE *forca*, *force* f. L *furca*]

■ *v.* **1** see SEPARATE *v.* 3, 4.

forked /fawrkt/ *adj.* **1** having a fork or forklike end or branches. **2** divergent; cleft. **3** (in *comb.*) having so many prongs (*three-forked*). □ **forked lightning** a lightning flash in the form of a zigzag or branching line.

forklift /fáwrklift/ *n.* a vehicle with a horizontal fork in front for lifting and carrying loads.

forlorn /fawrláwrn/ *adj.* **1** sad and abandoned or lonely. **2** in a pitiful state; of wretched appearance. □ **forlorn hope 1** a faint remaining hope or chance. **2** a desperate enterprise. □□ **forlornly** *adv.* **forlornness** *n.* [past part. of obs. *forlese* f. OE *forlēosan* (as FOR-, LOSE): *forlorn hope* f. Du. *verloren hoop* lost troop, orig. of a storming party, etc.]

■ **1** lonely, lonesome, abandoned, forsaken, deserted, neglected, friendless, comfortless, bereft, solitary, isolated; desolate, inconsolable, despairing, brokenhearted, sad, woebegone, woeful, cheerless, joyless, unhappy, depressed, miserable, disconsolate, gloomy, lugubrious, glum, despondent, dismal, doleful, dejected, dispirited, low-spirited, melancholy, sorrowful, mournful, *literary or joc.* dolorous. **2** miserable, wretched, pitiable, pitiful, pathetic, sad, sorry, hapless, unfortunate, *colloq.* down in the mouth.

form /fawrm/ *n.* & *v.* ● *n.* **1 a** a shape; an arrangement of parts. **b** the outward aspect (esp. apart from color) or shape of a body. **2** a person or animal as visible or tangible (*the familiar form of the teacher*). **3** the mode in which a thing exists or manifests itself (*took the form of a book*). **4** a species, kind, or variety. **5 a** a printed document with blank spaces for information to be inserted. **b** a regularly drawn document. **6** a class or grade, as in some private schools or a British school. **7** a customary method; what is usually done (*common form*). **8** a set order of words; a formula. **9** behavior according to a rule or custom. **10** (prec. by *the*) correct procedure (*knows the form*). **11 a** (of an athlete, horse, etc.) condition of health and training (*is in top form*). **b** *Racing* details of previous performances. **12** general state or disposition (*was in great form*). **13** *Brit. sl.* a criminal record. **14** formality or mere ceremony. **15** *Gram.* **a** one of the ways in which a word may be spelled or pronounced or inflected. **b** the external characteristics of words apart from meaning. **16** arrangement and style in literary or musical composition. **17** *Philos.* the essential nature of a species or thing. **18** *Brit.* a long bench without a back. **19** *Printing* **a** a body of type secured in a chase for printing at one impression. **b** a quantity of film arranged for making a plate, etc. **20** a hare's lair. **21** = FORMWORK. ● *v.* **1** *tr.* make or fashion into a certain shape or form. **2** *intr.* take a certain shape; be formed. **3** *tr.* be the material of; make up or constitute (*together form a unit*; *forms part of the structure*). **4** *tr.* train or instruct. **5** *tr.* develop or establish as a concept, institution, or practice (*form an idea*; *formed an alliance*; *form a habit*). **6** *tr.* (foll. by *into*) embody; organize. **7** *tr.* articulate (a word). **8** *tr.* & *intr.* (often foll. by *up*) esp. *Mil.* bring or be brought into a certain arrangement or formation. **9** *tr.* construct (a new word) by derivation, inflection, etc. □ **bad form** an offense against current social conventions. **form class** *Linguistics* a class of linguistic forms with grammatical or syntactical features in common. **form criticism** textual analysis of the Bible, etc., by tracing the history of its content by forms (e.g., proverbs, myths). **form letter** a standardized letter to deal with frequently occurring matters. **good form** what complies with current social conventions. **in form** fit for racing, etc. **off form** esp. *Brit.* not playing or performing well. **on form**

esp. *Brit.* playing or performing well. **out of form** not fit for racing, etc. [ME f. OF *forme* f. L *forma* mold, form]

■ *n.* **1 a** shape, figure; configuration, conformation, order, organization, arrangement, formation, construction, structure, composition. **b** build, shape, physique, body, cut, cast, mold, pattern, frame; silhouette, profile, contour(s); aspect, look, likeness, semblance, guise, appearance. **2** silhouette, figure, shape, image. **3** style, mode, character, manner, fashion, way, nature, state, stamp; aspect, look, likeness, semblance, guise, appearance. **4** type, kind, variety, version, sort, breed, species, genus, genre, make, brand, category, class, classification, order, strain, group, family. **7** custom, convention, code, rule, procedure, routine, style, tradition, protocol, ritual, observance, practice, technique, way, means, approach, mode, style. **8** form of words; see also FORMULA 3a. **9** behavior, manners, etiquette, conduct; propriety, seemliness, decency, decorum, convention(s). **10** protocol, practice, routine; see also PROCEDURE 1–3. **11 a** condition, state, order, shape, trim, fettle, health. **12** condition, shape, health; state, disposition, mood, temper. **14** see CEREMONY 2, 3. ● *v.* **1** make, fabricate, forge, shape, mold, turn, fashion, manufacture, construct, assemble, arrange, organize, cast, compose. **2** develop, grow, arise, appear, materialize, show up, take shape, emerge, spring up, brew; crystallize, *colloq.* jell. **3** make up, constitute, *disp.* comprise; serve as, function as, act as. **4** see INSTRUCT 1. **5** create, originate, establish, generate, devise, invent, design, compose, formulate, coin, concoct, conceive, contrive, dream up; acquire, develop, cultivate, contract. **6** embody; organize, arrange, assemble. **7** articulate, pronounce, utter, voice, vocalize, enunciate; say, speak. □ **bad form** see IMPROPER 1b. **good form** see CORRECT *adj.* 2, 3.

-form /fawrm/ *comb. form* (usu. as **-iform**) forming adjectives meaning: **1** having the form of (*cruciform*; *cuneiform*). **2** having such a number of (*uniform*; *multiform*). [from or after F *-forme* f. L *-formis* f. *forma* FORM]

formal /fáwrməl/ *adj. & n.* ● *adj.* **1** used or done or held in accordance with rules, convention, or ceremony (*formal dress*; *a formal occasion*). **2** ceremonial; required by convention (*a formal offer*). **3** precise or symmetrical (*a formal garden*). **4** prim or stiff in manner. **5** perfunctory; having the form without the spirit. **6** valid or correctly so called because of its form; explicit and definite (*a formal agreement*). **7** in accordance with recognized forms or rules. **8** of or concerned with (outward) form or appearance, esp. as distinct from content or matter. **9** *Logic* concerned with the form and not the matter of reasoning. **10** *Philos.* of the essence of a thing; essential not material. ● *n.* **1** evening dress. **2** an occasion on which evening dress is worn. □□ **formally** *adv.* **formalness** *n.* [ME f. L *formalis* (as FORM)]

■ *adj.* **1, 2, 7** correct, proper, set, prescribed, pro forma, formulaic, official, civic, diplomatic, civil, polite, ceremonious; conventional, customary, established; stately, courtly, dignified, solemn, ceremonial; professional, literary, specialized. **3** precise, symmetrical, orderly, ordered, well-ordered. **4** prim, rigid, stiff, exact, punctilious, strict, stilted, starched; straitlaced, stuffy, *colloq.* straight; impersonal, reserved, controlled, measured, reticent; pedantic, hidebound, particular. **5** nominal, perfunctory, routine, official, standard, formulaic. **6** formalized, authorized, official, structured, fixed, valid, authentic, legal, lawful; explicit, express, definite, exact, specific.

formaldehyde /fawrmáldihīd/ *n.* a colorless pungent gas used as a disinfectant and preservative and in the manufacture of synthetic resins. ¶ Chem. formula: CH_2O. Also called METHANAL. [FORMIC (ACID) + ALDEHYDE]

formalin /fáwrməlin/ *n.* a colorless solution of formaldehyde in water used as a preservative for biological specimens, etc.

formalism /fáwrməlizəm/ *n.* **1 a** excessive adherence to prescribed forms. **b** the use of forms without regard to inner

significance. **2** *derog.* an artist's concentration on form at the expense of content. **3** the treatment of mathematics as a manipulation of meaningless symbols. **4** *Theatr.* a symbolic and stylized manner of production. **5** *Physics & Math.* the mathematical description of a physical situation, etc. □□ **formalist** *n.* **formalistic** *adj.*

formality /fawrmálitee/ *n.* (*pl.* **-ies**) **1 a** a formal or ceremonial act, requirement of etiquette, regulation, or custom (often with an implied lack of real significance). **b** a thing done simply to comply with a rule. **2** the rigid observance of rules or convention. **3** ceremony; elaborate procedure. **4** being formal; precision of manners. **5** stiffness of design. [F *formalité* or med.L *formalitas* (as FORMAL)]

■ **1** form, (social) convention, practice, procedure, custom, observance, protocol, rule(s), regulation(s), ceremony, rite, ritual; (*formalities*) niceties, proprieties, etiquette, appearances, motions; rigmarole. **2** formalness, strictness, punctilio, exactness, precision, preciseness, correctness, stringency, inflexibility, rigidity. **3** see CEREMONY 2, 3. **4** formalness, politesse, punctilio, conformity, propriety, correctness, properness, punctiliousness, niceness, ceremoniousness, courtliness, courtesy, decorum, stateliness, seriousness, stuffiness, stiffness, gravity.

formalize /fáwrməliz/ *v.tr.* **1** give definite shape or legal formality to. **2** make ceremonious, precise, or rigid; imbue with formalism. □□ **formalization** /-lizáyshən/ *n.*

formant /fáwrmənt/ *n.* **1** the characteristic pitch constituent of a vowel. **2** a morpheme occurring only in combination in a word or word stem. [G f. L *formare* *formant-* to form]

format /fáwrmat/ *n. & v.* ● *n.* **1** the shape and size of a book, periodical, etc. **2** the style or manner of an arrangement or procedure. **3** *Computing* a defined structure for holding data, etc., in a record for processing or storage. ● *v.tr.* (**formatted, formatting**) **1** arrange or put into a format. **2** *Computing* prepare (a storage medium) to receive data. [F f. G f. L *formatus* (*liber*) shaped (book), past part. of *formare* FORM]

■ *n.* **1** shape, size, form, dimension(s), appearance, look, aspect, layout, plan, design, style, pattern, contour(s), composition. **2** structure, method, plan, organization, composition, makeup, constitution, arrangement, configuration, form, framework, system, order, setup, theme, character, style, manner. ● *v.* **1** see STRUCTURE *v.*

formate see FORMIC ACID.

formation /fawrmáyshən/ *n.* **1** the act or an instance of forming; the process of being formed. **2** a thing formed. **3** a structure or arrangement of parts. **4** a particular arrangement, e.g., of troops, aircraft in flight, etc. **5** *Geol.* an assemblage of rocks or series of strata having some common characteristic. □□ **formational** *adj.* [ME f. OF *formation* or L *formatio* (as FORM)]

■ **1, 2** foundation, development, appearance, materialization, generation, creation, genesis, crystallization, origination, fabrication, invention, production, establishment, institution, founding, composition. **3** arrangement, structure, setup, grouping, organization, configuration, disposition, pattern. **4** configuration, pattern, display, array.

formative /fáwrmətiv/ *adj. & n.* ● *adj.* **1** serving to form or fashion; of formation. **2** *Gram.* (of a flexional or derivative suffix or prefix) used in forming words. ● *n.* *Gram.* a formative element. □□ **formatively** *adv.* [ME f. OF *formatif* *-ive* or med.L *formativus* (as FORM)]

■ *adj.* **1** see SEMINAL 4.

forme /fawrm/ *n. Brit.* = FORM *n.* 19.

former[1] /fáwrmər/ *attrib.adj.* **1** of or occurring in the past or an earlier period (*in former times*). **2** having been previously

┌───┐
│ /. . ./ **pronunciation**   ● **part of speech** │
│ □ **phrases, idioms, and compounds** │
│ □□ **derivatives**   ■ **synonym section** │
│ **cross-references** appear in SMALL CAPITALS or *italics* │
└───┘

(*her former husband*). **3** (prec. by *the*; often *absol.*) the first or first mentioned of two (opp. LATTER). [ME f. *forme* first, after FOREMOST]

■ **1** old, past, bygone, ancient, *archaic* olden; obsolete; earlier, previous, prior; quondam, of old, *literary* of yore. **2** previous, earlier, ex-, one-time, sometime, erstwhile, late, ci-devant, *archaic* whilom.

former² /fáwrmər/ *n.* **1** a person or thing that forms. **2** *Electr.* a frame or core for winding a coil on. **3** *Aeron.* a transverse strengthening member in a wing or fuselage. **4** esp. *Brit.* (in *comb.*) a pupil of a specified form in a school (*fourth-former*).

formerly /fáwrmərlee/ *adv.* in the past; in former times.

■ once, before, previously, long ago, in the past, at one time, in the old days, once upon a time, in days gone by, hitherto, sometime, ci-devant, of old, *archaic* erst, erstwhile, *colloq.* way back, way back when, *formal* heretofore, *literary* of yore.

Formica /fawrmíkə/ *n. propr.* a hard durable plastic laminate used for working surfaces, cupboard doors, etc. [20th c.: orig. uncert.]

formic acid /fáwrmik/ *n.* a colorless irritant volatile acid (HCOOH) contained in the fluid emitted by some ants. □□ **formate** /-mayt/ *n.* [L *formica* ant]

formication /fáwrmikáyshən/ *n.* a sensation as of ants crawling over the skin. [L *formicatio* f. *formica* ant]

formidable /fáwrmidəbəl, *disp.* formídəbəl/ *adj.* **1** inspiring fear or dread. **2** inspiring respect or awe. **3** likely to be hard to overcome, resist, or deal with. □□ **formidableness** *n.* **formidably** *adv.* [F *formidable* or L *formidabilis* f. *formidare* fear]

■ **1** dreadful, fearful, fearsome, frightful, daunting, intimidating, alarming, frightening, startling, appalling, menacing, horrifying, petrifying, terrifying, terrible, shocking, dire. **2** impressive, awesome, awe-inspiring, imposing, redoubtable, *poet.* awful; breathtaking, amazing, marvelous, incredible, unbelievable, astonishing, *colloq.* stunning, mind-boggling. **3** arduous, difficult, daunting, challenging, burdensome, onerous, tough; indomitable, overwhelming, powerful, potent, strong, mighty, forbidding.

formless /fáwrmlis/ *adj.* shapeless; without determinate or regular form. □□ **formlessly** *adv.* **formlessness** *n.*

■ see SHAPELESS 1, *chaotic* (CHAOS).

formula /fáwrmyələ/ *n.* (*pl.* **formulas** or (esp. in senses 1, 2) **formulae** /-lee/) **1** *Chem.* a set of chemical symbols showing the constituents of a substance and their relative proportions. **2** *Math.* a mathematical rule expressed in symbols. **3 a** a fixed form of words, esp. one used on social or ceremonial occasions. **b** a rule unintelligently or slavishly followed; an established or conventional usage. **c** a form of words embodying or enabling agreement, resolution of a dispute, etc. **4 a** a list of ingredients; a recipe. **b** an infant's liquid food preparation given as a substitute for mother's milk. **5** a classification of racing car, esp. by the engine capacity. □ **formula weight** = *molecular weight.* □□ **formulaic** /-láyik/ *adj.* **formularize** /-ləriz/ *v.tr.* **formulize** *v.tr.* [L, dimin. of *forma* FORM]

■ **3 a** liturgy, rubric, observance, formulation, code; rite, ritual, spell, incantation, chant. **b** rule, protocol, convention, custom, practice, prescription, instruction, direction, directive; plan, routine, method, procedure, convention, form, technique, way, pattern, system, modus operandi, code; principle, axiom, theorem. **4 a** recipe, prescription; contents, ingredients.

formulary /fáwrmyələree/ *n. & adj.* ● *n.* (*pl.* **-ies**) **1** a collection of formulas or set forms, esp. for religious use. **2** *Pharm.* a compendium of formulae used in the preparation of medicinal drugs. ● *adj.* **1** using formulae. **2** in or of formulae. [(n.) F *formulaire* or f. med.L *formularius* (*liber* book) f. L (as FORMULA): (adj.) f. FORMULA]

formulate /fáwrmyəlayt/ *v.tr.* **1** express in a formula. **2** express clearly and precisely. **3** create or devise (a plan, etc.). **4** develop or prepare following a formula. □□ **formulation** /-láyshən/ *n.*

■ **1** program, systematize, codify, shape, draft, develop,

work out, form, frame, map out, block out, draw up; arrange, cast. **2** express, define, specify, particularize, articulate, vocalize, enunciate, pronounce, phrase, delineate. **3** devise, originate, initiate, create, dream up, hatch, conceive, concoct, invent, compose, improvise, *colloq.* think up, cook up.

formulism /fáwrmyəlizəm/ *n.* adherence to or dependence on conventional formulas. □□ **formulist** *n.* **formulistic** *adj.*

formwork /fáwrmwərk/ *n.* a temporary structure, usu. of wood, used to hold concrete during setting.

fornicate /fáwrnikayt/ *v.intr.* (of people not married or not married to each other) have sexual intercourse voluntarily. □□ **fornication** /-káyshən/ *n.* **fornicator** *n.* [eccl.L *fornicari* f. L *fornix -icis* brothel]

forrader /fáwrədər/ *Brit. colloq. compar.* of FORWARD.

forsake /fərsáyk, fawr-/ *v.tr.* (*past* **forsook** /-sŏŏk/; *past part.* **forsaken** /-sáykən/) **1** give up; break off from; renounce. **2** withdraw one's help, friendship, or companionship from; desert; abandon. □□ **forsakenness** *n.* **forsaker** *n.* [OE *forsacan* deny, renounce, refuse, f. WG; cf. OE *sacan* quarrel]

■ **1** give up, abstain from, relinquish, yield, forgo, waive, forfeit, resign, abdicate, secede from, surrender; renounce, reject, jettison, repudiate; abandon, pull out of, withdraw from, break off with, break with, have or be done with, quit, leave, flee, depart from, vacate. **2** abandon, desert, leave, maroon, jilt, reject, rebuff, snub, turn one's back on, leave in the lurch, brush off, drop, throw over, cast off *or* aside, *colloq.* dump, *sl.* ditch.

forsooth /fərsŏŏth, fawr-/ *adv. archaic* or *joc.* truly; in truth; no doubt. [OE *forsōth* (as FOR, SOOTH)]

forswear /fáwrswáir/ *v.tr.* (*past* **forswore** /-swáwr/; *past part.* **forsworn** /-swáwrn/) **1** abjure; renounce on oath. **2** (in *refl.* or *passive*) swear falsely; commit perjury. [OE *forswerian* (as FOR-, SWEAR)]

■ **1** see FORGO, RECANT 1.

forsythia /fawrsítheeə/ *n.* any ornamental shrub of the genus *Forsythia* bearing bright yellow flowers in early spring. [mod.L f. W. *Forsyth*, Engl. botanist d. 1804]

fort /fawrt/ *n.* **1** a fortified building or position. **2** *hist.* a trading post, orig. fortified. [F *fort* or It. *forte* f. L *fortis* strong]

forte¹ /fawrt, fáwrtay/ *n.* **1** a person's strong point; a thing in which a person excels. **2** *Fencing* the part of a sword blade from the hilt to the middle (cf. FOIBLE 2). [F *fort* strong f. L *fortis*]

■ **1** strong point, long *or* strong suit, strength, métier, specialty, esp. *Brit.* speciality; talent, gift, skill, knack, genius, flair, expertise.

forte² /fórtay/ *adj., adv., & n. Mus.* ● *adj.* performed loudly. ● *adv.* loudly. ● *n.* a passage to be performed loudly. □ **forte-piano** *adj. & adv.* loud and then immediately soft. [It., = strong, loud]

fortepiano /fórtaypiánō, -áanō/ *n.* (*pl.* **-os**) *Mus.* = PIANO-FORTE esp. with ref. to an instrument of the 18th to early 19th c. [FORTE² + PIANO²]

forth /fawrth/ *adv. archaic* except in set phrases and after certain verbs, esp. *bring, come, go,* and *set.* **1** forward; into view. **2** onward in time (*from this time forth; henceforth*). **3** forward. **4** out from a starting point (*set forth*). □ **and so forth** and so on; and the like. [OE f. Gmc]

■ **1, 3** see FORWARD *adv.* 2. **2** see ONWARD *adv.*

forthcoming /fáwrthkúming/ *attrib. adj.* **1 a** about or likely to appear or become available. **b** approaching. **2** produced when wanted (*no reply was forthcoming*). **3** (of a person) informative; responsive. □□ **forthcomingness** *n.*

■ **1** impending, approaching, coming, imminent, prospective, upcoming; near, pending, at hand, in the offing, on the horizon, in store, *archaic or dial.* nigh, *colloq.* just around the corner; likely, probable, possible, in the cards. **3** informative, responsive, outgoing, approachable, expansive, communicative, open, frank, candid, unreserved.

forthright /fáwrthrít/ *adj. & adv.* ● *adj.* **1** direct and outspoken; straightforward. **2** decisive; unhesitating. ● *adv.* in a direct manner; bluntly. □□ **forthrightly** adv. **forthright-ness** n. [OE forthriht (as FORTH, RIGHT)]

■ adj. **1** straightforward, straight, direct, blunt, outspoken, plainspoken, plain, explicit, unequivocal, candid, frank, honest, ingenuous, aboveboard, open, truthful, colloq. upfront; uninhibited, unreserved, unconstrained, unrestrained. **2** see UNHESITATING.

forthwith /fáwrthwíth, -wíth/ adv. immediately; without delay. [earlier forthwithal (as FORTH, WITH, ALL)]

fortification /fáwrtifikáyshən/ n. **1** the act or an instance of fortifying; the process of being fortified. **2** Mil. **a** the art or science of fortifying. **b** (usu. in pl.) defensive works fortifying a position. [ME f. F f. LL fortificatio -onis act of strengthening (as FORTIFY)]

fortify /fáwrtifí/ v.tr. (-ies, -ied) **1** provide or equip with defensive works so as to strengthen against attack. **2** strengthen or invigorate physically, mentally, or morally. **3** strengthen the structure of. **4** strengthen (wine) with alcohol. **5** increase the nutritive value of (food, esp. with vitamins). □□ **fortifiable** adj. **fortifier** n. [ME f. OF fortifier f. LL fortificare f. L fortis strong]

■ **1** arm, make ready; defend, strengthen, safeguard, secure, protect, shield, guard. **2** strengthen, invigorate, brace, stimulate, animate, vivify, quicken, enliven, energize; steel, harden, support, buoy (up), prop (up), uphold, sustain, encourage, hearten, embolden, cheer (on or up), uplift, inspire, reassure, colloq. boost. **3** reinforce, strengthen, toughen, brace, harden, stay, prop (up), shore (up), buttress (up), brace, bolster (up), literary stay. **4, 5** supplement, enhance, enrich, augment, lace, colloq. boost, spike.

fortissimo /fawrtísimō/ adj., adv., & n. Mus. ● adj. performed very loudly. ● adv. very loudly. ● n. (pl. -os or **fortissimi** /-mee/) a passage to be performed very loudly. [It., superl. of FORTE²]

■ adj. see LOUD adj. 1.

fortitude /fáwrtitōōd, -tyōōd/ n. courage in pain or adversity. [ME f. F f. L fortitudo -dinis f. fortis strong]

■ courage, bravery, daring, valor, boldness, intrepidity, stalwartness, stoutheartedness, resoluteness, resolution, pluck, nerve, mettle, colloq. grit, guts; stoicism, strength, backbone, endurance, willpower.

fortnight /fáwrtnít/ n. **1** a period of two weeks. **2** Brit. (prec. by a specified day) two weeks after (that day) (Tuesday fortnight). [OE fēowertīene niht fourteen nights]

fortnightly /fáwrtnítlee/ adj., adv., & n. esp. Brit. ● adj. done, produced, or occurring once a fortnight. ● adv. every fortnight. ● n. (pl. -ies) a magazine, etc., issued every fortnight.

Fortran /fáwrtran/ n. (also **FORTRAN**) Computing a high-level programming language used esp. for scientific calculations. [formula translation]

fortress /fáwrtris/ n. a military stronghold, esp. a strongly fortified town fit for a large garrison. [ME f. OF forteresse, ult. f. L fortis strong]

■ see STRONGHOLD 1.

fortuitous /fawrtōōitəs, -tyōō-/ adj. due to or characterized by chance; accidental; casual. □□ **fortuitously** adv. **fortuitousness** n. [L fortuitus f. forte by chance]

■ see ACCIDENTAL adj. 1.

fortuity /fawrtōōitee, -tyōō-/ n. (pl. -ies) **1** a chance occurrence. **2** accident or chance; fortuitousness.

■ **1** see COINCIDENCE 2. **2** see ACCIDENT 1, 3.

fortunate /fáwrchənət/ adj. **1** favored by fortune; lucky; prosperous. **2** auspicious; favorable. [ME f. L fortunatus (as FORTUNE)]

■ **1** lucky, blessed, charmed, favored; prosperous. **2** advantageous, promising, propitious, auspicious, providential, favorable, opportune, timely, well-timed, happy, serendipitous.

fortunately /fáwrchənətlee/ adv. **1** luckily; successfully. **2** (qualifying a whole sentence) it is fortunate that.

■ **1** see happily (HAPPY).

fortune /fáwrchən/ n. **1 a** chance or luck as a force in human affairs. **b** a person's destiny. **2** (**Fortune**) this force person-

ified, often as a deity. **3** (in sing. or pl.) the good or bad luck that befalls a person or an enterprise. **4** good luck. **5** prosperity; a prosperous condition. **6** (also colloq. **small fortune**) great wealth; a huge sum of money. □ **fortune hunter** colloq. a person seeking wealth by marriage. **fortune-teller** a person who claims to predict future events in a person's life. **fortune-telling** the practice of this. **make a** (or one's) **fortune** acquire wealth or prosperity. **tell a person's fortune** make predictions about a person's future. [ME f. OF f. L fortuna luck, chance]

■ **1 a** luck, chance, fate, destiny, hazard, accident, happenstance. **b** destiny, lot, fate, portion, kismet, Buddhism & Hinduism karma. **2** Fate, Chance, Providence. **3** circumstance(s), experience(s), adventures. **4** good luck, serendipity; fluke, stroke of luck, colloq. break. **5** prosperity, wealth, money, affluence, opulence, riches, plenty, literary weal; success. **6** colloq. packet, pile, Brit. sl. bomb; see also MINT² n. 2. □ **fortune-teller** clairvoyant, soothsayer, psychic, oracle, prophet, diviner, augur, seer, sibyl, haruspex, palmist, prognosticator, colloq. usu. derog. or joc. stargazer; futurologist.

forty /fáwrtee/ n. & adj. ● n. (pl. -ies) **1** the product of four and ten. **2** a symbol for this (40, xl, XL). **3** (in pl.) the numbers from 40 to 49, esp. the years of a century or of a person's life. **4** (**the Forties**) Brit. the sea area between the NE coast of Scotland and the SW coast of Norway (so called from its depth of forty fathoms or more). ● adj. that amount to forty. □ **forty-first, -second**, etc., the ordinal numbers between fortieth and fiftieth. **forty-five 1** a phonograph record played at 45 r.p.m. **2** a .45 caliber handgun. **the Forty-five** the Jacobite rebellion of 1745. **forty-niner** a seeker for gold, etc., in the California gold rush of 1849. **forty-one, -two**, etc., the cardinal numbers between forty and fifty. **forty winks** colloq. a short sleep. □□ **fortieth** adj. & n. **fortyfold** adj. & adv. [OE fēowertig (as FOUR, -TY²)]

forum /fáwrəm/ n. **1** a place of or meeting for public discussion. **2** a periodical, etc., giving an opportunity for discussion. **3** a court or tribunal. **4** hist. a public square or marketplace in an ancient Roman city used for judicial and other business. [L, in sense 4]

■ **1** see DISCUSSION 1. **2** see ORGAN 3.

forward /fáwrwərd/ adj., n., adv., & v. ● adj. **1** lying in one's line of motion. **2 a** onward or toward the front. **b** Naut. belonging to the fore part of a ship. **3** precocious; bold in manner; presumptuous. **4** Commerce relating to future produce, delivery, etc. (forward contract). **5 a** advanced; progressing toward or approaching maturity or completion. **b** (of a plant, etc.) well advanced or early. ● n. an attacking player positioned near the front of a team in football, hockey, etc. ● adv. **1** to the front; into prominence (come forward; move forward). **2** in advance; ahead (sent them forward). **3** onward so as to make progress (not getting any farther forward). **4** toward the future; continuously onward (from this time forward). **5** (also **forward**) **a** toward the front in the direction one is facing. **b** in the normal direction of motion or of traversal. **c** with continuous forward motion (backward and forward; rushing forward). **6** Naut. & Aeron. in, near, or toward the bow or nose. ● v.tr. **1 a** send (a letter, etc.) on to a further destination. **b** esp. Brit. dispatch (goods, etc.) (forwarding agent). **2** help to advance; promote. □ **forward-looking** progressive; favoring change. □□ **forwarder** n. **forwardly** adv. **forwardness** n. (esp. in sense 3 of adj.). [OE forweard, var. of forthweard (as FORTH, -WARD)]

■ adj. **1** (up) ahead, in front, colloq. up front. **2** advance, front, head, fore; foremost, leading, first; frontal. **3** precocious, presumptuous, presuming, familiar, confident, bold, brazen, audacious, saucy, colloq. fresh, pushy. **5** advanced, developed, well-developed, mature, ripe, precocious; early. ● *adv.* **1** ahead, in front, frontward(s), to the fore, up, out, (out) into the open, to the surface, into view, *colloq.* up front. **2** (up) ahead, in advance, in front, at the front, in the lead *or* vanguard, before, to the fore, *archaic* forth; onward(s). **3, 5** along, onward(s), forward, ahead; in front. ● *v.* **1 a** send on. **2** advance, further, promote, back, champion, favor, foster, support, benefit, aid, assist, help; propose, move, submit, suggest, advocate, recommend. □ **forward-looking** see PROGRESSIVE *adj.* 3.

forwards var. of FORWARD *adv.* 5.

forwent *past* of FORGO.

fossa /fósə/ *n.* (*pl.* **fossae** /-see/) *Anat.* a shallow depression or cavity. [L, = ditch, fem. past part. of *fodere* dig]

fosse /fos/ *n.* **1** a long narrow trench or excavation, esp. in a fortification. **2** *Anat.* = FOSSA. [ME f. OF f. L *fossa*: see FOSSA]

fossick /fósik/ *v.intr. Austral. & NZ colloq.* **1** (foll. by *about*, *around*) rummage; search. **2** search for gold, etc., in abandoned workings. □□ **fossicker** *n.* [19th c.: cf. dial. *fossick* bustle about]

fossil /fósəl/ *n. & adj.* ● *n.* **1** the remains or impression of a (usu. prehistoric) plant or animal hardened in rock (often *attrib.*: *fossil bones*; *fossil shells*). **2** *colloq.* an antiquated or unchanging person or thing. **3** a word that has become obsolete except in set phrases or forms, e.g., *hue* in *hue and cry*. ● *adj.* **1** of or like a fossil. **2** antiquated; out of date. □ **fossil fuel** a natural fuel such as coal or gas formed in the geological past from the remains of living organisms. **fossil ivory** see IVORY. □□ **fossiliferous** /fósilífərəs/ *adj.* **fossilize** *v.tr. & intr.* **fossilization** *n.* [F *fossile* f. L *fossilis* f. *fodere* foss- dig] ■ *n.* **2** see FOGY. ● *adj.* **2** see ANCIENT[1] *adj.* 2.

fossorial /fosáwreeəl/ *adj.* **1** (of animals) burrowing. **2** (of limbs, etc.) used in burrowing. [med.L *fossorius* f. *fossor* digger (as FOSSIL)]

foster /fáwstər, fós-/ *v. & adj.* ● *v.tr.* **1 a** promote the growth or development of. **b** encourage or harbor (a feeling). **2** (of circumstances) be favorable to. **3 a** bring up (a child that is not one's own by birth). **b** *Brit.* (of a local authority, etc.) place (a child) to be fostered. **4** cherish; have affectionate regard for (an idea, scheme, etc.). ● *adj.* **1** having a family connection by fostering and not by birth (*foster brother*; *foster child*; *foster parent*). **2** involving or concerned with fostering a child (*foster care*; *foster home*). □□ **fosterage** *n.* (esp. in sense 3 of *v.*). **fosterer** *n.* [OE *fōstrian*, *fōster*, rel. to FOOD] ■ *v.* **1 a** promote, encourage, stimulate, favor, further, forward, advance, aid, help, assist. **b** harbor, nurture; encourage, stimulate, arouse, awaken, excite, incite, stir up, inspire, fuel. **2** create, produce, generate, cultivate, encourage, stimulate. **3 a** bring up, rear, raise, take care of, look after, care for. **4** cherish, nurse, harbor, indulge, incubate; see also ENTERTAIN 3.

fosterling /fáwstərling, fós-/ *n.* a foster child; a nursling. [OE *fōsterling* (as FOSTER)]

fouetté /fwetáy/ *n. Ballet* a quick whipping movement of the raised leg. [F, past part. of *fouetter* whip]

fought *past* and *past part.* of FIGHT.

foul /fowl/ *adj., n., adv., & v.* ● *adj.* **1** offensive to the senses; loathsome; stinking. **2** dirty; soiled; filthy. **3** *colloq.* revolting; disgusting. **4 a** containing or charged with noxious matter (*foul air*). **b** clogged; choked. **5** morally polluted; disgustingly abusive or offensive (*foul language*; *foul deeds*). **6** unfair; against the rules of a game, etc. (*by fair means or foul*). **7** (of the weather) wet; rough; stormy. **8** (of a rope, etc.) entangled. **9** (of a ship's bottom) overgrown with weeds, barnacles, etc. ● *n.* **1** *Sports* an unfair or invalid stroke or action. **2** *Baseball* a batted ball not hit into fair territory. **3** a collision or entanglement, esp. in riding, rowing, or running. **4** a foul thing. ● *adv.* unfairly; contrary to the rules. ● *v.* **1** *tr. & intr.* make or become foul or dirty. **2** *tr.* (of an animal) make dirty with excrement. **3 a** *tr. Sports* commit a foul against (a player). **b** *intr.* commit a foul. **4** *tr. & intr. Sports* hit a ball foul. **5 a** *tr.* (often foll. by *up*) cause (an anchor,

cable, etc.) to become entangled or muddled. **b** *intr.* become entangled. **6** *tr.* jam or block (a crossing, railway line, or traffic). **7** *tr.* (usu. foll. by *up*) *colloq.* spoil or bungle. **8** *tr.* run foul of; collide with. **9** *tr.* pollute with guilt; dishonor. □ **foul ball** = sense 2 of *n.* **foul brood** a fatal disease of larval bees caused by bacteria. **foul mouth** a person who uses foul language. **foul play 1** unfair play in games. **2** treacherous or violent activity, esp. murder. **foul shot** = *free throw.* **foul-up** a muddled or bungled situation. □□ **foully** *adv.* **foulness** *n.* [OE *fūl* f. Gmc]
■ *adj.* **1** offensive, loathsome, vile, obnoxious, revolting, repulsive, repellent, repugnant, rank, sickening, nauseous, nauseating, *literary* noisome; stinking, malodorous, fetid, rancid, sour, putrid, rotten, smelly, rank. **2** filthy, dirty, grimy, mucky, unclean, squalid, sordid, soiled, *sl.* yucky. **3** revolting, disgusting, nauseating, sickening, repulsive, odious, execrable, detestable, hateful, abominable, hideous, horrid, distasteful, nasty, *colloq.* vile, horrible, beastly, *sl.* gross. **4 a** tainted, adulterated, contaminated, polluted, poisonous, impure, stale, musty, bad, mephitic. **b** choked, clogged (up), blocked, congested, obstructed; overgrown, rank. **5** vile, bad, base, depraved, reprobate, corrupt, squalid, sordid, seamy, shameful, low, sinful, immoral, nefarious, iniquitous, wicked, evil, diabolic, damnable, abominable, vicious, villainous, flagitious, atrocious, monstrous, disgraceful, ignominious; abusive, offensive, dirty, obscene, filthy, scatological, coarse, crude, gross, smutty, lewd, indecent, vulgar, rude, scurrilous, outrageous, profane, blasphemous. **6** dirty, dishonest, fraudulent, two-faced, dishonorable, unfair, unscrupulous, underhand, underhanded, unsporting, unsportsmanlike, double-dealing, *colloq.* crooked, esp. *Brit. sl.* bent; illegal, forbidden, prohibited, interdicted. **7** wet, rough, stormy, nasty, violent, atrocious, *colloq.* vile; adverse, hostile. **8** tangly, entangled, tangled, snarled (up), muddled (up), twisted; snagged, enmeshed, ensnared, entrapped, trapped, caught (up). ● *n.* **1** violation, breach, abuse, contravention, professional foul, infringement, infraction. **3** collision, entanglement, *Brit. colloq.* snarl-up; see also TANGLE[1] *n.* 1. **4** horror, abomination, anathema; see also *infamy* (INFAMOUS). ● *adv.* foully, unfairly, meanly, dishonestly, fraudulently, shabbily, dirtily, unsportingly; in violation. ● *v.* **1** dirty, defile, soil, besmirch, pollute, contaminate, taint, *poet.* sully, befoul. **5** tangle, entangle, catch (up), snare, ensnare, snarl (up), jam, twist. **6** jam, block, impede, obstruct, choke, stop (up), clog (up). **7** spoil, ruin, bungle, mismanage, mishandle, botch (up), mess up, make a mess of, muff, *colloq.* muck (up), make a muck of, *sl.* louse up, screw up, goof, blow. **8** strike, hit, collide with, bang *or* bump (into), crash *or* run *or* smash *or* slam into, dash against. **9** pollute, shame, degrade, debase, demean, disparage, abase, humiliate, belittle, besmirch, defile, tarnish, smear, taint, blacken, discredit; defame, dishonor, disgrace, sully; desecrate, violate. □ **foul play 1** cheating, unfairness, dirty tricks, dirty work. **2** trickery, perfidy, chicanery, duplicity, deceitfulness, deceit, guile, skulduggery; deception, dirty trick, crime, conspiracy; murder, manslaughter, homicide. **foul-up** see BLUNDER *n.*

foulard /foolaárd/ *n.* **1** a thin soft material of silk or silk and cotton. **2** an article made of this. [F]

found[1] *past* and *past part.* of FIND.

found[2] /fownd/ *v.* **1** *tr.* **a** establish (esp. with an endowment). **b** originate or initiate (an institution). **2** *tr.* be the original builder or begin the building of (a town, etc.). **3** *tr.* lay the base of (a building, etc.). **4** (foll. by *on*, *upon*) **a** *tr.* construct or base (a story, theory, rule, etc.) according to a specified principle or ground. **b** *intr.* have a basis in. □ **founding father** a person associated with a founding, esp. (usu. *cap.*) an American statesman at the time of the Revolution. [ME f. OF *fonder* f. L *fundare* f. *fundus* bottom]

■ **1** establish, constitute, set up, originate, institute, initiate, float, launch, organize, inaugurate, pioneer, start, create, begin, bring about, father. **2** build, erect, raise, construct, develop, establish. **4 a** construct, ground, build; rest; see also BASE¹ *v.* 1.

found³ /fownd/ *v.tr.* **1 a** melt and mold (metal). **b** fuse (materials for glass). **2** make by founding. □□ **founder** *n.* [ME f. OF *fondre* f. L *fundere fus-* pour]

foundation /fowndáyshən/ *n.* **1 a** the solid ground or base, natural or artificial, on which a building rests. **b** (usu. in *pl.*) the lowest load-bearing part of a building, usu. below ground level. **2** a body or ground on which other parts are overlaid. **3** a basis or underlying principle; groundwork (*the report has no foundation*). **4 a** the act or an instance of establishing or constituting (esp. an endowed institution) on a permanent basis. **b** such an institution, e.g., a college or hospital. **5** (in full **foundation garment**) a woman's supporting undergarment, e.g., a corset. □ **foundation cream** a cream used as a base for applying cosmetics. **foundation stone 1** a stone laid with ceremony to celebrate the founding of a building. **2** the main ground or basis of something. □□ **foundational** *adj.* [ME f. OF *fondation* f. L *fundatio -onis* (as FOUND²)]

■ **1** base, substructure. **2** background, body, ground, field, infrastructure. **3** basis, base, underlying principle, starting point, fundamental(s), grounds, groundwork, rationale, justification, raison d'être. **4** establishment, founding, instituting, institution, creation, origination, initiation, setting up, organizing, organization, inauguration, endowment.

founder¹ /fówndər/ *n.* a person who founds an institution. □□ **foundership** *n.*

■ originator, creator, progenitor, author, framer, father, architect, designer, builder, initiator, establisher.

founder² /fówndər/ *v. & n.* ● *v.* **1 a** *intr.* (of a ship) fill with water and sink. **b** *tr.* cause (a ship) to founder. **2** *intr.* (of a plan, etc.) fail. **3** *intr.* (of earth, a building, etc.) fall down or in; give way. **4 a** *intr.* (of a horse or its rider) fall to the ground, fall from lameness, stick fast in mud, etc. **b** *tr.* cause (a horse) to break down, esp. with founder. ● *n.* **1** inflammation of a horse's foot from overwork. **2** rheumatism of the chest muscles in horses. [ME f. OF *fondrer, esfondrer* submerge, collapse, ult. f. L *fundus* bottom]

■ *v.* **1 a** sink, go down *or* under, go to Davy Jones's locker; be wrecked *or* destroyed. **2** fail, miscarry, collapse, come to nothing *or* naught, fall through, abort, break down, come to grief, die, *sl.* come a cropper. **3** see *give way* 3 (WAY). **4 a** trip, stumble, lurch, fall, topple (over *or* down), collapse; go lame.

foundling /fówndling/ *n.* an abandoned infant of unknown parentage. [ME, perh. f. obs. *funding* (as FIND, -ING³), assim. to -LING¹]

■ orphan, waif; stray, outcast.

foundry /fówndree/ *n.* (*pl.* **-ies**) a workshop for or a business of casting metal.

■ see MILL¹ *n.* 3a.

fount¹ /fownt/ *n. poet.* a spring or fountain; a source. [back-form. f. FOUNTAIN after MOUNT²]

■ see FOUNTAIN 1–3, SPRING *n.* 6.

fount² /fownt/ *n. Brit.* = FONT.

fountain /fówntin/ *n.* **1 a** a jet or jets of water made to spout for ornamental purposes or for drinking. **b** a structure provided for this. **2** a structure for the constant public supply of drinking water. **3** a natural spring of water. **4** a source (in physical or abstract senses). **5** = *soda fountain*. **6** a reservoir for oil, ink, etc. □ **fountain pen** a pen with a reservoir or cartridge holding ink. □□ **fountained** *adj.* (also in *comb.*). [ME f. OF *fontaine* f. LL *fontana* fem. of L *fontanus* (adj.) f. *fons fontis* a spring]

■ **1–3** spring, jet, spout, spray, wellspring, wellhead, *archaic* well, *poet.* fount. **4** see SPRING *n.* 6, ORIGIN 1.

fountainhead /fównt'nhed/ *n.* an original source.

■ see SOURCE *n.* 1.

four /fawr/ *n. & adj.* ● *n.* **1** one more than three, or six less than ten; the product of two units and two units. **2** a symbol

for this (4, iv, IV, rarely iiii, IIII). **3** a size, etc., denoted by four. **4** a four-oared rowing boat or its crew. **5** the time of four o'clock (*is it four yet?*). **6** a card with four pips. ● *adj.* that amount to four. □ **four-eyes** *sl.* a person wearing glasses. **four flush** *Cards* a poker hand of little value, having four cards of the same suit and one of another. **four-flusher** a bluffer, one who makes false claims. **four hundred** the social élite of a community. **four-in-hand 1** a vehicle with four horses driven by one person. **2** a necktie worn with a knot and two hanging ends superposed. **four-leaf** (or **-leaved**) **clover** a clover leaf with four leaflets thought to bring good luck. **four-letter word** any of several short words referring to sexual or excretory functions, regarded as coarse or offensive. **four-part** *Mus.* arranged for four voices to sing or instruments to play. **four-poster** a bed with a post at each corner supporting a canopy. **four-stroke** (or **-cycle**) (of an internal combustion engine) having a cycle of four strokes (intake, compression, combustion, and exhaust). **four-wheel drive** drive powering all four wheels of a vehicle. **on all fours** on hands and knees. [OE *fēower* f. Gmc]

fourchette /fŏŏrshét/ *n. Anat.* a thin fold of skin at the back of the vulva. [F, dimin. of *fourche* (as FORK)]

fourfold /fáwrfōld/ *adj. & adv.* **1** four times as much or as many. **2** consisting of four parts. **3** amounting to four.

Fourier analysis /fŏŏreeay/ *n. Math.* the resolution of periodic data into harmonic functions using a Fourier series. [J. B. J. *Fourier*, Fr. mathematician d. 1830]

Fourier series /fŏŏreeay/ *n. Math.* an expansion of a periodic function as a series of trigonometric functions.

fourpence /fáwrpəns/ *n. Brit.* the sum of four pence.

fourpenny /fáwrpənee/ *adj. Brit.* costing four pence. □ **fourpenny one** *Brit. colloq.* a hit or blow.

fourscore /fáwrskáwr/ *n. archaic* eighty.

foursome /fáwrsəm/ *n.* **1** a group of four persons. **2 a** a golf match between two pairs with partners playing the same ball. **b** a golf match with four players.

foursquare /fáwrskwáir/ *adj. & adv.* *adj.* **1** solidly based. **2** steady; resolute; forthright. **3** square shaped. ● *adv.* steadily; resolutely.

fourteen /fáwrteen/ *n. & adj.* ● *n.* **1** one more than thirteen, or four more than ten; the product of two units and seven units. **2** a symbol for this (14, xiv, XIV). **3** a size, etc., denoted by fourteen. ● *adj.* that amount to fourteen. □□ **fourteenth** *adj. & n.* [OE *fēowertīene* (as FOUR, -TEEN)]

fourth /fawrth/ *n. & adj.* ● *n.* **1** the position in a sequence corresponding to that of the number 4 in the sequence 1–4. **2** something occupying this position. **3** the fourth person, etc., in a race or competition. **4** each of four equal parts of a thing; a quarter. **5** the fourth in a sequence of gears. **6** *Mus.* **a** an interval or chord spanning four consecutive notes in the diatonic scale (e.g., C to F). **b** a note separated from another by this interval. **7** (**Fourth**) the Fourth of July. ● *adj.* that is the fourth. □ **fourth dimension 1** a postulated dimension additional to those determining area and volume. **2** time regarded as equivalent to linear dimensions. **fourth estate** the press; journalism. □□ **fourthly** *adv.* [OE *fēortha, fēowertha* f. Gmc]

fovea /fóveeə/ *n.* (*pl.* **foveae** /-vee-ee/) *Anat.* a small depression or pit, esp. the pit in the retina of the eye for focusing images. □□ **foveal** *adj.* **foveate** /-veeayt/ *adj.* [L]

fowl /fowl/ *n. & v.* (*pl.* same or **fowls**) ● *n.* **1** any domestic cock or hen of various gallinaceous birds, kept for eggs and flesh. **2** the flesh of birds, esp. a domestic cock or hen, as food. **3** *archaic* (except in *comb.* or *collect.*) a bird (*guineafowl*; *wildfowl*). ● *v.intr.* catch or hunt wildfowl. □ **fowl cholera** see CHOLERA. **fowl pest** an infectious virus disease of fowls. **fowl-run** *Brit.* **1** a place where fowls may run. **2** a

---

/. . . ./ **pronunciation**	● **part of speech**
□ **phrases, idioms, and compounds**	
□□ **derivatives**	■ **synonym section**
cross-references appear in SMALL CAPITALS or *italics*	

breeding establishment for fowls. □□ **fowler** *n.* **fowling** *n.* [OE *fugol* f. Gmc]

Fox /foks/ *n.* **1 a** a N. American people native to the northeastern US. **b** a member of this people. **2** the language of this people.

fox /foks/ *n. & v.* ● *n.* **1 a** any of various wild flesh-eating mammals of the dog family, esp. of the genus *Vulpes*, with a sharp snout, bushy tail, and red or gray fur. **b** the fur of a fox. **2** a cunning or sly person. **3** *sl.* an attractive young woman or man. ● *v.* **1 a** *intr.* act craftily. **b** *tr.* deceive; baffle; trick. **2** *tr.* (usu. as **foxed** *adj.*) discolor (the leaves of a book, engraving, etc.) with brownish marks. □ **fox terrier 1** a terrier of a short-haired breed originally used for digging out foxes. **2** this breed. □□ **foxing** *n.* (in sense 2 of *v.*). **fox-like** *adj.* [OE f. WG]

■ *n.* **2** see DEVIL *n.* 3b. **3** see TEMPTER 1. ● *v.* **1 b** see FLUMMOX.

foxglove /fóksgluv/ *n.* any tall plant of the genus *Digitalis*, with erect spikes of purple or white flowers like glove fingers.

foxhole /fóks-hōl/ *n.* **1** *Mil.* a hole in the ground used as a shelter against enemy fire or as a firing point. **2** a place of refuge or concealment.

foxhound /fóks-hownd/ *n.* a kind of hound bred and trained to hunt foxes.

fox hunt /fóks-hunt/ *n. & v.* ● *n.* **1** the hunting of foxes with hounds. **2** a particular group of people engaged in this. ● *v.intr.* engage in a foxhunt. □□ **foxhunter** *n.* **foxhunting** *n. & adj.*

foxtail /fókstayl/ *n.* any of several grasses of the genus *Alopecurus*, with brushlike spikes.

foxtrot /fókstrot/ *n. & v.* ● *n.* **1** a ballroom dance with slow and quick steps. **2** the music for this. ● *v.intr.* (**foxtrotted, foxtrotting**) perform this dance.

foxy /fóksee/ *adj.* (**foxier, foxiest**) **1** of or like a fox. **2** sly or cunning. **3** reddish brown. **4** (of paper) damaged, esp. by mildew. **5** *sl.* sexually attractive. □□ **foxily** *adv.* **foxiness** *n.*

■ **1** foxlike, vulpine. **2** clever, sly, cunning, wily, crafty, tricky, guileful, devious, slippery, smooth, slick, artful, calculating, designing, plotting, scheming, disingenuous, knowing, shrewd, sharp, astute, *colloq.* shifty, *colloq.* wise. **3** see RED *adj.* 4. **5** attractive, alluring, seductive, vampish, sexy.

foyer /fóyər, fóyay, fwaáyay/ *n.* the entrance hall or other large area in a hotel, theater, etc. [F, = hearth, home, ult. f. L *focus* fire]

■ see HALL 1.

FP *abbr.* freezing point.

fp *abbr.* forte piano.

FPO *abbr.* **1** field post office. **2** fleet post office.

fps *abbr.* (also **f.p.s.**) **1** feet per second. **2** foot-pound-second.

Fr *symb. Chem.* the element francium.

Fr. *abbr.* (also **Fr**) **1** Father. **2** French.

fr. *abbr.* franc(s).

Fra /fraa/ *n.* a prefixed title given to an Italian monk or friar. [It., abbr. of *frate* brother]

frabjous /frábjəs/ *adj.* delightful; joyous. □□ **frabjously** *adv.* [devised by Lewis Carroll, app. to suggest *fair* and *joyous*]

fracas /fráykəs/ *n.* (*pl.* same, *pronunc.* /-kaaz/) a noisy disturbance or quarrel. [F f. *fracasser* f. It. *fracassare* make an uproar]

■ disturbance, commotion, fuss, spot of trouble *or* bother, hubbub, hullabaloo, uproar, scramble, turmoil, tumult, free-for-all, riot, fray, brouhaha, mêlée, affray, tussle, donnybrook, brawl, scuffle, fight, ruckus, *colloq.* scrap, rumpus, *Brit. colloq.* scrum, *sl.* roughhouse; argument, disagreement, quarrel, dispute, discord, wrangle, altercation, squabble, tiff, *colloq.* row, spat.

fraction /frákshən/ *n.* **1** a numerical quantity that is not a whole number (e.g., 0.5, $1/_2$). **2** a small, esp. very small, part, piece, or amount. **3** a portion of a mixture separated by distillation, etc. **4** *Polit.* any organized dissenting group, esp. a group of communists in a noncommunist organization. **5** *Eccl.* the division of the Eucharistic bread. □□ **fractionary** *adj.* **fractionize** *v.tr.* [ME f. OF f. LL *fractio -onis* f. L *frangere fract-* break]

■ **2** see SECTION *n.* 2.

fractional /frákshənəl/ *adj.* **1** of or relating to or being a fraction. **2** very slight; incomplete. **3** *Chem.* relating to the separation of parts of a mixture by making use of their different physical properties (*fractional crystallization; fractional distillation*). □□ **fractionalize** *v.tr.* **fractionally** *adv.* (esp. in sense 2).

■ **2** see LITTLE *adj.* 1, 2.

fractionate /frákshənayt/ *v.tr.* **1** break up into parts. **2** separate (a mixture) by fractional distillation, etc. □□ **fractionation** /-náyshən/ *n.*

fractious /frákshəs/ *adj.* **1** irritable; peevish. **2** unruly. □□ **fractiously** *adv.* **fractiousness** *n.* [FRACTION in obs. sense 'brawling,' prob. after *factious*, etc.]

■ **1** see IRRITABLE 1. **2** see UNRULY.

fracto- /fráktō/ *comb. form Meteorol.* (of a cloud form) broken or fragmentary (*fractocumulus; fractonimbus*). [L *fractus* broken: see FRACTION]

fracture /frákchər/ *n. & v.* ● *n.* **1 a** a breakage or breaking, esp. of a bone or cartilage. **b** the result of breaking; a crack or split. **2** the surface appearance of a freshly broken rock or mineral. **3** *Linguistics* **a** the substitution of a diphthong for a simple vowel owing to an influence esp. of a following consonant. **b** a diphthong substituted in this way. ● *v.intr. & tr.* **1** *Med.* undergo or cause to undergo a fracture. **2** break or cause to break. [ME f. F *fracture* or f. L *fractura* (as FRACTION)]

■ *n.* **1 a** break, breakage, breaking, separation, division. **b** break, crack, split, rupture, breach, cleavage, rift. ● *v.* break, rupture, crack, split, breach, separate, *literary* cleave.

fraenulum *Brit.* var. of FRENULUM.

fraenum *Brit.* var. of FRENUM.

fragile /frájil, -jīl/ *adj.* **1** easily broken; weak. **2** of delicate frame or constitution; not strong. □□ **fragilely** *adv.* **fragility** /frəjílitee/ *n.* [F *fragile* or L *fragilis* f. *frangere* break]

■ **1** breakable, brittle, rickety, frangible, frail, flimsy, weak, feeble, infirm, decrepit; tenuous, shaky, insubstantial. **2** delicate, dainty, thin, light, slight; frail, weak; see also FEEBLE 2.

fragment *n. & v.* ● *n.* /frágmənt/ **1** a part broken off; a detached piece. **2** an isolated or incomplete part. **3** the remains of an otherwise lost or destroyed whole, esp. the extant remains or unfinished portion of a book or work of art. ● *v.tr. & intr.* /fragmént/ break or separate into fragments. □□ **fragmental** /-mént'l/ *adj.* **fragmentize** *v.tr.* [ME f. F *fragment* or L *fragmentum* (as FRAGILE)]

■ *n.* **1, 2** piece, portion, part, chip, shard, splinter, sliver, scrap, bit, speck, snippet, morsel, crumb, particle, remnant, shred; snatch; (*fragments*) smithereens, debris, remains, disjecta membra. ● *v.* break (up), split (up), separate, shatter, splinter, explode, disintegrate; come apart.

fragmentary /frágmənteree/ *adj.* **1** consisting of fragments. **2** disconnected. **3** *Geol.* composed of fragments of previously existing rocks. □□ **fragmentarily** *adv.*

■ **1** piecemeal, incomplete, sketchy, bitty, scrappy, patchy, skimpy. **2** disconnected, scattered, disjointed; see also INCOHERENT 2.

fragmentation /frágməntáyshən/ *n.* the process or an instance of breaking into fragments. □ **fragmentation bomb** a bomb designed to break up into small rapidly-moving fragments when exploded.

■ see SEPARATION.

fragrance /fráygrəns/ *n.* **1** sweetness of smell. **2** a sweet scent. [F *fragrance* or L *fragrantia* (as FRAGRANT)]

■ **1** fragrancy, redolence, perfume. **2** fragrancy, scent, aroma, redolence, perfume, balm; bouquet.

fragrancy /fráygrənsee/ *n.* (*pl.* **-ies**) = FRAGRANCE.

fragrant /fráygrənt/ *adj.* sweet-smelling. □□ **fragrantly** *adv.* [ME f. F *fragrant* or L *fragrare* smell sweet]

■ aromatic, redolent, perfumed, odoriferous, ambrosial, sweet-scented, sweet-smelling.

frail /frayl/ *adj. & n.* ● *adj.* **1** fragile; delicate. **2** in weak health. **3** morally weak; unable to resist temptation. **4** transient; insubstantial. ● *n. Old-fash.* (usu. *derog.*) *sl.* a woman. ▫▫ **fraily** *adv.* **frailness** *n.* [ME f. OF *fraile, frele* f. L *fragilis* FRAGILE]

■ *adj.* **1** see FRAGILE 1. **2** ailing, unwell, ill, sick, sickly, poorly, wasting *or* fading away, languishing, infirm, feeble, fragile. **3** susceptible, weak, venal, corruptible; bribable, buyable, purchasable. ● *n.* see WOMAN 1.

frailty /fráyltee/ *n.* (*pl.* **-ies**) **1** the condition of being frail. **2** liability to err or yield to temptation. **3** a fault, weakness, or foible. [ME f. OF *fraileté* f. L *fragilitas -tatis* (as FRAGILE)]

■ **1** frailness, weakness, infirmity, feebleness, fragility, delicacy. **2** susceptibility, suggestibility, impressionability, vulnerability; fallibility. **3** weakness, foible, flaw, fault, defect, imperfection.

Fraktur /fráktŏŏr/ *n.* a German style of black letter type. [G]

frambesia /frambeezhə/ *n. Med.* = YAWS. [mod.L f. F *framboise* raspberry f. L *fraga ambrosia* ambrosial strawberry]

frame /fraym/ *n. & v.* ● *n.* **1** a case or border enclosing a picture, window, door, etc. **2** the basic rigid supporting structure of anything, e.g., of a building, motor vehicle, or aircraft. **3** (in *pl.*) the structure of spectacles holding the lenses. **4** a human or animal body, esp. with reference to its size or structure (*his frame shook with laughter*). **5** a framed work or structure (*the frame of heaven*). **6 a** an established order, plan, or system (*the frame of society*). **b** construction; constitution; build. **7** a temporary state (esp. in **frame of mind**). **8** a single complete image or picture on a movie or video film or transmitted in a series of lines by television. **9 a** a triangular structure for positioning the balls in pool, etc. **b** the balls positioned in this way. **c** a round of play in bowling, etc. **10** *Hort.* a boxlike structure of glass, etc., for protecting plants. **11** a removable box of slats for the building of a honeycomb in a beehive. **12** *sl.* = **frame-up.** ● *v.tr.* **1 a** set in or provide with a frame. **b** serve as a frame for. **2** construct by a combination of parts or in accordance with a design or plan. **3** formulate or devise the essentials of (a complex thing, idea, theory, etc.). **4** (foll. by *to, into*) adapt or fit. **5** *colloq.* concoct a false charge or evidence against; devise a plot with regard to. **6** articulate (words). ▫ **frame house** a house constructed of a wooden skeleton covered with boards, etc. **frame of reference 1** a set of standards or principles governing behavior, thought, etc. **2** *Geom.* a system of geometrical axes for defining position. **frame-up** *colloq.* a conspiracy, esp. to make an innocent person appear guilty. ▫▫ **framable** *adj.* (also **frameable**) **frameless** *adj.* **framer** *n.* [OE *framian* be of service f. *fram* forward: see FROM]

■ *n.* **1** border, casing, mount, edge, edging; setting. **2** framework, framing, body, structure, fabric, shell, form, skeleton, support; chassis; fuselage. **3** physique, build, bone structure, body, skeleton, figure. **6 a** system, form, pattern, scheme, schema, plan, order, organization, framework, scaffolding. **b** structure, construct, construction, build, arrangement, blueprint, design, layout, composition, constitution, context, makeup, configuration. **7** (**frame of mind**) mood, humor, state (of mind), condition, attitude, bent, disposition. ● *v.* **1** enclose, box (in). **2** construct, build, put together, make up, assemble, put up, erect, raise, elevate. **3** make, fashion, form, mold, carve out, forge, originate, set up, create, devise, compose, formulate, put together, conceive, draw up, draft, shape, block out, give form *or* shape to; contrive. **4** (*frame to or into*) see ADAPT 1a. ▫ **frame of reference 1** see CODE *n.* 5. **frame-up** see CONSPIRACY 1.

framework /fráymwərk/ *n.* **1** an essential supporting structure. **2** a basic system.

■ **1** see STRUCTURE *n.* 1b. **2** see FORMAT *n.* 2.

framing /fráyming/ *n.* a framework; a system of frames.

■ see FABRICATION 1.

franc /frangk/ *n.* the chief monetary unit of France, Belgium, Switzerland, Luxembourg, and several other countries. [ME f. OF f. *Francorum Rex* king of the Franks, the legend on the earliest gold coins so called (14th c.): see FRANK]

franchise /fránchīz/ *n. & v.* ● *n.* **1 a** the right to vote in governmental elections. **b** the principle of qualification for this. **2** full membership of a corporation or nation; citizenship. **3** authorization granted to an individual or group by a company to sell its goods or services in a particular way. **4** *hist.* legal immunity or exemption from a burden or jurisdiction. **5** a right or privilege granted to a person or corporation. **6** a professional sports team, esp. as part of a league. ● *v.tr.* grant a franchise to. ▫▫ **franchisee** /-zeé/ *n.* **franchiser** *n.* (also **franchisor**). [ME f. OF f. *franc, franche* free: see FRANK]

■ *n.* **1** see SUFFRAGE. **3** see LICENSE 2. **5** see PRIVILEGE *n.* 1a. ● *v.* see CHARTER *v.* 1.

Franciscan /fransískən/ *n. & adj.* ● *n.* a friar, sister, or lay member of an order founded in 1209 by St. Francis of Assisi (see also GREY FRIAR). ● *adj.* of St. Francis or his order. [F *franciscain* f. mod.L *Franciscanus* f. *Franciscus* Francis]

francium /fránseeəm/ *n. Chem.* a radioactive metallic element occurring naturally in uranium and thorium ores. ¶ Symb.: **Fr.** [mod.L f. *France* (the discoverer's country)]

Franco- /frángkō/ *comb. form* **1** French; French and (*Franco-German*). **2** regarding France or the French (*Francophile*). [med.L *Francus* FRANK]

francolin /frángkōlin/ *n.* any medium-sized partridge of the genus *Francolinus*. [F f. It. *francolino*]

Francophile /frángkəfīl/ *n.* a person who is fond of France or the French.

francophone /frángkəfōn/ *n. & adj.* ● *n.* a French-speaking person. ● *adj.* French-speaking. [FRANCO- + Gk *phōnē* voice]

frangible /fránjibəl/ *adj.* breakable; fragile. [OF *frangible* or med.L *frangibilis* f. L *frangere* to break]

frangipane /fránjipayn/ *n.* **1 a** an almond-flavored cream or paste. **b** a flan filled with this. **2** = FRANGIPANI. [F prob. f. Marquis *Frangipani*, 16th-c. It. inventor of the perfume]

frangipani /fránjipánee, -páanee/ *n.* (*pl.* **frangipanis**) **1** any tree or shrub of the genus *Plumeria*, native to tropical America, esp. *P. rubra* with clusters of fragrant white, pink, or yellow flowers. **2** the perfume from this plant. [var. of FRANGIPANE]

franglais /frónglay/ *n.* a version of French using many words and idioms borrowed from English. [F f. *français* French + *anglais* English]

Frank /frangk/ *n.* **1** a member of the Germanic nation or coalition that conquered Gaul in the 6th c. **2** (in the Levant) a person of Western nationality. ▫▫ **Frankish** *adj.* [OE *Franca*, OHG *Franko*, perh. f. the name of a weapon: cf. OE *franca* javelin]

frank /frangk/ *adj., v., & n.* ● *adj.* **1** candid; outspoken (*a frank opinion*). **2** undisguised; avowed (*frank admiration*). **3** ingenuous; open (*a frank face*). **4** *Med.* unmistakable. ● *v.tr.* **1** stamp (a letter) with an official mark (esp. other than a normal postage stamp) to record the payment of postage. **2** *hist.* superscribe (a letter, etc.) with a signature ensuring conveyance without charge; send without charge. **3** *archaic* facilitate the coming and going of (a person). ● *n.* **1** a franking signature or mark. **2** a franked cover. ▫▫ **frankable** *adj.* **franker** *n.* **frankness** *n.* [ME f. OF *franc* f. med.L *francus* free, f. FRANK (since only Franks had full freedom in Frankish Gaul)]

■ *adj.* **1** candid, direct, outspoken, blunt, plainspoken, forthright, *colloq.* upfront; explicit; truthful, *colloq.* on the level. **2** undisguised, avowed, open, free, unreserved, uninhibited, unrestrained, unchecked, unconstrained, unrestricted, unabashed. **3** ingenuous, open, honest, sincere, genuine, candid, naive, guileless, artless, innocent.

Frankenstein /frángkənstin/ *n.* (in full **Frankenstein's monster**) a thing that becomes terrifying to its maker; a

---

/. . ./ **pronunciation**	● **part of speech**
▫ **phrases, idioms, and compounds**	
▫▫ **derivatives**	■ **synonym section**
cross-references appear in SMALL CAPITALS or *italics*	

monster. [Baron *Frankenstein*, a character in and the title of a novel (1818) by Mary Shelley]

frankfurter /fráŋkfərtər/ *n.* a seasoned sausage made of beef or beef and other meat, such as pork. [G *Frankfurter Wurst* Frankfurt sausage]

frankincense /fráŋkinsens/ *n.* an aromatic gum resin obtained from trees of the genus *Boswellia*, used for burning as incense. [ME f. OF *franc encens* pure incense]

franklin /fráŋklin/ *n. hist.* a landowner of free but not noble birth in the 14th and 15th c. in England. [ME *francoleyn*, etc., f. AL *francalanus* f. *francalis* held without dues f. *francus* free: see FRANK]

Franklin stove /fráŋklin/ *n.* a cast-iron stove having the general shape of an open fireplace but often placed so as to be freestanding. [for its designer, US statesman Benjamin *Franklin* d. 1790]

frankly /fráŋklee/ *adv.* **1** in a frank manner. **2** (qualifying a whole sentence) to be frank.
■ **1** see OPENLY 1.

frantic /frántik/ *adj.* **1** wildly excited; frenzied. **2** characterized by great hurry or anxiety; desperate; violent. **3** *colloq.* extreme; very great. □□ **frantically** *adv.* **franticly** *adv.* **franticness** *n.* [ME *frentik*, *frantik* f. OF *frenetique* f. L *phreneticus*: see PHRENETIC]
■ **1** frenzied, excited, frenetic, hectic, hysterical, wild, mad, running amok, *literary* infuriate; *colloq.* in a state, all of a dither. **2** desperate, violent; upset, agitated, perturbed, at one's wit's end, disconcerted; overwrought, distraught, beside oneself, berserk, *colloq.* up the wall, in a tizzy.

frap /frap/ *v.tr.* (**frapped**, **frapping**) *Naut.* bind tightly. [F *frapper* bind, strike]

frappé /frapáy/ *adj. & n.* ● *adj.* (esp. of wine) iced, cooled.
● *n.* **1** an iced drink. **2** a soft semi-frozen drink or dessert. [F, past part. of *frapper* strike, ice (drinks)]

frass /fras/ *n.* **1** a fine powdery refuse left by insects boring. **2** the excrement of insect larvae. [G f. *fressen* devour (as FRET¹)]

frat /frat/ *n. colloq.* a student fraternity.

fraternal /frətə́rnəl/ *adj.* **1** of a brother or brothers. **2** suitable to a brother; brotherly. **3** (of twins) developed from separate ova and not necessarily closely similar. **4** of or concerning a fraternity (see FRATERNITY 3). □□ **fraternalism** *n.* **fraternally** *adv.* [med.L *fraternalis* f. L *fraternus* f. *frater* brother]
■ **2** friendly, comradely; see also *brotherly* (BROTHER).

fraternity /frətə́rnitee/ *n.* (*pl.* **-ies**) **1** a male students' society in a university or college. **2** a group or company with common interests, or of the same professional class. **3** a religious brotherhood. **4** being fraternal; brotherliness. [ME f. OF *fraternité* f. L *fraternitas -tatis* (as FRATERNAL)]
■ **2** community, brotherhood, crowd, set, clique, coterie, circle, society, club, company, guild, clan, league, union, association. **3** brotherhood, sodality. **4** brotherliness, fellowship, camaraderie, comradeship, friendship, companionship, association, solidarity, unity, esprit de corps, clannishness.

fraternize /frátərnīz/ *v.intr.* (often foll. by *with*) **1** associate; make friends; behave as intimates. **2** (of troops) enter into friendly relations with enemy troops or the inhabitants of an occupied country. □□ **fraternization** *n.* [F *fraterniser* & med.L *fraternizare* f. L *fraternus*: see FRATERNAL]
■ **1** consort, associate, hobnob, mingle, keep company, spend time (together), hang around (with), *sl.* hang out (with); (*fraternize with*) socialize with, go around with, spend time with, mix with, rub shoulders with; take up with, fall in with.

fratricide /frátrisīd/ *n.* **1** the killing of one's brother or sister. **2** a person who does this. □□ **fratricidal** /-síd'l/ *adj.* [F *fratricide* or LL *fratricidium*, L *fratricida*, f. *frater fratris* brother]

Frau /frow/ *n.* (*pl.* **Frauen** /frówən/) (often as a title) a married or widowed German woman. [G]

fraud /frawd/ *n.* **1** criminal deception; the use of false representations to gain an unjust advantage. **2** a dishonest artifice or trick. **3** a person or thing not fulfilling what is claimed or expected of it. [ME f. OF *fraude* f. L *fraus fraudis*]

■ **1** deception, trickery, cheating, subterfuge, sharp practice, chicanery, deceit, swindling, double-dealing, duplicity, artifice, craft, guile, bluff, humbug, humbuggery, treachery, *colloq.* monkey business, *sl.* funny business, hanky-panky. **2** trick, hoax, swindle, scam, deception, cheat, wile, stratagem, dodge, ruse, sham, fake, flimflam, *colloq.* rip-off, *sl.* scam, gyp. **3** deceiver, trickster, cheat(er), impostor, swindler, charlatan, humbug, sharper, quack, mountebank, fake(r), pretender, bluffer, confidence man, confidence trickster, defrauder, flimflammer, four-flusher, *colloq.* shark, phony, *sl.* con man, bilker.

fraudulent /fráwjələnt/ *adj.* **1** characterized or achieved by fraud. **2** guilty of fraud; intending to deceive. □□ **fraudulence** /-ləns/ *n.* **fraudulently** *adv.* [ME f. OF *fraudulent* or L *fraudulentus* (as FRAUD)]
■ **1** fake, counterfeit, forged, false, falsified, spurious, imitation, sham, misleading, pinchbeck, *colloq.* phony. **2** deceitful, dishonest, deceptive, tricky, artful, crafty, double-dealing, duplicitous, guileful, sharp, shady, *colloq.* crooked, shifty, esp. *Brit. sl.* bent.

fraught /frawt/ *adj.* **1** (foll. by *with*) filled or attended with (*fraught with danger*). **2** *colloq.* causing or affected by great anxiety or distress. [ME, past part. of obs. *fraught* (v.) load with cargo f. MDu. *vrachten* f. *vracht* FREIGHT]
■ **1** (*fraught with*) filled with, charged with, attended with, packed with, loaded with, replete with, overflowing with, abundant in. **2** tense, taut, stressed, strained, fretful, anxious; stressful, trying, distressing, distressful, upsetting, nerve-racking, traumatic.

Fräulein /fróylin, frów-/ *n.* (often as a title or form of address) an unmarried (esp. young) German woman. [G, dimin. of FRAU]

Fraunhofer lines /frównhōfər/ *n.pl.* the dark lines visible in solar and stellar spectra. [J. von *Fraunhofer*, Bavarian physicist d. 1826]

fraxinella /fráksinélə/ *n.* an aromatic plant *Dictamnus albus*, having foliage that emits an ethereal flammable oil. Also called DITTANY, *gas plant*, *burning bush*. [mod.L, dimin. of L *fraxinus* ash tree]

fray¹ /fray/ *v.* **1** *tr. & intr.* wear through or become worn, esp. (of woven material) unweave at the edges. **2** *intr.* (of nerves, temper, etc.) become strained; deteriorate. [F *frayer* f. L *fricare* rub]
■ **1** shred, wear thin, become threadbare, wear out, rub, unravel.

fray² /fray/ *n.* **1** conflict; fighting (*eager for the fray*). **2** a noisy quarrel or brawl. [ME f. *fray* to quarrel f. *affray* (v.) (as AFFRAY)]
■ **1** conflict, fight, fighting, action, battle, war. **2** see FRACAS.

frazil /fráyzil/ *n.* ice crystals that form in a stream or on its bed. [Can.F *frasil* snow floating in the water; cf. F *fraisil* cinders]

frazzle /frázəl/ *n. & v. colloq.* ● *n.* a worn or exhausted state (*burned to a frazzle*). ● *v.tr.* (usu. as **frazzled** *adj.*) wear out; exhaust. [orig. uncert.]

freak /freek/ *n. & v.* ● *n.* **1** (also **freak of nature**) a monstrosity; an abnormally developed individual or thing. **2** (often *attrib.*) an abnormal, irregular, or bizarre occurrence (*a freak storm*). **3** *colloq.* **a** an unconventional person. **b** a person with a specified enthusiasm or interest (*health freak*). **c** a person who undergoes hallucinations; a drug addict (see sense 2 of v.). **4 a** a caprice or vagary. **b** capriciousness. ● *v.* (often foll. by *out*) *colloq.* **1** *intr. & tr.* become or make very angry. **2** *intr. & tr.* undergo or cause to undergo hallucinations or a strong emotional experience, esp. from use of narcotics. **3** *intr.* adopt a wildly unconventional lifestyle. □ **freak-out** *colloq.* an act of freaking out; a hallucinatory or strong emotional experience. [16th c.: prob. f. dial.]
■ *n.* **1** monstrosity, mutant, lusus (naturae); see also MONSTER 3, 4. **2** anomaly, rarity, abnormality, irregularity, oddity, curiosity, quirk, rara avis, rare bird, *Brit. colloq.* one-off; (*attrib.*) freakish, freaky, abnormal, anomalous, extraordinary, unique, rare, atypical,

unusual, odd, queer, strange, exceptional, bizarre, weird, unparalleled, unforeseen, unexpected, unpredicted, unpredictable, *Brit. colloq.* one-off. **3 b** enthusiast, fan, devotee, aficionado, *colloq.* buff; fanatic, addict, *sl.* fiend, nut. **4 a** whim, caprice, vagary, crotchet, eccentricity, fancy, idiosyncrasy, peculiarity. ● *v.* **1** see RAGE *v.*, ANGER *v.* □ **freak-out** see TANTRUM, EXPERIENCE *n.* 3a.

freakish /fréekish/ *adj.* **1** of or like a freak. **2** bizarre, unconventional. □□ **freakishly** *adv.* **freakishness** *n.*
■ **1** see GROTESQUE *adj.* 1. **2** see BIZARRE.

freaky /fréekee/ *adj.* (**freakier**, **freakiest**) = FREAKISH. □□ **freakily** *adv.* **freakiness** *n.*

freckle /frékəl/ *n.* & *v.* ● *n.* (often in *pl.*) a light brown spot on the skin, usu. caused by exposure to the sun. ● *v.* **1** *tr.* (usu. as **freckled** *adj.*) spot with freckles. **2** *intr.* be spotted with freckles. □□ **freckly** /fréklee/ *adj.* [ME *fracel*, etc., f. dial. *freken* f. ON *freknur* (pl.)]

free /free/ *adj.*, *adv.*, & *v.* ● *adj.* (**freer** /fréeər/; **freest** /fréeist/) **1** not in bondage to or under the control of another; having personal rights and social and political liberty. **2** (of a nation, or its citizens or institutions) subject neither to foreign domination nor to despotic government; having national and civil liberty (*a free press*; *a free society*). **3 a** unrestricted; unimpeded; not restrained or fixed. **b** at liberty; not confined or imprisoned. **c** released from ties or duties; unimpeded. **d** unrestrained as to action; independent (*set free*). **4** (foll. by *of*, *from*) **a** not subject to; exempt from (*free of tax*). **b** not containing or subject to a specified (usu. undesirable) thing (*free of preservatives*; *free from disease*). **5** (foll. by *to* + infin.) able or permitted to take a specified action (*you are free to choose*). **6** unconstrained (*free gestures*). **7 a** available without charge; costing nothing. **b** not subject to tax, duty, trade restraint, or fees. **8 a** clear of engagements or obligations (*are you free tomorrow?*). **b** not occupied or in use (*the bathroom is free now*). **c** clear of obstructions. **9** spontaneous; unforced (*free compliments*). **10** open to all comers. **11** lavish; profuse; using or used without restraint (*very free with their money*). **12** frank; unreserved. **13** (of a literary, sporting, etc., style) not observing the strict laws of form. **14** (of a translation) conveying the broad sense; not literal. **15** forward; familiar; impudent. **16** (of talk, stories, etc.) slightly indecent. **17** *Physics* **a** not modified by an external force. **b** not bound in an atom or molecule. **18** *Chem.* not combined (*free oxygen*). **19** (of power or energy) disengaged or available. ● *adv.* **1** in a free manner. **2** without cost or payment. **3** *Naut.* not close-hauled. ● *v.tr.* **1** make free; set at liberty. **2** (foll. by *of*, *from*) relieve from (something undesirable). **3** disengage; disentangle. □ **free agent** a person with freedom of action, esp. a professional athlete to sign a contract with any team. **free and easy** informal; unceremonious. **free association** *Psychol.* a method of investigating a person's unconscious by eliciting from him or her spontaneous associations with ideas proposed by the examiner. **free church** a church dissenting or seceding from an established or state-controlled church. **free enterprise** a system in which private business operates in competition and largely free of government control. **free fall** movement under the force of gravity only, esp.: **1** the part of a parachute descent before the parachute opens. **2** the movement of a spacecraft in space without thrust from the engines. **free fight** a general fight in which all present join. **free-for-all** a free fight, unrestricted discussion, etc. **free-form** (*attrib.*) of an irregular shape or structure. **free hand** freedom to act at one's own discretion (see also FREEHAND). **free-handed** generous. **free-handedly** generously. **free-handedness** generosity. **free house** *Brit.* an inn or public house not controlled by a brewery and therefore not restricted to selling particular brands of beer or liquor. **free kick** *Soccer*, etc., a set kick allowed to be taken by one side without interference from the other. **free labor** *Brit.* the labor of workers not in a labor union. **free-living 1** indulgence in pleasures, esp. that of eating. **2** *Biol.* living freely and independently; not attached to a substrate; not parasitic or symbiotic. **free love** sexual relations according to choice

and unrestricted by marriage. **free market** a market in which prices are determined by unrestricted competition. **free on board** (or **rail**) without charge for delivery to a ship or railroad freight car. **free pass** an authorization of free admission, travel, etc. **free port 1** a port area where goods in transit are exempt from customs duty. **2** a port open to all traders. **free radical** *Chem.* an unchanged atom or group of atoms with one or more unpaired electrons. **free-range** (of hens, etc.) kept in natural conditions with freedom of movement. **free rein** see REIN. **free school 1** a school for which no fees are charged. **2** a school run on the basis of freedom from restriction for the pupils. **free speech** the right to express opinions freely. **free-spoken** speaking candidly; not concealing one's opinions. **free-standing** not supported by another structure. **Free State** a US state in which slavery was prohibited before the Civil War. **free throw** *Basketball* an unhindered shot at the basket made by a player after a foul has been called against the opposing team. **free trade** international trade left to its natural course without restriction on imports or exports. **free verse** verse without a fixed metrical pattern. **free vote** (in a parliamentary system) a vote not subject to party discipline. **free wheel 1** a device in a motor vehicle transmission allowing the drive shaft to spin faster than the engine. **2** the driving wheel of a bicycle, able to revolve with the pedals at rest. **free will 1** the power of acting without the constraint of necessity or fate. **2** the ability to act at one's own discretion (*I did it of my own free will*). **free world** the noncommunist countries, esp. during the Cold War. □□ **freely** *adv.* **freeness** *n.* [OE *frēo*, *frēon* f. Gmc]

■ *adj.* **1** freeborn. **2** independent, self-governing, self-governed, self-ruling, autonomous, democratic, sovereign. **3 a** unrestricted, unimpeded, unrestrained, untrammeled, unconstrained, uncontrolled, unencumbered; relaxed, casual, informal, free and easy, easy, natural, unceremonious, *colloq.* laid-back. **b** at liberty, at large, loose, out, unconfined, unfettered, unchained, unshackled, *sl.* sprung. **c** liberated, set free, let go, let off, emancipated, delivered, unshackled, unfettered, released, freed, *hist.* manumitted. **d** unattached, unconstrained, loose, independent, on the loose. **4** (*free of* or *from*) rid of, exempt(ed) from, relieved of, safe from, not liable *or* subject to, immune from, unaffected by, above, without, untouched by. **5** able, permitted, allowed, within one's rights. **6** unconstrained, unrestrained, relaxed. **7** cost-free, free of charge, complimentary, gratis, gratuitous, for nothing, without cost (or obligation), on the house, *Brit. sl.* buckshee. **8 a** at liberty; not busy, unoccupied, unengaged, available, accessible. **b** vacant, empty, not in use; unused, spare, extra; uninhabited, untenanted. **c** clear, empty; see also UNIMPEDED. **9** spontaneous, unforced, unasked for, unsolicited, unbidden, voluntary, unconditioned, unconditional; gratuitous. **10** see OPEN *adj.* 9–11. **11** generous, lavish, open, liberal, munificent, unstinting, bountiful, openhanded, unsparing; charitable. **12** frank, candid, plain, straight, unreserved, open, direct, outspoken, uninhibited. **15** forward, impudent; see also FAMILIAR *adj.* 4. **16** see INDECENT. ● *adv.* **1** freely, openly, at will, unrestrictedly, loose; loosely. **2** gratis, at no cost, free of charge, without charge. ● *v.* **1** set free, make free, set at liberty, release, let go, liberate, let out, let loose, emancipate, pardon, parole, furlough, *hist.* enfranchise, manumit, *literary* disenthrall; unloose, unchain, unfetter, uncage. **2** relieve, rid, unburden, disburden, discharge, disencumber, unbosom; rescue, redeem. **3** disengage, disentangle, untie, unbind, unfasten, undo, unshackle, unlock, open, release, loose, loosen, detach,

---

/ . . . / pronunciation   ● part of speech
□ phrases, idioms, and compounds
□□ derivatives   ■ synonym section
cross-references appear in SMALL CAPITALS or *italics*

extricate. □ **free and easy** see INFORMAL.. **free fight** see BRAWL *n.* **free-form** see IRREGULAR 1, 2. **free hand** CARTE BLANCHE. **free-handed** see GENEROUS 1. **free-living 1** see DISSIPATION 1, GLUTTONY. **free pass** pass, complimentary ticket, *colloq.* freebie. **free school** public school, non-fee-paying school. **free-spoken** see CANDID 1. **free will 2** see VOLITION. □□ **freely** unrestrainedly, unrestrictedly, without restriction, without let or hindrance, without interference; easily, smoothly, cleanly, unobstructedly; willingly, spontaneously, readily, voluntarily, on one's own, independently, of one's own accord, of one's own volition *or* free will; liberally, lavishly, unreservedly, generously, unstintingly, openhandedly, ungrudgingly, munificently, amply, plentifully, abundantly; candidly, frankly, openly, directly, plainly, outspokenly.

-free /freē/ *comb. form* free of or from (*duty-free*; *trouble-free*).

freebase /freēbays/ *n.* & *v. sl.* ● *n.* cocaine that has been purified by heating with ether, and is taken by inhaling the fumes or smoking the residue. ● *v.tr.* purify (cocaine) for smoking or inhaling.

freebie /freēbee/ *n. colloq.* a thing provided free of charge. [arbitrary f. FREE]

freeboard /freēbawrd/ *n.* the part of a ship's side between the waterline and the deck.

freebooter /freēbŏōtər/ *n.* a pirate or buccaneer. □□ **freeboot** *v.intr.* [Du. *vrijbuiter* (as FREE, BOOTY): cf. FILIBUSTER]
■ see THIEF.

freeborn /freēbawrn/ *adj.* inheriting a citizen's rights and liberty.

freedman /freēdmən/ *n.* (*pl.* **-men**) an emancipated slave.

freedom /freēdəm/ *n.* **1** the condition of being free or unrestricted. **2** personal or civic liberty; absence of slave status. **3** the power of self-determination; the quality of not being controlled by fate or necessity. **4** the state of being free to act (often foll. by *to* + infin.: *we have the freedom to leave*). **5** frankness; outspokenness; undue familiarity. **6** (foll. by *from*) the condition of being exempt from or not subject to (a defect, burden, etc.). **7** (foll. by *of*) **a** full or honorary participation in (membership, privileges, etc.). **b** unrestricted use of (facilities, etc.). **8** a privilege possessed by a city or corporation. **9** facility or ease in action. **10** boldness of conception. □ **the four freedoms** freedom of speech and religion, and freedom from fear and want. **freedom fighter** a person who takes part in violent resistance to an established political system, etc. [OE *frēodōm* (as FREE, -DOM)]
■ **1, 2** freeness, liberty; release, deliverance, liberation, emancipation, independence, self-government, self-determination, self-direction, autonomy, *hist.* manumission. **3** self-determination, independence. **4** ability, facility, license, permission, right, privilege, authority, discretion, authorization, power, free hand, carte blanche. **5** candor, honesty, openness, frankness, outspokenness, candidness, unconstraint, naturalness; boldness, audacity, audaciousness, forwardness, brazenness, impertinence, impudence, disrespect, arrogance, presumption, presumptuousness, *colloq.* brass, nerve, *sl.* gall. **6** exemption, immunity, deliverance, liberation, relief. **7** range, latitude, scope, play, run, liberty, free use. **9** facility, ease, easiness, effortlessness, simplicity. **10** see CONFIDENCE 2b.
□ **freedom fighter** see GUERRILLA.

freehand /freēhand/ *adj.* & *adv.* ● *adj.* (of a drawing or plan, etc.) done by hand without special instruments or guides. ● *adv.* in a freehand manner.

freehold /freēhōld/ *n.* & *adj.* ● *n.* **1** tenure of land or property in fee simple or fee tail or for life. **2** esp. *Brit.* land or property or an office held by such tenure. ● *adj.* held by or having the status of freehold. □□ **freeholder** *n.*

freelance /freēlans/ *n., v.,* & *adv.* ● *n.* **1 a** (also **freelancer**) a person, usu. self-employed, offering services on a temporary basis, esp. to several businesses, etc., for particular assignments. **b** (*attrib.*) (*a freelance editor*). **2** (usu. **free lance**) *hist.* a medieval mercenary. ● *v.intr.* act as a freelance. ● *adv.* as a freelance. [19th c.: orig. in sense 2 of *n.*]

freeloader /freēlōdər/ *n. sl.* a person who eats, drinks, or lives at others' expense; a sponger. □□ **freeload** /-lŏd/ *v.intr.*
■ see PARASITE.

freeman /freēmən/ *n.* (*pl.* **-men**) **1** a person who has the freedom of a city, company, etc. **2** a person who is not a slave or serf.

freemartin /freēmaartin/ *n.* a hermaphrodite or imperfect female calf of oppositely sexed twins. [17th c.: orig. unkn.]

Freemason /freēmaysən/ *n.* a member of an international fraternity for mutual help and fellowship (the *Free and Accepted Masons*), with elaborate secret rituals.

Freemasonry /freēmaysənree/ *n.* **1** the system and institutions of the Freemasons. **2** (**freemasonry**) instinctive sympathy or understanding.

freepost /freēpōst/ *n. Brit.* business reply mail.

freer *compar.* of FREE.

freesia /freēzhə, -zeeə/ *n.* any bulbous plant of the genus *Freesia*, native to Africa, having fragrant colored flowers. [mod.L f. F. H. T. *Freese*, Ger. physician d. 1876]

freest *superl.* of FREE.

freestone /freēstōn/ *n.* **1** any fine-grained stone which can be cut easily, esp. sandstone or limestone. **2** a stone fruit, esp. a peach, in which the stone is loose when the fruit is ripe (cf. CLINGSTONE).

freestyle /freēstil/ *adj.* & *n.* ● *adj.* (of a race or contest) in which all styles are allowed, esp.: **1** *Swimming* in which any stroke may be used. **2** *Wrestling* with few restrictions on the holds permitted. ● *n.* = CRAWL³.

freethinker /freēthingkər/ *n.* a person who rejects dogma or authority, esp. in religious belief. □□ **freethinking** *n.* & *adj.*
■ see *individualist* (INDIVIDUALISM), LIBERAL *n.* 1, NONBELIEVER.

freeware /freēwair/ *n. Computing* software that is distributed free and without technical support to users. [FREE + SOFTWARE]

freeway /freēway/ *n.* **1** an express highway, esp. with controlled access. **2** a toll-free highway.

freewheel /freēweel/ *v.intr.* **1** move freely with gears disengaged, esp. downhill. **2** move or act without constraint or effort.
■ **2** coast, drift, idle.

freeze /freez/ *v.* & *n.* ● *v.* (*past* **froze** /frōz/; *past part.* **frozen** /frōzən/) **1** *tr.* & *intr.* **a** turn or be turned into ice or another solid by cold. **b** (often foll. by *over, up*) make or become rigid or solid as a result of the cold. **2** *intr.* be or feel very cold. **3** *tr.* & *intr.* cover or become covered with ice. **4** *intr.* (foll. by *to, together*) adhere or be fastened by frost (*the curtains froze to the window*). **5** *tr.* preserve (food) by refrigeration below the freezing point. **6** *tr.* & *intr.* **a** make or become motionless or powerless through fear, surprise, etc. **b** react or cause to react with sudden aloofness or detachment. **7** *tr.* stiffen or harden, injure or kill, by chilling (*frozen to death*). **8** *tr.* make (credits, assets, etc.) temporarily or permanently unrealizable. **9** *tr.* fix or stabilize (prices, wages, etc.) at a certain level. **10** *tr.* arrest (an action) at a certain stage of development. **11** *tr.* arrest (a movement in a movie, video, etc.) by repeating a frame or stopping the film at a frame. ● *n.* **1** a state of frost; a period or the coming of frost or very cold weather. **2** the fixing or stabilization of prices, wages, etc. **3** a film shot in which movement is arrested by the repetition of a frame. □ **freeze-dry** (**-dries, -dried**) freeze and dry by the sublimation of ice in a high vacuum. **freeze-frame** = sense 3 of *n.* **freeze onto** *colloq.* take or keep tight hold of. **freeze out** *colloq.* exclude from business, society, etc., by competition or boycott, etc. **freeze up** obstruct or be obstructed by the formation of ice. **freeze-up** *n.* a period or conditions of extreme cold. **freezing point** the temperature at which a liquid, esp. water, freezes. **freezing works** *Austral.* & *NZ* a place where animals are slaughtered and carcasses frozen for export. **frozen mitt** *Brit. colloq.* a cool reception. □□ **freezable** *adj.* **frozenly** *adv.* [OE *frēosan* f. Gmc]
■ *v.* **1 a** ice; solidify, congeal, harden, stiffen. **b** ice. **2** be cold *or* icy *or* freezing *or* frozen *or* perished *or* perishing *or* chilled to the bone. **6 a** fix, immobilize, paralyze,

stop (dead), pin, transfix, gorgonize, *archaic or literary* stay. **b** see *pull back*. **10** see ARREST *v.* 2. ● *n.* **1** frost, freeze-up. **2** immobilization, stabilization. □ **freeze onto** see CLUTCH¹ *v.* 1. **freeze out** exclude, debar, ban, reject, ostracize; eject, drive away *or* out, expel, force out. **freeze-up** freeze, frost.

freezer /fréezər/ *n.* a refrigerated compartment, cabinet, or room for preserving food at very low temperatures; = *deep freeze n.*

freight /frayt/ *n.* & *v.* ● *n.* **1** the transport of goods in containers or by air or land or, esp. *Brit.*, water. **2** goods transported; cargo. **3** a charge for transportation of goods. **4** the lease of a ship or aircraft for transporting goods. **5** a load or burden. ● *v.tr.* **1** transport (goods) as freight. **2** load with freight. **3** lease out (a ship) for the carriage of goods and passengers. □ **freight car** a railroad car used for transporting freight. **freight ton** see TON¹. [MDu., MLG *vrecht* var. of *vracht*: cf. FRAUGHT]

■ *n.* **1** transport, transportation, carriage, conveyance, shipping, shipment, freightage. **2** goods, cargo, freightage; load, shipload, truckload, consignment, payload. **3** freightage, tonnage. **5** see LOAD *n.* 3.
● *v.* **1** see TRANSPORT *v.* 1. **2** see LOAD *v.* 1.

freightage /fráytij/ *n.* **1 a** the transportation of freight. **b** the cost of this. **2** freight transported.

■ **1 a** see FREIGHT *n.* 1. **b** see CARRIAGE 3b. **2** see FREIGHT *n.* 2.

freighter /fráytər/ *n.* **1** a ship or aircraft designed to carry freight. **2** a person who loads or charters and loads a ship. **3** a person who consigns goods for carriage inland. **4** a person whose business is to receive and forward freight.

freightliner /fráytlinər/ *n. Brit.* a train carrying goods in containers.

French /french/ *adj.* & *n.* ● *adj.* **1** of or relating to France or its people or language. **2** having the characteristics attributed to the French people. ● *n.* **1** the language of France, also used in Belgium, Switzerland, Canada, and elsewhere. **2** (*prec. by the*; treated as *pl.*) the people of France. **3** *colloq.* bad language (*excuse my French*). **4** *colloq.* dry vermouth (*gin and French*). □ **French bean** *Brit.* **1** a beanplant, *Phaseolus vulgaris*, having many varieties cultivated for their pods and seeds. **2 a** the pod used as food. **b** the seed used as food: also called HARICOT, *kidney bean*. **French bread** white bread in a long crisp loaf. **French Canadian** *n.* a Canadian whose principal language is French. ● *adj.* of or relating to French-speaking Canadians. **French chalk** a kind of steatite used for marking cloth and removing grease and as a dry lubricant. **French cuff** a double cuff formed by turning back a long cuff and fastening it. **French curve** a template used for drawing curved lines. **French door 1** a door with glass panes throughout its length. **2** = *French window*. **French dressing 1** a creamy orange salad dressing, usu. made with tomato. **2** a salad dressing of vinegar and oil, usu. seasoned. **French fries** (also **French fried potatoes**) a strip of potato, deep fried. **French horn** a coiled brass wind instrument with a wide bell. **French kiss** a kiss with one partner's tongue inserted in the other's mouth. **French leave** absence without permission. **French letter** *Brit. colloq.* a condom. **French mustard** *Brit.* a mild mustard mixed with vinegar. **French polish** shellac polish for wood. **French-polish** *v.tr.* polish with this. **French roof** a mansard. **French seam** a seam with the raw edges enclosed. **French toast 1** bread dipped in egg and milk and sautéed. **2** *Brit.* bread buttered on one side and toasted on the other. **French vermouth** *Brit.* dry vermouth. **French window** a pair of casement windows extending to the floor in an outside wall, serving as a window and door. □□ **Frenchness** *n.* [OE *frencisc* f. Gmc]

Frenchify /frénchifī/ *v.tr.* (**-ies, -ied**) (usu. as **Frenchified** *adj.*) make French in form, character, or manners.

Frenchman /frénchmən/ *n.* (*pl.* **-men**) a man who is French by birth or descent.

Frenchwoman /frénchwŏomən/ *n.* (*pl.* **-women**) a woman who is French by birth or descent.

frenetic /frənétik/ *adj.* **1** frantic; frenzied. **2** fanatic. □□ **fre-**

netically *adv.* [ME f. OF *frenetique* f. L *phreneticus* f. Gk *phrenitikos* f. *phrenitis* delirium f. *phrēn phrenos* mind]

■ **1** see HECTIC *adj.* 1. **2** see *fanatical* (FANATIC).

frenulum /frényələm/ *n.* (also *Brit.* **fraenulum**) (*pl.* **-la** /-lə/) *Anat.* a small frenum. [mod.L, dimin. of FRENUM]

frenum /frénəm/ *n.* (also *Brit.* **fraenum**) (*pl.* **-na** /-nə/) *Anat.* a fold of mucous membrane or skin, esp. under the tongue, checking the motion of an organ. [L, = bridle]

frenzy /frénzee/ *n.* & *v.* ● *n.* (*pl.* **-ies**) **1** mental derangement; wild excitement or agitation. **2** delirious fury. ● *v.tr.* (**-ies, -ied**) (usu. as **frenzied** *adj.*) drive to frenzy; infuriate. □□ **frenziedly** *adv.* [ME f. OF *frenesie* f. med.L *phrenesia* f. L *phrenesis* f. Gk *phrēn* mind]

■ *n.* **1** excitement, agitation, fever, passion, turmoil, transport. **2** fury, distraction; paroxysm, outburst, furor, bout, fit. ● *v.* (**frenzied**) see FEVERISH 2.

Freon /fréeon/ *n. propr.* any of a group of halogenated hydrocarbons containing fluorine, chlorine, and sometimes bromine, used in aerosols, refrigerants, etc. (see also CFC).

frequency /fréekwənsee/ *n.* (*pl.* **-ies**) **1** commonness of occurrence. **2 a** the state of being frequent; frequent occurrence. **b** the process of being repeated at short intervals. **3** *Physics* the rate of recurrence of a vibration, oscillation, cycle, etc.; the number of repetitions in a given time, esp. per second. ¶ Abbr.: f. **4** *Statistics* the ratio of the number of actual to possible occurrences of an event. □ **frequency band** *Electronics* = BAND¹ *n.* 3a. **frequency distribution** *Statistics* a measurement of the frequency of occurrence of the values of a variable. **frequency modulation** *Electronics* a modulation in which the frequency of the carrier wave is varied. ¶ Abbr.: FM. **frequency response** *Electronics* the dependence on signal frequency of the output–input ratio of an amplifier, etc. [L *frequentia* (as FREQUENT)]

■ *n.* **1** see INCIDENCE 1.

frequent /fréekwənt/ *adj.* & *v.* ● *adj.* **1** occurring often or in close succession. **2** habitual; constant (*a frequent caller*). **3** found near together; numerous; abundant. **4** (of the pulse) rapid. ● *v.tr.* (*also* frikwént/ attend or go to habitually. □□ **frequentation** *n.* **frequenter** /frikwéntər/ *n.* **frequently** /fréekwəntlee/ *adv.* [F *fréquent* or L *frequens -entis* crowded]

■ *adj.* **1** reiterative, continual. **2** habitual, constant, continual, continuing, recurrent, recurring, regular, familiar, everyday, customary, usual, ordinary, normal, common; persistent. **3** many, numerous, abundant, countless, innumerable, untold, numberless, infinite, *literary* myriad; see also UMPTEEN *adj.* ● *v.* haunt, patronize, visit, resort to, go to *or* attend regularly, *sl.* hang out at. □□ **frequently** often, regularly, continually, repeatedly, over and over (again), again and again, many times, many a time, time after time, time and (time) again, *archaic or literary* ofttimes; habitually, customarily, regularly, usually, ordinarily, generally, commonly, as often as not.

frequentative /frikwéntətiv/ *adj.* & *n. Gram.* ● *adj.* expressing frequent repetition or intensity of action. ● *n.* a verb or verbal form or conjugation expressing this (e.g., *chatter, twinkle*). [F *fréquentatif -ive* or L *frequentativus* (as FREQUENT)]

fresco /fréskō/ *n.* (*pl.* **-os** or **-oes**) **1** a painting done in watercolor on a wall or ceiling while the plaster is still wet. **2** this method of painting (*esp. in fresco*). □ **fresco secco** = SECCO. □□ **frescoed** *adj.* [It., = cool, fresh]

fresh /fresh/ *adj.*, *adv.*, & *n.* ● *adj.* **1** newly made or obtained (*fresh sandwiches*). **2 a** other; different; not previously known or used (*start a fresh page; we need fresh ideas*). **b** additional (*fresh supplies*). **3** (foll. by *from*) lately arrived from (a specified place or situation). **4** not stale or musty or faded (*fresh flowers; fresh memories*). **5** (of food) not preserved by

/.../	**pronunciation**	● **part of speech**
□ **phrases, idioms, and compounds**		
□□ **derivatives**		■ **synonym section**
cross-references appear in SMALL CAPITALS or *italics*		

salting, canning, freezing, etc. **6** not salty (*fresh water*). **7 a** pure; untainted; refreshing; invigorating (*fresh air*). **b** bright and pure in color (*a fresh complexion*). **8** (of the wind) brisk; of fair strength. **9** alert; vigorous; fit (*never felt fresher*). **10** *colloq.* **a** cheeky, presumptuous. **b** amorously impudent. **11** young and inexperienced. ● *adv.* newly; recently (esp. in *comb.*: *fresh-baked*; *fresh-cut*). ● *n.* the fresh part of the day, year, etc. (*in the fresh of the morning*). □□ **freshly** *adv.* **freshness** *n.* [ME f. OF *freis fresche* ult. f. Gmc]

■ *adj.* **1** new, today's, brand-new, most recent, latest. **2 a** new, modern, up-to-date, recent; novel, original, unusual, unconventional, different, alternative, unorthodox, *derog.* newfangled. **b** additional, new, further, renewed, extra, supplementary. **4** new, recent. **7 a** pure, clean, clear, cool, refreshing, invigorating, untainted, unpolluted; wholesome. **b** bright, pure, glowing, rosy, ruddy, blooming; peaches and cream. **8** moderate, fair, strong; see also BRISK 2. **9** alert, fit, well, refreshed, vigorous, energetic, invigorated, spry, lively, full of vim and vigor, keen, bright, brisk, active, sprightly, flourishing, *colloq.* bright-eyed and bushy-tailed. **10 a** bold, impudent, impertinent, brazen, brassy, forward, disrespectful, saucy, pert, cheeky, presumptuous, insolent, rude, *colloq.* flip, sassy. **b** see NAUGHTY 2. **11** young, raw, green, naive, callow, immature, inexperienced, untested, unsophisticated, untried, unfledged, untrained, wet behind the ears. □□ **freshly** newly, recently, just now, (just) a moment ago, fresh.

freshen /fréshən/ *v.* **1** *tr.* & *intr.* make or become fresh or fresher. **2** *intr.* & *tr.* (foll. by *up*) **a** wash, change one's clothes, etc. **b** revive; refresh; renew.

■ **1** ventilate, air out, deodorize, purify; strengthen, increase, blow harder. **2** (*freshen up*) **a** wash, wash up; titivate. **b** revive, refresh, renew, enliven, (re)vitalize, stimulate, invigorate, rouse, *colloq.* liven (up).

fresher /fréshər/ *n. Brit. colloq.* = FRESHMAN.

freshet /fréshit/ *n.* **1** a rush of fresh water flowing into the sea. **2** the flood of a river from heavy rain or melted snow. [prob. f. OF *freschete* f. *frais* FRESH]

freshman /fréshmən/ *n.* (*pl.* **-men**) a first-year student at a high school, college, or university.

■ see NEWCOMER 2.

freshwater /fréshwawtər, -wotər/ *adj.* **1** of or found in fresh water; not of the sea. **2** (esp. of a school or college) rustic or provincial. □ **freshwater flea** = DAPHNIA.

fret¹ /fret/ *v.* & *n.* ● *v.* (**fretted, fretting**) **1** *intr.* **a** be greatly and visibly worried or distressed. **b** be irritated or resentful. **2** *tr.* **a** cause anxiety or distress to. **b** irritate; annoy. **3** *tr.* wear or consume by gnawing or rubbing. **4** *tr.* form (a channel or passage) by wearing away. **5** *intr.* (of running water) flow or rise in little waves. ● *n. Brit.* irritation; vexation; querulousness (esp. *in a fret*). [OE *fretan* f. Gmc, rel. to EAT]

■ *v.* **1 a** worry, agonize, grieve, brood, be concerned, be upset, be distressed, be anxious, be disturbed, be in a state, tear one's hair out, *colloq.* stew. **b** see RESENT. **2 a** worry, concern; see also DISTRESS *v.* **b** annoy, irritate, vex, torment, provoke, rankle. **3** see WEAR¹ *v.* 5. **4** furrow, groove, channel, plow, bore.

fret² /fret/ *n.* & *v.* ● *n.* **1** an ornamental pattern made of continuous combinations of straight lines joined usu. at right angles. **2** *Heraldry* a device of narrow bands and a diamond interlaced. ● *v.tr.* (**fretted, fretting**) **1** embellish or decorate with a fret. **2** adorn (esp. a ceiling) with carved or embossed work. [ME f. OF *frete* trelliswork and *freter* (v.)]

fret³ /fret/ *n.* each of a sequence of bars or ridges on the fingerboard of some stringed musical instruments (esp. the guitar) fixing the positions of the fingers to produce the desired notes. □□ **fretless** *adj.* [15th c.: orig. unkn.]

fretful /frétfool/ *adj.* visibly anxious, distressed, or irritated. □□ **fretfully** *adv.* **fretfulness** *n.*

■ anxious, nervous, on edge, edgy, distressed, troubled, bothered, vexed, irritated, irked, upset, cross.

fretsaw /frétsaw/ *n.* a saw consisting of a narrow blade stretched on a frame, for cutting thin patterns in wood.

fretwork /frétwərk/ *n.* ornamental work in wood, done with a fretsaw.

Freudian /fróydeeən/ *adj.* & *n. Psychol.* ● *adj.* of or relating to the Austrian psychologist Sigmund Freud (d. 1939) or his methods of psychoanalysis, esp. with reference to the importance of sexuality in human behavior. ● *n.* a follower of Freud or his methods. □ **Freudian slip** an unintentional error regarded as revealing subconscious feelings. □□ **Freudianism** *n.*

F.R.G. *abbr.* Federal Republic of Germany.

Fri. *abbr.* Friday.

friable /fríəbəl/ *adj.* easily crumbled. □□ **friability** *n.* **friableness** *n.* [F *friable* or L *friabilis* f. *friare* crumble]

■ see BRITTLE *adj.* 1.

friar /fríər/ *n.* a member of any of certain religious orders of men, esp. the four mendicant orders (Augustinians, Carmelites, Dominicans, and Franciscans). □ **friar's** (or **friars'**) **balsam** a tincture of benzoin, etc., used esp. as an inhalant. □□ **friarly** *adj.* [ME & OF *frere* f. L *frater fratris* brother]

■ see MONK.

friary /fríəree/ *n.* (*pl.* **-ies**) a convent of friars.

■ see MONASTERY.

fricandeau /fríkəndō/ *n.* & *v.* ● *n.* (*pl.* **fricandeaux** /-dōz/) **1** a cushion-shaped piece of meat, esp. veal, cut from the leg. **2** a dish made from this, usu. braised or roasted and served with a sauce. ● *v.tr.* (**fricandeaus, fricandeaued, fricandeauing**) make into fricandeaux. [F]

fricassee /fríkəsee/ *n.* & *v.* ● *n.* a dish of stewed or fried pieces of meat served in a thick white sauce. ● *v.tr.* (**fricassees, fricasseed**) make a fricassee of. [F, fem. past part. of *fricasser* (v.)]

fricative /fríkətiv/ *adj.* & *n. Phonet.* ● *adj.* made by the friction of breath in a narrow opening. ● *n.* a consonant made in this way, e.g., *f* and *th*. [mod.L *fricativus* f. L *fricare* rub]

friction /fríkshən/ *n.* **1** the action of one object rubbing against another. **2** the resistance an object encounters in moving over another. **3** a clash of wills, temperaments, or opinions; mutual animosity arising from disagreement. **4** (in *comb.*) of devices that transmit motion by frictional contact (*friction clutch*; *friction disk*). □□ **frictional** *adj.* **frictionless** *adj.* [F f. L *frictio -onis* f. *fricare* frict-]

■ **1** rubbing, scraping, grating, chafing, fretting; abrasion, attrition, erosion. **2** grip. **3** clash, disagreement, discord, conflict, contention, argument, dispute, dissension, disharmony, controversy, wrangle, dissent, bickering, wrangling, ill feeling, ill will, bad feeling, bad blood, animosity, rivalry, hostility, antagonism, strife.

Friday /fríday, -dee/ *n.* & *adv.* ● *n.* the sixth day of the week, following Thursday. ● *adv. colloq.* **1** on Friday. **2** (**Fridays**) on Fridays; each Friday. □ **girl** (or **man**) **Friday** a helper or follower (after *Man Friday* in Defoe's *Robinson Crusoe*). [OE *frigedæg* f. Gmc (named after *Frigg* the wife of Odin)]

fridge /frij/ *n. colloq.* = REFRIGERATOR. [abbr.]

friend /frend/ *n.* & *v.* ● *n.* **1** a person with whom one enjoys mutual affection and regard (usu. exclusive of sexual or family bonds). **2** a sympathizer, helper, or patron (*no friend to virtue*; *a friend of order*). **3** a person who is not an enemy or who is on the same side (*friend or foe?*). **4 a** person already mentioned or under discussion (*my friend at the next table then left the room*). **b** a person known by sight. **c** used as a polite or ironic form of address. **5** (usu. in *pl.*) a regular contributor of money or other assistance to an institution. **6** (**Friend**) a member of the Society of Friends, a Quaker. **7** a helpful thing or quality. ● *v.tr.* befriend; help. □ **be** (or *Brit.* **keep**) **friends with** be friendly with. **friend at court** a friend whose influence may be made use of. **my honourable friend** *Brit.* used in the House of Commons to refer to another member of one's own party. **my learned friend** *Brit.* used by a lawyer in court to refer to another lawyer. **my noble friend** *Brit.* used in the House of Lords to refer to another member of one's own party. □□ **friended** *adj.* **friendless** *adj.* [OE *frēond* f. Gmc]

■ *n.* **1** (boon) companion, partner, comrade, crony, familiar, confidant, confidante, intimate, alter ego, ally, compeer, mate, playmate, *colloq.* chum, pal, (bosom) buddy, *Austral. & NZ colloq.* cobber, *Brit. sl.* (old) cock; pen pal; lover, sweetheart, escort; girl, girlfriend, lady friend, mistress, concubine; man, boy, boyfriend. **2** see SUPPORTER. **3** see *sympathizer* (SYMPATHIZE). **4 c** see DEAR *n.* **5** benefactor, patron, Maecenas, supporter, adherent, advocate. **7** asset, advantage, strength, benefit, plus, boon. □ **be friends with** see ASSOCIATE *v.* 5.

friendly /fréndlee/ *adj., n., & adv.* ● *adj.* (**friendlier, friendliest**) **1** acting as or like a friend; well-disposed; kindly. **2 a** (often foll. by *with*) on amicable terms. **b** not hostile. **3** characteristic of friends; showing or prompted by kindness. **4** favorably disposed; ready to approve or help. **5 a** (of a thing) serviceable; convenient; opportune. **b** = *user-friendly.* ● *n. Brit.* (*pl.* **-ies**) = *friendly match.* ● *adv.* in a friendly manner. □ **friendly action** *Brit. Law* an action brought merely to get a point decided. **friendly fire** *Mil.* fire coming from one's own side in a conflict, esp. as the cause of accidental injury or damage to one's forces. **friendly match** *Brit.* a match played for enjoyment and not in competition, etc. **Friendly Society** *Brit.* = *benefit society.* □□ **friendlily** *adv.* **friendliness** *n.*
   ■ *adj.* **1** well-disposed, kindly, kind, kindhearted, warmhearted, warm, affectionate, amiable, amicable, cordial, genial, sociable, agreeable, good-natured, pleasant, affable; approachable, accessible, unreserved, demonstrative, open. **2** congenial, companionable, comradely, convivial, familiar, close, on good terms, comfortable, at home, neighborly, chummy, clubby, esp. *Brit.* matey, *colloq.* pally, thick. **3** see KIND². **4** sympathetic, well-disposed, favorably disposed, supportive, approving, agreeable. **5** serviceable, convenient, useful, helpful, handy, expedient, suitable, *archaic* commodious; see also CONVENIENT 1.

friendship /fréndship/ *n.* **1** being friends; the relationship between friends. **2** a friendly disposition felt or shown. [OE *frēondscipe* (as FRIEND, -SHIP)]
   ■ **1** amity, harmony, alliance, companionability, comradeship, fellowship, neighborliness, familiarity, closeness, rapport, intimacy. **2** friendliness, amiability, amicability, congeniality, conviviality, sociability, warmth, devotion, affection, fondness, attachment, esteem, regard.

frier var. of FRYER.

Friesian /frée'zhən/ *n. & adj. Brit.* = HOLSTEIN.

frieze¹ /freez/ *n.* **1** *Archit.* the part of an entablature between the architrave and the cornice. **2** *Archit.* a horizontal band of sculpture filling this. **3** a band of decoration elsewhere, esp. along a wall near the ceiling. [F *frise* f. med.L *frisium, frigium* f. L *Phrygium* (*opus*) (work) of Phrygia]
   ■ **3** see BORDER *n.* 3.

frieze² /freez/ *n.* coarse woolen cloth with a nap, usu. on one side only. [ME f. F *frise*, prob. rel. to FRISIAN]

frig¹ /frig/ *v. & n. coarse sl.* ● *v.* (**frigged, frigging**) **1 a** *tr. & intr.* have sexual intercourse (with). **b** masturbate. **2** *tr.* (usu. as an exclamation) = FUCK *v.* 3. **3** *intr.* (foll. by *around, about*) mess around; fool around. **4** *intr.* (foll. by *off*) go away. ● *n.* an act of frigging. [perh. imit.: orig. senses 'move about, rub']

frig² /frij/ *n. colloq.* = REFRIGERATOR. [abbr.]

frigate /frígit/ *n.* **1 a** a naval vessel between a destroyer and a cruiser in size. **b** *Brit.* a similar ship between a corvette and a destroyer in size. **2** *hist.* a warship next in size to ships of the line. □ **frigate bird** any marine bird of the family Fregatidae, found in tropical seas, with a wide wingspan and deeply forked tail: also called *hurricane bird.* [F *frégate* f. It. *fregata,* of unkn. orig.]

fright /frit/ *n. & v.* ● *n.* **1 a** a sudden or extreme fear. **b** an instance of this (*gave me a fright*). **2** a person or thing looking grotesque or ridiculous. ● *v.tr.* frighten. □ **take fright** become frightened. [OE *fryhto,* metathetic form of *fyrhto,* f. Gmc]
   ■ *n.* **1 a** fear, alarm, terror, horror, panic, trepidation, dread, apprehension, *sl.* (blue) funk. **b** scare, shock,

surprise, start. **2** eyesore, mess, disaster, monstrosity, *colloq.* sight. ● *v.* see FRIGHTEN 1, 2.

frighten /frítən/ *v.* **1** *tr.* fill with fright; terrify (*was frightened at the bang; is frightened of dogs*). **2** *tr.* (foll. by *away, off, out of, into*) drive or force by fright (*frightened it out of the room; frightened them into submission; frightened me into agreeing*). **3** *intr.* become frightened (*I frighten easily*). □□ **frightening** *adj.* **frighteningly** *adv.*
   ■ **1** terrify, scare, alarm, intimidate, panic, petrify, horrify, startle, shock, daunt, cow, scare a person out of his *or* her wits, make a person's hair stand on end, scare the (living) daylights out of, scare stiff, *poet.* fright. **2** scare, terrify, *poet.* fright; see also INTIMIDATE. **3** scare. □□ **frightening** terrifying, alarming, startling, shocking, petrifying, horrifying, daunting, intimidating, formidable, hair-raising, harrowing, dreadful, *colloq.* scary, spooky.

frightener /frítnər/ *n.* a person or thing that frightens. □ **put the frighteners on** *Brit. sl.* intimidate.

frightful /frítfool/ *adj.* **1 a** dreadful; shocking; revolting. **b** ugly; hideous. **2** *colloq.* extremely bad (*a frightful idea*). **3** *colloq.* very great; extreme. □□ **frightfully** *adv.*
   ■ **1** awful, dreadful, terrible, disagreeable, atrocious, abhorrent, loathsome, grisly, ghastly, lurid, horrible, horrifying, horrid, horrendous, nasty, hideous, vile, unspeakable, nauseating, nauseous, repugnant, repulsive, shocking, revolting, abominable, offensive, ugly. **2** see AWFUL 1a, b. **3** see GREAT *adj.* 1a.
   □□ **frightfully** very, extremely, *colloq.* awfully; amazingly, surprisingly.

frightfulness /frítfoolnis/ *n.* **1** being frightful. **2** (transl. G *Schrecklichkeit*) the terrorizing of a civilian population as a military resource.

frigid /fríjid/ *adj.* **1 a** lacking friendliness or enthusiasm; apathetic; formal; forced. **b** dull; flat; insipid. **c** chilling; depressing. **2** (of a woman) sexually unresponsive. **3** (esp. of climate or air) cold. □ **frigid zones** the parts of the earth north of the Arctic Circle and south of the Antarctic Circle. □□ **frigidity** /-jíditee/ *n.* **frigidly** *adv.* **frigidness** *n.* [L *frigidus* f. *frigēre* be cold f. *frigus* (n.) cold]
   ■ **1 a** cold, cool, coldhearted, forbidding, austere, unemotional, unfeeling, stiff, rigid, formal, prim, straitlaced, stony, callous, steely, obdurate, thick-skinned, inaccessible, remote, unapproachable, unfriendly, standoffish, haughty, aloof, reserved; apathetic, unenthusiastic; forced. **b** see FLAT¹ *adj.* 3a. **2** unresponsive, cold. **3** cold, frosty, frozen, glacial, icy, hyperborean, polar, boreal, Siberian, freezing, wintry, chilly, *colloq.* arctic, *literary* chill, *poet.* frore.

frijoles /freehólays/ *n.pl.* beans. [Sp., pl. of *frijol* bean ult. f. L *phaseolus*]

frill /fril/ *n. & v.* ● *n.* **1 a** a strip of material with one side gathered or pleated and the other left loose with a fluted appearance, used as an ornamental edging. **b** a similar paper ornament on a lamb chop, etc. **c** a natural fringe of feathers, hair, etc., on an animal (esp. a bird) or a plant. **2** (in *pl.*) unnecessary embellishments or accomplishments. **b** airs; affectation (*put on frills*). ● *v.tr.* **1** decorate with a frill. **2** form into a frill. □ **frill** (or **frilled**) **lizard** a large N. Australian lizard, *Chlamydosaurus kingii,* with an erectile membrane round the neck. □□ **frilled** *adj.* **frillery** /-ləree/ *n.* [16th c.: orig. unkn.]
   ■ *n.* **1 a** trimming, edging, furbelow, flounce, ruffle, decoration, ornamentation. **2 a** (*frills*) embellishment(s), extras, additions, trimmings, gewgaws, *colloq.* bells and whistles; ornamentation, frippery, falderal, showiness, ostentation, superfluity.

frilly /frílee/ *adj. & n.* ● *adj.* (**frillier, frilliest**) **1** having a

---

/.../ **pronunciation**	● **part of speech**
□ **phrases, idioms, and compounds**	
□□ **derivatives**	■ **synonym section**
cross-references appear in SMALL CAPITALS or *italics*	

frill or frills. **2** resembling a frill. ● *n.* (*pl.* **-ies**) (in *pl.*) *Brit. colloq.* frilled underwear. □□ **frilliness** *n.*

fringe /frinj/ *n. & v.* ● *n.* **1 a** an ornamental bordering of threads left loose or formed into tassels or twists. **b** such a bordering made separately. **c** any border or edging. **2 a** *Brit.* a portion of the front hair hanging over the forehead; bangs. **b** a natural border of hair, etc., in an animal or plant. **3** an outer edge or margin; the outer limit of an area, population, etc. (often *attrib.: fringe theater*). **4** a thing, part, or area of secondary or minor importance. **5 a** a band of contrasting brightness or darkness produced by diffraction or interference of light. **b** a strip of false color in an optical image. **6** a fringe benefit. ● *v.tr.* **1** adorn or encircle with a fringe. **2** serve as a fringe to. □ **fringe benefit** an employee's benefit supplementing a money wage or salary. **fringing reef** a coral reef that fringes the shore. □□ **fringeless** *adj.* **fringy** *adj.* [ME & OF *frenge* ult. f. LL *fimbria* (earlier only in pl.) fibers, fringe]

■ *n.* **1** trimming, edge, edging, border, frill, flounce, ruffle, purfling, ruff, ruche, rickrack, decoration, furbelow, *archaic* purfle. **3** border, perimeter, edge, boundary, periphery, margin, limits, bounds, outskirts, *hist.* march(es). ● *v.* **1** bind, purfle, trim, edge, border. **2** edge, border, surround, ring, flank, skirt, circle.

fringing /frinjing/ *n.* material for a fringe or fringes.
frippery /friperee/ *n. & adj.* ● *n.* (*pl.* **-ies**) **1** showy, tawdry, or unnecessary finery or ornament, esp. in dress. **2** empty display in speech, literary style, etc. **3 a** knickknacks; trifles. **b** a knickknack or trifle. ● *adj.* **1** frivolous. **2** contemptible. [F *friperie* f. OF *freperie* f. *frepe* rag]
■ *n.* **1** see FINERY[1]. **3 b** see ORNAMENT *n.* 1, 2.
frippet /fripit/ *n. Brit. sl.* a frivolous or showy young woman. [20th c.: orig. unkn.]
Frisbee /frizbee/ *n. propr.* a molded plastic disk for sailing through the air as an outdoor game. [perh. f. *Frisbie* bakery (Bridgeport, Conn.), whose pie tins could be used similarly]
Frisian /frizhən, free-/ *adj. & n.* ● *adj.* of Friesland (an area comprising the NW Netherlands and adjacent islands). ● *n.* **1** a native or inhabitant of Friesland. **2** the language of Friesland. [L *Frisii* pl. f. OFris. *Frīsa, Frēsa*]
frisk /frisk/ *v. & n.* ● *v.* **1** *intr.* leap or skip playfully. **2** *tr. sl.* feel over or search (a person) for a weapon, etc. (usu. rapidly). ● *n.* **1** a playful leap or skip. **2** *sl.* the frisking of a person. □□ **frisker** *n.* [obs. *frisk* (adj.) f. OF *frisque* lively, of unkn. orig.]
■ *v.* **1** caper, gambol, frolic, skip, trip, romp, leap, dance, prance, play, rollick, curvet, *sl.* cavort. **2** feel (over), search, inspect, check, examine, go over, check out.
● *n.* **1** see CAPER[1] *n.* 1.
frisket /friskit/ *n. Printing* a thin iron frame keeping the sheet in position during printing on a hand press. [F *frisquette* f. Prov. *frisqueto* f. Sp. *frasqueta*]
frisky /friskee/ *adj.* (**friskier, friskiest**) lively; playful. □□ **friskily** *adv.* **friskiness** *n.*
■ lively, frolicsome, rollicking, playful, active, animated, (high-)spirited, coltish.
frisson /freesON/ *n.* an emotional thrill. [F, = shiver]
frit /frit/ *n. & v.* ● *n.* **1** a calcined mixture of sand and fluxes as material for glass-making. **2** a vitreous composition from which soft porcelain, enamel, etc., are made. ● *v.tr.* (**fritted, fritting**) make into frit; partially fuse; calcine. [It. *fritta* fem. past part. of *friggere* FRY[1]]
fritfly /fritfli/ *n.* (*pl.* **-flies**) a small fly, *Oscinella frit,* of which the larvae are destructive to grains. [19th c.: orig. unkn.]
frith var. of FIRTH.
fritillary /frit'leree/ *n.* (*pl.* **-ies**) **1** any liliaceous plant of the genus *Fritillaria,* esp. snake's head, having pendent bell-like flowers. **2** any of various butterflies, esp. of the genus *Argynnis,* having reddish brown wings checkered with black. [mod.L *fritillaria* f. L *fritillus* dice cup]
fritter[1] /fritər/ *n. & v.* ● *v.tr.* **1** (usu. foll. by *away*) waste (money, time, energy, etc.) triflingly, indiscriminately, or on divided aims. **2** *archaic* subdivide. [obs. n. *fritter(s)* fragments = obs. *fitters* (n.pl.), perh. rel. to MHG *vetze* rag]

■ **1** (*fritter away*) squander, waste, trifle away, idle away, frivol away, misspend, dissipate.
fritter[2] /fritər/ *n.* a piece of fruit, meat, etc., coated in batter and deep-fried (*apple fritter*). [ME f. OF *friture* ult. f. L *frigere* *frict*- FRY[1]]
fritto misto /freetō meestō/ *n.* a mixed grill. [It., = mixed fry]
fritz /frits/ *n.* □ **on the fritz** *sl.* out of order; unsatisfactory. [20th c.: orig. unkn.]
frivol /frivəl/ *v.* (**frivoled, frivoling**; also **frivolled, frivolling**) **1** *intr.* be a trifler; trifle. **2** *tr.* (foll. by *away*) spend (money or time) foolishly. [back-form. f. FRIVOLOUS]
frivolous /frivələs/ *adj.* **1** paltry; trifling; trumpery. **2** lacking seriousness; given to trifling; silly. □□ **frivolity** /-vólitee/ *n.* (*pl.* **-ies**). **frivolously** *adv.* **frivolousness** *n.* [L *frivolus* silly, trifling]
■ **1** trifling, paltry, trumpery, inconsequential, unimportant, trivial, nugatory, insignificant, minor, petty, niggling, peripheral, superficial, worthless, *colloq.* small-time, *colloq.* two-bit, twopenny. **2** scatterbrained, silly, featherbrained, irresponsible, flighty, giddy, puerile, flippant, superficial, casual, airy, light, slight, *colloq.* birdbrained, flip, esp. *Brit.* airy-fairy.
frizz /friz/ *v. & n.* ● *v.tr.* form (hair, etc.) into a mass of small curls. ● *n.* **1 a** frizzed hair. **b** a row of curls. **2** a frizzed state. [F *friser,* perh. f. the stem of *frire* FRY[1]]
frizzle[1] /frizəl/ *v.intr. & tr.* **1** fry, toast, or grill, with a sputtering noise. **2** (often foll. by *up*) burn or shrivel. [*frizz* (in the same sense) f. FRY[1], with imit. ending + -LE[4]]
frizzle[2] /frizəl/ *v. & n.* ● *v.* **1** *tr.* form (hair) into tight curls. **2** *intr.* (often foll. by *up*) (of hair, etc.) curl tightly. ● *n.* frizzled hair. [16th c.: orig. unkn. (earlier than FRIZZ)]
frizzly /frizlee/ *adj.* in tight curls.
frizzy /frizee/ *adj.* (**frizzier, frizziest**) in a mass of small curls. □□ **frizziness** *n.*
Frl. *abbr.* Fräulein.
fro /frō/ *adv.* back (now only in *to and fro*: see TO). [ME f. ON *frá* FROM]
frock /frok/ *n. & v.* ● *n.* **1** esp. *Brit.* a woman's or girl's dress. **2 a** a monk's or priest's long gown with loose sleeves. **b** priestly office. **3** a smock. **4 a** a frock coat. **b** a military coat of similar shape. **5** a sailor's woolen jersey. ● *v.tr.* invest with priestly office (cf. UNFROCK). □ **frock coat** a man's knee-length coat not cut away in front. [ME f. OF *froc* f. Frank.]
■ *n.* **1** dress, gown. ● *v.* see INAUGURATE 1.
froe /frō/ *n.* (also **frow**) a cleaving tool with a handle at right angles to the blade. [abbr. of *frower* f. FROWARD 'turned away']
Froebel system /frōbəl, frœbəl/ *n.* a system of education of children by means of kindergartens. □□ **Froebelian** /-beeleeən/ *adj.* **Froebelism** *n.* [F. W. A. *Fröbel,* Ger. teacher d. 1852]
frog[1] /frawg, frog/ *n.* **1** any of various small amphibians of the order Anura, having a tailless smooth-skinned body with legs developed for jumping. **2** (**Frog**) *sl. offens.* a French person. **3** a hollow in the top face of a brick for holding the mortar. **4** the nut of a violin bow, etc. □ **frog in the** (or **one's**) **throat** *colloq.* hoarseness. [OE *frogga* f. Gmc]
frog[2] /frawg, frog/ *n.* an elastic horny substance in the sole of a horse's foot. [17th c.: orig. uncert. (perh. a use of FROG[1])]
frog[3] /frawg, frog/ *n.* **1** an ornamental coat fastening of a spindle-shaped button and loop. **2** an attachment to a belt to support a sword, bayonet, etc. □□ **frogged** *adj.* **frogging** *n.* [18th c.: orig. unkn.]
frog[4] /frawg, frog/ *n.* a grooved piece of iron at a place in a railroad line where tracks cross. [19th c.: orig. unkn.]
frogfish /fráwgfish, fróg-/ *n.* = ANGLERFISH.
froggy /fráwgee, frógee/ *adj. & n.* ● *adj.* **1** of or like a frog or frogs. **2 a** cold as a frog. **b** abounding in frogs. **3** *sl. offens.* French. ● *n.* (**Froggy**) (*pl.* **-ies**) *sl. derog.* a French person.
froghopper /fráwghopər, fróg-/ *n.* any jumping insect of the family Cercopidae, sucking sap and as larvae producing a protective mass of froth (see *cuckoo spit*).
frogman /fráwgman, fróg-, -mən/ *n.* (*pl.* **-men**) a person

equipped with a rubber suit, flippers, and an oxygen supply for underwater swimming.

frogmarch /fráwgmaarch, fróg-/ v. & n. ● v.tr. **1** hustle (a person) forward holding and pinning the arms from behind. **2** carry (a person) in a frogmarch. ● n. the carrying of a person face downwards by four others each holding a limb.

frogmouth /fráwgmowth, fróg-/ n. any of various birds of Australia and SE Asia, esp. of the family Podargidae, having large wide mouths.

frolic /frólik/ v., n., & adj. ● v.intr. (**frolicked, frolicking**) play about cheerfully; gambol. ● n. **1** cheerful play. **2** a prank. **3** a merry party. **4** an outburst of gaiety. **5** merriment. ● adj. archaic **1** full of pranks; sportive. **2** joyous; mirthful. □□ **frolicker** n. [Du. vrolijk (adj.) f. vro glad + -lijk -LY¹]
■ v. frisk, caper, skylark, gambol, rollick, romp, cut a caper, play, skip, sport, have fun, party, horse around, colloq. make whoopee, sl. cavort. ● n. **1** play, horseplay, skylarking. **2** escapade, gambado, antic, caper; see also PRANK. **3** romp, party, revel, gambol, colloq. spree. **4** joke, laugh, colloq. lark, giggle, scream. **5** merriment, merrymaking, gaiety, sport, fun (and games), high jinks, jollity, mirth, jollification, festivity, celebration, revelry.

frolicsome /fróliksəm/ adj. merry; playful. □□ **frolicsomely** adv. **frolicsomeness** n.
■ playful, merry, frisky, sportive, gay, lively, sprightly, animated, spirited, coltish.

from /frum, from, frəm/ prep. expressing separation or origin, followed by: **1** a person, place, time, etc., that is the starting point of motion or action, or of extent in place or time (rain comes from the clouds; repeated from mouth to mouth; dinner is served from 8; from start to finish). **2** a place, object, etc., whose distance or remoteness is reckoned or stated (ten miles from Los Angeles; I am far from admitting it; absent from home; apart from its moral aspect). **3 a** a source (dig gravel from a pit; a man from Idaho; draw a conclusion from premises; quotations from Whitman). **b** a giver or sender (presents from their parents; have not heard from her). **4 a** a thing or person avoided, escaped, lost, etc. (released him from prison; cannot refrain from laughing; dissuaded from folly). **b** a person or thing deprived (took his gun from him). **5** a reason, cause, or motive (died from fatigue; suffering from mumps; did it from jealousy; from her looks you might not believe it). **6** a thing distinguished or unlike (know black from white). **7** a lower limit (saw from 10 to 20 boats; tickets from $5). **8** a state changed for another (from being the victim he became the attacker; raised the penalty from a fine to imprisonment). **9** an adverb or preposition of time or place (from long ago; from elsewhere; from under the bed). **10** the position of a person who observes or considers (saw it from the roof; from his point of view). **11** a model (painted it from nature). □ **from day to day** (or **hour to hour**, etc.) daily (or hourly, etc.); as the days (or hours, etc.) pass. **from home** out; away. **from now on** henceforward. **from time to time** occasionally. **from year to year** each year; as the years pass. [OE fram, from f. Gmc]

frond /frond/ n. **1** Bot. **a** a large usu. divided foliage leaf in various flowerless plants, esp. ferns and palms. **b** the leaflike thallus of some algae. **2** Zool. a leaflike expansion. □□ **frondage** n. **frondose** adj. [L frons frondis leaf]

frondeur /frondőr/ n. a political rebel. [F, = slinger, applied to a party (the Fronde) rebelling during the minority of Louis XIV of France]

front /frunt/ n., adj., & v. ● n. **1** the side or part normally nearer or toward the spectator or the direction of motion (the front of the car; the front of the chair; the front of the mouth). **2** any face of a building, esp. that of the main entrance. **3** Mil. **a** the foremost line or part of an army, etc. **b** line of battle. **c** the part of the ground toward a real or imaginary enemy. **d** a scene of actual fighting (go to the front). **e** the direction in which a formed line faces. **4 a** a sector of activity regarded as resembling a military front. **b** an organized political group. **5 a** demeanor; bearing (show a bold front). **b** outward appearance. **6** a forward or conspicuous position (come to the front). **7 a** a bluff. **b** a pretext. **8** a person, etc., serving to cover subversive or illegal activities. **9** esp. Brit. (prec. by the) the promenade of a seaside resort. **10** Meteorol. the forward edge of an advancing mass of cold or warm air. **11** (prec. by the) the audience or auditorium of a theater. **12 a** a face. **b** poet. or rhet. a forehead. **13 a** the breast of a man's shirt. **b** a false shirtfront. **14** impudence. ● attrib.adj. **1** of the front. **2** situated in front. **3** Phonet. formed at the front of the mouth. ● v. **1** intr. (foll. by on, to, toward, upon) have the front facing or directed. **2** intr. (foll. by for) sl. act as a front or cover for. **3** tr. furnish with a front (fronted with stone). **4** tr. lead (a band). **5** tr. **a** stand opposite to; front toward. **b** have its front on the side of (a street, etc.). **6** tr. archaic confront; meet; oppose. □ **front bench** Brit. the foremost seats in Parliament, occupied by leading members of the government and opposition. **front-bencher** Brit. such a member. **front door 1** the chief entrance of a house. **2** a chief means of approach or access to a place, situation, etc. **front line** Mil. = sense 3 of n. **front man** a person acting as a front or cover. **front matter** Printing the title page, preface, etc., preceding the text proper. **front office 1** the executives or executive branch of an organization. **2 a** a main office. **b** Brit. police headquarters. **front page** the first page of a newspaper, esp. as containing important or remarkable news. **front runner 1** the contestant most likely to succeed. **2** an athlete or horse running best when in the lead. **front-wheel drive** an automobile drive system in which power is transmitted from the engine to the front wheels. **in front 1** in an advanced position. **2** facing the spectator. **in front of 1** ahead of; in advance of. **2** in the presence of; confronting. **on the front burner** see BURNER. □□ **frontless** adj. **frontward** adj. & adv. **frontwards** adv. [ME f. OF front (n.), fronter (v.) f. L frons frontis]
■ n. **1** face, forepart, fore; obverse. **2** face, frontage, façade. **3** vanguard, van, formation, Mil. front line. **4 b** movement, organization, party, group, league; faction, wing. **5 a** bearing, demeanor, air, face, expression, countenance, literary mien. **b** façade, mask, show, guise, appearance, aspect, look, exterior. **6** beginning, head, forefront, fore. **7** bluff, disguise, guise, cover, show, pretext. **8** cover. **12 a** see FACE n. 1. **14** impudence, haughtiness, overconfidence, effrontery. ● attrib.adj. **2** first, advance, leading, head, anterior. ● v. **1, 5a** overlook, face, look out on or over; be opposite. **2** (front for) act for, represent; substitute for, cover for, replace. **6** see FACE v. 3. □ **in front 1** first, leading, in the lead, ahead, winning, in advance, in the vanguard or van, to the fore, in the forefront. **in front of 1** see ahead of.

frontage /frúntij/ n. **1** the front of a building. **2 a** a land abutting on a street or on water. **b** the land between the front of a building and the road. **3** extent of front (a store with little frontage). **4 a** the way a thing faces. **b** outlook. □ **frontage road** a road parallel to a main road, serving houses, stores, etc. □□ **frontager** n.
■ **1** see FACE n. 4e. **4** see EXPOSURE 5.

frontal¹ /frúnt'l/ adj. **1 a** of, at, or on the front (a frontal attack). **b** of the front as seen by an onlooker (a frontal view). **2** of the forehead or front part of the skull (frontal bone). □□ **frontally** adv. [mod.L frontalis (as FRONT)]

frontal² /frúnt'l/ n. **1** a covering for the front of an altar. **2** the façade of a building. [ME f. OF frontel f. L frontale (as FRONT)]

frontier /frúnteér/ n. **1 a** the border between two countries. **b** the district on each side of this. **2** the limits of attainment or knowledge in a subject. **3** the borders between settled and unsettled country. □□ **frontierless** adj. [ME f. AF frounter, OF frontiere ult. f. L frons frontis FRONT]
■ **1** border, boundary, bound(s), pale, archaic bourn, hist. march(es). **2** limit(s), bound(s), extreme(s), archaic bourn.

/.../ **pronunciation**	● **part of speech**
□ **phrases, idioms, and compounds**	
□□ **derivatives**	■ **synonym section**
cross-references appear in SMALL CAPITALS or italics	

frontiersman /frúnteĕrzmən/ n. (pl. **-men**) a person living in the region of a frontier, esp. between settled and unsettled country.
■ see PIONEER n. 2.

frontispiece /frúntispees/ n. **1** an illustration facing the title page of a book or of one of its divisions. **2** Archit. **a** the principal face of a building. **b** a decorated entrance. **c** a pediment over a door, etc. [F frontispice or LL frontispicium façade f. L frons frontis FRONT + -spicium f. specere look: assim. to PIECE]

frontlet /frúntlit/ n. **1** a piece of cloth hanging over the upper part of an altar frontal. **2** a band worn on the forehead. **3** a phylactery. **4** an animal's forehead. [OF frontelet (as FRONTAL²)]

frontline /frúntlin/ adj. **1** Mil. relating to or located at a front line. **2** relating to the forefront of any activity.

fronton /frónton, -tón/ n. **1** a jai alai court. **2** a pediment. [F f. It. frontone f. fronte forehead]

frore /frawr/ adj. poet. frozen; frosty. [archaic past part. of FREEZE]

frost /frawst, frost/ n. & v. ● n. **1 a** a white frozen dew coating esp. the ground at night (windows covered with frost). **b** a consistent temperature below freezing point causing frost to form. **2** a chilling dispiriting atmosphere. **3** Brit. sl. a failure. ● v. **1** intr. (usu. foll. by over, up) become covered with frost. **2** tr. **a** cover with or as if with frost, powder, etc. **b** injure (a plant, etc.) with frost. **3** tr. give a roughened or finely granulated surface to (glass, metal) (frosted glass). **4** tr. cover or decorate (a cake, etc.) with icing. □ **degrees of frost** Brit. degrees below the freezing point (ten degrees of frost tonight). **frost heave** Geol. an upthrust of soil or pavement caused by the freezing of moist soil underneath. □□ **frostless** adj. [OE f. Gmc]
■ n. **1 b** see FREEZE n. 1.

frostbite /fráwstbit, fróst-/ n. injury to body tissues, esp. the nose, fingers, or toes, due to freezing and often resulting in gangrene.

frosting /fráwsting, fróst-/ n. **1** icing. **2** a rough surface on glass, etc.

frostwork /fráwstwərk, frost-/ n. tracery made by frost on glass, etc.

frosty /fráwstee, fróstee/ adj. (**frostier, frostiest**) **1** cold with frost. **2** covered with or as with hoarfrost. **3** unfriendly in manner; lacking in warmth of feeling. □□ **frostily** adv. **frostiness** n.
■ **1** see COLD adj. 1. **3** see COLD adj. 4.

froth /frawth, froth/ n. & v. ● n. **1 a** a collection of small bubbles in liquid; caused by shaking, fermenting, etc.; foam. **b** impure matter on liquid; scum. **2 a** idle talk or ideas. **b** anything unsubstantial or of little worth. ● v. **1** intr. emit or gather froth (frothing at the mouth). **2** tr. cause (beer, etc.) to foam. □ **froth-blower** Brit. joc. a beer drinker (esp. as a designation of a member of a charitable organization). □□ **frothily** adv. **frothiness** n. **frothy** adj. (**frothier, frothiest**). [ME f. ON frotha, frauth f. Gmc]
■ n. **1** foam, spume, suds, lather, bubbles; head. **2** trivia, rubbish, nonsense, twaddle, babble, gibberish, drivel, colloq. gab, piffle, sl. hot air, gas. ● v. **1** foam, spume, bubble, fizz, effervesce; lather. **2** aerate.

frottage /frawtáazh/ n. **1** Psychol. an abnormal desire for contact between the clothed bodies of oneself and another. **2** Art the technique or process of taking a rubbing from an uneven surface to form the basis of a work of art. [F, = rubbing f. frotter rub f. OF froter]

froufrou /frōōfrōō/ n. **1** a rustling, esp. of a dress. **2** a frilly ornamentation. [F, imit.]

frow¹ /frow/ n. Brit. **1** a Dutchwoman. **2** a housewife. [ME f. Du. vrouw woman]

frow² var. of FROE.

froward /frṓərd/ adj. archaic perverse; difficult to deal with. □□ **frowardly** adv. **frowardness** n. [ME f. FRO + -WARD]

frown /frown/ v. & n. ● v. **1** intr. wrinkle one's brows, esp. in displeasure or deep thought. **2** intr. (foll. by at, on, upon) express disapproval. **3** intr. (of a thing) present a gloomy aspect. **4** tr. compel with a frown (frowned them into silence).

5 tr. express (defiance, etc.) with a frown. ● n. **1** an action of frowning; a vertically furrowed or wrinkled state of the brow. **2** a look expressing severity, disapproval, or deep thought. □□ **frowner** n. **frowningly** adv. [ME f. OF frongnier, froignier f. froigne surly look f. Celt.]
■ v. **1** scowl, glower, glare, knit one's brows, grimace, lower. **2** (frown on or upon) disapprove of, disfavor, discountenance, look askance at, not take kindly to, not think much of, look disapprovingly upon, colloq. take a dim view of. **3** look grim or gloomy. ● n. **2** scowl, glower, glare, grimace, lower, colloq. dirty look.

frowst /frowst/ n. & v. Brit. colloq. ● n. fusty warmth in a room. ● v.intr. stay in or enjoy frowst. □□ **frowster** n. [back-form. f. FROWSTY]

frowsty /frówstee/ adj. Brit. (**frowstier, frowstiest**) fusty; stuffy. □□ **frowstiness** n. [var. of FROWZY]

frowzy /frówzee/ adj. (also **frowsy**) (**-ier, -iest**) **1** fusty; musty; malodorous; close. **2** slatternly; unkempt; dingy. □□ **frowziness** n. [17th c.: orig. unkn.: cf. earlier frowy]
■ **1** see STUFFY 1. **2** see UNKEMPT 1.

froze past of FREEZE.

frozen past part. of FREEZE.

FRS abbr. **1** Federal Reserve System. **2** (in the UK) Fellow of the Royal Society.

fructiferous /fruktífərəs, frōōk-/ adj. bearing fruit. [L fructifer f. fructus FRUIT]

fructification /frúktifikáyshən, frōōk-/ n. Bot. **1** the process of fructifying. **2** any spore-bearing structure, esp. in ferns, fungi, and mosses. [LL fructificatio (as FRUCTIFY)]

fructify /frúktifī, frōōk-/ v. (**-ies, -ied**) **1** intr. bear fruit. **2** tr. make fruitful; impregnate. [ME f. OF fructifier f. L fructificare f. fructus FRUIT]
■ **2** see FERTILIZE 2.

fructose /frúktōs, frōōk-/ n. Chem. a simple sugar found in honey and fruits. Also called LEVULOSE, fruit sugar. [L fructus FRUIT + -OSE²]

fructuous /frúkchōōəs, frōōk-/ adj. full of or producing fruit. [ME f. OF fructuous or L fructuosus (as FRUIT)]

frugal /frōōgəl/ adj. **1** (often foll. by of) sparing or economical, esp. as regards food. **2** sparingly used or supplied; meager; costing little. □□ **frugality** /-gálitee/ n. **frugally** adv. **frugalness** n. [L frugalis f. frugi economical]
■ **1** thrifty, sparing, economical, careful, prudent, provident, moderate; abstemious. **2** meager, paltry, poor, skimpy, scanty, scant, small, negligible, colloq. piddling.

frugivorous /frōōjívərəs/ adj. feeding on fruit. [L frux frugis fruit + -VOROUS]

fruit /frōōt/ n. & v. ● n. **1 a** the usu. sweet and fleshy edible product of a plant or tree, containing seed. **b** (in sing.) these in quantity (eats fruit). **2** the seed of a plant or tree with its covering, e.g., an acorn, pea pod, cherry, etc. **3** (usu. in pl.) vegetables, grains, used for food (fruits of the earth). **4** (usu. in pl.) the result of action, etc., esp. as financial reward (fruits of his labors). **5** derog. sl. a male homosexual. **6** Bibl. an offspring (the fruit of the womb; the fruit of his loins). ● v.intr. & tr. bear or cause to bear fruit. □ **fruit bat** any large bat of the suborder Megachiroptera, feeding on fruit. **fruiting** (or **fruit**) **body** (pl. **-ies**) the spore-bearing part of a fungus. **fruit cocktail** a chopped usu. canned fruit salad. **fruit fly** (pl. **flies**) any of various flies, esp. of the genus Drosophila, having larvae that feed on fruit. **fruit machine** Brit. = slot machine. **fruit salad 1** various fruits cut up and served in syrup, juice, etc. **2** sl. a display of medals, etc. **fruit sugar** fructose. **fruit tree** a tree grown for its fruit. □□ **fruitage** n. **fruited** adj. (also in comb.). [ME f. OF f. L fructus fruit, enjoyment f. frui enjoy]
■ n. **4** product(s), result(s), revenue(s), outcome, consequence(s), return(s), advantage(s), benefit(s), profit(s), emolument, payment, income, deserts. **6** see OFFSPRING.

fruitarian /frōōtáireeən/ n. a person who eats only fruit. [FRUIT, after vegetarian]

fruitcake /frōōtkayk/ n. **1** a cake containing dried fruit. **2** sl. an eccentric or mad person.

■ **2** see ECCENTRIC *n.*

fruiter /frōōtər/ *n.* **1** a tree producing fruit, esp. with reference to its quality (*a poor fruiter*). **2** a fruit grower. **3** a ship carrying fruit. [ME f. OF *fruitier* (as FRUIT, -ER⁵): later f. FRUIT + -ER¹]

fruiterer /frōōtərər/ *n.* esp. *Brit.* a dealer in fruit.

fruitful /frōōtfŏŏl/ *adj.* **1** producing much fruit; fertile; causing fertility. **2** producing good results; successful; beneficial; remunerative. **3** producing offspring, esp. prolifically. □□ **fruitfully** *adv.* **fruitfulness** *n.*

■ **1** fertile, plentiful, abundant, fecund, copious, luxuriant, rich, flourishing, bountiful, *poet.* plenteous, bounteous; fructiferous, fructuous. **2** successful, effective, beneficial, profitable, remunerative, productive, advantageous, worthwhile, useful, rewarding, well-spent. **3** productive, fertile, prolific, fecund.

fruition /frōō-ĭshən/ *n.* **1 a** the bearing of fruit. **b** the production of results. **2** the realization of aims or hopes. **3** enjoyment. [ME f. OF f. LL *fruitio -onis* f. *frui* enjoy, erron. assoc. with FRUIT]

■ **1b, 2** production, completion; achievement, success, attainment, accomplishment, fulfillment, realization, consummation, materialization, perfection. **3** see *enjoyment* (ENJOY).

fruitless /frōōtlĭs/ *adj.* **1** not bearing fruit. **2** useless; unsuccessful; unprofitable. □□ **fruitlessly** *adv.* **fruitlessness** *n.*

■ **1** barren, unfruitful, unproductive, sterile, infertile. **2** worthless, futile, pointless, useless, vain, unavailing, ineffectual, ineffective, unprofitable, unsuccessful, unrewarding, abortive, *archaic* bootless; for naught, to no avail.

fruitlet /frōōtlĭt/ *n.* = DRUPEL.

fruitwood /frōōtwŏŏd/ *n.* the wood of a fruit tree, esp. when used in furniture.

fruity /frōōtee/ *adj.* (**fruitier, fruitiest**) **1 a** of fruit. **b** tasting or smelling like fruit, esp. (of wine) tasting of the grape. **2** (of a voice, etc.) of full rich quality. **3** *sl.* crazy; silly. **4** *offens. sl.* homosexual. **5** *Brit. colloq.* full of rough humor or (usu. scandalous) interest; suggestive. □□ **fruitily** *adv.* **fruitiness** *n.*

■ **1 b** see ROBUST 5.

frumenty /frōōməntee/ *n.* (also **furmety** /fɜ́rmitee/) hulled wheat boiled in milk and seasoned with cinnamon, sugar, etc. [ME f. OF *frumentee* f. *frument* f. L *frumentum* grain]

frump /frump/ *n.* a dowdy, unattractive, old-fashioned woman. □□ **frumpish** *adj.* **frumpishly** *adv.* [16th c.: perh. f. dial. *frumple* (v.) wrinkle f. MDu. *verrompelen* (as FOR-, RUMPLE)]

frumpy /frúmpee/ *adj.* (**frumpier, frumpiest**) dowdy, unattractive, and old-fashioned. □□ **frumpily** *adv.* **frumpiness** *n.*

■ see DOWDY *adj.* 2.

frustrate /frústrayt/ *v. & adj.* ● *v.tr.* **1** make (efforts) ineffective. **2** prevent (a person) from achieving a purpose. **3** (as **frustrated** *adj.*) **a** discontented because unable to achieve one's desire. **b** sexually unfulfilled. **4** disappoint (a hope). ● *adj. archaic* frustrated. □□ **frustratedly** /-stráytidlee/ *adv.* **frustrater** *n.* **frustrating** *adj.* **frustratingly** *adv.* **frustration** /-stráyshən/ *n.* [ME f. L *frustrari frustrat-* f. *frustra* in vain]

■ *v.* **1** counteract, neutralize, nullify, counter, negate. **2** prevent, defeat, forestall, stop, halt, cripple, hinder, hamper, disrupt, impede, hamstring, thwart, upset, foil, stymie, obstruct, block, baffle, check, balk; fight off, repel, repulse. **3** (**frustrated**) **a** see *discontented* (DISCONTENT). **b** unfulfilled, dissatisfied. **4** discourage, disappoint, foil, thwart, defeat, balk.

frustule /frúschŏŏl/ *n. Bot.* the siliceous cell wall of a diatom. [F f. L *frustulum* (as FRUSTUM)]

frustum /frústəm/ *n.* (*pl.* **frusta** /-tə/ or **frustums**) *Geom.* **1** the remainder of a cone or pyramid whose upper part has been cut off by a plane parallel to its base. **2** the part of a cone or pyramid intercepted between two planes. [L, = piece cut off]

frutescent /frōōtésʹənt/ *adj. Bot.* of the nature of a shrub. [irreg. f. L *frutex* bush]

frutex /frōōteks/ *n.* (*pl.* **frutices** /-tiseez/) *Bot.* a woody-stemmed plant smaller than a tree; a shrub. [L *frutex fruticis*]

fruticose /frōōtikōs/ *adj. Bot.* resembling a shrub. [L *fruticosus* (as FRUTEX)]

fry¹ /frī/ *v. & n.* ● *v.* (**fries, fried**) **1** *tr. & intr.* cook or be cooked in hot fat. **2** *tr. & intr. sl.* electrocute or be electrocuted. **3** *tr.* (as **fried** *adj.*) *sl.* drunk. **4** *intr. colloq.* be very hot. ● *n.* (*pl.* **fries**) **1** a French fry. **2** a social gathering serving fried food. **3** a dish of fried food, esp. meat. **4** various internal parts of animals usu. eaten fried (*lamb's fry*). □ **frying** (also **fry**) **pan** a shallow pan used in frying. **fry up** cook in a frying pan. **fry-up** *n. Brit. colloq.* a dish of miscellaneous fried food. **out of the frying pan into the fire** from a bad situation to a worse one. [ME f. OF *frire* f. L *frigere*]

■ *v.* **3** (**fried**) see DRUNK *adj.* 1. **4** see BOIL¹ *v.* 3c.

fry² /frī/ *n.pl.* **1** young or newly hatched fishes. **2** the young of other creatures produced in large numbers, e.g., bees or frogs. □ **small fry** people of little importance; children. [ME f. ON *frjó*]

fryer /frÍər/ *n.* (also **frier**) **1** a person who fries. **2** a vessel for frying, esp. deep frying. **3** a young chicken suitable for frying.

FSH *abbr.* follicle-stimulating hormone.

FSLIC *abbr.* Federal Savings and Loan Insurance Corporation.

f-stop /éf stop/ var. of F-NUMBER.

Ft. *abbr.* Fort.

ft. *abbr.* foot, feet.

FTC *abbr.* Federal Trade Commission.

fubsy /fúbzee/ *adj.* (**fubsier, fubsiest**) *Brit.* fat or squat. [obs. *fubs* small fat person + -Y¹]

fuchsia /fyōōshə/ *n.* any shrub of the genus *Fuchsia*, with drooping red or purple or white flowers. [mod.L f. L. *Fuchs*, Ger. botanist d. 1566]

fuchsin /fōōksin/ *n.* (also **fuchsine** /-seen/) a deep red aniline dye used in the pharmaceutical and textile-processing industries; rosaniline. [FUCHSIA (from its resemblance to the color of the flower)]

fuck /fuk/ *v., int., & n. coarse sl.* ● *v.* **1** *tr. & intr.* have sexual intercourse (with). **2** *intr.* (foll. by *around, about*) mess around; fool around. **3** *tr.* (usu. as an exclam.) curse; confound (*fuck the thing!*). **4** *intr.* (as **fucking** *adj., adv.*) used as an intensive to express annoyance, etc. ● *int.* expressing anger or annoyance. ● *n.* **1 a** an act of sexual intercourse. **b** a partner in sexual intercourse. **2** the slightest amount (*don't give a fuck*). □ **fuck off** go away. **fuck up** make a mess of. **fuck-up** *n.* a mess or muddle. ¶ A highly taboo word. □□ **fucker** *n.* (often as a term of abuse). [16th c.: orig. unkn.]

fucus /fyōōkəs/ *n.* (*pl.* **fuci** /fyōōsī/) any seaweed of the genus *Fucus*, with flat leathery fronds. □□ **fucoid** *adj.* [L, = rock lichen, f. Gk *phukos*, f. Semitic orig.]

fuddle /fúd'l/ *v. & n.* ● *v.* **1** *tr.* confuse or stupefy, esp. with alcoholic liquor. **2** *intr.* tipple; booze. ● *n.* **1** confusion. **2** intoxication. **3** *Brit.* a spell of drinking (*on the fuddle*). [16th c.: orig. unkn.]

fuddy-duddy /fúdeedúdee/ *adj. & n. sl.* ● *adj.* old-fashioned or quaintly fussy. ● *n.* (*pl.* **-ies**) a fuddy-duddy person. [20th c.: orig. unkn.]

■ *adj.* see SQUEAMISH 2, STUFFY 4. ● *n.* see FOGY.

fudge /fuj/ *n., v., & int.* ● *n.* **1** a soft toffee-like candy made with milk, sugar, butter, etc. **2** nonsense. **3** a piece of dishonesty or faking. **4** a piece of late news inserted in a newspaper page. ● *v.* **1** *tr.* put together in a makeshift or dishonest way; fake. **2** *tr.* deal with incompetently. **3** *intr.* practice such methods. ● *int.* expressing disbelief or annoyance. [perh. f. obs. *fadge* (v.) fit]

■ *v.* **1** see FALSIFY 1.

fuehrer var. of FÜHRER.

fuel /fyōōəl/ *n.* & *v.* ● *n.* **1** material, esp. coal, wood, oil, etc., burned or used as a source of heat or power. **2** food as a source of energy. **3** material used as a source of nuclear energy. **4** anything that sustains or inflames emotion or passion. ● *v.* (**fueled, fueling**; *Brit.* **fuelled, fuelling**) **1** *tr.* supply with fuel. **2** *tr.* sustain or inflame (an argument, feeling, etc.) (*liquor fueled his anger*). **3** *intr.* take in or get fuel. □ **fuel cell** a cell producing an electric current direct from a chemical reaction. **fuel element** an element of nuclear fuel, etc., for use in a reactor. **fuel injection** the direct introduction of fuel under pressure into the combustion units of an internal combustion engine. **fuel oil** oil used as fuel in an engine or furnace. [ME f. AF *fuaille, fewaile*, OF *fouaille*, ult. f. L *focus* hearth]
■ *n.* **2** nourishment, sustenance, nutriment, nutrition; food. **4** incitement, stimulus, stimulation, provocation; see also *encouragement* (ENCOURAGE), SPUR *n.* 2. ● *v.* **2** nourish, feed, sustain; stimulate, encourage, incite, provoke, inflame, exacerbate, excite.

fug /fug/ *n.* & *v. Brit. colloq.* ● *n.* stuffiness or fustiness of the air in a room. ● *v.intr.* (**fugged, fugging**) stay in or enjoy a fug. □□ **fuggy** *adj.* [19th c.: orig. unkn.]

fugacious /fyōōgáyshəs/ *adj.* fleeting; evanescent; hard to capture or keep. □□ **fugaciously** *adv.* **fugaciousness** *n.* **fugacity** /-gásitee/ *n.* [L *fugax fugacis* f. *fugere* flee]

fugal /fyōōgəl/ *adj.* of the nature of a fugue. □□ **fugally** *adv.*

-fuge /fyōōj/ *comb. form* forming adjectives and nouns denoting expelling or dispelling (*febrifuge*; *vermifuge*). [from or after mod.L *-fugus* f. L *fugare* put to flight]

fugitive /fyōōjitiv/ *adj.* & *n.* ● *adj.* **1** fleeing; that runs or has run away. **2** transient; fleeting; of short duration. **3** (of literature) of passing interest; ephemeral. **4** flitting; shifting. ● *n.* **1** (often foll. by *from*) a person who flees, esp. from justice, an enemy, danger, or a master. **2** an exile or refugee. □□ **fugitively** *adv.* [ME f. OF *fugitif -ive* f. L *fugitivus* f. *fugere* *fugit-* flee]
■ *adj.* **1** fleeing, escaped, running away, runaway. **2, 3** fleeting, passing, short-lived, transitory, transient, ephemeral, evanescent, momentary, volatile, *literary* fugacious. ● *n.* **1** runaway, escapee, deserter. **2** refugee, deportee; see also EXILE *n.* 3.

fugle /fyōōgəl/ *v.intr.* act as a fugleman. [back-form. f. FUGLEMAN]

fugleman /fyōōgəlmən/ *n.* (*pl.* **-men**) **1** *hist.* a soldier placed in front of a regiment, etc., while drilling to show the motions and time. **2** a leader, organizer, or spokesman. [G *Flügelmann* f. *Flügel* wing + *Mann* man]

fugue /fyōōg/ *n.* & *v.* ● *n.* **1** *Mus.* a contrapuntal composition in which a short melody or phrase (the subject) is introduced by one part and successively taken up by others and developed by interweaving the parts. **2** *Psychol.* loss of awareness of one's identity, often coupled with flight from one's usual environment. ● *v.intr.* (**fugues, fugued, fuguing**) *Mus.* compose or perform a fugue. □□ **fuguist** *n.* [F or It. f. L *fuga* flight]

fugued /fyōōgd/ *adj.* in the form of a fugue.

führer /fyōōrər/ *n.* (also **fuehrer**) a leader, esp. a tyrannical one. [G, = leader: part of the title assumed in 1934 by Hitler (see HITLER)]

-ful /fōōl/ *comb. form* forming: **1** adjectives from nouns, meaning: **a** full of (*beautiful*). **b** having the qualities of (*masterful*). **2** adjectives from adjectives or Latin stems with little change of sense (*direful*; *grateful*). **3** adjectives from verbs, meaning 'apt to,' 'able to,' 'accustomed to' (*forgetful*; *mournful*; *useful*). **4** nouns (*pl.* **-fuls**) meaning 'the amount needed to fill' (*handful*; *spoonful*).

fulcrum /fōōlkrəm, fúl-/ *n.* (*pl.* **fulcra** /-rə/ or **fulcrums**) **1** the point against which a lever is placed to get a purchase or on which it turns or is supported. **2** the means by which influence, etc., is brought to bear. [L, = post of a couch, f. *fulcire* to prop]
■ **1** see PIVOT *n.* 1.

fulfill /fōōlfíl/ *v.tr.* (**fulfilled, fulfilling**) **1** bring to consummation; carry out (a prophecy or promise). **2** satisfy (a desire or prayer). **3 a** execute; obey (a command or law). **b** perform; carry out (a task). **4** comply with (conditions). **5** answer (a purpose). **6** bring to an end; finish; complete (a period or piece of work). □ **fulfill oneself** develop one's gifts and character to the full. □□ **fulfillable** *adj.* **fulfiller** *n.* **fulfillment** *n.* [OE *fullfyllan* (as FULL[1], FILL)]
■ **1** bring about, consummate; see also REALIZE 4, KEEP *v.* 7a, b. **2** satisfy, live up to; see also ACHIEVE 2. **3 a** see OBEY. **b** perform, do, carry out, bring or carry off, see to, accomplish, effect, effectuate; implement. **4** abide by, comply with, conform to or achieve, observe, obey. **5** answer, satisfy, meet; see also SERVE *v.* 5a–c. **6** finish, complete, discharge, bring to an end, carry through, bring or carry to completion. □□ **fulfillment** completion, realization, implementation, execution, consummation, accomplishment, carrying out or through, discharge; performance, achievement, satisfaction; compliance, conformity or conformance, meeting (with).

fulgent /fúljənt/ *adj. poet.* or *rhet.* shining; brilliant. [ME f. L *fulgēre* shine]

fulguration /fúlgəráyshən/ *n. Surgery* the destruction of tissue by means of high-voltage electricity. [L *fulguratio* sheet lightning f. *fulgur* lightning]

fulgurite /fúlgərīt/ *n. Geol.* a rocky substance of sand fused or vitrified by lightning. [L *fulgur* lightning]

fuliginous /fyōōlíjinəs/ *adj.* sooty; dusky. [LL *fuliginosus* f. *fuligo -ginis* soot]

full[1] /fōōl/ *adj., adv., n.,* & *v.* ● *adj.* **1** (often foll. by *of*) holding all its limits will allow (*the bucket is full*; *full of water*). **2** having eaten to one's limits or satisfaction. **3** abundant; copious; satisfying; sufficient (*a full program of events*; *led a full life*; *turned it to full account*; *give full details*; *the book is very full on this point*). **4** (foll. by *of*) having or holding an abundance of; showing marked signs of (*full of vitality*; *full of interest*; *full of mistakes*). **5** (foll. by *of*) **a** engrossed in thinking about (*full of himself*; *full of his work*). **b** unable to refrain from talking about (*full of the news*). **6 a** complete; perfect; reaching the specified or usual or utmost limit (*full membership*; *full daylight*; *waited a full hour*; *it was full summer*; *in full bloom*). **b** *Bookbinding* used for the entire cover (*full leather*). **7 a** (of tone or color) deep and clear; mellow. **b** (of light) intense. **c** (of motion, etc.) vigorous (*a full pulse*; *at full gallop*). **8** plump; rounded; protuberant (*a full figure*). **9** (of clothes) made of much material arranged in folds or gathers. **10** (of the heart, etc.) overcharged with emotion. **11** *Brit. sl.* drunk. **12** (foll. by *of*) *archaic* having had plenty of (*full of years and honors*). ● *adv.* **1** very (*you know full well*). **2** quite; fully (*full six miles*). **3** exactly (*hit him full on the nose*). **4** more than sufficiently (*full early*). ● *n.* **1** height; acme (*season is past the full*). **2** the state or time of full moon. **3** the whole; the complete amount (*cannot tell you the full of it*; *paid in full*). ● *v.intr.* & *tr.* be or become or make (esp. clothes) full. □ **at full length 1** lying stretched out. **2** without abridgment. **come full circle** see CIRCLE. **full age** *Brit.* adult status (esp. with ref. to legal rights and duties). **full and by** *Naut.* close-hauled but with sails filling. **full blood** pure descent. **full-blooded 1** vigorous; hearty; sensual. **2** not hybrid. **full-bloodedly** forcefully; wholeheartedly. **full-bloodedness** being full-blooded. **full-blown** fully developed; complete; (of flowers) quite open. **full board** provision of accommodation and all meals at a hotel, etc. **full-bodied** rich in quality, tone, etc. **full brother** a brother born of the same parents. **full-court press** see PRESS[1]. **full dress** formal clothes worn on great occasions. **full-dress** *adj.* (of a debate, etc.) of major importance. **full employment 1** the condition in which there is no idle capital or labor of any kind that is in demand. **2** the condition in which virtually all who are able and willing to work are employed. **full face** with all the face visible to the spectator. **full-fashioned** (of women's clothing) shaped to fit the body. **full-fledged** mature. **full-frontal 1** (of nudity or a nude figure) with full exposure at the front. **2** unrestrained; explicit; with nothing concealed. **full-grown** having reached maturity. **full house 1** a maximum or large attendance at a theater, etc. **2** *Poker* a hand with three of a kind and a pair. **full-length 1** not shortened or abbreviated. **2** (of a mirror, portrait, etc.) showing the whole height of the human figure. **full lock** see LOCK[1]. **full marks** *Brit.* the maximum award in an examination, in assessment of a person, etc. **full measure** not less than the professed amount. **full moon 1** the moon with its whole disk illuminated. **2** the time when this occurs. **full-mouthed 1** (of cattle or sheep) having a full set of teeth. **2** (of a dog) baying loudly. **3** (of oratory, etc.) sonorous; vigorous. **full out 1** *Printing* flush with the margin. **2** at full power. **3** complete. **full page** an entire page of a newspaper, etc. **full point** = *full stop* 1. **full professor** a professor of the highest rank in a university, etc. **full-scale** not reduced in size; complete. **full score** *Mus.* a score giving the parts for all performers on separate staves. **full service** a church service performed by a choir without solos, or performed with music wherever possible. **full-service** (of a bank, service station, etc.) providing a wide range of service. **full sister** a sister born of the same parents. **full speed** (or **steam**) **ahead!** an order to proceed at maximum speed or to pursue a course of action energetically. **full stop 1** esp. *Brit.* = PERIOD *n.* 8. **2** a complete cessation. **full term** the completion of a normal pregnancy. **full tilt** see TILT. **full time 1** the total normal duration of work, etc. **2** *Brit.* the end of a soccer, etc., game. **full-time** *adj.* occupying or using the whole of the available working time. **full-timer** a person who holds a full-time job. **full up** *colloq.* completely full. **in full 1** without abridgment. **2** to or for the full amount (*paid in full*). **in full swing** at the height of activity. **in full view** entirely visible. **on a full stomach** see STOMACH. **to the full** to the utmost extent. [OE f. Gmc]

■ *adj.* **1** filled, replete, brimming, brimful, chockablock, chock-full, packed, loaded, crammed, crowded, stuffed, bursting, *colloq.* jam-packed; saturated. **2** gorged, sated, satiated, stuffed, replete, satisfied, filled up, *archaic* satiate. **3** copious, abundant, satisfying, sufficient, complete, thorough, detailed, broad, extensive, comprehensive, all-inclusive, all-encompassing, exhaustive, plenary. **4** (*be full of*) see TEEM[1] 2. **5** (*full of*) occupied in or with, engrossed in, absorbed in, immersed in, preoccupied with, obsessed with, consumed with, engaged with or in. **6** complete, maximum, top, unrestricted; entire, whole, unconditional, unqualified; greatest, highest, utmost; perfect. **7 b** unobscured, unshaded, undimmed, open, broad, bright, vivid, shining, brilliant, intense, blazing. **8** plump, rounded, protuberant, well-rounded, ample, shapely, buxom, busty, voluptuous, well-built, robust, *colloq.* curvaceous. **9** wide, ample, generous; see also LOOSE *adj.* 3–5. **10** overflowing. ● *adv.* **1** very, exceedingly, extremely, perfectly, quite, *colloq.* damned. **2** fully, completely, entirely, wholly, thoroughly, altogether, quite. **3** square(ly), directly, precisely, exactly, right, slap, *colloq.* bang, smack. ● *n.* **1** height, acme, maximum, greatest degree, fullest. □ **at full length 1** fully, completely, to the fullest extent. **2** in full, complete; see also UNABRIDGED. **full-blooded 1** see VIGOROUS 1, 3, 4. **2** pedigree, thoroughbred, purebred. **full-bodied** see RICH 8. **full-fledged** see MATURE *adj.* 1. **full-frontal 2** see EXPLICIT 3. **full-grown** see ADULT *adj.* 1. **full-length 1** in full, complete; see also UNABRIDGED. **full-mouthed 3** see LOUD 1, VIGOROUS 1, 3, 4. **full-scale** see COMPLETE *adj.* 1, 3. **in full** see UNABRIDGED. **2** completely, fully, entirely, wholly, thoroughly, in its entirety, totally, *in toto.* **in full swing** in (full) operation, under way, in progress, in business, animated, lively, on the move, moving, going, *colloq.* on the hop, cooking. **to the full** quite, to the utmost, to the greatest or fullest extent, a great deal; thoroughly, greatly, hugely, enormously.

full[2] /fool/ *v.tr.* cleanse and thicken (cloth). [ME, back-form. f. FULLER[1]: cf. OF *fouler* (FOIL[1])]

fullback /foolbak/ *n.* **1** an offensive player in the backfield in football. **2** a defensive player, or a position near the goal, in soccer, field hockey, etc.

fuller[1] /foolər/ *n.* a person who fulls cloth. □ **fuller's earth** a type of clay used in fulling cloth and as an adsorbent. [OE *fullere* f. L *fullo*]

fuller[2] /foolər/ *n.* & *v.* ● *n.* **1** a grooved or rounded tool on which iron is shaped. **2** a groove made by this, esp. in a horseshoe. ● *v.tr.* stamp with a fuller. [19th c.: orig. unkn.]

fullness /foolnis/ *n.* (also **fulness**) **1** being full. **2** (of sound, color, etc.) richness; volume; body. **3** all that is contained (in the world, etc.). □ **the fullness of the heart** emotion; genuine feelings. **the fullness of time** the appropriate or destined time.

■ **2** see BODY *n.* 8. **3** see ENTIRETY 1.

fully /foolee/ *adv.* **1** completely; entirely (*am fully aware*). **2** no less or fewer than (*fully 60*). □ **fully-fashioned** = *full-fashioned.* **fully-fledged** *Brit.* mature. [OE *fullice* (as FULL[1], -LY[2])]

■ **1** see *completely* (COMPLETE).

-fully /foolee/ *comb. form* forming adverbs corresp. to adjectives in *-ful.*

fulmar /foolmər/ *n.* any medium-sized sea bird of the genus *Fulmarus,* with stout body, robust bill, and rounded tail. [orig. Hebridean dial.: perh. f. ON *full* FOUL (with ref. to its smell) + *már* gull (cf. MEW[2])]

fulminant /fulminənt, fool-/ *adj.* **1** fulminating. **2** *Med.* (of a disease or symptom) developing suddenly. [F *fulminant* or L *fulminant-* (as FULMINATE)]

fulminate /fulminayt, fool-/ *v.* & *n.* ● *v.intr.* **1** (often foll. by *against*) express censure loudly and forcefully. **2** explode violently; flash like lightning (*fulminating mercury*). **3** *Med.* (of a disease or symptom) develop suddenly. ● *n. Chem.* a salt or ester of fulminic acid. □□ **fulmination** /-náyshən/ *n.* **fulminatory** /-nətáwree/ *adj.* [L *fulminare fulminat-* f. *fulmen -minis* lightning]

■ *v.* **1** (*fulminate against*) see RAIL[2].

fulminic acid /fulmínik, fool-/ *n. Chem.* an isomer of cyanic acid that is stable only in solution. ¶ Chem. formula: HONC. [L *fulmen*: see FULMINATE]

fulness var. of FULLNESS.

fulsome /foolsəm/ *adj.* **1** disgusting by excess of flattery, servility, or expressions of affection; excessive; cloying. **2** *disp.* copious. ¶ In *fulsome praise,* fulsome means 'excessive,' not 'generous.' □□ **fulsomely** *adv.* **fulsomeness** *n.* [ME f. FULL[1] + -SOME[1]]

■ **1** see EXCESSIVE.

fulvous /fulvəs/ *adj.* reddish yellow; tawny. □□ **fulvescent** /-vésənt/ *adj.* [L *fulvus*]

fumarole /fyoomərōl/ *n.* an opening in or near a volcano, through which hot vapors emerge. □□ **fumarolic** /-rólik/ *adj.* [F *fumarolle*]

fumble /fumbəl/ *v.* & *n.* ● *v.* **1** *intr.* (often foll. by *at, with, for, after*) use the hands awkwardly; grope about. **2** *tr.* **a** handle or deal with clumsily or nervously. **b** *Sports* fail to stop or catch (a ball) cleanly. ● *n.* an act of fumbling. □□ **fumbler** *n.* **fumblingly** *adv.* [LG *fummeln, fommeln,* Du. *fommelen*]

■ *v.* **1** grope, feel (about); (*fumble for*) search for, grope for, feel for, fish for. **2 a** mishandle, muff, bungle, botch, *colloq.* flub. ● *n.* grope, feel.

fume /fyoom/ *n.* & *v.* ● *n.* **1** (usu. in *pl.*) exuded gas or smoke or vapor, esp. when harmful or unpleasant. **2** a fit of anger (*in a fume*). ● *v.* **1 a** *intr.* emit fumes. **b** *tr.* give off as fumes. **2** *intr.* (often foll. by *at*) be affected by (esp. suppressed) anger (*was fuming at their inefficiency*). **3** *tr.* **a** fumigate. **b** subject to fumes, esp. those of ammonia (to darken tints in oak, photographic film, etc.). **4** *tr.* perfume with incense. □ **fume hood** (or *Brit.* **cupboard,** or **chamber,** etc.) a ventilated structure in a laboratory, for storing or experimenting with noxious chemicals. □□ **fumeless** *adj.* **fumingly** *adv.*

/.../ pronunciation	● part of speech
□ phrases, idioms, and compounds	
□□ derivatives	■ synonym section
cross-references appear in SMALL CAPITALS or *italics*	

fumy *adj.* (in sense 1 of *n.*). [ME f. OF *fum* f. L *fumus* smoke & OF *fume* f. *fumer* f. L *fumare* to smoke]

■ *n.* **1** smell, odor, stench, stink; (*fumes*) smoke, vapor, gas, exhalation, exhaust, pollution, smog, effluvium, *archaic* miasma. **2** see TANTRUM. ● *v.* **1** smoke, reek, steam, give off smoke. **2** seethe, smolder, chafe, rage, be hot under the collar, *colloq.* be steamed up. **3 a** see FUMIGATE 1.

fumigate /fyŏŏmigayt/ *v.tr.* **1** disinfect or purify with fumes. **2** apply fumes to. □□ **fumigant** /-gənt/ *n.* **fumigation** /-gáyshən/ *n.* **fumigator** *n.* [L *fumigare fumigat-* f. *fumus* smoke]

■ **1** disinfect, purify, sanitize, sterilize, *usu. formal* cleanse; fume. **2** fume.

fumitory /fyŏŏmitawree/ *n.* any plant of the genus *Fumaria*, esp. *F. officinalis*, formerly used against scurvy. [ME f. OF *fumeterre* f. med.L *fumus terrae* earth smoke]

fun /fun/ *n. & adj.* ● *n.* **1** amusement, esp. lively or playful. **2** a source of this. **3** (in full **fun and games**) exciting or amusing goings-on. ● *adj. disp. colloq.* amusing; entertaining; enjoyable (*a fun thing to do*). □ **be great** (or **good**) **fun** esp. *Brit.* be very amusing. **for fun** (or **for the fun of it**) not for a serious purpose. **fun run** *colloq.* an uncompetitive run, esp. for sponsored runners in support of a charity. **have fun** enjoy oneself. **in fun** as a joke; not seriously. **like fun 1** vigorously; quickly. **2** much. **3** *iron.* not at all. **make fun of** tease; ridicule. **what fun!** how amusing! [obs. *fun* (v.) var. of *fon* befool: cf. FOND]

■ *n.* **1** amusement, enjoyment, merriment, *colloq.* whoopee; joy, pleasure, gaiety, glee, jollity, playfulness, mirth, cheer, delight. **2** joy, pleasure, delight. **3** merrymaking, sport, recreation, entertainment, high jinks, horseplay, *colloq.* whoopee; festivity, frolic, diversion, pastime, prank(s), tomfoolery, joking, clowning, jesting, jocularity, nonsense, fooling around *or* about, skylarking. □ **for fun** (or **for the fun of it**) on impulse, *colloq.* for the hell of it; see also *in fun* below. **have fun** see *enjoy oneself*. **in fun** jokingly, in jest, facetiously, with tongue in cheek, playfully, for a joke *or* gag, for fun. **like fun 1** see *vigorously* (VIGOROUS). **3** in *or* under no circumstances, *colloq.* no way, like hell. **make fun of** poke fun at, tease, deride, (hold up to) ridicule, scoff at, lampoon, parody, satirize, make sport *or* game of, taunt, gibe, rag, *colloq.* kid, rib, send up, *Austral. sl.* mullock, poke borak at.

funambulist /fyŏŏnámbyŏlist/ *n.* a tightrope walker. [F *funambule* or L *funambulus* f. *funis* rope + *ambulare* walk]

function /fúngkshən/ *n. & v.* ● *n.* **1 a** an activity proper to a person or institution. **b** a mode of action or activity by which a thing fulfills its purpose. **c** an official or professional duty; an employment, profession, or calling. **2 a** a public ceremony or occasion. **b** a social gathering, esp. a large, formal, or important one. **3** *Math.* a variable quantity regarded in relation to another or others in terms of which it may be expressed or on which its value depends (*x is a function of y and z*). **4** a part of a program that corresponds to a single value. ● *v.intr.* fulfill a function; operate; be in working order. □□ **functionless** *adj.* [F *fonction* f. L *functio -onis* f. *fungi funct-* perform]

■ *n.* **1 a, b** activity, task, chore, assignment, commission; purpose, aim, use, role, raison d'être. **c** duty, job, occupation, work, employment, profession, calling; responsibility, mission, charge, concern, business, province, office. **2** reception, gathering, party, gala, ceremony; occasion, event, affair. ● *v.* serve, operate, act, act the part, take the role; perform, behave, work, go, run.

functional /fúngkshənəl/ *adj.* **1** of or serving a function. **2** (esp. of buildings) designed or intended to be practical rather than attractive; utilitarian. **3** *Physiol.* **a** (esp. of disease) of or affecting only the functions of an organ, etc., not structural or organic. **b** (of mental disorder) having no discernible organic cause. **c** (of an organ) having a function, not functionless or rudimentary. **4** *Math.* of a function. □ **functional group** *Chem.* a group of atoms that determine

the reactions of a compound containing the group. □□ **functionality** /-nálitee/ *n.* **functionally** *adv.*

■ **1** working, functioning, operating, running, going; operational. **2** utilitarian, practical, useful, serviceable, usable.

functionalism /fúngkshənəlizəm/ *n.* belief in or stress on the practical application of a thing. □□ **functionalist** *n.*

functionary /fúngkshənəree/ *n.* (*pl.* **-ies**) a person who has to perform official functions or duties; an official.

■ official, commissioner, bureaucrat, officeholder, officer, apparatchik.

fund /fund/ *n. & v.* ● *n.* **1** a permanent stock of something ready to be drawn upon (*a fund of knowledge*; *a fund of tenderness*). **2** a stock of money, esp. one set apart for a purpose. **3** (in *pl.*) money resources. **4** (in *pl.*; prec. by *the*) *Brit.* the stock of the National Debt (as a mode of investment). ● *v.tr.* **1** provide with money. **2** convert (a floating debt) into a more or less permanent debt at fixed interest. **3** put into a fund. □ **fund-raiser** a person who seeks financial support for a cause, enterprise, etc. **fund-raising** the seeking of financial support. **in funds** *Brit. colloq.* having money to spend. [L *fundus* bottom, piece of land]

■ *n.* **1** supply, stock, reserve, store, pool, reservoir, mine, repository. **2** stock, nest egg, endowment; see also CACHE *n.* 2. **3** (*funds*) assets, means, wealth, resources, capital, savings; money, ready money, (hard) cash, *colloq.* wherewithal, *derog. or joc.* pelf, *joc.* filthy lucre, *sl.* loot, green, bread, dough, scratch, bucks, jack, the ready, *Brit. sl.* lolly. ● *v.* **1** finance, pay for, support, endow, subsidize, back, capitalize, *colloq.* stake. □ **in funds** see *in the money* (MONEY).

fundament /fúndəmənt/ *n. joc.* the buttocks or anus. [ME f. OF *fondement* f. L *fundamentum* (as FOUND²)]

fundamental /fúndəmént'l/ *adj. & n.* ● *adj.* of, affecting, or serving as a base or foundation; essential; primary; original (*a fundamental change*; *the fundamental rules*; *the fundamental form*). ● *n.* **1** (usu. in *pl.*) a fundamental rule, principle, or article. **2** *Mus.* a fundamental note or tone. □ **fundamental note** *Mus.* the lowest note of a chord in its original (uninverted) form. **fundamental particle** *Physics* an elementary particle. **fundamental tone** *Mus.* the tone produced by vibration of the whole of a sonorous body (opp. HARMONIC). □□ **fundamentality** /-tálitee/ *n.* **fundamentally** *adv.* [ME f. F *fondamental* or LL *fundamentalis* (as FUNDAMENT)]

■ *adj.* essential, inherent, intrinsic, quintessential, rudimentary, elementary, basic, underlying, gut; main, prime, primary, first, principal, central, cardinal, crucial, critical, vital; original. ● *n.* **1** principle, axiom, essential, law, rule, sine qua non, cornerstone, keystone; (*fundamentals*) basics.

fundamentalism /fúndəméntəlizəm/ *n.* **1** (also **Fundamentalism**) strict maintenance of traditional Protestant beliefs such as the inerrancy of Scripture and literal acceptance of the creeds as fundamentals of Christianity. **2** strict maintenance of ancient or fundamental doctrines of any religion, esp. Islam. □□ **fundamentalist** *n.*

fundus /fúndəs/ *n.* (*pl.* **fundi** /-dī/) *Anat.* the base of a hollow organ; the part furthest from the opening. [L, = bottom]

funeral /fyŏŏnərəl/ *n. & adj.* ● *n.* **1 a** the burial or cremation of a dead person with its ceremonies. **b** a burial or cremation procession. **c** a burial or cremation service. **2** *sl.* one's (usu. unpleasant) concern (*that's your funeral*). ● *attrib.adj.* of or used, etc., at a funeral (*funeral oration*). □ **funeral director** an undertaker. **funeral parlor** (also **home**) an establishment where the dead are prepared for burial or cremation. **funeral urn** an urn holding the ashes of a cremated body. [ME f. OF *funeraille* f. med.L *funeralia* neut. pl. of LL *funeralis* f. L *funus -eris* funeral: (adj.) OF f. L *funeralis*]

■ *n.* **1** burial, interment, entombment, *literary* sepulture, inhumation; cremation; obsequies, exequies.

funerary /fyŏŏnəreree/ *adj.* of or used at a funeral or funerals. [LL *funerarius* (as FUNERAL)]

funereal /fyŏŏnéereeəl/ *adj.* **1** of or appropriate to a funeral.

2 gloomy; dismal; dark. □□ **funereally** adv. [L funereus (as FUNERAL)]

■ **2** gloomy, dismal, morose, somber, lugubrious, mournful, doleful, sorrowful, grave, solemn, sad, unhappy, melancholy, depressing, dreary, woeful, dark, sepulchral.

funfair /fúnfair/ n. Brit. = amusement park.

fungi pl. of FUNGUS.

fungible /fúnjibəl/ adj. Law (of goods, etc., contracted for, when an individual specimen is not meant) that can serve for, or be replaced by, another answering to the same definition. □□ **fungibility** n. [med.L fungibilis f. fungi (vice) serve (in place of)]

fungicide /fúnjisīd, fúnggi-/ n. a fungus-destroying substance. □□ **fungicidal** /-síd'l/ adj.

fungistatic /fúnjistátik, fúnggi-/ adj. inhibiting the growth of fungi. □□ **fungistatically** adv.

fungoid /fúnggoyd/ adj. & n. ● adj. **1** resembling a fungus in texture or in rapid growth. **2** Brit. of a fungus or fungi. ● n. a fungoid plant.

fungous /fúnggəs/ adj. **1** having the nature of a fungus. **2** springing up like a mushroom; transitory. [ME f. L fungosus (as FUNGUS)]

fungus /fúnggəs/ n. (pl. **fungi** /-gī, -jī/ or **funguses**) **1** any of a group of unicellular, multicellular, or multinucleate nonphotosynthetic organisms feeding on organic matter, which include molds, yeast, mushrooms, and toadstools. **2** anything similar usu. growing suddenly and rapidly. **3** Med. a spongy morbid growth. □□ **fungal** /fúnggəl/ adj. **fungiform** /fúnjifawrm, fúnggi-/ adj. **fungivorous** /funjívərəs, funggiv-/ adj. [L, perh. f. Gk sp(h)oggos SPONGE]

■ **1** see MOLD².

funicular /fyŏoníkyələr, fə-/ adj. & n. ● adj. **1** (of a railway, esp. on a mountainside) operating by cable with ascending and descending cars counterbalanced. **2** of a rope or its tension. ● n. a funicular railway. [L funiculus f. funis rope]

funk¹ /fungk/ n. & v. sl. ● n. **1** fear; panic. **2** Brit. a coward. ● v. Brit. **1** intr. flinch; shrink; show cowardice. **2** tr. try to evade (an undertaking); shirk. **3** tr. be afraid of. □ **in a funk** dejected. [18th-c. Oxford sl.: perh. f. sl. FUNK² = tobacco smoke]

■ n. **1** see FRIGHT n. 1a.

funk² /fungk/ n. sl. **1** funky music. **2** a strong smell. [funk blow smoke on, perh. f. F dial. funkier f. L (as FUMIGATE)]

funkia /fúngkeeə/ n. = HOSTA. [mod.L f. H. C. Funck, Prussian botanist d. 1839]

funky¹ /fúngkee/ adj. (**funkier, funkiest**) sl. **1** (esp. of jazz or rock music) earthy, bluesy, with a heavy rhythmical beat. **2** fashionable. **3** odd; unconventional. **4** having a strong smell. □□ **funkily** adv. **funkiness** n.

funky² /fúngkee/ adj. (**funkier, funkiest**) Brit. sl. **1** terrified. **2** cowardly.

funnel /fúnəl/ n. & v. ● n. **1** a narrow tube or pipe widening at the top, for pouring liquid, powder, etc., into a small opening. **2** a metal chimney on a steam engine or ship. **3** something resembling a funnel in shape or use. ● v.tr. & intr. (**funneled, funneling; funnelled, funnelling**) guide or move through or as through a funnel. □□ **funnellike** adj. [ME f. Prov. fonill f. LL fundibulum f. L infundibulum f. infundere (as IN-², fundere pour)]

■ n. **2** see STACK n. 4.

funny /fúnee/ adj. & n. ● adj. (**funnier, funniest**) **1** amusing; comical. **2** strange; perplexing; hard to account for. **3** colloq. slightly unwell, eccentric, etc. ● n. (pl. **-ies**) (usu. in pl.) colloq. **1** a comic strip in a newspaper. **2** a joke. □ **funny bone** the part of the elbow over which the ulnar nerve passes. **funny business 1** sl. misbehavior or deception. **2** comic behavior, comedy. **funny farm** sl. a mental hospital. **funny-ha-ha** colloq. = sense 1 of adj. **funny man** a clown or comedian, esp. a professional. **funny money** colloq. **1** counterfeit money. **2** foreign currency. **3** inflated currency. **funny paper** a newspaper, etc., containing humorous matter. **funny-peculiar** colloq. = senses 2, 3 of adj. □□ **funnily** adv. **funniness** n. [FUN + -Y¹]

■ adj. **1** comical, humorous, jocular, jocose, comic, droll,

witty, zany; amusing, entertaining, diverting, sidesplitting, hilarious, uproarious, colloq. hysterical; laughable, risible. **2** strange, peculiar, odd, queer, weird, bizarre, curious, mysterious, mystifying, puzzling, perplexing. **3** unwell, strange; unconventional, unusual, eccentric, sl. off-the-wall. ● n. **2** see JOKE n. 1. □ **funny business 1** see misbehavior (MISBEHAVE), DECEIT 1. **2** see JOKE n. 2. **funny farm** mental home or hospital, (mental) asylum or institution, archaic or colloq. madhouse, hist. lunatic asylum, sl. loony bin, nuthouse. **funny man** see CLOWN n. 1.

fur /fər/ n. & v. ● n. **1 a** the short fine soft hair of certain animals, distinguished from the longer hair. **b** the skin of such an animal with the fur on it; a pelt. **2 a** the coat of certain animals as material for making, trimming, or lining clothes. **b** a trimming or lining made of the dressed coat of such animals, or of material imitating this. **c** a garment made of or trimmed or lined with fur. **3** Brit. (collect.) furred animals. **4 a** a coating formed on the tongue in sickness. **b** Brit. a coating formed on the inside surface of a pipe, kettle, etc., by hard water. **c** a crust adhering to a surface, e.g., a deposit from wine. **5** Heraldry a representation of tufts on a plain ground. ● v. (**furred, furring**) **1** tr. (esp. as **furred** adj.) **a** line or trim (a garment) with fur. **b** provide (an animal) with fur. **c** clothe (a person) with fur. **d** coat (a tongue, the inside of a kettle) with fur. **2** intr. (often foll. by up) (of a kettle, etc.) become coated with fur. **3** tr. level (floorboards) by inserting strips of wood. □ **fur and feather** game animals and birds. **fur seal** a sea lion with a valuable undercoat. **make the fur fly** colloq. cause a disturbance; stir up trouble. □□ **furless** adj. [ME (earlier as v.) f. OF forrer f. forre, fuerre sheath f. Gmc]

■ n. **1b, 2a** see PELT².

fur. abbr. furlong(s).

furbelow /fərbilō/ n. & v. ● n. **1** a gathered strip or pleated border of a skirt or petticoat. **2** (in pl.) derog. showy ornaments. ● v.tr. adorn with a furbelow or furbelows. [18th-c. var. of falbala flounce, trimming]

■ n. **1** see FRILL n. 1a. **2** see ORNAMENT n. 1, 2.

furbish /fərbish/ v.tr. (often foll. by up) **1** remove rust from; polish; burnish. **2** give a new look to; renovate; revive (something antiquated). □□ **furbisher** n. [ME f. OF forbir f. Gmc]

■ **1** see POLISH v. 1. **2** see DECORATE 2.

furcate /fərkayt/ adj. & v. ● adj. /also fúrkət/ forked; branched. ● v.intr. form a fork; divide. □□ **furcation** /-káyshən/ n. [L furca fork: (adj.) f. LL furcatus]

furfuraceous /fərfəráyshəs/ adj. **1** Med. (of skin) resembling bran or dandruff; scaly. **2** Bot. covered with branlike scales. [furfur scurf f. L furfur bran]

furious /fyŏoreeəs/ adj. **1** extremely angry. **2** full of fury. **3** raging; violent; intense. □ **fast and furious** adv. **1** rapidly. **2** eagerly; uproariously. ● adj. (of mirth, etc.) eager; uproarious. □□ **furiously** adv. **furiousness** n. [ME f. OF furieus f. L furiosus (as FURY)]

■ **1, 2** angry, cross, irate, mad, enraged, infuriated, incensed, maddened, provoked, fuming, beside oneself, in high dudgeon, on the warpath, foaming at the mouth, archaic wroth, colloq. up the wall, steamed up, livid, wild, literary wrathful, infuriate, Austral. & NZ sl. ropable. **3** fierce, wild, raging, violent, savage, intense; unrestrained, frantic, frenzied. □ **fast and furious** (adv.) **1** see rapidly (RAPID). **2** see warmly (WARM). (adj.) see EAGER 1, UPROARIOUS.

furl /fərl/ v. **1** tr. roll up and secure (a sail, umbrella, flag, etc.). **2** intr. become furled. **3** tr. **a** close (a fan). **b** fold up (wings). **c** draw away (a curtain). **d** relinquish (hopes). □□ **furlable** adj. [F ferler f. OF fer(m) FIRM¹ + lier bind f. L ligare]

/.../	pronunciation	● part of speech
□	phrases, idioms, and compounds	
□□	derivatives	■ synonym section
cross-references	appear in SMALL CAPITALS or italics	

■ **1, 2** roll (up), wind up; see also WIND² *v.* 4.

furlong /fə́rlawng, -long/ *n.* an eighth of a mile, 220 yards. [OE *furlang* f. *furh* FURROW + *lang* LONG¹: orig. = length of a furrow in a common field]

furlough /fə́rlō/ *n. & v.* ● *n.* leave of absence, esp. granted to a member of the services or to a missionary. ● *v.* **1** *tr.* grant furlough to. **2** *intr.* spend furlough. **3** lay off. [Du. *verlof* after G *Verlaub* (as FOR-, LEAVE²)]
■ *n.* see HOLIDAY *n.* 1. ● *v.* **1** see FREE *v.* 1.

furmety (also **furmity**) vars. of FRUMENTY.

furn. *abbr.* **1** furnished. **2** furniture.

furnace /fə́rnis/ *n.* **1** an enclosed structure for intense heating by fire, esp. of metals or water. **2** a very hot place. [ME f. OF *fornais* f. L *fornax -acis* f. *fornus* oven]

furnish /fə́rnish/ *v.tr.* **1** provide (a house, room, etc.) with all necessary contents, esp. movable furniture. **2** (foll. by *with*) cause to have possession or use of. **3** provide; afford; yield. [OF *furnir* ult. f. WG]
■ **1** see EQUIP. **2** equip, rig (out *or* up), esp. *Brit.* kit (out *or* up); outfit, provision. **3** provide, afford, yield, give, supply.

furnished /fə́rnisht/ *adj.* (of a house, apartment, etc.) rented with furniture.

furnisher /fə́rnishər/ *n.* **1** a person who sells furniture. **2** a person who furnishes.

furnishings /fə́rnishingz/ *n.pl.* the furniture and utensils, etc., in a house, room, etc.
■ see FURNITURE 1.

furniture /fə́rnichər/ *n.* **1** the movable equipment of a house, room, etc., e.g., tables, chairs, and beds. **2** *Naut.* a ship's equipment, esp. tackle, etc. **3** accessories, e.g., the handles and lock of a door. **4** *Printing* pieces of wood or metal placed round or between type to make blank spaces and fasten the matter in the chase. □ **furniture beetle** a beetle, *Anobium punctatum*, the larvae of which bore into wood (see WOODWORM). **furniture van** *Brit.* = *moving van*. **part of the furniture** *colloq.* a person or thing taken for granted. [F *fourniture* f. *fournir* (as FURNISH)]
■ **1** furnishings; goods, movables, chattels, effects, possessions, belongings. **2** tackle, apparatus, gear, tack. **3** fittings, fitments, fixtures, attachments, accessories, appliances, equipment.

furor /fyŏórawr, -ər/ *n.* (*Brit.* **furore** /fyŏóráwree, fyŏórawr/) **1** an uproar; an outbreak of fury. **2** a wave of enthusiastic admiration; a craze. [It. f. L *furor -oris* f. *furere* be mad]
■ **1** uproar, outburst, commotion, brouhaha, to-do, hubbub, stir, fuss, disturbance; tumult, turmoil, ado, excitement. **2** rage, craze, mania, vogue, enthusiasm, fad.

furphy /fə́rfee/ *n.* (*pl.* **-ies**) *Austral. sl.* **1** a false report or rumor. **2** an absurd story. [water and sanitary *Furphy carts* of World War I, made at a foundry set up by the Furphy family]

furrier /fə́reeər/ *n.* a dealer in or dresser of furs. [ME *furrour* f. OF *forreor* f. *forrer* trim with fur, assim. to -IER]

furriery /fə́ree-əree/ *n.* the work of a furrier.

furrow /fə́rō, fúr-/ *n. & v.* ● *n.* **1** a narrow trench made in the ground by a plow. **2** a rut, groove, or deep wrinkle. **3** a ship's track. ● *v.tr.* **1** plow. **2 a** make furrows, grooves, etc., in. **b** mark with wrinkles. □□ **furrowless** *adj.* **furrowy** *adj.* [OE *furh* f. Gmc]
■ *n.* **2** groove, channel, rut, trench, track, ditch, gutter, trough, fosse, fissure, sulcation, flute, score, cut, gash, scratch, line; wrinkle, crinkle, crease, corrugation, crow's-foot, *Anat.* sulcus. ● *v.* **1** plow, harrow, till, cultivate, rib. **2 a** groove, channel, flute, score, cut, gash, scratch. **b** wrinkle, crease, corrugate, knit, pucker, crinkle.

furry /fə́ree, fúree/ *adj.* (**furrier, furriest**) **1** of or like fur. **2** covered with or wearing fur. □□ **furriness** *n.*
■ **1** see SOFT *adj.* 2, WOOLLY *adj.* 1.

further /fə́rthər/ *adv., adj., & v.* ● *adv.* **1** = FARTHER. **2** to a greater extent; more (*will inquire further*). **3** in addition; furthermore (*I may add further*). ● *adj.* **1** = FARTHER. **2** more;

additional; going beyond what exists or has been dealt with (*threats of further punishment*). ● *v.tr.* promote; favor; help; forward (a scheme, undertaking, movement, or cause). □ **further education** *Brit.* education for persons above school age but usu. below degree level. **till further notice** (or **orders**) to continue until explicitly changed. □□ **furtherer** *n.* **furthermost** *adj.* [OE *furthor* (adv.), *furthra* (adj.), *fyrthrian* (v.), formed as FORTH, -ER³]
■ *adv.* **3** furthermore, besides, moreover, too, also, additionally, in addition, what is more, to boot, yet, then (again), again. ● *adj.* **2** more, additional, other, new, supplemental, supplementary, accessory, auxiliary, extra, spare, fresh. ● *v.* advance, promote, favor, forward, foster, back, patronize, support, help, assist, aid.

furtherance /fə́rthərəns/ *n.* furthering or being furthered; the advancement of a scheme, etc.
■ promotion, advancement, championship, advocacy, patronage, backing, fostering, championing, advocating, *colloq.* boost(ing); support, help, aid, assistance.

furthermore /fə́rthərmáwr/ *adv.* in addition; besides (esp. introducing a fresh consideration in an argument).
■ see *in addition* (ADDITION).

furthest var. of FARTHEST.

furtive /fə́rtiv/ *adj.* **1** done by stealth; clandestine; meant to escape notice. **2** sly; stealthy. **3** stolen; taken secretly. **4** thievish; pilfering. □□ **furtively** *adv.* **furtiveness** *n.* [F *furtif -ive* or L *furtivus* f. *furtum* theft]
■ **1** secret, secretive, clandestine, conspiratorial, surreptitious, underhand(ed), covert, hidden, huggermugger, sneaky. **2** sly, foxy, cunning, crafty, wily, shifty, skulking, sneaky, untrustworthy, *colloq.* stealthy.

furuncle /fyŏórungkəl/ *n. Med.* = BOIL². □□ **furuncular** /-rúngkyələr/ *adj.* **furunculous** /-rúngkyələs/ *adj.* [L *furunculus* f. *fur* thief]

furunculosis /fyŏórúngkyəlṓsis/ *n.* **1** a diseased condition in which boils appear. **2** a bacterial disease of salmon and trout. [mod.L (as FURUNCLE)]

fury /fyŏóree/ *n.* (*pl.* **-ies**) **1 a** wild and passionate anger; rage. **b** a fit of rage (*in a blind fury*). **c** impetuosity in battle, etc. **2** violence of a storm, disease, etc. **3** (**Fury**) (usu. in *pl.*) (in Greek mythology) each of three goddesses sent from Tartarus to avenge crime, esp. against kinship. **4** an avenging spirit. **5** an angry or spiteful woman; a virago. □ **like fury** *colloq.* with great force or effect. [ME f. OF *furie* f. L *furia* f. *furere* be mad]
■ **1 a** rage, *literary* ire, wrath, *poet. or archaic* choler; see also ANGER *n.* **b** see TEMPER *n.* 2b. **c** impetuosity, vehemence; see also VIOLENCE 1. **2** ferocity, savagery, fierceness, tempestuousness, turbulence, violence. **5** virago, shrew, hellcat, termagant, vixen, she-devil, hag, witch, *archaic* beldam, *sl. offens.* bitch.

furze /fərz/ *n. Brit.* = GORSE. □□ **furzy** /fúrzee/ *adj.* [OE *fyrs*, of unkn. orig.]

fuscous /fúskəs/ *adj.* somber; dark-colored. [L *fuscus* dusky]

fuse¹ /fyŏoz/ *v. & n.* ● *v.* **1** *tr. & intr.* melt with intense heat; liquefy. **2** *tr. & intr.* blend or amalgamate into one whole by or as by melting. **3** *tr.* provide (a circuit, plug, etc.) with a fuse. **4** *Brit.* **a** *intr.* (of an appliance) cease to function when a fuse blows. **b** *tr.* cause (an appliance) to do this. ● *n.* a device or component for protecting an electric circuit, containing a strip of wire of easily melted metal and placed in the circuit so as to break it by melting when an excessive current passes through. □ **fuse box** a box housing the fuses for circuits in a building. [L *fundere fus-* pour, melt]
■ *v.* **2** blend, merge, unite, combine, mix, amalgamate, mingle, *literary* commingle; compound, consolidate; coalesce.

fuse² /fyŏoz/ *n. & v.* (also **fuze**) ● *n.* **1** a device for igniting a bomb or explosive charge, consisting of a tube or cord, etc., filled or saturated with combustible matter. **2** a component in a shell, mine, etc., designed to detonate an explosive charge on impact, after an interval, or when subjected to a magnetic or vibratory stimulation. ● *v.tr.* fit a fuse to. □□ **fuseless** *adj.* [It. *fuso* f. L *fusus* spindle]

fusee /fyŏŏzeé/ *n.* (also **fuzee**) **1** a conical pulley or wheel, esp. in a watch or clock. **2** a large-headed match for lighting a cigar or pipe in a wind. **3** a railroad signal flare. [F *fusée* spindle ult. f. L *fusus*]

fuselage /fyŏŏsəlaázh, -lij, -zə-/ *n.* the body of an airplane. [F f. *fuseler* cut into a spindle f. *fuseau* spindle f. OF *fusel* ult. f. L *fusus*]
■ see BODY *n.* 3a.

fusel oil /fyŏŏzəl/ *n.* a mixture of several alcohols, chiefly amyl alcohol, produced usu. in small amounts during alcoholic fermentation. [G *Fusel* bad brandy, etc.: cf. *fuseln* to bungle]

fusible /fyŏŏzibəl/ *adj.* that can be easily fused or melted. □□ **fusibility** *n.*

fusiform /fyŏŏzifawrm/ *adj. Bot. & Zool.* shaped like a spindle or cigar, tapering at both ends. [L *fusus* spindle + -FORM]

fusil /fyŏŏzil/ *n. hist.* a light musket. [F ult. f. L *focus* hearth, fire]

fusilier /fyŏŏzileér/ *n.* (also **fusileer**) **1** a member of any of several British regiments formerly armed with fusils. **2** *hist.* a soldier armed with a fusil. [F (as FUSIL)]

fusillade /fyŏŏsiláyd, -laád, -zi-/ *n. & v.* ● *n.* **1 a** a continuous discharge of firearms. **b** a wholesale execution by this means. **2** a sustained outburst of criticism, etc. ● *v.tr.* **1** assault (a place) by a fusillade. **2** shoot down (persons) with a fusillade. [F f. *fusiller* shoot]
■ *n.* **1 a** see DISCHARGE *n.* 4.

fusion /fyŏŏzhən/ *n.* **1** the act or an instance of fusing or melting. **2** a fused mass. **3** the blending of different things into one. **4** a coalition. **5** *Physics* = *nuclear fusion.* □ **fusion bomb** a bomb involving nuclear fusion, esp. a hydrogen bomb. □□ **fusional** *adj.* [F *fusion* or L *fusio* (as FUSE¹)]
■ **1–4** see *amalgamation* (AMALGAMATE).

fuss /fus/ *n. & v.* ● *n.* **1** excited commotion; bustle; ostentatious or nervous activity. **2 a** excessive concern about a trivial thing. **b** abundance of petty detail. **3** a sustained protest or dispute. **4** a person who fusses. ● *v.* **1** *intr.* **a** make a fuss. **b** busy oneself restlessly with trivial things. **c** move fussily. **2** *tr. Brit.* agitate; worry. □ **make a fuss** complain vigorously. **make a fuss over** (or *Brit.* **of**) treat (a person or animal) with great or excessive attention. □□ **fusser** *n.* [18th c.: perh. Anglo-Ir.]
■ *n.* **1, 2a** bother, fluster, flurry, commotion, bustle, to-do, furor, stir, uproar, disturbance, hubbub, brouhaha, excitement, ado, unrest, trouble, upset, agitation, *colloq.* flap, stink, *literary* pother, *sl.* hoo-ha, hoopla. **4** see *perfectionist* (PERFECTIONISM). ● *v.* **1 a** make a fuss, kick up a fuss; see also COMPLAIN 1, 2b. **c** rush about *or* around, flutter *or* fly about *or* around, run around in circles, bustle; see also TEAR¹ *v.* 5. □ **make a fuss** see COMPLAIN 1, 2b. **make a fuss over** (or *Brit.* **of**) see FÊTE *v.*

fussbudget /fúsbəjət/ *n.* a person who habitually frets over minor matters.

fusspot /fúspot/ *n. colloq.* a person given to fussing.
■ see BOTHER *n.* 1, *perfectionist* (PERFECTIONISM).

fussy /fúsee/ *adj.* (**fussier, fussiest**) **1** inclined to fuss. **2** full of unnecessary detail or decoration. **3** fastidious. □□ **fussily** *adv.* **fussiness** *n.*
■ **1** see CHOOSY. **2** fancy, elaborate, overdecorated, rococo, ornate, *Archit. & Painting* Byzantine. **3** particular, finicky, finical, dainty, fastidious, *colloq.* picky, choosy, persnickety, nitpicking.

fustanella /fústənélə/ *n.* a man's stiff white kilt worn in Albania and Greece. [It. dimin. of mod. Gk *phoustani* prob. f. It. *fustagno* FUSTIAN]

fustian /fúschən/ *n. & adj.* ● *n.* **1** thick twilled cotton cloth with a short nap, usu. dyed in dark colors. **2** turgid speech or writing; bombast. ● *adj.* **1** made of fustian. **2** bombastic. **3** worthless. [ME f. OF *fustaigne* f. med.L *fustaneus* (adj.) relating to cloth from *Fostat* a suburb of Cairo]
■ *n.* **2** see RHETORIC 2. ● *adj.* **2** see *bombastic* (BOMBAST).

fustic /fústik/ *n.* a yellow dye obtained from either of two kinds of wood, esp. old fustic. □ **old fustic 1** a tropical tree, *Chlorophora tinctoria*, native to America. **2** the wood of this tree. **young fustic 1** a sumac, *Cotinus coggyria*, native to Europe (also called *Venetian sumac*). **2** the wood of this tree. [F f. Sp. *fustoc* f. Arab. *fustuḳ* f. Gk *pistakē* pistachio]

fusty /fústee/ *adj.* (**fustier, fustiest**) **1** stale smelling; musty; moldy. **2** stuffy, close. **3** antiquated; old-fashioned. □□ **fustily** *adv.* **fustiness** *n.* [ME f. OF *fusté* smelling of the cask f. *fust* cask, tree trunk, f. L *fustis* cudgel]
■ **1** see MUSTY 1, 2. **2** see CLOSE¹ *adj.* 8.

futhark /fŏŏthaark/ *n.* (also **futhore, futhork**) the Scandinavian runic alphabet. [its first six letters *f, u, th, a* (or *ö*), *r, k*]

futile /fyŏŏt'l, -tīl/ *adj.* **1** useless; ineffectual, vain. **2** frivolous; trifling. □□ **futilely** *adv.* **futility** /-tílitee/ *n.* [L *futilis* leaky, futile, rel. to *fundere* pour]
■ **1** useless, vain, unavailing, unsuccessful, unprofitable, abortive, profitless, fruitless, unproductive, ineffective, ineffectual, *archaic* bootless. **2** frivolous, trifling; see also WORTHLESS.

futon /fŏŏton/ *n.* a Japanese quilted mattress rolled out on the floor for use as a bed; a type of low-slung wooden bed using this kind of mattress. [Jap.]

futtock /fútək/ *n.* each of the middle timbers of a ship's frame, between the floor and the top timbers. [ME *votekes,* etc., pl. f. MLG f. *fōt* FOOT + -*ken* -KIN]

future /fyŏŏchər/ *n. & adj.* ● *adj.* **1 a** going or expected to happen or be or become (*his future career*). **b** that will be something specified (*my future wife*). **c** that will be after death (*a future life*). **2 a** of time to come (*future years*). **b** *Gram.* (of a tense or participle) describing an event yet to happen. ● *n.* **1** time to come (*past, present, and future*). **2** what will happen in the future (*the future is uncertain*). **3** the future condition of a person, country, etc. **4** a prospect of success, etc. (*there's no future in it*). **5** *Gram.* the future tense. **6** (in *pl.*) *Stock Exch.* **a** goods and stocks sold for future delivery. **b** contracts for these. □ **for the future** from now onward. **future perfect** *Gram.* a tense giving the sense *will have done.* **future shock** inability to cope with rapid progress. **in future** = *for the future.* □□ **futureless** *adj.* [ME f. OF *futur* -*ure* f. L *futurus* future part. of *esse* be f. stem *fu-* be]
■ *adj.* **1 a** see PROSPECTIVE. **b** to be. **2 a** tomorrow's, coming; subsequent; to be, to come; see also PROSPECTIVE. ● *n.* **1** days *or* time to come; tomorrow; futurity. **3** see PROSPECT *n.* 1a. □ **for the future** hence, henceforth, as of now, from now (on *or* onward).

futurism /fyŏŏchərizəm/ *n.* a movement in art, literature, music, etc., with violent departure from traditional forms so as to express movement and growth. [FUTURE + -ISM, after It. *futurismo,* F *futurisme*]

futurist /fyŏŏchərist/ *n.* (often *attrib.*) **1** an adherent of futurism. **2** a believer in human progress. **3** a student of the future. **4** *Theol.* one who believes that biblical prophecies, esp. those of the Apocalypse, are still to be fulfilled.

futuristic /fyŏŏchərístik/ *adj.* **1** suitable for the future; ultramodern. **2** of futurism. **3** relating to the future. □□ **futuristically** *adv.*

futurity /fyŏŏtŏŏritee, -tyŏŏr-, chŏŏr-/ *n.* (*pl.* -**ies**) **1** future time. **2** (in *sing.* or *pl.*) future events. **3** future condition; existence after death. □ **futurity stakes** stakes raced for long after entries or nominations are made.

futurology /fyŏŏchəróləjee/ *n.* systematic forecasting of the future, esp. from present trends in society. □□ **futurologist** *n.*

fuze var. of FUSE².

fuzee var. of FUSEE.

fuzz /fuz/ *n.* **1** fluff. **2** fluffy or frizzled hair. **3** *sl.* **a** the police.

/. . ./ **pronunciation** ● **part of speech**
□ **phrases, idioms, and compounds**
□□ **derivatives** ■ **synonym section**
cross-references appear in SMALL CAPITALS or *italics*

b a policeman. [17th c.: prob. f. LG or Du.: sense 3 perh. a different word]
■ **1** see FLUFF *n*. 1. **3 a** see POLICE *n*. **b** see *police officer*.

fuzzball /fúzbawl/ *n*. a puffball fungus.

fuzzy /fúzee/ *adj*. (**fuzzier, fuzziest**) **1 a** like fuzz. **b** frayed; fluffy. **c** frizzy. **2** blurred; indistinct. □ **fuzzy-wuzzy** (*pl*. **-ies**) *Brit. offens*. **1** *colloq. hist*. a Sudanese soldier. **2** *sl*. a dark-skinned native of any country. □□ **fuzzily** *adv*. **fuzziness** *n*.
■ **1 a** woolly, furry, downy, flocculent, fluffy, linty. **b** see HAIRY 1. **c** see KINKY 3. **2** dim, faint, hazy, foggy, misty, blurred, blurry, indistinct, unclear, vague, shadowy, indefinite, obscure, ill-defined, woolly, distorted.

fwd *abbr*. forward.

f.w.d. *abbr*. **1** four-wheel drive. **2** front-wheel drive.

FY *abbr*. fiscal year.

-fy /fī/ *suffix* forming: **1** verbs from nouns, meaning: **a** make; produce (*pacify; satisfy*). **b** make into (*deify; petrify*). **2** verbs from adjectives, meaning 'bring or come into such a state' (*Frenchify; solidify*). **3** verbs in causative sense (*horrify; stupefy*). [from or after F *-fier* f. L *-ficare, -facere* f. *facere* do, make]

FYI *abbr*. for your information.

fylfot /fílfət/ *n*. a swastika. [perh. f. *fill-foot*, pattern to fill the foot of a painted window]

fyrd /fərd/ *n. hist*. **1** the Anglo-Saxon militia before 1066. **2** the duty to serve in this. [OE f. Gmc (as FARE)]

fytte var. of FIT³.

Gg

G¹ /jee/ *n.* (also **g**) (*pl.* **Gs** or **G's**) **1** the seventh letter of the alphabet. **2** *Mus.* the fifth note in the diatonic scale of C major.

G² *abbr.* (also **G.**) **1** gauss. **2** giga-. **3** gravitational constant. **4** *sl.* = GRAND *n.* 2.

g *abbr.* (also **g.**) **1** gelding. **2** gram(s). **3 a** gravity. **b** acceleration due to gravity.

GA *abbr.* Georgia (in official postal use).

Ga *symb. Chem.* the element gallium.

Ga. *abbr.* Georgia (US).

gab /gab/ *n. & v. colloq.* ● *n.* talk; chatter. ● *v.intr.* talk incessantly, trivially, or indiscreetly; chatter. □ **gift of gab** the facility of speaking eloquently or profusely. □□ **gabber** *n.* [17th-c. var. of GOB¹]
  ■ *n.* talk, chatter, prattle, jabber, blather, tittle-tattle, gossip, *colloq.* chitchat; cackle, drivel, twaddle, moonshine, blarney, nonsense, rubbish, bunkum, balderdash, garbage, *colloq.* hogwash, piffle, esp. *Brit. colloq.* tosh, *sl.* poppycock, bunk, eyewash, *Brit. sl.* codswallop. ● *v.* jabber, gabble, chatter, gibber, blather, prate, prattle, blab, gossip, *colloq.* natter, jaw, *Austral. colloq.* yabber, *sl. derog.* yak.

gabardine /gábərdeen/ *n.* (also **gaberdine**) **1** a smooth durable twilled cloth esp. of worsted or cotton. **2** *Brit.* a garment made of this, esp. a raincoat. [var. of GABERDINE]

gabble /gábəl/ *v. & n.* ● *v.* **1** *intr.* **a** talk volubly or inarticulately. **b** read aloud too fast. **2** *tr.* utter too fast, esp. in reading aloud. ● *n.* fast unintelligible talk. □□ **gabbler** *n.* [MDu. *gabbelen* (imit.)]
  ■ *v.* see PRATTLE *v.* ■ *n.* see PRATTLE *n.*

gabbro /gábrō/ *n.* (*pl.* **-os**) a dark granular plutonic rock of crystalline texture. □□ **gabbroic** /-brôik/ *adj.* **gabbroid** *adv.* [It. f. *Gabbro* in Tuscany]

gabby /gábee/ *adj.* (**gabbier, gabbiest**) *colloq.* talkative. [GAB + -Y¹]
  ■ see TALKATIVE.

gaberdine /gábərdeen/ *n.* **1** var. of GABARDINE. **2** *hist.* a loose long upper garment worn esp. by medieval Jews. [OF *gauvardine* perh. f. MHG *wallevart* pilgrimage]

gabion /gáybeeən/ *n.* a cylindrical wicker or metal basket for filling with earth or stones, used in engineering or (formerly) in fortification. □□ **gabionage** *n.* [F f. It. *gabbione* f. *gabbia* CAGE]

gable /gáybəl/ *n.* **1 a** the triangular upper part of a wall at the end of a ridged roof. **b** (in full **gable end**) a gable-topped wall. **2** a gable-shaped canopy over a window or door. □□ **gabled** *adj.* (also in *comb.*). [ME *gable* f. ON *gafl*]

gad¹ /gad/ *v. & n.* ● *v.intr.* (**gadded, gadding**) (foll. by *about*) go about idly or in search of pleasure. ● *n.* idle wandering or adventure. [back-form. f. obs. *gadling* companion f. OE *gǽdeling* f. *gǽd* fellowship]
  ■ *v.* (*gad about* or *around*) run around, flit, *colloq.* gallivant; see also IDLE *v.* 2, PHILANDER.

gad² /gad/ *int.* (also **by gad**) an expression of surprise or emphatic assertion. [= *God*]
  ■ *archaic* gadzooks, *archaic or joc.* egad.

gadabout /gádəbowt/ *n.* a person who gads about; an idle pleasure seeker.
  ■ see ROVER¹.

Gadarene /gádəreen/ *adj.* involving or engaged in headline

or suicidal rush or flight. [LL *Gadarenus* f. Gk *Gadarēnos* of Gadara in anc. Palestine, with ref. to Matthew 8:28–32]

gadfly /gádfli/ *n.* (*pl.* **-flies**) **1** a cattle-biting fly, esp. a warble fly, horsefly, or botfly. **2** an irritating or harassing person. [obs. *gad* goad, spike f. ON *gaddr*, rel. to YARD¹]
  ■ **2** see TROUBLEMAKER.

gadget /gájit/ *n.* any small and usu. ingenious mechanical or electronic device or tool. □□ **gadgeteer** /-teer/ *n.* **gadgetry** *n.* **gadgety** *adj.* [19th-c. Naut.: orig. unkn.]
  ■ device, contrivance, appliance, apparatus, mechanism, machine, instrument, implement, utensil, tool, what-do-you-call-it, what's-its-name, whatchamacallit, doodad, *colloq.* widget, thingamajig, thingy, hickey, doohickey, *usu. derog. or joc.* contraption, *sl.* gizmo.
  □□ **gadgetry** see APPARATUS.

gadoid /gáydoyd, gád-/ *n. & adj.* ● *n.* any marine fish of the cod family Gadidae, including haddock and whiting. ● *adj.* belonging to or resembling the Gadidae. [mod.L *gadus* f. Gk *gados* cod + -OID]

gadolinite /gád'linīt/ *n.* a dark crystalline mineral consisting of ferrous silicate of beryllium. [J. *Gadolin*, Finnish mineralogist d. 1852]

gadolinium /gád'líneeəm/ *n. Chem.* a soft silvery metallic element of the lanthanide series, occurring naturally in gadolinite. ¶ Symb.: **Gd**. [mod.L f. GADOLINITE]

gadroon /gədrōōn/ *n.* a decoration on silverware, etc., consisting of convex curves in a series forming an ornamental edge like inverted fluting. [F *godron*: cf. *goder* pucker]

gadwall /gádwawl/ *n.* a brownish gray freshwater duck, *Anas strepera*. [17th c.: orig. unkn.]

gadzooks /gadzōōks/ *int. archaic* an expression of surprise, etc. [GAD² + *zooks* of unkn. orig.]

Gael /gayl/ *n.* **1** a Scottish Celt. **2** a Gaelic-speaking Celt. □□ **Gaeldom** *n.* [Gael. *Gaidheal*]

Gaelic /gáylik, gálik/ *n. & adj.* ● *n.* any of the Celtic languages spoken in Ireland, Scotland, and the Isle of Man. ● *adj.* of or relating to the Celts or the Celtic languages.

Gaeltacht /gáyltəkht/ *n.* any of the regions in Ireland where the vernacular language is Irish. [Ir.]

gaff¹ /gaf/ *n. & v.* ● *n.* **1 a** a stick with an iron hook for landing large fish. **b** a barbed fishing spear. **2** a spar to which the head of a fore-and-aft sail is bent. ● *v.tr.* seize (a fish) with a gaff. [ME f. Prov. *gaf* hook]

gaff² /gaf/ *n. Brit. sl.* □ **blow the gaff** let out a plot or secret. [19th c., = nonsense: orig. unkn.]

gaffe /gaf/ *n.* a blunder; an indiscreet act or remark. [F]
  ■ see BLUNDER *n.*

gaffer /gáfər/ *n.* **1** an old fellow; an elderly rustic. **2** *Brit. colloq.* a foreman or boss. **3** *colloq.* the chief electrician in a movie or television production unit. [prob. contr. of GODFATHER]

gag /gag/ *n. & v.* ● *n.* **1** a piece of cloth, etc., thrust into or held over the mouth to prevent speaking or crying out, or to hold it open in surgery. **2** a joke or comic scene in a play, movie, etc., or as part of a comedian's act. **3** an actor's in-

---

/. . ./ **pronunciation**	● **part of speech**
□ **phrases, idioms, and compounds**	
□□ **derivatives**	■ **synonym section**
cross-references appear in SMALL CAPITALS or *italics*	

terpolation in a dramatic dialogue. **4** a thing or circumstance restricting free speech. **5 a** a joke or hoax. **b** a humorous action or situation. **6** an imposture or deception. **7** *Brit. Parl.* a closure or guillotine. • *v.* (**gagged, gagging**) **1** *tr.* apply a gag to. **2** *tr.* silence; deprive of free speech. **3** *tr.* apply a gag bit to (a horse). **4 a** *intr.* choke or retch. **b** *tr.* cause to do this. **5** *intr. Theatr.* make gags. □ **gag bit** a specially powerful bit for horse breaking. [ME, orig. as verb: orig. uncert.]

■ *n.* **1** muzzle. **4** restriction, ban, proscription; embargo, boycott. **5 a** joke, witticism, jest, quip, pun, *colloq.* wisecrack, crack; practical joke, hoax, prank, trick, *colloq.* fast one. **b** joke, frolic, *colloq.* giggle, lark, scream, hoot, laugh. **6** see MASQUERADE *n.* 1. • *v.* **2** silence, curb, put a lid on, suppress, repress, check, inhibit, restrain; stifle, still, muffle, muzzle. **4 a** retch, choke; see also HEAVE *v.* 6. **b** see CHOKE¹ *v.* 1.

gaga /gaágaa/ *adj. sl.* **1** senile. **2** infatuated; overly fond. **3** fatuous; slightly crazy. [F, = senile]

■ **3** see CRAZY 1.

gage¹ /gayj/ *n. & v.* • *n.* **1** a pledge; a thing deposited as security. **2 a** a challenge to fight. **b** a symbol of this, esp. a glove thrown down. • *v.tr. archaic* stake; pledge; offer as a guarantee. [ME f. OF *gage* (n.), F *gager* (v.) ult. f. Gmc, rel. to WED]

■ *n.* **1** see PLEDGE *n.* 2. **2** see CHALLENGE *n.* 1.

gage² var. of GAUGE.

gage³ /gayj/ *n.* = GREENGAGE. [abbr.]

gaggle /gágəl/ *n. & v.* • *n.* **1** a flock of geese. **2** *colloq.* a disorderly group of people. • *v.intr.* (of geese) cackle. [ME, imit.: cf. *gabble, cackle*]

gagman /gágman/ *n.* a deviser, writer, or performer of theatrical gags.

■ see COMEDIAN.

gagster /gágstər/ *n.* = GAGMAN.

gaiety /gáyətee/ *n.* (also **gayety**) **1** the state of being lighthearted or merry; mirth. **2** merrymaking; amusement. **3** a bright appearance, esp. of dress. [F *gaieté* (as GAY)]

■ **1** lightheartedness, cheerfulness, cheeriness, happiness, high spirits, *joie de vivre*, buoyancy, exhilaration, elation, glee, felicity, delight, pleasure, joy, joyfulness, joyousness, exultation, jubilation, merriment, mirth, mirthfulness, joviality, jollity, hilarity, *poet.* blitheness. **2** merrymaking, amusement, festivity, celebration, revelry, rejoicing, conviviality. **3** brightness, colorfulness, brilliance, glow; see also SPLENDOR 2.

gaillardia /gaylaárdeeə/ *n.* any composite plant of the genus *Gaillardia*, with showy flowers. [mod.L f. *Gaillard* de Marentoneau, 18th-c. Fr. botanist]

gaily /gáylee/ *adv.* **1** in a gay or lighthearted manner. **2** with a bright or colorful appearance.

■ **1** lightheartedly, happily, cheerfully, cheerily, gleefully, joyously, joyfully, jubilantly, merrily, jauntily, insouciantly, *poet.* blithely. **2** brightly, brilliantly, colorfully.

gain /gayn/ *v. & n.* • *v.* **1** *tr.* obtain or secure (usu. something desired or favorable) (*gain an advantage; gain recognition*). **2** *tr.* acquire (a sum) as profits or as a result of changed conditions; earn. **3** *tr.* obtain as an increment or addition (*gain momentum; gain weight*). **4** *tr.* **a** win (a victory). **b** reclaim (land from the sea). **5** *intr.* (foll. by *in*) make a specified advance or improvement (*gained in stature*). **6** *intr. & tr.* (of a clock, etc.) become fast, or be fast by (a specified amount of time). **7** *intr.* (often foll. by *on, upon*) come closer to a person or thing pursued. **8** *tr.* **a** bring over to one's interest or views. **b** (foll. by *over*) win by persuasion, etc. **9** *tr.* reach or arrive at (a desired place). • *n.* **1** something gained, achieved, etc. **2** an increase of possessions, etc.; a profit, advance, or improvement. **3** the acquisition of wealth. **4** (in *pl.*) sums of money acquired by trade, etc.; emoluments; winnings. **5** an increase in amount. **6** *Electronics* **a** the factor by which power, etc., is increased. **b** the logarithm of this. □ **gain ground** see GROUND¹. □□ **gainable** *adj.* **gainer** *n.* **gainings** *n.pl.* [OF *gaigner, gaaignier* to till, acquire, ult. f. Gmc]

■ *v.* **1** get, obtain, acquire, procure, attain, achieve, secure, earn, win, capture, net, reap, glean, collect, gather, come by, pick up, *colloq.* bag. **2** make, get, realize, clear; see also EARN 1. **3** gather, acquire, pick up; put on. **4** see WIN *v.* 1. **5** improve, progress, advance, increase. **7** gain ground, narrow the gap; (*gain on*) catch up (with), approach, get nearer to, overtake, close in on. **8** proselytize, change, switch, convert, win over. **9** arrive at, get to, come to; see also REACH *v.* 4. • *n.* **1** achievement, attainment, acquisition; see also ACCOMPLISHMENT 3, ADVANTAGE *n.* 1, 3. **2** profit, increase, advance, improvement, emolument, yield, return, dividend; proceeds, revenue, income, earnings, winnings, payout, take, *sl.* payoff. **4** (*gains*) see FRUIT *n.* 4. **5** increase, increment, rise, addition, advance, enhancement, elevation, augmentation; upward *or* forward movement, progress.

gainful /gáynfŏŏl/ *adj.* **1** (of employment) paid. **2** lucrative; remunerative. □□ **gainfully** *adv.* **gainfulness** *n.*

■ **2** lucrative, remunerative, moneymaking, profitable, advantageous, productive, fruitful.

gainsay /gáynsáy/ *v.tr.* (*past* and *past part.* **gainsaid** /-séd/) deny; contradict. □□ **gainsayer** *n.* [ME f. obs. *gain-* against f. ON *gegn* straight f. Gmc + SAY]

'gainst /genst/ *prep. poet.* = AGAINST. [abbr.]

gait /gayt/ *n.* **1** a manner of walking; one's bearing or carriage as one walks. **2** the manner of forward motion of a runner, horse, vehicle, etc. [var. of GATE²]

■ **1** see WALK *n.* 1.

gaiter /gáytər/ *n.* a covering of cloth, leather, etc., for the leg below the knee, for the ankle, for part of a machine, etc. □□ **gaitered** *adj.* [F *guêtre*, prob. rel. to WRIST]

gal¹ /gal/ *n. sl.* a girl. [repr. var. pronunc.]

■ see GIRL 1.

gal² /gal/ *n. Physics* a unit of acceleration for a gravitational field, equal to one centimeter per second per second. [*Galileo*: see GALILEAN¹]

Gal. *abbr.* Galatians (New Testament).

gal. *abbr.* gallon(s).

gala /gáylə, gaálə, gálə/ *n.* **1** (often *attrib.*) a festive or special occasion (*a gala performance*). **2** *Brit.* a festive gathering for sports, esp. swimming. [F or It. f. Sp. f. OF *gale* rejoicing f. Gmc]

■ **1** fete, festival, festivity, feast, celebration, holiday, carnival, pageant, party; (*attrib.*) festive, celebratory; special, commemorative.

galactagogue /gəláktəgawg, -gog/ *adj. & n.* • *adj.* inducing a flow of milk. • *n.* a galactagogue substance. [Gk *gala galaktos* milk, + *agōgos* leading]

galactic /gəláktik/ *adj.* of or relating to a galaxy or galaxies, esp. the Milky Way galaxy. [Gk *galaktias*, var. of *galaxias*: see GALAXY]

galago /gəláygō, -laá-/ *n.* (*pl.* **-os**) any small tree-climbing primate of the genus *Galago*, found in southern Africa, with large eyes and ears and a long tail. Also called *bush baby*. [mod.L]

galah /gəlaá/ *n. Austral.* **1** a small rosy-breasted gray-backed cockatoo, *Cacatua roseicapilla*. **2** *sl.* a fool. [Aboriginal]

Galahad /gálahad/ *n.* a person characterized by nobility, integrity, courtesy, etc. [name of a knight of the Round Table in Arthurian legend]

galantine /gálənteen/ *n.* white meat or fish boned, cooked, pressed, and served cold in aspic, etc. [ME f. OF, alt. f. *galatine* jellied meat f. med.L *galatina*]

galavant var. of GALLIVANT.

galaxy /gáləksee/ *n.* (*pl.* **-ies**) **1** any of many independent systems of stars, gas, dust, etc., held together by gravitational attraction. **2** (often **the Galaxy**) the galaxy of which the solar system is a part. **3** (often **the Galaxy**) the irregular luminous band of stars indistinguishable to the naked eye encircling the heavens; the Milky Way. **4** (foll. by *of*) a brilliant company or gathering. [ME f. OF *galaxie* f. med.L *galaxia*, LL *galaxias* f. Gk f. *gala galaktos* milk]

galbanum /gálbənəm/ *n.* a bitter aromatic gum resin produced from kinds of ferula. [ME f. L f. Gk *khalbanē*, prob. of Semitic orig.]

gale[1] /gayl/ *n.* **1** a very strong wind, esp. (on the Beaufort scale) one of 32–54 m.p.h. **2** *Naut.* a storm. **3** an outburst, esp. of laughter. [16th c.: orig. unkn.]
■ **2** see STORM *n.* 1. **3** outburst, burst, explosion, eruption; peal, roar, scream, shout, howl, shriek, hoot.

gale[2] /gayl/ *n.* (in full **sweet gale**) bog myrtle. [OE *gagel*(*le*), MDu. *gaghel*]

galea /gáyleeə/ *n.* (*pl.* **galeae** /-lee-ee/ or **-as**) *Bot.* & *Zool.* a structure like a helmet in shape, form, or function. □□ **galeate** /-lee-ayt/ *adj.* **galeated** *adj.* [L, = helmet]

galena /gəleénə/ *n.* a bluish, gray, or black mineral ore of lead sulfide. ¶ Chem. formula: PbS. [L, = lead ore (in a partly purified state)]

galenic var. of GALENICAL.

galenical /gəlénikəl/ *adj.* & *n.* (also **galenic** /-lénik/) ● *adj.* **1** of or relating to Galen, a Greek physician of the 2nd c. AD, or his methods. **2** made of natural as opposed to synthetic components. ● *n.* a drug or medicament produced directly from vegetable tissues.

Galilean[1] /gálileeáyən, -leéən/ *adj.* of or relating to Galileo, Italian astronomer d. 1642, or his methods.

Galilean[2] /gálileeən/ *adj.* & *n.* ● *adj.* **1** of Galilee in Palestine. **2** Christian. ● *n.* **1** a native of Galilee. **2** a Christian. **3** (prec. by *the*) *derog.* Christ.

galingale /gálinggayl/ *n.* **1** an aromatic rhizome of an E. Asian plant of the genus *Alpinia*, formerly used in cooking and medicine. **2** (in full **English galingale**) a sedge (*Cyperus longus*) having a root with similar properties. [OE *gallengar* OF *galingal* f. Arab. *k̠alanjān* f. Chin. *ge-liang-jiang* mild ginger from Ge in Canton]

galiot var. of GALLIOT.

galipot /gálipot/ *n.* a hardened deposit of resin formed on the stem of the cluster pine. [F: orig. unkn.]

gall[1] /gawl/ *n.* **1** *sl.* impudence. **2** asperity; rancor. **3** bitterness; anything bitter (*gall and wormwood*). **4** the bile of animals. **5** the gallbladder and its contents. □ **gallbladder** the vessel storing bile after its secretion by the liver and before release into the intestine. [ON, corresp. to OE *gealla*, f. Gmc]
■ **1** impudence, insolence, impertinence, audacity, brashness, brazenness, sauciness, effrontery, temerity, cheek, front, *colloq.* brass, nerve, guts, sauce, *sl.* crust, chutzpah. **2, 3** asperity, acerbity, causticity, harshness, rancor, acrimony, vitriol, bile, spleen; see also *bitterness* (BITTER).

gall[2] /gawl/ *n.* & *v.* ● *n.* **1** a sore on the skin made by chafing. **2 a** mental soreness or vexation. **b** a cause of this. **3** a place rubbed bare. ● *v.tr.* **1** rub sore; injure by rubbing. **2** vex; annoy; humiliate. □□ **gallingly** *adv.* [ME f. LG or Du. *galle*, corresp. to OE *gealla* sore on a horse]
■ *n.* **1** sore (spot), abrasion, scrape, graze, scratch, chafe. **2 a** soreness, vexation, exasperation; see also ANNOYANCE 1. **b** nuisance, bother, *disp.* aggravation; see also ANNOYANCE 2. ● *v.* **1** irritate, chafe, abrade, fret, scrape, rub, scratch. **2** vex, bother, humiliate, annoy, irritate, irk, exasperate, provoke, nettle, ruffle, fret, *colloq.* needle; anger, enrage, inflame, infuriate, incense.

gall[3] /gawl/ *n.* **1** a growth produced by insects or fungus, etc., on plants and trees, esp. on oak. **2** (*attrib.*) of insects producing galls. [ME f. OF *galle* f. L *galla*]

gallant *adj.*, *n.*, & *v.* ● *adj.* /gálənt/ **1** brave; chivalrous. **2 a** (of a ship, horse, etc.) grand; fine; stately. **b** *archaic* finely dressed. **3** /gálənt, gəlánt, -láənt/ *a* markedly attentive to women. **b** concerned with sexual love; amatory. ● *n.* /gálənt, gəlánt, -láənt/ **1** a ladies' man; a lover or paramour. **2** *archaic* a man of fashion; a fine gentleman. ● *v.* /gəlánt/ **1** *tr.* flirt with. **2** *tr.* escort; act as a cavalier to (a lady). **3** *intr.* **a** play the gallant. **b** (foll. by *with*) flirt. □□ **gallantly** /gáləntlee/ *adv.* [ME f. OF *galant* part. of *galer* make merry]
■ *adj.* **1** brave, courageous, bold, valiant, daring, dauntless, intrepid, plucky, fearless, valorous, unafraid, undaunted, manful, mettlesome, stouthearted, lionhearted, heroic; chivalrous, gracious, honorable, manly, courtly, courteous, polite, attentive, considerate, mannerly. **2 a** fine, elegant, imposing,

grand, noble, stately, dignified, glorious, splendid, majestic, magnificent. **b** see DAPPER 1. **3 b** see EROTIC.
● *n.* **1** lover, Romeo, ladies' man, seducer, *archaic or derog.* paramour; sweetheart, beloved, boyfriend, escort, suitor, admirer, beau, *poet.* swain. **2** see SWELL *n.* 4. ● *v.* **2** see ESCORT *v.* **3 a** see PHILANDER.

gallantry /gáləntree/ *n.* (*pl.* **-ies**) **1** bravery; dashing courage. **2** courtliness; devotion to women. **3** a polite act or speech. **4** the conduct of a gallant; sexual intrigue; immorality. [F *galanterie* (as GALLANT)]
■ **1** see BRAVERY. **2** see CHIVALRY 2.

galleon /gáleeən/ *n. hist.* **1** a ship of war (usu. Spanish). **2** a large Spanish merchant ship. **3** a vessel shorter and higher than a galley. [MDu. *galjoen* f. F *galion* f. *galie* galley, or f. Sp. *galeón*]

galleria /gáləreéə/ *n.* a collection of small shops under a single roof; an arcade. [It.]

gallery /gáləree/ *n.* (*pl.* **-ies**) **1** a room or building for showing works of art. **2** a balcony, esp. a platform projecting from the inner wall of a church, hall, etc., providing extra room for spectators, etc., or reserved for musicians, etc. (*minstrels' gallery*). **3 a** the highest balcony in a theater. **b** its occupants. **4 a** a covered space for walking in, partly open at the side; a portico or colonnade. **b** a long narrow passage in the thickness of a wall or supported on corbels, open toward the interior of the building. **5** a long narrow room, passage, or corridor. **6** *Mil.* & *Mining* a horizontal underground passage. **7** a group of spectators at a golf or tennis match, etc. □ **play to the gallery** seek to win approval by appealing to popular taste. □□ **galleried** *adj.* [F *galerie* f. It. *galleria* f. med.L *galeria*]
■ **4** see PORTICO.

galleryite /gáləree-īt/ *n.* a person occupying a seat in a gallery; a spectator at a play, tennis match, etc.

galley /gálee/ *n.* (*pl.* **-eys**) **1** *hist.* **a** a low flat single-decked vessel using sails and oars, and usu. rowed by slaves or criminals. **b** an ancient Greek or Roman warship with one or more banks of oars. **c** a large open rowing boat, e.g., that used by the captain of a man-of-war. **2** a ship's or aircraft's kitchen. **3** *Printing* **a** an oblong tray for set type. **b** the corresponding part of a composing machine. **c** (in full **galley proof**) a proof in the form of long single-column strips from type in a galley, not in sheets or pages. □ **galley slave 1** *hist.* a person condemned to row in a galley. **2** a drudge. [ME f. OF *galie* f. med.L *galea*, med.Gk *galaia*]
■ **2** see KITCHEN.

galliard /gályaard/ *n. hist.* **1** a lively dance usu. in triple time for two persons. **2** the music for this. [ME f. OF *gaillard* valiant]

Gallic /gálik/ *adj.* **1** French or typically French. **2** of the Gauls; Gaulish. □□ **Gallicize** /-lisīz/ *v.tr.* & *intr.* [L *Gallicus* f. *Gallus* a Gaul]

gallic acid /gálik/ *n. Chem.* an acid extracted from gallnuts, etc., formerly used in making ink. [F *gallique* f. *galle* GALL[3]]

Gallicism /gálisizəm/ *n.* a French idiom, esp. one adopted in another language. [F *gallicisme* (as GALLIC)]

galligaskins /gáligáskinz/ *n.pl. Brit. hist.* or *joc.* breeches; trousers; leggings. [orig. wide hose of the 16th–17th c., f. obs. F *garguesque* for *greguesque* f. It. *grechesca* fem. of *grechesco* Greek]

gallimaufry /gálimáwfree/ *n.* (*pl.* **-ies**) a heterogeneous mixture; a jumble or medley. [F *galimafrée*, of unkn. orig.]

gallinaceous /gálináyshəs/ *adj.* of or relating to the order Galliformes, which includes domestic poultry, pheasants, partridges, etc. [L *gallinaceus* f. *gallina* hen f. *gallus* cock]

gallinule /gálinool, -nyool/ *n.* **1** a small aquatic bird, *Gallinula chloropus*, with long legs and a short reddish-yellow bill. **2** any of various similar birds of the genus *Porphyrula* or *Por-*

/ . . . / pronunciation	● **part of speech**
□ **phrases, idioms, and compounds**	
□□ **derivatives**	■ **synonym section**
cross-references appear in SMALL CAPITALS or *italics*	

phyrio. [mod.L *gallinula*, dimin. of L *gallina* hen f. *gallus* cock]

galliot /gálleeət/ *n.* (also **galiot**) **1** a Dutch cargo boat or fishing vessel. **2** a small (usu. Mediterranean) galley. [ME f. OF *galiote* f. It. *galeotta* f. med.L *galea* galley]

gallipot /gálipot/ *n.* a small pot of earthenware, metal, etc., used for ointments, etc. [prob. GALLEY + POT[1], because brought in galleys from the Mediterranean]

gallium /gáleeəm/ *n. Chem.* a soft bluish white metallic element occurring naturally in coal, bauxite, and kaolin. ¶ Symb.: **Ga.** [mod.L f. L *Gallia* France (so named patriotically by its discoverer Lecoq de Boisbaudran d. 1912)]

gallivant /gálivant/ *v.intr. colloq.* **1** gad about. **2** flirt. [orig. uncert.]
▪ **1** see JOURNEY *v.* **2** see PHILANDER.

galliwasp /gáliwosp/ *n.* a W. Indian lizard, *Diploglossus monotropis.* [18th c.: orig. unkn.]

gallnut /gáwlnut/ *n.* = GALL[3].

Gallo- /gálō/ *comb. form* **1** French; French and. **2** Gaul (*Gallo-Roman*). [L *Gallus* a Gaul]

gallon /gálən/ *n.* **1 a** a measure of capacity equivalent to four quarts (3785 cc), used for liquids. **b** (in full **imperial gallon**) *Brit.* a measure of capacity equal to eight pints and equivalent to four quarts (4546 cc), used for liquids and grain, etc. **2** (usu. in *pl.*) *colloq.* a large amount. □ **gallonage** *n.* [ME f. ONF *galon*, OF *jalon*, f. base of med.L *gallēta*, *gallētum*, perh. of Celtic orig.]

galloon /gəlōōn/ *n.* a narrow braid of gold, silver, silk, cotton, nylon, etc., for trimming dresses, etc. [F *galon* f. *galonner* trim with braid, of unkn. orig.]

gallop /gáləp/ *n. & v.* ▪ *n.* **1** the fastest pace of a horse or other quadruped, with all the feet off the ground together in each stride. **2** a ride at this pace. **3** *Brit.* a track or ground for this. ▪ *v.* (**galloped, galloping**) **1 a** *intr.* (of a horse, etc., or its rider) go at the pace of a gallop. **b** *tr.* make (a horse, etc.) gallop. **2** *intr.* (foll. by *through, over*) read, recite, or talk at great speed. **3** *intr.* move or progress rapidly (*galloping inflation*). □ **at a gallop** at the pace of a gallop. □□ **galloper** *n.* [OF *galop, galoper*: see WALLOP]
▪ *v.* **1a, 3** see RUN *v.* 1, 3.

galloway /gáləway/ *n.* **1** an animal of a breed of hornless black beef cattle from Galloway in SW Scotland. **2** this breed.

gallows /gálōz/ *n.pl.* (usu. treated as *sing.*) **1** a structure, usu. of two uprights and a crosspiece, for the hanging of criminals. **2** (prec. by *the*) execution by hanging. □ **gallows humor** grim and ironic humor. [ME f. ON *gálgi*]
▪ **1** gibbet, *hist.* scaffold.

gallstone /gáwlstōn/ *n.* a small hard mass forming in the gallbladder.

Gallup poll /gáləp/ *n.* = *opinion poll.* [G. H. *Gallup*, US statistician d. 1984]

galluses /gáləsiz/ *n.pl. dial. & old-fashioned* suspenders. [pl. of *gallus* var. of GALLOWS]

galoot /gəlōōt/ *n. colloq.* a person, esp. a strange or clumsy one. [19th-c. Naut. sl.: orig. unkn.]

galop /gáləp/ *n. & v.* ▪ *n.* **1** a lively dance in duple time. **2** the music for this dance. ▪ *v.intr.* (**galoped, galoping**) perform this dance. [F: see GALLOP]

galore /gəláwr/ *adv.* in abundance (placed after noun: *flowers galore*). [Ir. *go leór* to sufficiency]
▪ aplenty, in abundance, in large quantity *or* quantities *or* number(s) *or* amounts, in profusion, à gogo; everywhere, all over.

galosh /gəlósh/ *n.* (also **golosh**) (usu. in *pl.*) a high, waterproof overshoe, usu. of rubber. [ME f. OF *galoche* f. LL *gallicula* small Gallic shoe]

galumph /gəlúmf/ *v.intr. colloq.* **1** move noisily or clumsily. **2** go prancing in triumph. [coined by Lewis Carroll (in sense 2), perh. f. GALLOP + TRIUMPH]
▪ **1** see PLOD *v.* 1. **2** see CAVORT.

galvanic /galvánik/ *adj.* **1 a** sudden and remarkable (*had a galvanic effect*). **b** stimulating; full of energy. **2** of or producing an electric current by chemical action. □□ **galvanically** *adv.*

galvanism /gálvənizəm/ *n.* **1** electricity produced by chemical action. **2** the use of electricity for medical purposes. □□ **galvanist** *n.* [F *galvanisme* f. L. *Galvani*, It. physiologist d. 1798]

galvanize /gálvəniz/ *v.tr.* **1** (often foll. by *into*) rouse forcefully, esp. by shock or excitement (*was galvanized into action*). **2** stimulate by or as if by electricity. **3** coat (iron) with zinc (usu. without the use of electricity) as a protection against rust. □□ **galvanization** *n.* **galvanizer** *n.* [F *galvaniser*: see GALVANISM]
▪ **1** see ROUSE 2a.

galvanometer /gálvənómitər/ *n.* an instrument for detecting and measuring small electric currents. □□ **galvanometric** /-nəmétrik/ *adj.*

gambade /gambaád/ *n.* (also **gambado** /-baádō/) (*pl.* **gambades; -os** or **-oes**) **1** a horse's leap or bound. **2** a capering movement. **3** an escapade. [F *gambade* & Sp. *gambado* f. It. & Sp. *gamba* leg]

gambier /gámbeeər/ *n.* an astringent extract of an Eastern plant used in tanning, etc. [Malay *gambir* name of the plant]

gambit /gámbit/ *n.* **1** a chess opening in which a player sacrifices a piece or pawn to secure an advantage. **2** an opening move in a discussion, etc. **3** a trick or device. [earlier *gambett* f. It. *gambetto* tripping up f. *gamba* leg]
▪ **3** see DEVICE 2.

gamble /gámbəl/ *v. & n.* ▪ *v.* **1** *intr.* play games of chance for money, esp. for high stakes. **2** *tr.* **a** bet (a sum of money) in gambling. **b** (often foll. by *away*) lose (assets) by gambling. **3** *intr.* take great risks in the hope of substantial gain. **4** *intr.* (foll. by *on*) act in the hope or expectation of (*gambled on fine weather*). ▪ *n.* **1** a risky undertaking or attempt. **2** a spell or an act of gambling. □□ **gambler** *n.* [obs. *gamel* to sport, *gamene* GAME[1]]
▪ *v.* **1, 3** play, game, wager, bet, *colloq.* punt; try one's luck; see also SPECULATE 3. **2 a** risk, venture, hazard, bet, wager, stake; play; place, put, lay. **4** (*gamble on*) take a chance on, count on, bargain on, rely on. ▪ *n.* **1** risk, venture, chance; uncertainty, speculation, leap in the dark. **2** bet, wager, stake, *colloq.* punt, *Brit. sl.* flutter.

gamboge /gambój, -boozh/ *n.* a gum resin produced by various E. Asian trees and used as a yellow pigment and as a purgative. [mod.L *gambaugium* f. *Cambodia* in SE Asia]

gambol /gámbəl/ *v. & n.* ▪ *v.intr.* (**gamboled, gamboling**; also **gambolled, gambolling**) skip or frolic playfully. ▪ *n.* a playful frolic. [GAMBADE]
▪ *v.* see SKIP[1] *v.* 1. ▪ *n.* see SKIP[1] *n.*

gambrel /gámbrəl/ *n.* (in full **gambrel roof**) **1** *US* a roof with gables and with each face having two slopes, the lower one steeper. **2** *Brit.* a roof like a hipped roof but with gablelike ends. [ONF *gamberel* f. *gambier* forked stick f. *gambe* leg (from the resemblance to the shape of a horse's hind leg)]

game[1] /gaym/ *n., adj., & v.* ▪ *n.* **1 a** a form or spell of play or sport, esp. a competitive one played according to rules and decided by skill, strength, or luck. **b** a specific instance of playing such a game; a match. **2** a single portion of play forming a scoring unit in some contests, e.g., bridge or tennis. **3** (in *pl.*) **a** *Brit.* athletics or sports as organized in a school, etc. **b** a meeting for athletic, etc., contests (*Olympic Games*). **4** a winning score in a game; the state of the score in a game (*the game is two all*). **5** the equipment for a game. **6** one's level of achievement in a game, as specified (*played a good game*). **7 a** a piece of fun; a jest (*was only playing a game with you*). **b** (in *pl.*) jokes; tricks (*none of your games!*). **8** a scheme or undertaking, etc., regarded as a game (*so that's your game*). **9 a** a policy or line of action. **b** an occupation or profession (*the fighting game*). **10** (*collect.*) a wild animals or birds hunted for sport or food. **b** the flesh of these. **11** a hunted animal; a quarry or object of pursuit or attack. **12** a kept flock of swans. ▪ *adj.* **1** spirited; eager and willing. **2** (foll. by *for*, or *to* + infin.) having the spirit or energy; eagerly prepared. ▪ *v.intr.* esp. *Brit.* play at games of chance for money; gamble. □ **the game is up** the scheme is revealed or foiled. **game plan 1** a winning strategy worked out in advance for a particular game. **2** a plan of campaign, esp. in politics. **game point** *Tennis*, etc., a point which, if won, would win the game. **game** (or **games**) **theory** the mathematical analysis of conflict in war, economics, games of skill, etc. **game warden** an official locally supervising game and hunting. **gaming house** a place frequented for gambling; a casino. **gaming table** a table used for gambling. **make game** (or **a game**) **of** mock; taunt. **off** (or **on**) **one's game** playing badly (or well). **on the game** *Brit. sl.* involved in prostitution or thieving. **play the game** behave fairly or according to the rules. □□ **gamely** *adv.* **gameness** *n.* **gamester** *n.* [OE *gamen*]

■ *n.* **1 a** amusement, pastime, diversion, distraction; recreation, sport. **2** round, bout; see also HEAT *n.* 6. **3 b** (*games*) contest, competition, meeting, meet, tournament, tourney, match, event. **7 a** see PRANK. **b** (*games*) jokes, dodges, tricks, ruses, ploys; mischief, horseplay, *colloq.* monkey business, shenanigans. **8** scheme, undertaking, plan, plot, design, stratagem, strategy, tactic, *sl.* racket. **9 a** policy, line of action, approach. **b** occupation, line (of work), field, business, trade, profession, *colloq.* racket. **11** quarry, prey; victim, target. ● *adj.* **1** spirited, high-spirited, devil-may-care, adventurous, plucky, daring, unflinching, courageous, brave, bold, *colloq.* gutsy. **2** eager, willing, ready, prepared; see also ENTHUSIASTIC. □ **game plan 2** see POLICY[1] **1. make game** (or **a game**) **of** see MOCK *v.* 1, 3. **play the game** play fair, be a sport.

game² /gaym/ *adj.* (of a leg, arm, etc.) lame; crippled. [18th-c. dial.: orig. unkn.]

gamecock /gáymkok/ *n.* (also **gamefowl** /-fowl/) a cock bred and trained for cockfighting.

gamekeeper /gáymkeepǝr/ *n.* a person employed to care for and protect game.

gamelan /gámǝlan/ *n.* **1** a type of orchestra found in SE Asia (esp. Indonesia), with string and woodwind instruments, and a wide range of percussion instruments. **2** a kind of xylophone used in this. [Jav.]

gamesman /gáymzmǝn/ *n.* (*pl.* **-men**) an exponent of gamesmanship.

gamesmanship /gáymzmǝnship/ *n.* the art or practice of winning games or other contests by gaining a psychological advantage over an opponent.

gamesome /gáymsǝm/ *adj.* merry; sportive. □□ **gamesomely** *adv.* **gamesomeness** *n.*

gametangium /gámitánjeeǝm/ *n.* (*pl.* **gametangia** /-jeeǝ/) *Bot.* an organ in which gametes are formed. [as GAMETE + *aggeion* vessel]

gamete /gámeet, gǝmeét/ *n. Biol.* a mature germ cell able to unite with another in sexual reproduction. □□ **gametic** /gǝmétik/ *adj.* [mod.L *gameta* f. Gk *gametē* wife f. *gamos* marriage]

gameto- /gǝmeétō/ *comb. form Biol.* gamete.

gametocyte /gǝmeétǝsīt/ *n. Biol.* any cell that is in the process of developing into one or more gametes.

gametogenesis /gǝmeétǝjénisis/ *n. Biol.* the process by which cells undergo meiosis to form gametes.

gametophyte /gǝmeétǝfīt/ *n.* the gamete-producing form of a plant that has alternation of generations between this and the asexual form. □□ **gametophytic** /-fítik/ *adj.*

gamin /gámin/ *n.* **1** a street urchin. **2** an impudent child. [F]
■ **1** see GUTTERSNIPE. **2** see DEVIL *n.* 3b.

gamine /gámeen/ *n.* **1** a girl gamin. **2** a girl with mischievous or boyish charm. [F]

gamma /gámǝ/ *n.* **1** the third letter of the Greek alphabet (Γ, γ). **2** *Brit.* a third-class mark given for a piece of work or in an examination. **3** *Astron.* the third brightest star in a constellation. **4** the third member of a series. □ **gamma radiation** (or **rays**) electromagnetic radiation of very short wavelength emitted by some radioactive substances. [ME f. Gk]

gammer /gámǝr/ *n. Brit. archaic* an old woman, esp. as a rustic name. [prob. contr. of GODMOTHER: cf. GAFFER]

gammon¹ /gámǝn/ *n.* & *v.* ● *n.* **1** the bottom piece of a side of bacon including a hind leg. **2** esp. *Brit.* the ham of a pig

cured like bacon. ● *v.tr.* cure (bacon). [ONF *gambon* f. *gambe* leg: cf. JAMB]
■ *n.* see LEG *n.* 2.

gammon² /gámǝn/ *n.* & *v.* ● *n.* a victory in backgammon in which the opponent removes no pieces from the board. ● *v.tr.* defeat in this way. [app. = ME *gamen* GAME¹]

gammon³ /gámǝn/ *n.* & *v. Brit. colloq.* ● *n.* humbug; deception. ● *v.* **1** *intr.* **a** talk speciously. **b** pretend. **2** *tr.* hoax; deceive. [18th c.: orig. uncert.]

gammy /gámee/ *adj.* (**gammier, gammiest**) *Brit. sl.* (esp. of a leg) lame; permanently injured. [dial. form of GAME²]

gamp /gamp/ *n. Brit. colloq.* an umbrella, esp. a large unwieldy one. [Mrs. *Gamp* in Dickens's *Martin Chuzzlewit*]

gamut /gámǝt/ *n.* **1** the whole series or range or scope of anything (*the whole gamut of crime*). **2** *Mus.* **a** the whole series of notes used in medieval or modern music. **b** a major diatonic scale. **c** a people's or a period's recognized scale. **d** a voice's or instrument's compass. **3** *Mus.* the lowest note in the medieval sequence of hexachords, = modern G on the lowest line of the bass staff. [med.L *gamma ut* f. GAMMA taken as the name for a note one tone lower than A of the classical scale + *ut* the first of six arbitrary names of notes forming the hexachord, being syllables (*ut, re, mi, fa, so, la*) of the Latin hymn beginning *Ut queant laxis*)]
■ **1** range, scale, spectrum, compass, spread, scope, sweep, field, series.

gamy /gáymee/ *adj.* (**gamier, gamiest**) **1** having the flavor or scent of game kept till it is high. **2** scandalous; sensational; racy. **3** = GAME¹ *adj.* □□ **gamily** *adv.* **gaminess** *n.*

gander /gándǝr/ *n.* & *v.* ● *n.* **1** a male goose. **2** *sl.* a look; a glance (*take a gander*). ● *v.intr.* look or glance. [OE *gandra*, rel. to GANNET]
■ *n.* **2** see GLANCE¹ *n.* 1. ● *v.* see PEEP *v.* 1.

gang¹ /gang/ *n.* & *v.* ● *n.* **1 a** a band of persons acting or going about together, esp. for criminal purposes. **b** *colloq.* such a band pursuing antisocial purposes. **2** a set of workers, slaves, or prisoners. **3** a set of tools arranged to work simultaneously. ● *v.tr.* arrange (tools, etc.) to work in coordination. □ **gang bang** *sl.* an occasion on which several men successively have sexual intercourse, often forcibly, with one partner. **gang up** *colloq.* **1** (often foll. by *with*) act in concert. **2** (foll. by *on*) combine against. [orig. = going, journey, f. ON *gangr, ganga* GOING, corresp. to OE *gang*]
■ *n.* **1** group, pack, mob, ring, company; crowd, band, set, party, team. □ **gang up 1** join together, join forces, get together, unite. **2** (*gang up on*) conspire *or* plot against, unite *or* unify against, club *or* band together against, join forces against.

gang² /gang/ *v.intr. Sc.* go. □ **gang agley** (of a plan, etc.) go wrong. [OE *gangan*: cf. GANG¹]

gangboard /gángbawrd/ *n.* = GANGPLANK.

ganger /gángǝr/ *n. Brit.* the foreman of a gang of workers.

gangland /gángland/ *n.* the world of organized crime.

gangle /gánggǝl/ *v.intr.* move ungracefully. [back-form. f. GANGLING]

gangling /gánggling/ *adj.* (of a person) loosely built; lanky. [frequent. of GANG²]
■ see LANKY.

ganglion /gánggleeǝn/ *n.* (*pl.* **ganglia** /-leeǝ/ or **ganglions**) **1 a** an enlargement or knot on a nerve, etc., containing an assemblage of nerve cells. **b** a mass of gray matter in the central nervous system forming a nerve nucleus. **2** *Med.* a cyst, esp. on a tendon sheath. **3** a center of activity or interest. □□ **gangliar** /-gleeǝr/ *adj.* **gangliform** /-glifawrm/ *adj.* **ganglionated** *adj.* **ganglionic** /-leeónik/ *adj.* [Gk *ganglion*]

gangly /gángglee/ *adj.* (**ganglier, gangliest**) = GANGLING.

gangplank /gángplangk/ *n.* a movable plank usu. with cleats nailed on it for boarding or disembarking from a ship, etc.

/. . ./ **pronunciation**	● **part of speech**
□ **phrases, idioms, and compounds**	
□□ **derivatives**	■ **synonym section**
cross-references appear in SMALL CAPITALS or *italics*	

gangrene /gánggreen/ *n. & v.* ● *n.* **1** *Med.* death and decomposition of a part of the body tissue, usu. resulting from obstructed circulation. **2** moral corruption. ● *v.tr. & intr.* affect or become affected with gangrene. □□ **gangrenous** /gánggrinəs/ *adj.* [F *gangrène* f. L *gangraena* f. Gk *gaggraina*] ■ *v.* see MORTIFY 3.

gangster /gángstər/ *n.* a member of a gang of violent criminals. □□ **gangsterism** *n.*
■ Mafioso, brigand, bandit, racketeer, *sl.* mobster, goon, hood, gunsel; see also CRIMINAL *n.*

gangue /gang/ *n.* valueless earth, rock, etc., in which ore is found. [F f. G *Gang* lode = GANG¹]

gangway /gángway/ *n. & int.* ● *n.* **1 a** an opening in the bulwarks for a gangplank by which a ship is entered or left. **b** a bridge laid from ship to shore. **c** a passage on a ship, esp. a platform connecting the quarterdeck and forecastle. **2** a temporary bridge on a building site, etc. **3** *Brit.* a passage, esp. between rows of seats; an aisle. ● *int.* make way!

ganister /gánistər/ *n.* a close-grained, hard, siliceous stone found in the coal measures of northern England, and used for furnace linings. [19th c.: orig. unkn.]

ganja /gaánjə/ *n.* marijuana. [Hindi *gāñjhā*]

gannet /gánit/ *n.* **1** any sea bird of the genus *Morus*, esp. *Morus bassanus*, catching fish by plunge-diving. **2** *Brit. sl.* a greedy person. □□ **gannetry** *n.* (*pl.* **-ies**). [OE *ganot* f. Gmc, rel. to GANDER]

ganoid /gánoyd/ *adj. & n.* ● *adj.* **1** (of fish scales) enameled; smooth and bright. **2** having ganoid scales. ● *n.* a fish having ganoid scales. [F *ganoïde* f. Gk *ganos* brightness]

gantlet var. of GAUNTLET².

gantry /gántree/ *n.* (*pl.* **-ies**) **1** an overhead structure with a platform supporting a traveling crane, or railroad or road signals. **2** a structure supporting a space rocket prior to launching. **3** (also **gauntry** /gáwntree/) a wooden stand for barrels. [prob. f. *gawn*, dial. form of GALLON + TREE]

GAO *abbr.* General Accounting Office.

gaol *Brit.* var. of JAIL.

gaoler *Brit.* var. of JAILER.

gap /gap/ *n.* **1** an unfilled space or interval; a blank; a break in continuity. **2** a breach in a hedge, fence, or wall. **3** a wide (usu. undesirable) divergence in views, sympathies, development, etc. (*generation gap*). **4** a gorge or pass. □ **fill** (or **close**, etc.) **a gap** make up a deficiency. **gap-toothed** having gaps between the teeth. □□ **gapped** *adj.* **gappy** *adj.* [ME f. ON, = chasm, rel. to GAPE]
■ **1** interval, space, blank, void, gulf, lacuna; lull, pause, cessation, intermission, rest, respite; wait, delay, halt, stop, break, hiatus, disruption, interruption, discontinuity, suspension. **2** opening, space, aperture, hole, cavity, crevice, chink, crack, cleft, breach, rift. **3** difference, distinction, divergence, disparity, discrepancy, inconsistency; division, split. **4** see GORGE *n.* 1.

gape /gayp/ *v. & n.* ● *v.intr.* **1 a** open one's mouth wide, esp. in amazement or wonder. **b** be or become wide open. **2** (foll. by *at*) gaze curiously or wondrously. **3** split; part asunder. **4** yawn. ● *n.* **1** an openmouthed stare. **2** a yawn. **3** (in *pl.*; prec. by *the*) **a** a disease of birds with gaping as a symptom, caused by infestation with gapeworm. **b** *joc.* a fit of yawning. **4 a** an expanse of open mouth or beak. **b** the part of a beak that opens. **5** a rent or opening. □□ **gapingly** *adv.* [ME f. ON *gapa*]
■ *v.* **1 b** yawn, open (wide), be (wide) open. **2** gaze, stare, goggle, *colloq.* gawk, rubberneck, *dial.* gawp. **3** see SPLIT *v.* 1a. ● *n.* **1** stare, goggle, gaze. **5** see SPLIT *n.* 2.

gaper /gáypər/ *n.* **1** any bivalve mollusk of the genus *Mya*, with the shell open at one or both ends. **2** the comber fish, which gapes when dead. **3** a person who gapes.

gapeworm /gáypwərm/ *n.* a nematode worm, *Syngamus tracheae*, that infests the trachea and bronchi of birds and causes the gapes.

gar /gaar/ *n.* **1** any mainly marine fish of the family *Belonidae*, esp. *Belone belone*, having long beaklike jaws with sharp teeth. Also called NEEDLEFISH. **2** any similar freshwater fish

of the genus *Lepisosteus*, with ganoid scales. Also called **garfish** or **garpike**. **3** *NZ & Austral.* either of two marine fish of the genus *Hemiramphus*. Also called HALFBEAK. [app. f. OE *gār* spear + *fisc* FISH¹]

garage /gəraázh, -raáj/ *n. & v.* ● *n.* **1** a building or shed for the storage of a motor vehicle or vehicles. **2** an establishment selling gasoline, etc., or repairing and selling motor vehicles. ● *v.tr.* put or keep (a motor vehicle) in a garage. □ **garage sale** a sale of miscellaneous household goods held in the garage or yard of a private house. [F f. *garer* shelter]

garb /gaarb/ *n. & v.* ● *n.* **1** clothing, esp. of a distinctive kind. **2** the way a person is dressed. ● *v.tr.* **1** (usu. in *passive* or *refl.*) put (esp. distinctive) clothes on (a person). **2** attire. [obs. F *garbe* f. It. *garbo* f. Gmc, rel. to GEAR]
■ *n.* see DRESS *n.* 2. ● *v.* see CLOTHE 1, 2.

garbage /gaárbij/ *n.* **1 a** refuse; filth. **b** domestic waste, esp. food wastes. **2** foul or inferior literature, etc. **3** nonsense. **4** incomprehensible or meaningless data, esp. in computing. □ **garbage can** a container for household refuse, esp. one kept outside. [AF: orig. unkn.]
■ **1 a** filth, dross, rubbish, junk, refuse, litter, debris, detritus, waste, offal, trash, *colloq.* muck; sweepings, slops, scraps. **2** rubbish, trash, *colloq.* tripe. **3** see NONSENSE.

garble /gaárbəl/ *v.tr.* **1** unintentionally distort or confuse (facts, messages, etc.). **2 a** mutilate in order to misrepresent. **b** make (usu. unfair or malicious) selections from (facts, statements, etc.). □□ **garbler** *n.* [It. *garbellare* f. Arab. *ġarbala* sift, perh. f. LL *cribellare* to sieve f. L *cribrum* sieve]
■ **1** distort, confuse, mix up, misconstrue, misunderstand, misread, jumble (up). **2** warp, twist, mangle, mutilate, falsify, misrepresent, misstate, misquote, misreport, mistranslate, misrender, slant, corrupt, color.

garboard /gaárbərd/ *n.* (in full **garboard strake**) the first range of planks or plates laid on a ship's bottom next to the keel. [Du. *gaarboord*, perh. f. *garen* GATHER + *boord* BOARD]

garçon /gaarsáwN/ *n.* a waiter in a French restaurant, hotel, etc. [F, lit. 'boy']

garden /gaárd'n/ *n. & v.* ● *n.* **1 a** a piece of ground used for growing esp. flowers or vegetables. **b** a piece of ground, usu. partly grassed and adjoining a private house, used for growing flowers, fruit, or vegetables, and as a place of recreation. **2** (esp. in *pl.*) ornamental grounds laid out for public enjoyment (*botanical gardens*). **3** a similar place with the service of refreshments (*tea garden*). **4** (*attrib.*) **a** (of plants) cultivated, not wild. **b** for use in a garden (*garden seat*). **5** (usu. in *pl.* prec. by a name) *Brit.* a street, square, etc. (*Onslow Gardens*). **6** an especially fertile region. **7** a large public hall. ● *v.intr.* cultivate or work in a garden. □ **garden center** an establishment where plants, garden equipment, etc., are sold. **garden city** an industrial or other town laid out systematically with spacious surroundings, parks, etc. **garden cress** a cruciferous plant, *Lepidium sativum*, used in salads. **garden party** a social event held on a lawn or in a garden. **garden suburb** *Brit.* a suburb laid out spaciously with open spaces, parks, etc. **garden warbler** a European woodland songbird, *Sylvia borin*. □□ **gardenesque** /-ésk/ *adj.* **gardening** *n.* [ME f. ONF *gardin* (OF *jardin*) ult. f. Gmc: cf. YARD²]

gardener /gaárdnər/ *n.* a person who gardens or is employed to tend a garden. □ **gardener bird** a bowerbird making a "garden" of moss, etc., in front of a bower. [ME ult. f. OF *jardinier* (as GARDEN)]

gardenia /gaardeényə/ *n.* any tree or shrub of the genus *Gardenia*, with large white or yellow flowers and usu. a fragrant scent. [mod.L f. Dr. A. *Garden*, Sc. naturalist d. 1791]

garfish /gaárfish/ *n.* (*pl.* same) = GAR.

gargantuan /gaargánchōōən/ *adj.* enormous; gigantic. [the name of a giant in Rabelais' book *Gargantua* (1534)]
■ see GIGANTIC.

garget /gaárgit/ *n.* **1** inflammation of a cow's or ewe's udder. **2** pokeweed. [perh. f. obs. *garget* throat f. OF *gargate, -guete*]

gargle /gaárgəl/ *v. & n.* ● *v.* **1** *tr.* (also *absol.*) wash (one's mouth and throat), esp. for medicinal purposes, with a liquid kept in motion by breathing through it. **2** *Brit. intr.* make a sound as when doing this. ● *n.* **1** a liquid used for gargling. **2** *sl.* an alcoholic drink. [F *gargouiller* f. *gargouille*: see GAR-GOYLE]

gargoyle /gáargoyl/ *n.* a grotesque carved human or animal face or figure projecting from the gutter of (esp. a Gothic) building usu. as a spout to carry water clear of a wall. [OF *gargouille* throat, gargoyle]

gargoylism /gáargoylizəm/ *n. Med.* = HURLER'S SYNDROME.

garibaldi /gáribáwldee/ *n.* (*pl.* **garibaldis**) **1** a kind of woman's or child's loose blouse, orig. of bright red material imitating the shirts worn by Garibaldi and his followers. **2** *Brit.* a cookie containing a layer of currants. **3** a small red Californian fish, *Hypsypops rubicundus.* [G. *Garibaldi*, It. patriot d. 1882]

garish /gáirish/ *adj.* **1** obtrusively bright; showy. **2** gaudy; over-decorated. □□ **garishly** *adv.* **garishness** *n.* [16th-c. *gaurish* app. f. obs. *gaure* stare]
■ **1** bright, showy, florid, flashy, harsh, loud, obtrusive. **2** gaudy, tawdry, raffish, meretricious, brummagem, showy, *colloq.* flash, *sl.* glitzy; overdecorated, overelaborate, overornate.

garland /gáarlənd/ *n. & v.* ● *n.* **1** a wreath of flowers, leaves, etc., worn on the head or hung as a decoration. **2** a prize or distinction. **3** a literary anthology or miscellany. ● *v.tr.* **1** adorn with garlands. **2** crown with a garland. [ME f. OF *garlande*, of unkn. orig.]
■ *n.* **1** wreath, crown, chaplet, circlet; festoon. **2** see PRIZE[1] *n.* 2. ● *v.* wreathe, festoon, crown, decorate; encircle, ring, circle.

garlic /gáarlik/ *n.* **1** any of various alliaceous plants, esp. *Allium sativum.* **2** the strong-smelling pungent bulb of this plant, used as a flavoring in cooking. □□ **garlicky** *adj.* [OE *gārleac* f. *gār* spear + *lēac* LEEK]

garment /gáarmənt/ *n. & v.* ● *n.* **1 a** an article of dress. **b** (in *pl.*) clothes. **2** the outward and visible covering of anything. ● *v.tr.* (usu. in *passive*) *rhet.* attire. [ME f. OF *garnement* (as GARNISH)]
■ *n.* **1 a** item *or* piece of clothing. **b** (*garments*) clothes, vestments, *colloq.* togs, *joc.* habiliments, *sl.* duds, threads; outfit, costume; garb, clothing, dress, rig, *archaic* raiment, habit, *colloq.* gear, *formal* attire, apparel. ● *v.* see DRESS *v.* 1a.

garner /gáarnər/ *v. & n.* ● *v.tr.* **1** collect. **2** store; deposit. ● *n. literary* a storehouse or granary. [ME (orig. as noun) f. OF *gernier* f. L *granarium* GRANARY]
■ *v.* **1** gather, collect, assemble, amass, accumulate, heap up, pile up. **2** store (up), stock (up), lay in *or* up *or* down, put away, put by, stow (away), cache, store. ● *n.* see STOREHOUSE.

garnet /gáarnit/ *n.* a vitreous silicate mineral, esp. a transparent deep red kind used as a gem. [ME f. OF *grenat* f. med.L *granatum* POMEGRANATE, from its resemblance to the pulp of the fruit]

garnish /gáarnish/ *v. & n.* ● *v.tr.* **1** decorate or embellish (esp. food). **2** *Law* **a** serve notice on (a person) for the purpose of legally seizing money belonging to a debtor or defendant. **b** summon (a person) as a party to litigation started between others. ● *n.* (also **garnishing**) a decoration or embellishment, esp. to food. □□ **garnishment** *n.* (in sense 2). [ME f. OF *garnir* f. Gmc]
■ *v.* **1** see DECORATE 1, 3. ● *n.* see DECORATION 2.

garnishee /gáarnishee/ *n. & v. Law* ● *n.* a person garnished. ● *v.tr.* (**garnishees, garnisheed**) **1** garnish (a person). **2** attach (money, etc.) by way of garnishment.

garniture /gáarnichər/ *n.* **1** decoration or trimmings, esp. of food. **2** accessories; appurtenances. [F (as GARNISH)]

garotte var. of GARROTE.

garpike /gáarpīk/ *n.* = GAR.

garret /gárit/ *n.* **1** a top floor or attic room, esp. a dismal or unfurnished one. **2** an attic. [ME f. OF *garite* watchtower f. Gmc]

garrison /gárisən/ *n. & v.* ● *n.* **1** the troops stationed in a fortress, town, etc., to defend it. **2** the building occupied by them. ● *v.tr.* **1** provide (a place) with or occupy as a garrison. **2** place on garrison duty. □ **garrison town** a town

having a permanent garrison. [ME f. OF *garison* f. *garir* defend, furnish f. Gmc]
■ *n.* **2** see STRONGHOLD 1. ● *v.* **1** see OCCUPY 4. **2** see STATION *v.* 1.

garrote /gərót/ *v. & n.* (also **garotte; garrotte**) ● *v.tr.* **1** execute or kill by strangulation, esp. with an iron or wire collar, etc. **2** throttle in order to rob. ● *n.* **1 a** a Spanish method of execution by garroting. **b** the apparatus used for this. **2** highway robbery in which the victim is throttled. [F *garrotter* or Sp. *garrotear* f. *garrote* a cudgel, of unkn. orig.]
■ *v.* **1** see CHOKE[1] *v.* 1.

garrulous /gárələs, gáryə-/ *adj.* **1** talkative, esp. on trivial matters. **2** loquacious; wordy. □□ **garrulity** /gərōōlitee/ *n.* **garrulously** *adv.* **garrulousness** *n.* [L *garrulus* f. *garrire* chatter]
■ see TALKATIVE.

garter /gáartər/ *n. & v.* ● *n.* **1** a band worn to keep a sock or stocking or shirt sleeve up. **2** a strap hanging from a girdle, etc., for holding up a stocking. **3** (**the Garter**) *Brit.* **a** the highest order of English knighthood. **b** the badge of this. **c** membership of this. ● *v.tr.* fasten (a stocking) or encircle (a leg) with a garter. □ **garter belt** a belt with hanging straps for holding up stockings. **garter snake** any water snake of the genus *Thamnophis*, native to N. America, having lengthwise stripes. **garter stitch** a plain knitting stitch or pattern, forming ridges in alternate rows. [ME f. OF *gartier* f. *garet* bend of the knee]

garth /gaarth/ *n. Brit.* **1** an open space within cloisters. **2** *archaic* **a** a close or yard. **b** a paddock. [ME f. ON *garthr* = OE *geard* YARD[2]]

gas /gas/ *n. & v.* ● *n.* (*pl.* **gases**) **1** any airlike substance which moves freely to fill any space available, irrespective of its quantity. **2 a** such a substance (esp. found naturally or extracted from coal) used as a domestic or industrial fuel (also *attrib.*: *gas stove*). **b** an explosive mixture of firedamp with air. **3** nitrous oxide or another gas used as an anesthetic (esp. in dentistry). **4** a gas or vapor used as a poisonous agent to disable an enemy in warfare. **5** *colloq.* **a** gasoline. **b** motor vehicle's accelerator. **6** *sl.* pointless idle talk; boasting. **7** *sl.* an enjoyable, attractive, or amusing thing or person. ● *v.* (**gases, gassed, gassing**) **1** *tr.* expose to gas, esp. to kill or make unconscious. **2** *intr.* give off gas. **3** *tr.* (usu. foll. by *up*) *colloq.* fill (the tank of a motor vehicle) with gasoline. **4** *intr. colloq.* talk idly or boastfully. □ **gas chamber** an airtight chamber that can be filled with poisonous gas to kill people or animals. **gas chromatography** chromatography employing gas as the eluent. **gas-cooled** (of a nuclear reactor, etc.) cooled by a current of gas. **gas fire** *Brit.* a domestic fire using gas as its fuel. **gas-fired** using gas as the fuel. **gas gangrene** a rapidly spreading gangrene of injured tissue infected by a soil bacterium and accompanied by the evolution of gas. **gas-guzzler** *colloq.* a motor vehicle that gets relatively poor gas mileage. **gas mask** a respirator used as a defense against poison gas. **gas meter** an apparatus recording the amount of gas consumed. **gas oil** a type of fuel oil distilled from petroleum and heavier than kerosene. **gas-permeable** (esp. of a contact lens) allowing the diffusion of gases. **gas plant** *Bot.* = FRAXINELLA. **gas-proof** impervious to gas. **gas ring** a hollow ring perforated with gas jets, used esp. for cooking. **gas station** a filling station. **gas-tight** proof against the leakage of gas. **gas turbine** a turbine driven by a flow of gas or by gas from combustion. [invented by J. B. van Helmont, Belgian chemist d. 1644, after Gk *khaos* chaos]
■ *n.* **1** see FUME *n.* 1. **6** see *hot air.* **7** see GIGGLE *n.* 2. ● *v.* **4** see JABBER *v.* 1.

gasbag /gásbag/ *n.* **1** a container of gas, esp. for holding the gas for a balloon or airship. **2** *sl.* an idle talker.
■ **2** see *talker* (TALK).

/..../ **pronunciation**	● **part of speech**
□ **phrases, idioms, and compounds**	
□□ **derivatives**	■ **synonym section**
cross-references appear in SMALL CAPITALS or *italics*	

Gascon /gáskən/ n. **1** a native of Gascony, a region of France. **2** (**gascon**) a braggart. [F f. L *Vasco -onis*]

gaseous /gáseeəs, gáshəs/ adj. of or like gas. □□ **gaseousness** n.

gash¹ /gash/ n. & v. ● n. **1** a long and deep slash, cut, or wound. **2 a** a cleft such as might be made by a slashing cut. **b** the act of making such a cut. ● v.tr. make a gash in; cut. [var. of ME *garse* f. OF *garcer* scarify, perh. ult. f. Gk *kharassō*]
■ n. **1** cut, slash, wound, incision, laceration. **2 a** score, slit, groove, split, cleft. **b** cut, slash, slice. ● v. cut, slash, lacerate, wound; score, incise, slit, groove, split, *literary* cleave.

gash² /gash/ adj. *Brit. sl.* spare; extra. [20th-c. Naut. sl.: orig. unkn.]

gasholder /gás-hōldər/ n. a large receptacle for storing gas.

gasify /gásifī/ v.tr. & intr. (**-ies, -ied**) convert or be converted into gas. □□ **gasification** /-fikáyshən/ n.

gasket /gáskit/ n. **1** a sheet or ring of rubber, etc., shaped to seal the junction of metal surfaces. **2** a small cord securing a furled sail to a yard. □ **blow a gasket** *sl.* lose one's temper. [perh. f. F *garcette* thin rope (orig. little girl)]

gaskin /gáskin/ n. the hinder part of a horse's thigh. [perh. erron. f. GALLIGASKINS]

gaslight /gáslīt/ n. **1** a jet of burning gas, usu. heating a mantle, to provide light. **2** light emanating from this.
■ see LIGHT¹ n. 2.

gasolene var. of GASOLINE.

gasoline /gásəleen/ n. (also **gasolene**) a volatile flammable liquid blended from petroleum and natural gas and used as a fuel. [GAS + -OL² + -INE⁴, -ENE]

gasometer /gasómitər/ n. *Brit.* a large tank in which gas is stored for distribution by pipes to users. [F *gazomètre* f. *gaz* gas + *-mètre* -METER]

gasp /gasp/ v. & n. ● v. **1** intr. catch one's breath with an open mouth as in exhaustion or astonishment. **2** intr. (foll. by *for*) strain to obtain by gasping (*gasped for air*). **3** tr. (often foll. by *out*) utter with gasps. ● n. a convulsive catching of breath. □ **at one's last gasp 1** at the point of death. **2** exhausted. [ME f. ON *geispa*: cf. *geip* idle talk]
■ v. **1** pant, catch one's breath, puff, huff, heave, wheeze. **2** (*gasp for*) gulp for, fight for, strain for. ● n. snort, puff, gulp, huff, heave, wheeze. □ **at one's last gasp 1** at death's door, on one's deathbed, with one foot in the grave, on one's last legs, *in extremis*, on the way out. **2** see *exhausted* (EXHAUST v. 2).

gasper /gáspər/ n. **1** a person who gasps. **2** *Brit. sl.* a cigarette.

gasser /gásər/ n. **1** *colloq.* an idle talker. **2** *sl.* a very attractive or impressive person or thing.

gassy /gásee/ adj. (**gassier, gassiest**) **1 a** of or like gas. **b** full of gas. **2** *colloq.* (of talk, etc.) pointless; verbose. □□ **gassiness** n.

gasthaus /gáast-hows/ n. a small inn or hotel in German-speaking countries. [G f. *Gast* GUEST + *Haus* HOUSE]

gastrectomy /gastréktəmee/ n. (pl. **-ies**) a surgical operation in which the whole or part of the stomach is removed. [GASTRO- + -ECTOMY]

gastric /gástrik/ adj. of the stomach. □ **gastric flu** a popular name for an intestinal disorder of unknown cause. **gastric juice** a thin clear virtually colorless acid fluid secreted by the stomach glands and active in promoting digestion. [mod.L *gastricus* f. Gk *gastēr gast(e)ros* stomach]

gastritis /gastrítis/ n. inflammation of the lining of the stomach.

gastro- /gástrō/ comb. form (also **gastr-** before a vowel) stomach. [Gk *gastēr gast(e)ros* stomach]

gastroenteric /gástrōentérik/ adj. of or relating to the stomach and intestines.

gastroenteritis /gástrō-éntərítis/ n. *Med.* inflammation of the stomach and intestines.

gastronome /gástrənōm/ n. a gourmet. [F f. *gastronomie* GASTRONOMY]
■ see GOURMET.

gastronomy /gastrónəmee/ n. the practice, study, or art of eating and drinking well. □□ **gastronomic** /gástrənómik/ adj. **gastronomical** adj. **gastronomically** adv. [F *gastronomie* f. Gk *gastronomia* (as GASTRO-, *-nomia* f. *nomos* law)]

gastropod /gástrəpod/ n. any mollusk of the class Gastropoda that moves along by means of a large muscular foot, e.g., a snail, slug, etc. □□ **gastropodous** /gastrópədəs/ adj. [F *gastéropode* f. mod.L *gasteropoda* (as GASTRO-, Gk *pous podos* foot)]

gastroscope /gástrəskōp/ n. an optical instrument used for inspecting the interior of the stomach.

gastrula /gástrələ/ n. (pl. **gastrulae** /-lee/) *Zool.* an embryonic stage developing from the blastula. [mod.L f. Gk *gastēr gast(e)ros* belly]

gasworks /gáswərks/ n. a place where gas is manufactured and processed.

gat¹ /gat/ n. *sl.* a revolver or other firearm. [abbr. of GATLING]

gat² /gat/ archaic past of GET v.

gate¹ /gayt/ n. & v. ● n. **1** a barrier, usu. hinged, used to close an opening made for entrance and exit through a wall, fence, tollbooth, etc. **2** such an opening, esp. in the wall of a city, enclosure, or large building. **3** a means of entrance or exit. **4** a numbered place of access to aircraft at an airport. **5** a mountain pass. **6** an arrangement of slots into which the gear lever of a motor vehicle moves to engage the required gear. **7** a device for holding the frame of a photographic film momentarily in position behind the lens of a camera or projector. **8 a** an electrical signal that causes or controls the passage of other signals. **b** an electrical circuit with an output which depends on the combination of several inputs. **9** a device regulating the passage of water in a lock, etc. **10 a** the number of people entering by payment at the gates of a sports stadium, etc. **b** (in full **gate money**) the proceeds taken for admission. **11** *Brit. sl.* the mouth. **12** *sl.* dismissal. **13** = *starting gate*. ● v.tr. **1** *Brit.* confine to college or school entirely or after certain hours. **2** (as **gated** adj.) (of a road) having a gate or gates to control the movement of traffic or animals. [OE *gæt, geat*, pl. *gatu*, f. Gmc]
■ n. **2, 3** gateway, opening, entrance, exit, access; see also MOUTH n. 2a, b. **5** see GORGE n. 1.
10 a admission(s), attendance, crowd, audience, assemblage. **b** see TAKE n. **12** see *dismissal* (DISMISS).

gate² /gayt/ n. (prec. or prefixed by a name) *Brit.* a street (*Westgate*). [ME f. ON *gata*, f. Gmc]

-gate /gayt/ suffix forming nouns denoting an actual or alleged scandal comparable in some way to the Watergate scandal of 1972 (*Irangate*). [f. (WATER)GATE]

gateau /gátō, gaa-/ n. (pl. **gateaus** or **gateaux** /-tōz/) any of various rich cakes, usu. containing cream or fruit. [F *gâteau* cake]

gatecrasher /gáytkrashər/ n. an uninvited guest at a party, etc. □□ **gatecrash** v.tr. & intr.
■ see INTRUDER.

gatefold /gáytfōld/ n. a page in a book or magazine, etc., that folds out to be larger than the page format.

gatehouse /gáyt-hows/ n. **1** a house standing by a gateway, esp. to a large house or park. **2** *hist.* a room over a city gate, often used as a prison. **3** a building in which the controls of a lock, dam, drawbridge, etc., are situated.

gatekeeper /gáytkeepər/ n. **1** an attendant at a gate, controlling entrance and exit. **2** any of several large brown species of butterfly, esp. *Maniola tithonus*, frequenting hedgerows and woodland.
■ **1** see PORTER².

gateleg /gáytleg/ n. (in full **gateleg table**) a table with drop leaves supported by legs swung open like a gate. □□ **gatelegged** adj.

gateman /gáytmən/ n. (pl. **-men**) = GATEKEEPER 1.

gatepost /gáytpōst/ n. a post on which a gate is hung or against which it shuts. □ **between you and me and the gatepost** in strict confidence.
■ □ **between you and me and the gatepost** between you and me, between ourselves, entre nous, in (strict) confidence.

gateway /gáytway/ n. **1** an entrance with or opening for a gate. **2** a frame or structure built over a gate. **3** an entrance or exit.

gather /gáthər/ v. & n. ● v. **1** tr. & intr. bring or come together; assemble; accumulate. **2** tr. (usu. foll. by *up*) **a** bring together from scattered places or sources. **b** take up together from the ground, a surface, etc. **c** draw into a smaller compass. **3** tr. acquire by gradually collecting; amass. **4** tr. **a** pick a quantity of (flowers, etc.). **b** collect (grain, etc.) as a harvest. **5** tr. (often foll. by *that* + clause) infer or understand. **6** tr. be subjected to or affected by the accumulation or increase of (*unread books gathering dust*; *gather speed*; *gather strength*). **7** tr. (often foll. by *up*) summon up (one's thoughts, energy, etc.) for a purpose. **8** tr. gain or recover (one's breath). **9** tr. **a** draw (material, or one's brow) together in folds or wrinkles. **b** pucker or draw together (part of a dress) by running a thread through. **10** intr. come to a head; develop a purulent swelling. ● n. (in *pl.*) a part of a garment that is gathered or drawn in. □ **gather way** (of a ship) begin to move. □□ **gatherer** n. [OE *gaderian* f. WG]
■ v. **1** collect, assemble, muster, convene, meet, forgather, get *or* come together, congregate, group; heap *or* pile (up), stockpile, stock, accumulate, amass, assemble, bring together. **2 a** collect, assemble, muster, get *or* bring *or* draw together. **3** acquire, collect, accumulate, amass, garner, glean. **4 a** see PICK¹ v. 2. **b** collect, harvest, reap, glean. **5** understand, infer, deduce, conclude, be led to believe, take it; hear. **6** gain, acquire, accumulate, pick up, increase. **9 a** draw *or* pull together, contract, pleat, tuck, fold; see also WRINKLE v. 1. **b** shirr, ruffle, pucker. ● n. (*gathers*) pleats, folds, ruffles, tucks.

gathering /gáthəring/ n. **1** an assembly or meeting. **2** a purulent swelling. **3** a group of leaves taken together in bookbinding.
■ **1** assembly, meeting, convocation, convention, congress, assemblage, rally, conclave, meet, conference, *colloq.* get-together.

Gatling /gátling/ n. (in full **Gatling gun**) a machine gun with clustered barrels. [R. J. *Gatling*, Amer. inventor d. 1903]

gator /gáytər/ n. (also **gater**) *colloq.* an alligator.

GATT /gat/ abbr. (also **Gatt**) General Agreement on Tariffs and Trade.

gauche /gōsh/ adj. **1** lacking ease or grace; socially awkward. **2** tactless. □□ **gauchely** adv. **gaucheness** n. [F, = left-handed, awkward]
■ **1** see AWKWARD 2. **2** see TACTLESS.

gaucherie /gṓshəree/ n. **1** gauche manners. **2** a gauche action. [F]

gaucho /gówchō/ n. (pl. **-os**) a cowboy from the S. American pampas. [Sp. f. Quechua]

gaud /gawd/ n. a gaudy thing; a showy ornament. [perh. through AF f. OF *gaudir* rejoice f. L *gaudēre*]

gaudy¹ /gáwdee/ adj. (**gaudier, gaudiest**) tastelessly or extravagantly bright or showy. □□ **gaudily** adv. **gaudiness** n. [prob. f. GAUD + -Y¹]
■ garish, flashy, loud, ostentatious, florid, showy, tawdry, raffish, vulgar, crude, brummagem, meretricious, tinselly, chintzy, trashy, tasteless, *colloq.* tarty, *sl.* glitzy.

gaudy² /gáwdee/ n. (pl. **-ies**) *Brit.* an annual feast or entertainment, esp. a college dinner for graduates, etc. [L *gaudium* joy or *gaude* imper. of *gaudēre* rejoice]

gauge /gayj/ n. & v. (also **gage**) ● n. **1** a standard measure to which certain things must conform, esp.: **a** the measure of the capacity or contents of a barrel. **b** the fineness of a textile. **c** the diameter of a bullet. **d** the thickness of sheet metal. **2** any of various instruments for measuring or determining this, or for measuring length, thickness, or other dimensions or properties. **3** the distance between a pair of rails or the wheels on one axle. **4** the capacity, extent, or scope of something. **5** a means of estimating; a criterion or test. **6** a graduated instrument measuring the force or quantity of rainfall, stream, tide, wind, etc. **7** *Naut.* a relative position with respect to the wind. ● v.tr. **1** measure exactly (esp. objects of standard size). **2** determine the capacity or content of. **3** estimate or form a judgment of (a person, temperament, situation, etc.). **4** make uniform; bring to a standard size or shape. □ **gauge pressure** the amount by which

a pressure exceeds that of the atmosphere. **take the gauge of** estimate. □□ **gaugeable** adj. **gauger** n. [ME f. ONF *gauge, gauger*, of unkn. orig.]
■ n. **1** yardstick, benchmark, measure, rule, pattern, guide. **4** scope, capacity, amount, extent, measure, size, dimension(s), magnitude, degree, limit. **5** criterion, standard, yardstick, measure, touchstone, model, guideline, guide, rule, norm, example; test. ● v. **1, 2** measure, calculate, compute, figure, reckon, determine, weigh. **3** judge, evaluate, appraise, assess, rate, estimate, take the gauge of; guess. **4** standardize, regularize.

Gaul /gawl/ n. a native or inhabitant of ancient Gaul. [*Gaul* the country f. F *Gaule* f. Gmc]

gauleiter /gówlītər/ n. **1** an official governing a district under Nazi rule. **2** a local or petty tyrant. [G f. *Gau* administrative district + *Leiter* leader]

Gaulish /gáwlish/ adj. & n. ● adj. of or relating to the ancient Gauls. ● n. their language.

Gaullism /gṓlizm, gáw-/ n. **1** the principles and policies of Charles de Gaulle, French military and political leader (d. 1970), characterized by their conservatism, nationalism, and advocacy of centralized government. **2** adherence to these. □□ **Gaullist** n. [F *Gaullisme*]

gault /gawlt/ n. *Geol. Brit.* **1** a series of clay and marl beds between the upper and lower greensand in S. England. **2** clay obtained from these beds. [16th c.: orig. unkn.]

gaunt /gawnt/ adj. **1** lean; haggard. **2** grim or desolate in appearance. □□ **gauntly** adv. **gauntness** n. [ME: orig. unkn.]
■ **1** lean, thin, scrawny, skinny, scraggy, haggard, rawboned, bony, angular, skeletal, cadaverous, hollow-cheeked, spare, pinched. **2** grim, dreary, dismal, bleak, deserted, forlorn, desolate, bare, stark, harsh, hostile, unfriendly, inimical, forbidding.

gauntlet¹ /gáwntlit/ n. **1** a stout glove with a long loose wrist. **2** *hist.* an armored glove. **3** the part of a glove covering the wrist. **4** a challenge (esp. in **throw down the gauntlet**). [ME f. OF *gantelet* dimin. of *gant* glove f. Gmc]

gauntlet² /gáwntlit/ n. (also **gantlet** /gánt-/) □ **run the gauntlet 1** be subjected to harsh criticism. **2** pass between two rows of people and receive blows from them, as a punishment or ordeal. [earlier *gantlope* f. Sw. *gatlopp* f. *gata* lane, *lopp* course, assim. to GAUNTLET¹]

gauntry var. of GANTRY 3.

gaur /gowr/ n. a wild species of E. Indian cattle, *Bos gaurus*. [Hind.]

gauss /gows/ n. (pl. same or **gausses**) a unit of magnetic induction, equal to one ten-thousandth of a tesla. ¶ Abbr.: G. [K. *Gauss*, Ger. mathematician d. 1855]

Gaussian distribution /gówseeən/ n. *Statistics* = *normal distribution*. [as GAUSS]

gauze /gawz/ n. **1** a thin transparent fabric of silk, cotton, etc. **2** a fine mesh of wire, etc. **3** a slight haze. [F *gaze* f. *Gaza* in Palestine]

gauzy /gáwzee/ adj. (**gauzier, gauziest**) **1** like gauze; thin and translucent. **2** flimsy; delicate. □□ **gauzily** adv. **gauziness** n.
■ see FILMY 1.

gave past of GIVE.

gavel /gávəl/ n. & v. ● n. a small hammer used by an auctioneer, or for calling a meeting, courtroom, etc., to order. ● v. (**gaveled, gaveling**; also **gavelled, gavelling**) **1** intr. use a gavel. **2** tr. (often foll. by *down*) end (a meeting) or dismiss (a speaker) by use of a gavel. [19th c.: orig. unkn.]

gavial /gáyveeəl/ n. (also **gharial** /gúreeəl/) a large crocodile of India, *Gavialis gangeticus*, having a long narrow snout widening at the nostrils. [Hind.]

gavotte /gəvót/ n. **1** an old French dance in moderately quick 4/4 time beginning on the third beat of the bar. **2** the music

---

/.../ pronunciation	● part of speech
□ phrases, idioms, and compounds	
□□ derivatives	■ synonym section
cross-references appear in SMALL CAPITALS or *italics*	

for this, or a piece of music in the rhythm of this as a movement in a suite. [F f. Prov. *gavoto* f. *Gavot* native of a region
in the Alps]

gawk /gawk/ *v. & n.* ● *v.intr. colloq.* stare stupidly. ● *n.* an
awkward or bashful person. □□ **gawkish** *adj.* [rel. to obs.
gaw gaze f. ON *gá* heed]
   ▪ *v.* stare, goggle, gape, *colloq.* rubberneck, *dial.* gawp.
   ● *n.* lout, churl, dolt, dunderhead, ignoramus, fool,
   simpleton, ass, clodhopper, oaf, bumpkin, boor,
   bungler, bumbler, *colloq.* galoot, lummox, *Brit. colloq.*
   clot, *sl.* clod, lug, *Austral. sl.* galah.

gawky /gáwkee/ *adj.* (**gawkier**, **gawkiest**) awkward or ungainly. □□ **gawkily** *adv.* **gawkiness** *n.*
   ▪ see CLUMSY 1.

gawp /gawp/ *v.intr. Brit. colloq.* stare stupidly or obtrusively.
   □□ **gawper** *n.* [earlier *gaup*, *galp* f. ME *galpen* yawn, rel. to
   YELP]

gay /gay/ *adj. & n.* ● *adj.* **1** lighthearted and carefree; mirthful. **2** characterized by cheerfulness or pleasure (*a gay life*).
3 a homosexual. **b** intended for or used by homosexuals (*a
gay bar*). ¶ Generally informal in use, but often favored by
esp. male homosexuals with ref. to themselves. **4** brightly
colored; showy, brilliant (*a gay scarf*). **5** *colloq.* dissolute;
immoral. ● *n.* a homosexual, esp. male. □□ **gayness** *n.* [ME
f. OF *gai*, of unkn. orig.]
   ▪ *adj.* **1** happy, jovial, lighthearted, debonair, cheerful,
   gleeful, bright, joyful, jubilant, high-spirited,
   gamesome, merry, mirthful, lively, carefree, vivacious,
   buoyant, effervescent, exuberant, bubbly, sparkling,
   colloq. chipper, *poet.* blithe. **2** see PLEASANT. **4** colorful,
   showy, bright, brilliant, vivid. **5** see DISSOLUTE.

gayal /gəyál/ *n.* a wild species of E. Indian cattle, *Bos frontalis.*
   [Hindi]

gayety var. of GAIETY.

gazania /gəzáyneeə/ *n.* any herbaceous plant of the genus
Gazania, with showy yellow or orange daisy-shaped flowers.
[18th c.: f. Theodore of *Gaza*, Greek scholar d. 1478]

gaze /gayz/ *v. & n.* ● *v.intr.* (foll. by *at*, *into*, *on*, *upon*, etc.)
look fixedly. ● *n.* a fixed or intent look. □□ **gazer** *n.* [ME:
orig. unkn.; cf. obs. *gaw* GAWK]
   ▪ *v.* gape, look; (*gaze at*) contemplate, regard, scrutinize,
   observe, watch, eye; see also STARE *v.* ● *n.* stare, look,
   goggle, fixed *or* intent *or* blank look.

gazebo /gəzeebō/ *n.* (*pl.* **-os** *or* **-oes**) a small building or
structure such as a summerhouse or turret, designed to give
a wide view. [perh. joc. f. GAZE, in imitation of L futures in
-ēbo: cf. LAVABO]

gazelle /gəzél/ *n.* any of various small graceful soft-eyed antelopes of Asia or Africa, esp. of the genus *Gazella*. [F prob.
f. Sp. *gacela* f. Arab. *ġazāl*]

gazette /gəzét/ *n. & v.* ● *n.* **1** a newspaper, esp. the official
one of an organization or institution (*University Gazette*). **2**
hist. a news sheet; a periodical publication giving current
events. **3** *Brit.* an official journal with a list of government
appointments, bankruptcies, and other public notices.
● *v.tr. Brit.* announce or publish in an official gazette. [F f.
It. *gazzetta* f. *gazeta*, a Venetian small coin]
   ▪ *n.* see JOURNAL 1.

gazetteer /gázitéer/ *n.* a geographical index or dictionary.
[earlier = journalist, for whom such an index was provided:
f. F *gazettier* f. It. *gazzettiere* (as GAZETTE)]

gazpacho /gəspaachō/ *n.* (*pl.* **-os**) a Spanish soup made with
tomatoes, oil, garlic, onions, etc., and served cold. [Sp.]

gazump /gəzúmp/ *v.tr.* (also *absol.*) *Brit. colloq.* **1** (of a seller)
raise the price of a property after having accepted an offer
by (an intending buyer). **2** swindle. □□ **gazumper** *n.* [20th
c.: orig. uncert.]

gazunder /gəzúndər/ *v.tr.* (also *absol.*) *Brit. colloq.* (of a
buyer) lower the amount of an offer made to (the seller) for
a property, esp. just before exchange of contracts. [GAZUMP
+ UNDER]

GB *abbr.* Great Britain.

Gd *symb. Chem.* the element gadolinium.

GDP *abbr.* gross domestic product.

GDR *abbr. hist.* German Democratic Republic.

Ge *symb. Chem.* the element germanium.

gear /geer/ *n. & v.* ● *n.* **1** (often in *pl.*) **a** a set of toothed
wheels that work together to transmit and control motion
from an engine, esp. to the road wheels of a vehicle. **b** a
mechanism for doing this. **2** a particular function or state of
adjustment of engaged gears (*low gear*; *second gear*). **3** a
mechanism of wheels, levers, etc., usu. for a special purpose
(*winding gear*). **4** a particular apparatus or mechanism, as
specified (*landing gear*). **5** equipment or tackle for a special
purpose. **6** *colloq.* **a** clothing, esp. when modern or fashionable. **b** possessions in general. **7** goods; household utensils.
8 rigging. **9** a harness for a draft animal. ● *v.* **1** *tr.* (foll. by
to) adjust or adapt to suit a special purpose or need. **2** *tr.*
(often foll. by *up*) equip with gears. **3** *tr.* (foll. by *up*) make
ready or prepared. **4** *tr.* put (machinery) in gear. **5** *intr.* **a**
Brit. be in gear. **b** (foll. by *with*) work smoothly with. □ **be
geared** (or **all geared**) **up** (often foll. by *for*, or *to* + infin.)
colloq. be ready or enthusiastic. **first** (or *Brit.* **bottom**) **gear**
the lowest gear in a series. **gear down** (or **up**) provide with
or shift into a low (or high) gear. **gear lever** *Brit.* = GEAR-
SHIFT. **high** (or **low**) **gear** a gear such that the driven end
of a transmission revolves faster (or slower) than the driving
end. **in gear** with a gear engaged. **out of gear 1** with no
gear engaged. **2** out of order. **top gear** the highest gear in
a series. [ME f. ON *gervi* f. Gmc]
   ▪ *n.* **1** (*gears*) **a** cogwheels. **b** gearbox. **4, 5** apparatus,
   mechanism, outfit, appliance; equipment, machinery,
   tackle, material. **6 a** clothing, clothes, garments, *colloq.*
   togs, *formal* apparel, attire, *joc.* habiliments, *sl.* duds,
   Brit. sl. clobber. **b** possessions, belongings, things,
   effects, chattels, goods, impedimenta, baggage,
   accoutrements, stuff, kit. **7** goods, materials, supplies,
   utensils, implements, tools, accoutrements,
   paraphernalia. ● *v.* **1** adjust, adapt, tailor, fit,
   accommodate, suit, alter. **3** (*gear up*) ready, make *or*
   get ready, set, equip, *colloq.* psych up; see also PREPARE
   3a. **5 b** (*gear with*) go together with, work well with,
   accord with, fit with. □ **be geared** (or **all geared**) **up**
   see READY *adj.* 1, 2.

gearbox /geerboks/ *n.* **1** the casing that encloses a set of
gears. **2** a set of gears with its casing, esp. in a motor vehicle;
a transmission.

gearing /geering/ *n.* **1** a set or arrangement of gears in a machine. **2** *Brit. Commerce* = LEVERAGE 5.

gearshift /geershift/ *n.* a lever used to engage or change gear,
esp. in a motor vehicle.

gearwheel /geerhweel, -weel/ *n.* **1** a toothed wheel in a set
of gears. **2** (in a bicycle) the cogwheel driven directly by the
chain.

gecko /gékō/ *n.* (*pl.* **-os** *or* **-oes**) any of various house lizards
found in warm climates, with adhesive feet for climbing ver-
tical surfaces. [Malay *chichak*, etc., imit. of its cry]

gee¹ /jee/ *int.* (also **gee whiz** /wiz/) *colloq.* a mild expression
of surprise, discovery, etc. [perh. abbr. of JESUS]

gee² /jee/ *int.* (often foll. by *up*) a command to a horse, etc.,
esp. to turn to the right or to go faster. [17th c.: orig. unkn.]

gee³ /jee/ *n. sl.* (usu. in *pl.*) a thousand dollars. [the letter *G*,
as initial of GRAND]

gee-gee /jéejee/ *n. Brit. colloq.* a horse. [orig. a child's word,
f. GEE²]

geek¹ /geek/ *n. sl.* **1** a person who is socially inept or tediously
conventional; a dupe. **2** a carnival performer who bites the
heads off live chickens in performance. [var. of dial. *geck*
fool, dupe]

geek² /geek/ *n. Austral. sl.* a look. [E dial.]

geese *pl.* of GOOSE.

gee-string var. of G-STRING 2.

geezer /geezər/ *n. sl.* a person, esp. an old man. [dial. pronunc. of *guiser* mummer]
   ▪ see FELLOW 1.

Gehenna /gihénə/ *n.* **1** (in the New Testament) hell. **2** a
place of burning, torment, or misery. [eccl.L f. Gk f. Heb.
gē' hinnōm hell, orig. the valley of Hinnom near Jerusalem,
where children were sacrificed]

Geiger counter /gígər/ *n.* a device for measuring radioactivity by detecting and counting ionizing particles. [H. *Geiger*, Ger. physicist d. 1945]

geisha /gáyshə, gée-/ *n.* (*pl.* same or **geishas**) a Japanese hostess trained in entertaining men with dance and song. [Jap.]

Geissler tube /gíslər/ *n.* a sealed tube of glass or quartz with a central constriction, filled with vapor for the production of a luminous electrical discharge. [H. *Geissler*, Ger. mechanic d. 1879]

gel /jel/ *n. & v.* • *n.* **1** a semisolid colloidal suspension or jelly, of a solid dispersed in a liquid. **2** a gelatinous hairstyling preparation. **3** *Theatr.* a thin sheet of colored gelatin used to color stage lights. • *v.intr.* (**gelled, gelling**) form a gel. □□ **gelation** /jeláyshən/ *n.* [abbr. of GELATIN]
■ *v.* see SET¹ *v.* 11, 26.

gelatin /jélətin/ *n.* (also **gelatine** /-teen/) **1** a virtually colorless, tasteless, transparent, water-soluble protein derived from collagen and used in food preparation, photography, etc. **2** a similar substance derived from vegetable matter. □□ **gelatinize** /jilát'niz/ *v.tr. & intr.* **gelatinization** /jilát'nizáyshən/ *n.* [F *gélatine* f. It. *gelatina* f. *gelata* JELLY]

gelatinous /jilát'nəs/ *adj.* **1** of or like gelatin. **2** of a jelly-like consistency. □□ **gelatinously** *adv.*
■ **2** see THICK *adj.* 5a.

gelation /jiláyshən/ *n.* solidification by freezing. [L *gelatio* f. *gelare* freeze]

gelato /jəláatō/ *n.* a kind of Italian ice cream. [It.]

geld /geld/ *v.tr.* **1** deprive (usu. a male animal) of the ability to reproduce. **2** castrate or spay; excise the testicles or ovaries of. [ME f. ON *gelda* f. *geldr* barren f. Gmc]
■ see STERILIZE 2.

gelding /gélding/ *n.* a gelded animal, esp. a male horse. [ME f. ON *geldingr*: see GELD]

gelid /jélid/ *adj.* **1** icy; ice cold. **2** chilly; cool. [L *gelidus* f. *gelu* frost]
■ see COLD *adj.* 1.

gelignite /jélignīt/ *n.* an explosive made from nitroglycerine, cellulose nitrate, sodium or potassium nitrate, and wood pulp. [GELATIN + L *ignis* fire + -ITE¹]

gelly /jélee/ *n. Brit. sl.* gelignite. [abbr.]

gem /jem/ *n. & v.* • *n.* **1** a precious stone, esp. when cut and polished or engraved. **2** an object or person of great beauty or worth. • *v.tr.* (**gemmed, gemming**) adorn with or as with gems. □□ **gemlike** *adj.* **gemmy** *adj.* [ME f. OF *gemme* f. L *gemma* bud, jewel]
■ *n.* **1** gemstone, jewel, precious stone, stone, *sl.* rock. **2** pearl, marvel, treasure; nonpareil, ideal, prize, masterpiece, chef-d'œuvre. • *v.* bejewel, bedeck, decorate, adorn.

Gemara /gimáarə, -máwrə, -maaraá/ *n.* a rabbinical commentary on the Mishnah, forming the second part of the Talmud. [Aram. *gᵉmārâ* completion]

geminal /jéminəl/ *adj. Chem.* (of molecules) having two functional groups attached to the same atom. □□ **geminally** *adv.* [as GEMINATE + -AL]

geminate *adj. & v.* • *adj.* /jéminət/ combined in pairs. • *v.tr.* /jéminayt/ **1** double; repeat. **2** arrange in pairs. □□ **gemination** *n.* [L *geminatus* past part. of *geminare* f. *geminus* twin]

Gemini /jémini, -nee/ *n.* **1** a constellation, traditionally regarded as contained in the figures of twins. **2 a** the third sign of the zodiac (the Twins). **b** a person born when the sun is in this sign. □□ **Geminean** /jémineéən, -níən/ *n. & adj.* [ME f. L, = twins]

gemma /jémə/ *n.* (*pl.* **gemmae** /-mee/) a small cellular body in cryptogams that separates from the mother plant and starts a new one; an asexual spore. [L: see GEM]

gemmation /jemáyshən/ *n.* reproduction by gemmae. [F f. *gemmer* to bud, *gemme* bud]

gemmiferous /jemífərəs/ *adj.* **1** producing precious stones. **2** bearing buds. [L *gemmifer* (as GEMMA, -FEROUS)]

gemmiparous /jemípərəs/ *adj.* of or propagating by gemmation. [mod.L *gemmiparus* f. L *gemma* bud + *parere* bring forth]

gemmule /jémyōōl/ *n.* an encysted embryonic cell cluster in sponges. [F *gemmule* or L *gemmula* little bud (as GEM)]

gemology /jemóləjee/ *n.* (also **gemmology**) the study of gems. □□ **gemologist** or **gemmologist** *n.* [L *gemma* gem + -LOGY]

gemstone /jémstōn/ *n.* a precious stone used as a gem.
■ see JEWEL *n.* 1a.

gemütlich /gəmóōtlikh/ *adj.* **1** pleasant and comfortable. **2** genial; agreeable. [G]

Gen. *abbr.* **1** General. **2** Genesis (Old Testament).

gen /jen/ *n. & v. Brit. sl.* • *n.* information. • *v.tr. & intr.* (**genned, genning**) (foll. by *up*) provide with or obtain information. [perh. f. first syll. of *general information*]

-gen /jən/ *comb. form* **1** *Chem.* that which produces (*hydrogen*; *antigen*). **2** *Bot.* growth (*endogen*; *exogen*; *acrogen*). [F *-gène* f. Gk *-genēs* -born, of a specified kind f. *gen-* root of *gignomai* be born, become]

gendarme /zhondaárm/ *n.* **1** a police officer, esp. in France. **2** a soldier, mounted or on foot, employed in police duties, esp. in France. **3** a rock tower on a mountain, occupying and blocking an arête. [F f. *gens d'armes* men of arms]
■ **1** see *police officer*.

gendarmerie /zhondaárməree/ *n.* **1** a force of gendarmes. **2** the headquarters of such a force.

gender /jéndər/ *n.* **1 a** the grammatical classification of nouns and related words, roughly corresponding to the two sexes and sexlessness. **b** each of the classes of nouns (see MASCULINE, FEMININE, NEUTER, COMMON *adj.* 6). **2** (of nouns and related words) the property of belonging to such a class. **3** *colloq.* a person's sex. [ME f. OF *gendre* ult. f. L GENUS]

gene /jeen/ *n.* a unit of heredity composed of DNA or RNA and forming part of a chromosome, etc., that determines a particular characteristic of an individual. □ **gene therapy** *Med.* the introduction of normal genes into cells in place of defective or missing ones in order to correct genetic disorders. [G *Gen*: see -GEN]

genealogical /jeeneeəlójikəl/ *adj.* **1** of or concerning genealogy. **2** tracing family descent. □ **genealogical tree** a chart like an inverted branching tree showing the descent of a family or of an animal species. □□ **genealogically** *adv.* [F *généalogique* f. Gk *genealogikos* (as GENEALOGY)]

genealogy /jeeneeáləjee/ *n.* (*pl.* **-ies**) **1 a** a line of descent traced continuously from an ancestor. **b** an account or exposition of this. **2** the study and investigation of lines of descent. **3** a plant's or animal's line of development from earlier forms. □□ **genealogist** *n.* **genealogize** *v.tr. & intr.* [ME f. OF *genealogie* f. LL *genealogia* f. Gk *genealogia* f. *genea* race]
■ **1** see LINEAGE.

genera *pl.* of GENUS.

general /jénərəl/ *adj. & n.* • *adj.* **1 a** completely or almost universal. **b** including or affecting all or nearly all parts or cases of things. **2** prevalent; widespread; usual. **3** not partial, particular, local, or sectional. **4** not limited in application; relating to whole classes or all cases. **5** including points common to the individuals of a class and neglecting the differences (*a general term*). **6** not restricted or specialized (*general knowledge*). **7** a roughly corresponding or adequate. **b** sufficient for practical purposes. **8** not detailed (*a general resemblance*; *a general idea*). **9** vague; indefinite (*spoke only in general terms*). **10** chief or principal; having overall authority (*general manager*; *Secretary General*). • *n.* **1 a** an army officer ranking next above lieutenant general. **b** = *brigadier general, lieutenant general, major general*. **2** a commander of an army. **3** a tactician or strategist of specified merit (*a great general*). **4** the head of a religious order, e.g., of the Jesuits or Dominicans or the Salvation Army. **5** (prec. by *the*) *archaic* the public. □ **as a general rule** in most cases. **General American** a form of US speech not markedly dialectal or

/.../ **pronunciation**   ● **part of speech**
□ **phrases, idioms, and compounds**
□□ **derivatives**   ■ **synonym section**
cross-references appear in SMALL CAPITALS or *italics*

regional. **general delivery** the delivery of letters to callers at a post office. **general election** the election of representatives to a legislature from constituencies throughout the country, esp. a final election between winners of earlier primary elections. **general headquarters** the headquarters of a military commander. **general meeting** a meeting open to all the members of a society, etc. **general of the army** (or **air force**) the officer of the highest rank in the army or air force. **general practice** the work of a general practitioner. **general practitioner** a doctor working in the community and treating cases of all kinds in the first instance, as distinct from a consultant or specialist. **general quarters** a condition of full readiness for combat on a warship. **general staff** the staff assisting a military commander in planning and administration. **general store** a store, usu. located in a rural area, that carries a wide variety of items, as food, clothing, housewares, etc., without being divided into departments. **general strike** a strike of workers in all or most trades. **General Synod** the highest governing body in the Church of England. **in general 1** as a normal rule; usually. **2** for the most part. □□ **generalness** n. [ME f. OF f. L *generalis* (as GENUS)]

▪ *adj.* **1** extensive, comprehensive, worldwide, global, ubiquitous; accepted, public, popular, shared, communal, well-known; see also UNIVERSAL *adj.* **2** common, usual, normal, regular, prevailing, prevalent, widespread, customary, habitual, everyday, familiar. **3** mixed, assorted, heterogeneous; see also MISCELLANEOUS. **4** inclusive, all-inclusive, nonexclusive, unrestricted; overall, across-the-board. **5** see SWEEPING *adj.* 1. **6** unspecialized, nonspecialized, encyclopedic, broad, comprehensive, catholic; sweeping, panoramic. **8, 9** vague, indefinite, ill-defined, loose, inexact, imprecise, unspecific, undetailed, generalized; overall, approximate, rough. □ **general practitioner** see DOCTOR *n.* 1a. **in general** see *usually* (USUAL).

generalissimo /jénərəlísimō/ *n.* (*pl.* **-os**) the commander of a combined military force in some countries consisting of army, navy, and air force units. [It., superl. of *generale* GENERAL]

generalist /jénərəlist/ *n.* a person competent in several different fields or activities (opp. SPECIALIST).

generality /jénərálitee/ *n.* (*pl.* **-ies**) **1** a statement or principle, etc.; having general validity or force. **2** applicability to a whole class of instances. **3** vagueness; lack of detail. **4** the state of being general. **5** (foll. by *of*) the main body or majority. [F *généralité* f. LL *generalitas -tatis* (as GENERAL)]

▪ **1** principle, law; generalization. **2** see *prevalence* (PREVALENT). **5** (*the generality of*) the great majority of, the vast majority of, the greater part of, most of.

generalization /jénərəlizáyshən/ *n.* **1** a general notion or proposition obtained by inference from (esp. limited or inadequate) particular cases. **2** the act or an instance of generalizing. [F *généralisation* (as GENERALIZE)]

generalize /jénərəliz/ *v.* **1** *intr.* **a** speak in general or indefinite terms. **b** form general principles or notions. **2** *tr.* reduce to a general statement, principle, or notion. **3** *tr.* **a** give a general character to. **b** call by a general name. **4** *tr.* infer (a law or conclusion) by induction. **5** *tr. Math. & Philos.* express in a general form; extend the application of. **6** *tr.* (in painting) render only the typical characteristics of. **7** *tr.* bring into general use. □□ **generalizable** *adj.* **generalizability** *n.* **generalizer** *n.* [F *généraliser* (as GENERAL)]

generally /jénərəlee/ *adv.* **1** usually; in most cases. **2** in a general sense; without regard to particulars or exceptions (*generally speaking*). **3** for the most part; extensively (*not generally known*). **4** in most respects (*they were generally well-behaved*).

▪ **1** usually, commonly, ordinarily, customarily, habitually, normally, typically; on average, as a rule, by and large, in general, for the most part, mostly, mainly, on the whole, predominantly. **2** roughly, broadly, loosely, approximately, unspecifically. **3** largely, extensively, widely. **4** see MAINLY.

generalship /jénərəlship/ *n.* **1** the art or practice of exercising

military command. **2** military skill; strategy. **3** skillful management; tact; diplomacy.

▪ **2** see TACTICS 1.

generate /jénərayt/ *v.tr.* **1** bring into existence; produce; evolve. **2** produce (electricity). **3** *Math.* (of a point or line or surface conceived as moving) make (a line or surface or solid). **4** *Math. & Linguistics* produce (a set or sequence of items) by the formulation and application of precise criteria. □□ **generable** /-rəbəl/ *adj.* [L *generare* beget (as GENUS)]

▪ **1** create, originate, initiate, invent, devise, coin; produce, evolve, develop, form, forge, make, manufacture; give rise to, bring about, engender, *literary* beget. **4** yield, produce, give.

generation /jénəráyshən/ *n.* **1** all the people born at a particular time, regarded collectively (*my generation; the next generation*). **2** a single step in descent or pedigree (*have known them for three generations*). **3** a stage in (esp. technological) development (*fourth-generation computers*). **4** the average time in which children are ready to take the place of their parents (usu. figured at about 30 years). **5** production by natural or artificial process, esp. the production of electricity or heat. **6 a** procreation; the propagation of species. **b** the act of begetting or being begotten. □ **generation gap** differences of outlook or opinion between those of different generations. **Generation X** term used for people born from about 1965 to 1975 (fr. a novel by Douglas Coupland). □□ **generational** *adj.* [ME f. OF f. L *generatio -onis* (as GENERATE)]

▪ **1** age (group), cohort; contemporaries, peers. **6 a** propagation, procreation, production, reproduction; breeding, spawning. **b** mothering, fathering, siring, *literary* begetting; conception.

generative /jénərətiv, -raytiv/ *adj.* **1** of or concerning procreation. **2** able to produce; productive. □ **generative grammar** a set of rules whereby permissible sentences may be generated from the elements of a language. [ME f. OF *generatif* or LL *generativus* (as GENERATE)]

▪ **2** see FERTILE 3.

generator /jénəraytər/ *n.* **1** a machine for converting mechanical into electrical energy. **2** an apparatus for producing gas, steam, etc. **3** a person who generates an idea, etc.; an originator.

generic /jinérik/ *adj.* **1** characteristic of or relating to a class; general, not specific or special. **2** *Biol.* characteristic of or belonging to a genus. **3** (of goods, esp. a drug) having no brand name; not protected by a registered trade mark. □□ **generically** *adv.* [F *générique* f. L GENUS]

generous /jénərəs/ *adj.* **1** giving or given freely. **2** magnanimous; noble-minded; unprejudiced. **3 a** ample; abundant; copious (*a generous portion*). **b** (of wine) rich and full. □□ **generosity** /-rósitee/ *n.* **generously** *adv.* **generousness** *n.* [OF *genereus* f. L *generosus* noble, magnanimous (as GENUS)]

▪ **1** bountiful, charitable, lavish, openhanded, free, liberal, unstinting, ungrudging, munificent, handsome, *poet.* bounteous. **2** magnanimous, benevolent, charitable, beneficent, benevolent, bighearted, unselfish, forgiving, humanitarian, philanthropic, humane, kindly, noble, noble-minded, good; disinterested, unprejudiced, unbiased, liberal-minded, broad-minded, tolerant, liberal. **3 a** ample, abundant, copious, plentiful, full, lavish, overflowing, bountiful, liberal; large, substantial, sizable, substantial, considerable, biggish, big.

genesis /jénisis/ *n.* **1** the origin, or mode of formation or generation, of a thing. **2** (**Genesis**) the first book of the Old Testament, with an account of the creation of the world. [L f. Gk f. *gen-* be produced, root of *gignomai* become]

▪ **1** see ORIGIN 1.

genet /jénit/ *n.* (also **genette** /jinét/) **1** any catlike mammal of the genus *Genetta*, native to Africa and S. Europe, with spotted fur and a long ringed bushy tail. **2** the fur of the genet. [ME f. OF *genete* f. Arab. *jarnait*]

genetic /jinétik/ *adj.* **1** of genetics or genes; inherited. **2** of, in, or concerning origin; causal. □ **genetic code** *Biochem.*

the means by which genetic information is stored as sequences of nucleotide bases in the chromosomal DNA. **genetic engineering** the deliberate modification of the characters of an organism by the manipulation of DNA and the transformation of certain genes. **genetic fingerprinting** (or **profiling**) the analysis of characteristic patterns in DNA as a means of identifying individuals. □□ **genetically** *adv.* [GENESIS after *antithetic*]

■ **1** see HEREDITARY 1.

genetics /jinétiks/ *n.pl.* (usu. treated as *sing.*) the study of heredity and the variation of inherited characteristics. □□ **geneticist** /-tisist/ *n.*

genette var. of GENET.

geneva /jineevə/ *n.* Dutch gin. [Du. *genever* f. OF *genevre* f. L *juniperus*, with assim. to the place name *Geneva*]

Geneva bands /jineevə/ *n.pl.* two white cloth strips attached to the collar of some Protestants' clerical dress. [*Geneva* in Switzerland, where orig. worn by Calvinists]

Geneva Convention /jineevə/ *n.* an international agreement first made at Geneva in 1864 and later revised, governing the status and treatment of prisoners and the sick, wounded, and dead in battle.

genial[1] /jeeneeəl/ *adj.* **1** jovial; sociable; kindly; cheerful. **2** (of the climate) mild and warm; conducive to growth. **3** cheering; enlivening. □□ **geniality** /-neeálitee/ *n.* **genially** *adv.* [L *genialis* (as GENIUS)]

■ **1** jovial, good-humored, cheerful, cheery, convivial, sociable, affable, amiable, cordial, warm, pleasant, nice, friendly, congenial, agreeable, hospitable, good-natured, kindly, kind. **2** see MILD 3. **3** cheering, good, enlivening, heartening, reassuring, uplifting, comforting, gladdening, refreshing.

genial[2] /jinfəl/ *adj.* *Anat.* of or relating to the chin. [Gk *geneion* chin f. *genus* jaw]

genic /jeenik/ *adj.* of or relating to genes.

-genic /jénik/ *comb. form* forming adjectives meaning: **1** producing (*carcinogenic*; *pathogenic*). **2** well suited to (*photogenic*; *radiogenic*). **3** produced by (*iatrogenic*). □□ **-genically** *suffix* forming adverbs. [-GEN + -IC]

genie /jeenee/ *n.* (*pl.* usu. **genii** /jeenee-ī/) a jinnee, goblin, or familiar spirit of Arabian folklore. [F *génie* f. L GENIUS: cf. JINNI]

genii *pl.* of GENIE, GENIUS.

genista /jinístə/ *n.* any almost leafless shrub of the genus *Genista*, with a profusion of yellow pea-shaped flowers, e.g., dyer's broom. [L]

genital /jénit'l/ *adj. & n.* ● *adj.* of or relating to animal reproduction. ● *n.* (in *pl.*) the external reproductive organs. [OF *génital* or L *genitalis* f. *gignere genit-* beget]

■ *adj.* see SEXUAL. ● *n.* (*genitals*) genitalia, reproductive organs, sex organs, private parts, *colloq.* privates, parts.

genitalia /jénitáyleeə/ *n.pl.* the genitals. [L, neut. pl. of *genitalis*: see GENITAL]

genitive /jénitiv/ *n. & adj. Gram.* ● *n.* the case of nouns and pronouns (and words in grammatical agreement with them) corresponding to *of*, *from*, and other prepositions and indicating possession or close association. ● *adj.* of or in the genitive. □□ **genitival** /-tívəl/ *adj.* **genitivally** *adv.* [ME f. OF *genetif*, *-ive* or L *genitivus* f. *gignere genit-* beget]

genito- /jénitō/ *comb. form* genital.

genitourinary /jénitōyŏŏrineree/ *adj.* of the genital and urinary organs.

genius /jeenyəs/ *n.* (*pl.* **geniuses** or **genii** /-nee-ī/) **1** (*pl.* **geniuses**) **a** an exceptional intellectual or creative power or other natural ability or tendency. **b** a person having this. **2** the tutelary spirit of a person, place, institution, etc. **3** a person or spirit regarded as powerfully influencing a person for good or evil. **4** the prevalent feeling or associations, etc., of a nation, age, etc. [L (in sense 2) f. the root of *gignere* beget]

■ **1 a** intellect, intelligence, brilliance; ingenuity, wit, brain(s); talent, gift, knack, flair, aptitude, forte; faculty, capacity, ability, capability. **b** mastermind, master, great, giant, luminary; virtuoso, maestro,

adept, expert, wizard; *colloq.* brain, whiz, whiz kid, Einstein, maven.

genizah /gənéezə, -neezaá/ *n.* a room attached to a synagogue and housing damaged, discarded, or heretical books, etc., and sacred relics. [Heb. *genīzāh*, lit. hiding place f. *gānaz* hide, set aside]

genl. *abbr.* general.

Genoa jib *n.* (also **genoa**, **jenny**) a large jib or foresail used esp. on yachts.

genocide /jénəsīd/ *n.* the deliberate extermination of a people or nation. □□ **genocidal** /-síd'l/ *adj.* [Gk *genos* race + -CIDE]

■ see MURDER *n.* 1.

genome /jeenōm/ *n.* **1** the haploid set of chromosomes of an organism. **2** the genetic material of an organism. [GENE + CHROMOSOME]

genotype /jeenətīp/ *n. Biol.* the genetic constitution of an individual. □□ **genotypic** /-típik/ *adj.* [G *Genotypus* (as GENE, TYPE)]

-genous /jénəs/ *comb. form* forming adjectives meaning 'produced' (*endogenous*).

genre /zhónrə/ *n.* **1** a kind or style, esp. of art or literature (e.g., novel, drama, satire). **2** (in full **genre painting**) the painting of scenes from ordinary life. [F, = a kind (as GENDER)]

■ **1** style, kind, genus, sort, type, class, category, variety, brand, species.

gens /jenz/ *n.* (*pl.* **gentes** /jénteez/) **1** *Rom.Hist.* a group of families sharing a name and claiming a common origin. **2** *Anthropol.* a number of people sharing descent through the male line. [L, f. the root of *gignere* beget]

gent /jent/ *n. colloq.* (often *joc.*) **1** a gentleman. **2** (in *pl.*) *Brit.* (in shop titles) men (*gents' outfitters*). **3** (**the Gents**) *Brit. colloq.* a men's public toilet. [abbr. of GENTLEMAN]

genteel /jenteel/ *adj.* **1** affectedly or ostentatiously refined or stylish. **2** often *iron.* of or appropriate to the upper classes. □□ **genteelly** *adv.* **genteelness** *n.* [earlier *gentile*, readoption of F *gentil* GENTLE]

■ **1** overpolite, overrefined, pretentious, affected, pompous, snobbish, *colloq.* posh, la-di-da, snooty, stuck-up, esp. *Brit. sl.* toffee-nosed. **2** well-bred, county, high-class, upper-class, aristocratic, thoroughbred, blue-blooded, patrician, gracious, refined, polished, sophisticated, debonair, suave, urbane, cultivated, cultured, elegant; courtly, polite, civil, well-mannered, courteous, ceremonious, mannerly, proper, respectable, decorous, *colloq.* classy, upper-crust, *US colloq.* tony.

genteelism /jenteelizəm/ *n.* a word used because it is thought to be less vulgar than the commoner word (e.g., *perspire* for *sweat*).

gentes *pl.* of GENS.

gentian /jénshən/ *n.* **1** any plant of the genus *Gentiana* or *Gentianella*, found esp. in mountainous regions, and having usu. vivid blue flowers. **2** (in full **gentian bitter**) a liquor extracted from the root of the gentian. □ **gentian violet** a violet dye used as an antiseptic, esp. in the treatment of burns. [OE f. L *gentiana* f. *Gentius* king of Illyria]

gentile /jéntil/ *adj. & n.* ● *adj.* **1** (**Gentile**) not Jewish; heathen. **2** of or relating to a nation or tribe. **3** *Gram.* (of a word) indicating nationality. **4** (**Gentile**) (in the Mormon Church) not Mormon. ● *n.* **1** (**Gentile**) a person who is not Jewish. **2** *Gram.* a word indicating nationality. **3** (**Gentile**) (in the Mormon Church) a person who is not Mormon. [ME f. L *gentilis* f. *gens gentis* family: see GENS]

■ *adj.* **1** (Gentile) heathen, *sl. derog.* goyish. ● *n.* **1** (Gentile) heathen, *sl. derog.* goy.

gentility /jentílitee/ *n.* **1** social superiority. **2** good manners;

/.../ **pronunciation**	● **part of speech**
□ **phrases, idioms, and compounds**	
□□ **derivatives**	■ **synonym section**
cross-references appear in SMALL CAPITALS or *italics*	

habits associated with the upper class. **3** people of high-class birth. [ME f. OF *gentilité* (as GENTLE)]

■ **2** see PROPRIETY 2. **3** see *the upper crust* (UPPER[1]).

gentle /jént'l/ *adj.*, *v.*, & *n.* ● *adj.* (**gentler, gentlest**) **1** not rough; mild or kind, esp. in temperament. **2** moderate; not severe or drastic (*a gentle rebuke; a gentle breeze*). **3** (of birth, pursuits, etc.) honorable, of or fit for people of good social position. **4** quiet; requiring patience (*gentle art*). **5** *archaic* generous; courteous. ● *v.tr.* **1** make gentle or docile. **2** handle (a horse, etc.) firmly but gently. ● *n.* *archaic* a person of high social status. □□ **gentleness** *n.* **gently** *adv.* [ME f. OF *gentil* f. L *gentilis*: see GENTILE]

■ *adj.* **1** kind, kindly, mild, tender, thoughtful, patient, indulgent, benign, gracious, compassionate, humane, tenderhearted, merciful, lenient; quiet, calm, still, temperate, unruffled, untroubled, undisturbed, tranquil, restful, peaceful, pacific, placid, smooth, soothing. **2** moderate, soft, light; balmy. **3** honorable, noble, high. **5** see COURTEOUS. ● *v.* **1** see TAME *v.* 1.

gentlefolk /jént'lfōk/ *n.pl. literary* people of good family.

gentleman /jént'lmən/ *n.* (*pl.* **-men**) **1** a man (in polite or formal use). **2** a chivalrous or well-bred man. **3** a man of good social position or of wealth and leisure (*country gentleman*). **4** esp. *Brit.* a man of gentle birth attached to a royal household (*gentleman in waiting*). **5** (in *pl.* as a form of address) a male audience or the male part of an audience. □ **gentleman-at-arms** (in the UK) one of a sovereign's bodyguard. **gentleman farmer** a country gentleman who farms. **gentleman's** (or **-men's**) **agreement** one which is binding in honor but not legally enforceable. [GENTLE + MÁN after OF *gentilz hom*]

■ **1** see MAN *n.* 1. **3** see NOBLE *n.*

gentlemanly /jént'lmənlee/ *adj.* like a gentleman in looks or behavior; befitting a gentleman. □□ **gentlemanliness** *n.*

■ see *well-bred* (WELL[1]).

gentlewoman /jént'lwŏomən/ *n.* (*pl.* **-women**) *archaic* a woman of good birth or breeding.

■ see NOBLE *n.*

gentoo /jéntŏo/ *n.* a penguin, *Pygoscelis papua* of the Antarctic region, esp. abundant in the Falkland Islands. [perh. f. Anglo-Ind. *Gentoo* = Hindu, f. Port. *gentio* GENTILE]

gentrification /jéntrifikáyshən/ *n.* the social advancement of an inner urban area by the refurbishing of buildings and arrival of affluent middle-class residents, usu. displacing poorer inhabitants. □□ **gentrify** /-fī/ *v.tr.* (**-ies, -ied**).

gentry /jéntree/ *n.pl.* **1** (in aristocratic societies) the people next below the nobility in position and birth. **2** people, esp. a specific group of people (*these gentry*). [prob. f. obs. *gentrice* f. OF *genterise* var. of *gentelise* nobility f. *gentil* GENTLE]

■ **1** landowners, squirearchy; ladies, gentlemen, *literary* gentlefolk. **2** see PEOPLE *n.* 2.

genuflect /jényəflekt/ *v.intr.* bend the knee, esp. in worship or as a sign of respect. □□ **genuflection** /-flékshən/ *n.* (also *Brit.* **genuflexion**). **genuflector** *n.* [eccl.L *genuflectere genuflex-* f. L *genu* the knee + *flectere* bend]

■ see BEND[1] *v.* 8a.

genuine /jényŏo-in/ *adj.* **1** really coming from its stated, advertised, or reputed source. **2** properly so called; not sham. **3** purebred. **4** (of a person) free from affectation or hypocrisy; honest. □□ **genuinely** *adv.* **genuineness** *n.* [L *genuinus* f. *genu* knee, with ref. to a father's acknowledging a newborn child by placing it on his knee: later associated with GENUS]

■ **1, 2** authentic, veritable, real, bona fide, legitimate, true, proper, pukka, unfeigned; original. **4** candid, frank, open, sincere, honest; decent, honorable, principled.

genus /jéenəs/ *n.* (*pl.* **genera** /jénərə/) **1** *Biol.* a taxonomic grouping of organisms having common characteristics distinct from those of other genera, usu. containing several or many species and being one of a series constituting a taxonomic family. **2** a kind or class having common characteristics. **3** *Logic* kinds of things including subordinate kinds or species. [L *genus -eris* birth, race, stock]

■ **1, 2** see SORT *n.* 1.

-geny /jənee/ *comb. form* forming nouns meaning 'mode of production or development of' (*anthropogeny; ontogeny; pathogeny*). [F *-génie* (as -GEN, -Y[3])]

Geo. *abbr.* George.

geo- /jée-ō/ *comb. form* earth. [Gk *geō-* f. *gē* earth]

geobotany /jéeōbót'nee/ *n.* the study of the geographical distribution of plants. □□ **geobotanist** *n.*

geocentric /jéeōséntrik/ *adj.* **1** considered as viewed from the center of the earth. **2** having or representing the earth as the center; not heliocentric. □ **geocentric latitude** the latitude at which a planet would appear if viewed from the center of the earth. □□ **geocentrically** *adv.*

geochemistry /jéeōkémistree/ *n.* the chemistry of the earth and its rocks, minerals, etc. □□ **geochemical** /-mikəl/ *adj.* **geochemist** /-mist/ *n.*

geochronology /jéeōkrənóləjee/ *n.* **1** the study and measurement of geological time by means of geological events. **2** the ordering of geological events. □□ **geochronological** /-krónəlójikəl/ *adj.* **geochronologist** *n.*

geode /jée-ōd/ *n.* **1** a small cavity lined with crystals or other mineral matter. **2** a rock containing such a cavity. □□ **geodic** /jee-ódik/ *adj.* [L *geodes* f. Gk *geōdēs* earthy f. *gē* earth]

geodesic /jéeədéezik, -désik/ *adj.* (also **geodetic** /-détik/) **1** of or relating to geodesy. **2** of, involving, or consisting of a geodesic line. □ **geodesic dome** a dome constructed of short struts along geodesic lines. **geodesic line** the shortest possible line between two points on a curved surface.

geodesy /jeeódisee/ *n.* the branch of mathematics dealing with the shape and area of the earth or large portions of it. □□ **geodesist** *n.* [mod.L f. Gk *geōdaisia* (as GEO-, *daiō* divide)]

geodetic var. of GEODESIC.

geog. *abbr.* **1** geographer. **2** geographic. **3** geographical. **4** geography.

geographic /jéeəgráfik/ *adj.* (also **geographical** /-gráfikəl/) of or relating to geography. □ **geographical latitude** the angle made with the plane of the equator by a perpendicular to the earth's surface at any point. **geographical mile** a distance equal to one minute of longitude or latitude at the equator (about 1850 meters; a nautical mile). **geographic information system(s)** a computerized system utilizing precise locational data for mapping, navigation, etc. ¶ Abbr.: **GIS.** □□ **geographically** *adv.* [*geographic* f. F *géographique* or LL *geographicus* f. Gk *geōgraphikos* (as GEO-, -GRAPHIC)]

geographical var. of GEOGRAPHIC.

geography /jeeógrəfee/ *n.* **1** the study of the earth's physical features, resources, and climate, and the physical aspects of its population. **2** the main physical features of an area. **3** the layout or arrangement of any set of constituent elements. □□ **geographer** *n.* [F *géographie* or L *geographia* f. Gk *geōgraphia* (as GEO-, -GRAPHY)]

geoid /jée-oyd/ *n.* **1** the shape of the earth. **2** a shape formed by the mean sea level and its imagined extension under land areas. **3** an oblate spheroid. [Gk *geōeidēs* (as GEO-, -OID)]

geol. *abbr.* **1** geologic. **2** geological. **3** geologist. **4** geology.

geology /jeeóləjee/ *n.* **1** the science of the earth, including the composition, structure, and origin of its rocks. **2** this science applied to any other planet or celestial body. **3** the geological features of a district. □□ **geologic** /jéeəlójik/ *adj.* **geological** *adj.* **geologically** *adv.* **geologist** /-ólǝjist/ *n.* **geologize** *v.tr.* & *intr.* [mod.L *geologia* (as GEO-, -LOGY)]

geom. *abbr.* **1** geometric. **2** geometrical. **3** geometry.

geomagnetism /jéeōmágnitizəm/ *n.* the study of the magnetic properties of the earth. □□ **geomagnetic** /-magnétik/ *adj.* **geomagnetically** *adv.*

geomancy /jéeōmánsee/ *n.* divination from the configuration of a handful of earth or random dots, lines, or figures. □□ **geomantic** /-mántik/ *adj.*

geometer /jeeómitər/ *n.* **1** a person skilled in geometry. **2** (also **geometrid** any moth, esp. of the family Geometridae, having twiglike larvae which move in a looping fashion, seeming to measure the ground. [ME f. LL *geometra* f. L *geometres* f. Gk *geōmetrēs* (as GEO-, *metrēs* measurer)]

geometric /jéeəmétrik/ *adj.* (also **geometrical**) **1** of, according to, or like geometry. **2** (of a design, architectural feature, etc.) characterized by or decorated with regular lines and shapes. □ **geometric mean** the central number in a geometric progression, also calculable as the nth root of a product of n numbers (as 9 from 3 and 27). **geometric progression** a progression of numbers with a constant ratio between each number and the one before (as 1, 3, 9, 27, 81). □□ **geometrically** adv. [F *géometrique* f. L *geometricus* f. Gk *geōmetrikos* (as GEOMETER)]

geometrid /jeeómitrid/ n. = GEOMETER 2.

geometry /jeeómitree/ n. **1** the branch of mathematics concerned with the properties and relations of points, lines, surfaces, and solids. **2** the relative arrangement of objects or parts. □□ **geometrician** /jeeəmitríshən/ n. [ME f. OF *geometrie* f. L *geometria* f. Gk (as GEO-, -METRY)]

geomorphology /jeeōmawrfóləjee/ n. the study of the physical features of the surface of the earth and their relation to its geological structures. □□ **geomorphological** /-fəlójikəl/ adj. **geomorphologist** n.

geophagy /jeeófəjee/ n. the practice of eating earth. [GEO- + Gk *phagō* eat]

geophysics /jee-ōfíziks/ n. the physics of the earth. □□ **geophysical** adj. **geophysicist** /-zisist/ n.

geopolitics /jee-ōpólitiks/ n. **1** the politics of a country as determined by its geographical features. **2** the study of this. □□ **geopolitical** /-pəlítikəl/ adj. **geopolitically** adv. **geopolitician** /-tíshən/ n.

George /jawrj/ n. Brit. sl. the automatic pilot of an aircraft. [the name *George*]

George Cross /jawrj/ n. (also **George Medal**) (in the UK) a decoration for bravery awarded esp. to civilians, instituted in 1940 by King George VI.

georgette /jawrjét/ n. a thin silk or crêpe dress material. [*Georgette* de la Plante, Fr. dressmaker]

Georgian[1] /jáwrjən/ adj. & n. ● adj. of or relating to the state of Georgia. ● n. a native of Georgia.

Georgian[2] /jáwrjən/ adj. **1** of or characteristic of the time of Kings George I–IV (1714–1830). **2** of or characteristic of the time of Kings George V and VI (1910–52), esp. of the literature of 1910–20.

Georgian[3] /jáwrjən/ adj. & n. ● adj. of or relating to Georgia in the Caucasus. ● n. **1** a native of Georgia; a person of Georgian descent. **2** the language of Georgia.

geosphere /jeeəsfeer/ n. **1** the solid surface of the earth. **2** any of the almost spherical concentric regions of the earth and its atmosphere.

geostationary /jee-ōstáyshəneree/ adj. Electronics (of an artificial satellite of the earth) moving in such an orbit as to remain above the same point on the earth's surface (see also GEOSYNCHRONOUS).

geostrophic /jee-ōstrófik/ adj. Meteorol. depending upon the rotation of the earth. [GEO- + Gk *strophē* a turning f. *strephō* to turn]

geosynchronous /jee-ōsíngkrənəs/ adj. (of an artificial satellite of the earth) moving in an orbit equal to the earth's period of rotation (see also GEOSTATIONARY).

geothermal /jee-ōthśrməl/ adj. relating to, originating from, or produced by the internal heat of the earth.

geotropism /jeeótrəpizəm/ n. plant growth in relation to gravity. □ **negative geotropism** the tendency of stems, etc., to grow away from the center of the earth. **positive geotropism** the tendency of roots to grow toward the center of the earth. □□ **geotropic** /jeeətrŏpik, -ótrópik/ adj. [GEO- + Gk *tropikos* f. *tropē* a turning f. *trepō* to turn]

Ger. abbr. German.

geranium /jəráyneeəm/ n. **1** any herb or shrub of the genus *Geranium* bearing fruit shaped like the bill of a crane, e.g., cranesbill. **2** (in general use) a cultivated pelargonium. **3** the color of the scarlet geranium. [L f. Gk *geranion* f. *geranos* crane]

gerbera /jśrbərə/ n. any composite plant of the genus *Gerbera* of Africa or Asia, esp. the Transvaal daisy. [T. *Gerber*, Ger. naturalist d. 1743]

gerbil /jśrbil/ n. (also **jerbil**) a mouselike desert rodent of the

subfamily Gerbillinae, with long hind legs. [F *gerbille* f. mod.L *gerbillus* dimin. of *gerbo* JERBOA]

gerenuk /gérənŏŏk/ n. an antelope, *Litocranius walleri*, native to E. Africa, with a very long neck and small head. [Somali]

gerfalcon var. of GYRFALCON.

geri /jéree/ n. Austral. colloq. a geriatric person. [abbr.]

geriatric /jéreeátrik/ adj. & n. ● adj. **1** of or relating to old people. **2** colloq. old; outdated. ● n. **1** an old person, esp. one receiving special care. **2** colloq. a person or thing considered as relatively old or outdated. [Gk *gēras* old age + *iatros* doctor]

geriatrics /jéreeátriks/ n.pl. (usu. treated as sing.) a branch of medicine or social science dealing with the health and care of old people. □□ **geriatrician** /-ətríshən/ n.

germ /jśrm/ n. **1** a microorganism, esp. one which causes disease. **2 a** a portion of an organism capable of developing into a new one; the rudiment of an animal or plant. **b** an embryo of a seed (*wheat germ*). **3** an original idea, etc., from which something may develop; an elementary principle. □ **germ cell 1** a cell containing half the number of chromosomes of a somatic cell and able to unite with one from the opposite sex to form a new individual; a gamete. **2** any embryonic cell with the potential of developing into a gamete. **germ warfare** the systematic spreading of microorganisms to cause disease in an enemy population. **in germ** not yet developed. □□ **germy** adj. [F *germe* f. L *germen germinis* sprout]

■ **1** microorganism, microbe, bacterium, virus, sl. bug. **3** embryo, seed, source, root, origin, beginning, start, poet. fount; principle, base, basis, rudiments.

German /jśrmən/ n. & adj. ● n. **1** a native or inhabitant of Germany; a person of German descent. **2** the language of Germany, also used in Austria and Switzerland. ● adj. of or relating to Germany or its people or language. □ **German measles** a contagious disease, rubella, with symptoms like mild measles. **German shepherd 1** a large breed of dog bred from the wolfhound, used in police work, as guide dogs for the blind, etc. **2** a dog of this breed. **German silver** a white alloy of nickel, zinc, and copper. **High German** a literary and cultured form of German. **Low German** German dialects other than High German. [L *Germanus* with ref. to related peoples of Central and N. Europe, a name perh. given by Celts to their neighbors: cf. OIr. *gair* neighbor]

german /jśrmən/ adj. (placed after *brother*, *sister*, or *cousin*) **1** having the same parents (*brother-german*). **2** having the same grandparents on one side (*cousin-german*). **3** archaic germane. [ME f. OF *germain* f. L *germanus* genuine, of the same parents]

germander /jərmándər/ n. any plant of the genus *Teucrium*. □ **germander speedwell** a creeping plant, *Veronica chamaedrys*, with germanderlike leaves and blue flowers. [ME f. med.L *germandra* ult. f. Gk *khamaidrus* f. *khamai* on the ground + *drus* oak]

germane /jərmáyn/ adj. (usu. foll. by *to*) relevant (to a subject under consideration). □□ **germanely** adv. **germaneness** n. [var. of GERMAN]

■ see RELEVANT.

Germanic /jərmánik/ adj. & n. ● adj. **1** having German characteristics. **2** hist. of the Germans. **3** of the Scandinavians, Anglo-Saxons, or Germans. **4** of the languages or language group called Germanic. ● n. **1** the branch of Indo-European languages including English, German, Dutch, and the Scandinavian languages. **2** the (unrecorded) early language from which other Germanic languages developed. □ **East Germanic** an extinct group including Gothic. **North Germanic** the Scandinavian languages. **West Germanic** a group including High and Low German, English, Frisian, and Dutch. [L *Germanicus* (as GERMAN)]

/.../ **pronunciation**	● **part of speech**
□ **phrases, idioms, and compounds**	
□□ **derivatives**	■ **synonym section**
cross-references appear in SMALL CAPITALS or *italics*	

germanic /jərmánik/ *adj. Chem.* of or containing germanium, esp. in its tetravalent state.

Germanist /jərmənist/ *n.* an expert in or student of the language, literature, and civilization of Germany, or Germanic languages.

germanium /jərmáyneeəm/ *n. Chem.* a lustrous brittle semimetallic element occurring naturally in sulfide ores and used in semiconductors. ¶ Symb.: **Ge**. [mod.L f. *Germanus* GERMAN]

Germanize /jə́rmənīz/ *v.tr. & intr.* make or become German; adopt or cause to adopt German customs, etc. □□ **Germanization** *n.* **Germanizer** *n.*

Germano- /jərmánō/ *comb. form* German; German and.

germanous /jə́rmáynəs/ *adj. Chem.* containing germanium in the bivalent state.

germicide /jə́rmisīd/ *n.* a substance destroying germs, esp. those causing disease. □□ **germicidal** /sídʹl/ *adj.*

■ see DISINFECTANT *n.*

germinal /jə́rminəl/ *adj.* **1** relating to or of the nature of a germ or germs (see GERM 1). **2** in the earliest stage of development. **3** productive of new ideas. □□ **germinally** *adv.* [L *germen germin-* sprout: see GERM]

■ **2** see PRIMARY *adj.* 2.

germinate /jə́rminayt/ *v.* **1 a** *intr.* sprout, bud, or put forth shoots. **b** *tr.* cause to sprout or shoot. **2 a** *tr.* cause (ideas, etc.) to originate or develop. **b** *intr.* come into existence. □□ **germination** /-náyshən/ *n.* **germinative** *adj.* **germinator** *n.* [L *germinare germinat-* (as GERM)]

■ **1 a** see SPROUT *v.* 2.

gerontology /jərontóləjee/ *n.* the scientific study of old age, the process of aging, and the special problems of old people. □□ **gerontological** /-təlójikəl/ *adj.* **gerontologist** *n.* [Gk *gerōn -ontos* old man + -LOGY]

-gerous /jərəs/ *comb. form* forming adjectives meaning 'bearing' (*lanigerous*).

gerrymander /jérimándər/ *v. & n.* ● *v.tr.* **1** manipulate the boundaries of (a constituency, etc.) so as to give undue influence to some party or class. **2** manipulate (a situation, etc.) to gain advantage. ● *n.* this practice. □□ **gerrymanderer** *n.* [the name of Governor *Gerry* of Massachusetts + (SALA)MANDER, from the shape of a political district drawn when he was in office (1812)]

gerund /jérənd/ *n. Gram.* a form of a verb functioning as a noun, orig. in Latin ending in *-ndum* (declinable), in English ending in *-ing* and used distinctly as a part of a verb (e.g., *do you mind my asking you?*). [LL *gerundium* f. *gerundum* var. of *gerendum*, the gerund of L *gerere* do]

gerundive /jərúndiv/ *n. Gram.* a form of a Latin verb, ending in *-ndus* (declinable) and functioning as an adjective meaning 'that should or must be done,' etc. [LL *gerundivus* (*modus* mood) f. *gerundium*: see GERUND]

gesso /jésō/ *n.* (*pl.* **-oes**) plaster of Paris or gypsum as used in painting or sculpture. [It. f. L *gypsum*: see GYPSUM]

gestalt /gəshtaált, -staált, -shtáwlt, -stawlt/ *n. Psychol.* an organized whole that is perceived as more than the sum of its parts. □ **gestalt psychology** a system maintaining that perceptions, reactions, etc., are gestalts. □□ **gestaltism** *n.* **gestaltist** *n.* [G, = form, shape]

Gestapo /gestaápō, -shtaá-/ *n.* **1** the German secret police under Nazi rule. **2** *derog.* an organization compared to this. [G, f. *Geheime Staatspolizei*]

gestate /jéstáyt/ *v.tr.* **1** carry (a fetus) in gestation. **2** develop (an idea, etc.).

gestation /jestáyshən/ *n.* **1 a** the process of carrying or being carried in the womb between conception and birth. **b** this period. **2** the private development of a plan, idea, etc. [L *gestatio* f. *gestare* frequent. of *gerere* carry]

gesticulate /jestíkyəlayt/ *v.* **1** *intr.* use gestures instead of or in addition to speech. **2** *tr.* express with gestures. □□ **gesticulation** /-láyshən/ *n.* **gesticulative** *adj.* **gesticulator** *n.* **gesticulatory** /-lətáwree/ *adj.* [L *gesticulari* f. *gesticulus* dimin. of *gestus* GESTURE]

■ see SIGNAL¹ *v.* 1, 2a.

gesture /jés-chər/ *n. & v.* ● *n.* **1** a significant movement of a limb or the body. **2** the use of such movements, esp. to convey feeling or as a rhetorical device. **3** an action to evoke a response or convey intention, usu. friendly. ● *v.tr. & intr.* gesticulate. □□ **gestural** *adj.* **gesturer** *n.* [ME f. med.L *gestura* f. L *gerere gest-* wield]

■ *n.* **1** movement, motion, gesticulation, action, move. **2** gesturing, gesticulation, movement, body language, kinesics; mime. **3** token, signal, indication; gambit, device, *colloq.* ploy, high sign. ● *v.* gesticulate, motion, signal, sign, indicate, *colloq.* give (a person) the high sign.

gesundheit /gəzŏŏnt-hīt/ *int.* expressing a wish of good health, esp. to a person who has sneezed. [G, = health]

get /get/ *v. & n.* ● *v.* (**getting**; *past* **got** /got/; *past part.* **got** or (and in *comb.*) **gotten** /gótʹn/) **1** *tr.* come into the possession of; receive or earn (*get a job; got $200 a week; got first prize*). **2** *tr.* **a** fetch; obtain; procure; purchase (*get my book for me; got a new car*). **b** capture; get hold of (a person). **3** *tr.* go to reach or catch (a bus, train, etc.). **4** *tr.* prepare (a meal, etc.). **5** *intr. & tr.* reach or cause to reach a certain state or condition; become or cause to become (*get rich; get one's feet wet; get to be famous; got them ready; got him into trouble; cannot get the key into the lock*). **6** *tr.* obtain as a result of calculation. **7** *tr.* contract (a disease, etc.). **8** *tr.* establish or be in communication with via telephone or radio; receive (a radio signal). **9** *tr.* experience or suffer; have inflicted on one; receive as one's lot or penalty (*got four years in prison*). **10 a** *tr.* succeed in bringing, placing, etc. (*get it around the corner; get it onto the agenda; flattery will get you nowhere*). **b** *intr. & tr.* succeed or cause to succeed in coming or going (*will get you there somehow; got absolutely nowhere*). **11** *tr.* (*prec. by have*) **a** possess (*haven't got a penny*). **b** (foll. by *to* + infin.) be bound or obliged (*have got to see you*). **12** *tr.* (foll. by *to* + infin.) induce; prevail upon (*got them to help me*). **13** *tr. colloq.* understand (a person or an argument) (*have you got that?; I get your point; do you get me?*). **14** *tr. colloq.* inflict punishment or retribution on, esp. in retaliation (*I'll get you for that*). **15** *tr. colloq.* **a** annoy. **b** move; affect emotionally. **c** attract; obsess. **d** amuse. **16** *tr.* (foll. by *to* + infin.) develop an inclination as specified (*am getting to like it*). **17** *intr.* (foll. by verbal noun) begin (*get going*). **18** *tr.* (esp. in *past* or *perfect*) catch in an argument; corner; puzzle. **19** *tr.* establish (an idea, etc.) in one's mind. **20** *intr. sl.* be off; go away. **21** *tr. archaic* beget. **22** *tr. archaic* learn; acquire (knowledge) by study. ● *n.* **1 a** an act of begetting (of animals). **b** an offspring (of animals). **2** *Brit. sl.* a fool or idiot. **3** *Tennis* an exceptional return. □ **get about** (or **around**) **1** travel extensively or fast; go from place to place. **2** manage to walk, move about, etc. (esp. after illness). **3** (of news) be circulated, esp. orally. **get across 1** manage to communicate (an idea, etc.). **2** (of an idea, etc.) be communicated successfully. **3** *Brit. colloq.* annoy; irritate. **get ahead** be or become successful. **get along** (or **on**) **1** (foll. by *together, with*) live harmoniously; accord. **2** *Brit.* be off! nonsense! **3** leave; depart (*I must be getting along*). **4** manage to survive; have sufficient means. **get around** (*Brit.* **round**) **1** successfully coax or cajole (a person) esp. to secure a favor. **2** evade (a law, etc.). **get around to** deal with (a task, etc.) in due course. **get at 1** reach; get hold of. **2** *colloq.* imply (*what are you getting at?*). **3** *colloq.* annoy; try to upset or irritate. **get away 1** escape. **2** leave, esp. on vacation. **3** (as *imper.*) *colloq.* expressing disbelief or skepticism. **4** (foll. by *with*) escape blame or punishment for. **get back at** *colloq.* retaliate against. **get by** *colloq.* **1** just manage, even with difficulty. **2** be acceptable. **get down 1** alight; descend (from a vehicle, ladder, etc.). **2** record in writing. **get a person down** depress or deject him or her. **get down to** begin working on or discussing. **get even** (often foll. by *with*) **1** achieve revenge; act in retaliation. **2** equalize the score. **get his** (or **hers**, etc.) *sl.* **1** be killed. **2** be avenged. **get hold** (or **ahold**) **of 1** grasp (physically). **2** grasp (intellectually); understand. **3** make contact with (a person). **4** acquire. **get in 1** enter. **2** be elected. **get into** become interested or involved in. **get it** *sl.* **1** understand. **2** be punished or in trouble. **get it into one's head** (foll. by *that* + clause) firmly believe or maintain; realize. **get off 1** *colloq.* be acquitted; escape with little or no punishment. **2** leave. **3** alight; alight from (a bus, etc.). **4** go, or cause to go, to sleep. **5** *sl.* to experience orgasm. **6** (foll. by *with*, *together*) *Brit. colloq.* form an amorous or sexual relationship, esp. abruptly or quickly. **get a person off** *colloq.* cause a person to be acquitted. **get off on** *sl.* be excited or aroused by; enjoy. **get on 1** make progress; manage. **2** enter (a bus, etc.). **3** esp. *Brit.* = *get along* 1. **4** *colloq.* become more advanced in time, age, etc. **get on to** *colloq.* **1** make contact with. **2** understand; become aware of. **get out 1** leave or escape. **2** manage to go outdoors. **3** alight from a vehicle. **4** transpire; become known. **5** succeed in uttering, publishing, etc. **6** *Brit.* solve or finish (a puzzle, etc.). **7** *Baseball, Cricket* be dismissed. **get-out** *n. Brit.* a means of avoiding something. **get a person out 1** help a person to leave or escape. **2** *Baseball, Cricket* dismiss (a batter or batsman). **get out of 1** avoid or escape (a duty, etc.). **2** abandon (a habit) gradually. **get a thing out of** manage to obtain it from (a person) esp. with difficulty. **get outside** (or **outside of**) *Brit. sl.* eat or drink. **get over 1** recover from (an illness, upset, etc.). **2** overcome (a difficulty). **3** manage to communicate (an idea, etc.). **get a thing over** (or **over with**) complete (a tedious task) promptly. **get one's own back** *colloq.* have one's revenge. **get-rich-quick** *adj.* designed to make a lot of money fast. **get rid of** see RID. **get somewhere** make progress; be initially successful. **get there** *colloq.* **1** succeed. **2** understand what is meant. **get through 1** pass or assist in passing (an examination, an ordeal, etc.). **2** finish or use up (esp. resources). **3** make contact by telephone. **4** (foll. by *to*) succeed in making (a person) listen or understand. **get a thing through** cause it to overcome obstacles, difficulties, etc. **get to 1** reach. **2** = *get down to*. **get together** gather; assemble. **get-together** *n. colloq.* a social gathering. **get up 1** rise or cause to rise from sitting, etc., or from bed after sleeping or an illness. **2** ascend or mount, e.g., on horseback. **3** (of fire, wind, or the sea) begin to be strong or agitated. **4** prepare or organize. **5** enhance or refine one's knowledge of (a subject). **6** work up (a feeling, e.g., anger). **7** produce or stimulate (*get up steam*; *get up speed*). **8** (often *refl.*) dress or arrange elaborately; make presentable; arrange the appearance of. **9** (foll. by *to*) esp. *Brit. colloq.* indulge or be involved in (*always getting up to mischief*). **get-up** *n. colloq.* **1** a style or arrangement of dress, etc., esp. an elaborate one. **2** a style of production or finish, esp. of a book. **get-up-and-go** *colloq.* energy; vim; enthusiasm. **get the wind up** see WIND¹. **get with child** *archaic* make pregnant. **have got it bad** (or **badly**) *sl.* be obsessed or affected emotionally. □□ **gettable** *adj.* [ME f. ON *geta* obtain, beget, guess, corresp. to OE *gietan* (recorded only in compounds), f. Gmc]

■ *v.* **1** obtain, secure, acquire, come by or into (the) possession of, pick up, collect, receive, be given, come by; earn, make, take (home), gross, clear, net, pocket, be paid, *colloq.* pull down; accede to, inherit, fall heir to, succeed to. **2 a** obtain, procure; fetch, go and get, go for or after, pick up; bring (back), retrieve; buy, purchase, engage; glean, absorb, take in. **b** capture, seize, arrest, take, apprehend, grab, lay or get hold of. **3** catch, take, make, come or go by, travel or journey by. **5** become, fall, turn, grow; put, place, set, fit, maneuver, manipulate; manage, arrange, come, succeed; contrive, fix it. **7** catch, contract, have, suffer from, come down with, fall ill or sick with, be afflicted with, become infected with, acquire, *Brit.* go down with. **8** reach, get in touch with, communicate with, get on or through to, contact; receive, pick up, tune in to or on to. **9** receive; suffer, endure, go through. **10 b** transport, carry, bear, bring, move; reach, arrive (at), come, go, travel, journey. **11 a** have, possess, own, be provided with. **b** (*have got to*) have to, be obliged to, be bound to, must, need to. **12** persuade, prevail upon, coax, induce, influence, cajole, wheedle, sway, bring around, cause. **13** understand, appreciate, see, grasp, apprehend, perceive, follow, comprehend, take in, work out, make head or tail of; catch, hear. **14** get even with, revenge oneself on, take vengeance on, pay

back, settle or even the score with, get back at, get one's own back on. **15 a** get at, irritate, annoy, vex, irk, nettle, pique, provoke, anger, exasperate, bother, perturb, rile, rub the wrong way, get or put a person's back up, *colloq.* get a person's goat, get in a person's hair, *disp.* aggravate, *sl.* bug; see also ANNOY 1. **b** affect, stir, move, touch, have an impact or effect on, make an impression on, impress, leave a mark on, get to. **c** see ATTRACT 1, OBSESS. **d** see AMUSE 1. **16** start, begin, come. **17** see BEGIN 2, 4. **18** baffle, confound, puzzle, perplex, bewilder; see also CONFUSE 1a. **20** see RUN *v.* 2. **22** see LEARN 3. □ **get about** (or **around**) **1** be active, go or get out; run about or around, gad about, move about. **3** spread, become known, leak (out), circulate, be bruited about or around, be noised abroad, go about or around. **get across 1** get or put over, put across, get through, communicate, make clear, impart. **get ahead** succeed, prosper, be or become successful, do well, thrive, flourish, make good, (make) progress, go far, go a long way, get on, go or come up or rise (up) in the world, *colloq.* go places. **get along 1** be friendly or compatible, agree, accord, be agreeable or congenial, *colloq.* hit it off. **3** leave, depart, go or move away, get going, get or be on one's way, go along, proceed. **get around 1** cajole, wheedle, persuade, coax, win over. **2** bypass, circumvent, skirt, evade; see also AVOID 2. **get around to** get or come to, reach, arrive at (finally), find time for. **get at 1** gain access to, access, reach, get hold of, put or lay one's hands on, get to. **2** intend, mean, suggest, hint (at), insinuate, imply, have in mind or view. **3** taunt, criticize, find fault with, carp, nag, pick on; see also TEASE *v.* **get away 1** escape, leave, break out or away, flee, depart, make good one's escape, elude one's captors, break free, disappear. **2** take a vacation or break, take a rest or respite. **3** see *go on!* (GO¹). **get back at** see GET *v.* 14 above. **get by 1** make ends meet, keep the wolf from the door, make do, keep one's head above water; see also MANAGE *v.* 2, 3, 5a. **get down 1** dismount, alight, descend, come or go down, climb or step down; (*get down from*) get off. **2** write (down), note (down), record, make a note of. **get a person down** (*get down*) depress, bring down, dispirit, sadden, dishearten, discourage, deject. **get down to** concentrate or focus on, turn one's attention to, turn to, attend to. **get even 1** (*get even with*) see GET *v.* 14 above. **2** draw level, even up, draw even, equalize. **get hold of** (or **ahold of**) **1** see GRASP *v.* 1a. **2** see UNDERSTAND 1, 2. **3** see CONTACT *v.* **4** see ACQUIRE 1. **get in 1** enter, get into or on or on to, embark, get or go aboard; arrive, return, come or go in. **get into** be or become involved in, take up, pursue, become enthusiastic about, *sl.* get off on. **get it into one's head** see REALIZE 2. **get off 1** be acquitted or set free or released, escape, get away, *sl.* walk. **2** leave, depart, go (off), set out or off, make a start, head off. **3** alight (from), disembark, dismount, descend (from); climb or step down off or from, get down from, get out of. **get on 1** manage, cope, shift, survive, make do, *colloq.* get by, make out, *literary* fare; make progress, proceed, advance, come on, move ahead or along or on. **4** age, get or become or grow older, advance; get or grow or become late. **get on to 1** see CONTACT *v.* **2** discover, learn about, become aware of, find out about, understand, *colloq.* cotton on to; *Brit. colloq.* twig. **get out 1** leave, depart, go out or away, be off, retire; escape, extricate or free oneself; be released. **4** see TRANSPIRE 1. **5** publish, put out, bring out; utter. **get out of 1** avoid, evade, sidestep, escape, shirk.

/ . . . / **pronunciation**   ● **part of speech**
□ **phrases, idioms, and compounds**
□□ **derivatives**   ■ **synonym section**
cross-references appear in SMALL CAPITALS or *italics*

get over 1 recover *or* recuperate from, get better from, convalesce from. **2** overcome, surmount, hurdle, cope with; see also SOLVE. **3** see COMMUNICATE 1a. **get one's own back** see GET *v.* 14 above. **get somewhere** make progress, do well. **get there 1** see SUCCEED 1a. **2** see UNDERSTAND 7. **get through 1** succeed in, complete, pass. **2** see *use up* 1. **3** (*get through to*) reach, contact, get, make contact with, get in touch with, get hold of. **4** (*get through to*) make oneself clear to. **get to 1** arrive at, come to, reach; near, approach. **get together** gather, accumulate, collect, assemble, convene, meet, congregate, socialize. **get-together** see PARTY¹ *n.* 1. **get up 1** awaken, awake, wake (up), bestir oneself, rise, get out of bed, come to, esp. *archaic & poet.* arise, *colloq.* surface; stand (up); get dressed. **2** mount, climb (up), ascend, scale, go up. **4** create, devise, organize; see also PREPARE 1, ARRANGE 2, 3. **5** brush up (on), study, learn, bring up to date, get up on, *Brit. colloq.* swot up (on). **8** dress, clothe, outfit, turn out, deck out, rig out, dress up, fit out *or* up, *archaic* apparel, *formal* attire. **get-up 1** see OUTFIT *n.* 1. **2** format, layout, arrangement, structure, look, style. **get-up-and-go** see ENERGY 1. **get with child** see IMPREGNATE *v.* 3.

getatable /gétátəbəl/ *adj. colloq.* accessible.
getaway /gétəway/ *n.* **1** an escape, esp. after committing a crime. **2 a** a vacation, esp. a brief one. **b** a place at which one spends such a vacation.
■ **1** flight, retreat; see also ESCAPE *n.* 1.
getter /gétər/ *n. & v.* ● *n.* **1** in senses of GET *v.* **2** *Physics* a substance used to remove residual gas from a vacuum tube. ● *v.tr. Physics* remove (gas) or evacuate (a vacuum tube) with a getter.
geum /jeéəm/ *n.* any rosaceous plant of the genus *Geum* including avens and herb bennet, with rosettes of leaves and yellow, red, or white flowers. [mod.L, var. of L *gaeum*]
GeV *abbr.* gigaelectronvolt (equivalent to 10⁹ electronvolts).
gewgaw /gyóōgaw, góō-/ *n.* a gaudy plaything or ornament; a bauble. [ME: orig. unkn.]
■ bauble, ornament, gimcrack, trifle, bagatelle, kickshaw, trinket, falderal, bijou, knickknack, plaything, toy, novelty; (*gewgaws*) bric-a-brac, frippery.
geyser /gízər/ *n.* **1** an intermittently gushing hot spring that throws up a tall column of water. **2** /geézər/ *Brit.* an apparatus for heating water rapidly for domestic use. [Icel. *Geysir*, the name of a particular spring in Iceland, rel. to *geysa* to gush]
■ **1** see STREAM *n.* 2.
Ghanaian /gaáneeən/ *adj. & n.* ● *adj.* of or relating to Ghana in W. Africa. ● *n.* a native or inhabitant of Ghana; a person of Ghanaian descent.
gharial var. of GAVIAL.
ghastly /gástlee/ *adj. & adv.* ● *adj.* (**ghastlier, ghastliest**) **1** horrible; frightful. **2** *colloq.* objectionable; unpleasant. **3** deathlike; pallid. ● *adv.* in a ghastly or sickly way (*ghastly pale*). □□ **ghastlily** *adv.* **ghastliness** *n.* [ME *gastlich* f. obs. *gast* terrify: *gh* after *ghost*]
■ *adj.* **1** horrible, horrendous, horrid, horrifying, frightful, shocking, appalling, dreadful, terrible, terrifying, grim, grisly, gruesome, loathsome, repulsive, repellent, hideous, ugly, *colloq.* scary. **2** objectionable, unpleasant, *sl.* gross; see also AWFUL 1a, b. **3** pallid, livid, ashen, wan, pale, pasty(-faced), ill, ailing, sick; deathlike, grim, cadaverous, haggard, drawn.
ghat /gaat, gat/ *n.* (also **ghaut**) in India: **1** steps leading down to a river. **2** a landing place. **3** a defile or mountain pass. [Hindi *ghāt*]
Ghazi /gaázee/ *n.* (*pl.* **Ghazis**) a Muslim fighter against non-Muslims. [Arab. *al-ġāzī* part. of *ġazā* raid]
ghee /gee/ *n.* (also **ghi**) clarified butter esp. from the milk of a buffalo or cow. [Hindi *ghī* f. Skr. *ghṛitá-* sprinkled]
gherao /gerów/ *n.* (*pl.* **-os**) (in India and Pakistan) coercion of employers, by which their workers prevent them from leaving the premises until certain demands are met. [Hind. *gherna* besiege]
gherkin /górkin/ *n.* **1** a small variety of cucumber, or a young

green cucumber, used for pickling. **2 a** a trailing plant, *Cucumis anguria*, with cucumber-like fruits used for pickling. **b** this fruit. [Du. *gurkkijn* (unrecorded), dimin. of *gurk*, f. Slavonic, ult. f. med. Gk *aggourion*]
ghetto /gétō/ *n. & v.* ● *n.* (*pl.* **-os**) **1** a part of a city, esp. a slum area, occupied by a minority group or groups. **2** *hist.* the Jewish quarter in a city. **3** a segregated group or area. ● *v.tr.* (**-oes, -oed**) put or keep (people) in a ghetto. □ **ghetto blaster** *sl.* a large portable radio, often with cassette player or CD player, esp. used to play loud pop music. [perh. f. It. *getto* foundry (applied to the site of the first ghetto in Venice in 1516)]
■ *n.* **1** see SLUM *n.* 1.
ghi var. of GHEE.
ghillie var. of GILLIE.
ghost /gōst/ *n. & v.* ● *n.* **1** the supposed apparition of a dead person or animal; a disembodied spirit. **2** a shadow or mere semblance (*not a ghost of a chance*). **3** an emaciated or pale person. **4** a secondary or duplicated image produced by defective television reception or by a telescope. **5** *archaic* a spirit or soul. ● *v.* **1** *intr.* (often foll. by *for*) act as ghost writer. **2** *tr.* act as ghost writer of (a work). □ **ghost town** a deserted town with few or no remaining inhabitants. **ghostwriter** a person who writes on behalf of the credited author of a work. □□ **ghostlike** *adj.* [OE *gāst* f. WG: *gh-* occurs first in Caxton, prob. infl. by Flem. *gheest*]
■ *n.* **1** apparition, phantom, specter, phantasm, spirit, wraith, doubleganger, doppelgänger, ghoul, manes, poltergeist, *Ir. & Sc.* banshee; *colloq.* spook, *literary* shade. **2** shadow, semblance, suggestion, hint, trace, scintilla, glimmer.
ghosting /gōsting/ *n.* the appearance of a "ghost" (see GHOST *n.* 4) or secondary image in a television picture.
ghostly /gōstlee/ *adj.* (**ghostlier, ghostliest**) like a ghost; spectral. □□ **ghostliness** *n.* [OE *gāstlic* (as GHOST)]
■ spectral, ghostlike, wraithlike, phantasmal; eerie, unearthly, *colloq.* spooky, creepy.
ghostwrite /gōstrit/ *v.tr. & intr.* act as ghost writer (of).
ghoul /gōōl/ *n.* **1** a person morbidly interested in death, etc. **2** an evil spirit or phantom. **3** a spirit in Muslim folklore preying on corpses. □□ **ghoulish** *adj.* **ghoulishly** *adv.* **ghoulishness** *n.* [Arab. *ġūl* protean desert demon]
■ **2** see GHOST *n.* 1. □□ **ghoulish** devilish, demonic, satanic, diabolic(al), fiendish, demoniac(al), Mephistophelian, malign; morbid, macabre, grisly, gruesome, *colloq.* sick.
GHQ *abbr.* General Headquarters.
ghyll *Brit.* var. of GILL³.
GI /jeé-í/ *n. & adj.* ● *n.* an enlisted soldier in the US armed forces, esp. the army. ● *adj.* of, for, or characteristic of US soldiers. [abbr. of *galvanized iron*, later taken as abbr. of *government* (or *general*) *issue*]
■ *n.* see SOLDIER *n.*
giant /jíənt/ *n. & adj.* ● *n.* **1** an imaginary or mythical being of human form but superhuman size. **2** (in Greek mythology) one of such beings who fought against the gods. **3** an abnormally tall or large person, animal, or plant. **4** a person of exceptional ability, integrity, courage, etc. **5** a large star. ● *attrib.adj.* **1** of extraordinary size or force; gigantic; monstrous. **2** *colloq.* extra large (*giant package*). **3** (of a plant or animal) of a very large kind. □□ **giantism** *n.* **giantlike** *adj.* [ME *geant* (later infl. by L) f. OF, ult. f. L *gigas gigant-* f. Gk]
■ *n.* **1** superhuman, colossus, ogre, Goliath; amazon. **2** Titan. **3** leviathan, behemoth, monster; see also JUMBO *n.* **4** see PRODIGY 1, WONDER *n.* 2. ● *attrib.adj.* **1, 2** see GIGANTIC.
giaour /jówər/ *n. derog. or literary* a non-Muslim, esp. a Christian (orig. a Turkish name). [Pers. *gaur, gōr*]
Gib. /jib/ *abbr.* Gibraltar.
gib /gib, jib/ *n.* a wood or metal bolt, wedge, or pin for holding a machine part, etc., in place. [18th c.: orig. unkn.]
gibber¹ /jíbər/ *v. & n.* ● *v.intr.* speak fast and inarticulately; chatter incoherently. ● *n.* such speech or sound. [imit.]
■ *v.* see PRATTLE *v.* ● *n.* see PRATTLE *n.*

gibber[2] /gíbər/ n. *Austral.* a boulder or large stone. [Aboriginal]

gibberellin /jíbərélin/ n. one of a group of plant hormones that stimulate the growth of leaves and shoots. [*Gibberella* a genus of fungi, dimin. of genus name *Gibbera* f. L *gibber* hump]

gibberish /jíbərish/ n. unintelligible or meaningless speech; nonsense. [perh. f. GIBBER[1] (but attested earlier) + -ISH[1] as used in *Spanish, Swedish,* etc.]

■ gibber, gabble, jabber, blather, babble, jabberwocky, mumbo jumbo; drivel, nonsense, rubbish, twaddle, balderdash, garbage, jargon, *colloq.* gobbledegook, tripe, piffle, *sl.* poppycock, bunk, *Brit. sl.* codswallop, bull; see also NONSENSE.

gibbet /jíbit/ n. & v. ● n. *hist.* **1 a** a gallows. **b** an upright post with an arm on which the bodies of executed criminals were hung up. **2** (prec. by *the*) death by hanging. ● v.tr. (**gibbeted, gibbeting**) **1** put to death by hanging. **2 a** expose on a gibbet. **b** hang up as on a gibbet. **3** hold up to contempt. [ME f. OF *gibet* gallows dimin. of *gibe* club, prob. f. Gmc]

■ v. 1 see HANG v. 7a.

gibbon /gíbən/ n. any small ape of the genus *Hylobates*, native to SE Asia, having a slender body and long arms. [F f. a native name]

gibbous /gíbəs/ adj. **1** convex or protuberant. **2** (of a moon or planet) having the bright part greater than a semicircle and less than a circle. **3** humped or humpbacked. □□ **gibbosity** /-bósitee/ n. **gibbously** adv. **gibbousness** n. [ME f. LL *gibbosus* f. *gibbus* hump]

gibe /jíb/ v. & n. (also **jibe**) ● v.intr. (often foll. by *at*) jeer; mock. ● n. an instance of gibing; a taunt. □□ **giber** n. [perh. f. OF *giber* handle roughly]

■ v. jeer, scoff, mock, sneer, make fun, poke fun, chaff; (*gibe at*) gird at, deride, tease, ridicule, twit, taunt, rag, heckle, *colloq.* rib, *sl.* razz. ● n. jeer, taunt, sneer, cutting remark, scoff, *colloq.* dig, crack, wisecrack; (*gibes*) mockery, raillery, derision, chaff, ridicule.

giblets /jíblits/ n.pl. the liver, gizzard, neck, etc., of a bird, usu. removed and kept separate when the bird is prepared for cooking. [OF *gibelet* game stew, perh. f. *gibier* game]

giddy /gídee/ adj. & v. ● adj. (**giddier, giddiest**) **1** having a sensation of whirling and a tendency to fall, stagger, or spin around. **2 a** overexcited as a result of success, pleasurable emotion, etc.; mentally intoxicated. **b** excitable; frivolous. **3** tending to make one giddy. ● v.tr. & intr. (**-ies, -ied**) make or become giddy. □□ **giddily** adv. **giddiness** n. [OE *gidig* insane, lit. 'possessed by a god']

■ adj. **1** dizzy, reeling, lightheaded, vertiginous, unsteady, *colloq.* woozy. **2 a** see OVERWROUGHT 1. **b** excitable, volatile, impulsive, capricious, whimsical, fickle, flighty, erratic; silly, frivolous, scatterbrained, irresponsible, reckless.

gift /gift/ n. & v. ● n. **1** a thing given; a present. **2** a natural ability or talent. **3** the power to give (*in his gift*). **4** the act or an instance of giving. **5** *colloq.* an easy task. ● v.tr. **1** endow with gifts. **2 a** (foll. by *with*) give to as a gift. **b** bestow as a gift. □ **gift certificate** (also *Brit.* **token** or **voucher**) a certificate used as a gift and exchangeable for goods. **gift of tongues** see TONGUE. **gift wrap** (**wrapped, wrapping**) wrap attractively as a gift. **look a gift horse in the mouth** (usu. *neg.*) find fault with what has been given. [ME f. ON *gipt* f. Gmc, rel. to GIVE]

■ n. **1** present, donation, benefaction, offering; premium, bonus, handout, tip, gratuity, *pourboire*; (*gifts*) largesse, bounty, charity, *hist.* alms. **2** talent, ability, aptitude, facility, capability, capacity, flair, knack, forte, strength, bent; (*gifts*) powers. **4** see PRESENTATION 1. **5** see BREEZE[1] n. 4.

gifted /gíftid/ adj. exceptionally talented or intelligent. □□ **giftedly** adv. **giftedness** n.

■ talented, intelligent, capable, able, skilled, skillful; outstanding, excellent, superb, brilliant, expert, master, masterful, virtuoso, first-class, first-rate, topflight, *colloq.* top-notch, crack, *sl.* ace, crackerjack.

gig[1] /gig/ n. **1** a light two-wheeled one-horse carriage. **2** a light ship's boat for rowing or sailing. **3** a rowing boat esp. for racing. [ME in var. senses: prob. imit.]

■ 2 see TENDER[3].

gig[2] /gig/ n. & v. *colloq.* ● n. an engagement of an entertainer, esp. a musician, usu. for a single appearance. ● v.intr. (**gigged, gigging**) perform a gig. [20th c.: orig. unkn.]

■ n. see PERFORMANCE 2.

gig[3] /gig/ n. a kind of fishing spear. [short for *fizgig, fishgig*: cf. 3р. *fisga* harpoon]

■ see LANCE n.

giga- /gígə, jígə/ comb. form denoting a factor of 10⁹. [Gk *gigas* giant]

gigabit /gígəbit, jígə-/ n. *Computing* a unit of information equal to one billion (10⁹) bits.

gigabyte /gígəbīt, jígə-/ n. *Computing* a unit of information equal to one billion (10⁹) bytes.

gigameter /gígəmeetər, jígə-/ n. a metric unit equal to 10⁹ meters.

gigantic /jīgántik/ adj. **1** very large; enormous. **2** like or suited to a giant. □□ **gigantesque** /-tésk/ adj. **gigantically** adv. [L *gigas gigantis* GIANT]

■ 1 huge, enormous, massive, immense, towering, vast, giant, colossal, mammoth, titanic, gargantuan, elephantine, *colloq.* jumbo, thumping, thundering, *sl.* walloping, whopping, humongous.

gigantism /jīgántizəm/ n. abnormal largeness, esp. *Med.* excessive growth due to hormonal imbalance, or to polyploidy in plants.

giggle /gígəl/ v. & n. ● v.intr. laugh in half-suppressed spasms, in an affected or silly manner. ● n. **1** such a laugh. **2** esp. *Brit. colloq.* an amusing person or thing; a joke. □□ **giggler** n. **giggly** adj. (**gigglier, giggliest**). **giggliness** n. [imit.: cf. Du. *gichelen*, G *gickeln*]

■ v. laugh, chuckle, titter, cackle, snicker, snigger, *colloq.* chortle. ● n. **1** laugh, chuckle, chortle, titter, snicker, snigger, cackle, *colloq.* chortle.

GIGO /gígō/ n. *Computing* abbr. for garbage *in*, garbage *out*, an informal rule stating that the quality of the data input determines the quality of the results.

gigolo /jígəlō, zhíg-/ n. (*pl.* **-os**) **1** a young man paid by an older woman to be her escort or lover. **2** a professional male dancing partner or escort. [F, formed as masc. of *gigole* dancehall woman]

■ 1 see PARAMOUR.

gigot /jígət, zheegó/ n. a leg of mutton or lamb. □ **gigot sleeve** a leg-of-mutton sleeve. [F, dimin. of dial. *gigue* leg]

gigue /zheeg/ n. **1** = JIG 1. **2** *Mus.* a lively dance usu. in a compound triple rhythm with two sections each repeated. [F: see JIG[1]]

Gila monster /heélə/ n. a large venomous lizard, *Heloderma suspectum,* of the southwestern US, having orange, yellow, and black scales like beads. [*Gila* River, Arizona]

gild[1] /gild/ v.tr. (*past part.* **gilded** or as adj. in sense 1 **gilt**) **1** cover thinly with gold. **2** tinge with a golden color or light. **3** give a specious or false brilliance to. □ **gilded cage** luxurious but restrictive surroundings. **gilded youth** young people of wealth, fashion, and flair. **gild the lily** try to improve what is already beautiful or excellent. □□ **gilder** n. [OE *gyldan* f. Gmc]

■ 1 see EMBELLISH 1.

gild[2] var. of GUILD.

gilding /gílding/ n. **1** the act or art of applying gilt. **2** material used in applying gilt.

■ 1 see embellishment (EMBELLISH).

gilgai /gílgī/ n. *Austral.* a saucershaped natural reservoir for rainwater. [Aboriginal]

gill[1] /gil/ n. & v. ● n. (usu. in *pl.*) **1** the respiratory organ in fishes and other aquatic animals. **2** the vertical radial plates

/.../	pronunciation	● part of speech
□ phrases, idioms, and compounds		
□□ derivatives	■ synonym section	
cross-references appear in SMALL CAPITALS or *italics*		

on the underside of mushrooms and other fungi. **3** the flesh below a person's jaws and ears (*green about the gills*). **4** the wattles or dewlap of fowls. ● *v.tr.* **1** gut (a fish). **2** cut off the gills of (a mushroom). **3** catch in a gill net. □ **gill cover** a bony case protecting a fish's gills; an operculum. **gill net** a net for entangling fishes by the gills. □□ **gilled** *adj.* (also in *comb.*). [ME f. ON *gil* (unrecorded) f. Gmc]

gill² /jil/ *n.* **1** a unit of liquid measure, equal to a quarter of a pint. **2** *Brit. dial.* half a pint. [ME f. OF *gille*, med.L *gillo* f. LL *gello*, *gillo* water pot]

gill³ /gil/ *n.* (also **ghyll**) *Brit.* **1** a deep usu. wooded ravine. **2** a narrow mountain torrent. [ME f. ON *gil* glen]

gillie /gílee/ *n.* (also **ghillie**) *Sc.* **1** a man or boy attending a person hunting or fishing. **2** *hist.* a Highland chief's attendant. [Gael. *gille* lad, servant]

gillion /jílyən/ *n. Brit.* **1** a thousand million. **2** a large number. ¶ Mainly used to avoid the ambiguity of *billion*. [GIGA- + MILLION]

gillyflower /jíleeflowr, gílee-/ *n.* **1** (in full **clove gillyflower**) a clove-scented pink (see CLOVE¹ 2). **2** any of various similarly scented flowers such as the wallflower, carnation, or white stock. [ME *gilofre*, *gerofle* f. OF *gilofre*, *girofle*, f. med.L f. Gk *karuophullon* clove tree f. *karuon* nut + *phullon* leaf, assim. to FLOWER]

gilt¹ /gilt/ *adj. & n.* ● *adj.* **1** covered thinly with gold. **2** gold-colored. ● *n.* **1** gold or a goldlike substance applied in a thin layer to a surface. **2** (often in *pl.*) *Brit.* a gilt-edged security. □ **gilt-edged 1** (of securities, stocks, etc.) having a high degree of reliability as an investment. **2** having a gilded edge. [past part. of GILD¹]
■ *adj.* see GOLDEN 1a.

gilt² /gilt/ *n.* a young unbred sow. [ME f. ON *gyltr*]

gimbals /gímbəlz, jím-/ *n.pl.* a contrivance, usu. of rings and pivots, for keeping a stove or instruments such as a compass and chronometer horizontal at sea, in the air, etc. [var. of earlier *gimmal* f. OF *gemel* double finger ring f. L *gemellus* dimin. of *geminus* twin]

gimcrack /jímkrak/ *adj. & n.* ● *adj.* showy but flimsy and worthless. ● *n.* a cheap showy ornament; a knickknack. □□ **gimcrackery** *n.* **gimcracky** *adj.* [ME *gibecrake* a kind of ornament, of unkn. orig.]
■ *adj.* see INFERIOR *adj.* 2. ● *n.* see GEWGAW.

gimlet /gímlit/ *n.* **1** a small tool with a screw tip for boring holes. **2** a cocktail usu. of gin and lime juice. □ **gimlet eye** an eye with a piercing glance. [ME f. OF *guimbelet*, dimin. of *guimble*]

gimmick /gímik/ *n. colloq.* a trick or device, esp. to attract attention, publicity, or trade. □□ **gimmickry** *n.* **gimmicky** *adj.* [20th-c. US: orig. unkn.]
■ trick, stratagem, ruse, wile, dodge; device, contrivance, gadget, *colloq.* ploy, *derog. or joc.* contraption, *sl.* gizmo; see also GADGET, TRICK *n.* 1.

gimp¹ /gimp/ *n.* (also **guimp, gymp**) **1** a twist of silk, etc., with cord or wire running through it, used esp. as trimming. **2** fishing line of silk, etc., bound with wire. **3** a coarser thread outlining the design of lace. [Du.: orig. unkn.]

gimp² /gimp/ *n. & v. sl.* ● *n.* a lame person, gait, or leg. ● *v.intr.* walk with a lame gait. □□ **gimpy** *adj.*

gin¹ /jin/ *n.* an alcoholic spirit distilled from grain or malt and flavored with juniper berries. □ **gin rummy** a form of the card game rummy. [abbr. of GENEVA]

gin² /jin/ *n. & v.* ● *n.* **1** a machine for separating cotton from its seeds. **2** a snare or trap. **3** a kind of crane and windlass. ● *v.tr.* (**ginned, ginning**) **1** treat (cotton) in a gin. **2** trap. □□ **ginner** *n.* [ME f. OF *engin* ENGINE]
■ *n.* 2 see TRAP¹ *n.* 1.

ginger /jínjər/ *n., adj., & v.* ● *n.* **1 a** a hot spicy root usu. powdered for use in cooking, or preserved in syrup, or candied. **b** the plant, *Zingiber officinale*, of SE Asia, having this root. **2** a light reddish yellow color. **3** spirit; mettle. **4** stimulation. ● *adj.* of a ginger color. ● *v.tr.* **1** flavor with ginger. **2** (foll. by *up*) rouse or enliven. **3** *Austral. colloq.* steal from (a person). □ **black ginger** unscraped ginger. **ginger ale** a carbonated nonalcoholic clear drink flavored with ginger ex-

tract. **ginger beer** a carbonated sometimes mildly alcoholic cloudy drink, made by fermenting a mixture of ginger and syrup. **ginger group** *Brit.* a group within a party or movement that presses for stronger or more radical policy or action. **ginger nut** *Brit.* a ginger flavored cookie. **ginger pop** *Brit. colloq.* = *ginger ale*. **ginger wine** a drink of fermented sugar, water, and bruised ginger. □□ **gingery** *adj.* [ME f. OE *gingiber* & OF *gingi(m)bre*, both f. med.L *gingiber* ult. f. Skr. *śṛṅgaveram* f. *śṛṅgam* horn + *-vera* body, with ref. to the antler shape of the root]

gingerbread /jínjərbred/ *n.* **1** a cake made with molasses or syrup and flavored with ginger. **2** (often *attrib.*) a gaudy, lavish, or superfluous decoration or ornament.
■ **2** see ORNAMENT *n.* 1, 2.

gingerly /jínjərlee/ *adv. & adj.* ● *adv.* in a careful or cautious manner. ● *adj.* showing great care or caution. □□ **gingerliness** *n.* [perh. f. OF *gensor* delicate, compar. of *gent* graceful f. L *genitus* (well-)born]
■ *adv.* cautiously, carefully, charily, tentatively, warily, circumspectly, guardedly, timidly, timorously, watchfully; delicately, daintily. ● *adj.* careful, cautious, wary, chary, tentative, circumspect, guarded, watchful, timid; fastidious, delicate, dainty.

gingersnap /jínjərsnap/ *n.* a thin brittle cookie flavored with ginger.

gingham /gíng-əm/ *n.* a plain-woven cotton cloth, esp. striped or checked. [Du. *gingang* f. Malay *ginggang* (orig. adj. = striped)]

gingiva /jinjívə, jínjivə/ *n.* (*pl.* **gingivae** /-vee/) the gum. □□ **gingival** /-jívəl, -jivəl/ *adj.* [L]

gingivitis /jínjivítis/ *n.* inflammation of the gums.

gingko var. of GINKGO.

ginglymus /jíngglıməs, ging-/ *n.* (*pl.* **ginglymi** /-mī/) *Anat.* a hingelike joint in the body with motion in one plane only, e.g., the elbow or knee. [mod.L f. Gk *gigglumos* hinge]

gink¹ /gingk/ *n. sl.* often *derog.* a fellow; a man. [20th-c. US: orig. unkn.]

gink² /gingk/ *n. Austral.* a scrutinizing look. [prob. alt. of GEEK]

ginkgo /gíngkgō/ *n.* (also **gingko**) (*pl.* **-os** or **-oes**) an orig. Chinese and Japanese tree, *Ginkgo biloba*, with fan-shaped leaves and yellow flowers. Also called *maidenhair tree*. [Jap. *ginkyo* f. Chin. *yinxing* silver apricot]

ginormous /jínáwrməs/ *adj. Brit. sl.* very large; enormous. [GIANT + ENORMOUS]

ginseng /jínseng/ *n.* **1** any of several medicinal plants of the genus *Panax*, found in E. Asia and N. America. **2** the root of this. [Chin. *renshen* perh. = man image, with allusion to its forked root]

gippy tummy /jípee/ *n.* (also **gyppy tummy**) *Brit. colloq.* diarrhea affecting visitors to hot countries. [abbr. of EGYPTIAN]

gipsy var. of GYPSY.

giraffe /jiráf/ *n.* (*pl.* same or **giraffes**) a ruminant mammal, *Giraffa camelopardalis* of Africa, the tallest living animal, with a long neck and forelegs and a skin of dark patches separated by lighter lines. [F *girafe*, It. *giraffa*, ult. f. Arab. *zarāfa*]

girandole /jírəndōl/ *n.* **1** a revolving cluster of fireworks. **2** a branched candle bracket or candlestick. **3** an earring or pendant with a large central stone surrounded by small ones. [F f. It. *girandola* f. *girare* GYRATE]

girasol /jírəsawl, -sōl/ *n.* (also **girasole** /-sōl/) **1** a kind of opal reflecting a reddish glow; a fire opal. **2** (usu. **girasole**) = JERUSALEM ARTICHOKE. [orig. = sunflower, f. F *girasol* or It. *girasole* f. *girare* (as GIRANDOLE) + *sole* sun]

gird¹ /gərd/ *v.tr.* (*past* and *past part.* **girded** or **girt**) **1** encircle, attach, or secure with a girdle or belt. **2** secure (clothes) on the body with a girdle or belt. **3** enclose or encircle. **4 a** (foll. by *with*) equip with a sword in a belt. **b** fasten (a sword) with a belt. **5** (foll. by *around*) place (cord, etc.) around. □ **gird** (or **gird up**) **one's loins** prepare for action. [OE *gyrdan* f. Gmc (as GIRTH)]
■ **1** see BAND¹ *v.* 1. **3** see ENCIRCLE 1.

gird² /gərd/ v. & n. ● v.intr. (foll. by at) jeer or gibe. ● n. a gibe or taunt. [ME, = strike, etc.: orig. unkn.]

girder /gərdər/ n. a large iron or steel beam or compound structure for bearing loads, esp. in a bridge or building. [GIRD¹ + -ER¹]
■ see BEAM n. 1.

girdle¹ /gərd'l/ n. & v. ● n. **1** a belt or cord worn around the waist. **2** a woman's corset extending from waist to thigh. **3** a thing that surrounds like a girdle. **4** the bony support for a limb (pelvic girdle). **5** the part of a cut gem dividing the crown from the base and embraced by the setting. **6** a ring around a tree made by the removal of bark. ● v.tr. **1** surround with a girdle. **2** remove a ring of bark from (a tree), esp. to make it more fruitful. [OE gyrdel: see GIRD¹]
■ n. **1** see BELT n. 1.

girdle² /gərd'l/ n. Sc. & No. of Engl. = GRIDDLE n. 1.

girl /gərl/ n. **1** a female child or youth. **2** colloq. a young (esp. unmarried) woman. **3** colloq. a girlfriend or sweetheart. **4** derog. a female servant. □ **girl Friday** see FRIDAY. **Girl Scout** a member of an organization of girls, esp. the Girl Scouts of America, that promotes character, outdoor activities, community service, etc. □□ **girlhood** n. [ME gurle, girle, gerle, perh. rel. to LG gör child]
■ **1** female child, young lady, miss, mademoiselle, Ir. colleen, esp. Sc. & No. of Engl. or poet. lass, archaic or poet. maid, maiden, colloq. lassie, sl. gal. **2** young woman, fräulein, archaic demoiselle, archaic or literary damsel, colloq. filly, Brit. colloq. popsy, joc. wench, sl. chick, frail, dame, broad, Austral. & NZ sl. sheila, Brit. sl. bird. **3** girlfriend, sweetheart, lover, inamorata, Brit. colloq. popsy, sl. moll, squeeze; betrothed, fiancée.

girlfriend /gərlfrend/ n. **1** a regular female companion or lover. **2** a female friend.
■ **1** see WOMAN 3.

girlie /gərlee/ adj. colloq. (of a magazine, etc.) depicting nude or partially nude young women in erotic poses.

girlish /gərlish/ adj. of or like a girl. □□ **girlishly** adv. **girlishness** n.
■ see YOUNG adj. 3.

giro /jīrō/ n. & v. ● n. (pl. -os) **1** a system of credit transfer between banks, post offices, etc., in Europe. **2** a check or payment by giro. ● v.tr. (-oes, -oed) pay by giro. [G f. It., = circulation (of money)]

girt¹ past part. of GIRD¹.

girt² var. of GIRTH.

girth /gərth/ n. & v. (also **girt** /gərt/) ● n. **1** the distance around a thing. **2** a band around the body of a horse to secure the saddle, etc. ● v. **1** tr. **a** secure (a saddle, etc.) with a girth. **b** put a girth on (a horse). **2** tr. surround; encircle. **3** intr. measure (an amount) in girth. [ME f. ON gjörth, Goth. gairda f. Gmc]
■ n. **1** circumference, ambit, periphery, circuit. **2** belt, girdle, cinch, archaic zone, literary cincture. ● v. **2** surround, encompass, encircle, enclose, envelop.

GIS abbr. geographic information system(s).

gist /jist/ n. **1** the substance or essence of a matter. **2** Law the real ground of an action, etc. [OF, 3rd sing. pres. of gesir lie f. L jacēre]
■ **1** substance, essence, pith, meat, marrow, core, heart, point, nub; significance, import, (main or basic) idea, meaning; direction, drift.

git /git/ n. Brit. sl. a silly or contemptible person. [var. of GET n.]

gittern /gitərn/ n. a medieval stringed instrument, a forerunner of the guitar. [ME f. OF guiterne: cf. CITTERN, GUITAR]

give /giv/ v. & n. ● v. (past **gave** /gayv/; past part. **given** /givən/) **1** tr. (also absol.; often foll. by to) transfer the possession of freely; hand over as a present (gave them her old curtains; gives to cancer research). **2** tr. **a** transfer the ownership of with or without actual delivery; bequeath (gave him $200 in her will). **b** transfer, esp. temporarily or for safe keeping; hand over; provide with (gave him the dog to hold; gave them a drink). **c** administer (medicine). **d** deliver (a message) (give her my best wishes). **3** tr. (usu. foll. by for) pay (gave him $30 for the bicycle). **b** sell (gave him the bicycle

for $30). **4** tr. **a** confer; grant (a benefit, an honor, etc.). **b** accord; bestow (one's affections, confidence, etc.). **c** award; administer (one's approval, blame, etc.); tell; offer (esp. something unpleasant) (gave him a talking-to; gave him my blessing). **d** pledge; assign as a guarantee (gave his word). **5** tr. **a** effect or perform (an action, etc.) (gave him a kiss; gave a jump). **b** utter (gave a shriek). **6** tr. allot; assign; grant (was given the contract). **7** tr. (in passive; foll. by to) be inclined to or fond of (is given to speculation). **8** tr. yield as a product or result (the lamp gives a bad light; the field gives fodder for twenty cows). **9** intr. **a** yield to pressure; become relaxed; lose firmness (this elastic doesn't give properly). **b** collapse (the roof gave under the pressure). **10** intr. (usu. foll. by of) grant; bestow (gave freely of his time). **11** tr. **a** commit, consign, or entrust (gave him into custody; give her into your care). **b** sanction the marriage of (a daughter, etc.). **12** tr. devote; dedicate (gave his life to croquet; shall give it my attention). **13** tr. (usu. absol.) colloq. tell what one knows (What happened? Come on, give!). **14** tr. present; offer; show; hold out (gives no sign of life; gave her his arm; give him your ear). **15** tr. Theatr. read, recite, perform, act, etc. (gave them Hamlet's soliloquy). **16** tr. impart; be a source of (gave him my sore throat; gave its name to the battle; gave them to understand; gives him a right to complain). **17** tr. allow (esp. a fixed amount of time) (can give you five minutes). **18** tr. (usu. foll. by for) value (something) (gives nothing for their opinions). **19** tr. concede; yield (I give you the victory). **20** tr. deliver (a judgment, etc.) authoritatively (gave his verdict). **21** tr. toast (a person, cause, etc.) (I give you our President). **22** tr. provide (a party, meal, etc.) as host (gave a banquet). ● n. **1** capacity to yield or bend under pressure; elasticity (there is no give in a stone floor). **2** ability to adapt or comply (no give in his attitudes). □ **give and take** v.tr. exchange (words, blows, or concessions). ● n. an exchange of words, etc.; a compromise. **give as good as one gets** retort adequately in words or blows. **give away 1** transfer as a gift. **2** hand over (a bride) ceremonially to a bridegroom. **3** betray or expose to ridicule or detection. **4** Austral. abandon; desist from; give up; lose faith or interest in. **give back** return (something) to its previous owner or in exchange. **give birth (to)** see BIRTH. **give chase** pursue a person, animal, etc.; hunt. **give down** (often absol.) (of a cow) let (milk) flow. **give forth** emit; publish; report. **give the game (or show) away** reveal a secret or intention. **give a hand** = lend a hand (see HAND). **give a person (or the devil) his or her due** acknowledge, esp. grudgingly, a person's rights, abilities, etc. **give in 1** cease fighting or arguing; yield. **2** Brit. hand in (a document, etc.) to an official, etc. **give in marriage** sanction the marriage of (one's daughter, etc.). **give it to a person** colloq. scold or punish. **give me** I prefer or admire (give me the Greek islands). **give off** emit (vapor, etc.). **give oneself** (of a woman) yield sexually. **give oneself airs** act pretentiously or snobbishly. **give oneself up to 1** abandon oneself to an emotion, esp. despair. **2** addict oneself to. **give onto** (or **into**) (of a window, corridor, etc.) overlook or lead into. **give or take** colloq. add or subtract (a specified amount or number) in estimating. **give out 1** announce; emit; distribute. **2** cease or break down from exhaustion, etc. **3** run short. **give over** Brit. **1** colloq. cease from doing; abandon (a habit, etc.); desist (give over sniffing). **2** hand over. **3** devote. **give rise to** cause; induce; suggest. **give tongue 1** speak one's thoughts. **2** (of hounds) bark, esp. on finding a scent. **give a person to understand** inform authoritatively. **give up 1** resign; surrender. **2** part with. **3** deliver (a wanted person, etc.). **4** pronounce incurable or insoluble; renounce hope of. **5** renounce or cease (an activity). **give up the ghost** archaic or colloq. die. **give way** see WAY. **give a person what for** colloq. punish or scold severely. **give one's word** (or **word of honor**) promise solemnly. **not give a damn** (or Brit. **monkey's** or **toss**, etc.)

/.../ **pronunciation**   ● **part of speech**
□ **phrases, idioms, and compounds**
□□ **derivatives**   ■ **synonym section**
cross-references appear in SMALL CAPITALS or italics

colloq. not care at all. **what gives?** *colloq.* what is the news?; what's happening? **would give the world** (or **one's ears, eyes,** etc.) **for** covet or wish for desperately. □□ **givable, giveable** *adj.* **giver** *n.* [OE *g(i)efan* f. Gmc]

■ *v.* **1, 2 a** provide, supply, present, offer, furnish; hand over, make over, contribute, grant, donate; see also BEQUEATH. **2 b** supply with, furnish with, provide with; transfer, hand over. **d** deliver, impart, pass on, transmit, send, convey, communicate, express. **3 b** sell, exchange, trade, barter, swap. **4** confer, grant, accord, bestow, pledge, award, offer. **5 b** utter, emit, give out. **6** see ASSIGN *v.* 1a. **7** (*be given*) be inclined, be prone, be liable. **8** yield, produce, make, furnish, provide. **9 b** give way, fail, collapse, buckle, break down, fall *or* come apart. **12** devote, dedicate; sacrifice, yield (up), surrender, give up, consign. **14** see SHOW *v.* 3. **15** present, offer, put on; recite, read, sing, act, perform. **16** cause, lead, induce, prompt, move, dispose; allow, provide with, furnish with, let have; impart, lend. **17** see ALLOW 2. **19** relinquish, concede, surrender, allow, cede, yield. ● *n.* **1** elasticity, flexibility, stretch, slack, play, leeway. **2** see *flexibility* (FLEXIBLE). □ **give and take** (*n.*) interaction, reciprocity, cooperation, teamwork, fair exchange; compromise. **give away 3** betray, inform on, *colloq.* blow the whistle on, *sl.* rat on, fink on; reveal, let out, divulge, disclose, expose, uncover, leak, let slip; (*give it away*) let the cat out of the bag, give the game *or* show away. **give forth** see EMIT 1. **give in 1** yield, submit, give ground, back off *or* down; give up, capitulate, surrender, admit defeat. **give it to a person** see SCOLD *v.* 1. **give off** give out, emit, exude, discharge, send *or* throw out, release; exhale. **give out 1** publish, announce, make public, make known, broadcast; impart, issue, reveal; disseminate, spread; distribute, dispense, hand out, dole (out), deal (out), pass around, allot, apportion, allocate, assign, *literary* mete out, *sl.* dish out; emit. **2** become exhausted, fail, collapse, break down, cease; see also FLAG[1] *v.* 1a. **3** become depleted, run short; see also *run out* 1. **give over 2** hand over, surrender, relinquish, pass over, give up. **give rise to** start, engender, generate, begin, produce, bring out, bring about, bring into being, *formal* commence; see also CAUSE *v.* 1. **give up 1** resign, surrender, capitulate, yield, cede, concede, give in, admit defeat, throw in the towel. **5** abandon, stop, cease, quit, leave off, *Austral.* give away, *literary* desist from; forgo, forsake, renounce, abstain from, *colloq.* swear off, chuck (in). **give up the ghost** see DIE[1]. **give a person what for** see SCOLD *v.* 1. **give one's word** (or **word of honor**) see PROMISE *v.* 1. **not give a damn** (or *Brit.* **monkey's** or **toss**) not care *or* mind at all, *sl.* not give *or* care a hoot.

giveaway /gívəway/ *n. colloq.* **1** an inadvertent betrayal or revelation. **2** an act of giving away. **3** a free gift; a low price.
■ **3** see BARGAIN *n.* 2.

given /gívən/ *adj. & n.* ● *adj.* **1** as previously stated or assumed; granted; specified (*given that he is a liar, we cannot trust him; a given number of people*). **2** *Law* (of a document) signed and dated (*given this day the 30th of June*). ● *n.* a known fact or situation. □ **given name** a name given as a first name. [past part. of GIVE]
■ *adj.* **1** assumed, understood, acknowledged, allowed, granted; stated, delineated, specified, set, confirmed, accepted, agreed; (pre)arranged, preordained, foreordained. ● *n.* assumption, donnée; fact, certainty, reality, actuality, certainty.

gizmo /gízmō/ *n.* (also **gismo**) (*pl.* **-os**) *sl.* a gadget. [20th c.: orig. unkn.]
■ see GADGET.

gizzard /gízərd/ *n.* **1** the second part of a bird's stomach, for grinding food usu. with grit. **2** a muscular stomach of some fish, insects, mollusks, and other invertebrates. □ **stick in one's gizzard** (or **craw**) *colloq.* be distasteful. [ME *giser* f. OF *giser, gesier*, etc., ult. f. L *gigeria* cooked entrails of fowl]

glabella /gləbélə/ *n.* (*pl.* **glabellae** /-lee/) the smooth part of the forehead above and between the eyebrows. □□ **glabellar** *adj.* [mod.L f. L *glabellus* (adj.) dimin. of *glaber* smooth]

glabrous /gláybrəs/ *adj.* free from hair or down; smooth skinned. [L *glaber glabri* hairless]

glacé /glasáy/ *adj.* **1** (of fruit, esp. cherries) preserved in sugar, usu. resulting in a glossy surface. **2** (of cloth, leather, etc.) smooth; polished. □ **glacé icing** icing made with confectioner's sugar and water. [F, past part. of *glacer* to ice, gloss f. *glace* ice: see GLACIER]

glacial /gláyshəl/ *adj.* **1** of ice; icy. **2** *Geol.* characterized or produced by the presence or agency of ice. **3** *colloq.* exceptionally slow. **4** *Chem.* forming icelike crystals upon freezing (*glacial acetic acid*). □ **glacial epoch** (or **period**) a period when ice-sheets were exceptionally extensive. □□ **glacially** *adv.* [F *glacial* or L *glacialis* icy f. *glacies* ice]
■ **1** see ICY 1, 2.

glaciated /gláyshee-aytid, -see-/ *adj.* **1** marked or polished by the action of ice. **2** covered or having been covered by glaciers or ice sheets. □□ **glaciation** /-áyshən/ *n.* [past part. of *glaciate* f. L *glaciare* freeze f. *glacies* ice]

glacier /gláyshər/ *n.* a mass of land ice formed by the accumulation of snow on high ground. [F f. *glace* ice ult. f. L *glacies*]

glaciology /gláysheeóləjee, -see-/ *n.* the science of the internal dynamics and effects of glaciers. □□ **glaciological** /-əlójikəl/ *adj.* **glaciologist** *n.* [L *glacies* ice + -LOGY]

glacis /gláysis, glás-/ *n.* (*pl.* same /-siz, -seez/) a bank sloping down from a fort, on which attackers are exposed to the defenders' missiles, etc. [F f. OF *glacier* to slip f. *glace* ice: see GLACIER]

glad[1] /glad/ *adj. & v.* ● *adj.* (**gladder, gladdest**) **1** (*predic.*; usu. foll. by *to* + infin. or *Brit. of*) pleased; willing (*shall be glad to come*). **2 a** marked by, filled with, or expressing, joy (*a glad expression*). **b** (of news, events, etc.) giving joy (*glad tidings*). **3** (of objects) bright; beautiful. ● *v.tr.* (**gladded, gladding**) *archaic* make glad. □ **the glad eye** *colloq.* an amorous glance. **glad hand** a hand of welcome, often insincere. **glad-hand** *v.tr.* greet cordially or welcome, esp. insincerely. **glad rags** *colloq.* best clothes; evening dress. □□ **gladly** *adv.* **gladness** *n.* **gladsome** *adj. poet.* [OE *glæd* f. Gmc]
■ *adj.* **1** pleased, willing, ready, keen, eager; thrilled, tickled, *colloq.* tickled pink *or* to death, pleased as Punch, *Brit. sl.* chuffed; see also HAPPY 1. **2 a** contented, gratified, satisfied; joyful, delighted. **b** joyful, satisfying, gratifying, delightful, cheering, *poet.* gladsome. □□ **gladly** cheerfully, happily, readily, with pleasure; see also *willingly* (WILLING).

glad[2] /glad/ *n.* (also *Austral.* **gladdie** /gládee/) *colloq.* a gladiolus. [abbr.]

gladden /glád'n/ *v.tr. & intr.* make or become glad. □□ **gladdener** *n.*
■ cheer (up), delight, enliven, brighten (up), hearten, buoy (up), exhilarate, elate, *archaic* glad.

gladdie *Austral.* var. of GLAD[2].

glade /glayd/ *n.* an open space in a wood or forest. [16th c.: orig. unkn.]

gladiator /gládee-aytər/ *n.* **1** *hist.* a man trained to fight with a sword or other weapons at ancient Roman shows. **2** a person defending or opposing a cause. □□ **gladiatorial** /-dee∂táwreeəl/ *adj.* [L f. *gladius* sword]

gladiolus /gládeeóləs/ *n.* (*pl.* **gladioli** /-lī/ or **gladioluses**) any iridaceous plant of the genus *Gladiolus* with sword-shaped leaves and usu. brightly colored flower spikes. [L, dimin. of *gladius* sword]

Gladstone bag /gládstōn, -stən/ *n.* a suitcase that opens flat into two equal compartments. [W. E. *Gladstone*, Engl. statesman d. 1898]

Glagolitic /glágəlítik/ *adj.* of or relating to the alphabet ascribed to St. Cyril and formerly used in writing some Slavonic languages. [mod.L *glagoliticus* f. Serbo-Croatian *glagolica* Glagolitic alphabet f. OSlav. *glagol* word]

glair /glair/ *n.* (also **glaire**) **1** white of egg. **2** an adhesive preparation made from this, used in bookbinding, etc. □□ **glaireous** adj. **glairy** adj. [ME f. OF glaire, ult. f. L clara fem. of clarus clear]

glaire var. of GLAIR.

glaive /glayv/ n. archaic poet. **1** a broadsword. **2** any sword. [ME f. OF, app. f. L gladius sword]

glamorize /glámərìz/ v.tr. (also **glamourize**) make glamorous or attractive. □□ **glamorization** n.

glamour /glámər/ n. & v. (also **glamor**) ● n. **1** physical attractiveness, esp. when achieved by makeup, etc. **2** alluring or exciting beauty or charm (the glamour of New York). ● v.tr. **1** poet. affect with glamour; bewitch; enchant. **2** colloq. make glamorous. □ **cast a glamour over** enchant. **glamour girl** (or **boy**) an attractive young woman (or man), esp. a model, etc. □□ **glamorous** adj. **glamorously** adv. [18th c.: var. of GRAMMAR, with ref. to the occult practices associated with learning in the Middle Ages]

■ n. **1** see elegance (ELEGANT), BEAUTY 1. **2** allure, beauty, brilliance, glitter, attractiveness, fascination, charm, charisma, enchantment, magic. ● v. **2** see PRIMP 2. □ **cast a glamour over** see ENCHANT 1. **glamour girl** (or **boy**) sex symbol, colloq. sex kitten, sl. dish; model; see also BEAUTY 3. □□ **glamorous** alluring, fascinating, intriguing, beguiling, charming, attractive, desirable; chic, smart, stylish, fashionable.

glance[1] /glans/ v. & n. ● v. **1** intr. (often foll. by down, up, etc.) cast a momentary look (glanced up at the sky). **2** intr. (often foll. by off) (esp. of a weapon) glide or bounce (off an object). **3** intr. (usu. foll. by over, off, from) (of talk or a talker) pass quickly over a subject or subjects (glanced over the question of payment). **4** intr. (of a bright object or light) flash, dart, or gleam; reflect (the sun glanced off the knife). **5** tr. (esp. of a weapon) strike (an object) obliquely. ● n. **1** (usu. foll. by at, into, over, etc.) a brief look (took a glance at the paper; threw a glance over her shoulder). **2 a** a flash or gleam (a glance of sunlight). **b** a sudden movement producing this. **3** a swift oblique movement or impact. □ **at a glance** immediately upon looking. **glance at 1** give a brief look at. **2** make a passing and usu. sarcastic allusion to. **glance one's eye** (foll. by at, over, etc.) look at briefly (esp. a document). **glance over** (or **through**) read cursorily. □□ **glancingly** adv. [ME glence, etc., prob. a nasalized form of obs. glace in the same sense, f. OF glacier to slip: see GLACIS]

■ v. **1** peek, look briefly; see also PEEP[1] v. 1. **2** glide, bounce, ricochet, rebound, Billiards carom, Brit. Billiards cannon. **3** see pass over 1 (PASS[1]). **4** flash, dart, glint, sparkle, flicker, glitter, glisten, gleam, shimmer, twinkle; reflect. ● n. **1** peek, peep, look, coup d'œil, sl. gander, Austral. & NZ sl. squiz, Brit. sl. dekko. **2 a** gleam, glint, twinkle, sparkle, glitter, flicker, flash. □ **glance at 1** see SCAN v. 1.

glance[2] /glans/ n. any lustrous sulfide ore (copper glance; lead glance). [G Glanz luster]

gland[1] /gland/ n. **1 a** an organ in an animal body secreting substances for use in the body or for ejection. **b** a structure resembling this, such as a lymph gland. **2** Bot. a secreting cell or group of cells on the surface of a plant structure. [F glande f. OF glandre f. L glandulae throat glands]

gland[2] /gland/ n. a sleeve used to produce a seal round a moving shaft. [19th c.: perh. var. of glam, glan a vice, rel. to CLAMP[1]]

glanders /glándərz/ n.pl. (also treated as sing.) **1** a contagious disease of horses, caused by a bacterium and characterized by swellings below the jaw and mucous discharge from the nostrils. **2** this disease in humans or other animals. □□ **glandered** adj. **glanderous** adj. [OF glandre: see GLAND[1]]

glandular /glánjələr/ adj. of or relating to a gland or glands. □ **glandular fever** = infectious mononucleosis (see MONONUCLEOSIS). [F glandulaire (as GLAND[1])]

glans /glanz/ n. (pl. **glandes** /glándeez/) the rounded part forming the end of the penis or clitoris. [L, = acorn]

glare[1] /glair/ v. & n. ● v. **1** intr. (usu. foll. by at, upon) look fiercely or fixedly. **2** intr. shine dazzlingly or disagreeably. **3** tr. express (hate, defiance, etc.) by a look. **4** intr. be overly

conspicuous or obtrusive. ● n. **1 a** strong fierce light, esp. sunshine. **b** oppressive public attention (the glare of fame). **2** a fierce or fixed look (a glare of defiance). **3** tawdry brilliance. □□ **glary** adj. [ME, prob. ult. rel. to GLASS: cf. MDu. and MLG glaren gleam, glare]

■ v. **1** frown, scowl, stare, glower, lower, look daggers. **2** dazzle, be blinding, be dazzling. **4** look out of place, stick out like a sore thumb, scream, stick out a mile. ● n. **1 a** brilliance, brightness, radiance, radiation, luminescence, fluorescence, luminosity; dazzle. **2** stare, frown, scowl, dirty look, black look, glower, lower. **3** garishness, tawdriness, gaudiness, floridity, flashiness.

glare[2] /glair/ adj. (esp. of ice) smooth and glassy. [perh. f. glare frost (16th c., of uncert. orig.)]

glaring /gláiring/ adj. **1** obvious; conspicuous (a glaring error). **2** shining oppressively. **3** staring fiercely. □□ **glaringly** adv. **glaringness** n.

■ **1** obvious, conspicuous, obtrusive, prominent, patent, manifest, blatant, flagrant, gross. **2** dazzling, brilliant, blinding, blazing, vivid, harsh, strong.

glasnost /gláasnəst, -nawst/ n. (in the former Soviet Union) the policy or practice of more open consultative government and wider dissemination of information. [Russ. glasnost', lit. = publicity, openness]

glass /glas/ n., v., & adj. ● n. **1 a** (often attrib.) a hard, brittle, usu. transparent, translucent, or shiny substance, made by fusing sand with soda and lime and sometimes other ingredients (a glass pitcher) (cf. crown glass, flint glass, plate glass). **b** a substance of similar properties or composition. **2** (often collect.) an object or objects made from, or partly from, or originally from, glass, esp.: **a** a drinking vessel. **b** esp. Brit. a mirror; a looking glass. **c** an hourglass or sandglass. **d** a window. **e** a greenhouse (rows of lettuce under glass). **f** glass ornaments. **g** a barometer. **h** Brit. a glass disk covering a watch face. **i** a magnifying lens. **j** a monocle. **3** (in pl.) a eyeglasses. **b** field glasses; opera glasses. **4** the amount of liquid contained in a glass; a drink (he likes a glass). **5** fiberglass. ● v.tr. **1** (usu. as **glassed** adj.) fit with glass; glaze. **2** poet. reflect as in a mirror. **3** Mil. look at or for with field glasses, etc. ● adj. of or made from glass. □ **glass case** an exhibition display case made mostly from glass. **glass ceiling** a barrier hindering promotion, esp. of women and minorities, to high executive positions. **glass cutter 1** a worker who cuts glass. **2** a tool used for cutting glass. **glass eye** a false eye made from glass. **glass fiber** Brit. **1** a filament or filaments of glass made into fabric; fiberglass. **2** such filaments embedded in plastic as reinforcement. **glass gall** = SANDIVER. **glass snake** any snakelike lizard of the genus Ophisaurus, with a very brittle tail. **glass wool** glass in the form of fine fibers used for packing and insulation. **has had a glass too much** is rather drunk. □□ **glassful** n. (pl. **-fuls**). **glassless** adj. **glasslike** adj. [OE glæs f. Gmc: cf. GLAZE]

■ n. **2 a** glassware; tumbler, flute, wineglass, goblet. **d** window, pane, windowpane. **i** lens, magnifying glass. **3** (glasses) **a** spectacles, eyeglasses, lorgnette(s), colloq. specs, goggles. **b** fieldglasses, binoculars; operaglasses. **4** see DRINK n. 1b, 2b.

glasshouse /gláss-hows/ n. **1** a building where glass is made. **2** Brit. a greenhouse. **3** Brit. sl. a military prison.

glassie var. of GLASSY n.

glassine /glaseén/ n. a glossy transparent paper. [GLASS]

glassblower /gláss-blōər/ n. a person who blows semimolten glass to make glassware.

glassblowing /gláss-blōing/ v. this occupation.

glassmaking /gláss-mayking/ n. the manufacture of glass.

glassware /gláss-wair/ n. articles made from glass, esp. drinking glasses, tableware, etc.

glasswort /gláss-wərt/ n. any plant of the genus Salicornia or Salsola formerly burned for use in glassmaking.

/.../ **pronunciation**	● **part of speech**
□ **phrases, idioms, and compounds**	
□□ **derivatives**	■ **synonym section**
cross-references appear in SMALL CAPITALS or italics	

glassy /glásee/ *adj. & n.* ● *adj.* (**glassier, glassiest**) **1** of or resembling glass, esp. in smoothness. **2** (of the eye, the expression, etc.) abstracted; dull; fixed (*fixed her with a glassy stare*). ● *n.* (also **glassie**) a glass marble. □ **the** (or **just the**) **glassy** *Austral.* the most excellent person or thing. □□ **glassily** *adv.* **glassiness** *n.*
■ *adj.* **1** smooth, gleaming, glossy, shining, shiny, slippery; icy. **2** fixed, staring, hypnotic, vacant, empty, abstracted, expressionless, blank, vacuous, dazed, dull, glazed, cold, lifeless.

Glaswegian /glazweéjən, glaas-/ *adj. & n.* ● *adj.* of or relating to Glasgow in Scotland. ● *n.* a native of Glasgow. [*Glasgow* after *Norwegian*, etc.]

Glauber's salt /glówbərz/ *n.* (also **Glauber's salts**) a crystalline hydrated form of sodium sulfate used esp. as a laxative. [J. R. *Glauber*, Ger. chemist d. 1668]

glaucoma /glawkṓmə, glou-/ *n.* an eye condition with increased pressure within the eyeball, causing gradual loss of sight. □□ **glaucomatous** *adj.* [L f. Gk *glaukōma -atos*, ult. f. *glaukos*: see GLAUCOUS]

glaucous /gláwkəs/ *adj.* **1** of a dull grayish green or blue. **2** covered with a powdery bloom as of grapes. [L *glaucus* f. Gk *glaukos*]

glaze /glayz/ *v. & n.* ● *v.* **1** *tr.* **a** fit (a window, picture, etc.) with glass. **b** provide (a building) with glass windows. **2** *tr.* **a** cover (pottery, etc.) with a glaze. **b** fix (paint) on pottery with a glaze. **3** *tr.* cover (pastry, meat, etc.) with a glaze. **4** *intr.* (often foll. by *over*) (of the eyes) become fixed or glassy (*his eyes glazed over*). **5** *tr.* cover (cloth, paper, leather, a painted surface, etc.) with a glaze or other similar finish. **6** *tr.* give a glassy surface to, e.g., by rubbing. ● *n.* **1** a vitreous substance, usu. a special glass, used to glaze pottery. **2** a smooth shiny coating of milk, sugar, gelatin, etc., on food. **3** a thin topcoat of transparent paint used to modify the tone of the underlying color. **4** a smooth surface formed by glazing. **5** a thin coating of ice. □ **glazed frost** a glassy coating of ice caused by freezing rain or a sudden thaw succeeded by a frost. **glaze in** enclose (a building, a window frame, etc.) with glass. □□ **glazer** *n.* **glazy** *adj.* [ME f. an oblique form of GLASS]
■ *v.* **4** see MIST *v.* **6** polish, burnish, shine, gloss, brighten, buff, furbish; varnish, lacquer, shellac. ● *n.* **4** coat, coating, covering; polish, shine, gloss, luster, patina.

glazier /gláyzhər/ *n.* a person whose trade is glazing windows, etc. □□ **glaziery** *n.*

glazing /gláyzing/ *n.* **1** the act or an instance of glazing. **2** windows (see also *double glazing*). **3** material used to produce a glaze.

gleam /gleem/ *n. & v.* ● *n.* **1** a faint or brief light (*a gleam of sunlight*). **2** a faint, sudden, intermittent, or temporary show (*not a gleam of hope*). ● *v.intr.* **1** emit gleams. **2** shine with a faint or intermittent brightness. **3** (of a quality) be indicated (*amusement gleamed in his eyes*). □□ **gleamingly** *adv.* **gleamy** *adj.* [OE *glǣm*: cf. GLIMMER]
■ *n.* **1** light, glimmer, glow, glint, flicker, shine, shimmer, glitter, twinkle, spark; beam, ray, shaft. **2** glimmer, ray, spark, flicker, hint, suggestion, indication, vestige, trace, scintilla. ● *v.* **2** glimmer, glint, shimmer, shine, twinkle, glitter, glisten.

glean /gleen/ *v.* **1** *tr.* collect or scrape together (news, facts, gossip, etc.) in small quantities. **2 a** *tr.* (also *absol.*) gather (ears of grain, etc.) after the harvest. **b** *tr.* strip (a field, etc.) after a harvest. □□ **gleaner** *n.* [ME f. OF *glener* f. LL *glennare*, prob. of Celt. orig.]
■ **1** see EXTRACT *v.* 4, 8. **2** see HARVEST *v.* 1.

gleanings /gleéningz/ *n.pl.* things gleaned, esp. facts.

glebe /gleeb/ *n.* **1** a piece of land serving as part of a clergyman's benefice and providing income. **2** *poet.* earth; land; a field. [ME f. L *gl(a)eba* clod, soil]

glee /glee/ *n.* **1** mirth; delight (*watched the enemy's defeat with glee*). **2** a song for three or more, esp. adult male, voices, singing different parts simultaneously, usu. unaccompanied. □ **glee club** a chorus for singing part-songs or other usu. short choral works. □□ **gleesome** *adj.* [OE *glīo, glēo* minstrelsy, jest f. Gmc]
■ **1** mirth, merriment, mirthfulness, joviality, jollity, gaiety, high spirits, cheerfulness, good cheer, exuberance, exhilaration, elation, exultation, delight, joy, joyfulness, joyousness, jubilation; schadenfreude.

gleeful /gleéfŏŏl/ *adj.* joyful. □□ **gleefully** *adv.* **gleefulness** *n.*
■ joyful, delighted, merry, mirthful, exuberant, cheerful, high-spirited, gamesome, exhilarated, elated, exultant, jubilant.

Gleichschaltung /glḯkh-shaltoong/ *n.* the standardization of political, economic, and social institutions in authoritarian countries. [G]

glen /glen/ *n.* a narrow valley. [Gael. & Ir. *gleann*]
■ see VALLEY.

glengarry /glengáree/ *n.* (*pl.* **-ies**) a brimless Scottish cap with a cleft down the center and usu. two ribbons hanging at the back. [*Glengarry* in Scotland]

glenoid cavity /gleénoyd/ *n.* a shallow depression on a bone, esp. the scapula and temporal bone, receiving the projection of another bone to form a joint. [F *glénoïde* f. Gk *glēnoeidēs* f. *glēnē* socket]

gley /glay/ *n.* a sticky waterlogged soil gray to blue in color. [Ukrainian, = sticky blue clay, rel. to CLAY]

glia /glḯə/ *n.* = NEUROGLIA. □□ **glial** *adj.* [Gk, = glue]

glib /glib/ *adj.* (**glibber, glibbest**) **1** (of a speaker, speech, etc.) fluent and voluble but insincere and shallow. **2** *archaic* smooth; unimpeded. □□ **glibly** *adv.* **glibness** *n.* [rel. to obs. *glibbery* slippery f. Gmc: perh. imit.]
■ **1** smooth, suave, smooth-spoken, smooth-tongued, smooth-talking, fast-talking; slick, superficial; ready, facile.

glide /glid/ *v. & n.* ● *v.* **1** *intr.* (of a stream, bird, snake, ship, train, skater, etc.) move with a smooth continuous motion. **2** *intr.* (of an aircraft, esp. a glider) fly without engine power. **3** *intr.* of time, etc.: **a** pass gently and imperceptibly. **b** (often foll. by *into*) pass and change gradually and imperceptibly (*night glided into day*). **4** *intr.* move quietly or stealthily. **5** *tr.* cause to glide (*breezes glided the boat on its course*). **6** *tr.* traverse or fly in a glider. ● *n.* **1 a** the act of gliding. **b** an instance of this. **2** *Phonet.* a gradually changing sound made in passing from one position of the speech organs to another. **3** a gliding dance or dance step. **4** a flight in a glider. □ **glide clip** *Austral.* a paper clip. **glide path** (also **slope**) an aircraft's line of descent to land, esp. as indicated by ground radar. □□ **glidingly** *adv.* [OE *glīdan* f. WG]
■ *v.* **1** slide, slip, stream, flow, coast, sail, soar; skate. **3** a slide by, pass by, disappear. **4** see SLITHER *v.*

glider /glḯdər/ *n.* **1 a** an aircraft that flies without an engine. **b** a glider pilot. **2** a type of porch swing with a gliding motion. **3** a person or thing that glides.

glim /glim/ *n.* **1** a faint light. **2** *archaic sl.* a candle; a lantern. [17th c.: perh. abbr. of GLIMMER or GLIMPSE]

glimmer /glímər/ *v. & n.* ● *v.intr.* shine faintly or intermittently. ● *n.* **1** a feeble or wavering light. **2** (usu. foll. by *of*) a faint gleam (of hope, understanding, etc.). **3** a glimpse. □□ **glimmeringly** *adv.* [ME prob. f. Scand. f. WG: see GLEAM]
■ *v.* see FLICKER[1] *v.* 1. ● *n.* **1** see FLICKER[1] *n.* 2 see GLEAM *n.* 2.

glimmering /glíməring/ *n.* **1** = GLIMMER *n.* 2 an act of glimmering.

glimpse /glimps/ *n. & v.* ● *n.* (often foll. by *of*) **1** a momentary or partial view (*caught a glimpse of her*). **2** a faint and transient appearance (*glimpses of the truth*). ● *v.* **1** *tr.* see faintly or partly (*glimpsed his face in the crowd*). **2** *intr.* (often foll. by *at*) cast a passing glance. **3** *intr.* **a** shine faintly or intermittently. **b** *poet.* appear faintly; dawn. [ME *glimse* corresp. to MHG *glimsen* f. WG (as GLIMMER)]
■ *n.* **1** see SIGHT *n.* 1b. ● *v.* **1** see SIGHT *v.* 1–3.

glint /glint/ *v. & n.* ● *v.intr. & tr.* flash or cause to flash; glitter; sparkle; reflect (*eyes glinted with amusement; the sword glinted fire*). ● *n.* a brief flash of light; a sparkle. [alt. of ME *glent*, prob. of Scand. orig.]
■ *v.* see SPARKLE *v.* 1a. ● *n.* see FLASH *n.* 1.

glissade /glisaád, -sáyd/ *n. & v.* • *n.* **1** an act of sliding down a steep slope of snow or ice, usu. on the feet with the support of an ice ax, etc. **2** a gliding step in ballet. • *v.intr.* perform a glissade. [F f. *glisser* slip, slide]

glissando /glisaándō/ *n.* (*pl.* **glissandi** /-dee/ or **-os**) *Mus.* a continuous slide of adjacent notes upwards or downwards. [It. f. F *glissant* sliding (as GLISSADE)]

glisten /glísən/ *v. & n.* • *v.intr.* shine, esp. like a wet object, snow, etc.; glitter. • *n.* a glitter; a sparkle. [OE *glisnian* f. *glisian* shine]

■ *v.* gleam, glint, sparkle, glitter; see also SHINE *v.* 1.
■ *n.* see GLEAM *n.* 1.

glister /glístər/ *v. & n. archaic* • *v.intr.* sparkle; glitter. • *n.* a sparkle; a gleam. [ME f. MLG *glistern*, MDu *glisteren*, rel. to GLISTEN]

glitch /glich/ *n. colloq.* a sudden irregularity or malfunction (of equipment, etc.). [20th c.: orig. unkn.]

■ see BUG *n.* 4.

glitter /glítər/ *v. & n.* • *v.intr.* **1** shine, esp. with a bright reflected light; sparkle. **2** (usu. foll. by *with*) **a** be a showy or splendid (*glittered with diamonds*). **b** be ostentatious or flashily brilliant (*glittering rhetoric*). • *n.* **1** a gleam; a sparkle. **2** showiness; splendor. **3** tiny pieces of sparkling material as on Christmas tree decorations. □□ **glitteringly** *adv.* **glittery** *adj.* [ME f. ON *glitra* f. Gmc]

■ *v.* **1** see GLISTEN *v.* **2** see SHINE *v.* 1. • *n.* **1** see GLEAM *n.* 1. **2** showiness, flashiness, splendor, brilliance, *colloq.* razzmatazz, *literary* refulgence, *sl.* pizzazz, razzle-dazzle, glitz, glitziness.

glitterati /glítəraátee/ *n.pl. sl.* the fashionable set of literary or show business people. [GLITTER + LITERATI]

glitz /glits/ *n. sl.* extravagant but superficial display; show business glamour. [back-form. f. GLITZY]

■ see GLITTER *n.* 2.

glitzy /glítsee/ *adj.* (**glitzier, glitziest**) *sl.* extravagant; ostentatious; tawdry; gaudy. □□ **glitzily** *adv.* **glitziness** *n.* [GLITTER, after RITZY: cf. G *glitzerig* glittering]

■ see GAUDY[1].

gloaming /glṓming/ *n. poet.* twilight; dusk. [OE *glōmung* f. *glōm* twilight, rel. to GLOW]

gloat /glōt/ *v. & n.* • *v.intr.* (often foll. by *on, upon, over*) consider or contemplate with lust, greed, malice, triumph, etc. (*gloated over his collection*). • *n.* **1** the act of gloating. **2** a look or expression of triumphant satisfaction. □□ **gloater** *n.* **gloatingly** *adv.* [16th c.: orig. unkn., but perh. rel. to ON *glotta* grin, MHG *glotzen* stare]

■ *v.* (*gloat over*) exult in, glory in, relish, revel in, delight in; crow over.

glob /glob/ *n.* a mass or lump of semiliquid substance, e.g., mud. [20th c.: perh. f. BLOB and GOB[1]]

global /glṓbəl/ *adj.* **1** worldwide (*global conflict*). **2** relating to or embracing a group of items, etc.; total. □ **global warming** the increase in temperature of the earth's atmosphere caused by the greenhouse effect. □□ **globally** *adv.* [F (as GLOBE)]

■ **1** worldwide, universal, international; cosmic. **2** broad, wide-ranging, far-reaching, all-embracing; total; see also EXTENSIVE 2.

globe /glōb/ *n. & v.* • *n.* **1 a** (prec. by *the*) the planet earth. **b** a planet, star, or sun. **c** any spherical body; a ball. **2** a spherical representation of the earth or of the constellations with a map on the surface. **3** a golden sphere as an emblem of sovereignty; an orb. **4** any spherical glass vessel, esp. a fish bowl, a lamp, etc. **5** the eyeball. • *v.tr. & intr.* make (usu. in *passive*) or become globular. □ **globe artichoke** the partly edible head of the artichoke plant. **globe lightning** = *ball lightning* (see BALL[1]). **globe-trotter** a person who travels widely. **globe-trotting** such travel. □□ **globelike** *adj.* **globoid** *adj. & n.* **globose** /-bōs/ *adj.* [F *globe* or L *globus*]

■ *n.* **1** a world, (mother) earth, planet. **b** planet, sun; see also STAR *n.* 1. **c** sphere, ball, orb; globule, spherule, spheroid. □ **globe-trotter** see TRAVELER 1.

globefish /glṓbfish/ = PUFFER 2.

globeflower /glṓbflowər/ *n.* any ranunculaceous plant of the genus *Trollius* with globular usu. yellow flowers.

globigerina /glōbíjərínə, -reénə/ *n.* any planktonic protozoan of the genus *Globigerina*, living near the surface of the sea. [mod.L f. L *globus* globe + *-ger* carrying + -INA]

globular /glóbyələr/ *adj.* **1** globe-shaped; spherical. **2** composed of globules. □□ **globularity** /-láritee/ *n.* **globularly** *adv.*

■ **1** see SPHERICAL.

globule /glóbyōol/ *n.* a small globe or round particle; a drop. □□ **globulous** *adj.* [F *globule* or L *globulus* (as GLOBE)]

■ **1** see DROP *n.* 1a.

globulin /glóbyəlin/ *n.* any of a group of proteins found in plant and animal tissues and esp. responsible for the transport of molecules, etc.

glockenspiel /glókənspeel, -shpeel/ *n.* a musical instrument consisting of a series of bells or metal bars or tubes suspended or mounted in a frame and struck by hammers. [G, = bell-play]

glom /glom/ *v. sl.* (**glommed, glomming**) **1** *tr.* steal; grab. **2** *intr.* (usu. foll. by *on to*) steal; grab. [var. of Sc. *glaum* (18th c., of unkn. orig.)]

glomerate /glómərət/ *adj. Bot. & Anat.* compactly clustered. [L *glomeratus* past part. of *glomerare* f. *glomus -eris* ball]

glomerule /glómərōol/ *n.* a clustered flower head.

glomerulus /glōméryələs/ *n.* (*pl.* **glomeruli** /-lī/) a cluster of small organisms, tissues, or blood vessels, esp. of the capillaries of the kidney. □□ **glomerular** *adj.* [mod.L, dimin. of L *glomus -eris* ball]

gloom /glōōm/ *n. & v.* • *n.* **1** darkness; obscurity. **2** melancholy; despondency. **3** *poet.* a dark place. • *v.* **1** *intr.* be gloomy or melancholy; frown. **2** *intr.* (of the sky, etc.) be dull or threatening; lower. **3** *intr.* appear darkly or obscurely. **4** *tr.* cover with gloom; make dark or dismal. [ME *gloum(b)e*, of unkn. orig.: cf. GLUM]

■ *n.* **1** darkness, dark, dusk, shadow(s), shade, shadowiness, dimness, gloominess, murkiness, murk, obscurity. **2** melancholy, sadness, blackness, downheartedness, sorrow, dejection, despondency, moroseness, depression, desolation, despair, misery, low spirits, *archaic or literary* woe, *literary* dolor; blues, doldrums, *colloq.* dumps. • *v.* **2** darken, threaten, menace, lower.

gloomy /glōōmee/ *adj.* (**gloomier, gloomiest**) **1** dark; unlighted. **2** depressed; sullen. **3** dismal; depressing. □□ **gloomily** *adv.* **gloominess** *n.*

■ **1** dark, black, shadowy, shaded, shady, obscure, unlighted, murky, dim, dusky, *literary* Stygian; dull, cloudy, overcast. **2** depressed, dejected, morose, glum, lugubrious, cheerless, dismal, moody, down, downcast, desolate, doleful, downhearted, crestfallen, chapfallen, forlorn, despondent, miserable, sullen, saturnine, joyless, dispirited, despairing, dreary, sorrowful, unhappy, melancholy, sad, distressed, blue, in the doldrums, *colloq.* down in the mouth, (down) in the dumps. **3** dismal, depressing, cheerless, dreary, dispiriting, sad, disheartening.

glop /glop/ *n. sl.* a liquid or sticky mess, esp. unappealing or inedible food. [imit.: cf. obs. *glop* swallow greedily]

Gloria /gláwreeə/ *n.* **1** any of various doxologies beginning with *Gloria*, esp. the hymn beginning with *Gloria in excelsis Deo* (Glory be to God in the highest). **2** an aureole. [L, = glory]

glorify /gláwrifī/ *v.tr.* (**-ies, -ied**) **1** exalt to heavenly glory; make glorious. **2** transform into something more splendid. **3** extol; praise. **4** (as **glorified** *adj.*) seeming or pretending to be better than in reality (*just a glorified office boy*). □□ **glorification** *n.* **glorifier** *n.* [ME f. OF *glorifier* f. eccl.L *glorificare* f. LL *glorificus* f. L *gloria* glory]

■ **2** elevate, exalt, raise (up), enhance, dignify, ennoble. **3** extol, praise, laud, lionize, applaud, commend, hail,

---

/.../ **pronunciation**	● **part of speech**
□ **phrases, idioms, and compounds**	
□□ **derivatives**	■ **synonym section**
cross-references appear in SMALL CAPITALS or *italics*	

acclaim, revere, venerate, pay tribute *or* homage to, honor, celebrate. **4** (**glorified**) exalted, high-flown, high-sounding, esp. *Brit. colloq.* jumped-up.

gloriole /gláwreeōl/ *n.* an aureole; a halo. [F f. L *gloriola* dimin. of *gloria* glory]

glorious /gláwreeəs/ *adj.* **1** possessing glory; illustrious. **2** conferring glory; honorable. **3** *colloq.* splendid; magnificent; delightful (*a glorious day*). **4** esp. *Brit. iron.* intense; unmitigated (*a glorious muddle*). **5** *Brit. colloq.* happily intoxicated. □□ **gloriously** *adv.* **gloriousness** *n.* [ME f. AF *glorious*, OF *glorios, -eus* f. L *gloriosus* (as GLORY)]

■ **1** illustrious, famed, famous, renowned, celebrated, distinguished, honored, eminent, excellent. **2** outstanding, splendid, magnificent, marvelous, memorable, wonderful, spectacular, dazzling; honorable, estimable, admirable, excellent, superior. **3** splendid, superb, magnificent, marvelous, wonderful, gorgeous; delightful, fine, excellent, beautiful, *colloq.* heavenly, great, fabulous; see also BRILLIANT *adj.* 4.

glory /gláwree/ *n. & v.* ● *n.* (*pl.* **-ies**) **1** high renown or fame; honor. **2** adoring praise and thanksgiving (*Glory to the Lord*). **3** resplendent majesty or magnificence; great beauty (*the glory of Versailles; the glory of the rose*). **4** a thing that brings renown or praise; a distinction. **5** the bliss and splendor of heaven. **6** *colloq.* a state of exaltation, prosperity, happiness, etc. (*is in his glory playing with his trains*). **7** an aureole; a halo. **8** an anthelion. ● *v.intr.* (often foll. by *in*, or *to* + infin.) pride oneself; exult (*glory in their skill*). □ **glory be!** **1** a devout ejaculation. **2** *colloq.* an exclamation of surprise or delight. **glory-box** *Austral.* & *NZ* a box for women's clothes, etc., stored in preparation for marriage; a hope chest. **glory hole 1** *Brit. colloq.* an untidy room, drawer, or receptacle. **2** an open quarry. **glory-of-the-snow** = CHIONODOXA. **go to glory** *sl.* die; be destroyed. [ME f. AF & OF *glorie* f. L *gloria*]

■ *n.* **1** honor, dignity, prestige, renown, eminence, distinction, illustriousness, celebrity, fame, exaltation, immortality. **2** worship, adoration, glorification, exaltation, praise, homage, thanksgiving, gratitude, *formal* laudation. **3** majesty, magnificence, excellence, splendor, pomp, pageantry, grandeur, greatness, beauty, radiance, brilliance, *literary* effulgence, refulgence. **4** distinction, merit, quality, credit; see also ACCOMPLISHMENT 3. **7** aureole, nimbus, aura, halo, gloriole; crown, circlet, corona, radiance, *Art* vesica, mandorla. ● *v.* revel, relish, delight, exult, pride oneself, rejoice. □ **glory be!** **2** see INDEED *int.*

gloss[1] /glaws, glos/ *n. & v.* ● *n.* **1** a surface shine or luster. **b** an instance of this; a smooth finish. **2 a** a deceptively attractive appearance. **b** an instance of this. **3** (in full **gloss paint**) paint formulated to give a hard glossy finish (cf. MATTE). ● *v.tr.* make glossy. □ **gloss over 1** seek to conceal beneath a false appearance. **2** conceal or evade by mentioning briefly or misleadingly. □□ **glosser** *n.* [16th c.: orig. unkn.]

■ *n.* **1** shine, sheen, luster, gleam, glow; glaze, polish, burnish; brightness. **2** façade, mask, surface, veneer, false appearance, disguise, camouflage, show, front, semblance. ● *v.* glaze, polish, burnish, shine, buff, furbish, brighten, clean. □ **gloss over** veil, cover up, conceal, hide, disguise, camouflage, mask; evade, explain away, gloss, gloze (over), smooth over, whitewash.

gloss[2] /glaws, glos/ *n. & v.* ● *n.* **1 a** an explanatory word or phrase inserted between the lines or in the margin of a text. **b** a comment, explanation, interpretation, or paraphrase. **2** a misrepresentation of another's words. **3 a** a glossary. **b** an interlinear translation or annotation. ● *v.* **1** *tr.* **a** add a gloss or glosses to (a text, word, etc.). **b** read a different sense into; explain away. **2** *intr.* (often foll. by *on*) make (esp. unfavorable) comments. **3** *intr.* write or introduce glosses. □□ **glosser** *n.* [alt. of GLOZE after med.L *glossa*]

■ *n.* **1, 3b** footnote; annotation, comment, commentary, critique, criticism, analysis; explanation, interpretation,

exegesis, explication, definition, elucidation; paraphrase, translation. **2** falsification, misrepresentation, distortion, misstatement, misquotation, perversion. ● *v.* **1 a** explain, interpret, explicate, define, elucidate; comment on, annotate, criticize, analyze, review, critique; translate. **b** see *gloss over* (GLOSS[1]).

glossal /gláwsəl, -glós/ *adj. Anat.* of the tongue; lingual. [Gk *glōssa* tongue]

glossary /gláwsəree, -glós/ *n.* (*pl.* **-ies**) **1** (also **gloss**) an alphabetical list of terms or words found in or relating to a specific subject or text, esp. dialect, with explanations; a brief dictionary. **2** a collection of glosses. □□ **glossarial** /-sáireeəl/ *adj.* **glossarist** *n.* [L *glossarium* f. *glossa* GLOSS[2]]

■ **1** word list, dictionary, wordbook, wordfinder.

glossator /glawsáytər, glo-/ *n.* **1** a writer of glosses or glossaries. **2** *hist.* a commentator on, or interpreter of, medieval law texts. [ME f. med.L f. *glossare* f. *glossa* GLOSS[2]]

glosseme /gláwseem, glós-/ *n.* any meaningful feature of a language that cannot be analyzed into smaller meaningful units. [Gk *glōssēma* f. *glōssa* GLOSS[2]]

glossitis /glawsítis, glo-/ *n.* inflammation of the tongue. [Gk *glōssa* tongue + -ITIS]

glossographer /glawsógrəfər, glo-/ *n.* a writer of glosses or commentaries. [GLOSS[2] + -GRAPHER]

glossolalia /gláwsəláyleeə, glós-/ *n.* = *gift of tongues* (see TONGUE). [mod.L f. Gk *glōssa* tongue + -*lalia* speaking]

glossolaryngeal /gláwsōlarínjeeəl, glós-/ *adj.* of the tongue and larynx. [Gk *glōssa* tongue + LARYNGEAL]

glossy /gláwsee, glós-/ *adj. & n.* ● *adj.* (**glossier, glossiest**) **1** having a shine; smooth. **2** (of paper, etc.) smooth and shiny. **3** (of a magazine, etc.) printed on such paper; expensively produced and attractively presented, but sometimes lacking in content or depth. ● *n.* (*pl.* **-ies**) *colloq.* **1** a glossy magazine. **2** a photograph with a glossy surface. □□ **glossily** *adv.* **glossiness** *n.*

■ *adj.* **1** shining, shiny, smooth, lustrous, sleek, glassy, glistening; polished, glazed, burnished, waxed. **3** coffee-table; upmarket; showy, *sl.* glitzy.

glottal /glót'l/ *adj.* of or produced by the glottis. □ **glottal stop** a sound produced by the sudden opening or shutting of the glottis.

glottis /glótis/ *n.* the space at the upper end of the windpipe and between the vocal cords, affecting voice modulation through expansion or contraction. □□ **glottic** /-tik/ *adj.* [mod.L f. Gk *glōttis* f. *glōtta* var. of *glōssa* tongue]

glove /gluv/ *n. & v.* ● *n.* **1** a covering for the hand, of wool, leather, cotton, etc., worn esp. for protection against cold or dirt, and usu. having separate fingers. **2** a padded protective glove, esp.: **a** a boxing glove. **b** *Baseball* a fielder's glove. ● *v.tr.* cover or provide with a glove or gloves. □ **fit like a glove** fit exactly. **glove box 1** a box for gloves. **2** a closed chamber with sealed-in gloves for handling radioactive material, etc. **3** = *glove compartment*. **glove compartment** a recess or cabinet for small articles in the dashboard of a motor vehicle. **glove puppet** a small cloth puppet fitted on the hand and worked by the fingers. **throw down** (or **take up**) **the glove** issue (or accept) a challenge. **with the gloves off** mercilessly; unfairly; with no compunction. □□ **gloveless** *adj.* **glover** *n.* [OE *glōf*, corresp. to ON *glófi*, perh. f. Gmc]

glow /glō/ *v. & n.* ● *v.intr.* **1 a** throw out light and heat without flame; be incandescent. **b** shine like something heated in this way. **2** (of the cheeks) redden, esp. from cold or exercise. **3** (often foll. by *with*) **a** (of the body) be heated, esp. from exertion; sweat. **b** express or experience strong emotion (*glowed with pride; glowing with indignation*). **4** show a warm color (*the painting glows with warmth*). **5** (as **glowing** *adj.*) expressing pride or satisfaction (*a glowing report*). ● *n.* **1** a glowing state. **2** a bright warm color, esp. the red of cheeks. **3** ardor; passion. **4** a feeling induced by good health, exercise, etc.; well-being. □ **glow discharge** a luminous sparkless electrical discharge from a pointed conductor in a gas at low pressure. **in a glow** *Brit. colloq.* hot or flushed; sweating. □□ **glowingly** *adv.* [OE *glōwan* f. Gmc]

■ *v.* **1** shine, glimmer, gleam, radiate, incandesce, phosphoresce. **2** flush, blush, color (up), redden, go red, burn. **5** (**glowing**) laudatory, complimentary, enthusiastic, eulogistic, rhapsodic, favorable, encomiastic, panegyrical. ● *n.* **1** luminosity, phosphorescence, incandescence, light, lambency, luster, brightness, gleam, luminousness, radiance. **2** flush, blush, redness, ruddiness; radiance, rosiness, bloom. **3** ardor, passion, excitement, warmth, fervor, fervency, enthusiasm, thrill. **4** well-being, (good) health.

glower /glowr/ *v. & n.* ● *v.intr.* (often foll. by *at*) stare or scowl, esp. angrily. ● *n.* a glowering look. □□ **gloweringly** *adv.* [orig. uncert.: perh. Sc. var. of ME *glore* f. LG or Scand., or f. obs. (ME) *glow* stare + -ER⁴]
■ *v.* see SCOWL *v.* ● *n.* see GLARE¹ *n.* 2.

glowworm /glṓwərm/ *n.* any beetle of the genus *Lampyris* whose wingless female emits light from the end of the abdomen.

gloxinia /gloksíneeə/ *n.* any tropical plant of the genus *Gloxinia*, native to S. America, with large bell flowers of various colors. [mod.L f. B. P. *Gloxin*, 18th-c. Ger. botanist]

gloze /glōz/ *v.* **1** *tr.* GLOSS², 1. **2** = *gloss over* (see GLOSS¹). **3** *intr. archaic* a (usu. foll. by *on, upon*) comment. b talk speciously; fawn. [ME f. OF *gloser* f. *glose* f. med.L *glosa, gloza* f. L *glossa* tongue, GLOSS²]

glucagon /glṓokəgon/ *n.* a polypeptide hormone formed in the pancreas, which aids the breakdown of glycogen. [Gk *glukus* sweet + *agōn* leading]

glucose /glṓokōs/ *n.* **1** a simple sugar containing six carbon atoms, found mainly in its dextrorotatory form (see DEXTROSE), which is an important energy source in living organisms and obtainable from some carbohydrates by hydrolysis. ¶ Chem. formula: $C_6H_{12}O_6$. **2** a syrup containing glucose sugars from the incomplete hydrolysis of starch. [F f. Gk *gleukos* sweet wine, rel. to *glukus* sweet]

glucoside /glṓokəsīd/ *n.* a compound giving glucose and other products upon hydrolysis. □□ **glucosidic** /-sídik/ *adj.*

glue /glṓo/ *n. & v.* ● *n.* an adhesive substance used for sticking objects or materials together. ● *v.tr.* (**glues, glued, gluing** or **glueing**) **1** fasten or join with glue. **2** keep or put very close (*an eye glued to the keyhole*). □ **glue sniffer** a person who inhales the fumes from adhesives as a drug. □□ **gluelike** *adj.* **gluer** *n.* **gluey** /glṓo-ee/ *adj.* (**gluier, gluiest**). **glueyness** *n.* [ME f. OF *glu* (n.), *gluer* (v.), f. LL *glus glutis* f. L *gluten*]
■ *n.* adhesive, gum, paste, cement, *colloq.* sticky. ● *v.* **1** gum, paste, fix, affix, cement; see also STICK² 4.

gluepot /glṓopot/ *n.* **1** a pot with an outer vessel holding water to heat glue. **2** *colloq.* an area of sticky mud, etc.

glug / glug/ *n. & v.* ● *n.* a hollow, usu. repetitive gurgling sound. ● *v.intr.* make a gurgling sound as of water from a bottle. [imit.]

glum /glum/ *adj.* (**glummer, glummest**) looking or feeling dejected; sullen; displeased. □□ **glumly** *adv.* **glumness** *n.* [rel. to dial. *glum* (v.) frown, var. of *gloume* GLOOM *v.*]
■ gloomy, dejected, dispirited, miserable, woebegone, crestfallen, doleful, down, lugubrious, morose, low, dismal, saturnine, sullen, sulky, dour, moody, displeased; see also SAD 1.

glume /glṓom/ *n.* **1** a membranous bract surrounding the spikelet of grasses or the florets of sedges. **2** the husk of grain. □□ **glumaceous** /-máyshəs/ *adj.* **glumose** *adj.* [L *gluma* husk]

gluon /glṓo-on/ *n. Physics* any of a group of elementary particles that are thought to bind quarks together. [GLUE + -ON]

glut /glut/ *v. & n.* ● *v.tr.* (**glutted, glutting**) **1** feed (a person, one's stomach, etc.) or indulge (an appetite, a desire, etc.) to the full; satiate; cloy. **2** fill to excess; choke up. **3** *Econ.* overstock (a market) with goods. ● *n.* **1** *Econ.* supply exceeding demand; a surfeit (*a glut in the market*). **2** full indulgence; one's fill. [ME prob. f. OF *gloutir* swallow f. L *gluttire*: cf. GLUTTON]
■ *v.* **1** gorge, stuff, cram, overfeed, surfeit, satiate, sate; indulge; sicken, cloy. **2, 3** overfill, overload,

oversupply, overstock; flood, saturate, swamp, inundate, deluge; clog, choke up. ● *n.* **1** surplus, excess, surfeit, saturation, oversupply, overabundance, superabundance, superfluity.

glutamate /glṓotəmayt/ *n.* any salt or ester of glutamic acid, esp. a sodium salt used to enhance the flavor of food.

glutamic acid /glṓotámik/ *n.* a naturally occurring amino acid, a constituent of many proteins. [GLUTEN + AMINE + -IC]

gluten /glṓotən/ *n.* **1** a mixture of proteins present in cereal grains. **2** *archaic* a sticky substance. [F f. L *gluten glutinis* glue]

gluteus /glṓoteeəs/ *n.* (*pl.* **glutei** /-teeī/) any of the three muscles in each buttock. □□ **gluteal** *adj.* [mod.L f. Gk *gloutos* buttock]

glutinous /glṓot'nəs/ *adj.* sticky; like glue. □□ **glutinously** *adv.* **glutinousness** *n.* [F *glutineux* or L *glutinosus* (as GLUTEN)]
■ see STICKY *adj.* 2.

glutton /glút'n/ *n.* **1** an excessively greedy eater. **2** (often foll. by *for*) *colloq.* a person insatiably eager (*a glutton for work*). **3** a voracious animal *Gulo gulo*, of the weasel family. Also called WOLVERINE. □ **a glutton for punishment** a person eager to take on hard or unpleasant tasks. □□ **gluttonize** *v.intr.* **gluttonous** *adj.* **gluttonously** *adv.* [ME f. OF *gluton, gloton* f. L *glutto -onis* f. *gluttire* swallow, *gluttus* greedy]
■ **1** gormandizer, gourmand, overeater, *colloq.* hog, pig, greedy-guts. **2** see ADDICT *n.* 2. □ **a glutton for punishment** see SUCKER *n.* 2. □□ **gluttonous** greedy, voracious, insatiable, *archaic or joc.* esurient, *colloq.* piggish, hoggish, swinish, piggy, *literary or joc.* edacious.

gluttony /glút'nee/ *n.* habitual greed or excess in eating. [OF *glutonie* (as GLUTTON)]
■ greed, greediness, gourmandism, voraciousness, voracity, insatiability, *colloq.* hoggishness, piggishness, pigginess.

glyceride /glísərīd/ *n.* any fatty acid ester of glycerol.

glycerin /glísərin/ *n.* (also **glycerine**) = GLYCEROL. [F *glycerin* f. Gk *glukeros* sweet]

glycerol /glísərawl, -rol/ *n.* a colorless sweet viscous liquid formed as a byproduct in the manufacture of soap, used as an emollient and laxative, in explosives, etc. ¶ Chem. formula: $C_3H_8O_3$. Also called GLYCERIN. [GLYCERIN + -OL¹]

glycine /glíseen/ *n.* the simplest naturally occurring amino acid, a general constituent of proteins. [G *Glycin* f. Gk *glukus* sweet]

glyco- /glíkō/ *comb. form* sugar. [Gk *glukus* sweet]

glycogen /glíkəjən/ *n.* a polysaccharide serving as a store of carbohydrates, esp. in animal tissues, and yielding glucose on hydrolysis. □□ **glycogenic** /-jénik/ *adj.*

glycogenesis /glíkəjénisis/ *n. Biochem.* the formation of glycogen from sugar.

glycol /glíkawl, -kol/ *n.* a diol, esp. ethylene glycol. □□ **glycolic** /-kólik/ *adj.* **glycollic** *adj.* [GLYCERIN + -OL¹, orig. as being intermediate between glycerine and alcohol]

glycolysis /glikólisis/ *n. Biochem.* the breakdown of glucose by enzymes in most living organisms to release energy and pyruvic or lactic acid.

glycoprotein /glíkōprṓteen/ *n.* any of a group of compounds consisting of a protein combined with a carbohydrate.

glycoside /glíkəsīd/ *n.* any compound giving sugar and other products on hydrolysis. □□ **glycosidic** /-sídik/ *adj.* [GLYCO-, after GLUCOSIDE]

glycosuria /glíkəsyŏoreeə, -shŏor-/ *n.* a condition characterized by an excess of sugar in the urine, associated with diabetes, kidney disease, etc. □□ **glycosuric** *adj.* [F *glycose* glucose + -URIA]

glyph /glif/ *n.* **1** a sculptured character or symbol. **2** a vertical

---

/ . . . / **pronunciation**   ● **part of speech**
□ **phrases, idioms, and compounds**
□□ **derivatives**   ■ **synonym section**
cross-references appear in SMALL CAPITALS or *italics*

groove, esp. that on a Greek frieze. □□ **glyphic** *adj.* [F *glyphe* f. Gk *gluphē* carving f. *gluphō* carve]

glyptic /glíptik/ *adj.* of or concerning carving, esp. on precious stones. [F *glyptique* or Gk *gluptikos* f. *gluptēs* carver f. *gluphō* carve]

glyptodont /glíptədont/ *n.* any extinct armadillolike edentate animal of the genus *Glyptodon* native to S. America, having fluted teeth and a body covered in a hard thick bony shell. [mod.L f. Gk *gluptos* carved + *odous odontos* tooth]

glyptography /gliptógrəfee/ *n.* the art or scientific study of engraving gems. [Gk *gluptos* carved + -GRAPHY]

GM *abbr.* **1** General Motors. **2** general manager. **3** (in the UK) George Medal.

gm *abbr.* gram(s).

G-man /jeéman/ *n.* (*pl.* **G-men**) **1** *US colloq.* a federal officer, esp. an FBI agent. **2** *Ir.* a political detective. [*Government* + MAN]

GMT *abbr.* Greenwich Mean Time.

gnamma /náma/ *n.* (also **namma**) *Austral.* a natural hole in a rock, containing water; a waterhole. [Aboriginal]

gnarled /naarld/ *adj.* (also **gnarly** /naárlee/) (of a tree, hands, etc.) knobbly; twisted; rugged. [var. of *knarled*, rel. to KNURL]
 ▪ knobbly, knotty, knotted, lumpy, bumpy, rugged, twisted, bent, crooked, distorted, contorted, warped.

gnash /nash/ *v. & n.* ● *v.* **1** *tr.* grind (the teeth). **2** *intr.* (of the teeth) strike together; grind. ● *n.* an act of grinding the teeth. [var. of obs. *gnacche* or *gnast*, rel. to ON *gnastan* a gnashing (imit.)]
 ▪ *v.* see GRIND *v.* 2b.

gnat /nat/ *n.* **1** any small two-winged biting fly of the genus *Culex*, esp. *C. pipiens*. **2** an insignificant annoyance. **3** a tiny thing. [OE *gnætt*]
 ▪ **2** see PEST 1.

gnathic /náthik/ *adj.* of or relating to the jaws. [Gk *gnathos* jaw]

gnaw /naw/ *v.* (*past part.* **gnawed** or **gnawn**) **1 a** *tr.* (usu. foll. by *away, off, in two*, etc.) bite persistently; wear away by biting. **b** *intr.* (often foll. by *at, into*) bite; nibble. **2 a** *intr.* (often foll. by *at, into*) (of a destructive agent, pain, fear, etc.) corrode; waste away; consume; torture. **b** *tr.* corrode, consume, torture, etc., with pain, fear, etc. (*was gnawed by doubt*). **3** *tr.* (as **gnawing** *adj.*) persistent; worrying. □□ **gnawingly** *adv.* [OE *gnagen*, ult. imit.]
 ▪ **1** bite, chew, nibble, champ, munch, masticate, *literary* manducate. **2 a** (*gnaw at*) worry, bother, haunt, trouble, distress, plague, torment, torture; consume, devour, wear down *or* away; erode, corrode, waste away. **3** (*gnawing*) nagging, lingering, niggling, worrying, worrisome; see also PERSISTENT 2, 3, *disturbing* (DISTURB).

gneiss /nīs/ *n.* a usu. coarse-grained metamorphic rock foliated by mineral layers, principally of feldspar, quartz, and ferromagnesian minerals. □□ **gneissic** *adj.* **gneissoid** *adj.* **gneissose** *adj.* [G]

GNMA /jínee may/ *n.* Government National Mortgage Association.

gnocchi /nyáwkee/ *n.pl.* an Italian dish of small dumplings usu. made from potato, semolina flour, etc., or from spinach and cheese. [It., pl. of *gnocco* f. *nocchio* knot in wood]

gnome[1] /nōm/ *n.* **1 a** a dwarfish legendary creature supposed to guard the earth's treasures underground; a goblin. **b** a figure of a gnome, esp. as a garden ornament. **2** (esp. in *pl.*) *colloq.* a person with sinister influence, esp. financial (*gnomes of Zurich*). □□ **gnomish** *adj.* [F f. mod.L *gnomus* (word invented by Paracelsus)]
 ▪ **1 a** see GOBLIN.

gnome[2] /nōm, nốmee/ *n.* a maxim; an aphorism. [Gk *gnōmē* opinion f. *gignōskō* know]

gnomic /nốmik/ *adj.* **1** of, consisting of, or using gnomes or aphorisms (see GNOME[2]). **2** *Gram.* (of a tense) used without the implication of time to express a general truth, e.g., *men were deceivers ever*. □□ **gnomically** *adv.* [Gk *gnōmikos* (as GNOME[2])]

gnomon /nốmon, -mən/ *n.* **1** the rod or pin, etc., on a sundial

that shows the time by the position of its shadow. **2** *Geom.* the part of a parallelogram left when a similar parallelogram has been taken from its corner. **3** *Astron.* a column, etc., used in observing the sun's meridian altitude. □□ **gnomonic** /-mónik/ *adj.* [F or L *gnomon* f. Gk *gnōmōn* indicator, etc., f. *gignōskō* know]

gnosis /nốsis/ *n.* knowledge of spiritual mysteries. [Gk *gnōsis* knowledge (as GNOMON)]

gnostic /nóstik/ *adj. & n.* ● *adj.* **1** relating to knowledge, esp. esoteric mystical knowledge. **2** (**Gnostic**) concerning the Gnostics; occult; mystic. ● *n.* (**Gnostic**) (usu. in *pl.*) a Christian heretic of the 1st–3rd c. claiming gnosis. □□ **Gnosticism** /-tisizəm/ *n.* **gnosticize** *v.tr. & intr.* [eccl.L *gnosticus* f. Gk *gnōstikos* (as GNOSIS)]

GNP *abbr.* gross national product.

gnu /nōō, nyōō/ *n.* any antelope of the genus *Connochaetes*, native to S. Africa, with a large erect head and brown stripes on the neck and shoulders. Also called WILDEBEEST. [Bushman *nqu*, prob. through Du. *gnoe*]

go[1] /gō/ *v., n., & adj.* ● *v.* (*3rd sing. present* **goes** /gōz/; *past* **went** /went/; *past part.* **gone** /gon/) **1** *intr.* **a** start moving or be moving from one place or point in time to another; travel; proceed. **b** (foll. by *to* + infin., or *and* + verb) proceed in order to (*went to find him; go and buy some bread*). **c** (foll. by *and* + verb) *colloq.* expressing annoyance (*you went and told him; they've gone and broken it; she went and won*). **2** *intr.* (foll. by verbal noun) make a special trip for; participate in; proceed to do (*went skiing; then went shopping; often goes running*). **3** *intr.* lie or extend in a certain direction; lead to (*the road goes to the shore; where does that door go?*). **4** *intr.* **a** leave; depart (*they had to go*). **b** *colloq.* disappear; vanish (*my bag has gone*). **5** *intr.* move, act, work, etc. (*the clock doesn't go; his brain is going all the time*). **6** *intr.* **a** make a specified movement (*go like this with your foot*). **b** make a sound (often of a specified kind) (*the gun went bang; the door bell went*). **c** *colloq.* say (*so he goes to me "Why didn't you like it?"*). **d** (of an animal) make (its characteristic cry) (*the cow went "moo"*). **7** *intr.* be in a specified state (*go hungry; went in fear of his life*). **8** *intr.* **a** pass into a specified condition (*gone bad; went mad; went to sleep*). **b** *colloq.* die. **c** proceed or escape in a specified condition (*the poet went unrecognized; the crime went unnoticed*). **9** *intr.* **a** (of time or distance) pass; elapse; be traversed (*ten days to go before Easter; the last mile went quickly*). **b** be finished (*the movie went quickly*). **10** *intr.* **a** (of a document, verse, song, etc.) have a specified content or wording; run (*the tune goes like this*). **b** be current or accepted (*so the story goes*). **c** be suitable; fit; match (*the shoes don't go with the hat*). **d** be regularly kept or put (*the forks go here*). **e** find room; fit (*this won't go into the cupboard*). **11** *intr.* **a** turn out; proceed; take a course or view (*things went well; Massachusetts went Democratic*). **b** be successful (*make the party go*). **c** progress (*we've still got a long way to go*). **12** *intr.* **a** be sold (*went for $1; went cheap*). **b** (of money) be spent (*$200 went on a new jacket*). **13** *intr.* **a** be relinquished, dismissed, or abolished (*the car will have to go*). **b** fail; decline; give way; collapse (*his sight is going; the bulb has gone*). **14** *intr.* be acceptable or permitted; be accepted without question (*anything goes; what I say goes*). **15** *intr.* (often foll. by *by, with, on, upon*) be guided by; judge or act on or in harmony with (*have nothing to go on; a good rule to go by*). **16** *intr.* attend or visit or travel to regularly (*goes to church; goes to school; this train goes to Paris*). **17** *intr.* (foll. by pres. part.) *colloq.* proceed (often foolishly) to do (*went running to the police; don't go making him angry*). **18** *intr.* act or proceed to a certain point (*will go so far and no further; went as high as $100*). **19** *intr.* (of a number) be capable of being contained in another (*6 into 12 goes twice; 6 into 5 won't go*). **20** *tr. Cards* bid; declare (*has gone two spades*). **21** *intr.* (usu. foll. by *to*) be allotted or awarded; pass (*first prize went to the girl; the job went to his rival*). **22** *intr.* (foll. by *to, toward*) amount to; contribute to (*12 inches go to make a foot; this will go toward your vacation*). **23** *intr.* (in *imper.*) begin motion (a starter's order in a race) (*ready, set, go!*). **24** *intr.* (usu. foll. by *to*) refer or appeal (*go to him for help*). **25** *intr.* (often foll. by *on*) take up a specified profession (*went on the stage; gone sol-*

diering; *went to sea*). **26** *intr.* (usu. foll. by *by, under*) be known or called (*goes by the name of Droopy*). **27** *tr. colloq.* proceed to (*go jump in the lake*). **28** *intr.* (foll. by *for*) apply to; have relevance for (*that goes for me too*). **29** *intr. colloq.* urinate or defecate. ● *n.* (*pl.* **goes**) **1** the act or an instance of going. **2** mettle; spirit; dash; animation (*she has a lot of go in her*). **3** vigorous activity (*it's all go*). **4** *colloq.* a success (*made a go of it*). **5** *colloq.* a turn; an attempt (*I'll have a go*; *it's my go*; *all in one go*). **6** permission; approval; go-ahead (*gave us a go on the new project*). **7** esp. *Brit. colloq.* a state of affairs (*a helluva go*). **8** esp. *Brit. colloq.* an attack of illness (*a bad go of flu*). **9** esp. *Brit. colloq.* a quantity of liquor, food, etc., served at one time. ● *adj. colloq.* **1** functioning properly (*all systems are go*). **2** fashionable; progressive. □ **all the go** *Brit. colloq.* in fashion. **as** (or **so**) **far as it goes** an expression of caution against taking a statement too positively (*the work is good as far as it goes*). **as** (**a person or thing**) **goes** as the average is (*a good actor as actors go*). **from the word go** *colloq.* from the very beginning. **give it a go** *colloq.* make an effort to succeed. **go about 1** busy oneself with; set to work at. **2** be socially active. **3** (foll. by pres. part.) make a habit of doing (*goes about telling lies*). **4** *Naut.* change to an opposite tack. **go ahead** proceed without hesitation. **go-ahead** *n.* permission to proceed. ● *adj.* enterprising. **go all the way 1** win a contest, one's ultimate goal, etc. **2** engage in sexual intercourse. **go along with** agree to; take the same view as. **go around 1** spin, revolve. **2** be long enough to encompass. **3** (of food, etc.) suffice for everybody. **4** (usu. foll. by *to*) visit informally. **5** (foll. by *with*) be regularly in the company of. **6** = *go about* 3. **7** = *go on* 4. **go-as-you-please** untrammeled; free. **go at** take in hand energetically; attack. **go away** depart, esp. from home for a vacation, etc. **go back 1** return; revert. **2** extend backward (in time or space). **3** (foll. by *to*) have a history extending back to. **go back on** fail to keep (one's word, promise, etc.). **go bail** see BAIL¹. **go begging** see BEG. **go-between** an intermediary; a negotiator. **go by 1** pass. **2** be dependent on; be guided by. **go-by** *colloq.* a snub; a slight (*gave it the go-by*). **go by default** see DEFAULT. **go-cart 1** a handcart; a stroller. **2** = *go-kart*. **3** *archaic* a baby walker. **go-devil** an instrument used to clean the inside of pipes, etc. **go down 1 a** (of an amount) become less (*the coffee has gone down a lot*). **b** subside (*the flood went down*). **c** decrease in price; lose value. **2 a** (of a ship) sink. **b** (of the sun) set. **3** (usu. foll. by *to*) be continued to a specified point. **4** deteriorate; fail; (of a computer network, etc.) cease to function. **5** be recorded in writing. **6** be swallowed. **7** (often foll. by *with*) be received (in a specified way). **8** *Brit. colloq.* leave university. **9** *Brit. colloq.* be sent to prison (*went down for ten years*). **10** (often foll. by *before*) fall (before a conqueror). **go down with** *Brit.* begin to suffer from (a disease). **go Dutch** see DUTCH. **go far** be very successful. **go fly a kite** stop annoying, irritating, etc., (someone), as with unwanted suggestions. **go for 1** go to fetch. **2** be accounted as or achieve (*went for nothing*). **3** prefer; choose (*that's the one I go for*). **4** *colloq.* strive to attain (*go for it!*). **5** *colloq.* attack (*the dog went for him*). **go for broke** exert all one's strength or risk all one's resources. **go-getter** *colloq.* an aggressively enterprising person, esp. a businessman. **go-go** *colloq.* **1** (of a dancer, music, etc.) in pop music style, lively, and rhythmic. **2** unrestrained; energetic. **3** (of investment) speculative. **go great guns** see GUN. **go halves** (or **shares**) (often foll. by *with*) share equally. **go in 1** enter a room, house, etc. **2** (usu. foll. by *for*) enter as a competitor. **3** (of the sun, etc.) become obscured by cloud. **go in for** take as one's object, style, pursuit, principle, etc. **going!, gone!** an auctioneer's announcement that bidding is closing or closed. **go into 1** enter (a profession, etc.). **2** take part in; be a part of. **3** investigate. **4** allow oneself to pass into (hysterics, etc.). **5** dress oneself in (mourning, etc.). **6** frequent (society). **go in with** join as a partner; share expenses for. (*decided to go in with some friends on a summer cottage*). **go it** *Brit. colloq.* **1** act vigorously, furiously, etc. **2** indulge in dissipation. **go it alone** see ALONE. **go it strong** *Brit. colloq.* go to great lengths; exaggerate. **go-kart** a miniature racing car. **go a**

long way 1 (often foll. by *toward*) have a great effect. **2** (of food, money, etc.) last a long time; buy much. **3** = *go far*. **go off 1** explode. **2 a** leave the stage. **b** leave; depart. **3** gradually cease to be felt. **4** (esp. of foodstuffs) deteriorate; decompose. **5** go to sleep; become unconscious. **6** be extinguished. **7** die. **8** be got rid of by sale, etc. **9** sound, as an alarm, siren, etc. **10** *Brit. colloq.* begin to dislike (*I've gone off him*). **go-off** *Brit. colloq.* a start (*at the first go-off*). **go off at** *Austral. & NZ sl.* reprimand; scold. **go off well** (or **badly**, etc.) (of an enterprise, etc.) be received or accomplished well (or badly, etc.). **go on 1** (often foll. by pres. part.) continue; persevere (*decided to go on with it*; *went on trying*; *unable to go on*). **2** *colloq.* **a** talk at great length. **b** (foll. by *at*) admonish (*went on and on at him*). **3** (foll. by *to* + infin.) proceed (*went on to become a star*). **4** happen. **5** conduct oneself (*shameful, the way they went on*). **6** *Theatr.* appear on stage. **7** (of a garment) be large enough for its wearer. **8** take one's turn to do something. **9** (also *Brit.* **go upon**) *colloq.* use as evidence (*police don't have anything to go on*). **10** *colloq.* (esp. in *neg.*) **a** concern oneself about. **b** care for (*don't go much on red hair*). **11** become chargeable to (an expense account, etc.). **go on!** *colloq.* an expression of encouragement or disbelief. **go out 1** leave a room, house, etc. **2** be broadcast. **3** be extinguished. **4** (often foll. by *with*) be courting. **5** (of a government or elected official) leave office. **6** cease to be fashionable. **7** (usu. foll. by *to*) depart, esp. to a colony, etc. **8** *colloq.* lose consciousness. **9** (of workers) strike. **10** (usu. foll. by *to*) (of the heart, etc.) expand with sympathy, etc., toward (*my heart goes out to them*). **11** *Golf* play the first nine holes in a round. **12** *Cards* be the first to dispose of one's hand. **13** (of a tide) turn to low tide. **14** mix socially; attend social events. **go over 1** inspect the details of; rehearse; retouch. **2** (often foll. by *to*) change one's allegiance or religion. **3** (of a play, etc.) be received in a specified way (*went over well in Dallas*). **go public 1** offer (a corporation's) shares for sale to the general public. **2** disclose or admit publicly. **go round** = *go around*. **go slow** *Brit.* work slowly, as a form of industrial action. **go-slow** *Brit.* such industrial action. **go through 1** be dealt with or completed. **2** discuss in detail; scrutinize in sequence. **3** perform (a ceremony, a recitation, etc.). **4** undergo. **5** *colloq.* use up; spend (money, etc.). **6** make holes in. **7** (of a book) be successively published (in so many editions). **8** *Austral. sl.* abscond. **go through with** not leave unfinished; complete. **go to!** *archaic* an exclamation of disbelief, impatience, admonition, etc. **go to the bar** become a lawyer. **go to blazes** (or **hell** or **Jericho**, etc.) *sl.* an exclamation of dismissal, contempt, etc. **go to the country** see COUNTRY. **go together 1** match; fit. **2** be courting. **go to it!** *colloq.* begin work! **go-to-meeting** (also **Sunday-go-to-meeting**) (of a hat, clothes, etc.) suitable for going to church in. **go to show** (or **prove**) serve to demonstrate (or prove). **go to town 1** expend great effort; attack (a project) vigorously. **2** spend time, effort, money, etc. lavishly or indulgently. (*the committee really went to town on the decorations*). **go under** sink; fail; succumb. **go up 1** increase in price. **2** *Brit. colloq.* enter a university. **3** be consumed (in flames, etc.); explode. **go up in the world** attain a higher social position. **go well** (or **ill**, etc.) (often foll. by *with*) turn out well, (or ill, etc.). **go with 1** be harmonious with; match. **2** agree to; take the same view as. **3 a** be a pair with. **b** be courting. **4** follow the drift of. **go without** manage without; forgo (also *absol.*: *we shall just have to go without*). **go with the tide** (or **times**) do as others do; follow the drift. **have a go at 1** esp. *Brit.* attack; criticize. **2** attempt; try. **no go 1** useless; unavailing. **2** canceled; not approved to proceed. **on the go** *colloq.* **1** in constant motion. **2** constantly working. **to go** (of food, etc.) to be eaten or drunk off the premises. **who goes there?** a sentry's challenge. [OE *gān* f. Gmc: *went* orig. past of WEND]

/.../ pronunciation	● part of speech
□ **phrases, idioms, and compounds**	
□□ **derivatives**	■ **synonym section**
cross-references appear in SMALL CAPITALS or *italics*	

■ *v.* **1 a** go off *or* along, move (ahead *or* forward *or* onward), proceed, advance, pass, travel, voyage, make headway, *literary or archaic* wend; set off, start off. **3** lead, open to, give access to, communicate to *or* with, connect with *or* to; run, extend. **4 a** depart, go out *or* away, move (out *or* away), decamp, make off, withdraw, repair, retire, retreat, take off; see also LEAVE[1] *v.* 1b, 3, 4. **b** see DISAPPEAR 1. **5** function, operate, work, move, run, perform, act. **6 c** say, utter. **7** live, continue, go on, survive, last (out), endure. **8 a** become, turn, grow, get, fall. **b** see DIE[1] 1. **c** pass, escape, continue, proceed, go on. **9** pass, elapse, slip *or* tick away, fly, glide by. **10 b** be told, run. **c** fit, belong (together), agree *or* conform, harmonize, blend, match, tone, be appropriate *or* suitable, complement each other; (*go with*) set off. **d** belong, be kept *or* put, live. **11 b** swing, *colloq.* be a hit. **c** see PROGRESS *v.* 1. **13 a** be disposed of *or* discarded *or* thrown away, be relinquished, be dismissed, be got rid of *or* abolished, be given up, be cast *or* set *or* put aside, be done with. **b** fail, fade, decline, flag, weaken, deteriorate, get worse, worsen, degenerate, wear out, give (out); give way, collapse, fall *or* come *or* go to pieces, break, disintegrate, crack. **15** see JUDGE *v.* 2, BEHAVE 1a. **16** see TRAVEL *v.* 1; (*go to*) see ATTEND 1a, 2a, VISIT *v.* 1. **24** (*go to*) see REFER 4. **28** see APPLY 2. ● *n.* **2** see ENERGY 1. **3** action; change; see also STIR[1] *n.* 2. **4** see TRIUMPH *n.* 1b. **5** chance, turn, opportunity, try, attempt, *colloq.* crack, whirl, shot, stab, bid, *formal* essay, *Brit. sl.* bash. ● *adj.* **2** see FASHIONABLE, PROGRESSIVE *adj.* 3b. □ **go about 1** approach, tackle, set about, undertake, begin, start. **go ahead** proceed, continue, move *or* go forward, advance, progress, go on. **go-ahead** (*n.*) permisssion, approval, leave, authorization, sanction, say-so, *colloq.* OK, green light, nod. (*adj.*) ambitious, enterprising, progressive, forward-looking, modern, advanced, resourceful, *colloq.* go. **go along with** agree to *or* with, concur with, acquiesce to *or* in, assent to. **go around 1** rotate, spin, whirl, twirl; see also REVOLVE 1, 2. **2** fit, extend, reach, span, stretch; see also ENCIRCLE 1. **3** suffice, be sufficient *or* adequate *or* enough, satisfy. **4** see VISIT *v.* 1. **5** (*go around with*) socialize with, frequent *or* seek the company of, spend time with, associate with, hang around *or* about with, *sl.* hang out with. **go-as-you-please** see FREE *adj.* 3a, b. **go at** attack, assault, assail, go for; launch into, throw oneself into, embark on, get going on *or* with. **go away** go (off), depart, withdraw, exit; retreat, recede, decamp, disappear, vanish; go on vacation, get away, take a break; see also LEAVE[1] *v.* 1b, 3, 4. **go back 3** (*go back to*) originate in, begin *or* start with, date back to. **go back on** renege (on), break, retract, repudiate, forsake, fail to keep. **go-between** intermediary, middleman, mediator, negotiator, intercessor, interceder, agent; messenger. **go by 1** pass (by), go past, move by *or* on, slip by *or* away, slide by, glide by; elapse. **2** rely *or* count *or* depend *or* bank on, put faith in, be guided by, judge from. **go-by** see INSULT *n.* **go down 1** decrease, decline, drop, sink, drop, fall; subside. **2 a** sink, go under, founder, become submerged, be engulfed, dive. **4** crash; see also DETERIORATE, FAIL *v.* 1, 2a. **5** be remembered *or* memorialized, *or* recalled *or* commemorated *or* recorded. **7** (*go down well*) find favor *or* acceptance *or* approval, be accepted. **go for 1** fetch, get, run for, go after, bring (back), retrieve, obtain. **3** fancy, favor, like, admire, be attracted to, prefer, choose, *sl.* dig. **4** target, strive for, try for, set one's sights on, aim for, focus attention *or* effort(s) on. **5** attack, assault, assail, set upon, go at. **go-go 2** see ENERGETIC 1, 2. **3** see SPECULATIVE 2. **go in 1** enter, come in. **2** (*go in for*) enter, enroll for, sign up for, put one's name down for. **go in for** embark on, pursue, take up, embrace, espouse, undertake, follow, adopt, go into, go out for; like, fancy, favor, practice, do, engage in. **go into 3** delve into, examine, pursue,

investigate, analyze, probe, scrutinize, inquire into, study; touch on, discuss, mention, talk about. **go it strong** see EXAGGERATE 1. **go off 1** explode, blow up, detonate, erupt, fly apart, burst; fire, be discharged. **2 a** leave, exit, walk off, go. **b** depart, leave, go (away), set out, exit, decamp, quit. **3** see DIMINISH 1. **4** deteriorate, rot, molder, decompose, go moldy, go stale, go bad, spoil, (go) sour, turn. **6** go out, cease to function, be extinguished, be put out *or* off. **7** see DIE[1] 1. **go on 1** continue, proceed, keep (on), carry on; go, persist, last, endure, persevere. **2 a** gabble, chatter, drone on, *colloq.* natter; see also CHATTER *v.* 1. **b** (*go on at*) see CRITICIZE 1. **4** occur, take place, come about; see also HAPPEN *v.* 1. **5** see BEHAVE 1a. **6** enter, make an *or* one's entrance, come on (stage), go on stage. **9** rely *or* depend on, use (as evidence). **10 b** see LIKE[2] *v.* 1. **go on!** you're kidding, you're not serious, get along, nonsense, rubbish, *Brit.* you're having me on, *archaic* go to, *colloq.* come off it, get away, tell that to the marines, you don't say so. **go out 1** depart, exit, go off; see also LEAVE[1] *v.* 1b, 3, 4. **3** fade *or* die (out), expire, cease functioning, go off, be extinguished. **4** court, go together, see (one another), *Brit. archaic* walk out, *colloq.* date. **9** see STRIKE *v.* 17a. **10** see SYMPATHIZE 1. **14** go about, socialize, mix. **go over 1** review, skim (through *or* over), go through, scan, look at, read, study; inspect, examine, scrutinize, investigate; rehearse, repeat, reiterate; retouch, redo. **2** convert, switch, change; (*go over to*) become, turn into. **3** go down, be received. **go through 1** be accepted *or* approved, pass (muster), be dealt with. **2** see *go over* 1 above. **4** experience, suffer, undergo, bear, take, stand, tolerate, put up with, submit to, endure, live through, brave, *literary* brook. **5** see *use up* 1. **go through with** follow through, finish; see also COMPLETE *v.* 1. **go to!** well I never, *colloq.* well I'm damned, well I'll be damned, you don't say, *sl.* well I'll be blowed; see also *go on!* above. **go to blazes** (or **hell** or **Jericho**) damn you; see also *drop dead!* **go together 1** match, harmonize, accord, agree, fit, go, suit each other, belong (with each other). **2** see *go out* 4 above. **go to it!** get cracking, buckle down; see also *jump to it*, *fall to*. **go to show** or (**prove**) see PROVE 1. **go under** sink, fail, collapse, subside, go bankrupt, succumb, go to the wall, *colloq.* fold, go belly up. **go up 1** rise, increase, climb, ascend, *colloq.* go through the roof; see also SOAR 2. **3** see EXPLODE 1. **go with 1** go together with, harmonize with, blend with, be suitable *or* suited for, fit (in) with, accord *or* agree with, match, suit. **2** go along with, concur with, acquiesce to *or* in, assent to; see also AGREE 4, 5. **3 b** socialize with, associate with, accompany, court, *archaic* walk out with, *colloq.* date. **go without** do *or* manage *or* get by without, forgo; lack, be deprived of, need; abstain from, survive *or* live *or* continue without. **go with the tide** (or **times**) go with the flow, follow the crowd *or* herd. **have a go at 2** see ESSAY *v.* **to go** take out *or* away, to carry out.

go[2] /gō/ *n.* a Japanese board game of territorial possession and capture. [Jap.]

goad /gōd/ *n.* & *v.* ● *n.* **1** a spiked stick used for urging cattle forward. **2** anything that torments, incites, or stimulates. ● *v.tr.* **1** urge on with a goad. **2** (usu. foll. by *on, into*) irritate; stimulate (*goaded him into retaliating*; *goaded me on to win*). [OE *gād*, rel. to Lombard *gaida* arrowhead f. Gmc]

■ *n.* **2** see SPUR *n.* 2. ● *v.* **2** see SPUR *v.*

goal /gōl/ *n.* **1** the object of a person's ambition or effort; a destination; an aim (*fame is his goal*; *Washington was our goal*). **2 a** *Football* a pair of posts with a crossbar between which the ball has to be sent to score. **b** *Soccer, Ice Hockey*, etc., a cage or basket similarly. **c** a point or points won (*scored 3 goals*). **3** a point marking the end of a race. □ **goal kick 1** *Soccer* a kick by the defending side after attackers send the ball over the goal line without scoring. **2** *Rugby* an attempt to kick a goal. **goal line** *Football, Soccer*, etc., a line between each pair of goalposts, extended to form the end

boundary of a field of play (cf. TOUCHLINE). **in goal** in the position of goalkeeper. □□ **goalless** *adj.* [16th c.: orig. unkn.: perh. identical with ME *gol* boundary]
■ **1** object, aim, purpose, end, objective, target; ambition, ideal, aspiration; destination.

goalball /gṓlbawl/ *n.* a team ball game for blind and visually handicapped players.

goalie /gṓlee/ *n. colloq.* = GOALKEEPER.

goalkeeper /gṓlkeepər/ *n.* a player stationed to protect the goal in various sports.

goalmouth /gṓlmowth/ *n. Soccer, Ice Hockey* the space between or near the goalposts.

goalpost /gṓlpōst/ *n.* either of the two upright posts of a goal. □ **move the goalposts** alter the basis or scope of a procedure during its course, so as to fit adverse circumstances encountered.

goaltender /gṓltendər/ *n.* a hockey goalkeeper.

goanna /gō-ánə/ *n. Austral.* a monitor lizard. [corrupt. of IGUANA]

goat /gōt/ *n.* **1 a** a hardy, lively, frisky short-haired domesticated mammal, *Capra aegagrus*, having horns and (in the male) a beard, and kept for its milk and meat. **b** either of two similar mammals, the mountain goat and the Spanish goat. **2** any other mammal of the genus *Capra*, including the ibex. **3** a lecherous man. **4** *Brit. colloq.* a foolish person. **5** (**the Goat**) the zodiacal sign or constellation Capricorn. **6** a scapegoat. □ **get a person's goat** *colloq.* irritate a person. **goat antelope** any antelopelike member of the goat family, including the chamois and goral. **goat god** Pan. **goat moth** any of various large moths of the family Cossidae. □□ **goatish** *adj.* **goaty** *adj.* [OE *gāt* she-goat f. Gmc]

goatee /gōteé/ *n.* a small pointed beard like that of a goat.

goatsbeard **1** a meadow plant, *Tragopogon pratensis.* **2** a herbaceous plant, *Aruncus dioicus*, with long spikes of white flowers.

goatherd /gṓt-hərd/ *n.* a person who tends goats.

goatskin /gṓtskin/ *n.* **1** the skin of a goat. **2** a garment or bottle made out of goatskin.

goatsucker /gṓtsukər/ *n.* = NIGHTJAR.

gob[1] /gob/ *n. esp. Brit. sl.* the mouth. □ **gob-stopper** a very large hard candy. [perh. f. Gael. & Ir., = beak, mouth]

gob[2] /gob/ *n. & v. sl.* ● *n.* **1** a lump or clot of slimy matter. **2** (in *pl.*) large amounts (*gobs of cash*) ● *v.intr.* (**gobbed, gobbing**) spit. [ME f. OF *go(u)be* mouthful]
■ *n.* **1** clot, blob, lump, gobbet, morsel, chunk, piece, fragment.

gob[3] /gob/ *n. sl.* a sailor. [20th c.: cf. GOBBY]

gobbet /góbit/ *n.* **1** a piece or lump of raw meat, flesh, food, etc. **2** an extract from a text, esp. one set for translation or comment in an examination. [ME f. OF *gobet* (as GOB[2])]
■ **1** see MORSEL.

gobble[1] /góbəl/ *v.tr. & intr.* eat hurriedly and noisily. □□ **gobbler** *n.* [prob. dial. f. GOB[2]]
■ see EAT 1a.

gobble[2] /góbəl/ *v.intr.* **1** (of a male turkey) make a characteristic swallowing sound in the throat. **2** make such a sound when speaking, esp. when excited, angry, etc. [imit.: perh. based on GOBBLE[1]]

gobbledygook /góbəldeegook/ *n.* (also **gobbledegook**) *colloq.* pompous or unintelligible jargon. [prob. imit. of a turkey]
■ jargon, mumbo jumbo, humbug, nonsense, gibberish, moonshine, rubbish, balderdash, drivel, garbage, *colloq.* hogwash, piffle, malarkey, esp. *Brit.* tosh, *sl.* bull, poppycock, eyewash, tommyrot, bunk, rot, bosh, bilge.

gobbler /góblər/ *n. colloq.* a male turkey.

gobby /góbee/ *n.* (*pl.* **-ies**) *Brit. sl.* **1** a coastguard. **2** an American sailor. [perh. f. GOB[2] + -Y[1]]

Gobelin /góbəlin, gṓbəlin, gawblán/ *n.* (in full **Gobelin tapestry**) **1** a tapestry made at the Gobelins factory. **2** a tapestry imitating this. [name of a factory in Paris, called *Gobelins* after its orig. owners]

gobemouche /góbmŏŏsh/ *n.* (*pl.* **gobemouches** *pronunc.* same) a gullible listener. [F *gobe-mouches*, = flycatcher f. *gober* swallow + *mouches* flies]

goblet /góblit/ *n.* **1** a drinking vessel with a foot and a stem, usu. of glass. **2** *archaic* a metal or glass bowl-shaped drinking cup without handles, sometimes with a foot and a cover. **3** *poet.* a drinking cup. [ME f. OF *gobelet* dimin. of *gobel* cup, of unkn. orig.]
■ see GLASS *n.* 2a.

goblin /góblin/ *n.* a mischievous, ugly, dwarflike creature of folklore. [ME prob. f. AF *gobelin*, med.L *gobelinus*, prob. f. name dimin. of *Gobel*, rel. to G *Kobold*: see COBALT]
■ elf, gnome, hobgoblin, imp, kobold, leprechaun, demon, brownie, pixie, nix, nixie.

gobsmacked /góbsmakt/ *adj. sl. Brit.* flabbergasted; struck dumb with awe or amazement. [GOB[1] + SMACK[1]]

goby /gṓbee/ *n.* (*pl.* **-ies**) any small marine fish of the family Gobiidae, having ventral fins joined to form a sucker or disk. [L *gobius, cobius* f. Gk *kōbios* GUDGEON[1]]

god /god/ *n. & int.* ● *n.* **1 a** (in many religions) a superhuman being or spirit worshiped as having power over nature, human fortunes, etc.; a deity. **b** an image, idol, animal, or other object worshiped as divine or symbolizing a god. **2** (**God**) (in Christian and other monotheistic religions) the creator and ruler of the universe; the supreme being. **3 a** an adored, admired, or influential person. **b** something worshiped like a god (*makes a god of success*). **4** *Theatr.* (in *pl.*) the gallery. **b** the people sitting in it. ● *int.* (**God!**) an exclamation of surprise, anger, etc. □ **by God!** an exclamation of surprise, etc. **for God's sake!** see SAKE[1]. **god-awful** *sl.* extremely unpleasant, nasty, etc. **God bless** an expression of good wishes on parting. **God bless me** (or **my soul**) see BLESS. **God damn (you, him**, etc.) may (you, etc.) be damned. **God the Father, Son, and Holy Spirit** (or **Ghost**) (in the Christian tradition) the Persons of the Trinity. **God-fearing** earnestly religious. **God forbid** (foll. by *that* + clause, or *absol.*) may it not happen! **God grant** (foll. by *that* + clause) may it happen. **God help (you, him**, etc.) an expression of concern for or sympathy with a person. **God knows 1** it is beyond all knowledge (*God knows what will become of him*). **2** I call God to witness that (*God knows we tried hard enough*). **God's acre** a churchyard. **God's book** the Bible. **God's gift** often *iron.* a godsend. **God's (own) country** an earthly paradise or beautiful wilderness, esp. the United States. **God squad** *sl.* **1** a religious organization, esp. an evangelical Christian group. **2** its members. **God's truth** the absolute truth. **God willing** if fate allows. **good God!** an exclamation of surprise, anger, etc. **in God's name** an appeal for help. **in the name of God** an expression of surprise or annoyance. **my** (or **oh**) **God!** an exclamation of surprise, anger, etc. **play God** assume importance or superiority. **thank God!** an exclamation of pleasure or relief. **with God** dead and in heaven. □□ **godhood** *n.* **godship** *n.* **godward** *adj. & adv.* **godwards** *adv.* [OE f. Gmc]
■ *n.* **1 a** deity, demigod, demiurge, divinity, spirit, power, numen; (*gods*) immortals. **b** see IDOL 1. **2** (**God**) the Creator, Supreme Being, the Deity, the Godhead; Allah, Jehovah, Yahweh. **3 a** see IDOL 3. ● *int.* (**God!**) by God, good God, my *or* oh God, Heavens, goodness, gracious, mercy, for Christ's *or* God's *or* goodness' *or* Heaven's *or* Pete's sake, good grief, Ir. begorra, *colloq.* hell, Jesus, *sl.* Christ; see also GRACIOUS *int.* □ **by God!** see GOD *int.* above. **god-awful** see NASTY 1, 5a, b;3. **God damn (you, him**, etc.) see CURSE *v.* 1b. **God-fearing** see DEVOUT 1. **God knows 1** Heaven (only) knows, God alone knows, goodness knows. **God's Acre** see GRAVEYARD. **God willing** Deo volente, DV, inshallah. **good God!** see GOD *int.* above. **my** (or **oh**) **God!** see GOD *int.* above. **thank God!** *Deo gratias*, phew, that was lucky, *colloq.* thank goodness or heavens.

godchild /gódchīld/ *n.* a person in relation to a godparent.

/.../ **pronunciation**	● **part of speech**
□ **phrases, idioms, and compounds**	
□□ **derivatives**	■ **synonym section**
cross-references appear in SMALL CAPITALS or *italics*	

goddamn /gódám/ *adj.* (or **goddam** or **goddamned** /-dámd/) *sl.* accursed; damnable.
- see DAMNABLE.

goddaughter /góddawtər/ *n.* a female godchild.

goddess /gódis/ *n.* **1** a female deity. **2** a woman who is adored, esp. for her beauty.
- **1** see DEITY 1.

godet /gōdét, gōdáy/ *n.* a triangular piece of material inserted in a dress, glove, etc. [F]

godfather /gódfaathər/ *n.* **1** a male godparent. **2** a person directing an illegal organization, esp. the Mafia.

godforsaken /gódfərsaykən/ *adj.* (also **Godforsaken**) devoid of all merit; dismal; dreary.
- see DISMAL 1, 2, BLEAK¹.

godhead /gódhed/ *n.* (also **Godhead**) **1 a** the state of being God or a god. **b** divine nature. **2** a deity. **3** (**the Godhead**) God.
- **1 a** godhood, godship, divinity. **3** (**the Godhead**) see GOD *n.* 2.

godless /gódlis/ *adj.* **1** impious; wicked. **2** without a god. **3** not recognizing a god or gods. □□ **godlessness** *n.*
- **1** wicked, evil, sinful, unrighteous, unholy; impious, blasphemous, profane, sacrilegious, ungodly. **3** atheistic, nullifidian, agnostic, unbelieving, skeptical; see also FAITHLESS 2, *heretical* (HERETIC).

godlike /gódlik/ *adj.* **1** resembling God or a god in some quality, esp. in physical beauty. **2** befitting or appropriate to a god.
- **1** divine; saintly, angelic, seraphic, deific, deiform; blessed, sainted, *poet.* blest. **2** holy, godly, heavenly, celestial, beatific, ethereal; see also SACRED 1b.

godly /gódlee/ *adj.* religious; pious; devout. □□ **godliness** *n.*
- religious, pious, devout, God-fearing, holy, reverent, saintly, pietistic, devoted, faithful, righteous, good, virtuous, moral, pure.

godmother /gódmuthər/ *n.* a female godparent.

godown /gódown/ *n.* a warehouse in parts of E. Asia. [Port. *gudāo* f. Malay *godong* perh. f. Telugu *gida&ndabove.gi* place where goods lie f. *kidu* lie]

godparent /gódpairənt/ *n.* a person who presents a child at baptism and responds on the child's behalf.

godsend /gódsend/ *n.* an unexpected but welcome event or acquisition.
- gift, blessing, boon, windfall, bonanza, stroke of (good) fortune, stroke of (good) luck, piece *or* bit of luck.

godson /gódsun/ *n.* a male godchild.

Godspeed /gódspeéd/ *int.* an expression of good wishes to a person starting a journey.

godwit /gódwit/ *n.* any wading bird of the genus *Limosa*, with long legs and a long straight or slightly upcurved bill. [16th c.: of unkn. orig.]

Godwottery /godwótəree/ *n. Brit. joc.* affected, archaic, or excessively elaborate speech or writing, esp. regarding gardens. [*God wot* (in a poem on gardens, by T. E. Brown 1876)]

goer /gōər/ *n.* **1** a person or thing that goes (*a slow goer*). **2** (often in *comb.*) a person who attends, esp. regularly (*a churchgoer*). **3** *Brit. colloq.* **a** a lively or persevering person. **b** a sexually promiscuous person. **4** *Austral. colloq.* a project likely to be accepted or to succeed.

goes *3rd sing. present of* GO¹.

goest /gōist/ *archaic 2nd sing. present of* GO¹.

goeth /gōith/ *archaic 3rd sing. present of* GO¹.

Goethean /gőteeən/ *adj. & n.* (also **Goethian**) ● *adj.* of, relating to, or characteristic of the German writer J. W. von Goethe (d. 1832). ● *n.* an admirer or follower of Goethe.

gofer /gófər/ *n. sl.* a person who runs errands, esp. on a movie set or in an office. [*go for* (see GO¹)]
- see MESSENGER.

goffer /gófər/ *v. & n.* ● *v.tr.* **1** make wavy, flute, or crimp (a lace edge, a trimming, etc.) with heated irons. **2** (as **goffered** *adj.*) (of the edges of a book) embossed. ● *n.* **1** an iron used for goffering. **2** ornamental braiding used for frills, etc. [F *gaufrer* stamp with a patterned tool f. *gaufre* honeycomb, rel. to WAFER, WAFFLE²]

goggle /gógəl/ *v., adj., & n.* ● *v.* **1** *intr.* **a** (often foll. by *at*) look with wide-open eyes. **b** (of the eyes) be rolled about; protrude. **2** *tr.* turn (the eyes) sideways or from side to side. ● *adj.* (usu. *attrib.*) (of the eyes) protuberant or rolling. ● *n.* **1** (in *pl.*) **a** eyeglasses for protecting the eyes from glare, dust, water, etc. **b** *colloq.* eyeglasses. **2** (in *pl.*) a sheep disease; the staggers. **3** a goggling expression. □ **goggle-box** *Brit. colloq.* a television set. **goggle-eyed** having staring or protuberant eyes, esp. through astonishment or disbelief. [ME, prob. from a base *gog* (unrecorded) expressive of oscillating movement]
- *v.* **1** see GAPE *v.* 2. **b** see PROTRUDE. ● *adj.* see PROTUBERANT. ● *n.* **1** (*goggles*) glasses, spectacles, eyeglasses, lorgnette(s), *colloq.* specs, shades; bifocals, trifocals. **3** gape, stare, gaze, ogle, fixed *or* blank look. □ **goggle-eyed** wide-eyed, staring, gawking, agape; openmouthed, awestruck, thunderstruck, dumbfounded, astonished, astounded, amazed, stupefied, dazed, surprised.

goglet /góglit/ *n. Ind.* a long-necked usu. porous earthenware vessel used for keeping water cool. [Port. *gorgoleta*]

Goidel /góyd'l/ *n.* a Celt who speaks Irish Gaelic, Scottish Gaelic, or Manx. □□ **Goidelic** /-délik/ *n.* [OIr. *Góidel*]

going /gōing/ *n. & adj.* ● *n.* **1 a** the act or process of going. **b** an instance of this; a departure. **2 a** the condition of the ground for walking, riding, etc. **b** progress affected by this (*found the going hard*). ● *adj.* **1** in or into action (*set the clock going*). **2** esp. *Brit.* existing; available; to be had (*there's hot soup going*; *one of the best writers going*). **3** current; prevalent (*the going rate*). □ **get going** start steadily talking, working, etc. (*can't stop him when he gets going*). **going away** a departure. **going concern** a thriving business. **going for one** *colloq.* acting in one's favor (*he's got a lot going for him*). **going on fifteen**, etc., approaching one's fifteenth, etc., birthday. **going on for** *Brit.* approaching (a time, an age, etc.) (*must be going on for 6 years*). **going-over 1** *colloq.* an inspection or overhaul. **2** *sl.* a beating. **3** *colloq.* a scolding. **goings-on** /gōingzón, -áwn/ behavior, esp. morally suspect. **going to** intending or intended to; about to; likely to (*it's going to sink!*). **heavy going** slow or difficult to progress with (*found Faulkner heavy going*). **to be going on with** to start with; for the time being. **while the going is good** while conditions are favorable. [GO¹: in some senses f. earlier *a-going*: see A²]
- *n.* **1** departure, leaving; see also RETREAT *n.* 1a. ● *adj.* **3** current, present, accepted, prevailing, prevalent, universal, common, usual, customary. □ **going concern** booming business; growth industry. **going-over 1** see CHECK¹ *n.* 1, OVERHAUL *n.* 2 see *thrashing* (THRASH). **3** see REPRIMAND *n.* **goings-on** see HANKY-PANKY. **heavy going** see TEDIOUS.

goiter /góytər/ *n.* (*Brit.* **goitre**) *Med.* a swelling of the neck resulting from enlargement of the thyroid gland. □□ **goitrous** /-trəs/ *adj.* [F, back-form. f. *goitreux* or f. Prov. *goitron*, ult. f. L *guttur* throat]

Golconda /golkóndə/ *n.* a mine or source of wealth, advantages, etc. [city near Hyderabad, India]

gold /gōld/ *n. & adj.* ● *n.* **1** a yellow, malleable, ductile, high density metallic element resistant to chemical reaction, occurring naturally in quartz veins and gravel, and precious as a monetary medium, in jewelry, etc. ¶ Symb.: **Au**. **2** the color of gold. **3 a** coins or articles made of gold. **b** money in large sums; wealth. **4** something precious, beautiful, or brilliant (*all that glitters is not gold*). **5** = *gold medal*. **6** gold used for coating a surface or as a pigment; gilding. **7** the bull's-eye of an archery target (usu. gilt). ● *adj.* **1** made wholly or chiefly of gold. **2** colored like gold. □ **age of gold** = *golden age*. **gold amalgam** an easily molded combination of gold with mercury. **gold bloc** a bloc of countries having a gold standard. **gold brick** *sl.* **1** a thing with only a surface appearance of value, a sham or fraud. **2** a lazy person. **gold card** a kind of preferential charge card giving privileges and benefits not available to holders of the standard card. **gold digger 1** *sl.* **a** a woman who wheedles money out of men. **b** a woman who strives to marry a rich man. **2** a person who digs for gold. **gold dust 1** gold in fine particles as often found naturally. **2** a plant, *Alyssum saxatile*, with many small yellow flowers. **gold field** a district in which gold is found as a mineral. **gold foil** gold beaten into a thin sheet. **gold leaf** gold beaten into a very thin sheet. **gold medal** a medal of gold, usu. awarded as first prize. **gold mine 1** a place where gold is mined. **2** *colloq.* a source of wealth. **gold of pleasure** an annual European yellow-flowered plant, *Camelina sativa*. **gold plate 1** vessels made of gold. **2** material plated with gold. **gold-plate** *v.tr.* plate with gold. **gold reserve** a reserve of gold coins or bullion held by a central bank, government, etc. **gold rush** a rush to a newly discovered gold field. **gold standard** a system by which the value of a currency is defined in terms of gold, for which the currency may be exchanged. **Gold Stick 1** (in the UK) a gilt rod carried on state occasions by the colonel of the Life Guards or the captain of the gentlemen-at-arms. **2** the officer carrying this rod. **gold thread 1** a thread of silk, etc., with gold wire wound around it. **2** a bitter plant, *Coptis tinfolia*. [OE f. Gmc]

goldbeater /góldbeetər/ *n.* a person who beats gold into gold leaf. □ **goldbeater's skin** a membrane used to separate leaves of gold during beating, or as a covering for slight wounds.

goldcrest /góldkrest/ *n.* a small bird, *Regulus regulus*, with a golden crest.

golden /góldən/ *adj.* **1 a** made or consisting of gold (*golden coin*). **b** yielding gold. **2** colored or shining like gold (*golden hair*). **3** precious; valuable; excellent; important (*a golden memory; a golden opportunity*). □ **golden age 1** a supposed past age when people were happy and innocent. **2** the period of a nation's greatest prosperity, literary merit, etc. **golden-ager** an old person. **golden balls** a pawnbroker's sign. **golden boy** (or **girl**) *colloq.* a popular or successful person. **golden calf** wealth as an object of worship (Exod. 32). **golden chain** the laburnum. **Golden Delicious** a variety of apple. **golden eagle** a large eagle, *Aquila chrysaetos*, with yellow-tipped head feathers. **Golden Fleece** (in Greek mythology) a fleece of gold sought and won by Jason. **golden goose** a continuing source of wealth or profit. **golden hamster** a usu. tawny hamster, *Mesocricetus auratus*, kept as a pet or laboratory animal. **golden handshake** *colloq.* a payment given on layoff or early retirement. **Golden Horde** the Tartar horde that overran E. Europe in the 13th c. (from the richness of the leader's tent). **Golden Horn** the harbor of Istanbul. **golden jubilee 1** the fiftieth anniversary of a sovereign's accession. **2** any other fiftieth anniversary. **golden mean 1** the principle of moderation, as opposed to excess. **2** = *golden section*. **golden oldie** *colloq.* an old hit record or movie, etc., that is still well known and popular. **golden oriole** a European oriole, *Oriolus oriolus*, of which the male has yellow and black plumage and the female has mainly green plumage. **golden parachute** an executive's contract that provides substantial severance pay, etc., in the event of job loss following the company's being sold or merged with another. **golden perch** *Austral.* = CALLOP. **golden retriever** a retriever with a thick, golden-colored coat. **golden rule** a basic principle of action, esp. "do unto others as you would have them do unto you." **golden section** the division of a line so that the whole is to the greater part as that part is to the smaller part. **golden share** the controlling interest in a company, esp. as retained by government after a nationalized industry is privatized. **Golden State** California. **golden syrup** *Brit.* a pale treacle. **golden wedding** the fiftieth anniversary of a wedding. □□ **goldenly** *adv.* **goldenness** *n.*

■ **1 a** gold, gilded, gilt. **b** auriferous. **2** gold, aureate, blond, yellow, flaxen; bright, shining, gleaming, lustrous, shiny, brilliant, sunny, glittering, dazzling, resplendent, radiant, glowing, sparkling. **3** precious, valuable, important; excellent, outstanding; happy, blissful, delightful, joyful, glorious, joyous; flourishing, halcyon, prosperous, thriving, favorable, blessed, palmy; advantageous, propitious, auspicious, promising, opportune, rosy. □ **golden age 2** see PRIME[1]

n. **1. golden-ager** senior, oldster, old dear, *colloq.* old girl, old boy, oldie; see also *senior citizen.* **golden boy** (or **girl**) see FAVORITE *n.* **golden rule** see MOTTO.

goldeneye /góldəní/ *n.* any marine duck of the genus *Bucephala*.

goldenrod /góldənrod/ *n.* any plant of the genus *Solidago* with a rodlike stem and small bright yellow flowerheads.

goldfinch /góldfinch/ *n.* any of various brightly colored songbirds of the genus *Carduelis*, esp. the Eurasian *C. carduelis* and the N. American *c. tristis*. [OE *goldfinc* (as GOLD, FINCH)]

goldfish /góldfish/ *n.* a small reddish golden Chinese carp kept for ornament, *Carassius auratus*. □ **goldfish bowl 1** a globular glass container for goldfish. **2** a situation lacking privacy.

goldilocks /góldeeloks/ *n.* **1** a person with golden hair. **2 a** a kind of buttercup, *Ranunculus auricomus*. **b** a composite plant, *Aster linosyris*, like the goldenrod. [*goldy* f. GOLD + LOCK[2]]

goldsmith /góldsmith/ *n.* a worker in gold; a manufacturer of gold articles. [OE (as GOLD, SMITH)]

golem /góləm/ *n.* **1** a clay figure supposedly brought to life in Jewish legend. **2** an automaton; a robot. [Yiddish *goylem* f. Heb. *gōlem* shapeless mass]

golf /golf, gawlf/ *n.* & *v.* ● *n.* a game played on a course set in open country, in which a small hard ball is driven with clubs into a series of 18 or 9 holes with the fewest possible strokes. ● *v.intr.* play golf. □ **golf bag** a bag used for carrying clubs and balls. **golf ball 1** a ball used in golf. **2** *colloq.* a small ball used in some electric typewriters to carry the type. **golf cart 1** a cart used for carrying golf clubs. **2** a motorized cart for one or two golfers and their equipment. **golf club 1** a club used in golf. **2** an association for playing golf. **3** the premises used by a golf club. **golf course** (or **links**) the course on which golf is played. [15th-c. Sc.: orig. unkn.]

golfer /gólfər/ *n.* **1** a golf player. **2** *Brit.* a cardigan.

Golgi body /gáwljee/ *n.* (also **Golgi apparatus**) *Biol.* an organelle of vesicles and folded membranes within the cytoplasm of most eukaryotic cells, involved esp. in the secretion of substances. [C. *Golgi*, It. cytologist d. 1926]

Goliath beetle /gəlíəth/ *n.* any large beetle of the genus *Goliathus*, esp. *G. giganteus* native to Africa. [LL f. Heb. *golyaṯ* giant slain by David (1 Sam. 17)]

golliwog /góleewog/ *n.* a black-faced brightly dressed soft doll with fuzzy hair. [19th c.: perh. f. GOLLY[1] + POLLIWOG]

gollop /góləp/ *v.* & *n. colloq.* ● *v.tr.* (**golloped**, **golloping**) swallow hastily or greedily. ● *n.* a hasty gulp. [perh. f. GULP, infl. by GOBBLE[1]]

golly[1] /gólee/ *int.* expressing surprise. [euphem. for GOD]

golly[2] /gólee/ *n.* (*pl.* **-ies**) *colloq.* = GOLLIWOG. [abbr.]

golosh *Brit.* var. of GALOSH.

gombeen /gombéen/ *n. Ir.* usury. □ **gombeen-man** a moneylender. [Ir. *gaimbín* perh. f. the same OCelt. source as med.L *cambire* CHANGE]

-gon /gən/ *comb. form* forming nouns denoting plane figures with a specified number of angles (*hexagon; polygon; n-gon*). [Gk *-gōnos* -angled]

gonad /gónad/ *n.* an animal organ producing gametes, e.g., the testis or ovary. □□ **gonadal** /-nád'l/ *adj.* [mod.L *gonas gonad-* f. Gk *gonē*, *gonos* generation, seed]

gonadotrophic hormone /gónádətrófik, -trófik/ *n.* (also **gonadotropic** /-trópik, -trópik/) *Biochem.* any of various hormones stimulating the activity of the gonads.

gonadotrophin /gónádətrófin, -trófin/ *n.* (also **gonadotropin**) = GONADOTROPHIC HORMONE.

gondola /góndələ, gondóla/ *n.* **1** a light flat-bottomed boat used on Venetian canals, with a central cabin and a high point at each end, worked by one oar at the stern. **2** a car suspended from an airship or balloon. **3** an island of shelves

---

/. . ./ **pronunciation**	● **part of speech**
□ **phrases, idioms, and compounds**	
□□ **derivatives**	■ **synonym section**
cross-references appear in SMALL CAPITALS or *italics*	

used to display goods in a supermarket. **4** (also **gondola car**) a flat-bottomed open railroad freight car. **5** a car attached to a ski lift. [Venetian It., of obscure orig.]

gondolier /góndəleér/ *n.* the oarsman on a gondola. [F f. It. *gondoliere* (as GONDOLA)]

gone /gawn, gon/ *adj.* **1 a** lost; hopeless. **b** dead. **2** *colloq.* pregnant for a specified time (*already three months gone*). **3** *sl.* completely enthralled or entranced, esp. by rhythmic music, drugs, etc. **4** *Brit.* (of time) past (*not until gone nine*). □ **all gone** consumed; finished; used up. **be gone** depart; leave temporarily (cf. BEGONE). **gone goose** (or **gosling**) *colloq.* a person or thing beyond hope. **gone on** *sl.* infatuated with. [past part. of GO¹]
■ **2 b** see DEAD *adj.* 1.

goner /gáwnər, gón-/ *n. sl.* a person or thing that is doomed, ended, irrevocably lost, etc.; a dead person.

gonfalon /gónfələn/ *n.* **1** a banner, often with streamers, hung from a crossbar. **2** *hist.* such a banner as the standard of some Italian republics. □□ **gonfalonier** /gónfələneér/ *n.* [It. *gonfalone* f. Gmc (cf. VANE)]

gong /gawng, gong/ *n. & v.* ● *n.* **1** a metal disk with a turned rim, giving a resonant note when struck. **2** a saucer-shaped bell. **3** *Brit. sl.* a medal; a decoration. ● *v.tr.* **1** summon with a gong. **2** (of traffic police in the UK) sound a gong, etc., to direct (a motorist) to stop. [Malay *gong, gung* of imit. orig.]

goniometer /gŏneeómitər/ *n.* an instrument for measuring angles. □□ **goniometry** *n.* **goniometric** /-neeəmétrik/ *adj.* **goniometrical** *adj.* [F *goniomètre* f. Gk *gōnia* angle]

gonococcus /gónəkókəs, -kó-/ *n.* (*pl.* **gonococci** /-kókī, -kóksī/) a bacterium causing gonorrhea. □□ **gonococcal** *adj.* [Gk *gonos* generation, semen + COCCUS]

gonorrhea /gónəreéə/ *n.* (*Brit.* **gonorrhoea**) a venereal disease with inflammatory discharge from the urethra or vagina. □□ **gonorrheal** *adj.* [LL f. Gk *gonorrhoia* f. *gonos* semen + *rhoia* flux]

goo /gōo/ *n.* **1** a sticky or viscous substance. **2** sickly sentiment. [20th c.: perh. f. *burgoo* (Naut. sl.) = porridge]
■ **1** see OOZE².

good /gŏod/ *adj., n., & adv.* ● *adj.* (**better, best**) **1** having the right or desired qualities; satisfactory; adequate. **2 a** (of a person) efficient; competent (*good at math; a good driver*). **b** (of a thing) reliable; efficient (*good brakes*). **c** (of health, etc.) strong (*good eyesight*). **3 a** kind; benevolent (*good of you to come*). **b** morally excellent; virtuous (*a good deed*). **c** charitable (*good works*). **d** well-behaved (*a good child*). **4** enjoyable, agreeable (*a good party*). **5** thorough; considerable (*gave it a good wash*). **6 a** not less than (*waited a good hour*). **b** considerable in number, quality, etc. (*a good many people*). **7** healthy; beneficial (*milk is good for you*). **8 a** valid; sound (*a good reason*). **b** financially sound (*his credit is good*). **9** in exclamations of surprise (*good heavens!*). **10** right; proper; expedient (*thought it good to have a try*). **11** fresh; eatable; untainted (*is the meat still good?*). **12** (sometimes patronizing) commendable; worthy (*good old George; good men and true; my good man*). **13** well shaped; attractive (*has good legs; good looks*). **14** in courteous greetings and farewells (*good afternoon*). **15** promising or favorable (*a good omen; good news*). **16** expressing approval; complimentary (*a good review*). ● *n.* **1** (only in *sing.*) that which is good; what is beneficial or morally right (*only good can come of it; did it for your own good; what good will it do?*). **2** (only in *sing.*) a desirable end or object; a thing worth attaining (*sacrificing the present for a future good*). **3** (in *pl.*) **a** movable property or merchandise. **b** *Brit.* things to be transported, as distinct from passengers; freight. **c** (prec. by *the*) *colloq.* what one has undertaken to supply (esp. *deliver the goods*). **d** (prec. by *the*) *sl.* the real thing; the genuine article. **4** proof, esp. of guilt. **5** (as *pl.*; prec. by *the*) virtuous people. ● *adv. colloq.* well (*doing pretty good*). □ **as good as** practically (*he as good as told me*). **be so good as** (or **be good enough**) **to** (often in a request) be kind and do (a favor) (*be so good as to open the window*). **be (a certain amount) to the good** have as net profit or advantage. **do good** show kindness; act philanthropically. **do a person good** be beneficial to. **for good**

(and all) finally; permanently. **good and** *colloq.* used as an intensifier before an adj. or adv. (*raining good and hard; was good and angry*). **the good book** the Bible. **good breeding** correct or courteous manners. **good faith** see FAITH. **good for 1** beneficial to; having a good effect on. **2** able to perform; inclined for (*good for a ten-mile walk*). **3** able to be trusted to pay (*is good for $100*). **good form** see FORM. **good-for-nothing** (or *Brit.* **-nought**) *adj.* worthless. ● *n.* a worthless person. **good for you!** (or **him!, her!,** etc.) exclamation of approval toward a person. **Good Friday** (in the Christian calender) the Friday before Easter commemorating the crucifixion of Christ. **good-hearted** kindly; well-meaning. **good humor** a genial mood. **a good job** esp. *Brit.* a fortunate state of affairs (*it's a good job you came early*). **good-looker** a handsome or attractive person. **good-looking** handsome; attractive. **good luck 1** good fortune; happy chance. **2** exclamation of well-wishing. **good money 1** genuine money; money that might usefully have been spent elsewhere. **2** *colloq.* high wages. **good nature** a friendly disposition. **good oil** *Austral. sl.* reliable information. **good on you!** (or **him!,** etc.) *Austral., NZ, & Brit.* = good for you! **goods and chattels** see CHATTEL. **good-time** recklessly pursuing pleasure. **good-timer** a person who recklessly pursues pleasure. **good times** a period of prosperity. **good will** the intention and hope that good will result (see also GOODWILL). **a good word** (often in phr. **put in a good word for**) words in recommendation or defense of a person. **good works** charitable acts. **have a good mind** see MIND. **have the goods on a person** *sl.* have advantageous information about a person. **have a good time** enjoy oneself. **in a person's good books** see BOOK. **in good faith** with honest or sincere intentions. **in good time 1** with no risk of being late. **2** (also **all in good time**) in due course but without haste. **make good 1** make up for; compensate for; pay (an expense). **2** fulfill (a promise); effect (a purpose or an intended action). **3** demonstrate the truth of (a statement); substantiate (a charge). **4** gain and hold (a position). **5** replace or restore (a thing lost or damaged). **6** (*absol.*) accomplish what one intended. **no good** mischief (*is up to no good*). **2** useless; to no advantage (*it is no good arguing*). **no-good** *adj.* useless. ● *n.* a useless thing or person. **take in good part** not be offended by. **to the good** having as profit or benefit. □□ **goodish** *adj.* [OE *gōd* f. Gmc]
■ *adj.* **1** commendable, acceptable, fair, adequate; see also SATISFACTORY. **2 a** efficient, competent, capable, accomplished, proficient, adept, adroit, skilled, skillful, gifted, talented, clever, admirable. **b** safe, secure, sound; efficient; see also RELIABLE. **c** see SOUND² *adj.* 1, HEALTHY 1. **3 a** kind, benevolent, beneficent, gracious, gentle, kindly, nice, considerate, friendly, solicitous, good-hearted, sympathetic, benign, charitable, humane, kindhearted, well-disposed. **b** moral, high-minded, righteous, noble, honorable, ethical, upstanding, upright, virtuous, worthy, saintly, godly, godlike; lofty, elevated; esteemed, respected, respectable, well-thought-of, reputable. **d** obedient, well-mannered; angelic; see also *well-behaved* (BEHAVE). **4** enjoyable, agreeable, fine, exemplary, choice, *Sc.* braw, *sl.* neat; welcome, propitious, favorable. **5** complete; penetrating, careful; see also THOROUGH 2. **6 b** considerable, extensive, sizable, large, substantial; ample, sufficient, adequate, fair. **7** healthy, salubrious, wholesome, healthful, salutary; see also BENEFICIAL. **8** genuine, valid, legitimate, authentic, proper, sensible, creditable, sound, solid, substantial, well-founded; credible, believable, convincing, compelling, cogent; reliable, secure, dependable, sound, safe. **10** right, proper, expedient; correct, decorous, orderly, seemly, fitting, suitable, appropriate; right, fit, all right, *archaic* meet. **11** fresh, palatable, eatable, edible, consumable; untainted, unspoiled. **13** see SHAPELY, ATTRACTIVE 2. **15** advantageous, propitious, promising, opportune, beneficial, profitable, favorable. **16** approving, complimentary, flattering, positive, favorable, enthusiastic, laudatory, eulogistic, encomiastic,

praising. ● *n.* **1, 2** goodness, virtue, merit, right, worth; advantage, profit, use, gain; avail; see also BENEFIT *n.* 1. **3** (*goods*) **a** commodities, wares, assets; merchandise, stock, produce. **d** (*the goods*) the real thing, the genuine article, *colloq.* the real McCoy. □ **for good** (**and all**) see *finally* (FINAL). **good breeding** see BREEDING 4. **good-for-nothing** (or *Brit.* **-nought**) (*adj.*) worthless, useless. (*n.*) ne'er-do-well, wastrel, idler, loafer, layabout, sluggard, *archaic* slugabed, *colloq.* waster, lazybones, *sl.* gold brick, goof-off. **good for you!** bravo, well done, congratulations. **good-hearted** see KIND[2]. **good-looker** see BEAUTY 3. **good-looking** see BEAUTIFUL 1. **good-timer** see SYBARITE *n.* **a good word** see *recommendation* (RECOMMEND). **have a good time** see *enjoy oneself.* **in good faith** see HONESTLY 1. **in good time 1** see EARLY *adj. & adv.* 1. **2** see PRESENTLY 1. **make good 1** see REDEEM 5, PAY[1] *v.* 1. **2** see KEEP *v.* 7b, EFFECT *v.* **3** see SUBSTANTIATE. **4** see *follow up* 1. **5** replace, put back; see also RESTORE 1, 3. **6** see SUCCEED 1a. **no good 1** see MISCHIEF 1–3, 4. **2** see POINTLESS. **no-good** (*adj.*) see USELESS 1. (*n.*) see *good-for-nothing n.* above.

good-bye /gŏŏdbī/ *int. & n.* (also **goodbye**, **good-by** or **goodby**) ● *int.* expressing good wishes on parting, ending a telephone conversation, etc., or said with reference to a thing gotten rid of or irrevocably lost. ● *n.* (*pl.* **good-byes**) the saying of "good-bye"; a parting; a farewell. [contr. of *God be with you!* with *good* substituted after *good night*, etc.]
■ *int.* farewell, adios, adieu, vale, au revoir, *colloq.* ciao, see you (later), bye, bye-bye, toodle-oo, so long, esp. *Brit. colloq.* ta ta, cheers, cheerio. ● *n.* see FAREWELL.

good-humored /gŏŏdhyŏŏmərd/ *adj.* genial; cheerful; amiable. □□ **good-humoredly** *adv.*
■ see GOOD-NATURED.

goodly /gŏŏdlee/ *adj.* (**goodlier**, **goodliest**) **1** comely; handsome. **2** of imposing size, etc. □□ **goodliness** *n.* [OE *gōdlic* (as GOOD, -LY[1])]
■ **1** see COMELY. **2** considerable, sizable, substantial, ample, great, large, significant.

goodman /gŏŏdmən/ *n.* (*pl.* **-men**) *archaic* the head of a household.

good-natured /gŏŏdnáychərd/ *adj.* kind; patient; easygoing. □□ **good-naturedly** *adv.*
■ kind, kindly, kindhearted, tenderhearted, charitable, tolerant, generous, good-humored, cheerful, good-tempered, friendly, agreeable, genial, gracious, good-hearted, pleasant, mellow, easygoing, considerate, nice, courteous, cordial, warm, warmhearted, amiable, amicable, cooperative, patient.

goodness /gŏŏdnis/ *n. & int.* ● *n.* **1** virtue; excellence, esp. moral. **2** kindness; generosity (*had the goodness to wait*). **3** what is good or beneficial in a thing (*vegetables with all the goodness boiled out*). ● *int.* (as a substitution for "God") expressing surprise, anger, etc. (*goodness me!; goodness knows; for goodness' sake!*). [OE *gōdnes* (as GOOD, -NESS)]
■ *n.* **1** see VIRTUE 1. **2** see KINDNESS 1. ● *int.* see INDEED *int.*

good-tempered /gŏŏdtémpərd/ *adj.* having a good temper; not easily annoyed. □□ **good-temperedly** *adv.*

goodwife /gŏŏdwīf/ *n.* (*pl.* **-wives**) *archaic* the mistress of a household.

goodwill /gŏŏdwíl/ *n.* **1** kindly feeling. **2** the established reputation of a business, etc., as enhancing its value. **3** cheerful consent or acquiescence; readiness; zeal.
■ **1** see AFFECTION 1.

goody[1] /gŏŏdee/ *n. & int.* ● *n.* (also **goodie**) (*pl.* **-ies**) **1** (usu. in *pl.*) something good or attractive, esp. to eat. **2** *colloq.* a good or favored person, esp. a hero in a story, movie, etc. **3** = *goody-goody n.* ● *int.* expressing childish delight. □ **goody-goody** *n.* a smug or obtrusively virtuous person. ● *adj.* obtrusively or smugly virtuous.
■ □ **goody-goody** *n.* see PRIG, PHARISEE. ● *adj.* smug, sanctimonious, self-righteous, priggish, prim, hypocritical, *colloq.* holier-than-thou.

goody[2] /gŏŏdee/ *n.* (*pl.* **goodies**) *archaic* (often as a title pre-

fixed to a surname) an elderly woman of humble station (*Goody Blake*). [for GOODWIFE: cf. HUSSY]

gooey /gŏŏ-ee/ *adj.* (**gooier**, **gooiest**) *sl.* **1** viscous; sticky. **2** sickly; sentimental. □□ **gooeyness** *n.* (also **gooiness**). [GOO + -Y[2]]
■ **1** viscous, gluey, sticky, tacky, glutinous, mucilaginous, gummy. **2** sickly, sentimental, sweet, sugary, saccharine, cloying, syrupy, sloppy, mushy, *colloq.* slushy; mawkish, maudlin.

goof /gŏŏf/ *n. & v. sl.* ● *n.* **1** a foolish or stupid person. **2** a mistake. ● *v.* **1** *tr.* bungle; mess up. **2** *intr.* blunder; make a mistake. **3** *intr.* (often foll. by *off*) idle. **4** *tr.* (as **goofed** *adj.*) stupefied with drugs. [var. of dial. *goff* f. F *goffe* f. It. *goffo* f. med.L *gufus* coarse]
■ *n.* **1** see SILLY *n.* **2** see MISTAKE *n.* ● *v.* **1, 2** see FOUL *v.* 6. **3** see IDLE *v.* 2.

goofball /gŏŏfbawl/ *n. sl.* **1** a pill containing a barbiturate or a tranquilizer. **2** a silly, ridiculous, or inept person.

goofy /gŏŏfee/ *adj.* (**goofier**, **goofiest**) *sl.* **1** stupid; silly. **2** *Brit.* having protruding or crooked front teeth. □□ **goofily** *adv.* **goofiness** *n.*
■ **1** see CRAZY 1.

goog /gŏŏg/ *n. Austral. sl.* an egg. □ **full as a goog** very drunk. [20th c.: orig. unkn.]

googly /gŏŏglee/ *n.* (*pl.* **-ies**) *Cricket* an off-break ball bowled with apparent leg-break action. [20th c.: orig. unkn.]

googol /gŏŏgawl/ *n.* ten raised to the hundredth power (10^{100}). ¶ Not in formal use. [arbitrary formation]

gook /gŏŏk, gŏŏk/ *n. sl. offens.* a foreigner, esp. a person from E. Asia. [20th c.: orig. unkn.]

goolie /gŏŏlee/ *n.* (also **gooly**) (*pl.* **-ies**) **1** (usu. in *pl.*) *Brit. sl.* a testicle. **2** *Austral. sl.* a stone or pebble. [app. of Ind. orig.; cf. Hind. *golī* bullet, ball, pill]

goon /gŏŏn/ *n. sl.* **1** a stupid or playful person. **2** a person hired by racketeers, etc., to terrorize political or industrial opponents. [perh. f. dial. *gooney* booby: infl. by the subhuman cartoon character "Alice the *Goon*"]
■ **1** see FOOL[1] *n.* 1. **2** see THUG.

goop[1] /gŏŏp/ *n. sl.* a stupid or fatuous person. [20th c.: cf. GOOF]

goop[2] /gŏŏp/ *n. colloq.* a viscous substance. [prob. f. GOO]

goopy[1] /gŏŏpee/ *adj. Brit. sl.* (**goopier**, **goopiest**) stupid; fatuous. □□ **goopiness** *n.*

goopy[2] /gŏŏpee/ *adj. colloq.* thick; viscous.

goosander /gŏŏsándər/ *n.* a large diving duck, *Mergus merganser*, with a narrow serrated bill; a common merganser. [prob. f. GOOSE + -*ander* in *bergander* sheldrake]

goose /gŏŏs/ *n. & v.* ● *n.* (*pl.* **geese** /gees/) **1 a** any of various large water birds of the family Anatidae, with short legs, webbed feet, and a broad bill. **b** the female of this (opp. GANDER). **c** the flesh of a goose as food. **2** *colloq.* a simpleton. **3** (*pl.* **gooses**) a tailor's smoothing iron, having a handle like a goose's neck. ● *v.tr. sl.* poke (a person) between the buttocks. □ **goose bumps** also **goose flesh** or **pimples** or **skin**) a bristling state of the skin produced by cold or fright. **goose egg** a zero score in a game. **goose step** a military marching step in which the knees are kept stiff. [OE *gōs* f. Gmc]
■ *n.* **2** see FOOL[1] *n.* 1.

gooseberry /gŏŏsberee, -bəree, gŏŏz-/ *n.* (*pl.* **-ies**) **1** a round edible yellowish green berry with a thin usu. translucent skin enclosing seeds in a juicy flesh. **2** the thorny shrub, *Ribes grossularia*, bearing this fruit. □ **play gooseberry** *Brit. colloq.* be an unwanted extra (usu. third) person. [perh. f. GOOSE + BERRY]

goosefoot /gŏŏsfŏŏt/ *n.* (*pl.* **-foots**) any plant of the genus *Chenopodium*, having leaves shaped like the foot of a goose.

goosegog /gŏŏzgog/ *n. Brit. colloq.* a gooseberry. [joc. corrupt.]

/.../ **pronunciation**	● **part of speech**
□ **phrases, idioms, and compounds**	
□□ **derivatives**	■ **synonym section**
cross-references appear in SMALL CAPITALS or *italics*	

goosegrass /gŏosgras/ n. cleavers.

GOP abbr. Grand Old Party (the Republican Party).

gopher[1] /gṓfər/ n. **1** (in full **pocket gopher**) any burrowing rodent of the family Geomyidae, native to N. America, having external cheek pouches and sharp front teeth. **2** a N. American ground squirrel. **3** a tortoise, Gopherus polyphemus, native to the southern US, that excavates tunnels as shelter from the sun. □ **gopher snake** a cribo. [18th c.: orig. uncert.]

gopher[2] /gṓfər/ n. **1** Bibl. a tree from the wood of which Noah's ark was made. **2** (in full **gopher wood**) a tree, Cladrastis lutea, yielding yellowish timber. [Heb. gōper]

goral /gáwrəl/ n. a goat antelope, Nemorhaedus goral, native to mountainous regions of N. India, having short horns curving to the rear. [native name]

gorblimey /gáwrblímee/ int. & n. Brit. sl. ● int. an expression of surprise, indignation, etc. ● n. (pl. **-eys**) a soft service cap. [corrupt. of God blind me]

Gordian knot /gáwrdeeən/ n. **1** an intricate knot. **2** a difficult problem or task. □ **cut the Gordian knot** solve a problem by force or by evasion. [Gordius, king of Phrygia, who tied an intricate knot that remained tied until cut by Alexander the Great]

gordo / gáwrdō/ n. Austral. a popular variety of grape. [Sp. gordo blanco fat white]

Gordon setter /gáwrd'n/ n. **1** a setter of a black and tan breed, used as a gun dog. **2** this breed. [4th Duke of Gordon, d. 1827, promoter of the breed]

gore[1] /gawr/ n. **1** blood shed and clotted. **2** slaughter; carnage. [OE gor dung, dirt]
■ **2** carnage, butchery, slaughter, bloodshed, killing, murder, violence, joc. bloodletting.

gore[2] /gawr/ v.tr. pierce with a horn, tusk, etc. [ME: orig. unkn.]
■ pierce, stab, poke, horn, penetrate, puncture, spear, gouge, spit, stick, impale.

gore[3] /gawr/ n. & v. ● n. **1** a wedge-shaped piece in a garment. **2** a triangular or tapering piece in an umbrella, etc. **3** a small often wedge-shaped plot of land, as between larger tracts. ● v.tr. shape with a gore. [OE gāra triangular piece of land, rel. to OE gār spear, a spearhead being triangular]

gorge /gawrj/ n. & v. ● n. **1** a narrow opening between hills or a rocky ravine, often with a stream running through it. **2** an act of gorging; a feast. **3** the contents of the stomach; what has been swallowed. **4** the neck of a bastion or other outwork; the rear entrance to a work. **5** a mass of ice, etc., blocking a narrow passage. ● v. **1** intr. feed greedily. **2** tr. **a** (often refl.) satiate; glut. **b** swallow; devour greedily. □ **one's gorge rises at** one is sickened by. □□ **gorger** n. [ME f. OF gorge throat ult. f. L gurges whirlpool]
■ n. **1** ravine, canyon, defile, pass, chasm, fissure, crevasse, gully, gap, notch, gulch, Brit. gill. **2** see FEAST n. 1. **3** vomit, Brit. colloq. sick, sl. puke, upchuck, Austral. sl. chunder. ● v. **1** feed, gormandize, gluttonize, overindulge, gobble, eat one's fill, guzzle, sl. nosh; see also OVEREAT. **2 a** satiate, glut, fill, stuff, cram, overfeed, surfeit, pall; (gorge oneself) gluttonize, colloq. make a hog of oneself; see also OVEREAT. **b** swallow, devour, gulp (down), gobble (down or up), bolt (down), wolf (down), gormandize.

gorgeous /gáwrjəs/ adj. **1** richly colored; sumptuous; magnificent. **2** colloq. very pleasant; splendid (gorgeous weather). **3** colloq. strikingly beautiful. □□ **gorgeously** adv. **gorgeousness** n. [earlier gorgayse, -yas f. OF gorgias fine, elegant, of unkn. orig.]
■ **1** rich, sumptuous, dazzling, radiant, brilliant, resplendent, splendid, magnificent, glorious, exquisite, beautiful, showy, colorful, colloq. or joc. splendiferous, literary refulgent. **2** splendid, wonderful, marvelous, glorious, spectacular, superb, excellent, colloq. great, terrific, fantastic, smashing, super, swell. **3** see BEAUTIFUL 1.

gorget /górjit/ n. **1** hist. **a** a piece of armor for the throat. **b** a woman's wimple. **2** a patch of color on the throat of a bird, insect, etc. [OF gorgete (as GORGE)]

gorgon /gáwrgən/ n. **1** (in Greek mythology) each of three snake-haired sisters (esp. Medusa) with the power to turn anyone who looked at them to stone. **2** a frightening or repulsive person, esp. a woman. □□ **gorgonian** /gawrgṓneeən/ adj. [L Gorgo -onis f. Gk Gorgō f. gorgos terrible]
■ **2** see HAG[1] 2.

gorgonian /gawrgṓneeən/ n. & adj. ● n. a usu. brightly colored horny coral of the order Gorgonacea, having a treelike skeleton bearing polyps, e.g., a sea fan. ● adj. of or relating to the Gorgonacea. [mod.L (as GORGON), with ref. to its petrifaction]

gorgonize /gáwrgəniz/ v.tr. **1** stare at like a gorgon. **2** paralyze with terror, etc.

Gorgonzola /gáwrgənzṓlə/ n. a type of rich cheese with bluish green veins. [Gorgonzola in Italy]

gorilla /gərílə/ n. the largest anthropoid ape, Gorilla gorilla, native to Central Africa, having a large head, short neck, and prominent mouth. [adopted as the specific name in 1847 f. Gk Gorillai an African tribe noted for hairiness]

gormandize /gáwrməndiz/ v. & n. ● v. **1** intr. & tr. eat or devour voraciously. **2** intr. indulge in good eating. ● n. = GOURMANDISE. □□ **gormandizer** n. [as GOURMANDISE]
■ v. **1** see DEVOUR 1. **2** see FEAST v. 1.

gormless /gáwrmlis/ adj. esp. Brit. colloq. foolish; lacking sense. □□ **gormlessly** adv. **gormlessness** n. [orig. gaumless f. dial. gaum understanding]

gorse /gawrs/ n. any spiny yellow-flowered shrub of the genus Ulex, esp. growing on European wastelands. Also called FURZE. □□ **gorsy** adj. [OE gors(t) rel. to OHG gersta, L hordeum, barley]

Gorsedd /gáwrseth/ n. a meeting of Welsh, etc., bards and druids (esp. as a daily preliminary to the eisteddfod). [Welsh, lit. 'throne']

gory /gáwree/ adj. (**gorier, goriest**) **1** involving bloodshed; bloodthirsty (a gory film). **2** covered in gore. □□ **gorily** adv. **goriness** n.
■ **1** bloodthirsty, bloody, sanguinary; gruesome, grisly, horrific, bloodcurdling. **2** bloody, blood-soaked, bloodstained.

gosh /gosh/ int. expressing surprise. [euphem. for GOD]

goshawk /gós-hawk/ n. a large short-winged hawk, Accipiter gentilis. [OE gōs-hafoc (as GOOSE, HAWK[1])]

gosling /gózling/ n. a young goose. [ME, orig. gesling f. ON gǽslingr]

gospel /góspəl/ n. **1** the teaching or revelation of Christ. **2** (**Gospel**) **a** the record of Christ's life and teaching in the first four books of the New Testament. **b** each of these books. **c** a portion from one of them read at a service. **d** a similar book in the Apocrypha. **3** a thing regarded as absolutely true (take my word as gospel). **4** a principle one acts on or advocates. **5** (in full **gospel music**) African-American evangelical religious singing. □ **Gospel side** the north side of the altar, at which the Gospel is read. **gospel truth** something considered to be unquestionably true. [OE gōdspel (as GOOD, spel news, SPELL[1]), rendering eccl.L bona annuntiatio, bonus nuntius = evangelium EVANGEL: assoc. with GOD]
■ **3** truth, fact, certainty, reality, actuality. **4** see PRINCIPLE 1.

gospeler /góspələr/ n. (also **gospeller**) the reader of the Gospel in the Mass. □ **hot gospeler** a zealous puritan; a rabid propagandist.

gossamer /gósəmər/ n. & adj. ● n. **1** a filmy substance of small spiders' webs. **2** delicate filmy material. **3** a thread of gossamer. ● adj. light and flimsy as gossamer. □□ **gossamered** adj. **gossamery** adj. [ME gos(e)somer(e), app. f. GOOSE + SUMMER[1] (goose summer = St Martin's summer, i.e. early November when geese were eaten, gossamer being common then)]
■ adj. see FLIMSY 4.

gossip /gósip/ n. & v. ● n. **1 a** easy or unconstrained talk or writing esp. about persons or social incidents. **b** idle talk; groundless rumor. **2** an informal chat, esp. about persons or social incidents. **3** a person who indulges in gossip. ● v.intr. (**gossiped, gossiping**) talk or write gossip. □ **gossip column** a section of a newspaper devoted to gossip about well-known people. **gossip columnist** a regular writer of gossip columns. □□ **gossiper** n. **gossipy** adj. [earlier sense 'godparent': f. OE *godsibb* person related to one in GOD: see SIB]

■ n. **1** talk, small talk, tittle-tattle, prattle, *colloq.* chitchat; see also CHATTER n. **2** chat, conversation, talk, *colloq.* natter, *sl.* chin-wag. **3** rumormonger, scandalmonger, gossipmonger, newsmonger, gossiper, busybody, blabber(mouth), blatherskite, telltale, talebearer, flibbertigibbet, tattletale, *archaic* quidnunc, *colloq.* bigmouth, *colloq.* Nosy Parker. ● v. tattle, whisper, blather, blab, tittle-tattle, tell tales, *colloq.* name names; see also *spill the beans* (SPILL¹), BABBLE v. 1a, b.

□□ **gossipy** see INDISCREET 1.

gossipmonger /gósipmongǝr/ n. a perpetrator of gossip.

■ see GOSSIP n. 3.

gossoon /gosoón/ n. Ir. a lad. [earlier *garsoon* f. F *garçon* boy]

got *past* and *past part.* of GET.

Goth /goth/ n. **1** a member of a Germanic tribe that invaded the Roman Empire in the 3rd–5th c. **2** an uncivilized or ignorant person. [LL *Gothi* (pl.) f. Gk *Go(t)thoi* f. Goth.]

goth /goth/ n. Brit. **1** a style of rock music with an intense or droning blend of guitars, bass, and drums, often with apocalyptic or mystical lyrics. **2** a performer or devotee of this music, often dressing in black clothing and wearing black make-up.

Gothic /góthik/ adj. & n. ● adj. **1** of the Goths or their language. **2** in the style of architecture prevalent in W. Europe in the 12th–16th c., characterized by pointed arches. **3** (of a novel, etc.) in a style popular in the 18th–19th c., with supernatural or horrifying events. **4** barbarous; uncouth. **5** *Printing* (of type) old-fashioned German, black letter, or sans serif. ● n. **1** the Gothic language. **2** Gothic architecture. **3** *Printing* Gothic type. □□ **Gothically** adv. **Gothicism** /-thisizǝm/ n. **Gothicize** /-thisiz/ v.tr. & intr. [F *gothique* or LL *gothicus* f. *Gothi*: see GOTH]

gotta /gótǝ/ *colloq.* have got to (*we gotta go*). [corrupt.]

gotten *past part.* of GET.

Götterdämmerung /gótǝrdámǝrung, gótǝrdémǝroong/ n. **1** the twilight (i.e., downfall) of the gods. **2** the complete downfall of a regime, etc. [G, esp. as the title of an opera by Wagner]

gouache /gwaash, goo-aásh/ n. **1** a method of painting in opaque pigments ground in water and thickened with a gluelike substance. **2** these pigments. **3** a picture painted in this way. [F f. It. *guazzo*]

Gouda /goódǝ, gów-/ n. a flat round usu. Dutch cheese with a yellow rind. [*Gouda* in Holland, where orig. made]

gouge /gowj/ n. & v. ● n. **1 a** a chisel with a concave blade, used in woodworking, sculpture, and surgery. **b** an indentation or groove made with or as with this. **2** *colloq.* a swindle. ● v. **1** tr. cut with or as with a gouge. **2** tr. **a** (foll. by *out*) force out (esp. an eye with the thumb) with or as with a gouge. **b** force out the eye of (a person). **3** tr. *colloq.* swindle; extort money from. **4** intr. *Austral.* dig for opal. □□ **gouger** n. [F f. LL *gubia*, perh. of Celt. orig.]

■ n. **1 b** groove, furrow, scratch, gash, score, channel, flute, cut; indentation, hollow. **2** see SWINDLE n. 1, 3. ● v. **1** chisel, gash, groove, incise, dig, scratch; scoop out, hollow out. **3** extort, extract, defraud, blackmail, cheat, swindle, squeeze, milk, bleed, fleece, *sl.* skin, bilk.

goulash /goólaash, -lash/ n. **1** a highly seasoned Hungarian dish of meat and vegetables, usu. flavored with paprika. **2** (in contract bridge) a re-deal, several cards at a time, of the four hands (unshuffled, but with each hand arranged in suits and order of value) when no player has bid. [Magyar *gulyáshús* f. *gulyás* herdsman + *hús* meat]

gourami /goóraamee, goórǝmee/ n. **1 a** a large freshwater fish, *Osphronemus goramy*, native to SE Asia, used as food. **b** any small fish of the family Osphronemidae, usu. kept in aquariums. **2** any small brightly colored freshwater fish of the family Belontiidae, usu. kept in aquariums. Also called *labyrinth fish*. [Malay *gurámi*]

gourd /goórd/ n. **1 a** any of various fleshy usu. large fruits with a hard skin, often used as containers, ornaments, etc. **b** any of various climbing or trailing plants of the family Cucurbitaceae bearing this fruit. Also called CUCURBIT. **2** the hollow hard skin of the gourd fruit, dried and used as a drinking vessel, water container, etc. □□ **gourdful** n. (*pl.* -fuls). [ME f. AF *gurde*, OF *gourde* ult. f. L *cucurbita*]

gourmand /goórmaánd/ n. & adj. ● n. **1** a glutton. **2** *disp.* a gourmet. ● adj. gluttonous; fond of eating, esp. to excess. □□ **gourmandism** n. [ME f. OF, of unkn. orig.]

■ n. **1** see GLUTTON 1. **2** see GOURMET.

gourmandise /goórmondeéz/ n. the habits of a gourmand; gluttony. [F (as GOURMAND)]

gourmet /goórmáy/ n. a connoisseur of good or delicate food. [F, = wine taster: sense infl. by GOURMAND]

■ epicure, gastronome, bon vivant, *bon viveur*, *colloq.* foodie, *disp.* gourmand.

gout /gowt/ n. **1** a disease with inflammation of the smaller joints, esp. the toe, as a result of excess uric acid salts in the blood. **2** *archaic* **a** a drop, esp. of blood. **b** a splash or spot. □□ **gouty** adj. **goutily** adv. **goutiness** n. [ME f. OF *goute* f. L *gutta* drop, with ref. to the medieval theory of the flowing down of humors]

Gov. abbr. **1** Government. **2** Governor.

gov. abbr. governor.

govern /gúvǝrn/ v. **1 a** tr. rule or control (a nation, subject, etc.) with authority; conduct the policy and affairs of (an organization, etc.). **b** intr. be in government. **2 a** tr. influence or determine (a person or a course of action). **b** intr. be the predominating influence. **3** tr. be a standard or principle for; constitute a law for; serve to decide (a case). **4** tr. check or control (esp. passions and machinery). **5** tr. Gram. (esp. of a verb or preposition) have (a noun or pronoun or its case) depending on it. **6** tr. be in military command of (a fort, town). □ **governing body** the managers of an institution. □□ **governable** adj. **governability** n. **governableness** n. [ME f. OF *governer* f. L *gubernare* steer, rule f. Gk *kubernaō*]

■ **1 a** rule, control, direct, manage, run, steer, lead, captain, pilot, command, head (up), look after, be in charge of, hold sway over, reign over. **b** wield power, exercise power, hold sway, be in power, have *or* hold the whip hand, be in charge, *colloq.* run the show, be in the saddle *or* driver's seat; reign, sit on the throne, wield the scepter, wear the crown. **2 a** see INFLUENCE v., DETERMINE 3. **b** predominate, dominate, hold sway. **3** see DETERMINE 3. **4** control, check, bridle, curb, master, subdue, restrain, contain, hold, suppress, repress.

governance /gúvǝrnǝns/ n. **1** the act or manner of governing. **2** the office or function of governing. **3** sway; control. [ME f. OF (as GOVERN)]

■ **1, 2** see MANAGEMENT 1.

governess /gúvǝrnis/ n. a woman employed to teach children in a private household. [earlier *governeress* f. OF *governeresse* (as GOVERNOR)]

■ see TEACHER.

governessy /gúvǝrnisee/ adj. characteristic of a governess; prim.

government /gúvǝrnmǝnt/ n. **1** the act or manner of governing. **2** the system by which a nation or community is governed. **3 a** a body of persons governing a nation. **b** (usu. **Government**) a particular party or group of people in office. **4** the nation as an agent. **5** Gram. the relation between a governed and a governing word. □ **Government House** (in certain countries) the official residence of a governor. **government issue** (of equipment) provided by the government. **government surplus** unused equipment sold by the government. □□ **governmental** /-mént'l/ adj. **governmentally** adv. [ME f. OF *governement* (as GOVERN)]

■ **1–3** rule, governance, command, regulation, control,

---

management, administration, direction, supervision, superintendence, domination, guidance, charge, operation, running, leadership, directorate, governorate, ministry; see also REGIME 1.

governor /gúvərnər/ *n.* **1** a person who governs; a ruler. **2** the executive head of each state of the US. **3 a** *hist.* an official governing a province, town, etc. **b** *Brit.* a representative of the British crown in a colony. **4** an officer commanding a fortress or garrison. **5** the head or a member of a governing body of an institution. **6** *Brit.* the official in charge of a prison. **7** *Brit.* **a** *sl.* one's employer. **b** *sl.* one's father. **c** *colloq.* (as a form of address) sir. **8** *Mech.* an automatic regulator controlling the speed of an engine, etc. □ **Governor-General 1** a high-ranking governor of a territory who presides over deputy governors. **2** the representative of the British crown in a Commonwealth country that regards the sovereign as head of state. □□ **governorate** /-rət, -rayt/ *n.* **governorship** *n.* [ME f. AF *gouvernour*, OF *governĕo(u)r* f. L *gubernator -oris* (as GOVERN)]

■ **1–4** see LEADER 1. **5** see HEAD *n.* 6a. **7 b** see FATHER *n.* 1a.

Govt. *abbr.* Government.

gowan /gówən/ *n.* *Sc.* **1** a daisy. **2** any white or yellow field flower. [prob. var. of dial. *gollan* ranunculus, etc., and rel. to *gold* in *marigold*]

gowk /gowk/ *n.* *Brit. dial.* **1** a cuckoo. **2** an awkward or half-witted person; a fool. [ME f. ON *gaukr* f. Gmc]

gown /gown/ *n. & v.* ● *n.* **1** a loose flowing garment, esp. a long dress worn by a woman. **2** the official robe of an alderman, judge, cleric, member of a university, etc. **3** a surgeon's robe, worn during surgery. **4** the members of a university as distinct from the permanent residents of the university town (cf. TOWN). ● *v.tr.* (usu. as **gowned** adj.) attire in a gown. [ME f. OF *goune, gon(n)e* f. LL *gunna* fur garment: cf. med. Gk *gouna* fur]

goy /goy/ *n.* (*pl.* **goyim** /góyim/ or **goys**) *sl.* sometimes *derog.* a Jewish name for a non-Jew. □□ **goyish** adj. (also **goyisch**). [Heb. *gōy* people, nation]

GP *abbr.* **1** general practitioner. **2** Grand Prix.

GPA *abbr.* grade point average.

GPO *abbr.* **1** General Post Office. **2** Government Printing Office.

gr *abbr.* (also **gr.**) **1** gram(s). **2** grain(s). **3** gross. **4** gray.

Graafian follicle /gráafeeən, gráf-/ *n.* a follicle in the mammalian ovary in which an ovum develops prior to ovulation. [R. de *Graaf*, Du. anatomist d. 1673]

grab /grab/ *v. & n.* ● *v.* (**grabbed, grabbing**) **1** *tr.* **a** seize suddenly. **b** capture; arrest. **2** *tr.* take greedily or unfairly. **3** *tr. sl.* attract the attention of; impress. **4** *intr.* (foll. by *at*) make a sudden snatch at. **5** *intr.* (of the brakes of a motor vehicle) act harshly or jerkily. ● *n.* **1** a sudden clutch or attempt to seize. **2** a mechanical device for clutching. **3** the practice of grabbing; rapacious proceedings, esp. in politics and commerce. **4** a children's card game in which certain cards may be snatched from the table. □ **grab bag 1** a container from which one removes a mystery gift, as at a party. **2** a miscellaneous group of items. **grab bar** (also **handle, rail,** etc.) a bar, handle or rail, etc., for aid in balance, as in a moving vehicle or a bathtub, etc. **up for grabs** *sl.* easily obtainable; inviting capture. □□ **grabber** *n.* [MLG, MDu. *grabben*: cf. GRIP, GRIPE, GROPE]

■ *v.* **1 a** snatch, lay *or* catch hold of, fasten upon, grasp, seize, catch, grip, clutch, snag. **b** seize, capture, catch, arrest, collar, apprehend, *sl.* nab, pinch. **2** appropriate, expropriate, arrogate, seize, commandeer, get one's hands *or* fingers on; usurp. **3** see IMPRESS[1] *v.* 1a. **4** (*grab at*) snatch at, make a grab for, *colloq.* go for. ● *n.* **1** snatch, clutch; grasp, grip. **3** money-grabbing, predaciousness; see also AVARICE. □ **up for grabs** see *on sale* (SALE).

grabble /grábəl/ *v.intr.* **1** grope about; feel for something. **2** (often foll. by *for*) sprawl on all fours; scramble (for something). [Du. & LG *grabbeln* scramble for a thing (as GRAB)]

■ **1** grope *or* feel about, *Austral. & NZ colloq.* fossick.

grabby /grábee/ *adj. colloq.* tending to grab; greedy; grasping.

graben /graabən/ *n.* (*pl.* same or **grabens**) *Geol.* a depression of the earth's surface between faults. [G, orig. = ditch]

grace /grays/ *n. & v.* ● *n.* **1** attractiveness, esp. in elegance of proportion or manner or movement; gracefulness. **2** courteous good will (*had the grace to apologize*). **3** an attractive feature; an accomplishment (*social graces*). **4 a** (in Christian belief) the unmerited favor of God; a divine saving and strengthening influence. **b** the state of receiving this. **c** a divinely given talent. **5** goodwill; favor (*fall from grace*). **6** delay granted as a favor (*a year's grace*). **7** a short thanksgiving before or after a meal. **8** (**Grace**) (in Greek mythology) each of three beautiful sister goddesses, bestowers of beauty and charm. **9** (**Grace**) (prec. by *His, Her, Your*) forms of description or address for a duke, duchess, or archbishop. ● *v.tr.* **1** lend or add grace to; enhance or embellish. **2** (often foll. by *with*) confer honor or dignity on (*graced us with his presence*). □ **days of grace** = *grace period.* **grace and favor house** etc., *Brit.* a house, etc., occupied by permission of a sovereign, etc. **grace note** *Mus.* an extra note as an embellishment not essential to the harmony or melody. **grace period** the time allowed by law for payment of an amount due. **in a person's good** (or **bad**) **graces** regarded by a person with favor (or disfavor). **with good** (or **bad**) **grace** as if willingly (or reluctantly). [ME f. OF f. L *gratia* f. *gratus* pleasing: cf. GRATEFUL]

■ *n.* **1** elegance, gracefulness, attractiveness, finesse, refinement, polish, poise, suppleness, ease; tastefulness, cultivation, suavity, suaveness, culture, savoir faire, discrimination, breeding, propriety, decorum, etiquette. **2** good will, courtesy, (good) taste, discernment, (good) manners, politeness, consideration, decency, tact, mannerliness; kindness, kindliness, benevolence, generosity, goodness, graciousness. **3** accomplishment, skill, talent, gift, ability. **4 a** goodwill, goodness, indulgence, forgiveness, favor, mercy, mercifulness, leniency, compassion, clemency, charity. **7** thanksgiving, prayer; blessing, benediction. ● *v.* **1** enhance, adorn, embellish, set off, decorate, ornament, beautify. **2** dignify, enhance, distinguish, enrich, honor, favor. □ **with good grace** see *willingly* (WILLING), KINDLY[1] 1. **with bad grace** see *begrudgingly* (BEGRUDGE).

graceful /gráysfŏŏl/ *adj.* having or showing grace or elegance. □□ **gracefully** *adv.* **gracefulness** *n.*

■ fluid, flowing, supple, lissome, lithe, smooth, nimble, agile; elegant, courtly, urbane, polished, refined, suave.

graceless /gráyslis/ *adj.* lacking grace or elegance or charm. □□ **gracelessly** *adv.* **gracelessness** *n.*

■ see UNGRACEFUL.

gracile /grásil, -sīl/ *adj.* slender; gracefully slender. [L *gracilis* slender]

gracility /grəsílitee/ *n.* **1** slenderness. **2** (of literary style) unornamented simplicity.

gracious /gráyshəs/ *adj. & int.* ● *adj.* **1** kind; indulgent and beneficent to others. **2** (of God) merciful; benign. **3** kindly; courteous. **4** *Brit.* a polite epithet used of royal persons or their acts (*the gracious speech from the throne*). ● *int.* expressing surprise. □ **gracious living** an elegant way of life. □□ **graciosity** /-sheeósitee/ *n.* **graciously** *adv.* **graciousness** *n.* [ME f. OF f. L *gratiosus* (as GRACE)]

■ *adj.* **1, 3** kind, kindly, benevolent, beneficent, indulgent, kindhearted, warmhearted, cordial, warm, friendly, sociable, good-natured, amiable, affable, benign, accommodating, obliging, agreeable, considerate; courteous, polite, well-mannered, tactful, mannerly. **2** see MERCIFUL. ● *int.* (upon) my word, by Jove, (well) I'm blessed, well I (do) declare, my (sainted) aunt, (my) goodness, (good) Lord, good heavens, well I never, mercy, *Brit.* I say, *colloq.* my stars, well I'm *or* I'll be damned, *Brit. sl.* crikey, blimey; see also GOD *int.*

grackle /grákəl/ *n.* **1** any of various orioles, esp. of the genus *Quiscalus*, native to America, the males of which are shiny black with a blue-green sheen. Also called BLACKBIRD. **2** any of various mynahs, esp. of the genus *Gracula*, native to Asia. [mod.L *Gracula* f. L *graculus* jackdaw]

grad /grad/ *n. colloq.* = GRADUATE *n.* 1. [abbr.]

gradate /gráydayt/ *v.* **1** *v.intr.* & *tr.* pass or cause to pass by gradations from one shade to another. **2** *tr.* arrange in steps or grades of size, etc. [back-form. f. GRADATION]
■ **1** see BLEND *v.* 4a.

gradation /gráydáyshən/ *n.* (usu. in *pl.*) **1** a stage of transition or advance. **2 a** a certain degree in rank, intensity, merit, divergence, etc. **b** such a degree; an arrangement in such degrees. **3** (of paint, etc.) the gradual passing from one shade, tone, etc., to another. **4** *Philol.* ablaut. □□ **gradational** *adj.* **gradationally** *adv.* [L *gradatio* f. *gradus* step]
■ **1, 2** see GRADE *n.* 1a.

grade /grayd/ *n.* & *v.* ● *n.* **1 a** a certain degree in rank, merit, proficiency, quality, etc. **b** a class of persons or things of the same grade. **2** a mark indicating the quality of a student's work. **3** a class in school, concerned with a particular year's work and usu. numbered from the first upwards. **4 a** a gradient or slope. **b** the rate of ascent or descent. **5 a** a variety of cattle produced by crossing native stock with a superior breed. **b** a group of animals at a similar level of development. **6** *Philol.* a relative position in a series of forms involving ablaut. ● *v.* **1** *tr.* arrange in or allocate to grades; class; sort. **2** *intr.* (foll. by *up, down, off, into,* etc.) pass gradually between grades, or into a grade. **3** *tr.* give a grade to (a student). **4** *tr.* blend so as to affect the grade of color with tints passing into each other. **5** *tr.* reduce (a road, etc.) to easy gradients. **6** *tr.* (often foll. by *up*) cross (livestock) with a better breed. □ **at grade** on the same level. **grade crossing** a crossing of a roadway, etc., with a railroad track at the same level. **grade point** the numerical equivalent of a scholastic letter grade. **grade point average** a scholastic average that is obtained by dividing the number of earned grade points by the number of credits taken. **grade school** elementary school. **make the grade** *colloq.* succeed; reach the desired standard. [F *grade* or L *gradus* step]
■ *n.* **1 a** degree, position, stage, station, gradation, echelon, class, level, category; rung, rank, status, standing. **b** see CATEGORY. **2** rating, mark, score, grading; result. **3** class, year, *Brit.* form. **4 a** slope, rise, gradient, acclivity, declivity, incline, decline, ascent, descent. ● *v.* **1** classify, class, order, organize, rank, sort, size, group, categorize. **3** mark, rate, evaluate, assess, judge; rank. □ **make the grade** measure up, succeed, qualify, pass muster, *colloq.* make it; see also PASS¹ *v.* 8a.

grader /gráydər/ *n.* **1** a person or thing that grades. **2** a wheeled machine for leveling the ground, esp. in road-making. **3** (in *comb.*) a pupil of a specified grade in a school (*third grader*).

gradient /gráydeeənt/ *n.* **1 a** a stretch of road, railroad, etc., that slopes from the horizontal. **b** the amount of such a slope. **2** the rate of rise or fall of temperature, pressure, etc., in passing from one region to another. [prob. formed on GRADE after *salient*]

gradin /gráydin/ *n.* (also **gradine** /-deen/) **1** each of a series of low steps or a tier of seats. **2** a ledge at the back of an altar. [It. *gradino* dimin. of *grado* GRADE]

gradual /grájōōəl/ *adj.* & *n.* ● *adj.* **1** taking place or progressing slowly or by degrees. **2** not rapid or steep or abrupt. ● *n. Eccl.* **1** a response sung or recited between the Epistle and Gospel in the Mass. **2** a book of music for the sung Mass. □□ **gradually** *adv.* **gradualness** *n.* [med.L *gradualis,* -*ale* f. L *gradus* step, the noun referring to the altar steps on which the response is sung]
■ *adj.* **1** piecemeal, inchmeal, steady; see also SLOW *adj.* 1. **2** easy, gentle, even, moderate, regular, steady. □□ **gradually** slowly, evenly, piecemeal, inchmeal, step by step, bit by bit, little by little, by degrees; cautiously, carefully.

gradualism /grájōōəlizəm/ *n.* a policy of gradual reform rather than sudden change or revolution. □□ **gradualist** *n.* **gradualistic** *adj.*

graduand /grájōōand/ *n. Brit.* a person about to receive an

academic degree. [med.L *graduandus* gerundive of *graduare* GRADUATE]

graduate *n.* & *v.* ● *n.* /grájōōət/ **1** a person who has been awarded an academic degree (also *attrib.: graduate student*). **2** a person who has completed a course of study. ● *v.* /grájōō-áyt/ **1 a** *intr.* take an academic degree. **b** *tr.* admit to an academic degree or a certificate of completion of school studies. **2** *intr.* **a** (foll. by *from*) be a graduate of a specified university. **b** (foll. by *in*) be a graduate in a specified subject. **3** *tr.* send out as a graduate from a university, etc. **4** *intr.* **a** (foll. by *to*) move up to (a higher grade of activity, etc.). **b** (foll. by *as, in*) gain specified qualifications. **5** *tr.* mark out in degrees or parts. **6** *tr.* arrange in gradations; apportion (e.g., tax) according to a scale. **7** *intr.* (foll. by *into, away*) pass by degrees. □ **graduated pension** (in the UK) a system of pension contributions by employees in proportion to their wages or salary. **graduate school** a division of a university for advanced work by graduates. □□ **graduator** *n.* [med.L *graduari* take a degree f. L *gradus* step]
■ *v.* **4 a** see ADVANCE *v.* 1, 2. **b** qualify, get *or* obtain qualifications, get a degree. **5** see CALIBRATE 1, 2. **6** gradate, scale, apportion; see also GRADE *v.* 1. **7** shade, merge, slip, blend, pass, move.

graduation /grájōōáyshən/ *n.* **1** the act or an instance of graduating or being graduated. **2** a ceremony at which degrees are conferred. **3** each or all of the marks on a vessel or instrument indicating degrees of quantity, etc.

Graecism var. of GRECISM.

Graecize var. of GRECIZE.

Graeco- var. of GRECO-.

Graeco-Roman var. of GRECO-ROMAN.

graffito /grəféetō/ *n.* (*pl.* **graffiti** /-tee/) **1** (usu. in *pl.*) a piece of writing or drawing scribbled, scratched, or sprayed on a surface. ¶ The plural form *graffiti* is sometimes used with a singular verb, even though it is not a mass noun in this sense, and so properly a plural construction is needed, e.g., *graffiti are an art form.* **2** *Art* a form of decoration made by scratches on wet plaster, showing a different colored underside. [It. f. *graffio* a scratch]

graft¹ /graft/ *n.* & *v.* ● *n.* **1** *Bot.* **a** a shoot or scion inserted into a slit of stock, from which it receives sap. **b** the place where a graft is inserted. **2** *Surgery* a piece of living tissue, organ, etc., transplanted surgically. **3** *Brit. sl.* hard work. ● *v.* **1** *tr.* **a** (often foll. by *into, on, together,* etc.) insert (a scion) as a graft. **b** insert a graft on (a stock). **2** *intr.* insert a graft. **3** *tr. Surgery* transplant (living tissue). **4** *tr.* (foll. by *in, on*) insert or fix (a thing) permanently to another. **5** *intr. Brit. sl.* work hard. □□ **grafter** *n.* [ME (earlier *graff*) f. OF *grafe, grefe* f. L *graphium* f. Gk *graphion* stylus f. *graphō* write]
■ *n.* **1 a** bud, scion; see also SHOOT *n.* 2. **2** implantation, implant, transplant. ● *v.* **1 a** insert, implant, splice, join. **4** fix, affix, join, secure, fasten; see also ATTACH 1.

graft² /graft/ *n.* & *v. colloq.* ● *n.* **1** practices, esp. bribery, used to secure illicit gains in politics or business. **2** such gains. ● *v.intr.* seek or make such gains. □□ **grafter** *n.* [19th c.: orig. unkn.]
■ *n.* **1** corruption, jobbery, bribery, extortion, payola. **2** payola, *colloq.* kickback; see also BLACKMAIL *n.* 1.

graham cracker /gram, gráyəm/ *n.* a crisp, slightly sweet cracker made from whole wheat flour. [after Sylvester *Graham* d. 1851, US dietary reformer]

Grail /grayl/ *n.* (in full **Holy Grail**) **1** (in medieval legend) the cup or platter used by Christ at the Last Supper, and in which Joseph of Arimathea received Christ's blood at the Cross, esp. as the object of quests by medieval knights. **2** any object of a quest. [ME f. OF *graal,* etc., f. med.L *gradalis* dish, of unkn. orig.]

grain /grayn/ *n.* & *v.* ● *n.* **1** a fruit or seed of a cereal. **2 a** (*collect.*) wheat or any related grass used as food. **b** (*collect.*)

/. . ./ pronunciation	● part of speech
□ phrases, idioms, and compounds	
□□ derivatives	■ synonym section
cross-references appear in SMALL CAPITALS or *italics*	

their fruit. **c** any particular species of a cereal crop. **3 a** a small hard particle of salt, sand, etc. **b** a discrete particle or crystal, usu. small, in a rock or metal. **c** a piece of solid propellant for use in a rocket engine. **4** the smallest unit of weight in the troy system (equivalent to $\frac{1}{480}$ of an ounce), and in the avoirdupois system (equivalent to $\frac{1}{437.5}$ of an ounce). **5** the smallest possible quantity (*not a grain of truth in it*). **6 a** roughness of surface. **b** *Photog.* a granular appearance on a photograph or picture. **7** the texture of skin, wood, stone, textile, etc.; the arrangement and size of constituent particles. **8 a** a pattern of lines of fiber in wood or paper. **b** lamination or planes of cleavage in stone, coal, etc. **9** nature; temper; tendency. **10 a** *hist.* kermes or cochineal, or dye made from either of these. **b** *poet.* dye; color. ● *v.* **1** *tr.* paint in imitation of the grain of wood or marble. **2** *tr.* give a granular surface to. **3** *tr.* dye in grain. **4** *tr.* & *intr.* form into grains. **5** *tr.* remove hair from (hides). □ **against the grain** (often in phr. **go against the grain**) contrary to one's natural inclination or feeling. **grain elevator** a building in which grain is stored, usu. with mechanical devices for lifting and lowering the grain. **grain leather** leather dressed with the grain side out. **grain side** the side of a hide on which the hair was. **grains of Paradise** capsules of a W. African plant (*Aframomum melegueta*), used as a spice and a drug. **in grain** thorough; genuine; by nature; downright; indelible. □□ **grained** *adj.* (also in *comb.*). **grainer** *n.* **grainless** *adj.* [ME f. OF f. L *granum*]
■ *n.* **1** kernel, fruit; see also SEED *n.* 1a. **2** cereal, grist, *Brit.* corn; wheat, barley, rice, oats. **3 a** particle, bit, fragment, crumb, crystal, speck, granule, molecule. **5** iota, scrap, trace, scintilla, hint, suggestion, whit, jot, jot or tittle, soupçon, *colloq.* smidgen. **6** graininess, lumpiness, roughness; see also INEQUALITY 3. **7** texture, pattern, fiber, weave, nap. **8 b** see SHEET¹ *n.* 2a, 3. **9** see NATURE 1, 7, TENDENCY. □ **against the grain** see ALIEN *adj.* 1a.

grainy /gráynee/ *adj.* (**grainier, grainiest**) **1** granular. **2** resembling the grain of wood. **3** *Photog.* having a granular appearance. □□ **graininess** *n.*
■ **1** see GRANULAR.

grallatorial /grálətáwreeəl/ *adj. Zool.* of or relating to long-legged wading birds, e.g., storks, flamingos, etc. [mod.L *grallatorius* f. L *grallator* stilt-walker f. *grallae* stilts]

gram¹ /gram/ *n.* (also *Brit.* **gramme**) a metric unit of mass equal to one-thousandth of a kilogram. □ **gram atom** *Chem.* the quantity of a chemical element equal to its relative atomic mass in grams (see MOLE⁴). **gram equivalent** *Chem.* the quantity of a substance equal to its equivalent weight in grams. **gram molecule** *Chem.* the quantity of a substance equal to its relative molecular mass in grams. [F *gramme* f. Gk *gramma* small weight]

gram² /gram/ *n.* any of various beans used as food. [Port. *grão* f. L *granum* grain]

-gram /gram/ *comb. form* forming nouns denoting a thing written or recorded (often in a special way) (*anagram*; *epigram*; *monogram*; *telegram*). □□ **-grammatic** /grəmátik/ *comb. form* forming adjectives. [from or after Gk *gramma -atos* thing written, letter of the alphabet, f. *graphō* write]

graminaceous /grámináyshəs/ *adj.* = GRAMINEOUS. [L *gramen -inis* grass]

gramineous /grəmíneeəs/ *adj.* of or like grass; grassy. [L *gramineus* f. *gramen -inis* grass]

graminivorous /gráminívərəs/ *adj.* feeding on grass, cereals, etc. [L *gramen -inis* grass + -VOROUS]

grammalogue /grámələwg, -log/ *n.* **1** a word represented by a single shorthand sign. **2** a logogram. [irreg. f. Gk *gramma* letter of the alphabet + *logos* word]

grammar /grámər/ *n.* **1 a** the study or rules of a language's inflections or other means of showing the relation between words, including its phonetic system. **b** a body of form and usages in a specified language (*Latin grammar*). **2** a person's manner or quality of observance or application of the rules of grammar (*bad grammar*). **3** a book on grammar. **4** the elements or rudiments of an art or science. **5** *Brit. colloq.* = *grammar school.* □ **grammar school 1** *US* an elementary

school. **2** *Brit. esp. hist.* a selective state-supported secondary school with a mainly academic curriculum. **3** *Brit. hist.* a school founded in or before the 16th c. for teaching Latin, later becoming a secondary school teaching academic subjects. □□ **grammarless** *adj.* [ME f. AF *gramere*, OF *gramaire* f. L *grammatica* f. Gk *grammatikē* (*tekhnē*) (art) of letters f. *gramma -atos* letter of the alphabet]

grammarian /grəmáireeən/ *n.* an expert in grammar or linguistics; a philologist. [ME f. OF *gramarien*]

grammatical /grəmátikəl/ *adj.* **1 a** of or relating to grammar. **b** determined by grammar, esp. by form or inflection (*grammatical gender*). **2** conforming to the rules of grammar, or to the formal principles of an art, science, etc. □□ **grammatically** *adv.* **grammaticalness** *n.* [F *grammatical* or LL *grammaticalis* f. L *grammaticus* f. Gk *grammatikos* (as GRAMMAR)]

gramme var. of GRAM¹.

gramophone /grámǝfōn/ *n.* = PHONOGRAPH. □□ **gramophonic** /-fónik/ *adj.* [formed by inversion of PHONOGRAM]

grampus /grámpəs/ *n.* (*pl.* **grampuses**) **1** a dolphin, *Grampus griseus*, with a blunt snout and long pointed black flippers. **2** a person breathing heavily and loudly. [earlier *graundepose*, *grapeys* f. OF *grapois*, etc., f. med.L *craspiscis* f. L *crassus piscis* fat fish]

Gram's stain /gramz/ *n.* (also **Gram stain, Gram's method**) *Biol.* a method of differentiating bacteria by staining with a dye, then attempting to remove the dye with a solvent, for purposes of identification. □ **Gram-positive** (or **-negative**) (of bacteria) that do (or do not) retain the dye. [H. C. J. *Gram*, Da. physician d. 1938]

gran /gran/ *n. colloq.* grandmother (cf. GRANNY). [abbr.]

granadilla /gránədílə, -deéyə/ *n.* (also **grenadilla** /grén-/) a passionfruit. [Sp., dimin. of *granada* pomegranate]

granary /gránəree, gráy-/ *n.* (*pl.* **-ies**) **1** a storehouse for threshed grain. **2** a region producing, and esp. exporting, much grain. [L *granarium* f. *granum* grain]

grand /grand/ *adj.* & *n.* ● *adj.* **1 a** splendid; magnificent; imposing; dignified. **b** solemn or lofty in conception, execution, or expression; noble. **2** main; of chief importance (*grand staircase*; *grand entrance*). **3** (**Grand**) of the highest rank, esp. in official titles (*Grand Cross*; *Grand Inquisitor*). **4** *colloq.* excellent; enjoyable (*had a grand time*). **5** belonging to high society; wealthy (*the grand folk at the manor*). **6** (in *comb.*) in names of family relationships, denoting the second degree of ascent or descent (*granddaughter*). **7** (**Grand**) (in French phrases or imitations) great (*Grand Monarch*; *Grand Hotel*). **8** *Law* serious; important (*grand larceny*) (cf. COMMON, PETTY). ● *n.* **1** = *grand piano.* **2** (*pl.* same) *sl.* a thousand dollars or pounds sterling. □ **grand aunt** a great-aunt (see GREAT *adj.* 11). **grand duchy** a nation ruled by a grand duke or duchess. **grand duke** (or **duchess**) **1** a prince (or princess) or noble person ruling over a territory. **2** (**Grand Duke**) *hist.* the son or grandson of a Russian czar. **grand jury** *Law* a jury selected to examine the validity of an accusation prior to trial. **grand master 1** a chess player of the highest class. **2** the head of a military order of knighthood, of Freemasons, etc. **Grand National** a steeplechase held annually at Aintree, Liverpool, England. **grand nephew** (or **niece**) a great-nephew or -niece (see GREAT *adj.* 11). **grand opera** opera on a serious theme, or in which the entire libretto (including dialogue) is sung. **grand piano** a large full-toned piano standing on three legs, with the body, strings, and soundboard arranged horizontally and in line with the keys. **grand slam 1** *Sports* the winning of all of a group of major championships. **2** *Bridge* the winning of all 13 tricks. **3** *Baseball* a home run hit with three runners on base. **grand total** the final amount after everything is added up; the sum of other totals. **grand tour** *hist.* a cultural tour of Europe, esp. in the 18th c. for educational purposes. □□ **grandly** *adv.* **grandness** *n.* [ME f. AF *graunt*, OF *grant* f. L *grandis* full-grown]
■ *adj.* **1 a** splendid, magnificent, imposing, impressive, fine, dignified, majestic, distinguished, stately, lofty, monumental, lavish, opulent, luxurious, palatial, sumptuous, *colloq.* posh; august, respected, eminent,

preeminent, outstanding, celebrated, illustrious, renowned, notable, exalted, revered, venerable. **b** solemn, lofty; see also NOBLE *adj.* 3, 4. **2** principal, chief, main, head, leading, foremost, highest. **4** marvelous, wonderful, outstanding, first-class, first-rate, splendid, excellent, superb, admirable, *colloq.* great, smashing, terrific, fantastic, fabulous, super; see also SUPERB. **5** see POSH *adj.* 2, RICH 1.

grandad /grándad/ *n.* (also **granddad**) *colloq.* **1** grandfather. **2** an elderly man.

granddaddy /grándadee/ *n.* (also **grandaddy**) (*pl.* -**dies**) **1** *colloq.* a grandfather. **2** the original and usu. most venerated of its kind (*the granddaddy of symphony orchestras*).

grandam /grándam/ *n.* **1** (also **grandame**) *archaic* grandmother. **2** an old woman. **3** an ancestress. [ME f. AF *graund dame* (as GRAND, DAME)]

grandchild /gránchild, gránd-/ *n.* (*pl.* -**children**) a child of one's son or daughter.

granddaughter /grándawtər/ *n.* a female grandchild.

grande dame /groND daám/ *n.* a dignified lady of high rank. [F]

grandee /grandeé/ *n.* **1** a Spanish or Portuguese nobleman of the highest rank. **2** a person of high rank or eminence. [Sp. & Port. *grande*, assim. TO -EE]

grandeur /gránjər, -jōōr/ *n.* **1** majesty; splendor; dignity of appearance or bearing. **2** high rank; eminence. **3** nobility of character. [F f. *grand* great, GRAND]
■ **1** magnificence, majesty, pomp; see also SPLENDOR 2. **2** see DISTINCTION 4. **3** see NOBILITY 1.

grandfather /gránfaathər, gránd-/ *n.* a male grandparent. □ **grandfather clock** a floor-standing pendulum clock in a tall wooden case. □□ **grandfatherly** *adj.*

Grand Guignol /groN geenyáwl/ *n.* a dramatic entertainment of a sensational or horrific nature. [the name (= Great Punch) of a theater in Paris]

grandiflora /grándifláwrə/ *adj.* bearing large flowers. [mod.L (often used in specific names of large-flowered plants) f. L *grandis* great + FLORA]

grandiloquent /grandíləkwənt/ *adj.* **1** pompous or inflated in language. **2** given to boastful talk. □□ **grandiloquence** /-kwəns/ *n.* **grandiloquently** *adv.* [L *grandiloquus* (as GRAND, *-loquus* -speaking f. *loqui* speak), after *eloquent*, etc.]
■ see POMPOUS 2.

grandiose /grándeeōs/ *adj.* **1** producing or meant to produce an imposing effect. **2** planned on an ambitious or magnificent scale. □□ **grandiosely** *adv.* **grandiosity** /-deeósitee/ *n.* [F f. It. *grandioso* (as GRAND, -OSE¹)]
■ **1** imposing, grand, monumental, magnificent; see also IMPRESSIVE 1. **2** ambitious, lofty, flamboyant, showy, bombastic, extravagant, pompous, high-flown, high-flying, melodramatic, flashy, *colloq.* highfalutin, flash.

grandma /gránmaa, gránd-/ *n. colloq.* grandmother.

grand mal /groN maál, gránd mál/ *n.* a serious form of epilepsy with loss of consciousness (cf. PETIT MAL). [F, = great sickness]

grandmama /gránməmaá, -maamə, gránd-/ *n. archaic colloq.* = GRANDMA.

grandmother /gránmuthər, gránd-/ *n.* a female grandparent. □ **grandmother clock** a clock like a grandfather clock but in a shorter case. **teach one's grandmother to suck eggs** presume to advise a more experienced person. □□ **grandmotherly** *adj.*

grandpa /gránpaa, gránd-/ *n. colloq.* grandfather.

grandpapa /gránpəpaá, -paapə, gránd-/ *n. archaic colloq.* = GRANDPA.

grandparent /gránpairənt, gránd-/ *n.* a parent of one's father or mother.

Grand Prix /groN preé/ *n.* any of several important international automobile or motorcycle racing events. [F, = great or chief prize]

grand siècle /groN syéklə/ *n.* the classical or golden age, esp. the 17th c. in France. [F, = great century or age]

grandsire /gránsīr, gránd-/ *n. archaic* **1** grandfather; old man; ancestor. **2** *Bell-ringing* a method of change-ringing.

grandson /gránsun, gránd-/ *n.* a male grandchild.

grandstand /gránstand, gránd-/ *n.* the main stand, usu. roofed, for spectators at a racecourse, etc. □ **grandstand finish** a close and exciting finish to a race, etc.

grange /graynj/ *n.* **1** esp. *Brit.* a country house with farm buildings. **2** (**Grange**) a farmer's social organization. **3** *archaic* a barn. [ME f. AF *graunge*, OF *grange* f. med.L *granica* (*villa*) ult. f. L *granum* GRAIN]

graniferous /grənífərəs/ *adj.* producing grain or a grainlike seed. □□ **graniform** /gránifawrm/ *adj.* [L *granum* GRAIN]

granite /gránit/ *n.* **1** a granular crystalline igneous rock of quartz, mica, feldspar, etc., used for building. **2** a determined or resolute quality, attitude, etc. □□ **granitic** /grənítik/ *adj.* **granitoid** *adj. & n.* [It. *granito*, lit. grained f. *grano* f. L *granum* GRAIN]

graniteware /gránitwair/ *n.* **1** a speckled form of earthenware imitating the appearance of granite. **2** a kind of enameled ironware.

granivorous /grənívərəs/ *adj.* feeding on grain. □□ **granivore** /gránivawr/ *n.* [L *granum* GRAIN]

granny /gránee/ *n.* (also **grannie**) (*pl.* -**ies**) *colloq.* grandmother. □ **granny glasses** wire-frame eyeglasses with small lenses, often round or oval. **granny knot** a square knot crossed the wrong way and therefore insecure. [obs. *grannam* for GRANDAM + -Y²]

Granny Smith /gránee smíth/ *n.* an orig. Australian green variety of apple. [Maria Ann ("Granny") Smith d. 1870]

granola /grənṓlə/ *n.* a breakfast or snack food consisting typically of a mixture of rolled oats, nuts, dried fruits, and brown sugar. [orig. f. *Granola*, a trademark]

grant /grant/ *v. & n.* ● *v.tr.* **1 a** consent to fulfill (a request, wish, etc.) (*granted all he asked*). **b** allow (a person) to have (a thing) (*granted me my freedom*). **c** (as **granted**) *colloq.* apology accepted; pardon given. **2** give (rights, property, etc.) formally; transfer legally. **3** (often foll. by *that* + clause) admit as true; concede, esp. as a basis for argument. ● *n.* **1** the process of granting or a thing granted. **2** a sum of money given by the government for any of various purposes, esp. to finance education. **3** *Law* **a** a legal conveyance by written instrument. **b** formal conferment. □ **grant-in-aid** (*pl.* **grants-in-aid**) a grant by central government to local government or an institution. **take for granted 1** assume something to be true or valid. **2** cease to appreciate through familiarity. □□ **grantable** *adj.* **grantee** /-teé/ *n.* (esp. in sense 2 of *v.*). **granter** *n.* **grantor** /-tór/ *n.* (esp. in sense 2 of *v.*). [ME f. OF *gr(e)anter* var. of *creanter* ult. f. part. of L *credere* entrust]
■ *v.* **1 a** agree to, consent to, concur with, assent to, concede to, admit, allow, accept, approve of, conform to. **b** allow, permit; give, award, offer, confer a thing on a person, bestow a thing on a person; supply with, furnish with; donate, allocate, assign. **2** see *make over* 1. **3** see CONCEDE 1a. ● *n.* **1, 2** gift, presentation, endowment, bequest, award, donation, contribution, concession, allowance; subvention, subsidy, grant-in-aid.

Granth /grunt/ *n.* (also **Grunth**) the sacred scriptures of the Sikhs. [Hindi, = book, code f. Skr. *grantha* tying, literary composition]

granular /grányələr/ *adj.* **1** of or like grains or granules. **2** having a granulated surface or structure. □□ **granularity** /-láritee/ *n.* **granularly** *adv.* [LL *granulum* GRANULE]
■ grainy, granulated, particulate, comminuted, sandy, gritty.

granulate /grányəlayt/ *v.* **1** *tr. & intr.* form into grains (*granulated sugar*). **2** *tr.* roughen the surface of. **3** *intr.* (of a wound, etc.) form small prominences as the beginning of healing; heal; join. □□ **granulation** /-láyshən/ *n.* **granulator** *n.*
■ **1** see GRIND *v.* 1a.

/.../	**pronunciation**	●	**part of speech**
□	**phrases, idioms, and compounds**		
□□	**derivatives**	■	**synonym section**
	cross-references appear in SMALL CAPITALS or *italics*		

granule /grányŏŏl/ n. a small grain. [LL granulum, dimin. of L granum grain]
■ see GRAIN n. 3a.

granulocyte /grányəlōsīt/ n. Physiol. any of various white blood cells having granules in their cytoplasm. □□ **granulocytic** /-sítik/ adj.

granulometric /grányəlōmétrik/ adj. relating to the distribution of grain sizes in sand, etc. [F granulométrique (as GRANULE, METRIC)]

grape /grayp/ n. **1** a berry (usu. green, purple, or black) growing in clusters on a vine, used as fruit and in making wine. **2** (prec. by the) colloq. wine. **3** = GRAPESHOT. **4** (in pl.) a diseased growth like a bunch of grapes on the pastern of a horse, etc., or on a pleura in cattle. □ **grape hyacinth** any liliaceous plant of the genus Muscari, with clusters of usu. blue flowers. **grape sugar** dextrose. □□ **grapy** adj. (also **grapey**). [ME f. OF grape bunch of grapes prob. f. graper gather (grapes) f. grap(p)e hook, ult. f. Gmc]

grapefruit /gráypfrŏŏt/ n. (pl. same) **1** a large round yellow citrus fruit with an acid juicy pulp. **2** the tree, Citrus paradisi, bearing this fruit.

grapeshot /gráypshot/ n. hist. small balls used as charge in a cannon and scattering when fired.

grapevine /gráypvīn/ n. **1** any of various vines of the genus Vitis, esp. Vitis vinifera. **2** colloq. the means of transmission of unofficial information or rumor (heard it through the grapevine).
■ **2** sl. network, bush telegraph.

graph[1] /graf/ n. & v. ● n. **1** a diagram showing the relation between variable quantities, usu. of two variables, each measured along one of a pair of axes at right angles. **2** Math. a collection of points whose coordinates satisfy a given relation. ● v.tr. plot or trace on a graph. □ **graph paper** paper printed with a network of lines as a basis for drawing graphs. [abbr. of graphic formula]
■ n. **1** see CHART n. 2.

graph[2] /graf/ n. Linguistics a visual symbol, esp. a letter or letters, representing a unit of sound or other feature of speech. [Gk graphē writing]

-graph /graf/ comb. form forming nouns and verbs meaning: **1** a thing written or drawn, etc., in a specified way (autograph; photograph). **2** an instrument that records (heliograph; seismograph; telegraph).

grapheme /gráfeem/ n. Linguistics **1** a class of letters, etc., representing a unit of sound. **2** a feature of a written expression that cannot be analyzed into smaller meaningful units. □□ **graphematic** /-mátik/ adj. **graphemic** /grəfeémik/ adj. **graphemically** adv. [GRAPH[2] + -EME]

-grapher /grəfər/ comb. form forming nouns denoting a person concerned with a subject (geographer; radiographer). [from or after Gk -graphos writer + -ER[1]]

graphic /gráfik/ adj. & n. ● adj. **1** of or relating to the visual or descriptive arts, esp. writing and drawing. **2** vividly descriptive; conveying all (esp. unwelcome or unpleasant) details; unequivocal. **3** (of minerals) showing marks like writing on the surface or in a fracture. **4** = GRAPHICAL. ● n. a product of the graphic arts (cf. GRAPHICS). □ **graphic arts** the visual and technical arts involving design, writing, drawing, printing, etc. **graphic equalizer** a device for the separate control of the strength and quality of selected audio frequency bands. □□ **graphically** adv. **graphicness** n. [L graphicus f. Gk graphikos f. graphē writing]
■ adj. **1** representational, visual, pictorial, descriptive. **2** vivid, picturesque, lifelike, telling, clear, explicit, realistic, true to life, descriptive, photographic, detailed, well-drawn; accurate, precise; clear, lucid, unambiguous, unequivocal.

-graphic /gráfik/ comb. form (also **-graphical** /gráfikəl/) forming adjectives corresponding to nouns in -graphy (see -GRAPHY). □□ **-graphically** /gráfiklee/ comb. form forming adverbs. [from or after Gk -graphikos (as GRAPHIC)]

graphicacy /gráfikəsee/ n. the ability to read a map, graph, etc., or to present information by means of diagrams. [GRAPHIC, after literacy, numeracy]

graphical /gráfikəl/ adj. **1** of or in the form of graphs (see GRAPH[1]). **2** graphic. □□ **graphically** adv.

graphics /gráfiks/ n.pl. (usu. treated as sing.) **1** the products of the graphic arts, esp. commercial design or illustration. **2** the use of diagrams in calculation and design. **3** (in full **computer graphics**) Computing a mode of processing and output in which a significant part of the information is in pictorial form.

graphite /gráfīt/ n. a crystalline allotropic form of carbon used as a solid lubricant, in pencils, and as a moderator in nuclear reactors, etc. Also called PLUMBAGO, black lead. □□ **graphitic** /-fítik/ adj. **graphitize** /-fītīz/ v.tr. & intr. [G Graphit f. Gk graphō write]

graphology /grəfóləjee/ n. **1** the study of handwriting esp. as a supposed guide to character. **2** a system of graphic formulae; notation for graphs (see GRAPH[1]). **3** Linguistics the study of systems of writing. □□ **graphological** /gráfəlójikəl/ adj. **graphologist** n. [Gk graphē writing]

-graphy /grəfee/ comb. form forming nouns denoting: **1** a descriptive science (bibliography; geography). **2** a technique of producing images (photography; radiography). **3** a style or method of writing, drawing, etc. (calligraphy). [from or after F or G -graphie f. L -graphia f. Gk -graphia writing]

grapnel /grápnəl/ n. **1** a device with iron claws, attached to a rope and used for dragging or grasping. **2** a small anchor with several flukes. [ME f. AF f. OF grapon f. Gmc: cf. GRAPE]

grappa /graápə/ n. a brandy distilled from the fermented residue of grapes after they have been pressed in wine-making. [It.]

grapple /grápəl/ v. & n. ● v. **1** intr. (often foll. by with) fight at close quarters or in close combat. **2** intr. (foll. by with) try to manage or overcome a difficult problem, etc. **3** tr. grip with the hands; come to close quarters with. **b** seize with or as with a grappel; grasp. ● n. **1 a** a hold or grip in or as in wrestling. **b** a contest at close quarters. **2** a clutching instrument; a grapnel. □ **grappling iron** (or **hook**) = GRAPNEL. □□ **grappler** n. [OF grapil (n.) f. Prov., dimin. of grapa hook (as GRAPNEL)]
■ v. **1** fight, wrestle, tussle, scuffle, skirmish; see also FIGHT v. 1a. **2** (grapple with) struggle with, contend with, wrestle with, tackle, face, take on, do battle with, combat, fight. **3** grip, hold, clutch, clasp; grab, seize, catch, snatch, grasp. ● n. **1 a** grip, hold, grasp, clutch, handgrip, clasp, handclasp. **b** see BOUT 2a. **2** grapnel, grappling iron or hook, grab. □ **grappling iron** (or **hook**) grapnel, grab, grapple.

graptolite /gráptəlīt/ n. an extinct marine invertebrate animal found as a fossil in lower Palaeozoic rocks. [Gk graptos marked with letters + -LITE]

grasp /grasp/ v. & n. ● v. **1** tr. **a** clutch at; seize greedily. **b** hold firmly; grip. **2** intr. (foll. by at) try to seize; accept avidly. **3** tr. understand or realize (a fact or meaning). ● n. **1** a firm hold; a grip. **2** (foll. by of) **a** mastery or control (a grasp of the situation). **b** a mental hold or understanding (a grasp of the facts). **3** mental agility (a quick grasp). □ **grasp at a straw** see STRAW. **grasp the nettle** Brit. tackle a difficulty boldly. **within one's grasp** capable of being grasped or comprehended by one. □□ **graspable** adj. **grasper** n. [ME graspe, grapse perh. f. OE grǣpsan (unrecorded) f. Gmc, rel. to GROPE: cf. LG grapsen]
■ v. **1 a** clutch at, seize, grab, snatch, take or lay or catch or get hold of. **b** clutch, grip, hold, clasp. **2** (grasp at) grab or snatch or clutch at, reach for; latch on to, snap up; see also JUMP at. **3** understand, comprehend, catch, follow, make head or tail of, get the point or drift of, colloq. get, sl. dig; appreciate, see, realize. ● n. **1** hold, grip, clasp, embrace, lock; clutches. **2 a** (grasp of) possession of, control of or over, power over, mastery of, hold of or over. **b** understanding, comprehension, apprehension, awareness, perception, sense. **3** see INTELLIGENCE 1b. □ **within one's grasp** graspable, possible, attainable, realizable, achievable, reachable, accomplishable; understandable, comprehensible, accessible.

grasping /grásping/ *adj.* avaricious; greedy. □□ **graspingly** *adv.* **graspingness** *n.*

■ greedy, avaricious, acquisitive, rapacious.

grass /gras/ *n. & v.* ● *n.* **1 a** vegetation belonging to a group of small plants with green blades that are eaten by cattle, horses, sheep, etc. **b** any species of this. **c** any plant of the family Gramineae, which includes cereals, reeds, and bamboos. **2** pasture land. **3** grass-covered ground; a lawn (*keep off the grass*). **4** grazing (*be at grass*). **5** *sl.* marijuana. **6** *Brit. sl.* an informer, esp. a police informer. **7** *sl.* asparagus; cress. ● *v.* **1** *tr.* cover with turf. **2** *tr.* provide with pasture. **3** *Brit. sl.* **a** *tr.* betray, esp. to the police. **b** *intr.* inform the police. **4** *Brit. tr.* knock down; fell (an opponent). **5** *tr.* **a** bring (a fish) to the bank. **b** bring down (a bird) by a shot. □ **at grass** *Brit.* out of work, on vacation, retired, etc. **grass bird** *Austral.* any of various warblers, esp. of the genus *Megalurus*, living among reeds. **grass catcher** (or *Brit.* **box**) a receptacle for cut grass on a lawnmower. **grass cloth** a linen-like cloth woven from ramie, etc. **grass court** a grass-covered tennis court. **grass of Parnassus** a herbaceous plant, *Parnassia palustris*. **grass parakeet** *Austral.* a parakeet, esp. of the genus *Neophema*, frequenting grassland. **grass roots 1** a fundamental level or source. **2** ordinary people, esp. as voters; the rank and file of an organization, esp. a political party. **grass skirt** *Polynesia* a skirt made of long grass and leaves fastened to a waistband. **grass snake 1** the common greensnake, *Opheodrys vernalis*. **2** *Brit.* the common ringed snake, *Natrix natrix*. **grass tree** = BLACKBOY. **grass widow** (or **widower**) **1** a person whose husband (or wife) is away for a prolonged period. **2** a divorced or separated woman (or man). **not let the grass grow under one's feet** be quick to act or to seize an opportunity. **out to grass 1** to pasture. **2** laid off; in retirement; on vacation. □□ **grassless** *adj.* **grasslike** *adj.* [OE *græs* f. Gmc, rel. to GREEN, GROW]

■ *n.* **2** see PASTURE *n.* **3** see LAWN¹. **4** grazing, feeding, feed. **5** cannabis, marijuana, hemp, hashish, ganja, *colloq.* hash, *sl.* pot, green, dope, the weed. ● *v.* **4** see FELL² *v.* **2**. □ **grass roots 1** see BOTTOM *n.* **5**. **2** see PEOPLE *n.* **2**.

grasshopper /grás-hoppər/ *n.* a jumping and chirping plant-eating insect of the order Saltatoria.

grassland /grásland/ *n.* a large open area covered with grass, esp. one used for grazing.

■ see PLAIN¹ *n.*

grassy /grásee/ *adj.* (**grassier, grassiest**) **1** covered with or abounding in grass. **2** resembling grass. **3** of grass. □□ **grassiness** *n.*

■ **1** see GREEN *adj.* 2a.

grate¹ /grayt/ *v.* **1** *tr.* reduce to small particles by rubbing on a serrated surface. **2** *intr.* (often foll. by *against, on*) rub with a harsh scraping sound. **3** *tr.* utter in a harsh tone. **4** *intr.* (often foll. by *on*) **a** sound harshly or discordantly. **b** have an irritating effect. **5** *tr.* grind (one's teeth). **6** *intr.* (of a hinge, etc.) creak. [ME f. OF *grater* ult. f. WG]

■ **1** shred, rasp, scrape, rub. **2** scrape, rasp, rub, grind, scratch; stridulate. **3** croak, rasp, growl, bark, snap; see also BAWL 1. **4 a** see JAR² *v.* 1, 2. **b** jar, go against the grain, rub a person the wrong way, *colloq.* get on a person's nerves; (*grate on*) annoy, vex, irk, irritate, fret, chafe. **5** grind, gnash, rub. **6** creak, squeak.

grate² /grayt/ *n.* **1** the recess of a fireplace or furnace. **2** a metal frame confining fuel in a grate. [ME, = grating f. OF ult. f. L *cratis* hurdle]

grateful /gráytfŏŏl/ *adj.* **1** thankful; feeling or showing gratitude (*am grateful to you for helping*). **2** pleasant, acceptable. □□ **gratefully** *adv.* **gratefulness** *n.* [obs. *grate* (adj.) f. L *gratus* + -FUL]

■ **1** thankful, appreciative; see also INDEBTED 1. **2** see PLEASANT.

grater /gráytər/ *n.* a device for reducing cheese or other food to small particles.

graticule /grátikyŏŏl/ *n.* **1** fine lines or fibers incorporated in a telescope or other optical instrument as a measuring scale or as an aid in locating objects. **2** *Surveying* a network of

lines on paper representing meridians and parallels. [F f. med.L *graticula* for *craticula* gridiron f. L *cratis* hurdle]

gratify /grátifī/ *v.tr.* (**-fies, -fied**) **1 a** please; delight. **b** please by compliance; assent to the wish of. **2** indulge in or yield to (a feeling or desire). □□ **gratification** *n.* **gratifier** *n.* **gratifying** *adj.* **gratifyingly** *adv.* [F *gratifier* or L *gratificari* do a favor to, make a present of, f. *gratus* pleasing]

■ **1 a** delight, cheer, gladden; see also PLEASE 1. **1b, 2** see SATISFY 2, 3. □□ **gratification** satisfaction, fulfillment, enjoyment, pleasure, delight; compensation, recompense, reward, return, requital.

grating¹ /gráyting/ *adj.* **1** sounding harsh or discordant (*a grating laugh*). **2** having an irritating effect. □□ **gratingly** *adv.*

■ **1** jarring, strident, raucous, harsh, shrill, discordant, dissonant, unharmonious; grinding, jangling, screeching, squawking, croaking, rasping. **2** irritating, offensive, irksome, annoying, vexatious, galling.

grating² /gráyting/ *n.* **1** a framework of parallel or crossed metal bars. **2** *Optics* a set of parallel wires, lines ruled on glass, etc., for producing spectra by diffraction.

■ **1** grate, grid, grille. **2** reticle, reticule; reticulation.

gratis /grátis, graa-/ *adv. & adj.* free; without charge. [L, contracted ablat. pl. of *gratia* favor]

■ see FREE *adj.* 7.

gratitude /grátitŏŏd, -tyŏŏd/ *n.* being thankful; readiness to show appreciation for and to return kindness. [F *gratitude* or med.L *gratitudo* f. *gratus* thankful]

■ thankfulness, appreciation, gratefulness, thanks, acknowledgment, recognition, thanksgiving.

gratuitous /grətŏŏitəs, tyŏŏ-/ *adj.* **1** given or done free of charge. **2** uncalled-for; unwarranted; lacking good reason (*a gratuitous insult*). □□ **gratuitously** *adv.* **gratuitousness** *n.* [L *gratuitus* spontaneous: cf. *fortuitous*]

■ **1** see FREE *adj.* 7. **2** unrequested, unprovoked, unsolicited, wanton, unlooked-for, uncalled-for, unjustified, unwarranted, baseless, groundless, needless, unfounded, ungrounded, unjustifiable, unreasonable.

gratuity /grətŏŏitee, -tyŏŏ-/ *n.* (*pl.* **-ies**) money given in recognition of services; a tip. [OF *gratuité* or med.L *gratuitas* gift f. L *gratus* grateful]

■ see TIP³ *n.*

gratulatory /gráchələtáwree/ *adj.* expressing congratulation. [LL *gratulatorius* f. L *gratus* grateful]

gravamen /grəváymen/ *n.* (*pl.* **gravamens** or **gravamina** /-váminə/) **1** the essence or most serious part of an argument. **2** a grievance. [LL, = inconvenience, f. L *gravare* to load f. *gravis* heavy]

grave¹ /grayv/ *n.* **1 a** a trench dug in the ground to receive a coffin for burial. **b** a mound or memorial stone placed over this. **2** (prec. by *the*) death, esp. as indicating mortal finality. **3** something compared to or regarded as a grave. □ **turn in one's grave** (of a dead person) be thought of in certain circumstances as likely to have been shocked or angry if still alive. □□ **graveless** *adj.* **graveward** *adv. & adj.* [OE *græf* f. WG]

■ **1 b** crypt, sepulcher, tomb, vault, mausoleum; tumulus, *Archaeol.* barrow; gravestone, headstone. **2** (*the grave*) see DEATH 1.

grave² /grayv/ *adj. & n.* ● *adj.* **1 a** serious; weighty; important (*a grave matter*). **b** dignified; solemn; somber (*a grave look*). **2** extremely serious or threatening (*grave danger*). **3** /graav/ (of sound) low-pitched; not acute. ● *n.* /graav/ = *grave accent.* □ **grave accent** /graav, grayv/ a mark (`) placed over a vowel in some languages to denote pronunciation, length, etc., orig. indicating low or falling pitch. □□ **gravely** *adv.* **graveness** *n.* [F *grave* or L *gravis* heavy, serious]

■ *adj.* **1 a** weighty, important, critical; see also SERIOUS 2,

---

/. . . / **pronunciation**	● **part of speech**
□ **phrases, idioms, and compounds**	
□□ **derivatives**	■ **synonym section**
cross-references appear in SMALL CAPITALS or *italics*	

3, 7. **b** dignified, somber, solemn, unsmiling, earnest, sober, gloomy, grim-faced, dour. **2** serious, vital, urgent, crucial, grim; perilous, dangerous, threatening, life-threatening.

grave³ /grayv/ *v.tr.* (*past part.* **graven** or **graved**) **1** (foll. by *in*, *on*) fix indelibly (on one's memory). **2** engrave; carve. □ **graven image** an idol. [OE *grafan* dig, engrave f. Gmc: cf. GROOVE]

grave⁴ /grayv/ *v.tr.* clean (a ship's bottom) by burning off accretions and by tarring. □ **graving dock** = *dry dock.* [perh. F dial. *grave* = OF *greve* shore]

gravedigger /gráyvdigər/ *n.* **1** a person who digs graves. **2** (in full **gravedigger beetle**) a sexton beetle.

gravel /grávəl/ *n. & v.* ● *n.* **1 a** a mixture of coarse sand and small waterworn or pounded stones, used for paths and roads and as an aggregate. **b** *Geol.* a stratum of this. **2** *Med.* aggregations of crystals formed in the urinary tract. ● *v.tr.* (**graveled, graveling**; also **gravelled, gravelling**) **1** lay or strew with gravel. **2** perplex; puzzle; nonplus (from an obs. sense 'run (a ship) aground'). □ **gravel-blind** *literary* almost completely blind ("more than sand-blind," in Shakesp. *Merchant of Venice* II. ii. 33). [ME f. OF *gravel(e)* dimin. of *grave* (as GRAVE⁴)]

gravelax var. of GRAVLAX.

gravelly /grávəlee/ *adj.* **1** of or like gravel. **2** having or containing gravel. **3** (of a voice) deep and rough sounding.
■ **1, 2** see *gritty* (GRIT). **3** see STRIDENT.

graven *past part.* of GRAVE³.

graver /gráyvər/ *n.* **1** an engraving tool; a burin. **2** an engraver; a carver.

Graves /graav/ *n.* a light usu. white wine from the Graves district in France.

Graves' disease /grayvz/ *n.* exophthalmic goiter with characteristic swelling of the neck and protrusion of the eyes, resulting from an overactive thyroid gland. [R. J. *Graves*, Ir. physician d. 1853]

gravestone /gráyvstōn/ *n.* a stone (usu. inscribed) marking a grave.
■ see MONUMENT 1–3.

graveyard /gráyvyaard/ *n.* a burial ground, esp. by a church. □ **graveyard shift** a work shift that usu. starts about midnight and ends about eight o'clock in the morning.
■ burial ground, churchyard, cemetery, God's acre, necropolis, potter's field, *sl.* boneyard.

gravid /grávid/ *adj. literary* or *Zool.* pregnant. [L *gravidus* f. *gravis* heavy]

gravimeter /grəvímitər/ *n.* an instrument for measuring the difference in the force of gravity from one place to another. [F *gravimètre* f. L *gravis* heavy]

gravimetric /grávimétrik/ *adj.* **1** of or relating to the measurement of weight. **2** denoting chemical analysis based on weight.

gravimetry /grəvímitree/ *n.* the measurement of weight.

gravitas /grávitaas/ *n.* solemn demeanor; seriousness. [L f. *gravis* serious]

gravitate /grávitayt/ *v.* **1** *intr.* (foll. by *to*, *toward*) move or be attracted to some source of influence. **2** *tr. & intr.* **a** move or tend by force of gravity toward. **b** sink by or as if by gravity. [mod.L *gravitatus* (as GRAVITAS)]
■ **1** see LEAN¹ *v.* 4. **2 b** see SETTLE¹ 13.

gravitation /grávitáyshən/ *n. Physics* **1** a force of attraction between any particle of matter in the universe and any other. **2** the effect of this, esp. the falling of bodies to the earth. [mod.L *gravitatio* (as GRAVITY)]
■ see ATTRACTION 2.

gravitational /grávitáyshənəl/ *adj.* of or relating to gravitation. □ **gravitational constant** the constant in Newton's law of gravitation relating gravity to the masses and separation of particles. ¶ Symb.: G. **gravitational field** the region of space surrounding a body in which another body experiences a force of attraction. □□ **gravitationally** *adv.*

gravity /grávitee/ *n.* **1 a** the force that attracts a body to the center of the earth or other celestial body. **b** the degree of intensity of this measured by acceleration. **c** gravitational force. **2** the property of having weight. **3 a** importance; se-

riousness; the quality of being grave. **b** solemnity; sobriety; serious demeanor. □ **gravity feed** the supply of material by its fall under gravity. [F *gravité* or L *gravitas* f. *gravis* heavy]
■ **1** gravitation; attraction. **2** see WEIGHT *n.* 2, 3.
3 a seriousness, acuteness, immediacy, importance, graveness, significance, magnitude, severity, urgency, exigency, momentousness, weight, weightiness.
b solemnity, dignity, somberness, sobriety, *gravitas*, soberness, graveness.

gravlax /graávlaaks/ *n.* (also **gravelax**) filleted salmon cured by marination in salt, sugar, and dill. [Sw.]

gravure /grəvyŏŏr/ *n.* = PHOTOGRAVURE. [abbr.]

gravy /gráyvee/ *n.* (*pl.* **-ies**) **1 a** the juices exuding from meat during and after cooking. **b** a sauce for food, made by thickening these, or from other materials. **2** *sl.* unearned or unexpected gains, esp. money. □ **gravy boat** a boat-shaped vessel for serving gravy. **gravy train** *sl.* a source of easy financial benefit. [ME, perh. from a misreading as *gravé* of OF *grané*, prob. f. *grain* spice: see GRAIN]

gray¹ /gray/ *adj., n., & v.* (also **grey**) ● *adj.* **1** of a color intermediate between black and white, as of ashes or lead. **2 a** (of the weather, etc.) dull; dismal; heavily overcast. **b** bleak; depressing; (of a person) depressed. **3 a** (of hair) turning white with age, etc. **b** (of a person) having gray hair. **4** anonymous; nondescript; unidentifiable. ● *n.* **1 a** a gray color or pigment. **b** gray clothes or material (*dressed in gray*). **2** a cold sunless light. **3** a gray or white horse. ● *v.tr. & intr.* make or become gray. □ **gray area 1** a situation or topic sharing features of more than one category and not clearly attributable to any one category. **2** *Brit.* an area in economic decline. **gray eminence** = ÉMINENCE GRISE. **gray goose** = GREYLAG. **gray matter 1** the darker tissues of the brain and spinal cord consisting of nerve cell bodies and branching dendrites. **2** *colloq.* intelligence. **gray squirrel** an American squirrel, *Sciurus carolinensis*, introduced to England in the 19th c. □□ **grayish** *adj.* **grayly** *adv.* **grayness** *n.* [OE *græg* f. Gmc]
■ *adj.* **1** ashen, leaden, livid, pearly, smoky, grizzly. **2** dark, murky, foggy, misty, cloudy, overcast, sunless; cheerless, gloomy, dull, dismal, drab, depressing; bleak, dreary, somber; glum; see also MISERABLE 3. **4** anonymous, unidentifiable; colorless; see also NONDESCRIPT *adj.* □ **gray matter 2** see BRAIN *n.* 3a, b.

gray² /gray/ *n. Physics* the SI unit of the absorbed dose of ionizing radiation, corresponding to one joule per kilogram. ¶ Abbr.: **Gy**. [L. H. *Gray*, Engl. radiobiologist d. 1965]

graybeard /gráybeerd/ *n. archaic* **1** an old man. **2** a large stoneware jug for alcohol. **3** *Brit.* clematis in seed.

grayling /gráyling/ *n.* **1** any silver-gray freshwater fish of the genus *Thymallus*, with a long high dorsal fin. **2** a butterfly, *Hipparchia semele*, having wings with gray undersides and bright eye-spots on the upper side. [GRAY¹ + -LING²]

graywacke /gráywakə, -wak/ *n.* (*Brit.* **greywacke**) *Geol.* a dark and coarse-grained sandstone, usu. with an admixture of clay. [Anglicized f. G *Grauwacke* f. *grau* gray: see WACKE]

graze¹ /grayz/ *v.* **1** *intr.* (of cattle, sheep, etc.) eat growing grass. **2** *tr.* **a** feed (cattle, etc.) on growing grass. **b** feed on (grass). **3** *intr.* pasture cattle. □□ **grazer** *n.* [OE *grasian* f. *græs* GRASS]
■ **1** see FEED *v.* 4.

graze² /grayz/ *v. & n.* ● *v.* **1** *tr.* rub or scrape (a part of the body, esp. the skin) so as to break the surface without causing bleeding or with only minor bleeding. **2 a** *tr.* touch lightly in passing. **b** *intr.* (foll. by *against*, *along*, etc.) move with a light passing contact. ● *n.* an act or instance of grazing. [perh. a specific use of GRAZE¹, as if 'take off the grass close to the ground' (of a shot, etc.)]
■ *v.* **1** see SCRAPE *v.* 3b. **2 a** see KISS *v.* 4. ● *n.* see SCRAPE *n.* 2.

grazier /gráyzhər/ *n.* **1** a person who feeds cattle for market. **2** *Austral.* a large-scale sheep farmer or cattle farmer. □□ **graziery** *n.* [GRASS + -IER]

grazing /gráyzing/ *n.* grassland suitable for pasturage.

grease /grees/ *n. & v.* ● *n.* **1** oily or fatty matter esp. as a lubricant. **2** the melted fat of a dead animal. **3** oily matter

in unprocessed wool. ● *v.tr.* /also greez/ smear or lubricate with grease. □ **grease gun** a device for pumping grease under pressure to a particular point. **grease monkey** *sl.* a mechanic, esp. one who works on motor vehicles. **grease the palm of** *colloq.* bribe. **like greased lightning** *colloq.* very fast. □□ **greaseless** *adj.* [ME f. AF *grece, gresse*, OF *graisse* ult. f. L *crassus* (adj.) fat]
■ *n.* see OIL *n.* ● *v.* see OIL *v.*

greasepaint /gréespaynt/ *n.* a waxy composition used as makeup for actors.

greaseproof /gréesproof/ *adj.* impervious to the penetration of grease.

greaser /gréesər/ *n.* **1** a person or thing that greases. **2** *sl.* a member of a gang of young street toughs. **3** *sl. offens.* a Mexican or Spanish-American. **4** *sl.* a gentle landing of an aircraft.

greasy /gréesee, gréezee/ *adj.* (**greasier, greasiest**) **1 a** of or like grease. **b** smeared or covered with grease. **c** containing or having too much grease. **2 a** slippery. **b** (of a person or manner) unpleasantly unctuous; smooth. **c** objectionable. □ **greasy spoon** *sl.* an inexpensive small restaurant that serves fried food and that is often dirty or unsanitary. □□ **greasily** *adv.* **greasiness** *n.*
■ **1** oily, sebaceous, fatty, fat, buttery, lardy, oleaginous, *formal or joc.* pinguid. **2 a** see SLIPPERY 1, 2. **b** unctuous, oily, slippery, fawning, slick, smooth, toadying, sycophantic, obsequious, *colloq.* smarmy.

great /grayt/ *adj. & n.* ● *adj.* **1 a** of a size, amount, extent, or intensity considerably above the normal or average; big (*made a great hole; take great care; lived to a great age*). **b** also with implied surprise, admiration, contempt, etc., esp. in exclamations (*great stuff!*). **c** reinforcing other words denoting size, quantity, etc. (*a great big hole; a great many*). **2** important; preeminent; worthy or most worthy of consideration. **3** grand; imposing (*a great occasion; the great hall*). **4 a** (esp. of a public or historic figure) distinguished; prominent. **b** (**the Great**) as a title denoting the most important of the name (*Alexander the Great*). **5 a** (of a person) remarkable in ability, character, achievement, etc. (*great men; a great thinker*). **b** (of a thing) outstanding of its kind (*the Great Depression*). **6** (foll. by *at*) competent; skilled; well-informed. **7** fully deserving the name of; doing a thing habitually or extensively (*a great reader; a great believer in tolerance; not a great one for traveling*). **8** (also **greater**) the larger of the name, species, etc. (*great auk; greater celandine*). **9** (**Greater**) (of a city, etc.) including adjacent urban areas (*Greater Boston*). **10** *colloq.* **a** very enjoyable or satisfactory; attractive; fine (*had a great time; it would be great if we won*). **b** (as an exclam.) fine; very good. **11** (in *comb.*) (in names of family relationships) denoting one degree further removed upwards or downwards (*great-uncle; great-great-grandmother*). ● *n.* **1** a great or outstanding person or thing. **2** (in *pl.*) (**Greats**) *colloq.* (at Oxford University) an honors course or final examinations in classics and philosophy. □ **great and small** all classes or types. **the Great Bear** Brit. = Big Dipper. **Great Britain** England, Wales, and Scotland. **great circle** see CIRCLE. **Great Dane** see DANE. **great deal** see DEAL¹. **the great majority** by far the most. **great northern diver** a diving sea bird, *Gavia immer*, of the northern hemisphere. **great organ** the chief manual in a large organ, with its related pipes and mechanism. **Great Russian** *n.* a member or the language of the principal East Slavonic ethnic group, inhabiting mainly the Russian Republic; (a) Russian. ● *adj.* of or relating to this people or language. **great tit** a Eurasian songbird, *Parus major*, with black and white head markings. **great toe** the big toe. **Great War** World War I (1914–18). **to a great extent** largely. □□ **greatness** *n.* [OE *grēat* f. WG]
■ *adj.* **1 a** big, large, huge, immense, enormous, stupendous, grand, extensive, colossal, gigantic, monstrous, mammoth, massive, vast, prodigious, tremendous; extreme, considerable, a lot of; marked, pronounced, inordinate, extraordinary, *colloq.* terrific; significant, profound, basic, cardinal. **2** critical, important, preeminent, crucial, vital, major, main,

chief. **3** grand, fine, imposing, lofty, elevated, exalted, noble, spectacular; momentous, significant, serious, weighty. **4 a** distinguished, prominent, important, eminent, celebrated, famous, famed, renowned, notable, illustrious, outstanding, well-known, weighty, influential. **5 a** gifted, talented, accomplished, skilled, excellent, brilliant, first-rate, outstanding, remarkable, exceptional, incomparable, matchless, peerless; leading. **b** extraordinary, outstanding. **6** (*great at* or *on*) competent at, well-informed on or about, expert at or in; talented at, skilled at, clever at, adept at, proficient at. **7** keen, zealous, eager, active, enthusiastic, devoted, ardent, passionate. **10** outstanding, first-rate, first-class, superior, marvelous, wonderful, splendid, *colloq.* tiptop, capital, super(-duper), smashing, A1, knockout, brilliant, grand, fantastic, terrific, fab, fabulous, crucial, A-OK, champion, *Brit. colloq.* tickety-boo, *sl.* cracking, ace, groovy, awesome, bad, *Austral. sl.* grouse; see also SUPERB. □ **to a great extent** see LARGELY.

greatcoat /gráytkōt/ *n.* a long heavy overcoat.

greathearted /gráyt-haártid/ *adj.* magnanimous; having a noble or generous mind. □□ **greatheartedness** *n.*
■ see NOBLE *adj.* 2, GENEROUS 2.

greatly /gráytlee/ *adv.* by a considerable amount; much (*greatly admired; greatly superior*).
■ see EXCEEDINGLY 1.

greave /greev/ *n.* (usu. in *pl.*) armor for the shin. [ME f. OF *greve* shin, greave, of unkn. orig.]

grebe /greeb/ *n.* any diving bird of the family Podicipedidae, with a long neck, lobed toes, and almost no tail. □ **little grebe** a small water bird of the grebe family, *Tachybaptus ruficollis*. [F *grèbe*, of unkn. orig.]

Grecian /gréeshən/ *adj.* (of architecture or facial outline) following Greek models or ideals. □ **Grecian nose** a straight nose that continues the line of the forehead without a dip. [OF *grecien* or med.L *graecianus* (unrecorded) f. L *Graecia* Greece]

Grecism /gréesizəm/ *n.* (also **Graecism**) **1** a Greek idiom, esp. as imitated in another language. **2 a** the Greek spirit, style, mode of expression, etc. **b** the imitation of these. [F *grécisme* or med.L *Graecismus* f. *Graecus* GREEK]

Grecize /gréesiz/ *v.tr.* (also **Graecize**) give a Greek character or form to. [L *Graecizare* (as GRAECISM)]

Greco- /grékō/ *comb. form* (also **Graeco-**) Greek; Greek and. [L *Graecus* GREEK]

Greco-Roman /greekō-rṓmən, grékō-/ *adj.* **1** of or relating to the Greeks and Romans. **2** *Wrestling* denoting a style attacking only the upper part of the body.

greed /greed/ *n.* an excessive desire, esp. for food or wealth. [back-form. f. GREEDY]
■ greediness, avarice, avariciousness, covetousness, acquisitiveness, cupidity, avidity; gluttony, piggishness, voraciousness, voracity, gormandizing.

greedy /gréedee/ *adj.* (**greedier, greediest**) **1** having or showing an excessive appetite for food or drink. **2** wanting wealth or pleasure to excess. **3** (foll. by *for*, or to + infin.) very keen or eager; needing intensely (*greedy for affection; greedy to learn*). □ **greedy-guts** *colloq.* a glutton. □□ **greedily** *adv.* **greediness** *n.* [OE *grǣdig* f. Gmc]
■ **1** voracious, gluttonous, esurient, *colloq.* piggish, hoggish, swinish, *literary or joc.* edacious. **2** avaricious, acquisitive, covetous, grasping, rapacious; materialistic, money hungry, mercenary. **3** see EAGER 2. □ **greedy-guts** see GLUTTON 1.

Greek /greek/ *n. & adj.* ● *n.* **1 a** a native or inhabitant of modern Greece; a person of Greek descent. **b** a native or citizen of any of the ancient nation-states of Greece; a member of the Greek people. **2** the Indo-European language of Greece. ● *adj.* of Greece or its people or language; Hellenic.

/.../ pronunciation	● part of speech
□ phrases, idioms, and compounds	
□□ derivatives	■ synonym section
cross-references appear in SMALL CAPITALS or *italics*	

□ **Greek** (or **Greek Orthodox**) **Church** the national church of Greece (see also *Orthodox Church*). **Greek cross** a cross with four equal arms. **Greek fire** *hist.* a combustible composition for igniting enemy ships, etc. **Greek** (or **greek**) **to me** *colloq.* incomprehensible to me. □□ **Greekness** *n.* [OE *Grēcas* (pl.) f. Gmc f. L *Graecus* Greek f. Gk *Graikoi*, the prehistoric name of the Hellenes (in Aristotle)]

green /green/ *adj., n.,* & *v.* ● *adj.* **1** of the color between blue and yellow in the spectrum; colored like grass, emeralds, etc. **2 a** covered with leaves or grass. **b** mild and without snow (*a green Christmas*). **3** (of fruit, etc., or wood) unripe or unseasoned. **4** not dried, smoked, or tanned. **5** inexperienced; naive; gullible. **6 a** (of the complexion) pale; sickly-hued. **b** jealous; envious. **7** young; flourishing. **8** not withered or worn out (*a green old age*). **9** vegetable (*green food; green salad*). **10** (also **Green**) concerned with or supporting protection of the environment as a political principle. **11** *archaic* fresh; not healed (*a green wound*). ● *n.* **1** a green color or pigment. **2** green clothes or material (*dressed in green*). **3 a** a piece of public or common grassy land (*village green*). **b** a grassy area used for a special purpose (*putting green; bowling green*). **c** *Golf* a putting green. **4** (in *pl.*) green vegetables. **5** vigor; youth; virility (*in the green*). **6** a green light. **7** a green ball, piece, etc., in a game or sport. **8** (also **Green**) a member or supporter of an environmentalist group or party. **9** (in *pl.*) *Brit. sl.* sexual intercourse. **10** *sl.* low-grade marijuana. **11** *sl.* money. **12** green foliage or growing plants. ● *v.* **1** *tr.* & *intr.* make or become green. **2** *tr. sl.* hoax; take in. □ **green** (or **string**) **bean** the green pods of a young kidney bean, eaten as a vegetable. **green belt** an area of open land round a city, designated for preservation. **Green Beret** *Mil.* a member of the U.S. Army Special Forces. **green card 1** a work and residence permit issued to permanent resident aliens in the US. **2** *Brit.* an international insurance document for motorists. **green cheese 1** *Brit.* cheese colored green with sage. **2** whey cheese. **3** unripened cheese. **green drake** the common British mayfly. **green earth** a hydrous silicate of potassium, iron, and other metals. **green-eyed** jealous. **the green-eyed monster** jealousy. **green fat** part of a turtle, highly regarded by gourmets. **green fee** (also **green fee**) *Golf* a charge for playing one round on a course. **green fingers** *Brit.* = **green thumb**. **green goose** a goose killed under four months old and eaten without stuffing. **green in a person's eye** *Brit.* a sign of gullibility (*do you see any green in my eye?*). **green leek** any of several green-faced Australian parakeets. **green light 1** a signal to proceed on a road, railroad, etc. **2** *colloq.* permission to go ahead with a project. **green linnet** = GREEN-FINCH. **green manure** growing plants plowed into the soil as fertilizer. **green meat** *Brit.* grass and green vegetables as food. **green pepper** the unripe bell or sweet pepper, *Capsicum annuum grossum*, eaten green as a vegetable. **green plover** a lapwing. **green pound** *Brit.* the exchange rate for the pound for payments for agricultural produce in the European Community. **green revolution** greatly increased crop production in underdeveloped countries. **green tea** tea made from dried, not fermented, leaves. **green thumb** skill in growing plants. **green turtle** a green-shelled sea turtle, *Chelonia mydas*, highly regarded as food. **green vitriol** ferrous sulfate crystals. □□ **greenish** *adj.* **greenly** *adv.* **greenness** *n.* [OE *grēne* (adj. & n.), *grēnian* (v.), f. Gmc, rel. to GROW]

■ *adj.* **1** emerald, jade, lime, lime green, bottle green, Lincoln green. **2 a** verdant, fresh, grassy; rural, pastoral, country-like; see also LEAFY. **b** see MILD 3. **3** immature, unripe, unripened, unseasoned, unready. **5** naive, callow, untested, untrained, unversed, inexperienced, new, raw, unsophisticated, *colloq.* wet behind the ears; gullible, amateur, unskilled, unskillful, amateurish, nonprofessional, inexpert. **6 a** see PALE¹ *adj.* 1. **b** see ENVIOUS. **7** young, youthful, flourishing, blooming, blossoming, thriving. **8** young, youthful; see also SPRIGHTLY. **10** (also **Green**) environmental, conservational, ecological, eco-, *attrib.* conservation. **11** fresh, new; see also RAW *adj.* 6a, b. ● *n.* **3 a** a common,

grassland; lawn(s), *archaic or literary* greensward, *literary* sward. **b** lawn, turf. **5** youth, youthfulness, salad days; see also VIGOR 1, MANHOOD 2a. **8** (also **Green**) see CONSERVATIONIST. **10** see GRASS *n.* 5. **11** see MONEY 1. **12** foliage; plants, shrubs, trees. ● *v.* **2** see *take in* 5. □ **green-eyed** see ENVIOUS. **the green-eyed monster** see ENVY *n.* **green light 2** see *go-ahead n.* (GO¹).

greenback /greenbak/ *n.* **1** a US legal tender note. **2** any of various green-backed animals.

greenbottle /greenbot'l/ *n.* any fly of the genus *Lucilia*, esp. *L. sericata* which lays eggs in the flesh of sheep.

greenery /greenaree/ *n.* green foliage or growing plants.

greenfeed /greenfeed/ *n. Austral.* & *NZ* forage grown to be fed fresh to livestock.

greenfield /greenfeeld/ *n.* (*attrib.*) (of a site, in terms of its potential development) having no previous building development on it.

greenfinch /greenfinch/ *n.* a finch, *Carduelis chloris*, with green and yellow plumage.

greenfly /greenflī/ *n.* (*pl.* **-flies**) **1** a green aphid. **2** these collectively.

greengage /greengayj/ *n.* a roundish green fine-flavored variety of plum. [Sir W. *Gage* d. 1727]

greengrocer /greengrōsər/ *n. Brit.* a retailer of fruit and vegetables.

greengrocery /greengrōsəree/ *n.* (*pl.* **-ies**) *Brit.* **1** the business of a greengrocer. **2** goods sold by a greengrocer.

greenhead /greenhed/ *n.* **1** any biting fly of the genus *Chrysops* or other genera. **2** an Australian ant, *Chalcoponera metallica*, with a painful sting.

greenheart /greenhaart/ *n.* **1** any of several tropical American trees, esp. *Ocotea rodiaei*. **2** the hard greenish wood of one of these.

greenhide /greehīd/ *n. Austral.* the untanned hide of an animal.

greenhorn /greenhawrn/ *n.* an inexperienced or foolish person; a new recruit.

■ newcomer, beginner, novice, tyro, learner, tenderfoot, neophyte, initiate, (new) recruit, *sl.* rookie.

greenhouse /greenhows/ *n.* a light structure with the sides and roof mainly of glass, for rearing delicate plants or hastening the growth of plants. □ **greenhouse effect** the trapping of the sun's warmth in the lower atmosphere of the earth caused by an increase in carbon dioxide, which is more transparent to solar radiation than to the reflected radiation from the earth. **greenhouse gas** any of various gases, esp. carbon dioxide, that contribute to the greenhouse effect.

greening /greening/ *n.* a variety of apple that is green when ripe. [prob. f. MDu. *groeninc* (as GREEN)]

greenkeeper var. of **greenskeeper**.

greenlet /greenlit/ *n.* = VIREO.

greenroom /greenrōōm/ *n.* a room in a theater for actors and actresses who are off stage.

greensand /greensand/ *n.* **1** a greenish kind of sandstone, often imperfectly cemented. **2** a stratum largely formed of this sandstone.

greenshank /greenshangk/ *n.* a large sandpiper, *Tringa nebularia*.

greensick /greensik/ *adj.* affected with chlorosis. □□ **greensickness** *n.*

greenskeeper /greenzkeepər/ *n.* the keeper of a golf course.

greenstick fracture /greenstik/ *n.* a bone fracture, esp. in children, in which one side of the bone is broken and one only bent.

greenstone /greenstōn/ *n.* **1** a greenish igneous rock containing feldspar and hornblende. **2** a variety of jade found in New Zealand, used for tools, ornaments, etc.

greenstuff /greenstuf/ *n.* vegetation; green vegetables.

greensward /greenswawrd/ *n. archaic* or *literary* **1** grassy turf. **2** an expanse of this.

greenweed /greenweed/ *n.* (in full **dyer's greenweed**) a bushy plant, *Genista tinctoria*, with deep yellow flowers.

Greenwich Mean Time /grénich, grínij/ *n.* (also **Greenwich Time**) the local time on the meridian of Greenwich, England, used as an international basis for reckoning time.

[*Greenwich* in London, former site of the Royal Observatory]

greenwood /greenwŏod/ *n.* a wood in summer, esp. as the scene of outlaw life.

greeny /greenee/ *adj.* greenish (*greeny-yellow*).

greenyard /greenyaard/ *n. Brit.* an enclosure for stray animals; a pound.

greet[1] /greet/ *v.tr.* **1** address politely or welcomingly on meeting or arrival. **2** receive or acknowledge in a specified way (*was greeted with derision*). **3** (of a sight, sound, etc.) become apparent to or noticed by. □□ **greeter** *n.* [OE *grētan* handle, attack, salute f. WG]
■ **1, 2** welcome, receive, hail, salute, meet; acknowledge.

greet[2] /greet/ *v.intr. Sc.* weep. [OE *grētan, grēotan*, of uncert. orig.]

greeting /greeting/ *n.* **1** the act or an instance of welcoming or addressing politely. **2** words, gestures, etc., used to greet a person. **3** (often in *pl.*) an expression of goodwill. □ **greeting card** a decorative card sent to convey greetings.
■ **1** welcome, salutation, reception. **3** (*greetings*) regards, respects, best *or* good wishes, compliments, *archaic* devoirs.

gregarious /grigáireeəs/ *adj.* **1** fond of company. **2** living in flocks or communities. **3** growing in clusters. □□ **gregariously** *adv.* **gregariousness** *n.* [L *gregarius* f. *grex gregis* flock]
■ **1** see SOCIABLE.

Gregorian calendar /grigáwreeən/ *n.* the calendar introduced in 1582 by Pope Gregory XIII, as a correction of the Julian calendar. [med.L *Gregorianus* f. LL *Gregorius* f. Gk *Grēgorios* Gregory]

Gregorian chant /grigáwreeən/ *n.* plainsong ritual music, named after Pope Gregory I.

Gregorian telescope /grigáwreeən/ *n.* a reflecting telescope in which light reflected from a secondary mirror passes through a hole in a primary mirror. [J. *Gregory*, Sc. mathematician d. 1675, who devised it]

gremlin /grémlin/ *n. colloq.* **1** an imaginary mischievous sprite regarded as responsible for mechanical faults, esp. in aircraft. **2** any similar cause of trouble. [20th c.: orig. unkn., but prob. after *goblin*]

grenade /grináyd/ *n.* **1** a small bomb thrown by hand (**hand grenade**) or shot from a rifle. **2** a glass receptacle containing chemicals which disperse on impact, for testing drains, extinguishing fires, etc. [F f. OF *grenate* and Sp. *granada* POMEGRANATE]

grenadier /grénədeer/ *n.* **1 a** *Brit.* (**Grenadiers** or **Grenadier Guards**) the first regiment of the royal household infantry. **b** *hist.* a soldier armed with grenades. **2** any deep-sea fish of the family Macrouridae, with a long tapering body and pointed tail, and secreting luminous bacteria when disturbed. [F (as GRENADE)]

grenadilla var. of GRANADILLA.

grenadine[1] /grénədeen/ *n.* a French syrup of pomegranates, etc., used in mixed drinks. [F f. *grenade*: see GRENADE]

grenadine[2] /grénədeen/ *n.* a dress fabric of loosely woven silk or silk and wool. [F, earlier *grenade* grained silk f. *grenu* grained]

Gresham's law /gréshəmz/ *n.* the tendency for money of lower intrinsic value to circulate more freely than money of higher intrinsic and equal nominal value. [Sir T. *Gresham*, Engl. financier d. 1579]

gressorial /gresáwreeəl/ *adj. Zool.* **1** walking. **2** adapted for walking. [mod.L *gressorius* f. L *gradi gress-* walk]

grew past of GROW.

grey var. of GRAY.

Grey Friar *n.* a Franciscan friar.

greyhound /gráyhownd/ *n.* **1** a dog of a tall slender breed having excellent sight and capable of high speed, used in racing and coursing. **2** this breed. [OE *grīghund* f. *grīeg* bitch (unrecorded: cf. ON *grey*) + *hund* dog, rel. to HOUND]

greylag /gráylag/ *n.* (in full **greylag goose**) a wild goose, *Anser anser*, native to Europe. [GREY + LAG[1] (because of its late migration)]

greywacke *Brit.* var. of GRAYWACKE.

grid /grid/ *n.* **1** a framework of spaced parallel bars; a grating. **2** a system of numbered squares printed on a map and forming the basis of map references. **3** a network of lines, electrical power connections, gas supply lines, etc. **4** a pattern of lines marking the starting places on a motor-racing track. **5** the wire network between the filament and the anode of a vacuum tube, etc. **6** an arrangement of city streets in a rectangular pattern. □ **grid bias** *Electr.* a fixed voltage applied between the cathode and the control grid of a vacuum tube which determines its operating conditions. □□ **gridded** *adj.* [back-form. f. GRIDIRON]
■ **1** see GRATING[2] 1. **3** see NETWORK *n.* 2.

griddle /grid'l/ *n. & v.* ● *n.* **1** a circular iron plate placed over a fire or otherwise heated for baking, toasting, etc. **2** a miner's wire-bottomed sieve. ● *v.tr.* **1** cook with a griddle; grill. **2** sieve with a griddle. [ME f. OF *gredil, gridil* griddle ult. f. L *craticula* dimin. of *cratis* hurdle; cf. GRATE[2], GRILL[1]]

gridiron /grídiərn/ *n.* **1** a cooking utensil of metal bars for broiling or grilling. **2** a frame of parallel beams for supporting a ship in dock. **3** a football field (with parallel lines marking out the area of play). **4** *Theatr.* a plank structure over a stage supporting the mechanism for drop scenery, etc. **5** = GRID 6. [ME *gredire*, var. of *gredil* GRIDDLE, later assoc. with IRON]

gridlock /grídlok/ *n.* **1** a traffic jam affecting a network of streets, caused by continuous lines of intersecting traffic. **2** a complete standstill in action or progress. □□ **gridlocked** *adj.*

grief /greef/ *n.* **1** deep or intense sorrow or mourning. **2** the cause of this. □ **come to grief** meet with disaster; fail. **good grief!** an exclamation of surprise, alarm, etc. [ME f. AF *gref*, OF *grief* f. *grever* GRIEVE[1]]
■ **1** anguish, suffering, agony, misery, distress, wretchedness, pain, hurt, sadness, sorrow, unhappiness, torment, desolation, heartbreak, heartache, *archaic or literary* woe; mourning. **2** tribulation, burden, ordeal, affliction, calamity, adversity, misfortune. □ **come to grief** fail, miscarry, meet with disaster, fall apart *or* to pieces, *colloq.* come unstuck, *sl.* come a cropper. **good grief!** see GRACIOUS *int.*

grievance /greevəns/ *n.* **1** a real or fancied cause for complaint. **2** a formal complaint.[ME, = injury, f. OF *grevance* (as GRIEF)]
■ complaint, objection, charge, allegation, grudge, gravamen, *Brit. Law* plaint, *colloq.* gripe, *sl.* beef; injustice, disservice, unfairness, injury, insult, outrage, affront, indignity, wrongdoing; wrong, ill, damage, harm.

grieve[1] /greev/ *v.* **1** *tr.* cause grief or great distress to. **2** *intr.* suffer grief, esp. at another's death. □□ **griever** *n.* [ME f. OF *grever* ult. f. L *gravare* f. *gravis* heavy]
■ **1** see DISTRESS *v.* **2** mourn, suffer, sorrow, mope, eat one's heart out; weep, cry, moan, keen, shed tears; (*grieve over*) bemoan, lament, deplore, regret, rue, bewail.

grieve[2] /greev/ *n. Sc.* a farm bailiff; an overseer. [OE *grǣfa*: cf. REEVE[1]]

grievous /greevəs/ *adj.* **1** (of pain, etc.) severe. **2** causing grief or suffering. **3** injurious. **4** flagrant; heinous. □ **grievous bodily harm** *Law* serious injury inflicted intentionally on a person. □□ **grievously** *adv.* **grievousness** *n.* [ME f. OF *grevos* (as GRIEVE[1])]
■ **1** severe, grave, serious; see also ACUTE *adj.* 1a. **2, 3** distressing, hurtful, harmful, wounding; injurious, damaging, wrongful. **4** flagrant, heinous, egregious, outrageous, atrocious, monstrous, deplorable, calamitous, lamentable, shameful, *colloq.* awful, appalling, terrible, shocking, dreadful.

/. . ./ **pronunciation**	● **part of speech**
	□ **phrases, idioms, and compounds**
□□ **derivatives**	■ **synonym section**
cross-references appear in SMALL CAPITALS or *italics*	

griffin /grífin/ *n.* (also **gryphon, griffon**) a mythical creature with an eagle's head and wings and a lion's body. [ME f. OF *grifoun* ult. f. LL *gryphus* f. L *gryps* f. Gk *grups*]

griffon /grífon/ *n.* **1 a** a dog of a small terrierlike breed with coarse or smooth hair. **b** this breed. **2** (in full **griffon vulture**) a large S. European vulture, *Gyps fulvus.* **3** = GRIFFIN. [F (in sense 1) or var. of GRIFFIN]

grig /grig/ *n.* **1** a small eel. **2** a grasshopper or cricket. □ **merry** (or **lively**) **as a grig** full of fun; extravagantly lively. [ME, orig. = dwarf: orig. unkn.]

grill[1] /gril/ *n. & v.* ● *n.* **1** = GRIDIRON 1. **2** a dish of food cooked on a grill. **3** (in full **grill room**) a restaurant serving grilled food. ● *v.* **1** *tr. & intr.* cook or be cooked under a boiler or on a gridiron. **2** *tr. & intr.* subject or be subjected to extreme heat, esp. from the sun. **3** *tr.* subject to severe questioning or interrogation. □□ **griller** *n.* **grilling** *n.* (in sense 3 of *v.*). [F *gril* (n.), *griller* (v.), f. OF forms of GRILLE]
■ *v.* **1** see BROIL[1] 1. **3** see QUESTION *v.* 1, 2.

grill[2] var. of GRILLE.

grillage /gríli̇j/ *n.* a heavy framework of cross-timbering or metal beams forming a foundation for building on difficult ground. [F (as GRILLE)]

grille /gril/ *n.* (also **grill**) **1** a grating or latticed screen, used as a partition or to allow discreet vision. **2** a metal grid protecting the radiator of a motor vehicle. [F f. OF *graille* f. med.L *graticula, craticula*: see GRIDDLE]
■ **1** see GRATING[2] 1.

grillwork /grílwərk/ *n.* metal fashioned to form a grille (*a balcony of ornate grillwork*).

grilse /grils/ *n.* a young salmon that has returned to fresh water from the sea for the first time. [ME: orig. unkn.]

grim /grim/ *adj.* (**grimmer, grimmest**) **1** of a stern or forbidding appearance. **2 a** harsh; merciless; severe. **b** resolute; uncompromising (*grim determination*). **3** ghastly; joyless; sinister (*has a grim truth in it*). **4** unpleasant; unattractive. □ **like grim death** with great determination. □□ **grimly** *adv.* **grimness** *n.* [OE f. Gmc]
■ **1** see FORBIDDING. **2 a** harsh, merciless, stern, severe, unrelenting, stony, iron, implacable, inexorable, formidable, ferocious, fierce, heartless, ruthless, pitiless, cruel, savage, vicious, brutal. **b** resolute, uncompromising, unyielding, inflexible, adamant, unbending, firm, intractable, unflinching, unmoving, unmoved, determined, steadfast, set, fixed, decided, obstinate, headstrong, stubborn, obdurate, dogged, unwavering. **3** ghastly, joyless, dreadful, frightful, frightening, sinister, hideous, horrid, horrible, horrendous, terrible, dread, alarming, gruesome, eerie, macabre, *poet.* awful. **4** see AWFUL 1a, b.

grimace /grímǝs, grimáys/ *n. & v.* ● *n.* a distortion of the face made in disgust, etc., or to amuse. ● *v.intr.* make a grimace. □□ **grimacer** *n.* [F f. Sp. *grimazo* f. *grima* fright]
■ *n.* see FROWN *n.* ● *v.* see FROWN *v.* 1.

grimalkin /grimálkin, -máwlkin/ *n. archaic* (esp. in fiction) **1** an old she-cat. **2** a spiteful old woman. [GRAY + *Malkin* dimin. of the name *Matilda*]

grime /grim/ *n. & v.* ● *n.* soot or dirt ingrained in a surface, esp. of buildings or the skin. ● *v.tr.* blacken with grime; befoul. [orig. as verb: f. MLG & MDu.]
■ *n.* filth, soot, *colloq.* muck; see also DIRT 1.
● *v.* blacken, dirty, soil, begrime, besmirch, muddy, defile, muck, *poet.* befoul.

grimy /grími/ *adj.* (**grimier, grimiest**) covered with grime; dirty. □□ **grimily** *adv.* **griminess** *n.*
■ see DIRTY *adj.* 1.

grin /grin/ *v. & n.* ● *v.* (**grinned, grinning**) **1** *intr.* **a** smile broadly, showing the teeth. **b** make a forced, unrestrained, or stupid smile. **2** *tr.* express by grinning (*grinned his satisfaction*). ● *n.* the act or action of grinning. □ **grin and bear it** take pain or misfortune stoically. □□ **grinner** *n.* **grinningly** *adv.* [OE *grennian* f. Gmc]
■ □ **grin and bear it** see *bite the bullet*.

grind /grind/ *v. & n.* ● *v.* (*past* and *past part.* **ground** /grownd/) **1 a** *tr.* reduce to small particles or powder by crushing esp. by passing through a mill. **b** *intr.* (of a mill,

machine, etc.) move with a crushing action. **2 a** *tr.* reduce, sharpen, or smooth by friction. **b** *tr. & intr.* rub or rub together gratingly (*grind one's teeth*). **3** *tr.* (often foll. by *down*) oppress; harass with exactions (*grinding poverty*). **4** *intr.* **a** (often foll. by *away*) work or study hard. **b** (foll. by *out*) produce with effort (*grinding out verses*). **c** (foll. by *on*) (of a sound) continue gratingly or monotonously. **5** *tr.* turn the handle of e.g., a coffee mill, barrel organ, etc. **6** *intr. sl.* (of a dancer) rotate the hips. **7** *intr. Brit. coarse sl.* have sexual intercourse. ● *n.* **1** the act or an instance of grinding. **2** *colloq.* hard dull work; a laborious task (*the daily grind*). **3** the size of ground particles. **4** *sl.* a dancer's rotary movement of the hips. **5** *Brit. coarse sl.* an act of sexual intercourse. □ **grind to a halt** stop laboriously. **ground glass 1** glass made nontransparent by grinding, etc. **2** glass ground to a powder. □□ **grindingly** *adv.* [OE *grindan*, of unkn. orig.]
■ *v.* **1** a pound, powder, pulverize, crush, mince, granulate, mill, kibble, triturate, *archaic* bray. **2 a** reduce; sharpen, whet; file, smooth, abrade, polish. **b** gnash, grate, rub. **3** (*grind down*) crush, wear down, oppress, harass, plague, subdue, suppress, tyrannize, persecute. **4 a** work, labor, toil, slave; study, burn the midnight oil, cram, *Brit. colloq.* swot, *literary* lucubrate. **b** (*grind out*) produce, generate, crank out. ● *n.* **2** work, toil, labor, drudgery, exertion, effort, *literary* travail; tasks, chores.

grinder /gríndǝr/ *n.* **1** a person or thing that grinds, esp. a machine (often in *comb.*: *coffee grinder; organ grinder*). **2** a molar tooth. **3** *US dial.* a submarine sandwich.
■ **1** see MILL[1] *n.* 1b, 2.

grindstone /gríndstōn/ *n.* **1** a thick revolving disk used for grinding, sharpening, and polishing. **2** a kind of stone used for this. □ **keep one's nose to the grindstone** work hard and continuously.

gringo /gríngō/ *n.* (*pl.* **-os**) *colloq.* a foreigner, esp. a non-Hispanic N. American, in a Spanish-speaking country. [Sp., = gibberish]

grip /grip/ *v. & n.* ● *v.* (**gripped, gripping**) **1 a** *tr.* grasp tightly; take a firm hold of. **b** *intr.* take a firm hold, esp. by friction. **2** *tr.* (of a feeling or emotion) deeply affect (a person) (*was gripped by fear*). **3** *tr.* compel the attention or interest of (*a gripping story*). ● *n.* **1 a** a firm hold; a tight grasp or clasp. **b** a manner of grasping or holding. **2** the power of holding attention. **3 a** mental or intellectual understanding or mastery. **b** effective control of a situation or one's behavior, etc. (*lose one's grip*). **4 a** a part of a machine that grips or holds something. **b** a part or attachment by which a tool, implement, weapon, etc., is held in the hand. **5** *Brit.* = HAIRGRIP. **6** a traveling bag. **7** an assistant in a theater, movie studio, etc. **8** *Austral. sl.* a job or occupation. □ **come** (or **get) to grips with** approach purposefully; begin to deal with. **get a grip (on oneself)** keep or recover one's self-control. **in the grip of** dominated or affected by (esp. an adverse circumstance or unpleasant sensation). **lose one's grip** lose control. □□ **gripper** *n.* **grippingly** *adv.* [OE *gripe, gripa* handful (as GRIPE)]
■ *v.* **1 a** grasp, clutch, clasp, hold. **b** hold, stay; see also STICK[2] 6. **2** see SEIZE 4, POSSESS 4b. **3** engross, engage, hold the attention of, fascinate, enthrall, entrance, absorb, mesmerize, hypnotize, spellbind, rivet.
● *n.* **1** hold, grasp, clutch, handgrip, clasp, handclasp. **2** control, command, hold, mastery; authority, influence, power. **3 a** grasp, understanding, mastery, apprehension, comprehension, awareness, perception. **b** see SELF-CONTROL. **6** valise, bag, holdall, carryall; see also SUITCASE. □ **come** (*or* **get) to grips with** tackle, confront, approach, meet head on, grapple with, deal with, cope with, handle, face, address. **in the grip of** under the control of, dominated or affected or controlled by; under the thumb of.

gripe /grip/ *v. & n.* ● *v.* **1** *intr. colloq.* complain, esp. peevishly. **2** *tr.* affect with gastric or intestinal pain. **3** *tr. archaic* clutch; grip. **4** *Naut.* **a** *tr.* secure with gripes. **b** *intr.* turn to face the wind in spite of the helm. ● *n.* **1** (usu. in *pl.*) gastric or intestinal pain; colic. **2** *colloq.* **a** a complaint. **b** the act of griping. **3** a grip or clutch. **4** (in *pl.*) *Naut.* lashings securing a boat in its place. □□ **griper** *n.* **gripingly** *adv.* [OE *grīpan* f. Gmc: cf. GROPE]

■ *v.* **1** complain, moan, grumble, whine, bleat, nag, cavil, carp, *colloq.* grouse, bitch, *Brit. colloq.* whinge, *sl.* beef, bellyache. ● *n.* **1** stomachache, cramp, twinge, pang, pain, *colloq.* bellyache; colic. **2** complaint, grievance, objection, protest, grumble, moan, whine, *sl.* beef; nagging, carping, grousing, *colloq.* bitching, *Brit. colloq.* whinging, *sl.* bellyaching. **3** grip, clasp, clutch, hold.

grippe /grip/ *n.* archaic or *colloq.* influenza. [F f. *gripper* seize]

grisaille /grizī́, -záyl/ *n.* **1** a method of painting in gray monochrome, often to imitate sculpture. **2** a painting or stained glass window of this kind. [F f. *gris* gray]

griseofulvin /grízeeəfoolvin/ *n.* an antibiotic used against fungal infections of the hair and skin. [mod.L *griseofulvum* f. med.L *griseus* gray + L *fulvus* reddish yellow]

grisette /grizét/ *n.* a young working-class Frenchwoman. [F, orig. a gray dress material, f. *gris* gray]

grisly /grízlee/ *adj.* (**grislier, grisliest**) causing horror, disgust, or fear. □□ **grisliness** *n.* [OE *grislic* terrifying]

■ gruesome, grim, gory, abhorrent, hideous, nasty, dreadful, repulsive, repellent, repugnant, disgusting, sickening, nauseating, horrific, horrendous, horrifying, awful, terrible, horrid, abominable, appalling.

grison /grísən, grízən/ *n.* any weasellike mammal of the genus *Galictis*, with dark fur and a white stripe across the forehead. [F, app. f. *grison* gray]

grist /grist/ *n.* **1** grain to grind. **2** malt crushed for brewing. □ **grist to the** (or **a person's**) **mill** a source of profit or advantage. [OE f. Gmc, rel. to GRIND]

gristle /grísəl/ *n.* tough flexible tissue in vertebrates; cartilage. □□ **gristly** /gríslee/ *adj.* [OE *gristle*]

grit /grit/ *n. & v.* ● *n.* **1** particles of stone or sand, esp. as causing discomfort, clogging machinery, etc. **2** coarse sandstone. **3** *colloq.* pluck; endurance; strength of character. ● *v.* (**gritted, gritting**) **1** *tr.* spread grit on (icy roads, etc.). **2** *tr.* clench (the teeth). **3** *intr.* make or move with a grating sound. □□ **gritter** *n.* **gritty** *adj.* (**grittier, grittiest**). **grittily** *adv.* **grittiness** *n.* [OE *grēot* f. Gmc: cf. GRITS, GROATS]

■ *n.* **3** pluck, courage, courageousness, valor, bravery, fortitude, endurance, resolution, resoluteness, resolve, toughness, mettle, spirit, backbone, nerve, gameness, intrepidity, dauntlessness, tenacity, determination, firmness, hardiness, staunchness, stalwartness, fearlessness, *archaic or joc.* doughtiness, *colloq.* guts, gutsiness, spunk, spunkiness, *sl.* moxie, *Brit.* bottle. □□ **gritty** sandy, gravelly, granular, grainy; rough, abrasive, rasping; courageous, valorous, brave, resolute, tough, mettlesome, plucky, spirited, game, intrepid, dauntless, tenacious, determined, persistent, firm, hardy, staunch, stalwart, fearless, *archaic or joc.* doughty, *colloq.* gutsy, spunky.

grits /grits/ *n.pl.* **1** coarsely ground hulled grain, esp. hominy prepared by boiling, then sometimes frying. **2** *Brit.* oats that have been husked but not ground. [OE *grytt(e)*: cf. GRIT, GROATS]

grizzle /grízəl/ *v.intr. Brit. colloq.* **1** (esp. of a child) cry fretfully. **2** complain whiningly. □□ **grizzler** *n.* **grizzly** *adj.* [19th c.: orig. unkn.]

grizzled /grízəld/ *adj.* having, or streaked with, gray hair. [*grizzle* gray f. OF *grisel* f. *gris* gray]

grizzly /grízlee/ *adj. & n.* ● *adj.* (**grizzlier, grizzliest**) gray, grayish, gray-haired. ● *n.* (*pl.* **-ies**) (in full **grizzly bear**) a large variety of brown bear found in N. America.

groan /grōn/ *v. & n.* ● *v.* **1 a** *intr.* make a deep sound expressing pain, grief, or disapproval. **b** *tr.* utter with groans. **2** *intr.* complain inarticulately. **3** *intr.* (usu. foll. by *under, beneath, with*) be loaded or oppressed. ● *n.* the sound made in groaning. □ **groan inwardly** be distressed. □□ **groaner** *n.* **groaningly** *adv.* [OE *grānian* f. Gmc, rel. to GRIN]

■ *v.* **1** moan, sigh, wail, whimper, whine. **2** complain, grumble, moan, object, protest, *colloq.* gripe, grouse, bitch, yammer, *Brit. colloq.* whinge, *sl.* beef. **3** be weighed down, be loaded or overloaded, be bowed

down; be oppressed, be burdened or saddled or pressured or lumbered, be overwhelmed. ● *n.* moan, sigh, murmur, wail, whimper, whine.

groat /grōt/ *n. hist.* **1** a silver coin worth four old English pence. **2** *archaic* a small sum (*don't care a groat*). [ME f. MDu. *groot*, orig. = great, i.e., thick (penny): cf. GROSCHEN]

groats /grōts/ *n.pl.* hulled or crushed grain, esp. oats. [OE *grotan* (pl.): cf. *grot* fragment, *grēot* GRIT, *grytt* bran]

grocer /grósər/ *n.* a dealer in food and household provisions. [ME & AF *grosser*, orig. one who sells in the gross, f. OF *grossier* f. med.L *grossarius* (as GROSS)]

grocery /grósəree/ *n.* (*pl.* **-ies**) **1** a grocer's trade or store. **2** (in *pl.*) provisions, esp. food, sold by a grocer.

■ **2** see PROVISION *n.* 2.

grog /grog/ *n.* **1** a drink of liquor (orig. rum) and water. **2** *Austral. & NZ colloq.* alcoholic liquor, esp. beer. [said to be from "Old Grog," the reputed nickname (f. his GROGRAM cloak) of Admiral Vernon, who in 1740 first had diluted instead of neat rum served out to sailors]

groggy /grógee/ *adj.* (**groggier, groggiest**) incapable or unsteady from being dazed or semiconscious. □□ **groggily** *adv.* **grogginess** *n.*

■ unsteady, shaky, wobbly, weak, stupefied, dazed, stunned, dizzy, faint, reeling, punch-drunk, muddleheaded, addled, confused, bewildered, befuddled, muzzy, *colloq.* dopey, woozy.

grogram /grógrəm, grṓ-/ *n.* a coarse fabric of silk, mohair and wool, or a mixture of these. [F *gros grain* coarse grain (as GROSS, GRAIN)]

groin[1] /groyn/ *n. & v.* ● *n.* **1** the depression between the belly and the thigh. **2** *Archit.* **a** an edge formed by intersecting vaults. **b** an arch supporting a vault. ● *v.tr. Archit.* build with groins. [ME *grynde*, perh. f. OE *grynde* depression]

groin[2] /groyn/ *n.* (also **groyn**) a wooden framework or low broad wall built out from a shore to check erosion of a beach. [dial. *groin* snout f. OF *groign* f. LL *grunium* pig's snout]

grommet /grómit/ *n.* (also **grummet** /grúmit/) **1** a metal, plastic, or rubber eyelet placed in a hole to protect or insulate a rope or cable, etc., passed through it. **2** a tube passed through the eardrum in surgery to make a connection with the middle ear. [obs. F *grommette* f. *gourmer* to curb, of unkn. orig.]

gromwell /grómwəl/ *n.* any of various plants of the genus *Lithospermum*, with hard seeds formerly used in medicine. [ME f. OF *gromil*, prob. f. med.L *gruinum milium* (unrecorded) crane's millet]

groom /groom/ *n. & v.* ● *n.* **1** = BRIDEGROOM. **2** a person employed to take care of horses. **3** *Brit. Mil.* any of certain officers of the Royal Household. ● *v.tr.* **1 a** curry or tend (a horse). **b** give a neat appearance to (a person, etc.). **2** (of an ape or monkey, etc.) clean and comb the fur of (its fellow) with the fingers. **3** prepare or train (a person) for a particular purpose or activity (*was groomed for the top job*). [ME, orig. = boy: orig. unkn.]

■ *n.* **1** stableboy, stable girl, stableman, stable lad, *hist.* equerry, *Brit. hist.* ostler. ● *v.* **1** spruce up, dress, tidy up, neaten or smarten up, preen, primp, *colloq.* titivate; tend; curry. **2** see CLEAN *v.* 1. **3** fit, train, prepare, coach, tutor, brief, drill, prime, (get or make) ready, shape.

groove /groov/ *n. & v.* ● *n.* **1 a** a channel or hollow, esp. one made to guide motion or receive a corresponding ridge. **b** a spiral track cut in a phonograph record. **2** an established routine or habit, esp. a monotonous one. ● *v.* **1** *tr.* make a groove or grooves in. **2** *intr. sl.* **a** enjoy oneself. **b** (often foll. by *with*) make progress; get on well. ¶ Often with ref. to popular music or jazz; now largely disused in general contexts. □ **in the groove** *sl.* **1** doing or performing well. **2** fash-

---

ionable. [ME, = mine shaft, f. obs. Du. *groeve* furrow f. Gmc]

■ *n.* **1 a** slot, cut, track, channel, furrow, flute, glyph, gouge, *Anat., Biol.,* & *Geol.* stria, striation. **2** routine, habit, rut, grind, treadmill. ● *v.* **1** furrow, flute; see SCORE *v.* 3. **2 a** see *enjoy oneself.* □ **in the groove 2** see TRENDY *adj.*

groovy / gró͞ovee/ *adj.* (**groovier, grooviest**) **1** *sl.* or *joc.* fashionable and exciting; enjoyable; excellent. **2** of or like a groove. □□ **groovily** *adv.* **grooviness** *n.*

■ **1** see MARVELOUS 2.

grope /grōp/ *v. & n.* ● *v.* **1** *intr.* (usu. foll. by *for*) feel about or search blindly or uncertainly with the hands. **2** *intr.* (foll. by *for, after*) search mentally (*was groping for the answer*). **3** *tr.* feel (one's way) toward something. **4** *tr. sl.* fondle clumsily for sexual pleasure. ● *n.* the process or an instance of groping. □□ **groper** *n.* **gropingly** *adv.* [OE *grāpian* f. Gmc]

■ *v.* **1** fumble, feel about, *Austral.* & *NZ colloq.* fossick about *or* around; (*grope for*) search for, feel for, fish for. **2** (*grope for*) seek, look for, search for, hunt for, quest for, pursue, be after, try to find. **4** see FONDLE, MOLEST 2. ● *n.* feel, fumble, search; fumbling, searching. □□ **gropingly** with difficulty; uncertainly, hesitantly, tentatively.

groper /grōpər/ *n. esp. Austral.* & *NZ* = GROUPER. [var. of GROUPER]

grosbeak /grōsbeek/ *n.* any of various finches of the families Cardinalidae and Fringillidae, having stout conical bills and usu. brightly colored plumage. [F *grosbec* (as GROSS)]

groschen /grōshən/ *n.* **1** an Austrian coin and monetary unit, one hundredth of a schilling. **2** a German 10-pfennig piece. **3** *hist.* a small German silver coin. [G f. MHG *gros, grosse* f. med.L (*denarius*) *grossus* thick (penny): cf. GROAT]

grosgrain /grōgrayn/ *n.* a corded fabric of silk, rayon, etc. [F, = coarse grain (as GROSS, GRAIN)]

gros point /grō póynt, pwán/ *n.* cross-stitch embroidery on large-holed canvas. [F (as GROSS, POINT)]

gross /grōs/ *adj., v., & n.* ● *adj.* **1** overfed; bloated; repulsively fat. **2** (of a person, manners, or morals) noticeably coarse, unrefined, or indecent. **3** flagrant; conspicuously wrong (*gross negligence*). **4** total; without deductions; not net (*gross tonnage; gross income*). **5 a** luxuriant; rank. **b** thick; solid; dense. **6** (of the senses, etc.) dull; lacking sensitivity. **7** *sl.* repulsive; disgusting. ● *v.tr.* produce or earn as gross profit or income. ● *n.* (*pl.* same) an amount equal to twelve dozen, or 144, things. □ **by the gross** in large quantities; wholesale. **gross domestic product** the total value of goods produced and services provided in a country in one year. **gross national product** the gross domestic product plus the total of net income from abroad. **gross out** *sl.* disgust, esp. by repulsive or obscene behavior. **gross up** increase (a net amount) to its value before deductions. □□ **grossly** *adv.* **grossness** *n.* [ME f. OF *gros grosse* large f. LL *grossus*: (n.) f. F *grosse douzaine* large dozen]

■ *adj.* **1** overfed, bloated, fat, overweight, big, large, bulky, heavy; see also OBESE. **2** coarse, vulgar, crude, unsophisticated, uncultured, crass, indelicate, inappropriate, unseemly, improper, unrefined, bawdy, ribald, Rabelaisian, rude, offensive, obscene, indecent, lewd, dirty, smutty, earthy, pornographic, filthy. **3** outrageous, flagrant, glaring, blatant, monstrous; obvious, plain, manifest, evident. **4** total, entire, inclusive, overall, whole; pretax. **5 a** see LUXURIANT 2. **6** see DULL *adj.* 1. **7** disgusting, repulsive, repellent, revolting, nauseating, *sl.* yucky. ● *v.* produce, bring in, make; see also EARN 1. □ **gross out** see DISGUST *v.*

grot /grot/ *n. & adj. Brit. sl.* ● *n.* rubbish; junk. ● *adj.* dirty. [back-form. f. GROTTY]

grotesque /grōtésk/ *adj. & n.* ● *adj.* **1** comically or repulsively distorted; monstrous; unnatural. **2** incongruous; ludicrous; absurd. ● *n.* **1** a decorative form interweaving human and animal features. **2** a comically distorted figure or design. **3** *Printing* a family of sans serif typefaces. □□ **grotesquely** *adv.* **grotesqueness** *n.* **grotesquerie** /-téskəree/

n. [earlier *crotesque* f. F *crotesque* f. It. *grottesca* grotto-like (painting, etc.) fem. of *grottesco* (as GROTTO, -ESQUE)]

■ *adj.* **1** distorted, gnarled, misshapen, malformed, deformed, unnatural, freakish, monstrous, gruesome. **2** absurd, incongruous, ludicrous, ridiculous, farcical, preposterous, bizarre, weird, odd, fantastic, strange, queer, peculiar, curious, outlandish, offbeat, abnormal, aberrant, *colloq.* crazy, insane. ● *n.* **1, 2** gargoyle; caricature; cartoon.

grotto /grótō/ *n.* (*pl.* **-oes** or **-os**) **1** a small esp. picturesque cave. **2** an artificial ornamental cave, e.g., in a park or large garden. □□ **grottoed** *adj.* [It. *grotta* ult. f. L *crypta* f. Gk *kruptē* CRYPT]

■ see CAVE *n.* 1.

grotty /grótee/ *adj.* (**grottier, grottiest**) *Brit. sl.* unpleasant; dirty; shabby; unattractive. □□ **grottiness** *n.* [shortening of GROTESQUE + -Y¹]

grouch /growch/ *v. & n. colloq.* ● *v.intr.* grumble. ● *n.* **1** a discontented person. **2** a fit of grumbling or the sulks. **3** a cause of discontent. [var. of *grutch*: see GRUDGE]

■ *v.* see COMPLAIN 1. ● *n.* **1** see KILLJOY. **2** see SQUAWK *n.* 2.

grouchy /grówchee/ *adj.* (**grouchier, grouchiest**) *colloq.* discontented; grumpy. □□ **grouchily** *adv.* **grouchiness** *n.*

■ see DISGRUNTLED.

ground¹ /grownd/ *n. & v.* ● *n.* **1 a** the surface of the earth, esp. as contrasted with the air around it. **b** a part of this specified in some way (*low ground*). **2** the substance of the earth's surface; soil; earth (*stony ground; dug deep into the ground*). **3 a** a position, area, or distance on the earth's surface. **b** the extent of activity, etc., achieved or of a subject dealt with (*the book covers a lot of ground*). **4** (often in *pl.*) a foundation, motive, or reason (*there is ground for concern; there are grounds for believing; excused on the grounds of poor health*). **5** an area of a special kind or designated for special use (often in *comb.*: *fishing-grounds*). **6** (in *pl.*) an area of sometimes enclosed land attached to a house, etc. **7** an area or basis for consideration, agreement, etc. (*common ground; on firm ground*). **8 a** (in painting) the prepared surface giving the predominant color or tone. **b** (in embroidery, ceramics, etc.) the undecorated surface. **9** (in full **ground bass**) *Mus.* a short theme in the bass constantly repeated with the upper parts of the music varied. **10** (in *pl.*) solid particles, esp. of coffee, forming a residue. **11** *Electr.* the connection to the ground that completes an electrical circuit. **12** the bottom of the sea (*the ship touched ground*). **13** *Brit.* the floor of a room, etc. **14** a piece of wood fixed to a wall as a base for boards, plaster, or joinery. **15** (*attrib.*) **a** (of animals) living on or in the ground; (of fish) living at the bottom of water; (of plants) dwarfish or trailing. **b** relating to or concerned with the ground (*ground staff*). ● *v.* **1** *tr.* **a** refuse authority for (a pilot or an aircraft) to fly. **b** restrict (esp. a child) from certain activities, places, etc., esp. as a form of punishment. **2 a** *tr.* run (a ship) aground; strand. **b** *intr.* (of a ship) run aground. **3** *tr.* (foll. by *in*) instruct thoroughly (in a subject). **4** *tr.* (often as **grounded** *adj.*) (foll. by *on*) base (a principle, conclusion, etc.) on. **5** *tr. Electr.* connect to the ground. **6** *intr.* alight on the ground. **7** *tr.* place or lay (esp. weapons) on the ground. □ **break new** (or **fresh**) **ground** treat a subject previously not dealt with. **cut the ground from under a person's feet** anticipate and preempt a person's arguments, plans, etc. **down to the ground** *Brit. colloq.* thoroughly; in every respect. **fall to the ground** (of a plan, etc.) fail. **from the ground up** gradually and thoroughly; from top to bottom. **gain** (or **make**) **ground 1** advance steadily; make progress. **2** (foll. by *on*) catch (a person) up. **get in on the ground floor** become part of an enterprise in its early stages. **get off the ground** *colloq.* make a successful start. **give** (or **lose**) **ground 1** retreat; decline. **2** lose the advantage or one's position in an argument, contest, etc. **go to ground 1** (of a fox, etc.) enter its burrow, etc. **2** (of a person) become inaccessible for a prolonged period. **ground bait** bait thrown to the bottom of a fishing ground. **ground ball** (or **grounder**) *Baseball* a ball batted such that it bounces on the ground. **ground**

control the personnel directing the landing, etc., of aircraft or spacecraft. **ground cover** plants covering the surface of the soil, esp. low-growing spreading plants that inhibit the growth of weeds. **ground crew** mechanics who maintain and service aircraft. **ground floor** the floor of a building at ground level. **ground frost** frost on the surface of the ground or in the top layer of soil. **ground level 1** the level of the ground; the ground floor. **2** *Physics* = ground state. **ground plan 1** the plan of a building at ground level. **2** the general outline of a scheme. **ground rent** esp. *Brit.* rent for land leased for building. **ground rule** a basic principle. **ground speed** an aircraft's speed relative to the ground. **ground squirrel 1** a squirrellike rodent, e.g., a chipmunk, gopher, etc. **2** any squirrel of the genus *Spermophilus* living in burrows. **ground state** *Physics* the lowest energy state of an atom, etc. **ground stroke** *Tennis* a stroke played near the ground after the ball has bounced. **ground swell 1** a heavy sea caused by a distant or past storm or an earthquake. **2** = GROUNDSWELL **ground zero** the point on the ground under an exploding (usu. nuclear) bomb. **hold one's ground** not retreat or give way. **into the ground** beyond what is reasonable, necessary, or productive. **on the ground** at the point of production or operation; in practical conditions. **on one's own ground** on one's own territory or subject; on one's own terms. **thin on the ground** not numerous. **work** (or **run**, etc.) **oneself into the ground** *colloq.* work, etc., to the point of exhaustion. □□ **grounder** *n.* [OE *grund* f. Gmc]

■ *n.* **1 a** (dry) land, earth, (solid) ground, terra firma. **b** land, terrain, country, territory. **2** earth, soil, sod, loam, clay, mold, dirt. **3** position, area, distance, range, scope, compass, territory. **4** reason, justification, rationale, argument, cause, motive, excuse, foundation. **7** base, basis, foundation, footing, position. **10** (*grounds*) particles, dregs, lees, settlings, grouts; sediment, deposit. ● *v.* **3** instruct, teach, train, coach, tutor, inform, prepare, initiate. **4** establish, found, organize; see also BASE¹ *v.* 1. □ **break new** (or **fresh**) **ground** innovate, pioneer, blaze a trail. **fall to the ground** see FAIL *v.* 1, 2a. **gain** (or **make**) **ground 1** see ADVANCE *v.* 1, 2, PROGRESS *v.* 1. **get off the ground** see START *v.* 1, 2. **give** (or **lose**) **ground 1** see RETREAT *v.* 1a **2** see LOSE 4, 5, 8, 10. **go to ground** see HIDE¹ *v.* 2. **ground rule** see PRINCIPLE 1. **hold one's ground** stand firm, stand pat, *colloq.* stick to one's guns; see also PERSEVERE. **thin on the ground** rare, uncommon, few (and far between), hard to come by *or* find; see also SCANTY. **work oneself into the ground** see SLAVE *v.*

ground² *past* and *past part.* of GRIND.

groundage /grówndij/ *n. Brit.* duty levied on a ship entering a port or lying on a shore.

groundbreaking /grówndbrayking/ *adj.* innovative in character; pioneering (*groundbreaking techniques in electronic communication*).

grounder /grówndər/ *n. Baseball* = ground ball.

groundfish /grówndfish/ *n.* a fish, as cod, flounder, etc., that lives at the bottom of oceans, lakes, rivers, etc.

groundhog /grówndhawg, -hog/ *n.* **1** a woodchuck; a marmot. **2** *Brit.* = AARDVARK.

grounding /grównding/ *n.* basic training or instruction in a subject.
■ see BACKGROUND 3.

groundless /grówndlis/ *adj.* without motive or foundation. □□ **groundlessly** *adv.* **groundlessness** *n.* [OE *grundlēas* (as GROUND¹, -LESS)]
■ baseless, without foundation, unfounded, unsupported; suppositional, hypothetical, tenuous, flimsy, illusory, imaginary; unsound, unjustified, unjustifiable, unwarranted, uncalled-for, unreasoned, unreasonable; unmotivated.

groundling /grówndling/ *n.* **1 a** a creeping or dwarf plant. **b** an animal that lives near the ground, at the bottom of a lake, etc., esp. a groundfish. **2** a person on the ground as opposed to one in an aircraft. **3** a spectator or reader of inferior taste (with ref. to Shakesp. *Hamlet* III. ii. 11).

groundnut /grówndnut/ *n.* **1 a** a N. American wild bean. **b** its edible tuber. **2** = PEANUT.

groundsel /grówndsəl/ *n.* any composite plant of the genus *Senecio*, esp. *S. vulgaris*, used as a food for cage birds. [OE *grundeswylige, gundæswelgiæ* (perh. = pus absorber f. *gund* pus, with ref. to use for poultices)]

groundsheet /grówndsheet/ *n.* a waterproof sheet for spreading on the ground, esp. in or under a tent.

groundskeeper /grówndzkeepər, grównz-/ *n.* a person who maintains the grounds of a sizable property, as a golf course or park.

groundsman /grówndzmən/ *n. Brit.* (*pl.* **-men**) a person who maintains a sports field; a groundskeeper.

groundswell /grówndswel/ *n.* an increasingly forceful presence (esp. of public opinion).
■ **2** see WAVE *n.* 6a.

groundwater /grówndwáwtər, -wotər/ *n.* water found in soil or in pores, crevices, etc., in rock.

groundwork /grówndwərk/ *n.* **1** preliminary or basic work. **2** a foundation or basis.
■ **1** spadework, preparation(s), preliminaries. **2** base, underpinning(s), cornerstone; see also FOUNDATION 3, BASIS 1, 2.

group /groop/ *n. & v.* ● *n.* **1** a number of persons or things located close together, or considered or classed together. **2** (*attrib.*) concerning or done by a group (*a group photograph*; *group therapy*). **3** a number of people working together or sharing beliefs, e.g., part of a political party. **4** a number of commercial companies under common ownership. **5** an ensemble playing popular music. **6** a division of an air force or air fleet. **7** *Math.* a set of elements, together with an associative binary operation, which contains an inverse for each element and an identity element. **8** *Chem.* **a** a set of ions or radicals giving a characteristic qualitative reaction. **b** a set of elements having similar properties. **c** a combination of atoms having a recognizable identity in a number of compounds. ● *v.* **1** *tr. & intr.* form or be formed into a group. **2** *tr.* (often foll. by *with*) place in a group or groups. **3** *tr.* form (colors, figures, etc.) into a well-arranged and harmonious whole. **4** *tr.* classify. □ **group dynamics** *Psychol.* the field of social psychology concerned with the nature, development, and interactions of human groups. **group practice** a medical practice in which several doctors are associated. **group therapy** therapy in which patients with a similar condition are brought together to assist one another psychologically. **group velocity** the speed of travel of the energy of a wave or wave group. □□ **groupage** *n.* [F *groupe* f. It. *gruppo* f. Gmc, rel. to CROP]

■ *n.* **1** batch, set, grouping, classification, collection, assemblage, number, accumulation, conglomeration, agglomeration, assortment, series; assembly, gathering, congregation, company, crowd, body, *colloq.* bunch. **2** (*attrib.*) see JOINT *adj.* **3** alliance, union, association, organization, league, society, coterie, clique, set, band, circle, club, party, body, faction, team, corps, guild, troupe, unit, troop, platoon, squad, gang. **4** see TRUST *n.* 8c. **5** see BAND² *n.* 2. ● *v.* **1, 2** collect, assemble, gather; arrange, place, organize, order, bring *or* put together. **3** see ARRANGE 1. **4** classify, class, sort, bracket, rank, assort, categorize, catalog.

grouper /groopər/ *n.* any marine fish of the family Serranidae, with heavy body, big head, and wide mouth. [Port. *garupa*, prob. f. native name in S. America]

groupie /groopee/ *n. sl.* an ardent follower of touring pop groups, esp. a young woman seeking sexual relations with them.
■ see FOLLOWER.

/ . . . / **pronunciation**   ● **part of speech**
□ **phrases, idioms, and compounds**
□□ **derivatives**   ■ **synonym section**
cross-references appear in SMALL CAPITALS or *italics*

grouping /gróoping/ n. **1** a process or system of allocation to groups. **2** the formation or arrangement so produced.
■ **2** see ARRANGEMENT 1–3.

grouse[1] /grows/ n. (pl. same) **1** any of various game birds of the family Tetraonidae, with a plump body and feathered legs. **2** the flesh of a grouse used as food. [16th c.: orig. uncert.]

grouse[2] /grows/ v.intr. & n. colloq. ● v.intr. grumble or complain pettily. ● n. a complaint. □□ **grouser** n. [19th c.: orig. unkn.]
■ v. see COMPLAIN 1. ● n. see COMPLAINT 2.

grouse[3] /grows/ adj. Austral. sl. very good or excellent (extra grouse). [20th c.: orig. unkn.]

grout[1] /growt/ n. & v. ● n. a thin fluid mortar for filling gaps in tiling, etc. ● v.tr. provide or fill with grout. □□ **grouter** n. [perh. f. GROUT[2], but cf. F dial. grouter grout a wall]

grout[2] /growt/ n. Brit. sediment; dregs. [OE grūt, rel. to GRITS, GROATS]

grouter /grówtər/ n. Austral. sl. an unfair advantage. [20th c.: orig. uncert.]

grove /grōv/ n. a small wood or group of trees. [OE grāf, rel. to grǣfa brushwood]
■ see THICKET.

grovel /gróvəl/ v.intr. (**groveled, groveling**; also **grovelled, grovelling**) **1** behave obsequiously in seeking favor or forgiveness. **2** lie prone in abject humility. □□ **groveler** n. **groveling** adj. **grovelingly** adv. [back-form. f. obs. grovelling (adv.) f. gruf face down f. on grufe f. ON á grúfu, later taken as pres. part.]
■ **1** see TRUCKLE v. **2** see PROSTRATE v. 2. □□ **groveling** obsequious, fawning, toadying, sycophantish, sycophantic, subservient, slavish, servile, submissive, cringing, cowering, sniveling, scraping, abject, crawling, colloq. bootlicking.

grow /grō/ v. (past **grew** /grōo/; past part. **grown** /grōn/) **1** intr. increase in size, height, quantity, degree, or in any way regarded as measurable (e.g., authority or reputation) (often foll. by in: grew in stature). **2** intr. **a** develop or exist as a living plant or natural product. **b** develop in a specific way or direction (began to grow sideways). **c** germinate; sprout; spring up. **3** intr. be produced; come naturally into existence; arise. **4** intr. (as **grown** adj.) fully matured; adult. **5** intr. **a** become gradually (grow rich; grow less). **b** (foll. by to + infin.) come by degrees (grew to like it). **6** intr. (foll. by into) **a** become; having grown or developed (the acorn has grown into a tall oak; will grow into a fine athlete). **b** become large enough for or suited to (will grow into the coat; grew into her new job). **7** intr. (foll. by on) become gradually more favored by. **8** tr. **a** produce (plants, fruit, wood, etc.) by cultivation. **b** bring forth. **c** cause (a beard, etc.) to develop. **9** tr. (in passive; foll. by over, up) be covered with a growth. □ **growing pains 1** early difficulties in the development of an enterprise, etc. **2** neuralgic pain in children's legs due to fatigue, etc. **grown-up** adj. adult. ● n. an adult person. **grow out of 1** become too large to wear (a garment). **2** become too mature to retain (a childish habit, etc.). **3** be the result or development of. **grow together** coalesce. **grow up 1 a** advance to maturity. **b** (esp. in imper.) begin to behave sensibly. **2** (of a custom) arise; become common. □□ **growable** adj. [OE grōwan f. Gmc, rel. to GRASS, GREEN]
■ **1** develop, increase, enlarge, wax, swell, expand, extend, broaden, thicken, spread, lengthen, multiply, intensify. **2 a, b** develop; exist, live. **c** see SPRING v. 4. **3** develop, evolve, arise, spring (up), originate, begin, start; see also OCCUR 1. **4** (**grown**) see MATURE adj. 1. **5 a** become, get. **b** come, get; start, begin. **6 a** (grow into) see BECOME 1. **b** see ADAPT 2. **7** (grow on) become accepted by, become liked by, become more pleasing to, become more favored by. **8 a** plant, sow, cultivate; breed, nurture, raise, propagate, produce. **9** (be grown over) be overgrown, be covered. □ **grown-up** (adj.) see MATURE adj. 1. **grow out of 3** be the result of, result or develop from, stem from, go back to, date back to, originate in, be caused by, start with. **grow up 1 a** mature, reach maturity or adulthood, come of age,

reach the age of majority. **b** be sensible, behave, act one's age, stop acting like a child, stop being a baby. **2** see ARISE 1.

grower /gróər/ n. **1** (often in comb.) a person growing produce (fruit-grower). **2** a plant that grows in a specified way (a fast grower).

growl /growl/ v. & n. ● v. **1** intr. **a** (often foll. by at) (esp. of a dog) make a low guttural sound, usu. of anger. **b** murmur angrily. **2** intr. rumble. **3** tr. (often foll. by out) utter with a growl. ● n. **1** a growling sound, esp. made by a dog. **2** an angry murmur; complaint. **3** a rumble. □□ **growlingly** adv. [prob. imit.]
■ v. **1, 3** see ROAR v. 3.

growler /grówlər/ n. **1** a person or thing that growls, esp. sl. a dog. **2** a small iceberg.

grown past part. of GROW.

growth /grōth/ n. **1** the act or process of growing. **2** an increase in size or value. **3** something that has grown or is growing. **4** Med. a morbid formation. **5** the cultivation of produce. **6** a crop or yield of grapes. □ **full growth** the size ultimately attained; maturity. **growth hormone** Biol. a substance which stimulates the growth of a plant or animal. **growth industry** an industry that is developing rapidly. **growth stock,** etc., stock, etc., that tends to increase in capital value rather than yield high income.
■ **1** development, evolution, evolvement; increase, expansion, broadening, extension, enlargement, spread, proliferation, flowering. **2** advance, advancement, increase, appreciation, improvement, expansion, rise, progress. **3** vegetation; see SPREAD n. 1. **4** excrescence, lump, tumor, swelling. **5** cultivation, culture, growing, farming. **6** crop, yield, harvest. □ **full growth** see maturity (MATURE).

groyne var. of GROIN[2].

grub /grub/ n. & v. ● n. **1** the larva of an insect, esp. of a beetle. **2** colloq. food. **3** a menial; a drudge. ● v. (**grubbed, grubbing**) **1** tr. & intr. dig superficially. **2** tr. **a** clear (the ground) of roots and stumps. **b** clear away (roots, etc.). **3** tr. (foll. by up, out) **a** fetch by digging (grubbing up weeds). **b** extract (information, etc.) by searching in books, etc. **4** intr. search; rummage. **5** intr. (foll. by on, along, away) toil; plod. □□ **grubber** n. (also in comb.). [ME, (v.) perh. corresp. to OE grybban (unrecorded) f. Gmc]
■ n. **2** see FOOD 1. ● v. **5** see PLOD v. 2.

grubby /grúbee/ adj. (**grubbier, grubbiest**) **1** dirty; grimy; slovenly. **2** of or infested with grubs. □□ **grubbily** adv. **grubbiness** n.

grubstake /grúbstayk/ n. & v. ● n. material or provisions supplied to an enterprise in return for a share in the resulting profits (orig. in prospecting for ore). ● v.tr. provide with a grubstake. □□ **grubstaker** n.

Grub Street /grub/ n. (often attrib.) the world or class of literary hacks and impoverished authors. [name of a street (later Milton St.) in Moorgate, London, inhabited by these in the 17th c.]

grudge /gruj/ n. & v. ● n. a persistent feeling of ill will or resentment, esp. one due to an insult or injury (bears a grudge against me). ● v.tr. **1** be resentfully unwilling to give, grant, or allow (a thing). **2** (foll. by verbal noun or to + infin.) be reluctant to do (a thing) (grudged paying so much). □□ **grudger** n. [ME grutch f. OF grouchier murmur, of unkn. orig.]
■ n. bitterness, resentment, rancor, ill will, hard feelings, pique, dislike, antipathy, animosity, enmity, malice, malevolence; grievance, aversion, animus. ● v. **1, 2** see BEGRUDGE 1, 2, MIND v. 1.

grudging /grújing/ adj. reluctant; not willing. □□ **grudgingly** adv. **grudgingness** n.

gruel /gróoəl/ n. a liquid food of oatmeal, etc., boiled in milk or water chiefly for invalids. [ME f. OF, ult. f. Gmc, rel. to GROUT[1]]

grueling /gróoling/ adj. & n. (also **gruelling**) ● adj. extremely demanding, severe, or tiring. ● n. a harsh or exhausting experience; punishment. □□ **gruelingly** adv. [GRUEL as verb, = exhaust, punish]

■ *adj.* see ARDUOUS.

gruesome /grōosəm/ *adj.* horrible; grisly; disgusting. □□ **gruesomely** *adv.* **gruesomeness** *n.* [Sc. *grue* to shudder f. Scand. + -SOME[1]]

■ ghastly, repugnant, horrible, horrid, horrific, horrendous, grisly, hideous, revolting, disgusting, repellent, repulsive, loathsome, grim, grotesque, macabre, frightful, fearsome, shocking, terrible, *colloq.* awful.

gruff /gruf/ *adj.* **1 a** (of a voice) low and harsh. **b** (of a person) having a gruff voice. **2** surly; laconic; rough-mannered. □□ **gruffly** *adv.* **gruffness** *n.* [Du., MLG *grof* coarse f. WG (rel. to ROUGH)]

■ **1 a** low, throaty, harsh, rough, guttural, rasping, hoarse, husky, deep. **2** laconic, terse, rough-mannered, surly, crusty, grumpy, curmudgeonly, cantankerous, churlish, rude, uncivil, bearish, testy, irritable, cross, irascible, bluff, abrupt, curt, blunt, brusque, short, short-tempered, bad-tempered, crabbed, sullen, sulky, ill-humored, *colloq.* grouchy, crotchety.

grumble /grúmbəl/ *v. & n.* ● *v.* **1** *intr.* **a** (often foll. by *at, about, over*) complain peevishly. **b** be discontented. **2** *intr.* **a** utter a dull inarticulate sound; murmur; growl faintly. **b** rumble. **3** *tr.* (often foll. by *out*) utter complainingly. **4** *intr.* (as **grumbling** *adj.*) *colloq.* giving intermittent discomfort without causing illness (*a grumbling appendix*). ● *n.* **1 a** complaint. **2 a** a dull inarticulate sound; a murmur. **b** a rumble. □□ **grumbler** *n.* **grumbling** *adj.* **grumblingly** *adv.* **grumbly** *adj.* [obs. *grumme*: cf. MDu. *grommen*, MLG *grommelen*, f. Gmc]

■ *v.* **1, 3** see COMPLAIN 1. ● *n.* **1** see COMPLAINT 2.

grummet var. of GROMMET.

grump /grump/ *n. colloq.* **1** a grumpy person. **2** (in *pl.*) a fit of sulks. □□ **grumpish** *adj.* **grumpishly** *adv.* [imit.]

■ **1** see KILLJOY.

grumpy /grúmpee/ *adj.* (**grumpier, grumpiest**) morosely irritable; surly. □□ **grumpily** *adv.* **grumpiness** *n.*

■ see SURLY.

Grundy /grúndee/ *n.* (*pl.* **-ies**) (in full **Mrs. Grundy**) a person embodying conventional propriety and prudery. □□ **Grundyism** *n.* [a person repeatedly mentioned in T. Morton's comedy *Speed the Plough* (1798)]

grunge /grunj/ *n. sl.* **1** grime; dirt. **2** an aggressive style of rock music characterized by a raucous guitar sound. **3** a style of youthful clothing and appearance marked by studied dishevelment. □□ **grungy** *adj.* [app. after GRUBBY, DINGY, etc.]

grunion /grúnyən/ *n.* a slender Californian marine fish, *Leuresthes tenuis*, that comes ashore to spawn. [prob. f. Sp. *gruñón* grunter]

grunt /grunt/ *n. & v.* ● *n.* **1** a low guttural sound made by a pig. **2** a sound resembling this. **3** any fish of the genus *Haemulon* that grunts when caught. ● *v.* **1** *intr.* (of a pig) make a grunt or grunts. **2** *intr.* (of a person) make a low inarticulate sound resembling this, esp. to express discontent, dissent, fatigue, etc. **3** *tr.* utter with a grunt. [OE *grunnettan*, prob. orig. imit.]

grunter /grúntər/ *n.* **1** a person or animal that grunts, esp. a pig. **2** a grunting fish, esp. = GRUNT *n.* 3.

Grunth var. of GRANTH.

Gruyère /grōō-yáir, gree-/ *n.* a firm pale cheese made from cow's milk. [*Gruyère*, a district in Switzerland where it was first made]

gr. wt. *abbr.* gross weight.

gryphon var. of GRIFFIN.

grysbok /grísbok/ *n.* any small antelope of the genus *Raphicerus*, native to S. Africa. [S.Afr. Du. f. Du. *grijs* gray + *bok* BUCK[1]]

GSA *abbr.* **1** General Services Administration. **2** Girl Scouts of America.

G-string /jeestring/ *n.* **1** *Mus.* a string sounding the note G. **2** (also **gee-string**) a narrow strip of cloth, etc., covering only the genitals and attached to a string around the waist, as worn esp. by striptease artists.

G suit /jeesōot/ *n.* a garment with inflatable pressurized pouches, worn by pilots and astronauts to enable them to withstand high acceleration. [*g* = gravity + SUIT]

GT *n.* a high-performance two-door automobile. [abbr. f. It. *gran turismo* great touring]

Gt. *abbr.* Great.

Gt. Brit. *abbr.* Great Britain.

guacamole /gwaákəmólee/ *n.* a dish of mashed avocado mixed with chopped onion, tomatoes, chili peppers, and seasoning. [Amer. Sp. f. Nahuatl *ahuacamolli* f. *ahuacatl* avocado + *molli* sauce]

guacharo /gwaáchərō/ *n.* (*pl.* **-os**) a nocturnal bird, *Steatornis caripensis*, native to S. America and feeding on fruit. Also called OILBIRD. [S.Amer. Sp.]

guaiac var. of GUAIACUM 2.

guaiacum /gwíakəm/ *n.* **1** any tree of the genus *Guaiacum*, native to tropical America. **2** (also **guaiac** /gwíak/) **a** the hard dense oily timber of some of these, esp. *G. officinale*. Also called LIGNUM VITAE. **b** the resin from this used medicinally. [mod.L f. Sp. *guayaco* of Haitian orig.]

guan /gwaan/ *n.* any of various game birds of the family Cracidae, of tropical America. [prob. f. a native name]

guanaco /gwənaákō/ *n.* (*pl.* **-os**) a llamalike camelid, *Lama guanicoe*, with a coat of soft pale brown hair used for wool. [Quechua *huanaco*]

guanine /gwáaneen/ *n. Biochem.* a purine derivative found in all living organisms as a component base of DNA and RNA. [GUANO + -INE[4]]

guano /gwaánō/ *n. & v.* (*pl.* **-os**) ● *n.* **1** the excrement of sea birds, used as manure. **2** an artificial manure, esp. that made from fish. ● *v.tr.* (**-oes, -oed**) fertilize with guano. [Sp. f. Quechua *huanu* dung]

■ **1** see DUNG *n.*

Guarani /gwaárənee/ *n.* **1 a** a member of a S. American Indian people. **b** the language of this people. **2** (**guarani**) the monetary unit of Paraguay. [Sp.]

guarantee /gárəntee/ *n. & v.* ● *n.* **1 a** a formal promise or assurance, esp. that an obligation will be fulfilled or that something is of a specified quality and durability. **b** a document giving such an undertaking. **2** = GUARANTY. **3** a person making a guaranty or giving a security. ● *v.tr.* (**guarantees, guaranteed**) **1 a** give or serve as a guarantee for; answer for the due fulfillment of (a contract, etc.) or the genuineness of (an article). **b** assure the permanence, etc., of. **c** provide with a guarantee. **2** (foll. by *that* + clause, or *to* + infin.) give a promise or assurance. **3 a** (foll. by *to*) secure the possession of (a thing) for a person. **b** make a (person) secure against a risk or in possession of a thing. [earlier *garante*, perh. f. Sp. *garante* = F *garant* WARRANT: later infl. by F *garantie* guaranty]

■ *n.* **1, 2** promise, assurance, word (of honor), oath, undertaking, pledge; guaranty, warranty, bond, security. **3** guarantor, assurer, insurer, warranter. ● *v.* **1** vouch for, answer for, stand behind, attest to; ensure, certify. **2** pledge, promise, undertake, make sure *or* certain, swear, attest. **3 a** see SECURE *v.* 3.

guarantor /gárəntáwr, -tər/ *n.* a person who gives a guarantee or guaranty.

guaranty /gárəntee/ *n.* (*pl.* **-ies**) **1** a written or other undertaking to answer for the payment of a debt or for the performance of an obligation by another person liable in the first instance. **2** a thing serving as security for a guaranty. [AF *guarantie*, var. of *warantie* WARRANTY]

guard /gaard/ *v. & n.* ● *v.* **1** *tr.* (often foll. by *from, against*) watch over and defend or protect from harm. **2** *tr.* keep watch by (a door, etc.) so as to control entry or exit. **3** *tr.* supervise (prisoners, etc.) and prevent from escaping. **4** *tr.* provide (machinery) with a protective device. **5** *tr.* keep (thoughts or speech) in check. **6** *tr.* provide with safeguards. **7** *intr.* (foll. by *against*) take precautions. **8** *tr.* (in various

/ . . . / **pronunciation** ● **part of speech**
□ **phrases, idioms, and compounds**
□□ **derivatives** ■ **synonym section**
cross-references appear in SMALL CAPITALS or *italics*

games) protect (a piece, card, etc.) with set moves. ● *n.* **1** a state of vigilance or watchfulness. **2** a person who protects or keeps watch. **3** a body of soldiers, etc. serving to protect a place or person; an escort. **4** a person who keeps watch over prisoners. **5** a part of an army detached for some purpose (*advance guard*). **6** (in *pl.*) (usu. **Guards**) any of various bodies of troops nominally employed to guard a ruler. **7** a thing that protects or defends. **8** (often in *comb.*) a device fitted to a machine, vehicle, weapon, etc., to prevent injury or accident to the user (*fire guard*). **9** *Brit.* an official who rides with and is in general charge of a train. **10** in some sports: **a** a protective or defensive player. **b** a defensive posture or motion. □ **be on** (or **keep** or **stand**) **guard** (of a sentry, etc.) keep watch. **guard cell** *Bot.* either of a pair of cells surrounding the stomata in plants. **lower one's guard** reduce vigilance against attack. **off** (or **off one's**) **guard** unprepared for some surprise or difficulty. **on** (or **on one's**) **guard** prepared for all contingencies; vigilant. **raise one's guard** become vigilant against attack. □□ **guarder** *n.* **guardless** *adj.* [ME f. OF *garde, garder* ult. f. WG, rel. to WARD *n.*]

■ *v.* **1** protect, shield, defend; safeguard, watch over, look after, tend, mind, supervise. **2** see WATCH *v.* 2a, 4. **3** see SUPERVISE. **5** see CONTROL *v.* 3. **7** see PREPARE 1. **8** see DEFEND 1. ● *n.* **1** watch, alert, vigil, lookout. **2** sentinel, watchman, sentry, security guard, *hist.* watch; custodian, guardian, protector; bodyguard, esp. *Brit. sl.* minder. **3** convoy, patrol; see also ESCORT *n.* 1. **4** turnkey, *Brit.* warder, wardress, *sl.* screw; see also JAILER. **5** see SQUAD. **7** defense, protection, safeguard, shield, screen, cover. **10 a** back, defender; *collect.* defense; see also BACK *n.* 4. □ **be on** (or **keep** or **stand**) **guard** see PATROL *v.* 2, WATCH *v.* 3. **lower one's guard** relax, lower one's defenses; see also *let up* 2 (LET¹). **off** (or **off one's**) **guard** see UNPREPARED. **on** (or **on one's**) **guard** see VIGILANT. **raise one's guard** raise *or* put up one's defenses.

guardant /gaárd'nt/ *adj. Heraldry* depicted with the body sideways and the face toward the viewer.

guarded /gaárdid/ *adj.* (of a remark, etc.) cautious; avoiding commitment. □□ **guardedly** *adv.* **guardedness** *n.*

■ careful, cautious, prudent, circumspect, wary, mindful, restrained, reticent, leery; noncommittal, *colloq.* cagey.

guardhouse /gaárdhows/ *n.* a building used to accommodate a military guard or to temporarily detain military prisoners.

■ see PRISON *n.* 1.

guardian /gaárdeeən/ *n.* **1** a defender, protector, or keeper. **2** a person having legal custody of another person and his or her property when that person is incapable of managing his or her own affairs. **3** the superior of a Franciscan convent. □ **guardian angel** a spirit conceived as watching over a person or place. □□ **guardianship** *n.* [ME f. AF *gardein,* OF *garden* f. Frank., rel. to WARD, WARDEN]

■ **1, 2** protector, defender, preserver, custodian, keeper, ward; trustee. □ **guardian angel** see PROTECTOR. □□ **guardianship** see CARE *n.* 4a.

guardrail /gaárdrayl/ *n.* a rail, e.g., a handrail, fitted as a support or to prevent an accident.

■ see RAIL¹ *n.* 1.

guardroom /gaárdroom, -room/ *n.* a room with the same purpose as a guardhouse.

guardsman /gaárdzmən/ *n.* (*pl.* **-men**) **1** a soldier belonging to a body of guards. **2** (in the UK) a soldier of a regiment of Guards.

guava /gwaávə/ *n.* **1** a small tropical American tree, *Psidium guajava,* bearing an edible pale yellow fruit with pink juicy flesh. **2** this fruit. [Sp. *guayaba* prob. f. a S. Amer. name]

guayule /gwiyoolee/ *n.* **1** a silver-leaved shrub, *Parthenium argentatum,* native to Mexico. **2** a rubber substitute made from the sap of this plant. [Amer. Sp. f. Nahuatl *cuauhuli*]

gubbins /gúbinz/ *n. Brit.* **1** a set of equipment or paraphernalia. **2** a gadget. **3** something of little value. **4** *colloq.* a foolish person (often with ref. to oneself). [orig. = fragments, f. obs. *gobbon*: perh. rel. to GOBBET]

gubernatorial /gŏoobərnətáwreeəl, gyŏo-/ *adj.* of or relating to a governor. [L *gubernator* governor]

gudgeon¹ /gújən/ *n.* **1** a small European freshwater fish, *Gobio gobio,* often used as bait. **2** a credulous or easily fooled person. [ME f. OF *goujon* f. L *gobio -onis* GOBY]

gudgeon² /gújən/ *n.* **1** any of various kinds of pivot working a wheel, bell, etc. **2** the tubular part of a hinge into which the pin fits to effect the joint. **3** a socket at the stern of a boat, into which a rudder is fitted. **4** a pin holding two blocks of stone, etc., together. □ **gudgeon pin** *Brit.* (in an internal combustion engine) a pin holding a piston rod and a connecting rod together; wrist pin. [ME f. OF *goujon* dimin. of *gouge* GOUGE]

guelder rose /géldər/ *n.* a deciduous shrub, *Viburnum opulus,* with round bunches of creamy white flowers. Also called *snowball bush.* [Du. *geldersch* f. *Gelderland* a province in the Netherlands]

guenon /gənón/ *n.* any African monkey of the genus *Cercopithecus,* having a characteristic long tail, e.g., the vervet. [F: orig. unkn.]

guerdon /gə́rdən/ *n. & v. poet.* ● *n.* a reward or recompense. ● *v.tr.* give a reward to. [ME f. OF *guerdon* f. med.L *widerdonum* f. WG *widarlōn* (as WITH, LOAN¹), assim. to L *donum* gift]

Guernsey /gə́rnzee/ *n.* (*pl.* **-eys**) **1 a** an animal of a breed of dairy cattle from Guernsey in the Channel Islands. **b** this breed. **2** (**guernsey**) **a** a thick (usu. blue) woolen sweater of a distinctive pattern. **b** *Austral.* a soccer or football shirt. □ **get a guernsey** *Austral. colloq.* **1** be selected for a soccer or football team. **2** gain recognition. **guernsey lily** a kind of nerine orig. from S. Africa, with large pink lilylike flowers.

guerrilla /gəríllə/ *n.* (also **guerilla**) a member of a small independently acting (usu. political) group taking part in irregular fighting, esp. against larger regular forces. □ **guerrilla war** (or **warfare**) fighting by or with guerrillas. [Sp. *guerrilla,* dimin. of *guerra* war]

■ partisan, freedom fighter, resistance *or* underground fighter, irregular; insurgent, revolutionary, saboteur, terrorist. □ **guerrilla war** (or **warfare**) terrorism, bush warfare, insurgency, freedom fighting.

guess /ges/ *v. & n.* ● *v.* **1** *tr.* (often *absol.*) estimate without calculation or measurement, or on the basis of inadequate data. **2** *tr.* (often foll. by *that,* etc. + clause, or *to* + infin.) form a hypothesis or opinion about; conjecture; think likely (*cannot guess how you did it*). **3** *tr.* conjecture or estimate correctly by guessing (*you have to guess the weight*). **4** *intr.* (foll. by *at*) make a conjecture about. ● *n.* an estimate or conjecture reached by guessing. □ **anybody's** (or **anyone's**) **guess** something very vague or difficult to determine. **I guess** *colloq.* I think it likely; I suppose. **keep a person guessing** *colloq.* withhold information. □□ **guessable** *adj.* **guesser** *n.* [ME *gesse,* of uncert. orig.: cf. OSw. *gissa,* MLG, MDu. *gissen*: f. the root of GET *v.*]

■ *v.* **1, 4** estimate, make a guess (at), *colloq.* make a stab (at). **2** conjecture, surmise, infer, deduce, conclude, judge, suppose, assume; believe, reckon, think, fancy, feel, suspect, divine, *formal* deem; hypothesize, speculate. ● *n.* estimate, assumption, supposition, judgment, feeling, suspicion, conjecture, speculation, surmise, shot in the dark, *colloq.* guesstimate. □ **anybody's** (or **anyone's**) **guess** poser, problem, moot point *or* issue, tricky one. **keep a person guessing** keep a person in the dark, not tell, not let on to.

guess-rope var. of GUEST-ROPE.

guesstimate /géstimət/ *n.* (also **guestimate**) *colloq.* an estimate based on a mixture of guesswork and calculation. [GUESS + ESTIMATE]

guesswork /géswərk/ *n.* the process of or results got by guessing.

guest /gest/ *n. & v.* ● *n.* **1** a person invited to visit another's house or have a meal, etc., at the expense of the inviter. **2** a person lodging at a hotel, boarding house, etc. **3 a** an outside performer invited to take part with a regular body of performers. **b** a person who takes part by invitation in a radio or television program (often *attrib.*: *guest artist*). **4** (*attrib.*) **a** serving or set aside for guests (*guest room*). **b** acting as a guest (*guest speaker*). **5** an organism living in close association with another. ● *v.intr.* be a guest on a radio or television show or in a theatrical performance, etc. □ **be my guest** *colloq.* make what use you wish of the available facilities. **guest of honor** the most important guest at an occasion. □□ **guestship** *n.* [ME f. ON *gestr* f. Gmc]

■ *n.* **1** visitor, caller; (*guests*) company. **2** patron, customer, lodger, boarder, roomer. **3b, 4b** (*attrib.*) visiting; outside, external.

guesthouse /gésthows/ *n.* a private house offering paid accommodation.

guest-rope /géstrōp, gésrōp/ *n.* (also **guess-rope**) **1** a second rope fastened to a boat in tow to steady it. **2** a rope slung outside a ship to give a hold for boats coming alongside. [17th c.: orig. uncert.]

guff /guf/ *n. sl.* empty talk; nonsense. [19th c., orig. = 'puff': imit.]

■ see MOONSHINE 1.

guffaw /gufáw/ *n. & v.* ● *n.* a loud or boisterous laugh. ● *v.* **1** *intr.* utter a guffaw. **2** *tr.* say with a guffaw. [orig. Sc.: imit.]

■ *n.* see LAUGH *n.* 1. ● *v.* see LAUGH *v.* 1.

guidance /gíd'ns/ *n.* **1** advice or information aimed at resolving a problem, difficulty, etc. **b** leadership or direction. **2** the process of guiding or being guided.

■ **1 a** advice, information, counsel, instruction, teaching, briefing. **b** leadership, direction, management, government, conduct, control, regulation, charge, handling, rule, auspices. **2** counseling, edification, preparation, guiding; see also INSTRUCTION 2.

guide /gīd/ *n. & v.* ● *n.* **1** a person who leads or shows the way, or directs the movements of a person or group. **2** a person who conducts travelers on tours, etc. **3** a professional mountain climber in charge of a group. **4** an adviser. **5** a directing principle or standard (*one's feelings are a bad guide*). **6** a book with essential information on a subject, esp. = GUIDEBOOK. **7** a thing marking a position or guiding the eye. **8** a soldier, vehicle, or ship whose position determines the movements of others. **9** *Mech.* **a** a bar, rod, etc., directing the motion of something. **b** a gauge, etc., controlling a tool. **10** (**Guide**) *Brit.* a member of an organization similar to the Girl Scouts. ● *v.tr.* **1 a** act as guide to; lead or direct. **b** arrange the course of (events). **2** be the principle, motive, or ground of (an action, judgment, etc.). **3** direct the affairs of (a government, etc.). □ **guided missile** a missile directed to its target by remote control or by equipment within itself. **guide dog** a dog trained to guide a blind person. **guide rope** a rope guiding the movement of a crane, airship, etc. **Queen's** (or **King's**) **Guide** *Brit.* a Guide (sense 10) who has reached the highest rank of proficiency. □□ **guidable** *adj.* **guider** *n.* [ME f. OF *guide* (n.), *guider* (v.), earlier *guier* ult. f. Gmc, rel. to WIT²]

■ *n.* **1–3** leader, conductor, director, guider, chaperon; cicerone. **4** adviser, mentor, counselor, guru, master, teacher. **5** principle, standard, model, criterion, exemplar, ideal, lodestar, inspiration. **6** guidebook, handbook, manual, vade mecum, *formal* enchiridion; Baedeker. **7** beacon, light, lodestar, guiding light, signal, sign, landmark, marker, indicator, signpost. ● *v.* **1, 3** lead, conduct, shepherd, direct, usher, steer, maneuver, pilot, channel, navigate; instruct, show, teach, tutor, train, counsel, advise; supervise, oversee, handle, manage, superintend, direct, control, regulate, govern. **2** steer, instruct, influence, sway, govern; see also MOTIVATE.

guidebook /gídbŏŏk/ *n.* a book of information about a place for visitors, tourists, etc.

guideline /gídlīn/ *n.* a principle or criterion guiding or directing action.

■ see STANDARD *n.* 1, 8.

guidepost /gídpōst/ *n.* = SIGNPOST.

guideway /gídway/ *n.* a groove or track that guides movement.

guidon /gíd'n/ *n.* **1** a pennant narrowing to a point or fork at

the free end, esp. one used as the standard of a military unit. **2** the soldier who carries it. [F f. It. *guidone* f. *guida* GUIDE]

guild /gild/ *n.* (also **gild**) **1** an association of people for mutual aid or the pursuit of a common goal. **2** a medieval association of craftsmen or merchants. [ME prob. f. MLG, MDu. *gilde* f. Gmc: rel. to OE *gild* payment, sacrifice]

■ see ASSOCIATION 1.

guilder /gíldər/ *n.* **1** the chief monetary unit of the Netherlands. **2** *hist.* a gold coin of the Netherlands and Germany. [ME, alt. of Du. *gulden*: see GULDEN]

guildhall /gíldhawl/ *n.* **1** the meeting place of a guild or corporation; (*Brit.*) a town hall. **2** (**the Guildhall**) the hall of the Corporation of the City of London, used for ceremonial occasions.

guildsman /gíldzmən/ *n.* (*pl.* **-men**; *fem.* **guildswoman**, *pl.* **-women**) a member of a guild.

guile /gīl/ *n.* treachery; deceit; cunning or sly behavior. □□ **guileful** *adj.* **guilefully** *adv.* **guilefulness** *n.* **guileless** *adj.* **guilelessly** *adv.* **guilelessness** *n.* [ME f. OF, prob. f. Gmc]

■ see DECEIT 1.

guillemot /gíləmot/ *n.* any fast-flying sea bird of the genus *Uria* or *Cepphus*, nesting on cliffs or islands. [F f. *Guillaume* William]

guilloche /gilósh, geeyósh/ *n.* an architectural or metalwork ornament imitating braided ribbons. [F *guillochis* (or *guilloche* the tool used)]

guillotine /gíləteen, gee'ə-/ *n. & v.* ● *n.* **1** a machine with a heavy knife blade dropping vertically in grooves, used for beheading. **2** a device for cutting paper, metal, etc. **3** a surgical instrument for excising the uvula, etc. **4** *Brit. Parl.* a method of preventing delay in the discussion of a legislative bill by fixing times at which various parts of it must be voted on. ● *v.tr.* **1** use a guillotine on. **2** *Brit. Parl.* end discussion of (a bill) by applying a guillotine. □□ **guillotiner** *n.* [F f. J.-I. *Guillotin*, Fr. physician d. 1814, who recommended its use for executions in 1789]

guilt /gilt/ *n.* **1** the fact of having committed a specified or implied offense. **2 a** culpability. **b** the feeling of this. □ **guilt complex** *Psychol.* a mental obsession with the idea of having done wrong. [OE *gylt*, of unkn. orig.]

■ **1** sinfulness, feloniousness, wrongdoing, criminality, misconduct. **2 a** culpability, guiltiness, blameworthiness, blame; responsibility. **b** remorse, self-reproach, regret, sorrow, contrition, penitence, repentance, shame, contriteness, self-condemnation.

guiltless /gíltlis/ *adj.* **1** (often foll. by *of*) innocent. **2** (foll. by *of*) not having knowledge or possession of. □□ **guiltlessly** *adv.* **guiltlessness** *n.* [OE *gyltlēas* (as GUILT, -LESS)]

■ **1** see INNOCENT *adj.* 2.

guilty /gíltee/ *adj.* (**guiltier, guiltiest**) **1** culpable of or responsible for a wrong. **2** conscious of or affected by guilt (*a guilty conscience*; *a guilty look*). **3** concerning guilt (*a guilty secret*). **4 a** (often foll. by *of*) having committed a (specified) offense. **b** *Law* adjudged to have committed a specified offense, esp. by a verdict in a trial. □□ **guiltily** *adv.* **guiltiness** *n.* [OE *gyltig* (as GUILT, -Y¹)]

■ **1, 4** culpable, blameworthy; responsible, answerable; at fault. **2** guilt-ridden, shamefaced, sheepish, red-faced; remorseful, contrite, regretful, repentant, sorrowful, conscience-stricken, rueful, penitent, sorry, ashamed. **3** see SORDID 2.

guimp var. of GIMP¹.

guinea /gínee/ *n.* **1** *Brit. hist.* the sum of 21 old shillings, used esp. in determining professional fees. **2** *hist.* a former British gold coin worth 21 shillings, first coined for the African trade. □ **guinea fowl** any African fowl of the family Numididae, esp. *Numida meleagris*, with slate-colored white-spotted plumage. **guinea pig 1** a domesticated S. American

/ . . . / **pronunciation** ● **part of speech**
□ **phrases, idioms, and compounds**
□□ **derivatives** ■ **synonym section**
cross-references appear in SMALL CAPITALS or *italics*

cavy, *Cavia porcellus*, kept as a pet or for research in biology, etc. **2** a person or thing used as a subject for experiment. [*Guinea* in W. Africa]

guipure /gipyŏŏr/ *n.* a heavy lace of linen pieces joined by embroidery. [F f. *guiper* cover with silk, etc., f. Gmc]

guise /gīz/ *n.* **1** an assumed appearance; a pretense (*in the guise of*; *under the guise of*). **2** external appearance. **3** *archaic* style of attire; garb. [ME f. OF ult. f. Gmc]

■ **1** disguise, pretense, cloak, cover; see also MASK *n.* 4. **2** appearance, aspect, semblance, façade, front, look, image, likeness. **3** see DRESS *n.* 2.

guitar /gitaar/ *n.* a usu. six-stringed musical instrument with a fretted fingerboard, played by plucking with the fingers or a plectrum. □□ **guitarist** *n.* [Sp. *guitarra* (partly through F *guitare*) f. Gk *kithara*: see CITTERN, GITTERN]

guiver /gívər/ *n.* (also **gyver**) *Austral. & NZ sl.* **1** plausible talk. **2** affectation of speech or manner. [19th c.: orig. unkn.]

Gujarati /gŏŏjəraatee/ *n. & adj.* ● *n.* (*pl.* **Gujaratis**) **1** the language of Gujarat in W. India. **2** a native of Gujarat. ● *adj.* of or relating to Gujarat or its language. [Hind.: see -I²]

gulch /gulch/ *n.* a ravine, esp. one in which a torrent flows. [perh. dial. *gulch* to swallow]

■ see RAVINE.

gulden /gŏŏldən, gŏŏl-/ *n.* = GUILDER. [Du. & G, = GOLDEN]

gules /gyŏŏlz/ *n. & adj.* (usu. placed after noun) *Heraldry* red. [ME f. OF *goules* red-dyed fur neck ornaments f. *gole* throat]

gulf /gulf/ *n. & v.* ● *n.* **1** a stretch of sea consisting of a deep inlet with a narrow mouth. **2** (**the Gulf**) **a** the Gulf of Mexico. **b** the Persian Gulf. **3** a deep hollow; a chasm or abyss. **4** a wide difference of feelings, opinion, etc. ● *v.tr.* engulf; swallow up. □ **Gulf Stream** an oceanic warm current flowing from the Gulf of Mexico to Newfoundland where it is deflected into the Atlantic Ocean. [ME f. OF *golfe* f. It. *golfo* ult. f. Gk *kolpos* bosom, gulf]

■ *n.* **1** cove, inlet, firth, fiord, *Brit.* creek, *Ir.* lough, *Sc.* loch; bay, bight. **3** hollow, deep, depths; chasm, abyss, rift, gap, split, *archaic or poet.* abysm; void, breach, space. **4** rift, gap; difference, disagreement, conflict, schism. ● *v.* see SWALLOW¹ *v.* 6.

gulfweed /gúlfweed/ *n.* = SARGASSO.

gull¹ /gul/ *n.* any of various long-winged web-footed sea birds of the family Laridae, usu. having white plumage with a mantle varying from pearly gray to black, and a bright bill. □□ **gullery** *n.* (*pl.* **-ies**). [ME ult. f. OCelt.]

gull² /gul/ *v.tr.* (usu. in *passive*; foll. by *into*) dupe; fool. [perh. f. obs. *gull* yellow f. ON *gulr*]

■ see DUPE *v.*

Gullah /gúlə/ *n.* **1** a member of a group of African-Americans living on the coast of S. Carolina or the nearby sea islands. **2** the Creole language spoken by them. [perh. a shortening of *Angola*, or f. a tribal name *Golas*]

gullet /gúlit/ *n.* **1** the food passage extending from the mouth to the stomach; the esophagus. **2** the throat. [ME f. OF dimin. of *go(u)le* throat f. L *gula*]

gullible /gúlibəl/ *adj.* easily persuaded or deceived; credulous. □□ **gullibility** *n.* **gullibly** *adv.* [GULL² + -IBLE]

■ credulous, persuadable, unsuspecting, unwary, unsuspicious; innocent, green, unsophisticated, naive, wide-eyed, inexperienced.

gully /gúlee/ *n. & v.* ● *n.* (*pl.* **-ies**) **1** a waterworn ravine. **2** a deep artificial channel; a gutter or drain. **3** *Austral. & NZ* a river valley. **4** *Cricket* **a** the fielding position between point and slips. **b** a fielder in this position. ● *v.tr.* (**-ies, -ied**) **1** form (channels) by water action. **2** make gullies in. [F *goulet* bottleneck (as GULLET)]

■ *n.* **1**, **3** channel, riverbed, river valley, gorge, ravine, canyon, defile, notch, arroyo, gulch, *Brit.* gill. **2** see DRAIN *n.* 1a. ● *v.* **1**, **2** see FURROW *v.* 2a.

gulp /gulp/ *v. & n.* ● *v.* **1** *tr.* (often foll. by *down*) swallow hastily, greedily, or with effort. **2** *intr.* swallow gaspingly or with difficulty; choke. **3** *tr.* (foll. by *down, back*) stifle; suppress (esp. tears). ● *n.* **1** an act of gulping (*drained it at one gulp*). **2** an effort to swallow. **3** a large mouthful of a drink.

□□ **gulper** *n.* **gulpingly** *adv.* **gulpy** *adj.* [ME prob. f. MDu. *gulpen* (imit.)]

■ *v.* **1** bolt, gobble, wolf, devour, gorge, guzzle, swallow, *sl.* knock back; swill, *colloq.* swig, *literary* quaff. **2** choke, catch one's breath, gasp (for breath), heave. **3** see STIFLE 1. ● *n.* **1** swallow, slurp, sip, sup, drink, *colloq.* swig. **3** mouthful, draft, swallow, *colloq.* swig.

gum¹ /gum/ *n. & v.* ● *n.* **1 a** a viscous secretion of some trees and shrubs that hardens on drying but is soluble in water (cf. RESIN). **b** an adhesive substance made from this. **2** chewing gum. **3** = GUMDROP. **4** = *gum arabic*. **5** = *gum tree*. **6** a secretion collecting in the corner of the eye. **7** = GUMBOOT. ● *v.* (**gummed, gumming**) **1** *tr.* smear or cover with gum. **2** *tr.* (usu. foll. by *down, together*, etc.) fasten with gum. **3** *intr.* exude gum. **4** *tr. & intr.* to clog or become clogged with or as if with gum. □ **gum arabic** a gum exuded by some kinds of acacia and used as glue and in incense. **gum benjamin** benzoin. **gum resin** a vegetable secretion of resin mixed with gum, e.g., gamboge. **gum tree** a tree exuding gum, esp. a eucalyptus. **gum up 1** (of a mechanism, etc.) become clogged or obstructed with stickiness. **2** *colloq.* interfere with the smooth running of (*gum up the works*). **up a gum tree** *Brit. colloq.* in great difficulties. [ME f. OF *gomme* ult. f. L *gummi, cummi* f. Gk *kommi* f. Egypt. *kemai*]

■ *n.* **1 b** see GLUE *n.* ● *v.* **2** see GLUE *v.*

gum² /gum/ *n.* (usu. in *pl.*) the firm flesh around the roots of the teeth. □ **gum shield** a pad protecting a boxer's teeth and gums. [OE *gōma* rel. to OHG *guomo*, ON *gómr* roof or floor of the mouth]

gum³ /gum/ *n. colloq.* (in oaths) God (*by gum!*). [corrupt. of *God*]

gumbo /gúmbō/ *n.* (*pl.* **-os**) **1** okra. **2** a soup thickened with okra pods. **3** (**Gumbo**) a patois of African-Americans and Creoles spoken esp. in Louisiana. [of Afr. orig.]

gumboil /gúmboyl/ *n.* a small abscess on the gums.

gumboot /gúmbŏŏt/ *n.* a rubber boot.

gumdrop /gúmdrop/ *n.* a soft, colored candy made with gelatin or gum arabic.

gumma /gúmə/ *n.* (*pl.* **gummas** or **gummata** /-mətə/) *Med.* a small soft swelling occurring in the connective tissue of the liver, brain, testes, and heart, and characteristic of the late stages of syphilis. □□ **gummatous** *adj.* [mod.L f. L *gummi* GUM¹]

gummy¹ /gúmee/ *adj.* (**gummier, gummiest**) **1** viscous; sticky. **2** abounding in or exuding gum. □□ **gumminess** *n.* [ME f. GUM¹ + -Y¹]

■ **1** see STICKY *adj.* 2.

gummy² /gúmee/ *adj. & n.* ● *adj.* (**gummier, gummiest**) toothless. ● *n.* (*pl.* **-ies**) **1** *Austral.* a small shark, *Mustelus antarcticus*, having rounded teeth with which it crushes hard-shelled prey. **2** *Austral. & NZ* a toothless sheep. □□ **gummily** *adv.* [GUM² + -Y¹]

gumption /gúmpshən/ *n. colloq.* **1** resourcefulness; initiative; enterprising spirit. **2** common sense. [18th-c. Sc.: orig. unkn.]

■ **1** resourcefulness, enterprise, initiative, gameness, backbone, pluck, mettle, courage, boldness, audacity, nerve, daring, spirit, vigor, energy, stamina, *colloq.* grit, spunk, guts, get-up-and-go, *Brit. sl.* bottle. **2** (common) sense, shrewdness, cleverness, mother wit, astuteness, judgment, *colloq.* horse sense.

gumshoe /gúmshŏŏ/ *n.* **1** *sl.* a detective. **2** a galosh.

gun /gun/ *n. & v.* ● *n.* **1** any kind of weapon consisting of a metal tube and often held in the hand with a grip at one end, from which bullets or other missiles are propelled with great force, esp. by a contained explosion. **2** any device imitative of this, e.g., a starting pistol. **3** a device for discharging insecticide, grease, electrons, etc., in the required direction (often in *comb.*: *grease gun*). **4** *Brit.* a member of a shooting party. **5** a gunman. **6** the firing of a gun. **7** (in *pl.*) *Naut. sl.* a gunnery officer. ● *v.* (**gunned, gunning**) **1** *tr.* **a** (usu. foll. by *down*) shoot (a person) with a gun. **b** shoot at with a gun. **2** *tr. colloq.* accelerate (an engine or vehicle). **3** *intr.* go shooting. **4** *intr.* (foll. by *for*) seek out determinedly to attack or rebuke. □ **go great guns** *colloq.* proceed forcefully or vigorously or successfully. **gun carriage** a wheeled support for a gun. **gun crew** a team manning a gun. **gun dog** a dog trained to follow hunters using guns. **gun-shy 1** (esp. of a sporting dog) alarmed at the report of a gun. **2** nervous; distrustful; wary. **jump the gun** *colloq.* start before a signal is given, or before an agreed time. **stick to one's guns** *colloq.* maintain one's position under attack. □□ **gunless** *adj.* **gunned** *adj.* [ME *gunne, gonne,* perh. f. the Scand. name *Gunnhildr*]

■ *n.* **1** see REVOLVER. **5** gunman, *sl.* hit man, hood, gunsel, gunslinger. ● *v.* **2** accelerate, speed up, open out *or* up, quicken; (*gun it*) *colloq.* put one's foot down, step on it, step on the gas. □ **stick to one's guns** see PERSEVERE.

gunboat /gúnbōt/ *n.* a small vessel of shallow draft and with relatively heavy guns. □ **gunboat diplomacy** political negotiation supported by the use or threat of military force.

guncotton /gúnkotən/ *n.* an explosive used for blasting, made by steeping cotton in nitric and sulfuric acids.

gundy /gúndee/ *n. Austral. colloq.* □ **no good to gundy** no good at all. [20th c.: orig. unkn.]

gunfight /gúnfīt/ *n.* a fight with firearms. □□ **gunfighter** *n.*

gunfire /gúnfīr/ *n.* **1** the firing of a gun or guns, esp. repeatedly. **2** the noise from this.

gunge /gunj/ *n. & v. Brit. colloq.* ● *n.* sticky or viscous matter, esp. when messy or indeterminate. ● *v.tr.* (usu. foll. by *up*) clog or obstruct with gunge. □□ **gungy** *adj.* [20th c.: orig. uncert.: cf. GOO, GUNK]

gung-ho /gúnghó/ *adj.* enthusiastic; eager. [Chin. *gonghe* work together, slogan adopted by US Marines in 1942]

gunk /gungk/ *n. sl.* viscous or liquid material. [20th c.: orig. the name of a detergent (propr.)]

■ see MUCK *n.* 1, 2.

gunlock /gúnlok/ *n.* a mechanism by which the charge of a gun is exploded.

gunman /gúnmən/ *n.* (*pl.* **-men**) a man armed with a gun, esp. in committing a crime.

gunmetal /gúnmetəl/ *n.* **1** a dull bluish gray color. **2** an alloy of copper and tin or zinc (formerly used for guns).

gunnel¹ /gúnəl/ *n.* any small eel-shaped marine fish of the family Pholidae, esp. *Pholis gunnellus.* Also called BUTTERFISH. [17th c.: orig. unkn.]

gunnel² var. of GUNWALE.

gunner /gúnər/ *n.* **1** an artillery soldier (esp. *Brit.* as an official term for a private). **2** *Naut.* a warrant officer in charge of a battery, magazine, etc. **3** a member of an aircraft crew who operates a gun. **4** a person who hunts game with a gun.

gunnera /gúnərə/ *n.* any plant of the genus *Gunnera* from S. America and New Zealand, having huge leaves and often grown for ornament. [J. E. *Gunnerus,* Norw. botanist d. 1773]

gunnery /gúnəree/ *n.* **1** the construction and management of large guns. **2** the firing of guns.

gunny /gúnee/ *n.* (*pl.* **-ies**) **1** coarse sacking, usu. of jute fiber. **2** a sack made of this. [Hindi & Marathi *gōnī* f. Skr. *gōṇi* sack]

gunplay /gúnplay/ *n.* the use of guns.

gunpoint /gúnpoynt/ *n.* the point of a gun. □ **at gunpoint** threatened with a gun or an ultimatum, etc.

gunpowder /gúnpowdər/ *n.* **1** an explosive made of saltpeter, sulfur, and charcoal. **2** a fine green tea of granular appearance.

gunpower /gúnpowər/ *n.* the strength or quantity of available guns.

gunroom /gúnrōōm, -rŏŏm/ *n.* **1** a room in a house for storing sporting guns. **2** *Brit.* quarters for junior officers (orig. for gunners) in a warship.

gunrunner /gúnrunər/ *n.* a person engaged in the illegal sale or importing of firearms. □□ **gunrunning** *n.*

gunsel /gúnsəl/ *n. sl.* a criminal, esp. a gunman. [Yiddish *gendzel* = G *Gänslein* gosling; infl. by GUN]

gunship /gúnship/ *n.* a heavily armed helicopter or other aircraft.

gunshot /gúnshot/ *n.* **1** a shot fired from a gun. **2** the range of a gun (*within gunshot*).

gunslinger /gúnslingər/ *n. sl.* a gunman. □□ **gunslinging** *n.*

gunsmith /gúnsmith/ *n.* a person who makes, sells, and repairs small firearms.

gunstock /gúnstok/ *n.* the wooden mounting of the barrel of a gun.

Gunter's chain /gúntərz/ *n. Surveying* **1** a measuring chain of 66 ft. **2** this length as a unit. [E. *Gunter,* Engl. mathematician d. 1626]

gunwale /gúnəl/ *n.* (also **gunnel**) the upper edge of the side of a boat or ship. [GUN + WALE (because formerly used to support guns)]

gunyah /gúnyaa/ *n. Austral.* an Aboriginal bush hut. [Aboriginal]

guppy /gúpee/ *n.* (*pl.* **-ies**) a freshwater fish, *Poecilia reticulata,* of the W. Indies and S. America, frequently kept in aquariums, and giving birth to live young. [R. J. L. *Guppy,* 19th-c. Trinidad clergyman who sent the first specimen to the British Museum]

gurdwara /gərdwáarə/ *n.* a Sikh temple. [Punjabi *gurduārā* f. Skr. *guru* teacher + *dvāra* door]

gurgle /gárgəl/ *v. & n.* ● *v.* **1** *intr.* make a bubbling sound as of water from a bottle. **2** *tr.* utter with such a sound. ● *n.* a gurgling sound. □□ **gurgler** *n.* [imit., or f. Du. *gorgelen,* G *gurgeln,* or med.L *gurgulare* f. L *gurgulio* gullet]

■ *v.* **1** bubble, burble, babble, ripple, splash, plash, lap, murmur, purl, glug. ● *n.* burble, bubble, purl, glug.

Gurkha /gárkə/ *n.* **1** a member of the dominant Hindu people in Nepal. **2** a Nepalese soldier serving in the British army. [native name, f. Skr. *gāus* cow + *raksh* protect]

gurnard /gárnərd/ *n.* (also **gurnet** /gárnit/) any marine fish of the family Triglidae, having a large spiny head with mailed sides, and three finger-like pectoral rays used for walking on the sea bed, etc. [ME f. OF *gornart* f. *grondir* to grunt f. L *grunnire*]

guru /gŏŏrōō/ *n.* **1** a Hindu spiritual teacher or head of a religious sect. **2 a** an influential teacher. **b** a revered mentor. [Hindi *gurū* teacher f. Skr. *gurús* grave, dignified]

■ see TEACHER.

gush /gush/ *v. & n.* ● *v.* **1** *tr. & intr.* emit or flow in a sudden and copious stream. **2** *intr.* speak or behave with effusiveness or sentimental affectation. ● *n.* **1** a sudden or copious stream. **2** an effusive or sentimental manner. □□ **gushing** *adj.* **gushingly** *adv.* [ME *gosshe, gusche,* prob. imit.]

■ *v.* **1** cascade, rush, flood, stream, spurt, jet, spout, burst; run, flow. **2** effervesce, bubble over, be ebullient *or* effusive, *colloq.* enthuse; go over the top. ● *n.* **1** cascade, rush, flood, flow, stream, spurt, jet, spout, burst, torrent; outburst, effusion. **2** effusiveness, animation; see also *exuberance* (EXUBERANT).

gusher /gúshər/ *n.* **1** an oil well from which oil flows without being pumped. **2** an effusive person.

gushy /gúshee/ *adj.* (**gushier, gushiest**) excessively effusive or sentimental. □□ **gushily** *adv.* **gushiness** *n.*

■ gushing, effusive, (over)sentimental, overenthusiastic, sloppy, *colloq.* slushy; fulsome, cloying, mawkish, excessive, over the top.

gusset /gúsit/ *n.* **1** a piece inserted into a garment, etc., to strengthen or enlarge a part. **2** a bracket strengthening an angle of a structure. □□ **gusseted** *adj.* [ME f. OF *gousset* flexible piece filling up a joint in armor f. *gousse* pod, shell]

gust /gust/ *n. & v.* ● *n.* **1** a sudden strong rush of wind. **2** a burst of rain, fire, smoke, or sound. **3** a passionate or emotional outburst. ● *v.intr.* blow in gusts. [ON *gustr,* rel. to *gjósa* to gush]

■ *n.* **1** rush, blast, puff, blow; see also BREEZE¹ *n.* 1. **2** burst, spurt, wave, surge, outbreak; see also OUTBURST. **3** see OUTBURST. ● *v.* puff, waft, blow, blast.

gustation /gustáyshən/ *n.* the act or capacity of tasting.

/. . ./ **pronunciation**	● **part of speech**
□ **phrases, idioms, and compounds**	
□□ **derivatives**	■ **synonym section**
cross-references appear in SMALL CAPITALS or *italics*	

□□ **gustative** /gústətiv/ *adj.* **gustatory** /gústətáwree/ *adj.* [F *gustation* or L *gustatio* f. *gustare* f. *gustus* taste]

gusto /gústō/ *n.* (*pl.* **-oes**) **1** zest; enjoyment or vigor in doing something. **2** (foll. by *for*) relish or liking. **3** *archaic* a style of artistic execution. [It. f. L *gustus* taste]

■ **1** zest, zeal, zealousness, avidity, eagerness, relish, vigor, enjoyment, enthusiasm, pleasure, delight, satisfaction, appreciation. **2** relish, appetite, liking, taste, fancy, preference.

gusty /gústee/ *adj.* (**gustier, gustiest**) **1** characterized by or blowing in strong winds. **2** characterized by gusto. □□ **gustily** *adv.* **gustiness** *n.*

■ **1** see WINDY 1. **2** see EAGER 1.

gut /gut/ *n. & v.* ● *n.* **1** the lower alimentary canal or a part of this; the intestine. **2** (in *pl.*) the bowel or entrails, esp. of animals. **3** (in *pl.*) *colloq.* personal courage and determination; vigorous application and perseverance. **4** (in *pl.*) the belly as the source of appetite. **b** the belly or abdomen. **5** (in *pl.*) **a** the contents of anything, esp. representing substantiality. **b** the essence of a thing, e.g., of an issue or problem. **6 a** material for violin or racket strings or surgical use made from the intestines of animals. **b** material for fishing lines made from the silk glands of silkworms. **7 a** a narrow water passage; a sound; straits. **b** a defile or narrow passage. **8** (*attrib.*) **a** instinctive (*a gut reaction*). **b** fundamental (*a gut issue*). ● *v.tr.* (**gutted, gutting**) **1** remove or destroy (esp. by fire) the internal fittings of (a house, etc.). **2** take out the guts of (a fish). **3** extract the essence of (a book, etc.). □ **hate a person's guts** *colloq.* dislike a person intensely. **sweat** (or **work**) **one's guts out** *colloq.* work extremely hard. [OE *guttas* (pl.), prob. rel. to *gēotan* pour]

■ *n.* **1, 2** intestine, alimentary canal, bowel; (*guts*) entrails, viscera, vitals, *colloq.* insides, innards. **3** (*guts*) backbone, bravery, boldness, audacity, pluck, courage, daring, spirit, mettle, nerve, *colloq.* grit, gumption, spunk, gutsiness, *Brit. sl.* bottle; application, perseverance, determination, willpower, stamina, endurance. **4 a** (*guts*) belly, *colloq.* tummy; see also STOMACH *n.* 3b. **b** stomach, abdomen, belly, beer belly, *joc.* corporation. **5** (*guts*) see SUBSTANCE 1. **8** (*attrib.*) **a** basic, heartfelt, instinctive, instinctual, intuitive, visceral, deep-seated, deep-rooted, emotional; see also INSTINCTIVE 2. **b** see FUNDAMENTAL *adj.* ● *v.* **1** destroy, devastate, ravage, *literary* despoil; ransack, pillage, plunder, loot; strip, empty, *sl.* clean out. **2** disembowel, draw, dress, clean, *formal* eviscerate. **3** see DIGEST *v.* 4a. □ **hate a person's guts** see LOATHE. **sweat** (or **work**) **one's guts out** see LABOR *v.* 1, 2, SLAVE *v.*

gutless /gútlis/ *adj. colloq.* lacking courage or determination; feeble. □ **gutless wonder** *colloq.* a person who lacks courage or determination. □□ **gutlessly** *adv.* **gutlessness** *n.*

■ see SPINELESS 2.

gutsy /gútsee/ *adj.* (**gutsier, gutsiest**) *colloq.* **1** courageous. **2** greedy. □□ **gutsily** *adv.* **gutsiness** *n.*

■ **1** see BRAVE *adj.* 1. **2** see GREEDY 1.

gutta-percha /gútəpérchə/ *n.* a tough plastic substance obtained from the latex of various Malaysian trees. [Malay *getah* gum + *percha* name of a tree]

guttate /gútayt/ *adj. Biol.* having droplike markings. [L *guttatus* speckled f. *gutta* drop]

gutted /gútid / *adj. sl.* utterly exhausted; devastated.

gutter /gútər/ *n. & v.* ● *n.* **1** a shallow trough along the eaves of a house, or a channel at the side of a street, to carry off rainwater. **2** (prec. by *the*) a poor or degraded background or environment. **3** an open conduit along which liquid flows out. **4** a groove. **5** a track made by the flow of water. **6** *Printing* the white space at the inside margin of two adjoining pages. ● *v.* **1** *intr.* flow in streams. **2** *tr.* furrow; channel. **3** *intr.* (of a candle) melt away as the wax forms channels down the side. □ **gutter press** esp. *Brit.* sensational journalism concerned esp. with the private lives of public figures. [ME f. AF *gotere*, OF *gotiere* ult. f. L *gutta* drop]

■ *n.* **1, 3** see DRAIN *n.* 1a.

guttering /gútəring/ *n.* **1 a** the gutters of a building, etc. **b** a section or length of a gutter. **2** material for gutters.

guttersnipe /gútərsnip/ *n.* a street urchin.

■ waif, (street) urchin, ragamuffin, gamin, *hist.* mudlark.

guttural /gútərəl/ *adj. & n.* ● *adj.* **1** throaty, harsh sounding. **2 a** *Phonet.* (of a consonant) produced in the throat or by the back of the tongue and palate. **b** (of a sound) coming from the throat. **c** of the throat. ● *n. Phonet.* a guttural consonant (e.g., *k, g*). □□ **gutturally** *adv.* [F *guttural* or med.L *gutturalis* f. L *guttur* throat]

■ *adj.* **1** see GRUFF 1a.

guv /guv/ *n. Brit. sl.* = GOVERNOR 7. [abbr.]

guy[1] /gī/ *n. & v.* ● *n.* **1** *colloq.* a man; a fellow. **2** (usu. in *pl.*) a person of either sex. **3** *Brit.* an effigy of Guy Fawkes in ragged clothing, burned on a bonfire on Nov. 5. **4** *Brit.* a grotesquely dressed person. ● *v.tr.* **1** ridicule. **2** *Brit.* exhibit in effigy. [*Guy Fawkes*, conspirator in the Gunpowder Plot to blow up Parliament in 1605]

■ *n.* **1** man, fellow, *colloq.* chap, dude, *sl.* geezer, *Brit. sl.* bloke, *sl. often derog.* gink. **2** person, individual, human (being), being, (living) soul, mortal, *Brit. colloq.* bod; (*guys*) people, folk(s). ● *v.* **1** mock, ridicule, make fun of, caricature, satirize, poke fun at, lampoon, *colloq.* rib, send up; see also RIDICULE *v.*

guy[2] /gī/ *n. & v.* ● *n.* a rope or chain to secure a tent or steady a crane load, etc. ● *v.tr.* secure with a guy or guys. [prob. of LG orig.: cf. LG & Du. *gei* brail, etc.]

guzzle /gúzəl/ *v.tr. & intr.* eat, drink, or consume excessively or greedily. □□ **guzzler** *n.* [perh. f. OF *gosiller* chatter, vomit f. *gosier* throat]

■ see SCOFF[2] *v.*

gybe /jīb/ *v. & n.* var. of JIBE[2].

gym /jim/ *n. colloq.* **1** a gymnasium. **2** gymnastics. [abbr.]

gymkhana /jimkaánə/ *n.* **1** a meeting for competition or display in a sport, esp. horse riding or automobile racing. **2** *Brit.* a public place with facilities for athletics. [Hind. *gendkhāna* ball house, racket court, assim. to GYMNASIUM]

gymnasium /jimnáyzeeəm/ *n.* (*pl.* **gymnasiums** or **gymnasia** /-zeeə/) **1** a room or building equipped for indoor sports, often including gymnastics. **2** a school in Germany or Scandinavia that prepares pupils for university entrance. □□ **gymnasial** /-zeeəl/ *adj.* [L f. Gk *gumnasion* f. *gumnazō* exercise f. *gumnos* naked]

gymnast /jímnast, -nəst/ *n.* an expert in gymnastics. [F *gymnaste* or Gk *gumnastēs* athlete trainer f. *gumnazō*: see GYMNASIUM]

gymnastic /jimnástik/ *adj.* of or involving gymnastics. □□ **gymnastically** *adv.* [L *gymnasticus* f. Gk *gumnastikos* (as GYMNASIUM)]

gymnastics /jimnástiks/ *n.pl.* (also treated as *sing.*) **1** exercises developing or displaying physical agility and coordination, usu. in competition. **2** other forms of physical or mental agility.

■ **1** see EXERCISE *n.* 3.

gymno- /jímnō/ *comb. form Biol.* bare; naked. [Gk *gumnos* naked]

gymnosophist /jimnósəfist/ *n.* a member of an ancient Hindu sect wearing little clothing and devoted to contemplation. □□ **gymnosophy** *n.* [ME f. F *gymnosophiste* f. L *gymnosophistae* (pl.) f. Gk *gumnosophistai*: see GYMNO-, SOPHIST]

gymnosperm /jímnəspórm/ *n.* any of various plants having seeds unprotected by an ovary, including conifers, cycads, and ginkgos (opp. ANGIOSPERM). □□ **gymnospermous** *adj.*

gymp var. of GIMP[1].

gyn. *abbr.* (also **gynecol.**) **1** gynecological. **2** gynecologist. **3** gynecology.

gynaeceum var. of GYNOECIUM.

gynandromorph /jinándrəmawrf, gī-/ *n. Biol.* an individual, esp. an insect, having male and female characteristics. □□ **gynandromorphic** *adj.* **gynandromorphism** *n.* [formed as GYNANDROUS + Gk *morphē* form]

gynandrous /jinándrəs, gī-/ *adj. Bot.* with stamens and pistil united in one column as in orchids. [Gk *gunandros* of doubtful sex, f. *gunē* woman + *anēr andros* man]

gyneco- /gínikō, jínə-/ *comb. form* (*Brit.* **gynaeco-**) woman; women; female. [Gk *gunē gunaikos* woman]

gynecology /gínikólǝjee, jínǝ-/ *n.* (*Brit.* **gynaecology**) the science of the physiological functions and diseases of women and girls, esp. those affecting the reproductive system. □□ **gynecologic** /-kǝlójik/ *adj.* **gynecological** *adj.* **gynecologically** *adv.* **gynecologist** /-kólǝjist/ *n.*

gynecomastia /gínikōmásteeǝ, jínǝ-/ *n.* (*Brit.* **gynaecomastia**) *Med.* enlargement of a man's breasts, usu. due to hormone imbalance or hormone therapy.

gynoecium /jineéseeǝm, -shee-, gī-/ *n.* (also **gynaecium**) (*pl.* **-cia** /-seeǝ, -sheeǝ/) *Bot.* the carpels of a flower taken collectively. [mod.L f. Gk *gunaikeion* women's apartments (as GYNECO-, Gk *oikos* house)]

-gynous /jinǝs, ginǝs/ *comb. form Bot.* forming adjectives meaning 'having specified female organs or pistils' (*monogynous*). [Gk *-gunos* f. *gunē* woman]

gyp[1] /jip/ *v. & n. sl.* ● *v.tr.* (**gypped, gypping**) cheat; swindle. ● *n.* an act of cheating; a swindle. [19th c.: perh. f. GYP[2]]

gyp[2] /jip/ *n. Brit. colloq.* **1** pain or severe discomfort. **2** a scolding (*gave them gyp*). [19th c.: perh. f. *gee-up* (see GEE[2])]

gyp[3] /jip/ *n. Brit.* a college servant at Cambridge and Durham. [perh. f. obs. *gippo* scullion, orig. a man's short tunic, f. obs. F *jupeau*]

gyppy tummy var. of GIPPY TUMMY.

gypsophila /jipsófilǝ/ *n.* any plant of the genus *Gypsophila*, with a profusion of small usu. white composite flowers, as baby's breath. [mod.L f. Gk *gupsos* chalk + *philos* loving]

gypsum /jípsǝm/ *n.* a hydrated form of calcium sulfate occurring naturally and used to make plaster of Paris and in the building industry. □□ **gypseous** *adj.* **gypsiferous** /-sífǝrǝs/ *adj.* [L f. Gk *gupsos*]

Gypsy /jípsee/ *n.* (also **Gipsy**) (*pl.* **-ies**) **1** a member of a nomadic people of Europe and N. America, of Hindu origin with dark skin and hair, and speaking a language related to Hindi. **2** (**gypsy**) a person resembling or living like a Gypsy. □ **gypsy moth** a kind of tussock moth, *Lymantria dispar*, of which the larvae are very destructive to foliage. □□ **Gypsydom** *n.* **Gypsyfied** *adj.* **Gypsyhood** *n.* **Gypsyish** *adj.* [earlier *gipcyan, gipsen* f. EGYPTIAN, from the supposed origin of Gypsies when they appeared in England in the early 16th c.]

■ **1** Romany, esp. *Brit.* traveler. **2** (**gypsy**) see MIGRANT *n.*

gyrate /jírayt/ *v. & adj.* ● *v.intr.* (also /jīráyt/) go in a circle or spiral; revolve; whirl. ● *adj. Bot.* arranged in rings or convolutions. □□ **gyration** /-ráyshǝn/ *n.* **gyrator** *n.* **gyratory** /-rǝtáwree/ *adj.* [L *gyrare gyrat-* revolve f. *gyrus* ring f. Gk *guros*]
■ *v.* rotate, spin, revolve, whirl, twirl, pirouette; swivel, turn around, turn, go around.

gyre /jīr/ *v. & n.* esp. *poet.* ● *v.intr.* whirl or gyrate. ● *n.* a gyration. [L *gyrus* ring f. Gk *guros*]

gyrfalcon /jǝrfalkǝn, -fawlkǝn/ *n.* (also **gerfalcon**) a large falcon, *Falco rusticolus*, of the northern hemisphere. [ME f. OF *gerfaucon* f. Frank. *gērfalco* f. ON *geirfálki*: see FALCON]

gyro /jírō/ *n.* (*pl.* **-os**) *colloq.* **1** = GYROSCOPE. **2** = GYROCOMPASS. [abbr.]

gyro- /jírō/ *comb. form* rotation. [Gk *guros* ring]

gyrocompass /jírōkumpǝs, -kom-/ *n.* a nonmagnetic compass giving true north and bearings from it by means of a gyroscope.

gyrograph /jírǝgraf/ *n.* an instrument for recording revolutions.

gyromagnetic /jírōmagnétik/ *adj.* **1** *Physics* of the magnetic and mechanical properties of a rotating charged particle. **2** (of a compass) combining a gyroscope and a normal magnetic compass.

gyropilot /jírōpílǝt/ *n.* a gyrocompass used for automatic steering.

gyroplane /jírǝplayn/ *n.* a form of aircraft deriving its lift mainly from freely rotating overhead vanes.

gyroscope /jírǝskōp/ *n.* a rotating wheel whose axis is free to turn but maintains a fixed direction unless perturbed, esp. used for stabilization or with the compass in an aircraft, ship, etc. □□ **gyroscopic** /-skópik/ *adj.* **gyroscopically** *adv.* [F (as GYRO-, SCOPE[2])]

gyrostabilizer /jírōstáybilizǝr/ *n.* a gyroscopic device for maintaining the equilibrium of a ship, aircraft, platform, etc.

gyrus /jírǝs/ *n.* (*pl.* **gyri** /-rī/) a fold or convolution, esp. of the brain. [L f. Gk *guros* ring]

gyttja /yíchǝ/ *n. Geol.* a lake deposit of a usu. black organic sediment. [Sw., = mud, ooze]

gyver var. of GUIVER.

/.../ **pronunciation** ● **part of speech**
□ **phrases, idioms, and compounds**
□□ **derivatives** ■ **synonym section**
cross-references appear in SMALL CAPITALS or *italics*

Hh

H¹ /aych/ *n.* (also **h**) (*pl.* **Hs** or **H's**) **1** the eighth letter of the alphabet (see AITCH). **2** anything having the form of an H (esp. in *comb.*: *H-girder*).

H² *abbr.* (also **H.**) **1** hardness. **2** (of a pencil lead) hard. **3** henry; henrys. **4** (water) hydrant. **5** *sl.* heroin.

H³ *symb. Chem.* the element hydrogen.

h. *abbr.* **1** hecto-. **2** height. **3** horse. **4** hot. **5** hour(s). **6** husband. **7** Planck's constant. **8** *Baseball* hit; hits.

Ha *symb. Chem.* the element hahnium.

ha¹ /haa/ *int.* (also **hah**) expressing surprise, suspicion, triumph, etc. (cf. HA HA). [ME]

ha² *abbr.* hectare(s).

haar /haar/ *n.* a cold sea fog on the east coast of England or Scotland. [perh. f. ON *hárr* hoar, hoary]

Hab. *abbr.* Habakkuk (Old Testament).

habanera /háabənáirə/ *n.* **1** a Cuban dance in slow duple time. **2** the music for this. [Sp., fem. of *habanero* of Havana in Cuba]

habeas corpus /háybeeəs káwrpəs/ *n.* a writ requiring a person to be brought before a judge or into court, esp. to investigate the lawfulness of his or her detention. [L, = you must have the body]

haberdasher /hábərdashər/ *n.* **1** a dealer in men's clothing. **2** *Brit.* a dealer in dress accessories and sewing goods. □□ **haberdashery** *n.* (*pl.* **-ies**). [ME prob. ult. f. AF *hapertas* perh. the name of a fabric]

habergeon /hábərjən/ *n. hist.* a sleeveless coat of mail. [ME f. OF *haubergeon* (as HAUBERK)]

habiliment /həbílimənt/ *n.* (usu. in *pl.*) **1** clothes suited to a particular purpose. **2** *joc.* ordinary clothes. [ME f. OF *habillement* f. *habiller* fit out f. *habile* ABLE]

habilitate /həbílitayt/ *v.intr.* qualify for office (esp. as a teacher in a German university). □□ **habilitation** /-táyshən/ *n.* [med.L *habilitare* (as ABILITY)]

habit /hábit/ *n. & v.* ● *n.* **1** a settled or regular tendency or practice (often foll. by *of* + verbal noun: *has a habit of ignoring me*). **2** a practice that is hard to give up. **3** a mental constitution or attitude. **4** *Psychol.* an automatic reaction to a specific situation. **5** *colloq.* an addictive practice, esp. of taking drugs. **6 a** the dress of a particular class, esp. of a religious order. **b** (in full **riding habit**) a woman's riding dress. **c** *archaic* dress; attire. **7** a bodily constitution. **8** *Biol. & Crystallog.* a mode of growth. ● *v.tr.* (usu. as **habited** *adj.*) clothe. □ **habit-forming** causing addiction. **make a habit of** do regularly. [ME f. OF *abit* f. L *habitus* f. *habēre habit-* have, be constituted]

■ *n.* **1** tendency, disposition, inclination, bent, penchant, propensity, proclivity; second nature; custom, routine, practice, convention, usage, ritual, pattern, mode, rule, praxis, *formal or joc.* wont; way, mannerism, quirk, peculiarity, idiosyncrasy. **2, 5** addiction, compulsion, obsession, fixation, vice; dependence. **3** see ATTITUDE 1. **6 a, c** costume, uniform, livery, garb; clothing, dress, *archaic* raiment, *colloq.* gear, getup, *formal* attire, apparel; clothes, garments, vestments, robe(s), *joc.* habiliments. **7** see SHAPE *n.* 6. ● *v.* see CLOTHE 1. □ **habit-forming** addictive, compulsive, (*of a drug*) hard; see also *obsessive* (OBSESS).

habitable /hábitəbəl/ *adj.* that can be inhabited. □□ **habita-**

bility *n.* **habitableness** *n.* **habitably** *adv.* [ME f. OF f. L *habitabilis* (as HABITANT)]

■ livable, inhabitable.

habitant *n.* **1** /hábit'nt/ an inhabitant. **2** /ábeetóN/ **a** an early French settler in Canada or Louisiana. **b** a descendant of these settlers. [F f. OF *habiter* f. L *habitare* inhabit (as HABIT)]

habitat /hábitat/ *n.* **1** the natural home of an organism. **2** a habitation. [L, = it dwells: see HABITANT]

■ **1** domain, range, terrain, territory, realm, element, environment, surroundings, haunt, home, *colloq.* stamping ground, *joc.* bailiwick. **2** habitation, *formal* dwelling (place); see also ABODE¹.

habitation /hábitáyshən/ *n.* **1** the process of inhabiting (*fit for human habitation*). **2** a house or home. [ME f. OF f. L *habitatio -onis* (as HABITANT)]

■ **2** see HOME *n.* 1.

habitual /həbíchŏŏəl/ *adj.* **1** done constantly or as a habit. **2** regular; usual. **3** given to a (specified) habit (*a habitual smoker*). □□ **habitually** *adv.* **habitualness** *n.* [med.L *habitualis* (as HABIT)]

■ **1** persistent, constant, continual, perpetual; frequent; automatic, mechanical, compulsive, obsessive. **2** settled, set, rooted, ingrained, fixed, established, regular, standard, routine, ritual, traditional, normal, usual, common, customary, accustomed, everyday, familiar, *attrib.* wonted. **3** inveterate, confirmed, compulsive, obsessional, hardened, established, *colloq. disp.* chronic.

habituate /həbíchŏŏ-ayt/ *v.tr.* (often foll. by *to*) accustom; make used to something. □□ **habituation** /-áyshən/ *n.* [LL *habituare* (as HABIT)]

■ see ACCUSTOM.

habitude /hábitŏŏd, -tyŏŏd/ *n.* **1** a mental or bodily disposition. **2** a custom or tendency. [ME f. OF f. L *habitudo -dinis* f. *habēre habit-* have]

habitué /həbíchŏŏ-áy/ *n.* a habitual visitor or resident. [F, past part. of *habituer* (as HABITUATE)]

■ frequent visitor, frequenter, patron, regular customer, *colloq.* regular; resident.

haček /háachek/ *n.* (also **háček**) a diacritical mark (ˇ) placed over letters to modify the sound in some Slavic and Baltic languages. [Czech, dimin. of *hák* hook]

hachures /hashyŏŏr/ *n.pl.* parallel lines used in shading hills on maps, their closeness indicating the steepness of gradient. [F f. *hacher* HATCH³]

hacienda /háasee-éndə/ *n.* in Spanish-speaking countries: **1** an estate or plantation with a dwelling house. **2** a factory. [Sp. f. L *facienda* things to be done]

hack¹ /hak/ *v. & n.* ● *v.* **1** *tr.* cut or chop roughly; mangle. **2** *Sports* strike illegally at an opponent's arms, legs, etc., during a game. **3** *intr.* (often foll. by *at*) deliver cutting blows. **4** *tr.* cut (one's way) through thick foliage, etc. **5** *tr. colloq.* gain unauthorized access to (data in a computer). **6** *tr. sl.* **a** manage; cope with. **b** tolerate. **c** (often foll. by *off* or as **hacked off** *adj.*) annoy; disconcert. ● *n.* **1** a kick with the toe of a boot. **2** a gash or wound, esp. from a kick. **3 a** a mattock. **b** a miner's pick. □ **hacking cough** a short dry frequent cough. [OE *haccian* cut in pieces f. WG]

■ *v.* **1** chop, cut, carve, hew; gash, slash; mangle,

658

lacerate, mutilate, butcher; (*hack off*) lop (off), sever, amputate. **2** kick, *colloq.* boot. **3** (*hack at*) stab (at), jab (at), thrust at, strike out at; cut, carve up, maim, mutilate, destroy, damage, deface. **4** cut, chop, carve, hew. **6 b** see TOLERATE 1, 3, 6. **c** (**hacked off**) see *discontented* (DISCONTENT *v.*). ● *n.* **1** kick, *colloq.* boot. □ **hacking cough** bark, (dry) cough.

hack² /hak/ *n., adj., & v.* ● *n.* **1 a** a horse for ordinary riding. **b** a horse let out for hire. **c** = JADE² 1. **2** a writer of mediocre literary work or journalism; *colloq.* usu. *derog.* a journalist. **3** a person hired to do dull routine work. **4** a taxi. ● *attrib.adj.* **1** used as a hack. **2** typical of a hack; commonplace (*hack work*). ● *v.* **1 a** *intr.* ride on horseback on a road at an ordinary pace. **b** *tr.* ride (a horse) in this way. **2** *tr.* make common or trite. **3** drive a taxi. [abbr. of HACKNEY]
■ *n.* **1** horse, saddle horse, mount, hackney, *archaic* palfrey, *colloq.* nag; jade. **2** esp. *Brit.* penny-a-liner, *often derog.* scribbler; see also WRITER 1. **3** drudge, plodder, toiler, menial, lackey, slave, *Brit.* fag, *usu. derog.* flunky. **4** see TAXI *n.* ● *attrib. adj.* **2** commonplace, hackneyed, trite, banal, humdrum, mediocre, stereotyped, stock, unoriginal, run-of-the-mill; tired, stale, tedious, overworked, overdone, *colloq.* old hat. ● *v.* **2** see PROSTITUTE *v.* 2b.

hack³ /hak/ *n.* **1** *Falconry* a board on which a hawk's meat is laid. **2** a rack holding fodder for cattle. □ **at hack** *Falconry* (of a young hawk) not yet allowed to prey for itself. [var. of HATCH¹]

hackberry /hákberee/ *n.* (*pl.* **-ies**) **1** any tree of the genus *Celtis*, native to N. America, bearing purple edible berries. **2** the berry of this tree. [var. of *hagberry*, of Norse orig.]

hacker /hákər/ *n.* **1** a person or thing that hacks or cuts roughly. **2** *colloq.* **a** a person who is very adept at programming and working with computers. **b** a person who uses computers to gain unauthorized access to data. **3** a golfer who plays poorly.

hackle /hákəl/ *n. & v.* ● *n.* **1** a long feather or series of feathers on the neck or saddle of a domestic fowl and other birds. **2** *Fishing* an artificial fly dressed with a hackle. **3** *Sc.* a feather in a Highland soldier's bonnet. **4** (in *pl.*) the erectile hairs along the back of a dog, which rise when it is angry or alarmed. **5** a steel comb for dressing flax. ● *v.tr.* dress or comb with a hackle. □ **raise a person's hackles** cause a person to be angry or indignant. [ME *hechele, hakele*, prob. f. OE f. WG]

hackney /háknee/ *n.* (*pl.* **-eys**) **1** a horse of average size and quality for ordinary riding. **2** (*attrib.*) designating any of various vehicles kept for hire. [ME, perh. f. *Hackney* (formerly *Hakenei*) in London, where horses were pastured]
■ **1** see HACK² *n.* 1. **2** see CAB.

hackneyed /hákneed/ *adj.* (of a phrase, etc.) made commonplace or trite by overuse.
■ see STALE¹ 2.

hacksaw /háksaw/ *n.* a saw with a narrow blade set in a frame, for cutting metal.

had *past and past part.* of HAVE.

haddock /hádək/ *n.* (*pl.* same) a marine fish, *Melanogrammus aeglefinus*, of the N. Atlantic, allied to cod, but smaller. [ME, prob. f. AF *hadoc*, OF (*h*)*adot*, of unkn. orig.]

hade /hayd/ *n. & v. Geol.* ● *n.* an incline from the vertical. ● *v.intr.* incline from the vertical. [17th c., perh. dial. form of *head*]

Hades /háydeez/ *n.* (in Greek mythology) the underworld; the abode of the spirits of the dead. □□ **Hadean** /-deeən/ *adj.* [Gk *haidēs*, orig. a name of Pluto]

Hadith /hádith/ *n. Relig.* a body of traditions relating to Muhammad. [Arab. *ḥadīt* tradition]

hadj var. of HAJJ.

hadji var. of HAJJI.

hadn't /hád'nt/ *contr.* had not.

hadron /hádron/ *n. Physics* any strongly interacting elementary particle. □□ **hadronic** /-drónik/ *adj.* [Gk *hadros* bulky]

hadst /hadst/ *archaic 2nd sing. past* of HAVE.

haere mai /hírə mì/ *int. NZ* welcome. [Maori, lit. 'come hither']

hafiz /háafiz/ *n.* a Muslim who knows the Koran by heart. [Pers. f. Arab. *ḥāfiz* guardian]

hafnium /háfneeəm/ *n. Chem.* a silvery lustrous metallic element occurring naturally with zirconium, used in tungsten alloys for filaments and electrodes. ¶ Symb.: **Hf**. [mod.L f. *Hafnia* Copenhagen]

haft /haft/ *n. & v.* ● *n.* the handle of a dagger, knife, etc. ● *v.tr.* provide with a haft. [OE *hæft* f. Gmc]
■ *n.* see HANDLE *n.* 1.

Hag. *abbr.* Haggai (Old Testament).

hag¹ /hag/ *n.* **1** an ugly old woman. **2** a witch. **3** = HAGFISH. □□ **haggish** *adj.* [ME *hegge, hagge*, perh. f. OE *hægtesse*, OHG *hagazissa*, of unkn. orig.]
■ **1** crone, fishwife, harridan, shrew, *archaic* beldam, *sl. derog.* (old) bag. **2** witch, fury, gorgon, harpy, sorceress, enchantress, magician, sibyl, pythoness.

hag² /hag/ *n. Sc. & No. of Engl.* **1** a soft place on a moor. **2** a firm place in a bog. [ON *högg* gap, orig. 'cutting blow,' rel. to HEW]

hagfish /hágfish/ *n.* any jawless fish of the family Myxinidae, with a rasp-like tongue used for feeding on dead or dying fish. [HAG¹]

Haggadah /həgáadə, -gáwdə, haagaadáa/ *n.* **1** a legend, etc., used to illustrate a point of the Law in the Talmud; the legendary element of the Talmud. **2** a book recited at the Passover Seder service. □□ **Haggadic** /həgádik, -gaà-, -gáw-/ *adj.* [Heb., = tale, f. *higgid* tell]

haggard /hágərd/ *adj. & n.* ● *adj.* **1** looking exhausted and distraught, esp. from fatigue, worry, privation, etc. **2** (of a hawk) caught and trained as an adult. ● *n.* a haggard hawk. □□ **haggardly** *adv.* **haggardness** *n.* [F *hagard*, of uncert. orig.: later infl. by HAG¹]
■ *adj.* **1** gaunt, drawn, distraught, hollow-eyed, hollow-cheeked, pinched, scrawny, scraggy, run-down, weary (-looking), careworn, spent, played out, exhausted, toilworn, worn out, worn(-looking); see also *emaciated* (EMACIATE).

haggis /hágis/ *n.* a Scottish dish consisting of a sheep's or calf's offal mixed with suet, oatmeal, etc., and boiled in a bag made from the animal's stomach or in an artificial bag. [ME: orig. unkn.]

haggle /hágəl/ *v. & n.* ● *v.intr.* (often foll. by *about, over*) dispute or bargain persistently. ● *n.* a dispute or wrangle. □□ **haggler** *n.* [earlier sense 'hack'. f. ON *höggva* HEW]
■ *v.* wrangle, higgle, bicker, chaffer, palter, dispute, squabble, quibble; bargain, negotiate, barter, dicker. ● *n.* see ARGUMENT 1.

hagio- /hágeeō, háyjeeō/ *comb. form* of saints or holiness. [Gk *hagios* holy]

Hagiographa /hágeeógrəfə, háyjee-/ *n.pl.* the twelve books comprising the last of the three major divisions of the Hebrew Scriptures, along with the Law and the Prophets.

hagiographer /hágeeógrəfər, háyjee-/ *n.* **1** a writer of the lives of saints. **2** a writer of any of the Hagiographa.

hagiography /hágeeógrəfee, háyjee-/ *n.* the writing of the lives of saints. □□ **hagiographic** /-geeəgráfik/ *adj.* **hagiographical** *adj.*

hagiolatry /hágeeólətree, háyjee-/ *n.* the worship of saints.

hagiology /hágeeóləjee/ *n.* literature dealing with the lives and legends of saints. □□ **hagiological** /-geeəlójikəl/ *adj.* **hagiologist** *n.*

hagridden /hágrid'n/ *adj.* afflicted by nightmares or anxieties.

hah var. of HA.

ha ha /háaháa/ *int.* repr. laughter. [OE: cf. HA]

ha-ha /háahaa/ *n.* a ditch with a wall on its inner side below ground level, forming a boundary to a park or garden without interrupting the view. [F, perh. from the cry of surprise on encountering it]

/.../ **pronunciation**   ● **part of speech**
□ **phrases, idioms, and compounds**
□□ **derivatives**   ■ **synonym section**
cross-references appear in SMALL CAPITALS or *italics*

hahnium /haániəm/ *n. Chem.* an artificially produced radioactive element. ¶ Symb.: **Ha**. [O. *Hahn*, Ger. chemist d. 1968 + -IUM]

haik /hīk, hayk/ *n.* (also **haick**) an outer covering for head and body worn by Arabs. [Moroccan Arab. *ḥāʾik*]

haiku /hīkoo/ *n.* (*pl.* same) **1** a Japanese three line poem of usu. 17 syllables. **2** an English imitation of this. [Jap.]

hail[1] /hayl/ *n. & v.* ● *n.* **1** pellets of frozen rain falling in showers from cumulonimbus clouds. **2** (foll. by *of*) a barrage or onslaught (of missiles, curses, questions, etc.). ● *v.* **1** *intr.* (prec. by *it* as subject) hail falls (*it is hailing*; *if it hails*). **2 a** *tr.* pour down (blows, words, etc.). **b** *intr.* come down forcefully. [OE *hagol*, *hægl*, *hagalian* f. Gmc]

■ *n.* sleet. **2** barrage, onslaught, volley, storm, shower, torrent, bombardment. ● *v.* **1** sleet. **2** rain, shower, pour, volley; pelt.

hail[2] /hayl/ *v., int.,* & *n.* ● *v.* **1** *tr.* greet enthusiastically. **2** *tr.* signal to or attract the attention of (*hailed a taxi*). **3** *tr.* acclaim (*hailed him king*; *was hailed as a prodigy*). **4** *intr.* (foll. by *from*) have one's home or origins in (a place) (*hails from Mexico*). ● *int. archaic* or *rhet.* expressing greeting. ● *n.* **1** a greeting or act of hailing. **2** distance as affecting the possibility of hailing (*was within hail*). □ **hail-fellow-well-met** jovially intimate, esp. too intimate. **Hail Mary** the Ave Maria (see AVE). □□ **hailer** *n.* [ellipt. use of obs. *hail* (adj.) f. ON *heill* sound, WHOLE]

■ *v.* **1** salute, greet; welcome, receive, meet, acknowledge, address, accost. **2** call, flag down, stop. **3** acclaim, acknowledge, *archaic* salute; cheer, applaud, approve, glorify, praise, laud, honor. **4** (*hail from*) come *or* be from; be a native *or* inhabitant *or* product of, trace one's roots to. ● *int.* see HELLO. ● *n.* **1** greeting, salutation; welcome, reception. **2** hailing distance.
□ **hail-fellow-well-met** see FAMILIAR *adj.* 4.

hailstone /háylstōn/ *n.* a pellet of hail.

hailstorm /háylstorm/ *n.* a period of heavy hail.

■ see STORM *n.* 1.

hair /hair/ *n.* **1 a** any of the fine threadlike strands growing from the skin of mammals, esp. from the human head. **b** these collectively (*his hair is falling out*). **c** a hairstyle or way of wearing the hair (*I like your hair today*). **2 a** an artificially produced hairlike strand, e.g., in a brush. **b** a mass of such hairs. **3** anything resembling a hair. **4** an elongated cell growing from the epidermis of a plant. **5** a very small quantity or extent (also *attrib.*: *a hair crack*). □ **get in a person's hair** *colloq.* encumber or annoy a person. **hair dryer** (or **drier**) an electrical device for drying the hair by blowing warm air over it. **hair grass** any of various grasses, esp. of the genus *Deschampsia, Corynephous, Aira*, etc., with slender stems. **hair of the dog** see DOG. **hair-raising** extremely alarming; terrifying. **hair's breadth** a very small amount or margin. **hair shirt** a shirt of haircloth, worn formerly by penitents and ascetics. **hair-shirt** *adj.* (*attrib.*) austere, harsh, self-sacrificing. **hair-slide** *Brit.* a (usu. ornamental) clip for keeping the hair in position; a barrette. **hair spray** a solution sprayed on the hair to keep it in place. **hair trigger** a trigger of a firearm set for release at the slightest pressure. **hair-trigger** reacting to the slightest pressure, stimulus, or provocation. **keep one's hair on** *Brit. colloq.* remain calm; not get angry. **let one's hair down** *colloq.* abandon restraint; behave freely or wildly. **make a person's hair stand on end** alarm or horrify a person. **not turn a hair** remain apparently unmoved or unaffected. □□ **haired** *adj.* (also in *comb.*). **hairless** *adj.* **hairlike** *adj.* [OE *hǣr* f. Gmc]

■ **1 b** tresses, locks, head of hair, mop, *colloq.* mane. **c** hairstyle, haircut, coiffure, cut, *colloq.* hairdo. **3** fiber, thread, filament, strand, fibril. **5** trifle, fraction, narrow margin, *colloq.* whisker; hair's breadth, hairbreadth, skin of one's teeth. □ **get in a person's hair** see ANNOY 1. **hair-raising** see *terrifying* (TERRIFY). **hair's breadth** see HAIR 5 above. **hair-shirt** self-sacrificing, self-immolating, self-punishing, masochistic, ascetic; see also HARSH 2. **let one's hair down** see REVEL *v.* 1, *enjoy oneself*. **make a person's hair stand on end** see

SCARE *v.* 1. **not turn a hair** be *or* remain calm, keep one's head, *colloq.* not *or* never bat an eyelid; keep one's shirt on, *sl.* cool it. □□ **hairless** bald, bald-headed, bald-pated, glabrous; see also SMOOTH *adj.* 2.

hairball /háirbawl/ *n.* (also **hair ball**) a compact ball of hair that accumulates in the stomach of a cat or other animal that grooms itself by licking its fur.

hairbreadth /háirbredth/ *n.* = *hair's breadth*; (esp. *attrib.*: *a hairbreadth escape*).

hairbrush /háirbrush/ *n.* a brush for arranging or smoothing the hair.

haircloth /háirklawth, -kloth/ *n.* stiff cloth woven from hair, used, e.g., in upholstery.

haircut /háirkut/ *n.* **1** a cutting of the hair. **2** the style in which the hair is cut.

hairdo /háirdoo/ *n.* (*pl.* **-dos**) *colloq.* the style or an act of styling a woman's hair.

■ hairstyle, haircut, coiffure, hair, cut.

hairdresser /háirdresər/ *n.* **1** a person who cuts and styles hair, esp. professionally. **2** the business or establishment of a hairdresser. □□ **hairdressing** *n.*

hairgrip /háirgrip/ *n. Brit.* a flat hairpin with the ends close together; a bobby pin.

hairline /háirlīn/ *n.* **1** the edge of a person's hair, esp. on the forehead. **2** a very thin line or crack, etc.

hairnet /háirnet/ *n.* a piece of fine mesh fabric for confining the hair.

hairpiece /háirpees/ *n.* a quantity or switch of detached hair used to augment a person's natural hair.

hairpin /háirpin/ *n.* a U-shaped pin for fastening the hair. □ **hairpin bend** (or **turn**) a sharp U-shaped bend in a road.

hairsplitting /háirspliting/ *adj. & n.* making overfine distinctions; quibbling. □□ **hairsplitter** *n.*

■ quibbling, (over)fussy, hypercritical, petty, captious, finicky, niggling, *colloq.* nitpicking.

hairspring /háirspring/ *n.* a fine spring regulating the balance wheel in a watch.

hairstreak /háirstreek/ *n.* a butterfly of the genus *Strymonidia*, etc., with fine streaks or rows of spots on its wings.

hairstyle /háirstīl/ *n.* a particular way of arranging or dressing the hair. □□ **hairstyling** *n.* **hairstylist** *n.*

■ see HAIRDO.

hairy /háiree/ *adj.* (**hairier, hairiest**) **1** made of or covered with hair. **2** having the feel of hair. **3** *sl.* **a** alarmingly unpleasant or difficult. **b** crude; clumsy. □□ **hairily** *adv.* **hairiness** *n.*

■ **1** hirsute, shaggy, downy, fleecy, fluffy, woolly, bristly, fringy, strigose; whiskered, whiskery, bearded, unshaven; *Bot.* comose, *Bot. & Zool.* setaceous, hispid. **2** downy, fluffy, woolly; rough, bristly. **3 a** unpleasant, dangerous, perilous, risky, uncertain, precarious, hazardous, frightening, worrying, nerve-racking, *colloq.* scary; tricky, difficult, knotty, complex, complicated, problematic.

hajj /haj/ *n.* (also **hadj**) the Islamic pilgrimage to Mecca. [Arab. *ḥajj* pilgrimage]

■ see PILGRIMAGE *n.* 1.

hajji /hájee/ *n.* (also **hadji**) (*pl.* **-is**) a Muslim who has been to Mecca as a pilgrim: also (**Hajji**) used as a title. [Pers. *ḥājī* (partly through Turk. *hacı*) f. Arab. *ḥajj*: see HAJJ]

■ see PILGRIM *n.*

hake /hayk/ *n.* any marine fish of the genus *Merluccius*, esp. *M. merluccius* with an elongate body and large head. [ME perh. ult. f. dial. *hake* hook + FISH[1]]

hakenkreuz /haákənkroyts/ *n.* a swastika, esp. as a Nazi symbol. [G f. *Haken* hook + *Kreuz* CROSS]

hakim[1] /haakéem/ *n.* (in India and Islamic countries) **1** a wise man. **2** a physician. [Arab. *ḥakīm* wise man, physician]

hakim[2] /haákeem/ *n.* (in India and Muslim countries) a judge, ruler, or governor. [Arab. *ḥākim* governor]

Halakah /haalaakhaá, həlaákhə, -láw-/ *n.* (also **Halachah**) Jewish law and jurisprudence, based on the Talmud. □□ **Halachic** /-laákhik/ *adj.* [Aram. *hᵃlākāh* law]

halal /haalaál/ *v. & n.* (also **hallal**) ● *v.tr.* (**halalled, halalling**) kill (an animal) as prescribed by Muslim law. ● *n.*

(often *attrib.*) meat prepared in this way; lawful food. [Arab. *ḥalāl* lawful]

halation /haláyshən/ *n. Photog.* the spreading of light beyond its proper extent in a developed image, caused by internal reflection in the support of the emulsion. [irreg. f. HALO + -ATION]

halberd /hálbərd/ *n.* (also **halbert** /-bərt/) *hist.* a combined spear and battleax. [ME f. F *hallebarde* f. It *alabarda* f. MHG *helmbarde* f. *helm* handle + *barde* hatchet]

halberdier /hálbərdeʹer/ *n. hist.* a man armed with a halberd. [F *hallebardier* (as HALBERD)]

halcyon /hálseeən/ *adj. & n.* ● *adj.* **1** calm; peaceful (*halcyon days*). **2** (of a period) happy, prosperous. ● *n.* **1** any kingfisher of the genus *Halcyon*, native to Europe, Africa, and Australasia, with brightly colored plumage. **2** *Mythol.* a bird thought in antiquity to breed in a nest floating at sea at the winter solstice, charming the wind and waves into calm. [ME f. L (*h*)*alcyon* f. Gk (*h*)*alkuōn* kingfisher]
■ *adj.* **1** see CALM *adj.* 1. **2** see GOLDEN 3.

hale[1] /hayl/ *adj.* (esp. of an old person) strong and healthy (esp. in **hale and hearty**). □□ **haleness** *n.* [OE *hāl* WHOLE]
■ strong, healthy, hearty, fit (as a fiddle), sound, able-bodied, hardy, robust, flourishing, in good *or* fine fettle, spry, sprightly, *colloq.* in the pink.

hale[2] /hayl/ *v.tr.* drag or draw forcibly. [ME f. OF *haler* f. ON *hala*]

half /haf/ *n., adj., & adv.* ● *n.* (*pl.* **halves** /havz/) **1** either of two equal or corresponding parts or groups into which a thing is or might be divided. **2** *colloq.* = HALFBACK. **3** *Brit. colloq.* half a pint, esp. of beer, etc. **4** either of two equal periods of play in sports. **5** *colloq.* a half-price fare or ticket, esp. for a child. **6** *Golf* a score that is the same as one's opponent's. ● *adj.* **1** of an amount or quantity equal to a half, or loosely to a part thought of as roughly a half (*take half the men; spent half the time reading; half a pint; a half pint; half-price*). **2** forming a half (*a half share*). ● *adv.* **1** (often in *comb.*) to the extent of half; partly (*only half cooked; half-frozen; half-laughing*). **2** to a certain extent; somewhat (esp. in idiomatic phrases: *half dead; am half inclined to agree*). **3** (in reckoning time) by the amount of half (an hour, etc.) (*half past two*). □ **at half cock** see COCK[1]. **by half** (prec. by *too* + adj.) excessively (*too clever by half*). **by halves** imperfectly or incompletely (*never does things by halves*). **half-and-half** being half one thing and half another, esp. a liquid of half cream and half milk. **half-baked 1** incompletely considered or planned. **2** (of enthusiasm, etc.) only partly committed. **3** foolish. **half the battle** see BATTLE. **half binding** a type of bookbinding in which the spine and corners are bound in one material (usu. leather) and the sides in another. **half-blood 1** a person having one parent in common with another. **2** this relationship. **3** = *half breed*. **half-blooded** born from parents of different races. **half board** *Brit.* provision of bed, breakfast, and one main meal at a hotel, etc. **half boot** a boot reaching up to the calf. **half breed** often *offens.* a person of mixed race. **half brother** a brother with only one parent in common. **half caste** often *offens. n.* a person whose parents are of different races, esp. the offspring of a European father and an E. Indian mother. ● *adj.* of or relating to such a person. **half a chance** *colloq.* the slightest opportunity (esp. *given half a chance*). **half crown** (or **half a crown**) (in the UK) a former coin and monetary unit worth two shillings and sixpence (12¹/₂p). **half-dozen** (or **half a dozen**) *colloq.* six, or about six. **half-duplex** see DUPLEX. **half an eye** the slightest degree of perceptiveness. **half-hardy** (of a plant) able to grow in the open air at all times except in severe frost. **half hitch** a noose or knot formed by passing the end of a rope around its standing part and then through the loop. **half-holiday** a day of which half (usu. the afternoon) is taken as a holiday. **half hour 1** (also **half an hour**) a period of 30 minutes. **2** a point of time 30 minutes after any hour o'clock. **half-hourly** at intervals of 30 minutes. **half-inch** *n.* a unit of length half as large as an inch. ● *v.tr. Brit. rhyming sl.* steal (= *pinch*). **half-landing** a landing part of the way up a flight of stairs, whose length is twice the width of the flight plus

the width of the well. **half-lap** the joining of rails, shafts, etc., by halving the thickness of each at one end and fitting them together. **half-length** a portrait of a person's upper half. **half-life** *Physics & Biochem.*, etc., the time taken for the radioactivity or some other property of a substance to fall to half its original value. **half-light** a dim imperfect light. **half-mast** the position of a flag halfway down the mast, as a mark of respect for a person who has died. **half measures** an unsatisfactory compromise or inadequate policy. **half a mind** see MIND. **half moon 1** the moon when only half its illuminated surface is visible from earth. **2** the time when this occurs. **3** a semicircular object. **half nelson** *Wrestling* see NELSON. **half note** *Mus.* a note whose duration is one half of a whole note; minim. **the half of it** *colloq.* the rest or more important part of something (usu. after *neg.*: *you don't know the half of it*). **half pay** reduced income, esp. on retirement. **half-pie** *NZ sl.* imperfect, mediocre. **half-seas-over** *Brit. sl.* partly drunk. **half sister** a sister with only one parent in common. **half sole** the sole of a boot or shoe from the shank to the toe. **half sovereign** a former British gold coin and monetary unit worth ten shillings (50p). **half-starved** poorly or insufficiently fed; malnourished. **half step** *Mus.* a semitone. **half-term** *Brit.* a period about halfway through a school term, when a short vacation is usually taken. **half-timbered** *Archit.* having walls with a timber frame and a brick or plaster filling. **half-time** *n.* **1** the time at which half of a game or contest is completed. **2** a short interval occurring at this time. ● *adj.* working half the usual or normal hours. **half the time** see TIME. **half title 1** the title or short title of a book, printed on the recto of the leaf preceding the title page. **2** the title of a section of a book printed on the recto of the leaf preceding it. **half-track 1** a propulsion system for land vehicles with wheels at the front and a continuous track at the back. **2** a vehicle equipped with this. **half-truth** a statement that, esp. deliberately, conveys only part of the truth. **half volley** (*pl.* -**eys**) (in ball games) the playing of a ball as soon as it bounces off the ground. **half-yearly** esp. *Brit.* at intervals of six months. **not half 1** not nearly (*not half long enough*). **2** *colloq.* not at all (*not half bad*). **3** *Brit. sl.* to an extreme degree (*he didn't half get angry*). [OE *half, healf* f. Gmc, orig. = 'side']

halfback /háfbak/ *n.* (in some sports) a player between the linemen and fullbacks, or behind the forward line.

halfbeak /háfbeek/ *n.* any fish of the family Hemirhamphidae with the lower jaw projecting beyond the upper.

halfhearted /háfhaártid/ *adj.* lacking enthusiasm; feeble. □□ **halfheartedly** *adv.* **halfheartedness** *n.*
■ feeble, lukewarm, unenthusiastic, indifferent, unconcerned, uninterested, half-baked, lackadaisical.

halfpenny /háypnee/ *n.* (also **ha'penny**) (*pl.* -**pennies** or -**pence** /háypəns/) (in the UK) a former bronze coin worth half a penny. ¶ Withdrawn in 1984 (cf. FARTHING).

halfpennyworth /háypəth/ *n. Brit.* (also **ha'p'orth**) **1** as much as could be bought for a halfpenny. **2** *colloq.* a negligible amount (esp. after *neg.*: *doesn't make a halfpennyworth of difference*).

halftone /háftōn/ *n.* **1** a reproduction printed from a block (produced by photographic means) in which the various tones of gray are produced from small and large black dots. **2** *Mus.* (**half tone**) a semitone.

halfway /háfway/ *adv. & adj.* ● *adv.* **1** at a point equidistant between two others (*we were halfway to Chicago*). **2** to some extent; more or less (*is halfway decent*). ● *adj.* situated halfway (*reached a halfway point*). □ **halfway house 1** a compromise. **2** the halfway point in a progression. **3** a center for rehabilitating ex-prisoners, mental patients, or others unused to normal life. **4** an inn midway between two towns. **halfway line** a line midway between the ends of a sports field, esp. in soccer.

/.../ **pronunciation**	● **part of speech**
□ **phrases, idioms, and compounds**	
□□ **derivatives**	■ **synonym section**
cross-references appear in SMALL CAPITALS or *italics*	

■ *adj.* see INTERMEDIATE *adj.*

halfwit /háfwit/ *n.* **1** *colloq.* an extremely foolish or stupid person. **2** a person who is mentally deficient. □□ **halfwitted** /wítid/ *adj.* **halfwittedly** *adv.* **halfwittedness** *n.*

■ **1** dunce, fool, idiot, simpleton, ninny, ass, dolt, dunderhead, nincompoop, dullard, numskull, *colloq.* moron, imbecile, nitwit, dimwit, birdbrain, cretin, esp. *Brit. sl.* nit, twit. □□ **halfwitted** stupid, foolish, silly, inane, asinine, doltish, feeble-minded, non compos (mentis), weak-minded, *colloq.* moronic, imbecilic, cretinous, thick, dotty, dim-witted, dumb, *sl.* balmy, esp. *Brit. sl.* barmy.

halibut /hálibət/ *n.* (also **holibut** /hól-/) (*pl.* same) a large marine flatfish, *Hippoglossus vulgaris*, used as food. [ME f. *haly* HOLY + BUTT³ flatfish, perh. because eaten on holy days]

halide /hálīd, háyl-/ *n. Chem.* **1** a binary compound of a halogen with another group or element. **2** any organic compound containing a halogen.

halieutic /hálee-ōotik/ *adj. formal* of or concerning fishing. [L *halieuticus* f. Gk *halieutikos* f. *halieutēs* fisherman]

haliotis /háleeōtis/ *n.* any edible gastropod mollusk of the genus *Haliotis* with an ear-shaped shell lined with mother-of-pearl. [Gk *hals hali*- sea + *ous ōt*- ear]

halite /hálīt, háy-/ *n.* rock salt. [mod.L *halites* f. Gk *hals* salt]

halitosis /hálitōsis/ *n.* = *bad breath*. [mod.L f. L *halitus* breath]

hall /hawl/ *n.* **1 a** a space or passage into which the front entrance of a house, etc., opens. **b** a corridor or passage in a building. **2 a** a large room or building for meetings, meals, concerts, etc. **b** *Brit.* (in *pl.*) music halls. **3** *Brit.* a large country house, esp. with a landed estate. **4** a university residence for students. **5 a** (in an English college, a residence hall, etc.) a common dining room. **b** *Brit.* dinner in this. **6** the building of a guild (*Fishmongers' Hall*). **7 a** a large public room in a palace, etc. **b** the principal living room of a medieval house. □ **Hall of Fame** a building with memorials to individuals who excelled in a sport, etc. **hall porter** *Brit.* a porter who carries baggage, etc., in a hotel. [OE = *hall* f. Gmc, rel. to HELL]

■ **1** passage, hallway, passageway, corridor; entrance (hall), entry(way), lobby, vestibule; foyer. **2 a** auditorium, amphitheater, theater; lecture room, lecture hall, lecture theater, concert hall, ballroom; assembly rooms. **b** (*halls*) music halls. **4** see ACCOMMODATION 1.

hallal var. of HALAL.

hallelujah var. of ALLELUIA.

halliard var. of HALYARD.

hallmark /háwlmaark/ *n. & v.* ● *n.* **1** a mark used at Goldsmiths' Hall in London (and by the UK assay offices) for marking the standard of gold, silver, and platinum. **2** any distinctive feature, esp. of excellence. ● *v.tr.* **1** stamp with a hallmark. **2** designate as excellent.

■ *n.* **1** stamp, mark, sign, symbol; plate mark, assay mark. **2** feature, stamp, mark, trademark, sign, characteristic.

hallo esp. *Brit.* var. of HELLO.

halloo /həlōo/ *int., n.,* & *v.* ● *int.* **1** inciting dogs to the chase. **2** calling attention. **3** expressing surprise. ● *n.* the cry "halloo." ● *v.* (**halloos, hallooed**) **1** *intr.* cry "halloo," esp. to dogs. **2** *intr.* shout to attract attention. **3** *tr.* urge on (dogs, etc.) with shouts. [perh. f. *hallow* pursue with shouts f. OF *halloer* (imit.)]

hallow /hálō/ *v. & n.* ● *v.tr.* **1** make holy; consecrate. **2** honor as holy. ● *n. archaic* a saint or holy person. □ **All Hallows** All Saints' Day, Nov. 1. [OE *hālgian, hālga* f. Gmc]

■ *v.* **1** consecrate, bless, sanctify; dedicate. **2** venerate, worship, revere, reverence, respect, honor, pay homage to, exalt, glorify. ● *n.* saint, holy man *or* woman, man *or* woman of God.

Halloween /hálōwéen/ *n.* (also **Hallowe'en**) the eve of All Saints' Day, Oct. 31, esp. as celebrated by children dressing in costumes and collecting treats door-to-door. [HALLOW + EVEN²]

Hallstatt /haálshtaat/ *adj.* of or relating to the early Iron Age in Europe as attested by archaeological finds at Hallstatt in Upper Austria.

halluces *pl.* of HALLUX.

hallucinate /həlōōsinayt/ *v.* **1** *tr.* produce illusions in the mind of (a person). **2** *intr.* experience hallucinations. □□ **hallucinant** /-nənt/ *adj. & n.* **hallucinator** *n.* [L (*h*)*allucinari* wander in mind f. Gk *alussō* be uneasy]

■ **2** see TRIP *v.* 7.

hallucination /həlōōsináyshən/ *n.* the apparent or alleged perception of an object not actually present. □□ **hallucinatory** /-sinətáwree/ *adj.* [L *hallucinatio* (as HALLUCINATE)]

■ mirage, illusion, vision, chimera, phantasm, phantom, figment, apparition. □□ **hallucinatory** dreamy, dreamlike, visionary; phantasmagorical, chimerical, fantastic, illusory, fanciful, fancied, imaginary, imagined, fictional, unreal, untrue, fallacious, false.

hallucinogen /həlōōsinəjən/ *n.* a drug causing hallucinations. □□ **hallucinogenic** /-jénik/ *adj.*

■ see DRUG *n.* 2.

hallux /háluks/ *n.* (*pl.* **halluces** /hályəseez/) **1** the big toe. **2** the innermost digit of the hind foot of vertebrates. [mod.L f. L *allex*]

hallway /háwlway/ *n.* an entrance hall or corridor.

■ see HALL 1.

halm var. of HAULM.

halma /hálmə/ *n.* a game played by two or four persons on a board of 256 squares, with men advancing from one corner to the opposite corner by being moved over other men into vacant squares. [Gk, = leap]

halo /háylō/ *n. & v.* ● *n.* (*pl.* **-oes**) **1** a disk or circle of light shown in art surrounding the head of a sacred person. **2** the glory associated with an idealized person, etc. **3** a circle of white or colored light around a luminous body, esp. the sun or moon. **4** a circle or ring. ● *v.tr.* (**-oes, -oed**) surround with a halo. [med.L f. L f. Gk *halōs* threshing floor, disk of the sun or moon]

■ *n.* **1, 3** nimbus, aura, aureole; corona, radiance, *Art* vesica, mandorla. **2** see GLORY *n.* 3. **4** ring, disk, circle; loop, wheel.

halogen /háləjən/ *n. Chem.* any of the group of nonmetallic elements: fluorine, chlorine, bromine, iodine, and astatine, which form halides (e.g., sodium chloride) by simple union with a metal. □□ **halogenic** /-jénik/ *adj.* [Gk *hals halos* salt]

halogenation /háləjináyshən/ *n.* the introduction of a halogen atom into a molecule.

halon /háylon/ *n. Chem.* any of various gaseous compounds of carbon, bromine, and other halogens, used to extinguish fires. [as HALOGEN + -ON]

halt¹ /hawlt/ *n. & v.* ● *n.* **1** a stop (usu. temporary); an interruption of progress (*come to a halt*). **2** a temporary stoppage on a march or journey. **3** *Brit.* a minor stopping place on a local railroad line, usu. without permanent buildings. ● *v.intr. & tr.* stop; come or bring to a halt. □ **call a halt (to)** decide to stop. [orig. in phr. *make halt* f. G *Halt machen* f. *halten* hold, stop]

■ *n.* **1** stop, standstill, stoppage, cessation, interruption, break; end, termination, close. **2** see PAUSE *n.*, HOLDUP 1. ● *v.* end, terminate, finish, cease, call a halt (to), discontinue, conclude, shut *or* close down; check, stem; see also STOP *v.* 1, 2. □ **call a halt (to)** see HALT¹ *v.* above and STOP *v.* 1, 2.

halt² /hawlt/ *v. & adj.* ● *v.intr.* **1** (esp. as **halting** *adj.*) lack smooth progress. **2** hesitate (*halt between two opinions*). **3** walk hesitatingly. **4** *archaic* be lame. ● *adj. archaic* lame or crippled. □□ **haltingly** *adv.* [OE *halt, healt, healtian* f. Gmc]

■ *v.* **1** (**halting**) hesitant, wavering, uneven, faltering, faulty, unsteady, awkward; stammering, stuttering. **2** see HESITATE 1. **3** dawdle, drag one's feet, scuff, shuffle, scrape along, shamble. ● *adj.* crippled, game; see also LAME *adj.* 1.

halter /háwltər/ *n. & v.* ● *n.* **1** a rope or strap with a noose or headstall for leading or tying up horses or cattle. **2 a** a strap around the back of a woman's neck holding her dress top or blouse and leaving her shoulders and back bare. **b** a dress top or blouse held by this. **3 a** a rope with a noose for hanging a person. **b** death by hanging. ● *v.tr.* **1** put a halter on (a horse, etc.). **2** hang (a person) with a halter. [OE *hælftre*: cf. HELVE]

■ *n.* **1** see TETHER *n.*

halterbreak /háwltərbrayk/ *v.tr.* accustom (a horse) to a halter.

halteres /haltéereez/ *n.pl.* the balancing organs of dipterous insects. [Gk, = weights used to aid leaping f. *hallomai* to leap]

halva /haálvaá/ *n.* (also **halvah**) a sweet confection of ground sesame seeds and honey. [Yiddish f. Turk. *helva* f. Arab. *ḥalwa*]

halve /hav/ *v.tr.* **1** divide into two halves or parts. **2** reduce by half. **3** share equally (with another person, etc.). **4** *Golf* use the same number of strokes as one's opponent in (a hole or match). **5** fit (two pieces of wood) together by cutting out half the thickness of each. [ME *halfen* f. HALF]

■ **1–3** see SPLIT *v.* 1a.

halves *pl.* of HALF.

halyard /hályərd/ *n.* (also **halliard, haulyard** /háwlyərd/) *Naut.* a rope or tackle for raising or lowering a sail or yard, etc. [ME *halier* f. HALE² + -IER, assoc. with YARD¹]

ham /ham/ *n. & v.* ● *n.* **1 a** the upper part of a pig's leg salted and dried or smoked for food. **b** the meat from this. **2** the back of the thigh; the thigh and buttock. **3** *sl.* (often *attrib.*) an inexpert or unsubtle actor or piece of acting. **4** (in full **radio ham**) *colloq.* the operator of an amateur radio station or holder of an amateur radio license. ● *v.intr.* & (often foll. by *up*) *tr.* (**hammed, hamming**) *sl.* overact; act or treat emotionally or sentimentally. [OE *ham, hom* f. a Gmc root meaning 'be crooked']

■ *n.* **1, 2** see LEG *n.* 1–3. **3** see THESPIAN *n.* ● *v.* see DRAMATIZE.

hamadryad /hámədríad/ *n.* **1** (in Greek and Roman mythology) a nymph who lives in a tree and dies when it dies. **2** the king cobra, *Naja bungarus*. [ME f. L *hamadryas* f. Gk *hamadruas* f. *hama* with + *drus* tree]

hamadryas /hámədríəs/ *n.* a large Arabian baboon, *Papio hamadryas*, with a silvery gray cape of hair over the shoulders, held sacred in ancient Egypt.

hamamelis /háməmeélis/ *n.* any shrub of the genus *Hamamelis*, e.g., witch hazel. [mod.L f. Gk *hamamēlis* medlar]

hamba /hámbə/ *int. S.Afr.* be off; go away. [Nguni *-hambe* go]

hambone /hámbōn/ *n. Austral. colloq.* a male striptease show. [20th c.: orig. uncert.]

hamburger /hámbərgər/ *n.* a patty of ground beef, usu. fried or grilled and eaten in a soft bread roll. [G, = of Hamburg in Germany]

hames /haymz/ *n.pl.* two curved pieces of iron or wood forming the collar or part of the collar of a draft horse, to which the traces are attached. [ME f. MDu. *hame*]

ham-fisted /hámfístid/ *adj. colloq.* clumsy; heavy-handed; bungling. ○○ **ham-fistedly** *adv.* **ham-fistedness** *n.*

■ see CLUMSY 1.

ham-handed /hámhándid/ *adj. colloq.* = HAM-FISTED. ○○ **ham-handedly** *adv.* **ham-handedness** *n.*

Hamitic /həmítik/ *n. & adj.* ● *n.* a group of African languages including ancient Egyptian and Berber. ● *adj.* **1** of or relating to this group of languages. **2** of or relating to the Hamites, a group of peoples in Egypt and N. Africa, by tradition descended from Noah's son Ham (Gen. 10:6 ff.).

hamlet /hámlit/ *n.* a small village. [ME f. AF *hamelet(t)e*, OF *hamelet* dimin. of *hamel* dimin. of *ham* f. MLG *hamm*]

■ see SETTLEMENT 2.

hammer /hámər/ *n. & v.* ● *n.* **1 a** a tool with a heavy metal head at right angles to the handle, used for breaking, driving nails, etc. **b** a machine with a metal block serving the same purpose. **c** a similar contrivance, as for exploding the charge in a gun, striking the strings of a piano, etc. **2** an auctioneer's mallet, indicating by a rap that an article is sold. **3 a** a metal ball of about 7 kg, attached to a wire for throwing in an athletic contest. **b** the sport of throwing the hammer. **4** a bone of the middle ear; the malleus. **5** *sl.* the accelerator of a motor vehicle. ● *v.* **1 a** *tr.* & *intr.* hit or beat with or as

with a hammer. **b** *intr.* strike loudly; knock violently (esp. on a door). **2** *tr.* **a** drive in (nails) with a hammer. **b** fasten or secure by hammering (*hammered the lid down*). **3** *tr.* (often foll. by *in*) inculcate (ideas, knowledge, etc.) forcefully or repeatedly. **4** *tr. colloq.* utterly defeat; inflict heavy damage on. **5** *intr.* (foll. by *at, away at*) work hard or persistently at. **6** *tr. Brit. Stock Exch.* declare (a person or a business) a defaulter. □ **come under the hammer** be sold at an auction. **hammer and sickle** the symbols of the industrial worker and the peasant used as the emblem of the former USSR and of international communism. **hammer and tongs** *colloq.* with great vigor and commotion. **hammer out 1** make flat or smooth by hammering. **2** work out the details of (a plan, agreement, etc.) laboriously. **3** play (a tune, esp. on the piano) loudly or clumsily. ○○ **hammering** *n.* (esp. in sense 4 of *v.*). **hammerless** *adj.* [OE *hamor, hamer*]

■ *v.* **1, 2a** see POUND² *v.* 1a, b. **3** see DIN *v.*

hammerbeam /hámərbeem/ *n.* a wooden beam (often carved) projecting from a wall to support the principal rafter or the end of an arch.

hammerhead /hámərhed/ *n.* **1** the striking head of a hammer. **2** any shark of the family Sphyrinidae, with a flattened head and eyes in lateral extensions of it. **3** a long-legged African marsh bird, *Scopus umbretta*, with a thick bill and an occipital crest.

hammerlock /hámərlok/ *n. Wrestling* a hold in which the arm is twisted and bent behind the back.

hammertoe /hámərtō/ *n.* a deformity in which the toe is bent permanently downwards.

hammock /hámək/ *n.* a bed of canvas or rope network, suspended by cords at the ends. [earlier *hamaca* f. Sp., of Carib orig.]

hammy /hámee/ *adj.* (**hammier, hammiest**) **1** of or like ham. **2** *colloq.* (of an actor or acting) over-theatrical.

■ **2** see *melodramatic* (MELODRAMA).

hamper¹ /hámpər/ *n.* **1** a large basket, usu. with a hinged lid and containing laundry or (esp. *Brit.*) food (*clothes hamper; picnic hamper*). **2** *Brit.* a selection of food, drink, etc., for an occasion. [ME f. obs. *hanaper*, AF f. OF *hanapier* case for a goblet f. *hanap* goblet]

hamper² /hámpər/ *v. & n.* ● *v.tr.* **1** prevent the free movement or activity of; impede; hinder. ● *n. Naut.* necessary but cumbersome equipment on a ship. [ME: orig. unkn.]

■ *v.* encumber, obstruct, block, impede, prevent; balk, thwart, hinder, delay, check, slow down, bog down, hold up, tie (up *or* down), retard, inhibit, interfere with, snarl (up), frustrate, restrict, curb, limit, handicap, trammel, bar, *archaic or literary* stay.

hamsin var. of KHAMSIN.

hamster /hámstər/ *n.* any of various rodents of the subfamily Cricetinae, esp. *Cricetus cricetus*, having a short tail and large cheek pouches for storing food, kept as a pet or laboratory animal. [G f. OHG *hamustro* weevil]

hamstring /hámstring/ *n. & v. Anat.* ● *n.* **1** each of five tendons at the back of the knee in humans. **2** the great tendon at the back of the hock in quadrupeds. ● *v.tr.* (*past* and *past part.* **hamstrung** or **hamstringed**) **1** cripple by cutting the hamstrings of (a person or animal). **2** prevent the activity or efficiency of (a person or enterprise).

■ *v.* **1** see LAME *v.* **2** see FRUSTRATE *v.* 2.

hamulus /hámyələs/ *n.* (*pl.* **hamuli** /-lī/) *Anat., Zool.,* & *Bot.* a hooklike process. [L, dimin. of *hamus* hook]

hand /hand/ *n. & v.* ● *n.* **1 a** the end part of the human arm beyond the wrist, including the fingers and thumb. **b** in other primates, the end part of a forelimb, also used as a foot. **2 a** (often in *pl.*) control; management; custody; disposal (*is in good hands*). **b** agency or influence (*suffered at their hands*). **c** a share in an action; active support. **3** a thing compared with a hand or its functions, esp. the pointer of a

---

/. . ./ **pronunciation**	● **part of speech**
□ **phrases, idioms, and compounds**	
○○ **derivatives**	■ **synonym section**
cross-references appear in SMALL CAPITALS or *italics*	

clock or watch. **4** the right or left side or direction relative to a person or thing. **5 a** a skill, esp. in something practical (*a hand for making pastry*). **b** a person skillful in some respect. **6** a person who does or makes something, esp. distinctively (*a picture by the same hand*). **7** an individual's writing or the style of this; a signature (*a legible hand; in one's own hand; witness the hand of . . .*). **8** a person, etc., as the source of information, etc. (*at first hand*). **9** a pledge of marriage. **10** a person as a source of manual labor, esp. in a factory, on a farm, or on board ship. **11 a** the playing cards dealt to a player. **b** the player holding these. **c** a round of play. **12** *colloq.* applause (*got a big hand*). **13** the unit of measure of a horse's height, equal to 4 inches (10.16 cm). **14** a forehock of pork. **15** a bunch of bananas. **16** (*attrib.*) **a** operated or held in the hand (*hand drill; hand luggage*). **b** done by hand and not by machine (*hand-knitted*). ● *v.tr.* **1** (foll. by *in, to, over*, etc.) deliver; transfer by hand or otherwise. **2** convey verbally (*handed me a lot of abuse*). **3** *colloq.* give away too readily (*handed them the advantage*). □ **all hands 1** the entire crew of a ship. **2** the entire workforce. **at hand 1** close by. **2** about to happen. **by hand 1** by a person and not a machine. **2** delivered privately and not by the public mail. **from hand to mouth** satisfying only one's immediate needs (also *attrib.*: *a hand-to-mouth existence*). **get** (or **have** or **keep**) **one's hand in** become (or be or remain) practiced in something. **hand and foot** completely; satisfying all demands (*waited on them hand and foot*). **hand around** distribute. **hand cream** a lotion for the hands. **hand down 1** pass the ownership or use of to another. **2 a** transmit (a decision) from a higher court, etc. **b** express (an opinion or verdict). **hand grenade** see GRENADE. **hand in glove** in collusion or association. **hand in hand** in close association. **hand it to** *colloq.* acknowledge the merit of (a person). **hand-me-down** an article of clothing, etc., passed on from another person. **hand off 1** *Football* hand (a football) to a teammate in the course of play. **2** pass along (responsibility, etc.) **3** *Rugby* push off (a tackling opponent) with the hand. **hand on** pass (a thing) to the next in a series or succession. **hand out 1** serve; distribute. **2** award; allocate (*the judges handed out stiff sentences*). **hand over** deliver; surrender possession of. **hand-over** *n.* the act or an instance of handing over. **hand-over-fist** *colloq.* with rapid progress. **hands down** (esp. of winning) with no difficulty. **hands off 1** a warning not to touch or interfere with something. **2** *Computing*, etc., not requiring manual use of controls. **hands on 1** *Computing* of or requiring personal operation at a keyboard. **2** direct; practical; involving or offering active participation rather than theory. **hands up!** an instruction to raise one's hands in surrender or to signify assent or participation. **hand-to-hand** (of fighting) at close quarters. **have** (or **take**) **a hand** (often foll. by *in*) share or take part. **have one's hands full** be fully occupied. **have one's hands tied** *colloq.* be unable to act. **hold one's hand** = *stay one's hand* (see HAND). **in hand 1** receiving attention. **2** in reserve; at one's disposal. **3** under one's control. **lay** (or **put**) **one's hands on** see LAY¹. **lend** (or **give**) **a hand** assist in an action or enterprise. **off one's hands** no longer one's responsibility. **on every hand** (or **all hands**) to or from all directions. **on hand** available. **on one's hands** resting on one as a responsibility. **on the one** (or **the other**) **hand** from one (or another) point of view. **out of hand 1** out of control. **2** peremptorily (*refused out of hand*). **put** (or **set**) **one's hand to** start work on; engage in. **stay one's hand** *archaic* or *literary* refrain from action. **to hand 1** within easy reach. **2** (of a letter) received. **turn one's hand to** undertake (as a new activity). □□ **handed** *adj.* **handless** *adj.* [OE *hand, hond*]

■ *n.* **1 a** fist, *colloq.* paw, *sl.* mitt, flipper. **b** paw. **2 a** (*hands*) control, hold, grasp, possession, custody, charge, clutches, keeping, power, disposal, authority, supervision, management, care. **b** see AGENCY 2b, INFLUENCE *n.* **c** part, share; participation, involvement; see also SUPPORT *n.* 1. **3** pointer, indicator. **5 a** touch, skill; see also TALENT 1. **b** see EXPERT *n.*, VIRTUOSO 1a. **7** writing, handwriting; signature; style. **10** laborer,

worker, workman, workwoman, man, drudge, employee, *colloq.* woman. **12** ovation, clap, (round of) applause. ● *v.* **1** (*hand in*) deliver, submit, give in, tender, present, proffer, offer; (*hand to*) pass to, give to, deliver to, present to or with; (*hand over*) deliver, submit, yield, give up, surrender, turn over; transfer. **2** give, convey; see also EXPRESS¹ 1, 2. □ **at hand 1** nearby, near, close, close by; handy, (readily) available, to or on hand, convenient, within reach, accessible, in sight. **2** imminent, impending, approaching, forthcoming, upcoming; in the offing, on the horizon, in store, in the cards. **hand and foot** see *completely* (COMPLETE). **hand around** see *hand out* 1 below, DISTRIBUTE 1. **hand down 1** see BEQUEATH. **2 a** see TRANSMIT 1a. **b** see DELIVER 4. **hand in glove** hand in hand, in league, in collusion, *sl.* in cahoots. **hand in hand** side by side, hand in glove, in close association. **hand it to** see RESPECT *v.* 1. **hand-me-down** secondhand, used, derivative, inferior. **hand out 1** distribute, disseminate, pass around, deal (out), dole (out); give out, disburse, serve. **2** award, allocate, dispense, *literary* mete. **hand over** see DELIVER 5. **hand-over** transfer, delivery, presentation, bestowal, conferral. **hand-over-fist** quickly, speedily, rapidly, swiftly, steadily. **hands down** readily, effortlessly; see also EASILY 1. **hands off 1** keep away (from), do not touch or interfere (with). **hands on 2** see PRACTICAL *adj.* 1. **have** (or **take**) **a hand** (**in**) see *take part* (PART). **have one's hands full** be swamped, be snowed under, *colloq.* have a lot on one's plate, be up to one's ears. **in hand 1** see *under way*. **2** in reserve, ready, available, on call, at one's disposal, accessible, in readiness, in store, *colloq.* on tap. **3** under control, in good hands; under a person's thumb. **lend** (or **give**) **a hand** see ASSIST *v.* 1. **on hand** see *at hand* 1 above. **out of hand 1** out of control, messy; see also *chaotic* (CHAOS). **2** categorically, peremptorily, flat(ly); see also ABSOLUTELY 1. **to hand 1** see *at hand* 1 above. **turn one's hand to** see UNDERTAKE 1.

handbag /hándbag/ *n. & v.* ● *n.* a small bag usu. with a handle or shoulder strap carried esp. by a woman and used to hold a wallet, cosmetics, etc. ● *v.tr. Brit.* (of a woman politician) treat (a person, idea, etc.) ruthlessly or insensitively.

■ *n.* see BAG *n.* 2b.

handball *n.* **1** /hándbawl/ one of several games with a ball thrown by hand among players or struck with an open hand against a wall. **2** /hándbáwl/ *Soccer* intentional touching of the ball with the hand or arm by a player other than the goalkeeper in the goal area, constituting a foul.

handbell /hándbel/ *n.* a small bell, usu. tuned to a particular note and rung by hand, esp. one of a set giving a range of notes.

handbill /hándbil/ *n.* a printed notice distributed by hand.

■ see LEAFLET *n.*

handbook /hándbŏok/ *n.* a short manual or guidebook.

■ see MANUAL *n.*

handbrake /hándbrayk/ *n.* a brake operated by hand.

handcart /hándkaart/ *n.* a small cart pushed or drawn by hand.

■ see CART *n.* 2.

handclap /hándklap/ *n.* a clapping of the hands.

handcraft /hándkraft/ *n. & v.* ● *n.* = HANDICRAFT. ● *v.tr.* make by handicraft.

handcuff /hándkuf/ *n. & v.* ● *n.* (in *pl.*) a pair of lockable linked metal rings for securing a person's wrists. ● *v.tr.* put handcuffs on.

■ *n.* (*handcuffs*) manacles, shackle(s), *colloq.* cuffs, *sl.* bracelets, *Brit. sl.* darbies. ● *v.* see SHACKLE *v.*

-handed /hándid/ *adj.* (in *comb.*) **1** for or involving a specified number of hands (in various senses) (*two-handed*). **2** using chiefly the hand specified (*left-handed*). □□ **-handedly** *adv.* **-handedness** *n.* (both in sense 2).

handful /hándfŏol/ *n.* (*pl.* **-fuls**) **1** a quantity that fills the

hand. 2 a small number or amount. 3 *colloq.* a troublesome person or task.

■ **1** fistful. **2** sprinkling, small number, small amount, scattering; a few. **3** see BOTHER *n.* 1.

handglass /hándglas/ *n.* **1** a magnifying glass held in the hand. **2** a small mirror with a handle.

handgrip /hándgrip/ *n.* **1** a grasp with the hand. **2** a handle designed for easy holding.

■ **1** see GRIP *n.* 1. **2** see HANDLE *n.* 1.

handgun /hándgun/ *n.* a small firearm held in and fired with one hand.

■ see PISTOL *n.*

handhold /hándhōld/ *n.* something for the hands to grip on (in climbing, sailing, etc.).

handicap /hándeekap/ *n. & v.* ● *n.* **1 a** a disadvantage imposed on a superior competitor in order to make the chances more equal. **b** a race or contest in which this is imposed. **2** the number of strokes by which a golfer normally exceeds par for the course. **3** a thing that makes progress or success difficult. **4** a physical or mental disability. ● *v.tr.* (**handicapped, handicapping**) **1** impose a handicap on. **2** place (a person) at a disadvantage. □□ **handicapper** *n.* [prob. from the phrase *hand i'* (= in) *cap* describing a kind of sporting lottery]

■ *n.* **3** hindrance, restraint, encumbrance, restriction, limitation, disability, disadvantage, impediment, barrier, bar, obstacle, block, stumbling block, constraint, check, curb, trammel (s). **4** see DISABILITY 1. ● *v.* hinder, hamper, encumber, restrict, limit, impede, bar, block, check, curb, trammel, disadvantage.

handicapped /hándeekapt/ *adj.* having a physical or mental disability.

■ see *disabled* (DISABLE).

handicraft /hándeekraft/ *n.* work that requires both manual and artistic skill. [ME, alt. of earlier HANDCRAFT after HANDIWORK]

handiwork /hándeewərk/ *n.* work done or a thing made by hand, or by a particular person. [OE *handgeweorc*]

■ see WORK *n.* 3.

handkerchief /hángkərchif, -cheef/ *n.* (*pl.* **handkerchiefs** or **-chieves** /-cheevz/) a square of cotton, linen, silk, etc., usu. carried in the pocket for wiping one's nose, etc.

handle /hánd'l/ *n. & v.* ● *n.* **1** the part by which a thing is held, carried, or controlled. **2** a fact that may be taken advantage of (*gave a handle to his critics*). **3** *colloq.* a personal title or nickname. **4** the feel of goods, esp. textiles, when handled. ● *v.tr.* **1** touch, feel, operate, or move with the hands. **2** manage or deal with; treat in a particular or correct way (*knows how to handle people*; *unable to handle the situation*). **3** deal in (goods). **4** discuss or write about (a subject). □ **get a handle on** *colloq.* understand the basis of or reason for a situation, circumstance, etc. □□ **handleable** *adj.* **handleability** *n.* **handled** *adj.* (also in *comb.*). [OE *handle, handlian* (as HAND)]

■ *n.* **1** grip, handgrip; hilt, haft, helve; lever, knob, switch, pull. **3** see TITLE *n.* 5. **4** see TEXTURE *n.* 1, 2. ● *v.* **1** feel, touch, finger; caress, fondle, pat; hold, move, operate, use. **2** manage, run, operate, direct, control; deal with, cope with, use, employ, utilize, manipulate; tackle, treat. **3** deal in, trade in, traffic in; market. **4** see TREAT *v.* 4. □ **get a handle on** see UNDERSTAND 1, 2.

handlebar /hánd'lbaar/ *n.* (often in *pl.*) the steering bar of a bicycle, etc., with a handgrip at each end. □ **handlebar mustache** a thick mustache with curved ends.

handler /hándlər/ *n.* **1** a person who handles or deals in certain commodities. **2** a person who trains and looks after an animal (esp. a working or show dog).

handlist /hándlist/ *n.* a short list of essential reading, reference books, etc.

handmade /hándmáyd/ *adj.* made by hand and not by machine, esp. as designating superior quality.

handmaid /hándmayd/ *n.* (also **handmaiden** /-máyd'n/) *archaic* a female servant or helper.

handout /hándowt/ *n.* **1** something given free to a needy per-

son. **2** a statement given to the press, printed information given to a lecture audience, etc.

■ **1** see GIFT *n.* 1. **2** statement, communiqué.

handpick /hándpik/ *v.tr.* choose carefully or personally. □□ **handpicked** *adj.*

■ see SELECT *v.* □□ **handpicked** see SELECT *adj.* 1.

handrail /hándrayl/ *n.* a narrow rail for holding as a support on stairs, etc.

handsaw /hándsaw/ *n.* a saw worked by one hand.

handsel /hánsəl/ *n. & v.* (also **hansel**) ● *n.* **1** a gift at the beginning of the new year, or on coming into new circumstances. **2** = EARNEST² 1. **3** a foretaste. ● *v.tr.* (**handseled, handseling**; or **handselled, handselling**) **1** give a handsel to. **2** inaugurate. **3** be the first to try. [ME, corresp. to OE *handselen* giving into a person's hands, ON *handsal* giving of the hand (esp. in promise), formed as HAND + OE *sellan* SELL]

handset /hándset/ *n.* a telephone mouthpiece and earpiece forming one unit.

■ see TELEPHONE *n.*

handshake /hándshayk/ *n.* the shaking of a person's hand by another's hand as a greeting, etc.

handsome /hánsəm/ *adj.* (**handsomer, handsomest**) **1** (of a person) good-looking. **2** (of a building, etc.) imposing; attractive. **3 a** generous; liberal (*a handsome present*; *handsome treatment*). **b** (of a price, fortune, etc., as assets gained) considerable. □□ **handsomeness** *n.* [ME, = easily handled, f. HAND + -SOME¹]

■ **1** good-looking, attractive, comely, goodly; see also BEAUTIFUL 1. **2** see IMPRESSIVE 1. **3 a** see GENEROUS 1. **b** sizable, large, big, substantial, considerable, good, goodly, ample, abundant.

handsomely /hánsəmlee/ *adv.* **1** generously; liberally. **2** finely; beautifully. **3** *Naut.* carefully.

handspike /hándspīk/ *n.* a wooden rod shod with iron, used on board ship and by artillery soldiers.

handspring /hándspring/ *n.* an aerobatic flip in which one lands first on the hands and then on the feet.

handstand /hándstand/ *n.* balancing on one's hands with the feet in the air or against a wall.

handwork /hándwərk/ *n.* work done with the hands, esp. as opposed to machinery. □□ **handworked** *adj.*

handwriting /hándrīting/ *n.* **1** writing with a pen, pencil, etc. **2** a person's particular style of writing. □□ **handwritten** /-rítən/ *adj.*

■ see WRITING 2.

handy /hándee/ *adj.* (**handier, handiest**) **1** convenient to handle or use; useful. **2** ready to hand; placed or occurring conveniently. **3** clever with the hands. □□ **handily** *adv.* **handiness** *n.*

■ **1** convenient, useful, clever, helpful, practical; usable, serviceable. **2** nearby, accessible, at *or* on *or* to hand, close by, convenient, within reach. **3** deft, dexterous, adroit, adept, skilled, skillful, proficient. □□ **handily** conveniently, readily, easily, comfortably; skillfully, capably, deftly, cleverly, dexterously, adroitly, expertly, proficiently, masterfully.

handyman /hándeeman/ *n.* (*pl.* **-men**) a person able or employed to do occasional domestic repairs and minor renovations.

hang /hang/ *v. & n.* ● *v.* (*past* and *past part.* **hung** /hung/ except in sense 7) **1** *tr.* **a** secure or cause to be supported from above, esp. with the lower part free. **b** (foll. by *up, on, onto,* etc.) attach loosely by suspending from the top. **2** *tr.* set up (a door, gate, etc.) on its hinges so that it moves freely. **3** *tr.* place (a picture) on a wall or in an exhibition. **4** *tr.* attach (wallpaper) in vertical strips to a wall. **5** *tr.* (foll. by *on*) *colloq.* attach the blame for (a thing) to (a person) (*you can't hang that on me*). **6** *tr.* (foll. by *with*) decorate by hanging pictures or decorations, etc. (*a hall hung with tapestries*). **7** *tr.* & *intr.* (*past* and *past part.* **hanged**) **a** suspend or be suspended by the neck, usu. with a noosed rope, until dead, esp. as a form of capital punishment. **b** as a mild oath (*hang the expense*; *let everything go hang*). **8** *tr.* let droop (*hang one's head*). **9** *tr.* suspend (meat or game) from a hook and leave it until dry or tender or high. **10** *intr.* be or remain hung (in various senses). **11** *intr.* remain static in the air. **12** *intr.* (often foll. by *over*) be present or imminent, esp. oppressively or threateningly (*a hush hung over the room*). **13** *intr.* (foll. by *on*) **a** be contingent or dependent on (*everything hangs on the discussions*). **b** listen closely to (*hangs on their every word*). **14** *tr. colloq.* make (a turn) (*hang a right at the corner*). ● *n.* **1** the way a thing hangs or falls. **2** a downward droop or bend. □ **get the hang of** *colloq.* understand the technique or meaning of. **hang around** (or *Brit.* **about**) **1** loiter or dally; not move away. **2** (foll. by *with*) associate with (a person, etc.). **hang back 1** show reluctance to act or move. **2** remain behind. **hang fire** be slow in taking action or in progressing. **hang glider** a frame with a fabric airfoil stretched over it, from which the operator is suspended and controls flight by body movement. **hang gliding** the sport of using a hang glider to launch oneself from a cliff or hill and glide. **hang heavily** (or **heavy**) (of time) pass slowly. **hang in** *colloq.* **1** persist; persevere. **2** linger. **hang loose** *colloq.* relax; stay calm. **hang on** *colloq.* **1** continue or persevere, esp. with difficulty. **2** (often foll. by *to*) cling; retain one's grip. **3** (foll. by *to*) retain; fail to give back. **4** a wait for a short time. **b** (in telephoning) continue to listen during a pause in the conversation. **hang out 1** hang from a window, clothesline, etc. **2** protrude or cause to protrude downwards. **3** (foll. by *of*) lean out of (a window, etc.). **4** *sl.* reside or be often present. **5** (foll. by *with*) *sl.* accompany; be friends with. **6** loiter; dally. **hang together 1** make sense. **2** remain associated. **hang up 1** hang from a hook, peg, etc. **2** (often foll. by *on*) end a telephone conversation, esp. abruptly (*then he hung up on me*). **3** cause delay or difficulty to. **4** (usu. in *passive*, foll. by *on*) *sl.* be a psychological or emotional obsession or problem to (*is really hung up on her teacher*). **hang-up** *n. sl.* an emotional problem or inhibition. **hung jury** a jury unable to reach unanimous agreement after extended deliberations. **hung-over** *colloq.* suffering from a hangover. **hung parliament** (in parliamentary governments) a parliament in which no party has a clear majority. **let it all hang out** *sl.* be uninhibited or relaxed. **not care** (or **give**) **a hang** *colloq.* not care at all. [ON *hanga* (tr.) = OE *hōn*, & f. OE *hangian* (intr.), f. Gmc]

■ *v.* **1** suspend, hang or hook up, sling; attach, fasten. **3** put up, show, exhibit. **5** see BLAME *v.* **2. 6** see DECORATE 1, 3. **7** a gibbet, string up; execute, kill, lynch. **b** damn, *sl.* stuff; see also CURSE *v.* 1b. **8** droop, drop, let down or fall, move or bring or put down. **9** suspend, hang up, hook up. **10** drape, swing, fall, dangle; be suspended or poised. **11** hover, be suspended, hang in the air, float, poise. **12** fall, descend, come down. **13** (*hang on*) **a** depend on, be dependent or contingent on, be subject to, be conditional on. **b** see LISTEN 1, 2. ● *n.* **1** drape, fall. **2** droop, fall. □ **get the hang of** see GRASP *v.* 3. **hang around** (or *Brit.* **about**) **1** loiter, wait (around), linger, dally, idle, loaf about, *archaic or literary* tarry. **2** (*hang around with*) associate with, socialize with, hobnob with, rub elbows with, rub shoulders with, consort with, fraternize with, mix with, *sl.* hang out with. **hang back 1** be reluctant, hesitate, falter, demur, think twice. **2** see LINGER 1. **hang fire** see POSTPONE, STALL[2] *v.* 1. **hang heavily** see DRAG *v.* 6. **hang in 1** see PERSEVERE. **2** see LINGER 1. **hang loose** see *let it all hang out* (HANG) below. **hang on 1** continue, persist, carry on, persevere, go on, hold out, endure. **2** (*hang on to*) hold on to, cling to, clutch, grip, grasp. **3** (*hang on to*) see RETAIN 1. **4** wait (a moment or minute or second), stay (here); hold on, hold the line. **hang out 1** put out or up, hang up, suspend, swing. **2** see PROTRUDE. **3** lean or bend out. **4** reside, live, be present; (*hang out at*)

frequent, haunt, visit, spend time at. **5** (*hang out with*) see ASSOCIATE *v.* 5. **hang together 1** make sense, be logical, be consistent, correspond, match (up), cohere, be coherent. **2** be or remain united, be or remain as or at one, remain associated, stick together; unite, join forces, cooperate, act in concert or harmony. **hang up 1** see SUSPEND 1. **2** break the connection, put down the receiver, esp. *Brit.* ring off; (*hang up on*) cut off. **4** (*be hung up on*) be obsessed by, *Psychol.* have a complex about, be fixated on, *colloq.* have a thing about. **hang-up** problem, difficulty, *Psychol.* complex, *colloq.* thing; see also INHIBITION 1, 2. **let it all hang out** open up, *colloq.* let one's hair down; relax, stay or keep calm or cool, cool off or down, sit back, take it easy, *colloq.* hang loose.

hangar /hángər/ *n.* a building with extensive floor area, for housing aircraft, etc. □□ **hangarage** *n.* [F, of unkn. orig.]

hangdog /hángdawg, -dog/ *adj.* having a dejected or guilty appearance; shamefaced.

hanger[1] /hángər/ *n.* **1** a person or thing that hangs. **2** (in full **coat hanger**) a shaped piece of wood or plastic, etc., from which clothes may be hung. □ **hanger-on** (*pl.* **hangers-on**) a follower or dependent, esp. an unwelcome one.

■ □ **hanger-on** follower, adherent, supporter, fan, dependent, parasite, toady, sycophant; *sl.* groupie, wanna-be; see also *yes-man*, *scrounger* (SCROUNGE).

hanger[2] /hángər/ *n. Brit.* a wood on the side of a steep hill. [OE *hangra* f. *hangian* HANG]

hanging /hánging/ *n.* & *adj.* ● *n.* **1** a the practice or an act of executing by hanging a person. **b** (*attrib.*) meriting or causing this (*a hanging offense*). **2** (usu. in *pl.*) draperies hung on a wall, etc. ● *adj.* that hangs or is hung; suspended. □ **hanging gardens** gardens laid out on a steep slope. **hanging valley** a valley, usu. tributary, above the level of the valleys or plains it joins.

■ *n.* **2** see DRAPERY. ● *adj.* see PENDULOUS 1.

hangman /hángmən/ *n.* (*pl.* **-men**) **1** an executioner who hangs condemned persons. **2** a word game for two players, in which the tally of failed guesses is kept by drawing a representation of a figure hanging from a gallows.

hangnail /hángnayl/ *n.* **1** a piece of torn skin at the root of a fingernail. **2** the soreness resulting from this. [alt. of AGNAIL, infl. by HANG and taking *nail* as = NAIL *n.* 2a]

hangout /hángowt/ *n. sl.* a place one lives in or frequently visits.

■ see LAIR[1] *n.* 1b.

hangover /hángōvər/ *n.* **1** a severe headache or other aftereffects caused by drinking an excess of liquor. **2** a survival from the past.

hank /hangk/ *n.* **1** a coil or skein of wool or thread, etc. **2** any of several measures of length of cloth or yarn, e.g., 840 yds. for cotton yarn and 560 yds. for worsted. **3** *Naut.* a ring of rope, iron, etc., for securing the staysails to the stays. [ME f. ON *hönk*: cf. Sw. *hank* string, Da. *hank* handle]

hanker /hángkər/ *v.intr.* (foll. by *to* + infin., *for*, or *after*) long for; crave. □□ **hankerer** *n.* **hankering** *n.* [obs. *hank*, prob. rel. to HANG]

■ (*hanker after or for or to*) crave, fancy, want (to), desire (to), yearn for or to, long for or to, thirst after or for, hunger after or for, pine for, lust after or for, have a hankering for, *colloq.* yen for, have a yen for; itch to.

hanky /hángkee/ *n.* (also **hankie**) (*pl.* **-ies**) *colloq.* a handkerchief. [abbr.]

hanky-panky /hángkeepángkee/ *n. sl.* **1** naughtiness, esp. sexual misbehavior. **2** dishonest dealing; trickery. [19th c.: perh. based on *hocus-pocus*]

■ **1** mischief, naughtiness, tomfoolery, goings-on, antics, *colloq.* monkey business, shenanigans. **2** trickery, double-dealing, deception, duplicity, deceit, legerdemain, chicanery, *Brit. colloq.* jiggery-pokery, *sl.* funny business.

Hanoverian /hánəveéreeən/ *adj.* of or relating to the British sovereigns from George I to Victoria (1714–1901). [*Hanover* in Germany, whose Elector became George I in 1714]

Hansa /hánsə/ *n.* (also **Hanse**) **1 a** a medieval guild of merchants. **b** the entrance fee to a guild. **2** (also **Hanseatic** /-seeátik/ **League**) a medieval political and commercial league of Germanic towns. □□ **Hanseatic** adj. [MHG hanse, OHG, Goth. hansa company]

Hansard /hánsaard/ n. the official verbatim record of debates in the British Parliament. [T. C. Hansard, Engl. printer d. 1833, who first printed it]

hansel var. of HANDSEL.

Hansen's disease /hánsənz/ n. leprosy. [G. H. A. Hansen, Norw. physician d. 1912]

hansom /hánsəm/ n. (in full **hansom cab**) hist. a two-wheeled horse-drawn carriage accommodating two inside, with the driver seated behind. [J. A. Hansom, Engl. architect d. 1882, who designed it]

Hants /hants/ abbr. Hampshire. [OE Hantescire]

Hanukkah /kháanəkə, haá-/ n. (also **Chanukkah**) the Jewish festival of lights, commemorating the purification of the Temple in 165 BC. [Heb. ḥānukkāh consecration]

hanuman /húnōōmaàn/ n. **1** an Indian langur venerated by Hindus. **2** (**Hanuman**) (in Hindu mythology) the monkey god, a loyal helper of Rama. [Hindi]

hap /hap/ n. & v. archaic ● n. **1** chance; luck. **2** a chance occurrence. ● v.intr. (**happed, happing**) **1** come about by chance. **2** (foll. by to + infin.) happen to. [ME f. ON happ]

hapax legomenon /hápaks ligóminon, háypaks/ n. (pl. **hapax legomena** /-minə/) a word of which only one instance of use is recorded in a document, a body of literature, etc. [Gk, = a thing said once]

ha'penny var. of HALFPENNY.

haphazard /hápházərd/ adj. & adv. ● adj. done, etc., by chance; random. ● adv. at random. □□ **haphazardly** adv. **haphazardness** n. [HAP + HAZARD]
■ adj. random, arbitrary, chance, aleatoric, accidental, adventitious, fortuitous, serendipitous. ● adv. see at random (RANDOM).

hapless /háplis/ adj. unlucky. □□ **haplessly** adv. **haplessness** n. [HAP + -LESS]
■ see UNHAPPY 2.

haplography /haplógrəfee/ n. the accidental omission of letters when these are repeated in a word (e.g., philogy for philology). [Gk haplous single + -GRAPHY]

haploid /háployd/ adj. & n. Biol. ● adj. (of an organism or cell) with a single set of chromosomes. ● n. a haploid organism or cell. [G f. Gk haplous single + eidos form]

haplology /haplóləjee/ n. the omission of a sound when this is repeated within a word (e.g., February pronounced /fébree/). [Gk haplous + -LOGY]

ha'p'orth Brit. var. of HALFPENNYWORTH.

happen /hápən/ v. & adv. ● v.intr. **1** occur (by chance or otherwise). **2** (foll. by to + infin.) have the (good or bad) fortune to (I happened to meet her). **3** (foll. by to) be the (esp. unwelcome) fate or experience of (what happened to you?; I hope nothing happens to them). **4** (foll. by on) encounter or discover by chance. ● adv. dial. perhaps; maybe (happen it'll rain). □ **as it happens** in fact; in reality (as it happens, it turned out well). [ME f. HAP + -EN¹]
■ v. **1** occur, take place, come about, go on, come to pass, come off, arise, poet. befall, betide; develop, materialize; disp. transpire. **2** chance. **3** (happen to) become of, come of, archaic hap to, poet. befall, betide. **4** (happen on) come upon, chance on or upon, hit on or upon, stumble on or upon or across, find; encounter, meet. ● adv. see PERHAPS. □ **as it happens** see in fact 1 (FACT).

happening /hápəning/ n. & adj. ● **1** an event or occurrence. **2** an improvised or spontaneous theatrical, etc., performance. ● adj. sl. exciting, fashionable, trendy.
■ n. **1** event, incident, occurrence, occasion, episode; phenomenon. **2** see improvisation (IMPROVISE).
● adj. see TRENDY adj.

happenstance /hápənstans/ n. a thing that happens by chance. [HAPPEN + CIRCUMSTANCE]
■ see COINCIDENCE 2.

happi /hápee/ n. (pl. **happis**) (also **happi coat**) a loose informal Japanese jacket, sometimes sashed. [Jap.]

happy /hápee/ adj. (**happier, happiest**) **1** feeling or showing pleasure or contentment. **2 a** fortunate; characterized by happiness. **b** (of words, behavior, etc.) apt; pleasing. **3** colloq. slightly drunk. **4** (in comb.) colloq. inclined to use excessively or at random (trigger-happy). □ **happy event** colloq. the birth of a child. **happy families** Brit. a card game the object of which is to acquire four members of the same "family." **happy-go-lucky** cheerfully casual. **happy hour** a period of the day when drinks are sold at reduced prices in bars, hotels, etc. **happy hunting ground 1** the conception of paradise for certain Native American tribes. **2** a place where success or enjoyment is obtained. **happy medium** a compromise; the avoidance of extremes. □□ **happily** adv. **happiness** n. [ME f. HAP + -Y¹]
■ **1** pleased, content(ed), glad, delighted, joyful, overjoyed, cheerful, cheery, lighthearted, thrilled, gleeful, elated, jubilant, exhilarated, exultant, exuberant, euphoric, ecstatic; pleased as Punch, in seventh heaven, over the moon, colloq. on top of the world, on cloud nine, tickled pink, poet. blithe. **2 a** lucky, fortunate; propitious, auspicious, favorable, blessed. **b** apt, pleasing, felicitous; see also APPROPRIATE adj. **3** see DRUNK adj. 2. □ **happy-go-lucky** see CAREFREE. **happy medium** balance, compromise, middle way or course, golden mean, literary via media; middle ground. □□ **happily** joyfully, delightedly, gleefully, cheerily, cheerfully, gaily, merrily, gladly, with pleasure, heartily, enthusiastically, willingly, contentedly, poet. blithely; luckily, propitiously, providentially, opportunely. **happiness** pleasure, delight, felicity, enjoyment, joy, joyousness, joyfulness, jubilation, cheerfulness, cheeriness, gladness, lightheartedness, exhilaration, elation, exuberance, high spirits, glee.

haptic /háptik/ adj. relating to the sense of touch. [Gk haptikos able to touch f. haptō fasten]

hara-kiri /hárəkeèree, háaree-/ n. (also **hari-kari**) ritual suicide by disembowelment with a sword, formerly practiced by samurai when disgraced or sentenced to death. [colloq. Jap. f. hara belly + kiri cutting]

harangue /həráng/ n. & v. ● n. a lengthy and earnest speech. ● v.tr. lecture or make a harangue to. □□ **haranguer** n. [ME f. F f. OF arenge f. med.L harenga, perh. f. Gmc]
■ n. speech, address, oration, declamation, exhortation, screed, diatribe, tirade, philippic. ● v. preach, sermonize; see also LECTURE v. 2.

harass /hərás, hárəs/ v.tr. **1** trouble and annoy continually or repeatedly. **2** make repeated attacks on (an enemy or opponent). □□ **harasser** n. **harassingly** adv. **harassment** n. [F harasser f. OF harer set a dog on]
■ **1** badger, harry, trouble, torment, bother, hound, persecute, annoy, irritate, pester, worry, beset, bait, nag, pick on, henpeck, Brit. chivvy, colloq. hassle, plague, disp. aggravate, sl. bug, ride, bullyrag. **2** see MOLEST 2.

harbinger /háarbinjər/ n. & v. ● n. **1** a person or thing that announces or signals the approach of another. **2** a forerunner. ● v.tr. announce the approach of. [earlier = 'one who provides lodging': ME herbergere f. OF f. herberge lodging f. Gmc]
■ n. omen, foretoken, sign, portent, augury; herald, forerunner, precursor. ● v. see ANNOUNCE 1.

harbor /háarbər/ n. & v. (Brit. **harbour**) ● n. **1** a place of shelter for ships. **2** a shelter; a place of refuge or protection. ● v. **1** tr. give shelter to (esp. a criminal or wanted person). **2** tr. keep in one's mind, esp. resentfully (harbor a grudge). **3** intr. come to anchor in a harbor. □ **harbor master** an official in charge of a harbor. □□ **harborless** adj. [OE herebeorg perh. f. ON, rel. to HARBINGER]

/.../ **pronunciation**	● **part of speech**
□ **phrases, idioms, and compounds**	
□□ **derivatives**	■ **synonym section**
cross-references appear in SMALL CAPITALS or italics	

■ *n.* **1** port, seaport, haven, harborage. **2** refuge, haven, asylum; see also SHELTER *n.* 1, 3. ● *v.* **1** shelter, protect, guard, shield; conceal, hide. **2** foster, nurture, cherish, nurse, retain, maintain, hold, cling to.

harborage /ha´arbərij/ *n.* (*Brit.* **harbourage**) a shelter or place of shelter, esp. for ships.

hard /haard/ *adj., adv.,* & *n.* ● *adj.* **1** (of a substance, material, etc.) firm and solid; unyielding to pressure; not easily cut. **2 a** difficult to understand or explain (*a hard problem*). **b** difficult to accomplish (*a hard decision*). **c** (foll. by *to* + infin.) not easy (*hard to believe; hard to please*). **3** difficult to bear; entailing suffering (*a hard life*). **4** (of a person) unfeeling; severely critical. **5** (of a season or the weather) severe; harsh (*a hard winter; a hard frost*). **6** harsh or unpleasant to the senses (*a hard voice; hard colors*). **7 a** strenuous; enthusiastic; intense (*a hard worker; a hard fight*). **b** severe; uncompromising (*a hard blow; a hard bargain; hard words*). **c** *Polit.* extreme; most radical (*the hard right*). **8 a** (of liquor) strongly alcoholic. **b** (of drugs) potent and addictive. **c** (of radiation) highly penetrating. **d** (of pornography) highly suggestive and explicit. **9** (of water) containing mineral salts that make lathering difficult. **10** established; not disputable; reliable (*hard facts; hard data*). **11** *Stock Exch.* (of currency, prices, etc.) high; not likely to fall in value. **12** *Phonet.* (of a consonant) guttural (as *c* in *cat, g* in *go*). **13** (of a shape, boundary, etc.) clearly defined; unambiguous. ● *adv.* **1** strenuously; intensely; copiously; with one's full effort (*try hard; look hard at; it is raining hard; hardworking*). **2** with difficulty or effort (*hard-earned*). **3** so as to be hard or firm (*hard-baked; the jelly set hard*). **4** *Naut.* fully; to the extreme (*hard to starboard*). ● *n. Brit.* **1** a sloping roadway across a foreshore. **2** *sl.* = hard labor (*got two years hard*). □ **be hard on 1** be difficult for. **2** be severe in one's treatment or criticism of. **3** be unpleasant to (the senses). **be hard put** (usu. foll. by *to* + infin.) find it difficult. **go hard with** turn out to (a person's) disadvantage. **hard and fast** (of a rule or a distinction made) definite; unalterable; strict. **hard at it** *colloq.* busily working or occupied. **hard-boiled 1** (of an egg) boiled until the white and the yolk are solid. **2** (of a person) tough; shrewd. **hard by** near; close by. **a hard case 1** *colloq.* **a** an intractable person. **b** *Austral.* & *NZ* an amusing or eccentric person. **2** a case of hardship. **hard cash** negotiable coins and paper money. **hard coal** anthracite. **hard copy** printed material produced by computer, usu. on paper, suitable for ordinary reading. **hard core 1** an irreducible nucleus. **2** *colloq.* **a** the most active or committed members of a society, etc. **b** a conservative or reactionary minority. **3** *Brit.* solid material, esp. rubble, forming the foundation of a road, etc. **hard-core** *adj.* blatant; uncompromising, esp.: **1** (of pornography) explicit; obscene. **2** (of drug addiction) relating to hard drugs, esp. heroin. **hard disk** (**drive**) *Computing* a large-capacity rigid usu. magnetic storage disk. **hard-done-by** *Brit.* harshly or unfairly treated. **hard error** *Computing* a permanent error. **hard feelings** feelings of resentment. **hard hat 1** a protective helmet worn on building sites, etc. **2** *colloq.* a reactionary person. **hard hit** badly affected. **hard-hitting** aggressively critical. **hard labor** heavy manual work as a punishment, esp. in a prison. **hard landing 1** a clumsy or rough landing of an aircraft. **2** an uncontrolled landing in which a spacecraft is destroyed. **hard line** unyielding adherence to a firm policy. **hard-liner** a person who adheres rigidly to a policy. **hard lines** *Brit. colloq.* = hard luck. **hard luck** worse fortune than one deserves. **hard-nosed** *colloq.* realistic; uncompromising. **a hard nut** *sl.* a tough, aggressive person. **a hard nut to crack** *colloq.* **1** a difficult problem. **2** a person or thing not easily understood or influenced. **hard of hearing** somewhat deaf. **hard on** (or **upon**) close to in pursuit, etc. **hard-on** *n. coarse sl.* an erection of the penis. **hard pad** a form of distemper in dogs, etc. **hard palate** the front part of the palate. **hard paste** denoting a Chinese or "true" porcelain made of fusible and infusible materials (usu. clay and stone) and fired at a high temperature. **hard-pressed 1** closely pursued. **2** burdened with urgent business. **hard rock** *colloq.* rock music with a heavy beat. **hard roe** see ROE[1]. **hard sauce** a

sauce of butter and sugar, often with brandy, etc., added. **hard sell** aggressive salesmanship or advertising. **hard shoulder** *Brit.* a hardened strip alongside a motorway for stopping on in an emergency. **hard stuff** *sl.* strong liquor, esp. whiskey. **hard up 1** short of money. **2** (foll. by *for*) at a loss for; lacking. **hard wheat** wheat with a hard grain rich in gluten. **hard-wired** involving or achieved by permanently connected circuits designed to perform a specific function. **put the hard word on** *Austral.* & *NZ sl.* ask a favor (esp. sexual or financial) of. □□ **hardish** *adj.* **hardness** *n.* [OE *hard, heard* f. Gmc]

■ *adj.* **1** rigid, stiff, solid, inflexible, tough, firm, dense, compressed, solidified, hardened; leathery, callous; stony, rocklike, flinty, steely, unyielding, adamantine, impenetrable, impervious. **2 a** perplexing, knotty, puzzling, baffling, enigmatic, intricate, complicated, complex, involved; see also DIFFICULT 1b. **b** thorny, problematic, tough, awkward, tricky; see also DIFFICULT 3. **c** difficult, tough, awkward, tricky. **3** difficult, laborious, arduous, backbreaking, burdensome, onerous, fatiguing, tiring, exhausting, wearying, strenuous, toilsome; bad, grievous, calamitous, racking, dark, grim, distressing, painful, unpleasant, severe, austere, rough, *colloq.* tough. **4** stern, cold, callous, intractable, adamant, exacting, strict, demanding, hardhearted, stony-hearted, severe, tyrannical, despotic, dictatorial, oppressive, cruel, ruthless, pitiless, merciless, savage, brutal, inhuman, unfeeling, heartless, harsh, unkind, implacable, unsympathetic, obdurate, insensitive, stony, unsparing; see also HARD *adj.* 7b below. **5** see SEVERE 3, 4. **6** see SEVERE 1, 5. **7 a** strenuous, sedulous, assiduous, conscientious, diligent, industrious, indefatigable, untiring, persistent, dogged, intent, intense, eager, enthusiastic, zealous, ardent, energetic, keen, avid, devoted. **b** severe, penetrating, searching, uncompromising, calculating, critical, methodical, systematic, practical, cool, unemotional, pragmatic, businesslike, realistic, hardheaded, hardboiled, *colloq.* hardbitten, hard-nosed, tough; see also HARD *adj.* 4 above. **8 a** alcoholic, spirituous, potent; see also STRONG *adj.* 14. **b** potent, addictive, habit-forming, hard-core. **10** established, reliable, real, plain, strict, straight, straightforward, cold, bare, unvarnished, unquestionable, verifiable, indisputable, undeniable, incontestable, incontrovertible, inescapable, ineluctable, unavoidable, unalterable, immutable. **13** sharp, well-defined, clearly defined, clear, distinct, stark, definite, unambiguous. ● *adv.* **1** vigorously, forcefully, copiously, energetically, arduously, laboriously, strenuously, earnestly, actively, dynamically, spiritedly, eagerly, intensely, ardently, heartily, zealously, intently, carefully, earnestly, diligently, assiduously, sedulously, studiously, determinedly, steadfastly, conscientiously, industriously, devotedly, urgently, persistently, untiringly, indefatigably, perseveringly, unfalteringly, relentlessly, doggedly, *colloq.* mightily. **2** well, thoroughly. **3** see FIRM[1] *adj.* 1a. □ **be hard on 1** see DIFFICULT 1a, 3. **2** keep in line, *colloq.* sit on; see also SEVERE 1, 5. **3** see HARSH 1. **hard and fast** see STRICT 2b. **hard at it** see BUSY *adj.* 1, 3. **hard-boiled 1** hard, firm, set. **2** see HARD *adj.* 7b above, TOUGH *adj.* 4a, SHREWD. **hard by** see NEAR *adj.* 1. **a hard case 1 a** mule, tartar, diehard, *sl.* hard nut. **hard cash** see MONEY 1. **hard-core 1** see OBSCENE 1. **2** hard, potent, addictive, habit-forming. **hard feelings** see RESENTMENT. **hard hit** hurt, damaged, harmed, badly affected, *colloq.* knocked sideways. **hard-hitting** see *scathing* (SCATHE *v.*). **hard labor** see SLAVERY 2. **hard line** tough stance, firm position. **hard-liner** stickler, bigot, partisan, sectionalist, intransigent, *colloq.* stick in the mud. **hard luck** misfortune, bad luck, ill luck, ill fortune, infelicity, adversity. **hard-nosed** see REALISTIC 2, INFLEXIBLE 2. **a hard nut** see *a hard case* 1 above, TOUGH *n.* **a hard nut to crack 1** see PROBLEM 1, 2. **2** enigma, puzzle, mystery, problem, conundrum, riddle. **hard on** (or **upon**) close behind, right behind, on a person's tail, in hot pursuit of, at *or* on the heels of. **hard-pressed 1** see TRACK[1] *v.* 1. **2** busy, occupied, engaged, tied up, wrapped up. **hard rock** rock, heavy metal. **hard stuff** see SPIRIT *n.* 4a. **hard up 1** poor, indigent, needy, poverty-stricken, impoverished, penniless, impecunious, in the red, *colloq.* broke, on one's uppers, *Brit. sl.* skint. **2** (*hard up for*) see DESTITUTE 2.

hardback /háardbak/ *adj.* & *n.* • *adj.* (of a book) bound in stiff covers. • *n.* a hardback book.

hardball /háardbawl/ *n.* & *v.* • *n.* **1** = BASEBALL. **2** *sl.* uncompromising methods or dealings, esp. in politics or business (*play hardball*). • *v.tr. sl.* pressure or coerce politically.

hardbitten /háardbítən/ *adj. colloq.* tough and cynical.
■ see HARD *adj.* 7b.

hardboard /háardbawrd/ *n.* stiff board made of compressed and treated wood pulp.

hardcover /hárdkəvər/ *adj.* & *n.* • *adj.* bound between rigid boards covered in cloth, paper, leather, or film (*a hardcover edition of the novel*). • *n.* a hardcover book.

harden /háardən/ *v.* **1** *tr.* & *intr.* make or become hard or harder. **2** *intr.* & *tr.* become, or make (one's attitude, etc.), uncompromising or less sympathetic. **3** *intr.* (of prices, etc.) cease to fall or fluctuate. □ **harden off** inure (a plant) to cold by gradually increasing its exposure. □□ **hardener** *n.*
■ **1** set, solidify, stiffen, freeze. **2** intensify, strengthen, toughen, stiffen; brace, fortify, reinforce. **3** stabilize, become fixed; freeze; level off, bottom out. □□ **hardener** coagulant; thermoplastic.

hardening /háardəning/ *n.* **1** the process or an instance of becoming hard. **2** (in full **hardening of the arteries**) *Med.* = ARTERIOSCLEROSIS.

hardheaded /háardhédid/ *adj.* practical; realistic; not sentimental. □□ **hardheadedly** *adv.* **hardheadedness** *n.*
■ see HARD *adj.* 7b.

hard-hearted /háardháartid/ *adj.* unfeeling; unsympathetic. □□ **hard-heartedly** *adv.* **hard-heartedness** *n.*
■ see HARD *adj.* 4.

hardihood /háardeehŏŏd/ *n.* boldness; daring.

hardly /háardlee/ *adv.* **1** scarcely; only just (*we hardly knew them*). **2** only with difficulty (*could hardly speak*). **3** harshly.
■ **1, 2** scarcely, barely, only just; seldom, rarely; with difficulty, with effort. **3** see ROUGHLY 1.

hardpan /háardpan/ *n. Geol.* a hardened layer of clay occurring in or below the soil profile.

hardshell /háardshel/ *adj.* **1** having a hard shell. **2** rigid; orthodox; uncompromising.

hardship /háardship/ *n.* **1** severe suffering or privation. **2** the circumstance causing this.
■ want, suffering, misery, distress, trouble, unhappiness; privation, deprivation, rigors, adversity, austerity, ill fortune, bad luck; affliction, misfortune, difficulty.

hardtack /háardtak/ *n.* a hard biscuit, as that formerly given to sailors and soldiers as rations.

hardtop /háardtop/ *n.* **1** an automobile without roof supports between the front and back windows. **2** an automobile with a rigid (usu. detachable) roof.

hardware /háardwair/ *n.* **1** tools and household articles of metal, etc. **2** heavy machinery or armaments. **3** the mechanical and electronic components of a computer, etc. (cf. SOFTWARE).
■ **1** tools, equipment, utensils, implements, kit, *Brit.* ironmongery, *colloq.* gear. **2** machinery, equipment; arms, munitions, armaments. **3** equipment, machinery; components, parts.

hardwearing /háardwáiring/ *adj.* able to stand much wear.
■ see DURABLE *adj.* 1.

hardwood /háardwŏŏd/ *n.* the wood from a deciduous broad-leaved tree as distinguished from that of conifers.

hardworking /háardwərking/ *adj.* diligent.
■ see DILIGENT.

hardy /háardee/ *adj.* (**hardier, hardiest**) **1** robust; capable of enduring difficult conditions. **2** (of a plant) able to grow in the open air all year round. □ **hardy annual 1** an annual plant that may be sown outdoors. **2** *Brit. joc.* a subject that comes up at regular intervals. □□ **hardily** *adv.* **hardiness** *n.* [ME f. OF *hardi* past part. of *hardir* become bold, f. Gmc, rel. to HARD]
■ **1** robust, strong, tough, vigorous, husky, able-bodied, fit, hale, healthy, stalwart, stout, sturdy, sound.

hare /hair/ *n.* & *v.* • *n.* **1** any of various mammals of the family Leporidae, esp. *Lepus europaeus*, like a large rabbit, with tawny fur, long ears, short tail, and hind legs longer than forelegs, inhabiting fields, hills, etc. **2** (in full **electric hare**) a dummy hare propelled by electricity, used in greyhound racing. • *v.intr.* run with great speed. □ **hare and hounds** a paper chase. **hare's-foot** (in full **hare's-foot clover**) a clover, *Trifolium arvense*, with soft hair around the flowers. **run with the hare and hunt with the hounds** *Brit.* try to remain on good terms with both sides. **start a hare** *Brit.* raise a topic of conversation. [OE *hara* f. Gmc]
• *v.* see TEAR[1] *v.* 5.

harebell /háirbel/ *n.* **1** a plant, *Campanula rotundifolia*, with slender stems and pale blue bell-shaped flowers. **2** = BLUEBELL 2.

harebrained /háirbraynd/ *adj.* rash; foolish; wild.
■ rash, foolhardy, foolish, stupid, silly, inane, asinine, witless, brainless, mindless, flighty, giddy, frivolous, scatterbrained; wild, madcap, reckless, *colloq.* crackpot, *Brit. colloq.* airy-fairy.

Hare Krishna /háaree kríshnə/ *n.* **1** a sect devoted to the worship of the Hindu deity Krishna (an incarnation of Vishnu). **2** (*pl.* **Hare Krishnas**) a member of this sect. [the title of a mantra based on the name *Krishna*, f. Skr. *O Hari!* an epithet of Krishna]

harelip /háirlip/ *n.* a congenital fissure of the upper lip. □□ **harelipped** *adj.*

harem /háirəm, hár-/ *n.* **1 a** the women of a Muslim household, living in a separate part of the house. **b** their quarters. **2** a group of female animals sharing a mate. [Arab. *ḥarām*, *ḥarīm*, orig. = prohibited, prohibited place, f. *ḥarama* prohibit]

harewood /háirwŏŏd/ *n.* stained sycamore wood used for making furniture. [G dial. *Ehre* f. L *acer* maple + WOOD]

haricot /árikō/ *n.* **1** (in full **haricot vert** /ver/) a variety of French bean with small white seeds. **2** the dried seed of this used as a vegetable. [F]

Harijan /hárijən/ *n.* a member of the class formerly called untouchables in India. [Skr., = a person dedicated to Vishnu, f. *Hari* Vishnu, *jana* person]

hark /haark/ *v.intr.* (usu. in *imper.*) *archaic* listen attentively. □ **hark back** revert to a topic discussed earlier. [ME *herkien* f. OE *heorcian* (unrecorded): cf. HEARKEN: *hark back* was orig. a hunting call to retrace steps]
■ see LISTEN 1, 2.

harken var. of HEARKEN.

harl /haarl/ *n.* (also **harle, herl** /herl/) fiber of flax or hemp. [MLG *herle, harle* fiber of flax or hemp]

harlequin /háarlikwin/ *n.* & *adj.* • *n.* **1** (**Harlequin**) **a** a mute character in pantomime, usu. masked and dressed in a diamond-patterned costume. **b** *hist.* a stock comic character in Italian *commedia dell'arte*. **2** (in full **harlequin duck**) an Icelandic duck, *Histrionicus histrionicus*, with variegated plumage. • *adj.* in varied colors; variegated. [F f. earlier *Herlequin* leader of a legendary troup of demon horsemen]
■ *n.* **1** see FOOL[1] *n.* 2. • *adj.* see *variegated* (VARIEGATE).

harlequinade /háarlikwináyd/ *n.* **1** the part of a pantomime featuring Harlequin. **2** a piece of buffoonery. [F *arlequinade* (as HARLEQUIN)]

harlot /háarlət/ *n. archaic* a prostitute. □□ **harlotry** *n.* [ME f. OF *harlot, herlot* lad, knave, vagabond]

/. . ./ **pronunciation**   • **part of speech**
□ **phrases, idioms, and compounds**
□□ **derivatives**   ■ **synonym section**
cross-references appear in SMALL CAPITALS or *italics*

■ see PROSTITUTE *n.* 1a.

harm /haarm/ *n.* & *v.* ● *n.* hurt; damage. ● *v.tr.* cause harm to. □ **out of harm's way** in safety. [OE *hearm, hearmian* f. Gmc]

■ *n.* hurt, injury, damage, mischief, abuse; see also SIN¹ *n.* 1, GRIEVANCE. ● *v.* hurt, damage, injure, abuse, maltreat, wound, impair, mar. □ **out of harm's way** see SAFE *adj.* 5.

harmattan /haármətán/ *n.* a parching dusty wind of the W. African coast occurring from December to February. [Fanti or Twi *haramata*]

■ see STORM *n.* 1.

harmful /haármfŏŏl/ *adj.* causing or likely to cause harm. □□ **harmfully** *adv.* **harmfulness** *n.*

■ dangerous, pernicious, deleterious, destructive, damaging, bad, detrimental, injurious; unhealthy, noxious, baleful, toxic, poisonous, venomous, malign, malignant, baneful.

harmless /haármlis/ *adj.* **1** not able or likely to cause harm. **2** inoffensive. □□ **harmlessly** *adv.* **harmlessness** *n.*

■ **1** benign, innocuous, gentle, mild, safe, nontoxic, nonpoisonous, nonvenomous. **2** see INOFFENSIVE.

harmonic /haarmónik/ *adj.* & *n.* ● *adj.* **1** of or characterized by harmony; harmonious. **2** *Mus.* **a** of or relating to harmony. **b** (of a tone) produced by vibration of a string, etc., in an exact fraction of its length. **3** *Math.* of or relating to quantities whose reciprocals are in arithmetical progression (*harmonic progression*). ● *n.* **1** *Mus.* an overtone accompanying at a fixed interval (and forming a note with) a fundamental. **2** *Physics* a component frequency of wave motion. □ **harmonic motion** (in full **simple harmonic motion**) oscillatory motion under a retarding force proportional to the amount of displacement from an equilibrium position. **harmonic progression** (or **series**) *Math.* a series of quantities whose reciprocals are in arithmetical progression. □□ **harmonically** *adv.* [L *harmonicus* f. Gk *harmonikos* (as HARMONY)]

■ *adj.* **1, 2a** see TUNEFUL.

harmonica /haarmónikə/ *n.* a small rectangular wind instrument with a row of metal reeds along its length, held against the lips and moved from side to side to produce different notes by blowing or sucking. [L, fem. sing. or neut. pl. of *harmonicus*: see HARMONIC]

harmonious /haarmṓneeəs/ *adj.* **1** pleasant sounding; tuneful. **2** forming a pleasing or consistent whole; concordant. **3** free from disagreement or dissent. □□ **harmoniously** *adv.* **harmoniousness** *n.*

■ **1** see TUNEFUL. **2** congruous, compatible, concordant, consonant, consistent, in accord, complementary; congenial, sympathetic, agreeable, simpatico. **3** see PEACEFUL 1.

harmonist /haármənist/ *n.* a person skilled in musical harmony; a harmonizer. □□ **harmonistic** *adj.*

harmonium /haarmṓneeəm/ *n.* a keyboard instrument in which the notes are produced by air driven through metal reeds by bellows operated by the feet. [F f. L (as HARMONY)]

harmonize /haármənīz/ *v.* **1** *tr.* add notes to (a melody) to produce harmony. **2** *tr.* & *intr.* (often foll. by *with*) bring into or be in harmony. **3** *intr.* make or form a pleasing or consistent whole. □□ **harmonization** *n.* [f. F *harmoniser* (as HARMONY)]

■ **2** see AGREE 3a. **3** see COORDINATE *v.* 1.

harmony /haármənee/ *n.* (*pl.* **-ies**) **1 a** a combination of simultaneously sounded musical notes to produce chords and chord progressions, esp. as having a pleasing effect. **b** the study of this. **2 a** an apt or aesthetic arrangement of parts. **b** the pleasing effect of this. **3** agreement; concord. **4** a collation of parallel narratives, esp. of the Gospels. □ **in harmony 1** (of singing, etc.) producing chords; not discordant. **2** (often foll. by *with*) in agreement. **harmony of the spheres** see SPHERE. [ME f. OF *harmonie* f. L *harmonia* f. Gk *harmonia* joining, concord, f. *harmos* joint]

■ **1 a** euphony, melodiousness, tunefulness. **2** see UNITY 1. **3** consonance, congruity, balance, consistency, agreement, accord, concord, chime, rapport,

unanimity, compatibility, suitability, harmoniousness; see also UNITY 2. □ **in harmony 1** in tune, harmonious; see also MUSICAL *adj.* **2** see AGREEABLE 2.

harness /haárnis/ *n.* & *v.* ● *n.* **1** the equipment of straps and fittings by which a horse is fastened to a cart, etc., and controlled. **2** a similar arrangement for fastening a thing to a person's body, for restraining a young child, etc. ● *v.tr.* **1 a** put a harness on (esp. a horse). **b** (foll. by *to*) attach by a harness. **2** make use of (natural resources) esp. to produce energy. □ **in harness** in the routine of daily work. □□ **harnesser** *n.* [ME f. OF *harneis* military equipment f. ON *hernest* (unrecorded) f. *herr* army + *nest* provisions]

■ *n.* **1** see TACK². ● *v.* **1** see HITCH *v.* 1.

harp /haarp/ *n.* & *v.* ● *n.* a large upright roughly triangular musical instrument consisting of a frame housing a graduated series of vertical strings, played by plucking with the fingers. ● *v.intr.* **1** (foll. by *on*) talk repeatedly and tediously about. **2** play on a harp. □ **harp seal** a Greenland seal, *Phoca groenlandica*, with a harp-shaped dark mark on its back. □□ **harper** *n.* **harpist** *n.* [OE *hearpe* f. Gmc]

harpoon /haarpŏŏn/ *n.* & *v.* ● *n.* a barbed spearlike missile with a rope attached, for killing whales, etc. ● *v.tr.* spear with a harpoon. □ **harpoon gun** a gun for firing a harpoon. □□ **harpooner** *n.* [F *harpon* f. *harpe* clamp f. L *harpa* f. Gk *harpē* sickle]

harpsichord /haárpsikawrd/ *n.* a keyboard instrument with horizontal strings which are plucked mechanically. □□ **harpsichordist** *n.* [obs. F *harpechorde* f. LL *harpa* harp, + *chorda* string, the *-s-* being unexplained]

harpy /haárpee/ *n.* (*pl.* **-ies**) **1** (in Greek and Roman mythology) a monster with a woman's head and body and bird's wings and claws. **2** a grasping unscrupulous person. □ **harpy eagle** a S. American crested bird of prey, *Harpia harpyja*, one of the largest of eagles. [F *harpie* or L *harpyia* f. Gk *harpuiai* snatchers (cf. *harpazō* snatch)]

harquebus /haárkwibəs/ *n.* (also **arquebus** /áar-/) *hist.* an early type of portable gun supported on a tripod or on a forked rest. [F (h)*arquebuse* ult. f. MLG *hakebusse* or MHG *hakenbühse*, f. *haken* hook + *busse* gun]

harridan /hárid'n/ *n.* a bad-tempered woman. [17th-c. cant, perhaps f. F *haridelle* old horse]

■ see HAG¹ 1.

harrier¹ /háreeər/ *n.* a person who harries or lays waste.

harrier² /háreeər/ *n.* **1 a** a hound used for hunting hares. **b** (in *pl.*) a pack of these with huntsmen. **2** a runner or group of cross-country runners. [HARE + -IER, assim. to HARRIER¹]

harrier³ /háreeər/ *n.* any bird of prey of the genus *Circus*, with long wings for swooping over the ground. [*harrower* f. *harrow* harry, rob, assim. to HARRIER¹]

Harris tweed /háris/ *n.* a kind of tweed woven by hand in Harris in the Outer Hebrides of Scotland.

harrow /hárō/ *n.* & *v.* ● *n.* a heavy frame with iron teeth dragged over plowed land to break up clods, remove weeds, cover seed, etc. ● *v.tr.* **1** draw a harrow over (land). **2** (usu. as **harrowing** *adj.*) distress greatly. □□ **harrower** *n.* **harrowingly** *adv.* [ME f. ON *hervi*]

■ *v.* **1** see PLOW *v.* 1. **2** (**harrowing**) distressing, disturbing, upsetting, worrying, alarming, unnerving, frightening, terrifying, horrifying, horrible, painful, torturous, heartrending, nerve-racking, traumatic, agonizing.

harrumph /hərúmf/ *v.intr.* clear the throat or make a similar sound, esp. ostentatiously or to signal disapproval. [imit.]

harry /háree/ *v.tr.* (**-ies, -ied**) **1** ravage or despoil. **2** harass; worry. [OE *herian, hergian* f. Gmc, rel. to OE *here* army]

■ **1** see OVERRUN *v.* **2** see WORRY *v.* 2.

harsh /haarsh/ *adj.* **1** unpleasantly rough or sharp, esp. to the senses. **2** severe; cruel. □□ **harshen** *v.tr.* & *intr.* **harshly** *adv.* **harshness** *n.* [MLG *harsch* rough, lit. 'hairy,' f. *haer* HAIR]

■ **1** rough, coarse, bristly, scratchy; grating, raucous, rasping, clashing, discordant, cacophonous, strident, shrill, *Mus.* dissonant, esp. *Mus.* inharmonious; bitter, acrid, sour, sharp. **2** severe, stern, stringent, tyrannical, merciless, pitiless, ruthless, unkind, cruel, unfeeling, unfriendly, hard, brutal; draconian, punitive; austere, bleak, dour, comfortless, grim, Spartan, stark, inhuman.

harslet var. of HASLET.

hart /haart/ n. esp. *Brit.* the male of the deer (esp. the red deer) usu. over five years old. □ **hart's tongue** a fern, *Phyllitis scolopendrium*, with narrow undivided fronds. [OE *heor(o)t* f. Gmc]

hartal /haárt'l/ n. the closing of shops and offices in India as a mark of protest or sorrow. [Hind. *hartāl, haṭṭāl* f. Skr. *haṭṭa* shop + *tālaka* lock]

hartebeest /haártəbeest, haártbeest/ n. any large African antelope of the genus *Alcelaphus*, with ringed horns bent back at the tips. [Afrik. f. Du. *hert* HART + *beest* BEAST]

hartshorn /haárts-hawrn/ n. *archaic* **1** an ammonious substance obtained from the horns of a hart. **2** (in full **spirit of hartshorn**) an aqueous solution of ammonia. [OE (as HART, HORN)]

harum-scarum /háirəmskáirəm/ adj. & n. *colloq.* • adj. wild and reckless. • n. such a person. [rhyming form. on HARE, SCARE]

haruspex /hərúspeks, hárəspeks/ n. (*pl.* **haruspices** /-spiseez/) a Roman religious official who interpreted omens from the inspection of animals' entrails. □□ **haruspicy** /-spisee/ n. [L]

■ see *fortune-teller*.

harvest /haárvist/ n. & v. • n. **1 a** the process of gathering in crops, etc. **b** the season when this takes place. **2** the season's yield or crop. **3** the product or result of any action. • v.tr. **1 a** gather as a harvest; reap. **b** earn; obtain as a result of harvesting. **2** experience (consequences). □ **harvest mite** any arachnid larvae of the genus *Trombicula*, a chigger. **harvest moon** the full moon nearest to the autumnal equinox (Sept. 22 or 23). **harvest mouse** a small rodent, *Micromys minutus*, that nests in the stalks of growing grain. □□ **harvestable** adj. [OE *hærfest* f. Gmc]

■ n. **1 a** ingathering, reaping, gathering; gleaning. **b** autumn, harvest home; Lammas, Pentecost. **2** crop, yield, produce, fruit; vintage; *Law* emblements. **3** see OUTCOME. • v. **1 a** reap, gather, pick, collect, garner, take in; glean. **b** earn, make, take in, collect, garner, get, receive, obtain, procure, net. **2** reap, experience; see also INCUR.

harvester /haárvistər/ n. **1** a reaper. **2** a reaping machine, esp. with sheaf-binding.

harvestman /haárvistmən/ n. (*pl.* **-men**) any of various arachnids of the family Opilionidae, with very long thin legs, found in humus and on tree trunks; a daddy-longlegs.

has *3rd sing. present* of HAVE.

has-been /házbin/ n. *colloq.* a person or thing that has lost a former importance or usefulness.

hash¹ /hash/ n. & v. • n. **1 a** a dish of cooked meat and potatoes cut into small pieces and recooked. **2 a** a mixture; a jumble. **b** a mess. **3** reused or recycled material. • v.tr. (often foll. by *up*) **1** make (meat, etc.) into a hash. **2** recycle (old material). □ **make a hash of** *colloq.* make a mess of; bungle. **settle a person's hash** *colloq.* deal with and subdue a person. [F *hacher* f. *hache* HATCHET]

■ n. **2 a** mixture, hodgepodge, mishmash, gallimaufry, farrago, jumble, olio, mélange, medley. **b** mess, shambles, confusion, bungle, botch, foul-up, *sl.* snafu. □ **make a hash of** bungle, make a mess *or* shambles of, mess *or* muddle up, botch, mishandle, mismanage, ruin, spoil, muff, *colloq.* foul up, *sl.* louse up, screw up. **settle a person's hash** see *put a person in his or her place* (PLACE).

hash² /hash/ n. *colloq.* hashish. [abbr.]

hashish /hásheesh, hasheésh/ n. a resinous product of the top leaves and tender parts of hemp, smoked or chewed for its narcotic effects. [f. Arab. *ḥašīš* dry herb; powdered hemp leaves]

Hasid /kháasid, kháw-, haá-/ (*pl.* **Hasidim** /-sídim, -seé-/) a member of any of several mystical Jewish sects, esp. one founded in the 18th c. □□ **Hasidic** /-sídik/ adj. [Heb. *ḥasíd* pious]

haslet /háslit, háyz-/ n. (also **harslet** /haár-/) pieces of (esp.

pig's) offal cooked together and usu. compressed into a meat loaf. [ME f. OF *hastelet* dimin. of *haste* roast meat, spit, f. OLG, OHG *harst* roast]

hasn't /házənt/ *contr.* has not.

hasp /hasp/ n. & v. • n. a hinged metal clasp that fits over a staple and can be secured by a padlock. • v.tr. fasten with a hasp. [OE *hæpse, hæsp*]

■ n. see LOCK¹ n. 1.

hassium /háseeəm/ n. a radioactive element. ¶ Symb.: **Hs**.

hassle /hásəl/ n. & v. *colloq.* • n. **1** a prolonged trouble or inconvenience. **2** an argument or involved struggle. • v. **1** tr. harass; annoy; cause trouble to. **2** intr. argue; quarrel. [20th c.: orig. dial.]

■ n. **1** see BOTHER n. 1. • v. **1** see BOTHER v. 1a.

hassock /hásək/ n. **1 a** a thick firm cushion for kneeling on, esp. in church. **b** a similar cushion used as a footrest, etc. **2** a tuft of matted grass, etc. [OE *hassuc*]

hast /hast/ *archaic 2nd sing. present* of HAVE.

hastate /hástayt/ adj. *Bot.* triangular; shaped like the head of a spear. [L *hastatus* f. *hasta* spear]

haste /hayst/ n. & v. • n. **1** urgency of movement or action. **2** excessive hurry. • v.intr. *archaic* = HASTEN. □ **in haste** quickly; hurriedly. **make haste** hurry; be quick. [ME f. OF *haste, haster* f. WG]

■ n. **1** swiftness, rapidity, quickness, speed, velocity, urgency, alacrity, briskness, *archaic or literary* celerity. **2** hurry, rush, rashness, hastiness, (hustle and) bustle, impetuousness, impetuosity, recklessness, precipitateness. □ **in haste** see *hastily* (HASTY). **make haste** see HURRY v. 1.

hasten /háysən/ v. **1** intr. (often foll. by *to* + infin.) make haste; hurry. **2** tr. cause to occur or be ready or be done sooner.

■ **1** hurry, rush, make haste, fly, flee, run, sprint, race, bolt, dash, scurry, scamper, scuttle, speed. **2** hurry (up), speed (up), quicken, accelerate, expedite, rush.

hasty /háystee/ adj. (**hastier, hastiest**) **1** hurried; acting quickly or hurriedly. **2** said, made, or done too quickly or too soon; rash; unconsidered. **3** quick-tempered. □□ **hastily** adv. **hastiness** n. [ME f. OF *hasti, hastif* (as HASTE, -IVE)]

■ **1** rushed, hurried, brief, speedy, fleeting; quick, swift, rapid, fast, brisk. **2** cursory, superficial, careless, slapdash, perfunctory; rash, precipitate, impetuous, impulsive, reckless, thoughtless, unthinking, incautious, heedless, ill-considered, unconsidered. **3** irritable, quick-tempered, irascible, testy, impatient, hot-tempered, volatile, choleric, short-tempered. □□ **hastily** quickly, speedily, swiftly, rapidly, posthaste, hurriedly, in haste; precipitately, impetuously, impulsively, rashly, recklessly, unthinkingly, thoughtlessly, heedlessly, incautiously; see also IMMEDIATELY adv. 1.

hat /hat/ n. & v. • n. **1** a covering for the head, often with a brim and worn out of doors. **2** *colloq.* a person's occupation or capacity, esp. one of several (*wearing his managerial hat*). • v.tr. (**hatted, hatting**) cover or provide with a hat. □ **hat trick** *Sports* the scoring of three goals, etc., in a single game, match, etc. **keep it under one's hat** *colloq.* keep it secret. **out of a hat** by random selection. **pass the hat** collect contributions of money. **take off one's hat to** (or **hats off to**) *colloq.* acknowledge admiration for. **throw one's hat in the ring** take up a challenge. □□ **hatful** n. (*pl.* **-fuls**). **hatless** adj. [OE *hætt* f. Gmc]

hatband /hátband/ n. a band of ribbon, etc., around a hat above the brim.

hatbox /hátboks/ n. a box to hold a hat, esp. for traveling.

hatch¹ /hach/ n. **1** an opening in the wall between two rooms, e.g., between a kitchen and a dining room for serving food. **2** an opening or door in an aircraft, spacecraft, etc. **3** *Naut.* **a** = HATCHWAY. **b** a trapdoor or cover for this (often in *pl.*:

/.../ pronunciation	• part of speech
□ phrases, idioms, and compounds	
□□ derivatives	■ synonym section
cross-references appear in SMALL CAPITALS or *italics*	

batten the hatches). **4** a floodgate. □ **down the hatch** *sl.* (as drinking a toast) drink up; cheers! [OE *hæcc* f. Gmc]

hatch² /hach/ *v. & n.* ● *v.* **1** *intr.* **a** (often foll. by *out*) (of a young bird or fish, etc.) emerge from the egg. **b** (of an egg) produce a young animal. **2** *tr.* incubate (an egg). **3** *tr.* (also foll. by *up*) devise (a plot, etc.). ● *n.* **1** the act or an instance of hatching. **2** a brood hatched. [ME *hacche*, of unkn. orig.]

■ *v.* **2** incubate, brood, sit on. **3** devise, contrive, concoct, design, formulate, originate, invent, dream up, *colloq.* cook up.

hatch³ /hach/ *v.tr.* mark (a surface, e.g., a map or drawing) with close parallel lines. [ME f. F *hacher* f. *hache* HATCHET]

hatchback /háchbak/ *n.* a car with a sloping back hinged at the top to form a door.

hatchery /hácharee/ *n.* (*pl.* **-ies**) a place for hatching eggs, esp. of fish or poultry.

hatchet /háchit/ *n.* a light short-handled ax. □ **hatchet-faced** *colloq.* sharp-featured or grim looking. **hatchet job** *colloq.* a fierce destructive critique of a person, esp. in print. **hatchet man** *colloq.* **1** a hired killer. **2** a person employed to carry out a hatchet job. [ME f. OF *hachette* dimin. of *hache* axe f. med.L *hapia* f. Gmc]

hatching /háching/ *n. Art & Archit.* close parallel lines forming shading, esp. on a map or an architectural drawing.

hatchling /háchling/ *n.* a bird or fish that has just hatched.

hatchment /háchmant/ *n. Heraldry* a large usu. diamond-shaped tablet with a deceased person's coat of arms, affixed to that person's house, tomb, etc. [contr. of ACHIEVEMENT]

hatchway /háchway/ *n.* an opening in a ship's deck for lowering cargo into the hold.

hate /hayt/ *v. & n.* ● *v.tr.* **1** dislike intensely; feel hatred toward. **2** *colloq.* **a** dislike. **b** (foll. by verbal noun or *to* + infin.) be reluctant (to do something) (*I hate to disturb you*). ● *n.* **1** hatred. **2** *colloq.* a hated person or thing. □□ **hatable** *adj.* (also **hateable**). **hater** *n.* [OE *hatian* f. Gmc]

■ *v.* **1** loathe, abhor, detest, have an aversion to, abominate, dislike, execrate, despise, scorn. **2 a** see DISLIKE *v.* **b** dislike, shrink from, be averse to, resist; (*hate to*) be loath to, be reluctant *or* unwilling *or* disinclined to. ● *n.* **1** hatred, abhorrence, detestation, loathing; animosity, antipathy, hostility, enmity, aversion; odium, animus. **2** enemy, bête noire, esp. *poet. or formal* foe; see also AVERSION 2.

hateful /háytfŏŏl/ *adj.* arousing hatred. □□ **hatefully** *adv.* **hatefulness** *n.*

■ loathsome, detestable, abhorrent, execrable, despicable, odious, abominable, obnoxious, heinous, foul, contemptible, repugnant, scurvy, repulsive, repellent, revolting, vile.

hath /hath/ *archaic 3rd sing. present* of HAVE.

hatha yoga /hátha/ *n.* a system of physical exercises and breathing control used in yoga. [Skr. *haṭha* force: see YOGA]

hatpin /hátpin/ *n.* a long pin, often decorative, for securing a hat to the head.

hatred /háytrid/ *n.* intense dislike or ill will. [ME f. HATE + -red f. OE *rēden* condition]

■ *n.* see DISLIKE *n.* 1.

hatstand /hátstand/ *n.* a stand with hooks on which to hang hats.

hatter /hátər/ *n.* **1** a maker or seller of hats. **2** *Austral. & NZ* a person (esp. a miner or bushman) who lives alone. □ **as mad as a hatter** wildly eccentric.

■ □ **as mad as a hatter** see INSANE 1.

hauberk /háwbərk/ *n. hist.* a coat of mail. [ME f. OF *hau(s)berc* f. Frank., = neck protection, f. *hals* neck + *berg-* f. *beorg* protection]

haughty /háwtee/ *adj.* (**haughtier**, **haughtiest**) arrogantly self-admiring and disdainful. □□ **haughtily** *adv.* **haughtiness** *n.* [extension of *haught* (adj.), earlier *haut* f. OF *haut* f. L *altus* high]

■ arrogant, proud, superior, self-important, self-admiring, pretentious, pompous, conceited, snobbish, lofty, aloof, supercilious, vain, disdainful, scornful, contemptuous, hoity-toity, *colloq.* highfalutin, stuck-up,

high and mighty, on one's high horse, snooty, la-di-da, snotty, uppity, esp. *Brit. colloq.* uppish.

haul /hawl/ *v. & n.* ● *v.* **1** *tr.* pull or drag forcibly. **2** *tr.* transport by truck, cart, etc. **3** *intr.* turn a ship's course. **4** *tr. colloq.* (usu. foll. by *up*) bring for reprimand or trial. ● *n.* **1** the act or an instance of hauling. **2** an amount gained or acquired. **3** a distance to be traversed (*a short haul*). □ **haul over the coals** see COAL. [var. of HALE²]

■ *v.* **1** drag, pull, tug, tow, trail, lug, heave, draw. **2** cart, transport, carry, convey, truck, move. **4** summon, subpoena, esp. *Law* summons. ● *n.* **1** pull, tug, drag, draw, heave, tow. **2** gain, catch, take, takings, yield, harvest; bag. **3** see DISTANCE *n.* 2.

haulage /háwlij/ *n.* **1** the commercial transport of goods. **2** a charge for this.

■ **1** see TRANSPORT *n.* 1a.

hauler /háwlər/ *n.* **1** a person or thing that hauls. **2** a miner who takes coal from the workface to the bottom of the shaft. **3** a person or business engaged in the transport of goods.

haulier /háwləər/ *n. Brit.* = HAULER.

haulm /hawm/ *n.* (also **halm**) **1** a stalk or stem. **2** the stalks or stems collectively of peas, beans, potatoes, etc., without the pods, etc. [OE *h(e)alm* f. Gmc]

haulyard var. of HALYARD.

haunch /hawnch/ *n.* **1** the fleshy part of the buttock with the thigh, esp. in animals. **2** the leg and loin of a deer, etc., as food. **3** the side of an arch between the crown and the pier. [ME f. OF *hanche*, of Gmc orig.: cf. LG *hanke* hind leg of a horse]

■ **1, 2** see LEG *n.* 2.

haunt /hawnt/ *v. & n.* ● *v.* **1** *tr.* (of a ghost) visit (a place) regularly, usu. reputedly giving signs of its presence. **2** *tr.* (of a person or animal) frequent or be persistently in (a place). **3** *tr.* (of a memory, etc.) be persistently in the mind of. **4** *intr.* (foll. by *with*, *in*) stay habitually. **5** trouble; distress (*their shady financial dealings came back to haunt them*) ● *n.* **1** (often in *pl.*) a place frequented by a person. **2** a place frequented by animals, esp. for food and drink. □□ **haunter** *n.* [ME f. OF *hanter* f. Gmc]

■ *v.* **2** visit, frequent, spend time at, *sl.* hang out at. **3** obsess, preoccupy, beset, harass, torment, trouble, possess, prey on, *colloq.* plague. ● *n.* **1** stamping ground, territory, domain, preserve, *colloq.* patch, *joc.* bailiwick, *sl.* hangout, turf.

haunting /háwnting/ *adj.* (of a memory, melody, etc.) poignant; wistful; evocative. □□ **hauntingly** *adv.*

Hausa /hówzə/ *n. & adj.* ● *n.* (*pl.* same or **Hausas**) **1 a** a people of W. Africa and the Sudan. **b** a member of this people. **2** the Hamitic language of this people, widely used in W. Africa. ● *adj.* of or relating to this people or language. [native name]

hausfrau /hówsfrowl/ *n.* a German housewife. [G f. *Haus* house + *Frau* woman]

hautboy *archaic* var. of OBOE.

haute couture /ŏt kōōtŏŏr/ *n.* high fashion; the leading fashion houses or their products. [F, lit. = high dressmaking]

haute cuisine /ŏt kwizeén/ *n.* cooking of a high standard, esp. of the French traditional school. [F, lit. = high cooking]

haute école /ŏt aykŏl/ *n.* the art or practice of advanced classical dressage. [F, = high school]

hauteur /hōtŏr/ *n.* haughtiness of manner. [F f. *haut* high]

■ see PRIDE *n.* 2.

haut monde /ō mawNd/ *n.* fashionable society. [F, lit. = high world]

■ see SOCIETY 5a.

Havana /həvánə/ *n.* a cigar made in Havana or elsewhere in Cuba.

have /hav/ *v. & n.* ● *v.* (*3rd sing. present* **has** /haz/; *past and past part.* **had** /had/) ● *v.tr.* **1** hold in possession as one's property or at one's disposal; be provided with (*has a car*; *had no time to read*; *has nothing to wear*). **2** hold in a certain relationship (*has a sister*; *had no equals*). **3** contain as a part or quality (*house has two floors*; *has green eyes*). **4 a** undergo; experience; enjoy; suffer (*had a good time*; *has a headache*).

b be subjected to a specified state (*had my car stolen; the book has a page missing*). **c** cause, instruct, or invite (a person or thing) to be in a particular state or take a particular action (*had him dismissed; had us worried; had my hair cut; had a copy made; had them stay*). **5 a** engage in (an activity) (*had an argument*). **b** hold (a meeting, party, etc.). **b** eat or drink (*had a beer*). **7** (usu. in *neg.*) accept or tolerate; permit to (*I won't have it; will not have you say such things*). **8 a** let (a feeling, etc.) be present (*have no doubt; has a lot of sympathy for me; have nothing against them*). **b** show or feel (mercy, pity, etc.) toward another person (*have pity on him; have mercy!*). **c** (foll. by *to* + infin.) show by action that one is influenced by (a feeling, quality, etc.) (*have the goodness to leave now*). **9 a** give birth to or beget (offspring). **b** conceive mentally (an idea, etc.). **10** receive; obtain (*had a letter from him; not a ticket to be had*). **11** be burdened with or committed to (*has a job to do; have my garden to attend to*). **12 a** have obtained (a qualification) (*has several degrees*). **b** know (a language) (*has no Latin*). **13** *sl.* **a** get the better of (*I had him there*). **b** (usu. in *passive*) cheat; deceive (*you were had*). **14** *coarse sl.* have sexual intercourse with. ● *v.aux.* (with *past part.* or *ellipt.*, to form the perfect, pluperfect, and future perfect tenses, and the conditional mood) (*have worked; had seen; will have been; had I known, I would have gone; have you met her? yes, I have*). ● *n.* **1** (usu. in *pl.*) *colloq.* a person who has wealth or resources. **2** *Brit. sl.* a swindle. □ **had best** see BEST. **had better** would find it prudent to. **had rather** see RATHER. **have a care** see CARE. **have done, have done with** see DONE. **have an eye for, have eyes for, have an eye to** see EYE. **have a good mind to** see MIND. **have got to** *colloq.* = **have to. have had it** *colloq.* **1** have missed one's chance. **2** (of a person) have passed one's prime; (of a thing) be worn out or broken. **3** have been killed, defeated, etc. **4** have suffered or endured enough. **have it 1** (foll. by *that* + clause) express the view that. **2** win a decision in a vote, etc. **3** *colloq.* have found the answer, etc. **have it away** (or **off**) *Brit. coarse sl.* have sexual intercourse. **have it both ways** see BOTH. **have it in for** *colloq.* be hostile or ill-disposed toward. **have it out** (often foll. by *with*) *colloq.* attempt to settle a dispute by discussion or argument. **have it one's own way** see WAY. **have-not** (usu. in *pl.*) *colloq.* a person lacking wealth or resources. **have nothing to do with** see DO¹. **have on 1** be wearing (clothes). **2** be committed to (an engagement); have plans for. **3** *Brit. colloq.* tease; play a trick on. **have out** get (a tooth, etc.) extracted (*had her tonsils out*). **have sex** (often foll. by *with*) *colloq.* have sexual intercourse. **have something** (or **nothing**) **on a person 1** know something (or nothing) discreditable or incriminating about a person. **2** have an (or no) advantage or superiority over a person. **have to** be obliged to; must. **have to do with** see DO¹. **have up** *Brit. colloq.* bring (a person) before a court of justice, interviewer, etc. [OE *habban* f. Gmc, prob. rel. to HEAVE]

■ *v.* **1** possess, hold, own, keep, be provided with. **3** possess, bear, contain, include. **4 a** undergo, suffer, endure, experience, enjoy. **c** cause to do or be, instruct to do or be, invite to do or be, induce to do or be, make a person do or be, make a thing do or be, force to do or be, oblige to do or be, press to do or be, require to do or be, compel to do or be, get to do, get done. **5 a** see ENGAGE 8. **b** hold, give, arrange, plan, organize, set (up), fix, prearrange, prepare, throw. **6** partake of, have a share or portion or part or bit of, consume; eat; drink. **7** see ALLOW 1. **8 b** see SHOW *v.* 3. **9 a** give birth to, bear, mother, deliver, bring into the world; procreate, sire, father, *literary* beget. **b** see CONCEIVE 3a. **10** receive, get, obtain, acquire, procure, secure; take, accept. **12 b** see KNOW *v.* 1a. **13 a** see BEAT *v.* 3a. **b** see DECEIVE 1. ● *n.* **1** (*haves*) winners, fortunate ones, the rich or affluent or prosperous or well off or moneyed or well-to-do or wealthy. □ **had better** ought to, must, should. **have had it 1** have missed the boat or bus, have missed one's chance, be too late. **2** see *on one's last legs* (LEG). **3** see DEAD *adj.* 1. **have it 1** see ARGUE 2. **2** see WIN *v.* 3a. **3** know, understand, see; *colloq.* get it,

catch on, cotton on, *Brit.* twig. **have it in for** see DISLIKE *v.* **have it out** see NEGOTIATE 1. **have-not** (*have-nots*) losers, the poor or needy or destitute or poverty-stricken or badly off or hard up or down and out. **have on 1** wear, be wearing, be dressed or clothed in, *formal* be attired in. **2** be committed to, have in the offing or pipeline, plan; see also ARRANGE 2, 3. **have sex** (**with**) see *make love* (LOVE). **have to** see MUST¹ *v.*

haven /háyvən/ *n.* **1** a harbor or port. **2** a place of refuge. [OE *hæfen* f. ON *höfn*]
■ **1** see HARBOR *n.* 1. **2** see REFUGE 1, 2.

haven't /hávənt/ *contr.* have not.

haver /hávər/ *v.* & *n.* ● *v.intr. Brit.* **1** talk foolishly; babble. **2** vacillate; hesitate. ● *n.* (usu. in *pl.*) *Sc.* foolish talk; nonsense. [18th c.: orig. unkn.]

haversack /hávərsak/ *n.* a stout bag for provisions, etc., carried on the back or over the shoulder. [F *havresac* f. G *Habersack* f. *Haber* oats + *Sack* SACK¹]
■ see PACK¹ *n.* 1.

haversine /hávərsin/ *n.* (also **haversin**) *Math.* half of a versed sine. [contr.]

havoc /hávək/ *n.* & *v.* ● *n.* widespread destruction; great confusion or disorder. ● *v.tr.* (**havocked, havocking**) devastate. □ **play havoc with** *colloq.* cause great confusion or difficulty to. [ME f. AF *havok* f. OF *havo(t)*, of unkn. orig.]
■ *n.* devastation, destruction, desolation, damage, (rack and) ruin, *literary* despoliation; confusion, chaos, disorder, mayhem, disruption. □ **play havoc with** see DISRUPT 1.

haw¹ /haw/ *n.* the hawthorn or its fruit. [OE *haga* f. Gmc, rel. to HEDGE]

haw² /haw/ *n.* the nictitating membrane of a horse, dog, etc., esp. when inflamed. [16th c.: orig. unkn.]

haw³ /haw/ *int.* & *v.* ● *int.* expressing hesitation. ● *v.intr.* (in **hem and haw**: see HEM²) [imit.: cf. HA]

haw⁴ /haw/ *int.* a command to a horse, etc., to turn to the left.

Hawaiian /həwíən/ *n.* & *adj.* ● *n.* **1 a** a native or inhabitant of Hawaii, an island or island group (comprising a US state) in the N. Pacific. **b** a person of Hawaiian descent. **2** the Malayo-Polynesian language of Hawaii. ● *adj.* of or relating to Hawaii or its people or language.

hawfinch /háwfinch/ *n.* any large stout finch of the genus *Coccothraustes*, with a thick beak for cracking seeds. [HAW¹ + FINCH]

hawk¹ /hawk/ *n.* & *v.* ● *n.* **1** any of various diurnal birds of prey of the family Accipitridae, having a characteristic curved beak, rounded short wings, and a long tail. **2** *Polit.* a person who advocates an aggressive or warlike policy, esp. in foreign affairs. **3** a rapacious person. ● *v.* **1** *intr.* hunt game with a hawk. **2** *intr.* (often foll. by *at*) & *tr.* attack, as a hawk does. **3** *intr.* (of a bird) hunt on the wing for food. □ **hawk-eyed** keen-sighted. **hawk moth** any darting and hovering moth of the family Sphingidae, having narrow forewings and a stout body. □□ **hawkish** *adj.* **hawkishness** *n.* **hawklike** *adj.* [OE *h(e)afoc, hæbuc* f. Gmc]
■ *n.* **2** see BELLIGERENT *n.*

hawk² /hawk/ *v.tr.* **1** carry about or offer around (goods) for sale. **2** (often foll. by *about*) relate (news, gossip, etc.) freely. [back-form. f. HAWKER¹]
■ **1** see SELL *v.* 2.

hawk³ /hawk/ *v.* **1** *intr.* clear the throat noisily. **2** *tr.* (foll. by *up*) bring (phlegm, etc.) up from the throat. [prob. imit.]

hawk⁴ /hawk/ *n.* a plasterer's square board with a handle underneath for carrying plaster or mortar. [17th c.: orig. unkn.]

hawker¹ /háwkər/ *n.* a person who travels about selling goods. [16th c.: prob. f. LG or Du.; cf. HUCKSTER]

/ . . . / **pronunciation**   ● **part of speech**
□ **phrases, idioms, and compounds**
□□ **derivatives**   ■ **synonym section**
cross-references appear in SMALL CAPITALS or *italics*

■ see SELLER.

hawker[2] /háwkər/ *n.* a falconer. [OE *hafocere*]

hawksbill /háwksbil/ *n.* (in full **hawksbill turtle**) a small turtle, *Eretmochelys imbricata*, yielding tortoiseshell.

hawkweed /háwkweed/ *n.* any composite plant of the genus *Hieracium*, with yellow flowers.

hawse /hawz/ *n.* **1** the part of a ship's bows in which hawse-holes or hawsepipes are placed. **2** the space between the head of an anchored vessel and the anchors. **3** the arrangement of cables when a ship is moored with port and starboard forward anchors. [ME *halse*, prob. f. ON *háls* neck, ship's bow]

hawsehole /háwzhōl/ *n.* a hole in the side of a ship through which a cable or anchor rope passes.

hawsepipe /háwzpīp/ *n.* a metal pipe lining a hawsehole.

hawser /háwzər/ *n. Naut.* a thick rope or cable for mooring or towing a ship. [ME f. AF *haucer*, *hauceour* f. OF *haucier* hoist ult. f. L *altus* high]

■ see ROPE *n.* 1a.

hawthorn /háwthawrn/ *n.* any thorny shrub or tree of the genus *Crataegus*, esp. *C. monogyna*, with white, red, or pink blossoms and small dark red fruit or haws. [OE *hagathorn* (as HAW[1], THORN)]

hay[1] /hay/ *n. & v.* ● *n.* grass mown and dried for fodder.
● *v.* **1** *intr.* make hay. **2** *tr.* put (land) under grass for hay.
3 *tr.* make into hay. □ **hay fever** a common allergy with respiratory symptoms, caused by pollen or dust. **make hay of** throw into confusion. **make hay (while the sun shines)** seize opportunities for profit or enjoyment. [OE *hēg*, *hīeg*, *hīg* f. Gmc]

■ *n.* see PROVENDER 1.

hay[2] /hay/ *n.* (also **hey**) **1** a country dance with interweaving steps. **2** a figure in this. [obs. F *haie*]

haycock /háykok/ *n.* a conical heap of hay in a field.

hayfield /háyfeeld/ *n.* a field where hay is being or is to be made.

haymaker /háymaykər/ *n.* **1** a person who tosses and spreads hay to dry after mowing. **2** an apparatus for shaking and drying hay. **3** *sl.* a forceful blow or punch. □□ **haymaking** *n.*

■ **3** see PUNCH[1] *n.* 1.

haymow /háymow/ *n.* hay stored in a stack or barn.

hayrick /háyrik/ *n.* = HAYSTACK.

hayseed /háyseed/ *n.* **1** grass seed obtained from hay. **2** *colloq.* a rustic or yokel.

■ **2** see PEASANT.

haystack /háystak/ *n.* a packed pile of hay with a pointed or ridged top.

■ see STACK *n.* 2.

haywire /háywir/ *adj. colloq.* **1** badly disorganized; out of control. **2** (of a person) badly disturbed; erratic. [HAY[1] + WIRE, from the use of hay-baling wire in makeshift repairs]

■ **1** see *out of order* 1 (ORDER).

hazard /házərd/ *n. & v.* ● *n.* **1** a danger or risk. **2** a source of this. **3** chance. **4** a dice game with a complicated arrangement of chances. **5** *Golf* an obstruction in playing a shot, e.g., a bunker, water, etc. ● *v.tr.* **1** venture on (*hazard a guess*). **2** run the risk of. **3** expose to hazard. [ME f. OF *hasard* f. Sp. *azar* f. Arab. *az-zahr* chance, luck]

■ *n.* **1, 2** peril, endangerment, threat, jeopardy; danger, risk, pitfall. **3** chance, uncertainty, luck; see also FORTUNE 1a. ● *v.* **1** venture, dare, stake, wager; make, (take the) risk (of). **2** (run the) risk (of), stake, chance, gamble on. **3** jeopardize, threaten, imperil; see also ENDANGER.

hazardous /házərdəs/ *adj.* **1** risky; dangerous. **2** dependent on chance. □□ **hazardously** *adv.* **hazardousness** *n.* [F *hasardeux* (as HAZARD)]

■ unsafe, unsound, risky, dangerous, shaky, questionable, unreliable, unpredictable, precarious, uncertain, chancy, *archaic or joc.* parlous, *sl.* dicey, hairy, *Brit. sl.* dickey.

haze[1] /hayz/ *n.* **1** obscuration of the atmosphere near the earth by fine particles of water, smoke, or dust. **2** mental obscurity or confusion. [prob. back-form. f. HAZY]

■ **1** see FOG[1] *n.* 1.

haze[2] /hayz/ *v.tr.* **1** *Naut.* harass with overwork. **2** seek to disconcert; ridicule. **3** subject (fraternity initiates, etc.) to tricks, humiliation, etc. [orig. uncert.: cf. obs. F *haser* tease, insult]

hazel /háyzəl/ *n.* **1** any shrub or small tree of the genus *Corylus*, esp. *C. avellana* bearing round brown edible nuts. **2 a** wood from the hazel. **b** a stick made of this. **3** a reddish brown or greenish brown color (esp. of the eyes). □ **hazel grouse** a European woodland grouse, *Tetrastes bonasia*. [OE *hæsel* f. Gmc]

hazelnut /háyzəlnut/ *n.* the fruit of the hazel.

hazy /háyzee/ *adj.* (**hazier**, **haziest**) **1** misty. **2** vague; indistinct. **3** confused; uncertain. □□ **hazily** *adv.* **haziness** *n.* [17th c. in Naut. use: orig. unkn.]

■ **1** misty, foggy. **2** indistinct, unclear, blurred, blurry, fuzzy, vague, dim, dark, murky, opaque, shadowy, obscure, faint, nebulous. **3** uncertain, unclear, indefinite, muddled; see also *confused* (CONFUSE 4b).

Hb *symb.* hemoglobin.

HBM *abbr.* Her or His Britannic Majesty (or Majesty's).

H-bomb /áychbom/ *n.* = hydrogen bomb. [H[3] + BOMB]

HC *abbr.* **1** Holy Communion. **2** (in the UK) House of Commons.

h.c. *abbr.* *honoris causa*.

HCF *abbr.* highest common factor.

hdbk. *abbr.* handbook.

HDTV *abbr.* high-definition television.

HE *abbr.* **1** high explosive. **2** His Eminence. **3** His or Her Excellency.

He *symb. Chem.* the element helium.

he /hee/ *pron. & n.* ● *pron.* (*obj.* **him** /him/; *poss.* **his** /hiz/; *pl.* **they** /thay/) **1** the man or boy or male animal previously named or in question. **2** a person, etc., of unspecified sex, esp. referring to one already named or identified (*if anyone comes he will have to wait*). ● *n.* **1** a male; a man. **2** (in *comb.*) male (*he-goat*). **3** *Brit.* a children's chasing game, with the chaser designated "he." □ **he-man** (*pl.* **-men**) a masterful or virile man. [OE f. Gmc]

head /hed/ *n., adj., & v.* ● *n.* **1** the upper part of the human body, or the foremost or upper part of an animal's body, containing the brain, mouth, and sense organs. **2 a** the head regarded as the seat of intellect or repository of comprehended information. **b** intelligence; imagination (*use your head*). **c** mental aptitude or tolerance (usu. foll. by *for*: *a good head for business*; *no head for heights*). **3** *colloq.* a headache, esp. resulting from a blow or from intoxication. **4** a thing like a head in form or position, esp.: **a** the operative part of a tool. **b** the flattened top of a nail. **c** the ornamented top of a pillar. **d** a mass of leaves or flowers at the top of a stem. **e** the flat end of a drum. **f** the foam on top of a glass of beer, etc. **g** the upper horizontal part of a window frame, door frame, etc. **5** life when regarded as vulnerable (*it cost him his head*). **6 a** a person in charge; a director or leader (esp. (usu. *Brit.*) the principal teacher at a school or college). **b** a position of leadership or command. **7** the front or forward part of something, e.g., a line. **8** the upper end of something, e.g., a table or bed. **9** the top or highest part of something, e.g., a page, stairs, etc. **10** a person or individual regarded as a numerical unit (*$10 per head*). **11** (*pl.* same) **a** an individual animal as a unit. **b** (as *pl.*) a number of cattle or game as specified (*20 head*). **12 a** the side of a coin bearing the image of a head. **b** (usu. in *pl.*) this side as a choice when tossing a coin. **13 a** the source of a river or stream, etc. **b** the end of a lake at which a river enters it. **14** the height or length of a head as a measure. **15** the component of a machine that is in contact with or very close to what is being processed or worked on, esp.: **a** the component on a tape recorder that touches the moving tape in play and converts the signals. **b** the part of a record player that holds the playing cartridge and stylus. **c** = PRINTHEAD. **16 a** a confined body of water behind a dam, or steam in an engine, etc. **b** the pressure exerted by this. **17** a promontory (esp. in place-names) (*Nags Head*). **18** *Naut.* **a** the bows of a ship. **b** a ship's latrine. **19** a main topic or category for consideration or discussion. **20** *Journalism* = HEADLINE *n*. **21** a culmination, climax, or crisis. **22** the fully developed top of a boil, etc. **23** *sl.* a habitual taker of drugs; a drug addict. ● *attrib.adj.* chief or principal (*head gardener; head office*). ● *v*. **1** *tr.* be at the head or front of. **2** *tr.* be in charge of (*headed a small team*). **3** *tr.* **a** provide with a head or heading. **b** (of an inscription, title, etc.) be at the top of; serve as a heading for. **4 a** *intr.* face or move in a specified direction or toward a specified result (often foll. by *for: is heading for trouble*). **b** *tr.* direct in a specified direction. **5** *tr. Soccer* strike (the ball) with the head. **6 a** *tr.* (often foll. by *down*) cut the head off (a plant, etc.). **b** *intr.* (of a plant, etc.) form a head. □ **above** (or **over**) **one's head** beyond one's ability to understand. **come to a head** reach a crisis. **enter** (or **come into**) **one's head** *colloq.* occur to one. **from head to toe** (or **foot**) all over a person's body. **get one's head down** *Brit. sl.* **1** go to bed. **2** concentrate on the task in hand. **give a person his** or **her head** allow a person to act freely. **go out of one's head** go mad. **go to one's head 1** (of liquor) make one dizzy or slightly drunk. **2** (of success) make one conceited. **head and shoulders** *colloq.* by a considerable amount. **head back 1** get ahead of so as to intercept and turn back. **2** return home, etc. **head-banger** *sl.* **1** a young person dancing violently to heavy metal music. **2** a crazy or eccentric person. **head-butt** *n*. a forceful thrust with the top or front of the head into the chin, head, or body of another person. ● *v.tr.* attack (another person) with a head-butt. **head first 1** with the head foremost. **2** precipitately. **head in the sand** refusal to acknowledge an obvious danger or difficulty. **head off 1** get ahead of so as to intercept and turn aside. **2** forestall. **a head of hair** the hair on a person's head, esp. as a distinctive feature. **head-on 1** with the front foremost (*a head-on crash*). **2** in direct confrontation. **head over heels 1** turning over completely in forward motion as in a somersault, etc. **2** topsy-turvy. **3** utterly; completely (*head over heels in love*). **head shrinker** *sl.* a psychiatrist. **head start** an advantage granted or gained at an early stage. **heads up** (as an interjection) watch out; be alert. **heads will roll** *colloq.* people will be disgraced or dismissed. **head teacher** the teacher in charge of a department or school. **head up** take charge of (a group of people). **head-up** *adj.* (of instrument readings in an aircraft, vehicle, etc.) shown so as to be visible without lowering the eyes. **head voice** the high register of the voice in speaking or singing. **head wind** a wind blowing from directly in front. **hold up one's head** be confident or unashamed. **in one's head 1** in one's thoughts or imagination. **2** by mental process without use of physical aids. **keep one's head** remain calm. **keep one's head above water** *colloq.* **1** keep out of debt. **2** avoid succumbing to difficulties. **keep one's head down** *colloq.* remain inconspicuous in difficult or dangerous times. **lose one's head** lose self-control; panic. **make head or tail of** (usu. with *neg.* or *interrog.*) understand at all. **off one's head** *sl.* crazy. **off the top of one's head** *colloq.* impromptu; without careful thought or investigation. **on one's** (or **one's own**) **head** as one's sole responsibility. **out of one's head 1** *sl.* crazy. **2** from one's imagination or memory. **over one's head 1** beyond one's ability to understand. **2** without one's knowledge or involvement, esp. when one has a right to this. **3** with disregard for one's own (stronger) claim (*was promoted over their heads*). **put heads together** consult together. **put into a person's head** suggest to a person. **take** (or **get**) **it into one's head** (foll. by *that* + clause or *to* + infin.) form a definite idea or plan. **turn a person's head 1** make a person conceited. **2** cause a person to be distracted, confused, etc. **with one's head in the clouds** see CLOUD. □□ **headed** *adj.* (also in *comb.*). **headless** *adj.* **headward** *adj. & adv.* [OE *hēafod* f. Gmc]

■ *n*. **1** *archaic* or *colloq.* pate, *colloq.* noddle, *sl.* dome, coconut, noggin, nut, noodle, conk, *archaic sl.* crumpet, *sl.* bean, *Brit. sl.* bonce, skull, cranium. **2** mind, brain(s), mentality, intellect, wit, intelligence, perception, imagination, *colloq.* gray matter; aptitude, talent, faculty, flair, perceptiveness; tolerance. **4** see TIP[1] *n*. 1. **6 a** chief, leader, headman, director,

managing director, president, chairman, chairwoman, superintendent, governor, principal, head teacher, headmaster, headmistress, *colloq.* boss, *sl.* (big) cheese, (chief) honcho, Mr. Big, *Brit. sl.* governor, guv. **b** top, first place, leading position, leadership, command, forefront. **7** front, vanguard, forefront, van. **9** see TOP[1] *n*. 1. **13 a** source, origin, fountainhead, wellspring, *poet.* fount. **17** promontory, headland; see also CLIFF. **21** crisis, (critical) point, (fever) pitch; climax, culmination, apex, peak, crest, conclusion, *disp.* crescendo. ● *attrib.adj.* first, leading, premier, chief, main, principal, foremost, prime, preeminent, cardinal, paramount, supreme; superior, senior. ● *v*. **1** top; see also LEAD[1] *v*. 5. **2** head up, be in charge of, direct, supervise, oversee, control, govern, run, lead, guide, manage, command, rule, conduct. **4 a** go, move, proceed, turn, steer, face, aim, point; (*head for*) make a beeline for, turn one's steps toward. See DIRECT *v*. 3b. □ **above** (or **over**) **one's head** see INCOMPREHENSIBLE. **come to a head** reach a crisis *or* climax, *disp.* come to *or* reach a crescendo; peak, culminate, *colloq.* climax. **enter** (or **come into**) **one's head** see OCCUR 3. **from head to toe** (or **foot**) see *completely* (COMPLETE). **go out of one's head** go mad, *sl.* go ape; see also CRAZY 1. **go to one's head 1** see INTOXICATE 1. **head and shoulders** see *substantially* (SUBSTANTIAL). **head first 2** see *prematurely* (PREMATURE). **head off 1** intercept, divert. **2** stop, forestall, cut off, block, prevent, inhibit, avert, ward *or* fend off. **head-on 2** see BLUNT *adj*. 2, OPENLY. **head over heels 3** completely, entirely, deeply, utterly, wholly, fully, wildly, *colloq.* madly. **head shrinker** see *therapist* (THERAPY). **head start** see ADVANTAGE *n*. 1, 3. **head up** see HEAD *v*. 2 above. **in one's head 2** mentally, in one's mind. **keep one's head** not turn a hair, stay calm *or* cool *or* calm and collected, not panic, *colloq.* not *or* never bat an eyelid. **lose one's head** see PANIC[1] *v*. **make head or tail of** see UNDERSTAND 1, 2. **off one's head** see CRAZY 1. **off the top of one's head** see OFFHAND *adv*. 2. **out of one's head 1** see CRAZY 1. **over one's head 1** see INCOMPREHENSIBLE. **2** see *behind a person's back*. **put heads together** see CONFER 2.

-head /hed/ *suffix* = -HOOD (*godhead; maidenhead*). [ME *-hed, -hede* = -HOOD]

headache /hédayk/ *n*. **1** a continuous pain in the head. **2** *colloq.* **a** a worrying problem. **b** a troublesome person. □□ **headachy** *adj*.

■ **2** worry, bother, vexation, inconvenience, nuisance, annoyance, problem, difficulty, trouble, bane; *colloq.* hassle, pain (in the neck), *sl.* pain in the butt.

headband /hédband/ *n*. a band worn around the head as decoration or to keep the hair off the face.

headboard /hédbawrd/ *n*. an upright panel forming the head of a bed.

headcount /hédkownt/ *n*. **1** a counting of individual people. **2** a total number of people, esp. the number of people employed in a particular organization.

headdress /héd-dres/ *n*. an ornamental covering or band for the head.

header /hédər/ *n*. **1** *Soccer* a shot or pass made with the head. **2** *colloq.* a headlong fall or dive. **3** a brick or stone laid at right angles to the face of a wall. **4** (in full **header tank**) a tank of water, etc., maintaining pressure in a plumbing system. **5** *Computing* line or lines of information printed at the top of the page throughout a document.

■ **2** see TUMBLE *n*. 1.

headgear /hédgeer/ *n*. a hat, headdress, or head covering.

head-hunting /hédhunting/ *n*. **1** the practice among some peoples of collecting the heads of dead enemies as trophies.

/.../ **pronunciation**	● **part of speech**
□ **phrases, idioms, and compounds**	
□□ **derivatives**	■ **synonym section**
cross-references appear in SMALL CAPITALS or *italics*	

2 the practice of filling a (usu. senior) business position by approaching a suitable person employed elsewhere. □□ **headhunt** v.tr. (also absol.). **headhunter** n.

heading /héding/ n. **1 a** a title at the head of a page or section of a book, etc. **b** a division or section of a subject of discourse, etc. **2 a** a horizontal passage made in preparation for building a tunnel. **b** Mining = DRIFT n. 6. **3** the extension of the top of a curtain above the tape that carries the hooks or the pocket for a rod. **4** the course of an aircraft, ship, etc. ■ **1 b** see CATEGORY.

headlamp /hédlamp/ n. = HEADLIGHT.

headland n. **1** /hédlənd/ a promontory. **2** /hédland/ a strip left unplowed at the end of a field, to allow machinery to pass through.
■ **1** see CAPE².

headlight /hédlīt/ n. **1** a strong light at the front of a motor vehicle or train engine. **2** the beam from this.
■ **1** see LIGHT¹ n. 4a.

headline /hédlīn/ n. & v. ● n. **1** a heading at the top of an article or page, esp. in a newspaper. **2** (in pl.) the most important items of news in a newspaper or broadcast news bulletin. ● v.tr. give a headline to. □ **hit** (or **make**) **the headlines** colloq. be given prominent attention as news.
■ n. **1** see TITLE n. 2.

headliner /hédlīnər/ n. a star performer.
■ see STAR n. 8a.

headlock /hédlok/ n. Wrestling a hold with an arm around the opponent's head.

headlong /hédlawng, -lóng/ adv. & adj. **1** with head foremost. **2** in a rush. [ME headling (as HEAD, -LING²), assim. to -LONG]
■ **2** see IMPULSIVE.

headman /hédmən/ n. (pl. **-men**) the chief man of a tribe, etc.
■ see CHIEF n.

headmaster /hédmástər/ n. (fem. **headmistress** /-místris/) (esp. in the UK or in private schools in the US) the person in charge of a school.
■ see PRINCIPAL n. 2.

headmost /hédmōst/ adj. (esp. of a ship) foremost.

headphone /hédfōn/ n. (usu. in pl.) a pair of earphones joined by a band placed over the head, for listening to audio equipment, etc.

headpiece /hédpees/ n. **1** an ornamental engraving at the head of a chapter, etc. **2 a** a helmet. **b** a ceremonial headdress. **3** intellect.

headquarters /hédkwáwrtərz/ n. (as sing. or pl.) **1** the administrative center of an organization. **2** the premises occupied by a military commander and the commander's staff.
■ **1** see SEAT n. 9. **2** see BASE¹ n. 3.

headrest /hédrest/ n. a support for the head, esp. on a seat or chair.

headroom /hédroom, -room/ n. **1** the space or clearance between the top of a vehicle and the underside of a bridge, etc., which it passes under. **2** the space above a driver's or passenger's head in a vehicle.

headscarf /hédskaarf/ n. a scarf worn around the head and tied under the chin, instead of a hat.

headset /hédset/ n. a set of headphones, often with a microphone attached, used esp. in telephone and radio communications.

headship /hédship/ n. the position of chief or leader, esp. of a headmaster or headmistress.

headsman /hédzmən/ n. (pl. **-men**) **1** hist. an executioner who beheads. **2** a person in command of a whaling boat.

headspring /hédspring/ n. **1** the main source of a stream. **2** a principal source of ideas, etc.

headsquare /hédskwair/ n. a rectangular scarf for wearing on the head.

headstall /hédstawl/ n. the part of a halter or bridle that fits around a horse's head.

headstock /hédstok/ n. a set of bearings in a machine, supporting a revolving part.

headstone /hédstōn/ n. a (usu. inscribed) stone set up at the head of a grave.

■ see TOMBSTONE.

headstrong /hédstrawng, -strong/ adj. self-willed and obstinate. □□ **headstrongly** adv. **headstrongness** n.
■ see SELF-WILLED.

headwater /hédwawtər, -woter/ n. (in sing. or pl.) streams flowing at the sources of a river.

headway /hédway/ n. **1** progress. **2** the rate of progress of a ship. **3** = HEADROOM 1. □ **make headway** see MAKE.
■ **1** progress, improvement; see also ADVANCE n. 1, 2. **2** speed, rate of progress; knots.

headword /hédwərd/ n. a word forming a heading, e.g., of an entry in a dictionary or encyclopedia.

headwork /hédwərk/ n. mental work or effort.

heady /hédee/ adj. (**headier**, **headiest**) **1** (of alcohol) potent; intoxicating. **2** (of success, etc.) likely to cause conceit. **3** (of a person, thing, or action) impetuous; violent. □□ **headily** adv. **headiness** n.

heal /heel/ v. **1** intr. (often foll. by up) (of a wound or injury) become sound or healthy again. **2** tr. cause (a wound, disease, or person) to heal or be healed. **3** tr. put right (differences, etc.). **4** tr. alleviate (sorrow, etc.). □ **heal-all 1** a universal remedy; a panacea. **2** a popular name of various medicinal plants. □□ **healable** adj. **healer** n. [OE hǣlan f. Gmc, rel. to WHOLE]
■ **1** mend, improve, get better. **2** cure, restore (to health); mend. **3** reconcile, settle, patch up, put or set straight, put or set right, remedy, repair, mend, rectify, make good. **4** see RELIEVE 2. □ **heal-all 1** cure, cure-all, panacea, universal remedy.

heald /heeld/ n. = HEDDLE. [app. f. OE hefel, hefeld, f. Gmc]

health /helth/ n. **1** the state of being well in body or mind. **2** a person's mental or physical condition (in poor health). **3** soundness, esp. financial or moral (the health of the nation). **4** a toast drunk in someone's honor. □ **health farm** a residential establishment where people seek improved health by a regimen of dieting, exercise, etc. **health food** food thought to have health-giving or -sustaining qualities. **health maintenance organization** an organization that provides medical care to subscribers who have paid in advance, usu. through a health insurance plan. **health service** Brit. a public service providing medical care. **health spa 1** a resort, club, gym, etc., providing facilities for exercise and conditioning. **2** = health farm. **health visitor** Brit. a trained nurse who visits those in need of medical attention in their homes. [OE hǣlth f. Gmc]
■ **1** healthiness, haleness, wholeness, fitness, robustness, vigor, vitality, well-being, strength. **2** condition, fitness, trim, fettle, form; constitution. **3** see STRENGTH 1. **4** see TOAST n. 2b.

healthful /hélthfool/ adj. conducive to good health; beneficial. □□ **healthfully** adv. **healthfulness** n.

healthy /hélthee/ adj. (**healthier**, **healthiest**) **1** having, showing, or promoting good health. **2** beneficial; helpful (a healthy respect for experience). □□ **healthily** adv. **healthiness** n.
■ **1** well, fit, trim, in good or fine fettle, in good shape, in good health, whole, robust, hale (and hearty), sturdy, strong, vigorous, thriving, flourishing, colloq. in the pink; healthful, wholesome, salubrious, nourishing, nutritious, tonic, bracing, invigorating, archaic salutary. **2** see BENEFICIAL.

heap /heep/ n. & v. ● n. **1** a collection of things lying haphazardly one on another. **2** (esp. Brit. in pl.) colloq. a large number or amount (there's heaps of time; is heaps better; a heap of chores to finish). **3** sl. an old or dilapidated thing, esp. a motor vehicle or building. ● v. **1** tr. & intr. (foll. by up, together, etc.) collect or be collected in a heap. **2** tr. (foll. by with) load copiously or to excess. **3** tr. (foll. by on, upon) accord or offer copiously to (heaped insults on them). **4** tr. (as **heaping**, **heaped** adj.) with the contents piled above the brim. □ **heap coals of fire on a person's head** Brit. cause a person remorse by returning good for evil. [OE hēap, hēapian f. Gmc]
■ n. **1** collection, pile, mound, stack, accumulation, agglomeration, congeries, conglomeration. **2**

abundance, mass, lot, mountain, peck, sea, *colloq.* good *or* great deal, pile, raft, slew; (*heaps*) lots, scores, plenty, *colloq.* loads, scads, oodles, tons, *Brit. colloq.* lashings, pots. **3** see WRECK *n.* 3. ● *v.* **1** collect, gather, accumulate, cumulate, amass, pile up, bank up. **2** see LOAD *v.* 3–5. **3** pile, pour; see also HURL *v.*

hear /heer/ *v.* (*past* and *past part.* **heard** /herd/) **1** *tr.* (also *absol.*) perceive (sound, etc.) with the ear. **2** *tr.* listen to (*heard them on the radio*). **3** *tr.* listen judicially to and judge (a case, plaintiff, etc.). **4** *intr.* (foll. by *about*, *of*, or *that* + clause) be told or informed. **5** *intr.* (foll. by *from*) be contacted by, esp. by letter or telephone. **6** *tr.* be ready to obey (an order). **7** *tr.* grant (a prayer). □ **have heard of** be aware of; know of the existence of. **hear! hear!** *int.* expressing agreement (esp. with something said in a speech). **hear a person out** listen to all that a person says. **hear say** (or **tell**) (usu. foll. by *of*, or *that* + clause) be informed. **will not hear** of will not allow or agree to. □□ **hearable** *adj.* **hearer** *n.* [OE *hīeran* f. Gmc]

■ **1** perceive, catch. **2** listen to, *archaic* hark at *or* to, *archaic or literary* hearken to. **3** see JUDGE *v.* 1a. **4** learn, discover, find out, be told *or* advised *or* informed; understand, gather; (*hear of*) get wind of, pick up rumors of, hear tell of, *colloq.* hear on the grapevine. **6** attend to, pay attention to; take note of, obey. **7** heed, grant, answer. □ **have heard of** know of, be aware of, be conscious of, be cognizant of, be informed of, be advised of, have knowledge of. **hear say** (or **tell**) see HEAR 4 above. **will not hear of** will not entertain *or* consider, will not sanction *or* condone, will not agree *or* consent *or* assent to.

hearing /heering/ *n.* **1** the faculty of perceiving sounds. **2** the range within which sounds may be heard; earshot (*within hearing*; *in my hearing*). **3** an opportunity to state one's case (*give them a fair hearing*). **4** the listening to evidence and pleadings in a court of law. □ **hearing aid** a small device to amplify sound, worn by a partially deaf person.

■ **3** see CHANCE *n.* 4. **4** see TRIAL 1.

hearken /haarkən/ *v.intr.* (also **harken**) *archaic* or *literary* (often foll. by *to*) listen. [OE *heorcnian* (as HARK)]

■ see LISTEN 1, 2.

hearsay /heersay/ *n.* rumor; gossip. □ **hearsay evidence** *Law* evidence given by a witness based on information received from others rather than personal knowledge.

■ see RUMOR *n.* 1.

hearse /hərs/ *n.* a vehicle for conveying the coffin at a funeral. [ME f. OF *herse* harrow f. med.L *herpica* ult. f. L *hirpex -icis* large rake]

heart /haart/ *n.* **1** a hollow muscular organ maintaining the circulation of blood by rhythmic contraction and dilation. **2** the region of the heart; the breast. **3 a** the heart regarded as the center of thought, feeling, and emotion (esp. love). **b** a person's capacity for feeling emotion (*has no heart*). **4 a** courage or enthusiasm (*take heart*; *lose heart*). **b** one's mood or feeling (*change of heart*). **5 a** the central or innermost part of something. **b** the vital part or essence (*the heart of the matter*). **6** the close compact center of a head of cabbage, lettuce, etc. **7 a** a heart-shaped thing. **b** a conventional representation of a heart with two equal curves meeting at a point at the bottom and a cusp at the top. **8 a** a playing card of a suit denoted by a red figure of a heart. **b** (in *pl.*) this suit. **c** (in *pl.*) a card game in which players avoid taking tricks containing a card of this suit. **9** condition of land as regards fertility (*in good heart*). □ **after one's own heart** such as one likes or desires. **at heart 1** in one's inmost feelings. **2** basically; essentially. **break a person's heart** overwhelm a person with sorrow. **by heart** in or from memory. **close to** (or **near**) **one's heart 1** dear to one. **2** affecting one deeply. **from the heart** (or **the bottom of one's heart**) sincerely; profoundly. **give** (or **lose**) **one's heart** (often foll. by *to*) fall in love (with). **have a heart** be merciful. **have the heart** (usu. with *neg.*; foll. by *to* + infin.) be insensitive or hard-hearted enough (*didn't have the heart to ask him*). **have** (or **put**) **one's heart in** be keenly involved in or committed to (an enterprise, etc.). **have one's heart**

in one's mouth be greatly alarmed or apprehensive. **have one's heart in the right place** be sincere or well-intentioned. **heart attack** a sudden occurrence of coronary thrombosis usu. resulting in the death of part of a heart muscle. **heart failure** a gradual failure of the heart to function properly, resulting in breathlessness, edema, etc. **heart-lung machine** a machine that temporarily takes over the functions of the heart and lungs, esp. in surgery. **heart of gold** a generous nature. **heart of oak** a courageous nature. **heart of stone** a stern or cruel nature. **heart-rending** very distressing. **heart-rendingly** in a heart-rending way. **heart-searching** the thorough examination of one's own feelings and motives. **heart to heart** candidly; intimately. **heart-to-heart** *adj.* (of a conversation, etc.) candid; intimate. ● *n.* a candid or personal conversation. **in one's heart of hearts** in one's inmost feelings. **take to heart** be much affected or distressed by. **to one's heart's content** see CONTENT[1]. **wear one's heart on one's sleeve** make one's feelings apparent. **with all one's heart** sincerely; with all goodwill. **with one's whole heart** with enthusiasm; without doubts or reservations. □□ **-hearted** *adj.* [OE *heorte* f. Gmc]

■ **1** *colloq.* ticker. **2** breast, chest. **3 a** core, heart of hearts, blood, bosom; midst, interior, core, center; see also SOUL 1, 2. **b** humanity, sympathy, kindness, kindliness, kindheartedness, compassion, goodness, consideration, concern, tenderness, magnanimity, generosity, sensitivity, sensibility, feeling, pity, love. **4 a** courage, stomach, nerve, bravery, boldness, pluck, resolution, determination, mettle, will, *colloq.* guts, spunk; enthusiasm, spirit, verve. **b** see MOOD[1] 1, FEELING 4. **5 a** kernel, core, center, hub, middle, marrow, nucleus. **b** essence, quintessence, nub, crux, pith; basics, fundamentals, *colloq.* bottom line, *sl.* nitty-gritty, brass tacks. □ **at heart 1** see INSIDE *adv.* 1. **2** see PRINCIPALLY. **close to** (or **near**) **one's heart 1** see DEAR *adj.* 3. **2** see IMPORTANT 1. **from the heart** (or **the bottom of one's heart**) see SINCERELY. **heart-rending** agonizing, heartbreaking, harrowing, tragic, distressing, painful. **heart-searching** soul-searching, introspection; psychoanalysis, *Psychol.* self-analysis; see also THOUGHT[1] 3a. **heart to heart** candidly, intimately, directly, frankly, freely, unrestrictedly; see also OPENLY 1. **with all one's heart** see SINCERELY. **with one's whole heart** see ABSOLUTELY 1.

heartache /haartayk/ *n.* mental anguish or grief.
■ see GRIEF 1.

heartbeat /haartbeet/ *n.* a pulsation of the heart.

heartbreak /haartbrayk/ *n.* overwhelming distress. □□ **heartbreaker** *n.* **heartbreaking** *adj.* **heartbroken** *adj.*
■ see GRIEF 1. □□ **heartbroken** brokenhearted, unhappy, grief-stricken, heartsick, disconsolate, distressed, doleful, sorrowful, mournful, crushed, devastated, *archaic or literary* heartsore, *sl.* gutted.

heartburn /haartbərn/ *n.* a burning sensation in the chest resulting from indigestion; pyrosis.
■ see INDIGESTION.

hearten /haart'n/ *v.tr. & intr.* make or become more cheerful. □□ **hearteningly** *adv.*
■ see CHEER *v.* 3.

heartfelt /haartfelt/ *adj.* sincere; deeply felt.
■ sincere, honest, genuine, unfeigned, earnest, serious, wholehearted, deep, profound, ardent, fervent, fervid, hearty, passionate.

hearth /haarth/ *n.* **1 a** the floor of a fireplace. **b** the area in front of a fireplace. **2** this symbolizing the home. **3** the bottom of a blast furnace where molten metal collects. [OE *heorth* f. WG]

hearthrug /haarthrug/ *n.* a rug laid before a fireplace.

hearthstone /haárthstōn/ n. **1** a flat stone forming a hearth. **2** a soft stone used to whiten hearths, doorsteps, etc.

heartily /haártilee/ adv. **1** in a hearty manner; with goodwill, appetite, or courage. **2** very; to a great degree (esp. with ref. to personal feelings) (am heartily sick of it; disliked him heartily).
■ **1** see happily (HAPPY).

heartland /haártland/ n. the central or most important part of an area.

heartless /haártlis/ adj. unfeeling; pitiless. □□ **heartlessly** adv. **heartlessness** n.
■ cruel, hard-hearted, pitiless, callous, unconcerned, inhuman, inhumane, unkind, unfeeling, unsympathetic, brutal, cold, merciless, ruthless, cold-blooded.

heartsease /haártseez/ n. (also **heart's-ease**) any plant of the genus Viola, esp. a pansy.

heartsick /haártsik/ adj. very despondent. □□ **heartsickness** n.
■ see SAD 1.

heartsore /haártsawr/ adj. archaic or literary grieving; heartsick.

heartstrings /haártstringz/ n.pl. one's deepest feelings or emotions.

heartthrob /haárt-throb/ n. **1** beating of the heart. **2** colloq. a person for whom one has (esp. immature) romantic feelings.
■ **2** see PASSION 3b.

heartwarming /haártwawrming/ adj. emotionally rewarding or uplifting.
■ moving, touching, affecting, uplifting, stirring, inspiriting, cheering, encouraging, rewarding, satisfying, gratifying, pleasing, comforting, pleasurable.

heartwood /haártwo͝od/ n. the dense inner part of a tree trunk, yielding the hardest timber.

hearty /haártee/ adj. & n. ● adj. (**heartier**, **heartiest**) **1** strong; vigorous. **2** spirited. **3** (of a meal or appetite) large. **4** warm; friendly. **5** genuine; sincere. ● n. **1** Brit. a hearty person, esp. one ostentatiously so. **2** (usu. in pl.) (as a form of address) fellows, esp. fellow sailors. □□ **heartiness** n.
■ adj. **1** strong, healthy, hale, vigorous, robust, energetic, active. **2** spirited, enthusiastic, vigorous, eager, zealous, exuberant. **3** (of a meal) abundant, ample, substantial, solid, sizable, satisfying, square; nourishing, invigorating, strengthening; (of appetite) healthy, robust, large, big, ample, good. **4** genial, warm, kindhearted, affectionate, amiable, amicable, friendly, affable, cordial, open, convivial. **5** genuine, unfeigned, authentic, sincere, heartfelt, warm, wholehearted, honest, earnest, devout, stalwart, stout.

heat /heet/ n. & v. ● n. **1 a** the condition of being hot. **b** the sensation or perception of this. **c** high temperature of the body. **2** Physics a a form of energy arising from the random motion of the molecules of bodies, which may be transferred by conduction, convection, or radiation. **b** the amount of this needed to cause a specific process, or evolved in a process (heat of formation; heat of solution). **3** hot weather (succumbed to the heat). **4 a** warmth of feeling. **b** anger or excitement (the heat of the argument). **5** (foll. by of) the most intense part or period of an activity (in the heat of the battle). **6** a (usu. preliminary or trial) round in a race or contest. **7** the receptive period of the sexual cycle, esp. in female mammals. **8** redness of the skin with a sensation of heat (prickly heat). **9** pungency of flavor. **10** sl. intensive pursuit, e.g., by the police. **11** sl. criticism. ● v. **1** tr. & intr. make or become hot or warm. **2** tr. inflame; excite or intensify. □ **heat barrier** the limitation of the speed of an aircraft, etc., by heat resulting from air friction. **heat capacity** thermal capacity. **heat death** Physics a state of uniform distribution of energy to which the universe is thought to be tending. **heat engine** a device for producing motive power from heat. **heat exchanger** a device for the transfer of heat from one medium to another. **heat exhaustion** (or **prostration**) a condition caused by prolonged exposure to or vigorous exercise in heat and characterized by faintness, nausea, and profuse sweating. **heat lighting** lightning seen as vivid flashes near the horizon, usu. without the sound of thunder and usu. occurring during late evening in summer. **heat pump** a device for the transfer of heat from a colder area to a hotter area by using mechanical energy. **heat-seeking** (of a missile, etc.) able to detect infrared radiation to guide it to its target. **heat shield** a device for protection from excessive heat, esp. fitted to a spacecraft. **heat sink** a device or substance for absorbing excessive or unwanted heat. **heat-treat** subject to heat treatment. **heat treatment** the use of heat to modify the properties of a metal, etc. **heat wave** a period of very hot weather. **in heat** (of mammals, esp. females) sexually receptive. **in the heat of the moment** during or resulting from intense activity, without pause for thought. **turn the heat on** colloq. concentrate an attack or criticism on (a person). [OE hǣtu f. Gmc]
■ n. **1 a, b** warmth, warmness, hotness; torridity. **c** fever, temperature, fieriness, feverishness, Med. pyrexia. **4** passion, ardor, fervor, intensity, arousal, stimulation, enthusiasm, zeal, excitement, exhilaration; fury, vehemence; see also ANGER n. **5** see CLIMAX n. **6** round, trial, preliminary, qualifier; game, stage, level. **8** see RASH[2] 1. **9** see SPICE n. 3a. ● v. **1** see WARM v. 1, THAW v. 1, 5. **2** excite, intensify, impassion, inflame; kindle, ignite, quicken, inspirit, rouse, waken, stir, animate, stimulate, activate, Brit. colloq. hot up. □ **turn the heat on** see ATTACK v. 3.

heated /heetid/ adj. **1** (of a person, discussions, etc.) angry; inflamed with passion or excitement. **2** made hot. □□ **heatedly** adv.
■ **1** angry, furious, stormy, tempestuous, violent, fiery, frenzied, frantic; impassioned, excited, inflamed, vehement, passionate, fervent, fervid, ardent, intense.

heater /heetər/ n. **1** a device for supplying heat to its environment. **2** a container with an element, etc., for heating the contents (water heater). **3** sl. a gun.
■ **3** see PISTOL n.

heath /heeth/ n. **1** an area of flattish uncultivated land with low shrubs. **2** a plant growing on a heath, esp. of the genus Erica or Calluna (e.g., heather). □□ **heathless** adj. **heathlike** adj. **heathy** adj. [OE hǣth f. Gmc]
■ **1** see MOOR¹ 1.

heathen /heethən/ n. & adj. ● n. **1** a person who does not belong to a widely-held religion (esp. who is not Christian, Jewish, or Muslim) as regarded by those that do. **2** an unenlightened person; a person regarded as lacking culture or moral principles. **3** (the heathen) heathen people collectively. **4** Bibl. a Gentile. ● adj. **1** of or relating to heathens. **2** having no religion. □□ **heathendom** n. **heathenism** n. [OE hǣthen f. Gmc]
■ n. **1** unbeliever, infidel, gentile, pagan, idolater, idolatress, polytheist, atheist, nullifidian, skeptic, agnostic, heretic. **2** barbarian, savage, brute. ● adj. **1** polytheistic, pantheistic, infidel, gentile, hist. heretical; savage, barbarian, barbaric, uncivilized, primitive, unenlightened. **2** pagan, atheistic, godless, nullifidian, skeptical, doubting, agnostic, irreligious.

heather /hethər/ n. **1** an evergreen shrub, Calluna vulgaris, with purple bell-shaped flowers. **2** any of various shrubs of the genus Erica or Daboecia, growing esp. on moors and heaths or in acid soil. **3** a fabric of mixed hues supposed to resemble heather. **b** the color of this. □□ **heathery** adj. [ME, Sc., & No. of Engl. hathir, etc., of unkn. orig.: assim. to heath]

Heath Robinson /heeth róbinsən/ adj. Brit. absurdly ingenious and impracticable in design or construction. [W. Heath Robinson, Engl. cartoonist d. 1944 who drew such contrivances]

heating /heeting/ n. **1** the imparting or generation of heat. **2** equipment or devices used to provide heat, esp. to a building.

heatstroke /heetstrōk/ n. a severe feverish condition caused by excessive exposure to high temperature.

heatwave /heetwayv/ n. a prolonged period of abnormally hot weather.

heave /heev/ v. & n. ● v. (past and past part. **heaved** or esp.

Naut. **hove** /hōv/ **1** *tr.* lift or haul (a heavy thing) with great effort. **2** *tr.* utter with effort or resignation (*heaved a sigh*). **3** *tr. colloq.* throw. **4** *intr.* rise and fall rhythmically or spasmodically. **5** *tr. Naut.* haul by rope. **6** *intr.* retch. ● *n.* **1** an instance of heaving. **2** *Geol.* a sideways displacement in a fault. **3** (in *pl.*) a disease of horses, with labored breathing. □ **heave-ho 1** a sailors' cry, esp. on raising the anchor. **2** *sl.* (usu. prec. by *the* or *the old*) a dismissal or rejection. **heave in sight** *Naut.* or *colloq.* come into view. **heave to** esp. *Naut.* bring or be brought to a standstill. □□ **heaver** *n.* [OE *hebban* f. Gmc, rel. to L *capere* take]

■ *v.* **1** lift, hoist, raise; haul, pull, draw, tug; move. **2** breathe, utter. **3** hurl, throw, toss, fling, cast, pitch, *colloq.* sling, chuck. **6** gag, retch, vomit, be sick, *colloq.* throw up, *sl.* puke, upchuck. ● *n.* **1** pull, draw, tug, jerk, wrench, *colloq.* yank.

heaven /hévən/ *n.* **1** a place regarded in some religions as the abode of God and the angels, and of the good after death, often characterized as above the sky. **2** a place or state of supreme bliss. **3** *colloq.* something delightful. **4** (usu. **Heaven**) **a** God; Providence. **b** (in *sing.* or *pl.*) an exclamation or mild oath (*by Heaven!*). **5** (**the heavens**) *poet.* the sky as the abode of the sun, moon, and stars and regarded from earth. □ **heaven-sent** providential; wonderfully opportune. **in heaven's name** *colloq.* used as an exclamation of surprise or annoyance. **in seventh heaven** in a state of ecstasy. **move heaven and earth** (foll. by *to* + infin.) make extraordinary efforts. □□ **heavenward** *adj.* & *adv.* **heavenwards** *adv.* [OE *heofon*]

■ **1** paradise, empyrean, kingdom (of heaven); Canaan, Zion, Valhalla. **2** paradise, bliss, nirvana, Elysium, Eden, Utopia, heaven on earth, paradise on earth; happiness, joy, rapture, ecstasy. **3** see DELIGHT *n.* **4 a** (**Heaven**) God, Providence, Fate. **b** (**Heaven!** or **Heavens!**) Jesus, *sl.* Christ; see also BOY *int.* **5** (**the heavens**) sky, skies, the blue, empyrean, *literary* firmament, *poet.* welkin.

heavenly /hévənlee/ *adj.* **1** of heaven; divine. **2** of the heavens or sky. **3** *colloq.* very pleasing; wonderful. □ **heavenly bodies** the sun, stars, planets, etc. □□ **heavenliness** *n.* [OE *heofonlic* (as HEAVEN)]

■ **1** divine, celestial, ethereal, paradisaical, unearthly; holy, immortal, blessed, beatific, spiritual, esp. *poet.* supernal; angelic, seraphic. **2** celestial. **3** delightful, wonderful, marvelous, sublime, paradisaical, glorious, splendid, superb, exquisite, perfect, excellent, rapturous, entrancing, blissful, *colloq.* fantastic, gorgeous, divine, smashing, great.

Heaviside layer /héveesīd/ *n.* (in full **Heaviside–Kennelly layer** /hévisīdkénəlee/) = E LAYER. [O. *Heaviside*, Engl. physicist d. 1925, and A. E. *Kennelly*, US physicist d. 1939]

heavy /hévee/ *adj., n., adv.,* & *v.* ● *adj.* (**heavier, heaviest**) **1 a** of great or exceptionally high weight; difficult to lift. **b** (of a person) fat; overweight. **2 a** of great density. **b** *Physics* having a greater than the usual mass (esp. of isotopes and compounds containing them). **3** abundant; considerable (*a heavy crop*). **4** severe; intense; extensive; excessive (*heavy fighting; a heavy sleep*). **5** doing something to excess (*a heavy drinker*). **6 a** striking or falling with force (*heavy blows; heavy rain*). **b** (of the sea) having large powerful waves. **7** (of machinery, artillery, etc.) very large of its kind; large in caliber, etc. **8** causing a strong impact (*a heavy fall*). **9** needing much physical effort (*heavy work*). **10** (foll. by *with*) laden. **11** carrying heavy weapons (*the heavy brigade*). **12 a** (of a person, writing, music, etc.) serious or somber in tone or attitude; dull; tedious. **b** (of an issue, etc.) grave; important; weighty. **13 a** (of food) hard to digest. **b** (of a literary work, etc.) hard to read or understand. **14** (of temperament) dignified; stern. **15** (of bread, etc.) too dense from not having risen. **16** (of ground) difficult to traverse or work. **17 a** oppressive; hard to endure (*a heavy fate; heavy demands*). **b** (of the atmosphere, weather, etc.) overcast; oppressive; sultry. **18 a** coarse; ungraceful (*heavy features*). **b** unwieldy. ● *n.* (*pl.* **-ies**) **1** *colloq.* a large violent person; a thug. **2** a villainous or tragic role or actor in a play, etc. **3** *Brit. colloq.* a

serious newspaper. **4** *colloq.* an important or influential person. **5** anything large or heavy of its kind, e.g., a vehicle. ● *adv.* heavily (esp. in *comb.*: *heavy-laden*). ● *v.tr. colloq.* harass or pressurize (a person). □ **heavier-than-air** (of an aircraft) weighing more than the air it displaces. **heavy chemicals** see CHEMICAL. **heavy-duty** *adj.* **1** intended to withstand hard use. **2** serious; grave. **heavy-footed** awkward; ponderous. **heavy going** slow or difficult progress. **heavy-hearted** sad; doleful. **heavy hydrogen** = DEUTERIUM. **heavy industry** industry producing metal, machinery, etc. **heavy-lidded** sleepy. **heavy metal 1** heavy guns. **2** metal of high density. **3** *colloq.* (often *attrib.*) a type of highly-amplified rock music with a strong beat. **heavy petting** erotic fondling between two people, stopping short of intercourse. **heavy sleeper** a person who sleeps deeply. **heavy water** a substance composed entirely or mainly of deuterium oxide. **make heavy weather of** see WEATHER. □□ **heavily** *adv.* **heaviness** *n.* **heavyish** *adj.* [OE *hefig* f. Gmc, rel. to HEAVE]

■ *adj.* **1 a** weighty, massive. **b** overweight, fat, obese, stout, chubby, plump, corpulent, portly, paunchy, tubby, pudgy, thickset, esp. *Brit.* podgy. **2 a** dense, solid. **3** abundant, considerable, copious, prodigious, ample, profuse. **4** intense, severe, concentrated, extensive, excessive, forceful, violent. **5** see IMMODERATE. **6 a** see FORCEFUL 1; (*of rain*) torrential, pouring. **b** see ROUGH *adj.* 5. **7** see LARGE *adj.* 1, 2. **8** see CONSIDERABLE 1, 2. **9** see HARD *adj.* 3. **10** burdened, laden, encumbered, loaded, overloaded, weighed down. **12 a** serious, somber, grave, ponderous; tedious, dull, dry, monotonous, dryasdust; prosaic, leaden, stodgy. **b** serious, grave, important, crucial, critical, acute; see also WEIGHTY 2. **13 a** see STODGY 1. **b** dense, weighty, difficult, complex, recondite, arcane, deep, profound, esoteric, impenetrable. **14** see DIGNIFIED, STERN¹. **15** stodgy, indigestible, solid, dense, filling. **16** see ROUGH *adj.* 1a. **17 a** burdensome, onerous, weighty, severe; see also OPPRESSIVE 1, 2. **b** gloomy, cloudy, overcast, bleak, dismal, dreary, leaden, gray, dark, lowering, threatening, oppressive; sultry, humid. **18 a** thick, coarse, broad, blunt, clumsy, ungraceful. **b** see UNWIELDY. ● *n.* **1** see THUG. ● *v.* see HARASS 1. □ **heavy-duty 1** see TOUGH *adj.* 1. **heavy-footed** see AWKWARD 2. **heavy-hearted** see SAD 1. **heavy-lidded** see DROWSY 1, 3.

heavy-handed /hévihándid/ *adj.* **1** clumsy. **2** overbearing; oppressive. □□ **heavy-handedly** *adv.* **heavy-handedness** *n.*

■ **1** awkward, clumsy, inept, maladroit, ungraceful, graceless, bungling. **2** overbearing, oppressive, domineering, autocratic, imperious, magisterial, despotic, dictatorial, tyrannical, harsh, severe.

heavyset /héveesét/ *adj.* stocky; thickset.

■ see STOCKY.

heavyweight /héveewayt/ *n.* **1 a** a weight in certain sports, differing for professional and amateur boxers, wrestlers, and weightlifters. **b** a sports participant of this weight. **2** a person, animal, or thing of above average weight. **3** *colloq.* a person of influence or importance. □ **light heavyweight 1** the weight in some sports between middleweight and heavyweight. **2** a sports participant of this weight.

Heb. *abbr.* **1** Hebrew. **2** Hebrews (New Testament).

hebdomadal /hebdóməd'l/ *adj.* weekly, esp. meeting weekly. [LL *hebdomadalis* f. Gk *hebdomas, -ados* f. *hepta* seven]

hebe /héebee/ *n.* any flowering shrub of the genus *Hebe*, with usu. overlapping scalelike leaves. [mod.L after the Gk goddess *Hēbē*]

hebetude /hébitōod, -tyōod/ *n. literary* dullness. [LL *hebetudo* f. *hebes, -etis* blunt]

/ ... / **pronunciation**   ● **part of speech**
□ **phrases, idioms, and compounds**
□□ **derivatives**   ■ **synonym section**
cross-references appear in SMALL CAPITALS or *italics*

■ see LETHARGY 1.

Hebraic /hibráyik/ *adj.* of Hebrew or the Hebrews. □□ **Hebraically** *adv.* [LL f. Gk *Hebraikos* (as HEBREW)]

Hebraism /heébrayízəm/ *n.* **1** a Hebrew idiom or expression, esp. in the Greek of the Bible. **2** an attribute of the Hebrews. **3** the Hebrew system of thought or religion. □□ **Hebraistic** *adj.* **Hebraize** *v.tr.* & *intr.* [F *hébraïsme* or mod.L *Hebraismus* f. late Gk *Hebraïsmos* (as HEBREW)]

Hebraist /heébrayist/ *n.* an expert in Hebrew.

Hebrew /heébroō/ *n.* & *adj.* ● *n.* **1** a member of a Semitic people orig. centered in ancient Palestine. **2 a** the language of this people. **b** a modern form of this used esp. in Israel. ● *adj.* **1** of or in Hebrew. **2** of the Hebrews or the Jews. [ME f. OF *Ebreu* f. med.L *Ebreus* f. L *hebraeus* f. Gk *Hebraios* f. Aram. *'ibray* f. Heb. *'ibrī* one from the other side (of the river)]

Hebridean /hébridéeən/ *adj.* & *n.* ● *adj.* of or relating to the Hebrides, an island group off the W. coast of Scotland. ● *n.* a native of the Hebrides.

hecatomb /hékətoōm/ *n.* **1** (in ancient Greece or Rome) a great public sacrifice, orig. of 100 oxen. **2** any extensive sacrifice. [L *hecatombe* f. Gk *hekatombē* f. *hekaton* hundred + *bous* ox]

■ see SLAUGHTER *n.* 2.

heck /hek/ *int. colloq.* a mild exclamation of surprise or dismay. [alt. f. HELL]

heckle /hékəl/ *v.tr.* **1** interrupt and harass (a public speaker). **2** dress (flax or hemp). □□ **heckler** *n.* [ME, northern and eastern form of HACKLE]

■ **1** interrupt, pester, bother, harass, harry, hector, taunt, *colloq.* hassle, plague, *Brit.* barrack.

hectare /héktair/ *n.* a metric unit of square measure, equal to 100 ares (2.471 acres or 10,000 square meters). □□ **hectarage** /-tərij/ *n.* [F (as HECTO-, ARE²)]

hectic /héktik/ *adj.* & *n.* ● *adj.* **1** busy and confused; excited. **2** having a hectic fever; morbidly flushed. ● *n.* **1** a hectic fever or flush. **2** a patient suffering from this. □ **hectic fever** (or **flush**) *hist.* a fever which accompanies consumption and similar diseases, with flushed cheeks and hot dry skin. □□ **hectically** *adv.* [ME *etik* f. OF *etique* f. LL *hecticus* f. Gk *hektikos* habitual f. *hexis* habit, assim. to F *hectique* or LL]

■ *adj.* **1** feverish, excited, agitated, busy, bustling, overactive, rushed, frenzied, frantic, chaotic, confused, wild, frenetic, riotous. **2** flushed, feverish, hot; febrile, pyretic, *Med.* pyrexic.

hecto- /héktə/ *comb. form* a hundred, esp. of a unit in the metric system. ¶ Abbr.: **ha**. [F, irreg. f. Gk *hekaton* hundred]

hectogram /héktəgram/ *n.* (also *Brit.* **hectogramme**) a metric unit of mass, equal to one hundred grams.

hectograph /héktəgraf/ *n.* an apparatus for copying documents by the use of a gelatin plate that receives an impression of the master copy.

hectoliter /héktəleetər/ *n.* a metric unit of capacity, equal to one hundred liters.

hectometer /héktəmeetər, hektómitər/ *n.* a metric unit of length, equal to one hundred meters.

hector /héktər/ *v.* & *n.* ● *v.tr.* bully; intimidate. ● *n.* a bully. □□ **hectoringly** *adv.* [*Hector,* L f. Gk *Hektōr,* Trojan hero and son of Priam in Homer's *Iliad,* f. its earlier use to mean 'swaggering fellow']

■ *v.* see BULLY¹ *v.* 1. ● *n.* see BULLY¹ *n.*

he'd /heed/ *contr.* **1** he had. **2** he would.

heddle /héd'l/ *n.* one of the sets of small cords or wires between which the warp is passed in a loom before going through the reed. [app. f. OE *hefeld*]

hedge /hej/ *n.* & *v.* ● *n.* **1** a fence or boundary formed by closely growing bushes or shrubs. **2** a protection against possible loss or diminution. ● *v.* **1** *tr.* surround or bound with a hedge. **2** *tr.* (foll. by *in*) enclose. **3 a** *tr.* reduce one's risk of loss on (a bet or speculation) by compensating transactions on the other side. **b** *intr.* avoid a definite decision or commitment. **4** *intr.* make or trim hedges. □ **hedge sparrow** a common gray and brown bird, *Prunella modularis;* the dunnock. □□ **hedger** *n.* [OE *hegg* f. Gmc]

■ *n.* **1** see ENCLOSURE 4. ● *v.* **1, 2** see ENCLOSE 1, 6. **3 b** see EQUIVOCATE.

hedgehog /héjhawg, -hog/ *n.* **1** any small nocturnal insect-eating mammal of the genus *Erinaceus,* esp. *E. europaeus,* having a piglike snout and a coat of spines, and rolling itself up into a ball for defense. **2** a porcupine or other animal similarly covered with spines. □□ **hedgehoggy** *adj.* [ME f. HEDGE (from its habitat) + HOG (from its snout)]

hedgehop /héjhop/ *v.intr.* fly at a very low altitude.

hedgerow /héjrō/ *n.* a row of bushes, etc., forming a hedge.

■ see SHRUBBERY.

hedonic /heedónik/ *adj.* **1** of or characterized by pleasure. **2** *Psychol.* of pleasant or unpleasant sensations. [Gk *hēdonikos* f. *hēdonē* pleasure]

hedonism /heéd'nizəm/ *n.* **1** belief in pleasure as the highest good and the proper aim of humans. **2** behavior based on this. □□ **hedonist** *n.* **hedonistic** *adj.* [Gk *hēdonē* pleasure]

■ **2** see DISSIPATION 1.

-hedron /heédrən, hédrən/ *comb. form* (*pl.* **-hedra**) forming nouns denoting geometrical solids with various numbers or shapes of faces (*dodecahedron; rhombohedron*). □□ **-hedral** *comb. form* forming adjectives. [Gk *hedra* seat]

heebie-jeebies /heébeejeébeez/ *n.pl.* (prec. by *the*) *sl.* a state of nervous depression or anxiety. [20th c.: orig. unkn.]

■ see NERVE *n.* 3b.

heed /heed/ *v.* & *n.* ● *v.tr.* attend to; take notice of. ● *n.* careful attention. □□ **heedful** *adj.* **heedfully** *adv.* **heedfulness** *n.* **heedless** *adj.* **heedlessly** *adv.* **heedlessness** *n.* [OE *hēdan* f. WG]

■ *v.* pay attention to, attend to, take note or notice of, listen to, mark, mind, bear in mind, consider; take, follow, obey, abide by. ● *n.* attention, notice, consideration, thought. □□ **heedless** unobservant, uncaring, inattentive; (*heedless of*) unmindful of, neglectful of, regardless of, oblivious of or to, deaf to, blind to.

hee-haw /heéhaw/ *n.* & *v.* ● *n.* the bray of a donkey. ● *v.intr.* (of or like a donkey) emit a braying sound, esp. a braying laugh. [imit.]

heel¹ /heel/ *n.* & *v.* ● *n.* **1** the back part of the foot below the ankle. **2** the corresponding part in vertebrate animals. **3 a** the part of a sock, etc., covering the heel. **b** the part of a shoe or boot supporting the heel. **4** a thing like a heel in form or position, e.g., the part of the palm next to the wrist, the end of a violin bow at which it is held, or the part of a golf club near where the head joins the shaft. **5** the crust end of a loaf of bread. **6** *colloq.* a person regarded with contempt or disapproval. **7** (as *int.*) a command to a dog to walk close to its owner's heel. ● *v.* **1** *tr.* fit or renew a heel on (a shoe or boot). **2** *intr.* touch the ground with the heel, as in dancing. **3** *intr.* (foll. by *out*) *Rugby* pass the ball with the heel. **4** *tr. Golf* strike (the ball) with the heel of the club. **5** *intr.* (of dog) follow at one's heels. □ **at heel 1** (of a dog) close behind. **2** (of a person, etc.) under control. **at** (or **on**) **the heels of** following closely after (a person or event). **cool** (or *Brit.* **kick**) **one's heels** be kept waiting. **down at** (**the**) **heel(s)** see DOWN¹. **take to one's heels** run away. **to heel 1** (of a dog) close behind. **2** (of a person, etc.) under control. **turn on one's heel** turn sharply around. **well-heeled** *colloq.* wealthy. □□ **heelless** *adj.* [OE *hēla, hæla* f. Gmc]

■ *n.* **5** end, crust; tail end, stump. **6** cad, scoundrel, rogue, worm, knave, blackguard, *colloq.* swine, *colloq.* or *joc.* bounder, *sl.* bastard, esp. *Brit. sl.* rotter. □ **take to one's heels** take flight, flee, run off or away, *Brit.* do a moonlight flit, *colloq.* show a clean pair of heels, skedaddle, fly the coop, *sl.* split, take a powder; see also RUN *v.* 2. **well-heeled** see WEALTHY.

heel² /heel/ *v.* & *n.* ● *v.* **1** *intr.* (of a ship, etc.) lean over owing to the pressure of wind or an uneven load (cf. LIST²). **2** *tr.* cause (a ship, etc.) to do this. ● *n.* the act or amount of heeling. [prob. f. obs. *heeld, hield* incline, f. OE *hieldan,* OS *-heldian* f. Gmc]

■ *v.* **1** list, lean (over), tip, incline; see also TILT *v.* 1. ■ *n.* see TILT *n.* 2.

heel³ /heel/ *v.tr.* (also **hele**) (foll. by *in*) set (a plant) temporarily in the ground at an angle and cover its roots. [OE *helian* f. Gmc]

heelball /héelbawl/ *n.* **1** a mixture of hard wax and lampblack used by shoemakers for polishing. **2** this or a similar mixture used in brass-rubbing.

heeltap /héeltap/ *n.* **1** a layer of leather, metal, etc., in a shoe heel. **2** liquor left at the bottom of a glass after drinking.

heft /heft/ *v. & n.* ● *v.tr.* lift (something heavy), esp. to judge its weight. ● *n.* weight; heaviness. [prob. f. HEAVE after *cleft, weft*]

■ *n.* see WEIGHT *n.* 2, 3.

hefty /héftee/ *adj.* (**heftier, heftiest**) **1** (of a person) big and strong. **2** (of a thing) large; heavy; powerful; sizable; considerable. □□ **heftily** *adv.* **heftiness** *n.*

■ **1** big, strong, powerful, strapping, robust, burly, husky, muscular, brawny, beefy, *colloq.* hunky. **2** big, large, enormous, huge, massive, bulky, substantial, heavy, powerful; considerable, sizable, *colloq.* thumping.

Hegelian /haygáyleeən, hijée-/ *adj. & n.* ● *adj.* of or relating to the German philosopher G. W. F. Hegel (d. 1831) or his philosophy of objective idealism. ● *n.* an adherent of Hegel or his philosophy. □□ **Hegelianism** *n.*

hegemonic /héjimónik/ *adj.* ruling; supreme. [Gk *hēgemonikos* (as HEGEMONY)]

hegemony /hijémənee, héjəmōnee/ *n.* leadership, esp. by one nation over others of a confederacy. [Gk *hēgemonia* f. *hēgemōn* leader f. *hēgeomai* lead]

■ see *leadership* (LEADER).

hegira /hijírə, héjirə/ *n.* (also **hejira, hijra** /híjrə/) **1** (**Hegira**) **a** Muhammad's departure from Mecca to Medina in AD 622. **b** the Muslim era reckoned from this date. **2** a general exodus or departure. [med.L *hegira* f. Arab. *hijra* departure from one's country f. *hajara* separate]

heifer /héfər/ *n.* **1 a** a young cow, esp. one that has not had more than one calf. **b** a female calf. **2** *Brit. sl. derog.* a woman. [OE *heahfore*]

heigh /hay, hī/ *int.* expressing encouragement or inquiry. □ **heigh-ho** /hí hố, háy-/ expressing boredom, resignation, etc. [imit.]

height /hīt/ *n.* **1** the measurement from base to top or (of a standing person) from head to foot. **2** the elevation above ground or a recognized level (usu. sea level). **3** any considerable elevation (*situated at a height*). **4 a** a high place or area. **b** rising ground. **5** the top of something. **6** *Printing* the distance from the foot to the face of type. **7 a** the most intense part or period of anything (*the battle was at its height*). **b** an extreme instance or example (*the height of fashion*). [OE *hēhthu* f. Gmc]

■ **1** tallness, size. **2, 3** altitude, elevation, level. **4** elevation, mound, hill, tor, cliff, bluff, peak, summit, promontory, headland, *No. of Eng.* fell; (*heights*) slopes. **5** crest, apex; see also TOP[1] *n.* 1. **7** pinnacle, acme, zenith, apogee, peak, high point, summit, climax, culmination; extreme.

heighten /hítən/ *v.tr. & intr.* make or become higher or more intense.

■ raise, elevate, lift, upraise, build up; intensify, deepen, strengthen, reinforce, amplify, magnify, enhance, augment, add to, supplement; see also RISE *v.* 2, INCREASE *v.* 1.

Heimlich maneuver /hímlik/ *n.* an emergency procedure for assisting a choking victim in which one applies sudden upward pressure with the fist against the victim's upper abdomen in order to dislodge the object causing the choking. [for US physician Henry J. *Heimlich* (b. 1920)]

heinous /háynəs/ *adj.* (of a crime or criminal) utterly odious or wicked. □□ **heinously** *adv.* **heinousness** *n.* [ME f. OF *haïneus* ult. f. *haïr* to hate f. Frank.]

■ see WICKED 1.

heir /air/ *n.* **1** a person entitled to property or rank as the legal successor of its former owner (often foll. by *to*: *heir to the throne*). **2** a person deriving or morally entitled to something, quality, etc., from a predecessor. □ **heir apparent** an heir whose claim cannot be set aside by the birth of another heir. **heir-at-law** (*pl.* **heirs-at-law**) an heir by right of

blood, esp. to the real property of an intestate. **heir presumptive** an heir whose claim may be set aside by the birth of another heir. □□ **heirdom** *n.* **heirless** *adj.* **heirship** *n.* [ME f. OF *eir* f. LL *herem* f. L *heres -edis*]

■ heiress, beneficiary, inheritor, successor, esp. *Sc. Law* heritor; legatee.

heiress /áiris/ *n.* a female heir, esp. to great wealth or high title.

heirloom /áirlōōm/ *n.* **1** a piece of personal property that has been in a family for several generations. **2** a piece of property received as part of an inheritance. [HEIR I LOOM[1] in the sense 'tool']

■ **1** see ANTIQUE *n.*

Heisenberg uncertainty principle /hízənbərg/ see *uncertainty principle.*

heist /hīst/ *n. & v. sl.* ● *n.* a robbery. ● *v.tr.* rob. [repr. a local pronunc. of HOIST]

■ *n.* see ROBBERY 1b. ● *v.* see STEAL *v.* 1.

hejira var. of HEGIRA.

HeLa /hélə/ *adj.* of a strain of human epithelial cells maintained in tissue culture. [*Henrietta Lacks*, whose cervical carcinoma provided the original cells]

held past and past part. of HOLD.

heldentenor /héld'ntenər/ *n.* **1** a powerful tenor voice suitable for heroic roles in opera. **2** a singer with this voice. [G f. *Held* a hero]

hele var. of HEEL[3].

helenium /heléeneeəm/ *n.* any composite plant of the genus *Helenium,* with daisy-like flowers having prominent central disks. [mod.L f. Gk *helenion,* possibly commemorating Helen of Troy]

heli- /hélee/ *comb. form* helicopter (*heliport*).

heliacal /hilíəkəl/ *adj. Astron.* relating to or near the sun. □ **heliacal rising** (or **setting**) the first rising (or setting) of a star after (or before) a period of invisibility due to conjunction with the sun. [LL *heliacus* f. Gk *hēliakos* f. *hēlios* sun]

helianthemum /héeleeánthəməm/ *n.* any evergreen shrub of the genus *Helianthemum,* with saucer-shaped flowers. Also called *rock rose.* [mod.L f. Gk *hēlios* sun + *anthemon* flower]

helianthus /héeleeánthəs/ *n.* any plant of the genus *Helianthus,* including the sunflower and Jerusalem artichoke. [mod.L f. Gk *hēlios* sun + *anthos* flower]

helical /hélikəl, héeli-/ *adj.* having the form of a helix. □□ **helically** *adv.* **helicoid** *adj. & n.*

■ see SPIRAL *adj.*

helices *pl.* of HELIX.

helichrysum /hélikrízəm, héeli-/ *n.* any composite plant of the genus *Helichrysum,* with flowers retaining their appearance when dried. [L f. Gk *helikhrusos* f. *helix* spiral + *khrusos* gold]

helicon /hélikən/ *n.* a large spiral bass tuba played encircling the player's head and resting on the shoulder. [L f. Gk *Helikōn* mountain sacred to the Muses: later assoc. with HELIX]

helicopter /hélikoptər/ *n. & v.* ● *n.* a type of aircraft without fixed wings, obtaining lift and propulsion from horizontally revolving overhead blades or rotors, and capable of moving vertically and horizontally. ● *v.tr. & intr.* transport or fly by helicopter. [F *hélicoptère* f. Gk *helix* (see HELIX) + *pteron* wing]

helio- /héeleeō/ *comb. form* the sun. [Gk *hēlios* sun]

heliocentric /héeleeōséntrik/ *adj.* **1** regarding the sun as center. **2** considered as viewed from the sun's center. □□ **heliocentrically** *adv.*

heliogram /héeleeəgram/ *n.* a message sent by heliograph.

heliograph /héeleeəgraf/ *n. & v.* ● *n.* **1 a** a signaling apparatus reflecting sunlight in flashes from a movable mirror. **b** a message sent by means of this; a heliogram. **2** an apparatus for photographing the sun. **3** an engraving obtained chem-

---

/.../ **pronunciation**	● **part of speech**
□ **phrases, idioms, and compounds**	
□□ **derivatives**	■ **synonym section**
cross-references appear in SMALL CAPITALS or *italics*	

ically by exposure to light. ● *v.tr.* send (a message) by heliograph. ◻◻ **heliography** /-leeógrəfee/ *n.*

heliogravure /heéeleeōgrəvyŏŏr/ *n.* = PHOTOGRAVURE.

heliolithic /heéeleeəlíthik/ *adj.* (of a civilization) characterized by sun worship and megaliths.

heliometer /heéeleeómitər/ *n.* an instrument used for finding the angular distance between two stars (orig. used for measuring the diameter of the sun).

heliostat /heéeleeəstat/ *n.* an apparatus with a mirror driven by clockwork to reflect sunlight in a fixed direction. ◻◻ **heliostatic** *adj.*

heliotherapy /heéeleeōthérəpee/ *n.* the use of sunlight in treating disease.

heliotrope /heéeleeətrōp/ *n.* **1 a** any plant of the genus *Heliotropium*, with fragrant purple flowers. **b** the scent of these. **2** a light purple color. **3** bloodstone. [L *heliotropium* f. Gk *hēliotropion* plant turning its flowers to the sun, f. *hēlios* sun + *-tropos* f. *trepō* turn]

heliotropism /heéeleeótrəpizəm/ *n.* the directional growth of a plant in response to sunlight (cf. PHOTOTROPISM). ◻◻ **heliotropic** /-leeətrŏpik, -trópik/ *adj.*

heliotype /heéeleeətíp/ *n.* a picture obtained from a sensitized gelatin film exposed to light.

heliport /heéeleepawrt/ *n.* a place where helicopters take off and land. [HELI-, after *airport*]

helium /heéeleeəm/ *n. Chem.* a colorless, light, inert, gaseous element occurring in deposits of natural gas, used in airships and balloons and as a refrigerant. ¶ Symb.: **He**. [Gk *hēlios* sun (having been first identified in the sun's atmosphere)]

helix /heéeliks/ *n.* (*pl.* **helices** /-seez, hél-/) **1** a spiral curve (like a corkscrew) or a coiled curve (like a watch spring). **2** *Geom.* a curve that cuts a line on a solid cone or cylinder, at a constant angle with the axis. **3** *Archit.* a spiral ornament. **4** *Anat.* the rim of the external ear. [L *helix -icis* f. Gk *helix -ikos*]

■ **1, 3** see SPIRAL *n.*

hell /hel/ *n.* **1** a place regarded in some religions as the abode of the dead, or of condemned sinners and devils. **2** a place or state of misery or wickedness. **3** *colloq.* used as an exclamation of surprise or annoyance (*who the hell are you?*; *a hell of a mess*). **4** *colloq.* fun; high spirits. ◻ **beat** (or **knock**, etc.) **the hell out of** *colloq.* beat, etc., without restraint. **come hell or high water** no matter what the difficulties. **for the hell of it** *colloq.* for fun; on impulse. **get** (or **catch**) **hell** *colloq.* be severely scolded or punished. **give a person hell** *colloq.* scold or punish or make things difficult for a person. **hell-bent** (foll. by *on*) recklessly determined. **hell of a** *colloq.* very much of a; extremely (*hell of a hot day*). **hell for leather** at full speed. **hell-raiser** a person who causes trouble or creates chaos. **Hell's Angel** a member of a gang of motorcyclists notorious for outrageous or violent behavior. **like hell** *colloq.* **1** not at all. **2** recklessly; exceedingly. **not a hope in hell** *colloq.* no chance at all. **play hell** (or *Brit.* **merry hell**) **with** *colloq.* be upsetting or disruptive to. **to hell with** *colloq.* (one is) finished with, disgusted with, or without a use for (something or someone). **what the hell** *colloq.* it is of no importance. ◻◻ **hell-like** *adj.* **hellward** *adv.* & *adj.* [OE *hel, hell* f. Gmc]

■ **1** underworld, abyss, inferno, (bottomless) pit, infernal regions, Hades, Tartarus, Gehenna, Abaddon, Sheol, abode of the damned, lower world, other place, *Bibl.* Tophet, *archaic* nether regions *or* world. **2** purgatory, chaos, misery, torment, agony, anguish, torture, pain; affliction, ordeal, nightmare, trial. **4** see FUN *n.* 3. ◻ **give a person hell** see SCOLD *v.* 1, PUNISH 1. **hell-bent on** intent *or* bent *or* set on, resolved *or* determined *or* decided on; keen on, enthusiastic *or* avid *or* passionate about. **like hell 2** see *dangerously* (DANGEROUS).

he'll /heel/ *contr.* he will; he shall.

hellacious /heláyshəs/ *adj. sl.* **1** impressive; terrific; tremendous; remarkable. **2** overwhelmingly powerful, severe, or difficult. [HELL + -ACIOUS]

Helladic /heládik/ *adj.* of or belonging to the Bronze Age

culture of mainland Greece. [Gk *Helladikos* f. *Hellas -ados* Greece]

hellcat /hélkat/ *n.* a spiteful violent woman.

■ see SHREW.

hellebore /hélibawr/ *n.* **1** any evergreen plant of the genus *Helleborus*, having large white, green, or purplish flowers, e.g., the Christmas rose. **2** a liliaceous plant, *Veratrum album*. **3** *hist.* any of various plants supposed to cure madness. [ME f. OF *ellebre, elebore* or med.L *eleborus* f. L *elleborus* f. Gk *(h)elleboros*]

helleborine /hélibəreen/ *n.* any orchid of the genus *Epipactis* or *Cephalanthera*. [F or L *helleborine* or L f. Gk *helleborinē* plant like hellebore (as HELLEBORE)]

Hellene /héleen/ *n.* **1** a native of modern Greece. **2** an ancient Greek. ◻◻ **Hellenic** /helénik/ *adj.* [Gk *Hellēn* a Greek]

Hellenism /hélinizəm/ *n.* **1** Greek character or culture (esp. of ancient Greece). **2** the study or imitation of Greek culture. ◻◻ **Hellenize** *v.tr.* & *intr.* **Hellenization** *n.* [Gk *hellēnismos* f. *hellēnizō* speak Greek, make Greek (as HELLENE)]

Hellenist /hélinist/ *n.* an expert on or admirer of Greek language or culture. [Gk *Hellēnistēs* (as HELLENISM)]

Hellenistic /hélinístik/ *adj.* of or relating to Greek history, language, and culture from the death of Alexander the Great to the time of Augustus (4th–1st c. BC).

hellfire /hélfīr/ *n.* the fire or fires regarded as existing in hell.

hellgrammite /hélgrəmīt/ *n.* an aquatic larva of an American fly, *Corydalus cornutus*, often used as fishing bait. [19th c.: orig. unkn.]

hellhole /hélhōl/ *n. colloq.* an oppressive or unbearable place.

■ see HOLE *n.* 4a.

hellhound /hélhownd/ *n.* a fiend.

■ see DEVIL *n.* 3a.

hellion /hélyən/ *n. colloq.* a mischievous or troublesome person, esp. a child. [perh. f. dial. *hallion* a worthless fellow, assim. to HELL]

hellish /hélish/ *adj.* & *adv.* ● *adj.* **1** of or like hell. **2** *colloq.* extremely difficult or unpleasant. ● *adv. Brit. colloq.* (as an intensifier) extremely (*hellish expensive*). ◻◻ **hellishly** *adv.* **hellishness** *n.*

■ *adj.* **1** see INFERNAL 1. **2** see ATROCIOUS 1.

hello /helō, hə-/ *int., n.,* & *v.* (also esp. *Brit.* (**hullo** /hə-/, **hallo**) /hə-/) ● *int.* **1 a** an expression of informal greeting, or esp. *Brit.* of surprise. **b** used to begin a telephone conversation. **2** a cry used to call attention. ● *n.* (*pl.* **-os**) a cry of "hello." ● *v.intr.* (**-oes, -oed**) cry "hello." [var. of earlier HOLLO]

■ *int.* hi, how do you do?, howdy, *archaic or literary* hail, *colloq.* ciao, hiya.

helm[1] /helm/ *n.* & *v.* ● *n.* **1** a tiller or wheel by which a ship's rudder is controlled. **2** the amount by which this is turned (*more helm needed*). ● *v.tr.* steer or guide as if with a helm. ◻ **at the helm** in control; at the head (of an organization, etc.). [OE *helma*, prob. related to HELVE]

■ *n.* **1** tiller, wheel, steering gear *or* apparatus. ● *v.* see STEER[1] *v.* 1. ◻ **at the helm** in control *or* command, in the chair *or* driver's seat *or* saddle; directing, presiding, leading, ruling.

helm[2] /helm/ *n. archaic* helmet. ◻◻ **helmed** *adj.* [OE f. Gmc]

helmet /hélmit/ *n.* **1** any of various protective head coverings worn by soldiers, police officers, firefighters, divers, cyclists, etc. **2** *Bot.* the arched upper part of the corolla in some flowers. **3** the shell of a gastropod mollusk of the genus *Cassis*, used in jewelry. ◻◻ **helmeted** *adj.* [ME f. OF, dimin. of *helme* f. WG (as HELM[2])]

helminth /hélminth/ *n.* any of various parasitic worms including flukes, tapeworms, and nematodes. ◻◻ **helminthic** /-mínthik/ *adj.* **helminthoid** *adj.* **helminthology** *n.* [Gk *helmins -inthos* intestinal worm]

helminthiasis /hélminthíəsis/ *n.* a disease characterized by the presence of any of several parasitic worms in the body.

helmsman /hélmzmən/ *n.* (*pl.* **-men**) a person who steers a vessel.

■ see PILOT *n.* 2, 6; NAVIGATOR.

helot /hélət/ *n.* a serf (esp. **Helot**), of a class in ancient Sparta. ◻◻ **helotism** *n.* **helotry** *n.* [L *helotes* pl. f. Gk *heilōtes*,

-*ōtai*, erron. taken as = inhabitants of *Helos*, a Laconian town]

■ see SLAVE *n.* 1.

help /help/ *v. & n.* ● *v.tr.* **1** provide (a person, etc.) with the means toward what is needed or sought (*helped me with my work*; *helped me (to) pay my debts*). **2** (foll. by *up*, *down*, etc.) assist or give support to (a person) in moving, etc., as specified (*helped her into the chair*; *helped him on with his coat*). **3** (often *absol.*) be of use or service to (a person) (*does that help?*). **4** contribute to alleviating (a pain or difficulty). **5** prevent or remedy (*it can't be helped*). **6** (usu. with *neg.*) **a** *tr.* refrain from (*can't help it*; *could not help laughing*). **b** *refl.* refrain from acting (*couldn't help himself*). **7** *tr.* (often foll. by *to*) serve (a person with food) (*shall I help you to more rice?*). ● *n.* **1** the act of helping or being helped (*we need your help*; *came to our help*). **2** a person or thing that helps. **3** a domestic servant or employee, or several collectively. **4** a remedy or escape (*there is no help for it*). □ **helping hand** assistance. **help oneself** (often foll. by *to*) **1** serve oneself (with food). **2** take without seeking help; take without permission; steal. **help a person out** give a person help, esp. in difficulty. **so help me** (or **help me God**) (as an invocation or oath) I am speaking the truth. □□ **helper** *n.* [OE *helpan* f. Gmc]

■ *v.* **1, 2** assist, aid, lend *or* give a hand; support. **3** serve, succor, aid, be of use *or* useful (to); be advantageous *or* of advantage (to), avail. **4, 5** relieve, alleviate, mitigate, ease, remedy, cure, make better, improve; prevent, avoid, obviate. **6 a** stop, refrain from, resist, keep from, *literary* forbear (from) *or* to do. **b** stop, control oneself. ● *n.* **1** aid, support, succor, assistance. **2** support; prop, helper, assistant, aide. **3** employee(s), worker(s), member(s) of staff, helper(s), hand(s), assistant(s), laborer(s), domestic(s), servant(s); *Brit. colloq.* daily help, daily; staff. **4** relief, escape; remedy, cure, balm. □ **helping hand** see *assistance* (ASSIST). **help oneself 2** take; appropriate, commandeer, steal, *colloq.* lift, *formal or joc.* purloin, *sl.* pinch, *Brit. sl.* nick.

helpful /hélpfŏŏl/ *adj.* (of a person or thing) giving help; useful. □□ **helpfully** *adv.* **helpfulness** *n.*

■ useful, serviceable, practical, beneficial, valuable, constructive, productive; supportive, reassuring, sympathetic, caring, kind, benevolent, considerate, cooperative, accommodating.

helping /hélping/ *n.* a portion of food esp. at a meal.

■ serving, portion, ration, plateful, dollop.

helpless /hélplis/ *adj.* **1** lacking help or protection; defenseless. **2** unable to act without help. □□ **helplessly** *adv.* **helplessness** *n.*

■ **1** vulnerable, dependent; see also *defenseless* (DEFENSE). **2** weak, feeble, infirm; confused, bewildered, muddled; incapable.

helpline /hélplin/ *n.* a telephone service providing help with problems.

helpmate /hélpmayt/ *n.* a helpful companion or partner (usu. a husband or wife).

■ see PARTNER *n.* 1, 4.

helter-skelter /héltərskéltər/ *adv., adj., & n.* ● *adv.* in disorderly haste; confusedly. ● *adj.* characterized by disorderly haste or confusion. ● *n. Brit.* a tall spiral slide around a tower, at a fairground or carnival. [imit., orig. in a rhyming jingle, perh. f. ME *skelte* hasten]

■ *adv.* hastily, hurriedly, confusedly, recklessly, pell-mell, headlong, unsystematically, chaotically, erratically, higgledy-piggledy, *colloq.* every which way. ● *adj.* hasty, hurried, reckless, headlong; disorderly, disorganized, confused, muddled, haphazard, careless, jumbled, random, topsy-turvy, higgledy-piggledy.

helve /helv/ *n.* the handle of a weapon or a tool. [OE *helfe* f. WG]

■ see HANDLE *n.* 1.

Helvetian /helvéeshən/ *adj. & n.* ● *adj.* Swiss. ● *n.* a native of Switzerland. [L *Helvetia* Switzerland]

hem[1] /hem/ *n. & v.* ● *n.* the border of a piece of cloth, esp. a cut edge turned under and sewn down. ● *v.tr.* (**hemmed,**

hemming) turn down and sew in the edge of (a piece of cloth, etc.). □ **hem in** confine; restrict the movement of. [OE, perh. rel. to dial. *ham* enclosure]

■ *n.* see BORDER *n.* 3. ● *v.* see SEW. □ **hem in** see BOX[1] *v.* 2.

hem[2] /hem, həm/ *int., n., & v.* ● *int.* (also **ahem**) calling attention to or expressing hesitation by a slight cough or clearing of the throat. ● *n.* an utterance of this. ● *v.intr.* (**hemmed, hemming**) say *hem*; hesitate in speech. □ **hem and haw** hesitate, esp. in speaking. [imit.]

hemal /héeməl/ *adj.* (*Brit.* **haemal**) *Anat.* **1** of or concerning the blood. **2 a** situated on the same side of the body as the heart and major blood vessels. **b** ventral. [Gk *haima* blood]

hematic /himátik/ *adj.* (*Brit.* **haematic**) *Med.* of or containing blood. [Gk *haimatikos* (as HEMATIN)]

hematin /héemətin, hém-/ *n.* (*Brit.* **haematin**) *Anat.* a bluish black derivative of hemoglobin, formed by removal of the protein part and oxidation of the iron atom. [Gk *haima -matos* blood]

hematite /héemətīt, hém-/ *n.* (*Brit.* **haematite**) a ferric oxide ore. [L *haematites* f. Gk *haimatitēs* (*lithos*) bloodlike (stone) (as HEMATIN)]

hemato- /héemətō, hém-/ *comb. form* (*Brit.* **haemato-**) blood. [Gk *haima haimat-* blood]

hematocele /himátəseel, héemətəseel, hém-/ *n.* (*Brit.* **haematocele**) *Med.* a swelling caused by blood collecting in a body cavity.

hematocrit /himátəkrit/ *n.* (*Brit.* **haematocrit**) *Physiol.* **1** the ratio of the volume of red blood cells to the total volume of blood. **2** an instrument for measuring this. [HEMATO- + Gk *kritēs* judge]

hematology /héemətóləjee, hém-/ *n.* (*Brit.* **haematology**) the study of the physiology of the blood. □□ **hematologic** /-təlójik/ *adj.* **hematological** *adj.* **hematologist** *n.*

hematoma /héemətṓmə, hém-/ *n.* (*Brit.* **haematoma**) *Med.* a solid swelling of clotted blood within the tissues.

hematuria /héemətyŏŏreeə, -tyŏŏr-, hém-/ *n.* (*Brit.* **haematuria**) *Med.* the presence of blood in urine.

heme /heem/ *n.* (also **haem**) a nonprotein compound containing iron, and responsible for the red color of hemoglobin. [Gk *haima* blood or f. HEMOGLOBIN]

hemerocallis /hémərōkális/ *n.* = DAYLILY. [L *hemerocalles* f. Gk *hēmerokalles* a kind of lily f. *hēmera* day + *kallos* beauty]

hemi- /hémee/ *comb. form* half. [Gk *hēmi-* = L *semi-*: see SEMI-]

-hemia *comb. form* var. of -EMIA.

hemianopsia /hémeeənópseeə/ *n.* (also **hemianopia** /-nŏpeeə/) blindness over half the field of vision.

hemicellulose /hémisélyəlōs/ *n.* any of various polysaccharides forming the matrix of plant cell walls in which cellulose is embedded. [G (as HEMI-, CELLULOSE)]

hemicycle /hémisīkəl/ *n.* a semicircular figure.

hemidemisemiquaver /hémeedémeesémeekwayvər/ *n. Mus. esp. Brit.* = sixty-fourth note.

hemihedral /hémiheedrəl/ *adj. Crystallog.* having half the number of planes required for symmetry of the holohedral form.

hemiplegia /hémipleejə, -jeeə/ *n. Med.* paralysis of one side of the body. □□ **hemiplegic** *n. & adj.* [mod.L f. Gk *hēmiplēgia* paralysis (as HEMI-, *plēgē* stroke)]

hemipterous /hemíptərəs/ *adj.* of the insect order Hemiptera, including aphids, bugs, and cicadas, with piercing or sucking mouthparts. [HEMI- + Gk *pteron* wing]

hemisphere /hémisfeer/ *n.* **1** half of a sphere. **2** a half of the earth, esp. as divided by the equator (into *northern* and *southern hemisphere*) or by a line passing through the poles (into *eastern* and *western hemisphere*). **3** either lateral half of the brain. □□ **hemispheric** /-sféerik, -sférik/ *adj.* **hemi-**

/.../ **pronunciation**	● **part of speech**
□ **phrases, idioms, and compounds**	
□□ **derivatives**	■ **synonym section**
cross-references appear in SMALL CAPITALS or *italics*	

spherical *adj.* [OF *emisphere* & L *hemisphaerium* f. Gk *hēmisphaira* (as HEMI-, SPHERE)]

hemistich /hémistik/ *n.* half of a line of verse. [LL *hemistichium* f. Gk *hēmistikhion* (as HEMI-, *stikhion* f. *stikhos* line)]

hemline /hémlin/ *n.* the line or level of the lower edge of a skirt, dress, or coat.

hemlock /hémlok/ *n.* **1 a** a poisonous umbelliferous plant, *Conium maculatum*, with fernlike leaves and small white flowers. **b** a poisonous potion obtained from this. **2** (in full **hemlock fir** or **spruce**) **a** any coniferous tree of the genus *Tsuga*, having foliage that smells like hemlock when crushed. **b** the lumber or pitch of these trees. [OE *hymlic(e)*]

hemo- /heémō, hémmō/ *comb. form* (*Brit.* **haemo-**) = HEMATO-. [abbr.]

hemocyanin /heéməsíənin, hém-/ *n.* (*Brit.* **haemocyanin**) an oxygen-carrying substance containing copper, present in the blood plasma of arthropods and mollusks. [HEMO- + *cyanin* blue pigment (as CYAN)]

hemodialysis /heémōdiálisis/ *n.* = DIALYSIS 2.

hemoglobin /heéməglóbin, hém-/ *n.* (*Brit.* **haemoglobin**) a red oxygen-carrying substance containing iron, present in the red blood cells of vertebrates. [shortened f. *hematoglobin*, compound of HEMATIN + GLOBULIN]

hemolysis /heemólisis, hem-/ *n.* (*Brit.* **haemolysis**) the loss of hemoglobin from red blood cells. □□ **hemolytic** /-məlítik/ *adj.*

hemophilia /heéməfíleeə, hém-/ *n.* (*Brit.* **haemophilia**) *Med.* a usu. hereditary disorder with a tendency to bleed severely from even a slight injury, through the failure of the blood to clot normally. □□ **hemophilic** *adj.* [mod.L (as HEMO-, -PHILIA)]

hemophiliac /heéməfíleeak, -feélee-, hém-/ *n.* (*Brit.* **haemophiliac**) a person suffering from hemophilia.

hemorrhage /hémərij, hémrij/ *n.* & *v.* (*Brit.* **haemorrhage**) • *n.* **1** an escape of blood from a ruptured blood vessel, esp. when profuse. **2** an extensive damaging loss suffered by a government, organization, etc., esp. of people or assets. • *v.intr.* undergo a hemorrhage. □□ **hemorrhagic** /hémərájik/ *adj.* [earlier *hemorrhagy* f. F *hémorr(h)agie* f. L *haemorrhagia* f. Gk *haimorrhagia* f. *haima* blood + stem of *rhēgnumi* burst]

hemorrhoid /héməroyd/ *n.* (*Brit.* **haemorrhoid**) (usu. in *pl.*) swollen veins at or near the anus; piles. □□ **hemorrhoidal** *adj.* [ME *emeroudis* (Bibl. *emerods*) f. OF *emeroyde* f. L f. Gk *haimorrhoides* (*phlebes*) bleeding (veins) f. *haima* blood, -*rhoos* -flowing]

hemostasis /himóstəsis, heémōstáysis, hém-/ *n.* (*Brit.* **haemostasis**) the stopping of the flow of blood. □□ **hemostatic** /heéməstátik/ *adj.*

hemp /hemp/ *n.* **1** (in full **Indian hemp**) a herbaceous plant, *Cannabis sativa*, native to Asia. **2** its fiber extracted from the stem and used to make rope and strong fabrics. **3** any of several narcotic drugs made from the hemp plant (cf. CANNABIS, MARIJUANA). **4** any of several other plants yielding fiber, including Manila hemp and sunn hemp. □ **hemp agrimony** a composite plant, *Eupatorium cannabinum*, with pale purple flowers and hairy leaves. **hemp nettle** any of various nettlelike plants of the genus *Galeopsis*. [OE *henep*, *hænep* f. Gmc, rel. to Gk *kannabis*]

hempen /hémpən/ *adj.* made from hemp.

hemstitch /hémstich/ *n.* & *v.* • *n.* a decorative stitch used in sewing hems. • *v.tr.* hem with this stitch.

hen /hen/ *n.* **1 a** a female bird, esp. of a domestic fowl. **b** (in *pl.*) domestic fowls of either sex. **2** a female lobster or crab or salmon. □ **hen and chickens** any of several succulent plants, esp. the houseleek. **hen party** *colloq.* often *derog.* a social gathering of women. [OE *henn* f. WG]

henbane /hénbayn/ *n.* **1** a poisonous herbaceous plant, *Hyoscyamus niger*, with sticky hairy leaves and an unpleasant smell. **2** a narcotic drug obtained from this.

hence /hens/ *adv.* **1** from this time (*two years hence*). **2** for this reason; as a result of inference (*hence we seem to be wrong*). **3** *archaic* from here; from this place. [ME *hens*, *hennes*, *henne* f. OE *heonan* f. the root of HE]

■ **1** from now, in the future. **2** therefore, consequently, accordingly, ergo, as a result, for that *or* this reason, so, *formal* thus.

henceforth /hénsfáwrth/ *adv.* (also **henceforward** /-fáwrwərd/) from this time onward.
■ hereafter, from now on, in future.

henchman /hénchmən/ *n.* (*pl.* **-men**) **1 a** a trusted supporter or attendant. **b** often *derog.* a political supporter; a partisan. **2** *hist.* a squire; a page of honor. **3** *Sc.* the principal attendant of a Highland chief. [ME *henxman*, *hengestman* f. OE *hengst* male horse]
■ **1** attendant, associate, supporter, partisan, confidant, crony, right-hand man, cohort, *colloq.* sidekick.

hencoop /hénkōop/ *n.* a coop for keeping fowls in.

hendeca- /hendékə/ *comb. form* eleven. [Gk *hendeka* eleven]

hendecagon /hendékəgon/ *n.* a plane figure with eleven sides and angles.

hendiadys /hendíədis/ *n.* the expression of an idea by two words connected with "and," instead of one modifying the other, e.g., *nice and warm* for *nicely warm*. [med.L f. Gk *hen dia duoin* one thing by two]

henequen /héniken/ *n.* **1** a Mexican agave, *Agave fourcroydes*. **2** the sisal-like fiber obtained from this. [Sp. *jeniquen*]

henge /henj/ *n.* a prehistoric monument consisting of a circle of massive stone or wood uprights. [back-form. f. *Stonehenge*, such a monument in S. England]

henhouse /hénhows/ *n.* a small shed for fowls to roost in.

henna /hénə/ *n.* **1** a tropical shrub, *Lawsonia inermis*, having small pink, red, or white flowers. **2** the reddish dye from its shoots and leaves esp. used to color hair. [Arab. *ḥinnā'*]

hennaed /hénəd/ *adj.* treated with henna.

henotheism /hénətheeízəm/ *n.* belief in or adoption of a particular god in a polytheistic system as the god of a tribe, class, etc. [Gk *heis henos* one + *theos* god]

henpeck /hénpek/ *v.tr.* (of a woman) constantly harass (a man, esp. her husband).
■ nag, harass, pester, torment, carp at, cavil at, *colloq.* go on at.

henry /hénree/ *n.* (*pl.* **-ies** or **henrys**) *Electr.* the SI unit of inductance that gives an electromotive force of one volt in a closed circuit with a uniform rate of change of current of one ampere per second. ¶ Abbr.: **H.** [J. *Henry*, Amer. physicist d. 1878]

heortology /heé-awrtóləjee/ *n.* the study of ecclesiatical festivals. [G *Heortologie*, F *héortologie* f. Gk *heortē* feast]

hep¹ var. of HIP³.

hep² var. of HIP².

heparin /hépərin/ *n.* *Biochem.* a substance produced in liver cells, etc., which inhibits blood coagulation, and is used as an anticoagulant in the treatment of thrombosis. □□ **heparinize** *v.tr.* [L f. Gk *hēpar* liver]

hepatic /hipátik/ *adj.* **1** of or relating to the liver. **2** dark brownish red; liver colored. [ME f. L *hepaticus* f. Gk *hēpatikos* f. *hēpar* -*atos* liver]

hepatica /hipátikə/ *n.* any plant of the genus *Hepatica*, with reddish brown lobed leaves resembling the liver. [med.L fem. of *hepaticus*: see HEPATIC]

hepatitis /hépətítis/ *n.* inflammation of the liver. [mod.L: see HEPATIC]

hepcat /hépkat/ *n.* a hip person of the 1930s or 40s; a devotee of jazz or swing.
■ *sl.* cat, hipster; see also TRENDY *n.*

Hepplewhite /hépəlwit/ *n.* a light and graceful style of furniture. [G. *Hepplewhite*, Engl. cabinetmaker d. 1786]

hepta- /héptə/ *comb. form* seven. [Gk *hepta* seven]

heptad /héptad/ *n.* a group of seven. [Gk *heptas* -*ados* set of seven (*hepta*)]

heptagon /héptəgon/ *n.* a plane figure with seven sides and angles. □□ **heptagonal** /-tágənəl/ *adj.* [F *heptagone* or med.L *heptagonum* f. Gk (as HEPTA-, -GON)]

heptahedron /héptəheédrən/ *n.* a solid figure with seven faces. □□ **heptahedral** *adj.* [HEPTA- + -HEDRON after POLYHEDRON]

heptameter /heptámitər/ *n.* a line or verse of seven metrical feet. [L *heptametrum* f. Gk (as HEPTA-, -METER)]

heptane /héptayn/ *n. Chem.* a liquid hydrocarbon of the alkane series, obtained from petroleum. ¶ *Chem.* formula: C_7H_{16}. [HEPTA- + -ANE[2]]

heptarchy /héptaarkee/ *n.* (*pl.* -ies) **1 a** a government by seven rulers. **b** an instance of this. **2** *hist.* the supposed seven kingdoms of the Angles and the Saxons in Britain in the 7th–8th c. □□ **heptarchic** /-taárkik/ *adj.* **heptarchical** *adj.* [HEPTA- after *tetrarchy*]

Heptateuch /héptatōōk, -tyōōk/ *n.* the first seven books of the Old Testament. [L f. Gk f. *hepta* seven + *teukhos* book, volume]

heptathlon /heptáthlon, -lən/ *n. Sports* a seven-event track and field competition esp. for women.

heptavalent /héptaváylənt/ *adj. Chem.* having a valence of seven; septivalent.

her /hər/ *pron. & poss.pron.* ● *pron.* **1** *objective case* of SHE (*I like her*). **2** *colloq.* she (*it's her all right*; *am older than her*). **3** *archaic* herself (*she fell and hurt her*). ● *poss.pron.* (*attrib.*) **1** of or belonging to her or herself (*her house*; *her own business*). **2** *Brit.* (**Her**) (in titles) that she is (*Her Majesty*). □ **her indoors** *Brit. colloq.* or *joc.* one's wife. [OE *hi(e)re* dative & genit. of *hio, hēo* fem. of HE]

herald /hérəld/ *n. & v.* ● *n.* **1** an official messenger bringing news. **2** a forerunner (*spring is the herald of summer*). **3 a** *Brit. hist.* an officer responsible for official ceremonies and etiquette. **b** *Brit.* an official of the Heralds' College. ● *v.tr.* proclaim the approach of; usher in (*the storm heralded trouble*). □ **Heralds' College** *Brit. colloq.* = *College of Arms*. [ME f. OF *herau(l)t, herauder* f. Gmc]

■ *n.* **1** see MESSENGER. **2** see FORERUNNER 2. ● *v.* see ANNOUNCE 1.

heraldic /hərɑ́ldik/ *adj.* of or concerning heraldry. □□ **heraldically** *adv.* [HERALD]

heraldist /hérəldist/ *n.* an expert in heraldry. [HERALD]

heraldry /hérəldree/ *n.* **1** the science or art of a herald, esp. in dealing with armorial bearings. **2** heraldic pomp. **3** armorial bearings.

herb /ərb, hərb/ *n.* **1** any nonwoody seed-bearing plant that dies down to the ground after flowering. **2** any plant with leaves, seeds, or flowers used for flavoring, food, medicine, scent, etc. **3** *sl.* marijuana. □ **give it the herbs** *Austral. colloq.* accelerate. **herb bennet** a common yellow-flowered European plant, *Geum urbanum.* **herb Christopher** a white-flowered baneberry, *Actaea spicata.* **herb Gerard** a white-flowered plant, *Aegopodium podagraria.* **herb Paris** a plant, *Paris quadrifolia,* with a single flower and four leaves in a cross shape on an unbranched stem. **herb Robert** a common cranesbill, *Geranium robertianum,* with red-stemmed leaves and pink flowers. **herb tea** an infusion of herbs. **herb tobacco** a mixture of herbs smoked as a substitute for tobacco. □□ **herbiferous** /-bífərəs/ *adj.* **herblike** *adj.* [ME f. OF *erbe* f. L *herba* grass, green crops, herb; *herb bennet* prob. f. med.L *herba benedicta* blessed herb (thought of as expelling the Devil)]

■ **2** see SPICE *n.* 1.

herbaceous /hərbáyshəs, ər-/ *adj.* of or like herbs (see HERB 1). □ **herbaceous border** a garden border containing esp. perennial flowering plants. **herbaceous perennial** a plant whose growth dies down annually but whose roots, etc., survive. [L *herbaceus* grassy (as HERB)]

herbage /ə́rbij, hər-/ *n.* **1** herbs collectively. **2** the succulent part of herbs, esp. as pasture. **3** *Law* the right of pasture on another person's land. [ME f. OF *erbage* f. med.L *herbaticum, herbagium* right of pasture, f. L *herba* herb]

herbal /ə́rbəl, hór-/ *adj. & n.* ● *adj.* of herbs in medicinal and culinary use. ● *n.* a book with descriptions and accounts of the properties of herbs. [med.L *herbalis* (as HERB)]

herbalist /ə́rbəlist, hór-/ *n.* **1** a dealer in medicinal herbs. **2** a person skilled in herbs, esp. an early botanical writer.

herbarium /hərbáireeəm, ər-/ *n.* (*pl.* **herbaria** /-reeə/) **1 a** systematically arranged collection of dried plants. **2** a book, room, or building for these. [LL (as HERB)]

herbicide /ə́rbisīd, ór-/ *n.* a substance toxic to plants and used to destroy unwanted vegetation.

herbivore /ə́rbivawr, ór-/ *n.* an animal that feeds on plants. □□ **herbivorous** /-bívərəs/ *adj.* [L *herba* herb + -*vore* (see -VOROUS)]

herby /ə́rbee, hór-/ *adj.* (**herbier, herbiest**) **1** abounding in herbs. **2** of the nature of a culinary or medicinal herb.

Herculean /hórkyəleéən, -kyōôleeən/ *adj.* having or requiring great strength or effort. [L *Herculeus* (as HERCULES)]

■ see SUPERHUMAN 1.

Hercules /hórkyəleez/ *n.* a man of exceptional strength or size. □ **Hercules beetle** *Zool.* a large S. American beetle, *Dynastes hercules,* with two horns extending from the head [ME f. L f. Gk *Hēraklēs* a hero noted for his great strength]

Hercynian /hərsíneeən/ *adj. Geol.* of a mountain-forming time in the E. hemisphere in the late Palaeozoic era. [L *Hercynia silva* forested mountains of central Germany]

herd /hərd/ *n. & v.* ● *n.* **1** a large number of animals, esp. cattle, feeding or traveling or kept together. **2** (often prec. by *the*) *derog.* a large number of people; a crowd; a mob (*prefers not to follow the herd*). **3** (esp. in *comb.*) a keeper of herds; a herdsman (*cowherd*). ● *v.* **1** *intr. & tr.* go or cause to go in a herd (*herded together for warmth*; *herded the cattle into the field*). **2** *tr.* tend (sheep, cattle, etc.) (*he herds the goats*). □ **the herd instinct** the tendency to associate or conform with one's own kind for support, etc. **ride herd on** keep watch on. □□ **herder** *n.* [OE *heord,* (in sense 3) *hirdi,* f. Gmc]

■ *n.* **1** see FLOCK[1] *n.* 1. **2** group, flock, crowd, multitude, host, throng, mass, swarm; *usu. derog.* mob, horde, common herd, masses, hoi polloi, riffraff, rabble, *colloq.* great unwashed. ● *v.* **1** gather (together), congregate, flock together, assemble, collect; round up, gather (together *or* up), wrangle, corral. **2** shepherd, look after; see also TEND[2] 1.

herdsman /hórdzmən/ *n.* (*pl.* -**men**) the owner or keeper of herds (of domesticated animals).

Herdwick /hórdwik/ *n.* **1** an animal of a hardy breed of mountain sheep from No. England. **2** this breed. [obs. *herdwick* pasture ground (as HERD, WICK[2]), perh. because this breed originated in Furness Abbey pastures]

here /heer/ *adv., n., & int.* ● *adv.* **1** in or at or to this place or position (*put it here*; *has lived here for many years*; *comes here every day*). **2** indicating a person's presence or a thing offered (*here is your coat*; *my son here will show you*). **3** at this point in the argument, situation, etc. (*here I have a question*). ● *n.* this place (*get out of here*; *lives near here*; *fill it up to here*). ● *int.* **1** calling attention: short for *come here, look here,* etc. (*here, where are you going with that?*). **2** indicating one's presence in a roll call: short for *I am here.* □ **here and now** at this very moment; immediately. **here and there** in various places. **here goes!** *colloq.* an expression indicating the start of a bold act. **here's** to I drink to the health of. **here we are** *colloq.* said on arrival at one's destination. **here we go again** *colloq.* the same, usu. undesirable, events are recurring. **here you are** said on handing something to somebody. **neither here nor there** of no importance or relevance. [OE *hēr* f. Gmc: cf. HE]

hereabouts /heérəbówts/ *adv.* (also **hereabout**) near this place.

hereafter /heeráftər/ *adv. & n.* ● *adv.* **1** from now on; in the future. **2** in the world to come (after death). ● *n.* **1** the future. **2** life after death.

hereat /heerát/ *adv. archaic* as a result of this.

hereby /heérbī/ *adv.* by this means; as a result of this.

hereditable /hirédit∍bəl/ *adj.* that can be inherited. [obs. F *héréditable* or med.L *hereditabilis* f. eccl.L *hereditare* f. L *heres -edis* heir]

hereditament /hérídítəmənt/ *n. Law* **1** any property that can be inherited. **2** inheritance. [med.L *hereditamentum* (as HEREDITABLE)]

---

hereditary /hiréditeree/ *adj.* **1** (of disease, instinct, etc.) able to be passed down from one generation to another. **2 a** descending by inheritance. **b** holding a position by inheritance. **3** the same as or resembling what one's parents had (*a hereditary hatred*). **4** of or relating to inheritance. □□ **hereditarily** *adv.* **hereditariness** *n.* [L *hereditarius* (as HEREDITY)]
■ **1** inheritable, transmissible, *Biol.* heritable; inherited, genetic, inborn, innate, bred in the bone. **2 a** ancestral, inherited, traditional, handed down. **3** inherited, ingrained; see also INBORN.

heredity /hiréditee/ *n.* **1 a** the passing on of physical or mental characteristics genetically from one generation to another. **b** these characteristics. **2** the genetic constitution of an individual. [F *hérédité* or L *hereditas* heirship (as HEIR)]

Hereford /hórfərd, hérifərd/ *n.* **1** an animal of a breed of red and white beef cattle. **2** this breed. [*Hereford* in England, where it originated]

herein /heeérin/ *adv. formal* in this matter, book, etc.

hereinafter /heeérináftər/ *adv.* esp. *Law formal* in a later part of this document, etc.

hereinbefore /heeérinbifáwr/ *adv.* esp. *Law formal* in a preceding part of this document, etc.

hereof /heeérúv, -óv/ *adv. formal* of this.

heresiarch /hereézeeaark, hérise-/ *n.* the leader or founder of a heresy. [eccl.L *haeresiarcha* f. Gk *hairesiarkhēs* (as HERESY + *arkhēs* ruler)]

heresy /hérəsee/ *n.* (*pl.* **-ies**) **1 a** belief or practice contrary to the orthodox doctrine of esp. the Christian church. **b** an instance of this. **2 a** opinion contrary to what is normally accepted or maintained (*it's heresy to suggest that instant coffee is as good as the real thing*). **b** an instance of this. □□ **heresiology** /hərəezeeólɔjee, -seeólɔjee/ *n.* [ME f. OF (*h*)*eresie*, f. eccl.L *haeresis*, in L = school of thought, f. Gk *hairesis* choice, sect f. *haireomai* choose]
■ **1** see SACRILEGE.

heretic /hérətik/ *n.* **1** the holder of an unorthodox opinion. **2** a person believing in or practicing religious heresy. □□ **heretical** /hirétikəl/ *adj.* **heretically** *adv.* [ME f. OF *heretique* f. eccl.L *haereticus* f. Gk *hairetikos* able to choose (as HERESY)]
■ **1** see NONCONFORMIST. **2** see INFIDEL *n.* □□ **heretical** unorthodox, heterodox, freethinking, iconoclastic; schismatic, apostatical, skeptical, agnostic, atheistic, infidel, idolatrous, heathen, pagan, godless; blasphemous, impious.

hereto /heeértoō/ *adv. formal* to this matter.

heretofore /heeértəfáwr/ *adv. formal* before this time.
■ see *previously* (PREVIOUS).

hereunder /heeérúndər/ *adv. formal* below (in a book, legal document, etc.).

hereunto /heeéruntoō/ *adv. archaic* to this.

hereupon /heeérəpón, -páwn/ *adv.* after this; in consequence of this.

herewith /heeérwíth, -wíth/ *adv.* with this (esp. of an enclosure in a letter, etc.).

heriot /héreeət/ *n. Brit. hist.* a tribute paid to a lord on the death of a tenant, consisting of a live animal, a chattel, or, orig., the return of borrowed equipment. [OE *heregeatwa* f. *here* army + *geatwa* trappings]

heritable /héritəbəl/ *adj.* **1** *Law* **a** (of property) capable of being inherited by heirs-at-law (cf. MOVABLE). **b** capable of inheriting. **2** *Biol.* (of a characteristic) transmissible from parent to offspring. □□ **heritability** *n.* **heritably** *adv.* [ME f. OF f. *heriter* f. eccl.L *hereditare*: see HEREDITABLE]
■ **2** see HEREDITARY 1.

heritage /héritij/ *n.* **1** anything that is or may be inherited. **2** inherited circumstances, benefits, etc. (*a heritage of confusion*). **3** a nation's, state's, etc., historic buildings, monuments, countryside, etc., esp. when regarded as worthy of preservation. **4** *Bibl.* **a** the ancient Israelites. **b** the church. [ME f. OF (as HERITABLE)]
■ **1** bequest, inheritance, legacy, patrimony; birthright. **2** legacy, inheritance.

heritor /héritər/ *n.* (esp. in Scottish Law) a person who in-

herits. [ME f. AF *heriter*, OF *heritier* (as HEREDITARY), assim. to words in -OR¹]

herky-jerky /hórkeejórkee/ *adj.* marked by fitful, spastic, or unpredictable movement or manner. [redupl. of JERKY]

herl var. of HARL.

herm /hərm/ *n. Gk Antiq.* a squared stone pillar with a head (esp. of Hermes) on top, used as a boundary marker, etc. (cf. TERMINUS 6). [L *Herma* f. Gk *Hermēs* messenger of the gods]

hermaphrodite /hərmáfrədit/ *n. & adj.* ● *n.* **1 a** *Zool.* an animal having both male and female sexual organs. **b** *Bot.* a plant having stamens and pistils in the same flower. **2 a** human being in which both male and female sex organs are present, or in which the sex organs contain both ovarian and testicular tissue. **3** a person or thing combining opposite qualities or characteristics. ● *adj.* **1** combining both sexes. **2** combining opposite qualities or characteristics. □ **hermaphrodite brig** *hist.* a two-masted sailing ship rigged on the foremast as a brig and on the mainmast as a schooner. □□ **hermaphroditic** /-dítik/ *adj.* **hermaphroditical** *adj.* **hermaphroditism** *n.* [L *hermaphroditus* f. Gk *hermaphroditos*, orig. the name of a son of Hermes and Aphrodite in Greek mythology, who became joined in one body with the nymph Salmacis]
■ *n.* **1, 2** see BISEXUAL *n.* ● *adj.* **1** see BISEXUAL *adj.*

hermeneutic /hórminoōtik, -nyoō-/ *adj.* concerning interpretation, esp. of Scripture or literary texts. □□ **hermeneutical** *adj.* **hermeneutically** *adv.* [Gk *hermēneutikos* f. *hermēneuō* interpret]

hermeneutics /hórminoōtiks, -nyoō-/ *n.pl.* (also treated as *sing.*) *Bibl.* interpretation, esp. of Scripture or literary texts.

hermetic /hərmétik/ *adj.* (also **hermetical**) **1** with an airtight closure. **2** protected from outside agencies. **3 a** of alchemy or other occult sciences (*hermetic art*). **b** esoteric. □ **hermetic seal** an airtight seal (orig. as used by alchemists). □□ **hermetically** *adv.* **hermetism** /hérmitizəm/ *n.* [mod.L *hermeticus* irreg. f. *Hermes Trismegistus* thrice greatest Hermes (as the founder of alchemy)]
■ **1** airtight, sealed; see also TIGHT *adj.* 4. **2** enclosed, protected, secured, sheltered, shielded, safe, impregnable. **3 a** see OCCULT *adj.* 1, 3. **b** see OCCULT *adj.* 2.

hermit /hórmit/ *n.* **1** an early Christian recluse. **2** any person living in solitude. □ **hermit crab** any crab of the family Paguridae that lives in a cast-off mollusk shell for protection. **hermit thrush** a migratory N. American thrush, *Catharus guttatus.* □□ **hermitic** /-mítik/ *adj.* [ME f. OF (*h*)*ermite* or f. LL *eremita* f. Gk *erēmitēs* f. *erēmia* desert f. *erēmos* solitary]
■ recluse, eremite, anchorite, anchoress, solitary.

hermitage /hórmitij/ *n.* **1** a hermit's dwelling. **2** a monastery. **3** a solitary dwelling. [ME f. OF (*h*)*ermitage* (as HERMIT)]

hernia /hórneeə/ *n.* (*pl.* **hernias** or **herniae** /-nee-ee/) the displacement and protrusion of part of an organ through the wall of the cavity containing it, esp. of the abdomen. □□ **hernial** *adj.* **herniary** *adj.* **herniated** *adj.* [L]

hero /heeérō/ *n.* (*pl.* **-oes**) **1 a** a person noted or admired for nobility, courage, outstanding achievements, etc. (*Newton, a hero of science*). **b** a great warrior. **2** the chief male character in a poem, play, story, etc. **3** *Gk Antiq.* a man of superhuman qualities, favored by the gods; a demigod. **4** *dial.* = *submarine sandwich.* □ **hero's welcome** a rapturous welcome, like that given to a successful warrior. **hero-worship** *n.* **1** idealization of an admired man. **2** *Gk Antiq.* worship of the ancient heroes. ● *v.tr.* (**-worshiped, -worshiping** or **-worshipped, -worshipping**) worship as a hero; idolize. **hero-worshiper** (or **-worshipper**) a person engaging in hero-worship. [ME f. L *heros* f. Gk *hērōs*]
■ **1 a** champion, exemplar, luminary, notable; celebrity, star, superstar, idol. **b** knight, warrior, *hist.* paladin. **2** protagonist; (male) lead, star, leading man, principal. □ **hero-worship** (*n.*) idolization, idealization, adoration; cultism; see also WORSHIP *n.* (*v.*) see WORSHIP *v.*

heroic /hirōik/ *adj. & n.* ● *adj.* **1 a** (of an act or a quality) of or fit for a hero. **b** (of a person) like a hero. **2 a** (of language)

grand; high-flown; dramatic. **b** (of a work of art) heroic in scale or subject; unusually large or impressive. **3** of the heroes of Greek antiquity; (of poetry) dealing with the ancient heroes. ● *n.* (in *pl.*) **1 a** high-flown language or sentiments. **b** unduly bold behavior. **2** = *heroic verse*. □ **the heroic age** the period in Greek history before the return from Troy. **heroic couplet** two lines of rhyming iambic pentameters. **heroic verse** a type of verse used for heroic poetry, esp. the hexameter, the iambic pentameter, or the alexandrine. □□ **heroically** *adv.* [F *héroïque* or L *heroicus* f. Gk *hērōikos* (as HERO)]
■ *adj.* **1** brave, courageous, bold, valiant, valorous, dauntless, stouthearted, noble, upstanding, honorable, virtuous, staunch, steadfast, stalwart, intrepid, gallant, daring, fearless, manly; majestic, grand, august, towering, eminent, distinguished, prominent. **2 a** grand, high-flown, dramatic, bombastic, exaggerated, magniloquent, grandiose, extravagant. **b** epic, Homeric, wonderful; prodigious, larger than life, enormous, huge, titanic, colossal, stupendous. **3** epic, mythological, legendary, classical, fabulous. ● *n.* **1 b** (*heroics*) see BRAVADO.

heroicomic /hirōikómik/ *adj.* (also **heroicomical**) combining the heroic with the comic. [F *héroïcomique* (as HERO, COMIC)]

heroin /hérōin/ *n.* a highly addictive white crystalline analgesic drug derived from morphine, often used as a narcotic. [G (as HERO, supposedly from its effects on the user's self-esteem)]

heroine /hérōin/ *n.* **1** a woman noted or admired for nobility, courage, outstanding achievements, etc. **2** the chief female character in a poem, play, story, etc. **3** *Gk Antiq.* a demigoddess. [F *héroïne* or L *heroina* f. Gk *hērōinē*, fem. of *hērōs* HERO]
■ **1** see HERO 1a. **2** protagonist; (female) lead, star, leading lady, principal; diva, prima donna.

heroism /hérōizəm/ *n.* heroic conduct or qualities. [F *héroïsme* f. *héros* HERO]
■ see BRAVERY.

heroize /hérō-iz/ *v.* **1** *tr.* **a** make a hero of. **b** make heroic. **2** *intr.* play the hero.

heron /hérən/ *n.* any of various large wading birds of the family Ardeidae, esp. *Ardea cinerea*, with long legs and a long S-shaped neck. □□ **heronry** *n.* (*pl.* -**ies**). [ME f. OF *hairon* f. Gmc]

herpes /hárpeez/ *n.* a virus disease with outbreaks of blisters on the skin, etc. □ **herpes simplex** a viral infection which may produce blisters or conjunctivitis. **herpes zoster** /zóstər/ = SHINGLES. □□ **herpetic** /-pétik/ *adj.* [ME f. L f. Gk *herpēs* -*ētos* shingles f. *herpō* creep: *zoster* f. Gk *zōstēr* belt, girdle]

herpetology /hárpitóləjee/ *n.* the study of reptiles. □□ **herpetological** /-təlójikəl/ *adj.* **herpetologist** *n.* [Gk *herpeton* reptile f. *herpō* creep]

Herr /hair/ *n.* (*pl.* **Herren** /hérən/) **1** the title of a German man; Mr. **2** a German man. [G f. OHG *hērro* compar. of *hēr* exalted]

Herrenvolk /hérənfawlk/ *n.* **1** the German nation characterized by the Nazis as born to mastery. **2** a group regarding itself as naturally superior. [G, = master race (as HERR, FOLK)]

herring /héring/ *n.* a N. Atlantic fish, *Clupea harengus*, coming near the coast in large shoals to spawn. □ **herring gull** a large gull, *Larus argentatus*, with dark wing tips. [OE *hæring, hēring* f. WG]

herringbone /héringbōn/ *n. & v.* ● *n.* **1** a stitch with a zigzag pattern, resembling the pattern of a herring's bones. **2** this pattern, or cloth woven in it. **3** any zigzag pattern, e.g., in building. **4** *Skiing* a method of ascending a slope with the skis pointing outwards. ● *v.* **1** *tr.* **a** work with a herringbone stitch. **b** mark with a herringbone pattern. **2** *intr. Skiing* ascend a slope using the herringbone technique.

hers /hərz/ *poss.pron.* the one or ones belonging to or associated with her (*it is hers; hers are over there*). □ **of hers** of or belonging to her (*a friend of hers*).

herself /hərsélf/ *pron.* **1 a** *emphat. form* of SHE or HER (*she herself will do it*). **b** *refl. form* of HER (*she has hurt herself*). **2** in her normal state of body or mind (*does not feel quite herself today*). □ **be herself** act in her normal unconstrained manner. **by herself** see *by oneself.* [OE *hire self* (as HER, SELF)]

hertz /herts/ *n.* (*pl.* same) a unit of frequency, equal to one cycle per second. ¶ Abbr.: **Hz.** [H. R. *Hertz*, Ger. physicist d. 1894]

Hertzian wave /hártseeən/ *n.* an electromagnetic wave of a length suitable for use in radio.

he's /heez/ *contr.* **1** he is. **2** he has.

hesitant /hézit'nt/ *adj.* **1** hesitating; irresolute. **2** (of speech) stammering; faltering. □□ **hesitance** /-təns/ *n.* **hesitancy** *n.* **hesitantly** *adv.*
■ **1** undecided, hesitating, irresolute, uncertain, unresolved, ambivalent, in *or* of two minds, *Brit.* havering; see also CAUTIOUS. **2** halting, stammering, stuttering, faltering.

hesitate /hézitayt/ *v.intr.* **1** (often foll. by *about, over*) show or feel indecision or uncertainty; pause in doubt (*hesitated over her choice*). **2** (often foll. by *to* + infin.) be deterred by scruples; be reluctant (*I hesitate to inform against him*). **3** stammer or falter in speech. □□ **hesitater** *n.* **hesitatingly** *adv.* **hesitation** /-táyshən/ *n.* **hesitative** *adj.* [L *haesitare* frequent. of *haerēre haes-* stick fast]
■ **1** vacillate, dither, shilly-shally, waver, be in *or* of two minds, *Brit.* haver, *colloq.* dillydally. **2** hang back, think twice, demur; (*hesitate to*) be reluctant to, hold back from, balk at, shrink from, scruple to, esp. *Brit.* jib at, *colloq.* boggle at. **3** stammer, stutter, falter, sputter, splutter, stumble, hem and haw.

Hesperian /hespéereeən/ *adj. poet.* **1** western. **2** (in Greek mythology) of or concerning the Hesperides (nymphs who guarded the garden of golden apples at the western extremity of the earth). [L *Hesperius* f. Gk *Hesperios* (as HESPERUS)]

hesperidium /héspəridéeəm/ *n.* (*pl.* **hesperidia** /-deeə/) a fruit with sectioned pulp inside a separable rind, e.g., an orange or grapefruit. [Gk *Hesperides* daughters of Hesperus, nymphs in Greek mythology who guarded a tree of golden apples]

Hesperus /héspərəs/ *n.* the evening star, Venus. [ME f. L f. Gk *hesperos* (adj. & n.) western, evening (star)]

hessian /héshən/ *n. & adj.* ● *n.* **1** esp. *Brit.* a strong coarse sacking made of hemp or jute. **2** (Hessian) a native of Hesse in Germany. **3** (Hessian) a soldier from Hesse fighting for Britain during the Revolutionary War. ● *adj.* (Hessian) of or concerning Hesse. □ **Hessian boot** a tasseled high boot first worn by Hessian troops. **Hessian fly** a midge, *Mayetiola destructor*, whose larva destroys growing wheat (thought to have been brought to America by Hessian troops). [*Hesse* in Germany]

hest /hest/ *n. archaic* behest. [OE *hǣs* (see HIGHT), assim. to ME nouns in -*t*]

hetaera /hiteérə/ *n.* (also **hetaira** /-tírə/) (*pl.* -**as, hetaerae** /-teéree/, or **hetairai** /-tírī/) a courtesan or mistress, esp. in ancient Greece. [Gk *hetaira*, fem. of *hetairos* companion]
■ see PROSTITUTE *n.* 1a.

hetaerism /hiteérizəm/ *n.* (also **hetairism** /-tírizəm/) **1** a recognized system of concubinage. **2** communal marriage in a tribe. [Gk *hetairismos* prostitution (as HETAERA)]

hetero /hétərō/ *n.* (*pl.* -**os**) *colloq.* a heterosexual. [abbr.]
■ see STRAIGHT *n.* 4b.

hetero- /hétərō/ *comb. form* other; different (often opp. HOMO-). [Gk *heteros* other]

heterochromatic /hétərōkrōmátik/ *adj.* of several colors.

heteroclite /hétərəklīt/ *adj. & n.* ● *adj.* **1** abnormal. **2** *Gram.* (esp. of a noun) irregularly declined. ● *n.* **1** an abnormal thing or person. **2** *Gram.* an irregularly declined word, esp.

/. . ./ **pronunciation** ● **part of speech**
□ **phrases, idioms, and compounds**
□□ **derivatives** ■ **synonym section**
cross-references appear in SMALL CAPITALS or *italics*

a noun. [LL *heteroclitus* f. Gk (as HETERO-, *klitos* f. *klinō* bend, inflect)]
■ *adj.* **1** see UNORTHODOX.

heterocyclic /hétərōsíklik, -síklik/ *adj. Chem.* (of a compound) with a bonded ring of atoms of more than one kind.

heterodox /hétərədoks/ *adj.* (of a person, opinion, etc.) not orthodox. □□ **heterodoxy** *n.* [LL *heterodoxus* f. Gk (as HETERO-, *doxos* f. *doxa* opinion)]
■ see *heretical* (HERETIC).

heterodyne /hétərədīn/ *adj. & v. Radio* ● *adj.* relating to the production of a lower frequency from the combination of two almost equal high frequencies. ● *v.intr.* produce a lower frequency in this way.

heterogamous /hétərógəməs/ *adj.* **1** *Bot.* irregular as regards stamens and pistils. **2** *Biol.* characterized by heterogamy or heterogony.

heterogamy /hétərógəmee/ *n.* **1** the alternation of generations, esp. of a sexual and parthenogenic generation. **2** sexual reproduction by fusion of unlike gametes. **3** *Bot.* a state in which the flowers of a plant are of two types.

heterogeneous /hétərōjéeneeəs, -nyəs/ *adj.* **1** diverse in character. **2** varied in content. **3** *Math.* incommensurable through being of different kinds or degrees. □□ **heterogeneity** /-jineéitee/ *n.* **heterogeneously** *adv.* **heterogeneousness** *n.* [med.L *heterogeneus* f. Gk *heterogenēs* (as HETERO-, *genos* kind)]
■ **1, 2** see DIVERSE.

heterogenesis /hétərōjénisis/ *n.* **1** the birth of a living being otherwise than from parents of the same kind. **2** spontaneous generation from inorganic matter. □□ **heterogenetic** /-jinétik/ *adj.*

heterogony /hétərógənee/ *n.* the alternation of generations, esp. of a sexual and hermaphroditic generation. □□ **heterogonous** *adj.*

heterograft /hétərōgraaft/ *n.* living tissue grafted from one individual to another of a different species.

heterologous /hétəróləgəs/ *adj.* not homologous. □□ **heterology** *n.*

heteromerous /hétərómərəs/ *adj.* not isomerous.

heteromorphic /hétərōmáwrfik/ *adj. Biol.* **1** of dissimilar forms. **2** (of insects) existing in different forms at different stages in their life cycle.

heteromorphism /hétərōmáwrfizəm/ *n.* existing in various forms.

heteronomous /hétərónəməs/ *adj.* **1** subject to an external law (cf. AUTONOMOUS). **2** *Biol.* subject to different laws (of growth, etc.).

heteronomy /hétərónəmee/ *n.* **1** the presence of a different law. **2** subjection to an external law.

heteropathic /hétərōpáthik/ *adj.* **1** allopathic. **2** differing in effect.

heterophyllous /hétərōfíləs/ *adj.* bearing leaves of different forms on the same plant. □□ **heterophylly** *n.* [HETERO- + Gk *phullon* leaf]

heteropolar /hétərōpốlər/ *adj.* having dissimilar poles, esp. *Electr.* with an armature passing north and south magnetic poles alternately.

heteropteran /hétəróptərən/ *n.* any insect of the suborder Heteroptera, including bugs, with nonuniform forewings having a thickened base and membranous tip (cf. HOMOPTERAN). □□ **heteropterous** *adj.* [HETERO- + Gk *pteron* wing]

heterosexual /hétərōséksh ōəl/ *adj. & n.* ● *adj.* **1** feeling or involving sexual attraction to persons of the opposite sex. **2** concerning heterosexual relations or people. **3** relating to the opposite sex. ● *n.* a heterosexual person. □□ **heterosexuality** /-shōóálitee/ *n.* **heterosexually** *adv.*
■ *adj.* **1, 2** see STRAIGHT *adj.* 9b. ● *n.* see STRAIGHT *n.* 4b.

heterosis /hétərōsis/ *n.* the tendency of a crossbred individual to show qualities superior to those of both parents. [Gk f. *heteros* different]

heterotaxy /hétərōtaksee/ *n.* the abnormal disposition of organs or parts. [HETERO- + Gk *taxis* arrangement]

heterotransplant /hétərōtránsplaant/ *n.* = HETEROGRAFT.

heterotrophic /hétərōtrốfik, -trófik/ *adj. Biol.* deriving its nourishment and carbon requirements from organic substances; not autotrophic. [HETERO- + Gk *trophos* feeder]

heterozygote /hétərōzígōt/ *n. Biol.* **1** a zygote resulting from the fusion of unlike gametes. **2** an individual with dominant and recessive alleles determining a particular characteristic. □□ **heterozygous** *adj.*

hetman /hétmən/ *n.* (*pl.* **-men**) a Polish or Cossack military commander. [Pol., prob. f. G *Hauptmann* captain]

het up /hét úp/ *adj. colloq.* excited; overwrought. [*het* dial. past part. of HEAT]
■ see JUMPY 1.

heuchera /hyóōkərə/ *n.* any N. American herbaceous plant of the genus *Heuchera*, with dark green round or heart-shaped leaves and tiny flowers. [mod.L f. J. H. von *Heucher*, Ger. botanist d. 1747]

heuristic /hyōōrístik/ *adj. & n.* ● *adj.* **1** allowing or assisting to discover. **2** *Computing* proceeding to a solution by trial and error. ● *n.* **1** the science of heuristic procedure. **2** a heuristic process or method. **3** (in *pl.*, usu. treated as *sing.*) *Computing* the study and use of heuristic techniques in data processing. □ **heuristic method** a system of education under which pupils are trained to find out things for themselves. □□ **heuristically** *adv.* [irreg. f. Gk *heuriskō* find]

hevea /héeveeə/ *n.* any S. American tree of the genus *Hevea*, yielding a milky sap used for making rubber. [mod.L f. native name *hevé*]

HEW *abbr. US hist.* Department of Health, Education, and Welfare (1953-79).

hew /hyōō/ *v.* (*past part.* **hewn** /hyōōn/ or **hewed**) **1** *tr.* **a** (often foll. by *down, away, off*) chop or cut (a thing) with an ax, a sword, etc. **b** cut (a block of wood, etc.) into shape. **2** *intr.* (often foll. by *at, among*, etc.) strike cutting blows. **3** *intr.* (usu. foll. by *to*) conform. □ **hew one's way** make a way for oneself by hewing. [OE *hēawan* f. Gmc]
■ **1, 2** see CHOP¹ *v.* 1.

hewer /hyóōər/ *n.* **1** a person who hews. **2** a person who cuts coal from a seam. □ **hewers of wood and drawers of water** menial drudges; laborers (Josh. 9:21).

hex /heks/ *v. & n.* ● *v.* **1** *intr.* practice witchcraft. **2** *tr.* cast a spell on; bewitch. ● *n.* **1** a magic spell; a curse. **2** a witch. [Pennsylvanian G *hexe* (v.), *Hex* (n.), f. G *hexen, Hexe*]
● *v.* **2** see BEWITCH 2. ● *n.* **1** see JINX *n.*

hexa- /héksə/ *comb. form* six. [Gk *hex* six]

hexachord /héksəkawrd/ *n.* a diatonic series of six notes with a semitone between the third and fourth, used at three different pitches in medieval music. [HEXA- + CHORD¹]

hexad /héksad/ *n.* a group of six. [Gk *hexas -ados* f. *hex* six]

hexadecimal /héksədésiməl/ *adj. & n.* (also **hex**) esp. *Computing* ● *adj.* relating to or using a system of numerical notation that has 16 rather than 10 as a base. ● *n.* the hexadecimal system; hexadecimal notation. □□ **hexadecimally** *adv.*

hexagon /héksəgən/ *n.* a plane figure with six sides and angles. □□ **hexagonal** /-ságənəl/ *adj.* [LL *hexagonum* f. Gk (as HEXA-, -GON)]

hexagram /héksəgram/ *n.* **1** a figure formed by two intersecting equilateral triangles. **2** a figure of six lines. [HEXA- + Gk *gramma* line]

hexahedron /héksəheédrən/ *n.* a solid figure with six faces. □□ **hexahedral** *adj.* [Gk (as HEXA-, -HEDRON)]

hexameter /heksámitər/ *n.* a line or verse of six metrical feet. □ **dactylic hexameter** a hexameter having five dactyls and a spondee or trochee, any of the first five feet, and sometimes the fifth, being replaceable by a spondee. □□ **hexametric** /-səmétrik/ *adj.* **hexametrist** *n.* [ME f. L f. Gk *hexametros* (as HEXA-, *metron* measure)]

hexane /héksayn/ *n. Chem.* a liquid hydrocarbon of the alkane series. ¶ *Chem. formula:* C_6H_{14}. [HEXA- + -ANE²]

hexapla /héksəplə/ *n.* a sixfold text, esp. of the Old Testament, in parallel columns. [Gk neut. pl. of *hexaploos* (as HEXA-, *ploos* -fold), orig. of Origen's OT text]

hexapod /héksəpod/ *n. & adj.* ● *n.* any arthropod with six legs; an insect. ● *adj.* having six legs. [Gk *hexapous, hexapod-* (as HEXA-, *pous pod-* foot)]

hexastyle /héksəstīl/ *n. & adj.* ● *n.* a six-columned portico.

• *adj.* having six columns. [Gk *hexastulos* (as HEXA-, *stulos* column)]

Hexateuch /héksətoۊok, -tyooۊok/ *n.* the first six books of the Old Testament. [Gk *hex* six + *teukhos* book]

hexavalent /héksəváylənt/ *adj.* having a valence of six; sexivalent.

hexose /héksōs/ *n. Biochem.* a monosaccharide with six carbon atoms in each molecule, e.g., glucose or fructose. [HEXA- + -OSE²]

hey¹ /hay/ *int.* calling attention or expressing joy, surprise, inquiry, enthusiasm, etc. □ **hey presto!** *Brit.* a phrase of command, or indicating a successful trick, used by a magician, etc. [ME: cf. OF *hay*, Du., G *hei*]

hey² var. of HAY².

heyday /háyday/ *n.* the flush or full bloom of youth, vigor, prosperity, etc. [archaic *heyday* expression of joy, surprise, etc.: cf. LG *heidi, heida*, excl. denoting gaiety]

■ see PRIME¹ *n.* 1.

HF *abbr.* high frequency.

Hf *symb. Chem.* the element hafnium.

hf. *abbr.* half.

HG *abbr.* Her or His Grace.

Hg *symb. Chem.* the element mercury. [mod.L *hydrargyrum*]

hg *abbr.* hectogram(s).

hgt. *abbr.* height.

hgwy. *abbr.* highway.

HH *abbr.* **1** His Holiness. **2** double hard (pencil lead). **3** *Brit.* Her or His Highness.

hh. *abbr.* hands (see HAND *n.* 13).

hhd. *abbr.* hogshead(s).

H-hour /áychowr/ *n.* the hour at which a military operation is scheduled to begin. [*H* for *hour* + HOUR]

HHS *abbr.* (Department of) Health and Human Services.

HI *abbr.* **1** Hawaii (also in official postal use). **2** the Hawaiian Islands.

hi /hī/ *int.* expression of greeting or (*Brit.*) to call attention. [parallel form to HEY¹]

hiatus /hīáytəs/ *n.* (*pl.* **hiatuses**) **1** a break or gap, esp. in a series, account, or chain of proof. **2** *Prosody & Gram.* a break between two vowels coming together but not in the same syllable, as in *though oft the ear.* □□ **hiatal** *adj.* [L, = gaping f. *hiare* gape]

■ **1** see SPACE *n.* 4.

hibachi /həbáachee/ *n.* a small charcoal-burning brazier for grilling food. [Jap.]

hibernate /híbərnayt/ *v.intr.* **1** (of some animals) spend the winter in a dormant state. **2** remain inactive. □□ **hibernation** /-náyshən/ *n.* **hibernator** *n.* [L *hibernare* f. *hibernus* wintry]

Hibernian /hībэ́rneeən/ *adj. & n. archaic poet.* • *adj.* of or concerning Ireland. • *n.* a native of Ireland. [L *Hibernia, Iverna* f. Gk *Iernē* f. OCelt.]

Hibernicism /hībэ́rnisizəm/ *n.* an Irish idiom or expression; = BULL³ 1. [as HIBERNIAN after *Anglicism*, etc.]

Hiberno- /hībэ́rnō/ *comb. form* Irish (*Hiberno-British*). [med.L *hibernus* Irish (as HIBERNIAN)]

hibiscus /hibískəs/ *n.* any tree or shrub of the genus *Hibiscus*, cultivated for its large bright-colored flowers. Also called *rose mallow*. [L f. Gk *hibiskos* marsh mallow]

hic /hik/ *int.* expressing the sound of a hiccup, esp. a drunken hiccup. [imit.]

hiccup /híkup/ *n. & v.* (also **hiccough**) • *n.* **1 a** an involuntary spasm of the diaphragm and respiratory organs, with sudden closure of the glottis and characteristic coughlike sound. **b** (in *pl.*) an attack of such spasms. **2** a temporary or minor stoppage or difficulty. • *v.* **1** *intr.* make a hiccup or series of hiccups. **2** *tr.* utter with a hiccup. □□ **hiccupy** *adj.* [imit.]

■ *n.* **2** see SETBACK 1.

hic jacet /hik jáyset, heek yáaket/ *n.* an epitaph. [L, = here lies]

hick /hik/ *n. colloq.* a country dweller; a provincial. [nickname for the name *Richard*: cf. DICK¹]

■ see PROVINCIAL *n.*

hickey /híkee/ *n.* (*pl.* **-eys**) *colloq.* **1** a gadget (cf. DOOHICKEY).

2 a reddish mark on the skin, esp. one produced by a sucking kiss. [20th c.: orig. unkn.]

■ **1** see GADGET.

hickory /híkəree/ *n.* (*pl.* **-ies**) **1** any N. American tree of the genus *Carya*, yielding tough heavy wood and bearing nutlike edible fruits (see PECAN). **2 a** the wood of these trees. **b** a stick made of this. [native Virginian *pohickery*]

hid *past* of HIDE¹.

hidalgo /hidálgō, eetháal-/ *n.* (*pl.* **-os**) a Spanish gentleman. [Sp. f. *hijo dalgo* son of something]

■ caballero, don.

hidden *past part.* of HIDE¹ □□ **hiddenness** *n.*

hide¹ /hīd/ *v. & n.* • *v.* (*past* **hid** /hid/; *past part.* **hidden** /hídən/ or *archaic* **hid**) **1** *tr.* put or keep out of sight (*hid it under the cushion; hid her in the closet*). **2** *intr.* conceal oneself. **3** *tr.* (usu. foll. by *from*) keep (a fact) secret (*hid his real motive from her*). **4** *tr.* conceal (a thing) from sight intentionally or not (*trees hid the house*). • *n. Brit.* = BLIND 6. □ **hidden agenda** a secret motivation behind a policy, statement, etc.; an ulterior motive. **hidden reserves** extra profits, resources, etc., kept concealed in reserve. **hide-and-seek** **1** a children's game in which one or more players seek a child or children hiding. **2** a process of attempting to find an evasive person or thing. **hide one's head** keep out of sight, esp. from shame. **hide one's light under a bushel** conceal one's merits (Matthew 5:15). **hide out** remain in concealment. **hide-out** *colloq.* a hiding place. □□ **hidden** *adj.* **hider** *n.* [OE *hȳdan* f. WG]

■ *v.* **1** conceal, secrete, cache, squirrel away, cover up. **2** go underground, take cover, lie low, lurk, go to ground, drop out of sight, go into hiding, hide out, *colloq.* hole up, *Brit. sl.* lie doggo. **3** conceal, cover (up), mask, camouflage, disguise, veil, shroud, screen, keep secret *or* quiet, suppress, hush (up), repress, silence; (*hide from*) keep from. **4** conceal, blot out; see also OBSCURE *v.* 3. □ **hide-out** see HIDEAWAY. □□ **hidden** concealed, secret, obscure(d), occult, veiled, cryptic, recondite, arcane, covert, esoteric, unseen, private.

hide² /hīd/ *n. & v.* • *n.* **1** the skin of an animal, esp. when tanned or dressed. **2** *colloq.* the human skin (*saved his own hide; I'll tan your hide*). **3** esp. *Austral. & NZ colloq.* impudence; effrontery; nerve. • *v.tr. colloq.* flog. □□ **hided** *adj.* (also in *comb.*). [OE *hȳd* f. Gmc]

■ *n.* **1** pelt, skin, fell. • *v.* whip, lash, flail, beat, thrash; see also FLOG 1a.

hide³ /hīd/ *n.* a former English measure of land large enough to support a family and its dependents, usu. between 60 and 120 acres. [OE *hī(gi)d* f. *hīw-, hīg-* household]

hideaway /hídəway/ *n.* a hiding place or place of retreat.

■ refuge, haven, retreat, sanctuary, hiding place, lair, den, hole, *colloq.* hidey-hole, hide-out.

hidebound /hídbownd/ *adj.* **1 a** narrow-minded; bigoted. **b** (of the law, rules, etc.) constricted by tradition. **2** (of cattle) with the skin clinging close as a result of bad feeding. [HIDE² + BOUND⁴]

■ **1 a** narrow-minded, bigoted, illiberal, intolerant; straitlaced, conventional, conservative, reactionary, rigid, set in one's ways, inflexible, intractable. **b** bound, constricted, constrained, limited, restricted, hemmed in.

hideosity /hídeeósitee/ *n.* (*pl.* **-ies**) **1** a hideous object. **2** hideousness.

hideous /hídeeəs/ *adj.* **1** frightful, repulsive, or revolting, to the senses or the mind (*a hideous monster; a hideous pattern*). **2** *colloq.* unpleasant. □□ **hideously** *adv.* **hideousness** *n.* [ME *hidous* f. AF *hidous*, OF *hidos, -eus*, f. OF *hide, hisde* fear, of unkn. orig.]

■ **1** frightful, grotesque, ugly, repulsive, revolting, disgusting, horrible, repellent, monstrous, beastly,

---

/.../ **pronunciation**	● **part of speech**
□ **phrases, idioms, and compounds**	
□□ **derivatives**	■ **synonym section**
cross-references appear in SMALL CAPITALS or *italics*	

gorgonian, unsightly, ghastly, grisly, gruesome, foul, abhorrent, heinous, horrifying, appalling, outrageous, abominable, vile, shocking, loathsome, contemptible, hateful, odious, atrocious, horrific, damnable, execrable. **2** see REVOLTING.

hidey-hole /hídeehōl/ n. colloq. a hiding place.

hiding[1] /hídiŋ/ n. colloq. a thrashing. □ **on a hiding to nothing** Brit. in a position from which there can be no successful outcome. [HIDE[2] + -ING[1]]
■ see thrashing (THRASH).

hiding[2] /hídiŋ/ n. **1** the act or an instance of hiding. **2** the state of remaining hidden (go into hiding). □ **hiding place** a place of concealment. [ME, f. HIDE[1] + -ING[1]]

hidrosis /hidrósis/ n. Med. perspiration. □□ **hidrotic** /-drótik/ adj. [mod.L f. Gk f. hidrōs sweat]

hie /hī/ v.intr. & refl. (**hies, hied, hieing** or **hying**) esp. archaic or poet. go quickly (hie to your chamber; hied him to the chase). [OE hīgian strive, pant, of unkn. orig.]
■ see RUN v. 1, 3.

hierarch /híəraark/ n. **1** a chief priest. **2** an archbishop. □□ **hierarchal** adj. [med.L f. Gk hierarkhēs f. hieros sacred + -arkhēs ruler]

hierarchy /híəraarkee/ n. (pl. -ies) **1 a** a system in which grades or classes of status or authority are ranked one above the other (ranks third in the hierarchy). **b** the hierarchical system (of government, management, etc.). **2 a** priestly government. **b** a priesthood organized in grades. **3 a** each of the three divisions of angels. **b** the angels. □□ **hierarchic** adj. /-raárkik/ **hierarchical** adj. **hierarchism** n. **hierarchize** v.tr. [ME f. OF ierarchie f. med.L (h)ierarchia f. Gk hierarkhia (as HIERARCH)]
■ **1** see ORDER n. 4.

hieratic /híərátik/ adj. **1** of or concerning priests; priestly. **2** of the ancient Egyptian writing of abridged hieroglyphics as used by priests (opp. DEMOTIC). **3** of or concerning Egyptian or Greek traditional styles of art. □□ **hieratically** adv. [L f. Gk hieratikos f. hieraomai be a priest f. hiereus priest]
■ **1** see PRIESTLY.

hiero- /híərō/ comb. form sacred; holy. [Gk hieros sacred + -o-]

hierocracy /hírókrəsee/ n. (pl. -ies) **1** priestly rule. **2** a body of ruling priests. [HIERO- + -CRACY]

hieroglyph /híərəglif/ n. **1 a** a picture of an object representing a word, syllable, or sound, as used in ancient Egyptian and other writing. **b** a writing consisting of characters of this kind. **2** a secret or enigmatic symbol. **3** (in pl.) = HIEROGLYPHIC n. 2. [back-form. f. HIEROGLYPHIC]
■ **1a, 2** see SIGN n. 2.

hieroglyphic /híərəglífik/ adj. & n. ● adj. **1** of or written in hieroglyphs. **2** symbolic. ● n. (in pl.) **1** hieroglyphs; hieroglyphic writing. **2** joc. writing difficult to read. □□ **hieroglyphical** adj. **hieroglyphically** adv. [F hiéroglyphique or LL hieroglyphicus f. Gk hieroglyphikos (as HIERO-, gluphikos f. gluphē carving)]

hierogram /híərəgram/ n. a sacred inscription or symbol.

hierograph /híərəgraf/ n. = HIEROGRAM.

hierolatry /hírólətree/ n. the worship of saints or sacred things.

hierology /híróləjee/ n. sacred literature or lore.

hierophant /híərəfant/ n. **1** Gk Antiq. an initiating or presiding priest; an official interpreter of sacred mysteries. **2** an interpreter of sacred mysteries or any esoteric principle. □□ **hierophantic** /-fántik/ adj. [LL hierophantes f. Gk hierophantēs (as HIERO-, phantēs f. phainō show)]

hi-fi /hífí/ adj. & n. colloq. ● adj. of high fidelity. ● n. (pl. **hi-fis**) a set of equipment for high fidelity sound reproduction. [abbr.]

higgle /hígəl/ v.intr. dispute about terms; haggle. [var. of HAGGLE]
■ see HAGGLE v.

higgledy-piggledy /hígəldeepígəldee/ adv., adj., & n. ● adv. & adj. in confusion or disorder. ● n. a state of disordered confusion. [rhyming jingle, prob. with ref. to the irregular herding together of pigs]
■ adv. & adj. see chaotic (CHAOS). ● n. see CHAOS 1a.

high /hī/ adj., n., & adv. ● adj. **1 a** of great vertical extent (a high building). **b** (predic.; often in comb.) of a specified height (one inch high; water was waist-high). **2 a** far above ground or sea level, etc. (a high altitude). **b** inland, esp. when raised (High Plains). **3** extending above the normal or average level (high boots; sweater with a high neck). **4** of exalted, esp. spiritual, quality (high minds; high principles; high art). **5 a** of exalted rank (in high society; is high in the government). **b** important; serious; grave. **6 a** great; intense; extreme; powerful (high praise; high temperature). **b** greater than normal (high prices). **c** extreme in religious or political opinion (high Tory). **7** (of physical action, esp. athletics) performed at, to, or from a considerable height (high diving; high flying). **8 a** elated; merry. **b** colloq. (often foll. by on) intoxicated by alcohol or esp. drugs. **9** (of a sound or note) of high frequency; shrill; at the top end of the scale. **10** (of a period, an age, a time, etc.) at its peak (high noon; high summer; High Renaissance). **11 a** (of meat) beginning to go bad; off. **b** (of game) well-hung and slightly decomposed. **12** Geog. (of latitude) near the North or South Pole. **13** Phonet. (of a vowel) close (see CLOSE[1] adj. 14). ● n. **1** a high, or the highest, level or figure. **2** an area of high barometric pressure; an anticyclone. **3** sl. a euphoric drug-induced state. **4** top gear in a motor vehicle. **5** colloq. high school. **6** (**the High**) Brit. colloq. a High Street, esp. that in Oxford. ● adv. **1** far up; aloft (flew the flag high). **2** in or to a high degree. **3** at a high price. **4** (of a sound) at or to a high pitch (sang high). □ **ace** (or **king** or **queen**, etc.) **high** (in card games) having the ace, etc., as the highest-ranking card. **from on high** from heaven or a high place. **High Admiral**, etc., Brit. a chief officer. **high altar** the chief altar of a church. **high and dry 1** out of the current of events; stranded. **2** (of a ship) out of the water. **high and low 1** everywhere (searched high and low). **2** (people) of all conditions. **high and mighty 1** colloq. arrogant. **2** archaic of exalted rank. **high beam** full, bright illumination from a motor vehicle's headlight. **high camp** sophisticated camp (cf. CAMP[2]). **high card** a card that outranks others, esp. the ace or a face card. **high chair** an infant's chair with long legs and a tray, for use at meals. **High Church** n. (in the Anglican communion) emphasizing Catholic tradition, as to ritual, church authority, and sacraments. ● adj. of or relating to this. **High Churchman** (pl. **-men**) an advocate of High Church principles. **high-class 1** of high quality. **2** characteristic of the upper class. **high color** a flushed complexion. **high command** an army commander-in-chief and associated staff. **High Commission** an embassy from one British Commonwealth country to another. **High Commissioner** the head of such an embassy. **High Court 1** the US Supreme Court. **2** (in England also **High Court of Justice**) a supreme court of justice for civil cases. **high day** a festal day. **High Dutch** see DUTCH. **high enema** an enema delivered into the colon. **higher animal** (or **plant**) an animal or plant evolved to a high degree. **higher court** Law a court that can overrule the decision of another. **the higher criticism** see CRITICISM. **higher education** education beyond high school, esp. to degree level. **higher mathematics** advanced mathematics as taught at the college level. **higher-up** colloq. a person of higher rank. **highest common factor** Math. the highest number that can be divided exactly into each of two or more numbers. **high explosive** an extremely explosive substance used in shells, bombs, etc. **high fashion** = HAUTE COUTURE. **high fidelity** the reproduction of sound with little distortion, giving a result very similar to the original. **High finance** financial transactions involving large sums. **high five** gesture in which two people slap each other's raised palm, esp. out of elation. **high-flown** (of language, etc.) extravagant; bombastic. **high-flyer** (or **-flier**) **1** an ambitious person. **2** a person or thing with great potential for achievement. **high-flying** reaching a great height; ambitious. **high frequency** a frequency, esp. in radio, of 3 to 30 megahertz. **high gear** see GEAR. **High German** see GERMAN. **high-grade** of high quality. **high hat 1** a tall hat; a top hat. **2** foot-operated cymbals. **3** a snobbish or overbearing person. **high-hat** adj. supercilious; snobbish. ● v. (**-hatted, -hat-**

ting) **1** *tr.* treat superciliously. **2** *intr.* assume a superior attitude. **High Holiday** (also **High Holy Day**) the Jewish New Year or the Day of Atonement. **high jinks** boisterous joking or merrymaking. **high jump 1** an athletic event consisting of jumping as high as possible over a bar of adjustable height. **2** *Brit. colloq.* a drastic punishment (*he's for the high jump*). **high-key** *Photog.* consisting of light tones only. **high kick** a dancer's kick high in the air. **high-level 1** (of negotiations, etc.) conducted by high-ranking people. **2** *Computing* (of a programming language) that is not machine-dependent and is usu. at a level of abstraction close to natural language. **high life** (or **living**) a luxurious existence ascribed to the upper classes. **high-lows** *archaic* boots reaching over the ankles. **High Mass** see MASS². **high-occupancy vehicle** a commuter vehicle carrying several (or many) passengers. ¶ Abbr.: **HOV. high-octane** (of gasoline, etc.) having good antiknock properties. **high old** *colloq.* most enjoyable (*had a high old time*). **high opinion** of a favorable opinion of. **high-pitched 1** (of a sound) high. **2** (of a roof) steep. **3** (of style, etc.) lofty. **4** at a high level of energy; intense. **high places** the upper ranks of an organization, etc. **high point** the maximum or best state reached. **high polymer** a polymer having a high molecular weight. **high-powered 1** having great power or energy. **2** important or influential. **high pressure 1** a high degree of activity or exertion. **2** a condition of the atmosphere with the pressure above average. **high priest 1** a chief priest, esp. in early Judaism. **2** the head of any cult. **high profile** exposure to attention or publicity. **high-profile** *adj.* (usu. *attrib.*) having a high profile. **high-ranking** of high rank; senior. **high relief** a method of molding or carving or stamping in which the design or figures stand clearly out from the surface. **high-rise 1** (of a building) having many stories. **2** such a building. **high-risk** (usu. *attrib.*) involving or exposed to danger (*high-risk sports*). **high road 1** (usu. foll. by *to*) a direct route (*on the high road to success*). **2** *Brit.* a main road. **high roller** *sl.* a person who gambles large sums or spends freely. **high school 1** a secondary school. **2** *Brit.* a grammar school. **high sea** (or **seas**) open seas not within any country's jurisdiction. **high season** the period of the greatest number of visitors at a vacation destination, etc. **High Sheriff** see SHERIFF. **high sign** *colloq.* a surreptitious gesture indicating that all is well or that the coast is clear. **high-sounding** pretentious; bombastic. **high-speed 1** operating at great speed. **2** (of steel) suitable for cutting tools even when red-hot. **high-spirited** vivacious; cheerful. **high-spiritedness** = *high spirits*. **high spirits** vivacity; energy; cheerfulness. **high spot** *sl.* an important place or feature. **high-stepper 1** a horse that lifts its feet high when walking or trotting. **2** a stately person. **High Steward** see STEWARD *n.* 6. **high street** *Brit.* a main road, esp. the principal shopping street of a town. **high-strung** very sensitive or nervous. **high table** *Brit.* a table on a platform at a public dinner or for the fellows of a college. **high tea** *Brit.* a main evening meal usu. consisting of a cooked dish, bread and butter, tea, etc. **high tech** *n.* = *high technology.* ● *adj.* **1** (of interior design, etc.) imitating styles more usual in industry, etc., esp. using steel, glass, or plastic in a functional way. **2** employing, requiring, or involved in high technology. **high technology** advanced technological development, esp. in electronics. **high-tensile** (of metal) having great tensile strength. **high tension** = *high-voltage* 1. **high tide** the time or level of the tide at its flow. **high time** a time that is late or overdue (*it is high time they arrived*). **high-toned** stylish; dignified; superior. **high tops** shoes, esp. sports shoes or sneakers, that cover the ankle. **high treason** see TREASON. **high-up** *colloq.* a person of high rank. **high-voltage 1** electrical potential causing some danger of injury or damage. **2** energetic; dynamic (*a high-voltage presentation*). **high water 1** the tide at its fullest. **2** the time of this. **high-water mark 1** the level reached at high water. **2** the maximum recorded value or highest point of excellence. **high, wide, and handsome** *colloq.* in a carefree or stylish manner. **high wire** a high tightrope. **high words** angry talk. **high yellow** *offens. sl.* a black person with palish skin. **in high feather** see

FEATHER. **the Most High** God. **on high** in or to heaven or a high place. **on one's high horse** *colloq.* behaving superciliously or arrogantly. **play high** *Brit.* **1** play for high stakes. **2** play a card of high value. **run high 1** (of the sea) have a strong current with high tide. **2** (of feelings) be strong. [OE *hēah* f. Gmc]

■ *adj.* **1 a** tall, elevated, towering, *literary* lofty. **4** exalted, elevated, lofty, superior, great; high-class. **5 a** chief, leading, important, principal, foremost; see also SUPERIOR *adj.* 1. **b** important, consequential, grave, serious, weighty, momentous. **6 a** great, intense, huge, enormous, considerable, strong, extreme, powerful. **b** extreme, excessive; exorbitant, *(predic.) colloq.* stiff, steep. **c** hard-line, extreme; see also *fanatical* (FANATIC). **8 a** cheerful, exuberant, merry, elated, boisterous, exhilarated, excited, *colloq.* switched-on. **b** intoxicated, inebriated, drunk, drugged, tipsy, *colloq.* turned-on, switched-on, on a trip, *sl.* loaded, stoned, spaced-out, squiffed, esp. *Brit. sl.* squiffy; euphoric. **9** high-pitched, shrill, squeaky, sharp, penetrating, piercing, ear-splitting, acute; treble, soprano. **10** mid-; late. **11** off, tainted, gamy, ripe, *Brit. colloq.* pongy. ● *n.* **1** peak, record, height, high point, maximum, acme, apex. **3** see TRANCE *n.* ● *adv.* **1** far up, aloft; see also ABOVE *adv.* 1. **2** well, far, greatly, highly. **3** dear, up, sky-high, *colloq.* through the roof. □ **high and dry** stranded, marooned, out on a limb, isolated, cut off. **high and low 1** see EVERYWHERE. **high and mighty 1** see ARROGANT. **high-class** first-rate, superior, high-grade, *colloq.* top-drawer, tiptop, A1; aristocratic, upper-class, elite, select, exclusive, upper crust, *colloq.* classy, tony. **high color** flush, blush, redness; glow, radiance, rosiness, bloom. **high day** feast, feast day, holy day, holiday, festal day, festival, celebration, fête, gala, red-letter day. **higher-up** see SUPERIOR *n.* **high-flown** see *bombastic* (BOMBAST). **high-flyer 1** high achiever, self-starter, arriviste, *colloq.* whiz kid. **high-flying** see AMBITIOUS 1a. **high-grade** see SUPERIOR *adj.* 2a. **high-hat** (*adj.*) see HAUGHTY. **high jinks** see FROLIC *n.* 5. **high-pitched 1** see HIGH *adj.* 9 above. **2** see STEEP¹ *adj.* 1. **3** see REFINED 1. **high point** see ZENITH. **high-powered 1** see POWERFUL 1. **2** see POWERFUL 2. **high-profile** see PROMINENT 2. **high-ranking** see SENIOR *adj.* **high-risk** see DANGEROUS. **high-sounding** see PRETENTIOUS 2. **high-spirited** see VIVACIOUS. **high spirits** see VITALITY 1. **high spot** see SIGHT *n.* 2. **high-strung** see NERVOUS 1-3, 5. **high-toned** see SUPERIOR *adj.* 2a. **high-up** see SUPERIOR *n.* **high, wide, and handsome** stylishly, with style; see also EASY *adv.*

highball /híbawl/ *n.* **1** a drink of liquor (esp. whiskey) and soda, etc., served with ice in a tall glass. **2** a railroad signal to proceed.

highbinder /híbindər/ *n.* a ruffian; a swindler; an assassin.
■ see THIEF.

highborn /híbawrn/ *adj.* of noble birth.
■ see NOBLE *adj.* 1.

highboy /híboy/ *n.* a tall chest of drawers on legs.
■ see *chest of drawers.*

highbrow /híbrow/ *adj.* & *n. colloq.* ● *adj.* intellectual; cultural. ● *n.* an intellectual or cultured person.
■ *adj.* scholarly, intellectual, learned, erudite, bookish, cultured, cultivated; cultural. ● *n.* scholar, *colloq.* egghead, brain; see also INTELLECTUAL *n.*

highfalutin /hífəlōōt'n/ *adj.* & *n.* (also **highfaluting** /-ing/) *colloq.* ● *adj.* absurdly pompous or pretentious. ● *n.* highfalutin speech or writing. [HIGH + -*falutin*, of unkn. orig.]
■ *adj.* see POMPOUS 1.

high-handed /híhándid/ *adj.* disregarding others' feelings; overbearing. □□ **high-handedly** *adv.* **high-handedness** *n.*

/.../ **pronunciation**	● **part of speech**
□ **phrases, idioms, and compounds**	
□□ **derivatives**	■ **synonym section**
cross-references appear in SMALL CAPITALS or *italics*	

■ see *overbearing* (OVERBEAR).

highland /hílənd/ *n. & adj.* ● *n.* (usu. in *pl.*) **1** an area of high land. **2** (**the Highlands**) the mountainous part of Scotland. ● *adj.* of or in a highland or the Highlands. □ **Highland cattle 1** cattle of a shaggy-haired breed with long curved widely-spaced horns. **2** this breed. **Highland dress** the kilt, etc. **Highland fling** see FLING *n.* 3. □□ **highlander** *n.* (also **Highlander**). **Highlandman** *n.* (*pl.* **-men**). [OE *hēahlond* promontory (as HIGH, LAND)]

■ *n.* **1** see RISE *n.* 2.

highlight /hílit/ *n. & v.* ● *n.* **1** (in a painting, etc.) a light area, or one seeming to reflect light. **2** a moment or detail of vivid interest; an outstanding feature. **3** (usu. in *pl.*) a bright tint in the hair produced by bleaching. ● *v.tr.* **1 a** bring into prominence; draw attention to. **b** mark with a highlighter. **2** create highlights in (the hair).

■ *n.* **2** see PIÈCE DE RÉSISTANCE. ● *v.* **1** see EMPHASIZE.

highlighter /hílitər/ *n.* a marker pen that overlays color on a printed word, etc., leaving it legible and emphasized.

highly /hílee/ *adv.* **1** in a high degree (*highly amusing; highly probable; commend it highly*). **2** honorably; favorably (*think highly of him*). **3** in a high position or rank (*highly placed*). □ **highly-strung** = *high-strung*. [OE *hēalīce* (as HIGH)]

■ **1** greatly, tremendously, enthusiastically, warmly, immensely, hugely; extremely, exceptionally, extraordinarily, incomparably, decidedly; very, much, well, quite. **2** honorably, favorably, enthusiastically, approvingly, warmly, well. **3** well, influentially, powerfully, strongly, authoritatively, importantly.

high-minded /hímíndid/ *adj.* **1** having high moral principles. **2** proud; pretentious. □□ **high-mindedly** *adv.* **high-mindedness** *n.*

■ **1** see MORAL *adj.* 2.

high-muck-a-muck /hímukəmuk/ *n.* (also **high-muckety-muck**) a person of great self-importance. [perh. f. Chinook *hiu* plenty + *muckamuck* food]

highness /hínis/ *n.* **1** the state of being high (cf. HEIGHT). **2** (**Highness**) a title used in addressing and referring to a prince or princess (*Her Highness; Your Royal Highness*). [OE *hēanes* (as HIGH)]

hight /hit/ *adj. archaic poet.*, or *joc.* called; named. [past part. (from 14th c.) of OE *hātan* command, call]

hightail /hítayl/ *v.intr. colloq.* move at high speed, esp. in retreat.

■ see HURRY *v.* 1.

highway /híway/ *n.* **1 a** a public road. **b** a main route (by land or water). **2** a direct course of action (*on the highway to success*). □ **highway patrol** an organization of state police officers who patrol state highways.

■ **1** see ROAD¹ 1.

highwayman /híwaymən/ *n.* (*pl.* **-men**) *hist.* a robber of passengers, travelers, etc., usu. mounted. [HIGHWAY]

■ see ROBBER.

HIH *abbr. Brit.* Her or His Imperial Highness.

hijack /híjak/ *v. & n.* ● *v.tr.* **1** seize control of (a loaded truck, an aircraft in flight, etc.), esp. to force it to a different destination. **2** seize (goods) in transit. **3** take over (an organization, etc.) by force or subterfuge in order to redirect it. ● *n.* an instance of hijacking. □□ **hijacker** *n.* [20th c.: orig. unkn.]

■ *v.* **2** see STEAL *v.* 1.

hijra var. of HEGIRA.

hike /hík/ *n. & v.* ● *n.* **1** a long walk, esp. in the country or wilderness with backpacks, etc. **2** an increase (of prices, etc.). ● *v.* **1** *intr.* walk, esp. across country, for a long distance, esp. with boots, backpack, etc. **2** (usu. foll. by *up*) **a** *tr.* hitch up (clothing, etc.); hoist; shove. **b** *intr.* work upwards out of place; become hitched up. **3** *tr.* increase (prices, etc.). **4** *Football* put the ball in play by passing it back to an offensive player in the backfield. □□ **hiker** *n.* [19th-c. dial.: orig. unkn.]

■ *n.* **1** see WALK *n.* 2b. **2** see JUMP *n.* 3. ● *v.* **1** see WALK *v.* 1, 2. **2 a** see *hitch up*. **3** see *mark up* 1 (MARK¹).

hila *pl.* of HILUM.

hilarious /hiláireeəs/ *adj.* **1** exceedingly funny. **2** boisterously

merry. □□ **hilariously** *adv.* **hilariousness** *n.* **hilarity** /-lár-itee/ *n.* [L *hilaris* f. Gk *hilaros* cheerful]

■ **1** funny, humorous, comical, amusing, entertaining, sidesplitting, uproarious; *colloq.* hysterical, killing. **2** merry, gay, jolly, jovial, cheerful, cheery, joyous, joyful, mirthful, rollicking. □□ **hilariousness, hilarity** laughter, gaiety, joviality, jollity, merriment, mirth, exuberance, glee, cheerfulness, joyfulness, jubilation, elation, revelry, high spirits, vivacity.

Hilary term /hílaree/ *n. Brit.* the university term beginning in January, esp. at Oxford. [*Hilarius* bishop of Poitiers d. 367, with a festival on Jan. 13.]

hill /hil/ *n. & v.* ● *n.* **1 a** a naturally raised area of land, not as high as a mountain. **b** (as **the hills**) *Anglo-Ind.* = *hill station*. **2** (often in *comb.*) a heap; a mound (*anthill; dunghill*). **3** a sloping piece of road. ● *v.tr.* **1** form into a hill. **2** (usu. foll. by *up*) bank up (plants) with soil. □ **hill climb** a race for vehicles up a steep hill. **hill station** *Anglo-Ind.* a government settlement, esp. for vacations, etc., during the hot season, in the low mountains of N. India. **old as the hills** very ancient. **over the hill** *colloq.* **1** past the prime of life; declining. **2** past the crisis. **up hill and down dale** see UP. [OE *hyll*]

■ *n.* **1** elevation, rise, mound, knoll, hillock, hummock, butte, foothill, tor, *No. of Eng.* fell, *Sc.* brae, *archaic* mount; (*hills*) highlands, uplands, downs, downlands. **2** heap, pile, mound, stack; mountain. **3** slope, incline, acclivity, declivity, gradient.

hillbilly /hílbilee/ *n.* (*pl.* **-ies**) **1** *colloq.*, often *derog.* a person from a remote or mountainous area, esp. in the Appalachian mountains of the eastern US (cf. HICK). **2** country music of or like that originating in the Appalachian region.

■ see RUSTIC *n.*

hillock /hílək/ *n.* a small hill or mound. □□ **hillocky** *adj.*

hillside /hílsid/ *n.* the sloping side of a hill.

hilltop /híltop/ *n.* the summit of a hill.

hillwalking /hílwawking/ *n.* the pastime of walking in hilly country. □□ **hillwalker** *n.*

hilly /hílee/ *adj.* (**hillier, hilliest**) having many hills. □□ **hilliness** *n.*

hilt /hilt/ *n. & v.* ● *n.* **1** the handle of a sword, dagger, etc. **2** the handle of a tool. ● *v.tr.* provide with a hilt. □ **up to the hilt** completely. [OE *hilt(e)* f. Gmc]

■ *n.* see HANDLE *n.* 1.

hilum /hílǝm/ *n.* (*pl.* **hila** /-lə/) **1** *Bot.* the point of attachment of a seed to its vessel. **2** *Anat.* a notch or indentation where a vessel enters an organ. [L, = little thing, trifle]

HIM *abbr. Brit.* Her or His Imperial Majesty.

him /him/ *pron.* **1** *objective case* of HE (*I saw him*). **2** *colloq.* he (*it's him again; is taller than him*). **3** *archaic* himself (*fell and hurt him*). [OE, masc. and neut. dative sing. of HE, IT¹]

Himalayan /híməláyən/ *adj.* of or relating to the Himalaya mountains in Nepal. [*Himalaya* Skr. f. *hima* snow + *ālaya* abode]

himation /himáteeon/ *n. hist.* the outer garment worn by the ancient Greeks over the left shoulder and under the right. [Gk]

himself /himsélf/ *pron.* **1 a** *emphat. form* of HE or HIM (*he himself will do it*). **b** *refl. form* of HIM (*he has hurt himself*). **2** in his normal state of body or mind (*does not feel quite himself today*). **3** *esp. Ir.* a third party of some importance; the master of the house. □ **be himself** act in his normal unconstrained manner. **by himself** see *by oneself*. [OE (as HIM, SELF)]

Hinayana /héenəyaánə/ *n.* = THERAVADA. [Skr. f. *hīna* lesser + *yāna* vehicle]

hind¹ /hind/ *adj.* (esp. of parts of the body) situated at the back; posterior (*hind leg*) (opp. FORE). □ **on one's hind legs** see LEG. [ME, perh. shortened f. OE *bihindan* BEHIND]

■ see POSTERIOR *adj.* 2.

hind² /hind/ *n.* a female deer (usu. a red deer or sika), esp. in and after the third year. [OE f. Gmc]

hind³ /hind/ *n. hist.* **1** esp. *Sc.* a skilled farm worker, usu. married and with a tied cottage, and formerly having charge of two horses. **2** *Brit.* a steward on a farm. **3** a rustic; a boor.

[ME *hine* f. OE *hīne* (pl.) app. f. *hī(g)na* genit. pl. of *hīgan*, *hīwan* 'members of a family' (cf. HIDE³): for *-d* cf. SOUND¹]

■ **1, 3** see PEASANT.

hinder¹ /híndər/ *v.tr.* (also *absol.*) impede; delay; prevent (*you will hinder him; hindered me from working*). [OE *hindrian* f. Gmc]

■ hamper, delay, interrupt, hold back; thwart, frustrate, impede, interfere with, stymie, balk, handicap, hobble, set back, put back, *archaic* let; stop, prevent, check, arrest, foil, forestall, bar, obstruct.

hinder² /híndər/ *adj.* rear; hind (*the hinder part*). [ME, perh. f. OE *hinderweard* backward: cf. HIND¹]

Hindi /híndee/ *n. & adj.* ● *n.* **1** a group of spoken dialects of N. India. **2** a literary form of Hindustani with a Sanskrit-based vocabulary and the Devanagari script, an official language of India. ● *adj.* of or concerning Hindi. [Urdu *hindī* f. *Hind* India]

hindmost /híndmōst/ *adj.* farthest behind; most remote.

■ see LAST¹ *adj.* 1, 5.

Hindoo *archaic* var. of HINDU.

hindquarters /híndkwáwrtərz/ *n.pl.* the hind legs and adjoining parts of a quadruped.

hindrance /híndrəns/ *n.* **1** the act or an instance of hindering; the state of being hindered. **2** a thing that hinders; an obstacle.

■ **2** obstruction, impediment, barrier, obstacle, restraint, encumbrance, *archaic* let; drawback, hitch, stumbling block.

hindsight /híndsīt/ *n.* **1** wisdom after the event (*realized with hindsight that they were wrong*) (opp. FORESIGHT). **2** the back-sight of a gun.

Hindu /híndōō/ *n. & adj.* ● *n.* **1** a follower of Hinduism. **2** *archaic* a person of India. ● *adj.* **1** of or concerning Hindus or Hinduism. **2** *archaic* of India. [Urdu f. Pers. f. *Hind* India]

Hinduism /híndōōizəm/ *n.* the main religious and social system of India, including belief in reincarnation and the worship of several gods. ▫▫ **Hinduize** *v.tr.*

Hindustani /híndōōstáanee, -stánee/ *n. & adj.* ● *n.* **1** a language based on Western Hindi, with elements of Arabic, Persian, etc., used as a lingua franca in much of India. **2** *archaic* Urdu. ● *adj.* of or relating to Hindustan or its people, or Hindustani. [Urdu f. Pers. *hindūstānī* (as HINDU, *stān* country)]

hinge /hinj/ *n. & v.* ● *n.* **1 a** a movable, usu. metal, joint or mechanism such as that by which a door is hung on a side post. **b** *Biol.* a natural joint performing a similar function, e.g., that of a bivalve shell. **2** a central point or principle on which everything depends. ● *v.* **1** *intr.* (foll. by *on*) **a** depend (*on a principle, an event, etc.*) (*all hinges on his acceptance*). **b** (of a door, etc.) hang and turn (on a post, etc.). **2** *tr.* attach with or as if with a hinge. ▫ **stamp hinge** a small piece of gummed transparent paper used for fixing postage stamps in an album, etc. ▫▫ **hinged** *adj.* **hingeless** *adj.* **hingewise** *adv.* [ME *heng*, etc., rel. to HANG]

■ *n.* **1 a** see PIVOT *n.* 1. ● *v.* **1 a** (*hinge on*) see DEPEND 1.

hinny¹ /hínee/ *n.* (*pl.* **-ies**) the offspring of a female donkey and a male horse. [L *hinnus* f. Gk *hinnos*]

hinny² /hínee/ *n.* (also **hinnie**) (*pl.* **-ies**) *Sc. & No. of Engl.* (esp. as a form of address) darling; sweetheart. ▫ **singing hinny** a currant cake baked on a griddle. [var. of HONEY]

hint /hint/ *n. & v.* ● *n.* **1** a slight or indirect indication or suggestion (*took the hint and left*). **2** a small piece of practical information (*handy hints on cooking*). **3** a very small trace; a suggestion (*a hint of perfume*). ● *v.tr.* (often foll. by *that* + clause) suggest slightly (*hinted that they were wrong*). ▫ **hint at** give a hint of; refer indirectly to. [app. f. obs. *hent* grasp, lay hold of, f. OE *hentan*, f. Gmc, rel. to HUNT]

■ *n.* **1** suggestion, clue, indication, tip, tip-off; intimation, allusion, innuendo, insinuation, implication, inkling; *colloq.* pointer. **2** clue, suggestion, tip, *colloq.* pointer; (*hints*) help, advice. **3** trace, suggestion, breath, whiff, undertone, tinge, whisper; taste, touch, dash, soupçon. ● *v.* suggest, imply,

indicate, intimate, insinuate, mention. ▫ **hint at** allude to; see also REFER 7, 8.

hinterland /híntərland/ *n.* **1** the often deserted or uncharted areas beyond a coastal district or a river's banks. **2** an area remote from but served by a port or other center. **3** a remote or fringe area. [G f. *hinter* behind + *Land* LAND]

■ **1** see INTERIOR *n.* 2. **3** see STICK¹ *n.* 12.

hip¹ /hip/ *n.* **1** a projection of the pelvis and upper thigh bone on each side of the body in human beings and quadrupeds. **2** (often in *pl.*) the circumference of the body at the buttocks. **3** *Archit.* the sharp edge of a roof from ridge to eaves where two sides meet. ▫ **hip-bath** *Brit.* = SITZ BATH. **hip flask** a flask for liquor, etc., carried in a hip pocket. **hip-huggers** (in *pl.*) trousers hanging from the hips. **hip-hugging** (of a garment) hanging from the hips rather than the waist. **hip joint** the articulation of the head of the thigh bone with the ilium. **hip pocket** a trouser pocket just behind the hip. **hip** (or **hipped**) **roof** a roof with the sides and the ends inclined. **on the hip** *archaic* at a disadvantage. ▫▫ **hipless** *adj.* **hipped** *adj.* (also in comb.). [OE *hype* f. Gmc, rel. to HOP¹]

hip² /hip/ *n.* (also **hep** /hep/) the fruit of a rose, esp. a wild kind. [OE *hēope, hīope* f. WG]

hip³ /hip/ *adj.* (also **hep** /hep/) (**hipper, hippest** or **hepper, heppest**) *sl.* **1** following the latest fashion in music, clothes, etc.; stylish. **2** (often foll. by *to*) understanding; aware. ▫ **hip-hop** a style of urban youth rock music or the street subculture that surrounds it (typically including graffiti art, rap, and break dancing). ▫▫ **hipness** *n.* [20th c.: orig. unkn.]

■ **1** see STYLISH 1. **2** understanding, informed, aware, knowledgeable, knowing, perceptive, streetwise, *colloq.* with it; (*hip to*) alert to, in *or* up on, on to, *colloq.* wise to.

hip⁴ /hip/ *int.* introducing a united cheer (*hip, hip, hooray*). [19th c.: orig. unkn.]

hipbone /hípbōn/ *n.* a bone forming the hip, esp. the ilium.

hippeastrum /hípeeáastrəm/ *n.* any S. American bulbous plant of the genus *Hippeastrum* with showy white or red flowers. [mod.L f. Gk *hippeus* horseman (the leaves appearing to ride on one another) + *astron* star (from the flower-shape)]

hipped /hipt/ *adj.* (usu. foll. by *on*) *sl.* obsessed; infatuated. [past part. of *hip* (v.) = make hip (HIP³)]

hipper /hípər/ *n. Austral.* a soft pad used to protect the hip when sleeping on hard ground.

hippie /hípee/ *n.* (also **hippy**) (*pl.* **-ies**) *colloq.* **1** (esp. in the 1960s) a person of unconventional appearance, typically with long hair, jeans, beads, etc., often associated with hallucinogenic drugs and a rejection of conventional values. **2** = HIPSTER². [HIP³]

■ **1** bohemian, longhair, flower person, *colloq.* dropout.

hippo /hípō/ *n.* (*pl.* **-os**) *colloq.* a hippopotamus. [abbr.]

hippocampus /hípəkámpəs/ *n.* (*pl.* **hippocampi** /-pī/) **1** any marine fish of the genus *Hippocampus*, swimming vertically and with a head suggestive of a horse; a sea horse. **2** *Anat.* the elongated ridges on the floor of each lateral ventricle of the brain, thought to be the center of emotion and the autonomic nervous system. [L f. Gk *hippokampos* f. *hippos* horse + *kampos* sea monster]

hippocras /hípəkras/ *n. hist.* wine flavored with spices. [ME f. OF *ipocras* Hippocrates (see HIPPOCRATIC OATH), prob. because strained through a filter called "Hippocrates' sleeve"]

Hippocratic oath /hípəkrátik/ *n.* an oath taken by doctors affirming their obligations and proper conduct. [med.L *Hippocraticus* f. *Hippocrates*, Gk physician of the 5th c. BC]

Hippocrene /hípəkreen/ *n. poet.* poetic or literary inspiration. [name of a fountain on Mount Helicon sacred to the

---

/.../ **pronunciation**	● **part of speech**
▫ **phrases, idioms, and compounds**	
▫▫ **derivatives**	■ **synonym section**
cross-references appear in SMALL CAPITALS or *italics*	

Muses: L f. Gk f. *hippos* horse + *krēnē* fountain, as having been produced by a stroke of Pegasus' hoof]

hippodrome /hípədrōm/ *n.* **1** an arena used for equestrian or other sporting events. **2** (in classical antiquity) a course for chariot races, etc. [F *hippodrome* or L *hippodromus* f. Gk *hippodromos* f. *hippos* horse + *dromos* race, course]
■ **1** see THEATER 1a. **2** see STADIUM.

hippogriff /hípəgrif/ *n.* (also **hippogryph**) a mythical griffin-like creature with the body of a horse. [F *hippogriffe* f. It. *ippogrifo* f. Gk *hippos* horse + It. *grifo* GRIFFIN]

hippopotamus /hípəpótəməs/ *n.* (*pl.* **hippopotamuses** or **hippopotami** /-mī/) **1** a large thick-skinned four-legged mammal, *Hippopotamus amphibius*, native to Africa, inhabiting rivers, lakes, etc. **2** (in full **pygmy hippopotamus**) a smaller related mammal, *Choeropsis liberiensis*, native to Africa, inhabiting forests and swamps. [ME f. L f. Gk *hippopotamos* f. *hippos* horse + *potamos* river]

hippy[1] var. of HIPPIE.

hippy[2] /hípee/ *adj.* having large hips.
■ see PLUMP[1] *adj.*

hipster[1] /hípstər/ *adj.* & *n. Brit.* ● *adj.* = hip-hugging. ● *n.* = hip-huggers.

hipster[2] /hípstər/ *n. sl.* a person who is stylish or hip. □□ **hipsterism** *n.*

hiragana /heèrəgáanə/ *n.* the cursive form of Japanese syllabic writing or kana (cf. KATAKANA). [Jap., = plain kana]

hircine /hɜ́rsin, -sin/ *adj.* goatlike. [L *hircinus* f. *hircus* goat]

hire /hīr/ *v.* & *n.* ● *v.tr.* **1** employ (a person) for wages or a fee. **2** (often foll. by *from*) procure the temporary use of (a thing) for an agreed payment; rent or lease. **3** *archaic* borrow (money). ● *n.* **1** hiring or being hired. **2** esp. *Brit.* payment for this. **3** a person who is hired. ● **for** (or **on**) **hire** ready to be hired. **hire-car** *Brit.* a car available for rent. **hired girl** (or **man**) a domestic servant, esp. on a farm. **hire out** grant the temporary use of (a thing) for an agreed payment. **hire purchase** *Brit.* a system by which a person may purchase a thing by regular payments while having the use of it. □□ **hirable** *adj.* (also **hireable**). **hirer** *n.* [OE *hȳrian*, *hȳr* f. WG]
■ *v.* **1** engage, employ, appoint, enlist, take on, sign on. **2** rent, lease, hire out; charter (out). ● *n.* **1** rent, rental, lease, *Brit.* let; charter. □ **hire out** rent (out), lease, *Brit.* let; charter.

hireling /hírling/ *n.* usu. *derog.* a person who works for hire. [OE *hȳrling* (as HIRE, -LING[1])]
■ see SUBORDINATE *n.*

hirsute /hɜ́rsyoōt/ *adj.* **1** hairy; shaggy. **2** untrimmed. □□ **hirsuteness** *n.* [L *hirsutus*]
■ **1** see HAIRY 1. **2** see SHAGGY.

hirsutism /hɜ́rsyoōtizəm/ *n.* the excessive growth of hair on the face and body.

his /hiz/ *poss.pron.* **1** (*attrib.*) of or belonging to him or himself (*his house*; *his own business*). **2** (**His**) (*attrib.*) (in titles) that he is (*His Majesty*). **3** the one or ones belonging to or associated with him (*it is his*; *his are over there*). □ **his and hers** *joc.* (of matching items) for husband and wife, or men and women. **of his** of or belonging to him (*a friend of his*). [OE, genit. of HE, IT[1]]

Hispanic /hispánik/ *adj.* & *n.* ● *adj.* **1** of or being a person of Latin-American or Spanish or Portuguese descent in the US. **2** of or relating to Spain or to Spain and Portugal. **3** of Spain and other Spanish-speaking countries. ● *n.* a Spanish-speaking person, esp. one of Latin-American descent, living in the US. □□ **Hispanicize** /-nisiz/ *v.tr.* [L *Hispanicus* f. *Hispania* Spain]

Hispanist /híspənist/ *n.* (also **Hispanicist** /hispánisist/) an expert in or student of the language, literature, and civilization of Spain.

Hispano- /hispánō/ *comb. form* Spanish. [L *Hispanus* Spanish]

hispid /híspid/ *adj. Bot.* & *Zool.* **1** rough with bristles; bristly. **2** shaggy. [L *hispidus*]
■ see HAIRY 1.

hiss /his/ *v.* & *n.* ● *v. intr.* **1** (of a person, snake, goose, etc.) make a sharp sibilant sound, esp. as a sign of disapproval or derision (*audience booed and hissed*; *the water hissed on the hotplate*). **2** *tr.* express disapproval of (a person, etc.) by hisses. **3** *tr.* whisper (a threat, etc.) urgently or angrily (*"Where's the door?" he hissed*). ● *n.* **1** a sharp sibilant sound as of the letter *s*, esp. as an expression of disapproval or derision. **2** *Electronics* unwanted interference at audio frequencies. □ **hiss away** (or **down**) drive off, etc., by hisses. **hiss off** hiss (actors, etc.) so that they leave the stage. [ME: imit.]
■ *v.* **1** sizzle, splutter, spit; whistle; see also SCOFF[1] *v.* **2** catcall; see also JEER *v.* 1. ● *n.* **1** sibilance, hissing; catcall, jeer, boo, hoot, *colloq.* raspberry. **2** see INTERFERENCE 2.

hist /hist/ *int. archaic* used to call attention, enjoin silence, incite a dog, etc. [16th c.: natural excl.]

hist. *abbr.* **1** historian. **2** historical. **3** history.

histamine /hístəmin, -meen/ *n. Biochem.* an organic compound occurring in injured body tissues, etc., and also associated with allergic reactions. □□ **histaminic** /-mínik/ *adj.* [HISTO- + AMINE]

histidine /hístideen/ *n. Biochem.* an amino acid from which histamine is derived. [Gk *histos* web, tissue]

histo- /hístō/ *comb. form* (before a vowel also **hist-**) *Biol.* tissue. [Gk *histos* web]

histochemistry /hístōkémistree/ *n.* the study of the identification and distribution of the chemical constituents of tissues by means of stains, indicators, and microscopy. □□ **histochemical** *adj.*

histogenesis /hístōjénisis/ *n.* the formation of tissues. □□ **histogenetic** /-jinétik/ *adj.*

histogeny /hístójinee/ *n.* = HISTOGENESIS. □□ **histogenic** /hístəjénik/ *adj.*

histogram /hístəgram/ *n. Statistics* a chart consisting of rectangles (usu. drawn vertically from a base line) whose areas and positions are proportional to the value or range of a number of variables. [Gk *histos* mast + -GRAM]

histology /hístóləjee/ *n.* the study of the structure of tissues. □□ **histological** /hístəlójikəl/ *adj.* **histologist** /hístóləjist/ *n.*

histolysis /hístólisis/ *n.* the breaking down of tissues. □□ **histolytic** /-təlítik/ *adj.*

histone /hístōn/ *n. Biochem.* any of a group of proteins found in chromatin. [G *Histon* perh. f. Gk *histamai* arrest, or as HISTO-]

histopathology /hístōpəthólǝjee/ *n.* **1** changes in tissues caused by disease. **2** the study of these.

historian /histáwreeən/ *n.* **1** a writer of history, esp. a critical analyst, rather than a compiler. **2** a person learned in or studying history (*English historian*; *ancient historian*). [F *historien* f. L (as HISTORY)]

historiated /histáwreeaytid/ *adj.* = STORIATED. [med.L *historiare* (as HISTORY)]

historic /histáwrik, -stór-/ *adj.* **1** famous or important in history or potentially so (*a historic moment*). **2** *Gram.* (of a tense) normally used in the narration of past events (esp. Latin & Greek imperfect and pluperfect; (cf. PRIMARY)). **3** = HISTORICAL. □ **historic infinitive** the infinitive when used instead of the indicative. **historic present** the present tense used instead of the past in vivid narration. [L *historicus* f. Gk *historikos* (as HISTORY)]
■ **1** momentous, important, noteworthy, significant, red-letter, notable, signal; celebrated, famous, distinguished, prominent, great, unforgettable, memorable.

historical /histáwrikəl, -stór-/ *adj.* **1** of or concerning history (*historical evidence*). **2** belonging to history, not to prehistory or legend. **3** (of the study of a subject) based on an analysis of its development over a period. **4** belonging to the past, not the present. **5** (of a novel, a movie, etc.) dealing or professing to deal with historical events. **6** in connection with history; from the historian's point of view (*of purely historical interest*). □□ **historically** *adv.*
■ **1, 2** factual, true, verifiable, reliable, real, authentic, recorded, documented. **3** period; chronological. **4** see PAST *adj.* 1. **5** period.

historicism /histáwrisizəm, -stór-/ *n.* **1 a** the theory that social and cultural phenomena are determined by history. **b** the belief that historical events are governed by laws. **2** the tendency to regard historical development as the most basic aspect of human existence. **3** an excessive regard for past styles, etc. ▫▫ **historicist** n. [HISTORIC after G *Historismus*]

historicity /hístərísitee/ n. the historical genuineness of an event, etc.

historiographer /histáwreeógrəfər/ n. **1** an expert in or student of historiography. **2** a writer of history, esp. an official historian. [ME f. F *historiographe* or f. LL *historiographus* f. Gk *historiographos* (as HISTORY, -GRAPHER)]

historiography /histáwreeógrəfee/ n. **1** the writing of history. **2** the study of historical writing. ▫▫ **historiographic** /-reeəgráfik/ adj. **historiographical** adj. [med.L *historiographia* f. Gk *historiographia* (as HISTORY, -GRAPHY)]

history /hístəree/ n. (pl. **-ies**) **1** a continuous, usu. chronological, record of important or public events. **2 a** the study of past events, esp. human affairs. **b** the total accumulation of past events, esp. relating to human affairs or to the accumulation of developments connected with a particular nation, person, thing, etc. (*our nation's history; the history of astronomy*). **c** the past in general; antiquity. **3** an eventful past (*this house has a history*). **4 a** a systematic or critical account of or research into a past event or events, etc. **b** a similar record or account of natural phenomena. **5** a historical play. ▫ **make history 1** influence the course of history. **2** do something memorable. [ME f. L *historia* f. Gk *historia* finding out, narrative, history f. *histōr* learned, wise man, rel. to WIT[2]]

■ **1** account, description, story, record, chronicle, narrative; annals. **2 b** tale, experience(s); biography, memoir; see also STORY[1] 2, 4. **c** ancient history, the past, yesterday, *archaic* olden days, antiquity, *literary* yesteryear. **3** past, reputation, background, life. **4** report; see also INQUIRY 1.

histrionic /hístreeónik/ adj. & n. ● adj. **1** of or concerning actors or acting. **2** (of behavior) theatrical; dramatic. ● n. **1** (in pl.) **a** insincere and dramatic behavior designed to impress. **b** theatricals; theatrical art. **2** *archaic* an actor. ▫▫ **histrionically** adv. [LL *histrionicus* f. L *histrio -onis* actor]

■ adj. **1** see DRAMATIC 1. **2** see DRAMATIC 4.

hit /hit/ v. & n. ● v. (**hitting**; past and past part. **hit**) **1** tr. **a** strike with a blow or a missile. **b** (of a moving body) strike (*the plane hit the ground*). **c** reach (a target, a person, etc.) with a directed missile (*hit the window with the ball*). **2** tr. cause to suffer or affect adversely; wound (*the loss hit him hard*). **3** intr. (often foll. by *at, against, upon*) direct a blow. **4** tr. (often foll. by *against, on*) knock (a part of the body) (*hit his head on the door frame*). **5** tr. light upon; get at (a thing aimed at) (*he's hit the truth at last; tried to hit the right tone in her apology*) (see hit on). **6** tr. colloq. **a** encounter (*hit a snag*). **b** arrive at (*hit an all-time low; hit the town*). **c** indulge in, esp. liquor, etc. (*hit the bottle*). **7** tr. sl. rob or kill. **8** tr. occur forcefully to (*the seriousness of the situation only hit him later*). **9** tr. *Sports* **a** propel (a ball, etc.) with a bat, etc. **b** score (runs, etc.) in this way. **c** (usu. foll. by *for*) strike (a ball or a pitcher, etc.) for a specific hit, result, etc. **10** tr. represent exactly. **11** tr. sl. (often foll. by *up*) ask (a person) for; beg. ● n. **1 a** a blow; a stroke. **b** a collision. **2** a shot, etc., that hits its target. **3** colloq. a popular success in entertainment. **4** a stroke of sarcasm, wit, etc. **5** a stroke of good luck. **6** sl. **a** a murder or other violent crime. **b** a drug injection, etc. **7** a successful attempt. **8** *Baseball* = base hit. ▫ **hit and run a** cause (accidental or willful) damage and escape or leave the scene before being discovered. **b** *Baseball* play in which a base runner begins running to the next base as the pitcher delivers the ball and the batter then tries to hit the thrown ball. **hit-and-run** *attrib.adj.* relating to or (of a person) committing an act or play of this kind. **hit back** retaliate. **hit below the belt 1** esp. *Boxing* give a foul blow. **2** treat or behave unfairly. **hit for six** *Brit.* defeat in an argument. **hit the hay** (or **sack**) colloq. go to bed. **hit the headlines** see HEADLINE. **hit home** make a salutary impression. **hit it off** (often foll. by *with, together*) agree or be

congenial. **hit list** sl. a list of prospective victims. **hit man** (pl. **hit men**) sl. a hired assassin. **hit the nail on the head** state the truth exactly. **hit on** (or **upon**) find (what is sought), esp. by chance. **hit-or-miss** aimed or done carelessly. **hit out** deal vigorous physical or verbal blows (*hit out at her enemies*). **hit parade** colloq. a list of the current best-selling records of popular music. **hit the road** (or **trail**) sl. depart. **hit the roof** see ROOF. **hit the spot** colloq. find out or do exactly what was needed. **hit up 1** sense 11 of v. **2** *Cricket* score (runs) energetically. **hit wicket** *Cricket* be out by striking the wicket with the bat, etc. **make a hit** (usu. foll. by *with*) be successful or popular. ▫▫ **hitter** n. [ME f. OE *hittan* f. ON *hitta* meet with, of unkn. orig.]

■ v. **1 a** strike, cuff, smack, knock, bash, thump, punch, buffet, slap, swat, spank, beat, batter, belabor, clout, *archaic or literary* smite, colloq. thwack, whack, sock, clip, swipe, bop, lambaste, sl. belt, wallop, whop, clobber, crown, conk, paste, zap; bludgeon, club, cudgel, thrash, pummel, flog, scourge, birch, cane, lash, flagellate, whip, horsewhip. **b** strike, collide with, smash or crash into, bump or bang into. **2** wound, hurt, touch; see also AFFECT[1] 2. **3** lash out; (*hit at*) swing at, colloq. swipe at. **4** see BEAT v. 2a. **5** light upon, discover; see also FIND v. 1a, 2a. **6 a** encounter, meet (with); see also FACE v. 3a. **b** reach, arrive at, come or get to, attain. **7** see ROB 1, KILL[1] v. 1a. **8** dawn on, enter a person's mind, occur to, strike. **9 a** propel, strike, bat, drive, colloq. swipe. **11** importune, beseech, petition, beg, implore, entreat, ask. ● n. **1 a** a blow, stroke, punch, knock, strike, swat, smack, bump, bust, colloq. whack, thwack, bop, sock, sl. conk. **b** impact, bump, bang; see also COLLISION 1. **2** shot, bull's-eye. **3** success, triumph, coup, winner, sensation, colloq. smash (hit), sellout. **6 a** murder, killing, slaying, assassination. **b** *Brit. sl.* bang. **7** see ACCOMPLISHMENT 3. ▫ **hit back** see RETALIATE 1. **hit the hay** (or **sack**) retire, go to bed, colloq. turn in, *Brit. sl.* kip (down). **hit home** strike home, affect; see also TOUCH v. 4. **hit it off** see *get along* 1. **hit man** see THUG. **hit the nail on the head** be accurate, correct, right, or precise, put one's finger on it **hit on** (or **upon**) come upon, happen on, chance on or upon, light on or upon, discover, find, uncover, unearth, stumble upon, arrive at, see, perceive, detect, discern; devise, think up, invent, dream up, come up with, work out. **hit-or-miss** see CASUAL adj. 3a, CARELESS 1, 2. **hit parade** top ten, top twenty, etc., colloq. charts. **hit the road** (or **trail**) see *beat it*.

hitch /hich/ v. & n. ● v. **1 a** tr. fasten with a loop, hook, etc.; tether (*hitched the horse to the cart*). **b** intr. (often foll. by *in, onto*, etc.) become fastened in this way (*the rod hitched in to the bracket*). **2** tr. move (a thing) with a jerk; shift slightly (*hitched the pillow to a comfortable position*). **3** colloq. **a** intr. = HITCHHIKE. **b** tr. obtain (a lift) by hitchhiking. **4** colloq. (as **hitched** adj.) married. ● n. **1** an impediment; a temporary obstacle. **2** an abrupt pull or push; a jerk. **3 a** a noose or knot of various kinds. **b** the connector assembly between a vehicle and something being towed. **4** colloq. a free ride in a vehicle. **5** sl. a period of service. ▫ **get hitched** colloq. marry. **half hitch** a knot formed by passing the end of a rope around its standing part and then through the bight. **hitch up** lift (esp. clothing) with a jerk. **hitch one's wagon to a star** make use of powers higher than one's own. ▫▫ **hitcher** n. [ME: orig. uncert.]

■ v. **1** fasten, connect, attach, join, unite, hook (up), link, fix; harness, tether. **2** jerk, tug, shift, pull, wrench, colloq. yank. ● n. **1** impediment, obstacle, snag, catch, difficulty, problem, hindrance, obstruction. **2** see JERK[1] n. 1, 2. **3 a** knot, noose; see also LOOP n. 4 lift, ride.

□ **get hitched** see MARRY 1, 2a. **hitch up** pull up, hike up, hoist, haul up, raise, lift (up).

hitchhike /hích-hīk/ v. & n. ● v.intr. travel by seeking free lifts in passing vehicles. ● n. a journey made by hitchhiking. □□ **hitchhiker** n.

■ v. hitchhike, thumb a lift or ride, sl. bum a ride.

hi-tech /híték/ n. = high tech. [abbr.]

hither /híthər/ adv. & adj. usu. formal or literary ● adv. to or toward this place. ● adj. situated on this side; the nearer (of two). □ **hither and thither** (or **yon**) in various directions; to and fro. [OE hider: cf. THITHER]

hitherto /híthərtoo/ adv. until this time; up to now.

■ see previously (PREVIOUS).

hitherward /híthərwərd/ adv. archaic in this direction.

Hitler /hítlər/ n. a person who embodies the authoritarian characteristics of Adolf Hitler, Ger. dictator d. 1945. □□ **Hitlerite** /-rīt/ n. & adj.

■ see TYRANT.

Hitlerism /hítlərizəm/ n. the political principles or policy of the Nazi Party in Germany. [HITLER]

Hittite /hítīt/ n. & adj. ● n. 1 a member of an ancient people of Asia Minor and Syria. 2 the extinct language of the Hittites. ● adj. of or relating to the Hittites or their language. [Heb. Ḥittīm]

HIV abbr. human immunodeficiency virus, either of two retroviruses causing AIDS.

hive /hiv/ n. & v. ● n. 1 a a beehive. b the bees in a hive. 2 a busy swarming place. 3 a swarming multitude. 4 a thing shaped like a hive in being domed. ● v. 1 tr. a place (bees) in a hive. b house (people, etc.) snugly. 2 intr. a enter a hive. b live together like bees. □ **hive off** esp. Brit. 1 separate from a larger group. 2 a from into or assign (work) to a subsidiary department or company. b denationalize or privatize (an industry, etc.). **hive up** hoard. [OE hȳf f. Gmc]

■ n. 3 see SWARM¹ n. 1–3.

hives /hivz/ n.pl. a skin eruption, esp. nettle rash. [16th c. (orig. Sc.): orig. unkn.]

hiya /híyə/ int. colloq. a word used in greeting. [corrupt. of how are you?]

HK abbr. Hong Kong.

HL abbr. (in the UK) House of Lords.

hl abbr. hectoliter(s).

HM abbr. Brit. 1 Her (or His) Majesty('s). 2 a headmaster. b headmistress.

hm abbr. hectometer(s).

h'm /hm/ int. & n. (also **hmm**) = HEM², HUM².

HMO abbr. health maintenance organization.

HMS abbr. Her or His Majesty's Ship.

Ho symb. Chem. the element holmium.

ho /hō/ int. 1 a an expression of surprise, admiration, triumph, or (often repeated as **ho! ho!**, etc.) derision. b (in comb.) (heigh-ho; what ho). 2 a call for attention. 3 (in comb.) Naut. an addition to the name of a destination, etc. (westward ho). [ME, imit.: cf. ON hó]

ho. abbr. house.

hoagie /hógee/ n. (also **hoagy**) (pl. **-ies**) = submarine sandwich. [orig. unknown]

hoar /hawr/ adj. & n. literary ● adj. 1 gray-haired with age. 2 grayish white. 3 (of a thing) gray with age. ● n. 1 = HOARFROST. 2 hoariness. [OE hār f. Gmc]

hoard /hawrd/ n. & v. ● n. 1 a stock or store (esp. of money) laid by. 2 an amassed store of facts, etc. 3 Archaeol. an ancient store of treasure, etc. ● v. 1 tr. (often absol.; often foll. by up) amass (money, etc.) and put away; store. 2 intr. accumulate more than one's current requirements of food, etc., in a time of scarcity. 3 tr. store in the mind. □□ **hoarder** n. [OE hord f. Gmc]

■ n. 1 supply, stock, store, stockpile, accumulation, collection; repertoire, fund, reserve, cache, reservoir. ● v. 1 amass, collect, accumulate, assemble, gather, stockpile, lay in, save (up); put away, store, reserve, set aside, squirrel away, colloq. stash (away). 3 see MEMORIZE.

hoarding /háwrding/ n. 1 a board fence erected around a building site, etc., often used for displaying posters, etc. 2 Brit. a large, usu. wooden, structure used to carry advertisements, etc.; a billboard. [obs. hoard f. AF h(o)urdis f. OF hourd, hort, rel. to HURDLE]

hoarfrost /háwrfrawst/ n. frozen water vapor deposited in clear still weather on vegetation, etc.

hoarhound var. of HOREHOUND.

hoarse /hawrs/ adj. 1 (of the voice) rough and deep; husky; croaking. 2 having such a voice. □□ **hoarsely** adv. **hoarsen** v.tr. & intr. **hoarseness** n. [ME f. ON hārs (unrecorded) f. Gmc]

■ see HUSKY¹ 1.

hoarstone /háwrstōn/ n. Brit. an ancient boundary stone.

hoary /háwree/ adj. (**hoarier, hoariest**) 1 a (of hair) gray or white with age. b having such hair; aged. 2 old and trite (a hoary joke). 3 Bot. & Zool. covered with short white hairs. □□ **hoarily** adv. **hoariness** n.

■ 1 a see WHITE adj. 1. b see AGED 2. 2 see MUSTY 3.

hoatzin /hwaatseén/ n. a tropical American bird, Opisthocomus hoatzin, whose young climb by means of hooked claws on their wings. [native name, imit.]

hoax /hōks/ n. & v. ● n. a humorous or malicious deception; a practical joke. ● v.tr. deceive (a person) with a hoax. □□ **hoaxer** n. [18th c.: prob. contr. f. HOCUS]

■ n. swindle, imposture, trick, (practical) joke, cheat, sl. con, gyp, scam, snow job; deception, fraud, flimflam, humbug. ● v. 2 deceive, defraud, cheat, swindle, trick, fool, dupe, take in, hoodwink, delude, gull, bluff, colloq. bamboozle, literary cozen, sl. con, gyp.

hob¹ /hob/ n. 1 a a flat metal shelf at the side of a fireplace, having its surface level with the top of the grate, used esp. for keeping things warm. b Brit. a flat heating surface for a pan on a stove. 2 a tool used for cutting gear teeth, etc. 3 a peg or pin used as a mark in quoits, etc. 4 = HOBNAIL. [perh. var. of HUB, orig. = lump]

hob² /hob/ n. 1 a male ferret. 2 a hobgoblin. □ **play** (or **raise**) **hob** cause mischief. [ME, familiar form of Rob, short for Robin or Robert]

hobbit /hóbit/ n. a member of an imaginary race of half-sized people in stories by Tolkien. □□ **hobbitry** n. [invented by J. R. R. Tolkien, Engl. writer d. 1973, and said by him to mean 'hole dweller']

hobble /hóbəl/ v. & n. ● v. 1 intr. a walk lamely; limp. b proceed haltingly in action or speech (hobbled lamely to his conclusion). 2 tr. a tie together the legs of (a horse, etc.) to prevent it from straying. b tie (a horse's, etc., legs). 3 tr. cause (a person, etc.) to limp. ● n. 1 an uneven or infirm gait. 2 a rope, etc., used for hobbling a horse, etc. □ **hobble skirt** a skirt so narrow at the hem as to impede walking. □□ **hobbler** n. [ME, prob. f. LG: cf. HOPPLE and Du. hobbelen rock from side to side]

■ v. 1 limp, dodder, totter, stumble, shuffle, falter, shamble. 2, 3 shackle, fetter, restrain, trammel, impede; see also HINDER¹. ● n. 1 shuffle, shamble, totter; see also LIMP¹ n.

hobbledehoy /hóbəldeehoy/ n. colloq. 1 a clumsy or awkward youth. 2 a hooligan. [16th c.: orig. unkn.]

■ see BOOR 1, 2.

hobby¹ /hóbee/ n. (pl. **-ies**) 1 a favorite leisure time activity or occupation. 2 archaic a small horse. □□ **hobbyist** n. [ME hobyn, hoby, f. nicknames for Robin: cf. DOBBIN]

■ 1 pastime, occupation, activity, sideline, pursuit, recreation, diversion.

hobby² /hóbee/ n. (pl. **-ies**) any of several small long-winged falcons, esp. Falco subbuteo, catching prey on the wing. [ME f. OF hobé, hobet dimin. of hobe small bird of prey]

hobbyhorse /hóbeehawrs/ n. 1 a child's toy consisting of a stick with a horse's head. 2 a preoccupation; a favorite topic of conversation. 3 a model of a horse, esp. of wicker, used in morris dancing, etc. 4 a rocking horse. 5 a horse on a merry-go-round.

hobgoblin /hóbgoblin/ n. a mischievous imp; a bogy; a bugbear. [HOB² + GOBLIN]

■ see IMP n. 2.

hobnail /hóbnayl/ n. a heavy-headed nail used for boot soles. □ **hobnail** (or **hobnailed**) **liver** a liver having many small knobbly projections due to cirrhosis. □□ **hobnailed** adj. [HOB¹ + NAIL]

hobnob /hóbnob/ v.intr. (**hobnobbed, hobnobbing**) **1** (usu. foll. by *with*) mix socially or informally. **2** drink together. [*hob or nob* = give or take, of alternate drinking; earlier *hab nab*, = have or not have]

■ **1** associate, fraternize, consort, mingle, mix, keep company; (*hobnob with*) hang about or around with, rub shoulders with

hobo /hóbō/ n. (pl. **-oes** or **-os**) a wandering worker; a tramp. [19th c.: orig. unkn.]

■ see TRAMP n. 1.

Hobson's choice /hóbsənz/ n. a choice of taking the thing offered or nothing. [T. *Hobson*, Cambridge liveryman d. 1631, who let out horses on the basis that customers must take the one nearest the door]

hock¹ /hok/ n. **1** the joint of a quadruped's hind leg between the knee and the fetlock. **2** a knuckle of pork; the lower joint of a ham. [obs. *hockshin* f. OE *hōhsinu*: see HOUGH]

hock² /hok/ n. Brit. a German white wine from the Rhineland (properly that of Hochheim on the river Main). [abbr. of obs. *hockamore* f. G *Hochheimer*]

hock³ /hok/ v. & n. colloq. ● v.tr. pawn; pledge. ● n. a pawnbroker's pledge. □ **in hock 1** in pawn. **2** in debt. **3** in prison. [Du. *hok* hutch, prison, debt]

■ v. see PAWN² v.

hockey¹ /hókee/ n. **1** = ice hockey. **2** = field hockey. [16th c.: orig. unkn.]

hockey² var. of OCHE.

Hocktide /hóktīd/ n. Brit. hist. a festival formerly kept on the second Monday and Tuesday after Easter, orig. for raising money. [ME: orig. unkn.]

hocus /hókəs/ v.tr. (**hocussed, hocussing**; also **hocused, hocusing**) **1** take in; hoax. **2** stupefy (a person, animal, etc.) with drugs. **3** drug (liquor). [obs. noun *hocus* = HOCUS-POCUS]

hocus-pocus /hókəspókəs/ n. & v. ● n. **1** deception; trickery. **2 a** a typical verbal formula used in conjuring. **b** language intended to mystify; mumbo-jumbo. **3** conjuring; sleight of hand. ● v. (**-pocussed, -pocussing**; also **-pocused, -pocusing**) **1** intr. (often foll. by *with*) play tricks. **2** tr. play tricks on; deceive. [17th-c. sham L]

■ n. **1** trickery, sophistry, legerdemain, chicanery, deceit, deception, artifice, duplicity, mischief, pretense, humbug, flimflam, esp. Brit. colloq. jiggery-pokery, sl. hanky-panky; sleight of hand. **2 a** abracadabra, hey presto. **b** mumbo-jumbo, incantation, nonsense, rigmarole, gibberish, colloq. gobbledygook. **3** magic, conjuring, jugglery, formal prestidigitation. ● v. **2** see DECEIVE 1.

hod /hod/ n. **1** a V-shaped open trough on a pole used for carrying bricks, mortar, etc. **2** a portable receptacle for coal. [prob. = dial. *hot* f. OF *hotte* pannier, f. Gmc]

hoddie /hódee/ n. Austral. a bricklayer's laborer; a hodman. [HOD + -IE]

Hodge /hoj/ n. Brit. a typical English agricultural laborer. [nickname for the name *Roger*]

hodgepodge /hójpoj/ n. a confused mixture, a jumble. [ME, assim. to HODGE]

■ miscellany, mixture, gallimaufry, jumble, farrago, mélange, mishmash, medley, hash, conglomeration, mixed bag or bunch, olio, olla podrida, potpourri, ragbag, welter, colloq. omnium gatherum.

Hodgkin's disease /hójkinz/ n. a malignant disease of lymphatic tissues usu. characterized by enlargement of the lymph nodes. [T. *Hodgkin*, Engl. physician d. 1866]

hodman /hódman/ n. Brit. (pl. **-men**) **1** a laborer who carries a hod. **2** a literary hack. **3** a person who works mechanically.

hodograph /hódəgraf/ n. a curve in which the radius vector represents the velocity of a moving particle. [Gk *hodos* way + -GRAPH]

hoe /hō/ n. & v. ● n. a long-handled tool with a thin metal blade, used for weeding, etc. ● v. (**hoes, hoed, hoeing**) **1** tr. weed (crops); loosen (earth); dig up or cut down with a hoe. **2** intr. use a hoe. □ **hoe in** Austral. & NZ sl. eat eagerly.

hoe into Austral. & NZ sl. attack (food, a person, a task). □□ **hoer** n. [ME *howe* f. OF *houe* f. Gmc]

■ v. see TILL³.

hoecake /hókayk/ n. a coarse cake of cornmeal orig. baked on the blade of a hoe.

hoedown /hódown/ n. a lively dance or dance party, esp. one with square dancing.

hog /hawg, hog/ n. & v. ● n. **1 a** a domesticated pig, esp. one over 120 pounds (54 kg.) and reared for slaughter. **b** any of several other pigs of the family Suidae, e.g., a warthog. **2** colloq. a greedy person. **3** (also **hogg**) Brit. dial. a young sheep before the first shearing. ● v. (**hogged, hogging**) **1** tr. colloq. take greedily; hoard selfishly. **2** tr. & intr. raise (the back), or rise in an arch in the center. □ **go the whole hog** colloq. do something completely or thoroughly. **hog-tie 1** secure by fastening the hands and feet or all four feet together. **2** restrain; impede. □□ **hogger** n. **hoggery** n. **hoggish** adj. **hoggishly** adv. **hoggishness** n. **hoglike** adj. [OE *hogg, hocg*, perh. of Celt. orig.]

■ n. **2** see GLUTTON 1. ● v. **1** see TAKE v. 1, MONOPOLIZE. □□ **hoggish** greedy, avaricious, insatiable; gluttonous, voracious, colloq. piggish, literary or joc. edacious; acquisitive, possessive, self-seeking, selfish.

hogan /hógaan, -gən/ n. a Navajo dwelling of logs, etc. [Navajo]

hogback /háwgbak, hóg-/ n. (also **hog's back**) a steep-sided ridge of a hill.

hogg var. of HOG n. 3.

hogget /hógit/ n. Brit. a yearling sheep. [HOG]

hoggin /hógin/ n. **1** a mixture of sand and gravel. **2** sifted gravel. [19th c.: orig. unkn.]

Hogmanay /hógmənáy/ n. Sc. **1** New Year's Eve. **2** a celebration on this day. **3** a gift of cake, etc., demanded by children at Hogmanay. [17th c.: perh. f. Norman F *hoguinané* f. OF *aguillanneuf* (also = new year's gift)]

hog's back var. of HOGBACK.

hogshead /háwgz-hed, hógz-/ n. **1** a large cask. **2** a liquid or dry measure, usu. about 63 gallons. [ME f. HOG, HEAD: reason for the name unkn.]

■ **1** see KEG.

hogwash /háwgwosh, -wawsh, hóg-/ n. **1** colloq. nonsense; rubbish. **2** kitchen swill, etc., for pigs.

■ **1** see NONSENSE. **2** see SWILL n. 2, 4.

hogweed /háwgweed, hóg-/ n. any of various coarse weeds of the genus *Heracleum*, esp. *H. sphondylium*.

ho-ho /hóhó/ int. expressing surprise, triumph, or derision. [redupl. of HO]

ho-hum /hóhúm/ int. expressing boredom. [imit. of yawn]

hoick¹ /hoyk/ v. & n. Brit. colloq. ● v.tr. (often foll. by *out*) lift or pull, esp. with a jerk. ● n. a jerky pull; a jerk. [perh. var. of HIKE]

hoick² /hoyk/ v.intr. Brit. sl. spit. [perh. var. of HAWK³]

hoicks var. of YOICKS.

hoi polloi /hóy pəlóy/ n. (often prec. by *the*: see note below) **1** the masses; the common people. **2** the majority. ¶ Use with *the* is strictly unnecessary, since *hoi* = 'the,' but this construction is very common. [Gk, = the many]

■ **1** masses, herd, common herd, riffraff, rabble, canaille, common people, crowd, multitude, rank and file, silent majority, colloq. great unwashed, colloq. derog. proles, colloq. usu. derog. plebs, derog. populace, esp. derog. proletariat, usu. derog. mob.

hoist /hoyst/ v. & n. ● v.tr. **1** raise or haul up. **2** raise by means of ropes and pulleys, etc. ● n. **1** an act of hoisting; a lift. **2** an apparatus for hoisting. **3 a** the part of a flag nearest the staff. **b** a group of flags raised as a signal. □ **hoist the flag** stake one's claim to discovered territory by displaying a flag. **hoist one's flag** signify that one takes command. **hoist with** (or **by**) **one's own petard** see PETARD.

/. . ./ pronunciation	● part of speech
□ phrases, idioms, and compounds	
□□ derivatives	■ synonym section
cross-references appear in SMALL CAPITALS or *italics*	

□□ **hoister** n. [16th c.: alt. of *hoise* f. (15th-c.) *hysse*, prob. of LG orig.: cf. LG *hissen*]

■ v. **1, 2** lift (up), haul up, elevate, raise, heave up, uplift; winch. ● n. **2** crane, lift, davit, winch, tackle, elevator.

hoity-toity /hóyteetóytee/ adj., int., & n. ● adj. **1** haughty; petulant; snobbish. **2** archaic frolicsome. ● int. expressing surprised protest at presumption, etc. ● n. archaic riotous or giddy conduct. [obs. *hoit* indulge in riotous mirth, of unkn. orig.]

■ adj. **1** haughty, arrogant, snobbish, disdainful, supercilious, conceited, petulant, lofty, superior, self-important, colloq. high and mighty, stuck-up, snooty, uppity, snotty, esp. Brit. colloq. uppish, esp. Brit. sl. toffee-nosed.

hokey /hṓkee/ adj. (also **hoky**) (**hokier, hokiest**) sl. sentimental; melodramatic; artificial. □□ **hokeyness** n. (also **hokiness**). **hokily** adv. [HOKUM + -Y²]

■ see *melodramatic* (MELODRAMA).

hokey-cokey /hṓkeekṓkee/ n. Brit. a dance similar to the hokey-pokey.

hokey-pokey /hṓkeepṓkee/ n. colloq. **1** = HOCUS-POCUS 1. **2** ice cream formerly sold esp. by Italian street vendors. **3** a communal dance performed in a circle with synchronized shaking of the limbs in turn. [perh. f. HOCUS-POCUS]

hokku /hṓkōō, hók-/ n. (pl. same) = HAIKU. [Jap.]

hokum /hṓkəm/ n. sl. **1** sentimental, popular, sensational, or unreal situations, dialogue, etc., in a movie or play, etc. **2** bunkum; rubbish. [20th c.: orig. unkn.]

■ **2** see RUBBISH n. 3.

hoky var. of HOKEY.

Holarctic /hōláarktik, -láartik/ adj. of or relating to the geographical distribution of animals in the whole northern or Arctic region. [HOLO- + ARCTIC]

hold¹ /hōld/ v. & n. ● v. (past and past part. **held** /held/) **1** tr. **a** keep fast; grasp (esp. in the hands or arms). **b** (also refl.) keep or sustain (a thing, oneself, one's head, etc.) in a particular position (*hold it to the light*; *held himself erect*). **c** grasp so as to control (*hold the reins*). **2** tr. (of a vessel, etc.) contain or be capable of containing (*the pitcher holds two pints*; *the hall holds 900*). **3** tr. possess, gain, or have, esp.: **a** be the owner or tenant of (land, property, stocks, etc.) (*holds the farm from the trust*). **b** gain or have gained (a degree, record, etc.) (*holds the long-jump record*). **c** have the position of (a job or office). **d** have (a specified card) in one's hand. **e** keep possession of (a place, a person's thoughts, etc.) esp. against attack (*held the fort against the enemy*; *held his place in her estimation*). **4** intr. remain unbroken; not give way (*the roof held under the storm*). **5** tr. observe; celebrate; conduct (a meeting, festival, conversation, etc.). **6** tr. **a** keep (a person, etc.) in a specified condition, place, etc. (*held her prisoner*; *held him at arm's length*). **b** detain, esp. in custody (*hold him until I arrive*). **7** tr. **a** engross (a person or a person's attention) (*the book held him for hours*). **b** dominate (*held the stage*). **8** tr. (foll. by *to*) make (a person, etc.) adhere to (terms, a promise, etc.). **9** intr. (of weather) continue fine. **10** tr. (often foll. by *to* + infin., or *that* + clause) think; believe (*held it to be self-evident*; *held that the earth was flat*). **11** tr. regard with a specified feeling (*held him in contempt*). **12** tr. **a** cease; restrain (*hold your fire*). **b** colloq. withhold; not use (*a burger please, and hold the onions!*). **13** tr. keep or reserve (*will you hold our seats please?*). **14** tr. be able to drink (liquor) without effect (*can hold his liquor*). **15** tr. (usu. foll. by *that* + clause) (of a judge, a court, etc.) lay down; decide. **16** intr. keep going (*held on his way*). **17** tr. Mus. sustain (a note). **18** intr. archaic restrain oneself. ● n. **1** a grasp (*catch hold of him*; *keep a hold on her*). **2** (often in *comb.*) a thing to hold by (*seized the handhold*). **3** (foll. by *on, over*) influence over (*has a strange hold over them*). **4** a manner of holding in wrestling, etc. **5** archaic a fortress. □ **hold (a thing) against (a person)** resent or regard it as discreditable to (a person). **hold aloof** avoid communication with people, etc. **hold back 1** impede the progress of; restrain. **2** keep (a thing) to or for oneself. **3** (often foll. by *from*) hesitate; refrain. **hold one's breath** see BREATH. **hold by** (or **to**) adhere to (a

choice, purpose, etc.). **hold cheap** Brit. not value highly; despise. **hold the clock on** time (a sporting event, etc.). **hold court** preside over one's admirers, etc.; be the center of attention. **hold dear** regard with affection. **hold down 1** repress. **2** colloq. be competent enough to keep (one's job, etc.). **hold everything!** (or **it!**) cease action or movement. **hold for ransom 1** keep (a person) prisoner until a ransom is paid. **2** demand concessions from by threats of esp. damaging action. **hold the fort 1** act as a temporary substitute. **2** cope in an emergency. **hold forth 1** offer (an inducement, etc.). **2** usu. derog. speak at length or tediously. **hold good** (or **true**) be valid; apply. **hold one's ground** see GROUND¹. **hold one's hand** see HAND. **hold a person's hand** give a person guidance or moral support. **hold hands** grasp one another by the hand as a sign of affection or for support or guidance. **hold hard!** Brit. stop!; wait! **hold harmless** Law indemnify. **hold one's head high** behave proudly and confidently. **hold one's horses** colloq. stop; slow down. **hold in** keep in check; confine. **hold it good** Brit. think it advisable. **hold the line 1** not yield. **2** maintain a telephone connection. **hold one's nose** compress the nostrils to avoid a bad smell. **hold off 1** delay; not begin. **2** keep one's distance. **3** keep at a distance; fend off. **hold on 1** keep one's grasp on something. **2** wait a moment. **3** (when telephoning) not hang up. **hold out 1** stretch forth (a hand, etc.). **2** offer (an inducement, etc.). **3** maintain resistance. **4** persist or last. **hold out for** continue to demand. **hold out on** colloq. refuse something to (a person). **hold over 1** postpone. **2** retain. **hold something over** threaten (a person) constantly with something. **hold one's own** see OWN. **hold sway** rule or dominate. **hold to bail** Law bind by bail. **hold to a draw** manage to achieve a draw against (an opponent thought likely to win). **hold together 1** cohere. **2** cause to cohere. **hold one's tongue** colloq. be silent. **hold up 1 a** support; sustain. **b** maintain (the head, etc.) erect. **c** last; endure. **2** exhibit; display. **3** arrest the progress of; obstruct. **4** stop and rob by violence or threats. **hold water** (of reasoning) be sound; bear examination. **hold with** (usu. with neg.) colloq. approve of (*don't hold with motorcycles*). **left holding the bag** (Brit. **baby**) left with unwelcome responsibility. **on hold 1** in abeyance; temporarily deferred. **2** (of a telephone call or caller) holding on (see *hold on* 3 above). **take hold** (of a custom or habit) become established. **there is no holding him** (or **her**, etc.) he (or she, etc.) is restive, high-spirited, determined, etc. **with no holds barred** with no restrictions; all methods being permitted. □□ **holdable** adj. [OE *h(e)aldan, heald*]

■ v. **1 a, c** seize, grasp, grip, clench, clasp, clutch, keep, colloq. hang on to; carry, cradle, enfold, hug, embrace. **b** maintain, sustain, keep, put. **2** contain, accommodate, support, carry. **3** possess, have; gain, achieve; maintain, keep, sustain. **4** stay, stick, remain, survive. **5** observe, celebrate; call, convene, assemble, formal convoke; run, conduct, engage in, participate in, have. **6** confine, restrain, contain; keep; imprison, detain, shut up, jail. **7 a** engross, possess, keep, absorb, occupy, engage, involve, monopolize. **9** see *carry on* 1. **10, 11** believe, judge, consider, regard, take, assume, formal deem, esteem; think, maintain. **12 a** see CEASE v. **b** see WITHHOLD 1 **13** see RESERVE v. 2. **15** decide, rule; see also *lay down* 3, 7 (LAY¹). **16** see PERSEVERE. ● n. **1** grasp, grip, clasp, clutch, purchase. **3** dominance, mastery, control, ascendancy, authority, influence, power; leverage, sway, pull, colloq. clout. □ **hold back 1** restrain, repress, suppress, curb, inhibit, control, check, hinder, impede. **2** withhold, reserve, deny, keep back, refuse. **3** see HESITATE 2. **hold by** (or **to**) see KEEP v. 7a. **hold dear** see APPRECIATE 1a. **hold down 1** control, restrain, check; see also REPRESS 1. **2** keep, maintain, manage. **hold forth 1** hold out, offer, proffer, tender, submit, advance, propose, propound, extend. **2** lecture, declaim, preach, sermonize, discourse, expatiate, pontificate, colloq. go on, witter on, Brit. colloq. rabbit on, joc. or derog. speechify, esp. joc. or derog. orate. **hold good** apply, stand or hold up,

hold *or* prove *or* be true, be the case, operate, be *or* remain *or* prove valid, be relevant *or* applicable *or* operative, hold water, wash. **hold in** control, curb, check, hold back, restrain, contain. **hold off 1** delay, defer, put off, postpone, avoid; (*hold off from*) refrain from. **3** repel, repulse, fend off, rebuff, resist, withstand. **hold on 1** (*hold on to*) grip, clutch (on to), cling to. **2** see WAIT *v.* 1a. **hold out 1, 2** offer, proffer, extend, present, hold up. **3** see RESIST *v.* 1, 2. **4** last, carry on, persist, persevere, continue, hang on, stand firm, stand pat. **hold over 1** postpone, delay, defer, put off, hold off, suspend, adjourn. **2** continue, retain, extend, prolong. **hold together 1** see JELL 2. **hold one's tongue** be *or* remain *or* keep silent, say nothing, not breathe *or* say a word, keep one's counsel, *colloq.* keep mum, shut up. **hold up 1 a, b** see SUPPORT *v.* 1, 2. **c** last, survive, bear up, endure, hold out. **2** present, show, exhibit, display, hold out. **3** obstruct, delay, impede, hinder, slow (down *or* up), set back. **4** rob, waylay, mug, *colloq.* stick up. **hold water** be logical *or* sound *or* valid *or* sensible *or* consistent, be believable *or* credible *or* defensible *or* feasible *or* workable; make sense, ring true; hold up under scrutiny *or* examination, bear scrutiny *or* examination. **hold with** support, approve (of), subscribe to, condone, concur with.

hold² /hōld/ *n.* a cavity in the lower part of a ship or aircraft in which the cargo is stowed. [obs. *holl* f. OE *hol* (orig. adj. = hollow), rel. to HOLE, assim. to HOLD¹]

holdall /hōldawl/ *n.* esp. *Brit.* a portable case for miscellaneous articles.
■ see SUITCASE.

holdback /hōldbak/ *n.* a hindrance or thing held back.
■ see HINDRANCE.

holder /hōldər/ *n.* **1** (often in *comb.*) a device or implement for holding something (*cigarette holder*). **2 a** the possessor of a title, etc. **b** the occupant of an office, etc. **3** = SMALL-HOLDER.
■ **1** see RECEPTACLE. **2** see INCUMBENT *n.*

holdfast /hōldfast/ *n.* **1** a firm grasp. **2** a staple or clamp securing an object to a wall, etc. **3** the attachment organ of an alga, etc.
■ **2** see BRACE *n.* 1a.

holding /hōlding/ *n.* **1 a** a land held by lease (cf. SMALLHOLD-ING). **b** the tenure of land. **2** stocks, property, etc., held. □ **holding company** a company created to hold the shares of other companies, which it then controls. **holding operation** a maneuver designed to maintain the status quo.
■ **1 a** see FARM *n.* **b** see TENURE 1, 2.

holdover /hōldōvər/ *n.* a relic.

holdup /hōldəp/ *n.* **1** a stoppage or delay by traffic, fog, etc. **2** a robbery, esp. by the use of threats or violence.
■ **1** delay, setback, hitch, snag, interruption, stoppage. **2** robbery, mugging, *colloq.* stickup, *sl.* heist.

hole /hōl/ *n. & v.* ● *n.* **1 a** an empty space in a solid body. **b** an aperture in or through something. **c** flaw; weakness; gap. **2** an animal's burrow. **3** a cavity or receptacle for a ball in various sports or games. **4 a** *colloq.* a small, mean, or dingy abode. **b** a dungeon; a prison cell. **5** *colloq.* an awkward situation. **6** *Golf* **a** a point scored by a player who gets the ball from tee to hole with the fewest strokes. **b** the terrain or distance from tee to hole. **7** a position from which an electron is absent, esp. acting as a mobile positive particle in a semiconductor. ● *v.tr.* **1** make a hole or holes in. **2** pierce the side of (a ship). **3** put into a hole. **4** (also *absol.*; often foll. by *out*) send (a golf ball) into a hole. □ **hole-and-corner** secret; underhand. **hole in the heart** a congenital defect in the heart septum. **hole in one** *Golf* a shot that enters the hole from the tee. **hole in the wall** a small dingy place (esp. of a business). **hole up** *colloq.* hide oneself. **in holes** worn so much that holes have formed. **make a hole in** use a large amount of. **a round** (or **square**) **peg in a square** (or **round**) **hole** see PEG. □□ **holey** adj. [OE *hol, holian* (as HOLD²)]
■ *n.* **1 a** cavity, pit, hollow, pocket, depression, indentation, dent, crater, recess, niche, nook. **b**

aperture, opening, orifice, perforation, puncture, slit, slot, breach, rip, tear, rent, break, crack, fissure. **2** warren, burrow, tunnel; den, set, lair. **4 a** a hole in the wall, shack, hovel, hut, shanty, slum, *colloq.* dump, hellhole. **b** cell, prison, dungeon, donjon, keep, jail, oubliette, brig. **5** difficulty, predicament, fix, plight, mess, muddle, cleft stick, tight corner *or* place *or* spot, *colloq.* scrape, pickle, bind, *disp.* dilemma; *colloq.* hot water, trouble. ● *v.* **1** puncture, pierce, perforate, prick, nick, penetrate, go through, rupture. □ **hole-and-corner** see SECRET *adj.* 1. **hole in the wall** see HOLE *n.* 4a above. **hole up** see HIDE¹ *v.* 2. **in holes** see TATTERED.

holibut var. of HALIBUT.

-holic var. of -AHOLIC.

holiday /hóliday/ *n. & v.* ● *n.* **1** a day of festivity or recreation when no work is done, esp. a religious festival, etc. **2** esp. *Brit.* (often in *pl.*) = VACATION. **3** (*attrib.*) (of clothes, etc.) festive. ● *v.intr. esp. Brit.* spend a holiday. □ **holiday camp** *Brit.* a vacation resort with accommodation, entertainment, and facilities on site. **holiday centre** *Brit.* a place with many tourist attractions. **holiday-maker** esp. *Brit.* a person on holiday. **on holiday** (or **one's holidays**) *Brit.* in the course of one's holiday. **take a** (or *archaic* **make**) **holiday** have a break from work. [OE *hāligdæg* (HOLY, DAY)]
■ *n.* **1** festival, feast, celebration, fête, fiesta, gala, red-letter day. **3** festive, best, Sunday.

holily /hólilee/ *adv.* in a holy manner. [OE *hāliglīce* (as HOLY)]

holiness /hóleenis/ *n.* **1** sanctity; the state of being holy. **2** (**Holiness**) a title used when referring to or addressing the Pope. [OE *hālignes* (as HOLY)]
■ **1** see SANCTITY 1, 2.

holism /hólizəm/ *n.* (also **wholism**) **1** *Philos.* the theory that certain wholes are to be regarded as greater than the sum of their parts (cf. REDUCTIONISM). **2** *Med.* the treating of the whole person including mental and social factors rather than just the symptoms of a disease. □□ **holistic** adj. **holistically** adv. [as HOLO- + -ISM]

holla /hóla/ *int., n., & v.* ● *int.* calling attention. ● *n.* a cry of "holla." ● *v.* (**hollas, hollaed** *or* **holla'd, hollaing**) **1** *intr.* shout. **2** *tr.* call to (hounds). [F *holà* (as HO, *là* there)]

holland /hóland/ *n.* a smooth, hard-wearing, linen fabric. □ **brown holland** unbleached holland. [*Holland* = Netherlands: Du., earlier *Holtlant* f. *holt* wood + *-lant* land, describing the Dordrecht district]

hollandaise sauce /hóləndáyz/ *n.* a creamy sauce of melted butter, egg yolks, and lemon juice or vinegar, etc., served esp. with fish, vegetables, etc. [F, fem. of *hollandais* Dutch f. *Hollande* Holland]

Hollander /hóləndər/ *n.* **1** a native of Holland (the Netherlands). **2** a Dutch ship.

Hollands /hóləndz/ *n.* gin made in Holland. [Du. *hollandsch genever* Dutch gin]

holler /hólər/ *v. & n. colloq.* ● *v.* **1** *intr.* make a loud cry or noise. **2** *tr.* express with a loud cry or shout. ● *n.* a loud cry, noise, or shout. [var. of HOLLO]
■ *v.* see BAWL 1. ■ *n.* see BELLOW *n.*

hollo /hólō/ *int., n., & v.* ● *int.* = HOLLA. ● *n.* (*pl.* **-os**) = HOLLA. ● *v.* (**-oes, -oed**) (also **hollow** *pronunc.* same) = HOLLA. [rel. to HOLLA]

hollow /hólō/ *adj., n., v., & adv.* ● *adj.* **1 a** having a hole or cavity inside; not solid throughout. **b** having a depression; sunken (*hollow cheeks*). **2** (of a sound) echoing, as though made in or on a hollow container. **3** empty; hungry. **4** without significance; meaningless (*a hollow triumph*). **5** insincere; cynical; false (*a hollow laugh; hollow promises*). ● *n.* **1** a hollow place; a hole. **2** a valley; a basin. ● *v.tr.* (often foll. by *out*) make hollow; excavate. ● *adv. colloq.* completely (*beaten hollow*). □ **hollow-eyed** with eyes deep sunk. **hol-**

low-hearted insincere. **hollow square** *Mil. hist.* a body of infantry drawn up in a square with a space in the middle. **in the hollow** (also **palm**) **of one's hand** entirely subservient to one. □□ **hollowly** *adv.* **hollowness** *n.* [ME *holg, holu, hol(e)we* f. OE *holh* cave, rel. to HOLE]

■ *adj.* **1 a** vacant, void, unfilled; see also EMPTY *adj.* 1. **b** sunken, concave, indented, recessed. **2** echoing, muffled, low, sepulchral. **3** hungry, ravenous, starved, empty, famished. **4** empty, futile, pyrrhic, worthless, vain, unavailing, fruitless, profitless, unprofitable, valueless, ineffective, pointless, senseless, meaningless, *archaic* bootless. **5** insincere, false, cynical, hypocritical, sham, artificial, feigned, fraudulent, spurious, deceitful, mendacious, deceptive. ● *n.* **1** hole, cavity, crater, pit, trough, furrow, indentation, dent, impression, dip; excavation. **2** basin, depression, dip, valley, dale, dell, glen, *Brit.* coomb, combe. ● *v.* excavate, dig, gouge, furrow; (*hollow out*) scoop out. ● *adv.* see *completely* (COMPLETE). □ **hollow-hearted** see INSINCERE.

hollowware /hólōwair/ *n.* hollow articles of metal, china, etc., such as pots, kettles, pitchers, etc. (opp. FLATWARE).

■ see SILVER *n.* 5, 6.

holly /hólee/ *n.* (*pl.* **-ies**) **1** any evergreen shrub of the genus *Ilex*, often with prickly usu. dark green leaves, small white flowers, and red berries. **2** its branches and foliage used as decorations at Christmas. □ **holly oak** a holm oak. [OE *hole(g)n*]

hollyhock /hóleehok/ *n.* a tall plant, *Alcea rosea*, with large showy flowers of various colors. [ME (orig. = marsh mallow) f. HOLY + obs. *hock* mallow, OE *hoc*, of unkn. orig.]

Hollywood /hóleewòod/ *n.* the American movie industry or its products, with its principal center at Hollywood, California.

holm[1] /hōm/ *n.* (also **holme**) *Brit.* **1** an islet, esp. in a river or near a mainland. **2** a piece of flat ground by a river, which is submerged in time of flood. [ON *holmr*]

holm[2] /hōm/ *n.* (in full **holm oak**) an evergreen oak, *Quercus ilex*, with hollylike young leaves. [ME alt. of obs. *holin* (as HOLLY)]

holmium /hólmeeəm/ *n. Chem.* a soft silvery metallic element of the lanthanide series occurring naturally in apatite. ¶ Symb.: **Ho.** [mod.L f. *Holmia* Stockholm]

holo- /hólō/ *comb. form* whole (*Holocene*; *holocaust*). [Gk *holos* whole]

holocaust /hóləkawst/ *n.* **1** a case of large-scale destruction or slaughter, esp. by fire or nuclear war. **2** (**the Holocaust**) the mass murder of the Jews by the Nazis in World War II. **3** a sacrifice wholly consumed by fire. [ME f. OF *holocauste* f. LL *holocaustum* f. Gk *holokauston* (as HOLO-, *kaustos* burned f. *kaiō* burn)]

■ **1** destruction, devastation; slaughter, genocide, mass murder, massacre, blood bath, pogrom, butchery, carnage, annihilation, extinction, extermination, eradication, elimination; conflagration, firestorm, inferno, fire.

Holocene /hóləseen/ *adj. & n. Geol.* ● *adj.* of or relating to the most recent epoch of the Quaternary period with evidence of human development and intervention, and the extinction of large mammals. ¶ Cf. Appendix VII. ● *n.* this period or system. Also called RECENT. [HOLO- + Gk *kainos* new]

holoenzyme /hólō-énzīm/ *n. Biochem.* a complex enzyme consisting of several components.

hologram /hóləgram/ *n. Physics* **1** a three-dimensional image formed by the interference of light beams from a coherent light source. **2** a photograph of the interference pattern, which when suitably illuminated produces a three-dimensional image.

holograph /hóləgraf/ *adj. & n.* ● *adj.* wholly written by hand by the person named as the author. ● *n.* a holograph document. [F *holographe* or LL *holographus* f. Gk *holographos* (as HOLO-, -GRAPH)]

holography /həlógrəfee/ *n. Physics* the study or production of holograms. □□ **holographic** /hóləgráfik/ *adj.* **holographically** *adv.*

holohedral /hóləheédrəl/ *adj. Crystallog.* having the full number of planes required by the symmetry of a crystal system.

holophyte /hóləfīt/ *n.* an organism that synthesizes complex organic compounds by photosynthesis. □□ **holophytic** /-fítik/ *adj.*

holothurian /hóləthōōreeən, -thyōōr-/ *n. & adj.* ● *n.* any echinoderm of the class Holothurioidea, with a wormlike body, e.g., a sea cucumber. ● *adj.* of or relating to this class. [mod.L *Holothuria* (n.pl.) f. Gk *holothourion*, a zoophyte]

holotype /hólətīp/ *n.* the specimen used for naming and describing a species.

hols /holz/ *n.pl. Brit. colloq.* holidays. [abbr.]

Holstein /hólstīn, -steen/ *n. & adj.* ● *n.* **1** a large animal of a usu. black and white breed of dairy cattle orig. from Friesland. **2** this breed. ● *adj.* of or concerning Holsteins. [*Holstein* in NW Germany]

holster /hólstər/ *n.* a leather case for a pistol or revolver, worn on a belt or under an arm or fixed to a saddle. [17th c., synonymous with Du. *holster*: orig. unkn.]

holt[1] /hōlt/ *n. Brit.* **1** an animal's (esp. an otter's) lair. **2** *colloq.* or *dial.* grip; hold. [var. of HOLD[1]]

holt[2] /hōlt/ *n. archaic* or *dial.* **1** a wood or copse. **2** a wooded hill. [OE f. Gmc]

holus-bolus /hóləsbóləs/ *adv.* all in a lump; altogether. [app. sham L]

holy /hólee/ *adj.* (**holier, holiest**) **1** morally and spiritually excellent or perfect, and to be revered. **2** belonging to, devoted to, or empowered by, God. **3** consecrated; sacred. **4** used as an intensive and in trivial exclamations (*holy cow!*; *holy mackerel!*; *holy Moses!*; *holy smoke!*). □ **holier-than-thou** *colloq.* self-righteous. **Holy City 1** a city held sacred by the adherents of a religion, esp. Jerusalem. **2** Heaven. **Holy Communion** see COMMUNION. **Holy Cross Day** the festival of the Exaltation of the Cross, Sept. 14. **holy day** a religious festival. **Holy Family** the young Jesus with his mother and St. Joseph (often with St. John the Baptist, St. Anne, etc.) as grouped in pictures, etc. **Holy Father** the Pope. **Holy Ghost** = *Holy Spirit*. **Holy Grail** see GRAIL. **holy Joe** *orig. Naut. sl.* **1** a clergyman. **2** a pious person. **Holy Land 1** W. Palestine, esp. Judaea. **2** a region similarly revered in non-Christian religions. **Holy Name** *RC Ch.* the name of Jesus as an object of formal devotion. **Holy Office** an office of the Roman Catholic Church succeeding the Inquisition and charged with the protection of faith and morals. **holy of holies 1** the inner chamber of the sanctuary in the Jewish temple, separated by a veil from the outer chamber. **2** an innermost shrine. **3** a thing regarded as most sacred. **holy orders** see ORDER. **holy place 1** (in *pl.*) places to which religious pilgrimage is made. **2** the outer chamber of the sanctuary in the Jewish temple. **Holy Roller** *sl.* a member of a religious group characterized by frenzied excitement or trances. **Holy Roman Empire** see ROMAN. **Holy Rood Day 1** the festival of the Invention (finding) of the Cross, May 3. **2** = *Holy Cross Day*. **Holy Sacrament** see SACRAMENT. **Holy Saturday** Saturday in Holy Week. **Holy Scripture** the Bible. **Holy See** the papacy or the papal court. **Holy Spirit** the third person of the Christian Trinity, God as spiritually acting. **holy terror** see TERROR. **Holy Thursday 1** Maundy Thursday. **2** Ascension Day. **Holy Trinity** see TRINITY. **holy war** a war waged in support of a religious cause. **holy water** water dedicated to holy uses, or blessed by a priest. **Holy Week** the week before Easter. **Holy Writ** holy writings collectively, esp. the Bible. **Holy Year** *RC Ch.* a period of remission from the penal consequences of sin, granted under certain conditions for a year usu. at intervals of 25 years. [OE *hālig* f. Gmc, rel. to WHOLE]

■ **1, 2** godly, godlike, saintly, saintlike, pious, devout, religious, reverent, faithful, God-fearing; chaste, pure, unsullied, clean, sinless, spotless, immaculate, undefiled, uncorrupted, untainted; sacred, divine, heavenly, celestial, esp. *poet.* supernal. **3** sacred, consecrated, sanctified, blessed, hallowed. □ **holier-than-thou** see SELF-RIGHTEOUS. **holy Joe 1** see

CLERGYMAN. **holy of holies 1** sanctum sanctorum. **2** sanctuary, shrine. **3** fetish, *colloq.* sacred cow.

holystone /hóleestōn/ *n. & v. Naut.* ● *n.* a piece of soft sandstone used for scouring decks. ● *v.tr.* scour with this. [19th c.: prob. f. HOLY + STONE: the stones were called *bibles*, etc., perh. because used while kneeling]

hom /hōm/ *n.* (also **homa** /hómə/) **1** the soma plant. **2** the juice of this plant as a sacred drink of the Parsees. [Pers. *hōm*, *hūm*, Avestan *haoma*]

homage /hómij/ *n.* **1** acknowledgment of superiority; respect; dutiful reverence (*pay homage to; do homage to*). **2** *hist.* formal public acknowledgment of feudal allegiance. [ME f. OF (*h*)*omage* f. med.L *hominaticum* f. L *homo -minis* man]
■ **1** obeisance, deference, reverence, veneration; respects, honor, tribute.

hombre /ómbray/ *n.* a man. [Sp.]

Homburg /hómbərg/ *n.* a man's felt hat with a narrow curled brim and a lengthwise dent in the crown. [*Homburg* in Germany, where first worn]

home /hōm/ *n., adj., adv., & v.* ● *n.* **1 a** the place where one lives; the fixed residence of a family or household. **b** a dwelling-house. **2** the members of a family collectively; one's family background (*comes from a good home*). **3** the native land of a person or of a person's ancestors. **4** an institution for persons needing care, rest, or refuge (*nursing home*). **5** the place where a thing originates or is native or most common. **6 a** the finishing point in a race. **b** (in games) the place where one is free from attack; the goal. **c** *Baseball* home plate. **d** *Lacrosse* a player in an attacking position near the opponents' goal. **7** *Sports* a home game or win. ● *attrib.adj.* **1 a** of or connected with one's home. **b** carried on, done, or made at home. **c** proceeding from home. **2 a** carried on or produced in one's own country (*home industries; the home market*). **b** dealing with the domestic affairs of a country. **3** *Sports* played on one's own field, etc. (*home game; home win*). **4** in the neighborhood of home. ● *adv.* **1 a** to one's home or country (*go home*). **b** arrived at home (*is he home yet?*). **c** at home (*stay home*). **2 a** to the point aimed at (*the thrust went home*). **b** as far as possible (*drove the nail home; pressed his advantage home*). ● *v.* **1** *intr.* (esp. of a trained pigeon) return home (cf. HOMING 1). **2** *intr.* (often foll. by *on, in on*) (of a vessel, missile, etc.) be guided toward a destination or target by a landmark, radio beam, etc. **3** *tr.* send or guide homewards. **4** *tr.* provide with a home. □ **at home 1** in one's own house or native land. **2** at ease as if in one's own home (*make yourself at home*). **3** (usu. foll. by *in, on, with*) familiar or well informed. **4** available to callers. ● *n.* a social reception in a person's home. **come home** to become fully realized by. **come home to roost** see ROOST. **home and dry** *Brit.* having achieved one's purpose. **home away from home** a place other than one's home where one feels at home; a place providing homelike amenities. **home-bird** *Brit.* a person who likes to stay at home. **home brew** beer or other alcoholic drink brewed at home. **home-brewed** (of beer, etc.) brewed at home. **Home Counties** (in the UK) the counties closest to London. **home economics** the study of household management. **home farm** *Brit.* a farm (one of several on an estate) set aside to provide produce for the owner. **home from home** = *home away from home*. **home guard** *hist.* a volunteer group that provides local military defense when the regular army is elsewhere. **home help** a person employed to help in a person's home. **home, James!** *joc.* drive home quickly! **home movie** a film made at home or of one's own activities. **Home Office 1** the British government department dealing with law and order, immigration, etc., in England and Wales. **2** the building used for this. **home of lost causes** Oxford University. **home perm** a permanent wave made with domestic equipment. **home plate** *Baseball* a plate beside which the batter stands and which the runner must cross to score a run. **home port** the port from which a ship originates. **home rule** the government of a country or region by its own citizens. **home run 1** *Baseball* a hit that allows the batter to make a complete circuit of the bases. **2** any singular success. **Home Secretary** (in the UK) the Secretary of State in charge of

the Home Office. **home signal** a signal indicating whether a train may proceed into a station or to the next section of the line. **home stretch** (*Brit.* **straight**) the concluding stretch of a racetrack. **home town** the town of one's birth or early life or present fixed residence. **home trade** trade carried on within a country. **home truth** basic but unwelcome information concerning oneself. **home unit** *Austral.* a private residence, usu. occupied by the owner, as one of several in a building. **near home** affecting one closely. □□ **homelike** *adj.* [OE *hām* f. Gmc]
■ *n.* **1** residence, domicile, abode, address, (living) quarters; house, habitation, place, *formal* dwelling (place), dwelling house. **2** family, household, ménage, background. **3** country, territory, (native) land *or* soil, homeland, fatherland, motherland, mother country. **4** institution, rest home, *Brit.* hospice, *hist.* almshouse, poorhouse; refuge, shelter, hostel. **5** see ENVIRONMENT 1, 2. ● *attrib.adj.* **1** family, domestic, household. **2** native, national, internal. **4** see NEIGHBORHOOD. ● *v.* **2** (*home in on*) zero in on, make a beeline for, head for, aim at *or* for, target. □ **at home 2** comfortable, at ease, relaxed, composed, tranquil, serene, untroubled. **3** (*at home with* or *in*) comfortable with, conversant with, knowledgeable about, familiar with, well-versed in, competent in, expert in, proficient in, skilled in, up on, current in, adroit in, informed in *or* on *or* about, *sl.* clued in on. **4** in, accessible, available, welcoming. ● *n.* see RECEPTION 3.

homebody /hómbodee/ *n.* (*pl.* **-ies**) a person who likes to stay at home.

homeboy /hómboy/ *n. colloq.* a person from one's own town or neighborhood.

homecoming /hómkəming/ *n.* **1** arrival at home. **2** a high school, college, or university game, dance, or other event to which alumni are invited to return.

homegrown /hómgrōn/ *adj.* grown or produced at home.

homeland /hómland/ *n.* **1** one's native land. **2** *hist.* an area in S. Africa formerly reserved for a particular African people (the official name for a Bantustan).
■ **1** see COUNTRY 3.

homeless /hómlis/ *adj. & n.* ● *adj.* lacking a home. ● *n.* (prec. by *the*) homeless people. □□ **homelessness** *n.*
■ *adj.* on the streets, dispossessed, *Brit.* sleeping out *or* rough.

homely /hómlee/ *adj.* (**homelier, homeliest**) **1** (of people or their features) not attractive in appearance; ugly. **2 a** simple; plain. **b** unpretentious. **c** primitive. **3** comfortable in the manner of a home; cozy. **4** skilled at housekeeping. □□ **homeliness** *n.*
■ **1** ugly, plain, uncomely, unattractive, unlovely. **2 a** basic, plain, natural; see also SIMPLE *adj.* 2. **b** unpretentious, modest, unassuming, unaffected, informal, unsophisticated, homespun, commonplace, ordinary, familiar, everyday. **3** homey, homelike, warm, cozy, snug, domestic, friendly, congenial, comfortable, easy.

homemade /hómmayd/ *adj.* made at home.

homemaker /hómmaykər/ *n.* a person who manages a household, esp. as a fulltime occupation.

homeopath /hómeeəpath/ *n.* (*Brit.* **homoeopath**) a person who practices homeopathy. [G *Homöopath* (as HOMEOPATHY)]

homeopathy /hómeeópəthee/ *n.* (*Brit.* **homoeopathy**) the treatment of disease by minute doses of drugs that in a healthy person would produce symptoms of the disease (cf. ALLOPATHY). □□ **homeopathic** /-meeəpáthik/ *adj.* **homeopathist** *n.* [G *Homöopathie* f. Gk *homoios* like + *patheia* -PATHY]

homeostasis /hómeeōstáysis/ *n.* (*Brit.* **homoeostasis**) (*pl.*

/. . ./ **pronunciation**	● **part of speech**
□ **phrases, idioms, and compounds**	
□□ **derivatives**	■ **synonym section**
cross-references appear in SMALL CAPITALS or *italics*	

-stases /-seez/) the tendency toward a relatively stable equilibrium between interdependent elements, esp. as maintained by physiological processes. □□ **homeostatic** /-státik/ adj. [mod.L f. Gk homoios like + -STASIS]

homeotherm /hŏmeeəthárm/ n. (also **homoeotherm** or **homoiotherm**) an organism that maintains its body temperature at a constant level, usu. above that of the environment, by its metabolic activity; a warm-blooded organism (cf. POIKILOTHERM). □□ **homeothermal** adj. **homeothermic** adj. **homeothermy** n. [mod.L f. Gk homoios like + thermē heat]

homeowner /hŏmōnər/ n. a person who owns his or her own home.

homer /hŏmər/ n. **1** Baseball a home run. **2** a homing pigeon.

Homeric /hōmérik/ adj. **1** of, or in the style of, Homer or the epic poems ascribed to him. **2** of Bronze Age Greece as described in these poems. **3** epic; large-scale; titanic (Homeric conflict). [L Homericus f. Gk Homērikos f. Homēros Homer, traditional author of the Iliad and the Odyssey]
■ **1, 3** see HEROIC adj. 2b.

homesick /hŏmsik/ adj. depressed by longing for one's home during absence from it. □□ **homesickness** n.
■ depressed, longing, pining, lonely, lonesome; nostalgic, wistful.

homespun /hŏmspun/ adj. & n. ● adj. **1 a** (of cloth) made of yarn spun at home. **b** (of yarn) spun at home. **2** plain; simple; unsophisticated; homely. ● n. **1** homespun cloth. **2** anything plain or homely.
■ adj. **2** rustic, homely, plain, simple, unrefined, unpolished, unsophisticated, down-to-earth.

homestead /hŏmsted/ n. **1** a house, esp. a farmhouse, and outbuildings. **2** Austral. & NZ the owner's residence on a sheep or cattle station. **3** an area of land (usu. 160 acres) granted to an early American settler as a home. □□ **homesteader** n. [OE hāmstede (as HOME, STEAD)]
■ **1** see HOUSE n. 1a.

homestyle /hŏmstil/ adj. (esp. of food) of a kind made or done at home; homey.

homeward /hŏmwərd/ adv. & adj. ● adv. (also **homewards** /-wərdz/) toward home. ● adj. going or leading toward home. □ **homeward bound** (esp. of a ship) preparing to go, or on the way, home. [OE hāmweard(es) (as HOME, -WARD)]

homework /hŏmwərk/ n. **1** work to be done at home, esp. by a school pupil. **2** preparatory work or study.
■ see ASSIGNMENT 1.

homey /hŏmee/ adj. (also **homy**) (**homier**, **homiest**) suggesting home; cozy. □□ **homeyness** n. (also **hominess**).
■ see HOMELY 3.

homicide /hŏmisid, hŏ-/ n. **1** the killing of a human being by another. **2** a person who kills a human being. □□ **homicidal** /-síd'l/ adj. [ME f. OF f. L homicidium (sense 1), homicida (sense 2) (HOMO man)]
■ **1** see MURDER n. 1. **2** see murderer, murderess (MURDER). □□ **homicidal** murderous, bloodthirsty, sanguinary, ferocious, death-dealing.

homiletic /hómilétik/ adj. & n. ● adj. of homilies. ● n. (usu. in pl.) the art of preaching. [LL homileticus f. Gk homilētikos f. homileō hold converse, consort (as HOMILY)]

homiliary /hómilee-eree/ n. (pl. **-ies**) a book of homilies. [med.L homeliarius (as HOMILY)]

homily /hómilee/ n. (pl. **-ies**) **1** a sermon. **2** a tedious moralizing discourse. □□ **homilist** n. [ME f. OF omelie f. eccl.L homilia f. Gk homilia f. homilos crowd]
■ see SERMON 1.

homing /hŏming/ attrib.adj. **1** (of a pigeon) trained to fly home; bred for long-distance racing. **2** (of a device) for guiding to a target, etc. **3** that goes home. □ **homing instinct** the instinct of certain animals to return to the territory from which they have been moved.

hominid /hóminid/ n. & adj. ● n. any member of the primate family Hominidae, including humans and their fossil ancestors. ● adj. of or relating to this family. [mod.L Hominidae f. L homini homo man]

hominoid /hóminoyd/ adj. & n. ● adj. **1** like a human. **2** hominid or pongid. ● n. an animal resembling a human.

■ adj. **1** see HUMAN adj. 1–3.

hominy /hóminee/ n. coarsely ground corn kernels soaked in lye then washed to remove the hulls. [Algonquian]

homo[1] /hŏmō/ n. any primate of the genus Homo, including modern humans and various extinct species. [L, = man]

homo[2] /hŏmō/ n. (pl. **-os**) offens. colloq. a homosexual. [abbr.]

homo- /hŏmō/ comb. form same (often opp. HETERO-). [Gk homos same]

homocentric /hŏmōséntrik/ adj. having the same center.

homoerotic /hŏmōərótik/ adj. homosexual.

homogametic /hŏmōgámeetik, -gəmét-/ adj. Biol. (of a sex or individuals of a sex) producing gametes that carry the same sex chromosome.

homogamy /həmógəmee/ n. Bot. **1** a state in which the flowers of a plant are hermaphrodite or of the same sex. **2** the simultaneous ripening of the stamens and pistils of a flower. □□ **homogamous** adj. [Gk homogamos (as HOMO-, gamos marriage)]

homogenate /həmójinayt/ n. a suspension produced by homogenizing.

homogeneous /hŏməjée'neeəs, -yəs/ adj. **1** of the same kind. **2** consisting of parts all of the same kind; uniform. **3** Math. containing terms all of the same degree. □□ **homogeneity** /-jinée'itee/ n. **homogeneously** adv. **homogeneousness** n. [med.L homogeneus f. Gk homogenēs (as HOMO-, genēs f. genos kind)]
■ **1** identical, alike, akin, similar, comparable. **2** uniform, constant, consistent, unvarying.

homogenetic /hŏmōjinétik/ adj. Biol. having a common descent or origin.

homogenize /həmójiniz/ v. **1** tr. & intr. make or become homogeneous. **2** tr. treat (milk) so that the fat droplets are emulsified and the cream does not separate. □□ **homogenization** n. **homogenizer** n.
■ **1** see STANDARDIZE.

homogeny /həmójinee/ n. Biol. similarity due to common descent. □□ **homogenous** adj.

homograft /hŏməgraft, hóm-/ n. a graft of living tissue from one to another of the same species but different genotype.

homograph /hóməgraf, hŏ-/ n. a word spelled like another but of different meaning or origin (e.g., POLE[1], POLE[2]).

homoiotherm var. of HOMEOTHERM.

homoiousian /hŏmoy-ōōseeən, -zee-, -ów-/ n. hist. a person who held that God the Father and God the Son are of like but not identical substance (cf. HOMOOUSIAN). [eccl.L f. Gk homoiousios f. homoios like + ousia essence]

homolog var. of HOMOLOGUE.

homologate /həmóləgayt/ v.tr. **1** acknowledge; admit. **2** confirm; accept. **3** approve (a car, boat, engine, etc.) for use in a particular class of racing. □□ **homologation** /-gáyshən/ n. [med.L homologare agree f. Gk homologeō (as HOMO-, logos word)]

homologize /həmóləjiz/ v. **1** intr. be homologous; correspond. **2** tr. make homologous.

homologous /həmóləgəs/ adj. **1 a** having the same relation, relative position, etc. **b** corresponding. **2** Biol. (of organs, etc.) similar in position and structure but not necessarily in function. **3** Biol. (of chromosomes) pairing at meiosis and having the same structural features and pattern of genes. **4** Chem. (of a series of chemical compounds) having the same functional group but differing in composition by a fixed group of atoms. [med.L homologus f. Gk (as HOMO-, logos ratio, proportion)]
■ see LIKE[1] adj. 1a.

homologue /hŏməlawg, -log, hŏ-/ n. (also **homolog**) a homologous thing. [F f. Gk homologon (neut. adj.) (as HOMOLOGOUS)]
■ see PARALLEL n. 1.

homology /həmóləjee/ n. a homologous state or relation; correspondence. □□ **homological** /hŏmələjikəl/ adj.

homomorphic /hŏmōmáwrfik, hóm-/ adj. (also **homomorphous**) of the same or similar form. □□ **homomorphically** adv. **homomorphism** n. **homomorphy** n.

homonym /hŏmənim/ n. **1** a word of the same spelling or sound as another but of different meaning; a homograph or homophone. **2** a namesake. □□ **homonymic** /-nímik/ *adj.* **homonymous** /həmóniməs/ *adj.* [L *homonymum* f. Gk *homōnumon* (neut. adj.) (as HOMO-, *onoma* name)]

homoousian /hómō-ōōseeən, -zee-, -ów-/ *n.* (also **homousian**) *hist.* a person who held that God the Father and God the Son are of the same substance (cf. HOMOIOUSIAN). [eccl.L *homoousianus* f. LL *homousius* f. Gk *homoousios* (as HOMO-, *ousia* essence)]

homophobia /hóməfōbeeə/ *n.* a hatred or fear of homosexuals. □□ **homophobe** /-əfōb/ *n.* **homophobic** *adj.*

homophone /hóməfōn, hō̃-/ *n.* **1** a word having the same sound as another but of different meaning or origin (e.g., *pair, pear*). **2** a symbol denoting the same sound as another.

homophonic /hóməfónik, hō̃-/ *adj. Mus.* in unison; characterized by movement of all parts to the same melody. □□ **homophonically** *adv.*

homophonous /həmófənəs/ *adj.* **1** (of music) homophonic. **2** (of a word or symbol) that is a homophone. □□ **homophony** *n.*

homopolar /hóməpólər, hóm-/ *adj.* **1** electrically symmetrical. **2** *Electr.* (of a generator) producing direct current without the use of commutators. **3** *Chem.* (of a covalent bond) in which one atom supplies both electrons.

homopteran /həmóptərən/ *n.* any insect of the suborder Homoptera, including aphids and cicadas, with wings of uniform texture (cf. HETEROPTERAN). □□ **homopterous** *adj.* [HOMO- + Gk *pteron* wing]

Homo sapiens /hṓmō sáypee-enz/ *n.* modern humans regarded as a species. [L, = wise man]
  ■ see HUMANITY 1a, b.

homosexual /hóməséksh ōōəl/ *adj. & n.* ● *adj.* **1** feeling or involving sexual attraction only to persons of the same sex. **2** concerning homosexual relations or people. **3** relating to the same sex. ● *n.* a homosexual person. □□ **homosexuality** /-shōōálitee/ *n.* **homosexually** *adv.*

homousian var. of HOMOOUSIAN.

homozygote /hómōzígōt/ *n. Biol.* **1** an individual with identical alleles determining a particular characteristic. **2** an individual that is homozygous and so breeds true. □□ **homozygous** *adj.*

homunculus /həmúngkyələs/ *n.* (also **homuncule** /-kyōōl/) (*pl.* **homunculi** /-lī/ or **homuncules**) a little man; a manikin. [L *homunculus* f. *homo -minis* man]

homy var. of HOMEY.

Hon. *abbr.* **1** Honorary. **2** Honorable.

hon /hun/ *n. colloq.* = HONEY 5. [abbr.]

honcho /hónchō/ *n. & v. sl.* ● *n.* (*pl.* **-os**) **1** a leader or manager; the person in charge. **2** an admirable man. ● *v.tr.* (**-oes, -oed**) be in charge of; oversee. [Jap. *han'chō* group leader]
  ■ *n.* **1** see BOSS¹ *n.*

hone /hōn/ *n. & v.* ● *n.* **1** a whetstone, esp. for razors. **2** any of various stones used as material for this. ● *v.tr.* sharpen on or as on a hone. [OE *hān* stone f. Gmc]
  ■ *v.* see SHARPEN.

honest /ónist/ *adj. & adv.* ● *adj.* **1** fair and just in character or behavior, not cheating or stealing. **2** free of deceit and untruthfulness; sincere. **3** fairly earned (*an honest living*). **4** (of an act or feeling) showing fairness. **5** (with patronizing effect) blameless but undistinguished (cf. WORTHY). **6** (of a thing) unadulterated; unsophisticated. ● *adv. colloq.* genuinely; really. □ **earn** (or **turn**) **an honest penny** (or **dollar**) earn money fairly. **honest broker** a mediator in international, industrial, etc., disputes (orig. of Bismarck). **honest-to-God** (or **-goodness**) *colloq. adj.* genuine; real. ● *adv.* genuinely; really. **make an honest woman of** *colloq.* marry (esp. a pregnant woman). [ME f. OF (*h*)*oneste* f. L *honestus* f. *honos* HONOR]
  ■ *adj.* **1** fair, just, trustworthy, truthful, honorable, decent, moral, virtuous, principled, upright, high-minded, *archaic* true, *archaic or joc.* trusty, *formal* veracious. **2** sincere, candid, frank, open, straightforward, forthright, direct, explicit, plainspoken, unambiguous, unequivocal, *colloq.* upfront. **3**

aboveboard, straight, square, square-dealing, proper, genuine, bona fide, legitimate, valid, rightful, sound, proper, *colloq* on the up and up. **4** fair, equitable; see also JUST *adj.* 2. **6** see UNSOPHISTICATED 2. ● *adv.* see REALLY 1. □ **honest-to-god** (or **goodness**) see GENUINE 1, 2.

honestly /ónistlee/ *adv.* **1** in an honest way. **2** really (*I don't honestly know*; *honestly, the nerve of them!*).
  ■ **1** truthfully, honorably, decently, morally, justly, fairly, equitably; in good faith, *colloq.* on the level; candidly, frankly, openly, straightforwardly, forthrightly, sincerely, unequivocally, plainly, simply; square, straight (out), in plain words *or* English. **2** see REALLY 1.

honesty /ónistee/ *n.* **1** being honest. **2** truthfulness. **3** a plant of the genus *Lunaria* with purple or white flowers, so called from its flat round semitransparent seed pods. [ME f. OF (*h*)*onesté* f. L *honestas -tatis* (as HONEST)]
  ■ **1** trustworthiness, uprightness, rectitude, probity, integrity, virtue, virtuousness, honor; fairness, equity, equitableness, evenhandedness, objectivity, impartiality, disinterestedness, justness, justice. **2** truthfulness, veracity, candor, openness, frankness, forthrightness, directness, straightforwardness, sincerity.

honey /húnee/ *n.* (*pl.* **-eys**) **1** a sweet sticky yellowish fluid made by bees and other insects from nectar collected from flowers. **2** the color of this. **3 a** a sweetness. **b** a sweet thing. **4** a person or thing excellent of its kind. **5** (usu. as a form of address) darling; sweetheart. □ **honey badger** a ratel. **honey bun** (or **bunch**) (esp. as a form of address) darling. **honey buzzard** any bird of prey of the genus *Pernis* feeding on the larvae of bees and wasps. **honey eater** any Australasian bird of the family Meliphagidae with a long tongue that can take nectar from flowers. **honey guide 1** any small bird of the family Indicatoridae which feeds on beeswax and insects. **2** a marking on the corolla of a flower thought to guide bees to nectar. **honey pot 1** a pot for honey. **2** a posture with the hands clasped under the hams. **3** something very attractive or tempting. **honey sac** an enlarged part of a bee's gullet where honey is formed. **honey-sweet** sweet as honey. [OE *hunig* f. Gmc]
  ■ **5** see DEAR *n.*

honeybee /húneebee/ *n.* any of various bees of the genus *Apis*, esp. the common hive bee (*A. mellifera*).

honeycomb /húneekōm/ *n. & v.* ● *n.* **1** a structure of hexagonal cells of wax, made by bees to store honey and eggs. **2 a** a pattern arranged hexagonally. **b** fabric made with a pattern of raised hexagons, etc. **3** tripe from the second stomach of a ruminant. **4** a cavernous flaw in metalwork, esp. in guns. ● *v.tr.* **1** fill with cavities or tunnels; undermine. **2** mark with a honeycomb pattern. [OE *hunigcamb* (as HONEY, COMB)]
  ■ *v.* **1** see RIDDLE² *v.* 1.

honeydew /húneedōō, -dyōō/ *n.* **1** a variety of melon with smooth pale skin and sweet green flesh. **2** a sweet sticky substance found on leaves and stems, excreted by aphids, fungus, etc. **3** an ideally sweet substance. **4** tobacco sweetened with molasses.

honeyed /húneed/ *adj.* (also **honied**) **1** of or containing honey. **2** sweet.

honeymoon /húneemōōn/ *n. & v.* ● *n.* **1** a vacation spent together by a newly married couple. **2** an initial period of enthusiasm or goodwill. ● *v.intr.* (usu. foll. by *in, at*) spend a honeymoon. □□ **honeymooner** *n.* [HONEY + MOON, orig. with ref. to waning affection, not to a period of a month]

honeysuckle /húneesukəl/ *n.* any climbing shrub of the genus *Lonicera* with fragrant yellow, pink, or red flowers. [ME

/.../ **pronunciation**	● **part of speech**
□ **phrases, idioms, and compounds**	
□□ **derivatives**	■ **synonym section**
cross-references appear in SMALL CAPITALS or *italics*	

703

hunisuccle, -soukel, extension of hunisucce, -souke, f. OE hunigsūce, -sūge (as HONEY, SUCK)]

honied var. of HONEYED.

honk /hawngk, hongk/ n. & v. ● n. **1** the cry of a wild goose. **2** the harsh sound of a car horn. ● v. **1** intr. emit or give a honk. **2** tr. cause to do this. [imit.]

honky /háwngkee, hóngkee/ n. (pl. **-ies**) black sl. offens. **1** a white person. **2** white people collectively. [20th c.: orig. unkn.]

honky-tonk /háwngkeetawngk, hóngkeetongk/ n. colloq. **1** ragtime piano music. **2** a cheap or disreputable nightclub, bar, dancehall, etc. [20th c.: orig. unkn.]
■ **2** see DIVE n. 4.

honor /ónər/ n. & v. (Brit. **honour**) ● n. **1** high respect; glory; credit; reputation; good name. **2** adherence to what is right or to a conventional standard of conduct. **3** nobleness of mind; magnanimity (honor among thieves). **4** a thing conferred as a distinction, esp. an official award for bravery or achievement. **5** (foll. by of + verbal noun, or to + infin.) privilege; special right (had the honor of being invited). **6 a** exalted position. **b** (**Honor**) (prec. by your, his, etc.) a title of a judge, a mayor, or Ir. in rustic speech any person of rank. **7** (foll. by to) a person or thing that brings honor (she is an honor to her profession). **8 a** (of a woman) chastity. **b** the reputation for this. **9** (in pl.) a special distinction for proficiency in an examination. **b** a course of degree studies more specialized than for a standard course or degree. **10 a** Bridge the ace, king, queen, jack, and ten, esp. of trumps, or the four aces at no trumps. **b** Whist the ace, king, queen, and jack, esp. of trumps. **11** Golf the right of driving off first as having won the last hole (it is my honor). ● v.tr. **1** respect highly. **2** confer honor on. **3** accept or pay (a bill or check) when due. **4** acknowledge. □ **do the honors** perform the duties of a host to guests, etc. **honor bright** colloq. = on my honor. **honor point** Heraldry the point halfway between the top of a shield and the fesse point. **honors are even** Brit. there is equality in the contest. **honors list** a list of persons awarded honors. **honors of war** privileges granted to a capitulating force, e.g., that of marching out with colors flying. **honor roll** a list of people who have attained an honor, esp., a list of students who have received academic honors. **honor system** a system of examinations, etc., without supervision, relying on the honor of those concerned. **in honor bound** = on one's honor. **in honor of** as a celebration of. **on one's honor** (usu. foll. by to + infin.) under a moral obligation. **on** (or **upon**) **my honor** an expression of sincerity. [ME f. OF (h)onor (n.), onorer (v.) f. L honor, honarare]
■ n. **1** respect, esteem, reverence, veneration, homage, regard, renown, glory, celebrity, distinction, prestige, illustriousness, reputation, credit, colloq. kudos. **2, 3** probity, uprightness, decency, righteousness, rectitude, morality, justice, virtuousness, virtue; nobleness, magnanimity, integrity, honesty, fairness, justness, goodness. **4** see AWARD n. 1a. **5** privilege, distinction, special right; blessing. **6 a** see DIGNITY 4. **8** virginity, chastity, virtue, purity, innocence, chasteness; reputation, (good) name. ● v. **1** respect, esteem, revere, venerate, prize, value, pay homage to. **2** praise, laud, glorify, eulogize, salute, hail, acclaim, exalt. **3** pay, redeem, accept, clear, settle. **4** carry out, discharge, fulfill, observe, meet; acknowledge.

honorable /ónərəbəl/ adj. (Brit. **honourable**) **1 a** worthy of honor. **b** bringing honor to its possessor. **c** showing honor, not base. **d** consistent with honor. **e** colloq. (of the intentions of a man courting a woman) directed toward marriage. **2** (**Honorable**) a title indicating eminence or distinction, given to certain government officials, members of Congress, and Brit. MPs and the children of certain ranks of the nobility. □ **honorable mention** an award of merit to a candidate in an examination, a work of art, etc., not awarded a prize. □□ **honorableness** n. **honorably** adv. [ME f. OF honorable f. L honorabilis (as HONOR)]
■ **1 a, b, c** upright, upstanding, trustworthy, honest, just, fair, moral, principled, uncorrupt, uncorrupted,

incorruptible, high-minded, noble, virtuous, chivalrous, righteous, right-minded, good, scrupulous, worthy, sterling, laudable, creditable, commendable, glorious, equitable, archaic or joc. trusty. **d** right, correct, proper, fitting, appropriate, virtuous, ethical, worthy, respectable, reputable, decent.

honorand /ónərand/ n. a person to be honored, esp. with an honorary degree. [L honorandus (as HONOR)]

honorarium /ónəráireeəm/ n. (pl. **honorariums** or **honoraria** /-reeə/) a fee, esp. a voluntary payment for professional services rendered without the normal fee. [L, neut. of honorarius: see HONORARY]
■ pay, payment, remuneration; emolument, fee.

honorary /ónəreree/ adj. **1 a** conferred as an honor, without the usual requirements, functions, etc. (honorary degree). **b** holding such a title or position (honorary colonel). **2** (of an office or its holder) unpaid (honorary secretaryship; honorary treasurer). **3** (of an obligation) depending on honor, not legally enforceable. [L honorarius (as HONOR)]
■ **1** see NOMINAL 1. **2** see UNPAID.

honorific /ónərifik/ adj. & n. ● adj. **1** conferring honor. **2** (esp. of forms of speech) implying respect. ● n. an honorific form of words. □□ **honorifically** adv. [L honorificus (as HONOR)]

honoris causa /onáwris kówzə/ adv. (esp. of a degree awarded without examination) as a mark of esteem. [L, = for the sake of honor]

honour Brit. var. of HONOR.

honourable Brit. var. of HONORABLE.

Hon. Sec. abbr. Honorary Secretary.

hooch /hōōch/ n. (also **hootch**) colloq. alcoholic liquor, esp. inferior or illicit whiskey. [abbr. of Alaskan hoochinoo, name of a liquor-making tribe]
■ see DRINK n. 2a.

hood¹ /hŏŏd/ n. & v. ● n. **1 a** a covering for the head and neck, whether part of a cloak, etc., or separate. **b** a separate hoodlike garment worn over a university gown or a surplice to indicate the wearer's degree. **2** the cover over the engine of a motor vehicle. **3** Brit. a folding waterproof top of an automobile, a baby carriage, etc. **4** a canopy to protect users of machinery or to remove fumes, etc. **5** the hoodlike part of a cobra, seal, etc. **6** a leather covering for a hawk's head. ● v.tr. cover with a hood. □ **hood mold** (or **molding**) Archit. a dripstone. □□ **hoodless** adj. **hoodlike** adj. [OE hōd f. WG, rel. to HAT]

hood² /hŏŏd/ n. sl. a gangster or gunman. [abbr. of HOODLUM]
■ see GANGSTER.

-hood /hŏŏd/ suffix forming nouns: **1** of condition or state (childhood; falsehood). **2** indicating a collection or group (sisterhood; neighborhood). [OE -hād, orig. an independent noun, = person, condition, quality]

hooded /hŏŏdid/ adj. having a hood; covered with a hood. □ **hooded crow** a piebald gray and black crow, Corvus cornix, native to Europe.

hoodie /hŏŏdee/ n. Sc. = hooded crow.

hoodlum /hŏŏdləm, hŏŏd-/ n. **1** a street hooligan; a young thug. **2** a gangster. [19th c.: orig. unkn.]
■ **1** thug, ruffian, tough, rowdy, knave, rogue, scoundrel, hooligan, Austral. larrikin, colloq. roughneck, sl. plugugly, mug, Brit. sl. yob, yobbo, bovver boy; see also BARBARIAN n. 1. **2** gangster, racketeer, desperado, terrorist, apache, crook, colloq. baddy, sl. mobster, goon, hood, gunsel.

hoodoo /hŏŏdōō/ n. & v. ● n. **1 a** bad luck. **b** a thing or person that brings or causes this. **2** voodoo. **3** a fantastic rock pinnacle or column of rock formed by erosion, etc. ● v.tr. (**hoodoos, hoodooed**) **1** make unlucky. **2** bewitch. [alt. of VOODOO]
■ n. **1** see JINX n. ● v. **2** see BEWITCH 2.

hoodwink /hŏŏdwingk/ v.tr. deceive; delude. [orig. 'blindfold,' f. HOOD¹ n. + WINK]
■ fool, trick, deceive, delude, mislead, dupe, gull, defraud, cheat, humbug, lead up or down the garden path, flimflam, take in, throw dust in a person's eyes, pull the wool over a person's eyes, beguile, archaic

chicane, *colloq.* do, bamboozle, diddle, pull a fast one on, string along, finagle, rip off, put one over on, *sl.* take for a ride, chisel, cross, clip, bilk, rook, con, gyp, take to the cleaners.

hooey /hŏŏ-ee/ *n. & int. sl.* nonsense; humbug. [20th c.: orig. unkn.]
■ see NONSENSE.

hoof /hŏŏf, hŏŏf/ *n. & v.* ● *n.* (*pl.* **hoofs** or **hooves** /hŏŏvz/) the horny part of the foot of a horse, antelope, and other ungulates. ● *v.* **1** *tr.* strike with a hoof. **2** *tr. sl.* kick or shove. □ **hoof it** *sl.* **1** go on foot. **2** dance. **on the hoof** (of cattle) not yet slaughtered. □□ **hoofed** *adj.* (also in *comb.*). [OE *hōf* f. Gmc]

hoofer /hŏŏfər, hŏŏfər/ *n. sl.* a professional dancer.

hoo-ha /hŏŏhaa/ *n. sl.* a commotion; a row; uproar; trouble. [20th c.: orig. unkn.]
■ see UPROAR.

hook /hŏŏk/ *n. & v.* ● *n.* **1 a** a piece of metal or other material bent back at an angle or with a round bend, for catching hold of or for hanging things on. **b** (in full **fishhook**) a bent piece of wire, usu. barbed and baited, for catching fish. **2** a curved cutting instrument (*reaping hook*). **3 a** a sharp bend, e.g., in a river. **b** a projecting point of land (*Hook of Holland*). **c** a sandspit with a curved end. **4 a** *Cricket & Golf* a hooking stroke (see sense 5 of *v.*). **b** *Boxing* a short swinging blow with the elbow bent and rigid. **5** a trap, a snare. **6 a** a curved stroke in handwriting, esp. as made in learning to write. **b** *Mus.* an added stroke transverse to the stem in the symbol for an eighth-note, etc. **7** (in *pl.*) *sl.* fingers. ● *v.* **1** *tr.* **a** grasp with a hook. **b** secure with a hook or hooks. **2** (often foll. by *on, up*) **a** *tr.* attach with or as with a hook. **b** *intr.* be or become attached with a hook. **3** *tr.* catch with or as with a hook (*he hooked a fish*; *she hooked a husband*). **4** *tr. sl.* steal. **5** *tr.* **a** *Cricket* play (the ball) around from the off to the on side with an upward stroke. **b** (also *absol.*) *Golf* strike (the ball) so that it deviates toward the striker. **6** *tr. Rugby* secure (the ball) and pass it backward with the foot in the scrum. **7** *tr. Boxing* strike (one's opponent) with the elbow bent and rigid. □ **be hooked on** *sl.* be addicted to or captivated by. **by hook or by crook** by one means or another; by fair means or foul. **hook and eye** a small metal hook and loop as a fastener on a garment. **hook it** *Brit. sl.* make off; run away. **hook, line, and sinker** entirely. **off the hook 1** *colloq.* no longer in difficulty or trouble. **2** (of a telephone receiver) not on its rest, and so preventing incoming calls. **off the hooks** *Brit. sl.* dead. **on one's own hook** *sl.* on one's own account. **sling** (or **take**) **one's hook** *Brit. sl.* = *hook it*. □□ **hookless** *adj.* **hooklet** *n.* **hooklike** *adj.* [OE *hōc*: sense 3 of *n.* prob. influenced by Du. *hoek* corner]
■ *n.* **1 a** hanger, peg, holder; fastener, catch, clasp, clip, pin. **5** see TRAP¹ *n.* 1. ● *v.* **3** catch, trap, entrap, snare, ensnare, bag, land; grab, capture, collar, seize, snag, *sl.* nab. **4** steal, pilfer, filch, *colloq.* lift, rip off, *sl.* snitch, pinch, liberate, *Brit. sl.* nick; see also APPROPRIATE *v.* 1. □ **be hooked on** be mad *or* crazy about, be addicted to; see also LOVE *v.* 2–4. **by hook or by crook** somehow (or other), some way, come what may, by fair means or foul, one way or another. **hook, line, and sinker** completely, entirely, all the way, through and through, thoroughly, totally, utterly, wholly. **off the hook 1** (set) free, (in the) clear, out of trouble, acquitted, exonerated, cleared.

hookah /hŏŏkə/ *n.* an oriental tobacco pipe with a long tube passing through water for cooling the smoke as it is drawn through. [Urdu f. Arab. *ḥukkah* casket]
■ see PIPE *n.* 2a.

hooked /hŏŏkt/ *adj.* **1** hook-shaped (*hooked nose*). **2** furnished with a hook or hooks. **3** in senses of HOOK *v.* **4** (of a rug or mat) made by pulling woolen yarn through canvas with a hook.

hooker¹ /hŏŏkər/ *n.* **1** *sl.* a prostitute. **2** a person or thing that hooks. **3** *Rugby* the player in the middle of the front row of the scrum who tries to hook the ball.
■ **1** see PROSTITUTE *n.* 1a.

hooker² /hŏŏkər/ *n.* **1** a small Dutch or Irish fishing vessel. **2** *derog.* any ship. [Du. *hoeker* f. *hoek* HOOK]

Hooke's law /hŏŏks/ *n.* the law that the strain in a solid is proportional to the applied stress within the elastic limit of that solid. [R. *Hooke*, Engl. scientist d. 1703]

hooknose /hŏŏknōz/ *n.* an aquiline nose. □□ **hook-nosed** *adj.*

hookup /hŏŏkəp/ *n.* **1** a connection, esp. an interconnection of broadcasting equipment for special transmissions. **2** a connection to a public water, sewer, electric, etc., line.

hookworm /hŏŏkwərm/ *n.* **1** any of various nematode worms, with hooklike mouthparts for attachment and feeding, infesting humans and animals. **2** a disease caused by one of these, often resulting in severe anemia.

hooky /hŏŏkee/ *n.* (also **hookey**) □ **play hooky** *sl.* play truant. [19th c.: orig. unkn.]

hooligan /hŏŏligən/ *n.* a young ruffian, esp. a member of a gang. □□ **hooliganism** *n.* [19th c.: orig. unkn.]
■ see THUG.

hoop¹ /hŏŏp/ *n. & v.* ● *n.* **1** a circular band of metal, wood, etc., esp. for binding the staves of casks, etc., or for forming part of a framework. **2 a** a circular usu. wood or plastic band used as a toy. **b** a large ring usu. with paper stretched over it for circus performers to jump through. **3** an arch of iron, etc., through which the balls are hit in croquet; a wicket. **4** (in *pl.*) the game of basketball. **5** *hist.* **a** a circle of flexible material for expanding a woman's petticoat or skirt. **b** (in full **hoop skirt**) a skirt expanded with this. **6 a** a band of contrasting color on a jockey's blouse, sleeves, or cap. **b** *Austral. colloq.* a jockey. ● *v.tr.* **1** bind with a hoop or hoops. **2** encircle with or as with a hoop. □ **be put** (or **go**) **through the hoop** (or **hoops**) undergo an ordeal. **hoop iron** iron in long thin strips for binding casks, etc. [OE *hōp* f. WG]
■ *n.* **1, 2** see RING¹ *n.* 2. ● *v.* **2** see CIRCLE *v.* 2.

hoop² var. of WHOOP.

hoopla /hŏŏplaa/ *n.* **1** *sl.* commotion; excitement. **2** *Brit.* a game in which rings are thrown in an attempt to encircle one of various prizes. **3** *sl.* pretentious nonsense. **4** noisy publicity; ballyhoo.

hoopoe /hŏŏpōō/ *n.* a salmon-pink bird, *Upupa epops*, with black and white wings and tail, a large erectile crest, and a long decurved bill. [alt. of ME *hoop* f. OF *huppe* f. L *upupa*, imit. of its cry]

hooray /hŏŏráy/ *int.* **1** = HURRAH. **2** *Austral. & NZ* good-bye. □ **Hooray Henry** /hŏŏray/ *Brit. sl.* a rich ineffectual young man, esp. one who is fashionable, extroverted, and conventional. [var. of HURRAH]

hooroo /hŏŏrōō/ *int. & n.* (also **hurroo**) *Austral. colloq.* = HURRAH. [alt. of HOORAY, HURRAH]

hoosegow /hŏŏsgow/ *n. sl.* a prison. [Amer. Sp. *juzgao*, Sp. *juzgado* tribunal f. L *judicatum* neut. past part. of *judicare* JUDGE]
■ see PRISON *n.* 1.

hoot /hŏŏt/ *n. & v.* ● *n.* **1** an owl's cry. **2** the sound made by a vehicle's horn or a steam whistle. **3** a shout expressing scorn or disapproval; an inarticulate shout. **4** *colloq.* **a** laughter. **b** a cause of this. **5** (also **two hoots**) *sl.* anything at all (*don't care a hoot*; *don't give a hoot*; *doesn't matter two hoots*). ● *v.* **1** *intr.* **a** (of an owl) utter its cry. **b** (of a vehicle horn or steam whistle) make a hoot. **c** (often foll. by *at*) make loud sounds, esp. of scorn or disapproval or *colloq.* merriment (*hooted with laughter*). **2** *tr.* **a** assail with scornful shouts. **b** (often foll. by *out, away*) drive away by hooting. **3** *tr.* sound (a vehicle horn or steam whistle). [ME *hūten* (v.), perh. imit.]
■ *n.* **1** see SQUAWK *n.* 1. **3** see JEER *n.* **4 a** see LAUGH *n.* 1. **5** see DAMN *n.* 2. ● *v.* **1 c** see LAUGH *v.* 1. **2** see SQUAWK *v.*

hootch var. of HOOCH.

/. . . / **pronunciation**	● **part of speech**
□ **phrases, idioms, and compounds**	
□□ **derivatives**	■ **synonym section**
cross-references appear in SMALL CAPITALS or *italics*	

hootenanny /hŏŏt'nanee/ n. (pl. -ies) colloq. an informal gathering with folk music. [orig. dial., = 'gadget']

hooter /hŏŏtər/ n. 1 sl. a nose. 2 (pl.) coarse sl. a women's breasts. 3 a person or animal that hoots. 4 Brit. a siren or steam whistle, esp. as a signal for work to begin or cease. 5 Brit. the horn of a motor vehicle.

hoots /hŏŏts/ int. Sc. & No. of Engl. expressing dissatisfaction or impatience. [natural exclam.: cf. Sw. hut begone, Welsh hwt away, Ir. ut out, all in similar sense]

Hoover /hŏŏvər/ n. & v. esp. Brit. ● n. propr. a vacuum cleaner (properly one made by the Hoover company). ● v. (**hoover**) 1 tr. (also absol.) clean (a carpet, etc.) with a vacuum cleaner. 2 (foll. by up) a tr. suck up with or as with a vacuum cleaner (hoovered up the crumbs). b absol. clean a room, etc., with a vacuum cleaner (decided to hoover up before they arrived). [W. H. Hoover, Amer. manufacturer d. 1932]

hooves pl. of HOOF.

hop¹ /hop/ v. & n. ● v. (**hopped, hopping**) 1 intr. (of a bird, frog, etc.) spring with two or all feet at once. 2 intr. (of a person) jump on one foot. 3 tr. cross (a ditch, etc.) by hopping. 4 intr. colloq. a make a quick trip. b make a quick change of position or location. 5 tr. colloq. a jump into (a vehicle). b obtain (a ride) in this way. 6 tr. (usu. as **hopping** n.) (esp. of aircraft) pass quickly from one (place of a specified type) to another (cloud-hopping; island-hopping). ● n. 1 a hopping movement. 2 colloq. an informal dance. 3 a short flight in an aircraft; the distance traveled by air without landing; a stage of a flight or journey. □ **hop in** (or out) colloq. get into (or out of) a car, etc. **hop it** Brit. sl. go away. **hopping mad** colloq. very angry. **hop, skip** (or **step**), **and jump** 1 a very short distance. 2 = triple jump. **hop the twig** (or **stick**) Brit. sl. 1 depart suddenly. 2 die. **on the hop** Brit. colloq. 1 unprepared (caught on the hop). 2 bustling about. [OE hoppian]

■ v. 1 jump, leap, bound, spring, vault. 4 a pop, nip, run, take a (short) trip, travel, come, go. ● n. 1 jump, leap, bound, spring, vault. 2 colloq. disco, bop; see also DANCE n. 3 (short) trip or flight or journey. □ **hop in** jump in, get in, climb in. **hopping mad** see FURIOUS 1, 2.

hop² /hop/ n. & v. ● n. 1 a climbing plant, Humulus lupulus, cultivated for the cones borne by the female. 2 (in pl.) a the ripe cones of this, used to give a bitter flavor to beer. b Austral. & NZ colloq. beer. 3 sl. opium or any other narcotic. ● v. (**hopped, hopping**) 1 tr. flavor with hops. 2 intr. produce or pick hops. 3 tr. sl. (foll. by up) stimulate with a drug. □ **hopped up** stimulated through the use of drugs (he was so hopped up he could barely stand still). [ME hoppe f. MLG, MDu. hoppe]

hope /hōp/ n. & v. ● n. 1 (in sing. or pl.; often foll. by of, that) expectation and desire combined, e.g., for a certain thing to occur (hope of getting the job). 2 a a person, thing, or circumstance that gives cause for hope. b ground of hope; promise. 3 what is hoped for. 4 archaic a feeling of trust. ● v. 1 intr. (often foll. by for) feel hope. 2 tr. expect and desire. 3 tr. feel fairly confident. □ **hope against hope** cling to a mere possibility. **hope chest** 1 a young woman's collection of clothes, linens, etc., in preparation for her marriage. 2 the chest in which it is stored. **not a** (or **some**) **hope!** colloq. no chance at all. □□ **hoper** n. [OE hopa]

■ n. 1, 3 desire, wish, expectation; ambition, dream; yearning, hankering, craving, longing, fancy; see also AMBITION 2. 2 b prospect, promise, expectation, expectancy, confidence, anticipation, security, faith, conviction, belief, trust. ● v. 1, 2 expect, wait, trust; anticipate, contemplate, foresee; (hope for) wish, want, desire, look for, seek. 3 (hope to) count or rely on or upon, expect or intend to; see also TRUST v. 1. □ **not a hope** no chance at all.

hopeful /hōpfŏŏl/ adj. & n. ● adj. 1 feeling hope. 2 causing or inspiring hope. 3 likely to succeed; promising. ● n. (in full **young hopeful**) 1 a person likely to succeed. 2 iron. a person likely to be disappointed. □□ **hopefulness** n.

■ adj. 1 wishful, desirous, anxious, expectant; sanguine, confident, assured, buoyant, bullish; see also optimistic

(OPTIMISM). 2, 3 promising, bright, rosy, cheering, reassuring, heartening, encouraging, auspicious, propitious, inspiriting, positive.

hopefully /hōpfŏŏlee/ adv. 1 in a hopeful manner. 2 disp. (qualifying a whole sentence) it is to be hoped (hopefully, the car will be ready by then).

■ 1 expectantly, optimistically, sanguinely, confidently. 2 with (any) luck, if things go well, all being well, it is hoped.

hopeless /hōplis/ adj. 1 feeling no hope. 2 admitting no hope (a hopeless case). 3 inadequate; incompetent (am hopeless at tennis). 4 without hope of success; futile. □□ **hopelessly** adv. **hopelessness** n.

■ 1 despairing, despondent, forlorn, disconsolate, inconsolable, depressed, dejected, melancholy, downcast, gloomy, miserable, discouraged, wretched, sorrowful, sad, unhappy. 2 desperate, beyond hope or saving, irreparable, beyond repair, irremediable, lost, irretrievable. 3 bad, poor, incompetent, inadequate, inept, unqualified, unfit, unskillful, deficient, feeble, ineffectual, esp. Brit. rubbishy, colloq. useless, sl. dud. 4 futile, vain, unavailing, impossible, impracticable, unworkable, pointless, worthless, useless, archaic bootless.

hophead /hóp-hed/ n. sl. 1 a drug addict. 2 Austral. & NZ a drunkard.

■ 1 see ADDICT n. 1.

Hopi /hŏpee/ n. 1 a a N. American people native to northeastern Arizona. b a member of this people. 2 the language of this people.

hoplite /hóplit/ n. a heavily armed foot-soldier of ancient Greece. [Gk hoplitēs f. hoplon weapon]

hopper¹ /hópər/ n. 1 a person who hops. 2 a hopping arthropod, esp. a flea or young locust. 3 a a container tapering downward (orig. having a hopping motion) through which grain passes into a mill. b a similar contrivance in various machines. 4 a a barge carrying away mud, etc., from a dredging machine and discharging it. b a railroad freight car able to discharge coal, etc., through its floor.

hopper² /hópər/ n. a hop picker.

hopple /hópəl/ v. & n. ● v.tr. fasten together the legs of (a horse, etc.) to prevent it from straying, etc. ● n. an apparatus for this. [prob. LG: cf. HOBBLE and early Flem. hoppelen = MDu. hobelen jump, dance]

hopsack /hópsak/ n. (or **sacking**) 1 a a coarse material made from hemp, etc. b sacking for hops made from this. 2 a coarse clothing fabric of a loose plain weave.

hopscotch /hópskoch/ n. a children's game of hopping over squares or oblongs marked on the ground to retrieve a flat stone, etc. [HOP¹ + SCOTCH¹]

horary /háwrəree/ adj. archaic 1 of the hours. 2 occurring every hour; hourly. [med.L horarius f. L hora HOUR]

horde /hawrd/ n. 1 a usu. derog. a large group; a gang. b a moving swarm or pack (of insects, wolves, etc.). 2 a troop of Tartar or other nomads. [Pol. horda f. Turki ordī, ordū camp: cf. URDU]

horehound /háwrhownd/ n. (also **hoarhound**) 1 a a herbaceous plant, Marrubium vulgare, with a white cottony covering on its stem and leaves. b its bitter aromatic juice used against coughs, etc. 2 a herbaceous plant, Ballota nigra, with an unpleasant aroma. [OE hāre hūne f. hār HOAR + hūne a plant]

horizon /hərīzən/ n. 1 a the line at which the earth and sky appear to meet. b (in full **sensible horizon**) the line at which the earth and sky would appear to meet but for irregularities and obstructions; a circle where the earth's surface touches a cone whose vertex is at the observer's eye. c (in full **celestial horizon**) a great circle of the celestial sphere, the plane of which passes through the center of the earth and is parallel to that of the apparent horizon of a place. 2 limit of mental perception, experience, interest, etc. 3 a geological stratum or set of strata, or layer of soil, with particular characteristics. 4 Archaeol. the level at which a particular set of remains is found. □ **on the horizon** (of an event) just imminent or becoming apparent. [ME f. OF or-

izon(te) f. LL *horizon -ontis* f. Gk *horizōn* (*kuklos*) limiting (circle)]
■ **2** view, purview, range, scope, vista, compass, perspective, ken, field of vision, limit(s). □ **on the horizon** see *in the pipeline* (PIPELINE).

horizontal /háwrizónt'l, hór-/ *adj.* & *n.* ● *adj.* **1 a** parallel to the plane of the horizon; at right angles to the vertical (*horizontal plane*). **b** (of machinery, etc.) having its parts working in a horizontal direction. **2 a** combining firms engaged in the same stage of production (*horizontal integration*). **b** involving social groups of equal status, etc. **3** of or at the horizon. ● *n.* a horizontal line, plane, etc. □ **horizontal stabilizer** a horizontal airfoil at the tail of an aircraft (*Brit.* also **tailplane**). □□ **horizontality** /-tálitee/ *n.* **horizontally** *adv.* **horizontalness** *n.* [F *horizontal* or mod.L *horizontalis* (as HORIZON)]
■ *adj.* **1 a** level, flat, plane; prone, supine, prostrate.

hormone /háwrmōn/ *n.* **1** *Biochem.* a regulatory substance produced in an organism and transported in tissue fluids such as blood or sap to stimulate cells or tissues into action. **2** a synthetic substance with a similar effect. □□ **hormonal** /-mōnəl/ *adj.* [Gk *hormōn* part. of *hormaō* impel]

horn /hawrn/ *n.* & *v.* ● *n.* **1 a** a hard permanent outgrowth, often curved and pointed, on the head of cattle, rhinoceroses, giraffes, and other esp. hoofed mammals, found singly, in pairs, or one in front of another. **b** the structure of a horn, consisting of a core of bone encased in keratinized skin. **2** each of two deciduous branched appendages on the head of (esp. male) deer. **3** a hornlike projection on the head of other animals, e.g., a snail's tentacle, the crest of a horned owl, etc. **4** the substance of which horns are composed. **5** anything resembling or compared to a horn in shape. **6** *Mus.* **a** = *French horn.* **b** a wind instrument played by lip vibration, orig. made of horn, now usu. of brass. **c** a horn player. **7** an instrument sounding a warning or other signal (*car horn*; *foghorn*). **8** a receptacle or instrument made of horn, e.g., a drinking vessel or powder flask, etc. **9** a horn-shaped projection. **10** the extremity of the moon or other crescent. **11 a** an arm or branch of a river, bay, etc. **b** (**the Horn**) Cape Horn. **12** a pyramidal peak formed by glacial action. **13** *sl.* the telephone. **14** *coarse sl.* an erect penis. **15** the hornlike emblem of a cuckold. ● *v.tr.* **1** (esp. as **horned** *adj.*) provide with horns. **2** gore with the horns. □ **horn in** *sl.* **1** (usu. foll. by *on*) intrude. **2** interfere. **horn of plenty** a cornucopia. **horn-rimmed** (esp. of spectacles) having rims made of horn or a substance resembling it. **on the horns of a dilemma** faced with a decision involving equally unfavorable alternatives. □□ **hornist** *n.* (in sense 6 of *n.*). **hornless** *adj.* **hornlike** *adj.* [OE f. Gmc, rel. to L *cornu*]
■ *n.* **7** see ALARM *n.* 2a. ● *v.* **2** see GORE[2].

hornbeam /háwrnbeem/ *n.* any tree of the genus *Carpinus*, with a smooth bark and a hard tough wood.

hornbill /háwrnbil/ *n.* any bird of the family Bucerotidae, with a hornlike excrescence on its large red or yellow curved bill.

hornblende /háwrnblend/ *n.* a dark brown, black, or green mineral occurring in many igneous and metamorphic rocks, and composed of calcium, magnesium, and iron silicates. [G (as HORN, BLENDE)]

hornbook /háwrnbŏŏk/ *n. hist.* a leaf of paper containing the alphabet, the Lord's Prayer, etc., mounted on a wooden tablet with a handle, and protected by a thin plate of horn.

horned /hawrnd/ *adj.* having a horn. □ **horned owl** an owl, *Bubo virginianus*, with hornlike feathers over the ears. **horned toad 1** an American lizard, *Phrynosoma cornutum*, covered with spiny scales. **2** any SE Asian toad of the family Pelobatidae, with horn-shaped extensions over the eyes.

hornet /háwrnit/ *n.* a large wasp, *Vespa crabro*, with a brown and yellow striped body, and capable of inflicting a serious sting. □ **stir up a hornets' nest** provoke or cause trouble or opposition. [prob. f. MLG, MDu. *horn(e)te*, corresp. to OE *hyrnet*, perh. rel. to HORN]

hornpipe /háwrnpip/ *n.* **1** a lively dance, usu. by one person (esp. associated with sailors). **2** the music for this. [name of an obs. wind instrument partly of horn: ME, f. HORN + PIPE]

hornstone /háwrnstōn/ *n.* a brittle siliceous rock.

hornswoggle /háwrnswogəl/ *v.tr. sl.* cheat; hoax. [19th c.: orig. unkn.]

hornwort /háwrnwərt/ *n.* any aquatic rootless plant of the genus *Ceratophyllum*, with forked leaves.

horny /háwrnee/ *adj.* (**hornier, horniest**) **1** of or like horn. **2** hard like horn; callous (*horny-handed*). **3** *sl.* sexually excited or frustrated. □□ **horniness** *n.*
■ **3** see *lustful* (LUST).

horologe /háwrələj, -loj, hór-/ *n. archaic* a timepiece. [ME f. OF *orloge* f. L *horologium* f. Gk *hōrologion* f. *hōra* time + *-logos* -telling]

horology /hawróləjee/ *n.* the art of measuring time or making clocks, watches, etc.; the study of this. □□ **horologer** *n.* **horologic** /háwrəlójik/ *adj.* **horological** *adj.* **horologist** /-rólǝjist/ *n.* [Gk *hōra* time + -LOGY]

horoscope /háwrəskōp, hór-/ *n. Astrol.* **1** a forecast of a person's future based on a diagram showing the relative positions of the stars and planets at that person's birth. **2** such a diagram (*cast a horoscope*). **3** observation of the sky and planets at a particular moment, esp. at a person's birth. □□ **horoscopic** /-skópik/ *adj.* **horoscopical** *adj.* **horoscopy** /həróskəpee/ *n.* [F f. L *horoscopus* f. Gk *hōroskopos* f. *hōra* time + *skopos* observer]

horrendous /həréndəs/ *adj.* horrifying; awful. □□ **horrendously** *adv.* **horrendousness** *n.* [L *horrendus* gerundive of *horrēre*: see HORRID]
■ see HORRIBLE 1.

horrent /háwrənt, hór-/ *adj. poet.* **1** bristling. **2** shuddering. [L *horrēre*: see HORRID]

horrible /háwribəl, hór-/ *adj.* **1** causing or likely to cause horror; hideous; shocking. **2** *colloq.* unpleasant; excessive (*horrible weather*; *horrible noise*). □□ **horribleness** *n.* **horribly** *adv.* [ME f. OF (*h*)*orrible* f. L *horribilis* f. *horrēre*: see HORRID]
■ **1** awful, horrendous, hideous, horrid, horrifying, horrific, terrible, terrifying, dreadful, abominable, abhorrent, appalling, frightening, frightful, ghastly, grim, grisly, ghoulish, gruesome, loathsome, repulsive, revolting, disgusting, sickening, shocking, atrocious, nauseating, nauseous, harrowing, bloodcurdling, unspeakable, monstrous, contemptible, despicable. **2** unpleasant, disagreeable, nasty, atrocious, objectionable, obnoxious, offensive, *colloq.* awful, detestable, horrid, terrible, dreadful, abominable, beastly, ghastly, frightful, shocking, accursed, infernal; see also REVOLTING.

horrid /háwrid, hór-/ *adj.* **1** horrible; revolting. **2** *colloq.* unpleasant; disagreeable (*horrid weather*; *horrid children*). **3** *archaic.* rough; bristling. □□ **horridly** *adv.* **horridness** *n.* [L *horridus* f. *horrēre* bristle, shudder]
■ **1, 2** see HORRIBLE.

horrific /hawrífik, hór-/ *adj.* horrifying. □□ **horrifically** *adv.* [F *horrifique* or L *horrificus* f. *horrēre*: see HORRID]
■ see HORRIBLE 1.

horrify /háwrifī, hór-/ *v.tr.* (**-ies, -ied**) arouse horror in; shock; scandalize. □□ **horrification** *n.* **horrifiedly** /-fīdlee/ *adv.* **horrifying** *adj.* **horrifyingly** *adv.* [L *horrificare* (as HORRIFIC)]
■ startle, upset, outrage, dismay, appall, distress, scandalize; see also SHOCK[1] *v.* 1.

horripilation /hawrípiláyshən, ho-/ *n.* = *goose flesh.* [LL *horripilatio* f. L *horrēre* to bristle + *pilus* hair]

horror /háwrər, hór-/ *n.* & *adj.* ● *n.* **1** a painful feeling of loathing and fear. **2 a** (often foll. by *of*) intense dislike. **b** (often foll. by *at*) *colloq.* intense dismay. **3 a** a person or thing causing horror. **b** *colloq.* a bad or mischievous person, etc. **4** (in *pl.*; prec. by *the*) a fit of horror, depression, or nervousness, esp. as in delirium tremens. **5** a terrified and revolted shuddering. **6** (in *pl.*) an exclamation of dismay.

/ . . . / **pronunciation** ● **part of speech**
□ **phrases, idioms, and compounds**
□□ **derivatives** ■ **synonym section**
cross-references appear in SMALL CAPITALS or *italics*

● *attrib. adj.* (of literature, movies, etc.) designed to attract by arousing pleasurable feelings of horror. □ **Chamber of Horrors** a place full of horrors (orig. a room of criminals, etc., in Madame Tussaud's waxworks). **horror-struck** (or **-stricken**) horrified; shocked. [ME f. OF (*h*)*orrour* f. L *horror -oris* (as HORRID)]

■ *n.* **1** fear, distress, dread, fright, alarm, upset, perturbation, panic, terror, trepidation, anxiety, angst, apprehension, uneasiness, queasiness, nervousness. **2 a** repugnance, dread, hatred, revulsion, detestation, abhorrence, distaste, dislike, aversion, antipathy, hostility, animosity, animus, rancor, odium. **3 b** see ROGUE *n.* 1, RASCAL. □ **horror-struck** (or **-stricken**) see *scared* (SCARE *v.* 2).

hors concours /áwr koɴkóor/ *adj.* **1** (of an exhibit or exhibitor) not competing for a prize. **2** unrivaled; unequaled. [F, lit. 'outside competition']

hors de combat /áwr də kawɴbaá/ *adj.* out of the fight; disabled. [F]

hors d'oeuvre /awrdŏrvrə, -dŏrv/ *n.* an appetizer served at the beginning of a meal or (occasionally) in place of or during a meal. [F, lit. 'outside the work']

■ appetizer, antipasto, smorgasbord, esp. *Brit.* starter.

horse /hawrs/ *n. & v.* ● *n.* **1 a** a solid-hoofed plant-eating quadruped, *Equus caballus*, with flowing mane and tail, used for riding and to carry and pull loads. **b** an adult male horse; a stallion or gelding. **c** a racehorse. **d** any other four-legged mammal of the genus *Equus*, including asses and zebras. **e** (*collect.*; as *sing.*) cavalry. **f** a representation of a horse. **2** a vaulting block. **3** a supporting frame esp. with legs (*clotheshorse*). **4** *sl.* heroin. **5** *colloq.* a unit of horsepower. **6** *Naut.* any of various ropes and bars. **7** *Mining* an obstruction in a vein. ● *v.* **1** *intr.* (foll. by *around*) fool around. **2** *tr.* provide (a person or vehicle) with a horse or horses. **3** *intr.* mount or go on horseback. □ **from the horse's mouth** (of information, etc.) from the person directly concerned or another authoritative source. **horse-and-buggy** old-fashioned; bygone. **horse block** a small platform of stone or wood for mounting a horse. **horse brass** see BRASS. **horse-breaker** one who breaks in horses. **horse chestnut 1** any large ornamental tree of the genus *Aesculus*, with upright conical clusters of white or pink or red flowers. **2** the dark brown fruit of this (like an edible chestnut, but with a coarse bitter taste). **horse-coper** *Brit.* a horse dealer. **horse doctor** a veterinary surgeon attending horses. **horse-drawn** (of a vehicle) pulled by a horse or horses. **Horse Guards 1** (in the UK) the cavalry brigade of the household troops. **2** the headquarters of such cavalry. **horse latitudes** a belt of calms in each hemisphere between the trade winds and the westerlies. **horse mackerel** any large fish of the mackerel type, e.g., the scad or the tuna. **horse mushroom** a large edible mushroom, *Agaricus arvensis*. **horse opera** *sl.* a western movie. **horse pistol** a pistol for use by a horseman. **horse-pond** a pond for watering and washing horses, proverbial as a place for ducking obnoxious persons. **horse race 1** a race between horses with riders. **2** *colloq.* a close contest. **horse racing** the sport of conducting horse races. **horse sense** *colloq.* plain common sense. **horses for courses** *Brit.* the matching of tasks and talents. **horse's neck** *Brit. sl.* a drink of flavored ginger ale usu. with liquor. **horse soldier** a soldier mounted on a horse. **horse-trading 1** dealing in horses. **2** shrewd bargaining. **to horse!** (as a command) mount your horses. □□ **horseless** *adj.* **horselike** *adj.* [OE *hors* f. Gmc]

horseback /háwrsbak/ *n.* the back of a horse, esp. as sat on in riding. □ **on horseback** mounted on a horse.

horsebean /háwrsbeen/ *n.* a broad bean used as fodder.

horsebox /háwrsboks/ *n. Brit.* a closed vehicle for transporting a horse or horses.

horseflesh /háwrsflesh/ *n.* **1** the flesh of a horse, esp. as food. **2** horses collectively.

horsefly /háwrsfli/ *n.* (*pl.* **-flies**) any of various biting dipterous insects of the family Tabanidae troublesome esp. to horses.

horsehair /háwrs-hair/ *n.* hair from the mane or tail of a horse, used for padding, etc.

horseleech /háwrsleech/ *n.* **1** a large kind of leech feeding by swallowing not sucking. **2** an insatiable person (cf. Prov. 30:15).

horseless /háwrslis/ *adj.* without a horse. □ **horseless carriage** *archaic* an automobile.

horseman /háwrsmən/ *n.* (*pl.* **-men**) **1** a rider on horseback. **2** a skilled rider.

horsemanship /háwrsmənship/ *n.* the art of riding on horseback; skill in doing this.

■ equestrianism, manège; seat.

horseplay /háwrsplay/ *n.* boisterous play.

■ see PLAY *n.* 1.

horsepower /háwrspowər/ *n.* (*pl.* same) **1** a unit of power equal to 550 foot-pounds per second (about 750 watts). ¶ Abbr.: **hp**. **2** the power of an engine, etc., measured in terms of this.

horseradish /háwrsradish/ *n.* **1** a cruciferous plant, *Armoracia rusticana*, with long lobed leaves. **2** the pungent root of this scraped or grated as a condiment, often made into a sauce.

horseshoe /háwrs-shoo/ *n.* **1** an iron shoe for a horse shaped like the outline of the hard part of the hoof. **2** a thing of this shape; an object shaped like C or U (e.g., a magnet, a table, a Spanish or Islamic arch). □ **horseshoe crab** a large marine arthropod, *Xiphosura polyphemus*, with a horseshoe-shaped shell and a long tail-spine: also called *king crab*.

horsetail /háwrstayl/ *n.* **1** the tail of a horse (formerly used in Turkey as a standard, or as an ensign denoting the rank of a pasha). **2** any cryptogamous plant of the genus *Equisetum*, like a horse's tail, with a hollow jointed stem and scalelike leaves. **3** = PONYTAIL.

horsewhip /háwrs-hwip, -wip/ *n. & v.* ● *n.* a whip for driving horses. ● *v.tr.* (**-whipped**, **-whipping**) beat with a horsewhip.

■ *n.* see WHIP *n.* ● *v.* see WHIP *v.* 1.

horsewoman /háwrswŏomən/ *n.* (*pl.* **-women**) **1** a woman who rides on horseback. **2** a skilled woman rider.

horst /hawrst/ *n. Geol.* a raised elongated block of land bounded by faults on both sides. [G, = heap]

horsy /háwrsee/ *adj.* (also **horsey**) (**horsier, horsiest**) **1** of or like a horse. **2** concerned with or devoted to horses or horse racing. **3** affectedly using the dress and language of a groom or jockey. **4** *colloq.* large; clumsy. □□ **horsily** *adv.* **horsiness** *n.*

hortative /háwrtətiv/ *adj.* (also **hortatory** /háwrtətawree/) tending or serving to exhort. □□ **hortation** /hawrtáyshən/ *n.* [L *hortativus* f. *hortari* exhort]

hortensia /hawrténseeə/ *n.* a kind of hydrangea, *Hydrangea macrophylla*, with large rounded infertile flower heads. [mod.L f. *Hortense* Lepaute, 18th-c. Frenchwoman]

horticulture /háwrtikúlchər/ *n.* the art of garden cultivation. □□ **horticultural** *adj.* **horticulturist** *n.* [L *hortus* garden, after AGRICULTURE]

hortus siccus /háwrtəs síkəs/ *n.* **1** an arranged collection of dried plants. **2** a collection of uninteresting facts, etc. [L, = dry garden]

Hos. *abbr.* Hosea (Old Testament).

hosanna /hōzánə/ *n. & int.* a shout of adoration (Matt. 21: 9, 15, etc.). [ME f. LL f. Gk *hōsanna* f. Heb. *hôša'nā* for *hôšî'a-nnā* save now!]

hose /hōz/ *n. & v.* ● *n.* **1** (also *Brit.* **hose-pipe**) a flexible tube conveying water for watering plants, etc., putting out fires, etc. **2 a** (*collect.*; as *pl.*) stockings and socks (esp. in trade use). **b** *hist.* breeches (*doublet and hose*). ● *v.tr.* **1** (often foll. by *down*) water or spray or drench with a hose. **2** provide with hose. [OE f. Gmc]

■ *n.* **1** see PIPE *n.* 1. ● *v.* **1** see WATER *v.* 1.

hosier /hŏzhər/ *n.* a dealer in hosiery.

hosiery /hŏzhəree/ *n.* **1** stockings and socks. **2** *Brit.* knitted or woven underwear.

hosp. *abbr.* **1** hospital. **2** hospice.

hospice /hóspis/ *n.* **1** a home or system of long-term care for

people who are terminally ill. **2** a lodging for travelers, esp. one kept by a religious order. [F f. L *hospitium* (as HOST²)]
■ **1** see HOME *n.* 4. **2** see MONASTERY.

hospitable /hóspitəbəl, hospít-/ *adj.* **1** giving or disposed to give welcome and entertainment to strangers or guests. **2** disposed to welcome something readily; receptive. □□ **hospitably** *adv.* [F f. *hospiter* f. med.L *hospitare* entertain (as HOST²)]
■ **1** welcoming, courteous, genial, friendly, agreeable, amicable, cordial, warm, congenial, generous. **2** openminded, receptive, amenable, approachable, tolerant.

hospital /hóspit'l/ *n.* **1** an institution providing medical and surgical treatment and nursing care for ill or injured people. **2** *hist.* **a** a hospice. **b** an establishment of the Knights Hospitallers. **3** *Brit. Law* a charitable institution (also in proper names, e.g., *Christ's Hospital*). □ **hospital corners** a way of tucking in sheets, used by nurses. **hospital fever** a kind of typhus formerly prevalent in crowded hospitals. **hospital ship** a ship to receive sick and wounded sailors, or to take sick and wounded soldiers home. **hospital train** a train taking wounded soldiers from a battlefield. [ME f. OF f. med.L *hospitale* neut. of L *hospitalis* (adj.) (as HOST²)]
■ **1** medical center, infirmary, dispensary, sanatorium, sanitarium, *Brit.* health center.

hospitaler var. of HOSPITALLER.

hospitalism /hóspit'lizəm/ *n.* the adverse effects of a prolonged stay in the hospital.

hospitality /hóspitálitee/ *n.* the friendly and generous reception and entertainment of guests or strangers. [ME f. OF *hospitalité* f. L *hospitalitas -tatis* (as HOSPITAL)]
■ friendliness, amicability, cordiality, warmth, congeniality, sociability, generosity.

hospitalize /hóspit'liz/ *v.tr.* send or admit (a patient) to the hospital. □□ **hospitalization** *n.*

hospitaller /hóspit'lər/ *n.* (also **hospitaler**) **1 a** a member of a charitable religious order. **b** (**Hospitaller**) a member of a military religious order, the Knights Hospitaller, established in 12th-c. Jerusalem. **2** a chaplain (in some London hospitals). [ME f. OF *hospitalier* f. med.L *hospitalarius* (as HOSPITAL)]

host¹ /hōst/ *n.* **1** (usu. foll. by *of*) a large number of people or things. **2** *archaic* an army. **3** (in full **heavenly host**) *Bibl.* **a** the sun, moon, and stars. **b** the angels. □ **host** (or **hosts**) **of heaven** = sense 3 of *n.* **Lord** (or **Lord God**) **of hosts** God as Lord over earthly or heavenly armies. [ME f. OF f. L *hostis* stranger, enemy, in med.L 'army']
■ **1, 2** army, swarm, crowd, horde, multitude, throng, mob, pack, herd, troop, legion, drove.

host² /hōst/ *n. & v.* ● *n.* **1** a person who receives or entertains another as a guest. **2** the landlord of an inn (*mine host*). **3** *Biol.* an animal or plant having a parasite or commensal. **4** an animal or person that has received a transplanted organ, etc. **5** the person who introduces and often interviews guests on a show, esp. a television or radio program. ● *v.tr.* act as host to (a person) or at (an event). [ME f. OF *oste* f. L *hospes -pitis* host, guest]
■ *n.* **2** innkeeper, hotelier, hotel keeper, landlord, landlady, manager, manageress, proprietor, *Brit.* publican. **5** master of ceremonies, MC, presenter, *Brit.* compère, *colloq.* emcee, announcer. ● *v.* entertain, act the host to, play host to; have, hold.

host³ /hōst/ *n.* the bread consecrated in the Eucharist. [ME f. OF (*h*)*oiste* f. L *hostia* victim]

hosta /hósta/ *n.* any perennial garden plant of the genus *Hosta* (formerly *Funkia*), including the plantain lily, with green or variegated ornamental leaves and loose clusters of tubular lavender or white flowers. [mod.L, f. N. T. *Host*, Austrian physician d. 1834]

hostage /hóstij/ *n.* **1** a person seized or held as security for the fulfillment of a condition. **2** a pledge or security. □ **a hostage to fortune** an acquisition, commitment, etc., regarded as endangered by unforeseen circumstances. □□ **hostageship** *n.* [ME f. OF (*h*)*ostage* ult. f. LL *obsidatus* hostageship f. L *obses obsidis* hostage]

■ **1** see CAPTIVE *n.* **2** security, surety, gage; see also PLEDGE *n.* 2.

hostel /hóst'l/ *n.* **1** = *youth hostel*. **2** *Brit.* **a** a house of residence or lodging for students, nurses, etc. **b** a place providing temporary accommodation for the homeless, etc. **3** *archaic* an inn. [ME f. OF (*h*)*ostel* f. med.L (as HOSPITAL)]

hosteling /hóst'ling/ *n.* the practice of staying in youth hostels, esp. while traveling. □□ **hosteler** *n.*

hostelry /hóst'lree/ *n.* (*pl.* **-ies**) *archaic* or *literary* an inn. [ME f. OF (*h*)*ostelerie* f. (*h*)*ostelier* innkeeper (as HOSTEL)]
■ inn, tavern, bar, saloon, *Brit.* pub, public house, *sl.* watering hole, joint.

hostess /hóstis/ *n.* **1** a woman who receives or entertains a guest. **2** a woman employed to welcome and entertain customers at a nightclub, etc. **3** a stewardess on an aircraft, train, etc. (*air hostess*). [ME f. OF (*h*)*ostesse* (as HOST²)]

hostile /hóstəl, -til/ *adj.* **1** of an enemy. **2** (often foll. by *to*) unfriendly; opposed. □ **hostile witness** *Law* a witness who appears hostile to the party calling him or her and therefore untrustworthy. □□ **hostilely** *adv.* [F *hostile* or L *hostilis* (as HOST¹)]
■ **1** enemy, warring, combative, opposing, militant, aggressive, fighting. **2** opposed, antagonistic, contrary, adverse; averse, loath; unfriendly, inimical, unsympathetic, inhospitable, unfavorable, unwelcoming; see also COLD *adj.* 4.

hostility /hóstílitee/ *n.* (*pl.* **-ies**) **1** being hostile; enmity. **2** a state of warfare. **3** (in *pl.*) acts of warfare. **4** opposition (in thought, etc.). [F *hostilité* or LL *hostilitas* (as HOSTILE)]
■ **1** antagonism, enmity, antipathy, animus, ill will, malevolence, malice, aversion, unfriendliness, hatred; see also ANIMOSITY. **3** (*hostilities*) war, warfare, fighting, combat, action, bloodshed. **4** see OPPOSITION 1–3.

hostler /hóslər, ós-/ *n.* **1** = OSTLER. **2** a person who services vehicles or machines, esp. train engines, when they are not in use. [ME f. *hosteler* (as OSTLER)]

hot /hot/ *adj., v., & adv.* ● *adj.* (**hotter, hottest**) **1 a** having a relatively or noticeably high temperature. **b** (of food or drink) prepared by heating and served without cooling. **2** producing the sensation of heat (*hot fever*; *hot flash*). **3** (of pepper, spices, etc.) pungent; piquant. **4** (of a person) feeling heat. **5 a** ardent; passionate; excited. **b** (often foll. by *for, on*) eager; keen (*in hot pursuit*). **c** angry or upset. **d** lustful. **e** exciting. **6 a** (of news, etc.) fresh; recent. **b** *Brit. colloq.* (of Treasury bills) newly issued. **7** *Hunting* (of the scent) fresh and strong, indicating that the quarry has passed recently. **8 a** (of a player) very skillful. **b** (of a competitor in a race or other sporting event) strongly favored to win (*a hot favorite*). **c** (of a hit, return, etc., in ball games) difficult for an opponent to deal with. **d** *colloq.* currently popular or in demand. **9** (of music, esp. jazz) strongly rhythmical and emotional. **10 a** difficult or awkward to deal with. **b** *sl.* (of goods) stolen, esp. easily identifiable and hence difficult to dispose of. **c** *sl.* (of a person) wanted by the police. **11 a** live, at a high voltage. **b** *sl.* radioactive. **12** *colloq.* (of information) unusually reliable (*hot tip*). **13** (of a color, shade, etc.) suggestive of heat; intense; bright. ● *v.* (**hotted, hotting**) (usu. foll. by *up*) *Brit. colloq.* **1** *tr. & intr.* make or become hot. **2** *tr. & intr.* make or become active, lively, exciting, or dangerous. ● *adv.* **1** *Brit.* angrily; severely (*give it him hot*). **2** eagerly. □ **go hot and cold 1** feel alternately hot and cold owing to fear, etc. **2** be alternately friendly then aloof. **have the hots for** *sl.* be sexually attracted to. **hot air** *sl.* empty, boastful, or excited talk. **hot-air balloon** a balloon (see BALLOON *n.* 2) consisting of a bag in which air is heated by burners located below it, causing it to rise. **hot blast** a blast of heated air forced into a furnace. **hotblooded** ardent; passionate. **hot cathode** a cathode heated to emit electrons. **hot cross bun** see BUN. **hot dog** *n.* **1** a

┌───┐
│ /. . ./ **pronunciation**   ● **part of speech** │
│ □ **phrases, idioms, and compounds**   │
│ □□ **derivatives**   ■ **synonym section** │
│ **cross-references** appear in SMALL CAPITALS or *italics* │
└───┘

= FRANKFURTER. **b** a frankfurter sandwiched in a soft roll. **2** *sl.* a person who is showy or shows off skills. ● *int. sl.* expressing approval. **hot flash** see FLASH. **hot gospeler** see GOSPELER. **hot line** a direct exclusive line of communication, esp. for emergencies. **hot metal** *Printing* using type made from molten metal. **hot money** capital transferred at frequent intervals. **hot plate** a heated metal plate, etc. (or a set of these), for cooking food or keeping it hot. **hot pot** *Brit.* a casserole of meat and vegetables, usu. with a layer of potato on top. **hot potato** *colloq.* a controversial or awkward matter or situation. **hot-press** *n.* a press of glazed boards and hot metal plates for smoothing paper or cloth or making plywood. ● *v.tr.* press (paper, etc.) in this. **hot rod** a motor vehicle modified to have extra power and speed. **hot seat** *sl.* **1** a position of difficult responsibility. **2** the electric chair. **hot spot 1** a small region or area that is relatively hot. **2** a lively or dangerous place. **hot spring** a spring of naturally hot water. **hot stuff** *colloq.* **1** a formidably capable person. **2** an important person or thing. **3** a sexually attractive person. **4** a spirited, strong-willed, or passionate person. **5** a book, movie, etc. with a strongly erotic content. **hot-tempered** impulsively angry. **hot tub** a tub of heated, circulating water for therapy or recreation, usu. able to accomodate several people. **hot under the collar** angry, resentful, or embarrassed. **hot war** an open war, with active hostilities. **hot water** *colloq.* difficulty, trouble, or disgrace (*be in hot water*; *get into hot water*). **hot-water bottle** (also **bag**) a container, usu. made of rubber, filled with hot water, esp. to warm the feet, a bed, etc. **hot well 1** = *hot spring.* **2** a reservoir in a condensing steam engine. **hot-wire** operated by the expansion of heated wire. **make it** (or **things**) **hot for a person** persecute a person. **not so hot** *colloq.* only mediocre. □□ **hotly** *adv.* **hotness** *n.* **hottish** *adj.* [OE *hāt* f. Gmc: cf. HEAT]

■ *adj.* **1** fiery, white-hot, red-hot, piping hot, burning, blistering, roasting, torrid, sultry, flaming, tropical, *colloq.* scorching, sizzling, boiling, baking, scalding, steaming, simmering, sweltering. **3** spicy, peppery, sharp, piquant, pungent. **5 a** intense, fervent, zealous, ardent, enthusiastic, passionate, fervid, feverish, vehement, excited, fiery, fierce, animated, earnest, violent. **b** eager, keen, avid, anxious, burning. **c** see ANGRY 1. **d** lustful, lecherous, libidinous, oversexed, sex-crazed, sex-mad, *archaic* lickerish, *formal* concupiscent; sexy, sensual, aroused, randy, *sl.* horny. **e** see EXCITING. **6 a** recent, fresh, new, latest, brand-new. **8 a** see SKILLFUL. **d** popular, sought-after, commercial, salable, marketable. **10 a** dangerous, precarious, risky, sensitive, delicate, unstable, touchy, unpredictable. **11 a** electrified, live, charged, powered. **12** see RELIABLE. **13** intense, vivid, striking, bright, brilliant, dazzling, loud. □ **have the hots for** see DESIRE *v.* 1. **hot air** blather, bunkum, verbiage, talk, bluff, bluster, wind, pretentiousness, pomposity, bombast, grandiloquence, magniloquence, flatulence, fluency, rodomontade, claptrap, *sl.* bosh, gas, guff; see also DRIVEL *n.* **hot-blooded** see PASSIONATE. **hot stuff 1** see GENIUS 1b. **3** see BEAUTY 3. **hot-tempered** see IRRITABLE 1. **hot under the collar** see ANGRY 1. **hot water** see DIFFICULTY 2b. **make it** (or **things**) **hot for a person** *colloq.* give a person hell; see also PERSECUTE 2, PUNISH 1. **not so hot** see MEDIOCRE 2. □□ **hotly** intensively, energetically, doggedly, persistently, zealously, fervently, fervidly, ardently, warmly, enthusiastically.

hotbed /hótbed/ *n.* **1** a bed of earth heated by fermenting manure. **2** (foll. by *of*) an environment promoting the growth of something, esp. something unwelcome (*hotbed of vice*).
■ **2** breeding ground, fertile source, hothouse.

hotcake /hótkayk/ *n.* a pancake. □ **like hotcakes** quickly and in great quantity, esp. because of popularity (*the new CD is selling like hotcakes*).

hotchpotch /hóchpoch/ *n.* (also (in sense 3) **hotchpot** /-pot/) **1** = HODGEPODGE. **2** a dish of many mixed ingredi-

ents, esp. a mutton broth or stew with vegetables. **3** *Law* the reunion and blending of properties for the purpose of securing equal division (esp. of the property of an intestate parent). [ME f. AF & OF *hochepot* f. OF *hocher* shake + POT¹: *-potch* by assim.]
■ **2** olio, olla podrida; see also STEW¹ *n.* 1.

hotdog /hótdawg, -dog/ *v.intr. sl.* show off, esp. one's skills.

hotel /hōtél/ *n.* **1** an establishment providing accommodation and meals for payment. **2** *Austral.* & *NZ* a public house; a bar. [F *hôtel*, later form of HOSTEL]
■ **1** inn; motel, motor hotel, bed and breakfast, auberge, gasthaus, pension, B & B, guesthouse, *archaic or literary* hostelry, *Austral. colloq.* pub.

hotelier /ōtelyáy, hōtˈleʹer/ *n.* a hotel-keeper. [F *hôtelier* f. OF *hostelier*: see HOSTELRY]
■ see PROPRIETOR 2.

hotfoot /hótfŏot/ *adv., v., & adj.* ● *adv.* in eager haste. ● *v.tr.* hurry eagerly (esp. *hotfoot it*). ● *adj.* acting quickly.
■ *v.* see HURRY *v.* 1.

hothead /hót-hed/ *n.* an impetuous person.

hotheaded /hót-hédid/ *adj.* impetuous; excitable. □□ **hotheadedly** *adv.* **hotheadedness** *n.*
■ impetuous, excitable, volatile, rash, hasty, wild, foolhardy, reckless, precipitate, thoughtless, heedless, madcap.

hothouse /hót-hows/ *n. & adj.* ● *n.* **1** a heated building, usu. largely of glass, for rearing plants out of season or in a climate colder than is natural for them. **2** an environment that encourages the rapid growth or development of something. ● *adj.* (*attrib.*) characteristic of something reared in a hothouse; sheltered; sensitive.
■ *n.* **1** hotbed, greenhouse, conservatory, esp. *Brit.* glasshouse. **2** see HOTBED 2. ● *adj.* dainty, delicate, sensitive, fragile, frail, pampered, overprotected, sheltered, shielded.

hotshot /hótshot/ *n. & adj. colloq.* ● *n.* an important or exceptionally able person. ● *adj.* (*attrib.*) important; able; expert; suddenly prominent.
■ *n.* see BIGWIG.

hotspur /hótspər/ *n.* a rash person. [sobriquet of Sir H. Percy, d. 1403]

Hottentot /hótˈntot/ *n. & adj.* ● *n.* **1** a member of a pastoral black people of SW Africa. **2** their language. ● *adj.* of this people. [Afrik., perh. = stammerer, with ref. to their mode of pronunc.]

hottie /hótee/ *n.* (also **hotty**) (*pl.* **-ies**) *Brit. colloq.* a hot-water bottle.

Houdini /hōodeénee/ *n.* **1** an ingenious escape. **2** a person skilled at escaping. [H. *Houdini*, professional name of E. Weiss, American escapologist d. 1926]

hough /hok/ *n. & v. Brit.* ● *n.* **1** = HOCK¹. **2** a cut of beef, etc., from this and the leg above it. ● *v.tr.* hamstring. □□ **hougher** *n.* [ME *ho(u)gh* = OE *hōh* (heel) in *hōhsinu* hamstring]

hoummos var. of HUMMUS.

hound /hownd/ *n. & v.* ● *n.* **1 a** a dog used for hunting, esp. one able to track by scent. **b** (**the hounds**) a pack of foxhounds. **2** *colloq.* a despicable man. **3** a runner who follows a trail in hare and hounds. **4** a person keen in pursuit of something (usu. in *comb.*: *newshound*). ● *v.tr.* **1** harass or pursue relentlessly. **2** chase or pursue with a hound. **3** (foll. by *at*) set (a dog or person) on (a quarry). **4** urge on or nag (a person). □ **hound's tongue** *Bot.* a tall plant, *Cynoglossum officinale*, with tongue-shaped leaves. **hound's-tooth** a check pattern with notched corners suggestive of a canine tooth. **ride to hounds** go fox-hunting on horseback. □□ **hounder** *n.* **houndish** *adj.* [OE *hund* f. Gmc]
■ *n.* **2** see WRETCH 2. ● *v.* **1** persecute, pursue, chase, annoy, pester, harry, badger, *colloq.* hassle; see also HARASS 1. **4** see URGE *v.* 2, NAG¹ *v.* 1, 3a, b.

hour /owr/ *n.* **1** a twenty-fourth part of a day and night, 60 minutes. **2** a time of day; a point in time (*a late hour*; *what is the hour?*). **3** (*pl.* with preceding numerals in form 18:00, 20:30, etc.) this number of hours and minutes past midnight on the 24-hour clock (*will assemble at 20:00 hours*).

4 a a period set aside for some purpose (*lunch hour*; *keep regular hours*). **b** (in *pl.*) a fixed period of time for work, use of a building, etc. (*office hours*; *opening hours*). **5** a short indefinite period of time (*an idle hour*). **6** the present time (*question of the hour*). **7** a time for action, etc. (*the hour has come*). **8** the distance traversed in one hour by a means of transport stated or implied (*we are an hour from San Francisco*). **9** *RC Ch.* **a** prayers to be said at one of seven fixed times of day (*book of hours*). **b** any of these times. **10** (prec. by *the*) each time o'clock of a whole number of hours (*buses leave on the hour*; *on the half hour*; *at quarter past the hour*). **11** *Astron.* 15° of longitude or right ascension. □ **after hours** after closing time. **hour hand** the hand on a clock or watch which shows the hour. **hour-long** *adj.* lasting for one hour. ● *adv.* for one hour. **till all hours** till very late. [ME *ure*, etc. f. AF *ure*, OF *ore*, *eure* f. L *hora* f. Gk *hōra* season, hour] ■ **2** see MOMENT 3.

hourglass /ówrglas/ *n.* & *adj.* ● *n.* a reversible device with two connected glass bulbs containing sand that takes an hour to pass from the upper to the lower bulb. ● *adj.* hourglass-shaped.

houri /hōoree/ *n.* a beautiful young woman, esp. in the Muslim Paradise. [F f. Pers. *ḥūrī* f. Arab. *ḥūr* pl. of *ḥawra'* gazelle-like (in the eyes)]

hourly /ówrlee/ *adj.* & *adv.* ● *adj.* **1** done or occurring every hour. **2** frequent; continual. **3** reckoned hour by hour (*hourly wage*). ● *adv.* **1** every hour. **2** frequently; continually.

house *n.* & *v.* ● *n.* /hows/ (*pl.* /hówziz, -siz/) **1 a** a building for human habitation. **b** (*attrib.*) (of an animal) kept in, frequenting, or infesting houses (*house cat*; *housefly*). **2** a building for a special purpose (*opera house*; *summer house*). **3** a building for keeping animals or goods (*henhouse*). **4 a** a religious community. **b** the buildings occupied by it. **5** esp. *Brit.* **a** a body of pupils living in the same building at a boarding school. **b** such a building. **c** a division of a day school for games, competitions, etc. **6** *Brit.* **a** a college of a university. **b** (**the House**) Christ Church, Oxford. **7** a family, esp. a royal family; a dynasty (*House of York*). **8 a** a business or institution. **b** *Brit.* its place of business. **c** (**the House**) *Brit. colloq.* the Stock Exchange. **9 a** a legislative or deliberative assembly. **b** the building where it meets. **c** (**the House**) the House of Representatives. **d** (**the House**) (in the UK) the House of Commons or Lords. **10 a** an audience in a theater, movie theater, etc. **b** *Brit.* a performance in a theater or movie theater (*second house starts at 9 o'clock*). **c** a theater. **11** *Astrol.* a twelfth part of the heavens. **12** (*attrib.*) staying in a hospital as a member of the staff (*house physician*; *house surgeon*). **13 a** a place of public refreshment; a restaurant or inn (*coffeehouse*). **b** (*attrib.*) (of wine) selected by the management of a restaurant, hotel, etc., to be offered at a special price. **14** a brothel. **15** *Sc.* a dwelling that is one of several in a building. **16** *Brit. sl.* = HOUSEY-HOUSEY. **17** an animal's den, shell, etc. **18** (**the House**) *Brit. hist. euphem.* the workhouse. ● *v.tr.* /howz/ **1** provide (a person, a population, etc.) with a house or houses or other accommodation. **2** store (goods, etc.). **3 a** serve as accommodation for; contain. **b** enclose or encase (a part or fitting). **4** fix in a socket, mortise, etc. □ **as safe as houses** *Brit.* thoroughly or completely safe. **house agent** *Brit.* an agent for the sale and renting of houses; a real estate agent. **house and home** (as an emphatic) home. **house arrest** detention in one's own house, etc., not in prison. **house church** *Brit.* **1** a charismatic church independent of traditional denominations. **2** a group meeting in a house as part of the activities of a church. **house dog** a dog kept to guard a house. **house flag** a flag indicating to what company a ship belongs. **house-hunting** seeking a house to live in. **house lights** the lights in the auditorium of a theater. **house magazine** a magazine published by a company and dealing mainly with its own activities. **house martin** a black and white swallow-like bird, *Delichon urbica*, which builds a mud nest on house walls, etc. **house music** a style of pop music typically using drum machines and synthesized bass lines with sparse repetitive vocals and a fast beat. **house of cards 1** an insecure

scheme, etc. **2** a structure built (usu. by a child) out of playing cards. **House of Commons** (in the UK) the elected chamber of Parliament. **house of God** a church; a place of worship. **house of ill repute** *archaic* a brothel. **House of Lords 1** (in the UK) the chamber of Parliament composed of peers and bishops. **2** a committee of specially qualified members of this appointed as the ultimate judicial appeal court. **House of Representatives** the lower house of the US Congress and other legislatures. **house party** a group of guests staying over one or more nights at a party. **house-proud** esp. *Brit.* attentive to, or unduly preoccupied with, the care and appearance of the home. **Houses of Parliament 1** the Houses of Lords and Commons regarded together. **2** the buildings where they meet. **house sparrow** a common brown and gray sparrow, *Passer domesticus*, which nests in the eaves and roofs of houses. **house style** a particular printer's or publisher's, etc., preferred way of presentation. **house-to-house** performed at or carried to each house in turn. **house-trained** *Brit.* = HOUSEBROKEN. **keep house** provide for or manage a household. **keep** (or **make**) **a House** *Brit.* secure the presence of enough members for a quorum in the House of Commons. **keep open house** provide general hospitality. **keep to the house** stay indoors. **like a house on fire 1** vigorously; fast. **2** successfully; excellently. **on the house** at the management's expense; free. **play house** play at being a family in its home. **put** (or **set**) **one's house in order** make necessary reforms. **set up house** begin to live in a separate dwelling. □□ **houseful** *n.* (*pl.* **-fuls**). **houseless** *adj.* [OE *hūs*, *hūsian*, f. Gmc] ■ *n.* **1** a residence, home, abode, homestead, domicile, lodging(s), *formal* dwelling (place); building, edifice, structure. **7** family, line, lineage, dynasty, clan. **8 a** establishment, institution, firm, concern, company, business, organization, enterprise, undertaking, *colloq.* outfit. **9 a** legislature, legislative body, congress, parliament, assembly, council, diet. **10 c** auditorium, theater, concert hall. **14** bawdy house, brothel, whorehouse, bagnio, bordello, *archaic* house of ill repute or fame, stews, *old-fashioned*, sporting house, *sl.* crib. **17** den, lair, burrow, hole, nest, set; shell. ● *v.* **1** shelter, accommodate, domicile, lodge, quarter, put up, board, harbor, *Mil.* billet. **2** see STORE *v.* 1. **3 a** contain, accommodate, quarter. **b** see ENCLOSE 1, 6. □ **house of God** church, chapel, place of worship. **house of ill repute** see HOUSE *n.* 14 above. **house-to-house** door-to-door. **like a house on fire 1** see FAST¹ *adv.* 1. **2** see WELL¹ *adv.* 9. **on the house** free, gratis, for nothing, without charge, at no charge, as a gift. **put one's house in order** see REFORM *v.* 1.

houseboat /hówsbōt/ *n.* a boat fitted for living in.

housebound /hówsbownd/ *adj.* unable to leave one's house due to illness, etc.

houseboy /hówsboy/ *n.* a boy or man as a servant in a house. ■ see SERVANT.

housebreak /hówsbrayk/ *v.tr.* train (a pet living indoors) to excrete outdoors.

housebreaker /hówsbraykər/ *n.* **1** a person guilty of housebreaking. **2** *Brit.* a person who is employed to demolish houses. ■ **1** see BURGLAR.

housebreaking /hówsbrayking/ *n.* the act of breaking into a building, esp. in a daytime, to commit a crime.

housebroken /hówsbrōkən/ *adj.* **1** (of animals) trained to be clean in the house. **2** *colloq.* well-mannered. ■ **1** see DOMESTIC *adj.* 3. **2** see COURTEOUS.

housecarl /hówskaarl/ *n.* (also **housecarle**) *hist.* a member of the bodyguard of a Danish or English king or noble. [OE *húscarl* f. ON *húskarl* f. *hús* HOUSE + *karl* man: cf. CARL]

/.../ **pronunciation**	● **part of speech**
□ **phrases, idioms, and compounds**	
□□ **derivatives**	■ **synonym section**
cross-references appear in SMALL CAPITALS or *italics*	

housecoat /hówskōt/ *n.* a woman's garment for informal wear in the house, usu. a long dresslike coat.
■ see ROBE *n.* 2.

housecraft /hówskraft/ *n. Brit.* skill in household management.

housedress /hówsdres/ *n.* an inexpensive dress of simple design suitable for wear while doing housework.

housefather /hówsfaathər/ *n.* a man in charge of a house, esp. of a home for children or a dormitory, etc.

housefly /hówsflī/ *n.* any fly of the family Muscidae, esp. *Musca domestica*, breeding in decaying organic matter and often entering houses.

houseguest /hówsgest/ *n.* a guest staying for some days in a private house.

household /hóws-hōld/ *n.* **1** the occupants of a house regarded as a unit. **2** a house and its affairs. **3** (prec. by *the*) (in the UK) the royal household. □ **household gods 1** gods presiding over a household, esp. (in Roman Antiquity) the lares and penates. **2** the essentials of home life. **household troops** (in the UK) troops nominally employed to guard the sovereign. **household word** (or **name**) **1** a familiar name or saying. **2** a familiar person or thing.
■ **1** family, ménage. **3** see TRAIN *n.* 4.

householder /hóws-hōldər/ *n.* **1** a person who owns or rents a house. **2** the head of a household.
■ **1** see LANDLORD 1, OCCUPANT.

househusband /hóws-həzbənd/ *n.* a husband who carries out the household duties traditionally carried out by a housewife.

housekeep /hówskeep/ *v.intr.* (*past* and *past part.* **-kept**) *colloq.* keep house.

housekeeper /hówskeepər/ *n.* **1** a person, esp. a woman, employed to manage a household. **2** a person in charge of a house, office, etc.
■ **1** see SERVANT 1.

housekeeping /hówskeeping/ *n.* **1** the management of household affairs. **2** money allowed for this. **3** operations of maintenance, record keeping, etc., in an organization.

houseleek /hówsleek/ *n.* a plant, *Sempervivum tectorum*, with pink flowers, growing on walls and roofs.

housemaid /hówsmayd/ *n.* a female servant in a house. □ **housemaid's knee** inflammation of the kneecap, often due to excessive kneeling.

houseman /hówsmən/ *n.* (*pl.* **-men**) **1** *Brit.* a resident doctor at a hospital, etc.; a medical intern **2** = HOUSEBOY.

housemaster /hówsmastər/ *n.* (*fem.* **housemistress** /-mistris/) the teacher in charge of a house at a boarding school.

housemother /hówsməthər/ *n.* a woman in charge of a house, esp. of a home for children or a dormitory, etc.

houseparent /hówspərənt/ *n.* a housemother or housefather.

houseplant /hówsplant/ *n.* a plant grown indoors.

houseroom /hówsrōōm, -rŏŏm/ *n.* space or accommodation in one's house. □ **not give houseroom to** *Brit.* not have in any circumstances.

housetop /hówstop/ *n.* the roof of a house. □ **proclaim** (or **shout**, etc.) **from the housetops** announce publicly.

housewares /hówswairz/ *n.pl.* small articles for furnishing a home, such as dishware, glassware, and small appliances.

housewarming /hówswawrming/ *n.* a party celebrating a move to a new home.

housewife /hówswīf/ *n.* (*pl.* **-wives**) **1** a woman (usu. married) managing a household. **2** *Brit.* /húzif/ a case for needles, thread, etc. □□ **housewifely** *adj.* **housewifeliness** *n.* [ME *hus(e)wif* f. HOUSE + WIFE]

housewifery /hówswifəree, -wīfree/ *n.* **1** housekeeping. **2** skill in household management and housekeeping.

housework /hówswərk/ *n.* regular work done in housekeeping, e.g., cleaning and cooking.

housey-housey /hówseehówsee, hówzeehówzee/ *n.* (also **housie-housie**) *Brit. sl.* a gambling form of lotto.

housing[1] /hówzing/ *n.* **1 a** dwelling houses collectively. **b** the provision of these. **2** shelter; lodging. **3** a rigid casing, esp. for moving or sensitive parts of a machine. **4** the hole or niche cut in one piece of wood to receive some part of another in order to join them. □ **housing development** (*Brit.* **estate**) a residential area planned as a unit.
■ **1, 2** homes, houses, lodging(s), quarters, habitation, accommodations, *Brit.* accommodation, *formal* dwellings, dwelling places; shelter, protection. **3** case, casing, cover, covering, enclosure, container, box, shield.

housing[2] /hówzing/ *n.* a cloth covering put on a horse for protection or ornament. [ME = covering, f. obs. *house* f. OF *houce* f. med.L *hultia* f. Gmc]

HOV *abbr.* high-occupancy vehicle.

hove *past* of HEAVE.

hovel /húvəl, hóv-/ *n.* **1** a small miserable dwelling. **2** a conical building enclosing a kiln. **3** an open shed or shelter. [ME: orig. unkn.]
■ **1** shack, shanty, hut, crib; pigsty, pigpen, *colloq.* dump. **3** hut, outhouse; see also SHED[1].

hover /húvər, hóvər/ *v. & n.* ● *v.intr.* **1** (of a bird, helicopter, etc.) remain in one place in the air. **2** (often foll. by *about, around*) wait close at hand; linger. **3** remain undecided. ● *n.* **1** hovering. **2** a state of suspense. □□ **hoverer** *n.* [ME f. obs. *hove* hover, linger]
■ *v.* **1** float, hang, poise, be *or* hang suspended, hang in the air. **2** linger, loiter, wait, hang about *or* around. **3** see HESITATE 1.

hovercraft /húvərkraft, hóv-/ *n.* (*pl.* same) a vehicle or craft that travels over land or water on a cushion of air provided by a downward blast.

hoverport /húvərpawrt, hóv-/ *n.* a terminal for hovercraft.

hovertrain /húvərtrayn, hóv-/ *n.* a train that travels on a cushion of air like a hovercraft.

how /how/ *adv., conj., & n.* ● *interrog. adv.* **1** by what means; in what way (*how do you do it?*; *tell me how you do it*; *how could you behave so disgracefully?*; *but how to bridge the gap?*). **2** in what condition, esp. of health (*how is the patient?*; *how do things stand?*). **3 a** to what extent (*how far is it?*; *how would you like to take my place?*; *how we laughed!*). **b** to what extent good or well, what . . . like (*how was the film?*; *how did they play?*). ● *rel. adv.* in whatever way; as (*do it how you like*). ● *conj. colloq.* that (*told us how he'd been in Canada*). ● *n.* the way a thing is done (*the how and why of it*). □ **and how!** *sl.* very much so (chiefly used ironically or intensively). **here's how!** *Brit.* I drink to your good health. **how about 1** would you like (*how about a game of chess?*). **2** what is to be done about. **3** what is the news about. **how are you? 1** what is your state of health? **2** = *how do you do?* **how come?** see COME. **how do?** an informal greeting on being introduced to a stranger. **how do you do?** a formal greeting. **how-do-you-do** (or **how-d'ye-do**) *n.* (*pl.* **-dos**) an awkward situation. **how many** what number. **how much 1** what amount (*how much do I owe you?*; *did not know how much to take*). **2** what price (*how much is it?*). **3** (as *interrog.*) esp. *Brit. joc.* what? (*"She is a hedonist." "A how much?"*). **how now?** *archaic* what is the meaning of this? **how so?** how can you show that that is so? **how's that?** what is your opinion or explanation of that? [OE *hū* f. WG]

howbeit /hówbeeit/ *adv. archaic* nevertheless.

howdah /hówdə/ *n.* a seat for two or more, usu. with a canopy, for riding on the back of an elephant. [Urdu *hawda* f. Arab. *hawdaj* litter]

howdy /hówdee/ *int.* = *how do you do?* [corrupt.]

however /hówevər/ *adv.* **1 a** in whatever way (*do it however you want*). **b** to whatever extent; no matter how (*however inconvenient*). **2** nevertheless. **3** *colloq.* (as an emphatic) in what way; by what means (*however did that happen?*).
■ **1 a** no matter how, in whatever way *or* manner, to whatever manner *or* extent *or* degree, howsoever, in any way *or* manner *or* respect, anyhow, how. **b** no matter how, regardless (of) how, notwithstanding how. **2** nevertheless, nonetheless, despite that, in spite of that, still, though, yet, even so, be that as it may, at any rate, anyway, anyhow, at all events, in any event, in any case, *Sc., Austral., & NZ* but. **3** how, in what way *or*

manner, by what means, *colloq.* how on earth, how in the world.

howitzer /hówitsər/ *n.* a short cannon for high-angle firing of shells at low velocities. [Du. *houwitser* f. G *Haubitze* f. Czech *houfnice* catapult]

howl /howl/ *n. & v.* ● *n.* **1** a long, loud, doleful cry uttered by a dog, wolf, etc. **2** a prolonged wailing noise, e.g., as made by a strong wind. **3** a loud cry of pain or rage. **4** a yell of derision or merriment. **5** *Electronics* a howling noise in a loudspeaker due to electrical or acoustic feedback. ● *v.* **1** *intr.* make a howl. **2** *intr.* weep loudly. **3** *tr.* utter (words) with a howl. □ **howl down** prevent (a speaker) from being heard by howls of derision. [ME *houle* (v.), prob. imit.: cf. OWL]
■ *n.* **1** yowl, ululation, wail, yelp, cry. **3** cry, shout, yell, bellow, scream, roar, *colloq.* holler. ● *v.* **1** yowl, cry, wail, ululate, bay; shout, yell, bellow, scream, roar, *colloq.* holler. **2** see CRY *v.* 2a.

howler /hówlər/ *n.* **1** *colloq.* a glaring mistake. **2** a S. American monkey of the genus *Alouatta.* **3** a person or animal that howls.
■ **1** blunder, mistake, error, gaffe, faux pas, *colloq.* slipup, *sl.* bloomer, boner, clanger, goof, screwup, clinker, boo-boo, *Brit. sl.* boob, cock-up.

howling /hówling/ *adj.* **1** that howls. **2** *sl.* extreme (*a howling shame*). **3** *archaic* dreary (*howling wilderness*). □ **howling dervish** see DERVISH.

howsoever /hówsō-évər/ *adv.* (also *poet.* **howsoe'er** /-sō-áir/) **1** in whatsoever way. **2** to whatsoever extent.
■ **1** see HOWEVER 1a.

hoy[1] /hoy/ *int. & n.* ● *int.* used to call attention, drive animals, or *Naut.* hail or call aloft. ● *n. Austral.* a game of chance resembling bingo, using playing cards. [ME: natural cry]

hoy[2] /hoy/ *n. hist.* a small vessel, usu. rigged as a sloop, carrying passengers and goods esp. for short distances. [MDu. *hoei, hoede,* of unkn. orig.]

hoy[3] /hoy/ *v.tr. Austral. sl.* throw. [Brit. dial.: orig. unkn.]

hoya /hóyə/ *n.* any climbing shrub of the genus *Hoya,* with pink, white, or yellow waxy flowers. [mod.L f. T. *Hoy,* Engl. gardener d. 1821]

hoyden /hóyd'n/ *n.* a boisterous girl. □□ **hoydenish** *adj.* [orig. = rude fellow, prob. f. MDu. *heiden* (= HEATHEN)]

Hoyle /hoyl/ *n.* □ **according to Hoyle** *adv.* correctly; exactly. ● *adj.* correct; exact. [E. *Hoyle,* Engl. writer on card games d. 1769]

h.p. *abbr.* **1** horsepower. **2** high pressure. **3** *Brit.* hire purchase.

HQ *abbr.* headquarters.

HR *abbr.* (also **H.R.**) **1** House of Representatives. **2** home run. **3** home rule.

hr. *abbr.* hour.

HRH *abbr. Brit.* Her or His Royal Highness.

hrs. *abbr.* hours.

HS *abbr.* high school.

Hs *symb. Chem.* the element hassium.

HSH *abbr. Brit.* Her or His Serene Highness.

HST *abbr.* **1** Hawaii(an) Standard Time. **2** hypersonic transport.

HT *abbr.* high tension.

hub /hub/ *n.* **1** the central part of a wheel, rotating on or with the axle, and from which the spokes radiate. **2** a central point of interest, activity, etc. [16th c.: perh. = HOB[1]]
■ **2** center, focus, focal point, pivot, heart, core, nucleus, navel.

hubble-bubble /húbəlbúbəl/ *n.* **1** a rudimentary form of hookah. **2** a bubbling sound. **3** confused talk. [redupl. of BUBBLE]
■ **1** see PIPE *n.* 2a.

hubbub /húbub/ *n.* **1** a confused din, esp. from a crowd of people. **2** a disturbance or riot. [perh. of Ir. orig.: cf. Gael. *ubub* int. of contempt, Ir. *abú,* used in battle cries]
■ **1** see NOISE *n.* **2** see DISTURBANCE 2.

hubby /húbee/ *n.* (*pl.* **-ies**) *colloq.* a husband. [abbr.]
■ see HUSBAND *n.*

hubcap /húbkap/ *n.* a cover for the hub of a vehicle's wheel.

hubris /hyoobris/ *n.* **1** arrogant pride or presumption. **2** (in Greek tragedy) excessive pride toward or defiance of the gods, leading to nemesis. □□ **hubristic** *adj.* [Gk]
■ **1** see PRIDE *n.* 2.

huckaback /húkəbak/ *n.* a stout linen or cotton fabric with a rough surface, used for toweling. [17th c.: orig. unkn.]

huckleberry /húkəlberee/ *n.* (*pl.* **-ies**) **1** any low-growing N. American shrub of the genus *Gaylussacia.* **2** the blue or black soft fruit of this plant. [prob. alt. of *hurtleberry,* WHORTLEBERRY]

huckster /húkstər/ *n. & v.* ● *n.* **1** a mercenary person. **2** a publicity agent, esp. for broadcast material. **3** a peddler or hawker. ● *v.* **1** *intr.* bargain; haggle. **2** *tr.* carry on a petty traffic in. **3** *tr.* adulterate. [ME prob. f. LG: cf. dial. *huck* to bargain, HAWKER[1]]
■ *n.* **3** see PEDDLER. ● *v.* **1** see BARGAIN *v.* **2** see PEDDLE.

HUD /hud/ *abbr.* (Department of) Housing and Urban Development.

huddle /húd'l/ *v. & n.* ● *v.* **1** *tr. & intr.* (often foll. by *up*) crowd together; nestle closely. **2** *intr. & refl.* (often foll. by *up*) coil one's body into a small space. **3** *tr. Brit.* heap together in a muddle. ● *n.* **1** a confused or crowded mass of people or things. **2** *colloq.* a close or secret conference (esp. in **go into a huddle**). **3** *Football* a gathering of the players of one team to receive instructions about the next play. **4** confusion; bustle. [16th c.: perh. f. LG and ult. rel. to HIDE[3]]
■ *v.* **1** cluster, gather, crowd *or* press together, throng *or* flock together, nestle, squeeze together. ● *n.* **1** cluster, group, bunch, clump, pack, herd, crowd, throng, mass. **2** meeting, conference, discussion, consultation, confabulation, *colloq.* confab. **3** see CONFUSION 2.

hue /hyoo/ *n.* **1 a** a color or tint. **b** a variety or shade of color caused by the admixture of another. **2** the attribute of a color by virtue of which it is discernible as red, green, etc. □□ **-hued** *adj.* **hueless** *adj.* [OE *hīew, hēw* form, beauty f. Gmc: cf. ON *hȳ* down on plants]
■ **1** color, tint, shade, tinge, tone, cast, tincture.

hue and cry /hyoo/ *n.* **1** a loud clamor or outcry. **2** *hist.* **a** a loud cry raised for the pursuit of a wrongdoer. **b** a proclamation for the capture of a criminal. [AF *hu e cri* f. OF *hu* outcry (f. *huer* shout) + *e* and + *cri* cry]
■ **1** see RACKET[2] 1a.

huff /huf/ *v. & n.* ● *v.* **1** *intr.* give out loud puffs of air, steam, etc. **2** *intr.* bluster loudly or threateningly (*huffing and puffing*). **3** *intr.* take or cause to take offense. **4** *tr. Checkers* remove (an opponent's man that could have made a capture) from the board as a forfeit (orig. after blowing on the piece). ● *n.* a fit of petty annoyance. □ **in a huff** annoyed and offended. □□ **huffish** *adj.* [imit. of the sound of blowing]
■ *v.* **1** see PUFF *v.* 4. **2** puff, bluster, storm about; see also RAGE *v.* ● *n.* see TANTRUM. □ **in a huff** piqued, irritated, annoyed, offended, in high dudgeon, in a pet, hot under the collar, furious, *colloq.* (all) het up, peeved, in a stink; see also ANGRY 1.

huffy /húfee/ *adj.* (**huffier, huffiest**) **1** apt to take offense. **2** offended. □□ **huffily** *adv.* **huffiness** *n.*
■ see IRRITABLE 1.

hug /hug/ *v. & n.* ● *v.tr.* (**hugged, hugging**) **1** squeeze tightly in one's arms, esp. with affection. **2** (of a bear) squeeze (a person) between its forelegs. **3** keep close to (the shore, curb, etc.). **4** cherish or cling to (prejudices, etc.). **5** *refl.* congratulate or be pleased with (oneself). ● *n.* **1** a strong clasp with the arms. **2** a squeezing grip in wrestling. □□ **huggable** *adj.* [16th c.: prob. f. Scand.: cf. ON *hugga* console]
■ *v.* **1** clasp, squeeze, cuddle; see also EMBRACE *v.* 1. **3** follow closely, cling to, stay *or* keep near *or* close

---

/.../ **pronunciation**	● **part of speech**
□ **phrases, idioms, and compounds**	
□□ **derivatives**	■ **synonym section**
cross-references appear in SMALL CAPITALS or *italics*	

to. ● *n.* **1** embrace, clasp, squeeze, *colloq.* clinch. **2** grip, clinch.

huge /hyōōj/ *adj.* **1** extremely large; enormous. **2** (of immaterial things) very great (*a huge success*). □□ **hugeness** *n.* [ME *huge* f. OF *ahuge*, *ahoge*, of unkn. orig.]
  ■ **1** large, great, enormous, gigantic, giant, immense, massive, gargantuan, mammoth, colossal, monumental, titanic, elephantine, leviathan, vast, *colloq.* jumbo, terrific, *sl.* whopping. **2** tremendous, prodigious, stupendous, colossal, immense, enormous, great, massive, *colloq.* terrific.

hugely /hyōōjlee/ *adv.* **1** enormously (*hugely successful*). **2** very much (*enjoyed it hugely*).
  ■ **1** see HIGHLY 1. **2** see VERY *adv.*

hugger-mugger /húgərmúgər/ *adj., adv., n.,* & *v.* ● *adj.* & *adv.* **1** in secret. **2** confused; in confusion. ● *n.* **1** secrecy. **2** confusion. ● *v.intr.* proceed in a secret or muddled fashion. [prob. rel. to ME *hoder* huddle, *mokere* conceal: cf. 15th-c. *hoder moder*, 16th-c. *hucker mucker* in the same sense]
  ■ *adj.* & *adv.* **1** see FURTIVE 1. **2** see *chaotic* (CHAOS).
  ● *n.* **2** see CHAOS 1a.

Hughie / hyōō-ee/ *n. Austral.* & *NZ sl.* the imaginary being responsible for the weather (esp. *send her down, Hughie!*). [male forename *Hugh* + -IE]

Huguenot /hyōōgənot/ *n. hist.* a French Protestant. [F, assim. of *eiguenot* (f. Du. *eedgenot* f. Swiss G *Eidgenoss* confederate) to the name of a Geneva burgomaster *Hugues*]

huh /hə/ *int.* expressing disgust, surprise, etc. [imit.]

hula /hōōlə/ *n.* (also **hula-hula**) a Polynesian dance with flowing movements of the arms and rhythmic hip movements, often accompanied by chants and drums. □ **hula hoop** a large hoop for spinning around the body with hula-like movements. **hula skirt** a long grass skirt. [Hawaiian]

hulk /hulk/ *n.* **1 a** the body of a dismantled ship, used as a storage vessel, etc. **b** (in *pl.*) *hist.* this used as a prison. **2** an unwieldy vessel. **3** *colloq.* a large clumsy-looking person or thing. [OE *hulc* & MLG, MDu. *hulk*: cf. Gk *holkas* cargo ship]
  ■ **1 a** shipwreck, wreck, shell, skeleton. **3** oaf, lout, lubber, lump, *colloq.* galoot, *sl.* clod, klutz.

hulking /húlking/ *adj. colloq.* bulky; large and clumsy.
  ■ clumsy, awkward, ungainly, ungraceful, inelegant, lubberly, oafish, loutish; unwieldy, cumbersome, bulky; see also MASSIVE 1–3.

hull¹ /hul/ *n.* & *v.* ● *n.* the body or frame of a ship, airship, flying boat, etc. ● *v.tr.* pierce the hull of (a ship) with gunshot, etc. [ME, perh. rel. to HOLD²]
  ■ *n.* framework, skeleton, frame, structure, body.
  ● *v.* pierce, hole, puncture, bore into, penetrate.

hull² /hul/ *n.* & *v.* ● *n.* **1** the outer covering of a fruit, esp. the pod of peas and beans, the husk of grain, or the green calyx of a strawberry. **2** a covering. ● *v.tr.* remove the hulls from (fruit, etc.). [OE *hulu* ult. f. *helan* cover: cf. HELE]
  ■ *n.* shell, pod, case, husk, skin, peel, rind, shuck; covering, casing. ● *v.* shell, peel, skin, husk, shuck.

hullabaloo /húləbəlōō/ *n.* (*pl.* **hullabaloos**) an uproar or clamor. [18th c.: redupl. of *hallo, hullo,* etc.]
  ■ see UPROAR.

hullo var. of HELLO.

hum¹ /hum/ *v.* & *n.* ● *v.* (**hummed, humming**) **1** *intr.* make a low steady continuous sound like that of a bee. **2** *tr.* (also *absol.*) sing (a wordless tune) with closed lips. **3** *intr.* utter a slight inarticulate sound. **4** *intr. colloq.* be in an active state (*really made things hum*). **5** *intr. Brit. colloq.* smell unpleasantly. ● *n.* **1** a humming sound. **2** an unwanted low-frequency noise caused by variation of electric current, usu. the alternating frequency of a power source, in an amplifier, etc. **3** *Brit. colloq.* a bad smell. □ **hum and haw** (or **ha**) *Brit.* = *hem and haw.* □□ **hummable** *adj.* **hummer** *n.* [ME, imit.]
  ■ *v.* **1** buzz, drone, murmur, whir, purr, vibrate. **4** bustle, stir, be active, move, happen. ● *n.* **1** buzz, drone, murmur, murmuring, whir, purr, vibration.

hum² /həm/ *int.* expressing hesitation or dissent. [imit.]

human /hyōōmən/ *adj.* & *n.* ● *adj.* **1** of or belonging to the genus *Homo.* **2** consisting of human beings (*the human race*). **3** of or characteristic of people as opposed to God or animals or machines, esp. susceptible to the weaknesses of human beings (*is only human*). **4** showing (esp. the better) qualities of man (*proved to be very human*). ● *n.* a human being. □ **human being** any man or woman or child of the species *Homo sapiens.* **human chain** a line of people formed for passing things along, e.g., buckets of water to the site of a fire. **human engineering 1** the management of industrial labor, esp. as regards relationships between humans and machines. **2** the study of this. **human interest** (in a newspaper story, etc.) reference to personal experience and emotions, etc. **human nature** the general characteristics and feelings of human beings. **human relations** relations with or between people or individuals. **human resources** = PERSONNEL. **human rights** rights held to be justifiably belonging to any person. **human shield** a person or persons placed in the line of fire in order to discourage attack. □□ **humanness** *n.* [ME *humain(e)* f. OF f. L *humanus* f. *homo* human being]
  ■ *adj.* **1–3** mortal, anthropoid, hominoid, manlike; defenseless, weak, vulnerable, fallible. **4** kind, kindly, kindhearted, considerate, charitable, compassionate, merciful, benign, benignant, tender, gentle, forgiving, lenient, benevolent, beneficent, generous, magnanimous, humanitarian, understanding, accommodating, sympathetic, good-natured, humane, sensitive. ● *n.* human being, person, individual, being, mortal, soul. □ **human being** see HUMAN *n.* above.

humane /hyōōmáyn/ *adj.* **1** benevolent; compassionate. **2** inflicting the minimum of pain. **3** (of a branch of learning) tending to civilize or confer refinement. □□ **humanely** *adv.* **humaneness** *n.* [var. of HUMAN, differentiated in sense in the 18th c.]
  ■ **1** see BENEVOLENT 1.

humanism /hyōōmənizəm/ *n.* **1** an outlook or system of thought concerned with human rather than divine or supernatural matters. **2** a belief or outlook emphasizing common human needs and seeking solely rational ways of solving human problems, and concerned with human beings as responsible and progressive intellectual beings. **3** (often **Humanism**) literary culture, esp. that of the Renaissance humanists.

humanist /hyōōmənist/ *n.* **1** an adherent of humanism. **2** a humanitarian. **3** a student (esp. in the 14th–16th c.) of Roman and Greek literature and antiquities. □□ **humanistic** *adj.* **humanistically** *adv.* [F *humaniste* f. It. *umanista* (as HUMAN)]

humanitarian /hyōōmánitáireeən/ *n.* & *adj.* ● *n.* **1** a person who seeks to promote human welfare. **2** a person who advocates or practices humane action; a philanthropist. ● *adj.* relating to or holding the views of humanitarians. □□ **humanitarianism** *n.*
  ■ *n.* good Samaritan, philanthropist, philanthrope, benefactor, benefactress, altruist, do-gooder. ● *adj.* see HUMAN *adj.* 4.

humanity /hyōōmánitee/ *n.* (*pl.* **-ies**) **1 a** the human race. **b** human beings collectively. **c** the fact or condition of being human. **2** humaneness; benevolence. **3** (in *pl.*) human attributes. **4** (in *pl.*) **a** learning or literature concerned with human culture as opposed to the sciences. **b** the study of Latin and Greek literature and philosophy. [ME f. OF *humanité* f. L *humanitas -tatis* (as HUMAN)]
  ■ **1 a, b** human race, human beings, people, society, humankind, Homo sapiens, man, mankind. **c** humanness, human nature, manhood. **2** humaneness, kindness, kindliness, kindheartedness, consideration, charitableness, openheartedness, warmheartedness, good will, benevolence, compassion, mercifulness, mercy, benignity, tenderness, warmth, beneficence, generosity, unselfishness, magnanimity, understanding, tact, tactfulness, sympathy, sensitivity. **4** (*the humanities*) see ART¹ 6.

humanize /hyōōmənīz/ v.tr. **1** make human; give a human character to. **2** make humane. □□ **humanization** n. [F humaniser (as HUMAN)]

■ **1** personify, personalize.

humankind /hyōōmənkind/ n. human beings collectively.

humanly /hyōōmənlee/ adv. **1** by human means (I will do it if it is humanly possible). **2** in a human manner. **3** from a human point of view. **4** with human feelings.

humble /húmbəl/ adj. & v. ● adj. **1 a** having or showing a low estimate of one's own importance. **b** offered with or affected by such an estimate (if you want my humble opinion). **2** of low social or political rank (humble origins). **3** (of a thing) of modest pretensions, dimensions, etc. ● v.tr. **1** make humble; bring low; abase. **2** lower the rank or status of. □ **eat humble pie** make a humble apology; accept humiliation. □□ **humbleness** n. **humbly** adv. [ME umble, humble f. OF umble f. L humilis lowly f. humus ground: humble pie f. UMBLES]

■ adj. **1** a modest, reserved, self-effacing, unassuming, unpresuming, retiring; submissive, meek, servile, obsequious, deferential, mild, respectful, subservient. **2** lowly, low, inferior, mean, ignoble, ordinary, plebeian, common, simple, obscure, unimportant, undistinguished, insignificant; low-born. **3** unpretentious, unostentatious, unprepossessing, small; see also MODEST 5. ● v. **1** chasten, bring or pull down, subdue, abase, demean, lower, reduce, make a person eat humble pie, shame, humiliate, crush, break, mortify, chagrin, take a person down a peg or notch, put a person in his or her place, colloq. put down. **2** debase, degrade, demote, downgrade; see also REDUCE 6.

humble-bee /húmbəlbee/ n. = BUMBLEBEE. [ME prob. f. MLG hummelbē, MDu. hommel, OHG humbal]

humbug /húmbug/ n. & v. ● n. **1** deceptive or false talk or behavior. **2** an impostor. **3** Brit. a hard boiled candy usu. flavored with peppermint. ● v. (**humbugged, humbugging**) **1** intr. be or behave like an impostor. **2** tr. deceive; hoax. □□ **humbuggery** /-búgəree/ n. [18th c.: orig. unkn.]

■ n. **1** see CANT[1] n. 1. **2** see IMPOSTOR 1. ● v. **2** see DUPE v.

humdinger /húmdíngər/ n. sl. an excellent or remarkable person or thing. [20th c.: orig. unkn.]

humdrum /húmdrum/ adj. & n. ● adj. **1** commonplace; dull. **2** monotonous. ● n. **1** commonplaceness; dullness. **2** a monotonous routine, etc. [16th c.: prob. f. HUM[1] by redupl.]

■ adj. dull, boring, tedious, tiresome, wearisome, monotonous, unvaried, unvarying, routine, undiversified, unchanging, repetitious, uneventful, unexciting, uninteresting, prosaic, mundane, ordinary, commonplace, banal, dry, insipid, jejune.

humectant /hyōōméktənt/ adj. & n. ● adj. retaining or preserving moisture. ● n. a substance, esp. a food additive, used to reduce loss of moisture. [L (h)umectant- part. stem of (h)umectare moisten f. umēre be moist]

humeral /hyōōmərəl/ adj. **1** of the humerus or shoulder. **2** worn on the shoulder. [F huméral & LL humeralis (as HUMERUS)]

humerus /hyōōmərəs/ n. (pl. **humeri** /-rī/) **1** the bone of the upper arm in humans. **2** the corresponding bone in other vertebrates. [L, = shoulder]

humic /hyōōmik/ adj. of or consisting of humus.

humid /hyōōmid/ adj. (of the air or climate) warm and damp. □□ **humidly** adv. [F humide or L humidus f. umēre be moist]

■ damp, moist, muggy, clammy, sticky, steamy, sultry, wet.

humidifier /hyōōmídifiər/ n. a device for keeping the atmosphere moist in a room, etc.

humidify /hyōōmídifi/ v.tr. (**-ies, -ied**) make (air, etc.) humid or damp. □□ **humidification** n.

humidity /hyōōmíditee/ n. (pl. **-ies**) **1** a humid state. **2** moisture. **3** the degree of moisture esp. in the atmosphere. □ **relative humidity** the proportion of moisture to the value for saturation at the same temperature. [ME f. OF humidité or L humiditas (as HUMID)]

■ see DAMP n. 1.

humidor /hyōōmidawr/ n. a room or container for keeping cigars or tobacco moist. [HUMID after cuspidor]

humify /hyōōmifi/ v.tr. & intr. (**-ies, -ied**) make or be made into humus. □□ **humification** n.

humiliate /hyōōmílee-ayt/ v.tr. make humble; injure the dignity or self-respect of. □□ **humiliating** adj. **humiliatingly** adv. **humiliation** /-áyshən/ n. **humiliator** n. [LL humiliare (as HUMBLE)]

■ disgrace, shame, discredit, abase, pull down, take down, put to shame, embarrass, humble, lower, demean, colloq. put down, flatten, score points off, show up; see also HUMBLE v. 1. □□ **humiliation** disgrace, shame, mortification, dishonor, ignominy, indignity, discredit, loss of face, obloquy, abasement, detraction, degradation, derogation, belittlement, disparagement, embarrassment.

humility /hyōōmílitee/ n. **1** humbleness; meekness. **2** a humble condition. [ME f. OF humilité f. L humilitas -tatis (as HUMBLE)]

■ **1** humbleness, modesty, meekness, self-effacement, shyness, diffidence, timidity, timorousness, bashfulness, mildness, unpretentiousness, submissiveness, servility, self-abasement. **2** modesty, lowliness, simplicity, ordinariness, plainness.

hummingbird /húmingbərd/ n. any tiny nectar-feeding bird of the family Trochilidae that makes a humming sound by the vibration of its wings when it hovers.

hummock /húmək/ n. **1** a hillock or knoll. **2** a piece of rising ground, esp. in a marsh. **3** a hump or ridge in an ice field. □□ **hummocky** adj. [16th c.: orig. unkn.]

■ see MOUND[1] n. 3.

hummus /hōōməs/ n. (also **hoummos**) a thick sauce or spread made from ground chickpeas and sesame oil flavored with lemon and garlic. [Turk. humus mashed chickpeas]

humongous /hyōōmónggəs, -múng-/ adj. (also **humungous**) sl. extremely large or massive. [20th c.: orig. uncert.]

humor /hyōōmər/ n. & v. (Brit. **humour**) ● n. **1 a** the condition of being amusing or comic (less intellectual and more sympathetic than wit). **b** the expression of humor in literature, speech, etc. **2** (in full **sense of humor**) the ability to perceive or express humor or take a joke. **3** a mood or state of mind (bad humor). **4** an inclination or whim (in the humor for fighting). **5** (in full **cardinal humor**) hist. each of the four chief fluids of the body (blood, phlegm, choler, melancholy), thought to determine a person's physical and mental qualities. ● v.tr. **1** gratify or indulge (a person or taste, etc.). **2** adapt oneself to; make concessions to. □ **out of humor** displeased. □□ **-humored** adj. **humorless** adj. **humorlessly** adv. **humorlessness** n. [ME f. AF umour, OF umor, humor f. L humor moisture (as HUMID)]

■ n. **1** a funniness, comedy, facetiousness, drollery; jocoseness, jocosity, jocularity, waggishness. **b** comedy, farce, jokes, jests, colloq. wisecracks, gags. **3** mood, frame or state of mind, temper, spirits, disposition, inclination, attitude. ● v. **1** soothe, gratify, placate, please, mollify, indulge, appease, pamper, cosset, coddle, mollycoddle, jolly, baby, spoil. □ **out of humor** in a (bad) mood, displeased; see also MOODY adj.

humoral /hyōōmərəl/ adj. **1** hist. of the four bodily humors. **2** Med. relating to body fluids, esp. as distinct from cells. [F humoral or med.L humoralis (as HUMOR)]

humoresque /hyōōmərésk/ n. a short lively piece of music. [G Humoreske f. Humor HUMOR]

humorist /hyōōmərist/ n. **1** a facetious person. **2** a humorous talker, actor, or writer. □□ **humoristic** adj.

■ **2** see COMEDIAN.

humorous /hyōōmərəs/ adj. **1** showing humor or a sense of

/.../ **pronunciation**	● **part of speech**
□ **phrases, idioms, and compounds**	
□□ **derivatives**	■ **synonym section**
cross-references appear in SMALL CAPITALS or italics	

humor. **2** facetious; comic. □□ **humorously** *adv.* **humorousness** *n.*

■ **1** amusing, witty, droll, whimsical, waggish, jocular, jocose, playful. **2** funny, comical, facetious, laughable, risible, farcical, sidesplitting, hilarious, uproarious, *colloq.* hysterical, killing.

humour *Brit.* var. of HUMOR.

humous /hyo͞oməs/ *adj.* like or consisting of humus.

hump /hump/ *n. & v.* ● *n.* **1** a rounded protuberance on the back of a camel, etc., or as an abnormality on a person's back. **2** a rounded raised mass of earth, etc. **3** a mound over which railroad cars are pushed so as to run by gravity to the required place in a switchyard. **4** a critical point in an undertaking, ordeal, etc. **5** (prec. by *the*) *Brit. sl.* a fit of depression or vexation (*it gives me the hump*). **6** *coarse sl.* an act of sexual intercourse; a sexual partner. ● *v.tr.* **1 a** *colloq.* lift or carry (heavy objects, etc.) with difficulty. **b** esp. *Austral.* hoist up; shoulder (one's pack, etc.). **2** make hump-shaped. **3** annoy; depress. **4** *coarse sl.* have sexual intercourse with. ¶ In sense 4 usually considered a taboo word. □ **hump bridge** = *humpback bridge.* **live on one's hump** *Brit. colloq.* be self-sufficient. **over the hump** over the worst; well begun. □□ **humped** *adj.* **humpless** *adj.* [17th c.: perh. rel. to LG *humpel* hump, LG *humpe*, Du. *homp* lump, hunk (of bread)]

■ *n.* **1** bulge, lump, bump, protuberance, protrusion, projection, knob, node, hunch, enlargement, swelling, growth, excrescence, tumescence. **2** mound, hummock, hillock. **4** crisis, critical time *or* moment *or* point, turning point, *colloq.* crunch. ● *v.* **1 a** drag, lug, haul, carry, heave, *colloq.* schlepp. **2** hunch, arch, curve, crook, bend. **3** see ANNOY 1, DEPRESS 2.

humpback /húmpbak/ *n.* **1 a** a deformed back with a hump. **b** a person having this. **2** a baleen whale, *Megaptera novaeangliae,* with a dorsal fin forming a hump. □ **humpback bridge** *Brit.* a small bridge with a steep ascent and descent. □□ **humpbacked** *adj.*

humph /humf/ *int. & n.* an inarticulate sound expressing doubt or dissatisfaction. [imit.]

humpty-dumpty /húmpteedúmptee/ *n.* (*pl.* **-ies**) **1** a short dumpy person. **2** a person or thing that once overthrown cannot be restored. [the nursery rhyme *Humpty-Dumpty,* perh. ult. f. HUMPY[1], DUMPY]

humpy[1] /húmpee/ *adj.* (**humpier, humpiest**) **1** having a hump or humps. **2** humplike.

humpy[2] /húmpee/ *n.* (*pl.* **-ies**) *Austral.* a primitive hut. [Aboriginal *oompi,* infl. by HUMP]

humus /hyo͞oməs/ *n.* the organic constituent of soil, usu. formed by the decomposition of plants and leaves by soil bacteria. □□ **humusify** *v.tr. & intr.* (**-ies, -ied**) [L, = soil]
■ see SOIL[1] 1.

Hun /hun/ *n.* **1** a member of a warlike Asiatic nomadic people who invaded and ravaged Europe in the 4th–5th c. **2** *offens.* a German (esp. in military contexts). **3** an uncivilized devastator; a vandal. □□ **Hunnish** *adj.* [OE *Hūne* pl. f. LL *Hunni* f. Gk *Hounnoi* f. Turki *Hun-yü*]

hunch /hunch/ *v. & n.* ● *v.* **1** *tr.* bend or arch into a hump. **2** *tr.* thrust out or up to form a hump. **3** *intr.* (usu. foll. by *up*) sit with the body hunched. ● *n.* **1** *colloq.* an intuitive feeling or conjecture. **2** *colloq.* a hint. **3** a hump. **4** a thick piece. [16th c.: orig. unkn.]

■ *v.* **1** see HUMP *v.* 2. ● *n.* **1** intuition, feeling, impression, suspicion, premonition, presentiment, idea. **2** see HINT *n.* 1. **3** see HUMP *n.* 1. **4** hunk, chunk; see also SLAB *n.*

hunchback /húnchbak/ *n.* = HUMPBACK. □□ **hunchbacked** *adj.*

hundred /húndrəd/ *n. & adj.* ● *n.* (*pl.* **hundreds** or (in sense 1) **hundred**) (in *sing.,* prec. by *a* or *one*) **1** the product of ten and ten. **2** a symbol for this (100, c, C). **3** a set of a hundred things. **4** (in *sing.* or *pl.*) *colloq.* a large number. **5** (in *pl.*) the years of a specified century (*the seventeen hundreds*). **6** *Brit. hist.* a subdivision of a county or shire, having its own court. ● *adj.* **1** that amount to a hundred. **2** used to express whole hours in the 24-hour system (*thirteen hun-*

dred hours). □ **a** (or **one**) **hundred per cent** *adv.* entirely; completely. ● *adj.* **1** entire; complete. **2** (usu. with *neg.*) fully recovered. **hundreds and thousands** *Brit.* tiny colored candies used chiefly for decorating cakes, etc. □□ **hundredfold** *adj. & adv.* **hundredth** *adj. & n.* [OE f. Gmc]
■ *n.* **4** (*hundreds*) see SCORE *n.* 3.

hundredweight /húndrədwayt/ *n.* (*pl.* same or **-weights**) **1** (in full **short hundredweight**) a unit of weight equal to 100 lb. (about 45.4 kg). **2** (in full **long hundredweight**) *Brit.* a unit of weight equal to 112 lb. (about 50.8 kg). **3** (in full **metric hundredweight**) a unit of weight equal to 50 kg.

hung *past* and *past part.* of HANG.

Hungarian /hunggáireeən/ *n. & adj.* ● *n.* **1 a** a native or inhabitant of Hungary in E. Europe. **b** a person of Hungarian descent. **2** the Finno-Ugric language of Hungary. ● *adj.* of or relating to Hungary or its people or language. [med.L *Hungaria* f. *Hungari* Magyar nation]

hunger /húnggər/ *n. & v.* ● *n.* **1** a feeling of pain or discomfort, or (in extremes) an exhausted condition, caused by lack of food. **2** (often foll. by *for, after*) a strong desire. ● *v.intr.* **1** (often foll. by *for, after*) have a craving or strong desire. **2** feel hunger. □ **hunger strike** the refusal of food as a form of protest, esp. by prisoners. **hunger striker** a person who takes part in a hunger strike. [OE *hungor, hyngran* f. Gmc]

■ *n.* **1** hungriness, emptiness, ravenousness, *archaic* famine. **2** yearning, desire, craving, itch, thirst, longing, hankering, *colloq.* yen. ● *v.* **1** (*hunger for* or *after*) long for, crave, yearn for, desire, thirst for, want, hanker after, *colloq.* have a yen for. **2** have an empty stomach, feel starving.

hungry /húnggree/ *adj.* (**hungrier, hungriest**) **1** feeling or showing hunger; needing food. **2** inducing hunger (*a hungry air*). **3 a** eager; greedy; craving. **b** *Austral.* mean; stingy. **4** (of soil) poor; barren. □□ **hungrily** *adv.* **hungriness** *n.* [OE *hungrig* (as HUNGER)]

■ **1** famished, ravenous, hollow, sharp-set, *archaic or joc.* esurient, *colloq.* empty, starving, starved, esp. *Brit. colloq.* peckish. **3 a** craving, eager, avid, greedy, keen, dying, yearning, desirous, longing, hungering, thirsting, thirsty, hankering, voracious, covetous. **4** see BARREN *adj.* 1b.

hunk /hungk/ *n.* **1 a** a large piece cut off (*a hunk of bread*). **b** a thick or clumsy piece. **2** *colloq.* **a** a sexually attractive man. **b** a very large person. □□ **hunky** *adj.* (**hunkier, hunkiest**). [19th c.: prob. f. Flem. *hunke*]

hunker /húngkər/ *n. & v.* ● *n.pl.* the haunches. ● *v.intr.* (foll. by *down*) **1** squat; crouch. **2** act defensively; hold to a position. [orig. Sc., f. *hunker* crouch, squat]

hunky-dory /húngkeedáwree/ *adj. colloq.* excellent. [19th c.: orig. unkn.]

hunt /hunt/ *v. & n.* ● *v.* **1** *tr.* (also *absol.*) **a** pursue and kill (wild animals, esp. game), *Brit.* esp. on horseback and with hounds, for sport or food. **b** (of an animal) chase (its prey). **2** *intr.* (foll. by *after, for*) seek; search (*hunting for a pen*). **3** *intr.* **a** oscillate. **b** *Brit.* (of an engine, etc.) run alternately too fast and too slow. **4** *tr.* (foll. by *away,* etc.) drive off by pursuit. **5** *tr.* scour (a district) in pursuit of game. **6** *tr.* (as **hunted** *adj.*) (of a look, etc.) expressing alarm or terror as of one being hunted. **7** *tr.* (foll. by *down, up*) move the place of (a bell) in ringing the changes. ● *n.* **1** the practice of hunting or an instance of this. **2 a** an association of people engaged in hunting with hounds. **b** an area where hunting takes place. **3** an oscillating motion. □ **hunt down** pursue and capture. **hunt out** find by searching; track down. [OE *huntian,* weak grade of *hentan* seize]

■ *v.* **1** chase, pursue, dog, hound, stalk, trail, track (down); shoot. **2** (*hunt for* or *after*) seek (out), search for, go in search of *or* for, look (high and low) for, quest for, go in quest of; (*hunt through*) see SEARCH *v.* 1, 3. **4** drive off *or* away; see also SHOO *v.* **5** see SCOUR[2]. **6** (**hunted**) see *scared* (SCARE *v.* 2). ● *n.* **1** chase, pursuit, tracking, stalking, hunting, pursuance; search, quest. □ **hunt down** see *track down* (TRACK¹). **hunt out** see *track down* (TRACK¹).

huntaway /húntaway/ *n. Austral.* & *NZ* a dog trained to drive sheep forward.

hunter /húntar/ *n.* **1 a** (*fem.* **huntress**) a person or animal that hunts. **b** a horse used in hunting. **2** a person who seeks something. **3** a watch with a hinged cover protecting the glass. □ **hunter's moon** the next full moon after the harvest moon.
■ **1 a** huntsman, stalker, tracker, nimrod. **2** seeker, searcher, quester.

hunting /húnting/ *n.* the practice of pursuing and killing wild animals, esp. for sport or food. □ **hunting crop** see CROP *n.* 3. **hunting ground 1** a place suitable for hunting. **2** a source of information or object of exploitation likely to be fruitful. **hunting horn** a straight horn used in hunting. **hunting pink** see PINK¹. [OE *huntung* (as HUNT)]

Huntington's chorea /húntingt'nz/ *n. Med.* see CHOREA. [G. *Huntington*, Amer. neurologist, d. 1916]

huntsman /húntsman/ *n.* (*pl.* **-men**) **1** a hunter. **2** a hunt official in charge of hounds.

hurdle /hórd'l/ *n.* & *v.* ● *n.* **1** *Track & Field* **a** each of a series of light frames to be cleared by athletes in a race. **b** (in *pl.*) a hurdle race. **2** an obstacle or difficulty. **3** a portable rectangular frame strengthened with withes or wooden bars, used as a temporary fence, etc. **4** *Brit. hist.* a frame on which traitors were dragged to execution. ● *v.* **1** *Track & Field* **a** *intr.* run in a hurdle race. **b** *tr.* clear (a hurdle). **2** *tr.* fence off, etc., with hurdles. **3** *tr.* overcome (a difficulty). [OE *hyrdel* f. Gmc]
■ *n.* **2** barrier, obstacle, impediment, hindrance, obstruction, bar, handicap, restraint, snag, (stumbling) block, difficulty, complication, problem. ● *v.* **1 b** clear, leap (over), vault (over), jump (over), bound over, spring over. **3** overcome, surmount, get over; see also SOLVE.

hurdler /hórdlar/ *n.* **1** *Track & Field* a person who runs in hurdle races. **2** a person who makes hurdles.

hurdy-gurdy /hórdeegórdee/ *n.* (*pl.* **-ies**) **1** a musical instrument with a droning sound, played by turning a handle, esp. one with a rosined wheel turned by the right hand to sound the drone strings, and keys played by the left hand. **2** *colloq.* a barrel organ. [prob. imit.]

hurl /hórl/ *v.* & *n.* ● *v.* **1** *tr.* throw with great force. **2** *tr.* utter (abuse, etc.) vehemently. **3** *intr.* play hurling. **4** *intr. sl.* vomit. ● *n.* **1** a forceful throw. **2** the act of hurling. [ME, prob. imit., but corresp. in form and partly in sense with LG *hurreln*]
■ *v.* **1** throw, toss, shy, sling, fling, pitch, cast, fire, propel, launch, let fly, *colloq.* chuck, heave. ● *n.* **1** see THROW *n.* 1.

Hurler's syndrome /hórlarz/ *n. Med.* a defect in metabolism resulting in mental retardation, a protruding abdomen, and deformities of the bones, including an abnormally large head. Also called GARGOYLISM. [G. *Hurler*, Ger. pediatrician]

hurling /hórling/ *n.* (also **hurley** /hórlee/) **1** an Irish game somewhat resembling field hockey, played with broad sticks. **2** a stick used in this.

hurly-burly /hórleebórlee/ *n.* boisterous activity; commotion. [redupl. f. HURL]
■ see DISTURBANCE 2.

Huron /hyóōran, -on/ *n.* **1 a** a N. American people native to the northeastern US. **b** a member of this people. **2** the language of this people.

hurrah /hŏōraá/ *int., n.,* & *v.* (also **hurray** /hŏōráy/) ● *int.* & *n.* an exclamation of joy or approval. ● *v.intr.* cry or shout "hurrah" or "hurray." [alt. of earlier *huzza*, perh. orig. a sailor's cry when hauling]
■ *int.* & *n.* see CHEER *n.* 1. ● *v.* see CHEER *v.* 2.

hurricane /hérikayn, húr-/ *n.* **1** a storm with a violent wind, esp. a cyclone in the W. Atlantic. **2** *Meteorol.* a wind of 65 knots (75 m.p.h.) or more, force 12 on the Beaufort scale. **3** a violent commotion. □ **hurricane bird** a frigate bird. **hurricane deck** a light upper deck on a ship, etc. **hurri-**

cane lamp an oil lamp designed to resist a high wind. [Sp. *huracan* & Port. *furacão* of Carib orig.]
■ **1, 2** cyclone, tornado, typhoon, whirlwind, twister, storm, gale. **3** see STIR¹ *n.* 2.

hurry /hóree, húree/ *n.* & *v.* ● *n.* (*pl.* **-ies**) **1 a** great haste. **b** (with *neg.* or *interrog.*) a need for haste (*there is no hurry*; *what's the hurry?*). **2** (often foll. by *for*, or *to* + infin.) eagerness to get a thing done quickly. ● *v.* (**-ies, -ied**) **1** *intr.* move or act with great or undue haste. **2** *tr.* (often foll. by *away*, *along*) cause to move or proceed in this way. **3** *tr.* (as **hurried** *adj.*) hasty; done rapidly owing to lack of time. □ **hurry up** (or **along**) make or cause to make haste. **in a hurry 1** hurrying; rushed; in a rushed manner. **2** *colloq.* easily or readily (*you will not beat that in a hurry*; *shall not ask again in a hurry*). □□ **hurriedly** *adv.* **hurriedness** *n.* [16th c.: imit.]
■ *n.* **1** a rush, hustle, (hustle and) bustle. **b** haste, pressure; see also *urgency* (URGENT). **2** see *eagerness* (EAGER). ● *v.* **1** rush, hasten, make haste, hotfoot (it), *colloq.* get cracking, get a move on, skedaddle, step on it, step on the gas, leg it, hightail (it), *sl.* get a wiggle on; speed, race, dash, hustle, scurry, fly, run, shoot, scuttle, go hell for leather, *colloq.* tear, scoot; speed up, accelerate. **2** push, press, drive; urge, egg on, spur (on). **3** (**hurried**) hasty, feverish, frantic, hectic, breakneck, frenetic, impetuous, rushed, precipitate, swift, quick, speedy; brief, short; superficial, cursory, offhand, perfunctory, slapdash. □ **hurry up** (or **along**) see HURRY *v.* 1, 2 above. **in a hurry 2** easily, readily, quickly.

hurry-scurry /hóreeskóree, húreeskúree/ *n., adj.,* & *adv.* ● *n.* disorderly haste. ● *adj.* & *adv.* in confusion. [jingling redupl. of HURRY]

hurst /hórst/ *n.* **1** a lillock. **2** a sandbank in the sea or river. **3** a wood or wooded eminence. [OE *hyrst*, rel. to OS, OHG *hurst horst*]

hurt /hórt/ *v, n.,* & *adj.* ● *v.* (*past* and *past part.* **hurt**) **1** *tr.* (also *absol.*) cause pain or injury to. **2** *tr.* cause mental pain or distress to (a person, feelings, etc.). **3** *intr.* suffer pain or harm (*my arm hurts*). **4** *tr.* cause damage to; be detrimental to. ● *n.* **1** bodily or material injury. **2** harm; wrong. **3** mental pain or distress. ● *adj.* expressing emotional pain; distressed; aggrieved. □□ **hurtless** *adj.* [ME f. OF *hurter, hurt* ult. perh. f. Gmc]
■ *v.* **1** harm, injure, wound. **2** distress, grieve, affect, afflict, depress, upset, disappoint, pain, cut to the quick, affront, offend. **3** ache, throb, pound, be sore *or* painful, sting, twinge; smart, burn. **4** damage, impair, mar, spoil, vitiate, ruin. ● *n.* **1** wound, damage; see also INJURY 1. **2** harm, injury, damage, wrong; see also GRIEVANCE. **3** pain, distress, discomfort, suffering, torment, torture, agony; anguish, misery, sadness, depression, *archaic or literary* woe, *literary* dolor. ● *adj.* injured, wronged, pained, rueful, grieved, unhappy, distressed, aggrieved, sad, wretched, woebegone, sorrowful, mournful.

hurtful /hórtfōōl/ *adj.* causing (esp. mental) hurt; causing damage or harm. □□ **hurtfully** *adv.* **hurtfulness** *n.*
■ nasty, cruel, cutting, malicious, mean, unkind, wounding, spiteful; harmful, injurious, detrimental, pernicious, disadvantageous, damaging, deleterious, destructive, noxious, baneful, mischievous, *literary* noisome.

hurtle /hórt'l/ *v.* **1** *intr.* & *tr.* move or hurl rapidly or with a clattering sound. **2** *intr.* come with a crash. [HURT in obs. sense 'strike forcibly']
■ **1** rush (headlong), plunge; tear, shoot, race, speed.

husband /húzband/ *n.* & *v.* ● *n.* a married man esp. in relation to his wife. ● *v.tr.* manage thriftily; use (resources)

/.../ **pronunciation** ● **part of speech**
□ **phrases, idioms, and compounds**
□□ **derivatives** ■ **synonym section**
cross-references appear in SMALL CAPITALS or *italics*

economically. □□ **husbander** *n.* **husbandhood** *n.* **husbandless** *adj.* **husbandlike** *adj.* **husbandly** *adj.* **husbandship** *n.* [OE *húsbonda* house dweller f. ON *húsbóndi* (as HOUSE, *bóndi* one who has a household)]

■ *n.* spouse, partner, *colloq.* mate, old man, hubby; groom, bridegroom. ● *v.* budget, economize on, manage.

husbandry /húzbəndree/ *n.* **1** farming. **2 a** management of resources. **b** careful management.

■ **1** see *farming* (FARM). **2** see ECONOMY 2a.

hush /hush/ *v., int.,* & *n.* ● *v.* **1** *tr.* & *intr.* (often as **hushed** *adj.*) make or become silent, quiet, or muted. **2** *tr.* calm (disturbance, disquiet, etc.); soothe; allay. ● *int.* calling for silence. ● *n.* an expectant stillness or silence. □ **hush money** money paid to prevent the disclosure of a discreditable matter. **hush puppy** a deep-fried ball of cornmeal dough. **hush up** suppress public mention of (a scandal). [back-form. f. obs. *husht* int., = quiet!, taken as a past part.]

■ *v.* **1** shush, silence, still, quiet, *Brit.* quieten; (**hushed**) muted, soft, quiet, *Mus.* piano. **2** soothe, allay, calm, quiet, mollify, pacify, placate, tranquilize, *Brit.* quieten. ● *int.* shush, quiet, be *or* keep quiet, hold your tongue *or* peace, *colloq.* shut up, clam up, button up, esp. *Sc.* & *Ir. dial.* whisht, *sl.* shut your face *or* trap *or* head *or* mouth, button your lip, esp. *Brit. sl.* shut your gob, put a sock in it, belt up. ● *n.* silence, quiet, stillness, peace, tranquillity. □ **hush up** suppress, repress, cover up, hide, conceal, keep quiet.

hushaby /húshəbī/ *int.* (also **hushabye**) used to lull a child.

hush-hush /húsh-húsh/ *adj. colloq.* (esp. of an official plan or enterprise, etc.) highly secret or confidential.

■ see SECRET *adj.* 3.

husk /husk/ *n.* & *v.* ● *n.* **1** the dry outer covering of some fruits or seeds, esp. of a nut or corn. **2** the worthless outside part of a thing. ● *v.tr.* remove a husk or husks from. [ME, prob. f. LG *húske* sheath, dimin. of *hús* HOUSE]

■ *n.* **1** see SKIN *n.* 4. ● *v.* see SHELL *v.* 1.

husky[1] /húskee/ *adj.* (**huskier, huskiest**) **1** (of a person or voice) dry in the throat; hoarse. **2** of or full of husks. **3** dry as a husk. **4** tough; strong; hefty. □□ **huskily** *adv.* **huskiness** *n.*

■ **1** hoarse, gruff, rasping, rough, raucous. **4** brawny, strapping, sturdy, burly, well-built, robust, hefty, rugged, powerful, strong, thickset, muscular, tough, beefy.

husky[2] /húskee/ *n.* (*pl.* **-ies**) **1** a dog of a powerful breed used in the Arctic for pulling sledges. **2** this breed. [perh. contr. f. ESKIMO]

hussar /hŏzaár, -saár/ *n.* **1** a soldier of a light cavalry regiment. **2** a Hungarian light horseman of the 15th c. [Magyar *huszár* f. OSerb. *husar* f. It. *corsaro* CORSAIR]

Hussite /húsīt/ *n. hist.* a member or follower of the movement begun by John *Huss*, Bohemian religious and nationalist reformer d. 1415. □□ **Hussitism** *n.*

hussy /húsee, -zee/ *n.* (*pl.* **-ies**) *derog.* an impudent or immoral girl or woman. [phonetic reduction of HOUSEWIFE (the orig. sense)]

■ see SLUT.

hustings /hústingz/ *n.* **1** political campaigning, esp. the appearances and activities involved with a campaign. **2** *Brit. hist.* a platform from which (before 1872) candidates for Parliament were nominated and addressed electors. [late OE *husting* f. ON *hústhing* house of assembly]

hustle /húsəl/ *v.* & *n.* ● *v.* **1** *tr.* push roughly; jostle. **2** *tr.* **a** (foll. by *into, out of,* etc.) force, coerce, or deal with hurriedly or unceremoniously (*hustled them out of the room*). **b** (foll. by *into*) coerce hurriedly (*was hustled into agreeing*). **3** *intr.* push one's way; hurry; bustle. **4** *tr. sl.* **a** obtain by forceful action. **b** swindle. **5** *intr. sl.* engage in prostitution. ● *n.* **1 a** an act or instance of hustling. **b** forceful or strenuous activity. **2** *colloq.* a fraud or swindle. [MDu. *husselen* shake, toss, frequent. of *hutsen*, orig. imit.]

■ *v.* **1** shove, push, jostle, elbow, thrust, force. **2 a** (*hustle into* or *out of,* etc.) force *or* coerce *or* drive into *or* out of *or* through, push *or* shove into *or* out of *or* through,

eject from, hasten into *or* out of *or* through, press through, expedite through, *sl.* bounce out of. **b** coerce, force, press, *colloq.* bounce. **3** rush, push, hurry, hasten, run, sprint, dash, scuttle, scurry, bustle. **4 b** see SWINDLE *v.* **5** walk the streets, *Brit. sl.* be *or* go on the game. ● *n.* **1 a** pushing, jostling, buffeting, jarring, elbowing, shoving, nudging. **b** action, activity, stir, movement. **2** see SWINDLE *n.* 1, 3.

hustler /húslər/ *n. sl.* **1** an active, enterprising, or unscrupulous individual. **2** a prostitute.

■ **2** see PROSTITUTE *n.*

hut /hut/ *n.* & *v.* ● *n.* **1** a small simple or crude house or shelter. **2** *Mil.* a temporary wooden, etc., house for troops. ● *v.* (**hutted, hutting**) **1** *tr.* provide with huts. **2** *tr. Mil.* place (troops, etc.) in huts. **3** *intr.* lodge in a hut. □□ **hutlike** *adj.* [F *hutte* f. MHG *hütte*]

■ *n.* **1** cabin, shack, shanty, *Austral.* gunyah, *poet.* cot.

hutch /huch/ *n.* **1** a box or cage, usu. with a wire mesh front, for keeping small pet animals. **2** *derog.* a small house. [ME, = coffer, f. OF *huche* f. med.L *hutica*, of unkn. orig.]

■ **1** see CAGE *n.*

hutment /hútmənt/ *n. Mil.* an encampment of huts.

HWM *abbr.* high-water mark.

hwy. *abbr.* highway.

hwyl /hŏŏil/ *n. Welsh* an emotional quality inspiring impassioned eloquence. [Welsh]

hyacinth /híəsinth/ *n.* **1** any bulbous plant of the genus *Hyacinthus* with racemes of usu. purplish blue, pink, or white bell-shaped fragrant flowers. **2** = *grape hyacinth.* **3** the purplish blue color of the hyacinth flower. **4** an orange variety of zircon used as a precious stone. **5** *poet.* hair or locks like the hyacinth flower (as a Homeric epithet of doubtful sense). □ **wild** (or **wood**) **hyacinth** = BLUEBELL 1. □□ **hyacinthine** /-sínthin, -in/ *adj.* [F *hyacinthe* f. L *hyacinthus* f. Gk *huakinthos*, flower and gem, also the name of a youth loved by Apollo]

Hyades /híədeez/ *n.pl.* a group of stars in Taurus near the Pleiades, whose heliacal rising was once thought to foretell rain. [ME f. Gk *Huades* (by popular etym. f. *huō* rain, but perh. f. *hus* pig)]

hyaena var. of HYENA.

hyalin /híəlin/ *n.* a clear glassy substance produced as a result of the degeneration of certain body tissues. [Gk *hualos* glass + -IN]

hyaline *adj.* & *n.* ● /híəlin, -lin/ *adj.* glasslike; vitreous; transparent. ● *n.* /híəleen, -lin/ *literary* a smooth sea, clear sky, etc. □ **hyaline cartilage** *n.* a common type of cartilage. [L *hyalinus* f. Gk *hualinos* f. *hualos* glass]

hyalite /híəlīt/ *n.* a colorless variety of opal. [Gk *hualos* glass]

hyaloid /híəloyd/ *adj. Anat.* glassy. □ **hyaloid membrane** a thin transparent membrane enveloping the vitreous humor of the eye. [F *hyaloïde* f. LL *hyaloides* f. Gk *hualoeidēs* (as HYALITE)]

hybrid /híbrid/ *n.* & *adj.* ● *n.* **1** *Biol.* the offspring of two plants or animals of different species or varieties. **2** often *offens.* a person of mixed racial or cultural origin. **3** a thing composed of incongruous elements, e.g., a word with parts taken from different languages. ● *adj.* **1** bred as a hybrid from different species or varieties. **2** *Biol.* heterogeneous. **3** of mixed character; derived from incongruous elements or unlike sources. □ **hybrid vigor** heterosis. □□ **hybridism** *n.* **hybridity** /-bríditee/ *n.* [L *hybrida,* (h)*ibrida* offspring of a tame sow and wild boar, child of a freeman and slave, etc.]

■ *n.* **1** crossbreed, cross, mongrel. **2** Creole, mestizo, *derog.* mongrel, *offens.* half-breed, *often offens.* half-caste. **3** mixture, composite, combination, compound, blend, amalgam, amalgamation, mix, union, conjunction, grouping. ● *adj.* **3** see DIVERSE.

hybridize /híbridīz/ *v.* **1** *tr.* subject (a species, etc.) to crossbreeding. **2** *intr.* **a** produce hybrids. **b** (of an animal or plant) interbreed. □□ **hybridizable** *adj.* **hybridization** *n.*

hydatid /hídətid/ *n. Med.* **1** a cyst containing watery fluid (esp. one formed by, and containing, a tapeworm larva). **2** a tapeworm larva. □□ **hydatidiform** /-tídiform/ *adj.* [mod.L *hydatis* f. Gk *hudatis -idos* watery vesicle f. *hudōr hudatos* water]

hydra /hídrǝ/ *n.* **1** a freshwater polyp of the genus *Hydra* with tubular body and tentacles around the mouth. **2** something that is hard to destroy. [ME f. L f. Gk *hudra* water snake, esp. a fabulous one with many heads that grew again when cut off]

hydrangea /hidráynjǝ, -dran-/ *n.* any shrub of the genus *Hydrangea* with large white, pink, or blue flowers. [mod.L f. Gk *hudōr* water + *aggos* vessel (from the cup shape of its seed capsule)]

hydrant /hídrǝnt/ *n.* a pipe (esp. in a street) with a nozzle to which a hose can be attached for drawing water from a water main. [irreg. f. HYDRO- + -ANT]
■ standpipe, fireplug.

hydrate /hídrayt/ *n. & v.* ● *n. Chem.* a compound of water combined with another compound or with an element. ● *v.tr.* **1 a** combine chemically with water. **b** (as **hydrated** *adj.*) chemically bonded to water. **2** cause to absorb water. □□ **hydratable** *adj.* **hydration** /-dráyshǝn/ *n.* **hydrator** *n.* [F f. Gk *hudōr* water]

hydraulic /hidráwlik, -drólik/ *adj.* **1** (of water, oil, etc.) conveyed through pipes or channels usu. by pressure. **2** (of a mechanism, etc.) operated by liquid moving in this manner (*hydraulic brakes*; *hydraulic elevator*). **3** of or concerned with hydraulics (*hydraulic engineer*). **4** hardening under water (*hydraulic cement*). □ **hydraulic press** a device in which the force applied to a fluid creates a pressure that when transmitted to a larger volume of fluid gives rise to a greater force. **hydraulic ram** an automatic pump in which the kinetic energy of a descending column of water raises some of the water above its original level. □□ **hydraulically** *adv.* **hydraulicity** /-lísitee/ *n.* [L *hydraulicus* f. Gk *hudraulikos* f. *hudōr* water + *aulos* pipe]

hydraulics /hidráwliks, -dróliks/ *n.pl.* (usu. treated as *sing.*) the science of the conveyance of liquids through pipes, etc., esp. as motive power.

hydrazine /hídrǝzeen/ *n. Chem.* a colorless alkaline liquid which is a powerful reducing agent and is used as a rocket propellant. ¶ Chem. formula: N_2H_4. [HYDROGEN + AZO- + -INE⁴]

hydride /hídrid/ *n. Chem.* a binary compound of hydrogen with an element, esp. with a metal.

hydriodic acid /hídreeódik/ *n. Chem.* a solution of the colorless gas hydrogen iodide in water. ¶ Chem. formula: HI. [HYDROGEN + IODINE]

hydro /hídrō/ *n.* (*pl.* **-os**) *colloq.* **1** *Brit.* a hotel or clinic, etc., orig. providing hydropathic treatment; a health spa. **2** a hydroelectric power plant. [abbr.]

hydro- /hídrō/ *comb. form* (also **hydr-** before a vowel) **1** having to do with water (*hydroelectric*). **2** *Med.* affected with an accumulation of serous fluid (*hydrocele*). **3** *Chem.* combined with hydrogen (*hydrochloric*). [Gk *hudro-* f. *hudōr* water]

hydrobromic acid /hídrǝbrōmik/ *n. Chem.* a solution of the colorless gas hydrogen bromide in water. ¶ Chem. formula: HBr.

hydrocarbon /hídrǝkáarbǝn/ *n.* a compound of hydrogen and carbon.

hydrocele /hídrǝseel/ *n. Med.* the accumulation of serous fluid in a body sac.

hydrocephalus /hídrǝséfǝlǝs/ *n. Med.* an abnormal amount of fluid within the brain, esp. in young children, which makes the head enlarge and can cause mental deficiency. □□ **hydrocephalic** /-sifálik/ *adj.*

hydrochloric acid /hídrǝkláwrik/ *n. Chem.* a solution of the colorless gas hydrogen chloride in water. ¶ Chem. formula: HCl.

hydrochloride /hídrǝkláwrid/ *n. Chem.* a compound of an organic base with hydrochloric acid.

hydrocortisone /hídrǝkáwrtizōn/ *n. Biochem.* a steroid hormone produced by the adrenal cortex, used medicinally to treat inflammation and rheumatism.

hydrocyanic acid /hídrōsiánik/ *n. Chem.* a highly poisonous volatile liquid with a characteristic odor of bitter almonds. ¶ Chem. formula: HCN. Also called *prussic acid*.

hydrodynamics /hídrōdīnámiks/ *n.* the science of forces acting on or exerted by fluids (esp. liquids). □□ **hydrodynamic** *adj.* **hydrodynamical** *adj.* **hydrodynamicist** /-misist/ *n.* [mod.L *hydrodynamicus* (as HYDRO-, DYNAMIC)]

hydroelectric /hídrōiléktrik/ *adj.* **1** generating electricity by utilization of waterpower. **2** (of electricity) generated in this way. □□ **hydroelectricity** /-trísitee/ *n.*

hydrofluoric acid /hídrǝflóorik, fláwr-/ *n. Chem.* a solution of the colorless liquid hydrogen fluoride in water. ¶ Chem. formula: HF.

hydrofoil /hídrǝfoyl/ *n.* **1** a boat equipped with a device consisting of planes for lifting its hull out of the water to increase its speed. **2** this device. [HYDRO-, after AIRFOIL]

hydrogen /hídrǝjǝn/ *n. Chem.* a colorless gaseous element, without taste or odor, the lightest of the elements and occurring in water and all organic compounds. ¶ Symb.: **H**. □ **hydrogen bomb** an immensely powerful bomb utilizing the explosive fusion of hydrogen nuclei: also called H BOMB. **hydrogen bond** a weak electrostatic interaction between an electronegative atom and a hydrogen atom bonded to a different electronegative atom. **hydrogen peroxide** a colorless viscous unstable liquid with strong oxidizing properties. ¶ Chem. formula: H_2O_2. **hydrogen sulfide** a colorless poisonous gas with a disagreeable smell, formed by rotting animal matter. ¶ Chem. formula: H_2S. □□ **hydrogenous** /-drójinǝs/ *adj.* [F *hydrogène* (as HYDRO-, -GEN)]

hydrogenase /hidrójinays, -nayz/ *n. Biochem.* any enzyme which catalyzes the oxidation of hydrogen and the reduction of protons.

hydrogenate /hidrójinayt, hídrǝjǝnayt/ *v.tr.* charge with or cause to combine with hydrogen. □□ **hydrogenation** /-náyshǝn/ *n.*

hydrography /hidrógrǝfee/ *n.* the science of surveying and charting seas, lakes, rivers, etc. □□ **hydrographer** *n.* **hydrographic** /hídrǝgráfik/ *adj.* **hydrographical** *adj.* **hydrographically** *adv.*

hydroid /hídroyd/ *adj. & n. Zool.* any usu. polypoid hydrozoan of the order Hydroida, including hydra.

hydrolase /hídrōlays, -layz/ *n. Biochem.* any enzyme which catalyzes the hydrolysis of a substrate.

hydrology /hidrólǝjee/ *n.* the science of the properties of the earth's water, esp. of its movement in relation to land. □□ **hydrologic** /hídrǝlójik/ *adj.* **hydrological** *adj.* **hydrologically** *adv.* **hydrologist** /-rólǝjist/ *n.*

hydrolysis /hidrólisis/ *n.* the chemical reaction of a substance with water, usu. resulting in decomposition. □□ **hydrolytic** /hídrǝlítik/ *adj.*

hydrolyze /hídrǝlīz/ *v.tr. & intr.* (*Brit.* **hydrolyse**) subject to or undergo the chemical action of water.

hydromagnetic /hídrōmagnétik/ *adj.* involving hydrodynamics and magnetism; magnetohydrodynamic.

hydromania /hídrǝmáyneeǝ/ *n.* a craving for water.

hydromechanics /hídrōmikániks/ *n.* the mechanics of liquids; hydrodynamics.

hydrometer /hidrómitǝr/ *n.* an instrument for measuring the density of liquids. □□ **hydrometric** /hídrǝmétrik/ *adj.* **hydrometry** *n.*

hydronium ion /hidrōneeǝm/ *n. Chem.* the hydrated hydrogen ion, H_3O^+.

hydropathy /hidrópǝthee/ *n.* the (medically unorthodox) treatment of disease by external and internal application of water. □□ **hydropathic** /hídrǝpáthik/ *adj.* **hydropathist** *n.* [HYDRO-, after HOMEOPATHY, etc.]

hydrophilic /hídrǝfílik/ *adj.* **1** having an affinity for water. **2** wettable by water. [HYDRO- + Gk *philos* loving]

hydrophobia /hídrǝfṓbeeǝ/ *n.* **1** a morbid aversion to water, esp. as a symptom of rabies in humans. **2** rabies, esp. in humans. [LL f. Gk *hudrophobia* (as HYDRO-, -PHOBIA)]

hydrophobic /hídrǝfóbik/ *adj.* **1** of or suffering from hydro-

---

/.../ **pronunciation**   ● **part of speech**
□ **phrases, idioms, and compounds**
□□ **derivatives**   ■ **synonym section**
cross-references appear in SMALL CAPITALS or *italics*

phobia. **2 a** lacking an affinity for water. **b** not readily wettable.

hydrophone /hídrəfōn/ *n.* an instrument for the detection of sound waves in water.

hydrophyte /hídrəfīt/ *n.* an aquatic plant, or a plant which needs much moisture.

hydroplane /hídrəplayn/ *n.* & *v.* ● *n.* **1** a light fast motor boat designed to skim over the surface of water. **2** a finlike attachment which enables a submarine to rise and submerge in water. ● *v.intr.* **1** (of a boat) skim over the surface of water with its hull lifted. **2** (of a vehicle) glide uncontrollably on the wet surface of a road.

hydroponics /hídrəpóniks/ *n.* the process of growing plants in sand, gravel, or liquid, without soil and with added nutrients. □□ **hydroponic** *adj.* **hydroponically** *adv.* [HYDRO- + Gk *ponos* labor]

hydroquinone /hídrəkwínōn/ *n.* a substance formed by the reduction of quinone, used as a photographic developer.

hydrosphere /hídrəsfeer/ *n.* the waters of the earth's surface.

hydrostatic /hídrəstátik/ *adj.* of the equilibrium of liquids and the pressure exerted by liquid at rest. □ **hydrostatic press** = hydraulic press. □□ **hydrostatical** *adj.* **hydrostatically** *adv.* [prob. f. Gk *hudrostatēs* hydrostatic balance (as HYDRO-, STATIC)]

hydrostatics /hídrəstátiks/ *n.pl.* (usu. treated as *sing.*) the branch of mechanics concerned with the hydrostatic properties of liquids.

hydrotherapy /hídrəthérəpee/ *n.* the use of water in the treatment of disorders, usu. exercises in swimming pools for arthritic or partially paralyzed patients. □□ **hydrotherapist** *n.* **hydrotherapeutic** /-pyōōtik/ *adj.*

hydrothermal /hídrəthérməl/ *adj.* of the action of heated water on the earth's crust. □□ **hydrothermally** *adv.*

hydrothorax /hídrətháwraks/ *n.* the condition of having fluid in the pleural cavity.

hydrotropism /hídrótrəpizəm/ *adj.* a tendency of plant roots, etc., to turn to or from moisture.

hydrous /hídrəs/ *adj. Chem.* & *Mineral.* containing water. [Gk *hudōr hudro-* water]

hydroxide /hidróksīd/ *n. Chem.* a metallic compound containing oxygen and hydrogen either in the form of the hydroxide ion (OH⁻) or the hydroxyl group (–OH).

hydroxy- /hidróksee/ *comb. form Chem.* having a hydroxide ion (or ions) or a hydroxyl group (or groups) (*hydroxybenzoic acid*). [HYDROGEN + OXYGEN]

hydroxyl /hidróksil/ *n. Chem.* the univalent group containing hydrogen and oxygen, as -OH. [HYDROGEN + OXYGEN + -YL]

hydrozoan /hídrəzṓən/ *n.* & *adj.* ● *n.* any aquatic coelenterate of the class *Hydrozoa* of mainly marine polyp or medusoid forms, including hydra and Portuguese man-of-war. [mod.L *Hydrozoa* (as HYDRA, Gk *zōion* animal)]

hyena /hī-éenə/ *n.* (also **hyaena**) any flesh-eating mammal of the order Hyaenidae, with hind limbs shorter than forelimbs. □ **laughing hyena** *n.* a hyena, *Crocuta crocuta*, whose howl is compared to a fiendish laugh. [ME f. OF *hyene* & L *hyaena* f. Gk *huaina* fem. of *hus* pig]

hygiene /hí̄jeen/ *n.* **1 a** a study, or set of principles, of maintaining health. **b** conditions or practices conducive to maintaining health. **2** sanitary science. [F *hygiène* f. mod.L *hygieina* f. Gk *hugieinē* (*tekhnē*) (art) of health f. *hugiēs* healthy]

hygienic /hījénik, hījéenik/ *adj.* conducive to hygiene; clean and sanitary. □□ **hygienically** *adv.*
■ clean, sanitary; sterile, disinfected, germfree, aseptic.

hygienics /hījéniks, hījéeniks/ *n.pl.* (usu. treated as *sing.*) = HYGIENE 1a.

hygienist /hījénist, -jée-, -hījeenist/ *n.* a specialist in the promotion and practice of cleanliness for the preservation of health, esp. (**dental hygienist**) a dental assistant who cleans the teeth.

hygro- /hígrō/ *comb. form* moisture. [Gk *hugro-* f. *hugros* wet, moist]

hygrology /hīgrólajee/ *n.* the study of the humidity of the atmosphere, etc.

hygrometer /hīgrómitər/ *n.* an instrument for measuring the humidity of the air or a gas. □□ **hygrometric** /hígrəmétrik/ *adj.* **hygrometry** *n.*

hygrophilous /hīgrófiləs/ *adj.* (of a plant) growing in a moist environment.

hygrophyte /hígrəfīt/ *n.* = HYDROPHYTE.

hygroscope /hígrəskōp/ *n.* an instrument that indicates but does not measure the humidity of the air.

hygroscopic /hígrəskópik/ *adj.* **1** of the hygroscope. **2** (of a substance) tending to absorb moisture from the air. □□ **hygroscopically** *adv.*

hying *pres. part.* of HIE.

hylic /hílik/ *adj.* of matter; material. [LL *hylicus* f. Gk *hulikos* f. *hulē* matter]

hylo- /hílō/ *comb. form* matter. [Gk *hulo-* f. *hulē* matter]

hylomorphism /híləmáwrfizəm/ *n.* the theory that physical objects are composed of matter and form. [HYLO- + Gk *morphē* form]

hylozoism /híləzóizəm/ *n.* the doctrine that all matter has life. [HYLO- + Gk *zōē* life]

hymen /híman/ *n. Anat.* a membrane that partially closes the opening of the vagina and is usu. broken at the first occurrence of sexual intercourse. □□ **hymenal** *adj.* [LL f. Gk *humēn* membrane]

hymeneal /hímineeəl/ *adj. literary* of or concerning marriage. [*Hymen* (L f. Gk *Humēn*) Greek and Roman god of marriage]
■ see NUPTIAL *adj.*

hymenium /himeeneeəm/ *n.* (*pl.* **hymenia** /-neeə/) the spore-bearing surface of certain fungi. [mod.L f. Gk *humenion* dimin. of *humēn* membrane]

hymenopteran /hímənóptərən/ *n.* any insect of the order *Hymenoptera* having four transparent wings, including bees, wasps, and ants. □□ **hymenopterous** *adj.* [mod.L *hymenoptera* f. Gk *humenopteros* membrane-winged (as HYMENIUM, *pteron* wing)]

hymn /him/ *n.* & *v.* ● *n.* **1** a song of praise, esp. to God in Christian worship, usu. a metrical composition sung in a religious service. **2** a song of praise in honor of a god or other exalted being or thing. ● *v.* **1** *tr.* praise or celebrate in hymns. **2** *intr.* sing hymns. □□ **hymnic** /hímnik/ *adj.* [ME *ymne*, etc. f. OF *ymne* f. L *hymnus* f. Gk *humnos*]
■ *n.* see SONG.

hymnal /hímnəl/ *n.* & *adj.* ● *n.* a hymnbook. ● *adj.* of hymns. [ME f. med.L *hymnale* (as HYMN)]

hymnary /hímnəree/ *n.* (*pl.* **-ies**) a hymnbook.

hymnbook /hímbŏŏk/ *n.* a book of hymns.

hymnody /hímnədee/ *n.* (*pl.* **-ies**) **1 a** the singing of hymns. **b** the composition of hymns. **2** hymns collectively. □□ **hymnodist** *n.* [med.L *hymnodia* f. Gk *humnōidia* f. *humnos* hymn: cf. PSALMODY]

hymnographer /himnógrəfər/ *n.* a writer of hymns. □□ **hymnography** *n.* [Gk *humnographos* f. *humnos* hymn]

hymnology /himnólajee/ *n.* (*pl.* **-ies**) **1** the composition or study of hymns. **2** hymns collectively. □□ **hymnologist** *n.*

hyoid /híoyd/ *n.* & *adj. Anat.* ● *n.* (in full **hyoid bone**) a U-shaped bone in the neck which supports the tongue. ● *adj.* of or relating to this. [F *hyoïde* f. mod.L *hyoïdes* f. Gk *huoeidēs* shaped like the letter upsilon (*hu*)]

hyoscine /hí̄əseen/ *n.* a poisonous alkaloid found in plants of the nightshade family, esp. of the genus *Scopolia*, and used as an antiemetic in motion sickness and a preoperative medication for examination of the eye. Also called SCOPOLAMINE. [f. HYOSCYAMINE]

hyoscyamine /hí̄əsíəmeen/ *n.* a poisonous alkaloid obtained from henbane, having similar properties to hyoscine. [mod.L *hyoscyamus* f. Gk *huoskuamos* henbane f. *hus huos* pig + *kuamos* bean]

hypaethral var. of HYPETHRAL.

hypallage /hīpáləjee/ *n. Rhet.* the transposition of the natural relations of two elements in a proposition (e.g., *Melissa shook her doubtful curls*). [LL f. Gk *hupallagē* (as HYPO-, *allassō* exchange)]

hype¹ /hīp/ *n.* & *v. sl.* ● *n.* **1** extravagant or intensive publicity promotion. **2** cheating; a trick. ● *v.tr.* **1** promote (a prod-

uct) with extravagant publicity. **2** cheat; trick. [20th c.: orig. unkn.]
■ *n.* **1** see ADVERTISEMENT 2. ● *v.* **1** see PROMOTE 3.

hype² /hip/ *n. sl.* **1** a drug addict. **2** a hypodermic needle or injection. □ **hyped up** stimulated by or as if by a hypodermic injection. [abbr. of HYPODERMIC]
■ **1** see ADDICT *n.* 1.

hyper /hípər/ *adj. sl.* excessively excited, nervous, stimulated, etc.

hyper- /hípər/ *prefix* meaning: **1** over; beyond; above (*hyperphysical*). **2** exceeding (*hypersonic*). **3** excessively; above normal (*hyperbole*; *hypersensitive*). [Gk *huper* over, beyond]

hyperactive /hípəráktiv/ *adj.* (of a person, esp. a child) abnormally active. □□ **hyperactivity** /-tívitee/ *n.*
■ see ACTIVE *adj.* 1a.

hyperbaric /hípərbárik/ *adj.* (of a gas) at a pressure greater than normal. [HYPER- + Gk *barus* heavy]

hyperbaton /hípərbəton/ *n. Rhet.* the inversion of the normal order of words, esp. for the sake of emphasis (e.g., *this I must see*). [L f. Gk *huperbaton* (as HYPER-, *bainō* go)]

hyperbola /hípórbələ/ *n.* (*pl.* **hyperbolas** or **hyperbolae** /-lee/) *Geom.* the plane curve of two equal branches, produced when a cone is cut by a plane that makes a larger angle with the base than the side of the cone (cf. ELLIPSE). [mod.L f. Gk *huperbolē* excess (as HYPER-, *ballō* to throw)]

hyperbole /hipórbəlee/ *n. Rhet.* an exaggerated statement not meant to be taken literally. □□ **hyperbolical** /hípərbólikəl/ *adj.* **hyperbolically** *adv.* **hyperbolism** *n.* [L (as HYPERBOLA)]
■ see *exaggeration* (EXAGGERATE).

hyperbolic /hípərbólik/ *adj. Geom.* of or relating to a hyperbola. □ **hyperbolic function** a function related to a rectangular hyperbola, e.g., a hyperbolic cosine.

hyperboloid /hípórbəloyd/ *n. Geom.* a solid or surface having plane sections that are hyperbolas, ellipses, or circles. □□ **hyperboloidal** *adj.*

hyperborean /hípərbáwreeən, -bəre'eən/ *n. & adj.* ● *n.* **1** an inhabitant of the extreme north of the earth. **2** (**Hyperborean**) (in Greek mythology) a member of a race worshiping Apollo and living in a land of sunshine and plenty beyond the north wind. ● *adj.* of the extreme north of the earth. [LL *hyperboreanus* f. L *hyperboreus* f. Gk *huperboreos* (as HYPER-, *Boreas* god of the north wind)]

hyperconscious /hípərkónshəs/ *adj.* (foll. by *of*) acutely or excessively aware.

hypercritical /hípərkrítikəl/ *adj.* excessively critical, esp. of small faults. □□ **hypercritically** *adv.*
■ see OVERCRITICAL.

hyperemia /hípəre'emeeə/ *n.* (*Brit.* **hyperaemia**) an excessive quantity of blood in the vessels supplying an organ or other part of the body. □□ **hyperemic** *adj.* [mod.L (as HYPER-, -EMIA)]

hyperesthesia /hípəris-theezhə/ *n.* (*Brit.* **hyperaesthesia**) an excessive physical sensibility, esp. of the skin. □□ **hyperesthetic** /-thétik/ *adj.* [mod.L (as HYPER-, Gk *-aisthēsia* f. *aisthanomai* perceive)]

hyperfocal distance /hípərfókəl/ *n.* the distance on which a camera lens can be focused to bring the maximum range of object distances into focus.

hypergamy /hīpárgəmee/ *n.* marriage to a person of equal or superior caste or class. [HYPER- + Gk *gamos* marriage]

hyperglycemia /hípərglíse'emeeə/ *n.* an excess of glucose in the bloodstream, often associated with diabetes mellitus. □□ **hyperglycemic** *adj.* [HYPER- + GLYCO- + -EMIA]

hypergolic /hípərgólik/ *adj.* (of a rocket propellant) igniting spontaneously on contact with an oxidant, etc. [G *Hypergol* (perh. as HYPO-, ERG¹, -OL)]

hypericum /hipérikəm/ *n.* any shrub of the genus *Hypericum* with five-petaled yellow flowers. Also called ST. JOHN'S WORT. [L f. Gk *hupereikon* (as HYPER-, *ereikē* heath)]

hypermarket /hípərmaarkit/ *n. Brit.* a very large self-service store with a wide range of goods and extensive parking facilities, usu. outside a town. [transl. F *hypermarché* (as HYPER-, MARKET)]

hypermetropia /hípərmitrŏpeeə/ *n.* the condition of being farsighted. □□ **hypermetropic** /-trópik/ *adj.* [mod.L f. HYPER- + Gk *metron* measure, *ōps* eye]
■ longsightedness, presbyopia, farsightedness.

hyperon /hípəron/ *n. Physics* an unstable elementary particle which is classified as a baryon apart from the neutron or proton. [HYPER- + -ON]

hyperopia /hípərŏpeeə/ *n.* = HYPERMETROPIA. □□ **hyperopic** /-rópik/ *adj.* [mod.L f. HYPER- + Gk *ōps* eye]

hyperphysical /hípərfízikəl/ *adj.* supernatural. □□ **hyperphysically** *adv.*

hyperplasia /hípərpláyzhə/ *n.* the enlargement of an organ or tissue from the increased production of cells. [HYPER- + Gk *plasis* formation]

hypersensitive /hípərsénsitiv/ *adj.* abnormally or excessively sensitive. □□ **hypersensitiveness** *n.* **hypersensitivity** /-tívitee/ *n.*
■ see SENSITIVE *adj.* 2.

hypersonic /hípərsónik/ *adj.* **1** relating to speeds of more than five times the speed of sound (Mach 5). **2** relating to sound frequencies above about a billion hertz. □□ **hypersonically** *adv.* [HYPER-, after SUPERSONIC, ULTRASONIC]

hypersthene /hípərs-theen/ *n.* a rock-forming mineral, magnesium iron silicate, of greenish color. [F *hyperstène* (as HYPER-, Gk *sthenos* strength, from its being harder than hornblende]

hypertension /hípərténshən/ *n.* **1** abnormally high blood pressure. **2** a state of great emotional tension. □□ **hypertensive** /-ténsiv/ *adj.*

hypertext /hípərtekst/ *n. Computing* computer software that links topics on the screen to related information, graphics, etc., usu. by a point-and-click method.

hyperthermia /hípərthórmeeə/ *n. Med.* the condition of having a body temperature greatly above normal. □□ **hyperthermic** *adj.* [HYPER- + Gk *thermē* heat]

hyperthyroidism /hípərthíroydizəm/ *n. Med.* overactivity of the thyroid gland, resulting in rapid heartbeat and an increased rate of metabolism. □□ **hyperthyroid** *n. & adj.* **hyperthyroidic** *adj.*

hypertonic /hípərtónik/ *adj.* **1** (of muscles) having high tension. **2** (of a solution) having a greater osmotic pressure than another solution. □□ **hypertonia** /-tŏneeə/ *n.* (in sense 1). **hypertonicity** /-tənisitee/ *n.*

hypertrophy /hīpártrəfee/ *n.* abnormal enlargement of an organ or part; excessive growth. □□ **hypertrophic** /-trŏfik, -trófik/ *adj.* **hypertrophied** *adj.* [mod.L *hypertrophia* (as HYPER-, Gk *-trophia* nourishment)]

hyperventilation /hípərvént'láyshən/ *n.* breathing at an abnormally rapid rate, resulting in an increased loss of carbon dioxide.

hypesthesia /hípis-theezhə, -zheeə, -zeeə/ *n.* a diminished capacity for sensation, esp. of the skin. □□ **hypesthetic** /-thétik/ *adj.* [mod.L (as HYPO-, Gk *-aisthēsia* f. *aisthanomai* perceive)]

hypethral /hipe'ethrəl/ *adj.* (also **hypaethral**) **1** open to the sky; roofless. **2** open-air. [L *hypaethrus* f. Gk *hupaithros* (as HYPO-, *aithēr* air)]

hypha /hífə/ *n.* (*pl.* **hyphae** /-fee/) a filament in the mycelium of a fungus. □□ **hyphal** *adj.* [mod.L f. Gk *huphē* web]

hyphen /hífən/ *n. & v.* ● *n.* the sign (-) used to join words semantically or syntactically (as in *pick-me-up, rock-forming*), to indicate the division of a word at the end of a line, or to indicate a missing or implied element (as in *man- and womankind*). ● *v.tr.* **1** write (a compound word) with a hyphen. **2** join (words) with a hyphen. [LL f. Gk *huphen* together f. *hupo* under + *hen* one]

hyphenate /hífənayt/ *v.tr.* = HYPHEN *v.* □□ **hyphenation** /-náyshən/ *n.*

hypno- /hípnō/ *comb. form* sleep; hypnosis. [Gk *hupnos* sleep]

/.../	**pronunciation**	● **part of speech**
□	**phrases, idioms, and compounds**	
□□	**derivatives**	■ **synonym section**
	cross-references appear in SMALL CAPITALS or *italics*	

hypnogenesis /hípnōjénisis/ *n.* the induction of a hypnotic state.

hypnology /hipnóləjee/ *n.* the science of the phenomena of sleep. □□ **hypnologist** *n.*

hypnopedia /hípnōpeédeeə/ *n.* learning by hearing while asleep.

hypnosis /hipnṓsis/ *n.* **1** a state like sleep in which the subject acts only on external suggestion. **2** artificially produced sleep. [mod.L f. Gk *hupnos* sleep + -OSIS]

hypnotherapy /hípnōthérəpee/ *n.* the treatment of disease by hypnosis.

hypnotic /hipnótik/ *adj. & n.* ● *adj.* **1** of or producing hypnosis. **2** (of a drug) soporific. ● *n.* **1** a thing, esp. a drug, that produces sleep. **2** a person under or open to the influence of hypnotism. □□ **hypnotically** *adv.* [F *hypnotique* f. LL *hypnoticus* f. Gk *hupnōtikos* f. *hupnoō* put to sleep]
■ *adj.* **1** see *enchanting* (ENCHANT). **2** see NARCOTIC *adj.*
● *n.* **1** see NARCOTIC *n.*

hypnotism /hípnətizəm/ *n.* the study or practice of hypnosis. □□ **hypnotist** *n.*

hypnotize /hípnətīz/ *v.tr.* **1** produce hypnosis in. **2** fascinate; capture the mind of (a person). □□ **hypnotizable** *adj.* **hypnotizer** *n.*
■ **2** fascinate, mesmerize, entrance, cast a spell over *or* on, captivate, enchant, charm, spellbind, bewitch.

hypo[1] /hípō/ *n. Photog.* the chemical sodium thiosulfate (incorrectly called hyposulfite) used as a photographic fixer. [abbr.]

hypo[2] /hípō/ *n.* (*pl.* **-os**) *colloq.* = HYPODERMIC *n.* [abbr.]

hypo- /hípō/ *prefix* (usu. **hyp-** before a vowel or *h*) **1** under (*hypodermic*). **2** below normal (*hypoxia*). **3** slightly (*hypomania*). **4** *Chem.* containing an element combined in low valence (*hypochlorous*). [Gk f. *hupo* under]

hypoallergenic /hípōàlərjénik/ *adj.* having little likelihood of causing an allergic reaction (*hypoallergenic foods*; *hypoallergenic cosmetics*).

hypoblast /hípəblast/ *n. Biol.* = ENDODERM. [mod.L *hypoblastus* (as HYPO-, -BLAST)]

hypocaust /hípəkawst/ *n.* a hollow space under the floor in ancient Roman houses, into which hot air was sent for heating a room or bath. [L *hypocaustum* f. Gk *hupokauston* place heated from below (as HYPO-, *kaiō, kau-* burn)]

hypochondria /hípəkóndreeə/ *n.* **1** abnormal anxiety about one's health. **2** morbid depression without real cause. [LL f. Gk *hupokhondria* soft parts of the body below the ribs, where melancholy was thought to arise (as HYPO-, *khondros* sternal cartilage)]
■ see VAPOR *n.* 4.

hypochondriac /hípəkóndreeak/ *n. & adj.* ● *n.* a person suffering from hypochondria. ● *adj.* (also **hypochondriacal** /-dríəkəl/) of or affected by hypochondria. [F *hypocondriaque* f. Gk *hupokhondriakos* (as HYPOCHONDRIA)]

hypocoristic /hípəkərístik/ *adj.* of the nature of a pet name. [Gk *hupokoristikos* f. *hupokorizomai* call by pet names]

hypocotyl /hípəkót'l/ *n. Bot.* the part of the stem of an embryo plant beneath the stalks of the seed leaves or cotyledons and directly above the root.

hypocrisy /hipókrisee/ *n.* (*pl.* **-ies**) **1** the assumption or postulation of moral standards to which one's own behavior does not conform; dissimulation, pretense. **2** an instance of this. [ME f. OF *ypocrisie* f. eccl.L *hypocrisis* f. Gk *hupokrisis* acting of a part, pretense (as HYPO-, *krinō* decide, judge)]
■ **1** deceit, deceitfulness, duplicity, double-dealing, deception, playacting, falseness, fakery, falsity, pharisaism, insincerity, sanctimony, sanctimoniousness, *colloq.* phoniness; dissumulation, pretense. **2** see DECEIT 2.

hypocrite /hípəkrit/ *n.* a person given to hypocrisy. □□ **hypocritical** /-krítikəl/ *adj.* **hypocritically** *adv.* [ME f. OF *ypocrite* f. eccl.L f. Gk *hupokritēs* actor (as HYPOCRISY)]
■ deceiver, double-dealer, faker, pretender, pharisee, whited sepulcher, *sl.* creeping Jesus. □□ **hypocritical** deceiving, dissembling, two-faced, dishonest; see also INSINCERE.

hypocycloid /hípəsíkloyd/ *n. Math.* the curve traced by a point on the circumference of a circle rolling on the interior of another circle. □□ **hypocycloidal** /-sīklóyd'l/ *adj.*

hypodermic /hípədérmik/ *adj. & n.* ● *adj. Med.* **1** of or relating to the area beneath the skin. **2 a** (of a drug, etc., or its application) injected beneath the skin. **b** (of a needle, syringe, etc.) used to do this. ● *n.* a hypodermic injection or syringe. □□ **hypodermically** *adv.* [HYPO- + Gk *derma* skin]

hypogastrium /hípəgástreeəm/ *n.* (*pl.* **hypogastria** /-treeə/) the part of the central abdomen which is situated below the region of the stomach. □□ **hypogastric** *adj.* [mod.L f. Gk *hupogastrion* (as HYPO-, *gastēr* belly)]

hypogean /hípəjeéən/ *adj.* (also **hypogeal** /-jeéəl/) **1** (existing or growing) underground. **2** (of seed germination) with the seed leaves remaining below the ground. [LL *hypogeus* f. Gk *hupogeios* (as HYPO-, *gē* earth)]

hypogene /hípəjeen/ *adj. Geol.* produced under the surface of the earth. [HYPO- + Gk *gen-* produce]

hypogeum /hípəjeéəm/ *n.* (*pl.* **hypogea** /-jeéə/) an underground chamber. [L f. Gk *hupogeion* neut. of *hupogeios*: see HYPOGEAN]

hypoglycemia /hípōgliseémeeə/ *n.* a deficiency of glucose in the bloodstream. □□ **hypoglycemic** *adj.* [HYPO- + GLYCO- + -EMIA]

hypoid /hípoyd/ *n.* a gear with the pinion offset from the centerline of the wheel, to connect nonintersecting shafts. [perh. f. HYPERBOLOID]

hypolimnion /hípəlímneeən/ *n.* (*pl.* **hypolimnia** /-neeə/) the lower layer of water in stratified lakes. [HYPO- + Gk *limnion* dimin. of *limnē* lake]

hypomania /hípəmáyneeə/ *n.* a minor form of mania. □□ **hypomanic** /-mánik/ *adj.* [mod.L f. G *Hypomanie* (as HYPO-, MANIA)]

hyponasty /hípənastee/ *n. Bot.* the tendency in plant organs for growth to be more rapid on the underside. □□ **hyponastic** /-nástik/ *adj.* [HYPO- + Gk *nastos* pressed]

hypophysis /hīpófisis/ *n.* (*pl.* **hypophyses** /-seez/) *Anat.* = *pituitary gland.* □□ **hypophyseal** /hípəfízeeəl/ *adj.* (also **-physial**). [mod.L f. Gk *hupophusis* offshoot (as HYPO-, *phusis* growth)]

hypostasis /hīpóstəsis/ *n.* (*pl.* **hypostases** /-seez/) **1** *Med.* an accumulation of fluid or blood in the lower parts of the body or organs under the influence of gravity, in cases of poor circulation. **2** *Metaphysics* an underlying substance, as opposed to attributes or to that which is unsubstantial. **3** *Theol.* **a** the person of Christ, combining human and divine natures. **b** each of the three persons of the Trinity. □□ **hypostasize** *v.tr.* (in senses 1, 2). [eccl.L f. Gk *hupostasis* (as HYPO-, STASIS standing, state)]

hypostatic /hípəstátik/ *adj.* (also **hypostatical**) *Theol.* relating to the three persons of the Trinity. □ **hypostatic union** the divine and human natures in Christ.

hypostyle /hípəstīl/ *adj. Archit.* having a roof supported by pillars. [Gk *hupostulos* (as HYPO-, STYLE)]

hypotaxis /hípətáksis/ *n. Gram.* the subordination of one clause to another. □□ **hypotactic** /-táktik/ *adj.* [Gk *hupotaxis* (as HYPO-, *taxis* arrangement)]

hypotension /hípəténshən/ *n.* abnormally low blood pressure. □□ **hypotensive** *adj.*

hypotenuse /hipót'nōōs, -nyōōs/ *n.* the side opposite the right angle of a right-angled triangle. [L *hypotenusa* f. Gk *hupoteinousa* (*grammē*) subtending (line) fem. part. of *hupoteinō* (as HYPO-, *teinō* stretch)]

hypothalamus /hípəthálləməs/ *n.* (*pl.* **-mi** /-mī/) *Anat.* the region of the brain that controls body temperature, thirst, hunger, etc. □□ **hypothalamic** /-thəlámik/ *adj.* [mod.L formed as HYPO-, THALAMUS]

hypothec /hipóthik/ *n.* (in Roman and Scottish law) a right established by law over property belonging to a debtor. □□ **hypothecary** /hipóthikeree/ *adj.* [F *hypothèque* f. LL *hypotheca* f. Gk *hupothēkē* deposit (as HYPO-, *tithēmi* place)]

hypothecate /hīpóthikayt/ *v.tr.* **1** pledge; mortgage. **2** hypothesize. □□ **hypothecation** /-káyshən/ *n.* **hypothecator** *n.* [med.L *hypothecare* (as HYPOTHEC)]
■ see PAWN[2] *v.*

hypothermia /hípōthə́rmeeə/ *n. Med.* the condition of having an abnormally low body temperature. [HYPO- + Gk *thermē* heat]

hypothesis /hipóthisis/ *n.* (*pl.* **hypotheses** /-seez/) **1** a proposition made as a basis for reasoning, without the assumption of its truth. **2** a supposition made as a starting point for further investigation from known facts (cf. THEORY). **3** a groundless assumption. [LL f. Gk *hupothesis* foundation (as HYPO-, THESIS)]

■ **1** postulate, premise, proposition. **2** assumption, theory; see also SUPPOSITION 1, 2. **3** see PRESUMPTION 2.

hypothesize /hipóthisiz/ *v.* **1** *intr.* frame a hypothesis. **2** *tr.* assume as a hypothesis. □□ **hypothesist** /-sist/ *n.* **hypothesizer** *n.*

■ see SPECULATE 1, 2.

hypothetical /hípəthétikəl/ *adj.* **1** of or based on or serving as a hypothesis. **2** supposed but not necessarily real or true. □□ **hypothetically** *adv.*

■ assumed, supposed, presumed, hypothesized, suppositional, suppositious; conjectural, conjectured, surmised, imagined, imaginary, speculative, theoretical.

hypothyroidism /hípōthíroydizəm/ *n. Med.* subnormal activity of the thyroid gland, resulting in cretinism in children, and mental and physical slowing in adults. □□ **hypothyroid** *n. & adj.* **hypothyroidic** /-róydik/ *adj.*

hypoventilation /hípōvént'láyshən/ *n.* breathing at an abnormally slow rate, resulting in an increased amount of carbon dioxide in the blood.

hypoxemia /hípokseémeeə/ *n. Med.* an abnormally low concentration of oxygen in the blood. [mod.L (as HYPO-, OXYGEN, -AEMIA)]

hypoxia /hipókseeə/ *n. Med.* a deficiency of oxygen reaching the tissues. □□ **hypoxic** *adj.* [HYPO- + OX- + -IA¹]

hypso- /hípsō/ *comb. form* height. [Gk *hupsos* height]

hypsography /hipsógrəfee/ *n.* a description or mapping of the contours of the earth's surface. □□ **hypsographic** /-səgráfik/ *adj.* **hypsographical** *adj.*

hypsometer /hipsómitər/ *n.* **1** a device for calibrating thermometers at the boiling point of water. **2** this instrument when used to estimate height above sea level using barometric pressure. □□ **hypsometric** /-səmétrik/ *adj.*

hyrax /híraks/ *n.* any small mammal of the order *Hyracoidea*, including the rock rabbit and dassie. [mod.L f. Gk *hurax* shrew mouse]

hyson /hísən/ *n.* a kind of green China tea. [Chin. *xichun*, lit. 'bright spring']

hyssop /hísəp/ *n.* **1** any small bushy aromatic herb of the genus *Hyssopus*, esp. *H. officinalis*, formerly used medicinally. **2** *Bibl.* **a** a plant whose twigs were used for sprinkling in Jewish rites. **b** a bunch of this used in purification. [OE (h)*ysope* (reinforced in ME by OF *ysope*) f. L *hyssopus* f. Gk *hyssōpos*, of Semitic orig.]

hysterectomy /hístəréktəmee/ *n.* (*pl.* **-ies**) the surgical removal of the uterus. □□ **hysterectomize** *v.tr.* [Gk *hustera* uterus + -ECTOMY]

hysteresis /hístəreésis/ *n. Physics* the lagging behind of an effect when its cause varies in amount, etc., esp. of magnetic induction behind the magnetizing force. [Gk *husterēsis* f. *hustereō* be behind f. *husteros* coming after]

hysteria /histéreeə, -steér-/ *n.* **1** a wild uncontrollable emotion or excitement. **2** a functional disturbance of the nervous system, of psychoneurotic origin. [mod.L (as HYSTERIC)]

■ **2** see MANIA 1.

hysteric /histérik/ *n. & adj.* ● *n.* **1** (in *pl.*) **a** a fit of hysteria. **b** *colloq.* overwhelming mirth or laughter (*we were in hysterics*). **2** a hysterical person. ● *adj.* = HYSTERICAL. [L f. Gk *husterikos* of the uterus (*hustera*), hysteria being thought to occur more frequently in women than in men and to be associated with the uterus]

hysterical /histérikəl/ *adj.* **1** of or affected with hysteria. **2** morbidly or uncontrolledly emotional. **3** *colloq.* extremely funny or amusing. □□ **hysterically** *adv.*

■ **1** see MAD *adj.* 1. **2** irrational, distracted, rabid, frantic, frenzied, wild, berserk, uncontrolled, uncontrollable, unrestrained, unrestrainable; beside oneself. **3** hilarious, sidesplitting, uproarious, farcical, comic(al), funny.

hysteron proteron /hístəron prótəron/ *n. Rhet.* a figure of speech in which what should come last is put first; an inversion of the natural order (e.g., *I die! I faint! I fail!*). [LL f. Gk *husteron proteron* the latter (put in place of) the former]

Hz *abbr.* hertz.

/.../ **pronunciation**   ● **part of speech**
□ **phrases, idioms, and compounds**
□□ **derivatives**   ■ **synonym section**
cross-references appear in SMALL CAPITALS or *italics*

I¹ /ī/ *n.* (also **i**) (*pl.* **Is** or **I's**) **1** the ninth letter of the alphabet. **2** (as a Roman numeral) 1. □ **I beam** a girder of I-shaped section.

I² /ī/ *pron. & n.* ● *pron.* (*obj.* **me**; *poss.* **my, mine**; *pl.* **we**) used by a speaker or writer to refer to himself or herself. ● *n.* (**the I**) *Metaphysics* the ego; the subject or object of self-consciousness. [OE f. Gmc]

I³ *symb. Chem.* the element iodine.

I⁴ *abbr.* (also **I.**) **1** Island(s). **2** Isle(s).

-i¹ /ee, ī/ *suffix* forming the plural of nouns from Latin in *-us* or from Italian in *-e* or *-o* (*foci; dilettanti; timpani*). ¶ Plural in *-s* or *-es* is often also possible.

-i² /ee/ *suffix* forming adjectives from names of countries or regions in the Near or Middle East (*Israeli; Pakistani*). [adj. suffix in Semitic and Indo-Iranian languages]

-i- a connecting vowel, esp. forming words in *-ana, -ferous, -fic, -form, -fy, -gerous, -vorous* (cf. -O-). [from or after F f. L]

IA *abbr.* Iowa (in official postal use).

Ia. *abbr.* Iowa.

-ia¹ /eeə, yə/ *suffix* **1** forming abstract nouns (*mania; utopia*), often in *Med.* (*anemia; pneumonia*). **2** *Bot.* forming names of classes and genera (*dahlia; fuchsia*). **3** forming names of countries (*Australia; India*). [from or after L & Gk]

-ia² /eeə, yə/ *suffix* forming plural nouns or the plural of nouns: **1** from Greek in *-ion* or Latin in *-ium* (*paraphernalia; regalia; amnia; labia*). **2** *Zool.* the names of groups (*Mammalia*).

IAA *abbr.* indoleacetic acid.

IAEA *abbr.* International Atomic Energy Agency.

-ial /eeəl, (ch)əl/ *suffix* forming adjectives (*celestial; dictatorial; trivial*). [from or after F *-iel* or L *-ialis*: cf. -AL]

iamb /íamb/ *n.* *Prosody* a foot consisting of one short (or unstressed) followed by one long (or stressed) syllable. [L f. Gk *iambos* iambus, lampoon, f. *iaptō* assail in words, from its use by Gk satirists]

iambic /iámbik/ *adj. & n.* *Prosody* ● *adj.* of or using iambuses. ● *n.* (usu. in *pl.*) iambic verse. [F *iambique* f. LL *iambicus* f. Gk *iambikos* (as IAMBUS)]

iambus /iámbəs/ *n.* (*pl.* **iambuses** or **-bi** /-bī/) an iamb.

-ian /eeən/ *suffix* var. of -AN. [from or after F *-ien* or L *-ianus*]

-iasis /íəsis/ *suffix* the usual form of -ASIS.

IATA /ī-aátə/ *abbr.* International Air Transport Association.

iatrogenic /íátrəjénik/ *adj.* (of a disease, etc.) caused by medical examination or treatment. [Gk *iatros* physician + -GENIC]

ib. var. of IBID.

Iberian /ībéereeən/ *adj. & n.* ● *adj.* of ancient Iberia, the peninsula now comprising Spain and Portugal; of Spain and Portugal. ● *n.* **1** a native of ancient Iberia. **2** any of the languages of ancient Iberia. [L *Iberia* f. Gk *Ibēres* Spaniards]

Ibero- /ibáirō/ *comb. form* Iberian; Iberian and (*Ibero-American*).

ibex /íbeks/ *n.* (*pl.* same or **ibexes**) a wild goat, *Capra ibex*, esp. of mountainous areas of Europe, N. Africa, and Asia, with a chin beard and thick curved ridged horns. [L]

ibid. /íbid/ *abbr.* (also **ib.**) in the same book or passage, etc. [L *ibidem* in the same place]

-ibility /ibílitee/ *suffix* forming nouns from, or corresponding to, adjectives in *-ible* (*possibility; credibility*). [F *-ibilité* or L *-ibilitas*]

ibis /íbis/ *n.* (*pl.* same or **ibises**) any wading bird of the family Threskiornithidae with a curved bill, long neck, and long legs, and nesting in colonies. □ **sacred ibis** an ibis, *Threskiornis aethiopica*, native to Africa and Madagascar, venerated by the ancient Egyptians. [ME f. L f. Gk]

-ible /ibəl/ *suffix* forming adjectives meaning 'that may or may be' (see -ABLE) (*terrible; forcible; possible*). [F *-ible* or L *-ibilis*]

-ibly /iblee/ *suffix* forming adverbs corresponding to adjectives in *-ible*.

IBM *abbr.* International Business Machines.

Ibo /eébō/ *n.* (also **Igbo**) (*pl.* same or **-os**) **1** a member of a black people of SE Nigeria. **2** the language of this people. [native name]

IBRD *abbr.* International Bank for Reconstruction and Development (also known as the *World Bank*).

ibuprofen /ibyŏoprōfən/ *n.* an anti-inflammatory medication used to relieve pain and reduce fever.

IC *abbr.* **1** integrated circuit. **2** intensive care.

i/c *abbr.* **1** in charge. **2** in command. **3** internal combustion.

-ic /ik/ *suffix* **1** forming adjectives (*Arabic; classic; public*) and nouns (*critic; epic; mechanic; music*). **2** *Chem.* in higher valence or degree of oxidation (*ferric; sulfuric*) (see also -OUS). **3** denoting a particular form or instance of a noun in *-ics* (*aesthetic; tactic*). [from or after F *-ique* or L *-icus* or Gk *-ikos*: cf. -ATIC, -ETIC, -FIC, -OTIC]

-ical /ikəl/ *suffix* **1** forming adjectives corresponding to nouns or adjectives, usu. in *-ic* (*classical; comical; farcical; musical*). **2** forming adjectives corresponding to nouns in *-y* (*pathological*).

-ically /iklee/ *suffix* forming adverbs corresponding to adjectives in *-ic* or *-ical* (*comically; musically; tragically*).

ICAO *abbr.* International Civil Aviation Organization.

ICBM *abbr.* intercontinental ballistic missile.

ICC *abbr.* **1** Interstate Commerce Commission. **2** International Claims Commission. **3** Indian Claims Commission.

ice /īs/ *n. & v.* ● *n.* **1 a** frozen water, a brittle transparent crystalline solid. **b** a sheet of this on the surface of water (*fell through the ice*). **2** *Brit.* a portion of ice cream, sherbet, etc. (*would you like an ice?*). **3** *sl.* diamonds. **4** *Austral.* an unemotional or cold-blooded person. ● *v.* **1** *tr.* mix with or cool in ice (*iced drinks*). **2** *tr. & intr.* (often foll. by *over, up*) **a** cover or become covered with ice. **b** freeze. **3** *tr.* cover (a cake, etc.) with icing. **4** *sl.* kill. □ **ice age** a glacial period, esp. (**the Ice Age**) in the Pleistocene epoch. **ice ax** a tool used by mountain climbers for cutting footholds. **ice bag** an ice-filled rubber bag for medical use. **ice blue** a very pale blue. **ice bucket** a bucketlike container with chunks of ice, used to keep a bottle of wine chilled. **ice cap** a permanent covering of ice, e.g., in polar regions. **ice-cold** as cold as ice. **ice cream** a sweet creamy frozen food, usu. flavored. **ice cube** a small block of ice made in a refrigerator. **ice field** an expanse of ice, esp. in polar regions. **ice floe** = FLOE. **ice hockey** a form of hockey played on ice with a puck. **ice (or iced) lolly** *Brit.* = POPSICLE. **ice pack 1** = *pack ice.* **2** a quantity of ice applied to the body for medical, etc., purposes. **ice pick** a needlelike implement with a handle for splitting up small pieces of ice. **ice plant** a plant, *Mesembryanthemum crystallinum*, with leaves covered with crystals or vesicles looking like ice specks. **ice rink** = RINK 1. **ice skate** a skate consisting of a boot with a blade be-

neath, for skating on ice. **ice-skate** *v.intr.* skate on ice. **ice-skater** a person who skates on ice. **ice station** a meteorological research center in polar regions. **on ice 1** (of an entertainment, sport, etc.) performed by skaters. **2** *colloq.* held in reserve; awaiting further attention. **on thin ice** in a risky situation. [OE *īs* f. Gmc]
■ *v.* **1** cool, chill, refrigerate. **2** see FREEZE *v.* 1. □ **ice-cold** see COLD *adj.* 1, 4. **on ice 2** see ABEYANCE.

-ice /is/ *suffix* forming (esp. abstract) nouns (*avarice*; *justice*; *service*) (cf. -ISE²).

iceberg /ísbərg/ *n.* **1** a large floating mass of ice detached from a glacier or ice sheet and carried out to sea. **2** an unemotional or cold-blooded person. □ **iceberg lettuce** any of various crisp lettuces with a freely blanching head. **the tip of the iceberg** a small perceptible part of something (esp. a difficulty) the greater part of which is hidden. [prob. f. Du. *ijsberg* f. *ijs* ice + *berg* hill]

iceblink /ísblingk/ *n.* a luminous appearance on the horizon, caused by a reflection from ice.

iceblock /ísblok/ *n.* *Austral.* & *NZ* = POPSICLE.

iceboat /ísbōt/ *n.* **1** a boat mounted on runners for traveling on ice. **2** a boat used for breaking ice on a river, etc.

icebound /ísbownd/ *adj.* confined by ice.

icebox /ísboks/ *n.* **1** a compartment in a refrigerator for making and storing ice. **2** a refrigerator.

icebreaker /ísbraykər/ *n.* **1** = ICEBOAT. **2** something that serves to relieve inhibitions, start a conversation, etc.

icefall /ísfawl/ *n.* a steep part of a glacier like a frozen waterfall.

icehouse /ís-hows/ *n.* a building often partly or wholly underground for storing ice.

Icelander /íslǝndǝr/ *n.* **1** a native or national of Iceland, an island in the N. Atlantic. **2** a person of Icelandic descent.

Icelandic /īslándik/ *adj.* & *n.* ● *adj.* of or relating to Iceland. ● *n.* the language of Iceland.

Iceland moss /íslǝnd/ *n.* (also **Iceland lichen**) a mountain and moorland lichen, *Cetraria islandica*, with edible branching fronds.

Iceland poppy /íslǝnd/ *n.* an arctic poppy, *Papaver nudicaule*, with red or yellow flowers.

Iceland spar /íslǝnd/ *n.* a transparent variety of calcite with the optical property of strong double refraction.

iceman /ísmǝn/ *n.* (*pl.* **-men**) **1** a person skilled in crossing ice. **2** a person who sells or delivers ice.

I Ching /ee chíng/ *n.* an ancient Chinese manual of divination based on symbolic trigrams and hexagrams. [Chin. *yijing* book of changes]

ichneumon /iknóōmǝn, -nyōō-/ *n.* **1** (in full **ichneumon fly**) any small hymenopterous insect of the family Ichneumonidae, depositing eggs in or on the larva of another insect as food for its own larva. **2** a mongoose of N. Africa, *Herpestes ichneumon*, noted for destroying crocodile eggs. [L f. Gk *ikhneūmōn* spider-hunting wasp f. *ikhneuō* trace f. *ikhnos* footstep]

ichnography /iknógrǝfee/ *n.* (*pl.* **-ies**) **1** the ground-plan of a building, map of a region, etc. **2** a drawing of this. [F *ichnographie* or L *ichnographia* f. Gk *ikhnographia* f. *ikhnos* track: see -GRAPHY]

ichor /íkawr, íkǝr/ *n.* **1** (in Greek mythology) fluid flowing like blood in the veins of the gods. **2** *poet.* bloodlike fluid. **3** *hist.* a watery fetid discharge from a wound, etc. □□ **ichorous** /íkǝrǝs/ *adj.* [Gk *ikhōr*]
■ **1, 2** see FLUID *n.* 1. **3** see DISCHARGE *n.* 5.

ichthyo- /íktheeō/ *comb. form* fish. [Gk *ikhthus* fish]

ichthyoid /íkthee-oyd/ *adj.* & *n.* ● *adj.* fishlike. ● *n.* any fishlike vertebrate.

ichthyolite /íkthee-ǝlít/ *n.* a fossil fish.

ichthyology /íktheeólǝjee/ *n.* the study of fishes. □□ **ichthyological** /-theeǝlójikǝl/ *adj.* **ichthyologist** *n.*

ichthyophagous /íktheeófǝgǝs/ *adj.* fish-eating. □□ **ichthyophagy** /-ófǝjee/ *n.*

ichthyosaur /íktheeǝsáwr/ *n.* (also **ichthyosaurus** /íktheeǝsáwrǝs/) any extinct marine reptile of the order Ichthyosauria, with long head, tapering body, four flippers, and usu. a large tail. [ICHTHYO- + Gk *sauros* lizard]

ichthyosis /íktheeósis/ *n.* a skin disease that causes the epidermis to become dry and horny like fish scales. □□ **ichthyotic** /-theeótik/ *adj.* [Gk *ikhthus* fish + -OSIS]

-ician /íshǝn/ *suffix* forming nouns denoting persons skilled in or concerned with subjects having nouns (usu.) in *-ic* or *-ics* (*magician*; *politician*). [from or after F *-icien* (as -IC, -IAN)]

icicle /ísikǝl/ *n.* a hanging tapering piece of ice, formed by the freezing of dripping water. [ME f. ICE + *ickle* (now dial.) icicle]

icing /ísing/ *n.* **1** a coating of sugar, etc., on a cake or cookie. **2** the formation of ice on a ship or aircraft. □ **icing on the cake** an attractive though inessential addition or enhancement. **icing sugar** *Brit.* = *confectioners' sugar* (*see* CONFECTIONER).
■ **1** glaze, coating, frosting. □ **icing on the cake** bonus, (fringe) benefit, added attraction, extra, reward, perquisite, *colloq.* perk.

-icist /isist/ *suffix* = -ICIAN (*classicist*). [-IC + -IST]

-icity /ísitee/ *suffix* forming abstract nouns, esp. from adjectives in *-ic* (*authenticity*; *publicity*). [-IC + -ITY]

-ick /ik/ *suffix* archaic var. of -IC.

icky /íkee/ *adj.* *colloq.* **1** sickly. **2** (as a general term of disapproval) nasty; repulsive. [20th c.: orig. unkn.]
■ **1** see SWEET *adj.* 1. **2** see REVOLTING.

-icle /ikǝl/ *suffix* forming (orig. diminutive) nouns (*article*; *particle*). [formed as -CULE]

icon /íkon/ *n.* (also **ikon**) **1** a devotional painting or carving, usu. on wood, of Christ or another holy figure, esp. in the Eastern Church. **2** an image or statue. **3** *Computing* a symbol or graphic representation that appears on the monitor in a program, option, or window, esp. one of several for selection. **4** *Linguistics* a sign which has a characteristic in common with the thing it signifies. [L f. Gk *eikōn* image]
■ **2** see IMAGE *n.* 1.

iconic /ikónik/ *adj.* **1** of or having the nature of an image or portrait. **2** (of a statue) following a conventional type. **3** *Linguistics* that is an icon. □□ **iconicity** /íkǝnísitee/ *n.* (esp. in sense 3). [L *iconicus* f. Gk *eikonikos* (as ICON)]

icono- /íkonō/ *comb. form* an image or likeness. [Gk *eikōn*]

iconoclasm /īkónǝklazǝm/ *n.* **1** the breaking of images. **2** the assailing of cherished beliefs. [ICONOCLAST after *enthusiasm*, etc.]

iconoclast /ikónǝklast/ *n.* **1** a person who attacks cherished beliefs. **2** a person who destroys images used in religious worship, esp. *hist.* during the 8th–9th c. in the churches of the East, or as a Puritan of the 16th–17th c. □□ **iconoclastic** /-klástik/ *adj.* **iconoclastically** *adv.* [med.L *iconoclastes* f. eccl.Gk *eikonoklastēs* (as ICONO-, *klaō* break)]
■ **1** see NONCONFORMIST.

iconography /íkǝnógrǝfee/ *n.* (*pl.* **-ies**) **1** the illustration of a subject by drawings or figures. **2 a** the study of portraits, esp. of an individual. **b** the study of artistic images or symbols. **3** a treatise on pictures or statuary. **4** a book whose essence is pictures. □□ **iconographer** *n.* **iconographic** /-nǝgráfik/ *adj.* **iconographical** *adj.* **iconographically** *adv.* [Gk *eikonographia* sketch (as ICONO- + -GRAPHY)]

iconolatry /íkǝnólǝtree/ *n.* the worship of images. □□ **iconolater** *n.* [eccl.Gk *eikonolatreia* (as ICONO-, -LATRY)]

iconology /íkǝnólǝjee/ *n.* **1** an artistic theory developed from iconography (see ICONOGRAPHY 2b). **2** symbolism.

iconostasis /íkǝnóstǝsis/ *n.* (*pl.* **iconostases** /-séez/) (in the Eastern Church) a screen bearing icons and separating the sanctuary from the nave. [mod.Gk *eikonostasis* (as ICONO-, STASIS)]

icosahedron /īkósǝheédrǝn, -íkós-/ *n.* a solid figure with twenty faces. □□ **icosahedral** *adj.* [LL *icosahedrum* f. Gk *eikosaedron* f. *eikosi* twenty + -HEDRON]

-ics /iks/ *suffix* (treated as *sing.* or *pl.*) forming nouns denoting arts or sciences or branches of study or action (*athletics*; *pol-*

/ . . . / pronunciation   ● part of speech
□ phrases, idioms, and compounds
□□ derivatives   ■ synonym section
cross-references appear in SMALL CAPITALS or *italics*

itics) (cf. -IC 3). [from or after F pl. *-iques* or L pl. *-ica* or Gk pl. *-ika*]

icterus /íktərəs/ *n. Med.* = JAUNDICE. □□ **icteric** /iktérik/ *adj.* [L f. Gk *ikteros*]

ictus /íktəs/ *n.* (*pl.* **ictuses** or same) **1** *Prosody* rhythmical or metrical stress. **2** *Med.* a stroke or seizure; a fit. [L, = blow f. *icere* strike]

■ **1** see STRESS *n.* 3b, c. **2** see SEIZURE 2.

ICU *abbr.* intensive care unit.

icy /ísee/ *adj.* (**icier**, **iciest**) **1** very cold. **2** covered with or abounding in ice. **3** (of a tone or manner) unfriendly; hostile (*an icy stare*). □□ **icily** *adv.* **iciness** *n.*

■ **1** ice-cold, frigid, glacial, freezing, frozen, gelid, hyperborean, wintry, bitter, raw, cold, chilling, chilly, *colloq.* perishing, arctic, nippy, polar, Siberian, *literary* chill. **2** frozen (over), glacial, icebound; glazed, glassy, slippery. **3** cold, cool, chilly, frigid, distant, aloof, remote, formal, reserved, unemotional, callous, forbidding, unfriendly, hostile, stony, flinty, steely, *literary* chill. □□ **icily** coldly, frostily, forbiddingly, stonily, unemotionally. **iciness** coldness, frost, slipperiness; frigidity, stiffness, formality, aloofness, hostility.

ID *abbr.* **1** identification, identity (*ID card*). **2** Idaho (in official postal use).

■ **1** see IDENTIFICATION 2, 3.

I'd /id/ *contr.* **1** I had. **2** I should; I would.

id /id/ *n. Psychol.* the inherited instinctive impulses of the individual as part of the unconscious. [L, = that, transl. G *es*]

id. *abbr.* = IDEM.

i.d. *abbr.* inner diameter.

-id[1] /id/ *suffix* forming adjectives (*arid*; *rapid*). [F *-ide* f. L *-idus*]

-id[2] /id/ *suffix* forming nouns: **1** general (*pyramid*). **2** *Biol.* of structural constituents (*plastid*). **3** *Bot.* of a plant belonging to a family with a name in *-aceae* (*orchid*). [from or after F *-ide* f. L *-is -idis* f. Gk *-is -ida* or *-idos*]

-id[3] /id/ *suffix* forming nouns denoting: **1** *Zool.* an animal belonging to a family with a name in *-idae* or a class with a name in *-ida* (*canid*; *arachnid*). **2** a member of a person's family (*Seleucid* from Seleucus). **3** *Astron.* **a** a meteor in a group radiating from a specified constellation (*Leonid* from Leo). **b** a star of a class like one in a specified constellation (*cepheid*). [from or after L *-ides*, pl. *-idae* or *-ida*]

-id[4] /id/ *suffix* var. of -IDE.

IDA *abbr.* International Development Association.

-ide /id/ *suffix* (also **-id**) *Chem.* forming nouns denoting: **1** binary compounds of an element (the suffix *-ide* being added to the abbreviated name of the more electronegative element, etc.) (*sodium chloride*; *lead sulfide*; *calcium carbide*). **2** various other compounds (*amide*; *anhydride*; *peptide*; *saccharide*). **3** elements of a series in the periodic table (*actinide*; *lanthanide*). [orig. in OXIDE]

idea /ideéə/ *n.* **1** a conception or plan formed by mental effort (*have you any ideas?*; *had the idea of writing a book*). **2 a** a mental impression or notion; a concept. **b** a vague belief or fancy (*had an idea you were married*; *had no idea where you were*). **c** an opinion; an outlook or point of view (*had some funny ideas about marriage*). **3** an intention, purpose, or essential feature (*the idea is to make money*). **4** an archetype or pattern as distinguished from its realization in individual cases. **5** *Philos.* **a** (in Platonism) an eternally existing pattern of which individual things in any class are imperfect copies. **b** a concept of pure reason which transcends experience. □ **get** (or **have**) **ideas** *colloq.* be ambitious, rebellious, etc. **have no idea** *colloq.* **1** not know at all. **2** be completely incompetent. **not one's idea of** *colloq.* not what one regards as (*not my idea of a pleasant evening*). **put ideas into a person's head** suggest ambitions, etc., he or she would not otherwise have had. **that's an idea** *colloq.* that proposal, etc., is worth considering. **the very idea!** *colloq.* an exclamation of disapproval or disagreement. □□ **ideaed** *adj.* **idealess** *adj.* [Gk *idea* form, pattern f. stem *id-* see]

■ **1** concept, conception, construct, thought, notion, plan, design, scheme, suggestion, recommendation.

2 a, b notion, impression, picture, (mental) image, concept, conception, fantasy, dream; belief, fancy, perception, understanding, awareness, apprehension, inkling, suspicion, hint, hunch, suggestion, clue, intimation, guess, estimate, estimation. **c** belief, opinion, hypothesis, theory, sentiment, feeling, teaching(s), doctrine, tenet, principle, philosophy, (point of) view, viewpoint, outlook, notion, conviction, position, stance. **3** intention, aim, goal, purpose, objective, object, end, point, essence, reason, raison d'être, motive. **4** see IDEAL *n.* 2a.

ideal /ideéəl/ *adj.* & *n.* ● *adj.* **1 a** answering to one's highest conception. **b** perfect or supremely excellent. **2 a** existing only in idea. **b** visionary. **3** embodying an idea. **4** relating to or consisting of ideas; dependent on the mind. ● *n.* **1 a** a perfect type, or a conception of this. **2 a** an actual thing as a standard for imitation. **b** (often in *pl.*) a moral principle or standard of behavior. □ **ideal gas** a hypothetical gas consisting of molecules occupying negligible space and without attraction for each other, thereby obeying simple laws. □□ **ideally** *adv.* [ME f. F *idéal* f. LL *idealis* (as IDEA)]

■ *adj.* **1** perfect, faultless, excellent, supreme, best, choice, consummate, complete, exemplary, model, idyllic; see also PERFECT *adj.* 2a. **2** conceptual, imagined, imaginary, unreal, abstract, notional, theoretical, illusory, fictitious, fanciful, fancied, utopian, idealistic, romantic, mythical, mythic, chimeric(al), visionary, fantastic. ● *n.* **1** acme, epitome, paragon, nonpareil, (standard of) perfection, optimum, quintessence, ideality. **2 a** model, standard, criterion, paradigm, exemplar, example, pattern, idea. **b** cause; (*ideals*) principles, morals, morality, (code of) ethics, standards; see also IDEOLOGY. □□ **ideally** under or in the best of circumstances, at best, in a perfect world, all things being equal or considered, if all goes well; theoretically, in theory, in principle; perfectly.

idealism /ideéəlizəm/ *n.* **1** the practice of forming or following after ideals, esp. unrealistically (cf. REALISM). **2** the representation of things in ideal or idealized form. **3** imaginative treatment. **4** *Philos.* any of various systems of thought in which the objects of knowledge are held to be in some way dependent on the activity of mind (cf. REALISM). □□ **idealist** *n.* **idealistic** *adj.* **idealistically** *adv.* [F *idéalisme* or G *Idealismus* (as IDEAL)]

■ **1** utopianism, quixotism, quixotry, romanticism, dreaming. □□ **idealist** idealizer, romantic, optimist, dreamer; see also VISIONARY *n.* **idealistic** romantic, utopian, optimistic, quixotic, impractical, unrealistic, romanticized, visionary, *colloq.* starry-eyed. **idealistically** unrealistically, impractically; romantically, optimistically, quixotically.

ideality /ideéálitee/ *n.* (*pl.* **-ies**) **1** the quality of being ideal. **2** an ideal thing.

idealize /ideéəliz/ *v.tr.* **1** regard or represent (a thing or person) in ideal form or character. **2** exalt in thought to ideal perfection or excellence. □□ **idealization** *n.* **idealizer** *n.*

■ exalt, elevate, glorify, worship, ennoble, deify, apotheosize, put on a pedestal, romanticize. □□ **idealization** see PERFECTION 3. **idealizer** see VISIONARY *n.*

ideate /ídeeayt/ *v. Psychol.* **1** *tr.* imagine; conceive. **2** *intr.* form ideas. □□ **ideation** /-áyshən/ *n.* **ideational** /-áyshənəl/ *adj.* **ideationally** /-áyshənəlee/ *adv.* [med.L *ideare* form an idea (as IDEA)]

idée fixe /eeday feéks/ *n.* (*pl.* **idées fixes** *pronunc.* same) an idea that dominates the mind; an obsession. [F, lit. 'fixed idea']

■ see OBSESSION.

idée reçue /eeday rəsőő/ *n.* (*pl.* **idées reçues** *pronunc.* same) a generally accepted notion or opinion. [F]

■ see OPINION 1.

idem /ídem/ *adv.* & *n.* ● *adv.* in the same author. ● *n.* the same word or author. [ME f. L]

identical /idéntikəl/ *adj.* **1** (often foll. by *with*) (of different things) agreeing in every detail. **2** (of one thing viewed at different times) one and the same. **3** (of twins) developed from a single fertilized ovum, therefore of the same sex and usu. very similar in appearance. **4** *Logic* & *Math.* expressing an identity. ▫▫ **identically** *adv.* **identicalness** *n.* [med.L *identicus* (as IDENTITY)]

■ **1** twin, duplicate, matching, corresponding, indistinguishable, interchangeable, equal, equivalent; the same, similar, like, alike, comparable, homogeneous, uniform; (*identical with*) the same as, interchangeable *or* of a piece *or* uniform with, equal *or* equivalent to. **2** (very) same, selfsame, one and the same. ▫▫ **identically** see ALIKE *adv.*

identification /idéntifikáyshən/ *n.* **1 a** the act or an instance of identifying; recognition; pinpointing. **b** association of oneself with the feelings, situation, characteristics, etc., of another person or group of people. **2** a means of identifying a person. **3** (*attrib.*) serving to identify (esp. the bearer) (*identification card*). ▫ **identification parade** *Brit.* a police lineup.

■ **1 a** classification, classifying, cataloging, categorization, categorizing, pigeonholing, recognition, distinguishing, indication, perception, detection, selection, naming, labeling, pinpointing, designation, characterization, denomination; authentication, verification, establishment, certification, substantiation, corroboration. **b** empathy, sympathy, involvement, rapport, relationship, connection, association, affiliation. **2** identity card, passport, driver's license, badge, credentials, papers, ID, ID card. **3** (*attrib.*) identity, ID.

identifier /idéntifīər/ *n.* **1** a person or thing that identifies. **2** *Computing* a sequence of characters used to identify or refer to a set of data.

■ **1** see LABEL *n.* 1.

identify /idéntifī/ *v.* (**-ies, -ied**) **1** *tr.* establish the identity of; recognize. **2** *tr.* establish or select by consideration or analysis of the circumstances (*identify the best method of solving the problem*). **3** *tr.* (foll. by *with*) associate (a person or oneself) inseparably or very closely (with a party, policy, etc.). **4** *tr.* (often foll. by *with*) treat (a thing) as identical. **5** *intr.* (foll. by *with*) **a** regard oneself as sharing characteristics of (another person). **b** associate oneself. ▫▫ **identifiable** /-fíəbəl/ *adj.* [med.L *identificare* (as IDENTITY)]

■ **1, 2** recognize, classify, categorize, catalog, pigeonhole, sort (out), specify, establish, pinpoint, home *or* zero in on, name, label, tag, place, mark, single out, point out, find, locate, isolate, work out, discover, decide on, select, choose, diagnose, *colloq.* put one's finger on. **3** associate, connect, link, equate. **4** equate, parallel, couple, connect, associate, relate. **5** (*identify with*) empathize with, sympathize with, relate to, appreciate, understand, *sl.* dig. ▫▫ **identifiable** see *discernible* (DISCERN).

Identi-Kit /idéntikit/ *n.* (often *attrib.*) *propr.* a reconstructed picture of a person (esp. one sought by the police) assembled from transparent strips showing typical facial features according to witnesses' descriptions. [IDENTITY + KIT[1]]

identity /idéntitee/ *n.* (*pl.* **-ies**) **1 a** the quality or condition of being a specified person or thing. **b** individuality; personality (*felt he had lost his identity*). **2** identification or the result of it (*a case of mistaken identity*; *identity card*). **3** the state of being the same in substance, nature, qualities, etc.; absolute sameness (*no identity of interests between them*). **4** *Algebra* **a** the equality of two expressions for all values of the quantities expressed by letters. **b** an equation expressing this, e.g., $(x + 1)^2 = x^2 + 2x + 1$. **5** *Math.* **a** (in full **identity element**) an element in a set, left unchanged by any operation to it. **b** a transformation that leaves an object unchanged. ▫ **identity crisis** a temporary period during which an individual experiences a feeling of loss or breakdown of identity. [LL *identitas* f. L *idem* same]

■ **1** personality, individuality, distinctiveness, uniqueness, particularity, singularity, selfhood. **2** see IDENTIFICATION 1a. **3** sameness, oneness, unity, equality;

indistinguishability, correspondence, interchangeability, agreement, accord, congruence.

ideogram /ídeeəgram/ *n.* a character symbolizing the idea of a thing without indicating the sequence of sounds in its name (e.g., a numeral, and many Chinese characters). [Gk *idea* form + -GRAM]

■ see SIGN *n.* 2.

ideograph /ídeeəgraf/ *n.* = IDEOGRAM. ▫▫ **ideographic** *adj.* **ideography** /ideeógrəfee/ *n.* [Gk *idea* form + -GRAPH]

ideologue /ídeeəlawg, -log, ídee-/ *n.* **1** a theorist; a visionary. **2** an adherent of an ideology. [F *idéologue* f. Gk *idea* (see IDEA) + -LOGUE]

ideology /ídeeóləjee, ídee-/ *n.* (*pl.* **-ies**) **1** the system of ideas at the basis of an economic or political theory (*Marxist ideology*). **2** the manner of thinking characteristic of a class or individual (*bourgeois ideology*). **3** visionary speculation. **4** *archaic* the science of ideas. ▫▫ **ideological** /-əlójikəl/ *adj.* **ideologically** *adv.* **ideologist** /-deeól-/ *n.* [F *idéologie* (as IDEOLOGUE)]

■ **1, 2** belief(s), convictions, tenets, credo, philosophy, principles, canons, creed, dogma, teachings, doctrine; see also IDEAL *n.* 2b.

ides /īdz/ *n.pl.* the eighth day after the nones in the ancient Roman calendar (the 15th day of March, May, July, October; the 13th of other months). [ME f. OF f. L *idus* (pl.), perh. f. Etruscan]

idiocy /ídeeəsee/ *n.* (*pl.* **-ies**) **1** utter foolishness; idiotic behavior or an idiotic action. **2** extreme mental imbecility. [ME f. IDIOT, prob. after *lunacy*]

■ **1** see *stupidity* (STUPID).

idiolect /ídeeəlekt/ *n.* the form of language used by an individual person. [Gk *idios* own + -*lect* in DIALECT]

■ see LANGUAGE 2, 3a, b.

idiom /ídeeəm/ *n.* **1** a group of words established by usage and having a meaning not deducible from those of the individual words (as in *at the drop of a hat*, *see the light*). **2** a form of expression peculiar to a language, person, or group of people. **3 a** the language of a people or country. **b** the specific character of this. **4** a characteristic mode of expression in music, art, etc. [F *idiome* or LL *idioma* f. Gk *idiōma -matos* private property f. *idios* own, private]

■ **1** expression, (set) phrase, phrasing, locution, cliché, collocation, saying. **2, 3** idiolect, phraseology, vernacular, dialect, argot, patois, jargon, cant, parlance, form *or* mode of expression; language, tongue, speech, *colloq.* lingo.

idiomatic /ídeeəmátik/ *adj.* **1** relating to or conforming to idiom. **2** characteristic of a particular language. ▫▫ **idiomatically** *adv.* [Gk *idiōmatikos* peculiar (as IDIOM)]

idiopathy /ídeeópəthee/ *n.* *Med.* any disease or condition of unknown cause or that arises spontaneously. ▫▫ **idiopathic** /ídeeəpáthik/ *adj.* [mod.L *idiopathia* f. Gk *idiopatheia* f. *idios* own + -PATHY]

idiosyncrasy /ídeeōsíngkrəsee/ *n.* (*pl.* **-ies**) **1** a mental constitution, view or feeling, or mode of behavior, peculiar to a person. **2** anything highly individualized or eccentric. **3** a mode of expression peculiar to an author. **4** *Med.* a physical constitution peculiar to a person. ▫▫ **idiosyncratic** /-krátik/ *adj.* **idiosyncratically** *adv.* [Gk *idiosugkrasia* f. *idios* own + *sun* together + *krasis* mixture]

■ **1** see CHARACTERISTIC *n.* **2** see *eccentricity* (ECCENTRIC). ▫▫ **idiosyncratic** see CHARACTERISTIC *adj.*, ECCENTRIC *adj.*

idiot /ídeeət/ *n.* **1** *colloq.* a stupid person; an utter fool. **2** a person deficient in mind and permanently incapable of rational conduct. ▫ **idiot box** *colloq.* a television set. **idiot card** esp. *Brit.* = *cue card* (see CUE[1]). ▫▫ **idiotic** /ídeeótik/ *adj.* **idiotically** /ídeeótiklee/ *adv.* [ME f. OF f. L *idiota* ig-

---

norant person f. Gk *idiōtēs* private person, layman, ignorant person f. *idios* own, private]
■ **1** see FOOL¹ *n*. 1. ▫▫ **idiotic** see STUPID *adj*. 1, 5; 2.
idiotically see MADLY 1.

idle /íd'l/ *adj. & v.* ● *adj.* (**idler, idlest**) **1** lazy; indolent. **2** not in use; not working; unemployed. **3** (of time, etc.) unoccupied. **4** having no special basis or purpose (*idle rumor*; *idle curiosity*). **5** useless. **6** (of an action, thought, or word) ineffective; worthless; vain. ● *v.* **1 a** *intr.* (of an engine) run slowly without doing any work. **b** *tr.* cause (an engine) to idle. **2** *intr.* be idle. **3** *tr.* (foll. by *away*) pass (time, etc.) in idleness. ▫ **idle wheel** an intermediate wheel between two geared wheels, esp. to allow them to rotate in the same direction. ▫▫ **idleness** *n*. **idly** *adv*. [OE *īdel* empty, useless]
■ *adj.* **1** lazy, indolent, listless, lethargic, slothful, languid, shiftless, lackadaisical, fainéant. **2** unused, not in use, inactive, unoccupied, nonoperative, not working, stationary; unemployed, out of work, redundant, jobless, workless, unwaged, at leisure, at liberty, between assignments, *Brit. euphem.* resting. **3** unoccupied, free, empty, vacant, unfilled, unused. **4** aimless, purposeless; baseless, groundless; offhand. **5, 6** useless, worthless, otiose, pointless, insignificant, meaningless, senseless, unimportant, trivial, trifling, nugatory, shallow, frivolous, superficial, *colloq.* piffling; ineffective, vain, unavailing, futile, unproductive, fruitless, unfruitful, abortive, *archaic* bootless. ● *v.* **2** laze (about), loiter, kill *or* mark time, loaf, loll, lounge, take it easy, mess around *or* about, fool around *or* about, putter *or Brit.* potter about *or* around, *Brit. colloq.* muck around *or* about, *sl.* goof off *or* around, lallygag. **3** (*idle away*) waste, fritter away, while away, kill, pass, spend, squander. ▫▫ **idleness** inactivity, inaction, unemployment, leisure; laziness, lethargy, torpor, indolence, sluggishness, sloth, slothfulness, shiftlessness, inertia, lassitude, flânerie, dolce far niente. **idly** lazily, listlessly, indolently, unproductively, purposelessly, worthlessly, pointlessly, meaninglessly, senselessly; unconsciously, unthinkingly, mechanically, indifferently, offhandedly, aimlessly, thoughtlessly, obliviously.

idler /ídlər/ *n*. **1** a habitually lazy person. **2** = *idle wheel*.
■ **1** layabout, loafer, lounger, slacker, shirker, drone, fainéant, clock-watcher, sluggard, dawdler, laggard, lazybones, ne'er-do-well, gold brick, *archaic* slugabed, *colloq.* lounge lizard, slob, *sl.* slouch, couch potato.

Ido /éedō/ *n*. an artificial universal language based on Esperanto. [Ido, = offspring]

idol /íd'l/ *n*. **1** an image of a deity, etc., used as an object of worship. **2** *Bibl.* a false god. **3** a person or thing that is the object of excessive or supreme adulation (*movie idol*). **4** *archaic* a phantom. [ME f. OF *idole* f. L *idolum* f. Gk *eidōlon* phantom f. *eidos* form]
■ **1** (graven) image, icon, effigy, symbol, fetish, totem, *NZ* tiki. **3** god, hero *or* heroine, star, superstar, celebrity, pinup, luminary, favorite, pet, darling, *colloq.* sacred cow.

idolater /ídólətər/ *n*. (*fem.* **idolatress** /-tris/) **1** a worshiper of idols. **2** (often foll. by *of*) a devoted admirer. ▫▫ **idolatrous** *adj.* [ME *idolatrer* f. OF or f. *idolatry* or f. OF *idolâtre*, ult. f. Gk *eidōlolatrēs* (as IDOL, -LATER)]
■ **1** see PAGAN *n*. ▫▫ **idolatrous** see HEATHEN *adj*.

idolatry /ídólətree/ *n*. **1** the worship of idols. **2** great adulation. [OF *idolatrie* (as IDOLATER)]
■ see WORSHIP *n*.

idolize /íd'līz/ *v*. **1** *tr.* venerate or love extremely or excessively. **2** *tr.* make an idol of. **3** *intr.* practice idolatry. ▫▫ **idolization** *n*. **idolizer** *n*.
■ **1, 2** venerate, deify, worship, apotheosize, adore, revere, reverence, exalt, glorify, put on a pedestal, lionize, adulate, honor, admire, look up to. ▫▫ **idolization** see *veneration* (VENERATE). **idolizer** worshiper, admirer, adulator, adorer; devotee, aficionado, fan, *sl.* groupie.

IDP *abbr.* **1** integrated data processing. **2** International Driving Permit.

idyll /íd'l/ *n*. (also **idyl**) **1** a short description in verse or prose of a picturesque scene or incident, esp. in rustic life. **2** an episode suitable for such treatment, usu. a love story. ▫▫ **idyllist** *n*. **idyllize** *v.tr.* [L *idyllium* f. Gk *eidullion*, dimin. of *eidos* form]
■ **1** pastoral, eclogue.

idyllic /ídílik/ *adj.* **1** blissfully peaceful and happy. **2** of or like an idyll. ▫▫ **idyllically** *adv*.
■ **1** blissful, heavenly, paradisal, paradisical, paradisaical, paradisiacal, heavenly, arcadian; halcyon, blessed, perfect, ideal, idealized; pastoral, rustic, bucolic, unspoiled *or* unspoilt, peaceful, pacific. ▫▫ **idyllically** blissfully; blessedly, perfectly, ideally; pastorally, rustically, bucolically, peacefully, pacifically.

IE *abbr.* **1** Indo-European. **2** industrial engineer(ing).

i.e. *abbr.* that is to say. [L *id est*]
■ see NAMELY.

-ie /ee/ *suffix* **1** var. of -Y² (*dearie; nightie*). **2** *archaic* var. of -Y¹, -Y³ (*litanie; prettie*). [earlier form of -Y]

-ier /eeər, eer/ *suffix* forming personal nouns denoting an occupation or interest: **1** with stress on the preceding element (*grazier*). **2** with stress on the suffix (*cashier; grenadier*). [sense 1 ME of various orig.; sense 2 F -*ier* f. L -*arius*]

IF *abbr.* intermediate frequency.

if /if/ *conj. & n.* ● *conj.* **1** introducing a conditional clause: **a** on the condition or supposition that; in the event that (*if he comes I will tell him; if you are tired we will rest*). **b** (with past tense) implying that the condition is not fulfilled (*if I were you; if I knew I would say*). **2** even though (*I'll finish it, if it takes me all day*). **3** whenever (*if I am not sure I ask*). **4** whether (*see if you can find it*). **5 a** expressing wish or surprise (*if I could just try!; if it isn't my old hat!*). **b** expressing a request (*if you wouldn't mind opening the door?*). **6** with implied reservation, = and perhaps not (*very rarely if at all*). **7** (with reduction of the protasis to its significant word) if there is or it is, etc. (*took little if any*). **8** despite being (*a useful if cumbersome device*). ● *n.* a condition or supposition (*too many ifs about it*). ▫ **if only 1** even if for no other reason than (*I'll come if only to see her*). **2** (often *ellipt.*) an expression of regret (*if only I had thought of it; if only I could swim!*). **if so** if that is the case. [OE *gif*]
■ *conj.* **1** see SUPPOSE 5.

IFC *abbr.* International Finance Corporation.

iff /if/ *conj. Logic & Math.* = if and only if. [arbitrary extension of *if*]

iffy /ífee/ *adj.* (**iffier, iffiest**) *colloq.* uncertain; doubtful.
■ see DOUBTFUL 2.

Igbo var. of IBO.

igloo /íglōō/ *n*. an Eskimo dome-shaped dwelling, esp. one built of snow. [Eskimo, = house]

igneous /ígneeəs/ *adj.* **1** of fire; fiery. **2** *Geol.* (esp. of rocks) produced by volcanic or magmatic action. [L *igneus* f. *ignis* fire]

ignis fatuus /ígnis fáchōōəs/ *n*. (*pl.* **ignes fatui** /ígneez fáchōō-ī/) a will-o'-the-wisp. [mod.L, = foolish fire, because of its erratic movement]
■ see ILLUSION 4.

ignite /ignít/ *v*. **1** *tr.* set fire to; cause to burn. **2** *intr.* catch fire. **3** *tr. Chem.* heat to the point of combustion or chemical change. **4** *tr.* provoke or excite (feelings, etc.). ▫▫ **ignitable** *adj.* **ignitability** /-təbílitee/ *n*. **ignitible** *adj.* **ignitibility** /-tibílitee/ *n*. [L *ignire* ignit- f. *ignis* fire]
■ **1** see FIRE *v.* 5a. **2** kindle, catch fire, burst into flame. **4** see EXCITE 1a, b.

igniter /ignítər/ *n*. **1** a device for igniting a fuel mixture in an engine. **2** a device for causing an electric arc.

ignition /igníshən/ *n*. **1** a mechanism for, or the action of, starting the combustion of fuel in the cylinder of an internal combustion engine. **2** the act or an instance of igniting or being ignited. ▫ **ignition key** a key to operate the ignition of a motor vehicle. [F *ignition* or med.L *ignitio* (as IGNITE)]

ignitron /ignítrən, ígni-/ *n. Electr.* a mercury-arc rectifier able to carry large currents. [IGNITE + -TRON]

ignoble /ignőbəl/ *adj.* (**ignobler, ignoblest**) **1** dishonorable; mean; base. **2** of low birth, position, or reputation. □□ **ignobility** *n.* **ignobly** *adv.* [F *ignoble* or L *ignobilis* (as IN-¹, *nobilis* noble)]
■ **1** see BASE² 1. **2** see HUMBLE *adj.* 2. □□ **ignobility** see VULGARITY.

ignominious /ígnəmíneeəs/ *adj.* **1** causing or deserving ignominy. **2** humiliating. □□ **ignominiously** *adv.* **ignominiousness** *n.* [ME f. F *ignominieux* or L *ignominiosus*]
■ **1** see INFAMOUS 1.

ignominy /ígnəminee/ *n.* **1** dishonor; infamy. **2** *archaic* infamous conduct. [F *ignominie* or L *ignominia* (as IN-¹, *nomen* name)]
■ **1** see *infamy* (INFAMOUS).

ignoramus /ígnəráyməs/ *n.* (*pl.* **ignoramuses** or **ignorami**) an ignorant person. [L, = we do not know: in legal use (formerly of a grand jury rejecting a bill) we take no notice of it; mod. sense perh. from a character in Ruggle's *Ignoramus* (1615) exposing lawyers' ignorance]

ignorance /ígnərəns/ *n.* (often foll. by *of*) lack of knowledge (about a thing). [ME f. OF f. L *ignorantia* (as IGNORANT)]
■ unawareness, obliviousness, unfamiliarity, unconsciousness, benightedness, *literary* nescience; inexperience, greenness, innocence, simplicity, naïveté.

ignorant /ígnərənt/ *adj.* **1 a** lacking knowledge or experience. **b** (foll. by *of*, *in*) uninformed (about a fact or subject). **2** *colloq.* ill-mannered; uncouth. □□ **ignorantly** *adv.* [ME f. OF f. L *ignorare ignorant-* (as IGNORE)]
■ **1 a** unknowing, unaware, unenlightened, unconscious, unwitting, benighted, in the dark, oblivious, *literary* nescient; uneducated, unschooled, uninitiated, uninformed, inexperienced, green, naive, fresh, innocent, unsophisticated, unread, unlearned, unlettered, unversed, untaught, illiterate. **b** (*ignorant of*) unaware of, unconscious of, uninformed about, unfamiliar with, unacquainted with, unschooled in, unversed in, untutored in, inexperienced in *or* with, unconversant with, unenlightened about, in the dark about *or* as to, oblivious to *or* of, innocent of. **2** ill-mannered, uncouth, rude, discourteous, unchivalrous, impolite, uncivil, boorish, gauche, ill-bred, bad-mannered.

ignore /ignáwr/ *v.tr.* **1** refuse to take notice of or accept. **2** intentionally disregard. □□ **ignorer** *n.* [F *ignorer* or L *ignorare* not know, ignore (as IN-¹, *gno-* know)]
■ **1** reject, snub, brush aside, cut, cold-shoulder, give the cold shoulder, send to Coventry, turn one's back on, *colloq.* give the go-by, turn up one's nose at, freeze out. **2** disregard, overlook, pass over *or* by, skip, omit, leave out, neglect; turn a blind eye to, turn a deaf ear to, be blind to, turn one's back on, wink at, brush off *or* aside.

iguana /igwáanə/ *n.* any of various large lizards of the family Iguanidae native to America, the W. Indies, and the Pacific islands, having a dorsal crest and throat appendages. [Sp. f. Carib *iwana*]

iguanodon /igwáanədon/ *n.* a large extinct plant-eating dinosaur of the genus *Iguanodon*, with forelimbs smaller than hind limbs. [IGUANA (from its resemblance to this), after *mastodon*, etc.]

i.h.p. *abbr.* indicated horsepower.

IHS *abbr.* Jesus. [ME f. LL, repr. Gk IHΣ = *Iēs(ous)* Jesus: often taken as an abbr. of various Latin words]

ikebana /íkəbaánə/ *n.* the art of Japanese flower arrangement, with formal display according to strict rules. [Jap., = living flowers]

ikon var. of ICON.

IL *abbr.* Illinois (in official postal use).

il- /il/ *prefix* assim. form of IN-¹, IN-² before *l*.

-il /il/ *suffix* (also **-ile** /il/) forming adjectives or nouns denoting relation (*civil*; *utensil*) or capability (*agile*; *sessile*). [OF f. L *-ilis*]

ilang-ilang var. of YLANG-YLANG.

ilea *pl.* of ILEUM.

ileostomy /íleeóstəmee/ *n.* (*pl.* **-ies**) a surgical operation in which the ileum is brought through the abdominal wall to create an artificial opening for the evacuation of the intestinal contents. [ILEUM + Gk *stoma* mouth]

ileum /íleeəm/ *n.* (*pl.* **ilea** /íleeə/) *Anat.* the third and last portion of the small intestine. □□ **ileac** *adj.* [var. of ILIUM]

ileus /íleeəs/ *n. Med.* any painful obstruction of the intestine, esp. of the ileum. [L f. Gk *(e)ileos* colic]

ilex /íleks/ *n.* **1** any tree or shrub of the genus *Ilex*, esp. the common holly. **2** the holm oak. [ME f. L]

ilia *pl.* of ILIUM.

iliac /íleeak/ *adj.* of the lower body or ilium (*iliac artery*). [LL *iliacus* (as ILIUM)]

ilium /íleeəm/ *n.* (*pl.* **ilia** /íleeə/) **1** the bone forming the upper part of each half of the human pelvis. **2** the corresponding bone in animals. [ME f. L]

ilk /ilk/ *n.* **1** a family, class, or set (*not of the same ilk as you*). **2** (in **of that ilk**) *Sc.* of the same (landed estate or place) (*Guthrie of that ilk* = of Guthrie). [OE *ilca* same]
■ **1** see TYPE *n.* 1.

Ill. *abbr.* Illinois.

ill. *abbr.* **1** illustrated. **2** illustration. **3** illustrator.

I'll /il/ *contr.* I shall; I will.

ill /il/ *adj.*, *adv.*, & *n.* ● *adj.* **1** (usu. *predic.*; often foll. by *with*) out of health; sick (*is ill*; *was taken ill with pneumonia*; *mentally ill people*). **2** (of health) unsound; disordered. **3** wretched; unfavorable (*ill fortune*; *ill luck*). **4** harmful (*ill effects*). **5** hostile; unkind (*ill feeling*). **6** *archaic* morally bad. **7** faulty; unskillful (*ill taste*; *ill management*). **8** (of manners or conduct) improper. ● *adv.* **1** badly; wrongly (*ill-matched*). **2 a** imperfectly (*ill-provided*). **b** scarcely (*can ill afford to do it*). **3** unfavorably (*it would have gone ill with them*). ● *n.* **1** injury; harm. **2** evil; the opposite of good. □ **do an ill turn to** harm (a person or a person's interests). **ill-advised 1** (of a person) foolish or imprudent. **2** (of a plan, etc.) not well formed or considered. **ill-advisedly** /-ədvízidlee/ in a foolish or badly considered manner. **ill-affected** (foll. by *toward*) not well disposed. **ill-assorted** not well matched. **ill at ease** embarrassed; uneasy. **ill-behaved** see BEHAVE. **ill blood** bad feeling; animosity. **ill-bred** badly brought up; rude. **ill breeding** bad manners. **ill-considered** = *ill-advised*. **ill-defined** not clearly defined. **ill-disposed 1** (often foll. by *toward*) unfavorably disposed. **2** disposed to evil; malevolent. **ill-equipped** (often foll. by *to* + infin.) not adequately equipped or qualified. **ill fame** see FAME. **ill-fated** destined to or bringing bad fortune. **ill-favored** unattractive; displeasing; objectionable. **ill feeling** bad feeling; animosity. **ill-founded** (of an idea, etc.) not well founded; baseless. **ill-gotten** gained by wicked or unlawful means. **ill humor** moroseness; irritability. **ill-humored** bad-tempered. **ill-judged** unwise; badly considered. **ill-mannered** having bad manners; rude. **ill nature** churlishness; unkindness. **ill-natured** churlish; unkind. **ill-naturedly** churlishly. **ill-omened** attended by bad omens. **ill-starred** unlucky; destined to failure. **ill success** partial or complete failure. **ill temper** moroseness. **ill-tempered** morose; irritable. **ill-timed** done or occurring at an inappropriate time. **ill-treat** (or **-use**) treat badly; abuse. **ill-treatment** (or **ill use**) abuse; bad treatment. **ill will** bad feeling; animosity. **an ill wind** an unfavorable or untoward circumstance (with ref. to the proverb *it's an ill wind that blows nobody good*). **speak ill of** say something unfavorable about. [ME f. ON *illr*, of unkn. orig.]
■ *adj.* **1** sick, unwell, not well, unhealthy, ailing, indisposed, infirm, poorly, bad, in bad health, in a bad way, the worse for wear, diseased, afflicted, out of sorts, off color, weak, sickly, invalid(ed), valetudinarian, nauseous, *colloq.* seedy, under the weather, *Brit. colloq.* a bit off, ropy. **2** bad, unsound, poor, mediocre, weak, frail, delicate, unstable,

disordered. **3** bad, adverse, unfavorable, unpropitious, untoward, unpromising, inauspicious, unlucky, unfortunate, miserable, wretched, disastrous; disturbing, ominous, sinister, unwholesome. **4** harmful, hurtful, injurious, detrimental, damaging, noxious, pernicious, deleterious, dangerous, destructive, bad, baleful, unfavorable, adverse, *literary* nocuous, *poet.* baneful; disastrous, catastrophic, ruinous, cataclysmic. **5** hostile, unfriendly, antagonistic, belligerent, malevolent, malicious, unkind, harsh, cruel. **6** bad, wicked, sinful, evil, iniquitous, nefarious, immoral, depraved, degenerate, vicious, vile, corrupt, wrong. **7** bad, poor, deficient, faulty; inadequate, unskillful, incompetent, inexpert, inept. **8** improper, unseemly, unsuitable, inappropriate. ● *adv.* **1** wrongly, badly, incorrectly, mistakenly, falsely, erroneously, inaccurately, imprecisely; wrongfully, awkwardly, improperly, unfairly, unjustly, unsatisfactorily, poorly, harshly, unkindly, maliciously, malevolently. **2 a** badly, imperfectly, insufficiently, unsatisfactorily, poorly, incompletely, patchily, faultily, defectively. **b** scarcely, hardly, barely, only just, not really; by no means, in no way. **3** badly, adversely, disastrously, unfavorably. ● *n.* **1** harm, damage, injury, hurt, mischief, trouble, misfortune, misery, affliction, pain, distress, woefulness, discomfort, unpleasantness, disaster, catastrophe, cataclysm, calamity, adversity, suffering, ruin, destruction, *archaic or literary* woe. **2** wrong, injustice, inequity, evil, sin, transgression, abuse. □ **do an ill turn to** see HARM *v.* **ill-advised 1** foolish, imprudent, foolhardy, unwise, reckless, rash, hasty, impetuous, incautious, shortsighted, improvident, ignorant, ill-informed, uninformed. **2** ill-considered, ill-judged, injudicious, misguided, unwise, imprudent, inadvisable, inappropriate, impolitic, wrongheaded, thoughtless, indiscreet, inexpedient. **ill-advisedly** foolishly, imprudently, unwisely, injudiciously, misguidedly, impetuously, rashly, recklessly, hastily, heedlessly, thoughtlessly, mindlessly. **ill-affected** (*ill-affected toward*) ill-disposed toward, antipathetic to, unsympathetic toward, opposed to, resistant to, against, anti. **ill-assorted** ill-matched, mismated, mismatched, incompatible, incongruous. **ill at ease** uncomfortable, embarrassed, uneasy, edgy, on edge, fidgety, nervous, anxious, disturbed, distressed, troubled, awkward, unsure, uncertain. **ill blood** see *ill will* below. **ill-bred** see *ill-mannered* below. **ill breeding** see INCIVILITY. **ill-defined** see INDEFINITE 1. **ill-disposed 1** see *ill-affected* above. **2** see EVIL *adj.* 1. **ill-equipped** see UNQUALIFIED 1. **ill-fated** see INAUSPICIOUS 1. **ill feeling** see *ill will* below. **ill-founded** groundless, baseless, without foundation, unsupported, unsubstantiated, empty, unjustified, unproven, uncorroborated, unsound, erroneous, invalid. **ill-gotten** see UNLAWFUL. **ill humor** ill temper, irritability, irascibility, crossness, grumpiness, moodiness, sulkiness, gloominess, sullenness, moroseness, peevishness, churlishness, surliness, petulance, huffiness; volatility. **ill-humored** see IRRITABLE 1. **ill-judged** see *ill-advised* 2 above. **ill-mannered** rude, discourteous, impolite, ill-bred, uncouth, boorish, uncivil, disrespectful, uncourtly, ungallant, ungracious, indecorous, ungentlemanly, unladylike, impudent, insolent, insulting, impertinent, brazen. **ill nature** see *ill humor* above. **ill-natured** see SURLY. **ill-naturedly** churlishly, irritably, bad-temperedly, surlily, meanly, crustily, sourly, peevishly, querulously, testily, grumpily, sulkily, rudely, uncivilly, acidly, caustically, *colloq.* grouchily. **ill-omened** see INAUSPICIOUS. **ill-starred** see INAUSPICIOUS 1. **ill temper** see *ill humor* above. **ill-tempered** see IRRITABLE 1. **ill-timed** see INOPPORTUNE. **ill-treat** (or **-use**) mistreat, maltreat, abuse, persecute, wrong, harm, hurt, injure, beat up, batter, knock about *or* around, *colloq.* manhandle; misuse, mishandle. **ill-**

treatment (or **ill use**) see ABUSE *n.* 4. **ill will** bad *or* ill feeling, resentment, bad *or* ill blood, dislike, animosity, hatred, hate, loathing, abhorrence, detestation, malevolence, malice, hostility, enmity, animus, antipathy, aversion, rancor, acrimony, spite, venom, vitriol, acerbity. **an ill wind** misfortune, adversity, mishap, calamity, catastrophe, disaster, tragedy, blow, shock, reverse, stroke of bad luck. **speak ill of** see VILIFY.

illation /iláyshən/ *n.* **1** a deduction or conclusion. **2** a thing deduced. [L *illatio* f. *illatus* past part. of *inferre* INFER]

illative /illáytiv, ílətiv/ *adj.* **1 a** (of a word) stating or introducing an inference. **b** inferential. **2** *Gram.* (of a case) denoting motion into. □□ **illatively** *adv.* [L *illativus* (as ILLATION)]

illegal /ileégəl/ *adj.* **1** not legal. **2** contrary to law. □□ **illegality** /-gálitee/ *n.* (*pl.* **-ies**). **illegally** *adv.* [F *illégal* or med.L *illegalis* (as IN-¹, LEGAL)]

■ **1** unlawful, unofficial, unsanctioned, unlicensed, unauthorized, unconstitutional, *attrib.* wildcat. **2** unlawful, illegitimate, criminal, felonious, illicit, outlawed, prohibited, banned, interdicted, forbidden, proscribed, wrong(ful), verboten, actionable; see also CROOKED 2, LAWLESS 2. □□ **illegality** unlawfulness, illegitimacy, criminality, illicitness. **illegally** unlawfully, criminally, illegitimately, feloniously, illicitly, wrongfully.

illegible /iléjibəl/ *adj.* not legible. □□ **illegibility** *n.* **illegibly** *adv.*

■ unreadable, unintelligible, indecipherable, indistinct, unclear; scrawled, scrawly, scribbled, scribbly.

illegitimate *adj.*, *n.*, & *v.* ● *adj.* /ílijítimət/ **1** (of a child) born of parents not married to each other. **2** not authorized by law; unlawful. **3** improper. **4** wrongly inferred. **5** physiologically abnormal. ● *n.* /ílijítimət/ a person whose position is illegitimate, esp. by birth. ● *v.tr.* /ílijítimayt/ declare or pronounce illegitimate. □□ **illegitimacy** /-məsee/ *n.* **illegitimately** *adv.* [LL *illegitimus*, after LEGITIMATE]

■ *adj.* **1** bastard, natural, fatherless, unfathered, adulterine, misbegotten, born out of wedlock, born on the wrong side of the blanket. **2** see ILLEGAL. **3** irregular, improper, incorrect, nonstandard, invalid, unauthorized, spurious. **5** see ABNORMAL. ● *n.* bastard, love child, natural child.

illiberal /ilíbərəl/ *adj.* **1** intolerant; narrow-minded. **2** without liberal culture. **3** not generous; stingy. **4** vulgar; sordid. □□ **illiberality** /-álitee/ *n.* (*pl.* **-ies**). **illiberally** *adv.* [F *illibéral* f. L *illiberalis* mean, sordid (as IN-¹, LIBERAL)]

■ **1** see INTOLERANT. **3** see SELFISH. □□ **illiberality** see *intolerance* (INTOLERANT).

illicit /ilísit/ *adj.* **1** unlawful; forbidden (*illicit dealings*). **2** secret; furtive (*an illicit cigarette*). □□ **illicitly** *adv.* **illicitness** *n.*

■ **1** see ILLEGAL 2. **2** underhand, underhanded, secret, furtive, clandestine, backdoor, sneaky, sly, shady. □□ **illicitly** see *illegally* (ILLEGAL), *secretly* (SECRET).

illimitable /ilímitəbəl/ *adj.* limitless. □□ **illimitability** *n.* **illimitableness** *n.* **illimitably** *adv.* [LL *illimitatus* f. L *limitatus* (as IN-¹, L *limitatus* past part. of *limitare* LIMIT)]

■ see LIMITLESS.

illiquid /ilíkwid/ *adj.* (of assets) not easily convertible into cash. □□ **illiquidity** /-kwíditee/ *n.*

illiterate /ilítərət/ *adj.* & *n.* ● *adj.* **1** unable to read. **2** uneducated. ● *n.* an illiterate person. □□ **illiteracy** *n.* **illiterately** *adv.* **illiterateness** *n.* [L *illitteratus* (as IN-¹, *litteratus* LITERATE)]

■ *adj.* **1** unlettered. **2** uneducated, unschooled, untaught, benighted, ignorant, unenlightened. ● *n.* nonreader; lowbrow, ignoramus. □□ **illiteracy, illiterateness** ignorance, unawareness, inexperience, lack of education.

illness /ílnis/ *n.* **1** a disease, ailment, or malady. **2** the state of being ill.

■ **1** disease, sickness, disorder, infection, affliction, ailment, malady, complaint, condition, trouble, infirmity, disability, indisposition, affection, *sl.* bug; malaise, queasiness, nausea. **2** ill health, bad health, valetudinarianism, indisposition, sickness, infirmity, disability.

illogical /ilójikəl/ *adj.* devoid of or contrary to logic. □□ **illogicality** /-kálitee/ *n.* (*pl.* **-ies**). **illogically** *adv.*
■ see UNREASONABLE 2. □□ **illogicality** see ABSURDITY 1, 2.

illude /ilŏŏd/ *v.tr. literary* trick or deceive. [ME, = mock, f. L *illudere* (as ILLUSION)]

illume /ilŏŏm/ *v.tr. poet.* light up; make bright. [shortening of ILLUMINE]

illuminant /ilŏŏminənt/ *n.* & *adj.* ● *n.* a means of illumination. ● *adj.* serving to illuminate. □□ **illuminance** /-nəns/ *n.* [L *illuminant-* part. stem of *illuminare* ILLUMINATE]

illuminate /ilŏŏminayt/ *v.tr.* **1** light up; make bright. **2** decorate (buildings, etc.) with lights as a sign of festivity. **3** decorate (an initial letter, a manuscript, etc.) with gold, silver, or brilliant colors. **4** help to explain (a subject, etc.). **5** enlighten spiritually or intellectually. **6** shed luster on. □□ **illuminating** *adj.* **illuminatingly** *adv.* **illumination** /-náyshən/ *n.* **illuminative** /-náytiv, -nətiv/ *adj.* **illuminator** *n.* [L *illuminare* (as IN-², *lumen luminis* light)]
■ **1** light (up), brighten, lighten, make bright *or* light, throw *or* cast light on *or* upon, inflame, *literary* illumine, *poet.* illume. **2** emblazon, deck out, light up, decorate, bedeck, make resplendent. **3** decorate, adorn, embellish, enrich, ornament, emblazon, rubricate, illustrate, highlight. **4** clarify, throw *or* cast *or* shed light on *or* upon, elucidate, explain, explicate, make plain, reveal, illustrate, *rhet. or poet.* enlighten. **5** see ENLIGHTEN 1a, 3b. **6** add luster to, shed luster on, enhance, enrich, highlight. □□ **illumination** lighting, light, brightness, radiance, luminosity, incandescence, fluorescence, phosphorescence; enlightenment, insight, revelation, edification, instruction, awareness, understanding, clarification, information, learning. **illuminator** illustrator, rubricator, decorator, embellisher, enhancer; clarifier, explainer, explicator, elucidator.

illuminati /ilŏŏmináatee/ *n.pl.* **1** persons claiming to possess special knowledge or enlightenment. **2** (**Illuminati**) *hist.* any of various intellectual movements or societies of illuminati. □□ **illuminism** /ilŏŏminizəm/ *n.* **illuminist** *n.* [pl. of L *illuminatus* or It. *illuminato* past part. (as ILLUMINATE)]

illumine /ilŏŏmin/ *v.tr. literary* **1** light up; make bright. **2** enlighten spiritually. [ME f. OF *illuminer* f. L (as ILLUMINATE)]

illusion /ilŏŏzhən/ *n.* **1** deception; delusion. **2** a misapprehension of the true state of affairs. **3 a** the faulty perception of an external object. **b** an instance of this. **4** a figment of the imagination. **5** = *optical illusion.* □ **be under the illusion** (foll. by *that* + clause) believe mistakenly. □□ **illusional** *adj.* [ME f. F f. L *illusio -onis* f. *illudere* mock (as IN-², *ludere* lusplay)]
■ **1** deception, deceiving, deceit, trick, trickery, *archaic* sleight (of hand); delusion, deluding, fancy. **2** misconception, misapprehension, misunderstanding, misjudgment, misbelief, fallacy, error, miscalculation, mistake, mistaken *or* false impression. **3** hallucination, delusion, misconstruction, mistake, error. **4** fantasy, hallucination, phantasm, phantom, chimera, phantasmagoria, mirage, daydream, aberration, vision, specter, figment of the imagination, will-o'-the-wisp, ignis fatuus. □ **be under the illusion** labor under the illusion *or* misapprehension, fancy, be convinced, convince oneself, believe, take it. □□ **illusional** see ILLUSORY.

illusionist /ilŏŏzhənist/ *n.* a person who produces illusions; a magician. □□ **illusionism** *n.* **illusionistic** *adj.*

illusive /ilŏŏsiv/ *adj.* = ILLUSORY. [med.L *illusivus* (as ILLUSION)]

illusory /ilŏŏsəree, -zəree/ *adj.* **1** deceptive (esp. as regards value or content). **2** having the character of an illusion. □□ **illusorily** *adv.* **illusoriness** *n.* [eccl.L *illusorius* (as ILLUSION)]
■ deceptive, misleading, illusive, delusive, illusional, beguiling, tricky, specious, seeming, apparent;

hallucinatory, fanciful, fancied, imaginary, imagined, fictional, unreal, untrue, fallacious, false. □□ **illusorily** deceptively, delusively, misleadingly, beguilingly, speciously, seemingly, apparently; see also *imaginarily* (IMAGINARY).

illustrate /iləstrayt/ *v.tr.* **1 a** provide (a book, newspaper, etc.) with pictures. **b** elucidate (a description, etc.) by drawings or pictures. **2** serve as an example of. **3** explain or make clear, esp. by examples. [L *illustrare* (as IN-², *lustrare* light up)]
■ **1 b** see ILLUMINATE 4. **2** exemplify, typify, represent, epitomize, instance, instantiate, embody, personify. **3** explain, explicate, elucidate, clarify, make plain; illuminate, shed *or* throw *or* cast light on *or* upon.

illustration /iləstráyshən/ *n.* **1** a drawing or picture illustrating a book, magazine article, etc. **2** an example serving to elucidate. **3** the act or an instance of illustrating. □□ **illustrational** *adj.* [ME f. OF f. L *illustratio -onis* (as ILLUSTRATE)]
■ **1** picture, (line) drawing, painting, sketch, diagram, image, figure, cartoon, artwork, design, graphic, *Computing* icon; engraving, etching, cut, woodcut, linocut, photogravure, duotone, halftone, print, plate; vignette, frontispiece. **2** example, case (in point), instance, exemplification; sample, specimen, exemplar. **3** depiction, representation, illumination; explanation, clarification, explication, elucidation.

illustrative /ilústrətiv, iləstray-/ *adj.* (often foll. by *of*) serving as an explanation or example. □□ **illustratively** *adv.*
■ see EXEMPLARY 3.

illustrator /íləstraytər/ *n.* a person who makes illustrations, esp. for magazines, books, advertising copy, etc.

illustrious /ilústreeəs/ *adj.* distinguished; renowned. □□ **illustriously** *adv.* **illustriousness** *n.* [L *illustris* (as ILLUSTRATE)]
■ distinguished, famous, noted, renowned, famed, eminent, well-known, prominent, important, notable, respected, esteemed, great, venerable, honored, acclaimed, celebrated, star, *colloq.* legendary.

Illyrian /ileéreeən/ *adj.* & *n.* ● *adj.* **1** of or relating to Illyria on the Balkan (east) coast of the Adriatic Sea (corresponding to parts of modern Albania and the former Yugoslavia). **2** of the language group represented by modern Albanian. ● *n.* **1** a native of Illyria; a person of Illyrian descent. **2 a** the language of Illyria. **b** the language group represented by modern Albanian.

illywhacker /íleewakər/ *n. Austral. sl.* a professional trickster. [20th c.: orig. unkn.]

ilmenite /ílmənīt/ *n.* a black ore of titanium. [*Ilmen* mountains in the Urals]

ILO *abbr.* International Labor Organization.

-ily /ilee/ *suffix* forming adverbs corresponding to adjectives in -y (see -Y¹, -LY²).

I'm /īm/ *contr.* I am.

im- /im/ *prefix* assim. form of IN-¹, IN-² before *b, m, p.*

image /ímij/ *n.* & *v.* ● *n.* **1** a representation of the external form of an object, e.g., a statue (esp. of a saint, etc., as an object of veneration). **2** the character or reputation of a person or thing as generally perceived. **3** an optical appearance or counterpart produced by light or other radiation from an object reflected in a mirror, refracted through a lens, etc. **4** semblance; likeness (*God created man in His own image*). **5** a person or thing that closely resembles another (*is the image of his father*). **6** a typical example. **7** a simile or metaphor. **8 a** a mental representation. **b** an idea or conception. **9** *Math.* a set formed by mapping from another set. ● *v.tr.* **1** make an image of; portray. **2** reflect; mirror. **3** describe or imagine vividly. **4** typify. □□ **imageable** *adj.* **imageless** *adj.* [ME f. OF f. L *imago -ginis*, rel. to IMITATE]
■ *n.* **1** representation, picture, sculpture, statue, effigy,

---

/.../	**pronunciation**	● **part of speech**
□	**phrases, idioms, and compounds**	
□□	**derivatives**	■ **synonym section**
cross-references	appear in SMALL CAPITALS or *italics*	

figure, portrait, icon; idol, graven image, fetish, totem, *NZ* tiki. **2** character, reputation, (public) face, persona, appearance, profile, aspect. **3** reflection, impression, picture, simulacrum. **4** likeness, semblance, appearance, aspect, guise; form, shape, mold, cast. **5** double, twin, duplicate, copy, counterpart, facsimile, replica, analog, mirror image, enantiomorph, doppelgänger, clone, simulacrum, (dead) ringer, *colloq.* spitting image; chip off the old block. **6** example, epitome, model, type, archetype, paradigm; embodiment, incarnation, personification, materialization. **7** figure (of speech), trope, metaphor, simile, *literary* conceit; word painting, word picture. **8** impression, concept, conception, perception, thought, idea, notion, vision, (mental) picture, *Psychol.* imago.
● *v.* **1** see PORTRAY 1, 2. **2** see REFLECT 1a. **3** picture, depict, portray, visualize, envisage, envision, conceive of, dream up, imagine, see in one's mind's eye. **4** see TYPIFY.

imagery /ímijree/ *n.* **1** figurative illustration, esp. as used by an author for particular effects. **2** images collectively. **3** statuary; carving. **4** mental images collectively. [ME f. OF *imagerie* (as IMAGE)]
■ **1** figurativeness, word painting, symbolism; metaphor(s), simile(s), conceit(s), figures (of speech). **2** artwork, graphics, design, illustration, representation; pictures, visuals, paintings, drawings, illustrations, sketches, figures, diagrams, cartoons. **4** (visual) perception, visualization; ideas, (mental) images, (mental) pictures, impressions, concepts, conceptions, notions, fancies, thoughts.

imaginable /ímájinəbəl/ *adj.* that can be imagined (*the greatest difficulty imaginable*). □□ **imaginably** *adv.* [ME f. LL *imaginabilis* (as IMAGINE)]
■ see *thinkable* (THINK).

imaginal /ímájinəl/ *adj.* **1** of an image or images. **2** *Zool.* of an imago. [L *imago imagin-*: see IMAGE]

imaginary /ímájinéree/ *adj.* **1** existing only in the imagination. **2** *Math.* being the square root of a negative quantity, and plotted graphically in a direction usu. perpendicular to the axis of real quantities (see REAL¹). □□ **imaginarily** *adv.* [ME f. L *imaginarius* (as IMAGE)]
■ **1** fictitious, fictive, fanciful, fancied, imagined, made-up, unreal, *colloq.* pretend; untrue, nonexistent, false, fallacious, notional, abstract, illusory, illusive, chimerical, visionary, mythical, mythic, fabulous, fantastic, legendary, mythological. □□ **imaginarily** fictitiously, fancifully, unreally, illusorily, fallaciously, falsely.

imagination /ímájináyshən/ *n.* **1** a mental faculty forming images or concepts of external objects not present to the senses. **2** the ability of the mind to be creative or resourceful. **3** the process of imagining. [ME f. OF f. L *imaginatio -onis* (as IMAGINE)]
■ **1** fantasy, mind's eye, fancy. **2** imaginativeness, creativity, creativeness, creative power(s), inventiveness, invention, innovation, innovativeness, ingenuity, insight, inspiration, vision; resourcefulness, lateral thinking, originality, unorthodoxy, individuality, nonconformity. **3** visualization, conception, vision.

imaginative /ímájinətiv/ *adj.* **1** having or showing in a high degree the faculty of imagination. **2** given to using the imagination. □□ **imaginatively** *adv.* **imaginativeness** *n.* [ME f. OF *imaginatif -ive* f. med.L *imaginativus* (as IMAGINE)]
■ **1** creative, original, ingenious, inventive, innovative, inspired, inspiring, insightful, inspirational, enterprising, clever, resourceful. **2** romantic, dreamy, dreaming, fanciful, poetic, poetical, visionary, whimsical. □□ **imaginatively** creatively, originally, ingeniously, inventively, innovatively, enterprisingly, resourcefully; fancifully, fantastically, dreamily, poetically, romantically, whimsically, fictionally. **imaginativeness** see IMAGINATION 2.

imagine /ímájin/ *v.tr.* **1 a** form a mental image or concept of. **b** picture to oneself (something nonexistent or not pres-

ent to the senses). **2** (often foll. by *to* + infin.) think or conceive (*imagined them to be soldiers*). **3** guess (*cannot imagine what they are doing*). **4** (often foll. by *that* + clause) suppose; be of the opinion (*I imagine you will need help*). **5** (in *imper.*) as an exclamation of surprise (*just imagine!*). □□ **imaginer** *n.* [ME f. OF *imaginer* f. L *imaginari* (as IMAGE)]
■ **1** picture, envisage, envision, contemplate, ponder, meditate (on), visualize, see (in one's mind's eye), think of, conceive of; think up, conceptualize, create, concoct, devise, invent, dream up, *colloq.* cook up. **2** think, understand, conceive, suppose, believe, assume, suspect, judge, consider, reckon, *formal* deem. **3** guess, conjecture, estimate, hypothesize, speculate, theorize. **4** suppose, expect, believe, think, be of the opinion, opine, consider, gather, surmise, fancy, guess, suspect, reckon, assume, presume, take it, infer, take it for granted *or* as given.

imagines *pl.* of IMAGO.

imaginings /ímájiningz/ *n.pl.* fancies; fantasies.

imagism /íməjizəm/ *n.* a movement in early 20th-c. poetry which sought clarity of expression through the use of precise images. □□ **imagist** *n.* **imagistic** *adj.*

imago /imáygō, imaá-/ *n.* (*pl.* **-oes** or **imagines** /imájineez/) **1** the final and fully developed stage of an insect after all metamorphoses, e.g., a butterfly or beetle. **2** *Psychol.* an idealized mental picture of oneself or others, esp. a parent. [mod.L sense of *imago* IMAGE]

imam /imaám/ *n.* **1** a leader of prayers in a mosque. **2** a title of various Muslim leaders, esp. of one succeeding Muhammad as leader of Islam. □□ **imamate** /-mayt/ *n.* [Arab. *'imām* leader f. *'amma* precede]

imbalance /imbáləns/ *n.* **1** lack of balance. **2** disproportion.
■ **2** see DISPROPORTION.

imbecile /ímbisil, -səl/ *n. & adj.* ● *n.* **1** a person of abnormally weak intellect, esp. an adult with a mental age of about five. **2** *colloq.* a stupid person. ● *adj.* mentally weak; stupid; idiotic. □□ **imbecilely** *adv.* **imbecilic** /-sílik/ *adj.* **imbecility** /-silitee/ *n.* (*pl.* **-ies**) [F *imbécil(l)e* f. L *imbecillus* (as IN-¹, *baculum* stick) orig. in sense 'without supporting staff']
■ *n.* **2** see FOOL¹ *n.* 1. ● *adj.* see STUPID *adj.* 1, 5. □□ **imbecilic** see STUPID *adj.* 1, 5. **imbecility** see *stupidity* (STUPID).

imbed var. of EMBED.

imbibe /imbíb/ *v.tr.* **1** (also *absol.*) drink (esp. alcoholic liquor). **2 a** absorb or assimilate (ideas, etc.). **b** absorb (moisture, etc.). **3** inhale (air, etc.). □□ **imbiber** *n.* **imbibition** /ímbibíshən/ *n.* [ME f. L *imbibere* (as IN-², *bibere* drink)]
■ **1** see DRINK *v.* 1.

imbricate *v. & adj.* ● *v.tr. & intr.* /ímbrikayt/ arrange (leaves, the scales of a fish, etc.), or be arranged, so as to overlap like roof tiles. ● *adj.* /ímbrikət/ having scales, etc., arranged in this way. □□ **imbrication** /-káyshən/ *n.* [L *imbricare imbricat-* cover with rain tiles f. *imbrex -icis* rain tile f. *imber* shower]
■ *v.* see OVERLAP *v.* 1, 2. □□ **imbrication** see OVERLAP *n.*

imbroglio /imbrólyō/ *n.* (*pl.* **-os**) **1** a confused or complicated situation. **2** a confused heap. [It. *imbrogliare* confuse (as EMBROIL)]
■ **1** see PREDICAMENT.

imbrue /imbroo/ *v.tr.* (foll. by *in*, *with*) *literary* stain (one's hand, sword, etc.). [OF *embruer* bedabble (as IN-², *breu* ult. f. Gmc, rel. to BROTH)]

imbue /imbyoo/ *v.tr.* (**imbues, imbued, imbuing**) (often foll. by *with*) **1** inspire or permeate (with feelings, opinions, or qualities). **2** saturate. **3** dye. [orig. as past part., f. F *imbu* or L *imbutus* f. *imbuere* moisten]
■ **1** see PERMEATE. **2** see SATURATE 1, 6.

IMF *abbr.* International Monetary Fund.

imide /ímid/ *n. Chem.* a compound containing the NH group formed by replacing two of the hydrogen atoms in ammonia by acid groups. [orig. F: arbitrary alt. of AMIDE]

imine /ímeen/ *n. Chem.* a compound containing the group (-NH-) formed by replacing two of the hydrogen atoms in ammonia by other groups. [G *Imin* arbitrary alt. of *Amin* AMINE]

imitate /ímitayt/ v.tr. **1** follow the example of; copy the action(s) of. **2** mimic. **3** make a copy of; reproduce. **4** be (consciously or not) like. □□ **imitable** adj. **imitator** n. [L imitari imitat-, rel. to imago IMAGE]

■ **1** emulate, copy, match, parallel, echo, mirror, reflect, pattern oneself on or after, model oneself on or after; take after, follow or tread in a person's footsteps, take a leaf out of a person's book. **2** mimic, copy, affect, ape, parrot, monkey, emulate, simulate, impersonate, do an impression of; parody, satirize, burlesque, caricature, travesty, mock, colloq. spoof, take off, send up. **3** copy, reproduce, duplicate, replicate, clone; counterfeit, fake, forge, simulate. **4** be like, mirror, reflect, match, take after, resemble, compare with, go with, accord with, coordinate with, correspond with. □□ **imitable** copiable, easy to copy, easily copied, reproducible, duplicable, replicable, forgeable; easy to impersonate, open to parody, mockable; matchable, comparable. **imitator** emulator, copier, simulator; forger, counterfeiter, faker; see also MIMIC n.

imitation /ímitáyshən/ n. & adj. ● n. **1** the act or an instance of imitating or being imitated. **2** a copy. **3** Mus. the repetition of a phrase, etc., usu. at a different pitch, in another part or voice. ● adj. made in imitation of something genuine; counterfeit; fake (imitation leather). [F imitation or L imitatio (as IMITATE)]

■ n. **1** reproduction, duplication, replication, simulation, mimicry, apery, emulation, impersonation, impression; parody, satirization, burlesque, caricature, mockery, travesty, colloq. takeoff, send-up. **2** copy, replica, replication, reproduction, simulation, dummy, facsimile, duplicate, duplication, simulacrum; fake, forgery, counterfeit. ● adj. counterfeit, fake, synthetic, artificial, simulated, reproduction, factitious, manmade, sham, ersatz, mock, bogus, colloq. phony.

imitative /ímitaytiv/ adj. **1** (often foll. by of) imitating; following a model or example. **2** counterfeit. **3** of a word: **a** that reproduces a natural sound (e.g., fizz). **b** whose sound is thought to correspond to the appearance, etc., of the object or action described (e.g., blob). □ **imitative arts** painting and sculpture. □□ **imitatively** adv. **imitativeness** n. [LL imitativus (as IMITATE)]

■ **2** see COUNTERFEIT adj. 2.

immaculate /imákyələt/ adj. **1** pure; spotless; perfectly clean or neat and tidy. **2** perfectly or extremely well executed (an immaculate performance). **3** free from fault; innocent. **4** Biol. not spotted. □ **Immaculate Conception** RC Ch. the doctrine that God preserved the Virgin Mary from the taint of original sin from the moment she was conceived. □□ **immaculacy** n. **immaculately** adv. **immaculateness** n. [ME f. L immaculatus (as IN-¹, maculatus f. macula spot)]

■ **1** spotless, stainless, unblemished, pure, clean, untarnished, unsullied, unsoiled, untainted, unblemished, pristine, snow-white, spick-and-span, tidy, neat, dapper, spruce; smart, trim, well-groomed. **2** faultless, flawless, perfect, errorless, unerring, impeccable; definitive, authoritative, infallible, irreproachable, consummate; exemplary; accurate, correct. **3** pure, faultless, innocent, blameless, sinless, impeccable, irreproachable, guileless, virtuous; virginal, virgin, intact, chaste, maidenly, vestal; pristine, undefiled, untainted, uncorrupted, unspoiled, unblemished, stainless, unadulterated.

immanent /ímənənt/ adj. **1** (often foll. by in) indwelling; inherent. **2** (of the Supreme Being) permanently pervading the universe (opp. TRANSCENDENT). □□ **immanence** /-nəns/ n. **immanency** n. **immanentism** n. **immanentist** n. [LL immanēre (as IN-², manēre remain)]

■ **1** see INHERENT 1.

immaterial /ímətéereeəl/ adj. **1** of no essential consequence; unimportant. **2** not material; incorporeal. □□ **immateriality** /-álitee/ n. **immaterialize** v.tr. **immaterially** adv. [ME f. LL immaterialis (as IN-¹, MATERIAL)]

■ **1** unimportant, inconsequential, insignificant, nugatory, trivial, trifling, petty, paltry, negligible,

minor, slight, flimsy, light, unessential, inessential, nonessential, of little account or value, colloq. footling, piffling, piddling. **2** airy, incorporeal, disembodied, discarnate, ethereal, ephemeral, evanescent, insubstantial, unsubstantial, impalpable, intangible; metaphysical, spiritual, transcendental, unearthly, supernatural, extramundane, otherworldly.

immaterialism /ímətéereeəlizəm/ n. the doctrine that matter has no objective existence. □□ **immaterialist** n.

immature /ímachŏŏr, -tŏŏr, -tyŏŏr/ adj. **1** not mature or fully developed. **2** lacking emotional or intellectual development. **3** unripe. □□ **immaturely** adv. **immaturity** n. [L immaturus (as IN-¹, MATURE)]

■ **1** undeveloped, pubescent, youthful, young, juvenile, teenage, teenaged; rudimentary, half-grown, unformed, unfledged, fledgling, budding, embryonic; unfinished, incomplete, imperfect, untried, maturing, raw, crude. **2** babyish, childish, childlike, puerile, juvenile, green, callow, unsophisticated, naive, inexperienced, (still) wet behind the ears, jejune, innocent, guileless, unfledged, fresh, tender. **3** unripe, unripened, undeveloped, green; unready, early, too early, unseasonable. □□ **immaturity** see YOUTH 1, INEXPERIENCE.

immeasurable /imézhərəbəl/ adj. not measurable; immense. □□ **immeasurability** /-bílitee/ n. **immeasurableness** n. **immeasurably** adv.

■ measureless, limitless, illimitable, indeterminable, boundless, unbounded, unlimited, inestimable, unfathomable, infinite, endless, never-ending, interminable, innumerable, unmeasurable, uncountable, incalculable, uncounted, untold, numberless; vast, immense, huge, great, enormous, giant, gigantic, massive, tremendous, colossal, titanic; see also GREAT 1a.

immediate /iméedeeət/ adj. **1** occurring or done at once or without delay (an immediate reply). **2** nearest; next; not separated by others (the immediate vicinity; the immediate future; my immediate neighbor). **3** most pressing or urgent; of current concern (our immediate concern was to get him to the hospital). **4** (of a relation or action) having direct effect; without an intervening medium or agency (the immediate cause of death). **5** (of knowledge, reactions, etc.) intuitive; gained or exhibited without reasoning. □□ **immediacy** n. **immediateness** n. [ME f. F immédiat or LL immediatus (as IN-¹, MEDIATE)]

■ **1** instantaneous, instant, prompt, swift, rapid, speedy, quick, express; unhesitating, spontaneous, abrupt, sudden. **2** nearest, next, closest, adjacent, proximate, near, nearby, close, imminent. **3** pressing, urgent, instant, critical, compelling, vital, important, serious; existing, present, current, actual. **4** direct, proximate. **5** intuitive, direct, basic, spontaneous, instinctive, visceral, emotional, irrational, unreasoned, unthinking, unhesitating, involuntary, mechanical, automatic, reflex, knee-jerk, gut.

immediately /iméedeeətlee/ adv. & conj. ● adv. **1** without pause or delay. **2** without intermediary. ● conj. Brit. as soon as.

■ adv. **1** at once, without delay, instantly, instantaneously, promptly, right away, now, right now, here and now, this (very) instant, this second, this minute, forthwith, directly, straightaway, unhesitatingly, without hesitation, then and there, there and then, on the spot, without more ado, posthaste, tout de suite, in a wink, in a twinkle, in the twinkling of an eye, in two shakes of a lamb's tail, in short order; archaic or joc. instanter, colloq. p.d.q., before you can say Jack Robinson, pronto, in a jiffy, lickety-split. **2** direct(ly); closely, intimately; at first hand, from the

/.../ **pronunciation**	● **part of speech**
□ **phrases, idioms, and compounds**	
□□ **derivatives**	■ **synonym section**
cross-references appear in SMALL CAPITALS or italics	

horse's mouth. ● *conj.* as soon as, the (very) moment
or second *or* instant *or* minute (that), once, when,
colloq. directly.

immedicable /imédikəbəl/ *adj.* that cannot be healed or
cured. □□ **immedicably** *adv.* [L *immedicabilis* (as IN-[1], MED-
ICABLE)]

immemorial /ímimáwreeəl/ *adj.* **1** ancient beyond memory
or record. **2** very old. □□ **immemorially** *adv.* [med.L *im-
memorialis* (as IN-[1], MEMORIAL)]

immense /iméns/ *adj.* **1** immeasurably large or great; huge.
2 very great; considerable (*made an immense difference*). **3**
colloq. very good. □□ **immenseness** *n.* **immensity** *n.* [ME
f. F f. L *immensus* immeasurable (as IN-[1], *mensus* past part.
of *metiri* measure)]
■ **1** enormous, extensive, vast, huge, massive,
voluminous, tremendous, staggering, stupendous,
mammoth, monstrous, gargantuan, colossal, gigantic,
giant, titanic, cyclopean, elephantine, *colloq.* jumbo,
sl. humongous; see also GREAT 1a. **2** see CONSIDERABLE
1, 2. **3** see FANTASTIC 1.

immensely /iménslee/ *adv.* **1** very much (*enjoyed myself immensely*). **2** to an immense degree.
■ **1** see HIGHLY 1.

immerse /imə́rs/ *v.tr.* **1 a** (often foll. by *in*) dip; plunge. **b**
cause (a person) to be completely under water. **2** (often *refl.*
or in *passive*; often foll. by *in*) absorb or involve deeply. **3**
(often foll. by *in*) bury; embed. [L *immergere* (as IN-[2], *mergere*
mers- dip)]
■ **1** plunge, sink, submerge, dip, dunk, duck, douse,
souse, steep, imbue, soak, bathe, drown, flood, swamp.
2 absorb, involve, engross, engage, occupy, plunge,
sink, submerge, bury; (*immersed*) preoccupied,
wrapped up, engrossed, involved, absorbed. **3** bury,
embed, enclose, envelop, cover (up *or* over).

immersion /imə́rzhən, -shən/ *n.* **1** the act or an instance of
immersing; the process of being immersed. **2** baptism by
immersing the whole person in water. **3** mental absorption.
4 *Astron.* the disappearance of a celestial body behind another or in its shadow. □ **immersion heater** an electric
heater designed for direct immersion in a liquid to be
heated, esp. as a fixture in a hot-water tank. [ME f. LL
immersio (as IMMERSE)]
■ **1** see PLUNGE *n.*

immigrant /ímigrənt/ *n.* & *adj.* ● *n.* a person who immi-
grates. ● *adj.* **1** immigrating. **2** of or concerning immigrants.
■ *n.* newcomer, migrant, settler, arrival, *Brit.* incomer,
derog. offens. wetback; alien, foreigner, nonnative,
outlander, outsider. ● *adj.* **1** immigratory, migrant,
Brit. incoming. **2** (ethnic) minority, alien, foreign,
nonnative.

immigrate /ímigrayt/ *v.* **1** *intr.* come as a permanent resident
to a country other than one's native land. **2** *tr.* bring in (a
person) as an immigrant. □□ **immigration** /-gráyshən/ *n.*
immigratory *adj.* [L *immigrare* (as IN-[2], MIGRATE)]
■ **1** see MIGRATE.

imminent /íminənt/ *adj.* **1** (of an event, esp. danger) impending; about to happen. **2** *archaic* overhanging. □□ **imminence** /-nəns/ *n.* **imminently** *adv.* [L *imminēre immi-
nent-* overhang, project]
■ **1** impending, looming, threatening, menacing, at hand,
immediate, close *or* near at hand, forthcoming, coming,
approaching, nearing, drawing near *or* close *or* nigh, in
the offing, on the horizon, in the wind, upcoming,
archaic or dial. nigh. □□ **imminence** forthcomingness,
nearness, closeness, immediacy, immediateness; threat,
menace. **imminently** threateningly, menacingly; see
also SOON *adv.* 1.

immiscible /imísibəl/ *adj.* (often foll. by *with*) that cannot be
mixed. □□ **immiscibility** *n.* **immiscibly** *adv.* [LL *immis-
cibilis* (as IN-[1], MISCIBLE)]

immitigable /imítigəbəl/ *adj.* that cannot be mitigated.
□□ **immitigably** *adv.* [LL *immitigabilis* (as IN-[1], MITIGATE)]

immittance /imít'ns/ *n.* *Electr.* admittance or impedance
(when not distinguished). [*impedance* + ad*mittance*]

immixture /imíks-chər/ *n.* **1** the process of mixing up. **2** (often foll. by *in*) being involved.

immobile /imṓbəl, -beel, -bīl/ *adj.* **1** not moving. **2** not able
to move or be moved. □□ **immobility** /-bílitee/ *n.* [ME f.
OF f. L *immobilis* (as IN-[1], MOBILE)]
■ **1** see STATIC *adj.* **2** see *fixed* (FIX *v.* 20a).
□□ **immobility** see *inactivity* (INACTIVE).

immobilize /imṓbiliz/ *v.tr.* **1** make or keep immobile. **2** make
(a vehicle or troops) incapable of being moved. **3** keep (a
limb or patient) restricted in movement for healing purposes. **4** restrict the free movement of. **5** withdraw (coins)
from circulation to support paper currency. □□ **immobilization** *n.* **immobilizer** *n.* [F *immobiliser* (as IMMOBILE)]
■ **1** see FREEZE *v.* 6a, ARREST *v.* 2. **2** see INCAPACITATE 1.

immoderate /imódərət/ *adj.* excessive; lacking moderation.
□□ **immoderately** *adv.* **immoderateness** *n.* **immoderation** /-ráyshən/ *n.* [ME f. L *immoderatus* (as IN-[1], MODERATE)]
■ excessive, extreme, exorbitant, unreasonable,
inordinate, extravagant, profligate, intemperate,
outrageous, preposterous, exaggerated, overblown,
unrestrained, undue, *colloq.* over-the-top.
□□ **immoderately** see OVERLY. **immoderateness**,
immoderation see EXCESS *n.* 4a.

immodest /imódist/ *adj.* **1** lacking modesty; forward; impudent. **2** lacking due decency. □□ **immodestly** *adv.* **immodesty** *n.* [F *immodeste* or L *immodestus* (as IN-[1], MODEST)]
■ **1** brazen, forward, bold, impudent, impertinent, brash,
arrogant, insolent, presumptuous, disrespectful, brassy,
as bold as brass, cheeky, *colloq.* fresh. **2** indecent,
shameless, shameful, indecorous, undignified,
indelicate, improper, wanton, loose, unrestrained,
provocative, flaunting, promiscuous, brassy, obscene,
lewd, smutty, dirty, lascivious, bawdy, coarse.
□□ **immodesty** see PRESUMPTION 1, IMPROPRIETY 1.

immolate /íməlayt/ *v.tr.* **1** kill or offer as a sacrifice. **2** *literary*
sacrifice (a valued thing). □□ **immolation** /-láyshən/ *n.* **im-
molator** *n.* [L *immolare* sprinkle with sacrificial meal (as
IN-[2], *mola* MEAL[2])]
■ **1** see SACRIFICE *v.* 3. **2** see SACRIFICE *v.* 1.
□□ **immolation** see SACRIFICE *n.* 1a, 2a.

immoral /imáwrəl, imór-/ *adj.* **1** not conforming to accepted
standards of morality (cf. AMORAL). **2** morally wrong (esp.
in sexual matters). **3** depraved; dissolute. □□ **immorality**
/-álitee/ *n.* (*pl.* **-ies**). **immorally** *adv.*
■ **1** unacceptable, unethical, unprincipled, reprobate,
disgraceful, reprehensible, taboo, indecent,
disreputable, indecorous, indelicate. **2** corrupt, bad,
wicked, evil, iniquitous, sinful, impure, unprincipled,
abandoned, base, wrong, vile, depraved, dissolute,
degenerate, reprobate, unregenerate, nefarious,
flagitious, villainous, treacherous, unscrupulous,
dishonest. **3** depraved, dissolute, unprincipled,
debauched, indecent, immodest, wanton, libertine,
loose, promiscuous, lecherous, lustful, libidinous,
carnal, salacious, lubricious, licentious, lascivious,
lewd, obscene, pornographic, dirty, perverted, smutty,
filthy, *formal* concupiscent. □□ **immorality**
unacceptability, amorality, unprincipledness,
reprobation, reprehensibility; see also VICE[1] 1, 2.
immorally see BADLY 1, FAST[1] *adv.* 5.

immortal /imáwrt'l/ *adj.* & *n.* ● *adj.* **1 a** living for ever; not
mortal. **b** divine. **2** unfading; incorruptible. **3** likely or worthy to be famous for all time. ● *n.* **1 a** an immortal being.
b (in *pl.*) the gods of antiquity. **2** a person (esp. an author)
of enduring fame. **3** (**Immortal**) a member of the French
Academy. □□ **immortality** /-tálitee/ *n.* **immortalize** *v.tr.*
immortalization *n.* **immortally** *adv.* [ME f. L *immortalis*
(as IN-[1], MORTAL)]
■ *adj.* **1 a** undying, eternal, deathless, everlasting,
imperishable, never-ending, endless, ceaseless,
perpetual, timeless, constant, permanent,
indestructible, *rhet.* sempiternal. **b** divine, godlike,
deiform; heavenly, celestial, supernal, unearthly,
extramundane; spiritual, superhuman, supernatural,
transcendent. **2** unfading, perpetual, lasting, constant,

imperishable, indestructible, incorruptible, indissoluble, enduring, abiding, perennial, evergreen; stable, steady, immutable, durable, unfaltering, unwavering. **3** famous, glorious, renowned, legendary, celebrated, lauded, honored; timeless, classic. ● *n.* **1 a** god, goddess, deity, divinity; demigod, demiurge; spirit, numen, angel. **b** (*immortals*) gods, Olympians, *collect.* pantheon; *Rom. Hist.* lares, penates. **2** legend, great, genius, phenomenon, luminary, giant. □□ **immortality** deathlessness, everlastingness, imperishability, endlessness, ceaselessness, perpetuity, timelessness, constancy, permanence, indestructibility, incorruptibility, indissolubility, immutability, durability; divinity, deity, heavenliness, unearthliness, spirituality, transcendence; see also GLORY *n.* 1. **immortalize** make immortal, apotheosize, deify, canonize; exalt, glorify, celebrate, honor, beatify, ennoble, extol. **immortalization** apotheosis, deification, canonization; exaltation, glorification, beatification, extolment. **immortally** eternally, deathlessly, everlastingly, imperishably, endlessly, ceaselessly, perpetually, constantly, permanently, indestructibly, unfadingly, enduringly, unwaveringly; divinely, celestially, supernally, superhumanly, transcendently; timelessly, famously, gloriously, classically.

immortelle /ímáwrtél/ *n.* a composite flower of papery texture retaining its shape and color after being dried, esp. a helichrysum. [F, fem. of *immortel* IMMORTAL]

immovable /imṓvəbəl/ *adj. & n.* (also **immoveable**) ● *adj.* **1** that cannot be moved. **2** steadfast; unyielding. **3** emotionless. **4** not subject to change (*immovable law*). **5** motionless. **6** *Law* (of property) consisting of land, houses, etc. ● *n.* (in *pl.*) *Law* immovable property. □ **immovable feast** a religious feast day that occurs on the same date each year. □□ **immovability** *n.* **immovableness** *n.* **immovably** *adv.* ■ *adj.* **1** unmovable, fixed, fast, rooted, planted, grounded, anchored, moored, set, riveted, frozen, rigid, stiff, immobile, motionless, stationary, static, stable. **2** steadfast, staunch, unshakable, unswerving, firm, determined, rigid, unyielding, unbending, unwavering, resolute, unflinching, dogged, stubborn, inflexible, obdurate, adamant, adamantine, stony. **3** emotionless, unemotional, unmoved, unfeeling, impassive, unresponsive, unsympathetic, inexorable, hard-hearted, cold, hard as nails, steely, stony, coldhearted. **4** unchangeable, immutable, unalterable, changeless, unchanging, invariable, unvarying, incommutable, irreversible, irrevocable, inexorable, inflexible. **5** motionless, unmoving, stationary, static, still, stock-still, at a standstill; jammed, wedged, stuck (fast), solid (as a rock), fixed, tight, stiff.

immune /imyṓn/ *adj.* **1 a** (often foll. by *against, from, to*) protected against an infection owing to the presence of specific antibodies, or through inoculation or inherited or acquired resistance. **b** relating to immunity (*immune mechanism*). **2** (foll. by *from, to*) free or exempt from or not subject to (some undesirable factor or circumstance). □ **immune response** the reaction of the body to the introduction into it of an antigen. [ME f. L *immunis* exempt from public service or charge (as IN-¹, *munis* ready for service): sense 1 f. F *immun*] ■ **1 a** inoculated, vaccinated, immunized; resistant, protected, shielded. **2** (*immune to* or *from*) free from, exempt from, safe from, protected from or against, proof against, insusceptible *or* unsusceptible to, impervious to, untouched by, unaffected by, unconcerned by; not liable to, excused from, absolved from.

immunity /imyṓnitee/ *n.* (*pl.* **-ies**) **1** *Med.* the ability of an organism to resist infection, by means of the presence of circulating antibodies and white blood cells. **2** freedom or exemption from an obligation, penalty, or unfavorable circumstance. [ME f. L *immunitas* (as IMMUNE): sense 1 f. F *immunité*]

■ **1** resistance, insusceptibility, unsusceptibility, protection, safety. **2** freedom, exemption, nonliability, invulnerability, protection, safety, excuse, release, exclusion, privilege, indemnity, amnesty, exoneration, absolution.

immunize /ímyəniz/ *v.tr.* make immune, esp. to infection, usu. by inoculation. □□ **immunization** *n.* **immunizer** *n.*

immuno- /ímyənō/ *comb. form* immunity to infection.

immunoassay /ímyənō-ásay, imyṓ-/ *n. Biochem.* the determination of the presence or quantity of a substance, esp. a protein, through its properties as an antigen or antibody.

immunochemistry /imyənōkémistree, imyṓ-/ *n.* the chemistry of immune systems, esp. in mammalian tissues.

immunodeficiency /ímyənōdifíshənsee, imyṓ-/ *n.* a reduction in a person's normal immune defenses.

immunogenic /ímyənōjénik, imyṓ-/ *adj. Biochem.* of, relating to, or possessing the ability to elicit an immune response.

immunoglobulin /ímyənōglóbyəlin, imyṓ-/ *n. Biochem.* any of a group of structurally related proteins which function as antibodies.

immunology /imyənóləjee/ *n.* the scientific study of immunity. □□ **immunologic** /-nəlójik/ **immunological** /-nəlójikəl/ *adj.* **immunologically** *adv.* **immunologist** /-nóləjist/ *n.*

immunosuppressed /ímyənōsəprést, imyṓ-/ *adj.* (of an individual) rendered partially or completely unable to react immunologically.

immunosuppression /ímyənōsəpréshən, imyṓ-/ *n. Biochem.* the partial or complete suppression of the immune response of an individual, esp. to maintain the survival of an organ after a transplant operation. □□ **immunosuppressant** *n.*

immunosuppressive /ímyənōsəprésiv, imyṓ-/ *adj. & n.* ● *adj.* partially or completely suppressing the immune response of an individual. ● *n.* an immunosuppressive drug.

immunotherapy /ímyənōthérəpee, imyṓ-/ *n. Med.* the prevention or treatment of disease with substances that stimulate the immune response.

immure /imyṓr/ *v.tr.* **1** enclose within walls; imprison. **2** *refl.* shut oneself away. □□ **immurement** *n.* [F *emmurer* or med.L *immurare* (as IN-², *murus* wall)] ■ **1** see ENCLOSE 1, 6.

immutable /imyṓtəbəl/ *adj.* **1** unchangeable. **2** not subject to variation in different cases. □□ **immutability** /-bílitee/ *n.* **immutably** *adv.* [ME f. L *immutabilis* (as IN-¹, MUTABLE)] ■ **2** see CHANGELESS. □□ **immutability** see FINALITY.

imp /imp/ *n. & v.* ● *n.* **1** a mischievous child. **2** a small mischievous devil or sprite. ● *v.tr.* **1** add feathers to (the wing of a falcon) to restore or improve its flight. **2** *archaic* enlarge; add by grafting. [OE *impa, impe* young shoot, scion, *impian* graft: ult. f. Gk *emphutos* implanted, past part. of *emphuō*] ■ *n.* **1** urchin, gamin, gamine, mischief-maker, (little) devil, (little) horror, (young *or* little) monkey, brat, hellion, *archaic* jackanapes, *colloq.* scamp, *often joc.* rascal, *joc.* rogue. **2** devil, demon, sprite, elf, gnome, pixie, leprechaun, puck, brownie, fairy, troll, kobold, *literary* fay; evil spirit, hobgoblin, goblin, hob, bogey, gremlin, *archaic* bugbear.

impact *n. & v.* ● *n.* /ímpakt/ **1** (often foll. by *on, against*) the action of one body coming forcibly into contact with another. **2** an effect or influence, esp. when strong. ● *v.* /impákt/ **1** *tr.* (often foll. by *in, into*) press or fix firmly. **2** *tr.* (as **impacted** *adj.*) **a** (of a tooth) wedged between another tooth and the jaw. **b** (of a fractured bone) with the parts crushed together. **c** (of feces) lodged in the intestine. **3** *intr.* **a** (foll. by *against, on*) come forcibly into contact with a (larger) body or surface. **b** (foll. by *on*) have a pronounced effect. □□ **impaction** /-pákshən/ *n.* [L *impact-* part. stem of *impingere* IMPINGE]

/ . . . / **pronunciation** ● **part of speech**
□ **phrases, idioms, and compounds**
□□ **derivatives** ■ **synonym section**
cross-references appear in SMALL CAPITALS or *italics*

■ *n.* **1** collision, contact, percussion, crash, smash, bump, bang, thump, slam, smack, blow, *colloq.* whack. **2** effect, impression, influence, import, meaning, bearing, force, thrust, weight, burden, brunt, repercussions, result(s), consequence(s). ● *v.* **1** compress, press in, force in, push in, wedge in, ram in *or* down. **2 a** (**impacted**) wedged, wedged in, compressed, forced in, rammed in *or* down. **3b** (*impact on*) affect, influence, modify, alter, change. □□ **impaction** see PRESSURE *n.* 1a, b.

impair /impáir/ *v.tr.* damage or weaken. □□ **impairment** *n.* [ME *empeire* f. OF *empeirier* (as IN-², LL *pejorare* f. L *pejor* worse)]

■ damage, cripple, harm, hurt, injure, spoil, mar, ruin, wreck; weaken, lessen, debilitate, enfeeble, enervate, attenuate. □□ **impairment** damage, harm, injury, marring; weakening, enfeeblement, debilitation, undermining, worsening, deterioration; reduction, decrease, diminution.

impala /impáalə, -pálə/ *n.* (*pl.* same) a small antelope, *Aepyceros melampus*, of S. and E. Africa, capable of long high jumps. [Zulu]

impale /impáyl/ *v.tr.* **1** (foll. by *on, upon, with*) transfix or pierce with a sharp instrument. **2** *Heraldry* combine (two coats of arms) by placing them side by side on one shield separated by a vertical line down the middle. □□ **impalement** *n.* [F *empaler* or med.L *impalare* (as IN-¹, *palus* stake)]

■ **1** transfix, spear, skewer, spit, spike, stick, run through; stab, pierce, perforate, puncture, prick. □□ **impalement** transfixion; see also PUNCTURE *n.* 1.

impalpable /impálpəbəl/ *adj.* **1** not easily grasped by the mind; intangible. **2** imperceptible to the touch. **3** (of powder) very fine; not containing grains that can be felt. □□ **impalpability** /-bílitee/ *n.* **impalpably** *adv.* [F *impalpable* or LL *impalpabilis* (as IN-¹, PALPABLE)]

■ **1** see INTANGIBLE *adj.* 2. **2** see INSUBSTANTIAL 1.

impanel /impán'l/ *v.tr.* (also **empanel**) (**-paneled, -paneling**; esp. *Brit.* **-panelled, -panelling**) enroll or enter on a panel (those eligible for jury service). □□ **impanelment** *n.* [AF *empaneller* (as EN-¹, PANEL)].

impark /impáark/ *v.tr.* **1** enclose (animals) in a park. **2** enclose (land) for a park. [ME f. AF *enparker*, OF *emparquer* (as IN-², *parc* PARK)]

impart /impáart/ *v.tr.* (often foll. by *to*) **1** communicate (news, etc.). **2** give a share of (a thing). □□ **impartable** *adj.* **impartation** /impaartáyshən/ *n.* **impartment** *n.* [ME f. OF *impartir* f. L *impartire* (as IN-², *pars* part)]

■ **1** communicate, tell, relate, report, convey, transmit, pass on; reveal, divulge, disclose, confide; mention, intimate, hint, suggest. **2** give, donate, bestow, convey, confer, transfer, grant, cede, afford, award.

impartial /impáarshəl/ *adj.* treating all sides in a dispute, etc., equally; unprejudiced; fair. □□ **impartiality** /-sheeálitee/ *n.* **impartially** *adv.*

■ equitable, evenhanded, neutral, unbiased, objective, uncolored, unprejudiced, fair, fair-minded, just, true, honest; disinterested, dispassionate, detached, uninvolved. □□ **impartiality** see *objectivity* (OBJECTIVE). **impartially** see FAIRLY 1.

impassable /impásəbəl/ *adj.* that cannot be traversed. □□ **impassability** *n.* **impassableness** *n.* **impassably** *adv.*

■ see DENSE 1, INACCESSIBLE 1.

impasse /ímpas/ *n.* a position from which progress is impossible; deadlock. [F (as IN-¹, *passer* PASS¹)]

■ deadlock, dead end, stalemate, nonplus, cul-de-sac, blind alley, standoff, *colloq.* catch-22; corner, dilemma, predicament, double bind, *colloq.* fix, hole; block, blockage, standstill.

impassible /impásibəl/ *adj.* **1** impassive. **2** incapable of feeling or emotion. **3** incapable of suffering injury. **4** *Theol.* not subject to suffering. □□ **impassibility** *n.* **impassibleness** *n.* **impassibly** *adv.* [ME f. OF f. eccl.L *impassibilis* (as IN-¹, PASSIBLE)]

impassion /impáshən/ *v.tr.* fill with passion; arouse emotionally. [It. *impassionare* (as IN-², PASSION)]

■ see INSPIRE 1, 2.

impassioned /impáshənd/ *adj.* deeply felt; ardent (*an impassioned plea*).

■ passionate, soulful, vehement, heartfelt, earnest, sincere, honest, wholehearted, full-hearted, profound, deep; ardent, intense, animated, fiery, inflamed, glowing, heated, warm, spirited, vigorous, inspired, emotional, stirring, rousing, aroused, fervent, fervid, feverish, fevered, zealous, eager, enthusiastic.

impassive /impásiv/ *adj.* **1 a** deficient in or incapable of feeling emotion. **b** undisturbed by passion; serene. **2** without sensation. **3** not subject to suffering. □□ **impassively** *adv.* **impassiveness** *n.* **impassivity** /-sívitee/ *n.*

■ **1 a** unfeeling, emotionless, unemotional, stolid, callous, stony, impassible, hard-hearted, coldhearted, cold-blooded, cold, uncaring, unsympathetic, heartless. **b** dispassionate, passionless, unemotional, emotionless, cold, objective, indifferent, detached, nonchalant, insouciant, unconcerned, remote, aloof, reserved, apathetic, cool; serene, calm, unruffled, undisturbed, unmoved, composed, controlled, contained, stoic(al); imperturbable, unimpressionable, phlegmatic, stolid. **2** insensible, insensate, insentient, unfeeling, unconscious, lifeless, dead, inanimate, wooden, mechanical; numb, benumbed, anesthetized, paralyzed, torpid. **3** anesthetized, numb, benumbed, deadened, frozen, dulled, *Theol.* impassible. □□ **impassiveness, impassivity** see INDIFFERENCE 1.

impasto /impástō, -páas-/ *n. Art* **1** the process of laying on paint thickly. **2** this technique of painting. [It. *impastare* (as IN-², *pastare* paste)]

impatiens /impáyshənz/ *n.* any plant of the genus *Impatiens*, including several known popularly as touch-me-not. [mod.L f. IMPATIENT]

impatient /impáyshənt/ *adj.* **1 a** (often foll. by *at, with*) lacking patience or tolerance. **b** (of an action) showing a lack of patience. **2** (often foll. by *for*, or *to* + infin.) restlessly eager. **3** (foll. by *of*) intolerant. □□ **impatience** /-shəns/ *n.* **impatiently** *adv.* [ME f. OF f. L *impatiens* (as IN-¹, PATIENT)]

■ **1 a** curt, short, abrupt, waspish, brusque, snappish, intolerant, *colloq.* uptight; irritable, irascible, testy, quick-tempered, short-tempered, hot-tempered, querulous, peevish. **b** hasty, precipitate, abrupt, rash, impetuous, unconsidered, cursory, hurried, rushed, headlong. **2** restless, uneasy, nervous, fidgety, agitated, restive, unquiet, fretful, agog, chafing, expectant, *poet.* athirst; (*impatient to*) eager to, anxious to, keen to, itching to, dying to, longing to, yearning to. **3** (*impatient of*) intolerant of, prejudiced against, biased against, unforgiving of, disapproving of. □□ **impatience** curtness, shortness, abruptness, waspishness, brusqueness, snappishness, intolerance; irritability, irascibility, testiness, temper, querulousness, peevishness; haste, hastiness, rashness, impetuosity, precipitateness, cursoriness, hurriedness; restlessness, uneasiness, nervousness, restiveness, fretfulness, expectancy; anxiousness, anxiety, keenness, longing, yearning, desire; prejudice, bias, unforgivingness, disapproval. **impatiently** curtly, shortly, abruptly, waspishly, brusquely, snappishly, intolerantly, irritably, irascibly, testily, querulously, peevishly; hastily, rashly, impetuously, precipitately, cursorily, hurriedly, headlong, in a rush; unforgivingly, disapprovingly; keenly.

impeach /impéech/ *v.tr.* **1** charge (the holder of a public office) with misconduct. **2** *Brit.* charge with a crime against the government, esp. treason. **3** call in question; disparage (a person's integrity, etc.). □□ **impeachable** *adj.* **impeachment** *n.* [ME f. OF *empecher* impede f. LL *impedicare* entangle (as IN-², *pedica* fetter f. *pes pedis* foot)]

■ **1** accuse, charge, arraign, indict, incriminate, implicate, inculpate, blame, censure. **3** challenge, call into *or* in question, question, attack, assail, denounce, inveigh against, declaim against, disparage, discredit, impugn, deprecate, belittle, asperse, cast aspersions on, deplore, slander, malign, vilify. □□ **impeachable** chargeable, arraignable, indictable, censurable; questionable, challengeable, assailable, discreditable, impugnable, deplorable. **impeachment** see ACCUSATION, CHALLENGE n. 3.

impeccable /impékəbəl/ adj. **1** (of behavior, performance, etc.) faultless; exemplary. **2** not liable to sin. □□ **impeccability** n. **impeccably** adv. [L impeccabilis (as IN-¹, peccare sin)]
■ **1** faultless, flawless, perfect, errorless, unerring, exemplary, ideal, consummate, correct, Brit. colloq. spot on; proper, spotless, immaculate, unblemished, pure, unimpeachable, blameless. **2** blameless, sinless, pure, immaculate, irreproachable; innocent, chaste, virginal, virtuous, decent, proper.

impecunious /ímpikyŏŏneeəs/ adj. having little or no money. □□ **impecuniosity** /-neeósitee/ n. **impecuniousness** n. [IN-¹ + obs. pecunious having money f. L pecuniosus f. pecunia money f. pecu cattle]
■ see POOR 1. □□ **impecuniosity, impecuniousness** see POVERTY 1.

impedance /impeéd'ns/ n. **1** Electr. the total effective resistance of an electric circuit, etc., to alternating current, arising from ohmic resistance and reactance. **2** an analogous mechanical property. [IMPEDE + -ANCE]

impede /impeéd/ v.tr. retard by obstructing; hinder. [L impedire shackle the feet of (as IN-², pes foot)]
■ obstruct, bar, block, thwart, check, hinder, balk, inhibit, hamper, handicap, encumber, shackle, stymie, check, curb, brake, restrain, retard, slow (down), hold up, delay, foil, confound, frustrate, spike, stop, archaic or literary stay.

impediment /impédimənt/ n. **1** a hindrance or obstruction. **2** a defect in speech, e.g., a lisp or stammer. □□ **impedimental** /-mént'l/ adj. [ME f. L impedimentum (as IMPEDE)]
■ **1** hindrance, obstacle, inhibition, obstruction, bar, barrier, block, check, curb, restraint, encumbrance, restriction, stricture, hitch, snag, bottleneck, holdup, delay.

impedimenta /impédiméntə/ n.pl. **1** encumbrances. **2** traveling equipment, esp. of an army. [L, pl. of impedimentum: see IMPEDIMENT]
■ **2** see PARAPHERNALIA.

impel /impél/ v.tr. (**impelled, impelling**) **1** drive, force, or urge into action. **2** drive forward; propel. □□ **impellent** adj. & n. **impeller** n. [ME f. L impellere (as IN-², pellere puls- drive)]
■ **1** see FORCE¹ v. 1. **2** see PROPEL 1.

impend /impénd/ v.intr. **1** be about to happen. **2** (often foll. by over) **a** (of a danger) be threatening. **b** hang; be suspended. □□ **impending** adj. [L impendēre (as IN-², pendēre hang)]
■ **1** be imminent, be close or near (at hand), be forthcoming, be about to happen, approach, brew, be in view, be in prospect, be in store, be in the offing, be on the horizon, be in the air, be on the cards. **2 a** threaten, loom, menace, lower. **b** hang, overhang, dangle, be suspended, archaic poet. depend. □□ **impending** imminent, approaching, close or near (at hand), forthcoming, to come, in view, in prospect, in store, in the offing, on the horizon, in the air, on the cards; menacing.

impenetrable /impénitrəbəl/ adj. **1** that cannot be penetrated. **2** inscrutable; unfathomable. **3** inaccessible to ideas, influences, etc. **4** Physics (of matter) having the property such that a body is incapable of occupying the same place as another body at the same time. □□ **impenetrability** n. **impenetrableness** n. **impenetrably** adv. [ME f. F impénétrable f. L impenetrabilis (as IN-¹, PENETRATE)]
■ **1** see DENSE 1, resistant (RESIST). **2** see INCOMPREHENSIBLE. □□ **impenetrability, impenetrableness** see PERPLEXITY 3.

impenitent /impénit'nt/ adj. not repentant or penitent. □□ **impenitence** n. **impenitency** n. **impenitently** adv. [eccl.L impaenitens (as IN-¹, PENITENT)]

■ see UNREPENTANT.

imperative /impérətiv/ adj. & n. ● adj. **1** urgent. **2** obligatory. **3** commanding; peremptory. **4** Gram. (of a mood) expressing a command (e.g., come here!). ● n. **1** Gram. the imperative mood. **2** a command. □□ **imperatival** /-ətívəl/ adj. **imperatively** adv. **imperativeness** n. [LL imperativus f. imperare command (as IN-², parare make ready)]
■ adj. **1** urgent, pressing, exigent; important, compelling, serious, high-priority, vital, essential, colloq. disp. crucial. **2** obligatory, mandatory, compulsory, necessary, indispensable, essential, vital, colloq. disp. crucial; required, demanded, de rigueur. **3** imperious, commanding, magisterial, lordly, high-handed, autocratic, dictatorial, tyrannical, despotic, authoritarian, arbitrary, prescriptive, dogmatic; peremptory, overbearing, domineering, colloq. bossy. ● n. **2** see COMMAND n. 1. □□ **imperativeness** imperiousness, lordliness, authoritarianism, highhandedness, peremptoriness, prescriptiveness, colloq. bossiness; see also urgency (URGENT), NECESSITY 2, 3.

imperator /ímpəraáatawr/ n. Rom.Hist. commander (a title conferred under the Republic on a victorious general and under the Empire on the emperor). □□ **imperatorial** /impérətáwreeəl/ adj. [L (as IMPERATIVE)]

imperceptible /ímpərséptibəl/ adj. **1** that cannot be perceived. **2** very slight, gradual, or subtle. □□ **imperceptibility** n. **imperceptibly** adv. [F imperceptible or med.L imperceptibilis (as IN-¹, PERCEPTIBLE)]
■ **1** indiscernible, unnoticeable, invisible, inaudible, indistinguishable, undetectable, inappreciable; illdefined, obscure, unclear, vague, shadowy, faint, muted, muffled. **2** inconsiderable, insignificant, unnoticeable, insensible, slight, subtle, gradual; minute, tiny, minuscule, infinitesimal, microscopic.

impercipient /ímpərsípeeənt/ adj. lacking in perception. □□ **impercipience** /-əns/ n.

imperfect /impárfikt/ adj. & n. ● adj. **1** not fully formed or done; faulty; incomplete. **2** Gram. (of a tense) denoting a (usu. past) action in progress but not completed at the time in question (e.g., they were singing). **3** Mus. (of a cadence) ending on the dominant chord. ● n. the imperfect tense. □ **imperfect rhyme** Prosody a rhyme that only partly satisfies the usual criteria (e.g., love and move). □□ **imperfectly** adv. [ME imparfit, etc., f. OF imparfait f. L imperfectus (as IN-¹, PERFECT)]
■ adj. **1** incomplete, unfinished, unformed, undeveloped, immature, unready, crude, rudimentary, raw; deficient, wanting, patchy, defective, flawed, faulty, not working, out of order, inoperative, unserviceable. □□ **imperfectly** see sketchily (SKETCHY), WRONG adv.

imperfection /ímpərfékshən/ n. **1** incompleteness. **2 a** faultiness. **b** a fault or blemish. [ME f. OF imperfection or LL imperfectio (as IMPERFECT)]
■ **1** incompleteness, patchiness, rudimentariness; insufficiency, inadequacy, deficiency, shortfall. **2** faultiness, fault, fallibility, failing, error, deficiency, defect, flaw, blemish, shortcoming, foible, weak spot, frailty, infirmity, weakness, Achilles' heel.

imperfective /ímpərféktiv/ adj. & n. Gram. ● adj. (of a verb aspect, etc.) expressing an action without reference to its completion (opp. PERFECTIVE). ● n. an imperfective aspect or form of a verb.

imperforate /impárfərət/ adj. **1** not perforated. **2** Anat. lacking the normal opening. **3** (of a postage stamp) lacking perforations.

imperial /impeéreeəl/ adj. & n. ● adj. **1** of or characteristic of an empire or comparable sovereign state. **2 a** of or characteristic of an emperor. **b** supreme in authority. **c** majestic; august. **d** magnificent. **3** (of nonmetric weights and mea-

/.../ **pronunciation**	● **part of speech**
□ **phrases, idioms, and compounds**	
□□ **derivatives**	■ **synonym section**
cross-references appear in SMALL CAPITALS or italics	

sures) used or formerly used by statute in the UK (*imperial gallon*). ● *n.* a former size of paper, 30 x 22 inches (762 x 559 mm). □□ **imperially** *adv.* [ME f. OF f. L *imperialis* f. *imperium* command, authority]

■ *adj.* **1** sovereign, crown, monarchal, monarchic, monarchical, royal, dynastic. **2 a** imperatorial, royal, regal, sovereign, majestic, kingly, kinglike, queenly, queenlike, princely, princelike, aristocratic. **b** supreme, absolute, commanding, preeminent, predominant, paramount, ruling, dominant, authoritative. **c** majestic, stately, dignified, exalted, grand, imposing, august, venerable, impressive. **d** magnificent, splendid, grand, superb, excellent, awe-inspiring; sumptuous, luxurious, gorgeous, lavish, rich, fine. **3** UK, British; nonmetric, *Brit.* predecimal; avoirdupois. □□ **imperially** magnificently, splendidly, grandly, superbly, excellently, sumptuously, luxuriously, gorgeously, lavishly, richly, fabulously; imposingly, impressively, majestically, royally, regally.

imperialism /impéereeəlizəm/ *n.* **1** an imperial rule or system. **2** usu. *derog.* a policy of acquiring dependent territories or extending a country's influence through trade, diplomacy, etc. □□ **imperialistic** *adj.* **imperialistically** *adv.* **imperialize** *v.tr.*

imperialist /impéereeəlist / *n. & adj.* ● *n.* usu. *derog.* an advocate or agent of imperial rule or of imperialism. ● *adj.* of or relating to imperialism or imperialists.

imperil /impéril/ *v.tr.* (**imperiled**, **imperiling**; esp. *Brit.* **imperilled**, **imperilling**) bring or put into danger.
■ see ENDANGER.

imperious /impéereeəs/ *adj.* **1** overbearing; domineering. **2** urgent; imperative. □□ **imperiously** *adv.* **imperiousness** *n.* [L *imperiosus* f. *imperium* command, authority]
■ **1** see *domineering* (DOMINEER).

imperishable /impérishəbəl/ *adj.* that cannot perish. □□ **imperishability** *n.* **imperishableness** *n.* **imperishably** *adv.*
■ see IMMORTAL *adj.* 2, PERMANENT.

imperium /impéereeəm/ *n.* absolute power or authority. [L, = command, authority]

impermanent /impə́rmənənt/ *adj.* not permanent; transient. □□ **impermanence** /-nəns/ *n.* **impermanency** *n.* **impermanently** *adv.*
■ see TRANSIENT *adj.*

impermeable /impə́rmeeəbəl/ *adj.* **1** that cannot be penetrated. **2** *Physics* that does not permit the passage of fluids. □□ **impermeability** *n.* [F *imperméable* or LL *impermeabilis* (as IN-¹, PERMEABLE)]
■ **1** impenetrable, impassable, impervious, inaccessible; closed, sealed, vitrified, hermetic, airtight, watertight, waterproof, dampproof. □□ **impermeability** impenetrability, impassability, imperviousness, inaccessibility.

impermissible /impərmísibəl/ *adj.* not allowable. □□ **impermissibility** *n.*

impersonal /impə́rsənəl/ *adj.* **1** having no personality. **2** having no personal feeling or reference. **3** *Gram.* **a** (of a verb) used only with a formal subject (usu. *it*) and expressing an action not attributable to a definite subject (e.g., *it is snowing*). **b** (of a pronoun) = INDEFINITE. □□ **impersonality** /-álitee/ *n.* **impersonally** *adv.* [LL *impersonalis* (as IN-¹, PERSONAL)]
■ **1** mechanical, machinelike, wooden, rigid, stiff, starchy, stilted, stuffy, prim, formal, cold, unfriendly, cool, unemotional, matter-of-fact, detached, objective. **2** disinterested, dispassionate, detached, aloof, neutral, objective, fair, equitable, unprejudiced, unbiased.

impersonate /impə́rsənayt/ *v.tr.* **1** pretend to be (another person) for the purpose of entertainment or fraud. **2** act (a character). □□ **impersonation** /-náyshən/ *n.* **impersonator** *n.* [IN-² + L *persona* PERSON]
■ **2** see ACT *v.* 5a. □□ **impersonation** see IMPRESSION 3. **impersonator** see MIMIC *n.*

impertinent /impə́rt'nənt/ *adj.* **1** rude or insolent; lacking proper respect. **2** out of place; absurd. **3** esp. *Law* irrelevant;

intrusive. □□ **impertinence** /-nəns/ *n.* **impertinently** *adv.* [ME f. OF or LL *impertinens* (as IN-¹, PERTINENT)]
■ **1** presumptuous, impudent, insolent, disrespectful, discourteous, uncivil, impolite, rude, cheeky, saucy, pert, brassy, brazen, brash, immodest, forward, audacious, bold, nervy, *colloq.* fresh, lippy; see also TACTLESS. **2** absurd, incongruous, preposterous, illogical, irrational, nonsensical, laughable, silly. **3** see IRRELEVANT. □□ **impertinence** presumption, presumptuousness, impudence, insolence, disrespect, discourtesy, incivility, impoliteness, rudeness, cheek, sauciness, pertness, brassiness, brazenness, effrontery, nerve, brashness, immodesty, forwardness, audacity, boldness, *colloq.* brass, *sl.* chutzpah, gall; absurdity, incongruousness, illogicality, irrationality, outlandishness, silliness; see also *irrelevance* (IRRELEVANT).

imperturbable /impərtə́rbəbəl/ *adj.* not excitable; calm. □□ **imperturbability** *n.* **imperturbableness** *n.* **imperturbably** *adv.* [ME f. LL *imperturbabilis* (as IN-¹, PERTURB)]
■ see CALM *adj.* 2. □□ **imperturbability** see SELF-CONTROL.

impervious /impə́rveeəs/ *adj.* (usu. foll. by *to*) **1** not responsive to an argument, etc. **2** not affording passage to a fluid. □□ **imperviously** *adv.* **imperviousness** *n.* [L *impervius* (as IN-¹, PERVIOUS)]
■ **1** see UNAFFECTED 1. **2** impermeable, watertight, waterproof. □□ **imperviousness** see TOLERANCE 4.

impetigo /impitígō/ *n.* a contagious bacterial skin infection forming pustules and yellow crusty sores. □□ **impetiginous** /impitíjinəs/ *adj.* [ME f. L *impetigo -ginis* f. *impetere* assail]

impetuous /impéchōōəs/ *adj.* **1** acting or done rashly or with sudden energy. **2** moving forcefully or rapidly. □□ **impetuosity** /-ósitee/ *n.* **impetuously** *adv.* **impetuousness** *n.* [ME f. OF *impetueux* f. LL *impetuosus* (as IMPETUS)]
■ **1** sudden, hasty, abrupt, quick, precipitate, spontaneous, unpremeditated, impulsive, unplanned, unreflective, unthinking, unreasoned, rash, spur-of-the-moment, offhand, reckless, headlong. □□ **impetuosity**, **impetuousness** see HASTE *n.* 2. **impetuously** see *hastily* (HASTY).

impetus /impitəs/ *n.* **1** the force or energy with which a body moves. **2** a driving force or impulse. [L, = assault, force, f. *impetere* assail (as IN-², *petere* seek)]
■ **1** force, energy, momentum; propulsion, impulsion, motion. **2** impulse, drive, thrust, driving force, stimulus, push, goad, stimulation, incentive, motivation, encouragement, inducement, inspiration, spark; see also SPUR *n.* 2.

impi /impee/ *n.* (*pl.* **impies** or **impis**) *S.Afr.* **1** a band of armed men. **2** *hist.* an African tribal army or regiment. [Zulu, = regiment, armed band]

impiety /impíətee/ *n.* (*pl.* **-ies**) **1** a lack of piety or reverence. **2** an act, etc. showing this. [ME f. OF *impieté* or L *impietas* (as IN-¹, PIETY)]
■ see SACRILEGE.

impinge /impínj/ *v.tr.* (usu. foll. by *on*, *upon*) **1** make an impact; have an effect. **2** encroach. □□ **impingement** *n.* **impinger** *n.* [L *impingere* drive (a thing) at (as IN-², *pangere* fix, drive)]
■ **2** see INFRINGE 2.

impious /ímpeeəs, impí-/ *adj.* **1** not pious. **2** wicked; profane. □□ **impiously** *adv.* **impiousness** *n.* [L *impius* (as IN-¹, PIOUS)]
■ **1** irreligious, irreverent, unholy, ungodly, godless; sacrilegious, blasphemous. **2** profane, unholy, godless, wicked, sinful, evil, iniquitous, satanic, diabolic, diabolical, perverted, reprobate; see also IMMORAL 2. □□ **impiousness** ungodliness, unholiness, godlessness, irreligion, profanity, sacrilege, blasphemy; see also SIN¹ *n.* 1.

impish /ímpish/ *adj.* of or like an imp; mischievous. □□ **impishly** *adv.* **impishness** *n.*
■ see MISCHIEVOUS 1, 2. □□ **impishness** see MISCHIEF 1–3.

implacable /implákəbəl/ adj. that cannot be appeased; inexorable. □□ **implacability** n. **implacably** adv. [ME f. F *implacable* or L *implacabilis* (as IN-¹, PLACABLE)]
- unappeasable, irreconcilable, unforgiving, intractable, uncompromising, inflexible, inexorable, unyielding, unrelenting, relentless, hard, rigid, unsympathetic, ruthless, cruel, pitiless, merciless; see also MORTAL adj. 5.

implant v. & n. ● v.tr. /implánt/ **1** (often foll. by *in*) insert or fix. **2** (often foll. by *in*) instill (a principle, idea, etc.) in a person's mind. **3** plant. **4** *Med.* **a** insert (tissue, etc.) in a living body. **b** (in *passive*) (of a fertilized ovum) become attached to the wall of the womb. ● n. /implant/ **1** a thing implanted. **2** a thing implanted in the body, e.g., a piece of tissue or a capsule containing material for radium therapy. □□ **implantation** n. [F *implanter* or LL *implantare* engraft (as IN-², PLANT)]
- v. **1** insert, inlay, embed, fix, fasten, introduce, put, place, graft, engraft. **2** instill, introduce, sow, plant, insinuate, inject; inoculate, indoctrinate, inculcate, engrain, impress, imprint. **3** plant, transplant, root, embed, inlay, graft, engraft. ● n. insert, inlay, fixture; graft, scion, transplant. □□ **implantation** insertion, introduction; insinuation, injection, inoculation, indoctrination, inculcation, impression; transplantation.

implausible /impláwzibəl/ adj. not plausible. □□ **implausibility** n. **implausibly** adv.
- improbable, unplausible, unlikely, doubtful, dubious, questionable, debatable, equivocal, unbelievable, incredible, farcical, far-fetched, unconvincing, unreasonable, suspect, suspicious, sl. fishy.

implead /impleéd/ v.tr. *Law* **1** prosecute or take proceedings against (a person). **2** involve (a person, etc.) in a suit. [ME f. AF *empleder*, OF *empleidier* (as EN-¹, PLEAD)]

implement n. & v. ● n. /implimənt/ **1** a tool, instrument, or utensil. **2** (in *pl.*) equipment; articles of furniture, dress, etc. **3** *Law* performance of an obligation. ● v.tr. /impliment/ **1 a** put (a decision, plan, etc.) into effect. **b** fulfill (an undertaking). **2** complete (a contract, etc.). **3** fill up; supplement. □□ **implementation** n. [ME f. med.L *implementa* (pl.) f. *implēre* employ (as IN-², L *plēre plet-* fill)]
- n. **1** utensil, tool, instrument, apparatus, device, appliance, contrivance, mechanism, (piece of) equipment, gadget, *derog. or joc.* contraption. **2** (*implements*) equipment, machinery, gadgetry, paraphernalia, gear, tackle, kit, set. ● v. **1, 2** carry out, execute, accomplish, perform, complete, achieve, (put into) effect, bring about, cause, fulfill, realize. **3** supplement, add to, augment, increase; see also FILL v. 1. □□ **implementation** see EXECUTION 2, *fulfillment* (FULFILL).

implicate v. & n. ● v.tr. /implikayt/ **1** (often foll. by *in*) show (a person) to be concerned or involved (in a charge, crime, etc.). **2** (in *passive*; often foll. by *in*) be affected or involved. **3** lead to as a consequence or inference. ● n. /implikət/ a thing implied. □□ **implicative** /implikaytiv, implíkə-/ adj. **implicatively** adv. [L *implicatus* past part. of *implicare* (as IN-², *plicare, plicat-* or *plicit-* fold)]
- v. **1** incriminate, inculpate, connect, involve, embroil, associate, sl. frame; inform on, colloq. rat on, sl., finger, squeal on, Brit. sl. grass (on). **2** (*be implicated*) be involved in, be included in, be connected in, be associated in, be embroiled, be ensnared, be entrapped, be enmeshed, be entangled. **3** imply, entail, mean, necessitate; suggest, hint at, intimate. ● n. see IMPLICATION.
  □□ **implicative** incriminatory, inculpative, inculpatory; see also CIRCUMSTANTIAL 2.

implication /implikáyshən/ n. **1** what is involved in or implied by something else. **2** the act of implicating or implying. □ **by implication** by what is implied or suggested rather than by formal expression. [ME f. L *implicatio* (as IMPLICATE)]
- consequence, import, purport, meaning, inference, substance, essence, sense, significance, drift, pith, denotation, connotation, conclusion, implicate;

incrimination, inculpation, association, involvement, entanglement; entailment, suggestion, intimation, hint, insinuation, innuendo. □ **by implication** see *implicitly* (IMPLICIT).

implicit /implísit/ adj. **1** implied though not plainly expressed. **2** (often foll. by *in*) virtually contained. **3** absolute; unquestioning; unreserved (*implicit obedience*). **4** *Math.* (of a function) not expressed directly in terms of independent variables. □□ **implicitly** adv. **implicitness** n. [F *implicite* or L *implicitus* (as IMPLICATE)]
- **1** implied, indirect, inferrable, understood, unspoken, undeclared, tacit, inferential, latent. **2** inherent, intrinsic, underlying, basic, integral, built-in. **3** absolute, unquestioning, unquestioned, unqualified, total, whole, complete, sheer, outright, out-and-out, all-out, categorical, unmitigated, unalloyed, undiluted, unlimited, unconditional, unreserved, utter, perfect, full, wholehearted. □□ **implicitly** indirectly, by implication, impliedly, tacitly, inferentially, latently; inherently, intrinsically, integrally; absolutely, unquestioningly, totally, wholly, completely, unmitigatedly, unconditionally, unreservedly, categorically, utterly, fully, wholeheartedly.

implode /implṓd/ v.intr. & tr. burst or cause to burst inward. □□ **implosion** /-plṓzhən/ n. **implosive** /-plṓsiv/ adj. [IN-² f. L *-plodere*, after EXPLODE]

implore /impláwr/ v.tr. **1** (often foll. by *to* + infin.) entreat (a person). **2** beg earnestly for. □□ **imploring** adj. **imploringly** adv. [F *implorer* or L *implorare* invoke with tears (as IN-², *plorare* weep)]
- see BEG 2.

imply /implí/ v.tr. (**-ies, -ied**) **1** (often foll. by *that* + clause) strongly suggest the truth or existence of (a thing not expressly asserted). **2** insinuate; hint (*what are you implying?*). **3** signify. □□ **implied** adj. **impliedly** adv. [ME f. OF *emplier* f. L *implicare* (as IMPLICATE)]
- **1** entail, point to, indicate, suggest, implicate, mean, necessitate; *disp.* infer. **2** hint (at), intimate, insinuate, suggest, *disp.* infer; allude to, refer to. **3** signify, signal, indicate, mean, express, denote, connote, betoken; involve, entail, evidence, necessitate, assume, presume. □□ **implied** see IMPLICIT 1. **impliedly** see *implicitly* (IMPLICIT).

impolite /ímpəlít/ adj. (**impolitest**) ill-mannered; uncivil; rude. □□ **impolitely** adv. **impoliteness** n. [L *impolitus* (as IN-¹, POLITE)]
- ill-mannered, uncivil, rude, discourteous, disrespectful, impudent, insolent, boorish, crude, indecorous, indelicate, unrefined, ill-bred, vulgar, coarse, ungracious, ungentlemanly, unladylike, unchivalrous, impertinent, pert, saucy, brassy, cheeky, colloq. fresh, lippy. □□ **impoliteness** see DISRESPECT.

impolitic /impólitik/ adj. **1** inexpedient; unwise. **2** not politic. □□ **impoliticly** adv.
- **1** see FOOLISH. **2** see TACTLESS.

imponderable /impóndərəbəl/ adj. & n. ● adj. **1** that cannot be estimated or assessed in any definite way. **2** very light. **3** *Physics* having no weight. ● n. (usu. in *pl.*) something difficult or impossible to assess. □□ **imponderability** n. **imponderably** adv.
- adj. **1** immeasurable, inestimable, inconceivable, unthinkable, incomprehensible; subtle, tenuous, rarefied, abstract. **2** light (as a feather), unsubstantial, insubstantial, tenuous, weightless; airy, ethereal. ● n. see INTANGIBLE.

import v. & n. ● v.tr. /impáwrt, ím-/ **1** bring in (esp. foreign goods or services) to a country. **2** (often foll. by *that* + clause) **a** imply; indicate; signify. **b** express; make known. ● n. /impawrt/ **1** the process of importing. **2 a** an imported

/.../ **pronunciation**	● **part of speech**
□ **phrases, idioms, and compounds**	
□□ **derivatives**	■ **synonym section**
cross-references appear in SMALL CAPITALS or *italics*	

article or service. **b** (in *pl.*) an amount imported (*imports exceeded $50 billion*). **3** what is implied; meaning. **4** importance. □□ **importable** *adj.* **importation** *n.* **importer** /-páwrtər/ *n.* (all in sense 1 of *v.*). [ME f. L *importare* bring in, in med.L = imply, be of consequence (as IN-², *portare* carry)]

■ *v.* **1** bring *or* carry in, bring into the country, convey (in), introduce; buy from abroad, source from abroad; smuggle (in), run. **2** imply, mean, indicate, convey, denote, betoken, signify, signal, express, show, make known, state, communicate, put *or* get across. ● *n.* **1** importation, introduction. **2 b** (*imports*) foreign goods, imported goods *or* articles, foreigners. **3** meaning, sense, denotation, signification, gist, drift, thrust, intention, implication, implicate, purport, connotation, suggestion, intimation. **4** importance, significance, weight, consequence, moment, substance. □□ **importation** see IMPORT *n.* 1 above. **importer** introducer, buyer, dealer; smuggler.

importance /impáwrt'ns/ *n.* **1** the state of being important. **2** weight; significance. **3** personal consequence; dignity. [F f. med.L *importantia* (as IMPORT)]

■ **1** momentousness, weightiness, gravity, seriousness, effect, authority, status, greatness, prominence, preeminence, precedence, consequence; pretentiousness, pomposity, grandness. **2** significance, consequence, import, value, worth, weight, account, concern, moment, substance, matter. **3** eminence, distinction, esteem, standing, status, station, position, rank, dignity, prominence, preeminence, grandeur, prestige, power, influence, note, worth; self-importance, arrogance, pomposity.

important /impáwrt'nt/ *adj.* **1** (often foll. by *to*) of great effect or consequence; momentous. **2** (of a person) having high rank or status, or great authority. **3** pretentious; pompous. **4** (*absol.* in parenthetic construction) what is a more important point or matter (*they are willing and, more important, able*). ¶ Use of *importantly* here is *disp.* □□ **importantly** *adv.* (see note above). [F f. med.L (as IMPORT)]

■ **1** significant, consequential, critical, all-important, urgent, portentous, weighty, grave, serious, pressing, substantial, momentous, world-shaking, material, signal, *colloq. disp.* crucial, *disp.* vital. **2** leading, prominent, notable, noted, noteworthy, worthy, eminent, distinguished, respected, high-ranking, top-level, high-level, superior, outstanding, foremost, conspicuous; impressive, influential, well-connected, powerful, formidable, mighty. **3** pretentious, pompous, consequential, grand, arrogant; see also *self-important* (SELF-IMPORTANCE).

importunate /impáwrchənət/ *adj.* **1** making persistent or pressing requests. **2** (of affairs) urgent. □□ **importunately** *adv.* **importunity** /-tŏŏnətee, -tyŏŏ-/ *n.* [L *importunus* inconvenient (as IN-¹, *portunus* f. *portus* harbor)]

■ **1** see INSISTENT 1. □□ **importunity** see *urgency* (URGENT).

importune /impáwrtŏŏn, -tyŏŏn, impáwrchən/ *v.tr.* **1** solicit (a person) pressingly. **2** solicit for an immoral purpose. [F *importuner* or med.L *importunari* (as IMPORTUNATE)]

■ **1** see SOLICIT 1, 2. **2** see SOLICIT 3.

impose /impóz/ *v.* **1** *tr.* (often foll. by *on, upon*) require (a tax, duty, charge, or obligation) to be paid or undertaken (by a person, etc.). **2** *tr.* enforce compliance with. **3** *intr.* & *refl.* (foll. by *on, upon,* or *absol.*) demand the attention or commitment of (a person); take advantage of (*I do not want to impose on you any longer; I did not want to impose*). **4** *tr.* (often foll. by *on, upon*) palm (a thing) off on (a person). **5** *tr. Printing* lay (pages of type) in the proper order ready for printing. **6** *intr.* (foll. by *on, upon*) exert influence by an impressive character or appearance. **7** *intr.* (often foll. by *on, upon*) practice deception. **8** *tr. archaic* (foll. by *upon*) place (a thing). [ME f. F *imposer* f. L *imponere imposit-* inflict, deceive (as IN-², *ponere* put)]

■ **1, 2** enjoin, prescribe, dictate, enforce, demand, require, saddle a person with, burden a person with;

administer, set, place, put, lay, *often joc.* inflict; (*impose a tax*) exact *or* levy *or* raise a tax. **3** (*impose on* or *upon*) take advantage of, exploit, force *or* foist oneself (up)on, presume (up)on, put upon, put a person out, *often joc.* inflict oneself (up)on; intrude (up)on, inconvenience, interrupt, trouble, bother, disturb, discommode, take up a person's time, *colloq.* hassle. **4** thrust, force, foist, palm off, fob off, *often joc.* inflict. **6** (*impose on* or *upon*) impress, make an impression on, have *or* exert an influence on, influence, persuade, convince. **7** see DISSIMULATE.

imposing /impózing/ *adj.* impressive or formidable, esp. in appearance. □□ **imposingly** *adv.* **imposingness** *n.*
■ see IMPRESSIVE 1.

imposition /ímpəzíshən/ *n.* **1** the act or an instance of imposing; the process of being imposed. **2** an unfair or resented demand or burden. **3** a tax or duty. **4** *Brit.* work set as a punishment at school. [ME f. OF *imposition* or L *impositio* f. *imponere*: see IMPOSE]

■ **1** enjoinment, prescription, dictation, infliction, enforcement, requirement, demand; administration, application, introduction. **2** demand, burden, onus, weight, trial, hardship, cross, affliction, oppression; intrusion, inconvenience, disturbance, bother, nuisance, *colloq.* hassle. **3** taxation, exaction, tax, duty, levy, tithe, charge.

impossibility /impósibílitee/ *n.* (*pl.* **-ies**) **1** the fact or condition of being impossible. **2** an impossible thing or circumstance. [F *impossibilité* or L *impossibilitas* (as IMPOSSIBLE)]

impossible /impósibəl/ *adj.* **1** not possible; that cannot be done, occur, or exist (*it is impossible to alter them; such a thing is impossible*). **2** (loosely) not easy; not convenient; not easily believable. **3** *colloq.* (of a person or thing) outrageous; intolerable. □□ **impossibly** *adv.* [ME f. OF *impossible* or L *impossibilis* (as IN-¹, POSSIBLE)]

■ **1** unrealizable, unattainable, impracticable, unworkable, infeasible, unfeasible, unresolvable, unsolvable, out of the question, impractical; self-contradictory, paradoxical, illogical, unreasonable, inconsistent, inconceivable, fantastic, unimaginable, unthinkable, absurd, nonsensical, ludicrous, preposterous, crazy. **2** difficult, problematic, problematical, awkward, inconvenient, inopportune, inexpedient, disruptive, troublesome, bothersome; unbelievable, implausible, unconvincing, far-fetched, improbable, unlikely, doubtful, dubious, questionable, debatable. **3** intolerable, unbearable, insupportable, unsupportable, unendurable, insufferable, unacceptable, unmanageable, impracticable; outrageous, absurd, preposterous, ridiculous, outlandish, crazy, weird, outré. □□ **impossibly** paradoxically, illogically, unreasonably, inconsistently, inconceivably, unimaginably, unthinkably, absurdly, nonsensically, ludicrously, preposterously, crazily; unattainably, unachievably, impracticably, unworkably; difficultly, problematically, awkwardly, inconveniently, inopportunely, inexpediently, disruptively, troublesomely; unbelievably, implausibly, unconvincingly, improbably, doubtfully, dubiously, questionably, debatably; intolerably, unbearably, insupportably, unsupportably, unendurably, insufferably, unacceptably, outrageously, ridiculously, outlandishly, weirdly.

impost¹ /ímpōst/ *n.* **1** a tax; duty; tribute. **2** a weight carried by a horse in a handicap race. [F f. med.L *impost-* part. stem of L *imponere*: see IMPOSE]
■ **1** see TAX *n.* 1.

impost² /ímpōst/ *n.* the upper course of a pillar, carrying an arch. [F *imposte* or It. *imposta* fem. past part. of *imporre* f. L *imponere*: see IMPOSE]

impostor /impóstər/ *n.* (also **imposter**) **1** a person who assumes a false character or pretends to be someone else. **2** a swindler. □□ **impostorous** *adj.* **impostrous** *adj.* [F *imposteur* f. LL *impostor* (as IMPOST¹)]
■ **1** impersonator, personator, humbug, fraud, phony,

Austral. bunyip. **2** swindler, deceiver, trickster, cheat, fraud, confidence man, mountebank, charlatan, hypocrite, humbug, flimflammer, four-flusher, *colloq.* shark, *sl.* con man, *Austral. sl.* illywhacker.

imposture /impós-chər/ *n.* the act or an instance of fraudulent deception. [F f. LL *impostura* (as IMPOST¹)]
■ see DECEIT.

impotent /ímpət'nt/ *adj.* **1 a** powerless; lacking all strength. **b** helpless. **c** ineffective. **2 a** (esp. of a male) unable, esp. for a prolonged period, to achieve a sexual erection or orgasm. **b** *colloq.* unable to procreate; infertile. □□ **impotence** /-t'ns/ *n.* **impotency** *n.* **impotently** *adv.* [ME f. OF f. L *impotens* (as IN-¹, POTENT¹)]
■ **1 a, b** weak, powerless, impuissant, enervated, enfeebled, spent, wasted, decrepit, debilitated, exhausted, worn out, effete, *colloq.* all in, *Brit. sl.* knackered; helpless, palsied, frail, feeble. **c** inadequate, ineffective, ineffectual, inept, incompetent, useless. **2 b** sterile, barren, infertile. □□ **impotence, impotency** weakness, powerlessness, impuissance, enervation, enfeeblement, wasting, decrepitude, debilitation, exhaustion, effeteness; helplessness, frailty, feebleness, inadequacy, inefficacy, ineffectualness, ineffectiveness, ineptness, incompetence; sterility, infertility.

impound /impównd/ *v.tr.* **1** confiscate. **2** take possession of. **3** shut up (animals) in a pound. **4** shut up (a person or thing) as in a pound. **5** (of a dam, etc.) collect or confine (water). □□ **impoundable** *adj.* **impounder** *n.* **impoundment** *n.*
■ **1, 2** see CONFISCATE. **3, 4** see PEN² *v.*

impoverish /impóvərish/ *v.tr.* (often as **impoverished** *adj.*) **1** make poor. **2** exhaust the strength or natural fertility of. □□ **impoverishment** *n.* [ME f. OF *empoverir* (as EN-¹, *povre* POOR)]
■ **1** see RUIN *v.* 1a; (**impoverished**) destitute, poor, poverty-stricken, penurious, beggared, needy, necessitous, impecunious, in desperate *or* dire straits, straitened, in distress, badly off, bankrupt, insolvent, ruined, (financially) embarrassed, stone-broke; *colloq.* (dead *or* flat) broke, pinched, up against it, on one's uppers, short, strapped (for cash), *Brit. sl.* skint. **2** see WEAKEN 1; (**impoverished**) stripped, barren, desolate, wasted, empty, depleted, denuded, drained, exhausted. □□ **impoverishment** see LOSS 3.

impracticable /impráktikəbəl/ *adj.* **1** impossible in practice. **2** (of a road, etc.) impassable. **3** (of a person or thing) unmanageable. □□ **impracticability** /-bílitee/ *n.* **impracticableness** *n.* **impracticably** *adv.*
■ **1** see IMPOSSIBLE 1. **2** impassable, impenetrable, inaccessible, closed, shut, blocked, barred, obstructed, clogged (up), jammed. **3** see IMPOSSIBLE 3.

impractical /impráktikəl/ *adj.* **1** not practical. **2** not practicable. □□ **impracticality** /-kálitee/ *n.* **impractically** *adv.*
■ **1** theoretical, idealistic, abstract, speculative, academic, doctrinaire, unrealistic, unpractical; unworldly, otherworldly, visionary, romantic, quixotic, *colloq.* starry-eyed, esp. *Brit. colloq.* airy-fairy, *sl.* crackpot; ineffective, ineffectual, useless, hopeless, vain. **2** see IMPOSSIBLE. □□ **impracticality** idealism, speculativeness, unworldliness, romanticism, quixotism, quixotry, ineffectuality, ineffectualness, ineffectiveness, uselessness; see also *madness* (MAD).

imprecate /ímprikayt/ *v.tr.* (often foll. by *upon*) invoke; call down (evil). □□ **imprecatory** /-kətáwree/ *adj.* [L *imprecari* (as IN-², *precari* pray)]
■ see SWEAR *v.* 4.

imprecation /ímprikáyshən/ *n.* **1** a spoken curse; a malediction. **2** imprecating.
■ **1** see CURSE *n.* 1.

imprecise /ímprisís/ *adj.* not precise. □□ **imprecisely** *adv.* **impreciseness** *n.* **imprecision** /-sízhən/ *n.*
■ inexact, inaccurate, inexplicit, indefinite, ill-defined, indistinct, vague, hazy, cloudy, blurred, fuzzy, woolly, ambiguous; incorrect, wrong, erroneous, wide of the mark, out, untrue, improper, mistaken, fallacious, false.

□□ **impreciseness, imprecision** inexactitude, inexactness, inaccuracy, inexplicitness, indefiniteness, indistinctness, vagueness, haziness, cloudiness, fuzziness, woolliness, ambiguity; incorrectness, wrongness, erroneousness, error, mistakenness, mistake, fallaciousness, fallacy, falseness, falsehood.

impregnable¹ /imprégnəbəl/ *adj.* **1** (of a fortified position) that cannot be taken by force. **2** resistant to attack or criticism. □□ **impregnability** /-bílitee/ *n.* **impregnably** *adv.* [ME f. OF *imprenable* (as IN-¹, *prendre* take)]
■ impenetrable, unassailable, well-fortified, thick-skinned, watertight, resistant, tenable; inviolable, invulnerable, invincible, unconquerable, unbeatable, insuperable, indomitable, immune, safe, secure; strong, stout, sturdy, staunch, solid, stable. □□ **impregnability** impenetrability, unassailability, unassailableness, resistance, tenability; inviolability, invulnerability, invincibility, unconquerableness, indomitability, indomitableness, immunity, safety, security.

impregnable² /imprégnəbəl/ *adj.* that can be impregnated.

impregnate /imprégnayt/ *v. & adj.* ● *v.tr.* **1** (often foll. by *with*) fill or saturate. **2** (often foll. by *with*) imbue; fill (with feelings, moral qualities, etc.). **3 a** make (a female) pregnant. **b** *Biol.* fertilize (a female reproductive cell or ovum). ● *adj.* also /-nət/ **1** pregnant. **2** (often foll. by *with*) permeated. □□ **impregnation** /-náyshən/ *n.* [LL *impregnare impregnat-* (as IN-², *pregnare* be pregnant)]
■ *v.* **1, 2** saturate, drench, soak, steep, permeate, penetrate, pervade, fill, suffuse, infuse, imbue. **3** fertilize, inseminate, fecundate, make pregnant, *archaic* get with child, get in an interesting *or* delicate condition, *colloq.* get in trouble *or* in the family way, *sl.* knock up, *Brit. sl.* put *or* get in the (pudding) club. ● *adj.* **1** see PREGNANT 1. □□ **impregnation** saturation, permeation, permeance, penetration, pervasion, suffusion, infusion; fertilization, insemination, fecundation.

impresario /ímprisáareeō, -sáir-/ *n.* (*pl.* **-os**) an organizer of public entertainments, esp. the manager of an operatic, theatrical, *or* concert company. [It. f. *impresa* undertaking]

imprescriptible /ímpriskríptibəl/ *adj. Law* (of rights) that cannot be taken away by prescription or lapse of time. [med.L *imprescriptibilis* (as IN-¹, PRESCRIBE)]
■ see INALIENABLE.

impress¹ *v. & n.* ● *v.tr.* /imprés/ **1** (often foll. by *with*) **a** affect or influence deeply. **b** evoke a favorable opinion or reaction from (a person) (*was most impressed with your efforts*). **2** (often foll. by *on*) emphasize (an idea, etc.) (*must impress on you the need to be prompt*). **3** (often foll. by *on*) **a** imprint or stamp. **b** apply (a mark, etc.) with pressure. **4** make a mark or design on (a thing) with a stamp, seal, etc. **5** *Electr.* apply (voltage, etc.) from outside. ● *n.* /ímpres/ **1** the act or an instance of impressing. **2** a mark made by a seal, stamp, etc. **3** a characteristic mark or quality. **4** = IMPRESSION 1. □□ **impressible** /-présibəl/ *adj.* [ME f. OF *empresser* (as EN-¹, PRESS¹)]
■ *v.* **1 a** affect, touch, move, reach, stir, strike, sway, influence, persuade, convince, *sl.* grab. **b** (*impressed with*) struck by *or* with, taken with, *sl.* grabbed by. **2** stress, emphasize, underline, bring home, draw a person's attention to. **3, 4** stamp, mark, imprint, print, engrave, emboss. ● *n.* **1** see IMPRESSION 4. **2** see STAMP *n.* 2, 4. **3** see STAMP *n.* 6a. □□ **impressible** see IMPRESSIONABLE.

impress² /imprés/ *v.tr. hist.* **1** force (men) to serve in the army or navy. **2** seize (goods, etc.) for public service. □□ **impressment** *n.* [IN-² + PRESS²]

impression /impréshən/ *n.* **1** an effect produced (esp. on the mind or feelings). **2** a notion or belief (esp. a vague or mis-

741

taken one) (*my impression is they are afraid*). **3** an imitation of a person or sound, esp. done to entertain. **4 a** the impressing of a mark. **b** a mark impressed. **5** an unaltered reprint from standing type or plates (esp. as distinct from *edition*). **6 a** the number of copies of a book, newspaper, etc., issued at one time. **b** the printing of these. **7** a print taken from a wood engraving. **8** *Dentistry* a negative copy of the teeth or mouth made by pressing them into a soft substance. □□ **impressional** *adj.* [ME f. OF f. L *impressio -onis* f. *imprimere impress-* (as IN-², PRESS¹)]

■ **1** sensation, feeling, sense, perception, awareness, consciousness; impact, effect, influence. **2** notion, belief, conception, idea, fancy, feeling, suspicion, hunch. **3** impersonation, imitation, parody, satire, *colloq.* takeoff, send-up. **4** stamp, impress, brand, mark; dent, indentation, depression, hollow. **5** printing, reprinting, reprint; copy. **6** issue, print, run, print run.

impressionable /impréshənəbəl/ *adj.* easily influenced; susceptible to impressions. □□ **impressionability** /-bílitee/ *n.* **impressionably** *adv.* [F *impressionnable* f. *impressionner* (as IMPRESSION)]

■ suggestible, susceptible, susceptive, persuadable, persuasible, convincible, receptive, responsive, impressible; soft, pliable, malleable, moldable.

impressionism /impréshənizəm/ *n.* **1** a style or movement in art concerned with expression of feeling by visual impression, esp. from the effect of light on objects. **2** a style of music or writing that seeks to describe a feeling or experience rather than achieve accurate depiction or systematic structure. □□ **impressionist** *n.* [F *impressionnisme* (after *Impression*: *Soleil levant*, title of a painting by Monet, 1872)]

impressionistic /impréshənístik/ *adj.* **1** in the style of impressionism. **2** subjective; unsystematic. □□ **impressionistically** *adv.*

impressive /imprésiv/ *adj.* **1** impressing the mind or senses, esp. so as to cause approval or admiration. **2** (of language, a scene, etc.) tending to excite deep feeling. □□ **impressively** *adv.* **impressiveness** *n.*

■ **1** imposing, formidable, awesome, awe-inspiring, portentous, redoubtable, powerful, striking; grand, august, dignified, stately, majestic, magnificent. **2** evocative, moving, affecting, stimulating, exciting, stirring, powerful, provocative, arousing, emotional. □□ **impressively** imposingly, formidably, awesomely, awe-inspiringly, redoubtably, powerfully, commandingly, augustly, grandly, majestically, magnificently; evocatively, movingly, affectingly, stimulatingly, excitingly, stirringly, provocatively, arousingly, emotionally. **impressiveness** imposingness, formidableness, awesomeness, power, dignity, stateliness, augustness, grandness, grandeur, majesty, magnificence; evocativeness, excitingness, provocativeness, emotion.

imprest /ímprest/ *n.* money advanced to a person, esp. for use in government business. [orig. *in prest* f. OF *prest* loan, advance pay: see PRESS²]

imprimatur /ímprimaátər, -máytər, -to͞or/ *n.* **1** *RC Ch.* an official license to print (an ecclesiastical or religious book, etc.). **2** official approval. [L, = let it be printed]

■ **2** see APPROVAL.

imprimatura /impréeməto͞orə/ *n.* (in painting) a colored transparent glaze as a primer. [It. *imprimitura* f. *imprimere* IMPRESS¹]

imprint *v. & n.* ● *v.tr.* /imprínt/ **1** (often foll. by *on*) impress or establish firmly, esp. on the mind. **2 a** (often foll. by *on*) make a stamp or impression of (a figure, etc.) on a thing. **b** make an impression on (a thing) with a stamp, etc. ● *n.* /ímprint/ **1** an impression or stamp. **2** the printer's or publisher's name and other details printed in a book. [ME f. OF *empreinter empreint* f. L *imprimere*: see IMPRESSION]

■ *v.* **2** see STAMP *v.* 2. ● *n.* **1** see IMPRESSION 4.

imprinting /imprínting/ *n.* **1** in senses of IMPRINT *v.* **2** *Zool.* the development in a young animal of a pattern of recognition and trust for its own species.

imprison /imprízən/ *v.tr.* **1** put into prison. **2** confine; shut

up. □□ **imprisonment** *n.* [ME f. OF *emprisoner* (as EN-¹, PRISON)]

■ **1** incarcerate, detain, remand, jail, lock up *or* away, intern, shut up, put behind bars, put away, put inside, put in *or* throw into irons, send up, *Brit.* send down, *poet.* prison, *sl.* jug, esp. *Brit. sl.* lag. **2** confine, shut in *or* up, block in *or* up, box in *or* up, hem in, circumscribe, immure, intern, impound, cloister, constrain, restrain, restrict, coop (up), cabin, mew (up), cage, encage, chain, fetter, trammel, *Brit.* gate. □□ **imprisonment** incarceration, detention, remand, internment, custody, *archaic* durance, *hist.* penal servitude, *sl.* time; confinement, circumscription, immurement, impoundment, constraint, restraint, restriction.

improbable /impróbəbəl/ *adj.* **1** not likely to be true or to happen. **2** difficult to believe. □□ **improbability** *n.* **improbably** *adv.* [F *improbable* or L *improbabilis* (as IN-¹, PROBABLE)]

■ **1** unlikely, doubtful, dubious, in doubt, questionable, debatable, unrealistic, unimaginable, unthinkable, inconceivable, impossible. **2** see IMPLAUSIBLE.

improbity /impróbitee/ *n.* (*pl.* **-ies**) **1** wickedness; lack of moral integrity. **2** dishonesty. **3** a wicked or dishonest act. [L *improbitas* (as IN-¹, PROBITY)]

impromptu /imprómpto͞o, -tyo͞o/ *adj., adv., & n.* ● *adj. & adv.* extempore; unrehearsed. ● *n.* **1** an extempore performance or speech. **2** a short piece of usu. solo instrumental music, often songlike. [F f. L *in promptu* in readiness: see PROMPT]

■ *adj. & adv.* see EXTEMPORANEOUS *adj.*

improper /imprópər/ *adj.* **1 a** unseemly; indecent. **b** not in accordance with accepted rules of behavior. **2** inaccurate; wrong. **3** not properly so called. □ **improper fraction** a fraction in which the numerator is greater than or equal to the denominator. □□ **improperly** *adv.* [F *impropre* or L *improprius* (as IN-¹, PROPER)]

■ **1 a** unseemly, unbecoming, untoward; indecent, indecorous, unladylike, ungentlemanly, indelicate, immodest, impolite, injudicious, indiscreet, tactless, rude, suggestive, risqué, blue, off color. **b** impolite, unacceptable, unsuitable, inappropriate, unfitting, unbefitting, incongruous, infelicitous, inapplicable, inapt, inapposite, malapropos, out of keeping, out of place, uncalled-for. **2** wrong, mistaken, erroneous, false, incorrect, inaccurate, inexact, imprecise, amiss, faulty, untrue; irregular, abnormal. **3** wrongly-named, miscalled, misnamed, so-called, nominal, spurious.

impropriate /impróʼpreeayt/ *v.tr. Brit.* **1** annex (an ecclesiastical benefice) to a corporation or person as property. **2** place (tithes or ecclesiastical property) in lay hands. □□ **impropriation** /-áyshən/ *n.* [AL *impropriare* (as IN-², *proprius* own)]

impropriator /impróʼpreeaytər/ *n. Brit.* a person to whom a benefice is impropriated.

impropriety /imprəprʼəee/ *n.* (*pl.* **-ies**) **1** lack of propriety; indecency. **2** an instance of improper conduct, etc. **3** incorrectness. **4** unfitness. [F *impropriété* or L *improprietas* (as IN-¹, *proprius* proper)]

■ **1** unseemliness, untowardness, indecorousness, indecorum, bad *or* poor taste, indelicacy, immodesty, impudicity, suggestiveness, indecency, immorality, sinfulness, wickedness, lewdness, lasciviousness. **2** gaffe, gaucherie, faux pas, slip, blunder, mistake, error. **3** incorrectness, erroneousness, falsity, falseness, inaccuracy, inaccurateness, inexactitude, inexactness, imprecision, impreciseness, irregularity, abnormality. **4** unfitness, unsuitableness, unsuitability, inappropriateness, inaptness, inaptitude, unaptness, inapplicability, infelicity, infelicitousness, incongruity, incongruousness, incompatibility, inopportuneness.

improvable /impro͞ovəbəl/ *adj.* **1** that can be improved. **2** suitable for cultivation. □□ **improvability** /-bílitee/ *n.*

improve /impro͞ov/ *v.* **1 a** *tr.* & *intr.* make or become better. **b** *intr.* (foll. by *on*, *upon*) produce something better than. **2**

absol. (as **improving** *adj.*) giving moral benefit (*improving literature*). [orig. *emprowe, improwe* f. AF *emprower* f. OF *emprou* f. *prou* profit, infl. by PROVE]

■ **1 a** better, upgrade, enhance, polish (up), refine, elaborate, add to, lift, develop, extend, increase, advance, heighten, intensify, perfect, *literary* meliorate, *formal* ameliorate; amend, repair, mend, put *or* set right, reform, recast, revise, revamp, refurbish, recondition, overhaul, renovate, modernize, update, remodel, retouch, touch up, give a new lease on (*or Brit.* of) life; redress, rectify, correct, emend, alter, edit; get better, pick up, look up, take a turn for the better, *Brit. colloq.* be on the up and up; recover, recuperate, revive, convalesce, rally, make progress, progress, come on, be on the upgrade, thrive, prosper, gain strength *or* ground, turn over a new leaf. **b** (*improve on* or *upon*) better, surpass, beat, exceed, excel, efface, eclipse, cap, *colloq.* best. **2** (**improving**) edifying, instructive, uplifting, regenerative, beneficial, salutary, healthy; heartwarming.

improvement /imprŏovmənt/ *n.* **1** the act or an instance of improving or being improved. **2** something that improves, esp. an addition or alteration that adds to value. **3** something that has been improved. [ME f. AF *emprowement* (as IMPROVE)]

■ **1, 2** betterment, enhancement, refinement, elaboration, development, extension, addition, increase, intensification, lift, *formal* amelioration; amendment, repair, reform, revision, revamp, refurbishment, overhaul, renovation, modernization, update, touch-up; rectification, correction, emendation, alteration; recovery, recuperation, convalescence, rally, progress. **3** advance, progression, change (for the better), breakthrough, upgrade.

improver /imprŏovər/ *n.* **1** a person who improves. **2** *Brit.* a person who works for low wages while acquiring skill and experience in a trade.

improvident /imprŏvid'nt/ *adj.* **1** lacking foresight or care for the future. **2** not frugal; thriftless. **3** heedless; incautious. □□ **improvidence** /-d'ns/ *n.* **improvidently** *adv.*

■ **1, 3** imprudent, injudicious, indiscreet, incautious, unwary, shortsighted, myopic, nearsighted; rash, impetuous, hasty, impulsive, reckless, heedless, careless, unthinking, unmindful, headlong. **2** thriftless, unthrifty, spendthrift, uneconomical, wasteful, profligate, prodigal, extravagant, lavish, profuse, penny-wise and pound-foolish. □□ **improvidence** see *imprudence* (IMPRUDENT), EXTRAVAGANCE 1.

improvise /ímprəviz/ *v.tr.* (also *absol.*) **1** compose or perform (music, verse, etc.) extempore. **2** provide or construct (a thing) extempore. □□ **improvisation** /-izáyshən/ *n.* **improvisational** *adj.* **improvisatorial** /impróvizətáwreeəl/ *adj.* **improvisatory** *adj.* **improviser** *n.* [F *improviser* or It. *improvvisare* f. *improvviso* extempore, f. L *improvisus* past part. (as IN-[1], PROVIDE)]

■ **1** ad lib, extemporize, vamp, scat, play (it) by ear, *colloq.* jam. **2** invent, concoct, devise, contrive, make up, throw together. □□ **improvisation** ad lib, extemporization, impromptu, happening, vamp, scat, *colloq.* jam (session); invention, concoction, device, contrivance; makeshift, lash-up, stopgap. **improvisational, improvisatorial, improvisatory** ad lib, extempore, extemporaneous, impromptu, unrehearsed, unprepared, *colloq.* off the cuff; made-up, thrown together, makeshift, stopgap, drumhead.

imprudent /improod'nt/ *adj.* rash; indiscreet. □□ **imprudence** /-d'ns/ *n.* **imprudently** *adv.* [ME f. L *imprudens* (as IN-[1], PRUDENT)]

■ rash, hasty, reckless, heedless, precipitate, unthinking, impulsive, incautious, inconsiderate, impetuous, improvident, indiscreet, injudicious, irresponsible, ill-judged, ill-considered, ill-advised, unadvised, inadvisable, unwise, impolitic, inexpedient, careless, foolish, foolhardy, inane, silly, perverse, wrong, wrongheaded, harebrained, mad, *colloq.* crazy, insane,

esp. *Brit. colloq.* daft. □□ **imprudence** indiscretion, injudiciousness, incautiousness, unguardedness, unwariness, improvidence, rashness, recklessness, audacity, boldness, temerity, impulsiveness, hastiness, haste, impetuousness, impetuosity, thoughtlessness, insensitivity, tactlessness, heedlessness, carelessness, naïveté, foolishness, foolhardiness, folly.

impudent /ímpyəd'nt/ *adj.* **1** insolently disrespectful; impertinent. **2** shamelessly presumptuous. **3** unblushing. □□ **impudence** /-d'ns/ *n.* **impudently** *adv.* [ME f. L *impudens* (as IN-[1], *pudēre* be ashamed)]

■ **1, 2** insolent, disrespectful, contemptuous, insulting, contumelious, ill-mannered, uncivil, discourteous, rude, impolite, impertinent, pert, saucy, brassy, cheeky, cocky, cocksure, nervy, *colloq.* fresh, lippy; arrogant, presumptuous, audacious, bold, brazen, brash, forward, immodest, *colloq.* pushy. **3** unblushing, unabashed, unashamed, shameless, immodest; blatant, flagrant, barefaced. □□ **impudence** insolence, disrespect, contempt, contumely, incivility, discourtesy, rudeness, impoliteness, impertinence, pertness, sauciness, brass, effrontery, cheek, cockiness, *colloq.* nerve, sauce, *sl.* chutzpah, gall; arrogance, presumption, presumptuousness, audacity, boldness, brazenness, brashness, forwardness, barefacedness, immodesty, shamelessness, *colloq.* pushiness; back talk, *colloq.* lip, mouth, *Austral. & NZ colloq.* hide, *Brit. colloq.* backchat.

impudicity /ímpyədísitee/ *n.* shamelessness; immodesty. [F *impudicité* f. L *impudicus* (as IMPUDENT)]

impugn /impyŏon/ *v.tr.* challenge or call in question (a statement, action, etc.). □□ **impugnable** *adj.* **impugnment** *n.* [ME f. L *impugnare* assail (as IN-[2], *pugnare* fight)]

■ see CHALLENGE *v.* 2.

impuissant /impyŏoisənt, impyŏo-ís-, impwís-/ *adj.* impotent; weak. □□ **impuissance** /-səns/ *n.* [F (as IN-[1], PUISSANT)]

■ see FEEBLE 1, 2.

impulse /ímpuls/ *n.* **1** the act or an instance of impelling; a push. **2** an impetus. **3** *Physics* **a** an indefinitely large force acting for a very short time but producing a finite change of momentum (e.g., the blow of a hammer). **b** the change of momentum produced by this or any force. **4** a wave of excitation in a nerve. **5** mental incitement. **6** a sudden desire or tendency to act without reflection (*did it on impulse*). □ **impulse buying** the unpremeditated buying of goods as a result of a whim or impulse. [L *impulsus* (as IMPEL)]

■ **1** see PUSH *n.* 1. **2** see IMPETUS 2. **5** see *incitation*, *incitement* (INCITE). **6** see FANCY *n.* 2.

impulsion /impúlshən/ *n.* **1** the act or an instance of impelling. **2** a mental impulse. **3** impetus. [ME f. OF f. L *impulsio -onis* (as IMPEL)]

impulsive /impúlsiv/ *adj.* **1** (of a person or conduct, etc.) apt to be affected or determined by sudden impulse. **2** tending to impel. **3** *Physics* acting as an impulse. □□ **impulsively** *adv.* **impulsiveness** *n.* [ME f. F *impulsif -ive* or LL *impulsivus* (as IMPULSION)]

■ **1** impetuous, spontaneous, spur-of-the-moment, snap, instinctive, involuntary, unthinking, unpremeditated, unplanned, unreasoned, unconsidered, extemporaneous, *Mus.* capriccioso; unpredictable, irregular, capricious; quick, sudden, immediate, precipitate, abrupt, hasty, rash, headlong, reckless, devil-may-care, madcap, wild, foolhardy. □□ **impulsively** impetuously, instinctively, spontaneously, unpredictably, capriciously; see also *hastily* (HASTY). **impulsiveness** impetuousness, impetuosity, spontaneity, unthinkingness;

/.../ **pronunciation**	● **part of speech**
□ **phrases, idioms, and compounds**	
□□ **derivatives**	■ **synonym section**
cross-references appear in SMALL CAPITALS or *italics*	

unpredictableness, unpredictability, capriciousness, caprice; see also HASTE *n.* 2.

impunity /impyŏŏnitee/ *n.* exemption from punishment or from the injurious consequences of an action. □ **with impunity** without having to suffer the normal injurious consequences (of an action). [L *impunitas* f. *impunis* (as IN-¹, *poena* penalty)]

■ see *exemption* (EXEMPT).

impure /impyŏŏr/ *adj.* **1** mixed with foreign matter; adulterated. **2 a** dirty. **b** ceremonially unclean. **3** unchaste. **4** (of a color) mixed with another color. □□ **impurely** *adv.* **impureness** *n.* [ME f. L *impurus* (as IN-¹, *purus* pure)]

■ **1** mixed, admixed, alloyed, base, debased, adulterated, cut. **2 a** see DIRTY *adj.* 1. **b** unclean, unhallowed, forbidden, disallowed, *Judaism* tref, not kosher. **3** unchaste, immoral, sinful, wicked, evil, vile, unvirtuous, unvirginal, corrupted, defiled, debased, vitiated, degenerate, depraved, loose, wanton, lustful, promiscuous, libidinous, dissolute, licentious, obscene, prurient, dirty, filthy, lubricious, salacious, lascivious, lewd, lecherous. □□ **impureness** see IMPURITY 1.

impurity /impyŏŏritee/ *n.* (*pl.* **-ies**) **1** the quality or condition of being impure. **2** an impure thing or constituent. [F *impurité* or L *impuritas* (as IMPURE)]

■ **1** impureness, baseness, adulteration, pollution, contamination, defilement; uncleanness, dirtiness, foulness, filthiness, muckiness, griminess, squalidness, sordidness, *colloq.* crumminess, *Brit. sl.* grottiness; unchasteness, unchastity, immorality, sinfulness, wickedness, evil, vileness, corruption, degeneration, depravity, looseness, wantonness, lust, lustfulness, promiscuity, promiscuousness, libidinousness, dissoluteness, licentiousness, obscenity, prurience, lubricity, salaciousness, lasciviousness, lewdness, lecherousness. **2** adulterant, admixture, contaminant, pollutant, foreign matter *or* body; see also DIRT *n.* 1.

impute /impyŏŏt/ *v.tr.* (foll. by *to*) **1** regard (esp. something undesirable) as being done or caused or possessed by. **2** *Theol.* ascribe (righteousness, guilt, etc.) to (a person) by virtue of a similar quality in another. □□ **imputable** *adj.* **imputation** *n.* **imputative** /-tətiv/ *adj.* [ME f. OF *imputer* f. L *imputare* enter in the account (as IN-², *putare* reckon)]

■ **1** (*impute to*) ascribe to, blame on, assign to, attribute to, put *or* set down to, lay on, lay at the door of. □□ **imputable** assignable, attributable, ascribable. **imputation** ascription, attribution, blame.

imshi /imshee/ *int. Austral. colloq.* be off! [colloq. (Egyptian) Arabic]

IN *abbr.* Indiana (in official postal use).

In *symb. Chem.* the element indium.

in /in/ *prep., adv.,* & *adj.* ● *prep.* **1** expressing inclusion or position within limits of space, time, circumstance, etc. (*in Nebraska*; *in bed*; *in the rain*). **2** during the time of (*in the night*; *in 1989*). **3** within the time of (*will be back in two hours*). **4 a** with respect to (*blind in one eye*; *good in parts*). **b** as a kind of (*the latest thing in luxury*). **5** as a proportionate part of (*one in three failed*; *a gradient of one in six*). **6** with the form or arrangement of (*packed in tens*; *falling in folds*). **7** as a member of (*in the army*). **8** concerned with (*is in politics*). **9** as or regarding the content of (*there is something in what you say*). **10** within the ability of (*does he have it in him?*). **11** having the condition of; affected by (*in bad health*; *in danger*). **12** having as a purpose (*in search of*; *in reply to*). **13** by means of or using as material (*drawn in pencil*; *modeled in bronze*). **14 a** using as the language of expression (*written in French*). **b** (of music) having as its key (*symphony in C*). **15** (of a word) having as a beginning or ending (*words beginning in un-*). **16** wearing as dress (*in blue*; *in a suit*). **17** with the identity of (*found a friend in Mary*). **18** (of an animal) pregnant with (*in calf*). **19** into (with a verb of motion or change: *put it in the box*; *cut it in two*). **20** introducing an indirect object after a verb (*believe in*; *engage in*; *share in*). **21** forming adverbial phrases (*in any case*; *in reality*; *in short*). ● *adv.* expressing position within limits, or motion to such a position: **1** into a room, house, etc. (*come in*). **2** at home, in

one's office, etc. (*is not in*). **3** so as to be enclosed or confined (*locked in*). **4** in a publication (*is the advertisement in?*). **5** in or to the inward side (*rub it in*). **6 a** in fashion, season, or office (*long skirts are in*; *strawberries are not yet in*). **b** elected (*the Democrat got in*). **7** exerting favorable action or influence (*their luck was in*). **8** *Cricket* (of a player or side) batting. **9** (of transport) at the platform, etc. (*the train is in*). **10** (of a season, harvest, order, etc.) having arrived or been received. **11** *Brit.* (of a fire) continuing to burn. **12** denoting effective action (*join in*). **13** (of the tide) at the highest point. **14** (in *comb.*) *colloq.* denoting prolonged or concerted action, esp. by large numbers (*sit-in*; *teach-in*). ● *adj.* **1** internal; living in; inside (*in-patient*). **2** fashionable; esoteric (*the in thing to do*). **3** confined to or shared by a group of people (*in-joke*). □ **in all** see ALL. **in at** present at; contributing to (*in at the kill*). **in between** see BETWEEN *adv.* **in-between** *attrib.adj. colloq.* intermediate (*at an in-between stage*). **in-box** a tray for documents, letters, etc., awaiting attention. **in for 1** about to undergo (esp. something unpleasant). **2** competing in or for. **3** involved in; committed to. **in on** sharing in; privy to (a secret, etc.). **ins and outs** (often foll. by *of*) all the details (of a procedure, etc.). **in that** because; in so far as. **in with** on good terms with. [OE *in, inn,* orig. as *adv.* with verbs of motion]

■ *prep.* **16** see WEAR¹ *v.* 1. ● *adv.* **6 a** see FASHIONABLE. □ **in-between** see INTERMEDIATE. **in on** see PRIVY *adj.* 1. **ins and outs** see ROPE *n.* 3a. **in with** on good terms with, en rapport with, tuned in to.

in. *abbr.* inch(es).

in-¹ /in/ *prefix* (also **il-, im-, ir-**) added to: **1** adjectives, meaning 'not' (*inedible*; *insane*). **2** nouns, meaning 'without; lacking' (*inaction*). [L]

in-² /in/ *prefix* (also **il-** before *l*, **im-** before *b, m, p*, **ir-** before *r*) in, on, into, toward, within (*induce*; *influx*; *insight*; *intrude*). [IN, or from or after L *in* in IN *prep.*]

-in /in/ *suffix Chem.* forming names of: **1** neutral substances (*gelatin*). **2** antibiotics (*penicillin*). [-INE⁴]

-ina /éenə/ *suffix* denoting: **1** feminine names and titles (*Georgina*; *tsarina*). **2** names of musical instruments (*concertina*). **3** names of zoological classification categories (*globigerina*). [It. or Sp. or L]

inability /ínəbílitee/ *n.* **1** the state of being unable. **2** a lack of power or means.

■ incapacity, incapability, disability, incompetence, impotence, powerlessness, helplessness, *Med.* insufficiency.

in absentia /ín absénshə/ *adv.* in (his, her, or their) absence. [L]

inaccessible /ínaksésibəl/ *adj.* **1** not accessible; that cannot be reached. **2** (of a person) not open to advances or influence; unapproachable. □□ **inaccessibility** *n.* **inaccessibleness** *n.* **inaccessibly** *adv.* [ME f. F *inaccessible* or LL *inaccessibilis* (as IN-¹, ACCESSIBLE)]

■ **1** unreachable, unapproachable, impenetrable, impassable, out of the way, beyond reach, out of reach, off the beaten track, remote, secluded, sequestered, rockbound, *colloq.* ungetatable; exclusive, restricted, select. **2** unreachable, unobtainable, unavailable; see also UNAPPROACHABLE 2. □□ **inaccessibility, inaccessibleness** unreachableness, unapproachability, unapproachableness, impenetrability, impassability, impassableness, remoteness, seclusion, sequestration; exclusivity, exclusiveness, restrictedness, selectness; unavailability, distance, aloofness, reserve, standoffishness, unfriendliness, coolness, coldness, frigidity.

inaccurate /ínákyərət/ *adj.* not accurate. □□ **inaccuracy** *n.* (*pl.* **-ies**). **inaccurately** *adv.*

■ inexact, imprecise, incorrect, erroneous, mistaken, wrong, false, untrue, fallacious, faulty, flawed, imperfect, improper, amiss, awry, out, off target, not on target, wide of the mark, *colloq.* off beam; careless, loose, sloppy, scrappy, scratchy, slapdash, slipshod, casual. □□ **inaccuracy** carelessness, looseness, sloppiness, scrappiness, scratchiness, casualness; see also *impreciseness* (IMPRECISE), ERROR 1.

inaction /inákshən/ n. **1** lack of action. **2** sluggishness; inertness.
■ **1** see *inactivity* (INACTIVE). **2** see *idleness* (IDLE).

inactivate /ináktivayt/ v.tr. make inactive or inoperative.
□□ **inactivation** /-váyshən/ n.
■ see INCAPACITATE 1.

inactive /ináktiv/ adj. **1** not active or inclined to act. **2** passive. **3** indolent. □□ **inactively** adv. **inactivity** /-tívitee/ n.
■ **1, 2** passive, unmoving, inert, motionless, immobile, immobilized, still, stationary, stagnant, static, lifeless, inanimate, dormant, abeyant, in abeyance, resting, supine; idle, nonfunctioning, inoperative, unoccupied, unemployed, jobless, out of work, out of a job; see also QUIET adj. 1. **3** indolent, lazy, idle, slothful, shiftless, fainéant, sluggish, listless, torpid, lethargic, lackadaisical, languid. □□ **inactivity** inaction, passiveness, passivity, motionlessness, immobility, stillness, stasis, stagnancy, inertia, inertness, lifelessness, inanimation; dormancy, hibernation, *Zool.* estivation; idleness, unemployment, joblessness; indolence, laziness, sloth, shiftlessness, sluggishness, listlessness, torpor, torpidity, lethargy, languidness; see also QUIET n. 1.

inadequate /inádikwət/ adj. (often foll. by *to*) **1** not adequate; insufficient. **2** (of a person) incompetent; unable to deal with a situation. □□ **inadequacy** /-kwəsee/ n. (pl. **-ies**). **inadequately** adv.
■ **1** unsatisfactory, unacceptable, no good, not good enough, imperfect, incomplete, deficient, deprived, defective, flawed, faulty, bad, poor, pathetic, meager, faint, slender, slight, scanty, sparse, skimpy, incommensurate; insufficient, not enough, too little, scarce, (in) short (supply). **2** incompetent, incapable, unqualified, inapt, unapt, impotent, powerless, useless, hopeless, inept, helpless, terrible, *sl. offens.* spastic. □□ **inadequacy** unsatisfactoriness, unacceptableness, imperfection, incompleteness, deficiency, defectiveness, flaw, fault, faultiness, poorness, poverty, meagerness, faintness, scantiness, sparseness, skimpiness, insufficiency, scarcity; see also *incompetence* (INCOMPETENT).

inadmissible /inədmísibəl/ adj. that cannot be admitted or allowed. □□ **inadmissibility** n. **inadmissibly** adv.
■ impermissible, unallowable, disallowed, unacceptable, intolerable, unendurable, exceptionable, objectionable, inapplicable, inappropriate, unsuitable, improper, illegitimate, invalid, incorrect, wrong, forbidden, prohibited.

inadvertent /inədvért'nt/ adj. **1** (of an action) unintentional. **2 a** not properly attentive. **b** negligent. □□ **inadvertence** /-t'ns/ n. **inadvertency** n. **inadvertently** adv. [IN-¹ + obs. *advertent* attentive (as ADVERT²)]
■ **1** unintentional, unintended, unpremeditated, unthinking, unwitting, unconscious, unplanned, unstudied, undesigned, uncalculated, *colloq.* off-the-cuff; accidental, chance. **2** inattentive, unobservant, unwary, unaware, unmindful, unheeding, unheedful, heedless, preoccupied, distracted, oblivious, negligent, forgetful, careless; see also ABSENTMINDED. □□ **inadvertence, inadvertency** unthinkingness, unwittingness, inattentiveness, unwariness, unawareness, unmindfulness, heedlessness, preoccupation, distraction, obliviousness, negligence, forgetfulness, carelessness; see also *absentmindedness* (ABSENTMINDED). **inadvertently** see *by accident* (ACCIDENT), *absentmindedly* (ABSENTMINDED).

inadvisable /inədvízəbəl/ adj. not advisable. □□ **inadvisability** n. [ADVISABLE]
■ see *ill-advised* 2 (ILL).

inalienable /ináyleeənəbəl/ adj. that cannot be transferred to another; not alienable. □□ **inalienability** n. **inalienably** adv.
■ untransferable, nontransferable, nonnegotiable;

inviolable, sacrosanct, unchallengeable, absolute, inherent, *Law* unalienable, imprescriptible, entailed, *literary* indefeasible.

inalterable /ináwltərəbəl/ adj. not alterable; that cannot be changed. □□ **inalterability** /-bílitee/ n. **inalterably** adv. [med.L *inalterabilis* (as IN-¹, *alterabilis* alterable)]

inamorato /ináməraátō/ n. (pl. **-os**; fem. **inamorata** /-tə/) a lover. [It., past part. of *inamorare* enamor (as IN-², *amore* f. L *amor* love)]

inane /ináyn/ adj. **1** silly; senseless. **2** empty; void. □□ **inanely** adv. **inaneness** n. **inanity** /-ánitee/ n. (pl. **-ies**). [L *inanis* empty, vain]
■ **1** silly, asinine, vacuous, absurd, fatuous, empty-headed, foolish, witless, pointless, senseless, nonsensical, unreasonable, preposterous, ludicrous, ridiculous, laughable, risible, mad, lunatic, stupid, idiotic, *colloq.* dopey, crazy, moronic, imbecilic, dumb, cretinous, dotty, esp. *Brit. colloq.* daft, *sl.* goofy, screwy, cracked, nutty, nuts, daffy, batty, dippy, wacky, cuckoo, kooky, loony, bonkers, *Brit. sl.* barmy, crackers. **2** empty, void, vacant, unfilled, hollow, vacuous.

inanimate /inánimət/ adj. **1** not animate; not endowed with (esp. animal) life. **2** lifeless; showing no sign of life. **3** spiritless; dull. □ **inanimate nature** everything other than the animal world. □□ **inanimately** adv. **inanimation** /-máyshən/ n. [LL *inanimatus* (as IN-¹, ANIMATE)]
■ **1** lifeless, insentient, dead, defunct; inorganic, nonorganic, mineral. **2** lifeless, exanimate, inert, inactive, motionless, immobile, unmoving, still. **3** spiritless, soulless, lifeless, cold, dead; flat, flaccid, dull, vapid, sluggish, slow, listless, torpid, inactive.

inanition /inəníshən/ n. emptiness, esp. exhaustion from lack of nourishment. [ME f. LL *inanitio* f. L *inanire* make empty (as INANE)]

inappellable /inəpéləbəl/ adj. that cannot be appealed against. [obs.F *inappelable* (as IN-¹, *appeler* APPEAL)]

inapplicable /ináplikəbəl, inəplík-/ adj. (often foll. by *to*) not applicable; unsuitable. □□ **inapplicability** n. **inapplicably** adv.
■ irrelevant, unrelated, unconnected, extraneous, beside the point, wide of or beside or off the mark, malapropos, impertinent; inappropriate, unsuitable, unsuited, inapt, inapposite.

inapposite /inápəzit/ adj. not apposite; out of place. □□ **inappositely** adv. **inappositeness** n.
■ see INAPPROPRIATE.

inappreciable /inəpreéshəbəl/ adj. **1** imperceptible; not worth reckoning. **2** that cannot be appreciated. □□ **inappreciably** adv.
■ **1** see IMPERCEPTIBLE 2.

inappreciation /inəpreesheeáyshən/ n. failure to appreciate. □□ **inappreciative** /-preéshətiv, -shee-áy-/ adj.

inappropriate /inəprópreeət/ adj. not appropriate. □□ **inappropriately** adv. **inappropriateness** n.
■ unsuitable, unsuited, unfitting, unbefitting, inapt, inapposite, out of keeping, incongruous, infelicitous, inopportune, untimely, irrelevant, inapplicable, malapropos, extraneous.

inapt /inápt/ adj. **1** not apt or suitable. **2** unskillful. □□ **inaptitude** n. **inaptly** adv. **inaptness** n.
■ **1** see INAPPROPRIATE. □□ **inaptitude, inaptness** see IMPROPRIETY 4.

inarch /inaárch/ v.tr. graft (a plant) by connecting a growing branch without separation from the parent stock. [IN-² + ARCH¹ v.]

inarguable /inaárgyōōəbəl/ adj. that cannot be argued about or disputed. □□ **inarguably** adv.

inarticulate /inaartíkyələt/ adj. **1** unable to speak distinctly

---

/.../ **pronunciation**	● **part of speech**
□ **phrases, idioms, and compounds**	
□□ **derivatives**	■ **synonym section**
cross-references appear in SMALL CAPITALS or *italics*	

or express oneself clearly. **2** (of speech) not articulate; indistinctly pronounced. **3** dumb. **4** esp. *Anat.* not jointed. □□ **inarticulately** *adv.* **inarticulateness** *n.* [LL *inarticulatus* (as IN-¹, ARTICULATE)]

■ **1** unclear, incomprehensible, unintelligible, incoherent, confused, muddled, mixed-up, jumbled, wild, irrational, illogical, disjointed, discursive, rambling, unconnected, digressive. **2** mumbled, muttered, murmurous, indistinct, unclear, unintelligible, muffled, blurred, garbled, scrambled, faltering, halting, jerky. **3** dumb, mute, voiceless, silent; speechless, tongue-tied, dumbstruck, dumbfounded, lost *or* at a loss for words.

inartistic /ínaartístik/ *adj.* **1** not following the principles of art. **2** lacking skill or talent in art; not appreciating art. □□ **inartistically** *adv.*

■ **1** see RUDE 3. **2** see UNGRACEFUL. □□ **inartistically** see BADLY 1.

inasmuch /ínəzmúch/ *adv.* (foll. by *as*) **1** since; because. **2** to the extent that. [ME, orig. *in as much*]

■ **1** (*inasmuch as*) see BECAUSE.

inattentive /ínətténtiv/ *adj.* **1** not paying due attention; heedless. **2** neglecting to show courtesy. □□ **inattention** *n.* **inattentively** *adv.* **inattentiveness** *n.*

■ heedless, careless, unthinking, unmindful, incautious, unwary, unguarded, inadvertent, unobservant; detached, distracted, distrait, absentminded, oblivious, abstracted, in a brown study, (with one's head) in the clouds, in a world of one's own, unconcerned, apathetic, uncaring, neglectful, negligent, slack, remiss. □□ **inattention, inattentiveness** incaution, unthinkingness, unmindfulness, unwariness, unguardedness, inadvertence, inadvertency; see also NEGLIGENCE, *absentmindedness* (ABSENTMINDED).

inaudible /ináwdibəl/ *adj.* that cannot be heard. □□ **inaudibility** *n.* **inaudibly** *adv.*

■ unheard, out of earshot, imperceptible, indistinct; low, faint, muted, quiet, soft, muffled, stifled, whispered. □□ **inaudibility** quietness, faintness, softness.

inaugural /ináwgyərəl/ *adj.* & *n.* ● *adj.* **1** of inauguration. **2** (of a lecture, etc.) given by a person being inaugurated. ● *n.* an inaugural speech, etc. [F f. *inaugurer* (as INAUGURATE)]

■ *adj.* see INTRODUCTORY.

inaugurate /ináwgyərayt/ *v.tr.* **1** admit (a person) formally to office. **2** initiate the public use of (a building, etc.). **3** begin; introduce. **4** enter with ceremony upon (an undertaking, etc.). □□ **inauguration** /-ráyshən/ *n.* **inaugurator** *n.* **inauguratory** /-rətáwree/ *adj.* [L *inaugurare* (as IN-², *augurare* take omens: see AUGUR)]

■ **1** install, induct, invest, instate, crown, enthrone, frock, ordain, chair. **2** open, declare open, establish, launch, unveil, take the wraps off. **3, 4** initiate, begin, start, originate, set up, launch, institute, introduce, usher in, enter upon, get under way, get going, get started, set rolling, *colloq.* get off the ground, *formal* commence. □□ **inauguration** installation, induction, investiture, instatement, coronation, enthronement, ordainment, ordination; establishment, launch, initiation, institution, introduction, *colloq.* kickoff.

inauspicious /ínawspíshəs/ *adj.* **1** ill-omened; unpropitious. **2** unlucky. □□ **inauspiciously** *adv.* **inauspiciousness** *n.*

■ **1** ill-omened, ill-starred, ill-fated, doomed, fateful, unpropitious, unpromising, unfavorable, unlucky, unfortunate, unhappy; sinister, ominous, menacing, dark, gloomy, black, threatening. **2** see UNFORTUNATE *adj.* 1.

inboard /ínbawrd/ *adv.* & *adj.* ● *adv.* within the sides of or toward the center of a ship, aircraft, or vehicle. ● *adj.* situated inboard.

inborn /ínbáwrn/ *adj.* existing from birth; implanted by nature.

■ innate, congenital, inherent, inherited, hereditary, inbred, natural, native, constitutional, deep-seated, deep-rooted, ingrained, instinctive, instinctual, connate.

inbreathe /inbréeth/ *v.tr.* **1** breathe in or absorb. **2** inspire (a person).

inbred /ínbréd/ *adj.* **1** inborn. **2** produced by inbreeding.

■ see INBORN.

inbreeding /ínbréeding/ *n.* breeding from closely related animals or persons. □□ **inbreed** *v.tr.* & *intr.* (*past* and *past part.* **inbred**).

inbuilt /ínbílt/ *adj.* incorporated as part of a structure.

inc. *abbr.* **1** (esp. **Inc.**) Incorporated. **2** incomplete.

Inca /íngkə/ *n.* a member of a Native American people in Peru before the Spanish conquest. □□ **Incaic** /ingkáyik/ *adj.* **Incan** *adj.* [Quechua, = lord, royal person]

incalculable /inkálkyələbəl/ *adj.* **1** too great for calculation. **2** that cannot be reckoned beforehand. **3** (of a person, character, etc.) uncertain. □□ **incalculability** *n.* **incalculably** *adv.*

■ **1** see IMMEASURABLE.

in camera see CAMERA.

incandesce /ínkandés/ *v.intr.* & *tr.* glow or cause to glow with heat. [back-form. f. INCANDESCENT]

■ see GLOW *v.* 1.

incandescent /ínkandésənt/ *adj.* **1** glowing with heat. **2** shining brightly. **3** (of an electric or other light) produced by a glowing white-hot filament. □□ **incandescence** /-səns/ *n.* **incandescently** *adv.* [F f. L *incandescere* (as IN-², *candescere* inceptive of *candere* be white)]

■ **1, 2** glowing, aglow, fervent, red-hot, white-hot, radiant, *poet.* fervid; alight, ablaze, aflame, ardent, flaming, burning, fiery, on fire. □□ **incandescence** glow, fervor, fervency, red heat, white heat, *poet.* fervidity; fire, blaze, flame, fieriness, ardency; see also *radiance* (RADIANT).

incantation /ínkantáyshən/ *n.* **1 a** a magical formula. **b** the use of this. **2** a spell or charm. □□ **incantational** *adj.* **incantatory** /-kántətáwree/ *adj.* [ME f. OF f. LL *incantatio* -*onis* f. *incantare* chant, bewitch (as IN-², *cantare* sing)]

■ **1a, 2** see SPELL² 1.

incapable /inkáypəbəl/ *adj.* **1** (often foll. by *of*) **a** not capable. **b** lacking the required quality or characteristic (favorable or adverse) (*incapable of hurting anyone*). **2** not capable of rational conduct or of managing one's own affairs (*drunk and incapable*). □□ **incapability** *n.* **incapably** *adv.* [F *incapable* or LL *incapabilis* (as IN-¹, *capabilis* CAPABLE)]

■ **1** (*incapable of*) **a** unable to, powerless to, incompetent to, unfit to, not equipped to, unqualified to, impotent to, unequal to, not up to. **b** unable to, not equipped to, not the type to, insusceptible to, resistant to, impervious to, ill-disposed to, disinclined to, not open to. **2** incapacitated, disabled, hors de combat, inoperative, immobilized, helpless, impuissant, paralyzed, paralytic.

incapacitate /ínkəpásitayt/ *v.tr.* **1** render incapable or unfit. **2** disqualify. □□ **incapacitant** *n.* **incapacitation** /-táyshən/ *n.*

■ **1** immobilize, inactivate, deactivate, put out of action *or* commission; indispose, disable, cripple, paralyze, lame, wound, maim, impair, weaken, enfeeble, enervate, exhaust, devitalize. **2** see DISQUALIFY.

incapacity /ínkəpásitee/ *n.* (*pl.* **-ies**) **1** inability; lack of the necessary power or resources. **2** legal disqualification. **3** an instance of incapacity. [F *incapacité* or LL *incapacitas* (as IN-¹, CAPACITY)]

■ **1** see INABILITY.

incarcerate /inkaársərayt/ *v.tr.* imprison or confine. □□ **incarceration** /-ráyshən/ *n.* **incarcerator** *n.* [med.L *incarcerare* (as IN-², L *carcer* prison)]

■ see IMPRISON. □□ **incarceration** see *imprisonment* (IMPRISON).

incarnadine /inkaárnədin/ *adj.* & *v. poet.* ● *adj.* flesh-colored or crimson. ● *v.tr.* dye this color. [F *incarnadin* -*ine* f. It. *incarnadino* (for -*tino*) f. *incarnato* INCARNATE *adj.*]

incarnate *adj.* & *v.* ● *adj.* /inkaárnət, -nayt/ **1** (of a person, spirit, quality, etc.) embodied in flesh, esp. in human form (*is the devil incarnate*). **2** represented in a recognizable or typical form (*folly incarnate*). ● *v.tr.* /inkaárnayt/ **1** embody in flesh. **2** put (an idea, etc.) into concrete form; realize. **3** (of a person, etc.) be the living embodiment of (a quality). [ME f. eccl.L *incarnare incarnat-* make flesh (as IN-², L *caro carnis* flesh)]

■ *adj.* **1** see PHYSICAL *adj.* 1. **2** see PHYSICAL *adj.* 2. ● *v.* **1** embody, flesh. **2** see EMBODY 1, 3. **3** see PERSONIFY 3.

incarnation /ínkaarnáyshən/ *n.* **1 a** embodiment in (esp. human) flesh. **b** (**the Incarnation**) *Theol.* the embodiment of God the Son in human flesh as Jesus Christ. **2** (often foll. by *of*) a living type (of a quality, etc.). **3** *Med.* the process of forming new flesh. [ME f. OF f. eccl.L *incarnatio -onis* (as INCARNATE)]

■ **1, 2** see *embodiment* (EMBODY).

incase var. of ENCASE.

incautious /inkáwshəs/ *adj.* heedless; rash. □□ **incaution** *n.* **incautiously** *adv.* **incautiousness** *n.*

■ see RASH¹. □□ **incautiously** see *hastily* (HASTY).

incendiary /inséndee-eree/ *adj.* & *n.* ● *adj.* **1** (of a substance or device, esp. a bomb) designed to cause fires. **2 a** of or relating to the malicious setting on fire of property. **b** guilty of this. **3** tending to stir up strife; inflammatory. ● *n.* (*pl.* **-ies**) **1** an incendiary bomb or device. **2** an incendiary person. □□ **incendiarism** *n.* [ME f. L *incendiarius* f. *incendium* conflagration f. *incendere incens-* set fire to]

■ *adj.* **3** see INFLAMMATORY 1. ● *n.* **2** see AGITATOR 1.

incense¹ /ínsens/ *n.* & *v.* ● *n.* **1** a gum or spice producing a sweet smell when burned. **2** the smoke of this, esp. in religious ceremonial. ● *v.tr.* **1** treat or perfume (a person or thing) with incense. **2** burn incense to (a deity, etc.). **3** suffuse with fragrance. □□ **incensation** *n.* [ME f. OF *encens, encenser* f. eccl.L *incensum* a thing burned, incense: see INCENDIARY]

incense² /inséns/ *v.tr.* (often foll. by *at, with, against*) enrage; make angry. [ME f. OF *incenser* (as INCENDIARY)]

■ see ENRAGE.

incensory /ínsensəree/ *n.* (*pl.* **-ies**) = CENSER. [med.L *incensorium* (as INCENSE¹)]

incentive /inséntiv/ *n.* & *adj.* ● *n.* **1** (often foll. by *to*) a motive or incitement, esp. to action. **2** a payment or concession to stimulate greater output by workers. ● *adj.* serving to motivate or incite. [ME f. L *incentivus* setting the tune f. *incinere incent-* sing to (as IN-², *canere* sing)]

■ *n.* **1** incitement, encouragement, promotion, motivation, enticement, lure, inducement, carrot, fillip, stimulus, goad, prod, provocation, spur, *sl.* come-on; motive, impetus, impulse, mainspring. **2** payment, bonus, reward, extra, perquisite, *colloq.* perk. ● *adj.* motivational, promotional.

incept /insépt/ *v.* **1** *tr. Biol.* (of an organism) take in (food, etc.). **2** *intr. Brit. hist.* take a master's or doctor's degree at a university. □□ **inceptor** *n.* (in sense 2). [L *incipere incept-* begin (as IN-², *capere* take)]

inception /insépshən/ *n.* a beginning. [ME f. OF *inception* or L *inceptio* (as INCEPT)]

■ see BEGINNING 1, 2.

inceptive /inséptiv/ *adj.* & *n.* ● *adj.* **1 a** beginning. **b** initial. **2** *Gram.* (of a verb) that denotes the beginning of an action. ● *n.* an inceptive verb. [LL *inceptivus* (as INCEPT)]

incertitude /insértitōōd, -tyōōd/ *n.* uncertainty; doubt. [F *incertitude* or LL *incertitudo* (as IN-¹, CERTITUDE)]

incessant /insésənt/ *adj.* unceasing; continual; repeated. □□ **incessancy** *n.* **incessantly** *adv.* **incessantness** *n.* [F *incessant* or LL *incessans* (as IN-¹, *cessans* pres. part. of L *cessare* CEASE)]

■ see CONTINUAL. □□ **incessantly** see *endlessly* (ENDLESS).

incest /ínsest/ *n.* sexual intercourse between persons regarded as too closely related to marry each other. [ME f. L *incestus* (as IN-¹, *castus* CHASTE)]

incestuous /inséschōōəs/ *adj.* **1** involving or guilty of incest. **2** (of human relations generally) excessively restricted or resistant to wider influence. □□ **incestuously** *adv.* **incestuousness** *n.* [LL *incestuosus* (as INCEST)]

inch¹ /inch/ *n.* & *v.* ● *n.* **1** a unit of linear measure equal to one-twelfth of a foot (2.54 cm). **2 a** (as a unit of rainfall) a quantity that would cover a horizontal surface to a depth of

1 inch. **b** (of atmospheric or other pressure) an amount that balances the weight of a column of mercury 1 inch high. **3** (as a unit of map scale) so many inches representing 1 mile on the ground (*a 4-inch map*). **4** a small amount (usu. with neg.: *would not yield an inch*). ● *v.tr. & intr.* move gradually in a specified way (*inched forward*). □ **every inch 1** entirely (*looked every inch a judge*). **2** the whole distance or area (*combed every inch of the garden*). **give a person an inch and he** or **she will take a mile** a person once conceded to will demand much. **inch by inch** gradually; bit by bit. **within an inch of** almost to the point of. [OE *ynce* f. L *uncia* twelfth part: cf. OUNCE¹]

■ *v.* crawl, creep, edge, work one's way; see also EASE *v.* **5b.** □ **inch by inch** see *by degrees* (DEGREE).

inch² /inch/ *n.* esp. *Sc.* a small island (esp. in place-names). [ME f. Gael. *innis*]

inchmeal /ínchmeel/ *adv.* by inches; little by little; gradually. [f. INCH¹ + MEAL¹]

■ see *gradually* (GRADUAL).

inchoate /inkóit/ *adj.* & *v.* ● *adj.* **1** just begun. **2** undeveloped; rudimentary; unformed. ● *v.tr.* begin; originate. □□ **inchoately** *adv.* **inchoateness** *n.* **inchoation** /-áyshən/ *n.* **inchoative** /-kŏətiv/ *adj.* [L *inchoatus* past part. of *inchoare* (as IN-², *choare* begin)]

■ *adj.* see UNDEVELOPED.

inchworm /ínchwərm/ *n.* = *measuring worm* (see MEASURE).

incidence /ínsidəns/ *n.* **1** (often foll. by *of*) the fact, manner, or rate, of occurrence or action. **2** the range, scope, or extent of influence of a thing. **3** *Physics* the falling of a line, or of a thing moving in a line, upon a surface. **4** the act or an instance of coming into contact with a thing. □ **angle of incidence** the angle which an incident line, ray, etc., makes with the perpendicular to the surface at the point of incidence. [ME f. OF *incidence* or med.L *incidentia* (as INCIDENT)]

■ **1** frequency, rate, degree, extent, occurrence, prevalence; quantity, amount, number. **2** see RANGE *n.* 1a–c.

incident /ínsidənt/ *n.* & *adj.* ● *n.* **1 a** an event or occurrence. **b** a minor or detached event attracting general attention or noteworthy in some way. **2** a hostile clash, esp. of troops of countries at war (*a frontier incident*). **3** a distinct piece of action in a play or a poem. **4** *Law* a privilege, burden, etc., attaching to an obligation or right. ● *adj.* **1 a** (often foll. by *to*) apt or liable to happen; naturally attaching or dependent. **b** (foll. by *to*) *Law* attaching to. **2** (often foll. by *on, upon*) (of light, etc.) falling or striking. [ME f. F *incident* or L *incidere* (as IN-², *cadere* fall)]

■ *n.* **1 a** event, occurrence, occasion, happening, proceeding, circumstance, fact, case, experience. **b** event, occasion, happening, function, scene, episode, to-do, *colloq.* affair, do. **2** clash, confrontation, disturbance, commotion, fracas, skirmish, fight, unpleasantness, upset, quarrel, scene, affair, dispute, altercation, argument, disagreement, *colloq.* dustup, set-to, scrap. ● *adj.* **1** (*incident to*) appurtenant to, pertinent to, pertaining to, attaching to, incidental to, liable to happen to, usual for, typical of; dependent on.

incidental /ínsidéntəl/ *adj.* **1** (often foll. by *to*) **a** having a minor role in relation to a more important thing, event, etc. **b** not essential. **c** casual; happening by chance. **2** (foll. by *to*) liable to happen. **3** (foll. by *on, upon*) following as a subordinate event. □ **incidental music** music used as a background to the action of a play, motion picture, broadcast, etc.

■ **1 a** secondary, subordinate, subsidiary, ancillary, auxiliary, supplementary, supplemental, peripheral, minor, inferior, lesser. **b** nonessential, unessential, inessential, unnecessary, dispensable, expendable, peripheral, extraneous, accidental; unimportant, inconsequential, trivial, lightweight, insignificant, negligible, petty, trifling, paltry. **c** casual, chance, fortuitous, aleatory, random, haphazard, serendipitous, unpredictable, accidental, coincidental, adventitious, unplanned, unlooked-for, *colloq.* fluky. **2** (*incidental to*) see INCIDENT *adj.* □ **incidental music** score, soundtrack; see also *background music*.

incidentally /ínsidént'lee/ *adv.* **1** by the way; as an unconnected remark. **2** in an incidental way.
■ **1** by the way, by the by, apropos, parenthetically, in passing, en passant. **2** secondarily, subordinately, subsidiarily, supplementarily, supplementally, peripherally, extraneously, unnecessarily; coincidentally, casually, as luck would have it, accidentally, by chance, *archaic or poet.* perchance.

incinerate /insínərayt/ *v.tr.* **1** consume (a body, etc.) by fire. **2** reduce to ashes. □□ **incineration** /-ráyshən/ *n.* [med.L *incinerare* (as IN-², *cinis -eris* ashes)]
■ see BURN¹ *v.* 1.

incinerator /insínəraytər/ *n.* a furnace or apparatus for burning, esp. refuse to ashes.

incipient /insípeeənt/ *adj.* **1** beginning. **2** in an initial stage. □□ **incipience** /-əns/ *n.* **incipiency** *n.* **incipiently** *adv.* [L *incipere incipient-* (as INCEPT)]
■ see INITIAL *adj.*

incise /insíz/ *v.tr.* **1** make a cut in. **2** engrave. [F *inciser* f. L *incidere incis-* (as IN-², *caedere* cut)]
■ **2** see CARVE 1, 2.

incision /insízhən/ *n.* **1** a cut; a division produced by cutting; a notch. **2** the act of cutting into a thing. [ME f. OF *incision* or LL *incisio* (as INCISE)]
■ **1** cut, slit, gash, slash, cleft, notch, score, nick, snick, scratch, scarification, *archaic* scotch.

incisive /insísiv/ *adj.* **1** mentally sharp; acute. **2** clear and effective. **3** cutting; penetrating. □□ **incisively** *adv.* **incisiveness** *n.* [med.L *incisivus* (as INCISE)]
■ **1** sharp, keen, acute, razor-sharp, piercing, perspicacious, perceptive, percipient, intelligent, clever, canny, shrewd, astute, smart, quick, alert, aware, *colloq.* on the ball. **2** clear, concise, succinct, terse, laconic, pithy, to the point, effective; aphoristic, epigrammatic, crisp, brisk, direct, plain, straightforward. **3** cutting, biting, mordant, trenchant, critical, caustic, sarcastic, ironic, cynical, sardonic, penetrating; pungent, acrid, stinging, corrosive, acerbic, acid, sharp, tart, bitter, acrimonious.

incisor /insízər/ *n.* a cutting tooth, esp. at the front of the mouth. [med.L, = cutter (as INCISE)]

incite /insít/ *v.tr.* (often foll. by *to*) urge or stir up. □□ **incitation** *n.* **incitement** *n.* **inciter** *n.* [ME f. F *inciter* f. L *incitare* (as IN-², *citare* rouse)]
■ urge, exhort, encourage, prompt, move, drive, push, egg on, excite, rally, rouse, arouse, wake, waken, awaken, instigate, stir, bestir, stir *or* whip *or* work up, agitate, stimulate, entice, goad, spur, prod, provoke, inspire, inflame, fire, *archaic* prick; foment.
□□ **incitation, incitement** exhortation, encouragement, motivation, instigation, persuasion, drive, push, excitement, arousal, agitation, stimulus, stimulation, enticement, persuasion, spur, provocation, inspiration, inflammation; fomentation; rabble-rousing; see also INCENTIVE *n.* 1. **inciter** see *arouser* (AROUSE), *rabble-rouser* (RABBLE¹).

incivility /ínsivílitee/ *n.* (*pl.* **-ies**) **1** rudeness; discourtesy. **2** a rude or discourteous act. [F *incivilité* or LL *incivilitas* (as IN-¹, CIVILITY)]
■ **1** rudeness, boorishness, coarseness, discourtesy, discourteousness, disrespect, unmannerliness, indecorum, indecorousness, impoliteness, tactlessness, ungentlemanliness, bad breeding, ill breeding, bad manners, misbehavior; see also *impertinence* (IMPERTINENT). **2** see MISSTEP 2.

inclement /inklémənt/ *adj.* (of the weather or climate) severe, esp. cold or stormy. □□ **inclemency** *n.* (*pl.* **-ies**). in-

clemently *adv.* [F *inclément* or L *inclemens* (as IN-¹, CLEMENT)]
■ extreme, intemperate, severe, adverse, harsh, rigorous, rough, violent; stormy, rainy, squally, blustery, raw, tempestuous; see also BAD *adj.* 2a. □□ **inclemency** see *severity* (SEVERE).

inclination /ínklináyshən/ *n.* **1** (often foll. by *to*) a disposition or propensity. **2** (often foll. by *for*) a liking or affection. **3** a leaning, slope, or slant. **4** the difference of direction of two lines or planes, esp. as measured by the angle between them. **5** the dip of a magnetic needle. [ME f. OF *inclination* or L *inclinatio* (as INCLINE)]
■ **1** disposition, predisposition, tendency, bent, bias, leaning, preference, turn, cast, proclivity, propensity, attitude, proneness, susceptibility, predilection, partiality, desire, *literary* velleity; see also WISH *n.* **2** affection, fondness, love, liking, penchant, weakness, soft spot, taste, fancy. **3** slope, slant, angle, bend, leaning, tilt, nod; see also INCLINE *n.*

incline *v. & n.* ● *v.* /inklín/ **1** *tr.* (usu. in *passive*; often foll. by *to, for,* or *to* + infin.) **a** make (a person, feelings, etc.) willing or favorably disposed (*am inclined to think so; does not incline me to agree*). **b** give a specified tendency to (a thing) (*the door is inclined to bang*). **2** *intr.* **a** be disposed (*I incline to think so*). **b** (often foll. by *to, toward*) tend. **3** *intr. & tr.* lean or turn away from a given direction, esp. the vertical. **4** *tr.* bend (the head, body, or oneself) forward or downward. ● *n.* /inklín/ **1** a slope. **2** an inclined plane. □ **inclined plane** a sloping plane (esp. as a means of reducing the force needed to raise a load). **incline one's ear** (often foll. by *to*) listen favorably. □□ **incliner** *n.* [ME *encline* f. OF *encliner* f. L *inclinare* (as IN-², *clinare* bend)]
■ *v.* **1** make, lead, get, persuade, convince, influence, dispose, predispose, prejudice, bias; (*inclined*) see WILLING *adj.*, LIKELY *adj.* 1. **2** be disposed *or* predisposed, have a mind, show favor *or* preference, be biased *or* prejudiced, gravitate; tend, be prone, be liable *or* likely *or* apt. **3, 4** lean, bend, bow, nod, stoop, slant, tilt, angle, bank, slope, tip, arch; (*inclined*) see OBLIQUE *adj.* 1. ● *n.* slope, pitch, grade, gradient, slant, ramp, hill, dip, descent, declivity, rise, ascent, acclivity.
□ **incline one's ear** lend an ear, give a fair hearing; give one's full *or* undivided attention, pay attention; (*incline one's ear to*) heed.

inclinometer /ínklinómitər/ *n.* **1** an instrument for measuring the angle between the direction of the earth's magnetic field and the horizontal. **2** an instrument for measuring the inclination of an aircraft or ship to the horizontal. **3** an instrument for measuring a slope. [L *inclinare* INCLINE *v.* + -METER]

inclose var. of ENCLOSE.

inclosure var. of ENCLOSURE.

include /inklōōd/ *v.tr.* **1** comprise or reckon in as part of a whole; place in a class or category. **2** (as **including** *prep.*) if we include (*six members, including the chairperson*). **3** treat or regard as so included. **4** (as **included** *adj.*) shut in; enclosed. □ **include out** *colloq.* or *joc.* specifically exclude. □□ **includable** *adj.* **includible** *adj.* **inclusion** /-klōōzhən/ *n.* [ME f. L *includere inclus-* (as IN-², *claudere* shut)]
■ **1** incorporate, embody, comprise, embrace, cover, encompass, number, take in, admit, subsume, comprehend, contain; classify, categorize, group, file, list, catalog, tabulate, register; see also SELECT *v.* **2** (**including**) see INCLUSIVE 1. **3** count, number, allow for, take into account, involve. **4** (**included**) enclosed, contained, wrapped, enveloped, packaged, inserted, encompassed, lodged. □ **include out** see EXCLUDE 3.
□□ **inclusion** incorporation, involvement, subsumption, embracement; admission, categorization, selection, choice; enclosure, packaging, insertion, encompassment.

inclusive /inklōōsiv/ *adj.* **1** (often foll. by *of*) including, comprising. **2** with the inclusion of the extreme limits stated (*pages 7 to 26 inclusive*). **3** including all the normal services, etc. (*a hotel offering inclusive terms*). □ **inclusive language**

language that is deliberately nonsexist, esp. avoiding the use of masculine pronouns to cover both men and women. □□ **inclusively** adv. **inclusiveness** n. [med.L inclusivus (as INCLUDE)]

■ **1** (inclusive of) including, embracing, comprising, taking in, covering, incorporating, embodying. **3** comprehensive, catchall, overall, full, thorough, across-the-board, all-in-one, all-encompassing, umbrella, blanket, Brit. all-in; general, wide, broad, deep, extensive.

incog /inkóg/ adj., adv., & n. Brit. colloq. = INCOGNITO. [abbr.]

incognito /inkogneétō, -kógni-/ adj., adv., & n. ● adj. & adv. with one's name or identity kept secret (was traveling incognito). ● n. (pl. -os) **1** a person who is incognito. **2** the pretended identity or anonymous character of such a person. [It., = unknown, f. L incognitus (as IN-[1], cognitus past part. of cognoscere know)]

■ adj. & adv. in disguise, in camouflage, under cover, under a false or assumed name, in plain clothes, colloq. incog; disguised, unidentified, unrecognized, camouflaged, masked; anonymous(ly), covert(ly), secret(ly), clandestine(ly); (adj.) plainclothes, unrecognizable, mysterious; (adv.) on the sly, colloq. on the q.t. ● n. **1** mystery man or woman, masquerader, Brit. colloq. incog. **2** false or assumed identity or name, alias, pseudonym, nom de guerre; disguise, masquerade, camouflage, mask, cover, smokescreen; act, charade, sham, pretense.

incognizant /inkógnizənt/ adj. (foll. by of) unaware; not knowing. □□ **incognizance** /-zəns/ n.

■ see UNAWARE adj. 1.

incoherent /inkōheérənt/ adj. **1** (of a person) unable to speak intelligibly. **2** (of speech, etc.) lacking logic or consistency. **3** Physics (of waves) having no definite or stable phase relationship. □□ **incoherence** /-əns/ n. **incoherency** n. (pl. -ies). **incoherently** adv.

■ **1** inarticulate, unintelligible, incomprehensible, delirious, raving, confused, rambling, obscure. **2** illogical, irrational, wild, unstructured, disconnected, disjointed, loose, unconnected, uncoordinated, disorganized, disordered, confused, garbled, mixed-up, jumbled, muddled, scrambled; rambling, discursive, digressive, raggle-taggle.

incombustible /inkəmbústibəl/ adj. that cannot be burned or consumed by fire. □□ **incombustibility** n. [ME f. med.L incombustibilis (as IN-[1], COMBUSTIBLE)]

■ nonflammable, not flammable, fireproof, fire-resistant, fire-retardant, asbestine; flameproof, heat-resistant, heatproof, ovenproof.

income /inkum/ n. the money or other assets received, esp. periodically or in a year, from one's business, lands, work, investments, etc. □ **income group** a section of the population determined by income. **income tax** a tax levied on income. [ME (orig. = arrival), prob. f. ON innkoma: in later use f. come in]

■ earnings, revenue(s), receipts, return(s), proceeds, turnover, incomings, takings, take; see also PROFIT n. 2. □ **income tax** see TAX n. 1.

incomer /inkumər/ n. **1** a person who comes in. **2** Brit. a person who arrives to settle in a place; an immigrant. **3** an intruder. **4** a successor.

-incomer /inkumər/ comb. form esp. Brit. earning a specified kind or level of income (middle-incomer).

incoming /inkuming/ adj. & n. ● adj. **1** coming in (the incoming tide; incoming telephone calls). **2** succeeding another person or persons (the incoming tenant). **3** Brit. immigrant. **4** (of profit) accruing. ● n. **1** (usu. in pl.) revenue; income. **2** the act of arriving or entering.

■ n. **1** see INCOME. **2** see ARRIVAL 1.

incommensurable /inkəménsərəbəl, -shərəbəl/ adj. (often foll. by with) **1** not comparable in respect of magnitude. **2** incapable of being measured. **3** Math. (of a magnitude or magnitudes) having no common factor, integral or fractional. **4** Math. irrational. □□ **incommensurability** n. **in-**

commensurably adv. [LL incommensurabilis (as IN-[1], COMMENSURABLE)]

incommensurate /inkəménsərət, -shərət/ adj. **1** (often foll. by with, to) out of proportion; inadequate. **2** = INCOMMENSURABLE. □□ **incommensurately** adv. **incommensurateness** n.

■ **1** see DISPROPORTIONATE.

incommode /inkəmód/ v.tr. **1** hinder; inconvenience. **2** trouble; annoy. [F incommoder or L incommodare (as IN-[1], commodus convenient)]

■ **1** see INCONVENIENCE v.

incommodious /inkəmódeeəs/ adj. not affording good accommodation; uncomfortable. □□ **incommodiously** adv. **incommodiousness** n.

■ see cramped (CRAMP v. 4).

incommunicable /inkəmyoonikəbəl/ adj. **1** that cannot be communicated or shared. **2** that cannot be uttered or told. **3** that does not communicate; uncommunicative. □□ **incommunicability** n. **incommunicableness** n. **incommunicably** adv. [LL incommunicabilis (as IN-[1], COMMUNICABLE)]

incommunicado /inkəmyoonikaádō/ adj. **1** without or deprived of the means of communication with others. **2** (of a prisoner) in solitary confinement. [Sp. incomunicado past part. of incomunicar deprive of communication]

incommunicative /inkəmyoonikətiv, -káytiv/ adj. not communicative; taciturn. □□ **incommunicatively** adv. **incommunicativeness** n.

incommutable /inkəmyootəbəl/ adj. **1** not changeable. **2** not commutable. □□ **incommutably** adv. [ME f. L incommutabilis (as IN-[1], COMMUTABLE)]

incomparable /inkómpərəbəl/ adj. **1** without an equal; matchless. **2** (often foll. by with, to) not to be compared. □□ **incomparability** n. **incomparableness** n. **incomparably** adv. [ME f. OF f. L incomparabilis (as IN-[1], COMPARABLE)]

■ **1** beyond compare, without equal, unequaled, matchless, peerless, unparalleled, unrivaled, hors concours, nonpareil, transcendent, perfect, surpassing, supreme, superior, superlative, unsurpassed, unsurpassable.

incompatible /inkəmpátibəl/ adj. **1** opposed in character; discordant. **2** (often foll. by with) inconsistent. **3** (of persons) unable to live, work, etc., together in harmony. **4** (of drugs) not suitable for taking at the same time. **5** (of equipment, machinery, etc.) not capable of being used in combination. □□ **incompatibility** n. **incompatibleness** n. **incompatibly** adv. [med.L incompatibilis (as IN-[1], COMPATIBLE)]

■ **1, 3** mismatched, unsuited, discordant, clashing, jarring, inconsistent, contradictory, conflicting, repugnant, uncongenial, inconsonant, irreconcilable, incongruous, out of keeping; antithetical, antithetic, opposed, opposite, contrary, antipathetic, antagonistic, hostile. **2** see UNLIKE adj. 1. □□ **incompatibility**, **incompatibleness** mismatch, discord, discordance, discordancy, inconsistency, contradictoriness, conflict, repugnance, uncongeniality, irreconcilability, incongruousness; disagreement, dissent, opposition, disaccord, dissimilarity, difference.

incompetent /inkómpit'nt/ adj. & n. ● adj. **1** (often foll. by to + infin.) not qualified or able to perform a particular task or function (an incompetent builder). **2** showing a lack of skill (an incompetent performance). **3** Med. (esp. of a valve or sphincter) not able to perform its function. ● n. an incompetent person. □□ **incompetence** /-t'ns/ n. **incompetency** n. **incompetently** adv. [F incompétent or LL incompetens (as IN-[1], COMPETENT)]

■ adj. **1** unqualified, inexpert, unfit, unable, incapable, *sl.* out to lunch; inadequate, insufficient, not good enough, deficient; unapt, inapt, unsuitable. **2** unskilled, unskillful, inept, maladroit, inexpert, awkward, clumsy, bungling, gauche, *Brit. colloq.* cack-handed, *sl.* klutzy; useless, hopeless, *colloq.* terrible, past it; inadequate, insufficient, ineffective, ineffectual, inefficient. ● *n.* bungler, botcher, blunderer, flounderer, bumbler, oaf, *colloq.* galoot, lummox, *sl.* duffer, slouch, klutz, *Brit. sl.* buffer. □□ **incompetence, incompetency** inability, incapability, incapacity, inexpertness, inadequacy, insufficiency, deficiency, inaptitude, inaptness, unaptness, unsuitability, unsuitableness; lack of skill, ineptitude, ineptness, maladroitness, awkwardness, clumsiness, gaucheness, *Brit. colloq.* cack-handedness; uselessness, hopelessness, inadequacy, insufficiency, inefficiency, ineffectiveness, ineffectuality, ineffectualness.

incomplete /ínkəmpleét/ *adj.* not complete. □□ **incompletely** *adv.* **incompleteness** *n.* [ME f. LL *incompletus* (as IN-¹, COMPLETE)]
■ unfinished, imperfect, undone, unaccomplished, unformed, undeveloped, deficient, defective, partial, sketchy, crude, rudimentary, rough, fragmentary, patchy. □□ **incompleteness** see IMPERFECTION 1.

incomprehensible /ínkomprihénsibəl/ *adj.* (often foll. by *to*) that cannot be understood. □□ **incomprehensibility** *n.* **incomprehensibleness** *n.* **incomprehensibly** *adv.* [ME f. L *incomprehensibilis* (as IN-¹, COMPREHENSIBLE)]
■ unintelligible, incoherent, inarticulate, unreadable, illegible, indecipherable, undecipherable, unfathomable, impenetrable, inscrutable; abstruse, arcane, recondite, cryptic, obscure, opaque, dark, occult, *colloq.* weird; enigmatic, mysterious, unaccountable, mystifying, puzzling, perplexing, baffling, deep, over a person's head; *attrib.* gibberish, *colloq.* (all) Greek to a person, gobbledygook *or* gobbledegook, double Dutch.

incomprehension /ínkomprihénshən/ *n.* failure to understand.

incompressible /ínkəmprésibəl/ *adj.* that cannot be compressed. □□ **incompressibility** *n.*

inconceivable /ínkənseévəbəl/ *adj.* **1** that cannot be imagined. **2** *colloq.* very remarkable. □□ **inconceivability** *n.* **inconceivableness** *n.* **inconceivably** *adv.*
■ **1** unimaginable, unthinkable, impossible, unrealistic, improbable; overwhelming, staggering, *colloq.* mind-boggling. **2** see MIRACULOUS 1, 3.

inconclusive /ínkənklōŏsiv/ *adj.* (of an argument, evidence, or action) not decisive or convincing. □□ **inconclusively** *adv.* **inconclusiveness** *n.*
■ indecisive, indefinite, unsettled, unestablished, undemonstrated, unproved, unproven, undecided, undetermined, moot, (still) open, indeterminate, unresolved, pending, in limbo, in the air; doubtful, vague, ambiguous, unfocused.

incondensable /ínkəndénsəbəl/ *adj.* that cannot be condensed, esp. that cannot be reduced to a liquid or solid condition.

incongruous /inkónggrōŏəs/ *adj.* **1** out of place; absurd. **2** (often foll. by *with*) disagreeing; out of keeping. □□ **incongruity** /-grōŏitee/ *n.* (*pl.* **-ies**). **incongruously** *adv.* **incongruousness** *n.* [L *incongruus* (as IN-¹, CONGRUOUS)]
■ inharmonious, disharmonious, disagreeing, out of place, out of keeping, discordant, dissonant, unapt, inappropriate, unsuitable, unbecoming, unseemly, unsuited, unfitting, unfit, improper, malapropos, not meet; out of step, out of line, inconsistent, discrepant, disparate, different, contrary; contradictory, paradoxical, nonsensical, illogical, absurd, ridiculous, preposterous, ludicrous.

inconsecutive /ínkənsékyətiv/ *adj.* lacking sequence; inconsequent. □□ **inconsecutively** *adv.* **inconsecutiveness** *n.*

inconsequent /ínkónsikwənt/ *adj.* **1** not following naturally; irrelevant. **2** lacking logical sequence. **3** disconnected. □□ **in-**consequence /-kwəns/ *n.* **inconsequently** *adv.* [L *inconsequens* (as IN-¹, CONSEQUENT)]

inconsequential /ínkónsikwénshəl, ínkon-/ *adj.* **1** unimportant. **2** = INCONSEQUENT. □□ **inconsequentiality** /-sheeáli-tee/ *n.* (*pl.* **-ies**). **inconsequentially** *adv.* **inconsequentialness** *n.*
■ **1** unimportant, insignificant, trivial, trifling, nugatory, inconsiderable, inappreciable, negligible, minor, little, small, paltry, petty, minuscule, immaterial, slight, lightweight, worthless, expendable, no-account, of no account, derisory, *colloq.* piddling, piffling, small-time.

inconsiderable /ínkənsídərəbəl/ *adj.* **1** of small size, value, etc. **2** not worth considering. □□ **inconsiderableness** *n.* **inconsiderably** *adv.* [obs. F *inconsidérable* or LL *inconsiderabilis* (as IN-¹, CONSIDERABLE)]
■ see INSIGNIFICANT 1.

inconsiderate /ínkənsídərət/ *adj.* **1** (of a person or action) thoughtless; rash. **2** lacking in regard for the feelings of others. □□ **inconsiderately** *adv.* **inconsiderateness** *n.* **inconsideration** /-ráyshən/ *n.* [L *inconsideratus* (as IN-¹, CONSIDERATE)]
■ **1** see IMPRUDENT. **2** thoughtless, unthoughtful, unconcerned, uncaring, selfish, callous, heartless, unsympathetic, insensitive, undiplomatic, tactless, rude, impolite.

inconsistent /ínkənsístənt/ *adj.* **1** acting at variance with one's own principles or former conduct. **2** (often foll. by *with*) not in keeping; discordant; incompatible. **3** (of a single thing) incompatible or discordant; having self-contradictory parts. □□ **inconsistency** *n.* (*pl.* **-ies**). **inconsistently** *adv.*
■ **1, 3** inconstant, irregular, changeable, variable, capricious, fickle, erratic, uneven, unstable, unsteady, unpredictable, unreliable, undependable; self-contradictory, paradoxical, incoherent, illogical, irrational, absurd, preposterous. **2** see INCONGRUOUS, STEP *n.* 9.

inconsolable /ínkənsŏləbəl/ *adj.* (of a person, grief, etc.) that cannot be consoled or comforted. □□ **inconsolability** /-bíl-itee/ *n.* **inconsolableness** *n.* **inconsolably** *adv.* [F *inconsolable* or L *inconsolabilis* (as IN-¹, *consolabilis* f. *consolari* CONSOLE¹)]
■ unconsolable, disconsolate, brokenhearted, heartbroken, desolated, desolate, forlorn, despairing, miserable, woebegone, wretched, heartsick, grief-stricken.

inconsonant /ínkónsənənt/ *adj.* (often foll. by *with, to*) not harmonious; not compatible. □□ **inconsonance** /-nəns/ *n.* **inconsonantly** *adv.*

inconspicuous /ínkənspíkyōŏəs/ *adj.* **1** not conspicuous; not easily noticed. **2** *Bot.* (of flowers) small, pale, or green. □□ **inconspicuously** *adv.* **inconspicuousness** *n.* [L *inconspicuus* (as IN-¹, CONSPICUOUS)]
■ **1** unnoticeable, unobtrusive, unostentatious, insignificant, indistinguishable, undistinguished, indefinite, faint; unseen, unnoticed, in the background, behind the scenes, backstage, out of *or* away from the public eye, out of the limelight *or* spotlight; modest, unassuming, discreet, sober, quiet, low-key, low-profile.

inconstant /inkónstənt/ *adj.* **1** (of a person) fickle; changeable. **2** frequently changing; variable; irregular. □□ **inconstancy** *n.* (*pl.* **-ies**). **inconstantly** *adv.* [ME f. OF f. L *inconstans -antis* (as IN-¹, CONSTANT)]
■ fickle, capricious, changeable, mercurial, volatile, flighty, moody, fitful, vacillating, fluctuating, wavering, irresolute, unsteady, unsteadfast, unreliable, undependable, erratic, irregular, unstable, unsettled, variable, *literary* mutable; see also INCONSISTENT 1, 3.
□□ **inconstancy** changeableness, changeability, irregularity, variability, unsteadiness, unsteadfastness, *literary* mutability; fickleness, capriciousness, caprice, volatility, mercuriality, unreliability, flightiness, moodiness; faithlessness, unfaithfulness.

incontestable /ínkəntéstəbəl/ *adj.* that cannot be disputed.

□□ **incontestability** /-bílitee/ *n.* **incontestably** *adv.* [F *in-contestable* or med.L *incontestabilis* (as IN-¹, *contestabilis* f. L *contestari* CONTEST)]

■ see INCONTROVERTIBLE. □□ **incontestably** see *undoubtedly* (UNDOUBTED).

incontinent /inkóntinənt/ *adj.* **1** unable to control movements of the bowels or bladder or both. **2** lacking self-restraint (esp. in regard to sexual desire). **3** (foll. by *of*) unable to control. □□ **incontinence** /-nəns/ *n.* **incontinently** *adv.* [ME f. OF or L *incontinens* (as IN-¹, CONTINENT²)]

■ **1** wet, *Med.* enuretic. **2** unrestrained, unconstrained, unrestricted, uncontrolled, uncontrollable, ungoverned, ungovernable, unbridled, uncurbed; lecherous, libidinous, lascivious, promiscuous, libertine, lustful, lewd, debauched, wanton, dissolute, loose, lubricious, salacious, profligate, obscene, dirty, filthy. □□ **incontinence** bedwetting, *Med.* enuresis; unrestrainedness, unrestrictedness, uncontrollableness, ungovernability; lechery, libidinousness, lasciviousness, lustfulness, lewdness, debauchery, wantonness, dissoluteness, salaciousness, profligacy, obscenity.

incontrovertible /ínkontrəvártibəl/ *adj.* indisputable; indubitable. □□ **incontrovertibility** *n.* **incontrovertibly** *adv.*

■ uncontrovertible, indisputable, indubitable, undeniable, incontestable, unquestionable, irrefutable, sure, certain, definite, definitive, final, established, absolute, positive. □□ **incontrovertibility** see FINALITY. **incontrovertibly** see *undoubtedly* (UNDOUBTED).

inconvenience /ínkənveényəns/ *n. & v.* ● *n.* **1** lack of suitability to personal requirements or ease. **2** a cause or instance of this. ● *v.tr.* cause inconvenience to. [ME f. OF f. LL *inconvenientia* (as INCONVENIENT)]

■ *n.* **1** troublesomeness, cumbersomeness, unwieldiness, burdensomeness, onerousness, disadvantageousness, awkwardness, inexpediency, inopportuneness, inappropriateness, untimeliness. **2** trouble, nuisance, bother, annoyance, irritation, awkwardness, burden, difficulty, hindrance, impediment, disturbance, disruption, discomfort, upset, disadvantage, drawback, *colloq.* hassle, pain (in the neck), *sl.* pain in the butt. ● *v.* discommode, incommode, trouble, disturb, disrupt, upset, put out, bother, annoy, irritate, irk, *colloq.* hassle.

inconvenient /ínkənveényənt/ *adj.* **1** unfavorable to ease or comfort; not convenient. **2** awkward; troublesome. □□ **inconveniently** *adv.* [ME f. OF f. L *inconveniens -entis* (as IN-¹, CONVENIENT)]

■ disadvantageous, troublesome, bothersome, annoying, irritating, irksome, unsettling, disturbing, upsetting, disrupting; cumbersome, unwieldy, burdensome, onerous, awkward; inappropriate, inexpedient, inopportune, untimely, ill-timed.

inconvertible /ínkənvártibəl/ *adj.* **1** not convertible. **2** (esp. of currency) not convertible into another form on demand. □□ **inconvertibility** *n.* **inconvertibly** *adv.* [F *inconvertible* or LL *inconvertibilis* (as IN-¹, CONVERTIBLE)]

incoordination /ínkō-awrd'náyshən/ *n.* lack of coordination, esp. of muscular action.

incorporate *v. & adj.* ● *v.* /inkáwrpərayt/ **1** *tr.* (often foll. by *in, with*) unite; form into one body or whole. **2** *intr.* become incorporated. **3** *tr.* combine (ingredients) into one substance. **4** *tr.* admit as a member of a company, etc. **5** *tr.* **a** constitute as a legal corporation. **b** (as **incorporated** *adj.*) forming a legal corporation. ● *adj.* /inkáwrpərət/ **1** (of a company, etc.) formed into a legal corporation. **2** embodied. □□ **incorporation** /-áyshən/ *n.* **incorporator** *n.* [ME f. LL *incorporare* (as IN-², L *corpus -oris* body)]

■ *v.* **1, 3** unite, unify, integrate, associate, amalgamate, combine, consolidate; assimilate, merge, mix, blend, fuse. **2** unite, integrate, amalgamate, combine, coalesce, assimilate, associate, merge, fuse, blend. **4** see INCLUDE 1. □□ **incorporation** union, unification, integration, association, amalgamation, combination, combine, consolidation, assimilation, merger, mixture, blend, fusion, coalescence; see also *inclusion* (INCLUDE).

incorporeal /ínkawrpáwreeəl/ *adj.* **1** not composed of matter. **2** of immaterial beings. **3** *Law* having no physical existence. □□ **incorporeality** /-reeálitee/ *n.* **incorporeally** *adv.* **incorporeity** /-pəreé-itee/ *n.* [L *incorporeus* (as INCORPORATE)]

■ **1, 2** see IMMATERIAL 2.

incorrect /ínkərékt/ *adj.* **1** not in accordance with fact; wrong. **2** (of style, etc.) improper; faulty. □□ **incorrectly** *adv.* **incorrectness** *n.* [ME f. OF or L *incorrectus* (as IN-¹, CORRECT)]

■ **1** wrong, mistaken, inaccurate, untrue, imprecise, inexact, erroneous, mistaken, out, off, false, fallacious, wide of the mark, *colloq.* off the beam. **2** see IMPROPER 2.

incorrigible /inkáwrijibəl, -kór-/ *adj.* **1** (of a person or habit) incurably bad or depraved. **2** not readily improved. □□ **incorrigibility** *n.* **incorrigibleness** *n.* **incorrigibly** *adv.* [ME f. OF *incorrigible* or L *incorrigibilis* (as IN-¹, CORRIGIBLE)]

■ **1** evil, bad, immoral, wicked, vicious, vile, sinful, depraved, corrupt, villainous, criminal; naughty, mischievous, ill-behaved. **2** inveterate, engrained, ingrained, hardened, habitual, incurable, unchangeable, dyed-in-the-wool, out-and-out, unalterable, intractable, stubborn, obdurate, *colloq.* *disp.* chronic.

incorruptible /inkəróptibəl/ *adj.* **1** that cannot be corrupted, esp. by bribery. **2** that cannot decay; everlasting. □□ **incorruptibility** /-bílitee/ *n.* **incorruptibly** *adv.* [ME f. OF *incorruptible* or eccl.L *incorruptibilis* (as IN-¹, CORRUPT)]

■ **1** moral, noble, upright, righteous, pure, upstanding, honorable, good, virtuous, honest, straightforward, straight, unimpeachable, rhadamanthine; see also TRUSTWORTHY. **2** everlasting, lasting, enduring; see also IMMORTAL *adj.* 2. □□ **incorruptibility** see INTEGRITY 1.

increase *v. & n.* ● *v.* /inkreés/ **1** *tr. & intr.* make or become greater in size, amount, etc., or more numerous. **2** *intr.* advance (in quality, attainment, etc.). **3** *tr.* intensify (a quality). ● *n.* /ínkrees/ **1** the act or process of becoming greater or more numerous; growth; enlargement. **2** (of people, animals, or plants) growth in numbers; multiplication. **3** the amount or extent of an increase. □ **on the increase** increasing, esp. in frequency. □□ **increasable** *adj.* **increaser** *n.* **increasingly** *adv.* [ME f. OF *encreiss-* stem of *encreistre* f. L *increscere* (as IN-², *crescere* grow)]

■ *v.* **1** (*tr. & intr.*) multiply, propagate, breed; augment, build up, enlarge, amplify, expand, extend, develop, broaden, widen, lengthen, heighten, escalate, accelerate, speed up; inflate, dilate, distend, swell; (*tr.*) add to, maximize, raise, lift, step up, *sl.* crank up; (*intr.*) grow, jump, soar, shoot up, rocket, explode, snowball, wax, flourish, proliferate, spread, *literary* burgeon. **2** appreciate, improve, get better, advance, progress, make progress, move (on *or* ahead *or* forward), climb. **3** intensify, enhance, sharpen, strengthen, reinforce, emphasize, point up, highlight; aggrandize, magnify, jazz up, *sl.* beef up. ● *n.* **1, 2** multiplication, propagation, proliferation, explosion; augmentation, increment, addition, enlargement, expansion, extension, development, amplification; acceleration, escalation, growth, jump, rise, spread, distension, inflation, dilation; appreciation, improvement, advance, progress; magnification, aggrandizement. **3** increment, gain, rise, growth, jump, lift, addition, advance, improvement, appreciation, *colloq.* boost. □ **on the increase** on the rise, on the way up, on the upgrade, increasing, growing, proliferating, escalating. □□ **increasingly** progressively, more and more, cumulatively; constantly, ever, still.

/. . ./ **pronunciation**	● **part of speech**
□ **phrases, idioms, and compounds**	
□□ **derivatives**	■ **synonym section**
cross-references appear in SMALL CAPITALS or *italics*	

incredible /inkrédibəl/ adj. **1** that cannot be believed. **2** *colloq.* hard to believe; amazing. □□ **incredibility** n. **incredibleness** n. **incredibly** adv. [ME f. L *incredibilis* (as IN-¹, CREDIBLE)]

■ **1, 2** unbelievable, beyond belief, inconceivable, unimaginable, unthinkable; impossible, absurd, preposterous, ridiculous, far-fetched, unrealistic, fictitious, fabulous, legendary, mythical, mythic, implausible, improbable, unlikely, doubtful, dubious, questionable, suspect, suspicious, *colloq.* funny, *sl.* fishy, unreal; see also *amazing* (AMAZE).

incredulous /inkréjələs/ adj. (often foll. by *of*) unwilling to believe. □□ **incredulity** /ínkridoॅolitee, -dyoॅo-/ n. **incredulously** adv. **incredulousness** n. [L *incredulus* (as IN-¹, CREDULOUS)]

■ disbelieving, unbelieving, mistrustful, distrustful, dubious, doubtful, skeptical, suspicious, interrogatory, questioning; cynical. □□ **incredulity, incredulousness** see DISTRUST n.

increment /ínkrimənt/ n. **1 a** an increase or addition, esp. one of a series on a fixed scale. **b** the amount of this. **2** *Math.* a small amount by which a variable quantity increases. □□ **incremental** /-ment'l/ adj. [ME f. L *incrementum* f. *increscere* INCREASE]

■ **1 a** see INCREASE n. 1, 2. **b** see INCREASE n. 3.

incriminate /inkríminayt/ v.tr. **1** tend to prove the guilt of (*incriminating evidence*). **2** involve in an accusation. **3** charge with a crime. □□ **incrimination** /-náyshən/ n. **incriminatory** /-nətáwree/ adj. [LL *incriminare* (as IN-², L *crimen* offense)]

■ **1** inculpate, point to, blame. **2** involve, embroil, enmesh, entangle, associate, connect, *sl.* frame. **3** accuse, charge, indict, arraign, impeach, inculpate, denounce, put in the dock. □□ **incrimination** see IMPLICATION, ACCUSATION.

incrust var. of ENCRUST.

incrustation /ínkrustáyshən/ n. **1** the process of encrusting or state of being encrusted. **2** a crust or hard coating, esp. of fine material. **3** a concretion or deposit on a surface. **4** a facing of marble, etc., on a building. [F *incrustation* or LL *incrustatio* (as ENCRUST)]

■ **2** see SKIN n. 4. **3** see DEPOSIT n. 3.

incubate /íngkyəbayt/ v. **1** tr. sit on or artificially heat (eggs) in order to bring forth young birds, etc. **2** tr. cause the development of (bacteria, etc.) by creating suitable conditions. **3** intr. sit on eggs; brood. [L *incubare* (as IN-², *cubare* cubit- or *cubat-* lie)]

■ **1, 3** hatch, sit on; brood. **2** breed, grow, raise, develop, nurse, nurture.

incubation /íngkyəbáyshən/ n. **1 a** the act of incubating. **b** brooding. **2** *Med.* **a** a phase through which the germs causing a disease pass before the development of the first symptoms. **b** the period of this. □□ **incubational** adj. **incubative** adj. **incubatory** /íngkyəbətáwree/ adj. [L *incubatio* (as INCUBATE)]

incubator /íngkyəbaytər/ n. **1** an apparatus used to provide a suitable temperature and environment for a premature baby or one of low birthweight. **2** an apparatus used to hatch eggs or grow microorganisms.

incubus /íngkyəbəs/ n. (pl. **incubi** /-bī/ or **incubuses**) **1** an evil spirit supposed to descend on sleeping persons. **2** a nightmare. **3** a person or thing that oppresses like a nightmare. [ME f. LL, = L *incubo* nightmare (as INCUBATE)]

incudes pl. of INCUS.

inculcate /inkúlkayt/ v.tr. (often foll. by *upon, in*) urge or impress (a fact, habit, or idea) persistently. □□ **inculcation** /-káyshən/ n. **inculcator** n. [L *inculcare* (as IN-², *calcare* tread f. *calx calcis* heel)]

■ see DIN v. □□ **inculcation** see DISCIPLINE n. 2a.

inculpate /inkúlpayt/ v.tr. **1** involve in a charge. **2** accuse; blame. □□ **inculpation** /-páyshən/ n. **inculpative** /inkúlpətiv/ adj. **inculpatory** /-pətáwree/ adj. [LL *inculpare* (as IN-², *culpare* blame f. *culpa* fault)]

■ **1** see INCRIMINATE 2, 3. **2** see INCRIMINATE 3.

incumbency /inkúmbənsee/ n. (pl. **-ies**) the office, tenure, or sphere of an incumbent.

■ place, position, office; see also TENURE 1, 2.

incumbent /inkúmbənt/ adj. & n. ● adj. **1** (foll. by *on, upon*) resting as a duty (*it is incumbent on you to warn them*). **2** (often foll. by *on*) lying; pressing. **3** in occupation or having the tenure of a post or position. ● n. the holder of an office or post, esp. an elected official. [ME f. AL *incumbens* pres. part. of L *incumbere* lie upon (as IN-², *cubare* lie)]

■ adj. **1** obligatory, necessary, required, requisite, mandatory, compulsory, binding; (*incumbent on*) expected of. **2** recumbent, prone, prostrate, supine; pressing. **3** in office, sitting, reigning, presiding; current. ● n. holder, officeholder, occupant; official, functionary, officer.

incunable /inkyoॅonəbəl/ n. = INCUNABULUM 1. [F, formed as INCUNABULUM]

incunabulum /ínkyənábyələm/ n. (pl. **incunabula** /-lə/) **1** a book printed at an early date, esp. before 1501. **2** (in pl.) the early stages of the development of a thing. [L *incunabula* swaddling clothes, cradle (as IN-², *cunae* cradle)]

incur /inkə́r/ v.tr. (**incurred, incurring**) suffer, experience, or become subject to (something unpleasant) as a result of one's own behavior, etc. (*incurred huge debts*). □□ **incurrable** adj. [ME f. L *incurrere incurs-* (as IN-², *currere* run)]

■ suffer, experience, undergo, face, sustain, meet (with), come in for; bring upon *or* on (oneself), draw, attract, arouse, provoke, invite, expose (oneself) to, lay (oneself) open to.

incurable /inkyoॅorəbəl/ adj. & n. ● adj. that cannot be cured. ● n. a person who cannot be cured. □□ **incurability** n. **incurableness** n. **incurably** adv. [ME f. OF *incurable* or LL *incurabilis* (as IN-¹, CURABLE)]

■ adj. irremediable, immedicable, inoperable, irreparable, irredeemable, irreversible; fatal, terminal, hopeless; see also INCORRIGIBLE 2. ● n. terminal, *sl.* goner.

incurious /inkyoॅoreeəs/ adj. **1** lacking curiosity. **2** heedless; careless. □□ **incuriosity** /-reeósitee/ n. **incuriously** adv. **incuriousness** n. [L *incuriosus* (as IN-¹, CURIOUS)]

incursion /inkə́rzhən, -shən/ n. an invasion or attack, esp. when sudden or brief. □□ **incursive** /-kə́rsiv/ adj. [ME f. L *incursio* (as INCUR)]

■ see ATTACK n. 1.

incurve /inkə́rv/ v.tr. **1** bend into a curve. **2** (as **incurved** adj.) curved inward. □□ **incurvation** /-váyshən/ n. [L *incurvare* (as IN-², CURVE)]

incus /íngkəs/ n. (pl. **incudes** /-kyoॅodeez/) the small anvil-shaped bone in the middle ear, in contact with the malleus and stapes. [L, = anvil]

incuse /inkyoॅoz, -kyoॅos/ n., v., & adj. ● n. an impression hammered or stamped on a coin. ● v.tr. **1** mark (a coin) with a figure by stamping. **2** impress (a figure) on a coin by stamping. ● adj. hammered or stamped on a coin. [L *incusus* past part. of *incudere* (as IN-², *cudere* forge)]

Ind. abbr. **1** Independent. **2** Indiana. **3 a** India. **b** Indian.

indaba /indaॅabə/ n. *S.Afr.* **1** a conference between or with members of S. African native tribes. **2** *colloq.* one's problem or concern. [Zulu, = business]

indebted /indétid/ adj. (usu. foll. by *to*) **1** owing gratitude or obligation. **2** owing money. □□ **indebtedness** n. [ME f. OF *endetté* past part. of *endetter* involve in debt (as EN-¹, *detter* f. *dette* DEBT)]

■ **1** obliged, beholden, bound, in a person's debt; liable, responsible, accountable; grateful, thankful, appreciative. **2** in debt, embarrassed, encumbered, overdrawn, in the red, *colloq.* in hock; insolvent, bankrupt. □□ **indebtedness** see DEBT.

indecent /indéesənt/ adj. **1** offending against recognized standards of decency. **2** unbecoming; highly unsuitable (*with indecent haste*). □ **indecent exposure** the intentional act of publicly and indecently exposing one's body, esp. the genitals. □□ **indecency** n. (pl. **-ies**). **indecently** adv. [F *indécent* or L *indecens* (as IN-¹, DECENT)]

■ **1** shameless, shameful, offensive, outrageous, repellent, repulsive, distasteful, ill-mannered, rude, suggestive, coarse, risqué, vulgar, blue, obscene, gross, rank, prurient, dirty, foul, filthy, pornographic, scatological, salacious, lascivious, licentious, lewd, lubricious, smutty, vile, degenerate, debauched, *Gk Hist.* ithyphallic, *Brit. colloq.* near the knuckle, *euphem.* adult. **2** unseemly, indecorous, indelicate, immodest, improper, unbecoming, unsuitable, unfit, inappropriate; in bad taste. □□ **indecency** shamelessness, shamefulness, offensiveness, outrageousness, repellence, repellency, repulsiveness, distastefulness, rudeness, suggestiveness, coarseness, vulgarity, obscenity, grossness, rankness, prurience, dirtiness, foulness, filthiness, pornography, salaciousness, lasciviousness, licentiousness, lewdness, lubricity, smuttiness, vileness, degeneracy; see also IMPROPRIETY 1.

indecipherable /índisífərəbəl/ *adj.* that cannot be deciphered.
■ see ILLEGIBLE.

indecision /índisízhən/ *n.* lack of decision; hesitation. [F *indécision* (as IN-¹, DECISION)]
■ indecisiveness, irresolution, irresoluteness, uncertainty, incertitude, doubt, ambivalence, tentativeness, hesitation, hesitance, hesitancy, tremulousness, vacillation, fluctuation, shilly-shally, *colloq.* dither.

indecisive /índisísiv/ *adj.* **1** not decisive. **2** undecided; hesitating. □□ **indecisively** *adv.* **indecisiveness** *n.*
■ **1** indefinite, indeterminate, undecided, undetermined, inconclusive, (still) open, unresolved, unsettled, moot, doubtful, vague, ambiguous. **2** undecided, irresolute, uncertain, of two minds, ambivalent, doubtful, dubious, tentative, hesitant, tremulous, shilly-shally, wishy-washy, *colloq.* dithery, all of a dither.

indeclinable /índiklínəbəl/ *adj. Gram.* **1** that cannot be declined. **2** having no inflections. [ME f. F *indéclinable* f. L *indeclinabilis* (as IN-¹, DECLINE)]

indecorous /indékərəs/ *adj.* **1** improper. **2** in bad taste. □□ **indecorously** *adv.* **indecorousness** *n.* [L *indecorus* (as IN-¹, *decorus* seemly)]
■ **1** see IMPROPER 1a. **2** see IMPROPER 1b.
□□ **indecorously** see FAST¹ *adv.* 5. **indecorousness** see IMPROPRIETY 1.

indecorum /indékáwrəm/ *n.* **1** lack of decorum. **2** improper behavior. [L, neut. of *indecorus*: see INDECOROUS]
■ **1** see INCIVILITY. **2** see IMPROPRIETY 1.

indeed /indeéd/ *adv. & int.* ● *adv.* **1** in truth; really; yes; that is so (*they are, indeed, a remarkable family*). **2** expressing emphasis or intensification (*I shall be very glad indeed; indeed it is; very, indeed inordinately, proud of it*). **3** admittedly (*there are indeed exceptions*). **4** in point of fact (*if indeed such a thing is possible*). **5** expressing an approving or ironic echo (*who is this Mr. Smith? — who is he indeed?*). ● *int.* expressing irony, contempt, incredulity, etc.
■ *adv.* **1** truly, truthfully, really, in reality, in fact, actually, *archaic* verily, yea, *archaic or joc.* forsooth, *literary* in truth; seriously, (all) joking aside *or* apart, on *or* upon my word, on *or* upon my honor, *colloq.* honor bright; exactly, precisely; yes, (that's) right, that's true, that is so, assuredly, check, *Brit.* rather, *colloq.* I'll say. **2** certainly, surely, to be sure, assuredly, doubtless, doubtlessly, undoubtedly, without doubt, no doubt, undeniably, definitely, positively, absolutely, by all means, *archaic* certes; not to say, nay, to say the least. **3** admittedly, undeniably, granted, (it is) true; of course, no doubt, certainly, naturally. **4** in (point of) fact, as a matter of fact, in reality, to be realistic. ● *int.* is that so *or* a fact?, really, *colloq.* you don't say (so), uh-huh, *sl.* no kidding; gracious, mercy, fancy (that), imagine, (upon) my word, by Jove, (well) I'm blessed, well I (do) declare, my (sainted) aunt, (my) goodness, (good) Lord, good heavens, *Brit.* I say, *colloq.* gee, gee whiz, my stars, well I'm *or* I'll be damned, *Brit. sl.* crikey, (cor) blimey, gorblimey; really?, bah, phooey, (stuff and) nonsense, rot, fudge, *archaic* go to, *colloq.*

come off it, go on, tell me another, pull the other one, tell that to the marines, oh yeah?, *Brit. sl.* cor, coo.

indef. *abbr.* indefinite.

indefatigable /índifátigəbəl/ *adj.* (of a person, quality, etc.) that cannot be tired out; unwearying; unremitting. □□ **indefatigability** *n.* **indefatigably** *adv.* [obs. F *indéfatigable* or L *indefatigabilis* (as IN-¹, *defatigare* wear out)]
■ see TIRELESS. □□ **indefatigably** see HARD *adv.* 1.

indefeasible /índifeézibəl/ *adj. literary* (esp. of a claim, rights, etc.) that cannot be lost. □□ **indefeasibility** *n.* **indefeasibly** *adv.*
■ see INALIENABLE.

indefectible /índiféktibəl/ *adj.* **1** unfailing; not liable to defect or decay. **2** faultless. [IN-¹ + *defectible* f. LL *defectibilis* (as DEFECT)]

indefensible /índifénsibəl/ *adj.* that cannot be defended or justified. □□ **indefensibility** *n.* **indefensibly** *adv.*
■ see INEXCUSABLE.

indefinable /índifínəbəl/ *adj.* that cannot be defined or exactly described. □□ **indefinably** *adv.*
■ see INEXPRESSIBLE.

indefinite /indéfinit/ *adj.* **1** vague; undefined. **2** unlimited. **3** *Gram.* not determining the person, thing, time, etc., referred to. □ **indefinite article** see ARTICLE. **indefinite integral** see INTEGRAL. **indefinite pronoun** *Gram.* a pronoun indicating a person, amount, etc., without being definite or particular, e.g., *any, some, anyone*. □□ **indefiniteness** *n.* [L *indefinitus* (as IN-¹, DEFINITE)]
■ **1** vague, uncertain, unsure, ambiguous, equivocal, doubtful, dubious, questionable, demurrable, debatable, moot, in doubt, open to question; inexplicit, nonspecific, unspecified, general, undefined, unsettled, indeterminate, imprecise, inexact; ill-defined, blurred, blurry, hazy, indistinct, obscure, dim, fuzzy, unrecognizable, indistinguishable; see also INDECISIVE 1. **2** unlimited, unrestricted, unbounded, indeterminate; unknown, uncounted, untold, undefined, uncountable, undefinable, indefinable, indeterminable, immeasurable, incalculable, limitless, boundless, endless, infinite.

indefinitely /indéfinitlee/ *adv.* **1** for an unlimited time (*was postponed indefinitely*). **2** in an indefinite manner.
■ **2** see *at random* (RANDOM), *vaguely* (VAGUE).

indehiscent /índihísənt/ *adj. Bot.* (of fruit) not splitting open when ripe. □□ **indehiscence** /-səns/ *n.*

indelible /indélibəl/ *adj.* **1** that cannot be rubbed out or (in abstract senses) removed. **2** (of ink, etc.) that makes indelible marks. □□ **indelibility** *n.* **indelibly** *adv.* [F *indélébile* or L *indelebilis* (as IN-¹, *delebilis* f. *delēre* efface)]
■ **1** ineradicable, ineffaceable, inexpungible; everlasting, permanent, enduring, abiding, lasting, constant, durable, fixed, ingrained, engrained, persistent; imperishable, indestructible, immortal, undying, eternal.

indelicate /indélikət/ *adj.* **1** coarse; unrefined. **2** tactless. **3** tending to indecency. □□ **indelicacy** *n.* (*pl.* **-ies**). **indelicately** *adv.*
■ **1** coarse, rough, crude, rough-hewn, unrefined, vulgar, common, gross; rude, boorish, loutish, uncivilized, uncouth, ill-mannered, offensive, impolite, discourteous, uncivil, unmannerly, ungentlemanly, unladylike, immodest, indecorous, unseemly, in poor *or* bad taste, tasteless, inelegant, ill-bred. **2** tactless, undiplomatic, gauche, clumsy, insensitive, unfeeling; crude, gruff, bluff, blunt, brusque, abrupt, surly, abrasive, churlish, rude, close to *or* near the bone. **3** see INDECENT 1.

indemnify /indémnifī/ *v.tr.* (**-ies, -ied**) **1** (often foll. by *from*, *against*) protect or secure (a person) in respect of harm, a

---

/.../ pronunciation	● part of speech
□ phrases, idioms, and compounds	
□□ derivatives	■ synonym section
cross-references appear in SMALL CAPITALS or *italics*	

loss, etc. **2** (often foll. by *for*) secure (a person) against legal responsibility for actions. **3** (often foll. by *for*) compensate (a person) for a loss, expenses, etc. □□ **indemnification** /-fikáyshən/ *n.* **indemnifier** *n.* [L *indemnis* unhurt (as IN-¹, *damnum* loss, damage)]

■ **3** see COMPENSATE 1. □□ **indemnification** see INSURANCE 1, RESTITUTION 2.

indemnity /indémnitee/ *n.* (*pl.* **-ies**) **1 a** compensation for loss incurred. **b** a sum paid for this, esp. a sum exacted by a victor in war, etc., as one condition of peace. **2** security against loss. **3** legal exemption from penalties, etc., incurred. [ME f. F *indemnité* or LL *indemnitas -tatis* (as INDEMNIFY)]

■ **1** compensation, consideration, restitution, reparation(s), redress, quid pro quo; atonement, expiation, satisfaction; indemnification, guarantee fund; recompense, repayment, reimbursement, remuneration, return. **2** security, protection, safety, insurance, assurance, guarantee, underwriting, warranty, endorsement, certification. **3** see *exemption* (EXEMPT).

indemonstrable /índimónstrəbəl, indémən-/ *adj.* that cannot be proved (esp. of primary or axiomatic truths).

indene /indeen/ *n.* *Chem.* a colorless, flammable liquid hydrocarbon obtained from coal tar and used in making synthetic resins. [INDOLE + -ENE]

indent¹ /indént/ *v. & n.* ● *v.* **1** *tr.* start (a line of print or writing) further from the margin than other lines, e.g., to mark a new paragraph. **2** *tr.* **a** divide (a document drawn up in duplicate) into its two copies with a zigzag line dividing them and ensuring identification. **b** draw up (usu. a legal document) in exact duplicate. **3** *Brit.* **a** *intr.* (often foll. by *on, upon* a person, *for* a thing) make a requisition (orig. a written order with a duplicate). **b** *tr.* order (goods) by requisition. **4** *tr.* make toothlike notches in. **5** *tr.* form deep recesses in (a coastline, etc.). ● *n.* also /índent/ **1** indentation. **2** an indented line. **3** *Brit.* **a** an order (esp. from abroad) for goods. **b** an official requisition for stores. **4** an indenture. □□ **indenter** *n.* **indentor** *n.* [ME f. AF *endenter* f. AL *indentare* (as IN-², L *dens dentis* tooth)]

■ *n.* **1** see INDENTATION 2.

indent² /indént/ *v.tr.* **1** make a dent in. **2** impress (a mark, etc.). [ME f. IN-² + DENT]

indentation /índentáyshən/ *n.* **1** the act or an instance of indenting; the process of being indented. **2** a cut or notch. **3** a zigzag. **4** a deep recess in a coastline, etc.

■ **2** notch, nick, snick, groove, joggle, gouge, cut, score, slash, *archaic* scotch; dent, depression, impression, cranny, hollow, dimple, pit, kick; serration, dentil, crenel, crenation, crenature; *Anat.* hilum, recess. **3** zigzag; scalloping, herringbone, stagger.

indention /indénshən/ *n.* **1** the indenting of a line in printing or writing. **2** = INDENTATION.

indenture /indénchər/ *n. & v.* ● *n.* **1** an indented document (see INDENT¹ *v.* 2). **2** (usu. in *pl.*) a sealed agreement or contract. **3** a formal list, certificate, etc. ● *v.tr. hist.* bind (a person) by indentures, esp. as an apprentice. □□ **indentureship** *n.* [ME (orig. Sc.) f. AF *endenture* (as INDENT¹)]

■ *n.* **2** see DEED *n.* 4. ● *v.* see APPRENTICE *v.*

independence /índipéndəns/ *n.* **1** (often foll. by *of, from*) the state of being independent. **2** independent income. □ **Independence Day** a day celebrating the anniversary of national independence; in the US July 4.

■ **1** freedom, liberty, *laissez-aller*, independency, autonomy, self-rule, home rule, self-determination, self-government, autarchy, sovereignty; confidence, self-confidence, self-sufficiency, self-reliance, self-dependence, self-assurance.

independency /índipéndənsee/ *n.* (*pl.* **-ies**) **1** an independent state, territory, etc. **2** = INDEPENDENCE.

independent /índipéndənt/ *adj. & n.* ● *adj.* **1 a** (often foll. by *of*) not depending on authority or control. **b** self-governing. **2 a** not depending on another person for one's opinion or livelihood. **b** (of income or resources) making it unnecessary to earn one's living. **3** unwilling to be under an ob-

ligation to others. **4** *Polit.* (usu. **Independent**) not belonging to or supported by a party. **5** not depending on something else for its validity, efficiency, value, etc. (*independent proof*). **6** (of broadcasting, a school, etc.) not supported by public funds. ● *n.* **1** (usu. **Independent**) a person who is politically independent. **2** (**Independent**) *hist.* a Congregationalist. □□ **independently** *adv.*

■ *adj.* **1 a** unregulated, uncontrolled; unrestrained, unrestricted, unfettered, untrammeled, unbound, unbridled, unconstrained, dégagé, *Law* sui juris; substantive, self-existent, freestanding, stand-alone. **b** self-governing, self-governed, self-determining, self-determined, autonomous, autarchic, autarchical, autocephalous, sovereign, plenipotentiary, *hist.* allodial; freelance. **2a, 3** self-reliant, self-contained, self-sufficient, autonomous, sufficient, *Biol.* free-living; self-willed, self-assured, (self-)confident, freethinking, bold, individualistic, bohemian, unconventional, unorthodox. **4** nonparty, unaffiliated, nonpartisan, nonaligned, unaligned; disinterested, neutral, impartial, unprejudiced, unbiased. **5** objective, external, outside, neutral, equitable, disinterested, dispassionate, unbiased, impartial; detached, uninvolved, separate, unconnected, unrelated, distinct. **6** nongovernmental, self-financing, private, voluntary. ● *n.* **1** individual, nonconformist, maverick, loner. □□ **independently** freely, unrestrictedly, without restriction, without let or hindrance; voluntarily, of one's own accord, of one's own volition *or* free will, in one's own name, on one's own responsibility, autonomously, autarchically; substantively, absolutely; self-reliantly, self-sufficiently, self-assuredly, (self-)confidently, boldly; externally, objectively, disinterestedly, impartially; separately, singly, individually, one by one, one at a time, severally, unconnectedly, unrelatedly, distinctly, apart; alone, on one's *or* its own, by oneself *or* itself, single-handed(ly), solo, under one's *or* its own steam; personally, privately.

in-depth see DEPTH.

indescribable /índiskríbəbəl/ *adj.* **1** too unusual or extreme to be described. **2** vague; indefinite. □□ **indescribability** *n.* **indescribably** *adv.*

■ **1** see INEXPRESSIBLE. **2** see NONDESCRIPT *adj.*

indestructible /índistrúktibəl/ *adj.* that cannot be destroyed. □□ **indestructibility** *n.* **indestructibly** *adv.*

■ everlasting, eternal, endless, undying, immortal, deathless, imperishable, indelible, ineradicable, inexpungible, ineffaceable; unchangeable, immutable, unalterable, permanent, fixed, unchanging, changeless, constant, perennial; unbreakable, nonbreakable, shatterproof; see also DURABLE.

indeterminable /índitérminəbəl/ *adj.* **1** that cannot be ascertained. **2** (of a dispute, etc.) that cannot be settled. □□ **indeterminably** *adv.* [ME f. LL *indeterminabilis* (as IN-¹, L *determinare* DETERMINE)]

■ **1** see INDEFINITE 1.

indeterminate /índitérminət/ *adj.* **1** not fixed in extent, character, etc. **2** left doubtful; vague. **3** *Math.* (of a quantity) not limited to a fixed value by the value of another quantity. **4** (of a judicial sentence) such that the convicted person's conduct determines the date of release. □ **indeterminate vowel** the obscure vowel /ə/ heard in '*a* moment *ago*'; a schwa. □□ **indeterminacy** *n.* **indeterminately** *adv.* **indeterminateness** *n.* [ME f. LL *indeterminatus* (as IN-¹, DETERMINATE)]

■ **1** see INDEFINITE. **2** see VAGUE 1.

indetermination /índitérmináyshən/ *n.* **1** lack of determination. **2** the state of being indeterminate.

indeterminism /índitérminizəm/ *n.* the belief that human action is not wholly determined by motives. □□ **indeterminist** *n.* **indeterministic** *adj.*

index /índeks/ *n. & v.* ● *n.* (*pl.* **indexes** or esp. in technical use **indices** /índiseez/) **1** an alphabetical list of names, subjects, etc., with references, usu. at the end of a book. **2** = *card index*. **3** (in full **index number**) a number showing the

variation of prices or wages as compared with a chosen base period (*retail price index*; *Dow-Jones index*). **4** *Math.* **a** the exponent of a number. **b** the power to which it is raised. **5 a** a pointer, esp. on an instrument, showing a quantity, a position on a scale, etc. **b** an indicator of a trend, direction, tendency, etc. **c** (usu. foll. by *of*) a sign, token, or indication of something. **6** *Physics* a number expressing a physical property, etc., in terms of a standard (*refractive index*). **7** *Computing* a set of items each of which specifies one of the records of a file and contains information about its address. **8** (**Index**) *RC Ch. hist.* a list of books forbidden to Roman Catholics to read. **9** *Printing* a symbol shaped like a pointing hand, used to draw attention to a note, etc. ● *v.tr.* **1** provide (a book, etc.) with an index. **2** enter in an index. **3** relate (wages, etc.) to the value of a price index. □ **index finger** the forefinger. **index-linked** esp. *Brit.* related to the value of a retail price index. **index of refraction** the ratio of the velocity of light in a vacuum to its velocity in a specified medium. □□ **indexation** *n.* **indexer** *n.* **indexible** /-déksibəl/ *adj.* **indexical** *adj.* **indexless** *adj.* [ME f. L *index indicis* forefinger, informer, sign: sense 8 f. L *Index librorum prohibitorum* list of prohibited books]
■ *n.* **1** table of contents, directory, catalog, register, inventory, itemization, list, listing, guide, key, ABC; gazetteer, dictionary, lexicon, vocabulary, concordance, thesaurus. **3** ratio, quotient, factor, measure, formula, figure. **5** pointer, indicator, needle, gnomon, guide, marker, *Computing* cursor; mark, sign, token, hint, clue. **9** fist. □ **index finger** forefinger, first finger.

india ink /índeeə/ *n.* (also **India ink**; *Brit.* **Indian ink**) **1** a black pigment made orig. in China and Japan. **2** a dark ink made from this, used esp. in drawing and technical graphics. [*India* in Asia: see INDIAN]

Indiaman /índeeəmən/ *n.* (*pl.* **-men**) *Naut. hist.* a ship engaged in trade with India or the East Indies.

Indian /índeeən/ *n.* & *adj.* ● *n.* **1 a** a native or national of India. **b** a person of Indian descent. **2** (in full **American Indian**) a member of the aboriginal peoples of America or their descendants. **3** any of the languages of the aboriginal peoples of America. ● *adj.* **1** of or relating to India, or to the subcontinent comprising India, Pakistan, and Bangladesh. **2** of or relating to the aboriginal peoples of America. □ **Indian clubs** a pair of bottle-shaped clubs swung to exercise the arms in gymnastics. **Indian corn** = CORN¹ 1. **Indian elephant** the elephant, *Elephas maximus*, of India, which is smaller than the African elephant. **Indian file** = *single file*. **Indian hemp** see HEMP 1. **Indian ink** *Brit.* = INDIA INK. **Indian Ocean** the ocean between Africa to the west, and Australia to the east. **Indian rope trick** a magician's trick, orig. from India, of climbing an upright unsupported length of rope. **Indian summer 1** a period of unusually dry, warm weather sometimes occurring in late autumn. **2** a late period of life characterized by comparative calm. [ME f. *India* ult. f. Gk *Indos* the River Indus f. Pers. *Hind*: cf. HINDU]

India paper *n.* **1** a soft absorbent kind of paper orig. imported from China, used for proofs of engravings. **2** a very thin, tough, opaque printing paper.

india rubber /índeeərúbər/ *n.* (also **India rubber**) = RUBBER¹ 2.

Indic /índik/ *adj.* & *n.* ● *adj.* of the group of Indo-European languages comprising Sanskrit and its modern descendants. ● *n.* this language group. [L *Indicus* f. Gk *Indikos* INDIAN]

indicate /índikayt/ *v.tr.* (often foll. by *that* + clause) **1** point out; make known; show. **2** be a sign or symptom of; express the presence of. **3** (often in *passive*) suggest; call for; require or show to be necessary (*stronger measures are indicated*). **4** admit to or state briefly (*indicated his disapproval*). **5** (of a gauge, etc.) give as a reading. [L *indicare* (as IN-², *dicare* make known)]
■ **1, 4** point out, designate, point to *or* at, mark, specify, identify, pinpoint, particularize, single out, call *or* direct attention to, show, display, exhibit, signal; manifest, demonstrate, make clear, make known; admit to, disclose, register, express, mention, state, say, tell.

2 signify, betoken, denote, manifest, imply, suggest, betoken, bespeak, reveal, evince, evidence. **3** call for, require, demand, need, recommend; suggest, hint (at), imply, intimate. **5** read, register, show, display, record.

indication /índikáyshən/ *n.* **1 a** the act or an instance of indicating. **b** something that suggests or indicates; a sign or symptom. **2** something indicated or suggested; esp. in *Med.*, a remedy or treatment that is suggested by the symptoms. **3** a reading given by a gauge or instrument. [F f. L *indicatio* (as INDICATE)]
■ **1 a** designation, specification, identification, particularization; show, display, exhibition, signal, manifestation, demonstration; admission, disclosure, registration, expression, mention, statement. **b** sign, signal, symptom, manifestation, token, *Computing* prompt; suggestion, hint, intimation, inkling, clue, implication; omen, portent, forewarning, warning, augury, foreshadowing, foretoken; (*indications*) evidence, data, indicia. **3** reading, readout, level, score; measure, degree.

indicative /indikətiv/ *adj.* & *n.* ● *adj.* **1** (foll. by *of*) suggestive; serving as an indication. **2** *Gram.* (of a mood) denoting simple statement of a fact. ● *n. Gram.* **1** the indicative mood. **2** a verb in this mood. □□ **indicatively** *adv.* [ME f. F *indicatif -ive* f. LL *indicativus* (as INDICATE)]
■ *adj.* **1** suggestive, symptomatic, indicatory, significative, denotative, indexical, indicial; characteristic, typical.

indicator /índikaytər/ *n.* **1** a person or thing that indicates. **2** a device indicating the condition of a machine, etc. **3** a recording instrument attached to an apparatus, etc. **4** esp. *Brit.* a board in a railroad station, etc., giving current information. **5** esp. *Brit.* a device (esp. a flashing light) on a vehicle to show that it is about to change direction; turn signal. **6** a substance that changes color at a given stage in a chemical reaction. **7** *Physics & Med.* a radioactive tracer.
■ **1** pointer, designator, marker, specifier, identifier, signaler; displayer; needle, gnomon, index, guide, *Computing* cursor. **2, 3** instrument, gauge, pressure gauge, meter, monitor, recorder, counter, log; flight recorder, black box; dial, display, panel, instrument panel, readout, LCD, LED. **6** litmus (paper); *Chem.* phenolphthalein, fluorescein.

indicatory /índikətawree/ *adj.* = INDICATIVE *adj.* 1.

indices *pl.* of INDEX.

indicia /indíshə/ *n.pl.* **1** distinguishing or identificatory marks. **2** signs; indications. [pl. of L *indicium* (as INDEX)]

indicial /indíshəl/ *adj.* **1** of the nature or form of an index. **2** of the nature of indicia; indicative.

indict /indít/ *v.tr.* accuse (a person) formally by legal process. □□ **indictee** /-tee/ *n.* **indicter** *n.* [ME f. AF *enditer* indict f. OF *enditier* declare f. Rmc *indictare* (unrecorded: as IN-², DICTATE)]
■ accuse, charge, arraign, impeach, incriminate, inculpate, prosecute, take to court, put in the dock, summon, summons; denounce, blame. □□ **indictee** (the) accused, defendant, respondent; corespondent. **indicter** see *accuser* (ACCUSE).

indictable /indítəbəl/ *adj.* **1** (of an offense) rendering the person who commits it liable to be charged with a crime. **2** (of a person) so liable.

indictment /indítmənt/ *n.* **1** the act of indicting. **2 a** a formal accusation. **b** a legal process in which this is made. **c** a document containing a charge. **3** something that serves to condemn or censure. [ME f. AF *enditement* (as INDICT)]
■ **1, 2a, c** see ACCUSATION.

indie /índee/ *n.* & *adj. colloq.* ● *n.* an independent record or motion-picture company. ● *adj.* (of a pop group or record label) independent, not belonging to one of the major companies.

/.../ **pronunciation**	● **part of speech**
□ **phrases, idioms, and compounds**	
□□ **derivatives**	■ **synonym section**
cross-references appear in SMALL CAPITALS or *italics*	

Indies /índeez/ *n.pl.* (prec. by *the*) archaic India and adjacent regions (see also *East Indies, West Indies*). [pl. of obs. *Indy* India]

indifference /indífrəns/ *n.* **1** lack of interest or attention. **2** unimportance (*a matter of indifference*). **3** neutrality. [L *indifferentia* (as INDIFFERENT)]

■ **1** unconcern, apathy, carelessness, pococurantism, listlessness, *disp.* disinterest; coolness, nonchalance, insouciance, aloofness, detachment, coldness, phlegm, stolidity, callousness, insensibility, impassiveness, impassivity; disregard, see also *absentmindedness* (ABSENTMINDED). **2** unimportance, insignificance, irrelevance, unconcern, inconsequence, inconsequentiality, triviality. **3** dispassion, disinterest, disinterestedness, impartiality, neutrality, objectivity, fairness, equitableness, evenhandedness.

indifferent /indífrənt/ *adj.* **1** neither good nor bad; average; mediocre. **2 a** not especially good. **b** fairly bad. **3** (often prec. by *very*) decidedly inferior. **4** (foll. by *to*) having no partiality for or against; having no interest in or sympathy for. **5** chemically, magnetically, etc., neutral. □□ **indifferently** *adv.* [ME f. OF *indifferent* or L *indifferens* (as IN-¹, DIFFERENT)]

■ **1** average, mediocre, fair (to middling), middling, neutral, ordinary, commonplace, everyday, *colloq.* common or garden; *comme ci, comme ça*; uninspired, undistinguished, colorless, bland; insipid, wishy-washy, dull, flat. **2 a** tolerable, passable, acceptable, satisfactory, all right, not bad, *colloq.* OK. **b** second-rate, so-so, lightweight, mediocre, lukewarm, poor, inferior, shoddy, substandard, unsatisfactory, not too good, *colloq.* not so hot; see also BAD *adj.* 1. **3** see BAD *adj.* 1. **4** impartial, neutral, evenhanded, objective, fair, fair-minded, equitable, unbiased, unprejudiced, uncolored, nonpartisan, disinterested, dispassionate, impassive, aloof, detached, distant, removed; unconcerned, apathetic, uninterested, listless, uncaring, cool, nonchalant, insouciant, blasé, lukewarm, Laodicean, lackadaisical; unsympathetic, insensitive, unfeeling, unemotional, inconsiderate, callous, cold, phlegmatic, stolid.

indifferentism /indífrəntizəm/ *n.* an attitude of indifference, esp. in religious matters. □□ **indifferentist** *n.*

indigenize /indíjiniz/ *v.tr.* **1** make indigenous; subject to native influence. **2** subject to increased use of indigenous people in government, etc. □□ **indigenization** *n.*

indigenous /indíjinəs/ *adj.* **1 a** (esp. of flora or fauna) originating naturally in a region. **b** (of people) born in a region. **2** (foll. by *to*) belonging naturally to a place. □□ **indigenously** *adv.* **indigenousness** *n.* [L *indigena* f. *indi-* = IN-² + *gen-* be born]

■ native, local, endemic; aboriginal, autochthonous, autochthonal, autochthonic.

indigent /indíjənt/ *adj.* needy; poor. □□ **indigence** /-jəns/ *n.* [ME f. OF f. LL *indigēre* f. *indi-* = IN-² + *egēre* need]

■ see POOR 1. □□ **indigence** see POVERTY 1.

indigested /índijéstid, -dī-/ *adj.* **1** shapeless. **2** ill-considered. **3** not digested.

indigestible /índijéstibəl/ *adj.* **1** difficult or impossible to digest. **2** too complex or awkward to read or comprehend easily. □□ **indigestibility** *n.* **indigestibly** *adv.* [F *indigestible* or LL *indigestibilis* (as IN-¹, DIGEST)]

indigestion /índijés-chən/ *n.* **1** difficulty in digesting food. **2** pain or discomfort caused by this. □□ **indigestive** *adj.* [ME f. OF *indigestion* or LL *indigestio* (as IN-¹, DIGESTION)]

■ dyspepsia, water brash, brash, acidity, heartburn, acidosis, *Med.* pyrosis; stomachache, upset stomach, stomach upset, *colloq.* bellyache, tummy ache, collywobbles; wind, flatulence.

indignant /indígnənt/ *adj.* feeling or showing scornful anger or a sense of injured innocence. □□ **indignantly** *adv.* [L *indignari indignant-* regard as unworthy (as IN-¹, *dignus* worthy)]

■ disgruntled, vexed, huffish, in a huff, in a pet, sore, displeased, resentful, up in arms, hot under the collar,

cross; piqued, irritated, irked, slighted, annoyed, exasperated, *colloq.* peeved, uptight, riled, miffed, *sl.* pissed, ticked off; see also ANGRY 1.

indignation /índignáyshən/ *n.* scornful anger at supposed unjust or unfair conduct or treatment. [ME f. OF *indignation* or L *indignatio* (as INDIGNANT)]

■ vexation, irritation, annoyance, exasperation, displeasure, resentment, pique, umbrage; anger, fury, rage, *literary* ire, wrath, *poet. or archaic* choler; see also ANGER *n.*

indignity /indígnitee/ *n.* (*pl.* -ies) **1** unworthy treatment. **2** a slight or insult. **3** the humiliating quality of something (*the indignity of my position*). [F *indignité* or L *indignitas* (as INDIGNANT)]

■ **1, 2** injustice, mistreatment; dishonor, embarrassment, disrespect, discourtesy, *colloq.* kick in the teeth; reproach, contumely, obloquy, offense, injury, abuse, outrage, affront, slap in the face, insult, slight, snub, *colloq.* put-down. **3** abjectness, wretchedness, miserableness, pitifulness.

indigo /índigō/ *n.* (*pl.* -os) **1 a** a natural blue dye obtained from the indigo plant. **b** a synthetic form of this dye. **2** any plant of the genus *Indigofera*. **3** (in full **indigo blue**) a color between blue and violet in the spectrum. □□ **indigotic** /-gótik/ *adj.* [16th-c. *indico* (f. Sp.), *indigo* (f. Port.) f. L *indicum* f. Gk *indikon* INDIAN (dye)]

indirect /índirékt, -dī-/ *adj.* **1** not going straight to the point. **2** (of a route, etc.) not straight. **3** not directly sought or aimed at (*an indirect result*). **4** (of lighting) from a concealed source and diffusely reflected. □ **indirect object** *Gram.* a person or thing affected by a verbal action but not primarily acted on (e.g., *him* in *give him the book*). **indirect question** *Gram.* a question in reported speech (e.g., *they asked who I was*). **indirect speech** (or **oration**) = *reported speech* (see REPORT). **indirect tax** a tax levied on goods and services and not on income or profits. □□ **indirectly** *adv.* **indirectness** *n.* [ME f. OF *indirect* or med.L *indirectus* (as IN-¹, DIRECT)]

■ **1, 2** oblique, circuitous, devious, tortuous, twisty, sinuous, winding, rambling, roundabout, erratic, crooked, zigzag, zigzagged; circumlocutory, circumlocutional, circumlocutionary, periphrastic, discursive, digressive, excursive. **3** secondary, ancillary, collateral, incidental, side, subordinate, subsidiary, accessory, additional, accidental, adventitious.
□ **indirect speech**, **indirect oration** reported speech, oblique oration *or* speech.

indiscernible /índisərnibəl/ *adj.* that cannot be discerned or distinguished from another. □□ **indiscernibility** *n.* **indiscernibly** *adv.*

■ see FAINT *adj.* 1, INDISTINGUISHABLE.

indiscipline /indísiplin/ *n.* lack of discipline.

indiscreet /índiskreét/ *adj.* **1** not discreet; revealing secrets. **2** injudicious; unwary. □□ **indiscreetly** *adv.* **indiscreetness** *n.* [ME f. LL *indiscretus* (as IN-¹, DISCREET)]

■ **1** garrulous, loquacious, talkative, gossipy, chattery, prating, *colloq.* gabby; untrustworthy, unreliable, undependable, irresponsible, feckless. **2** imprudent, injudicious, incautious, unguarded, unwary, improvident, impolitic, ill-advised, ill-judged, ill-considered, rash, reckless, audacious, bold, impulsive, hasty, impetuous, *literary* temerarious; thoughtless, insensitive, undiplomatic, tactless, heedless, careless, unthinking, mindless, unwise, naive, foolish, foolhardy.

indiscrete /índiskreét/ *adj.* not divided into distinct parts. [L *indiscretus* (as IN-¹, DISCRETE)]

indiscretion /índiskréshən/ *n.* **1** lack of discretion; indiscreet conduct. **2** an indiscreet action, remark, etc. [ME f. OF *indiscretion* or LL *indiscretio* (as IN-¹, DISCRETION)]

■ **1** garrulousness, loquaciousness, talkativeness; see also *imprudence* (IMPRUDENT). **2** gaffe, faux pas, misstep, blunder, error, mistake, slip, lapse, solecism, bull, *colloq.* (bad) break, slipup, howler, *sl.* booboo, boner, bloomer, *Brit. sl.* clanger.

indiscriminate /índiskrímínət/ *adj.* **1** making no distinc-

tions. **2** confused; promiscuous. □□ **indiscriminately** *adv.*
indiscriminateness *n.* **indiscrimination** /-náyshən/ *n.*
indiscriminative *adj.* [IN-¹ + *discriminate* (adj.) f. L *discriminatus* past part. (as DISCRIMINATE)]
■ **1** undiscriminating, indiscriminative, unselective, uncritical, arbitrary, random. **2** confused, haphazard, chaotic, erratic, random, disorganized, unorganized, jumbled, scrambled, mixed-up, promiscuous, uncoordinated, higgledy-piggledy; casual, unmethodical, unsystematic.

indispensable /índispénsəbəl/ *adj.* **1** (often foll. by *to, for*) that cannot be dispensed with; necessary. **2** (of a law, duty, etc.) that is not to be set aside. □□ **indispensability** *n.* **indispensableness** *n.* **indispensably** *adv.* [med.L *indispensabilis* (as IN-¹, DISPENSABLE)]
■ **1** necessary, obligatory, compulsory, mandatory, imperative, needful, requisite, essential, of the essence, vital, life-and-death, key, important, urgent, compelling, *colloq. disp.* crucial. **2** unavoidable, inescapable, ineluctable, overriding, incontestable, undeniable, inexorable.

indispose /índispōz/ *v.tr.* **1** (often foll. by *for,* or *to* + infin.) make unfit or unable. **2** (often foll. by *toward, from,* or *to* + infin.) make averse.
■ **1** see INCAPACITATE 1.

indisposed /índispōzd/ *adj.* **1** slightly unwell. **2** averse or unwilling.
■ **1** see ILL *adj.* 1. **2** averse, disinclined, loath, unwilling, reluctant, hesitant.

indisposition /índispəzíshən/ *n.* **1** ill health; a slight or temporary ailment. **2** disinclination. **3** aversion. [F *indisposition* or IN-¹ + DISPOSITION]
■ **1** see ILLNESS.

indisputable /índispyootəbəl/ *adj.* **1** that cannot be disputed. **2** unquestionable. □□ **indisputability** *n.* **indisputableness** *n.* **indisputably** *adv.* [LL *indisputabilis* (as IN-¹, DISPUTABLE)]
■ see INCONTROVERTIBLE.

indissoluble /índisólyəbəl/ *adj.* **1** that cannot be dissolved or decomposed. **2** lasting; stable (*an indissoluble bond*). □□ **indissolubility** *n.* **indissolubly** *adv.* [L *indissolubilis* (as IN-¹, DISSOLUBLE)]
■ □□ **indissolubly** see *inextricably* (INEXTRICABLE).

indistinct /índistíngkt/ *adj.* **1** not distinct. **2** confused; obscure. □□ **indistinctly** *adv.* **indistinctness** *n.* [ME f. L *indistinctus* (as IN-¹, DISTINCT)]
■ **1** uncertain, unsure, undecided, undetermined, indefinite, ambivalent, doubtful, vague; indistinguishable, undistinguishable, inseparable, undifferentiated. **2** confused, unclear, indeterminate, indefinite, ill-defined; blurred, blurry, fuzzy, hazy, foggy, misty, muddy, murky, dim, shadowy, bleary, obscure, vague; faint, imperceptible, indiscernible, indistinguishable; muffled, murmurous, garbled, scrambled, unintelligible, inarticulate, incomprehensible, illegible.

indistinctive /índistíngktiv/ *adj.* not having distinctive features. □□ **indistinctively** *adv.* **indistinctiveness** *n.*

indistinguishable /índistínggwishəbəl/ *adj.* (often foll. by *from*) not distinguishable. □□ **indistinguishableness** *n.* **indistinguishably** *adv.*
■ undistinguishable, inseparable, undifferentiated, indistinct; identical, (the) same, alike, similar, (two) of a kind; see also INDISTINCT 2.

indite /indít/ *v.tr. formal* or *joc.* **1** put (a speech, etc.) into words. **2** write (a letter, etc.). [ME f. OF *enditier*: see INDICT]
■ see WRITE 7.

indium /índeeəm/ *n. Chem.* a soft, silvery-white metallic element occurring naturally in sphalerite, etc., used for electroplating and in semiconductors. ¶ Symb.: **In**. [L *indicum* indigo with ref. to its characteristic spectral lines]

indivertible /índivértibəl/ *adj.* that cannot be turned aside. □□ **indivertibly** *adv.*

individual /índivíjooəl/ *adj. & n.* ● *adj.* **1** single. **2** particular; special; not general. **3** having a distinct character. **4** char-

acteristic of a particular person. **5** designed for use by one person. ● *n.* **1** a single member of a class. **2** a single human being as distinct from a family or group. **3** *colloq.* a person (*a most unpleasant individual*). □ **individual retirement account** a savings account that allows tax owed on interest to be deferred. [ME, = indivisible, f. med.L *individualis* (as IN-¹, *dividuus* f. *dividere* DIVIDE)]
■ *adj.* **1** single, sole, solitary, only, lone, one, alone; lonely, lonesome. **2, 3** particular, singular, specific, separate, distinct, discrete; special, peculiar, distinctive, different, unusual, odd, extraordinary, original, unique. **4** characteristic, typical, distinctive, idiosyncratic, peculiar; personal, own, *archaic* proper. **5** single, one-man; personal, custom-built, custom-made, made to measure, made to order. ● *n.* **1** person, human (being), (living) soul, mortal, man, woman, child. **2** one, customer; *colloq.* character, party, sort; see also FELLOW 1.

individualism /índivíjooəlizəm/ *n.* **1** the habit or principle of being independent and self-reliant. **2** a social theory favoring the free action of individuals. **3** self-centered feeling or conduct; egoism. □□ **individualist** *n.* **individualistic** *adj.* **individualistically** *adv.*
■ □□ **individualist** independent, freethinker, nonconformist, maverick, loner, lone wolf; *Philos.* solipsist. **individualistic** see INDEPENDENT *adj.* 2, 3.

individuality /índivíjoo-álitee/ *n.* (*pl.* -**ies**) **1** individual character, esp. when strongly marked. **2** (in *pl.*) individual tastes, etc. **3** separate existence.
■ **1** see *eccentricity* (ECCENTRIC). **2** (*individualities*) see DIVERSITY.

individualize /índivíjooəliz/ *v.tr.* **1** give an individual character to. **2** specify. □□ **individualization** *n.*
■ **1** see DISTINGUISH 2. **2** see SPECIFY.

individually /índivíjooəlee/ *adv.* **1** personally; in an individual capacity. **2** in a distinctive manner. **3** one by one; not collectively.
■ **1** see PERSONALLY 5, ALONE 1b. **3** one at a time, singly, one by one, separately, severally, apart.

individuate /índivíjoo-ayt/ *v.tr.* individualize; form into an individual. □□ **individuation** /-áyshən/ *n.* [med.L *individuare* (as INDIVIDUAL)]

indivisible /índivízibəl/ *adj.* **1** not divisible. **2** not distributable among a number. □□ **indivisibility** *n.* **indivisibly** *adv.* [ME f. LL *indivisibilis* (as IN-¹, DIVISIBLE)]

Indo- /índō/ *comb. form* Indian; Indian and. [L *Indus* f. Gk *Indos*]

Indo-Aryan /índō-áireeən/ *n. & adj.* ● *n.* **1** a member of any of the Aryan peoples of India. **2** the Indic group of languages. ● *adj.* of or relating to the Indo-Aryans or Indo-Aryan.

Indo-Chinese /índōchineéz/ *adj. & n.* (also **Indochinese**) ● *adj.* of or relating to Indochina in SE Asia. ● *n.* a native of Indochina; a person of Indo-Chinese descent.

indocile /índósil/ *adj.* not docile. □□ **indocility** /-sílitee/ *n.* [F *indocile* or L *indocilis* (as IN-¹, DOCILE)]

indoctrinate /índóktrinayt/ *v.tr.* **1** teach (a person or group) systematically or for a long period to accept (esp. partisan or tendentious) ideas uncritically. **2** teach; instruct. □□ **indoctrination** /-náyshən/ *n.* **indoctrinator** *n.* [IN-² + DOCTRINE + -ATE³]
■ train, teach, instruct, school, discipline, drill; brainwash, propagandize.

Indo-European /índō-yoorəpeéən/ *adj. & n.* ● *adj.* **1** of or relating to the family of languages spoken over the greater part of Europe and Asia as far as N. India. **2** of or relating to the hypothetical parent language of this family. ● *n.* **1** the Indo-European family of languages. **2** the hypothetical

---

/.../ pronunciation	● part of speech
□ phrases, idioms, and compounds	
□□ derivatives	■ synonym section
cross-references appear in SMALL CAPITALS or *italics*	

parent language of all languages belonging to this family. **3** (usu. in *pl.*) a speaker of an Indo-European language.

Indo-Iranian /índōiráyneeən/ *adj.* & *n.* ● *adj.* of or relating to the subfamily of Indo-European languages spoken chiefly in N. India and Iran. ● *n.* this subfamily.

indole /índōl/ *n. Chem.* an organic compound with a characteristic odor formed on the reduction of indigo. [INDIGO + L *oleum* oil]

indoleacetic acid /índōləseétik/ *n. Biochem.* any of the several isomeric acetic acid derivatives of indole, esp. one found as a natural growth hormone in plants. ¶ Abbr.: **IAA**. [INDOLE + ACETIC]

indolent /índələnt/ *adj.* **1** lazy; wishing to avoid activity or exertion. **2** *Med.* causing no pain (*an indolent tumor*). □□ **indolence** /-ləns/ *n.* **indolently** *adv.* [LL *indolens* (as IN-¹, *dolēre* suffer pain)]

■ **1** lazy, slothful, sluggish, idle, lethargic, shiftless, languorous, languid, torpid, inert, inactive, stagnant, fainéant, listless. □□ **indolence** laziness, slothfulness, sloth, sluggishness, idleness, lethargy, shiftlessness, languor, languidness, lassitude, listlessness, torpor, torpidity, inertia, inaction, inactivity, dolce far niente.

Indology /indóləjee/ *n.* the study of the history, literature, etc., of India. □□ **Indologist** *n.*

indomitable /indómitəbəl/ *adj.* **1** that cannot be subdued; unyielding. **2** stubbornly persistent. □□ **indomitability** *n.* **indomitableness** *n.* **indomitably** *adv.* [LL *indomitabilis* (as IN-¹, L *domitare* tame)]

■ **1** unconquerable, unbeatable, irrepressible, unstoppable, invincible, unyielding, unswerving, unwavering, unflinching. **2** resolute, resolved, determined, stubborn, steadfast, staunch, persistent, indefatigable, untiring, tireless, unflagging, undaunted, dauntless, fearless, unafraid, intrepid, brave, courageous, plucky, mettlesome.

Indonesian /índəneézhən, -shən/ *n.* & *adj.* ● *n.* **1 a** a native or national of Indonesia in SE Asia. **b** a person of Indonesian descent. **2** a member of the chief pre-Malay population of the E. Indies. **3** a language of the group spoken in the E. Indies, esp. the official language of the Indonesian Republic (see also BAHASA INDONESIA). ● *adj.* of or relating to Indonesia or its people or language. [*Indonesia* f. INDIES after *Polynesia*]

indoor /índáwr/ *adj.* situated, carried on, or used within a building or under cover (*indoor antenna; indoor games*). [earlier *within-door*: cf. INDOORS]

indoors /índáwrz/ *adv.* into or within a building. [earlier *within doors*]

indorse var. of ENDORSE.

indraft /índráft/ *n.* (*Brit.* **indraught**) **1** the drawing in of something. **2** an inward flow or current.

indrawn /índráwn/ *adj.* **1** (of breath, etc.) drawn in. **2** aloof.

indri /índree/ *n.* (*pl.* **indris**) a large lemur, *Indri indri*, of Madagascar. [Malagasy *indry* behold, mistaken for its name]

indubitable /indōobitəbəl, -dyōo-/ *adj.* that cannot be doubted. □□ **indubitably** *adv.* [F *indubitable* or L *indubitabilis* (as IN-¹, *dubitare* to doubt)]

■ see CERTAIN *adj.* 1b. □□ **indubitably** see *undoubtedly* (UNDOUBTED).

induce /indōos, -dyōos/ *v.tr.* **1** (often foll. by *to* + infin.) prevail on; persuade. **2** bring about; give rise to. **3** *Med.* bring on (labor) artificially, esp. by use of drugs. **4** *Electr.* produce (a current) by induction. **5** *Physics* cause (radioactivity) by bombardment. **6** infer; derive as a deduction. □□ **inducer** *n.* **inducible** *adj.* [ME f. L *inducere induct-* (as IN-², *ducere* lead)]

■ **1** lead, persuade, influence, prevail on *or* upon, sway, move, convince, get, talk into, prompt, incite, instigate, actuate, motivate, impel, encourage, inspire, stimulate, nudge, push, press, urge, prod, goad, spur, egg on, coax, cajole, lure, entice, inveigle, seduce. **2** cause, bring about *or* on, produce, give rise to, engender, create, generate, lead to; effect, occasion, set in motion.

inducement /indōosmənt, -dyōos-/ *n.* **1** (often foll. by *to*) an attraction that leads one on. **2** a thing that induces.

■ **1** attraction, lure, incentive, stimulus, enticement, bait, encouragement, incitement, provocation, spur. **2** lure, bait, carrot, spur, *sl.* come-on; see also INCENTIVE *n.* 2.

induct /indúkt/ *v.tr.* (often foll. by *to, into*) **1** introduce formally into possession of a benefice. **2** install into a room, office, etc. **3** introduce; initiate. **4** enlist (a person) for military service. □□ **inductee** /indúkteé/ *n.* [ME (as INDUCE)]

■ **1** install, inaugurate, invest, instate, establish, swear in; ordain. **2** install, move in, establish. **3** introduce, initiate, inaugurate, originate. **4** call up, enlist, conscript, enroll, recruit, register, draft.

inductance /indúktəns/ *n. Electr.* the property of an electric circuit that causes an electromotive force to be generated by a change in the current flowing.

induction /indúkshən/ *n.* **1** the act or an instance of inducting or inducing. **2** *Med.* the process of bringing on (esp. labor) by artificial means. **3** *Logic* **a** the inference of a general law from particular instances (cf. DEDUCTION). **b** *Math.* a means of proving a theorem by showing that, if it is true of any particular case, it is true of the next case in a series, and then showing that it is indeed true in one particular case. **c** (foll. by *of*) the production of (facts) to prove a general statement. **4** (often *attrib.*) a formal introduction to a new job, position, etc. (*attended an induction course*). **5** *Electr.* **a** the production of an electric or magnetic state by the proximity (without contact) of an electrified or magnetized body. **b** the production of an electric current in a conductor by a change of magnetic field. **6** the drawing of a fuel mixture into the cylinders of an internal combustion engine. **7** enlistment for military service. □ **induction coil** a coil for generating intermittent high voltage from a direct current. **induction heating** heating by an induced electric current. [ME f. OF *induction* or L *inductio* (as INDUCE)]

■ **1** see *initiation* (INITIATE), INSTALLATION 1.

inductive /indúktiv/ *adj.* **1** (of reasoning, etc.) of or based on induction. **2** of electric or magnetic induction. □□ **inductively** *adv.* **inductiveness** *n.* [LL *inductivus* (as INDUCE)]

■ **1** see LOGICAL 1–3.

inductor /indúktər/ *n.* **1** *Electr.* a component (in a circuit) which possesses inductance. **2** a person who inducts a member of the clergy. [L (as INDUCE)]

indue var. of ENDUE.

indulge /indúlj/ *v.* **1** *intr.* (often foll. by *in*) take pleasure freely. **2** *tr.* yield freely to (a desire, etc.). **3** *tr.* gratify the wishes of; favor (*indulged them with money*). **4** *intr. colloq.* take alcoholic liquor. □□ **indulger** *n.* [L *indulgēre indult-* give free rein to]

■ **1** wallow, luxuriate, be (self-)indulgent; gormandize, feast, carouse, banquet; (*indulge in*) yield to, succumb to, treat oneself to. **2** yield to, give in to, allow, gratify. **3** gratify, humor, oblige, minister to, cater to, pander to, treat; favor, pamper, baby, pet, cosset, mollycoddle, coddle, mother, spoil. **4** see DRINK *v.* 2.

indulgence /indúljəns/ *n.* **1 a** the act of indulging. **b** the state of being indulgent. **2** something indulged in. **3** *RC Ch.* the remission of temporal punishment in purgatory, still due for sins after absolution. **4** a privilege granted. □ **Declaration of Indulgence** the proclamation of religious liberties, esp. under Charles II in 1672 and James II in 1687. [ME f. OF f. L *indulgentia* (as INDULGENT)]

■ **1 a** self-indulgence, self-gratification; allowance, acceptance, forgiveness, remission, pardon. **b** self-indulgence, luxury, extravagance, profligacy, dissipation, self-satisfaction; tolerance, sufferance, understanding, patience, good will, forbearance, kindness, mercy, forgiveness. **2** treat, luxury, extravagance; fling.

indulgent /indúljənt/ *adj.* **1** ready or too ready to overlook faults, etc. **2** indulging or tending to indulge. □□ **indulgently** *adv.* [F *indulgent* or L *indulgere indulgent-* (as INDULGE)]

■ tolerant, permissive, patient, understanding, forbearing,

lenient, easygoing, relaxed, liberal, lax, soft, kind, kindly, well-disposed, agreeable.

indumentum /índŏŏméntəm, -dyŏŏ-/ n. (pl. **indumenta** /-tə/ or **indumentums**) Bot. the covering of hairs on part of a plant, esp. when dense. [L, = garment]

induna /indŏŏnə/ n. **1** S.Afr. a tribal councilor or headman. **2 a** an African foreman. **b** a person in authority. [Nguni inDuna captain, councilor]

indurate /índərayt, -dyə-/ v. **1** tr. & intr. make or become hard. **2** tr. make callous or unfeeling. **3** intr. become inveterate. □□ **induration** /-ráyshən/ n. **indurative** adj. [L indurare (as IN-², durus hard)]

indusium /indŏŏzeeəm, -zheeəm, -dyŏŏ-/ n. (pl. **indusia** /-zeeə/) **1** a membranous shield covering the fruit cluster of a fern. **2** a collection of hairs enclosing the stigma of some flowers. **3** the case of a larva. □□ **indusial** adj. [L, = tunic, f. induere put on (a garment)]

industrial /indústreeəl/ adj. & n. ● adj. **1** of or relating to industry or industries. **2** designed or suitable for industrial use (industrial alcohol). **3** characterized by highly developed industries (the industrial nations). ● n. (in pl.) shares in industrial companies. □ **industrial action** Brit. = job action. **industrial archaeology** the study of machines, factories, bridges, etc., formerly used in industry. **industrial estate** Brit. = industrial park. **industrial park** an area of land developed for a complex of factories and other businesses, usu. separate from an urban center. **industrial relations** the relations between management and workers in industries. **industrial revolution** the rapid development of a nation's industry (esp. the **Industrial Revolution**, in the late 18th and early 19th c.). □□ **industrially** adv. [INDUSTRY + -AL: in 19th c. partly f. F industriel]
■ adj. **1** see TECHNICAL 1.

industrialism /indústreeəlizəm/ n. a social or economic system in which manufacturing industries are prevalent.

industrialist /indústreeəlist/ n. a person engaged in the management of industry.
■ see manufacturer (MANUFACTURE).

industrialize /indústreeəlíz/ v. **1** tr. introduce industries to (a country or region, etc.). **2** intr. become industrialized. □□ **industrialization** n.

industrious /indústreeəs/ adj. diligent; hardworking. □□ **industriously** adv. **industriousness** n. [F industrieux or LL industriosus (as INDUSTRY)]
■ hardworking, diligent, sedulous, assiduous, Stakhanovist, workaholic; conscientious, earnest, painstaking; persistent, pertinacious, dogged, tenacious, untiring, tireless, indefatigable, unflagging; busy, energetic, vigorous, active, dynamic, enterprising, colloq. bustling. □□ **industriousness** see INDUSTRY 2, 3.

industry /índəstree/ n. (pl. **-ies**) **1 a** a branch of trade or manufacture. **b** trade and manufacture collectively (incentives to industry). **2** concerted or copious activity (the building was a hive of industry). **3 a** diligence. **b** colloq. the diligent study of a particular topic (the Shakespeare industry). **4** habitual employment in useful work. [ME, = skill, f. F industrie or L industria diligence]
■ **1** business, enterprise, commerce, trade, line, (line of) work; manufacture, production, fabrication. **2** busyness, industriousness, activity, (hustle and) bustle, dynamism, energy, vigor; work, labor, toil. **3** industriousness, diligence, assiduity, assiduousness, sedulity, sedulousness, Stakhanovism; conscientiousness, earnestness, painstakingness, application; persistence, persistency, perseverance, doggedness, determination, tenacity, tenaciousness, tirelessness, indefatigability; energy, vigor, exertion, effort, determination.

indwell /índwél/ v. (past and past part. **indwelt**) literary **1** intr. (often foll. by in) be permanently present as a spirit, principle, etc. **2** tr. inhabit spiritually. □□ **indweller** n.
■ □□ **indweller** see OCCUPANT 1.

-ine¹ /in, ín/ suffix forming adjectives, meaning 'belonging to, of the nature of' (Alpine; asinine). [from or after F -in -ine, or f. L -inus]

-ine² /ín/ suffix forming adjectives, esp. from names of minerals, plants, etc. (crystalline). [L -inus from or after Gk -inos]

-ine³ /in, een/ suffix forming feminine nouns (heroine; margravine). [F f. L -ina f. Gk -inē, or f. G -in]

-ine⁴ suffix **1** /ín/ forming (esp. abstract) nouns (discipline; medicine). **2** /een, in/ Chem. forming nouns denoting derived substances, esp. alkaloids, halogens, amines, and amino acids. [F f. L -ina (fem.) = -INE¹]

inebriate v., adj., & n. ● v.tr. /inéebreeayt/ **1** make drunk; intoxicate. **2** excite. ● adj. /inéebreeət/ drunken. ● n. /inéebreeət/ a drunken person, esp. a habitual drunkard. □□ **inebriation** /-áyshən/ n. **inebriety** /ínibríətee/ n. [ME f. L inebriatus past part. of inebriare (as IN-², ebrius drunk)]
■ v. **1** see INTOXICATE 1. **2** see INTOXICATE 2. □□ **inebriety** see drunkenness (DRUNKEN).

inedible /inédibəl/ adj. not edible, esp. not suitable for eating (cf. UNEATABLE). □□ **inedibility** n.
■ see UNPALATABLE.

inedited /inéditid/ adj. **1** not published. **2** published without editorial alterations or additions.

ineducable /inéjəkəbəl/ adj. incapable of being educated, esp. through mental retardation. □□ **ineducability** n.

ineffable /inéfəbəl/ adj. **1** unutterable; too great for description in words. **2** that must not be uttered. □□ **ineffability** n. **ineffably** adv. [ME f. OF ineffable or L ineffabilis (as IN-¹, effari speak out, utter)]
■ **1** unutterable, inexpressible, indefinable, undefinable, indescribable, incommunicable, unspeakable, beyond description, beyond words. **2** unmentionable, taboo.

ineffaceable /inifáysəbəl/ adj. that cannot be effaced. □□ **ineffaceability** n. **ineffaceably** adv.
■ see INDELIBLE.

ineffective /iniféktiv/ adj. **1** not producing any effect or the desired effect. **2** (of a person) inefficient; not achieving results. **3** lacking artistic effect. □□ **ineffectively** adv. **ineffectiveness** n.
■ **1** ineffectual, inefficacious, unsuccessful, unavailing; unproductive, unfruitful, fruitless, barren, vain, idle, futile, pointless, useless, archaic bootless; insufficient, inadequate; inoperative. **2** inefficient, incompetent, incapable, ineffectual; unskilled, unskillful, inexpert, inept; idle, otiose, redundant, shiftless.

ineffectual /inifékchŏŏəl/ adj. **1 a** without effect. **b** not producing the desired or expected effect. **2** (of a person) lacking the ability to achieve results (an ineffectual leader). □□ **ineffectuality** /-álitee/ n. **ineffectually** adv. **ineffectualness** n. [ME f. med.L ineffectualis (as IN-¹, EFFECTUAL)]
■ **1** see INEFFECTIVE 1. **2** incapable, incompetent, impotent, powerless, inefficient, inadequate, insufficient; weak, feeble, tame, lame; see also INEFFECTIVE 2.

inefficacious /inefikáyshəs/ adj. (of a remedy, etc.) not producing the desired effect. □□ **inefficaciously** adv. **inefficaciousness** n. **inefficacy** /inéfikəsee/ n.
■ see INEFFECTIVE 1.

inefficient /inifíshənt/ adj. **1** not efficient. **2** (of a person) not fully capable; not well qualified. □□ **inefficiency** n. **inefficiently** adv.
■ **1** uneconomical, uneconomic, wasteful, extravagant; unproductive, unprofitable, unfruitful, fruitless, ineffectual, inefficacious, ineffective; unprofessional, amateurish, disorganized, sloppy, lax, loose, slipshod. **2** ineffective, ineffectual, incompetent, incapable, unqualified, inexpert, unskilled, unskillful, inept, unfit. □□ **inefficiency** wastefulness, extravagance, unproductiveness, unprofitableness, unfruitfulness, fruitlessness; amateurishness, disorganization, sloppiness, laxity, laxness, looseness. **inefficiently** uneconomically, wastefully, extravagantly;

/. . ./ **pronunciation**	● **part of speech**
□ **phrases, idioms, and compounds**	
□□ **derivatives**	■ **synonym section**
cross-references appear in SMALL CAPITALS or italics	

unproductively, unprofitably, unfruitfully, fruitlessly; unprofessionally, amateurishly, sloppily, laxly, loosely.

inelastic /ínilástik/ *adj.* **1** not elastic. **2** unadaptable; inflexible; unyielding. □□ **inelastically** *adv.* **inelasticity** /-lastísitee/ *n.*

■ **1** see INFLEXIBLE 1. **2** see INFLEXIBLE 2.

inelegant /inélignt/ *adj.* **1** ungraceful. **2 a** unrefined. **b** (of a style) unpolished. □□ **inelegance** /-gns/ *n.* **inelegantly** *adv.* [F *inélégant* f. L *inelegans* (as IN-¹, ELEGANT)]

■ **1** see UNGRACEFUL. **2** see UNREFINED. □□ **inelegance** see *ineptitude* (INEPT).

ineligible /inélijibl/ *adj.* **1** not eligible. **2** undesirable. □□ **ineligibility** *n.* **ineligibly** *adv.*

■ unqualified, disqualified; unacceptable, unsuitable, unfit, inappropriate, improper.

ineluctable /ínilúktbl/ *adj.* **1** against which it is useless to struggle. **2** that cannot be escaped from. □□ **ineluctability** *n.* **ineluctably** *adv.* [L *ineluctabilis* (as IN-¹, *eluctari* struggle out)]

■ **2** see INEVITABLE 1. □□ **ineluctably** see NECESSARILY.

inept /inépt/ *adj.* **1** unskillful. **2** absurd; silly. **3** out of place. □□ **ineptitude** *n.* **ineptly** *adv.* **ineptness** *n.* [L *ineptus* (as IN-¹, APT)]

■ **1** unskillful, unskilled, inapt, inexpert, amateurish, inefficient, incompetent, maladroit, clumsy, awkward, bungling, bumbling, gauche, unhandy, ungainly, *Brit. colloq.* cack-handed, *sl.* out to lunch. **2** absurd, ridiculous, silly, preposterous, nonsensical, outlandish. **3** out of place, out of keeping, inappropriate, inexpedient, unsuitable, inapt, improper, outlandish. □□ **ineptitude, ineptness** unskillfulness, inaptitude, inaptness, inexpertness, amateurishness, inefficiency, incompetence, maladroitness, clumsiness, awkwardness, unhandiness, ungainliness, gaucherie, *Brit. colloq.* cack-handedness; absurdity, ridiculousness, silliness, preposterousness, outlandishness; inappropriateness, inexpediency, unsuitability, unsuitableness.

inequable /inékwbl/ *adj.* **1** not fairly distributed. **2** not uniform. [L *inaequabilis* uneven (as IN-¹, EQUABLE)]

inequality /íníkwólitee/ *n.* (*pl.* **-ies**) **1 a** lack of equality in any respect. **b** an instance of this. **2** the state of being variable. **3** (of a surface) irregularity. **4** *Math.* a formula affirming that two expressions are not equal. [ME f. OF *inequalité* or L *inaequalitas* (as IN-¹, EQUALITY)]

■ **1** disparity, difference, discrepancy, incongruence, incongruity, inconsistency, dissimilarity, imbalance; inequity, unfairness, injustice, partiality, bias, prejudice. **2** see *dissimilarity* (DISSIMILAR). **3** irregularity, unevenness, bumpiness, lumpiness, coarseness, roughness, jaggedness, cragginess.

inequitable /inékwitbl/ *adj.* unfair; unjust. □□ **inequitably** *adv.*

■ see UNREASONABLE 1.

inequity /inékwitee/ *n.* (*pl.* **-ies**) unfairness; bias.

■ see INEQUALITY 1.

ineradicable /ínirádikbl/ *adj.* that cannot be rooted out. □□ **ineradicably** *adv.*

■ see INDELIBLE.

inerrant /inérnt/ *adj.* not liable to err. □□ **inerrancy** *n.* [L *inerrans* (as IN-¹, ERR)]

inert /inrt/ *adj.* **1** without inherent power of action, motion, or resistance. **2** without active chemical or other properties. **3** sluggish; slow. □ **inert gas** = *noble gas*. □□ **inertly** *adv.* **inertness** *n.* [L *iners inert-* (as IN-¹, *ars* ART¹)]

■ **1** motionless, immobile, static, stationary, still, inanimate, dead, lifeless, nerveless, passive, quiet, quiescent. **2** inactive, unreactive, unresponsive, passive, neutral. **3** sluggish, slow, torpid, dull, inactive, leaden, slack, passive, supine, dormant, listless, languid, languorous, idle, indolent, lazy, slothful, *archaic* otiose. □□ **inertness** see INERTIA.

inertia /inórsh/ *n.* **1** *Physics* a property of matter by which it continues in its existing state of rest or uniform motion in a straight line, unless that state is changed by an external

force. **2** inertness; sloth. □ **inertia reel** esp. *Brit.* a reel device which allows a vehicle seat belt to unwind freely but which locks under force of impact or rapid deceleration. **inertia selling** esp. *Brit.* the sending of unsolicited goods in the hope of making a sale. □□ **inertial** *adj.* **inertialess** *adj.* [L (as INERT)]

■ **2** inertness, immobility, motionlessness, stasis, stationariness, stillness, inanimation, deadness, lifelessness, nervelessness, passivity, quiescence, quiescency, dormancy, inactivity, unresponsiveness; neutrality; apathy, sluggishness, slowness, torpor, torpidity, dullness, idleness, indolence, laziness, lassitude, listlessness, languor, slothfulness, sloth.

inescapable /ínisckáypbl/ *adj.* that cannot be escaped or avoided. □□ **inescapability** *n.* **inescapably** *adv.*

■ see UNAVOIDABLE. □□ **inescapably** see NECESSARILY.

-iness /eenis/ *suffix* forming nouns corresponding to adjectives in -*y* (see -Y¹, -LY²).

inessential /ínisénshl/ *adj. & n.* ● *adj.* **1** not necessary. **2** dispensable. ● *n.* an inessential thing.

■ *adj.* **1** see UNNECESSARY *adj.* 1. **2** see DISPENSABLE.

inestimable /inéstimbl/ *adj.* too great, intense, precious, etc., to be estimated. □□ **inestimably** *adv.* [ME f. OF f. L *inaestimabilis* (as IN-¹, ESTIMABLE)]

■ priceless, invaluable, above *or* beyond *or* without price, precious, costly, valuable; incalculable, uncountable, innumerable, countless, untold, numberless; immeasurable, measureless, unfathomable, limitless, illimitable, boundless, unbounded, infinite, endless, never-ending, interminable, vast, immense, huge, great, enormous, giant, gigantic, massive, colossal, titanic, prodigious, *colloq.* tremendous.

inevitable /inévitbl/ *adj.* **1 a** unavoidable; sure to happen. **b** that is bound to occur or appear. **2** *colloq.* that is tiresomely familiar. **3** (of character drawing, the development of a plot, etc.) so true to nature, etc., as to preclude alternative treatment or solution; convincing. □□ **inevitability** *n.* **inevitableness** *n.* **inevitably** *adv.* [L *inevitabilis* (as IN-¹, *evitare* avoid)]

■ **1** unavoidable, inescapable, ineluctable, inexorable, incontestable, irrevocable, unchangeable, destined, fated, ordained, decreed; assured, guaranteed, certain, sure, automatic. **2** familiar, usual, common, commonplace, everyday, frequent, traditional, customary, habitual, routine, typical. **3** see REALISTIC 1.

inexact /ínigzákt/ *adj.* not exact. □□ **inexactitude** /-títōōd, -tyōōd/ *n.* **inexactly** *adv.* **inexactness** *n.*

■ inaccurate, erroneous, incorrect, wrong, false, faulty, fallacious, mistaken, wide of the mark, out; imprecise, vague, indefinite, ill-defined, ambiguous, fuzzy, woolly, blurry, hazy, cloudy, muddled; approximate, rough, loose, estimated.

inexcusable /ínikskyóōzbl/ *adj.* (of a person, action, etc.) that cannot be excused or justified. □□ **inexcusably** *adv.* [ME f. L *inexcusabilis* (as IN-¹, EXCUSE)]

■ unpardonable, unforgivable, irremissible, inexpiable; reprehensible, blameworthy, censurable, reproachable, reprovable, condemnable; unjustifiable, unjustified, indefensible, unwarrantable.

inexhaustible /ínigzáwstibl/ *adj.* **1** that cannot be exhausted or used up. **2** that cannot be worn out. □□ **inexhaustibility** *n.* **inexhaustibly** *adv.*

■ **1** limitless, boundless, unlimited, unbounded, unrestricted, endless, infinite, never-ending; renewable. **2** untiring, tireless, indefatigable, unflagging, unfailing, unfaltering, unwearying, unwearied.

inexorable /inéksrbl/ *adj.* **1** relentless. **2** (of a person or attribute) that cannot be persuaded by request or entreaty. □□ **inexorability** /-bílitee/ *n.* **inexorably** *adv.* [F *inexorable* or L *inexorabilis* (as IN-¹, *exorare* entreat)]

■ **1** see RELENTLESS 1. **2** see OBSTINATE. □□ **inexorability** see NECESSITY 1. **inexorably** see NECESSARILY.

inexpedient /ínikspe̊édeent/ *adj.* not expedient. □□ **inexpediency** *n.*

■ see *ill-advised* 2 (ILL).

inexpensive /ínikspénsiv/ *adj.* **1** not expensive; cheap. **2** offering good value for the price. □□ **inexpensively** *adv.* **inexpensiveness** *n.*
■ cheap, economical, low-cost, cut-rate, economy, budget, reasonable, esp. *Brit.* cut-price, *colloq.* dirt cheap, *sl.* cheapo.

inexperience /ínikspeéreeəns/ *n.* lack of experience, or of the resulting knowledge or skill. □□ **inexperienced** *adj.* [F *inexpérience* f. LL *inexperientia* (as IN-¹, EXPERIENCE)]
■ immaturity, innocence, callowness, naïveté, greenness, rawness, unsophistication, unsophisticatedness, unworldliness, amateurishness, inexpertness.
□□ **inexperienced** untrained, unschooled, uninformed, uninitiated, unpracticed, untried, unseasoned, unskilled, unskillful, amateurish, inexpert; immature, callow, unsophisticated, unworldly, innocent, naive, green, fresh, raw, coltish, unfledged, new, young, (still) wet behind the ears.

inexpert /inékspərt/ *adj.* unskillful; lacking expertise. □□ **inexpertly** *adv.* **inexpertness** *n.* [OF f. L *inexpertus* (as IN-¹, EXPERT)]
■ see INEPT 1. □□ **inexpertly** see POORLY *adv.*

inexpiable /inékspeeəbəl/ *adj.* (of an act or feeling) that cannot be expiated or appeased. □□ **inexpiably** *adv.* [L *inexpiabilis* (as IN-¹, EXPIATE)]
■ see INEXCUSABLE.

inexplicable /íniksplíkəbəl, inéks-/ *adj.* that cannot be explained or accounted for. □□ **inexplicability** *n.* **inexplicably** *adv.* [F *inexplicable* or L *inexplicabilis* that cannot be unfolded (as IN-¹, EXPLICABLE)]
■ unexplainable, unaccountable, unintelligible, incomprehensible, unexplained, insoluble, inscrutable; enigmatic, cryptic, puzzling, mystifying, mysterious, perplexing, baffling, bewildering; phenomenal, miraculous, supernatural, preternatural, magical, occult, arcane, psychic, uncanny.

inexplicit /ínikspísit/ *adj.* not definitely or clearly expressed. □□ **inexplicitly** *adv.* **inexplicitness** *n.*
■ see INDEFINITE 1.

inexpressible /íniksprésibəl/ *adj.* that cannot be expressed in words. □□ **inexpressibly** *adv.*
■ unutterable, ineffable, indefinable, undefinable, indescribable, incommunicable, unspeakable, beyond description, beyond words.

inexpressive /íniksprésiv/ *adj.* not expressive. □□ **inexpressively** *adv.* **inexpressiveness** *n.*

inexpungible /ínikspúnjibəl/ *adj.* that cannot be expunged or obliterated.
■ see INDELIBLE.

in extenso /ín eksténsō/ *adv.* in full; at length. [L]

inextinguishable /ínikstínggwishəbəl/ *adj.* **1** not quenchable; indestructible. **2** (of laughter, etc.) irrepressible.
■ **1** unquenchable; indestructible, imperishable, inexpungible, ineffaceable, ineradicable, permanent, enduring, undying, eternal, everlasting. **2** see IRREPRESSIBLE.

in extremis /ín ekstreémis, -tré-/ *adj.* **1** at the point of death. **2** in great difficulties. [L]
■ **1** see DYING.

inextricable /inékstrikəbəl, ínikstrík-/ *adj.* **1** (of a circumstance) that cannot be escaped from. **2** (of a knot, problem, etc.) that cannot be unraveled or solved. **3** intricately confused. □□ **inextricability** *n.* **inextricably** *adv.* [ME f. L *inextricabilis* (as IN-¹, EXTRICATE)]
■ **1** mazy, labyrinthine, Daedalian, jungly; tricky, thorny, difficult, awkward, tough; impossible, paradoxical, *attrib.* catch-22. **2, 3** intricate, complex, complicated, involved, convoluted, convolutional, involute, involuted, confused, knotty, tangled, tangly; insoluble, unresolvable, insurmountable, unanswerable, impossible, difficult, tough, hard; perplexing, baffling, bewildering. □□ **inextricably** inescapably, ineluctably, unavoidably, irretrievably, inseparably, inevitably, necessarily; intricately; totally, completely.

inf. *abbr.* **1** infantry. **2** inferior. **3** infinitive.

infallible /infálibəl/ *adj.* **1** incapable of error. **2** (of a method, test, proof, etc.) unfailing; sure to succeed. **3** *RC Ch.* (of the pope) unable to err in pronouncing dogma as doctrinally defined. □□ **infallibility** /-bílitee/ *n.* **infallibly** *adv.* [ME f. F *infaillible* or LL *infallibilis* (as IN-¹, FALLIBLE)]
■ **1, 2** impeccable, perfect, incontestable, undisputable, unquestionable, incontrovertible, irrefutable, indubitable, undeniable; unerring, faultless, flawless, errorless, error-free; unfailing, dependable, reliable, trustworthy, guaranteed, assured, sure, certain, secure, sound, foolproof, *archaic or joc.* trusty, *colloq.* surefire.

infamous /ínfəməs/ *adj.* **1** notoriously bad; having a bad reputation. **2** abominable. **3** (in ancient law) deprived of all or some rights of a citizen on account of serious crime. □□ **infamously** *adv.* **infamy** /ínfəmee/ *n.* (*pl.* **-ies**). [ME f. med.L *infamosus* f. L *infamis* (as IN-¹, FAME)]
■ **1** notorious, disreputable, of ill fame *or* repute, discreditable, dishonorable, ignominious, scandalous. **2** bad, awful, wicked, evil, iniquitous, villainous, heinous, vile, abominable, execrable, abhorrent, opprobrious, misbegotten, despicable, loathsome, detestable, odious, foul, base, low, scurvy, seamy, rotten, atrocious, flagitious, revolting, monstrous, egregious, outrageous, shameful, disgraceful. □□ **infamy** notoriety, ill repute, ill fame, disrepute, shame, ignominy, obloquy, disgrace, dishonor, stigma, discredit; wickedness, evil, iniquity, villainy, heinousness, vileness, abomination, outrage, abhorrence, opprobrium, loathsomeness, hatefulness, odiousness, odium, atrocity, repulsiveness, monstrosity, egregiousness, shame, shamefulness, disgrace, disgracefulness.

infancy /ínfənsee/ *n.* (*pl.* **-ies**) **1** early childhood; babyhood. **2** an early state in the development of an idea, undertaking, etc. **3** *Law* the state of being a minor. [L *infantia* (as IN-FANT)]
■ **1** babyhood, early childhood *or* days *or* years; childhood, boyhood, girlhood, pupilage, juvenescence; cradle. **2** inception, incipience, incipiency, early *or* initial stage(s); beginning(s), start, outset, *formal* commencement; birth, nascency, emergence, dawn, cradle. **3** minority.

infant /ínfənt/ *n.* **1 a** a child during the earliest period of its life. **b** *Brit.* a schoolchild below the age of seven years. **2** (esp. *attrib.*) a child in an early stage of its development. **3** *Law* a minor; a person under 18. □ **infant mortality** death before the age of one. [ME f. OF *enfant* f. L *infans* unable to speak (as IN-¹, *fans fantis* pres. part. of *fari* speak)]
■ **1 a** see CHILD 1b. **3** see MINOR *n.*

infanta /infántə, -faán-/ *n. hist.* a daughter of the ruling monarch of Spain or Portugal (usu. the eldest daughter who is not heir to the throne). [Sp. & Port., fem. of INFANTE]

infante /infántee, -faántay/ *n. hist.* the second son of the ruling monarch of Spain or Portugal. [Sp. & Port. f. L (as INFANT)]

infanticide /infántisid/ *n.* **1** the killing of an infant soon after birth. **2** the practice of killing newborn infants. **3** a person who kills an infant. □□ **infanticidal** /-síd'l/ *adj.* [F f. LL *infanticidium, -cida* (as INFANT)]
■ **1, 2** see MURDER *n.* 1.

infantile /ínfəntīl/ *adj.* **1 a** like or characteristic of a child. **b** childish; immature (*infantile humor*). **2** in its infancy. □ **infantile paralysis** poliomyelitis. □□ **infantility** /-tílitee/ *n.* (*pl.* **-ies**). [F *infantile* or L *infantilis* (as INFANT)]
■ **1** childish, childlike, babyish, puerile, juvenile, prepubescent, pubescent, youthful, young, immature, unfledged, (still) wet behind the ears, green, tender. **2** incipient, inceptive, nascent, emergent, budding;

/. . ./ **pronunciation**	● **part of speech**
□ **phrases, idioms, and compounds**	
□□ **derivatives**	■ **synonym section**
cross-references appear in SMALL CAPITALS or *italics*	

embryonic, rudimentary, undeveloped, unformed, fledgling.

infantilism /ínfánt'lizəm/ n. **1** childish behavior. **2** *Psychol.* the persistence of infantile characteristics or behavior in adult life.

infantry /ínfəntree/ n. (pl. **-ies**) a body of soldiers who march and fight on foot; foot soldiers collectively. [F *infanterie* f. It. *infanteria* f. *infante* youth, infantryman (as INFANT)]

infantryman /ínfəntreemən/ n. (pl. **-men**) a soldier of an infantry unit.

■ see SOLDIER n.

infarct /ínfaarkt/ n. *Med.* a small localized area of dead tissue caused by an inadequate blood supply. □□ **infarction** /-fáarkshən/ n. [mod.L *infarctus* (as IN-², L *farcire farct-* stuff)]

infatuate /infáchoo-ayt/ v.tr. **1** inspire with intense, usu. transitory fondness or admiration. **2** affect with extreme folly. □□ **infatuation** /-áyshən/ n. [L *infatuare* (as IN-², *fatuus* foolish)]

■ **1** see CAPTIVATE. □□ **infatuation** /-áyshən/ see PASSION 1, 3a, 4a.

infatuated /infáchoo-aytid/ adj. (often foll. by *with*) affected by an intense fondness or admiration.

■ fascinated, spellbound, besotted, possessed, obsessed, *sl.* hipped; taken, beguiled, enchanted, bewitched, charmed, enraptured, hypnotized, mesmerized, captivated, enamored, *archaic or literary* smitten; (*infatuated with*) fond of, mad about *or* on, *colloq.* crazy about, struck on, stuck on, soft on, dotty about *or* over esp. *Brit. colloq.* daft about, *Brit. colloq.* soppy on, potty about, *sl.* gone on.

infauna /ínfawnə/ n. any animals that live just below the surface of the seabed. [Da. *ifauna* (as IN-², FAUNA)]

infeasible /infée'zibəl/ adj. not feasible; that cannot easily be done. □□ **infeasibility** n.

■ see IMPOSSIBLE 1, 2.

infect /infékt/ v.tr. **1** contaminate (air, water, etc.) with harmful organisms or noxious matter. **2** affect (a person) with disease, etc. **3** instill bad feeling or opinion into (a person). □□ **infector** n. [ME f. L *inficere infect-* taint (as IN-², *facere* make)]

■ **1** see CONTAMINATE. **2** see ATTACK v. 4.

infection /infékshən/ n. **1 a** the process of infecting or state of being infected. **b** an instance of this; an infectious disease. **2** communication of disease, esp. by the agency of air or water, etc. **3 a** moral contamination. **b** the diffusive influence of example, sympathy, etc. [ME f. OF *infection* or LL *infectio* (as INFECT)]

■ **1 b** see DISEASE 1, 3.

infectious /infékshəs/ adj. **1** infecting with disease. **2** (of a disease) liable to be transmitted by air, water, etc. **3** (of emotions, etc.) apt to spread; quickly affecting others. □ **infectious mononucleosis** an infectious viral disease characterized by swelling of the lymph glands and prolonged lassitude. □□ **infectiously** adv. **infectiousness** n.

■ **1** infective, corruptive, malignant, virulent; poisonous, toxic, *archaic* miasmic, miasmal, miasmatic. **2, 3** contagious, catching, taking, communicable, transmissible, transmittable.

infective /inféktiv/ adj. **1** capable of infecting with disease. **2** infectious. □□ **infectiveness** n. [L *infectivus* (as INFECT)]

infelicitous /ínfilísitəs/ adj. not felicitous; unfortunate. □□ **infelicitously** adv.

■ see INAPPROPRIATE.

infelicity /ínfilísitee/ n. (pl. **-ies**) **1 a** inaptness of expression, etc. **b** an instance of this. **2 a** unhappiness. **b** a misfortune. [ME f. L *infelicitas* (as IN-¹, FELICITY)]

■ **1 a** see IMPROPRIETY 1. **b** see IMPROPRIETY 2. **2 b** see MISFORTUNE.

infer /infór/ v.tr. (**inferred, inferring**) (often foll. by *that* + clause) **1** deduce or conclude from facts and reasoning. **2** *disp.* imply; suggest. □□ **inferable** adj. (also **infer(r)ible**). [L *inferre* (as IN-², *ferre* bring)]

■ **1** deduce, derive, conclude, draw the (*or* a) conclusion, take it; surmise, understand, gather. **2** see IMPLY 1.

inference /ínfərəns/ n. **1** the act or an instance of inferring. **2** *Logic* **a** the forming of a conclusion from premises. **b** a thing inferred. □□ **inferential** /-rénshəl/ adj. **inferentially** adv. [med.L *inferentia* (as INFER)]

■ deduction, conclusion, implication, implicate, derivation; understanding, surmise; *Law* presumption.

inferior /infée'reeər/ adj. & n. ● adj. **1** (often foll. by *to*) a lower; in a lower position. **b** of lower rank, quality, etc. **2** poor in quality. **3** (of a planet, specifically Venus or Mercury) having an orbit within Earth's. **4** *Bot.* situated below an ovary or calyx. **5** (of figures or letters) written or printed below the line. ● n. **1** a person inferior to another, esp. in rank. **2** an inferior letter or figure. □□ **inferiorly** adv. [ME f. L, compar. of *inferus* that is below]

■ adj. **1** lower, lesser, junior, minor, smaller, *archaic* nether; second, subordinate, secondary, ancillary, auxiliary, subsidiary, subaltern, petty, downscale. **2** second-rate, second-class, third-class, poor man's; poor, mean, bad, mediocre, common, coarse, (very) indifferent, low-grade, low-quality, low-class, cheap, cheapjack, cheap and nasty, trashy, tawdry, gimcrack, rubbishy, tinpot, *colloq.* crummy, lousy, tatty, measly, *sl.* cheesy; imperfect, inadequate, defective, faulty, flawed, substandard, shoddy, slipshod. **5** subscript. ● n. **1** subordinate, junior, satellite, doormat, *derog.* underling; menial, lackey, *colloq.* stooge, esp. *Brit.* dogsbody, *sl.* gofer. **2** subscript, *Math.* suffix.

inferiority /infée'reeə-áwritee, -ór-/ n. the state of being inferior. □ **inferiority complex** an unrealistic feeling of general inadequacy caused by actual or supposed inferiority in one sphere, sometimes marked by aggressive behavior in compensation.

■ juniority, subordination, secondariness, subsidiarity, pettiness; poverty, poorness, meanness, mediocrity, commonness, coarseness, cheapness, trashiness, tawdriness, *colloq.* crumminess, lousiness, tattiness, measliness, *sl.* cheesiness; imperfection, inadequacy, defectiveness, faultiness, shoddiness.

infernal /infórnəl/ adj. **1 a** of hell or the underworld. **b** hellish; fiendish. **2** *colloq.* detestable; tiresome. □□ **infernally** adv. [ME f. OF f. LL *infernalis* f. L *infernus* situated below]

■ **1** hellish, hell-like, Hadean, Stygian, plutonian, Tartarean, chthonic, chthonian; fiendish, fiendlike, devilish, diabolic, diabolical, demonic, demoniac, demoniacal, satanic, Mephistophelian; damnable, execrable, abominable, malicious, malevolent, wicked, evil, iniquitous, flagitious, *colloq.* damned, *literary* maleficent. **2** see TIRESOME 2.

inferno /infórnō/ n. (pl. **-os**) **1** a raging fire. **2** a scene of horror or distress. **3** hell, esp. with ref. to Dante's *Divine Comedy*. [It. f. LL *infernus* (as INFERNAL)]

■ **1** blaze, fire, conflagration, holocaust. **3** see HELL 1.

infertile /infórt'l/ adj. not fertile. □□ **infertility** /-tílitee/ n. [F *infertile* or LL *infertilis* (as IN-¹, FERTILE)]

■ unproductive, nonproductive, sterile, barren, unfruitful, fruitless, *Bot.* acarpous.

infest /infést/ v.tr. (of harmful persons or things, esp. vermin or disease) overrun (a place) in large numbers. □□ **infestation** n. [ME f. F *infester* or L *infestare* assail f. *infestus* hostile]

■ overrun, invade, plague, beset, take over; swarm over, overspread, pervade, permeate, penetrate, infiltrate, flood, inundate; parasitize.

infidel /ínfid'l, -del/ n. & adj. ● n. **1** a person who does not believe in religion or in a particular religion; an unbeliever. **2** usu. *hist.* an adherent of a religion other than Christianity, esp. a Muslim. ● adj. **1** that is an infidel. **2** of unbelievers. [ME f. F *infidèle* or L *infidelis* (as IN-¹, *fidelis* faithful)]

■ n. **1** unbeliever, heathen, heretic, pagan, agnostic, atheist, nullifidian, irreligionist, skeptic, disbeliever, freethinker. ● adj. unbelieving, heathen, heretic, pagan, agnostic, atheistic, atheistical, skeptic, skeptical, freethinking, *archaic* ethnic; gentile.

infidelity /ínfidélitee/ n. (pl. **-ies**) **1 a** disloyalty or unfaithfulness, esp. to a husband or wife. **b** an instance of this. **2**

disbelief in Christianity or another religion. [ME f. F *infidélité* or L *infidelitas* (as INFIDEL)]

■ **1 a** unfaithfulness, adultery, faithlessness, disloyalty, deceit, deception, betrayal, *colloq.* two-timing; duplicity, double-dealing, perfidy, treachery, falseness. **b** adultery, cuckoldry, (love) affair, *affaire*, liaison, amour, entanglement, romance, fling, *sl.* getting some on the side. **2** disbelief, unbelief, unbelievingness, heathenism, heresy, paganism, agnosticism, atheism, irreligionism, apostasy, skepticism, freethinking.

infield /ínfeeld/ *n.* **1** *Baseball* **a** the area enclosed by the three bases and home plate. **b** the four fielders stationed near the bases. **2** farmland around or near a homestead. **3 a** arable land. **b** land regularly manured and cropped. □□ **infielder** *n.* (in sense 1).
■ **1 a** diamond.

infighting /ínfīting/ *n.* **1** hidden conflict or competitiveness within an organization. **2** boxing at closer quarters than arm's length. □□ **infighter** *n.*
■ **1** see FACTION¹ 2.

infill /ínfil/ *n. & v.* ● *n.* **1** material used to fill a hole, gap, etc. **2** the placing of buildings to occupy the space between existing ones. ● *v.tr.* fill in (a cavity, etc.).

infiltrate /ínfiltrayt/ *v.* **1** *tr.* **a** gain entrance or access to surreptitiously and by degrees (as spies, etc.). **b** cause to do this. **2** *tr.* permeate by filtration. **3** *tr.* (often foll. by *into*, *through*) introduce (fluid) by filtration. □□ **infiltration** /-tráyshən/ *n.* **infiltrator** *n.* [IN-² + FILTRATE]
■ **1 a** see ENTER 2. **2** see PERMEATE. □□ **infiltration** see INVASION 1. **infiltrator** see INTRUDER.

infinite /ínfinit/ *adj. & n.* ● *adj.* **1** boundless; endless. **2** very great. **3** (usu. with *pl.*) innumerable; very many (*infinite resources*). **4** *Math.* **a** greater than any assignable quantity or countable number. **b** (of a series) that may be continued indefinitely. **5** *Gram.* (of a verb part) not limited by person or number, e.g., infinitive, gerund, and participle. ● *n.* **1** (**the Infinite**) God. **2** (**the infinite**) infinite space. □□ **infinitely** *adv.* **infiniteness** *n.* [ME f. L *infinitus* (as IN-¹, FINITE)]
■ *adj.* **1–3** boundless, unbounded, limitless, unlimited, illimitable, interminable, endless, never-ending, perpetual, undying, everlasting, eternal, unending, without end, inexhaustible, bottomless, unfathomable, indeterminable, indeterminate, inestimable, immeasurable, measureless, incalculable, innumerable, numberless, uncountable, countless, uncounted, untold, multitudinous, vast, immense, astronomical, enormous, huge, great, gigantic, giant, massive, colossal, titanic, prodigious, *colloq.* tremendous. ● *n.* **1** (**the Infinite**) see GOD *n.* 2. **2** (**the infinite**) see UNIVERSE 1a.

infinitesimal /ínfinitésiməl/ *adj. & n.* ● *adj.* infinitely or very small. ● *n.* an infinitesimal amount. □ **infinitesimal calculus** the differential and integral calculuses regarded as one subject. □□ **infinitesimally** *adv.* [mod.L *infinitesimus* f. INFINITE: cf. CENTESIMAL]
■ *adj.* see MINUTE² 1.

infinitive /ínfinitiv/ *n. & adj.* ● *n.* a form of a verb expressing the verbal notion without reference to a particular subject, tense, etc. (e.g., *see* in *we came to see, let him see*). ● *adj.* having this form. □□ **infinitival** /-tívəl/ *adj.* **infinitivally** /-tívəlee/ *adv.* [L *infinitivus* (as IN-¹, *finitivus* definite f. *finire finit-* define)]

infinitude /ínfinitōōd, -tyōōd/ *n.* **1** the state of being infinite; boundlessness. **2** (often foll. by *of*) a boundless number or extent. [L *infinitus*: see INFINITE, -TUDE]

infinity /ínfínitee/ *n.* (*pl.* **-ies**) **1** the state of being infinite. **2** an infinite number or extent. **3** infinite distance. **4** *Math.* infinite quantity. ¶ Symb.: ∞ [ME f. OF *infinité* or L *infinitas* (as INFINITE)]
■ **1** see ETERNITY 1, 3. **2** see LOT *n.* 1. **3** see ETERNITY 1, 3.

infirm /infórm/ *adj.* **1** physically weak, esp. through age. **2** (of a person, mind, judgment, etc.) weak; irresolute. □□ **infirmity** *n.* (*pl.* **-ies**). **infirmly** *adv.* [ME f. L *infirmus* (as IN-¹, FIRM¹)]

■ **1** weak, frail, decrepit, enfeebled, feeble, debilitated, weakened, fragile, withered, worn-out, *archaic* stricken in years; doddering, unstable, unsteady, unsound, shaky, wobbly; see also ILL *adj.* 1. **2** weak, irresolute, hesitant, undecided, uncertain, unsettled, indefinite, unresolved, undetermined, of two minds, ambivalent, inconstant. □□ **infirmity** weakness, feebleness, enfeeblement, frailness, frailty, debility, decrepitude, fragility; instability, unstableness, unsteadiness, unsoundness, shakiness, wobbliness, sickliness; irresoluteness, irresolution, hesitancy, indecision, uncertainty, indefiniteness, unresolvedness, ambivalence, inconstancy, vacillation; illness, affliction, ailment, malady, indisposition, complaint, disorder, defect, disability.

infirmary /infórməree/ *n.* (*pl.* **-ies**) **1** a hospital. **2** a place for those who are ill in a monastery, school, etc. [med.L *infirmaria* (as INFIRM)]
■ **1** hospital, health center, polyclinic, clinic, sanatorium, nursing home, lazaret, lazaretto, *hist.* pesthouse. **2** sick bay, first-aid post *or* station, sanitarium, esp. *Brit.* sanatorium, *Brit.* surgery; dispensary.

infix *v. & n.* ● *v.tr.* /ínfíks/ **1** (often foll. by *in*) **a** fix (a thing in another). **b** impress (a fact, etc., in the mind). **2** *Gram.* insert (a formative element) into the body of a word. ● *n.* /ínfiks/ *Gram.* a formative element inserted in a word. □□ **infixation** *n.* [L *infigere infix-* (as IN-², FIX): (n.) after *prefix, suffix*]

in flagrante delicto /in fləgrántee dilíktō/ *adv.* in the very act of committing an offense. [L, = in blazing crime]

inflame /infláym/ *v.* **1** *tr. & intr.* (often foll. by *with, by*) provoke or become provoked to strong feeling, esp. anger. **2** *Med.* **a** *intr.* become hot, reddened, and sore. **b** *tr.* (esp. as **inflamed** *adj.*) cause inflammation or fever in (a body, etc.); make hot. **3** *tr.* aggravate. **4** *intr. & tr.* catch or set on fire. **5** *tr.* light up with or as if with flames. □□ **inflamer** *n.* [ME f. OF *enflammer* f. L *inflammare* (as IN-², *flamma* flame)]
■ **1** provoke, incense, anger, enrage, madden, infuriate, impassion, whip *or* lash up, work up, exasperate, *colloq.* rile; arouse, rouse, incite, touch off, ignite, excite, foment, agitate, stir (up), fire (up), heat, *literary* enkindle; stimulate, animate, move, motivate, urge, prod, goad, spur (on), rally. **2 a** burn, redden, chafe, itch, smart, sting. **b** irritate, make sore, nettle; (**inflamed**) irritated, sore, angry, chafing, chafed, red, swollen, heated, hot, fevered, feverish, infected, septic. **3** aggravate, exacerbate, intensify, deepen, heighten, increase, augment, fan, fuel. **4** ignite, combust, light, set fire to, set on fire, set alight, set ablaze, kindle, *sl.* torch; catch fire, burst into flame(s), blaze up, flare, flash. **5** see ILLUMINATE 1.

inflammable /inflámməbəl/ *adj. & n.* ● *adj.* **1** easily set on fire; flammable. **2** easily excited. ● *n.* (usu. in *pl.*) a flammable substance. □□ **inflammability** *n.* **inflammableness** *n.* **inflammably** *adv.* [INFLAME after F *inflammable*]
■ *adj.* combustible, flammable, ignitable, explosive, fiery. **2** excitable, combustible, explosive, irascible, choleric, short-tempered, quick-tempered, irritable, nervous, edgy, high-strung, volatile, hotheaded, *Brit. sl.* waxy.

inflammation /ínfləmáyshən/ *n.* **1** the act or an instance of inflaming. **2** *Med.* a localized physical condition with heat, swelling, redness, and usu. pain, esp. as a reaction to injury or infection. [L *inflammatio* (as INFLAME)]
■ **1** provocation, enragement, infuriation; arousal, incitement, excitement, fomentation, agitation, stimulation, animation; aggravation, exacerbation, intensification; ignition, combustion. **2** irritation,

---

/.../ **pronunciation**   ● **part of speech**
□ **phrases, idioms, and compounds**
□□ **derivatives**   ■ **synonym section**
cross-references appear in SMALL CAPITALS or *italics*

redness, soreness, tenderness, swelling, eruption, rash, hives, prickly heat, *Med.* exanthema.

inflammatory /inflámətáwree/ *adj.* **1** (esp. of speeches, leaflets, etc.) tending to cause anger, etc. **2** of or tending to inflammation of the body.

■ **1** excitatory, provocative, maddening, infuriating, exasperating, irritating, rabble-rousing, seditious. **2** irritating, irritative, irritant, caustic.

inflatable /infláytəbəl/ *adj.* & *n.* ● *adj.* that can be inflated. ● *n.* an inflatable plastic or rubber object. ● *adj.* see EXPANSIVE 1.

inflate /infláyt/ *v.tr.* **1** distend (a balloon, etc.) with air. **2** (usu. foll. by *with*; usu. in *passive*) puff up (a person with pride, etc.). **3 a** (often *absol.*) bring about inflation (of the currency). **b** raise (prices) artificially. **4** (as **inflated** *adj.*) (esp. of language, sentiments, etc.) bombastic. □□ **inflatedly** *adv.* **inflatedness** *n.* **inflater** *n.* **inflator** *n.* [L *inflare inflat-* (as IN-², *flare* blow)]

■ **1** blow up, pump up, distend, expand, enlarge, swell. **2** puff up *or* out, swell; balloon, dilate, distend, expand, enlarge. **4** (**inflated**) grandiloquent, bombastic, tumid, orotund, high-flown, pompous, pretentious, extravagant, magniloquent; exaggerated, conceited, overblown, grandiose, puffed up, overstated.

inflation /infláyshən/ *n.* **1 a** the act or condition of inflating or being inflated. **b** an instance of this. **2** *Econ.* **a** a general increase in prices and fall in the purchasing value of money. **b** an increase in available currency regarded as causing this. □□ **inflationary** *adj.* **inflationism** *n.* **inflationist** *n.* & *adj.* [ME f. L *inflatio* (as INFLATE)]

■ **1** see *exaggeration* (EXAGGERATE), EXPANSION 1. **2 a** see INCREASE *n.* 1, 2.

inflect /inflékt/ *v.* **1** *tr.* change the pitch of (the voice, a musical note, etc.). **2** *Gram.* **a** *tr.* change the form of (a word) to express tense, gender, number, mood, etc. **b** *intr.* (of a word, language, etc.) undergo such change. **3** *tr.* bend inward; curve. □□ **inflective** *adj.* [ME f. L *inflectere inflex-* (as IN-², *flectere* bend)]

inflection /inflékshən/ *n.* (also esp. *Brit.* **inflexion**) **1 a** the act or condition of inflecting or being inflected. **b** an instance of this. **2** *Gram.* **a** the process or practice of inflecting words. **b** an inflected form of a word. **c** a suffix, etc., used to inflect, e.g., *-ed.* **3** a modulation of the voice. **4** *Geom.* a change of curvature from convex to concave at a particular point on a curve. □□ **inflectional** *adj.* **inflectionally** *adv.* **inflectionless** *adj.* [F *inflection* or L *inflexio* (as INFLECT)]

■ **1** see INTONATION 1.

inflexible /infléksibəl/ *adj.* **1** unbendable. **2** stiff; immovable; obstinate (*old and inflexible in his attitudes*). **3** unchangeable; inexorable. □□ **inflexibility** *n.* **inflexibly** *adv.* [L *inflexibilis* (as IN-¹, FLEXIBLE)]

■ **1** unbendable, unbending, stiff, rigid, inelastic, hard, steely, unmalleable, unyielding, solid. **2** stiff, unbending, rigid, firm, unyielding, stiff-necked, steely, stony, uncompromising, rigorous, severe, rhadamanthine; adamant, determined, fixed, resolute, resolved, unshakable, immovable; obdurate, obstinate, stubborn, pigheaded, mulish. **3** unchangeable, intractable, immutable, unadaptable, unaccommodating, uncompliant, invariable, unvaried, unvarying, hard and fast; inexorable, ineluctable, inescapable, unavoidable, definite, certain, sure, firm.

inflict /inflíkt/ *v.tr.* (usu. foll. by *on, upon*) **1** administer; deal (a stroke, wound, defeat, etc.). **2** (also *refl.*) often *joc.* impose (suffering, a penalty, oneself, one's company, etc.) on (*shall not inflict myself on you any longer*). □□ **inflictable** *adj.* **inflicter** *n.* **inflictor** *n.* [L *infligere inflict-* (as IN-², *fligere* strike)]

■ **1** administer, deal, serve, impose, apply, visit, levy, wreak, cause, force.

infliction /inflíkshən/ *n.* **1** the act or an instance of inflicting. **2** something inflicted, esp. a troublesome or boring experience. [LL *inflictio* (as INFLICT)]

■ **1** see IMPOSITION 1. **2** see IMPOSITION 2.

inflight /inflīt/ *attrib.adj.* occurring or provided during an aircraft flight.

inflorescence /inflərésəns/ *n.* **1** *Bot.* **a** the complete flower head of a plant including stems, stalks, bracts, and flowers. **b** the arrangement of this. **2** the process of flowering. [mod.L *inflorescentia* f. LL *inflorescere* (as IN-², FLORESCENCE)]

inflow /inflō/ *n.* **1** a flowing in. **2** something that flows in. □□ **inflowing** *n.* & *adj.*

influence /inflōōəns/ *n.* & *v.* ● *n.* **1 a** (usu. foll. by *on, upon*) the effect a person or thing has on another. **b** (usu. foll. by *over, with*) moral ascendancy or power. **c** a thing or person exercising such power (*is a good influence on them*). **2** *Astrol.* an ethereal fluid supposedly flowing from the stars and affecting character and destiny. **3** *Electr. archaic* = INDUCTION. ● *v.tr.* exert influence on; have an effect on. □ **under the influence** *colloq.* affected by alcoholic drink. □□ **influenceable** *adj.* **influencer** *n.* [ME f. OF *influence* or med.L *influentia* inflow f. L *influere* flow in (as IN-², *fluere* flow)]

■ *n.* **1** effect, impact, bearing, impression; power, force, potency, pressure, weight, leverage, pull, *colloq.* clout; hold, sway, control, mastery, authority, ascendancy; agent. ● *v.* affect, act *or* play *or* work on; sway, change, transform, modify, alter; move, drive, impel, force, urge; bias, persuade, motivate, induce, incline; impress (upon), bring pressure to bear on *or* upon, manipulate, pressurize, pressure. □ **under the influence** see DRUNK *adj.* 1.

influent /inflōōənt/ *adj.* & *n.* ● *adj.* flowing in. ● *n.* a tributary stream. [ME f. L (as INFLUENCE)]

influential /inflōō-énshəl/ *adj.* having a great influence or power (*influential in the financial world*). □□ **influentially** *adv.* [med.L *influentia* INFLUENCE]

■ powerful, weighty, strong, forceful, impressive; authoritative, important, substantial, significant, telling; dominant, leading, predominant; effective, effectual, efficacious; instrumental; persuasive.

influenza /inflōō-énzə/ *n.* a highly contagious virus infection causing fever, severe aching, and catarrh, often occurring in epidemics. □□ **influenzal** *adj.* [It. f. med.L *influentia* INFLUENCE]

influx /influks/ *n.* **1** a continual stream of people or things (*an influx of complaints*). **2** (usu. foll. by *into*) a flowing in, esp. of a stream, etc. [F *influx* or LL *influxus* (as IN-², FLUX)]

info /infō/ *n. colloq.* information. [abbr.]

infold var. of ENFOLD.

infomercial /infōmárshəl/ *n.* a television program promoting a commercial product.

inform /infáwrm/ *v.* **1** *tr.* (usu. foll. by *of, about, on,* or *that, how* + clause) tell (*informed them of their rights; informed us that the train was late*). **2** *intr.* (usu. foll. by *against, on*) make an accusation. **3** *tr.* (usu. foll. by *with*) *literary* inspire or imbue (a person, heart, or thing) with a feeling, principle, quality, etc. **4** *tr.* impart its quality to; permeate. □□ **informant** *n.* [ME f. OF *enfo(u)rmer* f. L *informare* give shape to, fashion, describe (as IN-², *forma* form)]

■ **1** tell, notify, apprise, enlighten, advise, brief, acquaint, tip off, report to, communicate to, *colloq.* fill in, put *or* set a person wise. **2** turn informer, name names, *sl.* sing, squeak, squeal, *Brit. school sl.* sneak; (*inform against* or *on*) accuse, incriminate, inculpate, implicate, identify, betray, denounce, *archaic* delate, peach, *colloq.* tell on, rat on, blow the whistle on, peach on *or* against, *sl.* snitch on, put the finger on, finger, fink on, *Brit. sl.* grass on, shop. **4** see PERMEATE. □□ **informant** see INFORMER.

informal /infáwrməl/ *adj.* **1** without ceremony or formality (*just an informal chat*). **2** (of language, clothing, etc.) everyday; normal. □□ **informality** /-málitee/ *n.* (*pl.* **-ies**). **informally** *adv.*

■ unceremonious, unstructured, unstilted, unaffected, unpretentious, unstuffy, casual, natural, free, free and easy, relaxed, unofficial, *colloq.* unbuttoned; colloquial, vernacular; familiar, ordinary, simple, everyday, folksy, *colloq.* common or garden. □□ **informality** see EASE *n.* 2b, c.

informatics /ínfərmátiks/ *n.pl.* (usu. treated as *sing.*) the science of processing data for storage and retrieval; information science. [transl. Russ. *informatika* (as INFORMATION, -ICS)]

information /infərmáyshən/ *n.* **1 a** something told; knowledge. **b** (usu. foll. by *on, about*) items of knowledge; news (*the latest information on the crisis*). **2** *Law* (usu. foll. by *against*) a charge or complaint lodged with a court or magistrate. **3 a** the act of informing or telling. **b** an instance of this. □ **information retrieval** the tracing of information stored in books, computers, etc. **information science** the study of the processes for storing and retrieving information. **information (super)highway** a putative worldwide computer network offering information, shopping, and other services. **information theory** *Math.* the quantitative study of the transmission of information by signals, etc. □□ **informational** *adj.* **informationally** *adv.* [ME f. OF f. L *informatio -onis* (as INFORM)]

■ **1** knowledge, news, data, report(s), communication, facts, details, message(s) *literary* tidings; word, advice, intelligence, *colloq.* info, lowdown, *sl.* dope, poop, *Austral. sl.* drum. **2** see CHARGE *n.* 2. **3** notification, advice, enlightenment, briefing, report, communication.

informative /infáwrmətiv/ *adj.* (also **informatory** /infáwrmətáwree/) giving information; instructive. □□ **informatively** *adv.* **informativeness** *n.* [med.L *informativus* (as INFORM)]

■ communicative, instructive, educational, edifying, revealing, illuminating, enlightening; clarificatory, explanatory, elucidatory, helpful; forthcoming.

informed /infáwrmd/ *adj.* **1** knowing the facts; instructed (*his answers show that he is badly informed*). **2** educated; intelligent. □□ **informedly** /infáwrmidlee/ *adv.* **informedness** /infáwrmidnis/ *n.*

■ **1** knowledgeable, aware, in touch, *au fait*, au courant, up to date, posted, in the picture, *colloq.* in the know, filled in; conversant (with), acquainted (with), (well-)versed (in), well up (on *or* in), cognizant (of). **2** (well-)educated, erudite, learned, well-read, cultured, cultivated, knowledgeable; intelligent, wise, smart, bright, clever, brainy, *sl.* savvy.

informer /infáwrmər/ *n.* **1** a person who informs against another. **2** a person who informs or advises.

■ **1** informant, telltale, taleteller, stool pigeon, tattletale, *colloq.* weasel, supergrass, *hist.* beagle, *sl.* ratfink, fink, stoolie, dog, snitch, finger, squealer, *Austral. sl.* fizgig, *Brit. sl.* grass, nark, shopper, *Brit. school sl.* sneak; traitor, betrayer, fifth columnist, spy, rat, *colloq.* mole. **2** informant, source, reporter, correspondent, communicator; consultant, adviser, counsel, counselor, guide, mentor.

infotainment /infótáynmənt/ *n.* **1** factual information presented in dramatized form on television. **2** a television program mixing news and entertainment.

infra /ínfrə/ *adv.* below, further on (in a book or writing). [L, = below]

■ see BELOW *adv.* 1.

infra- /ínfrə/ *comb. form* **1** below (opp. SUPRA-). **2** *Anat.* below or under a part of the body. [from or after L *infra* below, beneath]

infraction /infrákshən/ *n.* esp. *Law* a violation or infringement. □□ **infract** *v.tr.* **infractor** *n.* [L *infractio* (as INFRINGE)]

■ see *infringement* (INFRINGE).

infra dig /ínfrə díg/ *predic.adj. colloq.* beneath one's dignity; unbecoming. [abbr. of L *infra dignitatem*]

■ see BASE² 2.

infrangible /infránjibəl/ *adj.* **1** unbreakable. **2** inviolable. □□ **infrangibility** *n.* **infrangibleness** *n.* **infrangibly** *adv.* [obs.F *infrangible* or med.L *infrangibilis* (as IN-¹, FRANGIBLE)]

infrared /ínfrəréd/ *adj.* **1** having a wavelength just greater

than the red end of the visible light spectrum but less than that of radio waves. **2** of or using such radiation.

infrasonic /ínfrəsónik/ *adj.* of or relating to sound waves with a frequency below the lower limit of human audibility. □□ **infrasonically** *adv.*

infrasound /ínfrəsownd/ *n.* sound waves with frequencies below the lower limit of human audibility.

infrastructure /ínfrəstrukchər/ *n.* **1 a** the basic structural foundations of a society or enterprise; a substructure or foundation. **b** roads, bridges, sewers, etc., regarded as a country's economic foundation. **2** permanent installations as a basis for military, etc., operations. [F (as INFRA-, STRUCTURE)]

■ **1 a** see BASIS 1, 2.

infrequent /infréekwənt/ *adj.* not frequent. □□ **infrequency** *n.* **infrequently** *adv.* [L *infrequens* (as IN-¹, FREQUENT)]

■ occasional, rare, seldom; uncommon, unusual, unwonted, exceptional, stray; irregular, sporadic, intermittent. □□ **infrequently** occasionally, rarely, seldom, once in a blue moon, exceptionally; between times, sometimes, at times; irregularly, sporadically, intermittently, (every) now and then, (every) now and again, every so often, from time to time, (every) once in a while.

infringe /infrínj/ *v.* **1** *tr.* **a** act contrary to; violate (a law, an oath, etc.). **b** act in defiance of (another's rights, etc.). **2** *intr.* (usu. foll. by *on, upon*) encroach; trespass. □□ **infringement** *n.* **infringer** *n.* [L *infringere infract-* (as IN-², *frangere* break)]

■ **1** violate, contravene, break, disobey, transgress, overstep; flout, disregard, ignore, defy, challenge, thumb one's nose at, *sl.* cock a snook at. **2** (*infringe on* or *upon*) encroach on *or* upon, impinge on *or* upon, intrude on *or* upon, obtrude on *or* upon, trespass on *or* upon, break in on, butt in on, barge in on, interrupt, invade, *sl.* horn in on. □□ **infringement** violation, breach, contravention, infraction, disobedience, noncompliance, transgression; encroachment, impingement, intrusion, obtrusion, interruption, invasion, *Law* trespass.

infula /ínfyələ/ *n.* (*pl.* **infulae** /-lee/) *Eccl.* either of the two ribbons on a bishop's miter. [L, = woolen fillet worn by priest, etc.]

infundibular /ínfəndíbyələr/ *adj.* funnel-shaped. [L *infundibulum* funnel f. *infundere* pour in (as IN-², *fundere* pour)]

infuriate *v.* & *adj.* ● *v.tr.* /infyóoreeayt/ fill with fury; enrage. ● *adj.* /infyóoreeət/ *literary* excited to fury; frantic. □□ **infuriating** *adj.* **infuriatingly** *adv.* **infuriation** /-áyshən/ *n.* [med.L *infuriare infuriat-* (as IN-², L *furia* FURY)]

■ *v.* enrage, anger, madden, incense, make a person's blood boil, inflame, work *or* stir *or* fire up, arouse, provoke, vex, pique, gall, annoy, irritate, bother, chafe, fret, agitate, irk, nettle, goad, exasperate, exacerbate, make a person's hackles rise, get *or* put a person's back up, get on a person's nerves, *colloq.* needle, miff, peeve, rile, wind up, get under a person's skin, make a person see red, get a person's dander up, get a person's goat, *sl.* bug, burn up, *Brit. sl.* brown off, cheese off.

infuse /infyóoz/ *v.* **1** *tr.* (usu. foll. by *with*) imbue; pervade (*anger infused with resentment*). **2** *tr.* steep (herbs, tea, etc.) in liquid to extract the content. **3** *tr.* (usu. foll. by *into*) instill (grace, spirit, life, etc.). **4** *intr.* undergo infusion (*let it infuse for five minutes*). **5** *tr.* (usu. foll. by *into*) pour (a thing). □□ **infusable** *adj.* **infuser** *n.* **infusive** /-fyóosiv/ *adj.* [ME f. L *infundere infus-* (as IN-², *fundere* pour)]

■ **1** see SUFFUSE. **2**, **4** brew, soak. **3** see INSTILL 1.

infusible /infyóozibəl/ *adj.* not able to be fused or melted. □□ **infusibility** /-bílitee/ *n.*

infusion /infyóozhən/ *n.* **1** a liquid obtained by infusing. **2**

/.../ **pronunciation**   ● **part of speech**
□ **phrases, idioms, and compounds**
□□ **derivatives**   ■ **synonym section**
cross-references appear in SMALL CAPITALS or *italics*

an infused element; an admixture. **3** *Med.* a slow injection of a substance into a vein or tissue. **4 a** the act of infusing. **b** an instance of this. [ME f. F *infusion* or L *infusio* (as IN-FUSE)]
■ **1** see SOLUTION 2b.

infusorial earth /ínfyoōsáwreeəl/ *n.* = KIESELGUHR. [mod.L *infusoria*, formerly a class of protozoa found in decaying animal or vegetable matter (as INFUSE)]

-ing[1] /ing/ *suffix* forming gerunds and nouns from verbs (or occas. from nouns), denoting: **1 a** the verbal action or its result (*asking*; *carving*; *fighting*; *learning*). **b** the verbal action as described or classified in some way (*tough going*). **2** material used for or associated with a process, etc. (*piping*; *washing*). **3** an occupation or event (*banking*; *wedding*). **4** a set or arrangement of (*coloring*; *feathering*). [OE *-ung*, *-ing* f. Gmc]

-ing[2] /ing/ *suffix* **1** forming the present participle of verbs (*asking*; *fighting*), often as adjectives (*charming*; *strapping*). **2** forming adjectives from nouns (*hulking*) and verbs (*balding*). [ME alt. of OE *-ende*, later *-inde*]

-ing[3] /ing/ *suffix* forming nouns meaning 'one belonging to' or 'one having the quality of,' surviving esp. in names of coins and fractional parts (*farthing*; *gelding*; *riding*). [OE f. Gmc]

ingather /in-gáthər/ *v.tr.* gather in; assemble.

ingathering /in-gáthəring/ *n.* the act or an instance of gathering in, esp. of a harvest.

ingeminate /injéminayt/ *v.tr. literary* repeat; reiterate. □ **ingeminate peace** constantly urge peace. [L *ingeminare ingeminat-* (as IN-[2], GEMINATE)]

ingenious /injeényəs/ *adj.* **1** clever at inventing, constructing, organizing, etc.; skillful; resourceful. **2** (of a machine, theory, etc.) cleverly contrived. □□ **ingeniously** *adv.* **ingeniousness** *n.* [ME, = talented, f. F *ingénieux* or L *ingeniosus* f. *ingenium* cleverness: cf. ENGINE]
■ clever, skillful, skilled, adept, apt, adroit, dexterous, deft, slick, handy, inventive, *sl.* crackerjack; resourceful, creative, imaginative, original; gifted, talented, brilliant, bright, smart; acute, astute, sharp, shrewd, cunning, crafty, canny; neat, *colloq.* cute.

ingenue /ánzhənoō/ *n.* (also **ingénue**) **1** an innocent or unsophisticated young woman. **2** *Theatr.* **a** such a part in a play. **b** the actress who plays this part. [F, fem. of *ingénu* INGENUOUS]
■ **1** see INNOCENT *n.*

ingenuity /ínjinoōitee, -nyoō-/ *n.* skill in devising or contriving; ingeniousness. [L *ingenuitas* ingenuousness (as INGENUOUS): Engl. meaning by confusion of INGENIOUS with IN-GENUOUS]
■ ingeniousness, cleverness, skill, craft, art, artfulness, adeptness, aptness, dexterity, dexterousness, adroitness, deftness, handiness, inventiveness; resourcefulness, creativity, creativeness, imagination, imaginativeness, originality; giftedness, brilliance, brightness, smartness, acuteness, sharpness, canniness, shrewdness, cunning; genius, talent, flair, gift, knack, ability, capability, proficiency, prowess, facility, faculty.

ingenuous /injényoōəs/ *adj.* **1** innocent; artless. **2** open; frank. □□ **ingenuously** *adv.* **ingenuousness** *n.* [L *ingenuus* free-born, frank (as IN-[2], root of *gignere* beget)]
■ **1** naive, simple, innocent, unsophisticated, natural, childlike, suggestible, trusting, unsuspecting, gullible, credulous, green; artless, guileless, sincere, genuine, undeceitful, truthful, aboveboard, *colloq.* on the level; straight, plain, uncomplicated, unaffected. **2** frank, candid, open, transparent, straightforward, plain; forthright, direct, foursquare, outspoken, blunt, bluff, honest; free, uninhibited, unabashed, unreserved; trustworthy, honorable, (fair and) square, fair, just.

ingest /injést/ *v.tr.* **1** take in (food, etc.); eat. **2** absorb (facts, knowledge, etc.). □□ **ingestion** /injés-chən/ *n.* **ingestive** *adj.* [L *ingerere ingest-* (as IN-[2], *gerere* carry)]
■ **1** see SWALLOW[1] *v.* 1.

inglenook /ínggəlnoŏk/ *n.* a space within the opening on either side of a large fireplace; chimney corner. [dial. (orig.

Sc.) *ingle* fire burning on a hearth, perh. f. Gael. *aingeal* fire, light + NOOK]

inglorious /in-gláwreeəs/ *adj.* **1** shameful; ignominious. **2** not famous. □□ **ingloriously** *adv.* **ingloriousness** *n.*
■ **1** see SHAMEFUL. **2** see OBSCURE *adj.* 6.
□□ **ingloriousness** see OBSCURITY 1.

-ingly /inglee/ *suffix* forming adverbs esp. denoting manner of action or nature or condition (*dotingly*; *charmingly*; *slantingly*).

ingoing /ín-gōing/ *adj.* **1** going in; entering. **2** penetrating; thorough.

ingot /ínggət/ *n.* a usu. oblong piece of cast metal, esp. of gold, silver, or steel. [ME: perh. f. IN[1] + *goten* past part. of OE *geotan* cast]

ingraft var. of ENGRAFT.

ingrain *adj.* & *v.* ● *adj.* /ín-grayn/ **1** inherent; ingrained. **2** (of textiles) dyed in the fiber, before being woven. ● *v.tr.* /ín-gráyn/cause (a dye) to sink deeply into the texture of a fabric; cause to become embedded. □ **ingrain carpet** a reversible carpet, with different colors interwoven.

ingrained /ín-gráynd/ *attrib. adj.* ingrate1 deeply rooted; inveterate. **2** thorough. **3** (of dirt, etc.) deeply embedded. □□ **ingrainedly** /-gráynidlee/ *adv.* [var. of *engrained*: see ENGRAIN]
■ **1** engrained, deep-rooted, established, fixed, deep-seated, fundamental, basic, essential, inherent, inborn, innate, inbred, inherited, hereditary; inveterate, habitual, hardened, incurable, incorrigible, unchangeable, unalterable, dyed-in-the-wool, out-and-out. **2** see THOROUGH 3. **3** engrained, embedded, ground-in; indelible, ineradicable, ineffaceable, inexpungible, stubborn.

ingrate /ín-grayt/ *n.* & *adj. formal* or *literary* ● *n.* an ungrateful person. ● *adj.* ungrateful. [ME f. L *ingratus* (as IN-[1], *gratus* grateful)]

ingratiate /ín-gráysheeayt/ *v.refl.* (usu. foll. by *with*) bring oneself into favor. □□ **ingratiating** *adj.* **ingratiatingly** *adv.* **ingratiation** /-áyshən/ *n.* [L *in gratiam* into favor]
■ (*ingratiate oneself with*) flatter, adulate, cultivate, curry favor with, dance attendance on, fawn on *or* upon, grovel to, cringe to, toady to, bow and scrape to, kowtow to, shine up to, *colloq.* crawl to, creep to, suck up to, sweet-talk, cozy up to, *Brit. colloq.* chat up.
□□ **ingratiating** flattering, adulatory, fawning, groveling, toadyish, servile, obsequious, sycophantic, wheedling, unctuous, oily, buttery, slimy, sugary, saccharine, *colloq.* creepy, smarmy, bootlicking, sweet-talking.

ingratitude /in-grátitood, -tyood/ *n.* a lack of due gratitude. [ME f. OF *ingratitude* or LL *ingratitudo* (as INGRATE)]
■ unthankfulness, ungratefulness, thanklessness; snakiness.

ingravescent /ín-grəvésənt/ *adj. Med.* (of a disease, etc.) growing worse. □□ **ingravescence** /-səns/ *n.* [L *ingravescere* (as IN-[2], *gravescere* grow heavy f. *gravis* heavy)]

ingredient /in-greédeeənt/ *n.* a component part or element in a recipe, mixture, or combination. [ME f. L *ingredi ingress-* enter (as IN-[2], *gradi* step)]
■ constituent, element, part, component, factor, admixture; (*ingredients*) contents, makings.

ingress /ín-gres/ *n.* **1 a** the act or right of going in or entering. **b** an entrance. **2** *Astron.* the start of an eclipse or transit. □□ **ingression** /-greshən/ *n.* [ME f. L *ingressus* (as INGREDIENT)]
■ **1** see ENTRANCE[1] 1, 4; 3.

in-group /ín-groōp/ *n.* a small exclusive group of people with a common interest.

ingrowing /ín-grōing/ *adj.* growing inward, esp. (of a toenail) growing into the flesh. □□ **ingrown** *adj.* **ingrowth** *n.*

inguinal /ínggwinəl/ *adj.* of the groin. □□ **inguinally** *adv.* [L *inguinalis* f. *inguen -inis* groin]

ingurgitate /in-gə́rjitayt/ *v.tr.* **1** swallow greedily. **2** engulf. □□ **ingurgitation** /-táyshən/ *n.* [L *ingurgitare ingurgitat-* (as IN-[2], *gurges gurgitis* whirlpool)]

inhabit /inhábit/ v.tr. (of a person or animal) dwell in; occupy (a region, town, house, etc.). □□ **inhabitability** /-təbílitee/ n. **inhabitable** adj. **inhabitant** n. **inhabitation** /-táyshən/ n. [ME inhabite, enhabite f. OF enhabiter or L inhabitare (as IN-², habitare dwell): see HABIT]

■ reside in, live in, be domiciled in, occupy, tenant, archaic abide in, literary dwell in; populate, people; colonize. □□ **inhabitant** resident, householder, tenant, inmate, occupant, Brit. occupier; citizen, native, national, local, literary dweller, poet. denizen.

inhabitancy /inhábit'nsee/ n. (also **inhabitance** /-it'ns/) residence as an inhabitant, esp. during a specified period so as to acquire rights, etc.

inhalant /inháylənt/ n. a medicinal preparation for inhaling.

inhale /inháyl/ v.tr. (often absol.) breathe in (air, gas, tobacco smoke, etc.). □□ **inhalation** /-həláyshən/ n. [L inhalare breathe in (as IN-², halare breathe)]

■ breathe in, inspire, inbreathe, draw (in), suck in, take a breath of; sniff (up), sl. snort.

inhaler /inháylər/ n. a portable device used for relieving esp. asthma by inhaling.

inharmonic /ínhaarmónik/ adj. esp. Mus. not harmonic.

inharmonious /ínhaarmóneeəs/ adj. esp. Mus. not harmonious. □□ **inharmoniously** adv.

■ see mismatched (MISMATCH v.).

inhere /inheér/ v.intr. (often foll. by in) 1 exist essentially or permanently in (goodness inheres in that child). 2 (of rights, etc.) be vested in (a person, etc.). [L inhaerēre inhaes- (as IN-², haerēre to stick)]

inherent /inheérənt, inhér-/ adj. (often foll. by in) 1 existing in something, esp. as a permanent or characteristic attribute. 2 vested in (a person, etc.) as a right or privilege. □□ **inherence** /-rəns/ n. **inherently** adv. [L inhaerēre inhaerent- (as INHERE)]

■ 1 innate, connate, inborn, congenital, inherited, hereditary, inbred, natural, native, constitutional, ingrained, engrained, in one's blood, bred in the bone; essential, intrinsic, implicit, basic, fundamental, elementary, radical, structural, organic, integral, built-in; indwelling, immanent. 2 fundamental, basic, essential, elementary; inalienable, inviolable, sacrosanct, unchallengeable, absolute, Law unalienable, imprescriptible, entailed, literary indefeasible.

inherit /inhérit/ v. 1 tr. receive (property, rank, title, etc.) by legal descent or succession. 2 tr. derive (a quality or characteristic) genetically from one's ancestors. 3 absol. succeed as an heir (a younger son rarely inherits). □□ **inheritor** n. (fem. **inheritress** or **inheritrix**). [ME f. OF enheriter f. LL inhereditare (as IN-², L heres heredis heir)]

■ 1 come into, succeed to, fall or be or become heir to, be bequeathed, be left, be willed. 3 succeed, take over, become heir, receive an inheritance. □□ **inheritor**, etc. see HEIR.

inheritable /inhéritəbəl/ adj. 1 capable of being inherited. 2 capable of inheriting. □□ **inheritability** /-bílitee/ n. [ME f. AF (as INHERIT)]

■ 1 see HEREDITARY 1.

inheritance /inhérit'ns/ n. 1 something that is inherited. 2 a the act of inheriting. b an instance of this. □ **inheritance tax** a tax levied on property, etc., acquired by gift or inheritance. [ME f. AF inheritaunce f. OF enheriter: see INHERIT]

■ 1 patrimony, heritage, legacy, bequest, birthright. 2 endowment, succession, bequeathal.

inhesion /inheézhən/ n. formal the act or fact of inhering. [LL inhaesio (as INHERE)]

inhibit /inhíbit/ v.tr. 1 hinder, restrain, or prevent (an action or progress). 2 (as **inhibited** adj.) subject to inhibition. 3 a (usu. foll. by from + verbal noun) forbid or prohibit (a person, etc.). b (esp. in ecclesiastical law) forbid (an ecclesiastic) to exercise clerical functions. □□ **inhibitive** adj. **inhibitor** n. **inhibitory** adj. [L inhibēre (as IN-², habēre hold)]

■ 1 hinder, hamper, restrain, impede, obstruct, interfere with, check, prevent, stop, discourage, deter, repress, suppress, frustrate, hold back, bridle, shackle, muzzle,

cramp, curb, control. 2 (**inhibited**) pent up, repressed, restrained, suppressed, bottled up; shy, reticent, reserved, self-conscious, abashed, embarrassed, defensive, on the defensive, colloq. uptight, sl. hung up. 3 (inhibit from) forbid to, prohibit from, interdict from, bar from, ban from, keep from, stop, restrain from, discourage from, deter from.

inhibition /ínhibíshən/ n. 1 Psychol. a restraint on the direct expression of an instinct. 2 colloq. an emotional resistance to a thought, an action, etc. (has inhibitions about singing in public). 3 Law an order forbidding alteration to property rights. 4 a the act of inhibiting. b the process of being inhibited. [ME f. OF inhibition or L inhibitio (as INHIBIT)]

■ 1, 2 bar, barrier, defense mechanism, blockage, psychological block, mental block, check, curb, stricture, restraint, constraint, impediment, hindrance, interference, sl. hang-up; self-consciousness, defensiveness, shyness, reticence, embarrassment. 4 prohibition, interdiction, bar, ban, proscription; prevention, repression, suppression.

inhomogeneous /ínhōmōjeéneeəs, inhóma-/ adj. not homogeneous. □□ **inhomogeneity** /-jineé-itee/ n.

inhospitable /ínhóspitəbəl, inhóspi-/ adj. 1 not hospitable. 2 (of a region, coast, etc.) not affording shelter, etc. □□ **inhospitableness** n. **inhospitably** adv. [obs. F (as IN-¹, HOSPITABLE)]

■ 1 unwelcoming, unreceptive, uninviting, unsociable, unsocial, aloof, cold, icy, cool, standoffish, unfriendly, inimical, antisocial, hostile, intolerant, xenophobic. 2 uninviting, bleak, grim, harsh, barren, bare, cheerless, forbidding, hostile; unfavorable, unpromising, unpropitious, inauspicious; uninhabitable.

inhospitality /ínhóspitálitee/ n. the act or process of being inhospitable. [L inhospitalitas (as IN-¹, HOSPITALITY)]

in-house adj. & adv. ● adj. /ínhóws/ done or existing within an institution, company, etc. (an in-house project). ● adv. /inhóws/ internally, without outside assistance.

inhuman /inhyōōmən/ adj. 1 (of a person, conduct, etc.) brutal; unfeeling; barbarous. 2 not of a human type. □□ **inhumanly** adv. [L inhumanus (as IN-¹, HUMAN)]

■ 1 brutal, savage, barbaric, barbarous, beastly, bestial, ferocious, bloodthirsty, murderous; vicious, merciless, cruel, pitiless, ruthless, heartless, cold-blooded, stonyhearted, hard-hearted, unfeeling, unkind, unkindly, callous, insensitive, unsympathetic, severe, inhumane. 2 nonhuman, animal, bestial, brutal, brutish; devilish, fiendish, diabolic, diabolical, demonic, demoniac.

inhumane /ínhyōōmáyn/ adj. not humane. □□ **inhumanely** adv. [L inhumanus (see INHUMAN) & f. IN-¹ + HUMANE, orig. = INHUMAN]

■ see MERCILESS.

inhumanity /ínhyōōmánitee/ n. (pl. -ies) 1 brutality; barbarousness; callousness. 2 an inhumane act.

■ 1 see BARBARITY 1.

inhume /inhyōōm/ v.tr. literary bury. □□ **inhumation** n. [L inhumare (as IN-², humus ground)]

■ bury, inter, lay to rest. □□ **inhumation** see FUNERAL n.

inimical /inímikəl/ adj. (usu. foll. by to) 1 hostile. 2 harmful. □□ **inimically** adv. [LL inimicalis f. L inimicus (as IN-¹, amicus friend)]

■ 1 see HOSTILE 2. 2 see DETRIMENTAL.

inimitable /inímitəbəl/ adj. impossible to imitate. □□ **inimitability** n. **inimitableness** n. **inimitably** adv. [F inimitable or L inimitabilis (as IN-¹, imitabilis imitable)]

■ see UNPARALLELED. □□ **inimitability** see SUPERIORITY. **inimitably** see PERFECTLY 3.

iniquity /iníkwitee/ n. (pl. -ies) 1 wickedness; unrighteousness. 2 a gross injustice. □□ **iniquitous** adj. **iniquitously**

/.../ pronunciation	● part of speech
□ phrases, idioms, and compounds	
□□ derivatives	■ synonym section
cross-references appear in SMALL CAPITALS or italics	

adv. **iniquitousness** *n.* [ME f. OF *iniquité* f. L *iniquitas -tatis* f. *iniquus* (as IN-¹, *aequus* just)]

■ **1** see SIN¹ 1. **2** see SCANDAL 1b.

initial /iníshəl/ *adj., n.,* & *v.* ● *adj.* of, existing, or occurring at the beginning (*initial stage; initial expenses*). ● *n.* **1** = *initial letter.* **2** (usu. in *pl.*) the first letter or letters of the words of a (esp. a person's) name or names. ● *v.tr.* (**initialed, initialing**; esp. *Brit.* **initialled, initialling**) mark or sign with one's initials. □ **initial letter** the letter at the beginning of a word. **Initial Teaching Alphabet** a 44-letter phonetic alphabet used to help those beginning to read and write English. □□ **initially** *adv.* [L *initialis* f. *initium* beginning f. *inire init-* go in]

■ *adj.* first, prime, primary, original; aboriginal, autochthonal, autochthonic, autochthonous; incipient, nascent, inaugural, opening, starting, introductory, prefatory. ● *n.* **2** (*initials*) monogram. ● *v.* sign, endorse. □□ **initially** see *in the first instance* (INSTANCE).

initialism /iníshəlizəm/ *n.* a group of initial letters used as an abbreviation for a name or expression, each letter being pronounced separately (e.g., *CIA*) or the group of letters being pronounced as a word (e.g., *NATO*) (cf. ACRONYM).

■ see ABBREVIATION.

initialize /iníshəliz/ *v.tr. Computing* set to the value or put in the condition appropriate to the start of an operation. □□ **initialization** *n.*

initiate *v., n.,* & *adj.* ● *v.tr.* /inísheeayt/ **1** begin; set going; originate. **2 a** (usu. foll. by *into*) admit (a person) into a society, an office, a secret, etc., esp. with a ritual. **b** (usu. foll. by *in, into*) instruct (a person) in science, art, etc. ● *n.* /inísheeət/ a person who has been newly initiated. ● *adj.* /inísheeət/ (of a person) newly initiated (*an initiate member*). □□ **initiation** /-sheeáyshən/ *n.* **initiator** *n.* **initiatory** /inísheeətáwree/ *adj.* [L *initiare* f. *initium*: see INITIAL]

■ *v.* **1** begin, start, originate, pioneer, introduce, instigate, install, institute, set up, inaugurate, open, found, establish, set in motion, get under way, launch, float, get *or* set going, *colloq.* kick off, *formal* commence; create, generate, sow, cause, give rise to, spark (off), trigger, set off, touch off, actuate, activate. **2 a** admit, accept, introduce, induct, swear in, enroll, install; familiarize, break in, blood. **b** teach, instruct, train, tutor, drill, coach, school, ground, educate, guide, prepare. ● *n.* novice, beginner, apprentice, recruit, acolyte, neophyte, tyro, newcomer, new boy, new girl, greenhorn, tenderfoot, fledgling, learner, freshman, cub, punk, *Austral. colloq.* jackaroo, *Brit. colloq.* fresher, *sl.* rookie; novitiate, catechumen. ● *adj.* new, novice, apprentice, fledgling, *sl.* rookie. □□ **initiation** beginning, start, inception, origination, initiative, introduction, instigation, installation, institution, inauguration, opening, foundation, establishment, launch, flotation, debut, *colloq.* kickoff, *formal* commencement; creation, generation, actuation, activation; admittance, acceptance, introduction, induction, enrollment, investiture, ordination; education, teaching, instruction, training, preparation, schooling, grounding.

initiative /inísheeətiv/ *n.* & *adj.* ● *n.* **1** the ability to initiate things; enterprise (*I'm afraid he lacks all initiative*). **2** a first step; origination (*a peace initiative*). **3** the power or right to begin something. **4** *Polit.* (esp. in Switzerland and some US states) the right of citizens outside the legislature to originate legislation. ● *adj.* beginning; originating. □ **have the initiative** esp. *Mil.* be able to control the enemy's movements. **on one's own initiative** without being prompted by others. **take the initiative** (usu. foll. by *in* + verbal noun) be the first to take action. [F (as INITIATE)]

■ **1** leadership, enterprise, resourcefulness, self-motivation, aggressiveness, drive, push, dynamism, energy, vigor, dash, go, zip, snap, *colloq.* gumption, get-up-and-go, vim, pep, zing. **2** (first) move, (first) step, lead, opening move *or* gambit, *démarche*; see also *initiation* (INITIATE). □ **have the initiative** call the shots *or* tune, be in control, be in command, have the upper hand, pull the strings, be in the driver's seat, be in charge, be in the saddle, rule the roost, be at the wheel. **on one's own initiative** unprompted, unaided, independently, in one's own name, on one's own responsibility; see also VOLUNTARILY. **take the initiative** be the first, take the first step(s), make the first move, start *or* set the ball rolling, break the ice; see also *have the initiative* above.

inject /injékt/ *v.tr.* **1** *Med.* **a** (usu. foll. by *into*) drive or force (a solution, medicine, etc.) by or as if by a syringe. **b** (usu. foll. by *with*) fill (a cavity, etc.) by injecting. **c** administer medicine, etc., to (a person) by injection. **2** place or insert (an object, a quality, etc.) into something (*may I inject a note of realism?*). □□ **injectable** *adj.* & *n.* **injector** *n.* [L *injicere* (as IN-², *jacere* throw)]

■ **1** drive *or* force *or* shoot in, insert, introduce, intromit, transfuse; *sl.* fix, shoot (up), mainline, pop; inoculate, syringe. **2** introduce, insert, instill, bring in, interject, throw in.

injection /injékshən/ *n.* **1 a** the act of injecting. **b** an instance of this. **2** a liquid or solution (to be) injected (*prepare a morphine injection*). □ **injection molding** the shaping of rubber or plastic articles by injecting heated material into a mold. [F *injection* or L *injectio* (as INJECT)]

■ shot, inoculation, vaccination.

injudicious /injōōdíshəs/ *adj.* unwise; ill-judged. □□ **injudiciously** *adv.* **injudiciousness** *n.*

■ see *ill-advised* 2 (ILL). □□ **injudiciousness** see *imprudence* (IMPRUDENT).

Injun /ínjən/ *n. colloq. offens.* a Native American. [corrupt of INDIAN]

injunction /injúnkshən/ *n.* **1** an authoritative warning or order. **2** *Law* a judicial order restraining a person from an act or compelling redress to an injured party. □□ **injunctive** *adj.* [LL *injunctio* f. L *injungere* ENJOIN]

■ **1** prohibition, interdict, interdiction, restriction, restraint, order, mandate, directive, command, direction, instruction, ruling, dictate, diktat, ukase, exhortation; warning, admonition.

injure /ínjər/ *v.tr.* **1** do physical harm or damage to; hurt (*was injured in a road accident*). **2** harm or impair (*illness might injure her chances*). **3** do wrong to. □□ **injurer** *n.* [back-form. f. INJURY]

■ **1** harm, hurt, damage, wreck, maim, cripple, break, fracture; assault, molest, beat up; wound, spill a person's blood, cut, lacerate, gash, scrape, scratch, scar, disfigure; bruise, contuse, strain, pull, wrench, rip, tear, rack, wear, gall, chafe; burn, scorch, *poet.* scathe. **2** impair, harm, damage, ruin, cripple, mar, spoil, disable; vitiate, tarnish, weaken, undermine, shake, prejudice. **3** wrong, offend, abuse, insult, malign, vilify, calumniate, asperse, libel, slander, defame, smear, discredit, dishonor, outrage, affront, humiliate, slight, *sl.* do a person dirt; hurt, wound, mistreat, misuse, ill-treat, maltreat, oppress, persecute, *Law* damnify.

injured /ínjərd/ *adj.* **1** harmed or hurt (*the injured passengers*). **2** offended; wronged (*in an injured tone*).

injurious /injōōreeəs/ *adj.* **1** hurtful. **2** (of language) insulting; libelous. **3** wrongful. □□ **injuriously** *adv.* **injuriousness** *n.* [ME f. F *injurieux* or L *injuriosus* (as INJURY)]

■ **1** hurtful, malicious, nasty, spiteful, harsh, unpleasant, mischievous, *literary* maleficent; damaging, deleterious, detrimental, unfavorable, adverse, ruinous, bad; harmful, pernicious, noxious, toxic, poisonous, destructive, malignant, dangerous, insalubrious, unhealthy. **2** abusive, offensive, insulting, scathing, scornful, derogatory, deprecatory, contemptuous, catty, abrasive, barbed; slanderous, libelous, defamatory, calumnious, calumniatory, scurrilous, scandalous, malicious. **3** wrongful, unfair, unjust, underhand(ed), improper, dirty; iniquitous, nefarious, wicked, evil, sinful, unlawful, bad, wrong.

injury /ínjəree/ *n.* (*pl.* **-ies**) **1 a** physical harm or damage. **b** an instance of this (*suffered head injuries*). **2** esp. *Law* **a**

wrongful action or treatment. **b** an instance of this. **3** damage to one's good name, etc. [ME f. AF *injurie* f. L *injuria* a wrong (as IN-¹, *jus juris* right)]

■ **1** damage, hurt, harm, impairment, disablement, disfigurement, wreckage, mayhem; break, breakage, fracture, laceration, wound, cut, gash, scrape, scratch, scarring, scar; bruise, contusion, strain, pull, wrench, tear, rip. **2** wrong, abuse, maltreatment, mistreatment, ill-treatment, ill use; injustice, unjustness, wrongdoing, misdeed, outrage, offense, affront, insult, mischief, malice, ill, ill turn, disservice. **3** damage, insult, abuse, calumny, slander, libel, defamation, slur, smear, blot, aspersion.

injustice /injústis/ *n.* **1** a lack of fairness or justice. **2** an unjust act. □ **do a person an injustice** judge a person unfairly. [ME f. OF f. L *injustitia* (as IN-¹, JUSTICE)]

■ **1** unfairness, unjustness, wrong, inequity, inequality, iniquity, invidiousness, oppression, wrongfulness, unrighteousness; favoritism, discrimination, bias, partiality, partisanship, prejudice, bigotry, one-sidedness. **2** wrong, injury, outrage, abuse, ill turn, bad turn, disservice. □ **do a person an injustice** wrong a person, get a person wrong, misjudge a person, misread a person, underestimate a person, undervalue a person.

ink /ingk/ *n.* & *v.* ● *n.* **1 a** a colored fluid used for writing with a pen, marking with a rubber stamp, etc. **b** a thick paste used in printing, duplicating, in ballpoint pens, etc. **2** *Zool.* a black liquid ejected by a cuttlefish, octopus, etc., to confuse a predator. ● *v.tr.* **1** (usu. foll. by *in, over,* etc.) mark with ink. **2** cover (type, etc.) with ink before printing. **3** apply ink to. **4** (as **inked** *adj.*) *Austral. sl.* drunk. □ **ink-jet printer** a computer-controlled printer in which minute droplets of ink are projected onto the paper. **ink out** obliterate with ink. **ink pad** an ink-soaked pad, usu. in a box, used for inking a rubber stamp, etc. □□ **inker** *n.* [ME *enke, inke* f. OF *enque* f. LL *encau(s)tum* f. Gk *egkauston* purple ink used by Roman emperors for signature (as EN-², CAUSTIC)]

inkblot /íngkblot/ *n.* a spot or patten created by blotted ink. □ **inkblot test** a psychological test, esp. the Rorschach test, in which subjects must interpret inkblots.

inkhorn /íngkhawrn/ *n.* & *adj.* ● *n.* a small, portable container for ink, orig. of horn. ● *adj.* pretentiously learned.

inkling /íngkling/ *n.* (often foll. by *of*) a slight knowledge or suspicion; a hint. [ME *inkle* utter in an undertone, of unkn. orig.]

■ suspicion, clue, (the faintest *or* foggiest) idea, (the faintest) notion, glimmering; hint, intimation, indication, suggestion, tip, tip-off, whisper.

inkstand /íngkstand/ *n.* a stand for one or more ink bottles, often incorporating a pen tray, etc.

inkwell /íngkwel/ *n.* a pot for ink usu. housed in a hole in a desk.

inky /íngkee/ *adj.* (**inkier, inkiest**) of, as black as, or stained with ink. □□ **inkiness** *n.*

inlaid *past* and *past part.* of INLAY.

inland /ínlənd, ínland/ *adj., n.,* & *adv.* ● *adj.* **1** situated in the interior of a country. **2** esp. *Brit.* carried on within the limits of a country; domestic (*inland trade*). ● *n.* the parts of a country remote from the sea or frontiers; the interior. ● *adv.* in or toward the interior of a country. □ **inland duty** (in the UK) a tax payable on inland trade. **inland revenue** revenue consisting of taxes and inland duties. **Inland Revenue** (in the UK) the government department responsible for assessing and collecting income taxes, etc. □□ **inlander** *n.* **inlandish** *adj.*

■ *n.* **1** see INTERIOR *n.* 2.

in-law /ínlaw/ *n.* (often in *pl.*) a relative by marriage.

■ see RELATION 2.

inlay *v.* & *n.* ● *v.tr.* /ínláy/ (*past* and *past part.* **inlaid** /ínláyd/) **1 a** (usu. foll. by *in*) embed (a thing in another) so that the surfaces are even. **b** (usu. foll. by *with*) ornament (a thing with inlaid work). **2** (as **inlaid** *adj.*) (of a piece of furniture, etc.) ornamented by inlaying. **3** insert (a page, an

illustration, etc.) in a space cut in a larger thicker page. ● *n.* /ínlay/ **1** inlaid work. **2** material inlaid. **3** a filling shaped to fit a tooth cavity. □□ **inlayer** *n.* [IN-² + LAY¹]

■ *v.* **1 a** see IMPLANT *v.* 1.

inlet /ínlet, -lit/ *n.* **1** a small arm of the sea, a lake, or a river. **2** a piece inserted, esp. in dressmaking, etc. **3** a way of entry. [ME f. IN + LET¹ *v.*]

■ **1** see CREEK 1. **3** see ENTRY 3a.

inlier /ínliər/ *n. Geol.* a structure or area of older rocks completely surrounded by newer rocks. [IN, after *outlier*]

in-line /ínlín/ *adj.* **1** having parts arranged in a line. **2** constituting an integral part of a continuous sequence of operations or machines.

in loco parentis /in lṓkō pəréntis/ *adv.* in the place or position of a parent (used of a teacher, etc., responsible for children). [L]

inly /ínlee/ *adv. poet.* **1** inwardly; in the heart. **2** intimately; thoroughly. [OE *innlīce* (as IN, -LY²)]

inmate /ínmayt/ *n.* (usu. foll. by *of*) **1** an occupant of a hospital, prison, institution, etc. **2** an occupant of a house, etc., esp. one of several. [prob. orig. INN + MATE¹, assoc. with IN]

■ **1** prisoner, convict, captive, internee, detainee, jailbird, *sl.* con, esp. *Brit.* yardbird, (old) lag, patient, case. **2** inhabitant, occupant, resident, tenant; sharer.

in medias res /in meédiəs ráyz/ *adv.* **1** into the midst of things. **2** into the middle of a story, without preamble. [L]

in memoriam /in mímáwreeəm/ *prep.* & *n.* ● *prep.* in memory of (a dead person). ● *n.* a written article or notice, etc., in memory of a dead person; an obituary. [L]

inmost /ínmōst/ *adj.* **1** most inward. **2** most intimate; deepest. [OE *innemest* (as IN, -MOST)]

inn /in/ *n.* **1** a public house providing alcoholic liquor for consumption on the premises, and sometimes accommodation, etc. **2** *hist.* a house providing accommodation, esp. for travelers. □ **Inns of Court** *Brit. Law* **1** the four legal societies having the exclusive right of admitting people to the English bar. **2** any of the sets of buildings in London belonging to these societies. **3** a similar society in Ireland. [OE *inn* (as IN)]

■ **1** see BAR 4 **b**, **c**. **2** see HOTEL 1.

innards /ínərdz/ *n.pl. colloq.* **1** entrails. **2** works (of an engine, etc.). [dial., etc., pronunc. of *inwards*: see INWARD *n.*]

■ **1** see GUT *n.* 1, 2. **2** see WORK *n.* 8.

innate /ínáyt, ínayt/ *adj.* **1** inborn; natural. **2** *Philos.* originating in the mind. □□ **innately** *adv.* **innateness** *n.* [ME f. L *innatus* (as IN-², *natus* past part. of *nasci* be born)]

■ **1** see INBORN. □□ **innately** see NATURALLY 1.

inner /ínər/ *adj.* & *n.* ● *adj.* (usu. *attrib.*) **1** further in; inside; interior (*the inner compartment*). **2** (of thoughts, feelings, etc.) deeper; more secret. ● *n. Archery* esp. *Brit.* **1** a division of the target next to the bull's-eye. **2** a shot that strikes this. □ **inner bar** *Brit. Law* Queen's or King's Counsel collectively. **inner circle** an intimate, usu. influential small group of people. **inner city** the central most densely populated area of a city (also (with hyphen) *attrib.*: *inner-city housing*). **inner-directed** *Psychol.* governed by standards formed in childhood. **inner man** (or **woman** or **person**) **1** the soul or mind. **2** *joc.* the stomach. **inner planet** any of the four planets closest to the sun (i.e., Mercury, Venus, Earth, and Mars) (cf. *outer planet*). **inner space 1** the region between the earth and outer space, or below the surface of the sea. **2** the part of the mind not normally accessible to consciousness. **Inner Temple** one of the two Inns of Court on the site of the Temple in London (cf. *Middle Temple*). **inner tube** a separate inflatable tube inside the cover of a pneumatic tire. □□ **innerly** *adv.* **innermost** *adj.* **innerness** *n.* [OE *innera* (adj.), compar. of IN]

■ *adj.* **1** see INTERIOR *adj.* 1. **2** see INTERIOR *adj.* 5.

/ . . . / **pronunciation**　　● **part of speech**
□ **phrases, idioms, and compounds**
□□ **derivatives**　　■ **synonym section**
cross-references appear in SMALL CAPITALS or *italics*

□ **inner man** (or **woman** or **person**) **1** see SUBCONSCIOUS *n*. □□ **innermost** see SUBCONSCIOUS *adj*.

innerspring /ínərspring/ *adj*. (of a mattress, etc.) with internal springs.

innervate /ínərvayt, inər-/ *v.tr*. supply (an organ, etc.) with nerves. □□ **innervation** /-váyshən/ *n*. [IN-² + L *nervus* nerve + -ATE³]

inning /íning/ *n*. **1** *Baseball* **a** a division of a game in which the two teams alternate as offense and defense and during which each team is allowed three outs. **b** a single turn at bat for a team until they make three outs. **2** a similar division of play in other games, as horseshoes. **3** a period during which a person, group, etc., can achieve something. [*in* (v.) go in (f. IN)]

innings /íningz/ *n*. (*pl*. same; *Brit*. **inningses**) **1** *Cricket* **a** the part of a game during which a side is in or batting. **b** the play of or score achieved by a player during a turn at batting. **2** a period during which a government, party, cause, etc. is in office or effective. **3 a** = INNING 2. **b** *colloq*. a person's life span (*had her innings and died at 94*).

innkeeper /ínkeepər/ *n*. a person who keeps an inn.
■ see LANDLORD 2.

innocent /ínəsənt/ *adj. & n.* ● *adj*. **1** free from moral wrong; sinless. **2** (usu. foll. by *of*) not guilty (of a crime, etc.). **3 a** simple; guileless; naive. **b** pretending to be guileless. **4** harmless. **5** (foll. by *of*) *colloq*. without; lacking (*appeared, innocent of shoes*). ● *n*. **1** an innocent person, esp. a young child. **2** (in *pl*.) the young children killed by Herod after the birth of Jesus (Matt. 2:16). □ **Innocents'** (or **Holy Innocents'**) **Day** the day, Dec. 28, commemorating the massacre of the innocents. □□ **innocence** /-səns/ *n*. **innocency** *n*. **innocently** *adv*. [ME f. OF *innocent* or L *innocens inno-cent-* (as IN-¹, *nocēre* hurt)]
■ *adj*. **1** virtuous, moral, righteous, good, pure, chaste, virgin(al), undefiled, untainted, unstained, unsullied, pristine, sinless, uncorrupted, immaculate, spotless, unblemished, unpolluted, *colloq*. white. **2** not guilty, guiltless, blameless, (in the) clear, unimpeachable, above suspicion, above reproach, honest, faultless. **3 a** simple, unsuspecting, unsuspicious, ingenuous, trusting, trustful, gullible, credulous, dewy-eyed, *archaic* silly; guileless, artless, unaffected, unsophisticated, unworldly, naive, green, inexperienced, callow, childlike. **b** demure, coy, meek, *Brit*. twee. **4** harmless, well-intentioned, safe, tame, innocuous, innoxious, inoffensive, unoffending, unobjectionable; platonic. **5** see DESTITUTE 2. ● *n*. **1** infant, babe, child, cherub; ingénue, dove, virgin; simpleton, *Brit. colloq*. muggins, *sl*. sucker, soft *or* easy touch, *Brit. sl*. mug.

innocuous /inókyōōəs/ *adj*. **1** not injurious; harmless. **2** inoffensive. □□ **innocuity** /ínəkyōō-itee/ *n*. **innocuously** *adv*. **innocuousness** *n*. [L *innocuus* (as IN-¹, *nocuus* formed as INNOCENT)]
■ **1** see HARMLESS 1. **2** see INOFFENSIVE.
□□ **innocuousness** see PURITY 2.

innominate /inóminət/ *adj*. unnamed. □ **innominate bone** *n. Anat*. the bone formed from the fusion of the ilium, ischium, and pubis; the hipbone. [LL *innominatus* (as IN-¹, NOMINATE)]
■ see NAMELESS 1, 3, 5.

innovate /ínəvayt/ *v.intr*. **1** bring in new methods, ideas, etc. **2** (often foll. by *in*) make changes. □□ **innovation** /-váyshən/ *n*. **innovational** /-váyshənəl/ *adj*. **innovator** *n*. **innovative** *adj*. **innovativeness** *n*. **innovatory** /-vəytáwree/ *adj*. [L *innovare* make new, alter (as IN-², *novus* new)]
■ **1** break new ground, pioneer, blaze a trail. **2** make changes, make alterations, modernize, remodel, revamp. □□ **innovation** originality, inventiveness, creativity, imagination, imaginativeness; novelty, invention; modernization, alteration, change.
innovative see ORIGINAL *adj*. 2.

innoxious /inókshəs/ *adj*. harmless. □□ **innoxiously** *adv*. **innoxiousness** *n*. [L *innoxius* (as IN-¹, NOXIOUS)]

innuendo /ínyōō-éndō/ *n. & v.* ● *n*. (*pl*. **-os** or **-oes**) **1** an allusive or oblique remark or hint, usu. disparaging. **2** a remark with a double meaning, usu. suggestive. ● *v.intr*. (**-oes, -oed**) make innuendos. [L, = by nodding at, by pointing to: ablat. gerund of *innuere* nod at (as IN-², *nuere* nod)]
■ *n*. **1** allusion, insinuation, imputation, slur, suggestion, hint, intimation, implication, overtone. **2** double entendre; equivoque, pun, play on words, paronomasia, quibble. ● *v*. be suggestive; pun, equivocate, quibble.

Innuit var. of INUIT.

innumerable /inōōmərəbəl, inyōō-/ *adj*. too many to be counted. □□ **innumerability** /-bílitee/ *n*. **innumerably** *adv*. [ME f. L *innumerabilis* (as IN-¹, NUMERABLE)]
■ see MANY *adj*.

innumerate /inōōmərət, inyōō-/ *adj*. having no knowledge of or feeling for mathematical operations; not numerate. □□ **innumeracy** /-rəsee/ *n*. [IN-¹, NUMERATE]

innutrition /ínōōtríshən, -yōō-/ *n*. lack of nutrition. □□ **innutritious** *adj*.

inobservance /ínəbzórvəns/ *n*. **1** inattention. **2** (usu. foll. by *of*) nonobservance (of a law, etc.). [F *inobservance* or L *inobservantia* (as IN-¹, OBSERVANCE)]

inoculate /inókyəlayt/ *v.tr*. **1 a** treat (a person or animal) with a small quantity of the agent of a disease, in the form of vaccine or serum, usu. by injection, to promote immunity against the disease. **b** implant (a disease) by means of vaccine. **2** instill (a person) with ideas or opinions. □□ **inoculable** *adj*. **inoculation** /-láyshən/ *n*. **inoculative** *adj*. **inoculator** *n*. [orig. in sense 'insert (a bud) into a plant': L *inoculare inoculat-* engraft (as IN-², *oculus* eye, bud)]
■ **1** see INJECT 1. □□ **inoculation** shot, vaccination, injection; see IMMUNITY 1.

inoculum /inókyələm/ *n*. (*pl*. **inocula** /-lə/) any substance used for inoculation. [mod.L (as INOCULATE)]
■ see PREVENTIVE *n*.

inodorous /inódərəs/ *adj*. having no smell; odorless.

inoffensive /ínəfénsiv/ *adj*. not objectionable; harmless. □□ **inoffensively** *adv*. **inoffensiveness** *n*.
■ harmless, unobjectionable, innocuous, innoxious, unoffending; neutral, safe, tame; mild, bland, retiring; platonic.

inoperable /inópərəbəl/ *adj*. **1** *Surgery* that cannot suitably be operated on (*inoperable cancer*). **2** that cannot be operated; inoperative. □□ **inoperability** *n*. **inoperably** *adv*. [F *inopérable* (as IN-¹, OPERABLE)]
■ **1** see INCURABLE *adj*. **2** useless, unworkable, inoperative, broken, unusable, *colloq*. busted, *sl*. kaput.

inoperative /inópərətiv/ *adj*. not working or taking effect.
■ see *out of order* 1 (ORDER).

inopportune /inópərtōōn, -tyōōn/ *adj*. not appropriate, esp. as regards time; unseasonable. □□ **inopportunely** *adv*. **inopportuneness** *n*. [L *inopportunus* (as IN-¹, OPPORTUNE)]
■ inappropriate, malapropos, inconvenient, inexpedient, unsuited, unsuitable, out of place, unseemly, untoward, unpropitious, unfavorable, inauspicious, ill-chosen, unfortunate; ill-timed, untimely, unseasonable; premature, hasty, too early.

inordinate /ináwrd'nət/ *adj*. **1** immoderate; excessive. **2** intemperate. **3** disorderly. □□ **inordinately** *adv*. [ME f. L *inordinatus* (as IN-¹, *ordinatus* past part. of *ordinare* ORDAIN)]
■ **1, 2** immoderate, unrestrained, unbridled, untamed, intemperate, violent; extreme, excessive, exorbitant, disproportionate, out of all proportion, extravagant, overdone, overblown; outrageous, preposterous, unconscionable, unreasonable, unwarrantable, unjustifiable, undue, uncalled-for, unwarranted. **3** see DISORDERLY 1.

inorganic /ínawrgánik/ *adj*. **1** *Chem*. (of a compound) not organic, usu. of mineral origin (opp. ORGANIC). **2** without organized physical structure. **3** not arising by natural growth; extraneous. **4** *Philol*. not explainable by normal etymology. □ **inorganic chemistry** the chemistry of inorganic compounds. □□ **inorganically** *adv*.
■ **1** see INANIMATE 1.

inosculate /inóskyəlayt/ *v.intr.* & *tr.* **1** join by running together. **2** join closely. □□ **inosculation** /-láyshən/ *n.* [IN-² + L *osculare* provide with a mouth f. *osculum* dimin. of *os* mouth]

inpatient /ínpayshənt/ *n.* a patient who stays in the hospital while under treatment.

in propria persona /in própreeə pərsốnə/ *adv.* in his or her own person. [L]

input /ínpŏŏt/ *n.* & *v.* ● *n.* **1** what is put in or taken in, or operated on by any process or system. **2** *Electronics* **a** a place where, or a device through which, energy, information, etc., enters a system (*a tape recorder with inputs for microphone and radio*). **b** energy supplied to a device or system; an electrical signal. **3** the information fed into a computer. **4** the action or process of putting in or feeding in. **5** a contribution of information, etc. ● *v.tr.* (**inputting**; *past* and *past part.* **input** or **inputted**) (often foll. by *into*) **1** put in. **2** *Computing* supply (data, programs, etc., to a computer, program, etc.). □ **input-** (or **input/**) **output** *Computing* etc. of, relating to, or for input and output. □□ **inputter** *n.*

inquest /ínkwest, íng-/ *n.* **1** *Law* **a** an inquiry by a coroner's court into the cause of a death. **b** a judicial inquiry to ascertain the facts relating to an incident, etc. **c** a coroner's jury. **2** *colloq.* a discussion analyzing the outcome of a game, an election, etc. [ME f. OF *enqueste* (as INQUIRE)]
■ **1** see INQUIRY 1.

inquietude /inkwí-itŏŏd, -tyŏŏd/ *n.* uneasiness of mind or body. [ME f. OF *inquietude* or LL *inquietudo* f. L *inquietus* (as IN-¹, *quietus* quiet)]

inquiline /ínkwilīn, íng-/ *n.* an animal living in the home of another; a commensal. □□ **inquilinous** /-línəs/ *adj.* [L *inquilinus* sojourner (as IN-², *colere* dwell)]

inquire /inkwír, íng-/ *v.* **1** *intr.* (often foll. by *of*) seek information formally; make a formal investigation. **2** *intr.* (foll. by *about, after, for*) ask about a person, a person's health, etc. **3** *intr.* (foll. by *for*) ask about the availability of. **4** *tr.* ask for information as to (*inquired whether we were coming*). **5** *tr.* (foll. by *into*) investigate; look into. □□ **inquirer** *n.* [ME *enquere* f. OF *enquerre* ult. f. L *inquirere* (as IN-², *quaerere quaesit-* seek)]
■ **1** ask questions, make inquiries; (*inquire into*) investigate, research, explore, probe, look into, examine, study, explore, survey, inspect, scrutinize. **2–4** ask, query, question; request, demand, seek; ask about *or* after. **5** (*inquire into*) see INVESTIGATE 1.

inquiry /inkwíree, íng-, ínkwəree, íng-/ *n.* (*pl.* **-ies**) **1** an investigation, esp. an official one. **2** the act or an instance of asking or seeking information. □ **inquiry agent** *Brit.* a private detective.
■ **1** investigation, probe, examination, research, search, inspection, study, exploration, survey, scrutiny, inquest, interrogation, cross-examination, inquisition, grilling. **2** question, query, interrogation; request, demand.

inquisition /ínkwizíshən, íng-/ *n.* **1** usu. *derog.* an intensive search or investigation. **2** a judicial or official inquiry. **3** (**the Inquisition**) *RC Ch. hist.* an ecclesiastical tribunal for the suppression of heresy, esp. in Spain, operating through torture and execution. □□ **inquisitional** *adj.* [ME f. OF f. L *inquisitio -onis* examination (as INQUIRE)]
■ **1** see INVESTIGATION. **2** see INQUIRY 1.

inquisitive /inkwízitiv, íng-/ *adj.* **1** unduly curious; prying. **2** seeking knowledge; inquiring. □□ **inquisitively** *adv.* **inquisitiveness** *n.* [ME f. OF *inquisitif -ive* f. LL *inquisitivus* (as INQUISITION)]
■ **1** prying, curious, *colloq.* nosy, snoopy; intrusive, meddlesome, busy. **2** inquiring, curious, interested, investigative. □□ **inquisitiveness** see INTEREST *n.* 1a.

inquisitor /inkwízitər, íng-/ *n.* **1** an official investigator. **2** *hist.* an officer of the Inquisition. □ **Grand Inquisitor** the director of the court of Inquisition in some countries. **Inquisitor General** the head of the Spanish Inquisition. [F *inquisiteur* f. L *inquisitor -oris* (as INQUIRE)]

inquisitorial /inkwízitáwreeəl, íng-/ *adj.* **1** of or like an inquisitor. **2** offensively prying. **3** *Law* (of a trial, etc.) in which

the judge has a prosecuting role (opp. ACCUSATORIAL). □□ **inquisitorially** *adv.* [med.L *inquisitorius* (as INQUISITOR)]

inquorate /inkwáwrayt, ing-/ *adj.* not constituting a quorum.

in re /in rée, ráy/ *prep.* = RE¹. [L, = in the matter of]

INRI *abbr.* Jesus of Nazareth, King of the Jews. [L *Iesus Nazarenus Rex Iudaeorum*]

inroad /ínrōd/ *n.* **1** (often in *pl.*) **a** (usu. foll. by *on, into*) an encroachment; a using up of resources, etc. (*makes inroads on my time*). **b** (often foll. by *in, into*) progress; an advance (*making inroads into a difficult market*). **2** a hostile attack; a raid. [IN + ROAD¹ in sense 'riding']
■ **1 a** invasion, incursion, intrusion, encroachment. **b** advance, progress, breakthrough. **2** raid, attack, foray; penetration.

inrush /ínrush/ *n.* a rushing in; an influx. □□ **inrushing** *adj.* & *n.*

INS *abbr.* (US) Immigration and Naturalization Service.

ins. *abbr.* **1** inches. **2** insurance.

insalubrious /ínsəlŏŏbreeəs/ *adj.* (of a climate or place) unhealthy. □□ **insalubrity** *n.* [L *insalubris* (as IN-¹, SALUBRIOUS)]
■ see UNHEALTHY 2a, b.

insane /insáyn/ *adj.* **1** not of sound mind; mad. **2** *colloq.* extremely foolish; irrational. □□ **insanely** *adv.* **insaneness** *n.* **insanity** /-sánitee/ *n.* (*pl.* **-ies**). [L *insanus* (as IN-¹, *sanus* healthy)]
■ **1** psychotic, neurotic, schizophrenic, schizoid, psychoneurotic, *Psychol.* manic-depressive; mad, demented, out of one's mind *or* wits, manic, maniacal, lunatic, crazed, flighty, mad as a hatter *or* March hare, *colloq.* crackbrained, crazy, certifiable, mental, schizo, around the bend, up the wall, not all there, out to lunch, esp. *Brit. colloq.* daft, *sl.* cracked, screwy, loopy, loony, wacko, flaky, dippy, wacky, nutty (as a fruitcake), nuts, bats, batty, cuckoo, kooky, loco, gaga, off one's rocker *or* head *or* nut *or Brit.* chump, out of one's head *or* mind, off-the-wall, bonkers, *Brit. sl.* barmy, potty, crackers; (*be insane*) have bats in the belfry, *colloq.* have a screw loose; (*go insane*) take leave of one's senses, *sl.* lose one's marbles, go bananas, go ape, flip one's lid. **2** foolish, silly, fatuous, asinine, inane, stupid, brainless, senseless, witless, feebleminded, empty-headed, simple, *colloq.* crazy, idiotic, imbecilic, moronic, dumb, halfwitted, pinheaded, addlebrained, scatterbrained, esp. *Brit. colloq.* gormless, daft, *sl.* nutty, screwy, loopy, loony, dippy, nuts, bats, batty, bonkers, nerdy, *Brit. sl.* barmy, potty, crackers; mad, wild, reckless, harebrained, irresponsible, irrational, absurd, ridiculous, preposterous, ludicrous, nonsensical. □□ **insanity** madness, dementedness, lunacy, mental illness *or* disorder, dementia (praecox), psychosis, schizophrenia, (mental) derangement, mania, psychoneurosis, neurosis, *colloq.* craziness, esp. *Brit. colloq.* daftness, *sl.* screwiness, looniness, wackiness, nuttiness, battiness, flakiness, *Brit. sl.* barminess, pottiness, folly, foolishness, silliness, fatuity, asininity, stupidity, senselessness, witlessness, feeblemindedness, pinheadedness, *colloq.* idiocy, imbecility, dumbness, halfwittedness, esp. *Brit. colloq.* gormlessness; absurdity, nonsense, nonsensicality, ridiculousness, preposterousness, ludicrousness, irrationality, irresponsibility, wildness, recklessness.

insanitary /insániteree/ *adj.* not sanitary; dirty or germ-carrying.
■ see SORDID 1.

insatiable /insáyshəbəl/ *adj.* **1** unable to be satisfied. **2** (usu. foll. by *of*) extremely greedy. □□ **insatiability** *n.* **insatiably** *adv.* [ME f. OF *insaciable* or L *insatiabilis* (as IN-¹, SATIATE)]

/.../ pronunciation	● part of speech
□ phrases, idioms, and compounds	
□□ derivatives	■ synonym section
cross-references appear in SMALL CAPITALS or *italics*	

■ **1** see UNQUENCHABLE. **2** see GREEDY 1. □□ **insatiability** see GREED.

insatiate /insáysheeət/ *adj.* never satisfied. [L *insatiatus* (as IN-[1], SATIATE)]

inscape /ínskayp/ *n. literary* the unique inner quality or essence of an object, etc., as shown in a work of art, esp. a poem. [perh. f. IN-[2] + -SCAPE]

inscribe /inskríb/ *v.tr.* **1 a** (usu. foll. by *in, on*) write or carve (words, etc.) on stone, metal, paper, a book, etc. **b** (usu. foll. by *with*) mark (a sheet, tablet, etc.) with characters. **2** (usu. foll. by *to*) write an informal dedication (to a person) in or on (a book, etc.). **3** enter the name of (a person) on a list or in a book. **4** *Geom.* draw (a figure) within another so that some or all points of it lie on the boundary of the other (cf. CIRCUMSCRIBE). **5** (esp. as **inscribed** *adj.*) *Brit.* issue (stock, etc.) in the form of shares with registered holders. □□ **inscribable** *adj.* **inscriber** *n.* [L *inscribere inscript-* (as IN-[2], *scribere* write)]

■ **1 a** see WRITE 2–4. **2** dedicate, address, assign. **3** see ENTER 3.

inscription /inskrípshən/ *n.* **1** words inscribed, esp. on a monument, coin, stone, or in a book, etc. **2 a** the act of inscribing, esp. the informal dedication of a book, etc. **b** an instance of this. □□ **inscriptional** *adj.* **inscriptive** *adj.* [ME f. L *inscriptio* (as INSCRIBE)]

■ **1** dedication, address, message.

inscrutable /inskro̅o̅təbəl/ *adj.* wholly mysterious; impenetrable. □□ **inscrutability** *n.* **inscrutableness** *n.* **inscrutably** *adv.* [ME f. eccl.L *inscrutabilis* (as IN-[1], *scrutari* search: see SCRUTINY)]

■ see MYSTERIOUS. □□ **inscrutability** see MYSTERY[1] 2.

insect /ínsekt/ *n.* **1 a** any arthropod of the class Insecta, having a head, thorax, abdomen, two antennae, three pairs of thoracic legs, and usu. one or two pairs of thoracic wings. **b** (loosely) any other small segmented invertebrate animal. **2** an insignificant or contemptible person or creature. □□ **insectile** /-séktəl, -til/ *adj.* [L *insectum* (*animal*) notched (animal) f. *insecare insect-* (as IN-[2], *secare* cut)]

■ **1** see BUG *n.* 1.

insectarium /ínsektáireeəm/ *n.* (also **insectary** /ínséktəree/) (*pl.* **insectariums** or **insectaries**) a place for keeping insects.

insecticide /inséktisíd/ *n.* a substance used for killing insects. □□ **insecticidal** /-síd'l/ *adj.*

insectivore /inséktivawr/ *n.* **1** any mammal of the order Insectivora feeding on insects, etc., e.g., a hedgehog or mole. **2** any plant that captures and absorbs insects. □□ **insectivorous** /-tívərəs/ *adj.* [F f. mod.L *insectivorus* (as INSECT, -VORE: see -VOROUS)]

insecure /ínsikyo̅o̅r/ *adj.* **1** (of a person or state of mind) uncertain; lacking confidence. **2 a** unsafe; not firm or fixed. **b** (of ice, ground, etc.) liable to give way. **c** lacking security; unprotected. □□ **insecurely** *adv.* **insecurity** *n.*

■ **1** uncertain, unsure, irresolute, hesitant, undecided, unsettled; unsound, unreliable, untrustworthy; diffident, nervous, nervy, shaky, jumpy, jittery, unnerved, uncomfortable, disconcerted, apprehensive, anxious, worried. **2 a, b** unsafe, dangerous, perilous, precarious; unsound, weak, flimsy, unsubstantial, insubstantial, infirm, weak, frail; rickety, rocky, shaky, wobbly, unstable, unsteady, unreliable, untrustworthy, treacherous. **c** unprotected, vulnerable, unguarded, defenseless, undefended, exposed, open.

inselberg /ínsəlbərg, -zəl/ *n.* an isolated hill or mountain rising abruptly from its surroundings; monadnock. [G, = island mountain]

inseminate /inséminayt/ *v.tr.* **1** introduce semen into (a female) by natural or artificial means. **2** sow (seed, etc.). □□ **insemination** /-náyshən/ *n.* **inseminator** *n.* [L *inseminare* (as IN-[2], SEMEN)]

■ **1** see FERTILIZE 2.

insensate /insénsayt/ *adj.* **1** without physical sensation; unconscious. **2** without sensibility; unfeeling. **3** stupid. □□ **insensately** *adv.* [eccl.L *insensatus* (as IN-[1], *sensatus* f. *sensus* SENSE)]

■ **1** see SENSELESS 1, 4. **2** see *thick-skinned* (THICK).

insensibility /insénsibílitee/ *n.* **1** unconsciousness. **2** a lack of mental feeling or emotion; hardness. **3** (often foll. by *to*) indifference. [F *insensibilité* or LL *insensibilitas* (as INSENSIBLE)]

■ **1** see OBLIVION. **3** see INDIFFERENCE 1.

insensible /insénsibəl/ *adj.* **1 a** without one's mental faculties; unconscious. **b** (of the extremities, etc.) numb; without feeling. **2** (usu. foll. by *of, to*) unaware; indifferent (*insensible of her needs*). **3** without emotion; callous. **4** too small or gradual to be perceived; inappreciable. □□ **insensibly** *adv.* [ME f. OF *insensible* or L *insensibilis* (as IN-[1], SENSIBLE)]

■ **1** insensate, insentient, lifeless, inanimate, dead; unconscious, senseless, *colloq.* out, dead to the world; numb, benumbed, anesthetized, frozen, paralyzed, torpid, unfeeling. **2** (*insensible of* or *to*) unaware or unmindful of, oblivious to, blind or deaf to, heedless or unconscious of, unaffected or untouched or unmoved by; indifferent or insensitive or impervious to. **3** unfeeling, emotionless, unemotional, impassive, passionless, dispassionate, cold, clinical, objective, detached, unconcerned, nonchalant, insouciant, indifferent, apathetic; callous, coldhearted, hardhearted, steely, stony, heartless, uncaring, unsympathetic. **4** see IMPERCEPTIBLE 2.

insensitive /insénsitiv/ *adj.* (often foll. by *to*) **1** unfeeling; boorish; crass. **2** not sensitive to physical stimuli. □□ **insensitively** *adv.* **insensitiveness** *n.* **insensitivity** /-tívitee/ *n.*

■ **1** see THOUGHTLESS 1. □□ **insensitivity** see *imprudence* (IMPRUDENT).

insentient /insénshənt/ *adj.* not sentient; inanimate. □□ **insentience** /-shəns/ *n.*

■ see INSENSIBLE 1.

inseparable /insépərəbəl/ *adj.* & *n.* ● *adj.* **1** (esp. of friends) unable or unwilling to be separated. **2** *Gram.* (of a prefix, or a verb in respect of it) unable to be used as a separate word, e.g., *dis-, mis-, un-*. ● *n.* (usu. in *pl.*) an inseparable person or thing, esp. a friend. □□ **inseparability** *n.* **inseparably** *adv.* [ME f. L *inseparabilis* (as IN-[1], SEPARABLE)]

■ *adj.* **1** see CLOSE[1] *adj.* 2a, b, ONE *adj.* 5. □□ **inseparably** see *inextricably* (INEXTRICABLE).

insert *v.* & *n.* ● *v.tr.* /insə́rt/ **1** (usu. foll. by *in, into, between*, etc.) place, fit, or thrust (a thing) into another. **2** (usu. foll. by *in, into*) introduce (a letter, word, article, advertisement, etc.) into a newspaper, etc. **3** (as **inserted** *adj.*) *Anat.*, etc., (of a muscle, etc.), attached (at a specific point). ● *n.* /ínsərt/ something inserted, e.g., a loose page in a magazine, a piece of cloth in a garment, a motion-picture cut-in. □□ **insertable** *adj.* **inserter** *n.* [L *inserere* (as IN-[2], *serere sert-* join)]

■ *v.* **1** inset, inlay, place or put or stick in, feed, load, intromit, introduce; interpolate, interject, interpose, throw in. ● *n.* inset, inlay; interpolation, interjection; insertion, addition, addendum, supplement, advertisement, broadside, brochure, handbill, circular, flyer, *colloq.* ad, *Brit. colloq.* advert.

insertion /insə́rshən/ *n.* **1** the act or an instance of inserting. **2** an amendment, etc., inserted in writing or printing. **3** each appearance of an advertisement in a newspaper, etc. **4** an ornamental section of needlework inserted into plain material (*lace insertions*). **5** the manner or place of attachment of a muscle, an organ, etc. **6** the placing of a spacecraft in an orbit. [LL *insertio* (as INSERT)]

■ **2** see INSERT *n.*

in-service /ínsərvis/ *adj.* (of training) intended for those actively engaged in the profession or activity concerned.

inset *n.* & *v.* ● *n.* /ínset/ **1 a** an extra page or pages inserted in a folded sheet or in a book; an insert. **b** a small map, photograph, etc., inserted within the border of a larger one. **2** a piece let into a dress, etc. ● *v.tr.* /ínsét/ (**insetting**; *past* and *past part.* **inset** or **insetted**) **1** put in as an inset. **2** decorate with an inset. □□ **insetter** *n.*

inshore /ínsháwr/ *adv.* & *adj.* at sea but close to the shore. □ **inshore of** *esp. Brit.* nearer to shore than.

inside *n., adj., adv.,* & *prep.* ● *n.* /ínsíd/ **1 a** the inner side or surface of a thing. **b** the inner part; the interior. **2** (of a roadway, etc.) the side or lane nearer the center. **3** (usu. in *pl.*) *colloq.* **a** the stomach and bowels (*something wrong with my insides*). **b** the operative part of a machine, etc. **4** *colloq.* a position affording inside information (*knows someone on the inside*). ● *adj.* /ínsíd/ **1** situated on or in, or derived from, the inside; (of information, etc.) available only to those on the inside. **2** *Soccer & Field Hockey* nearer to the center of the field (*inside forward*; *inside left*; *inside right*). ● *adv.* /insíd/ **1** on, in, or to the inside. **2** *sl.* in prison. ● *prep.* /insíd/ **1** on the inner side of; within (*inside the house*). **2** in less than (*inside an hour*). □ **inside country** *Austral.* settled areas near the coast. **inside information** information not accessible to outsiders. **inside job** *colloq.* a crime committed by a person living or working on the premises burgled, etc. **inside of** *colloq.* **1** in less than (a week, etc.). **2** *Brit.* the middle part of. **inside out** with the inner surface turned outward. **inside story** = *inside information*. **inside track 1** the track which is shorter, because of the curve. **2** a position of advantage. **know a thing inside out** know a thing thoroughly. **turn inside out 1** turn the inner surface of outward. **2** *colloq.* ransack; cause confusion in. [IN + SIDE]

■ *n.* **1** inner side, inner surface; lining, backing, reverse; interior, center, middle, core, heart. **3** (*insides*) **a** bowels, entrails, viscera, gut(s), stomach, *colloq.* innards; *colloq.* works, doings. **b** see WORK *n.* 8. ● *adj.* **1** internal, interior; indoor; private, secret, confidential, clandestine, privileged, exclusive, *archaic* privy. **2** central, *attrib.* center. ● *adv.* **1** indoors; on *or* to the inside; centrally, at heart, fundamentally, basically, at bottom, by nature, deep down. **2** in prison *or* jail, behind bars, *colloq.* doing time, in hock, *sl.* in clink *or* jug *or* stir, in the can *or* cooler *or* slammer *or Brit.* nick, in hoosegow, in the slam, *Brit. sl.* banged up, in the choky. ● *prep.* within, *colloq.* inside of; in under, in less than. □ **inside of 1** see INSIDE *prep.* above. **inside out** outside in, wrong side out, reversed. **know a thing inside out** know a thing like the back of one's hand, know a thing backward. **turn inside out 1** reverse, invert, *Physiol.* evert, *Med. & Physiol.* evaginate. **2** see MESS *v.* 1.

insider /insídər/ *n.* **1** a person who is within a society, organization, etc. (cf. OUTSIDER). **2** a person privy to a secret, esp. when using it to gain advantage. □ **insider trading** *Stock Exch.* the illegal practice of trading to one's own advantage through having access to confidential information.

insidious /insídeeəs/ *adj.* **1** proceeding or progressing inconspicuously but harmfully (*an insidious disease*). **2** treacherous; crafty. □□ **insidiously** *adv.* **insidiousness** *n.* [L *insidiosus* cunning f. *insidiae* ambush (as IN-², *sedēre* sit)]

■ **2** see SINISTER 2. □□ **insidiously** see *behind a person's back* (BEHIND). **insidiousness** see PERFIDY.

insight /ínsít/ *n.* (usu. foll. by *into*) **1** the capacity of understanding hidden truths, etc., esp. of character or situations. **2** an instance of this. □□ **insightful** *adj.* **insightfully** *adv.* [ME, = 'discernment,' prob. of Scand. & LG orig. (as IN-², SIGHT)]

■ perception, percipience, sensitivity, perspicacity, perceptiveness, perspicaciousness, discernment, acuteness, acuity, acumen, sharpness, shrewdness, understanding, judgment, judiciousness, comprehension, vision, *sl.* savvy.

insignia /insígneeə/ *n.* (treated as *sing.* or *pl.* (formerly with *sing.* **insigne**); usu. foll. by *of*) **1** badges (*wore his insignia of office*). **2** distinguishing marks. [L, pl. of *insigne* neut. of *insignis* distinguished (as IN-², *signis* f. *signum* SIGN)]

■ **1** see SYMBOL *n.*

insignificant /insignífikənt/ *adj.* **1** unimportant; trifling. **2** (of a person) undistinguished. **3** meaningless. □□ **insignificance** /-kəns/ *n.* **insignificancy** *n.* **insignificantly** *adv.*

■ **1** unimportant, paltry, trifling, petty, trivial, nugatory, of no account, minor, inconsequential, insubstantial, unsubstantial, negligible, inconsiderable, niggling, puny, small, tinpot, dinky, picayune, *Brit.* twopenny-halfpenny, *colloq.* small-time, piddling, *Brit. sl.* potty; expendable, unessential, nonessential.

2 undistinguished, unexceptional, unremarkable, inconspicuous, unobtrusive, unnoticeable, low-key; ordinary, run-of-the-mill, mediocre, everyday, humble, simple; obscure, unheard-of, little-known, unknown, unsung. **3** meaningless, senseless, pointless, irrelevant, purposeless, vain, empty, vacuous, hollow; absurd, nonsensical, ridiculous, preposterous, fatuous.

insincere /insinseér/ *adj.* not sincere; not candid. □□ **insincerely** *adv.* **insincerity** /-séritee/ *n.* (*pl.* **-ies**). [L *insincerus* (as IN-¹, SINCERE)]

■ dishonest, deceitful, untruthful, false, lying, mendacious, deceptive, underhand, underhanded, *colloq.* crooked, phony; disingenuous, affected, synthetic, artificial, pseudo, hollow, empty, hypocritical; duplicitous, two-faced, double-faced, double-dealing, treacherous, faithless, perfidious; Machiavellian, sly, cunning, crafty, slick, glib, foxy, vulpine, wily, artful, evasive, tricky, *colloq.* shifty; unctuous, slimy, slippery. □□ **insincerity** see AFFECTATION 1, CANT¹ *n.* 1.

insinuate /insínyoō-ayt/ *v.tr.* **1** (often foll. by *that* + clause) convey indirectly or obliquely; hint (*insinuated that she was lying*). **2** (often *refl.*; usu. foll. by *into*) **a** introduce (oneself, a person, etc.) into favor, office, etc., by subtle manipulation. **b** introduce (a thing, an idea, oneself, etc.) subtly or deviously into a place (*insinuated himself into their inner circle*). □□ **insinuation** /-áyshən/ *n.* **insinuative** *adj.* **insinuator** *n.* **insinuatory** /-sínyoōətáwree/ *adj.* [L *insinuare insinuat-* (as IN-², *sinuare* to curve)]

■ **1** suggest, hint, intimate, imply, whisper, indicate. **2 a, b** (*insinuate oneself*) worm *or* work (one's way), insert oneself, maneuver oneself *or* one's way, infiltrate. **b** inject, infuse, instill, introduce, slip. □□ **insinuation** see IMPLICATION, INNUENDO *n.* 1.

insipid /insípid/ *adj.* **1** lacking vigor or interest; dull. **2** lacking flavor; tasteless. □□ **insipidity** /-píditee/ *n.* **insipidly** *adv.* **insipidness** *n.* [F *insipide* or LL *insipidus* (as IN-¹, *sapidus* SAPID)]

■ **1** see TEDIOUS. **2** see TASTELESS 1. □□ **insipidity**, **insipidness** see TEDIUM.

insist /insíst/ *v.tr.* (usu. foll. by *that* + clause; also *absol.*) maintain or demand positively and assertively (*insisted that he was innocent*; *give me the bag! I insist!*). □ **insist on** demand or maintain (*I insist on being present*; *insists on his suitability*). □□ **insister** *n.* **insistingly** *adv.* [L *insistere* stand on, persist (as IN-², *sistere* stand)]

■ demand, require, importune, urge, exhort; argue, remonstrate, expostulate; swear, asseverate, declare, assert, avow, emphasize, underline, stress, *formal* aver; maintain, persist. □ **insist on** demand, exact, stipulate, order, command; make a point of, stand on; maintain, assert, swear to, declare.

insistent /insístənt/ *adj.* **1** (often foll. by *on*) insisting; demanding positively or continually (*is insistent on taking me with him*). **2** obtruding itself on the attention (*the insistent rattle of the window frame*). □□ **insistence** /-təns/ *n.* **insistency** *n.* **insistently** *adv.*

■ **1** emphatic, firm, explicit, affirmative, positive, peremptory; assertive, importunate, urgent; dogged, persistent, tenacious, resolute, determined, uncompromising, unfaltering, unwavering, unrelenting, stubborn, obstinate, unyielding. **2** obtrusive, intrusive; importunate, persistent, nagging, unrelenting; clamorous, loud, noisy.

in situ /in seetoō, sí-/ *adv.* **1** in its place. **2** in its original place. [L]

insobriety /insəbrí-itee/ *n.* intemperance, esp. in drinking.

■ see *drunkenness* (DRUNKEN).

insofar as /insōfaár az/ *adv.* to the extent that.

/.../	**pronunciation**	●	**part of speech**
□	**phrases, idioms, and compounds**		
□□	**derivatives**	■	**synonym section**
cross-references appear in SMALL CAPITALS or *italics*			

insolation /ínsōláyshən/ *n.* exposure to the sun's rays, esp. for bleaching. [L *insolatio* f. *insolare* (as IN-², *solare* f. *sol* sun)]

insole /ínsōl/ *n.* **1** a removable sole worn in a boot or shoe for warmth, etc. **2** the fixed inner sole of a boot or shoe.

insolent /ínsələnt/ *adj.* offensively contemptuous or arrogant; insulting. □□ **insolence** /-ləns/ *n.* **insolently** *adv.* [ME, = 'arrogant,' f. L *insolens* (as IN-¹, *solens* pres. part. of *solēre* be accustomed)]

■ disrespectful, contemptuous, contumelious, insulting, rude, uncivil, offensive, insubordinate; arrogant, brazen, brassy, brash, bold, presumptuous, impertinent, impudent, pert, saucy, cheeky, cocky, cocksure, nervy, *colloq.* pushy, fresh, lippy. □□ **insolence** see BRASS *n.* 7, *impudence* (IMPUDENT).

insoluble /ínsólyəbəl/ *adj.* **1** incapable of being solved. **2** incapable of being dissolved. □□ **insolubility** *n.* **insolubilize** /-biliz/ *v.tr.* **insolubleness** *n.* **insolubly** *adv.* [ME f. OF *insoluble* or L *insolubilis* (as IN-¹, SOLUBLE)]

■ **1** see MYSTERIOUS.

insolvable /ínsólvəbəl/ *adj.* = INSOLUBLE.

insolvent /ínsólvənt/ *adj.* & *n.* ● *adj.* **1** unable to pay one's debts. **2** relating to insolvency (*insolvent laws*). ● *n.* a debtor. □□ **insolvency** *n.*

■ **1** bankrupt, in receivership, ruined, failed, collapsed, gone to the wall, embarrassed, *colloq.* (gone) bust, broke, on the rocks. □□ **insolvency** see FAILURE 6, POVERTY 1.

insomnia /ínsómneeə/ *n.* habitual sleeplessness; inability to sleep. □□ **insomniac** /-neeak/ *n.* & *adj.* [L f. *insomnis* sleepless (as IN-¹, *somnus* sleep)]

■ □□ **insomniac** (*adj.*) see SLEEPLESS.

insomuch /ínsōmúch/ *adv.* **1** (foll. by *that* + clause) to such an extent. **2** (foll. by *as*) inasmuch. [ME, orig. *in so much*]

■ see CONSIDERING 1.

insouciant /insōōseeənt, ANsōōsyaáN/ *adj.* carefree; unconcerned. □□ **insouciance** /-seeəns/ *n.* **insouciantly** *adv.* [F (as IN-¹, *souciant* pres. part. of *soucier* care)]

■ see CAREFREE. □□ **insouciance** see INDIFFERENCE 1. **insouciantly** see GAILY 1.

insp. *abbr.* **1** inspected. **2** inspector.

inspan /ínspán/ *v.* (**inspanned, inspanning**) *S.Afr.* **1** *tr.* (also *absol.*) **a** yoke (oxen, etc.) in a team to a vehicle. **b** harness an animal or animals to (a wagon). **2** *tr.* harness (people or resources) into service. [Du. *inspannen* stretch (as IN-², SPAN²)]

inspect /ínspékt/ *v.tr.* **1** look closely at or into. **2** examine (a document, etc.) officially. □□ **inspection** /-spékshən/ *n.* [L *inspicere inspect-* (as IN-², *specere* look at), or its frequent. *inspectare*]

■ examine, look at or into or over or around, see over, view, survey; observe, study, watch, eye; scrutinize, peruse, probe, pore over, audit, check (through), read through, go over, run one's eye over, scan; investigate, check up on, check out, *Brit.* run the rule over, *colloq.* have a look-see, *Brit. sl.* suss out. □□ **inspection** see EXAMINATION 1, 2.

inspector /ínspéktər/ *n.* **1** a person who inspects. **2** an official employed to supervise a service, a machine, etc., and make reports. **3** a police officer usu. ranking just below a superintendent. □ **inspector general** a chief inspector. □□ **inspectorate** /-təreeət/ *n.* **inspectorial** /-táwreeəl/ *adj.* **inspectorship** *n.* [L (as INSPECT)]

inspiration /ínspiráyshən/ *n.* **1 a** a supposed creative force or influence on poets, artists, musicians, etc., stimulating the production of works of art. **b** a person, principle, faith, etc., stimulating artistic or moral fervor and creativity. **c** a similar divine influence supposed to have led to the writing of Scripture, etc. **2** a sudden brilliant, creative, or timely idea. **3** a drawing in of breath; inhalation. □□ **inspirational** *adj.* **inspirationism** *n.* **inspirationist** *n.* [ME f. OF f. LL *inspiratio -onis* (as INSPIRE)]

■ **1 a** genius, oracle, afflatus, (the) Muse(s), *duende*, life force, fire, spark, *poet.* Hippocrene; stimulus, stimulation, encouragement, impetus, lift, fillip; spirit, passion, ardor, zeal, enthusiasm, energy, vigor, sparkle, imagination. **b** luminary, lamp, lodestar, rudder, guide, guiding light or star; watchword. **2** revelation, vision, stroke of genius, flash, spark, *colloq.* brainwave, brainstorm. **3** inhalation, sniff, gasp, pull, draw.

inspirator /ínspiraytər/ *n.* an apparatus for drawing in air or vapor. [LL (as INSPIRE)]

inspire /ínspír/ *v.tr.* **1** stimulate or arouse (a person) to esp. creative activity, esp. by supposed divine or supernatural agency (*your faith inspired him; inspired by God*). **2 a** (usu. foll. by *with*) animate (a person) with a feeling. **b** (usu. foll. by *into*) instill (a feeling) into a person, etc. **c** (usu. foll. by *in*) create (a feeling) in a person. **3** prompt; give rise to (*the poem was inspired by the autumn*). **4** (as **inspired** *adj.*) **a** (of a work of art, etc.) as if prompted by or emanating from a supernatural source; characterized by inspiration (*an inspired speech*). **b** (of a guess) intuitive but accurate. **5** (also *absol.*) breathe in (air, etc.); inhale. □□ **inspiratory** /-rətáwree/ *adj.* **inspiredly** /-ridlee/ *adv.* **inspirer** *n.* **inspiring** *adj.* **inspiringly** *adv.* [ME f. OF *inspirer* f. L *inspirare* breathe in (as IN-², *spirare* breathe)]

■ **1, 2** stimulate, move, arouse, rouse, stir, wake, awaken; uplift, buoy (up), buttress, encourage, rally, strengthen, support, reinforce, fortify, confirm, affirm, *colloq.* boost; inspirit, invigorate, energize, enliven, vitalize, animate, vivify, galvanize, carry away, excite, quicken, fire (up), provoke, *literary* enkindle. **3** activate, actuate, instigate, prompt, cause, create, trigger, set off, spark (off), provoke, excite, *literary* enkindle. **4** (**inspired**) creative, original, insightful, visionary, intuitive; ingenious, inventive, innovative, brilliant. **5** see INHALE.

inspirit /ínspírit/ *v.tr.* **1** put life into; animate. **2** (usu. foll. by *to*, or *to* + infin.) encourage (a person). □□ **inspiriting** *adj.* **inspiritingly** *adv.*

■ **1** see ANIMATE *v.* **2** see ANIMATE *v.* 3, 4, ENCOURAGE 1. □□ **inspiriting** see REFRESHING, ROUSING.

inspissate /inspísayt/ *v.tr. literary* thicken; condense. □□ **inspissation** /-sáyshən/ *n.* [LL *inspissare inspissat-* (as IN-², L *spissus* thick)]

■ see THICKEN.

inspissator /ínspísaytər/ *n.* an apparatus for thickening serum, etc., by heat.

inst. *abbr.* **1** = INSTANT *adj.* 4 (*the 6th inst.*). **2** instance. **3** institute. **4** institution. **5** instrument.

instability /ínstəbíliteeə/ *n.* (*pl.* **-ies**) **1** a lack of stability. **2** *Psychol.* unpredictability in behavior, etc. **3** an instance of instability. [ME f. F *instabilité* f. L *instabilitas -tatis* f. *instabilis* (as IN-¹, STABLE¹)]

■ **1, 3** see *fluctuation* (FLUCTUATE).

install /ínstáwl/ *v.tr.* (also esp. *Brit.* **instal**) (**installed, installing**) **1** place (equipment, machinery, etc.) in position ready for use. **2** place (a person) in an office or rank with ceremony (*installed in the office of attorney general*). **3** establish (oneself, a person, etc.) in a place, condition, etc. (*installed herself at the head of the table*). □□ **installant** *adj.* & *n.* **installer** *n.* [med.L *installare* (as IN-², *stallare* f. *stallum* STALL¹)]

■ **1** fit, set up, mount, site, fix or set (in place); connect (up), *Electr.* wire up. **2** invest, instate, enthrone, chair, inaugurate, induct, swear in, establish, institute, initiate. **3** place, put, position, settle, seat, sit, ensconce, establish.

installation /ínstəláyshən/ *n.* **1 a** the act or an instance of installing. **b** the process or an instance of being installed. **2** a piece of apparatus, a machine, etc., installed or the place where it is installed. [med.L *installatio* (as INSTALL)]

■ **1** investiture, instatement, enthronement, inauguration, induction, swearing-in, initiation, establishment, institution, ordination, coronation; placement, emplacement, settlement; installing, fitting, setting up, mounting, siting, fixing, building in; connection, plumbing in, wiring up. **2** fitting, fitment, machine, machinery, apparatus, equipment, gear; plant, factory, depot, station, warehouse, establishment.

installment /ínstáwlmənt/ *n.* (esp. *Brit.* **instalment**) **1** a sum of money due as one of several usu. equal payments for something, spread over an agreed period of time. **2** any of several parts, esp. of a television or radio serial or a magazine story, published or shown in sequence at intervals. □ **installment plan** payment by installments. [alt. f. obs. *estallment* f. AF *estalement* f. *estaler* fix: prob. assoc. with IN-STALLATION]

■ **2** episode, part, chapter.

instance /ínstəns/ *n. & v.* ● *n.* **1** an example or illustration of (*just another instance of his lack of determination*). **2** a particular case (*that's not true in this instance*). **3** *Law* a legal suit. ● *v.tr.* cite (a fact, case, etc.) as an instance. □ **at the instance of** at the request or suggestion of. **court of first instance** *Law* a court of primary jurisdiction. **for instance** as an example. **in the first** (or **second**, etc.) **instance** in the first (or second, etc.) place; at the first (or second, etc.) stage of a proceeding. [ME f. OF f. L *instantia* (as INSTANT)]

■ *n.* **1** case (in point), example, exemplar, exemplification, illustration. **2** case, situation, event, occasion, occurrence, (set of) circumstance(s). ● *v.* adduce, quote, cite, allude to. □ **at the instance of** at the request of, at the suggestion of, *literary* at the behest of; (as) per, in accordance with. **for instance** for example, e.g., like, (such) as, say, as an example, by way of illustration. **in the first instance** in the first place, for a start, *colloq.* for a kickoff; at the beginning *or* start, initially, originally, at first.

instancy /ínstənsee/ *n.* **1** urgency. **2** pressing nature. [L *instantia*: see INSTANCE]

instant /ínstənt/ *adj. & n.* ● *adj.* **1** occurring immediately (*gives an instant result*). **2 a** (of food, etc.) ready for immediate use, with little or no preparation. **b** prepared hastily and with little effort (*I have no instant solution*). **3** urgent; pressing. **4** *Commerce* of the current month (*the 6th instant*). **5** *archaic* of the present moment. ● *n.* **1** a precise moment of time, esp. the present (*come here this instant*; *went that instant*; *told you the instant I heard*). **2** a short space of time (*was there in an instant*; *not an instant too soon*). □ **instant replay** the immediate repetition of part of a videotaped sports event, often in slow motion. [ME f. F f. L *instare* *instant-* be present, press upon (as IN-², *stare* stand)]

■ *adj.* **1** instantaneous, immediate, direct, unhesitating, ready, spontaneous, unconsidered, on the spot, overnight; abrupt, precipitate, sudden, swift, speedy, quick. **2a** ready, ready-made, ready to serve, precooked, freeze-dried, *attrib.* convenience; ready-to-wear, *Brit.* off-the-peg; ready-mixed. **3** urgent, pressing, compelling, critical, imperative, exigent; crying. ● *n.* **1** moment, second, point (in time), minute; flash, twinkle, twinkling (of an eye), trice, *colloq.* jiffy, mo, sec, *Brit. colloq.* tick. □ **instant replay** (action *or* slow-motion) replay, playback, rerun.

instantaneous /ínstəntáyneeəs/ *adj.* **1** occurring or done in an instant or instantly. **2** *Physics* existing at a particular instant. □□ **instantaneity** /ínstəntənée-itee/ *n.* **instantaneously** *adv.* **instantaneousness** *n.* [med.L *instantaneus* f. L *instans* (as INSTANT) after eccl.L *momentaneus*]

■ **1** instant, immediate, direct, unhesitating, spontaneous, prompt, ready, on the spot, overnight; abrupt, precipitate, sudden, swift, speedy, quick; unconsidered. □□ **instantaneously** instantly, immediately, at once, (right) now, right *or* straight away, directly, forthwith, this (very) minute *or* second *or* instant *or* moment, here and now, then and there, there and then, on the spot, without more ado, without delay *or* hesitation, unhesitatingly, spontaneously, *tout de suite*, promptly, posthaste, in a wink *or* trice *or* twinkle, in the twinkling of an eye, in two shakes of a lamb's tail, momentarily, in short order, *archaic or joc.* instanter, *colloq.* pronto, in a jiffy, lickety-split, p.d.q., before you can say Jack Robinson. **instantaneousness** see *rapidity* (RAPID).

instanter /ínstántər/ *adv. archaic* or *joc.* immediately; at once. [L f. *instans* (as INSTANT)]

■ see IMMEDIATELY *adv.* 1.

instantiate /ínstánsheeayt/ *v.tr.* represent by an instance. □□ **instantiation** /-áyshən/ *n.* [L *instantia*: see INSTANCE]

instantly /ínstəntlee/ *adv.* **1** immediately; at once. **2** *archaic* urgently; pressingly.

■ **1** see IMMEDIATELY *adv.* 1.

instar /ínstaar/ *n.* a stage in the life of an insect, etc., between two periods of molting. [L, = form]

instate /ínstáyt/ *v.tr.* (often foll. by *in*) install; establish. [IN-² + STATE]

■ see INSTALL 2.

in statu pupillari /in stáytyōō pyōōpiláaree, stáchōō/ *adj.* **1** under guardianship, esp. as a pupil. **2** in a junior position at a university; not having a master's degree. [L]

instauration /ínstawráyshən/ *n. formal* **1** restoration; renewal. **2** an act of instauration. □□ **instaurator** *n.* [L *instauratio* f. *instaurare* (as IN-²; cf. RESTORE)]

instead /ínstéd/ *adv.* **1** (foll. by *of*) as a substitute or alternative to; in place of (*instead of this one*; *stayed instead of going*). **2** as an alternative (*took me instead*) (cf. STEAD). [ME, f. IN + STEAD]

■ **1** (*instead of*) in place of, in lieu of, in a person's *or* a thing's place *or* stead, as an alternative to, as a substitute to *or* for; rather than, in preference to; as opposed to, as contrasted with. **2** as an alternative, rather; by contrast.

instep /ínstep/ *n.* **1** the inner arch of the foot between the toes and the ankle. **2** the part of a shoe, etc., fitting over or under this. **3** a thing shaped like an instep. [16th c.: ult. formed as IN-² + STEP, but immed. orig. uncert.]

instigate /ínstigayt/ *v.tr.* **1** bring about by incitement or persuasion; provoke (*who instigated the inquiry?*). **2** (usu. foll. by *to*) urge on; incite (a person, etc.) to esp. an evil act. □□ **instigation** /-gáyshən/ *n.* **instigative** *adj.* **instigator** *n.* [L *instigare* *instigat-*]

■ **1** see PROVOKE 2. **2** see INDUCE 1. □□ **instigation** see *incitement* (INCITE). **instigator** see TROUBLEMAKER.

instill /ínstil/ *v.tr.* (esp. *Brit.* **instil**) (**instilled**, **instilling**) (often foll. by *into*) **1** introduce (a feeling, idea, etc.) into a person's mind, etc., gradually. **2** put (a liquid) into something in drops. □□ **instillation** *n.* **instiller** *n.* **instillment** *n.* [L *instillare* (as IN-², *stillare* drop): cf. DISTILL]

■ **1** infuse, insinuate, ingrain, engrain, implant, sow; inspire, inculcate, din. **2** drip, dribble, trickle, sprinkle.

instinct *n. & adj.* ● *n.* /ínstingkt/ **1 a** an innate, usu. fixed, pattern of behavior in most animals in response to certain stimuli. **b** a similar propensity in human beings to act without conscious intention; innate impulsion. **2** (usu. foll. by *for*) unconscious skill; intuition. ● *predic.adj.* /ínstíngkt/ (foll. by *with*) imbued; filled (with life, beauty, force, etc.). □□ **instinctual** /-stíngkchōōəl/ *adj.* **instinctually** *adv.* [ME, = 'impulse,' f. L *instinctus* f. *instinguere* incite (as IN-², *stinguere stinct-* prick)]

■ *n.* **1** impulsion, drive, (unconditional) reflex, *Biol.* tropism; nature, character, tendency, proclivity, inclination, propensity, predisposition; subconscious, unconscious, *Psychol.* id. **2** skill, bent, talent, flair, faculty, capacity, aptitude, facility, knack; feel, feeling, empathy, (sixth) sense, sensitivity, understanding, insight, awareness, grasp. ● *predic.adj.* (*instinct with*) replete with, full of; pregnant with, rich in *or* with, alive with. □□ **instinctual** see INSTINCTIVE.

instinctive /ínstíngktiv/ *adj.* **1** relating to or prompted by instinct. **2** apparently unconscious or automatic (*an instinctive reaction*). □□ **instinctively** *adv.*

■ **1** instinctual, natural, unconditioned; innate, native, inborn, inbred, inherent, intrinsic, congenital, constitutional, essential, fundamental, elementary, structural, organic. **2** unconscious, subconscious, automatic, mechanical, knee-jerk, spontaneous, immediate, involuntary, irrational, intuitional, intuitive; reflex, visceral, *attrib.* gut.

/.../ **pronunciation**	● **part of speech**
□ **phrases, idioms, and compounds**	
□□ **derivatives**	■ **synonym section**
cross-references appear in SMALL CAPITALS or *italics*	

institute /ínstitŏot, -tyŏot/ *n. & v.* ● *n.* **1 a** a society or organization for the promotion of science, education, etc. **b** a building used by an institute. **2** *Law* (usu. in *pl.*) a digest of the elements of a legal subject (*Institutes of Justinian*). **3** a principle of instruction. **4** a brief course of instruction for teachers, etc. ● *v.tr.* **1** establish; found. **2 a** initiate (an inquiry, etc.). **b** begin (proceedings) in a court. **3** (usu. foll. by *to, into*) appoint (a person) as a cleric in a church, etc. [ME f. L *institutum* design, precept, neut. past part. of *instituere* establish, arrange, teach (as IN-², *statuere* set up)]
  ■ *n.* **1** establishment, institution, foundation, society, company, organization, association, league, alliance, guild; school, college, academy, university, seminary; hospital, clinic, medical *or* health center; sanatorium, (nursing) home, asylum, sanitarium. **3** see PRINCIPLE *n.* 1. ● *v.* **1** establish, found, create, form, set up, inaugurate, launch, organize. **2** initiate, start, begin, set up, inaugurate, originate, pioneer, introduce, launch, usher in, instigate, set in motion, get going, get under way, *formal* commence. **3** install, induct, appoint, ordain, frock.

institution /ínstitŏoshən, -tyŏo-/ *n.* **1** the act or an instance of instituting. **2 a** a society or organization founded esp. for charitable, religious, educational, or social purposes. **b** a building used by an institution. **3** an established law, practice, or custom. **4** *colloq.* (of a person, a custom, etc.) a familiar object. **5** the establishment of a cleric, etc., in a church. [ME f. OF f. L *institutio -onis* (as INSTITUTE)]
  ■ **1** establishment, formation, creation, foundation, inauguration, launch, organization; initiation, start, beginning, origination, introduction, instigation, *formal* commencement. **2** see INSTITUTE *n.* 1. **3** custom, tradition, habit, practice, usage, routine, order (of the day), code (of practice), convention, principle, rule, regulation, law; doctrine, dogma, (received) wisdom. **4** fixture, regular, habitué, *colloq.* part of the furniture. **5** installation, induction, appointment, ordination, *archaic* sacring.

institutional /ínstitŏoshənəl, -tyŏo-/ *adj.* **1** of or like an institution. **2** typical of institutions, esp. in being regimented or unimaginative (*the food was dreadfully institutional*). **3** (of religion) expressed or organized through institutions (churches, etc.). **4** (of advertising) intended to create prestige rather than immediate sales. □□ **institutionalism** *n.* **institutionally** *adv.*

institutionalize /ínstitŏoshənəlīz, -tyŏo-/ *v.tr.* **1** (as **institutionalized** *adj.*) (of a prisoner, a long-term patient, etc.) made apathetic and dependent after a long period in an institution. **2** place or keep (a person) in an institution. **3** convert into an institution; make institutional. □□ **institutionalization** *n.*
  ■ **2** see *put away* 3 (PUT¹).

instruct /ínstrúkt/ *v.tr.* **1** (often foll. by *in*) teach (a person) a subject, etc. (*instructed her in French*). **2** (usu. foll. by *to* + infin.) direct; command (*instructed him to fill in the hole*). **3** (often foll. by *of*, or *that*, etc. + clause) inform (a person) of a fact, etc. **4** *Law* (of a judge) give information (esp. clarification of legal principles) to (a jury). [ME f. L *instruere instruct-* build, teach (as IN-², *struere* pile up)]
  ■ **1** teach, tutor, give lessons *or* classes; educate, school, train, drill, coach, prime, ground; guide, inform, prepare, edify, enlighten; indoctrinate, imbue. **2** direct, enjoin, counsel, advise, recommend, require, charge, tell, order, command, *archaic or literary* bid; give instructions, summon. **3** see INFORM *v.* 1.

instruction /ínstrúkshən/ *n.* **1** (often in *pl.*) a direction; an order (*gave him his instructions*). **2** teaching; education (*took a course of instruction*). **3** *Law* (in *pl.*) directions issued to a jury, etc. **4** *Computing* a direction in a computer program defining and effecting an operation. □□ **instructional** *adj.* [ME f. OF f. LL *instructio -onis* (as INSTRUCT)]
  ■ **1** direction, directive, bidding, enjoinment, injunction, advice, guidance, counsel, precept, recommendation, guideline, brief, prescription, requirement, order, command, dictate. **2** teaching, tuition, tutelage,

education, schooling, training, coaching, grounding, *Mil.* drill; lesson(s), class(es), apprenticeship; guidance, information, preparation, edification, enlightenment; indoctrination, inculcation.

instructive /ínstrúktiv/ *adj.* tending to instruct; conveying a lesson; enlightening (*found the experience instructive*). □□ **instructively** *adv.* **instructiveness** *n.*
  ■ didactic, prescriptive, educational, instructional; informative, informational, informatory, edifying, enlightening, illuminating, elucidatory, elucidative, explanatory, revealing, helpful.

instructor /ínstrúktər/ *n.* (*fem.* **instructress** /-strúktris/) **1** a person who instructs; a teacher, demonstrator, etc. **2** a university teacher ranking below assistant professor. □□ **instructorship** *n.*
  ■ **1** educator, preceptor, teacher, tutor, trainer, coach, demonstrator; professor, lecturer, don, schoolteacher, schoolmaster, schoolmistress, master, mistress, governess, *archaic* doctor, *archaic or derog.* pedagogue; mentor, adviser, guide, counselor.

instrument /ínstrəmənt/ *n. & v.* ● *n.* **1** a tool or implement, esp. for delicate or scientific work. **2** (in full **musical instrument**) a device for producing musical sounds by vibration, wind, percussion, etc. **3 a** a thing used in performing an action (*the meeting was an instrument in his success*). **b** a person made use of (*is merely their instrument*). **4** a measuring device, esp. in an airplane, serving to determine its position in darkness, etc. **5** a formal, esp. legal, document. ● *v.tr.* **1** arrange (music) for instruments. **2** equip with instruments (for measuring, recording, controlling, etc.). □ **instrument panel** (or **board**) a surface, esp. in a car or airplane, containing the dials, etc., of measuring devices. [ME f. OF *instrument* or L *instrumentum* (as INSTRUCT)]
  ■ *n.* **1** implement, tool, device, apparatus, utensil, appliance, contrivance, mechanism, gadget, doodah, *colloq.* widget, whatsit, hickey, *derog. or joc.* contraption, *sl.* jigger, gizmo; what-do-you-call-it, what's-its (*or* -his)-name, *colloq.* thingamabob, thingumajig, thingummy, thingy, whatnot. **3 a** agency, means, instrumentality, way, mechanism, *colloq.* wherewithal; factor, agent, (prime) mover, catalyst. **b** pawn, puppet, tool, cat's-paw, dummy; factotum, hack, drudge, *colloq.* stooge, *Brit. colloq.* dogsbody, *sl.* gofer. **4** gauge, meter, dial, indicator, monitor, (flight) recorder, log, black box. **5** contract, (legal) document, (written) agreement, pact, compact, paper, certificate. ● *v.* **1** score, arrange, orchestrate. **2** equip, fit out, kit out, rig out. □ **instrument panel** (or **board**) instrumentation, dash, dashboard, panel, control panel; display.

instrumental /ínstrəmént'l/ *adj. & n.* ● *adj.* **1** (usu. foll. by *to, in*, or *in* + verbal noun) serving as an instrument or means (*was instrumental in finding the money*). **2** (of music) performed on instruments, without singing (cf. VOCAL). **3** of, or arising from, an instrument (*instrumental error*). **4** *Gram.* of or in the instrumental. ● *n.* **1** a piece of music performed by instruments, not by the voice. **2** *Gram.* the case of nouns and pronouns (and words in grammatical agreement with them) indicating a means or instrument. □□ **instrumentalist** *n.* **instrumentality** /-mentálitee/ *n.* **instrumentally** *adv.* [ME f. F f. med.L *instrumentalis* (as INSTRUMENT)]
  ■ *adj.* **1** of service, influential, contributory, agential, subservient; catalytic, helpful, useful, conducive, effective, efficacious, beneficial, valuable, advantageous; significant, important.

instrumentation /ínstrəmentáyshən/ *n.* **1 a** the arrangement or composition of music for a particular group of musical instruments. **b** the instruments used in any one piece of music. **2 a** the design, provision, or use of instruments in industry, science, etc. **b** such instruments collectively. [F f. *instrumenter* (as INSTRUMENT)]
  ■ **1 a** see ARRANGEMENT 5.

insubordinate /ínsəbáwrd'nət/ *adj.* disobedient; rebellious. □□ **insubordinately** *adv.* **insubordination** /-náyshən/ *n.*
  ■ disobedient, recalcitrant, defiant, contumacious, uncooperative, fractious, *Brit.* unbiddable; rebellious,

insubstantial | insurmountable

refractory, mutinous, seditious, insurgent, insurrectional, insurrectionary, revolutionary; perverse, contrary, cross-grained, awkward, obstinate, stubborn, pigheaded, intractable, naughty, unruly, obstreperous, *Brit. colloq.* stroppy. □□ **insubordination** see REBELLION.

insubstantial /ˌinsəbstánshəl/ *adj.* **1** lacking solidity or substance. **2** not real. □□ **insubstantiality** /-sheeálitee/ *n.* **insubstantially** *adv.* [LL *insubstantialis* (as IN-¹, SUBSTANTIAL)]
■ **1** unsubstantial, flimsy, frail, weak, feeble, fragile, tenuous, meager, slight, paltry, puny, shaky, tinny, rickety, ramshackle, jerry-built, cardboard, *attrib.* pasteboard, *colloq. usu. derog.* itty-bitty; thin, light, fine, gossamer, wispy, fluffy, diaphanous, threadbare; airy, aeriform, frothy, *Brit. colloq.* airy-fairy. **2** unsubstantial, unreal, false, empty, illusory, illusive, imaginary, fanciful, fantastic, visionary, dreamlike, hallucinatory, chimerical, phantom, phantasmal, phantasmic; immaterial, intangible, impalpable, incorporeal, bodiless, spiritual, ethereal, airy.

insufferable /insúfərəbəl/ *adj.* **1** intolerable. **2** unbearably arrogant or conceited, etc. □□ **insufferableness** *n.* **insufferably** *adv.*
■ **1** intolerable, unbearable, insupportable, unsupportable, unendurable; unacceptable, *colloq.* too much, *Brit. colloq.* a bit thick. **2** arrogant, conceited, objectionable, unpleasant, obnoxious, awful, dreadful, unspeakable, *colloq.* impossible, ghastly.

insufficiency /ˌinsəfíshənsee/ *n.* **1** the condition of being insufficient. **2** *Med.* the inability of an organ to perform its normal function (*renal insufficiency*). [ME f. LL *insufficientia* (as INSUFFICIENT)]
■ **1** see LACK *n.*

insufficient /ˌinsəfíshənt/ *adj.* not sufficient; inadequate. □□ **insufficiently** *adv.* [ME f. OF f. LL *insufficiens* (as IN-¹, SUFFICIENT)]
■ deficient, skimpy, scanty, scant, scarce, meager, thin, too little, not enough, inadequate; unsatisfactory, disappointing, unacceptable, no good, not good enough.

insufflate /ínsəflayt/ *v.tr.* **1** *Med.* **a** blow or breathe (air, gas, powder, etc.) into a cavity of the body, etc. **b** treat (the nose, etc.) in this way. **2** *Theol.* blow or breathe on (a person) to symbolize spiritual influence. □□ **insufflation** /-fláyshən/ *n.* [LL *insufflare insufflat-* (as IN-², *sufflare* blow upon)]

insufflator /ínsəflaytər/ *n.* **1** a device for blowing powder on to a surface in order to make fingerprints visible. **2** an instrument for insufflating.

insular /ínsələr, ínsyə-/ *adj.* **1 a** of or like an island. **b** separated or remote, like an island. **2** ignorant of or indifferent to cultures, peoples, etc., outside one's own experience; narrow-minded. **3** of a British variant of Latin handwriting current in the Middle Ages. **4** (of climate) equable. □□ **insularism** *n.* **insularity** /-láritee/ *n.* **insularly** *adv.* [LL *insularis* (as INSULATE)]
■ **2** see PROVINCIAL *adj.* 2. □□ **insularity** see PROVINCIALISM 1.

insulate /ínsəlayt, ínsyə-/ *v.tr.* **1** prevent the passage of electricity, heat, or sound from (a thing, room, etc.) by interposing nonconductors. **2** detach (a person or thing) from its surroundings; isolate. **3** *archaic* make (land) into an island. □ **insulating tape** esp. *Brit.* = *electrical tape.* □□ **insulation** /-láyshən/ *n.* [L *insula* island + -ATE³]
■ **1** protect, shield, isolate; wrap, lag, cover. **2** detach, separate, isolate, segregate, set *or* keep apart, sequester, quarantine; shelter, cushion.

insulator /ínsəlaytər, ínsyə-/ *n.* **1** a thing or substance used for insulation against electricity, heat, or sound. **2** an insulating device to support telegraph wires, etc. **3** a device preventing contact between electrical conductors.

insulin /ínsəlin/ *n. Biochem.* a hormone produced in the pancreas by the islets of Langerhans, regulating the amount of glucose in the blood and the lack of which causes diabetes. [L *insula* island + -IN]

insult *v. & n.* ● *v.tr.* /insúlt/ **1** speak to or treat with scornful abuse or indignity. **2** offend the self-respect or modesty of. ● *n.* /ínsult/ **1** an insulting remark or action. **2** *colloq.* something so worthless or contemptible as to be offensive. **3** *Med.* **a** an agent causing damage to the body. **b** such damage. □□ **insulter** *n.* **insultingly** *adv.* [F *insulte* or L *insultare* (as IN-², *saltare* frequent. of *salire salt-* leap)]
■ *v.* **1** abuse, malign, revile, calumniate, call a person names, slander, libel, defame, vilify, bespatter, dishonor, be rude to, *colloq.* put down, *sl.* dump on; snub, cut (dead), spurn, shun, ignore, give the cold shoulder (to). **2** offend, give offense, affront, outrage, scandalize, injure, hurt, slight, pique, displease, chagrin, hurt a person's feelings, tread on a person's toes, humiliate, *colloq.* miff, put a person's nose out of joint. ● *n.* **1** offense, affront, indignity, discourtesy, rudeness, dishonor, outrage; vilification, calumniation, abuse, slander, calumny, libel, defamation, slur; slight, snub, cut, rebuff, slap in the face, *colloq.* put-down.

insuperable /insóopərəbəl/ *adj.* **1** (of a barrier) impossible to surmount. **2** (of a difficulty, etc.) impossible to overcome. □□ **insuperability** *n.* **insuperably** *adv.* [ME f. OF *insuperable* or L *insuperabilis* (as IN-¹, SUPERABLE)]
■ **1** see INVINCIBLE.

insupportable /ˌinsəpáwrtəbəl/ *adj.* **1** unable to be endured. **2** unjustifiable. □□ **insupportableness** *n.* **insupportably** *adv.* [F (as IN-¹, SUPPORT)]
■ **1** see INSUFFERABLE 1. **2** see UNTENABLE.

insurance /inshóorəns/ *n.* **1** the act or an instance of insuring. **2 a** a sum paid for this; a premium. **b** a sum paid out as compensation for theft, damage, loss, etc. **3** = *insurance policy.* **4** a measure taken to provide for a possible contingency (*take an umbrella as insurance*). □ **insurance agent a** a person authorized to sell insurance policies. **b** *Brit.* a person employed to collect premiums door to door. **insurance company** a company engaged in the business of insurance. **insurance policy 1** a contract of insurance. **2** a document detailing such a policy and constituting a contract. [earlier *ensurance* f. OF *enseürance* (as ENSURE)]
■ **1** indemnity, indemnification, guarantee, guaranty, warranty, bond, security, protection, cover, esp. *Brit.* assurance. **2 a** a premium; price, fee, charge; outlay, expenditure. **b** compensation, damages, reparation, reimbursement, recompense, redress. **4** precaution, provision, safety measure, safeguard, cover.

insure /inshóor/ *v.tr.* **1** (often foll. by *against*; also *absol.*) secure the payment of a sum of money in the event of loss or damage to (property, life, a person, etc.) by regular payments or premiums (*insured the house for $100,000; we have insured against flood damage*). **2** (of the owner of a property, an insurance company, etc.) secure the payment of (a sum of money) in this way. **3** (usu. foll. by *against*) provide for (a possible contingency) (*insured themselves against the rain by taking umbrellas*). **4** = ENSURE. □□ **insurable** *adj.* **insurability** /-shoorəbílitee/ *n.* [ME, var. of ENSURE]
■ **1** see COVER *v.* 7. **2** see UNDERWRITE 1.

insured /inshóord/ *adj. & n.* ● *adj.* covered by insurance. ● *n.* (usu. prec. by *the*) a person, etc., covered by insurance.

insurer /inshóorər/ *n.* **1** a person or company offering insurance policies for premiums; an underwriter. **2** a person that insures.

insurgent /insárjənt/ *adj. & n.* ● *adj.* **1** rising in active revolt. **2** (of the sea, etc.) rushing in. ● *n.* a rebel; a revolutionary. □□ **insurgence** /-jəns/ *n.* **insurgency** *n.* (*pl.* **-ies**) [F f. L *insurgere insurrect-* (as IN-², *surgere* rise)]
■ *adj.* **1** see REBELLIOUS 1. ● *n.* see REBEL. □□ **insurgence, insurgency** see REBELLION.

insurmountable /ˌinsərmówntəbəl/ *adj.* unable to be surmounted or overcome. □□ **insurmountably** *adv.*

/.../ **pronunciation** ● **part of speech**
□ **phrases, idioms, and compounds**
□□ **derivatives** ■ **synonym section**
cross-references appear in SMALL CAPITALS or *italics*

777

■ see INEXTRICABLE 2, 3.

insurrection /ínsərékshən/ *n.* a rising in open resistance to established authority; a rebellion. □□ **insurrectionary** *adj.* **insurrectionist** *n.* [ME f. OF f. LL *insurrectio -onis* (as IN-SURGENT)]

■ see REBELLION. □□ **insurrectionary** see REBELLIOUS 1. **insurrectionist** see REBEL.

insusceptible /ínsəséptibəl/ *adj.* (usu. foll. by *of, to*) not susceptible (of treatment, to an influence, etc.). □□ **insusceptibility** *n.*

■ see IMMUNE 1a. □□ **insusceptibility** see IMMUNITY 1.

inswinger /ínswingər/ *n.* **1** *Cricket* a ball bowled with a swing toward the batsman. **2** *Soccer* a pass or kick that sends the ball curving toward the goal.

int. *abbr.* **1** interior. **2** internal. **3** international.

intact /intákt/ *adj.* **1** entire; unimpaired. **2** untouched. □□ **intactness** *n.* [ME f. L *intactus* (as IN-1, *tactus* past part. of *tangere* touch)]

■ **1** whole, entire, complete, integral, solid, (all) in one piece, undivided, uncut, together, unabridged; unimpaired, perfect, flawless, sound, unbroken, undiminished. **2** untouched, inviolate, unblemished, unscathed, uninjured, unharmed, undamaged, unsullied, undefiled, untainted; maiden, virgin.

intagliated /intályaytid/ *adj.* decorated with surface carving. [It. *intagliato* past part. of *intagliare* cut into]

intaglio /intályō, -taál-/ *n. & v.* ● *n.* (*pl.* **-os**) **1** a gem with an incised design (cf. CAMEO). **2** an engraved design. **3** a carving, esp. incised, in hard material. **4** a process of printing from an engraved design. ● *v.tr.* (**-oes, -oed**) **1** engrave (material) with a sunk pattern or design. **2** engrave (such a design). [It. (as INTAGLIATED)]

intake /íntayk/ *n.* **1 a** the action of taking in. **b** an instance of this. **2** a number or the amount taken in or received. **3** a place where water is taken into a channel or pipe from a river, or fuel or air enters an engine, etc. **4** an airway into a mine.

■ **2** see DIET1 *n.* 1.

intangible /intánjibəl/ *adj. & n.* ● *adj.* **1** unable to be touched; not solid. **2** unable to be grasped mentally. ● *n.* something that cannot be precisely measured or assessed. □□ **intangibility** *n.* **intangibly** *adv.* [F *intangible* or med.L *intangibilis* (as IN-1, TANGIBLE)]

■ *adj.* **1** untouchable, impalpable, abstract, unsubstantial, insubstantial, immaterial, ethereal, spiritual, vaporous, airy, misty, incorporeal, bodiless, weightless. **2** incomprehensible, inconceivable, unintelligible, unfathomable, imponderable, inestimable, impenetrable; subtle, rarefied, vague, obscure, dim, imprecise, indefinite, shadowy, fleeting, elusive, evanescent. ● *n.* imponderable; abstract; abstraction.

intarsia /intaárseeə/ *n.* the craft of using wood inlays, esp. as practiced in 15th-c. Italy. [It. *intarsio*]

integer /íntijər/ *n.* **1** a whole number. **2** a thing complete in itself. [L (adj.) = untouched, whole: see ENTIRE]

■ **1** see NUMBER *n.* 1.

integral /íntigrəl, intégrəl/ *adj. & n.* ● *adj.* **1 a** of a whole or necessary to the completeness of a whole. **b** forming a whole (*integral design*). **c** whole; complete. **2** *Math.* **a** of or denoted by an integer. **b** involving only integers, esp. as coefficients of a function. ● *n.* /íntigrəl/ *Math.* **1** a quantity of which a given function is the derivative, either containing an indeterminate additive constant (**indefinite integral**), or calculated as the difference between its values at specified limits (**definite integral**). **2** a function satisfying a given differential equation. □ **integral calculus** mathematics concerned with finding integrals, their properties and application, etc. (cf. *differential calculus*). □□ **integrality** /-grálitee/ *n.* **integrally** *adv.* [LL *integralis* (as INTEGER)]

■ *adj.* **1 a** essential, necessary, indispensable; basic, elementary, elemental, fundamental, intrinsic, inherent, organic, built-in. **b,** *Brit.* in-line. **c** whole, complete, entire, intact, (all) in one piece.

integrand /íntigrand/ *n. Math.* a function that is to be integrated. [L *integrandus* gerundive of *integrare*: see INTEGRATE]

integrant /íntigrənt/ *adj.* (of parts) making up a whole; component. [F *intégrant* f. *intégrer* (as INTEGRATE)]

integrate *v. & adj.* ● *v.* /íntigrayt/ **1** *tr.* **a** combine (parts) into a whole. **b** complete (an imperfect thing) by the addition of parts. **2** *tr. & intr.* bring or come into equal participation in or membership of society, a school, etc. **3** *tr.* desegregate, esp. racially (a school, etc.). **4** *tr. Math.* **a** find the integral of. **b** (as **integrated** *adj.*) indicating the mean value or total sum of (temperature, an area, etc.). ● *adj.* /íntigrət/ **1** made up of parts. **2** whole; complete. □ **integrated circuit** *Electronics* a small chip, etc., of material replacing several separate components in a conventional electrical circuit. □□ **integrable** /íntigrəbəl/ *adj.* **integrability** *n.* **integrative** /íntigraytiv/ *adj.* [L *integrare integrat-* make whole (as INTEGER)]

■ *v.* **1–3** unite, unify, bring *or* put together, assemble, pool, coordinate; merge, blend, mix, mingle, compound, combine, coalesce, *literary* commingle; amalgamate, consolidate, embody, incorporate, desegregate; fuse, bind, bond, join, connect, knit, link, mesh.

integration /íntigráyshən/ *n.* **1** the act or an instance of integrating. **2** the intermixing of persons previously segregated. **3** *Psychol.* the combination of the diverse elements of perception, etc., in a personality. □□ **integrationist** *n.* [L *integratio* (as INTEGRATE)]

■ **1** see *amalgamation* (AMALGAMATE).

integrator /íntigraytər/ *n.* **1** an instrument for indicating or registering the total amount or mean value of some physical quality, as area, temperature, etc. **2** a person or thing that integrates.

integrity /intégritee/ *n.* **1** moral uprightness; honesty. **2** wholeness; soundness. [ME f. F *intégrité* or L *integritas* (as INTEGER)]

■ **1** rectitude, uprightness, righteousness, decency, honor, principle, morality, goodness, virtue, incorruptibility; probity, purity, honesty, veracity, trustworthiness. **2** wholeness, entirety, totality, completeness, unity, oneness, togetherness; soundness, coherence, consistency, validity.

integument /intégyəmənt/ *n.* a natural outer covering, as a skin, husk, rind, etc. □□ **integumental** /-mént'l/ *adj.* **integumentary** /-méntəree/ *adj.* [L *integumentum* f. *integere* (as IN-2, *tegere* cover)]

■ see SKIN *n.* 4.

intellect /íntilekt/ *n.* **1 a** the faculty of reasoning, knowing, and thinking, as distinct from feeling. **b** the understanding or mental powers (of a particular person, etc.) (*his intellect is not great*). **2 a** a clever or knowledgeable person. **b** the intelligentsia regarded collectively (*the combined intellect of four universities*). [ME f. OF *intellect* or L *intellectus* understanding (as INTELLIGENT)]

■ **1** rationality, reason, reasoning, understanding, insight, acumen, penetration, perspicacity, perception, percipience, discernment, judgment; intelligence, mind, brainpower, brain(s), braininess, wit(s), head, *archaic* headpiece, *colloq.* gray matter, *sl.* savvy. **2** see INTELLECTUAL *n.*

intellection /íntilékshən/ *n.* the action or process of understanding (opp. IMAGINATION). □□ **intellective** *adj.* [ME f. med.L *intellectio* (as INTELLIGENT)]

intellectual /íntilékchōōəl/ *adj. & n.* ● *adj.* **1** of or appealing to the intellect. **2** possessing a high level of understanding or intelligence; cultured. **3** requiring, or given to the exercise of, the intellect. ● *n.* a person possessing a highly developed intellect. □□ **intellectuality** /-chōōálitee/ *n.* **intellectualize** *v.tr. & intr.* **intellectually** *adv.* [ME f. L *intellectualis* (as INTELLECT)]

■ *adj.* **1** mental, cerebral, rational; abstract, noetic, academic, speculative, theoretical. **2** intelligent, insightful, analytical, perspicacious, percipient, clever, brainy, bright, smart, sharp, *sl.* savvy; thoughtful, academic, bookish, scholarly, donnish, scholastic, *derog.* Bloomsbury; cultured, erudite, learned, (well-)educated, *colloq.* highbrow. **3** profound, abstract, thought-provoking, *colloq.* highbrow; deep, unfathomable, abstruse, intricate, knotty, involved, tricky, difficult, hard. ● *n.* thinker, intellect, mastermind, genius, *colloq.* egghead, highbrow, brain, know-it-all, *Brit. colloq.* boffin, *derog.* bluestocking; scholar, academician, professor, savant, sage, guru, polymath, pundit, authority.

intellectualism /íntilékchōōəlizəm/ *n.* **1** the exercise, esp. when excessive, of the intellect at the expense of the emotions. **2** *Philos.* the theory that knowledge is wholly or mainly derived from pure reason. □□ **intellectualist** *n.*

intelligence /intélijəns/ *n.* **1 a** the intellect; the understanding. **b** (of a person or an animal) quickness of understanding; wisdom. **2 a** the collection of information, esp. of military or political value. **b** people employed in this. **c** information; news. **3** an intelligent or rational being. □ **intelligence agency** a usu. government bureau engaged in collecting esp. secret information. **intelligence quotient** a number denoting the ratio of a person's intelligence to the normal or average. **intelligence test** a test designed to measure intelligence rather than acquired knowledge. □□ **intelligential** /-jénshəl/ *adj.* [ME f. OF f. L *intelligentia* (as INTELLIGENT)]
■ **1 a** see INTELLECT 1. **b** cleverness, astuteness, brightness, smartness, sharpness, keenness, acuteness, acuity, incisiveness, quickness, alertness, quick-wittedness, shrewdness, wit, brainpower, IQ; (common) sense, mother *or* native wit; wisdom, sagacity, sageness, acumen, insight, perspicacity, perception, percipience, perspicaciousness, understanding, discernment, judgment, acumen, penetration, *literary* sapience. **2 a** espionage, spying. **b** secret service, CIA, *Brit.* MI5, MI6. **c** see INFORMATION 1.

intelligent /intélijənt/ *adj.* **1** having or showing intelligence, esp. of a high level. **2** quick of mind; clever. **3 a** (of a device or machine) able to vary its behavior in response to varying situations and requirements and past experience. **b** (esp. of a computer terminal) having its own data-processing capability; incorporating a microprocessor (opp. DUMB). □□ **intelligently** *adv.* [L *intelligere intellect-* understand (as INTER-, *legere* gather, pick out, read)]
■ **1** rational, cerebral, intellectual, analytical, logical, insightful, discerning, understanding, aware, receptive. **2** bright, brilliant, smart, clever, astute, quick, quick-witted, keen, sharp, sharp-witted, alert, shrewd, knowing, canny, perspicacious, perceptive, percipient, apt, gifted, brainy, *archaic* apprehensive; wise, sage, sagacious, discerning, judicious, sensible, informed, educated, enlightened, knowledgeable, *literary* sapient, *sl.* savvy.

intelligentsia /intélijéntseeə/ *n.* **1** the class of intellectuals regarded as possessing culture and political initiative. **2** people doing intellectual work; intellectuals. [Russ. f. Pol. *inteligencja* f. L *intelligentia* (as INTELLIGENT)]
■ intellectuals, literati, illuminati, brains, brain trust; see also INTELLECTUAL *n.*

intelligible /intélijibəl/ *adj.* **1** (often foll. by *to*) able to be understood; comprehensible. **2** *Philos.* able to be understood only by the intellect, not by the senses. □□ **intelligibility** *n.* **intelligibly** *adv.* [L *intelligibilis* (as INTELLIGENT)]
■ **1** understandable, comprehensible, perspicuous, apprehensible, coherent, articulate, rational, logical, clear, plain, lucid, distinct, unambiguous; accountable, fathomable, decipherable, decodable, legible, readable, audible; (*be intelligible*) make sense, fall into place, hang together, *colloq.* add up, figure, click.

Intelsat /íntelsat/ *n.* an international organization of countries operating a system of commercial communication satellites. [*International Telecommunications Satellite* Consortium]

intemperate /intémpərət/ *adj.* **1** (of a person, conduct, or speech) immoderate; unbridled; violent (*used intemperate language*). **2 a** given to excessive indulgence in alcohol. **b** excessively indulgent in one's appetites. □□ **intemperance**

/-rəns/ *n.* **intemperately** *adv.* **intemperateness** *n.* [ME f. L *intemperatus* (as IN-¹, TEMPERATE)]
■ **1** see IMMODERATE. **2 b** see SELF-INDULGENT.
□□ **intemperance** see EXCESS *n.* 4a. **intemperately** see FAST¹ *adj.* 9. **intemperateness** see *prodigality* (PRODIGAL).

intend /inténd/ *v.tr.* **1** have as one's purpose; propose (*we intend to go; we intend that it shall be done*). **2** (usu. foll. by *for, as*) design or destine (a person or a thing) (*I intend for him to go; I intend it as a warning*). **3** mean (*what does he intend by that?*). **4** (in *passive*; foll. by *for*) **a** be meant for a person to have or use, etc. (*they are intended for the children*). **b** be meant to represent (*the picture is intended for you*). **5** (as **intending** *adj.*) who intends to be (*an intending visitor*). [ME *entende, intende* f. OF *entendre, intendre* f. L *intendere intent-* or *intens-* strain, direct, purpose (as IN-², *tendere* stretch, tend)]
■ **1, 2** have (it) in mind *or* in view, be going, plan, set out, aim, purpose, design, mean, contemplate, think, propose, *colloq.* plan on; resolve, determine, destine, will. **3** mean, signify, indicate, express, imply, suggest, intimate, drive at, get at, refer to, denote, allude to, hint (at). **4 a** (*intended for*) for, meant for, designed for, destined for, supposed to be for, with a person *or* a thing in mind. **5** (**intending**) prospective, aspirant, aspiring, *often derog.* would-be.

intendant /inténdənt/ *n.* **1** (esp. as a title of foreign officials) a superintendent or manager of a department of public business, etc. **2** the administrator of an opera house or theater. □□ **intendancy** *n.* [F f. L *intendere* (as INTEND)]

intended /inténdid/ *adj.* & *n.* ● *adj.* **1** done on purpose; intentional. **2** designed; meant. ● *n. colloq.* the person one intends to marry; one's fiancé or fiancée (*is this your intended?*). □□ **intendedly** *adv.*
■ *adj.* **1** see INTENTIONAL. **2** see *destined* (DESTINE).
● *n.* see FIANCÉ.

intense /inténs/ *adj.* (**intenser, intensest**) **1** (of a quality, etc.) existing in a high degree; violent; forceful (*intense cold*). **2** (of a person) feeling, or apt to feel, strong emotion (*very intense about her music*). **3** (of a feeling or action, etc.) extreme (*intense joy; intense thought*). □□ **intensely** *adv.* **intenseness** *n.* [ME f. OF *intens* or L *intensus* (as INTEND)]
■ **1, 3** extreme, excessive, immoderate, intemperate, overpowering, acute, serious, severe, sharp, deep, profound, high, great, heavy, deadly, *colloq.* terrific, *Brit. colloq.* chronic; strong, fierce, harsh, violent, towering, consuming, powerful, forceful, concentrated, exquisite, hard, vehement, furious, frantic, fervent, fervid, heated, ardent, burning, torrid, unmitigated, *colloq.* flaming, *iron.* glorious; glaring, bright, full, vivid, acid. **2** emotional, passionate, impassioned, vehement, ardent, fervent, fervid, effusive, demonstrative, sentimental, *literary* perfervid; hysterical, overemotional, obsessive, *colloq.* manic, neurotic, *sl.* nutty, nuts; temperamental, high-strung, tense, touchy, sensitive, testy, *colloq.* uptight. □□ **intenseness** see INTENSITY 1.

intensifier /inténsifīər/ *n.* **1** a person or thing that intensifies. **2** *Gram.* = INTENSIVE *n.*

intensify /inténsifī/ *v.* (**-ies, -ied**) **1** *tr.* & *intr.* make or become intense or more intense. **2** *tr. Photog.* increase the opacity of (a negative). □□ **intensification** *n.*
■ **1** strengthen, reinforce, deepen; increase, inflate, magnify, enlarge, amplify, augment; extend, develop, build (up), *colloq.* boost; enhance, heighten, sharpen, whet, concentrate, focus, emphasize, point up, highlight; quicken, speed up, accelerate, escalate, step up, rev up, tone up, *sl.* crank up; heat (up), warm up, *Brit. colloq.* hot up; double, redouble, multiply,

proliferate; enliven, brighten, jazz up; exacerbate, aggravate, inflame, worsen, add to, stir up, fire up, excite, fan, fuel, *colloq.* blow up.

intension /inténshən/ *n.* **1** *Logic* the internal content of a concept. **2** *formal* the intensity, or high degree, of a quality. **3** *formal* the strenuous exertion of the mind or will. □□ **intensional** *adj.* **intensionally** *adv.* [L *intensio* (as INTEND)]

intensity /inténsitee/ *n.* (*pl.* **-ies**) **1** the quality or an instance of being intense. **2** esp. *Physics* the measurable amount of some quality, e.g., force, brightness, a magnetic field, etc.
■ **1** intenseness, extremeness, extremity, acuteness, seriousness, severity, sharpness, depth, profoundness, profundity, height, greatness, heaviness, strength, fierceness, ferocity, harshness, violence, power, force, forcefulness, vehemence, fervency, fervor, ardor, ardency, torridity; emotion, emotionality, passion, passionateness, devotion. **2** concentration, strength, force, power, potency, energy; brightness, vividness, brilliance, brilliancy, richness.

intensive /inténsiv/ *adj.* & *n.* ● *adj.* **1** thorough; vigorous; directed to a single point, area, or subject (*intensive study; intensive bombardment*). **2** of or relating to intensity as opp. to extent; producing intensity. **3** serving to increase production in relation to costs (*intensive farming methods*). **4** (usu. in *comb.*) *Econ.* making much use of (*a labor-intensive industry*). **5** *Gram.* (of an adjective, adverb, etc.) expressing intensity; giving force, as *really* in *my feet are really cold.* ● *n. Gram.* an intensive adjective, adverb, etc. □ **intensive care** medical treatment with constant monitoring, etc., of a dangerously ill patient (also (with hyphen) *attrib.*: *intensive-care unit*). □□ **intensively** *adv.* **intensiveness** *n.* [F *intensif -ive* or med.L *intensivus* (as INTEND)]
■ *adj.* **1** thorough, thoroughgoing, concentrated, exhaustive, in-depth; vigorous, energetic, dynamic, all-out; rigorous, painstaking, meticulous, assiduous, detailed.

intent /intént/ *n.* & *adj.* ● *n.* (usu. without article) intention; a purpose (*with intent to defraud; my intent to reach the top; with evil intent*). ● *adj.* **1** (usu. foll. by *on*) **a** resolved; bent; determined (*was intent on succeeding*). **b** attentively occupied (*intent on his books*). **2** (esp. of a look) earnest; eager; meaningful. □ **to** (or **for**) **all intents and purposes** practically; virtually. □□ **intently** *adv.* **intentness** *n.* [ME *entent* f. OF f. L *intentus* (as INTEND)]
■ *n.* see INTENTION 1. ● *adj.* **1 a** bent, set, resolved, determined, committed, decided, resolute, firm; keen, eager, zealous, avid, enthusiastic. **b** rapt, engrossed, absorbed, involved, wrapped up, deep. **2** earnest, sincere, serious, studious, thoughtful, solemn, grave, intense, steady, resolute, determined; diligent, eager, keen, zealous, conscientious, assiduous, industrious, hard-working, enthusiastic; meaningful, significant, expressive. □ **to** (or **for**) **all intents and purposes** virtually, practically, in effect, in all but name, more or less, (almost) as good as, pretty well, almost, *colloq.* just about. □□ **intently** avidly, eagerly, keenly, zealously, enthusiastically; closely, intensely, hard, searchingly, studiously, attentively, concentratedly, fixedly, raptly, steadily, steadfastly, diligently, conscientiously, assiduously, industriously; unflinchingly, continuously, doggedly, unremittingly, resolvedly, determinedly, resolutely, firmly; earnestly, sincerely, seriously, thoughtfully, solemnly, gravely.

intention /inténshən/ *n.* **1** (often foll. by *to* + infin., or *of* + verbal noun) a thing intended; an aim or purpose (*it was not her intention to interfere; have no intention of staying*). **2** the act of intending (*done without intention*). **3** *colloq.* (usu. in *pl.*) a person's, esp. a man's, designs in respect to marriage (*are his intentions strictly honorable?*). **4** *Logic* a conception. □ **first intention 1** *Med.* the healing of a wound by natural contact of the parts. **2** *Logic* one's primary conception of things (e.g., a tree, an oak). **intention tremor** *Med.* a trembling of a part of a body when commencing a movement. **second intention 1** *Med.* the healing of a wound by granulation. **2**

Logic one's secondary conception (e.g., difference, identity, species). **special** (or **particular**) **intention** *RC Ch.* a special aim or purpose for which a Mass is celebrated, prayers are said, etc. □□ **intentioned** *adj.* (usu. in *comb.*). [ME *entencion* f. OF f. L *intentio* stretching, purpose (as INTEND)]
■ **1** aim, purpose, intent, motive, design, goal, end, point, object, objective, target, ambition, aspiration. **2** premeditation, contemplation, resolution, determination; meaning, signification, indication, implication, intimation, suggestion, allusion.

intentional /inténshənəl/ *adj.* done on purpose. □□ **intentionality** /-álitee/ *n.* **intentionally** *adv.* [F *intentionnel* or med.L *intentionalis* (as INTENTION)]
■ intended, deliberate, willful, purposeful, voluntary, conscious; calculated, planned, premeditated, preconceived, meant. □□ **intentionally** deliberately, on purpose, purposely, willfully, consciously, wittingly, calculatedly, calculatingly, knowingly, pointedly, of one's (own) free will, on one's own, with one's eyes (wide) open.

inter /intǝr/ *v.tr.* (**interred, interring**) deposit (a corpse, etc.) in the earth, a tomb, etc.; bury. [ME f. OF *enterrer* f. Rmc (as IN-², L *terra* earth)]
■ bury, lay to rest, *literary* inhume.

inter. *abbr.* intermediate.

inter- /intǝr/ *comb. form* **1** between; among (*intercontinental*). **2** mutually; reciprocally (*interbreed*). [OF *entre-* or L *inter* between, among]

interact /intǝrákt/ *v.intr.* act reciprocally; act on each other. □□ **interactant** *adj.* & *n.*
■ see COOPERATE.

interaction /intǝrákshǝn/ *n.* **1** reciprocal action or influence. **2** *Physics* the action of atomic and subatomic particles on each other.
■ **1** see COOPERATION, INTERCOURSE 1.

interactive /intǝráktiv/ *adj.* **1** reciprocally active; acting upon or influencing each other. **2** (of a computer or other electronic device) allowing a two-way flow of information between it and a user, responding to the user's input. □□ **interactively** *adv.* [INTERACT, after *active*]
■ **1** see MUTUAL 1, 3.

inter alia /intǝr áyleeǝ, áaleeǝ/ *adv.* among other things. [L]

interallied /intǝrálid/ *adj.* relating to two or more allies (in war, etc.).

interarticular /intǝraartíkyǝlǝr/ *adj.* between the contiguous surfaces of a joint.

interatomic /intǝrǝtómik/ *adj.* between atoms.

interbank /intǝrbangk/ *adj.* agreed, arranged, or operating between banks (*interbank loan*).

interbed /intǝrbéd/ *v.tr.* (**-bedded, -bedding**) embed (one thing) among others.

interblend /intǝrblénd/ *v.* **1** *tr.* (usu. foll. by *with*) mingle (things) together. **2** *intr.* blend with each other.

interbreed /intǝrbreéd/ *v.* (*past* and *past part.* **-bred** /-bréd/) **1** *intr.* & *tr.* breed or cause to breed with members of a different race or species to produce a hybrid. **2** *tr.* breed within one family, etc., in order to produce desired characteristics (cf. CROSSBREED).

intercalary /intǝrkǝléree, -kálǝree/ *adj.* **1 a** (of a day or a month) inserted in the calendar to harmonize it with the solar year, e.g., Feb. 29 in leap years. **b** (of a year) having such an addition. **2** interpolated; intervening. [L *intercalari(u)s* (as INTERCALATE)]

intercalate /intǝrkǝlayt/ *v.tr.* **1** (also *absol.*) insert (an intercalary day, etc.). **2** interpose (anything out of the ordinary course). **3** (as **intercalated** *adj.*) (of strata, etc.) interposed. □□ **intercalation** /-láyshǝn/ *n.* [L *intercalare intercalat-* (as INTER-, *calare* proclaim)]
■ **1, 2** see INSERT *v.*

intercede /intǝrseéd/ *v.intr.* (usu. foll. by *with*) interpose or intervene on behalf of another; plead (*they interceded with the governor for his life*). □□ **interceder** *n.* [F *intercéder* or L *intercedere intercess-* intervene (as INTER-, *cedere* go)]
■ see INTERVENE. □□ **interceder** see *go-between* (GO¹).

intercellular /íntərsélyələr/ *adj. Biol.* located or occurring between cells.

intercensal /íntərsénsəl/ *adj.* between two censuses.

intercept *v.* & *n.* ● *v.tr.* /íntərsépt/ **1** seize, catch, or stop (a person, message, vehicle, ball, etc.) going from one place to another. **2** (usu. foll. by *from*) cut off (light, etc.). **3** check or stop (motion, etc.). **4** *Math.* mark off (a space) between two points, etc. ● *n.* /íntərsept/ *Math.* the part of a line between two points of intersection with usu. the coordinate axes or other lines. □□ **interception** /-sépshən/ *n.* **interceptive** /-séptiv/ *adj.* [L *intercipere intercept-* (as INTER-, *capere* take)]

■ *v.* **1–3** stop, halt, interrupt, arrest, trap, cut off, head off, thwart, ambush, waylay; check, block, bar, obstruct, dam, keep *or* hold back, prevent, hinder, impede, restrain, suppress; seize, catch, snatch, grab, take possession of, take a person prisoner, capture; take *or* carry away, appropriate, commandeer; deflect, reroute. □□ **interception** see *prevention* (PREVENT).

interceptor /íntərséptər/ *n.* **1** an aircraft used to intercept enemy raiders. **2** a person or thing that intercepts.

intercession /íntərséshən/ *n.* **1** the act of interceding, esp. by prayer. **2** an instance of this. **3** a prayer. □□ **intercessional** *adj.* **intercessor** *n.* **intercessorial** /-sesáwreeəl/ *adj.* **intercessory** *adj.* [F *intercession* or L *intercessio* (as INTERCEDE)]

interchange *v.* & *n.* ● *v.tr.* /íntərcháynj/ **1** (of two people) exchange (things) with each other. **2** put each of (two things) in the other's place; alternate. ● *n.* /íntərchaynj/ **1** (often foll. by *of*) a reciprocal exchange between two people, etc. **2** alternation (*the interchange of woods and fields*). **3** a road junction designed so that traffic streams do not intersect. □□ **interchangeable** *adj.* **interchangeability** /-cháynjəbílitee/ *n.* **interchangeableness** *n.* **interchangeably** *adv.* [ME f. OF *entrechangier* (as INTER-, CHANGE)]

■ *v.* **1** see EXCHANGE *v.* **2** see ALTERNATE *v.* **3.** ● *n.* **1** see EXCHANGE *n.* **1. 2** see ALTERNATION. **3** see JUNCTION 2. □□ **interchangeable** see COORDINATE *adj.* 1, SYNONYMOUS 1.

intercity /íntərsítee/ *adj.* existing or traveling between cities.

interclass /íntərklás/ *adj.* existing or conducted between different social classes.

intercollegiate /íntərkəleéjət/ *adj.* existing or conducted between colleges or universities.

intercolonial /íntərkəlőneeəl/ *adj.* existing or conducted between colonies.

intercom /íntərkom/ *n. colloq.* a system of intercommunication by radio or telephone between or within offices, aircraft, etc. [abbr.]

intercommunicate /íntərkəmyőőnikayt/ *v.intr.* **1** communicate reciprocally. **2** (of rooms, etc.) have free passage into each other; have a connecting door. □□ **intercommunication** /-káyshən/ *n.* **intercommunicative** /-kaytiv, -kətiv/ *adj.*

intercommunion /íntərkəmyőőnyən/ *n.* **1** mutual communion. **2** a mutual action or relationship, esp. between Christian denominations.

intercommunity /íntərkəmyőőnitee/ *n.* **1** the quality of being common to various groups, etc. **2** having things in common.

interconnect /íntərkənékt/ *v.tr.* & *intr.* connect with each other. □□ **interconnection** /-nékshən/ *n.*

■ □□ **interconnection** see RELATION 1a, c.

intercontinental /íntərkóntinént'l/ *adj.* connecting or traveling between continents. □□ **intercontinentally** *adv.*

■ see INTERNATIONAL.

interconvert /íntərkənvért/ *v.tr.* & *intr.* convert into each other. □□ **interconversion** /-vərzhən/ *n.* **interconvertible** *adj.*

intercooling /íntərkőőling/ *n.* the cooling of gas between successive compressions, esp. in a car or truck engine. □□ **intercool** *v.tr.* **intercooler** *n.*

intercorrelate /íntərkáwrələyt, -kór-/ *v.tr.* & *intr.* correlate with one another. □□ **intercorrelation** /-láyshən/ *n.*

intercostal /íntərkóst'l/ *adj.* between the ribs (of the body or a ship). □□ **intercostally** *adv.*

intercounty /íntərkówntee/ *adj.* existing or conducted between counties.

intercourse /íntərkawrs/ *n.* **1** communication or dealings between individuals, nations, etc. **2** = *sexual intercourse.* **3** communion between human beings and God. [ME f. OF *entrecours* exchange, commerce, f. L *intercursus* (as INTER-, *currere curs-* run)]

■ **1** communication, dealings, interaction, contact; relations, relationship; commerce, traffic, trade, business, exchange.

intercrop /íntərkróp/ *v.tr.* (also *absol.*) (**-cropped, -cropping**) raise (a crop) among plants of a different kind, usu. in the space between rows. □□ **intercropping** *n.*

intercross /íntərkráws, -krós/ *v.* **1** *tr.* & *intr.* lay or lie across each other. **2 a** *intr.* (of animals) breed with each other. **b** *tr.* cause to do this.

intercrural /íntərkrőőrəl/ *adj.* between the legs.

intercurrent /íntərkárənt, -kúr-/ *adj.* **1** (of a time or event) intervening. **2** *Med.* **a** (of a disease) occurring during the progress of another. **b** recurring at intervals. □□ **intercurrence** /-rəns/ *n.* [L *intercurrere intercurrent-* (as INTERCOURSE)]

intercut /íntərkút/ *v.tr.* (**-cutting**; *past* and *past part.* **-cut**) *Cinematog.* alternate (shots) with contrasting shots by cutting.

interdenominational /íntərdinómináyshənəl/ *adj.* concerning more than one (religious) denomination. □□ **interdenominationally** *adv.*

interdepartmental /íntərdeépaartmént'l/ *adj.* concerning more than one department. □□ **interdepartmentally** *adv.*

interdepend /íntərdipénd/ *v.intr.* depend on each other. □□ **interdependence** *n.* **interdependency** *n.* **interdependent** *adj.*

■ □□ **interdependence** see RELATION 1c. **interdependent** see RELATED 2.

interdict *n.* & *v.* ● *n.* /íntərdikt/ **1** an authoritative prohibition. **2** *RC Ch.* a sentence debarring a person, or esp. a place, from ecclesiastical functions and privileges. **3** *Sc. Law* an injunction. ● *v.tr.* /íntərdíkt/ **1** prohibit (an action). **2** forbid the use of. **3** (usu. foll. by *from* + verbal noun) restrain (a person). **4** (usu. foll. by *to*) forbid (a thing) to a person. □□ **interdiction** /-díkshən/ *n.* **interdictory** /-díktəree/ *adj.* [ME f. OF *entredit* f. L *interdictum* past part. of *interdicere* interpose, forbid by decree (as INTER-, *dicere* say)]

■ *n.* **1** see PROHIBITION. ● *v.* **1** see PROHIBIT 1. **4** see FORBID 2. □□ **interdiction** see PROHIBITION.

interdigital /íntərdíjit'l/ *adj.* between the fingers or toes. □□ **interdigitally** *adv.*

interdigitate /íntərdíjitayt/ *v.intr.* interlock like clasped fingers. [INTER- + L *digitus* finger + -ATE³]

interdisciplinary /íntərdísiplinéree/ *adj.* of or between more than one branch of learning.

interest /íntərist, -trist/ *n.* & *v.* ● *n.* **1 a** a feeling of curiosity or concern (*have no interest in fishing*). **b** a quality exciting curiosity or holding the attention (*this magazine lacks interest*). **c** the power of an issue, action, etc., to hold the attention; noteworthiness; importance (*findings of no particular interest*). **2** a subject, hobby, etc., in which one is concerned (*his interests are gardening and sports*). **3** advantage or profit, esp. when financial (*it is in your interest to go*; *look after your own interests*). **4** money paid for the use of money lent, or for not requiring the repayment of a debt. **5** (usu. foll. by *in*) **a** a financial stake (in an undertaking, etc.). **b** a legal concern, title, or right (in property). **6 a** a party or group having a common interest (*the mining interest*). **b** a principle in which a party or group is concerned. **7** the selfish pursuit of one's own welfare; self-interest. ● *v.tr.* **1** excite the curiosity or attention of (*your story interests me greatly*). **2** (usu.

/.../ **pronunciation**	● **part of speech**
□ **phrases, idioms, and compounds**	
□□ **derivatives**	■ **synonym section**
cross-references appear in SMALL CAPITALS or *italics*	

foll. by *in*) cause (a person) to take a personal interest or share (*can I interest you in a weekend cruise?*). **3** (as **interested** *adj.*) having a private interest; not impartial or disinterested (*an interested party*). □ **at interest** (of money borrowed) on the condition that interest is payable. **declare an** (or **one's**) **interest** make known one's financial, etc., interests in an undertaking before it is discussed. **in the interest** (or **interests**) **of** as something that is advantageous to. **lose interest** become bored or boring. **with interest** with increased force, etc. (*returned the blow with interest*). □□ **interestedly** *adv.* **interestedness** *n.* [ME, earlier *interesse* f. AF f. med.L, alt. app. after OF *interest*, both f. L *interest*, 3rd sing. pres. of *interesse* matter, make a difference (as INTER-, *esse* be)]

▪ *n.* **1 a** curiosity, concern, inquisitiveness, fascination, attention, attentiveness, enthusiasm, eagerness, keenness, avidity, zeal, excitement, passion, taste, relish. **b** appeal, excitement, attraction, attractiveness, allure, allurement, fascination. **c** noteworthiness, significance, importance, weight, moment, matter, note, import, concern, consequence. **2** hobby, pastime, recreation, diversion, avocation, pursuit, relaxation, amusement, entertainment, *sl.* bag; occupation, business. **3** profit, advantage, gain, benefit, good, use, avail, worth, value. **4** charge, fee, price, cost; percentage, rate, level, *sl.* vigorish. **5 a** stake, participation, involvement, investment, share, portion, piece, cut, percentage, *sl.* (piece of the) action. **b** title, entitlement, right, claim, concern, stake. **6a** industry, business, concern, field; fraternity, party, lobby, side, lot. **7** self-interest, egoism, egotism, egocentrism, selfishness. ● *v.* **1** engage, absorb, engross, fascinate, intrigue; distract, divert, amuse, entertain, attract, draw, catch, capture, captivate, hold, occupy; excite, incite, provoke, arouse, affect, quicken, infect, animate, kindle, fire. **2** influence, induce, persuade, talk a person into, move, tempt, dispose, incline, prevail (up)on; enroll, enlist, involve, concern. **3** (**interested**) concerned, involved, partial, biased, prejudiced, partisan. □ **in the interest of** for the benefit of, for the sake of; to a person *or* a thing's advantage; in *or Brit.* on behalf of (*or* in *or Brit.* on a person's behalf), in support of. **lose interest** become *or* get bored *or* tired, become *or* get fed up *or* impatient *or* sick and tired, *Brit. sl.* become *or* get browned off; become boring, go flat, lose one's sparkle, peter out, trail off, tail off, *colloq.* go downhill. **with interest** *sl.* in spades, *Brit. sl.* with knobs on.

interesting /íntristing, -tərĕsting/ *adj.* causing curiosity; holding the attention. □□ **interestingly** *adv.* **interestingness** *n.*

▪ fascinating, intriguing, attractive, tempting, inviting; provocative, stimulating, exciting, entertaining, eventful, *colloq.* juicy; absorbing, thought-provoking, engaging, gripping, riveting, engrossing, compelling, spellbinding, enchanting, captivating.

interface /íntərfays/ *n. & v.* ● *n.* **1** esp. *Physics* a surface forming a common boundary between two regions. **2** a point where interaction occurs between two systems, processes, subjects, etc. (*the interface between psychology and education*). **3** esp. *Computing* **a** an apparatus for connecting two pieces of equipment so that they can be operated jointly. **b** a means by which a user interacts with a program or utilizes an application. ● *v.tr. & intr.* (often foll. by *with*) connect with (another piece of equipment, etc.) by an interface.

▪ *n.* **1** see SURFACE *n.* 2.

interfacial /íntərfáyshəl/ *adj.* **1** included between two faces of a crystal or other solid. **2** of or forming an interface. □□ **interfacially** *adv.* (esp. in sense 2).

interfacing /íntərfaysing/ *n.* a stiffish material, esp. buckram, between two layers of fabric in collars, etc.

interfemoral /íntərfémərəl/ *adj.* between the thighs.

interfere /íntərféer/ *v.intr.* **1** (usu. foll. by *with*) **a** (of a person) meddle; obstruct a process, etc. **b** (of a thing) be a hindrance; get in the way. **2** (usu. foll. by *in*) take part or

intervene, esp. without invitation or necessity. **3** (foll. by *with*) *euphem.* molest or assault sexually. **4** *Physics* (of light or other waves) combine so as to cause interference. **5** (of a horse) knock one leg against another. □□ **interferer** *n.* **interfering** *adj.* **interferingly** *adv.* [OF *s'entreferir* strike each other (as INTER-, *ferir* f. L *ferire* strike)]

▪ **1** (*interfere with*) meddle with, hinder, get in the way of, impede, hamper, block, obstruct, inhibit, encumber, slow (down), hold back, retard, handicap, trammel, set back; disrupt, disturb, mess up, frustrate, subvert, sabotage; tinker with, fiddle with, monkey with, mess (about) with, *Brit. colloq.* muck about (*or* around) with. **2** intrude, interrupt, butt in, barge in, break in, intervene, intercede, interpose, put *or* stick one's oar in, thrust oneself *or* one's nose in, *sl.* horn in; pry, meddle, *colloq.* snoop, kibitz, poke one's nose in. **3** (*interfere with*) see MOLEST 2. □□ **interfering** see INTRUSIVE.

interference /íntərféerəns/ *n.* **1** (usu. foll. by *with*) **a** the act of interfering. **b** an instance of this. **2** the fading or disturbance of received radio signals by the interference of waves from different sources, or esp. by atmospherics or unwanted signals. **3** *Physics* the combination of two or more wave motions to form a resultant wave in which the displacement is reinforced or canceled. □□ **interferential** /-fərénshəl/ *adj.*

▪ **1** hindrance, obstruction, inhibition, encumbrance; disruption, disturbance, subversion; intrusion, interruption, intervention, intercession, interposition; impediment, block; meddlesomeness. **2** disturbance, static, noise, atmospherics, snow, ghosting, crosstalk, *Electronics* hiss, *Telephones* babble.

interferometer /íntərfərómitər/ *n.* an instrument for measuring wavelengths, etc., by means of interference phenomena. □□ **interferometric** /-férəmétrik/ *adj.* **interferometrically** *adv.* **interferometry** *n.*

interferon /íntərféeron/ *n.* *Biochem.* any of various proteins that can inhibit the development of a virus in a cell, etc. [INTERFERE + -ON]

interfibrillar /íntərfíbrilər/ *adj.* between fibrils.

interfile /íntərfíl/ *v.tr.* **1** file (two sequences) together. **2** file (one or more items) into an existing sequence.

▪ see FILE[1] *v.* 1.

interflow *v. & n.* ● *v.intr.* /íntərflṓ/ flow into each other. ● *n.* /íntərflō/ the process or result of this.

interfluent /íntərflṓoənt/ *adj.* flowing into each other. [L *interfluere interfluent-* (as INTER-, *fluere* flow)]

interfuse /íntərfyṓoz/ *v.* **1** *tr.* **a** (usu. foll. by *with*) mix (a thing) with; intersperse. **b** blend (things) together. **2** *intr.* (of two things) blend with each other. □□ **interfusion** /-fyṓozhən/ *n.* [L *interfundere interfus-* (as INTER-, *fundere* pour)]

intergalactic /íntərgəláktik/ *adj.* of or situated between two or more galaxies. □□ **intergalactically** *adv.*

interglacial /íntərgláyshəl/ *adj.* between glacial periods.

intergovernmental /íntərgúvərnmént'l/ *adj.* concerning or conducted between two or more governments. □□ **intergovernmentally** *adv.*

intergradation /íntərgrədáyshən/ *n.* the process of merging together by gradual change of the constituents.

intergrade *v. & n.* ● *v.intr.* /íntərgráyd/ pass into another form by intervening grades. ● *n.* /íntərgrayd/ such a grade.

intergrowth /íntərgrōth/ *n.* the growing of things into each other.

interim /íntərim/ *n., adj., & adv.* ● *n.* the intervening time (*in the interim he had died*). ● *adj.* intervening; provisional; temporary. ● *adv.* *archaic* meanwhile. □ **interim dividend** a dividend declared on the basis of less than a full year's results. [L, as INTER- + adv. suffix *-im*]

▪ *n.* meanwhile, meantime, interval. ● *adj.* see PROVISIONAL *adj.* ● *adv.* see MEANWHILE *adv.*

interior /intéereeər/ *adj. & n.* ● *adj.* **1** inner (opp. EXTERIOR). **2** remote from the coast or frontier; inland. **3** internal; domestic (opp. FOREIGN). **4** (usu. foll. by *to*) situated further in or within. **5** existing in the mind or soul; inward. **6** drawn, photographed, etc., within a building. **7** coming from inside.

● *n.* **1** the interior part; the inside. **2** the interior part of a country or region. **3 a** the home affairs of a country. **b** a department dealing with these (*Secretary of the Interior*). **4** a representation of the inside of a building or a room (*Dutch interior*). **5** the inner nature; the soul. □ **interior angle** the angle between adjacent sides of a rectilinear figure. **interior design** (or **decoration**) the design or decoration of the interior of a building, a room, etc. **interior monologue** a form of writing expressing a character's inner thoughts. **interior-sprung** *Brit.* = INNERSPRING. □□ **interiorize** *v.tr.* **interiorly** *adv.* [L, compar. f. *inter* among]

■ *adj.* **1** inside, internal, inner, inward. **2** inland, upland, up-country, high, midland, landlocked. **3** internal, domestic, national, civil, home, local, indigenous. **4** inner, inside, further in. **5** inner, innermost, inmost, inward, private, intimate, personal, individual; mental, intellectual, cerebral; secret, hidden, veiled, covert. **6** indoor, internal, inside; cross-sectional, cutaway. ● *n.* **1** inside; center, middle, heart, core, depths. **2** center, middle, heart; inland, heartland, upland, hinterland. **3** home affairs, internal affairs, domestic affairs. **5** see SOUL 1, 2.

interj. *abbr.* interjection.

interject /íntərjékt/ *v.tr.* **1** utter (words) abruptly or parenthetically. **2** interrupt with. □□ **interjectory** *adj.* [L *interjicere* (as INTER-, *jacere* throw)]

■ **2** see INTERPOSE 1.

interjection /íntərjékshən/ *n.* an exclamation, esp. as a part of speech (e.g., *ah!*, *dear me!*). □□ **interjectional** *adj.* [ME f. OF f. L *interjectio -onis* (as INTERJECT)]

■ exclamation, ejaculation, cry, utterance; interpolation, interruption.

interknit /íntərnít/ *v.tr.* & *intr.* (**-knitting**; *past* and *past part.* **-knitted** or **-knit**) knit together; intertwine.

interlace /íntərláys/ *v.* **1** *tr.* bind intricately together; interweave. **2** *tr.* mingle; intersperse. **3** *intr.* cross each other intricately. □□ **interlacement** *n.* [ME f. OF *entrelacier* (as INTER-, LACE *v.*)]

■ **1, 3** see WEAVE¹ *v.* 1b.

interlanguage /íntərlanggwij/ *n.* a language or use of language having features of two others, often a pidgin or dialect form.

interlap /íntərláp/ *v.intr.* (**-lapped**, **-lapping**) overlap.

interlard /íntərlaárd/ *v.tr.* (usu. foll. by *with*) mix (writing or speech) with unusual words or phrases. [F *entrelarder* (as INTER-, LARD *v.*)]

interleaf /íntərleéf/ *n.* (*pl.* **-leaves**) an extra (usu. blank) leaf between the leaves of a book.

interleave /íntərleév/ *v.tr.* insert (usu. blank) leaves between the leaves of (a book, etc.).

interleukin /íntərloökin/ *n.* *Biochem.* any of several glycoproteins produced by leukocytes for regulating immune responses. [INTER- + LEUKOCYTE]

interlibrary /íntərlíbreree/ *adj.* between libraries (esp. *interlibrary loan*).

interline¹ /íntərlín/ *v.tr.* **1** insert words between the lines of (a document, etc.). **2** insert (words) in this way. □□ **interlineation** /-línee-áyshən/ *n.* [ME f. med.L *interlineare* (as INTER-, LINE¹)]

interline² /íntərlín/ *v.tr.* put an extra lining between the ordinary lining and the fabric of (a garment).

■ line, face, cover.

interlinear /íntərlíneeər/ *adj.* written or printed between the lines of a text. [ME f. med.L *interlinearis* (as INTER-, LINEAR)]

interlining /íntərlíning/ *n.* material used to interline a garment.

interlink /íntərlíngk/ *v.tr.* & *intr.* link or be linked together.

interlobular /íntərlóbyələr/ *adj.* situated between lobes.

interlock /íntərlók/ *v.*, *adj.*, & *n.* ● *v.* **1** *intr.* engage with each other by overlapping or by the fitting together of projections and recesses. **2** *tr.* (usu. in *passive*) lock or clasp within each other. ● *adj.* (of a fabric) knitted with closely interlocking stitches. ● *n.* a device or mechanism for connecting or coordinating the function of different components. □□ **interlocker** *n.*

■ *v.* **2** see MESH *v.* 1.

interlocutor /íntərlókyətər/ *n.* (*fem.* **interlocutrix** /-triks/) a person who takes part in a dialogue or conversation. □□ **interlocution** /-ləkyoöshən/ *n.* [mod.L f. L *interloqui interlocut-* interrupt in speaking (as INTER-, *loqui* speak)]

interlocutory /íntərlókyətawree/ *adj.* **1** of dialogue or conversation. **2** *Law* (of a decree, etc.) given provisionally in a legal action. [med.L *interlocutorius* (as INTERLOCUTOR)]

interloper /íntərlópər/ *n.* **1** an intruder. **2** a person who interferes in others' affairs, esp. for profit. □□ **interlope** *v.intr.* [INTER- + *loper* as in *landloper* vagabond f. MDu. *landlooper*]

■ **1** see INTRUDER. □□ **interlope** see MEDDLE.

interlude /íntərloöd/ *n.* **1 a** a pause between the acts of a play. **b** something performed or done during this pause. **2 a** an intervening time, space, or event that contrasts with what goes before or after. **b** a temporary amusement or entertaining episode. **3** a piece of music played between other pieces, the verses of a hymn, etc. [ME, = a light dramatic item between the acts of a morality play, f. med.L *interludium* (as INTER-, *ludus* play)]

■ **1, 2** interval, intermission, pause, stop, stoppage, interruption, break, hiatus, lacuna, gap, halt, wait; breathing space, rest, spell, lull, respite, *colloq.* letup; parenthesis, entr'acte, divertissement, diversion, intermezzo, distraction; change. **3** symphony, *Mus.* verset, ritornello.

intermarriage /íntərmárij/ *n.* **1** marriage between people of different races, castes, families, etc. **2** (loosely) marriage between near relations.

intermarry /íntərmáree/ *v.intr.* (**-ies**, **-ied**) (foll. by *with*) (of races, castes, families, etc.) become connected by marriage.

intermediary /íntərmeédee-eree/ *n.* & *adj.* ● *n.* (*pl.* **-ies**) an intermediate person or thing, esp. a mediator. ● *adj.* acting as mediator; intermediate. [F *intermédiaire* f. It. *intermediario* f. L *intermedius* (as INTERMEDIATE)]

■ *n.* go-between, middleman, entrepreneur, mediator, intermediate, intermediator, broker, agent, factor, deputy, representative, messenger, third party; peacemaker, arbitrator, negotiator, arbiter, referee, umpire, judge. ● *adj.* mediatory, entrepreneurial; see also INTERMEDIATE *adj.*

intermediate *adj.*, *n.*, & *v.* ● *adj.* /íntərmeédeeət/ coming between two things in time, place, order, character, etc. ● *n.* /íntərmeédeeət/ **1** an intermediate thing. **2** a chemical compound formed by one reaction and then used in another, esp. during synthesis. ● *v.intr.* /íntərmeédeeáyt/ (foll. by *between*) act as intermediary; mediate. □ **intermediate frequency** the frequency to which a radio signal is converted during heterodyne reception. □□ **intermediacy** /-deeəsee/ *n.* **intermediately** *adv.* **intermediateness** *n.* **intermediation** /-deeáyshən/ *n.* **intermediator** /-deeaytər/ *n.* [med.L *intermediatus* (as INTER-, *medius* middle)]

■ *adj.* middle, medial, midway, halfway, transitional, intermediary, inter., inter-, meso-, mid-, *Law* mesne, *colloq.* in-between. ● *n.* **1** compromise, middle course or way, halfway house, *literary* via media. ● *v.* mediate, arbitrate, referee, umpire.

interment /íntərmənt/ *n.* the burial of a corpse, esp. with ceremony.

■ see BURIAL 1.

intermesh /íntərmésh/ *v.tr.* & *intr.* make or become meshed together.

intermezzo /íntərmétsō/ *n.* (*pl.* **intermezzi** /-see/ or **-os**) **a** a short connecting instrumental movement in an opera or other musical work. **b** a similar piece performed independently. **c** a short piece for a solo instrument. **2** a short, light dramatic or other performance inserted between the acts of a play. [It. f. L *intermedium* interval (as INTERMEDIATE)]

interminable /íntərminəbəl/ *adj.* **1** endless. **2** tediously long

---

/.../ **pronunciation**	● **part of speech**
□ **phrases, idioms, and compounds**	
□□ **derivatives**	■ **synonym section**
cross-references appear in SMALL CAPITALS or *italics*	

or habitual. **3** with no prospect of an end. □□ **interminableness** *n.* **interminably** *adv.* [ME f. OF *interminable* or LL *interminabilis* (as IN-[1], TERMINATE)]
▪ **1, 3** see ENDLESS 2. **2** see LENGTHY 2. □□ **interminably** see NONSTOP *adv.*

intermingle /íntərmínggəl/ *v.tr. & intr.* (often foll. by *with*) mix together; mingle.
▪ see MIX *v.* 1, 3, 4a.

intermission /íntərmíshən/ *n.* **1** a pause or cessation. **2** an interval between parts of a play, motion picture, concert, etc. **3** a period of inactivity. [F *intermission* or L *intermissio* (as INTERMIT)]
▪ **1, 3** pause, stop, stoppage, cessation, halt, break, interruption, hiatus, lacuna, interval, gap, wait; breathing space, rest, spell, lull, respite, *colloq.* letup. **2** interval, interlude, parenthesis, entr'acte.

intermit /íntərmít/ *v.* (**intermitted, intermitting**) **1** *intr.* esp. *Med.* stop or cease activity briefly (e.g., of a fever, or a pulse). **2** *tr.* suspend; discontinue for a time. [L *intermittere intermiss*- (as INTER-, *mittere* let go)]
▪ **2** suspend, interrupt, put in *or* into abeyance, shelve, stop *or* break off *or* discontinue temporarily.

intermittent /íntərmít'nt/ *adj.* occurring at intervals; not continuous or steady. □□ **intermittence** /-mít'ns/ *n.* **intermittency** *n.* **intermittently** *adv.* [L *intermittere intermittent*- (as INTERMIT)]
▪ sporadic, occasional, irregular, random, spasmodic, fitful, broken, on-off, stop-go; discontinuous, unsteady, variable, changeable, inconstant; periodic, cyclic(al), rhythmic(al), seasonal.

intermix /íntərmíks/ *v.tr. & intr.* mix together. □□ **intermixable** *adj.* **intermixture** *n.* [back-form. f. *intermixed, intermixt* f. L *intermixtus* past part. of *intermiscēre* mix together (as INTER-, *miscēre* mix)]
▪ see MINGLE.

intermolecular /íntərməlékyələr/ *adj.* between molecules.

intern *n. & v.* ● *n.* /íntərn/ (also **interne**) a recent graduate or advanced medical student living in a hospital and acting as an assistant physician or surgeon. ● *v.* **1** *tr.* /intə́rn/ confine; oblige (a prisoner, alien, etc.) to reside within prescribed limits. **2** *intr.* /íntərn/ serve as an intern. □□ **internment** /-tə́rn-/ *n.* **internship** /íntərn-/ *n.* [F *interne* f. L *internus* internal]
▪ *v.* **1** see IMPRISON. □□ **internment** see CAPTIVITY.

internal /intə́rnəl/ *adj. & n.* ● *adj.* **1** of or situated in the inside or invisible part. **2** relating or applied to the inside of the body (*internal injuries*). **3** of a nation's domestic affairs. **4** (of a student) attending a university, etc., as well as taking its examinations. **5** used or applying within an organization. **6 a** of the inner nature of a thing; intrinsic. **b** of the mind or soul. ● *n.* (in *pl.*) intrinsic qualities. □ **internal combustion engine** an engine with its motive power generated by the explosion of gases or vapor with air in a cylinder. **internal energy** the energy in a system arising from the relative positions and interactions of its parts. **internal evidence** evidence derived from the contents of the thing discussed. **internal exile** see EXILE *n.* 1. **internal medicine** a branch of medicine specializing in the diagnosis and nonsurgical treatment of diseases. **internal rhyme** a rhyme involving a word in the middle of a line and another at the end of the line or in the middle of the next. □□ **internality** /-nálitee/ *n.* **internalize** *v.tr.* **internalization** *n.* **internally** *adv.* [mod.L *internalis* (as INTERN)]
▪ *adj.* **1, 2** inside, interior, inward, inner; covert, hidden, secret, veiled, unseen, invisible. **3** domestic, interior, national, civil, home, local, indigenous. **5** in-house, intramural. **6** see INTRINSIC.

internat. *abbr.*

international /íntərnáshənəl/ *adj. & n.* ● *adj.* **1** existing, involving, or carried on between two or more nations. **2** agreed on or used by all or many nations (*international date line; international driver's license*). ● *n.* **1 a** a contest, esp. in sport, between teams representing different countries. **b** a member of such a team. **2 a** (**International**) any of four associations founded (1864–1936) to promote socialist or communist action. **b** a member of any of these. □ **international date line** (also **International Date Line**) see DATELINE 1. **international law** a body of rules established by custom or treaty and agreed as binding by nations in their relations with one another. **international system of units** a system of physical units based on the meter, kilogram, second, ampere, kelvin, candela, and mole, with prefixes to indicate multiplication or division by a power of ten. **international unit** a standard quantity of a vitamin, etc. □□ **internationality** /-nálitee/ *n.* **internationally** *adv.*
▪ *adj.* worldwide, world, global, universal, intercontinental, multinational, cosmopolitan; supranational, general, extensive; ecumenical; foreign.

Internationale /ANtərnaásyawnaál/ *n.* (prec. by *the*) an (orig. French) revolutionary song adopted by socialists. [F, fem. of *international* (adj.) f. INTERNATIONAL]

internationalism /íntərnáshənəlizəm/ *n.* **1** the advocacy of a community of interests among nations. **2** (**Internationalism**) the principles of any of the Internationals. □□ **internationalist** *n.*

internationalize /íntərnáshənəliz/ *v.tr.* **1** make international. **2** bring under the protection or control of two or more nations. □□ **internationalization** /-lizáyshən/ *n.*

interne var. of INTERN *n.*

internecine /íntərneéseen, -néseen/ *adj.* mutually destructive. [orig. = deadly, f. L *internecinus* f. *internecio* massacre f. *internecare* slaughter (as INTER-, *necare* kill)]

internee /íntərneé/ *n.* a person interned.
▪ see PRISONER.

Internet /íntərnét/ *n.* a communications network enabling the linking of computers worldwide for data interchange.

internist /intə́rnist/ *n.* *Med.* a specialist in internal medicine.

internode /íntərnōd/ *n.* **1** *Bot.* a part of a stem between two of the knobs from which leaves arise. **2** *Anat.* a slender part between two joints, esp. the bone of a finger or toe.

internuclear /íntərnoŏkleeər, -nyoŏ-/ *adj.* between nuclei.

internuncial /íntərnúnshəl/ *adj.* (of nerves) communicating between different parts of the system. [*internuncio* ambassador f. It. *internunzio*]

interoceanic /íntərōsheeánik/ *adj.* between or connecting two oceans.

interoceptive /íntərōséptiv/ *adj.* *Biol.* relating to stimuli produced within an organism, esp. in the viscera. [irreg. f. L *internus* interior + RECEPTIVE]

interosculate /íntəróskyəlayt/ *v.intr.* = INOSCULATE.

interosseous /íntəróseeəs/ *adj.* between bones.

interparietal /íntərpəríət'l/ *adj.* between the right and left parietal bones of the skull. □□ **interparietally** *adv.*

interpellate /intə́rpəlayt/ *v.tr.* (in European parliaments) interrupt the order of the day by demanding an explanation from (the minister concerned). □□ **interpellation** /-láyshən/ *n.* **interpellator** *n.* [L *interpellare interpellat*- (as INTER-, *pellere* drive)]

interpenetrate /íntərpénitrayt/ *v.* **1** *intr.* (of two things) penetrate each other. **2** *tr.* pervade; penetrate thoroughly. □□ **interpenetration** /-tráyshən/ *n.* **interpenetrative** *adj.*

interpersonal /íntərpə́rsənəl/ *adj.* (of relations) occurring between persons, esp. reciprocally. □□ **interpersonally** *adv.*

interplait /íntərpláyt, -plát/ *v.tr. & intr.* plait together.

interplanetary /íntərplániteree/ *adj.* **1** between planets. **2** relating to travel between planets.

interplay /íntərplay/ *n.* **1** reciprocal action. **2** the operation of two things on each other.

interplead /íntərpleéd/ *v.* **1** *intr.* litigate with each other to settle a point concerning a third party. **2** *tr.* cause to do this. □□ **interpleader** *n.* [ME f. AF *enterpleder* (as INTER-, PLEAD)]

Interpol /íntərpōl/ *n.* International Criminal Police Organization. [abbr.]

interpolate /intə́rpəlayt/ *v.tr.* **1 a** insert (words) in a book, etc., esp. to give false impressions as to its date, etc. **b** make such insertions in (a book, etc.). **2** interject (a remark) in a conversation. **3** estimate (values) from known ones in the same range. □□ **interpolation** /-láyshən/ *n.* **interpolative**

/-lətiv/ *adj.* **interpolator** *n.* [L *interpolare* furbish up (as INTER-, *polire* POLISH)]

■ **1** see INSERT *v.* **2** see INTERPOSE 2. □□ **interpolation** see INSERT *n.*, INTERJECTION.

interpose /íntərpōz/ *v.* **1** *tr.* (often foll. by *between*) place or insert (a thing) between others. **2** *tr.* say (words) as an interruption. **3** *tr.* exercise or advance (a veto or objection) so as to interfere. **4** *intr.* (foll. by *between*) intervene (between parties). [F *interposer* f. L *interponere* put (as INTER-, POSE¹)]

■ **1** see INSERT *v.* **2** interject, interpolate, put *or* throw in. **4** see INTERFERE 2.

interposition /íntərpəzíshən/ *n.* **1** the act of interposing. **2** a thing interposed. **3** an interference. [ME f. OF *interposition* or L *interpositio* (as INTER-, POSITION)]

■ see INTERFERENCE 1.

interpret /intə́rprit/ *v.* (**interpreted**, **interpreting**) **1** *tr.* explain the meaning of (foreign or abstruse words, a dream, etc.). **2** *tr.* make out or bring out the meaning of (creative work). **3** *intr.* act as an interpreter, esp. of foreign languages. **4** *tr.* explain or understand (behavior, etc.) in a specified manner (*interpreted his gesture as mocking*). □□ **interpretable** *adj.* **interpretability** *n.* **interpretation** *n.* **interpretational** *adj.* **interpretative** /-táytiv/ *adj.* **interpretive** *adj.* **interpretively** *adv.* [ME f. OF *interpreter* or L *interpretari* explain, translate f. *interpres -pretis* explainer]

■ **1, 2** explain, explicate, clarify, elucidate, illuminate, throw *or* shed light on; define, spell out, simplify, paraphrase; decipher, decode, translate, gloss, make sense (out) of, figure *or* work out, unravel. **3** translate; lip-read. **4** explain, understand, construe, take (to mean), read, see, analyze, diagnose. □□ **interpretation** explanation, explication, exegesis, clarification, elucidation, illumination, exposition, definition, simplification, paraphrase; performance, rendering, rendition, twist, treatment, approach; decipherment, translation, gloss; understanding, construal, reading, analysis, diagnosis.

interpreter /intə́rpritər/ *n.* a person who interprets, esp. one who translates speech orally. [ME f. AF *interpretour*, OF *interpreteur* f. LL *interpretator -oris* (as INTERPRET)]

interprovincial /íntərprəvínshəl/ *adj.* situated or carried on between provinces.

interracial /íntəráyshəl/ *adj.* existing between or affecting different races. □□ **interracially** *adv.*

interregnum /íntərrégnəm/ *n.* (*pl.* **interregnums** or **interregna** /-nə/) **1** an interval when the normal government is suspended, esp. between successive reigns or regimes. **2** an interval or pause. [L (as INTER-, *regnum* reign)]

■ see INTERVAL 1.

interrelate /íntəriláyt/ *v.tr.* relate (two or more things) to each other. □□ **interrelation** /-láyshən/ *n.* **interrelationship** *n.*

interrog. *abbr.* interrogative.

interrogate /intérəgayt/ *v.tr.* ask questions of (a person) esp. closely, thoroughly, or formally. □□ **interrogator** *n.* [ME f. L *interrogare interrogat-* ask (as INTER-, *rogare* ask)]

■ see QUESTION 1, 2.

interrogation /intérəgáyshən/ *n.* **1** the act or an instance of interrogating; the process of being interrogated. **2** a question or inquiry. □ **interrogation point** (or **mark**, etc.) = *question mark*. □□ **interrogational** *adj.* [ME f. F *interrogation* or L *interrogatio* (as INTERROGATE)]

■ questioning, examination, cross-examination, investigation, third degree, grilling; inquiry, query, inquest, probe, *usu. derog.* inquisition.

interrogative /íntərógətiv/ *adj. & n.* ● *adj.* **1 a** of or like a question; used in questions. **b** *Gram.* (of an adjective or pronoun) asking a question (e.g., *who?, which?*). **2** having the form or force of a question. **3** suggesting inquiry (*an interrogative tone*). ● *n.* an interrogative word (e.g., *what?, why?*). □□ **interrogatively** *adv.* [LL *interrogativus* (as INTERROGATE)]

interrogatory /íntərógətáwree/ *adj. & n.* ● *adj.* questioning; of or suggesting inquiry (*an interrogatory eyebrow*). ● *n.* (*pl.* **-ies**) a formal set of questions, esp. *Law* one formally put to an accused person, etc. [LL *interrogatorius* (as INTERROGATE)]

interrupt /íntərúpt/ *v.tr.* **1** act so as to break the continuous progress of (an action, speech, a person speaking, etc.). **2** obstruct (a person's view, etc.). **3** break or suspend the continuity of. □□ **interruptible** *adj.* **interruption** /-rúpshən/ *n.* **interruptive** *adj.* **interruptory** *adj.* [ME f. L *interrumpere interrupt-* (as INTER-, *rumpere* break)]

■ **1** break in on, intrude into, butt in on, barge in on, *sl.* horn in on; heckle, snap up, take up; punctuate; disturb, disrupt, derange; hold up, halt, cut off *or* short; (*absol.*) break in, strike in, cut in, *colloq.* chip in. **2** block, cut off, obstruct, impede, hinder, hamper, interfere with. **3** discontinue, suspend, break off, adjourn, leave off, cut short; halt, stop, end, arrest, terminate, cease, pause. □□ **interruption** intrusion, disturbance, interference, intervention, disruption, derangement; stoppage, holdup, halt, delay, check; obstruction, blockage, impediment, hindrance; break, adjournment, respite, rest, lull, stop, pause, intermission, interlude; gap, interval, lacuna, hiatus, space, *Prosody* caesura, *colloq.* letup; suspension, cessation, termination, cut, *literary* surcease.

interrupter /íntərúptər/ *n.* (also **interruptor**) **1** a person or thing that interrupts. **2** a device for interrupting, esp. an electric circuit.

intersect /íntərsékt/ *v.* **1** *tr.* divide (a thing) by passing or lying across it. **2** *intr.* (of lines, roads, etc.) cross or cut each other. [L *intersecare intersect-* (as INTER-, *secare* cut)]

■ **1** see CROSS *v.* 1. **2** see CROSS *v.* 2a.

intersection /íntərsékshən/ *n.* **1** the act of intersecting. **2** a place where two roads intersect. **3** a point or line common to lines or planes that intersect. □□ **intersectional** *adj.* [L *intersectio* (as INTERSECT)]

■ **1** see MEETING 1. **2** see JUNCTION 2.

interseptal /íntərséptəl/ *adj.* between septa or partitions.

intersex /íntərseks/ *n.* **1** the abnormal condition of being intermediate between male and female. **2** an individual in this condition.

intersexual /íntərséksho͞oəl/ *adj.* **1** existing between the sexes. **2** of intersex. □□ **intersexuality** /-álitee/ *n.* **intersexually** *adv.*

interspace *n. & v.* ● *n.* /íntərspáys/ an interval of space or time. ● *v.tr.* /íntərspáys/ put interspaces between.

■ *n.* see INTERVAL 1.

interspecific /íntərspəsífik/ *adj.* formed from different species.

intersperse /íntərspə́rs/ *v.tr.* **1** (often foll. by *between*, *among*) scatter; place here and there. **2** (foll. by *with*) diversify (a thing or things with others so scattered). □□ **interspersion** /-pérzhən/ *n.* [L *interspergere interspers-* (as INTER-, *spargere* scatter)]

■ **2** see PUNCTUATE.

interspinal /íntərspínəl/ *adj.* (also **interspinous** /-spínəs/) between spines or spinous processes.

interstate *adj. & n.* ● *adj.* /íntərstáyt/ existing or carried on between states, esp. of the US. ● *n.* /íntərstayt/ a highway that is part of the US Interstate Highway System. □□ **Interstate Highway System** a network of divided highways designed for fast intercity and urban travel.

■ *n.* autobahn, autoroute, autostrada, expressway, motorway, turnpike.

interstellar /íntərstélər/ *adj.* occurring or situated between stars.

interstice /intə́rstis/ *n.* **1** an intervening space. **2** a chink or crevice. [L *interstitium* (as INTER-, *sistere stit-* stand)]

■ **1** see INTERVAL 1.

interstitial /íntərstíshəl/ *adj.* of, forming, or occupying interstices. □□ **interstitially** *adv.*

/.../ **pronunciation**	● **part of speech**
□ **phrases, idioms, and compounds**	
□□ **derivatives**	■ **synonym section**
cross-references appear in SMALL CAPITALS or *italics*	

intertextuality /ìntərtékschōō-álitee/ *n.* the relationship between esp. literary texts.

intertidal /ìntərtíd'l/ *adj.* of or relating to the area which is covered at high tide and uncovered at low tide.

intertribal /ìntərtríbəl/ *adj.* existing or occurring between different tribes.

intertrigo /ìntərtrígō/ *n.* (*pl.* **-os**) *Med.* inflammation from the rubbing of one area of skin on another. [L f. *interterere intertrit-* (as INTER-, *terere* rub)]

intertwine /ìntərtwín/ *v.* **1** *tr.* (often foll. by *with*) entwine (together). **2** *intr.* become entwined. □□ **intertwinement** *n.*
- see ENTWINE 1, 3.

intertwist /ìntərtwíst/ *v.tr.* twist together.
- see TANGLE¹ *v.* 1.

interval /ìntərvəl/ *n.* **1** an intervening time or space. **2** *Brit.* a pause or break, esp. between the parts of a theatrical or musical performance. **3** the difference in pitch between two sounds. **4** the distance between persons or things in respect of qualities. □ **at intervals** here and there; now and then. □□ **intervallic** /-válik/ *adj.* [ME ult. f. L *intervallum* space between ramparts, interval (as INTER-, *vallum* rampart)]
- **1** meanwhile, meantime, interim, interregnum; interspace, interstice, space, gap, blank, opening, lacuna, hiatus, window, daylight, clearance; pause, time, spell, period, span, time lag, lapse, wait, delay. □ **at intervals** here and there, (all) around; (every) now and again, (every) now and then, periodically, (every) once in a while, occasionally, on occasion, off and on, on and off, intermittently, (every) so often, from time to time, sporadically.

intervene /ìntərveén/ *v.intr.* (often foll. by *between, in*) **1** occur in time between events. **2** interfere; come between so as to prevent or modify the result or course of events. **3** be situated between things. **4** come in as an extraneous factor or thing. **5** *Law* interpose in a lawsuit as a third party. □□ **intervener** *n.* **intervenient** *adj.* **intervenor** *n.* [L *intervenire* (as INTER-, *venire* come)]
- **2** interfere, meddle, intrude, strike in, put *or* stick one's oar in, *colloq.* poke one's nose in; interrupt, break in, barge in, butt in, strike in, *sl.* horn in; step in, intercede, mediate.

intervention /ìntərvénshən/ *n.* **1** the act or an instance of intervening. **2** interference, esp. by a state in another's affairs. **3** mediation. [ME f. F *intervention* or L *interventio* (as INTERVENE)]
- **1, 2** see INTERFERENCE 1. **3** see AGENCY 2b.

interventionist /ìntərvénshənist/ *n.* a person who favors intervention.

intervertebral /ìntərvértibrəl/ *adj.* between vertebrae.

interview /ìntərvyōō/ *n. & v.* ● *n.* **1** an oral examination of an applicant for employment, a college place, etc. **2** a conversation between a reporter, etc., and a person of public interest, used as a basis of a broadcast or publication. **3** a meeting of persons face to face, esp. for consultation. ● *v.tr.* **1** hold an interview with. **2** question to discover the opinions or experience of (a person). □□ **interviewee** /-vyōō-eé/ *n.* **interviewer** *n.* [F *entrevue* f. *s'entrevoir* see each other (as INTER-, *voir* f. L *vidère* see: see VIEW)]
- *n.* **1** examination, evaluation, appraisal, vetting, assessment, grilling; viva voce, *colloq.* oral; *Brit. colloq.* viva. **2** conversation, discussion, talk, chat, tête-à-tête; press conference, audience. **3** meeting, conference, discussion, consultation, colloquy, dialogue. ● *v.* **1** examine, appraise, evaluate, assess. **2** question, interrogate, sound out, quiz, pump, grill, check out, *colloq.* vet, *Brit. colloq.* viva; talk *or* chat with *or* to. □□ **interviewee** see CANDIDATE 1, 3.

interwar /ìntərwáwr/ *adj.* existing in the period between two wars, esp. the two world wars.

interweave /ìntərweév/ *v.tr.* (*past* **-wove** /-wóv/; *past part.* **-woven** /-wóvən/) **1** (often foll. by *with*) weave together. **2** blend intimately.
- **1** see WEAVE¹ *v.* 1b.

interwind /ìntərwínd/ *v.tr. & intr.* (*past* and *past part.* **-wound** /-wównd/) wind together.

interwork /ìntərwórk/ *v.* **1** *intr.* work together or interactively. **2** *tr.* interweave.

intestate /intéstayt, -tət/ *adj. & n.* ● *adj.* (of a person) not having made a will before death. ● *n.* a person who has died intestate. □□ **intestacy** /-téstəsee/ *n.* [ME f. L *intestatus* (as IN-¹, *testari testat-* make a will f. *testis* witness)]

intestine /intéstin/ *n.* (in *sing.* or *pl.*) the lower part of the alimentary canal from the end of the stomach to the anus. □ **large intestine** the cecum, colon, and rectum collectively. **small intestine** the duodenum, jejunum, and ileum collectively. □□ **intestinal** *adj.* [L *intestinum* f. *intestinus* internal]
- see BOWEL 1.

inthrall var. of ENTHRALL.

intifada /íntifaádə/ *n.* a movement of Palestinian uprising in the Israeli-occupied West Bank and Gaza Strip, beginning in 1987. [Arab., = uprising]

intimacy /íntiməsee/ *n.* (*pl.* **-ies**) **1** the state of being intimate. **2** an intimate act, esp. sexual intercourse. **3** an intimate remark; an endearment.
- **1** see FRIENDSHIP 1. **2** see SEX *n.* 5.

intimate¹ /íntimət/ *adj. & n.* ● *adj.* **1** closely acquainted; familiar; close (*an intimate friend*; *an intimate relationship*). **2** private and personal (*intimate thoughts*). **3** (usu. foll. by *with*) having sexual relations. **4** (of knowledge) detailed; thorough. **5** (of a relationship between things) close. **6** (of mixing, etc.) thorough. **7** essential; intrinsic. **8** (of a place, etc.) friendly; promoting close personal relationships. ● *n.* a very close friend. □□ **intimately** *adv.* [L *intimus* inmost]
- *adj.* **1** close, attached, inseparable, devoted, friendly, *colloq.* pally, chummy, thick; near, personal, familiar, bosom, boon, special, particular, dear, cherished. **2** private, personal, interior, secret, confidential, hidden, *archaic* privy; interesting; spicy, *colloq.* juicy. **4, 6** detailed, deep, profound, extensive, comprehensive, full, complete, total, thorough, exhaustive, meticulous, painstaking. **5** close, near, tight. **7** essential, intrinsic, inherent, fundamental, basic, elemental, elementary, organic, natural. **8** friendly, congenial, convivial, clubby, easy, relaxed, casual, informal, *colloq.* laid-back; cozy, snug, homely, comfortable, warm, welcoming, tête-à-tête, gemütlich, *colloq.* comfy. ● *n.* (best) friend, (boon) companion, second self, confidant, crony, familiar, partner, boyfriend, girlfriend, alter ego, *fidus Achates*, comrade, mate, soul mate, brother, sister, *colloq.* sidekick, chum, pal, buddy, amigo, *Austral. & NZ colloq.* cobber, *joc.* (old) retainer.

intimate² /íntimayt/ *v.tr.* **1** (often foll. by *that* + clause) state or make known. **2** imply; hint. □□ **intimater** *n.* **intimation** /-máyshən/ *n.* [LL *intimare* announce f. L *intimus* inmost]
- **1** state, make (it) known, announce, say, assert, asseverate, declare, affirm, mention, impart, *formal* aver; maintain, claim, allege. **2** hint, imply, suggest, insinuate; indicate, give a person to understand; warn, caution, tip a person off. □□ **intimation** see HINT *n.* 1.

intimidate /intímidayt/ *v.tr.* frighten or overawe, esp. to subdue or influence. □□ **intimidation** /-dáyshən/ *n.* **intimidator** *n.* [med.L *intimidare* (as IN-², *timidare* f. *timidus* TIMID)]
- frighten, terrify, petrify, scare, alarm, ruffle, unnerve, daunt, cow, dismay, awe, overawe, *archaic* concuss; terrorize, tyrannize, bully, menace, threaten, pressure, pressurize, railroad, browbeat, hector, haze, *colloq.* faze, psych (out), bulldoze, lean on, push around, put the screws on. □□ **intimidation** see TERROR 1, THREAT 1.

intinction /intíngkshən/ *n. Eccl.* the dipping of the Eucharistic bread in the wine so that the communicant receives both together. [LL *intinctio* f. L *intingere intinct-* (as IN-², TINGE)]

intitule /intíchōōl/ *v.tr. Brit.* entitle (an Act of Parliament, etc.). [OF *intituler* f. LL *intitulare* (as IN-², *titulare* f. *titulus* title)]

into /íntōō/ *prep.* **1** expressing motion or direction to a point on or within (*walked into a tree*; *ran into the house*). **2** expressing direction of attention or concern (*will look into it*).

3 expressing a change of state (*turned into a dragon*; *separated into groups*; *forced into cooperation*). **4** *colloq.* interested in; knowledgeable about (*is really into art*). [OE *intō* (as IN, TO)]

intolerable /intólərəbəl/ *adj.* that cannot be endured. □□ **intolerableness** *n.* **intolerably** *adv.* [ME f. OF *intolerable* or L *intolerabilis* (as IN-¹, TOLERABLE)]
- see UNBEARABLE.

intolerant /intólərənt/ *adj.* not tolerant, esp. of views, beliefs, or behavior differing from one's own. □□ **intolerance** /-rəns/ *n.* **intolerantly** *adv.* [L *intolerans* (as IN-¹, TOLERANT)]
- impatient, unforgiving, uncompromising, inflexible; (self-)opinionated, narrow-minded, blinkered, illiberal, dogmatic; biased, prejudiced, bigoted. □□ **intolerance** impatience, unforgivingness, uncompromisingness, inflexibility; opinionatedness, self-opinion, narrow-mindedness, illiberality, dogmatism; bias, prejudice, bigotry.

intonate /íntōnayt/ *v.tr.* intone. [med.L *intonare*: see INTONE]

intonation /íntōnáyshən/ *n.* **1** modulation of the voice; accent. **2** the act of intoning. **3** accuracy of pitch in playing or singing (*has good intonation*). **4** the opening phrase of a plainsong melody. □□ **intonational** *adj.* [med.L *intonatio* (as INTONE)]
- **1** accent, accentuation, (tonal) inflection, cadence, prosody, tone (of voice), tonicity, tonality, modulation, pitch. **2** chanting; articulation, pronunciation, phonation, vocalization, utterance. **3** (perfect *or* absolute) pitch.

intone /intōn/ *v.tr.* **1** recite (prayers, etc.) with prolonged sounds, esp. in a monotone. **2** utter with a particular tone. □□ **intoner** *n.* [med.L *intonare* (as IN-², L *tonus* TONE)]
- chant, sing, cantillate.

in toto /in tōtō/ *adv.* completely. [L]
- see ENTIRELY 1.

intoxicant /intóksikənt/ *adj.* & *n.* ● *adj.* intoxicating. ● *n.* an intoxicating substance.
- *n.* see LIQUOR *n.* 1.

intoxicate /intóksikayt/ *v.tr.* **1** make drunk. **2** excite or elate beyond self-control. □□ **intoxication** /-káyshən/ *n.* [med.L *intoxicare* (as IN-², *toxicare* poison f. L *toxicum*): see TOXIC]
- **1** inebriate, stupefy, befuddle, *sl.* zonk; fluster, mellow. **2** excite, arouse, overwhelm, elate, exhilarate, delight, enchant, transport, carry away, entrance, enrapture, captivate, ravish, thrill, galvanize, electrify, make one's head spin, take one's breath away, *colloq.* get, freak (out), bowl over, turn on, *sl.* send, zonk. □□ **intoxication** see *drunkenness* (DRUNKEN).

intoxicating /intóksikayting/ *adj.* **1** liable to cause intoxication; alcoholic. **2** exhilarating; exciting. □□ **intoxicatingly** *adv.*
- **1** alcoholic, spirituous, inebriant; potent. **2** exhilarating, invigorating, thrilling, exciting, heady, potent, stimulating, electrifying, entrancing, fascinating.

intr. *abbr.* intransitive.

intra- /íntrə/ *prefix* forming adjectives usu. from adjectives, meaning 'on the inside, within' (*intramural*). [L *intra* inside]

intracellular /íntrəsélyələr/ *adj.* Biol. located or occurring within a cell or cells.

intracranial /íntrəkráyneeəl/ *adj.* within the skull. □□ **intracranially** *adv.*

intractable /intráktəbəl/ *adj.* **1** hard to control or deal with. **2** difficult; stubborn. □□ **intractability** *n.* **intractableness** *n.* **intractably** *adv.* [L *intractabilis* (as INTRA-, TRACTABLE)]
- see STUBBORN. □□ **intractability** see *obstinacy* (OBSTINATE).

intrados /íntrədos, -dōs, intráydos, -dōs/ *n.* the lower or inner curve of an arch. [F (as INTRA-, *dos* back f. L *dorsum*)]

intramolecular /íntrəmələkyələr/ *adj.* within a molecule.

intramural /íntrəmyoŏrəl/ *adj.* **1** situated or done within walls. **2** forming part of normal university or college studies. □□ **intramurally** *adv.*

intramuscular /íntrəmúskyələr/ *adj.* in or into a muscle or muscles.

intransigent /intránsijənt, -tránz-/ *adj.* & *n.* ● *adj.* uncompromising; stubborn. ● *n.* an intransigent person. □□ **intransigence** /-jəns/ *n.* **intransigency** *n.* **intransigently** *adv.* [F *intransigeant* f. Sp. *los intransigentes* extreme republicans in Cortes, ult. formed as IN-¹ + L *transigere transigent*-come to an understanding (as TRANS-, *agere* act)]
- *adj.* see STUBBORN. □□ **intransigence** see *obstinacy* (OBSTINATE).

intransitive /intránsitiv, -tránz-/ *adj.* (of a verb or sense of a verb) that does not take or require a direct object (whether expressed or implied), e.g., *look* in *look at the sky* (opp. TRANSITIVE). □□ **intransitively** *adv.* **intransitivity** /-tívitee/ *n.* [LL *intransitivus* (as IN-¹, TRANSITIVE)]

intrauterine /íntrəyoŏtərin, -rin/ *adj.* within the uterus. □ **intrauterine device** a device inserted into the uterus that provides birth control by preventing implantation. ¶ Abbr.: IUD.

intravenous /íntrəvéeənəs/ *adj.* in or into a vein or veins. □□ **intravenously** *adv.* [INTRA- + L *vena* vein]

intrepid /intrépid/ *adj.* fearless; very brave. □□ **intrepidity** /-tripíditee/ *n.* **intrepidly** *adv.* [F *intrépide* or L *intrepidus* (as IN-¹, *trepidus* alarmed)]
- fearless, unafraid, dauntless, undaunted, unshrinking; courageous, brave, valiant, valorous, heroic, lionhearted, martial, manly, manful, *archaic or joc.* doughty, *colloq.* spunky, gutsy; bold, daring, audacious, spirited, plucky, game, gallant, dashing, adventurous, venturesome, daredevil; steadfast, resolute, indomitable, stout, tough, hardy, gritty, stalwart, stouthearted. □□ **intrepidity** see ASSURANCE 5a, BRAVERY.

intricate /íntrikit/ *adj.* very complicated; perplexingly detailed or obscure. □□ **intricacy** /-kəsee/ *n.* (*pl.* **-ies**). **intricately** *adv.* [ME f. L *intricare intricat*- (as IN-², *tricare* f. *tricae* tricks)]
- complicated, complex, involved, convoluted, convolutional, involute, involuted, tangled, tangly, knotty, tortuous, sinuous, labyrinthine; elaborate, Byzantine, fancy, ornate, rococo, flowery, busy, detailed; obscure, perplexing, puzzling, mystifying, enigmatic. □□ **intricacy** see SUBTLETY 1.

intrigant /íntrigənt/ *n.* (*fem.* **intrigante**) an intriguer. [F *intriguant* f. *intriguer*: see INTRIGUE]

intrigue *v.* & *n.* ● *v.* /intréeg/ (**intrigues**, **intrigued**, **intriguing**) **1** *intr.* (foll. by *with*) **a** carry on an underhand plot. **b** use secret influence. **2** *tr.* arouse the curiosity of; fascinate. ● *n.* /intréeg, ín-/ **1** an underhand plot or plotting. **2** *archaic* a secret love affair. □□ **intriguer** /intréegər/ *n.* **intriguing** /intréeging/*adj.* (esp. in sense 2 of *v.*). **intriguingly** *adv.* [F *intrigue* (n.), *intriguer* (v.) f. It. *intrigo, intrigare* f. L (as INTRICATE)]
- *v.* **1** conspire, plot, machinate, scheme, collude, connive, maneuver. **2** interest, engross, absorb, engage; fascinate, beguile, captivate, enthrall, allure, attract, charm. ● *n.* **1** conspiracy, plot, scheme, machination, collusion, cabal, maneuver, stratagem; connivance, trickery, chicanery, double-dealing, skulduggery, subterfuge. **2** see AFFAIR 3. □□ **intriguing** see INTERESTING.

intrinsic /intrínzik/ *adj.* inherent; essential; belonging naturally (*intrinsic value*). □□ **intrinsically** *adv.* [ME, = interior, f. F *intrinsèque* f. LL *intrinsecus* f. L *intrinsecus* (adv.) inwardly]
- inherent, essential, implicit, basic, fundamental, elemental, natural, native, innate, connate, proper, peculiar, inborn, inbred, congenital, inherited, hereditary, constitutional, organic, structural, underlying, built-in, integral, ingrained, engrained,

---

/.../ **pronunciation**	● **part of speech**
□ **phrases, idioms, and compounds**	
□□ **derivatives**	■ **synonym section**
cross-references appear in SMALL CAPITALS or *italics*	

instinctive, in one's blood; immanent, indwelling, internal.

intro /íntrō/ *n.* (*pl.* **-os**) *colloq.* an introduction. [abbr.]

intro- /íntrō/ *comb. form* into (*introgression*). [L *intro* to the inside]

intro. *abbr.* **1** introduction. **2** introductory.

introduce /íntrədōōs, -dyōōs/ *v.tr.* **1** (foll. by *to*) make (a person or oneself) known by name to another, esp. formally. **2** announce or present to an audience. **3** bring (a custom, idea, etc.) into use. **4** bring (a piece of legislation) before a legislative assembly. **5** (foll. by *to*) draw the attention or extend the understanding of (a person) to a subject. **6** insert; place in. **7** bring in; usher in; bring forward. **8** begin; occur just before the start of. □□ **introducer** *n.* **introducible** *adj.* [ME f. L *introducere introduct-* (as INTRO-, *ducere* lead)]

■ **1** (*introduce to*) acquaint with, present to, make known to. **2** present, give, offer; announce. **3** inaugurate, initiate, instigate, originate, pioneer, set *or* get going, get under way, bring in, set in motion; establish, institute, set up, put in, install, implant, induct. **4** put forward, propose, table, move, present. **5** (*introduce to*) acquaint with, familiarize with, inform of *or* about, tell about, make aware of, draw *or* direct a person's attention to, open a person's eyes to; notify of, apprise of, advise of *or* about. **6** see INSERT *v.* **7** bring in *or* forward *or* up, advance, present, raise, broach, mention, moot; drag in, foist in, lug in, trot out. **8** begin, start, open, get going *or* started, put into operation *or* motion, *colloq.* get off the ground, kick off, *formal* commence; precede, come *or* go before; preface, prelude, prologue.

introduction /íntrədúkshən/ *n.* **1** the act or an instance of introducing; the process of being introduced. **2** a formal presentation of one person to another. **3** an explanatory section at the beginning of a book, etc. **4** a preliminary section in a piece of music, often thematically different from the main section. **5** an introductory treatise on a subject. **6** a thing introduced. [ME f. OF *introduction* or L *introductio* (as INTRODUCE)]

■ **1** see INSTITUTION 1. **2** presentation, knockdown. **3, 5** see PREAMBLE.

introductory /íntrədúktəree/ *adj.* serving as an introduction; preliminary. [LL *introductorius* (as INTRODUCTION)]

■ opening, initial, inaugural, initiatory; prefatory, prodromal, prodromic, preambular, preludial, preliminary, precursory, preparatory; first, primary, basic, fundamental, elementary, rudimentary.

introit /íntroyt/ *n.* a psalm or antiphon sung or said while the priest approaches the altar for the Eucharist. [ME f. OF f. L *introitus* f. *introire introit-* enter (as INTRO-, *ire* go)]

introjection /íntrəjékshən/ *n.* the unconscious incorporation of external ideas into one's mind. [INTRO- after *projection*]

intromit /íntrəmít/ *v.tr.* (**intromitted, intromitting**) **1** *archaic* (foll. by *into*) let in; admit. **2** insert. □□ **intromission** /-míshən/ *n.* **intromittent** *adj.* [L *intromittere intromiss-* introduce (as INTRO-, *mittere* send)]

■ **2** see INJECT 1.

introspection /íntrəspékshən/ *n.* the examination or observation of one's own mental and emotional processes, etc. □□ **introspective** *adj.* **introspectively** *adv.* **introspectiveness** *n.* [L *introspicere introspect-* look inwards (as INTRO-, *specere* look)]

■ □□ **introspective** see THOUGHTFUL 1.

introvert *n.*, *adj.*, & *v.* ● *n.* /íntrəvərt/ **1** *Psychol.* a person predominantly concerned with his or her own thoughts and feelings rather than with external things. **2** a shy, inwardly thoughtful person. ● *adj.* /íntrəvərt/ (also **introverted** /-tid/) typical or characteristic of an introvert. ● *v.tr.* /íntrəvə́rt/ **1** *Psychol.* direct (one's thoughts or mind) inward. **2** *Zool.* withdraw (an organ, etc.) within its own tube or base, like the finger of a glove. □□ **introversion** /-vérzhən, -shən/ *n.* **introversive** /-vérsiv/ *adj.* **introverted** *adj.* **introvertive** /-vərtiv/ *adj.* [INTRO- + *vert* as in INVERT]

■ *adj.* (**introverted**) see SHY 1.

intrude /intrōod/ *v.* (foll. by *on, upon, into*) **1** *intr.* come uninvited or unwanted; force oneself abruptly on others. **2** *tr.* thrust or force (something unwelcome) on a person. □□ **intrudingly** *adv.* [L *intrudere intrus-* (as IN-², *trudere* thrust)]

■ **1** encroach, impinge, obtrude, trespass, infringe, invade; interfere, meddle, put or stick one's oar in, *colloq.* poke one's nose in; intervene, step in; (*intrude on or into*) break in on, interrupt, butt in on, barge in on, push in on, *colloq.* muscle in on, *sl.* horn in on. **2** see THRUST *v.* 2.

intruder /intrōodər/ *n.* a person who intrudes, esp. into a building with criminal intent.

■ housebreaker, (cat) burglar, thief, robber, *sl.* cracksman, yegg; incomer, interloper, encroacher, impinger, obtruder, trespasser, infringer, invader; gatecrasher, unwelcome visitor, cuckoo in the nest, squatter; interferer, meddler, busybody, *colloq.* snoop, snooper, kibitzer, Nosy Parker.

intrusion /intrōozhən/ *n.* **1** the act or an instance of intruding. **2** an unwanted interruption, etc. **3** *Geol.* an influx of molten rock between or through strata, etc., but not reaching the surface. **4** the occupation of a vacant estate, etc., to which one has no claim. [ME f. OF *intrusion* or med.L *intrusio* (as INTRUDE)]

■ **1** see IMPOSITION 2. **2** see interruption (INTERRUPT).

intrusive /intrōosiv/ *adj.* **1** that intrudes or tends to intrude. **2** characterized by intrusion. □□ **intrusively** *adv.* **intrusiveness** *n.*

■ interfering, interruptive, interruptory, intervenient, obtrusive, invasive; meddlesome, prying, inquisitive, busy, officious, *colloq.* nosy, snoopy; importunate, forward, presumptuous, *colloq.* pushy; uninvited, undesirable, unwelcome, uncalled-for, unwanted, unsought.

intrust var. of ENTRUST.

intubate /íntōobayt, -tyōō-/ *v.tr. Med.* insert a tube into the trachea for ventilation, usu. during anesthesia. □□ **intubation** /-báyshən/ *n.* [IN-² + L *tuba* tube]

intuit /intōoit, -tyōō-/ *v.* **1** *tr.* know by intuition. **2** *intr.* receive knowledge by direct perception. □□ **intuitable** *adj.* [L *intueri intuit-* consider (as IN-², *tueri* look)]

■ see SENSE *v.*

intuition /íntōo-íshən, -tyōō-/ *n.* **1** immediate apprehension by the mind without reasoning. **2** immediate apprehension by a sense. **3** immediate insight. □□ **intuitional** *adj.* [LL *intuitio* (as INTUIT)]

■ instinct, insight, inspiration, sixth sense, (extrasensory) perception, sensitivity, percipience, perceptiveness, perspicacity; presentiment, premonition, foreboding, hunch, sense, impression, notion, inkling, funny feeling, sneaking suspicion, *Buddhism* satori.

intuitionism /íntōo-íshənizəm, -tyōō-/ *n.* (also **intuitionalism**) *Philos.* the belief that primary truths and principles (esp. of ethics and metaphysics) are known directly by intuition. □□ **intuitionist** *n.*

intuitive /intōoitiv, -tyōō-/ *adj.* **1** of, characterized by, or possessing intuition. **2** perceived by intuition. □□ **intuitively** *adv.* **intuitiveness** *n.* [med.L *intuitivus* (as INTUIT)]

■ see INSTINCTIVE 1.

intuitivism /intōoitivizəm, -tyōō-/ *n.* the doctrine that ethical principles can be established by intuition. □□ **intuitivist** *n.*

intumesce /íntōomés, -tyōō-/ *v.intr.* swell up. □□ **intumescence** *n.* **intumescent** *adj.* [L *intumescere* (as IN-², *tumescere* incept. of *tumēre* swell)]

■ □□ **intumescence** see GROWTH 4.

intussusception /íntəsəsépshən/ *n.* **1** *Med.* the inversion of one portion of the intestine within another. **2** *Bot.* the deposition of new cellulose particles in a cell wall, to increase the surface area of the cell. [F *intussusception* or mod.L *intussusceptio* f. L *intus* within + *susceptio* f. *suscipere* take up]

intwine var. of ENTWINE.

Inuit /ínyōō-it/ *n.* (also **Innuit**) (*pl.* same or **Inuits**) a N. American Eskimo. [Eskimo *inuit* people]

inundate /ínəndayt/ *v.tr.* (often foll. by *with*) **1** flood. **2** over-

whelm (*inundated with inquiries*). □□ **inundation** /-dáyshən/ *n.* [L *inundare* flow (as IN-², *unda* wave)]
■ **1** see FLOOD *v.* 1. **2** see GLUT *v.* 2, 3. □□ **inundation** see FLOOD *n.* 1.

inure /inyŏŏr/ *v.* **1** *tr.* (often in *passive*; foll. by *to*) accustom (a person) to something esp. unpleasant. **2** *intr. Law* come into operation; take effect. □□ **inurement** *n.* [ME f. AF *eneurer* f. phr. *en eure* (both unrecorded) in use or practice, f. *en* in + OF *e(u)vre* work f. L *opera*]
■ **1** see CONDITION *v.* 2.

in utero /in yŏŏtərō/ *adv.* in the womb; before birth. [L]

in vacuo /in vákyŏŏ-ō/ *adv.* in a vacuum. [L]

invade /inváyd/ *v.tr.* (often *absol.*) **1** enter (a country, etc.) under arms to control or subdue it. **2** swarm into. **3** (of a disease) attack (a body, effect. etc.). **4** encroach upon (a person's rights, esp. privacy). □□ **invader** *n.* [L *invadere invas-* (as IN-², *vadere* go)]
■ **1** see OCCUPY 4. **2** see INFEST. **3** see ATTACK *v.* 4. **4** see ENCROACH 1. □□ **invader** see INTRUDER.

invaginate /invájinayt/ *v.tr.* **1** put in a sheath. **2** turn (a tube) inside out. □□ **invagination** /-náyshən/ *n.* [IN-² + L *vagina* sheath]

invalid¹ /ínvəlid/ *n. & v.* ● *n.* **1** a person enfeebled or disabled by illness or injury. **2** (*attrib.*) **a** of or for invalids (*invalid car; invalid diet*). **b** being an invalid (*caring for her invalid mother*). ● *v.* **1** *tr.* (often foll. by *out*, etc.) remove from active service (one who has become an invalid). **2** *tr.* (usu. in *passive*) disable (a person) by illness. **3** *intr.* become an invalid. □□ **invalidism** *n.* [L *invalidus* weak, infirm (as IN-¹, VALID)]
■ *n.* **1** valetudinarian, convalescent, patient, casualty, sufferer, cripple. **2 a** disabled. **b** disabled, handicapped, incapacitated, crippled, weakened, debilitated, lame; game, *archaic* halt; see also ILL *adj.* 1. ● *v.* **2** disable, incapacitate, indispose, immobilize, hospitalize, put out of action, lay up, cripple, paralyze, lame, wound, maim, weaken, enfeeble. **3** take to one's bed, keep one's bed, be(come) confined to a wheelchair, become housebound.

invalid² /inválid/ *adj.* not valid, esp. having no legal force. □□ **invalidly** *adv.* [L *invalidus* (as INVALID¹)]
■ (null and) void, null (and void), worthless, lapsed; false, spurious, bad, ineffective, *sl.* dud; illegitimate, illegal, unauthorized, irregular, nonstandard, improper, foul; untrue, erroneous, unsound, untenable, incorrect, wrong, faulty, imperfect, impaired.

invalidate /inválidayt/ *v.tr.* **1** make (esp. an argument, etc.) invalid. **2** remove the validity or force of (a treaty, contract, etc.). □□ **invalidation** /-dáyshən/ *n.* [med.L *invalidare invalidat-* (as IN-¹, *validus* VALID)]
■ **1** see DISPROVE. **2** see REVOKE *v.* □□ **invalidation** see REPEAL *n.*

invalidity /ínvəlíditee/ *n.* **1** lack of validity. **2** bodily infirmity. [F *invalidité* or med.L *invaliditas* (as INVALID¹)]

invaluable /invályŏŏəbəl/ *adj.* above valuation; inestimable. □□ **invaluableness** *n.* **invaluably** *adv.*
■ priceless, inestimable, above *or* beyond *or* without price, precious, costly, valuable, expensive, dear; irreplaceable, unique.

invar /inváar, ínvaar/ *n.* an iron-nickel alloy with a negligible coefficient of expansion, used in the manufacture of clocks and scientific instruments. [abbr. of INVARIABLE]

invariable /inváireeəbəl/ *adj.* **1** unchangeable. **2** always the same. **3** *Math.* constant; fixed. □□ **invariability** /-bílitee/ *n.* **invariableness** *n.* **invariably** *adv.* [F *invariable* or LL *invariabilis* (as IN-¹, VARIABLE)]
■ **1** immutable, unchangeable, unalterable, unmodifiable, hard and fast; incommutable, irreversible, irrevocable, inexorable, inflexible. **2** unchanging, changeless, unvarying, invariant, constant, static, steady, stable, flat, level, even, regular, uniform; unfailing, unwavering, certain; permanent, fixed, enduring, abiding, eternal, perpetual; unaltered, unchanged, unvaried, unmodified; fast, set, rigid.

invariant /inváireeənt/ *adj. & n.* ● *adj.* invariable. ● *n.*

Math. a function that remains unchanged when a specified transformation is applied. □□ **invariance** /-reeəns/ *n.*
■ *adj.* see INVARIABLE 2.

invasion /inváyzhən/ *n.* **1** the act of invading or process of being invaded. **2** an entry of a hostile army into a country. □□ **invasive** /-váysiv/ *adj.* [F *invasion* or LL *invasio* (as INVADE)]
■ **1** occupation, incursion, intrusion, infiltration, encroachment, infringement, transgression, violation. **2** occupation, incursion, raid, foray, inroad, attack, assault, onslaught, aggression, offensive, drive, push, advance, storming, blitzkrieg. □□ **invasive** see INTRUSIVE.

invective /invéktiv/ *n.* **1 a** strongly attacking words. **b** the use of these. **2** abusive rhetoric. [ME f. OF f. LL *invectivus* attacking (as INVEIGH)]
■ see ABUSE *n.* 2.

inveigh /inváy/ *v.intr.* (foll. by *against*) speak or write with strong hostility. [L *invehi* go into, assail (as IN-², *vehi* passive of *vehere vect-* carry)]
■ (*inveigh against*) see ATTACK *v.* 3.

inveigle /inváygəl, -veé-/ *v.tr.* (foll. by *into*, or *to* + infin.) entice; persuade by guile. □□ **inveiglement** *n.* [earlier *enve(u)gle* f. AF *envegler*, OF *aveugler* to blind f. *aveugle* blind prob. f. Rmc *ab oculis* (unrecorded) without eyes]
■ see ENTICE. □□ **inveiglement** see *cajolery* (CAJOLE).

invent /invént/ *v.tr.* **1** create by thought; devise; originate (a new method, an instrument, etc.). **2** concoct (a false story, etc.). □□ **inventable** *adj.* [ME, = discover, f. L *invenire invent-* find, contrive (as IN-², *venire vent-* come)]
■ **1** create, devise, contrive, think up, dream up, hatch, conceive, concoct, make up, imagine, formulate, improvise, design, mastermind; originate, generate, father, pioneer, innovate; coin, mint; strike, hit upon, discover. **2** fabricate, make up, concoct, trump up, manufacture, forge, *archaic* feign, *colloq.* cook up.

invention /invénshən/ *n.* **1** the process of inventing. **2** a thing invented; a contrivance, esp. one for which a patent is granted. **3** a fictitious story. **4** inventiveness. **5** *Mus.* a short piece for keyboard, developing a simple idea. [ME f. L *inventio* (as INVENT)]
■ **1** creation, conception, contrivance, concoction, formulation, improvisation, innovation, design, origination, generation; discovery; fabrication, manufacture. **2** creation, contrivance, concoction, design, discovery, device, gadget, innovation, *colloq.* gimmick, *derog. or joc.* contraption, *sl.* gizmo. **3** fiction, fabrication, figment, fantasy, tale, fable, fib, cock-and-bull story, fairy story *or* tale, *colloq.* story, yarn, tall story *or* tale; falsehood, lie, untruth, white lie, half-truth, *sl.* whopper; fake, sham, pretense, prevarication. **4** inventiveness, originality, creativeness, creativity, ingenuity, inspiration, ingeniousness, imagination, imaginativeness, resourcefulness, innovation; giftedness, cleverness, brilliance.

inventive /invéntiv/ *adj.* **1** able or inclined to invent; original in devising. **2** showing ingenuity of devising. □□ **inventively** *adv.* **inventiveness** *n.* [ME f. F *inventif -ive* or med.L *inventivus* (as INVENT)]
■ see ORIGINAL 2. □□ **inventiveness** see ORIGINALITY 1, 2, INVENTION 4.

inventor /invéntər/ *n.* a person who invents, esp. as an occupation.
■ see CREATOR 1.

inventory /ínvəntáwree/ *n. & v.* ● *n.* (*pl.* **-ies**) **1** a complete list of goods in stock, house contents, etc. **2** the goods listed in this. **3** the total of a firm's commercial assets. ● *v.tr.* (**-ies, -ied**) **1** make an inventory of. **2** enter (goods) in an

---

/.../ **pronunciation**	● **part of speech**
□ **phrases, idioms, and compounds**	
□□ **derivatives**	■ **synonym section**
cross-references appear in SMALL CAPITALS *or italics*

inventory. [ME f. med.L *inventorium* f. LL *inventarium* (as INVENT)]

■ *n.* **1** see LIST[1] *n.*

inverse /ínvərs, -və́rs/ *adj.* & *n.* ● *adj.* inverted in position, order, or relation. ● *n.* **1** the state of being inverted. **2** (often foll. by *of*) a thing that is the opposite or reverse of another. **3** *Math.* an element which, when combined with a given element in an operation, produces the identity element for that operation. □ **inverse proportion** (or **ratio**) a relation between two quantities such that one increases in proportion as the other decreases. **inverse square law** a law by which the intensity of an effect, such as gravitational force, illumination, etc., changes in inverse proportion to the square of the distance from the source. □□ **inversely** *adv.* [L *inversus* past part. of *invertere*: see INVERT]

■ *adj.* see REVERSE *adj.*

inversion /invə́rzhən, -shən/ *n.* **1** the act of turning upside down or inside out. **2** the reversal of a normal order, position, or relation. **3** the reversal of the order of words, for rhetorical effect. **4** the reversal of the normal variation of air temperature with altitude. **5** the process or result of inverting. **6** the reversal of direction of rotation of a plane of polarized light. **7** homosexuality. □□ **inversive** /-və́rsiv/ *adj.* [L *inversio* (as INVERT)]

invert *v.* & *n.* ● *v.tr.* /invə́rt/ **1** turn upside down. **2** reverse the position, order, or relation of. **3** *Mus.* change the relative position of the notes of (a chord or interval) by placing the lowest note higher, usu. by an octave. **4** subject to inversion. ● *n.* /ínvərt/ **1** a homosexual. **2** an inverted arch, as at the bottom of a sewer. □ **inverted comma** *Brit.* = *quotation mark.* **inverted snob** *Brit.* a person who likes or takes pride in what a snob might be expected to disapprove of. **invert sugar** a mixture of dextrose and levulose. □□ **inverter** *n.* **invertible** *adj.* **invertibility** *n.* [L *invertere invers-* (as IN-², *vertere* turn)]

■ *v.* **1, 2** see REVERSE *v.* 1.

invertebrate /invə́rtibrət, -brayt/ *adj.* & *n.* ● *adj.* **1** (of an animal) not having a backbone. **2** lacking firmness of character. ● *n.* an invertebrate animal. [mod.L *invertebrata* (pl.) (as IN-¹, VERTEBRA)]

■ *adj.* **1** spineless. **2** see SPINELESS 2.

invest /invést/ *v.* **1** *tr.* (often foll. by *in*) apply or use (money), esp. for profit. **2** *intr.* (foll. by *in*) **a** put money for profit (into stocks, etc.). **b** *colloq.* buy (*invested in a new car*). **3** *tr.* **a** (foll. by *with*) provide *or* endue (a person with qualities, insignia, or rank). **b** (foll. by *in*) attribute or entrust (qualities or feelings to a person). **4** *tr.* cover as a garment. **5** *tr.* lay siege to. □□ **investable** *adj.* **investible** *adj.* **investor** *n.* [ME f. F *investir* or L *investire investit-* (as IN-², *vestire* clothe f. *vestis* clothing): sense 1 f. It. *investire*]

■ **1** allot, put in *or* up, contribute, devote, supply, provide, sink, lay out, spend; venture, risk, stake, gamble, hazard, chance. **2** speculate, *Brit. colloq.* punt; (*invest in*) buy into, buy shares in, buy *or* take a stake in, back, finance, underwrite, *colloq.* stake. **b** (*invest in*) buy, purchase, esp. *Brit. colloq.* lash out on. **3 a** provide, endue, endow, furnish, supply; instate, install, inaugurate, induct, initiate, ordain. **b** entrust, attribute, assign, trust. **4** see COVER *v.* 3a. **5** besiege, lay siege to, beleaguer. □□ **investor** see *backer* (BACK).

investigate /invéstigayt/ *v.* **1** *tr.* **a** inquire into; examine; study carefully. **b** make an official inquiry into. **2** *intr.* make a systematic inquiry or search. □□ **investigator** *n.* **investigatory** /-gətáwree/ *adj.* [L *investigare investigat-* (as IN-², *vestigare* track)]

■ **1** inquire into, make inquiries into, check (up) on, probe, delve into, explore, look into, research, consider, study, analyze, examine, scrutinize, inspect, survey, look at, check, search, sift (through), winnow, go through *or* over (with a fine-tooth comb), check (out); follow up, pursue.

investigation /invéstigáyshən/ *n.* **1** the process or an instance of investigating. **2** a formal examination or study.

■ inquiry, check, probe, exploration, research, consideration, sounding, study, analysis, examination,

scrutiny, inspection, survey, review, look, search, poke, rummage; inquest, *usu. derog.* inquisition, *colloq.* postmortem.

investigative /invéstigaytiv/ *adj.* seeking or serving to investigate, esp. (of journalism) inquiring intensively into controversial issues.

■ see INQUISITIVE 2.

investiture /invéstichŏŏr, -chər/ *n.* **1** the formal investing of a person with honors or rank, esp. a ceremony at which a sovereign confers honors. **2** (often foll. by *with*) the act of enduing (with attributes). [ME f. med.L *investitura* (as INVEST)]

■ **1** see *initiation* (INITIATE).

investment /invéstmənt/ *n.* **1** the act or process of investing. **2** money invested. **3** property, etc., in which money is invested. **4** the act of besieging; a blockade. □ **investment trust** a trust that buys and sells shares in selected companies to make a profit for its members.

■ **2** see STAKE² *n.* 2. **3** see STOCK *n.* 5.

inveterate /invétərət/ *adj.* **1** (of a person) confirmed in an (esp. undesirable) habit, etc. (*an inveterate gambler*). **2 a** (of a habit, etc.) long-established. **b** (of an activity, esp. an undesirable one) habitual. □□ **inveteracy** /-rəsee/ *n.* **inveterately** *adv.* [ME f. L *inveterare inveterat-* make old (as IN-², *vetus veteris* old)]

■ **1** see INCORRIGIBLE 2. **2 b** see INGRAINED 1. □□ **inveterately** see *usually* (USUAL).

invidious /invídeeəs/ *adj.* (of an action, conduct, attitude, etc.) likely to excite resentment or indignation against the person responsible, esp. by real or seeming injustice (*an invidious position; an invidious task*). □□ **invidiously** *adv.* **invidiousness** *n.* [L *invidiosus* f. *invidia* ENVY]

invigilate /invíjilayt/ *v.intr.* **1** keep watch. **2** *Brit.* supervise candidates at an examination. □□ **invigilation** /-láyshən/ *n.* **invigilator** *n.* [orig. = keep watch, f. L *invigilare invigilat-* (as IN-², *vigilare* watch f. *vigil* watchful)]

■ □□ **invigilator** see MONITOR *n.*

invigorate /invígərayt/ *v.tr.* give vigor or strength to. □□ **invigorating** *adj.* **invigoratingly** *adv.* **invigoration** /-ráyshən/ *n.* **invigorative** /-vígərətiv/ *adj.* **invigorator** *n.* [IN-² + med.L *vigorare vigorat-* make strong]

■ fortify, strengthen, reinforce, bolster (up), brace, encourage, hearten, inspirit, animate, energize, enliven, vitalize, vivify, quicken, stimulate, perk up, tone up, *colloq.* boost, pep up; exhilarate, refresh, revive, restore, rejuvenate. □□ **invigorating** bracing, stimulating, exhilarating, tonic, restorative, refreshing, encouraging, rousing, heartening. **invigoration** see REFRESHMENT 1.

invincible /invínsibəl/ *adj.* unconquerable; that cannot be defeated. □□ **invincibility** *n.* **invincibleness** *n.* **invincibly** *adv.* [ME f. OF f. L *invincibilis* (as IN-¹, VINCIBLE)]

■ unconquerable, unbeatable, indomitable, insuperable, unstoppable; invulnerable, indestructible, unassailable, impregnable, impenetrable.

inviolable /invíələbəl/ *adj.* not to be violated or profaned. □□ **inviolability** /-bílitee/ *n.* **inviolably** *adv.* [F *inviolable* or L *inviolabilis* (as IN-¹, VIOLATE)]

■ see SACRED 2b.

inviolate /invíələt/ *adj.* not violated or profaned. □□ **inviolacy** /-ləsee/ *n.* **inviolately** *adv.* **inviolateness** *n.* [ME f. L *inviolatus* (as IN-¹, *violare, violat-* treat violently)]

■ see SACRED 2b.

invisible /invízibəl/ *adj.* **1** not visible to the eye, either characteristically or because hidden. **2** too small to be seen or noticed. **3** artfully concealed so as to be imperceptible. □ **invisible exports** (or **imports**, etc.) items, esp. services, involving payment between countries but not constituting tangible commodities. □□ **invisibility** *n.* **invisibleness** *n.* **invisibly** *adv.* [ME f. OF *invisible* or L *invisibilis* (as IN-¹, VISIBLE)]

■ **1, 2** unseeable, imperceptible, undetectable, indiscernible, unnoticeable, indistinguishable, *poet.* sightless; latent, hidden, blind, unseen, backstage, out of sight; microscopic, infinitesimal, minuscule.

3 veiled, covert, secret, masked, hidden, disguised, camouflaged; subtle, faint.

invitation /ínvitáyshən/ n. **1 a** the process of inviting or fact of being invited, esp. to a social occasion. **b** the spoken or written form in which a person is invited. **2** the action or an act of enticing; attraction; allurement.
■ **1** summons, request, call, bidding, challenge, colloq. invite. **2** attraction, inducement, allure, allurement, enticement, temptation, magnetism, bait, lure, draw, pull.

invite v. & n. • v. /invít/ **1** tr. (often foll. by to, or to + infin.) ask (a person) courteously to come, or to do something (were invited to lunch; invited them to reply). **2** tr. make a formal courteous request for (invited comments). **3** tr. tend to call forth unintentionally (something unwanted). **4 a** tr. attract. **b** intr. be attractive. • n. /ínvit/ colloq. an invitation. □□ **invitee** /-tée/ n. **inviter** n. [F inviter or L invitare]
■ v. **1** ask, summon, archaic or literary bid. **2** see BID v. 2b. **3** see INCUR. **4** see TEMPT 2. • n. see INVITATION 1.

inviting /invíting/ adj. **1** attractive. **2** enticing; tempting. □□ **invitingly** adv. **invitingness** n.
■ attractive, appealing, catching, taking, fetching, winsome, captivating, fascinating, intriguing, engaging; enticing, tempting, alluring, luring, seductive, beguiling, bewitching, entrancing, tantalizing, irresistible.

in vitro /in véetrō/ adv. Biol. (of processes or reactions) taking place in a test tube or other laboratory environment (opp. IN VIVO). [L, = in glass]

in vivo /in véevō/ adv. Biol. (of processes) taking place in a living organism. [L, = in a living thing]

invocation /ínvəkáyshən/ n. **1** the act or an instance of invoking, esp. in prayer. **2** an appeal to a supernatural being or beings, e.g., the Muses, for psychological or spiritual inspiration. **3** Eccl. the words "In the name of the Father," etc., used as the preface to a sermon, etc. □□ **invocatory** /invókətawree/ adj. [ME f. OF f. L invocatio -onis (as INVOKE)]
■ intercession, petition, prayer, supplication, entreaty, obsecration, litany, archaic orison.

invoice /ínvoys/ n. & v. • n. a list of goods shipped or sent, or services rendered, with prices and charges; a bill. • v.tr. **1** make an invoice of (goods and services). **2** send an invoice to (a person). [earlier invoyes pl. of invoy = ENVOY²]
■ n. see BILL¹ n. 1. • v. bill, charge, debit.

invoke /invók/ v.tr. **1** call on (a deity, etc.) in prayer or as a witness. **2** appeal to (the law, a person's authority, etc.). **3** summon (a spirit) by charms. **4** ask earnestly for (vengeance, help, etc.). □□ **invocable** adj. **invoker** n. [F invoquer f. L invocare (as IN-², vocare call)]
■ **1, 2, 4** see APPEAL v. 1.

involucre /ínvəlóokər/ n. **1** a covering or envelope. **2** Anat. a membranous envelope. **3** Bot. a whorl of bracts surrounding an inflorescence. □□ **involucral** /-lóokrəl/ adj. [F involucre or L involucrum (as INVOLVE)]

involuntary /invóləntéree/ adj. **1** done without the exercise of the will; unintentional. **2** (of a limb, muscle, or movement) not under the control of the will. □□ **involuntarily** /-térilee/ adv. **involuntariness** n. [LL involuntarius (as IN-¹, VOLUNTARY)]
■ unconscious, unthinking, unpremeditated, unintentional, unwitting, impulsive, instinctive, instinctual, natural, automatic, mechanical, spontaneous, reflex, convulsionary, knee-jerk, conditioned, uncontrollable.

involute /ínvəlŏŏt/ adj. & n. • adj. **1** involved; intricate. **2** curled spirally. **3** Bot. rolled inward at the edges. • n. Geom. the locus of a point fixed on a straight line that rolls without sliding on a curve and is in the plane of that curve (cf. EVOLUTE). [L involutus past part. of involvere (as INVOLVE)]

involuted /ínvəlŏŏtid/ adj. **1** complicated; abstruse. **2** = INVOLUTE adj. 2.
■ **1** see INTRICATE.

involution /ínvəlŏŏshən/ n. **1** the process of involving. **2** an entanglement. **3** intricacy. **4** curling inward. **5** a part that

curls upward. **6** Math. the raising of a quantity to any power. **7** Physiol. the reduction in size of an organ in old age, or when its purpose has been fulfilled (esp. the uterus after childbirth). □□ **involutional** adj. [L involutio (as INVOLVE)]

involve /invólv/ v.tr. **1** (often foll. by in) cause (a person or thing) to participate, or share the experience or effect (in a situation, activity, etc.). **2** imply; entail; make necessary. **3** (foll. by in) implicate (a person in a charge, crime, etc.). **4** include or affect in its operations. **5** (as **involved** adj.) **a** (often foll. by in) concerned or interested. **b** complicated in thought or form. [ME f. L involvere involut- (as IN-², volvere roll)]
■ **1** include, bring or take in, engage, engross, occupy, interest, absorb, immerse, employ. **2** imply, entail, necessitate, require, presuppose, assume; mean, suggest, indicate, implicate, betoken, point to, signify, evidence. **3** implicate, incriminate, inculpate; concern, connect, associate, draw in, mix up, catch up, entangle, enmesh, ensnare, embroil. **4** concern, affect, touch, relate to, bear on or upon, have a bearing on or upon, be relevant or germane to, apply to, influence, be of importance or interest to, have something to do with, regard; include, subsume, contain, comprise, cover, embrace, incorporate, encompass, embody, comprehend; number among, count in. **5** (**involved**) **a** concerned, included, implicated, affected; interested, engaged, absorbed, busy; partial, biased, prejudiced, partisan. **b** complicated, complex, intricate, convoluted, convolutional, involute, involuted, tangled, tangly, knotty, tortuous, sinuous, elaborate, Byzantine, labyrinthine.

involvement /invólvmənt/ n. **1** (often foll. by in, with) the act or an instance of involving; the process of being involved. **2** financial embarrassment. **3** a complicated affair or concern.
■ **1** see TIE n. 3. **3** complication, complexity, intricacy, convolution; see also PREDICAMENT.

invulnerable /invúlnərəbəl/ adj. that cannot be wounded or hurt, physically or mentally. □□ **invulnerability** n. **invulnerably** adv. [L invulnerabilis (as IN-¹, VULNERABLE)]
■ see INVINCIBLE. □□ **invulnerability** see IMMUNITY 2.

inward /ínwərd/ adj. & adv. • adj. **1** directed toward the inside; going in. **2** situated within. **3** mental; spiritual. • adv. (also **inwards**) **1** (of motion or position) toward the inside. **2** in the mind or soul. [OE innanweard (as IN, -WARD)]
■ adj. **1, 2** interior, inside, internal, inner.

inwardly /ínwərdlee/ adv. **1** on the inside. **2** in the mind or soul. **3** (of speaking) not aloud; inaudibly. [OE inweardlíce (as INWARD)]

inwardness /ínwərdnis/ n. **1** inner nature; essence. **2** the condition of being inward. **3** spirituality.

inwards var. of INWARD adv.

inweave /inwée'v/ v.tr. (also **enweave**) (past **-wove** /-wóv/; past part. **-woven** /-wóvən/) **1** weave (two or more things) together. **2** intermingle.

inwrap var. of ENWRAP.

inwreathe var. of ENWREATHE.

inwrought /ínráwt/ adj. **1 a** (often foll. by with) (of a fabric) decorated (with a pattern). **b** (often foll. by in, on) (of a pattern) wrought (in or on a fabric). **2** closely blended.

I/O abbr. Computing input/output.

IOC abbr. International Olympic Committee.

iodic /iódik/ adj. Chem. containing iodine in chemical combination (iodic acid). □□ **iodate** /íədayt/ n.

iodide /íədīd/ n. Chem. any compound of iodine with another element or group.

iodinate /iód'nayt, íəd'n-/ v.tr. treat or combine with iodine. □□ **iodination** /-náyshən/ n.

/.../ pronunciation	● part of speech
□ phrases, idioms, and compounds	
□□ derivatives	■ synonym section
cross-references appear in SMALL CAPITALS or italics	

iodine /íˈədin, -din, -deen/ *n.* **1** *Chem.* a non-metallic element of the halogen group, forming black crystals and a violet vapor, used in medicine and photography, and important as an essential element for living organisms. ¶ Symb.: I. **2** a solution of this in alcohol used as a mild antiseptic. [F *iode* f. Gk *iōdēs* violetlike f. *ion* violet + -INE⁴]

iodism /íˈədizəm/ *n.* *Med.* a condition caused by an overdose of iodides.

iodize /íˈədīz/ *v.tr.* treat or impregnate with iodine. □□ **iodization** *n.*

iodo- /ī-ˈŏdō/ *comb. form* (usu. **iod-** before a vowel) *Chem.* iodine.

iodoform /ī-ˈŏdəfawrm, -ˈódə-/ *n.* a pale yellow, volatile, sweet-smelling solid compound of iodine with antiseptic properties. ¶ Chem. formula: CHI₃. [IODINE after *chloroform*]

ion /íˈən, íˈon/ *n.* an atom or group of atoms that has lost one or more electrons (= CATION), or gained one or more electrons (= ANION). □ **ion exchange** the exchange of ions of the same charge between a usu. aqueous solution and a solid, used in water softening, etc. **ion exchanger** a substance or equipment for this process. [Gk, neut. pres. part. of *eimi* go]

-ion *suffix* (usu. as **-sion, -tion, -xion**; see -ATION, -ITION, -UTION) forming nouns denoting: **1** verbal action (*excision*). **2** an instance of this (*a suggestion*). **3** a resulting state or product (*vexation*; *concoction*). [from or after F *-ion* or L *-io -ionis*]

Ionian /ī-ˈóneeən/ *n. & adj.* ● *n.* a native or inhabitant of ancient Ionia in W. Asia Minor. ● *adj.* of or relating to Ionia or the Ionians. □ **Ionian mode** *Mus.* the mode represented by the natural diatonic scale C–C. [L *Ionius* f. Gk *Iōnios*]

Ionic /īˈónik/ *adj. & n.* ● *adj.* **1** of the order of Greek architecture characterized by a column with scroll shapes on either side of the capital. **2** of the ancient Greek dialect used in Ionia. ● *n.* the Ionic dialect. [L *Ionicus* f. Gk *Iōnikos*]

ionic /īˈónik/ *adj.* of, relating to, or using ions. □□ **ionically** *adv.*

ionization /íˈənizáyshən/ *n.* the process of producing ions as a result of solvation, heat, radiation, etc. □ **ionization chamber** an instrument for detecting ionizing radiation.

ionize /íˈənīz/ *v.tr. & intr.* convert or be converted into an ion or ions. □ **ionizing radiation** a radiation of sufficient energy to cause ionization in the medium through which it passes. □□ **ionizable** *adj.*

ionizer /íˈənīzər/ *n.* any thing which produces ionization, esp. a device used to improve the quality of the air in a room, etc.

ionosphere /īˈónəsfeer/ *n.* an ionized region of the atmosphere above the stratosphere, extending to about 600 miles (1,000 km) above the earth's surface and able to reflect radio waves, allowing long-distance transmission around the earth (cf. TROPOSPHERE). □□ **ionospheric** /-sfeérik, -sfér-/ *adj.*

-ior¹ /yər, eeər/ *suffix* forming adjectives of comparison (*senior*; *ulterior*). [L]

-ior² /yər, eeər/ *suffix* (also esp. *Brit.* **-iour**) forming nouns (*savior*; *warrior*). [-I- (as a stem element) + -OUR, -OR¹]

iota /ī-ˈōtə/ *n.* **1** the ninth letter of the Greek alphabet (I, ι). **2** (usu. with *neg.*) the smallest possible amount. [Gk *iōta*]
  ■ **2** see BIT¹ 1.

IOU /íˈ-ō-yˈŏo/ *n.* a signed document acknowledging a debt. [= I owe you]

-iour esp. *Brit.* var. of -IOR².

-ious /-eeəs, -əs/ *suffix* forming adjectives meaning 'characterized by, full of,' often corresponding to nouns in *-ion* (*cautious*; *curious*; *spacious*). [from or after F *-ieux* f. L *-iosus*]

IPA *abbr.* International Phonetic Alphabet (or Association).

ipecac /íˈpikak/ *n. colloq.* ipecacuanha. [abbr.]

ipecacuanha /íˈpikákyˈoo-áənə/ *n.* the root of a S. American shrub, *Cephaelis ipecacuanha*, used as an emetic and purgative. [Port. f. Tupi-Guarani *ipekaaguéne* emetic creeper]

ipomoea /íˈpəmeéə/ *n.* any twining plant of the genus *Ipomoea*, having trumpet-shaped flowers, e.g., the sweet potato and morning glory. [mod.L f. Gk *ips ipos* worm + *homoios* like]

ips *abbr.* (also **i.p.s.**) inches per second.

ipse dixit /ípsee díksit/ *n.* a dogmatic statement resting merely on the speaker's authority. [L, he himself said it (orig. of Pythagoras)]

ipsilateral /ípsilátərəl/ *adj.* belonging to or occurring on the same side of the body. [irreg. f. L *ipse* self + LATERAL]

ipsissima verba /ipsísimə vˈárbə/ *n.pl.* the precise words. [L]

ipso facto /ípsō fáktō/ *adv.* **1** by that very fact or act. **2** thereby. [L]

IQ *abbr.* intelligence quotient.
  ■ see MENTALITY 2.

-ique *archaic* var. of -IC.

IR *abbr.* infrared.

Ir *symb. Chem.* the element iridium.

ir- /ir/ *prefix* assim. form of IN-¹, IN-² before *r*.

IRA *abbr.* **1** individual retirement account. **2** Irish Republican Army.

irade /iraádee/ *n. hist.* a written decree of the sultan of Turkey. [Turk. f. Arab. *'irāda* will]

Iranian /iráyneeən/ *adj. & n.* ● *adj.* **1** of or relating to Iran (formerly Persia) in the Middle East. **2** of the Indo-European group of languages including Persian, Pashto, Avestan, and Kurdish. ● *n.* **1** a native or national of Iran. **2** a person of Iranian descent.

Iraqi /iraákee/ *adj. & n.* ● *adj.* of or relating to Iraq in the Middle East. ● *n.* (*pl.* **Iraqis**) **1 a** a native or national of Iraq. **b** a person of Iraqi descent. **2** the form of Arabic spoken in Iraq.

irascible /irásibəl/ *adj.* irritable; hot-tempered. □□ **irascibility** *n.* **irascibly** *adv.* [ME f. F f. LL *irascibilis* f. L *irasci* grow angry f. *ira* anger]
  ■ see IRRITABLE 1. □□ **irascibility** see TEMPER *n.* 3.

irate /īráyt/ *adj.* angry, enraged. □□ **irately** *adv.* **irateness** *n.* [L *iratus* f. *ira* anger]
  ■ see ANGRY 1.

IRBM *abbr.* intermediate range ballistic missile.

ire /īr/ *n. literary* anger. □□ **ireful** *adj.* [ME f. OF f. L *ira*]
  ■ see ANGER *n.* □□ **ireful** see ANGRY 1.

irenic /irénik, ireénik/ *adj.* (also **irenical**, esp. *Brit.* **eirenic**) *literary* aiming or aimed at peace. [Gk *eirēnikos* f. *eirēnē* peace]

iridaceous /íridáyshəs/ *adj. Bot.* of or relating to the family Iridaceae of plants growing from bulbs, corms, or rhizomes, e.g., iris, crocus, and gladiolus. [mod.L *iridaceus* (as IRIS)]

iridescent /íridésənt/ *adj.* **1** showing rainbowlike luminous or gleaming colors. **2** changing color with position. □□ **iridescence** /-səns/ *n.* **iridescently** *adv.* [L IRIS + -ESCENT]
  ■ see OPALESCENT.

iridium /irídeeəm/ *n. Chem.* a hard, white metallic element of the transition series used esp. in alloys. ¶ Symb.: **Ir**. [mod.L f. L IRIS + -IUM]

iris /íris/ *n.* **1** the flat, circular colored membrane behind the cornea of the eye, with a circular opening (pupil) in the center. **2** any herbaceous plant of the genus *Iris*, usu. with tuberous roots, sword-shaped leaves, and showy flowers. **3** (in full **iris diaphragm**) an adjustable diaphragm of thin overlapping plates for regulating the size of a central hole esp. for the admission of light to a lens. [ME f. L *iris iridis* f. Gk *iris iridos* rainbow, iris]

Irish /írish/ *adj. & n.* ● *adj.* of or relating to Ireland; of or like its people. ● *n.* **1** the Celtic language of Ireland. **2** (prec. by *the*; treated as *pl.*) the people of Ireland. □ **Irish bull** = BULL³. **Irish coffee** coffee mixed with Irish whiskey and served with cream on top. **Irish moss** dried carrageen. **Irish Sea** the sea between England and Wales and Ireland. **Irish setter** a silky-haired, dark red breed of setter. **Irish stew** a stew usu. of mutton, potato, and onion. **Irish terrier** a rough-haired, light reddish-brown breed of terrier. [ME f. OE *Iras* the Irish]

Irishman /írishmən/ *n.* (*pl.* **-men**) a person who is Irish by birth or descent.

Irishwoman /írishwˈoomən/ *n.* (*pl.* **-women**) a woman who is Irish by birth or descent.

iritis /irítis/ *n.* inflammation of the iris.

irk /ərk/ *v.tr.* (usu. *impers.*; often foll. by *that* + clause) irritate; bore; annoy. [ME: orig. unkn.]

■ irritate, anger, enrage, madden, infuriate, incense, make a person's blood boil, annoy, pique, vex, exasperate, chafe, nettle, gall, grate on, jar on, put out, get *or* put a person's back up, get on a person's nerves, *Brit.* get a person's blood up, *colloq.* get, rile, needle, miff, peeve, wind up, make a person see red, get a person's goat, *disp.* aggravate, *sl.* burn up, bug, *Brit. sl.* brown off, cheese off, nark; bother, worry, nag, pester, provoke, bait, goad, torment, fret, rub the wrong way, ride, *colloq.* hassle, get under a person's skin; bore, make a person fed up, get a person down.

irksome /ɔ́rksəm/ *adj.* tedious; annoying; tiresome. □□ **irksomely** *adv.* **irksomeness** *n.* [ME, = tired, etc., f. IRK + -SOME¹]

■ irritating, maddening, infuriating, annoying, vexing, vexatious, exasperating, galling, grating, bothersome, pestilential, *colloq.* pestilent, pesky, *disp.* aggravating, *Austral. sl.* on the nose; troublesome, burdensome, tiresome, trying, tedious, boring, wearisome, uninteresting; *colloq.* accursed, confounded, blasted, damned, damnable, darned.

IRO *abbr.* International Refugee Organization.

iroko /irókō/ *n.* (*pl.* -os) **1** either of two African trees, *Chlorophora excelsa* or *C. regia*. **2** the light-colored hardwood from these trees. [Ibo]

iron /íərn/ *n., adj., & v.* ● *n.* **1** *Chem.* a silver-white ductile metallic element occurring naturally as hematite, magnetite, etc., much used for tools and implements, and an essential element in all living organisms. ¶ Symb.: **Fe. 2** this as a type of unyieldingness or a symbol of firmness (*man of iron*; *will of iron*). **3** a tool or implement made of iron (*branding iron*; *curling iron*). **4** a household, now usu. electrical, implement with a flat base which is heated to smooth clothes, etc. **5** a golf club with an iron or steel sloping face used for lofting the ball. **6** (usu. in *pl.*) a fetter (*clapped in irons*). **7** (usu. in *pl.*) a stirrup. **8** (often in *pl.*) an iron support for a malformed leg. **9** a preparation of iron as a tonic or dietary supplement (*iron pills*). ● *adj.* **1** made of iron. **2** very robust. **3** unyielding; merciless (*iron determination*). ● *v.tr.* **1** smooth (clothes, etc.) with an iron. **2** furnish or cover with iron. **3** shackle with irons. □ **in irons** handcuffed, chained, etc. **Iron Age** *Archaeol.* the period following the Bronze Age when iron replaced bronze in the making of implements and weapons. **Iron Cross** the highest German military decoration for bravery. **Iron Curtain** *hist.* a notional barrier to the passage of people and information between the former Soviet bloc and the West. **iron hand** firmness or inflexibility (cf. *velvet glove*). **iron in the fire** an undertaking, opportunity, or commitment (usu. in *pl.*: *too many irons in the fire*). **ironing board** a flat surface usu. on legs and of adjustable height on which clothes, etc., are ironed. **iron lung** a rigid case fitted over a patient's body, used for administering prolonged artificial respiration by means of mechanical pumps. **iron maiden** *hist.* an instrument of torture consisting of a coffin-shaped box lined with iron spikes. **iron mold** a spot caused by iron rust or an ink stain, esp. on fabric. **iron-on** able to be fixed to the surface of a fabric, etc., by ironing. **iron out** remove or smooth over (difficulties, etc.). **iron pyrites** see PYRITES. **iron ration** a small emergency supply of food. □□ **ironer** *n.* **ironing** *n.* (in sense 1 of *v.*). **ironless** *adj.* **ironlike** *adj.* [OE *īren, īsern* f. Gmc, prob. f. Celt.]

■ *n.* 6 (*irons*) see MANACLE *n.* 1. ● *adj.* 3 see GRIM 2. ● *v.* 1 see PRESS¹ *v.* 2a. □ **iron hand** see *oppressor* (OPPRESS).

ironbark /íərnbaark/ *n.* any of various eucalyptus trees with a thick solid bark and hard dense timber.

ironbound /íərnbownd/ *adj.* **1** bound with iron. **2** rigorous; hard and fast. **3** (of a coast) rockbound.

ironclad *adj. & n.* ● *adj.* /íərnklád/ **1** clad or protected with iron. **2** impregnable; rigorous. ● *n.* /íərnklad/ *hist.* an early name for a 19th-c. warship built of iron or protected by iron plates.

ironic /irónik/ *adj.* (also **ironical**) **1** using or displaying irony. **2** in the nature of irony. □□ **ironically** *adv.* [F *ironique* or LL *ironicus* f. Gk *eirōnikos* dissembling (as IRONY¹)]

■ see SATIRICAL. □□ **ironically** see *tongue-in-cheek* (TONGUE).

ironist /írənist/ *n.* a person who uses irony. □□ **ironize** *v.intr.* [Gk *eirōn* dissembler + -IST]

ironmaster /íərnmastər/ *n. Brit.* a manufacturer of iron.

ironmonger /íərnmunggər, -mong-/ *n. Brit.* a dealer in hardware, etc. □□ **ironmongery** *n.* (*pl.* -ies).

ironside /íərnsid/ *n.* **1** a person of great bravery, strength, or endurance. **2** (usu. **Ironsides**) **a** a nickname of Oliver Cromwell. **b** Cromwell's troopers in the English Civil War. **3** (**ironsides**) (usu. treated as *sing.*) an ironclad.

ironstone /íərnstōn/ *n.* **1** any rock containing a substantial proportion of an iron compound. **2** a kind of hard, white, opaque stoneware.

ironware /íərnwair/ *n.* articles made of iron, esp. domestic implements.

ironwood /íərnwŏŏd/ *n.* **1** any of various tough-timbered trees and shrubs, esp. American hornbeam *Carpinus caroliniana*. **2** the wood from these trees.

ironwork /íərnwərk/ *n.* **1** things made of iron. **2** work in iron.

ironworks /íərnwərks/ *n.* (as *sing.* or *pl.*) a place where iron is smelted or iron goods are made.

irony¹ /írənee/ *n.* (*pl.* -ies) **1** an expression of meaning, often humorous or sarcastic, by the use of language of a different or opposite tendency. **2** an ill-timed or perverse arrival of an event or circumstance that is in itself desirable. **3** the use of language with one meaning for a privileged audience and another for those addressed or concerned. [L *ironia* f. Gk *eirōneia* simulated ignorance f. *eirōn* dissembler]

■ 1 see SATIRE 1.

irony² /í-ərnee/ *adj.* of or like iron.

Iroquoian /irəkwóyən/ *n. & adj.* ● *n.* **1** a language family of eastern N. America, including Cherokee and Mohawk. **2** a member of the Iroquois people. ● *adj.* of or relating to the Iroquois or the Iroquoian language family or one of its members.

Iroquois /írəkwoy/ *n. & adj.* ● *n.* (*pl.* same) **1 a** a Native American confederacy of five (later six) peoples formerly inhabiting New York State. **b** a member of any of these peoples. **2** any of the languages of these peoples. ● *adj.* of or relating to the Iroquois or their languages. [F f. Algonquian]

irradiant /iráydeeənt/ *adj. literary* shining brightly. □□ **irradiance** /-əns/ *n.*

irradiate /iráydee-áyt/ *v.tr.* **1** subject to (any form of) radiation. **2** shine upon; light up. **3** throw light on (a subject). □□ **irradiative** /-deeətiv/ *adj.* [L *irradiare irradiat-* (as IN-², *radiare* f. *radius* RAY¹)]

irradiation /iráydee-áyshən/ *n.* **1** the process of irradiating. **2** shining; illumination. **3** the apparent extension of the edges of an illuminated object seen against a dark background. [F *irradiation* or LL *irradiatio* (as IRRADIATE)]

irrational /iráshənəl/ *adj.* **1** illogical; unreasonable. **2** not endowed with reason. **3** *Math.* (of a root, etc.) not rational; not able to be expressed as a ratio between two integers; not commensurate with the natural numbers (e.g., a nonterminating decimal). □□ **irrationality** /-álitee/ *n.* **irrationalize** *v.tr.* **irrationally** *adv.* [L *irrationalis* (as IN-¹, RATIONAL)]

■ **1, 2** see UNREASONABLE 2. □□ **irrationality** see ABSURDITY 1, 2. **irrationally** see MADLY 1.

irreclaimable /írikláyməbəl/ *adj.* that cannot be reclaimed or reformed. □□ **irreclaimably** *adv.*

■ see IRRETRIEVABLE.

irreconcilable /irékənsiləbəl/ *adj. & n.* ● *adj.* **1** implacably hostile. **2** (of ideas, etc.) incompatible. ● *n.* **1** an uncompromising opponent of a political measure, etc. **2** (usu. in

---

/.../ **pronunciation**	● **part of speech**
□ **phrases, idioms, and compounds**	
□□ **derivatives**	■ **synonym section**
cross-references appear in SMALL CAPITALS or *italics*	

pl.) any of two or more items, ideas, etc., that cannot be made to agree. □□ **irreconcilability** *n.* **irreconcilableness** *n.* **irreconcilably** *adv.*
■ *adj.* **1** see IMPLACABLE. **2** see INCOMPATIBLE l, 3.
irrecoverable /írikúvərəbəl/ *adj.* that cannot be recovered or remedied. □□ **irrecoverably** *adv.*
■ see IRRETRIEVABLE.
irrecusable /írikyóōzəbəl/ *adj.* that must be accepted. [F *ir-récusable* or LL *irrecusabilis* (as IN-¹, *recusare* refuse)]
irredeemable /írideémǝbəl/ *adj.* **1** that cannot be redeemed. **2** hopeless; absolute. **3 a** (of a government annuity) not terminable by repayment. **b** (of paper currency) for which the issuing authority does not undertake ever to pay coin. □□ **irredeemability** *n.* **irredeemably** *adv.*
■ **1, 2** see INCURABLE *adj.*
irredentist /íridéntist/ *n.* a person, esp. in 19th-c. Italy, advocating the restoration to his or her country of any territory formerly belonging to it. □□ **irredentism** *n.* [It. *irredentista* f. (*Italia*) *irredenta* unredeemed (Italy)]
irreducible /íridōōsibǝl, -dyōō-/ *adj.* **1** that cannot be reduced or simplified. **2** (often foll. by *to*) that cannot be brought to a desired condition. □□ **irreducibility** *n.* **irreducibly** *adv.*
irrefragable /iréfrǝgǝbǝl/ *adj.* **1** (of a statement, argument, or person) unanswerable; indisputable. **2** (of rules, etc.) inviolable. □□ **irrefragably** *adv.* [LL *irrefragabilis* (as IN-¹, *refragari* oppose)]
irrefrangible /írifránjibǝl/ *adj.* **1** inviolable. **2** *Optics* incapable of being refracted.
irrefutable /iréfyǝtǝbǝl, írifyōō-/ *adj.* that cannot be refuted. □□ **irrefutability** *n.* **irrefutably** *adv.* [LL *irrefutabilis* (as IN-¹, REFUTE)]
■ see INCONTROVERTIBLE. □□ **irrefutability** see FINALITY. **irrefutably** see *undoubtedly* (UNDOUBTED).
irregardless /írigáardlis/ *adj.* & *adv.* *disp.* = REGARDLESS.
¶Though in widespread use, this word should be avoided in favor of *regardless*. [prob. blend of IRRESPECTIVE and REGARD-LESS]
irregular /irégyǝlǝr/ *adj.* & *n.* ● *adj.* **1** not regular; unsymmetrical; uneven; varying in form. **2** (of a surface) uneven. **3** contrary to a rule, moral principle, or custom; abnormal. **4** uneven in duration, order, etc. **5** (of troops) not belonging to the regular army. **6** *Gram.* (of a verb, noun, etc.) not inflected according to the usual rules. **7** disorderly. **8** (of a flower) having unequal petals, etc. ● *n.* (in *pl.*) irregular troops. □□ **irregularity** /-láritee/ *n.* (*pl.* **-ies**). **irregularly** *adv.* [ME f. OF *irreguler* f. LL *irregularis* (as IN-¹, REGULAR)]
■ *adj.* **1, 2** unequal, inequable, unsymmetrical, asymmetric(al), free-form, lopsided, skew, eccentric, deformed, bent, deviant; sprawling, ragged, rough-and-tumble; patchy, blotchy, scraggly, spotty, mottled, variegated, *colloq.* wiggly; uneven, bumpy, bulgy, lumpy, coarse, rough, pitted, jagged, craggy, rocky, rugged, broken, crazy. **3** illegitimate, improper, incorrect, nonstandard, invalid, unauthorized, spurious; abnormal, peculiar, unusual, uncommon, odd, strange, unconventional, divergent, exceptional, unnatural, untypical, extraordinary, singular, weird, eccentric, bizarre, quirky, wayward, anomalous, aberrant, queer, freakish, deformed, deviant, offbeat, *colloq.* oddball, kinky, way-out. **4** sporadic, aperiodic, episodic, random, erratic, haphazard, fitful, spasmodic, broken, uneven, abrupt, discontinuous, on-and-off, stop-and-go, stop-go, occasional; inconstant, unstable, changeable, variable, undependable, unpredictable, unreliable, mercurial, volatile, flighty, fickle, capricious; casual, *colloq.* promiscuous, *literary* mutable. **7** see DISORDERLY 1. □□ **irregularity** inequality, unevenness, bumpiness, lumpiness, coarseness, roughness, jaggedness, cragginess; anomaly, mistake, oversight; see also BUMP *n.* 2.
irrelative /irélǝtiv/ *adj.* **1** (often foll. by *to*) unconnected, unrelated. **2** having no relations; absolute. **3** irrelevant. □□ **irrelatively** *adv.*
irrelevant /irélivǝnt/ *adj.* (often foll. by *to*) not relevant; not

applicable (to a matter in hand). □□ **irrelevance** /-vǝns/ *n.* **irrelevancy** *n.* **irrelevantly** *adv.*
■ inappropriate, inapplicable, beside *or* off the point, beside *or* off *or* wide of the mark, out of the picture, beside the question, neither here nor there, inapposite, malapropos, out of place, inapt, unapt, inconsequent, inconsequential, irrelative, intrusive, esp. *Law* impertinent; unrelated, unconnected, extraneous, extrinsic, peripheral, tangential, gratuitous.
□□ **irrelevance, irrelevancy** impertinence, intrusiveness, inapplicability, inappropriateness, unrelatedness, gratuitousness.
irreligion /írilíjon/ *n.* disregard of or hostility to religion. □□ **irreligionist** *n.* [F *irréligion* or L *irreligio* (as IN-¹, RELIGION)]
irreligious /írilíjǝs/ *adj.* **1** indifferent or hostile to religion. **2** lacking a religion. □□ **irreligiously** *adv.* **irreligiousness** *n.*
■ **1** see IRREVERENT. **2** see HEATHEN 2.
irremediable /írimeédeeǝbǝl/ *adj.* that cannot be remedied. □□ **irremediably** *adv.* [L *irremediabilis* (as IN-¹, REMEDY)]
■ see HOPELESS 2.
irremissible /írimísibǝl/ *adj.* **1** unpardonable. **2** unalterably obligatory. □□ **irremissibly** *adv.* [ME f. OF *irremissible* or eccl.L *iremissibilis* (as IN-¹, REMISSIBLE)]
irremovable /írimōōvǝbǝl/ *adj.* that cannot be removed, esp. from office. □□ **irremovability** *n.* **irremovably** *adv.*
irreparable /iréparǝbǝl/ *adj.* (of an injury, loss, etc.) that cannot be rectified or made good. □□ **irreparability** *n.* **irreparableness** *n.* **irreparably** *adv.* [ME f. OF f. L *irreparabilis* (as IN-¹, REPARABLE)]
■ see HOPELESS 2.
irreplaceable /íripláysǝbǝl/ *adj.* **1** that cannot be replaced. **2** of which the loss cannot be made good. □□ **irreplaceably** *adv.*
■ **2** see INVALUABLE.
irrepressible /íripréssibǝl/ *adj.* that cannot be repressed or restrained. □□ **irrepressibility** *n.* **irrepressibleness** *n.* **irrepressibly** *adv.*
■ unrestrainable, inextinguishable, uncontainable, uncontrollable, unmanageable, ungovernable, unstoppable, indomitable, irresistible; incorrigible, headstrong, wayward; ebullient, buoyant, effervescent, bubbly, exuberant, boisterous.
irreproachable /íripróchǝbǝl/ *adj.* faultless; blameless. □□ **irreproachability** *n.* **irreproachableness** *n.* **irreproachably** *adv.* [F *irréprochable* (as IN-¹, REPROACH)]
■ blameless, unimpeachable, beyond reproach, innocent, above suspicion; faultless, impeccable, spotless, unblemished, flawless, perfect, exemplary, ideal; honest, pure, sinless, decent.
irresistible /írizístibǝl/ *adj.* **1** too strong or convincing to be resisted. **2** delightful; alluring. □□ **irresistibility** *n.* **irresistibleness** *n.* **irresistibly** *adv.* [med.L *irresistibilis* (as IN-¹, RESIST)]
■ **1** unstoppable, unconquerable, indomitable, inexorable, relentless, unavoidable, ineluctable, inescapable, overpowering, overwhelming, overriding, forceful, magnetic; irrepressible, uncontrollable, ungovernable, uncontainable, unmanageable; compulsive. **2** attractive, appealing, alluring, luring, enticing, seductive, inviting, tempting, tantalizing; charming, delightful, captivating, enchanting, ravishing, fascinating.
irresolute /irézǝlōōt/ *adj.* **1** hesitant; undecided. **2** lacking in resoluteness. □□ **irresolutely** *adv.* **irresoluteness** *n.* **irresolution** /-lōōshǝn/ *n.*
■ **1** hesitant, undecided, undetermined, unresolved, indecisive, uncertain, unsure, of two minds, wavering, ambivalent, doubtful, dubious, vague, tentative, tremulous, dithery, shilly-shally, wishy-washy, halfhearted. **2** unsteadfast, unstable, inconstant, erratic, fickle, changeable, capricious, flighty, moody, fitful; weak, infirm, spineless, fainthearted, half-baked, feeble, feckless, *Brit. colloq.* wet.

irresolvable /írizólvəbəl/ adj. **1** that cannot be resolved into its components. **2** (of a problem) that cannot be solved.

irrespective /írispéktiv/ adj. (foll. by of) not taking into account; regardless of. □□ **irrespectively** adv.

■ (irrespective of) regardless of, notwithstanding, despite, in spite of, without regard to, independent of, no matter; apart from, ignoring, discounting, disregarding, excluding, exclusive of.

irresponsible /írispónsibəl/ adj. **1** acting or done without due sense of responsibility. **2** not responsible for one's conduct. □□ **irresponsibility** n. **irresponsibly** adv.

■ **1** careless, reckless, feckless, devil-may-care; rash, unthinking, thoughtless, unconsidered, ill-considered, heedless, headlong, hasty, wild, hotheaded; unreliable, undependable, untrustworthy. **2** unaccountable, not responsible or answerable. □□ **irresponsibility** see stupidity (STUPID).

irresponsive /írispónsiv/ adj. (often foll. by to) not responsive. □□ **irresponsively** adv. **irresponsiveness** n.

irretrievable /íritreévəbəl/ adj. that cannot be retrieved or restored. □□ **irretrievability** n. **irretrievably** adv.

■ irrecoverable, irreclaimable, irreparable, beyond repair, incurable, irremediable, irredeemable, irreversible, irrevocable; hopeless, desperate, lost, gone.

irreverent /irévərənt/ adj. lacking reverence. □□ **irreverence** /-rəns/ n. **irreverential** /-rénshəl/ adj. **irreverently** adv. [L irreverens (as IN-¹, REVERENT)]

■ blasphemous, impious, profane, sacrilegious, unholy, ungodly, godless, irreligious; disrespectful, contemptuous, insulting, insolent, rude, discourteous, uncivil, offensive, derisive, impudent, impertinent, saucy, cheeky, pert, nervy, colloq. fresh, lippy.

irreversible /irivŕsibəl/ adj. not reversible or alterable. □□ **irreversibility** n. **irreversibly** adv.

■ irrevocable, unchangeable, unalterable, immutable, permanent, fixed, final, flat; irredeemable, irreparable, irretrievable; decided, unquestionable, indisputable, settled.

irrevocable /irévəkəbəl, irivók-/ adj. **1** unalterable. **2** gone beyond recall. □□ **irrevocability** /-bílitee/ n. **irrevocably** adv. [ME f. L irrevocabilis (as IN-¹, REVOKE)]

■ **1** irreversible, unchangeable, unalterable, inalterable, immutable, fixed, final, flat; permanent, everlasting; irredeemable, irreparable; settled, decided, unquestionable, indisputable. **2** irrecoverable, irretrievable, irreclaimable, lost, gone, beyond recall; desperate, hopeless.

irrigate /írigayt/ v.tr. **1 a** water (land) by means of channels. **b** (of a stream, etc.) supply (land) with water. **2** Med. supply (a wound, etc.) with a constant flow of liquid. **3** refresh as with moisture. □□ **irrigable** adj. **irrigation** /-gáyshən/ n. **irrigative** adj. **irrigator** n. [L irrigare (as IN-², rigare moisten)]

■ **1** see WATER v. 1.

irritable /íritəbəl/ adj. **1** easily annoyed or angered. **2** (of an organ, etc.) very sensitive to contact. **3** Biol. responding actively to physical stimulus. □□ **irritability** n. **irritably** adv. [L irritabilis (as IRRITATE)]

■ **1** irascible, testy, tetchy, touchy, oversensitive, prickly, huffy, waspish, snuffy, short-tempered, quick-tempered, hot-tempered, colloq. snappy, snappish, ratty, Brit. sl. waxy; peevish, cross, fiery, fractious, crabbed, crabby, crusty, bad-tempered, ill-tempered, ill-humored, cantankerous, curmudgeonly, quarrelsome, querulous, grumpy, crotchety, cranky, colloq. grouchy, peckish, Austral. & NZ colloq. crook, Brit. colloq. like a bear with a sore head, Austral. sl. snaky, lemony; impatient, petulant, intolerant, nervous, edgy, on edge, out of sorts. **2** sensitive, delicate, tender; hypersensitive. □□ **irritability** see impatience (IMPATIENT).

irritant /írit'nt/ adj. & n. ● adj. causing irritation. ● n. an irritant substance. □□ **irritancy** n.

irritate /íritayt/ v.tr. **1** excite to anger; annoy. **2** stimulate discomfort or pain in (a part of the body). **3** Biol. stimulate (an organ) to action. □□ **irritatedly** adv. **irritating** adj. **irritatingly** adv. **irritation** /-táyshən/ n. **irritative** adj. **irritator** n. [L irritare irritat-]

■ **1** anger, enrage, infuriate, madden, incense, make a person's blood boil; irk, annoy, pique, vex, exasperate, chafe, nettle, gall, grate on, jar on, put out, get or put a person's back up, get on a person's nerves, make a person's hackles rise, Brit. get a person's blood up, colloq. get, rile, needle, miff, peeve, make a person see red, get a person's goat, disp. aggravate, sl. burn up, bug, Brit. sl. brown off, cheese off, nark; bother, worry, nag, trouble, pester, provoke, bait, goad, torment, wind up, fret, rub the wrong way, ride, colloq. hassle, get under a person's skin, get on a person's nerves, get in a person's hair, drive a person up the wall. **2** hurt, pain, sting, burn, nettle, chafe, inflame, redden.

□□ **irritating** see IRKSOME. **irritation** see ANNOYANCE 1, BOTHER n. 1, INFLAMMATION 2.

irrupt /irúpt/ v.intr. (foll. by into) enter forcibly or violently. □□ **irruption** /irúpshən/ n. [L irrumpere irrupt- (as IN-², rumpere break)]

IRS abbr. Internal Revenue Service.

Is. abbr. **1 a** Island(s). **b** Isle(s). **2** (also **Isa.**) Isaiah (Old Testament).

is 3rd sing. present of BE.

isagogic /ísəgójik/ adj. introductory. [L isagogicus f. Gk eisagōgikos f. eisagōgē introduction f. eis into + agōgē leading f. agō lead]

isagogics /ísəgójiks/ n. an introductory study, esp. of the literary and external history of the Bible.

isatin /ísətin/ n. Chem. a red crystalline derivative of indole used in the manufacture of dyes. [L isatis woad f. Gk]

ISBN abbr. international standard book number.

ischemia /iskeémeeə/ n. (esp. Brit. **ischaemia**) Med. a reduction of the blood supply to part of the body. □□ **ischemic** adj. [mod.L f. Gk iskhaimos f. iskhō keep back]

ischium /ískeeəm/ n. (pl. **ischia** /-keeə/) the curved bone forming the base of each half of the pelvis. □□ **ischial** adj. [L f. Gk iskhion hip joint: cf. SCIATIC]

-ise¹ suffix var. of -IZE. ¶ See the note at -ize.

-ise² /íz, eez/ suffix forming nouns of quality, state, or function (exercise; expertise; franchise; merchandise). [from or after F or OF -ise f. L -itia, etc.]

-ise³ suffix var. of -ISH².

isentropic /ísentrŏpik, -trópik/ adj. having equal entropy. [ISO- + ENTROPY]

-ish¹ /ish/ suffix forming adjectives: **1** from nouns, meaning: **a** having the qualities or characteristics of (boyish). **b** of the nationality of (Danish). **2** from adjectives, meaning 'somewhat' (thickish). **3** colloq. denoting an approximate age or time of day (fortyish; six-thirtyish). [OE -isc]

-ish² /ish/ suffix forming verbs (vanish, finish). [from or after F -iss- (in extended stems of verbs in -ir) f. L -isc- incept. suffix]

isinglass /ízinglas/ n. **1** a kind of gelatin obtained from fish, esp. sturgeon, and used in making jellies, glue, etc. **2** mica. [corrupt. of obs. Du. huisenblas sturgeon's bladder, assim. to GLASS]

isl. abbr. island.

Islam /íslaam, íz-, islaám, iz-/ n. **1** the religion of the Muslims, a monotheistic faith regarded as revealed through Muhammad as the Prophet of Allah. **2** the Muslim world. □□ **Islamic** adj. **Islamism** n. **Islamist** n. **Islamize** v.tr. **Islamization** /-mizáyshən/ n. [Arab. islām submission (to God) f. aslama resign oneself]

island /ílənd/ n. **1** a piece of land surrounded by water. **2** anything compared to an island, esp. in being surrounded in some way. **3** = traffic island. **4 a** a detached or isolated thing. **b** Physiol. a detached portion of tissue or group of

---

/.../	pronunciation	● part of speech
□	phrases, idioms, and compounds	
□□	derivatives	■ synonym section
	cross-references appear in SMALL CAPITALS or italics	

cells (cf. ISLET). **5** *Naut.* a ship's superstructure, bridge, etc. [OE *īgland* f. *īg* island + LAND: first syll. infl. by ISLE] ■ **1** islet, cay, key, atoll, *Brit.* ait, holm, esp. *Sc.* inch, *Sc.* skerry, *poet.* isle.

islander /ílǝndǝr/ *n.* a native or inhabitant of an island.

isle /īl/ *n. poet.* (and in place-names) an island or peninsula, esp. a small one. [ME *ile* f. OF *ile* f. L *insula*: later ME & OF *isle* after L]

islet /ílit/ *n.* **1** a small island. **2** *Anat.* a portion of tissue structurally distinct from surrounding tissues. **3** an isolated place. □ **islets of Langerhans** /laánggǝrhaáns, -haánz/ *Physiol.* groups of pancreatic cells secreting insulin and glucagon. [OF, dimin. of *isle* ISLE]

ism /ízǝm/ *n. colloq.* usu. *derog.* any distinctive but unspecified doctrine or practice of a kind with a name in *-ism*. ■ see SECT 2.

-ism /ízǝm/ *suffix* forming nouns, esp. denoting: **1** an action or its result (*baptism*; *organism*). **2** a system, principle, or ideological movement (*Conservatism*; *jingoism*; *feminism*). **3** a state or quality (*heroism*; *barbarism*). **4** a basis of prejudice or discrimination (*racism*; *sexism*). **5** a peculiarity in language (*Americanism*). **6** a pathological condition (*alcoholism*; *Parkinsonism*). [from or after F *-isme* f. L *-ismus* f. Gk *-ismos* or *-isma* f. *-izō* -IZE]

Ismaili /ísmay-eélee, -maa-/ *n.* (*pl.* **Ismailis**) a member of a Muslim Shiite sect that arose in the 8th c. [*Ismail* a son of the patriarch Ibrāhim (= Abraham)]

isn't /ízǝnt/ *contr.* is not.

ISO *abbr.* **1** incentive stock option. **2** International Standardization Organization.

iso- /ísō/ *comb. form* **1** equal (*isometric*). **2** *Chem.* isomeric, esp. of a hydrocarbon with a branched chain of carbon atoms (*isobutane*). [Gk *isos* equal]

isobar /ísǝbaar/ *n.* **1** a line on a map connecting positions having the same atmospheric pressure at a given time or on average over a given period. **2** a curve for a physical system at constant pressure. **3** one of two or more isotopes of different elements, with the same atomic weight. □□ **isobaric** /-bárik/ *adj.* [Gk *isobarēs* of equal weight (as ISO-, *baros* weight)]

isocheim /ísǝkīm/ *n.* a line on a map connecting places having the same average temperature in winter. [ISO- + Gk *kheima* winter weather]

isochromatic /ísōkrōmátik/ *adj.* of the same color.

isochronous /ísókrǝnǝs/ *adj.* **1** occurring at the same time. **2** occupying equal time. □□ **isochronously** *adv.* [ISO- + Gk *khronos* time]

isoclinal /ísōklín'l/ *adj.* (also **isoclinic** /-klínik/) **1** *Geol.* (of a fold) in which the two limbs are parallel. **2** corresponding to equal values of magnetic dip. [ISO- + CLINE]

isoclinic var. of ISOCLINAL.

isodynamic /ísōdinámik/ *adj.* corresponding to equal values of (magnetic) force.

isoenzyme /ísō-énzīm/ *n. Biochem.* one of two or more enzymes with identical function but different structure.

isogeotherm /ísōjeé-ōthérm/ *n.* a line or surface connecting points in the interior of the earth having the same temperature. □□ **isogeothermal** *adj.*

isogloss /ísǝglaws, -glos/ *n.* a line on a map marking an area having a distinct linguistic feature.

isogonic /ísǝgónik/ *adj.* corresponding to equal values of magnetic declination.

isohel /ísōhel/ *n.* a line on a map connecting places having the same duration of sunshine. [ISO- + Gk *hēlios* sun]

isohyet /ísōhí-it/ *n.* a line on a map connecting places having the same amount of rainfall in a given period. [ISO- + Gk *huetos* rain]

isolate /ísǝláyt/ *v.tr.* **1 a** place apart or alone, cut off from society. **b** place (a patient thought to be contagious or infectious) in quarantine. **2 a** identify and separate for attention (*isolated the problem*). **b** *Chem.* separate (a substance) from a mixture. **3** insulate (electrical apparatus). □□ **isolable** /ísǝlǝbǝl/ *adj.* **isolatable** *adj.* **isolator** *n.* [orig. in past part., f. F *isolé* f. It. *isolato* f. LL *insulatus* f. L *insula* island] ■ **1** separate, detach, insulate, segregate, set *or* keep

apart, sequester, seclude, cloister, cut off, maroon, exclude, shut out; shun, cut, ostracize, send to Coventry, avoid, ignore, snub, cold-shoulder, boycott; quarantine; shelter, cushion. **2** see IDENTIFY 1, 2.

isolated /ísǝlaytid/ *adj.* **1** lonely; cut off from society or contact; remote (*feeling isolated*; *an isolated farmhouse*). **2** untypical; unique (*an isolated example*). ■ **1** lonesome, lonely, solitary, forlorn; alone, separate, secluded, remote, sequestered, cut off, out-of-the-way, cloistered, sheltered, unfrequented, lone, uninhabited; unconnected, detached; hermitic, eremitic(al), anchoretic, anchoritic, troglodytic(al), monastic, monkish, reclusive, withdrawn. **2** unique, single, solitary, singular; untypical, exceptional, particular, special, individual, *Brit. colloq.* one-off.

isolating /ísǝlayting/ *adj.* (of a language) having each element as an independent word without inflections.

isolation /ísǝláyshǝn/ *n.* the act or an instance of isolating; the state of being isolated or separated. □ **in isolation** considered singly and not relatively. **isolation hospital** (or **ward**, etc.) a hospital, ward, etc., for patients with contagious or infectious diseases. ■ see SECLUSION 1.

isolationism /ísǝláyshǝnizǝm/ *n.* the policy of holding aloof from the affairs of other countries or groups esp. in politics. □□ **isolationist** *n.*

isoleucine /ísōlōōseen/ *n. Biochem.* an amino acid that is a constituent of proteins and an essential nutrient. [G *Isoleucin* (see ISO-, LEUCINE)]

isomer /ísǝmǝr/ *n.* **1** *Chem.* one of two or more compounds with the same molecular formula but a different arrangement of atoms and different properties. **2** *Physics* one of two or more atomic nuclei that have the same atomic number and the same mass number but different energy states. □□ **isomeric** /-mérik/ *adj.* **isomerism** /ísómǝrizǝm/ *n.* **isomerize** *v.* [G f. Gk *isomerēs* sharing equally (as ISO-, *meros* share)]

isomerous /ísómǝrǝs/ *adj. Bot.* (of a flower) having the same number of petals in each whorl. [Gk *isomerēs*: see ISOMER]

isometric /ísǝmétrik/ *adj.* **1** of equal measure. **2** *Physiol.* (of muscle action) developing tension while the muscle is prevented from contracting. **3** (of a drawing, etc.) with the plane of projection at equal angles to the three principal axes of the object shown. **4** *Math.* (of a transformation) without change of shape or size. □□ **isometrically** *adv.* **isometry** /ísómitree/ *n.* (in sense 4). [Gk *isometria* equality of measure (as ISO-, -METRY)]

isometrics /ísǝmétriks/ *n.pl.* a system of physical exercises in which muscles are caused to act against each other or against a fixed object. ■ see EXERCISE *n.* 3.

isomorph /ísǝmawrf/ *n.* an isomorphic substance or organism. [ISO- + Gk *morphē* form]

isomorphic /ísǝmáwrfik/ *adj.* (also **isomorphous** /-fǝs/) **1** exactly corresponding in form and relations. **2** *Crystallog.* having the same form. □□ **isomorphism** *n.*

-ison /isǝn/ *suffix* forming nouns, = -ATION (*comparison*; *garrison*; *jettison*; *venison*). [OF *-aison*, etc., f. L *-atio*, etc.: see -ATION]

isophote /ísǝfōt/ *n.* a line (imaginary or in a diagram) of equal brightness or illumination. [ISO- + Gk *phōs phōtos* light]

isopleth /ísǝpleth/ *n.* a line on a map connecting places having equal incidence of a meteorological feature. [ISO- + Gk *plēthos* fullness]

isopod /ísǝpod/ *n.* any crustacean of the order *Isopoda*, including woodlice and slaters, often parasitic and having a flattened body with seven pairs of legs. [F *isopode* f. mod.L *Isopoda* (as ISO-, Gk *pous podos* foot)]

isosceles /īsósileez/ *adj.* (of a triangle) having two sides equal. [LL f. Gk *isoskelēs* (as ISO-, *skelos* leg)]

isoseismic /ísōsízmik/ *adj.* & *n.* (also **isoseismal** /-mǝl/) ● *adj.* having equal strength of earthquake shock. ● *n.* a line on a map connecting places having an equal strength of earthquake shock.

isostasy /īsóstəsee/ *n. Geol.* the general state of equilibrium of the earth's crust, with the rise and fall of land relative to sea. □□ **isostatic** /īsəstátik/ *adj.* [ISO- + Gk *stasis* station]

isothere /īsətheer/ *n.* a line on a map connecting places having the same average temperature in the summer. [ISO- + Gk *theros* summer]

isotherm /īsəthərm/ *n.* **1** a line on a map connecting places having the same temperature at a given time or on average over a given period. **2** a curve for changes in a physical system at a constant temperature. □□ **isothermal** *adj.* **isothermally** *adv.* [F *isotherme* (as ISO-, Gk *thermē* heat)]

isotonic /īsətónik/ *adj.* **1** having the same osmotic pressure. **2** *Physiol.* (of muscle action) taking place with normal contraction. □□ **isotonically** *adv.* **isotonicity** /-tənísitee/ *n.* [Gk *isotonos* (as ISO-, TONE)]

isotope /īsətōp/ *n. Chem.* one of two or more forms of an element differing from each other in relative atomic mass, and in nuclear but not chemical properties. □□ **isotopic** /-tópik/ *adj.* **isotopically** *adv.* **isotopy** /īsótəpee, īsətōpee/ *n.* [ISO- + Gk *topos* place (i.e. in the periodic table of elements)]

isotropic /īsōtrópik, -tróp-/ *adj.* having the same physical properties in all directions (opp. ANISOTROPIC). □□ **isotropically** *adv.* **isotropy** /īsótrəpee/ *n.* [ISO- + Gk *tropos* turn]

I-spy /ī-spī/ *n.* a game in which players try to identify something observed by one of them and referred to by its color, shape, etc.

Israeli /izráylee/ *adj.* & *n.* ● *adj.* of or relating to the modern state of Israel in the Middle East. ● *n.* **1** a native or national of Israel. **2** a person of Israeli descent. [*Israel*, a later name of Jacob, ult. f. Heb. *yisrā'ēl* he that strives with God (Gen. 32:28) + -I[2]]

Israelite /ízreeəlīt, -rəlīt/ *n. hist.* a native of ancient Israel; a Jew.

ISSN *abbr.* International Standard Serial Number.

issuant /íshōōənt/ *adj. Heraldry* (esp. of a beast with only the upper part shown) rising from the bottom or top of a bearing.

issue /íshōō/ *n.* & *v.* ● *n.* **1 a** a giving out or circulation of shares, notes, stamps, etc. **b** a quantity of coins, supplies, copies of a newspaper or book, etc., circulated or put on sale at one time. **c** an item or amount given out or distributed. **d** each of a regular series of a magazine, etc. (*the May issue*). **2 a** an outgoing; an outflow. **b** a way out; an outlet, esp. the place of the emergence of a stream, etc. **3** a point in question; an important subject of debate or litigation. **4** a result; an outcome; a decision. **5** *Law* children; progeny (*without male issue*). **6** *archaic* a discharge of blood, etc. ● *v.* (**issues, issued, issuing**) **1** *intr.* (often foll. by *out, forth*) *literary* go or come out. **2** *tr.* **a** send forth; publish; put into circulation. **b** supply, esp. officially or authoritatively (usu. foll. by *to*): *issued passports to them; issued orders to the staff*). **3** *intr.* **a** (often foll. by *from*) be derived or result. **b** (foll. by *in*) end; result. **4** *intr.* (foll. by *from*) emerge from a condition. □ **at issue 1** under discussion; in dispute. **2** at variance. **issue of fact** (or **law**) a dispute at law when the significance of a fact or facts is denied or when the application of the law is contested. **join issue** identify and submit an issue for formal argument (foll. by *with, on*). **make an issue of** make a fuss about; turn into a subject of contention. **take issue** disagree, esp. on a specific issue (foll. by *with, on*). □□ **issuable** *adj.* **issuance** *n.* **issueless** *adj.* **issuer** *n.* [ME f. OF ult. f. L *exitus* past part. of *exire* EXIT]

■ *n.* **1 a** output, circulation, production, publication, distribution, flotation, issuance, dissemination, promulgation. **b** printing, run, edition. **c** dividend, bonus, yield, payment. **d** copy, number, version, edition, installment. **2** outflow, outgoing, flux, efflux, effluxion, emanation, debouchment, issuance, emergence, emanation, discharge, outlet, vent, spout, egress, exit. **3** point (in question), topic, subject, talking point, matter, question, affair, business; problem, difficulty, crux, controversy, dispute, trouble, *colloq.* thing. **4** result, event, outcome, upshot, progeny, effect, consequence, end product, *sl.* payoff;

conclusion, decision, judgment, finding, ruling, verdict. **5** children, sons, daughters, descendants, heirs, offspring, progeny, scions; young, litter, brood, *archaic* seed. **6** see DISCHARGE *n.* 5. ● *v.* **1** go out *or* forth, come out *or* forth, emerge, emanate, flow out, discharge, pour, stream, escape, exit, *archaic* sally (forth). **2 a** send out *or* forth, put *or* give out, set out *or* forth, make known, make public, publicize, circulate, distribute, hand out, release, deliver, broadcast, disseminate; publish, announce, proclaim, promulgate; *Brit.* inscribe (*shares*). **b** supply, provide, furnish; equip, outfit, rig (out *or* up), fit (out *or* up). **3 a** arise, derive, result, originate, spring, stem, emerge, flow, proceed, emanate, come. **b** end (up), finish, result, conclude, culminate. **4** emerge, come out, appear, surface; come to life, hatch, peep out. □ **at issue** under discussion, in question, at stake, on the agenda, moot; the point, alive; in contention, in dispute. **make an issue of** kick up *or* make a fuss about, complain about, grumble *or* moan about, *colloq.* gripe *or* grouch *or* bitch *or Brit.* whinge about, kick up *or* make a stink about, *sl.* beef about. **take issue** disagree, argue, quarrel, contend; dispute, question, take exception to, query, challenge, contest, oppose, deny.

-ist /ist/ *suffix* forming personal nouns (and in some senses related adjectives) denoting: **1** an adherent of a system, etc., in *-ism*: see -ISM 2 (*Marxist; fatalist*). **2 a** a member of a profession (*pathologist*). **b** a person concerned with something (*pharmacist*). **3** a person who uses a thing (*violinist; balloonist; motorist*). **4** a person who does something expressed by a verb in *-ize* (*plagiarist*). **5** a person who subscribes to a prejudice or practices discrimination (*racist; sexist*). [OF *-iste*, L *-ista* f. Gk *-istēs*]

isthmian /ísmeeən/ *adj.* of or relating to an isthmus, esp. (**Isthmian**) to the Isthmus of Corinth in southern Greece.

isthmus /ísməs/ *n.* **1** a narrow piece of land connecting two larger bodies of land. **2** *Anat.* a narrow part connecting two larger parts. [L f. Gk *isthmos*]

-istic /ístik/ *suffix* forming adjectives from nouns and other stems generally denoting: of, pertaining to, referring to, or characteristic of that which is denoted by the noun or stem (*stylistic, puristic, fatalistic*) [F = *istique*, L = *isticus* f. Gk = *istikos*]

istle /ístlee/ *n.* a fiber used for cord, nets, etc., obtained from agave. [Mex. *ixtli*]

IT *abbr.* information technology.

It. *abbr.* Italian.

it[1] /it/ *pron.* (*poss.* **its**; *pl.* **they**) **1** the thing (or occas. the animal or child) previously named or in question (*took a stone and threw it*). **2** the person in question (*Who is it? It is I; is it a boy or a girl?*). **3** as the subject of an impersonal verb (*it is raining; it is winter; it is Tuesday; it is two miles to Denver*). **4** as a substitute for a deferred subject or object (*it is intolerable, this delay; it is silly to talk like that; I take it that you agree*). **5** as a substitute for a vague object (*tough it out; run for it!*). **6** as the antecedent to a relative word (*it was an owl I heard*). **7** exactly what is needed (*absolutely it*). **8** the extreme limit of achievement. **9** *colloq.* sexual intercourse; sex appeal. **10** (in children's games) a player who has to perform a required feat, esp. to catch the others. □ **that's it** *colloq.* that is: **1** what is required. **2** The difficulty. **3** the end; enough. **this is it** *colloq.* **1** the expected event is at hand. **2** this is the difficulty. [OE *hit* neut. of HE]

it[2] /it/ *n. Brit. colloq.* Italian vermouth (*gin and it*). [abbr.]

i.t.a. *abbr.* (also **ITA**) Initial Teaching Alphabet.

Ital. *abbr.* Italian.

ital. *abbr.* italic (type).

Italian /itályən/ *n.* & *adj.* ● *n.* **1 a** a native or national of Italy. **b** a person of Italian descent. **2** the Romance language

---

/.../ **pronunciation**	● **part of speech**
□ **phrases, idioms, and compounds**	
□□ **derivatives**	■ **synonym section**
cross-references appear in SMALL CAPITALS or *italics*	

used in Italy and parts of Switzerland. ● *adj.* of or relating to Italy or its people or language. [ME f. It. *Italiano* f. *Italia* Italy]

Italianate /itályənayt/ *adj.* of Italian style or appearance. [It. *Italianato*]

italic /itálik/ *adj.* & *n.* ● *adj.* **1 a** *Printing* of the sloping kind of letters now used esp. for emphasis or distinction and in foreign words. **b** (of handwriting) compact and pointed like early Italian handwriting. **2** (**Italic**) of ancient Italy. ● *n.* **1** a letter in italic type. **2** this type. [L *italicus* f. Gk *italikos* Italian (because introduced by Aldo Manuzio of Venice)]

italicize /itálisiz/ *v.tr.* print in italics. □□ **italicization** *n.*

Italiot /itáleeət/ *n.* & *adj.* ● *n.* an inhabitant of the Greek colonies in ancient Italy. ● *adj.* of or relating to the Italiots. [Gk *Italiōtēs* f. *Italia* Italy]

Italo- /itálō/ *comb. form* Italian; Italian and.

itch /ich/ *n.* & *v.* ● *n.* **1** an irritation in the skin. **2** an impatient desire; a hankering. **3** (prec. by *the*) (in general use) scabies. ● *v.intr.* **1** feel an irritation in the skin, causing a desire to scratch it. **2** (usu. foll. by *to* + infin.) (of a person) feel a desire to do something (*am itching to tell you the news*). □ **itching palm** avarice. **itch mite** a parasitic arthropod, *Sarcoptes scabiei*, which burrows under the skin causing scabies. [OE *gycce*, *gyccan* f. WG]

■ *n.* **1** itchiness, irritation, tickle, tingle, prickle. **2** desire, craving, hankering, hunger, thirst, yearning, longing, urge, impulse, compulsion, *colloq.* yen. ● *v.* **1** tickle; tingle, prickle. **2** desire, crave, hanker, hunger, thirst, yearn, pine, long, die, have an urge; wish, want, need.

itchy /íchee/ *adj.* (**itchier**, **itchiest**) having or causing an itch. □ **have itchy feet** *colloq.* **1** be restless. **2** have a strong urge to travel. □□ **itchiness** *n.*

■ see PRICKLY 3, RESTLESS 2, 3. □□ **itchiness** see PRICKLE *n.* 3.

it'd /ítəd/ *contr. colloq.* **1** it had. **2** it would.

-ite[1] /īt/ *suffix* forming nouns meaning 'a person or thing connected with': **1** in names of persons: **a** as natives of a country (*Israelite*). **b** often *derog.* as followers of a movement, etc. (*Pre-Raphaelite*; *Trotskyite*). **2** in names of things: **a** fossil organisms (*ammonite*). **b** minerals (*graphite*). **c** constituent parts of a body or organ (*somite*). **d** explosives (*dynamite*). **e** commercial products (*ebonite*; *vulcanite*). **f** salts of acids having names in *-ous* (*nitrite*; *sulfite*). [from or after F *-ite* f. L *-ita* f. Gk *-itēs*]

-ite[2] /īt, it/ *suffix* **1** forming adjectives (*erudite*; *favorite*). **2** forming nouns (*appetite*). **3** forming verbs (*expedite*; *unite*). [from or after L *-itus* past part. of verbs in *-ēre*, *-ere*, and *-ire*]

item /ítəm/ *n.* & *adv.* ● *n.* **1 a** any of a number of enumerated or listed things. **b** an entry in an account. **2** an article, esp. one for sale (*household items*). **3** a separate or distinct piece of news, information, etc. ● *adv. archaic* (introducing the mention of each item) likewise; also. [orig. as adv.: L, = in like manner, also]

■ *n.* **1, 2** thing, article, object; entry, point, detail, particular, subject, matter, element, component, ingredient, unit. **3** piece, article, feature, fact, story, filler; mention, notice, note.

itemize /ítəmiz/ *v.tr.* state or list item by item. □□ **itemization** *n.* **itemizer** *n.*

■ enumerate, list, particularize, detail, specify, document, schedule, inventory, catalog, take stock of; reel off, recite, rattle off; check off, tick off, run through, number, count, record.

iterate /ítərayt/ *v.tr.* repeat; state repeatedly. □□ **iteration** /-áyshən/ *n.* [L *iterare iterat-* f. *iterum* again]

■ see REITERATE. □□ **iteration** see ECHO *n.* 1.

iterative /ítəraytiv, -rətiv/ *adj. Gram.* = FREQUENTATIVE. □□ **iteratively** *adv.*

ithyphallic /íthifálik/ *adj. Gk Hist.* **1 a** of the phallus carried in Bacchic festivals. **b** (of a statue, etc.) having an erect penis. **2** lewd; licentious. **3** (of a poem or meter) used for Bacchic hymns. [LL *ithyphallicus* f. Gk *ithuphallikos* f. *ithus* straight, *phallos* PHALLUS]

■ **2** see INDECENT 1.

-itic /ítik/ *suffix* forming adjectives and nouns corresponding to nouns in *-ite*, *-itis*, etc. (*Semitic*; *arthritic*; *syphilitic*). [from or after F *-itique* f. L *-iticus* f. Gk *-itikos*: see -IC]

itinerant /ítínərənt, itín-/ *adj.* & *n.* ● *adj.* traveling from place to place. ● *n.* an itinerant person; a tramp. □ **itinerant judge** (or **minister**, etc.) a judge, minister, etc., traveling within a circuit. □□ **itineracy** *n.* **itinerancy** *n.* [LL *itinerari* travel f. L *iter itiner-* journey]

■ *adj.* see MIGRANT *adj.* ● *n.* see MIGRANT *n.*

itinerary /ítínəreree, itín-/ *n.* & *adj.* ● *n.* (*pl.* **-ies**) **1** a detailed route. **2** a record of travel. **3** a guidebook. ● *adj.* of roads or traveling. [LL *itinerarius* (adj.), *-um* (n.) f. L *iter*: see ITINERANT]

■ **1** see ROUTE.

itinerate /ítínərayt, itín-/ *v.intr.* travel from place to place or (of a minister, etc.) within a circuit. □□ **itineration** /-ráyshən/ *n.* [LL *itinerari*: see ITINERANT]

-ition /ishən/ *suffix* forming nouns, = -ATION (*admonition*; *perdition*; *position*). [from or after F *-ition* or L *-itio -itionis*]

-itious[1] /íshəs/ *suffix* forming adjectives corresponding to nouns in *-ition* (*ambitious*; *suppositious*). [L *-itio*, etc. + -OUS]

-itious[2] /íshəs/ *suffix* forming adjectives meaning 'related to, having the nature of' (*adventitious*; *supposititious*). [L *-icius* + -OUS, commonly written with *t* in med.L manuscripts]

-itis /ítis/ *suffix* forming nouns, esp.: **1** names of inflammatory diseases (*appendicitis*; *bronchitis*). **2** *colloq.* in extended uses with ref. to conditions compared to diseases (*electionitis*). [Gk *-itis*, forming fem. of adjectives in *-itēs* (with *nosos* 'disease' implied)]

-itive /itiv/ *suffix* forming adjectives, = -ATIVE (*positive*; *transitive*). [from or after F *-itif -itive* or L *-itivus* f. participial stems in *-it-*: see -IVE]

it'll /ít'l/ *contr. colloq.* it will; it shall.

ITO *abbr.* International Trade Organization.

-itor /ítər/ *suffix* forming agent nouns, usu. from Latin words (sometimes via French) (*creditor*). See also -OR[1].

-itory /itawree/ *suffix* forming adjectives meaning 'relating to or involving (a verbal action)' (*inhibitory*). See also -ORY[2]. [L *-itorius*]

-itous /ítəs/ *suffix* forming adjectives corresponding to nouns in *-ity* (*calamitous*; *felicitous*). [from or after F *-iteux* f. L *-itosus*]

its /its/ *poss.pron.* of it; of itself (*can see its advantages*).

it's /its/ *contr.* **1** it is. **2** it has.

itself /itsélf/ *pron.* emphatic and refl. form of IT[1]. □ **by itself** apart from its surroundings, automatically, spontaneously. **in itself** viewed in its essential qualities (*not in itself a bad thing*). [OE f. IT[1] + SELF, but often treated as ITS + SELF (cf. *its own self*)]

itty-bitty /íteebítee/ *adj.* (also **itsy-bitsy** /ítseebítsee/) *colloq.* usu. *derog.* tiny; insubstantial; slight. [redupl. of LITTLE, infl. by BIT[1]]

■ see TINY.

ITU *abbr.* **1** International Telecommunication Union. **2** International Typographical Union.

ITV *abbr.* instructional television.

-ity /itee/ *suffix* forming nouns denoting: **1** quality or condition (*authority*; *humility*; *purity*). **2** an instance or degree of this (*a monstrosity*; *humidity*). [from or after F *-ité* f. L *-itas -itatis*]

IU *abbr.* international unit.

IUD *abbr.* **1** intrauterine (contraceptive) device. **2** intra-uterine death (of the fetus before birth).

-ium /eeəm/ *suffix* forming nouns denoting esp.: **1** (also **-um**) names of metallic elements (*uranium*; *tantalum*). **2** a region of the body (*pericardium*; *hypogastrium*). **3** a biological structure (*mycelium*; *prothallium*). [from or after L *-ium* f. Gk *-ion*]

IUPAC /yóōpak/ *abbr.* International Union of Pure and Applied Chemistry.

IV /íveé/ *abbr.* intravenous(ly).

I've /iv/ *contr.* I have.

-ive /iv/ *suffix* forming adjectives meaning 'tending to, having the nature of,' and corresponding nouns (*suggestive*; *corrosive*; *palliative*; *coercive*; *talkative*). □□ **-ively** *suffix* forming adverbs. **-iveness** *suffix* forming nouns. [from or after F *-if -ive* f. L *-ivus*]

IVF *abbr.* in vitro fertilization.

ivied /íveed/ *adj.* overgrown with ivy.

ivory /ívəree, ívree/ *n.* (*pl.* **-ies**) **1** a hard, creamy-white substance composing the main part of the tusks of an elephant, hippopotamus, walrus, and narwhal. **2** the color of this. **3** (usu. in *pl.*) **a** an article made of ivory. **b** *sl.* anything made of or resembling ivory, esp. a piano key or a tooth. □ **fossil ivory** ivory from the tusks of a mammoth. **ivory black** black pigment from calcined ivory or bone. **ivory nut** the seed of a corozo palm, *Phytelephas macrocarpa*, used as a source of vegetable ivory for carving: also called *corozo nut*. **ivory tower** a state of seclusion or separation from the ordinary world and the harsh realities of life. **vegetable ivory** a hard, white material obtained from the endosperm of the ivory nut. □□ **ivoried** *adj.* [ME f. OF *yvoire* ult. f. L *ebur eboris*]

ivy /ívee/ *n.* (*pl.* **-ies**) **1** a climbing evergreen shrub, *Hedera helix*, with usu. dark-green, shining five-angled leaves. **2** any of various other climbing plants including ground ivy and poison ivy. □ **Ivy League** a group of prestigious universities in the eastern US. [OE *ifig*]

IWW *abbr.* Industrial Workers of the World.

ixia /íkseeə/ *n.* any iridaceous plant of the genus *Ixia* of S. Africa, with large showy flowers. [L f. Gk, a kind of thistle]

izard /ízaard/ *n.* a chamois. [F *isard*, of unkn. orig.]

-ize /īz/ *suffix* (also *Brit.* **-ise**) forming verbs, meaning: **1** make or become such (*Americanize; pulverize; realize*). **2** treat in such a way (*monopolize; pasteurize*). **3 a** follow a special practice (*economize*). **b** in verbs corresponding to feeling (*sympathize*). **4** affect with, provide with, or subject to (*oxidize; hospitalize*). ¶ The form *-ize* has been in use in English since the 16th c.; it is the regular form used in American English. The alternative spelling *-ise* (reflecting a French influence) is in common use in British English, and is obligatory in certain cases: (*a*) where it forms part of a larger word-element, such as *-mise* (= sending) in *compromise*, and *-prise* (= taking) in *surprise*; and (*b*) in verbs corresponding to nouns with *-i-* in the stem, such as *advertise* and *televise*. □□ **-ization** /-izáyshən/ *suffix* forming nouns. **-izer** *suffix* forming agent nouns. [from or after F *-iser* f. LL *-izare* f. Gk *-izō*]

/ . . . / **pronunciation**   ● **part of speech**
□ **phrases, idioms, and compounds**
□□ **derivatives**   ■ **synonym section**
cross-references appear in SMALL CAPITALS or *italics*

Jj

J¹ /jay/ *n.* (also **j**) (*pl.* **Js** or **J's**) **1** the tenth letter of the alphabet. **2** (as a Roman numeral) = *i* in a final position (*ij*; *vj*).

J² *abbr.* (also **J.**) **1** *Cards* jack. **2** Jewish. **3** joule(s). **4** Judge. **5** Justice.

jab /jab/ *v. & n.* ● *v.tr.* (**jabbed, jabbing**) **1 a** poke roughly. **b** stab. **2** (foll. by *into*) thrust (a thing) hard or abruptly. ● *n.* **1** an abrupt blow with one's fist or a pointed implement. **2** *colloq.* a hypodermic injection, esp. a vaccination. [orig. Sc. var. of JOB²]

■ *v.* **1 a** poke, dig, punch, job; nudge, elbow. **b** stab, stick; spear, lance, skewer, spike, spit, prick. **2** thrust, push, shove, lunge, drive, jam, ram, poke. ● *n.* **1** poke, dig, thrust, job, stab, shove, lunge, ram; punch, hit, cuff, thump, rap, blow, clout, slug, *colloq.* whack, thwack, sock, bop, bust, *sl.* wallop, biff, conk. **2** injection, inoculation, vaccination, *colloq.* shot, *sl.* hit.

jabber /jábər/ *v. & n.* ● *v.* **1** *intr.* chatter volubly and incoherently. **2** *tr.* utter (words) fast and indistinctly. ● *n.* meaningless jabbering; a gabble. [imit.]

■ *v.* **1** chatter, blather, babble, burble, gibber, gabble, drivel, prate, prattle, tattle, rattle (on), gush, cackle, *colloq. or dial.* yammer, yatter (on), *colloq.* natter, gas, jaw, yap, *Brit. colloq.* waffle, *sl. derog.* yak. **2** gabble, babble; prate, prattle, tattle. ● *n.* jabbering, chatter, blather, babble, gibber, burble, gabble, prate, prating, prattle, rattle, cackle, *colloq. or dial.* yammer, natter, *colloq.* jaw, yap, *Brit. colloq.* waffle, *sl. derog.* yak; gibberish, twaddle, nonsense, drivel, rubbish, jargon, gobbledegook, balderdash, claptrap, bunkum, wind, *colloq.* hogwash, tripe, malarkey, piffle, flapdoodle, double Dutch, *sl.* eyewash, hooey, bosh, baloney, hot air, gas, (tommy)rot.

jabberwocky /jábərwokee/ *n.* (*pl.* **-ies**) a piece of nonsensical writing or speech, esp. for comic effect. [title of a poem in Lewis Carroll's *Through the Looking Glass* (1871)]

■ see NONSENSE.

jabiru /jábirōō/ *n.* **1** a large stork, *Jabiru mycteria*, of Central and S. America. **2** a black-necked stork, *Xenorhyncus asiaticus*, of Asia and Australia. [Tupi-Guarani *jabirú*]

jaborandi /jábərándee/ *n.* (*pl.* **jaborandis**) **1** any shrub of the genus *Pilocarpus*, of S. America. **2** the dried leaflets of this, having diuretic and diaphoretic properties. [Tupi-Guarani *jaburandí*]

jabot /zhabố, ja-/ *n.* an ornamental frill or ruffle of lace, etc., on the front of a shirt or blouse. [F, orig. = crop of a bird]

jacana /zhaakənaá, -sənaá/ *n.* any of various small tropical wading birds of the family Jacanidae, with elongated toes and hind claws which enable them to walk on floating leaves, etc. [Port. *jaçanã* f. Tupi-Guarani *jasaná*]

jacaranda /jákərándə/ *n.* **1** any tropical American tree of the genus *Jacaranda*, with trumpet-shaped blue flowers. **2** any tropical American tree of the genus *Dalbergia*, with hard scented wood. [Tupi-Guarani *jacarandá*]

jacinth /jáysinth, jás-/ *n.* a reddish-orange variety of zircon used as a gem. [ME *iacynt*, etc., f. OF *iacinte* or med.L *jacint(h)us* f. L *hyacinthus* HYACINTH]

jack¹ /jak/ *n. & v.* ● *n.* **1** a device for lifting heavy objects, esp. the axle of a vehicle, off the ground while changing a wheel, etc. **2** a playing card with a picture of a man, esp. a

soldier, page, or knave, etc. **3** a ship's flag, esp. one flown from the bow and showing nationality. **4** a device using a single plug to connect an electrical circuit. **5** a small white ball in bowls, at which the players aim. **6 a** a small piece of metal, etc., used with others in tossing games. Also called JACKSTONE. **b** (in *pl.*) a game with a ball and jacks. **7** (**Jack**) the familiar form of *John* esp. typifying the common man or the male of a species (*I'm all right, Jack*). **8** the figure of a man striking the bell on a clock. **9** esp. *Brit. sl.* a detective; a policeman. **10** *sl.* money. **11** = LUMBERJACK. **12** = STEEPLEJACK. **13** a device for turning a spit. **14** any of various marine perchlike fish of the family Carangidae, including the amberjack. **15** a device for plucking the string of a harpsichord, etc., one being operated by each key. ● *v.tr.* **1** (usu. foll. by *up*) raise with or as with a jack (in sense 1). **2** (usu. foll. by *up*) *colloq.* raise, e.g., prices. **3** (foll. by *off*) **a** go away; depart. **b** *coarse sl.* masturbate. □ **before you can say Jack Robinson** *colloq.* very quickly or suddenly. **every man jack** each and every person. **Jack Frost** frost personified. **jack in** (or **up**) esp. *Brit. sl.* abandon (an attempt, etc.). **jack-in-the-box** a toy figure that springs out of a box when it is opened. **jack-in-office** *Brit.* a self-important minor official. **jack-in-the-pulpit** a N. American plant having an upright flower spike and an over-arching hoodlike spathe. **jack-of-all-trades** a person who can do many different kinds of work. **jack-o'-lantern 1** a will-o'-the wisp. **2** a lantern made esp. from a pumpkin with holes for facial features. **jack plane** a medium-sized plane for use in rough joinery. **jack plug** a plug for use with a jack (see sense 4 of *n.*). **jack-tar** a sailor. **Jack-the-lad** *Brit. colloq.* a brash, self-assured young man. **on one's jack** (or **Jack Jones**) *Brit. sl.* alone; on one's own. [ME *Iakke*, a pet name for *John*, erron. assoc. with F *Jacques* James]

■ *n.* **3** see FLAG¹ *n.* 1a. ● *v.* **2** see RAISE *v.* 3. **3 a** see LEAVE¹ *v.* 1b, 3, 4.

jack² /jak/ *n.* **1** = BLACKJACK³. **2** *hist.* a sleeveless padded tunic worn by foot soldiers. [ME f. OF *jaque*, of uncert. orig.]

jackal /jákəl/ *n.* **1** any of various wild doglike mammals of the genus *Canis*, esp. *C. aureus*, found in Africa and S. Asia, usu. hunting or scavenging for food in packs. **2** *colloq.* **a** a person who does preliminary drudgery for another. **b** a person who assists another's immoral behavior. [Turk. *çakal* f. Pers. *šagāl*]

■ **2** see YES-MAN.

jackanapes /jákənayps/ *n. archaic* **1** a pert or insolent fellow. **2** a mischievous child. **3** a tame monkey. [earliest as *Jack Napes* (1450): supposed to refer to the Duke of Suffolk, whose badge was an ape's clog and chain]

jackaroo var. of JACKEROO.

jackass /jákas/ *n.* **1** a male ass. **2** a stupid person.

■ **2** see FOOL¹ *n.* 1.

jackboot /jákbōōt/ *n.* **1** a large boot reaching above the knee. **2** this as a symbol of fascism or military oppression. □□ **jackbooted** *adj.*

jackdaw /jákdaw/ *n.* a small gray-headed crow, *Corvus monedula*, often frequenting rooftops and nesting in tall buildings, and noted for its inquisitiveness (cf. DAW).

jackeroo /jákərōō/ *n.* (also **jackaroo**) *Austral. colloq.* a novice on a sheep or cattle ranch. [JACK¹ + KANGAROO]

jacket /jákit/ *n. & v.* ● *n.* **1 a** a sleeved, short outer garment.

b a thing worn esp. around the torso for protection or support (*life jacket*). **2** a casing or covering, e.g., as insulation around a boiler. **3** = *dust jacket*. **4** the skin of a potato, esp. when baked whole. **5** an animal's coat. ● *v.tr.* cover with a jacket. □ **jacket potato** *Brit.* a baked potato served with the skin on. [ME f. OF *ja(c)quet* dimin. of *jaque* JACK²]
■ **1 a** see COAT *n.* 1. **2** see WRAPPER 1, 2.

jackfish /jákfish/ *n.* (*pl.* same) = PIKE¹.

jackfruit /jákfrōōt/ *n.* **1** an East Indian tree, *Artocarpus heterophyllus*, bearing fruit resembling breadfruit. **2** this fruit. [Port. *jaca* f. Malayalam *chakka* + FRUIT]

jackhammer /ják-hamər/ *n.* a pneumatic hammer or drill.

jackknife /jáknif/ *n.* & *v.* ● *n.* (*pl.* **-knives**) **1** a large pocketknife. **2** a dive in which the body is first bent at the waist and then straightened. ● *v.intr.* (**-knifed, -knifing**) (of an articulated vehicle) fold against itself in an accidental skidding movement.
■ **1** see KNIFE *n.* 1b.

jackpot /jákpot/ *n.* a large prize or amount of winnings, esp. accumulated in a game or lottery, etc. □ **hit the jackpot** *colloq.* **1** win a large prize. **2** have remarkable luck or success. [JACK¹ *n.* 2 + POT¹: orig. in a form of poker with two jacks as minimum to open the betting]
■ see WINDFALL.

jackrabbit /jákrabit/ *n.* any of various large prairie hares of the genus *Lepus* with very long ears and hind legs.

Jack Russell /jak rúsəl/ *n.* **1** a terrier of a breed with short legs. **2** this breed.

jackshaft /jákshaft/ *n.* = COUNTERSHAFT.

jacksnipe /jáksnīp/ *n.* a small snipe, *Lymnocryptes minimus*.

jackstaff /jákstaf/ *n. Naut.* **1** a staff at the bow of a ship for a jack. **2** a staff carrying the flag that is to show above the masthead.
■ see POLE¹ *n.*

jackstone /jákstōn/ *n.* **1** = JACK¹ 6. **2** (in *pl.*) the game of jacks.

jackstraw /jákstraw/ *n.* **1** a splinter of wood, straw, etc., esp. one of a bundle, pile, etc. **2** (in *pl.*) a game in which a heap of jackstraws is to be removed one at a time without moving the others.

Jacobean /jákəbéeən/ *adj.* & *n.* ● *adj.* **1** of or relating to the reign of James I of England. **2** (of furniture) in the style prevalent then, esp. of the color of dark oak. ● *n.* a Jacobean person. [mod.L *Jacobaeus* f. eccl.L *Jacobus* James f. Gk *Iakōbos* Jacob]

Jacobin /jákəbin/ *n.* **1 a** *hist.* a member of a radical democratic club established in Paris in 1789 in the old convent of the Jacobins (see sense 2). **b** any extreme radical. **2** *archaic* a Dominican friar. **3** (**jacobin**) a pigeon with reversed feathers on the back of its neck like a cowl. □□ **Jacobinic** /-bínik/ *adj.* **Jacobinical** *adj.* **Jacobinism** /ják-/ *n.* [orig. in sense 2 by assoc. with the Rue St. Jacques in Paris: ME f. F f. med.L *Jacobinus* f. eccl.L *Jacobus*]

Jacobite /jákəbit/ *n. hist.* a supporter of James II of England after his removal from the throne in 1688, or of his family, the Stuarts. □□ **Jacobitical** /-bítikəl/ *adj.* **Jacobitism** *n.* [L *Jacobus* James: see JACOBEAN]

Jacob's ladder /jáykəbz/ *n.* **1** a plant, *Polemonium caeruleum*, with corymbs of blue or white flowers, and leaves suggesting a ladder. **2** a rope ladder with wooden rungs. [f. Jacob's dream of a ladder reaching to heaven, as described in Gen. 28:12]

Jacob's staff /n.* **1** a surveyor's iron-shod rod used instead of a tripod. **2** an instrument for measuring distances and heights. [f. the staffs used by Jacob, as described in Gen. 30:37–43]

jaconet /jákənet/ *n.* a cotton cloth like cambric, esp. a dyed waterproof kind for poulticing, etc. [Urdu *jagannāthi* f. *Jagannath* (now Puri) in India, its place of origin: see JUGGERNAUT]

Jacquard /jákaard, jəkaárd/ *n.* **1** an apparatus using perforated cards that record a pattern and are fitted to a loom to mechanize the weaving of figured fabrics. **2** (in full **Jacquard loom**) a loom fitted with this. **3** a fabric or article

made with this, with an intricate variegated pattern. [J. M. *Jacquard*, Fr. inventor d. 1834]

jactitation /jáktitáyshən/ *n.* **1** *Med.* **a** the restless tossing of the body in illness. **b** the twitching of a limb or muscle. **2** *archaic* the offense of falsely claiming to be a person's wife or husband. [med.L *jactitatio* false declaration f. L *jactitare* boast, frequent. of *jactare* throw: sense 1 f. earlier *jactation*]

Jacuzzi /jəkōōzee/ *n.* (*pl.* **Jacuzzis**) *propr.* a large bath with underwater jets of water to massage the body. [name of the inventor and manufacturers]

jade¹ /jayd/ *n.* **1** a hard, usu. green stone composed of silicates of calcium and magnesium, or of sodium and aluminum, used for ornaments and implements. **2** the green color of jade. [F: *le jade* for *l'ejade* f. Sp. *piedra de ijada* stone of the flank, i.e., stone for colic (which it was believed to cure)]

jade² /jayd/ *n.* **1** an inferior or worn-out horse. **2** *derog.* a disreputable woman. [ME: orig. unkn.]
■ **1** nag, hack, esp. *Brit. sl.* screw. **2** trollop, slattern, drab, lady of easy virtue, whore, hussy, scarlet woman, *Brit.* slag, *colloq.* floozy, *derog.* slut, *sl.* tart, moll, broad.

jaded /jáydid/ *adj.* tired or worn out; surfeited. □□ **jadedly** *adv.* **jadedness** *n.*
■ exhausted, weary, tired (out), dead tired, dog-tired, spent, raddled, toilworn, broken down, decrepit, effete, *colloq.* fagged (out), done (in), dead beat, bushed, pooped, *Brit. sl.* knackered, clapped out; blasé, fed up, *Brit. sl.* browned off, cheesed (off); hackneyed, trite; sated, satiated, cloyed, surfeited, glutted, gorged, sick (and tired), slaked; dull, bored.

jadeite /jáydit/ *n.* a green, blue, or white sodium aluminum silicate form of jade.

jaeger /yáygər/ *n.* **1** (also **yager**) hunter. **2** /also jáy-/ any large predatory seabird of the family Stercorariidae that pursues other birds and makes them disgorge the fish they have caught. [G *Jäger* hunter f. *jagen* to hunt]

Jaffa /jáfə, jaá-/ *n.* a large, oval, thick-skinned variety of orange. [*Jaffa* in Israel, near where it was first grown]

jag¹ /jag/ *n.* & *v.* ● *n.* a sharp projection of rock, etc. ● *v.tr.* (**jagged, jagging**) **1** cut or tear unevenly. **2** make indentations in. □□ **jagger** *n.* [ME, prob. imit.]

jag² /jag/ *n. sl.* **1** a drinking bout; a spree. **2** a period of indulgence in an activity, emotion, etc. [orig. 16th c., = load for one horse: orig. unkn.]
■ **1** (drinking) bout, carouse, carousal, orgy, bacchanal, soak, *archaic* wassail, *colloq.* pub crawl, *sl.* binge, booze, drunk, bender, toot, *Brit. sl.* blind; frolic, romp, rollick, fling, debauch, *colloq.* lark, spree. **2** fit, spell, burst, stint, bout.

jagged /jágid/ *adj.* **1** with an unevenly cut or torn edge. **2** deeply indented; with sharp points. □□ **jaggedly** *adv.* **jaggedness** *n.*
■ **1** jaggy, rough, uneven, ragged, coarse; chipped; craggy, irregular. **2** jaggy, indented, serrated, crenellated, sawtooth(ed), toothed, spiky, notched, notchy, zigzag, *Bot.* & *Zool.* dentate, *Zool.* denticulate.

jaggy /jágee/ *adj.* (**jaggier, jaggiest**) **1** = JAGGED. **2** (also **jaggie**) *Sc.* prickly.

jaguar /jágwaar/ *n.* a large, flesh-eating spotted feline, *Panthera onca*, of Central and S. America. [Tupi-Guarani *jaguara*]

jaguarundi /jágwərúndee/ *n.* (*pl.* **jaguarundis**) a long-tailed slender feline, *Felis yaguarondi*, of Central and S. America. [Tupi-Guarani]

jai alai /hí lī, əlí/ *n.* an indoor court game somewhat resembling handball in which the ball is propelled with large curved wicker baskets. [Sp. f. Basque *jai* festival + *alai* merry]

jail /jayl/ *n.* & *v.* (also *Brit.* **gaol** *pronunc.* same) ● *n.* **1** a place to which persons are committed by a court for detention. **2**

/.../ **pronunciation**	● **part of speech**
□ **phrases, idioms, and compounds**	
□□ **derivatives**	■ **synonym section**
cross-references appear in SMALL CAPITALS or *italics*	

confinement in a jail. • *v.tr.* put in jail. [ME *gayole* f. OF *jaiole, jeole* & ONF *gaole* f. Rmc dimin. of L *cavea* CAGE]
■ *n.* **1** prison, coop, pen, labor camp, prison camp, lockup, bagnio, calaboose, penitentiary, brig, *archaic* bridewell, *hist.* bastille, roundhouse, stalag, *sl.* slammer, big house, can, clink, cooler, jug, stir, slammer, hoosegow, pen, pokey, slam, *Brit. sl.* choky, glasshouse, nick, quod; reform school, reformatory, *Brit.* detention center, youth custody center, *Brit. hist.* Borstal. **2** imprisonment, incarceration, internment, detention, detainer, confinement, custody, committal, remand, limbo, hard labor, *archaic* durance, *colloq.* time, *hist.* penal servitude. • *v.* imprison, incarcerate, detain, remand, lock up or away, intern, shut up, put behind bars, put away, put inside, put in or throw into irons, send up, *Brit.* send down, *poet.* prison, esp. *Brit. sl.* lag.
jailbait /jáylbayt/ *n. sl.* a girl under the age of consent.
jailbird /jáylbərd/ *n.* (also *Brit.* **gaolbird**) a prisoner or habitual criminal.
■ see PRISONER.
jailbreak /jáylbrayk/ *n.* (also *Brit.* **gaolbreak**) an escape from jail.
■ see ESCAPE *n.* 1.
jailer /jáylər/ *n.* (also **jailor**, *Brit.* **goaler**) a person in charge of a jail or of the prisoners in it.
■ governor, warden; prison officer, guard, *Brit.* warder, wardress, *archaic* turnkey, *sl.* screw.
Jain /jin/ *n.* & *adj.* (also **Jaina**) • *n.* an adherent of a non-Brahminical Indian religion. • *adj.* of or relating to this religion. □□ **Jainism** *n.* **Jainist** *n.* [Hindi f. Skr. *jainas* saint, victor f. *jīna* victorious]
jake /jayk/ *adj. sl.* all right; satisfactory. [20th c.: orig. uncert.]
■ see OK¹ *adj.*
jalap /jáləp, jaá-/ *n.* a purgative drug obtained esp. from the tuberous roots of a Mexican climbing plant, *Exogonium purga.* [F f. Sp. *jalapa* f. *Jalapa, Xalapa*, city in Mexico, f. Aztec *Xalapan* sand by the water]
jalapeño /halapáynyō, -peén-/ *n.* a variety of hot pepper commonly used in Mexican and other highly spiced cooking.
jalopy /jəlópee/ *n.* (*pl.* **-ies**) *colloq.* a dilapidated old motor vehicle. [20th c.: orig. unkn.]
■ see RATTLETRAP.
jalousie /jáləsee/ *n.* a blind or shutter made of a row of angled slats to keep out rain, etc., and control the influx of light. [F (as JEALOUSY)]
Jam. *abbr.* **1** Jamaica. **2** James (New Testament).
jam¹ /jam/ *v.* & *n.* • *v.tr.* & *intr.* (**jammed, jamming**) **1 a** *tr.* (usu. foll. by *into*) squeeze or wedge into a space. **b** *intr.* become wedged. **2 a** *tr.* cause (machinery or a component) to become wedged or immovable so that it cannot work. **b** *intr.* become jammed in this way. **3** *tr.* push or cram together in a compact mass. **4** *intr.* (foll. by *in, onto*) push or crowd (*they jammed onto the bus*). **5** *tr.* **a** block (a passage, road, etc.) by crowding or obstructing. **b** (foll. by *in*) obstruct the exit of (*we were jammed in*). **6** *tr.* (usu. foll. by *on*) apply (brakes, etc.) forcefully or abruptly. **7** *tr.* make (a radio transmission) unintelligible by causing interference. **8** *intr. colloq.* (in jazz, etc.) extemporize with other musicians. • *n.* **1** a squeeze or crush. **2** a crowded mass (*traffic jam*). **3** *colloq.* an awkward situation or predicament. **4** a stoppage (of a machine, etc.) due to jamming. **5** (in full **jam session**) *colloq.* improvised playing by a group of jazz musicians. □ **jam-packed** *colloq.* full to capacity. □□ **jammer** *n.* [imit.]
■ *v.* **1, 3, 4** cram, force, push, thrust, wedge, stuff, press, ram, squash, squeeze, shove, crush, pack, crowd, pile; crunch, scrunch, crumple, compact. **2** lock, seize, freeze; immobilize. **5** block, obstruct, congest, fill up, snarl up, foul (up), tangle up, clog, plug, stop up, barricade, hem in, shut in or off. **6** (*jam on*) slam on, ram on; apply, activate, actuate. **8** see IMPROVISE 1.
• *n.* **1** crush, squeeze, squash, press. **2** mass, crowd, pack, swarm, horde, throng, mob, multitude; obstruction, blockage, congestion, bottleneck, *colloq.* snarl-up. **3** trouble, difficulty, predicament, crisis,

emergency, plight, imbroglio, quandary, mess, *colloq.* bind, fix, hole, pickle, hot water, spot, scrape, *disp.* dilemma. **4** stoppage, blockage, seizure. **5** see *improvisation* (IMPROVISE). □ **jam-packed** full (up), replete, brimful, packed, bursting at the seams, chockablock, chock-full, solid.
jam² /jam/ *n.* & *v.* • *n.* **1** a conserve of fruit and sugar boiled to a thick consistency. **2** *Brit. colloq.* something easy or pleasant (*money for jam*). • *v.tr.* (**jammed, jamming**) **1** spread jam on. **2** make (fruit, etc.) into jam. □ **jam tomorrow** *Brit.* a pleasant thing often promised but usu. never forthcoming. [perh. = JAM¹]
jamb /jam/ *n. Archit.* a side post or surface of a doorway, window, or fireplace. [ME f. OF *jambe* ult. f. LL *gamba* hoof]
jambalaya /júmbəlíə/ *n.* a dish of rice with shrimp, chicken, etc. [Louisiana F f. mod. Prov. *jambalaia*]
jamberoo /jámbərōō/ *n. Austral.* a spree. [alt. of JAMBOREE]
jamboree /jámbəreé/ *n.* **1** a celebration or merrymaking. **2** a large rally of Boy Scouts or Girl Scouts. [19th c.: orig. unkn.]
■ **1** party, gathering, celebration, fête, fair, festival, carnival, frolic, revelry, revel, jubilee, cakes and ale, gaiety, high jinks, jollity, festivity, fun, *Austral.* jamberoo, *colloq.* get-together, spree, shindig, do, *Austral. colloq.* shivoo, *Brit. colloq.* jolly, rave(-up), beanfeast, knees-up, *sl.* bash, ball, wingding, *Brit. sl.* beano.
jamjar /jámjaar/ *n. Brit.* a glass jar for containing jam.
jammy /jámee/ *adj.* (**jammier, jammiest**) **1** covered with jam. **2** *Brit. colloq.* **a** lucky. **b** profitable.
Jan. *abbr.* January.
jane /jayn/ *n. sl.* a woman (*a plain jane*). [the name *Jane*]
jangle /jánggəl/ *v.* & *n.* • *v.* **1** *intr.* & *tr.* make, or cause (a bell, etc.) to make, a harsh metallic sound. **2** *tr.* irritate (the nerves, etc.) by discordant sound or speech, etc. • *n.* a harsh metallic sound. [ME f. OF *jangler*, of uncert. orig.]
■ *v.* **1** ring, jingle, tinkle, chime; clang, clank, clatter, rattle, clash, crash. **2** see JAR² *v.* 1. • *n.* ring, jingle, tinkle, tintinnabulation, chime; clang, clank, clatter, rattle, clash, crash, clangor.
Janglish /jángglish/ *n.* = JAPLISH. [*Ja*panese + E*nglish*]
janissary /jániseree/ *n.* (also **janizary** /-zeree/) (*pl.* **-ies**) **1** *hist.* a member of the Turkish infantry forming the Sultan's guard in the 14th–19th c. **2** a devoted follower or supporter. [ult. f. Turk. *yeniçeri* f. *yeni* new + *çeri* troops]
janitor /jánitər/ *n.* **1** a caretaker of a building. **2** *Brit.* a doorman. □□ **janitorial** /-táwreeəl/ *adj.* [L f. *janua* door]
■ **2** see PORTER².
janizary var. of JANISSARY.
jankers /jángkərz/ *n. Brit. Mil. sl.* punishment for defaulters. [20th c.: orig. unkn.]
January /jányōōeree/ *n.* (*pl.* **-ies**) the first month of the year. [ME f. AF *Jenever* f. L *Januarius* (*mensis*) (month) of Janus the guardian god of doors and beginnings]
Jap /jap/ *n.* & *adj. colloq.* often *offens.* = JAPANESE. [abbr.]
japan /jəpán/ *n.* & *v.* • *n.* **1** a hard, usu. black varnish, esp. of a kind brought orig. from Japan. **2** work in a Japanese style. • *v.tr.* (**japanned, japanning**) **1** varnish with japan. **2** make black and glossy as with japan. [Japan in E. Asia]
Japanese /jápəneéz/ *n.* & *adj.* • *n.* (*pl.* same) **1 a** a native or national of Japan. **b** a person of Japanese descent. **2** the language of Japan. • *adj.* of or relating to Japan, its people, or its language. □ **Japanese beetle** an iridescent green and brown beetle that is a garden and crop pest. **Japanese cedar** = CRYPTOMERIA. **Japanese print** a color print from woodblocks. **Japanese quince** any flowering shrub of the genus *Chaenomeles*, esp. *C. speciosa*, with round white, green, or yellow edible fruits and bright red flowers. [mod.L, fem. of *japonicus* Japanese]
jape /jayp/ *n.* & *v.* • *n.* a practical joke. • *v.intr.* play a joke. □□ **japery** *n.* [ME: orig. uncert.]
Japlish /jáplish/ *n.* a blend of Japanese and English, used in Japan. [*Ja*panese + E*nglish*]

japonica /jəpónikə/ *n.* **1** a camellia, *Camellia japonica*, with variously colored waxy flowers. **2** = *Japanese quince*.

jar[1] /jaar/ *n.* **1 a** a container of glass, earthenware, plastic, etc., usu. cylindrical. **b** the contents of this. **2** *Brit. colloq.* a glass of beer. □□ **jarful** *n.* (*pl.* **-fuls**). [F *jarre* f. Arab. *jarra*]
■ **1** receptacle, vessel, container, crock, urn, pot, vase, jug, pitcher, ewer, flagon, carafe, amphora, bottle, glass, *Archaeol.* pithos, *archaic* cruse.

jar[2] /jaar/ *v. & n.* ● *v.* (**jarred, jarring**) **1** *intr.* (often foll. by *on*) (of sound, words, manner, etc.) sound discordant or grating (on the nerves, etc.). **2 a** *tr.* (foll. by *against, on*) strike or cause to strike with vibration or a grating sound. **b** *intr.* (of a body affected) vibrate gratingly. **3** *tr.* send a shock through (a part of the body) (*the fall jarred his neck*). **4** *intr.* (often foll. by *with*) (of an opinion, fact, etc.) be at variance; be in conflict or in dispute. ● *n.* **1** a jarring sound or sensation. **2** a physical shock or jolt. **3** lack of harmony; disagreement. [16th c.: prob. imit.]
■ *v.* **1, 2** grate, jangle; stridulate, vibrate, rattle, clatter; rasp, scratch, scrape, grind, screech. **3** shock, jolt, jounce, jerk, bump, bounce, bang, knock, shake (up), jog, joggle, rock, disturb, agitate, esp. *Brit.* judder. **4** disagree, conflict, clash, discord, be at odds *or* variance. ● *n.* **1** discord, discordance, discordancy, cacophony, dissonance, clash, squall, jangle, crash, clatter, clang, clank. **2** jolt, lurch, bump, jerk, bounce, knock, start, shock, surprise. **3** disharmony, disagreement, discord, discordance, discordancy, disaccord, difference, dissent, conflict, dispute, argument, strife, contention, quarrel, feud, squabble, argument, altercation, dissension, clash.

jar[3] /jaar/ *n.* □ **on the jar** ajar. [late form of obs. *char* turn: see AJAR[1], CHAR[2]]

jardiniere /jaárd'néer, zhaárdinyáir/ *n.* (also **jardinière**) **1** an ornamental pot or stand for the display of growing plants. **2** a dish of mixed vegetables. [F]

jargon[1] /jaárgən/ *n.* **1** words or expressions used by a particular group or profession (*medical jargon*). **2** barbarous or debased language. **3** gibberish. □□ **jargonic** /-gónik/ *adj.* **jargonistic** *adj.* **jargonize** *v.tr. & intr.* [ME f. OF: orig. unkn.]
■ **1, 2** cant, argot, idiom, vernacular, terminology, slang, parlance, patter, *colloq.* lingo; patois, dialect, speech, talk; pidgin, *hist.* lingua franca. **3** gibberish, twaddle, nonsense, drivel, rubbish, gobbledegook, balderdash, claptrap, bunkum, wind, *colloq.* hogwash, tripe, malarkey, piffle, flapdoodle, double Dutch, *sl.* eyewash, hooey, bosh, baloney, hot air, gas, (tommy)rot, *Brit. sl.* codswallop; jabber, jabbering, chatter, blather, babble, gibber, burble, gabble, prate, prating, prattle, rattle, cackle, abracadabra, *colloq.* jaw, yap, gab, natter, yammer, yatter, esp. *Brit. colloq.* waffle, *sl. derog.* yak.

jargon[2] var. of JARGOON.

jargonelle /jaárgənél/ *n.* an early-ripening variety of pear. [F, dimin. of JARGON[2]]

jargoon /jaargoon/ *n.* (also **jargon** /jaárgən/) a translucent, colorless, or smoky variety of zircon. [F f. It. *giargone*, prob. ult. formed as ZIRCON]

jarl /yaarl/ *n. hist.* a Norse or Danish chief. [ON, orig. = man of noble birth, rel. to EARL]

jarrah /járə/ *n.* **1** an Australian hardwood tree, *Eucalyptus marginata*. **2** the durable wood of this. [Aboriginal *djarryl*]

Jas. *abbr.* James (also in New Testament).

jasmine /jázmin/ *n.* (also **jessamine** /jésəmin/) any of various fragrant ornamental shrubs of the genus *Jasminum* usu. with white or yellow flowers. □ **jasmine tea** a tea perfumed with dried jasmine blossom. [F *jasmin, jessemin* f. Arab. *yās(a)mīn* f. Pers. *yāsamīn*]

jaspé /jaspáy, zha-/ *adj.* like jasper; randomly colored (esp. of cotton fabric). [F, past part. of *jasper* marble f. *jaspe* JASPER]

jasper /jáspər/ *n.* an opaque variety of quartz, usu. red, yellow, or brown in color. [ME f. OF *jasp(r)e* f. L *iaspis* f. Gk. of Oriental orig.]

Jat /jaat/ *n.* a member of an Indo-Aryan people widely distributed in NW India. [Hindi *jāṭ*]

jato /jáytō/ *n.* (*pl.* **-os**) *Aeron.* **1** jet-assisted takeoff. **2** an auxiliary power unit providing extra thrust at takeoff. [abbr.]

jaundice /jáwndis/ *n. & v.* ● *n.* **1** *Med.* a condition with yellowing of the skin or whites of the eyes, often caused by obstruction of the bile duct or by liver disease. **2** disordered (esp. mental) vision. **3** envy. ● *v.tr.* **1** affect with jaundice. **2** (esp. as **jaundiced** *adj.*) affect (a person) with envy, resentment, or jealousy. [ME *iaunes* f. OF *jaunice* yellowness f. *jaune* yellow]
■ *n.* **2, 3** envy, jealousy, resentment, resentfulness, bitterness, spleen, spite. ● *v.* **2** see PREJUDICE *v.* 1; (**jaundiced**) envious, jealous, resentful, splenetic, yellow, bitter, disenchanted; cynical, spiteful, hostile, unfriendly, critical, disapproving; biased, prejudiced.

jaunt /jawnt/ *n. & v.* ● *n.* a short excursion for enjoyment. ● *v.intr.* take a jaunt. □ **jaunting car** a light, two-wheeled, horse-drawn vehicle formerly used in Ireland. [16th c.: orig. unkn.]
■ *n.* see EXCURSION 1.

jaunty /jáwntee/ *adj.* (**jauntier, jauntiest**) **1** cheerful and self-confident. **2** sprightly. □□ **jauntily** *adv.* **jauntiness** *n.* [earlier *jentee* f. F *gentil* GENTLE]
■ cheerful, buoyant, high-spirited, jovial, jolly, merry, gay, cheery, *colloq.* chirpy, chipper; self-confident, perky, frisky, lively, sprightly, brisk, vivacious, spry; dashing, rakish, debonair, dapper, *colloq.* natty, sporty.

Java Man /jaávə/ *n.* a prehistoric type of man whose remains were found in Java. [*Java* in Indonesia]

Javan /jaávən/ *n. & adj.* = JAVANESE.

Javanese /jávəneéz, jaa-/ *n. & adj.* ● *n.* (*pl.* same) **1 a** a native of Java in Indonesia. **b** a person of Javanese descent. **2** the language of Java. ● *adj.* of or relating to Java, its people, or its language.

Java sparrow /jaávə/ *n.* a finch, *Padda oryzivora*.

javelin /jávəlin, jávlin/ *n.* **1** a light spear thrown in a competitive sport or as a weapon. **2** the athletic event or sport of throwing the javelin. [F *javeline, javelot* f. Gallo-Roman *gabalottus*]
■ **1** see LANCE *n.* 1.

jaw /jaw/ *n. & v.* ● *n.* **1 a** each of the upper and lower bony structures in vertebrates forming the framework of the mouth and containing the teeth. **b** the parts of certain invertebrates used for the ingestion of food. **2 a** (in *pl.*) the mouth with its bones and teeth. **b** the narrow mouth of a valley, channel, etc. **c** the gripping parts of a tool or machine. **d** gripping power (*jaws of death*). **3** *colloq.* **a** talkativeness; tedious talk. **b** a sermonizing talk; a lecture. ● *v. colloq.* **1** *intr.* speak esp. at tedious length. **2** *tr.* **a** persuade by talking. **b** admonish or lecture. [ME f. OF *joe* cheek, jaw, of uncert. orig.]
■ *n.* **2 a** (*jaws*) see MOUTH *n.* 1. ● *v.* **1** see PRATTLE *v.*

jawbone /jáwbōn/ *n.* **1** each of the two bones forming the lower jaw in most mammals. **2** these two combined into one in other mammals.

jawbreaker /jáwbraykər/ *n.* **1** *colloq.* a word that is very long or hard to pronounce. **2** a round, very hard candy.

jay /jay/ *n.* **1 a** a noisy chattering European bird, *Garrulus glandarius*, with vivid pinkish-brown, blue, black, and white plumage. **b** any other bird of the subfamily Garrulinae. **2** a person who chatters impertinently. [ME f. OF f. LL *gaius, gaia*, perh. f. L praenomen *Gaius*: cf. *jackdaw, robin*]

jaywalk /jáywawk/ *v.intr.* cross or walk in the street or road without regard for traffic. □□ **jaywalker** *n.*

jazz /jaz/ *n. & v.* ● *n.* **1** music of American origin characterized by improvisation, syncopation, and usu. a regular or forceful rhythm. **2** *sl.* pretentious talk or behavior, nonsensical stuff (*all that jazz*). ● *v.intr.* play or dance to jazz.

/.../ **pronunciation** ● **part of speech**
□ **phrases, idioms, and compounds**
□□ **derivatives** ■ **synonym section**
cross-references appear in SMALL CAPITALS or *italics*

□ **jazz up** brighten or enliven. □□ **jazzer** *n.* [20th c.: orig. uncert.]

jazzman /jázman/ *n.* (*pl.* **-men**) a jazz musician.

jazzy /jázee/ *adj.* (**jazzier, jazziest**) **1** of or like jazz. **2** vivid; unrestrained; showy. □□ **jazzily** *adv.* **jazziness** *n.*
■ **2** see LOUD *adj.* 2.

JCB *abbr.* Bachelor of Canon Law. [mod.L *juris canonici baccalaureus*]

J.C.D. *abbr. Law* Doctor of Canon Law. [L *Juris Canonici Doctor*]

JCL *abbr. Computing* job control language.

JCS *abbr.* (also **J.C.S.**) Joint Chiefs of Staff.

jct. *abbr.* junction.

jealous /jélas/ *adj.* **1** (often foll. by *of*) fiercely protective (of rights, etc.). **2** afraid, suspicious, or resentful of rivalry in love or affection. **3** (often foll. by *of*) envious or resentful (of a person or a person's advantages, etc.). **4** (of God) intolerant of disloyalty. **5** (of inquiry, supervision, etc.) vigilant. □□ **jealously** *adv.* [ME f. OF *gelos* f. med.L *zelosus* ZEALOUS]
■ **1** protective, possessive, defensive. **2** distrustful, mistrustful, suspicious, resentful; anxious, afraid, insecure. **3** envious, resentful, bitter, jaundiced; green (with envy), green-eyed, covetous. **4** intolerant, impatient, uncompromising; demanding, tough, insistent. **5** vigilant, watchful, alert, sharp, observant, careful, wary, guarded, on one's guard. □□ **jealously** protectively, possessively, defensively; distrustfully, mistrustfully, suspiciously, resentfully, bitterly, anxiously; enviously, covetously; intolerantly, impatiently, uncompromisingly; vigilantly, watchfully, observantly, carefully, guardedly, warily.

jealousy /jélasee/ *n.* (*pl.* **-ies**) **1** a jealous state or feeling. **2** an instance of this. [ME f. OF *gelosie* (as JEALOUS)]
■ **1** see ENVY *n.*

jean /jeen/ *n.* twilled cotton cloth. [ME, attrib. use of *Jene* f. OF *Janne* f. med.L *Janua* Genoa]

jeans /jeenz/ *n.pl.* pants made of jean or (more usually) denim, for informal wear.

jeep /jeep/ *n.* (also *propr.* **Jeep**) a small, sturdy, esp. military motor vehicle with four-wheel drive. [orig. US, f. *gp* = general *p*urposes, infl. by 'Eugene the Jeep,' an animal in a comic strip]

jeepers /jeéparz/ *int. sl.* expressing surprise, etc. [corrupt. of *Jesus*]

jeer /jeer/ *v. & n.* ● *v.* **1** *intr.* (usu. foll. by *at*) scoff derisively. **2** *tr.* scoff at; deride. ● *n.* a scoff or taunt. □□ **jeeringly** *adv.* [16th c.: orig. unkn.]
■ *v.* **1** scoff, mock, laugh, fleer, flout, sneer, gibe, tease, heckle, boo, catcall, *Brit.* barrack; (*jeer at*) scoff at, mock (at), laugh at, fleer at, flout (at), ridicule, deride, make fun *or* sport of, poke fun at, have a fling at, twit, chaff, rag, tease, taunt, gibe at, gird at, sneer at, boo, heckle, catcall, *Brit.* barrack, *archaic* smoke, *colloq.* have a shy at, rib, *sl.* bullyrag. **2** scoff at, mock (at), laugh at, fleer at, flout (at), ridicule, deride, make fun *or* sport of, poke fun at, have a fling at, twit, chaff, rag, tease, taunt, gibe at, gird at, sneer at, boo, heckle, catcall, *Brit.* barrack, *archaic* smoke, *colloq.* have a shy at, rib, *sl.* bullyrag. ● *n.* scoff, taunt, gibe, fleer, flout, sneer, gird, boo, hoot, catcall, *colloq.* raspberry.

jeez /jeez/ *int. sl.* a mild expression of surprise, discovery, etc. (cf. GEE¹). [abbr. of JESUS]

jehad var. of JIHAD.

Jehovah /jahóva/ *n.* the Hebrew name of God in the Old Testament. □ **Jehovah's Witness** a member of a millenarian Christian sect rejecting the supremacy of government and religious institutions over personal conscience, faith, etc. [med.L *Iehoua(h)* f. Heb. *YHVH* (with the vowels of *adonai* 'my lord' included: see YAHWEH]
■ see LORD *n.* 4.

Jehovist /jahóvist/ *n.* = YAHWIST.

jejune /jijóon/ *adj.* **1** intellectually unsatisfying; shallow. **2** puerile. **3** (of ideas, writings, etc.) meager; scanty; dry and un-

interesting. **4** (of the land) barren, poor. □□ **jejunely** *adv.* **jejuneness** *n.* [orig. = fasting, f. L *jejunus*]
■ **1** see BANAL. **2** see IMMATURE 2. **3** see PROSAIC 2.

jejunum /jijóonam/ *n. Anat.* the part of the small intestine between the duodenum and ileum. [L, neut. of *jejunus* fasting]

Jekyll and Hyde /jékil and híd/ *n.* a person alternately displaying opposing good and evil personalities. [R. L. Stevenson's story *The Strange Case of Dr. Jekyll and Mr. Hyde*]

jell /jel/ *v.intr. colloq.* **1 a** set as a jelly. **b** (of ideas, etc.) take a definite form. **2** (of two different things) cohere. [backform. f. JELLY]
■ **1** set, congeal, solidify, harden, coagulate, thicken, stiffen, gelatinize; form, take form *or* shape, crystallize, materialize, come together, hang together, make sense, *colloq.* add up. **2** cohere, hang together, bond, connect, bind, marry, fuse, combine, unite.

jellaba var. of DJELLABA.

jellify /jélifī/ *v.tr. & intr.* (**-ies, -ied**) turn into jelly; make or become like jelly. □□ **jellification** *n.*

Jell-O /jélō/ *n. propr.* (often as **jello**) a type of gelatin, flavored and sweetened, served chilled as a dessert.

jelly /jélee/ *n. & v.* ● *n.* (*pl.* **-ies**) **1 a** a gelatinous preparation of fruit juice, etc., for use as a jam or a condiment (*grape jelly*). **b** esp. *Brit.* a soft, stiffish, semitransparent preparation of boiled sugar and fruit juice or milk, etc., often cooled in a mold and eaten as a dessert. **c** a similar preparation derived from meat, bones, etc., and gelatin (*marrowbone jelly*). **2** any substance of a similar consistency. **3** an inexpensive sandal or shoe made of molded plastic. *Brit. sl.* gelignite. ● *v.* (**-ies, -ied**) **1** *intr. & tr.* set or cause to set as a jelly; congeal. **2** *tr.* set (food) in a jelly (*jellied eels*). □ **jelly baby** *Brit.* a gelatinous candy in the stylized shape of a baby. **jelly bag** a bag for straining juice from fruit for jelly. **jelly bean** a chewy, gelationous candy in the shape of a bean with a hard sugar coating. **jelly roll** a rolled sponge cake with a jelly filling. □□ **jellylike** *adj.* [ME f. OF *gelee* frost, jelly, f. Rmc *gelata* f. L *gelare* freeze f. *gelu* frost]
■ *n.* **1 a** see PRESERVE *n.* 1.

jellyfish /jéleefish/ *n.* (*pl.* usu. **same**) **1** a marine coelenterate of the class Scyphozoa having an umbrella-shaped jellylike body and stinging tentacles. **2** *colloq.* a feeble person.
■ **2** see WEAKLING.

jemmy *Brit.* var. of JIMMY.

je ne sais quoi /zha na say kwa'a/ *n.* an indefinable something. [F, = I do not know what]

jennet /jénit/ *n.* a small Spanish horse. [F *genet* f. Sp. *jinete* light horseman f. Arab. *zenāta* Berber tribe famous as horsemen]

jenny /jénee/ *n.* (*pl.* **-ies**) **1** *hist.* = *spinning jenny*. **2** a female donkey or ass. **3** a locomotive crane. □ **jenny wren** a popular name for a female wren. [pet-form of the name *Janet*]

jeopardize /jépardīz/ *v.tr.* endanger; put into jeopardy.
■ endanger, imperil, threaten, menace, expose; risk, hazard, venture, stake, gamble.

jeopardy /jépardee/ *n.* **1** danger, esp. of severe harm or loss. **2** *Law* danger resulting from being on trial for a criminal offense. [ME *iuparti* f. OF *ieu parti* divided (i.e., even) game, f. L *jocus* game + *partitus* past part. of *partire* divide f. *pars partis* part]
■ **1** danger, peril; threat, menace, exposure, liability, vulnerability; risk, hazard, chance, uncertainty.

Jer. *abbr.* Jeremiah (Old Testament).

jerbil esp. *Brit.* var. of GERBIL.

jerboa /jarbóa/ *n.* any small desert rodent of the family Dipodidae with long hind legs and the ability to make long jumps. [mod.L f. Arab. *yarbū'* flesh of loins, jerboa]

jeremiad /jérimíad/ *n.* a doleful complaint or lamentation; a list of woes. [F *jérémiade* f. *Jérémie* Jeremiah f. eccl.L *Jeremias*, with ref. to the Lamentations of Jeremiah in the Old Testament]
■ see LAMENT *n.* 1.

Jeremiah /jérimía/ *n.* a dismal prophet, a denouncer of the times. [with ref. to *Jeremiah* (as JEREMIAD)]

jerk¹ /jark/ *n. & v.* ● *n.* **1** a sharp sudden pull, twist, twitch, start, etc. **2 a** spasmodic muscular twitch. **3** (in *pl.*) *Brit. colloq.* exercises (*physical jerks*). **4** *sl.* a fool; a stupid or contemptible person. ● *v.* **1** *intr.* move with a jerk. **2** *tr.* pull, thrust, twist, etc., with a jerk. **3** *tr.* throw with a suddenly arrested motion. **4** *tr. Weight Lifting* raise (a weight) from shoulder level to above the head. □ **jerk off** *coarse sl.* masturbate. ¶ Usually considered a taboo use. □□ **jerker** *n.* [16th c.: perh. imit.]

■ *n.* **1, 2** pull, wrench, tug, twist, tweak, *colloq.* yank; lurch, jolt, bump; start, jump, twitch, spasm, shudder. **4** fool, *sl.* creep, nerd, dweeb; see also DOLT. ● *v.* **1** lurch, jolt, jump, start, jig, jiggle, wriggle, twitch, shudder, recoil, *colloq.* wiggle. **2** wrench, pull, tug, whip, shove, thrust, push, jostle, nudge, twist, tweak, snatch, pluck, *colloq.* yank. **3** pitch, throw, propel, launch, cast, *colloq.* chuck.

jerk² /jərk/ *v.tr.* cure (beef) by cutting it in long slices and drying it in the sun. [Amer. Sp. *charquear* f. *charqui* f. Quechua *echarqui* dried flesh]

jerkin /jɔrkin/ *n.* **1** a sleeveless jacket. **2** *hist.* a man's close-fitting jacket, often of leather. [16th c.: orig. unkn.]

jerky /jɔrkee/ *adj.* (**jerkier, jerkiest**) **1** having sudden abrupt movements. **2** spasmodic. □□ **jerkily** *adv.* **jerkiness** *n.*

■ **1** see BUMPY 2. **2** see SPASMODIC 1.

jeroboam /jérəbṓəm/ *n.* a wine bottle of 4–12 times the ordinary size. [*Jeroboam* king of Israel (1 Kings 11:28, 14:16)]

Jerry /jéree/ *n.* (*pl.* **-ies**) *Brit. sl.* **1** a German (esp. in military contexts). **2** the Germans collectively. [prob. alt. of *German*]

jerry¹ /jéree/ *n.* (*pl.* **-ies**) *Brit. sl.* a chamber pot.

jerry² /jéree/ *v.intr. Austral. sl.* understand, realize. [20th c.: orig. unkn.]

jerry-builder /jéribildər/ *n.* a builder of unsubstantial houses, etc., with poor-quality materials. □□ **jerry-building** *n.* **jerry-built** *adj.*

■ □□ **jerry-built** see RAMSHACKLE.

jerry can /jérikan/ *n.* (also **jerrycan, jerrican**) a flat-sided 5-gallon container (orig. German) for liquids, usu. fuel or water. [JERRY + CAN²]

jerrymander var. *Brit.* var. of GERRYMANDER.

jersey /jɔrzee/ *n.* (*pl.* **-eys**) **1 a** a knitted, usu. woolen pullover or similar garment. **b** a plain-knitted (orig. woolen) fabric. **2** (**Jersey**) a light brown dairy cow from Jersey. [*Jersey*, largest of the Channel Islands]

Jerusalem artichoke /jərōōsələm/ *n.* **1** a species of sunflower, *Helianthus tuberosus*, with edible underground tubers. **2** this tuber used as a vegetable. [corrupt. of It. *girasole* sunflower]

jess /jes/ *n.* & *v.* ● *n.* a short strap of leather, silk, etc., put around the leg of a hawk in falconry. ● *v.tr.* put jesses on (a hawk, etc.). [ME *ges* f. OF *ges, get* ult. f. L *jactus* a throw f. *jacere jact-* to throw]

jessamine var. of JASMINE.

jest /jest/ *n.* & *v.* ● *n.* **1 a** a joke. **b** fun. **2 a** raillery; banter. **b** an object of derision (*a standing jest*). ● *v.intr.* **1** joke; make jests. **2** fool about; play or act triflingly. □ **in jest** in fun. □□ **jestful** *adj.* [orig. = exploit, f. OF *geste* f. L *gesta* neut. pl. past part. of *gerere* do]

■ *n.* **1 a** see JOKE *n.* 1. **b** see SPORT *n.* 3. **2 a** see BANTER *n.* ● *v.* see JOKE *v.* 1. □ **in jest** see *in fun* (FUN).

jester /jéstər/ *n.* a professional joker or 'fool' at a medieval court, etc., traditionally wearing a cap and bells and carrying a 'scepter.'

■ see FOOL¹ *n.* 2.

Jesuit /jézhōōit, jézōō-, jézyōō-/ *n.* a member of the Society of Jesus, a Roman Catholic order founded by St. Ignatius Loyola and others in 1534. [F *jésuite* or mod.L *Jesuita* f. *Jesus*: see JESUS]

Jesuitical /jézhōō-ítikəl, jézōō-, -yōō-/ *adj.* **1** of or concerning the Jesuits. **2** often *offens.* dissembling or equivocating, in the manner once associated with Jesuits. □□ **Jesuitically** *adv.*

■ **2** see EVASIVE 1, 3, 4.

Jesus /jeezəs/ *n.* the name of the source of the Christian religion d. *c.* AD 30.

■ see GOD *int.*

jet¹ /jet/ *n.* & *v.* ● *n.* **1** a stream of water, steam, gas, flame, etc., shot out esp. from a small opening. **2** a spout or nozzle for emitting water, etc., in this way. **3 a** a jet engine. **b** an aircraft powered by one or more jet engines. ● *v.* (**jetted, jetting**) **1** *intr.* spurt out in jets. **2** *tr.* & *intr. colloq.* send or travel by jet plane. □ **jet engine** an engine using jet propulsion for forward thrust, esp. of an aircraft. **jet lag** extreme tiredness and other bodily effects felt after a long flight involving marked differences of local time. **jet-propelled 1** having jet propulsion. **2** (of a person, etc.) very fast. **jet propulsion** propulsion by the backward ejection of a high-speed jet of gas, etc. **jet set** *colloq.* wealthy people frequently traveling by air, esp. for pleasure. **jet-setter** *colloq.* a member of the jet set. **jet stream 1** a narrow current of very strong winds encircling the globe several miles above the earth. **2** the stream of exhaust from a jet engine. [earlier as verb (in sense 1): F *jeter* throw ult. f. L *jactare* frequent. of *jacere jact-* throw]

■ *n.* **1** see GUSH *n.* 1. **3 b** see PLANE¹ *n.* 3. ● *v.* **1** see GUSH *v.* 1. □ **jet-setter** see TRAVELER 1.

jet² /jet/ *n.* & *adj.* ● *n.* **1 a** a hard black variety of lignite capable of being carved and highly polished. **b** (*attrib.*) made of this. **2** (in full **jet-black**) a deep glossy black color. [ME f. AF *geet*, OF *jaiet* f. L *gagates* f. Gk *gagatēs* f. *Gagai* in Asia Minor]

jeté /zhətáy/ *n. Ballet* a spring or leap with one leg forward and the other stretched backward. [F, past part. of *jeter* throw: see JET¹]

jetsam /jétsəm/ *n.* discarded material washed ashore, esp. that thrown overboard to lighten a ship, etc. (cf. FLOTSAM). [contr. of JETTISON]

jettison /jétisən, -zən/ *v.* & *n.* ● *v.tr.* **1 a** throw (esp. heavy material) overboard to lighten a ship, hot-air balloon, etc. **b** drop (goods) from an aircraft. **2** abandon; get rid of (something no longer wanted). ● *n.* the act of jettisoning. [ME f. AF *getteson*, OF *getaison* f. L *jactatio -onis* f. *jactare* throw: see JET¹]

■ **2** see *throw away* 1.

jetton /jét'n/ *n.* a counter with a stamped or engraved design esp. for insertion like a coin to operate a machine, etc. [F *jeton* f. *jeter* throw, add up accounts: see JET¹]

jetty /jétee/ *n.* (*pl.* **-ies**) **1** a pier or breakwater constructed to protect or defend a harbor, coast, etc. **2** a landing pier. [ME f. OF *jetee*, fem. past part. of *jeter* throw: see JET¹]

■ see PIER 1a.

jeu d'esprit /zhố despreé/ *n.* (*pl.* **jeux d'esprit** *pronunc.* same) a witty or humorous (usu. literary) trifle. [F, = game of the spirit]

jeunesse dorée /zhönes dawráy/ *n.* = *gilded youth* (see GILD¹). [F]

Jew /jōō/ *n.* & *v.* ● *n.* **1** a person of Hebrew descent or whose religion is Judaism. **2** *sl. offens.* (as a stereotype) a person considered as parsimonious or to drive a hard bargain in trading. ¶ The stereotype, which is deeply offensive, arose from historical associations of Jews as moneylenders in medieval England. ● *v.tr.* (**jew**) *sl. offens.* get a financial advantage over. □ **Jew's** (or **Jews'**) **harp** a small lyre-shaped musical instrument held between the teeth and struck with the finger. [ME f. OF *giu* f. L *judaeus* f. Gk *ioudaios* ult. f. Heb. *yᵉhûḏî* f. *yᵉhûḏâh* Judah]

jewel /jōōəl/ *n.* & *v.* ● *n.* **1 a** a precious stone. **b** this as used for its hardness as a bearing in watchmaking. **2** a personal ornament containing a jewel or jewels. **3** a precious person or thing. ● *v.tr.* (**jeweled, jeweling**; esp. *Brit.* **jewelled, jewelling**) **1** (esp. as **jeweled** *adj.*) adorn or set with jewels. **2** (in watchmaking) set with jewels. **jewel box 1** a small box in which jewelry is kept. **2** a plastic case for a compact disk or CD-ROM. □□ **jewellike** *adj.* [ME f. AF *juel, jeuel*, OF *joel*, of uncert. orig.]

■ *n.* **1a** gem, gemstone, brilliant, bijou, *colloq.* sparkler, *sl.* rock, shiner. **3** treasure, gem, pearl; marvel, find, godsend; prize, boon, blessing; masterpiece. ● *v.* **1** adorn, ornament, bedeck, gild, enrich, embellish.

jeweler /jŏŏələr/ *n.* (esp. *Brit.* **jeweller**) a maker of or dealer in jewels or jewelry. □ **jeweler's rouge** finely ground rouge for polishing. [ME f. AF *jueler*, OF *juelier* (as JEWEL)]

jewelry /jŏŏəlree/ *n.* (esp. *Brit.* **jewellery** /jŏŏəlree/) jewels or other ornamental objects, esp. for personal adornment, regarded collectively. [ME f. OF *juelerie* and f. JEWEL, JEWELER]
■ gems, precious stones, jewels, ornaments, adornments, finery, bijouterie, treasures, regalia.

jewelfish /jŏŏəlfish/ *n.* a scarlet and green tropical cichlid fish, *Hemichromis bimaculatus.*

Jewess /jŏŏ-is/ *n. offens.* a female Jew.

jewfish /jŏŏfish/ *n.* **1** a grouper, *Epinephelus itajara,* of N. American, Atlantic, and Pacific coasts. **2** any of various large Australian fish used as food, esp. the mulloway.

Jewish /jŏŏish/ *adj.* **1** of or relating to Jews. **2** of Judaism. □□ **Jewishly** *adv.* **Jewishness** *n.*

Jewry /jŏŏree/ *n.* (*pl.* **-ies**) **1** Jews collectively. **2** *hist.* a Jews' quarter in a town, etc. [ME f. AF *juerie,* OF *juierie* (as JEW)]

Jezebel /jézəbel/ *n.* a shameless or immoral woman. [*Jezebel,* wife of Ahab in the Old Testament (1 Kings 16, 19, 21)]
■ see WANTON *n.*

jg *abbr.* (also **J.G.**) *US Navy* junior grade.

jib[1] /jib/ *n. & v.* ● *n.* **1** a triangular staysail from the outer end of the jibboom to the top of the foremast or from the bowsprit to the masthead. **2** the projecting arm of a crane. ● *v.tr. & intr.* (**jibbed, jibbing**) (of a sail, etc.) pull or swing around from one side of the ship to the other; jibe. [17th c.: orig. unkn.]

jib[2] /jib/ *v.intr.* (**jibbed, jibbing**) esp. *Brit.* **1 a** (of an animal, esp. a horse) stop and refuse to go on; move backward or sideways instead of going on. **b** (of a person) refuse to continue. **2** (foll. by *at*) show aversion to (a person or course of action). □□ **jibber** *n.* [19th c.: orig. unkn.]

jibba /jibə/ *n.* (also **jibbah**) a long coat worn by Muslims. [Egypt. var. of Arab. *jubba*]

jibboom /jib-bōōm/ *n.* a spar run out from the end of the bowsprit.

jibe[1] var. of GIBE.

jibe[2] /jīb/ *v. & n.* (*Brit.* **gybe**) ● *v.* **1** *intr.* (of a fore-and-aft sail or boom) swing across in wearing or running before the winds. **2** *tr.* cause (a sail) to do this. **3** *intr.* (of a ship or its crew) change course so that this happens. ● *n.* a change of course causing jibing. [obs. Du. *gijben*]

jibe[3] /jīb/ *v.intr.* (usu. foll. by *with*) *colloq.* agree; be in accord. [19th c.: orig. unkn.]
■ see AGREE 3a.

jiff /jif/ *n.* (also **jiffy**, *pl.* **-ies**) *colloq.* a short time; a moment (*in a jiffy*; *half a jiff*). [18th c.: orig. unkn.]
■ see MOMENT 1, 2.

jig /jig/ *n. & v.* ● *n.* **1 a** a lively dance with leaping movements. **b** the music for this, usu. in triple time. **2** a device that holds a piece of work and guides the tools operating on it. ● *v.* (**jigged, jigging**) **1** *intr.* dance a jig. **2** *tr. & intr.* move quickly and jerkily up and down. **3** *tr.* work on or equip with a jig or jigs. □ **jig about** (esp. *Brit.*) fidget. **the jig is up** *sl.* all hope is gone, esp. of committing a wrong without being caught. [16th c.: orig. unkn.]
■ *v.* **2** see JERK[1] *v.* 1.

jigger[1] /jígər/ *n.* **1** *Naut.* **a** a small tackle consisting of a double and single block with a rope. **b** a small sail at the stern. **c** a small smack having this. **2** *sl.* a gadget. **3** *Golf* an iron club with a narrow face. **4** *Billiards colloq.* a cue rest. **5 a** a measure of spirits, etc. **b** a small glass holding this. **6** a person or thing that jigs.
■ **1 a** see SPAR[1]. **2** CONTRAPTION. **5 a** see DRINK *n.* 2b.

jigger[2] /jígər/ *n.* **1** = CHIGOE. **2** = CHIGGER 2. [corrupt.]

jiggered /jígərd/ *adj. colloq.* (as a mild oath) confounded (*I'll be jiggered*). [euphem.]

jiggery-pokery /jígəreepŏkəree/ *n. Brit. colloq.* deceitful or dishonest dealing; trickery. [cf. Sc. *joukery-pawkery* f. *jouk* dodge, skulk]

jiggle /jígəl/ *v.* (often foll. by *about,* etc.) **1** *tr.* shake lightly; rock jerkily. **2** *intr.* fidget. □□ **jiggly** *adj.* [JIG or JOGGLE[1]]
■ **1** jog, joggle, jig, shake, agitate, wriggle, jerk, wag, *colloq.* waggle, wiggle. **2** see FIDGET *v.* 1.

jigsaw /jígsaw/ *n.* **1 a** (in full **jigsaw puzzle**) a puzzle consisting of a picture on board or wood, etc., cut into irregular interlocking pieces to be reassembled. **b** a mental puzzle resolvable by assembling various pieces of information. **2** a machine saw with a fine blade enabling it to cut curved lines in a sheet of wood, metal, etc.

jihad /jihaád/ *n.* (also **jehad**) a holy war undertaken by Muslims against unbelievers. [Arab. *jihād*]
■ see CRUSADE *n.* 1b.

jill /jil/ *n. sl.* (also **Jill**) a young woman. [the name *Jill*]

jillion /jílyən/ *n. colloq.* a very large indefinite number.

jilt /jilt/ *v. & n.* ● *v.tr.* abruptly reject or abandon (a lover, etc.). ● *n.* a person (esp. a woman) who jilts a lover. [17th c.: orig. unkn.]
■ *v.* throw over, reject, abandon, discard, desert, break (up) with, walk *or* run out on, cast off *or* aside, finish with, leave in the lurch, forsake, dismiss, brush off, give a person the brush-off, *colloq.* drop, dump, chuck, give a person the elbow *or* push, *sl.* ditch.

jim crow /jim krō/ *n.* (also **Jim Crow**) **1** the practice of segregating blacks. **2** *offens.* a black person. **3** an implement for straightening iron bars or bending rails by screw pressure. □□ **jim crowism** *n.* (in sense 1). [nickname]
■ □□ **jim crowism** see SEGREGATION 1.

jimjams /jímjamz/ *n.pl.* **1** *sl.* = *delirium tremens.* **2** *colloq.* a fit of depression or nervousness. [fanciful redupl.]
■ **2** see NERVE *n.* 3b.

jimmy /jémee/ *n. & v.* (*Brit.* **jemmi** /jémee/) ● *n.* (*pl.* **-ies**) a burglar's short crowbar, usu. made in sections. ● *v.tr.* (**-ies, -ied**) force open with a jimmy. [pet-form of the name *James*]
■ *v.* see FORCE[1] *v.* 2.

jimmygrant /jímeegránt/ *n. Austral.* rhyming *sl.* an immigrant.

Jimmy Woodser /jímee wŏŏdzər/ *n. Austral.* **1** a person who drinks alone. **2** a drink taken on one's own. [Jimmy *Wood,* name of a character in the poem of that name by Barcroft Boake]

jimsonweed /jímsənweed/ *n.* = *thorn apple.* [*Jamestown* in Virginia]

jingle /jínggəl/ *n. & v.* ● *n.* **1** a mixed noise as of bells or light metal objects being shaken together. **2 a** a repetition of the same sound in words, esp. as an aid to memory or to attract attention. **b** a short verse of this kind used in advertising, etc. ● *v.* **1** *intr. & tr.* make or cause to make a jingling sound. **2** *intr.* (of writing) be full of alliterations, rhymes, etc. □□ **jingly** *adj.* (**jinglier, jingliest**). [ME: imit.]
■ *n.* **1** tinkle, ring, tintinnabulation, clink, chink, chime, jangle. **2 a** tautophony, alliteration, assonance, *Rhet.* anaphora. **b** tune, ditty, song, rhyme, verse, poem, lyric, doggerel, slogan, *sl.* buzzword. ● *v.* **1** tinkle, ring, clink, chink, chime, jangle.

jingo /jínggō/ *n.* (*pl.* **-oes**) a supporter of policy favoring war; a blustering patriot. □ **by jingo!** a mild oath. □□ **jingoism** *n.* **jingoist** *n.* **jingoistic** /-gō-ístik/ *adj.* [17th c.: orig. a magician's word: polit. sense from use of *by jingo* in a popular song, then applied to patriots]
■ jingoist, militarist, warmonger, *Polit.* hawk; patriot, nationalist, loyalist, chauvinist, flag-waver. □ **by jingo!** see INDEED *int.* □□ **jingoism** militarism, warmongering, belligerence, bellicosity, *Polit.* hawkishness; patriotism, nationalism, loyalism, chauvinism, flag-waving. **jingoist** see JINGO above. **jingoistic** militaristic, warmongering, belligerent, bellicose, warlike, *Polit.* hawkish; patriotic, nationalist, nationalistic, chauvinistic.

jink /jingk/ *v. & n.* ● *v.* **1** *intr.* move elusively; dodge. **2** *tr.* elude by dodging. ● *n.* an act of dodging or eluding. [orig. Sc.: prob. imit. of nimble motion]

jinker /jíngkər/ *n. & v. Austral.* ● *n.* **1** a wheeled conveyance for moving heavy logs. **2** a light, two-wheeled cart. ● *v.tr.*

convey by jinker. [Sc. *janker* long pole on wheels used for carrying logs]

jinni /jínee, jineé/ *n.* (also **jinn, djinn** /jin/) (*pl.* **jinn** or **jinns, djinn** or **djinns**) (in Muslim mythology) an intelligent being lower than the angels, able to appear in human and animal forms, and having power over people. [Arab. *jinnī*, pl. *jinn*: cf. GENIE]

jinx /jingks/ *n. & v. colloq.* ● *n.* a person or thing that seems to cause bad luck. ● *v.tr.* (often in *passive*) subject (a person) to an unlucky force. [perh. var. of *jynx* wryneck, charm]

■ *n.* (evil) spell, curse, (unlucky) charm, evil eye, voodoo, bogey, Jonah, hoodoo, hex, *sl.* kiss of death. ● *v.* curse, bewitch, cast a spell on, voodoo, damn, doom, condemn, sabotage, hoodoo, hex, *archaic* overlook, *Austral.* point the bone at, *sl.* give a person *or* thing the kiss of death.

jitter /jítər/ *n. & v. colloq.* ● *n.* (**the jitters**) extreme nervousness. ● *v.intr.* be nervous; act nervously. □□ **jittery** *adj.* **jitteriness** *n.* [20th c.: orig. unkn.]

■ *n.* (*the jitters*) nervousness, jitteriness, tension, anxiety, anxiousness, fretfulness, restlessness, uneasiness, skittishness, apprehension, the shakes, d.t.'s, (the) fidgets, nerves, the horrors, *colloq.* the creeps, the jimjams, the jumps, twitch, cold feet, the willies, *sl.* the heebie-jeebies; stage fright, buck fever. □□ **jittery** see NERVOUS 1–3, 5. **jitteriness** see JITTER *n.* above.

jitterbug /jítərbug/ *n. & v.* ● *n.* **1** a nervous person. **2** *hist.* **a** a fast popular dance. **b** a person fond of dancing this. ● *v.intr.* (**-bugged, -bugging**) dance the jitterbug.

jiujitsu var. of JUJITSU.

jive /jīv/ *n. & v.* ● *n.* **1** a jerky style of dance esp. popular in the 1950s. **2** music for this. **3** *sl.* talk, conversation, esp. when misleading or pretentious. ● *v.intr.* **1** dance the jive. **2** play jive music. □□ **jiver** *n.* [20th c.: orig. uncert.]

Jnr. *abbr.* esp. *Brit.* junior.

jo /jō/ *n.* (*pl.* **joes**) *Sc.* a sweetheart or beloved. [var. of JOY]

job[1] /job/ *n. & v.* ● *n.* **1** a piece of work, esp. one done for hire or profit. **2** a paid position of employment. **3** *colloq.* anything one has to do. **4** *colloq.* a difficult task (*had a job to find them*). **5** a product of work, esp. if well done. **6** *Computing* an item of work regarded separately. **7** *sl.* a crime, esp. a robbery. **8** a transaction in which private advantage prevails over duty or public interest. **9** a state of affairs or set of circumstances (*is a bad job*). ● *v.* (**jobbed, jobbing**) **1 a** do jobs; do piecework. **b** *tr.* (usu. foll. by *out*) let or deal with for profit; subcontract. **2 a** *intr.* deal in stocks. **b** *tr.* buy and sell (stocks or goods) as a middleman. **3 a** *intr.* turn a position of trust to private advantage. **b** *tr.* deal corruptly with (a matter). **4** *tr. sl.* swindle. □ **job action** any action, esp. a strike, taken by employees as a protest. **job control language** *Computing* a language enabling the user to determine the tasks to be undertaken by the operating system. **job-hunt** *colloq.* seek employment. **job lot** a miscellaneous group of articles, esp. bought together. **jobs for the boys** *colloq.* profitable situations, etc., to reward one's supporters. **job-sharing** an arrangement by which a full-time job is done jointly by several part-time employees who share the remuneration. **job work** work done and paid for by the job, esp. the miscellaneous work of a print shop. **just the job** esp. *Brit. colloq.* exactly what is wanted. **make a job** (or **good job**) **of** do thoroughly or successfully. **on the job** *colloq.* **1** at work; in the course of doing a piece of work. **2** *coarse* engaged in sexual intercourse. **out of a job** unemployed. [16th c.: orig. unkn.]

■ *n.* **1, 3** task, assignment, chore, (piece of) work, project, undertaking, charge; business, affair, matter, activity, operation. **2** employment, position, post, occupation, appointment, situation, vocation, calling, living, livelihood, *colloq.* berth; career, profession, métier, trade, craft, field, area, province, line; responsibility, concern, function, duty, role, mission. **4** problem, difficulty, hardship, hard time, strain, problem, obstacle; nuisance, bother, toil, grind, drudgery, hard work, *colloq.* headache, pain (in the

neck), hassle, *sl.* pain in the butt. **5** (end) result, (end) product, outcome, effect. **7** crime, felony; robbery, burglary, holdup, *colloq.* stickup, *sl.* caper. **8** scheme, enterprise, racket, game; swindle, dodge, trick, ruse, confidence game *or Brit.* trick, fraud, *colloq.* rip-off, *sl.* caper, con, gyp, scam. **9** see SITUATION 2. ● *v.* **1 a** work; freelance, *colloq.* temp. **b** (*job out*) let out, assign, apportion, allot, share out, contract, hire, employ, subcontract, farm out, consign, commission. **2** trade, deal, do business. **3** take advantage, cheat, *colloq.* cook the books; exploit, misemploy, misapply, misappropriate, misuse, manipulate, maneuver, rig, *colloq.* set up. **4** see SWINDLE *v.* □ **out of a job** see UNEMPLOYED 1.

job[2] /job/ *v. & n.* ● *v.* (**jobbed, jobbing**) **1** *tr.* prod; stab slightly. **2** *intr.* (foll. by *at*) thrust. ● *n.* a prod or thrust; a jerk at a horse's bit. [ME, app. imit.: cf. JAB]

jobber /jóbər/ *n.* **1 a** a wholesaler. **b** *derog.* a broker (see BROKER 2). **2** *Brit.* a principal or wholesaler dealing on the stock exchange. ¶ Up to Oct. 1986 permitted to deal only with brokers, not directly with the public. From Oct. 1986 the name has ceased to be in official use (see BROKER 2). **3** a person who jobs. [JOB[1]]

■ **2 a** see DEALER.

jobbery /jóbəree/ *n.* corrupt dealing.

■ see GRAFT[2] *n.* 1.

jobbing /jóbing/ *adj.* esp. *Brit.* working on separate or occasional jobs (esp. of a computer, gardener, or printer).

jobless /jóblis/ *adj.* without a job; unemployed. □□ **joblessness** *n.*

■ see UNEMPLOYED 1.

Job's comforter /jōbz/ *n.* a person who under the guise of comforting aggravates distress. [the patriarch *Job* in the Old Testament (Job 16:2)]

■ see MISERY 3.

Job's tears *n.pl.* the seeds of a grass, *Coix lacryma-jobi*, used as beads. [the patriarch *Job* in the Old Testament]

Jock /jok/ *n. Brit. sl.* a Scotsman. [Sc. form of the name *Jack* (see JACK[1])]

jock[1] /jok/ *n. colloq.* a jockey. [abbr.]

jock[2] /jok/ *n. sl.* **1** = JOCKSTRAP. **2** an athlete. [abbr.]

jockey /jókee/ *n. & v.* ● *n.* (*pl.* **-eys**) a rider in horse races, esp. a professional one. ● *v.* (**-eys, -eyed**) **1** *tr.* **a** trick or cheat (a person). **b** outwit. **2** *tr.* (foll. by *away, out, in,* etc.) draw (a person) by trickery. **3** *intr.* cheat. □ **jockey cap** a cap with a long peak, as worn by jockeys. **jockey for position** try to gain an advantageous position esp. by skillful maneuvering or unfair action. □□ **jockeydom** *n.* **jockeyship** *n.* [dimin. of JOCK]

■ *v.* **1, 2** see BEGUILE 3.

jockstrap /jókstrap/ *n.* a support or protection for the male genitals, worn esp. by athletes. [*sl. jock* genitals + STRAP]

jocose /jōkōs/ *adj.* **1** playful in style. **2** fond of joking; jocular. □□ **jocosely** *adv.* **jocoseness** *n.* **jocosity** /-kósitee/ *n.* (*pl.* **-ies**). [L *jocosus* f. *jocus* jest]

■ see HUMOROUS 1. □□ **jocoseness, jocosity** see HUMOR *n.* 1a.

jocular /jókyələr/ *adj.* **1** merry; fond of joking. **2** of the nature of a joke; humorous. □□ **jocularity** /-láritee/ *n.* (*pl.* **-ies**). **jocularly** *adv.* [L *jocularis* f. *joculus* dimin. of *jocus* jest]

■ see HUMOROUS 1. □□ **jocularity** see HUMOR *n.* 1. **jocularly** see *tongue-in-cheek* (TONGUE).

jocund /jókənd, jó-/ *adj. literary* merry; cheerful; sprightly. □□ **jocundity** /jəkúnditee/ *n.* (*pl.* **-ies**). **jocundly** *adv.* [ME f. OF f. L *jocundus, jucundus* f. *juvare* delight]

■ see JOYFUL. □□ **jocundity** see JOY *n.* 1.

jodhpurs /jódpərz/ *n.pl.* long breeches for riding, etc., close-fitting from the knee to the ankle. [*Jodhpur* in India]

Joe Bloggs /jō blógz/ *n. Brit. colloq.* = JOE BLOW.

┌───┐
│ /.../ **pronunciation**   ● **part of speech** │
│ □ **phrases, idioms, and compounds**   │
│ □□ **derivatives**   ■ **synonym section**   │
│ **cross-references** appear in SMALL CAPITALS or *italics* │
└───┘

Joe Blow /jō blṓ/ *n. colloq.* a hypothetical average man.
■ see PEOPLE *n.* 2.

joey /jṓee/ *n.* (*pl.* **-eys**) *Austral.* **1** a young kangaroo. **2** a young animal. [Aboriginal *joè*]

jog /jog/ *v. & n.* ● *v.* (**jogged, jogging**) **1** *intr.* run at a slow pace, esp. as physical exercise. **2** *intr.* (of a horse) move at a jog trot. **3** *intr.* (often foll. by *on, along*) proceed laboriously; trudge. **4** *intr.* go on one's way. **5** *intr.* proceed; get through the time (*we must jog on somehow*). **6** *intr.* move up and down with an unsteady motion. **7** *tr.* nudge (a person), esp. to arouse attention. **8** *tr.* shake with a push or jerk. **9** *tr.* stimulate (a person's or one's own memory). ● *n.* **1** a shake, push, or nudge. **2** a slow walk or trot. □ **jog trot 1** a slow regular trot. **2** a monotonous progression. [ME: app. imit.]

■ *v.* **1** run, trot, lope. **3** plod, labor, toil, slog, drag, trudge, tramp, crawl, creep, inch, shuffle. **4, 5** go on, continue, carry on, advance, proceed, push *or* press on. **6, 8** bounce, shake, jolt, joggle, jiggle, jounce, jerk, jar, pitch. **7** nudge, prod, push; poke, bump, shove, elbow. **9** stimulate, arouse, stir, prompt, activate; refresh. ● *n.* **1** shake, push, nudge, prod, poke, shove, jolt, jerk, joggle. **2** jogtrot, trot, run, dogtrot; walk, stroll, amble, ramble, saunter, tramp, trudge.

jogger /jógər/ *n.* a person who jogs, esp. one who runs for physical exercise.
■ see RUNNER 1.

joggle[1] /jógəl/ *v. & n.* ● *v.tr. & intr.* shake or move by or as if by repeated jerks. ● *n.* **1** a slight shake. **2** the act or action of joggling. [frequent. of JOG]

■ *v.* see SHAKE *v.* 1, 2, 5. ● *n.* see SHAKE *n.* 1.

joggle[2] /jógəl/ *n. & v.* ● *n.* **1** a joint of two pieces of stone or lumber, contrived to prevent their sliding on one another. **2** a notch in one of the two pieces, a projection in the other, or a small piece let in between the two, for this purpose. ● *v.tr.* join with a joggle. [perh. f. *jog* = JAG[1]]

john /jon/ *n. sl.* a toilet or bathroom. [the name *John*]

John Bull /bŏŏl/ *n.* a personification of England or the typical Englishman. [the name of a character repr. the English nation in J. Arbuthnot's satire *Law is a Bottomless Pit* (1712)]

John Dory /jon dáwree/ *n.* (*pl.* **-ies**) a European marine fish, *Zeus faber*, with a laterally flattened body and a black spot on each side.

John Hop /jon hóp/ *n. Austral. sl.* a police officer. [rhyming sl. for *cop*]

johnny /jónee/ *n.* (*pl.* **-ies**) **1** *colloq.* (also **Johnny**) a fellow; a man. **2** *sl.* a short-sleeved, collarless gown worn by patients in hospitals, examing rooms, etc. □ **johnny-come-lately** *colloq.* a recently arrived person. [familiar form of the name *John*]

Johnsonian /jonsṓneeən/ *adj.* **1** of or relating to Samuel Johnson, English man of letters and lexicographer (d. 1784). **2** typical of his style of writing.

joie de vivre /zhwaa də veévrə/ *n.* a feeling of healthy and exuberant enjoyment of life. [F, = joy of living]
■ see JOY *n.* 1.

join /joyn/ *v. & n.* ● *v.* **1** *tr.* (often foll. by *to, together*) put together; fasten; unite (one thing or person to another or several together). **2** *tr.* connect (points) by a line, etc. **3** *tr.* become a member of (an association, society, organization, etc.). **4** *tr.* take one's place with or in (a company, group, procession, etc.). **5** *tr.* **a** come into the company of (a person). **b** (foll. by *in*) take part with (others) in an activity, etc. (*joined me in condemnation of the outrage*). **c** (foll. by *for*) share the company of for a specified occasion (*may I join you for lunch?*). **6** *intr.* (often foll. by *with, to*) come together; be united. **7** *intr.* (often foll. by *in*) take part with others in an activity, etc. **8** *tr.* be or become connected or continuous with (*the Gila River joins the Colorado at Yuma*). ● *n.* a point, line, or surface at which two or more things are joined. □ **join battle** begin fighting. **join forces** combine efforts. **join hands 1 a** clasp each other's hands. **b** clasp one's hands together. **2** combine in an action or enterprise. **join up 1** enlist for military service. **2** (often foll. by *with*) unite;

connect. □□ **joinable** *adj.* [ME f. OF *joindre* (stem *joign-*) f. L *jungere junct-* join: cf. YOKE]

■ *v.* **1, 2** unite, unify, connect (up), conjoin, combine, add, couple, twin, marry, wed, mate, link, yoke; merge, fuse, knit, weld, solder, glue, stick, cement, tack; attach, fasten, nail, tie, tag on, knot, scarf, seam, sew (up), splice, bridge. **3, 4** enter, enlist in, enroll in, sign (up) with; ally *or* associate oneself with, fall in with, team up with, throw in one's lot with, attach oneself to. **5** go *or* come *or* be with, accompany, tag on *or* along with, team up with, *colloq.* string along with. **6** unite, combine, merge, mingle, integrate, amalgamate, coalesce; collaborate, cooperate, team up, join forces, club together. **7** (*join in*) participate, take part, share, get *or* become involved, climb *or* jump on the bandwagon. **8** meet, touch, abut (on), adjoin, converge with, coincide with, connect with, merge with, unite with, join up with, combine with, integrate with; reach, arrive at, hit. ● *n.* see JOINT *n.* 1. □ **join forces** see JOIN *v.* 6 above. **join up 1** see ENLIST 1. **2** see JOIN *v.* 8 above.

joinder /jóyndər/ *n. Law* the act of bringing together. [AF f. OF *joindre* to join]

joiner /jóynər/ *n.* **1** a person who makes furniture and light woodwork. **2** *colloq.* a person who readily joins societies, etc. □□ **joinery** *n.* (in sense 1). [ME f. AF *joignour*, OF *joigneor* (as JOIN)]

joint /joynt/ *n., adj., & v.* ● *n.* **1 a** a place at which two things are joined together. **b** a point at which, or a contrivance by which, two parts of an artificial structure are joined. **2** a structure in an animal body by which two bones are fitted together. **3 a** any of the parts into which an animal carcass is divided for food. **b** any of the parts of which a body is made up. **4** *sl.* a place of meeting for drinking, etc. **5** *sl.* a marijuana cigarette. **6** the part of a stem from which a leaf or branch grows. **7** a piece of flexible material forming the hinge of a book cover. **8** *Geol.* a fissure in a mass of rock. ● *adj.* **1** held or done by, or belonging to, two or more persons, etc., in conjunction (*a joint mortgage; joint action*). **2** sharing with another in some action, state, etc. (*joint author; joint favorite*). ● *v.tr.* **1** connect by joints. **2** divide (a body or member) at a joint or into joints. **3** fill up the joints of (masonry, etc.) with mortar, etc.; trim the surface of (a mortar joint). **4** prepare (a board, etc.) for being joined to another by planing its edge. □ **joint account** a bank account held by more than one person, each of whom has the right to deposit and withdraw funds. **joint and several** (of a bond, etc.) signed by more than one person, of whom each is liable for the whole sum. **Joint Chiefs of Staff** *Mil.* a military advisory group made up of the Army Chief of Staff, the Air Force Chief of Staff, the Marine Corps commandant, and the Chief of Naval Operations. **joint stock** capital held jointly; a common fund. **joint-stock company** one formed on the basis of a joint stock. **out of joint 1** (of a bone) dislocated. **2 a** out of order. **b** inappropriate. □□ **jointless** *adj.* **jointly** *adv.* [ME f. OF, past part. of *joindre* JOIN]

■ *n.* **1** join, union, juncture, connection, junction, intersection, commissure, linkage, articulation; link, weld, knot, splice, seam, gusset, bond, suture; bracket, brace, hinge. **4** bar, (night)club, drinking den, *colloq.* dive, honky-tonk, *sl.* clip joint, watering hole, *hist. sl.* speakeasy. **5** *sl.* reefer, spliff. ● *adj.* **1, 2** shared, common, communal, collective, combined, cooperative, collaborative; mutual, reciprocal. ● *v.* **1** articulate, hinge; link, couple, connect.

jointer /jóyntər/ *n.* **1 a** a plane for jointing. **b** a tool for jointing or pointing masonry. **2** a worker employed in jointing wires, pipes, etc.

jointress /jóyntris/ *n.* a widow who holds a jointure. [obs. *jointer* joint possessor]

jointure /jóynchər/ *n. & v.* ● *n.* an estate settled on a wife for the period during which she survives her husband. ● *v.tr.* provide (a wife) with a jointure. [ME f. OF f. L *junctura* (as JOIN)]

joist /joyst/ *n.* each of a series of parallel supporting beams of lumber, steel, etc., used in floors, ceilings, etc. □□ **joisted** *adj.* [ME f. OF *giste* ult. f. L *jacēre* lie]

jojoba /hōhṓbə/ *n.* a plant, *Simmondsia chinensis*, with seeds yielding an oily extract used in cosmetics, etc. [Mex. Sp.]

joke /jōk/ *n.* & *v.* ● *n.* **1 a** a thing said or done to excite laughter. **b** a witticism or jest. **2** a ridiculous thing, person, or circumstance. ● *v.* **1** *intr.* make jokes. **2** *tr.* poke fun at; banter. □ **no joke** *colloq.* a serious matter. □□ **jokingly** *adv.* **jokey** *adj.* (also **joky**). **jokily** *adv.* **jokiness** *n.* [17th c. (*joque*), orig. sl.: perh. f. L *jocus* jest]

■ *n.* **1** quip, gag, jest, waggery, witticism, *colloq.* crack, funny, wisecrack, one-liner, *sl.* josh; pun, wordplay, bon mot, double entendre; story, anecdote, shaggy-dog story, *colloq.* chestnut, old one; lark, frolic, laugh, *colloq.* giggle, scream; prank, jape, practical joke, trick, booby trap, hoax, *colloq.* put-on. **2** farce, mockery, absurdity, nonsense, travesty, charade, caricature, *colloq.* laugh; laughingstock, figure of fun, fool, ass, standing joke, *colloq.* goat. ● *v.* **1** jest, banter, tease, fool (about or around), *colloq.* kid, *sl.* josh; quip, pun, *colloq.* wisecrack; frolic, skylark. **2** see BANTER *v.* 1. □□ **jokingly** see *tongue-in-cheek* (TONGUE).

joker /jṓkər/ *n.* **1** a person who jokes. **2** *sl.* a fellow; a man. **3** a playing card usu. with a figure of a jester, used in some games esp. as a wild card. **4** a clause unobtrusively inserted in a bill or document and affecting its operation in a way not immediately apparent. **5** an unexpected factor or resource. □ **the joker in the deck** an unpredictable factor or participant.

■ **1** comic, (stand-up) comedian or comedienne, jokesmith, funny man, gag man, gagster, humorist, wag, wit, punster, buffoon, farceur, *colloq.* card, kidder; clown, mountebank, merry-andrew, *Theatr.* pierrot, *archaic* droll, *hist.* zany; jester, fool; trickster, prankster, practical joker. **2** see FELLOW 1. **4** fine or small print, catch, hitch, trap, twist, snag, pitfall. **5** unknown quantity, surprise package, the joker in the pack; trump (card).

jokesmith /jṓksmith/ *n.* a skilled user or inventor of jokes.
■ see JOKER 1.

jolie laide /zhōlee láyd/ *n.* (*pl.* **jolies laides** *pronunc.* same) a fascinatingly ugly woman. [F f. *jolie* pretty + *laide* ugly]

jollify /jólifī/ *v.tr.* & *intr.* (**-ies, -ied**) make or be merry, esp. in drinking. □□ **jollification** *n.*
■ □□ **jollification** see FESTIVITY 1.

jollity /jólitee/ *n.* (*pl.* **-ies**) **1** merrymaking; festiveness. **2** (in *pl.*) festivities. [ME f. OF *joliveté* (as JOLLY[1])]
■ see FESTIVITY 1.

jolly[1] /jólee/ *adj., adv., v.,* & *n.* ● *adj.* (**jollier, jolliest**) **1** cheerful and good-humored; merry. **2** festive; jovial. **3** slightly drunk. **4** esp. *Brit. colloq.* (of a person or thing) very pleasant; delightful (often *iron.: a jolly shame*). ● *adv.* esp. *Brit. colloq.* very (*they were jolly unlucky*). ● *v.tr.* (**-ies, -ied**) **1** (usu. foll. by *along*) *colloq.* coax or humor (a person) in a friendly way. **2** chaff; banter. ● *n.* (*pl.* **-ies**) *colloq.* a party or celebration; an outing. □ **Jolly Roger** a pirates' black flag, usu. with the skull and crossbones. □□ **jollily** *adv.* **jolliness** *n.* [ME f. OF *jolif* gay, pretty, perh. f. ON *jól* YULE]

■ *adj.* **1, 2** merry, cheerful, cheery, good-humored, happy, joyful, joyous, gleeful, gay, sunny; convivial, jovial, festive, jubilant, exuberant, vivacious, lively, high-spirited, *colloq.* chirpy; playful, frolicsome, frisky, sportive, jocose, jocular, light-hearted, buoyant, carefree, mirthful, *literary* jocund. **3** tipsy, *colloq.* woozy, happy, *Brit. colloq.* merry, tiddly, *sl.* squiffed; see also DRUNK *adj.* 1. ● *v.* **1** (*jolly along*) coax, humor, appease, cajole, wheedle, urge (on). **2** see BANTER *v.* 1. ● *n.* outing, jaunt, junket, trip; see also PARTY *n.* 1.

jolly[2] /jólee/ *n.* (*pl.* **-ies**) (in full **jolly boat**) a clinker-built ship's boat smaller than a cutter. [18th c.: orig. unkn.: perh. rel. to YAWL]
■ see TENDER[3].

jolt /jōlt/ *v.* & *n.* ● *v.* **1** *tr.* disturb or shake from the normal position (esp. in a moving vehicle) with a jerk. **2** *tr.* give a mental shock to; perturb. **3** *intr.* (of a vehicle) move along

with jerks, as on a rough road. ● *n.* **1** such a jerk. **2** a surprise or shock. □□ **jolty** *adj.* (**joltier, joltiest**). [16th c.: orig. unkn.]

■ *v.* **1** jar, jerk, jounce, bump, bang, knock, nudge, jog, joggle, shake, rock, bounce, rattle, disturb, agitate, *colloq.* yank. **2** shock, shake (up), disturb, perturb, rattle, agitate, unnerve, unsettle, disconcert; astonish, astound, amaze, surprise, startle, stun, dumbfound, stupefy, stagger, electrify, strike dumb, daze. **3** lurch, jerk, stagger, shudder, rock, rattle, esp. *Brit.* judder. ● *n.* **1** lurch, jerk, stagger, shudder, esp. *Brit.* judder; jar, jounce, bump, bang, knock, nudge, jog, joggle, shake, jump, bounce. **2** shock, surprise, blow, start, bolt from the blue, bombshell.

Jon. *abbr.* **1** Jonah (Old Testament). **2** Jonathan.

Jonah /jṓnə/ *n.* a person who seems to bring bad luck. [*Jonah* in the Old Testament]
■ see JINX *n.*

jongleur /zhoNglṓr/ *n. hist.* an itinerant minstrel. [F, var. of *jougleur* JUGGLER]
■ see MINSTREL.

jonquil /jóngkwil/ *n.* a bulbous plant, *Narcissus jonquilla*, with clusters of small fragrant yellow flowers. [mod.L *jonquilla* or F *jonquille* f. Sp. *junquillo* dimin. of *junco*: see JUNCO]

Jordanian /jawrdáyneeən/ *adj.* & *n.* ● *adj.* of or relating to the kingdom of Jordan in the Middle East. ● *n.* **1** a native or national of Jordan. **2** a person of Jordanian descent. [*Jordan*, river flowing into the Dead Sea]

jorum /jáwrəm/ *n.* **1** a large drinking bowl. **2** its contents, esp. punch. [perh. f. *Joram* (2 Sam. 8:10)]

Jos. *abbr.* Joseph.

Josh. *abbr.* Joshua (Old Testament).

josh /josh/ *n.* & *v. sl.* ● *n.* a good-natured or teasing joke. ● *v.* **1** *tr.* tease or banter. **2** *intr.* indulge in ridicule. □□ **josher** *n.* [19th c.: orig. unkn.]
■ *v.* **1** see TEASE *v.* 1a.

joss[1] /jos/ *n.* a Chinese idol. □ **joss house** a Chinese temple. **joss stick** a stick of fragrant tinder mixed with clay, burned as incense. [perh. ult. f. Port. *deos* f. L *deus* god]

joss[2] /jos/ *n. Austral.* a person of influence and importance. [Brit. dial.]

josser /jósər/ *n. Brit. sl.* **1** a fool. **2** a fellow. [JOSS + -ER[1]: cf. Austral. sense 'clergyman']

jostle /jósəl/ *v.* & *n.* ● *v.* **1** *tr.* push against; elbow. **2** *tr.* (often foll. by *away, from,* etc.) push (a person) abruptly or roughly. **3** *intr.* (foll. by *against*) knock or push, esp. in a crowd. **4** *intr.* (foll. by *with*) struggle; have a rough exchange. ● *n.* **1** the act or an instance of jostling. **2** a collision. [ME: earlier *justle* f. JOUST + -LE[4]]
■ *v.* **1–3** see PUSH *v.* 7. **4** see STRUGGLE *v.* 3.

jot /jot/ *v.* & *n.* ● *v.tr.* (**jotted, jotting**) (usu. foll. by *down*) write briefly or hastily. ● *n.* (usu. with *neg.* expressed or implied) a very small amount (*not one jot*). [earlier as noun: L f. Gk *iōta*: see IOTA]

■ *v.* (*jot down*) make a note of, write or note (down), put or set or take down, scribble (down), scrawl, pen, record. ● *n.* bit, scrap, grain, speck, mite, iota, whit, rap, hoot, particle, tittle, *colloq.* smidgen, tad, *sl.* two hoots; (*not a jot*) not in the slightest, not at all, not a whit.

jotter /jótər/ *n.* a small pad or notebook for making notes, etc.
■ see PAD[1] *n.* 2.

jotting /jóting/ *n.* (usu. in *pl.*) a note; something jotted down.
■ see NOTE *n.* 1.

joule /jōōl/ *n.* the SI unit of work or energy equal to the work done by a force of one newton when its point of application moves one meter in the direction of action of the force,

---

/.../ **pronunciation** ● **part of speech**
□ **phrases, idioms, and compounds**
□□ **derivatives** ■ **synonym section**
cross-references appear in SMALL CAPITALS or *italics*

equivalent to a watt-second. ¶ Symb.: **J**. [J. P. *Joule*, Engl. physicist d. 1889]

jounce /jowns/ *v.tr. & intr.* bump; bounce; jolt. [ME: orig. unkn.]

■ see JOLT *v.* 1.

journal /járnəl/ *n.* **1** a newspaper or periodical. **2** a daily record of events. **3** *Naut.* a logbook. **4** a book in which business transactions are entered, with a statement of the accounts to which each is to be debited and credited. **5** the part of a shaft or axle that rests on bearings. **6** a legislative body's record of daily proceedings. [ME f. OF *jurnal* f. LL *diurnalis* DIURNAL]

■ **1** newspaper, paper, organ, periodical, magazine, gazette, newsletter, review, tabloid, broadsheet, news sheet, pictorial, *colloq.* daily, *derog.* rag; weekly, fortnightly, monthly, quarterly. **2** diary, chronicle, record, log(book), yearbook, annal(s); almanac, calendar. **4** daybook, ledger.

journalese /járnəleez/ *n.* a hackneyed style of language characteristic of some newspaper writing.

journalism /járnəlizəm/ *n.* the business or practice of writing and producing newspapers.

journalist /járnəlist/ *n.* a person employed to report for or edit a newspaper, journal, or newscast. □□ **journalistic** *adj.* **journalistically** /-lístikəlee/ *adv.*

■ reporter, newspaperman, pressman, newsman, (gossip) columnist, publicist, (special) correspondent, commentator, newshound, hack, news gatherer, legman, wireman, staffer, *Austral.* roundsman, *colloq.* stringer, scribe; (*journalists*) the press, *Brit.* Fleet Street, the lobby, *joc.* the fourth estate; paparazzo; editor, subeditor, copy editor, city editor; newscaster, broadcaster, esp. *Brit.* newsreader.

journalize /járnəliz/ *v.tr.* record in a private journal.

journey /járnee/ *n. & v.* ● *n.* (*pl.* **-eys**) **1** an act of going from one place to another, esp. at a long distance. **2** the distance traveled in a specified time (*a day's journey*). **3** the traveling of a vehicle along a route at a stated time. ● *v.intr.* (**-eys, -eyed**) make a journey. □□ **journeyer** *n.* [ME f. OF *jornee* day, day's work or travel, ult. f. L *diurnus* daily]

■ *n.* voyage, expedition, odyssey, trek; trip, excursion, tour, outing, junket, jaunt, errand, *archaic or joc.* peregrination; cruise, flight, drive, ride, run, crossing, passage, hop, lap, circuit; walk, meander, ramble, tramp, stroll, march, *colloq. or dial.* traipse; pilgrimage, mission; course, route, career, way, transit, traverse, transition, progress, advance, travel. ● *v.* travel, tour, voyage, go (abroad or overseas), make *or* take a trip, make one's way, make a pilgrimage, trek, rove, range, wander, roam, cruise, gad (about), *archaic or joc.* peregrinate, *colloq.* gallivant, *literary or archaic* wend one's way. □□ **journeyer** see TRAVELER 1.

journeyman /járneemən/ *n.* (*pl.* **-men**) **1** a qualified mechanic or artisan who works for another. **2** *derog.* **a** a reliable but not outstanding worker. **b** a mere hireling. [JOURNEY in obs. sense 'day's work' + MAN]

■ **1** see TRADESMAN.

joust /jowst/ *n. & v. hist.* ● *n.* a combat between two knights on horseback with lances. ● *v.intr.* engage in a joust. □□ **jouster** *n.* [ME f. OF *juster* bring together ult. f. L *juxta* near]

■ *n.* see TOURNAMENT 3. ● *v.* see FIGHT *v.* 1a.

Jove /jōv/ *n.* (in Roman mythology) Jupiter. □ **by Jove!** an exclamation of surprise or approval. [ME f. L *Jovis* genit. of OL *Jovis* used as genit. of JUPITER]

jovial /jóveeəl/ *adj.* **1** merry. **2** convivial. **3** hearty and good-humored. □□ **joviality** /-álitee/ *n.* **jovially** *adv.* [F f. LL *jovialis* of Jupiter (as JOVE), with ref. to the supposed influence of the planet Jupiter on those born under it]

■ see MERRY 1. □□ **joviality** see MERRIMENT.

Jovian /jóveeən/ *adj.* **1** (in Roman mythology) of or like Jupiter. **2** of the planet Jupiter.

jowar /jow-waár/ *n.* = DURRA. [Hindi *jawār*]

jowl[1] /jowl/ *n.* **1** the jaw or jawbone. **2** the cheek (*cheek by*

jowl*). □□ **-jowled** *adj.* (in *comb.*). [ME *chavel* jaw f. OE *ceafl*]

jowl[2] /jowl/ *n.* **1** the external loose skin on the throat or neck when prominent. **2** the dewlap of oxen, wattle of a bird, etc. □□ **jowly** *adj.* [ME *cholle* neck f. OE *ceole*]

joy /joy/ *n. & v.* ● *n.* **1** (often foll. by *at, in*) a vivid emotion of pleasure; extreme gladness. **2** a thing that causes joy. **3** *Brit. colloq.* satisfaction; success (*got no joy*). ● *v.* esp. *poet.* **1** *intr.* rejoice. **2** *tr.* gladden. □ **wish a person joy of** *Brit. iron.* be gladly rid of (what that person has to deal with). □□ **joyless** *adj.* **joylessly** *adv.* [ME f. OF *joie* ult. f. L *gaudium* f. *gaudēre* rejoice]

■ *n.* **1** delight, elation, exaltation, ecstasy, exhilaration, exultation, rapture; bliss, heaven, paradise; gladness, felicity, happiness, contentment, pleasure, gratification, satisfaction, enjoyment; gaiety, fun, cheerfulness, sparkle, sunshine, radiance, cheer, glee, buoyancy, joviality, jollity, joyfulness, joyousness, jubilation, jubilee, merriment, lightheartedness, joie de vivre, *literary* jocundity. **2** delight, pleasure, treat; blessing, treasure, boon, godsend, gem, meat and drink.

● *v.* **1** see REJOICE 1. **2** see GLADDEN. □□ **joyless** sad, unhappy, miserable, depressed, dejected, mournful, downhearted, downcast, cast down, despondent, dispirited, melancholy, heavyhearted, cheerless, doleful, grief-stricken, crestfallen, wretched, disconsolate, inconsolable, morose, heartsick, sorrowful, woeful, woebegone; gloomy, depressing, dispiriting, disheartening, dreary, lugubrious, cheerless, dismal, bleak, inhospitable, desolate, grim, austere, severe.

Joycean /jóyseeən/ *adj. & n.* ● *adj.* of or characteristic of James Joyce, Irish poet and novelist (d. 1941) or his writings. ● *n.* a specialist in or admirer of Joyce's works.

joyful /jóyfŏŏl/ *adj.* full of, showing, or causing joy. □□ **joyfully** *adv.* **joyfulness** *n.*

■ cheerful, happy, buoyant, gleeful, merry, jovial, jolly, joyous, jubilant, gay, lighthearted, sunny, *literary* jocund, *poet.* blithe, blithesome; glad, pleased, delighted, happy, elated, ecstatic, exhilarated, exultant, overjoyed, jubilant, rapt, rapturous, in seventh heaven, *colloq.* on cloud nine, tickled (pink *or* to death), *Brit.* over the moon.

joyous /jóyəs/ *adj.* (of an occasion, circumstance, etc.) characterized by pleasure or joy; joyful. □□ **joyously** *adv.* **joyousness** *n.*

■ see JOYFUL. □□ **joyously** see *happily* (HAPPY). **joyousness** see JOY *n.* 1.

joyride /jóyrid/ *n. & v. colloq.* ● *n.* a ride for pleasure in an automobile, esp. without the owner's permission. ● *v.intr.* (*past* **-rode** /-rōd/; *past part.* **-ridden** /-rid'n/) go for a joyride. □□ **joyrider** *n.*

joystick /jóystik/ *n.* **1** *colloq.* the control column of an aircraft. **2** a lever that can be moved in several directions to control the movement of an image on a computer monitor.

JP *abbr.* **1** justice of the peace. **2** jet propulsion.

Jr. *abbr.* junior.

jt. *abbr.* joint.

jubilant /jŏŏbilənt/ *adj.* exultant; rejoicing; joyful. □□ **jubilance** /-ləns/ *n.* **jubilantly** *adv.* [L *jubilare jubilant-* shout for joy]

■ see JOYFUL. □□ **jubilantly** see GAILY 1.

jubilate /jŏŏbilayt/ *v.intr.* exult; be joyful. □□ **jubilation** /-láyshən/ *n.* [L *jubilare* (as JUBILANT)]

■ □□ **jubilation** see JOY *n.* 1.

jubilee /jŏŏbilee/ *n.* **1** a time or season of rejoicing. **2** an anniversary, esp. the 25th or 50th. **3** *Jewish Hist.* a year of emancipation and restoration, kept every 50 years. **4** *RC Ch.* a period of remission from the penal consequences of sin, granted under certain conditions for a year usu. at intervals of 25 years. **5** exultant joy. [ME f. OF *jubilé* f. LL *jubilaeus* (*annus*) (year) of jubilee ult. f. Heb. *yōbēl*, orig. = ram, ram's-horn trumpet]

■ **1** see JAMBOREE.

Jud. *abbr.* Judith (Apocrypha).

Judaeo- esp. *Brit.* var. of JUDEO-.

Judaic /jŏŏdáyik/ *adj.* of or characteristic of the Jews or Judaism. [L *Judaicus* f. Gk *Ioudaïkos* f. *Ioudaios* JEW]

Judaism /jŏŏdeeizəm, -day-/ *n.* **1** the religion of the Jews, with a belief in one God and a basis in Mosaic and rabbinical teachings. **2** the Jews collectively. □□ **Judaist** *n.* [ME f. LL *Judaismus* f. Gk *Ioudaïsmos* (as JUDAIC)]

Judaize /jŏŏdeeīz, -day-/ *v.* **1** *intr.* follow Jewish customs or rites. **2** *tr.* **a** make Jewish. **b** convert to Judaism. □□ **Judaization** *n.* [LL *judaizare* f. Gk *ioudaïzō* (as JUDAIC)]

Judas /jŏŏdəs/ *n.* **1** a person who betrays a friend. **2** (**judas**) (in full **judas hole**) a peephole in a door. □ **Judas tree** a Mediterranean tree, *Cercis siliquastrum*, with purple flowers usu. appearing before the leaves. [*Judas* Iscariot who betrayed Christ (Luke 22)]
■ **1** see TRAITOR.

judder /júdər/ *v.* & *n.* esp. *Brit.* ● *v.intr.* **1** (esp. of a mechanism) vibrate noisily or violently. **2** (of a singer's voice) oscillate in intensity. ● *n.* an instance of juddering. [imit.: cf. SHUDDER]

Judeo- /jŏŏdáy-ō, -dee-ō/ *comb. form* (esp. *Brit.* **Judaeo-**) Jewish; Jewish and. [L *judaeus* Jewish]

Judg. *abbr.* Judges (Old Testament).

judge /juj/ *n.* & *v.* ● *n.* **1** a public officer appointed to hear and try causes in a court of justice. **2** a person appointed to decide a dispute or contest. **3 a** a person who decides a question. **b** a person regarded in terms of capacity to decide on the merits of a thing or question (*am no judge of that*; *a good judge of art*). **4** *Jewish Hist.* a leader having temporary authority in the period between Joshua and the Kings. ● *v.* **1** *tr.* **a** try (a cause) in a court of justice. **b** pronounce sentence on (a person). **2** *tr.* form an opinion about; estimate, appraise. **3** *tr.* act as a judge of (a dispute or contest). **4** *tr.* (often foll. by *to* + infin. or *that* + clause) conclude, consider, or suppose. **5** *intr.* **a** form a judgment. **b** act as judge. □ **judge advocate general** an officer in supreme control of the courts martial in the armed forces. □□ **judgelike** *adj.* **judgeship** *n.* [ME f. OF *juge* (n.), *juger* (v.) f. L *judex judicis* f. *jus* law + *-dicus* speaking]
■ *n.* **1** justice, magistrate, jurist, the bench, official (principal), seneschal, deemster, alcalde, *Brit.* jurat, Common Serjeant, *Brit.* & *hist.* recorder, reeve, *Sc.* sheriff-depute, surrogate, squire, esp. *hist.* bailie, *Brit. sl.* beak. **2** arbitrator, arbiter, umpire, referee, adjudicator, mediator, moderator, assessor, examiner, appraiser, evaluator. **3 b** connoisseur, expert, authority, specialist, pundit, *arbiter elegantiae*; reviewer, critic.
● *v.* **1 a** try, hear, sit on, adjudicate, adjudge, decide; weigh. **b** sentence, pronounce *or* pass sentence on, pass judgment on. **2** reckon, estimate, figure, gauge, measure, weigh (up), size up, assess, evaluate, appraise, value, count, rate, rank; decide, determine. **3** adjudicate, adjudge, arbitrate, referee, umpire, mediate, moderate. **4** regard, hold, believe, perceive, suppose, consider, think, *formal* deem; find, conclude, infer, decide, determine. **5 a** make up one's mind, decide, take *or* reach *or* come to a conclusion *or* decision. **b** adjudicate, arbitrate, referee, umpire, mediate, moderate, officiate.

judgment /jújmənt/ *n.* (also **judgement**) **1** the critical faculty; discernment (*an error of judgment*). **2** good sense. **3** an opinion or estimate (*in my judgment*). **4** the sentence of a court of justice; a decision by a judge. **5** *joc.* a misfortune viewed as a deserved recompense (*it is a judgment on you for getting up late*). **6** criticism. □ **against one's better judgment** contrary to what one really feels to be advisable. **judgment by default** see DEFAULT. **Judgment Day** the day on which the Last Judgment is believed to take place. **judgment seat** a judge's seat; a tribunal. **the Last Judgment** (in some beliefs) the judgment of mankind expected to take place at the end of the world. [ME f. OF *jugement* (as JUDGE)]
■ **1, 2** discretion, discernment, discrimination, judiciousness, prudence, wisdom, sagacity, perspicacity, perception, percipience, acumen, acuity, insight, reason, reasoning, logic, intellect, mentality, understanding; intelligence, levelheadedness, (good) sense, common sense, (mother *or* native) wit, *colloq.* gumption, horse sense. **3** opinion, (point of) view, belief, (way of) thinking, conviction, feeling, sentiment, idea, notion, impression, conception, perception; estimate, evaluation, estimation, appraisal, analysis, assessment; criticism, critique, review. **4** decision, sentence, ruling, finding, adjudication, verdict, pronouncement, conclusion, determination, decree. **5** punishment, penalty, sentence, (just) deserts. **6** criticism, censure, disapproval, reproof, condemnation. □ **against one's better judgment** reluctantly, unwillingly, grudgingly. **Judgment Day** doomsday, doom; the Last Judgment. **the Last Judgment** see *Judgment Day* above.

judgmental /jujmént'l/ *adj.* (also **judgemental**) **1** of or concerning or by way of judgment. **2** condemning; critical. □□ **judgmentally** *adv.*
■ **2** see CRITICAL 1.

judicature /jŏŏdikəchər/ *n.* **1** the administration of justice. **2** a judge's office or term of office. **3** judges collectively; judiciary. **4** a court of justice. [med.L *judicatura* f. L *judicare* to judge]

judicial /jŏŏdíshəl/ *adj.* **1** of, done by, or proper to a court of law. **2** having the function of judgment (*a judicial assembly*). **3** of or proper to a judge. **4** expressing a judgment; critical. **5** impartial. **6** regarded as a divine judgment. □ **judicial factor** *Sc.* an official receiver. **judicial separation** the separation of man and wife by decision of a court. □□ **judicially** *adv.* [ME f. L *judicialis* f. *judicium* judgment f. *judex* JUDGE]
■ **1, 2** legal, judiciary, juridical, forensic; official. **3** judgelike, magisterial. **4** critical, judgmental; censorious, disparaging, deprecatory, deprecative, condemnatory. **5** impartial, equitable, evenhanded, neutral, unbiased, objective, uncolored, unprejudiced, fair, fair-minded, just, true, honest, disinterested, dispassionate, detached, uninvolved.

judiciary /jŏŏdíshee-eree, -díshəree/ *n.* (*pl.* **-ies**) the judges of a nation's judicial branch collectively. [L *judiciarius* (as JUDICIAL)]

judicious /jŏŏdíshəs/ *adj.* **1** sensible, prudent. **2** sound in discernment and judgment. □□ **judiciously** *adv.* **judiciousness** *n.* [F *judicieux* f. L *judicium* (as JUDICIAL)]
■ sensible, reasonable, logical, sane, prudent, careful, sound, sober, cautious, considered, (well-)advised, circumspect, provident, politic, diplomatic, discreet; wise, sage, sagacious, insightful, clear-sighted, intelligent, perceptive, percipient, perspicacious, discerning, canny, shrewd, astute, *literary* sapient.

judo /jŏŏdō/ *n.* a sport of unarmed combat derived from jujitsu. □□ **judoist** *n.* [Jap. f. *jū* gentle + *dō* way]

Judy /jŏŏdee/ *n.* (*pl.* **-ies**) **1** see PUNCH⁴. **2** (also **judy**) esp. *Brit. sl.* a woman. [pet-form of the name *Judith*]

jug /jug/ *n.* & *v.* ● *n.* **1 a** a deep vessel for holding liquids, with a handle and often with a spout or lip shaped for pouring. **b** the contents of this; a jugful. **2** a large jar with a narrow mouth. **3** *sl.* prison. **4** (in *pl.*) *coarse sl.* a woman's breasts. ● *v.tr.* (**jugged**, **jugging**) **1** (usu. as **jugged** *adj.*) stew or boil (a hare or rabbit) in a covered vessel. **2** *sl.* imprison. □□ **jugful** *n.* (*pl.* **-fuls**). [perh. f. *Jug*, pet-form of the name *Joan*, etc.]
■ *n.* **1, 2** pitcher, ewer, jar, boat, toby jug, creamer, *archaic* graybeard; urn, carafe, bottle, flask, decanter. **3** see PRISON *n.* 1. ● *v.* **1** stew, boil, simmer, steam, braise, casserole. **2** see IMPRISON 1.

Jugendstil /yŏŏgənt-shteel/ *n.* (also **jugendstil**) the German name for art nouveau. [G f. *Jugend* youth + *Stil* style]

juggernaut /júgərnawt/ *n.* **1** esp. *Brit.* a large heavy motor vehicle, esp. a tractor-trailer truck. **2** a huge or overwhelm-

┌───┐
│ /.../ **pronunciation**   ● **part of speech** │
│ □ **phrases, idioms, and compounds**   │
│ □□ **derivatives**   ■ **synonym section**   │
│ **cross-references** appear in SMALL CAPITALS or *italics* │
└───┘

ing force or object. **3** (**Juggernaut**) an institution or notion to which persons blindly sacrifice themselves or others. [Hindi *Jagannāth* f. Skr. *Jagannātha* = lord of the world: name of an idol of Krishna in Hindu mythol., carried in procession on a huge cart under which devotees are said to have formerly thrown themselves]

juggins /júginz/ *n. Brit. sl.* a simpleton. [perh. f. proper name *Juggins* (as JUG): cf. MUGGINS]

juggle /júgəl/ *v. & n.* ● *v.* **1 a** *intr.* (often foll. by *with*) perform feats of dexterity, esp. by tossing objects in the air and catching them, keeping several in the air at the same time. **b** *tr.* perform such feats with. **2** *tr.* continue to deal with (several activities) at once, esp. with ingenuity. **3** *intr.* (foll. by *with*) & *tr.* **a** deceive or cheat. **b** misrepresent (facts). **c** rearrange adroitly. ● *n.* **1** a piece of juggling. **2** a fraud. [ME, back-form. f. JUGGLER or f. OF *jogler, jugler* f. L *joculari* jest f. *joculus* dimin. of *jocus* jest]
■ *v.* **3 a** see DECEIVE 1. **b** misrepresent, misstate, distort, falsify, alter, manipulate, massage, tamper with, rig, *colloq.* fix, doctor, cook, *sl.* fiddle. **c** rearrange, reposition, reset, redo, reshuffle; shuffle, change, alter, modify, shift, switch, transpose. ● *n.* **1** prestidigitation, legerdemain; dexterity, wizardry, sleight of hand. **2** fraud, deception, deceit, trickery, swindle, legerdemain, sophistry, humbug, flimflam, hocus-pocus, hoax, trick, dodge, *colloq.* rip-off, *Brit. colloq.* jiggery-pokery, *sl.* funny business, gyp, scam.

juggler /júglər/ *n.* **1** a person who juggles. **2** a trickster or impostor. □□ **jugglery** *n.* [ME f. OF *jouglere -eor* f. L *joculator -oris* (as JUGGLE)]
■ □□ **jugglery** see HOCUS-POCUS *n.* 3.

Jugoslav var. of YUGOSLAV.

jugular /júgyələr/ *adj. & n.* ● *adj.* **1** of the neck or throat. **2** (of fish) having ventral fins in front of the pectoral fins. ● *n.* = *jugular vein.* □ **jugular vein** any of several large veins of the neck which carry blood from the head. [LL *jugularis* f. L *jugulum* collarbone, throat, dimin. of *jugum* YOKE]

jugulate /júgyəlayt/ *v.tr.* **1** kill by cutting the throat. **2** arrest the course of (a disease, etc.) by a powerful remedy. [L *jugulare* f. *jugulum* (as JUGULAR)]

juice /jōōs/ *n.* **1** the liquid part of vegetables or fruits. **2** the fluid part of an animal body or substance, esp. a secretion (*gastric juice*). **3** the essence or spirit of anything. **4** *colloq.* gasoline, etc., or electricity as a source of power. **5** *sl.* alcoholic liquor. □□ **juiceless** *adj.* [ME f. OF *jus* f. L *jus* broth, juice]
■ **1** sap, liquid, fluid; *Brit.* crush. **3** see ESSENCE 1. **4** gasoline, *Brit.* petrol, *colloq.* gas; electricity, current, power.

juicer /jōōsər/ *n.* **1** a kitchen tool or appliance for extracting the juice from fruits and vegetables. **2** *sl.* an alcoholic.

juicy /jōōsee/ *adj.* (**juicier, juiciest**) **1** full of juice; succulent. **2** *colloq.* substantial or interesting; racy; scandalous. **3** *colloq.* profitable. □□ **juicily** *adv.* **juiciness** *n.*
■ **1** succulent, lush, ripe, mellow, luscious. **2** substantial, significant, considerable, consequential; interesting, intriguing, fascinating, stirring, thrilling, exciting, entertaining, eventful, sensational, lurid, colorful, vivid, provocative, stimulating, suggestive, scandalous, racy, spicy, risqué. **3** see PROFITABLE 1.

jujitsu /jōōjítsōō/ *n.* (also **jiujitsu**) a Japanese system of unarmed combat and physical training. [Jap. *jūjutsu* f. *jū* gentle + *jutsu* skill]

juju /jōōjōō/ *n.* **1** a charm or fetish of some W. African peoples. **2** a supernatural power attributed to this. [perh. f. F *joujou* toy]
■ **1** see TALISMAN.

jujube /jōōjōōb/ *n.* **1 a** any plant of the genus *Zizyphus* bearing edible acidic berrylike fruits. **b** this fruit. **2** a small lozenge or candy of gelatin, etc., flavored with or imitating this. [F *jujube* or med.L *jujuba* ult. f. Gk *zizuphon*]

jukebox /jōōkboks/ *n.* a machine that automatically plays a selected musical recording when a coin is inserted. [Gullah *juke* disorderly + BOX¹]

Jul. *abbr.* July.

julep /jōōlip/ *n.* **1 a** a sweet drink, esp. as a vehicle for medicine. **b** a medicated drink as a mild stimulant, etc. **2** iced and flavored spirits and water (*mint julep*). [ME f. OF f. Arab. *julāb* f. Pers. *gulāb* f. *gul* rose + *āb* water]

Julian /jōōlyən/ *adj.* of or associated with Julius Caesar. □ **Julian calendar** a calendar introduced by Julius Caesar, in which the year consisted of 365 days, every fourth year having 366 (cf. GREGORIAN CALENDAR). [L *Julianus* f. *Julius*]

julienne /jōōlee-én/ *n. & adj.* ● *n.* foodstuff, esp. vegetables, cut into short, thin strips. ● *adj.* cut into thin strips. [F f. the name *Jules* or *Julien*]

Juliet cap /jōōleeət, -lee-et, jōōlee-ét/ *n.* a small network ornamental cap worn by brides, etc. [the heroine of Shakesp. *Romeo & Juliet*]

July /jōōlī/ *n.* (*pl.* **Julies** or **Julys**) the seventh month of the year. [ME f. AF *julie* f. L *Julius* (*mensis* month), named after Julius Caesar]

jumble /júmbəl/ *v. & n.* ● *v.* **1** *tr.* (often foll. by *up*) confuse; mix up. **2** *intr.* move about in disorder. ● *n.* **1** a confused state or heap; a muddle. **2** *Brit.* articles collected for a jumble sale. □ **jumble sale** *Brit.* a rummage sale, esp. for charity. □□ **jumbly** *adj.* [prob. imit.]
■ *v.* **1** confuse, disorder, mix (up), confound, muddle, shuffle, disarrange, disorganize, upset, mess (up), scramble, garble, tangle, entangle, snarl (up). **2** see MILL¹ *v.* 4. ● *n.* **1** muddle, tangle, mess, clutter, melee, imbroglio; disorder, confusion, disarray, chaos; gallimaufry, hash, hodgepodge, mishmash, assortment, medley, miscellany, mixture, patchwork.

jumbo /júmbō/ *n. & adj. colloq.* ● *n.* (*pl.* **-os**) **1** a large animal (esp. an elephant), person, or thing. **2** (in full **jumbo jet**) a large airliner with capacity for several hundred passengers. ● *adj.* **1** very large of its kind. **2** extra large (*jumbo packet*). [19th c. (orig. of a person): orig. unkn.: popularized as the name of a zoo elephant bought by US showman P.T. Barnum in 1882]
■ *n.* **1** giant, monster, colossus, behemoth, leviathan, *colloq.* hulk, *sl.* whopper. ● *adj.* huge, immense, gigantic, enormous, vast, massive, monstrous, gargantuan, colossal, mammoth, giant, titanic, elephantine, cyclopean; oversize, extra size, outsize, king-size, queen-size, economy(-size); large, big, *colloq.* thumping, hulking; *sl.* whopping, humongous; see also BIG *adj.* 1a.

jumbuck /júmbuk/ *n. Austral. colloq.* a sheep. [Aboriginal]

jump /jump/ *v. & n.* ● *v.* **1** *intr.* move off the ground or other surface (usu. upward, at least initially) by sudden muscular effort in the legs. **2** *intr.* (often foll. by *up, from, in, out,* etc.) move suddenly or hastily in a specified way (*we jumped into the car*). **3** *intr.* give a sudden bodily movement from shock or excitement, etc. **4** *intr.* undergo a rapid change, esp. an advance in status. **5** *intr.* (often foll. by *about*) change or move rapidly from one idea or subject to another. **6 a** *intr.* rise or increase suddenly (*prices jumped*). **b** *tr.* cause to do this. **7** *tr.* a pass over (an obstacle, barrier, etc.) by jumping. **b** move or pass over (an intervening thing) to a point beyond. **8** *tr.* skip or pass over (a passage in a book, etc.). **9** *tr.* cause (a thing, or an animal, esp. a horse) to jump. **10** *intr.* (foll. by *to, at*) reach a conclusion hastily. **11** *tr.* (of a train) leave (the rails) owing to a fault. **12** *tr.* esp. *Brit.* ignore and pass (a red traffic light, etc.). **13** *tr.* get on or off (a train, etc.) quickly, esp. illegally or dangerously. **14** *tr.* pounce on or attack (a person) unexpectedly. **15** *tr.* take summary possession of (a claim allegedly abandoned or forfeit by the former occupant). ● *n.* **1** the act or an instance of jumping. **2 a** a sudden bodily movement caused by shock or excitement. **b** (**the jumps**) *colloq.* extreme nervousness or anxiety. **3** an abrupt rise in amount, price, value, status, etc. **4** an obstacle to be jumped, esp. by a horse. **5 a** a sudden transition. **b** a gap in a series, logical sequence, etc. □ **get** (or **have**) **the jump on** *colloq.* get (or have) an advantage over (a person) by prompt action. **jump at** accept eagerly. **jump bail** see BAIL¹. **jump down a person's throat** *colloq.* reprimand or contradict a person fiercely. **jumped-up** *Brit. colloq.* upstart; presumptuously arrogant. **jump the gun** see

GUN. **jumping-off place** (or **point**, etc.) the place or point of starting. **jump-jet** a jet aircraft that can take off and land vertically. **jump-lead** a cable for conveying current from the battery of a motor vehicle to boost (or recharge) another. **jump-off** a deciding round in a show-jumping competition. **jump on** *colloq.* attack or criticize severely and without warning. **jump out of one's skin** *colloq.* be extremely startled. **jump the queue** *Brit.* **1** push forward out of one's turn. **2** take unfair precedence over others. **jump rope** a length of rope revolved over the head and under the feet while jumping as a game or exercise. **jump seat** a folding extra seat in a motor vehicle. **jump ship** (of a seaman) desert. **jump-start** *v.tr.* start (a motor vehicle) by pushing it or with jumper cables. ● *n.* the action of jump-starting. **jump to it** *colloq.* act promptly and energetically. **one jump ahead** one stage further on than a rival, etc. **on the jump** *colloq.* on the move; in a hurry. □□ **jumpable** *adj.* [16th c.: prob. imit.]

■ *v.* **1, 2** leap, bound, spring, hop, skip, dive, pounce; hurdle, vault; caper, gambol, prance, *sl.* cavort. **3** start, jerk, lurch, jolt, lunge, wince, flinch, recoil, shy, twitch, shudder. **4, 6** advance, increase, progress, improve, move (on *or* ahead *or* forward *or* up); climb, rise, gain, surge, soar, rocket, shoot up, escalate. **5** leap, skip, hop, pass, move, shift, switch, change. **7** hurdle, vault, clear, leap, hop, leapfrog. **8** skip (over *or* past), omit, pass over *or* by, bypass, go past, avoid, leave out, ignore, disregard, overlook, gloss over. **10** leap, rush, hasten. **14** see ATTACK *v.* 1. ● *n.* **1** leap, bound, spring, hop, skip, dive, pounce; hurdle, vault, caper, gambol, prance. **2 a** start, lurch, jolt, jerk, shy, spasm, twitch, recoil, wince, flinch, shudder. **b** (**the jumps**) nervousness, tension, anxiety, anxiousness, fretfulness, restlessness, uneasiness, skittishness, apprehension, the shakes, d.t.'s, (the) fidgets, nerves, the horrors, *colloq.* the jimjams, the jitters, twitch, cold feet, *sl.* the heebie-jeebies, stage fright, buck fever. **3** rise, increase, appreciation, advance, gain, surge, lift, escalation, upsurge, increment, elevation, leap, hike, *colloq.* boost. **4** obstacle, hurdle, fence, barricade, rail, obstruction; (*Show jumping*) gate, wall, ditch, water. **5** switch, shift, transition, change; break, gap, interval, hiatus, lacuna, space, hole, breach, rift, interruption, *Prosody* caesura. □ **get** (or **have**) **the jump on** get *or* have the advantage over, get *or* have the upper hand over. **jump at** snatch, seize (on), grab (at), leap at, pounce on, grasp, accept, *colloq.* swoop up. **jump down a person's throat** contradict, oppose, take issue with, *archaic or literary* gainsay, *colloq.* bite a person's head off; reprimand, rebuke, upbraid, castigate, give a person a tongue-lashing, give a person a rap on *or* over the knuckles, *colloq.* give a person a telling-off *or* dressing-down, give a person a slap on the wrist. **jump on** attack, berate, flay, launch into, have a go at, come down on (like a ton of bricks), crack down on, *colloq.* lay into, set about. **jump to it** look sharp, get on with it, *colloq.* get cracking, look lively, *sl.* get weaving.

jumper[1] /júmpər/ *n.* **1** sleeveless one-piece dress usu. worn over a blouse or shirt. **2** a loose outer jacket of canvas, etc., worn esp. by sailors. **3** *Brit.* a pullover sweater. [prob. f. (17th-c., now dial.) *jump* short coat perh. f. F *jupe* f. Arab. *jubba*]

jumper[2] /júmpər/ *n.* **1** a person or animal that jumps. **2** *Electr.* a short wire used to make or break a circuit. **3** a rope made fast to keep a yard, mast, etc., from jumping. **4** a heavy chisel-ended iron bar for drilling blast holes. □ **jumper cables** a pair of electrical cables attached to a battery and used to start a motor vehicle with a weak or discharged battery.

jumping bean /júmping/ *n.* the seed of a Mexican plant that jumps with the movement of the larva inside.

jumping jack /júmping/ *n.* **1** a jumping exercise performed by alternating the position of standing feet together with arms at sides with the position of standing feet apart with arms extended and hands above the head. **2** a toy figure of a man, with movable limbs.

jumpsuit /júmpsoot/ *n.* a one-piece garment for the whole body, of a kind orig. worn by paratroopers.

jumpy /júmpee/ *adj.* (**jumpier, jumpiest**) **1** nervous; easily startled. **2** making sudden movements, esp. of nervous excitement. □□ **jumpily** *adv.* **jumpiness** *n.*

■ **1** nervous, tense, agitated, anxious, fretful, uneasy, edgy, on edge, fidgety, ill at ease, restless, restive, panicky, overwrought, keyed up, nervy, flustered, agitated, rattled, *colloq.* jittery, het up, uptight, neurotic; high-strung, sensitive, temperamental, excitable, skittish, *sl.* spooky, *Austral. sl.* toey. **2** twitchy, jerky, tremulous, fluttery, *colloq.* all of a tremble, jittery.

Jun. *abbr.* **1** June. **2** Junior.

junco /júngkō/ *n.* (*pl.* **-os** or **-oes**) any small American finch of the genus *Junco.* [Sp. f. L *juncus* rush plant]

junction /júngkshən/ *n.* **1** a point at which two or more things are joined. **2** a place where two or more railroad lines or roads meet, unite, or cross. **3** the act or an instance of joining. **4** *Electronics* a region of transition in a semiconductor between regions where conduction is mainly by electrons and regions where it is mainly by holes. □ **junction box** a box containing a junction of electric cables, etc. [L *junctio* (as JOIN)]

■ **1** join, union, juncture, connection, contact, commissure, abutment, articulation; link, linkage, weld, knot, splice, seam, gusset, bond, suture; bracket, brace, hinge. **2** intersection, crossing, union, conjunction, meeting, meeting point, confluence, convergence, corner; crossroad(s), interchange, turnoff; *Brit.* point(s). **3** union, unification, connection, convergence, conjunction, juncture, combination, addition, coupling, twinning, marriage, merger, fusion, alliance, integration, amalgamation, coalition.

juncture /júngkchər/ *n.* **1** a critical convergence of events; a critical point of time (*at this juncture*). **2** a place where things join. **3** an act of joining. [ME f. L *junctura* (as JOIN)]

■ **1** pass, hump, situation, *colloq.* crunch; point, time, moment (in time), stage, period. **2** see JUNCTION 1. **3** see JUNCTION 3.

June /joon/ *n.* the sixth month of the year. □ **June bug** any of several large brown scarab beetles, esp. *Phyllophaga fusca.* [ME f. OF *juin* f. L *Junius* var. of *Junonius* sacred to Juno]

Jungian /yoongeeən/ *adj.* & *n.* ● *adj.* of the Swiss psychologist Carl Jung (d. 1961) or his system of analytical psychology. ● *n.* a supporter of Jung or of his system.

jungle /júnggəl/ *n.* **1 a** land overgrown with underwood or tangled vegetation, esp. in the tropics. **b** an area of such land. **2** a wild tangled mass. **3** a place of bewildering complexity or confusion, or of a struggle for survival (*blackboard jungle*). □ **jungle fever** a severe form of malaria. **jungle gym** a playground structure with bars, ladders, etc., for children to climb. **law of the jungle** a state of ruthless competition. □□ **jungled** *adj.* **jungly** *adj.* [Hindi *jangal* f. Skr. *jangala* desert, forest]

■ **1** rain forest. **2** see TANGLE[1] *n.* 2.

junior /joonyər/ *adj.* & *n.* ● *adj.* **1** less advanced in age. **2** (foll. by *to*) inferior in age, standing, or position. **3** the younger (esp. appended to a name for distinction from an older person of the same name). **4** of less or least standing; of the lower or lowest position (*junior partner*). **5** *Brit.* (of a school) having pupils in a younger age-range, usu. 7–11. **6** of the year before the final year at college, high school, etc. ● *n.* **1** a junior person. **2** one's inferior in length of service, etc. **3** a junior student. **4** *Brit.* a barrister who is not a Queen's Counsel. **5** *colloq.* a young male child, esp. in relation to his family. □ **junior college** a college offering a two-year course esp. in preparation for completion at senior college. **junior common** (or **combination**) **room** *Brit.* **1**

/.../ **pronunciation**	● **part of speech**

□ **phrases, idioms, and compounds**

□□ **derivatives**   ■ **synonym section**

cross-references appear in SMALL CAPITALS or *italics*

a room for social use by the junior members of a college. **2** the junior members collectively. **junior high school** school attended between elementary and high school and usu. consisting of grades seven and eight or seven, eight, and nine. **junior lightweight** see LIGHTWEIGHT. **junior middleweight** see MIDDLEWEIGHT. □□ **juniority** /-nyáwritee, -yór-/ *n.* [L, compar. of *juvenis* young]

■ *adj.* **2** (*junior to*) younger than; lower than, inferior to, subordinate to, secondary to, beneath, under, behind. **3** (the) younger, *Brit.* minor. **4** lower, lesser, minor, smaller, secondary, subordinate, inferior; lowest, least. ● *n.* **1, 2** subordinate, inferior, *derog.* underling; minor, youth, youngster, juvenile, child, boy, girl, baby, *archaic or colloq.* young thing. □□ **juniority** see INFERIORITY.

juniper /jóōnipər/ *n.* any evergreen shrub or tree of the genus *Juniperus*, esp. *J. communis* with prickly leaves and dark purple berrylike cones. □ **oil of juniper** oil from juniper cones used in medicine and in flavoring gin, etc. [ME f. L *juniperus*]

junk[1] /jungk/ *n. & v.* ● *n.* **1** discarded articles; rubbish. **2** anything regarded as of little value. **3** *sl.* a narcotic drug, esp. heroin. **4** old cables or ropes cut up for oakum, etc. **5** *Brit.* a lump or chunk. **6** *Naut.* hard salt meat. **7** a lump of fibrous tissue in the sperm whale's head, containing spermaceti. ● *v.tr.* discard as junk. □ **junk bond** *Stock Exch.* a bond bearing high interest but deemed to be a risky investment. **junk food** food with low nutritional value. **junk mail** unsolicited advertising matter sent through the mail. **junk shop** a store selling cheap secondhand goods or antiques. [ME: orig. unkn.]

■ *n.* **1, 2** rubbish, waste, refuse, litter, scrap, garbage, debris, detritus, dross, (the) dreg(s), lees, leavings, reject(s), flotsam and jetsam, trash, *sl.* dreck; lumber, rummage, paraphernalia, stuff, odds and ends, *colloq.* truck; see also NONSENSE. **3** heroin, *sl.* smack, dynamite, H, horse, speedball, sugar. ● *v.* discard, dispose of, dispense with, dump, get rid of, throw out *or* away, toss (out *or* aside *or* away), scrap, cast (aside), jettison, *colloq.* chuck (out *or* away), bin, get shot of, *sl.* ditch, *Brit. sl.* bung (out *or* away).

junk[2] /jungk/ *n.* a flat-bottomed sailing vessel used in the China seas, with a prominent stem and lugsails. [obs. F *juncque*, Port. *junco*, or Du. *jonk*, f. Jav. *djong*]

Junker /yóōngkər/ *n. hist.* **1** a young German nobleman. **2** a member of an exclusive (Prussian) aristocratic party. □□ **junkerdom** *n.* [G, earlier *Junkher* f. OHG (as YOUNG, HERR)]

junket /júngkit/ *n. & v.* ● *n.* **1** a dish of sweetened and flavored curds, often served with fruit or cream. **2** a feast. **3** a pleasure outing. **4** an official's tour at public expense. ● *v.intr.* feast; picnic. □□ **junketing** *n.* [ME *jonket* f. OF *jonquette* rush-basket (used to carry junket) f. *jonc* rush f. L *juncus*]

■ **3** see OUTING.

junkie /júngkee/ *n. sl.* a drug addict.

■ see ADDICT *n.* 1.

junkyard /júngkyard/ *n.* a yard in which junk is collected and sometimes resold.

junta /hŏōntə, júntə/ *n.* **1 a** a political or military clique or faction taking power after a revolution or coup d'état. **b** a secretive group; a cabal. **2** a deliberative or administrative council in Spain or Portugal. [Sp. & Port. f. L *juncta*, fem. past part. (as JOIN)]

■ **1** clique, faction, camarilla, cabal, mafia; coterie, gang, band, set, ring, party, group.

Jupiter /jóōpitər/ *n.* the largest planet of the solar system, orbiting about the sun between Mars and Saturn. [ME f. L *Jupiter* king of the gods f. OL *Jovis pater*]

jural /jóōrəl/ *adj.* **1** of law. **2** of rights and obligations. [L *jus juris* law, right]

Jurassic /jŏōrásik/ *adj. & n. Geol.* ● *adj.* of or relating to the second period of the Mesozoic era with evidence of many large dinosaurs, the first birds (including *Archaeopteryx*),

and mammals. ¶ Cf. Appendix VII. ● *n.* this era or system. [F *jurassique* f. *Jura* (Mountains): cf. *Triassic*]

jurat[1] /jóōrat/ *n.* a statement of the circumstances in which an affidavit was made. [L *juratum* neut. past part. (as JURAT[1])]

jurat[2] /jóōrat/ *n. Brit.* **1** a municipal officer (esp. of the Cinque Ports) holding a position similar to that of an alderman. **2** an honorary judge or magistrate in the Channel Islands. [ME f. med.L *juratus* past part. of L *jurare* swear]

juridical /jŏōrídikəl/ *adj.* **1** of judicial proceedings. **2** relating to the law. □□ **juridically** *adv.* [L *juridicus* f. *jus juris* law + *-dicus* saying f. *dicere* say]

■ see JUDICIAL 1, 2.

jurisconsult /jóōriskónsult/ *n.* a person learned in law; a jurist. [L *jurisconsultus* f. *jus juris* law + *consultus* skilled: see CONSULT]

jurisdiction /jóōrisdíkshən/ *n.* **1** (often foll. by *over, of*) the administration of justice. **2 a** legal or other authority. **b** the extent of this; the territory it extends over. □□ **jurisdictional** *adj.* [ME *jurisdiccioun* f. OF *jurediction, juridiction*, L *jurisdictio* f. *jus juris* law + *dictio* DICTION]

■ **1** authority, supervision, superintendence. **2** authority, power, prerogative, dominion, sovereignty, say, control, rule, ascendancy, hegemony, influence; province, district, area, territory, compass, realm, range, orbit, sphere (of influence), reach, clutches; shrievalty, *Law* bailiwick, *hist.* leet, *Brit. hist.* soke.

jurisprudence /jóōrisprŏōd'ns/ *n.* **1** the science or philosophy of law. **2** skill in law. □□ **jurisprudent** /-dənt/ *adj. & n.* **jurisprudential** /-dénshəl/ *adj.* [LL *jurisprudentia* f. L *jus juris* law + *prudentia* knowledge: see PRUDENT]

jurist /jóōrist/ *n.* **1** an expert in law. **2** a legal writer. **3** a lawyer. □□ **juristic** /-rístik/ *adj.* **juristical** /-rístikəl/ *adj.* [F *juriste* or med.L *jurista* f. *jus juris* law]

■ **3** see LAWYER.

juror /jóōrər/ *n.* **1** a member of a jury. **2** a person who takes an oath (cf. NONJUROR). [ME f. AF *jurour*, OF *jureor* f. L *jurator -oris* f. *jurare jurat-* swear]

jury /jóōree/ *n.* (*pl.* **-ies**) **1** a body of persons sworn to render a verdict on the basis of evidence submitted to them in a court of justice. **2** a body of persons selected to award prizes in a competition. □ **jury box** the enclosure for the jury in a court of law. [ME f. AF & OF *juree* oath, inquiry, f. *jurata* fem. past part. of L *jurare* swear]

juryman /jóōreemən/ *n.* (*pl.* **-men**) a member of a jury.

jury-rigged /jóōreerigd/ *adj. Naut.* having temporary makeshift rigging. [perh. ult. f. OF *ajurie* aid]

jurywoman /jóōreewŏōmən/ *n.* (*pl.* **-women**) a woman member of a jury.

jussive /júsiv/ *adj. Gram.* expressing a command. [L *jubēre juss-* command]

just /just/ *adj. & adv.* ● *adj.* **1** acting or done in accordance with what is morally right or fair. **2** (of treatment, etc.) deserved (*a just reward*). **3** (of feelings, opinions, etc.) well-grounded (*just resentment*). **4** right in amount, etc.; proper. ● *adv.* **1** exactly (*just what I need*). **2** exactly or nearly at this or that moment; a little time ago (*I have just seen them*). **3** *colloq.* simply; merely (*we were just good friends; it just doesn't make sense*). **4** barely; no more than (*I just managed it; just a minute*). **5** *colloq.* positively (*it is just splendid*). **6** quite (*not just yet; it is just as well that I checked*). **7** *colloq.* really; indeed (*won't I just tell him!*). **8** in questions, seeking precise information (*just how did you manage?*). □ **just about** *colloq.* almost exactly; almost completely. **just in case 1** lest. **2** as a precaution. **just now 1** at this moment. **2** a little time ago. **just so 1** exactly arranged (*they like everything just so*). **2** it is exactly as you say. □□ **justly** *adv.* **justness** *n.* [ME f. OF *juste* f. L *justus* f. *jus* right]

■ *adj.* **1** fair, equitable, impartial, reasonable, fair-minded, evenhanded, neutral, objective, nonpartisan, unbiased, unprejudiced, indifferent, disinterested, dispassionate; upright, righteous, right-minded, honorable, honest, ethical, moral, principled, conscientious, scrupulous, straight, square, decent,

good, correct, upstanding, virtuous, lawful, legitimate.
2 well-deserved, well-earned, due, rightful, merited;
condign. **3** well-grounded, justified, justifiable, well-
founded, legitimate, valid, reasonable, rightful. **4**
fitting, befitting, fit, proper, appropriate, due, right,
rightful, suitable, correct. ● *adv.* **1, 6** exactly,
precisely, completely, perfectly, totally, utterly, wholly,
fully, entirely, thoroughly, altogether, in every respect,
in all respects, perfectly, expressly, explicitly,
unreservedly, quite, *Brit. colloq.* bang on. **2** only *or* just
now, (just) a moment ago, (very) recently; lately,
latterly. **3, 4** only, merely, simply, solely, nothing but,
at best, at most, no more than; only just, barely,
hardly, scarcely, narrowly, by a hair's breadth, by the
skin of one's teeth. **5, 7** positively, absolutely,
emphatically, altogether, categorically, definitely,
utterly, thoroughly, entirely; certainly, unquestionably,
undeniably, assuredly, undoubtedly, unmistakably,
indubitably; really, truly, indeed. **8** exactly, accurately,
specifically. □ **just about** nearly, almost, virtually,
practically, for all practical purposes, as good as, all
but, more or less, approximately, *archaic or rhet.*
wellnigh, *colloq.* pretty much *or* nearly *or* well; not
quite. **just in case 1** lest, for fear that. **just now 1** see
NOW *adv.* 1, 4. **2** see JUST *adv.* 2 above. **just so 1** neat,
tidy, systematic, perfect, exact, accurate. **2** that's right,
that's it, quite so, even so, exactly, precisely, *colloq.*
absolutely, *Brit. colloq.* bang on.

justice /jústis/ *n.* **1** just conduct. **2** fairness. **3** the exercise of
authority in the maintenance of right. **4** judicial proceedings
(*was duly brought to justice*). **5 a** a magistrate. **b** a judge, esp.
of a supreme court. □ **do justice to** treat fairly or appropriately; show due appreciation of. **do oneself justice** perform
in a manner worthy of one's abilities. **in justice to** out of
fairness to. **justice of the peace** a local magistrate appointed to preserve the peace in a county, town, etc., hear
minor cases, grant licenses, perform marriages, etc. **with
justice** reasonably. □□ **justiceship** *n.* (in sense 5). [ME f.
OF f. L *justitia* (as JUST)]
■ **1–3** uprightness, righteousness, honorableness,
honesty, ethicality, morality, probity, principle,
conscientiousness, scrupulousness, scruple(s),
straightness, squareness, decency, goodness,
correctness, virtue; sportsmanship, fair play;
lawfulness, rightfulness, legitimacy; fairness, justness,
equity, equality, equitableness, impartiality, fair-
mindedness, evenhandedness, neutrality, objectivity,
objectiveness, indifference, disinterest,
dispassionateness; law, right. **4** court, law court,
courtroom, court of law, tribunal; bar, bench. **5** see
JUDGE *n.* 1.

justiciable /justíshəbəl/ *adj.* liable to legal consideration.
[OF f. *justicier* bring to trial f. med.L *justitiare* (as JUSTICE)]
justiciary /justíshee-eree/ *n.* & *adj.* ● *n.* (*pl.* **-ies**) an administrator of justice. ● *adj.* of the administration of justice.
[med.L *justitiarius* f. L *justitia*: see JUSTICE]
justifiable /jústifíəbəl/ *adj.* that can be justified or defended.
□ **justifiable homicide** killing regarded as lawful and without criminal guilt, esp. the execution of a death sentence.
□□ **justifiability** *n.* **justifiableness** *n.* **justifiably** *adv.* [F
f. *justifier*: see JUSTIFY]
■ see LEGITIMATE *adj.* □□ **justifiably** see TRULY 5.
justify /jústifī/ *v.tr.* (**-ies, -ied**) **1** show the justice or right-

ness of (a person, act, etc.). **2** demonstrate the correctness
of (an assertion, etc.). **3** adduce adequate grounds for (conduct, a claim, etc.). **4 a** (esp. in *passive*) (of circumstances)
be such as to justify. **b** vindicate. **5** (as **justified** *adj.*) just;
right (*am justified in assuming*). **6** *Theol.* declare (a person)
righteous. **7** *Printing* adjust (a line of type) to fill a space
evenly. □□ **justification** /-fikáyshən/ *n.* **justificatory** /-stíf-
íkətáwree/ *adj.* **justifier** *n.* [ME f. F *justifier* f. LL *justificare*
do justice to f. L *justus* JUST]
■ **1, 2, 4** vindicate, legitimate, legitimatize, legitimize,
legalize, rationalize, substantiate, defend, support,
uphold, sustain, validate, warrant, confirm, explain,
rationalize, account for. **3** excuse, explain, apologize
for, condone. **5** (**justified**) see RIGHT *adj.* 1.
□□ **justification** see ARGUMENT 2, BASIS 1, 2.
jut /jut/ *v.* & *n.* ● *v.intr.* (**jutted, jutting**) (often foll. by *out,
forth*) protrude; project. ● *n.* a projection; a protruding
point. [var. of JET[1]]
■ *v.* project, protrude, stick out, extend, overhang,
beetle.
Jute /joot/ *n.* a member of a Low-German tribe that settled
in Britain in the 5th–6th c. □□ **Jutish** *adj.* [repr. med.L *Jutae,
Juti*, in OE *Eotas, Iotas* = Icel. *Iótar* people of Jutland in
Denmark]
jute /joot/ *n.* **1** a rough fiber made from the bark of E. Indian
plants of the genus *Corchorus*, used for making twine and
rope, and woven into sacking, mats, etc. **2** either of two
plants *Corchorus capsularis* or *C. olitorius* yielding this fiber.
[Bengali *jhōṭo* f. Skr. *jūṭa* = *jaṭā* braid of hair]
juvenescence /joovinésəns/ *n.* **1** youth. **2** the transition
from infancy to youth. □□ **juvenescent** /-sənt/ *adj.* [L *juve-
nescere* reach the age of youth f. *juvenis* young]
■ see CHILDHOOD.
juvenile /joovənil/ *adj.* & *n.* ● *adj.* **1 a** young; youthful. **b** of
or for young persons. **2** suited to or characteristic of youth.
3 often *derog.* immature (*behaving in a very juvenile way*).
● *n.* **1** a young person. **2** *Commerce* a book intended for
young people. **3** an actor playing the part of a youthful person. □ **juvenile court** a court for the trial of children usu.
under 18. **juvenile delinquency** offenses committed by
a person or persons below the age of legal responsibility.
juvenile delinquent such an offender. □□ **juvenilely** *adv.*
juvenility /-nílitee/ *n.* [L *juvenilis* f. *juvenis* young]
■ *adj.* **1 a** young, youthful, adolescent, prepubescent,
pubescent, under age, minor, teenage(d); boyish,
girlish, childlike. **1b, 2** young person's *or* people's,
adolescent, junior, teenage, infant, children's. **3**
immature, adolescent, childish, infantile, babyish,
puerile, unsophisticated, green, callow, naive,
inexperienced, (still) wet behind the ears, jejune,
innocent, guileless, unfledged, raw, tender. ● *n.* **1**
youth, boy, girl, child, adolescent, minor, teenager,
youngster, schoolboy, schoolgirl, schoolchild, infant,
toddler, stripling, whippersnapper, lad, *Sc. & No. of
Engl. or poet.* lass, *archaic* younker, *colloq.* teenybopper,
kid.
juvenilia /joovəníleeə/ *n.pl.* works produced by an author or
artist in youth. [L, neut. pl. of *juvenilis* (as JUVENILE)]
juxtapose /júkstəpōz/ *v.tr.* **1** place (things) side by side. **2**
(foll. by *to, with*) place (a thing) beside another. □□ **juxtaposition** /-pəzíshən/ *n.* **juxtapositional** /-pəzíshənəl/ *adj.*
[F *juxtaposer* f. L *juxta* next: see POSE[1]]
JV *abbr.* junior varsity.

/.../ **pronunciation**   ● **part of speech**
□ **phrases, idioms, and compounds**
□□ **derivatives**   ■ **synonym section**
cross-references appear in SMALL CAPITALS or *italics*

K[1] /kay/ *n.* (also **k**) (*pl.* **Ks** or **K's**) the eleventh letter of the alphabet.

K[2] *abbr.* (also **K.**) **1** kelvin(s). **2** King, King's. **3** Köchel (catalogue of Mozart's works). **4** (also **k**) (prec. by a numeral) **a** *Computing* a unit of 1,024 (i.e., 2^{10}) bytes or bits, or loosely 1,000. **b** 1,000. **5** *Baseball* strikeout. [sense 4 as abbr. of KILO-]

K[3] *symb. Chem.* the element potassium.

k *abbr.* **1** kilo-. **2** knot(s).

Kaaba /ka'əbə/ *n.* (also **Caaba**) a sacred building at Mecca, the Muslim Holy of Holies containing the sacred black stone. [Arab. *Ka'ba*]

kabbala var. of CABALA.

kabob /kəbób/ *n.* (also **kebab, kebob**) (usu. in *pl.*) small pieces of meat, vegetables, etc., packed closely on a skewer and cooked. [Urdu f. Arab. *kabāb*]

kabuki /kəbo͞okee/ *n.* a form of popular traditional Japanese drama with highly stylized song, acted by males only. [Jap. f. *ka* song + *bu* dance + *ki* art]

kachina /kəcheenə/ *n.* **1** a Hopi ancestral spirit. **2** (in full **kachina dancer**) a person who represents a kachina in ceremonial dances. □ **kachina doll** a wooden doll representing a kachina. [Hopi, = supernatural]

Kaddish /ka'dish/ *n. Judaism* **1** a Jewish mourner's prayer. **2** a doxology in the synagogue service. [Aram. *ḳaddīš* holy]

kadi var. of QADI.

Kaffir /kafər/ *n.* **1 a** a member of the Xhosa-speaking peoples of S. Africa. **b** the language of these peoples. **2** *S.Afr. offens.* any black African. [Arab. *kāfir* infidel f. *kafara* not believe]

kaffiyeh /kəfee'ə/ *n.* (also **keffiyeh**) a Bedouin Arab's kerchief worn as a headdress. [Arab. *keffiya, kūfiyya,* perh. f. LL *cofea* COIF]

Kafir /kafər/ *n.* a native of the Hindu Kush mountains of NE Afghanistan. [formed as KAFFIR]

Kafkaesque /ka'afkəésk/ *adj.* (of a situation, atmosphere, etc.) impenetrably oppressive, nightmarish, in a manner characteristic of the fictional world of Franz Kafka, German-speaking novelist (d. 1924).
■ see *nightmarish* (NIGHTMARE).

kaftan var. of CAFTAN.

kai /ki/ *n. NZ colloq.* food. [Maori]

kail var. of KALE.

kailyard var. of KALEYARD.

kaiser /kīzər/ *n. hist.* an emperor, esp. the German emperor, the emperor of Austria, or the head of the Holy Roman Empire. □□ **kaisership** *n.* [in mod. Eng. f. G *Kaiser* and Du. *keizer*; in ME f. OE *cāsere* f. Gmc adoption (through Gk *kaisar*) of L *Caesar*: see CAESAR]

kaka /ka'akaa/ *n.* (*pl.* **kakas**) a large New Zealand parrot, *Nestor meridionalis*, with olive-brown plumage. [Maori]

kakapo /ka'akəpō/ *n.* (*pl.* **-os**) an owllike flightless New Zealand parrot, *Strigops habroptilus*. [Maori, = night kaka]

kakemono /ka'akəmṓnō/ *n.* (*pl.* **-os**) a vertical Japanese wall picture, usu. painted or inscribed on paper or silk and mounted on rollers. [Jap. f. *kake-* hang + *mono* thing]

kala-azar /ka'ala-əza'ar/ *n.* a tropical disease caused by the parasitic protozoan *Leishmania donovani*, which is transmitted to humans by sand flies. [Assamese f. *kālā* black + *āzār* disease]

kale /kayl/ *n.* (also **kail**) **1** a variety of cabbage, esp. one with wrinkled leaves and no compact head. Also called *curly kale.* **2** *sl.* money. [ME, northern form of COLE]
■ **2** see MONEY 1.

kaleidoscope /kəlídəskōp/ *n.* **1** a tube containing mirrors and pieces of colored glass, paper, plastic, etc., whose reflections produce changing patterns when the tube is rotated. **2** a constantly changing group of bright or interesting objects. □□ **kaleidoscopic** /-skópik/ *adj.* **kaleidoscopical** *adj.* [Gk *kalos* beautiful + *eidos* form + -SCOPE]
■ □□ **kaleidoscopic** see GAY *adj.* 3, PROTEAN 1.

kalends var. of CALENDS.

kaleyard /káyl-yaard/ *n.* (also **kailyard**) *Sc.* a kitchen garden. □ **kaleyard school** a group of 19th-c. fiction writers including J. M. Barrie, who described local town life in Scotland in a romantic vein and with much use of the vernacular. [KALE + YARD[2]]

kali /kálee, káylee/ *n.* a glasswort, *Salsola kali*, with fleshy jointed stems, having a high soda content. [Arab. *ḳalī* ALKALI]

kalmia /kálmeeə/ *n.* a N. American evergreen shrub of the genus *Kalmia* with showy flowers, as the mountain laurel. [mod.L f. P. *Kalm,* Sw. botanist d. 1779]

Kalmuck /kálmuk/ *adj. & n.* ● *adj.* of or relating to a people living on the north-western shores of the Caspian Sea. ● *n.* **1** a member of this people. **2** the language of this people. [Russ. *kalmyk*]

kalong /ka'alawng, -long/ *n.* any of various fruit-eating bats of the family Pteropodidae, esp. *Pteropus edulis*; a flying fox. [Malay]

kalpa /kálpə/ *n. Hinduism & Buddhism* the period between the beginning and the end of the world considered as the day of Brahma (4,320 million human years). [Skr.]

Kama /ka'amə/ *n.* the Hindu god of love. □ **Kama Sutra** /so͞otrə/ an ancient Sanskrit treatise on the art of erotic love. [Skr.]

kame /kaym/ *n.* a short ridge of sand and gravel deposited from the water of a melted glacier. [Sc. form of COMB]

kamikaze /kámikáazee/ *n. & adj.* ● *n. hist.* **1** a Japanese aircraft loaded with explosives and deliberately crashed by its pilot onto its target. **2** the pilot of such an aircraft. ● *adj.* **1** of or relating to a kamikaze. **2** reckless; dangerous; potentially self-destructive. [Jap. f. *kami* divinity + *kaze* wind]

kampong /ka'ampáwng, -póng/ *n.* a Malayan enclosure or village. [Malay: cf. COMPOUND[2]]

Kampuchean /kámpo͞ochee'ən/ *n. & adj.* = CAMBODIAN. [*Kampuchea,* native name for Cambodia]

Kan. *abbr.* Kansas.

kana /ka'anə/ *n.* any of various Japanese syllabaries. [Jap.]

kanaka /kənákə, -naákə/ *n.* **1** a native of Hawaii. **2** a South Sea islander, esp. (formerly) one employed in forced labor in Australia. [Hawaiian, = person]

Kanarese /kánərée'z/ *n.* (*pl.* same) **1** a member of a Dravidian people living in western India. **2** the language of this people. [*Kanara* in India]

kangaroo /kánggəro͞o/ *n.* a plant-eating marsupial of the genus *Macropus*, native to Australia and New Guinea, with a long tail and strongly developed hindquarters enabling it to travel by jumping. □ **kangaroo closure** *Brit. Parl.* a closure involving the chairperson of a committee selecting some amendments for discussion and excluding others. **kanga-**

816

roo court an improperly constituted or illegal court held by a mob, etc. **kangaroo mouse** any small rodent of the genus *Microdipodops*, native to N. America, with long hind legs for hopping. **kangaroo paw** any plant of the genus *Angiozanthos*, with green and red wooly flowers. **kangaroo rat** any burrowing rodent of the genus *Dipodomys*, having elongated hind feet. **kangaroo vine** an evergreen climbing plant, *Cissus antarctica*, with tooth-edged leaves. [Aboriginal name]

kanji /ka'anjee/ *n.* Japanese writing using Chinese characters. [Jap. f. *kan* Chinese + *ji* character]

Kannada /ka'anədə/ *n.* the Kanarese language. [Kanarese *kannaḍa*]

kanoon /kənoon/ *n.* an instrument like a zither, with fifty to sixty strings. [Pers. or Arab. *ḵānūn*]

Kans. *abbr.* Kansas.

Kansa /ka'anzə, -sə/ *n.* **1 a** a N. American people native to eastern Kansas. **b** a member of this people. **2** the language of this people. Also called **Kaw**.

kaolin /ka'yəlin/ *n.* a fine, soft, white clay produced by the decomposition of other clays or feldspar, used esp. for making porcelain and in medicines. Also called *china clay*. □□ **kaolinic** /-línik/ *adj.* **kaolinize** *v.tr.* [F f. Chin. *gaoling* the name of a mountain f. *gao* high + *ling* hill]

kaon /ka'yon/ *n. Physics* a meson having a mass several times that of a pion. [*ka* repr. the letter *K* (as symbol for the particle) + -ON]

kapellmeister /kəpélmīstər/ *n.* (*pl.* same) the conductor of an orchestra, opera, choir, etc., esp. in German contexts. [G f. *Kapelle* court orchestra f. It. *cappella* CHAPEL + *Meister* master]

kapok /ka'ypok/ *n.* a fine, fibrous, cottonlike substance found surrounding the seeds of a tropical tree, *Ceiba pentandra*, used for stuffing cushions, soft toys, etc. [ult. f. Malay *kāpoq*]

Kaposi's sarcoma /ka'pəseez, kapó-/ *n. Med.* a malignant neoplasm of connective tissue marked by bluish-red lesions on the skin; often associated with AIDS. [for Hungarian dermatologist M.K. *Kaposi* (1837–1902)]

kappa /ka'pə/ *n.* the tenth letter of the Greek alphabet (K, κ). [Gk]

kaput /kaapo͞ot/ *predic.adj. sl.* broken, ruined; done for. [G *kaputt*]

■ see BROKEN 1.

karabiner /ka'rəbéenər/ *n.* a coupling link with safety closure, used by mountaineers. [G, lit. 'carbine']

karakul /ka'rəko͞ol/ *n.* (also **Karakul, caracul**) **1** a variety of Asian sheep with a dark curled fleece when young. **2** fur made from or resembling this. Also called *Persian lamb*. [Russ.]

karaoke /ka'reeókee, ka'rə-/ *n.* a form of entertainment in which people sing popular songs as soloists against a prerecorded backing. □ **karaoke bar** (or **club**) a bar or club with this form of entertainment. [Jap., = empty orchestra]

karat /ka'rət/ *n.* (*Brit.* **carat**) a measure of purity of gold, pure gold being 24 karats. [cf. CARAT]

karate /kəra'atee/ *n.* a Japanese system of unarmed combat using the hands and feet as weapons. [Jap. f. *kara* empty + *te* hand]

karma /ka'armə/ *n. Buddhism & Hinduism* **1** the sum of a person's actions in previous states of existence, viewed as deciding his or her fate in future existences. **2** destiny. □□ **karmic** *adj.* [Skr., = action, fate]

■ **2** see DESTINY 2.

Karoo /kəroo/ *n.* (also **Karroo**) an elevated semidesert plateau in S. Africa. [Afrik. f. Hottentot *karo* dry]

karri /ka'ree/ *n.* (*pl.* **karris**) **1** a tall W. Australian tree, *Eucalyptus diversicolor*, with a hard, red wood. **2** the wood from this. [Aboriginal]

Karroo var. of KAROO.

karst /kaarst/ *n.* a limestone region with underground drainage and many cavities and passages caused by the dissolution of the rock. [the *Karst*, a limestone region in the northwest of the former Yugoslavia]

karyo- /ka'reeō/ *comb. form Biol.* denoting the nucleus of a cell. [Gk *karuon* kernel]

karyokinesis /ka'reeōkineésis/ *n. Biol.* the division of a cell nucleus during mitosis. [KARYO- + Gk *kinēsis* movement f. *kineō* move]

karyotype /ka'reeətīp/ *n.* the number and structure of the chromosomes in the nucleus of a cell.

Kasbah var. of CASBAH.

katabatic /ka'təbátik/ *adj. Meteorol.* (of wind) caused by air flowing downward (cf. ANABATIC). [Gk *katabatikos* f. *katabainō* go down]

katabolism esp. *Brit.* var. of CATABOLISM.

katakana /ka'təka'anə/ *n.* an angular form of Japanese kana. [Jap., = side kana]

katydid /ka'yteedid/ *n.* any of various green grasshoppers of the family Tettigoniidae, native to the US. [imit. of the sound it makes]

kauri /ko'wree/ *n.* (*pl.* **kauris**) a coniferous New Zealand tree, *Agathis australis*, which produces valuable timber and a resin. □ **kauri gum** (or **resin**) this resin. [Maori]

kava /ka'avə/ *n.* **1** a Polynesian shrub, *Piper methysticum*. **2** an intoxicating drink made from the crushed roots of this. [Polynesian]

kayak /kī'ak/ *n.* **1** an Eskimo canoe for one paddler, consisting of a light wooden frame covered with skins. **2** a small covered canoe resembling this. [Eskimo]

kayo /ka'yō, ka'yō/ *v. & n. colloq.* ● *v.tr.* (**-oes, -oed**) knock out; stun by a blow. ● *n.* (*pl.* **-os**) a knockout. [repr. pronunc. of KO]

■ *v.* see *knock out* 1. ● *n.* knockout, coup de grâce, *colloq.* K.O.

kazoo /kəzo͞o/ *n.* a toy musical instrument into which the player sings or hums. [19th c., app. with ref. to the sound produced]

KB *abbr.* (in the UK) King's Bench.

KBE *abbr.* (in the UK) Knight Commander of the Order of the British Empire.

KC *abbr.* **1** Kansas City. **2** Knights of Columbus. **3** King's Counsel.

kc *abbr.* kilocycle(s).

KCB *abbr.* (in the UK) Knight Commander of the Order of the Bath.

KCMG *abbr.* (in the UK) Knight Commander of the Order of St. Michael and St. George.

kc/s *abbr.* kilocycles per second.

KCVO *abbr.* (in the UK) Knight Commander of the Royal Victorian Order.

KE *abbr.* kinetic energy.

kea /ke'eə, ka'yə/ *n.* a parrot, *Nestor notabilis*, of New Zealand, with brownish-green and red plumage. [Maori, imit.]

kebab var. of KABOB.

kebob var. of KABOB.

kedge /kej/ *v. & n.* ● *v.* **1** *tr.* move (a ship) by means of a hawser attached to a small anchor that is dropped at some distance away. **2** *intr.* (of a ship) move in this way. ● *n.* (in full **kedge anchor**) a small anchor for this purpose. [perh. a specific use of obs. *cagge*, dial. *cadge* bind, tie]

kedgeree /ké'jəree/ *n.* **1** an E. Indian dish of rice, lentils, onions, eggs, etc. **2** a European dish of fish, rice, hard-boiled eggs, etc. [Hindi *khichṛī*, Skr. *k'rsara* dish of rice and sesame]

keek /keek/ *v. & n. Sc.* ● *v.intr.* peep. ● *n.* a peep. [ME *kike*: cf. MDu., MLG *kīken*]

keel[1] /keel/ *n. & v.* ● *n.* **1** the lengthwise timber or steel structure along the base of a ship, airship, or some aircraft, on which the framework of the whole is built up. **2** *poet.* a ship. **3** a ridge along the breastbone of many birds; a carina. **4** *Bot.* a prow-shaped pair of petals in a corolla, etc. ● *v.* **1** (often foll. by *over*) **a** *intr.* turn over or fall down. **b** *tr.* cause to do this. **2** *tr. & intr.* turn keel upward. □□ **keelless** *adj.* [ME *kele* f. ON *kjǫlr* f. Gmc]

/ . . . / **pronunciation**   ● **part of speech**

□ **phrases, idioms, and compounds**

□□ **derivatives**   ■ **synonym section**

cross-references appear in SMALL CAPITALS or *italics*

■ *v.* **1** see FALL *v.* 2a. **2** see CAPSIZE.

keel[2] /keel/ *n. Brit. hist.* **1** a flat-bottomed vessel, esp. of the kind formerly used on the Tyne River, etc., for loading coal ships. **2** an amount carried by such a vessel. [ME *kele* f. MLG *kēl*, MDu. *kiel* ship, boat, f. Gmc]

keelhaul /keelhawl/ *v.tr.* **1** *hist.* drag (a person) through the water under the keel of a ship as a punishment. **2** scold or rebuke severely.

■ **2** see CASTIGATE.

keelson /keelsən/ *n.* (also **kelson** /kelsən/) a line of timber fastening a ship's floor timbers to its keel. [ME *kelswayn*, perh. f. LG *kielswīn* f. *kiel* KEEL[1] + (prob.) *swīn* SWINE used as the name of a timber]

keen[1] /keen/ *adj.* **1** (of a person, desire, or interest) eager; ardent (*a keen sportsman; keen to be involved*). **2** (foll. by *on*) much attracted by; fond of or enthusiastic about. **3 a** (of the senses) sharp; highly sensitive. **b** (of memory, etc.) clear; vivid. **4** (of a person) intellectually acute; (of a remark, etc.) quick; sharp; biting. **5 a** having a sharp edge or point. **b** (of an edge, etc.) sharp. **6** (of a sound, light, etc.) penetrating; vivid; strong. **7** (of a wind, frost, etc.) piercingly cold. **8** (of a pain, etc.) acute; bitter. **9** *Brit.* (of a price) competitive. **10** *colloq.* excellent. □□ **keenly** *adv.* **keenness** *n.* [OE *cēne* f. Gmc]

■ **1** enthusiastic, avid, zealous, devoted, ardent, fervent, fervid, earnest, impassioned, passionate, enthused, intense, active, agog; eager, itching, bursting, raring, anxious. **2** (*keen on*) fond of, enthusiastic about, enamored of, devoted to, interested in, intent on, *colloq.* sweet on. **3 a** sharp, acute, sensitive, penetrating, discriminating, fine, discerning, perceptive. **b** vivid, clear, detailed, specific, unmistaken, unmistakable, distinct. **4** intelligent, sharp, acute, perceptive, perspicacious, percipient, sensitive, discerning, astute, smart, bright, discriminating, discriminative, quick(-witted), shrewd, clever, canny, cunning, crafty, wise; trenchant, incisive, cutting, rapierlike, pointed, mordant, acid, vitriolic, acerbic, astringent, biting, acrid, acrimonious, stinging, scorching, caustic, searing, withering, virulent, pungent, sarcastic, sardonic. **5** sharp, sharpened, honed, pointed, incisive, razor-sharp, razorlike, rapierlike, knife-edged. **7** piercing, penetrating, bitter, chilling, biting. **8** painful, bitter, acute, throbbing, searing, burning, fierce, grievous, severe, distressing, distressful, excruciating, strong, deep, profound, intense, extreme, poignant, heartfelt. □□ **keenness** see ENTHUSIASM 1, INTELLIGENCE 1b.

keen[2] /keen/ *n. & v.* ● *n.* an Irish funeral song accompanied with wailing. ● *v.* **1** *intr.* utter the keen. **2** *tr.* bewail (a person) in this way. **3** *tr.* utter in a wailing tone. □□ **keener** *n.* [Ir. *caoine* f. *caoinim* wail]

■ *n.* dirge, elegy, keening, knell, lament, lamentation, requiem, monody, threnody, epicedium, *Sc. & Ir.* coronach. ● *v.* **1** see MOAN *v.* 1, 3. **2** weep for, lament, mourn, grieve for, sorrow for, bewail, bemoan.

keep /keep/ *v. & n.* ● *v.* (*past* and *past part.* **kept** /kept/) **1** *tr.* have continuous charge of; retain possession of; save or hold on to. **2** *tr.* (foll. by *for*) retain or reserve for a future occasion or time (*will keep it for tomorrow*). **3** *tr. & intr.* retain or remain in a specified condition, position, course, etc. (*keep cool; keep off the grass; keep them happy*). **4** *tr.* put or store in a regular place (*knives are kept in this drawer*). **5** *tr.* (foll. by *from*) cause to avoid or abstain from something (*will keep you from going too fast*). **6** *tr.* detain; cause to be late (*what kept you?*). **7 a** observe or pay due regard to (a law, custom, etc.) (*keep one's word*). **b** honor or fulfill (a commitment, undertaking, etc.). **c** respect the commitment implied by (a secret, etc.). **d** act fittingly on the occasion of (*keep the Sabbath*). **8** *tr.* own and look after (animals) for amusement or profit (*keeps bees*). **9 a** provide for the sustenance of (a person, family, etc.). **b** (foll. by *in*) maintain (a person) with a supply of (etc.). **10** *tr.* manage (a shop, business, etc.). **11 a** *tr.* maintain (accounts, a diary, etc.) by making the requisite entries. **b** *tr.* maintain (a house) in proper or-

der. **12** *tr.* have (a commodity) regularly on sale (*do you keep buttons?*). **13** *tr.* **a** confine or detain (a person, animal, etc.). **b** guard or protect (a person or place, a goal in soccer, etc.). **14** *tr.* preserve in being; continue to have (*keep order*). **15** *intr.* (foll. by verbal noun) continue or do repeatedly or habitually (*why do you keep saying that?*). **16** *tr.* continue to follow (a way or course). **17** *intr.* **a** (esp. of perishable commodities) remain in good condition. **b** (of news or information, etc.) admit of being withheld for a time. **18** *tr.* esp. *Brit.* remain in (one's bed, room, house, etc.). **19** *tr.* retain one's place in (a seat or saddle, one's ground, etc.) against opposition or difficulty. **20** *tr.* maintain (a person) in return for sexual favors (*a kept woman*). ● *n.* **1** maintenance or the essentials for this (esp. food) (*hardly earn your keep*). **2** charge or control (*is in your keep*). **3** *hist.* a tower or stronghold. □ **for keeps** *colloq.* (esp. of something received or won) permanently; indefinitely. **how are you keeping?** *Brit.* how are you? **keep at** persist or cause to persist with. **keep away** (often foll. by *from*) **1** avoid being near. **2** prevent from being near. **keep back 1** remain or keep at a distance. **2** retard the progress of. **3** conceal; decline to disclose. **4** retain; withhold (*kept back $50*). **keep one's balance 1** remain stable; avoid falling. **2** retain one's composure. **keep down 1** hold in subjection. **2** keep low in amount. **3** lie low; stay hidden. **4** manage not to vomit (food eaten). **keep one's feet** manage not to fall. **keep-fit** *Brit.* regular exercises to promote personal fitness and health. **keep one's hair on** see HAIR. **keep one's hand in** see HAND. **keep in 1** confine or restrain (one's feelings, etc.). **2** remain or confine indoors. **3** esp. *Brit.* keep (a fire) burning. **keep in mind** take into account having remembered. **keep in with** remain on good terms with. **keep kosher** see KOSHER. **keep off 1** stay or cause to stay away from. **2** ward off; avert. **3** abstain from. **4** avoid (a subject) (*let's keep off religion*). **keep on 1** continue to do something; do continually (*kept on laughing*). **2** continue to use or employ. **3** (foll. by *at*) pester or harass. **keep out 1** keep or remain outside. **2** exclude. **keep state** esp. *Brit.* **1** maintain one's dignity. **2** be difficult of access. **keep to 1** adhere to (a course, schedule, etc.). **2** observe (a promise). **3** confine oneself to. **keep to oneself 1** avoid contact with others. **2** refuse to disclose or share. **keep together** remain or keep in harmony. **keep track of** see TRACK[1] *v.* **keep under** hold in subjection. **keep up 1** maintain (progress, etc.). **2** prevent (prices, one's spirits, etc.) from sinking. **3** keep in repair, in an efficient or proper state, etc. **4** carry on (a correspondence, etc.). **5** prevent (a person) from going to bed, esp. when late. **6** (often foll. by *with*) manage not to fall behind. **keep up with the Joneses** strive to compete socially with one's neighbors. **keep one's word** see WORD. **kept woman** a woman maintained or supported in return for sexual favors. □□ **keepable** *adj.* [OE *cēpan*, of unkn. orig.]

■ *v.* **1** retain, hold, hang *or* hold on to, preserve, conserve, have, save, maintain, control; accumulate, save (up), amass, hoard (up), husband, put *or* stow away; take care *or* charge of, mind, tend, care for, take care of, look after, guard, keep an eye on, watch over, protect, safeguard, have custody of, be responsible for. **3** stay, remain. **4** store, stow, maintain, preserve. **5** prevent, keep *or* hold back, restrain, (hold in) check, restrict, prohibit, forbid, inhibit, block, curb, deter, discourage. **6** detain, delay, slow up, hold (up), hold *or* set back. **7 a** keep to, abide by, follow, obey, mind, adhere to, stick to, attend to, pay attention to, heed, regard, observe, respect, acknowledge, defer to, accede to, agree to. **b** honor, fulfill, follow, carry out, conform to, keep faith with, respect. **c** harbor, maintain, safeguard, conceal, keep dark, keep hidden, hush up, bury; withhold, not breathe a word about, keep under wraps. **d** celebrate, observe, solemnize, honor, memorialize, commemorate. **8** raise, rear, look after. **9 a** maintain, feed, nourish, nurture, foster, provide for, support, sustain, provision, victual, board. **b** supply *or* stock *or* furnish with. **10** manage, run, have, maintain, supervise, superintend, be responsible for. **12** stock, have in stock, carry, store, trade in, deal in. **13** confine, detain; imprison, incarcerate, jail; defend, guard, protect, cover, safeguard, shield. **15** keep on, go on, continue, carry on, persist in, persevere in. **16** keep to, maintain, follow, stick to. **17** last, keep fresh, stay *or* remain fresh, be preserved, survive. **20** support, finance, provide for, subsidize, maintain. ● *n.* **1** upkeep, maintenance, support, room and board, subsistence, food, sustenance, living. **2** charge, control, care, custody, protection, keeping, safekeeping. **3** tower, stronghold, fortress, donjon, *archaic* dungeon. □ **for keeps** permanently, once and for all, for good, for ever, indefinitely. **keep at** persist in, persevere in, stick at, follow to a conclusion, peg away at, *colloq.* plug away at; (*keep at it*) hold out, keep going *or* trying, be steadfast, see it through, peg along, stay the distance *or* course; be determined, be firm, be unwavering, be resolute, *colloq.* hang on *or* in, stick it out. **keep away 1** (*keep away from*) see AVOID 1. **keep back 2** see *hold back* (HOLD[1]), SUPPRESS 2. **3, 4** see WITHHOLD 1. **keep down 1, 2** see SUPPRESS 2, TYRANNIZE. **3** see HIDE[1] *v.* 2. **keep in 1** keep *or* hold back, repress, suppress, stifle, smother, muzzle, bottle up, withhold, conceal, hide, shroud, mask, camouflage. **2** confine, shut in *or* up, coop up, fence in, detain. **keep in mind** see *bear in mind* (BEAR[1]). **keep off 1, 3, 4** see AVOID 1. **2** see *hold off*. **keep on 1** keep, continue, carry on, persist in, persevere in. **3** pester, harass, *colloq.* go on at. **keep to 1, 2** see KEEP *v.* 7 above.

keeper /kéepər/ *n.* **1** a person who keeps or looks after something or someone. **2** esp. *Brit.* a custodian of a museum, art gallery, forest, etc. **3 a** = GAMEKEEPER. **b** a person in charge of animals in a zoo. **4 a** = WICKETKEEPER. **b** = GOALKEEPER. **5** a fruit, etc., that remains in good condition. **6** a bar of soft iron across the poles of a horseshoe magnet to maintain its strength. **7 a** a plain ring to preserve a hole in a pierced ear lobe; a sleeper. **b** a ring worn to guard against the loss of a more valuable one. **8 a** a fish large enough to be kept without violating the law. **b** *colloq.* anything worth keeping. ■ **1** custodian, guardian, guard, warden, caretaker; warder, nurse, attendant, esp. *Brit. sl.* minder.

keeping /kéeping/ *n.* **1** custody; charge (*in safe keeping*). **2** agreement; harmony (esp. *in* or *out of keeping*). ■ **1** see CARE 4a. **2** see STEP 9a.

keepsake /kéepsayk/ *n.* a thing kept for the sake of or in remembrance of the giver. ■ memento, souvenir, token, reminder, remembrance, relic.

keeshond /káys-hond/ *n.* **1** a dog of a Dutch breed with long, thick hair like a large Pomeranian. **2** this breed. [Du.]

kef /kef, keef/ *n.* (also **kif** /kif/) **1** a drowsy state induced by marijuana, etc. **2** the enjoyment of idleness. **3** a substance smoked to produce kef. [Arab. *kayf* enjoyment, well-being]

keffiyeh var. of KAFFIYEH.

keg /keg/ *n.* a small barrel of less than 30 gallons (usu. 5–10 gallons). □ **keg beer** beer supplied from a sealed metal container. **keg party** a party at which keg beer is served. [ME *cag* f. ON *kaggi*, of unkn. orig.] ■ cask, barrel, butt, hogshead, tun, *hist.* puncheon.

keister /kéestər/ *n. sl.* **1** the buttocks. **2** a suitcase, satchel, handbag, etc. [orig. unkn.] ■ **1** see BUTTOCK. **2** see BAG *n.* 2a.

keloid /kéeloyd/ *n.* fibrous tissue formed at the site of a scar or injury. [Gk *khēlē* claw + -OID]

kelp /kelp/ *n.* **1** any of several large, broad-fronded brown seaweeds esp. of the genus *Laminaria*, suitable for use as manure. **2** the calcined ashes of seaweed formerly used in glassmaking and soap manufacture because of their high content of sodium, potassium, and magnesium salts. [ME *cúlp(e)*, of unkn. orig.]

kelpie /kélpee/ *n. Sc.* **1** a water spirit, usu. in the form of a horse, reputed to delight in the drowning of travelers, etc. **2** an Australian sheepdog orig. bred from a Scottish collie. [18th c.: orig. unkn.]

kelson var. of KEELSON.

Kelt var. of CELT.

kelt /kelt/ *n.* a salmon or sea trout after spawning. [ME: orig. unkn.]

kelter var. of KILTER.

kelvin /kélvin/ *n.* the SI unit of thermodynamic temperature, equal in magnitude to the degree celsius. ¶ Abbr.: **K.** □ **Kelvin scale** a scale of temperature with absolute zero as zero. [Lord *Kelvin*, Brit. physicist d. 1907]

kemp /kemp/ *n.* coarse hair in wool. □□ **kempy** *adj.* [ME f. ON *kampr* beard, whisker]

kempt /kempt/ *adj.* combed; neatly kept. [past part. of (now dial.) *kemb* COMB *v.* f. OE *cemban* f. Gmc] ■ (*well-kempt*) see TRIM *adj.* 1.

ken /ken/ *n. & v.* ● *n.* range of sight or knowledge (*it's beyond my ken*). ● *v.tr.* (**kenning**; *past* and *past part.* **kenned** or **kent**) *Sc. & No. of Engl.* **1** recognize at sight. **2** know. [OE *cennan* f. Gmc] ■ *n.* see HORIZON.

kendo /kéndō/ *n.* a Japanese form of fencing with bamboo swords. [Jap., = sword-way]

kennel /kénəl/ *n. & v.* ● *n.* **1** a small shelter for a dog. **2** (in *pl.*) a breeding or boarding establishment for dogs. **3** a mean dwelling. ● *v.* (**kenneled, kenneling**; esp. *Brit.* **kennelled, kennelling**) **1** *tr.* put into or keep in a kennel. **2** *intr.* live in or go to a kennel. [ME f. OF *chenil* f. med.L *canile* (unrecorded) f. L *canis* dog]

kenning /kéning/ *n.* a compound expression in Old English and Old Norse poetry, e.g., *oar-steed* = ship. [ME, = 'teaching,' etc., f. KEN]

kenosis /kinṓsis/ *n. Theol.* the doctrine of the renunciation of the divine nature, at least in part, by Christ in the Incarnation. □□ **kenotic** /-nótik/ *adj.* [Gk *kenōsis* f. *kenoō* to empty f. *kenos* empty]

kenspeckle /kénspekəl/ *adj. Sc.* conspicuous. [*kenspeck* of Scand. orig.: rel. to KEN]

kent *past* and *past part.* of KEN.

Kentish /kéntish/ *adj.* of Kent in England. □ **Kentish fire** *Brit.* a prolonged volley of rhythmic applause or a demonstration of dissent. [OE *Centisc* f. *Cent* f. L *Cantium*]

kentledge /kéntlij/ *n. Naut.* pig iron, etc., used as permanent ballast. [F *quintelage* ballast, with assim. to *kentle* obs. var. of QUINTAL]

Kenyan /kényən, kéen-/ *adj. & n.* ● *adj.* of or relating to Kenya in E. Africa. ● *n.* **a** a native or national of Kenya. **b** a person of Kenyan descent.

kepi /képee, káypee/ *n.* (*pl.* **kepis**) a French military cap with a horizontal peak. [F *képi* f. Swiss G *Käppi* dimin. of *Kappe* cap]

Kepler's laws /képlərz/ *n.pl.* three theorems describing orbital motion. □□ **Keplerian** /-léeriən/ *adj.* [J. *Kepler* Ger. astronomer d. 1630]

kept *past* and *past part.* of KEEP.

keratin /kérətin/ *n.* a fibrous protein which occurs in hair, feathers, hooves, claws, horns, etc. [Gk *keras keratos* horn + -IN]

keratinize /kérətinīz/ *v.tr. & intr.* cover or become covered with a deposit of keratin. □□ **keratinization** *n.*

keratose /kérətōs/ *adj.* (of sponge) composed of a horny substance. [Gk *keras keratos* horn + -OSE[1]]

kerb *Brit.* var. of CURB 2.

kerbstone *Brit.* var. of CURBSTONE.

kerchief /kárchif, -cheef/ *n.* **1** a cloth used to cover the head. **2** *poet.* a handkerchief. □□ **kerchiefed** *adj.* [ME *curchef* f. AF *courchef*, OF *couvrechief* f. *couvrir* COVER + CHIEF head]

kerf /kərf/ *n.* **1** a slit made by cutting, esp. with a saw. **2** the cut end of a felled tree. [OE *cyrf* f. Gmc (as CARVE)]

kerfuffle /kərfúffəl/ *n.* esp. *Brit. colloq.* a fuss or commotion. [Sc. *curfuffle* f. *fuffle* to disorder: imit.]

kermes /kármeez/ *n.* **1** the female of a bug, *Kermes ilicis*, with

/.../ **pronunciation**	● **part of speech**
□ **phrases, idioms, and compounds**	
□□ **derivatives**	■ **synonym section**
cross-references appear in SMALL CAPITALS or *italics*	

a berrylike appearance. **2** (in full **kermes oak**) an evergreen oak, *Quercus coccifera*, of S. Europe and N. Africa, on which this insect feeds. **3** a red dye made from the dried bodies of these insects. **4** (in full **kermes mineral**) a bright red hydrous trisulfide of antimony. [F *kermès* f. Arab. & Pers. *ḳirmiz*: rel. to CRIMSON]

kermis /kə́rmis/ *n.* **1** a periodical country fair, esp. in the Netherlands. **2** a charity bazaar. [Du., orig. = Mass on the anniversary of the dedication of a church, when yearly fair was held: f. *kerk* formed as CHURCH + *mis, misse* MASS²]
■ see FAIR² 2.

kern¹ /kərn/ *n. Printing* the part of a metal type projecting beyond its body or shank. □□ **kerned** *adj.* [perh. f. F *carne* corner f. OF *charne* f. L *cardo cardinis* hinge]

kern² /kərn/ *n.* (also **kerne**) **1** *hist.* a light-armed Irish foot soldier. **2** a peasant; a boor. [ME f. Ir. *ceithern*]

kernel /kə́rnəl/ *n.* **1** a central, softer, usu. edible part within a hard shell of a nut, fruit stone, seed, etc. **2** the whole seed of a cereal. **3** the nucleus or essential part of anything. [OE *cyrnel*, dimin. of CORN¹]
■ **1, 2** grain, seed, pip, stone; nut, (nut)meat. **3** center, core, nucleus, heart, essence, quintessence, substance, gist, pith, nub, crux, quiddity.

kero /kérō/ *n. Austral.* = KEROSENE. [abbr.]

kerosene /kérəseen/ *n.* (also **kerosine**) a liquid mixture obtained by distillation from petroleum or shale, used esp. as a fuel or solvent. [Gk *kēros* wax + -ENE]

kerry /kéree/ *n.* (also **Kerry**) (*pl.* **-ies**) **1** an animal of a breed of small, black dairy cattle. **2** this breed. [*Kerry* in Ireland]

Kerry blue *n.* **1** a terrier of a breed with a silky, wavy, blue-gray coat. **2** this breed.

kersey /kə́rzee/ *n.* (*pl.* **-eys**) **1** a kind of coarse narrow cloth woven from long wool, usu. ribbed. **2** a variety of this. [ME, prob. f. *Kersey* in Suffolk]

kerseymere /kə́rzeemeer/ *n.* a twilled fine woolen cloth. [alt. of *cassimere*, var. of CASHMERE, assim. to KERSEY]

keskidee var. of KISKADEE.

kestrel /késtrəl/ *n.* any small falcon, esp. *Falco tinnunculus*, that hovers while searching for its prey. [ME *castrell*, perh. f. F dial. *casserelle*, F *créc(er)elle*, perh. imit. of its cry]

ketch /kech/ *n.* a two-masted, fore-and-aft rigged sailing boat with a mizzenmast stepped forward of the rudder and smaller than its foremast. [ME *catche*, prob. f. CATCH]

ketchup /kéchup, káchup/ *n.* (also **catchup, catsup** /kátsəp/) a spicy sauce made from tomatoes, mushrooms, vinegar, etc., used as a condiment. [Chin. dial. *kōechiap* pickled-fish brine]

ketone /keétōn/ *n.* any of a class of organic compounds in which two hydrocarbon groups are linked by a carbonyl group, e.g., propanone (acetone). □ **ketone body** *Biochem.* any of several ketones produced in the body during the metabolism of fats. □□ **ketonic** /kitónik/ *adj.* [G *Keton* alt. of *Aketon* ACETONE]

ketonuria /keétōnŏŏreeə, -nyŏŏr-/ *n.* the excretion of abnormally large amounts of ketone bodies in the urine.

ketosis /keetōsis/ *n.* a condition characterized by raised levels of ketone bodies in the body, associated with fat metabolism and diabetes. □□ **ketotic** /-tótik/ *adj.*

kettle /két'l/ *n.* **1** a vessel, usu. of metal with a lid, spout, and handle, for boiling water in. **2** (in full **kettle hole**) a depression in the ground in a glaciated area. □ **a fine** (or **pretty**) **kettle of fish** an awkward state of affairs. □□ **kettleful** *n.* (*pl.* **-fuls**). [ME f. ON *ketill* ult. f. L *catillus* dimin. of *catinus* deep food-vessel]
■ □ **a fine** (or **pretty**) **kettle of fish** see MESS *n.* 2.

kettledrum /két'ldrum/ *n.* a large drum shaped like a bowl with a membrane adjustable for tension (and so pitch) stretched across. □□ **kettledrummer** *n.*

keV *abbr.* kilo-electronvolt.

Kevlar /kévlaar/ *n. propr.* a synthetic fiber of high tensile strength used esp. as a reinforcing agent in the manufacture of rubber products, e.g., tires.

Kewpie /kyŏŏpee/ *n.* /propr./ a small, chubby doll with a curl or topknot. [CUPID + -IE]

key¹ /kee/ *n., adj.,* & *v.* ● *n.* (*pl.* **keys**) **1** an instrument, usu.

of metal, for moving the bolt of a lock forward or backward to lock or unlock. **2** a similar implement for operating a switch in the form of a lock. **3** an instrument for grasping screws, pegs, nuts, etc., esp. one for winding a clock, etc. **4** a lever depressed by the finger in playing the organ, piano, flute, concertina, etc. **5** (often in *pl.*) each of several buttons for operating a typewriter, word processor, or computer terminal, etc. **6** what gives or precludes the opportunity for or access to something. **7** a place that by its position gives control of a sea, territory, etc. **8 a** a solution or explanation. **b** a word or system for solving a cipher or code. **c** an explanatory list of symbols used in a map, table, etc. **d** a book of solutions to mathematical problems, etc. **e** a literal translation of a book written in a foreign language. **f** the first move in a chess-problem solution. **9** *Mus.* a system of notes definitely related to each other, based on a particular note, and predominating in a piece of music; tone or pitch (*a study in the key of C major*). **10** a tone or style of thought or expression. **11** a piece of wood or metal inserted between others to secure them. **12** the part of a first coat of wall plaster that passes between the laths and so secures the rest. **13** the roughness of a surface, helping the adhesion of plaster, etc. **14** the samara of a sycamore, etc. **15** a mechanical device for making or breaking an electric circuit, e.g., in telegraphy. ● *adj.* essential; of vital importance (*the key element in the problem*). ● *v.tr.* (**keys, keyed**) **1** (foll. by *in, on,* etc.) fasten with a pin, wedge, bolt, etc. **2** (often foll. by *in*) enter (data) by means of a keyboard. **3** roughen (a surface) to help the adhesion of plaster, etc. **4** (foll. by *to*) align or link (one thing to another). **5** regulate the pitch of the strings of (a violin, etc.). **6** word (an advertisement in a particular periodical) so that answers to it can be identified (usu. by varying the form of address given). □ **key card** a card that operates an electronic door lock, used as a key at hotels, etc. **key industry** an industry essential to the carrying on of others, e.g., coal mining, dyeing. **key map** a map in bare outline, to simplify the use of a full map. **key money** *Brit.* a payment demanded from an incoming tenant for the provision of a key to the premises. **key ring** a ring for keeping keys on. **key signature** *Mus.* any of several combinations of sharps or flats after the clef at the beginning of each staff indicating the key of a composition. **key up** (often foll. by *to,* or *to* + infin.) make (a person) nervous or tense; excite. □□ **keyer** *n.* **keyless** *adj.* [OE *cǣg,* of unkn. orig.]
■ *n.* **1** latchkey, skeleton key, passkey, opener. **4** (*keys*) ivories. **5** button. **8 a** clue, cue, guide, solution, answer, indication, indicator, explanation, description, explication, clarification, translation. **b** keyword, password. **c** legend, code, table. **9** scale, mode, tonality, pitch, tone, timbre, level, frequency. **10** mood, tenor, tone, pitch, humor, style, vein, character. ● *adj.* important, essential, vital, necessary, crucial, critical, main, pivotal, fundamental, principal, chief, major, leading, criterial, central. ● *v.* **2** type, input, keyboard. □ **key up** see EXCITE *v.* 2. □□ **keyer** keyboarder, typist.

key² /kee/ *n.* a low-lying island or reef, esp. off the Florida coast (cf. CAY). [Sp. *cayo* shoal, reef, infl. by QUAY]

keyboard /keébawrd/ *n.* & *v.* ● *n.* **1** a set of keys on a typewriter, computer, piano, etc.; the keys of a computer terminal regarded as a person's place of work. **2** an electronic musical instrument with keys arranged as on a piano. ● *v.tr.* & *intr.* enter (data) by means of a keyboard; work at a keyboard. □□ **keyboarder** *n.* **keyboardist** *n.*
■ *n.* **1** ivories, keys; see also TERMINAL *n.* 5. **2** synthesizer, electric *or* electronic piano, electric *or* electronic organ. ● *v.* key (in), type, typewrite, input; transcribe.

keyhole /keéhōl/ *n.* a hole by which a key is put into a lock. □ **keyhole surgery** minimally invasive surgery carried out through a very small incision.

Keynesian /káynzeeən/ *adj.* & *n.* ● *adj.* of or relating to the economic theories of J. M. Keynes (d. 1946), esp. regarding government control of the economy through money and taxation. ● *n.* an adherent of these theories. □□ **Keynesianism** *n.*

keynote /keénōt/ *n.* **1** a prevailing tone or idea (*the keynote* *of the whole occasion).* **2** (*attrib.*) intended to set the prevailing tone at a meeting or conference (*keynote address*). **3** *Mus.* the note on which a key is based.

■ **1** see THEME 1.

keypad /kéepad/ *n.* a miniature keyboard or set of buttons for operating a portable electronic device, telephone, etc.

keypunch /kéepunch/ *n. & v.* ● *n.* a device for transferring data by means of punched holes or notches on a series of cards or paper tape. ● *v.tr.* transfer (data) by means of a keypunch. □□ **keypuncher** *n.*

keystone /kéestōn/ *n.* **1** the central principle of a system, policy, etc., on which all the rest depends. **2** a central stone at the summit of an arch locking the whole together.

■ crux, linchpin, basis, principle, foundation, base, bedrock, cornerstone.

keystroke /kéestrōk/ *n.* a single depression of a key on a keyboard, esp. as a measure of work.

keyway /kéeway/ *n.* a slot for receiving a machined key.

keyword /kéewərd/ *n.* (also **Key word**) **1** the key to a cipher, etc. **2 a** a word of great significance. **b** a significant word used in indexing.

■ see KEY[1] 8.

KG *abbr.* (in the UK) Knight of the Order of the Garter.

kg *abbr.* kilogram(s).

KGB /káyjeebée/ *n.* the state security police of the former USSR from 1954. [Russ., abbr. of *Komitet gosudarstvennoĭ bezopasnosti* committee of state security]

Kgs. *abbr.* Kings (Old Testament).

khaddar /káadər/ *n.* homespun cloth of India. [Hindi]

khaki /kákee, ká-/ *adj. & n.* ● *adj.* dust-colored; dull brownish-yellow. ● *n.* (*pl.* **khakis**) **1 a** khaki fabric of twilled cotton or wool, used esp. in military dress. **b** (in *pl.*) a garment, esp. pants or a military uniform, made of this fabric. **2** the dull brownish-yellow color of this. [Urdu *k̲h̲ākī* dust-colored f. *k̲h̲āk* dust]

khamsin /kámsin, kamseén/ *n.* (also **hamsin** /hám-/) an oppressive hot south or southeast wind occurring in Egypt for about 50 days in March, April, and May. [Arab. *k̲h̲amsīn* f. *k̲h̲amsūn* fifty]

■ see STORM *n.* 1.

khan[1] /kaan, kan/ *n.* **1** a title given to rulers and officials in Central Asia, Afghanistan, etc. **2** *hist.* **a** the supreme ruler of the Turkish, Tartar, and Mongol tribes. **b** the emperor of China in the Middle Ages. □□ **khanate** *n.* [Turki *k̲h̲ān* lord]

khan[2] /kaan, kan/ *n.* a caravansary. [Arab. *k̲h̲ān* inn]

khedive /kidéev/ *n. hist.* the title of the viceroy of Egypt under Turkish rule 1867–1914. □□ **khedival** *adj.* **khedivial** *adj.* [F *khédive*, ult. f. Pers. *k̲adīv* prince]

Khmer /kmair/ *n. & adj.* ● *n.* **1** a native of the ancient Khmer kingdom in SE Asia, or of modern Cambodia. **2** the language of this people. ● *adj.* of the Khmers or their language. [native name]

Khurta var. of KURTA.

kHz *abbr.* kilohertz.

kiang /keeáng/ *n.* a wild Tibetan ass, *Equus hemionus kiang*, with a thick, furry coat. [Tibetan *kyang*]

kibble[1] /kíbəl/ *v. & n.* ● *v.tr.* grind coarsely. ● *n.* coarsely ground pellets of meal, etc., used as a dry pet food. [18th c.: orig. unkn.]

■ *v.* see GRIND *v.* 1a.

kibble[2] /kíbəl/ *n. Brit.* an iron bucket used in mines for hoisting ore. [G *Kübel* (cf. OE *cyfel*) f. med.L *cupellus*, corn measure, dimin. of *cuppa* cup]

kibbutz /kibóöts/ *n.* (*pl.* **kibbutzim** /-bōotseém/) a communal, esp. farming, settlement in Israel. [mod.Heb. *kibbūṣ* gathering]

kibbutznik /kibóötsnik/ *n.* a member of a kibbutz. [Yiddish (as KIBBUTZ)]

kibe /kīb/ *n.* an ulcerated chilblain, esp. on the heel. [ME, prob. f. Welsh *cibi*]

kibitz /kíbits/ *v.intr. colloq.* act as a kibitzer. [Yiddish f. G *kiebitzen* (as KIBITZER)]

■ see MEDDLE.

kibitzer /kíbitsər/ *n. colloq.* **1** an onlooker at cards, etc., esp.

one who offers unwanted advice. **2** a busybody; a meddler. [Yiddish *kibitser* f. G *Kiebitz* lapwing, busybody]

■ **2** see BUSYBODY 1.

kiblah /kíblə/ *n.* (also **qibla**) **1** the direction of the Kaaba (the sacred building at Mecca), to which Muslims turn at prayer. **2** = MIHRAB. [Arab. *ḳibla* that which is opposite]

kibosh /kíbosh/ *n.* (also *Brit.* **kybosh**) *sl.* nonsense. □ **put the kibosh on** put an end to; finally dispose of. [19th c.: orig. unkn.]

■ see DRIVEL *n.* □ **put the kibosh on** see VETO *v.*

kick[1] /kik/ *v. & n.* ● *v.* **1** *tr.* strike or propel forcibly with the foot or hoof, etc. **2** *intr.* (usu. foll. by *at, against*) **a** strike out with the foot. **b** express annoyance at or dislike of (treatment, a proposal, etc.); rebel against. **3** *tr. sl.* give up (a habit). **4** *tr.* (often foll. by *out*, etc.) expel or dismiss forcibly. **5** *refl.* be annoyed with oneself (*I'll kick myself if I'm wrong*). **6** *tr. Football* score (a goal) by a kick. **7** *intr. Cricket* (of a ball) rise sharply from the field. ● *n.* **1 a** a blow with the foot or hoof, etc. **b** the delivery of such a blow. **2** *colloq.* **a** a sharp stimulant effect, esp. of alcohol (*has some kick in it; a cocktail with a kick in it*). **b** (often in *pl.*) a pleasurable thrill (*did it just for kicks; got a kick out of flying*). **3** strength; resilience (*have no kick left*). **4** *colloq.* a specified temporary interest or enthusiasm (*on a jogging kick*). **5** the recoil of a gun when discharged. **6** *Brit. Soccer colloq.* a player of specified kicking ability (*is a good kick*). □ **kick about** (or **around**) *colloq.* **1 a** drift idly from place to place. **b** be unused or unwanted. **2 a** treat roughly or scornfully. **b** discuss (an idea) unsystematically. **kick the bucket** *sl.* die. **kickdown** a device for changing gear in a motor vehicle by full depression of the accelerator. **kick one's heels** see HEEL. **kick in 1** knock down (a door, etc.) by kicking. **2** *sl.* contribute (esp. money); pay one's share. **kick in the pants** (or **teeth**) *colloq.* a humiliating punishment or setback. **kick off 1 a** *Football*, etc., begin or resume play. **b** *colloq.* begin. **2** remove (shoes, etc.) by kicking. **kick over the traces** see TRACE[2]. **kick pleat** a pleat in a narrow skirt to allow freedom of movement. **kick-start 1** start (a motorcycle, etc.) by the downward thrust of a pedal. **2** start or restart (a process, etc.) by providing some initial impetus. **kick starter** (or **start**) **1** a device to start the engine of a motorcycle, etc., by the downward thrust of a pedal. **2** a boost or push to start or restart a process, etc. **kick turn** a standing turn in skiing. **kick up** (or **kick up a fuss, dust**, etc.) create a disturbance; object or register strong disapproval. **kick up one's heels** frolic. **kick a person upstairs** shelve a person by giving him or her a promotion or a title. □□ **kickable** *adj.* **kicker** *n.* [ME *kike*, of unkn. orig.]

■ *v.* **1** punt, *archaic* foot, *colloq.* boot; strike, hit, shoot, pass. **2 b** see PROTEST 1. **3** see DISCONTINUE. **4** see *turn out* 1. ● *n.* **1** punt, hit, dropkick, strike, shot, pass, *colloq.* boot. **2** see THRILL *n.* 1. **3** see PUNCH[1] *n.* 3. **4** see FIXATION. **5** recoil, backlash, rebound. □ **kick about** (or **around**) **1 a** see *knock about* 2. **b** lie about *or* around, knock about *or* around, hang about *or* around. **2 a** see *knock about* 1. **b** discuss, debate, talk over. **kick the bucket** see DIE[1] 1. **kick in 1** knock down, smash in, throw down, demolish, destroy, wreck. **kick off 1** see START 1, 2. **kick-start 2** see BOOST *v.* 1a. **kick starter** (or **start**) **2** see BOOST *n.*. **kick up** fuss, make a fuss; see also COMPLAIN 1.

kick[2] /kik/ *n.* an indentation in the bottom of a glass bottle. [19th c.: orig. unkn.]

Kickapoo /kíkəpōō/ *n.* **1 a** a N. American people native to the upper Midwest. **b** a member of this people. **2** the language of this people.

kickback /kíkbak/ *n. colloq.* **1** the force of a recoil. **2** payment for collaboration, esp. collaboration for profit.

■ **1** see BACKLASH 2. **2** share, cut, compensation,

/.../ **pronunciation**	● **part of speech**
□ **phrases, idioms, and compounds**	
□□ **derivatives**	■ **synonym section**
cross-references appear in SMALL CAPITALS *or italics*	

remuneration, recompense, commission, percentage, reward; bribe, hush money, protection (money), payola, *colloq.* graft, plugola, *Brit. sl.* backhander; *sl.* boodle, payoff.

kickoff /kíkawf/ *n.* **1 a** *Football & Soccer* the start or resumption of play. **b** the start of something, esp. a campaign, drive, or project.

kickshaw /kíkshaw/ *n.* **1** *archaic*, usu. *derog.* a fancy dish in cookery. **2** something elegant but insubstantial; a toy or trinket. [F *quelque chose* something]

■ **2** see GEWGAW, TOY *n.* 2.

kickstand /kíkstand/ *n.* a rod attached to a bicycle or motor cycle and kicked into a vertical position to support the vehicle when stationary.

kid[1] /kid/ *n. & v.* ● *n.* **1** a young goat. **2** the leather made from its skin. **3** *colloq.* a child or young person. ● *v.intr.* (**kidded, kidding**) (of a goat) give birth. □ **handle with kid gloves** handle in a gentle, delicate, or gingerly manner. **kid brother** (or **sister**) *sl.* a younger brother or sister. **kidglove** (*attrib.*) dainty or delicate. **kid stuff** *sl.* something very simple. [ME *kide* f. ON *kith* f. Gmc]

■ *n.* **3** see CHILD 1a. □ **kid stuff** see BREEZE[1] *n.* 5.

kid[2] /kid/ *v.* (**kidded, kidding**) *colloq.* **1** *tr. & also refl.* deceive; trick (*don't kid yourself; kidded his mother that he was ill*). **2** *tr. & intr.* tease (*only kidding*). □ **no kidding** (or esp. *Brit.* *sl.*) that is the truth. □□ **kidder** *n.* **kiddingly** *adv.* [perh. f. KID[1]]

■ **1** see FOOL *v.* 2. **2** see TAUNT *v.* □ **no kidding** see INDEED *int.* □□ **kidder** see JOKER 1.

kid[3] /kid/ *n. hist.* a small wooden tub, esp. a sailor's mess tub for grog or rations. [perh. var. of KIT[1]]

Kidderminster /kídərminstər/ *n.* (in full **Kidderminster carpet**) a carpet made of two cloths of different colors woven together so that the carpet is reversible. [*Kidderminster* in S. England]

kiddie /kídee/ *n.* (also **kiddy**) (*pl.* **-ies**) *sl.* = KID[1] *n.* 3.

kiddle /kíd'l/ *n.* **1** a barrier in a river with an opening fitted with nets, etc. to catch fish. **2** an arrangement of fishing-nets hung on stakes along the seashore. [ME f. AF *kidel*, OF *quidel, guidel*]

kiddo /kídō/ *n.* (*pl.* **-os**) *sl.* = KID[1] *n.* 3.

kiddy var. of KIDDIE.

kidnap /kídnap/ *v.tr.* (**kidnapped, kidnapping** *or* **kidnaped, kidnaping**) **1** carry off (a person, etc.) by illegal force or fraud esp. to obtain a ransom. **2** steal (a child). □□ **kidnapper** *n.* [back-form. f. *kidnapper* f. KID[1] + *nap* = NAB]

■ abduct, capture, seize, carry off, hold as hostage, hold for ransom, snatch, make off with, take away. □□ **kidnapper** abductor, hostage taker.

kidney /kídnee/ *n.* (*pl.* **-eys**) **1** either of a pair of organs in the abdominal cavity of mammals, birds, and reptiles, which remove nitrogenous wastes from the blood and excrete urine. **2** the kidney of a sheep, ox, or pig as food. **3** temperament; nature; kind (*a man of that kidney; of the right kidney*). □ **kidney bean 1** a dwarf French bean. **2** a scarlet runner bean. **kidney machine** = *artificial kidney*. **kidney-shaped** shaped like a kidney, with one side concave and the other convex. **kidney vetch** a herbaceous plant, *Anthyllis vulneraria*. [ME *kidnei*, pl. *kidneiren*, app. partly f. *ei* EGG[1]]

■ **3** see NATURE 3, 5, CHARACTER *n.* 1.

kidskin /kídskin/ *n.* = KID[1] *n.* 2.

kiekie /keékee/ *n.* a New Zealand climbing plant with edible bracts, and leaves that are used for basket-making, etc. [Maori]

kielbasa /keelbaásə, kib-/ *n.* a variety of smoked, garlic-flavored sausage. [Pol., = sausage]

kieselguhr /keézəlgoor/ *n.* diatomaceous earth forming deposits in lakes and oceans and used as a filter, filler, insulator, etc., in various manufacturing processes. [G f. *Kiesel* gravel + dial. *Guhr* earthy deposit]

kif var. of KEF.

kike /kīk/ *n. sl. offens.* a Jew. [20th c.: orig. uncert.]

Kikuyu /kikóōyoō/ *n. & adj.* ● *n.* (*pl.* same or **Kikuyus**) **1** a member of an agricultural black African people, the largest Bantu-speaking group in Kenya. **2** the language of this people. ● *adj.* of or relating to this people or their language. [native name]

kilderkin /kíldərkin/ *n.* **1** a cask for liquids, etc., holding 18 imperial gallons. **2** *Brit.* this measure. [ME, alt. of *kinderkin* f. MDu. *kinde(r)kin, kinneken*, dimin. of *kintal* QUINTAL]

kill[1] /kil/ *v. & n.* ● *v.tr.* **1 a** deprive of life or vitality; put to death; cause the death of. **b** (*absol.*) cause or bring about death (*must kill to survive*). **2** destroy; put an end to (feelings, etc.) (*overwork killed my enthusiasm*). **3** *refl.* (often foll. by pres. part.) *colloq.* **a** overexert oneself (*don't kill yourself lifting them all at once*). **b** laugh heartily. **4** *colloq.* overwhelm (a person) with amusement, delight, etc. (*the things he says really kill me*). **5** switch off (a spotlight, engine, etc.). **6** *colloq.* delete (a line, paragraph, etc.) from a computer file. **7** *colloq.* cause pain or discomfort to (*my feet are killing me*). **8** pass (time, or a specified amount of it) usu. while waiting for a specific event (*had an hour to kill before the interview*). **9** defeat (a bill in Congress, etc.). **10** *colloq.* consume the entire contents of (a bottle of wine, etc.). **11 a** *Tennis*, etc., hit (the ball) so skillfully that it cannot be returned. **b** stop (the ball) dead. **12** neutralize or render ineffective (taste, sound, color, etc.) (*thick carpet killed the sound of footsteps*). ● *n.* **1** an act of killing (esp. an animal). **2** an animal or animals killed, esp. by a sportsman. **3** *colloq.* the destruction or disablement of an enemy aircraft, submarine, etc. □ **dressed to kill** dressed showily, alluringly, or impressively. **in at the kill** present at or benefiting from the successful conclusion of an enterprise. **kill off 1** get rid of or destroy completely (esp. a number of persons or things). **2** (of an author) bring about the death of (a fictional character). **kill or cure** (usu. *attrib.*) (of a remedy, etc.) drastic; extreme. **kill two birds with one stone** achieve two aims at once. **kill with kindness** spoil (a person) with overindulgence. [ME *cülle, kille*, perh. ult. rel. to QUELL]

■ *v.* **1 a** execute, murder, assassinate, put to death, cause the death of, liquidate, dispatch, take a person's life, put an end to, kill off, exterminate, put a person out of his *or* her misery, snuff out, extinguish, obliterate, eradicate, destroy, annihilate, ruin, waste, devastate, ravage, massacre, slaughter, decimate, butcher, *literary or joc.* slay; (*of animals*) put down, put to sleep; *colloq.* do away with, finish (off); *sl.* do in, bump *or* knock off, hit, rub out, ice. **2** destroy, put an end to, quash, suppress, stifle, crush, stamp out, extinguish, check, get rid of, eradicate, wipe out, eliminate, expunge, clear away, sweep away, remove, weed out, root out, defeat, veto, cancel, *colloq.* do away with. **3 a** exhaust, tire (out), fatigue, weary, fag (out); overexert, strain, tax, overtire, overwork. **b** (*kill oneself*) laugh oneself silly, split one's sides, roll on the floor, roll in the aisles, shake with laughter, be in fits, *colloq.* be in hysterics, have hysterics, be in stitches, crack up. **4** see AMUSE 1. **5** see *turn off* 1. **6** delete, erase, expunge, remove, cut out, strike out, withdraw. **7** hurt, pain, torment, torture. **8** consume, use up, spend, while away, occupy, fill, pass, idle away, take up, waste, fritter (away), squander. **10** see DEVOUR 1, SWALLOW *v.* 1. **12** muffle, neutralize, deaden, damp, silence, nullify, dull, absorb, smother, stifle, suppress, still. ● *n.* **1** death, killing, end, finish, deathblow, *coup de grâce*; termination, denouement, dispatch, conclusion. **2** game, prey; quarry; bag.

kill[2] /kil/ *n.* esp. New York State *dial.* a stream, creek, or tributary river. [Du. *kil* f. MDu. *kille* channel]

killdeer /kíldeer/ *n.* a large American plover, *Charadrius vociferus*, with a plaintive song. [imit.]

killer /kílər/ *n.* **1 a** a person, animal, or thing that kills. **b** a murderer. **2** *colloq.* **a** an impressive, formidable, or excellent thing (*this one is quite difficult, but the next one is a real killer*). **b** a hilarious joke. **c** a decisive blow (*his home run proved to be the killer*). □ **killer bee** a very aggressive honeybee, *Apis mellifera adansonii*, orig. from Africa. **Killer (T) cell** *Immunology* a cell that attacks and destroys a cell (as a tumor cell) that bears a specific antigen on its surface. **killer in-**

stinct **1** an innate tendency to kill. **2** a ruthless streak. **killer whale** a voracious cetacean, *Orcinus orca*, with a white belly and prominent dorsal fin.

■ **1** murderer, assassin, slayer, cutthroat, butcher, exterminator, bluebeard, ripper, *colloq.* hatchet man, *sl.* hit man. **2 a** wonder, marvel, prodigy, paragon, portent, *colloq.* beauty, dandy, pippin, ripsnorter, *Brit. colloq.* blinder, bobby dazzler, *sl.* corker, humdinger, daisy, lulu, the cat's whiskers *or* pajamas, beaut, dilly; *Austral.* & *NZ sl.* bottler; *colloq.* toughie, hard *or* tough nut to crack, *Brit. colloq.* facer.

killick /kílik/ *n.* **1** a heavy stone used by small craft as an anchor. **2** a small anchor. **3** *Brit. Naut. sl.* a leading seaman. [17th c.: orig. unkn.]

killifish /kíleefish/ *n.* **1** any small fresh- or brackish-water fish of the family Cyprinodontidae, many of which are brightly colored. **2** a brightly colored tropical aquarium fish, *Pterolebias peruensis.* [perh. f. KILL² + FISH¹]

killing /kíling/ *n.* & *adj.* ● *n.* **1 a** the causing of death. **b** an instance of this. **2** a great (esp. financial) success (*make a killing*). ● *adj. colloq.* **1** overwhelmingly funny. **2** exhausting; very strenuous. □ **killing bottle** a bottle containing poisonous vapor to kill insects collected as specimens. □□ **killingly** *adv.*

■ *n.* **1** murder, carnage, butchery, execution, slaughter, bloodshed, death, massacre, genocide, liquidation, mass murder *or* destruction, decimation, extermination, annihilation, blood bath, manslaughter; slaying, homicide, fatality. **2** coup, bonanza, success, windfall, stroke of luck, stroke of good fortune, gain, profit, *colloq.* hit, *Austral.* & *NZ sl.* spin. ● *adj.* **1** see UPROARIOUS 2. **2** devastating, ruinous, destructive, punishing, exhausting, debilitating, fatiguing, wearying, draining, tiring, enervating, difficult, hard, taxing, arduous, strenuous.

killjoy /kíljoy/ *n.* a person who throws gloom over or prevents other people's enjoyment.

■ spoilsport, damper, dampener, malcontent, pessimist, cynic, prophet of doom, Cassandra, *colloq.* grouch, grump, wet blanket, sourpuss, *sl.* party pooper.

kiln /kiln, kil-/ *n.* a furnace or oven for burning, baking, or drying, esp. for calcining lime or firing pottery, etc. [OE *cylene* f. L *culina* kitchen]

kiln-dry /kílndrī, kíl-/ *v.tr.* (**-ies, -ied**) dry in a kiln.

kilo /keelō/ *n.* (*pl.* **-os**) **1** a kilogram. **2** a kilometer. [F: abbr.]

kilo- /kílō/ *comb. form* denoting a factor of 1,000 (esp. in metric units). ¶ Abbr.: **k**, or **K** in *Computing.* [F f. Gk *khilioi* thousand]

kilobyte /kíləbīt/ *n. Computing* 1,024 (i.e. 2^{10}) bytes as a measure of memory size.

kilocalorie /kíləkáloree/ *n.* = CALORIE 2.

kilocycle /kíləsīkəl/ *n.* a former measure of frequency, equivalent to 1 kilohertz. ¶ Abbr.: **kc.**

kilogram /kíləgram/ *n.* (also *Brit.* **-gramme**) the SI unit of mass, equivalent to the international standard kept at Sèvres near Paris (approx. 2.205 lb.). ¶ Abbr.: **kg.** [F *kilogramme* (as KILO, GRAM¹)]

kilohertz /kíləhərts/ *n.* a measure of frequency equivalent to 1,000 cycles per second. ¶ Abbr.: **kHz.**

kilojoule /kíləjōōl/ *n.* 1,000 joules, esp. as a measure of the energy value of foods. ¶ Abbr.: **kJ.**

kiloliter /kíləleetər/ *n.* (*Brit.* **-litre**) 1,000 liters (equivalent to 220 imperial gallons). ¶ Abbr.: **kl.**

kilometer /kilómitər, kíləmeetər/ *n.* (*Brit.* **kilometre**) a metric unit of measurement equal to 1,000 meters (approx. 0.62 miles). ¶ Abbr.: **km.** □□ **kilometric** /kíləmétrik/ *adj.* [F *kilomètre* (as KILO-, METER¹)]

kiloton /kílətun/ *n.* a unit of explosive power equivalent to 1,000 tons of TNT.

kilovolt /kíləvōlt/ *n.* 1,000 volts. ¶ Abbr.: **kV.**

kilowatt /kíləwot/ *n.* 1,000 watts. ¶ Abbr.: **kW.**

kilowatt-hour /kíləwot-ówr/ *n.* a measure of electrical energy equivalent to a power consumption of 1,000 watts for one hour. ¶ Abbr.: **kWh.**

kilt /kilt/ *n.* & *v.* ● *n.* **1** a skirtlike garment, usu. of pleated tartan cloth and reaching to the knees, as traditionally worn in Scotland by Highland men. **2** a similar garment worn by women and children. ● *v.tr.* **1** tuck up (skirts) around the body. **2** (esp. as **kilted** *adj.*) gather in vertical pleats. □□ **kilted** *adj.* [orig. as verb: ME, of Scand. orig.]

kilter /kíltər/ *n.* (also *Brit.* **kelter** /kél-/) good working order (esp. *out of kilter*). [17th c.; orig. unkn.]

■ (*out of kilter*) see BROKEN 1.

kiltie /kíltee/ *n.* a wearer of a kilt, esp. a kilted Highland soldier.

kimberlite /kímbərlīt/ *n. Mineral.* a rare igneous blue-tinged rock sometimes containing diamonds, found in South Africa and Siberia. Also called *blue ground* (see BLUE¹). [*Kimberley* in S. Africa]

kimono /kimónō/ *n.* (*pl.* **-os**) **1** a long, loose Japanese robe worn with a sash. **2** a dressing gown modeled on this. □□ **kimonoed** *adj.* [Jap.]

■ see WRAPPER 4.

kin /kin/ *n.* & *adj.* ● *n.* one's relatives or family. ● *predic. adj.* (of a person) related (*we are kin; he is kin to me*) (see also AKIN). □ **kith and kin** see KITH. **near of kin** closely related by blood, or in character. **next of kin** see NEXT. □□ **kinless** *adj.* [OE *cynn* f. Gmc]

■ *n.* family, relatives, relations, folks, kindred, kinfolk, kinsfolk, kith and kin, kinsmen, kinswomen, stock, clan, people, blood relations, blood relatives.

● *adj.* related, akin (to), kindred, consanguineous, cognate, agnate.

-kin /kin/ *suffix* forming diminutive nouns (*catkin; manikin*). [from or after MDu. *-kijn, -ken,* OHG *-chin*]

kina /keénə/ *n.* the monetary unit of Papua New Guinea. [Papuan]

kinaesthesia esp. *Brit.* var. of KINESTHESIA.

kincob /kínkob/ *n.* a rich fabric of India embroidered with gold or silver. [Urdu f. Pers. *kamk̲āb* f. *kamk̲ā* damask]

kind¹ /kīnd/ *n.* **1 a** a race or species (*humankind*). **b** a natural group of animals, plants, etc. (*the wolf kind*). **2** class; type; sort; variety (*what kind of job are you looking for?*). ¶ In sense 2, *these* (or *those*) *kind* is often encountered when followed by a plural, as in *I don't like these kind of things*, but *this kind* and *these kinds* are usually preferred. **3** each of the elements of the Eucharist (*communion under* (or *in*) *both kinds*). **4** the manner or fashion natural to a person, etc. (*act after their kind; true to kind*). □ **kind of** *colloq.* to some extent (*felt kind of sorry; I kind of expected it*). **a kind of** used to imply looseness, vagueness, exaggeration, etc., in the term used (*a kind of Jane Austen of our times; I suppose he's a kind of doctor*). **in kind 1** in the same form; likewise (*was insulted and replied in kind*). **2** (of payment) in goods or labor as opposed to money (*received their wages in kind*). **3** in character or quality (*differ in degree but not in kind*). **law of kind** *archaic* nature in general; the natural order. **nothing of the kind 1** not at all like the thing in question. **2** (expressing denial) not at all. **of its kind** within the limitations of its own class (*good of its kind*). **of a kind 1** *derog.* scarcely deserving the name (*a choir of a kind*). **2** similar in some important respect (*they're two of a kind*). **one's own kind** those with whom one has much in common. **something of the kind** something like the thing in question. [OE *cynd(e), gecynd(e)* f. Gmc]

■ **1** race, species, genus, breed, type, group, order.

2 sort, type, variety, category, kidney, style, genre, species, set, class, cast, mold; brand, make, stamp. **4** nature, character, manner, description, persuasion. □ **kind of** see LITTLE *adv.* 3. **in kind 1** see LIKEWISE *adv.* 2. **of a kind 1** of sorts. **2** birds of a feather, of a *or* the same stripe, *colloq. disp.* of the same ilk.

kind² /kīnd/ *adj.* **1** of a friendly, generous, benevolent, or gentle nature. **2** (usu. foll. by *to*) showing friendliness, affection,

or consideration. **3 a** affectionate. **b** *archaic* loving. [OE *ge-cynde* (as KIND¹): orig. = 'natural, native']
- **1–3a** friendly, kindly, nice, congenial, affable, approachable, amiable, obliging, accommodating, amicable, well-disposed, courteous, good, good-natured, benevolent, well-meaning, well-wishing, thoughtful, well-intentioned, generous, bighearted, humanitarian, charitable, philanthropic, gentle, understanding, sympathetic, considerate, lenient, tolerant, indulgent, compassionate, kindhearted, gracious, warm, warmhearted, cordial, tenderhearted, affectionate.

kinda /kíndə/ *colloq.* = kind of. [corrupt.]

kindergarten /kíndərgaart'n/ *n.* an establishment or class for preschool learning. [G, = children's garden]
- nursery school, playgroup.

kindhearted /kíndhaártid/ *adj.* of a kind disposition. □□ **kindheartedly** *adv.* **kindheartedness** *n.*
- see KIND². □□ **kindheartedly** see KINDLY¹ 1. **kindheartedness** see KINDNESS 1.

kindle /kínd'l/ *v.* **1** *tr.* light or set on fire (a flame, fire, substance, etc.). **2** *intr.* catch fire, burst into flame. **3** *tr.* arouse or inspire (*kindle enthusiasm for the project*; *kindle jealousy in a rival*). **4** *intr.* (usu. foll. by *to*) respond; react (to a person, an action, etc.). **5** *intr.* become animated, glow with passion, etc. (*her imagination kindled*). **6** *tr.* & *intr.* make or become bright (*kindle the embers to a glow*). □□ **kindler** *n.* [ME f. ON *kynda*, kindle: cf. ON *kindill* candle, torch]
- **1** ignite, light, set alight, set fire to, set afire. **2** catch fire, burst into flame. **3** inflame, fire, foment, incite, instigate, provoke, prompt, goad, spur, whip up, stir (up), work up, excite, agitate, shake up, jolt, arouse, rouse, (a)waken, inspire, inspirit, stimulate, animate, enliven, energize, galvanize, *archaic* prick.

kindling /kíndling/ *n.* small sticks, etc., for lighting fires.

kindly¹ /kíndlee/ *adv.* **1** in a kind manner (*spoke to the child kindly*). **2** often *iron.* used in a polite request or demand (*kindly acknowledge this letter*; *kindly leave me alone*). □ **look kindly upon** regard sympathetically. **take a thing kindly** like or be pleased by it. **take kindly to** be pleased by or endeared to (a person or thing). **thank kindly** thank very much. [OE *gecyndelīce* (as KIND²)]
- **1** cordially, graciously, obligingly, amiably, amicably, kindheartedly, politely, genially, courteously, thoughtfully, considerately, hospitably, agreeably, pleasantly. **2** please, be so kind as to, be good enough to.

kindly² /kíndlee/ *adj.* (**kindlier, kindliest**) **1** kind; kindhearted. **2** (of climate, etc.) pleasant; genial. **3** *archaic* native-born (*a kindly Scot*). □□ **kindlily** *adv.* **kindliness** *n.* [OE *gecyndelic* (as KIND¹)]
- **1** see KIND². □□ **kindliness** see KINDNESS 1.

kindness /kíndnis/ *n.* **1** the state or quality of being kind. **2** a kind act.
- **1** friendliness, kindheartedness, warmheartedness, graciousness, goodness, good-naturedness, good-heartedness, goodwill, benevolence, benignity, humaneness, humanity, decency, tenderness, gentleness, kindliness, charity, charitableness, generosity, philanthropy, beneficence, compassion, sympathy, understanding, thoughtfulness, consideration, cordiality, hospitality, warmth, geniality, indulgence, tolerance, patience. **2** favor, good deed or turn, service, act of kindness *or* generosity; obligation.

kindred /kíndrid/ *n.* & *adj.* ● *n.* **1** one's relations, referred to collectively. **2** a relationship by blood. **3** a resemblance or affinity in character. ● *adj.* **1** related by blood or marriage. **2** allied or similar in character (*other kindred symptoms*). □ **kindred spirit** a person whose character and outlook have much in common with one's own. [ME f. KIN + -red f. OE *ræden* condition]
- *n.* **1** see KIN *n.* ● *adj.* **1** related, consanguineous, cognate, agnate. **2** close, associated, related, united, allied, analogous, like, similar, matching, parallel, common, related; akin.

kine /kin/ *archaic pl.* of COW¹.

kinematics /kínimátiks/ *n.pl.* (usu. treated as *sing.*) the branch of mechanics concerned with the motion of objects without reference to the forces which cause the motion. □□ **kinematic** *adj.* **kinematically** *adv.* [Gk *kinēma -matos* motion f. *kineō* move + -ICS]

kinematograph var. of CINEMATOGRAPH.

kinesics /kineésiks, -ziks/ *n.pl.* (usu. treated as *sing.*) **1** the study of body movements and gestures that contribute to communication. **2** these movements; body language. [Gk *kinēsis* motion (as KINETIC)]

kinesiology /kineéseeólǝjee, -zee-/ *n.* the study of the mechanics of body movements.

kinesthesia /kínǝs-theézhǝ/ *n.* (esp. *Brit.* **kinaesthesia**) (also **kinesthesis**) a sense of awareness of the position and movement of the voluntary muscles of the body. □□ **kinesthetic** /-thétik/ *adj.* [Gk *kineō* move + *aisthēsis* sensation]

kinetic /kinétik, ki-/ *adj.* of or due to motion. □ **kinetic art** a form of art that depends on movement for its effect. **kinetic energy** the energy of motion. **kinetic theory** a theory which explains the physical properties of matter in terms of the motions of its constituent particles. □□ **kinetically** *adv.* [Gk *kinētikos* f. *kineō* move]
- see MOTIVE *adj.*

kinetics /kinétiks, ki-/ *n.pl.* **1** = DYNAMICS 1a. **2** (usu. treated as *sing.*) the branch of physical chemistry concerned with measuring and studying the rates of chemical reactions.

kinetin /kínitin/ *n. Biochem.* a synthetic kinin used to stimulate cell division in plants. [as KINETIC + -IN]

kinfolk /kínfōk/ *n.pl.* (also **kinfolks, kinsfolk**) one's relations by blood.
- see KIN *n.*

king /king/ *n.* & *v.* ● *n.* **1** (as a title usu. **King**) a male sovereign, esp. the hereditary ruler of an independent nation. **2** a person or thing preeminent in a specified field or class (*railroad king*). **3** a large (or the largest) kind of plant, animal, etc. (*king penguin*). **4** *Chess* the piece on each side that the opposing side has to checkmate to win. **5** a piece in checkers with extra capacity of moving, made by crowning an ordinary piece that has reached the opponent's baseline. **6** a playing card bearing a representation of a king and usu. ranking next below an ace. **7** (**the King**) (in the UK) the national anthem when there is a male sovereign. **8** (**Kings** or **Books of Kings**) two Old Testament books dealing with history, esp. of the kingdom of Judah. ● *v.tr.* make (a person) king. □ **King Charles spaniel** a spaniel of a small black and tan breed. **king cobra** a large and venomous hooded Indian snake, *Ophiophagus hannah*. **king crab 1** = *horseshoe crab*. **2** any of various large edible spider crabs. **king it 1** play or act the king. **2** (usu. foll. by *over*) govern; control. **King James Bible** (or **Version**) = *Authorized Version* (see AUTHORIZE). **king of arms** *Heraldry* (in the UK) a title given to certain chief heralds. **king of (the) beasts** the lion. **king of birds** the eagle. **king of the hill** (or **mountain** or esp. *Brit.* **castle**) a children's game consisting of trying to displace a rival from a mound. **King of Kings 1** God. **2** Jesus Christ. **king post** an upright post from the tie beam of a roof to the apex of a truss. **King's Bench** see BENCH. **king's bishop, knight**, etc. *Chess* (of pieces that exist in pairs) the piece starting on the king's side of the board. **king's bounty** see BOUNTY. **king's color** see COLOR. **King's Counsel** see COUNSEL. **King's English** see ENGLISH. **king's evidence** see EVIDENCE. **king's evil** *hist.* scrofula, formerly held to be curable by the royal touch. **king's highway** see HIGHWAY. **king-size** (or **-sized**) larger than normal; very large. **king's pawn** *Chess* the pawn in front of the king at the beginning of a game. **King's Proctor** see PROCTOR. **king's ransom** a fortune. **king's scout** see SCOUT¹. **King's speech** see SPEECH. □□ **kinghood** *n.* **kingless** *adj.* **kinglike** *adj.* **kingly** *adj.* **kingliness** *n.* **kingship** *n.* [OE *cyning, cyng* f. Gmc]
- *n.* **1** prince, crowned head, majesty, sovereign, monarch, ruler, regent, *colloq.* royal. **2** see BIGWIG.
□ **King of Kings 1** see SAVIOR 2. **king-size** see BIG *adj.* 1a. **king's ransom** see MINT² *n.* 2. □□ **kinglike, kingly** see ROYAL 5. **kingship** see *sovereignty* (SOVEREIGN).

kingbird /kíngbərd/ n. any flycatcher of the genus *Tyrannus*, with olive-gray plumage and long pointed wings.

kingbolt /kíngbōlt/ n. = KINGPIN 1.

kingcraft /kíngkraft/ n. *archaic* the skillful exercise of kingship.

kingcup /kíngkup/ n. *Brit.* a marsh marigold.

kingdom /kíngdəm/ n. **1** an organized community headed by a king. **2** the territory subject to a king. **3 a** the spiritual reign attributed to God (*Thy kingdom come*). **b** the sphere of this (*kingdom of heaven*). **4** a domain belonging to a person, animal, etc. **5** a province of nature (*the vegetable kingdom*). **6** a specified mental or emotional province (*kingdom of the heart*; *kingdom of fantasy*). **7** *Biol.* the highest category in taxonomic classification. □ **come into** (or **to**) **one's kingdom** achieve recognition or supremacy. **kingdom come** *colloq.* eternity; the next world. **till kingdom come** *colloq.* for ever. □□ **kingdomed** *adj.* [OE *cyningdōm* (as KING)]

■ **1** empire, sovereignty, principality, monarchy, *formal esp. Law* realm. **2** see DOMINION 2. **4** field, area, domain, province, sphere (of influence), orbit, ambit, territory, home ground, *colloq.* patch, *joc.* bailiwick, *sl.* turf. □ **till kingdom come** for ever, eternally, everlastingly, in perpetuity, till doomsday, *colloq.* till the cows come home.

kingfish /kíngfish/ n. any of various large fish, esp. the opah or mulloway.

kingfisher /kíngfishər/ n. any bird of the family Alcedinidae esp. *Alcedo atthis* with a long sharp beak and brightly colored plumage, which dives for fish in rivers, etc.

kinglet /kínglit/ n. **1** a petty king. **2** any of various small birds of the family Regulidae, esp. the goldcrest.

kingmaker /kíngmaykər/ n. a person who makes kings, leaders, etc., through the exercise of political influence, orig. with ref. to the Earl of Warwick in the reign of Henry VI of England.

kingpin /kíngpin/ n. **1 a** a main or large bolt in a central position. **b** a vertical bolt used as a pivot. **2** an essential person or thing, esp. in a complex system; the most important person in an organization.

■ **1** see PIVOT n. 1. **2** see BIGWIG, LEADER 1.

kinin /kínin/ n. **1** any of a group of polypeptides present in the blood after tissue damage. **2** any of a group of compounds that promote cell division and inhibit aging in plants. [Gk *kineō* move + -IN]

kink /kingk/ n. & v. ● n. **1 a** a short backward twist in wire or tubing, etc., such as may cause an obstruction. **b** a tight wave in human or animal hair. **2** a mental twist or quirk. ● v.intr. & tr. form or cause to form a kink. [MLG *kinke* (v.) prob. f. Du. *kinken*]

■ n. **1** twist, crimp, tangle, knot, wrinkle, curl, coil, curlicue, crinkle. **2** crotchet, quirk, whim, caprice, fancy, vagary, eccentricity, idiosyncrasy, peculiarity; difficulty, complication, flaw, hitch, snag, defect, imperfection, distortion, deformity.

kinkajou /kíngkəjōō/ n. a Central and S. American nocturnal fruit-eating mammal, *Potos flavus*, with a prehensile tail and living in trees. [F *quincajou* perh. f. Ojibwa: cf. Algonquian *kwingwaage* wolverine]

kinky /kíngkee/ adj. (**kinkier, kinkiest**) **1** *colloq.* **a** given to or involving abnormal sexual behavior. **b** (of clothing, etc.) bizarre in a sexually provocative way. **2** strange; eccentric. **3** having kinks or twists. □□ **kinkily** adv. **kinkiness** n. [KINK + -Y¹]

■ **1 a** perverted, unnatural, deviant, degenerate, warped, abnormal, depraved. **b** suggestive, sexy. **2** outlandish, peculiar, odd, queer, quirky, bizarre, crotchety, eccentric, strange, peculiar, idiosyncratic, different, offbeat, unorthodox, capricious, irregular, erratic, unconventional, unique, freakish, weird, fantastic, whimsical. **3** crisp, frizzy, frizzed, frizzled, curly, crimped, wiry; knotted, tangled, twisted. □□ **kinkiness** see PERVERSION 3b, ODDITY 3.

kino /kéenō/ n. (pl. **-os**) a catechu-like gum produced by various trees and used in medicine and tanning as an astringent. [W. Afr.]

-kins /kinz/ suffix = -KIN, often with suggestions of endearment (*babykins*).

kinsfolk var. of KINFOLK.

kinship /kínship/ n. **1** blood relationship. **2** the sharing of characteristics or origins.

■ **1** consanguinity, (blood) relationship, (family) ties, (common) descent, lineage, flesh and blood. **2** affinity; connection, correspondence, closeness, concordance, parallelism, relationship, similarity, association, agreement, alliance.

kinsman /kínzmən/ n. (pl. **-men**; fem. **kinswoman**, pl. **-women**) **1** a blood relation or *disp.* a relation by marriage. **2** a member of one's own tribe or people.

■ **1** see RELATION 2.

kiosk /kéeosk, -ósk/ n. **1** a light, open-fronted booth or cubicle from which food, newspapers, tickets, etc. are sold. **2** *Brit.* a telephone booth. **3** a building in which refreshments are served in a park, zoo, etc. **4** a light, open pavilion in Turkey and Iran. [F *kiosque* f. Turk. *kiüshk* pavilion f. Pers. *guš*]

■ **1** booth, stall, stand, cubicle, shop. **2** telephone booth, telephone cubicle, *Brit.* call box, telephone box. **3** see STALL¹ n. 1.

Kiowa /kíəwə/ n. **1 a** a N. American people native to the southwest. **b** a member of this people. **2** the language of this people.

kip¹ /kip/ n. & v. *Brit. sl.* ● n. **1** a sleep or nap. **2** a bed or cheap motel, etc. **3** (also **kip-house** or **-shop**) a brothel. ● v.intr. (**kipped, kipping**) **1** sleep; take a nap. **2** (foll. by *down*) lie or settle down to sleep. [cf. Da. *kippe* mean hut]

kip² /kip/ n. the hide of a young or small animal as used for leather. [ME: orig. unkn.]

kip³ /kip/ n. (pl. same or **kips**) the basic monetary unit of Laos. [Thai]

kip⁴ /kip/ n. *Austral. sl.* a small piece of wood from which coins are spun in the game of two-up. [perh. f. E dial.: cf. *keper* a flat piece of wood preventing a horse from eating the corn, or Ir. dial. *kippeen* f. Ir. *cipín* a little stick]

kipper /kípər/ n. & v. ● n. **1** a kippered fish, esp. herring. **2** a male salmon in the spawning season. ● v.tr. cure (a herring, etc.) by splitting open, salting, and drying in the open air or smoke. [ME: orig. uncert.]

■ v. see PRESERVE v. 4a.

Kir /keer/ n. a drink made from dry white wine and crème de cassis. [Canon Felix *Kir* d. 1968, said to have invented the recipe]

Kirghiz /keergeez/ n. & adj. ● n. (pl. same) **1** a member of a Mongol people living in central Asia between the Volga and the Irtysh rivers. **2** the language of this people. ● adj. of or relating to this people or their language. [Kirghiz]

kirk /kurk/ n. *Sc. & No. of Engl.* **1** a church. **2** (**the Kirk** or **the Kirk of Scotland**) the Church of Scotland as distinct from the Church of England or from the Episcopal Church in Scotland. [ME f. ON *kirkja* f. OE *cir(i)ce* CHURCH]

kirkman /kɔ́rkmən/ n. (pl. **-men**) *Sc. & No. of Engl.* a member of the Church of Scotland.

kirsch /keersh/ n. (also **kirschwasser** /kéershvaasər/) a brandy distilled from the fermented juice of cherries. [G *Kirsche* cherry, *Wasser* water]

kirtle /kɔ́rt'l/ n. *archaic* **1** a woman's gown or outer petticoat. **2** a man's tunic or coat. [OE *cyrtel* f. Gmc, ult. perh. f. L *curtus* short]

kiskadee /kískədee/ n. (also **keskidee** /késkidee/) a tyrant flycatcher, *Pitangus sulphuratus*, of Central and S. America, with brown and yellow plumage. [imit. of its cry]

kismet /kízmet/ n. destiny; fate. [Turk. f. Arab. *ḳisma(t)* f. *ḳasama* divide]

/.../ **pronunciation**	● **part of speech**
□ **phrases, idioms, and compounds**	
□□ **derivatives**	■ **synonym section**
cross-references appear in SMALL CAPITALS or *italics*	

■ see DESTINY 2.

kiss /kis/ *v. & n.* ● *v.* **1** *tr.* touch with the lips, esp. as a sign of love, affection, greeting, or reverence. **2** *tr.* express (greeting or farewell) in this way. **3** *absol.* (of two persons) touch each others' lips in this way. **4** *tr.* (also *absol.*) (of a billiard ball, etc., in motion) lightly touch (another ball). ● *n.* **1** a touch with the lips in kissing. **2** the slight impact when one billiard ball, etc., lightly touches another. **3** a usu. droplet-shaped piece of candy or small cookie. □ **kiss and tell** recount one's sexual exploits. **kiss a person's ass** (or **butt**) *coarse sl.* act obsequiously toward a person. **kiss away** remove (tears, etc.) by kissing. **kiss curl** *Brit.* = *spit curl* (see SPIT¹). **kiss the dust** submit abjectly; be overthrown. **kiss good-bye to** *colloq.* accept the loss of. **kiss the ground** prostrate oneself as a token of homage. **kissing cousin** (or **kin**) a distant relative (given a formal kiss on occasional meetings). **kissing gate** *Brit.* a gate hung in a V- or U-shaped enclosure, to let one person through at a time. **kiss of death** an apparently friendly act which causes ruin. **kiss off** *sl.* **1** dismiss; get rid of. **2** go away; die. **kiss of life** mouth-to-mouth resuscitation. **kiss of peace** *Eccl.* a ceremonial kiss, esp. during the Eucharist, as a sign of unity. **kiss the rod** *Brit.* accept chastisement submissively. □□ **kissable** *adj.* [OE *cyssan* f. Gmc]

■ *v.* **1** peck (on the cheek), give a kiss to, plant a kiss on, caress, smother with kisses, *colloq.* buss, *colloq.* neck, *joc.* osculate. **3** *archaic* spoon, *colloq.* smooch, neck, *joc.* osculate, *Brit. sl.* snog. **4** touch, brush, graze. ● *n.* **1** peck, caress, smack, X, *colloq.* buss, *joc.* osculation, *sl.* smacker; *colloq.* smooch, *Brit. sl.* snog. □ **kiss good-bye to** say farewell to, give up, relinquish, abandon, forsake, desert, renounce, repudiate, forget (about), dismiss, disregard, ignore, *archaic or literary* bid adieu to. **kiss of death** see JINX *n.* **kiss off 2** see *beat it.*

kisser /kisər/ *n.* **1** a person who kisses. **2** (orig. *Boxing*) *sl.* the mouth; the face.

■ **2** see MOUTH *n.* 1.

kissy /kisee/ *adj. colloq.* given to kissing (*not the kissy type*).

kist var. of CIST¹.

Kiswahili /kiswaaheélee/ *n.* one of the six languages preferred for use in Africa by the Organization for African Unity. [Swahili *ki-* prefix for an abstract or inanimate object]

kit¹ /kit/ *n. & v.* ● *n.* **1** a set of articles, equipment, or clothing needed for a specific purpose (*first-aid kit*; *bicycle-repair kit*). **2** esp. *Brit.* the clothing, etc., needed for any activity, esp. sports (*hockey kit*). **3** a set of all the parts needed to assemble an item, e.g., a piece of furniture, a model, etc. **4** *Brit.* a wooden tub. ● *v.tr.* (**kitted**, **kitting**) (often foll. by *out*, *up*) esp. *Brit.* equip with the appropriate clothing or tools. □ **kit bag** a large, usu. cylindrical bag used for carrying a soldier's, traveler's, or sportsman's equipment. **the whole kit and caboodle** see CABOODLE. [ME f. MDu. *kitte* wooden vessel, of unkn. orig.]

■ *n.* **1** apparatus, gear, equipment, rig, outfit, set, paraphernalia, effects, appurtenances, accoutrements, tackle, trappings, supplies; instruments, tools, utensils, implements. □ **kit bag** see PACK¹ *n.* 1.

kit² /kit/ *n.* **1** a kitten. **2** a young fox, badger, etc. [abbr.]

kit³ /kit/ *n. hist.* a small fiddle esp. as used by a dancing master. [perh. f. L *cithara*; see CITTERN]

kit-cat /kitkat/ *n.* (in full **kit-cat portrait**) a portrait of less than half length, but including one hand; usu. 36 x 28 in. [named after a series of portraits of the members of the *Kit-Cat* Club in London, an early 18th-c. Whig society]

kitchen /kichin/ *n.* **1** the room or area where food is prepared and cooked. **2** (*attrib.*) of or belonging to the kitchen (*kitchen knife*; *kitchen table*). **3** *sl.* the percussion section of an orchestra. □ **everything but the kitchen sink** everything imaginable. **kitchen cabinet** a group of unofficial advisers thought to be unduly influential. **kitchen garden** a garden where vegetables and sometimes fruit or herbs are grown specifically for household use. **kitchen midden** a prehistoric refuse heap which marks an ancient settlement, chiefly containing bones, seashells, etc. **kitchen-sink** (in art

forms) depicting extreme realism, esp. drabness or sordidness (*kitchen-sink school of painting*; *kitchen-sink drama*). **kitchen tea** *Austral. & NZ* a bridal shower to which guests bring items of kitchen equipment as presents. [OE *cycene* f. L *coquere* cook]

■ **1** kitchenette, cookhouse, scullery; *Naut.* galley, caboose. □ **everything but the kitchen sink** see WORK *n.* 10. **kitchen garden** (garden) plot, patch.

kitchenette /kichinét/ *n.* a small kitchen or part of a room fitted as a kitchen.

kitchenware /kichinwair/ *n.* the utensils used in the kitchen.

kite /kīt/ *n. & v.* ● *n.* **1** a toy consisting of a light framework with thin material stretched over it, flown in the wind at the end of a long string. **2** any of various soaring birds of prey esp. of the genus *Milvus* with long wings and usu. a forked tail. **3** *Brit. sl.* an airplane. **4** *sl.* a fraudulent check, bill, or receipt. **5** *Geom.* a quadrilateral figure symmetrical about one diagonal. **6** *sl.* a letter or note, esp. one that is illicit or surreptitious. **7** (in *pl.*) the highest sail of a ship, set only in a light wind. **8** *archaic* a dishonest person; a sharper. ● *v.* **1** *intr.* soar like a kite. **2** *tr.* (also *absol.*) originate or pass (fraudulent checks, bills, or receipts). **3** *tr.* (also *absol.*) raise (money by dishonest means) (*kite a loan*). [OE *cȳta*, of unkn. orig.]

kith /kith/ *n.* □ **kith and kin** friends and relations. [OE *cȳthth* f. Gmc]

■ □ **kith and kin** see KIN *n.*

kitsch /kich/ *n.* (often *attrib.*) garish, pretentious, or sentimental art, usu. vulgar and worthless (*kitsch plastic models of the Lincoln Memorial*). □□ **kitschy** *adj.* (**kitschier**, **kitschiest**). **kitschiness** *n.* [G]

■ □□ **kitschy** tasteless, tawdry, garish, gaudy, coarse, crude, vulgar, unstylish, pretentious, sentimental, worthless.

kitten /kit'n/ *n. & v.* ● *n.* **1** a young cat. **2** a young ferret, etc. ● *v.intr. & tr.* (of a cat, etc.) give birth or give birth to. □ **have kittens** *colloq.* be extremely upset, anxious, or nervous. [ME *kito(u)n*, *ketoun* f. OF *chitoun*, *chetoun* dimin. of *chat* CAT]

kittenish /kit'nish/ *adj.* **1** like a young cat; playful and lively. **2** flirtatious. □□ **kittenishly** *adv.* **kittenishness** *n.* [KITTEN]

■ **1** playful, lively, sportive, (high-)spirited, frisky, sprightly. **2** coy, seductive, flirtatious, coquettish.

kittiwake /kiteewayk/ *n.* either of two small gulls, *Rissa tridactyla* and *R. brevirostris*, nesting on sea cliffs. [imit. of its cry]

kittle /kit'l/ *adj.* (also **kittle-cattle** /kit'lkat'l/) **1** *Brit.* (of a person) capricious, rash, or erratic in behavior. **2** difficult to deal with. [ME (now Sc. & dial.) *kittle* tickle, prob. f. ON *kitla*]

kitty¹ /kitee/ *n.* (*pl.* **-ies**) **1** a fund of money for communal use. **2** the pool in some card games. [19th c.: orig. unkn.]

■ **1** fund, reserve, pool, purse, bank, collection. **2** pool, pot, jackpot, stakes.

kitty² /kitee/ *n.* (*pl.* **-ies**) a pet name or a child's name for a kitten or cat. □ **Kitty Litter** *prop.* a granular clay used in boxes to absorb pet (esp. cat) waste.

kitty-corner var. of CATERCORNERED.

kiwi /keéwee/ *n.* (*pl.* **kiwis**) **1** a flightless New Zealand bird of the genus *Apteryx* with hairlike feathers and a long bill. Also called APTERYX. **2** (**Kiwi**) *colloq.* a New Zealander, esp. a soldier or member of a national sports team. □ **kiwi fruit** (or **berry**) the fruit of a climbing plant, *Actinidia chinensis*, having a thin hairy skin, green flesh, and black seeds: also called *Chinese gooseberry*. [Maori]

kJ *abbr.* kilojoule(s).

KKK *abbr.* Ku Klux Klan.

kl *abbr.* kiloliter(s).

Klaxon /kláksən/ *n.* a horn or warning hooter, orig. on a motor vehicle. [name of the manufacturing company]

Kleenex /kleéneks/ *n.* (*pl.* same or **Kleenexes**) *propr.* an absorbent disposable paper tissue, used esp. as a handkerchief.

Klein bottle /klīn/ *n. Math.* a closed surface with only one side, formed by passing the neck of a tube through the side of the tube to join the hole in the base. [F. *Klein*, Ger. mathematician d. 1925]

klepht /kleft/ *n.* **1** a member of the original body of Greeks who refused to submit to the Turks in the 15th c. **2** any of their descendants. **3** a brigand or bandit. [mod. Gk *klephtēs* f. Gk *kleptēs* thief]

kleptomania /kléptəmáyneeə/ *n.* a recurrent urge to steal, usu. without regard for need or profit. □□ **kleptomaniac** *n.* & *adj.* [Gk *kleptēs* thief + -MANIA]
■ □□ **kleptomaniac** (*n.*) see THIEF.

klieg /kleeg/ *n.* (also **klieg light**) a powerful lamp in a movie studio, etc. [A. T. & J. H. *Kliegl*, Amer. inventors d. 1927, 1959]

klipspringer /klípspringər/ *n.* a S. African dwarf antelope, *Oreotragus oreotragus*, which can bound up and down rocky slopes. [Afrik. f. *klip* rock + *springer* jumper]

Klondike /klóndīk/ *n.* a source of valuable material. [*Klondike* in Yukon, Canada, where gold was found in 1896]

kloof /kloof/ *n.* a steep-sided ravine or valley in S. Africa. [Du., = cleft]

kludge /kluj/ *n. sl.* **1** an ill-assorted collection of poorly matching parts. **2** *Computing* a machine, system, or program that has been badly put together.

klutz /kluts/ *n. sl.* **a** a clumsy awkward person. **b** a fool. □□ **klutzy** *adj.* [Yiddish f. G *Klotz* wooden block]

klystron /klístron/ *n.* an electron tube that generates or amplifies microwaves by velocity modulation. [Gk *kluzō kluswash* over]

km *abbr.* kilometer(s).

K-meson /kayméezon, -més-, -meézon, -son/ *n.* = KAON. [K (see KAON) + MESON]

kmph *abbr.* kilometers per hour.

kmps *abbr.* kilometers per second.

kn. *abbr. Naut.* knot(s).

knack /nak/ *n.* **1** an acquired or intuitive faculty of doing a thing adroitly. **2** a trick or habit of action or speech, etc. (*has a knack of offending people*). **3** *archaic* an ingenious device (see KNICKKNACK). [ME, prob. identical with *knack* sharp blow or sound f. LG, ult. imit.]
■ **1** genius, intuition, talent, gift, facility, faculty, skill, aptitude, bent; ability, flair, dexterity, capacity, adroitness, proficiency, expertise, skillfulness. **2** habit, trick, art, technique.

knacker /nákər/ *n.* & *v. Brit.* ● *n.* **1** a buyer of useless horses for slaughter. **2** a buyer of old houses, ships, etc. for the materials. ● *v.tr. sl.* **1** kill. **2** (esp. as **knackered** *adj.*) exhaust; wear out. [19th c.: orig. unkn.]

knackery /nákəree/ *n.* (*pl.* **-ies**) a knacker's yard or business.

knackwurst var. of KNOCKWURST.

knag /nag/ *n.* **1** a knot in wood; the base of a branch. **2** a short dead branch. **3** *esp. Brit.* a peg for hanging things on. □□ **knaggy** *adj.* [ME, perh. f. LG *Knagge*]

knap¹ /nap/ *n.* chiefly *dial.* the crest of a hill or of rising ground. [OE *cnæp(p)*, perh. rel. to ON *knappr* knob]

knap² /nap/ *v.tr.* (**knapped, knapping**) **1** break (stones for roads or building, flints, or *Austral.* ore) with a hammer. **2** *archaic* knock; rap; snap asunder. □□ **knapper** *n.* [ME, imit.]

knapsack /nápsak/ *n.* a soldier's or hiker's bag with shoulder straps, carried on the back, and usu. made of canvas or weatherproof material. [MLG, prob. f. *knappen* bite + SACK¹]
■ see PACK¹ *n.* 1.

knapweed /nápweed/ *n.* any of various plants of the genus *Centaurea*, having thistlelike purple flowers. [ME, orig. *knopweed* f. KNOP + WEED]

knar /naar/ *n.* a knot or protuberance in a tree trunk, root, etc. [ME *knarre*, rel. to MLG, M.Du., MHG *knorre* knobbed protuberance]

knave /nayv/ *n.* **1** a rogue; a scoundrel. **2** = JACK¹ *n.* 2. □□ **knavery** *n.* (*pl.* **-ies**). **knavish** *adj.* **knavishly** *adv.* **knavishness** *n.* [OE *cnafa* boy, servant, f. WG]
■ **1** see ROGUE *n.* 1. □□ **knavery, knavishness** see DEVILRY. **knavish** see DISHONEST.

knawel /náwəl/ *n.* any low-growing plant of the genus *Scleranthus*. [G *Knauel*]

knead /need/ *v.tr.* **1** work (a yeast mixture, clay, etc.) into dough, paste, etc., by pressing and folding. **b** make (bread, pottery, etc.) in this way. **2** blend or weld together (*kneaded them into a unified group*). **3** massage (muscles, etc.) as if kneading. □□ **kneadable** *adj.* **kneader** *n.* [OE *cnedan* f. Gmc]
■ **1 a** pummel, punch, pound, knock, thump, work, manipulate. **b** see MOLD¹ *v.* 1, 2. **3** massage, rub (down), manipulate.

knee /nee/ *n.* & *v.* ● *n.* **1 a** (often *attrib.*) the joint between the thigh and the lower leg in humans. **b** the corresponding joint in other animals. **c** the area around this. **d** the upper surface of the thigh of a sitting person; the lap (*held her on his knee*). **2** the part of a garment covering the knee. **3** anything resembling a knee in shape or position, esp. a piece of wood or iron bent at an angle, a sharp turn in a graph, etc. ● *v.tr.* (**knees, kneed, kneeing**) **1** touch or strike with the knee (*kneed him in the groin*). **2** *colloq.* cause (pants) to bulge at the knee. □ **bend** (or **bow**) **the knee** kneel, esp. in submission. **bring a person to his** or **her knees** reduce a person to submission. **knee bend** the action of bending the knee, esp. as a physical exercise in which the body is raised and lowered without the use of the hands. **knee breeches** close-fitting pants reaching to or just below the knee. **knee-deep 1** (usu. foll. by *in*) **a** immersed up to the knees. **b** deeply involved. **2** so deep as to reach the knees. **knee-high** so high as to reach the knees. **knee jerk** a sudden involuntary kick caused by a blow on the tendon just below the knee. **knee-jerk** (*attrib.*) predictable; automatic; stereotyped. **knee-length** reaching the knees. **knees-up** *Brit. colloq.* a lively party or gathering. **on** (or **on one's**) **bended knee** (or **knees**) kneeling, esp. in supplication, submission, or worship. [OE *cnēo(w)*]
■ □ **knee breeches** see SHORTS 1. **knee-deep 1 b** (*knee-deep in*) see AMONG 1. **knee-jerk** see AUTOMATIC *adj.* 2a.

kneecap /neékap/ *n.* & *v.* ● *n.* **1** the convex bone in front of the knee joint. **2** a protective covering for the knee. ● *v.tr.* (**-capped, -capping**) *colloq.* shoot (a person) in the knee or leg as a punishment, esp. for betraying a terrorist group. □□ **kneecapping** *n.*

kneehole /neéhōl/ *n.* a space for the knees, esp. under a desk.

kneel /neel/ *v.intr.* (*past* and *past part.* **knelt** /nelt/ or **kneeled**) fall or rest on the knees or a knee. [OE *cnēowlian* (as KNEE)]
■ bend the knee, bow the knee, get down on one's knees, genuflect, crouch, bow, stoop.

kneeler /neélər/ *n.* **1** a hassock or cushion used for kneeling, esp. in church. **2** a person who kneels.

kneepan /neépan/ *n.* the kneecap.

knell /nel/ *n.* & *v.* ● *n.* **1** the sound of a bell, esp. when rung solemnly for a death or funeral. **2** an announcement, event, etc., regarded as a solemn warning of disaster. ● *v.* **1** *intr.* **a** (of a bell) ring solemnly, esp. for a death or funeral. **b** make a doleful or ominous sound. **2** *tr.* proclaim by or as by a knell (*knelled the death of all their hopes*). □ **ring the knell of** announce or herald the end of. [OE *cnyll, cnyllan*: perh. infl. by *bell*]
■ *n.* **1** see TOLL² *n.* **2** see WARNING 2. ● *v.* **1** see RING² *v.* 1.

knelt *past* and *past part.* of KNEEL.

Knesset /knéset/ *n.* the parliament of modern Israel. [Heb., lit. gathering]

knew *past* of KNOW.

knickerbocker /níkərbokər/ *n.* **1** (in *pl.*) = KNICKERS 1 **2** (**Knickerbocker**) **a** a New Yorker. **b** a descendant of the original Dutch settlers in New York. [Diedrich *Knicker-*

/.../ **pronunciation**	● **part of speech**
□ **phrases, idioms, and compounds**	
□□ **derivatives**	■ **synonym section**
cross-references appear in SMALL CAPITALS or *italics*	

bocker, pretended author of W. Irving's *History of New York* (1809)]

knickers /níkərz/ *n.pl.* **1** loose-fitting pants gathered at the knee or calf. **2** *Brit.* = PANTIES. **3** (as *int.*) *Brit. sl.* an expression of contempt. [abbr. of KNICKERBOCKER]
▪ **2** see TROUSERS 1.

knickknack /níknak/ *n.* **1** a useless and usu. worthless ornament; a trinket. **2** a small, dainty article of furniture, dress, etc. ▫▫ **knickknackery** *n.* **knickknackish** *adj.* [redupl. of *knack* in obs. sense 'trinket']
▪ **1** see GEWGAW. **2** see ORNAMENT *n.* 1, 2.

knife /nif/ *n. & v.* ● *n.* (*pl.* **knives** /nivz/) **1 a** a metal blade used as a cutting tool with usu. one long, sharp edge fixed rigidly in a handle or hinged (cf. PENKNIFE). **b** a similar tool used as a weapon. **2** a cutting blade forming part of a machine. ● *v.tr.* **1** cut or stab with a knife. **2** *sl.* bring about the defeat of (a person) by underhand means. ▫ **before you can say knife** *Brit. colloq.* very quickly or suddenly. **get one's knife into** treat maliciously or vindictively; persecute. **knife-edge 1** the edge of a knife. **2** a position of extreme danger or uncertainty. **3** a steel wedge on which a pendulum, etc., oscillates. **4** = ARÊTE. **knife pleat** a narrow flat pleat on a skirt, etc., usu. overlapping another. **knife rest** a metal or glass support for a knife at the table. **knife-throwing** a circus, etc., act in which knives are thrown at targets. **that one could cut with a knife** *colloq.* (of an accent, atmosphere, etc.) very obvious, oppressive, etc. **under the knife** undergoing a surgical operation or operations. ▫▫ **knifelike** *adj.* **knifer** *n.* [OE *cnīf* f. ON *knifr* f. Gmc]
▪ *n.* **1 a** blade, cutting edge, cutter; penknife, pocket knife. **b** sword, rapier, saber, dagger, stiletto, cutlass, bayonet, switchblade, jackknife, *Brit.* flick-knife, *hist.* skean, *literary* poniard, *poet.* brand. ● *v.* **1** stab, pierce, slash, cut, slit, wound.

knifepoint /nifpoynt/ *n.* the point of a knife. ▫ **at knifepoint** threatened with a knife or an ultimatum, etc.

knight /nit/ *n. & v.* ● *n.* **1** a man awarded a non-hereditary title (*Sir*) by a sovereign in recognition of merit or service. **2** *hist.* **a** a man, usu. noble, raised esp. by a sovereign to honorable military rank after service as a page and squire. **b** a military follower or attendant, esp. of a lady as her champion in a war or tournament. **3** a man devoted to the service of a woman, cause, etc. **4** *Chess* a piece usu. shaped like a horse's head. **5 a** *Rom.Hist.* a member of the class of *equites*, orig. the cavalry of the Roman army. **b** *Gk Hist.* a citizen of the second class in Athens. **6** (in full **knight of the shire**) *Brit. hist.* a gentleman representing a shire or county in parliament. ● *v.tr.* confer a knighthood on. ▫ **knight bachelors** (*pl.* **knights bachelor**) a knight not belonging to a special order. **knight commander** see COMMANDER. **knight-errant 1** a medieval knight wandering in search of chivalrous adventures. **2** a man of a chivalrous or quixotic nature. **knight-errantry** the practice or conduct of a knight errant. **Knight Hospitaller** (*pl.* **Knights Hospitaller**) a member of an order of monks with a military history, founded at Jerusalem *c.*1050. **knight in shining armor** a chivalrous rescuer or helper, esp. of a woman. **knight of the road** *Brit. colloq.* **1** a highwayman. **2** a commercial traveler. **3** a tramp. **4** a truck driver or taxi driver. **Knight Templar** (*pl.* **Knights Templars** or **Knights Templar**) a member of a religious and military order for the protection of pilgrims to the Holy Land, suppressed in 1312. ▫▫ **knighthood** *n.* **knightlike** *adj.* **knightly** *adj. & adv. poet.* **knightliness** *n.* [OE *cniht* boy, youth, hero f. WG]
▪ *n.* **3** see PROTECTOR. ▫ **knight-errant 2** see SAVIOR *n.* 1. **knight-errantry** see CHIVALRY 2.

knightage /nítij/ *n.* **1** knights collectively. **2** a list and account of knights.

knish /knish/ *n.* a dumpling of flaky dough filled with potato, meat, cheese, etc., and baked or fried. [Yiddish f. Russ.]

knit /nit/ *v. & n.* ● *v.* (**knitting**; *past* and *past part.* **knitted** or (esp. in senses 2–4) **knit**) **1** *tr.* (also *absol.*) **a** make (a garment, blanket, etc.) by interlocking loops of yarn with knitting needles. **b** make (a garment, etc.) with a knitting machine. **c** make (a plain stitch) in knitting (*knit one, purl*

one). **2 a** *tr.* contract (the forehead) in vertical wrinkles. **b** *intr.* (of the forehead) contract; frown. **3** *tr. & intr.* (often foll. by *together*) make or become more close or compact esp. by common interests, etc. (*a close-knit group*). **4** *intr.* (often foll. by *together*) (of parts of a broken bone) become joined; heal. ● *n.* knitted material or a knitted garment. ▫ **knit up** *Brit.* **1** make or repair by knitting. **2** conclude, finish, or end. ▫▫ **knitter** *n.* [OE *cnyttan* f. WG: cf. KNOT¹]
▪ *v.* **2** furrow, contract, wrinkle, knot, crease; frown. **3** join *or* fasten *or* weave (together), interweave, interlace, interconnect, intertwine, link, bind, unite, tie (up *or* together), integrate, consolidate, combine, compact. **4** grow (together), heal, mend, join.

knitting /níting/ *n.* **1** a garment, etc., in the process of being knitted. **2 a** the act of knitting. **b** an instance of this. ▫ **knitting machine** a machine used for mechanically knitting garments, etc. **knitting needle** a thin pointed rod of steel, wood, plastic, etc., used esp. in pairs for knitting.

knitwear /nítwair/ *n.* knitted garments.

knives *pl.* of KNIFE.

knob /nob/ *n. & v.* ● *n.* **1 a** a rounded protuberance, esp. at the end or on the surface of a thing. **b** a handle of a door, drawer, etc., shaped like a knob. **c** a knob-shaped attachment for pulling, turning, etc. (*press the knob under the desk*). **2** *Brit.* a small, usu. round, piece (of butter, coal, sugar, etc.). ● *v.* (**knobbed, knobbing**) **1** *tr.* provide with knobs. **2** *intr.* (usu. foll. by *out*) bulge. ▫ **with knobs on** *Brit. sl.* that and more (used as a retort to an insult, in emphatic agreement, etc.) (*and the same to you with knobs on*). ▫▫ **knobby** *adj.* **knoblike** *adj.* [ME f. MLG *knobbe* knot, knob, bud: cf. KNOP, NOB², NUB]
▪ *n.* **1 a** boss, stud, protuberance, projection, protrusion, swelling, bump, node, knop. **b** handle. **c** button, control, switch, dial. ▫▫ **knobby** see BUMPY 1.

knobble /nóbəl/ *n.* a small knob. ▫▫ **knobbly** *adj.* [ME, dimin. of KNOB: cf. Du. & LG *knobbel*]
▪ ▫▫ **knobbly** see BUMPY 1.

knobkerrie /nóbkeree/ *n.* a short stick with a knobbed head used as a weapon esp. by S. African tribes. [after Afrik. *knopkierie*]

knock /nok/ *v. & n.* ● *v.* **1 a** *tr.* strike (a hard surface) with an audible sharp blow (*knocked the table three times*). **b** *intr.* strike, esp. a door to gain admittance (*can you hear someone knocking?*; *knocked at the door*). **2** *tr.* make (a hole, a dent, etc.) by knocking (*knock a hole in the fence*). **3** *tr.* (usu. foll. by *in, out, off*, etc.) drive (a thing, a person, etc.) by striking (*knocked the ball into the hole*; *knocked those ideas out of his head*; *knocked her hand away*). **4** *tr. sl.* criticize. **5** *intr.* **a** (of a motor or other engine) make a thumping or rattling noise esp. as the result of a loose bearing. **b** (of a vehicle engine) emit a series of high-pitched explosive sounds caused by faulty combustion. **6** *tr. Brit. sl.* make a strong impression on; astonish. **7** *tr. Brit. coarse sl. offens.* = knock off 7. ● *n.* **1** an act of knocking. **2** a sharp rap, esp. at a door. **3** an audible sharp blow. **4** the sound of knocking in esp. a motor engine. ▫ **knock about** (or **around**) **1** strike repeatedly; treat roughly. **2** lead a wandering adventurous life; wander aimlessly. **3** be present without design or volition (*there's a cup knocking about somewhere*). **4** (usu. foll. by *with*) be associated socially (*knocks about with his brother*). **knock against** *Brit.* **1** collide with. **2** come across casually. **knock back** *Brit.* **1** *sl.* eat or drink, esp. quickly. **2** *sl.* disconcert. **3** *Brit. colloq.* refuse; rebuff. **knock-back** *n. Brit. colloq.* a refusal; a rebuff. **knock the bottom out of** see BOTTOM. **knock down 1** strike (esp. a person) to the ground with a blow. **2** demolish. **3** (usu. foll. by *to*) (at an auction) dispose of (an article) to a bidder by a knock with a hammer (*knocked the Picasso down to him for a million*). **4** *colloq.* lower the price of (an article). **5** take (machinery, furniture, etc.) to pieces for transportation. **6** *sl.* steal. **knock one's head against** come into collision with (unfavorable facts or conditions). **knocking shop** *Brit. sl.* a brothel. **knock into a cocked hat** see COCK¹. **knock into the middle of next week** *colloq.* send (a person) flying, esp. with a blow. **knock into shape** see SHAPE. **knock-kneed** having knock-knees.

knock-knees a condition in which the legs curve inward at the knee. **knock off 1** strike off with a blow. **2** *colloq.* **a** finish work (*knocked off at 5:30*). **b** finish (work) (*knocked off work early*). **3** *colloq.* dispatch (business). **4** *colloq.* rapidly produce (a work of art, verses, etc.). **5** (often foll. by *from*) deduct (a sum) from a price, bill, etc. **6** *sl.* steal from (*knocked off a liquor store*). **7** *Brit. coarse sl. offens.* have sexual intercourse with (a woman). **8** *sl.* kill. **knock-on effect** *Brit.* a secondary, indirect, or cumulative effect. **knock on the head 1** stun or kill (a person) by a blow on the head. **2** *Brit. colloq.* put an end to (a scheme, etc.). **knock on** (or **knock**) **wood** knock something wooden with the knuckles to avert bad luck. **knock out 1** make (a person) unconscious by a blow on the head. **2** knock down (a boxer) for a count of 10, thereby winning the contest. **3** defeat, esp. in a knockout competition. **4** *sl.* astonish. **5** (*refl.*) *colloq.* exhaust (*knocked themselves out swimming*). **6** *colloq.* make or write (a plan, etc.) hastily. **7** empty (a tobacco pipe) by tapping. **knock sideways** *colloq.* disconcert; astonish. **knock spots off** esp. *Brit.* defeat easily. **knock together** put together or assemble hastily or roughly. **knock under** *Brit.* = *knuckle under.* **knock up 1** make or arrange hastily. **2** damage or mar. **3 a** become exhausted or ill. **b** exhaust or make ill. **4** *Brit.* arouse (a person) by a knock at the door. **5** *coarse sl.* make pregnant. **take a** (or **the**) **knock** esp. *Brit.* be hard hit financially or emotionally. [ME f. OE *cnocian*: prob. imit.]

■ *v.* **1** strike, hit, rap, thump, bang, bash, hammer, tap, *archaic or literary* smite, *colloq.* whack, thwack; see also BEAT *v.* 1, 2a. **4** criticize, deprecate, carp at, cavil at, disparage, run down, *colloq.* put down, pan, slate. ● *n.* **1, 2** rap, tap, thump, banging, pounding, hammering. **3** blow, punch, jab, smack, right, left, cuff, clout, *colloq.* thwack, whack, bop, *sl.* biff, conk. □ **knock about** (or **around**) **1** beat (up), maltreat, mistreat, maul, batter, abuse, hit, strike, *colloq.* manhandle. **2** wander, roam, ramble, rove, travel, gad about. **4** associate, consort, socialize, fraternize, keep company, *sl.* hang out. **knock down 1** strike down, fell, floor, cut down. **2** raze, demolish, destroy, level, wreck, lay in ruins, throw down, pull down, tear down. **4** see REDUCE 7. **5** dismantle, pull down, pull or take to pieces, take apart, take down. **6** see STEAL *v.* 1. **knock off 2 a** stop work(ing), quit, go home, clock off *or* out, lock up, close down. **b** stop, finish, cease, terminate, quit. **3** dispatch, make quick *or* short work of, complete, finish, bring to an end, polish off. **4** see *knock up* 1 below. **5** see DEDUCT. **6** steal, pilfer, thieve, rob, burglarize, *colloq.* hold up, lift, *sl.* heist, *Brit. sl.* nick. **8** see KILL[1] *v.* 1. **knock out 1, 2** knock *or* render unconscious, floor, prostrate, trounce, whip, *colloq.* flatten, KO, kayo. **3** see ELIMINATE 3. **4** overwhelm, overcome, daze, stagger, astound, astonish, bewilder, stun, *colloq.* bowl over, *sl.* blow a person's mind. **knock together** see *knock up* 1 below. **knock up 1** knock off *or* together, put together, throw together, whip up, improvise. **5** impregnate, make pregnant, *archaic* get with child.

knockabout /nókəbowt/ *adj. & n.* ● *attrib.adj.* **1** (of comedy) boisterous; slapstick. **2** (of clothes) suitable for rough use. **3** *Austral.* of a farm or station handyman. ● *n.* **1** *Austral.* a farm or station handyman. **2** a knockabout performer or performance.

■ *adj.* **1** see BOISTEROUS 1.

knockdown /nókdown/ *adj. & n.* ● *adj.* **1** (of a blow, misfortune, argument, etc.) overwhelming. **2** *Brit.* (of a price) very low. **3** (of a price at auction) reserve. **4** (of furniture, etc.) easily dismantled and reassembled. ● *n.* **1** a knockdown item. **2** *sl.* an introduction to a person.

knocker /nókər/ *n.* **1** a metal or wooden instrument hinged to a door for knocking to call attention. **2** a person or thing that knocks. **3** (in *pl.*) *coarse sl.* a woman's breasts. **4** *Brit.* a person who buys or sells door to door. □ **knocker-up** *Brit. hist.* a person employed to rouse early workers by knocking at their doors or windows. **on the knocker** *Brit.* **1** (buying or selling) from door to door. **2** (obtained) on credit. **up to the knocker** *Brit. sl.* in good condition; to perfection.

knockout /nókowt/ *n.* **1** the act of making unconscious by a blow. **2** *Boxing*, etc., a blow that knocks an opponent out. **3** a competition in which the loser in each round is eliminated (also *attrib.: a knockout round*). **4** *colloq.* an outstanding or irresistible person or thing. □ **knockout drops** a drug added to a drink to cause unconsciousness.

■ **2** coup de grâce, *colloq.* KO, kayo. **4** success, sensation, triumph, wonder, *colloq.* hit, winner, smash, smash hit, stunner. □ **knockout drops** SEE SEDATIVE *n.*

knockwurst /naákwərst/ *n.* a variety of thick, seasoned sausage. [Ger *knackwurst* f. *knacken* to crackle + *wurst* sausage]

knoll[1] /nōl/ *n.* a small hill or mound. [OE *cnoll* hilltop, rel. to MDu., MHG *knolle* clod, ON *knollr* hilltop]

■ hillock, hummock, mound, barrow, hill, elevation, rise.

knoll[2] /nōl/ *v. & n. archaic* ● *v.* **1** *tr. & intr.* = KNELL. **2** *tr.* summon by the sound of a bell. ● *n.* = KNELL. [ME, var. of KNELL: perh. imit.]

knop /nop/ *n.* **1** a knob, esp. ornamental. **2** an ornamental loop or tuft in yarn. **3** *archaic* a flower bud. [ME f. MLG, MDu. *knoppe*]

■ **1** see KNOB *n.* 1a.

knot[1] /not/ *n. & v.* ● *n.* **1 a** an intertwining of a rope, string, tress of hair, etc., with another, itself, or something else to join or fasten together. **b** a set method of tying a knot (*a reef knot*). **c** a ribbon, etc., tied as an ornament and worn on a dress, etc. **d** a tangle in hair, knitting, etc. **2 a** a unit of a ship's or aircraft's speed equivalent to one nautical mile per hour (see *nautical mile*). **b** a division marked by knots on a log line, as a measure of speed. **c** *colloq.* a nautical mile. **3** (usu. foll. by *of*) a group or cluster (*a small knot of journalists at the gate*). **4** something forming or maintaining a union; a bond or tie, esp. of wedlock. **5** a hard lump of tissue in an animal or human body. **6 a** a knob or protuberance in a stem, branch, or root. **b** a hard mass formed in a tree trunk at the intersection with a branch. **c** a round cross-grained piece in lumber where a branch has been cut through. **d** a node on the stem of a plant. **7** a difficulty; a problem. **8** a central point in a problem or the plot of a story, etc. ● *v.* (**knotted, knotting**) **1** *tr.* tie (a string, etc.) in a knot. **2** *tr.* entangle. **3** *tr.* esp. *Brit.* knit (the brows). **4** *tr.* unite closely or intricately (*knotted together in intrigue*). **5 a** *intr.* make knots for fringing. **b** *tr.* make (a fringe) with knots. □ **at a rate of knots** *Brit. colloq.* very fast. **get knotted!** *Brit. sl.* an expression of disbelief, annoyance, etc. **knot garden** an intricately designed formal garden, esp. of herbs. **tie in knots** *colloq.* baffle or confuse completely. **tie the knot** get married. □□ **knotless** *adj.* **knotter** *n.* **knotting** *n.* (esp. in sense 5 of *v.*). [OE *cnotta* f. WG]

■ *n.* **1 a** tie, bond, twist. **d** snarl, tangle. **3** collection, assemblage, group, aggregation, congregation, crowd, cluster, bunch, gathering, company, gang, crowd, throng, *archaic* band. **6 a** knob, protuberance, knar, knur, excrescence. **d** node, nodule. ● *v.* **1** fasten, tie, bind, secure, lash, tether, affix, fix, attach. **2** see ENTANGLE 1, 2. **4** unite, join, connect, link, bond. □ **tie in knots** see BEMUSE.

knot[2] /not/ *n.* a small sandpiper, *Calidris canutus.* [ME: orig. unkn.]

knotgrass /nótgras/ *n.* **1** a common weed, *Polygonum aviculare*, with creeping stems and small pink flowers. **2** = POLYGONUM. Also called KNOTWEED.

knothole /nóthōl/ *n.* a hole in a piece of lumber where a knot has fallen out.

knotty /nótee/ *adj.* (**knottier, knottiest**) **1** full of knots. **2** hard to explain; puzzling (*a knotty problem*). □□ **knottily** *adv.* **knottiness** *n.*

■ **1** see GNARLED. **2** see *perplexing* (PERPLEX), DIFFICULT 1b.

knotweed /nótweed/ *n.* = POLYGONUM.

/. . ./ **pronunciation**	● **part of speech**	
□ **phrases, idioms, and compounds**		
□□ **derivatives**	■ **synonym section**	
cross-references appear in SMALL CAPITALS or *italics*		

knotwork /nótwərk/ *n.* ornamental work representing or consisting of intertwined cords.

knout /nowt/ *n. & v.* ● *n. hist.* a scourge used in imperial Russia, often causing death. ● *v.tr.* flog with a knout. [F f. Russ. *knut* f. Icel. *knútr*, rel. to KNOT¹]

■ *n.* see LASH *n.* 2.

know /nō/ *v. & n.* ● *v.* (*past* **knew** /nōō, nyōō/; *past part.* **known** /nōn/) **1** *tr.* (often foll. by *that, how, what,* etc.) **a** have in the mind; have learned; be able to recall (*knows a lot about cars; knows what to do*). **b** (also *absol.*) be aware of (a fact) (*he knows I am waiting; I think she knows*). **c** have a good command of (a subject or language) (*knew German; knows his multiplication tables*). **2** *tr.* be acquainted or friendly with (a person or thing). **3** *tr.* **a** recognize; identify (*I knew him at once; knew him to be an Englishman*). **b** (foll. by *to* + infin.) be aware of (a person or thing) as being or doing what is specified (*knew them to be rogues*). **c** (foll. by *from*) be able to distinguish (one from another) (*did not know him from Adam*). **4** *tr.* be subject to (*her joy knew no bounds*). **5** *tr.* have personal experience of (fear, etc.). **6** *tr.* (as **known** *adj.*) **a** publicly acknowledged (*a known thief; a known fact*). **b** *Math.* (of a quantity, etc.) having a value that can be stated. **7** *intr.* have understanding or knowledge. **8** *tr. archaic* have sexual intercourse with. ● *n.* (in phr. **in the know**) *colloq.* well-informed; having special knowledge. □ **all one knows** (or **knows how**) **1** all one can (*did all she knew to stop it*). **2** *adv.* to the utmost of one's power (*tried all she knew*). **before one knows where one is** with baffling speed. **be not to know 1** have no way of learning (*wasn't to know they'd arrive late*). **2** be not to be told (*she's not to know about the party*). **don't I know it!** *colloq.* an expression of rueful assent. **don't you know** *colloq.* or *joc.* an expression used for emphasis (*such a bore, don't you know*). **for all I know** so far as my knowledge extends. **have been known to** be known to have done (*they have been known to not turn up*). **I knew it!** I was sure that this would happen. **I know what** I have a new idea, suggestion, etc. **know about** have information about. **know-all** esp. *Brit.* = **know-it-all**. **know best** be or claim to be better informed, etc., than others. **know better than** (foll. by *that,* or *to* + infin.) be wise, well-informed, or well-mannered enough to avoid (specified behavior, etc.). **know by name 1** have heard the name of. **2** be able to give the name of. **know by sight** recognize the appearance (only) of. **know how** know the way to do something. **know-how** *n.* **1** practical knowledge; technique; expertise. **2** natural skill or invention. **know-it-all** *colloq.* a person who acts as if he or she knows everything. **know-nothing 1** an ignorant person. **2** an agnostic. **3** (**Know-Nothing**) member of the Know-Nothing party. **Know-Nothing party** *US hist.* a short-lived 19th-century political party advocating intolerance toward immigrants and Roman Catholics esp. as political candidates. **know of** be aware of; have heard of (*not that I know of*). **know one's own mind** be decisive; not vacillate. **know the ropes** (or **one's stuff**) be fully knowledgeable or experienced. **know a thing or two** be experienced or shrewd. **know what's what** have adequate knowledge of the world, life, etc. **know who's who** be aware of who or what each person is. **not if I know it** only against my will. **not know that ...** *colloq.* be fairly sure that ... not (*I don't know that I want to go*). **not know what hit one** be suddenly injured, killed, disconcerted, etc. **not want to know** refuse to take any notice of. **what do you know** (or **know about that**)? *colloq.* an expression of surprise. **you know** *colloq.* **1** an expression implying something generally known or known to the hearer (*you know, the store on the corner*). **2** an expression used as a gap-filler in conversation. **you know something** (or **what**)? I am going to tell you something. **you-know-what** (or **-who**) a thing or person unspecified but understood. **you never know** nothing in the future is certain. □□ **knowable** *adj.* **knower** *n.* [OE (*ge*)*cnāwan*, rel. to CAN¹, KEN]

■ *v.* **1 a** understand, comprehend, be familiar with, grasp, be acquainted with, be versed in, be skilled in, have at one's fingertips. **b** be aware of, be conscious of, be cognizant of, be informed of, be advised of, have

knowledge of. **2** be acquainted with, be familiar with, be friendly with, be a friend of. **3 a** recognize, identify, place, recall, remember, recollect. **c** distinguish, separate, differentiate, discriminate. **5** see EXPERIENCE *v.* 2. **6** (**known**) **a** see *well-known*. ● *n.* (**in the know**) see *well-informed*. □ **know-how** (*n.*) see TECHNIQUE 1. **know-it-all** see *wise guy*. **know one's own mind** be decided, be resolved, be firm, be resolute, be decisive, be sure, be certain, be positive, be (self-)assured, be (self-)confident, be in touch with oneself.

knowing /nóing/ *n. & adj.* ● *n.* the state of being aware or informed of any thing. ● *adj.* **1** usu. *derog.* cunning; sly. **2** showing knowledge; shrewd. □ **there is no knowing** no one can tell. □□ **knowingness** *n.*

■ *n.* see KNOWLEDGE 1. ● *adj.* **1** conspiratorial, conspiratory, secret, private; significant, meaningful, eloquent, expressive; shrewd, canny, artful, sly, leery, wily, crafty, cunning. **2** wise, clever, shrewd, (well-)informed, knowledgeable, aware, expert, qualified, astute, perceptive, intelligent, sagacious.

knowingly /nóinglee/ *adv.* **1** consciously; intentionally (*had never knowingly injured him*). **2** in a knowing manner (*smiled knowingly*).

■ **1** see *deliberately* (DELIBERATE).

knowledge /nólij/ *n.* **1 a** (usu. foll. by *of*) awareness or familiarity gained by experience (of a person, fact, or thing) (*have no knowledge of their character*). **b** a person's range of information (*is not within his knowledge*). **c** specific information; facts or intelligence about something (*received knowledge of their imminent departure*). **2 a** (usu. foll. by *of*) a theoretical or practical understanding of a subject, language, etc. (*has a good knowledge of Greek*). **b** the sum of what is known (*every branch of knowledge*). **c** learning; scholarship. **3** *Philos.* true, justified belief; certain understanding, as opp. to opinion. **4** = *carnal knowledge*. □ **come to one's knowledge** become known to one. **to my knowledge 1** so far as I know. **2** as I know for certain. [ME *knaulege,* with earlier *knawlechen* (v.) formed as KNOW + OE *-lǣcan* f. *lāc* as in WEDLOCK]

■ **1** knowing, familiarity, awareness, apprehension, cognition, grasp, understanding, discernment, consciousness, conception, insight. **b** ken, perception. **c** facts, information, data, intelligence. **2 a** acquaintance, acquaintanceship, familiarity, understanding, appreciation, conversance, expertise, experience, adeptness, proficiency. **c** schooling, education, scholarship, instruction, learning, erudition.

knowledgeable /nólijəbəl/ *adj.* (also **knowledgable**) well-informed; intelligent. □□ **knowledgeability** *n.* **knowledgeableness** *n.* **knowledgeably** *adv.*

■ aware, *au fait,* au courant, up-to-date, (well-)informed, (well-)acquainted, cognizant, familiar, enlightened, expert, knowing, *colloq.* in the know; well-educated, erudite, learned, cultured, well-read, intelligent, sophisticated, (worldly-)wise, sage, sagacious.

known *past part.* of KNOW.

knuckle /núkəl/ *n. & v.* ● *n.* **1** the bone at a finger joint, esp. that adjoining the hand. **2 a** a projection of the carpal or tarsal joint of a quadruped. **b** a joint of meat consisting of this with the adjoining parts, esp. of bacon or pork. ● *v.tr.* strike, press, or rub with the knuckles. □ **go the knuckle** *Austral. sl.* fight, punch. **knuckle down** (often foll. by *to*) **1** apply oneself seriously (to a task, etc.). **2** give in; submit. **knuckle-duster** = *brass knuckles.* **knuckle sandwich** *sl.* a punch in the mouth. **knuckle under** give in; submit. **rap on** (or **over**) **the knuckles** see RAP¹. □□ **knuckly** *adj.* [ME *knokel* f. MLG, MDu. *knökel,* dimin. of *knoke* bone]

■ □ **knuckle down 1** see APPLY 5; (*knuckle down to*) see *buckle* (*down*) *to.* **2** see SUBMIT 1a, BUCKLE *v.* 2. **knuckle under** see SUBMIT 1a, BUCKLE *v.* 2. **rap on** (or **over**) **the knuckles** see CASTIGATE.

knuckleball /núkəlbawl/ *n. Baseball* a pitch delivered with the ball held by the knuckles or fingernails such that the thrown ball has minimal spin and moves erratically. □□ **knuckleballer** *n.*

knucklebone /núkəlbōn/ n. **1** bone forming a knuckle. **2** the bone of a sheep or other animal corresponding to or resembling a knuckle. **3** a knuckle of meat. **4** (in pl.) animal knucklebones used in the game of jacks. **5** (in pl.) the game of jacks.

knucklehead /núkəlhed/ n. colloq. a slow-witted or stupid person.

knur /nər/ n. **1** a hard excrescence on the trunk of a tree. **2** a hard concretion. [ME knorre, var. of KNAR]

knurl /nərl/ n. a small projecting knob, ridge, etc. □□ **knurled** /nərld/ adj. [KNUR]

KO abbr. **1** knockout. **2** kickoff.
■ **1** knockout, coup de grâce, colloq. kayo.

koa /kṓə/ n. **1** a Hawaiian tree, Acacia koa, which produces dark red wood. **2** this wood. [Hawaiian]

koala /kō-áálə/ n. an Australian bearlike marsupial, Phascolarctos cinereus, having thick, gray fur and feeding on eucalyptus leaves. ¶ The fuller form koala bear is now considered incorrect. [Aboriginal kūl(l)a]

koan /kṓ-aan/ n. a riddle used in Zen Buddhism to demonstrate the inadequacy of logical reasoning. [Jap., = public matter (for thought)]

kobold /kṓbawld/ n. (in Germanic mythology): **1** a familiar spirit; a brownie. **2** an underground spirit in mines, etc. [G]
■ **1** see IMP n. 2.

Köchel listing /kə́rshəl, kṓkhəl/ n. Mus. (also **Köchel number**) a number given to each of Mozart's compositions in the complete catalog of his works compiled by Köchel and his successors. [L. von Köchel, Austrian scientist d. 1877]

KO'd /kayṓd, káyōd/ adj. knocked out. [abbr.]

Kodiak /kṓdeeak/ n. (in full **Kodiak bear**) a large Alaskan brown bear, Ursus arctos middendorffi. [Kodiak Island, Alaska]

koel /kṓəl/ n. a dark-colored cuckoo, Eudynamys scolopacea. [Hindi kōïl f. Skr. kokila]

kohl /kōl/ n. a black powder, usu. antimony sulfide or lead sulfide, used as eye makeup esp. in Eastern countries. [Arab. kuḥl]

kohlrabi /kōlráabee/ n. (pl. **kohlrabies**) a variety of cabbage with an edible turniplike swollen stem. [G f. It. cavoli rape (pl.) f. med.L cauloropa (as COLE, RAPE²)]

koine /koynáy, kóynay/ n. **1** (usu. **Koine**) the common language of the Greeks from the close of the classical period to the Byzantine era. **2** a common language shared by various peoples; a lingua franca. [Gk koinē (dialektos) common (language)]

kola var. of COLA.

kolinsky /kəlínskee/ n. (pl. **-ies**) **1** the Siberian mink, Mustela sibirica, having a brown coat in winter. **2** the fur of this. [Russ. kolinskĭ f. Kola in NW Russia]

kolkhoz /kolkáwz, kulkhá́ws/ n. a collective farm in the former USSR. [Russ. f. kollektivnoe khozyaĭstvo collective farm]

komitadji (also **komitaji**) var. of COMITADJI.

Komodo dragon /kəmṓdō/ n. (also **Komodo lizard**) a large monitor lizard, Varanus komodoensis, native to the E. Indies. [Komodo Island in Indonesia]

Komsomol /kómsəmáwl/ n. hist. **1** an organization for Communist youth in the former Soviet Union. **2** a member of this. [Russ. f. Kommunisticheskĭ soyuz molodezhi Communist League of Youth]

koodoo var. of KUDU.

kook /kōōk/ n. & adj. sl. ● n. a crazy or eccentric person. ● adj. crazy; eccentric. [20th c.: prob. f. CUCKOO]
■ n. see WEIRDO.

kookaburra /kṓōkəbərə, -burə/ n. any Australian kingfisher of the genus Dacelo, esp. D. novaeguineae, which makes a strange laughing cry. Also called laughing jackass. [Aboriginal]

kooky /kṓōkee/ adj. (**kookier, kookiest**) sl. crazy or eccentric. □□ **kookily** adv. **kookiness** n.
■ see MAD adj. 1.

kop /kop/ n. S.Afr. a prominent hill or peak. [Afrik. f. Du., = head: cf. COP²]

kopeck /kṓpek, kópek/ n. (also **kopek, copeck**) a Russian coin and monetary unit worth one-hundredth of a ruble. [Russ. Kopeĭka dimin. of kop'ë lance (for the lance borne by the figure on the coin in former times)]

kopje /kópee/ n. (also **koppie**) S.Afr. a small hill. [Afrik. koppie, Du. kopje, dimin. of kop head]

koradji /kəraáajee/ n. (pl. **koradjis**) Austral. an Aboriginal medicine man. [Aboriginal]

Koran /kərán, -raán, kaw-/ n. (also **Qur'an** /kə-/) the Islamic sacred book, believed to be the word of God as dictated to Muhammad and written down in Arabic. □□ **Koranic** adj. [Arab. ḳur'ān recitation f. ḳara'a read]
■ see SCRIPTURE 2a.

Korean /kəreéan, kaw-/ n. & adj. ● n. **1** a native or national of N. or S. Korea in SE Asia. **2** the language of Korea. ● adj. of or relating to Korea or its people or language.

kosher /kṓshər/ adj. & n. ● adj. **1** (of food or premises in which food is sold, cooked, or eaten) fulfilling the requirements of Jewish law. **2** colloq. correct; genuine; legitimate. ● n. kosher food. □ **keep kosher** adhere to kosher practices. [Heb. kāšēr proper]
■ adj. 2 see AUTHENTIC, PERMISSIBLE.

koto /kṓtō/ n. (pl. **-os** or same) a Japanese musical instrument with usu. 7 or 13 long esp. silk strings. [Jap.]

kotow var. of KOWTOW.

koumiss /kṓōmis/ n. (also **kumiss**) a fermented liquor prepared from esp. mare's milk, used by Asian nomads and medicinally. [Tartar kumiz]

kourbash /kṓōrbash/ n. (also **kurbash**) a whip, esp. of hippopotamus hide, used as an instrument of punishment in Turkey and Egypt. [Arab. kurbāj f. Turk. kırbáç whip]

kowhai /kṓ-wi/ n. any of several trees or shrubs of the genus Sophora, esp. S. microphylla native to New Zealand, with pendant clusters of yellow flowers. [Maori]

kowtow /kowtów/ n. & v. (also **kotow** /kōtów/) ● n. hist. the Chinese custom of kneeling and touching the ground with the forehead in worship or submission. ● v.intr. **1** hist. perform the kowtow. **2** (usu. foll. by to) act obsequiously. [Chin. ketou f. ke knock + tou head]
■ v. 2 genuflect, salaam, prostrate oneself, bow (down), pay court, (bow and) scrape, cringe, fawn, grovel, toady, pander, truckle; (kowtow to) dance attendance on, play up to, lick a person's boots, shine up, colloq. butter up, suck up to.

KP n. Mil. colloq. **1** enlisted person detailed to help the cooks. **2** kitchen duty. [abbr. of kitchen police]

k.p.h. abbr. kilometers per hour.

Kr symb. Chem. the element krypton.

kraal /kraal/ n. S.Afr. **1** a village of huts enclosed by a fence. **2** an enclosure for cattle or sheep. [Afrik. f. Port. curral, of Hottentot orig.]

kraft /kraft/ n. (in full **kraft paper**) a kind of strong smooth brown wrapping paper. [G f. Sw., = strength]

krait /krit/ n. any venomous snake of the genus Bungarus of E. Asia. [Hindi karait]

kraken /kraákən/ n. a large mythical sea monster said to appear off the coast of Norway. [Norw.]

krans /kraans/ n. S.Afr. a precipitous or overhanging wall of rocks. [Afrik. f. Du. krans coronet]

kraut /krowt/ n. **1** colloq. sauerkraut. **2** (also **Kraut**) sl. offens. a German. [shortening of SAUERKRAUT]

kremlin /krémlin/ n. **1** a citadel within a Russian city or town. **2** (**the Kremlin**) **a** the citadel in Moscow. **b** the Russian or former USSR government housed within it. [F, f. Russ. Kreml', of Tartar orig.]

kriegspiel /kreégshpeel/ n. (also **Kriegspiel**) **1** a war game in which blocks representing armies, etc., are moved about on maps. **2** a form of chess with an umpire, in which each player has only limited information about the opponent's moves. [G f. Krieg war + Spiel game]

/.../ **pronunciation**	● **part of speech**
□ **phrases, idioms, and compounds**	
□□ **derivatives**	■ **synonym section**
cross-references appear in SMALL CAPITALS or italics	

....

■ **1** exercise, war game, training; maneuvers.

krill /kril/ *n.* tiny planktonic crustaceans found in the seas around the Antarctic and eaten by baleen whales. [Norw. *kril* tiny fish]

krimmer /krímər/ *n.* a gray or black fur obtained from the wool of young Crimean lambs. [G f. *Krim* Crimea]

kris /krees/ *n.* (also **crease, creese**) a Malay or Indonesian dagger with a wavy blade. [ult. f. Malay *k(i)rīs*]
■ see DAGGER.

Krishnaism /kríshnəizəm/ *n. Hinduism* the worship of Krishna as an incarnation of Vishnu.

kromesky /krəméskee/ *n.* (*pl.* **-ies**) a croquette of ground meat or fish, rolled in bacon and fried. [app. f. Pol. *krome-czka* small slice]

krona /krṓnə/ *n.* **1** (*pl.* **kronor** /krṓnər, -nawr/) the chief monetary unit of Sweden. **2** (*pl.* **kronur** /krṓnər/) the chief monetary unit of Iceland. [Sw. & Icel., = CROWN]

krone /krṓnə/ *n.* (*pl.* **kroner** /krṓnər/) the chief monetary unit of Denmark and of Norway. [Da. & Norw., = CROWN]

Kroo var. of KRU.

Kru /krōō/ *n. & adj.* (also **Kroo**) ● *n.* (*pl.* same) a member of a Black seafaring people on the coast of Liberia. ● *adj.* of or concerning the Kru. [W. Afr.]

Krugerrand /krṓōgərand, -raant/ *n.* (also **krugerrand**) a S. African gold coin depicting President Kruger. [S. J. P. *Kruger*, S. Afr. statesman d. 1904, + RAND[1]]

krummhorn /krúmhawrn/ *n.* (also **krumhorn, crumhorn**) a medieval wind instrument with a double reed and a curved end. [G f. *krumm* crooked + *Horn* HORN]

krypton /kríptən/ *n. Chem.* an inert gaseous element of the noble gas group, forming a small portion of the earth's atmosphere and used in fluorescent lamps, etc. ¶ Symb.: **Kr.** [Gk *krupton* hidden, neut. adj. f. *kruptō* hide]

KS *abbr.* Kansas (in official postal use).

Kshatriya /kshátreeə/ *n.* a member of the second of the four great Hindu castes, the military caste. [Skr. f. *kshatra* rule]

KT *abbr.* **1** Knight Templar. **2** (in the UK) Knight of the Order of the Thistle. **3** kiloton(s).

Kt. *abbr.* Knight.

kt. *abbr.* **1** karat(s). **2** kiloton(s). **3** knots.

Ku *symb. Chem.* the element kurchatovium.

kudos /kyṓōdōz, -dōs, -dos, kyṓō-/ *n. colloq.* glory; renown. [Gk]
■ praise, acclaim, glory, fame, renown, prestige, honor, plaudit(s), applause, admiration, acclamation, accolade, *formal* laudation.

kudu /kṓōdōō/ *n.* (also **koodoo**) either of two African antelopes, *Tragelaphus strepsiceros* or *T. imberbis*, with white stripes and corkscrew-shaped ridged horns. [Xhosa-Kaffir *iqudu*]

kudzu /kṓōdzōō, kúd-/ *n.* (in full **kudzu vine**) a quick-growing climbing plant, *Pueraria thunbergiana*, with reddish-purple flowers. [Jap. *kuzu*]

Kufic /kṓōfik, kyṓō-/ *n. & adj.* (also **Cufic**) ● *n.* an early angular form of the Arabic alphabet found chiefly in decorative inscriptions. ● *adj.* of or in this type of script. [*Cufa*, a city S. of Baghdad in Iraq]

Ku Klux Klan /kṓō kluks klán, kyṓō-/ *n.* a secret society founded in the southern US, orig. formed after the Civil War and dedicated to white supremacy. □□ **Ku Klux Klansman** *n.* (*pl.* **-men**). [perh. f. Gk *kuklos* circle + CLAN]

kukri /kṓōkree/ *n.* (*pl.* **kukris**) a curved knife broadening toward the point, used by Gurkhas. [Hindi *kukrī*]

kulak /kṓōlák, -laák/ *n. hist.* a peasant working for personal profit in Soviet Russia. [Russ., = fist, tight-fisted person]

kulan /kṓōlən/ *n.* a wild ass of SW Asia, closely related to the kiang. [Tartar]

kultur /kṓōltōŏr/ *n. esp. derog.* (also *Kultur*) German civilization and culture, seen as racist, authoritarian, and militaristic. [G f. L *cultura* CULTURE]

Kulturkampf /kṓōltōŏrkaampf/ *n. hist.* the conflict in 19th-c. Germany between the civil and ecclesiastical authorities, esp. as regards the control of schools. [G (as KULTUR, *Kampf* struggle)]

kumara /kṓōmərə/ *n. NZ* a sweet potato. [Maori]

kumiss var. of KOUMISS.

kümmel /kímǝl, kö-/ *n.* a sweet liqueur flavored with caraway and cumin seeds. [G (as CUMIN)]

kumquat /kúmkwot/ *n.* (also **cumquat**) **1** an orangelike fruit with a sweet rind and acid pulp, used in preserves. **2** any shrub or small tree of the genus *Fortunella* yielding this. [Cantonese var. of Chin. *kin kü* golden orange]

kung fu /kung fōō, kōōng/ *n.* the Chinese form of karate. [Chin. *gongfu* f. *gong* merit + *fu* master]

kurbash var. of KOURBASH.

kurchatovium /kərchətṓveeəm/ *n. Chem.* = RUTHERFORDIUM. ¶ Symb.: **Ku.** [I. V. *Kurchatov*, Russ. physicist d. 1960]

Kurd /kərd/ *n.* a member of a mainly pastoral Aryan Islamic people living in Kurdistan (contiguous areas of Iraq, Iran, and Turkey). [Kurdish]

kurdaitcha /kərdíchə/ *n. Austral.* **1** the tribal use of a bone in spells intended to cause sickness or death. **2** a man empowered to point the bone at a victim. [Aboriginal]

Kurdish /kə́rdish/ *adj. & n.* ● *adj.* of or relating to the Kurds or their language. ● *n.* the Iranian language of the Kurds.

kurrajong /kə́rəjawng, -jong, kúr-/ *n.* (also **currajong**) an Australian tree, *Brachychiton populneum*, which produces a tough bast fiber. [Aboriginal]

kurta /kártə/ *n.* (also **khurta**) a loose shirt or tunic worn by esp. Hindu men and women. [Hind.]

kurtosis /kərtṓsis/ *n. Statistics* the sharpness of the peak of a frequency-distribution curve. [mod.L f. Gk *kurtōsis* bulging f. *kurtos* convex]

kV *abbr.* kilovolt(s).

kvass /kvaas/ *n.* a Russian fermented beverage, low in alcohol, made from rye flour or bread with malt. [Russ. *kvas*]

kvetch /kvech/ *n. & v. sl.* ● *n.* an objectionable person, esp. one who complains a great deal. ● *v.* complain; whine. □□ **kvetcher** *n.*

kW *abbr.* kilowatt(s).

KWAC /kwak/ *n. Computing*, etc., keyword and context. [abbr.]

kwacha /kwaáchə/ *n.* the chief monetary unit of Zambia. [native word, = dawn]

kwashiorkor /kwóshee-áwrkawr/ *n.* a form of malnutrition caused by a protein deficiency of diet, esp. in young children in the tropics. [native name in Ghana]

kWh *abbr.* kilowatt-hour(s).

KY *abbr.* Kentucky (in official postal use).

Ky. *abbr.* Kentucky.

kyanite /kíənīt/ *n.* a blue crystalline mineral of aluminum silicate. □□ **kyanitic** /-nítik/ *adj.* [Gk *kuanos* dark blue]

kyanize /kíəniz/ *v.tr.* treat (wood) with a solution of corrosive sublimate to prevent decay. [J. H. *Kyan*, Ir. inventor d. 1850]

kybosh var. of KIBOSH.

kyle /kīl/ *n.* (in Scotland) a narrow channel between islands or between an island and the mainland. [Gael. *caol* strait]

kylie /kílee/ *n. W. Austral.* a boomerang. [Aboriginal]

kylin /keélin/ *n.* a mythical composite animal figured on Chinese and Japanese ceramics. [Chin. *qilin* f. *qi* male + *lin* female]

Kyloe /kílō/ *n. Brit.* **1** an animal of a breed of small usu. black long-horned highland cattle. **2** this breed. [*Kyloe* in Northumberland]

kymograph /kíməgraf/ *n.* an instrument for recording variations in pressure, e.g., in sound waves or in blood within blood vessels. □□ **kymographic** *adj.* [Gk *kuma* wave + -GRAPH]

kyphosis /kifṓsis/ *n. Med.* excessive outward curvature of the spine, causing hunching of the back (opp. LORDOSIS). □□ **kyphotic** /-fótik/ *adj.* [mod.L f. Gk *kuphōsis* f. *kuphos* bent]

Kyrie /keéreeay/ *n.* (in full **Kyrie eleison** /iláyizon, -son, eláy-/) *n.* **1 a** a short repeated invocation used in the RC and Greek Orthodox churches, esp. at the beginning of the Mass. **b** a response sometimes used in the Anglican communion service. **2** a musical setting of the Kyrie. [ME f. med.L f. Gk *Kurie eleēson* Lord, have mercy]

L¹ /el/ *n.* (also **l**) (*pl.* **Ls** or **L's**) **1** the twelfth letter of the alphabet. **2** (as a Roman numeral) 50. **3** a thing shaped like an L, esp. a joint connecting two pipes at right angles.

L² *abbr.* (also **L.**) **1** Lake. **2** Latin. **3** Liberal. **4** large. **5** *Biol.* Linnaeus. **6** lire.

l *abbr.* (also **l.**) **1** left. **2** line. **3** liter(s). **4** length. **5** *archaic* pound(s) (money).

£ *abbr.* (preceding a numeral) pound or pounds (of money). [L *libra*]

LA *abbr.* **1** Los Angeles. **2** Louisiana (in official postal use). **3** legislative assistant.

La *symb. Chem.* the element lanthanum.

La. *abbr.* Louisiana.

la /laa/ *n. Mus.* **1** (in tonic sol-fa) the sixth note of a major scale. **2** the note A in the fixed-do system. [ME f. L *labii*; see GAMUT]

laager /láagər/ *n. & v.* ● *n.* **1** esp. *S.Afr.* a camp or encampment, esp. formed by a circle of wagons. **2** *Mil.* a park for armored vehicles. ● *v.* **1** *tr.* **a** form (vehicles) into a laager. **b** encamp (people) in a laager. **2** *intr.* encamp. [Afrik. f. Du. *leger*: see LEAGUER²]

Lab. *abbr.* **1** *Brit.* Labour Party. **2** Labrador.

lab /lab/ *n. colloq.* a laboratory. [abbr.]

labarum /lábərəm/ *n.* **1** a symbolic banner. **2** Constantine the Great's imperial standard, with Christian symbols added to Roman military symbols. [LL: orig. unkn.]
■ **1** see STANDARD *n.* 4.

labdanum /lábdənəm/ *n.* (also **ladanum** /ládənəm/) a gum resin from plants of the genus *Cistus*, used in perfumery, etc. [L f. Gk *ladanon* f. *lēdon* mastic]

labefaction /lábifákshən/ *n. literary* a shaking, weakening, or downfall. [L *labefacere* weaken f. *labi* fall + *facere* make]

label /láybəl/ *n. & v.* ● *n.* **1** a usu. small piece of paper, card, linen, metal, etc., for attaching to an object and giving its name, information about it, instructions for use, etc. **2** esp. *derog.* a short classifying phrase or name applied to a person, a work of art, etc. **3 a** a small fabric label sewn into a garment bearing the maker's name. **b** the logo, title, or trademark of esp. a fashion or recording company (*brought it out under their own label*). **c** the piece of paper in the center of a phonograph record describing its contents, etc. **4** an adhesive stamp on a parcel, etc. **5** a word placed before, after, or in the course of a dictionary definition, etc., to specify its subject, register, nationality, etc. **6** *Archit.* a dripstone. **7** *Heraldry* the mark of an eldest son, consisting of a superimposed horizontal bar with usu. three downward projections. ● *v.tr.* (**labeled, labeling**; esp. *Brit.* **labelled, labelling**) **1** attach a label to. **2** (usu. foll. by *as*) assign to a category (*labeled them as irresponsible*). **3 a** replace (an atom) by an atom of a usu. radioactive isotope as a means of identification. **b** replace an atom in (a molecule) or atoms in the molecules of (a substance). **4** (as **labeled** *adj.*) made identifiable by the replacement of atoms. □□ **labeler** *n.* [ME f. OF, = ribbon, prob. f. Gmc (as LAP¹)]
■ *n.* **1** ticket, sticker, stamp, imprint, hallmark, earmark, mark, marker, (price) tag, tally, nametag, name tape, nameplate, identification, identifier, ID, *Brit.* docket, bookplate, ex libris; care label; bar code. **2** name, denomination, designation, category, classification, characterization, description, term, tag, epithet;

sobriquet, nickname, *colloq.* handle, *formal* appellation, *sl.* moniker. **3** trademark, trade name, brand, logo, mark, device, design, *Brit. archaic* chop. ● *v.* **1** ticket, tag, stamp, imprint, hallmark, earmark, brand, mark, identify, *Brit.* docket. **2** name, denominate, designate, call, term, dub, brand, classify, categorize, pigeonhole, class, characterize, describe, portray, identify.

labia *pl.* of LABIUM.

labial /láybeeəl/ *adj. & n.* ● *adj.* **1 a** of the lips. **b** *Zool.* of, like, or serving as a lip, a liplike part, or a labium. **2** *Dentistry* designating the surface of a tooth adjacent to the lips. **3** *Phonet.* (of a sound) requiring partial or complete closure of the lips (e.g., *p, b, f, v, m, w*; and vowels in which lips are rounded, e.g., *oo* in moon). ● *n. Phonet.* a labial sound. □ **labial pipe** *Mus.* an organ pipe having lips; a flue pipe. □□ **labialism** *n.* **labialize** *v.tr.* **labially** *adv.* [med.L *labialis* f. L *labia* lips]

labiate /láybeeət, -ayt/ *n. & adj.* ● *n.* any plant of the family Labiatae, including mint and rosemary, having square stems and a corolla or calyx divided into two parts suggesting lips. ● *adj.* **1** *Bot.* of or relating to the Labiatae. **2** *Bot. & Zool.* like a lip or labium. [mod.L *labiatus* (as LABIUM)]

labile /láybil, -bil/ *adj. Chem.* (of a compound) unstable; liable to displacement or change, esp. if an atom or group is easily replaced by other atoms or groups. □□ **lability** /ləbílitee, lay-/ *n.* [ME f. LL *labilis* f. *labi* to fall]
■ see CHANGEABLE 1.

labio- /láybeeō/ *comb. form* of the lips. [as LABIUM]

labiodental /láybeeōdént'l/ *adj.* (of a sound) made with the lips and teeth, e.g., *f* and *v*.

labiovelar /láybeeōveélər/ *adj.* (of a sound) made with the lips and soft palate, e.g., *w*.

labium /láybeeəm/ *n.* (*pl.* **labia** /-beeə/) **1** (usu. in *pl.*) *Anat.* each of the two pairs of skin folds that enclose the vulva. **2** the lower lip in the mouthparts of an insect or crustacean. **3** a lip, esp. the lower one of a labiate plant's corolla. □ **labia majora** /məjáwrə/ the larger outer pair of labia (in sense 1). **labia minora** /mináwrə/ the smaller inner pair of labia (in sense 1). [L, = lip]

labor /láybər/ *n. & v.* (*Brit.* **labour**) ● *n.* **1 a** physical or mental work; exertion; toil. **b** such work considered as supplying the needs of a community. **2 a** workers, esp. manual, considered as a class or political force (*a dispute between capital and labor*). **b** (in the UK) (**Labour**) the Labour Party. **3** the process of childbirth, esp. the period from the start of uterine contractions to delivery (*has been in labor for three hours*). **4** a particular task, esp. of a difficult nature. ● *v.* **1** *intr.* work hard; exert oneself. **2** *intr.* (usu. foll. by *for*, or *to* + infin.) strive for a purpose (*labored to fulfill his promise*). **3** *tr.* **a** treat at excessive length; elaborate needlessly (*I will not labor the point*). **b** (as **labored** *adj.*) done with great effort; not spontaneous or fluent. **4** *intr.* (often foll. by *under*) suffer under (a disadvantage or delusion) (*labored under universal disapproval*). **5** *intr.* proceed with trouble or difficulty (*la-*

/.../ **pronunciation**   ● **part of speech**
□ **phrases, idioms, and compounds**
□□ **derivatives**   ■ **synonym section**
cross-references appear in SMALL CAPITALS or *italics*

833

bored slowly up the hill). **6** *intr.* (of a ship) roll or pitch heavily. **7** *tr. archaic* or *poet.* till (the ground). □ **labor camp** a prison camp enforcing a regime of hard labor. **Labor Day** the first Monday in September (or in some other countries May 1), celebrated in honor of working people. **labor force** the body of workers employed, often that at a single plant. **labor-intensive** (of a form of work) needing a large workforce. **labor in vain** make a fruitless effort. **labor market** the supply of labor with reference to the demand on it. **labor of Hercules** a task needing enormous strength or effort. **labor of love** a task done for pleasure, not reward. **Labour Party 1** a British political party formed to represent the interests of ordinary working people. **2** any similar political party in other countries. **labor union** an organized association of workers, often in a trade or profession, formed to protect and further their rights and interests. **lost labor** fruitless effort. [ME f. OF *labo(u)r*, *laborer* f. L *labor*, *-oris*, *laborare*]

■ *n.* **1** toil, (hard) work, exertion, effort, industry, slog, strain, drudgery, donkeywork, pains, trouble, slavery, *colloq.* sweat, grind, elbow grease, *Brit. colloq.* fag, *literary* travail, *Austral. sl.* yakka, *Brit. sl.* (hard) graft. **2 a** workers, workforce, employees, laborers, workmen, workpeople, working people, (labor) force, (the) factory floor, (the) shop floor, men, help; wage earners, (the) working class. **b** (*Labour*) see *Labour party* below. **3** childbirth, accouchement, confinement, *archaic* childbed, *formal* parturition, *literary* travail; labor pains, contractions, throes; delivery. **4** task, job, chore, undertaking, mission, assignment, stint, trial. ● *v.* **1, 2** work, toil, exert oneself, sweat, slave (away), peg away, slog (away), beaver (away), grind (away), drudge, strain, strive, struggle, *Brit. colloq.* swot, *literary* travail. **3 a** belabor, dwell on, overdo, overemphasize, harp on, overstress, (over)strain, stretch, force, press, push. **b** (**labored**) strained, forced, difficult, hard, laborious, heavy; overdone, excessive, overwrought, ornate, elaborate, overworked, overembellished, contrived, affected, artificial, unnatural. **4** (*labor under*) suffer under, endure, struggle with or under, bear, undergo, live *or* go through, submit to, be disadvantaged by. **5** work (one's way), struggle, grind, slog, plow, lumber, plod, trudge, tramp, make one's way. **6** see PITCH¹ *v.* 6. □ **labor camp** prison camp, concentration camp, *hist.* stalag. **labor force** see LABOR *n.* 2a above. **Labour party** the left, left-wingers, socialists.

laboratory /lábrətáwree/ *n.* (*pl.* **-ies**) a room or building fitted out for scientific experiments, research, teaching, or the manufacture of drugs and chemicals. [med.L *laboratorium* f. L *laborare* LABOR]

laborer /láybərər/ *n.* (*Brit.* **labourer**) **1** a person doing unskilled, usu. manual, work for wages. **2** a person who labors. [ME f. OF *laboureur* (as LABOR)]

■ **1** worker, workman, working man, laboring man, artisan, hand, blue-collar worker, manual worker, slave, drudge, coolie, roustabout, *hist.* serf, *Brit.* navvy; peasant, peon, fellah, *hist.* muzhik, kulak.

laborious /ləbáwreeəs/ *adj.* **1** needing hard work or toil (*a laborious task*). **2** (esp. of literary style) showing signs of toil; pedestrian; not fluent. □□ **laboriously** *adv.* **laboriousness** *n.* [ME f. OF *laborieus* f. L *laboriosus* (as LABOR)]

■ **1** arduous, strenuous, toilsome, difficult, tough, hard, stiff, Herculean, burdensome, onerous, ponderous, backbreaking, grueling, painful, exhausting, taxing, tiring, fatiguing, wearying, wearisome, uphill. **2** labored, strained, forced, artificial, ponderous, stilted, pedestrian, stiff, unnatural, wooden; deliberate, affected, studied.

laborsaving /láybərsáyving/ *adj.* (of an appliance, etc.) designed to reduce or eliminate work.

labour, etc. *Brit.* var. of LABOR, etc.

Labourite /láybərīt/ *n.* (in the UK) a member or follower of the Labour Party.

labra *pl.* of LABRUM.

Labrador /lábrədawr/ *n.* (in full **Labrador retriever**) **1** a retriever of a breed with a black or golden coat often used as a gun dog or as a guide for a blind person. **2** this breed. [*Labrador* in Canada]

labret /láybrit/ *n.* a piece of shell, bone, etc., inserted in the lip as an ornament. [LABRUM]

labrum /láybrəm/ *n.* (*pl.* **labra** /-brə/) the upper lip in the mouthparts of an insect. [L, = lip: rel. to LABIUM]

laburnum /ləbə́rnəm/ *n.* any small tree of the genus *Laburnum* with racemes of golden flowers yielding poisonous seeds. Also called *golden chain*. [L]

labyrinth /lábərinth/ *n.* **1** a complicated irregular network of passages or paths, etc.; a maze. **2** an intricate or tangled arrangement. **3** *Anat.* the complex arrangement of bony and membranous canals and chambers of the inner ear which constitute the organs of hearing and balance. □ **labyrinth fish** = GOURAMI. □□ **labyrinthian** /-rintheeən/ *adj.* **labyrinthine** /-rínthin, -thin/ *adj.* [F *labyrinthe* or L *labyrinthus* f. Gk *laburinthos*]

■ **1** maze; complex, network, web, crisscross, plexus, warren. **2** tangle, jungle, snarl, knot; see also TANGLE¹ *n.* □□ **labyrinthian, labyrinthine** mazelike, mazy, tortuous, convoluted, intricate, involute, complicated, complex, Byzantine, tangled, knotty; confusing, perplexing, puzzling, enigmatic, baffling.

LAC *abbr.* leading aircraftsman.

lac¹ /lak/ *n.* a resinous substance secreted as a protective covering by the lac insect, and used to make varnish and shellac. □ **lac insect** an Asian scale insect, *Laccifer lacca*, living in trees. [ult. f. Hind. *lākh* f. Prakrit *lakkha* f. Skr. *lākṣā*]

lac² var. of LAKH.

laccolith /lákəlith/ *n.* *Geol.* a lens-shaped intrusion of igneous rock which thrusts the overlying strata into a dome. [Gk *lakkos* reservoir + -LITH]

lace /lays/ *n.* & *v.* ● *n.* **1** a fine open fabric, esp. of cotton or silk, made by weaving thread in patterns and used esp. to trim blouses, underwear, etc. **2** a cord or leather strip passed through eyelets or hooks on opposite sides of a shoe, corset, etc., pulled tight and fastened. **3** braid used for trimming esp. dress uniform (*gold lace*). ● *v.* **1** *tr.* (usu. foll. by *up*) **a** fasten or tighten (a shoe, corset, etc.) with a lace or laces. **b** compress the waist of (a person) with a laced corset. **2** *tr.* flavor or fortify (coffee, beer, etc.) with a dash of liquor. **3** *tr.* (usu. foll. by *with*) **a** streak with color (*cheek laced with blood*). **b** interlace or embroider (fabric) with thread, etc. **4** *tr.* & (foll. by *into*) *intr. colloq.* lash; beat; defeat. **5** *tr.* (often foll. by *through*) pass (a shoelace, etc.) through. **6** *tr.* trim with lace. □ **lace glass** Venetian glass with lacelike designs. **lace pillow** a cushion placed on the lap and providing support in lacemaking. **lace-up** ● *n.* a shoe fastened with a lace. ● *attrib.adj.* (of a shoe, etc.) fastened by a lace or laces. [ME f. OF *laz, las, lacier* ult. f. L *laqueus* noose]

■ *n.* **1** openwork, filigree, tracery, net, netting, bobbinet, mesh, web; needlepoint, needlepoint lace, point lace, filet, bobbin lace, pillow lace, crochet, tatting, macramé. **2** shoelace, shoestring, bootlace, cord, string, thong, tie, lacing. **3** braid, edging, trimming, braiding, passementerie, rickrack, soutache, fringe, ruff, ruffle, lacing, *archaic* purfling, *hist.* tucker, *colloq.* scrambled eggs. ● *v.* **1** fasten, tighten, tie (up), do up, secure, knot, truss. **2** fortify, strengthen, flavor, season, spice (up), enliven, liven up, *colloq.* doctor. **3 a** streak, stripe, striate, line, mark, smear, daub. **b** interlace, embroider, thread, weave, interweave. **4** (*lace into*) see BEAT *v.* 1, 3a. **5** thread, string, weave; loop. **6** trim, decorate, embellish, garnish, elaborate, adorn, ornament.

lacemaker /láysmaykər/ *n.* a person who makes lace, esp. professionally. □□ **lacemaking** *n.*

lacerate /lásərayt/ *v.tr.* **1** mangle or tear (esp. flesh or tissue). **2** distress or cause pain to (the feelings, the heart, etc.). □□ **lacerable** *adj.* **laceration** /-ráyshən/ *n.* [L *lacerare* f. *lacer* torn]

■ **1** mangle, tear, rip, gash, cut, hack, slash, claw, wound, *archaic* or *rhet.* rend. **2** see HURT *v.* 2. □□ **laceration** see INJURY 1, TEAR¹ *n.* 1.

lacertilian /lásərtíleeən/ *n.* & *adj.* (also **lacertian** /ləsə́rshən/, **lacertine** /lásərtīn/) • *n.* any reptile of the suborder Lacertilia, including lizards. • *adj.* of or relating to the Lacertilia; lizardlike; saurian. [L *lacerta* lizard]

lacewing /láyswing/ *n.* a neuropterous insect.

lacewood /láyswŏod/ *n.* the wood of the plane tree.

laches /láchiz/ *n. Law* delay in performing a legal duty, asserting a right, claiming a privilege, etc. [ME f. AF *laches(se)*, OF *laschesse* f. *lasche* ult. f. L *laxus* loose]

lachryma Christi /lákrimə krístee/ *n.* any of various wines from the slopes of Mt. Vesuvius. [L, = Christ's tear]

lachrymal /lákriməl/ *adj.* & *n.* (also **lacrimal**) • *adj.* 1 *literary* of or for tears. 2 (usu. as **lacrimal**) *Anat.* concerned in the secretion of tears (*lacrimal canal*; *lacrimal duct*). • *n.* 1 = *lachrymal vase.* 2 (in *pl.*) (usu. as **lacrimals**) the lacrimal organs. □ **lachrymal vase** *hist.* a vial holding the tears of mourners at a funeral. [ME f. med.L *lachrymalis* f. L *lacrima* tear]

lachrymation /lákrimáyshən/ *n.* (also **lacrimation**) *formal* the flow of tears. [L *lacrimatio* f. *lacrimare* weep (as LACHRYMAL)]

lachrymator /lákrimaytər/ *n.* an agent irritating the eyes, causing tears.

lachrymatory /lákrimətáwree/ *adj.* & *n.* • *adj. formal* of or causing tears. • *n.* (*pl.* **-ies**) a name applied to vials of a kind found in ancient Roman tombs and thought to be lachrymal vases.

lachrymose /lákrimōs/ *adj. formal* given to weeping; tearful. □□ **lachrymosely** *adv.* [L *lacrimosus* f. *lacrima* tear]

■ see TEARFUL 1.

lacing /láysing/ *n.* 1 lace trimming, esp. on a uniform. 2 a laced fastening on a shoe or corsets. 3 *colloq.* a beating. 4 a dash of spirits in a beverage. □ **lacing course** a strengthening course built into an arch or wall.

■ 2 see LACE *n.* 2.

laciniate /ləsíneeət, -neeayt/ *adj.* (also **laciniated** /-aytid/) *Bot.* & *Zool.* divided into deep narrow irregular segments; fringed. □□ **laciniation** /-neeáyshən/ *n.* [L *lacinia* flap of a garment]

lack /lak/ *n.* & *v.* • *n.* (usu. foll. by *of*) an absence, want, or deficiency (*a lack of talent*; *felt the lack of warmth*). • *v.tr.* be without or deficient in (*lacks courage*). □ **for lack of** owing to the absence of (*went hungry for lack of money*). **lack for** lack. [ME *lac*, *lacen*, corresp. to MDu., MLG *lak* deficiency, MDu. *laken* to lack]

■ *n.* absence, want, deficiency, need, dearth, famine, scarcity, shortage, paucity, poverty, insufficiency, deficit, inadequacy, defect. • *v.* want (for), be deficient in, be *or* fall short of, be without, be *or* stand in want *or* need of; need, require.

lackadaisical /lákədáyzikəl/ *adj.* 1 unenthusiastic; listless; idle. 2 feebly sentimental and affected. □□ **lackadaisically** *adv.* **lackadaisicalness** *n.* [archaic *lackaday*, *-daisy* (int.): see ALACK]

■ 1 unenthusiastic, dull, apathetic, insouciant, uncaring, careless, casual, unconcerned, indifferent, blasé, cold, cool, lukewarm, tepid, halfhearted, Laodicean, phlegmatic, unemotional, unexcitable, impassive, uninterested, unimpressed, uninspired, unmoved, unresponsive; listless, lethargic, languorous, languid, lazy, sluggish, lifeless, spiritless, weak, weary; idle, indolent, shiftless, inactive, torpid, slothful, fainéant.

2 see AFFECTED 3.

lacker var. of LACQUER.

lackey /lákee/ *n.* & *v.* (also **lacquey**) • *n.* (*pl.* **-eys**) 1 *derog.* **a** a servile political follower. **b** an obsequious parasitical person. 2 **a** a (usu. liveried) footman or manservant. **b** a servant. • *v.tr.* (**-eys**, **-eyed**) *archaic* behave servilely to; dance attendance on. [F *laquais*, obs. *alaquais* f. Cat. *alacay* = Sp. ALCALDE]

■ 2 see SERVANT 1.

lacking /láking/ *adj.* 1 absent or deficient (*money was lacking*; *is lacking in determination*). 2 *colloq.* deficient in intellect; mentally subnormal.

■ 1 see DEFICIENT 1.

lackland /láklənd/ *n.* & *adj.* • *n.* 1 a person having no land. 2 (**Lackland**) a nickname for King John of England. • *adj.* having no land.

lackluster /láklustər/ *adj.* (*Brit.* **lacklustre**) 1 lacking in vitality, force, or conviction. 2 (of the eye) dull.

■ 1 drab, dull, lifeless, colorless, lusterless, dingy, dismal, dreary; unexciting, boring, tedious, uninteresting; prosaic, unimaginative, flat, one-dimensional, two-dimensional, insipid, vapid, bland, wishy-washy; undistinguished, indifferent, mediocre; halfhearted, unenthusiastic; flimsy, feeble, weak, puny, pale, poor, lame, unconvincing. 2 see DULL *adj.* 4b.

Laconian /ləkőneeən/ *n.* & *adj.* • *n.* an inhabitant or the dialect of ancient Laconia. • *adj.* of the Laconian dialect or people; Spartan. [L *Laconia* Sparta f. Gk *Lakōn* Spartan]

laconic /ləkónik/ *adj.* 1 (of a style of speech or writing) brief; concise; terse. 2 (of a person) laconic in speech, etc. □□ **laconically** *adv.* **laconicism** /-sizəm/ *n.* [L f. Gk *Lakōnikos* f. *Lakōn* Spartan, the Spartans being known for their terse speech]

■ see CONCISE. □□ **laconicism** see BREVITY.

laconism /lákənizəm/ *n.* 1 brevity of speech. 2 a short pithy saying. [Gk *lakōnismos* f. *lakōnizō* behave like a Spartan: see LACONIC]

lacquer /lákər/ *n.* & *v.* (also **lacker**) • *n.* 1 a sometimes colored liquid made of shellac dissolved in alcohol, or of synthetic substances, that dries to form a hard protective coating for wood, brass, etc. 2 *Brit.* = *hair spray.* 3 the sap of the lacquer tree used to varnish wood, etc. • *v.tr.* coat with lacquer. □ **lacquer tree** an E. Asian tree, *Rhus verniciflua*, the sap of which is used as a hard-wearing varnish for wood. □□ **lacquerer** *n.* [obs. F *lacre* sealing wax, f. unexpl. var. of Port. *laca* LAC[1]]

■ *n.* 1 see GLAZE *n.* 1. • *v.* see GLAZE *v.* 6.

lacquey var. of LACKEY.

lacrimal var. of LACHRYMAL.

lacrimation var. of LACHRYMATION.

lacrosse /ləkraws, -krós/ *n.* a game like hockey, but with a ball driven by, caught, and carried in a crosse. [F f. *la* the + CROSSE]

lactase /láktays/ *n. Biochem.* any of a group of enzymes that catalyze the hydrolysis of lactose to glucose and galactose. [F f. *lactose* LACTOSE]

lactate[1] /láktayt/ *v.intr.* (of mammals) secrete milk. [as LACTATION]

lactate[2] /láktayt/ *n. Chem.* any salt or ester of lactic acid.

lactation /laktáyshən/ *n.* 1 the secretion of milk by the mammary glands. 2 the suckling of young. [L *lactare* suckle f. *lac lactis* milk]

lacteal /lákteeəl/ *adj.* & *n.* • *adj.* 1 of milk. 2 conveying chyle or other milky fluid. • *n.* (in *pl.*) the lymphatic vessels of the small intestine which absorb digested fats. [L *lacteus* f. *lac lactis* milk]

lactescence /laktésəns/ *n.* 1 a milky form or appearance. 2 a milky juice. [L *lactescere* f. *lactēre* be milky (as LACTIC)]

lactescent /laktésənt/ *adj.* 1 milky. 2 yielding a milky juice.

lactic /láktik/ *adj. Chem.* of, relating to, or obtained from milk. □ **lactic acid** a clear, odorless, syrupy carboxylic acid formed in sour milk, and produced in the muscle tissues during strenuous exercise. [L *lac lactis* milk]

lactiferous /laktífərəs/ *adj.* yielding milk or milky fluid. [LL *lactifer* (as LACTIC)]

lacto- /láktō/ *comb. form* milk. [L *lac lactis* milk]

lactobacillus /láktōbəsíləs/ *n.* (*pl.* **-bacilli** /-lī/) *Biol.* any gram-positive, rod-shaped bacterium of the genus *Lactobacillus*, producing lactic acid from the fermentation of carbohydrates.

/ . . . / **pronunciation**   • **part of speech**
□ **phrases, idioms, and compounds**
□□ **derivatives**   ■ **synonym section**
cross-references appear in SMALL CAPITALS or *italics*

lactometer /laktómitər/ *n.* an instrument for testing the density of milk.

lactone /láktōn/ *n. Chem.* any of a class of cyclic esters formed by the elimination of water from a hydroxy-carboxylic acid. [G *Lacton*]

lactoprotein /láktōprŏteen/ *n.* the albuminous constituent of milk.

lactose /láktōs/ *n. Chem.* a sugar that occurs in milk, and is less sweet than sucrose. [as LACTO-]

lacuna /ləkyŏŏnə/ *n.* (*pl.* **lacunae** /-nee/ or **lacunas**) **1** a hiatus, blank, or gap. **2** a missing portion or empty page, esp. in an ancient manuscript, book, etc. **3** *Anat.* a cavity or depression, esp. in bone. □□ **lacunal** *adj.* **lacunar** *adj.* **lacunary** /lákyŏŏnéree, ləkyŏŏnəree/ *adj.* **lacunose** *adj.* [L, = pool, f. *lacus* LAKE¹]
  ▪ **1** see GAP *n.* 1.

lacustrine /ləkústrin/ *adj. formal* or *Biol.* **1** of or relating to lakes. **2** living or growing in or beside a lake. [L *lacus* LAKE¹, after *palustris* marshy]

LACW *abbr.* leading aircraftswoman.

lacy /láysee/ *adj.* (**lacier, laciest**) of or resembling lace fabric. □□ **lacily** *adv.* **laciness** *n.*

lad /lad/ *n.* **1 a** a boy or youth. **b** a young son. **2** (esp. in *pl.*) *Brit. colloq.* a man; a fellow, esp. a workmate, drinking companion, etc. (*he's one of the lads*). **3** *Brit. colloq.* a high-spirited fellow; a rogue (*he's a bit of a lad*). **4** *Brit.* a stableman (regardless of age). [ME *ladde*, of unkn. orig.]
  ▪ **1** youth, boy, son, child, adolescent, minor, teenager, juvenile, young man, youngster, schoolboy, schoolchild, infant, toddler, stripling, whippersnapper, *Ir.* spalpeen, *Sc.* laddie, *archaic* younker, *archaic or colloq.* young thing, *colloq.* kid, fellow, shaver, *dial.* young'un, *joc.* little man, *Brit. sl.* sprog; (street) urchin, gamin, guttersnipe.

ladanum var. of LABDANUM.

ladder /ládər/ *n. & v.* ● *n.* **1** a set of horizontal bars of wood or metal fixed between two uprights and used for climbing up or down. **2** *Brit.* a run in a stocking or sheer hose. **3 a** a hierarchical structure. **b** such a structure as a means of advancement, promotion, etc. ● *v. Brit.* **1** *intr.* (of a stocking, etc.) develop a ladder. **2** *tr.* cause a ladder in (a stocking, etc.). □ **ladder-back** an upright chair with a back resembling a ladder. **ladder stitch** transverse bars in embroidery. **ladder tournament** a sporting contest with each participant listed and entitled to a higher place by defeating the one above. [OE *hlǣd(d)er*, ult. f. Gmc: cf. LEAN¹]

laddie /ládee/ *n. colloq.* a young boy or lad.

lade /layd/ *v.* (*past part.* **laden** /láyd'n/) **1** *tr.* **a** put cargo on board (a ship). **b** ship (goods) as cargo. **2** *intr.* (of a ship) take on cargo. **3** *tr.* (as **laden** *adj.*) (usu. foll. by *with*) **a** (of a vehicle, donkey, person, tree, table, etc.) heavily loaded. **b** (of the conscience, spirit, etc.) painfully burdened with sin, sorrow, etc. [OE *hladan*]
  ▪ **1a, 2** see LOAD *v.* 1, 2. **3 a** (**laden**) see LOADED 1.

la-di-da /láadeedáa/ *adj. & n. colloq.* (also **la-de-da**) ● *adj.* pretentious or snobbish, esp. in manner or speech. ● *n.* **1** a la-di-da person. **2** la-di-da speech or manners. [imit. of an affected manner of speech]
  ▪ *adj.* see SUPERCILIOUS.

ladies *pl.* of LADY.

Ladin /lədéen/ *n.* the Rhaeto-Romanic dialect of the Engadine Valley in Switzerland. [Romansh, f. L *latinus* LATIN]

lading /láyding/ *n.* **1** a cargo. **2** the act or process of lading.

Ladino /lədéenō/ *n.* (*pl.* **-os**) **1** the Spanish dialect of the Sephardic Jews. **2** a mestizo or Spanish-speaking white person in Central America. [Sp., orig. = Latin, f. L (as LADIN)]

ladle /láyd'l/ *n. & v.* ● *n.* **1** a large, long-handled spoon with a cup-shaped bowl used for serving esp. soups and gravy. **2** a vessel for transporting molten metal in a foundry. ● *v.tr.* (often foll. by *out*) transfer (liquid) from one receptacle to another. □ **ladle out** distribute, esp. lavishly. □□ **ladleful** *n.* (*pl.* **-fuls**). **ladler** *n.* [OE *hlǣdel* f. *hladan* LADE]
  ▪ *n.* **1** see SCOOP *n.* 1. ● *v.* see SCOOP *v.* 1.

lady /láydee/ *n.* (*pl.* **-ies**) **1 a** a woman regarded as being of superior social status or as having the refined manners associated with this (cf. GENTLEMAN). **b** (**Lady**) a title used by peeresses, female relatives of peers, the wives and widows of knights, etc. **2** (often *attrib.*) a woman; a female person or animal (*ask that lady over there*; *lady butcher*; *lady dog*). **3** *colloq.* **a** a wife. **b** a man's girlfriend. **4** a ruling woman (*lady of the house*; *lady of the manor*). **5** (in *pl.* as a form of address) a female audience or the female part of an audience. **6** *hist.* a woman to whom a man, esp. a knight, is chivalrously devoted; a mistress. □ **the Ladies** (or **Ladies'**) *Brit.* a women's public restroom. □ **ladies' fingers** *Brit.* = OKRA (cf. *lady's finger*). **Ladies' Gallery** *Brit.* a public gallery in the House of Commons, reserved for women. **ladies'** (or **lady's**) **man** a man fond of female company; a seducer. **ladies' night 1** a function at a men's club, etc., to which women are invited. **2** an evening concert, sports event, etc., at which women are admitted free or for a reduced rate, etc. **ladies' room** a women's restroom in a hotel, office, etc. **Lady Bountiful** a patronizingly generous lady of the manor, etc. (a character in Farquhar's *The Beaux' Stratagem*). **lady chapel** (or **Lady Chapel**) a chapel in a large church or cathedral, usu. behind the high altar, dedicated to the Virgin Mary. **Lady Day** the Feast of the Annunciation, Mar. 25. **lady fern** a slender fern, *Athyrium filix-femina*. **lady-in-waiting** a lady attending a queen or princess. **lady-killer 1** a man very attractive to women. **2** a practiced and habitual seducer. **lady of the bedchamber** = *lady-in-waiting*. **lady of easy virtue** a sexually promiscuous woman; a prostitute. **lady of the evening** a prostitute. **lady's finger** = LADYFINGER (cf. *ladies' fingers*). **lady's maid** a lady's personal maidservant. **lady's** (or **lady**) **slipper** any orchidaceous plant of the genus *Cypripedium*, with a usu. yellow or pink slipper-shaped lip on its flowers. **lady's tresses** any white-flowered orchid of the genus *Spiranthes*. **my lady** *Brit.* a form of address used chiefly by servants, etc., to holders of the title "Lady." **my lady wife** *Brit. joc.* my wife. **old lady** *colloq.* **1** my mother. **2** a wife or girlfriend. **Our Lady** the Virgin Mary. □□ **ladyhood** *n.* [OE *hlǣfdige* f. *hlāf* LOAF¹ + (unrecorded) *dig-* knead, rel. to DOUGH): in *Lady Day*, etc., f. OE genit. *hlǣfdigan* (Our) Lady's]
  ▪ **1** see NOBLE *n.* 1. **2** see WOMAN 1. **3** see WOMAN 3.
  □ **ladies' man** see *charmer* (CHARM). **ladies' room** see TOILET 1. **lady-in-waiting** see WOMAN 9. **lady-killer** see *charmer* (CHARM). **lady's maid** see SERVANT 1.

ladybird /láydeebərd/ *n.* esp. *Brit.* = LADYBUG.

ladybug /láydeebug/ *n.* a coleopterous insect of the family Coccinellidae, with wing covers usu. of a reddish-brown color with black spots.

ladyfinger /láydeefinggər/ *n.* a finger-shaped sponge cake.

ladylike /láydeelīk/ *adj.* **1 a** with the modesty, manners, etc., of a lady. **b** befitting a lady. **2** (of a man) effeminate.
  ▪ **1** refined, cultured, polished, elegant, gracious, genteel, nice, courteous, polite, courtly, mannerly, well-mannered, well-bred, dignified, respectable, proper, correct, decorous, seemly, *joc.* couth; well-born, highborn, aristocratic, patrician, noble, blue-blooded, top-drawer, upper-class, *Brit.* county, *colloq.* posh, esp. *Brit. colloq.* U. **2** effeminate, unmanly, unmasculine, emasculate, precious, epicene, milky, womanly, girlish, feminine, namby-pamby, niminy-piminy, *archaic* feminal, *colloq.* campy, sissy, usu. *derog.* womanish, *sl.* limp-wristed.

ladylove /láydeeluv/ *n.* a man's sweetheart.

ladyship /láydeeship/ *n. archaic* being a lady. □ **her** (or **your** or **their**) **ladyship** (or **ladyships**) **1** a respectful form of reference or address to a titled lady or ladies. **2** *iron.* a form of reference or address to a woman thought to be giving herself airs.

laevo- esp. *Brit.* var. of LEVO-.

laevorotatory esp. *Brit.* var. of LEVOROTATORY.

laevulose esp. *Brit.* var. of LEVULOSE.

lag¹ /lag/ *v. & n.* ● *v.intr.* (**lagged, lagging**) **1** (often foll. by *behind*) fall behind; not keep pace. **2** *Billiards* make the preliminary strokes that decide which player shall begin. ● *n.* **1** a delay. **2** *Physics* a retardation in a current or movement. **b** the amount of this. □ **lag of tide** the interval by which a tide falls behind mean time at the 1st and 3rd quarters of the moon (cf. PRIMING²). □□ **lagger** n. [orig. = hindmost person, hang back: perh. f. a fanciful distortion of LAST¹ in a children's game (*fog, seg, lag,* = 1st, 2nd, last, in dial.)] ■ v. **1** fall behind, straggle, trail, hang back, linger, be in arrears, tail off *or* away, dawdle, dally, *colloq.* dillydally. ● n. **1** delay, interval, gap, hiatus, interruption, interlude, stop, stoppage, wait, suspension, lull, deferment, deferral, postponement, holdup. □□ **lagger** see LAGGARD n.

lag² /lag/ v. & n. ● v.tr. (**lagged, lagging**) enclose or cover in lagging. ● n. **1** the non-heat-conducting cover of a boiler, etc.; lagging. **2** a piece of this. [prob. f. Scand.: cf. ON *lögg* barrel-rim, rel. to LAY¹]

lag³ /lag/ n. & v. *Brit. sl.* ● n. (esp. as **old lag**) a habitual convict. ● v.tr. (**lagged, lagging**) **1** send to prison. **2** apprehend; arrest. [19th c.: orig. unkn.]

lagan /lágən/ n. goods or wreckage lying on the bed of the sea, sometimes with a marking buoy, etc., for later retrieval. [OF, perh. of Scand. orig., f. root of LIE¹, LAY¹]

lager /laágər/ n. a kind of beer, effervescent and light in color and body. □ **lager lout** *Brit. colloq.* a youth who behaves badly as a result of excessive drinking. [G *Lagerbier* beer brewed for keeping f. *Lager* store]

lagerphone /laágərfōn/ n. *Austral.* an improvised musical instrument employing beer bottle tops.

laggard /lágərd/ n. & adj. ● n. a dawdler; a person who lags behind. ● adj. dawdling; slow. □□ **laggardly** adj. & adv. **laggardness** n. [LAG¹] ■ n. dawdler, straggler, loiterer, slouch, sluggard, loafer, snail, plodder, slowpoke, *Brit.* slowcoach. ● adj. see SLOW adj. 1. □□ **laggardness** see *sluggishness* (SLUGGISH).

lagging /láging/ n. material providing heat insulation for a boiler, pipes, etc. [LAG²]

lagomorph /lágəmawrf/ n. *Zool.* any mammal of the order Lagomorpha, including hares and rabbits. [Gk *lagōs* hare + *morphē* form]

lagoon /ləgōōn/ n. **1** a stretch of salt water separated from the sea by a low sandbank, coral reef, etc. **2** the enclosed water of an atoll. **3** a small freshwater lake near a larger lake or river. **4** an artificial pool for the treatment of effluent or to accommodate an overspill from surface drains during heavy rain. [F *lagune* or It. & Sp. *laguna* f. L *lacuna*: see LACUNA]

lahar /laáhaar/ n. a mudflow composed mainly of volcanic debris. [Jav.]

laic /láyik/ adj. & n. ● adj. nonclerical; lay; secular; temporal. ● n. formal a lay person; a noncleric. □□ **laical** adj. **laically** adv. [LL f. Gk *laïkos* f. *laos* people] ■ adj. see SECULAR adj. 1.

laicity /layísitee/ n. the status or influence of the laity.

laicize /láyisīz/ v.tr. **1** make (an office, etc.) tenable by lay people. **2** subject (a school or institution) to the control of lay people. **3** secularize. □□ **laicization** n.

laid *past* and *past part.* of LAY¹.

lain *past part.* of LIE¹.

lair¹ /lair/ n. & v. ● n. **1 a** a wild animal's resting place. **b** a person's hiding place; a den (*tracked him to his lair*). **2** a place where domestic animals lie down. **3** *Brit.* a shed or enclosure for cattle on the way to market. ● v. **1** *intr.* go to or rest in a lair. **2** *tr.* place (an animal) in a lair. [OE *leger* f. Gmc: cf. LIE¹] ■ n. **1 a** den, burrow, hole, nest, tunnel, cave, hollow, covert. **b** hideaway, hiding place, den, nest, refuge, cover, retreat, *Brit.* snuggery, *colloq.* hideout, hideyhole, sanctum.

lair² /lair/ n. & v. *Austral. sl.* ● n. a youth or man who dresses flashily and shows off. ● v.intr. (often foll. by *up*) behave or dress like a lair. □□ **lairy** adj. [*lair* back-form. f. *lairy*; *lairy* alt. f. LEERY]

laird /laird/ n. *Sc.* a landed proprietor. □□ **lairdship** n. [Sc. form of LORD]

laissez-aller /lesay-aaláy/ n. (also **laisser-aller**) unconstrained freedom; an absence of constraint. [F, = let go] ■ see LAISSEZ-FAIRE.

laissez-faire /lésayfáir/ n. (also **laisser-faire**) the theory or practice of governmental abstention from interference in the workings of the market, etc. [F, = let act] ■ free enterprise, free market economics, nonintervention, noninterference, deregulation, free trade; freedom, individualism, laissez-aller.

laissez-passer /lésaypaasáy/ n. (also **laisser-passer**) a document allowing the holder to pass; a permit. [F, = let pass]

laity /láy-itee/ n. (usu. prec. by *the*; usu. treated as *pl.*) **1** lay people, as distinct from the clergy. **2** nonprofessionals. [ME f. LAY² + -ITY]

lake¹ /layk/ n. a large body of water surrounded by land. □ **the Great Lakes** the Lakes Superior, Huron, Michigan, Erie, and Ontario, along the boundary of the US and Canada. **Lake District** (or **the Lakes**) the region of many lakes in NW England. **lake dweller** a prehistoric inhabitant of lake dwellings. **lake dwellings** prehistoric huts built on piles driven into the bed or shore of a lake. **Lake Poets** Coleridge, Southey, and Wordsworth, who lived in and were inspired by the Lake District. □□ **lakeless** adj. **lakelet** n. [ME f. OF *lac* f. L *lacus* basin, pool, lake] ■ see POOL¹ n. 1.

lake² /layk/ n. **1** a reddish coloring orig. made from lac (*crimson lake*). **2** a complex formed by the action of dye and mordants applied to fabric to fix color. **3** any insoluble product of a soluble dye and mordant. [var. of LAC¹]

Lakeland terrier /láyklənd/ n. **1** a terrier of a small stocky breed originating in the Lake District of NW England. **2** this breed.

lakeside /láyksīd/ *attrib.adj.* beside a lake.

lakh /laak/ n. (also **lac**) *Ind.* (usu. foll. by of) a hundred thousand (rupees, etc.). [Hind. *lākh* f. Skr. *lakṣa*]

Lallan /lálən/ n. & adj. *Sc.* ● n. (now usu. **Lallans**) a Lowland Scots dialect, esp. as a literary language. ● adj. of or concerning the Lowlands of Scotland. [var. of LOWLAND]

lallation /laláyshən/ n. **1** the pronunciation of *r* as *l*. **2** imperfect speech, esp. that of young children. [L *lallare* lallatsing a lullaby]

lallygag var. of LOLLYGAG.

Lam. *abbr.* Lamentations (Old Testament).

lam¹ /lam/ v. (**lammed, lamming**) *sl.* **1** *tr.* thrash; hit. **2** *intr.* (foll. by *into*) hit (a person, etc.) hard with a stick, etc. [perh. f. Scand.: cf. ON *lemja* beat so as to LAME]

lam² /lam/ n. □ **on the lam** *sl.* in flight, esp. from the police. [20th c.: orig. unkn.]

lama /laámə/ n. a Tibetan or Mongolian Buddhist monk. □□ **Lamaism** n. **Lamaist** n. & adj. [Tibetan *blama* (with silent b)]

Lamarckism /ləmaárkizəm/ n. the theory of evolution devised by Lamarck, French botanist and zoologist (d. 1829), based on the inheritance of acquired characteristics. □□ **Lamarckian** n. & adj.

lamasery /laáməseree/ n. (pl. **-ies**) a monastery of lamas. [F *lamaserie* irreg. f. *lama* LAMA] ■ see MONASTERY.

Lamaze method /ləmaáz/ n. *Med.* a method for childbirth in which breathing exercises and relaxation techniques are used to control pain and facilitate delivery. [for F physician Fernand *Lamaze* (1890-1957)]

lamb /lam/ n. & v. ● n. **1** a young sheep. **2** the flesh of a lamb as food. **3** a mild or gentle person, esp. a young child. ● v. **1 a** *tr.* (in *passive*) (of a lamb) be born. **b** *intr.* (of a ewe) give birth to lambs. **2** *tr.* tend (lambing ewes). □ **The Lamb** (or **The Lamb of God**) a name for Christ (see John 1:29) (cf. AGNUS DEI). **lamb's lettuce** esp. *Brit.* = *corn salad* (see CORN¹). **lamb's tails** = *burro's tail* (see BURRO). **lamb's**

/.../ **pronunciation** ● **part of speech**
□ **phrases, idioms, and compounds**
□□ **derivatives** ■ **synonym section**
cross-references appear in SMALL CAPITALS or *italics*

wool soft, fine wool from a young sheep used in knitted garments, etc. **like a lamb** meekly; obediently. □□ **lamber** *n.* **lambkin** *n.* **lamblike** *adj.* [OE *lamb* f. Gmc]
■ □□ **lamblike** see PASSIVE 2.

lambada /ləmbáːdə/ *n.* a fast erotic Brazilian dance in which couples dance with their hips touching each other.

lambaste /lambáyst/ *v.tr.* (also **lambast** /-bást/) *colloq.* **1** thrash; beat. **2** criticize severely. [LAM¹ + BASTE³]
■ **1** thrash, give a person a thrashing *or* beating, trounce, whip, scourge, flog, lash, strap, welt, leather, horsewhip, cane, birch, *colloq.* thwack, whack, give a person a hiding, whale, *sl.* belt, paste, tan a person's hide; beat, bludgeon, drub, maul, pummel, batter, bash, baste, belabor, cudgel, club, clout, thump, *sl.* clobber, whop, wallop, rough up, give a person a going-over. **2** censure, rebuke, berate, scold, rate, upbraid, chastise, reprimand, admonish, reprove, belabor, reproach, reprehend, revile, attack, abuse, rail at, harangue, excoriate, castigate, keelhaul, flay, rap a person over *or* on the knuckles, slap a person on the wrist, take to task, call down, rake over the coals, *archaic or literary* chide, *colloq.* dress down, give a person a dressing-down, call a person on the carpet, tell off, lay into, bawl out, chew out, esp. *Brit. colloq.* tick off, carpet, *literary* objurgate, *sl.* bullyrag, *Austral.* & *NZ sl.* go off at, *Brit. sl.* have a go at, slag off.

lambda /lámdə/ *n.* **1** the eleventh letter of the Greek alphabet (Λ, λ). **2** (as λ) the symbol for wavelength. [ME f. Gk *la(m)bda*]

lambent /lámbənt/ *adj.* **1** (of a flame or a light) playing on a surface with a soft radiance but without burning. **2** (of the eyes, sky, etc.) softly radiant. **3** (of wit, etc.) lightly brilliant. □□ **lambency** *n.* **lambently** *adv.* [L *lambere lambent-* lick]
■ **1** see BRIGHT *adj.* 1. □□ **lambency** see GLOW *n.* 1. **lambently** see BRIGHT *adv.*

lambert /lámbərt/ *n.* a former unit of luminance, equal to the emission or reflection of one lumen per square centimeter. [J. H. *Lambert*, Ger. physicist d. 1777]

lambrequin /lámbrikin, lámbər-/ *n.* **1** a short piece of drapery hung over the top of a door or a window or draped on a mantelpiece. **2** *Heraldry* = MANTLING. [F f. Du. (unrecorded) *lamperkin*, dimin. of *lamper* veil]
■ **1** see DRAPERY 2.

lambskin /lámskin/ *n.* a prepared skin from a lamb with the wool on or as leather.

lame /laym/ *adj.* & *v.* ● *adj.* **1** disabled, esp. in the foot or leg; limping; unable to walk normally (*lame in his right leg*). **2 a** (of an argument, story, excuse, etc.) unconvincing; unsatisfactory; weak. **b** (of verse, etc.) halting. ● *v.tr.* **1** make lame; disable. **2** harm permanently. □ **lame duck 1** a disabled or weak person. **2** a defaulter in the stock market. **3** esp. *Brit.* a firm, etc., in financial difficulties. **4** an official (esp. the president) in the final period of office, after the election of a successor. □□ **lamely** *adv.* **lameness** *n.* **lamish** *adj.* [OE *lama* f. Gmc]
■ *adj.* **1** disabled, handicapped, limping, game, *Vet.* spavined, *archaic* halt, *Brit. sl.* gammy. **2 a** unconvincing, unpersuasive, feeble, puny, weak, flimsy, thin, lackluster, halfhearted, half-baked, pale, poor, ineffective, unsatisfactory, unacceptable, inadequate, insufficient, disappointing. **b** halting, awkward, hesitant, uneven, stiff, stilted, stumbling. ● *v.* cripple, hamstring, disable, handicap, incapacitate, lay up, invalid; maim, damage, hurt, injure, impair, ruin, wreck, mar, spoil, mutilate, *colloq.* crock (up).

lamé /lamáy/ *n.* & *adj.* ● *n.* a fabric with gold or silver threads interwoven. ● *adj.* (of fabric, a dress, etc.) having such threads. [F]

lamebrain /láymbrayn/ *n. colloq.* a stupid person. □□ **lamebrain** or **lamebrained** *adj.*
■ see FOOL¹ *n.* 1.

lamella /ləmélə/ *n.* (*pl.* **lamellae** /-lee/ or **lamellas**) **1** a thin layer, membrane, scale, or platelike tissue or part, esp. in bone tissue. **2** *Bot.* a membranous fold in a chloroplast. □□ **lamellar** *adj.* **lamellate** /ləmélayt, lámə-/ *adj.* **lamelli-**

form *adj.* **lamellose** /-lōs/ *adj.* [L, dimin. of *lamina*: see LAMINA]
■ **1** see SCALE¹ *n.* 1. □□ **lamellar, lamellate** see SCALY.

lamellibranch /ləmélibrangk/ *n.* any aquatic mollusk having a shell formed of two pieces or valves, e.g., a mussel or oyster. Also called BIVALVE. [LAMELLA + Gk *bragkhia* gills]

lamellicorn /ləmélikawrn/ *n.* & *adj.* ● *n.* any beetle of the family Lamellicornia, having lamelliform antennae, including the stag beetle, cockchafer, dung beetle, etc. ● *adj.* having lamelliform antennae. [mod.L *lamellicornis* f. L *lamella* (see LAMELLA) + *cornu* horn]

lament /ləmént/ *n.* & *v.* ● *n.* **1** a passionate expression of grief. **2** a song or poem of mourning or sorrow. ● *v.tr.* (also *absol.*) **1** express or feel grief for or about; regret (*lamented the loss of his ticket*). **2** (as **lamented** *adj.*) a conventional expression referring to a recently dead person (*your late lamented father*). □ **lament for** (or **over**) mourn or regret. □□ **lamenter** *n.* **lamentingly** *adv.* [L *lamentum*]
■ *n.* **1** lamentation, moan, wail, ululation, whine, jeremiad, *colloq. or dial.* yammer, *literary or archaic* plaint; grief, sorrow, mourning, wake, *poet.* dole. **2** lamentation, keen, dirge, elegy, requiem, monody, threnody, epicedium, *Sc. & Ir.* coronach. ● *v.* **1** mourn, bemoan, bewail, wail, ululate, weep (over), grieve (for *or* over), keen (over), sorrow (for *or* over), sigh (for *or* over), *archaic or poet.* plain; regret, rue, deplore, deprecate, complain (of *or* about).

lamentable /ləméntəbəl, lámənt-/ *adj.* **1** (of an event, fate, condition, character, etc.) deplorable; regrettable. **2** *archaic* mournful. □□ **lamentably** *adv.* [ME f. OF *lamentable* or L *lamentabilis* (as LAMENT)]
■ **1** deplorable, wretched, piteous, miserable, regrettable, pitiful, forlorn, pitiable, pathetic, unfortunate, tragic, sad, sorrowful, terrible, awful, intolerable. **2** see MOURNFUL 1.

lamentation /láməntáyshən/ *n.* **1** the act or an instance of lamenting. **2** a lament. **3** (**Lamentations**) an Old Testament book concerning the destruction of Jerusalem in the 6th c. BC. [ME f. OF *lamentation* or L *lamentatio* (as LAMENT)]
■ **1, 2** see LAMENT *n.*

lamina /láminə/ *n.* (*pl.* **laminae** /-nee/ or **laminas**) a thin plate or scale, e.g., of bone, stratified rock, or vegetable tissue. □□ **laminose** *adj.* [L]
■ see SCALE¹ *n.* 1.

laminar /láminər/ *adj.* **1** consisting of laminae. **2** *Physics* (of a flow) taking place along constant streamlines, not turbulent.
■ **1** see SCALY.

laminate *v., n., & adj.* ● *v.* /láminayt/ **1** *tr.* beat or roll (metal) into thin plates. **2** *tr.* overlay with metal plates, a plastic layer, etc. **3** *tr.* manufacture by placing layer on layer. **4** *tr. & intr.* split or be split into layers or leaves. ● *n.* /láminət/ a laminated structure or material, esp. of layers fixed together to form rigid or flexible material. ● *adj.* /láminət/ in the form of lamina or laminae. □□ **lamination** /-náyshən/ *n.* **laminator** *n.* [LAMINA + -ATE², -ATE³]
■ *v.* **2** see PLATE *v.* 1.

lamington /lámingtən/ *n. Austral. & NZ* a square of sponge cake coated in chocolate icing and desiccated coconut. [C.W. Ballie, Baron *Lamington*, Governor of Queensland, d. 1940]

Lammas /láməs/ *n.* (in full **Lammas Day**) the first day of August, formerly observed as harvest festival. [OE *hlāfmæsse* (as LOAF¹, MASS²)]

lammergeier /lámərgiːər/ *n.* (also **lammergeyer**) a large vulture, *Gypaetus barbatus*, with a very large wingspan (often of 9–10 ft) and dark, beardlike feathers on either side of its beak. [G *Lämmergeier* f. *Lämmer* lambs + *Geier* vulture]

lamp /lamp/ *n.* & *v.* ● *n.* **1** a device for producing a steady light, esp.: **a** an electric bulb, and usu. its holder and shade or cover (*bedside lamp*; *bicycle lamp*). **b** an oil lamp. **c** a usu. glass holder for a candle. **d** a gas jet and mantle. **2** a source of spiritual or intellectual inspiration. **3** *poet.* the sun, the moon, or a star. **4** a device producing esp. ultraviolet or

infrared radiation as a treatment for various complaints.
● *v.* **1** *intr. poet.* shine. **2** *tr.* supply with lamps; illuminate.
3 *tr. sl.* look at. □ **lamp chimney** a glass cylinder enclosing and making a draft for an oil lamp's flame. **lamp standard** *Brit.* = LAMPPOST. □□ **lampless** *adj.* [ME f. OF *lampe* f. LL *lampada* f. accus. of L *lampas* torch f. Gk]
■ *n.* **1** see LIGHT[1] *n.* 4a.

lampblack /lámpblak/ *n.* a pigment made from soot.

lamplight /lámplit/ *n.* light given by a lamp or lamps.
■ see LIGHT[1] *n.* 2.

lamplighter /lámplitər/ *n. hist.* **1** a person who lights street lamps. **2** a spill for lighting lamps. □ **like a lamplighter** *Brit.* with great speed.

lampoon /lampoon/ *n.* & *v.* ● *n.* a satirical attack on a person, etc. ● *v.tr.* satirize. □□ **lampooner** *n.* **lampoonery** *n.* **lampoonist** *n.* [F *lampon,* conjectured to be f. *lampons* let us drink f. *lamper* gulp down f. *laper* LAP[3]]
■ *n.* burlesque, caricature, satire, satirization, parody, pasquinade, squib, mockery, *colloq.* takeoff, send-up.
● *v.* satirize, burlesque, caricature, parody, *archaic* squib, *colloq.* take off, send up; mock, ridicule, scoff at, laugh at, deride, guy, poke fun at, run down, have a go at.

lamppost /lámp-pōst/ *n.* a tall post supporting an outdoor light.

lamprey /lámpree, -pray/ *n.* (*pl.* **-eys**) any eellike aquatic vertebrate of the family Petromyzonidae, without scales, paired fins, or jaws, but having a sucker mouth with horny teeth and a rough tongue. [ME f. OF *lampreie* f. med.L *lampreda*: cf. LL *lampetra* perh. f. L *lambere* lick + *petra* stone]

lampshade /lámpshayd/ *n.* a translucent cover for a lamp used to soften or direct its light.
■ see SHADE *n.* 7, 8.

LAN /lan/ *abbr. local area network.*

Lancastrian /langkástreeən/ *n.* & *adj.* ● *n.* **1** a native of Lancashire or Lancaster in NW England. **2** *hist.* a follower of the House of Lancaster or of the Red Rose party supporting it in the Wars of the Roses (cf. YORKIST). ● *adj.* of or concerning Lancashire or Lancaster, or the House of Lancaster.

lance /lans/ *n.* & *v.* ● *n.* **1 a** a long weapon with a wooden shaft and a pointed steel head, used by a horseman in charging. **b** a similar weapon used for spearing a fish, killing a harpooned whale, etc. **2** a metal pipe supplying oxygen to burn metal. **3** = LANCER. ● *v.tr.* **1** *Surgery* prick or cut open with a lancet. **2** pierce with a lance. **3** *poet.* fling; launch. □ **break a lance** (usu. foll. by *for, with*) *Brit.* argue. **lance corporal 1** marine corps rank between private first class and corporal. **2** *Brit.* lowest ranked corporal in the army. **lance sergeant** *Brit.* a corporal acting as sergeant. **lance snake** = FER DE LANCE. [ME f. OF *lancier* f. L *lancea*: *lance corporal* on analogy of obs. *lancepesade* lowest grade of NCO ult. f. It. *lancia spezzata* broken lance]
■ *n.* **1** spear, pike, javelin, shaft, assegai, *literary* steel; gaff, gig, leister. ● *v.* **1** prick, cut (open), pierce, puncture, incise, slit. **2** pierce, impale, transfix, spear, run through, skewer, spit, spike, stick, stab, penetrate.

lancelet /lánslit/ *n.* any small, nonvertebrate fishlike chordate of the family Branchiostomidae, that burrows in sand. [LANCE *n.* + -LET, with ref. to its thin form]

lanceolate /lánseeəlayt/ *adj.* shaped like a lance head, tapering to each end. [LL *lanceolatus* f. *lanceola* dimin. of *lancea* lance]

lancer /lánsər/ *n.* **1** *hist.* a soldier of a cavalry regiment armed with lances. **2** (in *pl.*) **a** a quadrille for 8 or 16 pairs. **b** the music for this. [F *lancier* (as LANCE)]

lancet /lánsit/ *n.* a small, broad, two-edged surgical knife with a sharp point. □ **lancet arch** (or **window**) a narrow arch (or window) with a pointed head. □□ **lanceted** *adj.* [ME f. OF *lancette* (as LANCE)]

lancewood /lánswŏŏd/ *n.* a tough elastic wood from a W. Indian tree *Oxandra lanceolata,* used for carriage shafts, fishing rods, etc.

Land /laant/ *n.* (*pl.* **Länder** /léndər/) a province of Germany or Austria. [G (as LAND)]

land /land/ *n.* & *v.* ● *n.* **1** the solid part of the earth's surface (opp. SEA, WATER, AIR). **2 a** an expanse of country; ground; soil. **b** such land in relation to its use, quality, etc., or (often prec. by *the*) as a basis for agriculture (*building land; this is good land; works on the land*). **3** a country, nation, or state (*land of hope and glory*). **4 a** landed property. **b** (in *pl.*) estates. **5** the space between the rifling grooves in a gun. **6** *Sc.* a building containing several dwellings. **7** *S.Afr.* ground fenced off for tillage. **8** a strip of plow land or pastureland parted from others by drain furrows. ● *v.* **1 a** *tr. & intr.* set or go ashore. **b** *intr.* (often foll. by *at*) disembark (*landed at the harbor*). **2** *tr.* bring (an aircraft, its passengers, etc.) to the ground or the surface of water. **3** *intr.* (of an aircraft, bird, parachutist, etc.) alight on the ground or water. **4** *tr.* bring (a fish) to land. **5** *tr. & intr.* (also *refl.*; often foll. by *up*) *colloq.* bring to, reach, or find oneself in a certain situation, place, or state (*landed himself in jail; landed up in Alaska; landed her in trouble; landed up penniless*). **6** *tr. colloq.* **a** deal (a person, etc.) a blow, etc. (*landed him one in the eye*). **b** (foll. by *with*) present (a person) with (a problem, job, etc.). **7** *tr.* set down (a person, cargo, etc.) from a vehicle, ship, etc. **8** *tr. colloq.* win or obtain (a prize, job, etc.) esp. against strong competition. □ **how the land lies** what is the state of affairs. **in the land of the living** *joc.* still alive. **land agency** *Brit.* **1** the stewardship of an estate. **2** an agency for the sale, etc., of estates. **land agent** *Brit.* **1** the steward of an estate. **2** an agent for the sale of estates. **land bank** a bank that finances land development esp. for agriculture. **land breeze** a breeze blowing toward the sea from the land, esp. at night. **land bridge** a neck of land joining two large landmasses. **land crab** a crab, *Cardisoma guanhumi,* that lives in burrows inland and migrates in large numbers to the sea to breed. **land force** (or **forces**) armies, not naval or air forces. **land girl** *Brit.* a woman doing farmwork, esp. in wartime. **land-grabber** an illegal seizer of land, esp. a person who took the land of an evicted Irish tenant. **land mine 1** an explosive mine laid in or on the ground. **2** a parachute mine. **land of cakes** *Brit.* Scotland. **land office** a government office recording dealings in public land. **land-office business** enormous trade. **land of Nod** sleep (with pun on the phr. in Gen. 4:16). **land on one's feet** attain a good position, job, etc., by luck. **Land's End** the westernmost point of Cornwall and the SW tip of England. **land rail** = CORNCRAKE. **land tax** *hist.* a tax assessed on landed property. **land wind** = *land breeze.* **land yacht** a vehicle with wheels and sails for recreational use on a beach, etc. □□ **lander** *n.* **landless** *adj.* **landward** *adj.* & *adv.* **landward** *adv.* [OE f. Gmc]
■ *n.* **1** earth, (solid) ground, dry land, terra firma. **2 a** dirt, earth, soil, ground, turf, sod, loam. **b** plot, patch, tract, parcel (of land), property, area, lot, *Brit.* allotment. **3** country, nation, state, territory, domain, fatherland, motherland, homeland, native land, *formal esp. Law* realm. **4** property, ground(s), landed property, *Law* immovables, real property or estate; acreage, estate(s), *Law* realty. ● *v.* **1, 3** arrive, alight, light, touch or come or go down, splash down, settle (on or upon), come to rest; berth, dock, disembark, debark, go ashore, dismount, deplane. **2** bring or take down, *colloq.* ditch. **4** catch, hook, net, take, capture. **5** (*tr.*) get, bring, lead; (*intr.*) arrive, come, go, find oneself, appear, turn up, end up, finish up, *colloq.* show or roll up, blow in, fetch up. **6** deal, give, administer, dispense; present, leave, provide, supply, furnish, *literary* mete out. **7** set or put down, unload, offload, disembark, debark; discharge, empty, dump. **8** get, secure, obtain, acquire, procure, pick up, get hold of; win, gain, earn, receive, come into, *colloq.* pull down.

/.../ **pronunciation**   ● **part of speech**
□ **phrases, idioms, and compounds**
□□ **derivatives**   ■ **synonym section**
cross-references appear in SMALL CAPITALS or *italics*

□ **land on one's feet** strike oil, *colloq.* strike it rich, hit the jackpot.

landau /lándow, -daw/ *n.* a four-wheeled enclosed carriage with a removable front cover and a back cover that can be raised and lowered. [*Landau* near Karlsruhe in Germany, where it was first made]

landaulet /lánd'lét/ *n.* **1** a small landau. **2** *hist.* a car with a folding hood over the rear seats.

landed /lándid/ *adj.* **1** owning land (*landed gentry*). **2** consisting of, including, or relating to land (*landed property*).

Länder *pl.* of LAND.

landfall /lándfawl/ *n.* the approach to land, esp. for the first time on a sea or air journey.

landfill /lándfil/ *n.* **1** waste material, etc., used to landscape or reclaim areas of ground. **2** the process of disposing of rubbish in this way. □ **landfill site** a place where rubbish is disposed of by burying it in the ground.

landform /lándfawrm/ *n.* a natural feature of the earth's surface.

landgrave /lándgrayv/ *n.* (*fem.* **landgravine** /-grəveen/) *hist.* **1** a count having jurisdiction over a territory. **2** the title of certain German princes. □□ **landgraviate** /-gráyveeət, -veeayt/ *n.* [MLG *landgrave*, MHG *lantgrāve* (as LAND, G *Graf* COUNT²)]

landholder /lándhōldər/ *n.* the proprietor or, esp., the tenant of land. □□ **landholding** *n., adj.*
■ see PROPRIETOR 1.

landing /lánding/ *n.* **1 a** the act or process of coming to land. **b** an instance of this. **c** (also **landing place**) a place where ships, etc., land. **2 a** a platform between two flights of stairs, or at the top or bottom of a flight. **b** a passage leading to upstairs rooms. □ **landing craft** any of several types of craft esp. designed for putting troops and equipment ashore. **landing gear** the undercarriage of an aircraft. **landing net** a net for landing a large fish which has been hooked. **landing stage** a platform, often floating, on which goods and passengers are disembarked. **landing strip** an airstrip.
■ **1 a, b** touchdown, splashdown; belly landing, crash landing, forced landing, pancake landing, three-point landing; disembarkation, debarkation, arrival. **c** landing place, landing stage, dock, pier, jetty, wharf, quay, slipway.

landlady /lándlaydee/ *n.* (*pl.* **-ies**) **1** a woman who rents land, a building, part of a building, etc., to a tenant. **2** a woman who keeps a boardinghouse, an inn, etc.
■ **1** see LANDLORD 1. **2** proprietress, manageress, hostess, publican, innkeeper, hotelier, restaurateur, lady of the house, mistress.

ländler /léndlər/ *n.* (*pl.* same or **ländlers**) **1** an Austrian dance in triple time, a precursor of the waltz. **2** the music for a ländler. [G f. *Landl* Upper Austria]

landline /lándlin/ *n.* a means of telecommunication over land.

landlocked /lándlokt/ *adj.* almost or entirely enclosed by land.

landloper /lándlōpər/ *n.* esp. *Sc.* a vagabond. [MDu. *landlooper* (as LAND, *loopen* run, formed as LEAP)]

landlord /lándlawrd/ *n.* **1** a man who rents land, a building, part of a building, etc., to a tenant. **2** a man who keeps a boardinghouse, an inn, etc.
■ **1** (property) owner, lessor, landowner, householder, landholder, freeholder. **2** host, publican, proprietor, innkeeper, hotelier, manager, restaurateur, *archaic* mine host.

landlubber /lándlubər/ *n.* a person unfamiliar with the sea or sailing.

landmark /lándmaark/ *n.* **1 a** a conspicuous object in a district, etc. **b** an object marking the boundary of an estate, country, etc. **2** an event, change, etc., marking a stage or turning point in history, etc. **3** *attrib.* serving as a landmark; signifying an important change, development, etc.
■ **1** feature, oriflamme, monument; cairn, obelisk, *Archit.* terminus, *Gk Antiq.* herm. **2** turning point, watershed, divide, milestone. **3** (*attrib.*) critical, crucial, pivotal, seminal, important, historic, significant, ground

breaking, precedent-setting, momentous, notable, noteworthy, major.

landmass /lándmas/ *n.* a large area of land.

landowner /lándōnər/ *n.* an owner of land. □□ **landowning** *adj. & n.*
■ see PROPRIETOR 1.

landscape /lándskayp/ *n. & v.* ● *n.* **1** natural or imaginary scenery, as seen in a broad view. **2** (often *attrib.*) a picture representing this; the genre of landscape painting. **3** (in graphic design, etc.) a format in which the width of an illustration, etc., is greater than the height (cf. PORTRAIT). ● *v.tr.* (also *absol.*) improve (a piece of land) by landscape gardening. □ **landscape gardener** (or **architect**) a person who plans the layout of landscapes, esp. extensive grounds. **landscape gardening** (or **architecture**) the laying out of esp. extensive grounds to resemble natural scenery. [MDu. *landscap* (as LAND, -SHIP)]
■ *n.* **1** prospect, view, scene, aspect, vista, panorama; countryside, scenery, terrain.

landscapist /lándskaypist/ *n.* an artist who paints landscapes.

landslide /lándslid/ *n.* **1** the sliding down of a mass of land from a mountain, cliff, etc. **2** an overwhelming majority for one side in an election.
■ **1** landslip, earthslip, avalanche, mud slide.

landslip /lándslip/ *n.* = LANDSLIDE 1.

landsman /lándzmən/ *n.* (*pl.* **-men**) a nonsailor.

lane /layn/ *n.* **1** a narrow, often rural, road, street, or path. **2** a division of a road for a stream of traffic (*three-lane highway*). **3** a strip of track or water for a runner, rower, or swimmer in a race. **4** a path or course prescribed for and regularly followed by a ship, aircraft, etc. (*ocean lane*). **5** a gangway between crowds of people, objects, etc. □ **it's a long lane that has no turning** change is inevitable. [OE: orig. unkn.]
■ **1** see ROAD¹ 1, WALK *n.* 3a.

langlauf /laánglowf/ *n.* cross-country skiing; a cross-country skiing race. [G, = long run]

langouste /loNgoost, lónggōost/ *n.* a crawfish or spiny lobster. [F]

langoustine /lóNgōosteen, lángga-/ *n.* any of several varieties of small lobsters, used as food. [F]

lang syne /lang zin, sín/ *adv. & n. Sc.* ● *adv.* in the distant past. ● *n.* the old days (cf. AULD LANG SYNE). [= long since]

language /lánggwij/ *n.* **1** the method of human communication, either spoken or written, consisting of the use of words in an agreed way. **2** the language of a particular community or country, etc. (*speaks several languages*). **3 a** the faculty of speech. **b** a style or the faculty of expression; the use of words, etc. (*his language was poetic; hasn't the language to express it*). **c** (also **bad language**) coarse, crude, or abusive speech (*didn't like his language*). **4** a system of symbols and rules for writing computer programs or algorithms. **5** any method of expression (*the language of mime; sign language*). **6** a professional or specialized vocabulary. **7** literary style. □ **language laboratory** a room equipped with tape recorders, etc., for learning a foreign language. **language of flowers** a set of symbolic meanings attached to different flowers. **speak the same language** have a similar outlook, manner of expression, etc. [ME f. OF *langage* ult. f. L *lingua* tongue]
■ **1, 5** communication, intercourse, interaction; words, speech, diction, articulation, expression, talk. **2** tongue, dialect, idiolect, patois, idiom, parlance, argot, slang, vocabulary, terminology, vernacular, *colloq.* lingo. **3 a, b** speech, utterance, articulation; expression, diction, style, phraseology, phrasing, turn of phrase; vocabulary, wording; enunciation, pronunciation, accent; facility, fluency, *colloq.* gift of gab. **c** (**bad language**) see ABUSE *n.* 2. **6** jargon, cant, argot, idiom, slang, parlance, patter, idiolect, *colloq.* lingo; vocabulary, terminology. **7** see STYLE *n.* 2, 3. □ **speak the same language** see eye to eye, see things the same way, be two of a kind, be soul mates, be of one *or* the same mind, *colloq.* be on the same wavelength.

langue de chat /lóNG də shaá/ *n.* a very thin finger-shaped crisp cookie or piece of chocolate. [F, = cat's tongue]

langue d'oc /loNG dáw-ee, -eel/ *n.* the form of medieval French spoken south of the Loire, the basis of modern Provençal. [OF *langue* language f. L *lingua* tongue + *de* of + *oc* (f. L *hoc*) the form for *yes*]

langue d'oïl /loNG dáw-ee, -eel/ *n.* medieval French as spoken north of the Loire, the basis of modern French. [as LANGUE D´OC + *oïl* (f. L *hoc ille*) the form for *yes*]

languid /lánggwid/ *adj.* **1** lacking vigor; idle; inert; apathetic. **2** (of ideas, etc.) lacking force; uninteresting. **3** (of trade, etc.) slow-moving; sluggish. **4** faint; weak. □□ **languidly** *adv.* **languidness** *n.* [F *languide* or L *languidus* (as LANGUISH)]

  ■ **1** see IDLE *adj.* 1. **3** see LAZY 3. **4** see FEEBLE 1.
  □□ **languidness** see LETHARGY 1.

languish /lánggwish/ *v.intr.* **1** be or grow feeble; lose or lack vitality. **2** put on a sentimentally tender or languid look. □ **languish for** droop or pine for. **languish under** suffer under (esp. depression, confinement, etc.). □□ **languisher** *n.* **languishingly** *adv.* **languishment** *n.* [ME f. OF *languir*, ult. f. L *languēre*, rel. to LAX]

  ■ **1** see ROT *v.* 2b.

languor /lánggər/ *n.* **1** lack of energy or alertness; inertia; idleness; dullness. **2** faintness; fatigue. **3** a soft or tender mood or effect. **4** an oppressive stillness (of the air, etc.). □□ **languorous** *adj.* **languorously** *adv.* [ME f. OF f. L *languor -oris* (as LANGUISH)]

  ■ **1** see INERTIA 2. **2** see FATIGUE *n.* 1. □□ **languorous** see INERT 3.

langur /lunggŏŏr/ *n.* any of various Asian long-tailed monkeys esp. of the genus *Presbytis*. [Hindi]

laniary /láynee-eree, lán-/ *adj. & n.* ● *adj.* (of a tooth) adapted for tearing; canine. ● *n.* (*pl.* **-ies**) a laniary tooth. [L *laniarius* f. *lanius* butcher f. *laniare* to tear]

laniferous /lənífərəs/ *adj.* wool-bearing. [L *lanifer, -ger* f. *lana* wool]

  ■ see WOOLLY *adj.* 1.

lank /langk/ *adj.* **1** (of hair, grass, etc.) long, limp, and straight. **2** thin and tall. **3** shrunken; spare. □□ **lankly** *adv.* **lankness** *n.* [OE *hlanc* f. Gmc: cf. FLANK, LINK¹]

lanky /lángkee/ *adj.* (**lankier, lankiest**) (of limbs, a person, etc.) ungracefully thin and long or tall. □□ **lankily** *adv.* **lankiness** *n.*

  ■ spindly, gangling, gangly, rangy, lank; thin, lean, gaunt, skinny, twiggy, scraggy, bony.

lanner /lánər/ *n.* a S. European falcon, *Falco biarmicus*, esp. the female. [ME f. OF *lanier* perh. f. OF *lanier* cowardly, orig. = weaver f. L *lanarius* wool merchant f. *lana* wool]

lanneret /lánərét/ *n.* a male lanner, smaller than the female. [ME f. OF *laneret* (as LANNER)]

lanolin /lánəlin/ *n.* a fat found naturally on sheep's wool and used purified for cosmetics, etc. [G f. L *lana* wool + *oleum* oil]

lansquenet /lánskənət/ *n.* **1** a card game of German origin. **2** a German mercenary soldier in the 16th–17th c. [F f. G *Landsknecht* (as LAND, *Knecht* soldier f. OHG *knèht*: see KNIGHT)]

lantana /lántánə/ *n.* any evergreen shrub of the genus *Lantana*, with usu. yellow or orange flowers. [mod.L]

lantern /lántərn/ *n.* **1 a** a lamp with a transparent usu. glass case protecting a candle flame, etc. **b** a similar electric, etc., lamp. **c** its case. **2 a** a raised structure on a dome, room, etc., glazed to admit light. **b** a similar structure for ventilation, etc. **3** the light chamber of a lighthouse. **4** = *magic lantern*. □ **lantern fish** any marine fish of the family Myctophidae, having small light organs on the head and body. **lantern fly** (*pl.* **flies**) any tropical homopterous insect of the family Fulgoridae, formerly thought to be luminous. **lantern-jawed** having lantern jaws. **lantern jaws** long thin jaws and chin, giving a hollow look to the face. **lantern slide** a slide for projection by a magic lantern, etc. (see SLIDE *n.* 5b). **lantern wheel** a lantern-shaped gearwheel; a trundle. [ME f. OF *lanterne* f. L *lanterna* f. Gk *lamptēr* torch, lamp]

■ **1a, b** see LIGHT¹ *n.* 4a.

lanthanide /lánthənid/ *n. Chem.* an element of the lanthanide series. □ **lanthanide series** a series of 15 metallic elements from lanthanum to lutetium in the periodic table, having similar chemical properties: also called *rare earths* (see RARE¹). [G *Lanthanid* (as LANTHANUM)]

lanthanum /lánthənəm/ *n. Chem.* a silvery metallic element of the lanthanide series which occurs naturally and is used in the manufacture of alloys. ¶ Symb.: **La.** [Gk *lanthanō* escape notice, from having remained undetected in cerium oxide]

lanugo /lənŏŏgō, -nyŏŏ-/ *n.* fine, soft hair, esp. that which covers the body and limbs of a human fetus. [L, = down f. *lana* wool]

lanyard /lányərd/ *n.* **1** a cord hanging around the neck or looped around the shoulder, esp. of a scout or sailor, etc., to which a knife, a whistle, etc., may be attached. **2** *Naut.* a short rope or line used for securing, tightening, etc. **3** a cord attached to a breech mechanism for firing a gun. [ME f. OF *laniere, lasniere*: assim. to YARD¹]

Laodicean /layódiseeən/ *adj. & n.* ● *adj.* lukewarm or half-hearted, esp. in religion or politics. ● *n.* such a person. [L *Laodicea* in Asia Minor (with ref. to the early Christians there: see Rev. 3:16)]

  ■ *adj.* see LUKEWARM 2.

Laotian /layóshən, lóushən/ *n. & adj.* ● *n.* **1 a** a native or national of Laos in SE Asia. **b** a person of Laotian descent. **2** the language of Laos. ● *adj.* of or relating to Laos or its people or language.

lap¹ /lap/ *n.* **1 a** the front of the body from the waist to the knees of a sitting person (*sat on her lap; caught it in his lap*). **b** the clothing, esp. a skirt, covering the lap. **c** the front of a skirt held up to catch or contain something. **2** a hollow among hills. **3** a hanging flap on a garment, a saddle, etc. □ **in** (or **on**) **a person's lap** as a person's responsibility. **in the lap of the gods** (of an event, etc.) open to chance; beyond human control. **in the lap of luxury** in extremely luxurious surroundings. **lap robe** a blanket, etc., used for warmth on a journey. □□ **lapful** *n.* (*pl.* **-fuls**). [OE *læppa* fold, flap]

lap² /lap/ *n. & v.* ● *n.* **1 a** one circuit of a racetrack, etc. **b** a section of a journey, etc. (*finally we were on the last lap*). **2 a** an amount of overlapping. **b** an overlapping or projecting part. **3 a** a layer or sheet (of cotton, etc., being made) wound on a roller. **b** a single turn of rope, silk, thread, etc., around a drum or reel. **4** a rotating disk for polishing a gem or metal. ● *v.* (**lapped, lapping**) **1** *tr.* lead or overtake (a competitor in a race) by one or more laps. **2** *tr.* (often foll. by *about, around*) coil, fold, or wrap (a garment, etc.) around esp. a person. **3** *tr.* (usu. foll. by *in*) enfold or wrap (a person) in clothing, etc. **4** *tr.* (as **lapped** *adj.*) (usu. foll. by *in*) protectively encircled; enfolded caressingly. **5** *tr.* surround (a person) with an influence, etc. **6** *intr.* (usu. foll. by *over*) project; overlap. **7** *tr.* cause to overlap. **8** *tr.* polish (a gem, etc.) with a lap. □ **lap joint** the joining of rails, shafts, etc., by halving the thickness of each at the joint and fitting them together. **lap-weld** *v.tr.* weld with overlapping edges. ● *n.* such a weld. [ME, prob. f. LAP¹]

  ■ *n.* **1** a circuit, orbit, round, circle, tour, trip, revolution. **b** see LEG *n.* 7. **2** b flap, projection, overlap.
  ● *v.* **3** see SWATHE *v.* 6, **7** see OVERLAP *v.* 1, 2, PROJECT *v.* 2.

lap³ /lap/ *v. & n.* ● *v.* (**lapped, lapping**) **1** *tr.* **a** (also *absol.*) (usu. of an animal) drink (liquid) with the tongue. **b** (usu. foll. by *up, down*) consume (liquid) greedily. **c** (usu. foll. by *up*) consume (gossip, praise, etc.) greedily. **2 a** *tr.* (of water) move or beat upon (a shore) with a rippling sound as of lapping. **b** *intr.* (of waves, etc.) move in ripples; make a lapping sound. ● *n.* **1 a** the process or an act of lapping. **b** the

---

/.../ **pronunciation**	● **part of speech**
□ **phrases, idioms, and compounds**	
□□ **derivatives**	■ **synonym section**
cross-references appear in SMALL CAPITALS or *italics*	

amount of liquid taken up. **2** the sound of wavelets on a beach. **3** liquid food for dogs. **4** *sl.* **a** a weak beverage. **b** any liquor. [OE *lapian* f. Gmc]

■ *v.* **1 a, b** lick up, drink, slurp; gulp (down), swallow, swill, guzzle, toss off, *colloq.* swig, *literary* quaff, *sl.* knock back; consume, soak (up). **c** (*lap up*) enjoy, bask in; accept, believe, credit, swallow (whole), *colloq.* fall for, *sl.* buy. **2 b** wash, splash, ripple, plash, break, roll, purl. ● *n.* **1** lick, slurp, gulp, swill, *colloq.* swig. **2** wash, splash, ripple, plash.

laparoscope /lápərəskṓp/ *n. Surgery* a fiber-optic instrument inserted through the abdominal wall to give a view of the organs in the abdomen. □□ **laparoscopy** /-róskəpee/ *n.* (*pl.* **-ies**). [Gk *lapara* flank + -SCOPE]

laparotomy /lápərótəmee/ *n.* (*pl.* **-ies**) a surgical incision into the abdominal cavity for exploration or diagnosis. [Gk *lapara* flank + -TOMY]

lapdog /lápdawg/ *n.* a small pet dog.

lapel /ləpél/ *n.* the part of a coat, jacket, etc., folded back against the front around the neck opening. □□ **lapelled** or **lapeled** *adj.* [LAP¹ + -EL]

lapicide /lápisíd/ *n.* a person who cuts or engraves on stone. [L *lapicida* irreg. f. *lapis -idis* stone: see -CIDE]

lapidary /lápideree/ *adj. & n.* ● *adj.* **1** concerned with stone or stones. **2** engraved upon stone. **3** (of writing style) dignified and concise, suitable for inscriptions. ● *n.* (*pl.* **-ies**) a cutter, polisher, or engraver of gems. [ME f. L *lapidarius* f. *lapis -idis* stone]

lapilli /ləpílí/ *n.pl.* stone fragments ejected from volcanoes. [It. f. L, pl. dimin. of *lapis* stone]

lapis lazuli /lápis lázōōlee, lázyə-, lázhə-/ *n.* **1** a blue mineral containing sodium aluminum silicate and sulfur, used as a gemstone. **2** a bright blue pigment formerly made from this. **3** its color. [ME f. L *lapis* stone + med.L *lazuli* genit. of *lazulum* f. Pers. (as AZURE)]

Laplander /láplandər/ *n.* **1** a native or national of Lapland. **2** a person of this descent. [*Lapland* f. Sw. *Lappland* (as LAPP, LAND)]

Lapp /lap/ *n. & adj.* ● *n.* **1** a member of a nomadic Mongol people of N. Scandinavia. **2** the language of this people. ● *adj.* of or relating to the Lapps or their language. [Sw. *Lapp*, perh. orig. a term of contempt: cf. MHG *lappe* simpleton]

lappet /lápit/ *n.* **1** a small flap or fold of a garment, etc. **2** a hanging or loose piece of flesh, such as a lobe or wattle. □□ **lappeted** *adj.* [LAP¹ + -ET¹]
■ **1** see FLAP *n.* 1.

Lappish /lápish/ *adj. & n.* ● *adj.* = LAPP *adj.* ● *n.* the Lapp language.

lapse /laps/ *n. & v.* ● *n.* **1** a slight error; a slip of memory, etc. **2** a weak or careless decline into an inferior state. **3** (foll. by *of*) an interval or passage of time (*after a lapse of three years*). **4** *Law* the termination of a right or privilege through disuse or failure to follow appropriate procedures. ● *v.intr.* **1** fail to maintain a position or standard. **2** (foll. by *into*) fall back into an inferior or previous state. **3** (of a right or privilege, etc.) become invalid because it is not used or claimed or renewed. **4** (as **lapsed** *adj.*) (of a person or thing) that has lapsed. □ **lapse rate** *Meteorol.* the rate at which the temperature falls with increasing altitude. □□ **lapser** *n.* [L *lapsus* f. *labi laps-* glide, slip, fall]
■ *n.* **1** slip, error, mistake, fault, oversight, omission, peccadillo, *lapsus linguae or calami*; stumble, blunder, botch, gaffe, solecism, *colloq.* slipup, blooper, flub, *sl.* fluff, goof, boo-boo, bloomer, *Brit. sl.* clanger, boob. **2** decline, lowering, deterioration, degeneration, diminution, drop, fall, slump, descent. **3** gap, break, interval, intermission, interruption, pause, lull, lacuna, hiatus, space, time lag, period; wait, delay. ● *v.* **1, 2** relapse, slip (back), revert, fall (back *or* off), drop (off), diminish; sink, slump, decline, subside, deteriorate, degenerate; stumble, trip up. **3** run out, be up, be discontinued, become void, expire, terminate, end, come to an end, finish, cease, stop, peter out, die,

esp. *Law* determine. **4** (**lapsed**) invalid, (null and) void, worthless; fallen, failed.

lapstone /lápstōn/ *n.* a shoemaker's stone held in the lap and used to beat leather on.

lapstrake /lápstrayk/ *n. & adj.* ● *n.* a clinker-built boat. ● *adj.* clinker-built.

lapsus calami /lápsəs káləmī, -mee/ *n.* (*pl.* same) a slip of the pen. [L: see LAPSE]

lapsus linguae /lápsəs línggwee/ *n.* a slip of the tongue. [L: see LAPSE]
■ see TRIP *n.* 2.

laptop /láptop/ *n.* (often *attrib.*) a microcomputer that is portable and suitable for use while traveling.

lapwing /lápwing/ *n.* a plover, *Vanellus vanellus*, with black and white plumage, crested head, and a shrill cry. [OE *hléapewince* f. *hléapan* LEAP + WINK: assim. to LAP¹, WING]

larboard /laárbərd/ *n. & adj. Naut. archaic* = PORT³. [ME *lade-*, *ladde-*, *lathe-* (perh. = LADE + BOARD): later assim. to *starboard*]

larceny /laársənee/ *n.* (*pl.* **-ies**) the theft of personal property. **grand larceny** *Law* larceny in which the value of the stolen property exceeds a certain legally established limit. □□ **larcener** *n.* **larcenist** *n.* **larcenous** *adj.* [OF *larcin* f. L *latrocinium* f. *latro* robber, mercenary f. Gk *latreus*]
■ see THEFT 1. □□ **larcenous** see LAWLESS 2.

larch /laarch/ *n.* **1** a deciduous coniferous tree of the genus *Larix*, with bright foliage and producing tough wood. **2** (in full **larchwood**) its wood. [MHG *larche* ult. f. L *larix -icis*]

lard /laard/ *n. & v.* ● *n.* the internal fat of the abdomen of pigs, esp. when rendered and clarified for use in cooking and pharmacy. ● *v.tr.* **1** insert strips of fat or bacon in (meat, etc.) before cooking. **2** (foll. by *with*) embellish (talk or writing) with foreign or technical terms. [ME f. OF *lard* bacon f. L *lardum*, *laridum*, rel. to Gk *larinos* fat]

larder /laárdər/ *n.* **1** a room or cupboard for storing food. **2** a wild animal's store of food, esp. for winter. [ME f. OF *lardier* f. med.L *lardarium* (as LARD)]

lardoon /laárdoon/ *n.* (also **lardon** /-d'n/) a strip of fat bacon used to lard meat. [ME f. F *lardon* (as LARD)]

lardy /laárdee/ *adj.* like or with lard. □ **lardy-cake** *Brit.* a cake made with lard, currants, etc.
■ see GREASY 1.

lares /láreez, laár-/ *n.pl. Rom.Hist.* the household gods. □ **lares and penates** the home. [L]

large /laarj/ *adj. & n.* ● *adj.* **1** of considerable or relatively great size or extent. **2** of the larger kind (*the large intestine*). **3** of wide range; comprehensive. **4** pursuing an activity on a large scale (*large farmer*). ● *n.* (**at large**) **1** at liberty. **2** as a body or whole (*popular with the people at large*). **3** (of a narration, etc.) at full length and with all details. **4** without a specific target (*scatters insults at large*). **5** representing a whole area and not merely a part of it (*councilwoman at large*). □ **in large** on a large scale. **large as life** see LIFE. **large-minded** liberal; not narrow-minded. **larger than life** see LIFE. **large-scale** made or occurring on a large scale or in large amounts. □□ **largeness** *n.* **largish** *adj.* [ME f. OF f. fem. of L *largus* copious]
■ *adj.* **1, 2** big, great, wide, broad, beamy, long, tall, high, capacious, roomy, spacious, voluminous, king-size, extensive, sizable, substantial, considerable, ample, biggish, man-size(d); bigger, greater, major, main, principal; bulky, hefty, stout, thickset, chunky, stocky, heavyset, brawny, husky, sturdy, muscular, strapping, beefy, burly, solid, weighty, heavy, ponderous, mighty, *colloq.* hulking, hunky, whacking, thumping, *sl.* whopping; corpulent, fat, obese, rotund, portly, plump, adipose, overweight, gross, outsize, oversize(d); see also IMMENSE 1. **3** wide, wide-ranging, extensive, comprehensive, far-reaching, sweeping, widespread, broad, expansive, exhaustive, thorough, in-depth, all-out. **4** large-scale, grand, macro-, major, *attrib.* mass; epic, heroic, Homeric. ● *n.* (**at large**) **1** see FREE *adj.* 3b. **2** as a whole, collectively, in the aggregate, in the lump, in a body, altogether, over all,

overall. **3** see *at length* 1 (LENGTH). **4** see *at random* (RANDOM). □ **large-scale** see LARGE *adj.* 4 above.

largely /laárjlee/ *adv.* to a great extent; principally (*is largely due to laziness*).

■ to a great extent, in great part, in great measure, mostly, chiefly, mainly, principally, by and large; as a rule, generally, in general, in the main, on the whole, pretty much, essentially, at bottom, basically, in essence, fundamentally.

largesse /laarzhés/ *n.* (also **largess**) **1** money or gifts freely given, esp. on an occasion of rejoicing, by a person in high position. **2** generosity; beneficence. [ME f. OF *largesse* ult. f. L *largus* copious]

■ **1** gifts, presents, grants, bonuses, endowments, favor(s), contributions, donations, handouts, gratuities, bounty, *hist.* alms. **2** generosity, beneficence, munificence, bounty, liberality, openhandedness, lavishness, benevolence, *poet.* bounteousness; philanthropy, charity, support, subvention, aid, help, subsidy.

larghetto /laargétō/ *adv., adj., & n. Mus.* ● *adv. & adj.* in a fairly slow tempo. ● *n.* (*pl.* **-os**) a larghetto passage or movement. [It., dimin. of LARGO]

largo /laárgō/ *adv., adj., & n. Mus.* ● *adv. & adj.* in a slow tempo and dignified in style. ● *n.* (*pl.* **-os**) a largo passage or movement. [It., = broad]

lariat /láreeət/ *n.* **1** a lasso. **2** a tethering rope, esp. used by cowboys. [Sp. *la reata* f. *reatar* tie again (as RE-, L *aptare* adjust f. *aptus* APT, fit)]

■ **1** see LASSO *n.*

lark¹ /laark/ *n.* **1** any small bird of the family Alaudidae with brown plumage, elongated hind claws and tuneful song, esp. the skylark. **2** any of various similar birds such as the meadowlark. [OE *lāferce, lǣwerce*, of unkn. orig.]

lark² /laark/ *n. & v. colloq.* ● *n.* **1** a frolic or spree; an amusing incident; a joke. **2** *Brit.* a type of activity, affair, etc. (*fed up with this digging lark*). ● *v.intr.* (foll. by *about*) play tricks; frolic. □□ **larky** *adj.* **larkiness** *n.* [19th c.: orig. uncert.]

■ *n.* **1** frolic, escapade, adventure, caper, fling, romp, rollick, revel, antic, laugh, *colloq.* spree, giggle, scream; joke, gag, jape, game, trick, prank, horseplay, shenanigan(s), mischief, practical joke, booby trap, hoax, *colloq.* put-on. ● *v.* **1** (*lark about*) jape, fool (about *or* around), mess about *or* around, *colloq.* kid, *Brit. colloq.* muck about *or* around; frolic, caper, romp, revel, rollick, play (about *or* around), sport, gambol, skylark, *sl.* cavort.

larkspur /laárkspur/ *n.* any of various plants of the genus *Consolida*, with a spur-shaped calyx.

larn /laarn/ *v. colloq.* or *joc.* **1** *intr.* = LEARN. **2** *tr.* teach (*that'll larn you*). [dial. form of LEARN]

larrikin /lárikin/ *n. Austral.* a hooligan. [also Engl. dial.: perh. f. the name *Larry* (pet-form of *Lawrence*) + -KIN]

larrup /lárəp/ *v.tr. colloq.* thrash. [dial.: perh. f. LATHER]

larva /laárvə/ *n.* (*pl.* **larvae** /-vee/) **1** the stage of development of an insect between egg and pupa, e.g., a caterpillar. **2** an immature form of other animals that undergo some metamorphosis, e.g., a tadpole. □□ **larval** *adj.* **larvicide** /-visīd/ *n.* [L, = ghost, mask]

laryngeal /lərínjəl, -jeeəl/ *adj.* **1** of or relating to the larynx. **2** *Phonet.* (of a sound) made in the larynx.

laryngitis /lárinjítis/ *n.* inflammation of the larynx. □□ **laryngitic** /-jítik/ *adj.*

laryngoscope /lərínggəskōp, -rínjə-/ *n.* an instrument for examining the larynx, or for inserting a tube through it.

laryngotomy /láringgótəmee/ *n.* (*pl.* **-ies**) a surgical incision of the larynx, esp. to provide an air passage when breathing is obstructed.

larynx /láringks/ *n.* (*pl.* **larynges** /lərínjeez/ or **larynxes**) the hollow muscular organ forming an air passage to the lungs and holding the vocal cords in humans and other mammals. [mod.L f. Gk *larugx -ggos*]

lasagna /ləzaányə/ *n.* (also **lasagne**) pasta in the form of sheets or wide ribbons, esp. as cooked and layered with ground meat and cheese sauce. [It., pl. of *lasagna* f. L *lasanum* cooking pot]

lascar /láskər/ *n.* an E. Indian sailor. [ult. f. Urdu & Pers. *laškar* army]

lascivious /ləsíveeəs/ *adj.* **1** lustful. **2** inciting to or evoking lust. □□ **lasciviously** *adv.* **lasciviousness** *n.* [ME f. LL *lasciviosus* f. L *lascivia* lustfulness f. *lascivus* sportive, wanton]

■ **1** lustful, randy, lecherous, sexy, licentious, lewd, dirty, prurient, salacious, libidinous, erotic, sensual, lubricious, promiscuous, depraved, dissolute, ruttish, goatish, wanton, debauched, hot, *formal* concupiscent, *sl.* horny. **2** pornographic, obscene, blue, indecent, gross, coarse, vile, offensive, ribald, bawdy, suggestive, lurid, salacious, risqué, sexy, smutty, dirty, filthy, *euphem.* adult, *sl.* horny.

lase /layz/ *v.intr.* **1** function as or in a laser. **2** (of a substance) undergo the physical processes employed in a laser. [backform. f. LASER]

laser /láyzər/ *n.* a device that generates an intense beam of coherent monochromatic radiation in the infrared, visible, or ultraviolet region of the electromagnetic spectrum, by stimulated emission of photons from an excited source. □ **laser disc** = DISK 4b. [*l*ight *a*mplification by *s*timulated *e*mission of *r*adiation: cf. MASER]

laservision /láyzərvizhən/ *n.* a system for the reproduction of video signals recorded on a disk with a laser. [LASER + VISION, after TELEVISION]

lash /lash/ *v. & n.* ● *v.* **1** *intr.* make a sudden whiplike movement with a limb or flexible instrument. **2** *tr.* beat with a whip, rope, etc. **3** *intr.* pour or rush with great force. **4** *intr.* (foll. by *at, against*) strike violently. **5** *tr.* castigate in words. **6** *tr.* urge on as with a lash. **7** *tr.* (foll. by *down, together*, etc.) fasten with a cord, rope, etc. **8** *tr.* (of rain, wind, etc.) beat forcefully upon. ● *n.* **1 a** a sharp blow made by a whip, rope, etc. **b** (prec. by *the*) punishment by beating with a whip, etc. **2** the flexible end of a whip. **3** (usu. in *pl.*) an eyelash. □ **lash out 1** (often foll. by *at*) speak or hit out angrily. **2** *Brit.* spend money extravagantly; be lavish. **lash-up** a makeshift or improvised structure or arrangement. □□ **lasher** *n.* **lashingly** *adv.* (esp. in senses 4–5 of *v.*). **lashless** *adj.* [ME: prob. imit.]

■ *v.* **1, 2** whip, flail, thrash, thresh; (*tr.*) flog, beat, switch, scourge, horsewhip, strap, leather, flick, crack, *colloq.* thwack, lambaste, whack, give a person a (good) hiding *or* thrashing *or* drubbing *or* belting, whale, *sl.* belt, tan a person's hide. **3** pour, rush, gush, flow, flood, stream, spurt, spew, cascade, rain, teem, bucket, pelt. **4, 8** crash, beat, thrash, pound, dash, hit, strike, batter, pelt, *colloq.* thwack, whack. **5** see LAMBASTE 2. **6** see URGE *v.* 1. **7** fasten, tie, bind, attach, secure, rope, fix, strap, make fast. ● *n.* **1 a** stroke, blow, strike, clout, hit, smack, thump, crack, lick, *archaic* stripe, *colloq.* whack, thwack, *sl.* belt; slash, cut. **b** (*the lash*) whipping, flogging, flagellation. **2** whip, scourge, thong, quirt, bullwhip, horsewhip, kourbash, rawhide, sjambok, esp. *Austral.* pizzle, *Bibl.* scorpion, *hist.* rope's end, cat-o'-nine-tails, cat, knout. □ **lash out 1** (*lash out at*) hit out at, attack, tear into, *colloq.* lay into; berate, have a go at, rap, abuse, revile, inveigh against, flay, belabor, *colloq.* lambaste, jump on.

lashing /láshing/ *n.* **1** a beating. **2** cord used for lashing.

■ **1** see WHIPPING 1.

lashings /láshingz/ *n.pl. Brit. colloq.* (foll. by *of*) plenty; an abundance.

lass /las/ *n.* a girl or young woman. [ME *lasce* ult. f. ON *laskwa* unmarried (fem.)]

■ girl, young woman, young lady, woman, schoolgirl, miss, mademoiselle, fräulein, *Ir.* colleen, *archaic* demoiselle, *archaic or literary* damsel, *archaic or poet.*

/.../ **pronunciation**	● **part of speech**
□ **phrases, idioms, and compounds**	
□□ **derivatives**	■ **synonym section**
cross-references appear in SMALL CAPITALS or *italics*	

maiden, maid, *poet.* nymph, *colloq.* lassie, filly, floozy, nymphet, *Brit. colloq.* popsy, *joc.* wench, *joc. or derog.* baggage, chit, gill, *sl.* chick, gal, petticoat, frail, dame, broad, *Austral. & NZ sl.* sheila, brush, *Brit. sl.* bird, *sl. derog.* piece, heifer; gamine, tomboy, minx, sylph, rosebud, *colloq.* peach, sex kitten, puss, *Brit. colloq.* dolly-bird, madam, *sl.* baby, cutie, doll, babe, fox; see also YOUTH *n.* 4.

Lassa fever /lásə/ *n.* an acute and often fatal febrile viral disease of tropical Africa. [*Lassa* in Nigeria, where first reported]

lassie /lásee/ *n. colloq.* = LASS.

lassitude /lásitood, -tyood/ *n.* **1** languor; weariness. **2** disinclination to exert or interest oneself. [F *lassitude* or L *lassitudo* f. *lassus* tired]

▪ see LETHARGY 1.

lasso /lásō, lasoo/ *n. & v.* ● *n.* (*pl.* **-os** or **-oes**) a rope with a noose at one end, used esp. in N. America for catching cattle, etc. ● *v.tr.* (**-oes, -oed**) catch with a lasso. □□ **lassoer** *n.* [Sp. *lazo* LACE]

▪ *n.* lariat, noose, rope. ● *v.* noose, snare, rope.

last[1] /last/ *adj., adv., & n.* ● *adj.* **1** after all others; coming at or belonging to the end. **2 a** most recent; next before a specified time (*last Christmas; last week*). **b** preceding; previous in a sequence (*got on at the last station*). **3** only remaining (*the last cookie, our last chance*). **4** (prec. by *the*) least likely or suitable (*the last person I'd want; the last thing I'd have expected*). **5** the lowest in rank (*the last place*). ● *adv.* **1** after all others (esp. in *comb.*: *last-mentioned*). **2** on the last occasion before the present (*when did you last see him?*). **3** (esp. in enumerating) lastly. ● *n.* **1** a person or thing that is last, last-mentioned, most recent, etc. **2** (prec. by *the*) the last mention or sight, etc. (*shall never hear the last of it*). **3** the last performance of certain acts (*breathed his last*). **4** (prec. by *the*) **a** the end or last moment. **b** death. □ **at last** (or **long last**) in the end; after much delay. **last agony** the pangs of death. **last ditch** a place of final desperate defense (often (with hyphen) *attrib.*). **Last Judgment** see JUDGMENT. **last minute** (or **moment**) the time just before an important event (often (with hyphen) *attrib.*). **last name** surname. **last post** see POST[3]. **last rites** sacred rites for a person about to die. **the last straw** a slight addition to a burden or difficulty that makes it finally unbearable. **the Last Supper** that of Christ and his disciples on the eve of the Crucifixion, as recorded in the New Testament. **last thing** esp. *Brit. adv.* very late, esp. as a final act before going to bed. **the last word 1** a final or definitive statement (*always has the last word; is the last word on this subject*). **2** (often foll. by *in*) the latest fashion. **on one's last legs** see LEG. **pay one's last respects** see RESPECT. **to** (or **till**) **the last** till the end; esp. till death. [OE *latost* superl.: see LATE]

▪ *adj.* **1, 5** final, concluding, terminal, ultimate, extreme; hindmost, rearmost, aftermost, eventual; definitive, conclusive, decisive; bottom, lowest, worst. **2** latest, newest, most recent *or* up to date; precedent, preceding, previous, prior, former, foregoing, antecedent, earlier. **3** final, ultimate; residual, leftover, surviving, remaining, outstanding; see also ONLY *adj.* ● *adv.* **3** finally, lastly, in fine, in conclusion. ● *n.* **2** end, finish. **4 a** see END *n.* 3. **b** see DEATH *n.* 1. □ **at last** finally, eventually, ultimately, at length. **last ditch** (*attrib.*) final, extreme, desperate. **the last word 2** all the rage, the latest, state of the art, dernier cri.

last[2] /last/ *v.intr.* **1** remain unexhausted or adequate or alive for a specified or considerable time; suffice (*enough food to last us a week; the battery lasts and lasts*). **2** continue for a specified time (*the journey lasts an hour*). □ **last out** remain adequate or in existence for the whole of a period previously stated or implied. [OE *lǣstan* f. Gmc]

▪ continue, go on, keep on, carry on; survive, live, persist, remain, stay, hold out, last out, go the distance, stand up, wear, endure, withstand, resist, *archaic* abide, *colloq.* stick it out; keep, stay fresh; suffice, serve, do.

last[3] /last/ *n.* a shoemaker's model for shaping or repairing a shoe or boot. ▪ **stick to one's last** not meddle with what

one does not understand. [OE *lǣste* last, *lǣst* boot, *lāst* footprint f. Gmc]

▪ mold, matrix, form, model, pattern.

lasting /lásting/ *adj.* **1** continuing; permanent. **2** durable. □□ **lastingly** *adv.* **lastingness** *n.*

▪ permanent, constant, perpetual, imperishable, indestructible, incorruptible, indissoluble, long, everlasting, undying, unfading, perennial, evergreen, eternal, enduring, abiding, durable, persistent, continuing, long-lasting, long-lived, long-running, long-term, steady, steadfast, lifelong.

lastly /lástlee/ *adv.* finally; in the last place.

▪ see *finally* (FINAL).

lat. *abbr.* latitude.

latch /lach/ *n. & v.* ● *n.* **1** a bar with a catch and lever used as a fastening for a gate, etc. **2** a springlock preventing a door from being opened from the outside without a key after being shut. ● *v.tr. & intr.* fasten or be fastened with a latch. □ **latch on** (often foll. by *to*) *colloq.* **1** attach oneself (to). **2** understand. [prob. f. (now dial.) *latch* (v.) seize f. OE *læccan* f. Gmc]

▪ *n.* **2** see LOCK[1] *n.* 1. ● *v.* see LOCK[1] *v.* 1. □ **latch on 2** see UNDERSTAND 1, 2.

latchkey /láchkee/ *n.* (*pl.* **-eys**) a key of an outer door. □ **latchkey child** a child who is alone at home after school until a parent returns from work.

▪ see KEY[1] *n.* 1.

late /layt/ *adj. & adv.* ● *adj.* **1** after the due or usual time; occurring or done after the proper time (*late for dinner; a late milk delivery*). **2 a** far on in the day or night or in a specified time or period. **b** far on in development. **3** flowering or ripening toward the end of the season (*late strawberries*). **4** (prec. by *the* or *my, his*, etc.) no longer alive or having the specified status (*my late husband; the late president*). **5** of recent date (*the late storms*). **6** (as **latest**, prec. by *the*) fashionable, up to date. ● *adv.* **1** after the due or usual time (*arrived late*). **2** far on in time (*this happened later on*). **3** at or till a late hour. **4** at a late stage of development. **5** formerly but not now (*a family late of New England but now scattered throughout the South*). □ **at the latest** as the latest time envisaged (*will have done it by six at the latest*). **late in the day** *colloq.* at a late stage in the proceedings, esp. too late to be useful. **Late Latin** Latin of about AD 200–600. **the latest 1** the most recent news, etc. (*have you heard the latest?*). **2** the current fashion. □□ **lateness** *n.* [OE *lǣt* (adj.), *late* (adv.) f. Gmc]

▪ *adj.* **1** tardy, delayed, overdue, belated, behind time, latish, behindhand, in arrears, dilatory, unpunctual, past due. **4** dead, departed, lamented, *formal* deceased; former, past, ex-, one-time, erstwhile, sometime, ci-devant, *archaic* whilom. **5** recent, latest, last. **6** (**the latest**) fashionable, current, modern, stylish, à la mode, up-to-the-minute, up-to-date, in vogue, voguish, in, all the rage, *colloq.* with it, flash, swinging, *colloq. often derog.* trendy, *sl.* groovy, hip. ● *adv.* **1** tardily, unpunctually, belatedly, latish. **5** formerly, previously, once, at one time, sometime, ci-devant, *archaic* erstwhile, erst, whilom, *formal* heretofore; recently, lately, of late, latterly; hitherto. □ **the latest 2** see VOGUE 1.

latecomer /láytkumər/ *n.* a person who arrives late.

lateen /lateén/ *adj.* (of a ship) rigged with a lateen sail. □ **lateen sail** a triangular sail on a long yard at an angle of 45° to the mast. [F (*voile*) *latine* Latin (sail), because common in the Mediterranean]

lately /láytlee/ *adv.* not long ago; recently; in recent times. [OE *lǣtlīce* (as LATE, -LY[2])]

▪ recently, (of) late, latterly; just; hitherto.

La Tène /laa tén/ *adj.* of or relating to the second Iron Age culture of central and W. Europe. [*La Tène* in Switzerland, where remains of it were first identified]

latent /láyt'nt/ *adj.* **1** concealed; dormant. **2** existing but not developed or manifest. □ **latent heat** *Physics* the heat required to convert a solid into a liquid or vapor, or a liquid into a vapor, without change of temperature. **latent image**

Photog. an image not yet made visible by developing. □□ **latency** *n.* **latently** *adv.* [L *latēre latent-* be hidden]
■ **1** see DORMANT 2b. **2** see POTENTIAL *adj.*

-later /lətər/ *comb. form* denoting a person who worships a particular thing or person (*idolater*). [Gk: see LATRIA]

lateral /látərəl/ *adj. & n.* ● *adj.* **1** of, at, toward, or from the side or sides. **2** descended from a brother or sister of a person in direct line. ● *n.* a side part, etc., esp. a lateral shoot or branch. □ **lateral line** *Zool.* a visible line along the side of a fish consisting of a series of sense organs acting as vibration receptors. **lateral thinking** a method of solving problems indirectly or by apparently illogical methods. □□ **laterally** *adv.* [L *lateralis* f. *latus lateris* side]
■ □□ **laterally** see SIDEWAYS *adv.*

laterite /látərit/ *n.* a red or yellow ferruginous clay, friable and hardening in air, used for making roads in the tropics. □□ **lateritic** /-rítik/ *adj.* [L *later* brick + -ITE¹]

latex /láyteks/ *n.* (*pl.* **latices** /-tiseez/ or **latexes**) **1** a milky fluid of mixed composition found in various plants and trees, esp. the rubber tree, and used for commercial purposes. **2** a synthetic product resembling this. [L, = liquid]

lath /lath/ *n. & v.* ● *n.* (*pl.* **laths** /laths, lathz/) a thin flat strip of wood, esp. each of a series forming a framework or support for plaster, etc. ● *v.tr.* attach laths to (a wall or ceiling). □ **lath and plaster** a common material for interior walls and ceilings, etc. [OE *lætt*]

lathe /layth/ *n.* a machine for shaping wood, metal, etc., by means of a rotating drive which turns the piece being worked on against changeable cutting tools. [prob. rel. to ODa. *lad* structure, frame, f. ON *hlath*, rel. to *hlatha* LADE]

lather /láthər/ *n. & v.* ● *n.* **1** a froth produced by agitating soap, etc., and water. **2** frothy sweat, esp. of a horse. **3** a state of agitation. ● *v.* **1** *intr.* (of soap, etc.) form a lather. **2** *tr.* cover with lather. **3** *intr.* (of a horse, etc.) develop or become covered with lather. **4** *tr. colloq.* thrash. □□ **lathery** *adj.* [OE *lēathor* (n.), *lēthran* (v.)]
■ *n.* **1** froth, foam, spume, suds, bubbles. **3** fuss, flutter, panic, bother, *colloq.* dither, tizzy, state, flap, stew, sweat, *literary* pother. ● *v.* **1** soap (up), suds; foam, froth, spume; whip (up). **2** soap, suds. **3** sweat (up), foam, froth. **4** see BEAT *v.* 1.

lathi /láatee/ *n.* (*pl.* **lathis**) (in India) a long, heavy, iron-bound bamboo stick used as a weapon, esp. by police. [Hindi *lāṭhī*]

latices *pl.* of LATEX.

Latin /lát'n/ *n. & adj.* ● *n.* **1** the Italic language of ancient Rome and its empire, originating in Latium. **2** *Rom.Hist.* an inhabitant of ancient Latium in Central Italy. ● *adj.* **1** of or in Latin. **2** of the countries or peoples (e.g., France and Spain) using languages developed from Latin. **3** *Rom.Hist.* of or relating to ancient Latium or its inhabitants. **4** of the Roman Catholic Church. □ **Latin America** the parts of Central and S. America where Spanish or Portuguese is the main language. **Latin American** *n.* a native of Latin America. ● *adj.* of or relating to Latin America. **Latin Church** the Western Church. □□ **Latinism** *n.* **Latinist** *n.* [ME f. OF *Latin* or L *Latinus* f. *Latium*]
■ *adj.* **3** see CLASSICAL 1a.

Latinate /lát'nayt/ *adj.* having the character of Latin.

Latinize /lát'niz/ *v.* **1** *tr.* give a Latin or Latinate form to. **2** *tr.* translate into Latin. **3** *tr.* make conformable to the ideas, customs, etc., of the ancient Romans, Latin peoples, or Latin Church. **4** *intr.* use Latin forms, idioms, etc. □□ **Latinization** *n.* **Latinizer** *n.* [LL *latinizare* (as LATIN)]

Latino /lətéenō/ *n.* (*pl.* **Latinos**; *fem.* **Latina** /-nə/, *pl.* **Latinas**) **1** a native or inhabitant of Latin America. **2** a person of Spanish-speaking or Latin-American descent.

latish /láytish/ *adj. & adv.* fairly late.

latitude /látitōōd, -tyōōd/ *n.* **1** *Geog.* **a** the angular distance on a meridian north or south of the equator, expressed in degrees and minutes. **b** (usu. in *pl.*) regions or climes, esp. with reference to temperature (*warm latitudes*). **2** freedom from narrowness; liberality of interpretation. **3** tolerated variety of action or opinion (*was allowed much latitude*). **4** *Astron.* the angular distance of a celestial body or point from

the ecliptic. □ **high latitudes** regions near the poles. **low latitudes** regions near the equator. □□ **latitudinal** /-tōōd'nəl, -tyōōd-/ *adj.* **latitudinally** *adv.* [ME, = breadth, f. L *latitudo -dinis* f. *latus* broad]
■ **2, 3** see LEEWAY.

latitudinarian /látitōōd'náireeən, -tyōōd-/ *adj. & n.* ● *adj.* allowing latitude esp. in religion; showing no preference among varying creeds and forms of worship. ● *n.* a person with a latitudinarian attitude. □□ **latitudinarianism** *n.* [L *latitudo -dinis* breadth + -ARIAN]
■ *adj.* see TOLERANT 1. ● *n.* see LIBERAL *n.* 1.

latria /lətríə/ *n.* *Theol.* supreme worship allowed to God alone. [LL f. Gk *latreia* worship f. *latreuō* serve]

latrine /lətréen/ *n.* a communal toilet, esp. in a camp, barracks, etc. [F f. L *latrina*, shortening of *lavatrina* f. *lavare* wash]
■ see TOILET *n.* 1.

-latry /lətree/ *comb. form* denoting worship (*idolatry*). [Gk *latreia*: see LATRIA]

latten /lát'n/ *n.* an alloy of copper and zinc, often rolled into sheets, and formerly used for monumental brasses and church articles. [ME *latoun* f. OF *laton, leiton*]

latter /látər/ *adj.* **1 a** denoting the second-mentioned of two, or *disp.* the last-mentioned of three or more. **b** (prec. by *the*; usu. *absol.*) the second- or last-mentioned person or thing. **2** nearer to the end (*the latter part of the year*). **3** recent. **4** belonging to the end of a period, of the world, etc. □ **latter-day** modern; newfangled. **Latter-day Saints** the Mormons' name for themselves. [OE *lætra*, compar. of *læt* LATE]
■ □ **latter-day** see MODERN.

latterly /látərlee/ *adv.* **1** in the latter part of life or of a period. **2** recently.
■ **2** see LATELY.

lattice /látis/ *n.* **1 a** a structure of crossed laths or bars with spaces between, used as a screen, fence, etc. **b** = LATTICE-WORK. **2** *Crystallog.* a regular periodic arrangement of atoms, ions, or molecules in a crystalline solid. □ **lattice girder** a girder or truss made of top and bottom members connected by struts usu. crossing diagonally. **lattice window** a window with small panes set in diagonally crossing strips of lead. □□ **latticed** *adj.* **latticing** *n.* [ME f. OF *lattis* f. *latte* lath f. WG]
■ **1** see MESH *n.* 1, 2, 3a.

latticework /látiswərk/ *n.* laths arranged in lattice formation.

Latvian /látveeən/ *n. & adj.* ● *n.* **1 a** a native of Latvia, a Baltic republic. **b** a person of Latvian descent. **2** the language of Latvia. ● *adj.* of or relating to Latvia or its people or language.
■ **1** Lett.

laud /lawd/ *v. & n.* ● *v.tr.* praise or extol, esp. in hymns. ● *n.* **1** *literary* praise; a hymn of praise. **2** (in *pl.*) the traditional morning prayer of the Roman Catholic Church. [ME: (n.) f. OF *laude*, (v.) f. L *laudare*, f. L *laus laudis* praise]
■ *v.* praise, extol, acclaim, exalt, eulogize, panegyrize, hymn, celebrate, sing the praises of, honor, glorify, applaud; build up, cry up, write up, promote, advance, puff, recommend, commend, *colloq.* boost, crack up.

laudable /láwdəbəl/ *adj.* commendable; praiseworthy. □□ **laudability** /-bílitee/ *n.* **laudably** *adv.* [ME f. L *laudabilis* (as LAUD)]
■ praiseworthy, commendable, meritorious, creditable, admirable, estimable, worthy, good; outstanding, excellent, exemplary, noteworthy, notable.

laudanum /láwd'nəm/ *n.* a solution containing morphine and prepared from opium, formerly used as a narcotic painkiller. [mod.L, the name given by Paracelsus to a costly medicament, later applied to preparations containing opium: perh. var. of LADANUM]

/. . ./ **pronunciation**   ● **part of speech**
□ **phrases, idioms, and compounds**
□□ **derivatives**   ■ **synonym section**
cross-references appear in SMALL CAPITALS or *italics*

laudation /lawdáyshən/ *n. formal* praise. [L *laudatio -onis* (as LAUD)]
■ see TRIBUTE 1.

laudatory /láwdətáwree/ *adj.* (also **laudative** /-tiv/) expressing praise.
■ laudative, praiseful, eulogistic, panegyrical, encomiastic, complimentary, flattering; favorable, glowing, good.

laugh /laf/ *v. & n.* ● *v.* **1** *intr.* make the spontaneous sounds and movements usual in expressing lively amusement, scorn, derision, etc. **2** *tr.* express by laughing. **3** *tr.* bring (a person) into a certain state by laughing (*laughed them into agreeing*). **4** *intr.* (foll. by *at*) ridicule; make fun of (*laughed at us for going*). **5** *intr.* (**be laughing**) *colloq.* be in a fortunate or successful position. **6** *intr. esp. poet.* make sounds reminiscent of laughing. ● *n.* **1** the sound or act or manner of laughing. **2** *colloq.* a comical or ridiculous person or thing. □ **have the last laugh** be ultimately the winner. **laugh in a person's face** show open scorn for a person. **laugh off** get rid of (embarrassment or humiliation) with a jest. **laugh out of court** deprive of a hearing by ridicule. **laugh out of the other side of one's mouth** (or **on the other side of one's face**) change from enjoyment or amusement to displeasure, shame, apprehension, etc. **laugh up one's sleeve** be secretly or inwardly amused. **laugh track** recorded laughter added to a comedy show, esp. a television situation comedy. □□ **laugher** *n.* [OE *hlæhhan, hliehhan* f. Gmc]
■ *v.* **1** titter, giggle, te-hee, chuckle, chortle, guffaw, split one's sides, scream, shriek (with laughter), go into hysterics, roar (with laughter), *colloq.* crack up, kill oneself, roll about, *literary* cachinnate; snigger, snicker, fleer; bray, neigh, cackle, hoot. **4** (*laugh at*) deride, ridicule, mock (at), jeer (at), poke fun at, guy, make fun *or* sport of, make merry over, make a fool *or* monkey *or* ass of, scoff at, sneer at, chaff, twit, tease, pull a person's leg, taunt, rag, have a fling *or* go at, run down, heckle, catcall, *Brit.* barrack, *archaic* smoke, *colloq.* have a shy at, rib, *sl.* razz, bullyrag; see also LAMPOON *v.* **5** (*be laughing*) be in clover, be well off, ride high, *colloq.* have it made. ● *n.* **1** titter, giggle, te-hee, chuckle, chortle, snigger, snicker, cackle, guffaw, roar, scream, shriek, *literary* cachinnation. **2** joke, frolic, *colloq.* lark, giggle, hoot, scream, riot; prank, jape, practical joke, trick; farce, mockery, absurdity, nonsense, travesty, charade, caricature; laughingstock, figure of fun, fool, ass, standing joke, *colloq.* goat. □ **have the last laugh** have the last word; come out on top, come off best, come off the winner. **laugh in a person's face** see SCORN *v.* 1 **laugh off** brush aside, shrug off, pooh-pooh; spurn, dismiss, reject, disregard, ignore, belittle, minimize.

laughable /láfəbəl/ *adj.* ludicrous; highly amusing. □□ **laughably** *adv.*
■ see LUDICROUS.

laughing /láfing/ *n. & adj.* ● *n.* laughter. ● *adj.* in senses of LAUGH *v.* □ **laughing gas** nitrous oxide as an anesthetic, formerly used without oxygen and causing an exhilarating effect when inhaled. **laughing hyena** see HYENA. **laughing jackass** = KOOKABURRA. **no laughing matter** something serious. □□ **laughingly** *adv.*

laughingstock /láfingstok/ *n.* a person or thing open to general ridicule.
■ fool, exhibition, spectacle.

laughter /láftər/ *n.* the act or sound of laughing. [OE *hleahtor* f. Gmc]
■ see LAUGH *n.* 1.

launce /lans, laans/ *n.* = *sand lance.* [perh. f. LANCE: cf. *garfish*]

launch¹ /lawnch/ *v. & n.* ● *v.* **1** *tr.* set (a vessel) afloat. **2** *tr.* hurl or send forth (a weapon, rocket, etc.). **3** *tr.* start or set in motion (an enterprise, a person on a course of action, etc.). **4** *tr.* formally introduce (a new product) with publicity, etc. **5** *intr.* (often foll. by *out, into,* etc.) **a** make a start, esp. on an ambitious enterprise. **b** burst into strong language, etc. ● *n.* the act or an instance of launching.

□ **launching pad 1** = LAUNCHPAD. **2** = SPRINGBOARD 2. [ME f. AF *launcher*, ONF *lancher*, OF *lancier* LANCE *v.*]
■ *v.* **1, 3, 4** float; set in motion, get under way, get going, get started; initiate, begin, start (off), originate, pioneer, spearhead, inaugurate, institute, introduce, usher in, embark upon, enter upon, *colloq.* kick off, *formal* commence; establish, organize, set up, mount, found, open. **2** shoot, fire, discharge, propel, project, hurl, throw, toss, sling, pitch, fling, heave, catapult, send (off *or* up), dispatch, let go (with), deliver, release, *poet.* lance. **5 a** start, set out *or* off, begin, get under way, go. **b** burst, break, erupt, explode. ● *n.* flotation; initiation, start, beginning, début, origin, origination, conception, inauguration, institution, introduction, presentation, *colloq.* kickoff, *formal* commencement; establishment, organization, foundation, opening; firing, (moon)shot, takeoff, discharge, propulsion, dispatch, delivery.

launch² /lawnch/ *n.* **1** a motorboat, used esp. for pleasure. **2** a man-of-war's largest boat. [Sp. *lancha* pinnace perh. f. Malay *lancharan* f. *lanchār* swift]
■ **1** boat, skiff, tender, motor boat, runabout, gig, dinghy.

launcher /láwnchər/ *n.* a structure or device to hold a rocket during launching.

launchpad /láwnchpad/ *n.* a platform with a supporting structure, from which rockets are launched.

launder /láwndər, laán-/ *v. & n.* ● *v.tr.* **1** wash and iron (clothes, linen, etc.). **2** *colloq.* transfer (funds) to conceal a dubious or illegal origin. ● *n.* a channel for conveying liquids, esp. molten metal. □□ **launderer** *n.* [ME *launder* (n.) washer of linen, contr. of *lavander* f. OF *lavandier* ult. f. L *lavanda* things to be washed, neut. pl. gerundive of *lavare* wash]
■ *v.* **1** wash, clean, scrub, cleanse, rinse, soap, *literary* lave; starch; iron, press, smooth. **2** legitimize, legitimatize, legalize.

launderette /lawndərét, laán-/ *n.* (also **laundrette**) = LAUNDROMAT.

laundress /láwndris, laán-/ *n.* a woman who launders clothes, linen, etc., esp. professionally.

laundromat /láwndrəmat, laán-/ *n. propr.* an establishment with coin-operated washing machines and dryers for public use.

laundry /láwndree, laán-/ *n.* (*pl.* **-ies**) **1** an establishment for washing clothes or linen. **2** clothes or linen for laundering or newly laundered. □ **laundry list** *colloq.* a lengthy and often random list of items (*a laundry list of weekend projects; a laundry list of my flaws*). [contr. f. *lavendry* (f. OF *lavanderie*) after LAUNDER]

laureate /láwreeət, lór-/ *adj. & n.* ● *adj.* **1** wreathed with laurel as a mark of honor. **2** consisting of laurel; laurellike. ● *n.* **1** a person who is honored for outstanding creative or intellectual achievement (*Nobel laureate*). **2** = poet laureate. □□ **laureateship** *n.* [L *laureatus* f. *laurea* laurel wreath f. *laurus* laurel]

laurel /láwrəl, lór-/ *n. & v.* ● *n.* **1** = BAY². **2 a** (in *sing.* or *pl.*) the foliage of the bay tree used as an emblem of victory or distinction in poetry, usu. formed into a wreath or crown. **b** (in *pl.*) honor or distinction. **3** any plant with dark-green glossy leaves like a bay tree, e.g., cherry laurel, mountain laurel, spurge laurel. ● *v.tr.* (**laureled, laureling**; esp. *Brit.* **laurelled, laurelling**) wreathe with laurel. □ **look to one's laurels** beware of losing one's preeminence. **rest on one's laurels** be satisfied with what one has done and not seek further success. [ME *lorer* f. OF *lorier* f. *lorier* f. Prov. *laurier* f. *laur* f. L *laurus*]
■ *n.* **2 b** (*laurels*) honor(s), distinction(s), fame, awards, trophy, trophies, tributes, rewards; acclaim, acclamation, glory, renown, esteem, admiration, approbation, accolade(s), regard, respect, prestige, celebrity, popularity, reputation, *colloq.* kudos. □ **rest on one's laurels** be *or* get complacent *or* self-satisfied *or* smug *or* overconfident; sit back, relax, take it easy, ease up *or* off.

laurustinus /láwrəstínəs/ *n.* an evergreen winter-flowering shrub, *Viburnum tinus*, with dense glossy green leaves and white or pink flowers. [mod.L f. L *laurus* laurel + *tinus* wild laurel]

lav /lav/ *n. colloq.* lavatory. [abbr.]

lava /laávə, laávə/ *n.* **1** the molten matter which flows from a volcano. **2** the solid substance which it forms on cooling. [It. f. *lavare* wash f. L]

lavabo /ləvaábō/ *n.* (*pl.* **-os**) **1** *RC & Anglican Ch.* **a** the ritual washing of the celebrant's hands at the offertory of the Mass. **b** a towel or basin used for this. **2** a monastery washing trough. **3** a washbasin. [L, = I will wash, first word of Psalm 26:6]

■ **1b, 2, 3** see SINK *n.* 1.

lavage /ləvaázh, lávij/ *n. Med.* the washing out of a body cavity, such as the colon or stomach, with water or a medicated solution. [F f. *laver* wash: see LAVE]

lavation /ləváyshən/ *n. formal* washing. [L *lavatio* f. *lavare* wash]

lavatorial /lávətáwreeəl/ *adj. esp. Brit.* (esp. of humor) relating to bathrooms and their use.

lavatory /lávətawree/ *n.* (*pl.* **-ies**) **1** a sink or wash basin in a bathroom. **2** a room or compartment with a toilet and wash basin. **3** *Brit.* a flush toilet. □ **lavatory paper** *Brit.* = *toilet paper*. [ME, = washing vessel, f. LL *lavatorium* f. L *lavare lavat-* wash]

■ **2** toilet, ladies' room, men's room, powder room, latrine, bathroom, rest room, washroom, (little) boys' *or* girls' room, outhouse, *colloq.* can, john, throne, *Naut.* head(s), *Brit.* (public) convenience, the gents, water closet, WC, *Brit. colloq.* loo, lav, *Brit. euphem.* cloakroom, *Brit. sl.* bog.

lave /layv/ *v.tr. literary* **1** wash; bathe. **2** (of water) wash against; flow along. [ME f. OF *laver* f. L *lavare* wash, perh. coalescing with OE *lafian*]

■ **1** see WASH *v.* 1, 3.

lavender /lávindər/ *n. & v.* ● *n.* **1 a** any small evergreen shrub of the genus *Lavandula*, with narrow leaves and blue, purple, or pink aromatic flowers. **b** its flowers and stalks dried and used to scent linen, clothes, etc. **2** a pale blue color with a trace of red. ● *v.tr.* put lavender among (linen, etc.). □ **lavender water** a perfume made from distilled lavender, alcohol, and ambergris. [ME f. AF *lavendre*, ult. f. med.L *lavandula*]

laver[1] /láyvər/ *n.* any of various edible seaweeds, esp. *Porphyra umbilicalis*, having sheetlike fronds. □ **laver bread** a Welsh dish of laver which is boiled, dipped in oatmeal, and fried. [L]

laver[2] /láyvər/ *n.* **1** *Bibl.* a large brass vessel for Jewish priests' ritual ablutions. **2** *archaic* a washing or fountain basin; a font. [ME *lavo(u)r* f. OF *laveo(i)r* f. LL (as LAVATORY)]

lavish /lávish/ *adj. & v.* ● *adj.* **1** giving or producing in large quantities; profuse. **2** generous; unstinting. **3** excessive; overabundant. ● *v.tr.* (often foll. by *on*) bestow or spend (money, effort, praise, etc.) abundantly. □□ **lavishly** *adv.* **lavishness** *n.* [ME f. obs. *lavish, lavas* (n.) profusion f. OF *lavasse* deluge of rain f. *laver* wash]

■ *adj.* **1** profuse, abundant, plentiful, ample, copious, prolific, liberal, effusive, *disp.* fulsome, *poet.* plenteous; lush, luxuriant, luxurious, opulent, plush, sumptuous, rich, handsome, princely, generous. **2** generous, liberal, openhanded, free-handed, bountiful, munificent, unstinting, unsparing, unselfish, effusive, free, *poet.* bounteous; kind, beneficent, charitable, bighearted, greathearted, magnanimous, sporting, *Brit.* decent, *archaic* gentle. **3** excessive, immoderate, inordinate, uncurbed, unrestrained, intemperate, disproportionate, extravagant, exorbitant, exaggerated, undue, extreme, unreasonable, outrageous; wasteful, profligate, wanton, prodigal, improvident, overgenerous; overabundant, superabundant, overfull, bursting at the seams, superfluous, *colloq.* over-the-top. ● *v.* spend, expend, disburse, pay, esp. *Brit.* lash out, *colloq.* splurge; squander, waste, throw away, fritter (away), drivel

away, dissipate; shower, rain, pour, heap, bestow, *sl.* dish out, blow.

law /law/ *n.* **1 a** a rule enacted or customary in a community and recognized as enjoining or prohibiting certain actions and enforced by the imposition of penalties. **b** a body of such rules (*the law of the land*; *forbidden under state law*). **2** the controlling influence of laws; a state of respect for laws (*law and order*). **3** laws collectively as a social system or subject of study (*was reading law*). **4** (with defining word) any of the specific branches or applications of law (*commercial law*; *law of contract*). **5** binding force or effect (*their word is law*). **6** (prec. by *the*) **a** the legal profession. **b** *colloq.* the police. **7** the statute and common law (opp. EQUITY). **8** (in *pl.*) jurisprudence. **9 a** the judicial remedy; litigation. **b** courts of law as providing this (*go to law*). **10** a rule of action or procedure, e.g., in a game, social context, form of art, etc. **11** a regularity in natural occurrences, esp. as formulated or propounded in particular instances (*the laws of nature*; *the law of gravity*; *Parkinson's law*). **12 a** a divine commandments as expressed in the Bible or other sources. **b** (**Law of Moses**) the precepts of the Pentateuch. □ **at** (or **in**) **law** according to the laws. **be a law unto oneself** do what one feels is right; disregard custom. **go to law** *Brit.* take legal action; make use of the courts. **law-abiding** obedient to the laws. **law of diminishing returns** see DIMINISH. **law of nature** = *natural law*. **laws of war** the limitations on belligerents' action recognized by civilized nations. **lay down the law** be dogmatic or authoritarian. **take the law into one's own hands** redress a grievance by one's own means, esp. by force. [OE *lagu* f. ON *lag* something 'laid down' or fixed, rel. to LAY[1]]

■ **1 a** rule, regulation, ordinance, statute, act, enactment, measure, edict, decree, order, directive, injunction, command, commandment, precept, canon, mandate, ukase, *Brit.* bylaw, *hist.* constitution. **b** constitution, rules (and regulations), code, charter. **2** justice, right, equity, fairness, order, law and order; lawlessness, rightfulness, legitimacy, legality. **5** (*predic.*) final, conclusive, indisputable, binding, incontrovertible, definitive; irrevocable, immutable, unchangeable, unalterable, irreversible. **6 b** see POLICE *n.* 1, 2. **9** remedy, redress, reparation; litigation, suit (at law), lawsuit, (legal) action, case; (the) court(s), court of law, courtroom, tribunal, bench, bar, *Brit.* lawcourt. **10** rule, regulation, principle, direction, guide, guideline. **11** principle, proposition, theory, theorem, axiom; postulate, hypothesis; deduction, conclusion, inference, corollary, lemma, formula. □ **law-abiding** obedient, respectful, dutiful, decent, proper, upright, respectable, honest, virtuous, unimpeachable, peaceable, principled, disciplined, well-behaved, orderly, civilized, solid, *literary* duteous. **lay down the law** dictate, command, order, direct, give orders.

lawbreaker /láwbraykər/ *n.* a person who breaks the law. □□ **lawbreaking** *n. & adj.*

■ see *offender* (OFFEND).

lawcourt /láwkawrt/ *n.* a court of law.

lawful /láwfool/ *adj.* conforming with, permitted by, or recognized by law; not illegal or (of a child) illegitimate. □□ **lawfully** *adv.* **lawfulness** *n.*

■ legal, licit, legitimate, constitutional, just, rightful, de jure, valid, proper; permissible, allowable, justifiable, authorized.

lawgiver /láwgivər/ *n.* a person who lays down laws.

lawless /láwlis/ *adj.* **1** having no laws or enforcement of them. **2** disregarding laws. **3** unbridled; uncontrolled. □□ **lawlessly** *adv.* **lawlessness** *n.*

■ **1** anarchic, anarchical, anarchistic, chaotic, disorderly, unruly, unregulated. **2** unlawful, criminal, felonious,

---

/. . ./ **pronunciation**	● **part of speech**
□ **phrases, idioms, and compounds**	
□□ **derivatives**	■ **synonym section**
cross-references appear in SMALL CAPITALS or *italics*	

illegal, illicit, larcenous, *colloq.* crooked, esp. *Brit. sl.*
bent; dishonest, corrupt, venal; villainous, nefarious,
wicked, sinful, flagitious, iniquitous, treacherous. **3**
unbridled, uncontrolled, unconstrained, unrestrained,
unchecked, undisciplined, wild, unruly, rogue,
boisterous, riotous, rampant, out of hand *or* control.

lawmaker /láwmaykər/ *n.* a legislator.
  ■ see POLITICIAN 1.

lawman /láwman/ *n.* (*pl.* **-men**) a law-enforcement officer,
esp. a sheriff or policeman.
  ■ see OFFICER *n.* 2.

lawn[1] /lawn/ *n.* a piece of grass kept mown and smooth in a
yard, garden, park, etc. □ **lawn bowling** = BOWL[2] 2a. **lawn
tennis** the usual form of tennis, played with a soft ball on
outdoor grass or a hard court. **lawn mower** a machine for
cutting the grass on a lawn. [ME *laund* glade f. OF *launde*
f. OCelt., rel. to LAND]
  ■ grass, green, turf, sod, *archaic or literary* greensward,
  literary sward.

lawn[2] /lawn/ *n.* a fine linen or cotton fabric used for clothes.
  □□ **lawny** *adj.* [ME, prob. f. *Laon* in France]

lawrencium /lərénseeəm, law-/ *n. Chem.* an artificially made
transuranic radioactive metallic element. ¶ Symb.: **Lw.** [E.
O. *Lawrence*, Amer. physicist d. 1958]

lawsuit /láwsōot/ *n.* the process or an instance of making a
claim in a court of law.
  ■ see CASE[1] 5a.

lawyer /láwyər, lóyər/ *n.* a member of the legal profession.
  □□ **lawyerly** *adj.* [ME *law(i)er* f. LAW]
  ■ attorney(-at-law), jurist, counselor(-at-law), squire,
  counsel, advocate, member of the bar, legal
  practitioner, legal advisor, *Brit.* barrister(-at-law),
  Queen's Counsel, Q.C., bencher, recorder, solicitor,
  colloq. mouthpiece; pettifogger.

lax /laks/ *adj.* **1** lacking care, concern, or firmness. **2** loose,
relaxed; not compact. **3** *Phonet.* pronounced with the vocal
muscles relaxed. □□ **laxity** *n.* **laxly** *adv.* **laxness** *n.* [ME, =
loose, f. L *laxus*: rel. to SLACK[1]]
  ■ **1** careless, uncaring, devil-may-care, thoughtless,
  unthinking, negligent, neglectful, remiss, inattentive,
  unobservant, cursory, lackadaisical, perfunctory, loose,
  slipshod, slack, casual, untidy, hit-or-miss, scrappy,
  scratchy, sloppy; imprecise, inexact, inaccurate,
  indefinite, nonspecific, vague, shapeless, amorphous,
  general; permissive, weak, indulgent, lenient,
  easygoing, liberal, soft, relaxed, happy-go-lucky,
  nonchalant, carefree, insouciant, *colloq.* laid-back.
  2 loose, relaxed, open; supple, loose-limbed, flexible,
  slack, limp, soft.

laxative /láksətiv/ *adj. & n.* ● *adj.* tending to stimulate or
facilitate evacuation of the bowels. ● *n.* a laxative medicine.
[ME f. OF *laxatif -ive* or LL *laxativus* f. L *laxare* loosen (as
LAX)]
  ■ *adj.* see PURGATIVE *adj.* 2. ● *n.* see PURGATIVE *n.* 2.

lay[1] /lay/ *v. & n.* ● *v.* (*past* and *past part.* **laid** /layd/) **1** *tr.*
place on a surface, esp. horizontally or in the proper or spec-
ified place. **2** *tr.* put or bring into a certain or the required
position or state (*lay a carpet*). **3** *intr. dial.* or *erron.* lie. ¶
This use, incorrect in standard English, is probably partly
encouraged by confusion with *lay* as the past of *lie*, as in *the
dog lay on the floor* which is correct; *the dog is laying on the
floor* is not correct. **4** *tr.* make by laying (*lay the foundations*).
5 *tr.* (often *absol.*) (of a hen bird) produce (an egg). **6** *tr.* **a**
cause to subside or lie flat. **b** deal with to remove (a ghost,
fear, etc.). **7** *tr.* place or present for consideration (a case,
proposal, etc.). **8** *tr.* set down as a basis or starting point. **9**
tr. (usu. foll. by *on*) attribute or impute (blame, etc.). **10** *tr.*
locate (a scene, etc.) in a certain place. **11** *tr.* prepare or
make ready (a plan or a trap). **12** *tr.* prepare (a table) for a
meal. **13** *tr.* place or arrange the material for (a fire). **14** *tr.*
put down as a wager; stake. **15** *tr.* (foll. by *with*) coat or
strew (a surface). **16** *tr. sl. offens.* have sexual intercourse
with (esp. a woman). ● *n.* **1** the way, position, or direction
in which something lies. **2** *sl. offens.* a partner (esp. female)
in sexual intercourse. **3** the direction or amount of twist in

rope strands. □ **in lay** (of a hen) laying eggs regularly. **laid-
back** *colloq.* relaxed; unbothered; easygoing. **laid paper** paper with the surface marked in fine ribs. **laid up** confined
to bed or the house. **lay about one 1** hit out on all sides. **2**
criticize indiscriminately. **lay aside 1** put to one side. **2**
cease to practice or consider. **3** save (money, etc.) for future
needs. **lay at the door of** see DOOR. **lay back** cause to slope
back from the vertical. **lay bare** expose; reveal. **lay a
charge** make an accusation. **lay claim to** claim as one's
own. **lay down 1** put on the ground. **2** relinquish; give up
(an office). **3** formulate or insist on (a rule or principle). **4**
pay or wager (money). **5** esp. *Brit.* begin to construct (a ship
or railroad). **6** store (wine) in a cellar. **7** set down on paper.
8 sacrifice (one's life). **9** convert (land) into pasture. **10**
record (esp. popular music). **lay down the law** see LAW.
lay one's hands on obtain; acquire; locate. **lay hands on
1** seize or attack. **2** place one's hands on or over, esp. in
confirmation, ordination, or spiritual healing. **lay hold of**
seize or grasp. **lay in** provide oneself with a stock of. **lay
into** *colloq.* punish or scold severely. **lay it on thick** (or **with
a trowel**) *colloq.* flatter or exaggerate grossly. **lay low** overthrow, kill, or humble. **lay off 1** discharge (workers) temporarily because of a shortage of work. **2** *colloq.* desist. **the
lay of the land** the current state of affairs. **lay on 1** spread
on (paint, etc.). **2** inflict (blows). **3** impose (a penalty, obligation, etc.). **4** *Brit.* provide (a facility, amenity, etc.). **lay
on the table** see TABLE. **lay open 1** break the skin of. **2** (foll.
by *to*) expose (to criticism, etc.). **lay out 1** spread out. **2**
expose to view. **3** prepare (a corpse) for burial. **4** *colloq.*
knock unconscious. **5** prepare a layout. **6** expend (money).
7 *refl.* (foll. by *to* + infin.) take pains (to do something) (*laid
themselves out to help*). **lay store by** see STORE. **lay to rest**
bury in a grave. **lay up 1** store; save. **2** put (a ship, etc.) out
of service. **lay waste** see WASTE. [OE *lecgan* f. Gmc]
  ■ *v.* **1** place, put (down), set (down), lay down, position,
  deposit. **2** put down, fit. **3** see LIE[1] *v.* 1. **6 a** flatten,
  flat, pat (down), press, roll, planish, smooth, tamp.
  b (*lay to rest*) exorcize; destroy, drive out, get rid of,
  expel, eject, oust, remove; see also SUPPRESS *v.* 1. **7** see
  PRESENT[2] *v.* 1. **9** attribute, impute, ascribe, assign,
  direct, lodge, refer, aim, pin. **10** see LOCATE 2, 4.
  11 see PREPARE 1. **12, 13** set, arrange, prepare; spread.
  14 stake, bet, wager, gamble, hazard, risk, venture,
  chance, put up *or* down, lay down. **15** see COAT *v.* 1.
  16 copulate with, couple with, have (sexual)
  intercourse with, sleep with, go to bed with, make love
  to, possess, take, have one's (wicked) way with, *Law*
  have carnal knowledge of, *archaic* lie with, know,
  archaic or joc. fornicate with, *colloq.* bed, have sex with,
  go all the way with, *sl.* make, make it with. ● *n.* **1** see
  POSITION *n.* 1, 2. □ **laid-back** see *relaxed* (RELAX *v.* 5).
  laid up see SICK[1] *adj.* 2. **lay about one 1** hit out, lash
  out, strike out. **lay aside 2** see *put aside* 2. **3** see *put by*.
  lay bare see EXPOSE 5. **lay claim to** see CLAIM *v.* 1a.
  lay down 1 see LAY[1] *v.* 1 above. **2** see RELINQUISH 1, 2.
  3 formulate, set down, put down; insist on, stand on,
  exact. **4** see LAY[1] *v.* 14 above. **6** see STORE *v.* 2. **7** put *or*
  set down, put in writing, commit to writing *or* paper.
  8 see SACRIFICE *v.* 3. **lay one's hands on** see OBTAIN 1.
  lay hold of seize, grasp, grab, snatch, catch *or* get hold
  of, get, *sl.* nab. **lay in** see *stock up* 2. **lay it on thick**
  see EXAGGERATE, FLATTER 1. **lay low** see *put down* 1, 2
  (PUT[1]). **lay off 1** suspend; dismiss, discharge, release,
  let go, axe, boot (out), *colloq.* sack, kick out. **2** see
  CEASE *v.* **the lay of the land** state of affairs, condition,
  situation; atmosphere, mood, spirit, temper, character.
  lay on 1 see SPREAD *v.* 1b. **2** see INFLICT 1. **3** see IMPOSE
  1, 2. **lay open 2** see EXPOSE 3. **lay out 1** see SPREAD *v.*
  1a. **2** see EXPOSE 7. **4** see *knock out* 1. **6** see SPEND 1.
  lay up 1 see STORE *v.* 2.

lay[2] /lay/ *adj.* **1 a** nonclerical. **b** not ordained into the clergy.
2 a not professionally qualified, esp. in law or medicine. **b**
of or done by such persons. □ **lay brother** (or **sister**) a
person who has taken the vows of a religious order but is
not ordained and is employed in ancillary or manual work.

lay reader a lay person licensed to conduct some religious services. [ME f. OF *lai* f. eccl.L *laicus* f. Gk *laïkos* LAIC]
■ **1** laic, nonclerical, nonecclesiastical, civil; secular, profane, temporal, worldly. **2** amateur, nonprofessional, unprofessional, nonspecialist, popular.

lay³ /lay/ *n.* **1** a short lyric or narrative poem meant to be sung. **2** a song. [ME f. OF *lai*, Prov. *lais*, of unkn. orig.]
■ lyric, ballad, *hist.* ode; see also SONG 1.

lay⁴ *past* of LIE¹.

layabout /láyəbowt/ *n.* a habitual loafer or idler.
■ see IDLER 1.

lay-by /láybī/ *n.* (*pl.* **lay-bys**) **1** *Brit.* an area at the side of an open road where vehicles may stop. **2** a similar arrangement on a canal or railroad. **3** *Austral. & NZ* a system of paying a deposit to secure an article for later purchase.

layer /láyər/ *n. & v.* **1** a thickness of matter, esp. one of several, covering a surface. **2** a person or thing that lays. **3** a hen that lays eggs. **4** a shoot fastened down to take root while attached to the parent plant. ● *v.tr.* **1 a** arrange in layers. **b** cut (hair) in layers. **2** propagate (a plant) as a layer. □□ **layered** *adj.* [ME f. LAY¹ + -ER¹]
■ *n.* **1** see FILM *n.* 1. ● *v.* **1 a** see SPREAD *v.* 1b, 4a.

layette /layét/ *n.* a set of clothing, toilet articles, and bedclothes for a newborn child. [F, dimin. of OF *laie* drawer f. MDu. *laege*]

lay figure /lay/ *n.* **1** a dummy or jointed figure of a human body used by artists for arranging drapery on, etc. **2** an unrealistic character in a novel, etc. **3** a person lacking in individuality. [*lay* f. obs. *layman* f. Du. *leeman* f. obs. *led* joint]

layman /láymən/ *n.* (*pl.* **-men**; *fem.* **laywoman**, *pl.* **-women**) **1** any nonordained member of a church. **2** a person without professional or specialized knowledge in a particular subject.

layoff /láyawf/ *n.* **1** a temporary discharge of workers. **2** a period when this is in force.

layout /láyowt/ *n.* **1** the disposing or arrangement of a site, ground, etc. **2** the way in which plans, printed matter, etc., are arranged or set out. **3** something arranged or set out in a particular way. **4** the makeup of a book, newspaper, etc.

layover /láyōvər/ *n.* a period of rest or waiting before a further stage in a journey, etc.; a stopover.

lazar /lázər, láy-/ *n.* *archaic* a poor and diseased person, esp. a leper. [ME f. med.L *lazarus* f. the name in Luke 16:20]

lazaretto /lázərétō/ *n.* (also **lazaret** /-rét/; *pl.* **lazarettos** or **lazarets**) **1** a hospital for diseased people, esp. lepers. **2** a building or ship for quarantine. **3** the after part of a ship's hold, used for stores. [(F *lazaret*) f. It. *lazzaretto* f. *lazzaro* LAZAR]

laze /layz/ *v. & n.* ● *v.* **1** *intr.* spend time lazily or idly. **2** *tr.* (often foll. by *away*) pass (time) in this way. ● *n.* a spell of lazing. [back-form. f. LAZY]

lazuli /lázəlee, lázyə-, lázhə-/ *n.* = LAPIS LAZULI. [abbr.]

lazy /láyzee/ *adj.* (**lazier**, **laziest**) **1** disinclined to work; doing little work. **2** of or inducing idleness. **3** (of a river, etc.) slow-moving. □□ **lazily** *adv.* **laziness** *n.* [earlier *laysie*, *lasie*, *laesy*, perh. f. LG: cf. LG *lasich* idle]
■ **1** indolent, slothful, sluggish, idle, lethargic, shiftless, languorous, languid, torpid, inert, inactive, fainéant, listless, drowsy, dull, slack, lax, *archaic* otiose. **2** easy, easygoing, relaxed, nonchalant, happy-go-lucky, devil-may-care, carefree, dreamy, *colloq.* laid-back. **3** slow, slow-moving, languid, languorous, sluggish, torpid, stagnant, sullen, tortoiselike, snaillike.

lazybones /láyzeebōnz/ *n.* (*pl.* same) *colloq.* a lazy person.
■ see IDLER 1.

lb. *abbr.* a pound or pounds (weight). [L *libra*]

LC *abbr.* (also **L.C.** or **l.c.**) **1** landing craft. **2** left center. **3** letter of credit. **4** (LC or L.C.) Library of Congress. **5** lowercase. **6** in the passage, etc., cited. [sense 6 f. L *loco citato*]

LCD *abbr.* **1** liquid crystal display. **2** lowest (or least) common denominator.

LCM *abbr.* lowest (or least) common multiple.

LD *abbr.* lethal dose, usu. with a following numeral indicating the percentage of a group of animals killed by such a dose (LD_{50}).

Ld. *abbr.* Lord.

-le¹ /'l/ *suffix* forming nouns, esp.: **1** names of appliances or instruments (*handle*; *thimble*). **2** names of animals and plants (*beetle*; *thistle*). ¶ The suffix has ceased to be syllabic in *fowl*, *snail*, *stile*. [ult. from or repr. OE *-el*, etc. f. Gmc, with many IE cognates]

-le² /'l/ *suffix* (also **-el**) forming nouns with (or orig. with) diminutive sense, or = -AL (*angle*; *castle*; *mantle*; *syllable*; *novel*; *tunnel*). [ME *-el*, *-elle* f. OF ult. f. L forms *-ellus*, *-ella*, etc.]

-le³ /'l/ *suffix* forming adjectives, often with (or orig. with) the sense 'apt or liable to' (*brittle*; *fickle*; *little*; *nimble*). [ME f. OE *-el*, etc. f. Gmc, corresp. to L *-ulus*]

-le⁴ /'l/ *suffix* forming verbs, esp. expressing repeated action or movement or having diminutive sense (*bubble*; *crumple*; *wriggle*). ¶ Examples from OE are *handle*, *nestle*, *startle*, *twinkle*. [OE *-lian* f. Gmc]

lea /lee, láy/ *n. poet.* (also **ley**) a piece of meadow or pasture or arable land. [OE *lēa(h)* f. Gmc]
■ see MEADOW.

leach /leech/ *v.* **1** *tr.* make (a liquid) percolate through some material. **2** *tr.* subject (bark, ore, ash, or soil) to the action of percolating fluid. **3** *tr. & intr.* (foll. by *away*, *out*) remove (soluble matter) or be removed in this way. □□ **leacher** *n.* [prob. repr. OE *leccan* to water, f. WG]
■ **1, 3** see PERCOLATE 1.

lead¹ /leed/ *v., n., & adj.* ● *v.* (*past* and *past part.* **led** /led/) **1** *tr.* cause to go with one, esp. by guiding or showing the way or by going in front and taking a person's hand or an animal's halter, etc. **2** *tr.* **a** direct the actions or opinions of. **b** (often foll. by *to*, or *to* + infin.) guide by persuasion or example or argument (*what led you to that conclusion?*; *was led to think you may be right*). **3** *tr.* (also *absol.*) provide access to; bring to a certain position or destination (*this door leads you into a small room*; *the road leads to Atlanta*; *the path leads uphill*). **4** *tr.* pass or go through (a life, etc., of a specified kind) (*led a miserable existence*). **5** *tr.* **a** have the first place in (*lead the dance*; *leads the world in sugar production*). **b** (*absol.*) go first; be ahead in a race or game. **c** (*absol.*) be preeminent in some field. **6** *tr.* be in charge of (*leads a team of researchers*). **7** *tr.* **a** direct by example. **b** set (a fashion). **c** be the principal player of (a group of musicians). **8** *tr.* (also *absol.*) begin a round of play at cards by playing (a card) or a card of (a particular suit). **9** *intr.* (foll. by *to*) have as an end or outcome; result in (*what does all this lead to?*). **10** *intr.* (foll. by *with*) *Boxing* make an attack (with a particular hand or blow). **11 a** *intr.* (foll. by *with*) (of a newspaper) use a particular item as the main story (*led with the stock-market crash*). **b** *tr.* (of a story) be the main feature of (a newspaper or part of it) (*the governor's wedding will lead the front page*). **12** *tr.* (foll. by *through*) make (a liquid, strip of material, etc.) pass through a pulley, channel, etc. ● *n.* **1** guidance given by going in front; example. **2 a** a leading place; the leadership (*is in the lead*; *take the lead*). **b** the amount by which a competitor is ahead of the others (*a lead of ten yards*). **3** a clue, esp. an early indication of the resolution of a problem (*is the first real lead in the case*). **4** a strap or cord for leading a dog, etc. **5** esp. *Brit.* a conductor (usu. a wire) conveying electric current from a source to an appliance. **6 a** the chief part in a play, etc. **b** the person playing this. **7** (in full **lead story**) the item of news given the greatest prominence in a newspaper or magazine. **8 a** the act or right of playing first in a game or round of cards. **b** the card led. **9** the distance advanced by a screw in one turn. **10 a** an artificial watercourse, esp. one leading to a mill. **b** a channel of water in an icefield. ● *attrib.adj.* leading; principal; first. □ **lead astray** see ASTRAY. **lead by the nose** cajole (a person) into compliance. **lead a person a dance** see DANCE. **lead-in 1** an introduction, opening, etc. **2** a wire leading in from out-

---

/. . ./ **pronunciation**   ● **part of speech**

□ **phrases, idioms, and compounds**

□□ **derivatives**   ■ **synonym section**

cross-references appear in SMALL CAPITALS or *italics*

side, esp. from an aerial to a receiver or transmitter. **lead off 1 a** begin; make a start. **b** *Baseball* be the first batter in the batting order or the inning. **2** *colloq.* lose one's temper. **lead on 1** entice into going further than was intended. **2** mislead or deceive. **lead time** the time between the initiation and completion of a production process. **lead up the garden path** *colloq.* mislead. **lead up to 1** form an introduction to; precede; prepare for. **2** direct one's talk gradually or cautiously to a particular topic, etc. **lead the way** see WAY. □□ **leadable** *adj.* [OE *lædan* f. Gmc]

■ *v.* **1** conduct, take, convey, move, walk, steer, pilot, guide, show (the way), escort, accompany, usher, shepherd. **2** bring, guide, take, direct, move, induce, cause, influence, prompt, incline, persuade, dispose, convince. **3** go, run, communicate with, connect with; bring, take, carry, convey. **4** pass, spend, go through, experience, live through; suffer, bear, endure, undergo. **5** be *or* go first, be top, be in the lead; take the lead, be *or* move *or* go *or* forge ahead; excel, dominate, shine, be preeminent; surpass, exceed, precede, outstrip, distance, outrun, outpace, overshadow, outdo, beat. **6, 7a** be in charge of, run, head (up), direct, supervise, manage, be responsible for, superintend, oversee, govern, command, control, administer, preside, chair, spearhead; captain, skipper. **9** (*lead to*) result in, create, engender, cause, bring on *or* about, produce, give rise to, be conducive to, contribute to. ● *n.* **1** direction, guidance, leadership, precedent, example, model, exemplar, pattern, standard. **2** front, vanguard, van, pole position, first place; supremacy, priority, primacy, preeminence; advantage, edge, advance, margin, gap, distance. **3** tip, clue, indication, pointer, hint, suggestion, cue, intimation; evidence, information, advice, tip-off. **4** leash, tether, restraint, cord, rope, chain; strap, curb, halter, rein, leading strings *or* reins. **6** protagonist, principal, hero, heroine, leading role, leading lady *or* man, star; prima donna, diva; prima ballerina. ● *attrib. adj.* leading, foremost, first; main, chief, principal, premier, paramount. □ **lead-in 1** introduction, opening, overture, preamble, preface, prelude, prolegomenon, prologue, *colloq.* intro. **lead off 1 a** see BEGIN 1, 5. **lead on 1** lure, allure, entice, seduce, beguile, inveigle, tempt, draw on, suck in, *colloq.* sweet-talk, soft-soap. **2** see MISLEAD. **lead up the garden path** see MISLEAD. **lead up to 1** precede, introduce, usher in; prepare *or* pave *or* clear (the way) for, do the groundwork *or* spadework for. **2** approach, broach, bring up, present, introduce, work up *or* around to, get (up) to.

lead² /led/ *n. & v.* ● *n.* **1** *Chem.* a heavy, bluish-gray soft ductile metallic element occurring naturally in galena and used in building and the manufacture of alloys. ¶ Symb.: **Pb. 2 a** graphite. **b** a thin length of this for use in a pencil. **3** a lump of lead used in sounding water. **4** (in *pl.*) *Brit.* **a** strips of lead covering a roof. **b** a piece of lead-covered roof. **5** (in *pl.*) *Brit.* lead frames holding the glass of a lattice or stained-glass window. **6** *Printing* a blank space between lines of print (orig. with ref. to the metal strip used to give this space). **7** (*attrib.*) made of lead. ● *v.tr.* **1** cover, weight, or frame (a roof or window panes) with lead. **2** *Printing* separate lines of (printed matter) with leads. **3** add a lead compound to (gasoline, etc.). □ **lead acetate** a white crystalline compound of lead that dissolves in water to form a sweet-tasting solution. **lead balloon** a failure; an unsuccessful venture. **lead-free** (of gasoline) without added tetraethyl lead. **lead pencil** a pencil of graphite enclosed in wood. **lead poisoning** acute or chronic poisoning by absorption of lead into the body. **lead shot** = SHOT¹ 3b. **lead tetraethyl** = TETRAETHYL LEAD. □□ **leadless** *adj.* [OE *lēad* f. WG]

leaden /led'n/ *adj.* **1** of or like lead. **2** heavy; slow; burdensome (*leaden limbs*). **3** inert; depressing (*leaden rule*). **4** lead-colored (*leaden skies*). □□ **leadenly** *adv.* **leadenness** *n.* [OE *lēaden* (as LEAD²)]

■ **2** heavy, weighty, massive, dense, ponderous, slow, sluggish, slow-moving, onerous, burdensome,

oppressive. **3** inert, lifeless, inanimate, sluggish, listless, inactive, lethargic, languid, languorous, torpid, spiritless, stagnant, static, stationary, dense, heavy, dull, numbing, depressing, oppressive. **4** gray, ashen, smoky, livid, dull, drab, dingy, murky, gloomy, dark, somber, glowering, lowering, dreary, dismal, oppressive, sullen; cloudy, overcast, sunless.

leader /lēedər/ *n.* **1 a** a person or thing that leads. **b** a person followed by others. **2 a** the principal player in a music group or of the first violins in an orchestra. **b** a conductor of an orchestra. **3** esp. *Brit.* = *leading article.* **4** a short strip of nonfunctioning material at each end of a reel of film or recording tape for connection to the spool. **5** (in full **Leader of the House**) *Brit.* a member of the government officially responsible for initiating business in Parliament. **6** a shoot of a plant at the apex of a stem or of the main branch. **7** (in *pl.*) *Printing* a series of dots or dashes across the page to guide the eye, esp. in tabulated material. **8** the horse placed at the front in a team or pair. □□ **leaderless** *adj.* **leadership** *n.* [OE *lēdere* (as LEAD¹)]

■ **1** chief, head, director, chairman, chairwoman, chairperson, chair, principal, manager, executive, kingpin, esp. *Brit.* supremo, *colloq.* boss, number one, *Brit. colloq.* gaffer, *sl.* (big) cheese, (head) honcho, Mr. Big; king, queen, sovereign, monarch, ruler, governor, president, premier, head of state, prime minister; commander (in chief), commandant, admiral, warlord, chieftain, caudillo, duce, führer, *hist.* pendragon; initiator, pioneer, organizer, brain(s), fugleman, father, apostle, pillar; aga, ayatollah, imam, sharif, sheikh, maharishi, rabbi, *hist.* Mahdi, esp. *hist.* caliph; conductor, pilot, guide, escort; figurehead, flagship, standard-bearer, leading light, protagonist, pacesetter, trendsetter; tribune, sachem, *hist.* demagogue; captain, skipper. **2** conductor, director, bandmaster, bandleader; concertmaster. □□ **leadership** direction, guidance, lead, leading, command, regulation, control, management, executive, supervision, superintendence, running, administration, organization, operation, influence, initiative; governorship, directorship, chairmanship, headship; rule, sway, monarchy, government, presidency, premiership, regime, reign, sovereignty, hegemony; apostolate.

leading¹ /lēeding/ *adj. & n.* ● *adj.* chief; most important. ● *n.* guidance; leadership. □ **leading article** *Brit.* a newspaper article giving the editorial opinion. **leading edge 1** the foremost edge of an airfoil, esp. a wing or propeller blade. **2** *Electronics* the part of a pulse in which the amplitude increases (opp. *trailing edge*). **3** *colloq.* the forefront of development, esp. in technology. **leading lady** the actress playing the principal part. **leading light** a prominent and influential person. **leading man** the actor playing the principal part. **leading note** *Mus.* = *leading tone.* **leading question** a question that prompts the answer wanted. **leading strings** (or **reins**) **1** strings for guiding children learning to walk. **2** oppressive supervision or control. **leading tone** *Mus.* the seventh note of a diatonic scale.

■ *adj.* chief, principal, main, prime, cardinal, capital, foremost, head, premier, top, front, key, star, supreme, first, greatest, best, paramount, primary, preeminent, predominant, dominant, major, central, essential, banner; important, outstanding, prominent, influential, great, grand; peerless, matchless, unequaled, unrivaled, unsurpassed. ● *n.* see *leadership* (LEADER). □ **leading article** editorial, lead (story), esp. *Brit.* leader. **leading lady, leading man** see LEAD¹ *n.* 6. **leading light** see STAR *n.* 8a.

leading² /lēding/ *n. Printing* = LEAD² *n.* 6.

leadoff /lēedawf/ *n.* **1** an action beginning a process. **2** *Baseball* the first batter in the batting order or the inning.

leadwort /lēdwort, -wawrt/ *n.* = PLUMBAGO 2.

leaf /leef/ *n. & v.* ● *n.* (*pl.* **leaves** /leevz/) **1 a** each of several flattened usu. green structures of a plant, usu. on the side of a stem or branch and the main organ of photosynthesis. **b** other similar plant structures, e.g., bracts, sepals, and petals (*floral leaf*). **2 a** foliage regarded collectively. **b** the state of having leaves out (*a tree in leaf*). **3** the leaves of tobacco or tea. **4** a single thickness of paper, esp. in a book with each side forming a page. **5** a very thin sheet of metal, esp. gold or silver. **6 a** the hinged part or flap of a door, shutter, table, etc. **b** an extra section inserted to extend a table. ● *v.* **1** *intr.* put forth leaves. **2** *tr.* (foll. by *through*) turn over the pages of (a book, etc.). □ **leaf-green** the color of green leaves. **leaf insect** any insect of the family Phylliidae, having a flattened body leaflike in appearance. **leaf miner** any of various larvae burrowing in leaves, esp. moth caterpillars of the family Gracillariidae. **leaf mold** soil consisting chiefly of decayed leaves. **leaf spring** a spring made of strips of metal. □□ **leafage** *n.* **leafed** *adj.* (also in *comb.*). **leafless** *adj.* **leaflessness** *n.* **leaflike** *adj.* [OE *lēaf* f. Gmc]

■ *n.* **1** see BLADE 3. **4** see SHEET¹ *n.* 6. ● *v.* **2** see THUMB *v.* 2. □□ **leafless** see BARE *adj.* 2a.

leafhopper /leéfhopər/ *n.* any homopterous insect of the family Cicadellidae, which sucks the sap of plants and often causes damage and spreads disease.

leaflet /leéflit/ *n.* & *v.* ● *n.* **1** a young leaf. **2** *Bot.* any division of a compound leaf. **3** a sheet of (usu. printed) paper (sometimes folded but not stitched) giving information, esp. for free distribution. ● *v.tr.* (**leafleted, leafleting; leafletted, leafletting**) distribute leaflets to.

■ *n.* **3** pamphlet, folder, brochure, booklet, handbill, bill, circular, handout, flyer; advertisement, *colloq.* ad; (*leaflets*) documentation, junk mail, *colloq.* literature.

leafstalk /leéfstawk/ *n.* a petiole.

leafy /leéfee/ *adj.* (**leafier, leafiest**) **1** having many leaves; (of a place) rich in foliage; verdant. **2** resembling a leaf. □□ **leafiness** *n.*

■ **1** foliate; green, verdant, lush; tree-lined, woody, *literary* bosky; shady, shadowy.

league¹ /leeg/ *n.* & *v.* ● *n.* **1** a collection of people, countries, groups, etc., combining for a particular purpose, esp. mutual protection or cooperation. **2** an agreement to combine in this way. **3** a group of sports organizations that compete over a period for a championship. **4** a class of contestants. ● *v.intr.* (**leagues, leagued, leaguing**) (often foll. by *together*) join in a league. □ **in league** allied; conspiring. **League of Women Voters** an Amer. nonpartisan organization that promotes and sponsors programs, etc., that encourage voter awareness and participations. [F *ligue* or It. *liga*, var. of *lega* f. *legare* bind f. L *ligare*]

■ *n.* **1, 3** confederation, federation, union, association, coalition, alliance, combination, confederacy, organization; guild, society, institute, body, fraternity, band, fellowship, club, party; cabal, gang, group, ring, circle, syndicate, pool. **2** pact, bond, covenant, contract, agreement, arrangement, treaty. **4** class, grade, rank, level; division, category, group, classification. ● *v.* ally, unite, combine, associate, affiliate, confederate, collaborate, band together, join (forces), team up, get together, *colloq.* gang up; conspire, collude, plot, connive, scheme. □ **in league** allied, united, in alliance, in collusion, *sl.* in cahoots; conspiring.

league² /leeg/ *n. archaic* a varying measure of traveling distance by land, usu. about three miles. [ME, ult. f. LL *leuga, leuca,* of Gaulish orig.]

leaguer¹ /leégər/ *n.* a member of a league.

leaguer² /leégər/ *n.* & *v.* = LAAGER. [Du. *leger* camp, rel. to LAIR¹]

leak /leek/ *n.* & *v.* ● *n.* **1 a** a hole in a vessel, pipe, or container, etc., caused by wear or damage, through which matter, esp. liquid or gas, passes accidentally in or out. **b** the matter passing in or out through this. **c** the act or an instance of leaking. **2 a** a similar escape of electrical charge. **b** the charge that escapes. **3** the intentional disclosure of secret information. ● *v.* **1 a** *intr.* (of liquid, gas, etc.) pass in or out through a leak. **b** *tr.* lose or admit (liquid, gas, etc.) through a leak. **2** *tr.* intentionally disclose (secret information). **3** *intr.* (often foll. by *out*) (of a secret, secret infor-

mation) become known. □ **take a leak** *sl.* urinate. □□ **leaker** *n.* [ME prob. f. LG]

■ *n.* **1 a** hole, fissure, crack, chink, crevice, aperture, opening, puncture, perforation, cut, break, breach, rip, split, gash, rent, tear, gap, flaw. **b, c** leakage, discharge, trickle, escape, seepage, spillage, ooze, secretion, exudation, flow, outflow, effluence, efflux, emanation, *archaic* issue. **3** disclosure, revelation, leakage, exposure, divulgence, divulgement, divulgation, publication, release. ● *v.* **1 a** come *or* go *or* get out, escape, issue, emerge, spill (out), trickle (out), drip (out), dribble (out), seep (out), ooze (out), exude, pour *or* stream *or* flow out, extravasate. **b** discharge, spill, drip, ooze, exude, secrete, stream, pour, dribble, extravasate. **2** disclose, divulge, reveal, bring to light, impart, betray, tell, report, publish, release, give *or* let out, make known *or* public; let slip, blab, *colloq.* spill the beans about. **3** (*leak out*) transpire, come *or* get out, escape, emerge, trickle out, come to light, become known. □ **take a leak** see URINATE.

leakage /leékij/ *n.* **1** the action or result of leaking. **2** what leaks in or out. **3** an intentional disclosure of secret information.

■ **1, 2** see LEAK *n.* 1b, c. **3** see LEAK *n.* 3.

leaky /leékee/ *adj.* (**leakier, leakiest**) **1** having a leak or leaks. **2** given to letting out secrets. □□ **leakiness** *n.*

leal /leel/ *adj. Sc.* loyal; honest. [ME f. AF *leal*, OF *leel, loial* (as LOYAL)]

lean¹ /leen/ *v.* & *n.* ● *v.* (*past* and *past part.* **leaned** /leend, lent/ or **leant** /lent/) **1** *intr.* & *tr.* (often foll. by *across, back, over,* etc.) be or place in a sloping position; incline from the perpendicular. **2** *intr.* & *tr.* (foll. by *against, on, upon*) rest or cause to rest for support against, etc. **3** *intr.* (foll. by *on, upon*) rely on; derive support from. **4** *intr.* (foll. by *to, toward*) be inclined or partial to; have a tendency toward. ● *n.* a deviation from the perpendicular; an inclination (*has a decided lean to the right*). □ **lean on** put pressure on (a person) to act in a certain way. **lean over backward** see BACKWARD. **lean-to** (*pl.* **-tos**) **1** a building with its roof leaning against a larger building or a wall. **2** a shed with an inclined roof usu. leaning against trees, posts, etc. [OE *hleonian, hlinian* f. Gmc]

■ *v.* **1** slope, incline, slant, tilt, bend, tip. **2** (*tr.*) rest, prop, set, put, lay, place, position; (*intr.*) lie, rest, repose, recline, be propped *or* supported *or* sustained. **3** (*lean on*) rely on, depend on, count on, bank on, pin one's faith *or* hopes on; believe *or* trust in, have confidence in, be sure *or* certain of. **4** (*lean to* or *toward*) favor, gravitate toward, tend toward, be disposed toward, prefer, show *or* have a preference for, incline toward, be inclined *or* partial to, be *or* lean on the side of, be biased toward, have a tendency to *or* toward, be in favor of. ● *n.* inclination, slant, tilt, tip, slope, pitch, rake, cant, camber, ramp, angle, deviation. □ **lean on** pressure, pressurize, put pressure on, bring pressure to bear on; intimidate, squeeze, railroad, browbeat, threaten, menace, *colloq.* bulldoze, heavy, put the screws on. **lean-to** see SHED¹ 1.

lean² /leen/ *adj.* & *n.* ● *adj.* **1** (of a person or animal) thin; having no superfluous fat. **2** (of meat) containing little fat. **3 a** meager; of poor quality (*lean crop*). **b** not nourishing (*lean diet*). **4** unremunerative. ● *n.* the lean part of meat. □ **lean years** years of scarcity. □□ **leanly** *adv.* **leanness** *n.* [OE *hlǣne* f. Gmc]

■ *adj.* **1** thin, slim, slender, spare, skinny, bony, meager, skeletal, scraggy, scrawny, emaciated, wasted, gaunt, haggard, pinched, raw-boned, weasel-faced, hollow-cheeked, rangy, wiry, lanky, spindly, lank, angular, gangling, gangly, twiggy, reedy; *colloq.* nothing but *or* all skin and bone(s). **3 a** meager, poor, scanty, scant, skimpy, inadequate, deficient, insufficient, sparse; unfruitful, unproductive, barren, infertile, bare, arid. **4** unremunerative, unfruitful, unprofitable, fruitless; hard, bad, tough, difficult; impoverished, poverty-stricken, penurious.

leaning /lééning/ *n.* a tendency or partiality.
■ tendency, partiality, bent, inclination, bias, prejudice, predilection, liking, taste, preference, penchant, disposition, propensity, predisposition, proclivity, affinity, sympathy.

leap /leep/ *v. & n.* ● *v.* (*past and past part.* **leaped** /leept, lept/ or **leapt** /lept/) **1** *intr.* jump or spring forcefully. **2** *tr.* jump across. **3** *intr.* (of prices, etc.) increase dramatically. **4** *intr.* hurry; rush; proceed without pausing for thought (*leaped to the wrong conclusion; leapt to their defense*). ● *n.* a forceful jump. □ **by leaps and bounds** with startlingly rapid progress. **leap at 1** rush toward, pounce upon. **2** accept eagerly. **leap in the dark** a daring step or enterprise whose consequences are unpredictable. **leap to the eye** be immediately apparent. **leap of faith** an act or instance of accepting something on the basis of belief or trust not reason or fact. **leap year** a year, occurring once in four, with 366 days (including Feb. 29 as an intercalary day). □□ **leaper** *n.* [OE *hlýp, hléapan* f. Gmc: *leap year* prob. refers to the fact that feast days after Feb. in such a year fall two days later (instead of the normal one day later) than in the previous year]
■ *v.* **1** jump, spring, bound, hop, skip; gambol, caper, prance, curvet, *sl.* cavort. **2** jump, hurdle, vault, clear, leapfrog, hop (over), negotiate. **3** jump, increase, climb, rise, surge, soar, rocket, shoot up, escalate. **4** jump, rush, hurry, hasten. ● *n.* jump, spring, bound, vault, hurdle, hop, skip; climb, rise, hike, surge, upsurge, escalation, lift, *colloq.* boost. □ **by leaps and bounds** rapidly, quickly, swiftly, speedily, fast, at a gallop, *colloq.* like greased lightning, like blazes, like a house on fire, like a bat out of hell, *literary* apace. **leap at 2** jump at, accept, be eager for, take; seize (on), grab (at), pounce on, grasp, *colloq.* swoop up(on).

leapfrog /léepfrawg, -frog/ *n. & v.* ● *n.* a game in which players in turn vault with parted legs over another who is bending down. ● *v.* (**-frogged, -frogging**) **1** *intr.* (foll. by *over*) perform such a vault. **2** *tr.* vault over in this way. **3** *tr. & intr.* (of two or more people, vehicles, etc.) overtake alternately.

learn /lərn/ *v.* (*past and past part.* **learned** /lərnd, lərnt/ or esp. *Brit.* **learnt** /lərnt/) **1** *tr.* gain knowledge of or skill in by study, experience, or being taught. **2** *tr.* (foll. by *to* + infin.) acquire or develop a particular ability (*learn to swim*). **3** *tr.* commit to memory (*will try to learn your names*). **4** *intr.* (foll. by *of*) be informed about. **5** *tr.* (foll. by *that, how,* etc. + clause) become aware of by information or from observation. **6** *intr.* receive instruction; acquire knowledge or skill. **7** *tr. archaic* or *sl.* teach. □ **learn one's lesson** see LESSON. □□ **learnable** *adj.* **learnability** /lə́rnəbílitee/ *n.* [OE *leornian* f. Gmc: cf. LORE[1]]
■ **1, 2** be taught; be instructed in, have *or* take lessons in; master, study, get to know, get to grips with, get the hang of, *archaic* con. **3** memorize, commit to memory, learn by heart *or* rote; remember, retain, keep in mind. **4** (*learn of*) find out (about), discover, uncover, unearth, determine, identify, ascertain; hear of *or* about, gather, pick up, chance *or* hit upon, come across. **5** find out, discover, gather, hear, see, understand, grasp, comprehend, discern, perceive, realize, recognize, *Brit. colloq.* twig; conclude, infer, deduce. **6** study, train, practice, revise. **7** see TEACH 1.

learned /lə́rnid/ *adj.* **1** having much knowledge acquired by study. **2** showing or requiring learning (*a learned work*). **3** studied or pursued by learned persons. **4** concerned with the interests of learned persons; scholarly (*a learned journal*). **5** as a courteous description of a lawyer or colleague in certain formal contexts (*my learned friend*). □□ **learnedly** *adv.* **learnedness** *n.* [ME f. LEARN in the sense 'teach']

■ **1** knowledgeable, (well-)informed, erudite, (well-)educated, lettered, well-read, literate, cultured; scholarly, academic, intellectual, scholastic, *colloq.* highbrow; expert, authoritative, au fait, au courant, *colloq.* in the know; experienced, skilled, practiced, accomplished, (well-)versed, (well-)trained, (well-)grounded. **2–4** scholarly, academic, intellectual, cerebral, *colloq.* highbrow; abstract, theoretical, abstruse, formal, profound, deep, philosophical; educational, academical, collegiate; pedantic, scholastic, donnish, professorial, bookish, literary.

learner /lə́rnər/ *n.* **1** a person who is learning a subject or skill. **2** (in full **learner driver**) *Brit.* = *student driver.*
■ **1** student, pupil, trainee, apprentice; beginner, novice, tyro, initiate, neophyte, acolyte, newcomer, recruit, greenhorn, tenderfoot, punk, cub, *sl.* rookie.

learning /lə́rning/ *n.* knowledge acquired by study. □ **learning curve 1** a graph showing the time needed to acquire a new skill, knowledge of a subject, etc. **2** the time represented by such a graph. **learning disability** a disorder (such as dyslexia) that interferes with the learning process in a child of usu. normal intelligence. [OE *leornung* (as LEARN)]
■ knowledge, lore, wisdom, erudition; schooling, education, instruction, scholarship, illumination; information, facts, data, intelligence; culture.

lease /lees/ *n. & v.* ● *n.* an agreement by which the owner of a building or land allows another to use it for a specified time, usu. in return for payment. ● *v.tr.* grant or take on lease. □ **a new lease on life** a substantially improved prospect of living, or of use after repair. □□ **leasable** *adj.* **leaser** *n.* [ME f. AF *les*, OF *lais, leis* f. *lesser, laissier* leave f. L *laxare* make loose (*laxus*)]
■ *n.* rental, hire, charter, *Brit.* let, *Sc.* feu; sublease, sublet, underlet; agreement, contract, arrangement, settlement, deal. ● *v.* rent (out), let (out), hire (out), charter, *Law* demise; sublet, sublease.

leaseback /léesbak/ *n.* the leasing of a property back to the vendor.

leasehold /lées-hōld/ *n. & adj.* ● *n.* **1** the holding of property by lease. **2** property held by lease. ● *adj.* held by lease. □□ **leaseholder** *n.*
■ □□ **leaseholder** see TENANT *n.* 1.

leash /leesh/ *n. & v.* ● *n.* a thong for holding a dog; a dog's lead. ● *v.tr.* **1** put a leash on. **2** restrain. □ **straining at the leash** eager to begin. [ME f. OF *lesse, laisse* f. specific use of *laisser* let run on a slack lead: see LEASE]
■ *n.* see LEAD[1] *n.* 4. ● *v.* see TETHER *v.*

least /leest/ *adj., n., & adv.* ● *adj.* **1** smallest; slightest; most insignificant. **2** (prec. by *the*; esp. with *neg.*) any at all (*it does not make the least difference*). **3** (of a species or variety) very small (*least tern*). ● *n.* the least amount. ● *adv.* in the least degree. □ **at least 1** at all events; anyway; even if there is doubt about a more extended statement. **2** (also **at the least**) not less than. **in the least** (or **the least**) (usu. with *neg.*) in the smallest degree; at all (*not in the least offended*). **least common denominator, multiple** see DENOMINATOR, MULTIPLE. **to say the least** (or **the least of it**) used to imply the moderation of a statement (*that is doubtful to say the least*). [OE *lǣst, lǣsest* f. Gmc]
■ *adj.* **1** see MINIMUM *adj.* **3** see LITTLE *adj.* 7. ● *n.* see MINIMUM *n.*

leastways /léestwayz/ *adv.* (also **leastwise** /-wiz/) *dial.* or at least, or rather.

leat /leet/ *n. Brit.* an open watercourse conducting water to a mill, etc. [OE *-gelæt* (as Y- + root of LET[1])]

leather /léthər/ *n. & v.* ● *n.* **1 a** material made from the skin of an animal by tanning or a similar process. **b** (*attrib.*) made of leather. **2** a piece of leather for polishing with. **3** the leather part or parts of something. **4** *sl.* a football. **5** (in *pl.*) leather clothes, esp. leggings, breeches, or clothes for wearing on a motorcycle. **6** a thong (*stirrup-leather*). ● *v.tr.* **1** cover with leather. **2** polish or wipe with a leather. **3** beat; thrash (orig. with a leather thong). [OE *lether* f. Gmc]
■ *n.* **1** see HIDE[2] *n.* 1. ● *v.* **3** see BEAT *v.* 1.

leatherback /léthərbak/ *n.* a large marine turtle, *Dermochelys coriacea*, having a thick leathery carapace.

leathercloth /léthərklawth, -kloth/ *n.* strong fabric coated to resemble leather.

leatherette /léthərét/ *n.* imitation leather.

leatherjacket /léthərjakət/ *n.* **1** a crane-fly grub with a tough skin. **2** any of various tough-skinned marine fish of the family Monacanthidae.

leathern /léthərn/ *n. archaic* made of leather.

leatherneck /léthərnek/ *n. sl.* a US Marine (with reference to the leather collar formerly worn by them).

leathery /léthəree/ *adj.* **1** like leather. **2** (esp. of meat, etc.) tough. □□ **leatheriness** *n.*

■ **2** see TOUGH *adj.* 1.

leave¹ /leev/ *v.* (*past* and *past part.* **left** /left/) **1 a** *tr.* go away from; cease to remain in or on (*left him an hour ago; leave the track; leave here*). **b** *intr.* (often foll. by *for*) depart (*we leave tomorrow; has just left for Denver*). **2** *tr.* cause to or let remain; depart without taking (*has left his gloves; left a slimy trail; left a bad impression; six from seven leaves one*). **3** *tr.* (also *absol.*) cease to reside at or attend or belong to or work for (*has left the school; I am leaving for another firm*). **4** *tr.* abandon; forsake; desert. **5** *tr.* have remaining after one's death (*leaves a wife and two children*). **6** *tr.* bequeath. **7** *tr.* (foll. by *to* + infin.) allow (a person or thing) to do something without interference or assistance (*leave the future to take care of itself*). **8** *tr.* (foll. by *to*) commit or refer to another person (*leave that to me; nothing was left to chance*). **9** *tr.* **a** abstain from consuming or dealing with. **b** (in *passive*; often foll. by *over*) remain over. **10** *tr.* **a** deposit or entrust (a thing) to be attended to, collected, delivered, etc., in one's absence (*left a message with his assistant*). **b** depute (a person) to perform a function in one's absence. **11** *tr.* allow to remain or cause to be in a specified state or position (*left the door open; the performance left them unmoved; left nothing that was necessary undone*). **12** *tr.* pass (an object) so that it is in a specified relative direction (*leave the church on the left*). ● *n.* the position in which a player leaves the balls in billiards, croquet, etc. □ **be left with 1** retain (a feeling, etc.). **2** be burdened with (a responsibility, etc.). **be well left** be well provided for by a legacy, etc. **get left** *colloq.* be deserted. **have left** have remaining (*has no friends left*). **leave alone 1** refrain from disturbing; not interfere with. **2** not have dealings with. **leave be** *colloq.* refrain from disturbing; not interfere with. **leave behind 1** go away without. **2** leave as a consequence or a visible sign of passage. **3** pass. **leave a person cold** (or **cool**) not impress or excite a person. **leave go** *colloq.* relax one's hold. **leave hold of** cease holding. **leave it at that** *colloq.* abstain from comment or further action. **leave much** (or **a lot,** etc.) **to be desired** be highly unsatisfactory. **leave off 1** come to or make an end. **2** discontinue (*leave off work; leave off talking*). **3** not wear. **leave out** omit; not include. **leave over** *Brit.* leave to be considered, settled, or used later. **leave a person to himself** or **herself 1** not attempt to control a person. **2** leave a person solitary. **left at the gate** (**post**) beaten from the start of a race. **left for dead** abandoned as being beyond rescue. **left luggage** *Brit.* luggage deposited for later retrieval, esp. at a railroad station. □□ **leaver** *n.* [OE *lǣfan* f. Gmc]

■ *v.* **1b, 3, 4** depart, go or move (away *or* off), get *or* be away *or* off, be gone, be on one's way, go one's way, (make an) exit, get going, set off, check out, take off, *colloq.* fly, be off, push off, clear off, disappear, vanish, skedaddle, scram, *Brit. colloq.* flit, up sticks, *sl.* shove off, vamoose, buzz off, beat it, split, esp. *Brit. sl.* slope off, do a bunk, hop it; say good-bye, take one's leave, *archaic or literary* bid farewell *or* adieu; retire, (beat a) retreat, withdraw, decamp, pull out; quit, get *or* go *or* jump out of, disembark from, evacuate; desert, abandon, forsake; break (up) with, jilt, walk *or* run out on, throw over, cast off *or* aside, turn one's back on, leave in the lurch, discard, drop, *colloq.* dump, *sl.* ditch. **2** leave behind; forget, go without, mislay, lose. **6** see BEQUEATH 1, 2. **7** allow, let, permit, authorize, *archaic* suffer. **8** entrust, commit, consign, refer, assign, delegate, hand over, deliver, give. **9 a** abstain *or* refrain from, avoid, shun, keep *or* stay off *or* away from, keep *or* steer clear of, leave alone, *literary* eschew. **b** (*left over*) remaining, over; extra, spare, excess, unwanted. **10 a** deposit, entrust, consign, lodge, place, put, keep, store, stow, *colloq.* stash (away). □ **be left with 1** retain, keep, hold on to, preserve, *colloq.* hang on to. **2** be burdened *or* saddled *or* lumbered with. **leave alone 1** lay off, leave be, leave in peace. **2** see LEAVE¹ *v.* 9a above. **leave be** see *leave alone* 1 above. **leave behind 1, 2** see LEAVE¹ *v.* 2 above. **leave off 1, 2** see END *v.* 1. **leave out** see OMIT 1.

leave² /leev/ *n.* **1** (often foll. by *to* + infin.) permission. **2 a** (in full **leave of absence**) permission to be absent from duty. **b** the period for which this lasts. □ **by** (or **with**) **your leave** often *iron.* an expression of apology for taking a liberty or making an unwelcome statement. **on leave** legitimately absent from duty. **take one's leave** bid farewell. **take one's leave of** bid farewell to. **take leave of one's senses** see SENSE. **take leave to** venture or presume to. [OE *lēaf* f. WG: cf. LIEF, LOVE]

■ **1** permission, authority, authorization, license, consent, assent, agreement, acquiescence, sufferance, approval, blessing, sanction, dispensation, go-ahead, thumbs up, *colloq.* green light. **2** furlough, time off, holiday, vacation, sabbatical; R and R, free time; sick leave. □ **take one's leave** see LEAVE¹ *v.* 1b, 3, 4.

leaved /leevd/ *adj.* **1** having leaves. **2** (in *comb.*) having a leaf or leaves of a specified kind or number (*red-leaved maple*).

leaven /lévən/ *n. & v.* ● *n.* **1** a substance added to dough to make it ferment and rise, esp. yeast, or fermenting dough reserved for the purpose. **2 a** a pervasive transforming influence (cf. Matt. 13:33). **b** (foll. by *of*) a tinge or admixture of a specified quality. ● *v.tr.* **1** ferment (dough) with leaven. **2 a** permeate and transform. **b** (foll. by *with*) modify with a tempering element. □ **the old leaven** traces of the unregenerate state (cf. 1 Cor. 5:6–8). [ME f. OF *levain* f. Gallo-Roman spec. use of L *levamen* relief f. *levare* lift]

■ *v.* **1** see FERMENT *v.* 1.

leaves *pl.* of LEAF.

leavings /léevingz/ *n.pl.* things left over, esp. as worthless.

■ see LEFTOVER *n.*

Lebanese /lébəneéz/ *adj. & n.* ● *adj.* of or relating to Lebanon in the Middle East. ● *n.* (*pl.* same) **1** a native or national of Lebanon. **2** a person of Lebanese descent.

Lebensraum /láybənzrowm/ *n.* the territory which a nation believes is needed for its natural development. [G, = living space (orig. with reference to Germany, esp. in the 1930s)]

lech /lech/ *v. & n. colloq.* ● *v.intr.* feel lecherous; behave lustfully. ● *n.* **1** a strong desire, esp. sexual. **2** a lecher. [back-form. f. LECHER: (n.) perh. f. *letch* longing]

lecher /léchər/ *n.* a lecherous man; a debauchee. [ME f. OF *lecheor*, etc., f. *lechier* live in debauchery or gluttony f. Frank., rel. to LICK]

■ see LIBERTINE *n.* 1.

lecherous /léchərəs/ *adj.* lustful, having strong or excessive sexual desire. □□ **lecherously** *adv.* **lecherousness** *n.* [ME f. OF *lecheros*, etc. f. *lecheur* LECHER]

■ lustful, randy, lascivious, sexy, licentious, lewd, dirty, filthy, prurient, salacious, libidinous, erotic, sensual, lubricious, promiscuous, depraved, dissolute, ruttish, goatish, goaty, hot, fast, wanton, *formal* concupiscent, *sl.* horny.

lechery /léchəree/ *n.* unrestrained indulgence of sexual desire. [ME f. OF *lecherie* f. *lecheur* LECHER]

■ see DESIRE *n.* 2.

lecithin /lésithin/ *n.* **1** any of a group of phospholipids found naturally in animals, egg yolk, and some higher plants. **2** a

/.../ **pronunciation**	● **part of speech**
□ **phrases, idioms, and compounds**	
□□ **derivatives**	■ **synonym section**
cross-references appear in SMALL CAPITALS or *italics*	

preparation of this used to emulsify foods, etc. [Gk *lekithos* egg yolk + -IN]

lectern /léktərn/ *n.* **1** a stand for holding a book in a church or chapel, esp. for a bible from which lessons are to be read. **2** a similar stand for a lecturer, etc. [ME *lettorne* f. OF *let(t)run*, med.L *lectrum* f. *legere lect-* read]

lection /lékshən/ *n.* a reading of a text found in a particular copy or edition. [L *lectio* reading (as LECTERN)]

lectionary /lékshənéree/ *n.* (*pl.* **-ies**) **1** a list of portions of Scripture appointed to be read at divine service. **2** a book containing such portions. [ME f. med.L *lectionarium* (as LECTION)]

lector /léktər/ *n.* **1** a reader, esp. of lessons in a church service. **2** (esp. *Brit. fem.* **lectrice** /lektreés/) a lecturer or reader, esp. one employed in a foreign university to give instruction in his or her native language. [L f. *legere lect-* read]

lecture /lékchər/ *n. & v.* ● *n.* **1** a discourse giving information about a subject to a class or other audience. **2** a long, serious speech, esp. as a scolding or reprimand. ● *v.* **1** *intr.* (often foll. by *on*) deliver a lecture or lectures. **2** *tr.* talk seriously or reprovingly to (a person). **3** *tr.* instruct or entertain (a class or other audience) by a lecture. [ME f. OF *lecture* or med.L *lectura* f. L (as LECTOR)]

■ *n.* **1** speech, address, talk, presentation, demonstration, paper, dissertation, disquisition, lesson, instruction, declamation, harangue, screed, *literary* discourse, *sl.* spiel; seminar, workshop. **2** speech, sermon, scolding, tongue-lashing, upbraiding, castigation, reproof, reprimand, rebuke, reproach, remonstration, rap on *or* over the knuckles, *colloq.* talking-to, dressing-down, telling-off, chewing-out, esp. *Brit. colloq.* ticking off, *Brit. colloq.* wigging; *old-fashioned* curtain lecture; harangue, diatribe, philippic; censure, criticism. ● *v.* **1** make *or* deliver *or* give a speech *or* address *or* talk *or* presentation, give a paper, speak, talk, discourse, *colloq.* go on, *sl.* spiel; sermonize, hold forth, moralize, pontificate, preach, declaim, esp. *joc. or derog.* orate. **2** reprove, reprimand, rebuke, reproach, scold, upbraid, berate, rate, castigate, harangue, remonstrate with, give a person a tongue-lashing *or* dressing-down, give a person a rap on *or* over the knuckles, have a go at, *archaic or literary* chide, *colloq.* tell off, give a person a telling-off *or* talking-to *or* esp. *Brit.* ticking-off, lambaste, chew out, esp. *Brit. colloq.* tick off, *Brit. colloq.* wig, carpet; admonish, warn, caution, counsel, advise. **3** see INSTRUCT 1.

lecturer /lékchərər/ *n.* a person who lectures, esp. as a teacher in higher education.

■ see TEACHER.

lectureship /lékchərship/ *n.* the office of lecturer. ¶ The form *lecturership*, which is strictly more regular, is in official use at Oxford University and elsewhere, but is not widely current.

lecythus /lésithəs/ *n.* (*pl.* **lecythi** /-thī/) *Gk Antiq.* a thin narrow-necked vase or flask. [Gk *lēkuthos*]

LED *abbr.* light-emitting diode.

led *past* and *past part.* of LEAD[1].

lederhosen /láydərhōzən/ *n.pl.* leather shorts as worn in Bavaria, etc. [G, = leather trousers]

ledge /lej/ *n.* **1** a narrow horizontal surface projecting from a wall, etc. **2** a shelflike projection on the side of a rock or mountain. **3** a ridge of rocks, esp. below water. **4** *Mining* a stratum of metal-bearing rock. □□ **ledged** *adj.* **ledgy** *adj.* [perh. f. ME *legge* LAY[1]]

■ **1** shelf, ridge, projection, overhang, sill, step; mantelpiece, windowsill.

ledger /léjər/ *n.* **1** a tall, narrow book in which a firm's accounts are kept, esp. one which is the principal book of a set and contains debtor-and-creditor accounts. **2** a flat gravestone. **3** a horizontal timber in scaffolding, parallel to the face of the building. □ **ledger line 1** *Mus.* a short line added for notes above or below the range of a staff. **2** a kind of fishing tackle in which a lead weight keeps the bait on the bottom. [ME f. senses of Du. *ligger* and *legger* (f. *liggen* LIE[1], *leggen* LAY[1]) & pronunc. of ME *ligge*, *legge*]

■ **1** see JOURNAL 4.

lee /lee/ *n.* **1** shelter given by a neighboring object (*under the lee of*). **2** (in full **lee side**) the sheltered side, the side away from the wind (opp. *weather side*). □ **lee shore** the shore to leeward of a ship. [OE *hlēo* f. Gmc]

leeboard /leébawrd, -bōrd/ *n.* a plank frame fixed to the side of a flat-bottomed vessel and let down into the water to diminish leeway.

leech[1] /leech/ *n.* **1** any freshwater or terrestrial annelid worm of the class *Hirudinea* with suckers at both ends, esp. *Hirudo medicinalis*, a bloodsucking parasite of vertebrates formerly much used medically. **2** a person who extorts profit from or sponges on others. □ **like a leech** persistently or clingingly present. [OE *lǣce*, assim. to LEECH[2]]

■ **2** see BLOODSUCKER 2.

leech[2] /leech/ *n. archaic* or *joc.* a physician; a healer. [OE *lǣce* f. Gmc]

leech[3] /leech/ *n.* **1** a perpendicular or sloping side of a square sail. **2** the side of a fore-and-aft sail away from the mast or stay. [ME, perh. rel. to ON *lik*, a nautical term of uncert. meaning]

leechcraft /leéchkraft/ *n. archaic* the art of healing. [OE *lǣcecrǣft* (as LEECH[2], CRAFT)]

leek /leek/ *n.* **1** an alliaceous plant, *Allium porrum*, with flat overlapping leaves forming an elongated cylindrical bulb, used as food. **2** this as a Welsh national emblem. [OE *lēac* f. Gmc]

leer[1] /leer/ *v. & n.* ● *v.intr.* look slyly or lasciviously or maliciously. ● *n.* a leering look. □□ **leeringly** *adv.* [perh. f. obs. *leer* cheek f. OE *hlēor*, as though 'to glance over one's cheek']

■ *v.* (*leer at*) ogle, eye (up), make eyes at, give a person the (glad) eye. ● *n.* ogle, *colloq.* the (glad) eye, the once-over.

leer[2] var. of LEHR.

leery /leéree/ *adj.* (**leerier**, **leeriest**) *sl.* **1** knowing; sly. **2** (foll. by *of*) wary. □□ **leeriness** *n.* [perh. f. obs. *leer* looking askance f. LEER[1] + -Y[1]]

■ **1** knowing, sly, cunning, crafty, artful, clever, sharp, canny, wily, guileful, shrewd, devious, disingenuous, tricky, furtive, *colloq.* shifty. **2** wary, suspicious, skeptical, dubious, doubtful, distrustful, cautious, chary, careful, *colloq.* cagey.

lees /leez/ *n.pl.* **1** the sediment of wine, etc. (*drink to the lees*). **2** dregs; refuse. [pl. of ME *lie* f. OF *lie* f. med.L *lia* f. Gaulish]

■ **1** see SEDIMENT 1. **2** see RUBBISH *n.* 2.

leet[1] /leet/ *n. Brit. hist.* **1** (in full **Court leet**) a yearly or half-yearly court of record that lords of certain manors might hold. **2** its jurisdiction or district. [ME f. AF *lete* (= AL *leta*), of unkn. orig.]

leet[2] /leet/ *n. Sc.* a selected list of candidates for some office. □ **short leet** = SHORTLIST. [ME *lite*, etc., prob. f. AF & OF *lit(t)e*, var. of *liste* LIST[1]]

leeward /leéwərd, *Naut.* lōōərd/ *adj., adv., & n.* ● *adj. & adv.* on or toward the side sheltered from the wind (opp. WINDWARD). ● *n.* the leeward region, side, or direction (*to leeward; on the leeward of*).

leewardly /leéwərdlee, lōōərdlee/ *adj.* (of a ship) apt to drift to leeward.

leeway /leéway/ *n.* **1** the sideways drift of a ship to leeward of the desired course. **2 a** allowable deviation or freedom of action. **b** margin of safety. □ **make up leeway** struggle out of a bad position, recover lost time, etc.

■ **2** latitude, scope, freedom, range, play, (elbow)room, (breathing) space; safety factor, margin of error.

left[1] /left/ *adj., adv., & n.* (opp. RIGHT). ● *adj.* **1** on or toward the side of the human body which corresponds to the position of west if one regards oneself as facing north. **2** on or toward the part of an object which is analogous to a person's left side or (with opposite sense) which is nearer to an observer's left hand. **3** (also **Left**) *Polit.* of the Left. ● *adv.* on or to the left side. ● *n.* **1** the left-hand part or region or direction. **2** *Boxing* **a** the left hand. **b** a blow with this. **3 a**

(often **Left**) *Polit.* a group or section favoring liberalism, social reform, etc. (orig. the more radical section of a continental legislature, seated on the president's left); such persons collectively. **b** the more advanced or innovative section of any group. **4** the side of a stage which is to the left of a person facing the audience. **5** (esp. in marching) the left foot. **6** the left wing of an army. □ **have two left feet** be clumsy. **left and right** = *right and left*. **left bank** the bank of a river on the left facing downstream. **left field** *Baseball* the part of the outfield to the left of the batter as he or she faces the pitcher. **left hand 1** the hand of the left side. **2** (usu. prec. by *at*, *on*, *to*) the region or direction on the left side of a person. **left-hand** *adj.* **1** on or toward the left side of a person or thing (*left-hand drive*). **2** done with the left hand (*left-hand blow*). **3 a** (of rope) twisted counterclockwise. **b** (of a screw) = LEFT-HANDED. **left turn** a turn that brings one's front to face as one's left side did before. **left wing 1** the liberal or socialist section of a political party. **2** the left side of a soccer, etc., team on the field. **3** the left side of an army. **left-wing** *adj.* liberal; socialist; radical. **left-winger** a person on the left wing. **marry with the left hand** marry morganatically (see LEFT-HANDED). □□ **leftish** *adj.* [ME *lüft*, *lift*, *left*, f. OE, orig. sense 'weak, worthless']

■ *adj.* **1, 2** left-hand, sinistral, *Naut. archaic* larboard, *Heraldry & archaic* sinister. **3** left-wing, socialist(ic), *Brit.* Labour, *Polit.* leftist, *colloq.* red, esp. *derog.* pink, *sl.* Bolshie; progressive, progressivist, radical, liberal, democratic; communist(ic), Bolshevik, Marxist (-Leninist). ● *n.* **1, 4** left hand, port, *Naut. archaic* larboard; stage left. **3** left wing, left-wingers, socialists, *Brit.* Labour, *Polit.* leftists, *colloq.* lefties, reds, *sl.* Bolshies; progressives, progressivists, radicals, liberals, democrats; communists. □ **have two left feet** be clumsy *or* awkward *or* gauche *or* ungainly. **left hand 2** see LEFT¹ *n.* 1, 4 above. **left-hand 1** see LEFT¹ *adj.* 1, 2 above. **left wing 1** see LEFT¹ *n.* 3 above. **left-wing** see LEFT¹ *adj.* 3 above. **left-winger** socialist, Bolshevik, Bolshevist, *Polit.* leftist, *colloq.* red, *sl.* Bolshie; progressive, radical, liberal, democrat; communist.

left ² *past* and *past part.* of LEAVE¹.

left-handed /léft-hándid/ *adj.* **1** using the left hand by preference as more serviceable than the right. **2** (of a tool, etc.) made to be used with the left hand. **3** (of a blow) struck with the left hand. **4 a** turning to the left; toward the left. **b** (of a racecourse) turning counterclockwise. **c** (of a screw) advanced by turning to the left (counterclockwise). **5** awkward; clumsy. **6 a** (of a compliment) ambiguous. **b** of doubtful sincerity or validity. **7** (of a marriage) morganatic (from a German custom by which the bridegroom gave the bride his left hand in such marriages). □□ **left-handedly** *adv.* **left-handedness** *n.*

■ **1** sinistral, *colloq.* southpaw. **4** left-hand; counterclockwise, *Brit.* anticlockwise. **5** see AWKWARD 2. **6** ambiguous, backhanded, equivocal, questionable, dubious, doubtful; insincere, hollow, empty, false.

left-hander /léft-hándər/ *n.* **1** a left-handed person. **2** a left-handed blow.

leftie var. of LEFTY.

leftism /léftizəm/ *n. Polit.* the principles or policy of the left. □□ **leftist** *n.* & *adj.*

■ □□ **leftist** (*n.*) see PROGRESSIVE *n.* (*adj.*) see LEFT¹ *adj.* 3.

leftmost /léftmōst/ *adj.* furthest to the left.

leftover /léftōvər/ *adj.* & *n.* ● *adj.* remaining over; not used up or disposed of. ● *n.* (in *pl.*) items (esp. of food) remaining after the rest has been used.

■ *adj.* remaining, residual, extra, superfluous, excess, unused, uneaten. ● *n.* (*leftovers*) remains, remainders, remnants, scraps, leavings, crumbs, rejects, dregs, lees; rest, residue, residuum, balance; surplus, excess, superfluity, overage, odds and ends, flotsam and jetsam; debris, refuse, waste, rubbish, dross, junk.

leftward /léftwərd/ *adv.* & *adj.* ● *adv.* (also **leftwards** /-wərdz/) toward the left. ● *adj.* going toward or facing the left.

lefty /léftee/ *n.* (also **leftie**) (*pl.* **-ies**) *colloq.* **1** *Polit.* a left-winger. **2** a left-handed person.

leg /leg/ *n.* & *v.* ● *n.* **1 a** each of the limbs on which a person or animal walks and stands. **b** the part of this from the hip to the ankle. **2** a leg of an animal or bird as food. **3** an artificial leg (*wooden leg*). **4** a part of a garment covering a leg or part of a leg. **5 a** a support of a chair, table, bed, etc. **b** a long, thin support or prop, esp. a pole. **6** *Cricket* the half of the field (as divided lengthways through the pitch) in which the striker's feet are placed (opp. OFF). **7 a** a section of a journey. **b** a section of a relay race. **c** a stage in a competition. **d** one of two or more games constituting a round. **8** one branch of a forked object. **9** *Naut.* a run made on a single tack. **10** *archaic* an obeisance made by drawing back one leg and bending it while keeping the front leg straight. ● *v.tr.* (**legged**, **legging**) propel (a boat) through a canal tunnel by pushing with one's legs against the tunnel sides. □ **feel** (or **find**) **one's legs** become able to stand or walk. **give a person a leg up** help a person to mount a horse, etc. or get over an obstacle or difficulty. **have the legs of** esp. *Brit.* be able to go further than. **have no legs** *colloq.* (of a golf ball, etc.) have not enough momentum to reach the desired point. **keep one's legs** not fall. **leg iron** a shackle or fetter for the leg. **leg it** *colloq.* walk or run fast. **leg-of-mutton sail** a triangular mainsail. **leg-of-mutton sleeve** a sleeve which is full and loose on the upper arm but close-fitting on the forearm. **leg-pull** *colloq.* a hoax. **leg warmer** either of a pair of tubular knitted garments covering the leg from ankle to thigh. **not have a leg to stand on** be unable to support one's argument by facts or sound reasons. **on one's last legs** near death or the end of one's usefulness, etc. **on one's legs 1** (also **on one's hind legs**) standing, esp. to make a speech. **2** well enough to walk about. **take to one's legs** run away. □□ **legged** /legd, légid/ *adj.* (also in *comb.*). **legger** *n.* [ME f. ON *leggr* f. Gmc]

■ *n.* **1, 3** shank; calf, thigh, ham; limb, member, *Zool.* appendage; prosthesis, peg leg; (*legs*) *colloq.* pins, *joc.* stumps. **2** shank, ham, gammon, gigot, haunch, drumstick, hock, *Brit.* hough; joint. **4** trouser(s), pants, legging(s), stocking(s), hose. **5** cabriole, spindle; support, brace, prop, upright, standard, column, pillar, post. **7** section, part, stage, segment, portion, stretch, lap. **8** branch, fork, prong. □ **give a person a leg up** help a person (up), give a person a (helping) hand, lend a person a hand, aid, assist, support; push, *colloq.* boost. **leg it** see RUN *v.* 1, 3. **leg-pull** see HOAX *n.* **on one's last legs** decrepit, moribund, worn-out, spent, wasted, debilitated, exhausted, shattered, the worse for wear, *archaic* stricken in years, *colloq.* all in, *Brit. sl.* knackered, clapped out; weak, frail, enfeebled, feeble, infirm; run-down, falling apart *or* to pieces, broken-down, dilapidated, rickety, ramshackle, tumbledown.

legacy /légəsee/ *n.* (*pl.* **-ies**) **1** a gift left in a will. **2** something handed down by a predecessor (*legacy of corruption*). [ME f. OF *legacie* legateship f. med.L *legatia* f. L *legare* bequeath]

■ **1** see BEQUEST 2.

legal /léegəl/ *adj.* **1** of or based on law; concerned with law; falling within the province of law. **2** appointed or required by law. **3** permitted by law; lawful. **4** recognized by law, as distinct from equity. **5** *Theol.* **a** of the Mosaic law. **b** of salvation by works rather than by faith. □ **legal age** age at which a person assumes adult rights and privileges by law. **legal aid** payment from public funds allowed, in cases of need, to help pay for legal advice or proceedings. **legal holiday** a public holiday established by law. **legal proceedings** see PROCEEDING. **legal separation** see SEPARATION. **legal tender** currency that cannot legally be refused in payment of a debt (usu. up to a limited amount for coins

---

/.../ **pronunciation** ● **part of speech**
□ **phrases, idioms, and compounds**
□□ **derivatives** ■ **synonym section**
cross-references appear in SMALL CAPITALS or *italics*

not made of gold). □□ **legally** adv. [F légal or L legalis f. lex legis law: cf. LEAL, LOYAL]

■ **1** judicial, juridical, jurisprudent, jurisprudential, forensic. **2** constitutional, statutory, statutable. **3** lawful, legitimate, licit, acceptable, permissible, permitted, admissible, authorized, constitutional, de jure, right, proper, correct, valid, colloq. legit, kosher. □ **legal tender** see MONEY 1.

legalese /léegəléez/ n. colloq. the technical language of legal documents.

legalism /léegəlizəm/ n. **1** excessive adherence to law or formula. **2** Theol. adherence to the Law rather than to the Gospel, the doctrine of justification by works. □□ **legalist** n. **legalistic** /-lístik/ adj. **legalistically** /-lístikəlee/ adv.

■ **1** strictness, rigidity, fastidiousness, niceness, literalness, literality, pedantry, pettiness, pettifoggery, narrow-mindedness, hairsplitting, caviling, quibbling, colloq. nitpicking; litigiousness, disputatiousness, contentiousness. □□ **legalistic** literal, strict, rigid; fastidious, nice, pedantic, niggling, petty, pettifogging, narrow-minded, hairsplitting, caviling, quibbling, colloq. nitpicking, often offens. jesuitic; disputatious, contentious, litigious.

legality /ligálitee, leegál-/ n. (pl. **-ies**) **1** lawfulness. **2** legalism. **3** (in pl.) obligations imposed by law. [F légalité or med.L legalitas (as LEGAL)]

legalize /léegəliz/ v.tr. **1** make lawful. **2** bring into harmony with the law. □□ **legalization** n.

■ see LEGITIMATE v. 1. □□ **legalization** see SANCTION n. 2.

legate /légət/ n. **1** a member of the clergy representing the Pope. **2** Rom.Hist. **a** a deputy of a general. **b** a governor or deputy governor of a province. **3** archaic an ambassador or delegate. □ **legate a latere** /aa laáteray/ a papal legate of the highest class, with full powers. □□ **legateship** n. **legatine** /-teen, -tin/ adj. [OE f. OF legat f. L legatus past part. of legare depute, delegate]

legatee /légətée/ n. the recipient of a legacy. [as LEGATOR + -EE]

legation /ligáyshən/ n. **1** a body of deputies. **2 a** the office and staff of a diplomatic minister (esp. when not having ambassadorial rank). **b** the official residence of a diplomatic minister. **3** a legateship. **4** the sending of a legate or deputy. [ME f. OF legation or L legatio (as LEGATE)]

■ **1** see MISSION 3.

legato /ligaátō/ adv., adj., & n. Mus. • adv. & adj. in a smooth flowing manner, without breaks between notes (cf. STACCATO, TENUTO). • n. (pl. **-os**) **1** a legato passage. **2** legato playing. [It., = bound, past part. of legare f. L ligare bind]

legator /ligáytər/ n. the giver of a legacy. [archaic legate bequeath f. L legare (as LEGACY)]

legend /léjənd/ n. **1 a** a traditional story sometimes popularly regarded as historical but unauthenticated; a myth. **b** such stories collectively. **c** a popular but unfounded belief. **d** colloq. a subject of such beliefs (became a legend in his own lifetime). **2 a** an inscription, esp. on a coin or medal. **b** Printing a caption. **c** wording on a map, etc., explaining the symbols used. **3** hist. **a** the story of a saint's life. **b** a collection of lives of saints or similar stories. □□ **legendry** n. [ME (in sense 3) f. OF legende f. med.L legenda what is to be read, neut. pl. gerundive of L legere read]

■ **1 a–c** myth, folklore, fable, romance, tradition, fiction; story, (folk)tale, epic, saga, Edda, Haggadah. **d** immortal, hero, great, genius, phenomenon, wonder, luminary, giant, god, goddess, deity, divinity, demigod, demiurge; star, celebrity, idol, superstar, name, classic. **2** inscription, motto, slogan, title, caption, wording; key, code, table.

legendary /léjənderee/ adj. **1** of or connected with legends. **2** described in a legend. **3** colloq. remarkable enough to be a subject of legend. **4** based on a legend. □□ **legendarily** adv. [med.L legendarius (as LEGEND)]

■ **1, 2, 4** mythic, mythical, folkloric, folkloristic, traditional, romantic, epic, heroic, fabled, literary storied; fabulous, fictional, fictitious, storybook, fairy-

tale, unreal, imaginary, fanciful. **3** phenomenal, remarkable, extraordinary, wonderful, marvelous, exceptional, notable, noteworthy, eminent, prominent, great, classic, immortal, superhuman; illustrious, famous, fabled, celebrated, noted, famed, well-known, renowned, acclaimed.

legerdemain /léjərdəmáyn/ n. **1** sleight of hand; conjuring or juggling. **2** trickery; sophistry. [ME f. F léger de main light of hand, dexterous]

■ **1** see JUGGLE n. 1. **2** see TRICKERY.

leger line /léjər/ n. = ledger line.

legging /léging/ n. **1** (usu. in pl.) a stout protective outer covering for the leg from the knee to the ankle. **2** (pl.) a close-fitting stretch garment covering the legs and the lower part of the torso.

leggy /légee/ adj. (**leggier, leggiest**) **1 a** long-legged. **b** (of a woman) having attractively long legs. **2** long-stemmed. □□ **legginess** n.

■ **1 a** see TALL adj. 1.

leghorn /léghawrn, -ərn/ n. **1 a** fine plaited straw. **b** a hat of this. **2** (also **Leghorn**) **a** a bird of a small hardy breed of domestic fowl. **b** this breed. [Leghorn (Livorno) in Italy, from where the straw and fowls were imported]

legible /léjibəl/ adj. (of handwriting, print, etc.) clear enough to read; readable. □□ **legibility** n. **legibly** adv. [ME f. LL legibilis f. legere read]

■ clear, plain, distinct, unambiguous; readable, decipherable, understandable, intelligible, decodable.

legion /léejən/ n. & adj. • n. **1** a division of 3,000–6,000 men, including a complement of cavalry, in the ancient Roman army. **2** a large organized body. **3** a vast host, multitude, or number. • predic.adj. great in number (his good works have been legion). □ **American Legion** an association of US ex-servicemen formed in 1919. **foreign legion** a body of foreign volunteers in a modern, esp. French, army. **Legion of Honor** a French order of distinction founded in 1802. [ME f. OF f. L legio -onis f. legere choose]

■ **3** see HOST¹.

legionary /léejəneree/ adj. & n. • adj. of a legion or legions. • n. (pl. **-ies**) a member of a legion. [L legionarius (as LEGION)]

legioned /léejənd/ adj. poet. arrayed in legions.

legionella /léejənélə/ n. the bacterium Legionella pneumophila, which causes legionnaires' disease.

legionnaire /léejənáir/ n. **1** a member of a foreign legion. **2** a member of the American Legion. □ **legionnaires' disease** a form of bacterial pneumonia first identified after an outbreak at an American Legion meeting in 1976 (cf. LEGIONELLA). [F légionnaire (as LEGION)]

legislate /léjislayt/ v.intr. **1** make laws. **2** (foll. by for) make provision by law. [back-form. f. LEGISLATION]

legislation /léjisláyshən/ n. **1** the process of making laws. **2** laws collectively. [LL legis latio f. lex legis law + latio proposing f. lat- past part. stem of ferre bring]

■ **1** see PASSAGE¹ 7. **2** see MEASURE n. 9.

legislative /léjislaytiv/ adj. of or empowered to make legislation. □□ **legislatively** adv.

legislator /léjislaytər/ n. **1** a member of a legislative body. **2** a lawgiver. [L (as LEGISLATION)]

■ **1** see POLITICIAN 1.

legislature /léjislaychər/ n. the legislative body of a nation or state.

■ assembly, congress (or Congress), diet, council, parliament, house (or House), senate (or Senate).

legit /lijít/ adj. & n. colloq. • adj. legitimate. • n. **1** legitimate drama. **2** an actor in legitimate drama. [abbr.]

■ adj. see PERMISSIBLE.

legitimate adj. & v. • adj. /lijítimət/ **1 a** (of a child) born of parents lawfully married to each other. **b** (of a parent, birth, descent, etc.) with, of, through, etc., a legitimate child. **2** lawful; proper; regular; conforming to the standard type. **3** logically admissible. **4 a** (of a sovereign's title) based on strict hereditary right. **b** (of a sovereign) having a legitimate title. **5** constituting or relating to serious drama as distinct from musical comedy, revue, etc. • v.tr. /lijítimayt/ **1**

make legitimate by decree, enactment, or proof. **2** justify; serve as a justification for. □□ **legitimacy** /-məsee/ *n.* **legitimately** /-mətlee/ *adv.* **legitimation** /-máyshən/ *n.* [med.L *legitimare* f. L *legitimus* lawful f. *lex legis* law]

■ *adj.* **1, 2** lawful, licit, legal, proper; constitutional, de jure, statutory, statutable, permissible, allowable, justifiable, authorized, rightful; regular, standard, correct, conventional, established, orthodox, official; authentic, genuine, bona fide, real. **3** logical, justifiable, reasonable, rational, valid, sound, right, correct, proper. ● *v.* **1** legitimize, legitimatize, legalize, authorize, sanction, permit, allow, license. **2** justify, warrant, vindicate, validate, rationalize, account for, explain; substantiate, defend, uphold, confirm, certify; *colloq.* launder.

legitimatize /lijítimətiz/ *v.tr.* legitimize. □□ **legitimatization** *n.*

■ see AUTHORIZE 1. □□ **legitimatization** see SANCTION 2.

legitimism /lijítimizəm/ *n.* adherence to a sovereign or pretender whose claim is based on direct descent (esp. in French and Spanish history). □□ **legitimist** *n. & adj.* [F *légitimisme* f. *légitime* LEGITIMATE]

legitimize /lijítimiz/ *v.tr.* **1** make legitimate. **2** serve as a justification for. □□ **legitimization** *n.*

■ **1** see AUTHORIZE 1. **2** see JUSTIFY 1, 2, 4. □□ **legitimization** see SANCTION 2.

legless /léglis/ *adj.* **1** having no legs. **2** *sl.* drunk, esp. too drunk to stand.

legman /légman/ *n.* (*pl.* **-men**) a person employed to go about gathering news or running errands, etc.

■ see JOURNALIST.

Lego /légō/ *n. propr.* a construction toy consisting of interlocking plastic building blocks. [Da. *leg godt* play well f. *lege* to play]

legroom /légrŏŏm/ *n.* space for the legs of a seated person.

legume /légyŏŏm/ *n.* **1** the seedpod of a leguminous plant. **2** any seed, pod, or other edible part of a leguminous plant used as food. [F *légume* f. L *legumen -minis* f. *legere* pick, because pickable by hand]

leguminous /ligyŏŏminəs/ *adj.* of or like the family Leguminosae, including peas and beans, having seeds in pods and usu. root nodules able to fix nitrogen. [mod.L *leguminosus* (as LEGUME)]

legwork /légwərk/ *n.* work which involves a lot of walking, traveling, or physical activity.

lehr /leer/ *n.* (also **leer**) a furnace used for the annealing of glass. [17th c.: orig. unkn.]

lei[1] /láy-ee, lay/ *n.* a garland of flowers usu. worn on the head or shoulders. [Hawaiian]

lei[2] *pl.* of LEU.

Leibnizian /libnítseeən/ *adj. & n.* ● *adj.* of or relating to the philosophy of G. W. Leibniz, German philosopher (d. 1716), esp. regarding matter as a multitude of monads and assuming a preestablished harmony between spirit and matter. ● *n.* a follower of this philosophy.

Leicester /léstər/ *n.* a kind of mild firm cheese, usu. orange-colored and orig. made in Leicestershire, England.

leishmaniasis /leeshmənísosis/ *n.* any of several diseases caused by parasitic protozoans of the genus *Leishmania* transmitted by the bite of sandflies. [W. B. *Leishman*, Brit. physician d. 1926]

leister /léestər/ *n. & v.* ● *n.* a pronged salmon-spear. ● *v.tr.* pierce with a leister. [ON *ljóstr* f. *ljósta* to strike]

leisure /leézhər, lézh-/ *n.* **1** free time; time at one's own disposal. **2** enjoyment of free time. **3** (usu. foll. by *for*, or *to* + infin.) opportunity afforded by free time. □ **at leisure 1** not occupied. **2** in an unhurried manner. **at one's leisure** when one has time. □□ **leisureless** *adj.* [ME f. AF *leisour*, OF *leisir* ult. f. L *licēre* be allowed]

■ **1** spare *or* free time, time off; holiday, vacation, break, leave, furlough; respite, relief, rest, breathing space. **2** recreation, fun, entertainment, amusement, enjoyment, diversion, R and R; ease, (peace and) quiet, relaxation, tranquillity, repose. **3** see OPPORTUNITY 1, 2. □ **at leisure 1** see IDLE *adj.* 2. **2** unhurriedly, calmly,

steadily, deliberately; casually, easily, freely, in one's own time, at one's leisure, at one's convenience. **at one's leisure** see *at leisure* 2 above.

leisured /leézhərd, lézh-/ *adj.* having ample leisure.

■ leisurely, comfortable, easy, undemanding, restful, carefree.

leisurely /leézhərlee, lézh-/ *adj. & adv.* ● *adj.* having leisure; acting or done at leisure; unhurried; relaxed. ● *adv.* without hurry. □□ **leisureliness** *n.*

■ *adj.* see UNHURRIED. ● *adv.* see SLOW *adv.* 1.

leisurewear /leézhərwair, lézh-/ *n.* informal clothes, especially sportswear.

leitmotiv /lítmōteéf/ *n.* (also **leitmotif**) a recurrent theme associated throughout a musical, literary, etc., composition with a particular person, idea, or situation. [G *Leitmotiv* (as LEAD[1], MOTIVE)]

■ see MOTIF 1.

lek[1] /lek/ *n.* the chief monetary unit of Albania. [Albanian]

lek[2] /lek/ *n.* a patch of ground used by groups of certain birds during the breeding season as a setting for the males' display and their meeting with the females. [perh. f. Sw. *leka* to play]

LEM /lem/ *abbr.* lunar excursion module.

leman /lémən/ *n.* (*pl.* **lemans**) *archaic* **1** a lover or sweetheart. **2** an illicit lover, esp. a mistress. [ME *leofman* (as LIEF, MAN)]

■ see LOVE *n.* 4, 5.

lemma /lémə/ *n.* (*pl.* **lemmas** or **lemmata** /-mətə/) **1** an assumed or demonstrated proposition used in an argument or proof. **2 a** a heading indicating the subject or argument of a literary composition, a dictionary entry, etc. **b** a heading indicating the subject or argument of an annotation. **3** a motto appended to a picture, etc. [L f. Gk *lēmma -matos* thing assumed, f. the root of *lambanō* take]

lemme /lémee/ *colloq.* let me. [corrupt.]

lemming /léming/ *n.* any small arctic rodent of the genus *Lemmus*, esp. *L. lemmus* of Norway which is reputed to rush headlong into the sea and drown during periods of mass migration. [Norw.]

lemon /lémən/ *n.* **1 a** a pale-yellow, thick-skinned, oval citrus fruit with acidic juice. **b** a tree of the species *Citrus limon* which produces this fruit. **2** a pale-yellow color. **3** *colloq.* a person or thing regarded as feeble or unsatisfactory or disappointing. □ **lemon balm** a bushy plant, *Melissa officinalis*, with leaves smelling and tasting of lemon. **lemon drop** lemon-flavored hard candy. **lemon geranium** a lemon-scented pelargonium, *Pelargonium crispum*. **lemon squash** *Brit.* a soft drink made from lemons and other ingredients, often sold in concentrated form. **lemon thyme** an herb, *Thymus citriodorus*, with lemon-scented leaves used for flavoring. **lemon verbena** (or **plant**) a shrub, *Lippia citriodora*, with lemon-scented leaves. [ME f. OF *limon* f. Arab. *līma*: cf. LIME[2]]

■ **3** see FAILURE 2.

lemonade /lémonáyd/ *n.* **1** a beverage made from sweetened lemon juice. **2** a synthetic substitute for this.

■ see POP[1] *n.* 2.

lemongrass /lémongras/ *n.* any fragrant tropical grass of the genus *Cymbopogon*, yielding an oil smelling of lemon.

lemon sole /lémən/ *n.* a flatfish, *Microstomus kitt*, of the plaice family. [F *limande*]

lemony /lémənee/ *adj.* **1** tasting or smelling of lemons. **2** *Austral. & NZ sl.* irritable.

■ **1** see SOUR *adj.* 1.

lemur /leémər/ *n.* any arboreal primate of the family Lemuridae native to Madagascar, with a pointed snout and long tail. [mod.L f. L *lemures* (pl.) spirits of the dead, from its specterlike face]

Lenape /lénəpe, lənaápee/ *n.* see DELAWARE.

/.../ **pronunciation**	● **part of speech**
□ **phrases, idioms, and compounds**	
□□ **derivatives**	■ **synonym section**
cross-references appear in SMALL CAPITALS or *italics*	

lend /lend/ *v.tr.* (*past* and *past part.* **lent** /lent/) **1** (usu. foll. by *to*) grant (to a person) the use of (a thing) on the understanding that it or its equivalent shall be returned. **2** allow the use of (money) at interest. **3** bestow or contribute (something temporary) (*lend assistance*; *lends a certain charm*). □ **lend an ear** (or **one's ears**) listen. **lend a hand** see HAND. **lending library** a library from which books may be temporarily taken away with or *Brit.* without direct payment. **lend itself to** (of a thing) be suitable for. **Lend-Lease** *hist.* an arrangement made in 1941 whereby the US supplied equipment, etc., to the UK and its allies, orig. as a loan in return for the use of British-owned military bases. **lend oneself** to accommodate oneself to (a policy or purpose). □□ **lendable** *adj.* **lender** *n.* **lending** *n.* [ME, earlier *lēne(n)* f. OE *lǣnan* f. *lǣn* LOAN[1]]
■ **1, 2** loan, advance, put out; rent (out), lease (out), let (out), charter (out). **3** bestow, contribute, impart, furnish, provide, give, confer, add. □ **lend an ear** see LISTEN 1, 2. **lend itself to** be suitable *or* appropriate to *or* for, be applicable *or* adaptable to.

length /length, lengkth/ *n.* **1** measurement or extent from end to end; the greater of two or the greatest of three dimensions of a body. **2** extent in, of, or with regard to, time (*a stay of some length*; *the length of a speech*). **3** the distance a thing extends (*at arm's length*; *ships a cable's length apart*). **4** the length of a horse, boat, etc., as a measure of the lead in a race. **5** a long stretch or extent (*a length of hair*). **6** a degree of thoroughness in action (*went to great lengths*; *prepared to go to any length*). **7** a piece of material of a certain length (*a length of cloth*). **8** *Prosody* the quantity of a vowel or syllable. **9** the extent of a garment in a vertical direction when worn. **10** the full extent of one's body. □ **at length 1** (also **at full** or **great**, etc., **length**) in detail; without curtailment. **2** after a long time; at last. [OE *lengthu* f. Gmc (as LONG[1])]
■ **1, 3, 5** span, reach, extent, distance, stretch; measure, size, magnitude, dimension. **2** time, duration, stretch, term, period, while, span, interval. **6** trouble, inconvenience, bother, nuisance; (*lengths*) pains. □ **at length 1** in detail, in depth, comprehensively, thoroughly, completely, exhaustively, extensively, at large. **2** at last, finally, in the end, ultimately, eventually.

lengthen /léngthən, léngk-/ *v.* **1** *tr.* & *intr.* make or become longer. **2** *tr.* make (a vowel) long. □□ **lengthener** *n.*
■ **1** extend, elongate, stretch, expand, pad out; drag out, draw out, prolong, protract, continue; grow, enlarge, amplify; let down.

lengthways /léngthwayz, léngkth-/ *adv.* lengthwise.

lengthwise /léngthwīz, léngkth-/ *adv.* & *adj.* ● *adv.* in a direction parallel with a thing's length. ● *adj.* lying or moving lengthways.

lengthy /léngthee, léngkthee/ *adj.* (**lengthier**, **lengthiest**) **1** of unusual length. **2** (of speech, writing, style, a speaker, etc.) tedious; prolix. □□ **lengthily** *adv.* **lengthiness** *n.*
■ **1** long, extensive, extended, elongated, *Bot.* & *Zool.* elongate. **2** tedious, boring, dull, uninteresting, wearying, wearisome, tiresome, laborious, endless, unending, interminable; prolix, overlong, protracted, long-drawn(-out), long-winded, wordy, verbose, rambling, pleonastic.

lenient /léenyənt/ *adj.* **1** merciful; tolerant; not disposed to severity. **2** (of punishment, etc.) mild. **3** *archaic* emollient. □□ **lenience** /-yəns/ *n.* **leniency** *n.* **leniently** *adv.* [L *lenire lenit-* soothe f. *lenis* gentle]
■ **1, 2** merciful, compassionate, forgiving, clement, forbearing, indulgent, charitable, humane, tolerant, magnanimous, generous, patient, understanding, tenderhearted, kindhearted; liberal, latitudinarian, permissive, easygoing, easy, moderate; soft, mild, gentle, kind, tender.

Leninism /léninizəm/ *n.* Marxism as interpreted and applied by Lenin. □□ **Leninist** *n.* & *adj.* **Leninite** *n.* & *adj.* [V. I. *Lenin* (name assumed by V. I. Ulyanov), Russian statesman d. 1924]

lenition /liníshən/ *n.* (in Celtic languages) the process or result of articulating a consonant softly. [L *lenis* soft, after G *Lenierung*]

lenitive /lénitiv/ *adj.* & *n.* ● *adj.* *Med.* soothing. ● *n.* **1** *Med.* a soothing drug or appliance. **2** a palliative. [ME f. med.L *lenitivus* (as LENIENT)]
■ *adj.* see *soothing* (SOOTHE). ● *n.* see TRANQUILIZER.

lenity /lénitee/ *n.* (*pl.* **-ies**) *literary* **1** mercifulness; gentleness. **2** an act of mercy. [F *lénité* or L *lenitas* f. *lenis* gentle]
■ **1** see HUMANITY 2.

Lenni Lenape /lénee/ *n.* see DELAWARE.

leno /léenō/ *n.* (*pl.* **-os**) an openwork fabric with the warp threads twisted in pairs before weaving. [F *linon* f. *lin* flax f. L *linum*]

lens /lenz/ *n.* **1** a piece of a transparent substance with one or (usu.) both sides curved for concentrating or dispersing light rays, esp. in optical instruments. **2** a combination of lenses used in photography. **3** *Anat.* = *crystalline lens.* **4** *Physics* a device for focusing or otherwise modifying the direction of movement of light, sound, electrons, etc. □□ **lensed** *adj.* **lensless** *adj.* [L *lens lentis* lentil (from the similarity of shape)]
■ **1** see GLASS *n.* 2i.

Lent /lent/ *n.* *Eccl.* the period from Ash Wednesday to Holy Saturday, of which the 40 weekdays are devoted to fasting and penitence in commemoration of Christ's fasting in the wilderness. □ **Lent lily** *Brit.* a daffodil, esp. a wild one. **Lent term** *Brit.* the term at a university, etc., in which Lent falls. [ME f. LENTEN]

lent *past* and *past part.* of LEND.

-lent /lənt/ *suffix* forming adjectives (*pestilent*; *violent*) (cf. -ULENT). [L *-lentus* -ful]

Lenten /léntən/ *adj.* of, in, or appropriate to, Lent. □ **Lenten fare** a meager meal, esp. one without meat. [orig. as noun, = spring, f. OE *lencten* f. Gmc, rel. to LONG[1], perh. with ref. to lengthening of the day in spring: now regarded as adj. f. LENT + -EN[2]]

lenticel /léntisel/ *n.* *Bot.* any of the raised pores in the stems of woody plants that allow gas exchange between the atmosphere and the internal tissues. [mod.L *lenticella* dimin. of L *lens*: see LENS]

lenticular /lentíkyələr/ *adj.* **1** shaped like a lentil or a biconvex lens. **2** of the lens of the eye. [L *lenticularis* (as LENTIL)]

lentil /léntəl/ *n.* **1** a leguminous plant, *Lens culinaris*, yielding edible biconvex seeds. **2** this seed, esp. used as food with the husk removed. [ME f. OF *lentille* f. L *lenticula* (as LENS)]

lento /léntō/ *adj.* & *adv.* *Mus.* ● *adj.* slow. ● *adv.* slowly. [It.]

lentoid /léntoyd/ *adj.* = LENTICULAR 1. [L *lens* (see LENS) + -OID]

Leo /lée-ō/ *n.* (*pl.* **-os**) **1** a constellation, traditionally regarded as contained in the figure of a lion. **2 a** the fifth sign of the zodiac (the Lion). **b** a person born when the sun is in this sign. [OE f. L, = LION]

Leonid /lée-ənid/ *n.* any of the meteors that seem to radiate from the direction of the constellation Leo. [L *leo* (see LEO) *leonis* + -ID[3]]

Leonine /lée-ənīn/ *adj.* & *n.* ● *adj.* of Pope Leo; made or invented by Pope Leo. ● *n.* (in *pl.*) leonine verse. □ **Leonine City** the part of Rome around the Vatican fortified by Pope Leo IV. **leonine verse 1** medieval Latin verse in hexameter or elegiac meter with internal rhyme. **2** English verse with internal rhyme. [the name *Leo* (as LEONINE)]

leonine /lée-ənīn/ *adj.* **1** like a lion. **2** of or relating to lions. [ME f. OF *leonin -ine* f. L *leoninus* f. *leo leonis* lion]

leopard /lépərd/ *n.* (*fem.* **leopardess** /-dis/) **1** a large African or Asian feline, *Panthera pardus*, with either a black-spotted, yellowish-fawn or all black coat. Also called PANTHER. **2** *Heraldry* a lion passant guardant as in the arms of England. **3** (*attrib.*) spotted like a leopard (*leopard moth*). □ **leopard's-bane** any plant of the genus *Doronicum*, with large yellow daisylike flowers. [ME f. OF f. LL f. late Gk *leopardos* (as LION, PARD)]

leotard /lée-ətaard/ *n.* **1** a close-fitting one-piece garment worn by ballet dancers, acrobats, etc. **2** = TIGHTS. [J. *Léotard*, French trapeze artist d. 1870]

leper /lépər/ n. **1** a person suffering from leprosy. **2** a person shunned on moral grounds. [ME, prob. attrib. use of *leper* leprosy f. OF *lepre* f. L *lepra* f. Gk, fem. of *lepros* scaly f. *lepos* scale]
■ **2** see UNDESIRABLE *n.*

lepidopterous /lépidóptərəs/ adj. of the order Lepidoptera of insects, with four scale-covered wings often brightly colored, including butterflies and moths. □□ **lepidopteran** adj. & n. **lepidopterist** n. [Gk *lepis -idos* scale + *pteron* wing]

leporine /lépərin/ adj. of or like hares. [L *leporinus* f. *lepus -oris* hare]

leprechaun /léprəkon, -kawn/ n. a small mischievous sprite in Irish folklore. [OIr. *luchorpán* f. *lu* small + *corp* body]
■ see IMP *n.* 2.

leprosy /léprəsee/ n. **1** a contagious bacterial disease that affects the skin, mucous membranes, and nerves, causing disfigurement. Also called HANSEN′S DISEASE. **2** moral corruption or contagion. [LEPROUS + -Y³]

leprous /léprəs/ adj. **1** suffering from leprosy. **2** like or relating to leprosy. [ME f. OF f. LL *leprosus* f. *lepra*: see LEPER]

lepta pl. of LEPTON¹.

lepto- /léptō/ comb. form small; narrow. [Gk *leptos* fine, small, thin, delicate]

leptocephalic /léptəsifálik/ adj. (also **leptocephalous** /-séfələs/) narrow-skulled.

leptodactyl /léptōdáktil/ adj. & n. ● adj. having long, slender toes. ● n. a bird having these.

lepton¹ /lépton/ n. (pl. **lepta** /-tə/) a Greek coin worth one-hundredth of a drachma. [Gk *lepton* (*nomisma* coin) neut. of *leptos* small]

lepton² /lépton/ n. (pl. **leptons**) Physics any of a class of elementary particles which do not undergo strong interaction, e.g., an electron, muon, or neutrino. [LEPTO- + -ON]

leptospirosis /léptōspirṓsis/ n. an infectious disease caused by bacteria of the genus *Leptospira*, that occurs in rodents, dogs, and other mammals, and can be transmitted to humans. [LEPTO- + SPIRO-¹ + -OSIS]

leptotene /léptəteen/ n. Biol. the first stage of the prophase of meiosis in which each chromosome is apparent as two fine chromatids. [LEPTO- + Gk *tainia* band]

lesbian /lézbeeən/ n. & adj. ● n. a homosexual woman. ● adj. **1** of homosexuality in women. **2** (**Lesbian**) of Lesbos. □□ **lesbianism** n. [L *Lesbius* f. Gk *Lesbios* f. *Lesbos*, island in the Aegean Sea, home of Sappho (see SAPPHIC)]

lese-majesty /leez májistee/ n. (also **lèse-majesté** /layz mázhestay/) **1** treason. **2** an insult to a sovereign or ruler. **3** presumptuous conduct. [F *lèse-majesté* f. L *laesa majestas* injured sovereignty f. *laedere laes-* injure + *majestas* MAJESTY]

lesion /léezhən/ n. **1** damage. **2** injury. **3** Med. a morbid change in the functioning or texture of an organ, etc. [ME f. OF f. L *laesio -onis* f. *laedere laes-* injure]
■ **2** see WOUND¹ *n.* 1.

less /les/ adj., adv., n., & prep. ● adj. **1** smaller in extent, degree, duration, number, etc. (*of less importance*; *in a less degree*). **2** of smaller quantity; not so much (opp. MORE) (*find less difficulty*; *eat less meat*). **3** disp. fewer (*eat less cookies*). **4** of lower rank, etc. (*no less a person than*). ● adv. to a smaller extent, in a lower degree. ● n. a smaller amount or quantity or number (*cannot take less*; *for less than $10*; *is little less than disgraceful*). ● prep. minus (*made $1,000 less tax*). □ **in less than no time** joc. very quickly or soon. **much less** with even greater force of denial (*do not suspect him of negligence, much less of dishonesty*). [OE *lǣssa* (adj.), *lǣs* (adv.), f. Gmc]

-less /lis/ suffix forming adjectives and adverbs: **1** from nouns, meaning 'not having, without, free from' (*doubtless*; *powerless*). **2** from verbs, meaning 'not affected by or doing the action of the verb' (*fathomless*; *tireless*). □□ **-lessly** suffix forming adverbs. **-lessness** suffix forming nouns. [OE *-lēas* f. *lēas* devoid of]

lessee /lesée/ n. (often foll. by *of*) a person who holds a property by lease. □□ **lesseeship** n. [ME f. AF past part., OF *lessé* (as LEASE)]
■ see TENANT *n.* 1.

lessen /lésən/ v.tr. & intr. make or become less; diminish.
■ see DIMINISH 1.

lesser /lésər/ adj. (usu. *attrib.*) not so great as the other or the rest (*the lesser evil*; *the lesser celandine*). [double compar., f. LESS + -ER³]
■ see INFERIOR adj. 1.

lesson /lésən/ n. & v. ● n. **1 a** an amount of teaching given at one time. **b** the time assigned to this. **2** (in *pl.*; foll. by *in*) systematic instruction (*gives lessons in dancing*; *took lessons in French*). **3** a thing learned or to be learned by a pupil; an assignment. **4 a** an occurrence, example, rebuke, or punishment, that serves or should serve to warn or encourage (*let that be a lesson to you*). **b** a thing inculcated by experience or study. **5** a passage from the Bible read aloud during a church service. ● v.tr. archaic **1** instruct. **2** admonish; rebuke. □ **learn one's lesson** profit from or bear in mind a particular (usu. unpleasant) experience. **teach a person a lesson** punish a person, esp. as a deterrent. [ME f. OF *leçon* f. L *lectio -onis*: see LECTION]
■ **1 a** class, session, period. **2** (*lessons*) instruction, teaching, tutoring, schooling, classes, coaching, tutelage, tuition; course (of study); practice, drilling. **3** exercise, drill, reading, lecture, recitation; assignment, homework, task. **4** example, exemplar, model, guide, maxim, paragon; deterrent, discouragement; warning, admonition; message, moral, homily, precept; punishment, chastisement, chastening, castigation, scolding, chiding, rebuke, reprimand, reproof, *colloq.* talking-to. **5** reading, scripture passage, text, Epistle, lection, pericope.

lessor /lésawr/ n. a person who lets a property by lease. [AF f. *lesser*: see LEASE]
■ see LANDLORD 1.

lest /lest/ conj. **1** in order that not; for fear that (*lest we forget*). **2** that (*afraid lest we should be late*). [OE *thȳ lǣs the* whereby less that, later *the lǣste*, ME *lest(e)*]
■ see *in case* 2 (CASE¹).

let¹ /let/ v. & n. ● v. (**letting**; past and past part. **let**) **1** tr. **a** allow to; not prevent or forbid (*we let them go*). **b** cause to (*let me know*; *let it be known*). **2** tr. (foll. by *into*) **a** allow to enter. **b** make acquainted with (a secret, etc.). **c** inlay in. **3** tr. esp. Brit. grant the use of (rooms, land, etc.) for rent or hire (*was let to the new tenant for a year*). **4** tr. allow or cause (liquid or air) to escape (*let blood*). **5** tr. award (a contract for work). **6** aux. supplying the first and third persons of the imperative in exhortations (*let us pray*), commands (*let it be done at once*; *let there be light*), assumptions (*let AB be equal to CD*), and permission or challenge (*let him do his worst*). ● n. Brit. the act or an instance of letting a house, room, etc. (*a long let*). □ **let alone 1** not to mention (*hasn't got a television, let alone a VCR*). **2** = *let be.* **let be** not interfere with, attend to, or do. **let down 1** lower. **2** fail to support or satisfy; disappoint. **3** lengthen (a garment). **4** Brit. deflate (a tire). **let down gently** avoid humiliating abruptly. **let drop** (or **fall**) **1** drop (esp. a word or hint) intentionally or by accident. **2** (foll. by *on, upon, to*) Geom. draw (a perpendicular) from an outside point to a line. **let fly 1** (often foll. by *at*) attack physically or verbally. **2** discharge (a missile). **let go 1** release; set at liberty. **2 a** (often foll. by *of*) lose or relinquish one's hold. **b** lose hold of. **3** cease to think or talk about. **let oneself go 1** give way to enthusiasm, impulse, etc. **2** cease to take trouble; neglect one's appearance or habits. **let in 1** allow to enter (*let the dog in*; *let in a flood of light*; *this would let in all sorts of evils*). **2** (usu. foll. by *for*) involve (a person, often oneself) in loss or difficulty. **3** (foll. by *on*) allow (a person) to share privileges, information, etc. **4** inlay (a thing) in another. **let oneself in** unassistedly enter another person's home, office, etc., usu. with permission. **let loose** release or unchain (a dog, fury, a maniac, etc.). **let me see** see SEE¹. **let off 1 a** fire (a gun). **b** explode (a bomb or firework). **2** allow or cause (steam, liquid, etc.) to

---

/.../ **pronunciation**	● **part of speech**
□ **phrases, idioms, and compounds**	
□□ **derivatives**	■ **synonym section**
cross-references appear in SMALL CAPITALS or *italics*	

escape. **3** allow to alight from a vehicle, etc. **4 a** not punish or compel. **b** (foll. by *with*) punish lightly. **5** *Brit.* rent out (part of a house, etc.). **6** *Brit. colloq.* break wind. **let off steam** see STEAM. **let on** *colloq.* **1** reveal a secret. **2** pretend (*let on that he had succeeded*). **let out 1** allow to go out, esp. through a doorway. **2** release from restraint. **3** (often foll. by *that* + clause) reveal (a secret, etc.). **4** make (a garment) looser, esp. by adjustment at a seam. **5** put out to rent, esp. to several tenants, or to contract. **6** exculpate. **7** give vent or expression to; emit (a sound, etc.) **let-out** *n. Brit. colloq.* an opportunity to escape. **let rip** see RIP¹. **let slip** see SLIP¹. **let through** allow to pass. **let up** *colloq.* **1** become less intense or severe. **2** relax one's efforts. **to let** esp. *Brit.* available for rent. [OE *lǣtan* f. Gmc, rel. to LATE]

■ *v.* **1 a** allow (to), permit (to), sanction (to), give permission *or* leave (to), authorize (to), license (to), *archaic* suffer (to). **b** arrange for, enable *or* cause (to). **2** (*let into*) **a** admit to, allow into, take into, receive into. **b** acquaint with, make acquainted with, inform *or* notify *or* apprise *or* advise of, brief about, put a person in the picture about, update about, bring up to date about, *colloq.* fill in on. **5** contract (out), subcontract (out), farm (out), delegate. □ **let down 1** lower, move *or* bring *or* put down, drop. **2** fail, frustrate; disappoint, disenchant, dissatisfy, disillusion. **let fly 1** see *lash out* 1. **2** see *let off* 1 below. **let go 1** see *let out* 1, 2 below. **2** (*let go of*) leave (hold of), release, drop, give up, unloose, loose, loosen, relax one's grip on; abandon, relinquish, surrender, lose. **3** drop, give up, abandon, ignore, disregard, pay no heed *or* attention to. **let loose** see RELEASE *v.* 1. **let off 1** discharge, fire, let fly; detonate, explode, set off. **2** release, discharge; give vent to. **4 a** pardon, forgive, excuse, release, discharge, exempt (from), excuse *or* relieve from, spare (from), let go, exonerate, absolve, clear, acquit, vindicate, *colloq.* let off the hook, *formal* exculpate. **let on 1** talk, tell, blab, give the game *or* show away, let the cat out of the bag, *colloq.* spill the beans, blow the whistle, *sl.* squeal, *Brit. sl.* blow the gaff. **2** (*let on that*) pretend that, make as if, (put on an) act as if. **let out 1, 2** (let) loose, unloose, liberate, set at liberty, (set) free, release, let go, discharge, emancipate, *hist.* manumit. **3** reveal, divulge, disclose, confess, admit, give away, tell, leak; release, advertise, announce, publicize. **5** rent (out), hire (out), lease (out), charter (out), sublet (out). **7** give vent *or* expression to, express; give out, emit, produce. **let up 1** decrease, abate, ease (up), slacken (off), diminish, lessen, subside, moderate; soften, ebb, fade, weaken, peter out, run out of steam, die away *or* down. **2** take a break, have a rest, slow down, take time out, *colloq.* take *or* have a breather.

let² /let/ *n. & v.* ● *n.* **1** (in tennis, squash, etc.) an obstruction of a ball *or* a player in certain ways, requiring the ball to be served again. **2** (*archaic* except in **without let or hindrance**) obstruction; hindrance. ● *v.tr.* (**letting**; *past* and *past part.* **letted** *or* **let**) *archaic* hinder, obstruct. [OE *lettan* f. Gmc, rel. to LATE]

■ **2** impediment, obstacle, encumbrance, hurdle, block, stumbling block.

-let /lit, lət/ *suffix* forming nouns, usu. diminutives (*droplet*; *leaflet*) *or* denoting articles of ornament *or* dress (*anklet*). [orig. corresp. (in *bracelet*, *crosslet*, etc.) to F *-ette* added to nouns in *-el*]

letdown /létdown/ *n.* a disappointment.

■ see DISAPPOINTMENT.

lethal /léethəl/ *adj.* causing *or* sufficient to cause death. □ **lethal chamber** a chamber in which animals may be killed painlessly with gas. **lethal dose** the amount of a toxic compound *or* drug that causes death in humans *or* animals. □□ **lethality** /-álitee/ *n.* **lethally** *adv.* [L *let(h)alis* f. *letum* death]

■ deadly, fatal, mortal, terminal, deathly, murderous, life-threatening.

lethargy /léthərjee/ *n.* **1** lack of energy or vitality; a torpid, inert, or apathetic state. **2** *Med.* morbid drowsiness or pro-

longed and unnatural sleep. □□ **lethargic** /lithaárjik/ *adj.* **lethargically** *adv.* [ME f. OF *litargie* f. LL *lethargia* f. Gk *lēthargia* f. *lēthargos* forgetful f. *lēth-*, *lanthanomai* forget]

■ **1** sluggishness, sloth, dullness, heaviness, laziness, indolence, phlegm, idleness, languidness, languor, lassitude, listlessness, dolce far niente, inactivity, inertia, torpor, stupor, *literary* hebetude; unconcern, indifference, apathy. **2** weariness, tiredness, fatigue, weakness, exhaustion, drowsiness, sleepiness, somnolence, lassitude, debility. □□ **lethargic** sluggish, slow, dull, heavy, lazy, indolent, phlegmatic, slothful, idle, languid, languorous, listless, fainéant, inactive, torpid, stuporous, comatose; indifferent, apathetic, weary, tired, fatigued, enervated, weak, exhausted, drowsy, sleepy, somnolent, *colloq.* fagged (out), *Brit. sl.* knackered.

Lethe /léethee/ *n.* **1** (in Greek mythology) a river in Hades producing forgetfulness of the past. **2** (also **lethe**) such forgetfulness. □□ **Lethean** *adj.* [L, use of Gk *lēthē* forgetfulness (as LETHARGY)]

■ □□ **Lethean** see OBLIVIOUS.

let's /lets/ *contr.* let us (*let's go now*).

Lett /let/ *n.* = LATVIAN *n.* 1. [G *Lette* f. Latvian *Latvi*]

letter /létər/ *n. & v.* ● *n.* **1 a** a character representing one *or* more of the simple *or* compound sounds used in speech; any of the alphabetic symbols. **b** (in *pl.*) *colloq.* the initials of a degree, etc., after the holder's name. **c** a school *or* college initial as a mark of proficiency in sports, etc. **2 a** a written, typed, *or* printed communication, usu. sent by mail *or* messenger. **b** (in *pl.*) an addressed legal *or* formal document for any of various purposes. **3** the precise terms of a statement; the strict verbal interpretation (opp. SPIRIT *n.* 6) (*according to the letter of the law*). **4** (in *pl.*) **a** literature. **b** acquaintance with books; erudition. **c** authorship (*the profession of letters*). **5** *Printing* **a** types collectively. **b** a fount of type. ● *v.tr.* **1 a** inscribe letters on. **b** impress a title, etc., on (a book cover, etc.). **2** classify with letters. □ **letter bomb** a terrorist explosive device in the form of *or* enclosed in a posted envelope. **letter box** esp. *Brit.* a mailbox. **letter-card** *Brit.* a folded card with a gummed edge for mailing as a letter. **letter carrier** one who delivers mail, usu. as an employee of the postal service. **letter of comfort** an assurance about a debt, short of a legal guarantee, given to a bank by a third party. **letter of credit** see CREDIT. **letter-perfect 1** *Theatr.* knowing one's part perfectly. **2** precise; verbatim. **letter-quality** of the quality of printing suitable for a business letter; producing print of this quality. **letters missive** see MISSIVE. **letters of administration** authority to administer the estate of an intestate. **letters of marque** see MARQUE². **letters patent** see PATENT. **man** (or **woman**) **of letters** a scholar *or* author. **to the letter** with adherence to every detail. □□ **letterer** *n.* **letterless** *adj.* [ME f. OF *lettre* f. L *litera*, *littera* letter of alphabet, (in pl.) epistle, literature]

■ *n.* **1 a** character, symbol, sign, grapheme. **b** (*letters*) initials. **2 a** communication, note, line, message, dispatch, *formal or joc.* epistle, *joc.* missive; postcard, card, memorandum; (*letters*) correspondence, mail, post. **4** (*letters*) literature, (creative) writing, fiction; the humanities, belles lettres, the classics; culture, the world of letters, learning, scholarship. **5** fount(s), face(s), type; typeface. ● *v.* **1 a** inscribe, mark, initial. □ **to the letter** precisely, literally, exactly, accurately, strictly, unerringly, scrupulously, faithfully, sic, letter for letter, literatim, word for word, verbatim, closely, *formal* thus.

lettered /létərd/ *adj.* well-read *or* educated.

■ literate, literary, (well-)educated, well-read, erudite, scholarly, learned, well-informed, academic, (well-)schooled, enlightened, knowledgeable, (well-)versed, accomplished, refined, cultured, cultivated.

letterhead /létərhed/ *n.* **1** a printed heading on stationery. **2** stationery with this.

lettering /létəring/ *n.* **1** the process of inscribing letters. **2** letters inscribed.

letterpress /létərpres/ *n.* **1** printing from raised type, not from lithography or other planographic processes. **2** esp. *Brit.* **a** the contents of an illustrated book other than the illustrations. **b** printed matter relating to illustrations.

Lettic /létik/ *adj. & n.* ● *adj.* **1** = LATVIAN *adj.* **2** of or relating to the Baltic branch of languages. ● *n.* = LATVIAN *n.* 2.

Lettish /létish/ *adj. & n.* = LATVIAN *adj., n.* 2.

lettuce /létis/ *n.* **1** a composite plant, *Lactuca sativa*, with crisp edible leaves used in salads. **2** any of various plants resembling this. [ME *letus(e)*, rel. to OF *laitue* f. L *lactuca* f. *lac lactis* milk, with ref. to its milky juice]

letup /létup/ *n. colloq.* **1** a reduction in intensity. **2** a relaxation of effort.

■ abatement, slackening, weakening, lessening; stop, cessation, break, intermission, suspension, time out, remission, moderation, lull, respite, pause, breathing space, time off, *colloq.* breather, *literary* surcease.

leu /láy-oō/ *n.* (*pl.* **lei** /lay/) the basic monetary unit of Romania. [Romanian, = lion]

leucine /loōseen/ *n. Biochem.* an amino acid present in protein and essential in the diet of vertebrates. [F f. Gk *leukos* white + -IN]

leucocyte *Brit.* var. of LEUKOCYTE.

leucoma *Brit.* var. of LEUKOMA.

leucorrhoea *Brit.* var. of LEUKORRHEA.

leucotomy *Brit.* var. of LEUKOTOMY.

leukemia /loōkeèmeeə/ *n.* (*Brit.* **leukaemia**) *Med.* any of a group of malignant diseases in which the bone marrow and other blood-forming organs produce increased numbers of leukocytes. □□ **leukemic** *adj.* [mod.L f. G *Leukämie* f. Gk *leukos* white + *haima* blood]

leuko- /loōkō/ *comb. form* white. [Gk *leukos* white]

leukocyte /loōkəsīt/ *n.* (*Brit.* **leucocyte**) **1** a white blood cell. **2** any blood cell that contains a nucleus. □□ **leukocytic** /-sítik/ *adj.*

leukoma /loōkṓmə/ *n.* (*Brit.* **leucoma**) a white opacity in the cornea of the eye.

leukorrhea /loōkəreèə/ *n.* (*Brit.* **leucorrhoea**) a whitish or yellowish discharge of mucus from the vagina.

leukotomy /loōkótəmee/ *n.* (also **leucotomy**) (*pl.* **-ies**) *Brit.* = prefrontal lobotomy.

Lev. *abbr.* Leviticus (Old Testament).

Levant /livánt/ *n.* (prec. by *the*) the eastern part of the Mediterranean with its islands and neighboring countries. □ **Levant morocco** high-grade, large-grained morocco leather. [F, pres. part. of *lever* rise, used as noun = point of sunrise, east]

levant /livánt/ *v.intr. Brit. sl.* abscond or bolt, esp. with betting or gaming losses unpaid. [perh. f. LEVANT]

levanter[1] /livántər/ *n.* **1** a strong easterly Mediterranean wind. **2** (**Levanter**) a native or inhabitant of the Levant in the eastern Mediterranean.

levanter[2] /livántər/ *n. Brit. sl.* a person who levants.

Levantine /lévəntīn, -teen, ləván-/ *adj. & n.* ● *adj.* of or trading to the Levant. ● *n.* a native or inhabitant of the Levant.

levator /liváytər/ *n.* a muscle that lifts a body part. [L, = one who lifts f. *levare* raise]

levee[1] /lévee, liveè/ *n.* **1** an assembly of visitors or guests, esp. at a formal reception. **2** *hist.* (in the UK) an assembly held by the sovereign or sovereign's representative at which men only were received. **3** *hist.* a reception of visitors on rising from bed. [F *levé* var. of *lever* rising f. *lever* to rise: see LEVY]

■ **1, 2** see PARTY[1] *n.* 1.

levee[2] /lévee / *n.* **1** an embankment against river floods. **2** a natural embankment built up by a river. **3** a landing place; a quay. [F *levée* fem. past part. of *lever* raise: see LEVY]

level /lévəl/ *n., adj., & v.* ● *n.* **1** a horizontal line or plane. **2** a height or value reached, a position on a real or imaginary scale (*eye level; sugar level in the blood; danger level*). **3** a social, moral, or intellectual standard. **4** a plane of rank or authority (*discussions at cabinet level*). **5 a** an instrument giving a line parallel to the plane of the horizon for testing whether things are horizontal. **b** *Surveying* an instrument for giving a horizontal line of sight. **6** a more or less level sur-

face. **7** a flat tract of land. **8** a floor or story in a building, ship, etc. ● *adj.* **1** having a flat and even surface; not bumpy. **2** horizontal; perpendicular to the plumb line. **3** (often foll. by *with*) **a** on the same horizontal plane as something else. **b** having equality with something else. **c** (of a spoonful, etc.) with the contents flat with the brim. **4** even, uniform, equable, or well-balanced in quality, style, temper, judgment, etc. **5** (of a race) having the leading competitors close together. ● *v.* (**leveled, leveling**; esp. *Brit.* **levelled, levelling**) **1** *tr.* make level, even, or uniform. **2** *tr.* (often foll. by *to* (or *with*) *the ground, in the dust*) raze or demolish. **3** *tr.* (also *absol.*) aim (a missile or gun). **4** *tr.* (also *absol.*; foll. by *at, against*) direct (an accusation, criticism, or satire). **5** *tr.* abolish (distinctions). **6** *intr.* (usu. foll. by *with*) *sl.* be frank or honest. **7** *tr.* place on the same level. **8** *tr.* (also *absol.*) *Surveying* ascertain differences in the height of (land). □ **do one's level best** *colloq.* do one's utmost; make all possible efforts. **find one's level 1** reach the right social, intellectual, etc., place in relation to others. **2** (of a liquid) reach the same height in receptacles or regions which communicate with each other. **level crossing** *Brit.* = *grade crossing*. **level down** bring down to a standard. **leveling screw** a screw for adjusting parts of a machine, etc., to an exact level. **level off** make or become level or smooth. **level out** make or become level; remove differences from. **level up** esp. *Brit.* bring up to a standard. **on the level** *colloq. adv.* honestly; without deception. ● *adj.* honest; truthful. **on a level with 1** in the same horizontal plane as. **2** equal with. □□ **levelly** *adv.* **levelness** *n.* [ME f. OF *livel* ult. f. L *libella* dimin. of *libra* scales, balance]

■ *n.* **1** plane, horizontal. **2** position, grade; extent, measure, amount, quantity, size, magnitude; situation, stratum, tier, echelon, step, station, point, stage; elevation, height, altitude, depth. **3** class, position, status, standing, rank; plane; standard(s), (degree of) competence; see also TOUCHSTONE 2. **4** see RANK[1] *n.* 1a. **8** floor, story, tier, deck. ● *adj.* **1** even, smooth, plane, uniform, flat, flush, straight; uninterrupted, unbroken, unvarying, continuous, true. **2** horizontal, flat; prone, supine. **3 a** parallel, even, flush. **b** the same, equal, equivalent, on a par, consistent. **4** even, uniform, consistent, invariable, unvarying, unalterable, unchanging, unfluctuating; (well-)balanced, unruffled, imperturbable, constant, steady; equable, even-tempered, composed, calm, poised, placid, self-possessed, levelheaded. **5** even, tied, equal, neck and neck, fifty-fifty, nip and tuck, *colloq.* even-steven. ● *v.* **1** level off *or* out, plateau (out), even (out *or* up), smooth (out), flatten (out), iron (out). **2** raze, demolish, destroy, lay waste, devastate, knock down, tear down, pull down, flatten, wreck, bulldoze. **3** aim, point, direct, train, focus, turn; (*absol.*) take aim, draw a bead, zero in. **4** (*level at*) aim at, focus on, direct to, address to, turn on. **6** (*level with*) be *or* play fair with, be straight *or* open *or* straightforward *or* frank *or* honest with, tell the truth to, *colloq.* be up front with. □ **level off, level out** see LEVEL *v.* 1 above. **on the level** (*adv.*) straight (out), openly, candidly, fairly, freely, publicly, frankly, directly, sincerely, honestly, straightforwardly, plainly, *colloq.* upfront, on the up and up. (*adj.*) straight, straightforward, honest, direct, sincere, candid, frank, square, open, unbiased, fair, aboveboard, *colloq.* upfront, on the up and up.

levelheaded /lévəlhédid/ *adj.* mentally well-balanced, cool, sensible. □□ **levelheadedly** *adv.* **levelheadedness** *n.*

■ sensible, (well-)balanced, sane, reasonable, rational, commonsensical, level, unruffled, undisturbed, unperturbed, imperturbable, equable, even-tempered,

---

/.../ **pronunciation**	● **part of speech**
□ **phrases, idioms, and compounds**	
□□ **derivatives**	■ **synonym section**
cross-references appear in SMALL CAPITALS or *italics*	

composed, calm, collected, tranquil, serene, poised, cool, relaxed, self-possessed, *colloq.* unflappable.

leveler /lévələr/ *n.* (esp. *Brit.* **leveller**) **1** a person who advocates the abolition of social distinctions. **2** (**Leveler**) *hist.* an extreme radical dissenter in 17th-c. England. **3** a person or thing that levels.

lever /lévər, leev-/ *n.* & *v.* ● *n.* **1** a bar resting on a pivot, used to help lift a heavy or firmly fixed object. **2** *Mech.* a simple machine consisting of a rigid bar pivoted about a fulcrum (fixed point) which can be acted upon by a force (effort) in order to move a load. **3** a projecting handle moved to operate a mechanism. **4** a means of exerting moral pressure. ● *v.* **1** *intr.* use a lever. **2** *tr.* (often foll. by *away, out, up*, etc.) lift, move, or act on with a lever. □ **lever escapement** a mechanism connecting the escape wheel and the balance wheel using two levers. **lever watch** a watch with a lever escapement. [ME f. OF *levier, leveor* f. *lever* raise: see LEVY]

■ *n.* **3** see CONTROL *n.* 5. ● *v.* **2** see LIFT *v.* 1.

leverage /lévərij, lee-/ *n.* **1** the action of a lever; a way of applying a lever. **2** the power of a lever; the mechanical advantage gained by use of a lever. **3** a means of accomplishing a purpose; power; influence. **4** a set or system of levers. **5** *Commerce* the use of a relatively small investment or value in equity to acquire or control a much larger investment. □ **leveraged buyout** the buyout of a company by its management using outside capital.

■ **1, 2** see PURCHASE *n.* 4a. **3** see INFLUENCE *n.* 1.

leveret /lévərit/ *n.* a young hare, esp. one in its first year. [ME f. AF, dimin. of *levre*, OF *lievre* f. L *lepus leporis* hare]

leviable see LEVY.

leviathan /livíathən/ *n.* **1** *Bibl.* a sea monster. **2** anything very large or powerful, esp. a ship. **3** an autocratic monarch or state (in allusion to a book by Hobbes, 1651). [ME f. LL f. Heb. *liwyāṯān*]

■ **2** see JUMBO *n.*

levigate /lévigayt/ *v.tr.* **1** reduce to a fine, smooth powder. **2** make a smooth paste of. □□ **levigation** /-gáyshən/ *n.* [L *levigare levigat-* f. *levis* smooth]

■ **1** see POWDER *v.* 2. **2** see PULP *v.* 1.

levin /lévin/ *n. archaic* **1** lightning. **2** a flash of lightning. [ME *leven(e)*, prob. f. ON]

levirate /lévirət, -rayt, lee-/ *n.* a custom of the ancient Jews and some other peoples by which a man is obliged to marry his brother's widow. □□ **leviratic** /-rátik/ *adj.* **leviratical** *adj.* [L *levir* brother-in-law + -ATE[1]]

Levis /léeviz/ *n.pl. propr.* a type of (orig. blue) denim jeans or overalls reinforced with rivets. [*Levi* Strauss, orig. US manufacturer in 1860s]

levitate /lévitayt/ *v.* **1** *intr.* rise and float in the air (esp. with reference to spiritualism). **2** *tr.* cause to do this. □□ **levitation** /-táyshən/ *n.* **levitator** *n.* [L *levis* light, after GRAVITATE]

Levite /léevīt/ *n.* a member of the tribe of Levi, esp. of that part of it which provided assistants to the priests in the worship in the Jewish temple. [ME f. LL *levita* f. Gk *leuitēs* f. *Leui* f. Heb. *lēwī* Levi]

Levitical /livítikəl/ *adj.* **1** of the Levites or the tribe of Levi. **2** of the Levites' ritual. **3** of Leviticus. [LL *leviticus* f. Gk *leuitikos* (as LEVITE)]

levity /lévitee/ *n.* **1** lack of serious thought; frivolity; unbecoming jocularity. **2** inconstancy. **3** undignified behavior. **4** *archaic* lightness of weight. [L *levitas* f. *levis* light]

■ **1** lightheartedness, lightness, frivolity, frivolousness, flippancy, trivialization, triviality, trifling, facetiousness, silliness, hilarity. **2** fickleness, inconstancy, inconsistency, changeableness, unreliability, unreliableness, undependability, flightiness. **3** silliness, foolery, foolishness, tomfoolery, folly; antics. **4** lightness, unsubstantiality, thinness, weightlessness.

levo- /léevō/ *comb. form* (also esp. *Brit.* **laevo-**) on or to the left. [L *laevus* left]

levodopa /léevədópə/ *n.* levorotatory dopa.

levorotatory /léeva-rṓtətawree/ *adj.* (esp. *Brit.* **laevorotatory**) *Chem.* having the property of rotating the plane of a

polarized light ray to the left (counterclockwise facing the oncoming radiation).

levulose /léevyəlōs/ *n.* (esp. *Brit.* **laevulose**) = FRUCTOSE. [LEVO- + -ULE + -OSE[2]]

levy /lévee/ *v.* & *n.* ● *v.tr.* (**-ies, -ied**) **1 a** impose (a rate or toll). **b** raise (contributions or taxes). **c** (also *absol.*) raise (a sum of money) by legal execution or process (*the debt was levied on the debtor's goods*). **d** seize (goods) in this way. **e** extort (*levy blackmail*). **2** enlist or enroll (troops, etc.). **3** (usu. foll. by *upon, against*) wage; proceed to make (war). ● *n.* (*pl.* **-ies**) **1 a** the collecting of a contribution, tax, etc., or of property to satisfy a legal judgment. **b** a contribution, tax, etc., levied. **2 a** the act or an instance of enrolling troops, etc. **b** (in *pl.*) persons enrolled. **c** a body of persons enrolled. **d** the number of persons enrolled. □□ **leviable** *adj.* [ME f. OF *levee* fem. past part. of *lever* f. L *levare* raise f. *levis* light]

■ *v.* **1 a, b** impose, charge, exact, demand; raise. **2** see MOBILIZE *v.* 1a. **3** see INFLICT. ● *n.* **1 b** see TAX *n.* 1.

lewd /lood/ *adj.* **1** lascivious. **2** indecent; obscene. □□ **lewdly** *adv.* **lewdness** *n.* [OE *lǣwede* LAY[2], of unkn. orig.]

■ **1** lascivious, lustful, randy, lecherous, sexy, licentious, dirty, prurient, salacious, libidinous, erotic, sensual, lubricious, promiscuous, depraved, dissolute, ruttish, goatish, wanton, debauched, hot, *formal* concupiscent, *sl.* horny. **2** indecent, obscene, smutty, crude, coarse, foul, dirty, filthy, rude, pornographic, gross, bawdy, ribald, scurrilous, raw, blue, sexy, risqué, offensive, suggestive, (sexually) explicit, *euphem.* adult.

lewis /lóois/ *n.* an iron contrivance for gripping heavy blocks of stone or concrete for lifting. [18th c.: orig. unkn.]

Lewis gun /lóois/ *n.* a light machine gun with a magazine, air cooling, and operation by gas from its own firing. [I. N. *Lewis*, Amer. soldier d. 1931, its inventor]

lewisite /lóoisīt/ *n.* an irritant gas that produces blisters, developed for use in chemical warfare. [W. L. *Lewis*, Amer. chemist d. 1943 + -ITE[1]]

lex domicilii /léks domisíleeī/ *n. Law* the law of the country in which a person is domiciled. [L]

lexeme /lékseem/ *n. Linguistics* a basic lexical unit of a language comprising one or several words, the elements of which do not separately convey the meaning of the whole. [LEXICON + -EME]

lex fori /leks fáwrī/ *n. Law* the law of the country in which an action is brought. [L]

lexical /léksikəl/ *adj.* **1** of the words of a language. **2** of or as of a lexicon. □□ **lexically** *adv.* [Gk *lexikos, lexikon*: see LEXICON]

■ **1** see LITERAL *adj.* 1.

lexicography /léksikógrəfee/ *n.* the compiling of dictionaries. □□ **lexicographer** *n.* **lexicographic** /-kəgráfik/ *adj.* **lexicographical** *adj.* **lexicographically** *adv.*

lexicology /léksikóləjee/ *n.* the study of the form, history, and meaning of words. □□ **lexicological** /-kəlójikəl/ *adj.* **lexicologically** *adv.* **lexicologist** /-kóləjist/ *n.*

lexicon /léksikon/ *n.* **1** a dictionary, esp. of Greek, Latin, Hebrew, Syriac, or Arabic. **2** the vocabulary of a person, language, branch of knowledge, etc. [mod.L f. Gk *lexikon* (*biblion* book), neut. of *lexikos* f. *lexis* word f. *legō* speak]

■ **1** see DICTIONARY 1.

lexigraphy /leksígrəfee/ *n.* a system of writing in which each character represents a word. [Gk *lexis* (see LEXICON) + -GRAPHY]

lexis /léksis/ *n.* **1** words; vocabulary. **2** the total stock of words in a language. [Gk: see LEXICON]

lex loci /leks lṓsī, -kee, -kī/ *n. Law* the law of the country in which a transaction is performed, a tort is committed, or a property is situated. [L]

lex talionis /léks taleeónis/ *n.* the law of retaliation, whereby a punishment resembles the offense committed, in kind and degree. [L]

ley[1] /lay/ *n. Brit.* a field temporarily under grass. □ **ley farming** alternate growing of crops and grass. [ME (orig. adj.), perh. f. OE, rel. to LAY[1], LIE[1]]

ley[2] /lay, lee/ *n.* the supposed straight line of a prehistoric track, usu. between hilltops. [var. of LEA]

Leyden jar /líd'n/ *n.* an early form of capacitor consisting of a glass jar with layers of metal foil on the outside and inside. [*Leyden* (now *Leiden*) in Holland, where it was invented (1745)]

LF *abbr.* low frequency.

LH *abbr. Biochem.* luteinizing hormone.

l.h. *abbr.* left hand.

LI *abbr.* **1** Long Island. **2** *Brit.* light infantry.

Li *symb. Chem.* the element lithium.

liability /líəbílitee/ *n.* (*pl.* **-ies**) **1** the state of being liable. **2** a person or thing that is troublesome as an unwelcome responsibility; a handicap. **3** what a person is liable for, esp. (in *pl.*) debts or pecuniary obligations.
- **1** answerability, responsibility, accountability, accountableness; exposure, susceptibility, vulnerability. **2** burden, handicap, disadvantage, drawback, hindrance, impediment, encumbrance, millstone, cross (to bear), snag, hitch, difficulty, barrier, obstacle, obstruction, fly in the ointment, *colloq.* monkey wrench in the works. **3** (*liabilities*) obligations, debts, indebtedness, arrears, debits, dues.

liable /líəbəl/ *predic. adj.* **1** legally bound. **2** (foll. by *to*) subject to (a tax or penalty). **3** (foll. by *to* + infin.) under an obligation. **4** (foll. by *to*) exposed or open to (something undesirable). **5** *disp.* (foll. by *to* + infin.) apt; likely (*it is liable to rain*). **6** (foll. by *for*) answerable. [ME perh. f. AF f. OF *lier* f. L *ligare* bind]
- **1** (legally *or* statutorily) bound, responsible. **3** obliged, under an obligation, obligated, (duty-)bound, due, beholden. **4** exposed, susceptible, vulnerable, open, subject, given, predisposed, tending. **5** prone, apt, inclined, disposed, expected, due, likely, of a mind. **6** responsible, accountable, blameable, answerable, chargeable.

liaise /lee-áyz/ *v.intr.* (foll. by *with*, *between*) *colloq.* establish cooperation; act as a link. [back-form. f. LIAISON]

liaison /lee-áyzon, lée-ay-/ *n.* **1 a** communication or cooperation, esp. between military forces or units. **b** a person who initiates such. **2** an illicit sexual relationship. **3** the binding or thickening agent of a sauce. **4** the sounding of an ordinarily silent final consonant before a word beginning with a vowel (or a mute *h* in French). □ **liaison officer** an officer acting as a link between allied forces or units of the same force. [F f. *lier* bind f. L *ligare*]
- **1 a** connection, communication, contact, link(age), cooperation, relationship, relations, tie(s). **2** (love) affair, amour, relationship, *affaire* (*de cœur*), romance, entanglement, flirtation, fling, *archaic* intrigue.

liana /lee-aánə/ *n.* (also **liane** /-aán/) any of several climbing and twining plants of tropical forests. [F *liane*, *lierne* clematis, of uncert. orig.]

liar /líər/ *n.* a person who tells a lie or lies, esp. habitually. [OE *lēogere* (as LIE[2], -AR[4])]
- fibber, fibster, fabricator, prevaricator, perjurer, falsifier, teller of tales, romancer, fabulist, false witness, *colloq.* storyteller.

lias /líəs/ *n.* **1** (**Lias**) *Geol.* the lower strata of the Jurassic system of rocks, consisting of shales and limestones rich in fossils. **2** a blue limestone rock found in SW England. □□ **liassic** /líásik/ *adj.* (in sense 1). [ME f. OF *liois* hard limestone, prob. f. Gmc]

Lib. *abbr.* Liberal.

lib /lib/ *n. colloq.* liberation (*women's lib*). [abbr.]

libation /lībáyshən/ *n.* **1 a** the pouring out of a drink offering to a god. **b** such a drink offering. **2** *joc.* a drink. [ME f. L *libatio* f. *libare* pour as offering]

libber /líbər/ *n. colloq.* an advocate of women's liberation.

libel /líbəl/ *n. & v.* ● *n.* **1** *Law* **a** a published false statement damaging to a person's reputation (cf. SLANDER). **b** the act of publishing this. **2 a** a false and defamatory written statement. **b** (foll. by *on*) a thing that brings discredit by misrepresentation, etc. (*the portrait is a libel on him; the book is a libel on human nature*). **3 a** (in civil and ecclesiastical law) the

plaintiff's written declaration. **b** *Sc. Law* a statement of the grounds of a charge. ● *v.tr.* (**libeled, libeling**; esp. *Brit.* **libelled, libelling**) **1** defame by libelous statements. **2** accuse falsely and maliciously. **3** *Law* publish a libel against. **4** (in ecclesiastical law) bring a suit against. □□ **libeler** *n.* [ME f. OF f. L *libellus* dimin. of *liber* book]
- *n.* **2 a** defamation, vilification, denigration, slander, calumny, detraction, obloquy, misrepresentation, prevarication; aspersion, lie, untruth, false insinuation, falsehood, imputation, allegation, slur. **b** slur, smear, blot, stain, smirch. ● *v.* **1, 2** defame, vilify, denigrate, denounce, deprecate, decry, depreciate, belittle, disparage, disgrace, dishonor, shame, humiliate, mortify, abuse, *formal* derogate; slander, calumniate, lie about, misrepresent, asperse, cast aspersions on, give a bad name to, speak ill of, slur, smear, malign, stain, blacken, discredit, besmirch, stigmatize, traduce, badmouth.

libelous /líbələs/ *adj.* containing or constituting a libel. □□ **libelously** *adv.*
- see *slanderous* (SLANDER).

liber /líbər/ *n.* bast. [L, = bark]

liberal /líbərəl, líbrəl/ *adj. & n.* ● *adj.* **1** given freely; ample; abundant. **2** (often foll. by *of*) giving freely; generous; not sparing. **3** open-minded; not prejudiced. **4** not strict or rigorous; (of interpretation) not literal. **5** for general broadening of the mind; not professional or technical (*liberal studies*). **6 a** favoring individual liberty and political and social reform. **b** (**Liberal**) of or characteristic of Liberals or a Liberal party. **7** *Theol.* regarding many traditional beliefs as dispensable, invalidated by modern thought, or liable to change (*liberal Protestant; liberal Judaism*). ● *n.* **1** a person of liberal views. **2** (**Liberal**) a supporter or member of a Liberal party. □ **liberal arts 1** the arts as distinct from science and technology. **2** *hist.* the medieval trivium and quadrivium. **Liberal party** a political party advocating liberal policies. □□ **liberalism** *n.* **liberalist** *n.* **liberalistic** /-lístik/ *adj.* **liberally** *adv.* **liberalness** *n.* [ME, orig. = befitting a free man, f. OF f. L *liberalis* f. *liber* free (man)]
- *adj.* **1** lavish, handsome, ample, abundant, plentiful, profuse, copious, luxuriant, prolific, *poet.* bounteous. **2** bountiful, free, generous, openhearted, open, openhanded, giving, charitable, philanthropic, munificent, magnanimous, big, bighearted, unstinting, ungrudging, unselfish, unsparing, *poet.* bounteous. **3** fair, broad-minded, open-minded, large-minded, unprejudiced, unbigoted, unjaundiced, unbiased, tolerant, relaxed, permissive, lax, unopinionated, disinterested, impartial, dispassionate. **4** free, flexible, wide, lenient, loose, broad, open, nonrestrictive; casual, imprecise, inexact. **5** progressive, progressivist, libertine, freethinking, libertarian, reformist, humanistic, left (of center), latitudinarian. ● *n.* **1** progressive, libertarian, reformer, progressivist, latitudinarian, independent, freethinker, leftist, left-winger.

liberality /líbərálitee/ *n.* **1** free giving; munificence. **2** freedom from prejudice; breadth of mind. [ME f. OF *liberalite* or L *liberalitas* (as LIBERAL)]
- **1** see LARGESSE 2.

liberalize /líbərəlīz, líbrə-/ *v.tr. & intr.* make or become more liberal or less strict. □□ **liberalization** *n.* **liberalizer** *n.*
- broaden, widen, extend, expand, stretch, enlarge; loosen, ease, slacken, relax, modify, change, moderate, soften.

liberate /líbərayt/ *v.tr.* **1** (often foll. by *from*) set at liberty; set free. **2** free (a country, etc.) from an oppressor or an enemy occupation. **3** (often as **liberated** *adj.*) free (a person) from rigid social conventions, esp. in sexual behavior.

/.../ **pronunciation**	● **part of speech**
□ **phrases, idioms, and compounds**	
□□ **derivatives**	■ **synonym section**
cross-references appear in SMALL CAPITALS or *italics*	

4 *sl.* steal. **5** *Chem.* release (esp. a gas) from a state of combination. □□ **liberator** *n.* [L *liberare liberat-* f. *liber* free]
■ **1** (set) free, release, set at liberty, (let) loose, let go *or* out *or* off, deliver, rescue, unfetter, unshackle, emancipate, enfranchise, *hist.* manumit, *literary* disenthrall. **2** deliver, free, emancipate. **3** (**liberated**) emancipated, reformed; uninhibited, free, new. **4** steal, pilfer, filch, appropriate, *colloq.* lift, *formal or joc.* purloin, *Brit. sl.* nick; see also TAKE *v.* 14a.

liberation /líbəráyshən/ *n.* the act or an instance of liberating; the state of being liberated. □ **liberation theology** a theory that interprets liberation from social, political, and economic oppression as an anticipation of ultimate salvation. □□ **liberationist** *n.* [ME f. L *liberatio* f. *liberare*: see LIBERATE]
■ freeing, deliverance, emancipation, enfranchisement, affranchisement, rescue, release; freedom, liberty.

libertarian /líbərtáireeən/ *n.* & *adj.* ● *n.* **1** an advocate of liberty. **2** a believer in free will (opp. NECESSITARIAN). ● *adj.* believing in free will. □□ **libertarianism** *n.*
■ *n.* **1** see LIBERAL *n.* 1.

libertine /líbərteen, -tin/ *n.* & *adj.* ● *n.* **1** a dissolute or licentious person. **2** a free thinker on religion. **3** a person who follows his or her own inclinations. ● *adj.* **1** licentious; dissolute. **2** freethinking. **3** following one's own inclinations. □□ **libertinage** *n.* **libertinism** /-nízəm/ *n.* [L *libertinus* freedman f. *libertus* made free f. *liber* free]
■ *n.* **1** lecher, reprobate, profligate, rake, roué, debaucher, debauchee, dissipator, playboy, sport, *literary* wanton; womanizer, seducer, adulterer, philanderer, Don Juan, lothario, Casanova, Romeo, lady-killer, *archaic or joc.* fornicator, *colloq.* stud, *sl.* wolf. **2** freethinker, liberal, libertarian, latitudinarian. **3** liberal, independent, individualist. ● *adj.* **1** licentious, lecherous, reprobate, profligate, rakish, philandering, dissolute, immoral, degenerate, depraved, debauched, decadent, dirty, filthy, amoral, wanton, lewd, lascivious, prurient, lubricious, salacious, libidinous; see also LEWD 1. **2, 3** see LIBERAL *adj.* 6.

liberty /líbərtee/ *n.* (*pl.* **-ies**) **1 a** freedom from captivity, imprisonment, slavery, or despotic control. **b** a personification of this. **2 a** the right or power to do as one pleases. **b** (foll. by *to* + infin.) right; power; opportunity; permission. **c** *Philos.* freedom from control by fate or necessity. **3 a** (usu. in *pl.*) a right, privilege, or immunity, enjoyed by prescription or grant. **b** (in *sing.* or *pl.*) *hist.* an area having such privileges, etc., esp. a district controlled by a city though outside its boundary or an area outside a prison where some prisoners might reside. **4** setting aside of rules or convention. □ **at liberty 1** free; not imprisoned (*set at liberty*). **2** (foll. by *to* + infin.) entitled; permitted. **3** available; disengaged. **Liberty Bell** a bell in Philadelphia rung at the adoption of the Declaration of Independence. **liberty cap** *hist.* a conical knit cap worn as a symbol of liberty, esp. by American and French revolutionaries. **Liberty ship** *hist.* a prefabricated US-built freighter of World War II. **liberty pole** (or **tree**) *hist.* a pole, flagstaff, or tree atop of which a flag or liberty cap is displayed, esp. as a rallying symbol to American revolutionaries. **take liberties 1** (often foll. by *with*) behave in an unduly familiar manner. **2** (foll. by *with*) deal freely or superficially with rules or facts. **take the liberty** (foll. by *to* + infin., or *of* + verbal noun) presume; venture. [ME f. OF *liberté* f. L *libertas -tatis* f. *liber* free]
■ **1** freedom, independence, self-determination, autonomy, self-rule, self-government, sovereignty; emancipation, liberation. **2** freedom, license, leave, power, authority, prerogative, carte blanche; choice, option, alternative; latitude, elbowroom, margin, scope; free will. **3 a** freedom, franchise, privilege, prerogative; (*liberties*) (civil *or* human) rights. □ **at liberty 1** free, uninhibited, unfettered, unconstrained, unrestricted, unrestrained; see also FREE *adj.* 3. **2** free, permitted, allowed, given leave *or* permission, authorized, entitled, given the go-ahead, *colloq.* given the green light. **3** ready, disposed, on hand, available, disengaged. **take**

liberties 1 be unrestrained *or* overfamiliar *or* forward *or* aggressive *or* impudent *or* impertinent *or* audacious *or* improper; display *or* exercise boldness *or* impropriety *or* presumption *or* presumptuousness *or* indecorum *or* unseemliness *or* arrogance. **take the liberty** presume, venture, be presumptuous *or* bold *or* uninhibited, make (so) bold, go so far, have the audacity *or* effrontery, *colloq.* have the nerve.

libidinous /libídinəs/ *adj.* lustful. □□ **libidinously** *adv.* **libidinousness** *n.* [ME f. L *libidinosus* f. *libido -dinis* lust]
■ see *lustful* (LUST). □□ **libidinousness** see LUST *n.* 1, 3.

libido /libeedō, -bí-/ *n.* (*pl.* **-os**) *Psychol.* psychic drive or energy, esp. that associated with sexual desire. □□ **libidinal** /libídinəl/ *adj.* **libidinally** *adv.* [L: see LIBIDINOUS]
■ see LUST *n.* 3.

Lib-Lab /líbláb/ *adj. Brit. hist.* Liberal and Labour (parties). [abbr.]

Libra /léebrə, lí-/ *n.* **1** a constellation, traditionally regarded as contained in the figure of scales. **2 a** the seventh sign of the zodiac (the Balance or Scales). **b** a person born when the sun is in this sign. □□ **Libran** *n.* & *adj.* [ME f. L, orig. = pound weight]

librarian /líbráireeən/ *n.* a person in charge of, or an assistant in, a library. □□ **librarianship** *n.* [L *librarius*: see LIBRARY]

library /líbreree/ *n.* (*pl.* **-ies**) **1 a** a collection of books, etc., for use by the public or by members of a group. **b** a person's collection of books. **2** a room or building containing a collection of books (for reading or reference rather than for sale). **3 a** a similar collection of films, records, computer software, etc. **b** the place where these are kept. **4** a series of books issued by a publisher in similar bindings, etc., usu. as a set. **5** a public institution charged with the care of a collection of books, films, etc. □ **library edition** a strongly bound edition. **library science** the study of librarianship. [ME f. OF *librairie* f. L *libraria* (*taberna* shop), fem. of *librarius* bookseller's, of books, f. *liber libri* book]
■ **2** see STUDY *n.* 3.

libration /líbráyshən/ *n.* an apparent oscillation of a heavenly body, esp. the moon, by which the parts near the edge of the disk are alternately in view and out of view. [L *libratio* f. *librare* f. *libra* balance]
■ see SWING *n.* 1, 2.

libretto /librétō/ *n.* (*pl.* **-os** or **libretti** /-tee/) the text of an opera or other long musical vocal work. □□ **librettist** *n.* [It., dimin. of *libro* book f. L *liber libri*]
■ see LYRIC *n.* 3.

Librium /líbreeəm/ *n. propr.* a white crystalline drug used as a tranquilizer.

Libyan /líbeeən, líbyən/ *adj.* & *n.* ● *adj.* **1** of or relating to modern Libya in N. Africa. **2** of ancient N. Africa west of Egypt. **3** of or relating to the Berber group of languages. ● *n.* **1 a** a native or national of modern Libya. **b** a person of Libyan descent. **2** an ancient language of the Berber group.

lice *pl.* of LOUSE.

license /lísəns/ *n.* & *v.* (esp. *Brit.* **licence**) ● *n.* **1** a permit from an authority to own or use something (esp. a dog, gun, television set, or vehicle), do something (esp. marry, print something, preach, or drive on a public road), or carry on a business (esp. in alcoholic liquor). **2** leave; permission (*have I your license to remove the fence?*). **3 a** liberty of action, esp. when excessive; disregard of law or propriety; abuse of freedom. **b** licentiousness. **4** a writer's or artist's irregularity in grammar, meter, perspective, etc., or deviation from fact, esp. for effect (*poetic license*). **5** esp. *Brit.* a university certificate of competence in a faculty. ● *v.tr.* **1** grant a license to (a person). **2** authorize the use of (premises) for a certain purpose, esp. the sale and consumption of alcoholic liquor. **3** authorize the publication of (a book, etc.) or the performance of (a play). **4** *archaic* allow. □ **license plate** the usu. metal plate of a motor vehicle that attests to its registration. □□ **licensable** *adj.* **licenser** *n.* **licensor** *n.* [ME f. OF f. L *licentia* f. *licēre* be lawful]
■ *n.* **1** permit, pass, certificate, credential(s), paper(s), document(s), warrant, warranty, certification, authorization, dispensation. **2** leave, permission,

authorization, authority, entitlement, dispensation, empowerment, right, sanction, carte blanche, freedom, latitude, free choice, liberty, privilege; charter, franchise. **3** lack of control *or* restraint, laxness, laxity, looseness; libertinism, libertinage, profligateness, profligacy, excessiveness, immoderation, immoderateness, wantonness, debauchery, dissoluteness, dissipation. **4** disregard, deviation, departure, nonconformity, noncompliance, divergence, independence, individuality. ● *v.* **1** entitle, grant rights to, allow, permit, enable, empower. **3** authorize, allow, permit, certify, sanction, approve.

licensee /lísənsee/ *n.* the holder of a license, esp. to sell alcoholic liquor.

licentiate /līsénsheeət/ *n.* **1** a holder of a certificate of competence to practice a certain profession. **2** a licensed preacher not yet having an appointment, esp. in a Presbyterian church. [ME f. med.L *licentiatus* past part. of *licentiare* f. L *licentia*: see LICENSE]

licentious /līsénshəs/ *adj.* **1** immoral in sexual relations. **2** *archaic* disregarding accepted rules or conventions. □□ **licentiously** *adv.* **licentiousness** *n.* [L *licentiosus* f. *licentia*: see LICENSE]

■ **1** see IMMORAL 3. □□ **licentiousness** see *indecency* (INDECENT).

lichee var. of LITCHI.

lichen /líkən/ *n.* **1** any plant organism of the group Lichenes, composed of a fungus and an alga in symbiotic association, usu. of green, gray, or yellow tint and growing on and coloring rocks, tree trunks, roofs, walls, etc. **2** any of several types of skin disease in which small, round, hard lesions occur close together. □□ **lichened** *adj.* (in sense 1). **lichenology** *n.* (in sense 1). **lichenous** *adj.* (in sense 2). [L f. Gk *leikhēn*]

lich-gate /líchgayt/ *n.* (also **lych-gate**) a roofed gateway to a churchyard where a coffin awaits the clergyman's arrival. [ME f. OE *līc* corpse f. Gmc + GATE[1]]

licit /lísit/ *adj.* not forbidden; lawful. □□ **licitly** *adv.* [L *licitus* past part. of *licēre* be lawful]

■ see LEGAL 3.

lick /lik/ *v. & n.* ● *v.tr. & intr.* **1** *tr.* pass the tongue over, esp. to taste, moisten, or (of animals) clean. **2** *tr.* bring into a specified condition or position by licking (*licked it all up*; *licked it clean*). **3 a** *tr.* (of a flame, waves, etc.) touch; play lightly over. **b** *intr.* move gently or caressingly. **4** *tr. colloq.* **a** defeat; excel. **b** surpass the comprehension of (*has got me licked*). **5** *tr. colloq.* thrash. ● *n.* **1** an act of licking with the tongue. **2** = *salt lick*. **3** *colloq.* a fast pace (*at a lick*; *at full lick*). **4** *colloq.* **a** a small amount; quick treatment with (foll. by *of*: *a lick of paint*). **b** a quick wash. **5** a smart blow with a stick, etc. □ **a lick and a promise** *colloq.* a hasty performance of a task, esp. of washing oneself. **lick a person's boots** (or **shoes**) toady; be servile. **lick into shape** see SHAPE. **lick one's lips** (or **chops**) **1** look forward with relish. **2** show one's satisfaction. **lick one's wounds** be in retirement after defeat. □□ **licker** *n.* (also in *comb.*). [OE *liccian* f. WG]

■ *v.* **4** see OVERCOME 1. □ **lick a person's boots** see TRUCKLE *v.* **lick one's lips 2** see SAVOR *v.* 1.

lickerish /líkərish/ *adj.* (also **liquorish**) **1** lecherous. **2 a** fond of fine food. **b** greedy; longing. [ME *lickerous* f. OF *lecheros*: see LECHER]

■ **1** see LECHEROUS.

lickety-split /líkəteesplít/ *adv. colloq.* at full speed; headlong. [prob. f. LICK (cf. *at full lick*) + SPLIT]

■ see *quickly* (QUICK).

licking /líking/ *n. colloq.* **1** a thrashing. **2** a defeat.

lickspittle /líkspit'l/ *n.* a toady.

■ see *yes-man*.

licorice /líkərish, -ris/ *n.* (also esp. *Brit.* **liquorice**) **1** a black root extract used as a candy and in medicine. **2** the leguminous plant *Glycyrrhiza glabra* from which it is obtained. [ME f. AF *lycorys*, OF *licoresse* f. LL *liquiritia* f. Gk *glukurrhiza* f. *glukus* sweet + *rhiza* root]

lictor /líktər/ *n.* (usu. in *pl.*) *Rom.Hist.* an officer attending the consul or other magistrate, bearing the fasces, and executing sentence on offenders. [ME f. L, perh. rel. to *ligare* bind]

lid /lid/ *n.* **1** a hinged or removable cover, esp. for the top of a container. **2** = EYELID. **3** the operculum of a shell or a plant. **4** *sl.* a hat. □ **put a lid on** be quiet about; keep secret. **take the lid off** *colloq.* expose (a scandal, etc.). □□ **lidded** *adj.* (also in *comb.*). **lidless** *adj.* [OE *hlid* f. Gmc]

■ **1** see COVER *n.* 1a.

lido /leedō/ *n.* (*pl.* **-os**) esp. *Brit.* a public open-air swimming pool or beach resort. [It. f. *Lido*, the name of a beach resort near Venice, f. L *litus* shore]

lie[1] /lī/ *v. & n.* ● *v.intr.* (**lying** /lí-ing/; *past* **lay** /lay/; *past part.* **lain** /layn/) **1** be in or assume a horizontal position on a supporting surface; be at rest on something. **2** (of a thing) rest flat on a surface (*snow lay on the ground*). **3** (of abstract things) remain undisturbed or undiscussed, etc. (*let matters lie*). **4 a** be kept or remain or be in a specified, esp. concealed, state or place (*lie hidden*; *lie in wait*; *malice lay behind those words*; *they lay dying*; *the books lay unread*; *the money is lying in the bank*). **b** (of abstract things) exist; reside; be in a certain position or relation (foll. by *in*, *with*, etc.: *the answer lies in education*; *my sympathies lie with the family*). **5 a** be situated or stationed (*the village lay to the east*; *the ships are lying off the coast*). **b** (of a road, route, etc.) lead (*the road lies over mountains*). **c** be spread out to view (*the desert lay before us*). **6** (of the dead) be buried in a grave. **7** (foll. by *with*) *archaic* have sexual intercourse. **8** *Law* be admissible or sustainable (*the objection will not lie*). **9** (of a game bird) not rise. ● *n.* **1 a** the way or direction or position in which a thing lies. **b** *Golf* the position of a golf ball when about to be struck. **2** the place of cover of an animal or a bird. □ **as far as in me lies** to the best of my power. **let lie** not raise (a controversial matter, etc.) for discussion, etc. **lie about** (or **around**) be left carelessly out of place. **lie ahead** be going to happen; be in store. **lie back** recline so as to rest. **lie down** assume a lying position; have a short rest. **lie-down** *n.* esp. *Brit.* a short rest. **lie down under** esp. *Brit.* accept (an insult, etc.) without protest. **lie heavy** cause discomfort or anxiety. **lie in 1** remain in bed in the morning. **2** *archaic* be brought to bed in childbirth. **lie-in** *n.* **1** *Brit.* a prolonged stay in bed in the morning. **2** an organized protest in which demonstrators lie down (in a public place) refusing to be moved. **lie in state** (of a deceased great personage) be laid in a public place of honor before burial. **lie low 1** keep quiet or unseen. **2** be discreet about one's intentions. **lie off** *Naut.* stand some distance from shore or from another ship. **the lie of the land** esp. *Brit.* = *the lay of the land* (see LAY). **lie over** be deferred. **lie to** *Naut.* come almost to a stop facing the wind. **lie up** (of a ship) go into dock or be out of commission. **lie with** (often foll. by *to* + infin.) be the responsibility of (a person) (*it lies with you to answer*). **take lying down** (usu. with *neg.*) accept (defeat, rebuke, etc.) without resistance or protest, etc. [OE *licgan* f. Gmc]

■ *v.* **1** lie down, recline, stretch out, prostrate oneself, be prostrate *or* recumbent *or* prone *or* supine; rest, repose, lean, be supported. **2** rest, be level *or* flat. **3** rest, drop, cease, lapse. **4 b** exist, be, rest, remain, belong, reside. **5** be found, be, exist, be located *or* positioned *or* situated *or* placed *or* stationed. □ **lie ahead** see IMPEND 1. **lie back** see RECLINE 1. **lie down** prostrate oneself; have a rest *or* esp. *Brit.* lie-down, take to one's bed; see also LIE[1] *v.* 1 above, REST[1] *v.* 1, 2. **lie low** hide, remain concealed, stay in hiding, go into hiding, keep out of sight, go to ground, *Brit. sl.* lie doggo.

lie[2] /lī/ *n. & v.* ● *n.* **1** an intentionally false statement (*tell a lie*; *pack of lies*). **2** imposture; false belief (*live a lie*). ● *v.intr. & tr.* (**lies**, **lied**, **lying** /lí-ing/) **1** *intr.* **a** tell a lie or lies (*they lied to me*). **b** (of a thing) be deceptive (*the camera cannot*

---

lie). **2** *tr.* (usu. *refl.*; foll. by *into, out of*) get (oneself) into or out of a situation by lying (*lied themselves into trouble*; *lied my way out of danger*). □ **give the lie to** serve to show the falsity of (a supposition, etc.). **lie detector** an instrument for determining whether a person is telling the truth by testing for physiological changes considered to be symptomatic of lying. [OE *lyge lēogan* f. Gmc]

■ *n.* **1** falsehood, untruth, falsification, misrepresentation, false statement, fiction, invention, prevarication, fib, fabrication, stretching of the truth, half-truth, disinformation, exaggeration, overstatement, cock-and-bull story, fairy story *or* tale, *colloq.* (tall) story, (tall) tale, *sl.* whopper. ● *v.* **1 a** tell a lie, tell tales, prevaricate, fabricate *or* misrepresent *or* twist the evidence, invent stories, commit perjury, perjure *or* forswear oneself, exaggerate, fib. **b** deceive, misinform, misrepresent *or* distort *or* falsify *or* pervert the evidence. □ **give the lie to** see EXPLODE *v.* 4. **lie detector** polygraph.

Liebfraumilch /leebfrowmilk/ *n.* a light white wine from the Rhine region. [G f. *Liebfrau* the Virgin Mary, the patroness of the convent where it was first made + *Milch* milk]

lied /leed, leet/ *n.* (*pl.* **lieder** /leedər/) a type of German song, esp. of the Romantic period, usu. for solo voice with piano accompaniment. [G]

lief /leef/ *adv. archaic* gladly; willingly. (usu. **had lief, would lief**) [orig. as adj. f. OE *lēof* dear, pleasant, f. Gmc, rel. to LEAVE², LOVE]

■ see SOON 4.

liege /leej, leezh/ *adj. & n. usu. hist.* ● *adj.* (of a superior) entitled to receive or (of a vassal) bound to give feudal service or allegiance. ● *n.* **1** (in full **liege lord**) a feudal superior or sovereign. **2** (usu. in *pl.*) a vassal or subject. [ME f. OF *lige, liege* f. med.L *laeticus*, prob. f. Gmc]

liegeman /leejman, leezh-/ *n.* (*pl.* **-men**) *hist.* a sworn vassal; a faithful follower.

■ see SUBJECT *n.* 4.

lien /leen, leeən/ *n. Law* a right over another's property to protect a debt charged on that property. [F f. OF *loien* f. L *ligamen* bond f. *ligare* bind]

lierne /leeərn/ *n. Archit.* (in vaulting) a short rib connecting the bosses and intersections of the principal ribs. [ME f. F: see LIANA]

lieu /loo/ *n.* □ **in lieu 1** instead. **2** (foll. by *of*) in the place of. [ME f. F f. L *locus* place]

■ □ **in lieu 2** (*in lieu of*) see *in place of* (PLACE).

lieut. *abbr.* lieutenant.

lieutenant /looténənt/ *n.* **1** a deputy or substitute acting for a superior. **2 a** an army officer next in rank below captain. **b** a naval officer next in rank below lieutenant commander. **3** a police officer next in rank below captain. □ **lieutenant colonel** (or **commander** or **general**) officers ranking next below colonel, commander, or general. **lieutenant governor 1** (in the US) the elected official next in rank to a state's governor. **2** *Brit.* a deputy governor. □□ **lieutenancy** *n.* (*pl.* **-ies**). [ME f. OF (as LIEU, TENANT)]

■ **1** see AIDE, DEPUTY.

life /līf/ *n.* (*pl.* **lives** /līvz/) **1** the condition that distinguishes active animals and plants from inorganic matter, including the capacity for growth, functional activity, and continual change preceding death. **2 a** living things and their activity (*insect life*; *is there life on Mars?*). **b** human presence or activity (*no sign of life*). **3 a** the period during which life lasts, or the period from birth to the present time or from the present time to death (*have done it all my life*; *will regret it all my life*; *life membership*). **b** the duration of a thing's existence or of its ability to function; validity, efficacy, etc. (*the battery has a life of two years*). **4 a** a person's state of existence as a living individual (*sacrificed their lives*; *took many lives*). **b** a living person (*many lives were lost*). **5 a** an individual's occupation, actions, or fortunes; the manner of one's existence (*that would make life easy*; *start a new life*). **b** a particular aspect of this (*love life*; *private life*). **6** the active part of existence; the business and pleasures of the world (*travel is the best way to see life*). **7** a human's earthly or supposed future existence. **8 a** energy; liveliness; animation (*full of life*; *put some life into it!*). **b** an animating influence (*was the life of the party*). **c** (of an inanimate object) power; force; ability to perform its intended function. **9** the living, esp. nude, form or model (*drawn from life*). **10** a written account of a person's life; a biography. **11** *colloq.* a sentence of imprisonment for life (*they were all serving life*). **12** a chance; a fresh start (*cats have nine lives*; *gave the player three lives*). □ **come to life 1** emerge from unconsciousness or inactivity; begin operating. **2** (of an inanimate object) assume an imaginary animation. **for dear** (or **one's**) **life** as if or in order to escape death; as a matter of extreme urgency (*hanging on for dear life*; *run for your life*). **for life** for the rest of one's life. **for the life of** (foll. by pers. pron.) even if (one's) life depended on it (*cannot for the life of me remember*). **give one's life 1** (foll. by *for*) die; sacrifice oneself. **2** (foll. by *to*) dedicate oneself. **large as life** *colloq.* in person, esp. prominently (*stood there large as life*). **larger than life 1** exaggerated. **2** (of a person) having an exuberant personality. **life-and-death** vitally important; desperate (*a life-and-death struggle*). **life belt** a belt of buoyant or inflatable material for keeping a person afloat in water. **life buoy** a buoyant support (usu. a ring) for keeping a person afloat in water. **life cycle** the series of changes in the life of an organism including reproduction. **life expectancy** the average period that a person at a specified age may expect to live. **life force** inspiration or a driving force or influence. **life-form** an organism. **life-giving** that sustains life or uplifts and revitalizes. **Life Guards** (in the UK) a regiment of the royal household cavalry. **life history** the story of a person's life, esp. told at tedious length. **life insurance** insurance for a sum to be paid on the death of the insured person. **life jacket** a buoyant or inflatable jacket for keeping a person afloat in water. **life peer** *Brit.* a peer whose title lapses on death. **life preserver 1** a life jacket, etc. **2** *Brit.* a short stick with a heavily loaded end; blackjack. **life raft** an inflatable or log, etc., raft for use in an emergency instead of a boat. **life sciences** biology and related subjects. **life sentence 1** a sentence of imprisonment for life. **2** an illness or commitment, etc., perceived as a continuing threat to one's freedom. **life-size** (or **-sized**) of the same size as the person or thing represented. **life-support** *adj.* (of equipment) allowing vital functions to continue in an adverse environment or during severe disablement. **lose one's life** be killed. **a matter of life and** (or **or**) **death** a matter of vital importance. **not on your life** *colloq.* most certainly not. **save a person's life 1** prevent a person's death. **2** save a person from serious difficulty. **take one's life in one's hands** take a crucial personal risk. **to the life** true to the original. [OE *līf* f. Gmc]

■ **1** existence, being; sentience, animateness, animation, viability. **2** existence; animal life, plant life; human existence *or* life, people. **3** existence, lifetime, lifespan, time, duration, days; validity, efficacy, force, period of use. **4 b** person, mortal, being, human (being), individual, soul. **5** existence, living, way of life, walk of life, lifestyle; province, sphere, field, line, career, business; obsession, preoccupation, passion, fixation, compulsion, *colloq.* thing, *sl.* bag. **8** energy, liveliness, animation, vitality, sprightliness, vivacity, sparkle, dazzle, dash, vigor, verve, zest, flavor, pungency, freshness, effervescence, brio, flair, vim, exuberance, enthusiasm, *colloq.* pep, zing, get-up-and-go; soul, spirit, spark of life, vital spark, moving spirit, life-force, élan; lifeblood, dynamic force; power, force, bounce, resilience, elasticity. **10** biography, autobiography, memoir(s), (life) story, diary, journal. □ **come to life 1** see EMERGE 1, BEGIN 2, 4. **give one's life 1** (*give one's life for*) lay down one's life for, sacrifice oneself for *or* to; see also DIE¹ 1. **2** (*give one's life to*) dedicate oneself to, give oneself to, commit oneself to, devote oneself *or* one's life to, spend oneself for *or* on. **large as life** see *in person* (PERSON). **larger than life 1** see TALL 4. **2** see EXUBERANT 1. **life-and-death** see VITAL 2. **lose one's life** see DIE¹ 1. **a matter of life and** (or **or**) **death** see NECESSITY 2, 3.

lifeblood /lífblud/ n. **1** the blood, as being necessary to life. **2** the vital factor or influence.

■ **2** see LIFE 8.

lifeboat /lífbōt/ n. **1** a specially constructed boat launched from land to rescue those in distress at sea. **2** a ship's small boat for use in emergency.

lifeguard /lífgaard/ n. an expert swimmer employed to rescue bathers from drowning.

lifeless /líflis/ adj. **1** lacking life; no longer living. **2** unconscious. **3** lacking movement or vitality. □□ **lifelessly** adv. **lifelessness** n. [OE līflēas (as LIFE, -LESS)]

■ **1** dead, departed, demised, cold, stiff, dead as a doornail, formal deceased; inanimate, inorganic; barren, desert, desolate, bare, sterile, bleak, empty, uninhabited, unoccupied, dreary, waste. **2** unconscious, insensate, in a faint, inert, unmoving, corpselike, dead, insensible, immobile, inanimate, out for the count, colloq. (out) cold, dead to the world, literary in a swoon. **3** inactive, passive, dull, boring, tiresome, heavy, lackluster, torpid, tedious, flat, stale, uninteresting, colorless, uninspiring, vapid, wooden; spiritless, lethargic, enervated, exhausted.

lifelike /líflik/ adj. closely resembling the person or thing represented. □□ **lifelikeness** n.

■ authentic, realistic, natural, naturalistic, true to life, real, faithful, animated, lively, graphic, vivid.

lifeline /líflin/ n. **1 a** a rope, etc., used for lifesaving, e.g., that attached to a life buoy. **b** a diver's signaling line. **2** a sole means of communication or transport. **3** a fold in the palm of the hand, regarded as significant in palmistry. **4** an emergency telephone counseling service.

lifelong /líflawng, -long/ adj. lasting a lifetime.

■ see LASTING.

lifer /lífər/ n. sl. **1** a person serving a life sentence. **2** a person committed to a long or lifetime career in a profession, esp. the military.

lifesaver /lífsayvər/ n. **1** a person or thing that saves one from serious difficulty. **2** Austral. & NZ = LIFEGUARD.

■ □□ **lifesaving** n., adj.

lifestyle /lífstil/ n. the particular way of life of a person or group.

■ see CULTURE n. 2.

lifetime /líftim/ n. **1** the duration of a person's life. **2** the duration of a thing or its usefulness. **3** colloq. an exceptionally long time. □ **of a lifetime** such as does not occur more than once in a person's life (the chance of a lifetime; the journey of a lifetime).

■ **1, 2** see LIFE 3.

lifework /lífwórk/ n. a task, profession, etc., pursued throughout one's lifetime.

■ see VOCATION 2.

lift /lift/ v. & n. ● v. **1** tr. (often foll. by up, off, out, etc.) raise or remove to a higher position. **2** intr. go up; be raised; yield to an upward force (the window will not lift). **3** tr. give an upward direction to (the eyes or face). **4** tr. **a** elevate to a higher plane of thought or feeling (the news lifted their spirits). **b** make less heavy or dull; add interest to (something esp. artistic). **c** enhance; improve (lifted their game after halftime). **5** intr. (of a cloud, fog, etc.) rise; disperse. **6** tr. remove (a barrier or restriction). **7** tr. transport (supplies, troops, etc.) by air. **8** tr. colloq. **a** steal. **b** plagiarize (a passage of writing, etc.). **9** Phonet. **a** tr. make louder; raise the pitch of. **b** intr. (of the voice) rise. **10** tr. esp. Brit. dig up (esp. potatoes, etc., at harvest). **11** intr. (of a floor) swell upward, bulge. **12** tr. hold or have on high (the church lifts its spire). **13** tr. hit (a ball) into the air. **14** tr. (usu. in passive) perform cosmetic surgery on (esp. the face or breasts) to reduce sagging. ● n. **1** the act of lifting or process of being lifted. **2** a free ride in another person's vehicle (gave them a lift). **3 a** Brit. = ELEVATOR 3a. **b** an apparatus for carrying persons up or down a mountain, etc. (see ski lift). **4 a** transport by air (see AIRLIFT n.). **b** a quantity of goods transported by air. **5** the upward pressure that air exerts on an airfoil to counteract the force of gravity. **6** a supporting or elevating influence; a feeling of elation. **7** a layer of leather in the heel of a boot or shoe, esp. to correct shortening of a leg or increase height. **8 a** a rise in the level of the ground. **b** the extent to which water rises in a canal lock. □ **lift down** Brit. pick up and bring to a lower position. **lift a finger** (or **hand**, etc.) (in neg.) make the slightest effort (didn't lift a finger to help). **lift off** (of a spacecraft or rocket) rise from the launching pad. **lift up one's head** hold one's head high with pride. **lift up one's voice** sing out. □□ **liftable** adj. **lifter** n. [ME f. ON lypta f. Gmc]

■ v. **1** raise, elevate; hoist (up), heave (up), pull up, lever, put or pick up. **2** see RISE v. 1. **3** raise, elevate, tilt (upward). **4 a** raise, elevate, dignify, ennoble, uplift, upgrade, promote, advance, exalt, colloq. boost. **b** enliven, liven up, brighten, lighten, (re)vitalize, enhance, improve, jazz up, colloq. pep up. **c** enhance, improve, raise, make better, formal ameliorate. **5** rise, disperse, disappear, dissipate, disintegrate, vanish, break up, float away. **6** remove, raise, discontinue, end, terminate, stop, cease, put an end to, put a stop to; take away, get rid of, shift, transfer, withdraw, cancel, rescind, void, annul. **7** airlift. **8 a** steal, appropriate, pilfer, pocket, thieve, take, formal or joc. purloin, sl. pinch, liberate, Brit. sl. nick. **b** copy, imitate, plagiarize, appropriate, steal, pirate, formal or joc. purloin; abstract, borrow, colloq. crib, sl. pinch. **9 a** amplify, louden, make louder, increase; raise. **b** rise, go up. ● n. **1** raising, elevation, rise, increase, improvement; hoist, push, shove, heave, uplift. **2** ride, colloq. hitch. **4** airlift. **6** encouragement, stimulus, uplift, inducement, inspiration, hope, reassurance, cheering up, colloq. shot in the arm, boost. **8** incline, inclination, elevation, climb, rise, slope. □ **lift a finger** (or **hand**) make any attempt or effort, make a move, do one's part, do anything, contribute. **lift off** see take off 6.

liftoff /líftawf/ n. the vertical takeoff of a spacecraft or rocket.

■ see TAKEOFF 1.

ligament /lígəmənt/ n. **1** Anat. **a** a short band of tough, flexible, fibrous connective tissue linking bones together. **b** any membranous fold keeping an organ in position. **2** archaic a bond of union. □□ **ligamental** /-mént'l/ adj. **ligamentary** /-méntəree/ adj. **ligamentous** /-méntəs/ adj. [ME f. L ligamentum bond f. ligare bind]

■ **1** sinew, tendon, Anat. vinculum, Physiol. bridle.

ligand /lígənd, líg-/ n. Chem. an ion or molecule attached to a metal atom by covalent bonding in which both electrons are supplied by one atom. [L ligandus gerundive of ligare bind]

ligate /lígayt/ v.tr. Surgery tie up (a bleeding artery, etc.). □□ **ligation** /-gáyshən/ n. [L ligare ligat-]

ligature /lígəchər/ n. & v. ● n. **1** a tie or bandage, esp. in surgery for a bleeding artery, etc. **2** Mus. a slur; a tie. **3** Printing two or more letters joined, e.g., æ. **4** a bond; a thing that unites. **5** the act of tying or binding. ● v.tr. bind or connect with a ligature. [ME f. LL ligatura f. L ligare ligat-tie, bind]

■ **1** see TIE n. 1. **2** see TIE n. 7.

liger /lígər/ n. the offspring of a lion and a tigress (cf. TIGLON). [portmanteau word f. LION + TIGER]

light[1] /lit/ n., v., & adj. ● n. **1** the natural agent (electromagnetic radiation of wavelength between about 390 and 740 nm) that stimulates sight and makes things visible. **2** the medium or condition of the space in which this is present. **3** an appearance of brightness (saw a distant light). **4 a** a source of light, e.g., the sun, or a lamp, fire, etc. **b** (in pl.) illuminations. **5** (often in pl.) a traffic light (went through a red light; stop at the lights). **6 a** the amount or quality of illumination in a place (bad light stopped play). **b** one's fair or usual share of this (you are standing in my light). **7 a** a flame or spark serving to ignite (struck a light). **b** a device

/. . ./	**pronunciation**	●	**part of speech**
□	**phrases, idioms, and compounds**		
□□	**derivatives**	■	**synonym section**
cross-references appear in SMALL CAPITALS or italics			

producing this (*have you got a light?*). **8** the aspect in which a thing is regarded or considered (*appeared in a new light*). **9 a** mental illumination; elucidation; enlightenment. **b** hope; happiness; a happy outcome. **c** spiritual illumination by divine truth. **10** vivacity, enthusiasm, or inspiration visible in a person's face, esp. in the eyes. **11** (in *pl.*) a person's mental powers or ability (*according to one's lights*). **12** an eminent person (*a leading light*). **13 a** the bright part of a thing; a highlight. **b** the bright parts of a picture, etc., esp. suggesting illumination (*light and shade*). **14 a** a window or opening in a wall to let light in. **b** the perpendicular division of a mullioned window. **c** a pane of glass, esp. in the side or roof of a greenhouse. **15** *Brit.* (in a crossword, etc.) each of the items filling a space and to be deduced from the clues. **16** *Law* the light falling on windows, the obstruction of which by a neighbor is illegal. ● *v.* (*past* **lit** /lit/; *past part.* **lit** or (*attrib.*) **lighted**) **1** *tr.* & *intr.* set burning or begin to burn; ignite. **2** *tr.* provide with light or lighting. **3** *tr.* show (a person) the way or surroundings with a light. **4** *intr.* (usu. foll. by *up*) (of the face or eyes) brighten with animation. ● *adj.* **1** well provided with light; not dark. **2** (of a color) pale (*light blue*; *a light-blue ribbon*). □ **bring** (or **come**) **to light** reveal or be revealed. **festival of lights 1** = HANUKKAH. **2** = DIWALI. **in a good** (or **bad**) **light** giving a favorable (or unfavorable) impression. **in** (**the**) **light of** having regard to; drawing information from. **light meter** an instrument for measuring the intensity of the light, esp. to show the correct photographic exposure. **light of day 1** daylight; sunlight. **2** general notice; public attention. **light of one's life** usu. *joc.* a much-loved person. **light pen** (or **pencil**) **1** a penlike photosensitive device held to the screen of a computer terminal for passing information on to it. **2** a light-emitting device used for reading bar codes. **light show** a display of changing colored lights for entertainment. **light up 1** *colloq.* begin to smoke a cigarette, etc. **2** switch on lights or lighting; illuminate a scene. **light-year 1** *Astron.* the distance light travels in one year, nearly 6 trillion miles. **2** (in *pl.*) *colloq.* a long distance or great amount. **lit up** *colloq.* drunk. **out like a light** deeply asleep or unconscious. **throw** (or **shed**) **light on** help to explain. □□ **lightish** *adj.* **lightless** *adj.* **lightness** *n.* [OE *lēoht, līht, līhtan* f. Gmc]

▪ *n.* **2** illumination, brightness, brilliance, radiance, luminosity; daylight, lamplight, candlelight, firelight, gaslight, torchlight, starlight, moonlight, sunshine, sun, sunlight. **3** beam, ray, shaft of light, brilliance, brightness, radiance, radiation, luminescence, glare, gleam, glow, reflection, luminosity, shine, shining, sparkle, scintillation, incandescence, phosphorescence, fluorescence. **4 a** lamp, lightbulb, bulb, illuminant, beacon, lantern, torch, candle, sun, star, flame, blaze, flare, headlight, headlamp, streetlight, flashlight. **b** (*lights*) illuminations, light show, *son et lumière*. **5** (*lights*) traffic light(s), traffic signal(s), signals, stop light(s). **7** match, lighter, spill, taper, fire, flame, ignition. **8** see ASPECT 1b. **9 a** elucidaton, enlightenment, illumination; clarification, edification, insight, awareness, understanding, simplification, explanation. **b** see HOPE *n.* 2, *happiness* (HAPPY). ● *v.* **1** turn on, switch on, put on; set alight, set *or* put a match to, kindle, touch off, set fire to, set burning, fire; ignite; come on. **2** illuminate, light up, cast light on *or* upon, lighten, brighten, *literary* illumine, *poet.* illume. **3** direct, guide, escort, pilot. **4** (*light up*) lighten, brighten, cheer up, liven up, perk up. ● *adj.* **1** (well-)illuminated, bright, alight, (well-)lit, (well-)lighted, shining, luminous, brilliant, beaming, incandescent, phosphorescent, fluorescent, sunny, *literary* effulgent. **2** pale, light-hued, pastel, faded, subdued, washed-out. □ **bring** (or **come**) **to light** reveal, unearth, find, uncover, unveil, discover, expose, disclose, make known; be revealed, be unearthed, be uncovered, be unveiled, be discovered, be exposed, be disclosed, appear, come out, turn up, transpire, develop, evolve, emerge. **in** (**the**) **light of** having regard to, considering, in view of, in consideration of,

taking into account, keeping *or* bearing in mind, paying attention to. **light show** see LIGHT¹ *n.* 4b above. **out like a light** see UNCONSCIOUS *adj.* **throw** (or **shed**) **light on** explain, elucidate, simplify, clarify, clear up.

light² /līt/ *adj., adv., & v.* ● *adj.* **1** of little weight; not heavy; easy to lift. **2 a** relatively low in weight, amount, density, intensity, etc. (*light arms*; *light traffic*; *light metal*; *light rain*; *a light breeze*). **b** deficient in weight (*light coin*). **c** (of an isotope, etc.) having not more than the usual mass. **3 a** carrying or suitable for small loads (*light aircraft*; *light railroad*). **b** (of a ship) unladen. **c** carrying only light arms, armaments, etc. (*light brigade*; *light infantry*). **d** (of a locomotive) with no train attached. **4 a** (of food, a meal, etc.) small in amount; easy to digest (*had a light lunch*). **b** (of drink) not heavy on the stomach or strongly alcoholic. **5 a** (of entertainment, music, etc.) intended for amusement, rather than edification; not profound. **b** frivolous; thoughtless; trivial (*a light remark*). **6** (of sleep or a sleeper) easily disturbed. **7** easily borne or done (*light duties*). **8** nimble; quick-moving (*a light step*; *light of foot*; *a light rhythm*). **9** (of a building, etc.) graceful; elegant; delicate. **10** (of type) not heavy or bold. **11 a** free from sorrow; cheerful (*a light heart*). **b** giddy (*light in the head*). **12** (of soil) not dense; porous. **13** (of pastry, sponge cake, etc.) fluffy and well-aerated during cooking and with the fat fully absorbed. **14** (of a woman) unchaste or wanton; fickle. ● *adv.* **1** in a light manner (*tread light*; *sleep light*). **2** with a minimum load or minimum luggage (*travel light*). ● *v.intr.* (*past* and *past part.* **lit** /lit/ or **lighted**) **1** (foll. by *on, upon*) come upon or find by chance. **2** *archaic* **a** alight; descend. **b** (foll. by *on*) land on (shore, etc.). □ **lighter-than-air** (of an aircraft) weighing less than the air it displaces. **light-fingered** given to stealing. **light-footed** nimble. **light-footedly** nimbly. **light-headed** giddy; frivolous; delirious. **light-headedly** in a light-headed manner. **light-headedness** being light-headed. **light heavyweight** see HEAVYWEIGHT. **light industry** the manufacture of small or light articles. **light into** *colloq.* attack. **light out** *colloq.* depart. **light touch** delicate or tactful treatment. **make light of** treat as unimportant. **make light work of** do a thing quickly and easily. □□ **lightish** *adj.* **lightness** *n.* [OE *lēoht, līht, līhtan* f. Gmc, the verbal sense from the idea of relieving a horse, etc., of weight]

▪ *adj.* **1** lightweight, portable, transportable, manageable. **2 a** faint, gentle, mild, slight, delicate, insignificant. **b** lightweight, underweight, deficient, skinny, slight, gaunt; see also LEAN² *adj.* 1. **4 a** simple, digestible, modest, moderate. **5 a** amusing, entertaining, witty, diverting, pleasing, pleasurable, humorous; lightweight, middle-of-the-road. **b** frivolous, thoughtless, trivial; see also INCONSEQUENTIAL 1. **7** easy, not burdensome, endurable, bearable, tolerable, supportable, undemanding, effortless, untaxing, moderate, manageable, *colloq.* cushy. **8** nimble, quick-moving, agile, active, swift, spry, lithe, sprightly, lightsome, buoyant, light-footed, limber, lissome, deft, quick, esp. *Brit. colloq.* nippy. **11 a** cheerful, happy, gay, sunny, merry, lighthearted, happy-go-lucky, free and easy, untroubled, insouciant, easygoing, joyful, glad, optimistic, jovial, jolly, *poet.* blithe. **b** see DIZZY *adj.* 1a. ● *v.* **1** (*light on* or *upon*) chance or happen *or* stumble *or* hit (up)on, come across, encounter, find, meet up with, *colloq.* spot. □ **light-fingered** thieving; cunning, crafty, slick, furtive, dishonest, crooked. **light-footed** see LIGHT² *adj.* 8 above. **light-headed** see DIZZY *adj.* 1. **light into** assail, assault, pounce *or* fall on *or* upon, beat, belabor, *colloq.* lambaste; abuse, give a tongue-lashing to, harangue, upbraid, scold, berate, *colloq.* lace into; see also ATTACK *v.* 1, 3. **make light of** dismiss, write off, shrug off, gloss over, blink at, brush aside; trivialize; ridicule; see also DISREGARD *v.* 2, *play down.*

lightbulb /lītbulb/ *n.* a glass bulb containing an inert gas and a metal filament, providing light when an electric current is passed through.

lighten¹ /līt'n/ *v.* **1 a** *tr.* & *intr.* make or become lighter in

weight. **b** *tr.* reduce the weight or load of. **2** *tr.* bring relief to (the heart, mind, etc.). **3** *tr.* mitigate (a penalty).
■ **2** relieve, cheer (up), brighten, gladden, perk up, uplift, buoy up, hearten, comfort, reassure, restore. **3** see MITIGATE, TEMPER *v.* 2.

lighten² /líť'n/ *v.* **1 a** *tr.* shed light on. **b** *tr. & intr.* make or grow lighter or brighter. **2** *intr.* **a** shine brightly; flash. **b** emit lightning (*it is lightening*).
■ **1** illuminate, shed *or* cast light upon, brighten, light up, *literary* illumine, *poet.* illume.

lightening /líť'ning/ *n.* a drop in the level of the uterus during the last weeks of pregnancy.

lighter¹ /líťər/ *n.* a device for lighting cigarettes, etc.
■ see LIGHT¹ *n.* 7.

lighter² /líťər/ *n.* a boat, usu. flat-bottomed, for transferring goods from a ship to a wharf or another ship. [ME f. MDu. *lichter* (as LIGHT² in the sense 'unload')]

lighterage /líťərij/ *n.* **1** the transference of cargo by means of a lighter. **2** a charge made for this.

lighterman /líťərmən/ *n.* (*pl.* **-men**) a person who works on a lighter.

lighthearted /líť-haartid/ *adj.* **1** cheerful. **2** (unduly) casual; thoughtless. □□ **lightheartedly** *adv.* **lightheartedness** *n.*
■ see LIGHT² *adj.* 11a.

lighthouse /líť-hows/ *n.* a tower or other structure containing a beacon light to warn or guide ships at sea.
■ see BEACON 1a, 2.

lighting /líťing/ *n.* **1** equipment in a room or street, etc., for producing light. **2** the arrangement or effect of lights.
■ **2** see *illumination* (ILLUMINATE).

lightly /líťlee/ *adv.* in a light (esp. frivolous or unserious) manner. □ **get off lightly** escape with little or no punishment. **take lightly** not be serious about (a thing).

lightning /líťning/ *n. & adj.* ● *n.* a flash of bright light produced by an electric discharge between clouds or between clouds and the ground. ● *attrib.adj.* very quick (*with lightning speed*). □ **lightning bug** = FIREFLY. **lightning rod** (or **conductor**) a metal rod or wire fixed to an exposed part of a building or to a mast to divert lightning into the earth or sea. **lightning strike** *Brit.* a wildcat strike. [ME, differentiated from *lightening*, verbal noun f. LIGHTEN²]
■ *n.* see BOLT¹ *n.* 3. ● *attrib.adj.* see RAPID *adj.* 1, 2.

lightproof /líťprōōf/ *adj.* able to resist the harmful effects of (esp. excessive) light.

lights /lits/ *n.pl.* the lungs of sheep, pigs, bullocks, etc., used as a food, esp. for pets. [ME, noun use of LIGHT²: cf. LUNG]

lightship /líťship/ *n.* a moored or anchored ship with a beacon light.

lightsome /líťsəm/ *adj.* gracefully light; nimble; merry. □□ **lightsomely** *adv.* **lightsomeness** *n.*
■ see LIGHT² 8.

lightweight /líťwayt/ *adj. & n.* ● *adj.* **1** (of a person, animal, garment, etc.) of below average weight. **2** of little importance or influence. ● *n.* **1** a lightweight person, animal, or thing. **2 a** a weight in certain sports intermediate between featherweight and welterweight. **b** a sportsman of this weight.
■ *adj.* **1** see LIGHT² *adj.* 1. **2** see INCONSEQUENTIAL 1.
● *n.* **1** see WEAKLING *n.*

lightwood /líťwōōd/ *n.* wood used for kindling, esp. pine.

ligneous /lígneeəs/ *adj.* **1** (of a plant) woody (opp. HERBACEOUS). **2** of the nature of wood. [L *ligneus* (as LIGNI-)]
■ see WOODEN 1.

ligni- /lígni/ *comb. form* wood. [L *lignum* wood]

lignify /lígnifī/ *v.tr. & intr.* (**-ies, -ied**) *Bot.* make or become woody by the deposition of lignin.

lignin /lígnin/ *n. Bot.* a complex organic polymer deposited in the cell walls of many plants making them rigid and woody. [as LIGNI- + -IN]

lignite /lígnīt/ *n.* a soft brown coal showing traces of plant structure, intermediate between bituminous coal and peat. □□ **lignitic** /-nítik/ *adj.* [F (as LIGNI-, -ITE¹)]

lignocaine /lígnəkayn/ *n. Pharm.* a local anesthetic for the gums, mucous membranes, or skin, usu. given by injection. [*ligno-* (as LIGNI-) for XYLO- + COCA + -INE⁴]

lignum vitae /lígnəm víťee, vee'tī/ *n.* = GUAIACUM 2a. [L, = wood of life]

ligroin /lígrōin/ *n. Chem.* a volatile hydrocarbon mixture obtained from petroleum and used as a solvent. [20th c.: orig. unkn.]

ligulate /lígyələt, -layt/ *adj. Bot.* having strap-shaped florets. [formed as LIGULE + -ATE²]

ligule /lígyōōl/ *n. Bot.* a narrow projection from the sheath of a blade of grass. [L *ligula* strap, spoon f. *lingere* lick]

ligustrum /lígŭstrəm/ *n.* = PRIVET. [L]

likable /líkəbəl/ *adj.* (also **likeable**) pleasant; easy to like. □□ **likableness** *n.* **likably** /-blee/ *adv.*
■ genial, amiable, congenial, simpatico, agreeable, pleasing, attractive, appealing, nice, friendly, winning, charming, engaging, good-natured, winsome.

like¹ /līk/ *adj., prep., adv., conj., & n.* ● *adj.* (often governing a noun as if a transitive participle such as *resembling*) (**more like, most like**) **1 a** having some or all of the qualities of another or each other or an original; alike (*in like manner; as like as two peas; is very like her brother*). **b** resembling in some way, such as; in the same class as (*good writers like Poe*). **c** (usu. in pairs correlatively) as one is so will the other be (*like mother, like daughter*). **2** characteristic of (*it is not like them to be late*). **3** in a suitable state or mood for (doing or having something) (*felt like working; felt like a cup of coffee*). ● *prep.* in the manner of; to the same degree as (*drink like a fish; sell like hotcakes; acted like an idiot*). ● *adv.* **1** *archaic* likely (*they will come, like enough*). **2** *archaic* in the same manner (foll. by *as: sang like as a nightingale*). **3** *sl.* so to speak (*did a quick getaway, like; as I said, like, I'm no Shakespeare*). ● *conj. colloq. disp.* **1** as (*cannot do it like you do*). **2** as if (*ate like they were starving*). ● *n.* **1** a counterpart; an equal; a similar person or thing (*shall not see its like again; compare like with like*). **2** (prec. by *the*) a thing or things of the same kind (*will never do the like again*). □ **and the like** and similar things; et cetera (*music, painting, and the like*). **be nothing like** (usu. with compl.) be in no way similar or comparable or adequate. **like anything** see ANYTHING. **like** (or **as like**) **as not** *colloq.* probably. **like-minded** having the same tastes, opinions, etc. **like-mindedly** in accordance with the same tastes, etc. **like-mindedness** being like-minded. **like so** *colloq.* like this; in this manner. **the likes of** *colloq.* a person such as. **more like it** *colloq.* nearer what is required. [ME *līc, līk*, shortened form of OE *gelīc* ALIKE]
■ *adj.* **.1 a** similar (to), akin (to), allied (to), parallel (to *or* with), comparable (to *or* with), equivalent (to), equal (to), identical (to), cognate (with), analogous (to), correspondent (to), close (to), homologous (to *or* with), of a piece (with), (much) the same (as), along the same lines (as), not unlike, *archaic* corresponding (to). **b** resembling, in the same class as, comparable to *or* with; such as, for example, e.g., for instance. **2** typical of, in character with, indicative of, representative of, illustrative of. **3** in the mood for *or* to, disposed to, inclined to, willing to, eager for *or* to, anxious to. ● *prep.* similar to, identical to *or* with, in the same way as, in *or* after the manner of, similarly to, after the fashion of, along the same lines as. ● *adv.* **1** see LIKELY *adv.* 3. **so to speak, as it were, in a way, somehow, in some way or another.** ● *conj.* **1** as, just as, in the same way as. **2** as if, as though. ● *n.* **1** match, equal, peer, fellow, counterpart, twin, equivalent. **2** (*the like*) the same kind *or* sort *or* ilk *or* type *or* kidney *or* breed *or* mold *or* cast *or* strain of thing, a similar kind *or* sort *or* ilk *or* type *or* kidney *or* breed *or* mold *or* cast *or* strain of thing. □ **and the like** see *and all the rest* (REST²). **like as not** see LIKELY *adv.*

/.../ **pronunciation**	● **part of speech**
□ **phrases, idioms, and compounds**	
□□ **derivatives**	■ **synonym section**
cross-references appear in SMALL CAPITALS or *italics*	

like-minded see UNITED *adj.* 3. **like-mindedness** see UNITY 2. **like so** see THUS 1.

like² /lik/ *v. & n.* ● *v.tr.* **1 a** find agreeable or enjoyable or satisfactory (*like reading*; *like the sea*; *like to dance*). **b** be fond of (a person). **2 a** choose to have; prefer (*like my coffee black*; *do not like such things discussed*). **b** wish for or be inclined to (*would like a cup of tea*). **3** (usu. in *interrog.*; prec. by *how*) feel about; regard (*how would you like it if it happened to you?*). ● *n.* (in *pl.*) the things one likes or prefers. □ **I like that!** *iron.* as an exclamation expressing affront. **like it or not** *colloq.* whether it is acceptable or not. [OE *lician* f. Gmc]

■ *v.* **1** be fond of, approve of, appreciate, be partial to, have a fondness for, have a liking for, have a weakness for, take to, delight in, take pleasure in, derive *or* get pleasure from, find agreeable *or* congenial, be *or* feel attracted to, be *or* feel favorably impressed by, relish, love, adore, adulate, *colloq.* fancy, take a shine to, get a kick out of, *sl.* dig, get off on, groove on, get a charge out of, get a bang from *or* out of. **2** prefer, choose, go for, want, feel inclined to have, have (half) a mind to have, rather *or* sooner have, wish, desire. ● *n.* (*likes*) preference(s), favorite(s), *colloq.* thing, cup of tea, *sl.* bag; see also WEAKNESS 4.

-like /lik/ *comb. form* forming adjectives from nouns, meaning 'similar to, characteristic of' (*doglike*; *tortoiselike*). ¶ In (esp. polysyllabic) formations intended as nonce words, or not generally current, a hyphen is often used (*celebration-like*). Nouns ending in *-ll* always require it (*shell-like*).

likeable var. of LIKABLE.

likelihood /líkleehood/ *n.* probability; the quality or fact of being likely. □ **in all likelihood** very probably.

■ strong *or* distinct possibility, good chance, good prospect; probability, likeliness.

likely /líklee/ *adj. & adv.* ● *adj.* **1** probable; such as well might happen or be true (*it is not likely that they will come*; *the most likely place is California*; *a likely story*). **2** (foll. by *to* + infin.) to be reasonably expected (*he is not likely to come now*). **3** promising; apparently suitable (*this is a likely spot*; *three likely candidates*). ● *adv.* probably (*is very likely true*). □ **as likely as not** probably. **not likely!** *colloq.* certainly not; I refuse. □□ **likeliness** *n.* [ME f. ON *líkligr* (as LIKE¹, -LY¹)]

■ *adj.* **1** probable, expected, conceivable, reasonable, credible, believable, plausible, tenable. **2** disposed, apt, inclined, odds-on, expected, on the cards, *disp.* liable. **3** fitting, suitable, probable, seemly, right, proper, qualified, acceptable, appropriate, apposite, promising, applicable, relevant, *archaic* meet. ● *adv.* probably, no doubt, in all probability, *archaic* like enough, *colloq.* (as) like as not. □ **as likely as not** see LIKELY *adv.* above.

liken /líkən/ *v.tr.* (foll. by *to*) point out the resemblance of (a person or thing to another). [ME f. LIKE¹ + -EN¹]

■ compare, equate, match, juxtapose, associate, correlate.

likeness /líknis/ *n.* **1** (foll. by *between, to*) resemblance. **2** (foll. by *of*) a semblance or guise (*in the likeness of a ghost*). **3** a portrait or representation (*is a good likeness*). [OE *gelíknes* (as LIKE¹, -NESS)]

■ **1** similarity, resemblance, correspondence, analogy, agreement, similitude, closeness, sameness, parallelism. **2** appearance, semblance, guise, figure, image, look, outward form, shape, style, air, cast, *literary* mien. **3** copy, replica, facsimile, duplicate, reproduction, double, look-alike, clone, spitting image, model, painting, picture, portrait, portrayal, sketch, delineation, drawing, print, photograph, sculpture, statue, statuette, image, simulacrum, icon.

likewise /líkwiz/ *adv.* **1** also; moreover; too. **2** similarly (*do likewise*). [for *in like wise*]

■ **1** also, moreover, too, as well, furthermore, further, besides, in addition, additionally, to boot. **2** the same, in like manner, in the same manner *or* way, similarly.

liking /líking/ *n.* **1** what one likes; one's taste (*is it to your liking?*). **2** (foll. by *for*) regard or fondness; taste or fancy (*had a liking for chocolate*). [OE *licung* (as LIKE², -ING¹)]

■ **1** taste, fancy, preference, *formal* pleasure. **2** affinity,

affection, love, partiality, bias, preference, bent, predilection, predisposition, favor, fondness, inclination, propensity, appreciation, regard, taste, penchant; eye, relish, appetite, soft spot, weakness, fancy.

lilac /lílək, -lok, -lak/ *n. & adj.* ● *n.* **1** any shrub or small tree of the genus *Syringa*, esp. *S. vulgaris* with fragrant pale pinkish-violet or white blossoms. **2** a pale pinkish-violet color. ● *adj.* of this color. [obs. F f. Sp. f. Arab. *lilak* f. Pers. *lilak*, var. of *nilak* bluish f. *nil* blue]

liliaceous /lílee-áyshəs/ *adj.* **1** of or relating to the family Liliaceae of plants with elongated leaves growing from a corm, bulb, or rhizome, e.g., tulip, lily, or onion. **2** lilylike. [LL *liliaceus* f. L *lilium* lily]

lilliputian /lílipyōōshən/ *n. & adj.* (also **Lilliputian**) ● *n.* a diminutive person or thing. ● *adj.* diminutive. [*Lilliput* in Swift's *Gulliver's Travels*]

■ *adj.* see DIMINUTIVE *adj.* 1.

lilt /lilt/ *n. & v.* ● *n.* **1 a** a light springing rhythm or gait. **b** a song or tune marked by this. **2** (of the voice) a characteristic cadence or inflection; a pleasant accent. ● *v.intr.* (esp. as **lilting** *adj.*) move or speak, etc., with a lilt (*a lilting step*; *a lilting melody*). [ME *lilte, lülte*, of unkn. orig.]

■ *n.* **1 a** see RHYTHM 1, 2. ● *v.* (**lilting**) see MUSICAL *adj.* 2.

lily /lílee/ *n.* (*pl.* **-ies**) **1 a** any bulbous plant of the genus *Lilium* with large, trumpet-shaped, often spotted flowers on a tall, slender stem, e.g., the madonna lily and tiger lily. **b** any of several other plants of the family Liliaceae with similar flowers, e.g., the African lily. **c** the water lily. **2** a person or thing of special whiteness or purity. **3** a heraldic fleur-de-lis. **4** (*attrib.*) **a** delicately white (*a lily hand*). **b** pallid. □ **lily-livered** cowardly. **lily of the valley** any liliaceous plant of the genus *Convallaria*, with oval leaves in pairs and racemes of white, bell-shaped, fragrant flowers. **lily pad** a floating leaf of a water lily. **lily-white 1** as white as a lily. **2** faultless. □□ **lilied** *adj.* [OE *lilie* f. L *lilium* prob. f. Gk *leirion*]

■ □ **lily-livered** see COWARDLY *adj.* 1. **lily-white 1** see WHITE *adj.* 1. **2** see UNTARNISHED.

lima bean /líma/ *n.* **1** a tropical American bean plant, *Phaseolus limensis*, having large, flat, greenish-white edible seeds. **2** the seed of this plant. [*Lima* in Peru]

limb¹ /lim/ *n.* **1** any of the projecting parts of a person's or animal's body used for contact or movement. **2** a large branch of a tree. **3** a branch of a cross. **4** a spur of a mountain. **5** a clause of a sentence. □ **out on a limb 1** isolated; stranded. **2** at a disadvantage. **tear limb from limb** violently dismember. **with life and limb** (esp. escape) without grave injury. □□ **limbed** *adj.* (also in *comb.*). **limbless** *adj.* [OE *lim* f. Gmc]

■ **1** see LEG *n.* 1, 3. **2** see BRANCH *n.* 1.

limb² /lim/ *n.* **1** *Astron.* **a** a specified edge of the sun, moon, etc. (*eastern limb*; *lower limb*). **b** the graduated edge of a quadrant, etc. **2** *Bot.* the broad part of a petal, sepal, or leaf. [F *limbe* or L *limbus* hem, border]

limber¹ /límbər/ *adj. & v.* ● *adj.* **1** lithe; agile; nimble. **2** flexible. ● *v.* (usu. foll. by *up*) **1** *tr.* make (oneself or a part of the body, etc.) supple. **2** *intr.* warm up in preparation for athletic, etc., activity. □□ **limberness** *n.* [16th c.: orig. uncert.]

■ *adj.* **1** see NIMBLE 1. **2** see FLEXIBLE 1. ● *v.* see EXERCISE *v.* 3a. □□ **limberness** see *flexibility* (FLEXIBLE).

limber² /límbər/ *n. & v.* ● *n.* the detachable front part of a gun carriage, consisting of two wheels, axle, pole, and ammunition box. ● *v.* **1** *tr.* attach a limber to (a gun, etc.). **2** *intr.* fasten together the two parts of a gun carriage. [ME *limo(u)r*, app. rel. to med.L *limonarius* f. *limo -onis* shaft]

limbo¹ /límbō/ *n.* (*pl.* **-os**) **1** (in some Christian beliefs) the supposed abode of the souls of unbaptized infants, and of the just who died before Christ. **2** an intermediate state or condition of awaiting a decision, etc. **3** prison; confinement. **4** a state of neglect or oblivion. [ME f. med.L phr. *in limbo*, f. *limbus*: see LIMB²]

■ **2, 4** (*in limbo*) up in the air, consigned to oblivion, in abeyance, suspended, hanging (fire), neither here nor there, on hold, treading water, holding one's breath, on the shelf, on the back burner; see also OBSCURITY 1. **3** imprisonment, prison, confinement, incarceration, internment, detention, captivity.

limbo[2] /límbō/ n. (pl. **-os**) a W. Indian dance in which the dancer bends backward to pass under a horizontal bar that is progressively lowered to a position just above the ground. [a W. Indian word, perh. = LIMBER[1]]

Limburger /límbərgər/ n. a soft white cheese with a characteristic strong smell, orig. made in Limburg. [Du. f. *Limburg* in Belgium]

lime[1] /līm/ n. & v. ● n. **1** (in full **quicklime**) a white caustic alkaline substance (calcium oxide) obtained by heating limestone and used for making mortar or as a fertilizer or bleach, etc. **2** = BIRDLIME. ● v.tr. **1** treat (wood, skins, land, etc.) with lime. **2** *archaic* catch (a bird, etc.) with birdlime. □□ **limeless** adj. **limy** adj. (**limier**, **limiest**). [OE *līm* f. Gmc, rel. to LOAM]

lime[2] /līm/ n. **1 a** a round citrus fruit like a lemon but greener, smaller, and more acid. **b** the tree, *Citrus aurantifolia*, bearing this. **2** (in full **lime juice**) the juice of limes as a drink and formerly esp. as a cure for scurvy. **3** (in full **lime green**) a pale green color like a lime. [F f. mod.Prov. *limo*, Sp. *lima* f. Arab. *līma*: cf. LEMON]

lime[3] /līm/ n. **1** (in full **lime tree**) any ornamental tree of the genus *Tilia*, esp. *T. europaea* with heart-shaped leaves and fragrant yellow blossoms. Also called LINDEN. **2** the wood of this. [alt. of *line* = OE *lind* = LINDEN]

limekiln /límkiln, -kil / n. a kiln for heating limestone to produce lime.

limelight /límlīt/ n. **1** an intense white light obtained by heating a cylinder of lime in an oxyhydrogen flame, used formerly in theaters. **2** (prec. by *the*) the full glare of publicity; the focus of attention.
■ **2** see SPOTLIGHT n. 3.

limerick /límərik, límrik/ n. a humorous or comic form of five-line stanza with a rhyme scheme *aabba*. [said to be from the chorus "will you come up to Limerick?" sung between improvised verses at a gathering: f. *Limerick* in Ireland]

limestone /límstōn/ n. *Geol.* a sedimentary rock composed mainly of calcium carbonate, used as building material and in the making of cement.

limewash /límwosh, -wawsh/ n. a mixture of lime and water for coating walls.

limewater /límwawtər/ n. an aqueous solution of calcium hydroxide used esp. to detect the presence of carbon dioxide and as an antacid.

limey /límee/ n. (also **Limey**) (pl. **-eys**) *sl. offens.* a British person (orig. a sailor) or ship. [LIME[2], because of the former enforced consumption of lime juice in the British Navy]

limit /límit/ n. & v. ● n. **1** a point, line, or level beyond which something does not or may not extend or pass. **2** (often in *pl.*) the boundary of an area. **3** the greatest or smallest amount permissible or possible (*upper limit*; *lower limit*). **4** *Math.* a quantity that a function or sum of a series can be made to approach as closely as desired. ● v.tr. **1** set or serve as a limit to. **2** (foll. by *to*) restrict. □ **be the limit** *colloq.* be intolerable or extremely irritating. **off limits** out of bounds. **within limits** moderately; with some degree of freedom. **without limit** with no restriction. □□ **limitable** adj. **limitative** /-tətiv/ adj. **limiter** n. [ME f. L *limes limitis* boundary, frontier]
■ n. **1, 2** extent, end, limitation, check, curb, restriction, restraint; border, edge, boundary, bound(s), (boundary *or* border *or* partition) line, frontier, perimeter, periphery, fringe, verge, margin; area, ambit, territory, confines, zone, region, quarter, district, precinct(s). ● v. **1** check, curb, bridle, restrict, restrain, hold in check. **2** restrict, confine, delimit, narrow, focus, guide, channel; set, define, determine, fix. □ **be the limit** be the end, be the last straw, be the straw that broke the camel's back, be all (that) one can take, be (more than) enough, be too much, *colloq.* be it. **off limits** see TABOO adj. **within limits** see *moderately* (MODERATE).

limitary /límiteree/ adj. **1** subject to restriction. **2** of, on, or serving as a limit.

limitation /límitáyshən/ n. **1** the act or an instance of limiting; the process of being limited. **2** a condition of limited ability (often in *pl.*: *know one's limitations*). **3** a limiting rule or circumstance (often in *pl.*: *has its limitations*). **4** a legally specified period beyond which an action cannot be brought, or a property right is not to continue. [ME f. L *limitatio* (as LIMIT)]
■ **1** see CHECK[1] n. 2c. **3** see QUALIFICATION 3a.

limited /límitid/ adj. **1** confined within limits. **2** not great in scope or talents (*has limited experience*). **3 a** few; scanty; restricted (*limited accommodation*). **b** restricted to a few examples (*limited edition*). □ **limited** (or **limited liability**) **company** *Brit.* a company whose owners are legally responsible only to a limited amount for its debts. □□ **limitedly** adv. **limitedness** n.
■ **1** confined, circumscribed, restricted, fixed, predetermined, determinate, finite, checked, curbed, constrained. **2, 3a** narrow, restrictive, restricted, meager, sparing; small, little, few, scanty, reduced, minimal; unimaginative, unperceptive, slow-witted, dull, thick, slow, stupid.

limitless /límitlis/ adj. **1** extending or going on indefinitely (*a limitless expanse*). **2** unlimited (*limitless generosity*). □□ **limitlessly** adv. **limitlessness** n.
■ unlimited, unrestricted, unrestrained, unconfined, unbounded, boundless, uncircumscribed, extensive, vast, immense, enormous, illimitable; endless, interminable, never-ending, inexhaustible, unceasing, incessant, undefined, immeasurable, innumerable, numberless, incalculable, countless, unending, perpetual, everlasting, eternal, *literary* myriad.

limn /lim/ v.tr. **1** *archaic* paint (esp. a miniature portrait). **2** *hist.* illuminate (manuscripts). □□ **limner** n. [obs. *lumine* illuminate f. OF *luminer* f. L *luminare*: see LUMEN]
■ **1** see PAINT v. 2.

limnology /limnólǝjee/ n. the study of the physical phenomena of lakes and other fresh waters. □□ **limnological** /-nǝló-jikǝl/ adj. **limnologist** /-nól-/ n. [Gk *limnē* lake + -LOGY]

limo /límō/ n. (pl. **-os**) *colloq.* a limousine. [abbr.]

limousine /límǝzéen/ n. a large, luxurious automobile, often with a partition behind the driver. [F, orig. a caped cloak worn in the former French province of *Limousin*]

limp[1] /limp/ v. & n. ● v.intr. **1** walk lamely. **2** (of a damaged ship, aircraft, etc.) proceed with difficulty. **3** (of verse) be defective. ● n. a lame walk. □□ **limper** n. **limpingly** adv. [rel. to obs. *limphalt* lame, OE *lemp-healt*]
■ v. **1** hobble, stagger, totter, dodder, falter. ● n. hobble, stagger, totter; hobbling, staggering, tottering, doddering, faltering, *Med.* claudication.

limp[2] /limp/ adj. **1** not stiff or firm; easily bent. **2** without energy or will. **3** (of a book) having a soft cover. □ **limp-wristed** *sl. offens.* effeminate; weak; feeble. □□ **limply** adv. **limpness** n. [18th c.: orig. unkn.: perh. rel. to LIMP[1] in the sense 'hanging loose']
■ **1** slack, soft, drooping, floppy, loose, lax, flexible, pliable; relaxed, flaccid, flabby. **2** exhausted, tired, fatigued, worn out, spent, enervated, wasted, debilitated, frail; weak, feeble, halfhearted, lukewarm, spineless, namby-pamby, wishy-washy, *colloq.* gutless.

limpet /límpit/ n. **1** any of various marine gastropod mollusks, esp. the common limpet *Patella vulgata*, with a shallow conical shell and a broad muscular foot that sticks tightly to rocks. **2** a clinging person. □ **limpet mine** a mine designed to be attached to a ship's hull and set to explode after a certain time. [OE *lempedu* f. med.L *lampreda* limpet, LAMPREY]

limpid /límpid/ adj. **1** (of water, eyes, etc.) clear, transparent.

2 (of writing) clear and easily comprehended. □□ **limpidity** /-pídite/ *n.* **limpidness** *n.* [F *limpide* or L *limpidus*, perh. rel. to LYMPH]

■ **1** see CLEAR *adj.* 3a. □□ **limpidity** see CLARITY.

linage /línij/ *n.* **1** the number of lines in printed or written matter. **2** payment by the line.

linchpin /línchpin/ *n.* **1** a pin passed through the end of an axle to keep a wheel in position. **2** a person or thing vital to an enterprise, organization, etc. [ME *linch* f. OE *lynis* + PIN]

■ **2** see MAINSTAY 1.

Lincoln green /língkən/ *n.* **1** an olive-green color. **2** *Brit.* a bright green cloth of a kind orig. made at Lincoln, England.

lindane /líndayn/ *n.* *Chem.* a colorless, crystalline, chlorinated derivative of cyclohexane used as an insecticide. [T. van der *Linden*, Du. chemist b. 1884]

linden /líndən/ *n.* a lime tree. [(orig. adj.) f. OE *lind* lime tree: cf. LIME³]

line¹ /lin/ *n.* & *v.* ● *n.* **1** a continuous mark or band made on a surface (*drew a line*). **2** use of lines in art, esp. draftsmanship or engraving (*boldness of line*). **3** a thing resembling such a mark, esp. a furrow or wrinkle. **4** *Mus.* **a** each of (usu. five) horizontal marks forming a stave in musical notation. **b** a sequence of notes or tones forming an instrumental or vocal melody. **5 a** a straight or curved continuous extent of length without breadth. **b** the track of a moving point. **6 a** a contour or outline, esp. as a feature of design (*admired the sculpture's clean lines*; *this year's line is full at the back*; *the ship's lines*). **b** a facial feature (*the cruel line of his mouth*). **7 a** (on a map or graph) a curve connecting all points having a specified common property. **b** (**the Line**) the Equator. **8 a** a limit or boundary. **b** a mark limiting the area of play, the starting or finishing point in a race, etc. **c** the boundary between a credit and a debit in an account. **9 a** a row of persons or things. **b** a direction as indicated by them (*line of march*). **c** a queue. **10 a** a row of printed or written words. **b** a portion of verse written in one line. **11** (in *pl.*) **a** a piece of poetry. **b** the words of an actor's part. **c** a specified amount of text, etc., to be written out as a school punishment. **12** a short letter or note (*drop me a line*). **13** (in *pl.*) (in full **marriage lines**) *Brit.* a marriage certificate. **14** a length of cord, rope, wire, etc., usu. serving a specified purpose, esp. a fishing line or clothesline. **15 a** a wire or cable for a telephone or telegraph. **b** a connection by means of this (*am trying to get a line*). **16 a** a single track of a railroad. **b** one branch or route of a railroad system, or the whole system under one management. **17 a** a regular succession of buses, ships, aircraft, etc., plying between certain places. **b** a company conducting this (*shipping line*). **18** a connected series of persons following one another in time (esp. several generations of a family); stock; succession (*a long line of craftsmen*; *next in line to the throne*). **19 a** a course or manner of procedure, conduct, thought, etc. (*did it along these lines*; *don't take that line with me*). **b** policy (*the party line*). **c** conformity (*bring them into line*). **20** a direction, course, or channel (*lines of communication*). **21** a department of activity; a province; a branch of business (*accounting is not my line*). **22** a class of commercial goods (*a new line of hats*). **23** *colloq.* a false or exaggerated account or story; a dishonest approach (*gave me a line about missing the bus*). **24 a** a connected series of military fieldworks, defenses, etc. (*behind enemy lines*). **b** an arrangement of soldiers or ships side by side; a line of battle (*ship of the line*). **c** *Brit.* (prec. by *the*) regular army regiments (not auxiliary forces or guardsmen). **25** each of the very narrow horizontal sections forming a television picture. **26** a narrow range of the spectrum that is noticeably brighter or darker than the adjacent parts. **27** the level of the base of most letters in printing and writing. **28** (as a measure) one twelfth of an inch. ● *v.* **1** *tr.* mark with lines. **2** *tr.* cover with lines (*a face lined with pain*). **3** *tr.* & *intr.* position or stand at intervals along (*crowds lined the route*). □ **all along the line** at every point. **bring into line** make conform. **come into line** conform. **end of the line** the point at which further effort is unproductive or one can go no further. **get a line on** *colloq.* learn something about. **in line for** likely to receive. **in the line of** in the

course of (esp. duty). **in** (or **out of**) **line with** in (or not in) alignment or accordance with. **lay** (or **put**) **it on the line** speak frankly. **line drawing** a drawing in which images are produced from variations of lines. **line drive** *Baseball* a hard-hit ball that travels nearly parallel to the ground. **line of fire** the expected path of gunfire, a missile, etc. **line of force** *Physics* an imaginary line that represents the strength and direction of a magnetic, gravitational, or electric field at any point. **line of march** the route taken in marching. **line of vision** the straight line along which an observer looks. **line out** *Baseball* hit a line drive that is caught for an out. **line-out** *n.* *Rugby* parallel lines of opposing forwards at right angles to the touchline for the throwing in of the ball. **line printer** a machine that prints output from a computer a line at a time rather than character by character. **line up 1** arrange or be arranged in a line or lines. **2** have ready; organize (*had a job lined up*). **on the line 1** at risk (*put my reputation on the line*). **2** speaking on the telephone. **3** (of a picture in an exhibition) hung with its center about level with the spectator's eye. **out of line 1** not in alignment; discordant. **2** inappropriate; (of behavior, etc.) improper. **step out of line** behave inappropriately. [ME *line*, *ligne* f. OF *ligne* ult. f. L *linea* f. *linum* flax, & f. OE *line* rope, series]

■ *n.* **1** stroke, score; rule, underline, underscore; diagonal, slash, virgule, solidus, oblique, *hist.* shilling mark. **3** wrinkle, crease, crinkle, furrow, crow's-foot. **6** outline, contour, silhouette, profile. **8a** border, borderline, limit, boundary, frontier, edge; demarcation line; threshold. **9a** row, strip, belt, band, train, column, rank, file; *Brit. colloq.* crocodile. **c** row, esp. *Brit.* queue; *Brit.* tailback. **11b** (*lines*) part, role, script, words. **12** note, card, postcard, letter, postal card. **14** cord, string, wire, rope, cable, *Naut.* hawser. **16b** railroad, railway. **17b** company, firm; see also BUSINESS 8. **18** succession, series; ancestry, descent, stock, lineage, family, parentage, extraction, genealogy, clan, tribe; tradition. **19a** course, direction, path, way, route, road, track, procedure, tack, policy, game, strategy, tactic(s), approach, plan. **b** (party) policy, strategy, approach, plan; see also PLATFORM 6. **c** conformity, harmony, agreement, accord, keeping, consistency; obedience. **21** department, province, field, area, activity, forte, specialization, specialty, *Brit.* speciality; branch of business, profession, (line of) work, job, *colloq.* racket. **22** stock, brand, make, type, kind, variety. **23** story, (sales) pitch, *sl.* spiel. **24b** formation; vanguard, *Mil.* front (line). ● *v.* **1** rule, inscribe, score, underline, underscore; contour, hatch, crosshatch. **2** furrow, wrinkle, crease. **3** edge, border, fringe. □ **get a line on** see LEARN 4, 5, UNDERSTAND 1, 2. **in line for** likely to receive, ready for, up for, being considered for, under consideration for, a candidate for, in the running for, short-listed for, on the short list for. **in** (or **out of**) **line with** (*in line with*) in alignment with, aligned with, true to, plumb or flush with; in agreement or accord or accordance or conformity or step or harmony with, harmonious with; (*out of line with*) out of alignment with, not aligned with, misaligned with, out of true or balance with; out of step with, inconsistent with, discrepant or disparate or different from, contrary to. **line up 1** align, array, straighten, order; form a line, get in line, form ranks or columns, stand on line, esp. *Brit.* queue (up). **2** organize, prepare, ready, assemble, set up, put or set in place, develop, formulate, arrange (for), coordinate; secure, get (hold of), obtain, contract for; uncover, dig up, acquire, engage, hire, sign (up), contract with, employ.

line² /lin/ *v.tr.* **1 a** cover the inside surface of (a garment, box, etc.) with a layer of usu. different material. **b** serve as a lining for. **2** cover as if with a lining (*shelves lined with books*). **3** *colloq.* fill, esp. plentifully. □ **line one's pocket** (or **purse**) make money, usu. by corrupt means. [ME f. obs. *line* flax, with ref. to the use of linen for linings]

■ **1** interline, cover, face. **2, 3** fill, pack, pad, cram, crowd. □ **line one's pocket** make money, accept bribes, *colloq.* graft, be on the make.

lineage /línee-ij/ *n.* lineal descent; ancestry; pedigree. [ME f. OF *linage, lignage* f. Rmc f. L *linea* LINE[1]]

■ extraction, ancestry, family tree, pedigree, descent, stock, line, bloodline, parentage, genealogy; forebears, forefathers, family, people, clan, tribe; descendants, succession, progeny, offspring.

lineal /líneeəl/ *adj.* **1** in the direct line of descent or ancestry. **2** linear; of or in lines. □□ **lineally** *adv.* [ME f. OF f. LL *linealis* (as LINE[1])]

■ **1** see DIRECT *adj.* 4.

lineament /líneeəmənt/ *n.* (usu. in *pl.*) a distinctive feature or characteristic, esp. of the face. [ME f. L *lineamentum* f. *lineare* make straight f. *linea* LINE[1]]

■ see TRAIT.

linear /líneeər/ *adj.* **1 a** of or in lines; in lines rather than masses (*linear development*). **b** of length (*linear extent*). **2** long and narrow and of uniform breadth. **3** involving one dimension only. □ **linear accelerator** *Physics* an accelerator in which particles travel in straight lines, not in closed orbits. **Linear B** a form of Bronze Age writing found in Crete and parts of Greece and recording a form of Mycenaean Greek; an earlier undeciphered form (**Linear A**) also exists. **linear equation** an equation between two variables that gives a straight line when plotted on a graph. **linear motor** a motor producing straight-line (not rotary) motion by means of a magnetic field. □□ **linearity** /-neéaritee/ *n.* **linearize** *v.tr.* **linearly** *adv.* [L *linearis* f. *linea* LINE[1]]

■ **1a, 3** see STRAIGHT *adj.* 1.

lineation /línee-áyshən/ *n.* **1** a marking with or drawing of lines. **2** a division into lines. [ME f. L *lineatio* f. *lineare* make straight]

lineman /línmən/ *n.* (*pl.* **-men**) **1 a** a person who repairs and maintains telephone or electrical, etc., lines. **b** a person who tests the safety of railroad lines. **2** *Football* a player positioned along the line of scrimmage.

linen /línin/ *n. & adj.* ● *n.* **1 a** cloth woven from flax. **b** a particular kind of this. **2** (*collect.*) articles made or orig. made of linen, calico, etc., as sheets, cloths, etc. ● *adj.* made of linen or flax (*linen cloth*). □ **wash one's dirty linen in public** be indiscreet about one's domestic quarrels, etc. [OE *línen* f. WG, rel. to obs. *líne* flax]

■ **1** *archaic* flax. **2** *archaic* napery; bedclothes, bedlinen(s), sheets and pillowcases; table linen(s), tablecloths and napkins; towels and washcloths.

linenfold /líninfōld/ *n.* (often *attrib.*) a carved or molded ornament representing a fold or scroll of linen (*linenfold paneling*).

liner[1] /línər/ *n.* a ship or aircraft, etc., carrying passengers on a regular line. □ **liner train** *Brit.* a fast freight train with detachable containers on permanently coupled cars.

■ ship, boat, vessel; aircraft, airliner, jet, airplane.

liner[2] /línər/ *n.* a removable lining. □ **liner notes** printed information packaged with records, cassette tapes, and compact disks.

-liner /línər/ *comb. form* (prec. by a numeral, usu. *one* or *two*) *colloq.* a spoken passage of a specified number of lines in a play, etc. (*a one-liner*).

linesman /línzmən/ *n.* (*pl.* **-men**) **1** (in games played on a field or court) an umpire's or referee's assistant who decides whether a ball falls within the playing area or not. **2** *Brit.* = LINEMAN 1.

lineup /línup/ *n.* **1** a line of people for inspection or identification. **2** an arrangement of persons on a team, or of nations, etc., in an alliance.

ling[1] /ling/ *n.* a long slender marine fish, *Molva molva*, of N. Europe, used as food. [ME *leng(e)*, prob. f. MDu, rel. to LONG[1]]

ling[2] /ling/ *n.* any of various heathers, esp. *Calluna vulgaris*. □□ **lingy** *adj.* [ME f. ON *lyng*]

-ling[1] /ling/ *suffix* **1** denoting a person or thing: **a** connected with (*hireling; sapling*). **b** having the property of being (*weakling; underling*) or undergoing (*starveling*). **2** denoting

a diminutive (*duckling*), often derogatory (*lordling*). [OE (as -LE[1] + -ING[3]): sense 2 f. ON]

-ling[2] /ling/ *suffix* forming adverbs and adjectives (*darkling*) (cf. -LONG). [OE f. Gmc]

lingam /línggəm/ *n.* (also **linga** /línggə/) a phallus, esp. as the Hindu symbol of Siva. [Skr. *lingam*, lit. 'mark']

linger /línggər/ *v.intr.* **1 a** be slow or reluctant to depart. **b** stay about. **c** (foll. by *over, on,* etc.) dally (*lingered over dinner; lingered on what they said*). **2** (esp. of an illness) be protracted. **3** (foll. by *on*) (of a dying person or custom) be slow in dying; drag on feebly. □□ **lingerer** *n.* **lingering** *adj.* **lingeringly** *adv.* [ME *lenger*, frequent. of *leng* f. OE *lengan* f. Gmc, rel. to LENGTHEN]

■ **1** stay (behind), remain, loiter, delay, hang about *or* around, *archaic or literary* tarry, *colloq.* hang on, stick around; pause, idle, dally, dawdle, shilly-shally, *colloq.* dillydally; procrastinate, dither, temporize. **2** persist, endure, continue, drag on, be protracted. □□ **lingering** long, (long-)drawn-out, persistent, protracted, slow; remaining.

lingerie /laánzhəráy, lánzhəreé/ *n.* women's underwear and nightclothes. [F f. *linge* linen]

■ see UNDERCLOTHES.

lingo /línggō/ *n.* (*pl.* **-oes**) *colloq.* **1** a foreign language. **2** the vocabulary of a special subject or group of people. [prob. f. Port. *lingoa* f. L *lingua* tongue]

■ **1** language, tongue, speech; dialect, vernacular, patois, idiom, pidgin, creole. **2** jargon, argot, slang, cant, parlance, idiom, language; vocabulary, terminology; gobbledegook, gibberish, mumbo jumbo.

lingua franca /línggwə frángkə/ *n.* (*pl.* **lingua francas** or **linguae francae** /-gwee frángkee/) **1** a language adopted as a common language between speakers whose native languages are different. **2** a system for mutual understanding. **3** *hist.* a mixture of Italian with French, Greek, Arabic, and Spanish, used in the Levant. [It., = Frankish tongue]

■ **1, 2** see LANGUAGE *n.* 6.

lingual /línggwəl/ *adj.* **1** of or formed by the tongue. **2** of speech or languages. □□ **lingualize** *v.tr.* **lingually** *adv.* [med.L *lingualis* f. L *lingua* tongue, language]

linguiform /línggwifawrm/ *adj. Bot., Zool., & Anat.* tongue-shaped. [L *lingua* tongue + -FORM]

linguine /linggweénee/ *n.* (also **linguini**) a variety of pasta made in slender flattened strips. [It. dim. of *lingua* tongue]

linguist /línggwist/ *n.* a person skilled in languages or linguistics. [L *lingua* language]

linguistic /linggwístik/ *adj.* of or relating to language or the study of languages. □□ **linguistically** *adv.*

linguistics /linggwístiks/ *n.* the scientific study of language and its structure. □□ **linguistician** /-stíshən/ *n.* [F *linguistique* or G *Linguistik* (as LINGUIST)]

linguodental /línggwōdént'l, línggwə-/ *adj.* (of a sound) made with the tongue and teeth. [L *lingua* tongue + DENTAL]

liniment /línimənt/ *n.* an embrocation, usu. made with oil. [LL *linimentum* f. L *linire* smear]

■ see LOTION.

lining /líning/ *n.* **1** a layer of material used to line a surface, etc. **2** an inside layer or surface, etc. (*stomach lining*).

■ **2** see INSIDE *n.* 1.

link[1] /lingk/ *n. & v.* ● *n.* **1** one loop or ring of a chain, etc. **2 a** a connecting part, esp. a thing or person that unites or provides continuity; one in a series. **b** a state or means of connection. **3** a means of contact by radio or telephone between two points. **4** a means of travel or transport between two places. **5** = *cuff link* (see CUFF[1]). **6** a measure equal to one-hundredth of a surveying chain (7.92 inches). ● *v.* **1** *tr.* (foll. by *together, to, with*) connect or join (two things or one to another). **2** *tr.* clasp or intertwine (hands or arms). **3** *intr.* (foll. by *on, to, in to*) be joined; attach oneself to (a system, company, etc.). □ **link up** (foll. by *with*) connect or combine. [ME f. ON f. Gmc]

■ *n.* **2 a** tie, bond, coupling, connector, vinculum; element, constituent, component. **b** linkage, connection, tie-in, relation, relationship, association, affiliation, interdependence. **5** cuff link, stud.
● *v.* **1** connect, couple, join, fasten (together), unite; concatenate; tie (up *or* in *or* together), associate, relate, identify. **2** intertwine, clasp.

link² /lingk/ *n. hist.* a torch of pitch and tow for lighting the way in dark streets. [16th c.: perh. f. med.L *li(n)chinus* wick f. Gk *lukhnos* light]

linkage /língkij/ *n.* **1** a connection. **2** a system of links; a linking or link.

■ **1** see CONNECTION *n.* 1. **2** see JOINT *n.* 1.

linkman /língkman/ *n.* (*pl.* **-men**) *Brit.* **1** a person providing continuity in a broadcast program. **2** a player between the forwards and halfbacks or strikers and backs in soccer, etc.

links /lingks/ *n.pl.* **1** (treated as *sing.* or *pl.*) a golf course, esp. one having undulating ground, coarse grass, etc. **2** *Sc. dial.* level or undulating sandy ground near a seashore, with turf and coarse grass. [pl. of *link* 'rising ground' f. OE *hlinc*]

linkup /língkup/ *n.* an act or result of linking up.

linn /lin/ *n. Sc.* **1 a** a waterfall. **b** a pool below this. **2** a precipice; a ravine. [Gael. *linne*]

Linnaean /lineéən, -náyən/ *adj. & n.* (also **Linnean**) ● *adj.* of or relating to the Swedish naturalist Linnaeus (Linné, d. 1778) or his system of binary nomenclature in the classification of plants and animals. ● *n.* a follower of Linnaeus. ¶ Spelt *Linnean* in *Linnean Society*.

linnet /línit/ *n.* a finch, *Acanthis cannabina*, with brown and gray plumage. [OF *linette* f. *lin* flax (the bird feeding on flax seeds)]

lino /línō/ *n.* (*pl.* **-os**) esp. *Brit.* linoleum. [abbr.]

linocut /línōkut/ *n.* **1** a design or form carved in relief on a block of linoleum. **2** a print made from this. □□ **linocutting** *n.*

■ **2** see ILLUSTRATION 1.

linoleum /linṓleeəm/ *n.* a material consisting of a canvas backing thickly coated with a preparation of linseed oil and powdered cork, etc., used esp. as a floor covering. □□ **linoleumed** *adj.* [L *linum* flax + *oleum* oil]

Linotype /línətīp/ *n. Printing propr.* a composing machine producing lines of words as single strips of metal, used esp. for newspapers. [= *line o' type*]

linsang /línsang/ *n.* any of various civetlike cats, esp. of the genus *Poiana* of Africa. [Jav.]

linseed /línseed/ *n.* the seed of flax. □ **linseed cake** pressed linseed used as cattle feed. **linseed meal** ground linseed. **linseed oil** extracted from linseed and used esp. in paint and varnish. [OE *līnsǣd* f. *līn* flax + *sǣd* seed]

linsey-woolsey /línzeewŏŏlzee/ *n.* a fabric of coarse wool woven on a cotton warp. [ME f. *linsey* coarse linen, prob. f. *Lindsey* in Suffolk + WOOL, with jingling ending]

linstock /línstok/ *n. hist.* a match-holder used to fire cannon. [earlier *lintstock* f. Du. *lontstok* f. *lont* match + *stok* stick, with assim. to LINT]

lint /lint/ *n.* **1** a fabric, orig. of linen, with a raised nap on one side, used for dressing wounds. **2** fluff. **3** *Sc.* flax. □□ **linty** *adj.* [ME *lyn(n)et*, perh. f. OF *linette* linseed f. *lin* flax]

■ **2** see FLUFF *n.* 1. □□ **linty** see FUZZY 1a.

lintel /línt'l/ *n. Archit.* a horizontal supporting piece of wood, stone, etc., across the top of a door or window. □□ **linteled** *adj.* (esp. *Brit.* **intelled**). [ME f. OF *lintel* threshold f. Rmc *limitale* (unrecorded), infl. by LL *liminare* f. L *limen* threshold]

linter /líntər/ *n.* **1** a machine for removing the short fibers from cottonseed after ginning. **2** (in *pl.*) these fibers. [LINT + -ER¹]

liny /línee/ *adj.* (**linier, liniest**) marked with lines; wrinkled.

lion /líən/ *n.* **1** (*fem.* **lioness** /-nis/) a large feline, *Panthera leo*, of Africa and S. Asia, with a tawny coat and, in the male, a flowing shaggy mane. **2** (**the Lion**) the zodiacal sign or constellation Leo. **3** a brave or celebrated person. **4** the lion

as a national emblem of Great Britain or as a representation in heraldry. □ **the lion's share** the largest or best part. □□ **lionhood** *n.* **lionlike** *adj.* [ME f. AF *liun* f. L *leo -onis* f. Gk *leōn leontos*]

■ **3** see DIGNITARY. □ **the lion's share** see MAJORITY 1.

lionheart /líənhaart/ *n.* a courageous and generous person (esp. as a sobriquet of Richard I of England). □□ **lionhearted** *adj.*

■ □□ **lionhearted** see INTREPID.

lionize /líənīz/ *v.tr.* treat as a celebrity. □□ **lionization** *n.* **lionizer** *n.*

■ see GLORIFY 3.

lip /lip/ *n. & v.* ● *n.* **1 a** either of the two fleshy parts forming the edges of the mouth opening. **b** a thing resembling these. **c** = LABIUM. **2** the edge of a cup, vessel, etc., esp. the part shaped for pouring from. **3** *colloq.* impudent talk (*that's enough of your lip!*). ● *v.tr.* (**lipped, lipping**) **1 a** touch with the lips; apply the lips to. **b** touch lightly. **2** *Golf* **a** hit a ball just to the edge of (the cup). **b** (of a ball) reach the edge of (the cup) but fail to drop in. □ **bite one's lip** repress an emotion; stifle laughter, a retort, etc. **curl one's lip** express scorn. **hang on a person's lips** listen attentively to a person. **lick one's lips** see LICK. **lip-read** (*past* and *past part.* **-read** /-red/) practice lipreading. **lip-reader** a person who lip-reads. **lip service** an insincere expression of support, etc. **lip-sync** synchronize lip movements to recorded sound to appear to be singing or talking. **pass a person's lips** be eaten, drunk, spoken, etc. **smack one's lips** part the lips noisily in relish or anticipation, esp. of food. □□ **lipless** *adj.* **liplike** *adj.* **lipped** *adj.* (also in *comb.*). [OE *lippa* f. Gmc]

■ **2** see RIM *n.* 1. **3** see *impudence* (IMPUDENT). □ **lip service** see CANT¹ *n.* 1.

lipase /lípays, líp-/ *n. Biochem.* an enzyme that catalyzes the decomposition of fats. [Gk *lipos* fat + -ASE]

lipgloss /lípglos, -glaws/ *n.* a cosmetic preparation for adding shine or color to the lips.

lipid /lípid/ *n. Chem.* any of a group of organic compounds that are insoluble in water but soluble in organic solvents, including fatty acids, oils, waxes, and steroids. [F *lipide* (as LIPASE)]

lipidosis /lípidṓsis/ *n.* (also **lipoidosis** /lípoy-/) (*pl.* **-doses** /-seez/) any disorder of lipid metabolism in the body tissues.

Lipizzaner /lípitsáanər/ *n.* (also **Lippizaner**) **1** a horse of a fine white breed used esp. in displays of dressage. **2** this breed. [G f. *Lippiza* in Slovenia]

lipography /lipógrəfee/ *n.* the omission of letters or words in writing. [Gk *lip-* stem of *leipō* omit + -GRAPHY]

lipoid /lípoyd/ *adj.* resembling fat.

lipoprotein /lípōprṓteen, lí-/ *n. Biochem.* any of a group of proteins that are combined with fats or other lipids. [Gk *lipos* fat + PROTEIN]

liposome /lípōsōm, lí-/ *n. Biochem.* a minute artificial spherical sac usu. of a phospholipid membrane enclosing an aqueous core. [G. *Liposom*: see LIPID]

liposuction /lípōsúkshən, lí-/ *n.* a technique in cosmetic surgery for removing excess fat from under the skin by suction. [Gk *lipos* fat + SUCTION]

Lippizaner var. of LIPIZZANER.

lippy /lípee/ *adj.* (**lippier, lippiest**) *colloq.* **1** insolent; impertinent. **2** talkative.

lipreading /lípreeding/ *n.* (esp. of a deaf person) the practice of understanding (speech) entirely from observing a speaker's lip movements.

lipstick /lípstik/ *n.* a small stick of cosmetic for coloring the lips.

liquate /líkwáyt/ *v.tr.* separate or purify (metals) by liquefying. □□ **liquation** /-áyshən/ *n.* [L *liquare* melt, rel. to LIQUOR]

liquefy /líkwifī/ *v.tr. & intr.* (**-ies, -ied**) *Chem.* make or become liquid. □□ **liquefacient** /-fáyshənt/ *adj. & n.* **liquefaction** /-fákshən/ *n.* **liquefactive** /-fáktiv/ *adj.* **liquefiable** *adj.* **liquefier** *n.* [F *liquéfier* f. L *liquefacere* f. *liquēre* be liquid]

■ see DISSOLVE *v.* 1.

liquescent /likwésənt/ *adj.* becoming or apt to become liquid. [L *liquescere* (as LIQUEFY)]

liqueur /likə́r, -kyŏor/ *n.* any of several strong, sweet alcoholic liquors, variously flavored, usu. drunk after a meal. [F, = LIQUOR]

liquid /líkwid/ *adj.* & *n.* ● *adj.* **1** having a consistency like that of water or oil, flowing freely but of constant volume. **2** having the qualities of water in appearance; translucent (*liquid blue; a liquid luster*). **3** (of a gas, e.g., air, hydrogen) reduced to a liquid state by intense cold. **4** (of sounds) clear and pure; harmonious; fluent. **5** (of assets) easily converted into cash; also, having ready cash or liquid assets. **6** not fixed; fluid (*liquid opinions*). ● *n.* **1** a liquid substance. **2** *Phonet.* the sound of *l* or *r.* □ **liquid crystal** a turbid liquid with some order in its molecular arrangement. **liquid crystal display** a form of visual display in electronic devices, in which the reflectivity of a matrix of liquid crystals changes as a signal is applied. **liquid measure** a unit for measuring the volume of liquids. **liquid paraffin** *Brit.* = *mineral oil.* □□ **liquidly** *adv.* **liquidness** *n.* [ME f. L *liquidus* f. *liquēre* be liquid]
■ *adj.* **1, 3** fluid, liquefied; melted, runny, watery, aqueous; molten. **2** clear, transparent, translucent, limpid, pellucid; watery, aqueous. **4** clear, pure, distinct, clarion, bell-like; fluent, flowing, smooth, polished, harmonious, melodious, sweet(-sounding). **5** convertible, realizable, disposable; solvent, *colloq.* flush. **6** see FLUID *adj.* 2. ● *n.* **1** fluid, liquor, juice, sap, solution.

liquidambar /líkwidámbər/ *n.* **1** any tree of the genus *Liquidambar* yielding a resinous gum. **2** this gum. [mod.L app. f. L *liquidus* (see LIQUID) + med.L *ambar* amber]

liquidate /líkwidayt/ *v.* **1 a** *tr.* wind up the affairs of (a company or firm) by ascertaining liabilities and apportioning assets. **b** *intr.* (of a company) be liquidated. **2** *tr.* clear or pay off (a debt). **3** *tr.* put an end to or get rid of (esp. by violent means). [med.L *liquidare* make clear (as LIQUID)]
■ **1** see *wind up* 5 (WIND²). **2** see PAY¹ *v.* 2. **3** see KILL¹ *v.* 1.

liquidation /líkwidáyshən/ *n.* the process of liquidating a company, etc. □ **go into liquidation** (of a company, etc.) be wound up and have its assets apportioned.

liquidator /líkwidaytər/ *n.* a person called in to wind up the affairs of a company, etc.

liquidity /likwíditee/ *n.* (*pl.* **-ies**) **1** the state of being liquid. **2 a** availability of liquid assets. **b** (in *pl.*) liquid assets. [F *liquidité* or med.L *liquiditas* (as LIQUID)]

liquidize /líkwidīz/ *v.tr.* reduce (esp. food) to a liquid or puréed state.

liquidizer /líkwidīzər/ *n.* a machine for liquidizing.

liquify var. of LIQUEFY.

liquor /líkər/ *n.* & *v.* ● *n.* **1** an alcoholic (esp. distilled) drink. **2** water used in brewing. **3** other liquid, esp. that produced in cooking. **4** *Pharm.* a solution of a specified drug in water. ● *v.tr.* **1** dress (leather) with grease or oil. **2** steep (malt, etc.) in water. [ME f. OF *lic(o)ur* f. L *liquor -oris* (as LIQUID)]
■ *n.* **1** spirit(s), alcohol, (strong) drink, intoxicant(s), *colloq.* booze, firewater, grog, hooch, *sl.* hard stuff, rotgut, moonshine, lush, red-eye. **3** liquid, fluid, extract, stock, broth, infusion; distillate, concentrate.

liquorice esp. *Brit.* var. of LICORICE.

liquorish /líkərish/ *adj.* **1** = LICKERISH. **2** fond of or indicating a fondness for liquor. □□ **liquorishly** *adv.* **liquorishness** *n.* [var. of LICKERISH, misapplied]

lira /léerə/ *n.* (*pl.* **lire** /léere/ or **liras**) **1** the chief monetary unit of Italy. **2** the chief monetary unit of Turkey. [It. f. Prov. *liura* f. L *libra* pound (weight, etc.)]

lisle /līl/ *n.* (in full **lisle thread**) a fine, smooth cotton thread for stockings, etc. [*Lisle*, former spelling of *Lille* in France, where orig. made]

lisp /lisp/ *n.* & *v.* ● *n.* **1** a speech defect in which *s* is pronounced like *th* in *thick* and *z* is pronounced like *th* in *this*. **2** a rippling of waters; a rustling of leaves. ● *v.intr.* & *tr.* speak or utter with a lisp. □□ **lisper** *n.* **lispingly** *adv.* [OE

wlispian (recorded in *āwlyspian*) f. *wlisp* (adj.) lisping, of uncert. orig.]

lissome /lísəm/ *adj.* (also **lissom**) lithe; supple; agile. □□ **lissomely** *adv.* **lissomeness** *n.* [ult. f. LITHE + -SOME¹]
■ see SUPPLE *adj.* 1.

list¹ /list/ *n.* & *v.* ● *n.* **1** a number of connected items, names, etc., written or printed together usu. consecutively to form a record or aid to memory (*shopping list*). **2** (in *pl.*) **a** palisades enclosing an area for a tournament. **b** the scene of a contest. **3** *Brit.* **a** a selvage or edge of cloth, usu. of different material from the main body. **b** such edges used as a material. ● *v.* **1** *tr.* make a list of. **b** enumerate; name one by one as if in a list. **2** *tr.* enter in a list. **3** *tr.* (as **listed** *adj.*) **a** (of securities) approved for dealings on the stock exchange. **b** (of a building in the UK) officially designated as being of historical importance and having protection from demolition or major alterations. **4** *tr.* & *intr. archaic* enlist. □ esp. *Brit.* **enter the lists** issue or accept a challenge. **list price** the price of something as shown in a published list. □□ **listable** *adj.* [OE *liste* border, strip f. Gmc]
■ *n.* **1** listing, itemization, inventory, index, catalog, catalogue raisonné, program, schedule, register, roll, record, file, directory, roster, slate, esp. *Brit.* rota. ● *v.* **1 a** itemize, inventory, index, catalog, schedule, record. **b** enumerate, name, cite, quote, recount, recite, reel off, rattle off, itemize. **2** register, enter, enroll, inventory, log, book, note, record, catalog.

list² /list/ *v.* & *n.* ● *v.intr.* (of a ship, etc.) lean over to one side, esp. owing to a leak or shifting cargo (cf. HEEL²). ● *n.* the process or an instance of listing. [17th c.: orig. unkn.]
■ *v.* lean (over), tilt, slant, heel, lurch, tip, careen, cant, incline, slope. ● *n.* lean, tilt, slant, heel, lurch, tip, cant, slope, inclination, careenage, camber.

listen /lísən/ *v.intr.* **1 a** make an effort to hear something. **b** attentively hear a person speaking. **2** (foll. by *to*) **a** give attention with the ear (*listened to my story*). **b** take notice of; respond to advice or a request or to the person expressing it. **3** (also **listen out**) (often foll. by *for*) seek to hear or be aware of by waiting alertly. □ **listen in 1** eavesdrop; tap a private conversation, esp. one by telephone. **2** listen to a radio or television broadcast. **listening post 1 a** a point near an enemy's lines for detecting movements by sound. **b** a station for intercepting electronic communications. **2** a place for the gathering of information from reports, etc. [OE *hlysnan* f. WG]
■ **1, 2** pay attention, attend, take *or* pay heed, lend an ear, be all ears, prick up one's ears, keep one's ears open, *archaic* hark, *archaic or literary* hearken, *colloq.* tune in; (*listen to*) heed, take notice of, mind, hang upon; obey, follow, respect, accept. **3** (*listen (out) for*) wait for, await; look out for, watch out for, keep one's ears open for. □ **listen in 1** eavesdrop, apply a tap, spy, pry, *colloq.* snoop.

listenable /lísənəbəl/ *adj.* easy or pleasant to listen to. □□ **listenability** *n.*

listener /lísənər, lísnər/ *n.* **1** a person who listens. **2** a person receiving broadcast radio programs.

lister /lístər/ *n.* a plow with a double moldboard. [*list* prepare land for a crop + -ER¹]

listeria /listéereeə/ *n.* any motile rodlike bacterium of the genus *Listeria*, esp. *L. monocytogenes* infecting humans and animals eating contaminated food. [mod.L f. J. *Lister*, Engl. surgeon d. 1912]

listing /lísting/ *n.* **1** a list or catalog (see LIST¹ 1). **2** the drawing up of a list. **3** *Brit.* selvage (see LIST¹ *n.* 3).
■ **1** see LIST¹ *n.* 1.

listless /lístlis/ *adj.* lacking energy or enthusiasm; disinclined for exertion. □□ **listlessly** *adv.* **listlessness** *n.* [ME f. obs. *list* inclination + -LESS]

/.../ **pronunciation**   ● **part of speech**
□ **phrases, idioms, and compounds**
□□ **derivatives**   ■ **synonym section**
cross-references appear in SMALL CAPITALS or *italics*

■ sluggish, lethargic, languid, languorous, torpid, leaden, inanimate, lifeless, spiritless, weak, spent, weary, tired, exhausted, drained, enervated, *colloq.* fagged (out), knocked out, done in, all in, bushed, pooped, esp. *Brit. colloq.* whacked, *sl.* wiped out; shiftless, indolent, idle; unenthusiastic, indifferent, apathetic, lackadaisical, lukewarm, tepid, cool.

lit *past* and *past part.* of LIGHT¹, LIGHT².

litany /lítˈnee/ *n.* (*pl.* **-ies**) **1 a** a series of petitions for use in church services or processions, usu. recited by the clergy and responded to in a recurring formula by the people. **b** (**the Litany**) that contained in the Book of Common Prayer. **2** a tedious recital (*a litany of woes*). [ME f. OF *letanie* f. eccl.L *litania* f. Gk *litaneia* prayer f. *litē* supplication]
■ **1** petition, prayer, invocation, supplication, entreaty, obsecration. **2** recitation, recital, enumeration, listing, list, catalog, inventory.

litchi /leéchee/ *n.* (also **lichee, lychee**) **1** a sweet, fleshy fruit with a thin, spiny skin. **2** the tree, *Nephelium litchi*, orig. from China, bearing this. [Chin. *lizhi*]

-lite /līt/ *suffix* forming names of minerals (*rhyolite*; *zeolite*). [F f. Gk *lithos* stone]

liter /leétər/ *n.* (*Brit.* **litre**) a metric unit of capacity, formerly defined as the volume of one kilogram of water under standard conditions, now equal to 1 cubic decimeter (about 1.057 quarts). [F f. *litron*, an obs. measure of capacity, f. med.L f. Gk *litra* a Sicilian monetary unit]

literacy /lítərəsee/ *n.* the ability to read and write. [LITERATE + -ACY after *illiteracy*]

literal /lítərəl/ *adj.* & *n.* ● *adj.* **1** taking words in their usual or primary sense without metaphor or allegory (*literal interpretation*). **2** following the letter, text, or exact or original words (*literal translation*; *a literal transcript*). **3** (in full **literal-minded**) (of a person) prosaic; matter-of-fact. **4** a not exaggerated (*the literal truth*). **b** so called without exaggeration (*a literal extermination*). **5** *colloq. disp.* so called with some exaggeration or using metaphor (*a literal avalanche of mail*). **6** of, in, or expressed by a letter or the letters of the alphabet. **7** *Algebra* not numerical. ● *n. Printing* a misprint of a letter. □□ **literality** /-rálitee/ *n.* **literalize** *v.tr.* **literally** *adv.* **literalness** *n.* [ME f. OF *literal* or LL *litteralis* f. L *littera* (as LETTER)]
■ *adj.* **1** denotative, dictionary, lexical; see also LITERAL *adj.* **1** below. **2** verbatim, word-for-word; exact, precise, faithful, strict. **3** prosaic, colorless, dull, banal, unimaginative, pedestrian, humdrum, boring, tedious; down-to-earth, matter-of-fact. **4** basic, essential, pure, simple, simplistic, real, objective, true, actual, genuine, bona fide; unvarnished, unadulterated, unexaggerated, unembellished. □□ **literally** word for word, verbatim, literatim; faithfully, strictly, exactly, precisely, closely, rigorously; *sic, formal* thus; at one's word; actually, really, genuinely, truly; prosaically, colorlessly, dully, unimaginatively, boringly, tediously.

literalism /lítərəlizəm/ *n.* insistence on a literal interpretation; adherence to the letter. □□ **literalist** *n.* **literalistic** *adj.*

literary /lítəreree/ *adj.* **1** of, constituting, or occupied with books or literature or written composition, esp. of the kind valued for quality of form. **2** well informed about literature. **3** (of a word or idiom) used chiefly in literary works or other formal writing. ● **literary executor** see EXECUTOR. **literary history** the history of the treatment of a subject in literature. □□ **literarily** /-áirilee/ *adv.* **literariness** *n.* [L *litterarius* (as LETTER)]
■ **1** artistic, belletristic, poetic, dramatic. **2** well-read, lettered, bookish, bibliophilic; erudite, cultured, cultivated, refined, learned, knowledgeable, (well-)informed, (well-)educated, scholarly, *colloq.* highbrow. **3** poetic, dramatic; formal, written.

literate /lítərət/ *adj.* & *n.* ● *adj.* able to read and write. ● *n.* a literate person. □□ **literately** *adv.* [ME f. L *litteratus* (as LETTER)]
■ *adj.* see LEARNED 1.

literati /lítəráatee/ *n.pl.* **1** men of letters. **2** the learned class. [L, pl. of *literatus* (as LETTER)]

■ see INTELLIGENTSIA.

literatim /lítəráytim, -raá-/ *adv.* letter for letter; textually; literally. [med.L]

literation /lítəráyshən/ *n.* the representation of sounds, etc., by a letter or group of letters. [L *litera* LETTER]

literature /lítərəchər, -chōōr/ *n.* **1** written works, esp. those whose value lies in beauty of language or in emotional effect. **2** the realm of letters. **3** the writings of a country or period. **4** literary production. **5** *colloq.* printed matter, leaflets, etc. **6** the material in print on a particular subject (*there is a considerable literature on geraniums*). [ME, = literary culture, f. L *litteratura* (as LITERATE)]
■ **1, 3** (creative) writings, books, publications, work(s), texts, composition(s); poetry, drama, fiction, essays, novels. **2** (creative) writing, fiction; letters, belles lettres, the world of letters, the arts, the humanities, the classics; culture, learning, scholarship. **4** output, creation, *œuvre*, production. **5** documentation, paperwork, document(s), paper(s); brochure(s), pamphlet(s), leaflet(s), booklet(s), manuals, handout(s), publicity, blurb, prospectus(es), handbill(s), leaflet(s), circular(s); information, facts, data, details, instructions, specifications. **6** books, texts, work(s), publications; information, detail(s), data.

-lith /lith/ *suffix* denoting types of stone (*laccolith*; *monolith*). [Gk *lithos* stone]

litharge /líthaárj/ *n.* a red or yellow crystalline form of lead monoxide. [ME f. OF *litarge* f. L *lithargyrus* f. Gk *litharguros* f. *lithos* stone + *arguros* silver]

lithe /līth/ *adj.* flexible; supple. □□ **lithely** *adv.* **litheness** *n.* **lithesome** *adj.* [OE *līthe* f. Gmc]
■ see SUPPLE *adj.* 1.

lithia /lítheeə/ *n.* lithium oxide. □ **lithia water** water containing lithium salts and used against gout. [mod.L, alt. of earlier *lithion* f. Gk neut. of *litheios* f. *lithos* stone, after *soda*, etc.]

lithic /líthik/ *adj.* **1** of, like, or made of stone. **2** *Med.* of a calculus. [Gk *lithikos* (as LITHIA)]

lithium /lítheeəm/ *n. Chem.* a soft, silver-white metallic element, the lightest metal, used in alloys and in batteries. ¶ Symb.: **Li**. [LITHIA + -IUM]

litho /líthō/ *n.* & *v. colloq.* ● *n.* = LITHOGRAPHY. ● *v.tr.* (**-oes, -oed**) produce by lithography. [abbr.]

litho- /líthō/ *comb. form* stone. [Gk *lithos* stone]

lithograph /líthəgraf/ *n.* & *v.* ● *n.* a lithographic print. ● *v.tr.* **1** print by lithography. **2** write or engrave on stone. [back-form. f. LITHOGRAPHY]
■ *n.* see ENGRAVING.

lithography /lithógrəfee/ *n.* a process of obtaining prints from a stone or metal surface so treated that what is to be printed can be inked but the remaining area rejects ink. □□ **lithographer** *n.* **lithographic** /líthəgráfik/ *adj.* **lithographically** *adv.* [G *Lithographie* (as LITHO-, -GRAPHY)]

lithology /lithólɔjee/ *n.* the science of the nature and composition of rocks. □□ **lithological** /líthəlójikəl/ *adj.*

lithophyte /líthəfīt/ *n. Bot.* a plant that grows on stone.

lithopone /líthəpōn/ *n.* a white pigment of zinc sulfide, barium sulfate, and zinc oxide. [LITHO- + Gk *ponos* work]

lithosphere /líthəsfeer/ *n.* **1** the layer including the earth's crust and upper mantle. **2** solid earth (opp. HYDROSPHERE, ATMOSPHERE). □□ **lithospheric** /-sfeérik, -sfér-/ *adj.*

lithotomy /lithótəmee/ *n.* (*pl.* **-ies**) the surgical removal of a stone from the urinary tract, esp. the bladder. □□ **lithotomist** *n.* **lithotomize** *v.tr.* [LL f. Gk *lithotomia* (as LITHO-, -TOMY)]

lithotripsy /líthətripsee/ *n.* (*pl.* **-ies**) a treatment using ultrasound to shatter a stone in the bladder into small particles that can be passed through the urethra. □□ **lithotripter** /-triptər/ *n.* **lithotriptic** *adj.* [LITHO- + Gk *tripsis* rubbing f. *tribo* rub]

Lithuanian /líthōō-áyneeən/ *n.* & *adj.* ● *n.* **1 a** a native of Lithuania, a Baltic republic. **b** a person of Lithuanian descent. **2** the language of Lithuania. ● *adj.* of or relating to Lithuania or its people or language.

litigant /lítigənt/ n. & adj. ● n. a party to a lawsuit. ● adj. engaged in a lawsuit. [F (as LITIGATE)]
■ n. litigator, party; plaintiff, appellant, suitor, petitioner, suer, defendant, accused.

litigate /lítigayt/ v. **1** intr. go to law; be a party to a lawsuit. **2** tr. contest (a point) in a lawsuit. □□ **litigable** /-gəbəl/ adj. **litigation** /-gáyshən/ n. **litigator** n. [L litigare litigat- f. lis litis lawsuit]
■ **1** go to law or court, take (legal) action. **2** see CONTEST v. 1. □□ **litigation** lawsuit, suit (at law), case, (legal) action; (legal) remedy, redress, reparation. **litigator** see LITIGANT n.

litigious /litíjəs/ adj. **1** given to litigation; unreasonably fond of going to law. **2** disputable in a court of law; offering matter for a lawsuit. **3** of lawsuits. □□ **litigiously** adv. **litigiousness** n. [ME f. OF litigieux or L litigiosus f. litigium litigation: see LITIGATE]

litmus /lítməs/ n. a dye obtained from lichens that is red under acid conditions and blue under alkaline conditions. □ **litmus paper** a paper stained with litmus to be used as a test for acids or alkalis. **litmus test 1** a test for acids and alkalis using litmus paper. **2** a simple test to establish true character. [ME f. ONorw. litmosi f. ON litr dye + mosi moss]

litotes /lítəteez, lít-, lītóteez/ n. ironical understatement, esp. the expressing of an affirmative by the negative of its contrary (e.g., I won't be sorry for I will be glad). [LL f. Gk litotēs f. litos plain, meager]

litre Brit. var. of LITER.

Litt.D. abbr. Doctor of Letters. [L Litterarum Doctor]

litter /lítər/ n. & v. ● n. **1 a** refuse, esp. paper, discarded in an open or public place. **b** odds and ends lying about. **2** a state of untidiness, disorderly accumulation of papers, etc. **3** the young animals brought forth at a birth. **4** a vehicle containing a couch shut in by curtains and carried on men's shoulders or by beasts of burden. **5** a framework with a couch for transporting the sick and wounded. **6 a** straw, rushes, etc., as bedding, esp. for animals. **b** straw and dung in a farmyard. ● v.tr. **1** make (a place) untidy with litter. **2** scatter untidily and leave lying about. **3** give birth to (whelps, etc.). **4** (often foll. by down) **a** provide (a horse, etc.) with litter as bedding. **b** spread litter or straw on (a floor) or in (a stable). □ **litter-lout** Brit. = LITTERBUG. □□ **littery** adj. (in senses 1, 2 of n.). [ME f. AF litere, OF litiere f. med.L lectaria f. L lectus bed]
■ n. **1** rubbish, refuse, waste, garbage, trash; debris, detritus, scrap, dross, junk. **2** see MESS n. 1. **3** brood, offspring, young, progeny, Law issue; farrow. **4, 5** sedan chair, palanquin, hist. chair; stretcher. **6 a** bed, bedding, straw. ● v. **1** clutter (up), mess (up), muck up. **2** strew, scatter, spread, toss, throw.

litterae humaniores /lítəri hōōmáneeáwrez, lítəree/ n. the formal study of the humanities.

littérateur /lítəraatőr/ n. a literary person. [F]
■ see WRITER 2.

litterbag /lítərbag/ n. a bag used in a motor vehicle, etc., for trash disposal.

litterbug /lítərbug/ n. a person who carelessly leaves litter in a public place.

little /lít'l/ adj., n., & adv. ● adj. (**littler, littlest; less** /les/ or **lesser** /lésər/; **least** /leest/) **1** small in size, amount, degree, etc.; not great or big: often used to convey affectionate or emotional overtones, or condescension, not implied by small (a friendly little guy; a silly little fool; a nice little car). **2 a** short in stature (a little man). **b** of short distance or duration (will go a little way with you; wait a little while). **3** (prec. by a) a certain though small amount of (give me a little butter). **4** trivial; relatively unimportant (exaggerates every little difficulty). **5** not much; inconsiderable (gained little advantage from it). **6** operating on a small scale (the little storekeeper). **7** as a distinctive epithet: **a** of a smaller or the smallest size, etc. (little finger). **b** that is the smaller or smallest of the name (little auk; little grebe). **8** young or younger (a little boy; my little sister). **9** as of a child, evoking tenderness, condescension, amusement, etc. (we know their little ways). **10** mean; paltry; contemptible (you little sneak). ● n.

1 not much; only a small amount (got very little out of it; did what little I could). **2** (usu. prec. by a) **a** a certain but no great amount (knows a little of everything; every little bit helps). **b** a short time or distance (after a little). ● adv. (**less, least**) **1** to a small extent only (little-known authors; is little more than speculation). **2** not at all; hardly (they little thought). **3** (prec. by a) somewhat (is a little deaf). □ **in little** on a small scale. **Little Bear** = Little Dipper. **Little Dipper** the constellation of seven bright stars in Ursa Minor in the shape of a dipper. **little by little** by degrees; gradually. **little finger** the smallest finger, at the outer end of the hand. **Little League** an international organization that promotes youth baseball and softball. **Little Leaguer** a participant in Little League. **little man** esp. joc. (as a form of address) a boy. **little ones** young children or animals. **little or nothing** hardly anything. **the little people** fairies. **Little Russian** hist. n. a Ukrainian. ● adj. Ukrainian. **little slam** Bridge the winning of 12 tricks. **the little woman** colloq. often derog. one's wife. **no little** considerable; a good deal of (took no little trouble over it). **not a little** n. much; a great deal. ● adv. extremely (not a little concerned). □□ **littleness** n. [OE lȳtel f. Gmc]
■ adj. **1, 2a** small, short, slight, diminutive, compact, petite, bijou, esp. Sc. or colloq. wee; miniature, baby, toy, dwarf, pygmy, midget; undersized, puny; microscopic, minuscule, infinitesimal, mini-, micro-, colloq. teeny, teeny-weeny, teensy, teensy-weensy, colloq. usu. derog. itty-bitty. **2b** short, brief, fractional, infinitesimal. **3** (a little) some, a (little) bit of; a piece of, a spot of, a scrap of, a drop of, a dab of, a taste of, a trace of, a touch of, a suspicion of, a hint of. **4** trivial, trifling, small, minor, petty, paltry, slight, colloq. piddling, piffling; insignificant, inconsiderable, unimportant, inconsequential, negligible. **5** not much, hardly any, scant, meager, thin, poor, minimal, slender, inconsiderable, negligible. **6** small, small-scale, small-time; modest, unpretentious, humble, simple, plain, ordinary. **7** smaller, little, lesser, minor; smallest, littlest, least. **8** young, youthful, baby, small; younger, junior. **9** childlike, childish, innocent; silly, funny; dear, lovable, darling. **10** contemptible, wretched, despicable, loathsome, vile, scurvy, low, mean, paltry, cheap, petty, picayune, twopenny colloq. two-bit. ● n. **1** not much, hardly or scarcely anything; a pittance, colloq. peanuts, chicken feed. **2 a** bit, piece, spot, scrap, drop, dab, taste, trace, touch, suspicion, hint, colloq. smidgen, tad. **b** while, time, period, stretch. ● adv. **1, 2** scarcely, hardly, barely; not much; rarely, seldom; never, not at all, by no means, noway, nowise. **3** (a little) somewhat, slightly, a (little) bit, rather, quite, moderately, fairly, pretty, colloq. sort of, kind of, kinda. □ **little by little** see gradually (GRADUAL). **little man** see BOY n. 1, 2. **little ones** see YOUNG n. **no little** see CONSIDERABLE 2. **not a little** (n.) see LOT n. 1. (adv.) see extremely (EXTREME).

littoral /lítərəl/ adj. & n. ● adj. of or on the shore of the sea, a lake, etc. ● n. a region lying along a shore. [L littoralis f. litus litoris shore]
■ n. see COAST n. 1a.

liturgical /litə́rjikəl/ adj. of or related to liturgies or public worship. □□ **liturgically** adv. **liturgist** /lítərjist/ n. [med.L f. Gk leitourgikos (as LITURGY)]
■ see SOLEMN 2.

liturgy /lítərjee/ n. (pl. **-ies**) **1 a** a form of public worship. **b** a set of formularies for this. **c** public worship in accordance with a prescribed form. **2** Brit. (the Liturgy) the Book of Common Prayer. **3** (the Divine Liturgy) the Communion office of the Orthodox Church. **4** Gk Antiq. a public office or duty performed voluntarily by a rich Athenian. [F liturgie

---

/ . . . / pronunciation	**● part of speech**
□ phrases, idioms, and compounds	
□□ derivatives	**■ synonym section**
cross-references appear in SMALL CAPITALS or italics	

or LL *liturgia* f. Gk *leitourgia* public worship f. *leitourgos* minister f. *leit-* public + *ergon* work]
■ **1 b** see FORMULA 3a.

livable /lívəbəl/ *adj.* (also **liveable**) **1** (of a house, room, climate, etc.) fit to live in. **2** (of a life) worth living. **3** (of a person) companionable; easy to live with. □□ **livability** *n.* **livableness** *n.*
■ **1** see HABITABLE.

live¹ /liv/ *v.* **1** *intr.* have (esp. animal) life; be or remain alive. **2** *intr.* (foll. by *on*) subsist or feed (*lives on fruit*). **3** *intr.* (foll. by *on, off*) depend for subsistence (*lives off the family; lives on income from investments*). **4** *intr.* (foll. by *on, by*) sustain one's position or repute (*live on their reputation; lives by his wits*). **5** *tr.* **a** (with compl.) spend; pass; experience (*lived a happy life*). **b** express in one's life (*was living a lie*). **6** *intr.* conduct oneself in a specified way (*live quietly*). **7** *intr.* arrange one's habits, expenditure, feeding, etc. (*live modestly*). **8** *intr.* make or have one's abode. **9** *intr.* (foll. by *in*) spend the daytime (*the room does not seem to be lived in*). **10** *intr.* (of a person or thing) survive. **11** *intr.* (of a ship) escape destruction. **12** *intr.* enjoy life intensely or to the full (*you haven't lived till you've drunk champagne*). □ **live and let live** condone others' failings so as to be similarly tolerated. **live down** (usu. with *neg.*) cause (past guilt, embarrassment, etc.) to be forgotten by different conduct over a period of time (*you'll never live that down!*). **live in** (of a domestic employee) reside on the premises of one's work. **live-in** *attrib.adj.* **1** (of a domestic employee) living in (*live-in maid*). **2** (of a sexual partner) cohabiting. **live it up** *colloq.* live gaily and extravagantly. **live out 1** survive (a danger, difficulty, etc.). **2** (of a domestic employee) reside away from one's place of work. **live through** survive; remain alive at the end of. **live to** survive and reach (*lived to a great age*). **live to oneself** live in isolation. **live together** (esp. of a man and woman not married to each other) share a home and have a sexual relationship. **live up to** honor or fulfill; put into practice (principles, etc.). **live with 1** share a home with. **2** tolerate; find congenial. **long live …!** an exclamation of loyalty (to a person, etc., specified). [OE *libban, lifian,* f. Gmc]
■ **1–4** exist, be alive, breathe, draw breath, function; survive, thrive, subsist, stay alive, keep oneself alive, sustain oneself, keep going, persist, last, persevere, endure; (*live on*) feed on, eat, use, consume; depend on. **5 a** spend, pass, experience, lead, have, go through. **8, 9** reside, be, settle; remain, stay, sojourn, lodge, put up, room, *archaic* abide, *archaic or dial.* bide, *literary* dwell; (*live in*) occupy, inhabit, tenant, populate. **10, 11** survive, pull *or* come through; emerge, walk away; go on, continue. □ **live it up** see *enjoy oneself.* **live through** see WEATHER *v.* **live to** see REACH *v.* **5. live up to** see FULFILL 1, 2.

live² /liv/ *adj.* **1** (*attrib.*) that is alive; living. **2** (of a broadcast) heard or seen at the time of its performance, not from a recording. **3** full of power, energy, or importance; not obsolete or exhausted (*disarmament is still a live issue*). **4** expending or still able to expend energy in various forms, esp.: **a** (of coals) glowing; burning. **b** (of a shell) unexploded. **c** (of a match) unkindled. **d** (of a wire, etc.) connected to a source of electrical power. **5** (of rock) not detached, seeming to form part of the earth's frame. **6** (of a wheel or axle, etc., in machinery) moving or imparting motion. □ **live bait** small fish used to entice prey. **live load** the weight of persons or goods in a building or vehicle. **live oak** an American evergreen tree, *Quercus virginiana.* **live wire** an energetic and forceful person. [aphetic form of ALIVE]
■ **1** living, alive, breathing, animate, existent, *archaic* quick, *joc.* in the land of the living, among the living; viable. **3** energetic, lively, spirited, vigorous, active, dynamic, busy; current, contemporary; contemporaneous. **4 a** burning, glowing, aglow, ablaze, aflame, alight, unstruck, afire, on fire, in flames, flaming, red-hot, white-hot. **b** unexploded, explosive; loaded, charged, primed. **c** unkindled, unstruck, unused. **d** alive, charged, electrified. □ **live wire** fireball, tiger, demon, *colloq.* dynamo, ripsnorter.

liveable var. of LIVABLE.

livelihood /lívleehood/ *n.* a means of living; sustenance. [OE *līflād* f. *līf* LIFE + *lād* course (see LOAD): assim. to obs. *livelihood* liveliness]
■ see SUSTENANCE 2.

livelong¹ /lívlawng, -long/ *adj. poet.* or *rhet.* in its entire length or apparently so (*the livelong day*). [ME *lefe longe* (as LIEF, LONG¹): assim. to LIVE¹]

livelong² /lívlawng, -long/ *n.* an orpine. [LIVE¹ + LONG¹]

lively /lívlee/ *adj.* (**livelier, liveliest**) **1** full of life; vigorous, energetic. **2** brisk (*a lively pace*). **3** vigorous; stimulating (*a lively discussion*). **4** vivacious; jolly; sociable. **5** *joc.* exciting; dangerous; difficult (*the press is making things lively for them*). **6** (of a color) bright and vivid. **7** lifelike; realistic (*a lively description*). **8** (of a boat, etc.) rising lightly to the waves. □□ **livelily** *adv.* **liveliness** *n.* [OE *līflic* (as LIFE, -LY¹)]
■ **1** vital, animate, alive; spry, vivacious, frisky, sprightly, jaunty, pert, perky, cheery, bouncy, effervescent, bubbly, exuberant, volatile, skittish, kittenish, *colloq.* peppy, breezy, chirpy, full of beans, *dial.* peart; vigorous, energetic, active, dynamic, lusty, spirited, animated, eager, dashing, *colloq.* zappy, zippy; racy; busy, bustling; see also AGILE. **2** brisk, crisp, smart, keen, busy, spanking, sprightly, *colloq.* snappy; quick, fast, rapid, swift. **3** vigorous, stimulating, exciting, stirring; scintillating, sparkling; see also BOISTEROUS 1. **4** vivacious, jolly, jovial, sociable, convivial, festive, exuberant, hearty, high-spirited, *colloq.* swinging. **5** dangerous, precarious, risky, exciting, hot; difficult, tricky, awkward. **6** bright, brilliant, vivid, intense, bold, strong, loud, fluorescent; colorful, cheerful. **7** see LIFELIKE.

liven /lívən/ *v.tr.* & *intr.* (often foll. by *up*) *colloq.* brighten; cheer.
■ enliven, brighten (up), cheer (up), perk up; hearten, stimulate, *colloq.* pep up.

liver¹ /lívər/ *n.* **1 a** a large lobed glandular organ in the abdomen of vertebrates, functioning in many metabolic processes including the regulation of toxic materials in the blood, secreting bile, etc. **b** a similar organ in other animals. **2** the flesh of an animal's liver as food. **3** a dark reddish-brown color. □ **liver chestnut** see CHESTNUT. **liver fluke** either of two types of fluke, esp. *Fasciola hepatica,* the adults of which live within the liver tissues of vertebrates, and the larvae within snails. **liver of sulfur** a liver-colored mixture of potassium sulfides, etc., used as a lotion in skin disease. **liver salts** *Brit.* salts to cure dyspepsia or biliousness. **liver sausage** = LIVERWURST. **liver spots(s)** brownish pigmentation of the skin, esp. of older people. □□ **liverless** *adj.* [OE *lifer* f. Gmc]

liver² /lívər/ *n.* a person who lives in a specified way (*a clean liver*).

liverish /lívərish/ *adj.* **1** suffering from a disorder of the liver. **2** peevish; glum. **3** resembling liver. □□ **liverishly** *adv.* **liverishness** *n.*

Liverpudlian /lívərpúdleeən/ *n.* & *adj.* ● *n.* a native of Liverpool, England. ● *adj.* of or relating to Liverpool. [joc. f. *Liverpool* + PUDDLE]

liverwort /lívərwərt, -wawrt/ *n.* any small leafy or thalloid bryophyte of the class Hepaticae, of which some have liver-shaped parts.

liverwurst /lívərwərst, -vərst/ *n.* a sausage containing cooked liver, etc.

livery¹ /lívəree/ *n.* (*pl.* **-ies**) **1** a distinctive guise or marking or outward appearance (*birds in their winter livery*). **2** a distinctive color scheme in which the vehicles, aircraft, etc., of a particular company or line are painted. **3** a place where horses can be hired. **4** *hist.* a provision of food or clothing for retainers, etc. **5** *Law* **a** the legal delivery of property. **b** a writ allowing this. **6** *Brit.* distinctive clothing worn by a member of a City of London company or by a servant. **b** the membership of a City of London livery company. □ **at livery** (of a horse) kept for the owner and fed and groomed for a fixed charge. **livery stable** a stable where horses are kept at livery or let out for hire. □□ **liveried** *adj.* (esp. in senses 1, 2). [ME f. AF *liveré*, OF *livrée*, fem. past part. of *livrer* DELIVER]

livery[2] /lívəree/ *adj.* **1** of the consistency or color of liver. **2** *Brit.* (of soil) tenacious. **3** *colloq.* liverish.

liveryman /lívəreemən/ *n.* (*pl.* **-men**) **1** a keeper of or attendant in a livery stable. **2** *Brit.* a member of a livery company.

lives *pl.* of LIFE.

livestock /lívstok/ *n.* (usu. treated as *pl.*) animals, esp. on a farm, regarded as an asset.
■ see STOCK *n.* 4.

livid /lívid/ *adj.* **1** *colloq.* furiously angry. **2 a** of a bluish leaden color. **b** discolored as by a bruise. □□ **lividity** /-víditee/ *n.* **lividly** *adv.* **lividness** *n.* [F *livide* or L *lividus* f. *livēre* be bluish]
■ **1** see ANGRY 1. **2** see GRAY 1.

living /líving/ *n.* & *adj.* ● *n.* **1** a livelihood or means of maintenance (*made my living as a journalist*; *what does she do for a living?*). **2** *Brit. Eccl.* a position as a vicar or rector with an income or property. ● *adj.* **1** contemporary; now existent (*the greatest living poet*). **2** (of a likeness or image of a person) exact. **3** (of a language) still in vernacular use. **4** (of water) perennially flowing. **5** (of rock, etc.) = LIVE[2] 5. □ **living death** a state of hopeless misery. **living room** a room for general day use. **living will** a written statement of a person's desire not to be kept alive by artificial means in the event of terminal illness or accident. **within living memory** within the memory of people still living.
■ *n.* **1** see SUSTENANCE 2. ● *adj.* **1** see ALIVE 1. □ **living room** see PARLOR.

lixiviate /liksívee-ayt/ *v.tr.* separate (a substance) into soluble and insoluble constituents by the percolation of liquid. □□ **lixiviation** /-áyshən/ *n.* [L *lixivius* made into lye f. *lix* lye]

lizard /lízərd/ *n.* any reptile of the suborder Lacertilia, having usu. a long body and tail, four legs, movable eyelids, and a rough or scaly hide. [ME f. OF *lesard(e)* f. L *lacertus*]

LL *abbr.* **1** Late Latin. **2** Low Latin. **3** lower left.

ll. *abbr.* lines.

'll *v.* (usu. after pronouns) shall; will (*I'll*; *that'll*). [abbr.]

llama /laámə, yaá-/ *n.* **1 a** a S. American ruminant, *Lama glama*, kept as a beast of burden and for its soft, woolly fleece. **2** the wool from this animal, or cloth made from it. [Sp., prob. f. Quechua]

llanero /laanáirō, yaa-/ *n.* (*pl.* **-os**) an inhabitant of the llanos. [Sp.]

llano /laánō, yaá-/ *n.* (*pl.* **-os**) a treeless grassy plain or steppe, esp. in S. America. [Sp. f. L *planum* plain]
■ see PLAIN[1] *n.* 1.

LLB *abbr.* Bachelor of Laws. [L *legum baccalaureus*]

LLD *abbr.* Doctor of Laws. [L *legum doctor*]

LLM *abbr.* Master of Laws. [L *legum magister*]

Lloyd's /loydz/ *n.* an incorporated society of insurance underwriters in London. □ **Lloyd's List** a daily publication devoted to shipping news. **Lloyd's Register 1** an annual alphabetical list of ships assigned to various classes. **2** a society that produces this. [after the orig. meeting in a coffeehouse established in 1688 by Edward *Lloyd*]

LM *abbr.* **1** long meter. **2** lunar module.

lm *abbr.* lumen(s).

ln *abbr.* natural logarithm. [mod.L *logarithmus naturalis*]

lo /lō/ *int. archaic* calling attention to an amazing sight. □ **lo and behold** *joc.* a formula introducing a surprising or unexpected fact. [OE *lā* int. of surprise, etc., & ME *lō* = *lōke* LOOK]

loach /lōch/ *n.* any small edible freshwater fish of the family Cobitidae. [ME f. OF *loche*, of unkn. orig.]

load /lōd/ *n.* & *v.* ● *n.* **1 a** what is carried or is to be carried; a burden. **b** an amount usu. or actually carried (often in *comb.*: *a busload of tourists*; *a truckload of bricks*). **2** a unit of measure or weight of certain substances. **3** a burden or commitment of work, responsibility, care, grief, etc. **4** (in *pl.*; often foll. by *of*) *colloq.* plenty; a lot. **5 a** *Electr.* the amount of power supplied by a generating system at any given time. **b** *Electronics* an impedance or circuit that receives or develops the output of a transistor or other device. **6** the weight

or force borne by the supporting part of a structure. **7** a material object or force acting as a weight or clog. **8** the resistance of machinery to motive power. ● *v.* **1** *tr.* **a** put a load on or aboard (a person, vehicle, ship, etc.). **b** place (a load or cargo) aboard a ship, on a vehicle, etc. **2** *intr.* (often foll. by *up*) (of a ship, vehicle, or person) take a load aboard, pick up a load. **3** *tr.* (often foll. by *with*) **a** add weight to; be a weight or burden upon. **b** oppress. **4** *tr.* strain the bearing-capacity of (*a table loaded with food*). **5** *tr.* (also **load up**) (foll. by *with*) **a** supply overwhelmingly (*loaded us with work*). **b** assail overwhelmingly (*loaded us with abuse*). **6** *tr.* charge (a firearm) with ammunition. **7** *tr.* insert (the required operating medium) in a device, e.g., film in a camera, magnetic tape in a tape recorder, a program into a computer, etc. **8** *tr.* add an extra charge to (an insurance premium) in the case of a poorer risk. **9** *tr.* **a** weight with lead. **b** give a bias to (dice, a roulette wheel, etc.) with weights. □ **get a load of** *sl.* listen attentively to; notice. **load displacement** the displacement of a ship when laden. **load line** a Plimsoll line. [OE *lād* way, journey, conveyance, f. Gmc: rel. to LEAD[1], LODE]
■ *n.* **1** cargo, consignment, shipment, quantity; see also LOAD *n.* 2, 6, 7 below. **2, 6, 7** weight, charge, encumbrance, burden; impediment, *archaic* clog. **3** burden, pressure, strain, stress, commitment, imposition, responsibility, encumbrance, millstone, cross, albatross; care, anxiety, worry, trouble, hardship, trial. **4** (*loads*) see LOT *n.* 1. ● *v.* **1, 2** lade, charge, freight; fill, pack, stuff, cram, jam; stack, pile, heap, stow, install. **3–5** burden, weight, encumber, saddle, lumber; overload, overwhelm, oppress, crush, tax, strain; see also LOAD *v.* 1 above. **6** charge, arm, prime. □ **get a load of** listen to, pay attention to, lend an ear to, hear, take note of, notice, look at, watch, observe, examine, study, view, inspect, *colloq.* check out.

loaded /lōdid/ *adj.* **1** bearing or carrying a load. **2** *sl.* **a** wealthy. **b** drunk. **c** drugged. **3** (of dice, etc.) weighted or given a bias. **4** (of a question or statement) charged with some hidden or improper implication.
■ **1** laden, charged, filled, filled (up); packed, stuffed, crammed, cram-full, chockablock, chock-full; burdened, weighted (down), overloaded; (*of a gun*) primed, armed, ready. **2 a** see WEALTHY. **b** see DRUNK *adj.* 1. **c** drugged, intoxicated, stupefied, euphoric, *colloq.* turned on, tripping, on a trip, *sl.* stoned, spaced (out), (far) gone. **3** weighted, biased; crooked. **4** tricky, trick, insidious, devious; charged, pregnant; improper, misleading, disingenuous; biased, prejudiced, prejudicial.

loader /lōdər/ *n.* **1** a loading machine. **2** (in *comb.*) a gun, machine, truck, etc., loaded in a specified way (*breechloader*). **3** an attendant who loads guns at a shoot. □□ **-loading** *adj.* (in *comb.*) (in sense 2).

loading /lōding/ *n.* **1** *Electr.* the maximum current or power taken by an appliance. **2** an increase in an insurance premium due to a factor increasing the risk involved (see LOAD *v.* 8).

loadstar var. of LODESTAR.

loadstone var. of LODESTONE.

loaf[1] /lōf/ *n.* (*pl.* **loaves** /lōvz/) **1** a portion of baked bread, usu. of a standard size or shape. **2** (often in *comb.*) a quantity of other food formed into a particular shape (*sugarloaf*; *meat loaf*). **3** *Brit. sl.* the head, esp. as a source of common sense (*use your loaf*). [OE *hlāf* f. Gmc]
■ **1** bun, roll, bagel, pone, baguette, pita, twist, esp. *Austral.* & *NZ* damper, *Brit.* bap, *Ind.* chapati, *Sc.* & *No. of Engl.* bannock. **2** brick, cake, roll, block, chunk, hunk, slab, lump, cube, square.

loaf[2] /lōf/ *v.* & *n.* ● *v.* **1** *intr.* (often foll. by *about*, *around*) spend time idly; hang about. **2** *tr.* (foll. by *away*) waste (time) idly (*loafed away the morning*). **3** *intr.* saunter. ● *n.* an act or spell of loafing. [prob. a back-form. f. LOAFER]

■ *v.* **1** idle, lounge (about *or* around), hang about *or* around, loiter, loll, laze (about *or* around), mess about *or* around, potter (about *or* around), kill time, take it easy, *sl.* goof off *or* around, bum (about *or* around), lollygag, *Austral.* & *NZ sl.* bludge, *Brit. sl.* skive, *Brit. sl.* esp. *Mil.* scrimshank. **2** (*loaf away*) waste, fritter away, idle away, while away, kill; pass, spend. **3** see SAUNTER *v.*

loafer /lṓfər/ *n.* **1** an idle person. **2** (**Loafer**) *propr.* a leather shoe shaped like a moccasin with a flat heel. [perh. f. G *Landläufer* vagabond]

■ **1** idler, layabout, lounger, slacker, shirker, *flâneur*, drone, fainéant, sluggard, ne'er-do-well, good-for-nothing, wastrel, *archaic* slugabed, *colloq.* lazybones, lounge lizard, esp. *Brit. colloq.* waster, *sl.* bum, bummer, gold brick, *Austral.* & *NZ sl.* bludger, *Brit. sl.* skiver, *Brit. sl.* esp. *Mil.* scrimshanker.

loam /lōm/ *n.* **1** a fertile soil of clay and sand containing decayed vegetable matter. **2** a paste of clay and water with sand, chopped straw, etc., used in making bricks, plastering, etc. □□ **loamy** *adj.* **loaminess** *n.* [OE *lām* f. WG, rel. to LIME[1]]

■ **1** see SOIL[1] 1.

loan[1] /lōn/ *n.* & *v.* ● *n.* **1** something lent, esp. a sum of money to be returned normally with interest. **2** the act of lending or state of being lent. **3** a word, custom, etc., adopted by one people from another. ● *v.tr.* lend (esp. money). □ **loan shark** *colloq.* a person who lends money at exorbitant rates of interest. **loan translation** an expression adopted by one language from another in a more or less literally translated form. **on loan** acquired or given as a loan. □□ **loanable** *adj.* **loanee** /lōnée/ *n.* **loaner** *n.* [ME *lan* f. ON *lán* f. Gmc: cf. LEND]

■ *n.* **1, 2** advance, allowance, credit, accommodation; hire, rental, lease, charter; mortgage; imprest. ● *v.* lend, advance, allow, credit, put out; rent (out), hire (out), lease (out), charter (out).

loan[2] /lōn/ *n.* (also **loaning** /lṓning/) *Sc.* **1** a lane. **2** an open place where cows are milked. [ME var. of LANE]

loanword /lṓnwərd/ *n.* a word adopted, usu. with little modification, from a foreign language.

loath /lōth, lōth/ *predic.adj.* (also esp. *Brit.* **loth**) (usu. foll. by *to* + infin.) disinclined; reluctant; unwilling (*was loath to admit it*). □ **nothing loath** *adj.* quite willing. [OE *lāth* f. Gmc]

■ disinclined, reluctant, unwilling, indisposed, ill-disposed, resistant, averse, opposed.

loathe /lōth/ *v.tr.* regard with disgust; abominate; detest. □□ **loather** *n.* **loathing** *n.* [OE *lāthian* f. Gmc, rel. to LOATH]

■ detest, hate, dislike, abhor, abominate, execrate; regard *or* view with horror *or* repugnance *or* disgust, despise, shudder at, shrink *or* recoil from, have no use for, *literary* contemn. □□ **loathing** detestation, hatred, abhorrence, abomination, execration; horror, repugnance, revulsion, disgust, distaste, aversion, antipathy, phobia.

loathsome /lṓthsəm, lṓth-/ *adj.* arousing hatred or disgust; offensive; repulsive. □□ **loathsomely** *adv.* **loathsomeness** *n.* [ME f. *loath* disgust f. LOATHE]

■ detestable, abhorrent, odious, hateful, execrable, abominable, despicable, damnable, contemptible; obnoxious, offensive, horrible, disgusting, abhorrent, hideous, repellent, repulsive, repugnant, nauseating, sickening, revolting, nasty, ghastly, gruesome, *literary* noisome; vile, foul, rank.

loaves *pl.* of LOAF[1].

lob /lob/ *v.* & *n.* ● *v.tr.* (**lobbed, lobbing**) **1** hit or throw (a ball or missile, etc.) slowly or in a high arc. **2** send (an opponent) a lobbed ball. ● *n.* **1** a ball struck in a high arc. **2** a stroke producing this result. [earlier as noun, prob. f. LG or Du.]

■ *v.* **1** loft, toss; pitch, shy, heave, fling, hurl, throw,

launch, cast, propel, bowl, *colloq.* chuck, sling. ● *n.* **2** loft, toss; pitch, shy, heave, fling, throw; hit, shot, *colloq.* swipe.

lobar /lṓbər, -baar/ *adj.* **1** of the lungs (*lobar pneumonia*). **2** of, relating to, or affecting a lobe.

lobate /lṓbayt/ *adj.* *Biol.* having a lobe or lobes. □□ **lobation** /-áyshən/ *n.*

lobby /lóbee/ *n.* & *v.* ● *n.* (*pl.* **-ies**) **1** a porch, anteroom, entrance hall, or corridor. **2** *Brit.* **a** (in the House of Commons) a large hall used esp. for interviews between members of Parliament and the public. **b** (also **division lobby**) each of two corridors to which members of Parliament retire to vote. **3** a body of persons seeking to influence legislators on behalf of a particular interest (*the tobacco lobby*). **4** (prec. by *the*) (in the UK) a group of journalists who receive unattributable briefings from the government (*lobby correspondent*). ● *v.* (**-ies, -ied**) **1** *tr.* solicit the support of (an influential person). **2** *tr.* (of members of the public) seek to influence (the members of a legislature). **3** *intr.* frequent a parliamentary lobby. **4** *tr.* (foll. by *through*) get (a bill, etc.) through a legislature, by interviews, etc., in the lobby. □□ **lobbyer** *n.* **lobbyism** *n.* **lobbyist** *n.* [med.L *lobia, lobium* LODGE]

■ *n.* **1** porch, anteroom, foyer, (entrance) hall, vestibule, entry; reception (room), waiting room; corridor, hall, hallway, passage; *Archit.* tambour. **3** pressure group; faction, party, fraternity, group, interest; crusade.
● *v.* **1, 2** petition, appeal to, call on *or* upon, solicit, importune, push, press, pressure, pressurize, urge; persuade, influence, sway.

lobe /lōb/ *n.* **1** a roundish and flattish projecting or pendulous part, often each of two or more such parts divided by a fissure (*lobes of the brain*). **2** = EARLOBE. □□ **lobed** *adj.* **lobeless** *adj.* [LL f. Gk *lobos* lobe, pod]

lobectomy /lōbéktəmee/ *n.* (*pl.* **-ies**) *Surgery* the excision of a lobe of an organ such as the thyroid gland, lung, etc.

lobelia /lōbéelyə/ *n.* any plant of the genus *Lobelia*, with blue, scarlet, white, or purple flowers having a deeply cleft corolla. [M. de *Lobel*, Flemish botanist in England d. 1616]

lobotomy /ləbótəmee/ *n.* (*pl.* **-ies**) *Surgery* see *prefrontal lobotomy*. [LOBE + -TOMY]

lobscouse /lóbskows/ *n.* a sailor's dish of meat stewed with vegetables and ship's biscuit. [18th c.: orig. unkn.: cf. Du. *lapskous*, Da., Norw., G *Lapskaus*]

lobster /lóbstər/ *n.* & *v.* ● *n.* **1** any large marine crustacean of the family Nephropidae, with stalked eyes and two pincerlike claws as the first pair of ten limbs. **2** its flesh as food. ● *v.intr.* catch lobsters. □ **lobster pot** a basket in which lobsters are trapped. **lobster thermidor** /thérmidawr/ a mixture of lobster meat, mushrooms, cream, egg yolks, and sherry, cooked in a lobster shell. [OE *lopustre*, corrupt. of L *locusta* crustacean, locust: *thermidor* f. the name of the 11th month of the Fr. revolutionary calendar]

lobule /lóbyōōl/ *n.* a small lobe. □□ **lobular** *adj.* **lobulate** /-layt/ *adj.* [LOBE]

lobworm /lóbwərm/ *n.* **1** a large earthworm used as fishing bait. **2** = LUGWORM. [LOB in obs. sense 'pendulous object']

local /lṓkəl/ *adj.* & *n.* ● *adj.* **1** belonging to or existing in a particular place or places. **2** peculiar to or only encountered in a particular place or places. **3** of or belonging to the neighborhood (*the local doctor*). **4** of or affecting a part and not the whole, esp. of the body (*local pain; a local anesthetic*). **5** in regard to place. ● *n.* a local person or thing, esp.: **1** an inhabitant of a particular place regarded with reference to that place. **2** a local train, bus, etc. **3** (often prec. by *the*) *Brit. colloq.* a local pub; a local pub. **4** a local anesthetic. **4** a local branch of a labor union. □ **local area network** *Computing* a system for linking telecommunications or computer equipment in several offices, a group of buildings, etc. ¶ Abbr.: **LAN**. **local color** characteristics distinctive of a place, esp. as depicted in literature, film, etc. **local government** a system of administration of a county, etc., by the elected representatives of those who live there. **local option** a system whereby the inhabitants of a district may prohibit the sale of alcoholic liquor there. **local preacher** a Methodist lay

person authorized to conduct services in a particular circuit.
local time 1 time measured from the sun's transit over the meridian of a place. **2** the time as reckoned in a particular place, esp. with reference to an event recorded there. **local train** a train stopping at all the stations on its route. □□ **locally** adv. **localness** n. [ME f. OF f. LL localis f. L locus place]

■ adj. **1–3** indigenous, native, endemic; topical; regional, territorial, provincial, district, state, county, departmental, divisional, municipal, city, urban, town, village, neighborhood; neighboring, nearby. **4** localized, peculiar, particular, specific; restricted, limited. ● n. **1** resident, native, national, (fellow) citizen, townsman, townswoman, poet. denizen.

locale /lōkál/ n. a scene or locality, esp. with reference to an event or occurrence taking place there. [F local (n.) (as LOCAL), respelled to indicate stress: cf. MORALE]

■ scene, site, setting, locality, neighborhood, vicinity, environment, district, quarter; situation, location, spot, place, venue.

localism /lṓkəlizəm/ n. **1** preference for what is local. **2** a local idiom, custom, etc. **3 a** attachment to a place. **b** a limitation of ideas, etc., resulting from this.

■ **2** see PROVINCIALISM 2.

locality /lōkálitee/ n. (pl. **-ies**) **1** a district or neighborhood. **2** the site or scene of something, esp. in relation to its surroundings. **3** the position of a thing; the place where it is. [F localité or LL localitas (as LOCAL)]

■ **1** see NEIGHBORHOOD 1. **2, 3** see SPOT n. 2a, b.

localize /lṓkəlīz/ v.tr. **1** restrict or assign to a particular place. **2** invest with the characteristics of a particular place. **3** attach to districts; decentralize. □□ **localizable** adj. **localization** n.

locate /lṓkayt, lōkáyt/ v. **1** tr. discover the exact place or position of (locate the enemy's camp). **2** tr. establish or install in a place or in its proper place. **3** tr. state the locality of. **4** tr. (in passive) be situated. **5** intr. (often foll. by in) take up residence or business (in a place). □□ **locatable** adj. **locater, locator** n. [L locare locat- f. locus place]

■ **1, 3** discover, detect, find out, identify, determine, ascertain, pinpoint, track down, uncover, unearth, sniff or smoke or search out, lay or put one's hands on, point to, colloq. put one's finger on, Brit. sl. suss out; find, come across, chance or hit upon, turn up. **2, 4** establish, place, put, position, situate, site, set (up), fix, install, mount, lay, station, perch, settle, base. **5** see SETTLE[1] 1, 2a, b.

location /lōkáyshən/ n. **1** a particular place; the place or position in which a person or thing is. **2** the act of locating or process of being located. **3** an actual place or natural setting featured in a motion picture, etc., as distinct from a simulation in a studio (filmed entirely on location). [L locatio (as LOCATE)]

■ **1** place, position, spot, situation, site, scene, setting, locale, station, address, venue. **2** placement, establishment, orientation, situation, installation, mounting, settlement; discovery, detection, identification.

locative /lṓkətiv/ n. & adj. Gram. ● n. the case of nouns, pronouns, and adjectives, expressing location. ● adj. of or in the locative. [formed as LOCATE + -IVE, after vocative]

loc. cit. /lók sít/ abbr. in the passage already cited. [L loco citato]

loch /lok, lokh/ n. Sc. **1** a lake. **2** an arm of the sea, esp. when narrow or partially landlocked. [ME f. Gael.]

lochia /lókeeə, ló-/ n. a discharge from the uterus after childbirth. □□ **lochial** adj. [mod.L f. Gk lokhia neut. pl. of lokhios of childbirth]

loci pl. of LOCUS.

loci classici pl. of LOCUS CLASSICUS.

lock[1] /lok/ n. & v. ● n. **1** a mechanism for fastening a door, lid, etc., with a bolt that requires a key of a particular shape, or a combination of movements (see combination lock), to work it. **2** a confined section of a canal or river where the water level can be changed for raising and lowering boats

between adjacent sections by the use of gates and sluices. **3 a** the turning of the front wheels of a vehicle to change its direction of motion. **b** (in full **full lock**) the maximum extent of this. **4** an interlocked or jammed state. **5** Wrestling a hold that keeps an opponent's limb fixed. **6** an appliance to keep a wheel from revolving or slewing. **7** a mechanism for exploding the charge of a gun. **8** = airlock 2. ● v. **1 a** tr. fasten with a lock. **b** tr. (foll. by up) shut and secure (esp. a building) by locking. **c** intr. (of a door, window, box, etc.) have the means of being locked. **2** tr. (foll. by up, in, into) enclose (a person or thing) by locking or as if by locking. **3** tr. (often foll. by up, away) store or allocate inaccessibly (capital locked up in land). **4** tr. (foll. by in) hold fast (in sleep or enchantment, etc.). **5** tr. (usu. in passive) (of land, hills, etc.) enclose. **6** tr. & intr. make or become rigidly fixed or immovable. **7** intr. & tr. become or cause to become jammed or caught. **8** tr. (often in passive; foll. by in) entangle in an embrace or struggle. **9** tr. provide (a canal, etc.) with locks. **10** tr. (foll. by up, down) convey (a boat) through a lock. **11** intr. go through a lock on a canal, etc. □ **lock-knit** knitted with an interlocking stitch. **lock on to** locate or cause to locate by radar, etc., and then track. **lock out 1** keep (a person) out by locking the door. **2** (of an employer) submit (employees) to a lockout. **lock, stock, and barrel** n. the whole of a thing. ● adv. completely. **under lock and key** securely locked up. □□ **lockable** adj. **lockless** adj. [OE loc f. Gmc]

■ n. **1** padlock, deadlock, hasp, bolt, latch, bar, hook, clasp, catch, fastening; keyhole, mortise, selvage, tumbler. ● v. **1a, b** padlock, bolt, secure, fasten, seal, bar, latch; shut, close. **2** shut up or in or away, enclose, put away, put or keep under lock and key; imprison, jail, incarcerate, detain, remand, put or keep behind bars, put in or throw into irons, poet. prison, sl. put inside. **3** sink, put away, tie up, commit; invest. **4, 8** hold (fast), retain, secure, imprison, enchain; clasp, grip, seize, pin, engage, clutch, clench, entangle, entwine, enfold. **5** see ENCLOSE 1, 6. **6** jam, stick, seize (up), freeze, solidify; immobilize, fix. **7** catch, snag, lodge; see also LOCK[1] v. 6 above. □ **lock on to** locate, pinpoint, identify, fix; track, follow, pursue, keep track of, colloq. keep tabs or a tab on. **lock out 1** exclude, shut out, close out, keep out, bar, debar. **lock, stock, and barrel** (adv.) see completely (COMPLETE).

lock[2] /lok/ n. **1 a** a portion of hair that coils or hangs together. **b** (in pl.) the hair of the head. **2** a tuft of wool or cotton. □□ **-locked** adj. (in comb.). [OE locc f. Gmc]

■ **1 a** tress, curl, ringlet, coil, strand; forelock, cowlick, lovelock. **b** (locks) hair, tresses, colloq. mane. **2** tuft, aigrette, floccus, flock; tag.

lockage /lókij/ n. **1** the amount of rise and fall effected by canal locks. **2** a toll for the use of a lock. **3** the construction or use of locks. **4** locks collectively; the aggregate of locks constructed.

locker /lókər/ n. **1** a small lockable cupboard or compartment, esp. each of several for public use. **2** Naut. a chest or compartment for clothes, stores, ammunition, etc. **3** a person or thing that locks. □ **locker room** a room containing lockers (in sense 1), esp. in a sports facility.

■ **1** see COMPARTMENT n. 1. **2** see TRUNK 4.

locket /lókit/ n. **1** a small ornamental case holding a portrait, lock of hair, etc., and usu. hung from the neck. **2** a metal plate or band on a scabbard. [OF locquet dimin. of loc latch, lock, f. WG (as LOCK[1])]

■ **1** see PENDANT.

lockfast /lókfast/ adj. Sc. secured with a lock.

lockjaw /lókjaw/ n. = TRISMUS. ¶ Not in technical use.

lockkeeper /lók-keepər/ n. a keeper of a lock on a river or canal.

/.../ pronunciation	● part of speech
□ phrases, idioms, and compounds	
□□ derivatives	■ synonym section
cross-references appear in SMALL CAPITALS or italics	

locknut /lóknut/ *n. Mech.* a nut screwed down on another to keep it tight.

lockout /lókowt/ *n.* the exclusion of employees by their employer from their place of work until certain terms are agreed to.
■ see EXCLUSION.

locksman /lóksmən/ *n.* (*pl.* **-men**) a lockkeeper.

locksmith /lóksmith/ *n.* a maker and repairer of locks.

lockstep /lókstep/ *n.* marching with each person as close as possible to the one in front.

lockstitch /lókstich/ *n.* a stitch made by a sewing machine by firmly locking together two threads or stitches.

lockup /lókup/ *n. & adj.* ● *n.* **1** a house or room for the temporary detention of prisoners. **2** *Brit.* nonresidential premises, etc., that can be locked up, esp. a small store or storehouse. **3 a** the locking up of premises for the night. **b** the time of doing this. **4 a** the unrealizable state of invested capital. **b** an amount of capital locked up. ● *attrib.adj. Brit.* that can be locked up (*lockup shop*).
■ **1** see PRISON *n.* 1.

loco¹ /lókō/ *adj. & n.* ● *adj. sl.* crazy. ● *n.* (*pl.* **-os** or **-oes**) **1** *colloq.* = LOCOWEED. **2** *sl.* a crazy person; maniac.
■ *adj.* see CRAZY 1. ● *n.* **2** see MANIAC.

loco² /lókō/ *n.* (*pl.* **-os**) esp. *Brit. colloq.* a locomotive engine. [abbr.]

locomotion /lókəmōshən/ *n.* **1** motion or the power of motion from one place to another. **2** travel; a means of traveling, esp. an artificial one. [L *loco* ablat. of *locus* place + *motio* MOTION]

locomotive /lókəmōtiv/ *n. & adj.* ● *n.* (in full **locomotive engine**) an engine powered by steam, diesel fuel, or electricity, used for pulling trains. ● *adj.* **1** of or relating to or effecting locomotion (*locomotive power*). **2** having the power of or given to locomotion; not stationary.

locomotor /lókəmōtər/ *adj.* of or relating to locomotion. [LOCOMOTION + MOTOR]

locoweed /lókōweed/ *n.* a poisonous leguminous plant of the southwestern US, causing brain disease in cattle eating it. [Sp., = insane]

loculus /lókyələs/ *n.* (*pl.* **loculi** /-lī/) *Zool., Anat., & Bot.* each of a number of small separate cavities. □□ **locular** *adj.* [L, dimin. of *locus*: see LOCUS]

locum /lókəm/ *n. colloq.* = LOCUM TENENS. [abbr.]

locum tenens /teénenz, tén-/ *n.* (*pl.* **locum tenentes** /tinénteez/) esp. *Brit.* a deputy acting esp. for a clergyman or doctor. □□ **locum tenency** /ténənsee/ *n.* [med.L, one holding a place: see LOCUS, TENANT]
■ see SUBSTITUTE *n.* 1a.

locus /lókəs/ *n.* (*pl.* **loci** /lósī, -kee, -kī/) **1** a position or point, esp. in a text, treatise, etc. **2** *Math.* a curve, etc., formed by all the points satisfying a particular equation of the relation between coordinates, or by a point, line, or surface moving according to mathematically defined conditions. **3** *Biol.* the position of a gene, mutation, etc., on a chromosome. [L, = place]
■ **1** see PLACE *n.* 1a, b.

locus classicus /lókəs-klásikəs/ *n.* (*pl.* **loci classici** /klásisī, -kī/) the best known or most authoritative passage on a subject. [L]

locus standi /lókəs-stándī/ *n.* a recognized or identifiable (esp. legal) status.

locust /lókəst/ *n.* **1** any of various African and Asian grasshoppers of the family Acrididae, migrating in swarms and destroying vegetation. **2** a cicada. **3** (in full **locust bean**) a carob. **4** (in full **locust tree**) **a** a carob tree. **b** = ACACIA 2. **c** = KOWHAI. □ **locust-bird** (or **-eater**) any of various birds feeding on locusts. [ME f. OF *locuste* f. L *locusta* lobster, locust]

locution /lókyōōshən/ *n.* **1** a word or phrase, esp. considered in regard to style or idiom. **2** style of speech. [ME f. OF *locution* or L *locutio* f. *loqui locut-* speak]
■ **1** see PHRASE *n.* 1.

lode /lōd/ *n.* a vein of metal ore. [var. of LOAD]
■ see VEIN *n.* 5.

loden /lṓd'n/ *n.* **1** a thick, waterproof woolen cloth. **2** the dark green color in which this is often made. [G]

lodestar /lṓdstaar/ *n.* (also **loadstar**) **1** a star that a ship, etc., is steered by, esp. the pole star. **2 a** a guiding principle. **b** an object of pursuit. [LODE in obs. sense 'way, journey' + STAR]
■ **1** see GUIDE *n.* 7. **2** see GUIDE *n.* 5.

lodestone /lṓdstōn/ *n.* (also **loadstone**) **1** magnetic oxide of iron, magnetite. **2 a** a piece of this used as a magnet. **b** a thing that attracts.

lodge /loj/ *n. & v.* ● *n.* **1** a small house at the gates of a park or on the grounds of a large house, occupied by a gatekeeper, gardener, etc. **2** any large house or hotel, esp. in a resort. **3** a house occupied in the hunting or shooting season. **4 a** a porter's room or quarters at the gate of a college or other large building. **b** the residence of a head of a college, esp. at Cambridge University in England. **5** the members or the meeting place of a branch of a society such as the Freemasons. **6** *Brit.* a local branch of a labor union. **7 a** beaver's or otter's lair. **8** a type of Native American dwelling; a wigwam. ● *v.* **1** *tr.* deposit in court or with an official a formal statement of (complaint or information). **2** *tr.* deposit (money, etc.) for security. **3** *tr.* bring forward (an objection, etc.). **4** *tr.* (foll. by *in, with*) place (power, etc.) in a person or group. **5** *tr. & intr.* make or become fixed or caught without further movement (*the bullet lodged in his brain; the tide lodges mud in the cavities*). **6** *tr.* **a** provide with sleeping quarters. **b** receive as a guest or inmate. **c** establish as a resident in a house or room or rooms. **7** *intr.* reside or live, esp. as a guest paying for accommodation. **8** *tr.* serve as a habitation for; contain. **9** *tr.* (in *passive*; foll. by *in*) be contained in. **10 a** *tr.* (of wind or rain) flatten (crops). **b** *intr.* (of crops) be flattened in this way. [ME *loge* f. OF *loge* arbor, hut, f. med.L *laubia, lobia* (see LOBBY) f. Gmc]
■ *n.* **1** gatehouse, cottage. **2** house, grange, villa; hotel. **3** house, cottage, chalet, cabin, esp. *Brit.* shooting box. **4 a** gatehouse, lodgings, quarters. **5, 6** branch, chapter, order, fellowship, wing, group, local, *Printing* chapel. ● *v.* **1** deposit, set *or* put *or* lay down, leave, consign, entrust, place, put; see also LODGE *v.* 3 below. **2** lay *or* put away, set aside, store, keep, save, bank, pay in, *colloq.* stash (away); see also LODGE *v.* 1 above. **3** bring (forward), make, put, lay, submit, set forth *or* out, register, enter, record, file. **4** see PLACE *v.* 1. **5** wedge, catch, become *or* get fixed, embed *or* become embedded; see also STICK² 6. **6** accommodate, board, put up, quarter, house, *Mil.* billet; shelter, harbor, take in. **7** reside, live, stay, stop, put up, room, *archaic* abide, *literary* dwell. **8** see HOUSE *v.* 1, CONTAIN 1. **9** see INCLUDE 4.

lodger /lójər/ *n.* a person receiving accommodation in another's house for payment.
■ see GUEST *n.* 2.

lodging /lójing/ *n.* **1** temporary accommodation (*a lodging for the night*). **2** (in *pl.*) esp. *Brit.* a room or rooms (other than in a hotel) rented for lodging in. **3** a dwelling place. **4** *Brit.* (in *pl.*) the residence of a head of a college at Oxford. □ **lodging house** a house in which lodgings are let.
■ **1** see ACCOMMODATION 1. **3** see HOUSE *n.* 1.

lodgment /lójmənt/ *n.* (also esp. *Brit.* **lodgement**) **1** the act of lodging or process of being lodged. **2** the depositing or a deposit of money. **3** an accumulation of matter intercepted in fall or transit. **4** a place of lodging. [F *logement* (as LODGE)]

lodicule /lódikyōōl/ *n. Bot.* a small green or white scale below the ovary of a grass flower. [L *lodicula* dimin. of *lodix* coverlet]

loess /lóis, les, lus/ *n.* a deposit of fine, light-colored windblown dust found esp. in the basins of large rivers and very fertile when irrigated. □□ **loessial** /lō-éseeəl, léseeəl, lús-/ *adj.* [G *Löss* f. Swiss G *lösch* loose f. *lösen* loosen]

loft /lawft, loft/ *n. & v.* ● *n.* **1** the space under the roof of a house, above the ceiling of the top floor; an attic. **2** a room over a stable, esp. for hay and straw. **3** a gallery in a church or hall (*organ loft*). **4** an upstairs room. **5** a pigeon house. **6** *Golf* **a** a backward slope in a club head. **b** a lofting stroke.

● *v.tr.* **1 a** send (a ball, etc.) high up. **b** clear (an obstacle) in this way. **2** (esp. as **lofted** *adj.*) give a loft to (a golf club). [OE f. ON *lopt* air, sky, upper room, f. Gmc (as LIFT)]

■ **n. 6 b** see LOB *n.* 2. ● *v.* **1 a** see LOB *v.* 1.

lofter /láwftər, lóf-/ *n.* a golf club for lofting the ball.

lofty /láwftee, lóf-/ *adj.* (**loftier, loftiest**) **1** *literary* (of things) of imposing height; towering; soaring (*lofty heights*). **2** consciously haughty, aloof, or dignified (*lofty contempt*). **3** exalted or noble; sublime (*lofty ideals*). □□ **loftily** *adv.* **loftiness** *n.* [ME f. LOFT as in *aloft*]

■ **1** tall, high, elevated, towering, soaring. **2** haughty, aloof, grand, grandiose, dignified, arrogant, disdainful, condescending, contemptuous, scornful, supercilious, contumelious, patronizing, superior, overweening, pompous, snobbish, *colloq.* high and mighty, snotty, snooty, uppity, esp. *Brit. colloq.* uppish, *Brit. sl.* toffee-nosed, *literary* vainglorious. **3** exalted, noble, majestic, imposing, grand, magnificent, regal, imperial, thoroughbred, aristocratic, magisterial, august, stately, venerable, distinguished, dignified, elevated, eminent, celebrated, honored, honorable, respected, renowned, famous, prominent, illustrious, notable, leading, preeminent, sublime, immortal. □□ **loftiness** see *arrogance* (ARROGANT), NOBILITY 1.

log[1] /lawg/ *n. & v.* ● *n.* **1** an unhewn piece of a felled tree, or a similar rough mass of wood, esp. cut for firewood. **2 a** a float attached to a line wound on a reel for gauging the speed of a ship. **b** any other apparatus for the same purpose. **3** a record of events occurring during and affecting the voyage of a ship or aircraft (including the rate of a ship's progress shown by a log: see sense 2). **4** any systematic record of things done, experienced, etc. **5** = LOGBOOK. ● *v.tr.* (**logged, logging**) **1 a** enter (the distance made or other details) in a ship's logbook. **b** enter details about (a person or event) in a logbook. **c** (of a ship) achieve (a certain distance). **2 a** enter (information) in a regular record. **b** attain (a cumulative total of time, etc., recorded in this way) (*logged 50 hours on the computer*). **3** cut into logs. □ **like a log 1** in a helpless or stunned state (*fell like a log under the left hook*). **2** without stirring (*slept like a log*). **log cabin** a hut built of logs. **log in** = *log on.* **log line** a line to which a ship's log (see sense 2 a in *n.*) is attached. **log on** (or **off**) go through the procedures to begin (or conclude) use of a computer system. [ME: orig. unkn.]

■ **n. 3–5** see RECORD *n.* 1. ● *v.* **1a, b, 2a** see RECORD *v.* 1.

log[2] /lawg, log/ *n.* a logarithm (esp. prefixed to a number or algebraic symbol whose logarithm is to be indicated). □ **log table** (usu. in *pl.*) a table of logarithms. [abbr.]

-log var. of -LOGUE.

logan /lógən/ *n.* (in full **logan stone**) a poised heavy stone rocking at a touch. [= *logging* f. dial. *log* to rock + STONE]

loganberry /lógənberee/ *n.* (*pl.* **-ies**) **1** a hybrid, *Rubus loganobaccus*, between a blackberry and a raspberry with dull red acid fruits. **2** the fruit of this plant. [J. H. *Logan*, Amer. horticulturalist d. 1928 + BERRY]

logarithm /láwgərithəm, lóg-/ *n.* **1** one of a series of arithmetic exponents tabulated to simplify computation by making it possible to use addition and subtraction instead of multiplication and division. **2** the power to which a fixed number or base (see BASE[1] 7) must be raised to produce a given number (*the logarithm of 1,000 to base 10 is 3*). ¶ Abbr.: **log.** □ **common logarithm** a logarithm to the base 10. **natural** (or **Napierian**) **logarithm** a logarithm to the base of the irrational number *e* (2.71828.....). ¶ Abbr.: **ln** or **log**ₑ. □□ **logarithmic** /-ríthmik/ *adj.* **logarithmically** *adv.* [mod.L *logarithmus* f. Gk *logos* reckoning, ratio + *arithmos* number]

logbook /láwgbŏŏk, lóg-/ *n.* a book containing a detailed record or log.

■ see JOURNAL 2.

loge /lōzh/ *n.* (in a theater, etc.) **1** the front section of the first balcony. **2** a private box or enclosure. [F]

-loger /ləjər/ *comb. form* forming nouns, = -LOGIST. [after *astrologer*]

logger /láwgər, lóg-/ *n.* a lumberjack.

loggerhead /láwgərhed, lóg-/ *n.* **1** an iron instrument with a ball at the end heated for melting tar, etc. **2** any of various large-headed animals, esp. a turtle (*Caretta caretta*) or shrike (*Lanius ludovicianus*). **3** *archaic* a blockhead or fool. □ **at loggerheads** (often foll. by *with*) disagreeing or disputing. [prob. f. dial. *logger* block of wood for hobbling a horse + HEAD]

■ □ **at loggerheads** see *at odds* (ODDS).

loggia /lójeeə, láwj-/ *n.* **1** an open-sided gallery or arcade. **2** an open-sided extension of a house. [It., = LODGE]

logging /láwging, lóg-/ *n.* the work of cutting and preparing forest timber.

logia *pl.* of LOGION.

logic /lójik/ *n.* **1 a** the science of reasoning, proof, thinking, or inference. **b** a particular scheme of or treatise on this. **2 a** a chain of reasoning (*I don't follow your logic*). **b** the correct or incorrect use of reasoning (*your logic is flawed*). **c** ability in reasoning (*argues with great learning and logic*). **d** arguments (*is not governed by logic*). **3 a** the inexorable force or compulsion of a thing (*the logic of events*). **b** the necessary consequence of (an argument, decision, etc.). **4 a** a system or set of principles underlying the arrangements of elements in a computer or electronic device so as to perform a specified task. **b** logical operations collectively. □□ **logician** /ləjíshən/ *n.* [ME f. OF *logique* f. LL *logica* f. Gk *logikē* (*tekhnē*) (art) of reason: see LOGOS]

■ **1, 2** reasoning, thinking, argument, rationale, *literary* ratiocination; deduction, inference; philosophy, *Philos.* dialectics; reasonableness, rationality, intelligence, sense, judgment, judiciousness.

-logic /lójik/ *comb. form* (also **-logical** /lójikəl/) forming adjectives corresponding esp. to nouns in *-logy* (*analogic; theological*). [from or after Gk *-logikos*: see -IC, -ICAL]

logical /lójikəl/ *adj.* **1** of logic or formal argument. **2** not contravening the laws of thought; correctly reasoned. **3** deducible or defensible on the grounds of consistency; reasonably to be believed or done. **4** capable of correct reasoning. □ **logical atomism** *Philos.* the theory that all propositions can be analyzed into simple independent elements. **logical necessity** the compulsion to believe that of which the opposite is inconceivable. **logical positivism** (or **empiricism**) a form of positivism in which symbolic logic is used and linguistic problems of meaning are emphasized. □□ **logicality** /-kálitee/ *n.* **logically** *adv.* [med.L *logicalis* f. LL *logica* (as LOGIC)]

■ **1** syllogistic, inferential, deductive, inductive. **2, 3** valid, sound, legitimate, justifiable, deducible, defensible, tenable, reasonable, rational, consistent, coherent; correct, right, indisputable, irrefutable, incontrovertible, incontestable, unquestionable, undeniable; plausible, credible, believable; sensible, intelligent, well-thought-out, practical. **4** see INTELLIGENT 1.

logion /lógeeon, -jee-/ *n.* (*pl.* **logia** /-geeə/) a saying attributed to Christ, esp. one not recorded in the canonical Gospels. [Gk, = oracle f. *logos* word]

-logist /ləjist/ *comb. form* forming nouns denoting a person skilled or involved in a branch of study, etc., with a name in *-logy* (*archaeologist; etymologist*).

logistics /ləjístiks/ *n.pl.* **1** the organization of moving, lodging, and supplying troops and equipment. **2** the detailed organization and implementation of a plan or operation. □□ **logistic** *adj.* **logistical** *adj.* **logistically** *adv.* [F *logistique* f. *loger* lodge]

logjam /láwgjam, lóg-/ *n.* **1** a crowded mass of logs in a river. **2** a deadlock.

logo /lógō/ *n.* (*pl.* **-os**) *colloq.* **1** = LOGOTYPE 2. **2** a motto, esp. of a commercial product, etc. [abbr.]

logogram /láwgəgram, lóg-/ *n.* a sign or character representing a word, esp. in shorthand. [Gk *logos* word + -GRAM]

/. . ./ **pronunciation**	● **part of speech**
□ **phrases, idioms, and compounds**	
□□ **derivatives**	■ **synonym section**
cross-references appear in SMALL CAPITALS or *italics*	

logomachy /ləgómməkee/ *n.* (*pl.* **-ies**) *literary* a dispute about words; controversy turning on merely verbal points. [Gk *logomakhia* f. *logos* word + *makhia* fighting]

logorrhea /láwgəréeə, lóg-/ *n.* (*Brit.* **logorrhoea**) an excessive flow of words, esp. in mental illness. □□ **logorrheic** *adj.* [Gk *logos* word + *rhoia* flow]

Logos /lōgŏs, lógos/ *n. Theol.* the Word of God, associated with the second person of the Trinity. [Gk, = word, reason]

logotype /láwgətip, lóg-/ *n.* **1** *Printing* a single piece of type that prints a word or group of separate letters. **2 a** an emblem or device used as the badge of an organization in display material. **b** *Printing* a single piece of type that prints this. [Gk *logos* word + TYPE]
 ■ **2 a** see EMBLEM 1, 3.

logrolling /láwgrōling, lóg-/ *n.* **1** *colloq.* the practice of exchanging favors, esp. (in politics) of exchanging votes to mutual benefit. **2** a sport in which two contestants stand on a floating log and try to knock each other off. □□ **logroll** *v.intr.* & *tr.* **logroller** *n.* [polit. sense f. phr. *you roll my log and I'll roll yours*]

-logue /lawg, log/ *comb. form* (also **-log**) **1** forming nouns denoting talk (*dialogue*) or compilation (*catalog*). **2** = -LOGIST (*ideologue*). [from or after F *-logue* f. Gk *-logos, -logon*]

logwood /láwgwŏod, lóg-/ *n.* **1** a W. Indian tree, *Haematoxylon campechianum.* **2** the wood of this, producing a substance used in dyeing.

-logy /ləjee/ *comb. form* forming nouns denoting: **1** (usu. as **-ology**) a subject of study or interest (*archaeology*; *zoology*). **2** a characteristic of speech or language (*tautology*). **3** discourse (*trilogy*). [F *-logie* or med.L *-logia* f. Gk (as LOGOS)]

loin /loyn/ *n.* **1** (in *pl.*) the part of the body on both sides of the spine between the false ribs and the hipbones. **2** a joint of meat that includes the loin vertebrae. [ME f. OF *loigne* ult. f. L *lumbus*]
 ■ **1** (*loins*) flanks, sides.

loincloth /lóynklawth, -kloth/ *n.* a cloth worn around the loins, esp. as a sole garment.

loiter /lóytər/ *v.* **1** *intr.* hang around; linger idly. **2** *intr.* travel indolently and with long pauses. **3** *tr.* (foll. by *away*) pass (time, etc.) in loitering. □□ **loiterer** *n.* [ME f. MDu. *loteren* wag about]
 ■ **1, 2** see *hang around* 1. □□ **loiterer** see LAGGARD *n.*

loll /lol/ *v.* **1** *intr.* stand, sit, or recline in a lazy attitude. **2** *intr.* (foll. by *out*) (of the tongue) hang out. **3** *tr.* (foll. by *out*) hang (one's tongue) out. **4** *tr.* let (one's head or limbs) rest lazily on something. □□ **loller** *n.* [ME: prob. imit.]
 ■ **1** see LOUNGE *v.* **4** see SLOUCH *v.* 1.

Lollard /lólərd/ *n.* any of the followers of the 14th-c. religious reformer John Wyclif. □□ **Lollardism** *n.* [MDu. *lollaerd* f. *lollen* mumble]

lollipop /lóleepop/ *n.* a large, usu. flat, round candy on a small stick. □ **lollipop man** (or **lady** or **woman**) *Brit. colloq.* an official using a circular sign on a stick to stop traffic for children to cross the road, esp. near a school; crossing guard. [perh. f. dial. *lolly* tongue + POP¹]

lollop /lóləp/ *v.intr. colloq.* **1** flop about. **2** esp. *Brit.* move or proceed in a lounging or ungainly way. [prob. f. LOLL, assoc. with TROLLOP]

lolly /lólee/ *n.* (*pl.* **-ies**) **1** *colloq.* **a** a lollipop. **b** *Austral.* a piece of candy. **c** (in full **ice lolly**) *Brit.* = POPSICLE. **2** *Brit. sl.* money. [abbr. of LOLLIPOP]

lollygag /lóleegag/ *v.intr.* (also **lallygag** /láleegag/) (**-gagged**, **-gagging**) *sl.* **1** loiter. **2** cuddle amorously. [20th c.: orig. unkn.]
 ■ **1** see LOAF² *v.* 1.

Lombard /lómbaard, -bərd, lúm-/ *n.* & *adj.* ● *n.* **1** a member of a Germanic people who conquered Italy in the 6th c. **2** a native of Lombardy in N. Italy. **3** the dialect of Lombardy. ● *adj.* of or relating to the Lombards or Lombardy. □□ **Lombardic** /-bárdik/ *adj.* [ME f. OF *lombard* or MDu. *lombaerd*, f. It. *lombardo* f. med.L *Longobardus* f. L *Langobardus* f. Gmc]

Lombardy poplar /lómberdee, lúm-/ *n.* a variety of poplar with an especially tall slender form.

loment /lṓment/ *n. Bot.* a kind of pod that breaks up when mature into one-seeded joints. □□ **lomentaceous** /-táyshəs/ *adj.* [L *lomentum* bean meal (orig. cosmetic) f. *lavare* wash]

Londoner /lúndənər/ *n.* a native or inhabitant of London.

London plane /lúndən/ *n.* a hybrid plane tree resistant to air pollution and therefore often planted in cities.

lone /lōn/ *attrib.adj.* **1** (of a person) solitary; without a companion or supporter. **2** (of a place) unfrequented; uninhabited; lonely. **3** *literary* feeling or causing to feel lonely. □ **lone hand 1** a hand played or a player playing against the rest in certain card games. **2** a person or action without allies. **lone wolf** a person who prefers to act alone. [ME, f. ALONE]
 ■ **1, 3** see LONELY 1. **2** see ISOLATED 1. □ **lone wolf** see *individualist* (INDIVIDUALISM).

lonely /lṓnlee/ *adj.* (**lonelier, loneliest**) **1** solitary; companionless; isolated. **2** (of a place) unfrequented. **3** sad because without friends or company. □ **lonely heart** a lonely person (in sense 3). □□ **loneliness** *n.*
 ■ **1** solitary, sole, lone, one, single, solo, alone, unaccompanied, companionless, lonesome; isolated, separate, cut off, detached. **2** unfrequented, uninhabited, deserted, desolate, sequestered, remote, out-of-the-way, cut off, secluded, isolated. **3** see FORLORN 1. □□ **loneliness** lonesomeness, aloneness, solitude, desolation, isolation, seclusion.

loner /lṓnər/ *n.* a person or animal that prefers not to associate with others.
 ■ see *individualist* (INDIVIDUALISM).

lonesome /lṓnsəm/ *adj.* **1** solitary; lonely. **2** feeling lonely or forlorn. **3** causing such a feeling. □ **by** (or **on**) **one's lonesome** all alone. □□ **lonesomely** *adv.* **lonesomeness** *n.*
 ■ **1** see LONELY 1. **2** see FORLORN 1. □ **by** (or **on**) **one's lonesome** see ALONE 1a.

long¹ /lawng, long/ *adj., n.,* & *adv.* ● *adj.* (**longer** /láwnggər, lóng-/; **longest** /láwnggist, lóng-/) **1** measuring much from end to end in space or time; not soon traversed or finished (*a long line*; *a long journey*; *a long time ago*). **2** (following a measurement) in length or duration (*three miles long*; *the vacation is two months long*). **3** relatively great in extent or duration (*a long meeting*). **4 a** consisting of a large number of items (*a long list*). **b** seemingly more than the stated amount; tedious; lengthy (*ten long miles*; *tired after a long day*). **5** of elongated shape. **6 a** lasting or reaching far back or forward in time (*a long friendship*). **b** (of a person's memory) retaining things for a long time. **7** far-reaching; acting at a distance; involving a great interval or difference. **8** *Phonet.* & *Prosody* of a vowel or syllable: **a** having the greater of the two recognized durations. **b** stressed. **c** (of a vowel in English) having the pronunciation shown in the name of the letter (as in *pile* and *cute*, which have a long *i* and *u*, as distinct from *pill* and *cut*) (cf. SHORT *adj.* 6). **9** (of odds or a chance) reflecting or representing a low level of probability. **10** *Stock Exch.* **a** (of stocks) bought in large quantities in advance, with the expectation of a rise in price. **b** (of a broker, etc.) buying, etc., on this basis. **11** (of a bill of exchange) maturing at a distant date. **12** (of a cold drink) large and refreshing. **13** *colloq.* (of a person) tall. **14** (foll. by *on*) *colloq.* well supplied with. ● *n.* **1** a long interval or period (*shall not be away for long*; *it will not take long*). **2** *Phonet.* a long syllable or vowel. **b** a mark indicating that a vowel is long. **3 a** a long-dated stock. **b** a person who buys this. ● *adv.* (**longer** /lónggər/; **longest** /lónggist/) **1** by or for a long time (*long before*; *long ago*; *long live the king!*). **2** (following nouns of duration) throughout a specified time (*all day long*). **3** (in *compar.*; with *neg.*) after an implied point of time (*shall not wait any longer*). □ **as** (or **so**) **long as 1** during the whole time that. **2** provided that; only if. **at long last** see LAST¹. **before long** fairly soon (*shall see you before long*). **be long** (often foll. by *pres. part.* or *in* + verbal noun) take a long time; be slow (*was long finding it out*; *the chance was long in coming*; *I won't be long*). **by a long chalk** *Brit.* see CHALK. **in the long run 1** over a long period. **2** eventually; finally. **long ago** in the distant past. **long-ago** *adj.* that is in the distant past. **the long and the short of it 1** all that can or need be said. **2** the eventual outcome. **long-chain** (of a molecule) containing a chain of many carbon atoms. **long-**

day (of a plant) needing a long daily period of light to cause flowering. **long-distance 1** (of a telephone call, public transport, etc.) between distant places. **2** (of a weather forecast) long-range. **long division** division of numbers with details of the calculations written down. **long dozen** thirteen; baker's dozen. **long-drawn** (or **-drawn-out**) prolonged, esp. unduly. **long face** a dismal or disappointed expression. **long-faced** with a long face. **long haul 1** the transport of goods or passengers over a long distance. **2** a prolonged effort or task. **long hundredweight** see HUNDREDWEIGHT. **long in the tooth** rather old (orig. of horses, from the recession of the gums with age). **long johns** colloq. = long underwear. **long jump** a track-and-field contest of jumping as far as possible along the ground in one leap. **long-life** Brit. (of consumable goods) treated to preserve freshness. **long-lived** having a long life; durable. **long measure** a measure of length (meters, miles, etc.). **long meter** Mus. **1** a hymn stanza of four lines with eight syllables each. **2** a quatrain of iambic tetrameters with alternate lines rhyming. **long-playing** (of a phonograph record) playing for about 20–30 minutes on each side. **long-range 1** (of a missile, etc.) having a long range. **2** of or relating to a period of time far into the future. **long-running** continuing for a long time. **long shot 1** a wild guess or venture. **2** a bet at long odds. **3** Cinematog. a shot including objects at a distance. **long-sleeved** with sleeves reaching to the wrist. **long-standing** that has long existed; not recent. **long-suffering** bearing provocation patiently. **long-sufferingly** in a long-suffering manner. **long suit 1** many cards of one suit in a hand (esp. more than 3 or 4 in a hand of 13). **2** a thing at which one excels. **long-term** occurring in or relating to a long period of time (*long-term plans*). **long ton** see TON[1]. **long tongue** loquacity. **long underwear** a warm, close-fitting undergarment with ankle-length legs and often a long-sleeved top. **long vacation** Brit. the summer vacation of law courts and universities. **long waist** a low or deep waist of a dress or body. **long wave** a radio wave of frequency less than 300 kHz. **not by a long shot** by no means. □□ **longish** adj. [OE *long, lang*]
- adj. **1, 3–5, 7** lengthy, great, big, extensive, considerable; extended, elongated, *Bot. & Zool.* elongate; prolonged, sustained, protracted, long-drawn-out, prolix, long-winded; endless, interminable, unending; numerous, innumerable; time-consuming; far-reaching, long-distance. **6 a** see LASTING. **b** retentive, tenacious, good, photographic. **13** see TALL adj. **1.** □ **as** (or **so**) **long as 1** while, all the time (that). **2** provided (that), on condition that, (only) if. **before long** see SOON 1. **in the long run 2** see *finally* (FINAL). **not by a long shot** no way, in *or* under no circumstances, by no (manner of) means, on no account, never, *Brit.* not by a long chalk.

long² /lawng, long/ v.intr. (foll. by *for* or *to* + infin.) have a strong wish or desire for. [OE *langian* seem long to]
- wish, crave, want, yearn, desire, hunger, fancy, covet, dream, hanker, colloq. yen; eat one's heart out.

long. abbr. longitude.

-long /lawng, long/ comb. form forming adjectives and adverbs: **1** for the duration of (*lifelong*). **2** = -LING² (*headlong*).

longboard /láwngbawrd, lóng-/ n. a type of surfboard.

longboat /láwngbōt, lóng-/ n. a sailing ship's largest boat.

longbow /láwngbō, lóng-/ n. a bow drawn by hand and shooting a long feathered arrow.

longcase /láwngkays, lóng-/ adj.attrib. □ **longcase clock** a grandfather clock.

longe /lonj/ n. & v. (also **lunge** /lunj/) ● n. **1** a long rope on which a horse is held and made to move in a circle around its trainer. **2** a circular exercise ground for training horses. ● v.tr. exercise (a horse) with or in a lunge. [F *longe, allonge* (as LUNGE¹)]

longeron /lónjərən/ n. a longitudinal member of a plane's fuselage. [F, = girder]

longevity /lonjévitee, lawn-/ n. long life. [LL *longaevitas* f. L *longus* long + *aevum* age]

longhair /láwnghair, lóng-/ n. a person characterized by the associations of long hair, esp. a hippie or intellectual.
- see HIPPIE, SCHOLAR 1.

longhand /láwnghand, lóng-/ n. ordinary handwriting (as opposed to shorthand or typing or printing).
- see WRITING 2.

longheaded /láwnghedid, lóng-/ adj. shrewd; far-seeing; sagacious. □□ **longheadedness** n.

longhorn /láwnghawrn, lóng-/ n. **1** one of a breed of cattle with long horns. **2** any beetle of the family Cerambycidae with long antennae.

longhouse /láwnghows, lóng-/ n. a tribal communal dwelling, esp. in N. America and the Far East.

longicorn /lónjikawrn/ n. a longhorn beetle. [mod.L *longicornis* f. L *longus* long + *cornu* horn]

longing /láwnging, lóng-/ n. & adj. ● n. a feeling of intense desire. ● adj. having or showing this feeling. □□ **longingly** adv.
- n. craving, wish, yearning, hunger, fancy, desire, hankering, colloq. yen. ● adj. see DESIROUS 2.

longitude /lónjitōod, -tyōod, láwn-/ n. **1** Geog. the angular distance east or west from a standard meridian such as Greenwich to the meridian of any place. ¶ Symb.: λ. **2** Astron. the angular distance of a celestial body north or south of the ecliptic measured along a great circle through the body and the poles of the ecliptic. [ME f. L *longitudo -dinis* f. *longus* long]

longitudinal /lónjitōod'nəl, -tyōod-, láwn-/ adj. **1** of or in length. **2** running lengthwise. **3** of longitude. □ **longitudinal wave** a wave vibrating in the direction of propagation. □□ **longitudinally** adv.

longship /láwngship, lóng-/ n. hist. a long, narrow warship with many rowers, used esp. by the Vikings.

longshore /láwngshawr, lóng-/ adj. **1** existing on or frequenting the shore. **2** directed along the shore. [*along shore*]

longshoreman /láwngshawrmən, lóng-/ n. (*pl.* **-men**) a person employed to load and unload ships.

longsighted /láwngsítid, lóng-/ adj. **1** = FARSIGHTED. **2** having imagination or foresight. □□ **longsightedly** adv. **longsightedness** n.
- **longsightedness** see FORESIGHT 1.

longtime /láwngtīm, lóng-/ adj. that has been such for a long time.

longueur /lawnGŏr, lóng-/ n. **1** a tedious passage in a book, etc. **2** a tedious stretch of time. [F, = length]

longways /láwngwayz, lóng-/ adv. (also **longwise** /-wīz/) = LENGTHWAYS.

long-winded /láwngwíndid, lóng-/ adj. **1** (of speech or writing) tediously lengthy. **2** able to run a long distance without rest. □□ **long-windedly** adv. **long-windedness** n.
- **1** see TEDIOUS. □□ **long-windedness** see TEDIUM, TAUTOLOGY.

lonicera /lənísərə/ n. **1** a dense evergreen shrub, *Lonicera nitidum*, much used as hedging. **2** = HONEYSUCKLE. [A. *Lonicerus*, Ger. botanist d. 1586]

loo¹ /lōo/ n. Brit. colloq. a toilet. [20th c.: orig. uncert.]

loo² /lōo/ n. **1** a card game with penalties paid to the pool. **2** this penalty. [abbr. of obs. *lanterloo* f. F *lanturlu*, refrain of a song]

loof var. of LUFF.

loofah /lōofə/ n. (also **luffa** /lúfə/) **1** a climbing gourdlike plant, *Luffa cylindrica*, native to Asia, producing edible marrowlike fruits. **2** the dried fibrous vascular system of this fruit used as a sponge. [Egypt. Arab. *lūfa*, the plant]

look /lōok/ v., n., & int. ● v. **1 a** intr. (often foll. by *at*) use one's sight; turn one's eyes in some direction. **b** tr. turn one's eyes on; contemplate or examine (*looked me in the eyes*). **2** intr. **a** make a visual or mental search (*I'll look in the morning*). **b** (foll. by *at*) consider; examine (*we must look at*

/.../ pronunciation	● part of speech
□ phrases, idioms, and compounds	
□□ derivatives	■ synonym section
cross-references appear in SMALL CAPITALS or *italics*	

the facts). **3** *intr.* (foll. by *for*) **a** search for. **b** hope or be on the watch for. **c** expect. **4** *intr.* inquire (*when one looks deeper*). **5** *intr.* have a specified appearance; seem (*look a fool*; *look foolish*). **6** *intr.* (foll. by *to*) **a** consider; take care of; be careful about (*look to the future*). **b** rely on (a person or thing) (*you can look to me for support*). **c** expect. **7** *intr.* (foll. by *into*) investigate or examine. **8** *tr.* (foll. by *what, where,* etc. + clause) ascertain or observe by sight (*look where we are*). **9** *intr.* (of a thing) face or be turned, or have or afford an outlook, in a specified direction. **10** *tr.* express, threaten, or show (an emotion, etc.) by one's looks. **11** *intr.* (foll. by *that* + clause) take care; make sure. **12** *intr.* (foll. by *to* + infin.) expect (*am looking to finish this today*). ● *n.* **1** an act of looking; the directing of the eyes to look at a thing or person; a glance (*a scornful look*). **2** (in *sing.* or *pl.*) the appearance of a face; a person's expression or personal aspect. **3** the (esp. characteristic) appearance of a thing (*the place has a European look*). ● *int.* (also **look here!**) calling attention, expressing a protest, etc. □ **look after 1** attend to; take care of. **2** follow with the eye. **3** seek for. **look one's age** appear to be as old as one really is. **look-alike** a person or thing closely resembling another (*an Elvis look-alike*). **look alive** (or **lively**) *colloq.* be brisk and alert. **look around 1** look in every or another direction. **2** examine the objects of interest in a place (*you must come and look around sometime*). **3** examine the possibilities, etc., with a view to deciding on a course of action. **look as if** suggest by appearance the belief that (*it looks as if he's gone*). **look back 1** (foll. by *on, upon, to*) turn one's thoughts to (something past). **2** (usu. with *neg.*) cease to progress (*since then we have never looked back*). **3** *Brit.* make a further visit later. **look before you leap** avoid precipitate action. **look daggers** see DAGGER. **look down on** (or **upon** or **look down one's nose at**) regard with contempt or a feeling of superiority. **look for trouble** see TROUBLE. **look forward to** await (an expected event) eagerly or with specified feelings. **look in** make a short visit or call. **look-in** *n. colloq.* **1** an informal call or visit. **2** esp. *Brit.* a chance of participation or success (*never gets a look-in*). **3** *Football* a short pass pattern in which the receiver runs diagonally toward the center of the field. **look a person in the eye** (or **eyes** or **face**) look directly and unashamedly at him or her. **look like 1** have the appearance of. **2** *Brit.* seem to be (*they look like winning*). **3** threaten or promise (*it looks like rain*). **4** indicate the presence of (*it looks like woodworm*). **look on 1** (often foll. by *as*) regard (*looks on you as a friend; looked on them with disfavor*). **2** be a spectator; avoid participation. **look oneself** appear in good health (esp. after illness, etc.). **look out 1** direct one's sight or put one's head out of a window, etc. **2** (often foll. by *for*) be vigilant or prepared. **3** (foll. by *on, over,* etc.) have or afford a specified outlook. **4** search for and produce (*shall look one out for you*). **look over 1** inspect or survey (*looked over the house*). **2** examine (a document, etc.), esp. cursorily (*I'll look it over*). **look-see** *colloq.* a survey or inspection. **look sharp** act promptly; make haste (orig. = keep strict watch). **look small** see SMALL. **look through 1** examine the contents of, esp. cursorily. **2** penetrate (a pretense or pretender) with insight. **3** ignore by pretending not to see (*I waved, but you just looked through me*). **look up 1** search for (esp. information in a book). **2** *colloq.* go to visit (a person) (*had intended to look them up*). **3** raise one's eyes (*looked up when I went in*). **4** improve, esp. in price, prosperity, or well-being (*things are looking up*). **look a person up and down** scrutinize a person keenly or contemptuously. **look up to** respect or venerate. **not like the look of** find alarming or suspicious. □□ **-looking** *adj.* (in *comb.*). [OE *lōcian* f. WG]
■ *v.* **1a, 2b** (*look at*) observe, regard, view, scan, stare at; survey, inspect, scrutinize, study, examine, consider, contemplate, pay attention to, look over, attend, notice; watch, witness, see, *literary* behold, *sl.* eyeball. **2a, 3a** search, take *or* have a look, hunt, seek. **3b, c** (*look for*) expect, hope for, aim at, *disp.* anticipate; seek, demand, require. **4, 7** inquire; examine, study, investigate, inspect, delve, dig, probe, scrutinize, explore, search, research, check. **5** seem (to be), appear

(to be). **6** (*look to*) **a** consider, attend to, pay attention to, mind, heed, take care of, see to, deal with. **b, c** count on, reckon on, rely on, bank on; aim to. **8** see, observe, check, find out, ascertain, work out. **9** face, point, be turned; turn. **10** show, display, exhibit, express; threaten. ● *n.* **1** gaze, glance, glare, stare. **2, 3** appearance, aspect, bearing, manner, air, demeanor; expression, countenance, face, *literary* mien. ● *int.* (**look here!**) hey, listen to me. □ **look after 1** care for, take care of, be responsible for, attend (to), mind, watch (over), serve, wait on, nurse, protect, guard. **look-alike** twin, double, exact *or* perfect likeness *or* match, clone, doppelgänger, (dead) ringer, *colloq.* spitting image, spit and image. **look down on** disdain, despise, scorn, disparage, spurn, sneer at, *colloq.* turn up one's nose at, *formal* derogate, *literary* contemn, misprize. **look forward to** anticipate, await, wait for; expect, count *or* rely on *or* upon. **look out 2** be careful, be alert, be vigilant, be prepared, be on the qui vive, be watchful, watch out, beware, pay attention, be on (one's) guard. **3** (*look out on* or *over*) have a view over, front on, overlook, give (out) on to. **look over 1** inspect, survey, examine. **2** look at, examine, scan, study, check (out *or* over), *sl.* eyeball. **look up 1** seek, search for, look for, hunt for, try to find, track *or* run down. **2** visit, call on, look *or* drop in on, get in touch with. **4** improve, get better, pick up, show improvement, progress, gain, make headway *or* progress. **look up to** admire, regard highly, respect, esteem, honor, revere, worship, idolize, venerate.

looker /lóŏkər/ *n.* **1** a person having a specified appearance (*a good-looker*). **2** *colloq.* an attractive person. □ **looker-on** a person who is a mere spectator.
■ **2** see BEAUTY 3. □□ **looker-on** see SPECTATOR.

looking glass /lóŏking glas/ *n.* a mirror for looking at oneself.
■ see MIRROR *n.* 1.

lookout /lóŏkowt/ *n.* **1** a watch or looking out (*on the lookout for bargains*). **2 a** a post of observation. **b** a person or party or boat stationed to keep watch. **3** a view over a landscape. **4** esp. *Brit.* a prospect of luck (*it's a bad lookout for them*). **5** *colloq.* a person's own concern.
■ **1** alert, qui vive; guard, watch. **2 b** guard, sentry, sentinel, watchman. **5** responsibility, worry, concern, problem, difficulty, *colloq.* headache.

loom[1] /lóŏm/ *n.* an apparatus for weaving yarn or thread into fabric. [ME *lōme* f. OE *gelōma* tool]

loom[2] /lóŏm/ *v. & n.* ● *v.intr.* (often foll. by *up*) **1** come into sight dimly, esp. as a vague and often magnified or threatening shape. **2** (of an event or prospect) be ominously close. ● *n.* a vague often exaggerated first appearance of land at sea, etc. [prob. f. LG or Du.: cf. E Fris. *lōmen* move slowly, MHG *lüemen* be weary]
■ *v.* **1** appear, emerge, take shape *or* form, materialize, surface, arise. **2** menace, impend, threaten, hang, hover.

loon /lóŏn/ *n.* **1** any aquatic diving bird of the family Gaviidae, with a long, slender body and a sharp bill; a diver. **2** *colloq.* a crazy person (cf. LOONY). [alt. f. *loom* f. ON *lómr*]
■ **2** see FOOL[1] *n.* 1.

loony /lóŏnee/ *n. & adj. sl.* ● *n.* (*pl.* **-ies**) a mad or silly person; a lunatic. ● *adj.* (**loonier, looniest**) crazy; silly. □ **loony bin** *sl.* a mental home or hospital. □□ **looniness** *n.* [abbr. of LUNATIC]
■ *n.* see MADMAN. ● *adj.* see CRAZY 1.

loop /lóŏp/ *n. & v.* ● *n.* **1 a** a figure produced by a curve, or a doubled thread, etc., that crosses itself. **b** anything forming this figure. **2** a similarly shaped attachment or ornament formed of cord or thread, etc., and fastened at the crossing. **3** a ring or curved piece of material as a handle, etc. **4** a contraceptive coil. **5** a railroad or telegraph line that diverges from a main line and joins it again. **6** a maneuver in which an airplane describes a vertical loop. **7** *Skating* a maneuver describing a curve that crosses itself, made on a single edge. **8** *Electr.* a complete circuit for a current. **9** an endless strip

of tape or film allowing continuous repetition. **10** *Computing* a programmed sequence of instructions that is repeated until or while a particular condition is satisfied. ● *v.* **1** *tr.* form (thread, etc.) into a loop or loops. **2** *tr.* enclose with or as with a loop. **3** *tr.* (often foll. by *up, back, together*) fasten or join with a loop or loops. **4** *intr.* **a** form a loop. **b** move in looplike patterns. **5** *intr.* (also **loop the loop**) *Aeron.* perform an aerobatic loop. [ME: orig. unkn.]
■ *n.* **1–3** hoop, noose, ring, circle, bow, eye, eyelet, coil, whorl. ● *v.* **1–4** twist, coil, wind, circle, curl, turn, ring, *Naut.* bend.

looper /loōpər/ *n.* **1** a caterpillar of the geometer moth, which progresses by arching itself into loops. **2** a device for making loops. **3** *Baseball* a shallow fly ball to the outfield.

loophole /loōp-hōl/ *n. & v.* ● *n.* **1** a means of evading a rule, etc., without infringing the letter of it. **2** a narrow vertical slit in a wall for shooting or looking through or to admit light or air. ● *v.tr.* make loopholes in (a wall, etc.). [ME *loop* in the same sense + HOLE]
■ *n.* **1** outlet, way out, escape, cop-out, esp. *Brit.* get-out, let-out; *colloq.* dodge; subterfuge, pretext, evasion, quibble.

loopy /loōpee/ *adj.* (**loopier, loopiest**) **1** *sl.* crazy. **2** having many loops.
■ **1** see MAD *adj.* 1.

loose /loōs/ *adj., n., & v.* ● *adj.* **1 a** not or no longer held by bonds or restraint. **b** (of an animal) not confined or tethered, etc. **2** detached or detachable from its place (*has come loose*). **3** not held together or contained or fixed. **4** not specially fastened or packaged (*loose papers; had her hair loose*). **5** hanging partly free (*a loose end*). **6** slack; relaxed; not tense or tight. **7** not compact or dense (*loose soil*). **8** (of language, concepts, etc.) inexact; conveying only the general sense. **9** (preceding an agent noun) doing the expressed action in a loose or careless manner (*a loose thinker*). **10** morally lax; dissolute (*loose living*). **11** (of the tongue) likely to speak indiscreetly. **12** (of the bowels) tending to diarrhea. **13** *Sports* **a** (of a ball) in play but not in any player's possession. **b** (of play, etc.) with the players not close together. **14** *Cricket* **a** (of bowling) inaccurately pitched. **b** (of fielding) careless or bungling. **15** (in *comb.*) loosely (*loose-flowing; loose-fitting*). ● *n.* **1** a state of freedom or unrestrainedness. **2** loose play in soccer (*in the loose*). **3** free expression. ● *v.tr.* **1** release; set free; free from constraint. **2** untie or undo (something that constrains). **3** detach from moorings. **4** relax (*loosed my hold on it*). **5** discharge (a bullet or arrow, etc.). □ **at loose ends** (of a person) unoccupied, esp. temporarily. **loose box** *Brit.* = *box stall* (see BOX¹). **loose change** money as coins in the pocket, etc., for casual use. **loose-leaf** *adj.* (of a notebook, manual, etc.) with each leaf separate and removable. ● *n.* a loose-leaf notebook, etc. **loose-limbed** having supple limbs. **loose order** an arrangement of soldiers, etc., with wide intervals. **on the loose 1** escaped from captivity. **2** having a free enjoyable time. **play fast and loose** ignore one's obligations; be unreliable; trifle. □□ **loosely** *adv.* **looseness** *n.* **loosish** *adj.* [ME *lōs* f. ON *lauss* f. Gmc]
■ *adj.* **1** unconfined, untied, unfettered, released, freed, unshackled, unchained; free, at liberty, at large, on the loose, untrammeled; (*break loose*) see ESCAPE *v.* 1. **2** unattached, unconnected, disconnected, detached, free, unsecured, unfastened; movable, detachable. **3–5** untied, unbound, unsecured, unfastened, unpackaged, free; (*of clothing*) baggy, slack, flowing; (*of hair*) down; strewn *or* spread *or* tossed *or* thrown about *or* around, scattered (about *or* around), dispersed. **6** slack, relaxed, lax, limp, soft, floppy. **8, 9** general, broad, rough, free, vague, rambling, disconnected, unstructured, unconnected, discontinuous, nonspecific, unspecific, indefinite, imprecise, inexact, inaccurate; offhand, casual, untidy, slapdash, negligent, careless, sloppy, lax. **10** wanton, dissolute, lax, debauched, immoral, promiscuous, abandoned, fast, libertine, profligate, licentious, lewd, perverted, corrupt. ● *v.* **1** let go, (set) free, release, let *or* set *or* turn loose; liberate, deliver.

2–4 untie, undo, unfasten, let go, disengage, relax, release, ease, loosen, slacken; cast off. **5** let go, let fly, fire, discharge, shoot, unleash, release, deliver, emit, give out. □ **at loose ends** unoccupied, unemployed, purposeless, aimless, adrift, drifting, *colloq.* betwixt and between.

loosen /loōsən/ *v.* **1** *tr. & intr.* make or become less tight or compact or firm. **2** *tr.* make (a regime, etc.) less severe. **3** *tr.* release (the bowels) from constipation. **4** *tr.* relieve (a cough) from dryness. □ **loosen a person's tongue** make a person talk freely. **loosen up** = *limber up* (see LIMBER¹). □□ **loosener** *n.*
■ **1** loose, ease, release, undo, unfasten, unhook, unbutton, unlace, untie, unbind, unbuckle; unscrew; soften, weaken; detach, separate.

loosestrife /loōs-strif/ *n.* **1** any marsh plant of the genus *Lysimachia*, esp. the golden or yellow loosestrife, *L. vulgaris.* **2** any plant of the genus *Lythrum*, esp. the purple loosestrife, *L. salicaria*, with racemes of star-shaped purple flowers. [LOOSE + STRIFE, taking the Gk name *lusimakhion* (f. *Lusimakhos*, its discoverer) as if directly f. *luō* undo + *makhē* battle]

loot /loōt/ *n. & v.* ● *n.* **1** goods taken from an enemy; spoil. **2** booty; illicit gains made by an official. **3** *sl.* money. ● *v.tr.* **1** rob (premises) or steal (goods) left unprotected, esp. after riots or other violent events. **2** plunder or sack (a city, building, etc.). **3** carry off as booty. □□ **looter** *n.* [Hindi *lūṭ*]
■ *n.* **1, 2** booty, spoils, plunder, prize, haul, *sl.* swag, boodle. ● *v.* plunder, sack, ransack, rob, pillage, raid, ravage, maraud, *literary* despoil; see also STEAL *v.* 1.

lop¹ /lop/ *v. & n.* ● *v.* (**lopped, lopping**) **1** *tr.* **a** (often foll. by *off, away*) cut or remove (a part or parts) from a whole, esp. branches from a tree. **b** remove branches from (a tree). **2** *tr.* (often foll. by *off, away*) remove (items) as superfluous. **3** *intr.* (foll. by *at*) make lopping strokes on (a tree, etc.). ● *n.* parts lopped off, esp. branches and twigs of trees. □□ **lopper** *n.* [ME f. OE *loppian* (unrecorded): cf. obs. *lip* to prune]
■ *v.* **1, 2** chop (off), trim, top, head, crop, prune, dock, clip, snip (off), shear (off), cut (off), pare, shorten, hack (off), amputate.

lop² /lop/ *v.* (**lopped, lopping**) **1** *intr. & tr.* hang limply. **2** *intr.* (foll. by *about*) slouch; dawdle; hang about. **3** *intr.* move with short bounds. **4** *tr.* (of an animal) let (the ears) hang. □ **lop-eared** (of an animal) having drooping ears. □□ **loppy** *adj.* [rel. to LOB]

lope /lōp/ *v. & n.* ● *v.intr.* (esp. of animals) run with a long bounding stride. ● *n.* a long bounding stride. [ME, var. of Sc. *loup* f. ON *hlaupa* LEAP]
■ *v.* see RUN *v.* 1, 3.

lopho- /lofō, lō-fō/ *comb. form Zool.* crested. [Gk *lophos* crest]
lophobranch /lofəbrangk, lō-/ *adj.* (of a fish) having the gills arranged in tufts. [LOPHO- + BRANCHIA]
lophodont /lofədont, lō-/ *n. & adj.* ● *adj.* having transverse ridges on the grinding surface of molar teeth. ● *n.* an animal with these teeth. [LOPHO- + Gk *odous odont-* tooth]
lophophore /lofəfawr, lō-/ *n.* a tentacled disk at the mouth of bryozoans and brachiopods.
lopolith /lopəlith/ *n. Geol.* a large, saucer-shaped intrusion of igneous rock. [Gk *lopas* basin + -LITH]
lopsided /lopsfdid/ *adj.* with one side lower or smaller than the other; unevenly balanced. □□ **lopsidedly** *adv.* **lopsidedness** *n.* [LOP² + SIDE]
■ uneven, askew, one-sided, awry, unsymmetrical, asymmetric(al), unequal, crooked, irregular, *colloq.* cockeyed; unbalanced, biased, disproportionate, unfair, warped, twisted.

loquacious /lōkwáyshəs/ *adj.* **1** talkative. **2** (of birds or water) chattering; babbling. □□ **loquaciously** *adv.* **loqua-**

/.../ **pronunciation**	● **part of speech**
□ **phrases, idioms, and compounds**	
□□ **derivatives**	■ **synonym section**
cross-references appear in SMALL CAPITALS or *italics*	

ciousness *n.* **loquacity** /-kwásitee/ *n.* [L *loquax -acis* f. *loqui* talk]

■ **1** see TALKATIVE.

loquat /lṓkwot/ *n.* **1** a rosaceous tree, *Eriobotrya japonica*, bearing small, yellow egg-shaped fruits. **2** this fruit. [Chin. dial. *luh kwat* rush orange]

loquitur /lṓkwitōōr/ *v.intr.* (he or she) speaks (with the speaker's name following, as a stage direction or to inform the reader). [L]

lor /lawr/ *int. Brit. sl.* an exclamation of surprise or dismay. [abbr. of LORD]

loran /láwran/ *n.* a system of long-distance navigation in which position is determined from the intervals between signal pulses received from widely spaced radio transmitters. [*long-range navigation*]

lord /lawrd/ *n., int., & v.* ● *n.* **1** a master or ruler. **2** *hist.* a feudal superior, esp. of a manor. **3** (in the UK) a peer of the realm or a person entitled to the title *Lord*, esp. a marquess, earl, viscount, or baron. **4** (**Lord**) (often prec. by *the*) a name for God or Christ. **5** (**Lord**) **a** prefixed as the designation of a marquess, earl, viscount, or baron. **b** prefixed to the Christian name of the younger son of a duke or marquess. **c** (**the Lords**) = *House of Lords.* **6** *Astrol.* the ruling planet (of a sign, house, or chart). ● *int.* (**Lord**) expressing surprise, dismay, etc. ● *v.tr.* confer the title of Lord upon. □ **live like a lord** live sumptuously. **lord** (or **lord high**) **chancellor** (in the UK) the highest officer of the Crown, presiding in the House of Lords, etc. **Lord Chief Justice** (in the UK) the president of the Queen's Bench Division. **lord it over** domineer. **Lord Mayor** the title of the mayor in London and some other large cities. **lord over** (usu. in *passive*) domineer; rule over. **Lord Privy Seal** (in the UK) a senior cabinet minister without official duties. **Lord's Day** Sunday. **Lord's Prayer** the prayer taught by Jesus to his disciples. **Lords spiritual** the bishops in the House of Lords. **Lord's Supper** the Eucharist. **Lords temporal** the members of the House of Lords other than the bishops. **Our Lord** a name for Christ. □□ **lordless** *adj.* **lordlike** *adj.* [OE *hlāford* f. *hlāfweard* = loaf-keeper (as LOAF¹, WARD)]

■ *n.* **1** master, monarch, ruler, sovereign. **3** noble, nobleman, peer, aristocrat; marquess, earl, count, viscount, baron. **4** (**Lord** or **the Lord**) God, the Almighty, Our Lord, the Creator, the Supreme Being, Christ, Jesus, Jehovah. ● *int.* see GOD *int.* □ **lord it over** domineer, pull rank on, *colloq.* boss (about *or* around).

lordling /láwrdling/ *n.* usu. *derog.* a minor lord.

lordly /láwrdlee/ *adj.* (**lordlier, lordliest**) **1** haughty; imperious. **2** suitable for a lord. □□ **lordliness** *n.* [OE *hlāfordlic* (as LORD)]

■ **1** see *snobbish* (SNOB). **2** see NOBLE *adj.* 1. □□ **lordliness** see *snobbery* (SNOB).

lordosis /lawrdṓsis/ *n. Med.* inward curvature of the spine (opp. KYPHOSIS). □□ **lordotic** /-dótik/ *adj.* [mod.L f. Gk *lordōsis* f. *lordos* bent backward]

lordship /láwrdship/ *n.* **1** (usu. **Lordship**) a title used in addressing or referring to a man with the rank of Lord or a judge or a bishop (*Your Lordship*; *His Lordship*). **2** (foll. by *of, over*) dominion, rule, or ownership. **3** the condition of being a lord. [OE *hlāfordscipe* (as LORD, -SHIP)]

Lordy /láwrdee/ *int.* = LORD *int.*

lore¹ /lawr/ *n.* a body of traditions and knowledge on a subject or held by a particular group (*herbal lore*; *gypsy lore*). [OE *lār* f. Gmc, rel. to LEARN]

■ folklore, beliefs, culture, tradition(s), mythology, myths, *literary* mythi; teaching(s), doctrine, wisdom; knowledge, learning, erudition.

lore² /lawr/ *n. Zool.* a straplike surface between the eye and upper mandible in birds, or between the eye and nostril in snakes. [L *lorum* strap]

lorgnette /lawrnyét/ *n.* (in *sing.* or *pl.*) a pair of eyeglasses or opera glasses held by a long handle. [F f. *lorgner* to squint]

loricate /láwrikayt, -kit, lór-/ *adj. & n. Zool.* ● *adj.* having a defensive armor of bone, plates, scales, etc. ● *n.* an animal with this. [L *loricatus* f. *lorica* breastplate f. *lorum* strap]

lorikeet /láwrikeet, lór-/ *n.* any of various small, brightly colored parrots of the subfamily Loriinae, including the rainbow lorikeet. [dimin. of LORY, after *parakeet*]

loris /láwris/ *n.* (*pl.* same) either of two small, tailless nocturnal primates, *Loris tardigradus* of S. India (**slender loris**), and *Nycticebus coucang* of the E. Indies (**slow loris**). [F perh. f. obs. Du. *loeris* clown]

lorn /lawrn/ *adj. literary* desolate; forlorn; abandoned. [past part. of obs. *leese* f. OE *-lēosan* lose]

lorry /láwree, lór-/ *n. Brit.* (*pl.* **-ies**) **1** a large strong motor vehicle for transporting goods, etc.; a truck. **2** a long flat low wagon. **3** a railway freight car. [19th c.: orig. uncert.]

lory /láwree/ *n.* (*pl.* **-ies**) any of various brightly colored Australasian parrots of the subfamily Loriinae. [Malay *lūrī*]

lose /lōōz/ *v.* (*past* and *past part.* **lost** /lawst, lost/) **1** *tr.* be deprived of or cease to have, esp. by negligence or misadventure. **2** *tr.* **a** be deprived of (a person, esp. a close relative) by death. **b** suffer the loss of (a baby) in childbirth. **3** *tr.* become unable to find; fail to keep in sight or follow or mentally grasp (*lose one's way*). **4** *tr.* let or have pass from one's control or reach (*lose one's chance*; *lose one's bearings*). **5** *tr.* be defeated in (a game, race, lawsuit, battle, etc.). **6** *tr.* evade; get rid of (*lost our pursuers*). **7** *tr.* fail to obtain, catch, or perceive (*lose a train*; *lose a word*). **8** *tr.* forfeit (a stake, deposit, right to a thing, etc.). **9** *tr.* spend (time, efforts, etc.) to no purpose (*lost no time in raising the alarm*). **10** *intr.* **a** suffer loss or detriment; incur a disadvantage. **b** be worse off, esp. financially. **11** *tr.* cause (a person) the loss of (*will lose you your job*). **12** *intr. & tr.* (of a timepiece) become slow; become slow by (a specified amount of time). **13** *tr.* (in *passive*) **a** disappear; perish; be dead (*was lost in the war*). **b** fall, sin; be damned (*souls lost to drunkenness and greed*). **14** (as **lost** *adj.*) **a** gone; stray; mislaid; forgotten (*lost valuables*; *a lost art*). **b** dead; destroyed (*lost comrades*). **c** damned; fallen (*lost souls in hell*). □ **be lost** (or **lose oneself**) **in** be engrossed in. **be lost on** be wasted on, or not noticed or appreciated by. **be lost to** be no longer affected by or accessible to (*is lost to pity*; *is lost to the world*). **be lost without** have great difficulty if deprived of (*am lost without my diary*). **get lost** *sl.* (usu. in *imper.*) go away. **lose one's balance 1** fail to remain stable; fall. **2** fail to retain one's composure. **lose one's cool** *colloq.* lose one's composure. **lose face** be humiliated; lose one's credibility. **lose ground** see GROUND¹. **lose one's head** see HEAD. **lose heart** be discouraged. **lose one's heart** see HEART. **lose one's nerve** become timid or irresolute. **lose out** (often foll. by *on*) *colloq.* be unsuccessful; not get a fair chance or advantage (in). **lose sleep over a thing** lie awake worrying about a thing. **lose one's temper** become angry. **lose time** allow time to pass with something unachieved, etc. **lose touch** see TOUCH. **lose track of** see TRACK¹. **lose the** (or **one's**) **way** become lost; fail to reach one's destination. **losing battle** a contest or effort in which failure seems certain. **lost cause 1** an enterprise, etc., with no chance of success. **2** a person one can no longer hope to influence. **lost generation 1** a generation with many of its men killed in war, esp. (**the Lost Generation**) that of the World War I era. **2** an emotionally and culturally unstable generation coming to maturity, esp. the Lost Generation. □□ **losable** *adj.* [OE *losian* perish, destroy f. *los* loss]

■ **1–3** mislay, misplace, displace, part with; suffer the loss of, be deprived of. **4, 5, 8, 10** give up, forfeit; yield, capitulate, admit defeat, succumb, be defeated *or* conquered, suffer defeat, be beaten *or* overcome *or* worsted *or* bested, *colloq.* lose out. **6** elude, evade, escape, slip, throw *or* shake off, give a person the slip, get rid of. **7** miss. **9** waste, let slip, squander, dissipate, fritter *or* trifle away; consume, use (up), expend, spend. **13 a** (*be lost*) see DISAPPEAR, DIE¹ 1. **b** see SIN¹ *v.* 1. **14** (**lost**) **a** gone, departed, vanished, stray(ed); missing, mislaid, misplaced, irrecoverable; wasted, misspent, gone by the board, squandered, spent, *colloq.* out the window, down the drain; forgotten, past, bygone, extinct, obsolete, buried. **b** dead, departed, fallen, late; destroyed, demolished, devastated, ruined, wrecked, irreparable, unsalvageable, irreclaimable, irremediable.

c damned, cursed, accursed, abandoned, corrupt, fallen, wanton, unchaste, dissolute; hopeless, irredeemable. □ **get lost** see *beat it*. **lose one's balance 1** see SLIP[1] *v.* 1. **lose one's cool** see EXPLODE 2. **lose one's nerve** see PANIC[1] *v.* **lose out** see LOSE 4, 5, 8, 10 above. **lose one's temper** see EXPLODE 2. **lost cause** see DISASTER 2, FAILURE 1.

loser /loozər/ *n.* **1** a person or thing that loses or has lost (esp. a contest or game) (*is a poor loser; the loser pays*). **2** *colloq.* a person who regularly fails.

■ **2** also-ran, failure, lead balloon, *colloq.* washout, nonstarter, lemon, schlemiel, sad sack, *sl.* flop, dud, schnook, esp. *Brit. sl.* no-hoper.

loss /laws, los/ *n.* **1** the act or an instance of losing; the state of being lost. **2** a person, thing, or amount lost. **3** the detriment or disadvantage resulting from losing (*that is no great loss*). □ **at a loss** (sold, etc.) for less than was paid for it. **be at a loss** be puzzled or uncertain. **be at a loss for words** not know what to say. **loss adjuster** *Brit.* = *claims adjuster*. **loss leader** an item sold at a loss to attract customers. [ME *los, loss* prob. back-form. f. *lost*, past part. of LOSE]

■ **1** deprivation, bereavement, privation, denial, sacrifice, forfeiture, disappearance; defeat, setback, disadvantage, disappointment, failure, downfall, collapse, breakdown, ruin; drubbing, trouncing. **2** diminution, erosion, reduction, impoverishment, depletion, shrinkage, waste, wastage; debit, liability; casualty, death. **3** disadvantage, detriment, harm, impairment, injury, damage. □ **be at a loss** be confused *or* baffled *or* perplexed *or* puzzled *or* mystified *or* bewildered *or* confounded *or* adrift *or* helpless *or* disorient(at)ed *or* (all) at sea.

lost *past* and *past part.* of LOSE.

lot /lot/ *n.* & *v.* ● *n.* **1** *colloq.* (prec. by *a* or in *pl.*) **a** a large number or amount (*a lot of people; lots of chocolate*). **b** *colloq.* much (*a lot warmer; smiles a lot; is lots better*). **2 a** each of a set of objects used in making a chance selection. **b** this method of deciding (*chosen by lot*). **3** a share, or the responsibility resulting from it. **4** a person's destiny, fortune, or condition. **5** a plot; an allotment of land (*parking lot*). **6** an article or set of articles for sale at an auction, etc. **7** a number or quantity of associated persons or things. ● *v.tr.* (**lotted, lotting**) divide into lots. □ **bad lot** a person of bad character. **cast** (or **draw**) **lots** decide by means of lots. **throw in one's lot with** decide to share the fortunes of. **the** (or **the whole**) **lot** the whole number or quantity. **a whole lot** *colloq.* very much (*is a whole lot better*). [OE *hlot* portion, choice f. Gmc]

■ *n.* **1** (*a lot* or *lots*) a good *or* great deal, plenty, reams, a mass *or* masses, mountains *or* a mountain, *colloq.* oodles, zillions, loads, tons *or* a ton, stacks *or* a stack, piles *or* a pile, heaps *or* a heap, pots *or* a pot, *colloq.* scads; (*a lot of*) many, numerous, innumerable, countless, *literary* myriad; not a little. **2 b** lottery, raffle; drawing lots *or* straws. **3** share, portion, division, interest, part, allotment, assignment, apportionment, ration, allowance. **4** luck, fortune, destiny, fate, karma, plight, doom, end. **7** collection, batch, consignment, assortment, group, portion, set, quantity, grouping. □ **the** (or **the whole**) **lot** everything, *sl.* the whole (kit and) caboodle.

loth var. of LOATH.

lothario /lōtháreeō/ *n.* (also **Lothario**) (*pl.* **-os**) a rake or libertine. [a character in Rowe's *Fair Penitent* (1703)]

■ see LIBERTINE *n.* 1.

lotion /lōshən/ *n.* a medicinal or cosmetic liquid preparation applied externally. [ME f. OF *lotion* or L *lotio* f. *lavare* lot-wash]

■ cream, liniment, balm, salve, ointment, embrocation, unguent, pomade.

lottery /lótəree/ *n.* (*pl.* **-ies**) **1** a means of raising money by selling numbered tickets and giving prizes to the holders of numbers drawn at random. **2** an enterprise, process, etc., whose success is governed by chance (*life is a lottery*). [prob. f. Du. *loterij* (as LOT)]

■ **1** raffle, sweepstakes, drawing, pool.

lotto /lótō/ *n.* a game of chance like bingo, but with numbers drawn instead of called. [It.]

lotus /lōtəs/ *n.* **1** (in Greek mythology) a legendary plant inducing luxurious languor when eaten. **2 a** any water lily of the genus *Nelumbo*, esp. *N. nucifera* of India, with large pink flowers. **b** this flower used symbolically in Hinduism and Buddhism. **3** an Egyptian water lily, *Nymphaea lotus*, with white flowers. **4** any plant of the genus *Lotus*, e.g., bird's-foot trefoil. □ **lotus-eater** a person given to indolent enjoyment. **lotus position** a cross-legged position of meditation with the feet resting on the thighs. [L f. Gk *lōtos*, of Semitic orig.]

lotusland /lōtəsland/ *n.* a place of indolent enjoyment. [the land of lotus-eaters in Homer's *Odyssey*]

louche /loosh/ *adj.* disreputable; shifty. [F, = squinting]

■ see DISREPUTABLE 1.

loud /lowd/ *adj.* & *adv.* ● *adj.* **1 a** strongly audible, esp. noisily or oppressively so. **b** able or liable to produce loud sounds (*a loud engine*). **c** clamorous; insistent (*loud complaints*). **2** (of colors, design, etc.) gaudy; obtrusive. **3** (of behavior) aggressive and noisy. ● *adv.* in a loud manner. □ **loud-hailer** *Brit.* = BULLHORN. **out loud 1** aloud. **2** loudly (*laughed out loud*). □□ **louden** *v.tr.* & *intr.* **loudish** *adj.* **loudly** *adv.* **loudness** *n.* [OE *hlūd* f. WG]

■ *adj.* **1** deafening, earsplitting, ear-piercing, booming, blaring, stentorian, thunderous, sonorous, noisy, piercing, *Mus.* fortissimo; clamorous, insistent. **2** tawdry, garish, flashy, gaudy, tasteless, extravagant, showy, ostentatious, jazzy, *colloq.* splashy, *sl.* snazzy. **3** loudmouthed, brash, vociferous, raucous; see also ROWDY *adj.*

loudmouth /lówdmowth/ *n. colloq.* a noisily self-assertive, vociferous person. □□ **loudmouthed** *adj.*

loudspeaker /lówdspeékər/ *n.* an apparatus that converts electrical impulses into sound, esp. music and voice.

Lou Gehrig's disease /loo gérigz/ *n.* see AMYOTROPHIC LATERAL SCLEROSIS.

lough /lok, lokh/ *n. Ir.* = LAKE. [Ir. *loch* LAKE, assim. to the related obs. ME form *lough*]

louis /loo-ee/ *n.* (*pl.* same /loo-eez/) *hist.* (in full **louis d'or** /dawr/) a former French gold coin worth about 20 francs. [*Louis*, the name of kings of France]

lounge /lownj/ *v.* & *n.* ● *v.intr.* **1** recline comfortably and casually; loll. **2** stand or move about idly. ● *n.* **1 a** a place for lounging, esp.: **a** a public room (e.g., in a hotel). **b** a place in an airport, etc., with seats for waiting passengers. **c** *Brit.* a sitting room in a house; living room. **2** a spell of lounging. □ **lounge lizard** *colloq.* **1** a person, esp. a man, who frequents bars, etc. **2** an idler in fashionable society. **lounge suit** *Brit.* = *business suit*. [perh. f. obs. *lungis* lout]

■ *v.* idle, loaf, laze, loll, languish. ● *n.* **1 a, b** lobby, foyer, waiting room, reception (room).

lounger /lównjər/ *n.* **1** a person who lounges. **2** a piece of furniture for relaxing on. **3** a casual garment for wearing when relaxing.

loupe /loop/ *n.* a small magnifying glass used by jewelers, etc. [F]

lour var. of LOWER[3].

louse /lows/ *n.* & *v.* ● *n.* **1** (*pl.* **lice** /lis/) **a** a parasitic insect, *Pediculus humanus*, infesting the human hair and skin and transmitting various diseases. **b** any insect of the order Anoplura or Mallophaga parasitic on mammals, birds, fish, or plants. **2** *sl.* (*pl.* **louses**) a contemptible or unpleasant person. ● *v.tr.* remove lice from. □ **louse up** *sl.* make a mess of. [OE *lūs*, pl. *lȳs*]

■ **2** see WRETCH 2. □ **louse up** see BOTCH *v.* 1.

lousewort /lówswərt, -wawrt/ *n.* any plant of the genus *Ped-*

/.../ **pronunciation**	● **part of speech**
□ **phrases, idioms, and compounds**	
□□ **derivatives**	■ **synonym section**
cross-references appear in SMALL CAPITALS or *italics*	

icularis with purple-pink flowers found in marshes and wet places.

lousy /lówzee/ *adj.* (**lousier, lousiest**) **1** infested with lice. **2** *colloq.* very bad; disgusting (also as a term of general disparagement). **3** *colloq.* (often foll. by *with*) well supplied; teeming (with). □□ **lousily** *adv.* **lousiness** *n.*

■ **1** pedicular, pediculous. **2** awful, terrible, mean, contemptible, low, base, hateful, detestable, despicable, vile, wretched, miserable, scurvy, dirty, vicious, *sl.* rotten; bad, poor, inferior; low-quality, shoddy, shabby, miserable, second-rate. **3** (*lousy with*) alive with, awash with, overflowing with, overloaded with, swarming with, teeming with, crawling with, knee-deep in.

lout /lowt/ *n.* a rough, crude, or ill-mannered person (usu. a man). □□ **loutish** *adj.* **loutishly** *adv.* **loutishness** *n.* [perh. f. archaic *lout* to bow]

■ see ROWDY *n.* □□ **loutish** see ROUGH *adj.* 4a.

louver /loōvər/ *n.* (also esp. *Brit.* **louvre**) **1** each of a set of overlapping slats designed to admit air and some light and exclude rain. **2** a domed structure on a roof with side openings for ventilation, etc. □ **louver boards** the slats or boards making up a louver. □□ **louvered** *adj.* [ME f. OF *lover, lovier* skylight, prob. f. Gmc]

lovable /lúvəbəl/ *adj.* (also **loveable**) inspiring or deserving love or affection. □□ **lovability** *n.* **lovableness** *n.* **lovably** *adv.*

■ adorable, darling, dear, cherished, likable, attractive, engaging, fetching, taking, alluring, endearing, appealing, winsome, sweet, tender, cuddly, affectionate, charming, enchanting, cunning, *colloq.* cute, *literary* lovesome.

lovage /lúvij/ *n.* **1** a S. European herb, *Levisticum officinale*, used for flavoring, etc. **2** a white-flowered umbelliferous plant, *Ligusticum scoticum*. [ME *loveache* alt. f. OF *levesche* f. LL *levisticum* f. L *ligusticum* neut. of *ligusticus* Ligurian]

lovat /lúvət/ *n.* (also *attrib.*) a muted green color found esp. in tweed and woolen garments. [*Lovat* in Scotland]

love /luv/ *n. & v.* ● *n.* **1** an intense feeling of deep affection or fondness for a person or thing; great liking. **2** sexual passion. **3** sexual relations. **4 a** a beloved one; a sweetheart (often as a form of address). **b** *Brit. colloq.* a form of address regardless of affection. **5** *colloq.* a person of whom one is fond. **6** affectionate greetings (*give him my love*). **7** (often **Love**) a representation of Cupid. **8** (in some games) no score; nil. ● *v.tr.* **1** (also *absol.*) feel love or deep fondness for. **2** delight in; admire; greatly cherish. **3** *colloq.* like very much (*loves books*). **4** (foll. by verbal noun, or *to* + infin.) be inclined, esp. as a habit; greatly enjoy; find pleasure in (*children love dressing up; loves to find fault*). □ **fall in love** (often foll. by *with*) develop a great (esp. sexual) love (for). **for love** for pleasure not profit. **for the love of** for the sake of. **in love** (often foll. by *with*) deeply enamored (of). **love affair** a romantic or sexual relationship between two people in love; a passion for something. **love apple** *archaic* a tomato. **love child** a child born out of wedlock. **love feast** **1** a meal affirming brotherly love among early Christians. **2** a religious service of Methodists, etc., imitating this. **love game** a game in which the loser makes no score. **love-hate relationship** an intensely emotional relationship in which one or each party has ambivalent feelings of love and hate for the other. **love-in-a-mist** a blue-flowered garden plant, *Nigella damascena*, with many delicate green bracts. **love letter** a letter expressing feelings of sexual love. **love-lies-bleeding** a garden plant, *Amaranthus caudatus*, with drooping spikes of purple-red blooms. **love life** one's amorous or sexual relationships. **love match** a marriage made for love's sake. **love nest** a place of intimate lovemaking. **love seat** an armchair or small sofa for two. **make love** (often foll. by *to*) **1** have sexual intercourse (with). **2** *archaic* pay amorous attention (to). **not for love or money** *colloq.* not in any circumstances. **out of love** no longer in love. □□ **loveworthy** *adj.* [OE *lufu* f. Gmc]

■ *n.* **1** warmth, affection, attachment, fondness, tenderness, devotion, attraction, friendship, amity,

regard, admiration, fancy, adoration, adulation; liking, delight, enjoyment, pleasure, predilection, bent, leaning, proclivity, inclination, disposition, weakness, partiality, preference, taste, relish; sympathy, concern, charity, care, solicitude, affinity, rapport, harmony, brotherhood, sisterhood, fellow feeling. **2** ardor, passion, lust, fervor, rapture, infatuation. **4a, 5** darling, beloved, sweetheart, sweet, dear(est), honey, sweetie (pie), esp. *Brit. colloq.* lovey, *usu. joc.* light of one's life; lover, truelove, mate, *archaic* paramour; intended, betrothed; girlfriend, inamorata, ladylove, young lady, fiancée; boyfriend, beau, inamorato, suitor, young man, fiancé, *archaic* leman, *poet.* swain. ● *v.* **1** cherish, admire, adore, be in love with, lose one's heart to, worship, idolize, dote on, treasure, be infatuated with, think the world of, adulate, hold dear, like, be mad about, *colloq.* be crazy *or* nuts *or* wild about, have a crush on, *sl.* be hung up on. **2–4** cherish, delight in, take pleasure in, derive pleasure *or* enjoyment from, relish, be partial to, have a passion *or* preference *or* taste for, be attracted to, be captivated by, be fond of, like, enjoy, appreciate, value, be mad about, *colloq.* get a kick out of, be crazy *or* nuts *or* wild about, *sl.* get a bang from *or* out of. □ **love affair** amour, liaison, affair, *affaire (de cœur)*, romance, relationship, *archaic* intrigue; passion, mania. **love letter** *often joc.* billet-doux. **make love** embrace, cuddle, caress, fondle, *colloq.* neck, pet, canoodle; romance; have sexual intercourse, *colloq.* have sex; take, *archaic* know.

loveable var. of LOVABLE.

lovebird /lúvbərd/ *n.* **1** any of various African and Madagascan parrots, esp. *Agapornis personata*. **2** (in *pl.*) a pair of lovers who display much affection.

lovebite /lúvbīt/ *n.* esp. *Brit.* = HICKEY 2.

loveless /lúvlis/ *adj.* without love; unloving or unloved or both. □□ **lovelessly** *adv.* **lovelessness** *n.*

lovelock /lúvlok/ *n.* a curl or lock of hair worn on the temple or forehead.

lovelorn /lúvlawrn/ *adj.* pining from unrequited love.

lovely /lúvlee/ *adj. & n.* ● *adj.* (**lovelier, loveliest**) **1** exquisitely beautiful. **2** *colloq.* pleasing; delightful. ● *n.* (*pl.* **-ies**) *colloq.* a pretty woman. □ **lovely and** *colloq.* delightfully (*lovely and warm*). □□ **lovelily** *adv.* **loveliness** *n.* [OE *luflic* (as LOVE)]

■ *adj.* **1** good-looking, pretty, handsome, attractive, comely, fair, fetching, engaging, captivating, alluring, enticing, bewitching, ravishing, gorgeous, exquisite, beautiful, *literary* pulchritudinous, lovesome, *poet.* beauteous. **2** satisfying, satisfactory, agreeable, enjoyable, gratifying, nice, pleasing, pleasant, pleasurable, engaging, delightful.

lovemaking /lúvmayking/ *n.* **1** amorous sexual activity, esp. sexual intercourse. **2** *archaic* courtship.

■ **1** see SEX 5.

lover /lúvər/ *n.* **1** a person in love with another. **2** a person with whom another is having sexual relations. **3** (in *pl.*) a couple in love or having sexual relations. **4** a person who likes or enjoys something specified (*a music lover; a lover of words*). □□ **loverless** *adj.*

■ **1** see LOVE *n.* 4a, 5. **4** see ENTHUSIAST.

lovesick /lúvsik/ *adj.* languishing with romantic love. □□ **lovesickness** *n.*

lovesome /lúvsəm/ *adj. literary* lovely; lovable.

lovey /lúvee/ *n.* (*pl.* **-eys**) esp. *Brit. colloq.* love; sweetheart (esp. as a form of address).

lovey-dovey /lúveedúvee/ *adj. colloq.* fondly affectionate, esp. unduly sentimental.

loving /lúving/ *adj. & n.* ● *adj.* feeling or showing love; affectionate. ● *n.* affection; active love. □ **loving cup 1** a two-handled drinking cup passed around at banquets, etc. **2** a loving cup presented as a trophy. **loving-kindness** tenderness and consideration. □□ **lovingly** *adv.* **lovingness** *n.* [OE *lufiende* (as LOVE)]

■ *adj.* see AFFECTIONATE. □□ **lovingly** see *fondly* (FOND).

low[1] /lō/ *adj., n., & adv.* ● *adj.* **1** of less than average height;

not high or tall or reaching far up (*a low wall*). **2 a** situated close to ground or sea level, etc.; not elevated in position (*low altitude*). **b** (of the sun) near the horizon. **c** (of latitude) near the equator. **3** of or in humble rank or position (*of low birth*). **4** of small or less than normal amount or extent or intensity (*low price*; *low temperature*; *low in calories*). **5** small or reduced in quantity (*stocks are low*). **6** coming below the normal level (*a dress with a low neck*). **7 a** dejected; lacking vigor (*feeling low*; *in low spirits*). **b** poorly nourished; indicative of poor nutrition. **8** (of a sound) not shrill or loud or high-pitched. **9** not exalted or sublime; commonplace. **10** unfavorable (*a low opinion*). **11** abject; mean; vulgar (*low cunning*; *low slang*). **12** (in *compar.*) situated on less high land or to the south. **13** (of a geographical period) earlier. ● *n.* **1** a low or the lowest level or number (*the dollar has reached a new low*). **2** an area of low pressure. ● *adv.* **1** in or to a low position or state. **2** in a low tone (*speak low*). **3** (of a sound) at or to a low pitch. □ **low-ball** *n. Cards* a type of poker. ● *v.* underestimate or underbid a price (usu. for a service) deliberately. **low beam** an automobile headlight providing short-range illumination. **Low Church** the section of the Church of England giving a low place to ritual, priestly authority, and the sacraments. **low-class** of low quality or social class. **low comedy** that in which the subject and the treatment border on farce. **Low Countries** the Netherlands, Belgium, and Luxembourg. **low-cut** (of a dress, etc.) made with a low neckline. **low-down** *adj.* abject; mean; dishonorable. ● *n. colloq.* (usu. foll. by *on*) the relevant information (about). **lowest common denominator, multiple** see DENOMINATOR, MULTIPLE. **low frequency** (in radio) 30–300 kilohertz. **low gear** see GEAR. **Low German** see GERMAN. **low-grade** of low quality or strength. **low-key** lacking intensity or prominence; restrained. **Low Latin** medieval and later forms of Latin. **low-level** *Computing* (of a programming language) close in form to machine language. **low-lying** at low altitude (above sea level, etc.). **low mass** see MASS[2]. **low-pitched 1** (of a sound) low. **2** (of a roof) having only a slight slope. **low pressure 1** little demand for activity or exertion. **2** an atmospheric condition with pressure below average. **low profile** avoidance of attention or publicity. **low-profile** *adj.* **1** having a low profile. **2** (of a motor-vehicle tire) having a greater width than usual in relation to height. **low relief** = BAS-RELIEF. **low-rise** (of a building) having few stories. **low season** *Brit.* = off-season. **low-spirited** dejected; dispirited. **low-spiritedness** dejection; depression. **low spirits** dejection; depression. **Low Sunday** the Sunday after Easter. **low tide** the time or level of the tide at its ebb. **low water** the tide at its lowest. **low-water mark 1** the level reached at low water. **2** a minimum recorded level or value, etc. **Low Week** the week beginning with Low Sunday. □□ **lowish** *adj.* **lowness** *n.* [ME *lāh* f. ON *lágr* f. Gmc]

■ *adj.* **1** short, squat, little, small, stubby, stumpy, stunted. **2 a** low-lying. **3** humble, poor, lowborn, lowly, base, baseborn, inferior, plebeian, proletarian, ignoble. **4** small, reduced. **5** inadequate, insufficient, deficient, down, short, sparse, scanty, scant, limited. **7** weak, frail, feeble, debilitated, enervated, sickly, unhealthy, infirm, shaky, decrepit, ill, sick; ineffectual, ineffective; miserable, dismal, wretched, abysmal, sorry, abject, destitute; unhappy, depressed, dejected, sad, gloomy, melancholy, low-spirited, dispirited, despondent, disconsolate, blue, downcast, down, glum, morose, crestfallen, brokenhearted, heartbroken, tearful, sorrowful, mournful, heavyhearted, *formal* lachrymose. **8** quiet, hushed, soft, subdued, gentle, muted, low-pitched, muffled, stifled, indistinct, whispered, murmured, murmurous. **9** inferior, second-rate, poor, bad, low-grade, not up to par, worthless, shoddy, shabby, mediocre, substandard; commonplace. **10** unfavorable, critical, adverse. **11** base, vile, abject, contemptible, despicable, mean, menial, servile, ignoble, degraded, foul, dastardly, depraved, nasty, sordid; coarse, unrefined, indelicate, risqué, indecent, unseemly, vulgar, crude, common, rude, gross,

offensive, smutty, dirty. □ **low-cut** revealing, décolleté. **low-down** (*n.*) information, intelligence, data, facts, inside story *or* information, *colloq.* info, *sl.* dope. **low-pitched 1** see LOW[1] *adj.* 8 above. **low-spirited** see LOW[1] *adj.* 7 above.

low[2] /lō/ *n. & v.* ● *n.* a sound made by cattle; a moo. ● *v.intr.* utter this sound. [OE *hlōwan* f. Gmc]

■ *v.* moo, bellow.

lowborn /lṓbawrn/ *adj.* of humble birth.

■ see LOW[1] *adj.* 3.

lowboy /lṓboy/ *n.* a low chest or table with drawers and short legs.

■ see CABINET 1a.

lowbrow /lṓbrow/ *adj. & n.* ● *adj.* not highly intellectual or cultured. ● *n.* a lowbrow person. □□ **lowbrowed** *adj.*

■ *adj.* see PHILISTINE *adj.* ● *n.* see PHILISTINE *n.*

lower[1] /lṓər/ *adj. & adv.* ● *adj.* (*compar.* of LOW[1]). **1** less high in position or status. **2** situated below another part (*lower lip*; *lower atmosphere*). **3 a** situated on less high land (*Lower Egypt*). **b** situated to the south (*Lower California*). **4** (of a mammal, plant, etc.) evolved to a relatively small degree (e.g., a platypus or fungus). ● *adv.* in or to a lower position, status, etc. □ **lower class** working-class people and their families. **lower-class** *adj.* of the lower class. **lower deck 1** the deck of a ship situated immediately over the hold. **2** the petty officers and men of a ship collectively. **lower house** the usu. larger body in a legislature, esp. in Britain, the House of Commons. **lower regions** (or **world**) hell; the realm of the dead. □□ **lowermost** *adj.*

■ *adj.* **1** further down, under, *archaic* nether; see also INFERIOR *adj.* 1. **2, 3a** under, *archaic* nether; bottom, inferior. **3 b** southern, southerly, southernmost, south. **4** see PRIMITIVE *adj.* 7, 8. ● *adv.* see DOWNWARD *adv.* □ **lower-class** see PLEBEIAN *adj.* 1. **lower regions** see HELL 1.

lower[2] /lṓər/ *v.* **1** *tr.* let or haul down. **2** *tr. & intr.* make or become lower. **3** *tr.* reduce the height or pitch or elevation of (*lower your voice*; *lower one's eyes*). **4** *tr.* degrade. **5** *tr. & intr.* diminish.

■ **1** let *or* move *or* bring *or* put *or* haul down, drop. **2, 5** drop, reduce, decrease, mark down, discount, lessen, diminish, downgrade, cut, slash, lop, take down, crop, trim. **3** turn down, quiet, moderate, modulate, soften, tone down, *Brit.* quieten. **4** abase, debase, degrade, discredit, shame, disgrace, demean, belittle, humble, humiliate; (*lower oneself*) see CONDESCEND 1.

lower[3] /lowər/ *v. & n.* (also **lour**) ● *v.intr.* **1** frown; look sullen. **2** (of the sky, etc.) look dark and threatening. ● *n.* **1** a scowl. **2** a gloomy look (of the sky, etc.). □□ **loweringly** *adv.* **lowery** *adj.* [ME *loure*, of unkn. orig.]

■ *v.* **1** frown, scowl, glower; sulk, pout, mope. **2** darken; threaten, menace, loom.

lowercase /lṓərkays/ *n., adj., & v.* ● *n.* small letters (as in contrast to capital letters). ● *adj.* of or having small letters. *v.tr.* print or write in lowercase.

lowland /lṓlənd/ *n. & adj.* ● *n.* **1** (usu. in *pl.*) low-lying country. **2** (**Lowland**) (usu. in *pl.*) the region of Scotland lying south and east of the Highlands. ● *adj.* of or in lowland or the Scottish Lowlands. □□ **lowlander** *n.* (also **Lowlander**).

■ *n.* **1** see FLAT[1] *n.* 2.

lowlight /lṓlīt/ *n.* **1** a monotonous or dull period; a feature of little prominence (*one of the lowlights of the evening*). **2** (usu. in *pl.*) a dark tint in the hair produced by dyeing. [after HIGHLIGHT]

lowly /lṓlee/ *adj.* (**lowlier, lowliest**) **1** humble in feeling, behavior, or status. **2** modest; unpretentious. **3** (of an organism) evolved to only a slight degree. □□ **lowlily** *adv.* **lowliness** *n.*

/.../ **pronunciation**	● **part of speech**
□ **phrases, idioms, and compounds**	
□□ **derivatives**	■ **synonym section**
cross-references appear in SMALL CAPITALS or *italics*	

■ **1** see HUMBLE *adj.* 2. **2** see MODEST 5. **3** see PRIMITIVE *adj.* 7, 8.

low-minded /lṓmíndid/ *adj.* vulgar or ignoble in mind or character. □□ **low-mindedness** *n.*

lox¹ /loks/ *n.* liquid oxygen. [abbr.]

lox² /loks/ *n.* smoked salmon. [Yiddish *laks*]

loyal /lóyəl/ *adj.* **1** (often foll. by *to*) true or faithful (to duty, love, or obligation). **2** steadfast in allegiance; devoted to the legitimate sovereign or government of one's country. **3** showing loyalty. □□ **loyally** *adv.* [F f. OF *loial*, etc. f. L *legalis* LEGAL]

■ faithful, true, dependable, devoted, trustworthy, steady, steadfast, staunch, trusted, reliable, stable, unswerving, unwavering, dedicated, constant, *archaic* trusty; patriotic.

loyalist /lóyəlist/ *n.* **1** a person who remains loyal to the legitimate sovereign, etc., esp. in the face of rebellion or usurpation. **2** (**Loyalist**) *a hist.* a resident of N. America who supported Great Britain during the American Revolution. **b** a supporter of Parliamentary union between Great Britain and Northern Ireland. □□ **loyalism** *n.*

loyalty /lóyəltee/ *n.* (*pl.* **-ies**) **1** the state of being loyal. **2** (often in *pl.*) a feeling or application of loyalty.

■ faithfulness, fidelity, dependability, devotedness, devotion, allegiance, patriotism, trustworthiness, steadfastness, staunchness, firmness, reliability, stability, dedication, constancy.

lozenge /lózinj/ *n.* **1** a rhombus or diamond figure. **2** a small sweet or medicinal tablet, orig. lozenge-shaped, for dissolving in the mouth. **3** a lozenge-shaped pane in a window. **4** *Heraldry* a lozenge-shaped device. **5** the lozenge-shaped facet of a cut gem. □□ **lozenged** *adj.* (in sense 4). **lozengy** *adj.* [ME f. OF *losenge*, ult. of Gaulish or Iberian orig.]

■ **2** see TABLET 1a.

LP *abbr.* **1** long-playing (phonograph record). **2** low pressure.

■ **1** see RECORD *n.* 3a.

LPG *abbr.* liquefied petroleum gas.

LPN *abbr.* licensed practical nurse.

LSAT *abbr.* Law School Admissions Test.

LSD *abbr.* lysergic acid diethylamide.

l.s.d. *n.* (also **£.s.d.**) *Brit.* **1** pounds, shillings, and pence (in former British currency). **2** money; riches. [L *librae, solidi, denarii*]

Lt. *abbr.* **1** lieutenant. **2** light.

LTA *abbr.* (of aircraft) lighter-than-air.

Ltd. *abbr.* limited.

Lu *symb. Chem.* the element lutetium.

lubber /lúbər/ *n.* a big clumsy fellow; a lout. □ **lubber line** *Naut.* a line marked on a compass, showing the ship's forward direction. □□ **lubberlike** *adj.* **lubberly** *adj. & adv.* [ME, perh. f. OF *lobeor* swindler, parasite f. *lober* deceive]

■ □□ **lubberly** (*adj.*) see CLUMSY 1.

lubra /lṓbrə/ *n. Austral.* sometimes *derog.* an Aboriginal woman. [F *loubra* f. Tasmanian]

lubricant /lṓbrikənt/ *n. & adj.* ● *n.* a substance used to reduce friction. ● *adj.* lubricating.

■ *n.* see OIL *n.*

lubricate /lṓbrikayt/ *v.tr.* **1** reduce friction in (machinery, etc.) by applying oil or grease, etc. **2** make slippery or smooth with oil or grease. □□ **lubrication** /-káyshən/ *n.* **lubricative** *adj.* **lubricator** *n.* [L *lubricare lubricat-* f. *lubricus* slippery]

■ oil, grease.

lubricious /lṓbríshəs/ *adj.* (also **lubricous** /lṓbrikəs/) **1** slippery; smooth; oily. **2** lewd; prurient; evasive. □□ **lubricity** /-brísitee/ *n.* [L *lubricus* slippery]

■ **2** see LEWD. □□ **lubricity** see *indecency* (INDECENT).

Lucan /lṓkən/ *adj.* of or relating to St. Luke. [eccl.L *Lucas* f. Gk *Loukas* Luke]

luce /lṓos/ *n.* a pike (fish), esp. when full-grown. [ME f. OF *lus, luis* f. LL *lucius*]

lucent /lṓsənt/ *adj. literary* **1** shining; luminous. **2** translucent. □□ **lucency** *n.* **lucently** *adv.* [L *lucēre* shine (as LUX)]

lucerne /lṓsə́rn/ *n.* (also **lucern**) *Brit.* = ALFALFA. [F *luzerne* f. mod. Prov. *luzerno* glowworm, with ref. to its shiny seeds]

lucid /lṓsid/ *adj.* **1** expressing or expressed clearly; easy to understand. **2** of or denoting intervals of sanity between periods of insanity or dementia. **3** *Bot.* with a smooth shining surface. **4** *poet.* bright. □□ **lucidity** /-síditee/ *n.* **lucidly** *adv.* **lucidness** *n.* [L *lucidus* (perh. through F *lucide* or It. *lucido*) f. *lucēre* shine (as LUX)]

■ **1** see CLEAR *adj.* 6b. **2** see RIGHT *adj.* 5, SANE 1. **4** see VIVID 1. □□ **lucidity** see CLARITY.

Lucifer /lṓsifər/ *n.* **1** Satan. **2** *poet.* the morning star (the planet Venus). **3** (**lucifer**) *archaic* a friction match. [OE f. L, = light-bringing, morning star (as LUX, *-fer* f. *ferre* bring)]

■ **1** see DEVIL *n.* 1, 2.

luck /luk/ *n.* **1** chance regarded as the bringer of good or bad fortune. **2** circumstances of life (beneficial or not) brought by this. **3** good fortune; success due to chance (*in luck*; *out of luck*). □ **for luck** to bring good fortune. **good luck 1** good fortune. **2** an omen of this. **hard luck** worse fortune than one deserves. **no such luck** *colloq.* unfortunately not. **try one's luck** make a venture. **with luck** if all goes well. **worse luck** *colloq.* unfortunately. [ME f. LG *luk* f. MLG *geluke*]

■ **1, 2** fortune, chance; destiny, fate, accident, fortuity, happenstance; fluke. **3** good fortune, good luck, serendipity; stroke of luck, *colloq.* break; success.

luckily /lúkilee/ *adv.* **1** (qualifying a whole sentence or clause) fortunately (*luckily there was enough food*). **2** in a lucky or fortunate manner.

■ fortunately, mercifully, happily; opportunely, propitiously, well.

luckless /lúklis/ *adj.* having no luck; unfortunate. □□ **lucklessly** *adv.* **lucklessness** *n.*

■ see UNFORTUNATE *adj.* 1.

lucky /lúkee/ *adj.* (**luckier, luckiest**) **1** having or resulting from good luck, esp. as distinct from skill or design or merit. **2** bringing good luck (*a lucky mascot*). **3** fortunate; appropriate (*a lucky guess*). □ **lucky dip** *Brit.* = *grab bag.* □□ **luckiness** *n.*

■ **1** fortunate; favored, charmed, blessed. **2** providential, propitious, favorable, auspicious, advantageous. **3** fortunate, timely, opportune, convenient, fortuitous, appropriate, happy.

lucrative /lṓkrətiv/ *adj.* profitable; yielding financial gain. □□ **lucratively** *adv.* **lucrativeness** *n.* [ME f. L *lucrativus* f. *lucrari* to gain]

■ see PROFITABLE 1.

lucre /lṓkər/ *n. derog.* financial profit or gain. □ **filthy lucre** see FILTHY. [ME f. F *lucre* or L *lucrum*]

■ see PROFIT *n.* 2.

lucubrate /lṓkyoobrayt/ *v.intr. literary* **1** write or study, esp. by night. **2** express one's meditations in writing. □□ **lucubrator** *n.* [L *lucubrare lucubrat-* work by lamplight (as LUX)]

■ **1** see STUDY *v.* 2.

lucubration /lṓkyoobráyshən/ *n. literary* **1** nocturnal study or meditation. **2** (usu. in *pl.*) literary writings, esp. of a pedantic or elaborate character. [L *lucubratio* (as LUCUBRATE)]

Lucullan /lṓkúlən/ *adj.* profusely luxurious. [L. Licinius *Lucullus*, Roman general of 1st c. BC famous for his lavish banquets]

lud /lud/ *n. Brit.* □ **m'lud** (or **my lud**) a form of address to a judge in a court of law. [corrupt. of LORD]

Luddite /lúdīt/ *n. & adj.* ● *n.* **1** *hist.* a member of any of the bands of English artisans who rioted against mechanization and destroyed machinery (1811–16). **2** a person opposed to increased industrialization or new technology. ● *adj.* of the Luddites or their beliefs. □□ **Luddism** *n.* **Luddism** *n.* [perh. f. Ned *Lud*, who destroyed machinery *c.* 1779]

ludicrous /lṓdikrəs/ *adj.* absurd or ridiculous; laughable. □□ **ludicrously** *adv.* **ludicrousness** *n.* [L *ludicrus* prob. f. *ludicrum* stage play]

■ ridiculous, laughable, absurd, farcical, nonsensical, preposterous, incongruous, asinine, foolish, silly, zany, crazy, comical, risible; funny, facetious, droll, waggish, jocular, witty, jocose.

lues /lṓo-eez/ *n.* (in full **lues venerea** /vineéreeə/) syphilis. □□ **luetic** /loo-étik/ *adj.* [L]

luff /luf/ *n. & v.* (also **loof** /lṓof/) *Naut.* ● *n.* **1** the edge of the fore-and-aft sail next to the mast or stay. **2** *Brit.* the broadest part of the ship's bow where the sides begin to curve in. ● *v.tr.* (also *absol.*) **1** steer (a ship) nearer the wind. **2** turn (the helm) so as to achieve this. **3** obstruct (an opponent in yacht racing) by sailing closer to the wind. **4** raise or lower (the jib of a crane or derrick). [ME *lo(o)f* f. OF *lof*, prob. f. LG]

luffa var. of LOOFAH.

Luftwaffe /lŏŏftvaafə/ *n. hist.* the German air force. [G f. *Luft* air + *Waffe* weapon]

lug[1] /lug/ *v. & n.* ● *v.* (**lugged, lugging**) **1** *tr.* **a** drag or tug (a heavy object) with effort or violence. **b** (usu. foll. by *around, about*) carry (something heavy) around with one. **2** *tr.* (usu. foll. by *in, into*) introduce (a subject, etc.) irrelevantly. **3** *tr.* (usu. foll. by *along, to*) force (a person) to join in an activity. **4** *intr.* (usu. foll. by *at*) pull hard. ● *n.* **1** a hard or rough pull. **2** (in *pl.*) affectation (*put on lugs*). [ME, prob. f. Scand.: cf. Sw. *lugga* pull a person's hair f. *lugg* forelock]

  ■ *v.* **1, 4** drag, tug, tow, haul, heave, pull; carry, transport, *colloq.* schlep, tote.

lug[2] /lug/ *n.* **1** *Sc.* or *colloq.* an ear. **2** a projection on an object by which it may be carried, fixed in place, etc. **3** *sl.* a lout; a sponger; a stupid person. □ **lug nut** a nut that attaches to a heavy bolt, esp. as used to attach a wheel to a motor vehicle. [prob. of Scand. orig.: cf. LUG[1]]

lug[3] /lug/ *n.* = LUGWORM. [17th c.: orig. unkn.]

lug[4] /lug/ *n.* = LUGSAIL. [abbr.]

luge /lŏŏzh/ *n. & v.* ● *n.* a light toboggan for one or two people, ridden (usu. raced) in a supine position down a chute. ● *v.intr.* ride on a luge. [Swiss F]

Luger /lŏŏgər/ *n.* a type of German automatic pistol. [G. *Luger*, German firearms expert d. 1922]

luggage /lúgij/ *n.* suitcases, bags, etc., to hold a traveler's belongings. □ **luggage van** *Brit.* a baggage car on a train. [LUG[1] + -AGE]

  ■ baggage, bags, suitcases, gear, impedimenta, paraphernalia, things, belongings.

lugger /lúgər/ *n.* a small ship carrying two or three masts with a lugsail on each. [LUGSAIL + -ER[1]]

lugsail /lúgsayl, -səl/ *n. Naut.* a quadrilateral sail that is bent on and hoisted from a yard. [prob. f. LUG[2]]

lugubrious /lŏŏgŏŏbreeəs, -gyŏŏ-/ *adj.* doleful; mournful; dismal. □□ **lugubriously** *adv.* **lugubriousness** *n.* [L *lugubris* f. *lugēre* mourn]

  ■ see DISMAL 1, 2. □□ **lugubriously** see *sadly* (SAD).
  lugubriousness see MELANCHOLY *n.*

lugworm /lúgwərm/ *n.* any polychaete worm of the genus *Arenicola*, living in muddy sand and leaving characteristic worm-casts on lower shores, and often used as bait by fishermen. [LUG[3]]

lukewarm /lŏŏkwáwrm/ *adj.* **1** moderately warm; tepid. **2** unenthusiastic; indifferent. □□ **lukewarmly** *adv.* **lukewarmness** *n.* [ME f. (now dial.) *luke, lew* f. OE]

  ■ **1** tepid, cool, (at) room temperature, warm. **2** cool, indifferent, halfhearted, chilly, phlegmatic, unresponsive, unenthusiastic, unexcited, nonchalant, lackadaisical, apathetic, noncommittal, insouciant, Laodicean, unmoved, *colloq.* laid-back, unenthused.

lull /lul/ *v. & n.* ● *v.* **1** *tr.* soothe or send to sleep gently. **2** *tr.* (usu. foll. by *into*) deceive (a person) into confidence (*lulled into a false sense of security*). **3** *tr.* allay (suspicions, etc.) usu. by deception. **4** *intr.* (of noise, a storm, etc.) abate or fall quiet. ● *n.* a temporary quiet period in a storm or in any activity. [ME, imit. of sounds used to quiet a child]

  ■ *v.* **1** soothe, calm, quiet, hush, pacify, mollify, tranquilize, *Brit.* quieten. ● *n.* pause, respite, interlude, intermission, interval, break, hiatus, interruption, stop, halt, lapse, delay, *Prosody* caesura, *colloq.* letup; quiet, quiescence, hush, calm, calmness, stillness, silence, peace, peacefulness, tranquillity.

lullaby /lúləbī/ *n. & v.* ● *n.* (*pl.* **-ies**) **1** a soothing song to send a child to sleep. **2** the music for this. ● *v.tr.* (**-ies, -ied**) sing to sleep. [as LULL + -by as in BYE-BYE[2]]

lulu /lŏŏlŏŏ/ *n. sl.* a remarkable or excellent person or thing. [19th c., perh. f. *Lulu*, pet form of *Louise*]

  ■ see KILLER 2a.

lumbago /lumbáygō/ *n.* rheumatic pain in the muscles of the lower back. [L f. *lumbus* loin]

lumbar /lúmbər, -baar/ *adj. Anat.* relating to the loin, esp. the lower back area. □ **lumbar puncture** the withdrawal of spinal fluid from the lower back with a hollow needle, usu. for diagnosis. [med.L *lumbaris* f. L *lumbus* loin]

lumber[1] /lúmbər/ *v.intr.* (usu. foll. by *along, past, by*, etc.) move in a slow, clumsy, noisy way. □□ **lumbering** *adj.* [ME *lomere*, perh. imit.]

lumber[2] /lúmbər/ *n. & v.* ● *n.* **1** logs or timber cut and prepared for use. **2 a** disused articles of furniture, etc., inconveniently taking up space. **b** useless or cumbersome objects. ● *v.* **1** *intr.* cut and prepare forest timber for transport. **2** *tr.* **a** (usu. foll. by *with*) leave (a person, etc.) with something unwanted or unpleasant (*always lumbering me with the cleaning*). **b** (as **lumbered** *adj.*) in an unwanted or inconvenient situation (*afraid of being lumbered*). **3** *tr.* (usu. foll. by *together*) heap or group together carelessly. **4** *tr.* (usu. foll. by *up*) obstruct. □ **lumber jacket** *n.* a jacket, usu. of warm checked material, of the kind worn by lumberjacks. **lumber room** *Brit.* = STOREROOM. □□ **lumberer** *n.* (in sense 1 of *v.*). **lumbering** *n.* (in sense 1 of *v.*). [perh. f. LUMBER[1]: later assoc. with obs. *lumber* pawnbroker's shop]

  ■ *n.* **1** timber, wood, beams, planks, boards. **2** odds and ends, junk, clutter, jumble, rejects, white elephants.
  ● *v.* **2** encumber, burden, load, overload, saddle, impose upon, land.

lumberjack /lúmbərjak/ *n.* (also **lumberman** /-mən/ *pl.* **-men**) one who fells, prepares, or conveys lumber.

lumbersome /lúmbərsəm/ *adj.* unwieldy; awkward.

lumbrical muscle /lúmbrikəl/ *n.* any of the muscles flexing the fingers or toes. [mod.L *lumbricalis* f. L *lumbricus* earthworm, with ref. to its shape]

lumen /lŏŏmən/ *n.* **1** *Physics* the SI unit of luminous flux, equal to the amount of light emitted per second in a unit solid angle of one steradian from a uniform source of one candela. ¶ Abbr.: **lm. 2** *Anat.* (*pl.* **lumina** /-minə/) a cavity within a tube, cell, etc. □□ **luminal** /-minəl/ *adj.* [L *lumen luminis* a light, an opening]

Luminal /lŏŏminəl/ *n. propr.* phenobarbital. [as LUMEN + -al as in *veronal*]

luminance /lŏŏminəns/ *n. Physics* the intensity of light emitted from a surface per unit area in a given direction. [L *luminare* illuminate (as LUMEN)]

luminary /lŏŏmineree/ *n.* (*pl.* **-ies**) **1** *literary* a natural light-giving body, esp. the sun or moon. **2** a person as a source of intellectual light or moral inspiration. **3** a prominent member of a group or gathering (*a host of show-business luminaries*). [ME f. OF *luminarie* or LL *luminarium* f. L *LUMEN*]

  ■ **2** see INSPIRATION 1b. **3** see CELEBRITY 1.

luminescence /lŏŏminésəns/ *n.* the emission of light by a substance other than as a result of incandescence. □□ **luminescent** /-sənt/ *adj.* [as LUMEN + -escence (see -ESCENT)]

  ■ see LIGHT[1] *n.* 3. □□ **luminescent** see LUMINOUS 2, 4.

luminiferous /lŏŏminífərəs/ *adj.* producing or transmitting light.

luminous /lŏŏminəs/ *adj.* **1** full of or shedding light; radiant; bright; shining. **2** phosphorescent; visible in darkness (*luminous paint*). **3** (esp. of a writer or a writer's work) throwing light on a subject. **4** of visible radiation (*luminous intensity*). □□ **luminosity** /-nósitee/ *n.* **luminously** *adv.* **luminousness** *n.* [ME f. OF *lumineux* or L *luminosus*]

  ■ **1** shiny, shining, bright, brilliant, lighted (up), lit (up), illuminated, radiant, alight, resplendent, lustrous, gleaming, shimmering, glistening, sparkling, dazzling,

---

/.../ **pronunciation**	● **part of speech**
□ **phrases, idioms, and compounds**	
□□ **derivatives**	■ **synonym section**
cross-references appear in SMALL CAPITALS or *italics*	

literary refulgent, effulgent. **2, 4** glowing, aglow, luminescent, incandescent, phosphorescent, fluorescent. **3** illuminating, illuminative; clear, lucid, perspicuous, percipient, perspicacious, penetrating, discerning, descrying, clear-eyed, clearheaded, keen, acute, sharp, explicit, incisive.

lummox /lúmǝks/ *n. colloq.* a clumsy or stupid person. [19th c. in US & dial.: orig. unkn.]
■ see CLOD 2.

lump[1] /lump/ *n. & v.* ● *n.* **1** a compact shapeless or unshapely mass. **2** *sl.* a quantity or heap. **3** a tumor, swelling, or bruise. **4** a heavy, dull, or ungainly person. **5** (prec. by *the*) Brit. casual workers in the building and other trades. ● *v.* **1** *tr.* (usu. foll. by *together, with, in with, under*, etc.) mass together or group indiscriminately. **2** *tr.* carry or throw carelessly (*lumping crates around the yard*). **3** *intr.* become lumpy. **4** *intr.* (usu. foll. by *along*) proceed heavily or awkwardly. **5** *intr.* (usu. foll. by *down*) sit down heavily. □ **in the lump** taking things as a whole; in a general manner. **lump in the throat** a feeling of pressure there, caused by emotion. **lump sum 1** a sum covering a number of items. **2** money paid down at once (opp. INSTALLMENT). □□ **lumper** *n.* (in sense 2 of v.). [ME, perh. of Scand. orig.]
■ *n.* **1, 2** piece, gobbet, clod, chunk, clot, wad, clump, hunk, nugget; cube, wedge, cake; mass, heap, pile, quantity. **3** bump, growth, protuberance, protrusion, prominence, bulge, excrescence, tumor, swelling, tumescence, nodule, knob; wen, cyst, boil, carbuncle, blister, wart, corn, bruise. **4** see CLOD 2. ● *v.* **1** (*lump together*) combine, join, consolidate, collect, bunch, group, unite, mass, aggregate, blend, mix, throw *or* put together.

lump[2] /lump/ *v.tr. colloq.* endure or suffer (a situation) ungraciously. □ **like it or lump it** put up with something whether one likes it or not. [imit.: cf. *dump, grump*, etc.]
■ tolerate, suffer, put up with, bear, stand, endure, allow, *literary* brook.

lumpectomy /lumpéktǝmee/ *n.* (*pl.* **-ies**) the surgical removal of a usu. cancerous lump from the breast.

lumpenproletariat /lúmpǝnprōlitáireeǝt/ *n.* (esp. in Marxist terminology) the unorganized and unpolitical lower orders of society, not interested in revolutionary advancement. □□ **lumpen** *adj.* [G f. *Lumpen* rag, rogue: see PROLETARIAT]
■ □□ **lumpen** see RUSTIC *adj.* 2.

lumpfish /lúmpfish/ *n.* (*pl.* **-fishes** or **-fish**) a spiny-finned fish, *Cyclopterus lumpus*, of the N. Atlantic with modified pelvic fins for clinging to objects. [MLG *lumpen*, MDu. *lumpe* (perh. = LUMP[1]) + FISH[1]]

lumpish /lúmpish/ *adj.* **1** heavy and clumsy. **2** stupid; lethargic. □□ **lumpishly** *adv.* **lumpishness** *n.*
■ **1** see AWKWARD 2. **2** see STUPID *adj.* 1, 5.
□□ **lumpishness** see *stupidity* (STUPID).

lumpy /lúmpee/ *adj.* (**lumpier, lumpiest**) **1** full of or covered with lumps. **2** (of water) cut up by the wind into small waves. □□ **lumpily** *adv.* **lumpiness** *n.*
■ **1** chunky, bumpy, uneven, granular, grainy.

lunacy /lṓonǝsee/ *n.* (*pl.* **-ies**) **1** insanity (orig. of the intermittent kind attributed to changes of the moon); the state of being a lunatic. **2** *Law* such mental unsoundness as interferes with civil rights or transactions. **3** great folly or eccentricity; a foolish act.
■ **1, 2** madness, insanity, dementia, craziness, derangement, psychosis, mania; *Law* diminished responsibility. **3** folly, foolishness, bad *or* poor judgment, illogicality, senselessness, ridiculousness, irrationality, foolhardiness, stupidity; eccentricity.

luna moth /lṓonǝ/ *n.* a N. American moth, *Actias luna*, with crescent-shaped spots on its pale green wings. [L *luna*, = moon (from its markings)]

lunar /lṓonǝr/ *adj.* **1** of, relating to, or determined by the moon. **2** concerned with travel to the moon and related research. **3** (of light, glory, etc.) pale; feeble. **4** crescent-shaped; lunate. **5** of or containing silver (from alchemists' use of *luna* (= moon) for 'silver'). □ **lunar caustic** silver nitrate, esp. in stick form. **lunar cycle** = METONIC CYCLE.

lunar distance the angular distance of the moon from the sun, a planet, or a star, used in finding longitude at sea. **lunar module** a small craft used for traveling between the moon's surface and a spacecraft in orbit around the moon. **lunar month 1** the period of the moon's revolution, esp. the interval between new moons of about 292⁄x days. **2** (in general use) a period of four weeks. **lunar nodes** the points at which the moon's orbit cuts the ecliptic. **lunar observation** the finding of longitude by lunar distance. **lunar orbit 1** the orbit of the moon around the earth. **2** an orbit around the moon. **lunar year** a period of 12 lunar months. [L *lunaris* f. *luna* moon]

lunate /lṓonayt/ *adj. & n.* ● *adj.* crescent-shaped. ● *n.* a crescent-shaped prehistoric implement, etc. □ **lunate bone** a crescent-shaped bone in the wrist. [L *lunatus* f. *luna* moon]

lunatic /lṓonǝtik/ *n. & adj.* ● *n.* **1** an insane person. **2** someone foolish or eccentric. ● *adj.* mad; foolish. □ **lunatic asylum** *hist.* a mental home or hospital. **lunatic fringe** an extreme or eccentric minority group. [ME f. OF *lunatique* f. LL *lunaticus* f. L *luna* moon]
■ *n.* see MADMAN. ● *adj.* see MAD *adj.* 1.

lunation /loonáyshǝn/ *n.* the interval between new moons, about 292⁄x days. [ME f. med.L *lunatio* (as LUNATIC)]

lunch /lunch/ *n. & v.* ● *n.* **1** the meal eaten in the middle of the day. **2** a light meal eaten at any time. ● *v.* **1** *intr.* eat one's lunch. **2** *tr.* provide lunch for. □ **out to lunch** *sl.* unaware; incompetent. □□ **luncher** *n.* [LUNCHEON]
■ *n.* see MEAL[1].

lunchbox /lúnchboks/ *n.* a container for a packed lunch.

lunchtime /lúnchtim/ *n.* the time (usu. around noon) at which lunch is eaten.

luncheon /lúnchǝn/ *n. formal* lunch. □ **luncheon meat** sliced, cold prepared meats used for sandwiches, etc. [17th c.: orig. unkn.]
■ see MEAL[1].

luncheonette /lúnchǝnét/ *n.* a small restaurant or snack bar serving light lunches.

lune /loon/ *n. Geom.* a crescent-shaped figure formed on a sphere or plane by two arcs intersecting at two points. [F f. L *luna* moon]

lunette /loonét/ *n.* **1** an arched aperture in a domed ceiling to admit light. **2** a crescent-shaped or semicircular space or alcove that contains a painting, statue, etc. **3** a watch crystal of flattened shape. **4** a ring through which a hook is placed to attach a vehicle to the vehicle towing it. **5** a temporary fortification with two faces forming a salient angle, and two flanks. **6** *RC Ch.* a holder for the consecrated host in a monstrance. [F, dimin. of *lune* (see LUNE)]
■ **1, 2** see CRESCENT *n.* 2.

lung /lung/ *n.* either of the pair of respiratory organs, which bring air into contact with the blood in humans and many other vertebrates. □□ **lunged** *adj.* **lungful** *n.* (*pl.* **-fuls**). **lungless** *adj.* [OE *lungen* f. Gmc, rel. to LIGHT[2]]

lunge[1] /lunj/ *n. & v.* ● *n.* **1** a sudden movement forward. **2** a thrust with a sword, etc., esp. the basic attacking move in fencing. **3** a movement forward by bending the front leg at the knee while keeping the back leg straight. ● *v.* **1** *intr.* make a lunge. **2** *intr.* (usu. foll. by *at, out*) deliver a blow from the shoulder in boxing. **3** *tr.* drive (a weapon, etc.) violently in some direction. [earlier *allonge* f. F *allonger* lengthen f. *à* to + *long* LONG[1]]
■ *n.* **1** dive, plunge, rush, leap, jump, spring, pounce. **2** thrust, jab, strike. ● *v.* **1** dive, plunge, charge, pounce, dash, bound, jump. **2, 3** thrust, stab, jab; cut, strike, hit.

lunge[2] var. of LONGE.

lungfish /lúngfish/ *n.* any freshwater fish of the order Dipnoi, having gills and a modified swim bladder used as lungs, and able to estivate to survive drought.

lungi /lṓonggee/ *n.* (*pl.* **lungis**) a length of cotton cloth, usu. worn as a loincloth in India, or as a skirt in Burma where it is the national dress for both sexes. [Urdu]

lungwort /lúngwǝrt, -wawrt/ *n.* **1** any herbaceous plant of the genus *Pulmonaria*, esp. *P. officinalis* with white-spotted leaves likened to a diseased lung. **2** a lichen, *Lobaria pulmonaria*, used as a remedy for lung disease.

lunisolar /lōōnisōlər/ *adj.* of or concerning the sun and moon. □ **lunisolar period** a period of 532 years between the repetitions of both solar and lunar cycles. **lunisolar year** a year with divisions regulated by changes of the moon and an average length made to agree with the solar year. [L *luna* moon + *sol* sun]

lunula /lōōnyələ/ *n.* (*pl.* **lunulae** /-lee/) **1** a crescent-shaped mark, esp. the white area at the base of the fingernail. **2** a crescent-shaped Bronze Age ornament. [L, dimin. of *luna* moon]

lupine[1] /lōōpin/ *n.* (also **lupin**) **1** any plant of the genus *Lupinus*, with long tapering spikes of blue, purple, pink, white, or yellow flowers. **2** (in *pl.*) seeds of the lupine. [ME f. L *lupinus*]

lupine[2] /lōōpin/ *adj.* of or like a wolf or wolves. [L *lupinus* f. *lupus* wolf]
■ see RAPACIOUS.

lupus /lōōpəs/ *n.* any of various ulcerous skin diseases, esp. tuberculosis of the skin. □ **lupus vulgaris** /vulgáiris/ tuberculosis with dark red patches on the skin, usu. due to direct inoculation of the tuberculosis bacillus into the skin. □□ **lupoid** *adj.* **lupous** *adj.* [L, = wolf]

lur /lōōr/ *n.* (also **lure** /lyōōr/) a bronze S-shaped trumpet of prehistoric times, still used in Scandinavia to call cattle. [Da. & Norw.]

lurch[1] /lərch/ *n. & v.* ● *n.* a sudden unsteady movement or leaning. ● *v.intr.* stagger; move suddenly and unsteadily. [orig. Naut., *lee-lurch* alt. of *lee-latch* drifting to leeward]
■ *n.* stagger, sway, pitch; list, tilt, toss. ● *v.* stagger, sway, stumble, reel; roll, tilt, veer, pitch, list, heel, wallow.

lurch[2] /lərch/ *n.* □ **leave in the lurch** desert (a friend, etc.) in difficulties. [orig. = a severe defeat in a game, f. F *lourche* (also the game itself, like backgammon)]
■ □ **leave in the lurch** desert, abandon, forsake; drop, jilt.

lurcher /lərchər/ *n.* **1** *Brit.* a crossbred dog, usu. a retriever, collie, or sheepdog crossed with a greyhound, used esp. for hunting and by poachers. **2** *archaic* a petty thief, swindler, or spy. [f. obs. *lurch* (v.) var. of LURK]
■ **2** see BURGLAR *n.*

lure /lōōr/ *v. & n.* ● *v.tr.* **1** (usu. foll. by *away, into*) entice (a person, an animal, etc.) usu. with some form of bait. **2** attract back again or recall (a person, animal, etc.) with the promise of a reward. ● *n.* **1** a thing used to entice. **2** (usu. foll. by *of*) the attractive or compelling qualities (of a pursuit, etc.). **3** a falconer's apparatus for recalling a hawk, consisting of a bunch of feathers attached to a thong, within which the hawk finds food while being trained. □□ **luring** *adj.* **luringly** *adv.* [ME f. OE *luere* f. Gmc]
■ *v.* tempt, attract, induce, coax, inveigle, seduce, draw in, entice, lead on, decoy, charm, persuade, allure, catch. ● *n.* **1** bait, decoy, attraction, temptation, inducement, magnet, siren song, charm, carrot, *sl.* come-on.

Lurex /lōōreks/ *n. propr.* **1** a type of yarn that incorporates a glittering metallic thread. **2** fabric made from this yarn.

lurid /lōōrid/ *adj.* **1** vivid or glowing in color (*lurid orange*). **2** of an unnatural glare (*lurid nocturnal brilliance*). **3** sensational, horrifying, or terrible (*lurid details*). **4** showy; gaudy (*paperbacks with lurid covers*). **5** ghastly; wan (*lurid complexion*). **6** *Bot.* of a dingy yellowish brown. □ **cast a lurid light on** explain or reveal (facts or character) in a horrific, sensational, or shocking way. □□ **luridly** *adv.* **luridness** *n.* [L *luridus* f. *luror* wan or yellow color]
■ **1, 2** glaring, fiery, flaming, burning, aglow, glowing, glowering; fluorescent, loud, vivid, garish. **3** sensational, vivid, shocking, startling, graphic, melodramatic; ghastly, horrid, horrifying, horrendous, gory, grisly, gruesome, macabre, revolting, disgusting, appalling, frightful, terrible, awful. **4** showy, gaudy;

loud, cheap, garish. **5** pale, ghastly, ashen, sallow, wan, pallid, baleful.

lurk /lərk/ *v. & n.* ● *v.intr.* **1** linger furtively or unobtrusively. **2 a** lie in ambush. **b** (usu. foll. by *in, under, about*, etc.) hide, esp. for sinister purposes. **3** (as **lurking** *adj.*) latent; semiconscious (*a lurking suspicion*). ● *n. Austral. colloq.* a dodge, racket, or scheme; a method of profitable business. □□ **lurker** *n.* [ME perh. f. LOUR with frequent. *-k* as in TALK]
■ *v.* **1, 2** linger, loiter; skulk, slink, prowl, steal, sneak, hide, (lie in) wait, lie low. **3** (**lurking**) see *sneaking* (SNEAK *v.* 4).

luscious /lúshəs/ *adj.* **1 a** richly sweet in taste or smell. **b** *colloq.* delicious. **2** (of literary style, music, etc.) overrich in sound, imagery, or voluptuous suggestion. **3** voluptuously attractive. □□ **lusciously** *adv.* **lusciousness** *n.* [ME perh. alt. of obs. *licious* f. DELICIOUS]
■ **1** delicious, mouthwatering, tasty, toothsome, savory, appetizing, rich, sweet, epicurean, ambrosial, palatable, pleasant, *literary* delectable; succulent, juicy, *colloq.* scrumptious, yummy, esp. *Brit. colloq.* scrummy.

lush[1] /lush/ *adj.* **1** (of vegetation, esp. grass) luxuriant and succulent. **2** luxurious. □□ **lushly** *adv.* **lushness** *n.* [ME, perh. var. of obs. *lash* soft, f. OF *lasche* lax (see LACHES): assoc. with LUSCIOUS]
■ **1** luxuriant, thick, lavish, flourishing, verdant, green, dense, overgrown, exuberant; juicy, succulent, fresh, moist, ripe. **2** palatial, extravagant, elaborate, luxurious, opulent, sumptuous, *colloq.* ritzy, plush, plushy.

lush[2] /lush/ *n. & v. sl.* ● *n.* **1** alcohol; liquor. **2** an alcoholic; a drunkard. ● *v.* **1** *tr. & intr.* drink (alcohol). **2** *tr.* ply with alcohol. [18th c.: perh. joc. use of LUSH[1]]

lust /lust/ *n. & v.* ● *n.* **1** strong sexual desire. **2 a** (usu. foll. by *for, of*) a passionate desire for (*a lust for power*). **b** (usu. foll. by *of*) a passionate enjoyment of (*the lust of battle*). **3** (usu. in *pl.*) a sensuous appetite regarded as sinful (*the lusts of the flesh*). ● *v.intr.* (usu. foll. by *after, for*) have a strong or excessive (esp. sexual) desire. □□ **lustful** *adj.* **lustfully** *adv.* **lustfulness** *n.* [OE f. Gmc]
■ *n.* **1, 3** passion, desire, sensuality, libido, libidinousness, sexuality, lustfulness, sexual appetite, *formal* concupiscence, *sl.* horniness. **2** desire, drive, energy, voracity, avidity, avidness, ambition, ravenousness. ● *v.* (*lust after*) desire, crave, hunger or thirst or hanker for or after, ache for. □□ **lustful** libidinous, carnal, licentious, lewd, prurient, lascivious, salacious, randy, *formal* concupiscent, *sl.* horny.

luster[1] /lústər/ *n. & v.* (*Brit.* **lustre**) ● *n.* **1** gloss, brilliance, or sheen. **2** a shining or reflective surface. **3 a** a thin metallic coating giving an iridescent glaze to ceramics. **b** = LUSTERWARE. **4** a radiance or attractiveness; splendor; glory; distinction (of achievements, etc.) (*add luster to; shed luster on*). **5 a** a prismatic glass pendant on a chandelier, etc. **b** a cutglass chandelier or candelabra. **6 a** *Brit.* a thin dress material with a cotton warp, woolen weft, and a glossy surface. **b** any fabric with a sheen or gloss. ● *v.tr.* put luster on (pottery, a cloth, etc.). □□ **lusterless** *adj.* **lustrous** *adj.* **lustrously** *adv.* **lustrousness** *n.* [F f. It. *lustro* f. *lustrare* f. L *lustrare* illuminate]
■ *n.* **1** sheen, gleam, glow, gloss, luminosity, luminousness, radiance, brilliance, iridescence. **4** radiance, attractiveness; glory, splendor, renown, brilliance, honor, distinction, fame, illustriousness. □□ **lustrous** glossy, shiny, shined, polished, burnished.

luster[2] /lústər/ *n.* (*Brit.* **lustre**) = LUSTRUM. [ME, Anglicized f. LUSTRUM]

lusterware /lústərwair/ *n.* (*Brit.* **lustreware**) ceramics with an iridescent glaze. [LUSTER[1]]

lustra *pl.* of LUSTRUM.

/. . . / **pronunciation**	● **part of speech**
□ **phrases, idioms, and compounds**	
□□ **derivatives**	■ **synonym section**
cross-references appear in SMALL CAPITALS or *italics*	

lustral /lústrəl/ *adj.* relating to or used in ceremonial purification. [L *lustralis* (as LUSTRUM)]

lustrate /lústrayt/ *v.tr.* purify by expiatory sacrifice, ceremonial washing, or other such rite. □□ **lustration** /-tráy-shən/ *n.* [L *lustrare* (as LUSTRUM)]
■ see PURIFY.

lustre *Brit.* var. of LUSTER.

lustrum /lústrəm/ *n.* (*pl.* **lustra** /lústrə/ or **lustrums**) a period of five years. [L, an orig. purificatory sacrifice after a quinquennial census]

lusty /lústee/ *adj.* (**lustier, lustiest**) **1** healthy and strong. **2** vigorous or lively. □□ **lustily** *adv.* **lustiness** *n.* [ME f. LUST + -Y¹]
■ vigorous, healthy, strong, energetic, robust, hale and hearty, lively, husky, powerful; buxom, substantial.

lusus /lóosəs/ *n.* (in full **lusus naturae** /nətóoree, -tyóoree/) a freak of nature. [L]
■ see MONSTER 3, 4.

lutanist var. of LUTENIST.

lute¹ /loot/ *n.* a guitarlike instrument with a long neck and a pear-shaped body, much used in the 14th–17th c. [ME f. F *lut, leüt,* prob. f. Prov. *laüt* f. Arab. *al-'ūd*]

lute² /loot/ *n. & v.* ● *n.* **1** clay or cement used to stop a hole, make a joint airtight, coat a crucible, protect a graft, etc. **2** a rubber seal for a jar, etc. ● *v.tr.* apply lute to. [ME f. OF *lut* f. L *lutum* mud, clay]

lutecium var. of LUTETIUM.

lutein /looteein/ *n. Chem.* a pigment of a deep yellow color found in egg yolk, etc. [L *luteum* yolk of egg, neut. of *luteus* yellow]

luteinizing hormone /looteeinizing/ *n. Biochem.* a hormone secreted by the anterior pituitary gland that in females stimulates ovulation and in males stimulates the synthesis of androgen. ¶ Abbr.: **LH.** [LUTEIN]

lutenist /loot'nist/ *n.* (also **lutanist**) a lute player. [med.L *lutanista* f. *lutana* LUTE¹]

luteo- /looteeō/ *comb. form* orange-colored. [as LUTEOUS + -O-]

luteofulvous /looteeōfúlvəs/ *adj.* orange-tawny.

luteous /looteeəs/ *adj.* of a deep orange yellow or greenish yellow. [L *luteus* f. *lutum* WELD²]

lutestring /lootstring/ *n. archaic* a glossy silk fabric. [app. f. *lustring* f. F *lustrine* or It. *lustrino* f. *lustro* LUSTER]

lutetium /looteeshəm/ *n.* (also **lutecium**) *Chem.* a silvery metallic element of the lanthanide series. ¶ Symb.: **Lu.** [F *lutécium* f. L *Lutetia* the ancient name of Paris]

Lutheran /lootherən/ *n. & adj.* ● *n.* **1** a follower of Martin Luther, Ger. religious reformer d. 1546. **2** a member of the Lutheran Church, which accepts the Augsburg confession of 1530, with justification by faith alone as a cardinal doctrine. ● *adj.* of or characterized by the theology of Martin Luther. □□ **Lutheranism** *n.* **Lutheranize** *v.tr. & intr.*

Lutine bell /looteen/ *n.* a bell kept at Lloyd's in London and rung whenever there is an important announcement to be made to the underwriters. [HMS *Lutine,* which sank in 1799, whose bell it was]

luting /looting/ *n.* = LUTE² *n.*

lutz /luts/ *n.* a jump in figure skating in which the skater takes off from the outside back edge of one skate and lands, after a complete rotation in the air, on the outside back edge of the opposite skate. [prob. f. Swiss figure skater Gustave *Lussi* b. 1898, who invented it]

lux /luks/ *n.* (*pl.* same or **luxes**) *Physics* the SI unit of illumination, equivalent to one lumen per square meter. ¶ Abbr.: **lx.** [L *lux lucis* light]

luxe /looks, luks/ *n.* luxury (cf. DELUXE). [F f. L *luxus*]

Luxembourger /lúksəmbərgər/ *n.* **1** a native or national of Luxembourg. **2** a person of Luxembourg descent.

luxuriant /lugzhóoreeənt, lukshóor-/ *adj.* **1** (of vegetation, etc.) lush; profuse in growth. **2** prolific; exuberant; rank (*luxuriant imagination*). **3** (of literary or artistic style) florid; richly ornate. □□ **luxuriance** /-eeəns/ *n.* **luxuriantly** *adv.* [L *luxuriare* grow rank f. *luxuria* LUXURY]
■ **1** abundant, profuse, copious, lush, rich, *poet.* bounteous; overflowing, full, luxurious. **2** lavish, full,

rank, prolific, thriving, rife, exuberant, lush, abounding, abundant, superabundant, dense, fruitful, teeming, *poet.* plenteous. **3** ornate, elaborate, decorated, fancy, rococo, baroque, flowery, frilly, florid, overdone, flamboyant, showy, ostentatious, gaudy, garish, flashy.

luxuriate /lugzhóoreeayt, lukshóor-/ *v.intr.* **1** (foll. by *in*) take self-indulgent delight in; enjoy in a luxurious manner. **2** take one's ease; relax in comfort.
■ **1** (*luxuriate in*) wallow in, swim in, bask in, indulge in, delight in, relish, revel in, savor, enjoy, appreciate, like, love. **2** take one's ease, live in luxury *or* comfort, be *or* live in the lap of luxury, take it easy, enjoy oneself, live off *or* on the fat of the land, have the time of one's life, *colloq.* live the life of Riley, *sl.* have a ball.

luxurious /lugzhóoreeəs, lukshóor-/ *adj.* **1** supplied with luxuries. **2** extremely comfortable. **3** fond of luxury; self-indulgent; voluptuous. □□ **luxuriously** *adv.* **luxuriousness** *n.* [ME f. OF *luxurios* f. L *luxuriosus* (as LUXURY)]
■ **1** opulent, sumptuous, grand, extravagant, lavish, magnificent, splendid, voluptuous, deluxe, high-class, fancy, swanky, plush, *colloq.* ritzy, plushy, posh, swank; epicurean, gourmet. **3** self-indulgent, voluptuous, voluptuary, sybaritic, hedonistic, pampered.

luxury /lúgzhəree, lúkshəree/ *n.* (*pl.* **-ies**) **1** choice or costly surroundings, possessions, food, etc.; luxuriousness (*a life of luxury*). **2** something desirable for comfort or enjoyment, but not indispensable. **3** (*attrib.*) providing great comfort; expensive (*a luxury apartment; a luxury vacation*). [ME f. OF *luxurie, luxure* f. L *luxuria* f. *luxus* abundance]
■ **1** opulence, splendor, sumptuousness, grandeur, luxe, extravagance, magnificence, richness; luxuriousness, indulgence, self-indulgence, hedonism, sybaritism, voluptuousness. **2** frill, extravagance, extra, indulgence, treat. **3** (*attrib.*) see OPULENT 1, EXPENSIVE 1.

Lw *symb. Chem.* the element lawrencium.

LWM *abbr.* low-water mark.

LWV *abbr.* League of Women Voters.

lx *abbr.* lux.

LXX *abbr.* Septuagint.

-ly¹ /lee/ *suffix* forming adjectives esp. from nouns, meaning: **1** having the qualities of (*princely; manly*). **2** recurring at intervals of (*daily; hourly*). [from or after OE *-lic* f. Gmc, rel. to LIKE¹]

-ly² /lee/ *suffix* forming adverbs from adjectives, denoting esp. manner or degree (*boldly; happily; miserably; deservedly; amusingly*). [from or after OE *-lice* f. Gmc (as -LY¹)]

lycanthrope /líkənthrōp, likán-/ *n.* **1** a werewolf. **2** an insane person who believes that he or she is an animal, esp. a wolf. [mod.L *lycanthropus* f. Gk (as LYCANTHROPY)]

lycanthropy /líkánthrəpee/ *n.* **1** the mythical transformation of a person into a wolf (see also WEREWOLF). **2** a form of madness involving the delusion of being a wolf, with changed appetites, voice, etc. [mod.L *lycanthropia* f. Gk *lukanthrōpia* f. *lukos* wolf + *anthrōpos* man]

lycée /leesáy/ *n.* (*pl.* **lycées**) a government-sponsored secondary school, esp. in France. [F f. L (as LYCEUM)]

Lyceum /līseeəm/ *n.* **1 a** the garden at Athens in which Aristotle taught philosophy. **b** Aristotelian philosophy and its followers. **2** (**lyceum**) a literary institution, lecture hall, concert hall, etc. [L f. Gk *Lukeion* neut. of *Lukeios* epithet of Apollo (from whose neighboring temple the Lyceum was named)]

lychee var. of LITCHI.

lych-gate var. of LICH-GATE.

lychnis /líknis/ *n.* any herbaceous plant of the genus *Lychnis,* including ragged robin. [L f. Gk *lukhnis* a red flower f. *lukhnos* lamp]

lycopod /líkəpod/ *n.* any of various club mosses, esp. of the genus *Lycopodium.* [Anglicized form of LYCOPODIUM]

lycopodium /líkəpódeeəm/ *n.* **1** = LYCOPOD. **2** a fine powder of spores from this, used as an absorbent in surgery, and in making fireworks, etc. [mod.L f. Gk *lukos* wolf + *pous podos* foot]

Lycra /líkrə/ *n. propr.* an elastic polyurethane fiber or fabric used esp. for close-fitting sports clothing.

Lydian /lídeeən/ *adj. & n.* ● *n.* **1** a native or inhabitant of ancient Lydia in W. Asia Minor. **2** the language of this people. ● *adj.* of or relating to the people of Lydia or their language. □ **Lydian mode** *Mus.* the mode represented by the natural diatonic scale F–F. [L *Lydius* f. Gk *Ludios* of Lydia]

lye /lí/ *n.* **1** water that has been made alkaline by lixiviation of vegetable ashes. **2** any strong alkaline solution, esp. of potassium hydroxide used for washing or cleansing. [OE *lēag* f. Gmc: cf. LATHER]

lying[1] /lí-ing/ *pres. part.* of LIE[1]. *n.* a place to lie (*a dry lying*).

lying[2] /lí-ing/ *pres. part.* of LIE[2]. *adj.* deceitful; false. □□ **lyingly** *adv.*
■ untruthful, false, mendacious, hypocritical, dishonest, deceitful, deceptive, duplicitous, treacherous, perfidious.

lyke-wake /líkwayk/ *n. Brit.* a night watch over a dead body. [perh. f. ON: cf. LICH(-GATE), WAKE[1]]

Lyme disease /lím/ *n.* a disease transmitted by ticks, usually characterized by rash, fever, fatigue, and joint pain. [for Lyme, Connecticut, where first described]

lymph /limf/ *n.* **1** *Physiol.* a colorless fluid containing white blood cells, drained from the tissues and conveyed through the body in the lymphatic system. **2** this fluid used as a vaccine. **3** exudation from a sore, etc. **4** *poet.* pure water. □ **lymph node** (or **gland**) a small mass of tissue in the lymphatic system where lymph is purified and lymphocytes are formed. □□ **lymphoid** *adj.* **lymphous** *adj.* [F *lymphe* or L *lympha, limpa* water]

lymphatic /limfátik/ *adj. & n.* ● *adj.* **1** of or secreting or conveying lymph (*lymphatic gland*). **2** (of a person) pale, flabby, or sluggish. ● *n.* a veinlike vessel conveying lymph. □ **lymphatic system** a network of vessels conveying lymph. [orig. = frenzied, f. L *lymphaticus* mad f. Gk *numpholēptos* seized by nymphs: now assoc. with LYMPH (on the analogy of *spermatic*, etc.)]
■ *adj.* **2** see SUPINE *adj.* 3.

lymphocyte /límfəsīt/ *n.* a form of leukocyte occurring in the blood, in lymph, etc. □□ **lymphocytic** /-sítik/ *adj.*

lymphoma /limfṓmə/ *n.* (*pl.* **lymphomas** or **lymphomata** /-mətə/) any malignant tumor of the lymph nodes, excluding leukemia.

lyncean /linseeən/ *adj.* lynx-eyed; keen-sighted. [L *lynceus* f. Gk *lugkeios* f. *lugx* LYNX]

lynch /linch/ *v.tr.* (of a body of people) put (a person) to death for an alleged offense without a legal trial. □ **lynch law** the procedure of a self-constituted illegal court that punishes or executes. **lynch mob** a group of people intent on lynching someone. □□ **lyncher** *n.* **lynching** *n.* [*Lynch's law*, after Capt. W. *Lynch* of Virginia *c.*1780]
■ see HANG *v.* 7a.

lynchet /línchit/ *n.* (in the UK) a ridge or ledge formed by ancient plowing on a slope. [*linch* f. OE *hlinc*: cf. LINKS]

lynchpin var. of LINCHPIN.

lynx /lingks/ *n.* **1** a medium-sized feline, *Felis lynx*, with short tail, spotted fur, and tufted ear tips. **2** its fur. □ **lynx-eyed** keen-sighted. □□ **lynxlike** *adj.* [ME f. L f. Gk *lugx*]
■ □ **lynx-eyed** see *sharp-eyed*.

lyophilic /líəfílik/ *adj.* (of a colloid) readily dispersed by a solvent. [Gk *luō* loosen, dissolve + Gk *philos* loving]

lyophilize /líófilīz/ *v.tr.* freeze-dry.

lyophobic /líəfṓbik/ *adj.* (of a colloid) not lyophilic. [Gk *luō* loosen, dissolve + -*phobic* (see -PHOBIA)]

lyrate /lírayt, -rət/ *adj. Biol.* lyre-shaped.

lyre /lír/ *n. Gk Antiq.* an ancient stringed instrument like a small U-shaped harp, played usu. with a plectrum and accompanying the voice. [ME f. OF *lire* f. L *lyra* f. Gk *lura*]

lyrebird /lírbərd/ *n.* any Australian bird of the family Menuridae, the male of which has a lyre-shaped tail display.

lyric /lírik/ *adj. & n.* ● *adj.* **1** (of poetry) expressing the writer's emotions, usu. briefly and in stanzas or recognized forms. **2** (of a poet) writing in this manner. **3** of or for the lyre. **4** meant to be sung; fit to be expressed in song; songlike (*lyric drama*; *lyric opera*). ● *n.* **1** a lyric poem or verse. **2** (in *pl.*) lyric verses. **3** (usu. in *pl.*) the words of a song. [F *lyrique* or L *lyricus* f. Gk *lurikos* (as LYRE)]
■ *adj.* **1, 2** personal, subjective, individual; sentimental, rhapsodic, lyrical. **4** melodic, songlike, musical, melodious, lyrical; sweet, dulcet, graceful, silvery, lilting, mellifluous, mellow, light. ● *n.* **3** (*lyrics*) libretto, words.

lyrical /lírikəl/ *adj.* **1** = LYRIC *adj.* 1, 2. **2** resembling, couched in, or using language appropriate to, lyric poetry. **3** *colloq.* highly enthusiastic (*wax lyrical about*). □□ **lyrically** *adv.* **lyricalness** *n.*
■ **2** see LYRIC *adj.* 1, 2. **3** enthusiastic, ecstatic, encomiastic, rapturous, rhapsodic, effusive, impassioned, emotional, ebullient, exuberant, panegyrical, eulogistic.

lyricism /lírisizəm/ *n.* **1** the character or quality of being lyric or lyrical. **2** a lyrical expression. **3** high-flown sentiments.

lyricist /lírisist/ *n.* a person who writes the words to a song.

lyrist *n.* **1** /lírist/ a person who plays the lyre. **2** /lírist/ a lyric poet. [L *lyrista* f. Gk *luristēs* f. *lura* lyre]
■ **2** see POET.

lyse /līs/ *v.tr. & intr. Biol.* bring about or undergo lysis. [back-form. f. LYSIS]

lysergic acid /lisérjik/ *n.* a crystalline acid extracted from ergot or prepared synthetically. □ **lysergic acid diethylamide** /dī-éthilámíd/ a powerful hallucinogenic drug. ¶ Abbr.: **LSD**. [hydro*lysis* + *ergot* + -IC]

lysin /lísin/ *n. Biol.* a protein in the blood able to cause lysis. [G *Lysine*]

lysine /líseen/ *n. Biochem.* an amino acid present in protein and essential in the diet of vertebrates. [G *Lysin*, ult. f. LYSIS]

lysis /lísis/ *n.* (*pl.* **lyses** /-seez/) *Biol.* the disintegration of a cell. [L f. Gk *lusis* loosening f. *luō* loosen]

-lysis /lisis/ *comb. form* forming nouns denoting disintegration or decomposition (*electrolysis*; *hemolysis*).

lysosome /lísəsōm/ *n. Biol.* a cytoplasmic organelle in eukaryotic cells containing degradative enzymes enclosed in a membrane. [LYSIS + -SOME[3]]

lysozyme /lísəzīm/ *n. Biochem.* an enzyme found in tears and egg white that catalyzes the destruction of cell walls of certain bacteria. [LYSIS + ENZYME]

lytic /lítik/ *adj.* of, relating to, or causing lysis.

-lytic /litik/ *comb. form* forming adjectives corresponding to nouns in -*lysis*. [Gk *lutikos* (as LYSIS)]

/. . ./ pronunciation	● part of speech
□ phrases, idioms, and compounds	
□□ derivatives	■ synonym section
cross-references appear in SMALL CAPITALS or *italics*	

Mm

M¹ /em/ n. (pl. **Ms** or **M's**) **1** the thirteenth letter of the alphabet. **2** (as a Roman numeral) 1,000.

M² abbr. (also **M.**) **1** Master. **2** Monsieur. **3** mega-. **4** Chem. molar. **5** Mach. **6** Mus. major.

m abbr. (also **m.**) **1 a** masculine. **b** male. **2** married. **3** mile(s). **4** meter(s). **5** million(s). **6** minute(s). **7** Physics mass. **8** Currency mark(s). **9** milli-.

'm n. colloq. madam (in yes'm, etc.).

MA abbr. **1** Master of Arts. **2** Massachusetts (in official postal use).

ma /maa/ n. colloq. mother. [abbr. of MAMA]

ma'am /mam/ n. madam. [contr.]

Mac /mak/ n. colloq. man (esp. as a form of address).

mac /mak/ n. (also **mack**) colloq. mackintosh. [abbr.]

macabre /məkáabər/ adj. (also **macaber**) grim, gruesome. [ME f. OF macabré perh. f. Macabé a Maccabee, with ref. to a miracle play showing the slaughter of the Maccabees]
■ grim, ghastly, grisly, gory, gruesome, grotesque, ghoulish, fiendish, eerie, fearsome, frightful, frightening, terrifying, terrible, dreadful, dire; deathly, deadly, deathlike, ghostly, cadaverous.

macadam /məkádəm/ n. **1** material for making roads with successive layers of compacted broken stone. **2** a road made from such material. □□ **macadamize** v.tr. [J. L. McAdam, Brit. surveyor d. 1836, who advocated using this material]

macadamia /mákədáymeeə/ n. any Australian evergreen tree of the genus Macadamia, esp. M. ternifolia, bearing edible nutlike seeds. [J. Macadam, Austral. chemist d. 1865]

macaque /məkák/ n. any monkey of the genus Macaca, including the rhesus monkey and Barbary ape, having prominent cheek pouches and usu. a long tail. [F f. Port. macaco f. Bantu makaku some monkeys f. kaku monkey]

macaroni /mákərōnee/ n. **1** a tubular variety of pasta. **2** (pl. **macaronies**) hist. an 18th-c. British dandy affecting Continental fashions. [It. maccaroni f. late Gk makaria food made from barley]

macaronic /mákərónik/ n. & adj. ● n. (in pl.) burlesque verses containing Latin (or other foreign) words and vernacular words with Latin, etc., terminations. ● adj. (of verse) of this kind. [mod.L macaronicus f. obs. It. macaronico, joc. formed as MACARONI]

macaroon /mákərōōn/ n. a small light cake or cookie made with egg white, sugar, and ground almonds or coconut. [F macaron f. It. (as MACARONI]

Macassar /məkásər/ n. (in full **Macassar oil**) a kind of oil formerly used as a dressing for the hair. [Macassar, now in Indonesia, from where its ingredients were said to come]

macaw /məkáw/ n. any long-tailed brightly colored parrot of the genus Ara or Anodorhynchus, native to S. and Central America. [Port. macao, of unkn. orig.]

Macc. abbr. Maccabees (Apocrypha).

Maccabees /mákəbeez/ n.pl. (in full **Books of the Maccabees**) four books of Jewish history and theology, of which the first and second are in the Apocrypha. □□ **Maccabean** /-béeən/ adj. [the name of a Jewish family that led a revolt c.170 BC under Judas Maccabaeus]

Mace propr. aerosol spray used to disable an attacker temporarily. □□ **mace** v.

mace¹ /mays/ n. **1** a heavy club usu. having a metal head and spikes used esp. in the Middle Ages. **2** a ceremonial staff of office. **3** a stick used in the game of bagatelle. **4** = macebearer. □ **macebearer** an official who carries a mace on ceremonial occasions. [ME f. OF mace, masse f. Rmc mattea (unrecorded) club]

mace² /mays/ n. the fibrous layer between a nutmeg's shell and its husk, dried and ground as a spice. [ME macis (taken as pl.) f. OF macis f. L macir a red spicy bark]

macédoine /másidwaan/ n. mixed vegetables or fruit, esp. cut up small or in jelly. [F, = Macedonia, with ref. to the mixture of peoples there]

macerate /másərayt/ v. **1** tr. & intr. make or become soft by soaking. **2** intr. waste away, as by fasting. □□ **maceration** /-ráyshən/ n. macerator n. [L macerare macerat-]

Mach /maak, mak/ n. (in full **Mach number**) the ratio of the speed of a body to the speed of sound in the surrounding medium. □ **Mach one** (or **two**, etc.) the speed (or twice the speed) of sound. [E. Mach, Austrian physicist d. 1916]

machete /məshétee, məchétee/ n. a broad heavy knife used in Central America and the W. Indies as an implement and weapon. [Sp. f. macho hammer f. LL marcus]

Machiavellian /mákeeəvéleeən/ adj. elaborately cunning; scheming, unscrupulous. □□ **Machiavellianism** n. [N. dei Machiavelli, Florentine statesman and political writer d. 1527, who advocated resort to morally questionable methods in the interests of the state]
■ deceitful, cunning, shrewd, crafty, wily, foxy, scheming, tricky, perfidious, nefarious, treacherous, sneaky, unscrupulous.

machicolate /məchíkəlayt/ v.tr. (usu. as **machicolated** adj.) furnish (a parapet, etc.) with openings between supporting corbels for dropping stones, etc., on attackers. □□ **machicolation** /-láyshən/ n. [OF machicoler, ult. f. Prov. machacol f. macar crush + col neck]

machinable /məsheenəbəl/ adj. capable of being cut by machine tools. □□ **machinability** n.

machinate /mákinayt, másh-/ v.intr. lay plots; intrigue. □□ **machination** n. **machinator** n. [L machinari contrive (as MACHINE]
■ conspire, plot, scheme, collude, connive, intrigue, maneuver, design. □□ **machination** plot, scheme, intrigue, maneuver, design, stratagem, ruse, trick, trickery, device, artifice, dirty trick(s), wile, colloq. ploy; tactic(s), move, gambit.

machine /məsheen/ n. & v. ● n. **1** an apparatus using or applying mechanical power, having several parts each with a definite function and together performing certain kinds of work. **2** a particular kind of machine, esp. a vehicle, a piece of electrical or electronic apparatus, etc. **3** an instrument that transmits a force or directs its application. **4** the controlling system of an organization, etc. (the party machine). **5** a person who acts mechanically and with apparent lack of emotion. ● v.tr. make or operate on with a machine (esp. in sewing or manufacturing). □ **machine code** (or **language**) a computer language to which a particular computer can respond directly. **machine gun** an automatic gun giving continuous fire. **machine pistol** a pistol designed to fire automatically. **machine-readable** in a form that a computer can process. **machine tool** a mechanically operated tool for working on metal, wood, or plastics. **machine-tooled 1** shaped by a machine tool. **2** (of artistic presentation, etc.) precise, slick, esp. excessively so. [F f. L *machina* f. Gk *makhana* Doric form of *mēkhanē* f. *mēkhos* contrivance]

■ *n.* **1, 3** mechanism, device, apparatus, contrivance, appliance, instrument, implement, tool, utensil, gadget, *derog. or joc.* contraption, *sl.* gizmo. **2** engine, motor, prime mover, vehicle; car, motor car, automobile, *colloq.* auto. **4** organization, system; ring, gang, cabal, clique, party, faction. ● *v.* shape, make, manufacture; sew (up).

machinery /məsheénəree/ *n.* (*pl.* **-ies**) **1** machines collectively. **2** the components of a machine; a mechanism. **3** (foll. by *of*) an organized system. **4** (foll. by *for*) the means devised or available (*the machinery for decision making*).

■ **1** see APPARATUS. **2** see WORK *n.* 8.

machinist /məsheénist/ *n.* **1** a person who operates a machine, esp. a machine tool. **2** a person who makes machinery.

■ **1** see OPERATIVE *n.* 1.

machismo /məcheézmō, -chízmō/ *n.* exaggeratedly assertive manliness; a show of masculinity. [Sp. f. *macho* MALE f. L *masculus*]

■ manliness, virility, masculinity, *colloq.* grit, guts.

macho /maáchō/ *adj. & n.* ● *adj.* showily manly or virile. ● *n.* (*pl.* **-os**) **1** a macho man. **2** = MACHISMO. [MACHISMO]

■ *adj.* manly, masculine, virile; proud, arrogant.

macintosh var. of MACKINTOSH.

mack var. of MAC.

mackerel /mákərəl, mákrəl/ *n.* (*pl.* same or **mackerels**) a N. Atlantic marine fish, *Scomber scombrus*, with a greenish-blue body, used for food. □ **mackerel shark** any of the sharks of the family Lamnidae, incl. the mako and the great white. **mackerel sky** a sky dappled with rows of small white fleecy clouds, like the pattern on a mackerel's back. [ME f. AF *makerel*, OF *maquerel*]

mackintosh /mákintosh/ *n.* (also **macintosh**) **1** a waterproof, esp. rubberized, coat. **2** cloth waterproofed with rubber. [C. *Macintosh*, Sc. inventor d. 1843, who orig. patented the cloth]

mackle /mákəl/ *n.* a blurred impression in printing. [F *macule* f. L *macula* blemish: see MACULA]

macle /mákəl/ *n.* **1** a twin crystal. **2** a dark spot in a mineral. [F f. L (as MACKLE)]

macramé /mákrəmáy/ *n.* **1** the art of knotting cord or string in patterns to make decorative articles. **2** articles made in this way. [Turk. *makrama* bedspread f. Arab. *miḳrama*]

macro /mákrō/ *n.* (also **macroinstruction**) *Computing* a series of abbreviated instructions expanded automatically when required.

macro- /mákrō/ *comb. form* **1** long. **2** large; large-scale. [Gk *makro-* f. *makros* long, large]

macrobiotic /mákrōbiótik/ *adj. & n.* ● *adj.* relating to or following a diet intended to prolong life, comprising pure vegetable foods, brown rice, etc. ● *n.* (in *pl.*; treated as *sing.*) the use or theory of such a dietary system.

macrocephalic /mákrōsifálik/ *adj.* (also **macrocephalous** /-séfələs/) having a long or large head. □□ **macrocephaly** /-séfəlee/ *n.*

macrocosm /mákrōkozəm/ *n.* **1** the universe. **2** the whole of a complex structure. □□ **macrocosmic** /-kózmik/ *adj.* **macrocosmically** /-kózmiklee/ *adv.*

■ **1** see UNIVERSE 1a.

macroeconomics /mákrō-eékənómiks, -ék-/ *n.* the study of large-scale or general economic factors, e.g., national productivity. □□ **macroeconomic** *adj.*

macroinstruction /mákrō-instrúkshən/ *n.* = MACRO.

macromolecule /mákrōmólikyōōl/ *n.* *Chem.* a molecule containing a very large number of atoms. □□ **macromolecular** /-məlékyələr/ *adj.*

macron /máykraan, mák-/ *n.* a diacritical mark (ˉ) over a long or stressed vowel. [Gk *makron* neut. of *makros* large]

macrophage /mákrəfayj/ *n.* a large phagocytic white blood cell usu. occurring at points of infection.

macrophotography /mákrōfətógrəfee/ *n.* photography producing photographs larger than life.

macropod /mákrəpod/ *n.* any plant-eating mammal of the family Macropodidae native to Australia and New Guinea, including kangaroos and wallabies. [MACRO- + Gk *pous podos* foot]

macroscopic /mákrəskópik/ *adj.* **1** visible to the naked eye. **2** regarded in terms of large units. □□ **macroscopically** *adv.*

macula /mákyələ/ *n.* (*pl.* **maculae** /-lee/) **1** a dark spot, esp. a permanent one, in the skin. **2** (in full **macula lutea** /lōōteeə/) the region of greatest visual acuity in the retina. □□ **macular** *adj.* **maculation** /-láyshən/ *n.* [L, = spot, mesh]

mad /mad/ *adj. & v.* ● *adj.* (**madder, maddest**) **1** insane; having a disordered mind. **2** (of a person, conduct, or an idea) wildly foolish. **3** (often foll. by *about*, *Brit.* on) wildly excited or infatuated (*mad about football*; *is chess-mad*). **4** *colloq.* angry. **5** (of an animal) rabid. **6** wildly lighthearted. ● *v.* (**madded, madding**) **1** *intr. archaic* be mad; act madly (*the madding crowd*). □ **as mad as a hatter** see HATTER. **like mad** *colloq.* with great energy, intensity, or enthusiasm. □□ **madness** *n.* [OE *gemǣded* part. form f. *gemād* mad]

■ *adj.* **1** psychotic, neurotic, schizophrenic, schizoid, psychoneurotic, *Psychol.* manic-depressive; insane, deranged, certifiable, crazed, demented, lunatic, unhinged, delirious, out of one's mind *or* wits, manic, maniacal, (mentally) unbalanced, mentally ill, of unsound mind, *non compos* (*mentis*); (*often derog.*) touched, twisted, mad as a hatter *or* March hare, *colloq.* crazy, mental, dotty, not all there, out to lunch, (a)round the bend, esp. *Brit. colloq.* daft, *sl.* out of one's head, screwy, cuckoo, wacko, flaky, kooky, gaga, cracked, off-the-wall, nutty (as a fruit cake), nuts, loony, goofy, dippy, loopy, loco, wacky, batty, bats, off one's rocker *or* chump *or* head, bananas, bonkers, *Austral. sl.* dilly, *Brit. sl.* potty, round the twist, barmy, balmy, crackers. **2** foolish, silly, childish, immature, puerile, wild, nonsensical, foolhardy, madcap, heedless, senseless, absurd, imprudent, unwise, indiscreet, rash, ill-advised, ill-considered, harebrained, reckless, extravagant, irrational, fatuous, (*often derog.*) crackbrained, flighty. **3** crazy, infatuated, ardent, enthusiastic, eager, avid, zealous, passionate, fervent, fervid, keen, fanatical, wild, *colloq.* crazy, dotty, *sl.* nuts, nutty, *Brit. sl.* potty. **4** furious, angry, infuriated, incensed, enraged, irate, fuming, raging, berserk, irritated, provoked, exasperated, *archaic* wrathful, wroth. **5** wild, ferocious; rabid. □ **like mad** madly, feverishly, in a frenzy, frenziedly, desperately, excitedly, violently, wildly, hysterically, furiously, *colloq.* like crazy; enthusiastically, fervently, ardently. □□ **madness** insanity, lunacy, mania, dementia, psychosis, mental illness; lunacy, folly, foolishness, nonsense, senselessness, ridiculousness, pointlessness, illogicality, illogicalness, impracticality, preposterousness, futility, *colloq.* craziness.

madam /mádəm/ *n.* **1** a polite or respectful form of address or mode of reference to a woman. **2** a woman brothel-keeper. **3** *Brit. colloq.* a conceited or precocious girl or young woman. [ME f. OF *ma dame* my lady]

■ **2** see PROCURER. **3** miss, young lady.

Madame /mədaám, mádəm/ *n.* **1** (*pl.* **Mesdames** /maydaám, -dám/) a title or form of address used of or to a French-speaking woman, corresponding to Mrs. or madam. **2** (**madame**) = MADAM 1. [F (as MADAM)]

madcap /mádkap/ *adj. & n.* ● *adj.* **1** wildly impulsive. **2** undertaken without forethought. ● *n.* a wildly impulsive person.

■ *adj.* see IMPULSIVE.

MADD /mad/ *abbr.* Mothers Against Drunk Driving.

/ . . . / **pronunciation**   ● **part of speech**

□ **phrases, idioms, and compounds**

□□ **derivatives**   ■ **synonym section**

cross-references appear in SMALL CAPITALS or *italics*

madden /mádʼn/ v. **1** tr. & intr. make or become mad. **2** tr. irritate intensely. □□ **maddening** adj. **maddeningly** adv.

■ **2** infuriate, anger, enrage, incense, provoke, inflame, work or stir or fire up, arouse, vex, pique, gall, annoy, irritate, bother, irk, nettle, exasperate, goad, bait, badger, torment, plague, bedevil, make a person's blood boil, make a person's hackles rise, get or put a person's back up, drive a person mad, Brit. get a person's blood up, get on a person's nerves, colloq. drive a person crazy or up the wall or (a)round the bend, rile, needle, miff, peeve, wind up, get under a person's skin, make a person see red, get a person's dander up, get a person's goat, Brit. colloq. get across, sl. bug, burn up, tick off, Brit. sl. drive a person round the twist, brown off, cheese off.

madder /mádər/ n. **1** a herbaceous plant, Rubia tinctorum, with yellowish flowers. **2** a red dye obtained from the root of the madder, or its synthetic substitute. [OE mædere]

made /mayd/ **1** past and past part. of MAKE. **2** adj. (usu. in comb.) **a** (of a person or thing) built or formed (well-made; strongly made). **b** successful (a self-made man). □ **have it made** colloq. be sure of success. **made for** ideally suited to. **made of** consisting of. **made of money** colloq. very rich.

Madeira /mədéerə/ n. an amber-colored fortified white wine from the island of Madeira off the coast of N. Africa.

madeleine /mádəlin/ n. a small shell-shaped sponge cake. [F]

Mademoiselle /mádəməzél, mádmwə-/ n. (pl. **-s** or **Mesdemoiselles**) /máydmwə-/ **1** a title or form of address used of or to an unmarried French-speaking woman, corresponding to Miss. **2** (**mademoiselle**) **a** a young Frenchwoman. **b** a French governess. [F f. ma my + demoiselle DAMSEL]

■ **1, 2a** see MISS².

madhouse /mádhows/ n. **1** archaic or colloq. a home or hospital for the mentally disturbed. **2** colloq. a scene of extreme confusion or uproar.

■ **1** see BEDLAM 2. **2** see BEDLAM 1.

madly /mádlee/ adv. **1** in a mad manner. **2** colloq. **a** passionately. **b** extremely.

■ **1** insanely, hysterically, dementedly, wildly, distractedly, frenziedly; foolishly, stupidly, inanely, ridiculously, ludicrously, idiotically, absurdly, irrationally, senselessly, colloq. crazily. **2 a** passionately, ardently, fervently, furiously, fervidly, wildly, ferociously, fiercely, energetically, desperately, like mad, vehemently, feverishly, excitedly, fanatically, violently, impetuously. **b** excessively, extremely, desperately, intensely, wildly, exceedingly.

madman /mádmən, -man/ n. (pl. **-men**) a man who is insane or who behaves insanely.

■ lunatic, psychopath, psychotic, maniac, crazy, colloq. psycho, sl. crackpot, loony, nut, nutcase, screwball, kook, fruitcake, Brit. sl. nutter.

Madonna /mədónə/ n. Eccl. **1** (prec. by the) a name for the Virgin Mary. **2** a picture or statue of the Madonna. □ **Madonna lily** the white Lilium candidum, as shown in many pictures of the Madonna. [It. f. ma = mia my + donna lady f. L domina]

madras /mádrəs, mədrás/ n. a strong, lightweight cotton fabric with colored or white stripes, checks, etc. [Madras in India]

madrepore /mádripawr/ n. any perforated reef-building coral of the genus Madrepora. □□ **madreporic** /-páwrik/ adj. [F madrépore or mod.L madrepora f. It. madrepora f. madre mother + poro PORE¹]

madrigal /mádrigəl/ n. **1** a usu. 16th-c. or 17th-c. part song for several voices, usu. arranged in elaborate counterpoint and without instrumental accompaniment. **2** a short love poem. □□ **madrigalian** /-gáyleeən/ adj. **madrigalesque** /-gəlésk/ adj. **madrigalist** n. [It. madrigale f. med.L matricalis mother (church), formed as MATRIX]

madwoman /mádwoomən/ n. (pl. **-women**) a woman who is insane or who behaves insanely.

■ see MANIAC n. 1.

Maecenas /miséenəs/ n. a generous patron, esp. of literature, art, or music. [Gaius Maecenas, Roman statesman d. 8 BC, the patron of Horace and Virgil]

maelstrom /máylstrəm/ n. **1** a great whirlpool. **2** a state of confusion. [early mod.Du. f. malen grind, whirl + stroom STREAM]

■ **1** see WHIRLPOOL. **2** see CHAOS 1a.

maenad /méenad/ n. **1** a bacchante. **2** a frenzied woman. □□ **maenadic** /-nádik/ adj. [L Maenas Maenad- f. Gk Mainas -ados f. mainomai rave]

maestoso /mīstōsō/ adj., adv., & n. Mus. ● adj. & adv. to be performed majestically. ● n. (pl. **-os**) a piece of music to be performed in this way. [It.]

maestro /místrō/ n. (pl. **maestri** /-stree/ or **-os**) (often as a respectful form of address) **1** a distinguished musician, esp. a conductor or performer. **2** a great performer in any sphere, esp. artistic. [It., = master]

■ see VIRTUOSO 1a.

Mae West /may wést/ n. sl. an inflatable life jacket. [for the movie actress d. 1980, noted for her large bust]

Mafia /máafeeə, máf-/ n. **1** an organized international body of criminals, orig. in Sicily, now also in Italy, the US, and elsewhere. **2** (**mafia**) a group regarded as exerting a hidden sinister influence. [It. dial. (Sicilian), = bragging]

■ **1** see UNDERWORLD 1.

Mafioso /máafeeōsō, máf-/ n. (pl. **Mafiosi** /-see/) a member of the Mafia. [It. (as MAFIA)]

■ see GANGSTER.

mag¹ /mag/ n. colloq. a magazine (periodical). [abbr.]

mag² /mag/ v. & n. esp. Austral. ● v.intr. chatter or talk incessantly. ● n. a chatterbox. [f. MAGPIE]

mag. abbr. **1** magazine. **2** magnesium. **3** magneto. **4** magnetic.

magazine /mágəzéen/ n. **1** a periodical publication containing articles, stories, etc., usu. with photographs, illustrations, etc. **2** a chamber for holding a supply of cartridges to be fed automatically to the breech of a gun. **3** a similar device feeding a camera, slide projector, etc. **4** a store for arms, ammunition, and provisions for use in war. **5** a store for explosives. [F magasin f. It. magazzino f. Arab. makhāzin pl. of makhzan storehouse f. khazana store up]

■ **1** periodical, publication; see also JOURNAL 1. **4** arsenal, ammunition or munitions dump, armory.

Magdalenian /mágdəleeneeən/ adj. & n. Archaeol. ● adj. of the final Paleolithic period in Europe, characterized by horn and bone tools. ● n. the culture of this period. [F Magdalénien f. La Madeleine, Dordogne, France, where remains were found]

mage /mayj/ n. archaic **1** a magician. **2** a wise and learned person. [ME, Anglicized f. MAGUS]

Magellanic cloud /májilánik/ n. each of two galaxies visible in the southern sky. [F. Magellan, Port. explorer d. 1521]

magenta /məjéntə/ n. & adj. ● n. **1** a brilliant mauvish-crimson shade. **2** an aniline dye of this color; fuchsin. ● adj. of or colored with magenta. [Magenta in N. Italy, site of a battle (1859) fought shortly before the dye was discovered]

maggot /mágət/ n. **1** the soft-bodied larva of a dipterous insect, esp. the housefly or bluebottle. **2** archaic a whimsical fancy. □□ **maggoty** adj. [ME perh. alt. f. maddock, earlier mathek f. ON mathkr: cf. MAWKISH]

magi pl. of MAGUS.

magian /máyjeeən/ adj. & n. ● adj. of the magi or Magi. ● n. **1** a magus or Magus. **2** a magician. □□ **magianism** n. [L magus: see MAGUS]

magic /májik/ n., adj., & v. ● n. **1 a** the supposed art of influencing the course of events by the occult control of nature or of the spirits. **b** witchcraft. **2** conjuring tricks or sleight of hand. **3** an inexplicable or remarkable influence producing surprising results. **4** an enchanting quality or phenomenon. ● adj. **1** of or resulting from magic. **2** producing surprising results. **3** colloq. wonderful, exciting. ● v.tr. (**magicked**, **magicking**) change or create by magic, or apparently so. □ **like magic** very effectively or rapidly. **magic bullet** a medicine or treatment that is curative without incurring adverse side effects. **magic carpet** a mythical carpet able to transport a person on it to any desired place.

magic lantern a simple form of image projector using slides. **Magic Marker** *propr.* a felt-tipped pen. **magic mushroom** a mushroom producing psilocybin. **magic square** a square divided into smaller squares each containing a number such that the sums of all vertical, horizontal, or diagonal rows are equal. [ME f. OF *magique* f. L *magicus* adj., LL *magica* n., f. Gk *magikos* (as MAGUS)]
■ *n.* **1** witchcraft, sorcery, wizardry, black magic, necromancy, the black art, voodoo, devilry, diabolism, occultism, theurgy, white magic. **2** legerdemain, conjuring, prestidigitation, sleight of hand, illusion, hocus-pocus, trickery. **4** enchantment, allure, allurement, charm, bewitchment, spell, witchery, witchcraft, wizardry, glamour, fascination, magnetism.
● *adj.* **1** magical, miraculous, necromantic, occult, mystic, shamanistic, theurgical. **2** magical, miraculous, marvelous, amazing, surprising, awe-inspiring. **3** see MARVELOUS, EXCITING. □ **like magic** see FAST *adj.* 1, *like a charm* (CHARM).

magical /májikəl/ *adj.* **1** of or relating to magic. **2** resembling magic; produced as if by magic. **3** wonderful, enchanting. □□ **magically** *adv.*
■ **1** see MAGIC *adj.* 1. **2** miraculous. **3** magic, wonderful, enchanting, entrancing, bewitching, fascinating, spellbinding, charming, magnetic; see also MARVELOUS.

magician /məjíshən/ *n.* **1** a person skilled in or practicing magic. **2** a person who performs magic tricks for entertainment. **3** a person with exceptional skill. [ME f. OF *magicien* f. LL *magica* (as MAGIC)]
■ **1** wizard, sorcerer, sorceress, magus, necromancer, enchanter, enchantress, Houdini, Circe, witch, *archaic* warlock; thaumaturge, theurgist. **2** illusionist, *formal* prestidigitator. **3** virtuoso, wizard, genius, marvel, miracle worker, thaumaturge, *colloq.* whiz.

magilp var. of MEGILP.

Maginot line /mázhinō/ *n.* **1** a line of fortifications along the NE border of France begun in 1929, overrun by the German army in 1940 in World War II. **2** a line of defense on which one relies blindly. [A. *Maginot*, Fr. minister of war d. 1932]

magisterial /májistéereeəl/ *adj.* **1** imperious. **2** invested with authority. **3** of or conducted by a magistrate. **4** (of a work, opinion, etc.) highly authoritative. □□ **magisterially** *adv.* [med.L *magisterialis* f. LL *magisterius* f. L *magister* MASTER]
■ **1** see *overbearing* (OVERBEAR 1a), POMPOUS 1.

magisterium /májistéereeəm/ *n. RC Ch.* the official teaching of a bishop or pope. [L, = the office of a master (as MAGISTERIAL)]

magistracy /májistrəsee/ *n.* (*pl.* **-ies**) **1** the office or authority of a magistrate. **2** magistrates collectively.

magistral /májistrəl/ *adj.* **1** of a master or masters. **2** *Pharm.* (of a remedy, etc.) devised and made up for a particular case (cf. OFFICINAL). [F *magistral* or L *magistralis* f. *magister* MASTER]

magistrate /májistrayt, -strət/ *n.* **1** a civil officer administering the law. **2** an official conducting a court for minor cases and preliminary hearings (*magistrates' court*). □□ **magistrateship** *n.* **magistrature** /-chər/ *n.* [ME f. L *magistratus* (as MAGISTRAL)]
■ see JUDGE *n.* 1.

Maglemosian /mágləmōzeeən/ *n. & adj.* ● *n.* a N. European Mesolithic culture, characterized by bone and stone implements. ● *adj.* of or relating to this culture. [*Maglemose* in Denmark, where articles from it were found]

maglev /máglev/ *n.* (usu. *attrib.*) magnetic levitation, a system in which trains glide above the track in a magnetic field. [abbr.]

magma /mágmə/ *n.* (*pl.* **magmata** /-mətə/ or **magmas**) **1** fluid or semifluid material from which igneous rock is formed by cooling. **2** a crude pasty mixture of mineral or organic matter. □□ **magmatic** /-mátik/ *adj.* [ME, = a solid residue f. L f. Gk *magma -atos* f. the root of *massō* knead]

Magna Carta /mágnə kaártə/ *n.* (also **Magna Charta**) **1** a charter of liberty and political rights obtained from King John of England in 1215. **2** any similar document of rights. [med.L, = great charter]

magnanimous /magnánimэs/ *adj.* nobly generous; not petty in feelings or conduct. □□ **magnanimity** /mágnənímitee/ *n.* **magnanimously** *adv.* [L *magnanimus* f. *magnus* great + *animus* soul]
■ see GENEROUS 2. □□ **magnanimity** see HUMANITY 2.

magnate /mágnayt, -nət/ *n.* a wealthy and influential person, esp. in business (*shipping magnate; financial magnate*). [ME f. LL *magnas -atis* f. L *magnus* great]
■ see TYCOON.

magnesia /magnéezhə, -shə, -zyə/ *n.* **1** *Chem.* magnesium oxide. **2** (in general use) hydrated magnesium carbonate, a white powder used as an antacid and laxative. □□ **magnesian** *adj.* [ME f. med.L f. Gk *Magnēsia* (*lithos*) (stone) of Magnesia in Asia Minor, orig. referring to lodestone]

magnesite /mágnisīt/ *n.* a white or gray mineral form of magnesium carbonate.

magnesium /magnéezeeəm/ *n. Chem.* a silvery metallic element occurring naturally in magnesite and dolomite, used for making light alloys and important as an essential element in living organisms. ¶ Symb.: **Mg**. □ **magnesium light** (or **flare**) a blinding white light produced by burning magnesium wire.

magnet /mágnit/ *n.* **1** a piece of iron, steel, alloy, ore, etc., usu. in the form of a bar or horseshoe, having properties of attracting or repelling iron. **2** a lodestone. **3** a person or thing that attracts. □ **magnet school** a public school that draws students from throughout a district, offering superior facilities, specialized courses, etc. [ME f. L *magnes magnetis* f. Gk *magnēs = Magnēs -ētos* (*lithos*) (stone) of Magnesia: cf. MAGNESIA]
■ **3** see LURE *n.* 1.

magnetic /magnétik/ *adj.* **1 a** having the properties of a magnet. **b** producing, produced by, or acting by magnetism. **2** capable of being attracted by or acquiring the properties of a magnet. **3** very attractive or alluring (*a magnetic personality*). □ **magnetic compass** = COMPASS 1. **magnetic disk** see DISK. **magnetic equator** an imaginary line, near the equator, on which a magnetic needle has no dip. **magnetic field** a region of variable force around magnets, magnetic materials, or current-carrying conductors. **magnetic inclination** = DIP *n.* 8. **magnetic mine** a submarine mine detonated by the proximity of a magnetized body such as that of a ship. **magnetic moment** the property of a magnet that interacts with an applied field to give a mechanical moment. **magnetic needle** a piece of magnetized steel used as an indicator on the dial of a compass and in magnetic and electrical apparatus, esp. in telegraphy. **magnetic north** the point indicated by the north end of a compass needle. **magnetic pole 1** each of the points near the extremities of the axis of rotation of the earth or another body where a magnetic needle dips vertically. **2** each of the regions of an artificial or natural magnet, from which the magnetic forces appear to originate. **magnetic resonance imaging** a noninvasive diagnostic technique employing a scanner to obtain computerized images of internal body tissue. ¶ Abbr.: **MRI**. **magnetic storm** a disturbance of the earth's magnetic field caused by charged particles from the sun, etc. **magnetic tape** a tape coated with magnetic material for recording sound or pictures or for the storage of information. □□ **magnetically** *adv.* [LL *magneticus* (as MAGNET)]
■ **3** attractive, attracting, engaging, captivating, enthralling, seductive, alluring, entrancing, bewitching, beguiling, arresting, spellbinding, irresistible, charismatic, winning, winsome, inviting.

magnetism /mágnitizəm/ *n.* **1 a** magnetic phenomena and their study. **b** the property of producing these phenomena.

/.../ **pronunciation**	● **part of speech**
□ **phrases, idioms, and compounds**	
□□ **derivatives**	■ **synonym section**
cross-references appear in SMALL CAPITALS or *italics*	

2 attraction; personal charm. [mod.L *magnetismus* (as MAGNET)]

■ **2** attraction, appeal, allure, magic, lure, attractiveness, charm, pull, seductiveness, irresistibility, draw, charisma, sex appeal.

magnetite /mágnitit/ *n.* magnetic iron oxide. [G *Magnetit* (as MAGNET)]

magnetize /mágnitīz/ *v.tr.* **1** give magnetic properties to. **2** make into a magnet. **3** attract as or like a magnet. □□ **magnetizable** *adj.* **magnetization** *n.* **magnetizer** *n.*

magneto /magnéetō/ *n.* (*pl.* **-os**) an electric generator using permanent magnets and producing high voltage, esp. for the ignition of an internal combustion engine. [abbr. of MAGNETOELECTRIC]

magneto- /magnéetō/ *comb. form* indicating a magnet or magnetism. [Gk *magnēs*: see MAGNET]

magnetoelectric /magnéetō-iléktrik/ *adj.* (of an electric generator) using permanent magnets. □□ **magnetoelectricity** /-trísitee/ *n.*

magnetograph /magnéetəgraf/ *n.* an instrument for recording measurements of magnetic quantities.

magnetometer /mágnitómitər/ *n.* an instrument measuring magnetic forces, esp. the earth's magnetism. □□ **magnetometry** *n.*

magnetomotive /magnéetōmṓtiv/ *adj.* (of a force) being the sum of the magnetizing forces along a circuit.

magneton /mágniton/ *n.* a unit of magnetic moment in atomic and nuclear physics. [F *magnéton* (as MAGNETIC)]

magnetosphere /magnéetəsfeer/ *n.* the region surrounding a planet, star, etc., in which its magnetic field is effective.

magnetron /mágnitron/ *n.* an electron tube for amplifying or generating microwaves, with the flow of electrons controlled by an external magnetic field. [MAGNET + -TRON]

magnificat /magnífikat/ *n.* **1** a song of praise. **2** (**Magnificat**) the hymn of the Virgin Mary (Luke 1:46–55) used as a canticle. [f. the opening words *magnificat anima mea Dominum* my soul magnifies the Lord]

magnification /mágnifikáyshən/ *n.* **1** the act or an instance of magnifying; the process of being magnified. **2** the amount or degree of magnification. **3** the apparent enlargement of an object by a lens.

■ **1** enlargement, amplification; buildup, strengthening, enhancement, aggrandizement, raising, elevation, increase, expansion, heightening, glorification, ennoblement. **2** enlargement, amplification.

magnificent /magnífisənt/ *adj.* **1** splendid, stately. **2** sumptuously or lavishly constructed or adorned. **3** *colloq.* fine, excellent. □□ **magnificence** /-səns/ *n.* **magnificently** *adv.* [F *magnificent* or L *magnificus* f. *magnus* great]

■ **1** glorious, grand, impressive, imposing, awe-inspiring, brilliant, commanding, august, noble, majestic, regal, splendid, stately, distinguished, elegant, great, exalted, sublime, outstanding. **2** sumptuous, lavish, exquisite, gorgeous, resplendent, opulent, rich, luxurious. **3** see SUPERB.

magnifico /magnífikō/ *n.* (*pl.* **-oes**) a magnate or grandee. [It., = MAGNIFICENT: orig. with ref. to Venice]

magnify /mágnifī/ *v.tr.* (**-ies**, **-ied**) **1** make (a thing) appear larger than it is, as with a lens. **2** exaggerate. **3** intensify. **4** *archaic* extol, glorify. □ **magnifying glass** a lens used to produce an enlarged image. □□ **magnifiable** *adj.* **magnifier** *n.* [ME f. OF *magnifier* or L *magnificare* (as MAGNIFICENT)]

■ **1** enlarge, expand, amplify, inflate, increase, augment. **2** exaggerate, overstate, *colloq.* blow up. **3** intensify, heighten, build up, dramatize, *colloq.* boost; aggravate, worsen, exacerbate. **4** see GLORIFY 3.

magniloquent /magníləkwənt/ *adj.* **1** grand or grandiose in speech. **2** boastful. □□ **magniloquence** /-kwəns/ *n.* **magniloquently** *adv.* [L *magniloquus* f. *magnus* great + *-loquus* -speaking]

■ **1** see RHETORICAL 1a, 2, 3. **2** see BOASTFUL.
□□ **magniloquence** see RHETORIC 2a.

magnitude /mágnitōōd, -tyōōd/ *n.* **1** largeness. **2** size. **3** importance. **4 a** the degree of brightness of a star (see also *absolute magnitude*, *apparent magnitude*). **b** a class of stars

arranged according to this (*of the third magnitude*). □ **of the first magnitude** very important. [ME f. L *magnitudo* f. *magnus* great]

■ **1, 2** greatness, size, extent, bigness, immensity, enormousness, dimension(s). **3** significance, consequence, note; see also IMPORTANCE 1, 2.

magnolia /magnṓlyə/ *n.* **1** any tree or shrub of the genus *Magnolia*, cultivated for its dark-green foliage and large waxlike flowers in spring. **2** a pale creamy-pink color. [mod.L f. P. *Magnol*, Fr. botanist d. 1715]

magnum /mágnəm/ *n.* (*pl.* **magnums**) **1** a wine bottle of about twice the standard size. **2 a** a cartridge or shell that is especially powerful or large. **b** (often *attrib.*) a cartridge or gun adapted so as to be more powerful than its caliber suggests. [L, neut. of *magnus* great]

magnum opus /mágnəm ṓpəs/ *n.* **1** a great and usu. large work of art, literature, etc. **2** the most important work of an artist, writer, etc. [L, = great work: see OPUS]

■ see MASTERPIECE.

magpie /mágpī/ *n.* **1** a Eurasian crow (*Pica pica*) or a N. American crow (*P. nuttalli*) with a long pointed tail, black-and-white plumage, and noisy behavior. **2** any of various birds with plumage like a magpie, esp. *Gymnorhina tibicen* of Australia. **3** an idle chatterer. **4** a person who collects things indiscriminately. **5** *colloq.* a black-and-white cow or steer, esp. a Holstein. [*Mag*, abbr. of *Margaret* + PIE²]

magsman /mágzmən/ *n. Austral. sl.* **1** a confidence man. **2** a storyteller, a raconteur.

maguey /mágway/ *n.* an agave plant, esp. one yielding pulque. [Sp. f. Haitian]

magus /máygəs/ *n.* (*pl.* **magi** /máyjī/) **1** a member of a priestly caste of ancient Persia. **2** a sorcerer. **3** (**the Magi**) the "wise men" from the East who brought gifts to the infant Christ (Matt. 2:1). [ME f. L f. Gk *magos* f. OPers. *magus*]

Magyar /mágyaar/ *n. & adj.* ● *n.* **1** a member of a Ural-Altaic people now predominant in Hungary. **2** the language of this people. ● *adj.* of or relating to this people or language. [native name]

maharaja /maàhəraàjə, -zhə/ *n.* (also **maharajah**) *hist.* a title of some princes of India, esp. a ruler of one of the former states. [Hindi *mahārājā* f. *mahā* great + RAJA]

maharani /maàhəraànee/ *n.* (also **maharanee**) *hist.* a maharaja's wife or widow. [Hindi *mahārānī* f. *mahā* great + RANI]

maharishi /maàhəreeshi/ *n.* a great Hindu sage or spiritual leader. [Hindi f. *mahā* great + RISHI]

mahatma /məhaàtmə, -hát-/ *n.* **1 a** (esp. in India) a person regarded with reverence. **b** a sage. **2** each of a class of persons in India and Tibet supposed by some to have preternatural powers. [Skr. *mahātman* f. *mahā* great + *ātman* soul]

Mahayana /maàhəyaànə/ *n.* a school of Buddhism practiced in China, Japan, and Tibet. [Skr. f. *mahā* great + *yāna* vehicle]

Mahdi /maàdee/ *n.* (*pl.* **Mahdis**) **1** a spiritual and temporal messiah expected by Muslims. **2** esp. *hist.* a leader claiming to be this messiah. □□ **Mahdism** *n.* **Mahdist** *n.* [Arab. *mahdīy* he who is guided right, past part. of *hadā* guide]

Mahican /məhéekən/ *n. & adj.* (also **Mohican** /mō-/) ● *n.* **1** a N. American people native to the upper Hudson River Valley of New York state. **2** a member of this people. ● *adj.* of or relating to this people.

mah-jongg /maajóng, -jáwng, -zhóng, -zháwng/ *n.* (also **mahjong**) a Chinese game for four resembling rummy and played with 136 or 144 pieces called tiles. [Chin. dial. *matsiang*, lit. sparrows]

mahlstick var. of MAULSTICK.

mahogany /məhógənee/ *n.* (*pl.* **-ies**) **1 a** a reddish-brown wood used for furniture. **b** the color of this. **2** any tropical tree of the genus *Swietenia*, esp. *S. mahagoni*, yielding this wood. [17th c.: orig. unkn.]

mahonia /məhṓneeə/ *n.* any evergreen shrub of the genus *Mahonia*, with yellow bell-shaped or globular flowers. [F *mahonne*, Sp. *mahona*, It. *maona*, Turk. *māwuna*]

mahout /məhówt/ *n.* (esp. in India) an elephant driver or keeper. [Hindi *mahāut* f. Skr. *mahāmātra* high official, lit. "great in measure"]

Mahratta var. of MARATHA.

Mahratti var. of MARATHI.

maid /mayd/ *n.* **1** a female domestic servant. **2** *archaic* or *poet.* a girl or young woman. □ **maid of honor 1** a principal bridesmaid. **2** *Brit.* a kind of small custard tart. **3** an unmarried lady attending a queen or princess. □□ **maidish** *adj.* [ME, abbr. of MAIDEN]

■ **1** housemaid, maidservant, domestic, chambermaid, lady's maid, charwoman, *Brit.* daily. **2** girl, young woman, young lady, schoolgirl, miss, mademoiselle, signorina, Fräulein, *Ir.* colleen, esp. *Sc. & No. of Engl. or poet.* lass, *archaic* demoiselle, *archaic or literary* damsel, *archaic or poet.* maiden, *colloq.* nymphet, lassie, filly, *joc.* wench, *poet.* nymph. □ **maid of honor 3** lady-in-waiting, *archaic or hist.* woman.

maidan /mɪdáːn/ *n. Anglo-Ind.* **1** an open space in or near a town. **2** a parade ground. [Urdu f. Arab. *maydān*]

maiden /máyd'n/ *n. & adj.* ● *n.* **1** *archaic* or *poet.* a girl; a young unmarried woman. **2** *Cricket* = *maiden over.* **3** (often *attrib.*) **a** a horse that has never won a race. **b** a race open only to such horses. ● *adj.* **1** unmarried (*maiden aunt*). **2** being or involving the first attempt or occurrence (*maiden speech*; *maiden voyage*). **3** (of a female animal) unmated. □ **maiden name** a wife's surname before marriage. **maiden over** *Cricket* an over in which no runs are scored off the bat. □□ **maidenhood** *n.* **maidenish** *adj.* **maidenlike** *adj.* **maidenly** *adj.* [OE *mægden*, dimin. f. *mægeth* f. Gmc]

■ *n.* **1** see MAID 2 ● *adj.* **1** see UNMARRIED. **2** inaugural, first, initial.

maidenhair /máyd'nhair/ *n.* (in full **maidenhair fern**) a fern of the genus *Adiantum*, esp. *A. capillus-veneris*, with fine hairlike stalks and delicate fronds. □ **maidenhair tree** = GINKGO.

maidenhead /máyd'nhed/ *n.* **1** virginity. **2** the hymen.

maidservant /máydservənt/ *n.* a female domestic servant.

■ see SERVANT.

maieutic /may-ōōtik/ *adj.* (of the Socratic mode of inquiry) serving to bring a person's latent ideas into clear consciousness. [Gk *maieutikos* f. *maieuomai* act as a midwife f. *maia* midwife]

maigre /máygər/ *adj. RC Ch.* **1** (of a day) on which abstinence from meat is ordered. **2** (of food) suitable for eating on maigre days. [F, lit. lean: cf. MEAGER]

mail¹ /mayl/ *n. & v.* ● *n.* **1 a** letters and parcels, etc., conveyed by the postal system. **b** the postal system. **c** one complete delivery or collection of mail. **d** one delivery of letters to one place, esp. to a business on one occasion. **2** (usu. **the mails**) the system that delivers the mail. **3** a vehicle carrying mail. **4** *hist.* a bag of letters for conveyance by mail. ● *v.tr.* send (a letter, etc.) by mail. □ **mailboat** a boat carrying mail. **mail carrier** a person who delivers mail. **mail drop** a receptacle for mail. **mailing list** a list of people to whom advertising matter, information, etc., is to be mailed. **mail order** an order for goods sent by mail. **mail-order firm** a firm doing business primarily by mail. **mail train** a train carrying mail. [ME f. OF *male* wallet f. WG]

■ *n.* **1 a** correspondence, letters (and parcels), *Brit.* post. **b** postal system *or* service, post office, *Brit.* post. **c** delivery, collection, *Brit.* post. **d** delivery, *Brit.* post. ● *v.* send, dispatch, *Brit.* post.

mail² /mayl/ *n. & v.* ● *n.* **1** armor made of rings, chains, or plates, joined together flexibly. **2** the protective shell, scales, etc., of an animal. ● *v.tr.* clothe with or as if with mail. □ **coat of mail** a jacket covered with mail or composed of mail. **mailed fist** physical force. □□ **mailed** *adj.* [ME f. OF *maille* f. L *macula* spot, mesh]

mailable /máyləbəl/ *adj.* acceptable for conveyance by mail.

mailbag /máylbag/ *n.* a large sack or bag for carrying mail.

mailbox /máylboks/ *n.* **1** a public receptacle for depositing mail. **2** a private receptacle for at-home pickup and delivery of mail. **3** a computer file in which electronic mail is stored.

maillot /maayṓ/ *n.* **1** tights for dancing, gymnastics, etc. **2** a woman's one-piece bathing suit. **3** a jersey. [F]

mailman /máylmən/ *n.* (*pl.* **-men**) a mail carrier.

mailroom /máylrōōm, -rŏŏm/ *n.* a room for sorting incoming and outgoing mail in a business or an organization.

maim /maym/ *v.tr.* **1** cripple, disable, mutilate. **2** harm, impair (*emotionally maimed by neglect*). [ME *maime*, etc., f. OF *mahaignier*, etc., of unkn. orig.]

■ **1** cripple, disable, mutilate, lame, incapacitate, wound, wing, hamstring, put out of action *or* commission **2** harm, impair, injure, damage, deface.

main¹ /mayn/ *adj. & n.* ● *adj.* **1** chief in size, importance, extent, etc.; principal (*the main part*; *the main point*). **2** exerted to the full (*by main force*). ● *n.* **1** a principal channel, duct, etc., for water, sewage, etc. (*water main*). **2** *Brit.* (usu. in *pl.*; prec. by *the*) **a** the central distribution network for electricity, gas, water, etc. **b** a domestic electricity supply as distinct from batteries. **3** *archaic* or *poet.* **a** the ocean or oceans (*the Spanish Main*). **b** the mainland. □ **in the main** for the most part. **main brace** *Naut.* the brace attached to the main yard. **the main chance** one's own interests. **main course 1** the chief course of a meal. **2** *Naut.* the mainsail. **main deck** *Naut.* **1** the deck below the spar deck in a man-of-war. **2** the upper deck between the poop and the forecastle in a merchantman. **main drag** *US colloq.* = *main street*. **main line 1** a chief railway line. **2** *sl.* a principal vein, esp. as a site for a drug injection (cf. MAINLINE). **3** a chief road or street. **main man** *sl.* **1** best male friend **2** man who is most admired, relied upon, etc. **main street** the principal street of a town. **Main Street** *US* provincial, materialistic point of view (after Sinclair Lewis's novel, 1920). **main yard** *Naut.* the yard on which the mainsail is extended. **with might and main** with all one's force. [ME, partly f. ON *megenn, megn* (adj.), partly f. OE *mægen-* f. Gmc: (n.) orig. = physical force]

■ *adj.* **1** chief, primary, prime, (most) important, capital, principal, cardinal, paramount, first, foremost, leading, preeminent, predominant, predominating, dominant, ranking, major; outstanding; largest, biggest, greatest, strongest; necessary, essential, basic, particular, fundamental, critical, crucial, vital. **2** sheer, brute, utter, pure, out-and-out, absolute. ● *n.* **1** pipe, duct, channel, line, pipeline, conduit, water *or* gas main. **2** power (supply), grid. □ **in the main** see MAINLY.

main street *Brit.* high street.

main² /mayn/ *n.* a match between fighting cocks. [16th c.: prob. orig. *main chance*: see MAIN¹]

mainframe /máynfraym/ *n.* **1** the central processing unit and primary memory of a computer. **2** (often *attrib.*) a large computer system.

mainland /máynlənd/ *n.* a large continuous extent of land, excluding neighboring islands, etc. □□ **mainlander** *n.*

mainline /máynlīn/ *v. sl.* **1** *intr.* take drugs intravenously. **2** *tr.* inject (drugs) intravenously. □□ **mainliner** *n.*

mainly /máynlee/ *adv.* for the most part; chiefly.

■ in the main, chiefly, principally, predominantly, generally, above all, on the whole, in general, mostly, most of all, effectively, essentially, at bottom, first and foremost, for the most part, largely, by and large, primarily, as a rule, usually, all in all, on balance, for all practical purposes.

mainmast /máynmast, -məst/ *n. Naut.* the principal mast of a ship.

mainsail /máynsayl, -səl/ *n. Naut.* **1** (in a square-rigged vessel) the lowest sail on the mainmast. **2** (in a fore-and-aft rigged vessel) a sail set on the after part of the mainmast.

mainspring /máynspring/ *n.* **1** the principal spring of a mechanical watch, clock, etc. **2** a chief motive power; an incentive.

mainstay /máynstay/ *n.* **1** a chief support (*has been his main-*

/..../ pronunciation	● part of speech
□ phrases, idioms, and compounds	
□□ derivatives	■ synonym section
cross-references appear in SMALL CAPITALS or *italics*	

stay since his trouble). **2** *Naut.* a stay from the maintop to the foot of the foremast.

■ **1** (sheet) anchor, bulwark, buttress, support, pillar.

mainstream /máynstreem/ *n.* **1** (often *attrib.*) the prevailing trend in opinion, fashion, etc. **2** a type of jazz based on the 1930s swing style and consisting esp. of solo improvisation on chord sequences. **3** the principal current of a river.

■ **1** see CURRENT *n.* 3. **3** see CURRENT *n.* 1.

maintain /mayntáyn/ *v.tr.* **1** cause to continue; keep up, preserve (a state of affairs, an activity, etc.) (*maintained friendly relations*). **2** (often foll. by *in*; often *refl.*) support (life, a condition, etc.) by work, nourishment, expenditure, etc. (*maintained him in comfort*; *maintained themselves by fishing*). **3** (often foll. by *that* + clause) assert (an opinion, statement, etc.) as true (*maintained that she was the best*; *his story was true, he maintained*). **4** preserve or provide for the preservation of (a building, machine, road, etc.) in good repair. **5** give aid to (a cause, party, etc.). **6** provide means for (a garrison, etc., to be equipped). □ **maintained school** *Brit.* a school supported from public funds. □□ **maintainer** *n.* **maintainable** *adj.* **maintainability** *n.* [ME f. OF *maintenir* ult. f. L *manu tenēre* hold in the hand]

■ **1, 2** continue, preserve, persevere in, keep going, persist in, keep (up), carry on, retain, perpetuate, prolong, sustain, uphold; nurture, support. **3** hold, state, say, declare, claim, assert, allege, testify, contend, avow, announce, proclaim, profess, insist (on), affirm, *formal* aver. **4** look after, take care of, care for, preserve, keep up, service, keep in repair *or* service. **5** see SUPPORT *v.* 13.

maintenance /máyntənəns/ *n.* **1** the process of maintaining or being maintained. **2** the provision of the means to support life, esp. by work, etc. **3** *Law hist.* the offense of aiding a party in litigation without lawful cause. [ME f. OF f. *maintenir*: see MAINTAIN]

■ **1** upkeep, care, servicing, preservation, conservation, support, *formal* sustentation; continuation, continuance, perpetuation, prolongation. **2** upkeep, livelihood, subsistence, support, allowance, living, sustenance, stipend, subvention, contribution, keep.

maintop /máyntop/ *n. Naut.* a platform above the head of the lower mainmast.

main-topmast /mayntópmast, -məst/ *n. Naut.* a mast above the head of the lower mainmast.

maiolica /var. of MAJOLICA.

maisonette /máyzənét/ *n.* (also **maisonnette**) **1** a part of a house, apartment building, etc., forming separate living accommodation, usu. on two floors and having a separate entrance. **2** a small house. [F *maisonnette* dimin. of *maison* house]

maître d'hôtel /métrə dōtél, máyt-/ *n.* (*pl.* **maîtres d'hôtel** *pronunc.* same) **1** (also **maitre d'**) a headwaiter. **2** the manager, head steward, etc., of a hotel. [F, = master of (the) house]

■ **1** see WAITER.

maize /mayz/ *n.* **1** esp. *Brit.* = CORN¹ *n.* 1. **2** a pale golden-yellow color. [F *maïs* or Sp. *maíz*, of Carib orig.]

Maj. *abbr.* Major.

majestic /məjéstik/ *adj.* showing majesty; stately and dignified; grand, imposing. □□ **majestically** *adv.*

■ dignified, grand, imperial, regal, royal, kingly, queenly, princely, noble, lordly, lofty, elevated, exalted, glorious, magnificent, monumental, impressive, striking, imposing, awesome, splendid, marvelous.

majesty /májistee/ *n.* (*pl.* **-ies**) **1** impressive stateliness, dignity, or authority, esp. of bearing, language, the law, etc. **2** a royal power. **b** (**Majesty**) part of several titles given to a sovereign or a sovereign's wife or widow or used in addressing them (*Your Majesty*; *Her Majesty the Queen Mother*). **3** (also **Christ in Majesty**) a picture of God or Christ enthroned within an aureole. □ *Brit.* **Her** (or **His**) **Majesty's** part of the title of several government institutions (*Her Majesty's Stationery Office*). [ME f. OF *majesté* f. L *majestas -tatis* (as MAJOR)]

■ **1** authority, stateliness; see also DIGNITY 1. **2 b** Royal Highness, *archaic* Sire.

majlis /májlis/ *n. Polit.* the parliament of various N. African or Middle Eastern countries, esp. Iran. [Pers., = assembly]

majolica /məyólikə, məjól-/ *n.* (also **maiolica**) **1** a 19th-c. trade name for earthenware with colored decoration on an opaque white glaze. **2** a white tin-glazed earthenware decorated with metallic colors, orig. popular in the Mediterranean area during the Renaissance. [It. f. former name of Majorca]

major /máyjər/ *adj., n.,* & *v.* ● *adj.* **1** important, large, serious, significant (*a major road*; *a major war*; *the major consideration must be their health*). **2** (of an operation) serious or life-threatening. **3** *Mus.* **a** (of a scale) having intervals of a semitone between the third and fourth, and seventh and eighth degrees. **b** (of an interval) greater by a semitone than a minor interval (*major third*). **c** (of a key) based on a major scale, tending to produce a bright or joyful effect (*D major*). **4** of full legal age. **5** *Logic* **a** (of a term) occurring in the predicate or conclusion of a syllogism. **b** (of a premise) containing a major term. **6** *Brit.* (appended to a surname, esp. in public schools) the elder of two brothers or the first to enter the school (*Smith major*). ● *n.* **1 a** an army officer next below lieutenant colonel and above captain. **b** a person in charge of a section of band instruments (*drum major*). **2** a person of full legal age. **3** *US* **a** a student's most emphasized subject or course. **b** a student specializing in a specified subject (*a philosophy major*). **4** *Logic* a major term or premise. ● *v.intr.* (foll. by *in*) study or qualify in as a special subject (*majored in theology*). □ **major axis** the axis of an ellipse, passing through its foci. **major general** an officer next below a lieutenant general. **major league** a league of highest classification in baseball, etc. **major piece** *Chess* a rook or queen. **major planet** *Astron.* any of the nine large planets that revolve around the sun: Mercury, Venus, Earth, Mars, Jupiter, Saturn, Uranus, Neptune, or Pluto. **Major Prophet** Isaiah, Jeremiah, Ezekiel, or Daniel. **major suit** *Bridge* spades or hearts. □□ **majorship** *n.* [ME f. L, compar. of *magnus* great]

■ *adj.* **1** vital, important, critical, crucial, principal, foremost, paramount, primary, prime, main, big, large, biggest, preeminent, notable, noteworthy, significant, outstanding, dominant, dominating; serious, grave; larger, greater, bigger, chief. **4** see MATURE *adj.* 1.
● *n.* **2** adult, grown-up. **3 a** specialization. **b** specialist.
● *v.* specialize, *Brit.* read. □ **major part** bulk, greater part; see also MAJORITY 1.

majordomo /máyjərdómō/ *n.* (*pl.* **-os**) **1** the chief official of an Italian or Spanish princely household. **2** a house steward; a butler. [orig. *mayordome* f. Sp. *mayordomo*, It. *maggiordomo* f. med.L *major domus* highest official of the household (as MAJOR, DOME)]

■ **2** see SERVANT.

majorette /máyjərét/ *n.* = drum majorette. [abbr.]

majority /məjáwritee, -jór-/ *n.* (*pl.* **-ies**) **1** (usu. foll. by *of*) the greater number or part. ¶ Strictly used only with countable nouns, e.g., *a majority of people*, and not with mass nouns, e.g., *a majority of the work*. **2** *Polit.* **a** the number by which the votes cast for one party, candidate, etc., exceed those of the next in rank (*won by a majority of 151*). **b** a party, etc., receiving the greater number of votes. **3** full legal age (*attained his majority*). **4** the rank of major. □ **the great majority 1** much the greater number. **2** *euphem.* the dead (*has joined the great majority*). **in the majority** esp. *Polit.* belonging to or constituting a majority party, etc. **majority rule** the principle that the greater number should exercise greater power. **majority verdict** a verdict given by more than half of the jury, but not unanimous. [F *majorité* f. med.L *majoritas -tatis* (as MAJOR)]

■ **1** bulk, preponderance, mass, better *or* best part, lion's share. **3** adulthood, maturity, seniority, womanhood, manhood. □ **the great majority 1** the vast majority, (by far the) most people.

majuscule /májəskyool/ *n.* & *adj.* ● *n. Paleog.* **1** a large letter, whether capital or uncial. **2** large lettering. ● *adj.* of, written in, or concerning majuscules. □□ **majuscular** /məjúskyələr/ *adj.* [F f. L *majuscula* (*littera* letter), dimin. of MAJOR]

make /mayk/ *v. & n.* ● *v.* (*past* and *past part.* **made** /mayd/) **1** *tr.* construct; create; form from parts or other substances (*made a table*; *made it out of cardboard*; *made him a sweater*). **2** *tr.* (often foll. by *to* + infin.) cause or compel (a person, etc.) to do something (*make him repeat it*; *was made to confess*). **3** *tr.* **a** cause to exist; create; bring about (*made a noise*; *made an enemy*). **b** cause to become or seem (*made an exhibition of myself*; *made him angry*). **c** appoint; designate (*made him a cardinal*). **4** *tr.* compose; prepare; draw up (*made her will*; *made a film about Japan*). **5** *tr.* constitute; amount to (*makes a difference*; *2 and 2 make 4*; *this makes the tenth time*). **6** *tr.* **a** undertake or agree to (an aim or purpose) (*made a promise*; *make an effort*). **b** execute or perform (a bodily movement, a speech, etc.) (*made a face*; *made a bow*). **7** *tr.* gain, acquire, procure (money, a profit, etc.) (*made $20,000 on the deal*). **8** *tr.* prepare (tea, coffee, a dish, etc.) for consumption (*made apple pie*). **9** *tr.* **a** arrange bedding neatly on (a bed). **b** arrange and ignite materials for (a fire). **10** *intr.* **a** proceed (*made toward the river*). **b** (foll. by *to* + infin.) begin an action (*he made to go*). **11** *tr. colloq.* **a** arrive at (a place) or in time for (a train, etc.) (*made the border before dark*; *made the six o'clock train*). **b** manage to attend; manage to attend on (a certain day) or at (a certain time) (*couldn't make the meeting last week*; *can make any day except Friday*). **c** achieve a place in (*made the first team*; *made the six o'clock news*). **d** achieve the rank of (*made colonel in three years*). **12** *tr.* establish or enact (a distinction, rule, law, etc.). **13** *tr.* consider to be; estimate as (*I'd make the time to be 7:00 o'clock*; *do you make that a 1 or a 7?*). **14** *tr.* secure the success or advancement of (*his mother made him*; *it made my day*). **15** *tr.* accomplish (a distance, speed, score, etc.) (*made 60 m.p.h. on the freeway*). **16** *tr.* **a** become by development or training (*made a great leader*). **b** serve as (*a log makes a useful seat*). **17** *tr.* (usu. foll. by *out*) represent as; cause to appear as (*makes him out a liar*). **18** *tr.* form in the mind; feel (*I make no judgment*). **19** *tr.* (foll. by *it* + compl.) **a** determine, establish, or choose (*let's make it Tuesday*; *made it my business to know*). **b** bring to (a chosen value, etc.) (*decided to make it a dozen*). **20** *tr. sl.* have sexual relations with. **21** *tr. Cards* **a** win (a trick). **b** play (a card) to advantage. **c** win the number of tricks that fulfills (a contract). **d** shuffle (a pack of cards) for dealing. **22** *tr. Cricket* score (runs). **23** *tr. Electr.* complete or close (a circuit) (opp. BREAK¹). **24** *intr.* (of the tide) begin to flow or ebb. ● *n.* **1** (esp. of a product) a type, origin, brand, etc., of manufacture (*different make of car*; *our own make*). **2** a kind of mental, moral, or physical structure or composition. **3** an act of shuffling cards. **4** *Electr.* **a** the making of contact. **b** the position in which this is made. □ **be made for** be ideally suited to. **be made of** consist of (*cake made of marzipan*). **have it made** *colloq.* be sure of success; be successful. **made of money** *colloq.* very rich. **made to measure** (of a suit, etc.) made to a specific customer's measurements. **made to order** see ORDER. **make after** *archaic* pursue. **make against** be unfavorable to. **make as if** (or **though**) (foll. by *to* + infin. or conditional) act as if the specified circumstances applied (*made as if to leave*; *made as if he would hit me*; *made as if I had not noticed*). **make away with 1** get rid of; kill. **2** squander. **3** = *make off with.* **make-believe** (or **-belief**) **1** pretense. **2** pretended. **make believe** pretend. **make conversation** talk politely. **make a day** (or **night**, etc.) **of it** devote a whole day (or night, etc.) to an activity. **make do 1** manage with the limited or inadequate means available. **2** (foll. by *with*) manage with (something) as an inferior substitute. **make an entrance** see ENTRANCE¹. **make an example of** punish as a warning to others. **make a fool of** see FOOL¹. **make for 1** tend to result in (happiness, etc.). **2** proceed toward (a place). **3** assault; attack. **4** confirm (an opinion). **make friends** (often foll. by *with*) become friendly. **make fun of** see FUN. **make good** see GOOD. **make a habit of** see HABIT. **make a hash of** see HASH¹. **make hay** see HAY¹. **make head or tail** (or **heads or tails**) **of** see HEAD. **make headway** advance, progress. **make it 1** *colloq.* succeed in

reaching, esp. in time. **2** *colloq.* be successful. **3** (usu. foll. by *with*) *sl.* have sexual intercourse (with). **make it up 1** be reconciled, esp. after a quarrel. **2** fill in a deficit. **make it up to** remedy negligence, an injury, etc., to (a person). **make light of** see LIGHT². **make love** see LOVE. **make a meal of** see MEAL¹. **make merry** see MERRY. **make money** acquire wealth or an income. **make the most of** see MOST. **make much** (or **little** or **the best**) **of 1** derive much (or little, etc.) advantage from. **2** give much (or little, etc.) attention, importance, etc., to. **make a name for oneself** see NAME. **make no bones about** see BONE. **make nothing of 1** do without hesitation. **2** treat as a trifle. **3** be unable to understand, use, or deal with. **make of 1** construct from. **2** conclude to be the meaning or character of (*can you make anything of it?*). **make off** (or **away**) **with** carry away; steal. **make oneself scarce** see SCARCE. **make or break** or esp. *Brit.* **mar**) cause the success or ruin of. **make out 1 a** distinguish by sight or hearing. **b** decipher (handwriting, etc.). **2** understand (*can't make him out*). **3** assert; pretend (*made out he liked it*). **4** *colloq.* make progress; fare (*how did you make out?*). **5** (usu. foll. by *to*, in *favor of*) draw up; write out (*made out a check to her*). **6** prove or try to prove (*how do you make that out?*). **7** (often foll. by *with*). *colloq.* **a** engage in sexual play or petting. **b** form a sexual relationship. **make over 1** transfer the possession of (a thing) to a person. **2** refashion, restyle. **make a point of** see POINT. **make sail** *Naut.* **1** spread a sail or sails. **2** start a voyage. **make shift** see SHIFT. **make so bold as to** see BOLD. **make time 1** (usu. foll. by *for* or *to* + infin.) find an occasion when time is available. **2** (usu. foll. by *with*) *sl.* make sexual advances (to a person). **make up 1** serve or act to overcome (a deficiency). **2** complete (an amount, a party, etc.). **3** compensate. **4** be reconciled. **5** put together; compound; prepare (*made up the medicine*). **6** sew (parts of a garment, etc.) together. **7** get (a sum of money, a company, etc.) together. **8** concoct (a story). **9** (of parts) compose (a whole). **10 a** apply cosmetics. **b** apply cosmetics to. **11** settle (a dispute). **12** prepare (a bed) for use with fresh sheets, etc. **13** *Printing* arrange (type) in pages. **14** compile (a list, an account, a document, etc.). **15** arrange (a marriage, etc.). **make up one's mind** decide, resolve. **make up to** curry favor with; court. **make water 1** urinate. **2** (of a ship) take in water. **make way 1** (often foll. by *for*) allow room for others to proceed. **2** achieve progress. **make one's way** proceed. **make with** *colloq.* use; proceed with (*made with the feet and left in a hurry*). **on the make** *colloq.* **1** intent on gain. **2** looking for sexual partners. □□ **makable** *adj.* [OE *macian* f. WG: rel. to MATCH¹]

■ *v.* **1** build, assemble, construct, erect, put together, set up, fashion, form, mold, shape, frame, create, originate, fabricate, manufacture, produce, put out, forge, contrive, devise. **2** cause, compel, force, impel, coerce, provoke, urge, exhort, press, pressure, pressurize, require, command, order, induce, persuade, prevail (up)on, insist (up)on, oblige. **3** bring about, occasion, cause, give rise to; produce, create, generate; appoint, name, select, choose, elect, vote (in as), designate, authorize, commission, delegate, depute, deputize, assign, sanction, approve, affirm, certify, confirm. **4** make out or up, draw (up), create, write, sign, frame. **5** amount to, constitute, represent, add up to, total, come to. **6 a** see UNDERTAKE 1. **b** deliver, present; see also EXECUTE 2. **7** earn, reap, garner, take in, get, procure, gather, clear, realize, gross, net, pocket, acquire, obtain, receive, *Austral. & NZ sl.* knock out; win, gain, *colloq.* pull down; return, fetch. **8** prepare, cook, *colloq.* fix. **9 a** prepare, arrange, rearrange, tidy (up), neaten (up). **b** lay, prepare, arrange. **10 a** (*make for*) head for or toward, aim for, steer (a course) for, proceed toward, be bound for. **11 a** reach, arrive at, attain, get (to), win, achieve, accomplish. **c** achieve, get on *or* in. **12** enact, pass, frame, establish, institute; set up, organize. **13** judge, think, calculate, estimate, reckon, gauge, suppose. **15** reach, accomplish; do, go *or* travel *or* move at; score, get (to), achieve, earn. **16 a** become, change *or* turn *or* grow into, prove *or* come to be, turn out to be, perform as. **b** serve as, be suitable for *or* as. **17** present as, depict as, characterize as, describe as, delineate as, show as, define as, portray as, paint as; declare. **20** seduce, *sl.* make it with; see also LAY¹ *v.* 16. **22** score, get, earn, secure. ● *n.* **1** kind, brand, style, sort, type, mark, marque. **2** see MAKEUP 5. □ **have it made** see LAUGH *v.* 5. **made of money** see *in the money* (MONEY). **make after** see PURSUE 1. **make as if** (or **though**) pretend, feign, act as if *or* as though, affect, make a show *or* pretense of, give the impression of, make out, make believe. **make away** *or* **off** run away *or* off, flee, fly, abscond, take to one's heels, decamp, beat a (hasty) retreat, (make a) run for it, take off, *colloq.* clear out, skedaddle, skip (out *or* off), make tracks, scram, hightail (it), *sl.* beat it, skip it, cut and run, take a powder, vamoose. **make away with 1** see KILL *v.* 1a. **2** see WASTE *v.* 1. **make-believe** (or **belief**) **1** see PRETENSE 1. **2** see FICTITIOUS 2. **make believe** pretend, fancy, playact, dream, fantasize, imagine, act as if. **make conversation** make polite conversation, make small talk; see also CHAT¹ *v.* **make do 1, 2** get by *or* along, cope, scrape by *or* along, manage, muddle through, survive. **make for 1** promote, contribute to, be conducive to, favor, facilitate; see also LEAD¹ *v.* 9. **2** see MAKE *v.* 10a above. **3** assault, attack, set upon, charge, rush (at), pounce upon, fall upon *or* on, go for, lunge at, storm, assail. **make headway** advance, progress, make progress *or* way, move forward, go, gain (ground), get *or* go ahead, proceed, get going. **make it 1** arrive, get there, show up, appear, turn up. **2** succeed, prosper, triumph, win, make good, *colloq.* make the grade. **3** (*make it with*) see LAY¹ *v.* 16. **make it up 1** see *make up* 4 below. **make much of 2** emphasize, stress; see also MAXIMIZE. **make nothing of 1** think nothing of, make no bones about, not hesitate to. **2** play down, downplay; see also *make light of* (LIGHT²). **3** not make head or tail of, not understand. **make of 2** infer or deduce or derive or conclude or draw or surmise or understand or gather. **make off** see *make away* above. **make off with** steal, rob, filch, pilfer, walk away *or* off with, *colloq.* borrow, liberate, *formal or joc.* purloin, *sl.* pinch, hook, rip off, lift, swipe. **make out 1** see, discern, detect, discover, distinguish, *literary* descry, espy. **2** understand, fathom, comprehend, figure out, perceive, follow, grasp, see, decipher, read. **3** suggest, imply, hint, insinuate, indicate, intimate; pretend, make to appear, make as if *or* as though, make believe. **4** see FARE *v.* 1. **5** complete, fill in, fill out, *Brit.* fill up; draw (up), write (out). **6** see PROVE 1. **make over 1** transfer, hand over, sign over, convey, assign, turn over. **2** do over, remodel, refashion, redecorate, alter. **make sail 2** set sail, put (out) to sea. **make time 2** (*make time with*) see *chat up.* **make up 1** redress, overcome. **2** complete, fill out, finish (out), flesh out. **3** compensate, redress, make good, atone, make amends. **4** be reconciled, make peace, come to terms, bury the hatchet. **5** put together, construct, build; compound; prepare. **8** hatch, invent, concoct, devise, create, construct, dream up, originate, coin, compose, *colloq.* cook up. **9** compose, form, constitute, *disp.* comprise. **11** see SETTLE¹ 5–7, 8b. **12** see MAKE *v.* 9a above. **14** see COMPILE 1. **make up one's mind** see DECIDE 1. **make up to** see INGRATIATE. **make water 1** see URINATE. **2** leak, take *or* let in water. **make way 1** move aside, clear the way, allow to pass, make room *or* space. **2** see *get on* 1. **make one's way** see PROCEED 1. **on the**

make 1 aggressive, assertive, go-ahead, enterprising, vigorous, energetic, *colloq.* pushy. **2** *sl.* cruising.

makeover /máykōvər/ *n.* a complete transformation or restyling.

maker /máykər/ *n.* **1** (often in *comb.*) a person or thing that makes. **2** (**our, the**, etc., **Maker**) God. **3** *archaic* a poet.
   ■ **1** see CREATOR 1. **2** (**our** or **the Maker**) see CREATOR 2.

makeshift /máykshift/ *adj. & n.* ● *adj.* temporary; serving for the time being (*a makeshift arrangement*). ● *n.* a temporary substitute or device.
   ■ *adj.* temporary, ad interim, stopgap, expedient, emergency, improvised, ad hoc, tentative, standby, ersatz. ● *n.* expedient, improvisation, substitute, jury-rig; see also STOPGAP.

makeup /máykəp/ **1** cosmetics for the face, etc., either generally or to create an actor's appearance or disguise. **2** the appearance of the face, etc., when cosmetics have been applied (*his makeup was not convincing*). **3** *Printing* the making up of a type. **4** *Printing* the type made up. **5** a person's character, temperament, etc. **6** the composition or constitution of a thing.
   ■ **1** cosmetics, maquillage, greasepaint, *colloq.* warpaint. **5** temperament, constitution, character, cast, disposition, personality, make. **6** constitution, arrangement, construction, composition, format, configuration, build, form.

makeweight /máykwayt/ *n.* **1** a small quantity or thing added to make up the full weight. **2** an unimportant extra person. **3** an unimportant point added to make an argument seem stronger.

making /máyking/ *n.* **1** in senses of MAKE *v.* **2** (in *pl.*) **a** earnings; profit. **b** (foll. by *of*) essential qualities or ingredients (*has the makings of a general; we have the makings of a meal*). **c** *US & Austral. colloq.* paper and tobacco for rolling a cigarette. □ **be the making of** ensure the success or favorable development of. **in the making** in the course of being made or formed. [OE *macung* (as MAKE)]
   ■ **2 b** see INGREDIENT.

mako¹ /máykō, maákō/ *n.* (*pl.* **-os**) a blue shark, *Isurus oxyrinchus.* [Maori]

mako² /mákō/ *n.* (*pl.* **-os**) a small New Zealand tree, *Aristotelia serrata*, with clusters of dark-red berries and large racemes of pink flowers. Also called WINEBERRY. [Maori]

Mal. *abbr.* Malachi (Old Testament).

mal- /mal/ *comb. form* **1 a** bad, badly (*malpractice; maltreat*). **b** faulty, faultily (*malfunction*). **2** not (*maladroit*). [F *mal* badly f. L *male*]

malabsorption /máləbsáwrpshən, -záwrp-/ *n.* imperfect absorption of food material by the small intestine.

malacca /məlákə/ *n.* (in full **malacca cane**) a rich-brown cane from the stem of the palm tree *Calamus scipionum*, used for walking sticks, etc. [*Malacca* in Malaysia]

malachite /máləkit/ *n.* a bright-green mineral of hydrous copper carbonate, taking a high polish and used for ornament. [OF *melochite* f. L *molochites* f. Gk *molokhitis* f. *molokhē* = *malakhē* mallow]

malaco- /máləkō/ *comb. form* soft. [Gk *malakos* soft]

malacology /máləkóləjee/ *n.* the study of mollusks.

malacostracan /máləkóstrəkən/ *n. & adj.* ● *n.* any crustacean of the class Malacostraca, including crabs, shrimps, lobsters, and krill. ● *adj.* of or relating to this class. [MALACO- + Gk *ostrakon* shell]

maladaptive /máladáptiv/ *adj.* (of an individual, species, etc.) failing to adjust adequately to the environment, and undergoing emotional, behavioral, physical, or mental repercussions. □□ **maladaptation** /máladaptáyshən/ *n.*

maladjusted /máləjústid/ *adj.* **1** not correctly adjusted. **2** (of a person) unable to adapt to or cope with the demands of a social environment. □□ **maladjustment** *n.*
   ■ **2** see *disturbed* (DISTURB 4).

maladminister /máladminístər/ *v.tr.* manage or administer inefficiently, badly, or dishonestly. □□ **maladministration** /-stráyshən/ *n.*

maladroit /máladróyt/ *adj.* clumsy; bungling. □□ **maladroitly** *adv.* **maladroitness** *n.* [F (as MAL-, ADROIT)]

■ see CLUMSY 1. □□ **maladroitly** see ROUGHLY 1. **maladroitness** see *ineptitude* (INEPT).

malady /máladee/ *n.* (*pl.* **-ies**) **1** an ailment; a disease. **2** a morbid or depraved condition; something requiring a remedy. [ME f. OF *maladie* f. *malade* sick ult. f. L *male* ill + *habitus* past part. of *habēre* have]
■ **1** see DISEASE.

mala fide /máyla fídee, máalaa feéde/ *adj.* & *adv.* ● *adj.* acting or done in bad faith. ● *adv.* in bad faith. [L]

Malaga /málaga/ *n.* a sweet fortified wine from Málaga in S. Spain.

Malagasy /málagásee/ *adj.* & *n.* ● *adj.* of or relating to Madagascar, an island in the Indian Ocean. ● *n.* the language of Madagascar. [orig. *Malegass, Madegass* f. *Madagascar*]

malagueña /málagáynya/ *n.* **1** a Spanish dance resembling the fandango. **2** a piece of music for or in the style of a fandango. [Sp. (as MALAGA)]

malaise /maláyz/ *n.* **1** a non-specific bodily discomfort not associated with the development of a disease. **2** a feeling of uneasiness. [F f. OF *mal* bad + *aise* EASE]
■ **1** see AILMENT. **2** see DISCONTENT *n.*

malamute /málamyoot/ *n.* (also **malemute**) any of an Alaskan breed of large sled dogs. [name of a native Alaskan people]

malanders /málandərz/ *n.pl.* (also **mallenders**) a dry scabby eruption behind a horse's knee. [ME f. OF *malandre* (sing.) f. L *malandria* (pl.) neck pustules]

malapert /málapert/ *adj.* & *n. archaic* ● *adj.* impudent; saucy. ● *n.* an impudent or saucy person. [ME f. OF (as MAL-, *apert* = *espert* EXPERT)]

malapropism /málapropizəm/ *n.* (also **malaprop** /málaprop/) the use of a word in mistake for one sounding similar, to comic effect, e.g., *allegory* for *alligator*. [Mrs. *Malaprop* (f. MALAPROPOS) in Sheridan's *The Rivals* (1775)]

malapropos /málaprapó/ *adv., adj.,* & *n.* ● *adv.* inopportunely; inappropriately. ● *adj.* inopportune; inappropriate. ● *n.* something inappropriately said, done, etc. [F *mal à propos* f. *mal* ill: see APROPOS]
■ *adj.* see INAPPROPRIATE.

malar /máylər/ *adj.* & *n.* ● *adj.* of the cheek. ● *n.* (also **malar bone**) a bone of the cheek. [mod.L *malaris* f. L *mala* jaw]

malaria /maláireeə/ *n.* **1** an intermittent and remittent fever caused by a protozoan parasite of the genus *Plasmodium*, introduced by the bite of a mosquito. **2** *archaic* an unwholesome atmosphere caused by the exhalations of marshes, to which this fever was formerly attributed. □□ **malarial** *adj.* **malarian** *adj.* **malarious** *adj.* [It. *mal'aria* bad air]

malarkey /maláarkee/ *n. colloq.* humbug; nonsense. [20th c.: orig. unkn.]
■ see NONSENSE.

malathion /málathíon/ *n.* an insecticide containing phosphorus, with low toxicity to plants. [diethyl *maleate* + *thio*- acid + -ON]

Malay /máylay, maláy/ *n.* & *adj.* ● *n.* **1 a** a member of a people predominating in Malaysia and Indonesia. **b** a person of Malay descent. **2** the language of this people, the official language of Malaysia. ● *adj.* of or relating to this people or language. □□ **Malayan** *n.* & *adj.* [Malay *malāyu*]

Malayalam /málayáalam/ *n.* the Dravidian language of the state of Kerala in S. India. [native]

Malayo- /maláyō/ *comb. form* Malayan and (*Malayo-Chinese*). [MALAY]

malcontent /málkəntent/ *n.* & *adj.* ● *n.* a discontented person; a rebel. ● *adj.* discontented or rebellious. [F (as MAL-, CONTENT¹)]
■ *n.* see TROUBLEMAKER. ● *adj.* see DISGRUNTLED.

mal de mer /mál da máir/ *n.* seasickness. [F, = sickness of (the) sea]

male /mayl/ *adj.* & *n.* ● *adj.* **1** of the sex that can beget offspring by fertilization or insemination (*male child; male dog*). **2** of men or male animals, plants, etc.; masculine (*the male sex; a male-voice choir*). **3 a** (of plants or their parts) containing only fertilizing organs. **b** (of plants) thought of as male because of color, shape, etc. **4** (of parts of machinery,

etc.) designed to enter or fill the corresponding female part (*a male plug*). ● *n.* a male person or animal. □ **male chauvinist** (**pig**) a man who is prejudiced against women or regards women as inferior. **male fern** a common lowland fern, *Dryopteris filix-mas*. **male menopause** a crisis of potency, confidence, etc., supposed to afflict men in middle life. □□ **maleness** *n.* [ME f. OF *ma(s)le*, f. L *masculus* f. *mas* a male]
■ *adj.* **2** masculine, man's; virile, manful, macho; see also MANLY 1. ● *n.* see MAN *n.* 1. □ **male chauvinist** sexist, misogynist, chauvinist, woman-hater, *colloq.* MCP.

malediction /málidíkshən/ *n.* **1** a curse. **2** the utterance of a curse. □□ **maledictive** *adj.* **maledictory** *adj.* [ME f. L *maledictio* f. *maledicere* speak evil of f. *male* ill + *dicere dict*- speak]
■ see CURSE *n.* 1.

malefactor /málifaktər/ *n.* a criminal; an evildoer. □□ **malefaction** /-fákshən/ *n.* [ME f. L f. *malefacere malefact*- f. *male* ill + *facere* do]
■ see CRIMINAL *n.* □□ **malefaction** see OFFENSE 1.

malefic /məléfik/ *adj. literary* (of magical arts, etc.) harmful; baleful. [L *maleficus* f. *male* ill]

maleficent /məléfisənt/ *adj. literary* **1** (often foll. by *to*) hurtful. **2** criminal. □□ **maleficence** /-səns/ *n.* [*maleficence* formed as MALEFIC after *malevolence*]

maleic acid /máláyik/ *n.* a colorless crystalline organic acid used in making synthetic resins. [F *maléique* (as MALIC ACID)]

malemute var. of MALAMUTE.

malevolent /məlévələnt/ *adj.* wishing evil to others. □□ **malevolence** /-ləns/ *n.* **malevolently** *adv.* [OF *malivolent* or f. L *malevolens* f. *male* ill + *volens* willing, part. of *velle*]
■ see EVIL *adj.* 1. □□ **malevolence** see HOSTILITY 1.

malfeasance /malfeézəns/ *n. Law* evildoing. □□ **malfeasant** /-zənt/ *n.* & *adj.* [AF *malfaisance* f. OF *malfaisant* (as MAL-, *faisant* part. of *faire* do f. L *facere*): cf. MISFEASANCE]

malformation /málformáyshən/ *n.* faulty formation. □□ **malformed** /-fáwrmd/ *adj.*
■ see ABNORMALITY 2. □□ **malformed** see DEFORMED.

malfunction /málfúngkshən/ *n.* & *v.* ● *n.* a failure to function in a normal or satisfactory manner. ● *v.intr.* fail to function normally or satisfactorily.
■ *n.* see TROUBLE *n.* 4. ● *v.* see *go wrong* 2 (WRONG).

malic acid /málik/ *n.* an organic acid found in unripe apples and other fruits. [F *malique* f. L *malum* apple]

malice /mális/ *n.* **1 a** the intention to do evil. **b** a desire to tease, esp. cruelly. **2** *Law* wrongful intention, esp. as increasing the guilt of certain offenses. □ **malice aforethought** (or **prepense**) *Law* the intention to commit a crime, esp. murder. [ME f. OF f. L *malitia* f. *malus* bad]
■ **1** see HOSTILITY 1.

malicious /məlíshəs/ *adj.* characterized by malice; intending or intended to do harm. □□ **maliciously** *adv.* **maliciousness** *n.* [OF *malicius* f. L *malitiosus* (as MALICE)]
■ see VICIOUS 1, 3. □□ **maliciousness** see VENOM 2.

malign /məlín/ *adj.* & *v.* ● *adj.* **1** (of a thing) injurious. **2** (of a disease) malignant. **3** malevolent. ● *v.tr.* speak ill of; slander. □□ **maligner** *n.* **malignity** /məlígnitee/ *n.* (*pl.* **-ies**) **malignly** /-línlee/ *adv.* [ME f. OF *malin maligne, malignier* f. LL *malignare* contrive maliciously f. L *malignus* f. *malus* bad: cf. BENIGN]
■ *adj.* **1, 3** see EVIL *adj.* 2. ● *v.* see SLANDER *v.* □□ **malignity** see VENOM 2.

malignant /məlígnənt/ *adj.* **1 a** (of a disease) very virulent or infectious (*malignant cholera*). **b** (of a tumor) tending to invade normal tissue and recur after removal; cancerous. **2** harmful; feeling or showing intense ill will. □□ **malignancy** *n.* (*pl.* **-ies**). **malignantly** *adv.* [LL *malignare* (as MALIGN)]
■ **1** virulent, infectious, pernicious, harmful, injurious, life-threatening, invasive, cancerous. **2** harmful, injurious, malign, malevolent, evil, malicious,

/.../ **pronunciation**	● **part of speech**
□ **phrases, idioms, and compounds**	
□□ **derivatives**	■ **synonym section**
cross-references appear in SMALL CAPITALS or *italics*	

pernicious, vicious, spiteful, bitter, hateful, venomous; cankered.

malinger /məlíngɡər/ v.intr. exaggerate or feign illness in order to escape duty, work, etc. ▫▫ **malingerer** n. [back-form. f. malingerer app. f. F malingre, perh. formed as MAL- + haingre weak]

■ ▫▫ **malingerer** see TRUANT n.

mall /mawl/ n. **1** a sheltered walk or promenade. **2** an enclosed shopping center. **3** hist. **a** = PALL-MALL. **b** an alley used for this. [var. of MAUL: applied to The Mall in London (orig. a pall-mall alley)]

mallard /málərd/ n. (pl. same or **mallards**) **1** a wild duck or drake, Anas platyrhynchos, of the northern hemisphere. **2** the flesh of the mallard. [ME f. OF prob. f. maslart (unrecorded, as MALE)]

malleable /máleeəbəl/ adj. **1** (of metal, etc.) able to be hammered or pressed permanently out of shape without breaking or cracking. **2** adaptable; pliable, flexible. ▫▫ **malleability** n. **malleably** adv. [ME f. OF f. med.L malleabilis f. L malleare to hammer f. malleus hammer]

■ **1** see PLASTIC 1a. **2** see ADAPTABLE 1. ▫▫ **malleability** see flexibility (FLEXIBLE).

mallee /málee/ n. Austral. **1** any of several types of eucalyptus, esp. Eucalyptus dumosa, that flourish in arid areas. **2** a scrub formed by mallee. ▫ **mallee fowl** (or **bird** or **hen**) a megapode, Leipoa ocellata, resembling a turkey. [Aboriginal]

mallei pl. of MALLEUS.

mallemuck var. of MOLLYMAWK.

mallenders var. of MALANDERS.

malleolus /məleéələs/ n. (pl. **malleoli** /-lī/) Anat. a bone with the shape of a hammerhead, esp. each of those forming a projection on either side of the ankle. [L, dimin. of malleus hammer]

mallet /málit/ n. **1** a hammer, usu. of wood. **2** a long-handled wooden hammer for striking a croquet or polo ball. [ME f. OF maillet f. mailler to hammer f. mail hammer f. L malleus]

malleus /máleeəs/ n. (pl. **mallei** /-lee-ī/) Anat. a small bone in the middle ear transmitting the vibrations of the tympanum to the incus. [L, = hammer]

mallow /málō/ n. **1** any plant of the genus Malva, esp. M. sylvestris, with hairy stems and leaves and pink or purple flowers. **2** any of several other plants of the family Malvaceae, including marsh mallow and hollyhock. [OE meal(u)we f. L malva]

malm /maam/ n. **1** a soft chalky rock. **2** a loamy soil produced by the disintegration of this rock. **3** a fine-quality brick made originally from malm, marl, or a similar chalky clay. [OE mealm- (in compounds) f. Gmc]

malmsey /máamzee/ n. a strong sweet wine orig. from Greece, now chiefly from Madeira. [ME f. MDu., MLG malmesie, -eye, f. Monemvasia in S. Greece: cf. MALVOISIE]

malnourished /málnə́risht, -núr-/ adj. suffering from malnutrition.

malnourishment /málnə́rishmənt, -núr-/ n. = MALNUTRITION.

malnutrition /málnōōtríshən, -nyōō-/ n. a dietary condition resulting from the absence of some foods or essential elements necessary for health; insufficient nutrition.

malocclusion /maləklōōzhən/ n. Dentistry faulty contact of opposing teeth when the jaws are closed. [MAL- + OCCLUSION]

malodorous /malódərəs/ adj. having an unpleasant smell.

■ see SMELLY.

Malpighian layer /malpígeeən/ n. a layer of proliferating cells in the epidermis. [M. Malpighi, It. physician d. 1694]

malpractice /malpráktis/ n. **1** improper or negligent professional treatment, as by a medical practitioner. **2 a** criminal wrongdoing; misconduct. **b** an instance of this.

malt /mawlt/ n. & v. ● n. **1** barley or other grain that is steeped, germinated, and dried, esp. for brewing or distilling and vinegar making. **2** colloq. esp. Brit. malt whiskey; malt liquor. ● v. **1** tr. convert (grain) into malt. **2** intr. (of seeds) become malt when germination is checked by drought. ▫ **malted milk 1** a drink combining milk, a malt prepara-

tion, and ice cream or flavoring. **2** the powdered malt preparation used to make this. **malthouse** a building used for preparing and storing malt. **malt liquor** a kind of strong beer. **malt whiskey** whiskey made from malted barley. [OE m(e)alt f. Gmc, rel. to MELT]

maltase /mawltáys, -táyz/ n. Biochem. an enzyme found esp. in the small intestine that converts maltose into glucose.

Maltese /mawlteéz, -teés/ n. & adj. ● n. **1** (pl. same) **a** a native or national of Malta, an island in the W. Mediterranean. **b** a person of Maltese descent. **2** the language of Malta. ● adj. of or relating to Malta or its people or language. ▫ **Maltese cat** a variety of domestic cat with a blue-gray coat. **Maltese cross** a cross with arms of equal length broadening from the center, often indented at the ends. **Maltese dog** (or **terrier**) a small breed of spaniel or terrier.

maltha /máltha/ n. a cement made of pitch and wax or other ingredients. [L f. Gk]

Malthusian /malthōōzhən, -zeeən/ adj. & n. ● adj. of or relating to T. R. Malthus, English clergyman and economist (d. 1834) or his theories, esp. that sexual restraint should be exercised as a means of preventing an increase of the population beyond its means of subsistence. ● n. a follower of Malthus. ▫▫ **Malthusianism** n.

malting /máwlting/ n. **1** the process or an instance of brewing or distilling with malt. **2** = malthouse.

maltose /máwltōs, -tōz/ n. Chem. a sugar produced by the hydrolysis of starch under the action of the enzymes in malt, saliva, etc. [F (as MALT)]

maltreat /máltreét/ v.tr. ill-treat. ▫▫ **maltreater** n. **maltreatment** n. [F maltraiter (as MAL-, TREAT)]

■ see ill-treat. ▫▫ **maltreatment** see ABUSE n. 4.

maltster /máwltstər/ n. a person who makes or deals in malt.

malty /máwltee/ adj. (**maltier**, **maltiest**) of, containing, or resembling malt. ▫▫ **maltiness** n.

malvaceous /malváyshəs/ adj. Bot. of or relating to the Malvaceae, the mallow family. [L malvaceus f. malva MALLOW]

malversation /málvərsáyshən/ n. formal **1** corrupt behavior in a position of trust. **2** (often foll. by of) corrupt administration (of public money, etc.). [F f. malverser f. L male badly + versari behave]

malvoisie /málvwəzeé/ n. = MALMSEY. [ME f. OF malvesie f. F form of Monemvasia: see MALMSEY]

mama /maáma, məmaá/ n. colloq. (esp. as a child's term) mother [imit. of child's ma, ma]

■ see MOTHER n. 1.

mamba /maámba/ n. any venomous African snake of the genus Dendroaspis, esp. the green mamba (D. angusticeps) or black mamba (D. polylepis). [Zulu imamba]

mambo /maámbō/ n. & v. ● n. (pl. **-os**) **1** a Latin American dance like the rumba. **2** the music for this. ● v.intr. (**-oes**, **-oed**) perform the mambo. [Amer. Sp. prob. f. Haitian]

Mameluke /máməlōōk/ n. hist. a member of the military class (orig. Caucasian slaves) that ruled Egypt 1254–1811. [F mameluk, ult. f. Arab. mamlūk slave f. malaka possess]

mamilla /məmílə/ n. var. of MAMMILLA.

mamma[1] /maáma/ n. (also **momma**) colloq. (esp. as a child's term) MAMA.

mamma[2] /maáma/ n. (pl. **mammae** /-mee/) **1** a milk-secreting organ of female mammals. **2** a corresponding nonsecretory structure in male mammals. ▫▫ **mammiform** adj. [OE f. L]

mammal /mámal/ n. any vertebrate of the class Mammalia, usu. a warm-blooded quadruped with hair or fur, the females of which possess milk-secreting mammae for the nourishment of the young, and including human beings, dogs, rabbits, whales, etc. ▫▫ **mammalian** /-máylian/ adj. & n. **mammalogy** /-mólijee/ n. [mod.L mammalia neut. pl. of L mammalis (as MAMMA[2])]

mammaliferous /mámalifərəs/ adj. Geol. containing mammalian remains.

mammary /mámaree/ adj. of the human female breasts or milk-secreting organs of other mammals. ▫ **mammary gland** the milk-producing gland of female mammals. [MAMMA[2] + -ARY[1]]

mammee /mamee/ n. a tropical American tree, Mammea

americana, with large red-rinded yellow-pulped fruit. [Sp. *mamei* f. Haitian]

mammilla /məmílə/ *n.* (*pl.* **mammillae** /-lee/) **1** the nipple of a woman's breast. **2** a nipple-shaped organ, etc. □□ **mammillary** /mámmileree/ *adj.* **mammillate** /mámilayt/ *adj.* [L, dimin. of MAMMA²]

mammography /mamógrəfee/ *n. Med.* an X-ray technique of diagnosing and locating abnormalities (esp. tumors) of the breasts. [MAMMA² + -GRAPHY]

mammon /mámən/ *n.* (also **Mammon**) **1** wealth regarded as a god or as an evil influence. **2** the worldly rich. □□ **mammonish** *adj.* **mammonism** *n.* **mammonist** *n.* **mammonite** *n.* [ME f. LL *Mam(m)ona* f. Gk *mamōnas* f. Aram. *māmōn* riches: see Matt. 6:24, Luke 16:9–13]

mammoth /máməth/ *n. & adj.* ● *n.* any large extinct elephant of the genus *Mammuthus*, with a hairy coat and curved tusks. ● *adj.* huge. [Russ. *mamo(n)t*]

■ *adj.* see HUGE 1.

mammy /mámee/ *n.* (*pl.* **-ies**) **1** a child's word for mother. **2** *formerly southern US* an African-American nursemaid or nanny in charge of white children. [formed as MAMMA¹]

Man. *abbr.* Manitoba.

man /man/ *n. & v.* ● *n.* (*pl.* **men** /men/) **1** an adult human male, esp. as distinct from a woman or boy. **2 a** a human being; a person (*no man is perfect*). **b** human beings in general; the human race (*man is mortal*). **3** a person showing characteristics associated with males (*she's more of a man than he is*). **4 a** a worker; an employee (*the manager spoke to the men*). **b** esp. *Brit.* a manservant or valet. **c** *hist.* a vassal. **5 a** (usu. in *pl.*) soldiers, sailors, etc., esp. nonofficers (*was in command of 200 men*). **b** an individual, usu. male, person (*fought to the last man*). **c** (usu. prec. by *the*, or *poss. pron.*) a person regarded as suitable or appropriate in some way; a person fulfilling requirements (*I'm your man; not the man for the job*). **6 a** a husband (*man and wife*). **b** *colloq.* a boyfriend or lover. **7 a** a human being of a specified historical period or character (*Renaissance man*). **b** a type of prehistoric man named after the place where the remains were found (*Peking man*). **8** any one of a set of pieces used in playing chess, checkers, etc. **9** (as second element in *comb.*) a man of a specified nationality, profession, skill, etc. (*Dutchman; clergyman; horseman; gentleman*). **10 a** an expression of impatience, etc., used in addressing a male (*nonsense, man!*). **b** *colloq.* a general mode of address (*blew my mind, man!*). **11** (prec. by *a*) a person; one (*what can a man do?*). **12** a person pursued; an opponent, etc. (*the police have so far not caught their man*). **13** (**the Man**) *sl.* **a** the police. **b** *sl.* esp. *Afr.-Amer.* a person with power or authority. **14** (in *comb.*) a ship of a specified type (*merchantman; Indiaman*). ● *v.tr.* (**manned, manning**) **1** supply (a ship, fort, factory, etc.) with a person or people for work or defense, etc. **2** work or service or defend (a specified piece of equipment, a fortification, etc.) (*man the pumps*). **3** *Naut.* place men at (a part of a ship). **4** fill (a post or office). **5** (usu. *refl.*) fortify the spirits or courage of (*manned herself for the task*). □ **as one man** in unison; in agreement. **be a man** be courageous; not show fear. **be one's own man 1** be free to act; be independent. **2** be in full possession of one's faculties, etc. **man about town** a fashionable man of leisure. **man and boy** from childhood (*he's fished these waters, man and boy, for 60 years*). **man-at-arms** (*pl.* **men-at-arms**) *archaic* a soldier, esp. when heavily armed and mounted. **man Friday** see FRIDAY. **man-hour** (or **-day**, etc.) an hour (or day, etc.) regarded in terms of the amount of work that could be done by one person within this period. **man in the moon** the semblance of a face seen on the surface of a full moon. **man in** (*also* **on**) **the street** an ordinary average person, as distinct from an expert. **man-made** (esp. of a textile fiber) artificial; synthetic. **man of the cloth** a clergyman. **man of God 1** a clergyman. **2** a male saint. **man of honor** a man whose word can be trusted. **man of the house** the male head of a household. **man of letters** a scholar; an author. **man of the moment** a man of importance at a particular time. **man of straw** see *straw man.* **man-of-war** an armed ship, esp. of a specified country. **man of the world** see

WORLD. **man-size** (or **-sized**) **1** of the size of a man; very large. **2** big enough for a man. **man-to-man** with candor; honestly. **men's room** a usu. public restroom for men. **my** (or **my good**) **man** a patronizing mode of address to a man. **separate** (or **sort out**) **the men from the boys** *colloq.* find those who are truly virile, competent, etc. **to a man** all without exception. □□ **manless** *adj.* [OE *man(n)*, pl. *menn, mannian,* f. Gmc]

■ *n.* **1** gentleman, male, *colloq.* guy, fellow, chap, *sl.* dude, *Brit. sl.* bloke, *sl. often derog.* gink. **2 a** person, human being, mortal. **b** people, human beings, mankind, mortals, *Homo sapiens,* humanity, humankind, the human race. **4 a** see WORKER. **b** valet, manservant, servant, *joc.* retainer; houseboy, houseman. **c** see SLAVE *n.* 1. **5 b** see INDIVIDUAL *n.* 2, 3. **6 a** see HUSBAND *n.* **b** see LOVE *n.* 4a, 5. **11** see ONE *pron.* 1, 2. **12** see QUARRY². **13 a** (**the Man**) see POLICE *n.* ● *v.* **1** staff; crew. **5** see FORTIFY 2. □ **as one man** in unison, as one, together, in agreement, harmonious, in harmony. **man about town** see SWELL *n.* 4, TRENDY *n.* **man-at-arms** see SOLDIER *n.* **man in** (*also* **on**) **the street** layman, laywoman, man in the street. **man of God 1** see CLERGYMAN. **man of the house** patriarch, paterfamilias, father. **man of letters** see SCHOLAR 1, AUTHOR *n.* 1. **man-size** (or **-sized**) **1** see LARGE *adj.* 1, 2. **man-to-man** see HONESTLY 1.

mana /máanə/ *n.* **1** power; authority; prestige. **2** supernatural or magical power. [Maori]

manacle /mánəkəl/ *n. & v.* ● *n.* (usu. in *pl.*) **1** a fetter or shackle for the hand; a handcuff. **2** a restraint. ● *v.tr.* fetter with manacles. [ME f. OF *manicle* handcuff f. L *manicula* dimin. of *manus* hand]

■ *n.* **1** (*manacles*) shackles, fetters, handcuffs, chains, irons, *colloq.* cuffs, *sl.* bracelets, *Brit. sl.* darbies; see also RESTRAINT 6. **2** see RESTRAINT 2. ● *v.* shackle, fetter, handcuff, restrain, put *or* throw *or* clap in irons, chain (up).

manage /mánij/ *v. & n.* ● *v.* **1** *tr.* organize; regulate; be in charge of (a business, household, team, a person's career, etc.). **2** *tr.* (often foll. by *to* + infin.) succeed in achieving; contrive (*managed to arrive on time; managed a smile; managed to ruin the day*). **3** *intr.* **a** (often foll. by *with*) succeed in one's aim, esp. against heavy odds (*managed with one assistant*). **b** meet one's needs with limited resources, etc. (*just about manages on a pension*). **4** *tr.* gain influence with or maintain control over (a person, etc.) (*cannot manage their teenage son*). **5** *tr.* (also *absol.* ; often prec. by *can, be able to*) **a** cope with; make use of (*couldn't manage another bite; can you manage by yourself?*). **b** be free to attend on (a certain day) or at (a certain time) (*can you manage Thursday?*). **6** *tr.* handle or wield (a tool, weapon, etc.). **7** *tr.* take or have charge or control of (an animal or animals, esp. cattle). ● *n.* *archaic* **1 a** the training of a horse. **b** the trained movements of a horse. **2** a riding school (cf. MANÈGE). [It. *maneggiare, maneggio* ult. f. L *manus* hand]

■ *v.* **1** handle, administer, run, supervise, look after, watch over, direct, head, oversee, superintend, preside over, be in charge (of), take care of, control, organize, rule (over), govern, regulate. **2, 3, 5a** succeed, contrive; function, make do, make it, shift (for oneself), get along *or* by *or* on, make out, muddle through, survive, cope. **4** handle, cope *or* deal with, control, govern, manipulate. **6** see WIELD 1.

manageable /mánijəbəl/ *adj.* able to be easily managed, controlled, or accomplished, etc. □□ **manageability** *n.* **manageableness** *n.* **manageably** *adv.*

■ controllable; tractable, compliant, amenable, docile, tameable, tame, trainable, teachable, manipulable, submissive.

/. . ./ **pronunciation**	● **part of speech**
□ **phrases, idioms, and compounds**	
□□ **derivatives**	■ **synonym section**
cross-references appear in SMALL CAPITALS or *italics*	

management /mánijmənt/ n. **1** the process or an instance of managing or being managed. **2 a** the professional administration of business concerns, public undertakings, etc. **b** the people engaged in this. **c** (prec. by *the*) a governing body; a board of directors or the people in charge of running a business, regarded collectively. **3** (usu. foll. by *of*) *Med.* the technique of treating a disease, etc. **4** trickery; deceit. □ **management information system** *Computing* a computer system used in business for processing data related to management activities.
  ▪ **1** managing, control, supervision, manipulation, handling, direction, directing, directorship, administration, government, conduct, governance, operation, running, superintendence, command, guidance, stewardship. **2 b, c** administration, executive(s), bosses, directors, board (of directors), directorate, *colloq.* (top) brass. **4** see TRICKERY.

manager /mánijər/ n. **1** a person controlling or administering a business or part of a business. **2** a person controlling the affairs, training, etc., of a person or team in sports, entertainment, etc. **3** a person regarded in terms of skill in household or financial or other management (*a good manager*). □□ **managerial** /mánijéereeəl/ adj. **managerially** /-jéereeəlee/ adv. **managership** n.
  ▪ **1** supervisor, superintendent, director, executive, head, proprietor, overseer, foreman, forewoman, administrator, chief, manageress, straw boss, *colloq.* boss. **2** impresario, administrator; see also DIRECTOR 2.

managing /mánijing/ adj. **1** (in *comb.*) having executive control or authority (*managing partner*). **2** (*attrib.*) fond of controlling affairs, etc. **3** *archaic* economical.

manakin /mánəkin/ n. any small bird of the family Pipridae of Central and S. America, the males of which are often brightly colored. [var. of MANIKIN]

mañana /mənyáánə/ adv. & n. • adv. in the indefinite future (esp. to indicate procrastination). • n. an indefinite future time. [Sp., = tomorrow]

manatee /mánətee/ n. any large aquatic plant-eating mammal of the genus *Trichechus*, with paddlelike forelimbs, no hind limbs, and a powerful tail. [Sp. *manati* f. Carib *manattouï*]

manchineel /mánchineel/ n. a W. Indian tree, *Hippomane mancinella*, with a poisonous and caustic milky sap and acrid applelike fruit. [F *mancenille* f. Sp. *manzanilla* dimin. of *manzana* apple]

Manchu /manchōo/ n. & adj. • n. **1** a member of a people in China, descended from a Tartar people, who formed the last imperial dynasty (1644–1912). **2** the language of the Manchus, now spoken in part of NE China. • adj. of or relating to the Manchu people or their language. [Manchu, = pure]

manciple /mánsipəl/ n. esp. *Brit.* an officer who buys provisions for a college, an Inn of Court, etc. [ME f. AF & OF f. L *mancipium* purchase f. *manceps* buyer f. *manus* hand + *capere* take]

Mancunian /mangkyōōneeən/ n. & adj. • n. a native of Manchester in NW England. • adj. of or relating to Manchester. [L *Mancunium* Manchester]

-mancy /mansee/ comb. form forming nouns meaning 'divination by' (*geomancy; necromancy*). □□ **-mantic** comb. form forming adjectives. [OF *-mancie* f. LL *-mantia* f. Gk *manteia* divination]

Mandaean /mandéeən/ n. & adj. (also **Mandean**) • n. **1** a member of a Gnostic sect surviving in Iraq and claiming descent from John the Baptist. **2** the language of this sect. • adj. of or concerning the Mandaeans or their language. □□ **Mandaeanism** n. [Aram. *mandaiia* Gnostics f. *manda* knowledge]

mandala /mándələ, mún-/ n. **1** a symbolic circular figure representing the universe in various religions. **2** *Psychol.* such a symbol in a dream, representing the dreamer's search for completeness and self-unity. [Skr. *mándala* disk]

mandamus /mandáyməs/ n. *Law* a judicial writ issued as a command to an inferior court, or ordering a person to perform a public or statutory duty. [L, = we command]

mandarin[1] /mándərin/ n. **1** (**Mandarin**) the most widely spoken form of Chinese and the official language of China. **2** *hist.* a Chinese official in any of nine grades of the pre-Communist civil service. **3 a** a party leader; a bureaucrat. **b** a powerful member of the establishment. **4 a** a nodding Chinese figure, usu. of porcelain. **b** porcelain, etc., decorated with Chinese figures in mandarin dress. □ **mandarin collar** a small close-fitting upright collar. **mandarin duck** a small Chinese duck, *Aix galericulata*, noted for its bright plumage. **mandarin sleeve** a wide loose sleeve. □□ **mandarinate** n. [Port. *mandarim* f. Malay f. Hindi *mantrī* f. Skr. *mantrin* counselor]
  ▪ **3** see MOGUL.

mandarin[2] /mándərin/ n. (in full **mandarin orange**) **1** a small flattish deep-colored orange with a loose skin. **2** the tree, *Citrus reticulata*, yielding this. Also called TANGERINE. [F *mandarine* (perh. as MANDARIN[1], with ref. to the official's yellow robes)]

mandatary /mándətéree/ n. (*pl.* **-ies**) esp. *hist.* a person or country receiving a mandate. [LL *mandatarius* (as MANDATE)]

mandate /mándayt/ n. & v. • n. **1** an official command or instruction by an authority. **2** support for a policy or course of action, regarded by a victorious party, candidate, etc., as derived from the wishes of the people in an election. **3** a commission to act for another. **4** *Law* a commission by which a party is entrusted to perform a service, often gratuitously and with indemnity against loss by that party. **5** *hist.* a commission from the League of Nations to a member country to administer a territory. **6** a papal decree or decision. • v.tr. **1** instruct (a delegate) to act or vote in a certain way. **2** (usu. foll. by *to*) *hist.* commit (a territory, etc.) to a mandatary. □□ **mandator** n. [L *mandatum*, neut. past part. of *mandare* command f. *manus* hand + *dare* give: sense 2 of n. after F *mandat*]
  ▪ n. **1** see COMMAND n. 1. **2** see APPROVAL. **6** see DECREE n. 1. • v. **1** see DECREE v. **2** see REQUISITION v.

mandatory /mándətawree/ adj. & n. • adj. **1** of or conveying a command. **2** compulsory. • n. (*pl.* **-ies**) = MANDATARY. □□ **mandatorily** adv. [LL *mandatorius* f. L (as MANDATE)]
  ▪ adj. **2** compulsory, obligatory, requisite, required, essential, demanded, necessary, needed.

mandible /mándibəl/ n. **1** the jaw, esp. the lower jaw in mammals and fishes. **2** the upper or lower part of a bird's beak. **3** either half of the crushing organ in an arthropod's mouthparts. □□ **mandibular** /-díbyələr/ adj. **mandibulate** /-díbyəlät/ adj. [ME f. OF *mandible* or LL *mandibula* f. *mandere* chew]

mandolin /mándəlín/ n. (also **mandoline**) a musical instrument resembling a lute, having paired metal strings plucked with a plectrum. □□ **mandolinist** n. [F *mandoline* f. It. *mandolino* dimin. of *mandola* a large lute]

mandorla /mandawrlə/ n. = VESICA 2. [It., = almond]

mandragora /mandrágərə/ n. *hist.* the mandrake, esp. as a type of narcotic (Shakesp. *Othello* III. iii. 334). [OE f. med.L f. L f. Gk *mandragoras*]

mandrake /mándrayk/ n. **1** a poisonous plant, *Mandragora officinarum*, with white or purple flowers and large yellow fruit, having emetic and narcotic properties and possessing a root once thought to resemble the human form and to shriek when plucked. **2** = MAYAPPLE. [ME *mandrag(g)e*, prob. f. MDu. *mandrag(r)e* f. med.L (as MANDRAGORA): assoc. with MAN + *drake* dragon (cf. DRAKE)]

mandrel /mándrəl/ n. **1 a** a shaft in a lathe to which work is fixed while being turned. **b** a cylindrical rod around which metal or other material is forged or shaped. **2** *Brit.* a miner's pick. [16th c.: orig. unkn.]

mandrill /mándril/ n. a large W. African baboon, *Papio* (or *Mandrillus*) *sphinx*, the adult of which has a brilliantly colored face and blue-colored buttocks. [prob. f. MAN + DRILL[3]]

manducate /mánjōōkayt/ v.tr. *literary* chew; eat. □□ **manducation** /-káyshən/ n. **manducatory** /-kətáwree/ adj. [L *manducare manducat-* chew f. *manduco* guzzler f. *mandere* chew]

mane /mayn/ n. **1** long hair growing in a line on the neck of a horse, lion, etc. **2** *colloq.* a person's long hair. □□ **maned** *adj.* (also in *comb.*). **maneless** *adj.* [OE *manu* f. Gmc]

manège /manéźh/ *n.* (also **manege**) **1** a riding school. **2** the movements of a trained horse. **3** horsemanship. [F *manège* f. It. (as MANAGE)]

manes /maánayz, máyneez/ *n.pl.* **1** the deified souls of dead ancestors. **2** (as *sing.*) the revered ghost of a dead person. [ME f. L]

maneuver /mənóŏvər/ *n.* & *v.* (*Brit.* **manoeuvre**) ● *n.* **1** a planned and controlled movement or series of moves. **2** (in *pl.*) a large-scale exercise of troops, warships, etc. **3** a an often deceptive planned or controlled action designed to gain an objective. **b** a skillful plan. ● *v.* **1** *intr.* & *tr.* perform or cause to perform a maneuver (*maneuvered the car into the space*). **2** *intr.* & *tr.* perform or cause (troops, etc.) to perform military maneuvers. **3 a** *tr.* (usu. foll. by *into, out, away*) force, drive, or manipulate (a person, thing, etc.) by scheming or adroitness. **b** *intr.* use artifice. □□ **maneuverable** *adj.* **maneuverability** /-vrəbílitee, -vərə-/ *n.* **maneuverer** *n.* [F *manœuvre, manœuvrer* f. med.L *manuoperare* f. L *manus* hand + *operari* to work]

■ *n.* **1, 3** move, stratagem, tactic, trick, gambit, subterfuge, ruse, dodge, artifice, device, wile, démarche, strategy, plan, plot, scheme, intrigue, machination, *colloq.* ploy. **2** (*maneuvers*) exercise(s), war game(s). ● *v.* **1** manipulate, run, drive, guide, navigate, steer. **3** manipulate, contrive, plot, scheme, machinate, intrigue, trick, devise, engineer, finesse, manage, *colloq.* finagle, wangle.

manful /mánfŏŏl/ *adj.* brave; resolute. □□ **manfully** *adv.* **manfulness** *n.*

■ see INTREPID. □□ **manfulness** see SPIRIT *n.* 5c.

mangabey /mánggəbay/ *n.* any small long-tailed W. African monkey of the genus *Cercocebus*. [*Mangabey*, a region of Madagascar]

manganese /mánggəneéz/ *n.* **1** *Chem.* a gray brittle metallic transition element used with steel to make alloys. ¶ Symb.: **Mn. 2** (in full **manganese oxide**) the black mineral oxide of this used in the manufacture of glass. □□ **manganic** /-gánik/ *adj.* **manganous** /mánggənəs/ *adj.* [F *manganèse* f. It. *manganese*, alt. f. MAGNESIA]

mange /maynj/ *n.* a skin disease in hairy and woolly animals, caused by an arachnid parasite and occasionally communicated to people. [ME *mangie, maniewe* f. OF *manjue, mangeue* itch f. *mangier manju-* eat f. L *manducare* chew]

mangel /mánggəl/ *n.* esp. *Brit.* (also **mangold** /mánggōld/) (in full **mangel-wurzel, mangold-wurzel** /-wúrzəl/) a large kind of beet, *Beta vulgaris*, used as cattle food. [G *Mangoldwurzel* f. *Mangold* beet + *Wurzel* root]

manger /máynjər/ *n.* a long open box or trough in a stable, etc., for horses or cattle to eat from. [ME f. OF *mangeoire, mangeure* ult. f. L (as MANDUCATE)]

mangle[1] /mánggəl/ *v.tr.* **1** hack, cut, or mutilate by blows, etc. **2** spoil (a quotation, text, etc.) by misquoting, mispronouncing, etc. **3** cut roughly so as to disfigure. □□ **mangler** *n.* [AF *ma(ha)ngler*, app. frequent. of *mahaignier* MAIM]

■ **1** hack, cut, lacerate, chop (up), crush, damage, cripple, maim, destroy, mutilate, butcher, deform, disfigure, spoil, mar, ruin, wreck. **2** butcher, mutilate, spoil, mar, ruin, wreck. **3** hack, cut, lacerate, chop (up), disfigure, spoil, mar, ruin, wreck.

mangle[2] /mánggəl/ *n.* & *v.* ● *n.* a machine having two or more usu. heated revolving cylinders between which clothes, etc., are squeezed and pressed. ● *v.tr.* press (clothes, etc.) in a mangle. [Du. *mangel(stok)* f. *mangelen* to mangle, ult. f. Gk *magganon* + *stok* staff, STOCK]

mango /mánggō/ *n.* (*pl.* -**oes** or -**os**) **1** a fleshy yellowish-red fruit, eaten ripe or used green for pickles, etc. **2** the E. Indian evergreen tree, *Mangifera indica*, bearing this. [Port. *manga* f. Malay *mangā* f. Tamil *mānkāy* f. *mān* mango tree + *kāy* fruit]

mangold (also **mangold-wurzel**) var. of MANGEL.

mangonel /mánggənəl/ *n.* *Mil. hist.* a military engine for throwing stones, etc. [ME f. OF *mangonel(le)*, f. med.L *manganellus* dimin. of LL *manganum* f. Gk *magganon*]

mangosteen /mánggəsteen/ *n.* **1** a white juicy-pulped fruit with a thick reddish-brown rind. **2** the E. Indian tree, *Garcinia mangostana*, bearing this. [Malay *manggustan*]

mangrove /mánggrōv/ *n.* any tropical tree or shrub of the genus *Rhizophora*, growing in tidal-shore mud with many tangled roots above ground. [17th c.: orig. uncert.: assim. to GROVE]

mangy /máynjee/ *adj.* (**mangier, mangiest**) **1** (esp. of a domestic animal) having mange. **2** squalid; shabby. □□ **mangily** *adv.* **manginess** *n.*

■ **1** scabious, scabby. **2** scruffy, dirty, sleazy, sorry, squalid, slovenly, unkempt, slummy, dingy, seedy, poor, shabby, mean, low, bedraggled, raggedy, ragged, moth-eaten, the worse for wear, *Austral. sl.* warby.

manhandle /mánhánd'l/ *v.tr.* **1** move (heavy objects) by human effort. **2** *colloq.* handle (a person) roughly.

■ **2** hustle, jostle, tousle, molest, shove, maul, esp. *Brit.* frogmarch, *colloq.* paw, *sl.* bounce, roust.

manhattan /manhátən/ *n.* (also *cap.*) a cocktail made of vermouth and whiskey, usu. flavored with bitters. [*Manhattan*, borough of New York City]

manhole /mánhōl/ *n.* a covered opening in a floor, pavement, sewer, etc., for workers to gain access.

manhood /mánhŏŏd/ *n.* **1** the state of being a man rather than a child or woman. **2 a** manliness; courage. **b** a man's sexual potency. **3** the men of a country, etc. **4** the state of being human.

■ **2 a** masculinity, manliness, manfulness, virility, machismo, courage, bravery, pluck, boldness, determination, resolution, fortitude, spirit, *colloq.* guts, grit. **4** see HUMANITY 1c.

manhunt /mánhunt/ *n.* an organized search for a person, esp. a criminal.

mania /máyneeə/ *n.* **1** *Psychol.* mental illness marked by periods of great excitement and violence. **2** (often foll. by *for*) excessive enthusiasm; an obsession (*has a mania for jogging*). [ME f. LL f. Gk, = madness f. *mainomai* be mad, rel. to MIND]

■ **1** madness, lunacy, insanity, dementia, dementedness, derangement, hysteria, mental illness *or* disorder, *colloq.* craziness. **2** rage, craze, passion, fad; obsession, compulsion, urge, fascination, preoccupation, yearning, craving, desire, cacoëthes, *colloq.* yen.

-mania /máyneeə/ *comb. form* **1** *Psychol.* denoting a special type of mental abnormality or obsession (*megalomania; nymphomania*). **2** denoting extreme enthusiasm or admiration (*bibliomania; Anglomania*).

maniac /máyneeak/ *n.* & *adj.* ● *n.* **1** *colloq.* a person exhibiting extreme symptoms of wild behavior, etc.; a madman. **2** *colloq.* an obsessive enthusiast. **3** *Psychol. archaic* a person suffering from mania. ● *adj.* of or behaving like a maniac. □□ **maniacal** /mənī́əkəl/ *adj.* **maniacally** /mənī́əklee/ *adv.* [LL *maniacus* f. late Gk *maniakos* (as MANIA)]

■ *n.* **1** madman, madwoman, lunatic, psychopath, psychotic, *sl.* crackpot, nut, nutcase, loony, kook, crazy, *Brit. sl.* nutter. **2** fanatic, fan, enthusiast, zealot, nympholept, *colloq.* freak, *sl.* fiend, nut. ● *adj.* see *maniacal* below. □□ **maniacal** manic, maniac, insane, lunatic, mad, demented, deranged, mentally ill, non compos (mentis), psychotic; hysterical, berserk, wild, *colloq.* crazy, *sl.* loony.

-maniac /máyneeak/ *comb. form* forming adjectives and nouns meaning 'affected with -mania' or 'a person affected with -mania' (*nymphomaniac*).

manic /mánik/ *adj.* of or affected by mania. □ **manic-depressive** *Psychol.* *adj.* affected by or relating to a mental disorder with alternating periods of elation and depression. ● *n.* a person having such a disorder. □□ **manically** *adv.*

■ see MAD *adj.* 1.

┌───┐
│ /. . . / **pronunciation**   ● **part of speech** │
│ □ **phrases, idioms, and compounds**   │
│ □□ **derivatives**   ■ **synonym section**   │
│ **cross-references** appear in SMALL CAPITALS or *italics* │
└───┘

Manichee /mánikee/ n. **1** an adherent of a religious system of the 3rd–5th c., representing Satan in a state of everlasting conflict with God. **2** *Philos.* a dualist (see DUALISM). □□ **Manichean** /-kéeən/ adj. & n. (also **Manichaean**). **Manicheism** /-keé-izəm/ n. (also **Manichaeism**). [LL *Manichaeus* f. late Gk *Manikhaios*, f. *Manes* or *Manichaeus* Persian founder of the sect]

manicure /mánikyŏŏr/ n. & v. ● n. **1** a usu. professional cosmetic treatment of the hands and fingernails. **2** = MANICURIST. ● v.tr. give a manicure to (the hands or a person). [F f. L *manus* hand + *cura* care]

manicurist /mánikyŏŏrist/ n. a person who gives manicures professionally.

manifest[1] /mánifest/ adj. & v. ● adj. clear or obvious to the eye or mind (*his distress was manifest*). ● v. **1** tr. display or show (a quality, feeling, etc.) by one's acts, etc. **2** tr. show plainly to the eye or mind. **3** tr. be evidence of; prove. **4** refl. (of a thing) reveal itself. **5** intr. (of a ghost) appear. □ **Manifest Destiny** 19th-c. doctrine asserting that the United States was destined to expand westward to the Pacific and to exert economic and social control throughout N. America. □□ **manifestation** /-stáyshən/ n. **manifestative** /-féstətiv/ adj. **manifestly** adv. [ME f. OF *manifeste* (adj.), *manifester* (v.) or L *manifestus*, *manifestare* f. *manus* hand + *festus* (unrecorded) struck]

■ adj. apparent, clear, evident, obvious, plain, patent, blatant, conspicuous, unmistakable, discernible, recognizable, comprehensible, distinct, palpable, definite, explicit, unambiguous, unquestionable, indubitable, indisputable. ● v. **1, 2** show, demonstrate, exhibit, evince, reveal, disclose, display, betray; express, declare. **3** corroborate, substantiate, attest; see also PROVE 1. **4** reveal *or* show *or* exhibit itself. **5** materialize. □□ **manifestation** display, exhibition, demonstration, show, disclosure, appearance, exposure, presentation, sign, indication, mark, expression, example, instance; declaration, avowal, publication, announcement; materialization. **manifestly** evidently, clearly, obviously, plainly, apparently, patently, unmistakably, palpably, unquestionably, indubitably, undoubtedly, indisputably.

manifest[2] /mánifest/ n. & v. ● n. **1** a cargo list for the use of customs officers. **2** a list of passengers in an aircraft or of cars, etc., in a freight train. ● v.tr. record (names, cargo, etc.) in a manifest. [It. *manifesto*: see MANIFESTO]

manifesto /mániféstō/ n. (pl. **-os** or **-oes**) **1** a public declaration of policy and aims esp. political or social. **2** *Brit.* the platform of a political party or candidate. [It. f. *manifestare* f. L (as MANIFEST[1])]

■ declaration, platform, program.

manifold /mánifōld/ adj. & n. ● adj. *literary* **1** many and various (*manifold vexations*). **2** having various forms, parts, applications, etc. **3** performing several functions at once. ● n. **1** a thing with many different forms, parts, applications, etc. **2** *Mech.* a pipe or chamber branching into several openings. □□ **manifoldly** adv. **manifoldness** n. [OE *manigfeald* (as MANY, -FOLD)]

■ adj. **1, 2** diverse, diversified, multifarious, varied, various, assorted, multiplex, miscellaneous, sundry, many-sided, *archaic or literary* divers. ● n. **1** composite, amalgam; see also BLEND n.

manikin /mánikin/ n. (also **mannikin**) **1** a little man; a dwarf. **2** an artist's lay figure. **3** an anatomical model of the body. **4** (usu. **mannikin**) any small finchlike bird of the genus *Lonchura*, native to Africa and Australasia. [Du. *manneken*, dimin. of *man* MAN]

■ dwarf, midget, homunculus.

Manila /mənílə/ n. (also **Manilla**) **1** (in full **Manila hemp**) the strong fiber of a Philippine tree, *Musa textilis*, used for rope, etc. **2** (also **manila**) a strong brown paper made from Manila hemp or other material and used for wrapping paper, envelopes, etc. **3** a cigar or cheroot made in Manila. [*Manila* in the Philippines]

manilla /mənílə/ n. a metal bracelet used by African tribes

as a medium of exchange. [Sp., prob. dimin. of *mano* hand f. L *manus*]

manioc /máneeok/ n. **1** cassava. **2** the flour made from it. [Tupi *mandioca*]

maniple /mánipəl/ n. **1** *Rom.Hist.* a subdivision of a legion, containing 120 or 60 men. **2** a Eucharistic vestment consisting of a strip folded over the left arm. [OF *maniple* or L *manipulus* handful, troop f. *manus* hand]

manipulate /mənípyəlayt/ v.tr. **1** handle, treat, or use, esp. skillfully (a tool, question, material, etc.). **2** manage (a person, situation, etc.) to one's own advantage, esp. unfairly or unscrupulously. **3** manually examine and treat (a part of the body). **4** *Computing* alter, edit, or move (text, data, etc.). **5** stimulate (the genitals). □□ **manipulable** /-ləbəl/ adj. **manipulability** /-ləbílitee/ n. **manipulatable** adj. **manipulation** /-láyshən/ n. **manipulator** n. **manipulatory** /-lətáwree/ adj. [back-form. f. *manipulation* f. F *manipulation* f. mod.L *manipulatio* (as MANIPLE), after F *manipuler*]

■ **1** handle, control, operate, direct, work, use, treat, employ. **2** manage, handle, control, maneuver, orchestrate, choreograph, influence, use, exploit, play on, utilize; massage, rig, falsify, juggle, tamper with, doctor, *colloq.* cook, *sl.* fiddle. **5** see HANDLE v. 1.

manipulative /mənípyələtiv/ adj. **1** characterized by unscrupulous exploitation of a situation, person, etc., for one's own ends. **2** of or concerning manipulation. □□ **manipulatively** adv. **manipulativeness** n.

■ **1** see CALCULATING.

Manit. abbr. Manitoba.

manitou /mánitŏŏ/ n. **1** a good or evil spirit as an object of reverence. **2** something regarded as having supernatural power. [Algonquian *manito*, *-tu* he has surpassed]

mankind n. **1** /mánkínd/ the human species. **2** /mánkínd/ male people, as distinct from female.

■ **1** see HUMANITY 1a, b.

manlike /mánlīk/ adj. **1** having the qualities of a man. **2** (of a woman) mannish. **3** (of an animal, shape, etc.) resembling a human being.

■ **1** see MANLY 1.

manly /mánlee/ adj. (**manlier, manliest**) **1** having qualities regarded as admirable in a man, such as courage, frankness, etc. **2** (of a woman) mannish. **3** (of things, qualities, etc.) befitting a man. □□ **manliness** n.

■ **1** manful, virile, courageous, bold, brave, intrepid, valorous, valiant, dauntless, fearless, plucky, daring, venturesome, stout-hearted, resolute, stable, steadfast, unflinching, unwavering, unshrinking, chivalrous, gallant, noble, heroic; masculine, male, macho, red-blooded. **2** masculine, usu. derog. mannish, sl. butch.

manna /mánə/ n. **1** the substance miraculously supplied as food to the Israelites in the wilderness (Exod. 16). **2** an unexpected benefit (esp. *manna from heaven*). **3** spiritual nourishment, esp. the Eucharist. **4** the sweet dried juice from the manna ash and other related plants, used as a mild laxative. □ **manna ash** an ash tree native to S. Europe, *Fraxinus ornus*. □ **manna grass** any N. American marsh grass of the genus *Glyceria*. [OE f. LL f. Gk f. Aram. *mannā* f. Heb. *mān*, explained as = *mān hū?* what is it?, but prob. = Arab. *mann* exudation of common tamarisk (*Tamarix gallica*)]

manned /mand/ adj. (of an aircraft, spacecraft, etc.) having a human crew. [past part. of MAN]

mannequin /mánikin/ n. **1** a model employed by a dressmaker, etc., to show clothes to customers. **2** a window dummy. **3** an artist's lay figure. [F, = MANIKIN]

■ **2** dummy, model, figure.

manner /mánər/ n. **1** a way a thing is done or happens (*always dresses in that manner*). **2** (in pl.) **a** social behavior (*it is bad manners to stare*). **b** polite or well-bred behavior (*he has no manners*). **c** modes of life; conditions of society. **3** a person's outward bearing, way of speaking, etc. (*has an imperious manner*). **4 a** a style in literature, art, etc. (*in the manner of Rembrandt*). **b** = MANNERISM 2a. **5** *archaic* a kind or sort (*what manner of man is he?*). □ **all manner of** many different kinds of. **comedy of manners** satirical portrayal of social behavior, esp. of the upper classes. **in a manner of speak-**

ing in some sense; to some extent; so to speak. **manner of means** see MEANS. **to the manner born 1** *colloq.* naturally at ease in a specified job, situation, etc. **2** destined by birth to follow a custom or way of life (Shakesp. *Hamlet* I. iv. 17). □□ **mannerless** *adj.* (in sense 2b of *n.*). [ME f. AF *manere*, OF *maniere* ult. f. L *manuarius* of the hand (*manus*)]

■ **1** way, mode, style, technique, procedure, method, fashion; means, approach. **2** (*manners*) etiquette, decorum, (good) form, politeness, protocol, politesse, *colloq.* the done thing; civility, ceremony, social code, social graces, formalities, niceties, proprieties, convenances. **3** air, behavior, demeanor, bearing, deportment, conduct, attitude, aspect, *literary* comportment, mien. **5** see KIND[1] 1. □ **all manner of** all kinds of. **in a manner of speaking** so to speak, figuratively *or* metaphorically speaking; see also *partially* (PARTIAL).

mannered /mánərd/ *adj.* **1** (in *comb.*) behaving in a specified way (*ill-mannered*; *well-mannered*). **2** (of a style, artist, writer, etc.) showing idiosyncratic mannerisms. **3** (of a person) eccentrically affected in behavior.

■ **1** (*comb.*) -behaved. **2, 3** artificial, contrived, stilted, stiff, affected, insincere, pompous, pretentious, posed, unnatural, pseudo, *colloq.* phony.

mannerism /mánərizəm/ *n.* **1** a habitual gesture or way of speaking, etc.; an idiosyncrasy. **2 a** excessive addiction to a distinctive style in art or literature. **b** a stylistic trick. **3 a** style of Italian art preceding the Baroque, characterized by lengthened figures. □□ **mannerist** *n.* **manneristic** /-rístik/ *adj.* **manneristical** /-rístikəl/ *adj.* **manneristically** /-rístik-lee/ *adv.* [MANNER]

■ **1** quirk, peculiarity, idiosyncrasy, trait, characteristic, habit.

mannerly /mánərlee/ *adj. & adv.* ● *adj.* well-mannered; polite. ● *adv.* politely. □□ **mannerliness** *n.*

■ *adj.* see POLITE 1. □□ **mannerliness** see PROPRIETY 2.

mannikin var. of MANIKIN.

mannish /mánish/ *adj.* **1** usu. *derog.* (of a woman) masculine in appearance or manner. **2** characteristic of a man. □□ **mannishly** *adv.* **mannishness** *n.* [OE *mennisc* f. (and assim. to) MAN]

manoeuvre *Brit.* var. of MANEUVER.

manometer /mənómitər/ *n.* a pressure gauge for gases and liquids. □□ **manometric** /mánəmétrik/ *adj.* [F *manomètre* f. Gk *manos* thin]

ma non troppo see TROPPO[1].

manor /mánər/ *n.* **1** (also **manor house**) **a** a large country house with lands. **b** the house of the lord of the manor. **2** *Brit.* **a** a unit of land consisting of a lord's demesne and lands rented to tenants, etc. **b** *hist.* a feudal lordship over lands. **3** *Brit. colloq.* the district covered by a police station. □□ **manorial** /mənáwreeəl/ *adj.* [ME f. AF *maner*, OF *maneir*, f. L *manēre* remain]

■ **1a, 2a** see ESTATE 1. **1 b** see PALACE 2.

manpower /mánpowr/ *n.* **1** the power generated by a person working. **2** the number of people available or required for work, service, etc.

manqué /maaNkáy/ *adj.* (placed after noun) that might have been but is not; unfulfilled (*a comic actor manqué*). [F, past part. of *manquer* lack]

mansard /mánsaard/ *n.* a roof that has four sloping sides, each of which becomes steeper halfway down. [F *mansarde* f. F. *Mansart*, Fr. architect d. 1666]

manse /mans/ *n.* **1** the house of a minister, esp. a Presbyterian **2** a mansion. □ **son** (or **daughter**) **of the manse** the child of a Presbyterian, etc., minister. [ME f. med.L *mansus*, -*sa*, -*sum*, house f. *manēre mans*- remain]

manservant /mánsərvənt/ *n.* (*pl.* **menservants**) a male servant.

■ see SERVANT.

-manship /mənship/ *suffix* forming nouns denoting skill in a subject or activity (*craftsmanship*; *gamesmanship*).

mansion /mánshən/ *n.* **1** a large house. **2** (usu. in *pl.*) *Brit.* a large building divided into apartments. □ **mansion-house**

Brit. the house of a lord mayor or a landed proprietor. [ME f. OF f. L *mansio -onis* a staying (as MANSE)]

■ **1** see PALACE.

manslaughter /mánslawtər/ *n.* **1** the killing of one human being by another. **2** *Law* the unlawful killing of a human being without malice aforethought.

■ see KILLING *n.* 1.

mansuetude /mánswitōōd, -tyōōd/ *n.* *archaic* meekness, docility, gentleness. [ME f. OF *mansuetude* or L *mansuetudo* f. *mansuetus* gentle, tame f. *manus* hand + *suetus* accustomed]

manta /mántə/ *n.* **1** esp. *SW US* and *Latin Amer.* a cloak or shawl made from a square cloth. **2** any large ray of the family Mobulidae, esp. *Manta birostris*, having winglike pectoral fins and a whiplike tail. [Amer. Sp., = large blanket]

mantel /mánt'l/ *n.* **1** = MANTELPIECE 1. **2** = MANTELSHELF. [var. of MANTLE]

mantelet /mánt'lit/ *n.* (also **mantlet** /mántlit/) **1** *hist.* a woman's short loose sleeveless mantle. **2** a protective screen for gunners, etc. [ME f. OF, dimin. of *mantel* MANTLE]

mantelpiece /mánt'lpees/ *n.* **1** a structure of wood, marble, etc., above and around a fireplace. **2** = MANTELSHELF.

mantelshelf /mánt'lshelf/ *n.* a shelf above a fireplace.

mantic /mántik/ *adj.* *formal* of or concerning divination or prophecy. [Gk *mantikos* f. *mantis* prophet]

mantid /mántid/ *n.* = MANTIS.

mantilla /mántilə, -téeə/ *n.* a lace scarf worn by Spanish women over the hair and shoulders. [Sp., dimin. of *manta* MANTLE]

mantis /mántis/ *n.* (*pl.* same or **mantises**) any insect of the family Mantidae, feeding on other insects, etc. □ **praying mantis** a mantis, *Mantis religiosa*, that holds its forelegs in a position suggestive of hands folded in prayer, while waiting to pounce on its prey. [Gk, = prophet]

mantissa /mantísə/ *n.* the part of a logarithm after the decimal point. [L, = makeweight]

mantle /mánt'l/ *n. & v.* ● *n.* **1** a loose sleeveless cloak. **2** a covering (*a mantle of snow*). **3** responsibility or authority, esp. as passing from one person to another (see 2 Kings 2:13). **4** a fragile lacelike tube fixed around a gas jet to give an incandescent light. **5** an outer fold of skin enclosing a mollusk's viscera. **6** a bird's back, scapulars, and wing coverts, esp. if of a distinctive color. **7** the region between the crust and the core of the earth. ● *v.* **1** *tr.* clothe in or as if in a mantle; cover; conceal; envelop. **2** *intr.* **a** (of the blood) suffuse the cheeks. **b** (of the face) glow with a blush. **3** *intr.* (of a liquid) become covered with a coating or scum. [ME f. OF f. L *mantellum* cloak]

■ *n.* **1** cloak, cape, wrap, shawl, *hist.* pelisse. **2** covering, cover, sheet, veil, blanket, screen, cloak, shroud, pall, canopy, curtain. **3** responsibility, charge, burden, duty; power, right; see also AUSPICE 1. ● *v.* **1** cover, clothe, envelop, surround, encircle, shroud, veil, screen, obscure, cloak, conceal, hide, mask, wrap, disguise. **2 b** see GLOW *v.* 2.

mantlet var. of MANTELET.

mantling /mántling/ *n. Heraldry* **1** ornamental drapery, etc. behind and around a shield. **2** a representation of this. [MANTLE + -ING[1]]

mantra /mántrə, maán-, mún-/ *n.* **1** a word or sound repeated to aid concentration in meditation, orig. in Hinduism and Buddhism. **2** a Vedic hymn. [Skr., = instrument of thought f. *man* think]

■ **1** see CHANT *n.*

mantrap /mántrap/ *n.* a trap for catching poachers, trespassers, etc.

mantua /mánchōōə/ *n. hist.* a woman's loose gown of the 17th–18th c. [corrupt. of *manteau* (F, as MANTLE) after *Mantua* in Italy]

manual /mányōōəl/ *adj. & n.* ● *adj.* **1** of or done with the

---

/.../ **pronunciation**	● **part of speech**
□ **phrases, idioms, and compounds**	
□□ **derivatives**	■ **synonym section**
cross-references appear in SMALL CAPITALS or *italics*	

hands (*manual labor*). **2** (of a machine, etc.) worked by hand, not automatically. ● *n.* **1 a** a book of instructions, esp. for operating a machine or learning a subject; a handbook (*a computer manual*). **b** any small book. **2** a nonelectric typewriter. **3** an organ keyboard played only with the hands. **4** *Mil.* an exercise in handling a rifle, etc. **5** *hist.* a book of the forms to be used by priests in the administration of the sacraments. □ **manual alphabet** set of sign-language symbols used in fingerspelling. □□ **manually** *adv.* [ME f. OF *manuel*, f. (and later assim. to) L *manualis* f. *manus* hand]
■ *adj.* **1** hand, blue-collar. **2** hand-operated. ● *n.* **1** handbook, companion, vade mecum, *formal* enchiridion; directions, instructions, guide.

manufactory /mányəfáktəree/ *n.* (*pl.* **-ies**) *archaic* = FACTORY. [MANUFACTURE, after *factory*]

manufacture /mányəfákchər/ *n. & v.* ● *n.* **1 a** the making of articles, esp. in a factory, etc. **b** a branch of an industry (*woolen manufacture*). **2** esp. *derog.* the merely mechanical production of literature, art, etc. ● *v.tr.* **1** make (articles), esp. on an industrial scale. **2** invent or fabricate (evidence, a story, etc.). **3** esp. *derog.* make or produce (literature, art, etc.) in a mechanical way. □□ **manufacturable** *adj.* **manufacturability** /-chərəbílitee/ *n.* **manufacturer** *n.* [F f. It. *manifattura* & L *manufactum* made by hand]
■ *n.* **1** making, (mass) production, construction, building, assembly, fabrication, turning *or* putting out, putting together. ● *v.* **1** make, (mass-)produce, construct, build, assemble, fabricate, put together, turn out, create, originate. **2** concoct, create, contrive, invent, make up, fabricate, think up, *colloq.* cook up. **3** churn out, *colloq.* knock off. □□ **manufacturer** maker, producer, processor, industrialist; fabricator.

manuka /mannŏŏkə, maanəkə/ *n. Austral. & NZ* a small tree, *Leptospermum scoparium*, with aromatic leaves and hard timber. [Maori]

manumit /mányəmít/ *v.tr.* (**manumitted, manumitting**) *hist.* set (a slave) free. □□ **manumission** /-míshən/ *n.* [ME f. L *manumittere manumiss-* f. *manus* hand + *emittere* send forth]

manure /mənŏŏr, -nyŏŏr/ *n. & v.* ● *n.* **1** animal dung used for fertilizing land. **2** any compost or artificial fertilizer. ● *v.tr.* (also *absol.*) apply manure to (land, etc.). □□ **manurial** *adj.* [ME f. AF *mainoverer* = OF *manouvrer* MANEUVER]
■ *n.* **1** see DUNG *n.* ● *v.* see FERTILIZE *v.* 1.

manuscript /mányəskript/ *n. & adj.* ● *n.* **1** a book, document, etc., written by hand. **2** an author's handwritten or typed text, submitted for publication. **3** handwritten form (*produced in manuscript*). ● *adj.* written by hand. [med.L *manuscriptus* f. *manu* by hand + *scriptus* past part. of *scribere* write]
■ *adj.* handwritten, holograph.

Manx /mangks/ *adj. & n.* ● *adj.* of or relating to the Isle of Man. ● *n.* **1** the now extinct Celtic language formerly spoken in the Isle of Man. **2** (prec. by *the*; treated as *pl.*) the Manx people. □ **Manx cat** a breed of tailless cat. [ON f. OIr. *Manu* Isle of Man]

Manxman /mángksmən/ *n.* (*pl.* **-men**; *fem.* **Manxwoman**, *pl.* **-women**) a native of the Isle of Man.

many /ménee/ *adj. & n.* ● *adj.* (**more** /mawr/; **most** /mōst/) great in number; numerous (*many times*; *many people*; *many a person*; *his reasons were many*). ● *n.* (as *pl.*) **1** a large number (*many like skiing*; *many went*). **2** (prec. by *the*) the multitude of esp. working people. □ **as many** the same number of (*six mistakes in as many lines*). **as many again** the same number additionally (*sixty here and as many again there*). **be too** (or **one too**) **many for** outwit, baffle. **a good** (or **great**) **many** a large number. **many-sided** having many sides, aspects, interests, capabilities, etc. **many-sidedness** *n.* the fact or state of being many-sided. **many's the time** often (*many's the time we saw it*). **many a time** many times. [OE *manig*, ult. f. Gmc]
■ *adj.* numerous, multitudinous, profuse, innumerable, numberless, uncountable, *literary* myriad. ● *n.* **1** a good *or* great deal, hordes *or* a horde, crowds *or* a

crowd, swarms *or* a swarm, throngs *or* a throng, masses *or* a mass, mountains *or* a mountain, a profusion, multitudes *or* a multitude, a good *or* great many, an abundance, plenty, shoals *or* a shoal, flocks *or* a flock, droves *or* a drove, torrents *or* a torrent, floods *or* a flood, numbers *or* a number, scores, *or* a score, *colloq.* lots *or* a lot, hundreds *or* a hundred, oodles, zillions, loads *or* a load, stacks *or* a stack, piles *or* a pile, heaps *or* a heap, pots *or* a pot, tons *or* a ton, *US colloq.* scads. **2** (*the many*) see *the great unwashed* (UNWASHED). □ **be too** (or **one too**) **many for** outwit, *colloq.* outsmart; see also PERPLEX 1. **a good** (or **great**) **many** see MANY *n.* 1 above. **many-sided** see MANIFOLD *adj.*, VERSATILE 1. **many-sidedness** see VARIETY 1, versatility (VERSATILE). **many's the time, many a time** see OFTEN.

manzanilla /mánzəneélyə, -nee-ə/ *n.* a pale very dry Spanish sherry. [Sp., lit. 'camomile']

manzanita /mánzəneétə/ *n.* any of several evergreen shrubs of the genus *Arctostaphylos*, esp. *A. manzanita*, native to western N. America. [Sp., dimin. of *manzana* apple]

Maoism /mówizəm/ *n.* the Communist doctrines of Mao Zedong (d. 1976), Chinese statesman. □□ **Maoist** *n. & adj.*

Maori /mówree/ *n. & adj.* ● *n.* (*pl.* same or **Maoris**) **1** a member of the Polynesian aboriginal people of New Zealand. **2** the language of the Maori. ● *adj.* of or concerning the Maori or their language. [native name]

map /map/ *n. & v.* ● *n.* **1 a** a usu. flat representation of the earth's surface, or part of it, showing physical features, cities, etc. (cf. GLOBE). **b** a diagrammatic representation of a route, etc. (*drew a map of the journey*). **2** a two-dimensional representation of the stars, the heavens, etc., or of the surface of a planet, the moon, etc. **3** a diagram showing the arrangement or components of a thing. **4** *sl.* the face. ● *v.tr.* (**mapped, mapping**) **1** represent (a country, etc.) on a map. **2** *Math.* associate each element of (a set) with one element of another set. □ **map out** arrange in detail; plan (a course of conduct, etc.). **off the map** *colloq.* **1** of no account; obsolete. **2** very distant. **on the map** *colloq.* prominent, important. **wipe off the map** *colloq.* obliterate. □□ **mapless** *adj.* **mappable** *adj.* **mapper** *n.* [L *mappa* napkin: in med.L *mappa* (*mundi*) map (of the world)]
■ *n.* **1–3** see CHART *n.* ● *v.* **1** see CHART *v.*

maple /máypəl/ *n.* **1** any tree or shrub of the genus *Acer* grown for shade, ornament, wood, or its sugar. **2** the wood of the maple. □ **maple leaf** the leaf of the maple, used as an emblem of Canada. **maple sugar** a sugar produced by evaporating the sap of the sugar maple, etc. **maple syrup** a syrup produced from the sap of the sugar maple, etc. [ME *mapul*, etc., f. OE *mapeltrēow, mapulder*]

maquette /məkét/ *n.* **1** a sculptor's small preliminary model in wax, clay, etc. **2** a preliminary sketch. [F f. It. *machietta* dimin. of *macchia* spot]

maquillage /mákeeyaàzh/ *n.* **1** makeup; cosmetics. **2** the application of makeup. [F f. *maquiller* make up f. OF *masquiller* stain]
■ **1** see MAKEUP 1.

Maquis /makeé/ *n.* **1** the French resistance movement during the German occupation (1940–45). **2** a member of this. [F, = brushwood, f. Corsican It. *macchia* thicket]
■ **1** see UNDERGROUND *n.* 2.

Mar. *abbr.* March.

mar /maar/ *v.tr.* (**marred, marring**) **1** ruin. **2** impair the perfection of; spoil; disfigure. [OE *merran* hinder]
■ **1** damage, wreck, ruin, impair, harm, hurt. **2** impair, damage, mutilate, deface, deform, blight, blot, spoil, scar, disfigure, taint, stain, tarnish.

marabou /márəbōō/ *n.* (also **marabout**) **1** a large W. African stork, *Leptoptilos crumeniferus*. **2** a tuft of down from the wing or tail of the marabou used as a trimming for hats, etc. [F f. Arab. *murābiṭ* holy man (see MARABOUT), the stork being regarded as holy]

marabout /márəbōōt, -bōō/ *n.* **1** a Muslim hermit or monk, esp. in N. Africa. **2** a shrine marking a marabout's burial place. [F f. Port. *marabuto* f. Arab. *murābiṭ* holy man f. *ribāṭ* frontier station, where he acquired merit by combat against the infidel]

maraca /məraákə/ *n.* a hollow clublike gourd or gourd-shaped container filled with beans, etc., and usu. shaken in pairs as a percussion instrument in Latin American music. [Port. *maracá*, prob. f. Tupi]

maraschino /máraske'enō, -shée-/ *n.* (*pl.* **-os**) a strong, sweet liqueur made from a small black Dalmatian cherry. □ **maraschino cherry** a cherry preserved in or flavored with maraschino and used to decorate cocktails, etc. [It. f. *marasca* small black cherry, for *amarasca* f. *amaro* bitter f. L *amarus*]

marasmus /mərázməs/ *n.* a wasting away of the body. □□ **marasmic** *adj.* [mod.L f. Gk *marasmos* f. *marainō* wither]

Maratha /məraátə, -rátə/ *n.* (also **Mahratta**) a member of a warrior people native to the modern Indian state of Maharashtra. [Hindi *Marhaṭṭa* f. Skr. *Māhārāshṭra* great kingdom]

Marathi /məraátee, -rátee/ *n.* (also **Mahratti**) the language of the Marathas. [MARATHA]

marathon /márəthon/ *n.* **1** a long-distance running race, usu. of 26 miles 385 yards (42.195 km). **2** a long-lasting or difficult task, operation, etc. (often *attrib.: a marathon shopping expedition*). □□ **marathoner** *n.* [*Marathon* in Greece, scene of a victory over the Persians in 490 BC: a messenger was said to have run to Athens with the news, but the account has no authority]

maraud /məráwd/ *v.* **1** *intr.* **a** make a plundering raid. **b** pilfer systematically; plunder. **2** *tr.* plunder (a place). □□ **marauder** *n.* [F *marauder* f. *maraud* rogue]

■ see PLUNDER *v.* 2. □□ **marauder** see THIEF.

marble /maárbəl/ *n. & v.* ● *n.* **1** limestone in a metamorphic crystalline (or granular) state, and capable of taking a polish, used in sculpture and architecture. **2** (often *attrib.*) **a** anything made of marble (*a marble clock*). **b** anything resembling marble in hardness, coldness, durability, etc. (*her features were marble*). **3 a** a small ball of marble, glass, clay, etc., used as a toy. **b** (in *pl.*; treated as *sing.*) a game using these. **4** (in *pl.*) *sl.* one's mental faculties (*he's lost his marbles*). **5** (in *pl.*) a collection of sculptures (*Roman marbles*). ● *v.tr.* **1** (esp. as **marbled** *adj.*) stain or color (paper, the edges of a book, soap, etc.) to look like variegated marble. **2** (as **marbled** *adj.*) (of meat) streaked with alternating layers of lean and fat. □ **marble cake** a cake with a streaked appearance, made of light and dark batter. □□ **marbly** *adj.* [ME f. OF *marbre, marble,* f. L *marmor* f. Gk *marmaros* shining stone]

■ *v.* **1** (**marbled**) see *mottled* (MOTTLE).

marbling /maárbling/ *n.* **1** coloring or marking like marble. **2** streaks of fat in lean meat.

marc /maark/ *n.* **1** the refuse of pressed grapes, etc. **2** a brandy made from this. [F f. *marcher* tread, MARCH¹]

Marcan /maárkən/ *adj.* of or relating to St. Mark. [L *Marcus* Mark]

marcasite /maárkəsīt/ *n.* **1** a yellowish crystalline iron sulfide mineral. **2** these bronze-yellow crystals used in jewelry. [ME f. med.L *marcasita,* f. Arab. *marḳaṣīṭā* f. Pers.]

marcato /maarkaátō/ *adv. & adj. Mus.* played with emphasis. [It., = marked]

marcel /maarsél/ *n. & v.* ● *n.* (in full **marcel wave**) a deep wave in the hair. ● *v.tr.* (**marcelled, marcelling**) wave (hair) with a deep wave. [*Marcel* Grateau, Paris hairdresser d. 1936, who invented the method]

marcescent /maarsésənt/ *adj.* (of part of a plant) withering but not falling. □□ **marcescence** /-səns/ *n.* [L *marcescere* incept. of *marcēre* wither]

March /maarch/ *n.* the third month of the year. □ **March hare** a hare in the breeding season, characterized by excessive leaping, strange behavior, etc. (*mad as a March hare*). [ME f. OF *march(e),* dial. var. of *marz, mars,* f. L *Martius (mensis)* (month) of Mars]

march¹ /maarch/ *v. & n.* ● *v.* **1** *intr.* (usu. foll. by *away, off, out,* etc.) walk in a military manner with a regular measured tread. **2** *tr.* (often foll. by *away, on, off,* etc.) cause to march or walk (*marched the army to Moscow; marched him out of the room*). **3** *intr.* **a** walk or proceed steadily, esp. across country.

b (of events, etc.) continue unrelentingly (*time marches on*). **4** *intr.* take part in a protest march. ● *n.* **1 a** the act or an instance of marching. **b** the uniform step of troops, etc. (*a slow march*). **2** a long difficult walk. **3** a procession as a protest or demonstration. **4** (usu. foll. by *of*) progress or continuity (*the march of events*). **5 a** a piece of music composed to accompany a march. **b** a composition of similar character and form. □ **marching order** *Mil.* equipment or a formation for marching. **marching orders 1** *Mil.* the direction for troops to depart for war, etc. **2** a dismissal (*gave him his marching orders*). **march on 1** advance toward (a military objective). **2** proceed. **march past** *n.* the marching of troops past a saluting point at a review. ● *v.intr.* (of troops) carry out a march past. **on the march 1** marching. **2** in steady progress. □□ **marcher** *n.* [F *marche* (n.), *marcher* (v.), f. LL *marcus* hammer]

■ *v.* **1** parade, step, stride, strut, tread, pace, walk. **2** see *pack off.* **3 a** see WALK *v.* 1, 2. **4** see DEMONSTRATE 4. ● *n.* **1 a** parade, procession, cortege, walk. **2** walk, trek, slog, hike; see also TRAMP *n.* 3. **3** see DEMONSTRATION 2. **4** see PROGRESS *n.* 2. □ **marching orders 2** see *dismissal* (DISMISS). **march on 2** see PROCEED 1.

march² /maarch/ *n. & v.* ● *n. hist.* **1** (usu. in *pl.*) a boundary, a frontier (esp. of the borderland between England and Scotland or Wales). **2** a tract of often disputed land between two countries. ● *v.intr.* (foll. by *upon, with*) (of a country, an estate, etc.) have a common frontier with, border on. [ME f. OF *marche, marchir* ult. f. Gmc: cf. MARK¹]

marcher /maárchər/ *n.* an inhabitant of a march or border district.

marchioness /maárshənés/ *n.* **1** the wife or widow of a marquess. **2** a woman holding the rank of marquess in her own right (cf. MARQUISE). [med.L *marchionissa* f. *marchio -onis* captain of the marches (as MARCH²)]

■ see PEER² *n.* 1.

marchpane /maárchpayn/ *archaic* var. of MARZIPAN.

Mardi Gras /maárdee graá/ *n.* **1 a** the last day before Lent, celebrated in some places, as New Orleans; Shrove Tuesday. **b** merrymaking on this day. **2** the last day of a carnival, etc. **3** *Austral.* a carnival or fair at any time. [F, = fat Tuesday]

mare¹ /mair/ *n.* the female of any equine animal, esp. the horse. □ **mare's nest** an illusory discovery. **mare's tail 1** a tall slender marsh plant, *Hippuris vulgaris.* **2** (in *pl.*) long straight streaks of cirrus cloud. [ME f. OE *mearh* horse f. Gmc: cf. MARSHAL]

mare² /maáray/ *n.* (*pl.* **maria** /maáreeə/ or **mares**) **1** (in full **mare clausum** /klówsōōm/) *Law* the sea under the jurisdiction of a particular country. **2** (in full **mare liberum** /leébərōōm/) *Law* the sea open to all nations. **3 a** any of a number of large dark flat areas on the surface of the moon, once thought to be seas. **b** a similar area on Mars. [L, = sea]

maremma /mərémə/ *n.* (*pl.* **maremme** /-mee/) low marshy unhealthy land near a seashore. [It. f. L *maritima* (as MARITIME)]

margarine /maárjərin/ *n.* a butter substitute made from vegetable oils or animal fats with milk, etc. [F, misapplication of a chem. term, f. *margarique* f. Gk *margaron* pearl]

■ spread, oleo *or* oleomargarine.

margarita /maárgəreétə/ *n.* a cocktail made with tequila, lime or lemon juice, and orange-flavored liqueur, usu. served in a salt-rimmed glass.

margay /maárgay/ *n.* a small wild S. American cat, *Felis wiedii.* [F f. Tupi *mbaracaïa*]

marge¹ /maarj/ *n. Brit. colloq.* margarine. [abbr.]

marge² /maarj/ *n. poet.* a margin or edge. [F f. L *margo* (as MARGIN)]

margin /maárjin/ *n. & v.* ● *n.* **1** an edge or border. **2 a** the

/.../ pronunciation	● part of speech
□ phrases, idioms, and compounds	
□□ derivatives	■ synonym section
cross-references appear in SMALL CAPITALS or *italics*	

915

blank border on each side of the print on a page, etc. **b** a line or rule, as on paper, marking off a margin. **3** an amount (of time, money, etc.) by which a thing exceeds, falls short, etc. (*won by a narrow margin*; *a margin of profit*). **4** the lower limit of possibility, success, etc. (*his effort fell below the margin*). **5** an amount deposited with a stockbroker by the customer when borrowing from the broker to purchase securities. **6** in banking, the difference between the current market value of a loan's collateral and the face value of the loan. **7** *Austral.* an increment to a basic wage, paid for skill. ● *v.tr.* (**margined, margining**) provide with a margin or marginal notes. □ **margin of error** a usu. small difference allowed for miscalculation, change of circumstances, etc. **margin release** a device on a typewriter allowing a word to be typed beyond the margin normally set. [ME f. L *margo -ginis*]

■ *n.* **1** edge, border, perimeter, bound(s), boundary (line), frontier, line, periphery; rim, lip, side, brink, verge. **3** majority, amount, gap, difference, shortfall, deficit, surplus, excess, profit. **4** limit(s). **7** increment, increase, addition, bonus.

marginal /maárjinǝl/ *adj.* **1 a** of or written in a margin. **b** having marginal notes. **2 a** of or at the edge; not central. **b** not significant or decisive (*the work is of merely marginal interest*). **3** close to the limit, esp. of profitability. **4** (of the sea) adjacent to the shore of a state. **5** (of land) difficult to cultivate; unprofitable. **6** barely adequate; unprovided for. □ **marginal cost** the cost added by making one extra copy, etc. **7** *Brit.* (of a parliamentary seat or constituency) having a small majority at risk in an election. □□ **marginality** /-nálitee/ *n.* **marginally** *adv.* [med.L *marginalis* (as MARGIN)]

■ **2 b** borderline, minimal, small, slight, negligible, insignificant, tiny, infinitesimal; disputable, questionable, doubtful, dubious. **5** see UNPROFITABLE, BARREN *adj.* 1b.

marginalia /maárjináyleeǝ/ *n.pl.* marginal notes. [med.L, neut. pl. of *marginalis*]

■ see NOTE *n.* 2, 5.

marginalize /maárjinǝlīz/ *v.tr.* make or treat as insignificant. □□ **marginalization** *n.*

marginate *v. & adj.* ● *v.tr.* /maárjinayt/ **1** = MARGINALIZE. **2** provide with a margin or border. ● *adj.* /maárjinǝt/ *Biol.* having a distinct margin or border. □□ **margination** /-náyshǝn/ *n.*

margrave /maárgrayv/ *n. hist.* the hereditary title of some princes of the Holy Roman Empire (orig. of a military governor of a border province). □□ **margravate** /maárgrǝvǝt/ *n.* [MDu. *markgrave* border count (as MARK¹, *grave* COUNT² f. OLG *grēve*)]

margravine /maárgrǝveen/ *n. hist.* the wife of a margrave. [Du. *markgravin* (as MARGRAVE)]

marguerite /maárgǝrèet/ *n.* an oxeye daisy. [F f. L *margarita* f. Gk *margarītēs* f. *margaron* pearl]

maria *pl.* of MARE².

mariachi /maareeaáchee, mar-/ *n.* **1** a Mexican band of strolling street musicians. **2** the music played by such a band. [Mex. Sp.]

mariage de convenance /máriaázh dǝ kawnvǝnóns/ *n.* = marriage of convenience. [F]

Marian /máireeǝn/ *adj. RC Ch.* of or relating to the Virgin Mary (*Marian vespers*). [L *Maria* Mary]

marigold /márigōld/ *n.* any plant of the genus *Tagetes* or *Calendula*, with bright yellow, orange, or maroon flowers. [ME f. *Mary* (prob. the Virgin) + dial. *gold*, OE *golde*, prob. rel. to GOLD]

marijuana /máriwaánǝ/ *n.* (also **marihuana**) **1** the dried leaves, flowering tops, and stems of the hemp, used as an intoxicating or hallucinogenic drug, often smoked in cigarettes. **2** the plant yielding these (cf. HEMP). [Amer. Sp.]

■ **1** *slang* pot, grass, weed.

marimba /mǝrímbǝ/ *n.* **1** a xylophone of Africa and Central America. **2** a modern orchestral instrument derived from this. [Congo]

marina /mǝreénǝ/ *n.* a specially designed harbor with moor-

ings for pleasure yachts, etc. [It. & Sp. fem. adj. f. *marino* f. L (as MARINE)]

marinade /márináyd/ *n. & v.* ● *n.* **1** a mixture of wine, vinegar, oil, spices, etc., in which meat, fish, etc., is soaked before cooking. **2** meat, fish, etc., soaked in this liquid. ● *v.tr.* = MARINATE. [F f. Sp. *marinada* f. *marinar* pickle in brine f. *marino* (as MARINE)]

■ *v.* see SOAK *v.* 1.

marinara /marinaárǝ/ *adj.* (of a pasta sauce) made with tomatoes, spices, etc., usu. without meat. [It. *alla marinara* in sailor's style f. L (MARINE)]

marinate /márinayt/ *v.tr.* soak (meat, fish, etc.) in a marinade. □□ **marination** /-náyshǝn/ *n.* [It. *marinare* or F *mariner* (as MARINE)]

marine /mǝreén/ *adj. & n.* ● *adj.* **1** of, found in, or produced by the sea. **2 a** of or relating to shipping or naval matters (*marine insurance*). **b** for use at sea. ● *n.* **1** a country's shipping, fleet, or navy (*merchant marine*). **2 a** a member of the US Marine Corps. **b** a member of a body of troops trained to serve on land or sea. **3** a picture of a scene at sea. □ **marine stores** new or old ships' material, etc., sold as merchandise. **marine trumpet** a large single-stringed viol with a trumpetlike tone. **tell that** (or **it**) **to the marines** *colloq.* an expression of disbelief. [ME f. OF *marin* marine f. L *marinus* f. *mare* sea]

■ *adj.* **1** maritime, sea, oceanic, aquatic, saltwater, pelagic, thalassic. **2** maritime, nautical, naval, seafaring, seagoing, oceangoing, sea. ● *n.* **1** shipping, fleet, navy, flotilla, naval force, armada. □ **tell that** (or **it**) **to the marines** see *go on!* (GO¹).

mariner /márinǝr/ *n.* a seaman. □ **mariner's compass** a compass showing magnetic or true north and the bearings from it. [ME f. AF *mariner*, OF *marinier* f. med.L *marinarius* f. L (as MARINE)]

■ see SAILOR.

Mariolatry /máireeólǝtree/ *n. derog.* idolatrous worship of the Virgin Mary. [L *Maria* Mary + -LATRY, after *idolatry*]

marionette /máreeǝnét/ *n.* a puppet worked by strings. [F *marionnette* f. *Marion* dimin. of *Marie* Mary]

Marist /márist/ *n.* a member of the Roman Catholic Society of Mary. [F *Mariste* f. *Marie* Mary]

marital /máritǝl/ *adj.* **1** of marriage or the relations between husband and wife. **2** of or relating to a husband. □□ **maritally** *adv.* [L *maritalis* f. *maritus* husband]

■ **1** see NUPTIAL *adj.*

maritime /máritim/ *adj.* **1** connected with the sea or seafaring (*maritime insurance*). **2** living or found near the sea. [L *maritimus* f. *mare* sea]

■ **1** see MARINE 2. **2** see MARINE 1.

marjoram /maárjǝrǝm/ *n.* any aromatic herb of the genus *Origanum*, esp. *O. majorana* (**sweet marjoram**), the fresh or dried leaves of which are used as a flavoring in cooking. [ME & OF *majorane* f. med.L *majorana*, of unkn. orig.]

mark¹ /maark/ *n. & v.* ● *n.* **1** a trace, sign, stain, scar, etc., on a surface, face, page, etc. **2** (esp. in *comb.*) **a** a written or printed symbol (*punctuation mark*; *question mark*). **b** a numerical or alphabetical award denoting excellence, conduct, proficiency, etc. (*got a good mark for effort*; *gave him a black mark*). **3** (usu. foll. by *of*) a sign or indication of quality, character, feeling, etc. (*took off his hat as a mark of respect*). **4 a** a sign, seal, etc., used for distinction or identification. **b** a cross, etc., made in place of a signature by an illiterate person. **5 a** a target, object, goal, etc. (*missed the mark with his first shot*). **b** a standard for attainment (*his work falls below the mark*). **6** a line, etc., indicating a position; a marker. **7** (usu. **Mark**) (followed by a numeral) a particular design, model, etc., of a car, aircraft, etc. (*this is the Mark 2 model*). **8** a runner's starting point in a race. **9** *Naut.* a piece of material, etc., used to indicate a position on a sounding line. **10 a** *Rugby* a heel mark on the ground made by a player who has caught the ball direct from a kick or forward throw by an opponent. **b** *Austral. Rules Football* the catching before it reaches the ground of a ball kicked at least ten meters; the spot from which the subsequent kick is taken. **11** *sl.* the intended victim of a swindler, etc. **12** *Boxing* the pit of the stomach. **13** *hist.* a tract of land held in common by a Teutonic or medieval German village community. ● *v.tr.* **1 a** make a mark on (a thing or person), esp. by writing, cutting, scraping, etc. **b** put a distinguishing or identifying mark, initials, name, etc., on (clothes, etc.) (*marked the tree with their initials*). **2 a** allot marks to; correct (a student's work, etc.). **b** record (the points gained in games, etc.). **3** attach a price to (goods, etc.) (*marked the doll at $2*). **4** (often foll. by *by*) show or manifest (displeasure, etc.) (*marked his anger by leaving early*). **5** notice or observe (*she marked his agitation*). **6 a** characterize or be a feature of (*the day was marked by storms*). **b** acknowledge, recognize, celebrate (*marked the occasion with a toast*). **7** name or indicate (a place on a map, the length of a syllable, etc.) by a sign or mark. **8** characterize (a person or a thing) as (*marked them as weak*). **9 a** *Brit.* keep close to so as to prevent the free movement of (an opponent in sport). **b** *Austral. Rules Football* catch (the ball). **10** (as **marked** *adj.*) having natural marks (*is marked with silver spots*). **11** (of a graduated instrument) show, register (so many degrees, etc.). **12** *US & Austral.* castrate (a lamb). □ **one's mark** *Brit. colloq.* **1** what one prefers. **2** an opponent, object, etc., of one's own size, caliber, etc. (*the little one's more my mark*). **beside** (or **off** or **wide of**) **the mark 1** not to the point; irrelevant. **2** not accurate. **make one's mark** attain distinction. **mark down 1** mark (goods, etc.) at a lower price. **2** make a written note of. **3** choose (a person) as one's victim. **mark my words** heed my warning or prediction. **mark off** (often foll. by *from*) separate (one thing from another) by a boundary, etc. (*marked off the subjects for discussion*). **mark out 1** plan (a course of action, etc.). **2** destine (*marked out for success*). **3** trace out boundaries, a course, etc. **mark time 1** *Mil.* march on the spot, without moving forward. **2** act routinely; go through the motions. **3** await an opportunity to advance. **mark up 1** mark (goods, etc.) at a higher price. **2** mark or correct (text, etc.) for typesetting or alteration. **mark you** esp. *Brit.* please note (*without obligation, mark you*). **off the mark 1** having made a start. **2** = *beside the mark*. **of mark** noteworthy. **on the mark** ready to start. **on your mark** (or **marks**) (as an instruction) get ready to start (esp. a race). **up to the mark** reaching the usual or normal standard, esp. of health. [OE *me(a)rc* (n.), *mearcian* (v.), f. Gmc]

■ *n.* **1** spot, stain, scar, blemish, smear, smudge, trace, impression, dent, nick, scratch, pock(mark), streak, line, sign, splotch. **2a, 3, 4a** sign, symbol, emblem, device, hallmark, seal, earmark, fingerprint, badge, characteristic, token, brand, stamp, label, identification, indication; feature, attribute, trait, quality, property. **2 b** rating, grade, grading, score. **5 a** target, goal, objective, aim, purpose, end, object. **b** standard, criterion, norm, yardstick, level, measure; margin. **6** marker, indicator, guide, signpost, landmark. ● *v.* **1 a** spot, stain, blemish, smear, smudge, streak, dent, trace, pockmark, nick, scratch, cut, chip, pit, bruise. **2** correct; grade, evaluate, assess, appraise. **3** label; price, tag. **4** signify, indicate, show, manifest, express. **5** pay attention to, attend (to), pay heed to, note, notice, take notice of, heed, watch, see, look at, observe, eye. **6a, 8** brand, stamp, identify, characterize, distinguish. **6 b** acknowledge, observe, salute, honor, note; see also CELEBRATE *v.* 1. **7** signify, indicate, show, manifest, express, designate, identify, specify, label, *US* check, *Brit.* tick. **10** (**marked**) see SPOTTY 1. □ **beside** (or **off** or **wide of**) **the mark 1** see IRRELEVANT. **2** see INACCURATE. **make one's mark** succeed, get ahead, triumph, distinguish oneself, attain distinction, bring honor upon oneself, acquit oneself well, have an effect, *colloq.* make it big, make the grade. **mark down 1** reduce, devalue, discount. **2** write (down), record, register, make a note of, note (down). **mark off** see SEPARATE *v.* 6a. **mark out 1** see DESIGN *v.* 1. **2** see DESTINE. **mark time 2** act routinely *or* mechanically *or* perfunctorily, go through the motions. **3** see WAIT *v.* 1a. **mark up 1** increase, hike, *colloq.* up. **mark you** mind, note, I might add. **of mark** see NOTEWORTHY.

mark² /maark/ *n.* **1 a** = DEUTSCH MARK. **b** *hist.* = OSTMARK. **2** *hist.* **a** a European denomination of weight for gold and silver. **b** English money of account. [OE *marc*, prob. rel. to med.L *marca, marcus*]

markdown /máarkdown/ *n.* a reduction in price.

marked /maarkt/ *adj.* **1** having a visible mark. **2** clearly noticeable; evident (*a marked difference*). **3** (of playing cards) having distinctive marks on their backs to assist cheating. □ **marked man 1** a person whose conduct is watched with suspicion or hostility. **2** a person destined to succeed. □□ **markedly** /-kidlee/ *adv.* **markedness** /-kidnis/ *n.* [OE (past part. of MARK¹)]

■ **1** see SPOTTY 1. **2** noticeable, conspicuous, decided, pronounced, considerable, remarkable, significant, signal, unmistakable, prominent, obvious, patent, evident, apparent.

marker /máarkər/ *n.* **1** a stone, post, etc., used to mark a position, place reached, etc. **2** a person or thing that marks. **3** a felt-tipped pen with a broad tip. **4** a person who records a score, esp. in billiards. **5** a flare, etc., used to direct a pilot to a target. **6** a bookmark. **7** *US sl.* a promissory note; an IOU.

market /máarkit/ *n. & v.* ● *n.* **1 a** the gathering of people for the purchase and sale of provisions, livestock, etc., esp. with a number of different vendors. **b** the time of this. **2** an open space or covered building used for this. **3** (often foll. by *for*) a demand for a commodity or service (*goods find a ready market*). **4** a place or group providing such a demand. **5** conditions as regards, or opportunity for, buying or selling. **6** the rate of purchase and sale, market value (*the market fell*). **7** (prec. by *the*) the trade in a specified commodity (*the grain market*). **8** (**the Market**) *Brit.* the European Union (formerly known as the Common Market). ● *v.* **1** *tr.* sell. **2** *tr.* offer for sale. **3** *intr.* buy or sell goods in a market. □ **be in the market for** wish to buy. **be on** (or **come into**) **the market** be offered for sale. **make a market** *Stock Exch.* induce active dealing in a stock or shares. **market day** esp. *Brit.* a day on which a market is regularly held, usu. weekly. **market garden** esp. *Brit.* a place where vegetables and fruit are grown for the market, etc. **market gardener** esp. *Brit.* a person who owns or is employed in a market garden. **market maker** *Brit.* a member of the Stock Exchange granted certain privileges and trading to prescribed regulations. **market price** the price in current dealings. **market research** the study of consumers' needs and preferences. **market town** *Brit.* a town where a market is held. **market value** value as a salable thing (opp. *book value*). **mass-market** intended to be widely distributed through a variety of retail outlets. **put on the market** offer for sale. □□ **marketer** *n.* [ME ult. f. L *mercatus* f. *mercari* buy: see MERCHANT]

■ *n.* **1 a** marketplace, exchange. **2** shop, store, bazaar, supermarket, superstore, *Brit.* hypermarket. **3, 4** demand, call, trade; outlet; clientele. **7** see TRADE *n.* 1a, b. ● *v.* **1, 2** sell, merchandise, retail, vend, peddle, hawk, make available, furnish. □ **be on** (or **come into**) **the market** be on *or* for *or* up for sale, be on the block, *Brit.* be on offer. **put on the market** put on *or* up for sale, offer for sale, put on the block.

marketable /máarkitəbəl/ *adj.* able or fit to be sold. □□ **marketability** /-bílitee/ *n.*

marketeer /máarkiteér/ *n.* **1** *Brit.* a supporter of the European Union and British membership in it. **2** a marketer.

marketing /máarkiting/ *n.* **1** selling or buying in a market. **2** the activity or process involving research, promotion, sales, and distribution of a product or service.

marketplace /máarkitpláys/ *n.* **1** an open space where a market is held in a town. **2** the scene of actual dealings. **3** a forum or sphere for the exchange of ideas, etc.

markhor /máarkawr/ *n.* a large spiral-horned wild goat,

/.../ **pronunciation**	● **part of speech**
□ **phrases, idioms, and compounds**	
□□ **derivatives**	■ **synonym section**
cross-references appear in SMALL CAPITALS or *italics*	

Capra falconeri, of N. India. [Pers. *mār-ḵwār* f. *mār* serpent + *ḵwār* -eating]

marking /maárking/ *n.* (usu. in *pl.*) **1** an identification mark, esp. a symbol on an aircraft. **2** the coloring of an animal's fur, feathers, skin, etc. □ **marking-ink** *Brit.* indelible ink for marking linen, etc.

marksman /maárksmən/ *n.* (*pl.* **-men**; *fem.* **-woman**, *pl.* **-women**) a person skilled in shooting, esp. with a pistol or rifle. □□ **marksmanship** *n.*
■ see SHOT¹ *n.* 6.

markup /maárkup/ *n.* **1** the amount added to the cost price of goods to cover overhead charges, profit, etc. **2** the corrections made in marking up text.

marl¹ /maarl/ *n. & v.* ● *n.* soil consisting of clay and lime, with fertilizing properties. ● *v.tr.* apply marl to (the ground). □□ **marly** *adj.* [ME f. OF *marle* f. med.L *margila* f. L *marga*]

marl² /maarl/ *n.* **1** a mottled yarn of differently colored threads. **2** fabric made from this. [shortening of *marbled*: see MARBLE]

marlin /maárlin/ *n.* *US* any of various large long-nosed marine fish of the family Istophoridae, esp. the blue marlin *Makaira nigricans.* [MARLINSPIKE, with ref. to its pointed snout]

marline /maárlin/ *n.* *Naut.* a thin line of two strands. □ **marlinespike** = MARLINSPIKE. [ME f. Du. *marlijn* f. *marren* bind + *lijn* LINE¹]

marlinspike /maárlinspīk/ *n.* *Naut.* a pointed iron tool used to separate strands of rope or wire. [orig. app. *marling-spike* f. *marl* fasten with marline (f. Du. *marlen* frequent. of MDu. *marren* bind) + -ING¹ + SPIKE¹]

marmalade /maármǝlayd/ *n.* a preserve of citrus fruit, usu. bitter oranges, made like jam. □ **marmalade cat** a cat with orange fur. [F *marmelade* f. Port. *marmelada* quince jam f. *marmelo* quince f. L *melimelum* f. Gk *melimēlon* f. *meli* honey + *mēlon* apple]
■ see PRESERVE *n.* 1.

marmoreal /maarmáwreeǝl/ *adj. poet.* of or like marble. □□ **marmoreally** *adv.* [L *marmoreus* (as MARBLE)]

marmoset /maármǝset, -zet/ *n.* any of several small tropical American monkeys of the family Callitricidae, having a long bushy tail. [OF *marmouset* grotesque image, of unkn. orig.]

marmot /maármǝt/ *n.* any burrowing rodent of the genus *Marmota*, with a heavyset body and short bushy tail. [F *marmotte* prob. f. Romansh *murmont* f. L *murem* (nominative *mus*) *montis* mountain mouse]

marocain /márǝkayn/ *n.* a dress fabric of ribbed crepe. [F, = Moroccan f. *Maroc* Morocco]

Maronite /márǝnīt/ *n.* a member of a sect of Syrian Christians dwelling chiefly in Lebanon. [med.L *Maronita* f. *Maro* the 5th-c. Syrian founder]

maroon¹ /mǝrōōn/ *adj. & n.* ● *adj.* brownish-crimson. ● *n.* **1** this color. **2** esp. *Brit.* an explosive device giving a loud report. [F *marron* chestnut f. It. *marrone* f. med.Gk *maraon*]

maroon² /mǝrōōn/ *v. & n.* ● *v.tr.* **1** leave (a person) isolated in a desolate place (esp. an island). **2** (of a person or a natural phenomenon) cause (a person) to be unable to leave a place. ● *n.* **1** a person descended from a group of fugitive slaves in the remoter parts of Suriname and the W. Indies. **2** a marooned person. [F *marron* f. Sp. *cimarrón* wild f. *cima* peak]
■ *v.* abandon, cast away, desert, strand, forsake; isolate, seclude, cut off. ● *n.* **2** castaway.

marque¹ /maark/ *n.* a make of a product, as a sports car (*the Jaguar marque*). [F, = MARK¹]

marque² /maark/ *n. hist.* ● **letters of marque** (or **marque and reprisal**) **1** a license to fit out an armed vessel and employ it in the capture of an enemy's merchant shipping. **2** (in *sing.*) a ship carrying such a license. [ME f. F f. Prov. *marca* f. *marcar* seize as a pledge]

marquee /maarkée/ *n.* **1** a rooflike projection over the entrance to a theater, hotel, etc. **2** *Brit.* a large tent used for social or commercial functions. [MARQUISE, taken as pl. & assim. to -EE]

marquess /maárkwis/ *n.* a British nobleman ranking be-

tween a duke and an earl (cf. MARQUIS). □□ **marquessate** /-kwisǝt/ *n.* [var. of MARQUIS]

marquetry /maárkitree/ *n.* (also **marqueterie**) inlaid work in wood, ivory, etc. [F *marqueterie* f. *marqueter* variegate f. MARQUE¹]

marquis /maárkwis, -kée/ *n.* a nobleman ranking between a duke and a count (cf. MARQUESS). □□ **marquisate** /-kwisǝt/ *n.* [ME f. OF *marchis* f. Rmc (as MARCH², -ESE)]

marquise /maarkéez, -kée/ *n.* **1 a** the wife or widow of a marquis. **b** a woman holding the rank of marquis in her own right (cf. MARCHIONESS). **2 a** a finger ring set with a pointed oval cluster of gems. **b** (also **marquise cut**) an oval cut gem with many facets. **3** *archaic* = MARQUEE. [F, fem. of MARQUIS]

marquisette /maárkizét/ *n.* a fine light cotton, rayon, or silk fabric for net curtains, etc. [F, dimin. of MARQUISE]

marram /márǝm/ *n.* a shore grass, *Ammophila arenaria*, that binds sand with its tough rhizomes. [ON *marálmr* f. *marr* sea + *hálmr* HAULM]

marriage /márij/ *n.* **1** the legal union of a man and a woman in order to live together and often to have children. **2** an act or ceremony establishing this union. **3** one particular union of this kind (*by a previous marriage*). **4** an intimate union (*the marriage of true minds*). **5** *Cards* the union of a king and queen of the same suit. □ **by marriage** as a result of a marriage (*related by marriage*). **in marriage** as husband or wife (*give in marriage*; *take in marriage*). **marriage certificate** a certificate certifying the completion of a marriage ceremony. **marriage counseling** (or *Brit.* **guidance**) counseling of couples who have problems in married life. **marriage license** a license to marry. **marriage lines** *Brit.* a marriage certificate. **marriage of convenience** a marriage concluded to achieve some practical purpose, esp. financial or political. [ME f. OF *mariage* f. *marier* MARRY¹]
■ **1** matrimony, wedlock. **2** nuptials, wedding. **4** association, alliance, connection, coupling, union, merger, amalgamation, integration.

marriageable /márijǝbǝl/ *adj.* **1** fit for marriage, esp. old or rich enough to marry. **2** (of age) fit for marriage. □□ **marriageability** /-bílitee/ *n.*

married /máreed/ *adj. & n.* ● *adj.* **1** united in marriage. **2** of or relating to marriage (*married name*; *married life*). ● *n.* (usu. in *pl.*) a married person (*young marrieds*).
■ *adj.* **1** see ATTACHED 2. **2** see *matrimonial* (MATRIMONY).

marron glacé /marōN glaasáy/ *n.* (*pl.* **marrons glacés** *pronunc.* same) a chestnut preserved in and coated with sugar. [F, = iced chestnut: cf. GLACÉ]

marrow /márō/ *n.* **1** a soft fatty substance in the cavities of bones, often taken as typifying vitality. **2** the essential part. **3** *Brit.* (in full **vegetable marrow**) = *summer squash.* □ **to the marrow** right through. □□ **marrowless** *adj.* **marrowy** *adj.* [OE *mearg*, *mærg* f. Gmc]
■ **2** see ESSENCE 1.

marrowbone /márōbōn/ *n.* a bone containing edible marrow.

marrowfat /márōfat/ *n.* a kind of large pea.

marry¹ /máree/ *v.* (**-ies, -ied**) **1** *tr.* **a** take as one's wife or husband in marriage. **b** (often foll. by *to*) (of a priest, etc.) join (persons) in marriage. **c** (of a parent or guardian) give (a son, daughter, etc.) in marriage. **2** *intr.* **a** enter into marriage. **b** (foll. by *into*) become a member of (a family) by marriage. **3** *tr.* **a** unite intimately. **b** correlate (things) as a pair. **c** *Naut.* splice (rope ends) together without increasing their girth. □ **marry off** find a wife or husband for. [ME f. OF *marier* f. L *maritare* f. *maritus* husband]
■ **1 a** get married to, lead down the aisle *or* to the altar, *archaic* espouse, have *or* take to wife, *colloq.* get hitched *or* spliced to, *usu. formal or literary* wed. **b** join in wedlock *or* (holy) matrimony, *usu. formal or literary* wed. **c** give away, marry off, *archaic* espouse. **2 a** get married, become man and wife, *colloq.* get hitched *or* spliced, tie the knot, *usu. formal or literary* wed. **3 a** fit (together), unite, unify, bond, weld, fuse, put together, couple, join, link; ally, amalgamate, combine. **b** match (up).

marry[2] /máree/ *int. archaic* expressing surprise, asseveration, indignation, etc. [ME, = (the Virgin) *Mary*]

marrying /máree-ing/ *adj.* likely or inclined to marry (*not a marrying man*).

Mars /maarz/ *n.* a reddish planet, fourth in order of distance from the sun and next beyond the earth. [L *Mars Martis* the Roman god of war]

Marsala /maarsaálə/ *n.* a dark sweet fortified wine. [*Marsala* in Sicily, where orig. made]

Marseillaise /maársayéz, maársəláyz/ *n.* the national anthem of France, first sung in Paris by Marseilles patriots. [F, fem. adj. f. *Marseille* Marseilles]

marsh /maarsh/ *n.* **1** low land flooded in wet weather and usu. watery at all times. **2** (*attrib.*) of or inhabiting marshland. □ **marsh fever** malaria. **marsh gas** methane. **marsh hawk** the northern harrier, *Circus cyaneus* (see HARRIER[3]). **marsh mallow** a shrubby herbaceous plant, *Althaea officinalis*, the roots of which were formerly used to make marshmallow. **marsh marigold** a golden-flowered ranunculaceous plant, *Caltha palustris*, growing in moist meadows, etc.: also called COWSLIP; KINGCUP. **marsh trefoil** the buckbean. □□ **marshy** *adj.* (**marshier, marshiest**). **marshiness** *n.* [OE *mer(i)sc* f. WG]
■ **1** swamp, bog, wetland(s), marshland, fen, slough, quag, mire, quagmire.

marshal /maarshəl/ *n. & v.* ● *n.* **1** US an officer of a judicial district, similar to a sheriff. **2** US the head of a fire department. **3 a** a high-ranking officer in the armed forces of certain countries (*air marshal; field marshal*). **b** *Brit.* a high-ranking officer of state (*earl marshal*). **4** an officer arranging ceremonies, controlling procedure at races, etc. **5** (in full **judge's marshal**) *Brit.* an official accompanying a judge on circuit, with secretarial and social duties. **6** US a court officer who assists a judge. ● *v.* (**marshaled, marshaling;** *Brit.* **marshalled, marshalling**) **1** *tr.* arrange (soldiers, facts, one's thoughts, etc.) in due order. **2** *tr.* (often foll. by *into, to*) conduct (a person) ceremoniously. **3** *tr.* *Heraldry* combine (coats of arms). **4** *intr.* take up positions in due arrangement, etc., are assembled. □ **marshaling yard** a railroad yard in which trains, etc., are assembled. **Marshal of the Royal Air Force** (in the UK) an officer of the highest rank in the Royal Air Force. □□ **marshaler** *n.* **marshalship** *n.* [ME f. OF *mareschal* f. LL *mariscalcus* f. Gmc, lit. 'horse servant']
■ *v.* **1** see MUSTER *v.*

marshland /maarshland/ *n.* land consisting of marshes.
■ see SWAMP *n.*

marshmallow /maarshmélō, -máló/ *n.* a spongy confection made of sugar, albumen, gelatin, etc.

marsupial /maarsōōpeeəl/ *n. & adj.* ● *n.* any mammal of the order Marsupialia, characterized by being born incompletely developed and usu. carried and suckled in a pouch on the mother's belly. ● *adj.* **1** of or belonging to this order. **2** of or like a pouch (*marsupial muscle*). [mod.L *marsupialis* f. L *marsupium* f. Gk *marsupion* pouch, dimin. of *marsipos* purse]

mart /maart/ *n.* **1** a trade center. **2** an auction room. **3 a** a market. **b** a marketplace. [ME f. obs. Du. *mart*, var. of *markt* MARKET]

Martagon lily /maartəgən/ *n.* = Turk's-cap lily.

Martello /maartélō/ *n.* (*pl.* **-os**) (also **Martello tower**) a small circular fort, usu. on the coast to prevent a hostile landing. [alt. f. Cape *Mortella* in Corsica, where such a tower proved difficult to capture in 1794]

marten /maart'n/ *n.* any weasellike carnivore of the genus *Martes*, having valuable fur. [ME f. MDu. *martren* f. OF (*peau*) *martrine* marten (fur) f. *martre* f. WG]

martensite /maart'nzīt/ *n.* the chief constituent of hardened steel. [A. *Martens*, German metallurgist d. 1914 + -ITE[1]]

martial /maarshəl/ *adj.* **1** of or appropriate to warfare. **2** warlike; brave; fond of fighting. □ **martial arts** fighting sports such as judo and karate. **martial law** military government, involving the suspension of ordinary law. □□ **martially** *adv.* [ME f. OF *martial* or L *martialis* of the Roman god Mars: see MARS]
■ **1** military, soldierly, naval, fighting, service. **2** warlike,

belligerent, bellicose, pugnacious, militant; courageous, brave, valorous, valiant, stalwart, staunch, stouthearted.

Martian /maarshən/ *adj. & n.* ● *adj.* of the planet Mars. ● *n.* a hypothetical inhabitant of Mars. [ME f. OF *martien* or L *Martianus* f. *Mars*: see MARS]

martin /maart'n/ *n.* any of several swallows of the family Hirundinidae, esp. the house martin and purple martin. [prob. f. St. *Martin*: see MARTINMAS]

martinet /maart'nét/ *n.* a strict (esp. military or naval) disciplinarian. □□ **martinettish** *adj.* (also **martinetish**). [J. *Martinet*, 17th-c. French drillmaster]
■ see DISCIPLINARIAN.

martingale /maart'ngayl/ *n.* **1** a strap, or set of straps, fastened at one end to the noseband of a horse and at the other end to the girth, to prevent rearing, etc. **2** *Naut.* a rope for holding down the jib boom. **3** a gambling system of continually doubling the stakes after each loss. [F, of uncert. orig.]

martini /maarteénee/ *n.* a cocktail made of gin and dry vermouth, often garnished with a green olive, lemon peel, etc. [*Martini* & Rossi, Italian firm selling vermouth]

Martinmas /maart'nməs/ *n.* St. Martin's day, Nov. 11 [ME f. St. *Martin*, bishop of Tours in the 4th c., + MASS[2]]

martlet /maartlit/ *n.* **1** *Heraldry* an imaginary footless bird borne as a charge. **2** *archaic* **a** a swift. **b** a house martin. [F *martelet* alt. f. *martinet* dimin. f. MARTIN]

martyr /maartər/ *n. & v.* ● *n.* **1 a** a person who is put to death for refusing to renounce a faith or belief. **b** a person who suffers for adhering to a principle, cause, etc. **2** a person who feigns or complains of suffering to gain sympathy. **3** (foll. by *to*) a constant sufferer from (an ailment). ● *v.tr.* **1** put to death as a martyr. **2** torment. □ **make a martyr of oneself** accept or pretend to accept unnecessary discomfort, etc. [OE *martir* f. eccl.L *martyr* f. Gk *martur, martus -uros* witness]
■ *n.* **1** see VICTIM 1, 2. ● *v.* see PERSECUTE 1.

martyrdom /maartərdəm/ *n.* **1** the sufferings and death of a martyr. **2** torment. [OE *martyrdōm* (as MARTYR, -DOM)]
■ **1** see PASSION 5a.

martyrize /maartəriz/ *v.tr. & refl.* make a martyr of. □□ **martyrization** *n.*

martyrology /maartəróləjee/ *n.* (*pl.* **-ies**) **1** a list or register of martyrs. **2** the history of martyrs. □□ **martyrological** /-rəlójikəl/ *adj.* **martyrologist** /-rólə-/ *n.* [med.L *martyrologium* f. eccl.Gk *marturologion* (as MARTYR, *logos* account)]

martyry /maartəree/ *n.* (*pl.* **-ies**) a shrine or church erected in honor of a martyr. [ME f. med.L *martyrium* f. Gk *marturion* martyrdom (as MARTYR)]

marvel /maarvəl/ *n. & v.* ● *n.* **1** a wonderful thing or person. **2** (often foll. by *of*) a wonderful example (*a marvel of engineering; she's a marvel of patience*). ● *v.intr.* (**marveled, marveling;** *Brit.* **marvelled, marvelling;**) *literary* **1** (foll. by *at*, or *that* + clause) feel surprise or wonder. **2** (foll. by *how, why*, etc. + clause) wonder. □□ **marveler** *n.* [ME f. OF *merveille, merveiller* f. LL *mirabilia* neut. pl. of L *mirabilis* f. *mirari* wonder at: see MIRACLE]
■ *n.* **1** miracle, phenomenon; see also WONDER *n.* 2. **2** wonder, miracle, model, paragon. ● *v.* **1** wonder, be awed *or* amazed *or* agog *or* astonished, gape. **2** see WONDER *v.* 3.

marvelous /maarvələs/ *adj.* (*Brit.* **marvellous**) **1** astonishing. **2** excellent. **3** extremely improbable. □□ **marvelously** *adv.* **marvelousness** *n.* [ME f. OF *merveillos* f. *merveille*: see MARVEL]
■ **1, 3** wonderful, astonishing, amazing, astounding, surprising, remarkable, extraordinary, phenomenal, wondrous, miraculous, unbelievable, incredible, breathtaking, mind-boggling. **2** glorious, splendid, superb, excellent, spectacular, wonderful, sensational,

---

/.../ **pronunciation**	● **part of speech**

□ **phrases, idioms, and compounds**

□□ **derivatives** ■ **synonym section**

cross-references appear in SMALL CAPITALS or *italics*

unparalleled, *colloq.* terrific, great, fantastic, fabulous, out of this world, smashing, super, wild, *Brit. colloq.* spot *or* bang on, *sl.* crazy, awesome, wicked, far-out.

Marxism /maárksizəm/ *n.* the political and economic theories of Karl Marx, German political philosopher (d. 1883), predicting the overthrow of capitalism and the eventual attainment of a classless society with the state controlling the means of production. □ **Marxism-Leninism** Marxism as developed by Lenin. □□ **Marxist** *n.* & *adj.* **Marxist-Leninist** *n.* & *adj.*

marzipan /maárzipan/ *n.* & *v.* ● *n.* **1** a paste of ground almonds, sugar, etc., made up into small cakes, etc., or used to coat large cakes. **2** a piece of marzipan. ● *v.tr.* (**marzipanned, marzipanning**) cover with or as with marzipan. [G f. It. *marzapane*]

Masai /maasí, maásí/ *n.* & *adj.* ● *n.* (*pl.* same or **Masais**) **1 a** a pastoral people of mainly Hamitic stock living in Kenya and Tanzania. **b** a member of this people. **2** the Nilotic language of the Masai. ● *adj.* of or relating to the Masai or their language. [Bantu]

mascara /maskárə/ *n.* a cosmetic for darkening the eyelashes. [It. *mascara, maschera* MASK]

mascle /máskəl/ *n. Heraldry* a lozenge voided, with a central lozenge-shaped aperture. [ME f. AF f. AL *ma(s)cula* f. L MACULA]

mascon /máskon/ *n. Astron.* a concentration of dense matter below the moon's surface, producing a gravitational pull. [*mass concentration*]

mascot /máskot/ *n.* a person, animal, or thing that is supposed to bring good luck. [F *mascotte* f. mod. Prov. *mascotto* fem. dimin. of *masco* witch]

masculine /máskyəlin/ *adj.* & *n.* ● *adj.* **1** of or characteristic of men. **2** manly; vigorous. **3** (of a woman) having qualities considered appropriate to a man. **4** *Gram.* of or denoting the gender proper to men's names (e.g., *he, his.*) **5** *Prosody* (as of rhyme) occurring in a stressed final syllable. ● *n. Gram.* the masculine gender; a masculine word. □□ **masculinely** *adv.* **masculineness** *n.* **masculinity** /-línitee/ *n.* [ME f. OF *masculin -ine* f. L *masculinus* (as MALE)]

■ *adj.* **2** see MANLY 1. **3** see MANLY 2.

maser /máyzər/ *n.* a device using the stimulated emission of radiation by excited atoms to amplify or generate coherent monochromatic electromagnetic radiation in the microwave range (cf. LASER). [*microwave amplification by stimulated emission of radiation*]

MASH /mash/ *abbr.* Mobile Army Surgical Hospital.

mash /mash/ *n.* & *v.* ● *n.* **1** a soft mixture. **2** a mixture of boiled grain, bran, etc., given warm to horses, etc. **3** a mixture of malt or other grain and hot water used in brewing, distilling, etc. **4** *Brit. colloq.* mashed potatoes (*sausage and mash*). **5** a soft pulp made by crushing, mixing with water, etc. ● *v.tr.* **1** reduce (potatoes, etc.) to a uniform mass by crushing. **2** crush or pound to a pulp. **3** mix (malt) with hot water to form wort. □□ **masher** *n.* [OE *māsc* f. WG, perh. rel. to MIX]

■ **1, 5** see PULP *n.* 2. ● *v.* **1, 2** see CRUSH *v.* 1.

mashie /máshee/ *n. Golf* former name of an iron used for lofting or for medium distances; five iron. [perh. f. F *massue* club]

mask /mask/ *n.* & *v.* ● *n.* **1** a covering for all or part of the face: **a** worn as a disguise, or to appear grotesque and amuse or terrify. **b** made of wire, gauze, etc., and worn for protection (e.g., by a fencer) or by a surgeon to prevent infection of a patient. **c** worn to conceal the face at masquerades, etc. **2** a respirator used to filter inhaled air or to supply gas for inhalation. **3** a likeness of a person's face, esp. one made by taking a mold from the face (*death mask*). **4** a disguise or pretense (*throw off the mask*). **5** a hollow model of a human head worn by ancient Greek and Roman actors. **6** *Photog.* a screen used to exclude part of an image. **7** the face or head of an animal, esp. a fox. **8** a cosmetic preparation spread on the face and left to dry before removal. ● *v.tr.* **1** cover (the face, etc.) with a mask. **2** disguise or conceal (a taste, one's feelings, etc.). **3** protect from a process. **4** *Mil.* **a** conceal (a battery, etc.) from the enemy's view. **b** hinder (an army,

etc.) from action by observing with adequate force. **c** hinder (a friendly force) by standing in its line of fire. □ **masking tape** adhesive tape used in painting to cover areas on which paint is not wanted. □□ **masker** *n.* [F *masque* f. It. *maschera* f. Arab. *maskara* buffoon f. *sakira* to ridicule]

■ *n.* **1 c** domino. **4** disguise, guise, camouflage, show, semblance, pretense, cover, cover-up, false colors, concealment, cloak, facade, veil. ● *v.* **1** see VEIL *v.* **2** disguise, camouflage, cover (up), conceal, hide, cloak, obscure, veil, screen, shroud.

masked /maskt/ *adj.* wearing or disguised with a mask. □ **masked ball** a ball at which masks are worn.

■ see INCOGNITO *adj.* & *adv.* □ **masked ball** masquerade, fancy dress ball.

maskinonge /máskinonj/ *n.* = MUSKELLUNGE.

masochism /másəkizəm/ *n.* **1** a form of (esp. sexual) perversion characterized by gratification derived from one's own pain or humiliation (cf. SADISM). **2** *colloq.* the enjoyment of what appears to be painful or tiresome. □□ **masochist** *n.* **masochistic** *adj.* **masochistically** *adv.* [L. von Sacher-*Masoch*, Austrian novelist d. 1895, who described cases of it]

mason /máysən/ *n.* & *v.* ● *n.* **1** a person who builds with stone or brick. **2** (**Mason**) a Freemason. ● *v.tr.* build or strengthen with masonry. □ **mason's mark** a device carved on stone by the mason who dressed it. [ME f. OF *masson, maçonner*, ONF *machun*, prob. ult. f. Gmc]

Mason–Dixon line /máysən-díksən/ *n.* the boundary between Maryland and Pennsylvania, taken as the northern limit of the slave-owning states before the abolition of slavery. [C. *Mason* & J. *Dixon*, 18th-c. English astronomers who surveyed it]

Masonic /məsónik/ *adj.* of or relating to Freemasons.

mason jar /máysən/ *n.* (also **Mason jar**) a glass jar with a wide mouth and tight-sealing lid, used for canning. [for J. *Mason*, 19th-c. US inventor]

masonry /máysənree/ *n.* **1 a** the work of a mason. **b** stonework; brickwork. **2** (**Masonry**) Freemasonry. [ME f. OF *maçonerie* (as MASON)]

Masorah /məsáwrə/ *n.* (also **Masorah**) a body of traditional information and comment on the text of the Hebrew Bible. [Heb. *māsōret*, perh. = bond]

Masorete /másəreet/ *n.* (also **Massorete**) a Jewish scholar contributing to the Masorah. □□ **Masoretic** /-rétik/ *adj.* [F *Massoret* & mod.L *Massoreta*, orig. a misuse of Heb. (see MASORAH), assim. to -ETE]

masque /mask/ *n.* **1** a dramatic and musical entertainment esp. of the 16th and 17th c., orig. of pantomime, later with metrical dialogue. **2** a dramatic composition for this. □□ **masquer** *n.* [var. of MASK]

masquerade /máskəráyd/ *n.* & *v.* ● *n.* **1** a false show or pretense. **2** a masked ball. ● *v.intr.* (often foll. by *as*) appear in disguise, assume a false appearance. □□ **masquerader** *n.* [F *mascarade* f. Sp. *mascarada* f. *máscara* mask]

■ *n.* **1** disguise, deception, pose, pretense, dissimulation, bluff, subterfuge, fakery, imposture, playacting, act, (false) front, cover-up, camouflage, *colloq.* put-on.
● *v.* (*masquerade as*) pretend to be, pass oneself off as, impersonate, simulate, pose as.

Mass. *abbr.* Massachusetts.

mass[1] /mas/ *n.* & *v.* ● *n.* **1** a coherent body of matter of indefinite shape. **2** a dense aggregation of objects (*a mass of fibers*). **3** (in *sing.* or *pl.*; foll. by *of*) a large number or amount. **4** (usu. foll. by *of*) an unbroken expanse (of color, etc.). **5** (prec. by *a*; foll. by *of*) covered or abounding in (*was a mass of cuts and bruises*). **6** a main portion (of a painting, etc.) as perceived by the eye. **7** (prec. by *the*) **a** the majority. **b** (in *pl.*) the ordinary people. **8** *Physics* the quantity of matter a body contains. **9** (*attrib.*) relating to, done by, or affecting large numbers of people or things; large-scale (*mass audience; mass action; mass murder*). ● *v.tr.* & *intr.* **1** assemble into a mass or as one body (*the bands massed at dawn*). **2** *Mil.* (with ref. to troops) concentrate or be concentrated. □ **center of mass** a point representing the mean position of matter in a body or system. **in the mass** in the

aggregate. **law of mass action** the principle that the rate of a chemical reaction is proportional to the masses of the reacting substances. **mass defect** the difference between the mass of an isotope and its mass number. **mass energy** a body's ability to do work according to its mass. **mass-market** see MARKET. **mass media** = MEDIA[1] 2. **mass noun** *Gram.* a noun that is not countable and cannot be used with the indefinite article or in the plural (e.g., *happiness*). **mass number** the total number of protons and neutrons in a nucleus. **mass observation** *Brit.* the study and recording of the social habits and opinions of ordinary people. **mass-produce** produce by mass production. **mass production** the production of large quantities of a standardized article by a standardized mechanical process. **mass spectrograph** an apparatus separating isotopes, molecules, and molecular fragments according to mass by their passage in ionic form through electric and magnetic fields. **mass spectrometer** a device similar to a mass spectrograph but employing electrical detection. **mass spectrum** the distribution of ions shown by the use of a mass spectrograph or mass spectrometer. □□ **massless** *adj.* [ME f. OF *masse, masser* f. L *massa* f. Gk *maza* barley cake: perh. rel. to *massō* knead]
■ *n.* **1, 2** pile, heap, mountain, load, stack, mound, bunch, bundle, lot, batch, quantity, hoard, store, collection, accumulation, aggregation, conglomeration, agglomeration, congeries, assortment, miscellany, assemblage; block, concretion, chunk, lump, hunk, nugget. **3** abundance, quantity, profusion, multitude, horde, host, mob, crowd, throng, drove, herd, swarm, legion, score, number, *colloq.* bunch, ton, mountain, barrel, pile, load, bags, oodles, lots, oceans, scads, slew. **4** sea, pool, flood, sheet; see also EXPANSE. **5** (*be a mass of*) see ABOUND 2. **6, 7a** majority, best *or* better *or* greater part, bulk, body, preponderance, lion's share. **7 b** (*the masses*) the common people, the plebeians, (the) hoi polloi, the lower class(es), *colloq. usu. derog.* the plebs, *derog.* the (common) herd, esp. *derog.* the proletariat. ● *v.* amass, pile *or* heap up, gather, aggregate, accumulate, collect, assemble, congregate, group, cluster, concentrate; meet, get *or* come together, forgather, throng, convene, flock together; rally, marshal, muster, mobilize.

mass[2] /mas/ *n.* (often **Mass**) **1** the Eucharist, esp. in the Roman Catholic Church. **2** a celebration of this. **3** the liturgy used in the Mass. **4** a musical setting of parts of this. □ **high Mass** Mass with incense, music, and usu. the assistance of a deacon and subdeacon. **low Mass** Mass with no music and a minimum of ceremony. [OE *mæsse* f. eccl.L *missa* f. L *mittere miss-* dismiss, perh. f. the concluding dismissal *Ite, missa est* Go, it is the dismissal]

Massachuset /masəchōōsət, -zət/ *n. & adj.* ● *n.* **1 a** a N. American people, no longer in existence as a separate people, who occupied eastern Massachusetts in colonial times. **b** a member of this people. **2** the language of this people. ● *adj.* of or relating to this people or their language.

massacre /másəkər/ *n. & v.* ● *n.* **1** a general slaughter (of persons, occasionally of animals). **2** an utter defeat or destruction. ● *v.tr.* **1** make a massacre of. **2** murder (esp. a large number of people) cruelly or violently. [OF, of unkn. orig.]
■ *n.* **1** slaughter, carnage, annihilation, bloodbath, killing, execution, extermination, butchery, (mass) murder, slaying, liquidation, pogrom, holocaust, genocide. **2** see DEFEAT *n.*, DESTRUCTION 1. ● *v.* **1** see DEFEAT *v.* 1, *wipe out* 1a. **2** slaughter, annihilate, kill, execute, exterminate, butcher, murder, liquidate, destroy, eliminate, obliterate, eradicate, put to the sword, mow down, *disp.* decimate, *literary or joc.* slay, *sl.* bump off.

massage /məsáazh, -sáaj/ *n. & v.* ● *n.* **1** the rubbing, kneading, etc., of muscles and joints of the body with the hands for therapeutic benefit. **2** an instance of this. ● *v.tr.* **1** apply massage to. **2** manipulate (statistics) to give an acceptable result. □ **massage parlor 1** an establishment providing massage. **2** *euphem.* a brothel. □□ **massager** *n.* [F f. *masser*

treat with massage, perh. f. Port. *amassar* knead, f. *massa* dough: see MASS[1]]
■ *n.* rub, rubbing, rubdown, manipulation, kneading. ● *v.* **1** rub (down), manipulate, knead. **2** manipulate, doctor, falsify, *sl.* fiddle. □ **massage parlor 2** see BROTHEL.

massasauga /másəsáwgə/ *n.* a small N. American rattlesnake, *Sistrurus catenatus*. [irreg. f. *Mississagi* River, Ontario]

massé /masáy/ *n. Billiards* a stroke made with the cue held nearly vertical. [F, past part. of *masser* make such a stroke (as MACE[1])]

masseter /maseétər/ *n.* either of two chewing muscles which run from the temporal bone to the lower jaw. [Gk *masētēr* f. *masaomai* chew]

masseur /masőr/ *n.* (*fem.* **masseuse** /masőz/) a person who provides massage professionally. [F f. *masser*: see MASSAGE]

massicot /másikat/ *n.* yellow lead monoxide, used as a pigment. [F, perh. rel. to It. *marzacotto* unguent prob. f. Arab. *mashaḳūnyā*]

massif /maseéf, máseef/ *n.* a compact group of mountain heights. [F *massif* used as noun: see MASSIVE]

massive /másiv/ *adj.* **1** large and heavy or solid. **2** (of the features, head, etc.) relatively large; of solid build. **3** exceptionally large (*took a massive overdose*). **4** substantial, impressive (*a massive reputation*). **5** *Mineral.* not visibly crystalline. **6** *Geol.* without structural divisions. □□ **massively** *adv.* **massiveness** *n.* [ME f. F *massif -ive* f. OF *massiz* ult. f. L *massa* MASS[1]]
■ **1–3** big, large, oversized, huge, bulky, enormous, immense, gigantic, towering, mammoth, colossal, titanic, vast, tremendous, prodigious, mountainous, gargantuan, Cyclopean, elephantine, monster, monstrous, mighty, weighty, ponderous, strapping, *colloq.* jumbo, whacking, hulking, *sl.* walloping, whopping, humongous, *Brit. sl.* ginormous. **4** see IMPRESSIVE 1.

Massorah var. of MASORAH.

Massorete var. of MASORETE.

mast[1] /mast/ *n. & v.* ● *n.* **1** a long upright post of timber, iron, etc., set up from a ship's keel or deck, esp. to support sails. **2** a post or latticework upright for supporting a radio or television antenna. **3** a flagpole (*half-mast*). ● *v.tr.* furnish (a ship) with masts. □ **before the mast** serving as an ordinary seaman (quartered in the forecastle). □□ **masted** *adj.* (also in *comb.*). **master** *n.* (also in *comb.*). [OE *mæst* f. WG]
■ *n.* **1–3** see POLE[1] *n.* 1.

mast[2] /mast/ *n.* the fruit of the beech, oak, chestnut, and other forest trees, esp. as food for pigs. [OE *mæst* f. WG, prob. rel. to MEAT]

mastaba /mástəbə/ *n.* **1** *Archaeol.* an ancient Egyptian tomb with sloping sides and a flat roof. **2** a bench, usu. of stone, attached to a house in Islamic countries. [Arab. *maṣṭabah*]

mastectomy /mastéktəmee/ *n.* (*pl.* **-ies**) *Surgery* the removal of all or part of a breast. [Gk *mastos* breast + -ECTOMY]

master /mástər/ *n., adj., & v.* ● *n.* **1 a** a person having control of persons or things. **b** an employer, esp. of a servant. **c** a male head of a household (*master of the house*). **d** the owner of a dog, horse, etc. **e** the owner of a slave. **f** *Naut.* the captain of a merchant ship. **g** *Hunting* the person in control of a pack of hounds, etc. **2** esp. *Brit.* a male teacher or tutor, esp. a schoolmaster. **3 a** the head of a private school, etc. **b** the presiding officer of a Masonic lodge, etc. **4** a person who has or gets the upper hand (*we shall see which of us is master*). **5** a person skilled in a particular trade and able to teach others (often *attrib.*: *master carpenter*). **6** a holder of a university degree orig. giving authority to teach in the university (*Master of Arts*; *Master of Science*). **7 a** a revered teacher in philosophy, etc. **b** (**the Master**) Christ.

8 a great artist. **9** *Chess*, etc., a player of proven ability at international level. **10** an original version (e.g., of a film or audio recording) from which a series of copies can be made. **11** (**Master**) **a** a title prefixed to the name of a boy not old enough to be called *Mr.* (*Master T. Jones*; *Master Tom*). **b** *archaic* a title for a man of high rank, learning, etc. **12** a machine or device directly controlling another (cf. SLAVE). ● *adj.* **1** commanding, superior (*a master spirit*). **2** main, principal (*master bedroom*). **3** controlling others (*master plan*). ● *v.tr.* **1** overcome, defeat. **2** reduce to subjection. **3** acquire complete knowledge of (a subject) or facility in using (an instrument, etc.). **4** rule as a master. □ **be master of 1** have at one's disposal. **2** know how to control. **be one's own master** be independent or free to do as one wishes. **make oneself master of** acquire a thorough knowledge of or facility in using. **master-at-arms** (*pl.* **masters-at-arms**) a petty officer who enforces discipline aboard a naval vessel. **master class** a class given by a person of distinguished skill, esp. in music. **master hand 1** a person having commanding power or great skill. **2** the action of such a person. **master key** a key that opens several locks, each of which also has its own key. **master mariner 1** the captain of a merchant ship. **2** a seaman certified competent to be captain. **master mason 1** a skilled mason, or one in business on his or her own account. **2** a fully qualified Freemason, who has passed the third degree. **Master of Ceremonies** see CEREMONY. **masterstroke** an outstandingly skillful act of policy, etc. **master switch** a switch controlling the supply of electricity, etc., to an entire system. **master touch** a masterly manner of dealing with something. **masterwork** a masterpiece. □□ **masterdom** *n.* **masterhood** *n.* **masterless** *adj.* [OE *mægester* (later also f. OF *maistre*) f. L *magister*, prob. rel. to *magis* more]

■ *n.* **1** owner, head, chief, leader, chieftain, commander, lord, governor, director, controller, employer, manager, overseer, supervisor, superintendent, taskmaster, slavedriver, principal, sovereign, monarch, ruler, kingpin, skipper, Pooh-Bah, high muck-a-muck, *colloq.* boss, bigwig, top dog, *Brit. colloq.* gaffer; *sl.* (big) cheese, big wheel, Mr. Big, honcho. **2** teacher, tutor, schoolmaster, instructor, guide, leader, guru, swami. **3 a** see HEAD *n.* 6a. **4** chief, leader, *colloq.* boss. **5** expert, authority, craftsman, adept, maestro, mastermind, past master, old hand, virtuoso, genius, ace, wizard, *colloq.* maven, crackerjack, esp. *Brit. colloq.* dab hand.

7 b (**the Master**) Christ, Jesus; see also LORD *n.* 4.
● *adj.* **1** commanding, superior, controlling. **2** biggest, principal, chief; see also MAIN¹ *adj.* 1. **3** commanding, superior, controlling, prime, basic, chief, overall.
● *v.* **1, 2** control, overcome, repress, suppress, subdue, subjugate, bridle, check, quell, get the better of, defeat, conquer. **3** learn, grasp, become expert in, know a thing inside out, know, understand. **4** see CONTROL *v.* 1, 2. □ **be master of 2** see CONTROL *v.* 3. **be one's own master** be one's own man, *colloq.* do one's own thing. **master hand 1** see EXPERT *n.* **masterwork** see MASTERPIECE.

masterful /másterfool/ *adj.* **1** imperious, domineering. **2** masterly. ¶ Normally used of a person, whereas *masterly* is used of achievements, abilities, etc. □□ **masterfully** *adv.* **masterfulness** *n.*

■ **1** authoritarian, dictatorial, tyrannical, despotic, arbitrary, domineering, imperious, overbearing, arrogant, peremptory, dominating, autocratic, high-handed, magisterial, overweening, self-willed. **2** masterly, adept, expert, excellent, superior, superb, adroit, exquisite, superlative, supreme, consummate, accomplished, deft, skillful, skilled, *colloq.* crack.

masterly /másterlee/ *adj.* worthy of a master; very skillful (*a masterly piece of work*). □□ **masterliness** *n.*

■ see SKILLFUL. □□ **masterliness** see FACILITY 1, 2.

mastermind /mástermīnd/ *n.* & *v.* ● *n.* **1 a** a person with an outstanding intellect. **b** such an intellect. **2** the person directing an intricate operation. ● *v.tr.* plan and direct (a scheme or enterprise).

■ *n.* genius, mind, intellect, brain; planner, contriver, conceiver, creator, architect. ● *v.* plan, devise, conceive, think up, engineer, design, generate, create, manage, direct, organize, develop, work up *or* out.

masterpiece /másterpees/ *n.* **1** an outstanding piece of artistry or workmanship. **2** a person's best work.

■ **1** masterwork, magnum opus, tour de force, jewel, work of art, pièce de résistance. **2** chef-d'œuvre, masterwork, *magnum opus*, tour de force, jewel, pièce de résistance.

mastership /másterhip/ *n.* **1** the position or function of a master, esp. a schoolmaster. **2** dominion, control.

mastersinger /mástersingər/ *n.* = MEISTERSINGER.

mastery /másteree/ *n.* **1** dominion, sway. **2** masterly skill. **3** (often foll. by *of*) comprehensive knowledge or use of a subject or instrument. **4** (prec. by *the*) the upper hand. [ME f. OF *maistrie* (as MASTER)]

■ **1, 4** see SWAY *n.* 1. **2** see SKILL *n.* **3** see COMMAND *n.* 2.

masthead /mást-hed/ *n.* & *v.* ● *n.* **1** the highest part of a ship's mast, esp. that of a lower mast as a place of observation or punishment. **2 a** the title of a newspaper, etc., at the head of the front or editorial page. **b** the printed notice in a newspaper, magazine, etc., giving details of staff, ownership, etc. ● *v.tr.* **1** send (a sailor) to the masthead. **2** raise (a sail) to its position on the mast.

mastic /mástik/ *n.* **1** a gum or resin exuded from the bark of the mastic tree, used in making varnish. **2** (in full **mastic tree**) the evergreen tree, *Pistacia lentiscus*, yielding this. **3** a waterproof filler and sealant used in building. **4** a liquor flavored with mastic gum. [ME f. OF f. LL *mastichum* f. L *mastiche* f. Gk *mastikhē*, perh. f. *mastikhaō* (see MASTICATE) with ref. to its use as chewing gum]

masticate /mástikayt/ *v.tr.* grind or chew (food) with one's teeth. □□ **mastication** /-káyshən/ *n.* **masticator** *n.* **masticatory** /-kətáwree/ *adj.* [LL *masticare masticat-* f. Gk *mastikhaō* gnash the teeth]

■ see CHEW *v.*

mastiff /mástif/ *n.* **1** a dog of a large strong breed with drooping ears and pendulous lips. **2** this breed of dog. [ME ult. f. OF *mastin* ult. f. L *mansuetus* tame; see MANSUETUDE]

mastitis /mastítis/ *n.* an inflammation of the mammary gland (the breast or udder). [Gk *mastos* breast + -ITIS]

mastodon /mástədon/ *n.* a large extinct mammal of the genus *Mammut*, resembling the elephant but having nipple-shaped tubercles on the crowns of its molar teeth. □□ **mastodontic** /-dóntik/ *adj.* [mod.L f. Gk *mastos* breast + *odous odontos* tooth]

mastoid /mástoyd/ *adj.* & *n.* ● *adj.* shaped like a woman's breast. ● *n.* **1** = *mastoid process*. **2** *colloq.* mastoiditis. □ **mastoid process** a conical prominence on the temporal bone behind the ear, to which muscles are attached. [F *mastoïde* or mod.L *mastoides* f. Gk *mastoeidēs* f. *mastos* breast]

mastoiditis /mástoydítis/ *n.* inflammation of the mastoid process.

masturbate /másterbayt/ *v.intr.* & *tr.* arouse oneself sexually or cause (another person) to be aroused by manual stimulation of the genitals. □□ **masturbation** /-báyshən/ *n.* **masturbator** *n.* **masturbatory** /-tərbátáwree/ *adj.* [L *masturbari masturbat-*]

■ □□ **masturbation** onanism, self-gratification, *Psychol.* autoeroticism, *old-fashioned* self-abuse.

mat¹ /mat/ *n.* & *v.* ● *n.* **1** a piece of coarse material for wiping shoes on, esp. a doormat. **2** a piece of cork, rubber, plastic, etc., to protect a surface from the heat or moisture of an object placed on it. **3** a piece of resilient material for landing on in gymnastics, wrestling, etc. **4** a piece of coarse fabric of plaited rushes, straw, etc., for lying on, packing furniture, etc. **5** a small rug. ● *v.* (**matted**, **matting**) **1 a** *tr.* (esp. as **matted** *adj.*) entangle in a thick mass (*matted hair*). **b** *intr.* become matted. **2** *tr.* cover or furnish with mats. □ **on the mat** esp. *Brit. sl.* being reprimanded (orig. in the army, on the orderly-room mat before the commanding officer). [OE *m(e)att(e)* f. WG f. LL *matta*]

mat² var. of MATTE¹.

mat³ /mat/ *n.* = MATRIX 1. [abbr.]

matador /mátədawr/ *n.* **1** a bullfighter whose task is to kill the bull. **2** a principal card in omber, quadrille, etc. **3** a domino game in which the piece played must make a total of seven. [Sp. f. *matar* kill f. Pers. *māt* dead]

Mata Hari /maátə haáree/ *n.* a beautiful and seductive female spy. [name taken by Dutch spy M. G. Zelle, d. 1917, f. Malay *mata* eye + *hari* day]

match¹ /mach/ *n.* & *v.* ● *n.* **1** a contest or game of skill, etc., in which persons or teams compete against each other. **2 a** a person able to contend with another as an equal (*meet one's match; be more than a match for*). **b** a person equal to another in some quality (*we shall never see his match*). **c** a person or thing exactly like or corresponding to another. **3** a marriage. **4** a person viewed in regard to his or her eligibility for marriage, esp. as to rank or fortune (*an excellent match*). ● *v.* **1 a** *tr.* be equal to or harmonious with; correspond to in some essential respect (*the curtains match the wallpaper*). **b** *intr.* (often foll. by *with*) correspond; harmonize (*his socks do not match; does the ribbon match with your hat?*). **c** (as **matching** *adj.*) having correspondence in some essential respect (*matching curtains*). **2** *tr.* (foll. by *against, with*) place (a person, etc.) in conflict, contest, or competition with (another). **3** *tr.* find material, etc., that matches (another) (*can you match this silk?*). **4** *tr.* find a person or thing suitable for another (*matching unemployed workers to available jobs*). **5** *tr.* prove to be a match for. **6** *tr. Electronics* produce or have an adjustment of (circuits) such that maximum power is transmitted between them. **7** *tr.* (usu. foll. by *with*) *archaic* join (a person) with another in marriage. □ **make a match** bring about a marriage. **match play** *Golf* play in which the score is reckoned by counting the holes won by each side (cf. *stroke play*). **match point 1** *Tennis*, etc. **a** the state of a game when one side needs only one more point to win the match. **b** this point. **2** *Bridge* a unit of scoring in matches and tournaments. **to match** corresponding in some essential respect with what has been mentioned (*yellow dress with gloves to match*). **well-matched** fit to contend with each other, live together, etc., on equal terms. □□ **matchable** *adj.* [OE *gemecca* mate, companion, f. Gmc]

■ *n.* **1** contest, competition, game, meet, tourney, tournament, bout, duel, trial. **2 a, b** equal, equivalent, like, peer, fellow, mate. **c** parallel, replica, copy, double, twin, look-alike, facsimile, counterpart. **3** marriage, betrothal, alliance, combination, compact, contract, partnership, union, affiliation. **4** catch, prospect, candidate. ● *v.* **1 a, b** fit, suit; accord, agree, harmonize, go (together); coordinate, blend, correspond. **c** (**matching**) corresponding, comparable, equivalent, complementary; see also IDENTICAL 1. **2** (*match against* or *with*) pit or set or put against, play off against. **4** match up, join, marry, unite, link, combine, put together, pair up or off, conjoin. **5** equal, be equivalent to, resemble, compare with, measure up to, compete with, vie with, rival. **7** marry, join in wedlock or (holy) matrimony, *usu. formal or literary* wed. □ **well-matched** well-suited, compatible.

match² /mach/ *n.* **1** a short thin piece of flammable material tipped with a composition that can be ignited by friction. **2** a piece of wick, cord, etc., designed to burn at a uniform rate, for firing a cannon, etc. [ME f. OF *mesche, meiche*, perh. f. L *myxa* lamp nozzle]

matchboard /máchbawrd/ *n.* a board with a tongue cut along one edge and a groove along another, so as to fit with similar boards.

matchbox /máchboks/ *n.* a box for holding matches.

matchet var. of MACHETE.

matchless /máchlis/ *adj.* without an equal, incomparable. □□ **matchlessly** *adv.*

■ unique, original, peerless, unequaled, without equal, *hors concours*, inimitable, unmatched, incomparable, unparalleled, beyond compare.

matchlock /máchlok/ *n. hist.* **1** an old type of gun with a lock in which a match was placed for igniting the powder. **2** such a lock.

matchmaker /máchmaykər/ *n.* a person who tries to arrange an agreement or relationship between two parties, esp. a marriage partnership. □□ **matchmaking** *n.*

matchstick /máchstik/ *n.* the stem of a match.

matchwood /máchwŏod/ *n.* **1** wood suitable for matches. **2** minute splinters. □ **make matchwood of** smash utterly.

mate¹ /mayt/ *n.* & *v.* ● *n.* **1** a friend or fellow worker. **2** *Brit.*, etc. *colloq.* a general form of address, esp. to another man. **3 a** each of a pair, esp. of animals, birds, or socks. **b** *colloq.* a partner in marriage. **c** (in *comb.*) a fellow member or joint occupant of (*teammate; roommate*). **4** *Naut.* an officer on a merchant ship subordinate to the master. **5** an assistant to a skilled worker (*plumber's mate*). ● *v.* (often foll. by *with*) **1 a** *tr.* bring (animals or birds) together for breeding. **b** *intr.* (of animals or birds) come together for breeding. **2 a** *tr.* join (persons) in marriage. **b** *intr.* (of persons) be joined in marriage. **3** *intr. Mech.* fit well. □□ **mateless** *adj.* [ME f. MLG *mate* f. *gemate* messmate f. WG, rel. to MEAT]

■ *n.* **1** companion, associate, colleague, fellow worker, coworker, comrade, crony, ally, friend, alter ego, second self, cohort, *colloq.* chum, pal, buddy. **3 a** fellow, twin, counterpart. **b** spouse, partner, helpmate, consort, husband, wife, *colloq.* better half, hubby, old man or lady or woman, *Brit. rhyming sl.* trouble and strife, china. **5** see ASSISTANT. ● *v.* **1 a** pair (up), match (up), marry, join, unite, couple, link (up), *usu. formal or literary* wed. **b** breed, couple, copulate, pair (up). **2 a** marry, join in wedlock or (holy) matrimony, *usu. formal or literary* wed. **3** mesh, engage, dovetail, match (up), fit (together), synchronize, join.

mate² /mayt/ *n.* & *v.tr. Chess* = CHECKMATE. [ME f. F *mat(er)*: see CHECKMATE]

maté /maátay/ *n.* **1** an infusion of the leaves of a S. American shrub, *Ilex paraguayensis.* **2** this shrub, or its leaves. **3** a vessel in which these leaves are infused. [Sp. *mate* f. Quechua *mati*]

matelot /mátlō/ *n.* (also **matlow, matlo**) *Brit. sl.* a sailor. [F *matelot*]

matelote /mátəlōt/ *n.* a dish of fish, etc., with a sauce of wine and onions. [F (as MATELOT)]

mater /máytər/ *n. Brit. sl.* mother. ¶ Now only in jocular or affected use. [L]

materfamilias /máytərfəmíleeəs/ *n.* the woman head of a family or household (cf. PATERFAMILIAS). [L f. *mater* mother + *familia* FAMILY]

material /mətéereeəl/ *n.* & *adj.* ● *n.* **1** the matter from which a thing is made. **2** cloth, fabric. **3** (in *pl.*) things needed for an activity (*building materials; cleaning materials; writing materials*). **4** a person or thing of a specified kind or suitable for a purpose (*officer material*). **5** (in *sing.* or *pl.*) information, etc., to be used in writing a book, etc. (*experimental material; materials for a biography*). **6** (in *sing.* or *pl.*, often foll. by *of*) the elements or constituent parts of a substance. ● *adj.* **1** of matter; corporeal. **2** concerned with bodily comfort, etc. (*material well-being*). **3** (of conduct, points of view, etc.) not spiritual. **4** (often foll. by *to*) important, essential, relevant (*at the material time*). **5** concerned with the matter, not the form, of reasoning. □□ **materiality** /-reeálitee/ *n.* [ME f. OF *materiel, -al*, f. LL *materialis* f. L (as MATTER)]

■ *n.* **1** substance, fabric; matter, stuff. **2** cloth, fabric, textile, stuff. **3** (**materials**) constituents, elements, components. **5** information, data, facts, statistics, figures, documents, documentation, papers, notes, resources. **6** see ELEMENT 1. ● *adj.* **1** physical, tangible, concrete, solid, real, substantial, palpable, corporeal, bodily, *archaic* substantive. **2** bodily, physical, corporal. **3** worldly, earthly, mundane, temporal, secular, lay,

---

/.../	pronunciation	●	part of speech
□	phrases, idioms, and compounds		
□□	derivatives	■	synonym section
cross-references	appear in SMALL CAPITALS or *italics*		

materialistic. **4** consequential, important, significant, essential, relevant.

materialism /mətéereeəlizəm/ n. **1** a tendency to prefer material possessions and physical comfort to spiritual values. **2** *Philos.* **a** the opinion that nothing exists but matter and its movements and modifications. **b** the doctrine that consciousness and will are wholly due to material agency. **3** *Art* a tendency to lay stress on the material aspect of objects. □□ **materialist** n. **materialistic** /-lístik/ adj. **materialistically** /-lístiklee/ adv.

■ □□ **materialistic** greedy, acquisitive, selfish, commercial, sybaritic, *colloq. usu. derog.* yuppie.

materialize /mətéereeəliz/ v. **1** *intr.* become actual fact. **2 a** *tr.* cause (a spirit) to appear in bodily form. **b** *intr.* (of a spirit) appear in this way. **3** *intr. colloq.* appear or be present when expected. **4** *tr.* represent or express in material form. **5** *tr.* make materialistic. □□ **materialization** n.

■ **1** happen, come to pass, take place, occur, become manifest *or* real, be realized, be actualized. **3** appear, turn up; take shape *or* form, form, emerge.

materially /mətéereeəlee/ adv. **1** substantially, considerably. **2** in respect of matter.

■ **1** substantially, palpably, significantly, seriously, essentially, basically, considerably, greatly, much.

materia medica /mətéereeə médikə/ n. **1** the remedial substances used in the practice of medicine. **2** the study of the origin and properties of these substances. [mod.L, transl. Gk *hulē iatrikē* healing material]

matériel /mətéeree-él/ n. available means, esp. materials and equipment in warfare (opp. PERSONNEL). [F (as MATERIAL)]

maternal /mətə́rnəl/ adj. **1** of or like a mother. **2** motherly. **3** related through the mother (*maternal uncle*). **4** of the mother in pregnancy and childbirth. □□ **maternalism** n. **maternalistic** /-lístik/ adj. **maternally** adv. [ME f. OF *maternel* or L *maternus* f. *mater* mother]

■ **1, 2** motherly, warm, nurturing, caring, understanding, affectionate, tender, kind, kindly, devoted, fond, doting; maternalistic; matriarchal.

maternity /mətə́rnitee/ n. **1** motherhood. **2** motherliness. **3** (*attrib.*) **a** for women during and just after childbirth (*maternity hospital*; *maternity leave*). **b** suitable for a pregnant woman (*maternity dress*; *maternity wear*). [F *maternité* f. med.L *maternitas -tatis* f. L *maternus* f. *mater* mother]

■ **1** motherhood, parenthood.

mateship /máytship/ n. *Austral.* companionship, fellowship.

■ see COMPANIONSHIP.

matey /máytee/ adj. & n. ● adj. *Brit.* (**matier, matiest**) (often foll. by *with*) sociable; familiar and friendly. ● n. *Brit.* (*pl.* **-eys**) *colloq.* (usu. as a form of address) mate, companion. □□ **mateyness** n. (also **matiness**). **matily** adv.

■ adj. see FRIENDLY adj. 2.

math /math/ n. *US colloq.* mathematics (cf. MATHS). [abbr.]

mathematical /máthimátikəl/ adj. **1** of or relating to mathematics. **2** (of a proof, etc.) rigorously precise. □ **mathematical induction** = INDUCTION 3b. **mathematical tables** tables of logarithms and trigonometric values, etc. □□ **mathematically** adv. [F *mathématique* or L *mathematicus* f. Gk *mathēmatikos* f. *mathēma -matos* science f. *manthanō* learn]

■ **1** arithmetical. **2** precise, exact, rigorous.

mathematics /máthimátiks/ n.pl. **1** (also treated as *sing.*) the abstract science of number, quantity, and space studied in its own right (**pure mathematics**), or as applied to other disciplines such as physics, engineering, etc. (**applied mathematics**). **2** (as *pl.*) the use of mathematics in calculation, etc. □□ **mathematician** /-mətíshən/ n. [prob. f. F *mathématiques* pl. f. L *mathematica* f. Gk *mathēmatika*: see MATHEMATICAL]

maths /maths/ n. *Brit. colloq.* mathematics (cf. MATH). [abbr.]

Matilda /mətíldə/ n. *Austral. sl.* a bushman's bundle; a swag. □ **waltz** (or **walk**) **Matilda** carry a swag. [the name *Matilda*]

matinée /mat'náy/ n. (*US* also **matinee**) an afternoon performance in a theater, etc. □ **matinée coat** (or **jacket**) *Brit.* a baby's short coat. **matinée idol** a handsome actor admired esp. by women. [F, = what occupies a morning f. *matin* morning (as MATINS)]

matins /mát'nz/ n. (also **mattins**) (as *sing.* or *pl.*) **1 a** the office of one of the canonical hours of prayer, properly a night office, but also recited with lauds at daybreak or on the previous evening. **b** a service of morning prayer in churches of the Anglican communion. **2** (also **matin**) *poet.* the morning song of birds. [ME f. OF *matines* f. eccl.L *matutinas*, accus. fem. pl. adj. f. L *matutinus* of the morning f. *Matuta* dawn goddess]

matlo (also **matlow**) var. of MATELOT.

matrass /mátrəs/ n. *hist.* a long-necked glass vessel with a round or oval body, used for distilling, etc. [F *matras*, of uncert. orig.]

matriarch /máytreeaark/ n. a woman who is the head of a family or tribe. □□ **matriarchal** /-áarkəl/ adj. [L *mater* mother, on the false analogy of PATRIARCH]

■ see MOTHER n. 1.

matriarchy /máytreeaarkee/ n. (*pl.* **-ies**) a form of social organization in which the mother is the head of the family and descent is reckoned through the female line.

matrices *pl.* of MATRIX.

matricide /mátrisid, máy-/ n. **1** the killing of one's mother. **2** a person who does this. □□ **matricidal** adj. [L *matricida*, *matricidium* f. *mater matris* mother]

matriculate /mətríkyəlayt/ v. **1** *intr.* be enrolled at a college or university. **2** *tr.* admit (a student) to membership of a college or university. □□ **matriculatory** /-lətáwree/ adj. [med.L *matriculare matriculat-* enroll f. LL *matricula* register, dimin. of L MATRIX]

matriculation /mətríkyəláyshən/ n. **1** the act or an instance of matriculating. **2** an examination to qualify for this.

matrilineal /mátrilíneeəl/ adj. of or based on kinship with the mother or the female line. □□ **matrilineally** adv. [L *mater matris* mother + LINEAL]

matrilocal /mátrilókəl/ adj. of or denoting a custom in marriage where the husband goes to live with the wife's community. [L *mater matris* mother + LOCAL]

matrimony /mátrimōnee/ n. (*pl.* **-ies**) **1** the rite of marriage. **2** the state of being married. □□ **matrimonial** /-mōneeəl/ adj. **matrimonially** /-mōneeəlee/ adv. [ME f. AF *matrimonie*, OF *matremoi(g)ne* f. L *matrimonium* f. *mater matris* mother]

■ **1** marriage (service), wedding service. **2** marriage, wedlock. □□ **matrimonial** marital, marriage, wedding, conjugal, nuptial; married, wedded, connubial.

matrix /máytriks/ n. (*pl.* **matrices** /-triseez/ or **matrixes**) **1** a mold in which a thing is cast or shaped, such as a phonograph record, printing type, etc. **2 a** an environment or substance in which a thing is developed. **b** *archaic* a womb. **3** a mass of fine-grained rock in which gems, fossils, etc., are embedded. **4** *Math.* a rectangular array of elements in rows and columns that is treated as a single element. **5** *Biol.* the substance between cells or in which structures are embedded. **6** *Computing* a gridlike array of interconnected circuit elements. [L, = breeding female, womb, register f. *mater matris* mother]

■ **1** see MOLD[1] n. 1, 5.

matron /máytrən/ n. **1** a married woman, esp. a dignified and sober one. **2** a woman managing the domestic arrangements of a school, prison, etc. **3** *Brit.* a woman in charge of the nursing in a hospital. ¶ Now usu. called *senior nursing officer*. □ **matron of honor** a married woman attending the bride at a wedding. □□ **matronhood** n. [ME f. OF *matrone* f. L *matrona* f. *mater matris* mother]

matronly /máytrənlee/ adj. like or characteristic of a matron, esp. in respect of staidness or portliness.

Matt. *abbr.* Matthew (esp. in the New Testament).

matte[1] /mat/ adj., n., & v. (also **matt** or **mat**) ● adj. (of a color, surface, etc.) dull, without luster. ● n. **1** a border of dull gold around a framed picture. **2** (in full **matte paint**) paint formulated to give a dull flat finish (cf. GLOSS[1]). **3** the appearance of unburnished gold. ● v.tr. (**matted, matting**) **1** make (gilding, etc.) dull. **2** frost (glass). [F *mat*, *mater*, identical with *mat* MATE[2]]

■ *adj.* see FLAT¹ *adj.* 8a.

matte² /mat/ *n.* an impure product of the smelting of sulfide ores, esp. those of copper or nickel. [F]

matte³ /mat/ *n. Cinematog.* a mask to obscure part of an image and allow another image to be superimposed, giving a combined effect. [F]

matter /mátər/ *n. & v.* ● *n.* **1 a** physical substance in general, as distinct from mind and spirit. **b** that which has mass and occupies space. **2** a particular substance (*coloring matter*). **3** (*prec. by the*; often foll. by *with*) the thing that is amiss (*what is the matter?*; *there is something the matter with him*). **4** material for thought or expression. **5 a** the substance of a book, speech, etc., as distinct from its manner or form. **b** *Logic* the particular content of a proposition, as distinct from its form. **6** a thing or things of a specified kind (*printed matter*; *reading matter*). **7** an affair or situation being considered, esp. in a specified way (*a serious matter*; *a matter for concern*; *the matter of your overdraft*). **8** *Physiol.* **a** any substance in or discharged from the body (*fecal matter*; *gray matter*). **b** pus. **9** (foll. by *of*, *for*) what is or may be a good reason for (complaint, regret, etc.). **10** *Printing* the body of a printed work, as type or as printed sheets. ● *v.intr.* **1** (often foll. by *to*) be of importance; have significance (*it does not matter to me when it happened*). **2** secrete or discharge pus. □ **as a matter of fact** in reality (esp. to correct a falsehood or misunderstanding). **for that matter** (or **for the matter of that**) **1** as far as that is concerned. **2** and indeed also. **in the matter of** as regards. **a matter of 1** approximately (*for a matter of 40 years*). **2** a thing that relates to, depends on, or is determined by (*a matter of habit*; *only a matter of time before they agree*). **a matter of course** see COURSE. **a matter of fact 1** what belongs to the sphere of fact as distinct from opinion, etc. **2** *Law* the part of a judicial inquiry concerned with the truth of alleged facts (see also MATTER-OF-FACT). **a matter of form** a mere routine. **a matter of law** *Law* the part of a judicial inquiry concerned with the interpretation of the law. **a matter of life and death** something of critical or vital importance. **a matter of record** see RECORD. **no matter 1** (foll. by *when*, *how*, etc.) regardless of (*will do it no matter what the consequences*). **2** it is of no importance. **what is the matter with** surely there is no objection to. **what matter?** esp. *Brit.* that need not worry us. [ME f. AF *mater(i)e*, OF *matiere* f. L *materia* timber, substance, subject of discourse]

■ *n.* **1, 2** material, substance, stuff. **3** problem, difficulty, trouble; complication, worry. **4, 5** content, essentials, pith, theme, argument, purport, implication; signification, meaning, import. **7** situation, issue, question, affair, business, subject, topic, condition, thing, fact, concern; occurrence, episode, incident, event, occasion, proceeding. **8** see DISCHARGE *n.* 5. ● *v.* **1** be important *or* of importance, count, be of consequence, make a difference. □ **as a matter of fact** see *in fact* 1 (FACT). **in the matter of** see CONCERNING. **a matter of 1** see *approximately* (APPROXIMATE). **2** see QUESTION *n.* 3, 5. **a matter of fact 1** reality, actuality, certainty, truth. **a matter of form** see FORMALITY 1. **what matter?** *colloq.* so what?, so?

matter-of-fact /mátərəfákt/ *adj.* (see also MATTER). **1** unimaginative, prosaic. **2** unemotional. □□ **matter-of-factly** *adv.* **matter-of-factness** *n.*

■ **1** straightforward, direct, forthright, factual, unvarnished, unembellished, unadorned; sober, unimaginative, unartistic, prosaic, unpoetic, dry, dull, boring, tiresome, flat, mundane, lifeless, featureless, colorless. **2** see DISINTERESTED 1, HONEST *adj.* 2.

matting /máting/ *n.* **1** fabric of hemp, bast, grass, etc., for mats (*coconut matting*). **2** in senses of MAT¹ *v.*

mattins var. of MATINS.

mattock /mátək/ *n.* an agricultural tool shaped like a pickax, with an adze and a chisel edge as the ends of the head. [OE *mattuc*, of unkn. orig.]

mattoid /mátoyd/ *n.* a person of erratic mind, a mixture of genius and fool. [It. *mattoide* f. *matto* insane]

mattress /mátris/ *n.* a fabric case stuffed with soft, firm, or springy material, or a similar case filled with air or water,

used on or as a bed. [ME f. OF *materas* f. It. *materasso* f. Arab. *almaṭraḥ* the place, the cushion f. *ṭaraḥa* throw]

maturate /máchərayt/ *v.intr.* **1** *Med.* (of a boil, etc.) come to maturation. **2** mature [L *maturatus* (as MATURE *v.*)]

maturation /máchəráyshən/ *n.* **1 a** the act or an instance of maturing; the state of being matured. **b** the ripening of fruit. **2** *Med.* **a** the formation of purulent matter. **b** the causing of this. □□ **maturative** /məchŏŏrətiv/ *adj.* [ME f. F *maturation* or med.L *maturatio* f. L (as MATURE *v.*)]

■ **1 a** see DEVELOPMENT 1.

mature /məchŏŏr, -tyŏŏr, -tŏŏr/ *adj. & v.* ● *adj.* (**maturer**, **maturest**) **1** with fully developed powers of body and mind; adult. **2** complete in natural development; ripe. **3** (of thought, intentions, etc.) duly careful and adequate. **4** (of a bond, etc.) due for payment. ● *v.* **1 a** *tr. & intr.* develop fully. **b** *tr. & intr.* ripen. **c** *intr.* come to maturity. **2** *tr.* perfect (a plan, etc.). **3** *intr.* (of a bond, etc.) become due for payment. □□ **maturely** *adv.* **matureness** *n.* **maturity** *n.* [ME f. L *maturus* timely, early]

■ *adj.* **1** adult, grown (up), full-grown, fully grown, of age, full-fledged, fully fledged, developed, experienced, knowledgeable, sophisticated. **2** ripe, ready, ripened, mellow, aged, seasoned. **3** see MEASURED 2. ● *v.* **1 a, c** age, develop; grow up, come of age, *Med.* maturate. **b** mellow, age, season, come to maturity; ripen, bring to maturity. **2** develop, perfect, refine, polish, bring to fruition. □□ **maturity** adulthood, majority; ripeness, readiness, mellowness; perfection, completion, fullness, consummation.

matutinal /mətŏŏt'n'l, -tyŏŏt-, máchŏŏtínəl/ *adj.* **1** of or occurring in the morning. **2** early. [LL *matutinalis* f. L *matutinus*: see MATINS]

matzo /maátsə/ *n.* (also **matzoh**; *pl.* **-os** or **ohs** or **matzoth** /-sōt/) **1** a wafer of unleavened bread for the Passover. **2** such bread collectively. [Yiddish f. Heb. *maṣṣāh*]

maud /mawd/ *n.* **1** a Scots shepherd's gray-striped plaid. **2** a traveling robe or rug like this. [18th c.: orig. unkn.]

maudlin /máwdlin/ *adj. & n.* ● *adj.* weakly or tearfully sentimental, esp. in a tearful and effusive stage of drunkenness. ● *n.* weak or mawkish sentiment. [ME f. OF *Madeleine* f. eccl.L *Magdalena* Magdalen, with ref. to pictures of Mary Magdalen weeping]

■ *adj.* sentimental, (over)emotional, mawkish, tearful, weepy, mushy, romantic, *colloq.* soupy, slushy, *Brit. colloq.* soppy, *formal* lachrymose.

maul /mawl/ *v. & n.* ● *v.tr.* **1** beat and bruise. **2** handle roughly or carelessly. **3** damage by criticism. ● *n.* **1** a special heavy hammer, commonly of wood, esp. for driving in wedges or stakes. **2** *Rugby* a loose scrum with the ball off the ground. **3** *Brit.* a brawl. □□ **mauler** *n.* [ME f. OF *mail* f. L *malleus* hammer]

■ *v.* **1** see *knock about*. ● *n.* **3** see BRAWL *n.*

maulstick /máwlstik/ *n.* (also **mahlstick**) a light stick with a padded leather ball at one end, held by a painter in one hand to support the other hand. [Du. *maalstok* f. *malen* to paint + *stok* stick]

maunder /máwndər/ *v.intr.* **1** talk in a dreamy or rambling manner. **2** move or act listlessly or idly. [perh. f. obs. *maunder* beggar, to beg]

maundy /máwndee/ *n.* the ceremony of washing the feet of the poor, in commemoration of Jesus' washing of the disciples' feet at the Last Supper. □ **maundy money** alms distributed on Maundy Thursday or as part of the maundy ceremony. **Maundy Thursday** the Thursday before Easter. [ME f. OF *mandé* f. L *mandatum* MANDATE, commandment (see John 13:34)]

mausoleum /máwsəléeəm/ *n.* a large and grand tomb. [L f. Gk *Mausōleion* f. *Mausōlos* Mausolus king of Caria (4th c. BC), to whose tomb the name was orig. applied]

/. . ./ **pronunciation**	● **part of speech**
□ **phrases, idioms, and compounds**	
□□ **derivatives**	■ **synonym section**
cross-references appear in SMALL CAPITALS or *italics*	

■ see TOMB 3.

mauve /mōv/ *adj. & n.* ● *adj.* pale purple. ● *n.* **1** this color. **2** a bright but delicate pale purple dye from coal-tar aniline. □□ **mauvish** *adj.* [F, lit. = mallow, f. L *malva*]

maven /máyvən/ *n.* (also **mavin**) *colloq.* an expert or connoisseur. [Yiddish *meyvn* f. Heb. *mēḇīn*]

maverick /mávərik, mávrik/ *n.* **1** an unbranded calf or yearling. **2** an unorthodox or independent-minded person. [S. A. *Maverick*, Texas engineer and rancher d. 1870, who did not brand his cattle]

■ **2** see *individualist* (INDIVIDUALISM).

mavis /máyvis/ *n. esp. Brit. poet.* or *dial.* a song thrush. [ME f. OF *mauvis*, of uncert. orig.]

maw /maw/ *n.* **1 a** the stomach of an animal. **b** the jaws or throat of a voracious animal. **2** *colloq.* the stomach of a greedy person. [OE *maga* f. Gmc]

mawkish /máwkish/ *adj.* **1** sentimental in a feeble or sickly way. **2** having a faint sickly flavor. □□ **mawkishly** *adv.* **mawkishness** *n.* [obs. *mawk* maggot f. ON *mathkr* f. Gmc]

■ **1** see SENTIMENTAL.

max. *abbr.* maximum. □ **to the max** *sl.* to the utmost, to the fullest extent.

maxi /máksee/ *n.* (*pl.* **maxis**) *colloq.* a maxiskirt or other garment with a long skirt. [abbr.]

maxi- /máksee/ *comb. form* very large or long (*maxicoat, maxiskirt*). [abbr. of MAXIMUM: cf. MINI-]

maxilla /maksílə/ *n.* (*pl.* **maxillae** /-lee/ or **maxillas**) **1** the jaw or jawbone, esp. the upper jaw in most vertebrates. **2** the mouthpart of many arthropods used in chewing. □□ **maxillary** /máksəleeree/ *adj.* [L, = jaw]

maxim /máksim/ *n.* a general truth or rule of conduct expressed in a sentence. [ME f. F *maxime* or med.L *maxima* (*propositio*), fem. adj. (as MAXIMUM)]

■ saying, proverb, axiom, aphorism, adage, byword, saw, apothegm, epigram, motto, slogan; cliché, truism, platitude.

maxima *pl.* of MAXIMUM.

maximal /máksiməl/ *adj.* being or relating to a maximum; the greatest possible in size, duration, etc. □□ **maximally** *adv.*

maximalist /máksiməlist/ *n.* a person who rejects compromise and expects a full response to (esp. political) demands. [MAXIMAL, after Russ. *maksimalist*]

maximize /máksimiz/ *v.tr.* increase or enhance to the utmost. □□ **maximization** *n.* **maximizer** *n.* [L *maximus*: see MAXIMUM]

■ increase, broaden, improve, magnify, augment, add to, expand, build up, enlarge; enhance, embroider, embellish, elaborate; inflate, overplay, overdo, overstate, exaggerate, oversell, make much of, overstress.

maximum /máksiməm/ *n. & adj.* ● *n.* (*pl.* **maxima** /-mə/) the highest possible or attainable amount. ● *adj.* that is a maximum. [mod.L, neut. of L *maximus*, superl. of *magnus* great]

■ *n.* utmost, uttermost, greatest, most, highest, extreme, extremity, limit, peak, pinnacle, crest, top, summit, zenith, apex, acme, apogee, climax. ● *adj.* maximal, greatest, most, utmost, uttermost, superlative, supreme, paramount, extreme, highest, top, topmost, climactic, crowning.

maxwell /mákswel/ *n.* a unit of magnetic flux in the centimeter-gram-second system, equal to that induced through one square centimeter by a perpendicular magnetic field of one gauss. [J. C. *Maxwell*, Brit. physicist d. 1879]

May /may/ *n.* **1** the fifth month of the year. **2** (**may**) *esp. Brit.* the hawthorn or its blossom. **3** *poet.* bloom, prime. **May Day** May 1, esp. as a festival with dancing, or as an international holiday in honor of workers. **May queen** a girl chosen to preside over celebrations on May Day. **Queen of the May** = **May queen**. [ME f. OF *mai* f. L *Maius* (*mensis*) (month) of the goddess *Maia*]

may /may/ *v.aux.* (*3rd sing. present* **may**; *past* **might** /mit/) **1** (often foll. by *well* for emphasis) expressing possibility (*it may be true*; *I may have been wrong*; *you may well lose your way*). **2** expressing permission (*you may not go*; *may I come in?*). ¶ Both *can* and *may* are used to express permission; in more formal contexts *may* is usual since *can* also denotes capability (*can I move?* = am I physically able to move?; *may I move* = am I allowed to move?). **3** expressing a wish (*may he live to regret it*). **4** expressing uncertainty or irony in questions (*who may you be?*; *who are you, may I ask?*). **5** in purpose clauses and after *wish*, *fear*, etc. (*take such measures as may avert disaster*; *hope he may succeed*). □ **be that as it may** (or **that is as may be**) that may or may not be so (implying that there are other factors) (*be that as it may, I still want to go*). [OE *mæg* f. Gmc, rel. to MAIN¹, MIGHT²]

Maya /maayə/ *n.* **1** (*pl.* same or **Mayas**) a member of an ancient native people of Central America. **2** the language of this people. □□ **Mayan** *adj. & n.* [native name]

maya /maayə/ *n. Hinduism* a marvel or illusion, esp. in the phenomenal universe. [Skr. *māyā*]

mayapple /máyapəl/ *n.* (also **mandrake**) an American herbaceous plant, *Podophyllum peltatum*, bearing a yellow egg-shaped fruit in May.

maybe /máybee/ *adv.* perhaps, possibly. [ME f. *it may be*]

■ see PERHAPS.

Mayday /máyday/ *n.* an international radio-telephone distress signal used esp. by ships and aircraft. [repr. pronunc. of F *m'aidez* help me]

mayest /máyist/ *archaic* = MAYST.

mayflower /máyflowər/ *n.* **1** any of various flowers that bloom in May, esp. the trailing arbutus, *Epigaea repens*. **2** (*Mayflower*) the ship on which the Pilgrims traveled from England to N. America in 1620.

mayfly /máyflī/ *n.* (*pl.* **-flies**) **1** any insect of the order Ephemeroptera, living briefly in spring in the adult stage. **2** an imitation mayfly used by anglers.

mayhap /máyháp/ *adv. archaic* perhaps, possibly. [ME f. *it may hap*]

■ see PERHAPS.

mayhem /máyhem/ *n.* **1** violent or damaging action. **2** rowdy confusion, chaos. **3** *hist.* the crime of maiming a person so as to render him or her partly or wholly defenseless. [AF *mahem*, OF *mayhem* (as MAIM)]

■ **1** violence, havoc, destruction, devastation. **2** commotion, confusion, disorder, chaos.

maying /máying/ *n.* (also **Maying**) participation in May Day festivities. [ME f. MAY]

mayn't /máyənt/ *contr.* may not.

mayonnaise /máyənáyz/ *n.* a thick creamy dressing made of egg yolks, oil, vinegar, etc. [F, perh. f. *mahonnais -aise* of Port *Mahon* on Minorca]

mayor /máyər, mair/ *n.* the chief executive of a city or town. □□ **mayoral** *adj.* **mayorship** *n.* [ME f. OF *maire* f. L (as MAJOR)]

mayoralty /máyərəltee, máir-/ *n.* (*pl.* **-ies**) **1** the office of mayor. **2** a mayor's period of office. [ME f. OF *mairalté* (as MAYOR)]

mayoress /máyəris, máir-/ *n.* **1** a woman holding the office of mayor. **2** the wife of a mayor.

maypole /máypōl/ *n.* (also **Maypole**) a pole painted and decked with flowers and ribbons, for dancing around on May Day.

mayst /mayst/ *archaic 2nd sing. present* of MAY.

mayweed /máyweed/ *n.* the stinking chamomile, *Anthemis cotula*. [earlier *maidwede* f. obs. *maithe(n)* f. OE *magothe*, *mægtha* + WEED]

mazarine /mázəreén/ *n. & adj.* a rich deep blue. [17th c., perh. f. the name of Cardinal *Mazarin*, French statesman d. 1661, or Duchesse de *Mazarin*, French noblewoman d. 1699]

maze /mayz/ *n. & v.* ● *n.* **1** a network of paths and hedges designed as a puzzle for those who try to penetrate it. **2** a complex network of paths or passages; a labyrinth. **3** confusion, a confused mass, etc. ● *v.tr. Brit.* (esp. as **mazed** *adj.*) bewilder, confuse. □□ **mazy** *adj.* (**mazier, maziest**). [ME, orig. as *mased* (adj.): rel. to AMAZE]

■ *n.* **2** labyrinth, complex, network, warren. **3** see TANGLE¹ *n.*

mazer /máyzər/ *n. hist.* a hardwood drinking-bowl, usu. silver-mounted. [ME f. OF *masere* f. Gmc]

mazurka /məzə́rkə/ *n.* **1** a usu. lively Polish dance in triple time. **2** the music for this. [F *mazurka* or G *Masurka*, f. Pol. *mazurka* woman of the province *Mazovia*]

mazzard /mázzərd/ *b.* the wild sweet cherry, *Prunus avum*, of Europe. [alt. of MAZER]

MB *abbr.* **1** *Computing* megabyte(s). **2** esp. *Brit.* Bachelor of Medicine. [sense 2 f. L *Medicinae Baccalaureus*]

MBA *abbr.* Master of Business Administration.

MBE *abbr.* Member of the Order of the British Empire.

MC *abbr.* **1** master of ceremonies. **2** Marine Corps. **3** Medical Corps. **4** Member of Congress. **5** (in the UK) Military Cross.
- **1** see HOST² *n.* 5.

Mc *abbr.* **1** megacurie(s). **2** megacycle(s).

McCarthyism /məkáarthee-izəm/ *n.* the policy of hunting out suspected subversives or esp. Communists, usu. on the basis of weak evidence or false allegations. [J. R. *McCarthy*, US senator d. 1957]

McCoy /məkóy/ *n. colloq.* □ **the** (or **the real**) **McCoy** the real thing; the genuine article. [19th c.: orig. uncert.]

mCi *abbr.* millicurie(s).

MCP *abbr. colloq.* male chauvinist pig.

MCR *abbr.* Master of Comparative Religion.

MD *abbr.* **1** Doctor of Medicine. **2** Maryland (in official postal use). **3** Managing Director. **4** muscular dystrophy. [sense 1 f. L *Medicinae Doctor*]
- **1** see DOCTOR *n.* 1a. **2** see HEAD *n.* 6a.

Md *symb. Chem.* the element mendelevium.

Md. *abbr.* Maryland.

MDA *abbr.* methylene dioxymethamphetamine, an amphetamine-based drug that causes euphoric and hallucinatory effects, originally produced as an appetite suppressant (see ECSTASY 3).

ME *abbr.* **1** Maine (in official postal use). **2** Middle East. **3** Middle English.

Me. *abbr.* **1** Maine. **2** *Maître* (title of a French advocate).

me¹ /mee/ *pron.* **1** objective case of I² (*he saw me*). **2** *colloq.* = I² (*it's me all right; is taller than me*). **3** *colloq.* myself, to or for myself (*I got me a gun*). **4** *colloq.* used in exclamations (*ah me!; dear me!; silly me!*). □ **me and mine** me and my relatives. [OE *me, mē* accus. & dative of I² f. Gmc]

me² var. of MI.

mea culpa /máyə kǒŏlpə, meˊeə kúlpə/ *n. & int.* ● *n.* an acknowledgment of one's fault or error. ● *int.* expressing such an acknowledgment. [L, = by my fault]

mead¹ /meed/ *n.* an alcoholic drink of fermented honey and water. [OE *me(o)du* f. Gmc]

mead² /meed/ *n. poet.* or *archaic* = MEADOW. [OE *mæd* f. Gmc, rel. to MOW¹]

meadow /médō/ *n.* **1** a piece of grassland, esp. one used for hay. **2** a piece of low well-watered ground, esp. near a river. □ **meadow grass** a perennial creeping grass, esp. the Kentucky bluegrass, *Poa pratensis.* **meadow rue** any ranunculaceous plant of the genus *Thalictrum*, esp. *T. dioicum*, with drooping greenish white flowers. **meadow saffron** a perennial plant, *Colchicum autumnale*, abundant in meadows, with lilac flowers: also called *autumn crocus.* □□ **meadowy** *adj.* [OE *mædwe*, oblique case of *mæd*: see MEAD²]
- **1** field, pasture, *poet.* lea, *poet.* or *archaic* mead.

meadowlark /médōlaark/ *n.* any songbird of the genus *Sturnella*, esp. the yellow-breasted *S. magna* of N. America.

meadowsweet /médōsweet/ *n.* **1** any of several rosaceous plants of the genus *Spiraea*, native to N. America. **2** a rosaceous plant, *Filipendula ulmaria*, common in meadows and damp places, with creamy-white fragrant flowers.

meager /meeger/ *adj.* (*Brit.* **meagre**) **1** lacking in amount or quality (*a meager salary*). **2** (of literary composition, ideas, etc.) lacking fullness, unsatisfying. **3** (of a person or animal) lean, thin. □□ **meagerly** *adv.* **meagerness** *n.* [ME f. AF *megre*, OF *maigre* f. L *macer*]
- **1** scanty, poor, paltry, inadequate, skimpy, scrimpy, sparse, insufficient, bare, puny, trifling, niggardly, picayune, exiguous, *colloq.* piddling, measly, *Brit. colloq.*

pathetic. **2** spare, simplified, oversimplified, bare, inadequate, deficient, undetailed, unsatisfying. **3** spare, skinny, scrawny, bony, emaciated, gaunt, thin, lean, bareboned, (half-)starved, underfed, undernourished.

meal¹ /meel/ *n.* **1** an occasion when food is eaten. **2** the food eaten on one occasion. □ **make a meal of 1** treat (a task, etc.) too laboriously or fussily. **2** consume as a meal. **meals on wheels** a service by which meals are delivered to the elderly, invalids, etc. **meal ticket 1** a ticket entitling one to a meal, esp. at a specified place with reduced cost. **2** a person or thing that is a source of food or income. [OE *mæl* mark, fixed time, meal f. Gmc]
- spread, collation, *formal* repast, *literary* refection; dinner, supper, breakfast, lunch, brunch, *Brit.* tea, *formal* luncheon; food, victuals, nourishment. □ **make a meal of 1** overdo, overplay, carry to extremes, carry too far, do to excess.

meal² /meel/ *n.* **1** the edible part of any grain or pulse (usu. other than wheat) ground to powder. **2** *Sc.* oatmeal. **3** any powdery substance made by grinding. □ **meal beetle** an insect, *Tenebrio molitor*, infesting granaries, etc. [OE *melu* f. Gmc]

mealtime /meeltīm/ *n.* any of the usual times of eating.

mealworm /meelwórm/ *n.* the larva of the meal beetle.

mealy /meelee/ *adj.* (**mealier, mealiest**) **1 a** of or like meal; soft and powdery. **b** containing meal. **2** (of a complexion) pale. **3** (of a horse) spotty. **4** (in full **mealy-mouthed**) not outspoken; ingratiating; afraid to use plain expressions. □□ **mealiness** *n.*
- **2** see PALE¹ *adj.* 1. **3** see SPOTTY 1. **4** mincing, reticent, reluctant, hesitant, equivocal, ambiguous, indirect, euphemistic, roundabout, vague, circumlocutory, periphrastic; see also OBSEQUIOUS.

mealybug /meeleebúg/ *n.* any insect of the genus *Pseudococcus*, infesting plants, etc., whose body is covered with white powder.

mean¹ /meen/ *v.tr.* (*past* and *past part.* **meant** /ment/) **1 a** (often foll. by *to* + infin.) have as one's purpose or intention; have in mind (*they really mean mischief; I didn't mean to break it*). **b** (foll. by *by*) have as a motive in explanation (*what do you mean by that?*). **2** (often in *passive*) design or destine for a purpose (*mean it to be used; mean it for a stopgap; is meant to be a gift*). **3** intend to convey or indicate or refer to (a particular thing or notion) (*I mean we cannot go; I mean Springfield in Ohio*). **4** entail, involve (*it means catching the early train*). **5** (often foll. by *that* + clause) portend, signify (*this means trouble; your refusal means that we must look elsewhere*). **6** (of a word) have as its explanation in the same language or its equivalent in another language. **7** (foll. by *to*) be of some specified importance to (a person), esp. as a source of benefit or object of affection, etc. (*that means a lot to me*). □ **mean business** be in earnest. **mean it** not be joking or exaggerating. **mean to say** really admit (usu. in *interrog.*: *do you mean to say you have lost it?*). **mean well** (often foll. by *to, toward, by*) have good intentions. [OE *mǣnan* f. WG, rel. to MIND]
- **1, 2** intend, design, purpose, plan, aim, have in mind, contemplate, have in view; want, wish, expect, hope.
- **4, 6** denote, signify, connote, indicate, designate, represent, betoken, signal; imply, entail, involve.
- **5** portend, foretell, foreshadow, promise, presage, augur, herald; show, signify.

mean² /meen/ *adj.* **1** niggardly; not generous or liberal. **2** (of an action) ignoble, small-minded. **3** (of a person's capacity, understanding, etc.) inferior, poor. **4** (of housing) not imposing in appearance; shabby. **5 a** malicious, ill-tempered. **b** vicious or aggressive in behavior. **6** *colloq.* skillful, formidable (*is a mean fighter*). **7** *colloq.* ashamed (*feel mean*). □ **no**

/.../ **pronunciation**	● **part of speech**
□ **phrases, idioms, and compounds**	
□□ **derivatives**	■ **synonym section**
cross-references appear in SMALL CAPITALS or *italics*	

mean a very good (*that is no mean achievement*). □□ **meanly** *adv.* **meanness** *n.* [OE *mǽne, gemǽne* f. Gmc]

■ **1** stingy, miserly, tight, close, near, parsimonious, penurious, stinting, niggardly, penny-pinching, tightfisted, closefisted, uncharitable, ungenerous, mingy, *Austral.* hungry. **2** ignoble, small-minded, low, base, abject; meanspirited, small, petty, near. **3** inferior, poor, low. **4** inferior, poor, lowly, abject, modest, humble, run-down, sorry, miserable, scruffy, seedy, shabby, squalid, mangy, wretched, sordid, dismal, dreary. **5** unkind, malicious, cruel, unaccommodating, disobliging; cantankerous, churlish, nasty, hostile, ill-tempered, bad-tempered, sour, unpleasant. **6** formidable, excellent, wonderful, marvelous, great, exceptional, effective, skillful, skilled, esp. *US sl.* bad. **7** see ASHAMED 1.

mean³ /meen/ *n.* & *adj.* ● *n.* **1** a condition, quality, virtue, or course of action equally removed from two opposite (usu. unsatisfactory) extremes. **2** *Math.* **a** the term or one of the terms midway between the first and last terms of an arithmetical or geometrical, etc., progression (*2 and 8 have the arithmetic mean 5 and the geometric mean 4*). **b** the quotient of the sum of several quantities and their number, the average. ● *adj.* **1** (of a quantity) equally far from two extremes. **2** calculated as a mean. □ **mean free path** the average distance traveled by a gas molecule, etc., between collisions. **mean sea level** the sea level halfway between the mean levels of high and low water. **mean sun** an imaginary sun moving in the celestial equator at the mean rate of the real sun, used in calculating solar time. **mean time** the time based on the movement of the mean sun. [ME f. AF *meen* f. OF *meien, moien* f. L *medianus* MEDIAN]

■ *n.* average, middle, norm, (happy) medium; balance. ● *adj.* middle, center, intermediate, medial, medium, median, average, middling.

meander /meeándər/ *v.* & *n.* ● *v.intr.* **1** wander at random. **2** (of a stream) wind about. ● *n.* **1 a** a curve in a winding river, etc. **b** a crooked or winding path or passage. **2** a circuitous journey. **3** an ornamental pattern of lines winding in and out; a fret. □□ **meandrous** *adj.* [L *maeander* f. Gk *Maiandros*, the name of a winding river in Phrygia]

■ *v.* wander, ramble, zigzag, snake, coil, wind, twist, turn; stroll, amble, rove, *colloq.* swan around *or* about, *sl.* mosey. ● *n.* **1** turn, turning, twist, curve, loop, bend, coil, zigzag, convolution; oxbow; tortuosity, flexuosity, anfractuosity.

meandrine /meeándrin/ *adj.* full of windings (esp. of corals of the genus *Meandrina*, with a surface like a human brain). [MEANDER + -INE¹]

meanie /meenee/ *n.* (also **meany**) (*pl.* **-ies**) *colloq.* a mean, niggardly, or small-minded person.

meaning /meening/ *n.* & *adj.* ● *n.* **1** what is meant by a word, action, idea, etc. **2** significance. **3** importance. ● *adj.* expressive, significant (*a meaning glance*). □□ **meaningly** *adv.*

■ *n.* **1, 2** sense, import, content, signification, denotation, message, substance, gist; purport, implication, tenor, drift, spirit, connotation, significance, intention; interpretation, explanation. **3** see IMPORTANCE 2. ● *adj.* see EXPRESSIVE 1.

meaningful /meeningfŏŏl/ *adj.* **1** full of meaning; significant. **2** *Logic* able to be interpreted. □□ **meaningfully** *adv.* **meaningfulness** *n.*

■ **1** significant, important, consequential, serious, sober, deep, substantial, pithy, telling, weighty, valid, relevant, *archaic* substantive; suggestive, pregnant, telltale, revealing, pointed, sententious, expressive, eloquent.

meaningless /meeninglis/ *adj.* having no meaning or significance. □□ **meaninglessly** *adv.* **meaninglessness** *n.*

■ empty, hollow, vacuous, insubstantial, unsubstantial, absurd, silly, foolish, fatuous, asinine, ridiculous, preposterous, nonsensical; trivial, nugatory, trifling, puny, paltry, worthless, not worth anything *or* a straw *or* a rap, valueless, inconsequential, unimportant, of no

moment, vain, pointless, senseless, purposeless, undirected, irrelevant, insignificant.

means /meenz/ *n.pl.* **1** (often treated as *sing.*) that by which a result is brought about (*a means of quick travel*). **2 a** money resources (*live beyond one's means*). **b** wealth (*a man of means*). □ **by all means** (or **all manner of means**) **1** certainly. **2** in every possible way. **3** at any cost. **by any means** at all; in any way. **by means of** by the agency or instrumentality of (a thing or action). **by no means** (or **no manner of means**) not at all; certainly not. **means test** an official inquiry to establish need before financial assistance from public funds is given. [pl. of MEAN³]

■ **1** instrument, agency, method, process, technique, mode, manner, way(s), approach, course, procedure, avenue, medium, vehicle. **2** resources, funds, money, cash, wealth, capital, finances, backing, support, *colloq.* wherewithal. □ **by all means** (or **all manner of means**) **1** absolutely, definitely, certainly, surely, assuredly, of course, positively. **3** in any event, at all events, no matter what, without fail, at any cost, at all costs, in any case. **by means of** by dint of, via, through, by way of, with the help *or* aid of, employing, using, utilizing. **by no means** (or **no manner of means**) in no way, not at all, definitely *or* absolutely *or* certainly not, on no account, not conceivably, not in one's wildest dreams, not by any stretch of the imagination, *colloq.* no way.

meant *past* and *past part.* of MEAN¹.

meantime /meentim/ *adv.* & *n.* ● *adv.* = MEANWHILE. ¶ Less usual than *meanwhile*. ● *n.* the intervening period (esp. *in the meantime*). [MEAN³ + TIME]

■ *adv.* see MEANWHILE *adv.* ● *n.* see MEANWHILE *n.*

meanwhile /meenwil, -hwil/ *adv.* & *n.* ● *adv.* **1** in the intervening period of time. **2** at the same time. ● *n.* the intervening period (esp. *in the meanwhile*). [MEAN³ + WHILE]

■ *adv.* in the meanwhile, meantime, in the meantime, in the interim, *archaic* interim; for the moment, temporarily, for now, for the time being, ad interim. ● *n.* interim, meantime, interval.

meany var. of MEANIE.

measles /meezəlz/ *n.pl.* (also treated as *sing.*) **1 a** an acute infectious viral disease marked by red spots on the skin. **b** the spots of measles. **2** a tapeworm disease of pigs. [ME *masele(s)* prob. f. MLG *masele*, MDu. *masel* pustule (cf. Du. *mazelen* measles), OHG *masala*: change of form prob. due to assim. to ME *meser* leper]

measly /meezlee/ *adj.* (**measlier, measliest**) **1** *colloq.* inferior, contemptible, worthless. **2** *colloq. derog.* ridiculously small in size, amount, or value. **3** of or affected with measles. **4** (of pork) infested with tapeworms. [MEASLES + -Y¹]

■ **1** inferior, contemptible, worthless; see also WRETCHED 2. **2** sparse, scanty, meager, paltry, pathetic, skimpy, puny, miserly, niggardly, miserable, beggarly, stingy.

measurable /mézhərəbəl/ *adj.* that can be measured. □□ **measurability** /-bílitee/ *n.* **measurably** *adv.* [ME f. OF *mesurable* f. LL *mensurabilis* f. L *mensurare* (as MEASURE)]

measure /mézhər/ *n.* & *v.* ● *n.* **1** a size or quantity found by measuring. **2** a system of measuring (*liquid measure; linear measure*). **3** a rod or tape, etc., for measuring. **4** a vessel of standard capacity for transferring or determining fixed quantities of liquids, etc. (*a pint measure*). **5 a** the degree, extent, or amount of a thing. **b** (foll. by *of*) some degree of (*there was a measure of wit in her remark*). **6** a unit of capacity, e.g., a bushel (*20 measures of wheat*). **7** a factor by which a person or thing is reckoned or evaluated (*their success is a measure of their determination*). **8** (usu. in *pl.*) suitable action to achieve some end (*took measures to ensure a good profit*). **9** a legislative act. **10** a quantity contained in another an exact number of times. **11** a prescribed extent or quantity. **12** *Printing* the width of a page or column of type. **13 a** a poetical rhythm; meter. **b** a metrical group of a dactyl or two iambs, trochees, spondees, etc. **14** *US Mus.* a bar or the time content of a bar. **15** *archaic* a dance. **16** a mineral stratum (*coal measures*). ● *v.* **1** *tr.* ascertain the extent or quantity of (a thing) by comparison with a fixed unit or with an object of known size. **2** *intr.* be of a specified size (*it measures six inches*). **3** *tr.* ascertain the size and proportion of (a person) for clothes. **4** *tr.* estimate (a quality, person's character, etc.) by some standard or rule. **5** *tr.* (often foll. by *off*) mark (a line, etc., of a given length). **6** *tr.* (foll. by *out*) deal or distribute (a thing) in measured quantities. **7** *tr.* (foll. by *with, against*) bring (oneself or one's strength, etc.) into competition with. **8** *tr. poet.* traverse (a distance). □ **beyond measure** excessively. **for good measure** as something beyond the minimum; as a finishing touch. **in a** (or **some**) **measure** partly. **made to measure** see MAKE. **measure up 1 a** determine the size, etc., of by measurement. **b** take comprehensive measurements. **2** (often foll. by *to*) have the necessary qualifications (for). **measuring cup** a cup marked to measure its contents. **measuring worm** looper, the caterpillar of the geometer moth. [ME f. OF *mesure* f. L *mensura* f. *metiri mens-* measure]

■ *n.* **1** amount, quantity, magnitude, amplitude, size, bulk, mass, extent, reach, dimension(s), measurement(s), scope, proportions, range, spread; capacity, volume; width, length, breadth, height; weight. **2, 3** scale, gauge, yardstick, rule, ruler, tape measure; system, standard, criterion, method; barometer. **4** measuring cup. **5, 6** quota, allotment, ration, share, amount, degree, extent, proportion, quantity, allowance; portion, part, unit. **7** assessment, evaluation, valuation, appraisal, value, gauge, rank, rating, measurement, stamp, estimation. **8** (*measures*) step(s), action, course (of action); plan(s), method, means, avenue, tactic(s), way, direction, approach, technique, procedure(s). **9** bill, resolution, legislation, act, statute, law; plan, proposal. **13, 14** beat, rhythm, cadence, meter, time; bar. ● *v.* **1** rank, rate, gauge, meter, weigh, calculate, reckon, compute, calibrate, determine, ascertain, figure out *or* up, assess, appraise, estimate, evaluate, judge, value; survey, find out. **4** see JUDGE *v.* 2. **5** measure off, mark off *or* out, limit, delimit, fix, pace off *or* out. **6** (*measure out*) dole out, ration (out), parcel out, apportion, allot, share out, assign, allocate, *literary* mete out; give out, deal out, distribute, issue, pass out, hand out, dispense, disperse, spread around *or* about. **8** see TRAVERSE *v.* 1. □ **beyond measure** see *unduly* (UNDUE). **for good measure** to boot, as well, in addition, additionally, as a dividend, into the bargain, besides, as *or* for a bonus, moreover, furthermore. **in a** (or **some**) **measure** see *partially* (PARTIAL). **measure up 1** see MEASURE *v.* 1 above. **2** qualify (for), be suitable (for); (*measure up to*) meet, equal, fulfill, match, reach, attain, be equal to, be fit *or* fitted for, be up to. **measuring cup**) measure.

measured /mézhərd/ *adj.* **1** rhythmical; regular in movement (*a measured tread*). **2** (of language) carefully considered. □□ **measuredly** *adv.*

■ **1** rhythmic(al), regular, regulated, steady, uniform, even, monotonous. **2** careful, cautious, prudent, calculated, studied, considered, deliberate, systematic, sober, intentional, planned, regulated, premeditated, well-thought-out, reasoned.

measureless /mézhərlis/ *adj.* not measurable; infinite. □□ **measurelessly** *adv.*

measurement /mézhərmənt/ *n.* **1** the act or an instance of measuring. **2** an amount determined by measuring. **3** (in *pl.*) detailed dimensions.

■ **1** ascertainment, determination, assessment, estimation, appraisal, evaluation, valuation, judgment, calculation, computation, mensuration, commensuration, metage. **2** dimension, extent, size, amount, measure, magnitude, amplitude; length, breadth, height, width, depth; area; volume, capacity; weight, tonnage; (elapsed) time, period; (square *or* cubic) footage, (square) yardage, mileage, acreage.

meat /meet/ *n.* **1** the flesh of animals (esp. mammals) as food. **2** (foll. by *of*) the essence or chief part of. **3** the edible part of fruits, nuts, eggs, shellfish, etc. **4** *archaic* **a** food of any kind. **b** a meal. □ **meat and drink** *Brit.* a source of great

pleasure. **meat-and-potatoes** essential; fundamental; basic. **meat-ax 1** a butcher's cleaver. **2** drastic method of reducing something, esp. expenses. **meat hooks** *sl.* hands or fists. **meat loaf** seasoned ground meat molded into the shape of a loaf and baked. **meat market** *colloq.* a place (as a bar, club, etc.) in which people are evaluated on the basis of physical appearance. **meat safe** *Brit.* a cupboard for storing meat, usu. of wire gauze, etc. □□ **meatless** *adj.* [OE *mete* food f. Gmc]

■ **1** flesh. **2** pith, core, heart, marrow, kernel, essence, gist, substance, basics, essentials, crux. **3** flesh, pulp, marrow, kernel, soft part. **4** food, nourishment, sustenance, victuals, nutriment, provisions, edibles, eatables, *colloq.* eats, grub, *formal* viands, *formal or joc.* comestibles, *joc.* provender, *sl.* chow. □ **meat and drink 1** see JOY *n.* 2.

meatball /méetbawl/ *n.* seasoned ground meat formed into a small round ball.

meatpacking /méetpaking/ *n.* the business of slaughtering animals and processing the meat for sale as food.

meatus /meeáytəs/ *n.* (*pl.* same or **meatuses**) *Anat.* a channel or passage in the body or its opening. [L, = passage f. *meare* flow, run]

meaty /méetee/ *adj.* (**meatier, meatiest**) **1** full of meat; fleshy. **2** of or like meat. **3** full of substance. □□ **meatily** *adv.* **meatiness** *n.*

Mecca /mékə/ *n.* **1** a place one aspires to visit. **2** the birthplace of a faith, policy, pursuit, etc. [*Mecca* in Arabia, birthplace of Muhammad and chief place of Muslim pilgrimage]

mechanic /mikánik/ *n.* a skilled worker, esp. one who makes or uses or repairs machinery. [ME (orig. as adj.) f. OF *mecanique* or L *mechanicus* f. Gk *mēkhanikos* (as MACHINE)]

■ engineer, repairman, *Brit.* technician.

mechanical /mikánikəl/ *adj.* **1** of or relating to machines or mechanisms. **2** working or produced by machinery. **3** (of a person or action) like a machine; automatic; lacking originality. **4 a** (of an agency, principle, etc.) belonging to mechanics. **b** (of a theory, etc.) explaining phenomena by the assumption of mechanical action. **5** of or relating to mechanics as a science. □ **mechanical advantage** the ratio of exerted to applied force in a machine. **mechanical drawing** a scale drawing of machinery, etc., done with precision instruments. **mechanical engineer** a person skilled in the branch of engineering dealing with the design, construction, and repair of machines. **mechanical equivalent of heat** the conversion factor between heat energy and mechanical energy. □□ **mechanicalism** *n.* (in sense 4). **mechanically** *adv.* **mechanicalness** *n.* [ME f. L *mechanicus* (as MECHANIC)]

■ **2** automatic, automated, machine-driven, robotic; machine-made. **3** automatic, reflex, involuntary, instinctive, routine, habitual, unconscious, perfunctory, machinelike, robotlike.

mechanician /mékəníshən/ *n.* a person skilled in constructing machinery.

mechanics /mikániks/ *n.pl.* (usu. treated as *sing.*) **1** the branch of applied mathematics dealing with motion and tendencies to motion. **2** the science of machinery. **3** the method of construction or routine operation of a thing.

mechanism /mékənizəm/ *n.* **1** the structure or adaptation of parts of a machine. **2** a system of mutually adapted parts working together in or as in a machine. **3** the mode of operation of a process. **4** *Art* mechanical execution; technique. **5** *Philos.* the doctrine that all natural phenomena, including life, allow mechanical explanation by physics and chemistry. [mod.L *mechanismus* f. Gk (as MACHINE)]

■ **1** machinery, workings, works, structure, system, organization, arrangement. **2** movement, action, moving parts, gears; device, apparatus. **3** way, means,

---

/.../ **pronunciation**	● **part of speech**
□ **phrases, idioms, and compounds**	
□□ **derivatives**	■ **synonym section**
cross-references appear in SMALL CAPITALS or *italics*	

method, procedure, approach, technique, medium, process, agency. **5** materialism, mechanicalism.

mechanist /mékənist/ *n.* **1** a mechanician. **2** an expert in mechanics. **3** *Philos.* a person who holds the doctrine of mechanism. □□ **mechanistic** /-nístik/ *adj.* **mechanistically** /-nístiklee/ *adv.*

mechanize /mékənīz/ *v.tr.* **1** give a mechanical character to. **2** introduce machines in. **3** *Mil.* equip with tanks, armored cars, etc. (orig. as a substitute for horse-drawn vehicles and cavalry). □□ **mechanization** *n.* **mechanizer** *n.*

mechano- /mékənō/ *comb. form* mechanical. [Gk *mēkhano-* f. *mēkhanē* machine]

mechanoreceptor /mékənōriséptər/ *n. Biol.* a sensory receptor that responds to mechanical stimuli such as touch or sound.

mechatronics /mékətróniks/ *n.* the science of the combination of electronics and mechanics in developing new manufacturing techniques. [*mechanics* + *electronics*]

Mechlin /méklin/ *n.* (in full **Mechlin lace**) a fine lace originally made at Mechlin (now Mechelen or Malines) in Belgium.

M.Econ. *abbr.* Master of Economics.

meconium /mikōneeəm/ *n. Med.* a dark substance forming the first feces of a newborn infant. [L, lit. poppy juice, f. Gk *mēkōnion* f. *mēkōn* poppy]

M.Ed. *abbr.* Master of Education.

Med /med/ *n.* esp. *Brit. colloq.* the Mediterranean Sea. [abbr.]

med /med/ *adj.* medical (*med school*).

med. *abbr.* **1** medium. **2** medical. **3** medicine. **4** medieval.

medal /méd'l/ *n.* a piece of metal, usu. in the form of a disk, struck or cast with an inscription or device to commemorate an event, etc., or awarded as a distinction to a soldier, scholar, athlete, etc., for services rendered, for proficiency, etc. □ **medal play** *Golf* = *stroke play*. **Medal of Freedom** (also **Presidential Medal of Freedom**) medal awarded by the US president for achievement in various fields. **Medal of Honor** (also **Congressional Medal of Honor**) the highest US military decoration, awarded by Congress for exceptional bravery. □□ **medaled** *adj.* **medallic** /midálik/ *adj.* [F *médaille* f. It. *medaglia* ult. f. L *metallum* METAL]

■ see DECORATION 3.

medalist /méd'list/ *n.* (also esp. *Brit.* **medallist**) **1** a recipient of a (specified) medal (*gold medalist*). **2** an engraver or designer of medals.

medallion /midályən/ *n.* **1** a large medal. **2** a thing shaped like this, e.g., a decorative panel or tablet, portrait, etc. [F *médaillon* f. It. *medaglione* augment. of *medaglia* (as MEDAL)]

■ **1** see PENDANT 1, 2. **2** see PLAQUE.

meddle /méd'l/ *v.intr.* (often foll. by *with, in*) interfere in or busy oneself unduly with others' concerns. □□ **meddler** *n.* [ME f. OF *medler,* var. of *mesler* ult. f. L *miscēre* mix]

■ interfere, intrude, butt in, thrust one's nose in, pry, intervene, interlope, tamper, *colloq.* snoop, poke one's nose in, kibitz, *Austral. sl.* poke one's bib in.

meddlesome /méd'lsəm/ *adj.* fond of meddling; interfering. □□ **meddlesomely** *adv.* **meddlesomeness** *n.*

■ see NOSY *adj.* □□ **meddlesomeness** interference, interruption, intrusiveness, obtrusiveness, invasiveness, prying, inquisitiveness, officiousness, presumptuousness, *colloq.* nosiness, snooping.

Mede /meed/ *n. hist.* a member of an Indo-European people who established an empire in Media in Persia (modern Iran) in the 7th c. BC. □□ **Median** *adj.* [ME f. L *Medi* (pl.) f. Gk *Mēdoi*]

media¹ /méedeeə/ *n.pl.* **1** *pl.* of MEDIUM. **2** (usu. prec. by *the*) the main means of mass communication (esp. newspapers and broadcasting) regarded collectively. ¶ Use as a mass noun with a singular verb is common (e.g., *the media is on our side*), but is generally disfavored (cf. AGENDA, DATA). □ **media event** an event primarily intended to attract publicity.

media² /méedeeə/ *n.* (*pl.* **mediae** /-dee-ee/) **1** *Phonet.* a voiced stop, e.g., *g, b, d.* **2** *Anat.* a middle layer of the wall of an artery or other vessel. [L, fem. of *medius* middle]

mediaeval var. of MEDIEVAL.

medial /méedeeəl/ *adj.* **1** situated in the middle. **2** of average size. □□ **medially** *adv.* [LL *medialis* f. L *medius* middle]

■ **1** see MIDDLE *adj.* 1, 2. **2** see MEDIUM *adj.*

median /méedeeən/ *adj. & n.* ● *adj.* situated in the middle. ● *n.* **1** *Anat.* a median artery, vein, nerve, etc. **2** *Geom.* a straight line drawn from any vertex of a triangle to the middle of the opposite side. **3** *Math.* the middle value of a series of values arranged in order of size. **4** (also **median strip**) center divider separating opposing lanes on a divided highway. □□ **medianly** *adv.* [F *médiane* or L *medianus* (as MEDIAL)]

■ *adj.* see CENTRAL 1.

mediant /méedeeənt/ *n. Mus.* the third note of a diatonic scale of any key. [F *médiante* f. It. *mediante* part. of obs. *mediare* come between, f. L (as MEDIATE)]

mediastinum /méedeeəstínəm/ *n.* (*pl.* **mediastina** /-nə/) *Anat.* a membranous middle septum, esp. between the lungs. □□ **mediastinal** *adj.* [mod.L f. med.L *mediastinus* medial, after L *mediastinus* drudge f. *medius* middle]

mediate *v. & adj.* ● *v.* /méedeeayt/ **1** *intr.* (often foll. by *between*) intervene (between parties in a dispute) to produce agreement or reconciliation. **2** *tr.* be the medium for bringing about (a result) or for conveying (a gift, etc.). **3** *tr.* form a connecting link between. ● *adj.* /méedeeət/ **1** connected not directly but through some other person or thing. **2** involving an intermediate agency. □□ **mediately** /-ətlee/ *adv.* **mediation** /-áyshən/ *n.* **mediator** /méedeeaytər/ *n.* **mediatory** /méedeeətáwree/ *adj.* [LL *mediare mediat-* f. L *medius* middle]

■ *v.* **1** arbitrate, referee, umpire, moderate, liaise, intercede, *archaic* conciliate; see also NEGOTIATE 1, 2. **3** see CONNECT 1a, b. □□ **mediator** arbitrator, arbiter, referee, umpire, judge, negotiator, intermediary, go-between, middleman, moderator, liaison, intercessor, interceder, conciliator, appeaser, peacemaker.

medic¹ /médik/ *n. colloq.* a medical practitioner or student, esp. a member of a military medical corps. [L *medicus* physician f. *medēri* heal]

medic² /médik/ *n.* (also **medick**) any leguminous plant of the genus *Medicago,* esp. alfalfa. [ME f. L *medica* f. Gk *Mēdikē poa* Median grass]

medicable /médikəbəl/ *adj.* admitting of remedial treatment. [L *medicabilis* (as MEDICATE)]

Medicaid /médikayd/ *n.* a federal system of health insurance for those requiring financial assistance. [MEDICAL + AID]

medical /médikəl/ *adj. & n.* ● *adj.* **1** of or relating to the science of medicine in general. **2** of or relating to conditions requiring medical and not surgical treatment (*medical ward*). ● *n. colloq.* = *medical examination.* □ **medical examination** an examination to determine a person's physical fitness. **medical examiner** a person, usu. a physician, employed by a city, county, etc., to conduct autopsies and determine the cause of death. **medical jurisprudence** the law relating to medicine. **medical practitioner** a physician or surgeon. □□ **medically** *adv.* [F *médical* or med.L *medicalis* f. L *medicus:* see MEDIC¹]

□ **medical practitioner** see DOCTOR *n.* 1a.

medicament /médikəmənt, midíkə-/ *n.* a substance used for medical treatment. [F *médicament* or L *medicamentum* (as MEDICATE)]

■ see MEDICINE 2.

Medicare /médikair/ *n.* US federal government program for health insurance for persons esp. over 65 years of age. [MEDICAL + CARE]

medicate /médikayt/ *v.tr.* **1** treat medically. **2** impregnate with a medicinal substance. □□ **medicative** /médikáytiv/ *adj.* [L *medicari medicat-* administer remedies to f. *medicus:* see MEDIC¹]

■ **1** see TREAT *v.* 3.

medication /médikáyshən/ *n.* **1** a substance used for medical treatment. **2** treatment using drugs.

■ **1** see MEDICINE 2.

Medicean /medichéeən, -sée-/ *adj.* of the Medici family, rulers of Florence in the 15th c. [mod.L *Mediceus* f. It. *Medici*]

medicinal /mədísinəl/ *adj. & n.* ● *adj.* (of a substance) having healing properties. ● *n.* a medicinal substance. □□ **medicinally** *adv.* [ME f. OF f. L *medicinalis* (as MEDICINE)]

■ *adj.* healing, remedial, therapeutic, curative, restorative, sanative, medical, analeptic, *Med.* roborant. ● *n.* see MEDICINE 2.

medicine /médisin/ *n.* **1** the science or practice of the diagnosis, treatment, and prevention of disease, esp. as distinct from surgical methods. **2** any drug or preparation used for the treatment or prevention of disease, esp. one taken by mouth. **3** a spell, charm, or fetish which is thought to cure afflictions. □ **a dose** (or **taste**) **of one's own medicine** treatment such as one is accustomed to giving others. **medicine ball** a stuffed leather ball thrown and caught for exercise. **medicine chest** a box containing medicines, etc. **medicine man** a person believed to have magical powers of healing, esp. among Native Americans. **medicine show** a traveling show offering entertainment to entice a crowd to whom patent medicines, etc., would be sold. **take one's medicine** submit to something disagreeable. [ME f. OF *medecine* f. L *medicina* f. *medicus*: see MEDIC¹]

■ **1** esp. *archaic* physic. **2** medication, medicament, remedy, drug, pharmaceutical, prescription, esp. *archaic* physic; nostrum, panacea, cure-all. □ **medicine man** healer, witch doctor, shaman. **take one's medicine** face the music; see also *bite the bullet*.

medick var. of MEDIC².

medico /médikō/ *n.* (*pl.* **-os**) *colloq.* a medical practitioner or student. [It. f. L (as MEDIC¹)]

medico- /médikō/ *comb. form* medical; medical and (*medicolegal*). [L *medicus* (as MEDIC¹)]

medieval /meédee-eével, méd-, míd-/ *adj.* (also **mediaeval**) **1** of, or in the style of, the Middle Ages. **2** *colloq.* old-fashioned, archaic. □ **medieval history** the history of the 5th–15th c. **medieval Latin** Latin of about AD 600–1500. □□ **medievalism** *n.* **medievalist** *n.* **medievalize** *v.tr.* & *intr.* *adv.* [mod.L *medium aevum* f. L *medius* middle + *aevum* age]

■ **2** see ANTIQUATED.

mediocre /meédee-ōkər/ *adj.* **1** of middling quality, neither good nor bad. **2** second-rate. [F *médiocre* or f. L *mediocris* of middle height or degree f. *medius* middle + *ocris* rugged mountain]

■ **1** middling, indifferent, ordinary, commonplace, average, medium, everyday, run-of-the-mill, pedestrian, undistinguished, uninspired, unimaginative, unexceptional, tolerable, fair (to middling), not (that *or* too) good, not bad, so-so, *colloq.* common *or* garden. **2** second-rate, third-rate, inferior, poor, *colloq.* nothing to write home about, no great shakes.

mediocrity /meédee-ókritee/ *n.* (*pl.* **-ies**) **1** the state of being mediocre. **2** a mediocre person or thing.

■ **1** see INFERIORITY.

meditate /méditayt/ *v.* **1** *intr.* **a** exercise the mind in (esp. religious) contemplation. **b** (usu. foll. by *on, upon*) focus on a subject in this manner. **2** *tr.* plan mentally; design. □□ **meditation** /-táyshən/ *n.* **meditator** *n.* [L *meditari* contemplate]

■ **1** reflect, think, ponder, study, ruminate, cogitate, cerebrate, be lost in thought, be in a brown study, *literary* muse. **2** consider, contemplate, mull over, reflect on *or* upon, ponder on *or* over, chew over, plan, scheme, devise, contrive, design, conceive, frame, think up, have in mind.

meditative /méditaytiv/ *adj.* **1** inclined to meditate. **2** indicative of meditation. □□ **meditatively** *adv.* **meditativeness** *n.*

■ **1** thoughtful, pensive, contemplative, reflective, studious, cogitative, abstracted, rapt, engrossed, lost *or* deep in thought, ruminative, brooding.

Mediterranean /méditəráyneeən/ *n.* & *adj.* ● *n.* **1** a large landlocked sea bordered by S. Europe, SW Asia, and N. Africa. **2** a native of a country bordering on the Mediterranean Sea. ● *adj.* **1** of or characteristic of the Mediterranean or its surrounding region (*Mediterranean climate*; *Mediterranean cooking*). **2** (of a person) dark-complexioned and

not tall. [L *mediterraneus* inland f. *medius* middle + *terra* land]

medium /meédeeəm/ *n.* & *adj.* ● *n.* (*pl.* **media** or **mediums**) **1** the middle quality, degree, etc., between extremes (*find a happy medium*). **2** the means by which something is communicated (*the medium of sound*; *the medium of television*). **3** the intervening substance through which impressions are conveyed to the senses, etc. (*light passing from one medium into another*). **4** *Biol.* the physical environment or conditions of growth, storage, or transport of a living organism (*the shape of a fish is ideal for its fluid medium*; *growing mold on the surface of a medium*). **5** an agency or means of doing something (*the medium through which money is raised*). **6** the material or form used by an artist, composer, etc. (*language as an artistic medium*). **7** the liquid (e.g., oil or gel) with which pigments are mixed for use in painting. **8** (*pl.* **mediums**) a person claiming to be in contact with the spirits of the dead and to communicate between the dead and the living. ● *adj.* **1** between two qualities, degrees, etc. **2** average; moderate (*of medium height*). □ **medium dry** (of sherry, wine, etc.) having a flavor intermediate between dry and sweet. **medium frequency** a radio frequency between 300 kHz and 3 MHz. **medium of circulation** something that serves as an instrument of commercial transactions, e.g., coin. **medium-range** (of an aircraft, missile, etc.) able to travel a medium distance. **medium wave** esp. *Brit.* a radio wave of medium frequency. □□ **mediumism** *n.* (in sense 8 of *n.*). **mediumistic** /-místik/ *adj.* (in sense 8 of *n.*). **mediumship** *n.* (in sense 8 of *n.*). [L, = middle, neut. of *medius*]

■ *n.* **1** average, middle, midpoint, compromise, center, mean, norm. **2, 5, 6** means, method, mode, approach, instrument, device, mechanism, intermediation, technique, contrivance, agency, expedient, way, course, route, road, avenue, channel, conveyance, vehicle. **3** atmosphere, environment, ambience, milieu. **4** see ENVIRONMENT 1, 2. **8** see PSYCHIC *n.* ● *adj.* average, middle, middling, mid, medial, median, normal, standard, usual, everyday, ordinary.

medlar /médlər/ *n.* **1** a rosaceous tree, *Mespilus germanica*, bearing small brown applelike fruits. **2** the fruit of this tree that is eaten when decayed. [ME f. OF *medler* f. L *mespila* f. Gk *mespilē, -on*]

medley /médlee/ *n., adj.,* & *v.* ● *n.* (*pl.* **-eys**) **1** a varied mixture; a miscellany. **2** a collection of musical items from one work or various sources arranged as a continuous whole. ● *adj.* *archaic* mixed; motley. ● *v.tr.* (**-eys, -eyed**) *archaic* make a medley of; intermix. □ **medley relay** a relay race between teams in which each member runs a different distance, swims a different stroke, etc. [ME f. OF *medlee* var. of *meslee* f. Rmc (as MEDDLE)]

■ *n.* mixture, assortment, combination, miscellany, mélange, collection, conglomeration, agglomeration, hodgepodge, olio, blend, gallimaufry, pastiche, potpourri, salmagundi, olla podrida, mishmash, mixed bag, jumble, mess, farrago, stew, goulash, *colloq.* omnium gatherum. ● *adj.* see MIXED. ● *v.* see MIX *v.* 1, 3, 4a.

Medoc /maydók/ *n.* a fine red claret from the Médoc region of SW France.

medulla /midúlə/ *n.* **1** the inner region of certain organs or tissues, usu. when it is distinguishable from the outer region or cortex, as in hair or a kidney. **2** the myelin layer of certain nerve fibers. **3** the soft internal tissue of plants. □ **medulla oblongata** /óblonggaátə/ the continuation of the spinal cord within the skull, forming the lowest part of the brain stem. □□ **medullary** /méd'léree, mejə-, mədúləree/ *adj.* [L, = pith, marrow, prob. rel. to *medius* middle]

medusa /midōōsə, -zə, -dyōō-/ *n.* (*pl.* **medusae** /-see/ or

---

/.../ **pronunciation** ● **part of speech**
□ **phrases, idioms, and compounds**
□□ **derivatives** ■ **synonym section**
cross-references appear in SMALL CAPITALS or *italics*

medusas) **1** a jellyfish. **2** a free-swimming form of any coelenterate, having tentacles around the edge of a usu. umbrella-shaped jellylike body, e.g., a jellyfish. □□ **medusan** *adj.* [L f. Gk *Medousa*, name of a Gorgon with snakes instead of hair]

meed /meed/ *n. literary* or *archaic* **1** reward. **2** merited portion (of praise, etc.). [OE *mēd* f. WG, rel. to Goth. *mizdō*, Gk *misthos* reward]

meek /meek/ *adj.* **1** humble and submissive; suffering injury, etc., tamely. **2** piously gentle in nature. □□ **meekly** *adv.* **meekness** *n.* [ME *me(o)c* f. ON *mjúkr* soft, gentle]
■ modest, humble, submissive, unassuming, unambitious, unpretentious, mild, bland, patient, deferential, shy, retiring, lowly, tame, timid, weak, docile, compliant, yielding, acquiescent, unaggressive, nonmilitant, pacific, tractable, manageable, subdued, repressed, spiritless, suppressed, broken, *colloq.* wimpish.

meerkat /meerkat/ *n.* the suricate. [Du., = sea cat]

meerschaum /meershəm, -shawm/ *n.* **1** a soft white form of hydrated magnesium silicate, found chiefly in Turkey, which resembles clay. **2** a tobacco pipe with the bowl made from this. [G, = sea foam f. *Meer* sea + *Schaum* foam, transl. Pers. *kef-i-daryā*, with ref. to its frothiness]

meet¹ /meet/ *v. & n.* ● *v.* (*past* and *past part.* met /met/) **1 a** *tr.* encounter (a person or persons) by accident or design; come face to face with. **b** *intr.* (of two or more people) come into each other's company by accident or design (*decided to meet on the bridge*). **2** *tr.* go to a place to be present at the arrival of (a person, train, etc.). **3 a** *tr.* (of a moving object, line, feature of landscape, etc.) come together or into contact with (*where the road meets the river*). **b** *intr.* come together or into contact (*where the sea and the sky meet*). **4 a** *tr.* make the acquaintance of (*delighted to meet you*). **b** *intr.* (of two or more people) make each other's acquaintance. **5** *intr. & tr.* come together or come into contact with for the purposes of conference, business, worship, etc. (*the committee meets every week; the union met management yesterday*). **6** *tr.* **a** (of a person or a group) deal with or answer (a demand, objection, etc.) (*met the original proposal with hostility*). **b** satisfy or conform with (proposals, deadlines, a person, etc.) (*agreed to meet the new terms; did my best to meet them on that point*). **7** *tr.* pay (a bill, etc.); provide the funds required by (*meet the cost of the move*). **8** *tr.* & (foll. by *with*) *intr.* experience, encounter, or receive (*success, disaster, a difficulty, etc.*) (*met their death; met with many problems*). **9** *tr.* oppose in battle, contest, or confrontation. **10** *intr.* (of clothes, curtains, etc.) join or fasten correctly (*my jacket won't meet*). ● *n.* **1** the assembly of competitors for various sporting activities, as track, swimming, etc. **2** the assembly of riders and hounds for a hunt. □ **make ends meet** see END. **meet the case** be adequate. **meet the eye** (or **the ear**) be visible (or audible). **meet a person's eye** check if another person is watching and look into his or her eyes in return. **meet a person halfway** make a compromise, respond in a friendly way to the advances of another person. **meet up** *colloq.* happen to meet. **meet with 1** see sense 8 of *v.* **2** receive (a reaction) (*met with the committee's approval*). **3** see sense 1a of *v.* **more than meets the eye** possessing hidden qualities or complications. □□ **meeter** *n.* [OE *mētan* f. Gmc: cf. MOOT]
■ *v.* **1** encounter, come across, chance on *or* upon, happen on *or* upon, stumble on *or* into, see, run across *or* into, meet with, *colloq.* bump into; rendezvous (with), get together (with). **3** link up, join, come together, unite, touch, intersect. **4** make the acquaintance of, be introduced to. **5** convene, assemble, gather, get together, collect, forgather, congregate. **6** answer, deal with, handle, satisfy, fulfill, take care of, dispose of, heed, observe, carry out. **7** pay, settle, defray, liquidate. **8** encounter, be met by, experience; undergo, endure, suffer, have, go through. **9** see FIGHT *v.* 1a. ● *n.* competition, contest, meeting, match, tourney, tournament, rally. □ **meet the case** see SUFFICE 1. **meet with 2** see RECEIVE 4.

meet² /meet/ *adj. archaic* suitable; fit; proper. □□ **meetly** *adv.* **meetness** *n.* [ME (*i*)*mete* repr. OE *gemǣte* f. Gmc, rel. to METE¹]
■ fitting, appropriate, proper, fit, apt, congruous; see also SUITABLE.

meeting /meeting/ *n.* **1** in senses of MEET¹. **2** an assembly of people, esp. the members of a society, committee, etc., for discussion or entertainment. **3** an assembly (esp. of Quakers) for worship. **4** the persons assembled (*address the meeting*).
■ **1** appointment, engagement, rendezvous, encounter, assignation, *archaic* tryst; convergence, converging, confluence, joining, union, junction, conjunction, intersection. **2, 4** assembly, convention, conference, gathering, congress, conclave, session, congregation, convocation, caucus, *colloq.* get-together.

meetinghouse /meetinghows/ *n.* a place of worship, esp. of Quakers, etc.

mega /mégə/ *adj. & adv. sl.* ● *adj.* **1** excellent. **2** enormous. ● *adv.* extremely. [Gk f. as MEGA-]

mega- /mégə/ *comb. form* **1** large. **2** denoting a factor of one million (10^6) in the metric system of measurement. ¶ Abbr.: M. [Gk f. *megas* great]

megabuck /mégəbuk/ *n. colloq.* **1** a million dollars. **2** (in *pl.*) great sums of money.

megabyte /mégəbīt/ *n. Computing* 1,048,576 (i.e., 2^{20}) bytes as a measure of data capacity, or loosely 1,000,000 bytes. ¶ Abbr.: **MB**.

megadeath /mégədeth/ *n.* the death of one million people (esp. as a unit in estimating the casualties of war).

megahertz /mégəhərts/ *n.* one million hertz, esp. as a measure of frequency of radio transmissions. ¶ Abbr.: **MHz**.

megalith /mégəlith/ *n. Archaeol.* a large stone, esp. one placed upright as a monument or part of one. [MEGA- + Gk *lithos* stone]

megalithic /mégəlíthik/ *adj. Archaeol.* made of or marked by the use of large stones.

megalo- /mégəlō/ *comb. form* great (*megalomania*). [Gk f. *megas megal-* great]

megalomania /mégəlōmáyneeə/ *n.* **1** a mental disorder producing delusions of grandeur. **2** a passion for grandiose schemes. □□ **megalomaniac** *adj. & n.* **megalomaniacal** /-mənīəkəl/ *adj.* **megalomanic** /-mánik/ *adj.*

megalopolis /mégəlópəlis/ *n.* **1** a great city or its way of life. **2** an urban complex consisting of a city and its environs. □□ **megalopolitan** /-ləpólit'n/ *adj. & n.* [MEGA- + Gk *polis* city]

megalosaurus /mégələsáwrəs/ *n.* a large flesh-eating dinosaur of the genus *Megalosaurus*, with stout hind legs and small forelimbs. [MEGALO- + Gk *sauros* lizard]

megaphone /mégəfōn/ *n.* a large funnel-shaped device for amplifying the sound of the voice.

megapode /mégəpōd/ *n.* (also **megapod** /-pod/) any bird of the family Megapodidae, native to Australasia, that builds a mound of debris for the incubation of its eggs, e.g., a mallee fowl. [mod.L *Megapodius* (genus name) formed as MEGA- + Gk *pous podos* foot]

megaron /mégəron/ *n.* the central hall of a large Mycenaean house. [Gk, = hall]

megaspore /mégəspawr/ *n.* the larger of the two kinds of spores produced by some ferns (cf. MICROSPORE).

megastar /mégəstaar/ *n.* a very famous person, esp. in the world of entertainment.

megaton /mégətun/ *n.* a unit of explosive power equal to one million tons of TNT.

megavolt /mégəvōlt/ *n.* one million volts, esp. as a unit of electromotive force. ¶ Abbr.: **MV**.

megawatt /mégəwot/ *n.* one million watts, esp. as a measure of electrical power as generated by power stations. ¶ Abbr.: **MW**.

megilp /məgílp/ *n.* (also **magilp**) a mixture of mastic resin and linseed oil, added to oil paints, much used in the 19th c. [18th c.: orig. unkn.]

megohm /mégōm/ *n. Electr.* one million ohms. [MEGA- + OHM]

megrim[1] /meégrim/ n. **1** archaic migraine. **2** a whim, a fancy. **3** (in pl.) **a** depression; low spirits. **b** vertigo in horses, etc. [ME mygrane f. OF MIGRAINE]

megrim[2] /mégrim/ n. any deepwater flatfish of the family Lepidorhombus, esp. L. whiffiagonis. Also called sail fluke. [19th c.: orig. unkn.]

meiosis /mīōsis/ n. **1** Biol. a type of cell division that results in daughter cells with half the chromosome number of the parent cell (cf. MITOSIS). **2** = LITOTES. □□ **meiotic** /mīótik/ adj. **meiotically** /mīótiklee/ adv. [mod.L f. Gk meiōsis f. meioō lessen f. meiōn less]

Meissen /mísən/ n. a hard-paste porcelain made since 1710. [Meissen near Dresden in Germany]

Meistersinger /místərsingər/ n. (pl. same) a member of one of the 14th–16th-c. German guilds for lyric poets and musicians. [G f. Meister MASTER + Singer singer (see SING)]

meitnerium /mītnəreeəm/ n. Chem. an artificially produced chemical element, atomic number 109. ¶ Symb.: **Mt.** [for Austrian physicist Lise Meitner (1878–1968)]

melamine /méləmeen/ n. **1** a white crystalline compound that can be copolymerized with methanal to give thermosetting resins. **2** (in full **melamine resin**) a plastic made from melamine and used esp. for laminated coatings. [melam (arbitrary) + AMINE]

melancholia /mélənkőleeə/ n. a mental condition marked by depression and ill-founded fears. [LL: see MELANCHOLY]

melancholy /mélənkolee/ n. & adj. ● n. (pl. -ies) **1** a pensive sadness. **2 a** mental depression. **b** a habitual or constitutional tendency to this. **3** hist. one of the four humors; black bile (see HUMOR n. 5). ● adj. (of a person) sad, gloomy; (of a thing) saddening, depressing; (of words, a tune, etc.) expressing sadness. □□ **melancholic** /-kólik/ adj. **melancholically** /-kóliklee/ adv. [ME f. OF melancolie f. LL melancholia f. Gk melagkholia f. melas melanos black + kholē bile]

■ n. **1, 2** sadness, sorrow, misery, gloom, unhappiness, the blues, moroseness, melancholia, depression, dejection, dejectedness, despondence, despondency, downheartedness, glumness, gloominess, woefulness, lugubriousness, disconsolateness, dispiritedness, cheerlessness, mournfulness, sorrowfulness, miserableness, anguish, archaic or literary woe, literary dolor. ● adj. sad, morose, depressed, unhappy, dejected, despondent, blue, downhearted, glum, gloomy, woeful, woebegone, lugubrious, disconsolate, downcast, dispirited, low-spirited, cheerless, crestfallen, chapfallen, forlorn, heartbroken, mournful, sorrowful, miserable, dismal, low, colloq. down in the mouth, (down) in the dumps; saddening, depressing.

Melanesian /mélənéezhən, -shən/ n. & adj. ● n. **1** a member of the dominant Negroid people of Melanesia, an island group in the W. Pacific. **2** the language of this people. ● adj. of or relating to this people or their language. [Melanesia f. Gk melas black + nēsos island]

mélange /mayló́nzh/ n. a mixture, a medley. [F f. mêler mix (as MEDDLE)]

■ see MIXTURE 2.

melanin /mélənin/ n. a dark-brown to black pigment occurring in the hair, skin, and iris of the eye that is responsible for tanning of the skin when exposed to sunlight. [Gk melas melanos black + -IN]

melanism /mélənizəm/ n. an unusual darkening of body tissues caused by excessive production of melanin.

melanoma /mélənő́mə/ n. a malignant tumor of melanin-forming cells, usu. in the skin. [MELANIN + -OMA]

■ see TUMOR.

melanosis /mélənő́sis/ n. **1** = MELANISM. **2** a disorder in the body's production of melanin. □□ **melanotic** /-nótik/ adj. [mod.L f. Gk (as MELANIN)]

Melba /mélbə/ n. □ **do a Melba** Austral. sl. **1** return from retirement. **2** make several farewell appearances. **Melba sauce** a sauce made from puréed raspberries thickened with confectioners' sugar. **Melba toast** very thin crisp toast. **peach Melba** a dish of ice cream and peaches with liqueur or sauce. [Dame Nellie Melba, Austral. operatic soprano d. 1931]

meld[1] /meld/ v. & n. ● v.tr. (also absol.) (in rummy, canasta, etc.) lay down or declare (one's cards) in order to score points. ● n. a completed set or run of cards in any of these games. [G melden announce]

meld[2] /meld/ v.tr. & intr. merge, blend, combine. [perh. f. MELT + WELD[1]]

■ see BLEND v.

melee /máyláy/ n. (also **mêlée**) **1** a confused fight, skirmish, or scuffle. **2** a muddle. [F (as MEDLEY)]

■ **1** see SKIRMISH n. 1. **2** see JUMBLE n. 1.

melic /mélik/ adj. (of a poem, esp. a Gk lyric) meant to be sung. [L melicus f. Gk melikos f. melos song]

meliorate /meélyərayt, meéleeə-/ v.tr. & intr. literary improve (cf. AMELIORATE). □□ **melioration** /-ráyshən/ n. **meliorative** /-ráytiv, -rətiv/ adj. [LL meliorare (as MELIORISM)]

■ see IMPROVE 1a. □□ **melioration** see REFORM n.

meliorism /meélyərizəm, meéleeə-/ n. a doctrine that the world may be made better by human effort. □□ **meliorist** n. [L melior better + -ISM]

melisma /milízmə/ n. (pl. **melismata** /-mətə/ or **melismas**) Mus. a group of notes sung to one syllable of text. □□ **melismatic** /-mátik/ adj. [Gk]

melliferous /məlífərəs/ adj. yielding or producing honey. [L mellifer f. mel honey]

mellifluous /məlíflőōəs/ adj. (of a voice or words) pleasing, musical, flowing. □□ **mellifluence** n. **mellifluent** adj. **mellifluously** adv. **mellifluousness** n. [ME f. OF melliflue or LL mellifluus f. mel honey + fluere flow]

■ see TUNEFUL.

mellow /mélō/ adj. & v. ● adj. **1** (of sound, color, light) soft and rich, free from harshness. **2** (of character) softened or matured by age or experience. **3** genial, jovial. **4** partly intoxicated. **5** (of fruit) soft, sweet, and juicy. **6** (of wine) well-matured, smooth. **7** (of earth) rich, loamy. ● v.tr. & intr. make or become mellow. □ **mellow out** sl. relax. □□ **mellowly** adv. **mellowness** n. [ME, perh. f. attrib. use of OE melu, melw- MEAL[2]]

■ adj. **1** soft, softened, subtle, muted, pastel; musical, melodious, full, pure, rich, sweet, dulcet, mellifluous, euphonious, mature, deep. **2, 3** easygoing, genial, gentle, good-natured, easy, cordial, friendly, warm, amiable, agreeable, pleasant, cheerful, happy, jovial; see also MATURE adj. 1. **4** see DRUNK adj. 1. **5** soft, juicy, luscious, delicious, rich, sweet, flavorful, full-flavored, ready, ripe, mature, ripened, aged. **6** see SMOOTH adj. 8b. **7** see RICH 5. ● v. mature, ripen, age, season, sweeten, develop, soften.

melodeon /məlő́deeən/ n. (also **melodion**) **1** a small organ popular in the 19th c., similar to the harmonium. **2** a small German accordion, played esp. by folk musicians. [MELODY + HARMONIUM with Graecized ending]

melodic /məlódik/ adj. **1** of or relating to melody. **2** having or producing melody. □ **melodic minor** a scale with the sixth and seventh degrees raised when ascending and lowered when descending. □□ **melodically** adv. [F mélodique f. LL melodicus f. Gk melōidikos (as MELODY)]

■ see TUNEFUL.

melodious /məlő́deeəs/ adj. **1** of, producing, or having melody. **2** sweet-sounding. □□ **melodiously** adv. **melodiousness** n. [ME f. OF melodieus (as MELODY)]

■ **1** see TUNEFUL. **2** sweet(-sounding), dulcet, tuneful, euphonious, harmonious, melodic, lyrical, musical, mellifluous, mellifluent, silvery, golden.

melodist /mélədist/ n. **1** a composer of melodies. **2** a singer.

melodize /mélədīz/ v. **1** intr. make a melody or melodies; make sweet music. **2** tr. make melodious. □□ **melodizer** n.

melodrama /mélədraámə, -draámə/ n. **1** a sensational dra-

/.../ pronunciation ● part of speech
□ phrases, idioms, and compounds
□□ derivatives ■ synonym section
cross-references appear in SMALL CAPITALS or italics

matic piece with crude appeals to the emotions and usu. a happy ending. **2** the genre of drama of this type. **3** language, behavior, or an occurrence suggestive of this. **4** *hist.* a play with songs interspersed and with orchestral music accompanying the action. □□ **melodramatic** /-drəmátik/ *adj.* **melodramatically** /-drəmátiklee/ *adv.* **melodramatist** /-drámətist/ *n.* **melodramatize** /-drámətiz/ *v.tr.* [earlier *melodrame* f. F *mélodrame* f. Gk *melos* music + F *drame* DRAMA]

■ **2** fantasy, Gothic horror. **3** see DRAMA 4.
  □□ **melodramatic** sensational, sensationalistic, dramatic, stagy, theatrical, (over)sentimental, (over)sentimentalized, histrionic, overdrawn, overworked, overwrought, overdone, exaggerated, *colloq.* blood and thunder, hammy, *colloq.* schmaltzy, *sl.* hokey.

melodramatics /méldrəmátiks/ *n.pl.* melodramatic behavior, action, or writing.

melody /mélədee/ *n.* (*pl.* **-ies**) **1** an arrangement of single notes in a musically expressive succession. **2** the principal part in harmonized music. **3** a musical arrangement of words. **4** sweet music, tunefulness. [ME f. OF *melodie* f. LL *melodia* f. Gk *melōidia* f. *melos* song]

■ **1–3** song, tune, air, strain, measure, theme, refrain.
  4 tunefulness, melodiousness, euphony, harmony, musicality, sweetness.

melon /mélən/ *n.* **1** the sweet fruit of various gourds. **2** the gourd producing this (*honeydew melon*; *watermelon*). [ME f. OF f. LL *melo -onis* abbr. of L *melopepo* f. Gk *mēlopepōn* f. *mēlon* apple + *pepōn* gourd f. *pepōn* ripe]

melt[1] /melt/ *v.* & *n.* ● *v.* **1** *intr.* become liquefied by heat. **2** *tr.* change to a liquid condition by heat. **3** *tr.* (as **molten** *adj.*) (usu. of materials that require a great deal of heat to melt them) liquefied by heat (*molten lava*; *molten lead*). **4 a** *intr.* & *tr.* dissolve. **b** *intr.* (of food) be easily dissolved in the mouth. **5** *intr.* **a** (of a person, feelings, the heart, etc.) be softened as a result of pity, love, etc. **b** dissolve into tears. **6** *tr.* soften (a person, feelings, the heart, etc.) (*a look to melt a heart of stone*). **7** *intr.* (usu. foll. by *into*) change or merge imperceptibly into another form or state (*night melted into dawn*). **8** *intr.* (often foll. by *away*) (of a person) leave or disappear unobtrusively (*melted into the background*; *melted away into the crowd*). **9** *intr.* (usu. as **melting** *adj.*) (of sound) be soft and liquid (*melting chords*). **10** *intr. colloq.* (of a person) suffer extreme heat (*I'm melting in this thick sweater*). ● *n.* **1** liquid metal, etc. **2** an amount melted at any one time. **3** the process or an instance of melting. □ **melt away** disappear or make disappear by liquefaction. **melt down 1** melt (esp. metal articles) in order to reuse the raw material. **2** become liquid and lose structure (cf. MELT-DOWN). **melting point** the temperature at which any given solid will melt. **melting pot 1** a pot in which metals, etc., are melted and mixed. **2** a place where races, theories, etc., are mixed, or an imaginary pool where ideas are mixed together. □□ **meltable** *adj.* & *n.* **melter** *n.* **meltingly** *adv.* [OE *meltan, mieltan* f. Gmc, rel. to MALT]

■ *v.* **1, 2, 4** soften, thaw, liquefy, fuse, dissolve; liquidize; deliquesce. **5, 6** soften, thaw; mollify, assuage, touch, move, disarm, mellow. **7** blend, fade, merge, change, disappear, dissolve, shrink. **8** disappear, dissolve, vanish, evaporate, go away, fade, pass, shrink. **10** swelter, stifle, suffocate, burn, *colloq.* roast, bake, boil.

● *n.* **3** see THAW *n.* □ **melt away** see DISAPPEAR 1. **melt down** see MELT *v.* 1, 2, 4 above.

melt[2] /melt/ *n.* (also **milt**) the spleen in mammals, esp. cows, pigs, and other livestock.

meltdown /méltdown/ *n.* **1** the melting of (and consequent damage to) a structure, esp. the overheated core of a nuclear reactor. **2** a disastrous event, esp. a rapid fall in share prices.

melton /méltən/ *n.* cloth with a close-cut nap, used for overcoats, etc. [*Melton Mowbray* in central England]

meltwater /méltwawtər/ *n.* water formed by the melting of snow and ice, esp. from a glacier.

member /mémbər/ *n.* **1** a person, animal, plant, etc., belonging to a society, team, taxonomic group, etc. **2** a person

formally elected to take part in the proceedings of certain organizations (*Member of Congress*). **3** (also *attrib.*) a part or branch of a political body (*member state*; *a member of the United Nations*). **4** a constituent portion of a complex structure. **5** a part of a sentence, equation, group of figures, mathematical set, etc. **6 a** any part or organ of the body, esp. a limb. **b** = PENIS. □□ **membered** *adj.* (also in *comb.*). **memberless** *adj.* [ME f. OF *membre* f. L *membrum* limb]

■ **1, 3** associate, fellow. **4** see ELEMENT 1.

membership /mémbərship/ *n.* **1** being a member. **2** the number of members. **3** the body of members.

■ **1** see BELONGING 2. **2, 3** see FACULTY 4.

membrane /mémbrayn/ *n.* **1** any pliable sheetlike structure acting as a boundary, lining, or partition in an organism. **2** a thin pliable sheet or skin of various kinds. □□ **membranaceous** /-brənáyshəs/ *adj.* **membraneous** /-bráyneeəs/ *adj.* **membranous** /-brənəs/ *adj.* [L *membrana* skin of body, parchment (as MEMBER)]

■ see SHEET[1] *n.* 2a, 3.

memento /miméntō/ *n.* (*pl.* **-os** or **-oes**) an object kept as a reminder or a souvenir of a person or an event. [L, imper. of *meminisse* remember]

■ souvenir, keepsake, remembrance, reminder, relic, trophy, token; (*mementos*) memorabilia.

memento mori /məméntō máwree, -rī/ *n.* (*pl.* same) a warning or reminder of death (e.g., a skull). [L, = remember you must die]

memo /mémō/ *n.* (*pl.* **-os**) *colloq.* memorandum. [abbr.]

■ see MEMORANDUM.

memoir /mémwaar/ *n.* **1** a historical account or biography written from personal knowledge or special sources. **2** (in *pl.*) an autobiography or a written account of one's memory of certain events or people. **3 a** an essay on a learned subject specially studied by the writer. **b** (in *pl.*) the proceedings or transactions of a learned society (*Memoirs of the American Mathematical Society*). □□ **memoirist** *n.* [F *mémoire* (masc.), special use of *mémoire* (fem.) MEMORY]

■ **1** account, report, reportage, narrative, journal, record, biography, life; annals, history, chronology. **2** (*memoirs*) autobiography, reminiscences, recollections, memories, diary, journal, confessions, life story. **3 a** see ESSAY *n.* 1.

memorabilia /mémərəbileeə, -bílyə/ *n.pl.* **1** souvenirs of memorable events. **2** *archaic* memorable or noteworthy things. [L, neut. pl. (as MEMORABLE)]

■ **1** souvenirs, remembrances, reminders, relics, trophies, tokens.

memorable /mémərəbəl/ *adj.* **1** worth remembering, not to be forgotten. **2** easily remembered. □□ **memorability** /-bílitee/ *n.* **memorableness** *n.* **memorably** *adv.* [ME f. F *mémorable* or L *memorabilis* f. *memorare* bring to mind f. *memor* mindful]

■ unforgettable, catchy; noteworthy, notable, remarkable, significant, important, momentous, eventful, historic, illustrious, celebrated, worthy, great.

memorandum /mémərándəm/ *n.* (*pl.* **memoranda** /-də/ or **memorandums**) **1** a note or record made for future use. **2** an informal written message, esp. in business, diplomacy, etc. **3** *Law* a document recording the terms of a contract or other legal details. [ME f. L neut. sing. gerundive of *memorare*: see MEMORABLE]

■ **1, 2** note, record, minute, reminder, message, esp. *Brit.* chit, *colloq.* memo.

memorial /məmáwreeəl/ *n.* & *adj.* ● *n.* **1** an object, institution, or custom established in memory of a person or event (*the Albert Memorial*). **2** (often in *pl.*) *hist.* a statement of facts as the basis of a petition, etc.; a record; an informal diplomatic paper. ● *adj.* intending to commemorate a person or thing (*memorial service*). □ **Memorial Day** holiday on which those who died in war are remembered, usu. the last Monday in May. □□ **memorialist** *n.* [ME f. OF *memorial* or L *memorialis* (as MEMORY)]

■ *n.* **1** monument, marker, plaque, cenotaph, statue; remembrance, reminder. **2** see RECORD *n.* 1. ● *adj.* commemorative.

memorialize /məmáwreeəlïz/ *v.tr.* **1** commemorate. **2** address a memorial to (a person or body).
■ **1** honor, commemorate, pay homage *or* respect *or* tribute to, remember, celebrate, mark.

memorize /mémərïz/ *v.tr.* commit to memory. □□ **memorizable** *adj.* **memorization** *n.* **memorizer** *n.*
■ learn by heart *or* rote, commit to memory, learn word for word; retain, remember.

memory /méməree/ *n.* (*pl.* **-ies**) **1** the faculty by which things are recalled to or kept in the mind. **2 a** this faculty in an individual (*my memory is beginning to fail*). **b** one's store of things remembered (*buried deep in my memory*). **3** a recollection or remembrance (*the memory of better times*). **4** the storage capacity of a computer or other electronic machinery. **5** the remembrance of a person or thing (*his mother's memory haunted him*). **6 a** the reputation of a dead person (*his memory lives on*). **b** in formulaic phrases used of a dead sovereign, etc. (*of blessed memory*). **7** the length of time over which the memory or memories of any given person or group extends (*within living memory; within the memory of anyone still working here*). **8** the act of remembering (*a deed worthy of memory*). □ **commit to memory** learn (a thing) so as to be able to recall it. **from memory** without verification in books, etc. **in memory of** to keep alive the remembrance of. **memory lane** (usu. prec. by *down*, *along*) an imaginary and sentimental journey into the past. [ME f. OF *memorie*, *memoire* f. L *memoria* f. *memor* mindful, remembering, rel. to MOURN]
■ **1, 2a** recall, recollection, retention. **3, 5** recollection, remembrance; reminiscence, thought. **4** storage, RAM (random access memory), ROM (read-only memory), memory bank. **6 a** see NAME *n.* 4. **8** remembrance, recollection. □ **commit to memory** see LEARN 3.

memsahib /mémsaá-ib, -saáb/ *n. Anglo-Ind. hist.* form of address for a European married woman in India. [MA´AM + SAHIB]

men *pl.* of MAN.

menace /ménis/ *n. & v.* ● *n.* **1** a threat. **2** a dangerous or obnoxious thing or person. **3** *joc.* a pest, a nuisance. ● *v.tr. & intr.* threaten, esp. in a malignant or hostile manner. □□ **menacer** *n.* **menacing** *adj.* **menacingly** *adv.* [ME ult. f. L *minax -acis* threatening f. *minari* threaten]
■ *n.* **1** threat, danger, peril, hazard, risk; intimidation, scare, warning, commination. **2** threat, danger, peril. **3** see PEST 1. ● *v.* threaten, intimidate, daunt, terrorize, terrify, cow, bully, frighten, scare, alarm. □□ **menacing** threatening, ominous, minatory, baleful, black, dark, glowering, frightening, intimidating, lowering.

ménage /maynaázh/ *n.* the members of a household. [OF *manaige* ult. f. L (as MANSION)]
■ see FAMILY 1.

ménage à trois /maynaázh aa trwaá/ *n.* an arrangement in which three people live together, usu. a married couple and the lover of one of them. [F, = household of three (as MÉNAGE)]

menagerie /mənájəree, -názh-/ *n.* **1** a collection of wild animals in captivity for exhibition, etc. **2** the place where these are housed. [F *ménagerie* (as MÉNAGE)]
■ zoo, zoological garden, (safari) park.

menarche /menaárkee/ *n.* the onset of first menstruation. [mod.L formed as MENO- + Gk *arkhē* beginning]

mend /mend/ *v. & n.* ● *v.* **1** *tr.* restore to a sound condition; repair (a broken article, a damaged road, torn clothes, etc.). **2** *intr.* regain health; heal (as a bone). **3** *tr.* improve (*mend matters*). **4** *tr.* add fuel to (a fire). ● *n.* a darn or repair in material, etc. (*a mend in my shirt*). □ **mend one's fences** make peace with a person. **mend one's manners** improve one's behavior. **mend one's pace** go faster; alter one's pace to another's. **mend one's ways** reform, improve one's habits. **on the mend** improving in health or condition. □□ **mendable** *adj.* **mender** *n.* [ME f. AF *mender* f. *amender* AMEND]
■ *v.* **1** repair, fix, patch (up), rectify, correct, remedy, restore. **2** heal, improve, recover, convalesce, recuperate, rehabilitate, get better. **3** correct, improve,

better, reform, revise, rectify, set *or* put right, emend, *formal* ameliorate. **4** stoke, feed, fuel. ● *n.* repair, patch, darn. □ **mend one's fences** see *make up* 4. **mend one's pace** see *speed up*. **mend one's ways** reform, turn over a new leaf, go straight. **on the mend** recovering, recuperating, convalescing, convalescent, improving.

mendacious /mendáyshəs/ *adj.* lying, untruthful. □□ **mendaciously** *adv.* **mendaciousness** *n.* **mendacity** /-dásitee/ *n.* (*pl.* **-ies**). [L *mendax -dacis* perh. f. *mendum* fault]
■ see LYING². □□ **mendaciousness, mendacity** see *falsity* (FALSE).

mendelevium /méndəléeveeəm/ *n. Chem.* an artificially made transuranic radioactive metallic element. ¶ Symb.: **Md**. [D. I. *Mendeleev*, Russ. chemist d. 1907]

Mendelism /méndəlizəm/ *n.* the theory of heredity based on the recurrence of certain inherited characteristics transmitted by genes. □□ **Mendelian** /-déeleeən/ *adj. & n.* [G. J. *Mendel*, Austrian botanist d. 1884 + -ISM]

mendicant /méndikənt/ *adj. & n.* ● *adj.* **1** begging. **2** (of a friar) living solely on alms. ● *n.* **1** a beggar. **2** a mendicant friar. □□ **mendicancy** *n.* **mendicity** /-dísitee/ *n.* [L *mendicare* beg f. *mendicus* beggar f. *mendum* fault]
■ *n.* **1** see BEGGAR *n.* 1, 2.

mending /ménding/ *n.* **1** the action of a person who mends. **2** things, esp. clothes, to be mended.

menfolk /ménfōk/ *n.pl.* **1** men in general. **2** the men of one's family.

menhaden /menháyd'n/ *n.* (*pl.* same) any large herringlike fish of the genus *Brevoortia*, of the E. coast of N. America, yielding valuable oil and used for manure. [Algonquian: cf. Narragansett *munnawhatteaûg*]

menhir /ménheer/ *n. Archaeol.* a tall upright usu. prehistoric monumental stone. [Breton *men* stone + *hir* long]

menial /méeneeəl/ *adj. & n.* ● *adj.* **1** (esp. of unskilled domestic work) degrading, servile. **2** usu. *derog.* (of a servant) domestic. ● *n.* **1** a menial servant. **2** a servile person. □□ **menially** *adv.* [ME f. OF *meinee* household]
■ *adj.* lowly, servile, humble, subservient, base, low, mean, slavish, demeaning, degrading, ignoble; routine, unskilled, domestic. ● *n.* **1** lackey, serf, drudge, slave, hireling, gofer, underling, *Brit.* fag, *colloq.* dogsbody, *Brit. colloq. derog.* skivvy, *usu. derog.* flunky, *derog.* minion. **2** toady, sycophant, lickspittle, *colloq.* bootlicker, yes-man.

meningitis /méninjítis/ *n.* an inflammation of the meninges due to infection by viruses or bacteria. □□ **meningitic** /-jítik/ *adj.*

meninx /méeningks/ *n.* (*pl.* **meninges** /mənínjeez/) (usu. in *pl.*) any of the three membranes that line the skull and vertebral canal and enclose the brain and spinal cord (dura mater, arachnoid, pia mater). □□ **meningeal** /minínjeeəl/ *adj.* [mod.L f. Gk *mēnigx -iggos* membrane]

meniscus /mənískəs/ *n.* (*pl.* **menisci** /-nísï/ *or* **meniscuses**) **1** *Physics* the curved upper surface of a liquid in a tube. **2** a lens that is convex on one side and concave on the other. **3** *Math.* a crescent-shaped figure. **4** *Anat.* a cartilaginous disk within a joint, esp. the knee. □□ **meniscoid** *adj.* [mod.L f. Gk *mēniskos* crescent, dimin. of *mēnē* moon]

Mennonite /ménənït/ *n.* a member of a Protestant sect originating in Friesland in the 16th c., emphasizing adult baptism and rejecting church organization, military service, and public office. [*Menno* Simons, its founder, d. 1561]

meno- /ménō/ *comb. form* menstruation. [Gk *mēn mēnos* month]

menology /minóləjee/ *n.* (*pl.* **-ies**) a calendar, esp. that of the Greek Church, with biographies of the saints. [mod.L *menologium* f. eccl.Gk *mēnologion* f. *mēn* month + *logos* account]

/.../ **pronunciation**	● **part of speech**
□ **phrases, idioms, and compounds**	
□□ **derivatives**	■ **synonym section**
cross-references appear in SMALL CAPITALS or *italics*	

menopause /ménəpawz/ *n.* **1** the ceasing of menstruation. **2** the period in a woman's life (usu. between 45 and 50) when this occurs (see also *male menopause*). □□ **menopausal** /-páwzəl/ *adj.* [mod.L *menopausis* (as MENO-, PAUSE)]

menorah /mənáwrə, -nōrə/ *n.* a seven-armed candelabrum used in Jewish worship, esp. as a symbol of Judaism. [Heb., = candlestick]

menorrhagia /ménəráyjeeə/ *n.* abnormally heavy bleeding at menstruation. [MENO- + stem of Gk *rhēgnumi* burst]

menses /ménseez/ *n.pl.* **1** blood and other materials discharged from the uterus at menstruation. **2** the time of menstruation. [L, pl. of *mensis* month]

Menshevik /ménshəvik/ *n. hist.* a member of the non-Leninist wing of the Russian Social Democratic Workers' Party (cf. BOLSHEVIK). [Russ. *Men'shevik* a member of the minority (*men'she* less)]

mens rea /menz reéə/ *n.* criminal intent; the knowledge of wrongdoing. [L, = guilty mind]

menstrual /ménstrōōəl/ *adj.* of or relating to the menses or menstruation. □ **menstrual cycle** the process of ovulation and menstruation in female primates. [ME f. L *menstrualis* f. *mensis* month]

menstruate /ménstrōō-ayt/ *v.intr.* undergo menstruation. [LL *menstruare menstruat-* (as MENSTRUAL)]

menstruation /ménstrōō-áyshən/ *n.* the process of discharging blood and other materials from the uterus in sexually mature nonpregnant women at intervals of about one lunar month until the menopause.

menstruous /ménstrōōəs/ *adj.* **1** of or relating to the menses. **2** menstruating. [ME f. OF *menstrueus* or LL *menstruosus* (as MENSTRUAL)]

menstruum /ménstrōōəm/ *n.* (*pl.* **menstruums** or **menstrua** /-strōōə/) a solvent. [ME f. L, neut. of *menstruus* monthly f. *mensis* month f. the alchemical parallel between transmutation into gold and the supposed action of menses on the ovum]

mensurable /ménshərəbəl, -sə-/ *adj.* **1** measurable, having fixed limits. **2** *Mus.* = MENSURAL 2. [F *mensurable* or LL *mensurabilis* f. *mensurare* to measure f. L *mensura* MEASURE]

mensural /ménshərəl, -sə-/ *adj.* **1** of or involving measure. **2** *Mus.* of or involving a fixed rhythm or notes of definite duration (cf. PLAINSONG). [L *mensuralis* f. *mensura* MEASURE]

mensuration /ménshəráyshən, -sə-/ *n.* **1** measuring. **2** *Math.* the measuring of geometric magnitudes such as the lengths of lines, areas of surfaces, and volumes of solids. [LL *mensuratio* (as MENSURABLE)]

menswear /ménzwair/ *n.* clothes for men.

-ment /mənt/ *suffix* **1** forming nouns expressing the means or result of the action of a verb (*abridgment*; *embankment*). **2** forming nouns from adjectives (*merriment*; *oddment*). [from or after F f. L *-mentum*]

mental / mént'l/ *adj. & n.* ● *adj.* **1** of or in the mind. **2** done by the mind. **3** *colloq.* **a** insane. **b** crazy, wild, eccentric (*is mental about pop music*). □ **mental age** the degree of a person's mental development expressed as an age at which the same degree is attained by an average person. **mental cruelty** the infliction of suffering on another's mind, esp. *Law* as grounds for divorce. **mental deficiency** imperfect mental development leading to abnormally low intelligence. **mental hospital** (or **institution**) an establishment for the care of mental patients. **mental illness** a disorder of the mind. **mental patient** a sufferer from mental illness. **mental reservation** a qualification tacitly added in making a statement, etc. □□ **mentally** *adv.* [ME f. OF *mental* or LL *mentalis* f. L *mens -ntis* mind]

■ *adj.* **1, 2** intellectual, cognitive, cerebral, comprehensive, perceptual, rational, conceptual, theoretical, noetic, abstract. **3 a** lunatic, mad, psychotic, demented, mentally ill, unstable, unbalanced, deranged, disturbed; (*often derog.*) *colloq.* crazy, certifiable, dotty, esp. *Brit. colloq.* daft, *sl.* off one's rocker, nutty, batty, loony, screwy, bonkers, nuts, bananas, loco, *Austral. sl.* not the full quid, *Brit. sl.* barmy, crackers.

mentalism /mént'lizəm/ *n.* **1** *Philos.* the theory that physical

and psychological phenomena are ultimately only explicable in terms of a creative and interpretative mind. **2** *Psychol.* the primitive tendency to personify in spirit form the forces of nature, or endow inert objects with the quality of "soul." □□ **mentalist** *n.* **mentalistic** /-lístik/ *adj.*

mentality /mentálitee/ *n.* (*pl.* **-ies**) **1** mental character or disposition. **2** kind or degree of intelligence. **3** what is in or of the mind.

■ **1** inclination, attitude, bent, mind-set, disposition, character, frame of mind, temperament, outlook, view. **2** intelligence, brain, capacity, intellect, wit, sense, judgment, acuity, acumen, IQ, rationality, understanding, mental age. **3** intellectualism, intellectuality, rationality, rationalism, rationalization.

mentation /mentáyshən/ *n.* **1** mental action. **2** state of mind. [L *mens -ntis* mind]

menthol /ménthawl/ *n.* a mint-tasting organic alcohol found in oil of peppermint, etc., used as a flavoring and to relieve local pain. [G f. L *mentha* MINT¹]

mentholated /ménthəlaytid/ *adj.* treated with or containing menthol.

mention /ménshən/ *v. & n.* ● *v.tr.* **1** refer to briefly. **2** specify by name. **3** reveal or disclose (*do not mention this to anyone*). **4** *Brit.* (in dispatches) award (a person) an honor for meritorious, usu. gallant, military service. ● *n.* **1** a reference, esp. by name, to a person or thing. **2** *Brit.* (in dispatches) a military honor awarded for outstanding conduct. □ **don't mention it** said in polite dismissal of an apology or thanks. **make mention** (or **no mention**) **of** refer (or not refer) to. **not to mention** introducing a fact or thing of secondary or (as a rhetorical device) of primary importance. □□ **mentionable** *adj.* [OF f. L *mentio -onis* f. the root of *mens* mind]

■ *v.* **1, 2** speak *or* write about, refer to, allude to, touch on *or* upon, make mention of, talk of, bring up *or* in, introduce, broach, call *or* direct attention to, note, name, cite, acknowledge; point out, indicate, make known, adduce, report, quote. **3** divulge, reveal, intimate, disclose, impart, suggest, hint at, imply, insinuate. ● *n.* **1** reference, referral, allusion, note, citation, mentioning; announcement, remark. **2** citation; recognition, tribute, acknowledgment, praise. □ **don't mention it** (it was a) pleasure; see also *no sweat* (SWEAT). **make mention of** see REFER 7, 8. **make no mention of** see OMIT 1.

mentor /méntawr/ *n.* an experienced and trusted adviser. [F f. L f. Gk *Mentōr* adviser of the young Telemachus in Homer's *Odyssey* and Fénelon's *Télémaque*]

■ see ADVISER.

menu /ményōō/ *n.* **1 a** a list of dishes available in a restaurant, etc. **b** a list of items to be served at a meal. **2** *Computing* a list of options showing the commands or facilities available. □ **menu-driven** (of a program or computer) used by making selections from menus. [F, = detailed list, f. L *minutus* MINUTE²]

meow /mee-ów/ *n. & v.* ● *n.* the characteristic cry of a cat. ● *v.intr.* make this cry. [imit.]

■ *n.* meow, mew; caterwaul. ● *v.* meow, mew, miaul; caterwaul.

meperidine /mepérədeen/ *n.* a narcotic compound, $C_{15}H_{21}NO_2$, used as an analgesic, sedative, and antispasmodic.

Mephistopheles /méfistófəleez/ *n.* **1** an evil spirit to whom Faust, in the German legend, sold his soul. **2** a fiendish person. □□ **Mephistophelean** /-leéən/ *adj.* **Mephistophelian** /-feéleeən/ *adj.* [G (16th c.), of unkn. orig.]

■ □□ **Mephistophelian** see SATANIC.

mephitis /məfítis/ *n.* **1** a noxious emanation, esp. from the earth. **2** a foul-smelling or poisonous stench. □□ **mephitic** /-fítik/ *adj.* [L]

■ see STENCH. □□ **mephitic** see STINKING *adj.* 1.

-mer /mər/ *comb. form* denoting a substance of a specified class, esp. a polymer (*dimer*; *isomer*; *tautomer*). [Gk *meros* part, share]

mercantile /mérkəntil/ *adj.* **1** of trade, trading. **2** commercial. **3** mercenary, fond of bargaining. □ **mercantile ma-**

rine shipping employed in commerce not war. [F f. It. f. *mercante* MERCHANT]

■ **1, 2** commercial, business, trade, trading, marketing, market. **3** see MERCENARY *adj.*

mercantilism /mərkəntilizəm/ *n.* an old economic theory that money is the only form of wealth. □□ **mercantilist** *n.*

mercaptan /mərkáptən/ *n.* = THIOL. [mod.L *mercurium captans* capturing mercury]

Mercator projection /mərkáytər/ *n.* (also **Mercator's projection**) a projection of a map of the world onto a cylinder so that all the parallels of latitude have the same length as the equator, first published in 1569 and used esp. for marine charts and certain climatological maps. [G. *Mercator* (Latinized f. Kremer), Flemish-born geographer d. 1594]

mercenary /mársəneree/ *adj. & n.* ● *adj.* primarily concerned with money or other reward (*mercenary motives*). ● *n.* (*pl.* **-ies**) a hired soldier in foreign service. □□ **mercenariness** *n.* [ME f. L *mercenarius* f. *merces -edis* reward]

■ *adj.* grasping, greedy, acquisitive, covetous, predatory, avaricious, moneygrubbing. ● *n.* soldier of fortune, *usu. derog.* hireling.

mercer /mársər/ *n. Brit.* a dealer in textile fabrics, esp. silk and other costly materials. □□ **mercery** *n.* (*pl.* **-ies**). [ME f. AF *mercer*, OF *mercier* ult. f. L *merx mercis* goods]

mercerize /mársəriz/ *v.tr.* treat (cotton fabric or thread) under tension with caustic alkali to give greater strength and impart luster. □□ **mercerization** *n.* [J. *Mercer*, alleged inventor of the process d. 1866]

merchandise /márchəndiz/ *n. & v.* ● *n.* goods for sale. ● *v.* **1** *intr.* trade, traffic. **2** *tr.* trade or traffic in. **3** *tr.* **a** put on the market, promote the sale of (goods, etc.). **b** advertise, publicize (an idea or person). □□ **merchandisable** *adj.* **merchandiser** *n.* [ME f. OF *marchandise* f. *marchand*: see MERCHANT]

■ *n.* goods, commodities, products, stock, staples, produce. ● *v.* **1, 2** trade, deal, traffic, distribute, retail, (buy and) sell. **3** promote, advertise, publicize, market.

merchant /márchənt/ *n.* **1** a retail trader; dealer; storekeeper. **2** esp. *Brit.* a wholesale trader, esp. with foreign countries. **3** *colloq.* usu. *derog.* a person showing a partiality for a specified activity or practice (*speed merchant*). □ **merchant bank** esp. *Brit.* a bank dealing in commercial loans and finance. **merchant marine** a nation's commercial shipping. **merchant ship** = MERCHANTMAN. [ME f. OF *marchand, marchant* ult. f. L *mercari* trade f. *merx mercis* merchandise]

■ **1** dealer, retailer, seller, shopkeeper, store owner, trader, tradesman, tradeswoman, vendor. **2** distributor, wholesaler, broker, agent, factor, forwarder; businessman, businesswoman, merchant prince, tycoon, magnate, baron, *US* jobber, *colloq.* mogul. **3** see FREAK *n.* 3b.

merchantable /márchəntəbəl/ *adj.* salable; marketable. [ME f. *merchant* (v.) f. OF *marchander* f. *marchand*: see MERCHANT]

merchantman /márchəntmən/ *n.* (*pl.* **-men**) a ship conveying merchandise.

merciful /mársifool/ *adj.* having, showing, or feeling mercy. □□ **mercifulness** *n.*

■ compassionate, sympathetic, forgiving, kind, kindly, clement, kindhearted, forbearing, sparing, lenient, tender, humane, mild, tenderhearted, softhearted, gracious, generous, magnanimous, benignant, beneficent, charitable, considerate, indulgent, *often iron.* big.

mercifully /mársifoolee/ *adv.* **1** in a merciful manner. **2** (qualifying a whole sentence) fortunately (*mercifully, the sun came out*).

■ **2** see *happily* (HAPPY).

merciless /mársilis/ *adj.* **1** pitiless. **2** showing no mercy. □□ **mercilessly** *adv.* **mercilessness** *n.*

■ cruel, pitiless, ruthless, heartless, unmerciful, inhumane, inhuman, brutal, savage, barbarous, barbaric, barbarian, crude, rude, rough, harsh, tough, callous, hard, hard-hearted, tyrannical, stonyhearted, cold, severe, unsparing, unsympathetic, unforgiving,

malevolent, uncharitable, unmoved, unbending, inflexible, relentless, unrelenting, inexorable.

mercurial /mərkyŏŏreeəl/ *adj. & n.* ● *adj.* **1** (of a person) sprightly, ready-witted, volatile. **2** of or containing mercury. **3** (**Mercurial**) of the planet Mercury. ● *n.* a drug containing mercury. □□ **mercurialism** *n.* **mercuriality** /-reeálitee/ *n.* **mercurially** *adv.* [ME f. OF *mercuriel* or L *mercurialis* (as MERCURY)]

■ *adj.* **1** see VOLATILE *adj.* 2. □□ **mercuriality** see *inconstancy* (INCONSTANT).

mercury /márkyəree/ *n.* **1** *Chem.* a silvery-white heavy liquid metallic element occurring naturally in cinnabar and used in barometers, thermometers, and amalgams; quicksilver. ¶ Symb.: **Hg. 2** (**Mercury**) the planet nearest to the sun. **3** any plant of the genus *Mercurialis*, esp. *M. perenne*. □ **mercury vapor lamp** a lamp in which light is produced by an electric discharge through mercury vapor. □□ **mercuric** /-kyŏŏrik/ *adj.* **mercurous** *adj.* [ME f. L *Mercurius* messenger of the gods and god of traders f. *merx mercis* merchandise]

mercy /mársee/ *n. & int.* ● *n.* (*pl.* **-ies**) **1** compassion or forbearance shown to enemies or offenders in one's power. **2** the quality of compassion. **3** an act of mercy. **4** (*attrib.*) administered or performed out of mercy or pity for a suffering person (*mercy killing*). **5** something to be thankful for (*small mercies*). ● *int.* expressing surprise or fear. □ **at the mercy of 1** wholly in the power of. **2** liable to danger or harm from. **have mercy on** (or **upon**) show mercy to. **mercy killing** = EUTHANASIA. [ME f. OF *merci* f. L *merces -edis* reward, in LL pity, thanks]

■ *n.* **1, 2** compassion, forbearance, pity, quarter, tolerance, sympathy, favor, forgiveness, kindness, kindliness, leniency, tenderness, humanity, humaneness, liberality, kindheartedness, tenderheartedness, softheartedness, graciousness, generosity, magnanimity, benignity, beneficence, charity, thoughtfulness, consideration, indulgence. **3** errand of mercy, kindness, favor. **4** see MERCIFUL. **5** see LUCK 3. ● *int.* see BOY *int.* □ **at the mercy of 1** in the power of, under a person's thumb. **have mercy on** (or **upon**) see SPARE *v.* 2a.

mere[1] /meer/ *attrib.adj.* (**merest**) that is solely or no more or better than what is specified (*a mere boy; no mere theory*). □ **mere right** *Law* a right in theory. □□ **merely** *adv.* [ME f. AF *meer*, OF *mier* f. L *merus* unmixed]

■ bare, basic, sheer, simple, very; least, nothing but. □□ **merely** only, simply, solely, purely, no more than; barely, scarcely.

mere[2] /meer/ *n. archaic* or *poet.* a lake or pond. [OE f. Gmc]

meretricious /méritríshəs/ *adj.* **1** (of decorations, literary style, etc.) showily but falsely attractive. **2** of or befitting a prostitute. □□ **meretriciously** *adv.* **meretriciousness** *n.* [L *meretricius* f. *meretrix -tricis* prostitute f. *merēri* be hired]

■ **1** see GAUDY[1].

merganser /mərgánsər/ *n.* any of various diving fish-eating northern ducks of the genus *Mergus*, with a long narrow serrated hooked bill. [mod.L f. L *mergus* diver f. *mergere* dive + *anser* goose]

merge /mərj/ *v.* **1** *tr. & intr.* (often foll. by *with*) **a** combine or be combined. **b** join or blend gradually. **2** *intr. & tr.* (foll. by *in*) lose or cause to lose character and identity in (something else). **3** *tr.* (foll. by *in*) embody (a title or estate) in (a larger one). □□ **mergence** *n.* [L *mergere mers-* dip, plunge, partly through legal AF *merger*]

■ **1** combine, coalesce, unite, join, amalgamate, consolidate, blend, mix, mingle, fuse, conflate, *literary* commingle; pool.

merger /márjər/ *n.* **1** the combining of two commercial companies, etc., into one. **2** a merging, esp. of one estate in another. **3** *Law* the absorbing of a minor offense in a greater one. [AF (as MERGE)]

■ **1, 2** combination, coalescence, union, amalgamation, consolidation, coalition, merging, pooling, blending, mixing, mingling, fusing, fusion, *literary* commingling.

meridian /mərídeeən/ *n. & adj.* ● *n.* **1** a circle passing through the celestial poles and zenith of any place on the earth's surface. **2 a** a circle of constant longitude, passing through a given place and the terrestrial poles. **b** the corresponding line on a map. **3** *archaic* the point at which a sun or star attains its highest altitude. **4** prime; full splendor. ● *adj.* **1** of noon. **2** of the period of greatest splendor, vigor, etc. [ME f. OF *meridien* or L *meridianus* (adj.) f. *meridies* midday f. *medius* middle + *dies* day]

■ *n.* **3, 4** see ZENITH.

meridional /mərídeeənəl/ *adj. & n.* ● *adj.* **1** of or in the south (esp. of Europe). **2** of or relating to a meridian. ● *n.* an inhabitant of the south (esp. of France). [ME f. OF f. LL *meridionalis* irreg. f. L *meridies*: see MERIDIAN]

meringue /məráng/ *n.* **1** a confection of sugar, egg whites, etc., baked crisp. **2** a small cake or shell of this, usu. decorated or filled with whipped cream, etc. [F, of unkn. orig.]

merino /məreenō/ *n.* (*pl.* **-os**) **1** (in full **merino sheep**) a variety of sheep with long fine wool. **2** a soft woolen or wool-and-cotton material like cashmere, orig. of merino wool. **3** a fine woolen yarn. [Sp., of uncert. orig.]

meristem /méristem/ *n. Bot.* a plant tissue consisting of actively dividing cells forming new tissue. □□ **meristematic** /-stəmátik/ *adj.* [Gk *meristos* divisible f. *merizō* divide f. *meros* part, after *xylem*]

merit /mérit/ *n. & v.* ● *n.* **1** the quality of deserving well. **2** excellence, worth. **3** (usu. in *pl.*) **a** a thing that entitles one to reward or gratitude. **b** esp. *Law* intrinsic rights and wrongs (*the merits of a case*). **4** *Theol.* good deeds as entitling to a future reward. ● *v.tr.* deserve or be worthy of (reward, punishment, consideration, etc.). □ **make a merit of** regard or represent (one's own conduct) as praiseworthy. **merit system** a policy of hiring and promoting (esp. public) employees based on their abilities rather than political favoritism, seniority, etc. **on its merits** with regard only to its intrinsic worth. [ME f. OF *merite* f. L *meritum* price, value, = past part. of *merēri* earn, deserve]

■ *n.* **1, 2** worth, worthiness, value, excellence, quality, virtue, good, goodness. **3** (*merits*) **a** assets, advantage(s). **b** rights and wrongs. ● *v.* earn, deserve, warrant, rate, have a right *or* claim to, be entitled to, be qualified for, be worthy of. □ **make a merit of** sing the praises of, praise; see GLORIFY 3.

meritocracy /méritókrəsee/ *n.* (*pl.* **-ies**) **1** government by persons selected competitively according to merit. **2** a group of persons selected in this way. **3** a society governed by meritocracy.

meritorious /méritáwreeəs/ *adj.* **1** (of a person or act) having merit; deserving reward, praise, or gratitude. **2** deserving commendation for thoroughness, etc. □□ **meritoriously** *adv.* **meritoriousness** *n.* [ME f. L *meritorius* f. *merēri* merit-earn]

■ honorable, laudable, praiseworthy, commendable, creditable, admirable, estimable, excellent, exemplary, outstanding.

merle /mərl/ *n.* (also **merl**) *Sc.* or *archaic* a blackbird. [ME f. F f. L *merula*]

merlin /mərlin/ *n.* a small European or N. American falcon, *Falco columbarius*, that hunts small birds. [ME f. AF *merilun* f. OF *esmerillon* augment. f. *esmeril* f. Frank.]

merlon /mərlən/ *n.* the solid part of an embattled parapet between two embrasures. [F f. It. *merlone* f. *merlo* battlement]

mermaid /mərmayd/ *n.* an imaginary half-human sea creature, with the head and trunk of a woman and the tail of a fish. [ME f. MERE[2] in obs. sense 'sea' + MAID]

merman /mərman/ *n.* (*pl.* **-men**) the male equivalent of a mermaid.

mero- /mérō/ *comb. form* partly, partial. [Gk *meros* part]

-merous /mərəs/ *comb. form* esp. *Bot.* having so many parts (*dimerous*). [Gk (as MERO-)]

Merovingian /mérəvínjeeən, -jən/ *adj. & n.* ● *adj.* of or relating to the Frankish dynasty founded by Clovis and reigning in Gaul and Germany *c.*500–750. ● *n.* a member of this dynasty. [F *mérovingien* f. med.L *Merovingi* f. L *Meroveus* name of the reputed founder]

merriment /mérimənt/ *n.* **1** exuberant enjoyment; being merry. **2** mirth, fun.

■ jollity, joviality, merrymaking, revelry, gaiety, high *or* good spirits, mirth, mirthfulness, joyfulness, felicity, jubilation, festivity, exhilaration, buoyancy, exuberance, cheer, cheerfulness, glee, fun, hilarity, enjoyment, happiness.

merry /méree/ *adj.* (**merrier, merriest**) **1 a** joyous. **b** full of laughter or gaiety. **2** *Brit. colloq.* slightly drunk. □ **make merry 1** be festive; enjoy oneself. **2** (foll. by *over*) make fun of. □□ **merrily** *adv.* **merriness** *n.* [OE *myrige* f. Gmc]

■ **1** cheerful, happy, gay, cheery, jolly, jovial, in high *or* good spirits, mirthful, joyful, joyous, hilarious, jubilant, gamesome, festive, exuberant, vivacious, convivial, buoyant, gleeful, carefree, lighthearted, delighted, *poet.* blithe. □ **make merry 1** celebrate, carouse, frolic; see also REVEL *v.* 1. **2** see TEASE *v.* **merry andrew** see CLOWN *n.* 1.

merry-go-round /méreegōrownd/ *n.* **1** a revolving machine with wooden horses or other animals, etc., for riding on at an amusement park, etc. **2** a cycle of bustling activities.

■ **1** carousel, whirligig, *Brit.* roundabout.

merrymaking /méreemayking/ *n.* festivity, fun. □□ **merrymaker** *n.*

■ see FUN *n.* 3.

merrythought /méreethawt/ *n.* esp. *Brit.* the wishbone of a cooked chicken, etc.

mesa /máysə/ *n.* an isolated flat-topped hill with steep sides, found in landscapes with horizontal strata. [Sp., lit. table, f. L *mensa*]

mésalliance /mayzáleeəns, máyzalyaáns/ *n.* a marriage with a person of a lower social position. [F (as MIS-[2], ALLIANCE)]

mescal /méskal/ *n.* **1 a** a maguey. **b** liquor obtained from this. **2** a peyote cactus. □ **mescal buttons** disk-shaped dried tops from the peyote cactus, eaten or chewed as an intoxicant and hallucinogen. [Sp. *mezcal* f. Nahuatl *mexcalli*]

mescaline /méskəleen, -lin/ *n.* (also **mescalin** /-lin/) a hallucinogenic alkaloid present in mescal buttons.

mesdames *pl.* of MADAME.

mesdemoiselles *pl.* of MADEMOISELLE.

mesembryanthemum /mizémbreeánthiməm/ *n.* any of various succulent plants of the genus *Mesembryanthemum* of S. Africa, having daisylike flowers in a wide range of bright colors that open fully in sunlight. [mod.L f. Gk *mesembria* noon + *anthemon* flower]

mesencephalon /mésenséfəlon, méz-/ *n.* the part of the brain developing from the middle of the primitive or embryonic brain. Also called MIDBRAIN. [Gk *mesos* middle + *encephalon* brain: see ENCEPHALIC]

mesentery /mésəntéree, méz-/ *n.* (*pl.* **-ies**) a double layer of peritoneum attaching the stomach, small intestine, pancreas, spleen, and other abdominal organs to the posterior wall of the abdomen. □□ **mesenteric** /-térik/ *adj.* **mesenteritis** /-rítis/ *n.* [med.L *mesenterium* f. Gk *mesenterion* (as MESO-, *enteron* intestine)]

mesh /mesh/ *n. & v.* ● *n.* **1** a network fabric or structure. **2** each of the open spaces or interstices between the strands of a net or sieve, etc. **3** (in *pl.*) **a** a network. **b** a snare. **4** (in *pl.*) *Physiol.* an interlaced structure. ● *v.* **1** *intr.* (often foll. by *with*) (of the teeth of a wheel) be engaged (with others). **2** *intr.* be harmonious. **3** *tr.* catch in or as in a net. □ **in mesh** (of the teeth of wheels) engaged. [earlier *meish*, etc. f. MDu. *maesche* f. Gmc]

■ *n.* **1–3a** meshwork, network, netting, net, web, webbing, lattice, latticework, screen, screening, interlacing, lacework, grid, grate, grating, trellis, trelliswork, decussation, reticulation, reticle, reticulum, graticule, plexus, *Anat.* rete; interstice. **3 b** (*meshes*) grip, clutch(es), grasp, web, trap, snare, entanglement, tangle. ● *v.* **1** engage, fit (together), dovetail, knit, enmesh, match, interlock. **2** see JELL 2. **3** catch, entangle, enmesh, grab, trap, entrap, snare, ensnare; involve, implicate.

mesial /méezeeəl/ *adj. Anat.* of, in, or directed toward the middle line of a body. □□ **mesially** *adv.* [irreg. f. Gk *mesos* middle]

mesmerism /mézmərizəm/ *n.* **1** *Psychol.* **a** a hypnotic state produced in a person by another's influence over the will and nervous system. **b** a doctrine concerning this. **c** an influence producing this. **2** fascination. □□ **mesmeric** /mezmérik/ *adj.* **mesmerically** /-mériklee/ *adv.* **mesmerist** *n.* [F. A. *Mesmer*, Austrian physician d. 1815]
■ **2** see SPELL² 2.

mesmerize /mézməriz/ *v.tr.* **1** *Psychol.* hypnotize; exercise mesmerism on. **2** fascinate, spellbind. □□ **mesmerization** *n.* **mesmerizer** *n.* **mesmerizingly** *adv.*
■ **2** see FASCINATE 1.

mesne /meen/ *adj. Law* intermediate. □ **mesne lord** *Engl. hist.* a lord holding an estate from a superior feudal lord. **mesne profits** profits received from an estate by a tenant between two dates. [ME f. law F, var. of AF *meen*, MEAN³: cf. DEMESNE]

meso- /mésō, méz-/ *comb. form* middle, intermediate. [Gk *mesos* middle]

mesoblast /mésəblast, méz-/ *n. Biol.* the middle germ layer of an embryo.

mesoderm /mésəderm, méz-/ *n. Biol.* = MESOBLAST. [MESO- + Gk *derma* skin]

mesolithic /mézəlíthik, més-/ *adj. Archaeol.* of or concerning the Stone Age between the Paleolithic and Neolithic periods. [MESO- + Gk *lithos* stone]

mesomorph /mézəmawrf, més-/ *n.* a person with a compact and muscular build of body (cf. ECTOMORPH, ENDOMORPH). □□ **mesomorphic** /-máwrfik/ *adj.* [MESO- + Gk *morphē* form]
■ □□ **mesomorphic** see MUSCULAR.

meson /mézon, més-, méezon, -son/ *n. Physics* any of a class of elementary particles believed to participate in the forces that hold nucleons together in the atomic nucleus. □□ **mesic** /mézik, més-, méezik, -sik/ *adj.* **mesonic** /mezónik/ *adj.* [earlier *mesotron*: cf. MESO-, -ON]

mesophyll /mésəfil, méz-/ *n.* the inner tissue of a leaf. [MESO- + Gk *phullon* leaf]

mesophyte /mésəfit, méz-/ *n.* a plant needing only a moderate amount of water.

mesosphere /mésəsfeer, méz-/ *n.* the region of the atmosphere extending from the top of the stratosphere to an altitude of about 50 miles.

Mesozoic /mésəzṓ-ik, méz-/ *adj. & n. Geol.* ● *adj.* of or relating to an era of geological time marked by the development of dinosaurs, and with evidence of the first mammals, birds, and flowering plants. ¶ Cf. Appendix VII. ● *n.* this era (cf. CENOZOIC, PALEOZOIC). [MESO- + Gk *zōion* animal]

mesquite /meskéet/ *n.* **1** any N. American leguminous tree of the genus *Prosopis*, esp. *P. juliflora*. **2** the wood of the mesquite, as used in grilling food. □ **mesquite bean** a pod from the mesquite, used as fodder. [Mex. Sp. *mezquite*]

mess /mes/ *n. & v.* ● *n.* **1** a dirty or untidy state of things (*the room is a mess*). **2** a state of confusion, embarrassment, or trouble. **3** something causing a mess, e.g., spilled liquid, etc. **4** a domestic animal's excreta. **5 a** a company of persons who take meals together, esp. in the armed forces. **b** a place where such meals or recreation take place communally. **c** a meal taken there. **6** *derog.* a disagreeable concoction or medley. **7** *Brit.* a liquid or mixed food for hounds, etc. **8** a portion of liquid or pulpy food. ● *v.* **1** *tr.* (often foll. by *up*) **a** make a mess of; dirty. **b** muddle; make into a state of confusion. **2** *intr.* (foll. by *with*) interfere with. **3** *intr.* take one's meals. **4** *intr. colloq.* defecate. □ **make a mess of** bungle (an undertaking). **mess about** (or **around**) **1** act desultorily. **2** *colloq.* make things awkward for; cause arbitrary inconvenience to (a person). **3** philander. **4** associate, esp. for immoral purposes. **mess hall** a communal, esp. military, din-

ing area. **mess jacket** a short close-fitting coat worn as part of a military, etc. uniform. **mess kit** a soldier's cooking and eating utensils. [ME f. OF *mes* portion of food f. LL *missus* course at dinner, past part. of *mittere* send]
■ *n.* **1** chaos, disorder, disarray, disorganization, muddle, disarrangement, clutter, hodgepodge, litter, tangle, jumble, confusion, mishmash, *colloq.* shambles; untidiness. **2** predicament, difficulty, plight, trouble, quandary, imbroglio, foul-up, pretty kettle of fish, *colloq.* stew, fix, hot water, pickle, jam, can of worms, *disp.* dilemma, *sl.* screwup, snafu. **5 b** mess hall, canteen, refectory. **6** concoction, mixture, medley, miscellany, hash, hodgepodge, gallimaufry, farrago, olio, olla podrida. ● *v.* **1** dirty, clutter up, make untidy, turn upside down, pull to pieces, upset, muddle, disarrange, disarray, dishevel, tousle, *colloq.* muss (up); ruin, destroy, wreck, bungle, botch, foul up, *colloq.* make a hash or shambles of, *Brit. colloq.* muck up. **2** (*mess with*) interfere in or with, intervene in, meddle with or in, intrude in, butt in or into, tinker with, tamper with, get involved in or with. **3** see EAT 1b. **4** see DEFECATE. □ **make a mess of** see BOTCH *v.* 1. **mess about** (or **around**) **1** fool or play (about or around), poke or fiddle about or around, potter (about or around), *Brit. colloq.* muck about or around; dally, waste time, dawdle, loiter, *sl.* lollygag. **2** cause trouble, cause complications for, create difficulties for, *Brit. colloq.* muck about or around. **mess hall** mess, canteen, refectory.

message /mésij/ *n. & v.* ● *n.* **1** an oral or written communication sent by one person to another. **2 a** an inspired or significant communication from a prophet, writer, or preacher. **b** the central import or meaning of an artistic work, etc. **3** a mission or errand. ● *v.tr.* **1** send as a message. **2** transmit (a plan, etc.) by signaling, etc. □ **get the message** *colloq.* understand what is meant. **message center** area, or system as in an office, for the receiving and dispatching of telephone, electronic, and postal communications. **message stick** *Austral.* a stick carved with significant marks, carried as identification by aboriginal messengers. **message unit** a measurement of time and distance of telephone calls, usu. for billing purposes. [ME f. OF ult. f. L *mittere miss-* send]
■ *n.* **1** communication, bulletin, report, communiqué, news, dispatch, information, word, intelligence, *literary* tidings; note, letter, memorandum, *joc.* missive. **2 b** idea, point, import, meaning, essence, implication. **3** see MISSION 1a.

messeigneurs *pl.* of MONSEIGNEUR.

messenger /mésinjər/ *n.* **1** a person who carries a message. **2** a person employed to carry messages. □ **King's** (or **Queen's**) **Messenger** (in the UK) a courier in the diplomatic service. **messenger RNA** a form of RNA carrying genetic information from DNA to a ribosome. ¶ Abbr.: **mRNA**. [ME & OF *messager* (as MESSAGE): -*n*- as in *harbinger*, *passenger*, etc.]
■ envoy, emissary, nuncio, intermediary, go-between, *archaic* legate; page, courier, runner, *sl.* gofer; herald, harbinger.

Messiah /misíə/ *n.* **1** (also **messiah**) a liberator or would-be liberator of an oppressed people or country. **2 a** the promised deliverer of the Jews. **b** (usu. prec. by *the*) Christ regarded as this. □□ **Messiahship** *n.* [ME f. OF *Messie* ult. f. Heb. *māšīaḥ* anointed]
■ **1** deliverer, liberator, emancipator, savior, redeemer, rescuer.

Messianic /méseeánik/ *adj.* **1** of the Messiah. **2** inspired by hope or belief in a Messiah. □□ **Messianism** /mesíənizəm/ *n.* [F *messianique* (as MESSIAH) after *rabbinique* rabbinical]

/.../ pronunciation	● part of speech
□ phrases, idioms, and compounds	
□□ derivatives	■ synonym section
cross-references appear in SMALL CAPITALS or *italics*	

939

messieurs *pl.* of MONSIEUR.

messmate /mésmayt/ *n.* a person with whom one regularly takes meals, esp. in the armed forces.

messrs. /mésərz/ *pl.* of MR. [abbr. of MESSIEURS]

messuage /méswij/ *n. Law* a dwelling house with outbuildings and land assigned to its use. [ME f. AF: perh. an alternative form of *mesnage* dwelling]

messy /mésee/ *adj.* (**messier, messiest**) **1** untidy or dirty. **2** causing or accompanied by a mess. **3** difficult to deal with; full of awkward complications. □□ **messily** *adv.* **messiness** *n.*

■ **1, 2** see UNTIDY.

mestizo /mesteézō/ *n.* (*pl.* **-os**; *fem.* **mestiza** /-zə/, *pl.* **-as**) a Spaniard or Portuguese of mixed race, esp. the offspring of a Spaniard and a Native American. [Sp. ult. f. L *mixtus* past part. of *miscēre* mix]

Met /met/ *n.* (in full **the Met**) *colloq.* the Metropolitan Opera House in New York. [abbr.]

met *past* and *past part.* of MEET[1].

met. /met/ *abbr.* **1** meteorology; meteorological. **2** metropolitan. **3** metaphor; metaphoric.

meta- /métə/ *comb. form* (usu. **met-** before a vowel or *h*) **1** denoting change of position or condition (*metabolism*). **2** denoting position: **a** behind. **b** after or beyond (*metaphysics*; *metacarpus*). **c** of a higher or second-order kind (*metalanguage*). **3** *Chem.* **a** relating to two carbon atoms separated by one another in a benzene ring. **b** relating to a compound formed by dehydration (*metaphosphate*). [Gk *meta-*, *met-*, *meth-* f. *meta* with, after]

metabolism /mətábəlizəm/ *n.* all the chemical processes that occur within a living organism, resulting in energy production (CATABOLISM) and growth (ANABOLISM). □□ **metabolic** /métəbólik/ *adj.* **metabolically** /métəbóliklee/ *adv.* [Gk *metabolē* change (as META-, *bolē* f. *ballō* throw)]

metabolite /mətábəlīt/ *n. Physiol.* a substance formed in or necessary for metabolism.

metabolize /mətábəlīz/ *v.tr. & intr.* process or be processed by metabolism. □□ **metabolizable** *adj.*

metacarpus /métəkaárpəs/ *n.* (*pl.* **metacarpi** /-pī/) **1** the set of five bones of the hand that connects the wrist to the fingers. **2** this part of the hand. □□ **metacarpal** *adj.* [mod.L f. Gk *metakarpon* (as META-, CARPUS)]

metacenter /métəsentər/ *n.* the point of intersection between a line (vertical in equilibrium) through the center of gravity of a floating body and a vertical line through the center of pressure after a slight angular displacement, which must be above the center of gravity to ensure stability. □□ **metacentric** /-séntrik/ *adj.* [F *métacentre* (as META-, CENTER)]

metage /meétij/ *n.* **1** the official measuring of a load of coal, etc. **2** the duty paid for this. [METE[1] + -AGE]

metagenesis /métəjénisis/ *n.* the alternation of generations between sexual and asexual reproduction. □□ **metagenetic** /-jinétik/ *adj.* [mod.L (as META-, GENESIS)]

metal /mét'l/ *n., adj., & v.* • *n.* **1 a** any of a class of chemical elements such as gold, silver, iron, and tin, usu. lustrous ductile solids and good conductors of heat and electricity and forming basic oxides. **b** an alloy of any of these. **2** material used for making glass, in a molten state. **3** *Heraldry* gold or silver as tincture. **4** (in *pl.*) the rails of a railroad line. **5** *Brit.* = *road metal* (see ROAD[1]). • *adj.* made of metal. • *v.tr.* (**metaled, metaling**; esp. *Brit.* **metalled, metalling**) **1** provide or fit with metal. **2** *Brit.* make or mend (a road) with road metal. □ **metal detector** an electronic device giving a signal when it locates metal. **metal fatigue** fatigue (see FATIGUE *n.* 2) in metal. [ME f. OF *metal* or L *metallum* f. Gk *metallon* mine]

metalanguage /métəlanggwij/ *n.* **1** a form of language used to discuss a language. **2** a system of propositions about propositions.

metalize /mét'līz/ *v.tr.* (esp. *Brit.* **metallize**) **1** render metallic. **2** coat with a thin layer of metal. □□ **metalization** *n.*

metallic /mətálik/ *adj.* **1** of, consisting of, or characteristic of metal or metals. **2** sounding sharp and ringing, like struck

metal. **3** having the sheen or luster of metals. □□ **metallically** *adv.* [L *metallicus* f. Gk *metallikos* (as METAL)]

■ **2** see TINNY *adj.* 3b.

metalliferous /mét'lífərəs/ *adj.* bearing or producing metal. [L *metallifer* (as METAL, -FEROUS)]

metallography /mét'lógrəfee/ *n.* the descriptive science of the structure and properties of metals. □□ **metallographic** /metáləgráfik/ *adj.* **metallographical** *adj.* **metallographically** *adv.*

metalloid /mét'loyd/ *adj. & n.* • *adj.* having the form or appearance of a metal. • *n.* any element intermediate in properties between metals and nonmetals, e.g., boron, silicon, and germanium.

metallurgy /mét'lərjee/ *n.* the science concerned with the production, purification, and properties of metals and their application. □□ **metallurgic** /mét'lərjik/ *adj.* **metallurgical** *adj.* **metallurgically** *adv.* **metallurgist** *n.* [Gk *metallon* metal + -*ourgia* working]

metalwork /mét'lwərk/ *n.* **1** the art of working in metal. **2** metal objects collectively. □□ **metalworker** *n.*

metamere /métəmeer/ *n. Zool.* each of several similar segments, that contain the same internal structures, of an animal body. [META- + Gk *meros* part]

metameric /métəmérik/ *adj.* **1** *Chem.* having the same proportional composition and molecular weight, but different functional groups and chemical properties. **2** *Zool.* or relating to metameres. □□ **metamer** /métəmər/ *n.* **metamerism** /métámərizəm/ *n.*

metamorphic /métəmáwrfik/ *adj.* **1** of or marked by metamorphosis. **2** *Geol.* (of rock) that has undergone transformation by natural agencies such as heat and pressure. □□ **metamorphism** *n.* [META- + Gk *morphē* form]

metamorphose /métəmawrfōz/ *v.tr.* **1** change in form. **2** (foll. by *to, into*) **a** turn (into a new form). **b** change the nature of. [F *métamorphoser* f. *métamorphose* METAMORPHOSIS]

■ see CHANGE *v.* 1.

metamorphosis /métəmáwrfəsis/ *n.* (*pl.* **metamorphoses** /-seez/) **1** a change of form (by natural or supernatural means). **2** a changed form. **3** a change of character, conditions, etc. **4** *Zool.* the transformation between an immature form and an adult form, e.g., from a pupa to an insect, or from a tadpole to a frog. [L f. Gk *metamorphōsis* f. *metamorphoō* transform (as META-, *morphoō* f. *morphē* form)]

■ **1, 3, 4** see CHANGE *n.* 1.

metaphase /métəfayz/ *n. Biol.* the stage of meiotic or mitotic cell division when the chromosomes become attached to the spindle fibers.

metaphor /métəfawr/ *n.* **1** the application of a name or descriptive term or phrase to an object or action to which it is imaginatively but not literally applicable (e.g., *killing him with kindness*). **2** an instance of this. □□ **metaphoric** /-fáwrik, -fórik/ *adj.* **metaphorical** /-fáwrikəl, -fórikəl/ *adj.* **metaphorically** /-fáwriklee, -fóriklee/ *adv.* [F *métaphore* or L *metaphora* f. Gk *metaphora* f. *metapherō* transfer]

■ figure (of speech), analogy, image, trope, symbol; simile; symbolism, imagery. □□ **metaphoric**, **metaphorical** nonliteral, analogical, analogous, figurative, symbolic, tropological.

metaphrase /métəfrayz/ *n. & v.* • *n.* literal translation. • *v.tr.* put into other words. □□ **metaphrastic** /-frástik/ *adj.* [mod.L *metaphrasis* f. Gk *metaphrasis* f. *metaphrazō* translate]

■ *v.* see PARAPHRASE *v.*

metaphysic /métəfízik/ *n.* a system of metaphysics.

metaphysical /métəfízikəl/ *adj. & n.* • *adj.* **1** of or relating to metaphysics. **2** based on abstract general reasoning. **3** excessively subtle or theoretical. **4** incorporeal; supernatural. **5** visionary. **6** (of poetry, esp. in the 17th c. in England) characterized by subtlety of thought and complex imagery. • *n.* (**the Metaphysicals**) the metaphysical poets. □□ **metaphysically** *adv.*

■ *adj.* **2** see ABSTRACT *adj.* 1a. **3** see SUBTLE 1, THEORETICAL. **4** see SUPERNATURAL *adj.*

metaphysics /métəfíziks/ *n.pl.* (usu. treated as *sing.*) **1** the

theoretical philosophy of being and knowing. **2** the philosophy of mind. **3** *colloq.* abstract or subtle talk; mere theory. □□ **metaphysician** /-zíshən/ *n.* **metaphysicize** /-fízisiz/ *v.intr.* [ME *metaphysic* f. OF *metaphysique* f. med.L *metaphysica* ult. f. Gk *ta meta ta phusika* the things after the Physics, from the sequence of Aristotle's works]
■ **1, 2** see PHILOSOPHY 1.

metaplasia /métəpláyzhə, -zeeə/ *n. Physiol.* an abnormal change in the nature of a tissue. □□ **metaplastic** /-plástik/ *adj.* [mod.L f. G *Metaplase* f. Gk *metaplasis* (as META-, *plasis* f. *plassō* to mold)]

metapsychology /métəsīkóləjee/ *n.* the study of the nature and functions of the mind beyond what can be studied experimentally. □□ **metapsychological** /-kəlójikəl/ *adj.*

metastable /métəstáybəl/ *adj.* **1** (of a state of equilibrium) stable only under small disturbances. **2** passing to another state so slowly as to seem stable. □□ **metastability** /-stəbílitee/ *n.*

metastasis /métástəsis/ *n.* (*pl.* **metastases** /-seez/) *Physiol.* **1** the transference of a bodily function, disease, etc., from one part or organ to another. **2** the transformation of chemical compounds into others in the process of assimilation by an organism. □□ **metastasize** *v.intr.* **metastatic** /métəstátik/ *adj.* [LL f. Gk f. *methistēmi* change]
■ **2** see TRANSITION. □□ **metastasize** see SPREAD *v.* 2.

metatarsus /métətaársəs/ *n.* (*pl.* **metatarsi** /-sī/) **1** the part of the foot between the ankle and the toes. **2** the set of bones in this. □□ **metatarsal** *adj.* [mod.L (as META-, TARSUS)]

metathesis /mitáthisis/ *n.* (*pl.* **metatheses** /-seez/) **1** *Gram.* the transposition of sounds or letters in a word. **2** *Chem.* the interchange of atoms or groups of atoms between two molecules. **3** an instance of either of these. □□ **metathetic** /métəthétik/ *adj.* **metathetical** /métəthétikəl/ *adj.* [LL f. Gk *metatithēmi* transpose]

metazoan /métəzóən/ *n. & adj. Zool.* ● *n.* any animal of the subkingdom Metazoa, having multicellular and differentiated tissues. ● *adj.* of or relating to the Metazoans. [*Metazoa* f. Gk META- + *zōia* pl. of *zōion* animal]

mete[1] /meet/ *v.tr.* **1** (usu. foll. by *out*) *literary* apportion or allot (a punishment or reward). **2** *poet.* or *Bibl.* measure. [OE *metan* f. Gmc., rel. to MEET[1]]
■ **1** (*mete out*) deal (out), apportion, distribute, dole (out), allot, assign, allocate, parcel out, share (out), ration (out), measure out, dispense, hand out, give out, pass out, *sl.* dish out. **2** see MEASURE *v.* 1.

mete[2] /meet/ *n.* a boundary or boundary stone. [ME f. OF f. L *meta* boundary, goal]

metempsychosis /mətémsikōsis, métəm-/ *n.* (*pl.* **-psychoses** /-seez/) **1** the supposed transmigration of the soul of a human being or animal at death into a new body of the same or a different species. **2** an instance of this. □□ **metempsychosist** *n.* [LL f. Gk *metempsukhōsis* (as META-, EN-[2], *psukhē* soul)]
■ transmigration, reincarnation, rebirth.

meteor /meeteeər, -eeawr/ *n.* **1** a small body of matter from outer space that becomes incandescent as a result of friction with the earth's atmosphere. **2** a streak of light emanating from a meteor. □ **meteor shower** a group of meteors appearing to come from one point in the sky. [ME f. mod.L *meteorum* f. Gk *meteōron* neut. of *meteōros* lofty, (as META-, *aeirō* raise)]

meteoric /meetee-áwrik, -ór-/ *adj.* **1 a** of or relating to the atmosphere. **b** dependent on atmospheric conditions. **2** of meteors. **3** rapid like a meteor; dazzling, transient (*meteoric rise to fame*). □ **meteoric stone** a meteorite. □□ **meteorically** *adv.*
■ **3** brief, short-lived, temporary, transitory, transient, ephemeral, evanescent, impermanent, fleeting, momentary, swift, overnight; brilliant, dazzling, flashing, spectacular, sensational.

meteorite /meeteeərīt/ *n.* a fallen meteor, or fragment of natural rock or metal, that reaches the earth's surface from outer space. □□ **meteoritic** /-rítik/ *adj.*

meteorograph /meeteeərəgraf/ *n.* an apparatus that records

several meteorological phenomena at the same time. [F *météorographe* (as METEOR, -GRAPH)]

meteoroid /meeteeəróyd/ *n.* any small body moving in the solar system that becomes visible as it passes through the earth's atmosphere as a meteor. □□ **meteoroidal** /-róyd'l/ *adj.*

meteorology /meeteeəróləjee/ *n.* **1** the study of the processes and phenomena of the atmosphere, esp. as a means of forecasting the weather. **2** the atmospheric character of a region. □□ **meteorological** /-rəlójikəl/ *adj.* **meteorologically** *adv.* **meteorologist** *n.* [Gk *meteōrologia* (as METEOR)]

meter[1] /meetər/ *n.* (*Brit.* **metre**) a metric unit and the base SI unit of linear measure, equal to about 39.4 inches, and reckoned as the length of the path traveled by light in a vacuum during $1/299{,}792{,}458$ of a second. □ **meter-kilogram-second** denoting a system of measure using the meter, kilogram, and second as the basic units of length, mass, and time. ¶ Abbr.: **mks**. □□ **meterage** /meetərij/ *n.* [F *mètre* f. Gk *metron* measure]

meter[2] /meetər/ *n.* (*Brit.* **metre**) **1 a** any form of poetic rhythm, determined by the number and length of feet in a line. **b** a metrical group or measure. **2** the basic pulse and rhythm of a piece of music. [OF *metre* f. L *metrum* f. Gk *metron* MEASURE]
■ see RHYTHM 1, 2.

meter[3] /meetər/ *n. & v.* ● *n.* **1** an instrument that measures, esp. one for recording a quantity of gas, electricity, postage, etc., supplied, present, or needed. **2** = *parking meter* (see PARK). ● *v.tr.* measure by means of a meter. [ME f. METE[1] + -ER[1]]
■ *n.* **1** see INDICATOR 2, 3. ● *v.* see MEASURE *v.* 1.

-meter /mitər, meetər/ *comb. form* **1** forming nouns denoting measuring instruments (*barometer*). **2** *Prosody* forming nouns denoting lines of poetry with a specified number of measures (*pentameter*).

methadone /méthədōn/ *n.* a potent narcotic analgesic drug used to relieve severe pain, as a cough suppressant and as a substitute for morphine or heroin. [6-dimethylamino-4,4-diphenyl-3-heptanone]

methamphetamine /méthamfétəmin, -meen/ *n.* an amphetamine derivative with quicker and longer action, used as a stimulant. [METHYL + AMPHETAMINE]

methanal /méthənal/ *n. Chem.* = FORMALDEHYDE. [METHANE + ALDEHYDE]

methane /méthayn/ *n. Chem.* a colorless, odorless, flammable, gaseous hydrocarbon, the simplest in the alkane series, and the main constituent of natural gas. ¶ Chem. formula: CH_4. [METHYL + -ANE[2]]

methanol /méthənawl, -nol/ *n. Chem.* a colorless, volatile, flammable liquid, used as a solvent. ¶ Chem. formula: CH_3OH. Also called *methyl alcohol*. [METHANE + ALCOHOL]

methinks /mithíngks/ *v.intr.* (*past* **methought** /mitháwt/) *archaic* it seems to me. [OE *mē thyncth* f. *mē* dative of ME[1] + *thyncth* 3rd sing. of *thyncan* seem, THINK]

methionine /methíəneen/ *n. Biochem.* an amino acid containing sulfur and an important constituent of proteins. [METHYL + Gk *theion* sulfur]

method /méthəd/ *n.* **1** a special form of procedure esp. in any branch of mental activity. **2** orderliness; regular habits. **3** the orderly arrangement of ideas. **4** a scheme of classification. **5** *Theatr.* a technique of acting based on the actor's thorough emotional identification with the character. □ **method in** (or **to**) **one's madness** sense in what appears to be foolish or strange behavior. [F *méthode* or L *methodus* f. Gk *methodos* pursuit of knowledge (as META-, *hodos* way)]
■ **1** way, means, procedure, approach, route, avenue, road, mode, manner, technique, process, routine, modus operandi; plan, scheme, program, course, practice, pattern, system, heuristic, *Math.* algorithm;

/.../ **pronunciation**	● **part of speech**
□ **phrases, idioms, and compounds**	
□□ **derivatives**	■ **synonym section**
cross-references appear in SMALL CAPITALS or *italics*	

methodology. **2, 3** arrangement, order, system, structure, organization, design, pattern, orderliness, neatness, regularity, discipline. **4** see SCHEME *n.* 1a, SYSTEM 4a.

methodical /mithódikəl/ *adj.* (also **methodic**) characterized by method or order. □□ **methodically** *adv.* [LL *methodicus* f. Gk *methodikos* (as METHOD)]
■ organized, ordered, systematic, structured, businesslike, orderly, neat, tidy, regular, routine, balanced, disciplined, painstaking, meticulous, deliberate; plodding, labored.

Methodist /méthədist/ *n.* **1** a member of any of several Protestant religious bodies (now united) originating in the 18th-c. evangelistic movement of Charles and John Wesley and George Whitefield. **2** (**methodist**) a person who follows or advocates a particular method or system of procedure. □□ **Methodism** *n.* **Methodistic** /-dístik/ *adj.* **Methodistical** /-dístikəl/ *adj.* [mod.L *methodista* (as METHOD): sense 1 prob. from following a specified "method" of devotional study]

methodize /méthədiz/ *v.tr.* **1** reduce to order. **2** arrange in an orderly manner. □□ **methodizer** *n.*

methodology /méthədólojee/ *n.* (*pl.* **-ies**) **1** the science of method. **2** a body of methods used in a particular branch of activity. □□ **methodological** /-dəlójikəl/ *adj.* **methodologically** *adv.* **methodologist** *n.* [mod.L *methodologia* or F *méthodologie* (as METHOD)]
■ **2** see SYSTEM 4a.

methought *past* of METHINKS.

Methuselah /mithŏŏzələ/ *n.* **1** a very old person or thing. **2** (also **methuselah**) a large wine bottle with a capacity of approx. 6 liters. [ME: the name of a patriarch said to have lived 969 years (Gen. 5:27)]

methyl /méthil/ *n. Chem.* the univalent hydrocarbon radical CH_3, present in many organic compounds. □ **methyl alcohol** = METHANOL. **methyl benzene** = TOLUENE. □□ **methylic** /methílik/ *adj.* [G *Methyl* or F *méthyle*, back-form. f. G *Methylen*, F *méthylène*: see METHYLENE]

methylate /méthilayt/ *v.tr.* **1** mix or impregnate with methanol. **2** introduce a methyl group into (a molecule or compound). □ **methylated spirit** (or **spirits**) alcohol impregnated with methanol to make it unfit for drinking and exempt from duty. □□ **methylation** /-láyshən/ *n.*

methylene /méthileen/ *n. Chem.* the highly reactive divalent group of atoms CH_2. [F *méthylène* f. Gk *methu* wine + *hulē* wood + -ENE]

metic /métik/ *n. Gk Antiq.* an alien living in a Greek city with some privileges of citizenship. [irreg. f. Gk *metoikos* (as META-, *oikos* dwelling)]

meticulous /mətíkyələs/ *adj.* **1** giving great or excessive attention to details. **2** very careful and precise. □□ **meticulously** *adv.* **meticulousness** *n.* [L *meticulosus* f. *metus* fear]
■ careful, precise, accurate, exact, fastidious, scrupulous, thorough, particular, painstaking, punctilious, fussy, finicky, demanding, strict, critical, exacting, perfectionist, *colloq.* persnickety.

métier /métyáy/ *n.* (also **metier**) **1** one's trade, profession, or department of activity. **2** one's forte. [F ult. f. L *ministerium* service]
■ **1** see TRADE *n.* 2.

métis /maytées/ *n.* (*pl.* **métis**; *fem.* **métisse**, *pl.* **métisses**) a person of mixed race, esp. the offspring of a white person and a Native American in Canada. [F *métis*, OF *mestis* f. Rmc, rel. to MESTIZO]

Metol /méetawl/ *n. propr.* a white soluble powder used as a photographic developer. [G, arbitrary name]

Metonic cycle /mitónik/ *n.* a period of 19 years (235 lunar months) covering all the changes of the moon's position relative to the sun and the earth. [Gk *Metōn*, Athenian astronomer of the 5th c. BC]

metonym /métanim/ *n.* a word used in metonymy. [back-form. f. METONYMY, after *synonym*]

metonymy /mitónimee/ *n.* the substitution of the name of an attribute or adjunct for that of the thing meant (e.g., *White House* for *president*, *the turf* for *horse racing*). □□ **met-**

onymic /métənímik/ *adj.* **metonymical** /métənímikəl/ *adj.* [LL *metonymia* f. Gk *metōnumia* (as META-, *onoma*, *onuma* name)]

metope /métəpee, métōp/ *n. Archit.* a square space between triglyphs in a Doric frieze. [L *metopa* f. Gk *metopē* (as META-, *opē* hole for a beam end)]

metre *Brit.* var. of METER.

metric /métrik/ *adj.* of or based on the meter. □ **metric system** the decimal measuring system with the meter, liter, and gram (or kilogram) as units of length, volume, and mass (see also SI). **metric ton** (or **tonne**) 1,000 kilograms (2,205 lb.). [F *métrique* (as METER[1])]

-metric /métrik/ *comb. form* (also **-metrical**) forming adjectives corresponding to nouns in *-meter* and *-metry* (*thermometric*; *geometric*). □□ **-metrically** *comb. form* forming adverbs. [from or after F *-métrique* f. L (as METRICAL)]

metrical /métrikəl/ *adj.* **1** of, relating to, or composed in meter (*metrical psalms*). **2** of or involving measurement (*metrical geometry*). □□ **metrically** *adv.* [ME f. L *metricus* f. Gk *metrikos* (as METER[2])]
■ **1** see POETIC 1b.

metricate /métrikayt/ *v.intr.* & *tr.* change or adapt to a metric system of measurement. □□ **metrication** /-káyshən/ *n.* **metricize** /-trisiz/ *v.tr.*

metritis /mitrítis/ *n.* inflammation of the womb. [Gk *mētra* womb + -ITIS]

metro /métrō/ *n.* (*pl.* **-os**) a subway system in a city, esp. Paris. [F *métro*, abbr. of *métropolitain* METROPOLITAN]
■ see UNDERGROUND *n.* 1.

metrology /mitrólojee/ *n.* the scientific study of measurement. □□ **metrologic** /métrəlójik/ *adj.* **metrological** /métrəlójikəl/ *adj.* [Gk *metron* measure + -LOGY]

metronome /métrənōm/ *n. Mus.* an instrument marking time at a selected rate by giving a regular tick. □□ **metronomic** /-nómik/ *adj.* [Gk *metron* measure + *nomos* law]

metronymic /métrənímik/ *adj.* & *n.* ● *adj.* (of a name) derived from the name of a mother or female ancestor. ● *n.* a metronymic name. [Gk *mētēr mētros* mother, after *patronymic*]

metropolis /mitrópəlis/ *n.* **1** the chief city of a country; a capital city. **2** a metropolitan bishop's see. **3** a center of activity. [LL f. Gk *mētropolis* parent state f. *mētēr mētros* mother + *polis* city]
■ **1** capital, (capital) city, megalopolis, municipality. **3** see HUB.

metropolitan /métrəpólit'n/ *adj.* & *n.* ● *adj.* **1** of or relating to a metropolis, esp. as distinct from its environs (*metropolitan New York*). **2** belonging to, forming or forming part of, a mother country as distinct from its colonies, etc. (*metropolitan France*). **3** of an ecclesiastical metropolis. ● *n.* **1** (in full **metropolitan bishop**) a bishop having authority over the bishops of a province, in the Western Church equivalent to archbishop, in the Orthodox Church ranking above archbishop and below patriarch. **2** an inhabitant of a metropolis. □□ **metropolitanate** *n.* (in sense 1 of *n.*). **metropolitanism** *n.* [ME f. LL *metropolitanus* f. Gk *mētropolitēs* (as METROPOLIS)]
■ *adj.* **1** see MUNICIPAL.

metrorrhagia /meetrō-ráyjeeə, -jə/ *n.* abnormal bleeding from the womb. [mod.L f. Gk *mētra* womb + *-rrhage* as HEMORRHAGE]

-metry /mitree/ *comb. form* forming nouns denoting procedures and systems corresponding to instruments in *-meter* (*calorimetry*; *thermometry*). [after *geometry*, etc., f. Gk *-metria* f. *-metrēs* measurer]

mettle /mét'l/ *n.* **1** the quality of a person's disposition or temperament (*a chance to show your mettle*). **2** natural ardor. **3** spirit, courage. □ **on one's mettle** incited to do one's best. □□ **mettled** *adj.* (also in *comb.*). **mettlesome** *adj.* [var. of METAL *n.*]
■ **1** see DISPOSITION 1b. **2, 3** see SPIRIT *n.* 5c. □□ **mettlesome** see SPIRITED.

meunière /mónyáir/ *adj.* (esp. of fish) cooked or served in lightly browned butter with lemon juice and parsley (*sole* *meunière*). [F (*à la*) *meunière* (in the manner of) a miller's wife]

MeV *abbr.* megaelectronvolt(s).

mew[1] /myoō/ *v. & n.* ● *v.intr.* (of a cat, gull, etc.) utter its characteristic cry. ● *n.* this sound, esp. of a cat. [ME: imit.]

mew[2] /myoō/ *n.* a gull, esp. the common gull, *Larus canus*. Also called **mew gull**. [OE *mǣw* f. Gmc]

mew[3] /myoō/ *n. & v.* ● *n.* a cage for hawks, esp. while molting. ● *v.tr.* **1** put (a hawk) in a cage. **2** (often foll. by *up*) shut up; confine. [ME f. OF *mue* f. *muer* molt f. L *mutare* change]

mewl /myoōl/ *v.intr.* **1** cry feebly; whimper. **2** mew like a cat. [imit.]

■ **1** see CRY *v.* 2a.

mews /myoōz/ *n.* esp. *Brit.* a set of stables around an open yard or along a lane, now often converted into dwellings. [pl. (now used as sing.) of MEW[3], orig. of the royal stables on the site of hawks' mews at Charing Cross, London]

Mexican /méksikən/ *n. & adj.* ● *n.* **1 a** a native or national of Mexico, a country in southern N. America. **b** a person of Mexican descent. **2** a language spoken in Mexico, esp. Nahuatl. ● *adj.* **1** of or relating to Mexico or its people. **2** of Mexican descent. [Sp. *mexicano*]

mezereon /mizéereeən/ *n.* (also **mezereum**) a small European and Asian shrub, *Daphne mezereum*, with fragrant purplish red flowers and red berries. [med.L f. Arab. *māzaryūn*]

mezuzah /mezoōzə, -zoōzaá/ *n.* (also **mezuza**; *pl.* **-s**; also **mezuzot** or **mezuzoth** /-zoōzŏt/) a parchment inscribed with religious texts and attached in a case to the doorpost of a Jewish house as a sign of faith. [Heb. *mʿzûzāh* doorpost]

mezzanine /mézzəneén/ *n.* **1** a low story between two others (usu. between the first and second floors). **2 a** the lowest balcony in a theater. **b** the first several rows of this balcony. [F f. It. *mezzanino* dimin. of *mezzano* middle f. L *medianus* MEDIAN]

mezza voce /métsə vŏchay/ *adv. Mus.* with less than the full strength of the voice or sound. [It., = half voice]

mezzo /métsō/ *adv. & n. Mus.* ● *adv.* half, moderately. ● *n.* (in full **mezzo-soprano**) (*pl.* **-os**) **1 a** a female singing voice between soprano and contralto. **b** a singer with this voice. **2** a part written for mezzo-soprano. □ **mezzo forte** fairly loud. **mezzo piano** fairly soft. [It., f. L *medius* middle]

mezzo-relievo /métsō-rileévō/ *n.* (also **mezzo-rilievo** /-rilyáyvō/) (*pl.* **-os**) a raised surface in the form of half-relief, in which the figures project half their true proportions. [It. *mezzo-rilievo* = half-relief]

mezzo-rilievo var. of MEZZO-RELIEVO.

mezzotint /métsōtint/ *n. & v.* ● *n.* **1** a method of printing or engraving in which the surface of a plate is roughened by scraping so that it produces tones and halftones. **2** a print produced by this process. ● *v.tr.* engrave in mezzotint. □□ **mezzotinter** *n.* [It. *mezzotinto* f. *mezzo* half + *tinto* tint]

MF *abbr.* medium frequency.

mf *abbr.* mezzo forte.

M.F.A. *abbr.* Master of Fine Arts.

mfg. *abbr.* manufacturing.

m.f.n. *abbr.* most favored nation.

mfr. *abbr.* **1** manufacture. **2** manufacturer.

MG *abbr.* **1** machine gun. **2** major general. **3** myasthenia gravis.

Mg *symb. Chem.* the element magnesium.

mg *abbr.* milligram(s).

Mgr. *abbr.* **1** Manager. **2** Monseigneur. **3** Monsignor.

mho /mō/ *n.* (*pl.* **-os**) *Electr.* the reciprocal of an ohm, a former unit of conductance. [OHM reversed]

MHR *abbr.* (in the US and Australia) Member of the House of Representatives.

MHz *abbr.* megahertz.

MI *abbr.* **1** Michigan (in official postal use). **2** myocardial infarction.

M.I.5 *abbr.* (in the UK) the department of Military Intelligence concerned with government security. ¶ Not in official use.

M.I.6 *abbr.* (in the UK) the department of Military Intelligence concerned with espionage. ¶ Not in official use.

mi /mee/ *n.* (also **me**) *Mus.* **1** the third tone of the diatonic scale. **2** the note E in the fixed solmization system. [ME f. L *mira*: see GAMUT]

mi. *abbr.* mile(s).

MIA *abbr.* missing in action.

Miami /mīámee/ *n. & adj.* ● *n.* **1 a** a N. American people native to the midwestern United States. **b** a member of this people. **2** the language of this people. ● *adj.* of or relating to this people or their language.

miasma /mī-ázmə, mee-/ *n.* (*pl.* **miasmata** /-mətə/ or **miasmas**) *archaic* an infectious or noxious vapor. □□ **miasmal** *adj.* **miasmatic** /-mátik/ *adj.* **miasmic** *adj.* **miasmically** *adv.* [Gk, = defilement, f. *mainō* pollute]

■ see VAPOR *n.* 1. □□ **miasmal, miasmatic, miasmic** see SMELLY.

Mic. *abbr.* Micah (Old Testament).

mica /míkə/ *n.* any of a group of silicate minerals with a layered structure, esp. muscovite. □□ **micaceous** /-káyshəs/ *adj.* [L, = crumb]

mice *pl.* of MOUSE.

micelle /misél, mī-/ *n. Chem.* an aggregate of molecules in a colloidal solution, as occurs, e.g., when soap dissolves in water. [mod.L *micella* dimin. of L *mica* crumb]

Mich. *abbr.* **1** Michigan. **2** Michaelmas.

Michaelmas /míkəlməs/ *n.* the feast of St. Michael, September 29. □ **Michaelmas daisy** an autumn-flowering aster. **Michaelmas term** *Brit.* (in some universities) the autumn term. [OE *sancte Micheles mæsse* Saint Michael's mass: see MASS[2]]

mick /mik/ *n. sl. offens.* an Irishman. [pet form of the name *Michael*]

mickery /míkəree/ *n. Austral.* (also **mickerie**) a water hole or excavated well, esp. in a dry riverbed. [Aborig. *migri*]

Mickey Finn /míkee fín/ (often **Mickey**) *n. sl.* **1** an alcoholic drink, adulterated with a narcotic or laxative. **2** the adulterant itself. [20th c.: orig. uncert.]

mickle /míkəl/ *adj. & n. archaic* or *Sc.* ● *adj.* much, great. ● *n.* a large amount. □ **many a little makes a mickle** many small amounts accumulate to make a large amount. [ME f. ON *mikell* f. Gmc]

micro /míkrō/ *n.* (*pl.* **-os**) *colloq.* **1** = MICROCOMPUTER. **2** = MICROPROCESSOR.

micro- /míkrō/ *comb. form* **1** small (*microchip*). **2** denoting a factor of one millionth (10⁻⁶) (*microgram*). ¶ Symb.: μ. [Gk *mikro-* f. *mikros* small]

■ **1** mini-.

microanalysis /míkrōənálisis/ *n.* the quantitative analysis of chemical compounds using a sample of a few milligrams.

microbe /míkrōb/ *n.* a minute living being; a microorganism (esp. bacteria causing disease and fermentation). □□ **microbial** /-krōbeeəl/ *adj.* **microbic** /-krōbik/ *adj.* [F f. Gk *mikros* small + *bios* life]

■ microorganism, germ, bacterium, *sl.* bug.

microbiology /míkrōbīóləjee/ *n.* the scientific study of microorganisms, e.g., bacteria, viruses, and fungi. □□ **microbiological** /-bīəlójikəl/ *adj.* **microbiologically** /-bīəlójiklee/ *adv.* **microbiologist** *n.*

microbrewery /míkrōbroōəree/ *n.* a limited-production brewery, often selling only locally.

microburst /míkrōbərst/ *n.* a particularly violent wind shear, esp. during a thunderstorm.

microcephaly /míkrōséfəlee/ *n.* an abnormal smallness of the head in relation to the rest of the body. □□ **microcephalic** /-sifálik/ *adj. & n.* **microcephalous** /-séfələs/ *adj.*

microchip /míkrōchip/ *n.* a small piece of semiconductor (usu. silicon) used to carry electronic circuits.

microcircuit /míkrōsərkit/ *n.* an integrated circuit on a microchip. □□ **microcircuitry** *n.*

microclimate /míkrōklimit/ *n.* the climate of a small local

/ . . . / **pronunciation** ● **part of speech**

□ **phrases, idioms, and compounds**

□□ **derivatives** ■ **synonym section**

cross-references appear in SMALL CAPITALS or *italics*

area, e.g., inside a greenhouse. □□ **microclimatic** /-mátik/ *adj.* **microclimatically** /-mátiklee/ *adv.*

microcode /míkrōkōd/ *n.* **1** = MICROINSTRUCTION. **2** = MICROPROGRAM.

microcomputer /míkrōkəmpyŏŏtər/ *n.* a small computer that contains a microprocessor as its central processor.

microcopy /míkrōkópee/ *n. & v.* ● *n.* (*pl.* **-ies**) a copy of printed matter that has been reduced by microphotography. ● *v.tr.* (**-ies, -ied**) make a microcopy of.

microcosm /míkrəkozəm/ *n.* **1** (often foll. by *of*) a miniature representation. **2** mankind viewed as the epitome of the universe. **3** any community or complex unity viewed in this way. □□ **microcosmic** /-kózmik/ *adj.* **microcosmically** /-kózmiklee/ *adv.* [ME f. F *microcosme* or med.L *microcosmus* f. Gk *mikros kosmos* little world]

microdot /míkrōdot/ *n.* a microphotograph of a document, etc., reduced to the size of a dot.

microeconomics /míkrō-eékənómiks, -ék-/ *n.* the branch of economics dealing with individual commodities, producers, etc.

microelectronics /míkrō-ílektróniks/ *n.* the design, manufacture, and use of microchips and microcircuits.

microfiche /míkrōfeesh/ *n.* (*pl.* same or **microfiches**) a flat rectangular piece of film bearing microphotographs of the pages of a printed text or document.

microfilm /míkrəfilm/ *n. & v.* ● *n.* a length of film bearing microphotographs of documents, etc. ● *v.tr.* photograph (a document, etc.) on microfilm.

microform /míkrōfawrm/ *n.* microphotographic reproduction on film or paper of a manuscript, etc.

microgram /míkrōgram/ *n.* one-millionth of a gram.

micrograph /míkrōgraf/ *n.* a photograph taken by means of a microscope.

microinstruction /míkrō-instrúkshən/ *n.* a machine-code instruction that effects a basic operation in a computer system.

microlight /míkrōlit/ *n.* a kind of motorized hang glider.

microlith /míkrōlith/ *n. Archaeol.* a minute worked flint usu. as part of a composite tool. □□ **microlithic** /-líthik/ *adj.*

micromesh /míkrōmesh/ *n.* (often *attrib.*) material, esp. nylon, consisting of a very fine mesh.

micrometer[1] /mikrómitər/ *n.* a gauge for accurately measuring small distances, thicknesses, etc. □□ **micrometry** *n.*

micrometer[2] /míkrōmeétər/ *n.* = MICRON.

microminiaturization /míkrōmínee-əchərizáyshən/ *n.* the manufacture of very small electronic devices by using integrated circuits.

micron /míkron/ *n.* one-millionth of a meter. Also called **micrometer.** [Gk *mikron* neut. of *mikros* small: cf. MICRO-]

Micronesian /míkrəneéezhən/ *adj. & n.* ● *adj.* of or relating to Micronesia, an island group in the W. Pacific. ● *n.* a native of Micronesia. [*Micronesia*, formed as MICRO- + Gk *nēsos* island]

microorganism /míkrō-áwrgənizəm/ *n.* any of various microscopic organisms, including algae, bacteria, fungi, protozoa, and viruses.
■ see MICROBE.

microphone /míkrəfōn/ *n.* an instrument for converting sound waves into electrical energy variations that may be reconverted into sound after transmission by wire or radio or after recording. □□ **microphonic** /-fónik/ *adj.*
■ bug, transmitter, *colloq.* mike.

microphotograph /míkrōfótəgraf/ *n.* a photograph reduced to a very small size.

microphyte /míkrōfīt/ *n.* a microscopic plant.

microprocessor /míkrōprósesər/ *n.* an integrated circuit that contains all the functions of a central processing unit of a computer.

microprogram /míkrōprógram/ *n.* a microinstruction program that controls the functions of a central processing unit of a computer.

micropyle /míkrōpīl/ *n. Bot.* a small opening in the surface of an ovule, through which pollen passes. [MICRO- + Gk *pulē* gate]

microscope /míkrəskōp/ *n.* an instrument magnifying small

objects by means of a lens or lenses so as to reveal details invisible to the naked eye. [mod.L *microscopium* (as MICRO-, -SCOPE)]

microscopic /míkrəskópik/ *adj.* **1** so small as to be visible only with a microscope. **2** extremely small. **3** regarded in terms of small units. **4** of the microscope. □□ **microscopical** *adj.* (in sense 4). **microscopically** *adv.*
■ **1, 2** see TINY.

microscopy /mikróskəpee/ *n.* the use of the microscope. □□ **microscopist** *n.*

microsecond /míkrōsekənd/ *n.* one-millionth of a second.

microsome /míkrəsōm/ *n. Biol.* a small particle of organelle fragments obtained by centrifugation of homogenized cells. [MICRO- + -SOME³]

microspore /míkrəspawr/ *n.* the smaller of the two kinds of spore produced by some ferns.

microstructure /míkrōstrúkchər/ *n.* (in a metal or other material) the arrangement of crystals, etc., that can be made visible and examined with a microscope.

microsurgery /míkrōsúrjəree/ *n.* intricate surgery performed using microscopes, enabling the tissue to be operated on with miniaturized precision instruments. □□ **microsurgical** /-súrjikəl/ *adj.*

microswitch /míkrōswich/ *n.* a switch that can be operated rapidly by a small movement.

microtome /míkrətōm/ *n.* an instrument for cutting extremely thin sections of material for examination under a microscope. [MICRO- + -TOME]

microtone /míkrətōn/ *n. Mus.* an interval smaller than a semitone.

microtubule /míkrōtóōbyŏōl, -tyōō-/ *n. Biol.* a minute protein filament occurring in cytoplasm and involved in forming the spindles during cell division, etc.

microwave /míkrəwayv/ *n. & v.* ● *n.* **1** an electromagnetic wave with a wavelength in the range 0.001–0.3m. **2** (in full **microwave oven**) an oven that uses microwaves to cook or heat food quickly. ● *v.tr.* (**-ving**) cook in a microwave oven.

micturition /míkchəríshən/ *n. formal* or *Med.* urination. [L *micturire micturit-*, desiderative f. *mingere mict-* urinate]

mid[1] /mid/ *attrib.adj.* **1** (usu. in *comb.*) that is the middle of (*in midair; from mid-June to mid-July*). **2** that is in the middle; medium, half. **3** *Phonet.* (of a vowel) pronounced with the tongue neither high nor low. [OE *midd* (recorded only in oblique cases), rel. to L *medius*, Gk *mesos*]
■ **1, 2** see MIDDLE *adj.* 1, 2.

mid[2] /mid/ *prep. poet.* = AMID. [abbr. f. AMID]

midair /midáir/ *n.* a place or point in the air far removed from the ground or other solid surface.

Midas touch /mídəs/ *n.* the ability to turn one's activities to financial advantage. [*Midas*, king of Phrygia, whose touch was said to turn all things to gold]

midbrain /mídbrayn/ *n.* the part of the brain developing from the middle of the primitive or embryonic brain.

midday /míd-dáy/ *n.* the middle of the day; noon. [OE *middæg* (as MID¹, DAY)]
■ noon, noontide, twelve noon, 1200 hours, high noon.

midden /míd'n/ *n.* **1** a dunghill. **2** a refuse heap near a dwelling. **3** = *kitchen midden.* [ME *myddyng*, of Scand. orig.: cf. Da. *mødding* muck heap]

middle /míd'l/ *adj., n., & v.* ● *attrib.adj.* **1** at an equal distance from the extremities of a thing. **2** (of a member of a group) so placed as to have the same number of members on each side. **3** intermediate in rank, quality, etc. **4** average (*of middle height*). **5** (of a language) of the period between the old and modern forms. **6** *Gram.* designating the voice of (esp. Greek) verbs that expresses reciprocal or reflexive action. ● *n.* **1** (often foll. by *of*) the middle point or position or part. **2** a person's waist. **3** *Gram.* the middle form or voice of a verb. **4** = *middle term.* ● *v.tr.* **1** place in the middle. **2** *Soccer* return (the ball) from the wing to the midfield. **3** *Naut.* fold in the middle. □ **in the middle of** (often foll. by *verbal noun*) in the process of; during. **middle age** the period between youth and old age, about 45 to 60. **middle-aged** in middle age. **the Middle Ages** the period of Eu-

ropean history from the fall of the Roman Empire in the West (5th c.) to the fall of Constantinople (1453), or more narrowly from *c.*1000 to 1453. **middle-age** (or **-aged**) **spread** the increased bodily girth often associated with middle age. **Middle America 1** the N. American region that includes Mexico and Central America, and often the West Indies. **2** the middle class in the US, esp. as a conservative political force. **3** the US Middle West. **middle C** *Mus.* the C near the middle of the piano keyboard, the note between the treble and bass staves, at about 260 Hz. **middle class** the class of society between the upper and the lower, including professional and business workers and their families. **middle-class** *adj.* of the middle class. **middle course** a compromise between two extremes. **middle distance 1** (in a painted or actual landscape) the part between the foreground and the background. **2** *Track* a race distance of esp. 800 or 1500 meters. **middle ear** the cavity of the central part of the ear behind the eardrum. **the Middle East** the area covered by countries from Egypt to Iran inclusive. **Middle Eastern** of or in the Middle East. **Middle English** the English language from *c.*1150 to 1500. **middle finger** the finger between the forefinger and the ring finger. **middle game** the central phase of a chess game, when strategies are developed. **middle ground** a neutral position between two opposing extremes. **middle-income** of the wages earned by the middle class. **middle management** in business and industry, the mid-level positions in administration. **middle name 1** a person's name placed after the first name and before the surname. **2** a person's most characteristic quality (*sobriety is my middle name*). **middle-of-the-road** (of a person, course of action, etc.) moderate; avoiding extremes. **middle passage** the sea journey between W. Africa and the W. Indies (with ref. to the slave trade). **middle school** a school for children from about 10 to 13 years old (grades 5–8). **middle-sized** of medium size. **Middle Temple** one of the two Inns of Court on the site of the Temple in London (cf. *Inner Temple*). **middle term** *Logic* the term common to both premises of a syllogism. **middle watch** the watch from midnight to 4 a.m. **middle way 1** = *middle course*. **2** the eightfold path of Buddhism between indulgence and asceticism. **Middle West** = MIDWEST [OE *middel* f. Gmc]
■ *adj.* **1, 2** central, center, medial, median, *Anat.* mesial; midway, mid, halfway; inner, inside. **3** see INTERMEDIATE *adj.* **4** normal, mean; see also AVERAGE *adj.* 1a. ● *n.* **1** center, midpoint, midst, halfway point; heart, bull's-eye. **2** midriff, waist, stomach. □ **in the middle of** halfway *or* midway through, in the midst of; during. **middle class** (petty *or* petite) bourgeoisie; Middle America. **middle-class** see BOURGEOIS *adj.* 1a. **middle name 2** see HALLMARK *n.* 2. **middle-of-the-road** see MODERATE *adj.* 1. **middle-sized** average, medium-sized; see also MEDIUM *adj.*

middlebrow /míd'lbrow/ *adj.* & *n. colloq.* ● *adj.* claiming to be or regarded as only moderately intellectual. ● *n.* a middlebrow person.

middleman /míd'lman/ *n.* (*pl.* **-men**) **1** any of the traders who handle a commodity between its producer and its consumer. **2** an intermediary.
■ see INTERMEDIARY *n.*

middleweight /míd'lwayt/ *n.* **1** a weight in certain sports intermediate between welterweight and light heavyweight. **2** a sportsman of this weight.

middling /mídling/ *adj., n.,* & *adv.* ● *adj.* **1 a** moderately good (esp. *fair to middling*). **b** second-rate. **2** (of goods) of the second of three grades. ● *n.* (in *pl.*) middling goods, esp. flour of medium fineness. ● *adv.* **1** fairly or moderately (*middling good*). **2** *colloq.* fairly well (esp. in health). □□ **middlingly** *adv.* [ME, of Sc. orig.: prob. f. MID¹ + -LING²]
■ *adj.* **1** see MODERATE *adj.* 2, 4.

middy¹ /mídee/ *n.* (*pl.* **-ies**) **1** *colloq.* a midshipman. **2** (in full **middy blouse**) a woman's or child's loose blouse with a collar like that worn by sailors.

middy² /mídee/ *n.* (*pl.* **-ies**) *Austral. sl.* a measure of beer of varying size, often a half a pint. [20th c.: orig. unkn.]

Mideast /mídeést/ *n. Middle East.*

midfield /mídfeéld/ *n.* in certain sports, esp. football and soccer, the area of the field midway between the two goals. □□ **midfielder** *n.*

midge /mij/ *n.* **1** *colloq.* **a** a gnatlike insect. **b** a small person. **2 a** any dipterous nonbiting insect of the family Chironomidae. **b** any similar insect of the family Ceratopogonidae with piercing mouthparts for sucking blood or eating smaller insects. [OE *mycg(e)* f. Gmc]

midget /míjit/ *n.* **1** an extremely small person or thing. **2** (*attrib.*) very small. [MIDGE + -ET¹]
■ **2** (*attrib.*) see SMALL *adj.* 1.

midgut /mídgút/ *n.* the middle part of the alimentary canal, including the small intestine.

MIDI /mídee/ *n.* a system for using combinations of electronic equipment, esp. audio and computer equipment. [acronym of *musical instrument digital interface*]

midi /mídee/ *n.* (*pl.* **midis**) a garment of medium length, usu. reaching to mid-calf. [MID¹ after MINI]

midinette /mídinét/ *n.* a Parisian shopgirl, esp. a milliner's assistant. [F f. *midi* midday + *dinette* light dinner]

midland /mídlənd/ *n.* & *adj.* ● *n.* **1** the middle part of a country. **2** the dialect of American English spoken in the east-central US, from southern New Jersey and northern Delaware west across the Appalachians and the Ohio and Mississippi river valleys. **3** (**the Midlands**) the inland counties of central England. ● *adj.* of or in the midland or Midlands. □□ **midlander** *n.*

midlife /mídlíf/ *n.* middle age. □ **midlife crisis** an emotional crisis of self-confidence that can occur in early middle age.

midline /mídlín/ *n.* a median line, or plane of bilateral symmetry.

midmost /mídmōst/ *adj.* & *adv.* in the very middle.

midnight /mídnīt/ *n.* **1** the middle of the night; 12 o'clock at night. **2** intense darkness. □ **midnight blue** a very dark blue. **midnight sun** the sun visible at midnight during the summer in polar regions. [OE *midniht* (as MID¹, NIGHT)]

midrash /mídraash/ *n.* (*pl.* **midrashim** /-shím/) an ancient commentary on part of the Hebrew scriptures. [Bibl. Heb. *midrāš* commentary]

midrib /mídrib/ *n.* the central rib of a leaf.

midriff /mídrif/ *n.* **1 a** the region of the front of the body between the thorax and abdomen. **b** the diaphragm. **2** a garment or part of a garment covering the abdomen. [OE *midhrif* (as MID¹, *hrif* belly)]
■ **1a** see MIDDLE *n.* 2.

midship /mídship/ *n.* the middle part of a ship or boat.

midshipman /mídshípmən/ *n.* (*pl.* **-men**) **1** a cadet in the U.S. Naval Academy. **2** *Brit.* a naval officer of rank between naval cadet and sublieutenant.

midships /mídships/ *adv.* = AMIDSHIPS.

midst /midst/ *prep.* & *n.* ● *prep. poet.* amidst. ● *n.* middle (now only in phrases as below). □ **in the midst of** among; in the middle of. **in our** (or **your** or **their**) **midst** among us (or you or them). [ME *middest, middes* f. *in middes, in middan* (as IN, MID¹)]
■ □ **in the midst of** in the middle of, halfway *or* midway through; during; see also AMONG 1.

midsummer /mídsúmər/ *n.* the period of or near the summer solstice, around June 21. □ **Midsummer** (or **Midsummer's**) **Day** esp. *Brit.* June 24. **midsummer madness** extreme, usu. temporary, folly. [OE *midsumor* (as MID¹, SUMMER¹)]

midtown /mídtown/ *n.* the central part of a city between the downtown and uptown areas.

midway /mídwáy/ *n.* & *adv.* ● *n.* area for concessions and amusements at a carnival, fair, etc. ● *adv.* in or toward the middle of the distance between two points.

/.../ **pronunciation**   ● **part of speech**
□ **phrases, idioms, and compounds**
□□ **derivatives**   ■ **synonym section**
cross-references appear in SMALL CAPITALS or *italics*

Midwest /mídwést/ *n.* region of northern US states from Ohio west to the Rocky Mountains.

midwife /mídwīf/ *n.* (*pl.* **-wives** /-wīvz/) **1** a person (usu. a woman) trained to assist women in childbirth. **2** a person who helps in producing or bringing something forth. □□ **midwifery** /-wífəree/ *n.* [ME, prob. f. obs. prep. *mid* with + WIFE woman, in the sense of 'one who is with the mother']

midwinter /mídwíntər/ *n.* the period of or near the winter solstice, around Dec. 22 [OE (as MID¹, WINTER)]

mien /meen/ *n.* *literary* a person's look or bearing, as showing character or mood. [prob. f. obs. *demean* f. DEMEAN², assim. to F *mine* expression]
■ see LOOK *n.* 2, 3.

miff /mif/ *v.* & *n.* *colloq.* ● *v.tr.* (usu. in *passive*) put out of humor; offend. ● *n.* **1** a petty quarrel. **2** a huff. [perh. imit.: cf. G *muff*, exclam. of disgust]
■ *v.* see OFFEND 1, 2.

might¹ /mīt/ *past* of MAY, used esp.: **1** in reported speech, expressing possibility (*said he might come*) or permission (*asked if I might leave*) (cf. MAY 1, 2). **2** expressing a possibility based on a condition not fulfilled (*if you'd looked you might have found it*; *but for the radio we might not have known*). **3** expressing complaint that an obligation or expectation is not or has not been fulfilled (*he might offer to help*; *they might have asked*; *you might have known they wouldn't come*). **4** expressing a request (*you might call in at the butcher's*). **5** *colloq.* **a** = MAY 1 (*it might be true*). **b** (in tentative questions) = MAY 2 (*might I have the pleasure of this dance?*). **c** = MAY 4 (*who might you be?*). □ **might as well** expressing that it is probably at least as desirable to do a thing as not to do it (*finished the work and decided they might as well go to lunch*; *won't win but might as well try*). **might-have-been** *colloq.* esp. *Brit.* **1** a past possibility that no longer applies. **2** a person who could have been more eminent.

might² /mīt/ *n.* **1** great bodily or mental strength. **2** power to enforce one's will (usu. in contrast with *right*). □ **with all one's might** to the utmost of one's power. **with might and main** see MAIN¹. [OE *miht, mieht* f. Gmc, rel. to MAY]
■ **1** strength, power, energy, force, muscle, mightiness, potency, *archaic* puissance. **2** influence, authority, weight, sway, dominion, ascendancy, superiority, capability, capacity, power, effectiveness, *colloq.* clout.

mightn't /mít'nt/ *contr.* might not.

mighty /mítee/ *adj.* & *adv.* ● *adj.* (**mightier, mightiest**) **1** powerful or strong, in body, mind, or influence. **2** massive, bulky. **3** *colloq.* great, considerable. ● *adv.* *colloq.* very (*a mighty difficult task*). □□ **mightily** *adv.* **mightiness** *n.* [OE *mihtig* (as MIGHT²)]
■ *adj.* **1** powerful, strong, potent, influential, dominant, predominant, ascendant, weighty, authoritarian, autocratic, indomitable; muscular, robust, strapping, sturdy, brawny, burly, well-built, able-bodied, hardy, hefty, *archaic or joc.* doughty, *colloq.* hunky. **2** big, large, huge, grand, great, enormous, gargantuan, gigantic, tremendous, towering, monumental, prodigious, massive, bulky. **3** see CONSIDERABLE 1, 2. ● *adv.* see VERY *adv.*

mignonette /mínyənét/ *n.* **1 a** any of various plants of the genus *Reseda*, esp. *R. odorata*, with fragrant greenish-white flowers. **b** the color of these. **2** a light, fine, narrow pillow lace. [F *mignonnette* dimin. of *mignon* small]

migraine /mígrayn/ *n.* a recurrent throbbing headache that usually affects one side of the head, often accompanied by nausea and disturbance of vision. □□ **migrainous** /-gráynis/ *adj.* [F f. LL *hemicrania* f. Gk *hēmikrania* (as HEMI-, CRANIUM): orig. of a headache confined to one side of the head]

migrant /mígrənt/ *adj.* & *n.* ● *adj.* that migrates. ● *n.* **1** a person who moves regularly, as for work. **2** an animal that changes habitats, as with the seasons.
■ *adj.* transient, migratory, itinerant, peripatetic, nomadic, gypsy, vagrant. ● *n.* wanderer, rover, drifter, gypsy, nomad, itinerant, transient, migrator, wayfarer, bird of passage, traveler, vagrant, *archaic or joc.* peregrinator, *sl. offens.* wetback.

migrate /mígrayt/ *v.intr.* **1** (of people) move from one place of abode to another, esp. in a different country. **2** (of a bird or fish) change its area of habitation with the seasons. **3** move under natural forces. □□ **migration** /-gráyshən/ *n.* **migrational** /-gráyshənəl/ *adj.* **migrator** *n.* **migratory** /-grətáwree/ *adj.* [L *migrare migrat-*]
■ go, move, travel, settle, resettle, relocate, move house; emigrate, immigrate; wander, roam, voyage, rove, drift, range.

mihrab /meéraab/ *n.* a niche or slab in a mosque, used to show the direction of Mecca. [Arab. *miḥrāb* praying place]

mikado /mikaadō/ *n.* (*pl.* **-os**) *hist.* the emperor of Japan. [Jap. f. *mi* august + *kado* door]

mike /mīk/ *n.* *colloq.* a microphone. [abbr.]

mil /mil/ *n.* one-thousandth of an inch, as a unit of measure for the diameter of wire, etc. [L *millesimum* thousandth f. *mille* thousand]

milady /miláydee/ *n.* (*pl.* **-ies**) **1** an English noblewoman or great lady. **2** a form used in speaking of or to such a person. [F f. E *my lady*: cf. MILORD]

milage var. of MILEAGE.

Milanese /míləneéz/ *adj.* & *n.* ● *adj.* of or relating to Milan in N. Italy. ● *n.* (*pl.* same) a native of Milan. □ **Milanese silk** a finely woven silk or rayon.

milch /milch/ *adj.* (of a domestic mammal) giving or kept for milk. □ **milch cow** = *milk cow*. [ME *m(i)elche* repr. OE *mielce* (unrecorded) f. Gmc: see MILK]

mild /mīld/ *adj.* **1** (esp. of a person) gentle and conciliatory. **2** (of a rule, punishment, illness, feeling, etc.) moderate; not severe. **3** (of the weather, esp. in winter) moderately warm. **4** (of food, tobacco, etc.) not sharp or strong in taste, etc. **5** (of medicine) operating gently. **6** tame; feeble; lacking energy or vivacity. □ **mild steel** steel containing a small percentage of carbon, strong and tough but not readily tempered. □□ **milden** *v.tr.* & *intr.* **mildish** *adj.* **mildness** *n.* [OE *milde* f. Gmc]
■ **1** placid, peaceful, calm, tranquil, tolerant, mellow, inoffensive, gentle, serene, good-natured, affable, amiable, kind, kindly, equable, easygoing, temperate, nonviolent, conciliatory, indulgent, merciful, forgiving, compassionate, lenient, forbearing, peaceable, pacific, passive, submissive, yielding, tractable, meek, unassuming, modest, quiet, subdued. **2** see LENIENT. **3** clement, balmy, warm, fair, pleasant, temperate, placid, moderate. **5** soothing, demulcent, emollient, gentle, calming, *Med.* lenitive. **6** see TAME *adj.* 3.

mildew /míldōo, -dyōo/ *n.* & *v.* ● *n.* **1** a destructive growth of minute fungi on plants. **2** a similar growth on paper, leather, etc., exposed to damp. ● *v.tr.* & *intr.* taint or be tainted with mildew. □□ **mildewy** *adj.* [OE *mildēaw* f. Gmc]
■ *n.* see MOLD². ● *v.* see SPOIL *v.* 3a. □□ **mildewy** see MOLDY 1.

mildly /míldlee/ *adv.* in a mild fashion. □ **to put it mildly** as an understatement (implying the reality is more extreme).
■ see *quietly* (QUIET).

mile /mīl/ *n.* **1** (also **statute mile**) a unit of linear measure equal to 1,760 yards (approx. 1.609 kilometers). **2** *hist.* a Roman measure of 1,000 paces (approx. 1,620 yards). **3** (in *pl.*) *colloq.* a great distance or amount (*miles better*; *beat them by miles*). **4** a race extending over a mile. [OE *mīl* ult. f. L *mil(l)ia* pl. of *mille* thousand (see sense 2)]

mileage /mílij/ *n.* (also **milage**) **1 a** a number of miles traveled, used, etc. **b** the number of miles traveled by a vehicle per unit of fuel. **2** traveling expenses (per mile). **3** *colloq.* benefit, profit, advantage (*we got a lot of mileage out of that old chair*).
■ **1 a** see DISTANCE *n.* 2.

milepost /mílpōst/ *n.* **1** a post or sign giving distance in miles, as along a highway. **2** a post one mile from the finish line of a race, etc.

miler /mílər/ *n.* *colloq.* a person or horse qualified or trained specially to run a mile.

milestone /mílstōn/ *n.* **1** a stone set up beside a road to mark a distance in miles. **2** a significant event or stage in a life, history, project, etc.

■ **2** see LANDMARK 2.

milfoil /mílfoyl/ *n.* the common yarrow, *Achillea millefolium*, with small white flowers and finely divided leaves. [ME f. OF f. L *millefolium* f. *mille* thousand + *folium* leaf, after Gk *muriophullon*]

miliary /mílee-éree, mílyəree/ *adj.* **1** like a millet seed in size or form. **2** (of a disease) having as a symptom a rash with lesions resembling millet seed. [L *miliarius* f. *milium* millet]

milieu /milyő, meélyö/ *n.* (*pl.* **milieus** or **milieux** /-lyőz/) one's environment or social surroundings. [F f. *mi* MID[1] + *lieu* place]

■ environment, climate, surroundings, environs, background, neighborhood, precincts; ambience, sphere, setting, atmosphere, medium, element.

militant /mílit'nt/ *adj. & n.* ● *adj.* **1** combative; aggressively active, esp. in support of a (usu. political) cause. **2** engaged in warfare. ● *n.* **1** a militant person, esp. a political activist. **2** a person engaged in warfare. □□ **militancy** *n.* **militantly** *adv.* [ME f. OF f. L (as MILITATE)]

■ *adj.* **1** aggressive, combative, pugnacious, belligerent, hostile, contentious, antagonistic, offensive, truculent, fierce, ferocious, warlike, bellicose, martial, jingoistic, hawkish. **2** warring, fighting, combatant, embattled; at war, up in arms. ● *n.* **1** activist, fighter, campaigner. **2** aggressor, combatant, belligerent, warrior, soldier.

militarism /mílitərizəm/ *n.* **1** the spirit or tendencies of a professional soldier. **2** undue prevalence of the military spirit or ideals. □□ **militaristic** /-rístik/ *adj.* **militaristically** /-rístiklee/ *adv.* [F *militarisme* (as MILITARY)]

■ □□ **militaristic** see WARLIKE 1.

militarist /mílitərist/ *n.* **1** a person dominated by militaristic ideas. **2** a student of military science.

militarize /mílitəriz/ *v.tr.* **1** equip with military resources. **2** make military or warlike. **3** imbue with militarism. □□ **militarization** *n.*

military /mílitéree/ *adj. & n.* ● *adj.* of, relating to, or characteristic of soldiers or armed forces. ● *n.* (as *sing.* or *pl.*; prec. by *the*) members of the armed forces, as distinct from civilians and the police. □ **military honors** marks of respect paid by troops at the burial of a soldier, to royalty, etc. **military police** a corps responsible for police and disciplinary duties in the army. **military policeman** a member of the military police. □□ **militarily** /-táirəlee/ *adv.* **militariness** *n.* [F *militaire* or L *militaris* f. *miles militis* soldier]

■ *adj.* martial, soldierly, army, fighting, service. ● *n.* (*the military*) (armed) services *or* forces, army, air force, soldiery.

militate /mílitayt/ *v.intr.* (usu. foll. by *against*) (of facts or evidence) have force or effect (*what you say militates against our opinion*). ¶ Often confused with *mitigate*. [L *militare militat-* f. *miles militis* soldier]

■ (*militate against*) work *or* go *or* operate against, foil, counter, countervail (against), cancel (out); resist, oppose.

militia /milíshə/ *n.* a military force, esp. one raised from the civil population and supplementing a regular army in an emergency. [L, = military service f. *miles militis* soldier]

militiaman /milíshəmən/ *n.* (*pl.* **-men**) a member of a militia.

milk /milk/ *n. & v.* ● *n.* **1** an opaque white fluid secreted by female mammals for the nourishment of their young. **2** the milk of cows, goats, or sheep as food. **3** the milklike juice of plants, e.g., in the coconut. **4** a milklike preparation of herbs, drugs, etc. ● *v.tr.* **1** draw milk from (a cow, ewe, goat, etc.). **2 a** exploit (a person) esp. financially. **b** get all possible advantage from (a situation). **3** extract sap, venom, etc., from. **4** *sl.* tap (telegraph or telephone wires, etc.). □ **cry over spilled milk** lament an irremediable loss or error. **in milk** secreting milk. **milk and honey** abundant means of prosperity. **milk bar** a snack bar selling milk drinks and other refreshments. **milk chocolate** chocolate made with milk. **milk float** *Brit.* a small usu. electric vehicle used in delivering milk. **milk leg** a painful swelling, esp. of the legs, after childbirth. **milk of human kindness** kindness regarded as natural to humanity. **milk of magnesia** a

white suspension of magnesium hydroxide usu. in water as an antacid or laxative. **milk pudding** *Brit.* a pudding of rice, sago, tapioca, etc., baked with milk in a dish. **milk round** *Brit.* = *milk route.* **milk route 1** a fixed route on which milk is delivered regularly. **2** a regular trip or tour involving calls at several places. **milk run** a routine expedition or service journey. **milk shake** a drink of milk, flavoring, and usu. ice cream, mixed by shaking or blending. **milk snake** any of various harmless snakes, *Lampropeltis triangulum*, common to N. America, with colorful markings on a grayish or tan body. **milk sugar** lactose. **milk-toast** *adj.* lacking assertiveness; timid. ● *n.* = MILQUETOAST. **milk tooth** a temporary tooth in young mammals. **milk vetch** any leguminous yellow-flowered plant of the genus *Astragalus*. **milk-white** white like milk. □□ **milker** *n.* [OE *milc, milcian* f. Gmc]

■ *n.* **3** latex; see also JUICE 1. **4** see SOLUTION 2b. ● *v.* **2** exploit, bleed, drain, take advantage of. □ **milk and honey** prosperity, riches, wealth, opulence. **milk route 2** rounds, circuit.

milkmaid /mílkmayd/ *n.* a girl or woman who milks cows or works in a dairy.

milkman /mílkman/ *n.* (*pl.* **-men**) a person who sells or delivers milk.

milksop /mílksop/ *n.* a spiritless or meek person, esp. a man.

■ coward, weakling, namby-pamby, crybaby, *poet. or archaic* caitiff, *Austral. & NZ sl. derog.* sook. *colloq.* sissy, mama's boy, *colloq. derog.* pansy, *Brit.* mollycoddle, chinless wonder.

milkweed /mílkweed/ *n.* any of various wild plants with milky juice.

milkwort /mílkwərt/ *n.* any plant of the genus *Polygala*, formerly supposed to increase women's milk.

milky /mílkee/ *adj.* (**milkier, milkiest**) **1** of, like, or mixed with milk. **2** (of a gem or liquid) cloudy; not clear. **3** effeminate; weakly amiable. □ **Milky Way** a faintly luminous band of light emitted by countless stars encircling the heavens; the Galaxy. □□ **milkiness** *n.*

■ **2** see FILMY 2. **3** see EFFEMINATE.

mill[1] /mil/ *n. & v.* ● *n.* **1 a** a building fitted with a mechanical apparatus for grinding grain. **b** such an apparatus. **2** an apparatus for grinding any solid substance to powder or pulp (*pepper mill*). **3 a** a building fitted with machinery for manufacturing processes, etc. (*cotton mill*). **b** such machinery. **4 a** a boxing match. **b** a fistfight. **5** a place that processes things or people in a mechanical way (*diploma mill*). ● *v.* **1** *tr.* grind (grain), produce (flour), or hull (seeds) in a mill. **2** *tr.* produce regular ribbed markings on the edge of (a coin). **3** *tr.* cut or shape (metal) with a rotating tool. **4** *intr.* (often foll. by *about, around*) (of people or animals) move in an aimless manner, esp. in a confused mass. **5** *tr.* thicken (cloth, etc.) by fulling. **6** *tr.* beat (chocolate, etc.) to froth. **7** *tr. sl.* beat, strike, fight. □ **go** (or **put**) **through the mill** undergo (or cause to undergo) intensive work or training, etc. □□ **millable** *adj.* [OE *mylen* ult. f. LL *molinum* f. L *mola* grindstone, mill f. *molere* grind]

■ *n.* **1b, 2** grinder, quern, crusher, roller. **3 a** plant, factory, works, workshop, shop, foundry. **4** see BOUT 2a. ● *v.* **1** grind, crush, hull, comminute, powder, pulverize, granulate, pound, triturate, crunch, *archaic* bray. **4** (*mill about or around*) crowd, throng, swarm. **7** see BEAT *v.* 1, FIGHT *v.* 1a.

mill[2] /mil/ *n.* one-thousandth of a US dollar as money of account. [L *millesimum* thousandth: cf. CENT]

millboard /mílbawrd/ *n.* stout pasteboard for bookbinding, etc.

mille-feuille /meelfő-yə/ *n.* a rich confection of puff pastry split and filled with custard, whipped cream, etc. [F, = thousand-leaf]

/.../ **pronunciation**   ● **part of speech**
□ **phrases, idioms, and compounds**
□□ **derivatives**   ■ **synonym section**
cross-references appear in SMALL CAPITALS or *italics*

millenarian /mílináireeən/ *adj. & n.* ● *adj.* **1** of or related to the millennium. **2** believing in the millennium. ● *n.* a person who believes in the millennium. [as MILLENARY]
■ *adj.* chiliastic, millenary, millenialist. ● *n.* chiliast, millenary, millenialist.

millenary /mílənéree/ *n. & adj.* ● *n.* (*pl.* **-ies**) **1** a period of 1,000 years. **2** the festival of the 1,000th anniversary of a person or thing. **3** a person who believes in the millennium. ● *adj.* of or relating to a millenary. [LL *millenarius* consisting of a thousand f. *milleni* distrib. of *mille* thousand]

millennium /míléneeəm/ *n.* (*pl.* **millennia** /-neeə/ or **millenniums**) **1** a period of 1,000 years, esp. that of Christ's prophesied reign in person on earth (Rev. 20:1–5). **2** a period of good government, great happiness, and prosperity. □□ **millennial** *adj.* **millennialist** *n. & adj.* [mod.L f. L *mille* thousand after BIENNIUM]

millepede var. of MILLIPEDE.

millepore /mílipawr/ *n.* a reef-building coral of the order Milleporina, with polyps protruding through pores in the calcareous exoskeleton. [F *millépore* or mod.L *millepora* f. L *mille* thousand + *porus* PORE¹]

miller /mílər/ *n.* **1** the proprietor or tenant of a mill. **2** a person who works or owns a mill. □ **miller's-thumb** a small spiny freshwater fish, *Cottus gobio*: also called BULLHEAD. [ME *mylnere*, prob. f. MLG, MDu. *molner, mulner*, OS *mulineri* f. LL *molinarius* f. *molina* MILL¹, assim. to MILL¹]

millesimal /mílésimǝl/ *adj. & n.* ● *adj.* **1** thousandth. **2** of or belonging to a thousandth. **3** of or dealing with thousandths. ● *n.* a thousandth part. □□ **millesimally** *adv.* [L *millesimus* f. *mille* thousand]

millet /mílit/ *n.* **1** any of various cereal plants, esp. *Panicum miliaceum*, bearing a large crop of small nutritious seeds. **2** the seed of this. □ **millet grass** a tall woodland grass, *Milium effusum*. [ME f. F, dimin. of *mil* f. L *milium*]

milli- /mílee, -i, -ə/ *comb. form* a thousand, esp. denoting a factor of one thousandth. ¶ Abbr.: **m**. [L *mille* thousand]

milliammeter /míleeámitǝr/ *n.* an instrument for measuring electrical current in milliamperes.

milliampere /míleeámpir/ *n.* one-thousandth of an ampere, a measure for small electrical currents.

milliard /mílyǝrd, -yaard/ *n. Brit.* one thousand million. ¶ Now largely superseded by *billion*. [F f. *mille* thousand]

millibar /mílǝbaar/ *n.* one-thousandth of a bar, the cgs unit of atmospheric pressure equivalent to 100 pascals.

milligram /míligram/ *n.* one-thousandth of a gram.

milliliter /mílileetǝr/ *n.* one-thousandth of a liter (0.002 pint).

millimeter /mílimeetǝr/ *n.* one-thousandth of a meter (0.039 in.).

milliner /mílinǝr/ *n.* a person who makes or sells women's hats. □□ **millinery** /-eree/ *n.* [orig. = vendor of goods from *Milan*]

million /mílyǝn/ *n. & adj.* ● *n.* (*pl.* same or (in sense 2) **millions**) (in *sing.* prec. by *a* or *one*) **1** a thousand thousand. **2** (in *pl.*) *colloq.* a very large number (*millions of years*). **3** (prec. by *the*) the bulk of the population. **4** (prec. by *a*) a million dollars. ● *adj.* that amount to a million. □ **gone a million** *Austral. sl.* completely defeated. □□ **millionfold** *adj. & adv.* **millionth** *adj. & n.* [ME f. OF, prob. f. It. *millione* f. *mille* thousand + *-one* augment. suffix]
■ *n.* **2** (*millions*) see SCORE *n.* 3.

millionaire /mílyǝnáir/ *n.* (*fem.* **millionairess** /-ris/) **1** a person whose assets are worth at least one million dollars, pounds, etc. **2** a person of great wealth. [F *millionnaire* (as MILLION)]
■ see TYCOON.

millipede /mílǝpeed/ *n.* (also **millepede**) any arthropod of the class Diplopoda, having a long segmented body with two pairs of legs on each segment. [L *millepeda* wood louse f. *mille* thousand + *pes pedis* foot]

millisecond /mílisekǝnd/ *n.* one-thousandth of a second.

millpond /mílpond/ *n.* a pool of water retained by a dam for the operation of a mill. □ **like a millpond** (of a stretch of water) very calm.

millrace /mílrays/ *n.* a current of water that drives a mill wheel.

millstone /mílstōn/ *n.* **1** each of two circular stones used for grinding grain. **2** a heavy burden or responsibility (cf. Matt. 18:6).
■ **2** see BURDEN *n.* 1, 2.

millwright /mílrit/ *n.* a person who designs, builds, or operates a mill or milling machinery.

milometer /mílómitǝr/ *n. Brit.* an instrument for measuring the number of miles traveled by a vehicle.

milord /miláwrd/ *n. hist.* an English gentleman, esp. one traveling in Europe in aristocratic style. [F f. E *my lord*: cf. MILADY]

milquetoast /mílktōst/ *n.* a meek, unassertive person. [for Casper *Milquetoast*, character in comic strip by US cartoonist H.T. Webster (1885–1952)]

milt /milt/ *n.* **1** a sperm-filled reproductive gland of a male fish. **2** the sperm-filled secretion of this gland. **3** var. of MELT². [OE *milt(e)* f. Gmc, perh. rel. to MELT]

milter /míltǝr/ *n.* a male fish in spawning time.

mimbar /mímbaar/ *n.* (also **minbar** /mín-/) a stepped platform for preaching in a mosque. [Arab. *minbar*]

mime /mim/ *n. & v.* ● *n.* **1** the theatrical technique of suggesting action, character, etc., by gesture and expression without using words. **2** a theatrical performance using this technique. **3** *Gk & Rom. Antiq.* a simple farcical drama including mimicry. **4** (also **mime artist**) a practitioner of mime. ● *v.* **1** *tr.* (also *absol.*) convey (an idea or emotion) by gesture without words. **2** *intr.* esp. *Brit.* (often foll. by *to*) (of singers, etc.) mouth the words of a song, etc., along with a soundtrack; lip-sync (*mime to a record*). □□ **mimer** *n.* [L *mimus* f. Gk *mimos*]

mimeograph /mímeeǝgraf/ *n. & v.* ● *n.* **1** (often *attrib.*) a duplicating machine that produces copies from a stencil. **2** a copy produced in this way. ● *v.tr.* reproduce (text or diagrams) by this process. [irreg. f. Gk *mimeomai* imitate: see -GRAPH]

mimesis /mimeésis, mī-/ *n. Biol.* a close external resemblance of an animal to another that is distasteful or harmful to predators of the first. [Gk *mimēsis* imitation]

mimetic /mimétik/ *adj.* **1** relating to or habitually practicing imitation or mimicry. **2** *Biol.* of or exhibiting mimesis. □□ **mimetically** *adv.* [Gk *mimētikos* imitation (as MIMESIS)]
■ **1** see MIMIC *adj.*

mimic /mímik/ *v., n., & adj.* ● *v.tr.* (**mimicked, mimicking**) **1** imitate (a person, gesture, etc.) esp. to entertain or ridicule. **2** copy minutely or servilely. **3** (of a thing) resemble closely. ● *n.* a person skilled in imitation. ● *adj.* having an aptitude for mimicry; imitating; imitative of a thing, esp. for amusement. □□ **mimicker** *n.* [L *mimicus* f. Gk *mimikos* (as MIME)]
■ *v.* **1** mock, ridicule, satirize, caricature, parody, make fun of, lampoon, impersonate, *colloq.* take off; imitate, ape, copy, simulate. **2** reproduce, duplicate, copy; see also IMITATE 3. **3** mirror, echo; see also RESEMBLE. ● *n.* impersonator, imitator, impressionist, caricaturist, parodist; *colloq.* copycat. ● *adj.* imitative, mimetic; imitation, mock, simulated, sham, make-believe, pretend(ed).

mimicry /mímikree/ *n.* (*pl.* **-ies**) **1** the act or art of mimicking. **2** a thing that mimics another. **3** *Zool.* mimesis.
■ **1** see IMITATION *n.* 1.

mimosa /mimōsǝ, -zǝ/ *n.* **1** any leguminous shrub of the genus *Mimosa*, esp. *M. pudica*, having globular usu. yellow flowers and sensitive leaflets that droop when touched. **2** any of various acacia plants with showy yellow flowers. **3** a cocktail of champagne and orange juice. [mod.L, app. f. L (as MIME, from being as sensitive as animals) + *-osa* fem. suffix]

mimulus /mímyǝlǝs/ *n.* any flowering plant of the genus *Mimulus*, including musk and the monkey flower. [mod.L, app. dimin. of L (as MIME, perh. with ref. to its masklike flowers)]

Min /min/ *n.* any of the Chinese languages or dialects spoken in the Fukien province in SE China. [Chin.]

Min. *abbr.* esp. *Brit.* **1** Minister. **2** Ministry.

min. *abbr.* **1** minute(s). **2** minimum. **3** minim (fluid measure).

mina var. of MYNA.

minaret /mínərét/ *n.* a slender turret connected to a mosque and having a balcony from which the muezzin calls at hours of prayer. □□ **minareted** *adj.* [F *minaret* or Sp. *minarete* f. Turk. *minare* f. Arab. *manār(a)* lighthouse, minaret f. *nār* fire, light]
■ see TOWER *n.* 1a.

minatory /mínətəwree/ *adj.* threatening, menacing. [LL *minatorius* f. *minari minat-* threaten]
■ see *threatening* (THREATEN).

minbar var. of MIMBAR.

mince /mins/ *v.* & *n.* ● *v.* **1** *tr.* cut up or grind into very small pieces. **2** *tr.* (usu. with *neg.*) restrain (one's words, etc.) within the bounds of politeness. **3** *intr.* (usu. as **mincing** *adj.*) speak or walk with an affected delicacy. ● *n.* esp. *Brit.* ground meat. □ **mince matters** (usu. with *neg.*) use polite expressions, etc. **mince pie** a pie containing mincemeat. □□ **mincer** *n.* **mincingly** *adv.* (in sense 3 of *v.*). [ME f. OF *mincier* ult. f. L (as MINUTIA)]
■ *v.* **1** see *cut up* 1, GRIND *v.* 1a. **3** (**mincing**) effeminate, dainty, delicate, foppish, dandyish, affected, precious, chichi, *Brit. usu. derog.* twee.

mincemeat /mínsmeet/ *n.* a mixture of currants, raisins, sugar, apples, candied peel, spices, often suet, and sometimes meat. □ **make mincemeat of** utterly defeat (a person, argument, etc.).

mind /mind/ *n.* & *v.* ● *n.* **1 a** the seat of consciousness, thought, volition, and feeling. **b** attention, concentration (*my mind keeps wandering*). **2** the intellect; intellectual powers; aptitude. **3** remembrance, memory (*it went out of my mind; I can't call it to mind*). **4** one's opinion (*we're of the same mind*). **5** a way of thinking or feeling (*shocking to the Victorian mind*). **6** the focus of one's thoughts or desires (*put one's mind to it*). **7** the state of normal mental functioning (*lose one's mind; in one's right mind*). **8** a person as embodying mental faculties (*a great mind*). ● *v.tr.* **1** (usu. with *neg.* or *interrog.*) object to (*do you mind if I smoke?; I don't mind your being late*). **2 a** remember; take care to (*mind you come on time*). **b** (*Brit.* often foll. by *out*) take care; be careful. **3** have charge of temporarily (*mind the house while I'm away*). **4** apply oneself to, concern oneself with (business, affairs, etc.) (*I try to mind my own business*). **5** give heed to; notice (*mind the step; don't mind the expense; mind how you go*). **6** be obedient to (*mind what your mother says*). □ **be of two minds** be undecided. **be of a mind** (often foll. by *to* + infin.) be prepared or disposed. **cast one's mind back** think back; recall an earlier time. **come into a person's mind** be remembered. **come to mind** (of a thought, idea, etc.) suggest itself. **cross one's mind** happen to occur to one. **don't mind me** *iron.* do as you please. **do you mind!** *iron.* an expression of annoyance. **give a person a piece of one's mind** scold or reproach a person. **have a good** (or **half a**) **mind to** (often as a threat, usu. unfulfilled) feel tempted to (*I've a good mind to report you*). **have (it) in mind** intend. **have a mind of one's own** be capable of independent opinion. **have on one's mind** be troubled by the thought of. **meeting of minds** accord; agreement. **in one's mind's eye** in one's imagination or mental view. **mind-bending** *colloq.* (esp. of a psychedelic drug) influencing or altering one's state of mind. **mind-blowing** *sl.* **1** confusing, shattering. **2** (esp. of drugs, etc.) inducing hallucinations. **mind-boggling** *colloq.* overwhelming, startling. **mind-expanding** causing heightened perceptions, as from psychedelic drugs. **mind over matter** the power of the mind asserted over the physical universe. **mind one's Ps & Qs** be careful in one's behavior. **mind-read** discern the thoughts of (another person). **mind reader** a person capable of mind reading. **mind-set** habits of mind formed by earlier events. **mind the store** have charge of affairs temporarily. **mind you** an expression used to qualify a previous statement (*I found it quite quickly—mind you, it wasn't easy*). **never mind 1** an expression used to comfort or console. **2** (also **never you mind**) an expression used to evade a ques-

tion. **3** disregard (*never mind the cost*). **open** (or **close**) **one's mind to** be receptive (or unreceptive) to (changes, new ideas, etc.). **out of one's mind** crazy. **presence of mind** ability to think, act constructively, etc., during a crisis. **put a person in mind of** remind a person of. **put** (or **set**) **a person's mind at rest** reassure a person. **put a person** (or **thing**) **out of one's mind** deliberately forget. **read a person's mind** discern a person's thoughts. **to my mind** in my opinion. [ME *mynd* f. OE *gemynd* f. Gmc]
■ *n.* **1b, 6** consciousness, awareness; attention, thoughts, concentration, attentiveness; see also PERCEPTION, SENSITIVITY. **2** intelligence, intellect, wit(s), mentality, brain, brains, brainpower, sense, sagacity, wisdom, perception, percipience, reason, astuteness, insight, shrewdness, sapience, *colloq.* gray matter; aptitude, head, perception, capacity. **3** memory, recollection; remembrance. **4** opinion, sentiment, attitude, (point of) view, feeling, judgment, belief, viewpoint, standpoint, position. **5** intention, disposition, temper, temperament, humor, fancy, tendency, bent, inclination, bias, persuasion, mentality. **7** see SANITY 1. **8** intellect, intellectual, sage, genius, thinker, *colloq.* brain. ● *v.* **1** object to, resent, take offense at, be offended by, dislike, be troubled *or* annoyed by, care about, disapprove of, be bothered *or* affronted by. **2 a** remember, not forget to, take care to, make sure to, be sure to. **b** (*mind out*) watch out, look out, take care, be careful. **3** watch over, take care of, care for, look after, sit with, babysit, guard, keep an eye on *or* out for, have *or* take charge of, attend to. **4** see *address oneself to* 2, *mind one's own business* (BUSINESS). **5, 6** heed, give heed to, attend to, pay attention to, obey, listen to, make *or* take note of, mark, note, notice; watch, be careful of, take care with, be cautious of, be concerned about *or* over. □ **be of two minds** vacillate, waver, shilly-shally, dither, be uncertain *or* unsure, be undecided *or* ambivalent, hesitate, *Brit.* haver, *colloq.* dillydally. **cast one's mind back** see REMINISCE. **come to mind** see OCCUR 3. **give a person a piece of one's mind** castigate, scold, rebuke, reprimand, rail at, reprove, reproach, chastise, upbraid, berate, read a person the riot act, haul *or* call over the coals, *colloq.* tell off, dress down, bawl out, give a person hell, chew out. **have (it) in mind** see INTEND 1, 2. **have on one's mind** be preoccupied by, be troubled *or* plagued by the thought of. **mind-bending** mind-altering, *sl.* mind-blowing; psychedelic, hallucinogenic. **mind-blowing 1** see OVERWHELMING. **2** see *mind-bending* above. **mind-boggling** see OVERWHELMING. **mind-read** read a person's mind. **mind you** see THOUGH *adv.* **never mind 2** see *mind one's own business* (BUSINESS). **3** ignore, disregard, forget, pay no attention to, do not think twice about, do not give a second thought to, erase *or* obliterate *or* cancel from the mind. **out of one's mind** see CRAZY 1. **put a person in mind of** remind of, cause to remember. **put** (or **set**) **a person's mind at rest** see REASSURE. **put a thing out of one's mind** see FORGET 4. **read a person's mind** mind read. **to my mind** as I see it, in my opinion *or* judgment *or* view, in my book, for my money, if you ask me, from my point of view, to my way of thinking, personally.

minded /míndid/ *adj.* **1** (in *comb.*) **a** inclined to think in some specified way (*mathematically minded; fair-minded*). **b** having a specified kind of mind (*high-minded*). **c** interested in or enthusiastic about a specified thing (*car-minded*). **2** (usu. foll. by *to* + infin.) disposed or inclined (to an action).

minder /míndər/ *n.* **1 a** a person whose job it is to attend to a person or thing. **b** (in *comb.*) *Brit.* (*child-minder; machine-*

minder). **2** esp. *Brit. sl.* **a** a bodyguard, esp. a person employed to protect a criminal. **b** a thief's assistant.
■ **1** babysitter, sitter, nanny, nurse, governess, *Brit.* childminder. **2 a** bodyguard, protector; see also ESCORT *n.* 1.

mindful /míndfŏŏl/ *adj.* (often foll. by *of*) taking heed or care; being conscious. □□ **mindfully** *adv.* **mindfulness** *n.*
■ aware, alert, attentive, alive, conscious, heedful, careful, conscientious, watchful, vigilant, on the qui vive, on the lookout, circumspect, cautious.

mindless /míndlis/ *adj.* **1** lacking intelligence; stupid. **2** not requiring thought or skill (*totally mindless work*). **3** (usu. foll. by *of*) heedless of (advice, etc.). □□ **mindlessly** *adv.* **mindlessness** *n.*
■ **1** stupid, asinine, obtuse, idiotic, thoughtless, witless, senseless, brainless, feebleminded, fatuous, *colloq.* thick, thickheaded, moronic, imbecilic, esp. *Brit. colloq.* gormless. **2** perfunctory, unthinking; see also MECHANICAL 3. **3** heedless, unaware; see also INATTENTIVE.

mindset /míndset/ *n.* **1** a mental attitude that can influence one's interpretation of events or situations. **2** an inclination or a fixed way of thinking.

mine[1] /mīn/ *poss. pron.* **1** the one or ones belonging to or associated with me (*it is mine; mine are over there*). **2** (*attrib.* before a vowel) *archaic* = MY (*mine eyes have seen; mine host*). □ **of mine** of or belonging to me (*a friend of mine*). [OE *mīn* f. Gmc]

mine[2] /mīn/ *n. & v.* ● *n.* **1** an excavation in the earth for extracting metal, coal, salt, etc. **2** an abundant source (of information, etc.). **3** a receptacle filled with explosive and placed in the ground or in the water for destroying enemy personnel, ships, etc. **4 a** a subterranean gallery in which explosive is placed to blow up fortifications. **b** *hist.* a subterranean passage under the wall of a besieged fortress. ● *v.tr.* **1** obtain (metal, coal, etc.) from a mine. **2** (also *absol.*, often foll. by *for*) dig in (the earth, etc.) for ore, etc. **3 a** dig or burrow in (usu. the earth). **b** delve into (an abundant source) for information, etc. **c** make (a hole, passage, etc.) underground. **4** lay explosive mines under or in. **5** = UNDERMINE. □ **mine detector** an instrument for detecting the presence of mines. □□ **mining** *n.* [ME f. OF *mine, miner*, perh. f. Celt.]
■ *n.* **1** pit, excavation; colliery, coalfield. **2** source, quarry, store, storehouse, supply, deposit, depository, repository, reserve, hoard, reservoir, well-spring; fund, mint, gold mine, treasury. ● *v.* **1, 2** excavate, dig, quarry, extract, scoop out *or* up, remove, unearth; derive, extract, draw. **3 a, c** dig *or* burrow in; gouge (out), scoop (out), hollow out. **b** ransack, search, rake through, scour, scan, read, survey, look through, probe.

minefield /mínfeeld/ *n.* **1** an area planted with explosive mines. **2** a subject or situation presenting unseen hazards.

minelayer /mínlayər/ *n.* a ship or aircraft for laying mines.

miner /mínər/ *n.* **1** a person who works in a mine. **2** any burrowing insect or grub. [ME f. OF *minēor, minour* (as MINE[2])]

mineral /mínərəl/ *n. & adj.* ● *n.* **1** any of the species into which inorganic substances are classified. **2** a substance obtained by mining. **3** (often in *pl.*) *Brit.* an artificial mineral water or other effervescent drink. ● *adj.* **1** of or containing a mineral or minerals. **2** obtained by mining. □ **mineral oil** *Pharm.* a colorless, odorless, oily liquid obtained from petroleum and used as a laxative, in manufacturing cosmetics, etc. **mineral water 1** water found in nature with some dissolved salts present. **2** an artificial imitation of this, esp. soda water. **3** *Brit.* any effervescent nonalcoholic drink. **mineral wax** a fossil resin, esp. ozocerite. **mineral wool** a woollike substance made from inorganic material, used for packing, etc. [ME f. OF *mineral* or med.L *mineralis* f. *minera* ore f. OF *miniere* mine]

mineralize /mínərəlīz/ *v.* **1** *v.tr. & intr.* change wholly or partly into a mineral. **2** *v.tr.* impregnate (water, etc.) with a mineral substance.

mineralogy /mínəráləjee/ *n.* the scientific study of minerals. □□ **mineralogical** /-rəlójikəl/ *adj.* **mineralogist** *n.*

minestrone /mínistrōnee/ *n.* a soup containing vegetables and pasta, beans, or rice. [It.]

minesweeper /mínsweepər/ *n.* a ship for clearing away floating and submarine mines.

minever var. of MINIVER.

mineworker /mínwərkər/ *n.* a person who works in a mine.

Ming /ming/ *n.* **1** the dynasty ruling China 1368–1644. **2** Chinese porcelain made during the rule of this dynasty. [Chin.]

mingle /mínggəl/ *v.* **1** *tr. & intr.* mix, blend. **2** *intr.* (often foll. by *with*) (of a person) move about, associate. □ **mingle their** (etc.) **tears** *literary* weep together. □□ **mingler** *n.* [ME *mengel* f. obs. *meng* f. OE *mengan*, rel. to AMONG]
■ **1** mix, blend, intermingle, intermix, combine, amalgamate, merge, compound, marry, join, unite, *literary* commingle. **2** mix, socialize, associate, fraternize, hobnob, consort, spend time, hang about *or* around, rub shoulders, *Brit. colloq.* pal up, *sl.* hang out; (*mingle with*) join, circulate among, move *or* go about among.

mingy /mínjee/ *adj.* (**mingier, mingiest**) *colloq.* mean, stingy. □□ **mingily** *adv.* [perh. f. MEAN[2] and STINGY]
■ see MEAN[2] 1.

mini /mínee/ *n.* (*pl.* **minis**) *colloq.* a miniskirt, minidress, etc.

mini- /mínee/ *comb. form* miniature; very small or minor of its kind (*minibus; mini-budget*). [abbr. of MINIATURE]
■ micro-.

miniature /míneeəchər, mínichər/ *adj., n., & v.* ● *adj.* **1** much smaller than normal. **2** represented on a small scale. ● *n.* **1** any object reduced in size. **2** a small-scale minutely finished portrait. **3** this branch of painting (*portrait in miniature*). **4** a picture or decorated letters in an illuminated manuscript. ● *v.tr.* represent on a smaller scale. □ **in miniature** on a small scale. **miniature golf** game similar to golf, played with a golf ball and putter, on a confined, usu. carpeted course featuring obstacles, etc. □□ **miniaturist** *n.* (in senses 2 and 3 of *n.*). [It. *miniatura* f. med.L *miniatura* f. L *miniare* rubricate, illuminate f. L *minium* red lead, vermilion]
■ *adj.* small, small-scale, little, tiny, diminutive, minute, minimal, minuscule, mini-, microscopic, midget, dwarf, baby, pygmy, pocket, Lilliputian, esp. *Sc. or colloq.* wee.

miniaturize /míneeəchərīz, mínichə-/ *v.tr.* produce in a smaller version; make small. □□ **miniaturization** *n.*

minibike /míneebīk/ *n.* a motorbike designed for off-road use, esp. with elevated handlebars.

minibus /míneebus/ *n.* a small bus or van.

minicab /míneekab/ *n. Brit.* a small car used as a taxi.

minicam /míneekam/ *n.* a portable lightweight video camera.

minicomputer /míneekəmpyŏŏtər/ *n.* a computer of medium power, more than a microcomputer but less than a mainframe.

minikin /mínikin/ *adj. & n.* ● *adj.* **1** diminutive. **2** affected, mincing. ● *n.* a diminutive creature. [obs. Du. *minneken* f. *minne* love + *-ken, -kijn* -KIN]

minim /mínim/ *n.* **1** one-sixtieth of a fluid dram, about a drop. **2** *Mus.* esp. *Brit.* = *half note.* **3** an object or portion of the smallest size or importance. **4** a single downstroke of the pen. [ME f. L *minimus* smallest]

minima *pl.* of MINIMUM.

minimal /mínimɔl/ *adj.* **1** very minute or slight. **2** being or related to a minimum. **3** the least possible in size, duration, etc. **4** *Art*, etc., characterized by the use of simple or primary forms or structures, etc., often geometric or massive (*huge minimal forms in a few colors*). □□ **minimalism** *n.* (in sense 4). **minimally** *adv.* (in senses 1–3). [L *minimus* smallest]
■ **1** see MINUTE[2] 1. **2, 3** least, smallest, minutest, littlest, tiniest, slightest; minimum, nominal, token.

minimalist /mínimɔlist/ *n.* **1** (also *attrib.*) a person advocating small or moderate reform in politics (opp. MAXIMALIST). **2** = MENSHEVIK. **3** a person who advocates or practices minimal art. □□ **minimalism** *n.*

minimax /míneemaks/ *n.* **1** *Math.* the lowest of a set of maximum values. **2** (usu. *attrib.*) **a** a strategy that minimizes the greatest risk to a participant in a game, etc. **b** the theory that in a game with two players, a player's smallest possible maximum loss is equal to the same player's greatest possible minimum gain. [MINIMUM + MAXIMUM]

minimize /mínimīz/ *v.* **1** *tr.* reduce to, or estimate at, the smallest possible amount or degree. **2** *tr.* estimate or represent at less than the true value or importance. **3** *intr.* attain a minimum value. □□ **minimization** *n.* **minimizer** *n.*

■ **1** reduce, shrink, lessen, diminish, prune, abbreviate, pare (down), cut (down), curtail, abridge, shorten, decrease. **2** belittle, de-emphasize, downplay, play down, make little *or* light of, disparage, decry, deprecate, depreciate, devalue, undervalue, underrate, underestimate, talk down, *literary* misprize.

minimum /mínimǝm/ *n.* & *adj.* (*pl.* **minima** /-mǝ/) ● *n.* the least possible or attainable amount (*reduced to a minimum*). ● *adj.* that is a minimum. **minimum wage** the lowest wage permitted by law. [L, neut. of *minimus* least]

■ *n.* (rock) bottom, base, floor, lower limit. ● *adj.* minimal, minutest, littlest, least, slightest, lowest, rock-bottom.

minion /mínyǝn/ *n.* **1** *derog.* a servile agent; a slave. **2** a favorite servant, animal, etc. **3** a favorite of a sovereign, etc. [F *mignon*, OF *mignot*, of Gaulish orig.]

■ **1** see FLUNKY 1.

miniseries /míneeseereez/ *n.* a short series of television programs on a common theme.

miniskirt /míneeskǝrt/ *n.* a very short skirt.

minister /mínistǝr/ *n.* & *v.* ● *n.* **1** a member of the clergy; a person authorized to officiate in religious worship. **2** a head of a government department (in some countries). **3** a diplomatic agent, usu. ranking below an ambassador. **4** (usu. foll. by *of*) a person employed in the execution of a purpose, will, etc.) (*a minister of justice*). **5** (in full **minister general**) the superior of some religious orders. ● *v.* **1** *intr.* (usu. foll. by *to*) render aid or service (to a person, cause, etc.). **2** *tr.* (usu. foll. by *with*) *archaic* furnish, supply, etc. □ **ministering angel** a kindhearted person, esp. a woman, who nurses or comforts others (with ref. to Mark 1:13). **Minister of the Crown** *Brit. Parl.* a member of the Cabinet. □□ **ministrable** *adj.* [ME f. OF *ministre* f. L *minister* servant f. *minus* less]

■ *n.* **1** cleric, clergyman, clergywoman, ecclesiastic, pastor, reverend, churchman, divine, parson, preacher, man of the cloth, evangelist, curate, curé, chaplain, padre, *sl.* sky pilot, *orig. Naut. sl.* holy Joe. **2, 3** envoy, delegate, diplomat, ambassador, emissary, (minister) plenipotentiary, envoy extraordinary, consul, agent, chargé d'affaires, *archaic* legate; *Brit.* Cabinet Minister. **4** see OFFICER 1, 3, 4. ● *v.* **1** (*minister to*) attend (to *or* on *or* upon), wait on, care for, look after, see to, accommodate; serve, supply, aid, help, assist, support. **2** see SUPPLY[1] *v.* 1, 2. □ **ministering angel** angel, saint, comforter; see also NURSE *n.*

ministerial /mínisteereeǝl/ *adj.* **1** of a minister of religion or a minister's office. **2** instrumental or subsidiary in achieving a purpose (*ministerial in bringing about a settlement*). **3** of a government minister. □□ **ministerialist** *n.* (in sense 3b). **ministerially** *adv.* [F *ministériel* or LL *ministerialis* f. L (as MINISTRY)]

■ **1** see CLERICAL 1.

ministration /mínistráyshǝn/ *n.* **1** (usu. in *pl.*) aid or service (*the kind ministrations of his neighbors*). **2** ministering, esp. in religious matters. **3** (usu. foll. by *of*) the supplying (of help, justice, etc.). □□ **ministrant** /mínistrǝnt/ *adj.* & *n.* **ministrative** /mínistráytiv/ *adj.* [ME f. OF *ministration* or L *ministratio* (as MINISTER)]

ministry /mínistree/ *n.* (*pl.* **-ies**) **1 a** (prec. by *the*) the vocation or profession of a religious minister (*called to the ministry*). **b** the office of a religious minister, priest, etc. **c** the period of tenure of this. **2** (prec. by *the*) the body of ministers of a government or of a religion. **3 a** a government department headed by a minister. **b** the building which it occupies (*the Ministry of Transportation*). **4** a period of gov-

ernment under one Prime Minister. **5** ministering, ministration. [ME f. L *ministerium* (as MINISTER)]

■ **1, 2** (*the ministry*) priesthood, the church, the pulpit, the cloth, holy orders; clergy, clergymen, clergywomen; see also CABINET 2. **3** office, bureau, agency; see also DEPARTMENT 1a. **4** term (of office); see also ADMINISTRATION 2, 3.

minivan /míneevan/ *n.* a vehicle, smaller than a full-sized van, for passengers, cargo, etc.

miniver /mínivǝr/ *n.* (also **minever**) plain white fur used in ceremonial costume. [ME f. AF *menuver*, OF *menu vair* (as MENU, VAIR)]

mink /mingk/ *n.* **1** either of two small semiaquatic stoatlike animals of the genus *Mustela*, *M. vison* of N. America and *M. intreola* of Europe. **2** the thick brown fur of these. **3** a coat made of this. [cf. Sw. *mänk, menk*]

minke /míngkǝ/ *n.* a small baleen whale, *Balaenoptera acutorostrata*, with a pointed snout. [prob. f. *Meincke*, the name of a Norw. whaler]

Minn. *abbr.* Minnesota.

minnesinger /mínisíngǝr/ *n.* a German lyric poet and singer of the 12th–14th c. [G, = love-singer]

minnow /mínō/ *n.* any of various small freshwater fish of the carp family, esp. *Phoxinus phoxinus*. [late ME *menow*, perh. repr. OE *mynwe* (unrecorded), *myne*: infl. by ME *menuse*, *menise* f. OF *menuise*, ult. rel. to MINUTIA]

Minoan /minóǝn/ *adj.* & *n. Archaeol.* ● *adj.* of or relating to the Bronze Age civilization centered on Crete (*c.*3000–1100 BC). ● *n.* **1** an inhabitant of Minoan Crete or the Minoan world. **2** the language or scripts associated with the Minoans. [named after the legendary Cretan king *Minos* (Gk *Minōs*), to whom the palace excavated at Knossos was attributed]

minor /mínǝr/ *adj.*, *n.*, & *v.* ● *adj.* **1** lesser or comparatively small in size or importance (*minor poet; minor operation*). **2** *Mus.* **a** (of a scale) having intervals of a semitone between the second and third, fifth and sixth, and seventh and eighth degrees. **b** (of an interval) less by a semitone than a major interval. **c** (of a key) based on a minor scale, tending to produce a melancholy effect. **3** pertaining to a student's secondary field of study. **4** *Logic* **a** (of a term) occurring as the subject of the conclusion of a categorical syllogism. **b** (of a premise) containing the minor term in a categorical syllogism. **5 Minor** *Brit.* (in schools) indicating the younger of two children from the same family or the second to enter the school (usu. put after the name). ● *n.* **1** a person under the legal age limit or majority (*no unaccompanied minors*). **2** *Mus.* a minor key, etc. **3** a student's subsidiary subject or course (cf. MAJOR). **4** *Logic* a minor term or premise. ● *v.intr.* (foll. by *in*) (of a student) undertake study in (a subject) as a subsidiary to a main subject. □ **in a minor key** (of novels, events, people's lives, etc.) understated, uneventful. **minor axis** *Geom.* (of a conic) the axis perpendicular to the major axis. **minor canon** a cleric who is not a member of the chapter, who assists in daily cathedral services. **minor key** *Mus.* a key based on a minor scale. **minor league** (in baseball, basketball, etc.) a league of professional clubs other than the major leagues. **minor orders** see ORDER. **minor piece** *Chess* a bishop or a knight. **minor planet** an asteroid. **Minor Prophet** any of the Old Testament prophets from Hosea to Malachi, whose surviving writings are not lengthy. **minor scale** *Mus.* a scale with half steps between the second and third, fifth and sixth, and seventh and eighth degrees. **minor suit** *Bridge* diamonds or clubs. [L, = smaller, less, rel. to *minuere* lessen]

■ *adj.* **1** lesser, smaller, secondary, subordinate, subsidiary; insignificant, obscure, inconsequential, unimportant, trifling, trivial, negligible, inconsiderable, slight, petty, paltry, small, minor league, picayune, *colloq.* small-time, one-horse, two-bit. ● *n.* **1** child, youngster, youth, stripling, teenager, adolescent, schoolboy, schoolgirl, boy, girl, lad, infant, ward, esp. *Sc. & No. of Engl. or poet.* lass, *colloq.* laddie, lassie.

minority /mínáwritee, -nór-/ *n.* (*pl.* **-ies**) **1** (often foll. by *of*) a smaller number or part, esp. within a political party or structure. **2** the number of votes cast for this (*a minority of two*). **3** the state of having less than half the votes or of being supported by less than half of the body of opinion (*in the minority*). **4** a relatively small group of people differing from others in the society of which they are a part in race, religion, language, political persuasion, etc. **5** (*attrib.*) relating to or done by the minority (*minority interests*). **6 a** the state of being under full legal age. **b** the period of this. □ **minority leader** the leader of the minority political party in a legislature. [F *minorité* or med.L *minoritas* f. L *minor*: see MINOR] ■ **6** see CHILDHOOD.

Minotaur /mínətawr/ *n.* (in Greek mythology) a man with a bull's head, kept in a Cretan labyrinth and fed with human flesh. [ME f. OF f. L *Minotaurus* f. Gk *Minōtauros* f. *Minōs*, legendary king of Crete (see MINOAN) + *tauros* bull]

minoxidil /mənóksədil/ *n.* a vasodilator drug taken orally to treat hypertension or applied topically to stimulate hair growth in certain types of baldness.

minster /mínstər/ *n.* **1** a large or important church (*York Minster*). **2** the church of a monastery. [OE *mynster* f. eccl.L *monasterium* f. Gk *monastērion* MONASTERY]

minstrel /mínstrəl/ *n.* **1** a medieval singer or musician, esp. singing or reciting poetry. **2** *hist.* a person who entertained patrons with singing, buffoonery, etc. **3** (usu. in *pl.*) a member of a band of public entertainers with blackened faces, etc., performing songs and music ostensibly of African-American origin. [ME f. OF *menestral* entertainer, servant, f. Prov. *menest(ai)ral* officer, employee, musician, f. LL *ministerialis* official, officer: see MINISTERIAL] ■ **1, 2** troubadour, balladeer, *hist.* skald, minnesinger, bard, jongleur.

minstrelsy /mínstrəlsee/ *n.* (*pl.* **-ies**) **1** the minstrel's art. **2** a body of minstrels. **3** minstrel poetry. [ME f. OF *menestralsie* (as MINSTREL)]

mint¹ /mint/ *n.* **1** any aromatic plant of the genus *Mentha.* **2** a peppermint sweet or lozenge. □ **mint julep** a sweet iced alcoholic drink of bourbon flavored with mint. □□ **minty** *adj.* (**mintier, mintiest**). [OE *minte* ult. f. L *ment(h)a* f. Gk *minthē*]

mint² /mint/ *n. & v.* ● *n.* **1** a place where money is coined, usu. under government authority. **2** a vast sum of money (*making a mint*). **3** a source of invention, etc. (*a mint of ideas*). ● *v.tr.* **1** make (coin) by stamping metal. **2** invent, coin (a word, phrase, etc.). □ **in mint condition** freshly minted; (of books, etc.) as new. □□ **mintage** *n.* [OE *mynet* f. WG f. L *moneta* MONEY] ■ *n.* **2** (small) fortune, king's ransom, millions, billions, wad(s), *colloq.* pile, heap(s), packet, pot(s), loads, *sl.* bundle, big bucks, *Brit. sl.* bomb. **3** see MINE² *n.* 2. ● *v.* **1** stamp, coin, produce. **2** see COIN *v.* 3.

minuend /mínyōō-énd/ *n. Math.* a quantity or number from which another is to be subtracted. [L *minuendus* gerundive of *minuere* diminish]

minuet /mínyōō-ét/ *n. & v.* ● *n.* **1** a slow stately dance for two in triple time. **2** *Mus.* the music for this, or music in the same rhythm and style, often as a movement in a suite, sonata, or symphony. ● *v.intr.* (**minueted, minueting**) dance a minuet. [F *menuet*, orig. adj. = fine, delicate, dimin. of *menu*: see MENU]

minus /mínəs/ *prep., adj., & n.* ● *prep.* **1** with the subtraction of (*7 minus 4 equals 3*). ¶ Symb.: –. **2** (of temperature) below zero (*minus 2°*). **3** *colloq.* lacking; deprived of (*returned minus their dog*). ● *adj.* **1** *Math.* negative. **2** *Electronics* having a negative charge. ● *n.* **1** = minus sign. **2** *Math.* a negative quantity. **3** a disadvantage. □ **minus sign** the symbol (−) indicating subtraction or a negative value. [L, neut. of *minor* less]

minuscule /mínəskyōōl/ *n. & adj.* ● *n.* **1** *Paleog.* a kind of cursive script developed in the 7th c. **2** a lowercase letter.

● *adj.* **1** lowercase. **2** *colloq.* extremely small or unimportant. □□ **minuscular** /minúskyōōlər/ *adj.* [F f. L *minuscula* (*littera* letter) dimin. of *minor*: see MINOR] ■ *adj.* **2** see MINUTE² 1.

minute¹ /mínit/ *n. & v.* ● *n.* **1** the sixtieth part of an hour. **2** a distance covered in one minute (*twenty minutes from the station*). **3 a** a moment; an instant; a point of time (*expecting her any minute; the train leaves in a minute*). **b** (prec. by *this*) *colloq.* the present time (*what are you doing at this minute?*). **c** (foll. by clause) as soon as (*call me the minute you get back*). **4** the sixtieth part of an angular degree. **5** (in *pl.*) a brief summary of the proceedings at a meeting. **6** an official memorandum authorizing or recommending a course of action. ● *v.tr.* **1** record (proceedings) in the minutes. **2** send the minutes to (a person). □ **just** (or **wait**) **a minute 1** a request to wait for a short time. **2** as a prelude to a query or objection. **minute hand** the hand on a watch or clock that indicates minutes. **minute steak** a thin slice of steak to be cooked quickly. **up-to-the-minute** completely up to date. [ME f. OF f. LL *minuta* (n.), f. fem. of *minutus* MINUTE²: senses 1 & 4 of noun f. med.L *pars minuta prima* first minute part (cf. SECOND²): senses 5 & 6 perh. f. med.L *minuta scriptura* draft in small writing] ■ *n.* **3 a** instant, (split) second, flash, moment, trice, *colloq.* sec, jiff, mo, *Brit. colloq.* tick, two ticks. **b** (*at this minute*) at present, at the present moment or time, now, at the moment, this moment. **5** (*minutes*) log, record, journal, transcript, notes, summary, résumé, proceedings, transactions. **6** see MEMORANDUM. ● *v.* **1** record, transcribe, take down, write down, note, make a note of, document, log. □ **just** (or **wait**) **a minute** wait (a moment or second), hold on, *colloq.* hang on. **up to the minute** latest, newest, modern, up to date, fashionable, smart, all the rage, in vogue, stylish, in fashion, à la mode, in, *colloq.* with it, *colloq. often derog.* trendy, *sl.* hip.

minute² /mínōōt, -yōōt/ *adj.* (**minutest**) **1** very small. **2** trifling, petty. **3** (of an inquiry, inquirer, etc.) accurate, detailed, precise. □□ **minutely** *adv.* **minuteness** *n.* [ME f. L *minutus* past part. of *minuere* lessen] ■ **1** small, little, tiny, minuscule, minimal, miniature, infinitesimal, microscopic, diminutive, mini-, baby, Lilliputian, esp. *Sc. or colloq.* wee, *colloq.* pint-sized, teensy, teensy-weensy, teeny, teeny-weeny, *colloq. usu. derog.* itsy-bitsy. **2** unimportant, petty, insignificant, slight, mere, trifling, trivial, minor, small, little, picayune, *colloq.* piffling, piddling. **3** see PRECISE 2.

minuteman /mínitman/ *n.* (*pl.* **-men**) **1** *US hist.* (also **Minuteman**) an American militiaman of the Revolutionary War period (ready to march at a minute's notice). **2** a type of three-stage intercontinental ballistic missile.

minutia /minōōsheeə, -shə, -nyōō-/ *n.* (*pl.* **-iae** /-shee-ee/) (usu. in *pl.*) a precise, trivial, or minor detail. [L, = smallness, in pl. trifles f. *minutus*: see MINUTE²] ■ see REFINEMENT 6.

minx /mingks/ *n.* a pert, sly, or playful girl. □□ **minxish** *adj.* **minxishly** *adv.* [16th c.: orig. unkn.] ■ see FLIRT *n.*

Miocene /míəseen/ *adj. & n. Geol.* ● *adj.* of or relating to the fourth epoch of the Tertiary period with evidence for the diversification of primates, including early apes. ¶ Cf. Appendix VII. ● *n.* this epoch or system. [irreg. f. Gk *meiōn* less + *kainos* new]

miosis /mīṓsis/ *n.* (also **myosis**) (*pl.* **-ses** /-seez/) excessive constriction of the pupil of the eye. □□ **miotic** /mīótik/ *adj.* [Gk *muō* shut the eyes + -OSIS]

mirabelle /mírəbél/ *n.* **1 a** a European variety of plum tree, *Prunus insititia*, bearing small round yellow fruit. **b** a fruit from this tree. **2** a liqueur distilled from this fruit. [F]

miracle /mírəkəl/ *n.* **1** an extraordinary event attributed to some supernatural agency. **2 a** any remarkable occurrence. **b** a remarkable development in some specified area (*an economic miracle; the German miracle*). **3** (usu. foll. by *of*) a remarkable or outstanding specimen (*the plan was a miracle of ingenuity*). □ **miracle drug** a drug that represents a break-

through in medical science. **miracle play** a medieval play based on the Bible or the lives of the saints. [ME f. OF f. L *miraculum* object of wonder f. *mirari* wonder f. *mirus* wonderful]
■ see WONDER *n.* 2. □ **miracle drug** see ELIXIR 1c.
miraculous /mirákyələs/ *adj.* **1** of the nature of a miracle. **2** supernatural. **3** remarkable, surprising. □□ **miraculously** *adv.* **miraculousness** *n.* [F *miraculeux* or med.L *miraculosus* f. L (as MIRACLE)]
■ **1, 3** marvelous, wonderful, incredible, unbelievable, inexplicable, unexplainable, extraordinary, spectacular, amazing, astounding, astonishing, mind-boggling, surprising, remarkable, phenomenal, fantastic, fabulous, far-out, *colloq.* out of this world, *poet.* wondrous, *sl.* crazy. **2** magical, preternatural, superhuman; see also SUPERNATURAL *adj.*
mirador /mírədáwr/ *n.* a turret or tower, etc., attached to a building and commanding an excellent view. [Sp. f. *mirar* to look at]
mirage /miráazh/ *n.* **1** an optical illusion caused by atmospheric conditions, esp. the appearance of a sheet of water in a desert or on a hot road from the reflection of light. **2** an illusory thing. [F f. *se mirer* be reflected, f. L *mirare* look at]
■ see ILLUSION 3.
mire /mīr/ *n. & v.* ● *n.* **1** a stretch of swampy or boggy ground. **2** mud, dirt. ● *v.* **1** *tr. & intr.* plunge or sink in a mire. **2** *tr.* involve in difficulties. □ **in the mire** in difficulties. [ME f. ON *mýrr* f. Gmc, rel. to MOSS]
■ *n.* **1** swamp, bog, fen, marsh, quag, quagmire, slough, *literary* morass. **2** mud, ooze, muck, slime, dirt. ● *v.* **2** bog down, entangle, tangle, enmesh, mesh, involve, ensnare, trap. □ **in the mire** see *in trouble* 1 (TROUBLE).
mirepoix /meerpwáa/ *n.* (also **mirepois**) sautéed diced vegetables, used in sauces, etc. [F, f. Duc de *Mirepoix*, Fr. general d. 1757]
mirk var. of MURK.
mirky var. of MURKY.
mirror /mírər/ *n. & v.* ● *n.* **1** a polished surface, usu. of amalgam-coated glass or metal, which reflects an image; a looking glass. **2** anything regarded as giving an accurate reflection or description of something else. ● *v.tr.* reflect as in a mirror. □ **mirror finish** a reflective surface. **mirror image** an identical image, but with the structure reversed, as in a mirror. **mirror-writing** backward writing, like ordinary writing reflected in a mirror. [ME f. OF *mirour* ult. f. L *mirare* look at]
■ *n.* **1** looking glass, glass, speculum, reflector. **2** reflection, reproduction, picture, representation, replication, image, *colloq.* spitting image. ● *v.* reflect, reproduce, represent, depict, repeat, echo, send back. □ **mirror image** enantiomorph.
mirth /mərth/ *n.* merriment, laughter. □□ **mirthful** *adj.* **mirthfully** *adv.* **mirthfulness** *n.* **mirthless** *adj.* **mirthlessly** *adv.* **mirthlessness** *n.* [OE *myrgth* (as MERRY)]
■ merriment, merrymaking, jollity, gaiety, fun, laughter, amusement, frolic, joviality, joyousness, revelry, rejoicing, glee, high spirits, mirthfulness, hilarity, buoyancy, *literary* jocundity.
MIRV /mərv/ *abbr.* multiple independently targeted reentry vehicle (a type of missile).
MIS *abbr. Computing* management information system.
mis-¹ /mis/ *prefix* added to verbs and verbal derivatives: meaning 'amiss,' 'badly,' 'wrongly,' 'unfavorably' (*mislead; misshapen; mistrust*). [OE f. Gmc]
mis-² /mis/ *prefix* occurring in a few words adopted from French meaning 'badly,' 'wrongly,' 'amiss,' 'ill-,' or having a negative force (*misadventure; mischief*). [OF *mes-* ult. f. L *minus* (see MINUS): assim. to MIS-¹]
misaddress /mísədrés/ *v.tr.* **1** address (a letter, etc.) wrongly. **2** address (a person) wrongly, esp. impertinently.
■ **1** see MISDIRECT.
misadventure /mísədvénchər/ *n.* **1** *Law* an accident without concomitant crime or negligence (*death by misadventure*). **2**

bad luck. **3** a misfortune. [ME f. OF *mesaventure* f. *mesavenir* turn out badly (as MIS-², ADVENT: cf. ADVENTURE)]
■ **1** see ACCIDENT 2. **2, 3** see MISFORTUNE 2.
misalign /mísəlín/ *v.tr.* give the wrong alignment to. □□ **misalignment** *n.*
misalliance /mísəlíəns/ *n.* an unsuitable alliance, esp. an unsuitable marriage. □□ **misally** /-əlí/ *v.tr.* (**-ies, -ied**). [MIS-¹ + ALLIANCE, after MÉSALLIANCE]
■ mésalliance, mismarriage, mismatch, bad match.
misanthrope /mísənthrōp, míz-/ *n.* (also **misanthropist** /misánthrəpist/) **1** a person who hates mankind. **2** a person who avoids human society. □□ **misanthropic** /-thrópik/ *adj.* **misanthropical** *adj.* **misanthropically** *adv.* **misanthropy** /misánthrəpee/ *n.* **misanthropize** /misánthrəpiz/ *v.intr.* [F f. Gk *misanthrōpos* f. *misos* hatred + *anthrōpos* man]
■ **2** loner, hermit, recluse, anchorite, lone wolf.
□□ **misanthropic** antisocial, unsocial, unsociable, unfriendly.
misapply /mísəplí/ *v.tr.* (**-ies, -ied**) apply (esp. funds) wrongly. □□ **misapplication** /mísaplikáyshən/ *n.*
■ see MISUSE *v.* 1. □□ **misapplication** see MISUSE *n.*
misapprehend /mísaprihénd/ *v.tr.* misunderstand (words, a person). □□ **misapprehension** /-hénshən/ *n.* **misapprehensive** *adj.*
■ see MISUNDERSTAND.
misappropriate /mísəprópreeayt/ *v.tr.* apply (usu. another's money) to one's own use, or to a wrong use. □□ **misappropriation** /-áyshən/ *n.*
■ embezzle, steal, filch, pilfer, pocket, peculate; *formal* defalcate; misapply, misuse, pervert, misemploy.
misbegotten /mísbigót'n/ *adj.* **1** illegitimate, bastard. **2** contemptible, disreputable.
■ **1** see ILLEGITIMATE *adj.* 1. **2** see CONTEMPTIBLE.
misbehave /mísbiháyv/ *v.intr. & refl.* (of a person or machine) behave badly. □□ **misbehaver** *n.* **misbehavior** *n.*
■ behave badly or improperly, be bad or naughty or mischievous or disobedient, cause trouble, *Brit.* play up, *colloq.* carry on, act up, raise hell, raise Cain.
□□ **misbehavior** naughtiness, badness, misconduct, misdemeanor(s), disorderliness, disobedience, delinquency, disorderly conduct, rowdyism.
misbelief /mísbileéf/ *n.* **1** wrong or unorthodox religious belief. **2** a false opinion or notion.
■ **2** see DELUSION.
misc. *abbr.* miscellaneous.
miscalculate /mískálkyəlayt/ *v.tr.* (also *absol.*) calculate (amounts, results, etc.) wrongly. □□ **miscalculation** /-láyshən/ *n.*
■ misjudge, miscount, misread; underestimate, undervalue, underrate; overestimate, overvalue, overrate. □□ **miscalculation** see ERROR 1.
miscall /mískáwl/ *v.tr.* **1** call by a wrong or inappropriate name. **2** *archaic or dial.* call (a person) names.
miscarriage /mískárij/ *n.* **1** a spontaneous abortion, esp. before the 28th week of pregnancy. **2** the failure (of a plan, letter, etc.) to reach completion or its destination. □ **miscarriage of justice** any failure of the judicial system to attain the ends of justice. [MISCARRY, after CARRIAGE]
■ **1** *colloq.* miss. **2** failure, abortion, collapse, breakdown, failing, nonfulfillment; defeat, frustration.
miscarry /mískáree/ *v.intr.* (**-ies, -ied**) **1** (of a woman) have a miscarriage. **2** (of a letter, etc.) fail to reach its destination. **3** (of a business, plan, etc.) fail, be unsuccessful.
■ **3** abort; fail, fall through, break down, go wrong, founder, come to nothing or naught, go awry, come to grief, go amiss, misfire, go up or end up in smoke, *colloq.* go belly up.
miscast /mískást/ *v.tr.* (*past* and *past part.* **-cast**) allot an unsuitable part to (an actor).

/.../ **pronunciation**	● **part of speech**
□ **phrases, idioms, and compounds**	
□□ **derivatives**	■ **synonym section**
cross-references appear in SMALL CAPITALS or *italics*	

miscegenation /miséjináyshən, mísəjə-/ n. the interbreeding of races, esp. of whites and nonwhites. [irreg. f. L *miscēre* mix + *genus* race]

miscellanea /mísəláyneeə/ n.pl. **1** a literary miscellany. **2** a collection of miscellaneous items. [L neut. pl. (as MISCELLANEOUS)]
■ **2** see SUNDRY n.

miscellaneous /mísəláyneeəs/ adj. **1** of mixed composition or character. **2** (foll. by pl. noun) of various kinds. **3** (of a person) many-sided. □□ **miscellaneously** adv. **miscellaneousness** n. [L *miscellaneus* f. *miscellus* mixed f. *miscēre* mix]
■ **1, 2** varied, heterogeneous, diverse, mixed, diversified, motley, sundry, assorted, various, varying, multifarious, multiform, multiplex, *archaic or literary* divers, *literary* manifold.

miscellany /mísəláynee/ n. (pl. **-ies**) **1** a mixture, a medley. **2** a book containing a collection of stories, etc., or various literary compositions. □□ **miscellanist** n. [F *miscellanées* (fem. pl.) or L MISCELLANEA]
■ **1** mixture, assortment, variety, medley, diversity, mixed bag, job lot, ragbag, mélange, potpourri, gallimaufry, motley, hodgepodge, salmagundi, olio, olla podrida, hash, jumble, *colloq.* omnium gatherum, *derog.* mess.

mischance /míscháns/ n. **1** bad luck. **2** an instance of this. [ME f. OF *mesch(e)ance* f. *mescheoir* (as MIS-², CHANCE)]
■ see MISFORTUNE 2.

mischief /míschif/ n. **1** conduct that is troublesome, but not malicious, esp. in children. **2** pranks, scrapes (*get into mischief*; *keep out of mischief*). **3** playful malice; archness; satire (*eyes full of mischief*). **4** harm or injury caused by a person or thing. **5** a person or thing responsible for harm or annoyance (*that loose connection is the mischief*). **6** (prec. by *the*) the annoying part or aspect (*the mischief of it is that*, etc.). [ME f. OF *meschief* f. *meschever* (as MIS-², *chever* come to an end f. *chef* head: see CHIEF)]
■ **1–3** misbehavior, naughtiness, impishness, roguishness, devilry, mischievousness, playfulness, devilment, pranks, scrapes, *colloq.* monkey business, shenanigan(s), monkeyshines, *often joc.* rascality. **4** harm, injury, damage, detriment, trouble, hurt, wrong, difficulty, disruption, destruction, misfortune, evil. **5, 6** trouble, worry, bother, *colloq.* hassle; see also NUISANCE.

mischievous /míschivəs/ adj. **1** (of a person) disposed to mischief. **2** (of conduct) playfully malicious. **3** (of a thing) having harmful effects. □□ **mischievously** adv. **mischievousness** n. [ME f. AF *meschevous* f. OF *meschever*: see MISCHIEF]
■ **1, 2** naughty, impish, roguish, devilish, elfish, puckish, pucklike, *colloq.* scampish, *often joc.* rascally. **3** harmful, injurious, hurtful, damaging, pernicious, detrimental, destructive, deleterious, dangerous, spiteful, malicious, vicious, malign, baleful, baneful, noxious, wicked, evil, bad.

misch metal /mish/ n. an alloy of lanthanide metals, usu. added to iron to improve its malleability. [G *mischen* mix + *Metall* metal]

miscible /mísibəl/ adj. (often foll. by *with*) capable of being mixed. □□ **miscibility** /-bílitee/ n. [med.L *miscibilis* f. L *miscēre* mix]

misconceive /mískənseév/ v. **1** intr. (often foll. by *of*) have a wrong idea or conception. **2** tr. (as **misconceived** adj.) badly planned, organized, etc. **3** tr. misunderstand (a word, person, etc.). □□ **misconceiver** n. **misconception** /-sépshən/ n.
■ **1, 3** misunderstand, misconstrue, misjudge, miscalculate, mistake, misapprehend, misinterpret, misread; get *or* have the wrong idea, get (hold of) the wrong end of the stick. **2** (**misconceived**) badly planned, ill-organized; ill-judged, ill thought out.
□□ **misconception** false *or* wrong notion *or* idea, misunderstanding, misconstruction, misjudgment, miscalculation, misapprehension, mistaken belief, error, mistake, delusion.

misconduct n. & v. ● n. /mískóndukt/ **1** improper or unprofessional behavior. **2** bad management. ● v. /mískəndúkt/ **1** *refl.* misbehave. **2** tr. mismanage.
■ n. **1** see *misbehavior* (MISBEHAVE). ● v. **2** see MISHANDLE 1.

misconstrue /mískənstroo/ v.tr. (**-construes**, **-construed**, **-construing**) **1** interpret (a word, action, etc.) wrongly. **2** mistake the meaning of (a person). □□ **misconstruction** /-strúkshən/ n.
■ see MISINTERPRET. □□ **misconstruction** see MISUNDERSTANDING 1.

miscopy /mískópee/ v.tr. (**-ies**, **-ied**) copy (text, etc.) incorrectly.

miscount /mískównt/ v. & n. ● v.tr. (also *absol.*) count wrongly. ● n. a wrong count.
■ v. see MISCALCULATE.

miscreant /mískreeənt/ n. & adj. ● n. **1** a vile wretch, a villain. **2** *archaic* a heretic. ● adj. **1** depraved, villainous. **2** *archaic* heretical. [ME f. OF *mescreant* (as MIS-², *creant* part. of *croire* f. L *credere* believe)]
■ n. **1** villain, criminal, wrongdoer, felon, malefactor, rogue, reprobate, scoundrel, knave, scalawag, blackguard, wretch, hooligan, ruffian, hoodlum, thug, *Austral.* larrikin, *archaic or joc.* varlet, rapscallion, *colloq.* scamp, crook, baddy, *often joc.* rascal, *poet. or archaic* caitiff, *sl.* hood, mug. ● adj. **1** villainous, criminal, felonious, corrupt, malevolent, evil, wicked, depraved, base, nefarious, iniquitous, vicious, unprincipled, wretched, reprobate, scoundrelly, mischievous, *often joc.* rascally, *literary* malefic.

miscue /mískyoo/ n. & v. ● n. (in billiards, etc.) the failure to strike the ball properly with the cue. ● v.intr. (**-cues**, **-cued**, **-cueing** or **-cuing**) make a miscue.

misdate /misdáyt/ v.tr. date (an event, a letter, etc.) wrongly.

misdeal /mísdeél/ v. & n. ● v.tr. (also *absol.*) (*past* and *past part.* **-dealt** /-délt/) make a mistake in dealing (cards). ● n. **1** a mistake in dealing cards. **2** a misdealt hand.

misdeed /mísdeéd/ n. an evil deed, a wrongdoing; a crime. [OE *misdēd* (as MIS-¹, DEED)]
■ offense, crime, felony, wrongdoing, misdoing, transgression, misdemeanor, fault, misconduct, sin, trespass, wrong, peccadillo.

misdemeanant /mísdimeénənt/ n. a person convicted of a misdemeanor or guilty of misconduct. [archaic *misdemean* misbehave]

misdemeanor /mísdimeénər/ n. (*Brit.* **misdemeanour**) **1** an offense, a misdeed. **2** *Law* an indictable offense, less heinous than a felony.
■ see OFFENSE 1.

misdiagnose /mísdiəgnos, -noz/ v.tr. diagnose incorrectly. □□ **misdiagnosis** /-nosis/ n.

misdial /mísdiəl/ v.tr. (also *absol.*) (**-dialed**, **-dialing**; esp. *Brit.* **-dialled**, **-dialling**) dial (a telephone number, etc.) incorrectly.

misdirect /mísdirékt, -dī-/ v.tr. **1** direct (a person, letter, blow, etc.) wrongly. **2** (of a judge) instruct (the jury) wrongly. □□ **misdirection** /-rékshən/ n.
■ misguide, misadvise; misaddress; see also MISINFORM.

misdoing /mísdooing/ n. a misdeed.

misdoubt /mísdówt/ v.tr. **1** have doubts or misgivings about the truth or existence of. **2** be suspicious about; suspect that.

miseducation /mísejəkáyshən/ n. wrong or faulty education. □□ **miseducate** /-éjəkayt/ v.tr.

mise-en-scène /meéz ON sén/ n. **1** *Theatr.* the scenery and properties of a play. **2** the setting or surroundings of an event. [F]
■ **1** see SET² 18. **2** see SETTING.

misemploy /mísemplóy/ v.tr. employ or use wrongly or improperly. □□ **misemployment** n.
■ see MISUSE v. 1.

miser /mízər/ n. **1** a person who hoards wealth and lives miserably. **2** an avaricious person. [L, = wretched]
■ skinflint, hoarder, niggard, penny-pincher, pinchpenny, cheeseparer, Scrooge, *colloq.* money-grubber, cheapskate.

miserable /mízərəbəl/ *adj.* **1** wretchedly unhappy or uncomfortable (*felt miserable*). **2** unworthy, inadequate (*a miserable hovel*); contemptible. **3** causing wretchedness or discomfort (*miserable weather*). **4** stingy; mean. □□ **miserableness** *n.* **miserably** *adv.* [ME f. F *misérable* f. L *miserabilis* pitiable f. *miserari* to pity f. *miser* wretched]
 ■ **1** wretched, unhappy, depressed, woeful, woebegone, sad, dejected, forlorn, disconsolate, despondent, heartbroken, sorrowful, brokenhearted, mournful, abject, desolate, desperate, despairing, downhearted, melancholy, glum, low-spirited, dispirited, gloomy, dismal, tearful, upset, torn up, *colloq.* down, *formal* lachrymose. **2** inadequate, unworthy, poor, sorry, pitiful, pathetic, lamentable, squalid, wretched, shabby, mean, contemptible. **3** unpleasant, inclement, untoward, bad, unfavorable, awful, terrible, adverse, *colloq.* lousy, *sl.* rotten. **4** see MEAN² 1.

miserere /mízəráiree, -réeree/ *n.* **1** (**Miserere**) Psalm 50 (in the Vulgate) and 51 (in the Authorized Version). **2** a cry for mercy. **3** = MISERICORD 1. [ME f. L, imper. of *misereri* have mercy (as MISER); first word of Ps. 50 in Latin]

misericord /mízərikawrd, -mízér-/ *n.* **1** a shelving projection on the underside of a hinged seat in a choir stall serving (when the seat is turned up) to help support a person standing. **2** an apartment in a monastery in which some relaxations of discipline are permitted. **3** a dagger for dealing the death stroke. [ME f. OF *misericorde* f. L *misericordia* f. *misericors* compassionate f. stem of *misereri* pity + *cor cordis* heart]

miserly /mízərlee/ *adj.* like a miser, niggardly. □□ **miserliness** *n.* [MISER]
 ■ stingy, niggardly, penny-pinching, parsimonious, mean, cheeseparing, tightfisted, close, closefisted, mercenary, avaricious, greedy, covetous, penurious, *Austral.* hungry, *colloq.* moneygrubbing, tight, *Brit. colloq.* mingy.

misery /mízəree/ *n.* (*pl.* **-ies**) **1** a wretched state of mind, or of outward circumstances. **2** a thing causing this. **3** *Brit. colloq.* a constantly depressed or discontented person. □ **put out of its**, etc., **misery 1** release (a person, animal, etc.) from suffering or suspense. **2** kill (an animal in pain). [ME f. OF *misere* or L *miseria* (as MISER)]
 ■ **1** unhappiness, distress, discomfort, wretchedness, sadness, melancholy, sorrow, heartache, grief, anguish, depression, despair, desperation, desolation, despondency, gloom, *archaic or literary* woe, *literary* dolor; squalor, poverty, destitution, privation, indigence, penury, sordidness. **2** hardship, suffering, calamity, disaster, curse, misfortune, ordeal, trouble, catastrophe, trial, tribulation, adversity, burden, affliction, *archaic or literary* woe. **3** spoilsport, damper, killjoy, Job's comforter, malcontent, pessimist, cynic, prophet of doom, Cassandra, *colloq.* wet blanket, grouch, grump, sourpuss, *sl.* party pooper. □ **put out of its**, etc., **misery 1** release, relieve, free, deliver, rescue, save, spare. **2** see *put down* 7 (PUT¹).

misfeasance /mísféezəns/ *n. Law* a transgression, esp. the wrongful exercise of lawful authority. [ME f. OF *mesfaisance* f. *mesfaire* misdo (as MIS-², *faire* do f. L *facere*): cf. MALFEASANCE]

misfire /mísfír/ *v. & n.* ● *v.intr.* **1** (of a gun, motor engine, etc.) fail to go off or start or function regularly. **2** (of an action, etc.) fail to have the intended effect. ● *n.* a failure of function or intention.
 ■ *v.* **2** fail, abort, miscarry, go wrong, fizzle out, fall through, *Brit. colloq.* go phut, *sl.* flop, come a cropper. ● *n.* miscarriage, failure, malfunction, *sl.* dud, flop.

misfit /mísfit/ *n.* **1** a person unsuited to a particular kind of environment, occupation, etc. **2** a garment, etc., that does not fit.
 ■ **1** eccentric, individual, nonconformist, maverick, round (*or* square) peg in a square (*or* round) hole.

misfortune /misfáwrchən/ *n.* **1** bad luck. **2** an instance of this.
 ■ **1** bad luck, ill luck, ill fortune, hard luck, infelicity,

adversity. **2** accident, misadventure, mishap, calamity, catastrophe, mischance, disaster, contretemps, tragedy, blow, shock, loss; reverse, stroke of bad luck.

misgive /misgív/ *v.tr.* (*past* **-gave** /-gáyv/; *past part.* **-given** /-gívən/) (often foll. by *about, that*) (of a person's mind, heart, etc.) fill (a person) with suspicion or foreboding.

misgiving /misgíving/ *n.* (usu. in *pl.*) a feeling of mistrust or apprehension.
 ■ apprehension, mistrust, worry, concern, anxiety, qualm, scruple, disquiet, hesitation, doubt, question, uncertainty, suspicion, unease, uneasiness, discomfort; dread, premonition, foreboding, (funny) feeling.

misgovern /misgúvərn/ *v.tr.* govern (a state, a nation, etc.) badly. □□ **misgovernment** *n.*

misguide /misgíd/ *v.tr.* **1** (as **misguided** *adj.*) mistaken in thought or action. **2** mislead, misdirect. □□ **misguidance** *n.* **misguidedly** *adv.* **misguidedness** *n.*
 ■ **1** (**misguided**) mistaken, wrong, misdirected, foolish, unreasoning, erroneous, misled, misplaced, imprudent, unwise, impolitic, ill-advised, ill-judged, beside *or* off *or* wide of the mark. **2** see MISLEAD.

mishandle /mis-hánd'l/ *v.tr.* **1** deal with incorrectly or ineffectively. **2** handle (a person or thing) roughly or rudely; ill-treat.
 ■ **1** mismanage, bungle, botch, misconduct, mess up, muddle, muff, make a mess of, *colloq.* make a hash of, *sl.* screw up, *Brit. sl.* cock up. **2** abuse, mistreat, maltreat, ill-treat, brutalize, maul, molest, injure, hurt, harm, knock about *or* around, *colloq.* manhandle.

mishap /mis-hap/ *n.* an unlucky accident.
 ■ see MISFORTUNE 2.

mishear /mis-heer/ *v.tr.* (*past* and *past part.* **-heard** /-hérd/) hear incorrectly or imperfectly.

mishit *v. & n.* ● *v.tr.* /mis-hít/ (**-hitting**; *past* and *past part.* **-hit**) hit (a tennis ball, etc.) faultily. ● *n.* /mís-hit/ a faulty or bad hit.

mishmash /míshmash, -maash/ *n.* a confused mixture. [ME, reduplication of MASH]
 ■ mess, medley, hash, gallimaufry, farrago, potpourri, jumble, pastiche, mixture, salmagundi, hodgepodge, mélange, olio, olla podrida, *colloq.* omnium gatherum.

Mishnah /míshnə/ *n.* a collection of precepts forming the basis of the Talmud, and embodying Jewish oral law. □□ **Mishnaic** /-náyik/ *adj.* [Heb. *mišnāh* (teaching by) repetition]

misidentify /mísídéntifī/ *v.tr.* (**-ies, -ied**) identify erroneously. □□ **misidentification** /-fikáyshən/ *n.*
 ■ (*misidentify as*) see MISTAKE *v.* 2.

misinform /mísinfórm/ *v.tr.* give wrong information to; mislead. □□ **misinformation** /-fərmáyshən/ *n.*
 ■ misguide, mislead, misadvise, misdirect, delude, deceive, dupe, fool, gull, lead astray, put *or* throw off the scent, *colloq.* slip *or* put one over on, pull a fast one on, *sl.* con, *sl.* give a bum steer to. □□ **misinformation** disinformation; (*piece of misinformation*) red herring, false trail, false scent.

misinterpret /mísintórprit/ *v.tr.* (**-interpreted, -interpreting**) **1** interpret wrongly. **2** draw a wrong inference from. □□ **misinterpretation** /-táyshən/ *n.* **misinterpreter** *n.*
 ■ misunderstand, misconstrue, misconceive, misread, misjudge, misapprehend, mistake.

misjudge /mísjúj/ *v.tr.* (also *absol.*) **1** judge wrongly. **2** have a wrong opinion of. □□ **misjudgment** *n.* (also **misjudgement**).
 ■ see MISTAKE *v.* 1.

miskey /mískée/ *v.tr.* (**-keys, -keyed**) key (data) wrongly.

mislay /misláy/ *v.tr.* (*past* and *past part.* **-laid** /-láyd/) **1** unintentionally put (a thing) where it cannot readily be found. **2** *euphem.* lose.
 ■ misplace, lose.

/.../ **pronunciation**	● **part of speech**
□ **phrases, idioms, and compounds**	
□□ **derivatives**	■ **synonym section**
cross-references appear in SMALL CAPITALS or *italics*	

mislead /misleéd/ *v.tr.* (*past* and *past part.* **-led** /-léd/) **1** cause (a person) to go wrong, in conduct, belief, etc. **2** lead astray or in the wrong direction. □□ **misleader** *n.*

■ misinform, lead astray, misguide, misdirect, put *or* throw off the scent, pull the wool over a person's eyes, fool, outwit, bluff, hoodwink, trick, humbug, deceive, dupe, gull, flimflam, take in, *archaic* wilder, *colloq.* bamboozle, lead up the garden path, slip *or* put one over on, *literary* cozen, *sl.* con, take, give a bum steer to.

misleading /misleéding/ *adj.* causing to err or go astray; imprecise; confusing. □□ **misleadingly** *adv.* **misleadingness** *n.*

■ see FALSE *adj.* 2b.

mislike /mislík/ *v.tr.* & *n. archaic* dislike. [OE *mislīcian* (as MIS-[1], LIKE[2])]

mismanage /mismánij/ *v.tr.* manage badly or wrongly. □□ **mismanagement** *n.*

■ see MISHANDLE 1.

mismarriage /mismárij/ *n.* an unsuitable marriage or alliance. [MIS-[1] + MARRIAGE]

mismatch *v.* & *n.* ● *v.tr.* /mismách/ (usu. as **mismatched** *adj.*) match unsuitably or incorrectly, esp. in marriage. ● *n.* /mísmach/ a bad match.

■ *v.* (**mismatched**) mismated, ill-matched, incompatible, unfit, inappropriate, unsuited, unsuitable, incongruous, disparate, uncongenial, inconsistent, inharmonious, discordant. ● *n.* see MISALLIANCE.

mismated /mismáytid/ *adj.* **1** (of people) not suited to each other, esp. in marriage. **2** (of objects) not matching.

mismeasure /mismézhər/ *v.tr.* measure or estimate incorrectly. □□ **mismeasurement** *n.*

misname /misnáym/ *v.tr.* = MISCALL.

misnomer /misnṓmər/ *n.* **1** a name or term used wrongly. **2** the wrong use of a name or term. [ME f. AF f. OF *mesnom(m)er* (as MIS-[2], *nommer* name f. L *nominare* formed as NOMINATE)]

misogamy /misógəmee/ *n.* the hatred of marriage. □□ **misogamist** *n.* [Gk *misos* hatred + *gamos* marriage]

misogyny /misójinee/ *n.* the hatred of women. □□ **misogynist** *n.* **misogynous** *adj.* [Gk *misos* hatred + *gunē* woman]

mispickel /míspikəl/ *n. Mineral.* arsenical pyrite.

misplace /mispláys/ *v.tr.* **1** put in the wrong place. **2** bestow (affections, confidence, etc.) on an inappropriate object. **3** time (words, actions, etc.) badly. □□ **misplacement** *n.*

■ **1** see LOSE 1–3.

misplay *v.* & *n.* ● *v.tr.* /mispláy/ play (a ball, card, etc.) in a wrong or ineffective manner. ● *n.* /mispláy, míspláy/ an instance of this.

misprint *v.* & *n.* ● *n.* /mísprint/ a mistake in printing. ● *v.tr.* /misprínt/ print wrongly.

■ *n.* error, mistake, erratum, typographical error, printer's *or* printing error, *Printing* literal, *colloq.* typo.

misprision[1] /misprízhən/ *n. Law* **1** (in full **misprision of a felony** or **of treason**) the deliberate concealment of one's knowledge of a crime, treason, etc. **2** a wrong action or omission. [ME f. AF *mesprisioun* f. OF *mesprison* error f. *mesprendre* to mistake (as MIS-[2], *prendre* take)]

misprision[2] /misprízhən/ *n.* **1** a misreading, misunderstanding, etc. **2** (usu. foll. by *of*) a failure to appreciate the value of a thing. **3** *archaic* contempt. [MISPRIZE after MISPRISION[1]]

misprize /mispríz/ *v.tr. literary* despise, scorn; fail to appreciate. [ME f. OF *mesprisier* (as MIS-[1], PRIZE[1])]

mispronounce /mísprənówns/ *v.tr.* pronounce (a word, etc.) wrongly. □□ **mispronunciation** /-nunseeáyshən/ *n.*

misquote /mískwṓt/ *v.tr.* quote wrongly. □□ **misquotation** /-táyshən/ *n.*

■ see TWIST *v.* 5. □□ **misquotation** see MISSTATEMENT.

misread /mísreéd/ *v.tr.* (*past* and *past part.* **-read** /-réd/) read or interpret (text, a situation, etc.) wrongly.

■ see MISINTERPRET.

misremember /mísrimémbər/ *v.tr.* remember imperfectly or incorrectly.

misreport /mísripáwrt/ *v.* & *n.* ● *v.tr.* give a false or incorrect report of. ● *n.* a false or incorrect report.

■ *v.* see GARBLE 2. ● *n.* see MISSTATEMENT.

misrepresent /mísreprizént/ *v.tr.* represent wrongly; give a false or misleading account or idea of. □□ **misrepresentation** /-táyshən/ *n.* **misrepresentative** *adj.*

■ distort, twist, pervert, garble, misstate, mangle; falsify, belie, disguise, color.

misrule /mísroōl/ *n.* & *v.* ● *n.* bad government; disorder. ● *v.tr.* govern badly.

Miss. *abbr.* Mississippi.

miss[1] /mis/ *v.* & *n.* ● *v.* **1** *tr.* (also *absol.*) fail to hit, reach, find, catch, etc. (an object or goal). **2** *tr.* fail to catch (a bus, train, etc.). **3** *tr.* fail to experience, see, or attend (an occurrence or event). **4** *tr.* fail to meet (a person); fail to keep (an appointment). **5** *tr.* fail to seize (an opportunity, etc.) (*I missed my chance*). **6** *tr.* fail to hear or understand (*I'm sorry, I missed what you said*). **7** *tr.* **a** regret the loss or absence of (a person or thing) (*did you miss me while I was away?*). **b** notice the loss or absence of (an object) (*bound to miss the key if it isn't there*). **8** *tr.* avoid (*go early to miss the traffic*). **9** *tr.* = miss out 1. **10** *intr.* (of an engine, etc.) fail, misfire. ● *n.* **1** a failure to hit, reach, attain, connect, etc. **2** *colloq.* = MISCARRIAGE 1. □ **be missing** see MISSING *adj.* **give** (a thing) **a miss** esp. *Brit.* avoid, leave alone (*gave the party a miss*). **miss the boat** (or **bus**) lose an opportunity. **miss fire** (of a gun) fail to go off or hit the mark (cf. MISFIRE). **a miss is as good as a mile** the fact of failure or escape is not affected by the narrowness of the margin. **miss out 1** (usu. foll. by *on*) *colloq.* fail to get or experience (*always misses out on the good times*). **2** *Brit.* omit, leave out (*missed out my name from the list*). **not miss much** be alert. **not miss a trick** never fail to seize an opportunity, advantage, etc. □□ **missable** *adj.* [OE *missan* f. Gmc]

■ *v.* **3** absent oneself from, be absent from; see also CUT *v.* 12. **6** misunderstand, misinterpret, misconstrue, misapprehend, mistake. **7** long for, yearn for, pine for, want, need, wish for. **8** see AVOID 1. □ **give** (**a thing**) **a miss** see AVOID 1. **miss out 1** omit, leave out, pass up, pass over, overlook, disregard, ignore. **2** (*miss out on*) let slip (by), let pass, miss.

miss[2] /mis/ *n.* **1** a young or unmarried woman. **2** (**Miss**) **a** respectful title of an unmarried woman or girl, or of a married woman retaining her maiden name for professional purposes (cf. **Ms.**). **b** the title of a beauty queen (*Miss World*). **3** usu. *derog.* or *joc.* a girl, esp. a schoolgirl. **4** the title used to address a young woman or girl. □□ **missish** *adj.* (in sense 3). [abbr. of MISTRESS]

■ **1, 3** girl, (young) lady, (young) woman, bachelor girl, mademoiselle, Fräulein, signorina, señorita, *Ir.* colleen, esp. *Sc.* & *No. of Engl.* lass, *archaic* demoiselle, *archaic or literary* damsel, *archaic or poet.* maid, maiden, *colloq.* lassie, filly, *Brit. colloq.* nymphet, popsy, *joc.* wench, *poet.* nymph, *sl.* gal, chick, petticoat, *Austral.* & *NZ sl.* sheila, brush, *Brit. sl.* schoolgirl, teenager, coed, *colloq.* teenybopper; spinster, *derog.* old maid.

missal /mísəl/ *n. RC Ch.*, *Anglican Ch.* **1** a book containing the texts used in the service of the Mass throughout the year. **2** a book of prayers, esp. an illuminated one. [ME f. med.L *missale* neut. of eccl.L *missalis* of the mass f. *missa* MASS[2]]

misshape /mís-sháyp/ *v.tr.* give a bad shape or form to; distort.

■ see DISTORT 1a.

misshapen /mís-sháypən/ *adj.* ill-shaped, deformed, distorted. □□ **misshapenly** *adv.* **misshapenness** *n.*

■ ill-shaped, distorted, twisted, contorted, crooked, deformed, crippled, malformed, grotesque, awry, warped, gnarled, ill-made, monstrous.

missile /mísəl/ *n.* **1** an object or weapon suitable for throwing at a target or for discharge from a machine. **2** a weapon directed by remote control or automatically. □□ **missilery** /-əlree/ *n.* [L *missilis* f. *mittere miss-* send]

■ projectile, brickbat; guided missile, ballistic missile, cruise missile.

missing /mísing/ *adj.* **1** not in its place; lost. **2** (of a person)

not yet traced or confirmed as alive but not known to be dead. **3** not present. □ **missing link 1** a thing lacking to complete a series. **2** a hypothetical intermediate type, esp. between humans and apes.
■ **3** see ABSENT *adj.* 1.

mission /míshən/ *n.* **1 a** a particular task or goal assigned to a person or group. **b** a journey undertaken as part of this. **c** a person's vocation (*mission in life*). **2** a military or scientific operation or expedition for a particular purpose. **3** a body of persons sent, esp. to a foreign country, to conduct negotiations, etc. **4 a** a body sent to propagate a religious faith. **b** a field of missionary activity. **c** a missionary post or organization. **d** a place of worship attached to a mission. **5** a particular course or period of preaching, services, etc., undertaken by a parish or community. [F *mission* or L *missio* f. *mittere miss-* send]
■ **1 a** task, duty, function, purpose, job, office, work, assignment, errand, charge, business, commission, undertaking, aim, goal, objective. **c** calling, occupation, vocation, trade, line (of work), profession, métier. **2** see EXPEDITION 1. **3** delegation, legation, deputation, commission, committee, group.

missionary /míshəneree/ *adj. & n.* ● *adj.* of, concerned with, or characteristic of, religious missions. ● *n.* (*pl.* **-ies**) a person doing missionary work. □ **missionary position** *colloq.* a position for sexual intercourse with the woman lying on her back and the man lying on top and facing her. [mod.L *missionarius* f. L (as MISSION)]
■ *n.* evangelist, preacher, proselytizer.

missioner /míshənər/ *n.* **1** a missionary. **2** a person in charge of a religious mission.

missis var. of MISSUS.

missive /mísiv/ *n.* **1** *joc.* a letter, esp. a long and serious one. **2** an official letter. □ **letter** (or **letters**) **missive** a letter from a sovereign to a dean and chapter nominating a person to be elected bishop. [ME f. med.L *missivus* f. L (as MISSION)]
■ letter, communication, message, dispatch, *formal* or *joc.* epistle.

Missouri /mizóoree, -zóorə/ *n. & adj.* ● *n.* **1** a N. American tribe native to the Missouri River valley. **2** a member of this people. ● *adj.* of or relating to this people.

misspell /mís-spél/ *v.tr.* (*past* and *past part.* **-spelled** or esp. *Brit.* **-spelt**) spell wrongly.

misspelling /mís-spéling/ *n.* a wrong spelling.

misspend /mís-spénd/ *v.tr.* (*past* and *past part.* **-spent** /-spént/) (esp. as **misspent** *adj.*) spend amiss or wastefully.
■ see WASTE *v.* 1; (**misspent**) wasted, squandered, idle, dissipated, thrown away, profitless, prodigal.

misstate /mís-stáyt/ *v.tr.* state wrongly or inaccurately.
■ see TWIST *v.* 5.

misstatement /mís-stáytmənt/ *n.* a wrong or inaccurate statement.
■ falsification, misreport, misquotation, distortion, misrepresentation, misconstruction, misinterpretation, perversion, lie, falsehood, untruth, fabrication; error, inaccuracy.

misstep /mís-stép/ *n.* **1** a wrong step or action. **2** a faux pas.
■ **1** false step, blunder, mistake, error, bad *or* wrong *or* false move, trip, stumble, slip. **2** indiscretion, mistake, lapse, faux pas, oversight, error, gaffe, *colloq.* slipup, howler, *colloq.* blooper, flub, *sl.* goof, booboo, *Brit. sl.* clanger, bloomer, boob.

missus /mísəz/ *n.* (also **missis** /-siz/) *sl.* or *joc.* **1** a form of address to a woman. **2** a wife. □ **the missus** my or your wife. [corrupt. of MISTRESS: cf. MRS.]

missy /mísee/ *n.* (*pl.* **-ies**) an affectionate or derogatory form of address to a young girl.

mist /mist/ *n. & v.* ● *n.* **1** a water vapor near the ground in minute droplets limiting visibility. **b** condensed vapor settling on a surface and obscuring glass, etc. **2** dimness or blurring of the sight caused by tears, etc. **3** a cloud of particles resembling mist. ● *v.tr. & intr.* (usu. foll. by *up*, *over*) cover or become covered with mist or as with mist. □□ **mistful** *adj.* **mistlike** *adj.* [OE f. Gmc]
■ *n.* **1, 3** fog, haze, smog, cloud, vapor; drizzle, mizzle,

literary brume. ● *v.* (*mist up* or *over*) cloud (up *or* over), fog, dim, blur, film, steam up; becloud, befog.

mistake /mistáyk/ *n. & v.* ● *n.* **1** an incorrect idea or opinion; a thing incorrectly done or thought. **2** an error of judgment. ● *v.tr.* (*past* **mistook** /-tŏŏk/; *past part.* **mistaken** /-táykən/) **1** misunderstand the meaning or intention of (a person, a statement, etc.). **2** (foll. by *for*) wrongly take or identify (*mistook me for you*). **3** choose wrongly (*mistake one's vocation*). □ **and** (or **make**) **no mistake** *colloq.* undoubtedly. **by mistake** accidentally; in error. **there is no mistaking** one is sure to recognize (a person or thing). □□ **mistakable** *adj.* **mistakably** *adv.* [ME f. ON *mistaka* (as MIS-¹, TAKE)]
■ *n.* misconception, misapprehension, miscalculation, misjudgment; error, fault, slip, erratum; bad move, false step, misstep, gaffe, blunder, botch, fumble, faux pas, indiscretion, *colloq.* slip-up, howler, blooper, flub, *sl.* booboo, bloomer, goof, *Brit. sl.* clanger, boob. ● *v.* **1** misunderstand, misinterpret, misjudge, misconstrue, take the wrong way, get wrong, misread, misapprehend. **2** (*mistake for*) mix up with, confuse with, take for, misidentify as. □ **by mistake** see *by accident* (ACCIDENT).

mistaken /mistáykən/ *adj.* **1** wrong in opinion or judgment. **2** based on or resulting from this (*mistaken loyalty*; *mistaken identity*). □□ **mistakenly** *adv.* **mistakenness** *n.*
■ wrong, erroneous, fallacious, false, inaccurate, incorrect, misconceived, amiss, misinformed, faulty, in error, off, out, wide of the mark, in the wrong, barking up the wrong tree, on the wrong track, *colloq.* off beam; flawed, warped, distorted, twisted, misguided, *colloq.* cockeyed.

misteach /mís-téech/ *v.tr.* (*past* and *past part.* **-taught** /-táwt/) teach wrongly or incorrectly.

mister /místər/ *n.* **1** (**Mister**) respectful title for a man, usu. abbr. (as **Mr.**). **2** *sl.* or *joc.* sir; a form of address to a man (*Hey, mister!*). **3** a husband. [weakened form of MASTER in unstressed use before a name: cf. MR.]

mistime /mís-tím/ *v.tr.* say or do at the wrong time. [OE *mistīmian* (as MIS-¹, TIME)]

mistitle /mís-tít'l/ *v.tr.* give the wrong title or name to.

mistletoe /mísəltō/ *n.* **1** a parasitic plant, *Viscum album*, growing on apple and other trees and bearing white glutinous berries in winter. **2** a similar plant, genus *Phoradendron*, native to N. America. [OE *misteltān*]

mistook *past of* MISTAKE.

mistral /místrəl, mistraál/ *n.* a cold northerly wind that blows down the Rhône valley and S. France into the Mediterranean. [F & Prov. f. L (as MAGISTRAL)]

mistranslate /místranzláyt, -trans-, mistránzlayt, -tráns-/ *v.tr.* translate incorrectly. □□ **mistranslation** /-láyshən/ *n.*
■ see TWIST *v.* 5.

mistreat /místréet/ *v.tr.* treat badly. □□ **mistreatment** *n.*
■ abuse, maltreat, wrong, ill-use, ill-treat, misuse, *colloq.* manhandle; damage, harm, hurt, injure; molest, maul, brutalize, *sl.* rough up. □□ **mistreatment** abuse, maltreatment, ill use, ill-treatment, misuse, *colloq.* manhandling; molestation, brutalization, *sl.* roughing-up.

mistress /místris/ *n.* **1** a female head of a household. **2 a** a woman in authority over others. **b** the female owner of a pet. **3** a woman with power to control, etc. (often foll. by of: *mistress of the situation*). **4** *Brit.* **a** a female teacher (*music mistress*). **b** a female head of a college, etc. **5 a** a woman (other than his wife) with whom a married man has a (usu. prolonged) sexual relationship. **b** *archaic* or *poet.* a woman loved and courted by a man. **6** *archaic* or *dial.* (as a title) = MRS. [ME f. OF *maistresse* f. *maistre* MASTER]
■ **4** schoolmistress, instructress, governess, teacher, headmistress. **5** lover, girlfriend, kept woman, the other

---

/. . ./ **pronunciation**   ● **part of speech**
□ **phrases, idioms, and compounds**
□□ **derivatives**   ■ **synonym section**
cross-references appear in SMALL CAPITALS or *italics*

woman, concubine, inamorata, *archaic or derog.* paramour, *literary* doxy, *sl. derog.* fancy woman.

mistrial /mís-tríəl/ *n.* **1** a trial rendered invalid through some error in the proceedings. **2** a trial in which the jury cannot agree on a verdict.

mistrust /mís-trúst/ *v. & n.* ● *v.tr.* **1** be suspicious of. **2** feel no confidence in (a person, oneself, one's powers, etc.). ● *n.* **1** suspicion. **2** lack of confidence.

■ *v.* suspect, distrust, be suspicious of, doubt, misdoubt, be *or* feel wary *or* doubtful of *or* about, have (one's) doubts about, question, have reservations about, *sl.* be leery of. ● *n.* suspicion, distrust, doubt, skepticism, wariness, reservation, chariness, misgiving(s), uncertainty, unsureness, apprehension, apprehensiveness, caution, *sl.* leeriness.

mistrustful /mís-trústfŏŏl/ *adj.* **1** (foll. by *of*) suspicious. **2** lacking confidence or trust. □□ **mistrustfully** *adv.* **mistrustfulness** *n.*

■ **1** see SUSPICIOUS 1, 2.

misty /místee/ *adj.* (**mistier, mistiest**) **1** of or covered with mist. **2** indistinct or dim in outline. **3** obscure, vague (*a misty idea*). □□ **mistily** *adv.* **mistiness** *n.* [OE *mistig* (as MIST)]

■ cloudy, foggy, hazy; fuzzy, dim, blurred, blurry; unclear, indistinct, vague, dark, murky, opaque, shadowy, obscure.

mistype /mís-típ/ *v.tr.* type wrongly. [MIS-¹ + TYPE]

misunderstand /mísundərstánd/ *v.tr.* (*past* and *past part.* **-understood** /-stŏŏd/) **1** fail to understand correctly. **2** (usu. as **misunderstood** *adj.*) misinterpret the words or actions of (a person).

■ misconceive, misconstrue, misinterpret, misapprehend, get wrong, get the wrong idea about, get (hold of) the wrong end of the stick about, misread, misjudge, miscalculate, miss the point of.

misunderstanding /mísundərstánding/ *n.* **1** a failure to understand correctly. **2** a slight disagreement or quarrel.

■ **1** misconception, misconstruction, misinterpretation, misapprehension, misreading, misjudgment, miscalculation, error, wrong idea, wrong *or* false impression. **2** disagreement, discord, dispute, argument, difference, dissension, controversy, quarrel, rift, falling out.

misusage /mísyŏŏsij/ *n.* **1** wrong or improper usage. **2** ill-treatment.

misuse *v. & n.* ● *v.tr.* /mísyŏŏz/ **1** use wrongly; apply to the wrong purpose. **2** ill-treat. ● *n.* /mísyŏŏs/ wrong or improper use or application. □□ **misuser** *n.*

■ *v.* **1** abuse, misapply, misemploy, misappropriate; pervert. **2** see MISTREAT. ● *n.* misapplication, misusage, misappropriation, misemployment; perversion; corruption, solecism, malapropism, barbarism, catachresis, ungrammaticality, infelicity; see also *mistreatment* (MISTREAT).

MIT *abbr.* Massachusetts Institute of Technology.

mite¹ /mít/ *n.* any small arachnid of the order Acari, having four pairs of legs when adult. □□ **mity** *adj.* [OE *míte* f. Gmc]

mite² /mít/ *n. & adv.* ● *n.* **1** *hist.* a Flemish copper coin of small value. **2** any small monetary unit. **3** a small object or person, esp. a child. **4** a modest contribution; the best one can do (*offered my mite of comfort*). ● *adv.* (usu. prec. by *a*) *colloq.* somewhat (*is a mite shy*). [ME f. MLG, MDu. *míte* f. Gmc: prob. the same as MITE¹]

■ *n.* **3** see PARTICLE 2.

miter /mítər/ *n. & v.* (*Brit.* **mitre**) ● *n.* **1** a tall deeply-cleft headdress worn by bishops and abbots, esp. as a symbol of office. **2** the joint of two pieces of wood or other material at an angle of 90°, such that the line of junction bisects this angle. **3** a diagonal join of two pieces of fabric that meet at a corner, made by folding. ● *v.* **1** *tr.* bestow the miter on. **2** *tr. & intr.* join with a miter. □ **miter box** a guide for a saw in cutting miter-joints. □□ **mitered** *adj.* [ME f. OF f. L *mitra* f. Gk *mitra* girdle, turban]

Mithraism /míthrayizəm/ *n.* the cult of the ancient Persian god Mithras associated with the sun. □□ **Mithraic** /-ráyik/

adj. **Mithraist** *n.* [L *Mithras* f. Gk *Mithras* f. OPers. *Mithra* f. Skr. *Mitra*]

mithridatize /mithrídətīz/ *v.tr.* render proof against a poison by administering gradually increasing doses of it. □□ **mithridatic** /-dátik/ *adj.* **mithridatism** /-dətizəm/ *n.* [f. *mithridate* a supposed universal antidote attributed to *Mithridates* VI, king of Pontus d. 63 BC]

mitigate /mítigayt/ *v.tr.* make milder or less intense or severe; moderate (*your offer certainly mitigated their hostility*). ¶ Often confused with *militate.* □ **mitigating circumstances** *Law* circumstances permitting greater leniency. □□ **mitigable** *adj.* **mitigation** /-gáyshən/ *n.* **mitigator** *n.* **mitigatory** /-gətáwree/ *adj.* [ME f. L *mitigare mitigat-* f. *mitis* mild]

■ moderate, temper, reduce, abate, lessen, decrease, relieve, ease, relax, alleviate, remit, assuage, allay, slacken, tone down, lighten, appease, palliate, mollify, calm, tranquilize, soothe, placate, still, soften, dull, blunt, take the edge off, quiet, *Brit.* quieten.

mitochondrion /mítəkóndreeən/ *n.* (*pl.* **mitochondria** /-dreeə/) *Biol.* an organelle found in most eukaryotic cells, containing enzymes for respiration and energy production. [mod.L f. Gk *mitos* thread + *khondrion* dimin. of *khondros* granule]

mitosis /mītósis/ *n. Biol.* a type of cell division that results in two daughter cells each having the same number and kind of chromosomes as the parent nucleus (cf. MEIOSIS). □□ **mitotic** /-tótik/ *adj.* [mod.L f. Gk *mitos* thread]

mitral /mítrəl/ *adj.* of or like a miter. □ **mitral valve** a two-cusped valve between the left atrium and the left ventricle of the heart. [mod.L *mitralis* f. L *mitra* girdle]

mitre *Brit* var. of MITER.

mitt /mit/ *n.* **1** a baseball glove for catching the ball. **2** = MITTEN. **3** *sl.* a hand or fist. **4** a glove leaving the fingers and thumb-tip exposed. [abbr. of MITTEN]

■ **3** see HAND *n.* 1a.

mitten /mít'n/ *n.* a glove with two sections, one for the thumb and the other for all four fingers. □□ **mittened** *adj.* [ME f. OF *mitaine* ult. f. L *medietas* half: see MOIETY]

mittimus /mítiməs/ *n.* a warrant committing a person to prison. [ME f. L, = we send]

mitzvah /mítsvə/ *n.* (*pl.* **mitzvoth** /-vōt/ or **mitzvahs**) in Judaism: **1** a precept or commandment. **2** a good deed done from religious duty. [Heb. *miṣwāh* commandment]

mix /miks/ *v. & n.* ● *v.* **1** *tr.* combine or put together (two or more substances or things) so that the constituents of each are diffused among those of the other(s). **2** *tr.* prepare (a compound, cocktail, etc.) by combining the ingredients. **3** *tr.* combine an activity, etc., with another simultaneously (*mix business and pleasure*). **4** *intr.* **a** join, be mixed, or combine, esp. readily (*oil and water will not mix*). **b** be compatible. **c** be sociable (*must learn to mix*). **5** *intr.* **a** (foll. by *with*) (of a person) be harmonious or sociable with; have regular dealings with. **b** (foll. by *in*) participate in. **6** *tr.* drink different kinds of (alcoholic liquor) in close succession. ● *n.* **1 a** the act or an instance of mixing; a mixture. **b** the proportion of materials, etc., in a mixture. **2** *colloq.* a group of persons of different types (*social mix*). **3** the ingredients prepared commercially for making a cake, etc., or for a process such as making concrete. **4** the merging of film pictures or sound. □ **be mixed up in** (or **with**) be involved in or with (esp. something undesirable). **mix in** be harmonious or sociable. **mix it** (usu. foll. by *up*) *colloq.* start fighting. **mix up** **1** mix thoroughly. **2** confuse; mistake the identity of. **mix-up** *n.* a confusion, misunderstanding, or mistake. □□ **mixable** *adj.* [back-form. f. MIXED (taken as past part.)]

■ *v.* **1, 3** combine, blend, merge, unite, alloy, mingle, intermingle, amalgamate, join, *literary* commingle; incorporate, put together, stir, mix up. **2** see PREPARE 2. **4 a** combine, blend, merge, unite, mingle, intermingle, amalgamate, coalesce, join, incorporate, *literary* commingle. **b** be compatible, go together. **4c, 5** socialize, be sociable, mix in; fraternize, consort, hobnob, go around *or* about, keep company, associate, *colloq.* hang about *or* around, *sl.* hang out. ● *n.* **1 a** see

MIXTURE. □ **be mixed up in** *or* **with** be involved in, be implicated in, be included in, be connected with, be drawn *or* dragged into. **mix in** see MIX *v.* 4c, 5 above. **mix up 1** see MIX *v.* 1, 3 above. **2** confuse, confound, bewilder, muddle, perplex, puzzle, fluster, upset, addle, disturb, *joc.* discombobulate; snarl, ensnarl, tangle, entangle, scramble, jumble; mistake, misidentify, get the wrong way around; interchange, exchange, swap (over *or* around). **mix-up** confusion, misunderstanding, mess, muddle, hodgepodge, tangle, jumble, botch, mistake, mishmash, foul-up, *sl.* screwup, snafu, *Brit. sl.* cock-up.

mixed /mikst/ *adj.* **1** of diverse qualities or elements. **2** containing persons from various backgrounds, etc. **3** for or involving persons of both sexes (*a mixed school*; *mixed swimming*). □ **mixed bag** a diverse assortment of things or persons. **mixed blessing** a thing having advantages and disadvantages. **mixed crystal** one formed from more than one substance. **mixed doubles** *Tennis* a doubles game with a man and a woman as partners on each side. **mixed drink** an alcoholic beverage containing two or more ingredients, esp. one made according to a standard recipe. **mixed economy** an economic system combining private and public enterprise. **mixed farming** farming of both crops and livestock. **mixed feelings** a mixture of pleasure and dismay about something. **mixed grill** a dish of various grilled meats and vegetables, etc. **mixed marriage** a marriage between persons of different races or religions. **mixed metaphor** a combination of inconsistent metaphors (e.g., *this tower of strength will forge ahead*). **mixed number** an integer and a proper fraction. **mixed-up** *colloq.* mentally or emotionally confused; socially ill-adjusted. □□ **mixedness** /miksidnis/ *n*, [ME *mixt* f. OF *mixte* f. L *mixtus* past part. of *miscēre* mix] ■ **1** diverse, diversified, assorted, heterogeneous, sundry, miscellaneous, varied, various, multiform, *archaic* medley, *archaic or literary* divers; (*of ancestry, etc.*) hybrid, half-bred, mongrel, interbred, crossbred; (*of feelings, etc.*) confused, muddled, conflicting, contradictory, opposing, clashing, opposite. □ **mixed bag** or **bunch** see MEDLEY *n*. **mixed-up** see *confused* (CONFUSE 4).

mixer /miksər/ *n.* **1** a device for mixing foods, etc. or for processing other materials. **2** a person who manages socially in a specified way (*a good mixer*). **3** a (usu. soft) drink to be mixed with another. **4** *Broadcasting & Cinematog.* **a** a device for merging input signals to produce a combined output in the form of sound or pictures. **b** a person who operates it.

mixology /miksólajee/ *n.* the art or skill of preparing mixed drinks. □□ **mixologist** *n*.

mixture /miks-chər/ *n.* **1** the process of mixing or being mixed. **2** the result of mixing; something mixed; a combination. **3** *Chem.* the product of the random distribution of one substance through another without any chemical reaction taking place between the components, as distinct from a chemical compound. **4** ingredients mixed together to produce a substance, esp. a medicine (*cough mixture*). **5** a person regarded as a combination of qualities and attributes. **6** gas or vaporized gasoline or oil mixed with air, forming an explosive charge in an internal-combustion engine. □ **the mixture as before** *Brit.* the same treatment repeated. [ME f. F *mixture* or L *mixtura* (as MIXED)] ■ **1** mixing, amalgamation, combination, blend, association, synthesis, interweaving, merger, fusion. **2** assortment, amalgam, amalgamation, medley, compound, alloy, combination, composite, blend, jumble, mix, miscellany, mélange, mess, mishmash, conglomeration, hodgepodge, gallimaufry, farrago, olio, olla podrida, hash, potpourri, salmagundi, *colloq.* omnium gatherum.

mizzen /mizən/ *n.* (also **mizen**) *Naut.* (in full **mizzen sail**) the lowest fore-and-aft sail of a fully rigged ship's mizzenmast. □ **mizzen yard** the spar on which the mizzen is extended. [ME f. F *misaine* f. It. *mezzana* mizen-sail, fem. of *mezzano* middle: see MEZZANINE]

mizzenmast /mizənmast/ *n.* the mast next aft of a ship's mainmast.

mizzle[1] /mizəl/ *n. & v.intr.* drizzle. □□ **mizzly** *adj.* [ME, prob. f. LG *miseln*: cf. MDu. *miezelen*] ■ *n.* see MIST *n*. ● *v.* see RAIN *v.* 1.

mizzle[2] /mizəl/ *v.intr. Brit. sl.* run away; decamp. [18th c.: orig. unkn.] ■ see ESCAPE *v.* 1.

Mk. *abbr.* **1** the German mark. **2** Mark (esp. in the New Testament).

mks *abbr.* meter-kilogram-second.

mkt. *abbr.* market.

ml *abbr.* milliliter(s).

MLA *abbr.* Modern Language Association (of America).

MLD *abbr.* minimum lethal dose.

M.Litt. *abbr.* Master of Letters. [L *Magister Litterarum*]

Mlle. *abbr.* (*pl.* **Mlles.**) Mademoiselle.

MM *abbr.* **1** (as **MM.**) Messieurs. **2** (in the UK) Military Medal.

mm *abbr.* millimeter(s).

Mme. *abbr.* (*pl.* **Mmes.**) Madame.

m.m.f. *abbr.* magnetomotive force.

MN *abbr.* Minnesota (in official postal use).

Mn *symb. Chem.* the element manganese.

mnemonic /nimónik/ *adj. & n.* ● *adj.* of or designed to aid the memory. ● *n.* a mnemonic device. □□ **mnemonically** *adv.* **mnemonist** /neémənist/ *n.* [med.L *mnemonicus* f. Gk *mnēmonikos* f. *mnēmōn* mindful]

mnemonics /nimóniks/ *n.pl.* (usu. treated as *sing.*) **1** the art of improving memory. **2** a system for this.

MO *abbr.* **1** Missouri (in official postal use). **2** money order.

Mo *symb. Chem.* the element molybdenum.

Mo. *abbr.* Missouri.

mo. *abbr.* month.

m.o. *abbr.* modus operandi.

moa /móə/ *n.* any extinct flightless New Zealand bird of the family Dinornithidae, resembling the ostrich. [Maori]

moan /mōn/ *n. & v.* ● *n.* **1** a long murmur expressing physical or mental suffering. **2** a low plaintive sound of wind, etc. **3** a complaint; a grievance. ● *v.* **1** *intr.* make a moan or moans. **2** *intr. colloq.* complain or grumble. **3** *tr.* **a** utter with moans. **b** lament. □□ **moaner** *n.* **moanful** *adj.* **moaningly** *adv.* [ME f. OE *mān* (unrecorded) f. Gmc] ■ *n.* **1, 2** lament, lamentation, groan, wail, ululation, sigh, sob, cry; sough, soughing. **3** complaint, grievance, grumble, *colloq.* grouse, gripe, *sl.* beef. ● *v.* **1, 3** sigh, cry, wail, sob, snivel, bawl, keen; mourn, lament, bemoan, weep, sorrow, grieve, mewl, ululate, *literary* pule. **2** complain, lament, groan, wail, grumble, whine, whimper, *colloq.* bitch, grouse, gripe, *sl.* beef.

moat /mōt/ *n. & v.* ● *n.* a deep defensive ditch around a castle, town, etc., usu. filled with water. ● *v.tr.* surround with or as with a moat. [ME *mot(e)* f. OF *mote, motte* mound] ■ *n.* see CHANNEL[1] *n.* 5a, 6.

mob /mob/ *n. & v.* ● *n.* **1** a disorderly crowd; a rabble. **2** (prec. by *the*) usu. *derog.* the populace. **3** *colloq.* a gang; an associated group of persons. **4** = MAFIA. **5** esp. *Austral.* a flock or herd. ● *v.tr. & intr.* (**mobbed, mobbing**) **1** *tr.* **a** crowd around in order to attack or admire. **b** (of a mob) attack. **c** crowd into (a building). **2** *intr.* assemble in a mob. □ **mob law** law or rule imposed and enforced by a mob. □□ **mobber** *n. & adj.* [abbr. of *mobile*, short for L *mobile vulgus* excitable crowd: see MOBILE] ■ *n.* **1** rabble, horde, host, legion, press, throng, crowd, pack, herd, swarm, crush, jam, multitude, mass, body, assemblage, collection, group, *colloq.* gaggle. **2** (*the mob*) the rabble, the riffraff, the proletariat, the populace, the (general) public, the masses, the rank and file, the hoi polloi, canaille, the lower class, *colloq.*

/.../ **pronunciation**	● **part of speech**
□ **phrases, idioms, and compounds**	
□□ **derivatives**	■ **synonym section**
cross-references appear in SMALL CAPITALS or *italics*	

the (great) unwashed. **3** see GANG¹ *n.* ● *v.* **1 a** crowd (around), jostle, throng, surround, beset, clamor over, swoop down on *or* upon. **b** see ATTACK *v.* 1. **2** see UNITE 2.

mobcap /móbkap/ *n. hist.* a woman's large indoor cap covering all the hair, worn in the 18th and early 19th c. [obs. (18th-c.) *mob*, orig. = *slut* + CAP]

mobile /móbəl, -beel, -bil/ *adj. & n.* ● *adj.* **1** movable; not fixed; free or able to move or flow easily. **2** (of the face, etc.) readily changing its expression. **3** (of a shop, library, etc.) accommodated in a vehicle so as to serve various places. **4** (of a person) able to change his or her social status. ● *n.* /-beel/ a decorative structure that may be hung so as to turn freely. □ **mobile home** a transportable structure usu. parked and used as a residence. **mobile sculpture** a sculpture having moving parts. □□ **mobility** /mōbílitee/ *n.* [ME f. F f. L *mobilis* f. *movēre* move]

■ *adj.* **1, 3** movable, nonstationary, unfixed, *Zool. & Bot.* motile; portable, transportable; motorized, traveling; ambulatory, *Med.* ambulant; agile, versatile, nimble, quick, alert, active, responsive. **2** expressive, sensitive, animated, plastic, flexible. □□ **mobility** see MOTION *n.* 1.

mobilize /móbiliz/ *v.* **1 a** *tr.* organize for service or action (esp. troops in time of war). **b** *intr.* be organized in this way. **2** *tr.* render movable; bring into circulation. □□ **mobilizable** *adj.* **mobilization** *n.* **mobilizer** *n.* [F *mobiliser* (as MOBILE)]

■ **1 a** assemble, marshal, conscript, enroll, enlist, organize, muster, levy, rally, activate, call up, prepare, ready, draft.

Möbius strip /móbias, máy-, mṍ-/ *n. Math.* a one-sided surface formed by joining the ends of a rectangle after twisting one end through 180°. [A. F. *Möbius*, Ger. mathematician d. 1868]

mobocracy /mobókrəsee/ *n.* (*pl.* **-ies**) *colloq.* **1** rule by a mob. **2** a ruling mob.

mobster /móbstər/ *n. sl.* a gangster.

■ see GANGSTER.

moccasin /mókəsin/ *n.* **1** a type of soft leather slipper or shoe with combined sole and heel, as orig. worn by Native Americans. **2** (in full **water moccasin**) a poisonous American snake of the genus *Agkistrodon*, esp. the cottonmouth, *A. piscivorus*. [Algonquian *mockasin, makisin*]

mocha /mókə/ *n.* **1** a coffee of fine quality. **2** a beverage or flavoring made with this, often with chocolate added. **3** a soft kind of sheepskin. [*Mocha*, a port on the Red Sea, from where the coffee first came]

mock /mok/ *v., adj., & n.* ● *v.* **1 a** *tr.* ridicule; scoff at. **b** *intr.* (foll. by *at*) act with scorn or contempt for. **2** *tr.* mimic contemptuously. **3** *tr.* jeer, defy, or delude contemptuously. ● *attrib.adj.* sham, imitation (esp. without intention to deceive); pretended (*a mock battle*; *mock cream*). ● *n.* **1** a thing deserving scorn. **2** (in *pl.*) *colloq.* mock examinations. □ **make mock** (or **a mock**) of ridicule. **mock-heroic** *adj.* (of a literary style) burlesquing a heroic style. ● *n.* such a style. **mock moon** paraselene. **mock orange** a white-flowered heavy-scented shrub, *Philadelphus coronarius.* **mock sun** parhelion. **mock turtle soup** soup made from a calf's head, etc., to resemble turtle soup. **mock-up** an experimental model or replica of a proposed structure, etc. □□ **mockable** *adj.* **mocker** *n.* **mockingly** *adv.* [ME *mokke, mocque* f. OF *mo(c)quer* deride f. Rmc]

■ *v.* **1, 3** deride, ridicule, make fun of, tease, taunt, tantalize, jeer (at), gibe (at), chaff, laugh at, poke fun at, make sport of, guy, scorn, abuse, delude, scoff at, sneer at, fleer at, disdain, disparage, decry, defy, flout, *colloq.* rib, kid, *sl.* rag, thumb one's nose at, razz, give the Bronx cheer to, give the raspberry to, *Austral. & NZ sl.* sling off at. **2** ape, mimic, imitate, caricature, lampoon, satirize, parody, burlesque, travesty, copy, *colloq.* spoof, take off, *Brit. colloq.* send up. ● *adj.* substitute, artificial, simulated, fake, synthetic, imitation, false, ersatz, sham, feigned, *colloq.* phony, pseudo; pretended, make-believe, *colloq.* pretend.

mockery /mókəree/ *n.* (*pl.* **-ies**) **1 a** derision, ridicule. **b** a

subject or occasion of this. **2** (often foll. by *of*) a counterfeit or absurdly inadequate representation. **3** a ludicrously or insultingly futile action, etc. [ME f. OF *moquerie* (as MOCK)]

■ **1 a** ridicule, derision, disdain, taunting, disparagement, abuse, scorn, contempt, contumely, decrial, belittlement. **1b, 2** caricature, parody, mimicry, burlesque, travesty, farce, *colloq.* spoof, take-off, *Brit. colloq.* send-up. **3** absurdity; see also JOKE *n.* 2.

mockingbird /mókingbərd/ *n.* a bird that mimics the notes of other birds, esp. the American songbird *Mimus polyglottos.*

mod /mod/ *adj. & n. colloq.* ● *adj.* modern, esp. in style of dress. ● *n. Brit.* a young person (esp. in the 1960s) of a group aiming at sophistication and smart modern dress.

modal /mṓd'l/ *adj.* **1** of or relating to mode or form as opposed to substance. **2** *Gram.* **a** of or denoting the mood of a verb. **b** (of an auxiliary verb, e.g., *would*) used to express the mood of another verb. **c** (of a particle) denoting manner. **3** *Statistics* of or relating to a mode; occurring most frequently in a sample or population. **4** *Mus.* denoting a style of music using a particular mode. **5** *Logic* (of a proposition) in which the predicate is affirmed of the subject with some qualification, or which involves the affirmation of possibility, impossibility, necessity, or contingency. □□ **modally** *adv.* [med.L *modalis* f. L (as MODE)]

modality /mōdálitee/ *n.* (*pl.* **-ies**) **1** the state of being modal. **2** (in *sing.* or *pl.*) a prescribed method of procedure. [med.L *modalitas* (as MODAL)]

mode /mōd/ *n.* **1** a way or manner in which a thing is done; a method of procedure. **2** a prevailing fashion or custom. **3** *Computing* a way of operating or using a system (*print mode*). **4** *Statistics* the value that occurs most frequently in a given set of data. **5** *Mus.* **a** each of the scale systems that result when the white notes of the piano are played consecutively over an octave (*Lydian mode*). **b** each of the two main modern scale systems, the major and minor (*minor mode*). **6** *Logic* **a** the character of a modal proposition. **b** = MOOD². **7** *Physics* any of the distinct kinds or patterns of vibration of an oscillating system. **8** *Gram.* = MOOD². [F *mode* and L *modus* measure]

■ **1** way, manner, method, approach, form, course, fashion, procedure, technique, system, modus operandi, m.o., methodology, standard operating procedure, SOP, *archaic* wise. **2** fashion, style, look, vogue; trend, rage, craze, fad. **3** status, condition, state, configuration, set-up.

model /mṓd'l/ *n. & v.* ● *n.* **1** a representation in three dimensions of an existing person or thing or of a proposed structure, esp. on a smaller scale (often *attrib.: a model train*). **2** a simplified (often mathematical) description of a system, etc., to assist calculations and predictions. **3** a figure in clay, wax, etc., to be reproduced in another material. **4** a particular design or style of a structure or commodity, esp. of a car. **5 a** an exemplary person or thing (*a model of self-discipline*). **b** (*attrib.*) ideal, exemplary (*a model student*). **6** a person employed to pose for an artist or photographer or to display clothes, etc., by wearing them. **7** a garment, etc., by a well-known designer, or a copy of this. ● *v.* (**modeled, modeling;** *Brit.* **modelled, modelling**) **1** *tr.* **a** fashion or shape (a figure) in clay, wax, etc. **b** (foll. by *after, on,* etc.) form (a thing in imitation of). **2 a** *intr.* act or pose as a model. **b** *tr.* (of a person acting as a model) display (a garment). **3** *tr.* devise a (usu. mathematical) model of (a phenomenon, system, etc.). **4** *tr. Painting* cause to appear three-dimensional. □□ **modeler** *n.* [F *modelle* f. It. *modello* ult. f. L *modulus:* see MODULUS]

■ *n.* **1, 3** representation, replica, mock-up, maquette, scale model, working model, miniature, dummy, mannequin; image, likeness, facsimile, copy, imitation. **4** design, kind, type, style, version; variety, sort, form, fashion; brand, mark. **5 a** original, archetype, prototype, pattern, paragon, ideal, exemplar, example, standard, epitome, acme, perfection, cream, crème de la crème, ne plus ultra, nonpareil, nonesuch. **b** ideal, exemplary, perfect, archetypal, unequaled, consummate, inimitable. **6** subject, sitter, poser. ● *v.*

1 a fashion, mold, shape, form, sculpt, design, carve (out); make, fabricate, produce. **b** (*model after* or *on*) imitate, copy, pattern on or after, emulate, follow. **2** pose, sit; display, show (off), exhibit; wear, sport.

modem /mṓdem/ *n.* a combined device for modulation and demodulation, e.g., between a computer and a telephone line. [*modulator* + *demodulator*]

moderate *adj., n.,* & *v.* ● *adj.* /módərət/ **1** avoiding extremes; temperate in conduct or expression. **2** fairly or tolerably large or good. **3** (of the wind) of medium strength. **4** (of prices) fairly low. ● *n.* /módərət/ a person who holds moderate views, esp. in politics. ● *v.* /módərayt/ **1** *tr.* & *intr.* make or become less violent, intense, rigorous, etc. **2** *tr.* (also *absol.*) act as a moderator of or to. **3** *tr. Physics* retard (neutrons) with a moderator. □□ **moderately** /-rətlee/ *adv.* **moderateness** /-rətnis/ *n.* **moderatism** /módərətizəm/ *n.* [ME f. L *moderatus* past part. of *moderare* reduce, control: rel. to MODEST]

■ *adj.* **1** temperate, calm, reasonable, cool, judicious, rational, balanced, unexcessive, modest, sober, sensible, commonsensical, controlled, deliberate, steady; center, middle-of-the-road, mainstream, nonradical, nonreactionary. **2, 4** fair, middling, average, ordinary, medium, middle, modest, mediocre, unexceptional, fair to middling; lowish. ● *n.* nonradical, nonreactionary, *Polit. often derog.* centrist. ● *v.* **1** abate, calm, mollify, soothe, ease, relax, alleviate, pacify, mitigate, soften, dull, blunt, cushion, relieve, reduce, lessen, remit, slacken, diminish, decrease, defuse, temper, *colloq.* let up. **2** mediate, arbitrate, referee, judge, chair, supervise, preside (over), coordinate, run, regulate, manage, direct. □□ **moderately** somewhat, rather, quite, fairly, comparatively, slightly, passably, more or less, *colloq.* pretty; to some extent, within reason, to a certain extent, to a degree, to some degree, in some measure, *colloq.* sort of, kind of; in moderation, within limits, temperately.

moderation /módəráyshən/ *n.* **1** the process or an instance of moderating. **2** the quality of being moderate. **3** *Physics* the retardation of neutrons by a moderator (see MODERATOR 4). □ **in moderation** in a moderate manner or degree. [ME f. OF f. L *moderatio -onis* (as MODERATE)]

■ **1** see RELAXATION 3, 4. **2** see TEMPERANCE 1.

moderato /módəra̋atō/ *adj., adv.,* & *n. Mus.* ● *adj.* & *adv.* performed at a moderate pace. ● *n.* (*pl.* **-os**) a piece of music to be performed in this way. [It. (as MODERATE)]

moderator /módəraytər/ *n.* **1** an arbitrator or mediator. **2** a presiding officer. **3** *Eccl.* a Presbyterian minister presiding over an ecclesiastical body. **4** *Physics* a substance used in a nuclear reactor to retard neutrons. □□ **moderatorship** *n.* [ME f. L (as MODERATE)]

■ **1** mediator, arbiter, arbitrator, judge, referee, umpire. **2** chair, chairperson, chairman, chairwoman, presiding officer, president, coordinator, leader, facilitator; anchorman, anchorwoman, anchor; master of ceremonies, MC, toastmaster, *Brit.* compère, *colloq.* emcee.

modern /módərn/ *adj.* & *n.* ● *adj.* **1** of the present and recent times. **2** in current fashion; not antiquated. ● *n.* (usu. in *pl.*) a person living in modern times. □ **modern English** English from about 1500 onward. **modern history** history from the end of the Middle Ages to the present day. □□ **modernity** /-dérnitee/ *n.* **modernly** *adv.* **modernness** *n.* [F *moderne* or LL *modernus* f. L *modo* just now]

■ *adj.* up-to-date, current, contemporary, today's, new, fresh, novel, brand-new, up to the minute, present-day, latest, new-fashioned, *derog.* newfangled; à la mode, modish, in vogue, fashionable, in fashion, stylish, in style, chic, in, *colloq.* hot, with it, mod, *colloq. often derog.* trendy, *sl.* hip, hep.

modernism /módərnizəm/ *n.* **1 a** modern ideas or methods. **b** the tendency of religious belief to harmonize with modern ideas. **2** a modern term or expression. □□ **modernist** *n.*

modernistic /-nístik/ *adj.* **modernistically** /-nístiklee/ *adv.*

■ □□ **modernistic** see *streamlined* (STREAMLINE *v.* 3b).

modernize /módərnīz/ *v.* **1** *tr.* make modern; adapt to modern needs or habits. **2** *intr.* adopt modern ways or views. □□ **modernization** /-záyshən/ *n.* **modernizer** *n.*

■ **1** renovate, streamline, redo, redecorate, refurbish, refurnish, update, rejuvenate, refresh, revamp, redesign, remodel, refashion, remake, *colloq.* do over; develop. □□ **modernization** see IMPROVEMENT, DEVELOPMENT 1.

modest /módist/ *adj.* **1** having or expressing a humble or moderate estimate of one's own merits or achievements. **2** diffident, bashful, retiring. **3** decorous in manner and conduct. **4** moderate or restrained in amount, extent, severity, etc.; not excessive or exaggerated (*a modest sum*). **5** (of a thing) unpretentious in appearance, etc. □□ **modestly** *adv.* [F *modeste* f. L *modestus* keeping due measure]

■ **1, 2** unassuming, unpresuming, humble, unpretentious, unobtrusive, reserved, retiring, diffident, shy, bashful, demure, coy, self-effacing, self-conscious, reticent, reluctant, timid, meek, timorous. **3** see DECOROUS. **4** moderate, limited, understated, unexaggerated, reasonable, sensible, constrained, restricted, restrained. **5** humble, simple, plain, ordinary, unpretentious, homely, lowly, unexceptional, unostentatious; bare, spartan; inconspicuous, unobtrusive.

modesty /módistee/ *n.* the quality of being modest.

■ see HUMILITY, PURITY 2.

modicum /módikəm/ *n.* (foll. by *of*) a small quantity. [L, = short distance or time, neut. of *modicus* moderate f. *modus* measure]

■ bit, trifle, jot, (jot or) tittle, atom, scintilla, spark, particle, iota, speck, grain, whit, scrap, shred, snippet, sliver, fragment, splinter, morsel, crumb, ounce, dram, drop, dash, spot, touch, tinge, hint, suggestion, *colloq.* smidgen, tad.

modification /módifikáyshən/ *n.* **1** the act or an instance of modifying or being modified. **2** a change made. [F or f. L *modificatio* (as MODIFY)]

■ see ADAPTATION.

modifier /módifiər/ *n.* **1** a person or thing that modifies. **2** *Gram.* a word, esp. an adjective or noun used attributively, that qualifies the sense of another word (e.g., *good* and *family* in *a good family house*).

modify /módifī/ *v.tr.* (**-ies, -ied**) **1** make less severe or extreme; tone down (*modify one's demands*). **2** make partial changes in; make different. **3** *Gram.* qualify or expand the sense of (a word, etc.). **4** *Phonet.* change (a vowel) by umlaut. **5** *Chem.* change or replace all the substituent radicals of a polymer, thereby changing its physical properties such as solubility, etc. (*modified starch*). □□ **modifiable** *adj.* **modificatory** /-fikətáwree/ *adj.* [ME f. OF *modifier* f. L *modificare* (as MODE)]

■ **1** reduce, decrease, diminish, lessen, moderate, temper, soften, lower, abate, tone down, modulate; qualify, limit, restrict. **2** adjust, adapt, change, vary, transform, alter, revise, amend, redo, remake, remold, reshape, reconstruct, reform, revamp, refashion, remodel, rework, reword, reorient(ate), reorganize.

modillion /mədílyən/ *n. Archit.* a projecting bracket under the corona of a cornice in the Corinthian and other orders. [F *modillon* f. It. *modiglione* ult. f. L *mutulus* mutule]

modish /mṓdish/ *adj.* fashionable. □□ **modishly** *adv.* **modishness** *n.*

■ see FASHIONABLE. □□ **modishness** see CHIC *n.*

modiste /mōdéest/ *n.* a milliner; a dressmaker. [F (as MODE)]

■ see DRESSMAKER.

/. . ./ pronunciation	● part of speech
□ phrases, idioms, and compounds	
□□ derivatives	■ synonym section
cross-references appear in SMALL CAPITALS or *italics*	

modular /mójələr/ *adj.* of or consisting of modules or moduli. □□ **modularity** /-láritee/ *n.* [mod.L *modularis* f. L *modulus*: see MODULUS]

modulate /mójəlayt/ *v.* **1** *tr.* **a** regulate or adjust. **b** moderate. **2** *tr.* adjust or vary the tone or pitch of (the speaking voice). **3** *tr.* alter the amplitude or frequency of (a wave) by a wave of a lower frequency to convey a signal. **4** *intr.* & *tr.* *Mus.* (often foll. by *from*, *to*) change or cause to change from one key to another. □□ **modulation** /-láyshən/ *n.* **modulator** *n.* [L *modulari modulat-* to measure f. *modus* measure]
  ■ **1, 2** adjust, regulate, set, tune, balance, temper, moderate, modify, vary; lower, tune *or* tone down, turn down, soften.

module /mójōōl/ *n.* **1** a standardized part or independent unit used in construction, esp. of furniture, a building, or an electronic system. **2** an independent self-contained unit of a spacecraft (*lunar module*). **3** a unit or period of training or education. **4 a** a standard or unit of measurement. **b** *Archit.* a unit of length for expressing proportions, e.g., the semi-diameter of a column at the base. [F *module* or L *modulus*: see MODULUS]

modulo /mójəlō/ *prep.* & *adj.* *Math.* using, or with respect to, a modulus (see MODULUS 2). [L, ablat. of MODULUS]

modulus /mójələs/ *n.* (*pl.* **moduli** /-lī/) *Math.* **1 a** the magnitude of a real number without regard to its sign. **b** the positive square root of the sum of the squares of the real and imaginary parts of a complex number. **2** a constant factor or ratio. **3** (in number theory) a number used as a divisor for considering numbers in sets giving the same remainder when divided by it. **4** a constant indicating the relation between a physical effect and the force producing it. [L, = measure, dimin. of *modus*]

modus operandi /módəs ópərándee, -dī/ *n.* (*pl.* **modi operandi** /módee, -dī/) **1** the particular way in which a person performs a task or action. **2** the way a thing operates. [L, = way of operating: see MODE]
  ■ see WAY *n.* 4a.

modus vivendi /módəs vivéndee, -dī/ *n.* (*pl.* **modi vivendi** /módee, -dī/) **1** a way of living or coping. **2 a** an arrangement whereby those in dispute can carry on pending a settlement. **b** an arrangement between people who agree to differ. [L, = way of living: see MODE]

mofette /mōfét/ *n.* **1** a fumarole. **2** an exhalation of vapor from this. [F *mofette* or Neapolitan It. *mofetta*]

mogul /mṓgəl/ *n.* **1** *colloq.* an important or influential person. **2** (**Mogul**) *hist.* **a** = MUGHAL. **b** (often **the Great Mogul**) any of the emperors of Delhi in the 16th–19th c. [Pers. *mugūl*: see MUGHAL]
  ■ **1** magnate, tycoon, baron, mandarin, nabob, VIP, *colloq.* big shot, bigwig, hotshot, *sl.* big gun, big cheese, big daddy, *sl.* (big) wheel, Mr. Big.

mohair /mṓhair/ *n.* **1** the hair of the angora goat. **2** a yarn or fabric from this, either pure or mixed with wool or cotton. [ult. f. Arab. *mukayyar*, lit. choice, select]

Mohammedan var. of MUHAMMADAN.

Mohawk /mṓhawk/ *n.* **1 a** a member of a Native American people of New York State. **b** the language of this people. **2** (of a hairstyle) with the head shaved except for a strip of hair from the middle of the forehead to the back of the neck, often worn in tall spikes.

Mohegan /mōhéegən/ *n.* & *adj.* ● *n.* a member of a Native American people of Connecticut. ● *adj.* **1** of or relating to this people.

Mohican var. of **Mahican.**

moho /mṓhō/ *n.* (*pl.* **-os**) *Geol.* a boundary of discontinuity separating the earth's crust and mantle. [A. *Mohorovičić*, Yugoslav seismologist d. 1936]

moidore /móydawr/ *n.* *hist.* a Portuguese gold coin, current in England in the 18th c. [Port. *moeda d'ouro* money of gold]

moiety /móyətee/ *n.* (*pl.* **-ies**) *Law* or *literary* **1** a half. **2** each of the two parts into which a thing is divided. [ME f. OF *moité*, *moitié* f. L *medietas -tatis* middle f. *medius* (adj.) middle]

moil /moyl/ *v.* & *n.* *archaic* ● *v.intr.* drudge (esp. *toil and*

moil). ● *n.* drudgery. [ME f. OF *moillier* moisten, paddle in mud, ult. f. L *mollis* soft]

moire /mwaar, mawr/ *n.* (in full **moire antique**) watered fabric, orig. mohair, now usu. silk. [F (earlier *mouaire*) f. MOHAIR]

moiré /mwaaráy, máwray/ *adj.* & *n.* ● *adj.* **1** (of silk) watered. **2** (of metal) having a patterned appearance like watered silk. ● *n.* **1** this patterned appearance. **2** = MOIRE. [F, past part. of *moirer* (as MOIRE)]

moist /moyst/ *adj.* **1 a** slightly wet; damp. **b** (of the season, etc.) rainy. **2** (of a disease) marked by a discharge of matter, etc. **3** (of the eyes) wet with tears. □□ **moistly** *adv.* **moistness** *n.* [ME f. OF *moiste*, ult. from or rel. to L *mucidus* (see MUCUS) and *musteus* fresh (see MUST²)]
  ■ **1 a** damp, wet, wettish, dampish, dewy, dank, humid, soggy, moisture-laden, clammy, muggy, steamy, misty, foggy. **b** damp, wet, rainy, drizzly. **3** tearful, teary, misty, wet.

moisten /móysən/ *v.tr.* & *intr.* make or become moist.
  ■ see WATER *v.* 1.

moisture /móys-chər/ *n.* water or other liquid diffused in a small quantity as vapor, or within a solid, or condensed on a surface. □□ **moistureless** *adj.* [ME f. OF *moistour* (as MOIST)]
  ■ see WET *n.* 1.

moisturize /móys-chərīz/ *v.tr.* make less dry (esp. the skin by use of a cosmetic). □□ **moisturizer** *n.*

Mojave /mōháavee/ *n.* & *adj.* (also **Mohave**) ● *n.* **1** a N. American people native to Arizona and California. **2** a member of this people. ● *adj.* of or relating to this people.

moke /mōk/ *n.* *sl.* **1** *Brit.* a donkey. **2** *Austral.* a very poor horse. [19th c.: orig. unkn.]

moksha /mókshə/ *n.* (also **moksa**) *Hinduism*, etc., release from the cycle of rebirth. [Skr. *mokṣa*]

mol /mōl/ *abbr.* = MOLE⁴.

molal /mṓləl/ *adj.* *Chem.* (of a solution) containing one mole of solute per kilogram of solvent. □□ **molality** /məlálitee/ *n.* [MOLE⁴ + -AL]

molar¹ /mṓlər/ *adj.* & *n.* ● *adj.* (usu. of a mammal's back teeth) serving to grind. ● *n.* a molar tooth. [L *molaris* f. *mola* millstone]

molar² /mṓlər/ *adj.* **1** of or relating to mass. **2** acting on or by means of large masses or units. [L *moles* mass]

molar³ /mṓlər/ *adj.* *Chem.* **1** of a mass of substance usu. per mole (*molar latent heat*). **2** (of a solution) containing one mole per liter of solvent. □□ **molarity** /məláritee/ *n.* [MOLE⁴ + -AR¹]

molasses /məlásiz/ *n.pl.* (treated as *sing.*) **1** uncrystallized syrup extracted from raw sugar during refining. **2** treacle. [Port. *melaço* f. LL *mellaceum* MUST² f. *mel* honey]

mold¹ /mōld/ *n.* & *v.* (*Brit.* **mould**) ● *n.* **1** a hollow container into which molten metal, etc., is poured or soft material is pressed to harden into a required shape. **2 a** a metal or earthenware vessel used to give shape to cakes, etc. **b** a dessert, etc., made in this way. **3** a form or shape, esp. of an animal body. **4** *Archit.* a molding or group of moldings. **5** a frame or template for producing moldings. **6** character or disposition (*in heroic mold*). ● *v.tr.* **1** make (an object) in a required shape or from certain ingredients (*was molded out of clay*). **2** give a shape to. **3** influence the formation or development of (*consultation helps to mold policies*). **4** (esp. of clothing) fit closely to (*the gloves molded his hands*). □□ **moldable** *adj.* **molder** *n.* [ME *mold(e)*, app. f. OF *modle* f. L *modulus*: see MODULUS]
  ■ *n.* **1, 5** form, cast, matrix, die; template, pattern, frame. **3** form, shape, pattern, format, structure, build, construction, design, arrangement, organization, configuration, kind, brand, make, line, type, stamp, cut. **6** character, nature, disposition, stamp, type, kind, kidney, sort, *colloq.* disp. ilk. ● *v.* **1, 2** shape, form, make, work, fashion, configure, sculpture, sculpt, model, knead, construct; carve, cut; forge, cast, stamp, die-cast. **3** influence, shape, form, affect, make, control, direct, guide, lead.

mold² /mōld/ *n.* (*Brit.* **mould**) a woolly or furry growth of minute fungi occurring esp. in moist warm conditions. [ME prob. f. obs. *mold* adj.; past part. of *moul* grow moldy f. ON *mygla*]

■ mildew, fungus, must, mustiness; blight, smut.

mold³ /mōld/ *n.* (*Brit.* **mould**) **1** loose earth. **2** the upper soil of cultivated land, esp. when rich in organic matter.

■ soil, earth, dirt, loam, topsoil, humus.

molder /mōldər/ *v.intr.* (*Brit.* **moulder**) **1** decay to dust. **2** (foll. by *away*) rot or crumble. **3** deteriorate. [perh. f. MOLD³, but cf. Norw. dial. *muldra* crumble]

■ **1, 2** see DECAY *v.* 1a.

molding /mōlding/ *n.* (*Brit.* **moulding**) **1 a** an ornamentally shaped outline as an architectural feature, esp. in a cornice. **b** a strip of material in wood or stone, etc., for use as molding. **2** similar material in wood or plastic, etc., used for other decorative purposes, e.g., in picture framing.

■ see BORDER *n.* 3.

moldy /mōldee/ *adj.* (*Brit.* **mouldy**) (**-ier, -iest**) **1** covered with mold. **2** stale; out of date. **3** *colloq.* (as a general term of disparagement) dull, miserable, boring. □□ **moldiness** *n.*

■ **1** musty, mildewy, mildewed, moldering, blighted, smutty; decayed, decaying, carious, spoiled, rotten, rotting, putrid, putrescent, putrefying, rancid, rank, decomposed, decomposing. **2** aged, ancient, outdated, old-fashioned, antediluvian, unused, stale. **3** see DULL *adj.* 2.

mole¹ /mōl/ *n.* **1** any small burrowing insect-eating mammal of the family Talpidae, esp. *Talpa europaea*, with dark velvety fur and very small eyes. **2** *colloq.* **a** a spy established deep within an organization and usu. dormant for a long period while attaining a position of trust. **b** a betrayer of confidential information. [ME *molle*, prob. f. MDu. *moll(e)*, *mol*, MLG *mol*, *mul*]

■ **2 a** see SPY *n.*

mole² /mōl/ *n.* a small often slightly raised dark blemish on the skin caused by a high concentration of melanin. [OE *māl* f. Gmc]

mole³ /mōl/ *n.* **1** a massive structure serving as a pier, breakwater, or causeway. **2** an artificial harbor. [F *môle* f. L *moles* mass]

mole⁴ /mōl/ *n. Chem.* the SI unit of amount of substance equal to the quantity containing as many elementary units as there are atoms in 0.012 kg of carbon 12. [G *Mol* f. *Molekül* MOLECULE]

mole⁵ /mōl/ *n. Med.* an abnormal mass of tissue in the uterus. [F *môle* f. L *mola* millstone]

molecular /məlékyələr/ *adj.* of, relating to, or consisting of molecules. □ **molecular biology** the study of the structure and function of large molecules associated with living organisms. **molecular sieve** a crystalline substance with pores of molecular dimensions that permit the entry of certain molecules but are impervious to others. **molecular weight** the ratio of the average mass of one molecule of an element or compound to one twelfth of the mass of an atom of carbon-12; also called *relative molecular mass*. □□ **molecularity** /-láritee/ *n.* **molecularly** *adv.*

molecule /mólikyōōl/ *n.* **1** *Chem.* the smallest fundamental unit (usu. a group of atoms) of a chemical compound that can take part in a chemical reaction. **2** (in general use) a small particle. [F *molécule* f. mod.L *molecula* dimin. of L *moles* mass]

■ **2** see PARTICLE 2.

molehill /mólhil/ *n.* a small mound thrown up by a mole in burrowing. □ **make a mountain out of a molehill** exaggerate the importance of a minor difficulty.

moleskin /mólskin/ *n.* **1** the skin of a mole used as fur. **2 a** a kind of cotton fustian with its surface shaved before dyeing. **b** (in *pl.*) clothes, esp. trousers, made of this.

molest /məlést/ *v.tr.* **1** annoy or pester (a person) in a hostile or injurious way. **2** attack or interfere with (a person), esp. sexually. □□ **molestation** /mōlestáyshən, mól-/ *n.* **molester** *n.* [OF *molester* or L *molestare* annoy f. *molestus* troublesome]

■ **1** annoy, irritate, vex, disturb, pester, badger, provoke, nettle, tease, harass, harry, worry, hector, irk, bother, gall, chafe, torment, beleaguer, roil, *colloq.* needle,

plague. **2** accost, meddle with, interfere with, abuse, attack, assault, ill-treat, harm, maltreat, *colloq.* manhandle, paw, *sl.* grope; rape, ravish, violate.

moline /məlín/ *adj. Heraldry* (of a cross) having each extremity broadened and curved back. [prob. f. AF *moliné* f. *molin* MILL¹, because of the resemblance to the iron support of a millstone]

moll /mol/ *n. sl.* **1** a gangster's female companion. **2** a prostitute. [pet form of the name *Mary*]

■ **2** see PROSTITUTE *n.* 1a.

mollify /mólifī/ *v.tr.* (**-ies, -ied**) **1** appease, pacify. **2** reduce the severity of; soften. □□ **mollification** /-fikáyshən/ *n.* **mollifier** *n.* [ME f. F *mollifier* or L *mollificare* f. *mollis* soft]

■ **1** see CALM *v.* **2** see MODERATE *v.* 1.

mollusk /móləsk/ *n.* (also esp. *Brit.* **mollusc**) any invertebrate of the phylum Mollusca, with a soft body and usu. a hard shell, including limpets, snails, cuttlefish, oysters, mussels, etc. □□ **molluskan** or **molluscan** /məlúskən/ *n. & adj.* **mollusklike** *adj.* [mod.L *mollusca* neut. pl. of L *molluscus* f. *mollis* soft]

mollycoddle /móleekodəl/ *v. & n.* ● *v.tr.* coddle, pamper. ● *n.* an effeminate man or boy; a milksop. [formed as MOLL + CODDLE]

● *v.* see PAMPER. ● *n.* see MILKSOP.

mollymawk /móleemawk/ *n.* (also **mallemuck** /málimuk/) any of various small kinds of albatross or similar birds. [Du. *mallemok* f. *mal* foolish + *mok* gull]

Moloch /mōlok, mólək/ *n.* **1 a** a Canaanite idol to whom children were sacrificed. **b** a tyrannical object of sacrifices. **2** (**moloch**) the spiny slow-moving grotesque Australian reptile, *Moloch horridus.* [LL f. Gk *Molokh* f. Heb. *mōlek̠*]

Molotov cocktail /mólətáwf/ *n.* a crude incendiary device usu. consisting of a bottle filled with flammable liquid. [V. M. *Molotov*, Russian statesman d. 1986]

molt /mōlt/ *v. & n.* (*Brit.* **moult**) ● *v.* **1** *intr.* shed feathers, hair, a shell, etc., in the process of renewing plumage, a coat, etc. **2** *tr.* (of an animal) shed (feathers, hair, etc.). ● *n.* the act or an instance of molting (*is in molt once a year*). □□ **molter** *n.* [ME *moute* f. OE *mutian* (unrecorded) f. L *mutare* change: *-l-* after *fault*, etc.]

● *v.* see SHED².

molten /mōltən/ *adj.* melted, esp. made liquid by heat. [past part. of MELT]

■ see LIQUID *adj.* 1, 3.

molto /mōltō/ *adv. Mus.* very (*molto sostenuto; allegro molto*). [It. f. L *multus* much]

moly /mōlee/ *n.* (*pl.* **-ies**) **1** an alliaceous plant, *Allium moly*, with small yellow flowers. **2** a mythical herb with white flowers and black roots, endowed with magic properties. [L f. Gk *mōlu*]

molybdenite /məlíbdinīt/ *n.* molybdenum disulfide as an ore.

molybdenum /məlíbdinəm/ *n. Chem.* a silver-white brittle metallic transition element occurring naturally in molybdenite and used in steel to give strength and resistance to corrosion. ¶ Symb.: **Mo**. [mod.L, earlier *molybdena*, orig. = molybdenite, lead ore: L *molybdena* f. Gk *molubdaina* plummet f. *molubdos* lead]

mom /mom/ *n. colloq.* mother. □ **mom-and-pop** (**store**) of or pertaining to a small retail business, as a grocery store, owned and operated by members of a family. [abbr. of MOMMA]

moment /mōmənt/ *n.* **1** a very brief portion of time; an instant. **2** a short period of time (*wait a moment*) (see also MINUTE¹). **3** an exact or particular point of time (*at last the moment arrived; I came the moment you called*). **4** importance (*of no great moment*). **5** *Physics & Mech.*, etc. **a** the turning effect produced by a force acting at a distance on an object. **b** this effect expressed as the product of the force and the

/.../ **pronunciation**	● **part of speech**
□ **phrases, idioms, and compounds**	
□□ **derivatives**	■ **synonym section**
cross-references appear in SMALL CAPITALS or *italics*	

distance from its line of action to a point. □ **at the moment** at this time; now. **in a moment 1** very soon. **2** instantly. **man** (or **woman**, etc.) **of the moment** the one of importance at the time in question. **moment of inertia** *Physics* the quantity by which the angular acceleration of a body must be multiplied to give corresponding torque. **moment of truth** a time of crisis or test (orig. the final sword thrust in a bullfight). **not for a** (or **one**) **moment** never; not at all. **this moment** immediately; at once (*come here this moment*). [ME f. OF f. L *momentum*: see MOMENTUM]

■ **1, 2** instant, second, minute, flash, half a second, two seconds, *colloq*. jiff, jiffy, mo, tick. **3** instant, time, second, minute; point (in time), juncture, stage. **4** importance, weight, consequence, significance, import, gravity, seriousness, prominence, concern, note, interest, consideration. □ **at the moment** see NOW *adv*. 1, 4. **in a moment** see SOON 1. **this moment** see IMMEDIATELY *adv*. 1.

momenta *pl.* of MOMENTUM.

momentarily /mṓməntairilee/ *adv*. **1** for a moment. **2 a** at any moment. **b** instantly.

■ **1** see *briefly* (BRIEF). **2 a** see SOON 1. **b** see *instantaneously* (INSTANTANEOUS).

momentary /mṓmənteree/ *adj*. **1** lasting only a moment. **2** short-lived; transitory. □□ **momentariness** *n*. [L *momentarius* (as MOMENT)]

■ fleeting, temporary, ephemeral, evanescent, impermanent, fugitive, passing, transitory, brief, short-lived, quick, short.

momently /mṓməntlee/ *adv. literary* **1** from moment to moment. **2** every moment. **3** for a moment.

momentous /mōméntəs/ *adj*. having great importance. □□ **momentously** *adv*. **momentousness** *n*.

■ important, weighty, consequential, significant, grave, serious, decisive, crucial, critical, vital, pivotal, portentous.

momentum /mōméntəm/ *n*. (*pl.* **momenta** /-tə/) **1** *Physics* the quantity of motion of a moving body, measured as a product of its mass and velocity. **2** the impetus gained by movement. **3** strength or continuity derived from an initial effort. [L f. *movimentum* f. *movēre* move]

■ energy, force, drive, strength, impetus, power, impulse, thrust, push.

momma /mómə/ *n*. var. of MAMMA[1].

mommy /mómee/ *n*. (*pl.* **-ies**) *colloq*. mother. [imit. of a child's pronunc.: cf. MAMMA[1]]

■ see MOTHER *n*. 1

Mon. *abbr*. Monday.

monad /mónad, mṓ-/ *n*. **1** the number one; a unit. **2** *Philos*. any ultimate unit of being (e.g., a soul, an atom, a person, God). **3** *Biol*. a simple organism, e.g., one assumed as the first in the genealogy of living beings. □□ **monadic** /mənádik/ *adj*. **monadism** *n*. (in sense 2). [F *monade* or LL *monas* *monad*- f. Gk *monas -ados* unit f. *monos* alone]

monadelphous /mónədélfəs/ *adj. Bot*. **1** (of stamens) having filaments united into one bundle. **2** (of a plant) with such stamens. [Gk *monos* one + *adelphos* brother]

monadnock /mənádnok/ *n*. a steep-sided isolated hill resistant to erosion and rising above a plain. [Mount *Monadnock* in New Hampshire]

monandry /mənándree/ *n*. **1** the custom of having only one husband at a time. **2** *Bot*. the state of having a single stamen. □□ **monandrous** *adj*. [MONO- after *polyandry*]

monarch /mónərk, -aark/ *n*. **1** a sovereign with the title of king, queen, emperor, empress, or the equivalent. **2** a supreme ruler. **3** a powerful or preeminent person. **4** a large orange and black butterfly, *Danaus plexippus*. □□ **monarchal** /mənaárkəl/ *adj*. **monarchic** /mənaárkik/ *adj*. **monarchical** /mənaárkikəl/ *adj*. **monarchically** /mənaárkiklee/ *adv*. [ME f. F *monarque* or LL *monarcha* f. Gk *monarkhēs, -os*, f. *monos* alone + *arkhō* to rule]

■ **1, 2** ruler, sovereign, potentate, crowned head; emperor, empress, queen, king. **3** ruler, sovereign, chief, lord, master, owner, czar, *Brit*. supremo, *colloq*. boss.

monarchism /mónərkizəm/ *n*. the advocacy of or the principles of monarchy. □□ **monarchist** *n*. [F *monarchisme* (as MONARCHY)]

monarchy /mónərkee/ *n*. (*pl.* **-ies**) **1** a form of government with a monarch at the head. **2** a nation with this. □□ **monarchial** /mənaárkeeəl/ *adj*. [ME f. OF *monarchie* f. LL *monarchia* f. Gk *monarkhia* the rule of one (as MONARCH)]

■ **1** monocracy, autocracy; royalism, monarchism. **2** kingdom, empire, domain, principality, *formal esp. Law* realm.

monastery /mónəsteree/ *n*. (*pl.* **-ies**) the residence of a religious community, esp. of monks living in seclusion. [ME f. eccl.L *monasterium* f. eccl.Gk *monastērion* f. *monazō* live alone f. *monos* alone]

■ abbey, cloister, priory, friary, *Buddhism* vihara, lamasery, *Ind*. ashram.

monastic /mənástik/ *adj. & n.* ● *adj*. **1** of or relating to monasteries or the religious communities living in them. **2** resembling these or their way of life; solitary and celibate. ● *n*. a monk or other follower of a monastic rule. □□ **monastically** *adv*. **monasticism** /-tisizəm/ *n*. **monasticize** /-tisiz/ *v.tr*. [F *monastique* or LL *monasticus* f. Gk *monastikos* (as MONASTERY)]

■ *adj*. **2** see ISOLATED 1. ● *n*. see MONK. □□ **monastically** see *severely* (SEVERE).

monatomic /mónətómik/ *adj. Chem*. **1** (esp. of a molecule) consisting of one atom. **2** having one replaceable atom or radical.

monaural /mónáwrəl/ *adj*. **1** = MONOPHONIC. **2** of or involving one ear. □□ **monaurally** *adv*. [MONO- + AURAL[1]]

monazite /mónəzit/ *n*. a phosphate mineral containing rare-earth elements and thorium. [G *Monazit* f. Gk *monazō* live alone (because of its rarity)]

Monday /múnday, -dee/ *n. & adv.* ● *n*. the second day of the week, following Sunday. ● *adv. colloq*. **1** on Monday. **2** (**Mondays**) on Mondays; each Monday. [OE *mōnandæg* day of the moon, transl. LL *lunae dies*]

Monel /mōnél/ *n*. (in full **Monel metal**) *propr*. a nickel-copper alloy with high tensile strength and resisting corrosion. [A. *Monell*, US businessman d. 1921]

monetarism /mónitərizəm, mún-/ *n*. the theory or practice of controlling the supply of money as the chief method of stabilizing the economy.

monetarist /mónitərist, mún-/ *n. & adj.* ● *n*. an advocate of monetarism. ● *adj*. in accordance with the principles of monetarism.

monetary /móniteree, -mún/ *adj*. **1** of the currency in use. **2** of or consisting of money. □□ **monetarily** /-táirəlee/ *adv*. [F *monétaire* or LL *monetarius* f. L (as MONEY)]

■ **2** pecuniary, fiscal, financial, capital, cash, money; numismatic.

monetize /mónitiz, mún-/ *v.tr*. **1** give a fixed value as currency. **2** put (a metal) into circulation as money. □□ **monetization** *n*. [F *monétiser* f. L (as MONEY)]

money /múnee/ *n*. **1 a** a current medium of exchange in the form of coins and paper currency. **b** a particular form of this (*silver money*). **2** (*pl.* **-eys** or **-ies**) (in *pl.*) sums of money. **3 a** wealth; property viewed as convertible into money. **b** wealth as giving power or influence (*money speaks*). **c** a rich person or family (*has married into money*). **4 a** money as a resource (*time is money*). **b** profit, remuneration (*in it for the money*). □ **for my money** in my opinion or judgment; for my preference (*is too aggressive for my money*). **have money to burn** see BURN[1]. **in the money** *colloq*. having or winning a lot of money. **money box** *Brit*. a box for saving money dropped through a slit. **money changer** a person whose business it is to change money, esp. at an official rate. **money for jam** (or **old rope**) *Brit. colloq*. profit for little or no trouble. **money-grubber** *colloq*. a person greedily intent on amassing money. **money-grubbing** *n*. this practice. ● *adj*. given to this. **money market** *Stock Exch*. trade in short-term stocks, loans, etc. **money of account** see ACCOUNT. **money order** an order for payment of a specified sum, issued by a bank or post office. **money-spinner** esp. *Brit*. a thing that brings in a profit. **money's worth** good value for one's money. **put money into** invest in. □□ **moneyless** adj. [ME f. OF moneie f. L moneta mint, money, orig. a title of Juno, in whose temple at Rome money was minted]

■ **1** currency, legal tender, medium of exchange, specie, (hard) cash, ready money, paper currency, paper money, coin(s), (small) change, bills, greenbacks, Brit. notes, esp. Sc. silver, US & Austral. roll, colloq. shekels, folding money, derog. or joc. pelf, joc. filthy lucre, sl. loot, dough, bread, boodle, scratch, stuff, readies, the ready, moolah, green, kale, bucks, Brit. sl. lolly, rhino, brass. **3** resources, wealth, fortune, funds, finance(s), capital, affluence, means, (liquid) assets, riches, colloq. wherewithal, sl. bundle. **4 b** gain, remuneration, (net) profit, take, colloq. percentage, rake-off; see also PAY¹ n. □ **for my money** in my opinion or view or judgment, to my mind, as I see it; for my liking or preference. **in the money** rich, wealthy, affluent, moneyed, well off, well-to-do, prosperous, in clover, colloq. flush, in or on easy street, well-heeled, rolling in it, rolling in money or dough, filthy rich, sl. loaded, stinking rich. **money-grubber** see MISER. **moneygrubbing** see MISERLY. **put money into** see INVEST 2a.

moneybags /múneebagz/ n.pl. (treated as sing.) colloq. usu. derog. a wealthy person.

moneyed /múneed/ adj. **1** having much money; wealthy. **2** consisting of money (moneyed assistance).

■ **1** see WEALTHY.

moneylender /múneelendər/ n. a person who lends money, esp. as a business, at interest. □□ **moneylending** n. & adj.

moneymaker /múneemaykər/ n. **1** a person who earns much money. **2** a thing, idea, etc., that produces much money. □□ **moneymaking** n. & adj.

■ □□ **moneymaking** (adj.) see SUCCESSFUL.

moneywort /múneewərt/ n. a trailing evergreen plant, Lysimachia nummularia, with round glossy leaves and yellow flowers.

monger /múnggər, móng-/ n. (usu. in comb.) **1** esp. Brit. a dealer or trader (fishmonger; ironmonger). **2** usu. derog. a person who promotes or deals in something specified (warmonger; scaremonger). [OE mangere f. mangian to traffic f. Gmc, ult. f. L mango dealer]

■ **1** see SELLER.

Mongol /móngɡəl, -gōl/ adj. & n. ● adj. **1** of or relating to the Asian people now inhabiting Mongolia in Central Asia. **2** resembling this people, esp. in appearance. ● n. **1** a Mongolian. [native name: perh. f. mong brave]

Mongolian /monggóleeən/ n. & adj. ● n. a native or inhabitant of Mongolia; the language of Mongolia. ● adj. of or relating to Mongolia or its people or language.

mongolism /móngɡəlizəm/ n. = DOWN'S SYNDROME. ¶ The term Down's syndrome is now preferred. [MONGOL + -ISM, because its physical characteristics were thought to be reminiscent of Mongolians]

Mongoloid /móngɡəloyd/ adj. & n. ● adj. **1** characteristic of the Mongolians, esp. in having a broad flat yellowish face. **2** (**mongoloid**) often offens. having the characteristic symptoms of Down's syndrome. ● n. a Mongoloid or mongoloid person.

mongoose /móngɡōōs/ n. (pl. **mongooses** or **mongeese**) any of various small flesh-eating civetlike mammals of the family Viverridae, esp. of the genus Herpestes. [Marathi mangūs]

mongrel /múngɡrəl, móng-/ n. & adj. ● n. **1** a dog of no definable type or breed. **2** any other animal or plant resulting from the crossing of different breeds or types. **3** derog. a person of mixed race. ● adj. of mixed origin, nature, or character. □□ **mongrelism** n. **mongrelize** v.tr. **mongrelization** /-lizáyshən/ n. **mongrelly** adj. [earlier meng-, mang- f. Gmc: prob. rel. to MINGLE]

■ **1** crossbreed, mixed breed, half-breed, Biol. hybrid, Brit. lurcher, derog. mutt,

'mongst poet. var. of AMONG. [see AMONG]

monial /mōneeəl/ n. a mullion. [ME f. OF moinel middle f. moien MEAN³]

monicker var. of MONIKER.

monies see MONEY 2.

moniker /mónikər/ n. (also **monicker**) sl. a name. [19th c.: orig. unkn.]

moniliform /mōnílifawrm/ adj. with a form suggesting a string of beads. [F moniliforme or mod.L moniliformis f. L monile necklace]

monism /mónizəm, mṓ-/ n. **1** any theory denying the duality of matter and mind. **2** the doctrine that only one ultimate principle or being exists. □□ **monist** n. **monistic** /-nístik/ adj. [mod.L monismus f. Gk monos single]

monition /məníshən/ n. **1** (foll. by of) literary a warning (of danger). **2** Eccl. a formal notice from a bishop or ecclesiastical court admonishing a person not to commit an offense. [ME f. OF f. L monitio -onis (as MONITOR)]

■ **1** see CAUTION n. 2.

monitor /mónitər/ n. & v. ● n. **1** any of various persons or devices for checking or warning about a situation, operation, etc. **2** a school pupil with disciplinary or other special duties. **3** a cathode-ray tube used as a television receiver or computer display device. **4** a person who listens to and reports on foreign broadcasts, etc. **5** a detector of radioactive contamination. **6** Zool. any tropical lizard of the genus Varanus, supposed to give warning of the approach of crocodiles. **7** a heavily armed shallow-draft warship. ● v.tr. **1** act as a monitor of. **2** maintain regular surveillance over. **3** regulate the strength of (a recorded or transmitted signal). □□ **monitorial** /-táwreeəl/ adj. **monitorship** n. [L f. monēre monit- warn]

■ n. **1** watchdog, supervisor, sentinel, guard, guardian, custodian; proctor, Brit. invigilator. ● v. **1, 2** watch, oversee, observe, check (out or up on), audit, supervise, superintend, scan, examine, study, follow, keep an eye on, survey, keep track of, track, trace, record, vet, colloq. keep tabs on.

monitory /mónitáwree/ adj. & n. ● adj. literary giving or serving as a warning. ● n. (pl. **-ies**) Eccl. a letter of admonition from the pope or a bishop. [L monitorius (as MONITION)]

■ adj. see EXEMPLARY 2a.

monk /mungk/ n. a member of a religious community of men living under certain vows, esp. of poverty, chastity, and obedience. □□ **monkish** adj. [OE munuc ult. f. Gk monakhos solitary f. monos alone]

■ brother, religious, cenobite, monastic, friar.

monkey /múngkee/ n. & v. ● n. (pl. **-eys**) **1** any of various New World and Old World primates esp. of the families Cebidae (including capuchins), Callitrichidae (including marmosets and tamarins), and Cercopithecidae (including baboons and apes). **2** a mischievous person, esp. a child (young monkey). **3** Brit. sl. £500. **4** (in full **monkey engine**) a machine hammer for pile driving, etc. ● v. (**-eys, -eyed**) **1** tr. mimic or mock. **2** intr. (often foll. by with) tamper or play mischievous tricks. **3** intr. (foll. by around, about) fool around. □ **have a monkey on one's back 1** sl. be a drug addict. **2** have a persistent problem or hindrance. **make a monkey of** humiliate by making appear ridiculous. **monkey business** colloq. mischief. **monkey jacket** a short close-fitting jacket worn by sailors, etc., or at a mess. **monkey puzzle** a coniferous tree, Araucaria araucana, native to Chile, with downward-pointing branches and small close-set leaves. **monkey suit** colloq. formal attire, esp. a tuxedo. **monkey tricks** Brit. colloq. mischief. **monkey wrench** a wrench with an adjustable jaw. □□ **monkeyish** adj. [16th c.: orig. unkn. (perh. LG)]

■ n. **1** simian, ape, primate. **2** imp, devil, mischief-maker, archaic or joc. rapscallion, colloq. scamp, often joc. rascal.
● v. **1** mimic, imitate, impersonate, copy, ape; see also MOCK v. 2. **2, 3** fool around, play, fiddle, meddle, interfere, mess (about or around),

---

/.../ **pronunciation**	● **part of speech**
□ **phrases, idioms, and compounds**	
□□ **derivatives**	■ **synonym section**
cross-references appear in SMALL CAPITALS or italics	

tinker, tamper, *Brit. colloq.* muck about *or* around. □ **make a monkey of** make a fool *or* laughingstock of; see also PARODY *v.* **monkey business, monkey tricks** see MISCHIEF 1–3.

monkeyshine /múngkeeshĭn/ *n.* (usu. in *pl.*) *US colloq.* = *monkey business.*

monkfish /múnkfish/ *n.* **1** an anglerfish, esp. *Lophius piscatorius*, often used as food. **2** a large cartilaginous fish, *Squatina squatina*, with a flattened body and large pectoral fins. Also called *angel shark.*

monkshood /múngks-hŏŏd/ *n. Bot.* a poisonous garden plant *Aconitum napellus*, with hood-shaped blue or purple flowers.

mono¹ /mónō/ *n. colloq.* infectious mononucleosis. [abbr.]

mono² /mónō/ *adj. & n. colloq.* ● *adj.* monophonic. ● *n.* (*pl.* **-os**) a monophonic record, reproduction, etc. [abbr.]

mono- /mónō/ *comb. form* (usu. **mon-** before a vowel) **1** one, alone, single. **2** *Chem.* (forming names of compounds) containing one atom or group of a specified kind. [Gk f. *monos* alone]

monoacid /mónōásid/ *adj. Chem.* (of a base) having one replaceable hydroxide ion.

monobasic /mónōbáysik/ *adj. Chem.* (of an acid) having one replaceable hydrogen atom.

monocarpic /mónōkaárpik/ *adj.* (also **monocarpous** /-kaárpəs/) *Bot.* bearing fruit only once. [MONO- + Gk *karpos* fruit]

monocausal /mónōkáwzəl/ *adj.* in terms of a sole cause.

monocephalous /mónōséfələs/ *adj. Bot.* having only one head.

monochord /mónəkawrd/ *n. Mus.* an instrument with a single string and a movable bridge, used esp. to determine intervals. [ME f. OF *monocorde* f. LL *monochordon* f. Gk *monokhordon* (as MONO-, CHORD¹)]

monochromatic /mónəkrəmátik/ *adj.* **1** *Physics* (of light or other radiation) of a single wavelength or frequency. **2** containing only one color. □□ **monochromatically** *adv.*

monochromatism /mónōkrṓmətizəm/ *n.* complete color blindness in which all colors appear as shades of one color.

monochrome /mónəkrōm/ *n. & adj.* ● *n.* a photograph or picture done in one color or different tones of this, or in black and white only. ● *adj.* having or using only one color or in black and white only. □□ **monochromic** /-krṓmik/ *adj.* [ult. f. Gk *monokhrōmatos* (as MONO-, *khrōmatos* f. *khrōma* color)]

monocle /mónəkəl/ *n.* a single eyeglass. □□ **monocled** *adj.* [F, orig. adj. f. LL *monoculus* one-eyed (as MONO-, *oculus* eye)]

monocline /mónōklīn/ *n. Geol.* a bend in rock strata that are otherwise uniformly dipping or horizontal. □□ **monoclinal** /-klín'l/ *adj.* [MONO- + Gk *klinō* lean, dip]

monoclinic /mónōklínik/ *adj.* (of a crystal) having one axial intersection oblique. [MONO- + Gk *klinō* lean, slope]

monoclonal /mónōklṓnəl/ *adj.* forming a single clone; derived from a single individual or cell. □ **monoclonal antibodies** antibodies produced artificially by a single clone and consisting of identical antibody molecules.

monocoque /mónəkok/ *n. Aeron.* an aircraft or vehicle structure in which the chassis is integral with the body. [F (as MONO-, *coque* shell)]

monocot /mónōkot, -kōt/ *n.* = MONOCOTYLEDON. [abbr.]

monocotyledon /mónəkót'leéd'n/ *n. Bot.* any flowering plant with a single cotyledon. □□ **monocotyledonous** *adj.*

monocracy /mənókrəsee/ *n.* (*pl.* **-ies**) government by one person only. □□ **monocratic** /mónəkrátik/ *adj.*

monocular /mənókyələr/ *adj.* with or for one eye. □□ **monocularly** *adj.* [LL *monoculus* having one eye]

monoculture /mónōkulchər/ *n.* the cultivation of a single crop.

monocycle /mónəsīkəl/ *n.* a one-wheeled vehicle, esp. a unicycle.

monocyte /mónəsīt/ *n. Biol.* a large type of leukocyte.

monodactylous /mónədáktiləs/ *adj.* having one finger, toe, or claw.

monodrama /mónōdraamə, -dramə/ *n.* a dramatic piece for one performer.

monody /mónədee/ *n.* (*pl.* **-ies**) **1** an ode sung by a single actor in a Greek tragedy. **2** a poem lamenting a person's death. **3** *Mus.* a composition with only one melodic line. □□ **monodic** /mónódik/ *adj.* **monodist** /mónə-/ *n.* [LL *monodia* f. Gk *monōidia* f. *monōidos* singing alone (as MONO-, ODE)]

■ **2** see LAMENT *n.* 2.

monoecious /mənéeshəs/ *adj.* **1** *Bot.* with unisexual male and female organs on the same plant. **2** *Zool.* hermaphroditic. [mod.L *Monoecia* the class of such plants (Linnaeus) f. Gk *monos* single + *oikos* house]

monofilament /mónōfíləmənt/ *n.* **1** a single strand of manmade fiber. **2** a type of fishing line using this.

monogamy /mənógəmee/ *n.* **1** the practice or state of being married to one person at a time. **2** *Zool.* the habit of having only one mate at a time. □□ **monogamist** *n.* **monogamous** *adj.* **monogamously** *adv.* [F *monogamie* f. eccl.L f. Gk *monogamia* (as MONO-, *gamos* marriage)]

monogenesis /mónōjénisis/ *n.* (also **monogeny** /mənóji-nee/) **1** the theory of the development of all beings from a single cell. **2** the theory that mankind descended from one pair of ancestors. □□ **monogenetic** /-jinétik/ *adj.*

monoglot /mónəglot/ *adj. & n.* ● *adj.* using only one language. ● *n.* a monoglot person.

monogram /mónəgram/ *n.* two or more letters, esp. a person's initials, interwoven as a device. □□ **monogrammatic** /-grəmátik/ *adj.* **monogrammed** *adj.* [F *monogramme* f. LL *monogramma* f. Gk (as MONO-, -GRAM)]

■ see SIGN *n.* 2.

monograph /mónəgraf/ *n. & v.* ● *n.* a separate treatise on a single subject or an aspect of it. ● *v.tr.* write a monograph on. □□ **monographer** /mənógrəfər/ *n.* **monographist** /mənógrəfist/ *n.* **monographic** /mónəgráfik/ *adj.* [earlier *monography* f. mod.L *monographia* f. *monographus* writer on a single genus or species (as MONO-, -GRAPH, -GRAPHY)]

■ *n.* treatise, dissertation, disquisition, essay, paper.

monogynous /mənójinəs/ *adj. Bot.* having only one pistil.

monogyny /mənójinee/ *n.* the custom of having only one wife at a time.

monohull /mónōhul/ *n.* a boat with a single hull.

monohybrid /mónōhíbrid/ *n.* a hybrid with respect to only one allele.

monohydric /mónōhídrik/ *adj. Chem.* containing one hydroxyl group.

monokini /mónōkeénee/ *n.* a woman's bathing suit equivalent to the lower half of a bikini. [MONO- + BIKINI, by false assoc. with BI-]

monolayer /mónōlayər/ *n. Chem.* a layer only one molecule in thickness.

monolingual /mónōlínggwəl/ *adj.* speaking or using only one language.

monolith /mónəlith/ *n.* **1** a single block of stone, esp. shaped into a pillar or monument. **2** a person or thing like a monolith in being massive, immovable, or solidly uniform. **3** a large block of concrete. □□ **monolithic** /-líthik/ *adj.* [F *monolithe* f. Gk *monolithos* (as MONO-, *lithos* stone)]

■ □□ **monolithic** massive, huge, enormous, monumental, imposing, colossal, gigantic, giant; featureless, uniform, undifferentiated, characterless; rigid, impenetrable, invulnerable, unbending, inflexible, solid, stolid, intractable, immovable.

monologue /mónəlawg, -log/ *n.* **1 a** a scene in a drama in which a person speaks alone. **b** a dramatic composition for one performer. **2** a long speech by one person in a conversation, etc. □□ **monologic** /-lójik/ *adj.* **monological** /-lójikəl/ *adj.* **monologist** /mənóləjist/ *n.* (also **-loguist**). **monologize** /mənóləjīz/ *v.intr.* [F f. Gk *monologos* speaking alone (as MONO-, -LOGUE)]

■ see SPEECH 2.

monomania /mónəmáyneeə/ *n.* obsession of the mind by one idea or interest. □□ **monomaniac** *n. & adj.* **monomaniacal** /-mənfákəl/ *adj.* [F *monomanie* (as MONO-, -MANIA)]

■ see *fanaticism* (FANATIC). □□ **monomaniac** (*n.*) see CRANK[2].

monomer /mónəmər/ *n. Chem.* **1** a unit in a dimer, trimer, or polymer. **2** a molecule or compound that can be polymerized. □□ **monomeric** /-mérik/ *adj.*

monomial /mənṓmeeəl/ *adj. & n. Math.* ● *adj.* (of an algebraic expression) consisting of one term. ● *n.* a monomial expression. [MONO- after *binomial*]

monomolecular /mónōmələ́kyələr/ *adj. Chem.* (of a layer) only one molecule in thickness.

monomorphic /mónəmáwrfik/ *adj.* (also **monomorphous** /-máwrfəs/) *Biochem.* not changing form during development. □□ **monomorphism** *n.*

mononucleosis /mónōnṓōkleeṓsis, -nyṓō-/ *n.* an abnormally high proportion of monocytes in the blood, esp. = *infectious mononucleosis.* [MONO- + NUCLEO- + -OSIS]

monopetalous /mónəpét'ləs/ *adj. Bot.* having the corolla in one piece, or the petals united into a tube.

monophonic /mónəfónik/ *adj.* **1** (of sound reproduction) using only one channel of transmission (cf. STEREOPHONIC). **2** *Mus.* homophonic. □□ **monophonically** *adv.* [MONO- + Gk *phōnē* sound]

monophthong /mónəf-tháwng, -thong/ *n. Phonet.* a single vowel sound. □□ **monophthongal** /-thónggəl/ *adj.* [Gk *monophthoggos* (as MONO-, *phthoggos* sound)]

Monophysite /mənófisit/ *n.* a person who holds that there is only one nature (partly divine, partly and subordinately human) in the person of Christ. [eccl.L *monophysita* f. eccl.Gk *monophusitēs* (as MONO-, *phusis* nature)]

monoplane /mónōplayn/ *n.* an airplane with one set of wings (cf. BIPLANE).

monopolist /mənópəlist/ *n.* a person who has or advocates a monopoly. □□ **monopolistic** /-lístik/ *adj.*

monopolize /mənópəliz/ *v.tr.* **1** obtain exclusive possession or control of (a trade or commodity, etc.). **2** dominate or prevent others from sharing in (a conversation, person's attention, etc.). □□ **monopolization** *n.* **monopolizer** *n.*
■ corner, control, dominate, *colloq.* hog.

monopoly /mənópəlee/ *n.* (*pl.* **-ies**) **1 a** the exclusive possession or control of the trade in a commodity or service. **b** this conferred as a privilege by the government. **2 a** a commodity or service that is subject to a monopoly. **b** a company, etc., that possesses a monopoly. **3** (foll. by *on*) exclusive possession, control, or exercise. [L *monopolium* f. Gk *monopōlion* (as MONO-, *pōleō* sell)]
■ **3** exclusive *or* supreme control.

monorail /mónōrayl/ *n.* a railway in which the track consists of a single rail, usu. elevated with the cars suspended from it.

monosaccharide /mónōsákərid/ *n. Chem.* a sugar that cannot be hydrolyzed to give a simpler sugar, e.g., glucose.

monosodium glutamate /mónəsṓdiəm glṓōtəmayt/ *n. Chem.* a sodium salt of glutamic acid used to flavor food (cf. GLUTAMATE).

monospermous /mónəspérməs/ *adj. Bot.* having one seed. [MONO- + Gk *sperma* seed]

monostichous /mənóstikəs/ *adj. Bot. & Zool.* arranged in or consisting of one layer or row. [MONO- + Gk *stikhos* row]

monosyllabic /mónəsilábik/ *adj.* **1** (of a word) having one syllable. **2** (of a person or statement) using or expressed in monosyllables. □□ **monosyllabically** *adv.*

monosyllable /mónəsiləbəl/ *n.* a word of one syllable. □ **in monosyllables** in simple direct words.

monotheism /mónəthe'eizəm/ *n.* the doctrine that there is only one God. □□ **monotheist** *n.* **monotheistic** /-ístik/ *adj.* **monotheistically** /-ístiklee/ *adv.* [MONO- + Gk *theos* god]

monotint /mónōtint/ *n.* = MONOCHROME.

monotone /mónōtōn/ *n. & adj.* ● *n.* **1** a sound or utterance continuing or repeated on one note without change of pitch. **2** sameness of style in writing. ● *adj.* without change of pitch. [mod.L *monotonus* f. late Gk *monotonos* (as MONO-, TONE)]

monotonic /mónətónik/ *adj.* **1** uttered in a monotone. **2** *Math.* (of a function or quantity) varying in such a way that it either never decreases or never increases. □□ **monotonically** *adv.*

monotonous /mənót'nəs/ *adj.* **1** lacking in variety; tedious through sameness. **2** (of a sound or utterance) without variation in tone or pitch. □□ **monotonize** *v.tr.* **monotonously** *adv.* **monotonousness** *n.*
■ boring, tedious, dull, tiresome, humdrum, sleep-inducing, soporific, wearisome, wearying, tiring, repetitious, prosaic, banal, dry, dryasdust, uninteresting, dreary, colorless, unexciting, run-of-the-mill, ordinary, commonplace, routine, uneventful, everyday, mechanical; unvaried, unvarying, unchanging.

monotony /mənót'nee/ *n.* **1** the state of being monotonous. **2** dull or tedious routine.
■ **1** see TEDIUM.

monotreme /mónətreem/ *n.* any mammal of the order Monotremata, native to Australia and New Guinea, including the duckbill and spiny anteater, laying large yolky eggs through a common opening for urine, feces, etc. [MONO- + Gk *trēma -matos* hole]

monotype /mónətip/ *n.* **1** (**Monotype**) *Printing propr.* a typesetting machine that casts and sets up types in individual characters. **2** an impression on paper made from an inked design painted on glass or metal.

monotypic /mónətípik/ *adj.* having only one type or representative.

monovalent /mónəváylənt/ *adj. Chem.* having a valence of one; univalent. □□ **monovalence** /-ləns/ *n.* **monovalency** *n.*

monoxide /mənóksid/ *n. Chem.* an oxide containing one oxygen atom (*carbon monoxide*). [MONO- + OXIDE]

Monroe doctrine /munrṓ/ *n.* the US policy of objecting to intervention by European powers in the affairs of the Western Hemisphere. [J. *Monroe*, US president d. 1831, who formulated it]

Monseigneur /máwNsenyṓr/ *n.* (*pl.* **Messeigneurs** /méssenyṓr/) a title given to an eminent French person, esp. a prince, cardinal, archbishop, or bishop. [F f. *mon* my + *seigneur* lord]

Monsieur /məsyṓ/ *n.* (*pl.* **Messieurs** /mesyṓ/) **1** the title or form of address used of or to a French-speaking man, corresponding to Mr. or sir. **2** a Frenchman. [F f. *mon* my + *sieur* lord]

Monsignor /monseényər/ *n.* (*pl.* **Monsignors** or **Monsignori** /-nyáwree/) the title of various Roman Catholic prelates, officers of the papal court, etc. [It., after MONSEIGNEUR: see SIGNOR]

monsoon /monsṓōn, món-/ *n.* **1** a wind in S. Asia, esp. in the Indian Ocean, blowing from the southwest in summer (**wet monsoon**) and the northeast in winter (**dry monsoon**). **2** a rainy season accompanying a wet monsoon. **3** any other wind with periodic alternations. □□ **monsoonal** *adj.* [obs. Du. *monssoen* f. Port. *monção* f. Arab. *mawsim* fixed season f. *wasama* to mark]

mons pubis /monz pyṓōbis/ *n.* a rounded mass of fatty tissue lying over the joint of the pubic bones. [L, = mount of the pubes]

monster /mónstər/ *n.* **1** an imaginary creature, usu. large and frightening, compounded of incongruous elements. **2** an inhumanly cruel or wicked person. **3** a misshapen animal or plant. **4** a large hideous animal or thing (e.g., a building). **5** (*attrib.*) huge; extremely large of its kind. [ME f. OF *monstre* f. L *monstrum* portent, monster f. *monēre* warn]
■ **1** beast, fiend, ogre, giant, dragon, brute, demon, troll, bogeyman. **2** see DEVIL *n.* 3a. **3, 4** mutant, mutation, freak, deformity, lusus (naturae); monstrosity, eyesore, horror. **5** (*attrib.*) see HUGE 1, GIGANTIC.

monstera /mónstərə/ *n.* any tropical American climbing

/ . . . / **pronunciation**   ● **part of speech**
□ **phrases, idioms, and compounds**
□□ **derivatives**   ■ **synonym section**
cross-references appear in SMALL CAPITALS or *italics*

plant of the genus *Monstera*, esp. *M. deliciosa*. [mod.L, perh. f. L *monstrum* monster (from the odd appearance of its leaves)]

monstrance /mónstrəns/ *n.* RC Ch. a vessel in which the consecrated Host is displayed for veneration. [ME, = demonstration, f. med.L *monstrantia* f. L *monstrare* show]

monstrosity /monstrósitee/ *n.* (*pl.* -ies) **1** a huge or outrageous thing. **2** monstrousness. **3** = MONSTER 3. [LL *monstrositas* (as MONSTROUS)]
■ **1** see MONSTER 3, 4. **2** monstrousness, heinousness, horribleness, horridness, hideousness, awfulness, nightmarishness, dreadfulness, frightfulness, horror, hellishness, ghoulishness, fiendishness, barbarity.

monstrous /mónstrəs/ *adj.* **1** like a monster; abnormally formed. **2** huge. **3 a** outrageously wrong or absurd. **b** atrocious. □□ **monstrously** *adv.* **monstrousness** *n.* [ME f. OF *monstreux* or L *monstrosus* (as MONSTER)]
■ **1** awful, horrible, horrid, horrific, horrendous, horrifying, hideous, ugly, nightmarish, dreadful, grisly, gruesome, disgusting, nauseous, nauseating, repulsive, repellent, revolting, frightful, grotesque, hellish, ghoulish, freakish, fiendish. **2** gigantic, giant, huge, vast, enormous, colossal, monster, gargantuan, immense, tremendous, titanic, prodigious, massive, towering, elephantine, mammoth, *colloq.* jumbo. **3** outrageous, shocking, scandalous, atrocious, appalling, wicked, villainous, evil, ugly, vile, insensitive, cruel, base, debased, shameful, shameless, infamous, barbaric, barbarous, savage, inhuman, brutish, beastly, disgraceful, nefarious, egregious, heinous, foul, flagitious, loathsome, depraved; merciless, ruthless, brutal, vicious.

mons veneris /monz vénəris/ *n.* the human female's mons pubis. [L, = mount of Venus]

Mont. *abbr.* Montana.

montage /montaázh, mawn-/ *n.* **1 a** a process of selecting, editing, and piecing together separate sections of movie or television film to form a continuous whole. **b** a sequence of such film as a section of a longer film. **2 a** the technique of producing a new composite whole from fragments of pictures, words, music, etc. **b** a composition produced in this way. [F f. *monter* MOUNT[1]]

montane /móntayn/ *adj.* of or inhabiting mountainous country. [L *montanus* (as MOUNT[2], -ANE[1])]

montbretia /monbreésha/ *n.* a hybrid plant of the genus *Crocosmia*, with bright orange-yellow trumpet-shaped flowers. [mod.L f. A. F. E. Coquebert de *Montbret*, Fr. botanist d. 1801]

monte /móntee/ *n.* Cards **1** (also **monte bank**) a Spanish game of chance, played with 40 cards. **2** (in full **three-card monte**) a game of Mexican origin played with three cards. [Sp., = mountain, heap of cards]

Monte Carlo method /móntee kaárlō/ *n.* Statistics a method of using the random sampling of numbers in order to estimate the solution to a numerical problem. [*Monte Carlo* in Monaco, famous for its gambling casino]

Montessori /móntisáwree/ *n.* (usu. *attrib.*) a system of education (esp. of young children) that seeks to develop natural interests and activities rather than use formal teaching methods. [Maria *Montessori*, It. educationist d. 1952, who initiated it]

month /munth/ *n.* **1** (in full **calendar month**) **a** each of usu. twelve periods into which a year is divided. **b** a period of time between the same dates in successive calendar months. **2** a period of 28 days or of four weeks. **3** = *lunar month*. □ **month of Sundays** a very long period. [OE *mōnath* f. Gmc, rel. to MOON]

monthly /múnthlee/ *adj.*, *adv.*, & *n.* ● *adj.* done, produced, or occurring once a month. ● *adv.* once a month; from month to month. ● *n.* (*pl.* -ies) **1** a monthly periodical. **2** (in *pl.*) *colloq.* a menstrual period.
■ *n.* **1** see PERIODICAL *n.*

monticule /móntikyōōl/ *n.* **1** a small hill. **2** a small mound caused by a volcanic eruption. [F f. LL *monticulus* dimin. of *mons* MOUNT[2]]

monument /mónyəmənt/ *n.* **1** anything enduring that serves to commemorate or make celebrated, esp. a structure or building. **2** a stone or other structure placed over a grave or in a church, etc., in memory of the dead. **3** an ancient building or site, etc., that has survived or been preserved. **4** (foll. by *of*, *to*) a typical or outstanding example (*a monument of indiscretion*). **5** a written record. [ME f. F f. L *monumentum* f. *monēre* remind]
■ **1–3** marker, memorial, tablet, shrine, cairn; sepulcher, gravestone, tombstone, headstone, tomb, mausoleum, cenotaph. **4** model, archetype, pattern, paragon, nonpareil, perfect specimen, example, exemplar. **5** see RECORD *n.* 1.

monumental /mónyəmént'l/ *adj.* **1 a** extremely great; stupendous (*a monumental achievement*). **b** (of a literary work) massive and permanent. **2** of or serving as a monument. **3** *colloq.* (as an intensifier) very great; calamitous (*a monumental blunder*). □ **monumental mason** a maker of tombstones, etc. □□ **monumentality** /-tálitee/ *n.* **monumentally** *adv.*
■ **1 a** staggering, awe-inspiring, outstanding, prominent, immense, colossal, stupendous, vast, awesome, epoch-making, historic, history-making, memorable, lasting, permanent, unforgettable, significant, notable, noteworthy, impressive, marvelous, prodigious, wonderful, spectacular, magnificent, grand, striking, glorious, enduring, classic, *poet.* wondrous. **b** massive, huge, gigantic, enormous, prodigious, colossal, immense, vast, tremendous. **2** commemorative, memorial. **3** egregious, catastrophic, calamitous, huge, enormous, abject, unforgivable, unbelievable, monstrous, *colloq.* awful, terrible, *sl.* whopping.

monumentalize /mónyəmént'līz/ *v.tr.* record or commemorate by or as by a monument.

-mony /mónee/ *suffix* forming nouns, esp. denoting an abstract state or quality (*acrimony*; *testimony*). [L -*monia*, -*monium*, rel. to -MENT]

moo /mōō/ *v.* & *n.* ● *v.intr.* (**moos**, **mooed**) make the characteristic vocal sound of cattle; = LOW[2]. ● *n.* (*pl.* **moos**) this sound. □ **moo-cow** a childish name for a cow. [imit.]

mooch /mōōch/ *v.* *colloq.* **1** borrow (an item, service, etc.) with no intention of making repayment. **2** beg. **3** steal. **4** sneak around; skulk. **5** *intr.* loiter or saunter desultorily. □□ **moocher** *n.* [ME, prob. f. OF *muchier* hide, skulk]
■ **5** see WANDER *v.* 1. **2** see BEG 1b, c.

mood[1] /mōōd/ *n.* **1** a state of mind or feeling. **2** (in *pl.*) fits of melancholy or bad temper. **3** (*attrib.*) inducing a particular mood (*mood music*). □ **in the** (or **no**) **mood** (foll. by *for*, or *to* + infin.) inclined or (disinclined) (*was in no mood to agree*). [OE *mōd* mind, thought, f. Gmc]
■ **1** humor, attitude, inclination, disposition, nature, temper, frame of mind, spirit, atmosphere, sense, feeling. **2** (*moods*) see TEMPER *n.* 2b. □ **in the mood** ready, willing, eager, keen, (well-)disposed, inclined, minded. **in no mood** unwilling, disinclined, not happy or willing or keen.

mood[2] /mōōd/ *n.* **1** Gram. **a** a form or set of forms of a verb serving to indicate whether it is to express fact, command, wish, etc. (*subjunctive mood*). **b** the distinction of meaning expressed by different moods. **2** Logic any of the classes into which each of the figures of a valid categorical syllogism is subdivided. [var. of MODE, assoc. with MOOD[1]]

moodswing /mōōdswing/ *n.* a marked change in temperament, as from euphoria to depression.

moody /mōōdee/ *adj.* & *n.* ● *adj.* (**moodier**, **moodiest**) given to changes of mood; gloomy, sullen. ● *n. colloq.* a bad mood; a tantrum. □□ **moodily** *adv.* **moodiness** *n.* [OE *mōdig* brave (as MOOD[1])]
■ *adj.* fickle, volatile, capricious, mercurial, unstable, fitful, flighty, unsteady, changeable, erratic, inconstant, undependable, unreliable, unpredictable, *Sc.* kittle; testy, crotchety, short-tempered, abrupt, short, curt, impatient, crabby, crusty, huffy, huffish, crabbed, cantankerous, curmudgeonly, ill-humored, ill-tempered, cranky, petulant, waspish, temperamental, snappish, snappy, irritable, peevish, touchy; sullen,

gloomy, glum, moping, mopy, mopish, sulky, sulking, morose, brooding, broody, dour, cheerless, dismal, lugubrious, saturnine. ● *n.* see TEMPER *n.* 2b.

Moog /mōog/ *n.* (in full **Moog synthesizer**) *propr.* an electronic instrument with a keyboard, for producing a wide variety of musical sounds: see SYNTHESIZER. [R. A. *Moog*, Amer. engineer b. 1934, who invented it]

moola /mōolə/ *n. sl.* money. [20th c.: orig. unkn.]

moon /mōon/ *n. & v.* ● *n.* **1 a** the natural satellite of the earth, orbiting it monthly, illuminated by the sun and reflecting some light to the earth. **b** this regarded in terms of its waxing and waning in a particular month (*new moon*). **c** the moon when visible (*there is no moon tonight*). **2** a satellite of any planet. **3** (prec. by *the*) something desirable but unattainable (*promised them the moon*). **4** *poet.* a month. ● *v.* **1** *intr.* (often foll. by *about, around,* etc.) move or look listlessly. **2** *tr.* (foll. by *away*) spend (time) in a listless manner. **3** *intr.* (foll. by *over*) act aimlessly or inattentively from infatuation for (a person). **4** *tr. sl.* expose one's naked buttocks publicly as a joke, sign of disrespect, etc. □ **moon-faced** having a round face. **over the moon** esp. *Brit.* extremely happy or delighted. □□ **moonless** *adj.* [OE *mōna* f. Gmc, rel. to MONTH]
  ■ □ **over the moon** see OVERJOYED.

moonbeam /mōonbeem/ *n.* a ray of moonlight.

mooncalf /mōonkaf/ *n.* a born fool.
  ■ see FOOL[1] *n.* 1.

moonfish /mōonfish/ *n.* = OPAH.

Moonie /mōonee/ *n. sl.* a member of the Unification Church. [Sun Myung *Moon*, its founder]

moonlight /mōonlit/ *n. & v.* ● *n.* **1** the light of the moon. **2** (*attrib.*) lighted by the moon. ● *v.intr.* (**-lighted**) *colloq.* have two paid occupations, esp. one by day and one by night. □ **moonlight flit** *Brit.* a hurried departure by night, esp. to avoid paying a debt. □□ **moonlighter** *n.*
  ■ **1** see LIGHT[1] *n.* 2.

moonlit /mōonlit/ *adj.* lighted by the moon.

moonquake /mōonkwayk/ *n.* a tremor of the moon's surface.

moonrise /mōonriz/ *n.* **1** the rising of the moon. **2** the time of this.

moonscape /mōonskayp/ *n.* **1** the surface or landscape of the moon. **2** an area resembling this; a wasteland.

moonset /mōonset/ *n.* **1** the setting of the moon. **2** the time of this.

moonshine /mōonshin/ *n.* **1** foolish or unrealistic talk or ideas. **2** *sl.* illicitly distilled or smuggled alcoholic liquor. **3** moonlight.
  ■ **1** (stuff and) nonsense, rubbish, humbug, drivel, twaddle, balderdash, blather, claptrap, garbage, *colloq.* hogwash, malarkey, piffle, tripe, line, razzmatazz, *sl.* hot air, bosh, gas, eyewash, bunk, guff, bilge, (tommy)rot, bull, hooey, hokum, jive. **2** *Ir.* poteen, *colloq.* hooch. **3** moonlight, moonbeams.

moonshiner /mōonshinər/ *n. sl.* an illicit distiller or smuggler of alcoholic liquor.

moonshot /mōonshot/ *n.* the launching of a spacecraft to the moon.

moonstone /mōonstōn/ *n.* feldspar of pearly appearance.

moonstruck /mōonstruk/ *adj.* **1** mentally deranged. **2** romantically distracted.

moony /mōonee/ *adj.* (**moonier, mooniest**) **1** listless; stupidly dreamy. **2** of or like the moon.

Moor /mōor/ *n.* a member of a Muslim people of mixed Berber and Arab descent, inhabiting NW Africa. [ME f. OF *More* f. L *Maurus* f. Gk *Mauros* inhabitant of Mauretania, a region of N. Africa]

moor[1] /mōor/ *n.* **1** a tract of open uncultivated upland, esp. when covered with heather. **2** a tract of ground preserved for shooting. **3** a marsh □□ **moorish** *adj.* **moory** *adj.* [OE *mōr* waste land, marsh, mountain, f. Gmc]
  ■ **1** heath, moorland, wasteland, *No. of Engl.* fell. **3** fen, marsh.

moor[2] /mōor/ *v.* **1** *tr.* make fast (a boat, buoy, etc.) by attaching a cable, etc., to a fixed object. **2** *intr.* (of a boat) be

moored. □□ **moorage** *n.* [ME *more*, prob. f. LG or MLG *mōren*]
  ■ secure, tie up, make fast, dock, berth, anchor; fix.

moorhen /mōorhen/ *n.* **1** = GALLINULE 1. **2** esp. *Brit.* a female red grouse.

mooring /mōoring/ *n.* **1 a** a fixed object to which a boat, buoy, etc., is moored. **b** (often in *pl.*) a place where a boat, etc., is moored. **2** (in *pl.*) a set of permanent anchors and chains laid down for ships to be moored to.
  ■ **1a, 2** anchor, sheet anchor.

Moorish /mōorish/ *adj.* of or relating to the Moors. □ **Moorish idol** a brightly colored Pacific fish of the genus *Zanclus*.

moorland /mōorlənd/ *n.* an extensive area of moor.
  ■ see PLAIN[1] *n.*

moose /mōos/ *n.* (*pl.* same) largest variety of N. American deer. [Narragansett *moos*]

moot /mōot/ *adj., v., & n.* ● *adj.* (orig. the noun used *attrib.*) **1** debatable, undecided (*a moot point*). **2** *Law* having no practical significance. ● *v.tr.* raise (a question) for discussion. ● *n.* **1** *hist.* an assembly. **2** *Law* a discussion of a hypothetical case as an academic exercise. [OE *mōt*, and *mōtian* converse, f. Gmc, rel. to MEET[1]]
  ■ *adj.* **1** debatable, arguable, undecided, undetermined, controversial, doubtful, disputable, open to debate, at issue, indefinite, problematic(al), questionable, open (to question *or* to discussion), contestable, unsettled, disputed, unresolved, (up) in the air, unconcluded. ● *v.* raise, bring up *or* forward, introduce, broach, put forward, proffer, posit, propound, advance, submit, suggest.

mop /mop/ *n. & v.* ● *n.* **1** a wad or bundle of cotton or synthetic material fastened to the end of a stick, for cleaning floors, etc. **2** a similarly shaped large or small implement for various purposes. **3** anything resembling a mop, esp. a thick mass of hair. **4** an act of mopping or being mopped (*gave it a mop*). ● *v.tr.* (**mopped, mopping**) **1** wipe or clean with or as with a mop. **2 a** wipe tears or sweat, etc., from (one's face or brow, etc.). **b** wipe away (tears, etc.). □ **mop up 1** wipe up with or as with a mop. **2** *colloq.* absorb (profits, etc.). **3** dispatch; make an end of. **4** *Mil.* **a** complete the occupation of (a district, etc.) by capturing or killing enemy troops left there. **b** capture or kill (stragglers). □□ **moppy** *adj.* [ME *mappe*, perh. ult. rel. to L *mappa* napkin]
  ■ *n.* **4** see WIPE *n.* ● *v.* see WIPE *v.* 1.

mope /mōp/ *v. & n.* ● *v.intr.* be gloomily depressed or listless; behave sulkily. ● *n.* **1** a person who mopes. **2** (**the mopes**) low spirits. □□ **moper** *n.* **mopish** *adj.* **mopy** *adj.* (**mopier, mopiest**). **mopily** *adv.* **mopiness** *n.* [16th c.: prob. rel. to *mope, mopp(e)* fool]
  ■ *v.* see SULK *v.* □□ **mopy** see MOODY *adj.*

moped /mōped/ *n.* a low-power, lightweight motorized bicycle with pedals. [Sw. (as MOTOR, PEDAL[1])]

mophead /mop-hed/ *n.* a person with thick matted hair.

moppet /mopit/ *n. colloq.* (esp. as a term of endearment) a baby or small child. [obs. *moppe* baby, doll]

moquette /mōkét/ *n.* a thick pile or looped material used for carpets and upholstery. [F, perh. f. obs. It. *mocaiardo* mohair]

moraine /məráyn/ *n.* an area covered by rocks and debris carried down and deposited by a glacier. □□ **morainal** *adj.* **morainic** *adj.* [F f. It. dial. *morena* f. F dial. *mor(re)* snout f. Rmc]

moral /máwrəl, mór-/ *adj. & n.* ● *adj.* **1 a** concerned with goodness or badness of human character or behavior, or with the distinction between right and wrong. **b** concerned with accepted rules and standards of human behavior. **2 a** conforming to accepted standards of general conduct. **b** capable of moral action (*man is a moral agent*). **3** (of rights or duties, etc.) founded on moral law. **4 a** concerned with mor-

/ . . . / **pronunciation**   ● **part of speech**
□ **phrases, idioms, and compounds**
□□ **derivatives**   ■ **synonym section**
cross-references appear in SMALL CAPITALS or *italics*

969

als or ethics (*moral philosophy*). **b** (of a literary work, etc.) dealing with moral conduct. **5** concerned with or leading to a psychological effect associated with confidence in a right action (*moral courage*; *moral support*; *moral victory*). ● *n.* **1 a** a moral lesson (esp. at the end) of a fable, story, event, etc. **b** a moral maxim or principle. **2** (in *pl.*) moral behavior, e.g., in sexual conduct. □ **moral certainty** probability so great as to allow no reasonable doubt. **moral law** the conditions to be satisfied by any right course of action. **moral majority** the majority of people, regarded as favoring firm moral standards (orig. *Moral Majority*, name of a right-wing movement). **moral philosophy** the branch of philosophy concerned with ethics. **moral pressure** persuasion by appealing to a person's moral sense. **moral science** systematic knowledge as applied to morals. **moral sense** the ability to distinguish right and wrong. □□ **morally** *adv.* [ME f. L *moralis* f. *mos moris* custom, pl. *mores* morals]

■ *adj.* **1, 4** ethical; moralizing, moralistic, deontic, prescriptive. **2** ethical, right, good, pure, honest, proper, upright, honorable, decent, respectable, high-minded, virtuous, upstanding, righteous, principled, scrupulous, incorruptible, noble, just. ● *n.* **1** lesson, homily, teaching, point, message; aphorism, maxim, precept, apothegm, adage, saw, proverb, motto, slogan. **2** (*morals*) behavior, conduct, mores, beliefs, habits, customs, practices, principles, scruples, ethics, ideals, standards; probity, morality, rectitude, integrity.

morale /mərál/ *n.* the mental attitude or bearing of a person or group, esp. as regards confidence, discipline, etc. [F *moral* respelled to preserve the pronunciation]

■ dedication, spirit(s), unity, esprit de corps; disposition, attitude, confidence, self-confidence, self-esteem.

moralism /máwrəlizəm, mór-/ *n.* **1** a natural system of morality. **2** religion regarded as moral practice.

moralist /máwrəlist, mór-/ *n.* **1** a person who practices or teaches morality. **2** a person who follows a natural system of ethics. □□ **moralistic** /-lístik/ *adj.* **moralistically** /-lístiklee/ *adv.*

■ see PURITAN *n.*

morality /mərálitee/ *n.* (*pl.* **-ies**) **1** the degree of conformity of an idea, practice, etc., to moral principles. **2** right moral conduct. **3** a lesson in morals. **4** the science of morals. **5** a particular system of morals (*commercial morality*). **6** (in *pl.*) moral principles; points of ethics. **7** (in full **morality play**) *hist.* a kind of drama with personified abstract qualities as the main characters and inculcating a moral lesson, popular in the 16th c. [ME f. OF *moralité* or LL *moralitas* f. L (as MORAL)]

■ **1, 2, 6** ethics, morals, principle(s), mores, standards, ideals; honesty, right, rightness, righteousness, rectitude, integrity, propriety, justice, fair play, fairness, decency, probity, uprightness. **5** behavior, conduct, habit(s), custom(s), mores, attitude; see also ETIQUETTE.

moralize /máwrəliz, mór-/ *v.* **1** *intr.* (often foll. by *on*) indulge in moral reflection or talk. **2** *tr.* interpret morally; point the moral of. **3** *tr.* make moral or more moral. □□ **moralization** *n.* **moralizer** *n.* **moralizingly** *adv.* [F *moraliser* or med.L *moralizare* f. L (as MORAL)]

■ **1** see PREACH 2.

morass /mərás/ *n.* **1** an entanglement; a disordered situation, esp. one impeding progress. **2** *literary* a bog or marsh. [Du. *moeras* (assim. to *moer* MOOR)[1] f. MDu. *marasch* f. OF *marais* marsh f. med.L *mariscus*]

■ **1** entanglement, confusion, muddle, mess, quagmire, tangle. **2** bog, marsh, swamp, fen, quag, mire, quagmire, slough, marshland, quicksand, *Sc.* & *No. of Engl.* moss.

moratorium /máwrətáwreeəm, mór-/ *n.* (*pl.* **moratoriums** or **moratoria** /-reeə/) **1** (often foll. by *on*) a temporary prohibition or suspension (of an activity). **2 a** a legal authorization to debtors to postpone payment. **b** the period of this postponement. [mod.L, neut. of LL *moratorius* delaying f. L *morari morat-* to delay f. *mora* delay]

■ **1** halt, prohibition, freeze, suspension, stay, postponement, delay, waiting period, respite, hiatus.

Moravian /məráyveeən/ *n.* & *adj.* ● *n.* **1** a native of Moravia, now part of the Czech Republic. **2** a member of a Protestant sect founded in Saxony by emigrants from Moravia, holding views derived from the Hussites and accepting the Bible as the only source of faith. ● *adj.* of, relating to, or characteristic of Moravia or its people.

moray /máwray/ *n.* any tropical eellike fish of the family Muraenidae, esp. *Muraena helena* found in Mediterranean waters. [Port. *moreia* f. L f. Gk *muraina*]

morbid /máwrbid/ *adj.* **1 a** (of the mind, ideas, etc.) unwholesome; sickly; macabre. **b** given to morbid feelings. **2** *colloq.* melancholy. **3** *Med.* of the nature of or indicative of disease. □ **morbid anatomy** the anatomy of diseased organs, tissues, etc. □□ **morbidity** /-bíditee/ *n.* **morbidly** *adv.* **morbidness** *n.* [L *morbidus* f. *morbus* disease]

■ **1 a** unhealthy, unwholesome, disordered, unsound, sick, sickly; grim, ghoulish, macabre, monstrous, ghastly, grotesque, grisly, gruesome. **2** gloomy, lugubrious, glum, morose, somber, blue, sad, despondent, depressed, dejected, downcast; see also MELANCHOLY *adj.*

morbific /mawrbífik/ *adj.* causing disease. [F *morbifique* or mod.L *morbificus* f. L *morbus* disease]

morbilli /mawrbíli/ *n.pl.* **1** measles. **2** the spots characteristic of measles. [L, pl. of *morbillus* pustule f. *morbus* disease]

mordant /máwrd'nt/ *adj.* & *n.* ● *adj.* **1** (of sarcasm, etc.) caustic; biting. **2** pungent; smarting. **3** corrosive; cleansing. **4** (of a substance) serving to fix coloring matter or gold leaf on another substance. ● *n.* a mordant substance (in senses 3, 4 of *adj.*). □□ **mordancy** *n.* **mordantly** *adv.* [ME f. F, part. of *mordre* bite f. L *mordēre*]

■ **1** see BITING 2.

mordent /máwrd'nt/ *n. Mus.* **1** an ornament consisting of one rapid alternation of a written note with the note immediately below it. **2** a pralltriller. [G f. It. *mordente* part. of *mordēre* bite]

more /mawr/ *adj.*, *n.*, & *adv.* ● *adj.* **1** existing in a greater or additional quantity, amount, or degree (*more problems than last time*; *bring some more water*). **2** greater in degree (*more's the pity*; *the more fool you*). ● *n.* a greater quantity, number, or amount (*more than three people*; *more to it than meets the eye*). ● *adv.* **1** in a greater degree (*do it more carefully*). **2** to a greater extent (*people like to walk more these days*). **3** forming the comparative of adjectives and adverbs, esp. those of more than one syllable (*more absurd*; *more easily*). **4** again (*once more*; *never more*). **5** moreover. □ **more and more** in an increasing degree. **more like it** see LIKE[1]. **more of** to a greater extent (*more of a poet than a musician*). **more or less 1** in a greater or less degree. **2** approximately; as an estimate. **more so** of the same kind to a greater degree. [OE *māra* f. Gmc]

■ □ **more or less 1** see SOMEWHAT *adv.* **2** see *approximately* (APPROXIMATE).

moreen /mawreen/ *n.* a strong ribbed woolen or cotton material for curtains, etc. [perh. fanciful f. MOIRE]

morel[1] /mərél/ *n.* an edible fungus of the genus *Morchella*, esp. *M. esculenta*, with ridged mushroom caps. [F *morille* f. Du. *morilje*]

morel[2] /mərél/ *n.* (also **morelle**) a nightshade, esp. the black nightshade. [ME f. OF *morele* fem. of *morel* dark brown ult. f. L *Maurus* MOOR]

morello /mərélō/ *n.* (*pl.* **-os**) a sour kind of dark cherry. [It. *morello* blackish f. med.L *morellus* f. L (as MOREL[1])]

moreover /máwrṓvər/ *adv.* (introducing or accompanying a new statement) further, besides.

■ furthermore, further, besides, not only that, more than that, what is more; to boot, into the bargain, in addition, additionally, as well, also, too, *archaic* withal.

mores /máwrayz, -reez/ *n.pl.* customs or conventions regarded as essential to or characteristic of a community. [L, pl. of *mos* custom]

■ see CULTURE *n.* 2.

Moresco var. of MORISCO.

Moresque /mawrésk/ *adj.* (of art or architecture) Moorish in style or design. [F f. It. *moresco* f. *Moro* MOOR]

morganatic /máwrgənátik/ *adj.* **1** (of a marriage) between a person of high rank and another of lower rank, the spouse and children having no claim to the possessions or title of the person of higher rank. **2** (of a wife) married in this way. □□ **morganatically** *adv.* [F *morganatique* or G *morganatisch* f. med.L *matrimonium ad morganaticam* 'marriage with a morning gift,' the husband's gift to the wife after consummation being his only obligation in such a marriage]

morgue /mawrg/ *n.* **1** a mortuary. **2** (in a newspaper office, etc.) a room or file of miscellaneous information, esp. for future obituaries. [F, orig. the name of a Paris mortuary]

moribund /máwribund, mór-/ *adj.* **1** at the point of death. **2** lacking vitality. **3** on the decline, stagnant. □□ **moribundity** /-búnditee/ *n.* [L *moribundus* f. *mori* die]

■ **1** dying, in extremis, at death's door, failing, fading, with one foot in the grave, half-dead, breathing one's last, expiring, on one's last legs, on one's deathbed, on the way out. **2** see LIFELESS 1, 3. **3** declining, obsolescent, weak, waning, on the wane *or* decline, dying out; stagnating, stagnant.

Morisco /mərískō/ *n. & adj.* (also **Moresco** /-réskō/) ● *n.* (*pl.* **-os** *or* **-oes**) **1** a Moor, esp. in Spain. **2** a morris dance. ● *adj.* Moorish. [Sp. f. *Moro* MOOR]

Mormon /máwrmən/ *n.* a member of the Church of Jesus Christ of Latter-day Saints, a millenary religion founded in 1830 by Joseph Smith on the basis of revelations in the Book of Mormon. □□ **Mormonism** *n.*

morn /mawrn/ *n. poet.* morning. [OE *morgen* f. Gmc]

mornay /mawrnáy/ *n.* a cheese-flavored white sauce. [20th c.: orig. uncert.]

morning /mawrning/ *n. & int.* ● *n.* **1** the early part of the day, esp. from sunrise to noon (*this morning*; *during the morning*; *morning coffee*). **2** this time spent in a particular way (*had a busy morning*). **3** sunrise, daybreak. **4** a time compared with the morning, esp. the early part of one's life, etc. ● *int.* = good morning (see GOOD *adj.* 14). □ **in the morning 1** during or in the course of the morning. **2** *colloq.* tomorrow. **morning after** *colloq.* a hangover. **morning-after pill** a contraceptive pill effective when taken some hours after intercourse. **morning coat** a coat with tails, and with the front cut away below the waist. **morning dress** a man's morning coat and striped trousers. **morning glory** any of various twining plants of the genus *Ipomoea*, with trumpet-shaped flowers. **morning sickness** nausea felt in the morning in pregnancy. **morning star** a planet or bright star, usu. Venus, seen in the east before sunrise. **morning watch** *Naut.* the 4–8 a.m. watch. [ME *mor(we)ning* f. *morwen* MORN + -ING[1] after *evening*]

■ *n.* **1, 2** a.m., *Naut. or Law or archaic* forenoon, *poet.* morn. **3** dawn, daybreak, sunrise, cock crow, sunup.

Moro /máwrō/ *n.* (*pl.* **-os**) a Muslim living in the Philippines. [Sp., = MOOR]

Moroccan /mərókən/ *n. & adj.* ● *n.* **1** a native or national of Morocco in N. Africa. **2** a person of Moroccan descent. ● *adj.* of or relating to Morocco.

morocco /mərókō/ *n.* (*pl.* **-os**) **1** a fine flexible leather made (orig. in Morocco) from goatskins tanned with sumac, used esp. in bookbinding and shoemaking. **2** an imitation of this in grained calf, etc.

moron /máwron/ *n.* **1** *colloq.* a very stupid or foolish person. **2** an adult with a mental age of about 8–12. □□ **moronic** /mərónik/ *adj.* **moronically** /məróniklee/ *adv.* **moronism** *n.* [Gk *mōron*, neut. of *mōros* foolish]

■ **1** see FOOL[1] *n.* 1.

morose /mərós/ *adj.* sullen and ill-tempered. □□ **morosely** *adv.* **moroseness** *n.* [L *morosus* peevish, etc. f. *mos moris* manner]

■ see SULLEN *adj.* 1.

morph[1] /mawrf/ *n.* = ALLOMORPH. [back-form.]

morph[2] /mawrf/ *v. intr. Cinematog.* change form or appearance, as from person to animal, by computer-controlled special effects.

morpheme /máwrfeem/ *n. Linguistics* **1** a morphological element considered in respect of its functional relations in a linguistic system. **2** a meaningful morphological unit of a language that cannot be further divided (e.g., *in, come, -ing,* forming *incoming*). □□ **morphemic** /-feémik/ *adj.* **morphemically** /-feémiklee/ *adv.* [F *morphème* f. Gk *morphē* form, after PHONEME]

morphemics /mawrfeémiks/ *n.pl.* (usu. treated as *sing.*) Linguistics the study of word structure.

morphia /máwrfeeə/ *n.* = MORPHINE.

morphine /máwrfeen/ *n.* an analgesic and narcotic drug obtained from opium and used medicinally to relieve pain. □□ **morphinism** /-finizəm/ *n.* [G *Morphin* & mod.L *morphia* f. *Morpheus* god of sleep]

morphing /máwrfing/ *n.* a computer graphics technique used in filmmaking, whereby an image is apparently transformed into another by a smooth progression; the act or process of changing one image into another using this technique. [shortened f. METAMORPHOSIS + -ING[1]]

morphogenesis /máwrfəjénisis/ *n. Biol.* the development of form in organisms. □□ **morphogenetic** /-jinétik/ *adj.* **morphogenic** *adj.* [mod.L f. Gk *morphē* form + GENESIS]

morphology /mawrfóləjee/ *n.* the study of the forms of things, esp.: **1** *Biol.* the study of the forms of organisms. **2** *Philol.* **a** the study of the forms of words. **b** the system of forms in a language. □□ **morphological** /mawrfəlójikəl/ *adj.* **morphologically** /-fəlójiklee/ *adv.* **morphologist** *n.* [Gk *morphē* form + -LOGY]

Morris chair /máwris, móris/ *n.* a type of plain easy chair with an adjustable back. [William *Morris*, Engl. poet and craftsman d. 1896]

morris dance /máwris, mór-/ *n.* a traditional English dance by groups of people in fancy costume, usu. as characters in legend, with ribbons and bells. □□ **morris dancer** *n.* **morris dancing** *n.* [*morys*, var. of MOORISH]

morrow /máwrō, mór-/ *n.* (usu. prec. by *the*) *literary* **1** the following day. **2** the time following an event. [ME *morwe, moru* (as MORN)]

Morse /mawrs/ *n. & v.* ● *n.* (in full **Morse code**) an alphabet or code in which letters are represented by combinations of long and short light or sound signals. ● *v.tr. & intr.* signal by Morse code. [S. F. B. *Morse*, Amer. inventor d. 1872, who devised it]

morsel /máwrsəl/ *n.* a mouthful; a small piece (esp. of food). [ME f. OF, dimin. of *mors* a bite f. *mordēre mors-* to bite]

■ mouthful, bite, gobbet, spoonful, taste, sample, nibble, bit, drop, dollop, soupçon; crumb, fragment, scrap, sliver, splinter, shard, shred, particle, atom, speck, whit, fraction, grain, granule, pinch, piece, *colloq.* smidgen, *Austral. colloq.* skerrick.

mort /mawrt/ *n.* Hunting a note sounded when the quarry is killed. [ME f. OF f. L *mors mortis* death]

mortadella /mawrtədélə/ *n.* (*pl.* **mortadelle** /-déle/) a large spiced pork sausage. [It. dimin., irreg. f. L *murtatum* seasoned with myrtle berries]

mortal /mawrt'l/ *adj. & n.* ● *adj.* **1 a** (of a living being, esp. a human) subject to death. **b** (of material or earthly existence) temporal, ephemeral. **2** (often foll. by *to*) causing death; fatal. **3** (of a battle) fought to the death. **4** associated with death (*mortal agony*). **5** (of an enemy) implacable. **6** (of pain, fear, an affront, etc.) intense, very serious. **7** *colloq.* a very great (*in a mortal hurry*). **b** long and tedious (*for two mortal hours*). **8** *colloq.* conceivable, imaginable (*every mortal thing*; *of no mortal use*). ● *n.* **1** a mortal being, esp. a human. **2** *joc.* a person described in some specified way (*a thirsty mortal*). □ **mortal sin** *Theol.* a grave sin that is regarded as depriving the soul of divine grace. □□ **mortally** *adv.* [ME f. OF *mortal, mortel* or L *mortalis* f. *mors mortis* death]

■ *adj.* **1** human; physical, bodily, corporeal, corporal, fleshly, earthly, worldly, perishable; transitory, temporal, transient, ephemeral. **2** deadly, fatal, lethal, terminal. **5** relentless, implacable, unrelenting, bitter,

/ . . . / **pronunciation** ● **part of speech**
□ **phrases, idioms, and compounds**
□□ **derivatives** ■ **synonym section**
cross-references appear in SMALL CAPITALS or *italics*

deadly, unappeasable. **6** abject, extreme, awful, great, enormous, severe, intense, terrible, inordinate, dire, serious. ● *n.* human (being), man, woman, person, soul, individual, creature.

mortality /mawrtálitee/ *n.* (*pl.* **-ies**) **1** the state of being subject to death. **2** loss of life on a large scale. **3 a** the number of deaths in a given period, etc. **b** (in full **mortality rate**) a death rate. [ME f. OF *mortalité* f. L *mortalitas -tatis* (as MORTAL)]

mortar /mawrtər/ *n. & v.* ● *n.* **1** a mixture of lime with cement, sand, and water, used in building to bond bricks or stones. **2** a short large-bore cannon for firing shells at high angles. **3** a contrivance for firing a lifeline or firework. **4** a vessel made of hard material, in which ingredients are pounded with a pestle. ● *v.tr.* **1** plaster or join with mortar. **2** attack or bombard with mortar shells. □□ **mortarless** *adj.* (in sense 1). **mortary** *adj.* (in sense 1). [ME f. AF *morter*, OF *mortier* f. L *mortarium*: partly from LG]

■ *n.* **1** see CEMENT *n.*

mortarboard /mawrtərbawrd/ *n.* **1** an academic cap with a stiff, flat square top. **2** a flat board with a handle on the undersurface, for holding mortar in bricklaying, etc.

mortgage /mawrgij/ *n. & v.* ● *n.* **1 a** a conveyance of property by a debtor to a creditor as security for a debt (esp. one incurred by the purchase of the property), on the condition that it shall be returned on payment of the debt within a certain period. **b** a deed effecting this. **2 a** a debt secured by a mortgage. **b** a loan resulting in such a debt. ● *v.tr.* **1** convey (a property) by mortgage. **2** (often foll. by *to*) pledge (oneself, one's powers, etc.). □ **mortgage rate** the rate of interest charged by a mortgagee. □□ **mortgageable** *adj.* [ME f. OF, = dead pledge f. *mort* f. L *mortuus* dead + *gage* GAGE¹]

■ *n.* **2** see LOAN¹ *n.* ● *v.* see PAWN² *v.*

mortgagee /mawrgijée/ *n.* the creditor in a mortgage, usu. a bank or other lending institution.

mortgagor /mawrgijər/ *n.* (also **mortgager** /-jər/) the debtor in a mortgage.

mortice var. of MORTISE.

mortician /mawrtíshən/ *n.* an undertaker; a manager of funerals. [L *mors mortis* death + -ICIAN]

■ see UNDERTAKER.

mortify /mawrtifī/ *v.* (**-ies, -ied**) **1** *tr.* **a** cause (a person) to feel shamed or humiliated. **b** wound (a person's feelings). **2** *tr.* bring (the body, the flesh, the passions, etc.) into subjection by self-denial or discipline. **3** *intr.* (of flesh) be affected by gangrene or necrosis. □□ **mortification** /-fikáyshən/ *n.* **mortifying** *adj.* **mortifyingly** *adv.* [ME f. OF *mortifier* f. eccl.L *mortificare* kill, subdue f. *mors mortis* death]

■ **1** humiliate, abase, shame, humble, embarrass, abash, chagrin, rebuff, crush, wound, discomfit, deflate, bring down, degrade, chasten, subdue, restrain, suppress, make a person eat humble pie, *colloq.* put down. **2** punish, castigate, discipline, control, subdue, restrain, subjugate. **3** gangrene, fester, putrefy, rot, decompose, decay, *Med. & Physiol.* necrose.

mortise /mawrtis/ *n. & v.* (also **mortice**) ● *n.* a hole in a framework designed to receive the end of another part, esp. a tenon. ● *v.tr.* **1** join securely, esp. by mortise and tenon. **2** cut a mortise in. □ **mortise lock** a lock recessed into a mortise in the frame of a door or window, etc. [ME f. OF *mortoise* f. Arab. *murtazz* fixed in]

mortmain /mawrtmayn/ *n. Law* **1** the status of lands or tenements held inalienably by an ecclesiastical or other corporation. **2** the land or tenements themselves. [ME f. AF, OF *mortemain* f. med.L *mortua manus* dead hand, prob. in allusion to impersonal ownership]

mortuary /mawrchoo-eree/ *n. & adj.* ● *n.* (*pl.* **-ies**) a room or building in which dead bodies may be kept until burial or cremation. ● *adj.* of or concerning death or burial. [ME f. AF *mortuarie* f. med.L *mortuarium* f. L *mortuarius* f. *mortuus* dead]

morula /mawryələ, mawrə-/ *n.* (*pl.* **morulae** /-lee/) a fully segmented ovum from which a blastula is formed. [mod.L, dimin. of L *morum* mulberry]

Mosaic /mōzáyik/ *adj.* of or associated with Moses (in the Old Testament). □ **Mosaic Law** the laws attributed to Moses and listed in the Pentateuch. [F *mosaïque* or mod.L *Mosaicus* f. *Moses* f. Heb. *Mōšeh*]

mosaic /mōzáyik/ *n. & v.* ● *n.* **1 a** a picture or pattern produced by an arrangement of small variously colored pieces of glass or stone, etc. **b** work of this kind as an art form. **2** a diversified thing. **3** an arrangement of photosensitive elements in a television camera. **4** *Biol.* a chimera. **5** (in full **mosaic disease**) a virus disease causing leaf-mottling in plants, esp. tobacco, corn, and sugar cane. **6** (*attrib.*) **a** of or like a mosaic. **b** diversified. ● *v.tr.* (**mosaicked, mosaicking**) **1** adorn with mosaics. **2** combine into or as into a mosaic. □ **mosaic gold 1** tin disulfide. **2** an alloy of copper and zinc used in cheap jewelry, etc. □□ **mosaicist** /-záyisist/ *n.* [ME f. F *mosaïque* f. It. *mosaico* f. med.L *mosaicus, musaicus* f. Gk *mous(e)ion* mosaic work f. *mousa* MUSE¹]

mosasaurus /mōsəsáwrəs/ *n.* any large extinct marine reptile of the genus *Mosasaurus*, with a long slender body and flipperlike limbs. [mod.L f. *Mosa* river Meuse (near which it was first discovered) + Gk *sauros* lizard]

moschatel /móskətél/ *n.* a small plant, *Adoxa moschatellina*, with pale-green flowers and a musky smell. [F *moscatelle* f. It. *moscatella* f. *moscato* musk]

Moselle /mōzél/ *n.* a light medium-dry white wine produced in the valley of the Moselle River in Germany.

mosey /mōzee/ *v.intr.* (**-eys, -eyed**) (often foll. by *along*) *sl.* walk in a leisurely or aimless manner. [19th c.: orig. unkn.]

■ see STROLL *v.*

moshav /mōsháav/ *n.* (*pl.* **moshavim**) a cooperative association of Israeli farmers. [Heb. *mošāb*, lit. 'dwelling']

Moslem var. of MUSLIM.

mosque /mosk/ *n.* a Muslim place of worship. [F *mosquée* f. It. *moschea* f. Arab. *masjid*]

■ see TEMPLE¹.

mosquito /məskeétō/ *n.* (*pl.* **-oes** or **-os**) any of various slender biting insects, esp. of the genus *Culex, Anopheles,* or *Aedes*, the female of which punctures the skin of humans and other animals with a long proboscis to suck their blood and transmits diseases such as filariasis and malaria. □ **mosquito boat** a motor torpedo-boat. **mosquito net** a net designed to keep out mosquitoes. [Sp. & Port., dimin. of *mosca* f. L *musca* fly]

moss /maws/ *n. & v.* ● *n.* **1** any small cryptogamous plant of the class Musci, growing in dense clusters on the surface of the ground, in bogs, on trees, stones, etc. **2** *Sc. & No. of Engl.* a bog, esp. a peatbog. ● *v.tr.* cover with moss. □ **moss agate** agate with mosslike dendritic markings. **moss-grown** overgrown with moss. **moss hag** *Sc.* broken ground from which peat has been taken. □□ **mosslike** *adj.* [OE *mos* bog, moss f. Gmc]

■ *n.* **2** see SWAMP *n.*

mossie /mózee/ *n.* esp. *Austral. sl.* = MOSQUITO.

mosso /mawsō/ *adv. Mus.* with animation or speed. [It., past part. of *muovere* move]

mosstrooper /maws-tróōpər/ *n.* **1** a freebooter of the Scottish-English border in the 17th c. **2** any such freebooter.

mossy /mawsee/ *adj.* (**mossier, mossiest**) **1** covered in or resembling moss. **2** *sl.* antiquated, old-fashioned. □□ **mossiness** *n.*

most /mōst/ *adj., n., & adv.* ● *adj.* **1** existing in the greatest quantity or degree (*you have made the most mistakes; see who can make the most noise*). **2** the majority of; nearly all of (*most people think so*). ● *n.* **1** the greatest quantity or number (*this is the most I can do*). **2** (**the most**) *sl.* the best of all. **3** the majority (*most of them are missing*). ● *adv.* **1** in the highest degree (*this is most interesting; what most annoys me*). **2** forming the superlative of adjectives and adverbs, esp. those of more than one syllable (*most certain; most easily*). **3** *colloq.* almost. □ **at most** no more or better than (*this is at most a makeshift*). **at the most 1** as the greatest amount. **2** not more than. **for the most part 1** as regards the greater part. **2** usually. **make the most of 1** employ to the best advantage. **2** represent at its best or worst. **Most Reverend** a title given to archbishops and to Roman Catholic bishops. [OE *mǣst* f. Gmc]

■ □ **at most** see JUST *adv.* 3, 4. **for the most part** 2 see *usually* (USUAL).

-most /mōst/ *suffix* forming superlative adjectives and adverbs from prepositions and other words indicating relative position (*foremost*; *uttermost*). [OE *-mest* f. Gmc]

mostly /mōstlee/ *adv.* **1** as regards the greater part. **2** usually. ■ **2** see *usually* (USUAL).

mot /mō/ *n.* (*pl.* **mots** *pronunc.* same) a witty saying. □ **mot juste** /zhYst/ (*pl.* **mots justes** *pronunc.* same) the most appropriate expression. [F, = word, ult. f. L *muttum* uttered sound f. *muttire* murmur]

■ see EPIGRAM 3.

mote /mōt/ *n.* a speck of dust. [OE *mot*, corresp. to Du. *mot* dust, sawdust, of unkn. orig.]

■ see SPECK *n.* 2.

motel /mōtél/ *n.* a roadside hotel providing accommodation for motorists and parking for their vehicles. [portmanteau word f. MOTOR + HOTEL]

■ see HOTEL 1.

motet /mōtét/ *n.* *Mus.* a short sacred choral composition. [ME f. OF, dimin. of *mot*: see MOT]

moth /mawth, moth-/ *n.* **1** any usu. nocturnal insect of the order Lepidoptera excluding butterflies, having a stout body and without clubbed antennae. **2** any small lepidopterous insect of the family Tineidae breeding in cloth, etc., on which its larva feeds. □ **moth-eaten 1** damaged or destroyed by moths. **2** antiquated, timeworn. [OE *moththe*]

■ □□ **moth-eaten 2** see TIMEWORN.

mothball /máwthbawl, moth-/ *n.* & *v.* ● *n.* a ball of naphthalene, etc. placed in stored clothes to keep away moths. ● *v.tr.* **1** place in mothballs. **2** leave unused. □ **in mothballs** stored unused for a considerable time.

■ *v.* **2** see TABLE *v.* 2.

mother /múthər/ *n.* & *v.* ● *n.* **1 a** a woman in relation to a child or children to whom she has given birth. **b** (in full **adoptive mother**) a woman who has continuous care of a child, esp. by adoption. **2** any female animal in relation to its offspring. **3** a quality or condition, etc., that gives rise to another (*necessity is the mother of invention*). **4** (in full **Mother Superior**) the head of a female religious community. **5** *archaic* (esp. as a form of address) an elderly woman. **6** (*attrib.*) **a** designating an institution, etc., regarded as having maternal authority (*Mother Church*; *mother earth*). **b** designating the main ship, spacecraft, etc., in a convoy or mission (*the mother craft*). ● *v.tr.* **1** give birth to; be the mother of. **2** protect as a mother. **3** give rise to; be the source of. **4** acknowledge or profess oneself the mother of. □ **Mother Carey's chicken** = *storm petrel* 1. **mother country** a country in relation to its colonies. **mother figure** an older woman who is regarded as a source of nurture, support, etc. **Mother Goose rhyme** a nursery rhyme. **mother-in-law** (*pl.* **mothers-in-law**) the mother of one's husband or wife. **mother lode** *Mining* the main vein of a system. **mother-of-pearl** a smooth iridescent substance forming the inner layer of the shell of some mollusks. **Mother's Day 1** the second Sunday in May, traditionally a day for honoring mothers. **2** *Brit.* = MOTHERING SUNDAY. **mother's son** *colloq.* a man (*every mother's son of you*). **mother tongue 1** one's native language. **2** a language from which others have evolved. **mother wit** native wit; common sense. □□ **motherless** *adj.* **motherlessness** *n.* **motherlike** *adj.* & *adv.* [OE *mōdor* f. Gmc]

■ *n.* **1** parent, matriarch, materfamilias, *colloq.* ma, mam, mama, mamma, old lady, old woman, *colloq.* mom, mommy, mammy, *Brit. colloq.* mummy, mum, *Brit. sl.* mater; nourisher, nurturer. **2** dam. **3** origin, genesis; see also SOURCE *n.* 1, 2. ● *v.* **1** give birth to, have, deliver, bear, bring forth *or* into the world, birth, *derog.* whelp. **2** nurture, nourish, nurse, care for, look after, protect, shelter, watch over, take care of; pamper, baby, coddle, spoil, indulge, fuss over, overprotect. **3** see CAUSE *v.* 1.

motherboard /múthərbawrd/ *n.* a computer's main circuit board, into which other boards can be plugged or wired.

motherhood /múthərhŏŏd/ *n.* **1** the condition or fact of being a mother. **2** (*attrib.*) (of an issue, report, etc.) protective, withholding the worst aspects.

Mothering Sunday /múthəring/ *n.* *Brit.* the fourth Sunday in Lent, traditionally a day for honoring mothers.

motherland /múthərland/ *n.* one's native country.

■ see COUNTRY 3.

motherly /múthərlee/ *adj.* **1** like or characteristic of a mother in affection, care, etc. **2** of or relating to a mother. □□ **motherliness** *n.* [OE *mōdorlic* (as MOTHER)]

■ see MATERNAL 1, 2.

mothproof /máwthprŏŏf, moth-/ *adj.* & *v.* ● *adj.* (of clothes) treated so as to repel moths. ● *v.tr.* treat (clothes) in this way.

mothy /máwthee, móthee/ *adj.* (**mothier, mothiest**) infested with moths.

motif /mōtéef/ *n.* **1** a distinctive feature or dominant idea in artistic or literary composition. **2** *Mus.* = FIGURE *n.* 10. **3** an ornament of lace, etc., sewn separately on a garment. **4** *Brit.* an ornament on a vehicle identifying the maker, model, etc. [F (as MOTIVE)]

■ **1** theme, idea, topic, subject, concept, leitmotif; pattern, figure, refrain, device, element, convention.

motile /mōt'l, -tīl, -til/ *adj.* *Zool.* & *Bot.* capable of motion. □□ **motility** /-tílitee/ *n.* [L *motus* motion (as MOVE)]

motion /mōshən/ *n.* & *v.* ● *n.* **1** the act or process of moving or of changing position. **2** a particular manner of moving the body in walking, etc. **3** a change of posture. **4** a gesture. **5** a formal proposal put to a committee, legislature, etc. **6** *Law* an application for a rule or order of court. **7** esp. *Brit.* **a** an evacuation of the bowels. **b** (in *sing.* or *pl.*) feces. **8** a piece of moving mechanism. ● *v.* (often foll. by *to* + infin.) **1** *tr.* direct (a person) by a sign or gesture. **2** *intr.* (often foll. by *to* a person) make a gesture directing (*motioned to me to leave*). □ **go through the motions 1** make a pretense; do something perfunctorily or superficially. **2** simulate an action by gestures. **in motion** moving; not at rest. **motion picture** (often (with hyphen) *attrib.*) a film or movie with the illusion of movement (see FILM *n.* 3). **put** (or **set**) **in motion** set going or working. □□ **motional** *adj.* **motionless** *adj.* [ME f. OF f. L *motio -onis* (as MOVE)]

■ *n.* **1** movement, moving, change, shift, shifting, action, going, traveling, travel, progress, passage, transit; activity, commotion, stir, agitation, turmoil, turbulence. **2** gait, bearing, carriage, tread, walk, step, pace. **4** gesture, gesticulation, signal, sign. **5** proposal, suggestion, proposition, recommendation, offering, submission. ● *v.* gesture, beckon, signal, wave; gesticulate, sign. □ **go through the motions 1** see PRETEND *v.* 2b. □□ **motionless** see STILL[1] *adj.* 1.

motivate /mótivayt/ *v.tr.* **1** supply a motive to; be the motive of. **2** cause (a person) to act in a particular way. **3** stimulate the interest of (a person in an activity). □□ **motivation** /-váyshən/ *n.* **motivational** /-váyshənəl/ *adj.* **motivationally** /-váyshənəlee/ *adv.*

■ prompt, activate, move, inspire, incite, induce, actuate, stimulate, provoke, influence, encourage, occasion, bring about, cause; excite, egg (on), urge, prod, spur, galvanize, goad, rouse, arouse, stir (up), wheedle, coax, persuade, cajole, tempt, push, impel, drive, instigate. □□ **motivation** inducement, incentive, stimulus, motivating force, stimulation, incitement, influence, cause, reason, motive, rationale, ground(s); attraction, lure, enticement, goad, spur, urge, prod.

motive /mótiv/ *n.*, *adj.*, & *v.* ● *n.* **1** a factor or circumstance that induces a person to act in a particular way. **2** = MOTIF. ● *adj.* **1** tending to initiate movement. **2** concerned with

---

/.../ **pronunciation**	● **part of speech**
□ **phrases, idioms, and compounds**	
□□ **derivatives**	■ **synonym section**
cross-references appear in SMALL CAPITALS or *italics*	

movement. ● *v.tr.* = MOTIVATE. □ **motive power** a moving or impelling power, esp. a source of energy used to drive machinery. □□ **motiveless** *adj.* **motivelessly** *adv.* **motivelessness** *n.* **motivity** /-tívitee/ *n.* [ME f. OF *motif* (adj. & n.) f. LL *motivus* (adj.) (as MOVE)]

■ *n.* **1** motivating force, stimulus, inducement, incentive, motivation; cause, reason, justification, rationale, spur, ground(s), explanation. ● *adj.* **1** driving, impelling, propelling, propulsive, kinetic, activating, operative, moving.

motley /mótlee/ *adj. & n.* ● *adj.* (**motlier, motliest**) **1** diversified in color. **2** of varied character (*a motley crew*). ● *n.* **1** an incongruous mixture. **2** *hist.* the parti-colored costume of a jester. □ **wear motley** play the fool. [ME *mottelay*, perh. ult. rel. to MOTE]

■ *adj.* **1** see *variegated* (VARIEGATE). **2** see MISCELLANEOUS. ● *n.* **1** see MISCELLANY.

motocross /mótōkraws, -kros/ *n.* cross-country racing on motor cycles. [MOTOR + CROSS-]

moto perpetuo /mótō pərpétyōō-ō/ *n. Mus.* a usu. fast-moving instrumental composition consisting mainly of notes of equal value. [It., = perpetual motion]

motor /mótər/ *n., adj., & v.* ● *n.* **1** a thing that imparts motion. **2** a machine (esp. one using electricity or internal combustion) supplying motive power for a vehicle, etc., or for some other device with moving parts. **3** *Brit.* = CAR 1. ● *adj.* **1** giving, imparting, or producing motion. **2** driven by a motor. **3** of or for motor vehicles. **4** *Anat.* relating to muscular movement or the nerves activating it. ● *v.intr. & tr.* esp. *Brit.* go or convey in a motor vehicle. □ **motor area** the part of the frontal lobe of the brain associated with the initiation of muscular action. **motor bicycle** a motor cycle or moped. **motor home** a vehicle built on a truck frame that includes kitchen facilities, beds, etc. (see also TRAILER, *mobile home*). **motor neuron** a nerve carrying impulses from the brain or spinal cord to a muscle. **motor pool** a group of vehicles maintained by a government agency, military installation, etc., for use by personnel as needed. **motor scooter** see SCOOTER. **motor vehicle** a road vehicle powered by an internal-combustion engine. □□ **motorial** /mōtáwreeəl/ *adj.* (in sense 4a of *n.*). **motory** *adj.* (in sense 4a of *n.*). [L, = mover (as MOVE)]

■ *n.* **1** see ENGINE. ● *v.* see DRIVE *v.* 3b.

motorable /mótərəbəl/ *adj. Brit.* (of a road) that can be used by motor vehicles.

motorbike /mótərbīk/ *n.* **1** lightweight motorcyle. **2** motorized bicycle.

motorboat /mótərbōt/ *n.* a motor-driven boat, esp. a recreational boat. *v.* travel by motorboat.

■ see BOAT *n.*

motorbus /mótərbus/ *n.* = BUS 1.

motorcade /mótərkayd/ *n.* a procession of motor vehicles. [MOTOR, after *cavalcade*]

■ see PROCESSION 1.

motorcar /mótərkaar/ *n.* esp. *Brit.* see CAR 1.

motorcycle /mótərsīkəl/ *n.* two-wheeled motor-driven road vehicle without pedal propulsion. □□ **motorcyclist** *n.*

motorist /mótərist/ *n.* the driver or passenger of an automobile.

motorize /mótəriz/ *v.tr.* **1** equip (troops, etc.) with motor transport. **2** provide with a motor for propulsion, etc. □□ **motorization** *n.*

motorman /mótərmən/ *n.* (*pl.* **-men**) the driver of a subway train, streetcar, etc.

motormouth /mótərmówth/ *n. sl.* a person who talks incessantly and trivially.

motorway /mótərwáy/ *n. Brit.* an expressway.

Motown /mótown/ *n.* music with rhythm and blues elements, associated with Detroit. [a nickname for Detroit, shortening of *Motor Town*]

motte /mot/ *n.* **1** a mound forming the site of a castle, camp, etc. **2** *SW US* (also **mott**) clump of trees; grove. [ME f. OF *mote* (as MOAT)]

mottle /mót'l/ *v. & n.* ● *v.tr.* (esp. as **mottled** *adj.*) mark with spots or smears of color. ● *n.* **1** an irregular arrangement of spots or patches of color. **2** any of these spots or patches. [prob. back-form. f. MOTLEY]

■ *v.* see DAPPLE *v.*; (**mottled**) dappled, brindled, marbled, streaked, splotchy, blotched, blotchy, freckled, spotted, spotty, patchy, speckled, flecked, sprinkled, spattered, splashed, streaky, stippled, pied, piebald, *colloq.* multicolored, variegated, parti-colored.

motto /mótō/ *n.* (*pl.* **-oes** or **-os**) **1** a maxim adopted as a rule of conduct. **2** a phrase or sentence accompanying a coat of arms or crest. **3** a sentence inscribed on some object and expressing an appropriate sentiment. **4** quotation prefixed to a book or chapter. [It. (as MOT)]

■ **1, 3, 4** maxim, proverb, saying, adage, saw, aphorism, apothegm, gnome, slogan; catchword, war *or* battle cry, byword, guide, moral, principle, rule, precept.

moue /mōō/ *n.* = POUT[1] *n.* [F]

mouflon /mōōflon/ *n.* (also **moufflon**) a wild mountain sheep, *Ovis musimon*, of S. Europe. [F *mouflon* f. It. *muflone* f. Rmc]

mouillé /mōō-yáy/ *adj. Phonet.* (of a consonant) palatalized. [F, = wetted]

moujik var. of MUZHIK.

mould *Brit.* var. of MOLD[1], MOLD[2], MOLD[3].

moulder *Brit.* var. of MOLDER.

moulding *Brit.* var. of MOLDING.

mouldy *Brit.* var. of MOLDY.

moulin /mōōlán/ *n.* a nearly vertical shaft in a glacier, formed by surface water percolating through a crack in the ice. [F, lit. = mill]

moult *Brit.* var. of MOLT.

mound[1] /mownd/ *n. & v.* ● *n.* **1** a raised mass of earth, stones, or other compacted material. **2** a heap or pile. **3** a hillock. ● *v.tr.* **1** heap up in a mound or mounds. **2** enclose with mounds. [16th c. (orig. = hedge or fence): orig. unkn.]

■ *n.* **1, 2** heap, pile, stack; tumulus, (kitchen) midden, *Archaeol.* tell, barrow. **3** hillock, rise, hummock, hill, hump, bank, elevation, knoll, swell, butte, dune, slope, tor. ● *v.* **1** see PILE[1] *v.* 1.

mound[2] /mownd/ *n. Heraldry* a ball of gold, etc., representing the earth, and usu. surmounting a crown. [ME f. OF *monde* f. L *mundus* world]

Mound Builders /mownd bíldərz/ *n.* prehistoric Native American peoples of the Mississippi River Valley who left behind earthworks and burial mounds.

mount[1] /mownt/ *v. & n.* ● *v.* **1** *tr.* ascend or climb (a hill, stairs, etc.). **2** *tr.* **a** get up on (an animal, esp. a horse) to ride it. **b** set (a person) on horseback. **c** provide (a person) with a horse. **d** (as **mounted** *adj.*) serving on horseback (*mounted police*). **3** *tr.* go up or climb on to (a raised surface). **4** *intr.* **a** move upward. **b** (often foll. by *up*) increase, accumulate. **c** (of a feeling) become stronger or more intense (*excitement was mounting*). **d** (of the blood) rise into the cheeks. **5** *tr.* (esp. of a male animal) get on to (a female) to copulate. **6** *tr.* (often foll. by *on*) place (an object) on an elevated support. **7** *tr.* **a** set in or attach to a backing, setting, or other support. **b** attach (a picture, etc.) to a mount or frame. **c** fix (an object for viewing) on a microscope slide. **8** *tr.* **a** arrange (a play, exhibition, etc.) or present for public view or display. **b** take action to initiate (a program, campaign, etc.). **9** *tr.* prepare (specimens) for preservation. **10** *tr.* **a** bring into readiness for operation. **b** raise (guns) into position on a fixed mounting. **11** *intr.* rise to a higher level of rank, power, etc. ● *n.* **1** a backing, setting, or other support on which a picture, etc., is set for display. **2** the margin surrounding a picture or photograph. **3 a** a horse available for riding. **b** an opportunity to ride a horse, esp. as a jockey. **4** = *stamp hinge* (see HINGE). □ **mount guard** esp. *Brit.* (often foll. by *over*) perform the duty of guarding; take up sentry duty. □□ **mountable** *adj.* **mounter** *n.* [ME f. OF *munter, monter* ult. f. L (as MOUNT[2])]

■ *v.* **1** climb (up), go up, ascend, scale, clamber up, make one's way up. **2a, 3** climb *or* get *or* clamber (up) on (to); bestride, straddle, bestraddle. **4 a** rise (up), ascend, soar, fly (up), rocket (upward), esp. *archaic & poet.* arise. **b, c** increase, wax, rise, escalate, intensify, swell, expand, grow; multiply, pile up, build up, accumulate. **6–8, 10** display, exhibit, put on display *or* exhibit *or* exhibition, present, install; stage, prepare, ready, put on, put in place, set up; arrange, coordinate, compose, organize, set in motion, launch; frame, set off, back. ● *n.* **1, 2** backing, setting, support, mounting, background, set, arrangement, backdrop, scene. **3 a** horse, *archaic* palfrey, *archaic or poet.* steed, *poet.* charger. **b** ride.

mount² /mownt/ *n. archaic* (except before a name): mountain, hill (*Mount Everest; Mount of Olives*). [ME f. OE *munt* & OF *mont* f. L *mons montis* mountain]
■ see MOUNTAIN 1.

mountain /mównt'n/ *n.* **1** a large natural elevation of the earth's surface rising abruptly from the surrounding level; a large or high and steep hill. **2** a large heap or pile; a huge quantity (*a mountain of work*). **3** a large surplus stock of a commodity (*butter mountain*). □ **make a mountain out of a molehill** see MOLEHILL. **mountain ash 1** a tree, *Sorbus aucuparia*, with delicate pinnate leaves and scarlet berries; also called ROWAN. **2** any of several Australian eucalypti. **mountain bike** a bicycle with a light sturdy frame, broad deep-treaded tires, and multiple gears, originally designed for riding on mountainous terrain. **mountain goat** a white goatlike animal, *Oreamnos americanus*, of the Rocky Mountains, etc. **mountain laurel** a N. American shrub, *Kalmia latifolia*. **mountain lion** a puma. **mountain panther** = OUNCE². **mountain range** a line of mountains connected by high ground. **mountain sickness** a sickness caused by the rarefaction of the air at great heights. **mountain time** (also **Mountain Standard Time**) the standard time of parts of Canada and the US in or near the Rocky Mountains. **move mountains 1** achieve spectacular results. **2** make every possible effort. □□ **mountainy** *adj.* [ME f. OF *montaigne* ult. f. L (as MOUNT²)]
■ **1** height, elevation, eminence, prominence, peak, alp, tor, summit, *No. of Engl.* fell, *Sc.* ben, *S. Afr.* berg, *archaic* mount. **2, 3** heap, pile, stack, mound, accumulation, abundance, mass, *colloq.* ton(s), heaps, piles, stacks; surplus, surfeit, plethora, excess, oversupply, glut. □ **move mountains 1** work *or* perform miracles *or* a miracle, work *or* do wonders, achieve the impossible, do the unheard of. **2** pull all the stops out, bend over backward, do one's utmost *or* best, make every effort.

mountaineer /mównt'neér/ *n. & v.* ● *n.* **1** a person skilled in mountain climbing. **2** a person living in an area of high mountains. ● *v.intr.* climb mountains as a sport. □□ **mountaineering** *n.*

mountainous /mównt'nəs/ *adj.* **1** (of a region) having many mountains. **2** huge.
■ **1** craggy, alpine, hilly, *Austral.* rangy. **2** huge, towering, high, steep, enormous, immense, formidable, mighty, monumental, prodigious, staggering; see also GIGANTIC.

mountainside /mównt'nsìd/ *n.* the slope of a mountain below the summit.

mountebank /mówntibángk/ *n.* **1** a swindler; a charlatan. **2** a clown. **3** *hist.* an itinerant quack appealing to an audience from a platform. □□ **mountebankery** *n.* [It. *montambanco* = *monta in banco* climb on bench: see MOUNT¹, BENCH]
■ **1** see *swindler* (SWINDLE). **2** see JOKER 1.

Mountie /mówntee/ *n. colloq.* a member of the Royal Canadian Mounted Police.

mounting /mównting/ *n.* **1** = MOUNT¹ *n.* 1. **2** in senses of MOUNT¹ *v.* □ **mounting block** a block of stone placed to help a rider mount a horse.

mourn /mawrn/ *v.* **1** *tr.* & (foll. by *for*) *intr.* feel *or* show deep sorrow *or* regret for (*a dead person, a lost thing, a past event, etc.*). **2** *intr.* show conventional signs of grief for a period after a person's death. [OE *murnan*]
■ grieve, lament, sorrow, bemoan, bewail, keen, weep; regret, rue.

mourner /mawrnər/ *n.* **1** a person who mourns, esp. at a funeral. **2** a person hired to attend a funeral.

mournful /máwrnfŏŏl/ *adj.* **1** doleful, sad, sorrowing. **2** ex-

pressing or suggestive of mourning. □□ **mournfully** *adv.* **mournfulness** *n.*
■ sad, sorrowful, sorrowing, dismal, melancholy, blue, afflicted, doleful, grief-stricken, rueful, forlorn, woebegone, somber, lugubrious, funereal, joyless, dispirited, cheerless, unhappy, downhearted, heavyhearted, disconsolate, heartbroken, inconsolable, despondent, desolate, despairing, heartsick, overcome, prostrate, *literary or joc.* dolorous; grievous, distressing, upsetting, tragic, saddening, disheartening, depressing, lamentable.

mourning /mawrning/ *n.* **1** the expression of deep sorrow, esp. for a dead person, by the wearing of solemn dress. **2** the clothes worn in mourning. □ **in mourning** assuming the signs of mourning, esp. in dress. **mourning band** a band of black crepe, etc., around a person's sleeve or hat as a token of mourning. **mourning dove** an American dove with a plaintive note, *Zenaida macroura*.
■ **1** grief, lament, grieving, lamentation, sorrowing, keening, weeping, wailing; anguish, sorrow, misery, sadness, woefulness, melancholy, heartache, despondency, despair, desolation, *archaic or literary* woe. **2** black, sackcloth (and ashes), *archaic* (widow's) weeds.

mousaka var. of MOUSSAKA.

mouse /mows/ *n. & v.* ● *n.* (*pl.* **mice** /mīs/) **1 a** any of various small rodents of the family Muridae, esp. of the genus *Mus*. **b** any of several similar rodents such as a small shrew or vole. **2** a timid or feeble person. **3** *Computing* a small hand-held device that controls the cursor on a computer monitor. **4** *sl.* a black eye. ● *v.intr.* /also mowz/ **1** (esp. of a cat, owl, etc.) hunt for or catch mice. **2** (foll. by *about*) search industriously; prowl about as if searching. □ **mouse-colored 1** dark gray with a yellow tinge. **2** nondescript light brown. **mouse deer** a chevrotain. **mouse hare** esp. *Brit.* a pika. □□ **mouselike** *adj. & adv.* **mouser** *n.* [OE *mūs, pl. mŷs* f. Gmc]
■ *n.* **2** see COWARD *n.* ● *v.* **2** see PROWL *v.* □ **mouse-colored 2** mousy, dun, gray, grayish-brown, brownish-gray, brownish, brown, dull-colored, drab.

mousetrap /mówstrap/ *n.* a spring trap with bait for catching and usu. killing mice.

moussaka /mōōsaáka, -saakaá/ *n.* (also **mousaka**) a Greek dish of ground meat, eggplant, etc., with a cheese sauce. [mod. Gk or Turk.]

mousse /mōōs/ *n.* **1 a** a dessert of whipped cream, eggs, etc., usu. flavored with fruit or chocolate. **b** a meat or fish purée made with whipped cream, etc. **2** a preparation applied to the hair enabling it to be styled more easily. **3** a mixture of oil and seawater which forms a froth on the surface of the water after an oil spill. [F, = moss, froth]

mousseline /mōōsleén/ *n.* **1** a muslinlike fabric of silk, etc. **2** a sauce lightened by the addition of whipped cream or eggs. [F: see MUSLIN]

moustache var. of MUSTACHE.

Mousterian /mōōsteéreeən/ *adj. Archaeol.* of or relating to the flint workings of the Middle Paleolithic epoch, dated to *c.*70,000–30,000 BC, and attributed to Neanderthal peoples. [F *moustérien* f. *Le Moustier* in SW France, where remains were found]

mousy /mówsee/ *adj.* (**mousier, mousiest**) **1** of or like a mouse. **2** (of a person) shy or timid; ineffectual. **3** = *mouse-colored*. □□ **mousily** *adv.* **mousiness** *n.*
■ **2** timid, cowering, timorous, shy, self-effacing, bashful, diffident, ineffectual.

mouth *n. & v.* ● *n.* /mowth/ (*pl.* **mouths** /mowthz/) **1 a** an external opening in the head, through which most animals admit food and emit communicative sounds. **b** (in humans and some animals) the cavity behind it containing the means

---

/. . ./ pronunciation	● **part of speech**
□ **phrases, idioms, and compounds**	
□□ **derivatives**	■ **synonym section**
cross-references appear in SMALL CAPITALS or *italics*	

of biting and chewing and the vocal organs. **2 a** the opening of a container such as a bag or sack. **b** the opening of a cave, volcano, etc. **c** the open end of a woodwind or brass instrument. **d** the muzzle of a gun. **3** the place where a river enters the sea. **4** *colloq.* **a** talkativeness. **b** impudent talk; cheek. **5** an individual regarded as needing sustenance (*an extra mouth to feed*). **6** a horse's readiness to feel and obey the pressure of the bit. **7** an expression of displeasure; a grimace ● *v.* /mowth/ **1** *tr.* & *intr.* utter or speak solemnly or with affectations; rant, declaim (*mouthing platitudes*). **2** *tr.* utter very distinctly. **3** *intr.* a move the lips silently. **b** grimace. **4** *tr.* take (food) in the mouth. **5** *tr.* touch with the mouth. **6** *tr.* train the mouth of (a horse). □ **keep one's mouth shut** *colloq.* not reveal a secret. **mouth organ** = HARMONICA. **mouth-to-mouth** (of resuscitation) in which a person breathes into a subject's lungs through the mouth. **put words into a person's mouth** represent a person as having said something in a particular way. **take the words out of a person's mouth** say what another was about to say. □□ **mouthed** /mowthd/ *adj.* (also in *comb.*). **mouther** /mówthər/ *n.* **mouthless** /mówthlis/ *adj.* [OE *mūth* f. Gmc]

■ *n.* **1** lips, jaws, orifice, *sl.* trap, kisser, chops, yap; muzzle, maw, esp. *Brit. sl.* gob, *Zool.* stoma. **2 a, b** opening, aperture, doorway, door, gateway, gate, access, entrance, entry, entryway, way in; exit, way out; passage, passageway, orifice, vent. **3** outfall, debouchment, embouchure, outlet. **4** talkativeness, garrulousness, loquaciousness; bragging, boasting, braggadocio, bombast, rodomontade, fustian, claptrap, *sl.* hot air, gas; disrespect, impudence, insolence, sauciness, rudeness, impertinence, pertness, boldness, audacity, presumptuousness, brashness, flippancy, cheek, *colloq.* lip, sauce, freshness, sass, back talk, *Brit. colloq.* backchat. **7** grimace, pout, moue, face. ● *v.* **1, 2** utter, say, speak, pronounce, announce, enunciate, articulate, voice, sound, express, vocalize; rant, declaim, esp. *joc. or derog.* orate. □ **keep one's mouth shut** play one's cards close to one's chest, give nothing away, not give the game away, keep quiet, say nothing, keep to oneself, tell no one, play dumb, not tell a soul, *colloq.* keep it under one's hat.

mouthful /mówthfool/ *n.* (*pl.* **-fuls**) **1** a quantity, esp. of food, that fills the mouth. **2** a small quantity. **3** a long or complicated word or phrase. **4** *colloq.* something important said.

■ **1** morsel, bite, spoonful, lump, chunk, hunk. **2** see MODICUM. **3** tongue-twister.

mouthpiece /mówthpees/ *n.* **1 a** the part of a musical instrument placed between or against the lips. **b** the part of a telephone for speaking into. **c** the part of a tobacco pipe placed between the lips. **2 a** a person who speaks for another or others. **b** *colloq.* a lawyer. **3** a part attached as an outlet.

■ **1 a** embouchure. **b** receiver, handset. **2 a** spokesman, spokeswoman, spokesperson, agent, representative, intermediator, mediator, delegate. **b** attorney, *colloq.* shyster; see also LAWYER.

mouthwash /mówthwosh, -wawsh/ *n.* **1** a liquid antiseptic, etc., for rinsing the mouth or gargling. **2** esp. *Brit. colloq.* nonsense.

■ **1** see WASH *n.* 7, 10.

mouthwatering /mówthwawtəring/ *adj.* **1** (of food, etc.) having a delicious smell or appearance. **2** tempting; alluring. □□ **mouthwateringly** *adv.*

mouthy /mówthee, -thee/ *adj.* (**mouthier, mouthiest**) **1** ranting, railing. **2** bombastic.

movable /móovəbəl/ *adj.* & *n.* (*also* **moveable**) ● *adj.* **1** that can be moved. **2** *Law* (of property) of the nature of a chattel, as distinct from land or buildings. **3** (of a feast or festival) variable in date from year to year. ● *n.* **1** an article of furniture that may be removed from a house, as distinct from a fixture. **2** (in *pl.*) personal property. □ **movable-do** *Mus.* applied to a system of sight-singing in which do is the keynote of any major scale (cf. *fixed-do*). **movable type** type in which each character is on a separate piece of metal.

□□ **movability** /-bílitee/ *n.* **movableness** *n.* **movably** *adv.* [ME f. OF (*as* MOVE)]

■ *adj.* **1** portable, transportable, transferable. **3** floating, variable, changeable, unfixed.

move /moov/ *v.* & *n.* ● *v.* **1** *intr.* & *tr.* change one's position or posture, or cause to do this. **2** *tr.* & *intr.* put or keep in motion; rouse, stir. **3 a** *intr.* make a move in a board game. **b** *tr.* change the position of (a piece) in a board game. **4** *intr.* (often foll. by *about, away*, etc.) go or pass from place to place. **5** *intr.* take action, esp. promptly (*moved to reduce unemployment*). **6** *intr.* make progress (*the project is moving fast*). **7** *intr.* **a** change one's place of residence. **b** (of a business, etc.) change to new premises (also *tr.*: *move offices*). **8** *intr.* (foll. by *in*) live or be socially active in (a specified place or group, etc.) (*moves in the best circles*). **9** *tr.* affect (a person) with (usu. tender or sympathetic) emotion. **10** *tr.* **a** (foll. by *in*) stimulate (laughter, anger, etc., in a person). **b** (foll. by *to*) provoke (a person to laughter, etc.). **11** *tr.* (foll. by *to*, or *to* + infin.) prompt or incline (a person to a feeling or action). **12 a** *tr.* cause (the bowels) to be evacuated. **b** *intr.* (of the bowels) be evacuated. **13** *tr.* (often foll. by *that* + clause) propose in a meeting, deliberative assembly, etc. **14** *intr.* (foll. by *for*) make a formal request or application. **15** *intr.* (of merchandise) be sold. ● *n.* **1** the act or an instance of moving. **2** a change of house, business premises, etc. **3** a step taken to secure some action or effect; an initiative. **4 a** the changing of the position of a piece in a board game. **b** a player's turn to do this. □ **get a move on** *colloq.* **1** hurry up. **2** make a start. **make a move** take action. **move along** (*or* **on**) change to a new position, esp. to avoid crowding, getting in the way, etc. **move heaven and earth** see HEAVEN. **move in 1** take possession of a new house. **2** get into a position of influence, interference, etc. **3** get into a position of readiness or proximity (for an offensive action, etc.). **move mountains** see MOUNTAIN. **move out 1** leave one's home; change one's place of residence. **2** leave a position, job, etc. **move over** (*or* **up**) adjust one's position to make room for another. **on the move 1** progressing. **2** moving about. [ME f. AF *mover*, OF *moveir* f. L *movēre mot-*]

■ *v.* **1, 4** shift, stir, budge, make a move, go, set off, start off; proceed, advance, progress, make headway, pass, travel, voyage, migrate, transfer; see also LEAVE[1] *v.* 1b, 3, 4. **2, 10, 11** arouse, rouse, provoke, actuate, lead, prompt, spur, motivate, influence, impel, inspire, incline, make, excite, stir (up); stimulate; prod, remind. **5** make a move, take action, take the initiative, begin *or* start to act, proceed, do something. **6** see PROGRESS *v.* 1. **7** move house, move out, move away, relocate, decamp, pull (up) stakes, leave, depart, change residence, emigrate, go *or* make *or* take off, transfer, *Brit. colloq.* up sticks, *formal* remove, *sl.* split. **8** circulate, mix, mingle, go around, move around, socialize, fraternize, keep company, hobnob, associate, *colloq.* hang around *or* about, *sl.* hang out. **9** affect, touch, stir (up), shake (up), agitate, hit (hard), upset, strike, disturb, ruffle, disquiet, have an effect on, make an impression on, *archaic or literary* smite; stir, agitate. **13, 14** propose, put forward *or* forth, forward, advance, submit, suggest, advocate, propound, request. ● *n.* **1, 2** gesture, gesticulation, action, motion, movement; stirring, change, changeover, relocation, transfer, shift, removal. **3** step, initiative; maneuver, device, trick, caper, dodge, stratagem, artifice, ruse, action, act, deed, gambit, *colloq.* ploy. **4 b** turn, time, opportunity, chance, *colloq.* shot, go. □ **get a move on 1** hurry (up), hasten, make haste, rush, run, *colloq.* step on it *or* on the gas. **2** begin, start, make a start, get started, get going, get moving, get under way, stir *or* bestir oneself, *colloq.* get cracking, get *or* set *or* start the ball rolling, get the show on the road, *formal* commence. **make a move** see MOVE *v.* 5 above. **move in 2** step in, intercede, intervene, become involved; see also INTRUDE 1. **move over** (*or* **up**) see SHIFT *v.* 1. **on the move 1** proceeding, progressing, advancing, moving ahead, succeeding, *colloq.* on the go. **2** traveling, in transit, on the way, on one's way, on the road, moving, *colloq.* on the go.

moveable var. of MOVABLE.

movement /mo͞ovmənt/ *n.* **1** the act or an instance of moving or being moved. **2 a** the moving parts of a mechanism (esp. a clock or watch). **b** a particular group of these. **3 a** a body of persons with a common object (*the peace movement*). **b** a campaign undertaken by such a body. **4** (usu. in *pl.*) a person's activities and whereabouts, esp. at a particular time. **5** *Mus.* a principal division of a longer musical work, self-sufficient in terms of key, tempo, structure, etc. **6** the progressive development of a poem, story, etc. **7** motion of the bowels. **8 a** an activity in a market for some commodity. **b** a rise or fall in price. **9** a mental impulse. **10** a development of position by a military force or unit. **11** a prevailing tendency in the course of events or conditions; trend. [ME f. OF f. med.L *movimentum* (as MOVE)]

■ **1** move, motion, relocation, repositioning, moving, migration, shift, transfer, flow, displacement; maneuver, maneuvering; action, activity, stir, stirring; gesture, gesticulation, flicker, sign, signal. **2** mechanism, works, workings, moving parts, machinery, action, gears, *colloq.* innards. **3** front, faction, party, group, wing, lobby; campaign, crusade, drive. **6** development, unfolding, progression, progress, momentum, advancement. **8** change, advance, activity, action, shift, decline, increase, decrease, rise, fall; progress, development. **11** drift, trend, tendency, course, swing.

mover /mo͞ovər/ *n.* **1** a person or thing that moves. **2** a person or company that moves household goods, etc., from one location to another as a business. **3** the author of a fruitful idea.

■ **3** see INSTRUMENT *n.* 3a.

movie /mo͞ovee/ *n.* esp. *colloq.* **1** a motion picture. **2** (**the movies**) **a** the motion-picture industry or medium. **b** the showing of a movie (*going to the movies*). □ **movie house** a theater that shows movies [abbr. of moving picture]

■ motion picture, film, moving picture, *colloq.* flick, talkie; cinema.

moviedom /mo͞oveedəm/ *n.* the movie industry and its associated businesses, personnel, etc.

moving /mo͞oving/ *adj.* **1** that moves or causes to move. **2** affecting with emotion. □ **moving picture** a continuous picture of events obtained by projecting a sequence of photographs taken at very short intervals. **moving staircase** esp. *Brit.* an escalator. **moving van** a large van used to move furniture, household goods, etc., from one house to another. □□ **movingly** *adv.* (in sense 2).

■ **1** active, mobile, unfixed, traveling, going, operating, working, in motion, on the move. **2** touching, poignant, emotive, affecting, pathetic, heartbreaking, heartrending, emotional, telling, effective, impressive, striking, compelling; stirring, exciting, thrilling, inspiring, inspirational, persuasive.

mow¹ /mō/ *v.tr.* (*past part.* **mowed** or **mown**) **1** cut down (grass, hay, etc.) with a scythe or machine. **2** cut down the produce of (a field) or the grass, etc., of (a lawn) by mowing. □ **mow down** kill or destroy randomly or in great numbers. □□ **mowable** *adj.* **mower** *n.* [OE *māwan* f. Gmc, rel. to MEAD²]

■ cut (down), scythe, trim, shear. □ **mow down** annihilate, kill, massacre, butcher, slaughter, exterminate, liquidate, eradicate, wipe out, cut down, cut to pieces, destroy, *disp.* decimate.

mow² /mow/ *n. dial.* **1** a stack of hay, wheat, etc. **2** a place in a barn where hay, etc., is heaped. [OE *mūga*]

moxa /móksə/ *n.* a downy substance from the dried leaves of *Artemisia moxa*, etc., burned on the skin in Eastern medicine as a counterirritant. [Jap. *mogusa* f. *moe kusa* burning herb]

moxie /móksee/ *n. sl.* energy, courage, daring. [trade name of a drink]

mozzarella /mótsərélə/ *n.* an Italian semisoft cheese. [It.]

mozzle /mózəl/ *n. Austral. colloq.* luck, fortune. [Heb. *mazzā*]

MP *abbr.* **1 a** military police. **b** military policeman. **2** Member of Parliament.

■ **2** see POLITICIAN.

mp *abbr.* mezzo piano.

m.p. *abbr.* melting point.

m.p.g. *abbr.* miles per gallon.

m.p.h. *abbr.* miles per hour.

■ see VELOCITY 3.

Mr. /místər/ *n.* (*pl.* **Messrs.**) **1** the respectful title of a man without a higher title (*Mr. Jones*). **2** a title prefixed to a designation of office, etc. (*Mr. President; Mr. Speaker*). □ **Mr. Big** *sl.* the head of an organization; any important person. **Mr. Right** *joc.* a woman's destined husband. [abbr. of MISTER]

MRI *abbr.* magnetic resonance imaging.

mRNA *abbr. Biol.* messenger RNA.

Mrs. /mísiz/ *n.* (*pl.* same or **Mesdames**) the respectful title of a married woman without a higher title (*Mrs. Jones*). [abbr. of MISTRESS: cf. MISSUS]

MS *abbr.* **1** Mississippi (in official postal use). **2** Master of Science. **3** multiple sclerosis. **4** (also **ms.**) manuscript.

Ms. /miz/ *n.* form of address for a woman, used regardless of marital status. [combination of MRS., MISS²]

M.Sc. *abbr.* Master of Science.

MS-DOS /émesdáws, -dós/ *abbr. propr.* a microcomputer disk operating system.

MSG *abbr.* monosodium glutamate.

Msgr. *abbr.* **1** Monseigneur. **2** Monsignor.

MSS *abbr.* (also **mss.**) manuscripts.

MST *abbr.* Mountain Standard Time.

MT *abbr.* **1** Montana (in official postal use). **2** Mountain Time. **3** mechanical transport.

Mt *abbr.* MEITNERIUM.

Mt. *abbr.* **1** mount. **2** mountain

mu /myo͞o, mo͞o/ *n.* **1** the twelfth Greek letter (M, μ). **2** (μ, as a symbol) = MICRO- 2. □ **mu-meson** = MUON. [Gk]

much /much/ *adj., n.,* & *adv.* ● *adj.* **1** existing or occurring in a great quantity (*much trouble; not much rain; too much noise*). **2** (prec. by *as, how, that*, etc.) with relative rather than distinctive sense (*I don't know how much money you want*). ● *n.* **1** a great quantity (*much of that is true*). **2** (prec. by *as, how, that*, etc.) with relative rather than distinctive sense (*we do not need that much*). **3** (usu. in *neg.*) a noteworthy or outstanding example (*not much to look at; not much of a party*). ● *adv.* **1 a** in a great degree (*much to my surprise; is much the same*). **b** (qualifying a verb or past participle) greatly (*they much regret the mistake; I was much annoyed*). ¶ *Much* implies a strong verbal element in the participle, whereas *very* implies a strong adjectival element: compare the second example above with *I was very annoyed*. **c** qualifying a comparative or superlative adjective (*much better; much the most likely*). **2** for a large part of one's time (*is much away from home*). □ **as much** the extent or quantity just specified; the idea just mentioned (*I thought as much; as much as that?*). **a bit much** *colloq.* somewhat excessive or immoderate. **make much of** see MAKE. **much as** even though (*cannot come, much as I would like to*). **much less** see LESS. **much obliged** see OBLIGE. **not much** *colloq.* **1** *iron.* very much. **2** certainly not. **not much in it** see IN. **too much** *colloq.* an intolerable situation, etc. (*that really is too much*). **too much for 1** more than a match for. **2** beyond what is endurable by. □□ **muchly** *adv. joc.* [ME f. *muchel* MICKLE: for loss of *el* cf. BAD, WENCH]

■ *n.* **1** see LOT *n.* 1. ● *adv.* **2** see OFTEN.

muchness /múchnis/ *n.* greatness in quantity or degree. □ **much of a muchness** very nearly the same or alike.

mucilage /myo͞osilij/ *n.* **1** a viscous substance obtained from plant seeds, etc., by maceration. **2** a solution of gum, glue,

---

/.../ **pronunciation**	● **part of speech**
□ **phrases, idioms, and compounds**	
□□ **derivatives**	■ **synonym section**
cross-references appear in SMALL CAPITALS or *italics*	

etc. ▫▫ **mucilaginous** /-lájinəs/ *adj.* [ME f. F f. LL *mucilago -ginis* musty juice (MUCUS)]

muck /muk/ *n. & v.* ● *n.* **1** farmyard manure. **2** *colloq.* dirt or filth; anything disgusting. **3** *colloq.* an untidy state; a mess. ● *v.tr.* **1** (usu. foll. by *up*) *colloq.* bungle (a job). **2** (often foll. by *out*) remove muck from. **3** make dirty or untidy. **4** manure with muck. ▫ **make a muck of** *colloq.* bungle. **muck about** (or **around**) esp. *Brit. colloq.* **1** putter or fool about. **2** (foll. by *with*) fool or interfere with. [ME *muk* prob. f. Scand.: cf. ON *myki* dung, rel. to MEEK]
■ *n.* **1, 2** ordure, manure, dung, excrement, feces, droppings, guano; dirt, filth, bilge, slime, sludge, ooze, scum, sewage, mire, mud, feculence, *Brit. colloq.* gunge, *sl.* gunk, grunge. **3** see MESS *n.* 1. ● *v.* **1** (*muck up*) muff (up), spoil, make a mess of, botch, mess up, bungle, *colloq.* make a muck of, foul up, *sl.* screw up, *Brit. sl.* cock up. ▫ **make a muck of** see MUCK *v.* above. **muck about 1** putter *or* fool about *or* around, waste time, idle, loiter, mess around *or* about. **2** (*muck about with*) see INTERFERE 1.

muckle var. of MICKLE.

muckrake /múkrayk/ *v.intr.* search out and reveal scandal, esp. among famous people. ▫▫ **muckraker** *n.* **muckraking** *n.*

mucky /múkee/ *adj.* (**muckier, muckiest**) **1** covered with muck. **2** dirty. ▫▫ **muckiness** *n.*
■ see DIRTY *adj.* 1.

muco- /myo͞okō/ *comb. form Biochem.* mucus, mucous.

mucopolysaccharide /myo͞okōpóleesákərid/ *n. Biochem.* any of a group of polysaccharides whose molecules contain sugar residues and are often found as components of connective tissue.

mucosa /myo͞okṓsə/ *n.* (*pl.* **mucosae** /-see/) a mucous membrane. [mod.L, fem. of *mucosus*: see MUCOUS]

mucous /myo͞okəs/ *adj.* of or covered with mucus. ▫ **mucous membrane** a mucus-secreting epithelial tissue lining many body cavities and tubular organs. ▫▫ **mucosity** /-kósitee/ *n.* [L *mucosus* (as MUCUS)]
■ see SLIMY 1, 2.

mucro /myo͞okrō/ *n.* (*pl.* **mucrones** /-krṓneez/) *Bot. & Zool.* a sharp-pointed part or organ. ▫▫ **mucronate** /-krənət, -nayt/ *adj.* [L *mucro -onis* sharp point]

mucus /myo͞okəs/ *n.* **1** a slimy substance secreted by a mucous membrane. **2** a gummy substance found in all plants. **3** a slimy substance exuded by some animals, esp. fishes. [L]

mud /mud/ *n.* **1** wet, soft, earthy matter. **2** hard ground from the drying of an area of this. **3** what is worthless or polluting. ▫ **as clear as mud** *colloq.* not at all clear. **fling** (or **sling** or **throw**) **mud** speak disparagingly or slanderously. **here's mud in your eye!** *colloq.* a drinking toast. **mud bath 1** a bath in the mud of mineral springs, esp. to relieve rheumatism, etc. **2** a muddy scene or occasion. **mud brick** a brick made from baked mud; adobe. **mud flat** a stretch of muddy land left uncovered at low tide. **mud puppy** a large nocturnal salamander, *Necturus maculosus*, of eastern US. **mud volcano** a volcano discharging mud. **one's name is mud** one is unpopular or in disgrace. [ME *mode, mudde*, prob. f. MLG *mudde*, MHG *mot* bog]
■ **1** muck, ooze, slime, mire, clay, sludge, silt, dirt.
▫ **fling** (or **sling** or **throw**) **mud** see DISPARAGE *v.*

muddle /múd'l/ *v. & n.* ● *v.* **1** *tr.* (often foll. by *up, together*) bring into disorder. **2** *tr.* bewilder, confuse. **3** *tr.* mismanage (an affair). **4** *tr.* crush and mix (the ingredients for a drink). **5** *intr.* (often foll. by *with*) busy oneself in a confused and ineffective way. ● *n.* **1** disorder. **2** a muddled condition. ▫ **make a muddle of 1** bring into disorder. **2** bungle. **muddle along** (or **on**) progress in a haphazard way. **muddle-headed** stupid, confused. **muddle-headedness** stupidity; a confused state. **muddle through** succeed by perseverance rather than skill or efficiency. **muddle up** confuse (two or more things). ▫▫ **muddler** *n.* **muddlingly** *adv.* [perh. f. MDu. *moddelen*, frequent. of *modden* dabble in mud (as MUD)]
■ *v.* **1, 3** confuse, mix up, jumble, scramble, entangle,

tangle, mess up, disorder, muddle up, disarrange, disorganize; bungle, botch, mismanage, muff. **2** bewilder, confuse, confound, mystify, baffle, mix up, disorient(ate), befuddle, perplex, bemuse, puzzle, befog. ● *n.* mess, confusion, mix-up, jumble, tangle, disorder, hodgepodge, mishmash, *colloq.* stew, *sl.* screw-up, snafu, *Brit. sl.* cock-up. ▫ **muddle along** (or **on**) see MANAGE *v.* 2, 3, 5a. **muddle-headed** see STUPID *adj.* 1, 5, *confused* (CONFUSE 4). **muddle-headedness** see *stupidity* (STUPID). **muddle through** manage, cope, make it, scrape by *or* through *or* along, contrive, make do, get by *or* along. **muddle up** see MUDDLE *v.* 1, 3 above.

muddy /múdee/ *adj. & v.* ● *adj.* (**muddier, muddiest**) **1** like mud. **2** covered in or full of mud. **3** (of liquid) turbid. **4** mentally confused. **5** obscure. **6** (of light) dull. **7** (of color) impure. ● *v.tr.* (**-ies, -ied**) make muddy. ▫▫ **muddily** *adv.* **muddiness** *n.*
■ *adj.* **2** fouled, muddied, mud-spattered, dirty, grubby, grimy, soiled, mud-caked, slimy, mucky, miry, *poet.* befouled; oozy, squelchy, squishy, squashy, boggy, fenny, marshy, swampy, feculent. **4, 5** confused, muddled, addled, mixed-up; unclear, vague, obscure, dull, dim, fuzzy. **6, 7** drab, dull, subdued, blurred, dingy, matte, washed out, flat; murky, impure. ● *v.* dirty, soil, begrime, smirch, besmirch, spatter, bespatter; obscure, dull, dim, confuse, mix up, befog, cloud.

mudfish /múdfish/ *n.* any fish that burrows in mud, as the bowfin.

mudflap /múdflap/ *n.* a flap hanging behind the wheel of a vehicle, to catch mud and stones, etc., thrown up from the road.

mudguard /múdgaard/ *n.* a curved strip or cover over a wheel of a bicycle or motorcycle to reduce the amount of mud, etc., thrown up from the road.

mudlark /múdlaark/ *n. Brit.* **1** *hist.* a destitute person, esp. a child, searching in river mud for objects of value. **2** *hist.* a street urchin.
■ **2** see GUTTERSNIPE.

mudstone /múdstōn/ *n.* a dark clay rock.

muesli /mo͞oslee, myóoz-/ *n.* a breakfast food of crushed cereals, dried fruits, nuts, etc., eaten with milk. [Swiss G]

muezzin /myo͞o-ézin, moō-/ *n.* a Muslim crier who proclaims the hours of prayer, usu. from a minaret. [Arab. *mu'addin* part. of '*addana* proclaim]

muff[1] /muf/ *n.* a fur or other covering, usu. in the form of a tube with an opening at each end for the hands to be inserted for warmth. [Du. *mof*, MDu. *moffel, muffel* f. med.L *muff(u)la*, of unkn. orig.]

muff[2] /muf/ *v. & n.* ● *v.tr.* **1** bungle; deal clumsily with. **2** fail to catch or receive (a ball, etc.). **3** blunder in (a theatrical part, etc.). ● *n.* **1** esp. *Brit.* a person who is awkward or stupid, orig. in some athletic sport. **2** a failure, esp. to catch a ball in baseball, etc. ▫▫ **muffish** *adj.* [19th c.: orig. unkn.]
■ *v.* **1** see BOTCH *v.* 1.

muffin /múfin/ *n.* a small cake or quick bread made from batter or dough and baked in a muffin pan. [18th c.: orig. unkn.]

muffle[1] /múfəl/ *v. & n.* ● *v.tr.* **1** (often foll. by *up*) wrap or cover for warmth. **2** cover or wrap up (a source of sound) to reduce its loudness. **2** (usu. as **muffled** *adj.*) stifle (an utterance, e.g., a curse). **4** prevent from speaking. ● *n.* **1** a receptacle in a furnace where substances may be heated without contact with combustion products. **2** a similar chamber in a kiln for baking painted pottery. [ME: (n.) f. OF *moufle* thick glove; (v.) perh. f. OF *enmoufler* f. *moufle*]
■ *v.* **1** wrap, swathe, swaddle, cloak, envelop, cover (up), enfold, shroud, conceal, protect, *literary* enshroud. **2–4** deaden, silence, suppress, stifle, subdue, damp (down), dampen, mute, hush, quiet(en), tone down, still.

muffle[2] /múfəl/ *n.* the thick part of the upper lip and nose of ruminants and rodents. [F *mufle*, of unkn. orig.]

muffler /múflər/ *n.* **1** a wrap or scarf worn for warmth. **2** a noise-reducing device on a motor vehicle's exhaust system. **3 a** *Brit.* any of various devices used to deaden sound in musical instruments. **b** a mute. ■ **1** scarf, shawl, wrap, stole, boa.

mufti[1] /múftee/ *n.* a Muslim legal expert empowered to give rulings on religious matters. [Arab. *muftī*, part. of *'aftā* decide a point of law]

mufti[2] /múftee/ *n.* plain clothes worn by a person who also wears (esp. military) uniform (*in mufti*). [19th c.: perh. f. MUFTI[1]]

mug[1] /mug/ *n. & v.* ● *n.* **1 a** a drinking vessel, usu. cylindrical and with a handle and used without a saucer. **b** its contents. **2** *sl.* the face or mouth of a person. **3** *sl.* a hoodlum or thug. **4** *Brit. sl.* **a** a simpleton. **b** a gullible person. ● *v.* (**mugged, mugging**) **1** *tr.* rob (a person) with violence, esp. in a public place. **2** *tr.* fight; thrash. **3** *tr.* strangle. **4** *intr. sl.* make faces, esp. before an audience, a camera, etc. □ **a mug's game** *colloq.* a foolish or unprofitable activity. **mug shot** *sl.* a photograph of a face, esp. for official purposes. □□ **mugger** *n.* (esp. in sense 1 of *v.*). **mugful** *n.* (*pl.* **-fuls**). **mugging** *n.* (in sense 1 of *v.*). [prob. f. Scand.: sense 2 of *n.* prob. f. the representation of faces on mugs, and sense 3 prob. from this]

■ *n.* **1** jug, tankard, stein, toby jug, pot, schooner, beaker, cup, jar, flagon, *archaic* stoup. **2** face, features, countenance, mouth, *Brit. colloq.* phiz, phizog, *literary* visage, *sl.* pan, kisser, mush, *Brit. sl.* clock, dial. **3** see THUG. **4** fool, simpleton, dupe, gull, innocent, *colloq.* chump, soft *or* easy touch, *Brit. colloq.* muggins, *sl.* sucker, duffer, *Austral. sl.* dill. ● *v.* **1** set upon, rob, assault; see also ATTACK *v.* 1. **2** see BEAT *v.* 1. **3** strangle, garrotte, throttle; stifle, suffocate, smother, choke, asphyxiate. **4** make *or* pull a face, grimace.

mug[2] /mug/ *v.tr.* (**mugged, mugging**) *Brit.* (usu. foll. by *up*) *sl.* learn (a subject) by concentrated study. [19th c.: orig. unkn.]

■ (*mug up*) study, get up, *Brit. colloq.* swot (up), bone up, *literary* lucubrate.

mugger[1] see MUG[1].

mugger[2] /múgər/ *n.* a broad-nosed E. Indian crocodile, *Crocodylus palustris*, venerated by many Hindus. [Hindi *magar*]

muggins /múginz/ *n. Brit.* (*pl.* same or **mugginses**) **1** *colloq.* **a** a simpleton. **b** a person who is easily outwitted (often with allusion to oneself: *so muggins had to pay*). **2** a card game like snap. [perh. the surname *Muggins*, with allusion to MUG[1]]

■ **1** see DOLT.

muggy /múgee/ *adj.* (**muggier, muggiest**) (of the weather, a day, etc.) oppressively damp and warm; humid. □□ **mugginess** *n.* [dial. *mug* mist, drizzle f. ON *mugga*]

■ humid, damp, sticky, sultry, oppressive, steamy, close, stuffy; moist, soggy.

Mughal /mo͞ogaal/ *n.* **1** a Mongolian. **2** (*attrib.*) denoting the Muslim dynasty in India in the 16th–19th c. (cf. MOGUL 2b). [Pers. *mugūl* MONGOL]

mugwort /múgwərt, -wawrt/ *n.* any of various plants of the genus *Artemisia*, esp. *A. vulgaris*, with silver-gray aromatic foliage. [OE *mucgwyrt* (as MIDGE, WORT)]

mugwump /múgwump/ *n.* **1** a great man; a boss. **2** a person who remains aloof, esp. from party politics. [Algonquian *mugquomp* great chief]

Muhammadan /məhámád'n/ *n. & adj.* (also **Mohammedan**) = MUSLIM. ¶ A term not used or favored by Muslims, and often regarded as *offens.* □□ **Muhammadanism** *n.* [*Muhammad*, Arabian prophet d. 632]

mujahidin /mo͞ojaahidéen/ *n.pl.* (also **mujahedin, -deen**) guerrilla fighters in Islamic countries, esp. supporting Muslim fundamentalism. [Pers. & Arab. *mujāhidīn* pl. of *mujāhid* one who fights a JIHAD]

mulatto /mo͞olátó, -laá-, myo͞o-/ *n. & adj.* ● *n.* (*pl.* **-oes** or **-os**) a person of mixed white and black parentage. ● *adj.* of the color of mulattoes; tawny. [Sp. *mulato* young mule, *mulatto*, irreg. f. *mulo* MULE[1]]

mulberry /múlberee, -bəree/ *n.* (*pl.* **-ies**) **1** any deciduous tree of the genus *Morus*, grown originally for feeding silkworms, and now for its fruit and ornamental qualities. **2** its dark-red or white berry. **3** a dark-red or purple color. [ME *mol-*, *mool-*, *mulberry*, dissim. f. *murberie* f. OE *mōrberie*, f. L *morum*: see BERRY]

mulch /mulch/ *n. & v.* ● *n.* a mixture of straw, leaves, etc., spread around or over a plant to enrich or insulate the soil. ● *v.tr.* treat with mulch. [prob. use as noun of *mulsh* soft: cf. dial. *melsh* mild f. OE *melsc*]

■ *v.* see FERTILIZE 1.

mulct /mulkt/ *v. & n.* ● *v.tr.* **1** extract money from by fine or taxation. **2 a** (often foll. by *of*) deprive by fraudulent means; swindle. **b** obtain by swindling. ● *n.* a fine. [earlier *mult(e)* f. L *multa, mulcta*: (v.) through F *mulcter* & L *mulctare*]

■ *v.* **1** see FINE[2] *v.* **2** see SWINDLE *v.* ● *n.* see FINE[2] *n.*

mule[1] /myo͞ol/ *n.* **1** the offspring (usu. sterile) of a male donkey and a female horse, or (in general use) of a female donkey and a male horse (cf. HINNY[1]), used as a beast of burden. **2** a stupid or obstinate person. **3** (often *attrib.*) a hybrid and usu. sterile plant or animal (*mule canary*). **4** (in full **spinning mule**) a kind of spinning machine producing yarn on spindles. [ME f. OF *mul(e)* f. L *mulus mula*]

mule[2] /myo͞ol/ *n.* a light shoe or slipper without a back. [F]

muleteer /myo͞olitéer/ *n.* a mule driver. [F *muletier* f. *mulet* dimin. of OF *mul* MULE[1]]

mulga /múlgə/ *n. Austral.* **1** a small spreading tree, *Acacia aneura*. **2** the wood of this tree. **3** scrub or bush. **4** *colloq.* the outback. [Aboriginal]

muliebrity /myo͞olee-ébrite/ *n. literary* **1** womanhood. **2** the normal characteristics of a woman. **3** softness, effeminacy. [LL *muliebritas* f. L *mulier* woman]

mulish /myo͞olish/ *adj.* **1** like a mule. **2** stubborn. □□ **mulishly** *adv.* **mulishness** *n.*

■ **2** see STUBBORN.

mull[1] /mul/ *v.tr. & intr.* (often foll. by *over*) ponder or consider. [perh. f. *mull* grind to powder, ME *mul* dust f. MDu.]

■ (*mull over*) ponder, consider, study, think over *or* about, cerebrate, cogitate (on *or* over *or* about), evaluate, turn over, weigh (up), deliberate (on *or* over), reflect on, review, examine, contemplate, meditate (on), chew over, ruminate (on *or* over), *archaic* con (over), *literary* muse on.

mull[2] /mul/ *v.tr.* warm (wine or beer) with added sugar, spices, etc. [17th c.: orig. unkn.]

mull[3] /mul/ *n. Sc.* a promontory. [ME: cf. Gael. *maol*, Icel. *múli*]

mull[4] /mul/ *n.* humus formed under nonacid conditions. [G f. Da. *muld*]

mull[5] /mul/ *n.* a thin, soft, plain muslin. [abbr. of *mulmull* Hindi *malmal*]

mullah /múlə, mo͞ol-/ *n.* a Muslim learned in Islamic theology and sacred law. [Pers., Turk., Urdu *mullā* f. Arab. *mawlā*]

mullein /múlin/ *n.* any herbaceous plant of the genus *Verbascum*, with woolly leaves and yellow flowers. [ME f. OF *moleine* f. Gaulish]

muller /múlər/ *n.* a stone or other heavy weight used for grinding material on a slab. [ME, perh. f. AF *moldre* grind]

mullet /múlit/ *n.* any fish of the family Mullidae (**red mullet**) or Mugilidae (**gray mullet**), usu. with a thick body and a large blunt-nosed head, commonly used as food. [ME f. OF *mulet* dimin. f. L *mullus* red mullet f. Gk *mollos*]

mulligatawny /múligətáwnee/ *n.* a highly seasoned soup orig. from India. [Tamil *milagutannir* pepper water]

mullion /múlyən/ *n.* (also **munnion** /mún-/) a vertical bar dividing the panes in a window (cf. TRANSOM). □□ **mullioned** *adj.* [prob. an altered form of MONIAL]

mulloway /múləway/ *n. Austral.* a large marine fish, *Sciaena antarctica*, used as food. [19th c.: orig. unkn.]

/. . ./ **pronunciation**	● **part of speech**
□ **phrases, idioms, and compounds**	
□□ **derivatives**	■ **synonym section**
cross-references appear in SMALL CAPITALS or *italics*	

multangular /multánggyələr/ *adj.* having many angles. [med.L *multangularis* (as MULTI-, ANGULAR)]

multi- /múltee, -tī/ *comb. form* many; more than one. [L f. *multus* much, many]

multi-access /múlteeákses, -tī-/ *n.* (often *attrib.*) the simultaneous connection to a computer of a number of terminals.

multiaxial /múlteeákseeəl/ *adj.* of or involving several axes.

multicellular /múlteesélyələr, -tī-/ *adj. Biol.* having many cells.

multichannel /múlteechánəl, -tī-/ *adj.* employing or possessing many communication or television channels.

multicolor /múltikúlər/ *adj.* (also **multicolored**) of many colors.

■ see *variegated* (VARIEGATE 1, 3).

multicultural /múlteekúlchərəl/ *adj.* of or relating to or constituting several cultural or ethnic groups within a society. □□ **multiculturalism** *n.* **multiculturally** *adv.*

multidimensional /múlteedimén shənəl, -dī-/ *adj.* of or involving more than three dimensions. □□ **multidimensionality** /-nálitee/ *n.* **multidimensionally** *adv.*

multidirectional /múlteedirékshənəl, -dī-, -tī-/ *adj.* of, involving, or operating in several directions.

multifaceted /múlteefásitid, -tī-/ *adj.* having several facets.

■ see SOPHISTICATED 2.

multifarious /múltifáireeəs/ *adj.* **1** (foll. by pl. noun) many and various. **2** having great variety. □□ **multifariously** *adv.* **multifariousness** *n.* [L *multifarius*]

■ see VARIOUS 2.

multifid /múltifid/ *adj. Bot. & Zool.* divided into many parts. [L *multifidus* (as MULTI-, *fid-* stem of *findere* cleave)]

multifoil /múltifoyl/ *n. Archit.* an ornament consisting of more than five foils.

multiform /múltifawrm/ *n.* (usu. *attrib.*) **1** having many forms. **2** of many kinds. □□ **multiformity** /-fáwrmitee/ *n.*

■ see DIVERS.

multifunctional /múlteefúngkshənəl, -tī-/ *adj.* having or fulfilling several functions.

multigrade /múltigrayd/ *n.* (usu. *attrib.*) an engine oil, etc., meeting the requirements of several standard grades.

multilateral /múltilátərəl/ *adj.* **1 a** (of an agreement, treaty, conference, etc.) in which three or more parties participate. **b** performed by more than two parties (*multilateral disarmament*). **2** having many sides. □□ **multilaterally** *adv.*

multilingual /múlteelínggwəl, -tī-/ *adj.* in or using several languages. □□ **multilingually** *adv.*

multimedia /múltimeédeeə/ *adj. & n.* ● *attrib. adj.* involving several media. ● *n.* the combined use of several media, such as film, print, sound, etc.

multimillion /múlteemílyən, -tī-/ *attrib. adj.* costing or involving several million (dollars, pounds, etc.) (*multimillion-dollar fraud*).

multimillionaire /múlteemílyənáir, -tī-/ *n.* a person with a fortune of several millions.

multinational /múlteenáshənəl, -tī-/ *adj. & n.* ● *adj.* **1** (of a business organization) operating in several countries. **2** relating to or including several nationalities or ethnic groups. ● *n.* a multinational company. □□ **multinationally** *adv.*

multinomial /múltinṓmeeəl/ *adj. & n. Math.* = POLYNOMIAL. [MULTI-, after *binomial*]

multiparous /multípərəs/ *adj.* **1** bringing forth many young at a birth. **2** having borne more than one child. [MULTI- + -PAROUS]

multipartite /múltipáartīt/ *adj.* divided into many parts.

multiphase /múltifayz/ *n. Electr.* = POLYPHASE.

multiple /múltipəl/ *adj. & n.* ● *adj.* **1** having several or many parts, elements, or individual components. **2** (foll. by pl. noun) many and various. **3** *Bot.* (of fruit) collective. ● *n.* a number that may be divided by another a certain number of times without a remainder (*56 is a multiple of 7*). □ **least** (or **lowest**) **common multiple** the least quantity that is a multiple of two or more given quantities. **multiple-choice** (of a question in an examination) accompanied by several possible answers from which the correct one has to be chosen. **multiple personality** *Psychol.* the apparent existence

of two or more distinct personalities in one individual. **multiple sclerosis** see SCLEROSIS. **multiple shop** (or **store**) *Brit.* = *chain store*. **multiple standard** see STANDARD. **multiple star** several stars so close as to seem one, esp. when forming a connected system. □□ **multiply** *adv.* [F f. LL *multiplus* f. L (as MULTIPLEX)]

multiplex /múltipleks/ *adj., v., & n.* ● *adj.* **1** manifold; of many elements. **2** involving simultaneous transmission of several messages along a single channel of communication. ● *v.tr.* incorporate into a multiplex signal or system. ● *n.* a building that houses several movie theaters □□ **multiplexer** *n.* (also **multiplexor**). [L (as MULTI-, *-plex -plicis* -fold)]

■ *adj.* **1** see MANIFOLD *adj.*

multipliable /múltipliəbəl/ *adj.* that can be multiplied.

multiplicable /múltiplíkəbəl/ *adj.* = MULTIPLIABLE. [OF *multiplicable* or med.L *multiplicabilis* f. L (as MULTIPLY)]

multiplicand /múltiplikánd/ *n.* a quantity to be multiplied by a multiplier. [med.L *multiplicandus* gerundive of L *multiplicare* (as MULTIPLY)]

multiplication /múltiplikáyshən/ *n.* **1** the arithmetical process of multiplying. **2** the act or an instance of multiplying. □ **multiplication sign** the sign (×) to indicate that one quantity is to be multiplied by another, as in $2 \times 3 = 6$. **multiplication table** a list of multiples of a particular number, usu. from 1 to 12. □□ **multiplicative** /-plíkətiv/ *adj.* [ME f. OF *multiplication* or L *multiplicatio* (as MULTIPLY)]

■ **2** see INCREASE *n.* 1, 2.

multiplicity /múltiplísitee/ *n.* (*pl.* **-ies**) **1** manifold variety. **2** (foll. by *of*) a great number. [LL *multiplicitas* (as MULTIPLEX)]

■ **1** see VARIETY 2.

multiplier /múltipliər/ *n.* **1** a quantity by which a given number is multiplied. **2** *Econ.* a factor by which an increment of income exceeds the resulting increment of saving or investment. **3** *Electr.* an instrument for increasing by repetition the intensity of a current, force, etc.

multiply /múltipli/ *v.* (**-ies, -ied**) **1** *tr.* (also *absol.*) obtain from (a number) another that is a specified number of times its value (*multiply 6 by 4 and you get 24*). **2** *intr.* increase in number esp. by procreation. **3** *tr.* produce a large number of (instances, etc.). **4** *tr.* **a** breed (animals). **b** propagate (plants). [ME f. OF *multiplier* f. L *multiplicare* (as MULTIPLEX)]

■ **2** see INCREASE *v.* 1.

multipolar /múltipṓlər/ *adj.* having many poles (see POLE²).

multiprocessing /múlteeprṓsesing/ *n. Computing* processing by a number of processors sharing a common memory and common peripherals.

multiprogramming /múlteeprṓgraming/ *n. Computing* the execution of two or more independent programs concurrently.

multipurpose /múlteepə́rpəs, -tī-/ *n.* (*attrib.*) having several purposes.

■ see VERSATILE 2.

multiracial /múlteeráyshəl, -tī-/ *adj.* relating to or made up of many human races. □□ **multiracially** *adv.*

multirole /múlteerṓl/ *n.* (*attrib.*) having several roles or functions.

multistage /múltistayj/ *n.* (*attrib.*) (of a rocket, etc.) having several stages of operation.

multistory /múltistáwree/ *n.* (*attrib.*) (of a building) having several (esp. similarly designed) stories.

multitude /múltitōōd, -tyōōd/ *n.* **1** (often foll. by *of*) a great number. **2** a large gathering of people; a crowd. **3** (**the multitude**) the common people. **4** the state of being numerous. [ME f. OF f. L *multitudo -dinis* f. *multus* many]

■ **1** see MANY *n.* 1. **2** see CROWD *n.* 1. **3** see PEOPLE *n.* 2.

multitudinous /múltitōōd'nəs, -tyōōd-/ *adj.* **1** very numerous. **2** consisting of many individuals or elements. **3** (of an ocean, etc.) vast. □□ **multitudinously** *adv.* **multitudinousness** *n.* [L (as MULTITUDE)]

■ **1, 2** see MANY *adj.*

multiuser /múltiyōōzər/ *n.* (*attrib.*) (of a computer system) having a number of simultaneous users (cf. MULTI-ACCESS).

multivalent /múltiváylənt, multívə-/ *adj. Chem.* **1** having a valence of more than two. **2** having a variable valency. □□ **multivalency** *n.*

multivalve /múltivalv/ *n.* (*attrib.*) (of a shell, etc.) having several valves.

multiversity /múltivérsitee/ *n.* (*pl.* **-ies**) a large university with many different departments. [MULTI- + UNIVERSITY]

multivocal /multívəkəl/ *adj.* having many meanings.

mum¹ /mum/ *adj. colloq.* silent (*keep mum*). □ **mum's the word** say nothing. [ME: imit. of closed lips]

■ silent, mute, close-mouthed, quiet, tight-lipped. □ **mum's the word** don't tell a soul, keep quiet, keep it to yourself, say nothing, tell no one, play dumb, *colloq.* keep it under one's hat, *sl.* button one's lip.

mum² /mum/ *v.intr.* (**mummed, mumming**) act in a traditional masked mime. [cf. MUM² and MLG *mummen*]

mum³ /mum/ *n.* = CHRYSANTHEMUM.

mum⁴ /mum/ *n. Brit. colloq.* mother. [abbr. of MUMMY]

mumble /múmbəl/ *v. & n.* ● *v.* **1** *intr. & tr.* speak or utter indistinctly. **2** *tr.* bite or chew with or as with toothless gums. ● *n.* an indistinct utterance. □□ **mumbler** *n.* **mumblingly** *adv.* [ME *momele*, as MUM²: cf. LG *mummelen*]

■ *v.* **1** murmur, mutter, slur, swallow one's words.

mumbo jumbo /múmbōjúmbō/ *n.* (*pl.* **jumbos**) **1** meaningless or ignorant ritual. **2** language or action intended to mystify or confuse. **3** an object of senseless veneration. [*Mumbo Jumbo*, a supposed African idol]

■ **1** spell, incantation, chant, formula, charm, abracadabra, rite, ritual, rigmarole, conjuration, magic. **2** gibberish, nonsense, rubbish, hocus-pocus, gobbledegook, drivel, humbug, bunkum, jargon, double-talk, mystique, rigmarole, jabberwocky, blather, moonshine, claptrap, *colloq.* hogwash, malarkey, piffle, *Brit. colloq.* tosh, *sl.* eyewash, poppycock, rot, tommyrot, bilge, bull, hooey, bunk.

mummer /múmər/ *n.* **1** an actor in a traditional masked mime. **2** *archaic* or *derog.* an actor in the theater. [ME f. OF *momeur* f. *momer* MUM³]

mummery /múməree/ *n.* (*pl.* **-ies**) **1** ridiculous (esp. religious) ceremonial. **2** a performance by mummers. [OF *momerie* (as MUMMER)]

mummify /múmifī/ *v.tr.* (**-ies, -ied**) **1** embalm and preserve (a body) in the form of a mummy (see MUMMY¹). **2** (usu. as **mummified** *adj.*) shrivel or dry up (tissues, etc.). □□ **mummification** /-fikáyshən/ *n.*

mummy¹ /múmee/ *n.* (*pl.* **-ies**) esp. *Brit.* = MOMMY.

mummy² /múmee/ *n.* (*pl.* **-ies**) **1** a body of a human being or animal embalmed for burial, esp. in ancient Egypt. **2** a dried-up body. **3** *Brit.* a pulpy mass (*beat it to a mummy*). **4** a rich brown pigment. [F *momie* f. med.L *mumia* f. Arab. *mūmiyā* f. Pers. *mūm* wax]

mumps /mumps/ *n.pl.* **1** (treated as *sing.*) a contagious and infectious viral disease with swelling of the parotid salivary glands in the face. **2** *Brit.* a fit of sulks. □□ **mumpish** *adj.* (in sense 2). [archaic *mump* be sullen]

munch /munch/ *v.tr.* eat steadily with a marked action of the jaws. [ME, imit.: cf. CRUNCH]

■ chew, crunch, masticate, champ, chomp, scrunch.

munchies /mə́ncheez/ *n. pl. colloq.* **1** snack foods. **2** the urge to snack.

mundane /múndáyn/ *adj.* **1** dull, routine. **2** of this world; worldly. □□ **mundanely** *adv.* **mundaneness** *n.* **mundanity** /-dánitee/ *n.* (*pl.* **-ies**). [ME f. OF *mondain* f. LL *mundanus* f. L *mundus* world]

■ **1** see HUMDRUM *adj.* **2** see WORLDLY 1.

mung /mung/ *n.* (in full **mung bean**) a leguminous plant, *Phaseolus aureus*, native to India and used as food. [Hindi *mūng*]

mungo /múnggō/ *n.* (*pl.* **-os**) the short fibers recovered from heavily felted material. [19th c.: orig. uncert.]

municipal /myoonísipəl/ *adj.* of or concerning a municipality or its self-government. □ **municipal bond** a bond issued by a city, county, state, etc., to finance public projects. □□ **municipalize** *v.tr.* **municipalization** /-lizáyshən/ *n.* **municipally** *adv.* [L *municipalis* f. *municipium* free city f. *municeps*

-cipis citizen with privileges f. *munia* civic offices + *capere* take]

■ civic, civil, metropolitan, urban, city, town, borough, parish, council.

municipality /myoonísipálitee/ *n.* (*pl.* **-ies**) **1** a town or district having local government. **2** the governing body of this area. [F *municipalité* f. *municipal* (as MUNICIPAL)]

■ **1** city, metropolis, town, borough, district, *Brit. hist.* or *Austral. & NZ* township.

munificent /myoonífisənt/ *adj.* (of a giver or a gift) splendidly generous, bountiful. □□ **munificence** *n.* /-səns/ **munificently** *adv.* [L *munificent-*, var. stem of *munificus* f. *munus* gift]

■ see GENEROUS 1.

muniment /myoonimənt/ *n.* (usu. in *pl.*) **1** a document kept as evidence of rights or privileges, etc. **2** an archive. [ME f. OF f. L *munimentum* defense, in med.L title deed f. *munire munit-* fortify]

munition /myoonishən/ *n. & v.* ● *n.* (usu. in *pl.*) military weapons, ammunition, equipment, and stores. ● *v.tr.* supply with munitions. [F f. L *munitio -onis* fortification (as MUNIMENT)]

■ *n.* (*munitions*) see HARDWARE 2.

munitioner /myoonishənər/ *n.* a person who makes or supplies munitions.

munnion var. of MULLION.

muntjac /múntjak/ *n.* (also **muntjak**) any small deer of the genus *Muntiacus* native to SE Asia, the male having tusks and small antlers. [Sundanese *minchek*]

Muntz metal /munts/ *n.* an alloy (approx. 60% copper, 40% zinc) used for sheathing ships, etc. Also called **alpha-beta brass**. [G. F. *Muntz*, Engl. manufacturer d. 1857]

muon /myoo-on/ *n. Physics* an unstable elementary particle like an electron, but with a much greater mass. [μ (MU), as the symbol for it]

murage /myoorij/ *n. Brit. hist.* a tax levied for building or repairing the walls of a town. [ME f. OF, in med.L *muragium* f. OF *mur* f. L *murus* wall]

mural /myoorəl/ *n. & adj.* ● *n.* a painting executed directly on a wall. ● *adj.* **1** of or like a wall. **2** on a wall. □ **mural crown** *Rom. Antiq.* a crown or garland given to the soldier who was first to scale the wall of a besieged town. □□ **muralist** *n.* [F f. L *muralis* f. *murus* wall]

murder /mə́rdər/ *n. & v.* ● *n.* **1** the unlawful premeditated killing of a human being by another (cf. MANSLAUGHTER). **2** *colloq.* an unpleasant, troublesome, or dangerous state of affairs (*it was murder here on Saturday*). ● *v.tr.* **1** kill (a human being) unlawfully, esp. wickedly or inhumanly. **2** *Law* kill (a human being) with a premeditated motive. **3** *colloq.* utterly defeat or spoil by a bad performance, mispronunciation, etc. (*murdered the soliloquy in the second act*). □ **cry bloody murder** *sl.* make an extravagant outcry. **get away with murder** do whatever one wishes and escape punishment. **murder will out** murder cannot remain undetected. □□ **murderer** *n.* **murderess** *n.* [OE *morthor* & OF *murdre* f. Gmc]

■ *n.* **1** homicide, killing, slaying, assassination; slaughter, butchery, genocide, massacre, liquidation, extermination, eradication, *disp.* decimation; bloodshed, carnage; regicide, patricide, matricide, parricide, fratricide, uxoricide, infanticide. **2** see HELL 2. ● *v.* **1** kill, assassinate, put to death, destroy, butcher, massacre, liquidate, exterminate, eradicate, annihilate, extinguish, slaughter, lay low, eliminate, take out, snuff out, *colloq.* polish off, *literary or joc.* slay, *sl.* wipe out, bump off, knock off, do in, rub out, waste, ice. **3** spoil, ruin, mar, destroy, wreck, kill, mangle, butcher, mutilate. □□ **murderer, murderess** killer,

/.../ pronunciation	● part of speech
□ phrases, idioms, and compounds	
□□ derivatives	■ synonym section
cross-references appear in SMALL CAPITALS or *italics*	

assassin, homicide, cutthroat, executioner, butcher, *literary or joc.* slayer, *sl.* hit man.

murderous /mɜ́rdərəs/ *adj.* **1** (of a person, weapon, action, etc.) capable of, intending, or involving murder or great harm. **2** *colloq.* extremely troublesome, unpleasant, or dangerous. □□ **murderously** *adv.* **murderousness** *n.*
■ **1** fatal, lethal, deadly, deathly, mortal; destructive, devastating, sanguinary, bloody, brutal, savage, bloodthirsty, barbarous, cruel, inhuman, *poet. or rhet.* fell. **2** strenuous, stressful, difficult, arduous, exhausting, harrowing, rigorous, intolerable, unbearable, *colloq.* hellish, killing.

mure /myŏŏr/ *v.tr. archaic* **1** immure. **2** (foll. by *up*) wall up or shut up in an enclosed space. [ME f. OF *murer* f. *mur*: see MURAGE]

murex /myŏŏreks/ *n.* (*pl.* **murices** /-riseez/ or **murexes**) any gastropod mollusk of the genus *Murex*, yielding a purple dye. [L]

murine /myŏŏrīn/ *adj.* of or like a mouse or mice. [L *murinus* f. *mus muris* mouse]

murk /mɜrk/ *n. & adj.* (also **mirk**) ● *n.* **1** darkness, poor visibility. **2** air obscured by fog, etc. ● *adj. archaic* (of night, day, place, etc.) = MURKY. [prob. f. Scand.: cf. ON *myrkr*]
■ *n.* **1** see GLOOM *n.* 1.

murky /mɜ́rkee/ *adj.* (also **mirky**) (**-ier, -iest**) **1** dark, gloomy. **2** (of darkness) thick, dirty. **3** suspiciously obscure (*murky past*). □□ **murkily** *adv.* **murkiness** *n.*
■ **1, 2** dark, gloomy, threatening, dim, clouded, cloudy, overcast, gray, dismal, dreary, bleak, somber, grim, funereal, shady, shadowy; thick, dirty. **3** see SHADY 3.

murmur /mɜ́rmər/ *n. & v.* ● *n.* **1** a subdued continuous sound, as made by waves, a brook, etc. **2** a softly spoken or nearly inarticulate utterance. **3** *Med.* a recurring sound heard in the auscultation of the heart and usu. indicating abnormality. **4** a subdued expression of discontent. ● *v.* **1** *intr.* make a subdued continuous sound. **2** *tr.* utter (words) in a low voice. **3** *intr.* (usu. foll. by *at, against*) complain in low tones, grumble. □□ **murmurer** *n.* **murmuringly** *adv.* **murmurous** *adj.* [ME f. OF *murmurer* f. L *murmurare*: cf. Gk *mormurō* (of water) roar, Skr. *marmaras* noisy]
■ *n.* **1** undercurrent, undertone, background noise *or* sound, rumble, mumble, drone, buzz, murmuring, hum, *literary* susurration, susurrus. **2** see WHISPER *n.* 1. **4** mutter, complaint, grumble, *colloq.* grouse; see also MOAN *n.* 3. ● *v.* **1, 2** mumble, mutter; whisper, drone, buzz, hum. **3** complain, grumble, mutter, moan, *colloq.* grouse, grouch, gripe, *Brit. colloq.* chunter.

murphy /mɜ́rfee/ *n.* (*pl.* **-ies**) *sl.* a potato. [Ir. surname]

Murphy's Law /mɜ́rfeez/ *n. joc.* any of various maxims about the perverseness of things.

murrain /mɜ́rin/ *n.* **1** an infectious disease of cattle, carried by parasites. **2** *archaic* a plague, esp. the potato blight during the Irish famine in the mid-19th c. [ME f. AF *moryn*, OF *morine* f. *morir* f. L *mori* die]

murrey /mɜ́ree/ *n. & adj. archaic* ● *n.* the color of a mulberry; a deep red or purple. ● *adj.* of this color. [ME f. OF *moré* f. med.L *moratus* f. *morum* mulberry]

murther /mɜ́rthər/ *archaic* var. of MURDER.

Mus.B. *abbr.* (also **Mus. Bac.**) Bachelor of Music. [L *Musicae Baccalaureus*]

muscadel var. of MUSCATEL.

Muscadet /mɜ́skəday/ *n.* **1** a white wine from the Loire region of France. **2** a variety of grape from which the wine is made. [*Muscadet* variety of grape]

muscadine /mɜ́skədin, -dīn/ *n.* a variety of grape with a musk flavor, used chiefly in wine making. [perh. Engl. form f. Prov. MUSCAT]

muscarine /mɜ́skərin/ *n.* a poisonous alkaloid from the fungus *Amanita muscaria*. [L *muscarius* f. *musca* fly]

muscat /mɜ́skat, -kət/ *n.* **1** = MUSCATEL. **2** a muscadine. [F f. Prov. *muscat muscade* (adj.) f. *musc* MUSK]

muscatel /mɜ́skətél/ *n.* (also **muscadel** /-dél/) **1** a sweet fortified white wine made from muscadines. **2** a raisin from a muscadine grape. [ME f. OF f. Prov. dimin. of *muscat*: see MUSCAT]

muscle /mɜ́səl/ *n. & v.* ● *n.* **1** a fibrous tissue with the ability to contract, producing movement in or maintaining the position of an animal body. **2** the part of an animal body that is composed of muscles. **3** physical power or strength. ● *v.intr.* (usu. foll. by *in*) *colloq.* force oneself on others; intrude by forceful means. □ **muscle-bound** with muscles stiff and inelastic through excessive exercise or training. **muscle man** a man with highly developed muscles, esp. one employed as an intimidator. **not move a muscle** be completely motionless. □□ **muscled** *adj.* (usu. in *comb.*). **muscleless** *adj.* **muscly** *adj.* [F f. L *musculus* dimin. of *mus* mouse, from the fancied mouselike form of some muscles]
■ *n.* **3** see STRENGTH 1.

muscology /mɜskóləjee/ *n.* the study of mosses. □□ **muscologist** *n.* [mod.L *muscologia* f. L *muscus* moss]

muscovado /mɜ́skəvaádō/ *n.* (*pl.* **-os**) an unrefined sugar made from the juice of sugar cane by evaporation and draining off the molasses. [Sp. *mascabado* (sugar) of the lowest quality]

Muscovite /mɜ́skəvīt/ *n. & adj.* ● *n.* **1** a native or citizen of Moscow. **2** *archaic* a Russian. ● *adj.* **1** of or relating to Moscow. **2** *archaic* of or relating to Russia. [mod.L *Muscovita* f. *Muscovia* = MUSCOVY]

muscovite /mɜ́skəvīt/ *n.* a silver-gray form of mica with a sheetlike crystalline structure that is used in the manufacture of electrical equipment, etc. [obs. MUSCOVY *glass* (in the same sense) + -ITE[1]]

Muscovy /mɜ́skəvee/ *n. archaic* Russia. □ **Muscovy duck** a tropical American duck, *Cairina moschata*, having a small crest and red markings on its head. [obs. F *Muscovie* f. mod.L *Moscovia* f. Russ. *Moskva* Moscow]

muscular /mɜ́skyələr/ *adj.* **1** of or affecting the muscles. **2** having well-developed muscles. □ **muscular Christianity** a Christian life of cheerful physical activity as described in the writings of Charles Kingsley. **muscular dystrophy** see DYSTROPHY. **muscular rheumatism** = MYALGIA. **muscular stomach** see STOMACH. □□ **muscularity** /-láritee/ *n.* **muscularly** *adv.* [earlier *musculous* (as MUSCLE)]
■ **2** sinewy, brawny, burly, powerful, well-built, strapping, rugged, husky, robust, athletic, sturdy, well-muscled, broad-shouldered, *colloq.* hunky.

musculature /mɜ́skyələchər/ *n.* the muscular system of a body or organ. [F f. L (as MUSCLE)]

musculoskeletal /mɜskyəlōskélət'l/ *adj.* of or involving both the muscles and the skeleton.

Mus.D. *abbr.* (also **Mus. Doc.**) Doctor of Music. [L *Musicae Doctor*]

muse[1] /myŏŏz/ *n.* **1** (as **the Muses**) (in Greek and Roman mythology) nine goddesses, the daughters of Zeus and Mnemosyne, who inspire poetry, music, drama, etc. **2** (usu. prec. by *the*) **a** a poet's inspiring goddess. **b** a poet's genius. [ME f. OF *muse* or L *musa* f. Gk *mousa*]

muse[2] /myŏŏz/ *v. & n.* ● *v. literary* **1** *intr.* **a** (usu. foll. by *on, upon*) ponder, reflect. **b** (usu. foll. by *on*) gaze meditatively (on a scene, etc.). **2** *tr.* say meditatively. ● *n. archaic* a fit of abstraction. [ME f. OF *muser* to waste time f. Rmc perh. f. med.L *musum* muzzle]
■ *v.* **1** cogitate, meditate, reflect, contemplate, ruminate, think, consider, deliberate, mull, brood, ponder; be absorbed (in thought), be in a brown study, dream, daydream, be in a trance *or* reverie; (*muse on*) weigh, evaluate, study, chew over, revolve.

musette /myŏŏzét/ *n.* **1 a** a kind of small bagpipe with bellows, common in the French court in the 17th–18th c. **b** a tune imitating the sound of this. **2** a small oboelike double-reed instrument in 19th-c. France. **3** a popular dance in the courts of Louis XIV and XV. **4** a small knapsack. [ME f. OF, dimin. of *muse* bagpipe]

museum /myŏŏzeéəm/ *n.* a building used for storing and exhibiting objects of historical, scientific, or cultural interest. □ **museum piece 1** a specimen of art, etc., fit for a museum. **2** *often derog.* an old-fashioned or quaint person or object. □□ **museology** /myŏŏzeeóləjee/ *n.* [L f. Gk *mouseion* seat of the Muses: see MUSE[1]]

mush[1] /mush/ *n.* **1** soft pulp. **2** feeble sentimentality. **3** a boiled cornmeal dish. **4** *sl.* the mouth; the face. □□ **mushy** *adj.* (**mushier, mushiest**). **mushily** *adv.* **mushiness** *n.* [app. var. of MASH]

■ **1** see PULP *n.* 2. **2** see *sentimentality* (SENTIMENTAL). **4** see FACE *n.* 1, MOUTH *n.* 1. □□ **mushy** soft, pulpy, doughy, spongy, sloppy, slushy, *colloq.* squishy, squashy, *sl.* gooey; mawkish, maudlin, sentimental, romantic, saccharine, sugary, syrupy, *colloq.* corny, schmaltzy, *Brit. colloq.* wet. **mushiness** see *sentimentality* (SENTIMENTAL).

mush² /mush/ *v. & n.* ● *v.intr.* **1** (in *imper.*) used as a command to dogs pulling a sled to urge them forward. **2** go on a journey across snow with a dogsled. ● *n.* a journey across snow with a dogsled. [prob. corrupt. f. F *marchons* imper. of *marcher* advance]

mushroom /múshrōōm, -rŏŏm/ *n. & v.* ● *n.* **1** the usu. edible, spore-producing body of various fungi, esp. *Agaricus campestris*, with a stem and domed cap, proverbial for its rapid growth. **2** the pinkish-brown color of this. **3** any item resembling a mushroom in shape (*darning mushroom*). **4** (usu. *attrib.*) something that appears or develops suddenly or is ephemeral; an upstart. ● *v.intr.* **1** appear or develop rapidly. **2** expand and flatten like a mushroom cap. **3** gather mushrooms. □ **mushroom cloud** a cloud suggesting the shape of a mushroom, esp. from a nuclear explosion. **mushroom growth 1** a sudden development or expansion. **2** anything undergoing this. □□ **mushroomy** *adj.* [ME f. OF *mousseron* f. LL *mussirio -onis*]

■ *v.* **1** see PROLIFERATE. **2** see SWELL *v.* 1.

music /myóŏzik/ *n.* **1** the art of combining vocal or instrumental sounds (or both) to produce beauty of form, harmony, and expression of emotion. **2** the sounds so produced. **3** musical compositions. **4** the written or printed score of a musical composition. **5** certain pleasant sounds, e.g., birdsong, the sound of a stream, etc. □ **music box** a mechanical instrument playing a tune by causing a toothed cylinder to strike a comblike metal plate within a box. **music center** *Brit.* = *entertainment center*. **music drama** Wagnerian-type opera without formal arias, etc., and governed by dramatic considerations. **music hall** *Brit.* a theater featuring variety entertainment, esp. singing, dancing, and novelty acts. **music of the spheres** see SPHERE. **music paper** paper printed with staves for writing music. **music stand** a rest or frame on which sheet music or a score is supported. **music theater** in late 20th-c. music, the combination of elements from music and drama in new forms distinct from traditional opera, esp. as designed for small groups of performers. **music to one's ears** something very pleasant to hear. [ME f. OF *musique* f. L *musica* f. Gk *mousikē* (*tekhnē* art) of the Muses (*mousa* Muse: see MUSE¹)]

■ **2** see STRAIN¹ *n.* 4. **4** see SCORE *n.* 5a.

musical /myóŏzikəl/ *adj. & n.* ● *adj.* **1** of or relating to music. **2** (of sounds, a voice, etc.) melodious, harmonious. **3** fond of or skilled in music (*the musical one of the family*). **4** set to or accompanied by music. ● *n.* a movie or drama that features songs. □ **musical box** *Brit.* = *music box* **musical bumps** *Brit.* a game similar to musical chairs, with players sitting on the floor and the one left standing eliminated. **musical chairs 1** a party game in which the players compete in successive rounds for a decreasing number of chairs. **2** a series of changes or political maneuvering, etc., after the manner of the game. □□ **musicality** /-kálitee/ *n.* **musicalize** *v.tr.* **musically** *adv.* **musicalness** *n.* [ME f. OF f. med.L *musicalis* f. L *musica*: see MUSIC]

■ *adj.* **2** tuneful, melodic, harmonious, lilting, lyrical, melodious, mellifluous, dulcet, sweet, euphonious, sonorous.

musicale /myōŏzikál/ *n.* a musical party. [F fem. adj. (as MUSICAL)]

musician /myōŏzíshən/ *n.* a person who plays a musical instrument, esp. professionally, or is otherwise musically gifted. □□ **musicianly** *adj.* **musicianship** *n.* [ME f. OF *musicien* f. *musique* (as MUSIC, -ICIAN)]

■ see PLAYER 2.

musicology /myōŏzikóləjee/ *n.* the study of music other than

that directed to proficiency in performance or composition. □□ **musicologist** *n.* **musicological** /-kəlójikəl/ *adj.* [F *musicologie* or MUSIC + -LOGY]

musique concrète /myzéek kawnkrét/ *n.* music constructed by mixing recorded sounds. [F]

musk /musk/ *n.* **1** a strong-smelling reddish-brown substance produced by a gland in the male musk deer and used as an ingredient in perfumes. **2** the plant, *Mimulus moschatus*, with pale-green ovate leaves and yellow flowers (orig. with a smell of musk that is no longer perceptible in modern varieties). □ **musk deer** any small Asian deer of the genus *Moschus*, having no antlers and in the male having long protruding canine teeth. **musk duck** the Australian duck *Biziura lobata*, having a musky smell. **musk ox** a large goat-antelope, *Ovibos moschatus*, native to N. America, with a thick shaggy coat and small curved horns. **musk rose** a rambling rose, *Rosa moschata*, with large white flowers smelling of musk. **musk thistle** a nodding thistle, *Carduus nutans*, whose flowers have a musky fragrance. □□ **musky** *adj.* (**muskier, muskiest**). **muskiness** *n.* [ME f. LL *muscus* f. Pers. *mušk*, perh. f. Skr. *muṣka* scrotum (from the shape of the musk deer's gland)]

muskeg /múskeg/ *n.* a level swamp or bog in Canada. [Cree]

muskellunge /múskəlunj/ *n.* a large N. American pike, *Esox masquinongy*, found esp. in the Great Lakes. Also **maskinonge**. [ult. f. Ojibwa 'great fish']

musket /múskit/ *n. hist.* an infantryman's (esp. smooth-bored) light gun, often supported on the shoulder. □ **musket-shot 1** a shot fired from a musket. **2** the range of this shot. [F *mousquet* f. It. *moschetto* crossbow bolt f. *mosca* fly]

musketeer /múskiteer/ *n. hist.* a soldier armed with a musket.

musketry /múskitree/ *n.* **1** muskets, or soldiers armed with muskets, referred to collectively. **2** the knowledge of handling muskets.

muskmelon /múskmelən/ *n.* the common yellow or green melon, *Cucumis melo*, usu. with a raised network of markings on the skin.

muskrat /múskrat/ *n.* **1** a large aquatic rodent, *Ondatra zibethica*, native to N. America, having a musky smell. Also called MUSQUASH. **2** the fur of this.

Muslim /múzlim, mŏŏz-, mŏŏs-/ *n. & adj.* (also **Moslem** /mózləm/) ● *n.* a follower of the Islamic religion. ● *adj.* of or relating to the Muslims or their religion. [Arab. *muslim*, part. of *aslama*: see ISLAM]

muslin /múzlin/ *n.* **1** a fine delicately woven cotton fabric. **2** a cotton cloth in plain weave. □□ **muslined** *adj.* [F *mousseline* f. It. *mussolina* f. *Mussolo* Mosul in Iraq, where it was made]

musmon /múzmən/ *n. Zool.* = MOUFLON. [L *musimo* f. Gk *mousmōn*]

musquash /múskwosh/ *n.* = MUSKRAT. [Algonquian]

muss /mus/ *v. & n. colloq.* ● *v.tr.* (often foll. by *up*) disarrange; throw into disorder. ● *n.* a state of confusion; untidiness, mess. □□ **mussy** *adj.* [app. var. of MESS]

■ *v.* see MESS *v.* 1. □□ **mussy** see UNTIDY.

mussel /músəl/ *n.* **1** any bivalve mollusk of the genus *Mytilus*, living in seawater and often used for food. **2** any similar freshwater mollusk of the genus *Margaritifer* or *Anodonta*, forming pearls. [ME f. OE *mus(c)le* & MLG *mussel*, ult. rel. to L *musculus* (as MUSCLE)]

Mussulman /músəlmən/ *n. & adj. archaic* ● *n.* (*pl.* **-mans** or **-men**) a Muslim. ● *adj.* of or concerning Muslims. [Pers. *musulmān* orig. adj. f. *muslim* (as MUSLIM)]

must¹ /must/ *v. & n.* ● *v.aux.* (*3rd sing. present* **must**; *past* **had to** or in indirect speech **must**) (foll. by infin., or *absol.*) **1 a** be obliged to (*you must go to school; must we leave now?; said he must go; I must away*). ¶ The negative (i.e., lack of obligation) is expressed by *not have to* or *need not; must not*

/.../ **pronunciation**	● **part of speech**
□ **phrases, idioms, and compounds**	
□□ **derivatives**	■ **synonym section**
cross-references appear in SMALL CAPITALS or *italics*	

denotes positive forbidding, as in *you must not smoke*. **b** in ironic questions (*must you slam the door?*). **2** be certain to (*we must win in the end; you must be her sister; he must be mad; they must have left by now; seemed as if the roof must blow off*). **3** ought to (*we must see what can be done; it must be said that*). **4** expressing insistence (*I must ask you to leave*). **5** (foll. by *not* + infin.) **a** not be permitted to, be forbidden to (*you must not smoke*). **b** ought not; need not (*you mustn't think he's angry; you must not worry*). **c** expressing insistence that something should not be done (*they must not be told*). **6** (as past or historic present) expressing the perversity of destiny (*what must I do but break my leg*). ● *n. colloq.* a thing that cannot or should not be overlooked or missed (*if you go to London, St. Paul's is a must*). □ **I must say** often *iron.* I cannot refrain from saying (*I must say he made a good attempt; a fine way to behave, I must say*). **must needs** see NEEDS. [OE *mōste* past of *mōt* may]

■ *v.* **1, 3, 4** ought to, should, have to, need to, be obliged to, be required to, be *or* feel compelled *or* forced to.
● *n.* necessity, requisite, requirement, obligation, sine qua non, essential.

must² /must/ *n.* grape juice before fermentation is complete. [OE f. L *mustum* neut. of *mustus* new]

must³ /must/ *n.* mustiness, mold. [back-form. f. MUSTY]

must⁴ var. of MUSTH.

mustache /mústash, məstásh/ *n.* (also **moustache**) **1** hair left to grow on a man's upper lip. **2** a similar growth around the mouth of some animals. □ **mustache cup** a cup with a partial cover to protect the mustache when drinking. □□ **mustached** *adj.* [F f. It. *mostaccio* f. Gk *mustax -akos*]

mustachio /məstaásheeō, -stásheeō, -shō/ *n.* (*pl.* **-os**) (often in *pl.*) *archaic* a mustache. □□ **mustachioed** *adj.* [Sp. *mostacho* & It. *mostaccio* (as MUSTACHE)]

mustang /mústang/ *n.* a small wild horse native to Mexico and California. □ **mustang grape** a grape from the wild vine *Vitis candicans*, of the southern US, used for making wine. [Sp. *mestengo* f. *mesta* company of graziers, & Sp. *mostrenco*]

mustard /mústərd/ *n.* **1 a** any of various plants of the genus *Brassica* with slender pods and yellow flowers, esp. *B. nigra*. **b** any of various plants of the genus *Sinapis*, esp. *S. alba*, eaten at the seedling stage, often with cress. **2** the seeds of these which are crushed, made into a paste, and used as a spicy condiment. **3** the brownish-yellow color of this condiment. **4** *sl.* a thing that adds piquancy or zest. □ **cut the mustard** *sl.* be able to reach an expected level of performance. **mustard gas** a colorless oily liquid whose vapor is a powerful irritant and vesicant. **mustard plaster** a poultice made with mustard. **mustard seed 1** the seed of the mustard plant. **2** a small thing capable of great development (Matt. 13:31). [ME f. OF *mo(u)starde*: orig. the condiment as prepared with MUSTARD²]

muster /mústər/ *v. & n.* ● *v.* **1** *tr.* collect (orig. soldiers) for inspection, to check numbers, etc. **2** *tr. & intr.* collect, gather together. **3** *tr. Austral.* round up (livestock). ● *n.* **1** the assembly of persons for inspection. **2** an assembly, a collection. **3** *Austral.* a rounding up of livestock. **4** *Austral. sl.* the number of people attending (a meeting, etc.) (*had a good muster*). **5** a muster roll. □ **muster book** a book for registering military personnel. **muster in** enroll (recruits). **muster out** discharge (soldiers, etc.). **muster roll** an official list of officers and men in a regiment or ship's company. **muster up** collect or summon (courage, strength, etc.). **pass muster** be accepted as adequate. □□ **musterer** *n.* (in sense 3 of *n. & v.*). [ME f. OF *mo(u)stre* ult. f. L *monstrare* show]

■ *v.* **1, 2** call together, assemble, convene, collect, mobilize, rally, round up, gather, marshal; muster up, summon (up), *formal* convoke; come together. ● *n.* **1, 2** rally, assembly, assemblage, convocation, meet, meeting, convention, congress, roundup, gathering, congregation, aggregation, turnout. □ **pass muster** come *or* be up to scratch, measure up, be acceptable *or* adequate, be good enough, *colloq.* make thc grade, come *or* be up to snuff.

musth /must/ *adj. & n.* (also **must**) ● *adj.* (of a male elephant or camel) in a state of frenzy. ● *n.* this state. [Urdu f. Pers. *mast* intoxicated]

mustn't /músənt/ *contr.* must not.

musty /mústee/ *adj.* (**mustier, mustiest**) **1** moldy. **2** of a moldy or stale smell or taste. **3** stale, antiquated (*musty old books*). □□ **mustily** *adv.* **mustiness** *n.* [perh. alt. f. *moisty* (MOIST) by assoc. with MUST²]

■ **1, 2** moldy, damp, mildewed, mildewy, rancid, spoiled, decayed, rotten, putrid, fetid, fusty, stale. **3** stale, old-fashioned, antiquated, ancient, out-of-date, bygone, passé, obsolete, archaic, *colloq.* antediluvian; tired, hoary, worn out, trite, clichéd, *colloq.* old hat.

mutable /myōōtəbəl/ *adj. literary* **1** liable to change. **2** fickle. □□ **mutability** /-bílitee/ *n.* [L *mutabilis* f. *mutare* change]

■ **1** see CHANGEABLE 1. **2** see FICKLE.

mutagen /myōōtəjən/ *n.* an agent promoting mutation, e.g., radiation. □□ **mutagenic** /-jénik/ *adj.* **mutagenesis** /-jénisis/ *n.* [MUTATION + -GEN]

mutant /myōōt'nt/ *adj. & n.* ● *adj.* resulting from mutation. ● *n.* a mutant form. [L *mutant-* part. f. *mutare* change]

mutate /myōōtáyt/ *v.intr. & tr.* undergo or cause to undergo mutation. [back-form. f. MUTATION]

■ see TRANSFORM *v.*

mutation /myōōtáyshən/ *n.* **1** the process or an instance of change or alteration. **2** a genetic change which, when transmitted to offspring, gives rise to heritable variations. **3** a mutant. **4 a** an umlaut. **b** (in a Celtic language) a change of a consonant, etc., determined by a preceding word. □□ **mutational** *adj.* **mutationally** *adv.* [ME f. L *mutatio* f. *mutare* change]

■ **1** change, alteration, modification, transformation, metamorphosis, transmutation, transfiguration, evolution, variation. **3** deformity, monstrosity, freak, mutant; anomaly, departure.

mutatis mutandis /mōōtaátis mōōtaándis, myōō-/ *adv.* (in comparing cases) making the necessary alterations. [L]

mutch /much/ *n. Brit. dial.* a woman's or child's linen cap. [ME f. MDu. *mutse* MHG *mütze* f. med.L *almucia* AMICE²]

mute /myōōt/ *adj., n., & v.* ● *adj.* **1** silent, refraining from or temporarily bereft of speech. **2** not emitting articulate sound. **3** (of a person or animal) dumb; speechless. **4** not expressed in speech (*mute protest*). **5 a** (of a letter) not pronounced. **b** (of a consonant) plosive. **6** (of hounds) not giving tongue. ● *n.* **1** a dumb person (*a deaf mute*). **2** *Mus.* **a** a clamp for damping the resonance of the strings of a violin, etc. **b** a pad or cone for damping the sound of a wind instrument. **3** an unsounded consonant. **4** an actor whose part is in a dumb show. **5** a hired mourner. ● *v.tr.* **1** deaden, muffle, or soften the sound of (a thing, esp. a musical instrument). **2 a** tone down, make less intense. **b** (as **muted** *adj.*) (of colors, etc.) subdued (*a muted green*). □ **mute button** a device on a telephone, etc., to temporarily prevent the caller from hearing what is being said at the receiver's end. **mute swan** the common white swan, *Cygnus olor*. □□ **mutely** *adv.* **muteness** *n.* [ME f. OF *muet*, dimin. of *mu* f. L *mutus*, assim. to L]

■ *adj.* **1-3** silent, dumb, speechless, voiceless, wordless, tight-lipped, taciturn, tacit, reserved, quiet, *colloq.* mum. **4** unspoken, unsaid, silent; see also TACIT. ● *v.* **1, 2a** deaden, silence, muffle, stifle, dampen, damp (down), subdue, soften, suppress, quiet, hush, restrain, soft-pedal, turn down, tone down, esp. *Brit.* quieten (down).

mutilate /myōōt'layt/ *v.tr.* **1 a** deprive (a person or animal) of a limb or organ. **b** destroy the use of (a limb or organ). **2** render (a book, etc.) imperfect by excision or some act of destruction. □□ **mutilation** /-láyshən/ *n.* **mutilative** /-láytiv/ *adj.* **mutilator** *n.* [L *mutilare* f. *mutilus* maimed]

■ **1** maim, disfigure, mangle, cripple, lame, butcher, disable; dismember, hack *or* cut *or* tear *or* rip to pieces. **2** deface, vandalize, spoil, mar, ruin, damage, destroy; bowdlerize, censor.

mutineer /myōōt'neér/ *n.* a person who mutinies. [F *mutinier*

f. *mutin* rebellious f. *muete* movement ult. f. L *movēre* move]

■ see REBEL *n.*

mutinous /myŏŏt'nəs/ *adj.* rebellious; tending to mutiny. □□ **mutinously** *adv.* [obs. *mutine* rebellion f. F *mutin*: see MUTINEER]

■ rebellious, revolutionary, subversive, seditious, insurgent, insurrectionary; recalcitrant, refractory, contumacious, obstinate, defiant, insubordinate, disobedient, unruly, unmanageable, ungovernable, uncontrollable.

mutiny /myŏŏt'nee/ *n.* & *v.* ● *n.* (*pl.* **-ies**) an open revolt against constituted authority, esp. by soldiers or sailors against their officers. ● *v.intr.* (**-ies, -ied**) (often foll. by *against*) revolt; engage in mutiny. [obs. *mutine* (as MUTINOUS)]

■ *n.* revolt, rebellion, revolution, insurgency, insurgence, insurrection, uprising. ● *v.* rebel, rise up, revolt; disobey, subvert, agitate.

mutism /myŏŏtizəm/ *n.* muteness; silence; dumbness. [F *mutisme* f. L (as MUTE)]

muton /myŏŏton/ *n. Biol.* the smallest element of genetic material capable of giving rise to a mutant individual.

mutt /mut/ *n.* **1** a dog. **2** *sl.* an ignorant, stupid, or blundering person. [abbr. of *muttonhead*]

■ **2** see MONGREL *n.*

mutter /mútər/ *v.* & *n.* ● *v.* **1** *intr.* speak low in a barely audible manner. **2** *intr.* (often foll. by *against, at*) murmur or grumble about. **3** *tr.* utter (words, etc.) in a low tone. **4** *tr.* say in secret. ● *n.* **1** muttered words or sounds. **2** muttering. □□ **mutterer** *n.* **mutteringly** *adv.* [ME, rel. to MUTE]

■ *v.* **1, 3** mumble, murmur, grunt; see also WHISPER *v.* 1. **2** grumble, complain, moan, *colloq.* grouch, grouse, gripe, *Brit. colloq.* chunter.

mutton /mút'n/ *n.* **1** the flesh of sheep used for food. **2** *joc.* a sheep. □ **mutton bird** *Austral.* **1** any bird of the genus *Puffinus*, esp. the short-tailed shearwater, *P. tenuirostris*. **2** any of various petrels. **mutton dressed as lamb** *Brit. colloq.* a usu. middle-aged or elderly woman dressed or made up to appear younger. □□ **muttony** *adj.* [ME f. OF *moton* f. med.L *multo -onis* prob. f. Gaulish]

muttonchops /mút'nchops/ *n.* side whiskers trimmed narrow at the temples and broad along the cheeks.

mutual /myŏŏchŏŏəl/ *adj.* **1** (of feelings, actions, etc.) experienced or done by each of two or more parties with reference to the other or others (*mutual affection*). **2** *colloq. disp.* common to two or more persons (*a mutual friend*; *a mutual interest*). **3** standing in a (specified) relation to each other (*mutual well-wishers*; *mutual beneficiaries*). □ **mutual fund** an investment program funded by shareholders that trades in diversified holdings and is professionally managed. **mutual inductance** the property of an electric circuit that causes an electromotive force to be generated in it by change in the current flowing through a magnetically linked circuit. **mutual induction** the production of an electromotive force between adjacent circuits that are magnetically linked. **mutual insurance** insurance in which some or all the profits are divided among the policyholders. □□ **mutuality** /-chŏŏ-álitee, -tyŏŏ-álitee/ *n.* **mutually** *adv.* [ME f. OF *mutuel* f. L *mutuus* mutual, borrowed, rel. to *mutare* change]

■ **1, 3** reciprocal, reciprocated; interactive, complementary. **2** communal, joint, shared; see also COMMON *adj.* 2.

mutualism /myŏŏchŏŏəlizəm/ *n.* **1** the doctrine that mutual dependence is necessary to social well-being. **2** mutually beneficial symbiosis. □□ **mutualist** *n.* & *adj.* **mutualistic** /-lístik/ *adj.* **mutualistically** /-lístiklee/ *adv.*

mutuel /myŏŏchŏŏəl/ *n.* a totalizator; a *pari-mutuel.* [abbr. of PARI-MUTUEL]

mutule /myŏŏchŏŏl/ *n. Archit.* a block derived from the ends of wooden beams projecting under a Doric cornice. [F f. L *mutulus*]

muumuu /mŏŏmŏŏ/ *n.* a woman's loose brightly colored dress. [Hawaiian]

Muzak /myŏŏzak/ *n.* **1** *propr.* a system of music transmission for playing in public places. **2** (**muzak**) recorded light background music. [alt. f. MUSIC]

muzhik /mŏŏzhik/ *n.* (also **moujik**) *hist.* a Russian peasant. [Russ. *muzhik*]

■ see PEASANT.

muzzle /múzəl/ *n.* & *v.* ● *n.* **1** the projecting part of an animal's face, including the nose and mouth. **2** a guard, usu. made of straps or wire, fitted over an animal's nose and mouth to stop it biting or feeding. **3** the open end of a firearm. ● *v.tr.* **1** put a muzzle on (an animal, etc.). **2** impose silence upon. **3** *Naut.* take in (a sail). □ **muzzle velocity** the velocity with which a projectile leaves the muzzle of a gun. □□ **muzzler** *n.* [ME f. OF *musel* ult. f. med.L *musum*: cf. MUSE²]

■ *n.* **1** snout, trunk, proboscis. ● *v.* **2** see SILENCE *v.*

muzzy /múzee/ *adj.* (**muzzier, muzziest**) **1 a** mentally hazy; dull, spiritless. **b** esp. *Brit.* stupid from drinking alcohol. **2** blurred, indistinct. □□ **muzzily** *adv.* **muzziness** *n.* [18th c.: orig. unkn.]

■ **1** see GROGGY. **2** see FAINT *adj.* 1.

MV *abbr.* **1** megavolt(s). **2** motor vessel. **3** muzzle velocity.

MVP *abbr. Sports* most valuable player.

MW *abbr.* **1** megawatt(s). **2** medium wave.

mW *abbr.* milliwatt(s).

Mx. *abbr.* maxwell(s).

my /mī/ *poss.pron.* (*attrib.*) **1** of or belonging to me or myself (*my house*; *my own business*). **2** as a form of address in affectionate, sympathetic, jocular, or patronizing contexts (*my dear boy*). **3** in various expressions of surprise (*my God!*; *oh my!*). **4** *colloq.* indicating the speaker's husband, wife, child, etc. (*my Johnny's ill again*). □ **my Lady** (or **Lord**) the form of address to certain titled persons. [ME *mī*, reduced f. *mīn* MINE¹]

my- *comb. form* var. of MYO-.

myalgia /mīáljə/ *n.* a pain in a muscle or group of muscles. □□ **myalgic** *adj.* [mod.L f. Gk *mus* muscle]

myalism /mīəlizəm/ *n.* a kind of sorcery akin to obeah, practiced esp. in the W. Indies. [*myal*, prob. f. W.Afr. orig.]

myall /mīəl/ *n.* **1 a** any tree of the genus *Acacia*, esp. *A. pendula*, native to Australia. **b** the hard scented wood of this, used for fences and tobacco pipes. **2** an Aboriginal living in a traditional way. [Aboriginal *maiāl*]

myasthenia /mīəs-theéneeə/ *n.* a condition causing abnormal weakness of certain muscles. □ **myasthenia gravis** a disease characterized by fatigue and muscle weakness, caused by an autoimmune attack on acetylcholine receptors. [mod.L f. Gk *mus* muscle: cf. ASTHENIA]

mycelium /mīseéleeəm/ *n.* (*pl.* **mycelia** /-leeə/) the vegetative part of a fungus, consisting of microscopic threadlike hyphae. □□ **mycelial** *adj.* [mod.L f. Gk *mukēs* mushroom, after EPITHELIUM]

Mycenaean /mīsineéən/ *adj.* & *n.* ● *adj. Archaeol.* of or relating to the late Bronze Age civilization in Greece (*c.*1580–1100 BC), depicted in the Homeric poems and represented by finds at Mycenae and elsewhere. ● *n.* an inhabitant of Mycenae or the Mycenaean world. [L *Mycenaeus*]

-mycin /mísin/ *comb. form* used to form the names of antibiotic compounds derived from fungi. [Gk *mukēs* fungus + -IN]

mycology /mīkóləjee/ *n.* **1** the study of fungi. **2** the fungi of a particular region. □□ **mycological** /-kəlójikəl/ *adj.* **mycologically** /-kəlójiklee/ *adv.* **mycologist** *n.* [Gk *mukēs* mushroom + -LOGY]

mycorrhiza /mīkərīzə/ *n.* (*pl.* **mycorrhizae** /-zee/) a symbiotic association of a fungus and the roots of a plant. □□ **mycorrhizal** *adj.* [mod.L f. Gk *mukēs* mushroom + *rhiza* root]

mycosis /mīkṓsis/ *n.* any disease caused by a fungus, e.g.,

/.../ pronunciation	● part of speech
□ phrases, idioms, and compounds	
□□ derivatives	■ synonym section
cross-references appear in SMALL CAPITALS or *italics*	

985

ringworm. □□ **mycotic** /-kótik/ *adj.* [Gk *mukēs* mushroom + -OSIS]

mycotoxin /míkətóksin/ *n.* any toxic substance produced by a fungus.

mycotrophy /mīkótrəfee/ *n.* the condition of a plant which has mycorrhizae and is perhaps helped to assimilate nutrients as a result. [G *Mykotrophie* f. Gk *mukēs* mushroom + *trophē* nourishment]

mydriasis /midríəsis/ *n.* excessive dilation of the pupil of the eye. [L f. Gk *mudriasis*]

myelin /mí-ilin/ *n.* a white substance which forms a sheath around certain nerve fibers. □□ **myelination** *n.* [Gk *muelos* marrow + -IN]

myelitis /mī-ilítis/ *n.* inflammation of the spinal cord. [mod.L f. Gk *muelos* marrow]

myeloid /mí-iloyd/ *adj.* of or relating to bone marrow or the spinal cord. [Gk *muelos* marrow]

myeloma /mí-ilṓmə/ *n.* (*pl.* **myelomas** or **myelomata** /-mətə/) a malignant tumor of the bone marrow. [mod.L, as MYELITIS + -OMA]

Mylar /mílaar/ *n. propr.* an extremely strong polyester film made in thin sheets and used for recording tapes, insulation, etc.

mylodon /mílədon/ *n.* an extinct gigantic ground sloth of the genus *Mylodon*, with cylindrical teeth and found in deposits formed during the ice age of the Pleistocene epoch in South America. [mod.L f. Gk *mulē* mill, molar + *odous odontos* tooth]

mynah /mínə/ *n.* (also **myna, mina**) any of various SE Asian starlings, esp. those such as *Gracula religiosa*, which are able to mimic the human voice. [Hindi *mainā*]

myo- /mío/ *comb. form* (also **my-** before a vowel) muscle. [Gk *mus muos* muscle]

myocardium /míōkaárdeeəm/ *n.* (*pl.* **myocardia** /-deeə/) the muscular tissue of the heart. □ **myocardial infarction** a heart attack. □□ **myocardiac** *adj.* **myocardial** *adj.* [MYO- + Gk *kardia* heart]

myofibril /míōfíbril/ *n.* any of the elongated contractile threads found in striated muscle cells.

myogenic /míəjénik/ *adj.* originating in muscle tissue.

myoglobin /míōglṓbin/ *n.* an oxygen-carrying protein containing iron and found in muscle cells.

myology /mīóləjee/ *n.* the study of the structure and function of muscles.

myope /míōp/ *n.* a myopic person. [F f. LL *myops* f. Gk *muōps* f. *muō* shut + *ōps* eye]

myopia /mīṓpeeə/ *n.* **1** nearsightedness. **2** lack of imagination or intellectual insight. □□ **myopic** /miópik/ *adj.* **myopically** /miópiklee/ *adv.* [mod.L (as MYOPE)]

  ■ □□ **myopic** see NEARSIGHTED 1, SMALL-MINDED.

myosis var. of MIOSIS.

myosotis /míəsṓtis/ *n.* (*also* **myosote** /míəsōt/) any plant of the genus *Myosotis* with blue, pink, or white flowers, esp. a forget-me-not. [L f. Gk *muosōtis* f. *mus muos* mouse + *ous ōtos* ear]

myotonia /míətṓneeə/ *n.* the inability to relax voluntary muscle after vigorous effort. □□ **myotonic** /-tónik/ *adj.* [MYO- + Gk *tonos* tone]

myriad /míreeəd/ *n. & adj. literary* ● *n.* **1** an indefinitely great number. **2** ten thousand. ● *adj.* of an indefinitely great number. [LL *mirias miriad-* f. Gk *murias -ados* f. *murioi* 10,000]

  ■ *n.* **1** see LOT *n.* 1. ● *adj.* see UNLIMITED.

myriapod /míreeəpód/ *n. & adj.* ● *n.* any land-living arthropod of the group Myriapoda, with numerous leg-bearing segments, e.g., centipedes and millipedes. ● *adj.* of or relating to this group. [mod.L *Myriapoda* (as MYRIAD, Gk *pous podos* foot)]

myrmidon /mṓrmid'n, -don/ *n.* **1** a hired ruffian. **2** a base servant. [L *Myrmidones* (pl.) f. Gk *Murmidones*, warlike Thessalian people who went with Achilles to Troy]

myrobalan /mirṓbələn/ *n.* **1** (in full **myrobalan plum**) = *cherry plum*. **2** (in full **myrobalan nut**) the fruit of an Asian tree, *Terminalia chebula*, used in medicines, for tanning leather, and to produce inks and dyes. [F *myrobolan* or L

myrobalanum f. Gk *murobalanos* f. *muron* unguent + *balanos* acorn]

myrrh[1] /mər/ *n.* a gum resin from several trees of the genus *Commiphora* used, esp. in the Near East, in perfumery, medicine, incense, etc. □□ **myrrhic** *adj.* **myrrhy** *adj.* [OE *myrra*, *myrre* f. L *myrr(h)a* f. Gk *murra*, of Semitic orig.]

myrrh[2] /mər/ *n.* = *sweet cicely.* [L *myrris* f. Gk *murris*]

myrtaceous /mərtáyshəs/ *adj.* of or relating to the plant family Myrtaceae, including myrtles.

myrtle /mṓrtəl/ *n.* **1** an evergreen shrub of the genus *Myrtus* with aromatic foliage and white flowers, esp. *M. communis*, bearing purple-black ovoid berries. **2** = PERIWINKLE[1]. [ME f. med.L *myrtilla*, *-us* dimin. of L *myrta*, *myrtus* f. Gk *murtos*]

myself /misélf/ *pron.* **1** *emphat.* form of I[2] or ME[1] (*I saw it myself*; *I like to do it myself*). **2** *refl.* form of ME[1] (*I was angry with myself*; *able to dress myself*; *as bad as myself*). **3** in my normal state of body and mind (*I'm not myself today*). **4** *poet.* = I[2]. □ **by myself** see *by oneself*. **I myself** I for my part (*I myself am doubtful*). [ME[1] + SELF: *my-* partly after *herself* with *her* regarded as poss. pron.]

mysterious /mistéereeəs/ *adj.* **1** full of or wrapped in mystery. **2** (of a person) delighting in mystery. □□ **mysteriously** *adv.* **mysteriousness** *n.* [F *mystérieux* f. *mystère* f. OF (as MYSTERY[1])]

  ■ puzzling, enigmatic, baffling, insoluble, unsolvable, bewildering, confounding, confusing, perplexing, mystifying, weird, bizarre, strange, uncanny, curious; cryptic, arcane, secret, inscrutable, covert, hidden, furtive, unclear, dark, concealed, occult, inexplicable, incomprehensible, mystic(al), unknown, unfathomable, recondite, abstruse.

mystery[1] /místəree/ *n.* (*pl.* **-ies**) **1** a secret, hidden, or inexplicable matter (*the reason remains a mystery*). **2** secrecy or obscurity (*wrapped in mystery*). **3** (*attrib.*) secret, undisclosed (*mystery guest*). **4** the practice of making a secret of (esp. unimportant) things (*engaged in mystery and intrigue*). **5** (in full **mystery story**) a fictional work dealing with a puzzling event, esp. a crime (*a well-known mystery writer*). **6 a** a religious truth divinely revealed, esp. one beyond human reason. **b** *RC Ch.* a decade of the rosary. **7** (in *pl.*) **a** the secret religious rites of the ancient Greeks, Romans, etc. **b** *archaic* the Eucharist. □ **make a mystery of** treat as an impressive secret. **mystery play** a miracle play. **mystery tour** (or **trip**) *Brit.* a pleasure excursion to an unspecified destination. [ME f. OF *mistere* or L *mysterium* f. Gk *mustērion*, rel. to MYSTIC]

  ■ **1** puzzle, enigma, conundrum, riddle, question, secret. **2** obscurity, secrecy, indefiniteness, vagueness, nebulousness, ambiguity, ambiguousness, inscrutability, inscrutableness. **3** see SECRET *adj.* 1. **4** secrecy, intrigue, stealth, stealthiness, furtiveness, concealment, covertness, surreptitiousness, clandestinity. **5** detective story *or* novel, murder story *or* mystery, thriller, *colloq.* whodunit.

mystery[2] /místəree/ *n.* (*pl.* **-ies**) *archaic* a handicraft or trade, esp. as referred to in indentures, etc. (*art and mystery*). [ME f. med.L *misterium* contr. of *ministerium* MINISTRY, assoc. with MYSTERY[1]]

mystic /místik/ *n. & adj.* ● *n.* a person who seeks by contemplation and self-surrender to obtain unity or identity with or absorption into the Deity or the ultimate reality, or who believes in the spiritual apprehension of truths that are beyond the understanding. ● *adj.* **1** mysterious and awe-inspiring. **2** spiritually allegorical or symbolic. **3** occult, esoteric. **4** of hidden meaning. □□ **mysticism** /-tisizəm/ *n.* [ME f. OF *mystique* or L *mysticus* f. Gk *mustikos* f. *mustēs* initiated person f. *muō* close the eyes or lips, initiate]

  ■ *adj.* **1, 3** see OCCULT *adj.* 1, 3. **4** see CRYPTIC 1c.

mystical /místikəl/ *adj.* of mystics or mysticism. □□ **mystically** *adv.*

  ■ allegorical, symbolic(al), mystic, cabalistic, arcane, unrevealed, secret, occult, supernatural, esoteric, otherworldly, preternatural, cryptic, concealed, hidden, clandestine, private, veiled, ineffable, mysterious.

mystify /místifī/ *v.tr.* (**-ies, -ied**) **1** bewilder, confuse. **2**

hoax, take advantage of the credulity of. **3** wrap up in mystery. □□ **mystification** /-fikáyshən/ *n.* [F *mystifier* (irreg. formed as MYSTIC or MYSTERY[1])]

■ **1, 2** confuse, confound, mix up, bewilder, stump, puzzle, baffle, beat, *colloq.* flummox; fool, mislead, hoax, humbug, *colloq.* bamboozle.

mystique /misteék/ *n.* **1** an atmosphere of mystery and veneration attending some activity or person. **2** any skill or technique impressive or mystifying to the layman. [F f. OF (as MYSTIC)]

■ **1** mystery, magic, charisma, aura, inscrutability, charm, inscrutableness. **2** see MUMBO JUMBO 2.

myth /mith/ *n.* **1** a traditional narrative usu. involving supernatural or imaginary persons and embodying popular ideas on natural or social phenomena, etc. **2** such narratives collectively. **3** a widely held but false notion. **4** a fictitious person, thing, or idea. **5** an allegory (*the Platonic myth*). □□ **mythic** *adj.* **mythical** *adj.* **mythically** *adv.* [mod.L *mythus* f. LL *mythos* f. Gk *muthos*]

■ **1, 2, 5** legend, fable, allegory, parable, (folk)tale, (folk)story, *literary* mythus. **3** see *misconception* (MISCONCEIVE). **4** fable, lie, (tall) tale, fiction, untruth, falsehood, fabrication, fantasy, fairy story *or* tale, cock-and-bull story, *sl.* whopper. □□ **mythic, mythical** mythological, fabled, legendary, traditional, folkloric, romantic, fairy-tale, storybook, *literary* storied; allegorical, symbolic, parabolic(al); fanciful, imaginary, fictitious, make-believe, made-up, chimerical, untrue.

mythicize /míthisiz/ *v.tr.* treat (a story, etc.) as a myth; interpret mythically. □□ **mythicism** /-sizəm/ *n.* **mythicist** /-sist/ *n.*

mytho- /míthō/ *comb. form* myth.

mythogenesis /míthōjénisis/ *n.* the production of myths.

mythographer /mithógrəfər/ *n.* a compiler of myths.

mythography /mithógrəfee/ *n.* the representation of myths in plastic art.

mythoi *pl.* of MYTHOS.

mythology /mithóləjee/ *n.* (*pl.* **-ies**) **1** a body of myths (*Greek mythology*). **2** the study of myths. □□ **mythologer** *n.* **mythologic** /-thəlójik/ *adj.* **mythological** /-thəlójikəl/ *adj.* **mythologically** /-thəlójiklee/ *adv.* **mythologist** *n.* **mythologize** *v.tr. & intr.* **mythologizer** *n.* [ME f. F *mythologie* or LL *mythologia* f. Gk *muthologia* (as MYTHO-, -LOGY)]

■ **1** myth(s), folklore, fable, legend, tradition, lore, stories.

mythomania /míthōmáyneə/ *n.* an abnormal tendency to exaggerate or tell lies. □□ **mythomaniac** /-neeak/ *n. & adj.*

mythopoeia /míthōpeéə/ *n.* the making of myths. □□ **mythopoeic** *adj.* (also **mythopoetic** /-pō-étik/).

mythos /míthos/ *n.* (*pl.* **mythoi** /-thoy/) *literary* a myth. [mod.L: see MYTH]

myxedema /míksədeémə/ *n.* a syndrome caused by hypothyroidism, resulting in thickening of the skin, weight gain, mental dullness, loss of energy, and sensitivity to cold.

myxo- /míksō/ *comb. form* (also **myx-** before a vowel) mucus. [Gk *muxa* mucus]

myxoma /miksōmə/ *n.* (*pl.* **myxomas** or **myxomata** /-mətə/) a benign tumor of mucous or gelatinous tissue. □□ **myxomatous** /-sómətəs/ *adj.* [mod.L (as MYXO-, -OMA)]

myxomatosis /míksəmətōsis/ *n.* an infectious usu. fatal viral disease in rabbits, causing swelling of the mucous membranes.

myxomycete /míksōmiseét/ *n.* any of a group of small acellular organisms inhabiting damp areas.

myxovirus /míksōvirəs/ *n.* any of a group of viruses including the influenza virus.

/ . . . / **pronunciation** ● **part of speech**
□ **phrases, idioms, and compounds**
□□ **derivatives** ■ **synonym section**
cross-references appear in SMALL CAPITALS or *italics*

Nn

N¹ /en/ *n.* (also **n**) (*pl.* **Ns** or **N's**) **1** the fourteenth letter of the alphabet. **2** *Printing* en. **3** *Math.* (**n**) an indefinite number. □ **to the nth** (or **nth degree**) **1** *Math.* to any required power. **2** to any extent; to the utmost.

N² *abbr.* (also **N.**) **1** north; northern. **2** newton(s). **3** *Chess* knight. **4** New. **5** nuclear.

N³ *symb. Chem.* the element nitrogen.

n *abbr.* (also **n.**) **1** name. **2** nano-. **3** neuter. **4** noon. **5** note. **6** noun.

'n *conj.* (also **'n'**) *colloq.* and. [abbr.]

-n¹ *suffix* see -EN².

-n² *suffix* see -EN³.

Na *symb. Chem.* the element sodium.

na /nə/ *adv. Sc.* (in *comb.*; usu. with an auxiliary verb) = NOT (*I canna do it*; *they didna go*).

N.A. *abbr.* North America.

n/a *abbr.* **1** not applicable. **2** not available.

NAACP /endəbəláyseepee/ *abbr.* National Association for the Advancement of Colored People.

NAAFI /náfee/ *abbr. Brit.* **1** Navy, Army, and Air Force Institutes. **2** a canteen for servicemen run by the NAAFI.

nab /nab/ *v.tr.* *sl.* **1** arrest; catch in wrongdoing. **2** seize, grab. [17th c., also *napp*, as in KIDNAP: orig. unkn.]

■ **1** catch, capture, arrest, put *or* place under arrest, seize, apprehend, pick up, bring in, take into custody, collar, nail, *colloq.* run in, *sl.* pinch, *Brit. sl.* nick.

nabob /náybob/ *n.* **1** *hist.* a Muslim official or governor under the Mughal empire. **2** (formerly) a conspicuously wealthy person, esp. one returned from India with a fortune. **3** any wealthy person of influence. [Port. *nababo* or Sp. *nabab*, f. Urdu (as NAWAB)]

nacarat /nákərat/ *n.* a bright orange-red color. [F, perh. f. Sp. & Port. *nacardo* (*nacar* NACRE)]

nacelle /nəsél/ *n.* **1** the outer casing of the engine of an aircraft. **2** the car of an airship. [F, f. LL *navicella* dimin. of L *navis* ship]

nacho /naachṓ/ *n.* (*pl.* **-os**) (usu. in *pl.*) a tortilla chip, usu. topped with melted cheese and spices, etc. [20th c.: orig. uncert.]

nacre /náykər/ *n.* mother-of-pearl from any shelled mollusk. □□ **nacred** *adj.* **nacreous** /náykreeəs/ *adj.* **nacrous** /-krəs/ *adj.* [F]

nadir /náydər, -deer/ *n.* **1** the part of the celestial sphere directly below an observer (opp. ZENITH). **2** the lowest point in one's fortunes; a time of deep despair. [ME f. OF f. Arab. *naẓīr* (*as-samt*) opposite (to the zenith)]

■ **2** abyss, down, low point, extreme; rock bottom; (*the nadir*) the depths (of despair), *sl.* the pits.

naff¹ /naf/ *v.intr. Brit. sl.* **1** (in *imper.*, foll. by *off*) go away. **2** (as **naffing** *adj.*) used as an intensive to express annoyance, etc.

naff² /naf/ *adj. Brit. sl.* **1** unfashionable; socially awkward. **2** worthless, rubbishy. [20th c.: orig. unkn.]

■ **1** see OBSOLETE, AWKWARD 2. **2** see WORTHLESS.

NAFTA /náftə/ *abbr.* North American Free Trade Agreement.

nag¹ /nag/ *v. & n.* ● *v.* (**nagged, nagging**) **1 a** *tr.* annoy or irritate (a person) with persistent faultfinding or continuous urging. **b** *intr.* (often foll. by *at*) find fault, complain, or urge, esp. persistently. **2** *intr.* (of a pain) ache dully but persis-

tently. **3 a** *tr.* worry or preoccupy (a person, the mind, etc.) (*his mistake nagged him*). **b** *intr.* (often foll. by *at*) worry or gnaw. **c** (as **nagging** *adj.*) persistently worrying or painful.
● *n.* a persistently nagging person. □□ **nagger** *n.* **naggingly** *adv.* [of dial., perh. Scand. or LG, orig.: cf. Norw. & Sw. *nagga* gnaw, irritate, LG (*g*)*naggen* provoke]

■ *v.* **1, 3a, b** annoy, irritate, irk, pester, criticize, scold, carp at, upbraid, badger, harass, harry, vex, henpeck, torment, hector, pick at, goad, pick on, find fault with, berate, nettle, bully, provoke, worry, bother, ride, *Brit.* chivvy, *colloq.* needle, plague, *Austral. colloq.* heavy. **3 c** (**nagging**) persistent, continuing, continual, unrelenting, relentless; worrying, distressing. ● *n.* pest, shrew, virago, termagant, harridan, *archaic* scold.

nag² /nag/ *n.* **1** *colloq.* a horse. **2** a small riding horse or pony. [ME: orig. unkn.]

■ jade; horse, hack, pony, dobbin, bangtail, racehorse, thoroughbred.

Nah. *abbr.* Nahum (Old Testament).

Nahuatl /naáwaát'l/ *n. & adj.* ● *n.* **1** a member of a group of peoples native to S. Mexico and Central America, including the Aztecs. **2** the language of these people. ● *adj.* of or concerning the Nahuatl peoples or language. □□ **Nahuatlan** *adj.* [Sp. f. Nahuatl]

naiad /níad/ *n.* (*pl.* **naiads** or **-des** /níədeez/) **1** *Mythol.* a water nymph. **2** the larva of a dragonfly, etc. **3** any aquatic plant of the genus *Najas*, with narrow leaves and small flowers. [L *Naïas Naïad-* f. Gk *Naias -ados* f. naō flow]

nail /nayl/ *n. & v.* ● *n.* **1** a small usu. sharpened metal spike with a broadened flat head, driven in with a hammer to join things together or to serve as a peg, protection (cf. HOBNAIL), or decoration. **2 a** a horny covering on the upper surface of the tip of the human finger or toe. **b** a claw or talon. **c** a hard growth on the upper mandible of some soft-billed birds. **3** *hist.* a measure of cloth length (equal to 2¹/₄ inches).
● *v.tr.* **1** fasten with a nail or nails (*nailed it to the beam*; *nailed the planks together*). **2** fix or keep (a person, attention, etc.) fixed. **3 a** secure, catch, or get hold of (a person or thing). **b** expose or discover (a lie or a liar). □ **hard as nails** **1** callous; unfeeling. **2** in good physical condition. **nail-biting** causing severe anxiety or tension. **nail one's colors to the mast** persist; refuse to give in. **nail down 1** bind (a person) to a promise, etc. **2** define precisely. **3** fasten (a thing) with nails. **nail enamel** = *nail polish.* **nail file** a roughened metal or emery strip used for smoothing the nails. **nail in a person's coffin** something thought to increase the risk of death. **nail polish** a varnish applied to the nails to color them or make them shiny. **nail scissors** small curved scissors for trimming the nails. **nail set** a tool for sinking the head of a nail below a surface. **nail up 1** close (a door, etc.) with nails. **2** fix (a thing) at a height with nails. **nail varnish** *Brit.* = *nail polish.* **on the nail** (esp. of payment) without delay (*cash on the nail*). □□ **nailed** *adj.* (also in *comb.*). **nailless** *adj.* [OE *nægel, næglan* f. Gmc]

■ *n.* **1** tack, brad, staple, clout, spike, pin; peg, fastener, fastening. **2** fingernail, toenail; claw, talon. ● *v.* **1** fasten, attach, secure, join, pin, tack, peg, clinch, clench, fix, rivet. **2** see HOLD¹ *v.* 7a. **3 a** see CATCH *v.* 1. **b** see EXPOSE 5. □ **hard as nails 1** cold, unsentimental, unsympathetic; unfeeling, callous. **2** see HARDY. **nail-**

biting see *nerve-racking*. **nail down 1** see BIND *v.* 5.
2 see *pin down* 4. **3** see FASTEN 1. **on the nail**
immediately, at once, straight *or* right away, promptly,
without delay, on the spot.

nailer /náylər/ *n.* a nail driver, esp. an automatic device.

nainsook /náynsŏŏk/ *n.* a fine soft cotton fabric, orig. from
India. [Hindi *nainsukh* f. *nain* eye + *sukh* pleasure]

naira /nírə/ *n.* the chief monetary unit of Nigeria. [contr. of
Nigeria]

naïve /naa-éev/ *adj.* (also **naive**) **1** artless; innocent; unaffected. **2** foolishly credulous; simple. □□ **naïvely** *adv.* **na-
ïveness** *n.* [F, fem. of *naïf* f. L *nativus* NATIVE]
■ innocent, unaffected, unsophisticated, artless, guileless,
unpretentious, unpretending, candid, natural,
ingenuous, childlike; unsuspecting, unsuspicious,
trusting, trustful, credulous, gullible, green,
inexperienced, unworldly, unenlightened, simple,
simplistic, simple-minded.

naïveté /naa-eevtáy, -éevtáy/ *n.* (also **naivete**, **naiveté** esp.
Brit. **naïvety** /naa-éevətee/) **1** the state or quality of being
naïve. **2** a naïve action. [F *naïveté* (as NAÏVE)]
■ **1** ingenuousness, innocence, credulity, credulousness,
inexperience, trust, gullibility, artlessness, callowness,
guilelessness, simplicity, unpretentiousness, candor,
naturalness, frankness, openness, sincerity.

naked /náykid/ *adj.* **1** without clothes; nude. **2** plain; undisguised; exposed (*the naked truth; his naked soul*). **3** (of a
light, flame, etc.) unprotected from the wind, etc.; unshaded. **4** defenseless. **5** without addition, comment, support, evidence, etc. (*his naked word; naked assertion*). **6 a** (of
landscape) barren; treeless. **b** (of rock) exposed; without
soil, etc. **7** (of a sword, etc.) unsheathed. **8** (usu. foll. by *of*)
devoid; without. **9** without leaves, hairs, scales, shell, etc.
10 (of a room, wall, etc.) without decoration, furnishings,
etc.; empty; plain. □ **naked boys** (or **lady** or **ladies**) *Brit.*
the meadow saffron, which flowers while leafless: also called
autumn crocus. **the naked eye** unassisted vision, e.g., without a telescope, microscope, etc. □□ **nakedly** *adv.* **nakedness** *n.* [OE *nacod* f. Gmc]
■ **1** unclothed, undraped, bare, stripped, undressed,
unclad, uncovered, bared, nude, in the nude, in the
raw, in a state of nature, stark (naked), *colloq.* in the
altogether, in the buff, *joc.* in one's birthday suit,
Austral. sl. bollocky, *Brit. sl.* starkers. **2** plain,
unadorned, evident, unembellished, stark, overt,
patent, obvious, conspicuous, manifest, sheer, exposed,
undisguised, unvarnished, unmitigated, evident,
palpable, unconcealed, in plain sight *or* view; blatant,
barefaced, undeniable, glaring, flagrant; unmistakable,
unalloyed, unmixed, blunt, unadulterated, pure. **3** see
OPEN *adj.* 1–4, 13, 20. **5** unaided, unsupported,
unassisted; see also BARE *adj.* 3. **7** unsheathed, drawn,
bare.

namby-pamby /námbeepámbee/ *adj. & n.* ● *adj.* **1** lacking
vigor or vitality; weak. **2** insipidly pretty or sentimental. ● *n.*
(*pl.* **-ies**) **1** a namby-pamby person. **2** namby-pamby talk.
[fanciful formulation on name of *Ambrose* Philips, Engl. pastoral writer d. 1749]
■ *adj.* **1** see WEAK *adj.* 3a. ● *n.* **1** see WEAKLING.

name /naym/ *n. & v.* ● *n.* **1 a** the word by which an individual person, animal, place, or thing is known, spoken of, etc.
(*mentioned him by name; her name is Joanna*). **b** all who go
under one name; a family, clan, or people in terms of its
name (*the Scottish name*). **2 a** a usu. abusive term used of a
person, etc. (*called him names*). **b** a word denoting an object
or esp. a class of objects, ideas, etc. (*what is the name of that
kind of vase?; that sort of behavior has no name*). **3** a famous
person (*many great names were there*). **4** a reputation, esp. a
good one (*has a name for honesty; their name is guarantee
enough*). **5** something existing only nominally (opp. FACT,
REALITY). **6** (*attrib.*) widely known (*a name brand of shampoo*). ● *v.tr.* **1** give a usu. specified name to (*named the dog
Spot*). **2** call (a person or thing) by the right name (*named
the man in the photograph*). **3** mention; specify; cite (*named

her requirements). **4** nominate, appoint, etc. (*was named the
new chairman*). **5** specify as something desired (*named it as
her dearest wish*). **6** *Brit. Parl.* (of the Speaker) mention (an
MP) as disobedient to the chair. □ **by name** called (*Tom by
name*). **have to one's name** possess. **in name** (or **name only**)
as a mere formality; hardly
at all (*is the leader in name only*). **in a person's name** = *in
the name of*. **in the name of** calling to witness; invoking (*in
the name of goodness*). **in one's own name** independently;
without authority. **make a name for oneself** become famous. **name after** (also **for**) call (a person) by the name of
(a specified person) (*named him after his uncle Roger*). **name-
calling** abusive language. **name the day** arrange a date
(esp. of a woman fixing the date for her wedding). **name-
drop** (**-dropped**, **-dropping**) indulge in name-dropping.
name-dropper a person who name-drops. **name-dropping** the familiar mention of famous people as a form of
boasting. **name names** mention specific names, esp. in accusation. **name of the game** *colloq.* the purpose or essence
of an action, etc. **name tape** a tape fixed to a garment, etc.,
and bearing the name of the owner. **of** (or **by**) **the name
of** called. **put one's name down for 1** apply for. **2** promise
to subscribe (a sum). **what's in a name?** names are arbitrary labels. **you name it** *colloq.* no matter what; whatever
you like. □□ **nameable** *adj.* [OE *nama, noma*, (*ge*)*namian* f.
Gmc, rel. to L *nomen*, Gk *onoma*]
■ *n.* **1, 2** designation, label, term, tag, style, *colloq.*
handle, *formal* appellation, *sl.* moniker. **3** personage,
somebody, celebrity, star, superstar, hero, VIP,
dignitary, luminary, big name, *colloq.* big shot, bigwig,
(big) cheese, big noise. **4** reputation; repute, honor,
rank, standing, rating, preeminence, superiority,
eminence, notability, prominence, prestige, distinction,
renown, fame, popularity, celebrity. **6** (*attrib.*) see *well-
known* (WELL¹). ● *v.* **1** label, tag, style, call, dub,
archaic entitle; christen, baptize. **3–5** choose, elect,
select, delegate, nominate, designate, appoint; identify,
denominate, pinpoint, specify; mention, cite. □ **by
name** see CALL *v.* 7. **in all but name** see *virtually*
(VIRTUAL). **name-calling** see ABUSE *n.* 2. **name of the
game** see IDEA 3. **you name it** see *I'm easy* (EASY).

nameless /náymlis/ *adj.* **1** having no name or name inscription. **2** inexpressible; indefinable (*a nameless sensation*). **3**
unnamed; anonymous, esp. deliberately (*our informant, who
shall be nameless*). **4** too loathsome or horrific to be named
(*nameless vices*). **5** obscure; inglorious. **6** illegitimate.
□□ **namelessly** *adv.* **namelessness** *n.*
■ **1, 3, 5** unnamed, innominate; unidentified,
anonymous, incognito; unknown, unheard-of, unsung;
obscure, inglorious. **2** inexpressible, indefinable,
unidentifiable, unspecified, unspecifiable, ineffable.
4 ineffable, unutterable, unspeakable, unmentionable,
abominable, horrible, indescribable, repulsive.

namely /náymlee/ *adv.* that is to say; in other words.
■ specifically, that is (to say), i.e., in other words,
videlicet, viz., scilicet, sc., to wit.

namesake /náymsayk/ *n.* a person or thing having the same
name as another (*was her aunt's namesake*). [prob. f. phr. *for
the name's sake*]

namma var. of GNAMMA.

nana /nánə/ *n. colloq.* **1** grandmother. **2** godmother. **3** nursemaid. [f. NANNY]

nance /nans/ *n. & adj.* (also **nancy** /nánsee/) *derog. sl.* ● *n.*
(*pl.* **-ies**) (in full **nancy boy**) an effeminate man, esp. a
homosexual. ● *adj.* effeminate. [f. name *Nancy*]

nankeen /nangkéen/ *n.* **1** a yellowish cotton cloth. **2** a yellowish buff color. **3** (in *pl.*) trousers of nankeen. [*Nankin*(*g*)
in China, where orig. made]

nanny /nánee/ *n. & v.* ● *n.* (*pl.* **-ies**) **1 a** a child's nursemaid.

/. . ./ pronunciation	● part of speech
□ phrases, idioms, and compounds	
□□ derivatives	■ synonym section
cross-references appear in SMALL CAPITALS or *italics*	

b *Brit.* an unduly protective person, institution, etc. (*the nanny state*). **2** (in full **nanny goat**) a female goat. ● *v.tr.* (**-ies, -ied**) be unduly protective toward. [pet form of name *Ann*]

■ *n.* **1 a** see MINDER 1.

nano- /nánō, náynō/ *comb. form* denoting a factor of 10⁻⁹ (*nanosecond*). [L f. Gk *nanos* dwarf]

nanometer /nánōmeetər/ *n.* one billionth of a meter. ¶ Abbr.: **nm**.

nanosecond /nánōsekənd/ *n.* one billionth of a second. ¶ Abbr.: **ns**.

naos /náyos/ *n.* (*pl.* **naoi** /náyoy/) *Gk Hist.* the inner part of a temple. [Gk, = temple]

nap¹ /nap/ *v. & n.* ● *v.intr.* (**napped, napping**) sleep lightly or briefly. ● *n.* a short sleep or doze, esp. by day (*took a nap*). □ **catch a person napping 1** find a person asleep or off guard. **2** detect in negligence or error. [OE *hnappian*, rel. to OHG (*h*)*naffezan* to slumber]

■ *v.* sleep, doze, nod (off), catnap, *colloq.* catch *or* get forty winks, drop off, get some shut-eye, snooze, *Brit. sl.* kip, have a *or* some kip. ● *n.* sleep, doze, catnap, siesta, lie-down, *colloq.* forty winks, shut-eye, snooze, *Brit. sl.* kip. □ **catch a person napping 1** catch a person unawares *or* off guard *or* in an unguarded moment; see also SURPRISE *v.* 3, 4.

nap² /nap/ *n. & v.* ● *n.* **1** the raised pile on textiles, esp. velvet. **2** a soft downy surface. **3** *Austral. colloq.* blankets, bedding, swag. ● *v.tr.* (**napped, napping**) raise a nap on (cloth). □□ **napless** *adj.* [ME *noppe* f. MDu., MLG *noppe* nap, *noppen* trim nap from]

■ *n.* **1** pile, fiber, texture, weave, down, shag; see also TEXTURE *n.* 1, 2.

nap³ /nap/ *n. & v.* ● *n.* **1 a** a form of whist in which players declare the number of tricks they expect to take, up to five. **b** a call of five in this game. **2** *Brit.* **a** the betting of all one's money on one horse, etc. **b** a tipster's choice for this. ● *v.tr. Brit.* (**napped, napping**) name (a horse, etc.) as a probable winner. □ **go nap** *Brit.* **1** attempt to take all five tricks in nap. **2** risk everything in one attempt. **3** win all the matches, etc., in a series. **not go nap on** *Austral. colloq.* not be too keen on; not care much for. [abbr. of orig. name of game NAPOLEON]

napa var. of NAPPA.

napalm /náypaam/ *n. & v.* ● *n.* **1** a thickening agent produced from naphthenic acid, other fatty acids, and aluminum. **2** a jellied substance made from this, used in incendiary bombs. ● *v.tr.* attack with napalm bombs. [NAPHTHENIC + *palmitic acid* in coconut oil]

nape /nayp/ *n.* the back of the neck. [ME: orig. unkn.]

napery /náypəree/ *n. Sc.* or *archaic* household linen, esp. table linen. [ME f. OF *naperie* f. *nape* (as NAPKIN)]

naphtha /náf-thə, náp-/ *n.* a flammable oil obtained by the dry distillation of organic substances such as coal, shale, or petroleum. [L f. Gk, = flammable volatile liquid issuing from the earth, of Oriental origin]

naphthalene /náf-thəleen, náp-/ *n.* a white crystalline aromatic substance produced by the distillation of coal tar and used in mothballs and the manufacture of dyes, etc. □□ **naphthalic** /-thálik/ *adj.* [NAPHTHA + -ENE]

naphthene /náf-theen, náp-/ *n.* any of a group of cycloalkanes. [NAPHTHA + -ENE]

naphthenic /naf-theénik, náp-/ *adj.* of a naphthene or its radical. □ **naphthenic acid** any carboxylic acid resulting from the refining of petroleum.

Napierian logarithm /naypéereeən, nə-/ *n.* see LOGARITHM. [J. *Napier*, Sc. mathematician d. 1617]

napkin /nápkin/ *n.* **1** (in full **table napkin**) a square piece of linen, paper, etc. used for wiping the lips, fingers, etc., at meals; a serviette. **2** *Brit.* a baby's diaper. **3** a small towel. □ **napkin ring** a ring used to hold (and distinguish) a person's table napkin when not in use. [ME f. OF *nappe* f. L *mappa* (MAP)]

napoleon /nəpóleeən/ *n.* **1** *hist.* a gold twenty-franc piece minted in the reign of Napoleon I. **2** *hist.* a 19th-c. high boot. **3** = NAP³. **4** = MILLE-FEUILLE. □ **double napoleon** *hist.*

a forty-franc piece. [F *napoléon* f. *Napoléon*, name of 19th-c. French emperors]

Napoleonic /nəpōleeónik/ *adj.* of, relating to, or characteristic of Napoleon I or his time.

nappa /nápə/ *n.* (also **napa**) a soft leather made by a special process from the skin of sheep or goats. [*Napa* in California]

nappe /nap/ *n. Geol.* a sheet of rock that has moved sideways over neighboring strata, usu. as a result of overthrust. [F *nappe* tablecloth]

nappy /nápee/ *n.* (*pl.* **-ies**) *Brit.* a baby's diaper. [abbr. of NAPKIN]

narc /nark/ *n.* (also **narc**) *sl.* a federal agent or police officer who enforces the laws regarding illicit sale or use of drugs and narcotics.

narceine /naársee-eén, -in/ *n.* a narcotic alkaloid obtained from opium. [F *narcéine* f. Gk *narkē* numbness]

narcissism /naársisizəm/ *n. Psychol.* excessive or erotic interest in oneself, one's physical features, etc. □□ **narcissist** *n.* **narcissistic** *adj.* **narcissistically** *adv.* [*Narcissus* (Gk *Narkissos*), youth who fell in love with his reflection in water]

■ see VANITY 1. □□ **narcissistic** see VAIN 1.

narcissus /naársísəs/ *n.* (*pl.* **narcissi** /-sī/ or **narcissuses**) any bulbous plant of the genus *Narcissus*, esp. *N. poeticus* bearing a heavily scented single flower with an undivided corona edged with crimson and yellow. [L f. Gk *narkissos*, perh. f. *narkē* numbness, with ref. to its narcotic effects]

narcolepsy /naárkəlepsee/ *n. Med.* a disease with fits of sleepiness and drowsiness. □□ **narcoleptic** /-léptik/ *adj. & n.* [Gk *narkoō* make numb, after EPILEPSY]

narcosis /naarkōsis/ *n.* **1** *Med.* the working or effects of soporific narcotics. **2** a state of insensibility. [Gk *narkōsis* f. *narkoō* make numb]

narcoterrorism /náarkōtérərizəm/ *n.* violent crime associated with illicit drugs. □□ **narcoterrorist** *adj. & n.* [NARCOTIC + *terrorism*]

narcotic /naarkótik/ *adj. & n.* ● *adj.* **1** (of a substance) inducing drowsiness, sleep, stupor, or insensibility. **2** (of a drug) affecting the mind. **3** of or involving narcosis. **4** soporific. ● *n.* a narcotic substance, drug, or influence. □□ **narcotically** *adv.* **narcotism** /naárkətizəm/ *n.* **narcotize** /naárkətiz/ *v.tr.* **narcotization** /-tizáyshən/ *n.* [ME f. OF *narcotique* or med.L f. Gk *narkōtikos* (as NARCOSIS)]

■ *adj.* **1, 4** soporific, hypnotic, sedative, sleep-inducing, opiate, dulling, numbing, anesthetic, stupefacient, stupefying, stupefactive, tranquilizing, lethean. ● *n.* drug, soporific, hypnotic, sedative, opiate, anesthetic, stupefacient, tranquilizer.

nard /naard/ *n.* **1** any of various plants yielding an aromatic balsam used by the ancients. **2** = SPIKENARD. [ME f. L *nardus* f. Gk *nardos* ult. f. Skr.]

nares /náireez/ *n.pl. Anat.* the nostrils. □□ **narial** *adj.* [pl. of L *naris*]

narghile /naárgilee/ *n.* a Middle Eastern tobacco pipe with the smoke drawn through water; a hookah. [Pers. *nārgīleh* (*nārgīl* coconut)]

nark /naark/ *n. & v. sl.* ● *n.* **1** *Brit.* a police informer or decoy. **2** *Austral.* an annoying person or thing. ● *v.tr.* (usu. in *passive*) *Brit.* annoy; infuriate (*was narked by their attitude*). □ **nark it!** *Brit.* stop that! [Romany *nāk* nose]

Narragansett /narəgánsət, -gánt-/ *n.* **1 a** a N. American people native to Rhode Island. **b** a member of this people. **2** the language of this people.

narrate /nárayt, naráyt/ *v.tr.* (also *absol.*) **1** give a continuous story or account of. **2** provide a spoken commentary or accompaniment for (a film, etc.). □□ **narratable** *adj.* **narration** /-ráyshən/ *n.* [L *narrare narrat-*]

■ relate, tell, recount, report, give an account of, recite, rehearse, repeat, review, unfold, chronicle, describe, detail, reveal, retail; speak, read, *disp.* commentate. □□ **narration** telling; report, recital, recitation, rehearsal, relation, chronicle, description, portrayal, detailing, revelation, story, tale, narrative; reading, voice-over.

narrative /nárətiv/ *n. & adj.* ● *n.* **1** a spoken or written account of connected events in order of happening. **2** the

practice or art of narration. ● *adj.* in the form of, or concerned with, narration (*narrative verse*). □□ **narratively** *adv.* [F *narratif -ive* f. LL *narrativus* (as NARRATE)]
■ *n.* **1** story, tale, chronicle, description, revelation, portrayal, account, report, record, history, recital, statement. **2** storytelling.

narrator /náraytər/ *n.* **1** an actor, announcer, etc., who delivers a commentary in a film, broadcast, etc. **2** a person who narrates. [L (as NARRATE)]
■ commentator, announcer, reader; reporter, storyteller, raconteur, taleteller, anecdotist, anecdotalist, relator, annalist, chronicler, describer, *Austral. sl.* magsman.

narrow /nárō/ *adj., n., & v.* ● *adj.* (**narrower, narrowest**) **1 a** of small width in proportion to length; lacking breadth. **b** confined or confining; constricted (*within narrow bounds*). **2** of limited scope; restricted (*in the narrowest sense*). **3** with little margin (*a narrow escape*). **4** searching; precise; exact (*a narrow examination*). **5** = NARROW-MINDED. **6** (of a vowel) tense. **7** of small size. ● *n.* **1** (usu. in *pl.*) the narrow part of a strait, river, sound, etc. **2** a narrow pass or street. ● *v.* **1** *intr.* become narrow; diminish; contract; lessen. **2** *tr.* make narrow; constrict; restrict. □ **narrow circumstances** poverty. **narrow gauge** a railroad track that has a smaller gauge than the standard one. **narrow seas** *Brit.* the English Channel and the Irish Sea. **narrow squeak** *Brit.* **1** a narrow escape. **2** a success barely attained. □□ **narrowish** *adj.* **narrowly** *adv.* **narrowness** *n.* [OE *nearu nearw-* f. Gmc]
■ *adj.* **1 a** slender, slim, thin, straitened, attenuated, narrowed; narrowing, tapering. **b** confined, confining, limited, cramped, close, meager, pinched, tight, incommodious; constricted, restricted. **2** restricted, limited, circumscribed, prescribed, denotative; see also STRAIT *adj.* 1. **3** close, near, hairbreadth; lucky. **4** strict, careful, close, precise, exact, exacting, demanding, finicky, finical, fastidious, sharp, meticulous, scrupulous, fussy, rigid, stringent, rigorous, searching, critical. ● *n.* strait, channel, passage. ● *v.* **1** diminish, contract, lessen, decrease, reduce, get *or* become smaller *or* thinner *or* narrower. **2** constrict, limit, qualify, reduce, lessen, diminish, decrease, restrict, focus, confine, concentrate, narrow down.
□□ **narrowly** barely, (only) just, scarcely, hardly, by a hair's breadth, by the skin of one's teeth, *colloq.* by a whisker; closely, carefully, meticulously, scrupulously, searchingly, critically.

narrow-minded /nárōmíndid/ *adj.* rigid or restricted in one's views; intolerant; prejudiced; illiberal. □□ **narrow-mindedly** *adv.* **narrow-mindedness** *n.*
■ bigoted, prejudiced, illiberal, narrow, limited, biased, opinionated, one-sided, intolerant, conservative, parochial, conventional, hidebound, petty, shallow, pettifogging, small-minded, puritanical, rigid, restricted, unprogressive, strait-laced, stuffy, close-minded, *sl.* square.

narthex /náartheks/ *n.* **1** a railed-off antechamber or porch, etc., at the western entrance of some early Christian churches, used by catechumens, penitents, etc. **2** a similar antechamber in a modern church. [L f. Gk *narthēx* giant fennel, stick, casket, narthex]

narwhal /náarwəl/ *n.* an Arctic white whale, *Monodon monoceros*, the male of which has a long straight spirally fluted tusk developed from one of its teeth. Also called BELUGA. [Du. *narwal* f. Da. *narhval* f. *hval* whale: cf. ON *náhvalr* (perh. f. *nár* corpse, with ref. to its skin color)]

nary /náiree/ *adj. colloq.* or *dial.* not any; no (*nary a one*). [f. *ne'er a*]

NAS *abbr.* National Academy of Sciences.

NASA /násə/ *abbr.* National Aeronautics and Space Administration.

nasal /náyzəl/ *adj. & n.* ● *adj.* **1** of, for, or relating to the nose. **2** *Phonet.* (of a letter or a sound) pronounced with the breath passing through the nose, e.g., *m, n, ng,* or French *en, un,* etc. **3** (of the voice or speech) having an intonation caused by breathing through the nose. ● *n.* **1** *Phonet.* a nasal letter or sound. **2** *hist.* a nosepiece on a helmet. □□ **nasality**

/-zálitee/ *n.* **nasalize** *v.intr.* & *tr.* **nasalization** *n.* **nasally** *adv.* [F *nasal* or med.L *nasalis* f. L *nasus* nose]

nascent /násənt, náy-/ *adj.* **1** in the act of being born. **2** just beginning to be; not yet mature. **3** *Chem.* just being formed and therefore unusually reactive (*nascent hydrogen*). □□ **nascency** /násənsee, náy-/ *n.* [L *nasci nascent-* be born]

NASDAQ /názdak, nás-/ *abbr.* National Association of Securities Dealers Automated Quotations.

naseberry /náyzberee/ *n.* (*pl.* **-ies**) a sapodilla. [Sp. & Port. *néspera* medlar f. L (see MEDLAR): assim. to BERRY]

naso- /náyzō/ *comb. form* nose. [L *nasus* nose]

nasofrontal /náyzōfrúnt'l/ *adj.* of or relating to the nose and forehead.

nastic /nástik/ *adj. Bot.* (of the movement of plant parts) not determined by an external stimulus. [Gk *nastos* squeezed together f. *nassō* to press]

nasturtium /nəstárshəm/ *n.* **1** (in general use) a trailing plant, *Tropaeolum majus*, with rounded edible leaves and bright orange, yellow, or red flowers. **2** any cruciferous plant of the genus *Nasturtium*, including watercress. [L]

nasty /nástee/ *adj. & n.* ● *adj.* (**nastier, nastiest**) **1 a** highly unpleasant (*a nasty experience*). **b** annoying; objectionable (*the car has a nasty habit of breaking down*). **2** difficult to negotiate; dangerous, serious (*a nasty fence; a nasty question; a nasty illness*). **3** (of a person or animal) ill-natured, ill-tempered, spiteful; violent, offensive (*nasty to his mother; turns nasty when he's drunk*). **4** (of the weather) foul, wet, stormy. **5 a** disgustingly dirty, filthy. **b** unpalatable; disagreeable (*nasty smell*). **c** (of a wound) septic. **6 a** obscene. **b** delighting in obscenity. ● *n.* (*pl.* **-ies**) *colloq.* a horror film, esp. one on video and depicting cruelty or killing. □ **a nasty bit** (or **piece**) **of work** esp. *Brit. colloq.* an unpleasant or contemptible person. □□ **nastily** *adv.* **nastiness** *n.* [ME: orig. unkn.]
■ **1, 5a, b** disagreeable, unsavory, painful, annoying, untoward, awkward, difficult, bad, serious; foul, filthy, dirty, unclean, offensive, disgusting, repulsive, unpalatable, unpleasant, nauseating, revolting, horrible, loathsome, repugnant, repellent, vile, odious, obnoxious, objectionable, nauseous, sickening, fetid, mephitic, rank, stinking, malodorous, rancid, noxious, *literary* noisome. **2** bad, severe, acute, dangerous, critical, painful, serious; hard, tricky, problematical, difficult. **3** unpleasant, disagreeable, ugly, bad-tempered, vicious, violent, offensive, surly, abusive, spiteful, irascible, ill-natured, malicious, ill-tempered, cruel, mean, inconsiderate, rude, churlish, obnoxious, crotchety, curmudgeonly, cantankerous, crabbed, cranky. **4** see DIRTY *adj.* 6, FOUL *adj.* 7. **5c** septic. **6** obscene, dirty, filthy, pornographic, blue, smutty, lewd, vulgar, sordid, indecent, licentious, gross, coarse, crude, rude, ribald, bawdy, risqué, suggestive, off-color, *colloq.* raunchy.

nat. *abbr.* **1** national. **2** native. **3** natural.

natal /náytəl/ *adj.* of or from one's birth. [ME f. L *natalis* (as NATION)]
■ see INHERENT 1, INBORN.

natality /naytálitee, nə-/ *n.* (*pl.* **-ies**) birth rate. [F *natalité* (as NATAL)]

natation /naytáyshən, na-/ *n. formal* or *literary* the act or art of swimming. [L *natatio* f. *natare* swim]

natatorial /náytətáwreeəl, nát-/ *adj.* (also **natatory** /-táwree/) *formal* **1** swimming. **2** of or concerning swimming. [LL *natatorius* f. L *natator* swimmer (as NATATION)]

natatorium /náytətawreeəm/ *n.* (*pl.* **-ums** or **-ria** /-ree-ə/) a swimming pool, esp. indoors. [LL neut. of *natatorius* (see NATATORIAL)]

natch /nach/ *adv. colloq.* = NATURALLY. [abbr.]

Natchez /náchiz/ *n.* **1 a** a N. American people native to Mis-

/.../	pronunciation	● part of speech
□ phrases, idioms, and compounds		
□□ derivatives	■ synonym section	
cross-references appear in SMALL CAPITALS or *italics*		

sissippi. **b** a member of this people. **2** the language of this people.

nates /náyteez/ *n.pl. Anat.* the buttocks. [L]

natheless /náythlis/ *adv.* (also **nathless**) *archaic* nevertheless. [ME f. OE *nā* not (f. *ne* not + *ā* ever) + THE + *lǣs* LESS]

nation /náyshən/ *n.* **1** a community of people of mainly common descent, history, language, etc., forming a unified government or inhabiting a territory. **2** a tribe or confederation of tribes of Native Americans. □ **law of nations** *Law* international law. □□ **nationhood** *n.* [ME f. OF f. L *natio -onis* f. *nasci nat-* be born]

■ **1** country, state, land, polity, domain, *formal esp. Law* realm.

national /náshənəl/ *adj. & n.* ● *adj.* **1** of or common to a nation or the nation. **2** peculiar to or characteristic of a particular nation. ● *n.* **1** a citizen of a specified country, usu. entitled to hold that country's passport (*French nationals*). **2** a fellow countryman. **3** (**the National**) = *Grand National*. □ **national anthem** a song adopted by a nation, expressive of its identity, etc., and intended to inspire patriotism. **National Assembly 1** an elected house of legislature in various countries. **2** *hist.* the elected legislature in France 1789–91. **national bank** a bank chartered under the federal government. **national debt** the money owed by a country because of loans to it. **national football** *Austral.* Australian Rules football. **National Front** a UK political party with extreme reactionary views on immigration, etc. **national grid** *Brit.* **1** the network of high-voltage electric power lines between major power stations. **2** the metric system of geographical coordinates used in maps of the British Isles. **National Guard** the primary reserve force partly maintained by the states of the United States but available for federal use. **National Health** (or **Health Service**) (in the UK) a system of national medical care paid for mainly by taxation and started in 1948. **national income** the total money earned within a nation. **national park** an area of natural beauty protected by the government for the use of the general public. **national service** *Brit. hist.* service in the army, etc., under conscription. **National Socialism** *hist.* the doctrines of nationalism, racial purity, etc., adopted by the Nazis. **National Socialist** *hist.* a member of the fascist party implementing National Socialism in Germany, 1933–45. **National Trust** (in the UK, Australia, etc.) an organization for maintaining and preserving historic buildings, etc. □□ **nationally** *adv.* [F (as NATION)]

■ *adj.* nationwide, countrywide, governmental, civil, federal, *Brit.* state; public, popular. ● *n.* **1** citizen, subject, resident, native; voter. □ **national service** draft, conscription, call-up, *US hist.* selective service.

nationalism /náshənəlizəm/ *n.* **1** a patriotic feeling, principles, etc. **b** an extreme form of this; chauvinism. **2** a policy of national independence. □□ **nationalist** *n. & adj.* **nationalistic** *adj.* **nationalistically** *adv.*

■ **1 b** flag-waving, chauvinism; see also *jingoism* (JINGO). □□ **nationalist** (*n.*) see PATRIOT. **nationalistic** nationalist, patriotic, jingoistic, chauvinistic, xenophobic, isolationist.

nationality /náshənálitee/ *n.* (*pl.* -**ies**) **1 a** the status of belonging to a particular nation (*what is your nationality?*; *has Austrian nationality*). **b** a nation (*people of all nationalities*). **2** the condition of being national; distinctive national qualities. **3** an ethnic group forming a part of one or more political nations. **4** existence as a nation; nationhood. **5** patriotic sentiment.

■ **1** citizenship. **3** race, nation, ethnic group, ethnic minority, clan, tribe; strain, stock, pedigree, heritage, extraction, bloodline, breed.

nationalize /náshənəlíz/ *v.tr.* **1** take over (railways, coal-mines, the steel industry, land, etc.) from private ownership on behalf of the government. **2 a** make national. **b** make into a nation. **3** naturalize (a foreigner). □□ **nationalization** *n.* **nationalizer** *n.* [F *nationaliser* (as NATIONAL)]

nationwide /náyshənwíd/ *adj.* extending over the whole nation.

■ see NATIONAL *adj.*

native /náytiv/ *n. & adj.* ● *n.* **1 a** (usu. foll. by *of*) a person born in a specified place, or whose parents are domiciled in that place at the time of the birth (*a native of Chicago*). **b** a local inhabitant. **2** often *offens.* a member of a nonwhite indigenous people, as regarded by the colonial settlers. **3** (usu. foll. by *of*) an indigenous animal or plant. ● *adj.* **1** (usu. foll. by *to*) belonging to a person or thing by nature; inherent; innate (*spoke with the facility native to him*). **2** of one's birth or birthplace (*native dress*; *native country*). **3** belonging to one by right of birth. **4** (usu. foll. by *to*) belonging to a specified place (*the anteater is native to S. America*). **5 a** (esp. of a non-European) indigenous; born in a place. **b** of the natives of a place (*native customs*). **6** in a natural state; unadorned; simple. **7** *Geol.* (of metal, etc.) found in a pure or uncombined state. □ **go native** esp. *Brit.* (of a settler) adopt the local way of life, esp. in a non-European country. **Native American** a member of the aboriginal peoples of America or their descendants. **native bear** *Austral. & NZ* = KOALA. **native rock** rock in its original place. □□ **natively** *adv.* **nativeness** *n.* [ME (earlier as adj.) f. OF *natif -ive* or L *nativus* f. *nasci nat-* be born]

■ *n.* **1** aborigine, indigene, autochthon; national, citizen, resident, inhabitant; local. ● *adj.* **1** see INHERENT 1, INBORN. **2, 5** domestic, local, home, homegrown; indigenous, autochthonous, aboriginal; national, ethnic, clan, tribal; provincial, local. **3** inherited, hereditary; constitutional. **4** see INDIGENOUS. **6** unadorned, real, genuine, untouched, unaffected; simple, plain.

nativism /náytivizəm/ *n. Philos.* the doctrine of innate ideas. □□ **nativist** *n.*

nativity /nətívitee, nay-/ *n.* (*pl.* -**ies**) **1** (esp. **the Nativity**) **a** the birth of Christ. **b** the festival of Christ's birth; Christmas. **2** a picture of the Nativity. **3** birth. **4** the horoscope at a person's birth. **5 a** the birth of the Virgin Mary or St. John the Baptist. **b** the festival of the nativity of the Virgin (Sept. 8) or St. John (June 24). □ **nativity play** a play usu. performed by children at Christmas dealing with the birth of Christ. [ME f. OF *nativité* f. LL *nativitas -tatis* f. L (as NATIVE)]

■ **3** see BIRTH *n.* 1

natl. *abbr.* national.

NATO /náytō/ *abbr.* North Atlantic Treaty Organization.

natron /náytrən/ *n.* a mineral form of hydrated sodium salts found in dried lake beds. [F f. Sp. *natrón* f. Arab. *naṭrūn* f. Gk *nitron* NITER]

natter /nátər/ *v. & n. colloq.* ● *v.intr. Brit.* **1** chatter idly. **2** grumble; talk fretfully. ● *n.* **1** aimless chatter. **2** grumbling talk. □□ **natterer** *n.* [orig. Sc., imit.]

■ *v.* **1** see CHATTER *v.* 1. ● *n.* **1** see CHAT¹ *n.* 2.

natterjack /nátərjak/ *n.* a European toad, *Bufo calamita*, with a bright yellow stripe down its back, and moving by running not hopping. [perh. f. NATTER, from its loud croak, + JACK¹]

nattier blue /náteeər/ *n.* a soft shade of blue. [much used by J. M. *Nattier*, Fr. painter d. 1766]

natty /nátee/ *adj.* (**nattier**, **nattiest**) *colloq.* **1 a** smartly or neatly dressed, dapper. **b** spruce; trim; smart (*a natty blouse*). **2** deft. □□ **nattily** *adv.* **nattiness** *n.* [orig. sl., perh. rel. to NEAT¹]

■ **1** see SMART *adj.* 2.

natural /nácharəl/ *adj. & n.* ● *adj.* **1 a** existing in or caused by nature; not artificial (*natural landscape*). **b** uncultivated; wild (*existing in its natural state*). **2** in the course of nature; not exceptional or miraculous (*died of natural causes*; *a natural occurrence*). **3** (of human nature, etc.) not surprising; to be expected (*natural for her to be upset*). **4 a** (of a person or a person's behavior) unaffected, easy, spontaneous. **b** (foll. by *to*) spontaneous; easy (*friendliness is natural to him*). **5 a** (of qualities, etc.) inherent; innate (*a natural talent for music*). **b** (of a person) having such qualities (*a natural linguist*). **6** not disguised or altered (as by makeup, etc.). **7** lifelike; as if in nature (*the portrait looked very natural*). **8** likely by its or their nature to be such (*natural enemies*; *the natural antithesis*). **9** having a physical existence as opposed to what is spiritual, intellectual, etc. (*the natural world*). **10 a** related by nature, out of wedlock, esp. in a specified manner (*her natural son*). **b** illegitimate (*a natural child*). **11** based on the innate moral sense; instinctive (*natural justice*). **12** *Mus.* **a** (of a note) not sharpened or flattened (*B natural*). **b** (of a scale) not containing any sharps or flats. **13** not enlightened or communicated by revelation (*the natural man*). ● *n.* **1** *colloq.* (usu. foll. by *for*) a person or thing naturally suitable, adept, expert, etc. (*a natural for the championship*). **2** *archaic* a person mentally deficient from birth. **3** *Mus.* **a** a sign (♮) denoting a return to natural pitch after a sharp or a flat. **b** a natural note. **c** a white key on a piano. **4 a** *Cards* a hand with no wild card nor joker. **b** *Cards* a hand making 21 in the first deal in blackjack. **c** a throw of 7 or 11 at craps. **5** a pale fawn color. □ **natural-born** having a character or position by birth. **natural childbirth** *Med.* childbirth with minimal medical or technological intervention. **natural classification** a scientific classification according to natural features. **natural death** death by age or disease, not by accident, poison, violence, etc. **natural food** food without preservatives, etc. **natural gas** a flammable mainly methane gas found in the earth's crust, not manufactured. **natural history 1** the study of animals or plants esp. as set forth for popular use. **2** an aggregate of the facts concerning the flora and fauna, etc., of a particular place or class (*a natural history of the Florida Keys*). **natural key** (or **scale**) *Mus.* a key or scale having no sharps or flats, i.e., C major and A minor. **natural language** a language that has developed naturally. **natural law 1** *Philos.* unchanging moral principles common to all people by virtue of their nature as human beings. **2** a correct statement of an invariable sequence between specified conditions and a specified phenomenon. **3** the laws of nature; regularity in nature (*where they saw chance, we see natural law*). **natural life** the duration of one's life on earth. **natural logarithm** see LOGARITHM. **natural magic** magic involving the supposed invocation of impersonal spirits. **natural note** *Mus.* a note that is neither sharp nor flat. **natural numbers** the integers 1, 2, 3, etc. **natural philosopher** *archaic* a physicist. **natural philosophy** *archaic* physics. **natural religion** a religion based on reason (opp. *revealed religion*); deism. **natural resources** materials or conditions occurring in nature and capable of economic exploitation. **natural science** the sciences used in the study of the physical world, e.g., physics, chemistry, geology, biology, botany. **natural selection** the Darwinian theory of the survival and propagation of organisms best adapted to their environment. **natural theology** the knowledge of God as gained by the light of natural reason. **natural uranium** unenriched uranium. **natural virtues** *Philos.* justice, prudence, temperance, fortitude. **natural year** the time taken by one revolution of the earth around the sun, 365 days 5 hours 48 minutes. □□ **naturalness** *n.* [ME f. OF *naturel* f. L *naturalis* (as NATURE)]

■ *adj.* **1a, 2, 6** ordinary, common, commonplace, normal, standard, regular, usual, customary, unsurprising, unexceptional, routine, habitual, typical, everyday; reasonable, understandable, logical, sensible, accepted, obvious; expected; simple, basic, fundamental, real, genuine, unembellished, unadorned; true, actual, authentic, bona fide. **4** unstudied, unconstrained, candid, frank, spontaneous, unaffected, genuine, easy, honest, straight, straightforward, artless, guileless, impulsive, unpremeditated, ingenuous, unsophisticated. **5 a** see INHERENT 1, INBORN. **7** see LIFELIKE. **8** logical, reasonable, fitting, appropriate, expected, understandable, obvious. **10** see ILLEGITIMATE *adj.* 1. ● *n.* **2** see FOOL[1] *n.* 1. □ **natural history 1** ecology, biology, botany, zoology, geology.

naturalism /náchərəlizəm/ *n.* **1** the theory or practice in art and literature of representing nature, character, etc. realistically and in great detail. **2 a** *Philos.* a theory of the world that excludes the supernatural or spiritual. **b** any moral or religious system based on this theory. **3** action based on natural instincts. **4** indifference to conventions. [NATURAL, in Philos. after F *naturalisme*]

naturalist /náchərəlist/ *n. & adj.* ● *n.* **1** an expert in natural

history. **2** a person who believes in or practices naturalism. ● *adj.* = NATURALISTIC.

■ *n.* **1** ecologist, biologist, botanist, zoologist, ornithologist, entomologist; natural historian, wildlife expert, bird-watcher, conservationist, environmentalist, ecologist, preservationist.

naturalistic /náchərəlístik/ *adj.* **1** imitating nature closely; lifelike. **2** of or according to naturalism. **3** of natural history. □□ **naturalistically** *adv.*

■ **1** see REALISTIC 1.

naturalize /náchərəliz/ *v.* **1** *tr.* admit (a foreigner) to the citizenship of a country. **2** *tr.* introduce (an animal, plant, etc.) into another region so that it flourishes in the wild. **3** *tr.* adopt (a foreign word, custom, etc.). **4** *intr.* become naturalized. **5** *tr. Philos.* exclude from the miraculous; explain naturalistically. **6** *tr.* free from conventions; make natural. **7** *tr.* cause to appear natural. **8** *intr.* study natural history. □□ **naturalization** *n.* [F *naturaliser* (as NATURAL)]

naturally /náchərəlee, náchrə-/ *adv.* **1** in a natural manner. **2** as a natural result. **3** (qualifying a whole sentence) as might be expected; of course.

■ **1** normally, by nature, by character, genuinely; inherently, instinctively, innately, congenitally; unaffectedly, unpretentiously, easily, candidly, openly, simply, plainly, honestly, straightforwardly. **2, 3** (as a matter) of course, needless to say, to be sure, certainly, not unexpectedly, as expected, *disp.* as anticipated; obviously, clearly, logically.

nature /náychər/ *n.* **1** a thing's or person's innate or essential qualities or character (*not in their nature to be cruel*; *is the nature of iron to rust*). **2** (often **Nature**) **a** the physical power causing all the phenomena of the material world (*Nature is the best physician*). **b** these phenomena, including plants, animals, landscape, etc. (*nature gives him comfort*). **3** a kind, sort, or class (*things of this nature*). **4** = *human nature*. **5 a** a specified element of human character (*the rational nature*; *our animal nature*). **b** a person of a specified character (*even strong natures quail*). **6 a** an uncultivated or wild area, condition, community, etc. **b** the countryside, esp. when picturesque. **7** inherent impulses determining character or action. **8** heredity as an influence on or determinant of personality (opp. NURTURE). **9** a living thing's vital functions or needs (*such a diet will not support nature*). □ **against nature** unnatural; immoral. **against** (or **contrary to**) **nature** miraculous; miraculously. **back to nature** returning to a precivilized or natural state. **by nature** innately. **from nature** *Art* using natural objects as models. **human nature** general human characteristics, feelings, etc. **in nature 1** actually existing. **2** anywhere; at all. **in** (or **of**) **the nature of** characteristically resembling or belonging to the class of (*the answer was in the nature of an excuse*). **in a state of nature 1** in an uncivilized or uncultivated state. **2** totally naked. **3** in an unregenerate state. **law of nature** = *natural law* 2. **nature cure** = NATUROPATHY. **nature printing** a method of producing a print of leaves, etc., by pressing them on a prepared plate. **nature reserve** a tract of land managed so as to preserve its flora, fauna, physical features, etc. **nature study** the practical study of plant and animal life, etc., as a school subject. **nature trail** a signposted path through the countryside designed to draw attention to natural phenomena. [ME f. OF f. L *natura* f. *nasci nat-* be born]

■ **1, 7** quality, properties, features, character, personality, makeup, essence, constitution, identity, reality, attributes, disposition, temperament, complexion. **2 a** Mother Nature. **b** wildlife, fauna and flora, environment, landscape, countryside. **3** kind, variety, description, sort, class, category, type, genre, species; stamp, cast, mold, kidney, color, stripe; character, constitution. **6** scenery, countryside, wilderness;

/.../ **pronunciation**	● **part of speech**
□ **phrases, idioms, and compounds**	
□□ **derivatives**	■ **synonym section**
cross-references appear in SMALL CAPITALS or *italics*	

wildness, primitiveness, simplicity. □ **by nature** see
NATURALLY 1.

natured /náychərd/ *adj.* (in *comb.*) having a specified disposition (*good-natured*; *ill-natured*).

naturism /náychərizəm/ *n.* **1** nudism. **2** naturalism in regard
to religion. **3** the worship of natural objects. □□ **naturist** *n.*

naturopathy /náychərópəthee/ *n.* **1** the treatment of disease,
etc., without drugs, usu. involving diet, exercise, massage,
etc. **2** this regimen used preventively. □□ **naturopath**
/-əpáth/ *n.* **naturopathic** *adj.*

naught /nawt/ *n. & adj.* ● *n.* **1** *archaic* or *literary* nothing;
nothingness. **2** zero; cipher. ● *adj.* (usu. *predic.*) *archaic* or
literary worthless; useless. □ **bring to naught** ruin; baffle.
come to naught be ruined or baffled. **set at naught** disregard; despise. [OE *nāwiht, -wuht* f. *nā* (see NO²) + *wiht*
WIGHT]

■ *n.* **1** nothing, nil, *sl.* zilch. **2** zero, *Brit.* nought.

naughty /náwtee/ *adj.* (**naughtier, naughtiest**) **1** (esp. of
children) disobedient; badly behaved. **2** *colloq. joc.* indecent.
3 *archaic* wicked. □□ **naughtily** *adv.* **naughtiness** *n.* [ME
f. NAUGHT + -Y¹]

■ **1** mischievous, misbehaving, impish, puckish, roguish,
devilish, *colloq.* scampish; disobedient, refractory,
insubordinate, bad, perverse, wicked, fractious,
unruly, wayward, ill-behaved, wild, unmanageable,
ungovernable, undisciplined, defiant, obstreperous.
2 improper, offensive, vulgar, rude, indecent,
immoral, risqué, ribald, bawdy, blue, pornographic,
smutty, lewd, obscene, dirty, off-color, *colloq.* raunchy,
x-rated.

nauplius /náwpleeəs/ *n.* (*pl.* **nauplii** /-plee-ī/) the first larval
stage of some crustaceans. [L, = a kind of shellfish, or f.
Gk *Nauplios* son of Poseidon]

nausea /náwzeeə, -zhə, -seeə, -shə/ *n.* **1** a feeling of sickness
with an inclination to vomit. **2** loathing; revulsion. [L f. Gk
nausia f. *naus* ship]

■ **2** see DISGUST *n.* 1.

nauseate /náwzeeayt, -zhee-, -see-, -shee/ *v.* **1** *tr.* affect with
nausea (*was nauseated by the smell*); disgust. **2** *intr.* (usu. foll.
by *at*) loathe food, an occupation, etc.; feel sick. □□ **nauseating** *adj.* **nauseatingly** *adv.* [L *nauseare* (as NAUSEA)]

■ **1** sicken, disgust, repel, revolt, offend. □□ **nauseating**
see DISGUSTING.

nauseous /náwshəs, -zeeəs/ *adj.* **1** affected with nausea; sick.
2 causing nausea; offensive to the taste or smell. **3** disgusting; loathsome. □□ **nauseously** *adv.* **nauseousness** *n.* [L
nauseosus (as NAUSEA)]

■ **2, 3** nauseating, loathsome, sickening, disgusting,
repellent, offensive, revolting, repugnant, repulsive,
abhorrent, nasty, foul, unpleasant, stomach-turning;
emetic.

nautch /nawch/ *n.* a performance of professional dancing
girls from India. □ **nautch girl** a professional dancing girl
from India. [Urdu (Hindi) *nāch* f. Prakrit *nachcha* f. Skr.
nṛitja dancing]

nautical /náwtikəl/ *adj.* of or concerning sailors or navigation; naval; maritime. □ **nautical almanac** a yearbook containing astronomical and tidal information for navigators,
etc. **nautical mile** a unit of approx. 2,025 yards (1,852
meters): also called *sea mile.* □□ **nautically** *adv.* [F *nautique*
or f. L *nauticus* f. Gk *nautikos* f. *nautēs* sailor f. *naus* ship]

■ maritime, marine, seafaring, seagoing; naval; boating,
yachting, sailing; navigational.

nautilus /náwt'ləs/ *n.* (*pl.* **nautiluses** or **nautili** /-lī/) **1** any
cephalopod of the genus *Nautilus* with a light brittle spiral
shell, esp. (**pearly nautilus**) one having a chambered shell
with nacreous septa. **2** (in full **paper nautilus**) any small
floating octopus of the genus *Argonauta*, of which the female
has a very thin shell and webbed saillike arms. [L f. Gk
nautilos, lit. sailor (as NAUTICAL)]

Navajo /návəhō, náa-/ *n.* (also **Navaho**) (*pl.* **-os**) **1** a member of a N. American people native to New Mexico and
Arizona. **2** the language of this people. [Sp., = pueblo]

naval /náyvəl/ *adj.* **1** of, in, for, etc., the navy or a navy. **2** of
or concerning ships (*a naval battle*). □ **naval academy** a

college for training naval officers. **naval architect** a designer of ships. **naval architecture** the designing of ships.
naval officer an officer in a navy. **naval stores** all materials
used in shipping. □□ **navally** *adv.* [L *navalis* f. *navis* ship]

■ see NAUTICAL.

nave¹ /nayv/ *n.* the central part of a church, usu. from the
west door to the chancel and excluding the side aisles.
[med.L *navis* f. L *navis* ship]

nave² /nayv/ *n.* the hub of a wheel. [OE *nafu, nafa* f. Gmc,
rel. to NAVEL]

navel /náyvəl/ *n.* **1** a depression in the center of the belly
caused by the detachment of the umbilical cord. **2** a central
point. □ **navel orange** a large seedless orange with a navellike formation at the top. [OE *nafela* f. Gmc, rel. to NAVE²]

■ **1** *Anat.* umbilicus, *colloq.* belly button. **2** center, nub,
Gk Antiq. omphalos; see also HUB.

navelwort /náyvəlwərt/ *n.* a pennywort.

navicular /nəvíkyələr/ *adj. & n.* ● *adj.* boat-shaped. ● *n.* (in
full **navicular bone**) a boat-shaped bone in the foot or
hand. □ **navicular disease** an inflammatory disease of the
navicular bone in horses, causing lameness. [F *naviculaire*
or LL *navicularis* f. L *navicula* dimin. of *navis* ship]

navigable /návigəbəl/ *adj.* **1** (of a river, the sea, etc.) affording a passage for ships. **2** (of a ship, etc.) seaworthy (*in
navigable condition*). **3** (of a balloon, airship, etc.) steerable.
□□ **navigability** *n.* [F *navigable* or L *navigabilis* (as NAVI
GATE)]

■ **1** passable, traversable, negotiable; unblocked,
unobstructed, clear, open. **2, 3** seaworthy, sailable;
maneuverable, controllable, steerable.

navigate /návigayt/ *v.* **1** *tr.* manage or direct the course of (a
ship, aircraft, etc.). **2** *tr.* **a** sail on (a sea, river, etc.). **b** travel
or fly through (the air). **3** *intr.* (of a passenger in a vehicle)
assist the driver by map-reading, etc. **4** *intr.* sail a ship; sail
in a ship. **5** *tr.* (often *refl.*) *colloq.* steer (oneself, a course,
etc.) through a crowd, etc. [L *navigare* f. *navis* ship + *agere*
drive]

■ **1** maneuver, handle, sail, guide, pilot, steer, direct;
skipper, captain, *Naut.* con. **2, 4** sail, voyage, cruise,
journey; cross, traverse.

navigation /návigáyshən/ *n.* **1** the act or process of navigating. **2** any of several methods of determining or planning a
ship's or aircraft's position and course by geometry, astronomy, radio signals, etc. **3** a voyage. □ **inland navigation**
communication by canals and rivers. **navigation light** *Brit.*
= *running light.* □□ **navigational** *adj.* [F or f. L *navigatio* (as
NAVIGATE)]

■ **1** pilotage, seamanship, steering, sailing.

navigator /návigaytər/ *n.* **1** a person skilled or engaged in
navigation. **2** an explorer by sea. [L (as NAVIGATE)]

■ **1** helmsman, seaman, steersman, skipper, wheelman,
pilot.

navvy /návee/ *n. & v. Brit.* ● *n.* (*pl.* **-ies**) a laborer employed
in building or excavating roads, canals, etc. ● *v.intr.* (**-ies,
-ied**) work as a navvy. [abbr. of NAVIGATOR]

■ *n.* see LABORER.

navy /náyvee/ *n.* (*pl.* **-ies**) **1** (often **the Navy**) **a** the whole
body of a nation's ships of war, including crews, maintenance systems, etc. **b** the officers, men, and women of a
navy. **2** (in full **navy blue**) a dark-blue color. **3** *poet.* a fleet
of ships. □ **Department of the Navy** the government department in charge of the US Navy. **navy bean** a small
white kidney bean, usu. dried for storage and then soaked
and cooked before being eaten. **Navy Cross** a US Navy
decoration awarded for extraordinary heroism against an
enemy. **navy yard** a government shipyard where naval vessels are built, maintained, etc., and where naval supplies are
stored. [ME, = fleet f. OF *navie* ship, fleet f. Rmc & pop.L
navia ship f. L *navis*]

■ **1a, 3** naval force(s); see also FLEET¹.

nawab /nəwaáb, -wáwb/ *n.* **1** the title of a distinguished Muslim in Pakistan. **2** *hist.* the title of a governor or nobleman
in India. [Urdu *nawwāb* pl. f. Arab. *nā'ib* deputy: cf. NABOB]

nay /nay/ *adv. & n.* ● *adv.* **1** or rather; and even; and more
than that (*impressive, nay, magnificent*). **2** *archaic* = NO² *adv.*

1. ● *n.* **1** the word 'nay'. **2** a negative vote (*counted 16 nays*). **3** a person who votes nay. [ME f. ON *nei* f. *ne* not + *ei* AYE²]

naysay /náysay/ *v.* (*3rd sing. present* **-says**; *past* and *past part.* **-said**) **1** *intr.* utter a denial or refusal. **2** *tr.* refuse or contradict. □□ **naysayer** *n.*

■ □□ **naysayer** denier, refuser, rejecter, dissenter, dissident, recusant.

Nazarene /názəreén/ *n. & adj.* ● *n.* **1 a** (prec. by *the*) Christ. **b** (esp. in Jewish or Muslim use) a Christian. **2** a native or inhabitant of Nazareth. **3** a member of an early Jewish-Christian sect. ● *adj.* of or concerning Nazareth, the Nazarenes, etc. [ME f. LL *Nazarenus* f. Gk *Nazarēnos* f. *Nazaret* Nazareth]

Nazarite /názərit/ *n.* (also **Nazirite**) *hist.* a Hebrew who had taken certain vows of abstinence; an ascetic (Num. 6). [LL *Nazaraeus* f. Heb. *nāzir* f. *nāzar* to separate or consecrate oneself]

Nazi /naátsee, nát-/ *n. & adj.* ● *n.* (*pl.* **Nazis**) **1** *hist.* a member of the German National Socialist party. **2** *derog.* a person holding extreme racist or authoritarian views or behaving brutally. **3** a person belonging to any organization similar to the Nazis. ● *adj.* of or concerning the Nazis, Nazism, etc. □□ **Nazidom** *n.* **Nazify** /-sifi/ *v.tr.* (**-ies, -ied**). **Naziism** /-see-izəm/ *n.* **Nazism** /naátsizəm, nát-/ *n.* [repr. pronunc. of *Nati-* in G *Nationalsozialist*]

■ *n.* **2** see SUPREMACIST. ● *adj.* see TOTALITARIAN *adj.*

Nazirite var. of NAZARITE.

NB *abbr.* **1** New Brunswick. **2** nota bene. **3** Scotland (North Britain).

Nb *symb. Chem.* the element niobium.

NBC *abbr.* National Broadcasting Company.

NbE *abbr.* north by east.

NbW *abbr.* north by west.

NC *abbr.* North Carolina (also in official postal use).

NCO *abbr.* noncommissioned officer.

ND *abbr.* North Dakota (in official postal use).

Nd *symb. Chem.* the element neodymium.

n.d. *abbr.* no date.

-nd *suffix* see -AND, -END.

N.Dak. *abbr.* North Dakota.

NE *abbr.* **1** Nebraska (in official postal use). **2** northeast. **3** northeastern.

Ne *symb. Chem.* the element neon.

né /nay/ *adj.* born (indicating a man's previous name) (*Lord Beaconsfield, né Benjamin Disraeli*). [F, past part. of *naître* be born: cf. NÉE]

NEA *abbr.* National Education Association.

Neanderthal /neeándərthawl, -tawl, -taal/ (also **Neandertal**) *adj.* of or belonging to the type of human widely distributed in Paleolithic Europe, with a retreating forehead and massive brow ridges. [*Neanderthal*, a region in Germany where remains were found]

neap /neep/ *n. & v.* ● *n.* (in full **neap tide**) a tide just after the first and third quarters of the moon when there is least difference between high and low water. ● *v.* **1** *intr.* (of a tide) tend toward or reach the highest point of a neap tide. **2** *tr.* (in *passive*) (of a ship) be kept aground, in harbor, etc., by a neap tide. [OE *nēpflōd* (cf. FLOOD), of unkn. orig.]

Neapolitan /neeəpólitən/ *n. & adj.* ● *n.* a native or citizen of Naples in Italy. ● *adj.* of or relating to Naples. □ **Neapolitan ice cream** ice cream made in layers of different colors and flavors, esp. vanilla, chocolate, and strawberry. **Neapolitan violet** a sweet-scented double viola. [ME f. L *Neapolitanus* f. L *Neapolis* Naples f. Gk f. *neos* new + *polis* city]

near /neer/ *adv., prep., adj., & v.* ● *adv.* **1** (often foll. by *to*) to or at a short distance in space or time; close by (*the time drew near; dropped near to them*). **2** closely (*as near as one can guess*). **3** *archaic* almost, nearly (*very near died*). **4** *archaic* parsimoniously; meanly (*lives very near*). ● *prep.* (compar. & superl. also used) **1** to or at a short distance (in space, time, condition, or resemblance) from (*stood near the back; occurs nearer the end; the sun is near setting*). **2** (in *comb.*) **a** that is almost (*near-hysterical; a near-Communist*). **b** intended as a substitute for; resembling (*near beer*). ● *adj.* **1**

(usu. *predic.*) close at hand; close to, in place or time (*the man nearest you; in the near future*). **2 a** closely related (*a near relation*). **b** intimate (*a near friend*). **3** (of a part of a vehicle, animal, or road) left (*the near foreleg; near side front wheel* [orig. of the side from which one mounted]) (opp. OFF). **4** close; narrow (*a near escape; a near guess*). **5** (of a road or way) direct. **6** niggardly, mean. ● *v.* **1** *tr.* approach; draw near to (*neared the harbor*). **2** *intr.* draw near (*could distinguish them as they neared*). □ **come** (or **go**) **near** (foll. by verbal noun, or *to* + verbal noun) be on the point of, almost succeed in (*came near to falling*). **go near** (foll. by *to* + infin.) narrowly fail. **near at hand 1** within easy reach. **2** in the immediate future. **the Near East** the region comprising the countries of the eastern Mediterranean. **Near Eastern** of the Near East. **near go** *Brit. colloq.* a narrow escape. **near the knuckle** *Brit. colloq.* verging on the indecent. **near miss 1** a bomb, etc., that is close to the target. **2** a situation in which a collision is narrowly avoided. **3** an attempt that is almost but not quite successful. **near upon** *archaic* not far in time from. □□ **nearness** *n.* [ME f. ON *nær*, orig. compar. of *ná* = OE *nēah* NIGH]

■ *adv.* **1** close (by *or* at hand), not far (off *or* away), nearby, in the vicinity *or* neighborhood, within reach, *archaic or dial.* nigh. **2** close, closely. **3** nearly, almost, just about, all but, virtually, practically, *archaic or rhet.* wellnigh; not quite. ● *prep.* **1** close to, in the vicinity *or* neighborhood of, next to, adjacent to, within reach of, a stone's throw from, not far (away) from. ● *adj.* **1** close, imminent, immediate, impending, looming, coming, approaching, forthcoming, in the offing, at hand, upcoming; nearby, adjacent, next-door, adjoining, neighboring, contiguous. **2 a** close, intimate, connected, related, attached. **b** see INTIMATE¹ *adj.* 1. **4** close, narrow, hairbreadth; lucky. **6** stingy, mean, niggardly, miserly, tight, parsimonious, penurious, cheap, penny-pinching, cheeseparing, selfish, close, tightfisted, closefisted. ● *v.* approach, draw near, come close *or* closer to; verge on, approximate to, lean toward. □ **near at hand 1** see NEARBY *adj.* **2** see SOON 1. **the Near East** *obs.* region comprising countries in the eastern Mediterranean basin. **near the knuckle** see RISQUÉ. **near miss 2** close *or* near thing, shave, narrow escape, narrow squeak, *colloq.* close shave. **near thing** see *near miss* above.

nearby /neerbí/ *adj. & adv.* ● *adj.* situated in a near position (*a nearby hotel*). ● *adv.* close; not far away.

■ *adj.* close, within reach, handy, accessible, at *or* to hand, adjacent. ● *adv.* close by, close at hand, not far (off *or* away), in the vicinity *or* neighborhood, within reach, about, around.

Nearctic /neeaárktik/ *adj.* of or relating to the Arctic and the temperate parts of N. America as a zoogeographical region. [NEO- + ARCTIC]

nearly /neerlee/ *adv.* **1** almost (*we are nearly there*). **2** closely (*they are nearly related*). □ **not nearly** nothing like; far from (*not nearly enough*).

■ **1** almost, not quite, about, approximately, around, approaching, nearing, close to, all but, just about, virtually, practically, as good as, more or less, next to, *archaic or rhet.* well-nigh, *colloq.* next; barely, hardly, scarcely.

nearsighted /neersítid/ *adj.* having the inability to focus the eyes except on comparatively near objects. □□ **nearsightedly** *adv.* **nearsightedness** *n.*

■ shortsighted, myopic, dim-sighted.

neat¹ /neet/ *adj.* **1** tidy and methodical. **2** elegantly simple in form, etc.; well-proportioned. **3** (of language, style, etc.) brief, clear, and pointed; epigrammatic. **4 a** a cleverly executed (*a neat piece of work*). **b** deft; dexterous. **5** (of esp.

/.../ **pronunciation**	● **part of speech**
□ **phrases, idioms, and compounds**	
□□ **derivatives**	■ **synonym section**
cross-references appear in SMALL CAPITALS or *italics*	

alcoholic liquor) undiluted. **6** *sl.* (as a general term of approval) good, pleasing, excellent. □□ **neatly** *adv.* **neatness** *n.* [F *net* f. L *nitidus* shining f. *nitēre* shine]

■ **1** tidy, orderly, clean, uncluttered, trim, smart, spruce, fastidious, spick-and-span, shipshape, organized, well-organized, well-ordered, systematic, methodical, esp. *Brit. archaic or dial.* trig, *colloq.* natty, *Brit. colloq.* dinky. **2** unembellished, unadorned, unornamented, simple, elegant, well-proportioned, graceful, smart, uncomplicated; regular, precise. **3** distinct, clear, witty, lucid, crisp, emphatic; see also *epigrammatic* (EPIGRAM). **4** deft, adroit, clever, efficient, ingenious, expert, practiced, skillful, dexterous, *colloq.* nifty. **5** straight, unadulterated, unmixed, undiluted, unblended, pure, uncut. **6** good, fine, wonderful, marvelous, splendid, excellent, exceptional, first-class, first-rate, *colloq.* far-out, capital, grand, great, smashing, keen, top-notch, A1, *Brit. colloq.* top-hole, *colloq.* A-OK, swell, *sl.* cool, spiffy, *Brit. archaic sl.* spiffing, topping.

neat² /neet/ *n. archaic* **1** a bovine animal. **2** (as *pl.*) cattle. □ **neat's-foot oil** oil made from boiled cow heel and used to dress leather. [OE *nēat* f. Gmc]

neaten /néet'n/ *v.tr.* make neat.

■ tidy (up), straighten (up *or* out), clean (up), spruce up, trim (up), (put in) order, smarten, esp. *Brit. archaic or dial.* trig.

neath /neeth/ *prep. poet.* beneath. [BENEATH]

NEB *abbr.* New English Bible.

Neb. *abbr.* Nebraska.

neb /neb/ *n. Sc. & No. of Engl.* **1** a beak or bill. **2** a nose; a snout. **3** a tip, spout, or point. [OE *nebb* ult. f. Gmc: cf. NIB]

nebbish /nébish/ *n. & adj. colloq.* ● *n.* a submissive or timid person. ● *adj.* submissive; timid. [Yiddish *nebach* poor thing!]

Nebr. *abbr.* Nebraska.

Nebuchadnezzar /nébəkədnézər, nébyŏo-/ *n.* a wine bottle of about 20 times the standard size. [name of a king of Babylonia (6th c. BC)]

nebula /nébyələ/ *n.* (*pl.* **nebulae** /-lee/ or **nebulas**) **1** *Astron.* **a** a cloud of gas and dust, sometimes glowing and sometimes appearing as a dark silhouette against other glowing matter. **b** a bright area caused by a galaxy, or a large cloud of distant stars. **2** *Med.* a clouded spot on the cornea causing defective vision. [L, = mist]

nebular /nébyələr/ *adj.* of or relating to a nebula or nebulae. □ **nebular theory** (or **hypothesis**) the theory that the solar and stellar systems were developed from a primeval nebula.

nebulous /nébyələs/ *adj.* **1** cloudlike. **2 a** formless, clouded. **b** hazy, indistinct, vague (*put forward a few nebulous ideas*). **3** *Astron.* of or like a nebula or nebulae. □ **nebulous star** a small cluster of indistinct stars, or a star in a luminous haze. □□ **nebulosity** /-lósitee/ *n.* **nebulously** *adv.* **nebulousness** *n.* [ME f. F *nébuleux* or L *nebulosus* (as NEBULA)]

■ **2** vague, hazy, clouded, unclear, obscure, indistinct, fuzzy, muddy, ill-defined, shapeless, amorphous, formless, blurred, indeterminate, murky, opaque, turbid, dim, foggy, faint, pale.

nebuly /nébyəlee/ *adj. Heraldry* wavy in form; cloudlike. [F *nébulé* f. med.L *nebulatus* f. L NEBULA]

necessarian /nésisáireeən/ *n. & adj.* = NECESSITARIAN. □□ **necessarianism** *n.*

necessarily /nésəsérilee/ *adv.* as a necessary result; inevitably.

■ inevitably, unavoidably, inescapably, incontrovertibly, automatically, naturally, (as a matter) of course, of necessity, as a result, by definition, axiomatically, certainly, surely, to be sure, willy-nilly, *archaic* perforce, *colloq.* like it or not, *literary* nolens volens.

necessary /nésəseree/ *adj. & n.* ● *adj.* **1** requiring to be done, achieved, etc.; requisite; essential (*it is necessary to work*; *lacks the necessary documents*). **2** determined, existing, or happening by natural laws, predestination, etc., not by free will; inevitable (*a necessary evil*). **3** *Philos.* (of a concept or a mental process) inevitably resulting from or produced by the nature of things, etc., so that the contrary is impos-

sible. **4** *Philos.* (of an agent) having no independent volition. ● *n.* (*pl.* **-ies**) (usu. in *pl.*) any of the basic requirements of life, such as food, warmth, etc. □ **the necessary** *colloq.* **1** money. **2** an action, item, etc., needed for a purpose (*they will do the necessary*). [ME f. OF *necessaire* f. L *necessarius* f. *necesse* needful]

■ *adj.* **1** indispensable, essential, required, needed, compulsory, requisite, vital, demanded, imperative, obligatory, needful, of the essence. **2** sure, certain, predetermined, predestined, fated, inexorable; inevitable, unavoidable, inescapable, ineluctable. ● *n.* **1** see NECESSITY 1a. □ **the necessary 1** see MONEY 3. **2** resources, means, material, essential(s), basics, requisite(s), tools, *colloq.* the needful; (*have the necessary*) have potential, *colloq.* have what it takes.

necessitarian /nisésitáireeən/ *n. & adj. Philos.* ● *n.* a person who holds that all action is predetermined and that free will is impossible. ● *adj.* of or concerning such a person or theory (opp. LIBERTARIAN). □□ **necessitarianism** *n.*

necessitate /nisésitayt/ *v.tr.* **1** make necessary (esp. as a result) (*will necessitate some sacrifice*). **2** (usu. foll. by *to* + infin.) force or compel (a person) to do something. [med.L *necessitare* compel (as NECESSITY)]

■ **1** see ENTAIL *v.*

necessitous /nisésitəs/ *adj.* poor; needy. [F *nécessiteux* or f. NECESSITY + -OUS]

■ see POOR 1.

necessity /nisésitee/ *n.* (*pl.* **-ies**) **1 a** an indispensible thing; a necessary (*central heating is a necessity*). **b** (usu. foll. by *of*) indispensability (*the necessity of a warm overcoat*). **2** a state of things or circumstances enforcing a certain course (*there was a necessity to hurry*). **3** imperative need (*necessity is the mother of invention*). **4** want; poverty; hardship (*stole because of necessity*). **5** constraint or compulsion regarded as a natural law governing all human action. □ **of necessity** unavoidably. [ME f. OF *necessité* f. L *necessitas -tatis* f. *necesse* needful]

■ **1 a** requirement, essential, necessary, requisite, need, prerequisite, basic, fundamental, sine qua non. **b** indispensability, needfulness; unavoidability, inevitability, inexorability. **2, 3** urgency, need, emergency, crisis, misfortune, exigency. **4** poverty, want, indigence, need, destitution, penury, straits, hardship, difficulty, difficulties, pauperism, neediness. □ **of necessity** see NECESSARILY.

neck /nek/ *n. & v.* ● *n.* **1 a** the part of the body connecting the head to the shoulders. **b** the part of a shirt, dress, etc., around or close to the neck. **2 a** something resembling a neck, such as the narrow part of a cavity or vessel, a passage, channel, pass, isthmus, etc. **b** the narrow part of a bottle near the mouth. **3** the part of a violin, etc., bearing the fingerboard. **4** the length of a horse's head and neck as a measure of its lead in a race. **5** the flesh of an animal's neck (*neck of lamb*). **6** *Geol.* solidified lava or igneous rock in an old volcano crater or pipe. **7** *Archit.* the lower part of a capital. **8** *Brit. sl.* impudence (*you've got a neck, asking that*). ● *v.* **1** *intr. & tr. colloq.* kiss and caress amorously. **2 a** *tr.* form a narrowed part in. **b** *intr.* form a narrowed part. □ **get it in the neck** *colloq.* **1** receive a severe reprimand or punishment. **2** suffer a fatal or severe blow. **neck and neck** running even in a race, etc. **neck of the woods** *colloq.* **1** region; neighborhood. **2** esp. *Brit.* a usu. remote locality. **neck or nothing** risking everything on success. **up to one's neck** (often foll. by *in*) *colloq.* very deeply involved; very busy. □□ **necked** *adj.* (also in *comb.*). **necker** *n.* (in sense 1 of *v.*).

neckless *adj.* [OE *hnecca* ult. f. Gmc]

■ *n.* **2 a** see CAPE² *n.* ● *v.* **1** see KISS *v.* 1, 3. □ **neck and neck** see LEVEL *adj.* 5. **neck of the woods** see PART *n.* 11.

neckband /nékband/ *n.* a strip of material around the neck of a garment.

neckcloth /nék-klawth, -kloth/ *n. hist.* a cravat.

neckerchief /nékərchif, -cheef/ *n.* a square of cloth worn around the neck.

necking /néking/ *n. Archit.* = NECK *n.* 7.

necklace /nékləs/ *n.* a chain or string of beads, precious stones, links, etc., worn as an ornament around the neck. ■ beads, chain, choker, *hist.* torque.

necklet /néklit/ *n.* **1** = NECKLACE. **2** a strip of fur worn around the neck.

neckline /néklin/ *n.* the edge or shape of the opening of a garment at the neck (*a square neckline*).

necktie /nékti/ *n.* = TIE *n.* 2. □ **necktie party** *sl.* a lynching or hanging.

neckwear /nékwair/ *n.* collars, ties, etc.

necro- /nékrō/ *comb. form* corpse. [from or after Gk *nekro-* f. *nekros* corpse]

necrobiosis /nékrōbĭósis/ *n.* decay in the tissues of the body, esp. swelling of the collagen bundles in the dermis. □□ **necrobiotic** /-bĭótik/ *adj.*

necrolatry /nekrólətree/ *n.* worship of, or excessive reverence toward, the dead.

necrology /nekróləjee/ *n.* (*pl.* **-ies**) **1** a list of recently dead people. **2** an obituary notice. □□ **necrological** /-rəlójikəl/ *adj.*

necromancy /nékrōmansee/ *n.* **1** the prediction of the future by the supposed communication with the dead. **2** witchcraft. □□ **necromancer** *n.* **necromantic** /-mántik/ *adj.* [ME f. OF *nigromancie* f. med.L *nigromantia* changed (by assoc. with L *niger nigri* black) f. LL *necromantia* f. Gk *nekromanteia* (as NECRO-, -MANCY)]
■ see MAGIC *n.* 1. □□ **necromancer** see MAGICIAN 1. **necromantic** see MAGIC *adj.* 1.

necrophilia /nékrəfíleeə/ *n.* (also **necrophily** /nikrófilee/) a morbid and esp. erotic attraction to corpses. □□ **necrophile** /nékrəfil/ *n.* **necrophiliac** /-fíleeak/ *n.* **necrophilic** *adj.* **necrophilism** /-krófilizəm/ *n.* **necrophilist** /-krófilist/ *n.* [NECRO- + Gk *-philia* loving]

necrophobia /nékrəfōbeeə/ *n.* an abnormal fear of death or dead bodies.

necropolis /nekrópəlis/ *n.* an ancient cemetery or burial place.
■ see GRAVEYARD.

necropsy /nékropsee/ *n.* (also **necroscopy** /-króskəpee/) (*pl.* **-ies**) = AUTOPSY 1. [NECRO- after AUTOPSY, or + -SCOPY]

necrosis /nekrósis/ *n. Med. & Physiol.* the death of tissue caused by disease or injury, esp. as one of the symptoms of gangrene or pulmonary tuberculosis. □□ **necrose** *v.intr.* **necrotic** /-krótik/ *adj.* **necrotize** /nékrətīz/ *v.intr.* [mod.L f. Gk *nekrōsis* (as NECRO-, -OSIS)]

nectar /néktər/ *n.* **1** a sugary substance produced by plants and made into honey by bees. **2** (in Greek and Roman mythology) the drink of the gods. **3** a drink compared to this. □□ **nectarean** /-táireeən/ *adj.* **nectareous** /-táireeəs/ *adj.* **nectariferous** /-rífərəs/ *adj.* **nectarous** *adj.* [L f. Gk *nektar*]

nectarine /nektəreén/ *n.* **1** a variety of peach with a thin brightly colored smooth skin and firm flesh. **2** the tree bearing this. [orig. as adj. = nectarlike, f. NECTAR + -INE⁴]

nectary /néktəree/ *n.* (*pl.* **-ies**) the nectar-secreting organ of a flower or plant. [mod.L *nectarium* (as NECTAR)]

neddy /nédee/ *n.* (*pl.* **-ies**) *Brit. colloq.* a donkey. [dimin. of *Ned*, pet form of the name *Edward*]

Ned Kelly /ned kélee/ *n. Austral.* a person of reckless courage or unscrupulous business dealings. [the name of the most famous Australian bushranger (1857–80)]

née /nay/ *adj.* (also **nee**) (used in adding a married woman's maiden name after her surname) born (*Mrs. Ann Smith, née Jones*). [F, fem. past part. of *naître* be born]

need /need/ *v. & n.* ● *v.* **1** *tr.* stand in want of; require (*needs a new coat*). **2** *tr.* (foll. by *to* + infin.; *3rd sing. present neg. or interrog.* **need** without *to*) be under the necessity or obligation (*it needs to be done carefully; he need not come; need you ask?*). **3** *intr. archaic* be necessary. ● *n.* **1 a** a want or requirement (*my needs are few; the need for greater freedom*). **b** a thing wanted (*my greatest need is a car*). **2** circumstances requiring some course of action; necessity (*there is no need to worry; if need arise*). **3** destitution; poverty. **4** a crisis; an emergency (*failed them in their need*). □ **at need** in time of

need. **had need** *archaic* ought to (*had need remember*). **have need of** require; want. **have need to** require to (*has need to be warned*). **in need** requiring help. **in need of** requiring. **need not have** did not need to (but did). [OE *nēodian, nēd* f. Gmc]
■ *v.* **1** require, demand, want, be *or* stand in want of, be *or* stand in need of, call for, have need of, cry out for; lack, miss, have occasion for. **2** (*need to*) see GET *v.* 11b, *cannot choose but* (CHOOSE). ● *n.* **1, 2** necessity, requirement; call, demand, want; constraint; essential, necessary, requisite, prerequisite, basic(s), fundamental(s), sine qua non; lack, dearth, shortage, paucity, scarcity, insufficiency. **3, 4** distress, difficulty, trouble, (dire *or* desperate) straits, stress, crisis, emergency, exigency, extremity; neediness, needfulness; poverty, penury, impecuniousness, destitution, privation, deprivation, indigence, beggary. □ **have need of** see NEED *v.* 1 above. **in need** see *deprived* (DEPRIVE 2).

needful /néedfŏŏl/ *adj.* **1** requisite; necessary; indispensable. **2** (prec. by *the*) **a** what is necessary. **b** *colloq.* money or action needed for a purpose. □□ **needfully** *adv.* **needfulness** *n.*
■ **1** see NECESSARY *adj.* 1. **2 a** (*the needful*) see *the necessary* 2 (NECESSARY). **b** see MONEY 3. □□ **needfulness** see NECESSITY 1b.

needle /néed'l/ *n. & v.* ● *n.* **1 a** a very thin small piece of smooth steel, etc., pointed at one end and with a slit (eye) for thread at the other, used in sewing. **b** a larger plastic, wooden, etc., slender stick without an eye, used in knitting. **c** a slender hooked stick used in crochet. **2** a pointer on a dial (see *magnetic needle*). **3** any of several small thin pointed instruments, esp.: **a** a surgical instrument for stitching. **b** the end of a hypodermic syringe. **c** = STYLUS. **d** an etching tool. **e** a steel pin exploding the cartridge of a breech-loading gun. **4 a** an obelisk (*Cleopatra's Needle*). **b** a pointed rock or peak. **5** the leaf of a fir or pine tree. **6** a beam used as a temporary support during underpinning. **7** *Brit. sl.* a fit of bad temper or nervousness (*got the needle while waiting*). ● *v.tr.* **1** *colloq.* incite or irritate; provoke (*the silence needled him*). **2** sew, pierce, or operate on with a needle. □ **needle in a haystack** something almost impossible to find because it is concealed by so many other things, etc. **needle's eye** (or **eye of a needle**) the least possible aperture, esp. with ref. to Matt. 19:24. **needle time** *Brit.* an agreed maximum allowance of time for broadcasting music from records. **needle valve** a valve closed by a thin tapering part. [OE *nǣdl* f. Gmc]
■ *n.* **2** see INDICATOR 1. **5** see SPINE 2. ● *v.* see IRRITATE 1.

needlecraft /néed'lkraft/ *n.* skill in needlework.

needlefish /néed'lfish/ *n.* a garfish.

needlepoint /néed'lpoynt/ *n.* decorative needlework or lace made with a needle.

needless /néedlis/ *adj.* **1** unnecessary. **2** uncalled-for; gratuitous. □ **needless to say** of course; it goes without saying. □□ **needlessly** *adv.* **needlessness** *n.*
■ unnecessary, nonessential, unessential, inessential, unneeded, unwanted, uncalled-for, gratuitous, superfluous, redundant, pointless, useless, excess, excessive, tautological, dispensable, expendable, supererogatory, de trop; pleonastic. □ **needless to say** (as a matter of) course, obviously, it goes without saying, manifestly, clearly; see also NATURALLY 2, 3. □□ **needlessly** see *unduly* (UNDUE).

needlewoman /néed'lwŏŏmən/ *n.* (*pl.* **-women**) **1** a seamstress. **2** a woman or girl with specified sewing skill (*a good needlewoman*).

needlework /néed'lwərk/ *n.* sewing or embroidery.

/.../ **pronunciation** ● **part of speech**
□ **phrases, idioms, and compounds**
□□ **derivatives** ■ **synonym section**
cross-references appear in SMALL CAPITALS or *italics*

needs /needz/ *adv. archaic* (usu. prec. or foll. by *must*) of necessity (*must needs decide*). [OE *nēdes* (as NEED, -s³)]

needy /néedee/ *adj.* (**needier, neediest**) **1** (of a person) poor; destitute. **2** (of circumstances) characterized by poverty. **3** emotionally impoverished or demanding. □□ **neediness** *n.*

■ **1** poor, indigent, poverty-stricken, destitute, impoverished, penniless, impecunious, necessitous, underprivileged, deprived, disadvantaged, in dire straits, in reduced circumstances, down-and-out, insolvent, hard up, pinched, on the breadline, *colloq.* on one's uppers, flat broke, strapped (for cash), up against it.

neep /neep/ *n. Sc. & No. of Engl.* a turnip. [OE *nǣp* f. L *napus*]

ne'er /nair/ *adv. poet.* = NEVER. □ **ne'er-do-well** *n.* a good-for-nothing person. ● *adj.* good-for-nothing. [ME contr. of NEVER]

■ □ **ne'er-do-well** (*n.*) see *good-for-nothing n.* (*adj.*) see SHIFTLESS.

nefarious /nifáireeəs/ *adj.* wicked; iniquitous. □□ **nefariously** *adv.* **nefariousness** *n.* [L *nefarius* f. *nefas* wrong f. *ne-* not + *fas* divine law]

■ see EVIL *adj.* 1. □□ **nefariousness** see EVIL *n.* 2.

neg. *abbr.* negative.

negate /nigáyt/ *v.tr.* **1** nullify; invalidate. **2** imply, involve, or assert the nonexistence of. **3** be the negation of. □□ **negator** *n.* [L *negare negat-* deny]

■ **1** see NEUTRALIZE.

negation /nigáyshən/ *n.* **1** the absence or opposite of something actual or positive. **2 a** the act of denying. **b** an instance of this. **3** (usu. foll. by *of*) a refusal, contradiction, or denial. **4** a negative statement or doctrine. **5** a negative or unreal thing; a nonentity. **6** *Logic* the assertion that a certain proposition is false. □□ **negatory** /négətáwree/ *adj.* [F *negation* or L *negatio* (as NEGATE)]

■ **2** see DENIAL 1. **3** see DENIAL 3.

negative /négətiv/ *adj., n., & v.* ● *adj.* **1** expressing or implying denial, prohibition, or refusal (*a negative vote; a negative answer*). **2** (of a person or attitude): **a** lacking positive attributes; apathetic; pessimistic. **b** opposing or resisting; uncooperative. **3** marked by the absence of qualities (*a negative reaction; a negative result from the test*). **4** of the opposite nature to a thing regarded as positive (*debt is negative capital*). **5** *Algebra* (of a quantity) less than zero, to be subtracted from others or from zero (opp. POSITIVE). **6** *Electr.* **a** of the kind of charge carried by electrons (opp. POSITIVE). **b** containing or producing such a charge. ● *n.* **1** a negative statement, reply, or word (*hard to prove a negative*). **2** *Photog.* **a** an image with black and white reversed or colors replaced by complementary ones, from which positive pictures are obtained. **b** a developed film or plate bearing such an image. **3** a negative quality; an absence of something. **4** (prec. by *the*) a position opposing the affirmative. **5** *Logic* = NEGATION 6. ● *v.tr.* **1** refuse to accept or countenance; veto; reject. **2** disprove (an inference or hypothesis). **3** contradict (a statement). **4** neutralize (an effect). □ **in the negative** with negative effect; so as to reject a proposal, etc.; no (*the answer was in the negative*). **negative evidence** (or **instance**) evidence of the nonoccurrence of something. **negative feedback 1** the return of part of an output signal to the input, tending to decrease the amplification, etc. **2** feedback that tends to diminish or counteract the process giving rise to it. **negative geotropism** see GEOTROPISM. **negative income tax** an amount credited as allowance to a taxed income, and paid as benefit when it exceeds debited tax. **negative pole** the south-seeking pole of a magnet. **negative proposition** *Logic* = NEGATION 6. **negative quantity** *joc.* nothing. **negative sign** a symbol (-) indicating subtraction or a value less than zero. **negative virtue** abstention from vice. □□ **negatively** *adv.* **negativeness** *n.* **negativity** /-tívitee/ *n.* [ME f. OF *negatif -ive* or LL *negativus* (as NEGATE)]

■ *adj.* **1** contradictory, anti, contrary, dissenting, opposing, denying. **2 a** apathetic, unenthusiastic, cool, cold, uninterested, unresponsive, *disp.* disinterested; pessimistic. **b** opposing, resisting, refusing, denying, gainsaying; uncooperative, disputatious, argumentative, adversarial, antagonistic, antipathetic, adverse. **3** see INERT 2. □ **in the negative** negatively; no.

negativism /négətivizəm/ *n.* **1** a negative position or attitude; extreme skepticism, criticism, etc. **2** denial of accepted beliefs. □□ **negativist** *n.* **negativistic** /-vístik/ *adj.*

neglect /niglékt/ *v. & n.* ● *v.tr.* **1** fail to care for or to do; be remiss about (*neglected their duty; neglected his children*). **2** (foll. by verbal noun, or *to* + infin.) fail; overlook or forget the need to (*neglected to inform them; neglected telling them*). **3** not pay attention to; disregard (*neglected the obvious warning*). ● *n.* **1** lack of caring; negligence (*the house suffered from neglect*). **2 a** the act of neglecting. **b** the state of being neglected (*the house fell into neglect*). **3** (usu. foll. by *of*) disregard. □□ **neglectful** *adj.* **neglectfully** *adv.* **neglectfulness** *n.* [L *neglegere neglect-* f. *neg-* not + *legere* choose, pick up]

■ *v.* **1, 2** disregard, let slide *or* pass, be remiss about, abandon, lose sight of, forget, shirk; fail to do, omit. **3** disregard, ignore, slight, pay no attention *or* heed to, be inattentive to, overlook; pass by, spurn, rebuff, scorn, disdain, cold-shoulder. ● *n.* **1** negligence, laxity, laxness, slackness, neglectfulness, lack of care, inactivity, inaction, dereliction, default, failure, failing, remissness. **3** disregard, disrespect, inattention, indifference, slighting, unconcern, oversight, heedlessness, neglectfulness, carelessness, inadvertence.

negligee /néglizháy/ *n.* (also **negligée, négligé**) **1** a woman's dressing gown of sheer fabric. **2** unceremonious or informal attire. [F, past part. of *négliger* NEGLECT]

■ **1** see WRAPPER 4.

negligence /néglijəns/ *n.* **1 a** a lack of proper care and attention; carelessness. **b** an act of carelessness. **2** *Law* = *contributory negligence*. **3** *Art* freedom from restraint or artificiality. □□ **negligent** /-jənt/ *adj.* **negligently** *adv.* [ME f. OF *negligence* or L *negligentia* f. *negligere* = *neglegere*: see NEGLECT]

■ **1** inattention, inattentiveness, indifference, carelessness, unconcern, dereliction, failure, failing, heedlessness, laxity, laxness, disregard, oversight, omission, inadvertence, neglect, neglectfulness, remissness, forgetfulness, *formal* oscitation.

negligible /néglijibəl/ *adj.* not worth considering; insignificant. □□ **negligibility** *n.* **negligibly** *adv.* [obs. F f. *négliger* NEGLECT]

■ insignificant, minor, unimportant, trifling, trivial, inconsequential, inappreciable, small, slight, paltry, nugatory, worthless, petty, niggling, not worth mentioning *or* talking about, *colloq.* small-time, piddling, piffling, *sl.* small potatoes.

negotiable /nigṓshəbəl, -sheeə-/ *adj.* **1** open to discussion or modification. **2** able to be negotiated. □□ **negotiability** *n.*

■ **2** see NAVIGABLE 1.

negotiate /nigṓsheeayt, -seeayt/ *v.* **1** *intr.* (usu. foll. by *with*) confer with others in order to reach a compromise or agreement. **2** *tr.* arrange (an affair) or bring about (a result) by negotiating (*negotiated a settlement*). **3** *tr.* find a way over, through, etc. (an obstacle, difficulty, fence, etc.). **4** *tr.* **a** transfer (a check, etc.) to another for a consideration. **b** convert (a check, etc.) into cash or notes. **c** get or give value for (a check, etc.) in money. □□ **negotiant** /-sheeənt, -seeənt/ *n.* **negotiation** /-áyshən/ *n.* **negotiator** *n.* [L *negotiari* f. *negotium* business f. *neg-* not + *otium* leisure]

■ **1** deal, bargain, haggle, chaffer, palter, dicker; discuss, debate, mediate, consult, parley, speak, talk, transact, come to terms. **2** arrange (for), organize, orchestrate, conduct, handle, maneuver, manage, engineer, work out, settle; get, obtain, bring off *or* about, accomplish, pull off, do, execute, effect, complete, conclude. **3** clear, maneuver one's way through *or* past *or* around *or* over, get through *or* past *or* around *or* over, pass, cross, *colloq.* make it through *or* past *or* around *or* over. □□ **negotiation** discussion, mediation, arbitration, bargaining, parley, talk; deal, bargain, transaction. **negotiator** arbitrator, arbiter, mediator, moderator, diplomat, ambassador, go-between, middleman, intercessor, interceder, intervener, agent, broker.

Negress /néegris/ *n.* often *offens.* a female Negro (black person).

Negrillo /nigrílō/ *n.* (*pl.* **-os**) a member of a very small Negroid people native to Central and S. Africa. [Sp., dimin. of NEGRO]

Negrito /nigréetō/ *n.* (*pl.* **-os**) a member of a small Negroid people native to the Malayo-Polynesian region. [as NEGRILLO]

negritude /néegritōōd, -tyōōd, nég-/ (also **Negritude**) *n.* **1** the quality or state of being a Negro (black person). **2** the affirmation or consciousness of the value of Negro (black) culture. [F *négritude* NIGRITUDE]

Negro /néegrō/ *n.* & *adj.* ● *n.* (*pl.* **-oes**) a member of a dark-skinned race orig. native to Africa. ● *adj.* **1** of or concerning Negroes (black people). **2** (as **negro**) *Zool.* black or dark (*negro ant*). ¶ The term *black* or *African American* is usually preferred when referring to people. [Sp. & Port., f. L *niger nigri* black]
■ *adj.* **1** see BLACK *adj.* 3.

Negroid /néegroyd/ *adj.* & *n.* ● *adj.* **1** (of features, etc.) characterizing a member of the Negro (black) race, esp. in having dark skin, tightly curled hair, and a broad flattish nose. **2** of or concerning Negroes (black people). ● *n.* a Negro (black person). [NEGRO]
■ *adj.* see BLACK *adj.* 3.

Negus /néegas/ *n. hist.* the title of the ruler of Ethiopia. [Amh. *n'gus* king]

negus /néegas/ *n. hist.* a hot drink of port, sugar, lemon, and spice. [Col. F. *Negus* d. 1732, its inventor]

Neh. *abbr.* Nehemiah (Old Testament).

neigh /nay/ *n.* & *v.* ● *n.* **1** the high whinnying sound of a horse. **2** any similar sound, e.g., a laugh. ● *v.* **1** *intr.* make such a sound. **2** *tr.* say, cry, etc., with such a sound. [OE *hnǽgan*, of imit. orig.]

neighbor /náybər/ *n.* & *v.* ● *n.* **1** a person living next door to or near or nearest another (*my next-door neighbor; his nearest neighbor is 10 miles away; they are neighbors*). **2 a** a person regarded as having the duties or claims of friendliness, consideration, etc., of a neighbor. **b** a fellow human being, esp. as having claims on friendship. **3** a person or thing near or next to another (*my neighbor at dinner*). **4** (*attrib.*) neighboring. ● *v.* **1** *tr.* border on; adjoin. **2** *intr.* (often foll. by *on, upon*) border; adjoin. □□ **neighboring** *adj.* **neighborless** *adj.* **neighborship** *n.* [OE *néahgebūr* (as NIGH: *gebūr*, cf. BOOR)]
■ *v.* see BORDER *v.* 3a. □□ **neighboring** nearby, adjacent, surrounding, adjoining, contiguous, bordering, next, nearest.

neighborhood /náybərhŏŏd/ *n.* **1 a** a district, esp. one forming a community within a town or city. **b** the people of a district; one's neighbors. **2** neighborly feeling or conduct. □ **in the neighborhood of** roughly; about (*paid in the neighborhood of $100*). **neighborhood watch** systematic local vigilance by householders to discourage crime, esp. against children and property.
■ **1** locality, community, area, region, vicinity, vicinage, environs, quarter, district, precinct(s), purlieus, locale; surroundings, confines. **2** neighborliness. □ **in the neighborhood of** approximately, about, around, nearly, practically, close to, almost, more or less, in the region of, as near as dammit to, not far off, *colloq.* getting on for, in the ballpark of.

neighborly /náybərlee/ *adj.* characteristic of a good neighbor; friendly; kind. □□ **neighborliness** *n.*
■ friendly, cordial, warm, amiable, agreeable, affable, companionable, well-disposed, kindly, kind, sociable, social, considerate, thoughtful, helpful, courteous, harmonious, civil.

neither /néethər, níth-/ *adj., pron., adv.,* & *conj.* ● *adj.* & *pron.* (foll. by sing. verb) **1** not the one nor the other (of two things); not either (*neither of the accusations is true; neither of them knows; neither wish was granted; neither went to the fair*). **2** *disp.* none of any number of specified things. ● *adv.* **1** not

either; not on the one hand (foll. by *nor*; introducing the first of two or more things in the negative: *neither knowing nor caring; would neither come in nor go out; neither the teachers nor the parents nor the children*). **2** not either; also not (*if you do not, neither shall I*). **3** (with *neg.*) *disp.* either (*I don't know that neither*). ● *conj. archaic* nor yet; nor (*I know not, neither can I guess*). [ME *naither, neither* f. OE *nowther* contr. of *nōhwæther* (as NO², WHETHER): assim. to EITHER]

nekton /néktən/ *n. Zool.* any aquatic animal able to swim and move independently. [G f. Gk *nēkton* neut. of *nēktos* swimming f. *nēkhō* swim]

nellie /nélee/ *n.* a silly or effeminate person. □ **not on your nellie** *sl.* certainly not. [perh. f. the name *Nelly*: idiom f. rhyming sl. *Nelly Duff* = puff = breath: cf. *not on your life*]

nelson /nélsən/ *n.* a wrestling hold in which one arm is passed under the opponent's arm from behind and the hand is applied to the neck (**half nelson**), or both arms and hands are applied (**full nelson**). [app. f. the name *Nelson*]

nelumbo /nilúmbō/ *n.* (*pl.* **-os**) any water lily of the genus *Nelumbo*, native to India and China, bearing small pink flowers. Also called LOTUS. [mod.L f. Sinh. *nelum*(*bu*)]

nematocyst /nimátəsist, némə-/ *n.* a specialized cell in a jellyfish, etc., containing a coiled thread that can be projected as a sting. [as NEMATODE + CYST]

nematode /némətōd/ *n.* any parasitic or free-living worm of the phylum Nematoda, with a slender unsegmented cylindrical shape. Also called ROUNDWORM. [Gk *nēma -matos* thread + -ODE¹]

Nembutal /némbyətawl, -taal/ *n. propr.* a sodium salt of pentobarbitone, used as a sedative and anticonvulsant. [Na (= sodium) + 5-*ethyl*-5-(1-*methylbutyl*) barbiturate + -AL]

nem. con. *abbr.* with no one dissenting. [L *nemine contradicente*]

nemertean /nimə́rteeən/ *n.* & *adj.* (also **nemertine** /-tin/) ● *n.* any marine ribbon worm of the phylum Nemertea, often very long and brightly colored, found in tangled knots in coastal waters of Europe and the Mediterranean. ● *adj.* of or relating to this class. [mod.L *Nemertes* f. Gk *Nēmertēs* name of a sea nymph]

nemesia /niméezhə/ *n.* any S. African plant of the genus *Nemesia*, cultivated for its variously colored and irregular flowers. [mod.L f. Gk *nemesion*, the name of a similar plant]

nemesis /némisis/ *n.* (*pl.* **nemeses** /-seez/) **1** retributive justice. **2 a** a downfall caused by this. **b** an agent of such a downfall. [Gk, = righteous indignation, personified as goddess of retribution f. *nemō* give what is due]

neo- /née-ō/ *comb. form* **1** new, modern. **2** a new or revived form of. [Gk f. *neos* new]

neoclassical /née-ōklásikəl/ *adj.* (also **neoclassic** /-ik/) of or relating to a revival of a classical style or treatment in art, literature, music, etc. □□ **neoclassicism** /-sisizəm/ *n.* **neoclassicist** *n.*

neocolonialism /née-ōkələlōneeəlizəm/ *n.* the use of economic, political, or other pressures to control or influence other countries, esp. former dependencies. □□ **neocolonialist** *n.* & *adj.*

neodymium /née-ōdímeeəm/ *n. Chem.* a silver-gray naturally occurring metallic element of the lanthanide series used in coloring glass, etc. ¶ Symb.: **Nd**. [NEO- + DIDYMIUM]

neolithic /née-ōlíthik/ *adj.* of or relating to the later Stone Age, when ground or polished stone weapons and implements prevailed. [NEO- + Gk *lithos* stone]

neologism /nee-óləjizəm/ *n.* **1** a new word or expression. **2** the coining or use of new words. □□ **neologist** *n.* **neologize** /-jiz/ *v.intr.* [F *néologisme* (as NEO-, -LOGY, -ISM)]
■ coinage.

neomycin /née-ōmísin/ *n.* an antibiotic related to streptomycin.

neon /née-on/ *n. Chem.* an inert gaseous element occurring

/.../ **pronunciation**	● **part of speech**
□ **phrases, idioms, and compounds**	
□□ **derivatives**	■ **synonym section**
cross-references appear in SMALL CAPITALS or *italics*	

in traces in the atmosphere and giving an orange glow when electricity is passed through it in a sealed low-pressure tube, used in lights and illuminated advertisements (*neon light*; *neon sign*). ¶ Symb.: **Ne**. [Gk, neut. of *neos* new]

neonate /néeənayt/ *n.* a newborn child. □□ **neonatal** /-náyt'l/ *adj.* [mod.L *neonatus* (as NEO-, L *nasci nat-* be born)]

neophyte /néeəfīt/ *n.* **1** a new convert, esp. to a religious faith. **2** *RC Ch.* **a** a novice of a religious order. **b** a newly ordained priest. **3** a beginner; a novice. [eccl.L *neophytus* f. NT Gk *neophutos* newly planted (as NEO- *phuton* plant)]
  ■ **1** convert, proselyte. **2, 3** see NOVICE.

neoplasm /néeə-əplazəm/ *n.* a new and abnormal growth of tissue in some part of the body, esp. a tumor. □□ **neoplastic** /-plástik/ *adj.* [NEO- + Gk *plasma* formation: see PLASMA]

Neoplatonism /néeə-ōpláyt'nizəm/ *n.* a philosophical and religious system developed by the followers of Plotinus in the third c., combining Platonic thought with oriental mysticism. □□ **Neoplatonic** /-plətónik/ *adj.* **Neoplatonist** *n.*

neoprene /néeə-əpreen/ *n.* a synthetic rubberlike polymer. [NEO- + *chloroprene*, etc. (perh. f. PROPYL + -ENE)]

neoteny /neeót'nee/ *n.* the retention of juvenile features in the adult form of some animals, e.g., an axolotl. □□ **neotenic** /néeə-ōténik/ *adj.* **neotenous** *adj.* [G *Neotenie* (as NEO- + Gk *teinō* extend)]

neoteric /néeə-ōtérik/ *adj. literary* recent; newfangled; modern. [LL *neotericus* f. Gk *neōterikos* (*neōteros* compar. of *neos* new)]

neotropical /néeə-ōtrópikəl/ *adj.* of or relating to tropical and S. America as a biogeographical region.

Nepalese /népəleez, -lees/ *adj. & n.* (*pl.* same) = NEPALI.

Nepali /nipáwlee/ *n. & adj.* ● *n.* (*pl.* same or **Nepalis**) **1 a** a native or national of Nepal in Central Asia. **b** a person of Nepali descent. **2** the language of Nepal. ● *adj.* of or relating to Nepal or its language or people.

nepenthe /nipénthee/ *n.* = NEPENTHES 1. [var. of NEPENTHES, after It. *nepente*]

nepenthes /nipéntheez/ *n.* **1** *poet.* a drug causing forgetfulness of grief. **2** any pitcher plant of the genus *Nepenthes*. [L f. Gk *nēpenthes* (*pharmakon* drug), neut. of *nēpenthēs* f. *nē-* not + *penthos* grief]

nephew /néfyoo/ *n.* a son of one's brother or sister, or of one's brother-in-law or sister-in-law. [ME f. OF *neveu* f. L *nepos nepotis* grandson, nephew]

nephology /nefóləjee/ *n.* the study of clouds. [Gk *nephos* cloud + -LOGY]

nephrite /néfrīt/ *n.* a green, yellow, or white calcium magnesium silicate form of jade. [G *Nephrit* f. Gk *nephros* kidney, with ref. to its supposed efficacy in treating kidney disease]

nephritic /nəfrítik/ *adj.* **1** of or in the kidneys; renal. **2** of or relating to nephritis. [LL *nephriticus* f. Gk *nephritikos* (as NE-PHRITIS)]

nephritis /nefrítis/ *n.* inflammation of the kidneys. Also called *Bright's disease*. [LL f. Gk *nephros* kidney]

nephro- /néfrō/ *comb. form* (usu. **nephr-** before a vowel) kidney. [Gk f. *nephros* kidney]

ne plus ultra /náy ploõs oõltraa, nē plus últrə/ *n.* **1** the furthest attainable point. **2** the culmination, acme, or perfection. [L, = not further beyond, the supposed inscription on the Pillars of Hercules (the Strait of Gibraltar) prohibiting passage by ships]

nepotism /népə-tizəm/ *n.* favoritism shown to relatives in conferring offices or privileges. □□ **nepotist** *n.* **nepotistic** *adj.* [F *népotisme* f. It. *nepotismo* f. *nepote* NEPHEW: orig. with ref. to popes with illegitimate sons called nephews]
  ■ see FAVORITISM.

Neptune /néptoōn, -tyoōn/ *n.* a distant planet of the solar system, eighth from the sun, discovered in 1846 from mathematical computations. [ME f. F *Neptune* or L *Neptunus* god of the sea]

neptunium /neptoõneeəm, -tyoõ-/ *n. Chem.* a radioactive transuranic metallic element produced when uranium atoms absorb bombarding neutrons. ¶ Symb.: **Np**. [NEPTUNE, as the next planet beyond Uranus, + -IUM]

nerd /nərd/ *n.* (also **nurd**) *sl.* **1** a foolish, feeble, or uninteresting person. **2** a person academically or intellectually tal-

ented but socially unskilled. □□ **nerdy** *adj.* [20th c.: orig. uncert.]
  ■ see JERK¹ *n.* 4.

nereid /néereeid/ *n. Mythol.* a sea nymph. [L *Nereïs Nereïd-* f. Gk *Nēreïs -idos* daughter of the sea god Nereus]

nerine /nirínee/ *n.* any S. African plant of the genus *Nerine*, bearing flowers with usu. six narrow strap-shaped petals, often crimped and twisted. [mod.L f. the L name of a water nymph]

neroli /nérəlee, neér-/ *n.* (in full **neroli oil**) an essential oil from the flowers of the Seville orange, used in perfumery. [F *néroli* f. It. *neroli*, perh. f. the name of an Italian princess]

nervate /nárvayt/ *adj.* (of a leaf) having veins. □□ **nervation** /-váyshən/ *n.* [NERVE + -ATE²]

nerve /nərv/ *n. & v.* ● *n.* **1 a** a fiber or bundle of fibers that transmits impulses of sensation or motion between the brain or spinal cord and other parts of the body. **b** the material constituting these. **2 a** coolness in danger; bravery; assurance. **b** *colloq.* impudence; audacity (*they've got a nerve*). **3** (in *pl.*) **a** the bodily state in regard to physical sensitiveness and the interaction between the brain and other parts. **b** a state of heightened nervousness or sensitivity; a condition of mental or physical stress (*need to calm my nerves*). **4** a rib of a leaf, esp. the midrib. **5** *poet. archaic* a sinew or tendon. ● *v.tr.* **1** (usu. *refl.*) brace (oneself) to face danger, suffering, etc. **2** give strength, vigor, or courage to. □ **get on a person's nerves** irritate or annoy a person. **have nerves of iron** (or **steel**) (of a person, etc.) be not easily upset or frightened. **nerve cell** an elongated branched cell transmitting impulses in nerve tissue. **nerve center 1** a group of closely connected nerve cells associated in performing some function. **2** the center of control of an organization, etc. **nerve gas** a poisonous gas affecting the nervous system. **nerve-racking** (also **nerve-wracking**) stressful, frightening; straining the nerves. □□ **nerved** *adj.* (also in *comb.*). [ME, = sinew, f. L *nervus*, rel. to Gk *neuron*]
  ■ *n.* **1** (*attrib.*) nervo-, neuro-. **2 a** courage, coolness, boldness, bravery, intrepidity, determination, valor, daring, fearlessness, nervelessness, dauntlessness, pluck, mettle, spirit, fortitude; assurance, will, tenacity, steadfastness, staunchness, firmness, resoluteness, *archaic or joc.* doughtiness, *colloq.* guts, grit, gumption, spunk, sand, *sl.* moxie. **b** effrontery, brazenness, impertinence, impudence, insolence, audacity, brashness, presumption, presumptuousness, temerity, face, front, cheek, *colloq.* sauce, brass, esp. *Austral. & NZ colloq.* hide, *sl.* gall, chutzpah, crust. **3 b** (*nerves*) tension, nervousness, hysteria, anxiety, fretfulness, stress, worry, apprehension, fright, the shakes, *colloq.* the jitters, the willies, *sl.* the heebie-jeebies, jimjams. □ **get on a person's nerves** annoy, irritate, upset; see also IRK. **nerve-racking** stressful, frightening, harrowing, worrying, nail-biting, agonizing, distressing, trying, vexing, vexatious, troublesome, worrisome, irksome, irritating.

nerveless /nárvlis/ *adj.* **1** inert; lacking vigor or spirit. **2** confident; not nervous. **3** (of style) diffuse. **4** *Bot. & Entomol.* without nervures. **5** *Anat. & Zool.* without nerves. □□ **nervelessly** *adv.* **nervelessness** *n.*

nervine /nárvīn/ *adj. & n.* ● *adj.* relieving nerve disorders. ● *n.* a nervine drug. [F *nervin* (as NERVE)]

nervo- /nárvō/ *comb. form* (also **nerv-** before a vowel) a nerve or the nerves.

nervous /nárvəs/ *adj.* **1** having delicate or disordered nerves. **2** timid or anxious. **3 a** excitable; highly strung; easily agitated. **b** resulting from this temperament (*nervous tension*; *a nervous headache*). **4** affecting or acting on the nerves. **5** (foll. by *about* + verbal noun) reluctant; afraid (*am nervous about meeting them*). □ **nervous breakdown** a period of mental illness, usu. resulting from severe depression or anxiety. **nervous system** the body's network of specialized cells that transmit nerve impulses between parts of the body (cf. *central nervous system*, *peripheral nervous system*). **nervous wreck** *colloq.* a person suffering from mental stress, exhaustion, etc. □□ **nervously** adv. **nervousness** n. [ME f. L nervosus (as NERVE)]

■ **1–3, 5** highly strung, high-strung, excitable, sensitive, tense, agitated, overwrought, worked up, upset, flustered, ruffled, disturbed, perturbed, distressed, worried, anxious, troubled, concerned, disquieted, edgy, on edge, on tenterhooks, fidgety, fretful, uneasy, apprehensive, frightened, fearful, timid, shaky, jumpy, nervy, scared, skittish, on pins and needles, colloq. jittery, windy, in a stew, all of a dither, in a sweat, in a tizzy, in a flap, uptight, Austral. sl. toey. **4** neurological.

nervure /nɔ́rvyər/ n. **1** each of the hollow tubes that form the framework of an insect's wing; a venule. **2** the principal vein of a leaf. [F nerf nerve]

nervy /nɔ́rvee/ adj. (**nervier, nerviest**) **1** bold, impudent, pushy. **2** esp. Brit. nervous; easily excited or disturbed. **3** archaic sinewy, strong. □□ **nervily** adv. **nerviness** n.

■ **1** see NERVOUS 1–3, 5. **2** see IMPERTINENT 1.

nescient /néshənt, -eeənt/ adj. literary (foll. by of) lacking knowledge; ignorant. □□ **nescience** n. [LL nescientia f. L nescire not know f. ne- not + scire know]

ness /nes/ n. a headland or promontory. [OE næs, rel. to OE nasu NOSE]

■ see CAPE².

-ness /nis/ suffix forming nouns from adjectives and occas. other words, expressing: **1** state or condition, or an instance of this (bitterness; conceitedness; happiness; a kindness). **2** something in a certain state (wilderness). [OE -nes, -ness f. Gmc]

nest /nest/ n. & v. ● n. **1** a structure or place where a bird lays eggs and shelters its young. **2** an animal's or insect's breeding place or lair. **3** a snug or secluded retreat or shelter. **4** (often foll. by of) a place fostering something undesirable (a nest of vice). **5** a brood or swarm. **6** a group or set of similar objects, often of different sizes and fitting together for storage (a nest of tables). ● v. **1** intr. use or build a nest. **2** intr. take wild birds' nests or eggs. **3** intr. (of objects) fit together or one inside another. **4** tr. (usu. as **nested** adj.) establish in or as in a nest. □ **nest egg 1** a sum of money saved for the future. **2** a real or artificial egg left in a nest to induce hens to lay eggs there. □□ **nestful** n. (pl. **-fuls**). **nesting** n. (in sense 2 of v.). **nestlike** adj. [OE nest]

■ n. **1** roost, perch, aerie. **2, 3** den, lair, nidus, retreat, refuge, haunt, hideaway, nook, Brit. snuggery, colloq. hideout. **4** breeding ground, den; cradle, nidus.

nestle /nésəl/ v. **1** intr. (often foll. by down, in, etc.) settle oneself comfortably. **2** intr. press oneself against another in affection, etc. **3** tr. (foll. by in, into, etc.) push (a head or shoulder, etc.) affectionately or snugly. **4** intr. lie half hidden or embedded. [OE nestlian (as NEST)]

■ **1, 2** cuddle, snuggle, huddle, curl up, nuzzle, settle down, snug down.

nestling /nésling, nést-/ n. a bird that is too young to leave its nest.

net¹ /net/ n. & v. ● n. **1** an open-meshed fabric of cord, rope, fiber, etc.; a structure resembling this. **2** a piece of net used esp. to restrain, contain, or delimit, or to catch fish or other animals. **3** a structure with net to enclose an area of ground, esp. in sport. **4 a** a structure with net used in various games, esp. forming the goal in soccer, hockey, etc., and dividing the court in tennis, etc. **b** (often in pl.) a practice ground in cricket, surrounded by nets. **5** a system or procedure for catching or entrapping a person or persons. **6** = NETWORK. ● v. (**netted, netting**) **1** tr. a cover, confine, or catch with a net. **b** procure as with a net. **2** tr. hit (a ball) into the net, esp. of a goal. **3** intr. make netting. **4** tr. make (a purse, hammock, etc.) by knotting, etc., threads together to form a net. **5** tr. fish with nets, or set nets, in (a river). **6** tr. (usu. as **netted** adj.) mark with a netlike pattern; reticulate. □□ **netful** n. (pl. **-fuls**). [OE net, nett]

■ n. **1** network, netting, mesh, meshwork, web, webbing, openwork, lattice, latticework, trellis, trelliswork, lacework, reticulum, reticle, plexus, grid, grille, grate, grating, fretwork, Anat. rete. **2** trammel, trawl, trawl net, fishnet, dragnet, drift net, landing net, butterfly

net, mosquito net. ● v. **1** catch, capture, trap, entrap, snare, ensnare, bag.

net² /net/ adj. & v. ● adj. **1** (esp. of money) remaining after all necessary deductions, or free from deductions. **2** (of a price) to be paid in full; not reducible. **3** (of a weight) excluding that of the packaging or container, etc. **4** (of an effect, result, etc.) ultimate, effective. ● v.tr. (**netted, netting**) gain or yield (a sum) as net profit. □ **net profit** the effective profit; the actual gain after expenses have been paid. **net ton** see TON¹. [F net NEAT¹]

■ adj. **1** clear, after deductions, after taxes, take-home, final. **4** final, end, closing, concluding, conclusive, effective, ultimate. ● v. gain, yield, fetch; make, realize, clear, take home, bring in, earn, pocket, take in, get.

nether /néthər/ adj. archaic = LOWER¹. □ **nether regions** (or **world**) hell; the underworld. □□ **nethermost** adj. [OE nithera, etc. f. Gmc]

■ □ **nether regions** see HELL 1.

Netherlander /néthərlandər/ n. **1** a native or national of the Netherlands. **2** a person of Dutch descent. □□ **Netherlandish** adj. [Du. Nederlander, Nederlandsch]

Netherlands /néthərləndz/ n. **1** (usu. prec. by the) Holland. **2** hist. the Low Countries. [Du. Nederland (as NETHER, LAND)]

netsuke /nétsōōkee/ n. (pl. same or **netsukes**) (in Japan) a carved buttonlike ornament, esp. of ivory or wood, formerly worn to suspend articles from a girdle. [Jap.]

netting /néting/ n. **1** netted fabric. **2** a piece of this.

■ see MESH n. 1–3a.

nettle /nét'l/ n. & v. ● n. **1** any plant of the genus Urtica, esp. U. dioica, with jagged leaves covered with stinging hairs. **2** any of various plants resembling this. ● v.tr. **1** irritate; provoke; annoy. **2** sting with nettles. □ **nettle rash** a skin eruption like nettle stings. [OE netle, netele]

■ v. **1** see IRRITATE 1.

nettlesome /nét'lsəm/ adj. **1** awkward, difficult. **2** causing annoyance.

■ **1** see TROUBLESOME 1. **2** see TROUBLESOME 2.

network /nétwərk/ n. & v. ● n. **1** an arrangement of intersecting horizontal and vertical lines, like the structure of a net. **2** a complex system of railways, roads, canals, etc. **3** a group of people who exchange information, contacts, and experience for professional or social purposes. **4** a chain of interconnected computers, machines, or operations. **5** a system of connected electrical conductors. **6** a group of broadcasting stations connected for a simultaneous broadcast of a program. ● v. **1** tr. link (machines, esp. computers) to operate interactively. **2** intr. establish a network. **3** Brit. tr. broadcast on a network. **4** intr. be a member of a network (see sense 3 of n.).

■ n. **1** see NET¹ n. 1. **2** system, arrangement, structure, organization, complex, grid, crisscross, web, plexus; maze, labyrinth, jungle, tangle. **3** see UNION 2.

networker /nétwərkər/ n. **1** Computing a member of an organization or computer network who operates from home, from an external office, or from one of several computer terminals within an office. **2** a member of a professional or social network.

neume /nōōm, nyōōm/ n. (also **neum**) Mus. a sign in plainsong indicating a note or group of notes to be sung to a syllable. [ME f. OF neume f. med.L neu(p)ma f. Gk pneuma breath]

neural /nŏŏrəl, nyŏŏr-/ adj. of or relating to a nerve or the central nervous system. □ **neural network** (or **neural net**) Computing a computer system modeled on the human brain and nervous system. □□ **neurally** adv. [Gk neuron nerve]

neuralgia /nŏŏráljə, nyŏŏ-/ n. an intense intermittent pain along the course of a nerve, esp. in the head or face. □□ **neuralgic** *adj.* [as NEURAL + -ALGIA]

neurasthenia /nŏŏrəsthéeneeə, nyŏŏr-/ *n.* a general term for fatigue, anxiety, listlessness, etc. (not in medical use). □□ **neurasthenic** /-thénik/ *adj.* & *n.* [Gk *neuron* nerve + AS-THENIA]

neuritis /nŏŏrítis, nyŏŏ-/ *n.* inflammation of a nerve or nerves. □□ **neuritic** /-rítik/ *adj.* [formed as NEURO- + -ITIS]

neuro- /nŏŏrō, nyŏŏrō/ *comb. form* a nerve or the nerves. [Gk *neuron* nerve]

neurogenesis /nŏŏrōjénisis, nyŏŏr-/ *n.* the growth and development of nervous tissue.

neurogenic /nŏŏrōjénik, nyŏŏr-/ *adj.* caused by or arising in nervous tissue.

neuroglia /nŏŏráagleeə, nyŏŏr-/ *n.* the connective tissue supporting the central nervous system. [NEURO- + Gk *glia* glue]

neurohormone /nŏŏrōháwrmōn, nyŏŏr-/ *n.* a hormone produced by nerve cells and secreted into the circulation.

neurology /nŏŏráaləjee, nyŏŏr-/ *n.* the scientific study of the nervous system. □□ **neurological** /-rəlójikəl/ *adj.* **neurologically** *adv.* **neurologist** *n.* [mod.L *neurologia* f. mod. Gk (as NEURO-, -LOGY)]

neuroma /nŏŏrōmə, nyŏŏ-/ *n.* (*pl.* **neuromas** or **neuromata** /-mətə/) a tumor on a nerve or in nerve tissue. [Gk *neuron* nerve + -OMA]

neuromuscular /nŏŏrōmúskyələr, nyŏŏr-/ *adj.* of or relating to nerves and muscles.

neuron /nŏŏron, nyŏŏr-/ *n.* (also **neurone** /-ōn/) a specialized cell transmitting nerve impulses; a nerve cell. □□ **neuronal** *adj.* **neuronic** /-rónik/ *adj.* [Gk *neuron* nerve]

neuropath /nŏŏrōpath, nyŏŏr-/ *n.* a person affected by nervous disease, or with an abnormally sensitive nervous system. □□ **neuropathic** *adj.* **neuropathy** /-rópəthee/ *n.*

neuropathology /nŏŏrōpəthóləjee, nyŏŏr-/ *n.* the pathology of the nervous system. □□ **neuropathologist** *n.*

neurophysiology /nŏŏrōfízeeóləjee, nyŏŏr-/ *n.* the physiology of the nervous system. □□ **neurophysiological** /-zeeəlójikəl/ *adj.* **neurophysiologist** *n.*

neuropteran /nŏŏróptərən, nyŏŏ-/ *n.* any insect of the order Neuroptera, including lacewings, having four finely veined membranous leaflike wings. □□ **neuropterous** *adj.* [NEURO- + Gk *pteron* wing]

neurosis /nŏŏrōsis, nyŏŏ-/ *n.* (*pl.* **neuroses** /-seez/) a mental illness characterized by irrational or depressive thought or behavior, caused by a disorder of the nervous system usu. without organic change. [mod.L (as NEURO-, -OSIS)]

neurosurgery /nŏŏrōsúrjəree, nyŏŏr-/ *n.* surgery performed on the nervous system, esp. the brain and spinal cord. □□ **neurosurgeon** *n.* **neurosurgical** *adj.*

neurotic /nŏŏrótik, nyŏŏ-/ *adj.* & *n.* ● *adj.* **1** caused by or relating to neurosis. **2** (of a person) suffering from neurosis. **3** *colloq.* abnormally sensitive or obsessive. ● *n.* a neurotic person. □□ **neurotically** *adv.* **neuroticism** /-isizəm/ *n.*
   ■ *adj.* **2, 3** psychoneurotic; unstable, disturbed, confused, irrational, disordered, maladjusted, distraught, oversensitive, overwrought, anxious, nervous, obsessive.

neurotomy /nŏŏrótəmee, nyŏŏ-/ *n.* (*pl.* **-ies**) the operation of cutting a nerve, esp. to produce sensory loss.

neurotransmitter /nŏŏrōtránsmitər, -tránz-, nyŏŏr-/ *n.* *Biochem.* a chemical substance released from a nerve fiber that effects the transfer of an impulse to another nerve or muscle.

neut. *abbr.* neuter.

neuter /nŏŏtər, nyŏŏ-/ *adj.*, *n.*, & *v.* ● *adj.* **1** *Gram.* (of a noun, etc.) neither masculine nor feminine. **2** (of a plant) having neither pistils nor stamen. **3** (of an insect, animal, etc.) sexually undeveloped; castrated or spayed. ● *n.* **1** *Gram.* a neuter word. **2 a** a nonfertile insect, esp. a worker bee or ant. **b** a castrated animal. ● *v.tr.* castrate or spay. [ME f. OF *neutre* or L *neuter* neither f. *ne-* not + *uter* either]
   ■ *adj.* **2** asexual, sexless. **3** asexual, sexless, neutral, androgyne, undeveloped, epicene; neutered, castrated, desexed, emasculated, gelded, caponized, spayed.

● *v.* desex, castrate, emasculate, cut, fix, geld, caponize, spay, *US & Austral.* alter, mark.

neutral /nŏŏtrəl, nyŏŏ-/ *adj.* & *n.* ● *adj.* **1** not helping nor supporting either of two opposing sides, esp. nations at war or in dispute; impartial. **2** belonging to a neutral party, nation, etc. (*neutral ships*). **3** indistinct, vague, indeterminate. **4** (of a gear) in which the engine is disconnected from the driven parts. **5** (of colors) not strong nor positive; gray or beige. **6** *Chem.* neither acid nor alkaline. **7** *Electr.* neither positive nor negative. **8** *Biol.* sexually undeveloped; asexual. ● *n.* **1 a** a neutral nation, person, etc. **b** a subject of a neutral nation. **2** a neutral gear. □□ **neutrality** /-trálitee/ *n.* **neutrally** *adv.* [ME f. obs. F *neutral* or L *neutralis* of neuter gender (as NEUTER)]
   ■ *adj.* **1, 2** nonbelligerent, noncombatant; unaligned, nonaligned, unaffiliated, uninvolved, unallied, nonallied, nonpartisan, impartial, disinterested; indifferent, dispassionate, unbiased, uncommitted, noncommittal, aloof, withdrawn, detached, remote, removed. **3, 5** dull, drab, colorless, achromatic, toneless, washed-out, pale, indefinite, indistinct, indistinguishable, indeterminate, vague; gray, beige, taupe, ecru.

neutralism /nŏŏtrəlizəm, nyŏŏ-/ *n.* a policy of political neutrality. □□ **neutralist** *n.*

neutralize /nŏŏtrəliz, nyŏŏ-/ *v.tr.* **1** make neutral. **2** counterbalance; render ineffective by an opposite force or effect. **3** exempt or exclude (a place) from the sphere of hostilities. □□ **neutralization** *n.* **neutralizer** *n.* [F *neutraliser* f. med.L *neutralizare* (as NEUTRAL)]
   ■ **2** void, annul, cancel (out), nullify, invalidate, negate, delete, undo, make *or* render ineffective, counterbalance, counteract, offset; equalize, even, square; compensate for, make up for.

neutrino /nŏŏtréenō, nyŏŏ-/ *n.* (*pl.* **-os**) any of a group of stable elementary particles with zero electric charge and probably zero mass, which travel at the speed of light. [It., dimin. of *neutro* neutral (as NEUTER)]

neutron /nŏŏtron, nyŏŏ-/ *n.* an elementary particle of about the same mass as a proton but without an electric charge, present in all atomic nuclei except those of ordinary hydrogen. □ **neutron bomb** a bomb producing neutrons and little blast, causing damage to life but little destruction to property. **neutron star** a very dense star composed mainly of neutrons. [NEUTRAL + -ON]

Nev. *abbr.* Nevada.

névé /náyváy/ *n.* an expanse of granular snow not yet compressed into ice at the head of a glacier. [Swiss F, = glacier, ult. f. L *nix nivis* snow]

never /névər/ *adv.* **1 a** at no time; on no occasion; not ever (*have never been to Paris; never saw them again*). **b** *colloq.* as an emphatic negative (*I never heard you come in*). **2** not at all (*never fear*). **3** *Brit. colloq.* (expressing surprise) surely not (*you never left the key in the lock!*). □ **never-ending** eternal, undying; immeasurable. **never-never** (often prec. by *the*) *Brit. colloq.* hire purchase. **never-never land** an imaginary utopian place. **never a one** none. **never say die** see DIE[1]. **well I never!** expressing great surprise. [OE *næfre* f. *ne* not + *æfre* EVER]
   ■ **1 a** at no time, not ever, not at any time, on no occasion, not at all. **1b, 2** by no means, on no account, by no chance, in no circumstances, under no circumstances *or* condition(s), *colloq.* no way, not in a million years; in no case, in no way, not in any way, not in the least, not in any degree, not under any condition(s), nohow. □ **never-ending** see ENDLESS 1, 2; IMMEASURABLE. **well I never!** blow me down, good gracious, goodness me, you don't say, well I declare, *colloq.* I'll be damned, *sl.* well I'll be blowed; see also BOY *int.*

nevermore /névərmáwr/ *adv.* at no future time.

nevertheless /névərthəlés/ *adv.* in spite of that; notwithstanding; all the same.
   ■ still, notwithstanding, yet, in spite of that, despite that, nonetheless, regardless, be that as it may, for all that,

even so, but, however, just *or* all the same, anyway, in any case.

nevus /nēevəs/ *n.* (*pl.* **nevi** /-vī/) **1** a birthmark in the form of a raised red patch on the skin. **2** = MOLE². □□ **nevoid** *adj.* [L]

new /nōō, nyōō/ *adj. & adv.* ● *adj.* **1 a** of recent origin or arrival. **b** made, invented, discovered, acquired, or experienced recently or now for the first time (*a new star; has many new ideas*). **2** in original condition; not worn or used. **3 a** renewed or reformed (*a new life; the new order*). **b** reinvigorated (*felt like a new person*). **4** different from a recent previous one (*has a new job*). **5** in addition to others already existing (*have you been to the new supermarket?*). **6** (often foll. by *to*) unfamiliar or strange (*a new sensation; the idea was new to me*). **7** (often foll. by *at*) (of a person) inexperienced, unaccustomed (to doing something) (*am new at this business*). **8** (usu. prec. by *the*) often *derog.* **a** later, modern. **b** newfangled. **c** given to new or modern ideas (*the new man*). **d** recently affected by social change (*the new rich*). **9** (often prec. by *the*) advanced in method or theory (*the new formula*). **10** (in place names) discovered or founded later than and named after (*New York; New Zealand*). ● *adv.* (usu. in *comb.*) **1** newly, recently (*new-fashioned; new-baked*). **2** anew, afresh. □ **New Age** a set of beliefs intended to replace traditional Western Culture, with alternative approaches to religion, medicine, the environment, music, etc. **new birth** *Theol.* spiritual regeneration. **new broom** see BROOM. **new deal** new arrangements or conditions, esp. when better than the earlier ones. **new look** a new or revised appearance or presentation, esp. of something familiar. **the new mathematics** (or *Brit.* **maths**) a system of teaching mathematics to children, with emphasis on investigation by them and on set theory. **new moon 1** the moon when first seen as a crescent after conjunction with the sun. **2** the time of its appearance. **a new one** (often foll. by *on*) *colloq.* an account or idea not previously encountered (by a person). **new potatoes** the earliest potatoes of a new crop. **new star** a nova. **New Style** dating reckoned by the Gregorian Calendar. **New Testament** the part of the Bible concerned with the life and teachings of Christ and his earliest followers. **new town** a self-sufficient, planned town established as a completely new settlement. **new wave 1** = NOUVELLE VAGUE. **2** a style of rock music popular in the 1970s. **New World** N. and S. America regarded collectively in relation to Europe. **new year 1** the calendar year just begun or about to begin. **2** the first few days of a year. **New Year's Day** January 1. **New Year's Eve** December 31. □□ **newish** *adj.* **newness** *n.* [OE *nīwe* f. Gmc]

■ *adj.* **1 a** brand-new, recent, newly arrived. **b** novel, original, unique, different, fresh, innovative. **2** original, fresh, mint, unworn, unused. **3** revitalized, reinvigorated, reformed, reborn, renewed, rejuvenated, changed, altered, redone, restored, redesigned, remodeled. **4** different, fresh, (an)other. **5** further, additional, supplemental, supplementary. **6** unfamiliar, unknown, strange, different, unusual; unheard-of; uncharted, unexplored, untrodden; experimental. **7** inexperienced, green, fresh, callow, unfledged, untrained, unaccustomed; immature. **8, 9** latest, late, modern, avant-garde, innovative, contemporary, modish, stylish, fashionable, chic, *colloq.* mod, *colloq. often derog.* trendy, *formal* hodiernal, *sl.* hip, with it; recent, advanced, up-to-date, brand-new; *derog.* newfangled.

newborn/nōōbawrn, nyōō-/ *adj.* **1** (of a child, etc.) recently born. **2** spiritually reborn; regenerated.

newcomer /nōōkumər, nyōō-/ *n.* **1** a person who has recently arrived. **2** a beginner in some activity.

■ **1** alien, immigrant, foreigner, outlander, stranger, settler, colonist, outsider. **2** beginner, amateur, novice, proselyte, neophyte, tyro, initiate, trainee, learner, fledgling, greenhorn, freshman, *Brit. colloq.* fresher.

newel /nōōəl, nyōō-/ *n.* **1** the supporting central post of winding stairs. **2** the top or bottom supporting post of a stair rail.

[ME f. OF *noel, nouel,* knob f. med.L *nodellus* dimin. of L *nodus* knot]

newfangled /nōōfánggəld, nyōō-/ *adj. derog.* different from what one is used to; objectionably new. [ME *newfangle* (now dial.) liking what is new f. *newe* NEW *adv.* + *-fangel* f. OE *fangol* (unrecorded) inclined to take]

■ see MODERN *adj.*

Newfoundland /nōōfəndlənd, noofówndlənd, nyōō-, -land, -fənd-, nyōō-/ *n.* (in full **Newfoundland dog**) **1** a dog of a very large breed with a thick, usu. black, coarse coat. **2** this breed. [the name of a Canadian province, an island at the mouth of the St. Lawrence River]

newly /nōōlee, nyōō-/ *adv.* **1** recently (*a friend newly arrived; a newly discovered country*). **2** afresh, anew (*newly painted*). **3** in a new or different manner (*newly arranged*).

newlywed /nōōleewed, nyōō-/ *n.* a recently married person.

news /nōōz, nyōōz/ *n.pl.* (usu. treated as *sing.*) **1** information about important or interesting recent events, esp. when published or broadcast. **2** (prec. by *the*) a broadcast report of news. **3** newly received or noteworthy information. **4** (foll. by *to*) *colloq.* information not previously known (to a person) (*that's news to me*). □ **news agency** an organization that collects and distributes news items. **news bulletin 1** *US* brief item of news broadcast almost as soon as received. **2** *Brit.* a collection of items of news, esp. for broadcasting. **news conference** a press conference. □□ **newsless** *adj.* [ME, pl. of NEW after OF *noveles* or med.L *nova* neut. pl. of *novus* new]

■ **1, 3** word, information, advice, *archaic* intelligence, *colloq.* info, *literary* tidings; dispatch, report, account, story, communication, bulletin, flash, news flash, communiqué, announcement, message, statement, (press) release, newsbrief; rumor, talk, gossip, hearsay, dirt, scandal, exposé, *colloq.* lowdown, scuttlebutt, *sl.* dope; (good) copy, front-page news, (hot) item, scoop. **2** (*the news*) newscast, broadcast, telecast, news program, newsreel; news flash, news brief, (news) bulletin.

newsagent /nōōzayjənt, nyōōz-/ *n. Brit.* a seller of or shop selling newspapers and usu. related items, e.g., stationery.

newsboy /nōōzboy, nyōōz-/ *n.* a boy who sells or delivers newspapers.

news brief /nōōzbreef, nyōōz-/ *n.* a short item of news, esp. on television; a news flash.

newscast /nōōzkast, nyōōz-/ *n.* a radio or television broadcast of news reports.

newscaster /nōōzkastər, nyōōz-/ *n.* a person who reads the news broadcast on radio or television.

■ see ANNOUNCER.

newsdealer /nōōzdeelər, nyōōz-/ *n.* a person who sells newspapers, magazines, etc.

news flash /nōōzflash, nyōōz-/ *n.* a single item of important news, broadcast separately and often interrupting other programs.

newsgirl /nōōzgərl, nyōōz-/ *n.* a girl who sells or delivers newspapers.

newsletter /nōōzletər, nyōōz-/ *n.* an informal printed report issued periodically to the members of a society, business, organization, etc.

■ see PUBLICATION 1b.

newsman /nōōzman, -mən, nyōōz-/ *n.* (*pl.* **-men**) a newspaper reporter; a journalist.

■ see JOURNALIST.

newsmonger /nōōzmonggər, nyōōz-/ *n.* a gossip.

■ see GOSSIP *n.* 3.

newspaper /nōōzpaypər, nyōōz-, nōōs-, nyōōs-/ *n.* **1** a printed publication (usu. daily or weekly) containing news, advertisements, correspondence, etc. **2** the sheets of paper forming this (*wrapped in newspaper*).

/ . . ./ **pronunciation**	● **part of speech**
□ **phrases, idioms, and compounds**	
□□ **derivatives**	■ **synonym section**
cross-references appear in SMALL CAPITALS or *italics*	

■ **1** see PUBLICATION 1b.

newspaperman /nŏŏzpaypərmən, -mən, nyŏŏz-, nŏŏs-, nyŏŏs-/ *n.* (*pl.* **-men**) a journalist.

■ see JOURNALIST.

newspeak /nŏŏspeek, nyŏŏ-/ *n.* (also **Newspeak**) ambiguous euphemistic language used esp. in political propaganda. [an artificial official language in George Orwell's *Nineteen Eighty-Four* (1949)]

newsprint /nŏŏzprint, nyŏŏ-/ *n.* a type of low-quality paper on which newspapers are printed.

newsreader /nŏŏzreedər, nyŏŏz-/ *n. Brit.* = NEWSCASTER.

■ see ANNOUNCER.

newsreel /nŏŏzreel, nyŏŏz-/ *n.* a short movie of recent events.

newsroom /nŏŏzroom, nyŏŏz-/ *n.* a room in a newspaper or broadcasting office where news stories are prepared.

newsstand /nŏŏzstand, nyŏŏz-/ *n.* a stall for the sale of newspapers, magazines, etc.

newsweekly /nŏŏzweeklee, nyŏŏz-/ *n.* a periodical published weekly that summarizes current events.

newsworthy /nŏŏzwərthee, nyŏŏz-/ *adj.* topical; noteworthy as news. □□ **newsworthiness** *n.*

newsy /nŏŏzee, nyŏŏ-/ *adj.* (**newsier**, **newsiest**) *colloq.* full of news.

newt /nŏŏt, nyŏŏt/ *n.* any of various small amphibians, esp. of the genus *Triturus*, having a well-developed tail. [ME f. *ewt*, with *n* from *an* (cf. NICKNAME): var. of *evet* EFT]

New Test. *abbr.* New Testament.

newton /nŏŏt'n, nyŏŏ-/ *n. Physics* the SI unit of force that, acting on a mass of one kilogram, increases its velocity by one meter per second every second along the direction that it acts. ¶ Abbr.: N. [Sir Isaac *Newton*, Engl. scientist d. 1727]

Newtonian /nŏŏtŏneeən, nyŏŏ-/ *adj.* of or devised by Isaac Newton (see NEWTON). □ **Newtonian mechanics** the system of mechanics that relies on Newton's laws of motion concerning the relations between forces acting and motions occurring. **Newtonian telescope** a reflecting telescope with a small secondary mirror at 45° to the main beam of light to reflect it into a magnifying eyepiece.

New Zealander /nŏŏzeeələndər, nyŏŏ-/ *n.* **1** a native or national of New Zealand, an island group in the Pacific. **2** a person of New Zealand descent.

next /nekst/ *adj., adv., n., & prep.* ● *adj.* **1** (often foll. by *to*) being or positioned or living nearest (*in the next house*; *the chair next to the fire*). **2** the nearest in order of time; the first or soonest encountered or considered (*next Friday*; *ask the next person you see*). ● *adv.* **1** (often foll. by *to*) in the nearest place or degree (*put it next to mine*; *came next to last*). **2** on the first or soonest occasion (*when we next meet*). ● *n.* the next person or thing. ● *prep. colloq.* next to. □ **next-best** the next in order of preference. **next door** see DOOR. **next of kin** the closest living relative or relatives. **next to almost** (*next to nothing left*). **the next world** see WORLD. [OE *nēhsta* superl. (as NIGH)]

■ *adj.* **1** see *adjoining* (ADJOIN). **2** see SUBSEQUENT. □ **next of kin** see FAMILY 1.

nexus /néksəs/ *n.* (*pl.* same) **1** a connected group or series. **2** a bond; a connection. [L f. *nectere nex-* bind]

Nez Percé /náy persáy/ *n.* (also **Nez Perce** /néz pórs/, nés pérs/) **1 a** a N. American people native to the northwestern US. **b** a member of this people. **2** the language of this people.

Nfld. *abbr.* (also **NF**) Newfoundland.

n.g. *abbr.* no good.

NH *abbr.* New Hampshire (also in official postal use).

NHI *abbr.* (in the UK) National Health Insurance.

NHS *abbr.* (in the UK) National Health Service.

NI *abbr.* Northern Ireland.

Ni *symb. Chem.* the element nickel.

niacin /nísin/ *n.* = NICOTINIC ACID. [*nicotinic acid* + -IN]

nib /nib/ *n. & v.* ● *n.* **1** the point of a pen, which touches the writing surface. **2** (in *pl.*) shelled and crushed coffee or cocoa beans. **3** the point of a tool, etc. ● *v.* (**nibbed**, **nibbing**) **1** *tr.* provide with a nib. **2** *tr.* mend the nib of. **3** *tr. & intr.* nibble. [prob. f. MDu. *nib* or MLG *nibbe*, var. of *nebbe* NEB]

■ *n.* **1, 3** see TIP¹ *n.* 1.

nibble /níbəl/ *v. & n.* ● *v.* **1** *tr.* & (foll. by *at*) *intr.* **a** take small bites at. **b** eat in small amounts. **c** bite at gently or cautiously or playfully. **2** *intr.* (foll. by *at*) show cautious interest in. ● *n.* **1** an instance of nibbling. **2** a very small amount of food. **3** *Computing* half a byte, i.e., 4 bits. □□ **nibbler** *n.* [prob. of LG or Du. orig.: cf. LG *nibbeln* gnaw]

■ *v.* **1** see *pick at* (PICK¹). ● *n.* **2** see MORSEL.

niblick /níblik/ *n. Golf* an iron with a large round heavy head, used esp. for playing out of bunkers. [19th c.: orig. unkn.]

nibs /nibz/ *n.* □ **his nibs** *joc. colloq.* a mock title used with reference to an important or self-important person. [19th c.: orig. unkn. (cf. earlier *nabs*)]

nicad /nícad/ *adj. & n.* ● *adj.* nickel and cadmium. ● *n.* a nickel and cadmium battery. [NICKEL + CADMIUM]

nice /nis/ *adj.* **1** pleasant, agreeable, satisfactory. **2** (of a person) kind, good-natured. **3** *iron.* bad or awkward (*a nice mess you've made*). **4 a** fine or subtle (*a nice distinction*). **b** requiring careful thought or attention (*a nice problem*). **5** fastidious; delicately sensitive. **6** punctilious, scrupulous (*were not too nice about their methods*). **7** (foll. by an adj., often with *and*) satisfactory or adequate in terms of the quality described (*a nice long time*; *nice and warm*). □ **nice work** a task well done. □□ **nicely** *adv.* **niceness** *n.* [ME, = stupid, wanton f. OF, = silly, simple f. L *nescius* ignorant (as *nescience*: see NESCIENT)]

■ **1, 2** pleasant, agreeable, good, satisfactory, commendable, worthy, worthwhile; amiable, amicable, friendly, good-natured, cordial, warm, gracious, warmhearted, kind, kindly, outgoing, charming, genial, delightful, courteous, polite, refined, gentlemanly, ladylike, winsome, likable, attractive; trim, well turned out, tidy, neat, fine. **3** see AWFUL 1a, b. **4–6** fine, delicate, sensitive, exquisite, flawless, faultless, subtle; attentive, sharp, acute, keen, fastidious, hairsplitting, careful, strict, close, small, exact, minute, exacting, rigorous, precise, accurate, unerring, scrupulous, critical, meticulous, punctilious, discriminating, discriminative, perceptive; complex, complicated, intricate. **7** pleasantly, delightfully, pleasingly, agreeably, enjoyably, gratifyingly, satisfyingly, comfortably, adequately, satisfactorily.

Nicene Creed /níseen/ *n.* a formal statement of Christian belief based on that adopted at the first Council of Nicaea in 325. [*Nicene* ME f. LL *Nicenus* of Nicaea in Asia Minor]

nicety /nísitee/ *n.* (*pl.* **-ies**) **1** a subtle distinction or detail. **2** precision, accuracy. **3** intricate or subtle quality (*a point of great nicety*). **4** (in *pl.*) **a** minutiae; fine details. **b** refinements, trimmings. □ **to a nicety** with exactness. [ME f. OF *niceté* (as NICE)]

■ **2** see PRECISION 2. **3** see SUBTLETY 1.

niche /nich, neesh/ *n. & v.* ● *n.* **1** a shallow recess, esp. in a wall to contain a statue, etc. **2** a comfortable or suitable position in life or employment. **3** an appropriate combination of conditions for a species to thrive. ● *v.tr.* (often as **niched** *adj.*) **1** place in a niche. **2** ensconce (esp. oneself) in a recess or corner. [F f. *nicher* make a nest, ult. f. L *nidus* nest]

■ *n.* **1** bay, slot, cell, hole, pigeonhole, cubbyhole; see also NOOK. **2** pigeonhole; see also PLACE *n.* 5.

Nichrome /níkrōm/ *n. propr.* a group of nickel-chromium alloys used for making wire in heating elements, etc. [NICKEL + CHROME]

Nick /nik/ *n.* □ **Old Nick** the Devil. [prob. f. a pet form of the name *Nicholas*]

■ □ **Old Nick** see DEVIL *n.* 1, 2.

nick /nik/ *n. & v.* ● *n.* **1** a small cut or notch. **2** *Brit. sl.* **a** a prison. **b** a police station. **3** (prec. by *in* with adj.) *Brit. colloq.* condition (*in reasonable nick*). **4** the junction between the floor and walls in a squash court. ● *v.tr.* **1** make a nick or nicks in. **2** *Brit. sl.* **a** steal. **b** arrest, catch. □ **in the nick of time** only just in time; just at the right moment. [ME: orig. uncert.]

■ *n.* **1** cut, notch, chip, gouge, gash, score; dent, indentation; flaw, mark, blemish, defect. **2 a** see PRISON

n. **1. b** police station, station house, *Brit. sl.* cop-shop. **3** trim, (state of) health; see also CONDITION *n.* 2a.
● *v.* **1** cut, notch, chip, gouge, gash, scratch, dent, score. **2 a** steal, take, appropriate, make off with, *colloq.* lift, swipe, *formal or joc.* purloin, *sl.* pinch. **b** see ARREST *v.* 1a.

nickel /níkəl/ *n. & v.* ● *n.* **1** *Chem.* a malleable ductile silver-white metallic transition element, occurring naturally in various minerals and used in special steels, in magnetic alloys, and as a catalyst. ¶ Symb.: **Ni. 2** a five-cent coin. ● *v.tr.* (**nickeled, nickeling**) coat with nickel. □ **nickel-and-dime** *adj.* involving a small amount of money; insignificant; trivial. ● *v.tr.* weaken (one's financial position) by continued small expenses, bills, etc. **nickel brass** an alloy of copper, zinc, and a small amount of nickel. **nickel-plated** coated with nickel by plating. **nickel silver** = *German silver.* **nickel steel** a type of stainless steel with chromium and nickel. [abbr. of G *Kupfernickel* copper-colored ore, from which nickel was first obtained, f. *Kupfer* copper + *Nickel* demon, with ref. to the ore's failure to yield copper]

nickelodeon /níkəlṓdeeən/ *n. colloq.* **1** an early movie theater, esp. one with admission priced at 5 cents. **2** a jukebox. [NICKEL + MELODEON]

nicknack var. of KNICKKNACK.

nickname /níknaym/ *n. & v.* ● *n.* a familiar or humorous name given to a person or thing instead of or as well as the real name. ● *v.tr.* **1** give a nickname to. **2** call (a person or thing) by a nickname. [ME f. *eke-name*, with *n* from *an* (cf. NEWT): *eke* = addition, f. OE *ēaca* (as EKE)]
■ *n.* pet name, sobriquet, epithet, *colloq.* handle, tag, *formal* appellation, *sl.* moniker.

Nicol /níkəl/ *n.* (in full **Nicol prism**) a device for producing plane-polarized light, consisting of two pieces of cut calcite cemented together with Canada balsam. [W. *Nicol,* Sc. physicist d. 1851, its inventor]

nicotine /níkəteen/ *n.* a colorless poisonous alkaloid present in tobacco. [F f. mod.L *nicotiana* (*herba*) tobacco plant, f. J. *Nicot,* Fr. diplomat & introducer of tobacco into France in the 16th c.]

nicotinic acid /níkətínik/ *n.* a vitamin of the B complex, found in milk, liver, and yeast, a deficiency of which causes pellagra. Also called NIACIN.

nictitate /níktitayt/ *v.intr.* close and open the eyes; blink or wink. □ **nictitating membrane** a clear membrane forming a third eyelid in amphibians, birds, and some other animals, that can be drawn across the eye to give protection without loss of vision. □□ **nictitation** /-táyshən/ *n.* [med.L *nictitare* frequent. of L *nictare* blink]

nide /nid/ *n.* (*Brit.* **nye** /ni/) a brood of pheasants. [F *nid* or L *nidus:* see NIDUS]

nidificate /nídifikayt/ *v.intr.* (of a bird) build a nest. □□ **nidification** /-fikáyshən/ *n.* [L *nidificare* f. NIDUS nest]

nidify /nídifi/ *v.intr.* (**-ies, -ied**) = NIDIFICATE.

nidus /nídəs/ *n.* (*pl.* **nidi** /-di/ or **niduses**) **1** a place in which an insect, etc., deposits its eggs, or in which spores or seeds develop. **2** a place in which something is nurtured or developed. [L, rel. to NEST]

niece /nees/ *n.* a daughter of one's brother or sister, or of one's brother-in-law or sister-in-law. [ME f. OF ult. f. L *neptis* granddaughter]

niello /nee-élṓ/ *n.* (*pl.* **nielli** /-lee/ or **-os**) **1** a black composition of sulfur with silver, lead, or copper, for filling engraved lines in silver or other metal. **2 a** such ornamental work. **b** an object decorated with this. □□ **nielloed** *adj.* [It. f. L *nigellus* dimin. of *niger* black]

nielsbohrium /neelzbáwreeəm/ *n.* an artificially produced radioactive element; atomic number 107. ¶ Symb.: **Ns.** [for Danish physicist *Niels Bohr* (1885–1962)]

nifty /níftee/ *adj.* (**niftier, niftiest**) *colloq.* **1** clever, adroit. **2** smart, stylish. □□ **niftily** *adv.* **niftiness** *n.* [19th c.: orig. uncert.]
■ **1** clever, adroit, skillful, neat; healthy, in good form, spry, energetic, agile, quick; apt, suitable; excellent, great, splendid, fine. **2** smart, stylish, modish, chic,

spruce, elegant, well turned out, fashionable, snappy, *colloq.* classy, *Brit. colloq.* swish; see also DAPPER 1.

niggard /nígərd/ *n. & adj.* ● *n.* a mean or stingy person. ● *adj. archaic* = NIGGARDLY. [ME, alt. f. earlier (obs.) *nigon,* prob. of Scand. orig.: cf. NIGGLE]
■ *n.* see MISER.

niggardly /nígərdlee/ *adj. & adv.* ● *adj.* **1** stingy, parsimonious. **2** meager, scanty. ● *adv.* in a stingy or meager manner. □□ **niggardliness** *n.*
■ *adj.* **1** see MEAN² 1. **2** see MEAGER 1. □□ **niggardliness** see THRIFT.

nigger /nígər/ *n. offens.* **1** a black person. **2** a dark-skinned person. □ **a nigger in the woodpile** *offens.* a hidden cause of trouble or inconvenience. [earlier *neger* f. F *nègre* f. Sp. *negro* NEGRO]

niggle /nígəl/ *v. & n.* ● *v.* **1** *intr.* be overattentive to details. **2** *intr.* find fault in a petty way. **3** *tr. colloq.* irritate; nag pettily. ● *n.* a trifling complaint or criticism; a worry or annoyance. [app. of Scand. orig.: cf. Norw. *nigla*]
■ *v.* **1, 2** find fault, moan, nag, carp, fuss, cavil, criticize; complain, *colloq.* grouse, bitch, *sl.* kvetch.

niggling /nígling/ *adj.* **1** troublesome or irritating in a petty way. **2** trifling or petty. □□ **nigglingly** *adv.*
■ **1** irritating, worrying, worrisome, irksome, vexing, vexatious, annoying, troublesome, bothersome, *colloq.* pesky. **2** petty, nugatory, trifling, trivial, insignificant, unimportant, inconsequential, frivolous, picayune, *colloq.* piddling, piffling, nit-picking, fussy.

nigh /ni/ *adv., prep., & adj. archaic* or *dial.* near. □ **nigh on** nearly, almost. [OE *nēh, nēah*]

night /nit/ *n.* **1** the period of darkness between one day and the next; the time from sunset to sunrise. **2** nightfall (*shall not reach home before night*). **3** the darkness of night (*as black as night*). **4** a night or evening appointed for some activity, or spent or regarded in a certain way (*last night of the performance; a great night out*). □ **night blindness** = NYCTALOPIA. **night fighter** an airplane used for interception at night. **night-light** a dim light kept on in a bedroom at night. **night nurse** a nurse on duty during the night. **night owl** *colloq.* a person active at night. **night safe** *Brit.* a safe with access from the outer wall of a bank for the deposit of money, etc., when the bank is closed. **night school** an institution providing evening classes for those working by day. **night shift** a shift of workers employed during the night. **night soil** the contents of cesspools, etc., removed at night, esp. for use as manure. **night watchman 1** a person whose job is to keep watch by night. **2** *Cricket* an inferior batsman sent in when a wicket falls near the close of a day's play. □□ **nightless** *adj.* [OE *neaht, niht* f. Gmc]
■ **1, 3** nighttime, evening, dark; darkness, blackness, gloom. **2** nightfall, sunset, sundown, twilight, dusk, dark, evening, *archaic* or *poet.* eventide, *poet.* gloaming, vesper. □ **nighttime** see NIGHT 1, 3 above.

nightbird /nítbərd/ *n. Brit. colloq.* = night owl.

nightcap /nítkap/ *n.* **1** *hist.* a cap worn in bed. **2** a hot or alcoholic drink taken at bedtime.
■ **2** see DRINK *n.* 2b.

nightclothes /nítklōz, -klōthz/ *n.* clothes worn in bed.

nightclub /nítklub/ *n.* a club that is open at night and provides refreshment and entertainment.
■ see CABARET 2.

nightdress /nítdres/ *n.* = NIGHTGOWN.

nightfall /nítfawl/ *n.* the onset of night; the end of daylight.
■ see DUSK *n.* 1.

nightgown /nítgown/ *n.* **1** a woman's or child's loose garment worn in bed. **2** *hist.* a dressing gown.

nighthawk /níthawk/ *n.* **1** a nocturnal prowler, esp. a thief. **2** a nightjar.

nightie /nítee/ *n. colloq.* a nightgown. [abbr.]

/.../	**pronunciation**	● **part of speech**
□	**phrases, idioms, and compounds**	
□□	**derivatives**	■ **synonym section**
	cross-references appear in SMALL CAPITALS or *italics*	

nightingale /nít'ngayl/ *n.* any small reddish-brown bird of the genus *Luscinia*, esp. *L. megarhynchos*, of which the male sings melodiously, esp. at night. [OE *nihtegala* (whence obs. *nightgale*) f. Gmc: for -*n*- cf. FARTHINGALE]

nightjar /nítjaar/ *n.* any nocturnal bird of the family Caprimulgidae, having a characteristic harsh cry.

nightlife /nítlif/ *n.* entertainment available at night in a town.

nightlong /nítlawng/ *adj. & adv.* • *adj.* lasting all night. • *adv.* throughout the night.

nightly /nítlee/ *adj. & adv.* • *adj.* **1** happening, done, or existing in the night. **2** recurring every night. • *adv.* every night. [OE *nihtlic* (as NIGHT)]

▪ *adj.* **1** nocturnal, bedtime. • *adv.* every night, each (and every) night, night after night; after dark, after sunset; nocturnally.

nightmare /nítmair/ *n.* **1** a frightening or unpleasant dream. **2** *colloq.* a terrifying or very unpleasant experience or situation. **3** a haunting or obsessive fear. □□ **nightmarish** *adj.* **nightmarishly** *adv.* [an evil spirit (incubus) once thought to lie on and suffocate sleepers: OE *mære* incubus]

▪ **2** see ORDEAL. **3** see FEAR *n.* 3. □□ **nightmarish** frightening, terrifying, alarming, horrific, horrible, dreadful, awful, ghastly, dismaying, agonizing, worrisome, exasperating, frustrating, Kafkaesque, *colloq.* creepy, scary.

nightshade /nítshayd/ *n.* any of various poisonous plants, esp. of the genus *Solanum*, including *S. nigrum* (**black nightshade**) with black berries, and *S. dulcamara* (**woody nightshade**) with red berries. □ **deadly nightshade** = BELLADONNA. [OE *nihtscada* app. formed as NIGHT + SHADE, prob. with ref. to its poisonous properties]

nightshirt /nítshərt/ *n.* a long shirt worn in bed.

nightspot /nítspot/ *n.* a nightclub.

▪ see CABARET 2.

nightstick /nítstik/ *n.* a policeman's club.

nighttime /níttim/ *n.* the time of darkness.

nigrescent /nigrésənt/ *adj.* blackish. □□ **nigrescence** /-səns/ *n.* [L *nigrescere* grow black f. *niger nigri* black]

nigritude /nígritood, -tyood, ní-/ *n.* blackness. [L *nigritudo* (as NIGRESCENT)]

NIH *abbr.* National Institutes of Health.

nihilism /ní-ilizəm, neé-/ *n.* **1** the rejection of all religious and moral principles. **2** an extreme form of skepticism maintaining that nothing has a real existence. □□ **nihilist** *n.* **nihilistic** *adj.* [L *nihil* nothing]

▪ □□ **nihilist** skeptic, doubter, cynic.

nihility /nihílitee, neé-/ *n.* (*pl.* -**ies**) **1** nonexistence, nothingness. **2** a mere nothing; a trifle. [med.L *nihilitas* (as NIHILISM)]

▪ **1** see OBLIVION.

nihil obstat /níhil óbstat, neé-/ *n.* **1** *RC Ch.* a certificate that a book is not open to objection on doctrinal or moral grounds. **2** an authorization or official approval. [L, = nothing hinders]

-nik /nik/ *suffix* forming nouns denoting a person associated with a specified thing or quality (*beatnik*; *refusenik*). [Russ. (as SPUTNIK) and Yiddish]

nil /nil/ *n.* nothing; no number or amount (esp. *Brit.* as a score in games). [L, = *nihil* nothing]

▪ nothing, zero, love, naught, goose-egg, *poet.* or *archaic* naught, *sl.* zilch.

Nile /nil/ *n. & adj.* (in full **Nile blue, Nile green**) pale greenish blue or green. [the river *Nile* in NE Africa]

nilgai /nílgi/ *n.* a large short-horned E. Indian antelope, *Boselaphus tragocamelus*. [Hindi *nīlgāī* f. *nīl* blue + *gāī* cow]

Nilotic /nilótik/ *adj.* **1** of or relating to the Nile or the Nile region of Africa. **2** of or relating to a group of E. African Negroid peoples, or the languages spoken by them. [L *Niloticus* f. Gk *Neilōtikos* f. *Neilos* Nile]

nim /nim/ *n.* a game in which two players must alternately take one or more objects from one of several heaps and seek either to avoid taking or to take the last remaining object. [20th c.: perh. f. archaic *nim* take (as NIMBLE), or G *nimm* imper. of *nehmen* take]

nimble /nímbəl/ *adj.* (**nimbler, nimblest**) **1** quick and light in movement or action; agile. **2** (of the mind) quick to comprehend; clever, versatile. □□ **nimbleness** *n.* **nimbly** *adv.* [OE *næmel* quick to seize f. *niman* take f. Gmc, with -*b*- as in THIMBLE]

▪ **1** agile, lively, active, light, lithe, limber, spry, sprightly, brisk, smart, energetic, rapid, quick, swift, adroit, deft, dexterous, *literary* volant. **2** agile, clever, versatile, alert, acute, quick-witted, quick, ready-witted, intelligent, keen, sharp, smart, brilliant.

nimbostratus /nímbōstráytəs, -strátəs/ *n.* (*pl.* **nimbostrati** /-tī/) *Meteorol.* a low dark-gray layer of cloud. [mod.L, f. NIMBUS + STRATUS]

nimbus /nímbəs/ *n.* (*pl.* **nimbi** /-bī/ or **nimbuses**) **1 a** a bright cloud or halo investing a deity or person or thing. **b** the halo of a saint, etc. **2** *Meteorol.* a rain cloud. □□ **nimbused** *adj.* [L, = cloud, aureole]

NIMBY /nímbee/ *abbr. colloq.* not in my backyard.

niminy-piminy /níminee-píminee/ *adj.* feeble, affected; lacking in vigor. [cf. NAMBY-PAMBY]

▪ see AFFECTED 3, FEEBLE 2.

Nimrod /nímrod/ *n.* a great hunter or sportsman. [Heb. *Nimrōd* valiant: see Gen. 10:8-9]

nincompoop /nínkəmpoop/ *n.* a simpleton; a fool. [17th c.: orig. unkn.]

▪ see FOOL¹ *n.* 1.

nine /nin/ *n. & adj.* • *n.* **1** one more than eight, or one less than ten; the sum of five units and four units. **2** a symbol for this (9, ix, IX). **3** a size, etc., denoted by nine. **4** a set or team of nine individuals. **5** the time of nine o'clock (*is it nine yet?*). **6** a card with nine pips. **7** (**the Nine**) the nine muses. • *adj.* that amount to nine. □ **dressed** (*Brit.* **up**) **to the nines** dressed very elaborately. **nine days' wonder** a person or thing that is briefly famous. **nine times out of ten** nearly always. **nine to five** a designation of typical office hours. [OE *nigon* f. Gmc]

ninefold /nínfōld/ *adj. & adv.* **1** nine times as much or as many. **2** consisting of nine parts.

ninepin /nínpin/ *n.* **1** (in *pl.*; usu. treated as *sing.*) a game in which nine pins are set up at the end of an alley and bowled at in an attempt to knock them down. **2** a pin used in this game.

nineteen /nínteen/ *n. & adj.* • *n.* **1** one more than eighteen, nine more than ten. **2** the symbol for this (19, xix, XIX). **3** a size, etc., denoted by nineteen. • *adj.* that amount to nineteen. □ **talk nineteen to the dozen** see DOZEN. □□ **nineteenth** *adj. & n.* [OE *nigontyne*]

ninety /níntee/ *n. & adj.* • *n.* (*pl.* -**ies**) **1** the product of nine and ten. **2** a symbol for this (90, xc, XC). **3** (in *pl.*) the numbers from 90 to 99, esp. the years of a century or of a person's life. • *adj.* that amount to ninety. □ **ninety-first, -second,** etc., the ordinal numbers between ninetieth and hundredth. **ninety-one, -two,** etc., the cardinal numbers between ninety and a hundred. □□ **ninetieth** *adj. & n.* **ninetyfold** *adj. & adv.* [OE *nigontig*]

ninja /nínjə/ *n.* a person skilled in ninjutsu. [Jap.]

ninjutsu /ninjŏŏtsoo/ *n.* one of the Japanese martial arts, characterized by stealthy movement and camouflage. [Jap.]

ninny /nínee/ *n.* (*pl.* -**ies**) a foolish or simpleminded person. [perh. f. *innocent*]

▪ see FOOL¹ *n.* 1.

ninon /neénon, neenáwN/ *n.* a lightweight silk dress fabric. [F]

ninth /ninth/ *n. & adj.* • *n.* **1** the position in a sequence corresponding to the number 9 in the sequence 1–9. **2** something occupying this position. **3** each of nine equal parts of a thing. **4** *Mus.* **a** an interval or chord spanning nine consecutive notes in the diatonic scale (e.g., C to D an octave higher). **b** a note separated from another by this interval. • *adj.* that is the ninth. □□ **ninthly** *adv.*

niobium /nīōbeeəm/ *n. Chem.* a rare gray-blue metallic transition element occurring naturally in several minerals and used in alloys for superconductors. ¶ Symb.: **Nb**. Also called COLUMBIUM. □□ **niobic** *adj.* **niobous** *adj.* [*Niobe* daughter of Tantalus: so-called because first found in TANTALITE]

Nip /nip/ *n. sl. offens.* a Japanese person. [abbr. of NIPPONESE]

nip¹ /nip/ *v. & n.* ● *v.* (**nipped, nipping**) **1** *tr.* pinch, squeeze, or bite sharply. **2** *tr.* (often foll. by *off*) remove by pinching, etc. **3** *tr.* (of the cold, frost, etc.) cause pain or harm to. **4** *intr.* (foll. by *in, out*, etc.) *Brit. colloq.* go nimbly or quickly. **5** *tr. sl.* steal, snatch. ● *n.* **1 a** a pinch, a sharp squeeze. **b** a bite. **2 a** biting cold. **b** a check to vegetation caused by this. □ **nip and tuck** neck and neck. **nip in the bud** suppress or destroy (esp. an idea) at an early stage. □□ **nipping** *adj.* [ME, prob. of LG or Du. orig.]

■ *v.* **1, 2** bite, nibble; pinch, snip, clip, cut, snap, tweak, twitch, trim, lop, crop, shear; grip, squeeze. **3** sting, bite, hurt, pain, pinch; grip. **4** dart, zip, dash, sprint, fly, shoot, speed, skip, hop, leap, flick, whisk, flash, hurry, pop, run, *Austral. sl.* nick. **5** see STEAL *v.* 1.
● *n.* **1** pinch, squeeze, tweak, snip; bite, nibble, morsel. **2 a** chill, coldness, iciness, frost; sharpness, tang, bite. □ **nip and tuck** tied, equal, even, *colloq.* even-steven; see also CLOSE¹ *adj.* 5. **nip in the bud** stop, arrest, check, thwart, obstruct, frustrate, stymie, forestall; quash, squash, crush, stamp on, squelch, suppress, extinguish, put down; scotch.

nip² /nip/ *n. & v.* ● *n.* a small quantity of liquor. ● *v.intr.* (**nipped, nipping**) drink liquor. [prob. abbr. of *nipperkin* small measure: cf. LG, Du. *nippen* to sip]

■ *n.* taste, drop, sip, soupçon, portion, swallow, gulp, mouthful, finger, tot, thimbleful, dram, draft, *Brit.* peg, *colloq.* snort, shot, *sl.* snifter.

nipa /néepə/ *n.* **1** an E. Indian palm tree, *Nipa fruticans*, with a creeping trunk and large feathery leaves. **2** an alcoholic drink made from its sap. [Sp. & Port. f. Malay *nīpah*]

nipper /nípər/ *n.* **1** a person or thing that nips. **2** the claw of a crab, lobster, etc. **3** *Brit. colloq.* a young child. **4** (in *pl.*) any tool for gripping or cutting, e.g., forceps or pincers.
■ **3** see CHILD 1a. **4** (*nippers*) pincers, tweezers, pliers.

nipple /nípəl/ *n.* **1** a small projection in which the mammary ducts of either sex of mammals terminate and from which in females milk is secreted for the young. **2** the mouthpiece of a feeding bottle or pacifier. **3** a device like a nipple in function, e.g., the tip of a grease gun. **4** a nipplelike protuberance. **5** a short section of pipe with a screw thread at each end for coupling. [16th c., also *neble, nible*, perh. dimin. f. *neb*]

Nipponese /nípənéez, -née's/ *n. & adj.* ● *n.* (*pl.* same) a Japanese person. ● *adj.* Japanese. [Jap. *Nippon* Japan, lit. "land of the rising sun"]

nippy /nípee/ *adj.* (**nippier, nippiest**) *colloq.* **1** esp. *Brit.* quick, nimble, active. **2** chilly, cold. **3** tending to nip, as a dog. □□ **nippily** *adv.* [NIP¹ + -Y¹]
■ **2** see CHILLY 1.

nirvana /nərvaánə, neer-/ *n.* (in Buddhism) perfect bliss and release from karma, attained by the extinction of individuality. [Skr. *nirvāṇa* f. *nirvā* be extinguished f. *nis* out + *vā-* to blow]
■ see PARADISE 2.

nisei /néesay, neesáy/ (also **Nisei**) *n.* an American whose parents were immigrants from Japan. [Jap., lit. 'second generation']

nisi /nísī/ *adj. Law* that takes effect only on certain conditions (*decree nisi*). [L, = 'unless']

Nissen hut /nísən/ *n.* a tunnel-shaped hut of corrugated iron with a cement floor. [P. N. *Nissen*, British engineer d. 1930, its inventor]

nit /nit/ *n.* **1** the egg or young form of a louse or other parasitic insect, esp. of human head lice or body lice. **2** *Brit. sl.* a stupid person. [OE *hnitu* f. WG]
■ **2** see FOOL¹ *n.* 1.

niter /nítər/ *n.* (*Brit.* **nitre**) saltpeter, potassium nitrate. [ME f. OF f. L *nitrum* f. Gk *nitron*, of Semitic orig.]

nitinol /nít'nawl, -nōl/ *n.* an alloy of nickel and titanium. [*Ni* + *Ti* + Naval Ordnance Laboratory, Maryland]

nitpick /nítpik/ *v.intr. colloq.* find fault in a petty manner; criticize. □□ **nitpicker** *n.* **nitpicking** *n.*
■ see QUIBBLE *v.*

nitrate /nítrayt/ *n. & v.* ● *n.* **1** any salt or ester of nitric acid. **2** potassium or sodium nitrate when used as a fertilizer.

● *v.tr. Chem.* treat, combine, or impregnate with nitric acid. □□ **nitration** /-áyshən/ *n.* [F (AS NITER, -ATE¹)]

nitre *Brit.* var. of NITER.

nitric /nítrik/ *adj.* of or containing nitrogen, esp. in the quinquevalent state. □ **nitric acid** a colorless corrosive poisonous liquid. ¶ *Chem.* formula: HNO₃. **nitric oxide** a colorless gas. ¶ *Chem.* formula: NO. [F *nitrique* (AS NITER)]

nitride /nítrīd/ *n. Chem.* a binary compound of nitrogen with a more electropositive element. [NITER + -IDE]

nitrify /nítrifī/ *v.tr.* (**-ies, -ied**) **1** impregnate with nitrogen. **2** convert (nitrogen, usu. in the form of ammonia) into nitrites or nitrates. □□ **nitrifiable** *adj.* **nitrification** /-fi-kayshən/ *n.* [F *nitrifier* (AS NITER)]

nitrile /nítrīl/ *n. Chem.* an organic compound consisting of an alkyl radical bound to a cyanide radical.

nitrite /nítrīt/ *n.* any salt or ester of nitrous acid.

nitro- /nítrō/ *comb. form* **1** of or containing nitric acid, niter, or nitrogen. **2** made with or by use of any of these. **3** of or containing the monovalent -NO₂ group (*the nitro groups in TNT*). [Gk (AS NITER)]

nitrobenzene /nítrōbénzeen/ *n.* a yellow oily liquid made by the nitration of benzene and used to make aniline, etc.

nitrocellulose /nítrōsélyəlōs/ *n.* a highly flammable material made by treating cellulose with concentrated nitric acid, used in the manufacture of explosives and celluloid.

nitrogen /nítrəjən/ *n. Chem.* a colorless, tasteless, odorless gaseous element that forms four-fifths of the atmosphere and is an essential constituent of proteins and nucleic acids. ¶ Symb.: N. □ **nitrogen cycle** the interconversion of nitrogen and its compounds, usu. in the form of nitrates, in nature. **nitrogen fixation** a chemical process in which atmospheric nitrogen is assimilated into organic compounds in living organisms and hence into the nitrogen cycle. □□ **ni-**

nitroglycerin /nítrōglísərin/ *n.* (also **nitroglycerine**) an explosive yellow liquid made by reacting glycerol with a mixture of concentrated sulfuric and nitric acids.

nitrous /nítrəs/ *adj.* of, like, or impregnated with nitrogen, esp. in the tervalent state. □ **nitrous acid** a weak acid existing only in solution and in the gas phase. ¶ Chem. formula: HNO₂. **nitrous oxide** a colorless gas used as an anesthetic (= *laughing gas*) and as an aerosol propellant. ¶ Chem. formula: N₂O. [L *nitrosus* (AS NITER), partly through F *nitreux*]

nitty-gritty /níteegrítee/ *n. sl.* the realities or practical details of a matter. [20th c.: orig. uncert.]
■ see POINT *n.* 13a.

nitwit /nítwit/ *n. colloq.* a stupid person. □□ **nitwittery** /-witəree/ *n.* [perh. f. NIT + WIT¹]
■ see FOOL¹ *n.* 1.

nitwitted /nítwitid/ *adj.* stupid. □□ **nitwittedness** /-witidnis/ *n.*

nix¹ /niks/ *n. & v. sl.* ● *n.* **1** nothing. **2** a denial or refusal. ● *v.tr.* **1** cancel. **2** reject. [G, colloq. var. of *nichts* nothing]
■ *n.* **1** see ZERO *n.* 1. ● *v.* **2** see VETO *v.*

nix² /niks/ *n.* (*fem.* **nixie** /níksee/) a water spirit of German folklore. [G (AS *Nixe*)]

nix³ /niks/ *int.* esp. *Brit. sl.* giving warning to confederates, etc., that a person in authority is approaching. [19th c.: perh. = NIX¹]

NJ *abbr.* New Jersey (also in official postal use).

NLRB *abbr.* National Labor Relations Board.

NM *abbr.* New Mexico (in official postal use).

nm *abbr.* nanometer.

n.m. *abbr.* nautical mile.

N.Mex. *abbr.* New Mexico.

NMR *abbr.* (also **nmr**) nuclear magnetic resonance.

NNE *abbr.* north-northeast.

NNW *abbr.* north-northwest.

/.../ pronunciation	● part of speech
□ phrases, idioms, and compounds	
□□ derivatives	■ synonym section
cross-references appear in SMALL CAPITALS or *italics*	

No[1] *symb. Chem.* the element nobelium.

No[2] /nō/ *n.* (also **Noh**) traditional Japanese drama with dance and song, evolved from Shinto rites. [Jap. *nō*]

No. *abbr.* **1** number. **2** North. [sense 1 f. L *numero*, ablat. of *numerus* number]

no[1] /nō/ *adj.* **1** not any (*there is no excuse; no circumstances could justify it; no two of them are alike*). **2** not a, quite other than (*is no fool; is no part of my plan; caused no slight inconvenience*). **3** hardly any (*is no distance; did it in no time*). **4** used elliptically as a slogan, notice, etc., to forbid, reject, or deplore the thing specified (*no parking; no surrender*). □ **by no means** see MEANS. **no-account** unimportant, worthless. **no ball** *Cricket n.* an unlawfully delivered ball. ● *v.tr.* pronounce (a bowler) to have bowled a no ball. **no-brainer** a problem, question, examination, etc., that requires very little thought. **no dice** see DICE. **no doubt** see DOUBT. **no end** see END. **no entry** (of a notice) prohibiting vehicles or persons from entering a road or place. **no-fault** (of insurance) valid regardless of the allocation of blame for an accident, etc. **no fear** see FEAR. **no-frills** lacking ornament or embellishment. **no-go** impossible, hopeless. **no-good** see GOOD. **no-hitter** *Baseball* a game in which a pitcher allows no hits. **no-hoper** *sl.* esp. *Brit.* a useless person. **no joke** see JOKE. **no joy** see JOY n. 3. **no little** see LITTLE. **no man** no person, nobody. **no man's land 1** *Mil.* the space between two opposing armies. **2** an area not assigned to any owner. **3** an area not clearly belonging to any one subject, etc. **no-no** *colloq.* a thing not possible or acceptable. **no-nonsense** serious, without flippancy. **no-show** a person who has reserved a seat, etc., but neither uses it nor cancels the reservation. **no side** *Rugby* **1** the end of a game. **2** the referee's announcement of this. **no small** see SMALL. **no sweat** *colloq.* no bother, no trouble. **no thoroughfare** *Brit.* an indication that passage along a street, path, etc., is blocked or prohibited. **no time** see TIME. **no trumps** (or **trump**) *Bridge* a declaration or bid involving playing without a trump suit. **no-trumper** *Bridge* a hand on which a no-trump bid can suitably be, or has been, made. **no way** *colloq.* **1** it is impossible. **2** I will not agree, etc. **no whit** see WHIT. **no-win** of or designating a situation in which success is impossible. **no wonder** see WONDER. **. . . or no . . .** regardless of the . . . (*rain or no rain, I shall go out*). **there is no . . .ing** it is impossible to . . . (*there is no accounting for tastes; there was no mistaking what he meant*). [ME f. *nān, nōn* NONE[1], orig. only before consonants]
■ □ **no entry** no access, no right of way; no thoroughfare, no through road. **no-nonsense** serious, unfrivolous, businesslike, practical, down-to-earth.

no[2] /nō/ *adv. & n.* ● *adv.* **1** equivalent to a negative sentence: the answer to your question is negative; your request or command will not be complied with; the statement made or course of action intended or conclusion arrived at is not correct or satisfactory; the negative statement made is correct. **2** (foll. by *compar.*) by no amount; not at all (*no better than before*). **3** *Sc.* not (*will ye no come back again?*). ● *n.* (*pl.* **noes** or **nos**) **1** an utterance of the word *no.* **2** a denial or refusal. **3** a negative vote. □ **is no more** has died or ceased to exist. **no can do** *colloq.* I am unable to do it. **the noes have it** the negative voters are in the majority. **no less** (often foll. by *than*) **1** as much (*gave me $50, no less; gave me no less than $50; is no less than a scandal; a no less fatal victory*). **2** as important (*no less a person than the president*). **3** *disp.* no fewer (*no less than ten people have told me*). **no longer** not now or henceforth as formerly. **no more** *n.* nothing further (*have no more to say; want no more of it*). ● *adj.* not any more (*no more wine?*). ● *adv.* **1** no longer. **2** never again. **3** to no greater extent (*is no more an authority than I am; could no more do it than fly in the air*). **4** just as little, neither (*you did not come, and no more did he*). **no, no** an emphatic equivalent of a negative sentence (cf. sense 1 of *adv.*). **no-see-um** (or **-em**) a small bloodsucking insect, esp. a midge of the family *Ceratopogonidae.* **no sooner . . . than** see SOON. **not take no for an answer** persist in spite of refusals. **or no** or not (*pleasant or no, it is true*). **whether or no** (or **not**) **1** in either case. **2** (as an indirect question) which of a case and its

negative (*tell me whether or no*). [OE *nō, nā* f. *ne* not + *ō, ā* ever]

NOAA /nóə/ *abbr.* National Oceanic and Atmospheric Administration.

Noah's ark /nóəz/ *n.* **1 a** the ship in which (according to the Bible) Noah, his family, and the animals were saved. **b** an imitation of this as a child's toy. **2 a** large or cumbrous or old-fashioned trunk or vehicle. **3** a bivalve mollusk, *Arca noae,* with a boat-shaped shell. [*Noah,* Hebrew patriarch in Gen. 6]

nob[1] /nob/ *n. sl.* the head. □ **his nob** *Cribbage* a score of one point for holding the jack of the same suit as a card turned up by the dealer. [perh. var. of KNOB]

nob[2] /nob/ *n. Brit. sl.* a person of wealth or high social position. [orig. Sc. *knabb, nab;* 18th c., of unkn. orig.]
■ see SWELL n. 4.

nobble /nóbəl/ *v.tr. Brit. sl.* **1** tamper with (a racehorse) to prevent its winning. **2** get hold of (money, etc.) dishonestly. **3** catch (a criminal). **4** secure the support of or weaken (a person) esp. by underhand means. **5** seize, grab. **6** try to influence (e.g., a judge) unfairly. [prob. = dial. *knobble, knubble* knock, beat, f. KNOB]
■ **2** see ROB 1.

nobbler /nóblər/ *n. Austral. sl.* a glass or drink of liquor. [19th c.: orig. unkn.]

Nobelist /nóbəlist/ *n.* a winner of a Nobel prize.

nobelium /nōbéeleeəm/ *n. Chem.* a radioactive transuranic metallic element. ¶ Symb.: **No.** [*Nobel* (see NOBEL PRIZE) + -IUM]

Nobel prize /nōbél/ *n.* any of six international prizes awarded annually for physics, chemistry, physiology or medicine, literature, economics, and the promotion of peace. [Alfred *Nobel* (d. 1896), Swedish chemist and engineer, who endowed them]

nobiliary /nōbílee-eree, -bílyəree/ *adj.* of the nobility. □ **nobiliary particle** a preposition forming part of a title of nobility (e.g., French *de,* German *von*). [F *nobiliaire* (as NOBLE)]

nobility /nōbílitee/ *n.* (*pl.* **-ies**) **1** nobleness of character, mind, birth, or rank. **2** (prec. by *a, the*) a class of nobles, an aristocracy. [ME f. OF *nobilité* or L *nobilitas* (as NOBLE)]
■ **1** nobleness, dignity, grandeur, illustriousness, greatness, glory, influence, authority, leadership, distinction; probity, integrity, excellence, goodness, character, rectitude, righteousness, ethics, honesty, honorableness, decency, justness, high-mindedness, magnanimity; prestige, loftiness, primacy, significance; rank, position, class, birth, blue blood. **2** (*the nobility*) the élite, the aristocracy, the plutocracy, the ruling class(es), the four hundred, *Brit.* the peerage, *colloq.* the upper crust.

noble /nóbəl/ *adj. & n.* ● *adj.* (**nobler, noblest**) **1** belonging by rank, title, or birth to the aristocracy. **2** of excellent character; having lofty ideals; free from pettiness and meanness; magnanimous. **3** of imposing appearance; splendid; magnificent; stately. **4** excellent; admirable (*noble horse; noble cellar*). ● *n.* **1** a nobleman or noblewoman. **2** *hist.* a former English gold coin first issued in 1351. □ **noble gas** any one of a group of gaseous elements that almost never combine with other elements. **noble metal** a metal (e.g., gold, silver, or platinum) that resists chemical action, does not corrode or tarnish in air or water, and is not easily attacked by acids. **noble savage** primitive man idealized as in Romantic literature. **the noble science** boxing. □□ **nobleness** *n.* **nobly** *adv.* [ME f. OF f. L (*g*)*nobilis,* rel. to KNOW]
■ *adj.* **1** highborn, high-class, upper-class, aristocratic, titled, high-ranking, lordly, patrician, blue-blood(ed). **2** upright, righteous, honorable, honest, virtuous, incorruptible, chivalrous, staunch, steadfast, true, loyal, faithful, trustworthy, true, principled, moral, good, decent, self-sacrificing, magnanimous, generous. **3, 4** splendid, magnificent, imposing, impressive, stately, fine, sublime, grand, striking, superb, excellent, admirable, elegant, rich, lordly, sumptuous, luxurious, *colloq.* stunning; dignified, eminent, distinguished,

august, lofty, elevated, illustrious, prestigious, preeminent, noted, honored, esteemed, celebrated, renowned, acclaimed, respected, venerated. ● *n.* **1** nobleman, noblewoman, aristocrat, patrician, lord, lady, peer, peeress.

nobleman /nṓbəlmən/ *n.* (*pl.* **-men**) a man of noble rank or birth; a peer.
■ see PEER² *n.* 1.

noblesse /nōblés/ *n.* the class of nobles (as of France, etc.). □ **noblesse oblige** /ōbléězh/ privilege entails responsibility. [ME = nobility, f. OF (as NOBLE)]

noblewoman /nṓbəlwŏŏmən/ *n.* (*pl.* **-women**) a woman of noble rank or birth; a peeress.
■ see PEER² *n.* 1.

nobody /nṓbodee, -budee, -bədee/ *pron. & n.* ● *pron.* no person. ● *n.* (*pl.* **-ies**) a person of no importance, authority, or position. □ **like nobody's business** see BUSINESS. **nobody's fool** see FOOL. [ME f. NO¹ + BODY (= person)]
■ *pron.* no one, not anyone, no person. ● *n.* nonentity, unknown, zero, cipher, nothing; see also COG 2.

nock /nok/ *n. & v.* ● *n.* **1** a notch at either end of a bow for holding the string. **2 a** a notch at the butt end of an arrow for receiving the bowstring. **b** a notched piece of horn serving this purpose. ● *v.tr.* set (an arrow) on the string. [ME, perh. = *nock* forward upper corner of some sails, f. MDu. *nocke*]

noctambulist /noktámbyəlist/ *n.* a sleepwalker. □□ **noctambulism** *n.* [L *nox noctis* night + *ambulare* walk]

noctule /nókchŏŏl/ *n.* a large W. European bat, *Nyctalus noctula*. [F f. It. *nottola* bat]

nocturn /nóktərn/ *n. RC Ch.* a part of matins orig. said at night. [ME f. OF *nocturne* or eccl.L *nocturnum* neut. of L *nocturnus*: see NOCTURNAL]

nocturnal /noktə́rnəl/ *adj.* of or in the night; done or active by night. □ **nocturnal emission** involuntary emission of semen during sleep. □□ **nocturnally** *adv.* [LL *nocturnalis* f. L *nocturnus* of the night f. *nox noctis* night]
■ nightly, nighttime, bedtime. □□ **nocturnally** see NIGHTLY *adv.*

nocturne /nóktərn/ *n.* **1** *Mus.* a short composition of a romantic nature, usu. for piano. **2** a picture of a night scene. [F (as NOCTURN)]

nocuous /nókyŏŏəs/ *adj. literary* noxious, harmful. [L *nocuus* f. *nocēre* hurt]
■ see *poisonous* (POISON).

nod /nod/ *v. & n.* ● *v.* (**nodded, nodding**) **1** *intr.* incline one's head slightly and briefly in greeting, assent, or command. **2** *intr.* let one's head fall forward in drowsiness; be drowsy. **3** *tr.* incline (one's head). **4** *tr.* signify (assent, etc.) by a nod. **5** *intr.* (of flowers, plumes, etc.) bend downward and sway, or move up and down. **6** *intr.* make a mistake due to a momentary lack of alertness or attention. **7** *intr.* (of a building, etc.) incline from the perpendicular (*nodding to its fall*). ● *n.* a nodding of the head, esp. as a sign to proceed, etc. □ **get the nod** be chosen or approved. **nodding acquaintance** (usu. foll. by *with*) a very slight acquaintance with a person or subject. **nod off** *colloq.* fall asleep. **on the nod** *colloq.* **1** with merely formal assent and no discussion. **2** *Brit. sl.* on credit. □□ **noddingly** *adv.* [ME *nodde*, of unkn. orig.]
■ *v.* **1, 4** say yes; consent, assent, agree, concur, acquiesce; (*nod at*) greet, acknowledge, recognize. **2** doze (off), nod off, nap, drowse, drop off, fall asleep. **3, 5, 7** see INCLINE *v.* 3, 4; SWAY *v.* 1. **6** slip (up), err, make a mistake, be mistaken *or* wrong; be careless *or* negligent *or* lax *or* inattentive. ● *n.* signal, sign, cue, indication, gesture; approval; consent, acquiescence, concurrence, assent, agreement, *colloq.* OK. □ **get the nod** see *make the grade* (GRADE). **nodding acquaintance** casual *or* slight *or* superficial *or* distant *or* passing acquaintance *or* knowledge *or* understanding; *Brit.* bowing acquaintance. **nod off** see NOD *v.* 2 above.

noddle¹ /nód'l/ *n. colloq.* the head. [ME *nodle*, of unkn. orig.]
■ see HEAD *n.* 1.

noddle² /nód'l/ *v.tr. colloq.* nod or wag (one's head). [NOD + -LE⁴]

noddy /nódee/ *n.* (*pl.* **-ies**) **1** a simpleton. **2** any of various tropical seabirds of the genus *Anous*, resembling terns. [prob. f. obs. *noddy* foolish, which is perh. f. NOD]
■ **1** see SAP³.

node /nōd/ *n.* **1** *Bot.* **a** the part of a plant stem from which one or more leaves emerge. **b** a knob on a root or branch. **2** *Anat.* a natural swelling or bulge in an organ or part of the body. **3** *Astron.* either of two points at which a planet's orbit intersects the plane of the ecliptic or the celestial equator. **4** *Physics* a point of minimum disturbance in a standing wave system. **5** *Electr.* a point of zero current or voltage. **6** *Math.* **a** a point at which a curve intersects itself. **b** a vertex in a graph. **7** a component in a computer network. □□ **nodal** *adj.* **nodical** *adj.* (in sense 3). [L *nodus* knot]
■ **2** see SWELLING.

nodi *pl.* of NODUS.

nodose /nṓdōs/ *adj.* (also **nodous**) knotty, knotted. □□ **nodosity** /-dósitee/ *n.* [L *nodosus* (as NODE)]

nodule /nójŏŏl/ *n.* **1** a small, rounded lump of anything, e.g., flint in chalk, carbon in cast iron, or a mineral on the seabed. **2** a small swelling or aggregation of cells, e.g., a small tumor, node, or ganglion, or a swelling on a root of a legume containing bacteria. □□ **nodular** /-jələr/ *adj.* **nodulated** /-jəlaytid/ *adj.* **nodulation** /-jəláyshən/ *n.* **nodulose** /-jolōs/ *adj.* **nodulous** /-jələs/ *adj.* [L *nodulus* dimin. of *nodus*: see NODUS]
■ **2** see SWELLING.

nodus /nṓdəs/ *n.* (*pl.* **nodi** /-dī/) a knotty point, a difficulty, a complication in the plot of a story, etc. [L, = knot]

Noel /nō-él/ *n.* **1** Christmas (esp. as a refrain in carols); the Christmas season. **2** (also **noel**) a Christmas carol. [F f. L (as NATAL)]

noetic /nō-étik/ *adj. & n.* ● *adj.* **1** of the intellect. **2** purely intellectual or abstract. **3** given to intellectual speculation. ● *n.* (in *sing.* or *pl.*) the science of the intellect. [Gk *noētikos* f. *noētos* intellectual f. *noeō* apprehend]

nog¹ /nog/ *n. & v.* ● *n.* **1** a small block or peg of wood. **2** a snag or stump on a tree. **3** nogging. ● *v.tr.* (**nogged, nogging**) **1** secure with nogs. **2** build in the form of nogging. [17th c.: orig. unkn.]

nog² /nog/ *n.* **1** = EGGNOG. **2** *Brit.* a strong beer formerly brewed in Norfolk, England. [17th c.: orig. unkn.]

noggin /nógin/ *n.* **1** a small mug. **2** a small measure, usu. 1 pint, of liquor. **3** *sl.* the head. [17th c.: orig. unkn.]
■ **3** see HEAD *n.* 1.

nogging /nóging/ *n.* brickwork or timber braces in a timber frame. [NOG¹ + -ING¹]

Noh var. of No².

nohow /nṓhow/ *adv.* **1** in no way; by no means. **2** *dial.* out of order; out of sorts.

noil /noyl/ *n.* (in *sing.* or *pl.*) short wool-combings. [perh. f. OF *noel* f. med.L *nodellus* dimin. of L *nodus* knot]

noise /noyz/ *n. & v.* ● *n.* **1** a sound, esp. a loud or unpleasant or undesired one. **2** a series of loud sounds, esp. shouts; a confused sound of voices and movements. **3** irregular fluctuations accompanying a transmitted signal but not relevant to it. **4** (in *pl.*) conventional remarks, or speechlike sounds without actual words (*made sympathetic noises*). ● *v.* **1** *tr.* (usu. in *passive*) make public; spread abroad (a person's fame or a fact). **2** *intr. archaic* make much noise. ■ **make a noise** **1** (usu. foll. by *about*) talk or complain much. **2** be much talked of; attain notoriety. **noise pollution** harmful or annoying noise. **noises off** esp. *Brit.* sounds made offstage to be heard by the audience of a play. [ME f. OF, = outcry, disturbance, f. L *nausea*: see NAUSEA]
■ *n.* **1, 2** sound, clamor, crash, clap, clash, clangor, din, thunder, thundering, rumble, rumbling, outcry, hubbub, uproar, hullabaloo, racket, rattle,

/. . ./ **pronunciation**	● **part of speech**
□ **phrases, idioms, and compounds**	
□□ **derivatives**	■ **synonym section**
cross-references appear in SMALL CAPITALS or *italics*	

caterwauling, blare, blast, blasting, bawling, babel, commotion, bedlam, fracas, tumult, pandemonium, turmoil; discordance, dissonance, cacophony, ruckus, shivaree, *colloq.* rumpus, ruction, ballyhoo, *joc.* alarums and excursions. ● *v.* **1** make public, make known, circulate, spread (abroad), rumor, bruit (abroad *or* about). □ **make a noise 1** see PROTEST *v.* 1. **2** see *make a splash* (SPLASH).

noiseless /nóyzlis/ *adj.* **1** silent. **2** making no avoidable noise. □□ **noiselessly** *adv.* **noiselessness** *n.*
■ silent, mute, still, inaudible, soundless; muted, quiet, soft, hushed, muffled, deadened, dampened, damped.

noisemaker /nóyzmākər/ *n.* a device for making a loud noise at a party, etc.

noisette /nwaazét/ *n.* a small, lean, usu. round piece of meat, etc. [F, dimin. of *noix* nut]

noisome /nóysəm/ *adj. literary* **1** harmful, noxious. **2** evil-smelling. **3** objectionable, offensive. □□ **noisomeness** *n.* [ME f. obs. *noy* f. ANNOY]
■ **1** see BAD *adj.* 3. **2** see SMELLY. **3** see OBNOXIOUS.
□□ **noisomeness** see STENCH.

noisy /nóyzee/ *adj.* (**noisier**, **noisiest**) **1** full of or attended with noise. **2** making or given to making much noise. **3** clamorous; turbulent. **4** (of a color, garment, etc.) loud; conspicuous. □□ **noisily** *adv.* **noisiness** *n.*
■ **1–3** loud, deafening, ear-splitting, jarring, grating, harsh, piercing, shrill, discordant, unmusical, dissonant, cacophonous, resounding, clarion, clamorous, clangorous, thunderous, uproarious, blaring, blasting, obstreperous, vociferous, boisterous, tumultuous, turbulent, riotous, *literary* clamant. **4** see LOUD *adj.* 2.

nolens volens /nólenz vólenz, nólens wólens/ *adv. literary* willy-nilly; perforce. [L participles, = unwilling, willing]

nolle prosequi /nólee prósikwī, -kwee/ *n. Law* **1** the relinquishment by a plaintiff or prosecutor of all or part of a suit. **2** the entry of this on record. *abbr.* **nol pros** [L, = refuse to pursue]

nom. *abbr.* nominal.

nomad /nómad/ *n. & adj.* ● *n.* **1** a member of a tribe roaming from place to place for pasture. **2** a wanderer. ● *adj.* **1** living as a nomad. **2** wandering. □□ **nomadic** /-mádik/ *adj.* **nomadically** *adv.* **nomadism** *n.* **nomadize** *v.intr.* [F *nomade* f. L *nomas* nomad- f. Gk *nomas -ados* f. *nemō* to pasture]
■ **2** see ROVER. □□ **nomadic** see *traveling* (TRAVEL).

nombril /nómbril/ *n. Heraldry* the point halfway between fess point and the base of the shield. [F, = navel]

nom de guerre /nóm də gáir/ *n.* (*pl.* **noms de guerre** *pronunc.* same) an assumed name under which a person fights, plays, writes, etc. [F, = war name]
■ see PSEUDONYM.

nom de plume /nóm də plóom/ *n.* (*pl.* **noms de plume** *pronunc.* same) an assumed name under which a person writes. [formed in E of F words, = pen name, after NOM DE GUERRE]
■ see PSEUDONYM.

nomen /nómen/ *n.* (*pl.* **nomina** /nómənə/) an ancient Roman's second name, indicating the gens, as in Marcus *Tullius* Cicero. [L, = name]

nomenclature /nómənklaychər, nōménkləchər/ *n.* **1** a person's or community's system of names for things. **2** the terminology of a science, etc. **3** systematic naming. **4** a catalog or register. □□ **nomenclative** *adj.* **nomenclatural** /-kláchərəl/ *adj.* [F f. L *nomenclatura* f. *nomen* + *calare* call]
■ **2** see TERMINOLOGY.

nominal /nóminəl/ *adj.* **1** existing in name only; not real or actual (*nominal and real prices*; *nominal ruler*). **2** (of a sum of money, rent, etc.) virtually nothing; much below the actual value of a thing. **3** of or in names (*nominal and essential distinctions*). **4** consisting of or giving the names (*nominal list of officers*). **5** of or as or like a noun. □ **nominal definition** a statement of all that is connoted in the name of a concept. **nominal value** the face value (of a coin, shares, etc.). □□ **nominally** *adv.* [ME f. F *nominal* or L *nominalis* f. *nomen -inis* name]

■ **1** titular, in name only, formal, pretended, so-called, self-styled, soi-disant, professed, purported, supposed, would-be, representational, represented, supposititious; proposed, propositional; puppet, figurehead. **2** insignificant, trivial, trifling, minor, minuscule, tiny, small, insubstantial, minimal, inconsiderable, token; derisory.

nominalism /nóminəlizəm/ *n. Philos.* the doctrine that universals or general ideas are mere names (opp. REALISM). □□ **nominalist** *n.* **nominalistic** *adj.* [F *nominalisme* (as NOMINAL)]

nominalize /nóminəliz/ *v.tr.* form a noun from (a verb, adjective, etc.), e.g., *output*, *truth*, from *put out*, *true*. □□ **nominalization** *n.*

nominate /nóminayt/ *v.tr.* **1** propose (a candidate) for election. **2** appoint to an office (*a board of six nominated and six elected members*). **3** name or appoint (a date or place). **4** mention by name. **5** call by the name of, designate. □□ **nominator** *n.* [L *nominare nominat-* (as NOMINAL)]
■ **1–3** choose, select, name, appoint, designate, suggest, offer, submit, recommend, propose, present, put up *or* forward, forward, *formal* put forth.

nomination /nóminάyshən/ *n.* **1** the act or an instance of nominating; the state of being nominated. **2** the right of nominating for an appointment (*have a nomination at your disposal*). [ME f. OF *nomination* or L *nominatio* (as NOMINATE)]
■ **1** see APPOINTMENT 2c.

nominative /nóminətiv/ *n. & adj.* ● *n. Gram.* **1** the case of nouns, pronouns, and adjectives, expressing the subject of a verb. **2** a word in this case. ● *adj.* **1** *Gram.* of or in this case. **2** /-naytiv/ of, or appointed by, nomination (as distinct from election). □□ **nominatival** /-tívəl/ *adj.* [ME f. OF *nominatif -ive* or L *nominativus* (as NOMINATE), transl. Gk *onomastikē* (*ptōsis* case)]
■ *n.* subjective (case).

nominee /nóminée/ *n.* **1** a person who is nominated for an office or as the recipient of a grant, etc. **2** *Commerce* a person (not necessarily the owner) in whose name a stock, etc., is registered. [NOMINATE]
■ **1** candidate, appointee; assignee.

nomogram /nóməgram, nó̄-/ *n.* (also **nomograph** /-graf/) a graphical presentation of relations between quantities whereby the value of one may be found by simple geometrical construction (e.g., drawing a straight line) from those of others. □□ **nomographic** *adj.* **nomographically** *adv.* **nomography** /nəmógrəfee/ *n.* [Gk *nomo-* f. *nomos* law + -GRAM]

nomothetic /nóməthétik, nó̄-/ *adj.* **1** stating (esp. scientific) laws. **2** legislative. [obs. *nomothete* legislator f. Gk *nomothetēs*]

-nomy /nəmee/ *comb. form* denoting an area of knowledge or the laws governing it (*astronomy*; *economy*).

non- /non/ *prefix* giving the negative sense of words with which it is combined, esp.: **1** not doing or having or involved with (*nonattendance*; *nonpayment*; *nonproductive*). **2 a** not of the kind or class described (*nonalcoholic*; *nonmember*; *nonevent*). **b** forming terms used adjectivally (*nonunion*; *nonparty*). **3** a lack of (*nonaccess*). **4** (with adverbs) not in the way described (*nonaggressively*). **5** forming adjectives from verbs, meaning "that does not" or "that is not meant to (or to be)" (*nonskid*; *noniron*). **6** used to form a neutral negative sense when a form in *in-* or *un-* has a special sense or (usu. unfavorable) connotation (*noncontroversial*; *noneffective*; *nonhuman*). ¶ The number of words that can be formed with this prefix is unlimited; consequently only a selection, considered the most current or semantically noteworthy, can be given here. [from or after ME *no(u)n-* f. AF *noun-*, OF *non-*, *nom-* f. L *non* not]

nona- /nónə/ *comb. form* nine. [L f. *nonus* ninth]

nonabstainer /nónəbstáynər/ *n.* a person who does not abstain (esp. from alcohol).

nonacceptance /nónəkséptəns/ *n.* a lack of acceptance.

nonaccess /nónákses/ *n.* a lack of access.

nonaddictive /nónədíktiv/ *adj.* (of a drug, habit, etc.) not causing addiction.

nonage /nónij, nố-/ *n.* **1** *hist.* the state of being under full legal age, minority. **2** a period of immaturity. [ME f. AF *nounage*, OF *nonage* (as NON-, AGE)]

nonagenarian /nónəjináireeən, nố-/ *n.* & *adj.* • *n.* a person from 90 to 99 years old. • *adj.* of this age. [L *nonagenarius* f. *nonageni* distributive of *nonaginta* ninety]

nonaggression /nónəgréshən/ *n.* lack of or restraint from aggression (often *attrib.*: *nonaggression pact*).

nonagon /nónəgon/ *n.* a plane figure with nine sides and angles. [L *nonus* ninth, after HEXAGON]

nonalcoholic /nónalkəhólik/ *adj.* (of a drink, etc.) not containing alcohol.

■ see NONINTOXICATING.

nonaligned /nónəlínd/ *adj.* (of nations, etc.) not aligned with another (esp. major) power. □□ **nonalignment** *n.*

■ uncommitted, nonallied, nonaffiliated, unaligned, unaffiliated, unallied; neutral, impartial.

nonallergic /nónəlérjik/ *adj.* not causing allergy; not allergic.

nonambiguous /nónambígyōōəs/ *adj.* not ambiguous. ¶ Neutral in sense: see NON- 6, UNAMBIGUOUS.

nonappearance /nónəpeérəns/ *n.* failure to appear or be present.

■ see ABSENCE 1, 2.

nonart /nónaart/ *n.* something that avoids the normal forms of art.

nonary /nónəree/ *adj.* & *n.* • *adj. Math.* (of a scale of notation) having nine as its base. • *n.* (*pl.* **-ies**) a group of nine. [L *nonus* ninth]

non-Aryan /nónáireeən/ *adj.* & *n.* • *adj.* (of a person or language) not Aryan or of Aryan descent. • *n.* a non-Aryan person.

nonattached /nónətácht/ *adj.* that is not attached. ¶ Neutral in sense: see NON- 6, UNATTACHED.

nonattendance /nónəténdəns/ *n.* failure to attend.

■ see ABSENCE 1, 2.

nonattributable /nónətríbyōōtəbəl/ *adj.* that cannot or may not be attributed to a particular source, etc. □□ **nonattributably** *adv.*

nonavailability /nónəváyləbílitee/ *n.* a state of not being available.

nonbeliever /nónbileévər/ *n.* a person who does not believe or has no (esp. religious) faith.

■ unbeliever, disbeliever, cynic, doubting Thomas, doubter, skeptic, freethinker, agnostic, atheist, nullifidian; infidel, heathen, pagan.

nonbelligerency /nónbəlíjərənsee/ *n.* a lack of belligerency.

nonbelligerent /nónbəlíjərənt/ *adj.* & *n.* • *adj.* not engaged in hostilities. • *n.* a nonbelligerent nation, etc.

nonbiological /nónbīəlójikəl/ *adj.* not concerned with biology or living organisms.

nonblack /nónblák/ *adj.* & *n.* • *adj.* **1** (of a person) not black. **2** of or relating to nonblack people. • *n.* a nonblack person.

nonbreakable /nónbráykəbəl/ *adj.* not breakable.

■ see INDESTRUCTIBLE.

noncapital /nónkápit'l/ *adj.* (of an offense) not punishable by death.

non-Catholic /nónkáthəlik, -káthlik/ *adj.* & *n.* • *adj.* not Roman Catholic. • *n.* a non-Catholic person.

nonce /nons/ *n.* □ **for the nonce** for the time being; for the present occasion. **nonce word** a word coined for one occasion. [ME *for than anes* (unrecorded) = for the one, altered by wrong division (cf. NEWT)]

■ □ **for the nonce** see *for the time being* (TIME).

nonchalant /nónshəláant/ *adj.* calm and casual, unmoved, unexcited, indifferent. □□ **nonchalance** /-áans/ *n.* **nonchalantly** *adv.* [F, part. of *nonchaloir* f. *chaloir* be concerned]

■ cool, unexcited, unexcitable, unperturbed, imperturbable, undisturbed, untroubled, unruffled, dispassionate, unemotional, phlegmatic, detached, distant, unconcerned, indifferent, insouciant, uninterested, aloof, blasé, offhand, calm, collected, composed, serene, easygoing, free and easy, happy-go-

lucky, casual, relaxed, at ease, *colloq.* unflappable, laid-back, together; unenthusiastic, apathetic.

non-Christian /nónkrís-chən, / *adj.* & *n.* • *adj.* not Christian. • *n.* a non-Christian person.

noncitizen /nónsítizən/ *n.* a person who is not a citizen (of a particular nation, town, etc.).

nonclassified /nónklásif'id/ *adj.* (esp. of information) that is not classified. ¶ Neutral in sense: see NON- 6, UNCLASSIFIED.

nonclerical /nónklérikəl/ *adj.* not doing or involving clerical work.

noncollegiate /nónkəleéjət/ *adj.* **1** not attached to a college. **2** not having colleges.

noncom /nónkom/ *n. colloq.* a noncommissioned officer. [abbr.]

noncombatant /nónkəmbát'nt, -kómbət'nt/ *n.* a person not fighting in a war, esp. a civilian, army chaplain, etc.

noncommissioned /nónkəmíshənd/ *adj. Mil.* (of an officer) not holding a commission. ¶ *Abbr.*: NCO.

noncommittal /nónkəmít'l/ *adj.* avoiding commitment to a definite opinion or course of action. □□ **noncommittally** *adv.*

■ wary, cautious, careful, gingerly, guarded, circumspect, watchful, prudent, canny, tentative, on guard, reserved, cool.

noncommunicant /nónkəmyōōnikənt/ *n.* a person who is not a communicant (esp. in the religious sense).

noncommunicating /nónkəmyōōnikayting/ *adj.* that does not communicate.

noncommunist /nónkómyənist/ *adj.* & *n.* (also **non-Communist** with ref. to a particular party) • *adj.* not advocating or practicing communism. • *n.* a noncommunist person.

noncompliance /nónkəmplíəns/ *n.* failure to comply; a lack of compliance.

■ disobedience, nonconformity, nonobservance, nonfeasance, disregard, noncooperation, rejection, refusal, denial.

non compos mentis /nón kompəs méntis/ *adj.* (also **non compos**) not in one's right mind. [L, = not having control of one's mind]

nonconductor /nónkəndúktər/ *n.* a substance that does not conduct heat or electricity. □□ **nonconducting** *adj.*

nonconfidential /nónkonfidénshəl/ *adj.* not confidential. □□ **nonconfidentially** *adv.*

nonconformist /nónkənfáwrmist/ *n.* **1** a person who does not conform to the doctrine or discipline of an established Church, esp. (**Nonconformist**) a member of a (usu. Protestant) sect dissenting from the Anglican Church. **2** a person who does not conform to a prevailing principle. □□ **nonconformism** *n.* **Nonconformism** *n.*

■ **2** renegade, maverick, rebel, radical, individualist, heretic, dissenter, dissident, iconoclast, loner, exception, anomaly; eccentric.

nonconformity /nónkənfáwrmitee/ *n.* **1 a** nonconformists as a body, esp. (**Nonconformity**) Protestants dissenting from the Anglican Church. **b** the principles or practice of nonconformists, esp. (**Nonconformity**) Protestant dissent. **2** (usu. foll. by *to*) failure to conform to a rule, etc. **3** lack of correspondence between things.

■ **2** see NONCOMPLIANCE. **3** see *disagreement* (DISAGREE).

noncontagious /nónkəntáyjəs/ *adj.* not contagious.

noncontentious /nónkənténshəs/ *adj.* not contentious.

noncontributory /nónkəntríbyətawree/ *adj.* not contributing or (esp. of a pension plan) involving contributions.

noncontroversial /nónkóntrəvérshəl/ *adj.* not controversial. ¶ Neutral in sense: see NON- 6, UNCONTROVERSIAL.

noncooperation /nónkō-ópəráyshən/ *n.* failure to cooperate; a lack of cooperation.

■ see NONCOMPLIANCE.

nondelivery /nóndilívəree/ *n.* failure to deliver.

/.../ pronunciation	● part of speech
□ phrases, idioms, and compounds	
□□ derivatives	■ synonym section
cross-references appear in SMALL CAPITALS or *italics*	

nondenominational /nóndinómináyshənəl/ *adj.* not restricted as regards religious denomination.
■ ecumenical.

nondescript /nóndiskript/ *adj. & n.* ● *adj.* lacking distinctive characteristics; not easily classified; neither one thing nor another. ● *n.* a nondescript person or thing. □□ **nondescriptly** *adv.* **nondescriptness** *n.* [NON- + *descript* described f. L *descriptus* (as DESCRIBE)]
■ *adj.* indescribable, unclassifiable, unclassified; ordinary, common, commonplace, unremarkable, colorless, drab, everyday, bland, uninteresting, insipid, characterless, undistinctive, unexceptional.

nondestructive /nóndistrúktiv/ *adj.* that does not involve destruction or damage.

nondrinker /nóndríngkər/ *n.* a person who does not drink alcoholic liquor.
■ abstainer, teetotaler, *Austral. sl.* wowser.

nondriver /nóndrívər/ *n.* a person who does not drive a motor vehicle.

none[1] /nun/ *pron., adj., & adv.* ● *pron.* **1** (foll. by *of*) **a** not any of (*none of this concerns me; none of them has found it; none of your impudence!*). **b** not any one of (*none of them has come; none were recovered*). ¶ The verb following *none* in this sense can be singular or plural according to the sense. **2 a** no persons (*none but fools have ever believed it*). **b** no person (*none can tell*). ● *adj.* (usu. with a preceding noun implied) **1** no; not any (*you have money and I have none; would rather have a bad reputation than none at all*). **2** not to be counted in a specified class (*his understanding is none of the clearest; if a linguist is wanted, I am none*). ● *adv.* (foll. by *the* + compar., or *so, too*) by no amount; not at all (*am none the wiser; are none too fond of him*). □ **none other** (usu. foll. by *than*) no other person. [OE *nān* f. *ne* not + *ān* ONE]
■ *pron.* no one, not anyone, nobody, no person; not one; not any. □ **none the less** see NEVERTHELESS.

none[2] /nōn/ *n.* (also in *pl.*) **1** the office of the fifth of the canonical hours of prayer, orig. said at the ninth hour (3 p.m.). **2** this hour. [F f. L *nona* fem. sing. of *nonus* ninth: cf. NOON]

nonearning /non-ə́rning/ *adj.* not earning (esp. a regular wage or salary).
■ unwaged.

noneffective /nóniféktiv/ *adj.* that does not have an effect. ¶ Neutral in sense: see NON- 6, INEFFECTIVE.

nonego /nóneègō/ *n. Philos.* all that is not the conscious self.

nonentity /nonéntitee/ *n.* (*pl.* **-ies**) **1** a person or thing of no importance. **2 a** a nonexistence. **b** a nonexistent thing, a figment. [med.L *nonentitas* nonexistence]
■ **1** see NOBODY *n.*

nones /nōnz/ *n.pl.* in the ancient Roman calendar, the ninth day before the ides by inclusive reckoning—i.e., the 7th day of March, May, July, and October, and the 5th of the other months. [OF *nones* f. L *nonae* fem. pl. of *nonus* ninth]

nonessential /nónisénshəl/ *adj.* not essential. ¶ Neutral in sense: see NON- 6, INESSENTIAL.
■ unessential, inessential, nonrequisite; dispensable, expendable; extra, optional; luxury.

nonesuch /núnsuch/ *n.* (also **nonsuch**) **1** a person or thing that is unrivaled, a paragon. **2** a leguminous plant, *Medicago lupulina*, with black pods. [NONE[1] + SUCH, usu. now assim. to NON-]

nonet /nōnét/ *n.* **1** *Mus.* **a** a composition for nine voices or instruments. **b** the performers of such a piece. **2** a group of nine. [It. *nonetto* f. *nono* ninth f. L *nonus*]

nonetheless /núnthələs/ *adv.* nevertheless.

non-Euclidean /nónyōōklídeeən/ *adj.* denying or going beyond Euclidean principles in geometry.

nonevent /nónivént/ *n.* an unimportant or anticlimactic occurrence.
■ anticlimax, lead balloon, *Brit.* damp squib, *colloq.* nonstarter, *sl.* dud.

nonexistent /nónigzístənt/ *adj.* not existing. □□ **nonexistence** /-təns/ *n.*
■ unreal, imaginary, imagined, fictional, fictive, fanciful, fancied, mythical, fabulous, fabled, illusory, chimerical,

delusive. □□ **nonexistence** nonentity; see also NOTHING *n.* 4.

nonexplosive /nóniksplósiv/ *adj.* (of a substance) that does not explode.

nonfattening /nónfát'ning/ *adj.* (of food) that does not fatten.
■ low-calorie, low-fat, low-sugar; diet, light, healthy.

nonfeasance /nónfeézəns/ *n.* failure to perform an act required by law. [NON-: see MISFEASANCE]

nonferrous /nónférəs/ *adj.* (of a metal) other than iron or steel.

nonfiction /nónfíkshən/ *n.* literary work other than fiction, including biography and reference books. □□ **nonfictional** *adj.*

nonflammable /nónflámbəl/ *adj.* not flammable.
■ see INCOMBUSTIBLE.

nonfulfillment /nónfŏŏlfílmənt/ *n.* failure to fulfill (an obligation).
■ noncompletion, breach; failure.

nonfunctional /nónfúngkshənəl/ *adj.* not having a function.

nong /nong/ *n. Austral. sl.* a foolish or stupid person. [20th c.: orig. unkn.]
■ see SILLY *n.*

nongovernmental /nón-gy̌vərnmént'l/ *adj.* not belonging to or associated with a government.

nonhuman /nónhyŏŏmən/ *adj. & n.* ● *adj.* (of a being) not human. ● *n.* a nonhuman being. ¶ Neutral in sense: see NON- 6, INHUMAN, UNHUMAN.

noninfectious /nóninfékshəs/ *adj.* (of a disease) not infectious.

noninflected /nóninfléktid/ *adj.* (of a language) not having inflections.

noninterference /nónintərfeérəns/ *n.* a lack of interference.
■ see LAISSEZ-FAIRE.

nonintervention /nónintərvénshən/ *n.* the principle or practice of not becoming involved in others' affairs, esp. by one nation in regard to another.

nonintoxicating /nónintóksikayting/ *adj.* (of drink) not causing intoxication.
■ soft, nonalcoholic, low-alcohol, *Brit.* dealcoholized.

noniron /nónfərn/ *adj. Brit.* (of a fabric) that needs no ironing.

nonjoinder /nónjóyndər/ *n. Law* the failure of a partner, etc., to become a party to a suit.

nonjuror /nónjŏŏrər/ *n.* a person who refuses to take an oath, esp. *hist.* also **Nonjuror**) a member of the clergy refusing to take the oath of allegiance to King William and Queen Mary of Great Britain in 1689. □□ **nonjuring** *adj.*

nonjury /nónjŏŏree/ *adj.* (of a trial) without a jury.

nonlinear /nónlíneeər/ *adj.* not linear, esp. with regard to dimension.

nonliterary /nónlítərereee/ *adj.* (of writing, a text, etc.) not literary in character.

nonlogical /nónlójikəl/ *adj.* not involving logic. ¶ Neutral in sense: see NON- 6, ILLOGICAL. □□ **nonlogically** *adv.*

nonmagnetic /nónmagnétik/ *adj.* (of a substance) not magnetic.

nonmember /nónmémbər/ *n.* a person who is not a member (of a particular association, club, etc.). □□ **nonmembership** *n.*
■ see OUTSIDER 1, 2.

nonmetal /nónmét'l/ *adj.* not made of metal. □□ **nonmetallic** /-mətálik/ *adj.*

nonmilitant /nónmílitənt/ *adj.* not militant.
■ moderate, middle-of-the-road; see also MEEK, MODERATE *adj.* 1.

nonmilitary /nónmíliteree/ *adj.* not military; not involving armed forces, civilian.
■ civil, civilian.

nonministerial /nónministeéreeəl/ *adj.* not ministerial (esp. in political senses).

nonmoral /nónmáwrəl, -mór-/ *adj.* not concerned with morality. ¶ Neutral in sense: see NON- 6, AMORAL, IMMORAL. □□ **nonmorally** *adv.*

nonnatural /nón-nácherel/ *adj.* not involving natural means nor processes. ¶ Neutral in sense: see NON- 6, UNNATURAL.

nonnegotiable /nón-nigőshəbəl, -sheeə-/ *adj.* that cannot be negotiated (esp. in financial senses).
- see INALIENABLE.

nonnuclear /nón-nőőkleeər, -nyőő-/ *adj.* **1** not involving nuclei nor nuclear energy. **2** (of a nation, etc.) not having nuclear weapons.

nonobservance /nónəbzárvəns/ *n.* failure to observe (esp. an agreement, requirement, etc.).
- see NONCOMPLIANCE.

nonoperational /nónopəráyshənəl/ *adj.* **1** that does not operate. **2** out of order.

nonorganic /nóawrgánik/ *adj.* not organic. ¶ Neutral in sense: see NON- 6, INORGANIC.

nonpareil /nónpərél/ *adj.* & *n.* ● *adj.* unrivaled or unique. ● *n.* **1** such a person or thing. **2** a candy made from a chocolate disk, decorated with sugar pellets. [F f. *pareil* equal f. pop.L *pariculus* dimin. of L *par*]
- *n.* paragon, model, standard, ne plus ultra, exemplar, ideal, nonesuch, *colloq.* one of a kind, *Brit. sl.* oner.

nonparticipating /nónpaartísipayting/ *adj.* not taking part.

nonpartisan /nónpaartizən/ *adj.* not partisan.
- nonaligned, unaligned, unaffiliated, independent, uncommitted, neutral, uninvolved, free, on the fence; impartial, evenhanded, fair, just, objective, unbiased, unprejudiced, equitable, dispassionate, disinterested.

nonparty /nónpáartee/ *adj.* independent of political parties.

nonpayment /nónpáymənt/ *n.* failure to pay; a lack of payment.
- see DEFAULT *n.* 1.

nonperson /nónpə́rsən/ *n.* a person regarded as nonexistent or insignificant (cf. UNPERSON).

nonpersonal /nónpə́rsənəl/ *adj.* not personal. ¶ Neutral in sense: see NON- 6, IMPERSONAL.

nonphysical /nónfízikəl/ *adj.* not physical. □□ **nonphysically** *adv.*
- incorporeal, immaterial; mental, psychological; spiritual, ethereal; platonic.

non placet /non pláyset/ *n.* a negative vote in a church or university assembly. [L, = it does not please]

nonplaying /nónpláying/ *adj.* that does not play or take part (in a game, etc.).

nonplus /nonplús/ *v.* & *n.* ● *v.tr.* (**nonplussed** or **nonplused**, **nonplussing** or **nonplusing**) completely perplex. ● *n.* a state of perplexity, a standstill (*at a nonplus; reduce to a nonplus*). [L *non plus* not more]
- *v.* confound, perplex, puzzle, confuse, dismay, baffle, stop, check, stun, shock, dumbfound, take aback, astonish, astound, stump, *colloq.* faze, flummox.

nonpoisonous /nónpóyzənəs/ *adj.* (of a substance) not poisonous.
- see HARMLESS *n.*

nonpolitical /nónpəlítikəl/ *adj.* not political; not involved in politics.

nonporous /nónpáwrəs/ *adj.* (of a substance) not porous.

non possumus /non pósəməs/ *n.* a statement of inability to act in a matter. [L, = we cannot]

nonproductive /nónprədúktiv/ *adj.* not productive. ¶ Neutral in sense: see NON- 6, UNPRODUCTIVE. □□ **nonproductively** *adv.*
- unproductive; nonoperational.

nonprofessional /nónprəféshənəl/ *adj.* not professional (esp. in status). ¶ Neutral in sense: see NON- 6, UNPROFESSIONAL.
- see AMATEUR *adj.*

nonprofit /nónprófit/ *adj.* not involving nor making a profit.
- self-financing, noncommercial, uncommercial, charitable.

nonproliferation /nónprəlifəráyshən/ *n.* the prevention of an increase in something, esp. possession of nuclear weapons.

nonracial /nónráyshəl/ *adj.* not involving race or racial factors.

nonreader /nónreédər/ *n.* a person who cannot or does not read.

nonresident /nónrézidənt/ *adj.* & *n.* ● *adj.* **1** not residing in a particular place, esp. (of a member of the clergy) not residing where his or her duties require. **2** (of a post) not requiring the holder to reside at the place of work. ● *n.* a nonresident person. □□ **nonresidence** /-dəns/ *n.* **nonresidential** /-dénshəl/ *adj.*

nonresistance /nónrizístəns/ *n.* failure to resist; a lack of resistance.

nonreturnable /nónritə́rnəbəl/ *adj.* that may or need or will not be returned.
- see DISPOSABLE *adj.* 1.

nonrigid /nónríjid/ *adj.* (esp. of materials) not rigid.
- see FLEXIBLE.

nonscientific /nónsīəntifik/ *adj.* not involving science or scientific methods. ¶ Neutral in sense: see NON- 6, UNSCIENTIFIC. □□ **nonscientist** /-síəntist/ *n.*

nonsectarian /nónsektáireeən/ *adj.* not sectarian.

nonsense /nónsens, -səns/ *n.* **1 a** (often as *int.*) absurd or meaningless words or ideas; foolish or extravagant conduct. **b** an instance of this. **2** a scheme, arrangement, etc., that one disapproves of. **3** (often *attrib.*) a form of literature meant to amuse by absurdity (*nonsense verse*). □□ **nonsensical** /-sénsikəl/ *adj.* **nonsensicality** /nónsensikálitee/ *n.* (*pl.* **-ies**). **nonsensically** /-sénsiklee/ *adv.*
- **1** rubbish, drivel, gibberish, stuff and nonsense, garbage, twaddle, trash, babble, balderdash, moonshine, puffery, flummery, blather, cackle, bunkum, jargon, mumbo jumbo, palaver, claptrap, jabberwocky, *colloq.* gobbledegook, piffle, hogwash, malarkey, tripe, esp. *Brit. colloq.* waffle, *sl.* double Dutch, poppycock, gas, bunk, rot, (Irish) bull, hooey, bosh, eyewash, bilge, baloney, hot air; mischief, clowning, antics, capering, horseplay, pranks, tricks, jokes, silliness, foolishness, inanity, frivolity, tomfoolery, joking, jesting, waggishness, buffoonery, *colloq.* shenanigan(s), monkey business, monkey tricks, monkeyshines. □□ **nonsensical** senseless, meaningless, absurd, ridiculous, ludicrous, laughable, preposterous, irrational, askew, mad, silly, foolish, harebrained, asinine, idiotic, stupid, dumb, *colloq.* crazy, moronic, imbecilic, cockeyed, fool, *sl.* nutty, screwy, loony, screwball.

non sequitur /non sékwitər/ *n.* a conclusion that does not logically follow from the premises. [L, = it does not follow]

nonsexual /nónsekshőől/ *adj.* not based on or involving sex. □□ **nonsexually** *adv.*
- see PLATONIC 2.

nonskid /nónskid/ *adj.* **1** that does not skid. **2** that inhibits skidding.

nonslip /nónslíp/ *adj.* **1** that does not slip. **2** that inhibits slipping.

nonsmoker /nónsmőkər/ *n.* **1** a person who does not smoke. **2** a train compartment, etc., in which smoking is forbidden. □□ **nonsmoking** *adj.* & *n.*

nonsoluble /nónsólyəbəl/ *adj.* (esp. of a substance) not soluble. ¶ Neutral in sense: see NON- 6, INSOLUBLE.

nonspecialist /nónspéshəlist/ *n.* a person who is not a specialist (in a particular subject).
- see AMATEUR *n.*

nonspecific /nónspisifik/ *adj.* that cannot be specified.
- see VAGUE 1.

nonstandard /nónstándərd/ *adj.* **1** not standard. **2** *Gram.* not conforming to standard usage.

nonstarter /nónstaártər/ *n.* **1** a person or animal that does not start in a race. **2** *colloq.* a person or thing that is unlikely to succeed or be effective.
- **2** see FAILURE *n.* 2.

nonstick /nónstik/ *adj.* **1** that does not stick. **2** that does not allow things to stick to it.

/.../ **pronunciation**	● **part of speech**
□ **phrases, idioms, and compounds**	
□□ **derivatives**	■ **synonym section**
cross-references appear in SMALL CAPITALS or *italics*	

nonstop /nónstóp/ *adj., adv.,* & *n.* ● *adj.* **1** (of a train, etc.) not stopping at intermediate places. **2** (of a journey, performance, etc.) done without a stop or intermission. ● *adv.* without stopping or pausing (*flying nonstop to Chicago*). ● *n.* a nonstop train, etc.

■ *adj.* uninterrupted, continuous, unbroken, direct; unending, endless, interminable, unceasing, ceaseless, continual, persistent, relentless, constant, unremitting, steady, round-the-clock, ongoing, continuing, unhesitating, unfaltering, tireless; regular, habitual. ● *adv.* unendingly, endlessly, interminably, unceasingly, ceaselessly, continually, continuously, uninterruptedly, persistently, relentlessly, constantly, unremittingly, steadily, round-the-clock, day in day out, tirelessly; regularly, habitually.

nonsubscriber /nónsəbskríbər/ *n.* a person who is not a subscriber.

nonsuch var. of NONESUCH.

nonsuit /nónsŏt, -syŏŏt/ *n.* & *v. Law* ● *n.* the stoppage of a suit by the judge when the plaintiff fails to make out a legal case or to bring sufficient evidence. ● *v.tr.* subject (a plaintiff) to a nonsuit. [ME f. AF *no(u)nsuit*]

nonswimmer /nónswímər/ *n.* a person who cannot swim.

nontechnical /nóntéknikəl/ *adj.* **1** not technical. **2** without technical knowledge.

■ **1** unspecialized, nonspecialist, everyday, ordinary; understandable, accessible. **2** lay, amateur; uninitiated, untrained; unskilled.

nontoxic /nóntóksik/ *adj.* not toxic.

■ see HARMLESS 1.

nontransferable /nóntransfərəbəl/ *adj.* that may not be transferred.

non-U /nónyŏŏ/ *adj. esp. Brit. colloq.* not characteristic of the upper class. [NON- + U²]

nonuniform /nónyŏŏnifawrm/ *adj.* not uniform.

nonunion /nónyŏŏnyən/ *adj.* **1** not belonging to a labor union. **2** not done or produced by members of a labor union.

nonusage /nónyŏŏsij, -yŏŏzij/ *n.* failure to use.

nonuse /nónyŏŏs/ *n.* failure to use.

nonuser /nónyŏŏzər/ *n. Law* the failure to use a right, by which it may be lost. [AF *nounuser* (unrecorded) (as NON-, USER)]

nonverbal /nónvə́rbəl/ *adj.* not involving words or speech. □□ **nonverbally** *adv.*

nonvintage /nónvíntij/ *adj.* (of wine, etc.) not vintage.

nonviolence /nónvíələns/ *n.* the avoidance of violence, esp. as a principle. □□ **nonviolent** /-lənt/ *adj.*

■ nonresistance; ahimsa; pacifism; passive resistance, *Ind.* satyagraha. □□ **nonviolent** see PEACEABLE 1.

nonvolatile /nónvólət'l, -til/ *adj.* (esp. of a substance) not volatile.

nonvoting /nónvṓting/ *adj.* not having or using a vote. □□ **nonvoter** *n.*

nonwhite /nónhwīt, -wīt/ *adj.* & *n.* ● *adj.* **1** (of a person) not white. **2** of or relating to nonwhite people. ● *n.* a nonwhite person.

nonword /nónwərd/ *n.* an unrecorded or unused word.

noodle¹ /nŏŏd'l/ *n.* a strip or ring of pasta. [G *Nudel*]

noodle² /nŏŏd'l/ *n.* **1** a simpleton. **2** *sl.* the head. [18th c.: orig. unkn.]

■ **1** see SAP³. **2** see HEAD *n.* 1.

nook /nŏŏk/ *n.* a corner or recess; a secluded place. □ **in every nook and cranny** everywhere. [ME *nok(e)* corner, of unkn. orig.]

■ cranny, recess, niche, alcove, corner, cavity, crevice, crack, opening; retreat, hideaway, nest, esp. *Brit.* bolthole, *colloq.* hideout; inglenook.

nooky /nŏŏkee/ *n.* (also **nookie**) *coarse sl.* sexual intercourse. [20th c.: perh. f. NOOK]

noon /nŏŏn/ *n.* **1** twelve o'clock in the day; midday. **2** the culminating point. [OE *nōn* f. L *nona* (*hora*) ninth hour: orig. = 3 p.m. (cf. NONE²)]

■ **1** twelve o'clock, midday, 1200 hours, twelve noon, noontide, noontime, noonday, high noon.

noonday /nŏŏnday/ *n.* midday.

■ see NOON.

no one /nŏ wun/ *n.* no person; nobody.

noontime /nŏŏntīm/ *n.* (also **noontide** /-tīd/) midday.

■ see NOON.

noose /nŏŏs/ *n.* & *v.* ● *n.* **1** a loop with a running knot, tightening as the rope or wire is pulled, esp. in a snare, lasso, or hangman's halter. **2** a snare or bond. **3** *joc.* the marriage tie. ● *v.tr.* **1** catch with or enclose in a noose, ensnare. **2 a** make a noose on (a cord). **b** (often foll. by *around*) arrange (a cord) in a noose. □ **put one's head in a noose** bring about one's own downfall. [ME *nose*, perh. f. OF *no(u)s* f. L *nodus* knot]

■ *n.* **1** see LOOP *n.* **2** see SNARE *n.* 1.

nopal /nṓpəl, -paál/ *n.* any American cactus of the genus *Nopalea*, esp. *N. cochinellifera* grown in plantations for breeding cochineal. [F & Sp. f. Nahuatl *nopalli* cactus]

nope /nṓp/ *adv. colloq.* = NO² *adv.* 1. [NO²]

nor /nawr, nər/ *conj.* **1** and not; and not either (*neither one thing nor the other; not a man nor a child was to be seen; I said I had not seen it, nor had I; can neither read nor write*). **2** and no more; neither ("*I cannot go*" – "*Nor can I*"). □ **nor . . . nor . . .** *poet.* or *archaic* neither . . . nor . . . [ME, contr. f. obs. *nother* f. OE *nawther*, *nāhwæther* (as NO², WHETHER)]

nor' /nawr/ *n., adj.,* & *adv.* (esp. in compounds) = NORTH (*nor'ward*; *nor'wester*). [abbr.]

noradrenaline /nawrədrénəlin/ *n.* (also **noradrenalin**) = NOREPINEPHRINE. [normal + ADRENALIN]

Nordic /náwrdik/ *adj.* & *n.* ● *adj.* **1** of or relating to the tall blond dolichocephalic Germanic people found in N. Europe, esp. in Scandinavia. **2** of or relating to Scandinavia or Finland. **3** (of skiing) with cross-country work and jumping. ● *n.* a Nordic person, esp. a native of Scandinavia or Finland. [F *nordique* f. *nord* north]

nor'easter /noreéstər/ *n.* a northeaster.

norepinephrine /náwrepinéfrin, -reen/ *n.* a hormone released by the adrenal medulla and by sympathetic nerve endings as a neurotransmitter. Also called **noradrenaline**. [*normal* + EPINEPHRINE]

Norfolk jacket /nawrfək/ *n.* a man's loose belted jacket, with box pleats. [*Norfolk* in S. England]

norland /náwrlənd/ *n. Brit.* a northern region. [contr. of NORTHLAND]

norm /nawrm/ *n.* **1** a standard or pattern or type. **2** a standard quantity to be produced or amount of work to be done. **3** customary behavior, etc. [L *norma* carpenter's square]

■ model, standard, type, pattern, criterion, rule, measure, gauge, yardstick, benchmark; average, mean.

normal /náwrməl/ *adj.* & *n.* ● *adj.* **1** conforming to a standard; regular; usual; typical. **2** free from mental or emotional disorder. **3** *Geom.* (of a line) at right angles; perpendicular. **4** *Chem.* (of a solution) containing one gram-equivalent of solute per liter. ● *n.* **1 a** the normal value of a temperature, etc., esp. that of blood. **b** the usual state, level, etc. **2** *Geom.* a line at right angles. □ **normal distribution** *Statistics* a function that represents the distribution of many random variables as a symmetrical bell-shaped graph. **normal school** (in the US, France, etc.) formerly, a school or college for training teachers. □□ **normalcy** *n.* **normality** /-málitee/ *n.* [F *normal* or L *normalis* (as NORM)]

■ *adj.* **1** standard, regular, average, conventional, usual, run-of-the-mill, ordinary, routine, universal, general, common, customary, natural, typical, conformist, orthodox. **2** sane, stable, rational, reasonable, well-adjusted; healthy. □ **normal school** teacher training-college, *Brit.* college of education.

normalize /náwrməlīz/ *v.* **1** *tr.* make normal. **2** *intr.* become normal. **3** *tr.* cause to conform. □□ **normalization** *n.* **normalizer** *n.*

■ regularize, standardize, regulate, control; conform.

normally /náwrməlee/ *adv.* **1** in a normal manner. **2** usually.

■ **2** see *usually* (USUAL).

Norman /náwrmən/ *n.* & *adj.* ● *n.* **1** a native or inhabitant of medieval Normandy (now part of France). **2** a descendant of the people of mixed Scandinavian and Frankish origin established there in the 10th c., who conquered England in 1066. **3** Norman French. **4** *Archit.* the style of Romanesque architecture found in Britain under the Normans. **5** any of the English kings from William I to Stephen. ● *adj.* **1** of or relating to the Normans. **2** of or relating to the Norman style of architecture. □ **Norman Conquest** see CONQUEST. **Norman English** English as spoken or influenced by the Normans. **Norman French** French as spoken by the Normans or (after 1066) in English courts of law. □□ **Normanesque** /-nésk/ *adj.* **Normanism** *n.* **Normanize** *v.tr.* & *intr.* [OF *Normans* pl. of *Normant* f. ON *Northmathr* (as NORTH, MAN)]

normative /náwrmətiv/ *adj.* of or establishing a norm. □□ **normatively** *adv.* **normativeness** *n.* [F *normatif -ive* f. L *norma* (see NORM)]

Norn /nawrn/ *n.* any of three goddesses of destiny in Scandinavian mythology. [ON: orig. unkn.]

Norse /nawrs/ *n.* & *adj.* ● *n.* **1 a** the Norwegian language. **b** the Scandinavian language group. **2** (prec. by *the;* treated as *pl.*) **a** the Norwegians. **b** the Vikings. ● *adj.* of ancient Scandinavia, esp. Norway. □ **Old Norse 1** the Germanic language from which the Scandinavian languages are derived. **2** the language of Norway and its colonies until the 14th c. □□ **Norseman** *n.* (*pl.* **-men**). [Du. *noor(d)sch* f. *noord* north]

north /nawrth/ *n.,* *adj.,* & *adv.* ● *n.* **1 a** the point of the horizon 90° counterclockwise from east. **b** the compass point corresponding to this. **c** the direction in which this lies. **2** (usu. **the North**) **a** the part of the world or a country or a town lying to the north (*the North Atlantic; northern states*). **b** the arctic. **3** (**North**) *Bridge* a player occupying the position designated "north." ● *adj.* **1** toward, at, near, or facing north. **2** coming from the north (*north wind*). ● *adv.* **1** toward, at, or near the north. **2** (foll. by *of*) further north than. □ **North American** *adj.* of North America. ● *n.* a native or inhabitant of North America, esp. a citizen of the US or Canada. **north and south** lengthwise along a line from north to south. **north by east** (or **west**) between north and north-northeast (or north-northwest). **North Country 1** the geographical region including Alaska and the Canadian Yukon. **2** the northern part of England (north of the Humber estuary). **north light** light from the north, esp. as desired by painters and in factory design. **north-northeast** the point or direction midway between north and northeast. **north-northwest** the point or direction midway between north and northwest. **north pole** (also **North Pole**) **1** the northernmost point of the earth's axis of rotation. **2** the northernmost point about which the stars appear to revolve. **North Star** the polestar. **to the north** (often foll. by *of*) in a northerly direction. [OE f. Gmc]

northbound /náwrthbownd/ *adj.* traveling or leading northward.

northeast /nawrtheést/ *n.,* *adj.,* & *adv.* ● *n.* **1** the point of the horizon midway between north and east. **2** the compass point corresponding to this. **3** the direction in which this lies. ● *adj.* of, toward, or coming from the northeast. ● *adv.* toward, at, or near the northeast.

northeaster /náwrtheéstər, náwréestər/ *n.* (also **nor'easter**) **1** a northeast wind. **2** a strong storm from the northeast, esp. in New England.

norther /náwrthər/ *n.* a strong cold north wind blowing in autumn and winter over Texas, Florida, and the Gulf of Mexico.

northerly /náwrthərlee/ *adj.,* *adv.,* & *n.* ● *adj.* & *adv.* **1** in a northern position or direction. **2** (of wind) blowing from the north. ● *n.* (*pl.* **-ies**) (usu. in *pl.*) a wind blowing from the north.

■ *adj.* **1** north, northern, northward, northbound.

northern /náwrthərn/ *adj.* **1** of or in the north; inhabiting the north. **2** lying or directed toward the north. □ **northern** (or **hen**) **harrier** a hawk, *Circus cyaneus,* that inhabits marshy regions of N. America and Europe. **northern hemisphere** (also **Northern Hemisphere**) the half of the earth north of the equator. **northern lights** the aurora borealis. **north-**

ern states the states in the north of the US. □□ **northernmost** *adj.* [OE *northerne* (as NORTH, -ERN)]

■ northerly, north; northward, northbound.

northerner /náwrthərnər/ *n.* a native or inhabitant of the north.

northing /náwrthing, -thing/ *n. Naut.* the distance traveled or measured northward.

northland /náwrthlənd/ *n. poet.* (also **Northland**) the northern lands; the northern part of a country. [OE (as NORTH, LAND)]

Northman /náwrthmən/ *n.* (*pl.* **-men**) a native of Scandinavia, esp. of Norway. [OE]

Northumbrian /nawrthúmbreeən/ *adj.* & *n.* ● *adj.* of or relating to ancient Northumbria (England north of the Humber) or modern Northumberland. ● *n.* **1** a native of ancient Northumbria or modern Northumberland. **2** the dialect of ancient Northumbria or modern Northumberland. [obs. *Northumber,* persons living beyond the Humber, f. OE *Northhymbre*]

northward /náwrthwərd/ *adj.,* *adv.,* & *n.* ● *adj.* & *adv.* (also **northwards**) toward the north. ● *n.* a northward direction or region.

northwest /náwrthwést/ *n.,* *adj.,* & *adv.* ● *n.* **1** the point of the horizon midway between north and west. **2** the compass point corresponding to this. **3** the direction in which this lies. ● *adj.* of, toward, or coming from the northwest. ● *adv.* toward, at, or near the northwest.

northwester /náwrthwéstər, náwrwés-/ *n.* (also **nor'wester**) a northwest wind.

Norway rat /náwrway/ *n.* the common brown rat, *Rattus norvegicus.*

Norwegian /nawrweéjən/ *n.* & *adj.* ● *n.* **1 a** a native or national of Norway. **b** a person of Norwegian descent. **2** the language of Norway. ● *adj.* of or relating to Norway or its people or language. [med.L *Norvegia* f. ON *Norvegr* (as NORTH, WAY), assim. to *Norway*]

Nos. *abbr.* (also **nos.**) numbers. [cf. No.]

nose /nōz/ *n.* & *v.* ● *n.* **1** an organ above the mouth on the face or head of a human or animal, containing nostrils and used for smelling and breathing. **2 a** the sense of smell (*dogs have a good nose*). **b** the ability to detect a particular thing (*a nose for scandal*). **3** the odor or perfume of wine, tea, tobacco, hay, etc. **4** the open end or nozzle of a tube, pipe, pair of bellows, retort, etc. **5 a** the front end or projecting part of a thing, e.g., of a car or aircraft. **b** = NOSING. **6** *Brit. sl.* an informer of the police. ● *v.* **1** *tr.* (often foll. by *out*) **a** perceive the smell of, discover by smell. **b** detect. **2** *tr.* thrust or rub one's nose against or into, esp. in order to smell. **3** *intr.* (usu. foll. by *about, around,* etc.) pry or search. **4 a** *intr.* make one's way cautiously forward. **b** *tr.* make (one's or its way). □ **as plain as the nose on your face** easily seen. **by a nose** by a very narrow margin (*won the race by a nose*). **count noses** count those present, one's supporters, etc.; decide a question by mere numbers. **cut off one's nose to spite one's face** disadvantage oneself in the course of trying to disadvantage another. **get up a person's nose** *Brit. sl.* annoy a person. **keep one's nose clean** *sl.* stay out of trouble; behave properly. **keep one's nose to the grindstone** see GRINDSTONE. **nose cone** the cone-shaped nose of a rocket, etc. **nose flute** a musical instrument blown with the nose. **nose job** *sl.* surgery on the nose, esp. for cosmetic reasons; rhinoplasty. **nose leaf** a fleshy part on the nostrils of some bats, used for echo location. **nose rag** *sl.* a pocket handkerchief. **nose ring** a ring fixed in the nose. **on the nose 1** precisely. **2** *Austral. sl.* annoying. **3** *Austral. sl.* stinking. **put a person's nose out of joint** *colloq.* embarrass, disconcert, frustrate, or supplant a person. **rub a person's nose in it** see RUB. **see no further than one's nose** be shortsighted, esp. in foreseeing the consequences of one's actions, etc. **speak through one's nose** pronounce words with a nasal twang. **turn up one's nose** (usu. foll. by *at*) *colloq.* show disdain. **under a person's nose** *colloq.* right before a person (esp. of defiant or unnoticed actions). **with one's nose in the air** haughtily. □□ **nosed** *adj.* (also in *comb.*). **noseless** *adj.* [OE *nosu*]

■ *n.* 3 see PERFUME *n.* 1. ● *v.* 3 see ROOT[2] *v.* 2a. □ **on the nose 1** exactly. **put a person's nose out of joint** see OFFEND 1, 2; DISPOSSESS 1.

nosebag /nṓzbag/ *n.* a bag containing fodder, hung on a horse's head.

noseband /nṓzband/ *n.* the lower band of a bridle, passing over the horse's nose.

nosebleed /nṓzbleed/ *n.* an instance of bleeding from the nose.

nosedive /nṓzdīv/ *n. & v.* ● *n.* 1 a steep downward plunge by an airplane. 2 a sudden plunge or drop. ● *v.intr.* make a nosedive.

■ *n.* see PLUNGE *n.* ● *v.* see PLUNGE *v.* 1b.

nosegay /nṓzgay/ *n.* a bunch of flowers, esp. a sweet-scented posy. [NOSE + GAY in obs. use = ornament]

■ see BOUQUET *n.* 1.

nosepiece /nṓzpees/ *n.* 1 = NOSEBAND. 2 the part of a helmet, etc., protecting the nose. 3 the part of a microscope to which the objective is attached. 4 the bridge on the frame of eyeglasses.

nosey var. of NOSY.

nosh /nosh/ *v. & n. sl.* ● *v.tr. & intr.* 1 eat or drink. 2 eat between meals. ● *n.* 1 food or drink. 2 a snack. □ **nosh-up** *Brit.* a large meal. [Yiddish]

■ *v.* 1 see EAT *v.* 1. 2 snack, nibble, pick. ● *n.* 1 see REFRESHMENT 2. 2 see SNACK *n.* 1, 2.

noshery /nóshəree/ *n.* (*pl.* **-ies**) *sl.* a restaurant or snack bar.

nosing /nṓzing/ *n.* a rounded edge of a step, molding, etc., or a metal shield for it.

nosography /nōsógrəfee/ *n.* the systematic description of diseases. [Gk *nosos* disease + -GRAPHY]

nosology /nōsóləjee/ *n.* the branch of medical science dealing with the classification of diseases. □□ **nosological** /nósəlójikəl/ *adj.* [Gk *nosos* disease + -LOGY]

nostalgia /nostáljə, -jeeə, nə-/ *n.* 1 (often foll. by *for*) sentimental yearning for a period of the past. 2 regretful or wistful memory of an earlier time. 3 severe homesickness. □□ **nostalgic** *adj.* **nostalgically** *adv.* [mod.L f. Gk *nostos* return home]

■ 1, 2 see *sentimentality* (SENTIMENTAL), LONGING *n.* □□ **nostalgic** see HOMESICK, WISTFUL.

nostoc /nóstok/ *n.* any gelatinous blue-green unicellular alga of the genus *Nostoc,* which fix nitrogen from the atmosphere. [name invented by Paracelsus]

Nostradamus /nóstrədáaməs, -dáy-, nō-/ *n.* a person who claims to foretell future events. [Latinized form of the name of M. de *Nostredame,* French astrologer and physician d. 1566]

nostril /nóstrəl/ *n.* either of two external openings of the nasal cavity in vertebrates that admit air to the lungs and smells to the olfactory nerves. □□ **nostrilled** *adj.* (also in *comb.*). [OE *nosthyrl, nosterl* f. *nosu* NOSE + *thyr(e)l* hole: cf. THRILL]

nostrum /nóstrəm/ *n.* 1 a quack remedy, a patent medicine, esp. one prepared by the person recommending it. 2 a panacean plan or scheme, esp. for political or social reform. [L, neut. of *noster* our, used in sense "of our own make"]

■ 1 see MEDICINE 2, ELIXIR 1c.

nosy /nṓzee/ *adj. & n.* (also **nosey**) ● *adj.* (**nosier, nosiest**) 1 *colloq.* inquisitive, prying. 2 *Brit.* having a large nose. 3 *Brit.* having a distinctive (good or bad) smell. ● *n.* (*pl.* **-ies**) a person with a large nose. □ **Nosy Parker** esp. *Brit. colloq.* (also **Nosey Parker**) a busybody. □□ **nosily** *adv.* **nosiness** *n.*

■ *adj.* 1 curious, inquisitive, prying, meddlesome, spying, peeping, eavesdropping, *colloq.* snooping, snoopy. □ **Nosy Parker** see BUSYBODY 1.

not /not/ *adv.* expressing negation, esp.: 1 (also **n't** joined to a preceding verb) following an auxiliary verb or *be* or (in a question) the subject of such a verb (*she isn't there; didn't*

you tell me?; am I not right?; aren't we smart?). ¶ Use with other verbs is now *archaic* (*I know not; fear not*), except with participles and infinitives (*not knowing, I cannot say; we asked them not to come*). 2 used elliptically for a negative sentence or verb or phrase (*Is she coming? — I hope not; Do you want it? — Certainly not!*). 3 used to express the negative of other words (*not a single one was left; Are they pleased? — Not they; he is not my cousin, but my nephew*). □ **not at all** (in polite reply to thanks) there is no need for thanks. **not but what** *archaic* 1 all the same; nevertheless (*I cannot do it, not but what a stronger man might*). 2 not such . . . or so . . . that . . . not (*not such a fool but what he can see it*). **not half** see HALF. **not least** with considerable importance, notably. **not much** see MUCH. **not quite 1** almost (*am not quite there*). 2 noticeably not (*not quite proper*). **not that** (foll. by clause) it is not to be inferred that (*if he said so — not that he ever did — he lied*). **not a thing** nothing at all. **not very** see VERY. [ME contr. of NOUGHT]

■ □ **not quite 1** see ALMOST. 2 see *a far cry* 2 (CRY).

nota bene /nṓtə bénay/ *v.tr.* (as *imper.*) observe what follows, take notice (usu. drawing attention to a following qualification of what has preceded). [L, = note well]

notability /nṓtəbílitee/ *n.* (*pl.* **-ies**) 1 the state of being notable (*names of no historical notability*). 2 a prominent person. [ME f. OF *notabilité* or LL *notabilitas* (as NOTABLE)]

■ 1 see PROMINENCE 1.

notable /nṓtəbəl/ *adj. & n.* ● *adj.* worthy of note; striking; remarkable; eminent. ● *n.* an eminent person. □□ **notableness** *n.* **notably** *adv.* [ME f. OF f. L *notabilis* (as NOTE)]

■ *adj.* noteworthy, remarkable, different, distinctive, singular, unusual, uncommon, extraordinary, conspicuous, striking, preeminent, peerless, matchless, unmatched, unequaled, unparalleled, outstanding, memorable, unforgettable; noted, famous, famed, well-known, renowned, illustrious, important, prominent, eminent, great, distinguished, celebrated, acclaimed. ● *n.* dignitary, personage, notability, worthy, VIP; celebrity, luminary, (big) name, *colloq.* big shot, bigwig, big noise, *sl.* brass hat, big gun, (big) cheese, big wheel, *Brit. sl.* nob. □□ **notably** particularly, especially, markedly, noticeably, signally, distinctly, remarkably, unusually, uncommonly, outstandingly, conspicuously, clearly, obviously, evidently, manifestly, specifically, curiously, oddly, strangely, strikingly, shockingly, surprisingly, stunningly, *disp.* uniquely; meaningfully, significantly, importantly, prominently.

notarize /nṓtəriz/ *v.tr.* certify (a document) as a notary.

■ see SANCTION *v.* 2.

notary /nṓtəree/ *n.* (*pl.* **-ies**) (in full **notary public**) a person authorized to perform certain legal formalities, esp. to draw up or certify contracts, deeds, etc. □□ **notarial** /nōtáireeəl/ *adj.* **notarially** /nōtáireeəlee/ *adv.* [ME f. L *notarius* secretary (as NOTE)]

notate /nṓtayt/ *v.tr.* write in notation. [back-form. f. NOTATION]

notation /nōtáyshən/ *n.* 1 a the representation of numbers, quantities, pitch and duration, etc., of musical notes, etc., by symbols. b any set of such symbols. 2 a set of symbols used to represent chess moves, dance steps, etc. 3 a a note or annotation. b a record. 4 = *scale of notation* (see SCALE[3]). □□ **notational** *adj.* [F *notation* or L *notatio* (as NOTE)]

■ 1, 2 symbols, signs, code, characters; symbolism. 3 note, memorandum, jotting, record, reminder, minute(s), abstract, *colloq.* memo.

notch /noch/ *n. & v.* ● *n.* 1 a V-shaped indentation on an edge or surface. 2 a nick made on a stick, etc., in order to keep count. 3 *colloq.* a step or degree (*move up a notch*). 4 a deep, narrow mountain pass or gap. ● *v.tr.* 1 make notches in. 2 (foll. by *up*) record or score with or as with notches. 3 secure or insert by notches. □□ **notched** *adj.* **notcher** *n.* **notchy** *adj.* (**notchier, notchiest**). [AF *noche* perh. f. a verbal form *nocher* (unrecorded), of uncert. orig.]

■ *n.* 1, 2 nick, cut, dent, indentation, groove, cleft, score, mark, gouge, gash. 3 step, grade, level, degree, stage, gradation, tier, echelon. ● *v.* 1 nick, cut, dent, indent, groove, score, mark, gash, gouge. **2** (*notch up*) score, gain, win, accomplish, achieve, register, mark (up), tally. □□ **notched** serrated, sawtooth(ed), crenellated, pinked, scalloped, zigzag, toothed, *Bot.* & *Zool.* crenate(d), dentate, esp. *Anat.*, *Biol.*, & *Zool.* serrate.

note /nōt/ *n.* & *v.* ● *n.* **1** a brief record of facts, topics, thoughts, etc., as an aid to memory, for use in writing, public speaking, etc. (often in *pl.*: *make notes*; *spoke without notes*). **2** an observation, usu. unwritten, of experiences, etc. (*compare notes*). **3** a short or informal letter. **4** a formal diplomatic or parliamentary communication. **5** a short annotation or additional explanation in a book, etc.; a footnote. **6 a** *Brit.* = BANKNOTE (*a five-pound note*). **b** a written promise or notice of payment of various kinds. **7 a** a notice, attention (*worthy of note*). **b** distinction, eminence (*a person of note*). **8 a** a written sign representing the pitch and duration of a musical sound. **b** a single tone of definite pitch made by a musical instrument, the human voice, etc. **c** a key of a piano, etc. **9 a** a bird's song or call. **b** a single tone in this. **10** a quality or tone of speaking, expressing mood or attitude, etc.; a hint or suggestion (*sound a note of warning*; *ended on a note of optimism*). **11** a characteristic; a distinguishing feature. ● *v.tr.* **1** observe, notice; give or draw attention to. **2** record as a thing to be remembered or observed. **3** (in *passive*; often foll. by *for*) be famous or well known (for a quality, activity, etc.) (*were noted for their generosity*). □ **hit** (or **strike**) **the right note** speak or act in exactly the right manner. **of note** important, distinguished (*a person of note*). **take note** (often foll. by *of*) observe; pay attention (to). □□ **noted** *adj.* (in sense 3 of *v.*). **noteless** *adj.* [ME f. OF *note* (n.), *noter* (v.) f. L *nota* mark]

■ *n.* **1** memorandum, jotting, record, reminder, aide-mémoire, minute(s), abstract, *colloq.* memo. **2, 5** comment, remark, observation, explanation, annotation, footnote, endnote, side-note, gloss, critique, criticism, scholium; (*notes*) marginalia. **3** message, letter, communication, postcard, card, word, line, memorandum, *colloq.* memo, *formal or joc.* epistle; fan letter, love letter, bread-and-butter letter, thank-you note, *often joc.* billet-doux. **6 b** promissory note, letter of credit, (bank) draft, demand note, *Econ.* bill of exchange. **7 a** heed, attention, notice, regard, respect, thought. **b** mark, consequence, substance, importance, moment, weight, distinction, merit, prestige, (high) rank *or* standing, eminence, prominence, repute, reputation, renown. **8** tone, sound; key. **10, 11** theme, characteristic, motif, element, quality, mood, tone, tenor; hint, suggestion, signal, cue, intimation, inkling, suspicion, clue, idea. ● *v.* **1** observe, perceive, see, spot, mark, think about, give thought to, consider, contemplate, study, pay attention to, attend to; call *or* draw attention to, remark on *or* about, mention, report, touch on, comment on *or* about. **2** record, register, write down, put *or* set down, put on record, jot down, put in writing, chronicle. □ **of note** see NOTABLE *adj.* **take note** take heed, attend, listen, pay attention, incline one's ear, beware; (*take note of*) see HEED *v.* □□ **noted** respected, eminent, distinguished, illustrious, esteemed, acclaimed; well-known, famous, famed, prominent, celebrated, notable, popular; notorious.

notebook /nōtbŏŏk/ *n.* a small book for making or taking notes. □ **notebook computer** a lightweight computer that closes to notebook size for portability.

■ see TABLET 5.

notecase /nōtkays/ *n. Brit.* a billfold.

■ see WALLET.

notelet /nōtlit/ *n. Brit.* a small folded sheet of paper, usu. with a decorative design, for an informal letter; note paper.

notepaper /nōtpaypər/ *n.* paper for writing notes.

noteworthy /nōtwərthee/ *adj.* worthy of attention; remarkable. □□ **noteworthiness** *n.*

■ notable, remarkable; exceptional, extraordinary, out of the ordinary, unusual, rare, uncommon, singular, different, *disp.* unique.

nothing /núthing/ *n.* & *adv.* ● *n.* **1** not anything (*nothing has*

been done; *have nothing to do*). **2** no thing (often foll. by compl.: *I see nothing that I want*; *can find nothing useful*). **3 a** a person or thing of no importance or concern; a trivial event or remark (*was nothing to me*; *the little nothings of life*). **b** (*attrib.*) *colloq.* of no value; indeterminate (*a nothing sort of day*). **4** nonexistence; what does not exist. **5** (in calculations) no amount; naught (*a third of nothing is nothing*). ● *adv.* **1** not at all, in no way (*is nothing like what we expected*). **2** *colloq.* not at all (*Is he ill? — Ill nothing, he's dead.*). □ **be nothing to 1** not concern. **2** not compare with. **be** (or **have**) **nothing to do with 1** have no connection with. **2** not be involved or associated with. **for nothing 1** at no cost; without payment. **2** to no purpose. **have nothing on 1** be naked. **2** have no engagements. **no nothing** *colloq.* (concluding a list of negatives) nothing at all. **nothing doing** *colloq.* **1 a** there is no prospect of success or agreement. **b** I refuse. **2** nothing is happening. **nothing** (or **nothing else**) **for it** (often foll. by *but* to + infin.) *Brit.* no alternative (*nothing for it but to pay up*). **nothing** (or **not much**) **in it** (or **to it**) **1** untrue or unimportant. **2** simple to do. **3** no (or little) advantage to be seen in one possibility over another. **nothing less than** at least (*nothing less than a disaster*). **think nothing of it** do not apologize or feel bound to show gratitude. [OE *nān thing* (as NO[1], THING)]

■ *n.* **1, 2** no thing, not anything, nil, *archaic, literary, or poet.* naught, *sl.* nix, zilch. **3** cipher, zero, nobody, nonentity; trifle, bagatelle, *colloq.* peanuts. **4** nonexistence, nothingness, nihility, nonentity, void, emptiness, vacuum. **5** see ZERO *n.* 1 □ **be** (or **have**) **nothing to do with 1** be remote from, be extrinsic to, be extraneous to, be unrelated to, be inapposite to, be irrelevant to, be unconnected with, be inappropriate to, be inapplicable to, be malapropos of. **2** have no truck with, be unknown to, be a stranger to, be unfamiliar with. **for nothing 2** to no avail; see also *in vain* (VAIN).

nothingness /núthingnis/ *n.* **1** nonexistence; the nonexistent. **2** worthlessness, triviality, insignificance.

■ **1** see OBLIVION.

notice /nōtis/ *n.* & *v.* ● *n.* **1** attention; observation (*it escaped my notice*). **2** a displayed sheet, etc., bearing an announcement or other information. **3 a** an intimation or warning, esp. a formal one to allow preparations to be made (*give notice*; *at a moment's notice*). **b** (often foll. by *to* + infin.) a formal announcement or declaration of intention to end an agreement or leave employment at a specified time (*hand in one's notice*; *notice to quit*). **4** a short published review or comment about a new play, book, etc. ● *v.tr.* **1** (often foll. by *that, how,* etc., + clause) perceive; observe; take notice of. **2** remark upon; speak of. □ **at short** (or **a moment's**) **notice** with little warning. **notice-board** *Brit.* a board for displaying notices; bulletin board. **put a person on notice** alert or warn a person. **take notice** (or **no notice**) show signs (or no signs) of interest. **take notice of 1** observe; pay attention to. **2** act upon. **under notice** served with a formal notice. [ME f. OF f. L *notitia* being known f. *notus* past part. of *noscere* know]

■ *n.* **1** attention, awareness, consciousness, perception, observation, cognizance; regard, consideration, respect, note, heed. **2** bill, handbill, *affiche*, leaflet, flyer, broadside; see also SIGN *n.* 4. **3** notification, announcement; warning, intimation. **4** criticism, critique, *compte rendu*, review, comment, commentary, write-up. ● *v.* **1** note, take *or* make note of, take notice of, pay attention to, attend to, heed, take heed of, pay heed to, mark, remark, mind, observe, perceive, see, discern, detect, make out, identify, recognize, *colloq.* spot. □ **at short** (or **a moment's**) **notice** summarily, straightaway, on the spur of the moment, on the spot, impromptu; see also PLUMP[2] *adv.* **notice-board**

/.../ **pronunciation**	● **part of speech**
□ **phrases, idioms, and compounds**	
□□ **derivatives**	■ **synonym section**
cross-references appear in SMALL CAPITALS or *italics*	

bulletin board. **put a person on notice** see WARN.
take notice of 1 see NOTICE *v.* above.

noticeable /nṓtisəbəl/ *adj.* **1** easily seen or noticed; perceptible. **2** noteworthy. □□ **noticeably** *adv.*
- **1** discernible, perceivable, observable, perceptible, recognizable, distinguishable, visible, palpable, manifest, distinct, evident, clear, clear-cut, conspicuous, obvious; patent, unmistakable, undisguised, unconcealed. **2** noteworthy, notable, significant, signal, remarkable, important, singular, exceptional, pronounced, distinct, especial, considerable, major.

notifiable /nṓtifīəbəl/ *adj.* (of a disease) that must be reported to the health authorities.

notify /nṓtifī/ *v.tr.* (**-ies**, **-ied**) **1** (often foll. by *of*, or *that* + clause) inform or give notice to (a person). **2** make known; announce or report (a thing). □□ **notification** /-fikáyshən/ *n.* [ME f. OF *notifier* f. L *notificare* f. *notus* known: see NOTICE]
- **1** inform, tell, advise, alert, apprise, warn. **2** make known, announce, report, publish, declare, proclaim, give notice of. □□ **notification** word, intimation, warning; see also ADVICE 2.

notion /nṓshən/ *n.* **1 a** a concept or idea; a conception (*it was an absurd notion*). **b** an opinion (*has the notion that people are honest*). **c** a vague view or understanding (*have no notion what you mean*). **2** an inclination, impulse, or intention (*has no notion of conforming*). **3** (in *pl.*) small, useful articles, esp. thread, needles, buttons, etc.; sundries. [L *notio* idea f. *notus* past part. of *noscere* know]
- **1** idea, thought, concept, conception, image, impression, (mental) picture; view, understanding; opinion; inkling, clue. **2** fancy, whim, crotchet, whimsy, caprice, impulse, inclination, vagary, conceit; intention.

notional /nṓshənəl/ *adj.* **1 a** hypothetical, imaginary. **b** (of knowledge, etc.) speculative; not based on experiment, etc. **2** *Gram.* (of a verb) conveying its own meaning, not auxiliary. □□ **notionally** *adv.* [obs. F *notional* or med.L *notionalis* (as NOTION)]
- **1 a** see IMAGINARY.

notochord /nṓtəkawrd/ *n.* a cartilaginous skeletal rod supporting the body in all embryo and some adult chordate animals. [Gk *nōton* back + CHORD²]

notorious /nōtáwreeəs/ *adj.* well-known, esp. unfavorably (*a notorious criminal*; *notorious for its climate*). □□ **notoriety** /-təríətee/ *n.* **notoriously** *adv.* [med.L *notorius* f. L *notus* (as NOTION)]
- infamous, disreputable, dishonorable, disgraceful, shameful, shaming, embarrassing, discreditable, scandalous, flagrant, ignominious, opprobrious; celebrated, renowned, famous, well-known, fabled, legendary, memorable. □□ **notoriety** infamy, disrepute, dishonor, disgrace, shame, discredit, scandal, stain, blot, obloquy, ignominy, opprobrium; fame, renown.

notornis /nətáwrnis/ *n.* a rare flightless New Zealand bird, *Porphyrio mantelli*, with a large bill and brightly colored plumage. Also called TAKAHE. [Gk *notos* south + *ornis* bird]

notwithstanding /nótwithstánding, -with-/ *prep.*, *adv.*, & *conj.* ● *prep.* in spite of; without prevention by (*notwithstanding your objections*; *this fact notwithstanding*). ● *adv.* nevertheless; all the same. ● *conj.* (usu. foll. by *that* + clause) although. [ME, orig. absol. part. f. NOT + WITHSTAND + -ING²]
- *prep.* despite, in spite of, regardless of, in the face of, against. ● *adv.* nevertheless, nonetheless, all the same, despite that, in spite of that, still, yet, anyway. ● *conj.* although, though, even though, despite the fact that.

nougat /nṓogət/ *n.* a usu. chewy candy made from sugar or honey, nuts, egg white, and often fruit pieces. [F f. Prov. *nogat* f. *noga* nut]

nought var. of NAUGHT. □ **noughts and crosses** *Brit.* tick-tack-toe.

noun /nown/ *n. Gram.* a word (other than a pronoun) or group of words used to name or identify any of a class of persons, places, or things (**common noun**), or a particular one of these (**proper noun**). □□ **nounal** *adj.* [ME f. AF f. L *nomen* name]

nourish /nə́rish, núr-/ *v.tr.* **1 a** sustain with food. **b** enrich; promote the development of (the soil, etc.). **c** provide with intellectual or emotional sustenance or enrichment. **2** foster or cherish (a feeling, etc.). □□ **nourisher** *n.* [ME f. OF *norir* f. L *nutrire*]
- **1** feed, sustain, support, maintain, keep, provide for, care for, take care of, look after, nurture, nurse; strengthen, enrich, fortify, encourage, promote, stimulate, cultivate, help, advance, aid. **2** foster, cherish, nurse, maintain, harbor, keep, nurture, sustain.

nourishing /nə́rishing, núr-/ *adj.* (esp. of food) containing much nourishment; sustaining. □□ **nourishingly** *adv.*
- see WHOLESOME 1.

nourishment /nə́rishmənt, núr-/ *n.* sustenance, food.
- food, sustenance, nutriment, nutrition, victuals, *colloq.* grub.

nous *n.* **1** /nōos/ *Philos.* the mind or intellect. **2** /nows/ *Brit. colloq.* common sense; gumption. [Gk]
- **1** see GUMPTION 2. **2** see INTELLIGENCE 1b.

nouveau riche /nōovṓ reésh/ *n.* (*pl.* **nouveaux riches** *pronunc.* same) a person who has recently acquired (usu. ostentatious) wealth. [F, = new rich]
- see PARVENU 1.

nouvelle cuisine /nōovél kwizeén/ *n.* a modern style of cookery avoiding heaviness and emphasizing presentation. [F, = new cookery]

nouvelle vague /nōovél vaág/ *n.* a new trend, esp. in French filmmaking of the early 1960s. [F, fem. of *nouveau* new + *vague* wave]

Nov. *abbr.* November.

nova /nṓvə/ *n.* (*pl.* **novas** or **novae** /-vee/) a star showing a sudden large increase of brightness that then subsides. [L, fem. of *novus* new, because orig. thought to be a new star]
- see STAR *n.* 1.

novel¹ /nóvəl/ *n.* **1** a fictitious prose story of book length. **2** (*prec.* by *the*) this type of literature. [It. *novella* (*storia* story) fem. of *novello* new f. L *novellus* f. *novus*]
- story, tale, narrative, romance, fiction; novella, novelette, best-seller, *sl.* blockbuster.

novel² /nóvəl/ *adj.* of a new kind or nature; strange; previously unknown. [ME f. OF f. L *novellus* f. *novus* new]
- new, unusual, unfamiliar, unconventional, fresh, different, original, creative; untested, untried, unknown, strange.

novelette /nóvəlét/ *n.* **1 a** a short novel. **b** esp. *Brit. derog.* a light romantic novel. **2** *Mus.* a piano piece in free form with several themes.

novelist /nóvəlist/ *n.* a writer of novels. □□ **novelistic** *adj.*
- see WRITER 2.

novelize /nóvəliz/ *v.tr.* make into a novel, as a screenplay. □□ **novelization** *n.*

novella /nəvélə/ *n.* (*pl.* **novellas** or **novelle**) a short novel or narrative story; a tale. [It.: see NOVEL¹]

novelty /nóvəltee/ *n.* & *adj.* ● *n.* (*pl.* **-ies**) **1 a** newness; new character. **b** originality. **2** a new or unusual thing or occurrence. **3** a small toy or decoration, etc., of novel design. **4** (*attrib.*) having novelty (*novelty toys*). [ME f. OF *novelté* (as NOVEL²)]
- **1** originality, newness, uniqueness, freshness, innovativeness. **3** gimcrack, trifle, gewgaw, bauble, knickknack, toy, trinket, ornament, plaything, kickshaw, *colloq.* gimmick. **4** (*attrib.*) see NEW *adj.* 1b.

November /nōvémbər/ *n.* the eleventh month of the year. [ME f. OF *novembre* f. L *November* f. *novem* nine (orig. the ninth month of the Roman year)]

novena /nōveénə, nə-/ *n. RC Ch.* a devotion consisting of special prayers or services on nine successive days. [med.L f. L *novem* nine]

novice /nóvis/ *n.* **1 a** a probationary member of a religious order, before the taking of vows. **b** a new convert. **2** a beginner; an inexperienced person. **3** an animal that has not won a major prize in a competition. [ME f. OF f. L *novicius* f. *novus* new]

■ **1, 2** beginner, neophyte, newcomer, proselyte, tyro, novitiate, learner, amateur, initiate, apprentice, trainee, probationer, greenhorn, fledgling, freshman, rookie.

novitiate /nōvisheeət, -ayt/ *n.* (also **noviciate**) **1** the period of being a novice. **2** a religious novice. **3** novices' quarters. [F *noviciat* or med.L *noviciatus* (as NOVICE)]

Novocaine /nṓvəkayn/ *n.* (also **novocaine**) *propr.* a local anesthetic derived from benzoic acid. [L *novus* new + COCAINE]

now /now/ *adv., conj.,* & *n.* ● *adv.* **1** at the present or mentioned time. **2** immediately (*I must go now*). **3** by this or that time (*it was now clear*). **4** under the present circumstances (*I cannot now agree*). **5** on this further occasion (*what do you want now?*). **6** in the immediate past (*just now*). **7** (esp. in a narrative or discourse) then, next (*the police now arrived; now to consider the next point*). **8** (without reference to time, giving various tones to a sentence) surely, I insist, I wonder, etc. (*now what do you mean by that?*; *oh come now!*). ● *conj.* (often foll. by *that* + clause) as a consequence of the fact (*now that I am older; now you mention it*). ● *n.* this time; the present (*should be there by now; has happened before now*). □ **as of now** from or at this time. **for now** until a later time (*goodbye for now*). **now and again** (or **then**) from time to time; intermittently. **now or never** an expression of urgency. [OE *nū*]

■ *adv.* **1, 4** at present, at the moment, just now, right now, as of now, at the present time *or* moment, at this (very) moment *or* minute *or* second *or* instant; these days, nowadays, today, in these times, in this day and age, under *or* in the present circumstances *or* conditions, in the present climate, things being what they are; contemporarily; any more, any longer. **2** at once, immediately, right away, straightaway, without delay, instantly, promptly, archaic straightway, *archaic or joc.* instanter. **6** see JUST *adv.* 2. **7** then, next, at this *or* that point. ● *conj.* see FOR *conj.* ● *n.* the present, the time being, right now, this moment. □ **as of now** hence, henceforward, in (the) future, from now (on *or* onward), hereafter. **for now** for the time being, for a little while, for the present. **now and again** occasionally, from time to time, at times, on occasion, sometimes, sporadically, once in a while, every now and then *or* again, randomly, intermittently; infrequently, seldom, rarely, once in a blue moon.

nowadays /nówədayz/ *adv.* & *n.* ● *adv.* at the present time or age; in these times. ● *n.* the present time.

■ *adv.* see NOW *adv.* 1, 4.

noway /nṓway/ *adv.* (also **noways**) = NOWISE; see *no way*.

nowel (also **nowell**) *archaic* var. of NOEL.

nowhere /nṓhwair, -wair/ *adv.* & *pron.* ● *adv.* in or to no place. ● *pron.* no place. □ **be** (or **come in**) **nowhere** esp. *Brit.* be unplaced in a race or competition. **come from nowhere** be suddenly evident or successful. **get nowhere** make or cause to make no progress. **in the middle of nowhere** *colloq.* remote from urban life. **nowhere near** not nearly. [OE *nāhwǣr* (as NO¹, WHERE)]

nowise /nṓwiz/ *adv.* in no manner; not at all.

■ see SCARCELY 2.

nowt /nowt/ *n. Brit. colloq.* or *dial.* nothing. [var. of NOUGHT]

noxious /nókshəs/ *adj.* harmful, unwholesome. □□ **noxiously** *adv.* **noxiousness** *n.* [f. L *noxius* f. *noxa* harm]

■ see HARMFUL. □□ **noxiousness** see *virulence* (VIRULENT).

nozzle /nózəl/ *n.* a spout on a hose, etc., from which a jet issues. [NOSE + -LE²]

NP *abbr.* **1** notary public. **2** nurse-practitioner.

Np *symb. Chem.* the element neptunium.

n.p. *abbr.* **1** new paragraph. **2** no place of publication.

nr. *abbr.* near.

NRC *abbr.* Nuclear Regulatory Commission.

NS *abbr.* **1** new style. **2** new series. **3** Nova Scotia.

Ns *abbr.* NIELSBOHRIUM.

ns *abbr.* nanosecond.

NSA *abbr.* National Security Agency.

NSC *abbr.* National Security Council.

NSF *abbr.* **1** National Science Foundation. **2** not sufficient funds.

NSPCA *abbr. Brit.* National Society for the Prevention of Cruelty to Animals.

NSW *abbr.* New South Wales.

NT *abbr.* **1** New Testament. **2** Northern Territory (of Australia). **3** *Cards* no trump.

-n't /ənt/ *adv.* (in *comb.*) = NOT (usu. with *is, are, have, must*, and the auxiliary verbs *can, do, should, would*: *isn't*; *mustn't*) (see also CAN'T, DON'T, WON'T) [*contr.*]

nth see N¹.

NTP *abbr.* normal temperature and pressure.

nt. wt. *abbr.* net weight.

nu /nōo, nyōo/ *n.* the thirteenth letter of the Greek alphabet (N, ν). [Gk]

nuance /nōo-áans, nyōo-/ *n.* & *v.* ● *n.* a subtle difference in or shade of meaning, feeling, color, etc. ● *v.tr.* give a nuance or nuances to. [F f. *nuer* to shade, ult. f. L *nubes* cloud]

■ *n.* see SHADE *n.* 11.

nub /nub/ *n.* **1** the point or gist (of a matter or story). **2** a small lump, esp. of coal. **3** a stub; a small residue. □□ **nubby** *adj.* [app. var. of *knub*, f. MLG *knubbe, knobbe* KNOB]

■ **1** essence, core, heart, nucleus, crux, point, gist, pith, kernel, nucleus, meat, (sum and) substance, main issue, gravamen. **2, 3** projection, protuberance, knob, boss, nubble, lump, bump, knop, protrusion, bulge, node, knot, stub; excrescence, swelling, tumescence.

nubble /núbəl/ *n.* a small knob or lump. □□ **nubbly** *adj.* [dimin. of NUB]

nubile /nōobil, -bil, nyōo-/ *adj.* (of a woman) marriageable or sexually attractive. □□ **nubility** /-bílitee/ *n.* [L *nubilis* f. *nubere* become the wife of]

nuchal /nōokəl, nyōo-/ *adj.* of or relating to the nape of the neck. [*nucha* nape f. med.L *nucha* medulla oblongata f. Arab. *nuka'* spinal marrow]

nuci- /nōosee, nyōo-/ *comb. form* nut. [L *nux nucis* nut]

nuciferous /nōosífərəs, nyōo-/ *adj. Bot.* bearing nuts.

nucivorous /nōosívərəs, nyōo-/ *adj.* nut-eating.

nuclear /nōokleeər, nyōo-/ *adj.* **1** of, relating to, or constituting a nucleus. **2** using nuclear energy (*nuclear reactor*). **3** having nuclear weapons. □ **nuclear bomb** a bomb involving the release of energy by nuclear fission or fusion or both. **nuclear disarmament** the gradual or total reduction by a nation of its nuclear weapons. **nuclear energy** energy obtained by nuclear fission or fusion. **nuclear family** a couple and their children, regarded as a basic social unit. **nuclear fission** a nuclear reaction in which a heavy nucleus splits spontaneously or on impact with another particle, with the release of energy. **nuclear force** a strong attractive force between nucleons in the atomic nucleus that holds the nucleus together. **nuclear-free** free from nuclear weapons, power, etc. **nuclear fuel** a substance that will sustain a fission chain reaction so that it can be used as a source of nuclear energy. **nuclear fusion** a nuclear reaction in which atomic nuclei of low atomic number fuse to form a heavier nucleus with the release of energy. **nuclear magnetic resonance** the absorption of electromagnetic radiation by a nucleus having a magnetic moment when in an external magnetic field, used mainly as an analytical technique and in body imaging for diagnosis. ¶ Abbr.: NMR, nmr. **nuclear medicine** *Med.* a specialty that uses radioactive materials for diagnosis and treatment. **nuclear physics** the physics of atomic nuclei and their interactions, esp. in the generation of nuclear energy. **nuclear power** **1** electric or motive power generated by a nuclear reactor. **2** a country that has nuclear weapons. **nuclear reactor** a device in which a nuclear fission chain reaction is sustained and controlled in order to produce energy. **nuclear warfare** warfare in which nuclear weapons are used. **nuclear waste** any

---

/.../ **pronunciation**	● **part of speech**
□ **phrases, idioms, and compounds**	
□□ **derivatives**	■ **synonym section**
cross-references appear in SMALL CAPITALS or *italics*	

radioactive waste material from the reprocessing of spent nuclear fuel. **nuclear winter** obstruction of sunlight as a potential result of nuclear warfare, causing extreme cold. [NUCLEUS + -AR¹]

■ **2** atomic, fission, fusion; atom, hydrogen, neutron. □ **nuclear bomb** H-bomb, A-bomb, atom bomb, atomic bomb, hydrogen bomb, neutron bomb, the bomb. **nuclear energy** nuclear power, atomic power, atomic energy.

nuclease /nŏōkleeays, -ayz, nyŏō-/ *n.* an enzyme that catalyzes the breakdown of nucleic acids.

nucleate /nŏōkleeayt, nyŏō-/ *adj. & v.* ● *adj.* having a nucleus. ● *v.intr. & tr.* form or form into a nucleus. □□ **nucleation** /-áyshən/ *n.* [LL *nucleare nucleat-* form a kernel (as NUCLEUS)]

nuclei *pl.* of NUCLEUS.

nucleic acid /nŏōkleéik, -kláyik, nyŏō-/ *n.* either of two complex organic molecules (DNA and RNA), consisting of many nucleotides linked in a long chain, and present in all living cells.

nucleo- /nŏōkleeō, nyŏō-/ *comb. form* nucleus; nucleic acid (*nucleoprotein*).

nucleolus /nŏōkleeələs, nyŏō-/ *n.* (*pl.* **nucleoli** /-lī/) a small dense spherical structure within a nondividing nucleus. □□ **nucleolar** *adj.* [LL, dimin. of L *nucleus*: see NUCLEUS]

nucleon /nŏōkleeon, nyŏō-/ *n. Physics* a proton or neutron.

nucleonics /nŏōkleeóniks, nyŏō-/ *n.pl.* (treated as *sing.*) the branch of science and technology concerned with atomic nuclei and nucleons, esp. the exploitation of nuclear power. □□ **nucleonic** *adj.* [NUCLEAR, after *electronics*]

nucleoprotein /nŏōkleeōprṓteen, nyŏō-/ *n.* a complex of nucleic acid and protein.

nucleoside /nŏōkleeəsīd, nyŏō-/ *n. Biochem.* an organic compound consisting of a purine or pyrimidine base linked to a sugar, e.g., adenosine.

nucleotide /nŏōkleeətid, nyŏō-/ *n. Biochem.* an organic compound consisting of a nucleoside linked to a phosphate group.

nucleus /nŏōkleeəs/ *n.* (*pl.* **nuclei** /-lee-ī/) **1 a** the central part or thing around which others are collected. **b** the kernel of an aggregate or mass. **2** an initial part meant to receive additions. **3** *Astron.* the solid part of a comet's head. **4** *Physics* the positively charged central core of an atom that contains most of its mass. **5** *Biol.* a large dense organelle of eukaryotic cells, containing the genetic material. **6** a discrete mass of gray matter in the central nervous system. [L, = kernel, inner part, dimin. of *nux nucis* nut]

■ **1** core, heart, center, kernel, pith, focus, nub.

nuclide /nŏōklid, nyŏō-/ *n. Physics* a certain type of atom characterized by the number of protons and neutrons in its nucleus. □□ **nuclidic** /nŏōklídik, nyŏō-/ *adj.* [NUCLEUS + Gk *eidos* form]

nude /nŏōd, nyŏōd/ *adj. & n.* ● *adj.* naked, bare, unclothed. ● *n.* **1** a painting, sculpture, photograph, etc., of a nude human figure; such a figure. **2** a nude person. **3** (prec. by *the*) **a** an unclothed state. **b** the representation of an undraped human figure as a genre in art. [L *nudus*]

■ *adj.* unclothed, undressed, uncovered, bare, naked, in the nude, stark naked, undraped, without a stitch (on), *colloq.* in the buff, in the altogether, *joc.* in one's birthday suit, *Brit. sl.* starkers.

nudge /nuj/ *v. & n.* ● *v.tr.* **1** prod gently with the elbow to attract attention. **2** push gently or gradually. **3** give a gentle reminder or encouragement to (a person). ● *n.* the act or an instance of nudging; a gentle push. □□ **nudger** *n.* [17th c.: orig. unkn.: cf. Norw. dial. *nugga*, *nyggja* to push, rub]

■ *v.* jog, poke, elbow, jab, dig, bump, shove; prod, push, prompt, encourage; remind. ● *n.* jog, poke, elbow, jab, dig, bump, shove; prod, push, prompt, encouragement; reminder.

nudist /nŏōdist, nyŏō-/ *n.* a person who advocates or practices going unclothed. □□ **nudism** *n.*

■ naturist.

nudity /nŏōditee, nyŏō-/ *n.* the state of being nude; nakedness.

nugatory /nŏōgətáwree, nyŏō-/ *adj.* **1** futile; trifling; worthless. **2** inoperative; not valid. [L *nugatorius* f. *nugari* to trifle f. *nugae* jests]

■ **1** see INSIGNIFICANT 1.

nugget /núgit/ *n.* **1 a** a lump of gold, platinum, etc., as found in the earth. **b** a lump of anything compared to this. **2** something valuable for its size (often abstract in sense: *a little nugget of information*). [app. f. dial. *nug* lump, etc.]

■ **1** see LUMP¹ *n.* 1, 2.

nuisance /nŏōsəns, nyŏō-/ *n.* **1** a person, thing, or circumstance causing trouble or annoyance. **2** anything harmful or offensive to the community or a member of it and for which a legal remedy exists. □ **nuisance value** esp. *Brit.* an advantage resulting from the capacity to harass or frustrate. [ME f. OF, = hurt, f. *nuire nuis-* f. L *nocēre* to hurt]

■ **1** annoyance, inconvenience, trial, ordeal, burden, irritation, irritant, thorn in one's flesh *or* side, difficulty, bother, *colloq.* pain (in the neck), headache, hassle, *sl.* pain in the butt; bore, pest, nag, tease, tormentor, *Austral. sl.* nark.

nuke /nŏōk, nyŏōk/ *n. & v. colloq.* ● *n.* a nuclear weapon. ● *v.tr.* **1** *colloq.* bomb or destroy with nuclear weapons. **2** *colloq.* to cook (something) in a microwave oven. [abbr.]

null /nul/ *adj. & n.* ● *adj.* **1** (esp. **null and void**) invalid; not binding. **2** nonexistent; amounting to nothing. **3** having or associated with the value zero. **4** *Computing* **a** empty; having no elements (*null list*). **b** all the elements of which are zeros (*null matrix*). **5** without character or expression. ● *n. Brit.* a dummy letter in a code. □ **null character** *Computing* a character denoting nothing, usu. represented by a zero. **null hypothesis** a hypothesis suggesting that the difference between statistical samples does not imply a difference between populations. **null link** *Computing* a reference incorporated into the last item in a list to indicate there are no further items in the list. [F *nul nulle* or L *nullus* none f. *ne* not + *ullus* any]

■ *adj.* **1** see INVALID².

nullah /núlə/ *n. Anglo-Ind.* a dry riverbed or ravine. [Hindi *nālā*]

nulla-nulla /núlənulə/ *n.* (also **nulla**) *Austral.* a hardwood club used by Aborigines. [Aboriginal]

nullifidian /núlifídeeən/ *n. & adj.* (a person) having no religious faith or belief. [med.L *nullifidius* f. L *nullus* none + *fides* faith]

nullify /núlifī/ *v.tr.* (**-ies, -ied**) make null; neutralize; invalidate; cancel. □□ **nullification** /-fikáyshən/ *n.* **nullifier** *n.*

■ see NEUTRALIZE. □□ **nullification** see CANCELLATION.

nullipara /núlípərə/ *n.* a woman who has never borne a child. □□ **nulliparous** *adj.* [mod.L f. L *nullus* none + *-para* fem. of *-parus* f. *parere* bear children]

nullipore /núlipawr/ *n.* any of various seaweeds able to secrete lime. [L *nullus* none + PORE¹]

nullity /núlitee/ *n.* (*pl.* **-ies**) **1** *Law* a being null; invalidity, esp. of marriage. **b** an act, document, etc., that is null. **2 a** nothingness. **b** a mere nothing; a nonentity. [F *nullité* or med.L *nullitas* f. L *nullus* none]

Num. *abbr.* Numbers (Old Testament).

num. *abbr.* **1** number. **2** numerical.

numb /num/ *adj. & v.* ● *adj.* (often foll. by *with*) deprived of feeling or the power of motion (*numb with cold*). ● *v.tr.* **1** make numb. **2** stupefy; paralyze. □□ **numbly** *adv.* **numbness** *n.* [ME *nome(n)* past part. of *nim* take: for *-b* cf. THUMB]

■ *adj.* numbed, benumbed, insensible, insensate, dead, deadened, without feeling, senseless; asleep. ● *v.* benumb, anesthetize, drug, deaden, dull, freeze, paralyze, immobilize, stun, stupefy. □□ **numbness** anesthesia, paralysis, torpidity; see also STUPOR.

numbat /númbat/ *n.* a small Australian marsupial, *Myrmecobius fasciatus*, with a bushy tail and black and white striped back. [Aboriginal]

number /númbər/ *n. & v.* ● *n.* **1 a** an arithmetical value representing a particular quantity and used in counting and making calculations. **b** a word, symbol, or figure representing this; a numeral. **c** an arithmetical value showing position in a series, esp. for identification, reference, etc. (*registration number*). **2** (often foll. by *of*) the total count or aggregate (*the number of accidents has decreased*; *twenty in number*). **3 a** the study of the behavior of numbers; numerical reckoning (*the laws of number*). **b** (in *pl.*) arithmetic (*not good at numbers*). **4 a** (in *sing.* or *pl.*) a quantity or amount; a total; a count (*a large number of people*; *only in small numbers*). **b** (in *pl.*) numerical preponderance (*force of numbers*; *there is safety in numbers*). **5 a** a person or thing having a place in a series, esp. a single issue of a magazine, an item in a program, etc. **b** a song, dance, musical item, etc. **6** company, collection, group (*among our number*). **7** *Gram.* **a** the classification of words by their singular or plural forms. **b** a particular such form. **8** *colloq.* a person or thing regarded familiarly or affectionately (usu. qualified in some way: *an attractive little number*). **9** (**Numbers**) the Old Testament book containing a census. ● *v.tr.* **1** include (*I number you among my friends*). **2** assign a number or numbers to. **3** have or amount to (a specified number). **4 a** count. **b** comprise (*numbering forty thousand men*). □ **by numbers** following simple instructions (as if) identified by numbers. **do a number on** *sl.* injure, cheat, criticize, or humiliate. **one's days are numbered** one does not have long to live. **have a person's number** *colloq.* understand a person's real motives, character, etc. **have a person's number on it** (of a bomb, bullet, etc.) be destined to hit a specified person. **number cruncher** *Computing & Math. sl.* a machine or person capable of complex calculations, etc. **number crunching** the act or process of making these calculations. **one's number is up** *colloq.* one is finished or doomed to die. **a number of** some, several. ¶ Use with a plural verb is now standard: *a number of problems remain*. **number one** *n. colloq.* oneself (*always takes care of number one*). ● *adj.* most important (*the number-one priority*). **number plate** *Brit.* = *license plate.* **numbers game** an illegal lottery based on the occurrence of unpredictable numbers in the results of races, etc. **number two** a second in command. **without number** innumerable. [ME F. of *nombre* (N.), *nombrer* (v.) f. L *numerus, numerare*]

■ *n.* **1** numeral, integer, figure, digit. **2** see SUM *n.* 1, 2. **3 b** (*numbers*) see SUM *n.* 3b. **4** amount, quantity. **5 a** issue; edition, copy; item. **b** see ACT *n.* 3a. **6** see GROUP *n.* 1, COMPANY *n.* 1a. ● *v.* **1** see INCLUDE 3. **3** see AMOUNT *v.* 1. **4 a** see COUNT *v.* 1. **b** see INCLUDE 1. □ **a number of** see SEVERAL *adj.* **number plate** license plate. **number two** deputy, second in command, lieutenant; see also AIDE. **without number** see NUMBERLESS.

numberless /númbərlis/ *adj.* innumerable.
■ uncountable, uncounted, countless, innumerable, incalculable, immeasurable, numerous, untold, without number, infinite, *literary* myriad.

numbles /númbəlz/ *n.pl.* (also **nombles**) the edible entrails of a deer, etc. [ME f. OF *numbles, nombles* loin, etc., f. L *lumbulus* dimin. of *lumbus* loin: cf. UMBLES]

numbskull var. of NUMSKULL.

numen /nóōmən, nyóō-/ *n.* (*pl.* **numina** /-minə/) a presiding deity or spirit. [L *numen -minis*]

numerable /nóōmərəbəl, nyóō-/ *adj.* that can be counted. □□ **numerably** *adv.* [L *numerabilis* f. *numerare* NUMBER *v.*]

numeral /nóōmərəl, nyóō-/ *n.* & *adj.* ● *n.* a word, figure, or group of figures denoting a number. ● *adj.* of or denoting a number. [LL *numeralis* f. L (as NUMBER)]
■ *n.* see NUMBER *n.* 1.

numerate *v.* & *adj.* ● *v.* /nóōmərayt, nyóō-/ **1** = ENUMERATE. **2.** represent numbers by numerals. ● *adj.* /nóōmərət, nyóō-/ acquainted with the basic principles of mathematics. □□ **numeracy** /-əsee/ *n.* [L *numerus* number + -ATE² after *literate*]

numeration /nóōməráyshən, nyóō-/ *n.* **1 a** a method or process of numbering or computing. **b** calculation. **2** the expression in words of a number written in figures. [ME f. L *numeratio* payment, in LL numbering (as NUMBER)]

numerator /nóōməraytər, nyóō-/ *n.* **1** the number above the line in a common fraction showing how many of the parts indicated by the denominator are taken (e.g., 2 in $^2/_3$). **2** a

person or device that numbers. [F *numérateur* or LL *numerator* (as NUMBER)]

numerical /nóōmérikəl, nyóō-/ *adj.* (also **numeric**) of or relating to a number or numbers (*numerical superiority*). □ **numerical analysis** the branch of mathematics that deals with the development and use of numerical methods for solving problems. □□ **numerically** *adv.* [med.L *numericus* (as NUMBER)]

numerology /nóōmərólòjee, nyóō-/ *n.* (*pl.* **-ies**) the study of the supposed occult significance of numbers. □□ **numerological** /-rəlójikəl/ *adj.* **numerologist** *n.* [L *numerus* number + -LOGY]

numerous /nóōmərəs, nyóō-/ *adj.* **1** (with *pl.*) great in number (*received numerous gifts*). **2** consisting of many (*the rose family is a numerous one*). □□ **numerously** *adv.* **numerousness** *n.* [L *numerosus* (as NUMBER)]
■ *adj.* **1** see MANY *adj.*

numina *pl.* of NUMEN.

numinous /nóōminəs, nyóō-/ *adj.* **1** indicating the presence of a divinity. **2** spiritual. **3** awe-inspiring. [L *numen*: see NUMEN]

numismatic /nóōmizmátik, nyóō-/ *adj.* of or relating to coins or medals. □□ **numismatically** *adv.* [F *numismatique* f. L *numisma* f. Gk *nomisma -atos* current coin f. *nomizō* use currently]

numismatics /nóōmizmátiks, nyóō-/ *n.pl.* (usu. treated as *sing.*) the study of coins or medals. □□ **numismatist** /nóōmízmətist, nyóō-/ *n.*

numismatology /nóōmízmətólòjee, nyóō-/ *n.* = NUMISMATICS.

nummulite /númyəlīt/ *n.* a disk-shaped fossil shell of a foraminiferous protozoan found in Tertiary strata. [L *nummulus* dimin. of *nummus* coin]

numskull /númskul/ *n.* (also **numbskull**) a stupid or foolish person. [NUMB + SKULL]
■ see FOOL *n.* 1.

nun /nun/ *n.* a member of a community of women living apart under religious vows. □□ **nunhood** *n.* **nunlike** *adj.* **nunnish** *adj.* [ME f. OE *nunne* and OF *nonne* f. eccl.L *nonna* fem. of *nonnus* monk, orig. a title given to an elderly person]

nunatak /núnətak/ *n.* an isolated peak of rock projecting above a surface of glaciated land, e.g., in Greenland. [Inuit]

nun buoy /nún boy, bóōee/ *n.* a conical buoy. [obs. *nun* child's top + BUOY]

Nunc Dimittis /núngk dimítis/ *n.* the song of Simeon (Luke 2:29–32) used as a canticle. [f. the opening words *nunc dimittis* now let (your servant) depart]

nunciature /núnsheechōōr, -chər, nóōn-/ *n.* *RC Ch.* the office or tenure of a nuncio. [It. *nunziatura* (as NUNCIO)]

nuncio /núnsheeō/ *n.* (*pl.* **-os**) *RC Ch.* a papal ambassador. [It. f. L *nuntius* messenger]

nuncupate /núngkyəpayt/ *v.tr.* declare (a will or testament) orally, not in writing. □□ **nuncupation** /-páyshən/ *n.* **nuncupative** /-páytiv/ *adj.* [L *nuncupare nuncupat-* name]

nunnery /núnəree/ *n.* (*pl.* **-ies**) a religious house of nuns; a convent.

nuptial /núpshəl/ *adj.* & *n.* ● *adj.* of or relating to marriage or weddings. ● *n.* (usu. in *pl.*) a wedding. [F *nuptial* or L *nuptialis* f. *nuptiae* wedding f. *nubere nupt-* wed]
■ *adj.* bridal, matrimonial, wedding, wedded, marital, connubial, conjugal, *literary* hymeneal.

nurd var. of NERD.

nurse /nərs/ *n.* & *v.* ● *n.* **1** a person trained to care for the sick or infirm. **2** (formerly) a person employed or trained to take charge of young children. **3** *archaic* = *wet nurse.* **4** *Forestry* a tree planted as a shelter to others. **5** *Zool.* a nonreproductive bee, ant, etc., caring for a young brood; a worker. ● *v.* **1 a** *intr.* work as a nurse. **b** *tr.* attend to (a sick person). **c** *tr.* give medical attention to (an illness or injury).

/.../ **pronunciation**	● **part of speech**
□ **phrases, idioms, and compounds**	
□□ **derivatives**	■ **synonym section**
cross-references appear in SMALL CAPITALS or *italics*	

2 *tr.* & *intr.* feed or be fed at the breast. **3** *tr.* (in *passive*; foll. by *in*) be brought up in (a specified condition) (*nursed in poverty*). **4** *tr.* esp. *Brit.* hold or treat carefully or caressingly (*sat nursing my feet*). **5** *tr.* **a** foster; promote the development of (the arts, plants, etc.). **b** harbor or nurture (a grievance, hatred, etc.). **c** esp. *Brit.* pay special attention to (*nursed the voters*). **6** *tr.* consume slowly or over a long time. □ **licensed practical nurse** a person licensed to provide basic nursing care. **nurse-midwife** a registered nurse who assists women during childbirth. **nurse-practitioner** a registered nurse who has received advanced training in diagnosing and treating illness. **registered nurse** a nurse with graduate training who has passed a state certification exam and is licensed to practice nursing. **visiting nurse** a nurse, often employed by a public health agency, who visits the sick at home. [reduced f. ME and OF *norice, nurice* f. LL *nutricia* fem. of L *nutricius* f. *nutrix -icis* f. *nutrire* NOURISH]

■ *n.* **1** matron, paramedic, attendant, ministering angel. ● *v.* **1 b** care for, look after, tend, attend, minister to, treat. **2** wet-nurse, suckle, breast-feed, nourish. **5** nurture, foster, cherish, preserve, keep alive, cultivate, develop; harbor, coddle, baby, pamper.

nurseling var. of NURSLING.

nursemaid /nɔ́rsmayd/ *n.* & *v.* ● *n.* **1** a woman in charge of a child or children. **2** a person who watches over or guides another carefully. ● *v. tr.* act as nursemaid to.

■ **1** au pair, nurserymaid, nanny, mammy, *Brit.* childminder.

nursery /nɔ́rsəree/ *n.* (*pl.* **-ies**) **1 a** a room or place equipped for young children. **b** = *day nursery*. **2** a place where plants, trees, etc., are reared for sale or transplantation. **3** any sphere or place in or by which qualities or types of people are fostered or bred. □ **nursery rhyme** a simple traditional song or story in rhyme for children. **nursery school** a school for children from the age of about three to five.

■ □ **nursery school** kindergarten, playgroup, day care.

nurseryman /nɔ́rsəreemən/ *n.* (*pl.* **-men**) an owner of or worker in a plant nursery.

nursing /nɔ́rsing/ *n.* **1** the practice or profession of caring for the sick as a nurse. **2** (*attrib.*) concerned with or suitable for nursing the sick or elderly, etc. (*nursing home*). □ **nursing officer** *Brit.* a senior nurse.

nursling /nɔ́rsling/ *n.* (also **nurseling**) an infant that is being suckled.

nurture /nɔ́rchər/ *n.* & *v.* ● *n.* **1** the process of bringing up or training (esp. children); fostering care. **2** nourishment. **3** sociological factors as an influence on or determinant of personality (opp. NATURE). ● *v.tr.* **1** bring up; rear. **2** nourish. □□ **nurturer** *n.* [ME f. OF *nour(e)ture* (as NOURISH)]

■ *n.* **1** see UPBRINGING. ● *v.* **1** see *bring up* 1. **2** see NOURISH. □□ **nurturer** see MOTHER *n.* 1.

nut /nut/ *n.* & *v.* ● *n.* **1 a** a fruit consisting of a hard or tough shell around an edible kernel. **b** this kernel. **2** a pod containing hard seeds. **3** a small usu. square or hexagonal flat piece of metal or other material with a threaded hole through it for screwing on the end of a bolt to secure it. **4** *sl.* a person's head. **5** *sl.* **a** a crazy or eccentric person. **b** an obsessive enthusiast or devotee (*a health-food nut*). **6** esp. *Brit.* small lump of coal, butter, etc. **7 a** a device fitted to the bow of a violin for adjusting its tension. **b** the fixed ridge on the neck of a stringed instrument over which the strings pass. **8** (in *pl.*) *coarse sl.* the testicles. ● *v.intr.* (**nutted, nutting**) seek or gather nuts (*go nutting*). □ **do one's nut** *Brit. sl.* be extremely angry or agitated. **for nuts** *Brit. colloq.* even tolerably well (*cannot sing for nuts*). **nut cutlet** *Brit.* a cutlet-shaped portion of meat substitute, made from nuts, etc. **nut oil** an oil obtained from hazelnuts and walnuts and used in paints and varnishes. **nuts and bolts** *colloq.* the practical details. **nut tree** any tree bearing nuts. **off one's nut** *sl.* crazy. □□ **nutlike** *adj.* [OE *hnutu* f. Gmc]

■ *n.* **1 b** see KERNEL 1, 2. **4** see HEAD *n.* 1. **5 a** see MADMAN. **b** see ENTHUSIAST.

nutant /nóōt'nt, nyōō-/ *adj. Bot.* nodding, drooping. [L *nutare* nod]

nutation /nōōtáyshən, nyōō-/ *n.* **1** the act or an instance of nodding. **2** *Astron.* a periodic oscillation of the earth's poles. **3** oscillation of a spinning top. **4** the spiral movement of a plant organ during growth. [L *nutatio* (as NUTANT)]

nutcase /nútkays/ *n. sl.* a crazy or foolish person.

■ see MADMAN.

nutcracker /nútkrakər/ *n.* a device for cracking nuts.

nutgall /nútgawl/ *n.* a gall found esp. on oak, often used as a dyestuff.

nuthatch /nút-hach/ *n.* any small bird of the family Sittidae, climbing up and down tree trunks and feeding on nuts, insects, etc. [NUT + *hatch* rel. to HATCH²]

nuthouse /núthows/ *n. sl.* a mental home or hospital.

nutlet /nútlit/ *n.* a small nut or nutlike fruit.

nutmeg /nútmeg/ *n.* **1** an evergreen E. Indian tree, *Myristica fragrans*, yielding a hard aromatic spheroidal seed. **2** the seed of this used as a spice and in medicine. [ME: partial transl. of OF *nois mug(u)ede* ult. f. L *nux* nut + LL *muscus* MUSK]

nutria /nóōtreeə, nyōō-/ *n.* **1** an aquatic beaverlike rodent, *Myocastor Coypus*, native to S. America and kept in captivity for its fur. **2** its skin or fur. [Sp., = otter]

nutrient /nóōtreeənt, nyōō-/ *n.* & *adj.* ● *n.* any substance that provides essential nourishment for the maintenance of life. ● *adj.* serving as or providing nourishment. [L *nutrire* nourish]

nutriment /nóōtrimənt, nyōō-/ *n.* **1** nourishing food. **2** an intellectual or artistic, etc., nourishment or stimulus. □□ **nutrimental** /-mént'l/ *adj.* [L *nutrimentum* (as NUTRIENT)]

■ **1** see NOURISHMENT. □□ **nutrimental** see NUTRITIOUS.

nutrition /nōōtríshən, nyōō-/ *n.* **1 a** the process of providing or receiving nourishing substances. **b** food, nourishment. **2** the study of nutrients and nutrition. □□ **nutritional** *adj.* [F *nutrition* or LL *nutritio* (as NUTRIENT)]

■ **1 b** see NOURISHMENT.

nutritionist /nōōtríshənist, nyōō-/ *n.* a person who studies or is an expert on the processes of human nourishment.

nutritious /nōōtríshəs, nyōō-/ *adj.* efficient as food; nourishing. □□ **nutritiously** *adv.* **nutritiousness** *n.* [L *nutritius* (as NURSE)]

■ healthful, healthy, nutritive, nourishing, wholesome, life-giving, beneficial, salutary, alimentary, nutrimental.

nutritive /nóōtritiv, nyōō-/ *adj.* & *n.* ● *adj.* **1** of or concerned in nutrition. **2** serving as nutritious food. ● *n.* a nutritious article of food. [ME f. F *nutritif -ive* f. med.L *nutritivus* (as NUTRIENT)]

■ *adj.* **2** see NUTRITIOUS.

nuts /nuts/ *adj.* & *int.* ● *adj. sl.* crazy, mad, eccentric. ● *int. sl.* an expression of contempt or derision (*nuts to you*). □ **be nuts about** (or *Brit.* **on**) *colloq.* be enthusiastic about or very fond of.

■ *adj.* see CRAZY 1.

nutshell /nútshel/ *n.* the hard exterior covering of a nut. □ **in a nutshell** in a few words.

■ □ **in a nutshell** see *in a word* (WORD).

nutter /nútər/ *n. Brit. sl.* a crazy or eccentric person.

■ see MADMAN.

nutty /nútee/ *adj.* (**nuttier, nuttiest**) **1 a** full of nuts. **b** tasting like nuts. **2** *sl.* = NUTS *adj.* □□ **nuttiness** *n.*

■ **2** see CRAZY 1. □□ **nuttiness** see FOLLY 1.

nux vomica /nuks vómikə/ *n.* **1** an E. Indian tree, *Strychnos nux-vomica*, yielding a poisonous fruit. **2** the seeds of this tree, containing strychnine. [med.L f. L *nux* nut + *vomicus* f. *vomere* vomit]

nuzzle /núzəl/ *v.* **1** *tr.* prod or rub gently with the nose. **2** *intr.* (foll. by *into, against, up to*) press the nose gently. **3** *tr.* (also *refl.*) nestle; lie snug. [ME f. NOSE + -LE⁴]

■ **1, 2** see CARESS *v.* **3** see NESTLE.

NV *abbr.* Nevada (in official postal use).

NW *abbr.* **1** northwest. **2** northwestern.

NY *abbr.* New York (also in official postal use).

nyala /nyáálə/ *n.* (also **inyala** /in-/) (*pl.* **nyalas** or same) a large antelope, *Tragelaphus angasi*, native to S. Africa, with curved horns having a single complete turn. [Zulu]

NYC *abbr.* New York City.

nyctalopia /níktəlṓpeeə/ *n.* the inability to see in dim light or at night. Also called *night blindness*. [LL f. Gk *nuktalōps* f. *nux nuktos* night + *alaos* blind + *ōps* eye]

nyctitropic /níktitrṓpik, -trópˊ-/ *adj. Bot.* (of plant movements) occurring at night and caused by changes in light and temperature. [Gk *nukti-* comb. form of *nux nuktos* night + *tropos* turn]

nylghau /nílgaw/ *n.* = NILGAI. [Hind. f. Pers. *nīlgāw* f. *nīl* blue + *gāw* cow]

nylon /nílon/ *n.* **1** any of various synthetic polyamide fibers having a proteinlike structure, with tough, lightweight, elastic properties, used in industry and for textiles, etc. **2** a nylon fabric. **3** (in *pl.*) stockings made of nylon. [invented word, after *cotton, rayon*]

nymph /nimf/ *n.* **1** any of various mythological semidivine spirits regarded as maidens and associated with aspects of nature, esp. rivers and woods. **2** *poet.* a beautiful young woman. **3 a** an immature form of some insects. **b** a young dragonfly or damselfly. □□ **nymphal** *adj.* **nymphean** /-feeən/ *adj.* **nymphlike** *adj.* [ME f. OF *nimphe* f. L *nympha* f. Gk *numphē*]

■ **2** see MISS², BEAUTY 3.

nymphae /nímfee/ *n.pl. Anat.* the labia minora. [L, pl. of *nympha*: see NYMPH]

nymphet /nímfét/ *n.* **1** a young nymph. **2** *colloq.* a sexually precocious or provocative young woman.

■ **2** see MISS².

nympho /nímfṓ/ *n.* (*pl.* **-os**) *colloq.* a nymphomaniac. [abbr.]

nympholepsy /nímfəlepsee/ *n.* ecstasy or frenzy caused by desire of the unattainable. [NYMPHOLEPT after *epilepsy*]

nympholept /nímfəlept/ *n.* a person inspired by violent enthusiasm, esp. for an ideal. □□ **nympholeptic** /-léptik/ *adj.* [Gk *numpholēptos* caught by nymphs (as NYMPH, *lambanō* take)]

nymphomania /nímfəmáyneeə/ *n.* excessive sexual desire in women. □□ **nymphomaniac** *n.* & *adj.* [mod.L (as NYMPH, -MANIA)]

NYSE *abbr.* New York Stock Exchange.

nystagmus /nistágməs/ *n.* rapid involuntary movements of the eyes. □□ **nystagmic** *adj.* [Gk *nustagmos* nodding f. *nustazō* nod]

NZ *abbr.* New Zealand.

/.../ **pronunciation**	● **part of speech**
□ **phrases, idioms, and compounds**	
□□ **derivatives**	■ **synonym section**
cross-references appear in SMALL CAPITALS or *italics*	

O¹ /ō/ *n.* (also **o**) (*pl.* **Os** or **O's**) **1** the fifteenth letter of the alphabet. **2** (0) naught; zero (in a sequence of numerals, esp. when spoken). **3** a human blood type of the ABO system.

O² *abbr.* (also **O.**) Old.

O³ *symb. Chem.* the element oxygen.

O⁴ /ō/ *int.* **1** var. of OH¹. **2** prefixed to a name in the vocative (*O God*). [ME, natural excl.]

O' /ō, ə/ *prefix* of Irish patronymic names (*O'Connor*). [Ir. *ó, ua*, descendant]

o' /ə/ *prep.* of, on (esp. in phrases: *o'clock*; *will-o'-the-wisp*). [abbr.]

-o /ō/ *suffix* forming usu. *sl.* or *colloq.* variants or derivatives (*weirdo*; *wino*). [perh. OH¹ as joc. suffix]

-o- /ō/ *suffix* the terminal vowel of combining forms (*spectro-*; *chemico-*; *Franco-*). ¶ Often elided before a vowel, as in *neuralgia*. [orig. Gk]

oaf /ōf/ *n.* (*pl.* **oafs**) **1** an awkward lout. **2** a stupid person. □□ **oafish** *adj.* **oafishly** *adv.* **oafishness** *n.* [orig. = elf's child, var. of obs. *auf* f. ON *álfr* elf]
■ **1** see HULK 3. **2** see FOOL¹ *n.* 1. □□ **oafish** see CLUMSY 1. **oafishness** see *stupidity* (STUPID).

oak /ōk/ *n.* **1** any tree or shrub of the genus *Quercus* usu. having lobed leaves and bearing acorns. **2** the durable wood of this tree, used esp. for furniture and in building. **3** (*attrib.*) made of oak (*oak table*). **4** *Brit.* a heavy outer door of a set of university college rooms. **5** (**the Oaks**) (treated as *sing.*) an annual race at Epsom Downs (in Surrey, England) for three-year-old fillies (from the name of a nearby estate). □ **oak apple** (or **oak gall**) an applelike gall containing larvae of certain wasps, found on oak trees. □□ **oaken** *adj.* [OE *āc* f. Gmc]

oakum /ōkəm/ *n.* a loose fiber obtained by picking old rope to pieces and used esp. in caulking. [OE *ǣcumbe, ācumbe*, lit. "off-combings"]

oar /awr/ *n.* **1** a pole with a blade used for rowing or steering a boat by leverage against the water. **2** a rower. □ **put** (or **stick**) **one's oar in** interfere; meddle. **rest on one's oars** relax one's efforts. □□ **oared** *adj.* (also in *comb.*). **oarless** *adj.* [OE *ār* f. Gmc, perh. rel. to Gk *eretmos* oar]
■ **1** paddle, scull, sweep. **2** oarsman, oarswoman, sculler, rower, paddler. □ **put** (or **stick**) **one's oar in** see INTERFERE 2.

oarfish /áwrfish/ *n.* a ribbonfish, esp. *Regalecus glesne*.

oarlock /áwrlok/ *n.* a device on a boat's gunwale, esp. a pair of tholepins, serving as a fulcrum for an oar and keeping it in place. [OE *ārloc*]

oarsman /áwrzmən/ *n.* (*pl.* **-men**; *fem.* **oarswoman**, *pl.* **-women**) a rower. □□ **oarsmanship** *n.*
■ see OAR 2.

OAS *abbr.* Organization of American States.

oasis /ō-áysis/ *n.* (*pl.* **oases** /-seez/) **1** a fertile spot in a desert, where water is found. **2** an area or period of calm in the midst of turbulence. [LL f. Gk, app. f. Egypt. orig.]
■ **1** watering hole, water hole, watering place. **2** haven, refuge, (safe) harbor, sanctuary, retreat, asylum, resort, *colloq.* sanctum.

oast /ōst/ *n.* a kiln for drying hops. □ **oast-house** esp. *Brit.* a building containing this. [OE *āst* f. Gmc]

oat /ōt/ *n.* **1 a** a cereal plant, *Avena sativa*, cultivated in cool climates. **b** (in *pl.*) the grain yielded by this, used as food. **2** any other cereal of the genus *Avena*, esp. the wild oat, *A. fatua.* **3** *poet.* the oat stem used as a musical pipe by shepherds, etc., usu. in pastoral or bucolic poetry. **4** (in *pl.*) esp. *Brit. sl.* sexual gratification. □ **feel one's oats** *colloq.* **1** be lively. **2** feel self-important. **oat grass** any of various grasses, esp. of the genus *Arrhenatherum.* **off one's oats** *colloq.* not hungry. **sow one's oats** (or **wild oats**) indulge in youthful excess or promiscuity. □□ **oaten** *adj.* [OE *āte*, pl. *ātan*, of unkn. orig.]

oatcake /ōtkayk/ *n.* a thin unleavened cake made of oatmeal, common in Scotland and the north of England.

oath /ōth/ *n.* (*pl.* **oaths** /ō̄thz, ōths/) **1** a solemn declaration or undertaking (often naming God) as to the truth of something or as a commitment to future action. **2** a statement or promise contained in an oath (*oath of allegiance*). **3** a profane or blasphemous utterance; a curse. □ **under** (or **on**) **oath** having sworn a solemn oath. **take** (or **swear**) **an oath** make such a declaration or undertaking. [OE *āth* f. Gmc]
■ **1, 2** vow, avowal, pledge, promise, word (of honor), guarantee, guaranty, warranty, (sworn) statement, *archaic* plight, troth. **3** curse, profanity, blasphemy, imprecation, malediction, swearword, expletive, four-letter word, obscenity, dirty word. □ **take** (or **swear**) **an oath** see SWEAR *v.* 1a, 2.

oatmeal /ōtmeel/ *n.* **1** meal made from ground or rolled oats used esp. in breakfast cereal, cookies, etc. **2** a cooked breakfast cereal made from this. **3** a grayish-fawn color flecked with brown.

OAU *abbr.* Organization of African Unity.

OB *abbr.* **1 a** obstetric. **b** obstetrician. **c** obstetrics. **2** off Broadway.

ob. *abbr.* he or she died. [L *obiit*]

ob- /ob/ *prefix* (also **oc-** before *c*, **of-** before *f*, **op-** before *p*) occurring mainly in words of Latin origin, meaning: **1** exposure, openness (*object*; *obverse*). **2** meeting or facing (*occasion*; *obvious*). **3** direction (*oblong*; *offer*). **4** opposition, hostility, or resistance (*obstreperous*; *opponent*; *obstinate*). **5** hindrance, blocking, or concealment (*obese*; *obstacle*; *occult*). **6** finality or completeness (*obsolete*; *occupy*). **7** (in modern technical words) inversely; in a direction or manner contrary to the usual (*obconical*; *obovate*). [L f. *ob* toward, against, in the way of]

Obad. *abbr.* Obadiah (Old Testament).

obbligato /óbligáatō/ *n.* (*pl.* **-os**) *Mus.* an accompaniment, usu. special and unusual in effect, forming an integral part of a composition (*with violin obbligato*). [It., = obligatory, f. L *obligatus* past part. (as OBLIGE)]

obconical /obkónikəl/ *adj.* (also **obconic**) in the form of an inverted cone.

obcordate /obkáwrdayt/ *adj. Biol.* in the shape of a heart and attached at the pointed end.

obdurate /óbdoorit, -dyoor-/ *adj.* **1** stubborn. **2** hardened against persuasion or influence. □□ **obduracy** /-doorəsee, -dyoor-/ *n.* **obdurately** *adv.* **obdurateness** *n.* [ME f. L *obduratus* past part. of *obdurare* (as OB-, *durare* harden f. *durus* hard)]
■ **1** see OBSTINATE. **2** see DOGMATIC 1. □□ **obduracy** see *obstinacy* (OBSTINATE). **obdurateness** see *severity* (SEVERE).

OBE *abbr.* (in the UK) Officer (of the Order) of the British Empire.

obeah /óbeeə/ *n.* (also **obi** /óbee/) a kind of sorcery practiced esp. in the West Indies. [W. Afr.]

obeche /ōbéechee/ *n.* **1** a West African tree, *Triplochiton scleroxylon.* **2** the light-colored timber from this. [Nigerian name]

obedience /ōbéedeeəns/ *n.* **1** obeying as an act or practice or quality. **2** submission to another's rule or authority. **3** compliance with a law or command. **4** *Eccl.* **a** compliance with a monastic rule. **b** a sphere of authority (*the Roman obedience*). □ **in obedience to** actuated by or in accordance with. [ME f. OF f. L *obedientia* (as OBEY)]

■ **1–3** compliance, dutifulness, observance, respect, respectfulness, tractability, conformity, conformance, yielding, conformability, adaptability, agreement, agreeableness, acquiescence, submissiveness, submission, subservience, docility, passiveness, passivity.

obedient /ōbéedeeənt/ *adj.* **1** obeying or ready to obey. **2** (often foll. by *to*) submissive to another's will; dutiful (*obedient to the law*). □□ **obediently** *adv.* [ME f. OF f. L *obediens -entis* (as OBEY)]

■ compliant, dutiful, observant, respectful, tractable, yielding, conformable, adaptable, agreeable, amenable, acquiescent, submissive, subservient, docile, passive, timid, biddable, pliant, *literary* duteous.

obeisance /ōbáysəns, ōbée-/ *n.* **1** a bow, curtsy, or other respectful, or submissive gesture (*make an obeisance*). **2** homage; submission; deference (*pay obeisance*). □□ **obeisant** /-sənt/ *adj.* **obeisantly** *adv.* [ME f. OF *obeissance* (as OBEY)]

■ **1** see BOW² *n.* **2** deference, respect, respectfulness, homage, submission, reverence, honor.

obeli *pl.* of OBELUS.

obelisk /óbəlisk/ *n.* **1 a** a tapering, usu. four-sided stone pillar set up as a monument or landmark, etc. **b** a mountain, tree, etc., of similar shape. **2** = OBELUS. [L *obeliscus* f. Gk *obeliskos* dimin. of *obelos* SPIT²]

■ **1 a** pillar, needle.

obelize /óbəlīz/ *v.tr.* mark with an obelus as spurious, etc. [Gk *obelizō* f. *obelos*: see OBELISK]

obelus /óbələs/ *n.* (*pl.* **obeli** /-lī/) **1** a dagger-shaped reference mark in printed matter. **2** a mark (− or ÷) used in ancient manuscripts to mark a word or passage, esp. as spurious. [L f. Gk *obelos* SPIT²]

obese /ōbées/ *adj.* very fat; corpulent. □□ **obeseness** *n.* **obesity** *n.* [L *obesus* (as OB-, *edere* eat)]

■ fat, overweight, stout, fleshy, gross, corpulent, heavy, plump, portly, tubby, chubby, paunchy, rotund, abdominous, potbellied, esp. *Brit.* podgy, *colloq.* pudgy, *Austral. colloq.* poddy. □□ **obesity** corpulence, plumpness, tubbiness, chubbiness, grossness, embonpoint, rotundity, portliness, paunchiness; size, bulk, weight, avoirdupois.

obey /ōbáy/ *v.* **1** *tr.* **a** carry out the command of (*you will obey me*). **b** carry out (a command) (*obey orders*). **2** *intr.* do what one is told to do. **3** *tr.* be actuated by (a force or impulse). □□ **obeyer** *n.* [ME f. OF *obeir* f. L *obedire* (as OB-, *audire* hear)]

■ comply (with), agree (to), consent (to), submit (to), abide by, observe, respect, adhere to, follow, conform (to *or* with), acquiesce (to *or* in), mind, accept, heed, defer (to), yield (to), knuckle down *or* under, give way (to), surrender (to), succumb (to), give in (to), truckle to, bow (to), bend (to), take *or* accept orders (from); discharge, execute, effect, carry out, fulfill, meet, satisfy, do, perform; serve, act.

obfuscate /óbfuskayt/ *v.tr.* **1** obscure or confuse (a mind, topic, etc.). **2** stupefy, bewilder. □□ **obfuscation** /-káyshən/ *n.* **obfuscatory** /obfúskətawree/ *adj.* [LL *obfuscare* (as OB-, *fuscus* dark)]

■ **1** see OBSCURE *v.* 1, 2.

ob-gyn /óbee-jeewién/ *abbr.* **1** obstetrician-gynecologist. **2** obstetrics-gynecology.

obi¹ *var.* of OBEAH.

obi² /óbee/ *n.* (*pl.* same or **obis**) a broad sash worn with a Japanese kimono. [Jap. *obi* belt]

obit /óbit, ōbit/ *n. colloq.* an obituary. [abbr.]

obiter dictum /óbitər díktəm/ *n.* (*pl.* **obiter dicta** /-tə/) **1** a judge's expression of opinion uttered in court or giving judgment, but not essential to the decision and therefore without binding authority. **2** an incidental remark. [L f. *obiter* by the way + *dictum* a thing said]

obituary /ōbíchōō-eree/ *n.* (*pl.* **-ies**) **1** a notice of a death or deaths esp. in a newspaper. **2** an account of the life of a deceased person. **3** (*attrib.*) of or serving as an obituary. □□ **obituarial** /-áireeəl/ *adj.* **obituarist** *n.* [med.L *obituarius* f. L *obitus* death f. *obire obit-* die (as OB-, *ire* go)]

■ necrology, death notice, eulogy, *colloq.* obit.

obj. *abbr.* **1** object. **2** objective. **3** objection.

object *n.* & *v.* ● *n.* /óbjikt, -jekt/ **1** a material thing that can be seen or touched. **2** (foll. by *of*) a person or thing to which action or feeling is directed (*the object of attention; the object of our study*). **3** a thing sought or aimed at; a purpose. **4** *Gram.* a noun or its equivalent governed by an active transitive verb or by a preposition. **5** *Philos.* a thing external to the thinking mind or subject. **6** *derog.* a person or thing of esp. a pathetic or ridiculous appearance. **7** *Computing* a package of information and a description of its manipulation. ● *v.* /əbjékt/ **1** *intr.* (often foll. by *to*) express or feel opposition, disapproval, or reluctance; protest (*I object to being treated like this*). **2** *tr.* (foll. by *that* + clause) state as an objection (*objected that they were kept waiting*). **3** *tr.* (foll. by *to* or *that* + clause) adduce (a quality or fact) as contrary or damaging (to a case). □ **no object** not forming an important or restricting factor (*money no object*). **object ball** *Billiards*, etc., that at which a player aims the cue ball. **object glass** the lens in a telescope, etc., nearest to the object observed. **object language 1** a language described by means of another language (see METALANGUAGE). **2** *Computing* a language into which a program is translated by means of a compiler or assembler. **object lesson** a striking practical example of some principle. **object of the exercise** the main point of an activity. □□ **objectless** /óbjiktlis/ *adj.* **objector** /əbjéktər/ *n.* [ME f. med.L *objectum* thing presented to the mind, past part. of L *objicere* (as OB-, *jacere ject-* throw)]

■ *n.* **1** thing, item; reality, entity. **2** focus, target, butt, aim, destination, quarry, goal. **3** purpose, end, intention, objective, reason, intent, idea, goal, plan, object of the exercise, *colloq.* name of the game. ● *v.* **1, 2** protest, raise objection(s), argue, take exception, disapprove, draw the line, complain, remonstrate, take a stand, refuse.

objectify /əbjéktifī/ *v.tr.* (**-ies, -ied**) **1** make objective; embody. **2** present as an object of perception. □□ **objectification** /-fikáyshən/ *n.*

objection /əbjékshən/ *n.* **1** an expression or feeling of opposition or disapproval. **2** the act of objecting. **3** an adverse reason or statement. [ME f. OF *objection* or LL *objectio* (as OBJECT)]

■ protest, remonstration, remonstrance, demur, demurral, interference, opposition, disapproval, dislike, antipathy, exception, argument, challenge, complaint, question, doubt, stand, refusal, *Law* demurrer.

objectionable /əbjékshənəbəl/ *adj.* **1** open to objection. **2** unpleasant, offensive. □□ **objectionableness** *n.* **objectionably** *adv.*

■ **1** see EXCEPTIONABLE. **2** OFFENSIVE *adj.* 1.

objective /əbjéktiv/ *adj.* & *n.* ● *adj.* **1** external to the mind; actually existing; real. **2** (of a person, writing, art, etc.) dealing with outward things or exhibiting facts uncolored by feelings or opinions; not subjective. **3** *Gram.* (of a case or word) constructed as or appropriate to the object of a tran-

---

/ . . . / **pronunciation** ● **part of speech**
□ **phrases, idioms, and compounds**
□□ **derivatives** ■ **synonym section**
cross-references appear in SMALL CAPITALS or *italics*

sitive verb or preposition (cf. ACCUSATIVE). **4** aimed at (*objective point*). **5** (of symptoms) observed by another and not only felt by the patient. ● *n.* **1** something sought or aimed at; an objective point. **2** *Gram.* the objective case. **3** = *object glass*. □□ **objectival** /óbjektívəl/ *adj.* **objectively** *adv.* **objectiveness** *n.* **objectivity** /-tívitee/ *n.* **objectivize** *v.tr.* **objectivization** *n.* [med.L *objectivus* (as OBJECT)]

■ *adj.* **1** manifest, palpable, existing, real; see also FACTUAL, ACTUAL 1. **2** fair, impartial, just, judicious, equitable, neutral, disinterested, dispassionate, open-minded, detached, unbiased, unprejudiced, evenhanded, uncolored. ● *n.* **1** target, goal, object, aim, purpose, end, intent, intention, design, aspiration, ambition, hope. □□ **objectivity, objectiveness** impartiality, fairness, fair-mindedness, equitableness, equitability, evenhandedness, neutrality, disinterest, detachment, dispassion.

objectivism /əbjéktivizəm/ *n.* **1** the tendency to lay stress on what is objective. **2** *Philos.* the belief that certain things (esp. moral truths) exist apart from human knowledge or perception of them. □□ **objectivist** *n.* **objectivistic** *adj.*

objet d'art /áwbzhay daár/ *n.* (*pl.* **objets d'art** *pronunc.* same) a small decorative object. [F, lit. 'object of art']

objurgate /óbjərgayt, objə́r-/ *v.tr. literary* chide or scold. □□ **objurgation** /-gáyshən/ *n.* **objurgatory** /-jə́rgətáwree/ *adj.* [L *objurgare objurgat-* (as OB-, *jurgare* quarrel f. *jurgium* strife)]

oblanceolate /oblánseeəlayt/ *adj. Bot.* (esp. of leaves) lanceolate with the more pointed end at the base.

oblate[1] /óblayt/ *n.* a person dedicated to a monastic or religious life or work. [F f. med.L *oblatus* f. *offerre oblat-* offer (as OB-, *ferre* bring)]

oblate[2] /óblayt/ *adj. Geom.* (of a spheroid) flattened at the poles (cf. PROLATE). [mod.L *oblatus* (as OBLATE[1])]

oblation /əbláyshən, ob-/ *n. Relig.* **1** a thing offered to a divine being. **2** the presentation of bread and wine to God in the Eucharist. □□ **oblational** *adj.* **oblatory** /óblətáwree/ *adj.* [ME f. OF *oblation* or LL *oblatio* (as OBLATE[1])]

■ **1** see OFFERING.

obligate *v.* & *adj.* ● *v.tr.* /óbligayt/ **1** (usu. in *passive*; foll. by *to* + infin.) bind (a person) legally or morally. **2** commit (assets) as security. ● *adj.* /óbligət/ *Biol.* that has to be as described (*obligate parasite*). □□ **obligator** *n.* [L *obligare obligat-* (as OBLIGE)]

■ *v.* **1** oblige, commit, bind; require, compel, constrain, force.

obligation /óbligáyshən/ *n.* **1** the constraining power of a law, precept, duty, contract, etc. **2** a duty; a burdensome task. **3** a binding agreement, esp. one enforceable under legal penalty; a written contract or bond. **4 a** a service or benefit; a kindness done or received (*repay an obligation*). **b** indebtedness for this (*be under an obligation*). □ **day of obligation** *Eccl.* a day on which all are required to attend Mass or Communion. **of obligation** obligatory. □□ **obligational** *adj.* [ME f. OF f. L *obligatio -onis* (as OBLIGE)]

■ **1, 3** indebtedness, constraint, compulsion; requirement, demand; contract, promise, pledge, bond, agreement, covenant. **2** responsibility, duty, *archaic* devoir; charge, burden, onus; liability, trust. **4** debt, liability; see also KINDNESS 2.

obligatory /əblígətáwree/ *adj.* **1** legally or morally binding. **2** compulsory and not merely permissive. **3** constituting an obligation. □□ **obligatorily** *adv.* [ME f. LL *obligatorius* (as OBLIGE)]

■ required, demanded, necessary, requisite, compulsory, mandatory; incumbent; indispensable, essential.

oblige /əblíj/ *v.* **1** *tr.* (foll. by *to* + infin.) constrain; compel. **2** *tr.* be binding on. **3** *tr.* **a** make indebted by conferring a favor. **b** (foll. by *with*, or *by* + verbal noun) gratify (*oblige me by leaving*). **c** perform a service for (often *absol.*: *will you oblige?*). **4** *tr.* (in *passive*; foll. by *to*) be indebted (*am obliged to you for your help*). **5** *intr. colloq.* (foll. by *with*) make a contribution of a specified kind (*Doris obliged with a song*). **6** *tr. archaic* or *Law* (foll. by *to*, or *to* + infin.) bind by oath, promise, contract, etc. □ **much obliged** an expression of

thanks. □□ **obliger** *n.* [ME f. OF *obliger* f. L *obligare* (as OB-, *ligare* bind)]

■ **1, 2** make, require, demand, force, compel, constrain, coerce, bind, obligate. **3** accommodate, indulge, favor, serve, please, humor, gratify. **4** (*obliged*) thankful, grateful, appreciative, beholden, indebted, obligated. □ **much obliged** thank you, thanks, thanks a lot, thanks very much, *Brit. colloq.* thanks *or* ta (ever so *or joc.* muchly).

obligee /óblijeé/ *n. Law* a person to whom another is bound by contract or other legal procedure (cf. OBLIGOR).

obliging /əblíjing/ *adj.* courteous, accommodating; ready to do a service or kindness. □□ **obligingly** *adv.* **obligingness** *n.*

■ accommodating, willing, indulgent, gracious, courteous, civil, considerate, polite, agreeable, amenable, kind, kindly, helpful, friendly, amiable, neighborly, supportive.

obligor /óbligáwr/ *n. Law* a person who is bound to another by contract or other legal procedure (cf. OBLIGEE).

oblique /əbleék/ *adj., n.,* & *v.* ● *adj.* **1 a** slanting; declining from the vertical or horizontal. **b** diverging from a straight line or course. **2** not going straight to the point; roundabout; indirect. **3** *Geom.* **a** (of a line, plane figure, or surface) inclined at other than a right angle. **b** (of an angle) acute or obtuse. **c** (of a cone, cylinder, etc.) with an axis not perpendicular to the plane of its base. **4** *Anat.* neither parallel nor perpendicular to the long axis of a body or limb. **5** *Bot.* (of a leaf) with unequal sides. **6** *Gram.* denoting any case other than the nominative or vocative. ● *n.* **1** an oblique muscle. **2** *Brit.* an oblique stroke (/). ● *v.intr.* (**obliques, obliqued, obliquing**) esp. *Mil.* advance obliquely. □ **oblique sphere** see SPHERE. □□ **obliquely** *adv.* **obliqueness** *n.* **obliquity** /əblíkwitee/ *n.* [ME f. F f. L *obliquus*]

■ *adj.* **1** slanting, slanted, sloping, aslant, slant, inclined, diagonal, inclining, angled, canted, banked, banking, cambered, crooked, askew, divergent, diverging, tilted, atilt, tilting. **2** roundabout, indirect, circuitous, circumlocutionary, evasive, sly, devious, sidelong, offhand, surreptitious, furtive, implied, clandestine, underhand(ed), deceitful, deceptive, false. ● *n.* **2** solidus, virgule, slash, stroke.

obliterate /əblítərayt/ *v.tr.* **1 a** blot out; efface; erase; destroy. **b** leave no clear traces of. **2** deface (a postage stamp, etc.) to prevent further use. □□ **obliteration** /-ráyshən/ *n.* **obliterative** /-rətiv/ *adj.* **obliterator** *n.* [L *obliterare* (as OB-, *litera* LETTER)]

■ **1** erase, expunge, rub out, efface, eradicate, wipe out, delete, strike off *or* out, block out, rule out, eliminate; annihilate, blot out, extirpate, destroy, kill, exterminate.

oblivion /əblíveeən/ *n.* **1 a** the state of having or being forgotten. **b** disregard; an unregarded state. **2** an amnesty or pardon. □ **fall into oblivion** be forgotten or disused. [ME f. OF f. L *oblivio -onis* f. *oblivisci* forget]

■ **1** blankness, blackness, darkness, obscurity, nothingness, nonentity, nihility, anonymity, extinction, nonexistence, void, limbo; unawareness, obliviousness, forgetfulness, heedlessness, disregard, unconsciousness, insensibility.

oblivious /əblíveeəs/ *adj.* **1** (often foll. by *of*) forgetful; unmindful. **2** (foll. by *to, of*) unaware or unconscious of. □□ **obliviously** *adv.* **obliviousness** *n.* [ME f. L *obliviosus* (as OBLIVION)]

■ absentminded, forgetful, lethean; unaware, unconscious, unmindful, disregardful, insensible, insensitive, distant, unconcerned, detached, removed, unfeeling, abstracted. □□ **obliviousness** unawareness, heedlessness, disregard, unconsciousness, insensibility, oblivion; absentmindedness, forgetfulness.

oblong /óblawng/ *adj.* & *n.* ● *adj.* **1** deviating from a square form by having one long axis, esp. rectangular with adjacent sides unequal. **2** greater in breadth than in height. ● *n.* an oblong figure or object. [ME f. L *oblongus* longish (as OB-, *longus* long)]

obloquy /óbləkwee/ n. **1** the state of being generally ill spoken of. **2** abuse, detraction. [ME f. LL *obloquium* contradiction f. L *obloqui* deny (as OB-, *loqui* speak)]

■ **1** see *notoriety* (NOTORIOUS). **2** see ABUSE n. 2.

obnoxious /əbnókshəs/ adj. offensive, objectionable, disliked. □□ **obnoxiously** adv. **obnoxiousness** n. [orig. = vulnerable (to harm), f. L *obnoxiosus* or *obnoxius* (as OB-, *noxa* harm: assoc. with NOXIOUS)]

■ revolting, repulsive, repugnant, disgusting, offensive, objectionable, fulsome, vile, repellent, nauseous, nauseating, sickening, foul, noxious, mephitic, unsavory, execrable, abominable, abhorrent, loathsome, detestable, hateful, odious, scurvy, base, obscene, despicable, awful, terrible, unpalatable, distasteful, unlikable, disliked, unpleasant, nasty, *colloq.* beastly, *literary* noisome.

oboe /ṓbō/ n. **1 a** a woodwind double-reed instrument of treble pitch and plaintive incisive tone. **b** its player. **2** an organ stop with a quality resembling an oboe. □ **oboe d'amour** /dəmóor/ an oboe with a pear-shaped bell and mellow tone, pitched a minor third below a normal oboe, commonly used in baroque music. □□ **oboist** /ṓbō-ist/ n. [It. *oboe* or F *hautbois* f. *haut* high + *bois* wood: F *d'amour* = of love]

obol /óbəl/ n. an ancient Greek coin, equal to one-sixth of a drachma. [L *obolus* f. Gk *obolos*, var. of *obelos* OBELUS]

obovate /obṓvayt/ adj. *Biol.* (of a leaf) ovate with the narrower end at the base.

obscene /əbseén/ adj. **1** offensively or repulsively indecent, esp. by offending accepted sexual morality. **2** *colloq.* highly offensive or repugnant (*an obscene accumulation of wealth*). **3** esp. *Brit. Law* (of a publication) tending to deprave or corrupt. □□ **obscenely** adv. **obsceneness** n. [F *obscène* or L *obsc(a)enus* ill-omened, abominable]

■ **1** improper, rude, shameless, shameful, indecent, immodest, indecorous, indelicate, risqué, vulgar, immoral, degenerate, amoral, dissolute, broad, suggestive, erotic, sensual, ribald, debauched, wanton, loose, libertine, bawdy, blue, X(-rated), scabrous, coarse, dirty, filthy, smutty, pornographic, hard-core, libidinous, lewd, licentious, lecherous, lustful, goatish, carnal, ruttish, lascivious, salacious, prurient, disgusting, offensive, repulsive, foul, abominable, vile, loathsome, gross, foulmouthed, scurrilous, scatological, off-color, *colloq.* raunchy; *euphem.* adult. **2** offensive, outrageous, repulsive, shocking, repellent, repugnant, obnoxious, off-putting, objectionable, intolerable, insufferable, unpalatable, distasteful, nauseous, nauseating, sickening, execrable, despicable, nasty, evil, wicked, heinous, atrocious, *colloq.* awful.

obscenity /əbsénitee/ n. (*pl.* **-ies**) **1** the state or quality of being obscene. **2** an obscene action, word, etc. [L *obscaenitas* (as OBSCENE)]

■ **1** see RIBALDRY. **2** see CURSE n. 3.

obscurantism /əbskyōórəntizəm, óbskyŏórán-/ n. opposition to knowledge and enlightenment. □□ **obscurant** /əbskyóorənt/ n. **obscurantist** n. [*obscurant* f. G f. L *obscurans* f. *obscurare*: see OBSCURE]

obscure /əbskyóor/ adj. & v. ● adj. **1** not clearly expressed nor easily understood. **2** unexplained; doubtful. **3** dark; dim. **4** indistinct; not clear. **5** hidden; remote from observation. **6 a** unnoticed. **b** (of a person) undistinguished; hardly known. **7** (of a color) dingy; dull; indefinite. ● v.tr. **1** make obscure, dark, indistinct, or unintelligible. **2** dim the glory of; outshine. **3** conceal from sight. □□ **obscuration** n. **obscurely** adv. [ME f. OF *obscur* f. L *obscurus* dark]

■ adj. **1, 2, 4** unclear, uncertain, ambiguous, vague, hazy, doubtful, dubious, equivocal, indefinite, indistinct, fuzzy, blurred, confused, confusing, Delphic, puzzling, enigmatic, perplexing, baffling, mystifying, mysterious, cryptic, unexplained, incomprehensible, unfamiliar, foreign, strange; abstruse, arcane, recondite, esoteric, intricate, complex, occult, out of the ordinary, unfamiliar, *sl.* far-out. **3** dark, unlit, gloomy, somber, dismal, murky, dusky, black, dim, faint, blurred, veiled,

shadowy, umbral, shady, hazy, foggy, befogged, clouded, nebulous, overcast, cloudy, *formal* subfusc, *literary* tenebrous. **5** secret, concealed, hidden, remote, out-of-the-way, inconspicuous, unnoticeable, secluded. **6** unknown, unheard-of, anonymous, unnamed, insignificant, unimportant, inconsequential, humble, lowly, mean, inglorious, inconspicuous, undistinguished, unnoticed, unsung, minor, little-known. **7** muddy, murky, dull, indefinite; see also SOBER adj. 5, DINGY. ● v. **1, 2** dim, cloud, becloud, dull, shroud, shade, darken, obfuscate, block, *poet.* bedim; eclipse, adumbrate, overshadow, outshine, put in the shade. **3** cover, conceal, hide, veil, shroud, cloak, mask, screen, disguise.

obscurity /əbskyŏóritee/ n. (*pl.* **-ies**) **1** the state of being obscure. **2** an obscure person or thing. [F *obscurité* f. L *obscuritas* (as OBSCURE)]

■ **1** dimness, darkness, gloom, murk, murkiness, duskiness, dusk, blackness, faintness, blurriness, shade, shadow, haze, fog, cloudiness, nebulousness; abstruseness, ambiguousness, intricacy, complexity, unintelligibility; insignificance, unimportance, ingloriousness, inconspicuousness, anonymity, namelessness, limbo. **2** nobody, nonentity, nullity, nothing, zero, cipher, pawn, *colloq.* nebbish; mystery, arcanum, secret.

obsecration /óbsikráyshən/ n. earnest entreaty. [ME f. L *obsecratio* f. *obsecrare* entreat (as OB-, *sacrare* f. *sacer sacri* sacred)]

obsequies /óbsikweez/ n.pl. **1** funeral rites. **2** a funeral. □□ **obsequial** /əbseékweeəl/ adj. [ME, pl. of obs. *obsequy* f. AF *obsequie*, OF *obseque* f. med.L *obsequiae* f. L *exsequiae* funeral rites (see EXEQUIES): assoc. with *obsequium* (see OBSEQUIOUS)]

■ see FUNERAL n.

obsequious /əbseékweeəs/ adj. servilely obedient or attentive. □□ **obsequiously** adv. **obsequiousness** n. [ME f. L *obsequiosus* f. *obsequium* compliance (as OB-, *sequi* follow)]

■ low, cringing, toadying, toadyish, sycophantic, sycophantish, unctuous, truckling, groveling, crawling, fawning, deferential, ingratiating, menial, flattering, servile, slavish, subservient, submissive, abject, mealymouthed, slimy, *colloq.* bootlicking, smarmy.

observance /əbzérvəns/ n. **1** the act or process of keeping or performing a law, duty, custom, ritual, etc. **2** an act of a religious or ceremonial character; a customary rite. **3** the rule of a religious order. **4** *archaic* respect; deference. **5** *archaic* the act of observing or watching; observation. [ME f. OF f. L *observantia* (as OBSERVE)]

■ **1** observation, obedience, compliance, conformity, adherence, keeping, accordance, regard, recognition, respect, heed, attention. **2** ceremony, celebration, ceremonial, practice, rite, ritual, service, performance; form, custom, convention, tradition, formality, usage, habit, institution. **5** observation, examination, inspection, scrutiny, looking, watching.

observant /əbzérvənt/ adj. & n. ● adj. **1 a** acute or diligent in taking notice. **b** (often foll. by *of*) carefully particular; heedful. **2** attentive in esp. religious observances (*an observant Jew*). ● n. (**Observant**) a member of the branch of the Franciscan order that observes the strict rule. □□ **observantly** adv. [F (as OBSERVE)]

■ **1 a** watchful, alert, attentive, vigilant, on the lookout, on the qui vive, on guard, regardful, mindful, aware, keen, keen-eyed, sharp-eyed, eagle-eyed, perceptive, sharp, shrewd, acute, diligent, *colloq.* wide awake. **b** heedful, attentive, particular. **2** obedient, compliant, respectful, conformist, adherent.

observation /óbzərváyshən/ n. **1** the act or an instance of noticing; the condition of being noticed. **2** perception; the faculty of taking notice. **3** a remark or statement, esp. one that is of the nature of a comment. **4 a** the accurate watching and noting of phenomena as they occur in nature with regard to cause and effect or mutual relations. **b** the noting of the symptoms of a patient, the behavior of a suspect, etc. **5** the taking of the sun's or another heavenly body's altitude to find a latitude or longitude. **6** *Mil.* the watching of a fortress or hostile position or movements. □ **observation car** esp. *US* a railroad car built so as to afford good views. **observation post** *Mil.* a post for watching the effect of artillery fire, etc. **under observation** being watched. □□ **observational** *adj.* **observationally** *adv.* [ME f. L *observatio* (as OBSERVE)]

■ **1, 2, 4** watching, examination, scrutiny, inspection, viewing, survey, surveillance; notice, perception, discovery, attention, awareness. **3** comment, remark, note, reflection, opinion, sentiment, point of view, impression, feeling, commentary, criticism; utterance, word, announcement, pronouncement, proclamation, declaration.

observatory /əbzérvətawree/ *n.* (*pl.* **-ies**) a room or building equipped for the observation of natural, esp. astronomical or meteorological, phenomena. [mod.L *observatorium* f. L *observare* (as OBSERVE)]

observe /əbzérv/ *v.* **1** *tr.* (often foll. by *that* or *how* + clause) perceive; note; take notice of; become conscious of. **2** *tr.* watch carefully. **3** *tr.* **a** follow or adhere to (a law, command, method, principle, etc.). **b** keep or adhere to (an appointed time). **c** maintain (silence). **d** duly perform (a rite). **e** celebrate (an anniversary). **4** *tr.* examine and note (phenomena) without the aid of experiment. **5** *tr.* (often foll. by *that* + clause) say, esp. by way of comment. **6** *intr.* (foll. by *on*) make a remark or remarks about. □□ **observable** *adj.* **observably** *adv.* [ME f. OF *observer* f. L *observare* watch (as OB-, *servare* keep)]

■ **1** see NOTICE *v.* **2, 4** watch, look at, examine, monitor, scrutinize, study, regard, view, inspect, pore over, contemplate, consider, check (over), check out, *sl.* case. **3 a, b** obey, abide by, comply with, be heedful of, attend to, conform to, regard, keep, follow, adhere to, respect, pay attention to. **c** see MAINTAIN 1, 2. **d, e** celebrate, keep, solemnize, mark, commemorate, memorialize, remember, recognize. **5** comment, remark, mention, say, note, make reference; state, declare. □□ **observable** perceptible, perceivable, noticeable, discernible, recognizable, detectable, visible, apparent, distinct, evident, manifest, plain, obvious, clear, explicit, transparent, patent, tangible, unmistakable.

observer /əbzérvər/ *n.* **1** a person who observes. **2** an interested spectator. **3** a person who attends a conference, etc., to note the proceedings but does not participate. **4 a** a person trained to notice and identify aircraft. **b** a person carried in an airplane to note the enemy's position, etc.

■ **1–3** witness, eyewitness, spectator, viewer, onlooker, beholder, watcher, looker-on; nonparticipant, bystander.

obsess /əbsés/ *v.tr.* & *intr.* (often in *passive*) preoccupy; haunt; fill the mind of (a person) continually. □ **obsessive-compulsive** relating to a neurosis characterized by the persistence of an obsessive thought and the desire to engage in compulsive behavior, such as repeated hand washing. □□ **obsessive** *adj.* & *n.* **obsessively** *adv.* **obsessiveness** *n.* [L *obsidēre obsess-* (as OB-, *sedēre* sit)]

■ haunt, take control of, torment, take over, preoccupy, dominate, control, grip, possess, hold, *colloq.* plague. □□ **obsessive** (*adj.*) dominating, controlling, compulsive, addictive; haunting, harassing, tormenting.

obsession /əbséshən/ *n.* **1** the act of obsessing or the state of being obsessed. **2** a persistent idea or thought dominating a person's mind. **3** a condition in which such ideas are present. □□ **obsessional** *adj.* **obsessionalism** *n.* **obsessionally** *adv.* [L *obsessio* (as OBSESS)]

■ fixed idea, idée fixe, fixation, conviction,

preoccupation, prepossession, passion, mania, phobia, *colloq.* thing, *sl.* hang-up.

obsidian /əbsídeeən/ *n.* a dark glassy volcanic rock formed from hardened lava. [L *obsidianus*, error for *obsianus* f. *Obsius*, the name (in Pliny) of the discoverer of a similar stone]

obsolescent /óbsəlésənt/ *adj.* becoming obsolete; going out of use or date. □□ **obsolescence** /-səns/ *n.* [L *obsolescere obsolescent-* (as OB-, *solēre* be accustomed)]

■ fading, waning, on the wane, declining, dying, on the way out, on the decline; see also OBSOLETE.

obsolete /óbsəleét/ *adj.* **1** disused; discarded; antiquated. **2** *Biol.* less developed than formerly or than in a cognate species; rudimentary. □□ **obsoletely** *adv.* **obsoleteness** *n.* **obsoletism** *n.* [L *obsoletus* past part. (as OBSOLESCENT)]

■ **1** out-of-date, out of fashion, outdated, passé, out, dead, outmoded, old, antiquated, ancient, superannuated, dated, archaic, old-fashioned, *démodé*, superseded, extinct, *colloq.* old hat, antediluvian; unused, disused, discarded.

obstacle /óbstəkəl/ *n.* a person or thing that obstructs progress. □ **obstacle course 1** a training course through which a series of obstacles (walls, ditches, etc.) must be overcome in succession. **2** any situation that presents a series of challenges or obstacles. [ME f. OF f. L *obstaculum* f. *obstare* impede (as OB-, *stare* stand)]

■ impediment, hindrance, obstruction, hurdle, hitch, catch, snag, stumbling block, barrier, bar, check.

obstetric /əbstétrik, ob-/ *adj.* (also **obstetrical**) of or relating to childbirth and associated processes. □□ **obstetrically** *adv.* **obstetrician** /-stətríshən/ *n.* [mod.L *obstetricus* for L *obstetricius* f. *obstetrix* midwife f. *obstare* be present (as OB-, *stare* stand)]

obstetrics /əbstétriks, ob-/ *n.pl.* (usu. treated as *sing.*) the branch of medicine and surgery concerned with childbirth and midwifery.

obstinate /óbstinət/ *adj.* **1** stubborn, intractable. **2** firmly adhering to one's chosen course of action or opinion despite dissuasion. **3** inflexible, self-willed. **4** unyielding; not readily responding to treatment, etc. □□ **obstinacy** *n.* **obstinately** *adv.* [ME f. L *obstinatus* past part. of *obstinare* persist (as OB-, *stare* stand)]

■ stubborn, dogged, tenacious, persistent, mulish, bullheaded, hardheaded, perverse, headstrong, pigheaded, single-minded, willful, strong-willed, self-willed, contrary, recalcitrant, uncooperative, rebellious, contumacious, refractory, intransigent, pertinacious, obdurate, fixed, inflexible, stony, adamant, set, unmoving, immovable, inexorable, intractable, unchangeable, resolute, steadfast, unyielding, persevering, stiff, rigid, hard, *archaic* froward, esp. *Brit. colloq.* bloody-minded. □□ **obstinacy** stubbornness, doggedness, tenacity, persistence, persistency, mulishness, bullheadedness, hardheadedness, pigheadedness, willfulness, contrariness, perverseness, perversity, recalcitrance, uncooperativeness, rebelliousness, contumacy, refractoriness, intractability, intransigence, pertinacity, pertinaciousness, obduracy, fixedness, stolidity, inflexibility, firmness, *archaic* frowardness, esp. *Brit. colloq.* bloody-mindedness.

obstreperous /əbstrépərəs/ *adj.* **1** turbulent; unruly; noisily resisting control. **2** noisy; vociferous. □□ **obstreperously** *adv.* **obstreperousness** *n.* [L *obstreperus* f. *obstrepere* (as OB-, *strepere* make a noise)]

■ riotous, uproarious, tumultuous, boisterous, rowdy, tempestuous, unruly, disorderly, unmanageable, uncontrollable, uncontrolled, unrestrained, irrepressible, out of control, undisciplined, roisterous, wild, turbulent, rambunctious, *Brit. colloq.* rumbustious; vociferous, clamorous, noisy, loud, raucous.

obstruct /əbstrúkt/ *v.tr.* **1** block up; make hard or impossible to pass. **2** prevent or retard the progress of; impede. □□ **obstructor** *n.* [L *obstruere obstruct-* (as OB-, *struere* build)]

■ **1** block (up), clog, stop (up), bar, blockade, barricade, shut off, get *or* stand in the way of. **2** balk, block, check, hamper, slow, impede, retard, hinder, interrupt, delay, stay, stall, frustrate, inhibit, thwart, handicap, trammel, encumber.

obstruction /əbstrúkshən/ *n.* **1** the act or an instance of blocking; the state of being blocked. **2** the act of making or the state of becoming more or less impassable. **3** an obstacle or blockage. **4** the retarding of progress by deliberate delays, esp. within a legislative assembly. **5** *Sports* the act of unlawfully obstructing another player. **6** *Med.* a blockage in a bodily passage, esp. in an intestine. □□ **obstructionism** *n.* (in sense 4). **obstructionist** *n.* (in sense 4). [L *obstructio* (as OBSTRUCT)]

■ **1, 2** blocking, barring, barricading; hindering, delaying, stalling; frustration. **3** obstacle, barrier, hurdle, bar, check, hindrance, impediment, constraint, restriction; blockage, bottleneck. **4** obstructiveness, delaying tactics.

obstructive /əbstrúktiv/ *adj. & n.* ● *adj.* causing or intended to cause an obstruction. ● *n.* an obstructive person or thing. □□ **obstructively** *adv.* **obstructiveness** *n.*

■ *adj.* see DIFFICULT 2.

obtain /əbtáyn/ *v.* **1** *tr.* acquire; secure; have granted to one. **2** *intr.* be prevalent or established or in vogue. □□ **obtainable** *adj.* **obtainability** *n.* **obtainer** *n.* **obtainment** *n.* **obtention** /əbténshən/ *n.* [ME f. OF *obtenir* f. L *obtinēre obtent-* keep (as OB-, *tenēre* hold)]

■ **1** get, procure, acquire, come by, come into (the) possession of, secure, get hold of, lay *or* get one's hands on, grasp, capture, take possession of, seize; buy, purchase; earn, gain. **2** prevail, be in force, be in vogue, exist, have (a) place, be prevalent, be established, be customary, apply, be relevant.

obtrude /əbtróōd/ *v.* **1** *intr.* be or become obtrusive. **2** *tr.* (often foll. by *on, upon*) thrust forward (oneself, one's opinion, etc.) importunately. □□ **obtruder** *n.* **obtrusion** /-tróōzhən/ *n.* [L *obtrudere obtrus-* (as OB-, *trudere* push)]

■ stick *or* stand out, impinge, trespass, push *or* shove *or* thrust forward *or* in, intrude, impose.

obtrusive /əbtróōsiv/ *adj.* **1** unpleasantly or unduly noticeable. **2** obtruding oneself. □□ **obtrusively** *adv.* **obtrusiveness** *n.* [as OBTRUDE]

■ **1** loud, showy, garish, flashy, *colloq.* flash; see also GLARING 1. **2** interfering, intrusive, meddling, officious, meddlesome, importunate, forward, presumptuous, forceful, *colloq.* pushy.

obtund /əbtúnd/ *v.tr.* blunt or deaden (a sense or faculty). [ME f. L *obtundere obtus-* (as OB-, *tundere* beat)]

obtuse /əbtóōs, -tyóōs/ *adj.* **1** dull-witted; slow to understand. **2** of blunt form; not sharp-pointed nor sharp-edged. **3** (of an angle) more than 90° and less than 180°. **4** (of pain or the senses) dull; not acute. □□ **obtusely** *adv.* **obtuseness** *n.* **obtusity** *n.* [L *obtusus* past part. (as OBTUND)]

■ **1** dull, insensitive, unfeeling, imperceptive, thick-skinned, stolid, thick, dense, doltish, cloddish, thickheaded, dull-witted, dim-witted, slow-witted, boneheaded, lumpish, loutish, oafish, simple, simpleminded, stupid, dopey. **2** rounded; see also BLUNT *adj.* 1.

obverse /óbvərs/ *n. & adj.* ● *n.* **1 a** the side of a coin or medal, etc., bearing the head or principal design. **b** this design (cf. REVERSE). **2** the front or proper or top side of a thing. **3** the counterpart of a fact or truth. ● *adj.* **1** *Biol.* narrower at the base or point of attachment than at the apex or top (see OB- 7). **2** answering as the counterpart to something else. □□ **obversely** *adv.* [L *obversus* past part. (as OBVERT)]

■ *n.* **2** see FRONT *n.* 1.

obvert /əbvərt/ *v.tr. Logic* alter (a proposition) so as to infer another proposition with a contradictory predicate, e.g., *no men are immortal* to *all men are mortal*. □□ **obversion** /-zhən/ *n.* [L *obvertere obvers-* (as OB-, *vertere* turn)]

obviate /óbveeayt/ *v.tr.* get around or do away with (a need, inconvenience, etc.). □□ **obviation** /-áyshən/ *n.* [LL *obviare* oppose (as OB-, *via* way)]

■ see PRECLUDE 2. □□ **obviation** see *prevention* (PREVENT).

obvious /óbveeəs/ *adj.* easily seen or recognized or under-

stood; palpable; indubitable. □□ **obviously** *adv.* **obviousness** *n.* [L *obvius* f. *ob viam* in the way]

■ clear, plain, apparent, patent, perceptible, evident, self-evident, clear-cut, manifest, palpable, (much) in evidence, conspicuous, open, visible, overt, pronounced, prominent, glaring, undeniable, unconcealed, unhidden, unsubtle, distinct, simple, bald, bald-faced, straightforward, direct, self-explanatory, indisputable, indubitable, unmistakable; see also CERTAIN *adj.* 1b. □□ **obviously** clearly, plainly, apparently, patently, evidently, simply, certainly, of course, undeniably, unmistakably, indubitably, doubtless(ly).

OC *abbr.* officer candidate.

oc- /ok/ *prefix* assim. form of OB- before *c.*

o.c. *abbr.* in the work cited. [L *opere citato*]

ocarina /ókəréenə/ *n.* a small egg-shaped ceramic (usu. terracotta) or metal wind instrument. [It. f. *oca* goose (from its shape)]

Occam's razor /ókəmz/ *n.* the principle attributed to the English philosopher William of Occam (d. *c.*1350) that the fewest possible assumptions are to be made in explaining a thing.

occasion /əkáyzhən/ *n. & v.* ● *n.* **1 a** a special or noteworthy event or happening (*dressed for the occasion*). **b** the time or occurrence of this (*on the occasion of their marriage*). **2** (often foll. by *for,* or *to* + infin.) a reason, ground, or justification (*there is no occasion to be angry*). **3** a juncture suitable for doing something; an opportunity. **4** an immediate but subordinate or incidental cause (*the assassination was the occasion of the war*). ● *v.tr.* **1** be the occasion or cause of; bring about esp. incidentally. **2** (foll. by *to* + infin.) cause (a person or thing to do something). □ **on occasion** now and then; when the need arises. **rise to the occasion** produce the necessary will, energy, ability, etc., in unusually demanding circumstances. **take occasion** (foll. by *to* + infin.) make use of the opportunity. [ME f. OF *occasion* or L *occasio* juncture, reason, f. *occidere occas-* go down (as OB-, *cadere* fall)]

■ *n.* **1 a** event, function, happening, occurrence, affair; observance, commemoration, ceremony, celebration. **2** reason, cause, call, justification, ground(s), warrant, provocation, stimulus, incitement, inducement. **3** time, moment, circumstance, opportunity, chance, opening, advantage. ● *v.* give rise to, bring about, cause, bring on, effect, prompt, provoke, evoke, call forth, elicit, call up, induce, impel, create, generate, engender, produce, make (for). □ **on occasion** see *occasionally* (OCCASIONAL).

occasional /əkáyzhənəl/ *adj.* **1** happening irregularly and infrequently. **2 a** made or meant for, or associated with, a special occasion. **b** (of furniture, etc.) made or adapted for infrequent and varied use. **3** acting on a special occasion. □ **occasional cause** a secondary cause; an occasion (see OCCASION *n.* 4). **occasional table** a small table for infrequent and varied use. □□ **occasionality** /-nálitee/ *n.* **occasionally** *adv.*

■ **1** intermittent, irregular, periodic, random, sporadic, infrequent, casual, incidental. **2 a** special, particular, solemn, official; see also CEREMONIAL *adj.* 1. **b** additional, extra, spare, supplementary, incidental, auxiliary, accessory. □□ **occasionally** sometimes, on occasion, (every) now and then, from time to time, at times, (every) now and again, once in a while, every so often, periodically, intermittently, sporadically, irregularly, off and on.

Occident /óksidənt, -dent/ *n. poet.* or *rhet.* **1** (prec. by *the*) the West. **2** western Europe. **3** Europe, America, or both, as distinct from the Orient. **4** European, in contrast to Ori-

---

/.../ **pronunciation**	● **part of speech**
□ **phrases, idioms, and compounds**	
□□ **derivatives**	■ **synonym section**
cross-references appear in SMALL CAPITALS or *italics*	

ental, civilization. [ME f. OF f. L *occidens -entis* setting, sunset, west (as OCCASION)]

occidental /óksidént'l/ *adj. & n.* ● *adj.* **1** of the Occident. **2** western. **3** of Western nations. ● *n.* (**Occidental**) a native of the Occident. □□ **occidentalism** *n.* **occidentalist** *n.* **occidentalize** *v.tr.* **occidentally** *adv.* [ME f. OF *occidental* or L *occidentalis* (as OCCIDENT)]

occipito- /oksípitō/ *comb. form* the back of the head. [as OCCIPUT]

occiput /óksiput/ *n.* the back of the head. □□ **occipital** /-síp-it'l/ *adj.* [ME f. L *occiput* (as OB-, *caput* head)]

Occitan /óksitan/ *n.* (also *attrib.*) the Provençal language. □□ **Occitanian** /-táyneeən/ *n. & adj.* [F: cf. LANGUE D´OC]

occlude /əklōōd/ *v.tr.* **1** stop up or close (pores or an orifice). **2** *Chem.* absorb and retain (gases or impurities). □ **occluded front** *Meteorol.* a front resulting from occlusion. [L *occludere occlus-* (as OB-, *claudere* shut)]

occlusion /əklōōzhən/ *n.* **1** the act or process of occluding. **2** *Meteorol.* a phenomenon in which the cold front of a depression overtakes the warm front, causing upward displacement of warm air between them. **3** *Dentistry* the position of the teeth when the jaws are closed. **4** the blockage or closing of a hollow organ, etc. (*coronary occlusion*). **5** *Phonet.* the momentary closure of the vocal passage. □□ **occlusive** *adj.*

occult /əkúlt, ókult/ *adj. & v.* ● *adj.* **1** involving the supernatural; mystical; magical. **2** kept secret; esoteric. **3** recondite; mysterious; beyond the range of ordinary knowledge. **4** *Med.* not obvious on inspection. ● *v.tr. Astron.* (of a concealing body much greater in size than the concealed body) hide from view by passing in front; conceal by being in front. □ **the occult** occult phenomena generally. **occulting light** a light, esp. of a lighthouse, that is cut off at regular intervals. □□ **occultation** /-táyshən/ *n.* **occultism** *n.* **occultist** *n.* **occultly** *adv.* **occultness** *n.* [L *occulere occult-* (as OB-, *celare* hide)]

■ *adj.* **1, 3** magical, mystical, mystic, alchemic(al), unexplained, unexplainable, inexplicable, puzzling, baffling, perplexing, mystifying, mysterious, recondite, incomprehensible, inscrutable, indecipherable, impenetrable, unfathomable, transcendental, supernatural, preternatural. **2** secret, dark, concealed, private, hidden, obscure, veiled, obscured, shrouded, vague, abstruse, shadowy, mystical, mysterious, cabalistic, esoteric, recondite, arcane, *archaic* privy. □ **the occult** the supernatural, the paranormal, the unknown, the black arts; arcana, cabala; cabalism, occultism, sorcery, witchcraft, (black) magic.

occupant /ókyəpənt/ *n.* **1** a person who occupies, resides in, or is in a place, etc. (*both occupants of the car were unhurt*). **2** a person holding property, esp. land, in actual possession. **3** a person who establishes a title by taking possession of something previously without an established owner. □□ **occupancy** /-pənsee/ *n.* (*pl.* **-ies**). [F *occupant* or L *occupans -antis* (as OCCUPY)]

■ **1, 2** resident, inhabitant, tenant, lessee, leaseholder, renter, owner, householder, owner-occupier, dweller, lodger, boarder, roomer, *Brit.* occupier, *poet.* denizen; addressee; incumbent.

occupation /ókyəpáyshən/ *n.* **1** what occupies one; a means of passing one's time. **2** a person's temporary or regular employment; a business, calling, or pursuit. **3** the act of occupying or state of being occupied. **4 a** the act of taking or holding possession of (a country, district, etc.) by military force. **b** the state or time of this. **5** tenure, occupancy. **6** (*attrib.*) for the sole use of the occupiers of the land concerned (*occupation road*). [ME f. AF *occupacioun*, OF *occupation* f. L *occupatio -onis* (as OCCUPY)]

■ **2** job, position, post, situation, appointment, employment, vocation, line (of work), career, field, calling, trade, pursuit, métier, craft, skill, profession, business, work. **3, 5** possession, tenure, occupancy; rule, control, suzerainty; subjugation, subjection, oppression, bondage. **4 a** conquest, seizure, appropriation, takeover.

occupational /ókyəpáyshənəl/ *adj.* **1** of or in the nature of an occupation or occupations. **2** (of a disease, hazard, etc.) rendered more likely by one's occupation. □ **occupational therapy** mental or physical activity designed to assist recovery from disease or injury.
■ **2** work-related.

occupier /ókyəpīər/ *n. Brit.* a person residing in a property as its owner or tenant.
■ see OCCUPANT.

occupy /ókyəpī/ *v.tr.* (**-ies, -ied**) **1** reside in; be the tenant of. **2** take up or fill (space or time or a place). **3** hold (a position or office). **4** take military possession of (a country, region, town, strategic position). **5** place oneself in (a building, etc.) forcibly or without authority. **6** (usu. in *passive*; often foll. by *in, with*) keep busy or engaged. [ME f. OF *occuper* f. L *occupare* seize (as OB-, *capere* take)]

■ **1** live *or* reside in, tenant, be established *or* ensconced *or* situated in, establish *or* ensconce *or* situate oneself in, inhabit, be settled in *or* into, settle in *or* into, take up residence in, make one's home in, move in *or* into, *literary* dwell in; be located in. **2** take up, fill, cover, extend over, consume, use (up), eat up. **3** see HOLD¹ *v.* 3. **4** capture, seize, take possession of, conquer, invade, take over, overrun, garrison, dominate, hold. **6** engage, busy, absorb, monopolize, hold, take up *or* over, catch, grab, seize, grip; divert, amuse, entertain, distract, beguile, preoccupy, interest, engross, involve.

occur /əkér/ *v.intr.* (**occurred, occurring**) **1** come into being as an event or process at or during some time; happen. **2** exist or be encountered in some place or conditions. **3** (foll. by *to*; usu. foll. by *that* + clause) come into the mind of, esp. as an unexpected or casual thought (*it occurred to me that you were right*). [L *occurrere* go to meet, present itself (as OB-, *currere* run)]

■ **1** happen, take place, arise, come about, come to pass, appear, surface, materialize, develop, become manifest, manifest itself, crop up, turn up, *colloq.* come off, *disp.* transpire, *poet.* befall. **3** (*occur to*) dawn on, strike, hit, come to, come to a person's mind, suggest itself to, cross a person's mind, enter a person's head.

occurrence /əkérəns, əkúr-/ *n.* **1** the act or an instance of occurring. **2** an incident or event. □ **of frequent occurrence** often occurring. [*occurrent* that occurs f. F f. L *occurrens -entis* (as OCCUR)]

■ **1** existence, instance, manifestation, materialization, appearance, development; frequency, incidence, rate, *Statistics* distribution. **2** happening, event, incident, phenomenon, affair, matter, experience.

ocean /ṓshən/ *n.* **1 a** a large expanse of sea, esp. each of the main areas called the Atlantic, Pacific, Indian, Arctic, and Antarctic Oceans. **b** these regarded cumulatively as the body of water surrounding the land of the globe. **2** (usu. prec. by *the*) the sea. **3** (often in *pl.*) a very large expanse or quantity of anything (*oceans of time*). □ **ocean tramp** *Brit.* = TRAMP *n.* 6. □□ **oceanward** *adv.* (also esp. *Brit.* **-wards**). [ME f. OF *ocean* f. L *oceanus* f. Gk *ōkeanos* stream encircling the earth's disk, Atlantic]

■ **1b, 2** (deep blue) sea, high sea(s), depths, brine, *archaic or poet.* main, *colloq.* the drink, *poet.* the deep, *sl.* Davy Jones('s locker), the briny deep. **3** (*oceans*) plenty, mass(es), an abundance, a multitude, a profusion, a flood, a plethora, *colloq.* loads, a lot, lots, tons, oodles, zillions, scads.

oceanarium /ṓshənáireeəm/ *n.* (*pl.* **oceanariums** or **-ria** /-reeə/) a large seawater aquarium for keeping sea animals. [OCEAN + -ARIUM, after *aquarium*]

oceangoing /ṓshən-gṓing/ *adj.* (of a ship) able to cross oceans.

Oceania /ṓsheeáneeə, -áaneeə/ *n.* the islands of the Pacific and adjacent seas. □□ **Oceanian** *adj. & n.* [mod.L f. F *Océanie* f. L (as OCEAN)]

oceanic /ṓsheeánik/ *adj.* **1** of, like, or near the ocean. **2** (of a climate) governed by the ocean. **3** of the part of the ocean distant from the continents. **4** (**Oceanic**) of Oceania.

■ **1, 2** marine, pelagic, thalassic; saltwater, deepwater, aquatic, maritime, sea, ocean.

Oceanid /ōseéənid/ n. (pl. **Oceanids** or **-ides** /ōseeáni-deez/) (in Greek mythology) an ocean nymph. [Gk ōkeanis -idos daughter of Oceanus]

oceanography /ṓshənógrəfee/ n. the study of the oceans. □□ **oceanographer** n. **oceanographic** /-nəgráfik/ adj. **oceanographical** adj.

ocellus /ōséləs/ n. (pl. **ocelli** /-lī/) **1** each of the simple, as opposed to compound, eyes of insects, etc. **2** a spot of color surrounded by a ring of a different color on the wing of a butterfly, etc. □□ **ocellar** adj. **ocellate** /ósilayt/ adj. **ocellated** adj. [L, dimin. of oculus eye]

ocelot /ósilot, ṓsi-/ n. **1** a medium-sized feline, Felis pardalis, native to S. and Central America, having a deep yellow or orange coat with black striped and spotted markings. **2** its fur. [F f. Nahuatl ocelotl jaguar]

och /okh/ int. Sc. & Ir. expressing surprise or regret. [Gael. & Ir.]

ocher /ṓkər/ n. (Brit. **ochre**) **1** a mineral of clay and ferric oxide, used as a pigment varying from light yellow to brown or red. **2** a pale brownish yellow. □□ **ocherous** adj. **ochery** adj. [ME f. OF ocre f. L ochra f. Gk ōkhra yellow ocher]

ochlocracy /oklókrəsee/ n. (pl. **-ies**) mob rule. □□ **ochlocrat** /óklōkrat/ n. **ochlocratic** /óklōkrátik/ adj. [F ochlocratie f. Gk okhlokratia f. okhlos mob]

ochone /okhṓn/ int. (also **ohone**) Sc. & Ir. expressing regret or lament. [Gael. & Ir. ochóin]

ochre Brit. var. of OCHER.

-ock /ək/ suffix forming nouns orig. with diminutive sense (hillock; bullock). [from or after OE -uc, -oc]

ocker /ókər/ n. Austral. sl. a boorish or aggressive Australian (esp. as a stereotype). [20th c.: orig. uncert.]

o'clock /əklók/ adv. of the clock (used to specify the hour) (6 o'clock).

OCR abbr. optical character recognition.

OCS abbr. officer candidate school.

Oct. abbr. October.

oct. abbr. octavo.

oct- /okt/ comb. form assim. form of OCTA-, OCTO- before a vowel.

octa- /óktə/ comb. form (also **oct-** before a vowel) eight. [Gk okta- f. oktō eight]

octad /óktad/ n. a group of eight. [LL octas octad- f. Gk oktas -ados f. oktō eight]

octagon /óktəgon, -gən/ n. **1** a plane figure with eight sides and angles. **2** an object or building with this cross section. □□ **octagonal** /-tágənəl/ adj. **octagonally** adv. [L octagonos f. Gk octagṓnos (as OCTA-, -GON)]

octahedron /óktəheédrən/ n. (pl. **octahedrons** or **octahedra** /-drə/) **1** a solid figure contained by eight (esp. triangular) plane faces. **2** a body, esp. a crystal, in the form of a regular octahedron. □ **regular octahedron** an octahedron contained by equal and equilateral triangles. □□ **octahedral** adj. [Gk oktaedron (as OCTA-, -HEDRON)]

octal /óktəl/ adj. reckoning or proceeding by eights (octal scale).

octamerous /oktámərəs/ adj. **1** esp. Bot. having eight parts. **2** Zool. having organs arranged in eights.

octane /óktayn/ n. a colorless flammable hydrocarbon of the alkane series. ¶ Chem. formula: C_8H_{18}. □ **high-octane** (of fuel used in internal-combustion engines) having good antiknock properties, not detonating readily during the power stroke. **octane number** (or **rating**) a figure indicating the antiknock properties of a fuel. [OCT- + -ANE²]

octant /óktənt/ n. **1** an arc of a circle equal to one-eighth of the circumference. **2** such an arc with two radii, forming an area equal to one eighth of the circle. **3** each of eight parts into which three planes intersecting (esp. at right angles) at a point divide the space or the solid body round it. **4** Astron. a point in a body's apparent course 45° distant from a given point, esp. a point at which the moon is 45° from conjunction or opposition with the sun. **5** an instrument in the form of a graduated eighth of a circle, used in astronomy and navigation. [L octans octant- half-quadrant f. octo eight]

octaroon var. of OCTOROON.

octastyle /óktəstil/ adj. & n. ● adj. having eight columns at the end or in front. ● n. an octastyle portico or building. [L octastylus f. Gk oktastulos (as OCTA- + stulos pillar)]

octavalent /óktəváylənt/ adj. Chem. having a valence of eight. [OCTA- + VALENCE¹]

octave /óktiv, -tayv/ n. **1** Mus. **a** a series of eight notes occupying the interval between (and including) two notes, one having twice or half the frequency of vibration of the other. **b** this interval. **c** each of the two notes at the extremes of this interval. **d** these two notes sounding together. **2** a group or stanza of eight lines; an octet. **3** a the seventh day after a festival. **b** a period of eight days including a festival and its octave. **4** a group of eight. **5** the last of eight parrying positions in fencing. **6** esp. Brit. a wine cask holding an eighth of a pipe. [ME f. OF f. L octava dies eighth day (reckoned inclusively)]

octavo /oktáyvō, oktaávō/ n. (pl. **-os**) **1** a size of book or page given by folding a standard sheet three times to form a quire of eight leaves. **2** a book or sheet of this size. ¶ Abbr.: **8vo.** [L in octavo in an eighth f. octavus eighth]

octennial /okténeeəl/ adj. **1** lasting eight years. **2** occurring every eight years. [LL octennium period of eight years (as OCT-, annus year)]

octet /oktét/ n. (also **octette**) **1** Mus. **a** a composition for eight voices or instruments. **b** the performers of such a piece. **2** a group of eight. **3** the first eight lines of a sonnet. **4** Chem. a stable group of eight electrons. [It. ottetto or G Oktett: assim. to OCT-, DUET, QUARTET]

octo- /óktō/ comb. form (also **oct-** before a vowel) eight. [L octo or Gk oktō eight]

October /oktṓbər/ n. the tenth month of the year. [OE f. L (as OCTO-): cf. DECEMBER, SEPTEMBER]

Octobrist /oktṓbrist/ n. hist. a member of the moderate party in the Russian Duma, supporting the Imperial Constitutional Manifesto of Oct. 30, 1905. [OCTOBER, after Russ. oktyabrist]

octocentenary /óktōsenténəree, -sént'neree/ n. & adj. ● n. (pl. **-ies**) **1** an eight-hundredth anniversary. **2** a celebration of this. ● adj. of or relating to an octocentenary.

octodecimo /óktōdésimō/ n. (pl. **-os**) **1** a size of book or page given by folding a standard sheet into eighteen leaves. **2** a book or sheet of this size. [in octodecimo f. L octodecimus eighteenth]

octogenarian /óktəjináireeən/ n. & adj. ● n. a person from 80 to 89 years old. ● adj. of this age. [L octogenarius f. octogeni distributive of octoginta eighty]

octopod /óktəpod/ n. any cephalopod of the order Octopoda, with eight arms usu. having suckers, and a round saclike body, including octopuses. [Gk oktṓpous -podos f. oktō eight + pous foot]

octopus /óktəpəs/ n. (pl. **octopuses**) **1** any cephalopod mollusk of the genus Octopus having eight suckered arms, a soft saclike body, and strong beaklike jaws. **2** an organized and usu. harmful ramified power or influence. [Gk oktṓpous: see OCTOPOD]

octoroon /óktərṓon/ n. (also **octaroon**) the offspring of a quadroon and a white person; a person of one-eighth black ancestry. [OCTO- after QUADROON]

octosyllabic /óktōsilábik/ adj. & n. ● adj. having eight syllables. ● n. an octosyllabic verse. [LL octosyllabus (as OCTO-, SYLLABLE)]

octosyllable /óktōsíləbəl/ n. & adj. ● n. an octosyllabic verse or word. ● adj. = OCTOSYLLABIC.

octroi /óktroi, áwktrwaa/ n. **1** a duty levied in some European countries on goods entering a town. **2 a** the place where this is levied. **b** the officials by whom it is levied. [F f. octroyer grant, f. med.L auctorizare: see AUTHORIZE]

octuple /óktəpəl, oktōō-, -tyōō-/ adj., n., & v. ● adj. eight-

---

/.../ **pronunciation**	● **part of speech**
□ **phrases, idioms, and compounds**	
□□ **derivatives**	■ **synonym section**
cross-references appear in SMALL CAPITALS or italics	

fold. ● *n.* an eightfold amount. ● *v.tr. & intr.* multiply by eight. [F *octuple* or L *octuplus* (adj.) f. *octo* eight: cf. DOUBLE]

ocular /ókyoolər/ *adj. & n.* ● *adj.* of or connected with the eyes or sight; visual. ● *n.* the eyepiece of an optical instrument. □ **ocular spectrum** see SPECTRUM. □□ **ocularly** *adv.* [F *oculaire* f. LL *ocularis* f. L *oculus* eye]

ocularist /ókyələrist/ *n.* a maker of artificial eyes. [F *oculariste* (as OCULAR)]

oculate /ókyəlayt/ *adj.* = *ocellate* (see OCELLUS). [L *oculatus* f. *oculus* eye]

oculist /ókyəlist/ *n. formerly* **1** an ophthalmologist. **2** an optometrist. □□ **oculistic** /-lístik/ *adj.* [F *oculiste* f. L *oculus* eye]

oculo- /ókyəlō/ *comb. form* eye (*oculonasal*). [L *oculus* eye]

OD[1] *abbr.* **1** doctor of optometry. **2** *oculus dexter* (right eye). **3** officer of the day. **4 a** overdraft. **b** overdrawn.

OD[2] /ṓdeé/ *n. & v. sl.* ● *n.* an overdose, esp. of a narcotic drug. ● *v.intr.* (**OD's, OD'd, OD'ing**) take an overdose. [abbr.]

od[1] /od/ *n.* a hypothetical power once thought to pervade nature and account for various scientific phenomena. [arbitrary term coined in G by Baron von Reichenbach, Ger. scientist d. 1869]

od[2] /od/ *n.* (as *int.* or in oaths) *archaic* = GOD. [corruption]

o.d. *abbr.* outside diameter.

odalisque /ṓdəlisk/ *n. hist.* an Eastern female slave or concubine, esp. in the Turkish sultan's seraglio. [F f. Turk. *odalik* f. *oda* chamber + *lik* function]

odd /od/ *adj. & n.* ● *adj.* **1** extraordinary, strange, queer, remarkable, eccentric. **2** casual, occasional, unconnected (*odd jobs*; *odd moments*). **3** not normally noticed or considered; unpredictable (*in some odd corner*; *picks up odd bargains*). **4** additional; besides the calculated amount (*a few odd cents*). **5 a** (of numbers) not integrally divisible by two. **b** (of things or persons numbered consecutively) bearing such a number (*no parking on odd dates*). **6** left over when the rest have been distributed or divided into pairs (*have got an odd sock*). **7** detached from a set or series (*a few odd volumes*). **8** (appended to a number, sum, weight, etc.) somewhat more than (*forty odd*; *forty-odd people*). **9** by which a round number, given sum, etc., is exceeded (*we have 102 — what shall we do with the odd 2?*). ● *n.* Golf **1** one stroke more than the opponent's. **2** *Brit.* a handicap of one stroke at each hole. □ **odd job** a casual isolated piece of work. **odd job man** (or **odd jobber**) a person who does odd jobs. **odd man out 1** a person or thing differing from all the others in a group in some respect. **2** a method of selecting one of three or more persons, e.g., by tossing a coin. □□ **oddish** *adj.* **oddly** *adv.* **oddness** *n.* [ME f. ON *odda-* in *odda-mathr* third man, odd man, f. *oddi* angle]

■ *adj.* **1** strange, peculiar, unusual, uncommon, different, unexpected, unfamiliar, extraordinary, remarkable, atypical, untypical, exotic, out of the ordinary, unparalleled, unconventional, exceptional, unique, singular, individual, anomalous, idiosyncratic, rare, deviant, outlandish, uncanny, queer, curious, bizarre, weird, eccentric, funny, quaint, fantastic, freak, abnormal, freakish, offbeat, kinky, freaky, *colloq.* oddball, *Brit. colloq.* rum, *sl.* screwy, bent, kooky. **2, 7** occasional, casual, part-time, irregular, random, sporadic, discontinuous, disconnected, unconnected, various, varied, miscellaneous, sundry, incidental. **4, 6, 9** leftover, surplus, remaining, unused, spare, superfluous, extra, additional; uneven, unmatched, unpaired.

oddball /ódbawl/ *n. colloq.* **1** an odd or eccentric person. **2** (*attrib.*) strange, bizarre.

■ **1** see ECCENTRIC *n.* 1. **2** (*attrib.*) see ODD *adj.* 1.

Odd Fellow /ód fellō/ *n.* a member of a fraternity similar to the Freemasons.

oddity /óditee/ *n.* (*pl.* **-ies**) **1** a strange person, thing, or occurrence. **2** a peculiar trait. **3** the state of being odd.

■ **1** peculiarity, curiosity, rarity, freak, original, phenomenon, character, eccentric, nonconformist, fish out of water, rara avis, misfit, round *or* square peg in a square *or* round hole, maverick, crank, *colloq.* weirdo,

oddball, odd fish, *sl.* kook, screwball. **2** peculiarity, irregularity, anomaly, idiosyncrasy, eccentricity, deviation, quirk, mannerism, twist, kink. **3** peculiarity, strangeness, unnaturalness, curiousness, curiosity, incongruity, incongruousness, eccentricity, outlandishness, extraordinariness, unconventionality, bizarreness, weirdness, queerness, oddness, unusualness, individuality, singularity, distinctiveness, anomalousness, anomaly, *colloq.* kinkiness, *sl.* kookiness.

oddment /ódmənt/ *n.* **1** an odd article; something left over. **2** (in *pl.*) miscellaneous articles. **3** *Printing* matter other than the main text.

■ **2** (**oddments**) see *odds and ends*.

odds /odz/ *n.pl.* **1** the ratio between the amounts staked by the parties to a bet, based on the expected probability either way. **2** the chances or balance of probability in favor of or against some result (*the odds are against it*; *the odds are that it will rain*). **3** the balance of advantage (*the odds are in your favor*; *won against all the odds*). **4** an equalizing allowance to a weaker competitor. **5** a difference giving an advantage (*makes no odds*). □ **at odds** (often foll. by *with*) in conflict or at variance. **by all odds** certainly. **lay** (or **give**) **odds** offer a bet with odds favorable to the other bettor. **odds and ends** miscellaneous articles or remnants. **odds-on** a state when success is more likely than failure, esp. as indicated by the betting odds. **take odds** offer a bet with odds unfavorable to the other bettor. **what's** (or **what are**) **the odds?** *colloq.* what are the chances? (implying a slim likelihood). [app. pl. of ODD *n.*: cf. NEWS]

■ **1, 2** chances, likelihood, probability. □ **at odds** at variance, at loggerheads, at daggers drawn, at sixes and sevens, at cross purposes, at each other's throats, in disagreement, in opposition, on bad terms; not in keeping, out of line, inharmonious, conflicting, clashing, disagreeing, differing. **odds and ends** oddments, fragments, leftovers, leavings, remnants, bits (and pieces), shreds, snippets, scraps, rummage, *Brit.* jumble.

ode /ōd/ *n.* **1** a lyric poem, usu. rhymed and in the form of an address, in varied or irregular meter. **2** *hist.* a poem meant to be sung. [F f. LL *oda* f. Gk *ōidē* Attic form of *aoidē* song f. *aeidō* sing]

■ see POEM.

-ode[1] /ōd/ *suffix* forming nouns meaning 'thing of the nature of' (*geode*; *trematode*). [Gk *-ōdēs* adj. ending]

-ode[2] /ōd/ *comb. form Electr.* forming names of electrodes, or devices having them (*cathode*; *diode*). [Gk *hodos* way]

odeum /ṓdeeəm/ *n.* (*pl.* **odea** /-deeə/ or **odeums**) a building for musical performances, esp. among the ancient Greeks and Romans. [F *odéum* or L *odeum* f. Gk *ōideion* (as ODE)]

odious /ṓdeeəs/ *adj.* hateful; repulsive. □□ **odiously** *adv.* **odiousness** *n.* [ME f. OF *odieus* f. L *odiosus* (as ODIUM)]

■ see REPULSIVE.

odium /ṓdeeəm/ *n.* a general or widespread dislike or reprobation incurred by a person or associated with an action. [L, = hatred f. *odi* to hate]

■ see AVERSION 1.

odometer /ōdómitər/ *n.* an instrument for measuring the distance traveled by a wheeled vehicle. □□ **odometry** *n.* [F *odomètre* f. Gk *hodos* way: see -METER]

odonto- /ōdóntō/ *comb. form* tooth. [Gk *odous odont-* tooth]

odontoglossum /ōdóntəglósəm/ *n.* any of various orchids bearing flowers with jagged edges like tooth marks. [ODONTO- + Gk *glōssa* tongue]

odontoid /ōdóntoyd/ *adj.* toothlike. □ **odontoid process** a projection from the second cervical vertebra. [Gk *odontoeidēs* (as ODONTO- + Gk *eidos* form)]

odontology /ōdóntóləjee/ *n.* the scientific study of the structure and diseases of teeth. □□ **odontological** /-təlójikəl/ *adj.* **odontologist** *n.*

odor /ṓdər/ *n.* (*Brit.* **odour**) **1** the property of a substance that has an effect on the nasal sense of smell. **2** a lasting quality or trace attaching to something (*an odor of intolerance*). **3** regard, repute (*in bad odor*). □□ **odorless** *adj.* (in sense 1). [ME f. AF *odour*, OF *odor* f. L *odor -oris* smell, scent]

■ **1** smell, scent, aroma, bouquet, fragrance, perfume, redolence; stench, stink, fetor. **2** air, breath, hint, suggestion, whiff, atmosphere, spirit, quality, redolence, flavor, savor, aura, tone. **3** standing, esteem, repute, regard.

odoriferous /ṓdərífərəs/ *adj.* diffusing a scent, esp. an agreeable one; fragrant. □□ **odoriferously** *adv.* [ME f. L *odorifer* (as ODOR)]

■ see FRAGRANT.

odorous /ṓdərəs/ *adj.* **1** having a scent. **2** = ODORIFEROUS. □□ **odorously** *adv.* [L *odorus* fragrant (as ODOR)]

■ **1** redolent, aromatic.

odour *Brit.* var. of ODOR.

odyssey /ódisee/ *n.* (*pl.* **-eys**) a series of wanderings; a long adventurous journey. □□ **Odyssean** *adj.* [L *Odyssea* f. Gk *Odusseia*, title of an epic poem attributed to Homer describing the adventures of Odysseus (Ulysses) on his journey home from Troy]

■ see JOURNEY *n.*

OECD *abbr.* Organization for Economic Cooperation and Development.

OED *abbr.* Oxford English Dictionary.

oedema *Brit.* var. of EDEMA.

Oedipus complex /édipəs, éedi-/ *n.* *Psychol.* (according to Freud, etc.) the complex of emotions aroused in a young (esp. male) child by a subconscious sexual desire for the parent of the opposite sex and by a wish to exclude the parent of the same sex. □□ **Oedipal** *adj.* [Gk *Oidipous*, legendary king of Thebes who unknowingly killed his father and married his mother]

OEM *abbr.* original equipment manufacturer.

oenology var. of ENOLOGY.

oenophile /éenəfil/ *n.* a connoisseur of wines. □□ **oenophilist** /eenófilist/ *n.* [as ENOLOGY]

o'er /ôər/ *adv. & prep. poet.* = OVER. [contr.]

oersted /ə́rsted/ *n.* a unit of magnetic field strength equivalent to 79.58 amperes per meter. [H. C. *Oersted*, Da. physicist d. 1851]

oesophagus *Brit.* var. of ESOPHAGUS.

oestrogen *Brit.* var. of ESTROGEN.

oestrus *Brit.* var. of ESTRUS.

oeuvre /ȫvrə/ *n.* the works of an author, painter, composer, etc., esp. regarded collectively. [F, = work, f. L *opera*]

■ see WORK *n.* 5.

of /uv, ov, əv/ *prep.* connecting a noun (often a verbal noun) or pronoun with a preceding noun, adjective, adverb, or verb, expressing a wide range of relations broadly describable as follows: **1** origin, cause, or authorship (*paintings of Turner; people of Rome; died of malnutrition*). **2** the material or substance constituting or identifying a thing (*a house of cards; was built of bricks*). **3** belonging, connection, or possession (*a thing of the past; articles of clothing; the head of the business; the tip of the iceberg*). **4** identity or close relation (*the city of Rome; a pound of apples; a fool of a man*). **5** removal, separation, or privation (*north of the city; got rid of them; robbed us of $500*). **6** reference, direction, or respect (*beware of the dog; suspected of lying; very good of you; short of money; the selling of goods*). **7** objective relation (*love of music; in search of peace*). **8** partition, classification, or inclusion (*no more of that; part of the story; a friend of mine; this sort of book; some of us will stay*). **9** description, quality, or condition (*the hour of prayer; a person of tact; a girl of ten; on the point of leaving*). **10** time in relation to the following hour (*a quarter of three*). □ **be of** possess intrinsically; give rise to (*is of great interest*). **of all** designating the (nominally) least likely or expected example (*you of all people!*). **of all the nerve** (or *Brit.* **cheek**, etc.) an exclamation of indignation at a person's impudence, etc. **of an evening** (or **morning**, etc.) *colloq.* **1** on most evenings (or mornings, etc.). **2** at some time in the evenings (or mornings, etc.). **of late** recently. **of old** formerly; long ago. [OE, unaccented form of *æf*, f. Gmc]

of- /of/ *prefix* assim. form of OB- before *f*.

ofay /ṓfay/ *n.* *US sl. offens.* a white person (esp. used by black persons). [20th c.: prob. of Afr. orig.]

off. *abbr.* **1** office. **2** officer.

off /awf, of/ *adv., prep., adj., & n.* ● *adv.* **1 a** away; at or to a distance (*drove off; is three miles off*). **b** distant or remote in fact, nature, likelihood, etc. **2** out of position; not on or touching or attached; loose; separate; gone (*has come off; take your coat off*). **3** so as to be rid of (*sleep it off*). **4** so as to break continuity or continuance; discontinued; stopped (*turn off the radio; take a day off; the game is off*). **5** esp. *Brit.* not available as a choice, e.g., on a menu (*swordfish is off*). **6** to the end; entirely; so as to be clear (*clear off; finish off; pay off*). **7** situated as regards money, supplies, etc. (*is badly off; is not very well off*). **8** esp. *Brit.* offstage (*noises off*). **9 a** (of food, etc.) beginning to decay. **b** in error; abnormal; odd. **10** esp. *Brit.* (with preceding numeral) denoting a quantity produced or made at one time (*esp. one-off*). **11** away or free from a regular commitment (*How about tomorrow? I'm off then*). ● *prep.* **1 a** from; away or down or up from (*fell off the chair; took something off the price; jumped off the edge*). **b** not on (*was already off the pitch*). **2 a** (temporarily) relieved of or abstaining from (*off duty; am off my diet*). **b** not attracted by for the time being (*off their food; off smoking*). **c** not achieving or doing one's best in (*off form; off one's game*). **3** using as a source or means of support (*live off the land*). **4** leading from; not far from (*a street off 1st Avenue*). **5** at a short distance to sea from (*sank off Cape Horn*). ● *adj.* **1** far, further (*the off side of the wall*). **2** (of a part of a vehicle, animal, or road) right (*the off front wheel*). ● *n. Brit.* the start of a race. □ **a bit off** *Brit. colloq.* **1** rather annoying or unfair. **2** somewhat unwell (*am feeling a bit off*). **off and on** intermittently; now and then. **off-center** not quite coinciding with a central position. **the off chance** see CHANCE. **off-color 1** somewhat indecent. **2** *Brit.* not in good health. **off-the-cuff** see CUFF[1]. **off day** a day when one is not at one's best. **off one's feet** see FOOT. **off form** see FORM. **off guard** see GUARD. **off-key 1** out of tune. **2** not quite suitable or fitting. **off-licence** *Brit.* a shop selling alcoholic drink for consumption elsewhere. **off limits** see LIMIT. **off-line** *Computing* (of a computer terminal or process) not directly controlled by or connected to a central processor. **off-load** = UNLOAD. **off of** *sl. disp.* = OFF *prep.* (*picked it off of the floor*). **off-peak** used so at times other than those of greatest demand. **off the point** *adj.* irrelevant. ● *adv.* irrelevantly. **off-putting** disconcerting; repellent. **off-the-rack** (of clothes) ready-made. **off the record** see RECORD. **off-road** *attrib.adj.* **1** away from the road, on rough terrain. **2** (of a vehicle, etc.) designed for rough terrain or for cross-country driving. **off-roading** driving on dirt tracks and other unpaved surfaces as a sport or leisure activity. **off-season** a time when business, etc., is slack. **off time** a time when business, etc., is slack. **off the wall** see WALL. **off-white** white with a gray or yellowish tinge. [orig. var. of OF, to distinguish the sense]

■ *adv.* **1 a** away, out, elsewhere; distant, afar, far off. **2** away; loose, separate, removed, gone. **4** canceled, postponed, discontinued, stopped. **6** up, entirely; see also THROUGH *adv.* **7** situated, fixed, supplied. **9 a** sour, moldy, bad, rotten, rancid, turned, high. **b** incorrect, wrong, inaccurate, in error, mistaken, misguided, misled, off the mark; mad, insane, eccentric, *colloq.* dotty, dippy, crazy, nutty, esp. *Brit. colloq.* potty; unlikely, odd, abnormal, *sl.* off the wall. **11** off work, at leisure, idle, free; on vacation *or Brit.* holiday. ● *prep.* **1** (away *or* down *or* up) from, out of. **2 c** not up to, not on. **3** on, by, from. **4, 5** near, adjoining, next to, connecting with, leading from, contiguous with, adjacent to, abutting, bordering. ● *adj.* **1** see FAR 1 *adj.* □ **off and on** on and off; see also *by fits and starts*

/ . . . / **pronunciation**   ● **part of speech**
□ **phrases, idioms, and compounds**
□□ **derivatives**   ■ **synonym section**
cross-references appear in SMALL CAPITALS or *italics*

(FIT²). **off-color 1** unwell, ill, out of sorts, queasy, sick, run-down, poorly, lousy, *colloq.* awful, under the weather, seedy, *sl.* rotten. **2** indelicate, risqué, ribald, bawdy, indecent, suggestive, broad, inelegant, improper, inappropriate, unseemly, blue. **off-key 1** out of tune, tuneless, flat, unmelodic, unmusical; see also DISCORDANT 2. **2** see INCONGRUOUS. **off the point** see IRRELEVANT. **off-putting** see DISAGREEABLE 1.

offal /áwfəl, óf-/ *n.* **1** the less valuable edible parts of a carcass, esp. the entrails and internal organs. **2** refuse or waste stuff. **3** carrion; putrid flesh. [ME f. MDu. *afval* f. *af* OFF + *vallen* FALL]

■ **2** see RUBBISH 1.

offbeat *adj. & n.* ● *adj.* /áwfbeét, óf-/ **1** not coinciding with the beat. **2** eccentric, unconventional. ● *n.* /ófbeet/ any of the unaccented beats in a bar.

■ *adj.* **2** strange, eccentric, bizarre, weird, peculiar, odd, queer, unconventional, unorthodox, Bohemian, idiosyncratic, unusual, unexpected, outré, outlandish, deviant, novel, innovative, freaky, *colloq.* kinky, way-out, *sl.* off-the-wall, far-out.

offcut /áwfkut, óf-/ *n. esp. Brit.* a remnant of lumber, paper, etc., after cutting.

offence *Brit.* var. of OFFENSE.

offend /əfénd/ *v.* **1** *tr.* cause offense to or resentment in; wound the feelings of. **2** *tr.* displease or anger. **3** *intr.* (often foll. by *against*) do wrong; transgress. □□ **offendedly** *adv.* **offender** *n.* **offending** *adj.* [ME f. OF *offendre* f. L (as OFFENSE)]

■ **1, 2** hurt a person's feelings, affront, insult, slight, snub, give offense, hurt, pain, wound, displease, disgruntle, chagrin, humiliate, embarrass; pique, fret, gall, vex, annoy, irritate, nettle, needle, provoke, ruffle, outrage, anger, put out, get *or* put a person's back up, *colloq.* miff, rile, put a person's nose out of joint, tread on a person's toes, rattle; disgust, sicken, turn a person's stomach, nauseate, repel, repulse, revolt, *colloq.* turn off. **3** see TRANSGRESS. □□ **offender** criminal, malefactor, lawbreaker, outlaw, wrongdoer, culprit, miscreant, transgressor, sinner, evildoer, *colloq.* crook.

offense /əféns/ *n.* (*Brit.* **offence**) **1** an illegal act; a transgression or misdemeanor. **2** a wounding of the feelings; resentment or umbrage (*no offense was meant*). **3** /áwfens, óf-/ the act of attacking or taking the offensive; aggressive action. **4** /áwfens, óf-/ *Sports* the team in possession of the ball, puck, etc. ■ **give offense** cause hurt feelings. **take offense** suffer hurt feelings. □□ **offenseless** *adj.* [orig. = stumbling, stumbling block: ME & OF *offens* f. L *offensus* annoyance, and ME & F *offense* f. L *offensa* a striking against; hurt; displeasure, both f. *offendere* (as OB-, *fendere fens-* strike)]

■ **1** violation, breach, crime, felony, misdemeanor, infraction, transgression, trespass, wrong, wrongdoing, sin, peccadillo, misdeed, fault, infringement, malefaction; dereliction, lapse, slip, error. **2** resentment, annoyance, umbrage. **3** see AGGRESSION 2. □ **give offense** injure, harm; see also OFFEND 1, 2. **take offense** take umbrage, feel displeased *or* annoyed *or* resentful *or* indignant, be angered *or* enraged *or* hurt; see also *take exception* (EXCEPTION).

offensive /əfénsiv/ *adj. & n.* ● *adj.* **1** giving or meant or likely to give offense; insulting (*offensive language*). **2** disgusting, foul-smelling, nauseous, repulsive. **3 a** aggressive, attacking. **b** (of a weapon) meant for use in attack. **4** *Sports* designating the team in possession of the ball, puck, etc. ● *n.* **1** an aggressive action or attitude (*take the offensive*). **2** an attack; an offensive campaign or stroke. **3** aggressive or forceful action in pursuit of a cause (*a peace offensive*). □□ **offensively** *adv.* **offensiveness** *n.* [F *offensif -ive* or med.L *offensivus* (as OFFENSE)]

■ *adj.* **1** insulting, rude, disrespectful, uncivil, insolent, discourteous, impolite, unmannerly, impertinent, impudent, objectionable, displeasing. **2** disgusting, unsavory, unpalatable, nauseating, nauseous, noxious, obnoxious, repugnant, repulsive, repellent, revolting,

abominable, foul, loathsome, vile, sickening, fetid, rank, malodorous, mephitic, putrid, putrescent, putrefying, rancid, rotten, *literary* noisome. **3 a** antagonistic, hostile, contentious, quarrelsome, attacking, aggressive, threatening, provocative, combative, martial, belligerent, warlike, bellicose. ● *n.* **2, 3** attack, onslaught, drive, assault, offense, push.

offer /áwfər, óf-/ *v. & n.* ● *v.* **1** *tr.* present for acceptance or refusal or consideration (*offered me a drink; was offered a ride; offer one's services; offer no apology*). **2** *intr.* (foll. by *to* + infin.) express readiness or show intention (*offered to take the children*). **3** *tr.* provide; give an opportunity for. **4** *tr.* make available for sale. **5** *tr.* (of a thing) present to one's attention or consideration (*each day offers new opportunities*). **6** *tr.* present (a sacrifice, prayer, etc.) to a deity. **7** *intr.* present itself; occur (*as opportunity offers*). **8** *tr.* give an opportunity for (battle) to an enemy. **9** *tr.* attempt, or try to show (violence, resistance, etc.). ● *n.* **1** an expression of readiness to do or give if desired, or to buy or sell (for a certain amount). **2** an amount offered. **3** a proposal (esp. of marriage). **4** a bid. □ **on offer** *Brit.* for sale at a certain (esp. reduced) price. □□ **offerer** *n.* **offeror** *n.* [OE *offrian* in religious sense, f. L *offerre* (as OB-, *ferre* bring)]

■ *v.* **1** proffer, propose, tender; see also VENTURE *v.* 3. **2** volunteer, present oneself, step *or* come forward. **3, 5** proffer, provide, submit, put forward *or* forth, advance, present, tender, extend; suggest. **4** make available, present, put on the market, sell, put up for sale, put up, furnish. ● *n.* proposal, bid, tender, offering, presentation, proposition, *literary* proffer.

offering /áwfəring, óf-/ *n.* **1** a contribution, esp. of money, to a church. **2** a thing offered as a religious sacrifice or token of devotion. **3** anything, esp. money, contributed or offered.

■ contribution, donation, gift, present; sacrifice, *Relig.* oblation.

offertory /áwfərtawree, óf-/ *n.* (*pl.* **-ies**) **1** *Eccl.* **a** the offering of the bread and wine at the Eucharist. **b** an anthem accompanying this. **2 a** the collection of money at a religious service. **b** the money collected. [ME f. eccl.L *offertorium* offering f. LL *offert-* for L *oblat-* past part. stem of *offerre* OFFER]

offhand /áwfhánd, óf-/ *adj. & adv.* ● *adj.* curt or casual in manner. ● *adv.* **1** in an offhand manner. **2** without preparation or premeditation. □□ **offhanded** *adj.* **offhandedly** *adv.* **offhandedness** *n.*

■ *adj.* curt, brusque, abrupt, perfunctory, ungracious, glib, smooth; casual, informal, nonchalant, cool, distant, aloof, easygoing, blasé, unceremonious, relaxed, easy, smooth, unconcerned, insouciant, light-hearted, uninterested, superficial, cursory, cavalier, careless; extempore, impromptu, unpremeditated, unstudied, extemporaneous, informal, off-the-cuff, ad lib. ● *adv.* **1** casually, informally, incidentally, by the way, offhandedly, by the by, parenthetically, in passing, en passant, cursorily, superficially. **2** extempore, impromptu, extemporaneously, informally, off-the-cuff, ad lib, on the spur of the moment, at the drop of a hat.

office /áwfis, óf-/ *n.* **1** a room or building used as a place of business, esp. for clerical or administrative work. **2** a room or department or building for a particular kind of business (*ticket office; post office*). **3** the local center of a large business (*our Honolulu office*). **4** the consulting room of a professional person. **5** a position with duties attached to it; a place of authority or trust or service, esp. of a public nature. **6** tenure of an official position, esp. that of government (*hold office*; *out of office for 13 years*). **7** (**Office**) *Brit.* the quarters or staff or collective authority of a government department, etc. (*Foreign Office*). **8** a duty attaching to one's position; a task or function. **9** (usu. in *pl.*) a piece of kindness or attention; a service (esp. *through the good offices of*). **10** *Eccl.* **a** an authorized form of worship (*Office for the Dead*). **b** (in full **divine office**) the daily service of the Roman Catholic breviary (*say the office*). **11** a ceremonial duty. **12** (in *pl.*) *Brit.* the parts of a house devoted to household work, storage, etc. **13** *sl.* a hint or signal. □ **office block** *Brit.* a large building designed to contain business offices. **office boy** (or **girl**) a young man (or woman) employed to do minor jobs in a business office. **office hours** the hours during which business is normally conducted. **office park** a commercial property with usu. several office buildings situated in or near a park-like setting. **office worker** an employee in a business office. [ME f. OF f. L *officium* performance of a task (in med.L also office, divine service), f. *opus* work + *facere* fic-do]

■ **1** workplace, workroom, studio, study; headquarters, station, base, center. **2, 3, 7** department, branch; commission; section, division; business, organization, firm, house, establishment, company, corporation. **5, 6, 8** duty, obligation, responsibility, charge, commission, service, employment, occupation, position, station, post, appointment, assignment, chore, task, job, place, berth, work, role, function, purpose, part, bit. **9** (*offices*) intermediation, auspices, support, advocacy, aegis, help, aid, intercession, mediation, patronage, favor, backing, backup.

officer /áwfisər, óf-/ *n. & v.* ● *n.* **1** a person holding a position of authority or trust, esp. one with a commission in the armed services, in the merchant marine, or on a passenger ship. **2** a policeman or policewoman. **3** a holder of a post in a society or business enterprise (e.g., the president or secretary). **4** a holder of a public, civil, or ecclesiastical office; a sovereign's minister; an appointed or elected functionary (usu. with a qualifying word: *medical officer; probation officer; returning officer*). **5** a bailiff (*the sheriff's officer*). **6** a member of the grade below commander in the Order of the British Empire, etc. ● *v.tr.* **1** provide with officers. **2** act as the commander of. □ **officer of arms** a herald or pursuivant. [ME f. AF *officer*, OF *officier* f. med.L *officiarius* f. L *officium*: see OFFICE]

■ *n.* **1, 3, 4** (public) official, dignitary, officeholder, public servant, (political) appointee, (government) agent, bureaucrat, functionary, commissioner, administrator, manager, director, minister; apparatchik. **2** policeman, policewoman, police officer, officer of the law, constable, gendarme, lawman, peace officer, *colloq.* G-man, *sl.* cop, gumshoe, flatfoot, dick, copper, fuzz, *Austral. sl.* demon, John Hop.

official /əfíshəl/ *adj. & n.* ● *adj.* **1** of or relating to an office (see OFFICE n. 5, 6) or its tenure or duties. **2** characteristic of officials and bureaucracy. **3** emanating from or attributable to a person in office; properly authorized. **4** holding office; employed in a public capacity. **5** *Med.* according to the pharmacopoeia; officinal. ● *n.* **1** a person holding office or engaged in official duties. **2** *Brit.* (in full **official principal**) the presiding officer or judge of an archbishop's, bishop's, or esp. archdeacon's court. □ **official birthday** *Brit.* a day in June chosen for the observance of the sovereign's birthday. **official secrets** *Brit.* confidential information involving national security. □□ **officialdom** *n.* **officialism** *n.* **officially** *adv.* [ME (as noun) f. OF f. L *officialis* (as OFFICE)]

■ *adj.* **1, 2** ceremonial, formal, solemn, ritualistic, ceremonious, pompous, stiff, proper, seemly, decorous; bureaucratic. **3, 4** authorized, legitimate, lawful, legal, authentic, bona fide, proper, true, accredited, valid, documented, licensed, sanctioned, endorsed, certified, verified, recognized, accepted. ● *n.* **1** see OFFICER n. 1, 3, 4.

officialese /əfíshəleéz/ *n. derog.* the formal precise language characteristic of official documents.

officiant /əfíshənt/ *n.* a person who officiates at a religious ceremony.

officiate /əfísheeáyt/ *v.intr.* **1** act in an official capacity, esp. on a particular occasion. **2** perform a divine service or ceremony. □□ **officiation** /-áyshən/ *n.* **officiator** *n.* [med.L *officiare* perform a divine service (*officium*): see OFFICE]

■ **1** umpire, referee, judge, adjudicate, moderate, mediate; (*officiate at*) preside (over), direct, manage, chair, conduct, oversee, head (up), run, lead, supervise, superintend.

officinal /əfísinəl/ *adj.* **1 a** (of a medicine) kept ready for immediate dispensing. **b** made from the pharmacopoeia recipe (cf. MAGISTRAL). **c** (of a name) adopted in the pharmacopoeia. **2** (of an herb or drug) used in medicine. □□ **officinally** *adv.* [med.L *officinalis* f. L *officina* workshop]

officious /əfíshəs/ *adj.* **1** asserting one's authority aggressively; domineering. **2** intrusive or excessively enthusiastic in offering help, etc.; meddlesome. **3** *Diplomacy* informal, unofficial. □□ **officiously** *adv.* **officiousness** *n.* [L *officiosus* obliging f. *officium*: see OFFICE]

■ **1, 2** dictatorial, domineering, aggressive, insistent, persistent, demanding, importunate, intrusive, intruding, meddlesome, meddling, obtrusive, forward, bold, interfering.

offing /áwfing, óf-/ *n.* the more distant part of the sea in view. □ **in the offing** not far away; likely to appear or happen soon. [perh. f. OFF + -ING[1]]

■ □ **in the offing** see *impending* (IMPEND).

offish /áwfish, óf-/ *adj. colloq.* inclined to be aloof. □□ **offishly** *adv.* **offishness** *n.* [OFF: cf. *uppish*]

off-price /áwfprís, óf-/ *adj.* involving merchandise sold at a lower price than that recommended by the manufacturer.

offprint /áwfprint, óf-/ *n.* a printed copy of an article, etc., originally forming part of a larger publication.

offscreen /áwfskreén, óf-/ *adj. & adv.* ● *adj.* not appearing on a movie, television, or computer screen. ● *adv.* **1** without use of a screen. **2** outside the view presented by a filmed scene.

offset *n. & v.* ● *n.* /áwfset, óf-/ **1** a side shoot from a plant serving for propagation. **2** an offshoot or scion. **3** a compensation; a consideration or amount diminishing or neutralizing the effect of a contrary one. **4** *Archit.* a sloping ledge in a wall, etc., where the thickness of the part above is diminished. **5** a mountain spur. **6** a bend in a pipe, etc., to carry it past an obstacle. **7** (often *attrib.*) a method of printing in which ink is transferred from a plate or stone to a uniform rubber surface and from there to paper, etc. (*offset lithography*). **8** *Surveying* a short distance measured perpendicularly from the main line of measurement. ● *v.tr.* /áwfsét, óf-/ (**-setting**; *past* and *past part.* **-set**) **1** counterbalance, compensate. **2** place out of line. **3** print by the offset process.

■ *n.* **3** compensation, consideration, counterbalance, counteraction, check, equalizer, neutralizer. ● *v.* **1** compensate, counterbalance, countervail, counterpoise, counteract, balance (out), equalize, even (out or up), square, cancel (out), neutralize, nullify, make up (for), atone for, redress; repay, make amends or restitution for, make good, reimburse.

offshoot /áwfshoot, óf-/ *n.* **1 a** a side shoot or branch. **b** a collateral branch or descendant of a family. **2** something derivative.

■ **1 a** branch, spur; shoot, limb, bough, twig, stem, appendage, sucker, sprout, sprig, tendril, scion, offset. **b** descendant, relation, relative, kin, kindred. **2** outgrowth, development, branch, spin-off, by-product, derivative.

offshore /áwfsháwr, óf-/ *adj.* **1** situated at sea some distance from the shore. **2** (of the wind) blowing seaward. **3** (of goods, funds, etc.) made or registered abroad.

offside *adj. & n.* ● *adj.* /áwfsíd, óf-/ *Sports* (of a player in a field game or ice hockey) in a position, usu. ahead of the ball, that is not allowed if it affects play. ● *n.* /áwfsíd, óf-/ (often *attrib.*) esp. *Brit.* the right side of a vehicle, animal, etc.

offsider /áwfsídər, of-/ *n. Austral. colloq.* a partner, assistant, or deputy.

■ see DEPUTY 1.

offspring /áwfspring, óf-/ *n.* (*pl.* same) **1** a person's child or

/.../ **pronunciation**	● **part of speech**
□ **phrases, idioms, and compounds**	
□□ **derivatives**	■ **synonym section**
cross-references appear in SMALL CAPITALS or *italics*	

children or descendant(s). **2** an animal's young or descendant(s). **3** a result. [OE *offspring* f. OF from + *springan* SPRING *v.*]

■ **1, 2** child(ren), progeny, youngster(s), brood, young, successor(s), heir(s), descendant(s), *Law* issue, *archaic* seed.

offstage /áwfstayj, óf-/ *adj. & adv. Theatr.* not on the stage and so not visible to the audience.

oft /awft, oft/ *adv. archaic* or *literary* often (usu. in *comb.*: *oft-recurring*). [OE]

often /áwfən, áwftən, óf-/ *adv.* (**oftener, oftenest**) **1 a** frequently; many times. **b** at short intervals. **2** in many instances. □ **as often as not** in roughly half the instances. [ME: extended f. OFT, prob. after *selden* = SELDOM]

■ frequently, regularly, much, many times, usually, habitually, commonly, ordinarily, again and again, over and over again, time after time, repeatedly, time and (time) again, in many cases *or* instances, on numerous occasions, day in (and) day out, continually, *archaic or literary* oft, *colloq.* a lot. □ **as often as not** many a time, every so often, frequently, many times, *archaic or literary* oftentimes.

oftentimes /áwfəntimz, óf-/ *adv.* (also **ofttimes**) often.

ogam var. of OGHAM.

ogdoad /ógdō-ad/ *n.* a group of eight. [LL *ogdoas ogdoad-* f. Gk *ogdoas -ados* f. *ogdoos* eighth f. *oktō* eight]

ogee /ṓjeé, ṓjee/ *adj. & n. Archit.* ● *adj.* showing in section a double continuous S-shaped curve. ● *n.* an S-shaped line or molding. □ **ogee arch** an arch with two ogee curves meeting at the apex. □□ **ogee'd** *adj.* [app. f. OGIVE, as being the usu. molding in groin ribs]

ogham /ógəm, áw-/ *n.* (also **ogam**) **1** an ancient British and Irish alphabet of twenty characters formed by parallel strokes on either side of or across a continuous line. **2** an inscription in this alphabet. **3** each of its characters. [OIr. *ogam*, referred to the Irish god *Ogma*, its supposed inventor]

ogive /ṓjīv, ṓjív/ *n.* **1** a pointed or Gothic arch. **2** one of the diagonal groins or ribs of a vault. **3** an S-shaped line. **4** *Statistics* a cumulative frequency graph. □□ **ogival** *adj.* [ME f. F, of unkn. orig.]

ogle /ógəl/ *v. & n.* ● *v.* **1** *tr.* eye amorously or lecherously. **2** *intr.* look amorously. ● *n.* an amorous or lecherous look. □□ **ogler** *n.* [prob. LG or Du.: cf. LG *oegeln*, frequent. of *oegen* look at]

■ *v.* **1** eye, make (sheep's) eyes at, leer at, *colloq.* give a person the glad eye, look a person over, eye a person up. **2** leer, gape, gaze, goggle, stare, *colloq.* gawk. ● *n.* leer, stare, gape, goggle, *colloq.* glad eye.

ogre /ṓgər/ *n.* (*fem.* **ogress** /ṓgris/) **1** a human-eating giant in folklore, etc. **2** a terrifying person. □□ **ogreish** *adj.* (also **ogrish**). [F, first used by Perrault in 1697, of unkn. orig.]

■ monster, giant, fiend, demon, troll, man-eater, bogey, bogeyman, specter, gorgon, *archaic* bugbear; brute, sadist, villain, cad, scoundrel.

OH *abbr.* Ohio (in official postal use).

oh[1] /ō/ *int.* (also **O**) expressing surprise, pain, entreaty, etc. (*oh, what a mess*; *oh for a holiday*). □ **oh boy** expressing surprise, excitement, etc. **oh well** expressing resignation. [var. of o[4]]

oh[2] /ō/ *n.* = o[1] 2.

o.h.c. *abbr.* overhead camshaft.

ohm /ōm/ *n. Electr.* the SI unit of resistance, transmitting a current of one ampere when subjected to a potential difference of one volt. ¶ Symb.: Ω. □□ **ohmage** *n.* [G. S. *Ohm*, Ger. physicist d. 1854]

ohmmeter /ṓm-meetər/ *n.* an instrument for measuring electrical resistance.

OHMS *abbr.* on Her (or His) Majesty's Service.

Ohm's law /ōmz/ *n. Electr.* a law stating that current is proportional to voltage and inversely proportional to resistance. [see OHM]

oho /ōhṓ/ *int.* expressing surprise or exultation. [ME f. o[4] + HO]

-oholic var. of -AHOLIC.

ohone var. of OCHONE.

oi var. of OY.

-oid /oyd/ *suffix* forming adjectives and nouns, denoting form or resemblance (*asteroid*; *rhomboid*; *thyroid*). □□ **-oidal** *suffix* forming adjectives. **-oidally** *suffix* forming adverbs. [mod.L *-oides* f. Gk *-oeidēs* f. *eidos* form]

oidium /ō-ídeeəm/ *n.* (*pl.* **oidia** /-eeə/) spores formed by the breaking up of fungal hyphae into cells. [mod.L f. Gk *ōion* egg + *-idion* dimin. suffix]

oil /oyl/ *n. & v.* ● *n.* **1** any of various thick, viscous, usu. flammable liquids insoluble in water but soluble in organic solvents (see also *essential oil, fixed oil, mineral oil, volatile oil*). **2** petroleum. **3** using oil as fuel (*oil heater*). **4 a** (usu. in *pl.*) = *oil paint.* **b** *colloq.* a picture painted in oil paints. **5** (in *pl.*) = OILSKIN. ● *v.* **1** *tr.* apply oil to; lubricate. **2** *tr.* impregnate or treat with oil (*oiled silk*). **3** *tr. & intr.* supply with or take on oil as fuel. **4** *tr. & intr.* make (butter, grease, etc.) into or (of butter, etc.) become an oily liquid. □ **oil cake** a mass of compressed linseed, etc., left after oil has been extracted, used as fodder or manure. **oiled silk** silk made waterproof with oil. **oil-fired** using oil as fuel. **oil a person's palm** (or **hand**) bribe a person. **oil lamp** a lamp using oil as fuel. **oil meal** ground oil cake. **oil of vitriol** concentrated sulfuric acid. **oil paint** (or **color**) a mix of ground color pigment and oil. **oil painting 1** the art of painting in oil paints. **2** a picture painted in oil paints. **oil palm** either of two trees, *Elaeis guineensis* of W. Africa, or *E. oleifera* of the US, from which palm oil is extracted. **oil pan** the bottom section of an internal combustion engine's crankcase. **oil press** an apparatus for pressing oil from seeds, etc. **oil rig** esp. *Brit.* = *drill rig.* **oil sand** a stratum of porous rock yielding petroleum. **oil shale** a fine-grained rock from which oil can be extracted. **oil slick** a smooth patch of oil, esp. one on the sea. **oil tanker** a ship designed to carry oil in bulk. **oil well** a well from which petroleum is drawn. **oil the wheels** help make things go smoothly. **well-oiled 1** operating smoothly. **2** *colloq.* drunk. □□ **oilless** *adj.* [ME *oli, oile* f. AF, ONF *olie* = OF *oile*, etc. f. L *oleum* (olive) oil f. *olea* olive]

■ *n.* **1, 2** lubricant, grease, lubrication, unguent; fuel; petroleum. ● *v.* **1** lubricate, grease; see also SLICK *v.* □ **oil cake** linseed cake; cotton cake. **oil a person's palm** (or **hand**) see BRIBE *v.* **well-oiled 2** see DRUNK *adj.* 1.

oilbird /óylbərd/ *n.* a guacharo.

oilcan /óylkan/ *n.* a can containing oil, esp. one with a long spout for oiling machinery.

oilcloth /óylklawth, -kloth/ *n.* **1** a fabric waterproofed with oil. **2** an oilskin. **3** a canvas coated with linseed or other oil and used to cover a table or floor.

oiler /óylər/ *n.* **1** an oilcan for oiling machinery. **2** an oil tanker. **3 a** an oil well. **b** (in *pl.*) oilskin.

oilman /óylmən/ *n.* (*pl.* **-men**) a person who deals in oil.

oilpaper /óylpáypər/ *n.* a paper made transparent or waterproof by soaking in oil.

oilseed /óylseéd/ *n.* any of various seeds from cultivated crops yielding oil, e.g., rape, peanut, or cotton.

oilskin /óylskin/ *n.* **1** cloth waterproofed with oil. **2 a** a garment made of this. **b** (in *pl.*) a suit made of this.

■ **2 a** see SLICKER 2.

oilstone /óylstōn/ *n.* a fine-grained flat stone used with oil for sharpening flat tools, e.g., chisels, planes, etc. (cf. WHETSTONE).

oily /óylee/ *adj.* (**oilier, oiliest**) **1** of, like, or containing much oil. **2** covered or soaked with oil. **3** (of a manner, etc.) fawning, insinuating, unctuous. □□ **oilily** *adv.* **oiliness** *n.*

■ **1, 2** greasy, oleaginous, fat, fatty, adipose, sebaceous, soapy, buttery, *formal or joc.* pinguid; slippery, slimy, slithery, smooth, unctuous. **3** glib, smooth, unctuous, servile, fawning, bootlicking, obsequious, sycophantic, ingratiating, insinuating, flattering, hypocritical, *colloq.* smarmy, *joc.* saponaceous; suave, urbane, sophisticated.

oink /oyngk/ *v.intr.* (of a pig) make its characteristic grunt. [imit.]

ointment /óyntmənt/ *n.* a smooth greasy healing or cosmetic preparation for the skin. [ME *oignement, ointment*, f. OF *oignement* ult. f. L (as UNGUENT): *oint-* after obs. *oint* anoint f. OF, past part. of *oindre* ANOINT]

■ unguent, balm, salve, emollient, embrocation, demulcent, pomade, pomatum; *propr*. Vaseline; lotion, cream.

Oireachtas /awráwkhtəs/ *n.* the legislature of the Irish Republic: the president, the Dáil, and the Seanad. [Ir.]

Ojibwa /ōjíbway/ *n. & adj.* ● *n.* **1 a** a N. American people native to Canada and the eastern and central northern United States. **b** a member of this people. **2** the language of this people. ● *adj.* of or relating to this people or their language. Also called CHIPPEWA.

OK[1] /ốkáy/ *adj., adv., n., & v.* (also **okay**) *colloq.* ● *adj.* (often as *int.* expressing agreement or acquiescence) all right; satisfactory. ● *adv.* well; satisfactorily (*that worked out OK*). ● *n.* (*pl.* **OKs**) approval, sanction. ● *v.tr.* (**OK's, OK'd, OK'ing**) give an OK to; approve, sanction. [orig. US: prob. abbr. of *orl* (or *oll*) *korrect*, joc. form of 'all correct']

■ *adj.* satisfactory, acceptable, correct, suitable, all right, fine, good, in order, *Austral. & NZ sl.* jake; well, healthy, sound, in good condition, in fine fettle; adequate, mediocre, fair, middling, passable, tolerable, so-so, pretty good, not bad. ● *adv.* all right, reasonably, passably, tolerably; see also WELL[1] *adv.* 1. ● *n.* approval, sanction, ratification, authorization, endorsement, agreement, support, permission, consent, go-ahead, thumbs-up, *colloq.* green light. ● *v.* approve, sanction, ratify, authorize, endorse, support, allow, consent to, agree (to), rubber-stamp, give the go-ahead to, give the thumbs-up to, *colloq.* give the green light to.

OK[2] *abbr.* Oklahoma (in official postal use).

okapi /ōkáapee/ *n.* (*pl.* same or **okapis**) a ruminant mammal, *Okapia johnstoni*, native to N. and NE Zaïre, with a head resembling that of a giraffe and a body resembling that of a zebra, having a dark chestnut coat and transverse stripes on the hindquarters and upper legs only. [Mbuba]

okay var. of OK[1].

okeydoke /ốkeedốk/ *adj. & adv.* (also **okeydokey** /-dốkee/) *sl.* = OK[1]. [redupl.]

Okla. *abbr.* Oklahoma.

okra /ốkrə/ *n.* **1** a malvaceous African plant, *Abelmoschus esculentus*, yielding long ridged seedpods. **2** the seedpods eaten as a vegetable and used to thicken soups and stews. Also called GUMBO. [W.Afr. native name]

-ol[1] /awl, ol/ *suffix Chem.* the termination of *alcohol*, used in names of alcohols or analogous compounds (*methanol; phenol*).

-ol[2] /ol/ *comb. form* = -OLE. [L *oleum* oil]

old /ōld/ *adj.* (**older, oldest**) (cf. ELDER, ELDEST). **1 a** advanced in age; far on in the natural period of existence. **b** not young or near its beginning. **2** made long ago. **3** long in use. **4** worn or dilapidated or shabby from the passage of time. **5** having the characteristics (experience, feebleness, etc.) of age (*the child has an old face*). **6** practiced, inveterate (*an old offender; old in crime*). **7** belonging only or chiefly to the past; lingering on; former (*old times; haunted by old memories*). **8** dating from far back; long established or known; ancient; primeval (*old as the hills; old friends; an old family*). **9** (appended to a period of time) of age (*is four years old; a four-year-old boy; a four-year-old*). **10** (of language) as used in former or earliest times. **11** *colloq.* as a term of affection or casual reference (*good old Charlie; old shipmate*). **12** the former or first of two or more similar things (*our old house; wants his old job back*). □ **old age** the later part of normal life. **Old Bailey** the Central Criminal Court in London. **Old Bill** *Brit. sl.* the police. **old bird** a wary person. **old boy 1** *Brit.* a former male pupil of a school. **2** *colloq.* **a** an elderly man. **b** an affectionate form of address to a boy or man. **old-boy network** preferment in employment of those from a similar social background, esp. fellow alumni. **Old Church Slavonic** the Slavic language of *c.* 800–1000, as found in the Biblical translations of Cyril and Methodius. **the old country** the native country of colonists, etc. **Old**

English the English language up to *c.*1150. **old-fashioned** in or according to a fashion or tastes no longer current; antiquated. **Old French** the French language of the period before *c.*1400. **old fustic** see FUSTIC. **old girl 1** *colloq.* **a** an elderly woman. **b** an affectionate term of address to a girl or woman. **2** *Brit.* a former female pupil of a school. **Old Glory** the US national flag. **old gold** a dull brownish-gold color. **old guard** the original or past or conservative members of a group. **old hand** a person with much experience. **old hat** *colloq. adj.* tediously familiar or out-of-date. ● *n.* something tediously familiar or out-of-date. **Old High German** High German (see GERMAN) up to *c.*1200. **old lady** *colloq.* one's mother or wife. **old lag** *Brit.* see LAG[3]. **old maid 1** *derog.* an elderly unmarried woman. **2** a prim and fussy person. **3** a card game in which players try not to be left with an unpaired queen. **old-maidish** like an old maid. **old man** *colloq.* **1** one's husband or father. **2** one's employer or other person in authority over one. **3** esp. *Brit.* an affectionate form of address to a boy or man. **old-man's beard** a wild clematis, *Clematis vitalba*, with gray fluffy hairs around the seeds: also called *traveler's-joy*. **old master 1** a great artist of former times, esp. of the 13th–17th c. in Europe. **2** a painting by such a painter. **old moon** the moon in its last quarter, before the new moon. **Old Nick** *colloq.* the Devil. **Old Norse** see NORSE. **an old one** a familiar joke. **Old Pretender** James Stuart (1688–1766), son of James II and claimant to the British throne. **old school 1** traditional attitudes. **2** people having such attitudes. **old school tie** esp. *Brit.* **1** a necktie with a characteristic pattern worn by the pupils of a particular school. **2** the principle of excessive loyalty to traditional values. **old soldier** an experienced person, esp. in an arduous activity. **old stager** an experienced person, an old hand. **old style** of a date reckoned by the Julian calendar. **Old Testament** the part of the Christian Bible containing the scriptures of the Hebrews. **old-time** belonging to former times. **old-timer** a person with long experience or standing. **old wives' tale** a foolish or unscientific tradition or belief. **old woman** *colloq.* **1** one's wife or mother. **2** a fussy or timid man. **old-womanish** fussy and timid. **Old World** Europe, Asia, and Africa. **old-world** belonging to or associated with old times. □□ **oldish** *adj.* **oldness** *n.* [OE *ald* f. WG]

■ **1** elderly, aging, aged, advanced in years *or* age, long-lived, past one's *or* its prime, gray, getting on (in years), hoary, superannuated, *archaic* full of years, *colloq.* over-the-hill, past it. **2, 3, 10** ancient, antiquated, old-fashioned, fossil, prehistoric, obsolete, antique, outdated, out-of-date, old-time, dated, archaic, stale, outmoded, passé, *colloq.* antediluvian. **4** timeworn, decayed, dilapidated, ramshackle, disintegrated, crumbling, shabby, worn out, dusty, broken-down, tumbledown; disused, unused, cast-off, cast aside. **6** experienced, veteran, practiced, (well-)versed, knowledgeable, proficient, accomplished, adept, skilled, expert, old-time; inveterate. **7, 12** previous, preceding, prior, former, quondam, erstwhile, onetime, sometime, ex-. **8** long-standing, well-established, enduring, lasting, age-old, time-honored; former, bygone; early, ancient, primordial, primitive, *archaic* olden. □ **old age** see AGE *n.* 3. **old boy 2 b** friend, *colloq.* chum, pal, *Brit. sl.* old bean. **old-fashioned** old, antiquated, antique, passé, outmoded, outdated, unfashionable, stale, dated, out-of-date, tired, old-time, obsolete, obsolescent, dead, superseded, replaced, disused, out, *colloq.* old hat. **old hand** past master; see also ADEPT *n.* **old hat** (*adj.*) see *old-fashioned* above.

olden /ốldən/ *adj. archaic* of old; of a former age (esp. *in olden times*).

oldie /ốldee/ n. colloq. an old person or thing.
  ■ old person, senior citizen, senior, geriatric; retiree, pensioner, golden-ager, colloq. old-timer, old geezer, old fogey, geri.

oldster /ốldstər/ n. an old person. [OLD + -STER, after youngster]

-ole /ōl/ comb. form forming names of esp. heterocyclic compounds (indole). [L oleum oil]

oleaceous /ốleeáyshəs/ adj. of the plant family Oleaceae, including olive and jasmine. [mod.L Oleaceae f. L olea olive tree]

oleaginous /ốleeájinəs/ adj. 1 having the properties of or producing oil. 2 oily, greasy. 3 obsequious, ingratiating. [F oléagineux f. L oleaginus f. oleum oil]
  ■ 2 see OILY 1, 2.

oleander /ốleeándər/ n. an evergreen poisonous shrub, Nerium oleander, native to the Mediterranean and bearing clusters of white, pink, or red flowers. [med.L]

oleaster /ốleeástər/ n. any of various trees of the genus Elaeagnus, often thorny and with evergreen leathery foliage, esp. E. angustifolia bearing olive-shaped yellowish fruits. Also called Russian olive. [ME f. L f. olea olive tree: see -ASTER]

olecranon /ōlékrənon, ốlikráynən/ n. a bony prominence on the upper end of the ulna at the elbow. [Gk ōle(no)kranon f. ōlenē elbow + kranion head]

olefin /ốlifin/ n. (also **olefine**) Chem. = ALKENE. [F oléfiant oil-forming (with ref. to oily ethylene dichloride)]

oleic acid /ōleˈeik/ n. an unsaturated fatty acid present in many fats and soaps. □□ **oleate** /ốleeət/ n. [L oleum oil]

oleiferous /ốleeífərəs/ adj. yielding oil. [L oleum oil + -FEROUS]

oleo- /ốleeō/ comb. form oil. [L oleum oil]

oleograph /ốleeəgraf/ n. a print made to resemble an oil painting.

oleomargarine /ốleeōmaárjərin/ n. 1 a margarine made from vegetable oils. 2 a fatty substance extracted from beef fat and used in margarine.

oleometer /ốleeómitər/ n. an instrument for determining the density and purity of oils.

oleoresin /ốleeōrézin/ n. a natural or artificial mixture of essential oils and a resin, e.g., balsam.

oleum /ốleeəm/ n. concentrated sulfuric acid containing excess sulfur trioxide in solution forming a dense corrosive liquid. [L, = oil]

olfaction /olfákshən, ōl-/ n. the act or capacity of smelling; the sense of smell. □□ **olfactive** adj. [L olfactus a smell f. olēre to smell + facere fact- make]

olfactory /olfáktəree, ōl-/ adj. of or relating to the sense of smell (olfactory nerves). [L olfactare frequent. of olfacere (as OLFACTION)]

olibanum /ōlíbənəm/ n. an aromatic gum resin from any tree of the genus Boswellia, used as incense. [ME f. med.L f. LL libanus f. Gk libanos frankincense, of Semitic orig.]

oligarch /óligaark, ốli-/ n. a member of an oligarchy. [Gk oligarkhēs f. oligoi few + arkhō to rule]

oligarchy /óligaarkee, ốli-/ n. (pl. **-ies**) 1 government by a small group of people. 2 a nation governed in this way. 3 the members of such a government. □□ **oligarchic** /-gaárkik/ adj. **oligarchical** adj. **oligarchically** adv. [F oligarchie or med.L oligarchia f. Gk oligarkhia (as OLIGARCH)]

oligo- /óligō, ốli-/ comb. form few, slight. [Gk oligos small, oligoi few]

Oligocene /óligəseen, ốli-/ adj. & n. Geol. • adj. of or relating to the third epoch of the Tertiary period, with evidence of the first primates. ¶ Cf. Appendix VII. • n. this epoch or system. [as OLIGO- + Gk kainos new]

oligopoly /óligópəlee, ốli-/ n. (pl. **-ies**) a state of limited competition between a small number of producers or sellers. □□ **oligopolist** n. **oligopolistic** /-lístik/ adj. [OLIGO-, after MONOPOLY]

oligosaccharide /óligōsákərīd, ốli-/ n. any carbohydrate whose molecules are composed of a relatively small number of monosaccharide units.

oligotrophic /óligōtrốfik, -tróf-, ốli-/ adj. (of a lake, etc.) relatively poor in plant nutrients. □□ **oligotrophy** /-igótrəfee/ n.

olio /ốleeō/ n. (pl. **-os**) 1 a mixed dish; a stew of various meats and vegetables. 2 a hodgepodge or miscellany. [Sp. olla stew f. L olla cooking pot]
  ■ 1 see STEW¹ n. 1. 2 see MISCELLANY.

olivaceous /ốliváyshəs/ adj. olive-green; of a dusky yellowish green.

olivary /óliveree/ adj. Anat. olive-shaped; oval. [L olivarius (as OLIVE)]

olive /óliv/ n. & adj. • n. 1 (in full **olive tree**) any evergreen tree of the genus Olea, having dark-green, lance-shaped leathery leaves with silvery undersides, esp. O. europaea of the Mediterranean, and O. africana native to S. Africa. 2 the small oval fruit of this, having a hard stone and bitter flesh, green when unripe and bluish-black when ripe. 3 (in full **olive-green**) the grayish-green color of an unripe olive. 4 the wood of the olive tree. 5 Anat. each of a pair of olive-shaped swellings in the medulla oblongata. 6 a any olive-shaped gastropod of the genus Oliva. b the shell of this. 7 Brit. a slice of beef or veal made into a roll with stuffing inside and stewed. • adj. 1 colored like an unripe olive. 2 (of the complexion) yellowish-brown, sallow. □ **olive branch 1** the branch of an olive tree as a symbol of peace. 2 a gesture of reconciliation or friendship. **olive drab** the dull olive color of US Army uniforms. **olive oil** an oil extracted from olives used esp. in cookery. [ME f. OF f. L oliva f. Gk elaia f. elaion oil]

olivine /ốliveen/ n. Mineral. a naturally occurring form of magnesium-iron silicate, usu. olive-green and found in igneous rocks.

olla podrida /ốlə pədreédə, ốlyə/ n. = OLIO. [Sp., lit. 'rotten pot' (as OLIO + L putridus: cf. PUTRID]

Olmec /ốlmek, ốl-/ n. & adj. • n. 1 a N. American people native to the Gulf coast of Mexico. 2 a member of this people. • adj. of or relating to this people.

-ology /óləjee/ comb. form see -LOGY.

oloroso /ốlərốsō/ n. (pl. **-os**) a heavy dark medium-sweet sherry. [Sp., lit. 'fragrant']

Olympiad /ōlímpeead/ n. 1 a a period of four years between Olympic games, used by the ancient Greeks in dating events. b a four-yearly celebration of the ancient Olympic Games. 2 a celebration of the modern Olympic Games. 3 a regular international contest in chess, etc. [ME f. F Olympiade f. L Olympias Olympiad- f. Gk Olumpias Olumpiad- f. Olumpios: see OLYMPIAN, OLYMPIC]

Olympian /əlímpeeən, ōlím-/ adj. & n. • adj. 1 a of or associated with Mount Olympus in NE Greece, traditionally the home of the Greek gods. b celestial; godlike. 2 (of manners, etc.) magnificent; condescending; superior. 3 a of or relating to ancient Olympia in S. Greece. b = OLYMPIC. • n. 1 any of the pantheon of twelve gods regarded as living on Olympus. 2 a person of great attainments or of superhuman calm and detachment. [L Olympus or Olympia: see OLYMPIC]
  ■ adj. 2 see STANDOFFISH. • n. 1 (Olympians) see IMMORTAL n. 1b.

Olympic /əlímpik, ōlím-/ adj. & n. • adj. of ancient Olympia or the Olympic games. • n.pl. (**the Olympics**) the Olympic games. □ **Olympic games 1** an ancient Greek festival held at Olympia every four years, with athletic, literary, and musical competitions. 2 a modern international revival of this as a sports festival usu. held every four years since 1896 in different venues. [L Olympicus f. Gk Olumpikos of Olympus or Olympia (the latter being named from the games in honor of Zeus of Olympus)]

OM abbr. (in the UK) Order of Merit.

-oma /ốmə/ n. forming nouns denoting tumors and other abnormal growths (carcinoma). [mod.L f. Gk -ōma suffix denoting the result of verbal action]

Omaha /ốməhaw, -haa/ n. & adj. • n. 1 a a N. American people native to Nebraska. b a member of this people. 2 the language of this people. • adj. of or relating to this people or their language.

omasum /ōmáysəm/ n. (pl. **omasa** /-sə/) the third stomach of a ruminant. [L, = bullock's tripe]

OMB abbr. Office of Management and Budget.

ombre /ómbər/ n. (also **hombre**) a card game for three, popular in Europe in the 17th–18th c. [Sp. hombre man, with ref. to one player seeking to win the pool]

ombré /awnbráy/ adj. (of a fabric, etc.) having gradual shading of color from light to dark. [F, past part. of ombrer to shadow (as UMBER)]

ombro- /ómbrō/ comb. form rain. [Gk ombros rain shower]

ombudsman /ómbŏŏdzmən/ n. (pl. **-men**) an official appointed by a government to investigate individuals' complaints against public authorities, etc. [Sw., = legal representative]

-ome /ōm/ suffix forming nouns denoting objects or parts of a specified nature (rhizome; trichome). [var. of -OMA]

omega /ōmáygə, ŏmeegə, ōmégə/ n. **1** the last (24th) letter of the Greek alphabet (Ω, ω). **2** the last of a series; the final development. [Gk, ō mega = great O]

omelette /ómlit/ n. (also **omelet**) a dish of beaten eggs cooked in a frying pan and served plain or with a savory or sweet filling. [F omelette, obs. amelette by metathesis f. alumette var. of alumelle f. lemele knife blade f. L lamella: see LAMELLA]

omen /ōmən/ n. & v. ● n. **1** an occurrence or object regarded as portending good or evil. **2** prophetic significance (of good omen). ● v.tr. (usu. in passive) portend; foreshow. □□ **omened** adj. (also in comb.). [L omen ominis]
■ n. portent, augury, sign, token, foretoken, indication, harbinger, forewarning, premonition, foreshadowing, writing on the wall, prognostic, presage.

omentum /ōméntəm/ n. (pl. **omenta** /-tə/) a fold of peritoneum connecting the stomach with other abdominal organs. □□ **omental** adj. [L]

omertà /ōmairtaá/ n. a code of silence, esp. as practiced by the Mafia. [It., = conspiracy of silence]

omicron /ómikron, ŏmi-/ n. the fifteenth letter of the Greek alphabet (O, o). [Gk, o mikron = small o]

ominous /óminəs/ adj. **1** threatening; indicating disaster or difficulty. **2** of evil omen; inauspicious. **3** giving or being an omen. □□ **ominously** adv. **ominousness** n. [L ominosus (as OMEN)]
■ **1, 2** foreboding, threatening, fateful, dark, black, gloomy, lowering, menacing, sinister; unpropitious, unfavorable, ill-omened, ill-starred, unpromising, inauspicious, archaic star-crossed; minatory, warning, admonitory, cautionary. **3** portentous, prophetic, oracular, predictive, prognostic, augural, meaningful, premonitory, foreshadowing, foretelling, foretokening, indicative, formal vaticinal, mantic.

omission /ōmíshən/ n. **1** the act or an instance of omitting or being omitted. **2** something that has been omitted or overlooked. □□ **omissive** /-siv/ adj. [ME f. OF omission or LL omissio (as OMIT)]
■ **1, 2** noninclusion, leaving out or off, dropping, skipping, exclusion, exception, deletion, elimination, excision; failure, default, neglect, dereliction, oversight, shortcoming, negligence.

omit /ōmít/ v.tr. (**omitted**, **omitting**) **1** leave out; not insert or include. **2** leave undone. **3** (foll. by verbal noun or to + infin.) fail or neglect (omitted saying anything; omitted to say). □□ **omissible** /-mísəbəl/ adj. [ME f. L omittere omiss- (as OB-, mittere send)]
■ **1** leave out, exclude, skip, except, pass over. **2, 3** neglect, disregard, fail, forget, overlook, let slide, ignore.

ommatidium /ómətídeeəm/ n. (pl. **ommatidia** /-eeə/) a structural element in the compound eye of an insect. [mod.L f. Gk ommatidion dimin. of omma ommat- eye]

omni- /ómnee/ comb. form **1** all; of all things. **2** in all ways or places. [L f. omnis all]

omnibus /ómnibəs/ n. & adj. ● n. **1** formal = BUS. **2** a volume containing several novels, etc., previously published separately. ● adj. **1** serving several purposes at once. **2** comprising several items. [F f. L (dative pl. of omnis), = for all]

■ n. **1** see COACH n. 1.

omnicompetent /ómnikómpit'nt/ adj. **1** able to deal with all matters. **2** having jurisdiction in all cases. □□ **omnicompetence** /-t'ns/ n.

omnidirectional /ómneedirékshən'l/ adj. (of an antenna, etc.) receiving or transmitting in all directions.

omnifarious /ómnifáireeəs/ adj. of all sorts or varieties. [LL omnifarius (as OMNI-): cf. MULTIFARIOUS]

omnipotent /omnípət'nt/ adj. **1** having great or absolute power. **2** having great influence. □□ **omnipotence** /-t'ns/ n. **omnipotently** adv. [ME f. OF f. L omnipotens (as OMNI-, POTENT[1])]
■ **1** see DICTATORIAL 1. □□ **omnipotence** see SUPREMACY 1.

omnipresent /ómniprézənt/ adj. **1** present everywhere at the same time. **2** widely or constantly encountered. □□ **omnipresence** /-zəns/ n. [med.L omnipraesens (as OMNI-, PRESENT[1])]
■ **1** see UNIVERSAL adj. **2** see PREVALENT 1.
□□ **omnipresence** see prevalence (PREVALENT).

omniscient /omníshənt/ adj. knowing everything or much. □□ **omniscience** /-shəns/ n. **omnisciently** adv. [med.L omnisciens -entis (as OMNI-, scire know)]
■ all-knowing.

omnium gatherum /ómneeəm gáthərəm/ n. colloq. a miscellany or strange mixture. [mock L f. L omnium of all + GATHER]

omnivorous /omnívərəs/ adj. **1** feeding on many kinds of food, esp. on both plants and flesh. **2** making use of everything available. □□ **omnivore** /ómnivawr/ n. **omnivorously** adv. **omnivorousness** n. [L omnivorus (as OMNI-, -VOROUS)]

omphalo- /ómfəlō/ comb. form navel. [Gk (as OMPHALOS)]

omphalos /ómfələs/ n. Gk Antiq. **1** a conical stone (esp. that at Delphi) representing the navel of the earth. **2** a boss on a shield. **3** a center or hub. [Gk, = navel, boss, hub]

on /on, awn/ prep., adv., & adj. ● prep. **1** (so as to be) supported by or attached to or covering or enclosing (sat on a chair; stuck on the wall; rings on her fingers; leaned on his elbow). **2** carried with; about the person of (do you have a pen on you?). **3** (of time) exactly at; during; contemporaneously with (on May 29; on the hour; on schedule; working on Tuesday). **4** immediately after or before (I saw them on my return). **5** as a result of (on further examination I found this). **6** (so as to be) having membership, etc., of or residence at or in (she is on the board of directors; lives on the waterfront). **7** supported financially by (lives on $200 a week; lives on his wits). **8** close to; just by (a house on the sea; lives on the main road). **9** in the direction of; against. **10** so as to threaten; touching or striking (advanced on him; pulled a knife on me; a punch on the nose). **11** having as an axis or pivot (turned on his heels). **12** having as a basis or motive (works on a transmission; arrested on suspicion). **13** having as a standard, confirmation, or guarantee (had it on good authority; did it on purpose; I promise on my word). **14** concerning or about (writes on finance). **15** using or engaged with (is on the pill; here on business). **16** so as to affect (walked out on her). **17** at the expense of (the drinks are on me; the joke is on him). **18** added to (disaster on disaster). **19** in a specified manner or style (often foll. by the + adj. or noun: on the cheap; on the run). ● adv. **1** (so as to be) covering or in contact with something, esp. of clothes (put your boots on). **2** in the appropriate direction; toward something (look on). **3** further forward; in an advanced position or state (is getting on in years; it happened later on). **4** with continued movement or action (went plodding on; keeps on complaining). **5** in operation or activity (the light is on; the chase was on). **6** due to take place as planned (is the party still on?). **7** colloq. **a** (of a person) willing to participate or approve, or make a bet. **b** esp. Brit. (of an idea, proposal, etc.) practicable or acceptable (that's just not

/. . ./ pronunciation	● part of speech
□ phrases, idioms, and compounds	
□□ derivatives	■ synonym section
cross-references appear in SMALL CAPITALS or italics	

on). **8** being shown or performed (*a good movie on tonight*). **9** (of an actor) on stage. **10** (of an employee) on duty. **11** forward (*head on*). ● *adj. Baseball* positioned at a base as a runner. □ **be on about** refer to or discuss esp. tediously or persistently (*what are they on about?*). **be on at** *colloq.* nag or grumble at. **be on to 1** realize the significance or intentions of. **2** get in touch with (esp. by telephone). **on and off** intermittently; now and then. **on and on** continually; at tedious length. **on-line** *Computing* (of equipment or a process) directly controlled by or connected to a central processor. **on-off 1** (of a switch) having two positions, 'on' and 'off.' **2** = *on and off*. **on-screen** *adj.* appearing in a movie or on television. ● *adv.* **1** on or by means of a screen. **2** within the view presented by a filmed scene. **on time 1** punctual; punctually; in good time. **2** by means of installment payments (*buying new furniture on time*). **on to** to a position or state on or in contact with (cf. ONTO). [OE *on*, *an* f. Gmc]

-on /on/ *suffix Physics, Biochem., & Chem.* forming nouns denoting: **1** elementary particles (*meson*; *neutron*). **2** quanta (*photon*). **3** molecular units (*codon*). **4** substances (*interferon*; *parathion*). [ION, orig. in *electron*]

onager /ónəgər/ *n.* **1** a wild ass, esp. *Equus hemionus* of Central Asia. **2** *hist.* an ancient military engine for throwing rocks. [ME f. L f. Gk *onagros* f. *onos* ass + *agrios* wild]

onanism /ónənizəm/ *n.* **1** masturbation. **2** coitus interruptus. □□ **onanist** *n.* **onanistic** /-nístik/ *adj.* [F *onanisme* or mod.L *onanismus* f. *Onan* (Gen. 38:9)]

once /wuns/ *adv., conj., & n.* ● *adv.* **1** on one occasion or for one time only (*did not once say please; have read it once*). **2** at some point or period in the past (*could once play chess*). **3** ever or at all (*if you once forget it*). **4** multiplied by one; by one degree. ● *conj.* as soon as (*once they have gone we can relax*). ● *n.* one time or occasion (*just the once*). □ **all at once 1** without warning; suddenly. **2** all together. **at once 1** immediately. **2** simultaneously. **for once** on this (or that) occasion, even if at no other. **once again** (or **more**) another time. **once and for all** (or **once for all**) (done) in a final or conclusive manner, esp. so as to end hesitation or uncertainty. **once** (or **every once**) **in a while** from time to time; occasionally. **once or twice** a few times. **once-over** *colloq.* **1** a rapid preliminary inspection or piece of work. **2** an appraising glance. **once upon a time** at some vague time in the past. [ME *ānes*, *ōnes*, genit. of ONE]

■ *adv.* **1** one time, on one occasion, a single time. **2** once upon a time, formerly, (at) one time, on a former occasion, previously, before, in days gone by, in the (good) old days, long ago, some time ago, years *or* ages ago, *archaic* in olden days, *literary* in days of yore. **3** see EVER 2. ● *conj.* as soon as, when, the minute *or* moment. □ **all at once** see *suddenly* (SUDDEN). **at once 1** immediately, straightaway, right away, directly, without delay, promptly, instantly, posthaste; in a wink, in the twinkling of an eye, in a minute *or* moment *or* second *or* split second, in no time (at all), in a trice, in two shakes (of a lamb's tail), *colloq.* before you can say Jack Robinson, in a jiff *or* jiffy. **2** together, at the same time, simultaneously, at a stroke, in the same instant, in the same breath, *colloq.* at *or* in one go, at a go. **once again** (or **more**) again, one more time, another time, over (again), all over again. **once and for all** (or **once for all**) finally, positively, definitely, decidedly, conclusively, for good. **once** (or **every once**) **in a while** occasionally, (every) now and then, now and again, at times, sometimes, periodically, from time to time, at intervals, sporadically. **once-over** examination, assessment, check, inspection, survey, scrutiny, vetting, appraisal, evaluation; see also SCAN *n.* 1, LEER[1] *n.*

oncer /wúnsər/ *n.* **1** *Brit. hist. sl.* a one-pound note. **2** *Brit. colloq.* a thing that occurs only once. **3** *Austral. colloq.* an election of an MP likely to serve only one term.

onchocerciasis /óngkōsərkíəsis/ *n.* a tropical disease of the skin caused by a parasitic worm, the larvae of which can

migrate into the eye and cause blindness. Also called *river blindness*.

onco- /óngkō/ *comb. form Med.* tumor. [Gk *onkos* mass]

oncogene /óngkəjeen/ *n.* a gene that can transform a cell into a tumor cell. □□ **oncogenic** /-jénik/ *adj.* **oncogenous** /-kójinəs/ *adj.*

oncology /ongkóləjee/ *n. Med.* the study of tumors.

oncoming /ónkuming, áwn-/ *adj. & n.* ● *adj.* approaching from the front. ● *n.* an approach or onset.
■ *adj.* advancing, arriving, coming, nearing, approaching, imminent. ● *n.* onset, beginning, nearing, arrival, advance, approach.

oncost /ónkawst, áwn-/ *n. Brit.* an overhead expense.

one /wun/ *adj., n., & pron.* ● *adj.* **1** single and integral in number. **2** (with a noun implied) a single person or thing of the kind expressed or implied (*one of the best; a nasty one*). **3** a particular but undefined, esp. as contrasted with another (*that is one view; one thing after another*). **b** *colloq.* (as an emphatic) a noteworthy example of (*that is one difficult question*). **4** only such (*the one man who can do it*). **5** forming a unity (*one and undivided*). **6** identical; the same (*of one opinion*). ● *n.* **1 a** the lowest cardinal number. **b** a thing numbered with it. **2** unity; a unit (*one is half of two; came in ones and twos*). **3** a single thing or person or example (often referring to a noun previously expressed or implied: *the big dog and the small one*). **4** *colloq.* an alcoholic drink (*have a quick one; have one on me*). **5** a story or joke (*the one about the frog*). ● *pron.* **1** a person of a specified kind (*loved ones; like one possessed*). **2** any person, as representing people in general (*one is bound to lose in the end*). **3** I, me (*one would like to help*). ¶ Often regarded as an affectation. □ **all one** (often foll. by *to*) a matter of indifference. **at one** in agreement. **for one** being one, even if the only one (*I for one do not believe it*). **for one thing** as a single consideration, ignoring others. **one and the same** the same; (the) identical. **one another** each the other or others (as a formula of reciprocity: *love one another*). **one-armed bandit** *colloq.* a slot machine worked by a long handle at the side. **one by one** singly, successively. **one day 1** on an unspecified day. **2** at some unspecified future date. **one-horse 1** using a single horse. **2** *colloq.* small, poorly equipped. **one-liner** *colloq.* a single brief sentence, often witty or apposite. **one-man** involving, done, or operated by only one person. **one-night stand 1** a single performance of a play, etc., in a place. **2** *colloq.* a sexual liaison lasting only one night. **one-off** esp. *Brit. colloq. adj.* made or done as the only one; not repeated. ● *n.* the only example of a manufactured product; something not repeated. **one-on-one 1** of or involving a direct confrontation or communication between two persons. **2** *Sports* playing directly against one opposing player. **one or two** see OR[1]. **one-piece** (of a bathing suit, etc.) made as a single garment. **one-sided 1** favoring one side in a dispute; unfair; partial. **2** having or occurring on one side only. **3** larger or more developed on one side. **one-sidedly** in a one-sided manner. **one-sidedness** the act or state of being one-sided. **one-step** *Dancing* a vigorous kind of foxtrot in three-quarter time. **one-to-one** with one member of one group corresponding to one of another. **one-track mind** a mind preoccupied with one subject. **one-two** *colloq.* **1** *Boxing* the delivery of two punches in quick succession. **2** *Soccer*, etc. a series of reciprocal passes between two advancing players. **one up** (often foll. by *on*) *colloq.* having a particular advantage. **one-upmanship** *colloq.* the art of maintaining a psychological advantage. **one-way** allowing movement or travel in one direction only. [OE *ān* f. Gmc]
■ *adj.* **3 a** a particular, a certain, a given, a specific. **b** *colloq.* some. **4** single, lone, solitary, individual, sole, only. **5** unified, united, inseparable, joined, undivided, one and the same, identical, equal, at one, harmonious, in unison, whole, entire, complete. ● *n.* **5** joke, story, anecdote, chestnut, one-liner, gag, *colloq.* funny. ● *pron.* **1, 2** a person, an individual, a man *or* a woman, everybody, everyone, anybody, anyone; people. □ **at one** agreed, united, in accord *or* agreement, in harmony. **one by one** see *singly* (SINGLE). **one-off**

(*adj.*) see UNIQUE *adj.* 1. (*n.*) rarity, special, exclusive, original. **one-sided 1** partial, biased, partisan, prejudiced, bigoted, unfair, unjust, inequitable, close-minded, narrow-minded, intolerant. **2** unilateral, independent; exclusionary, exclusive. **3** lopsided, unbalanced, unequal, unequalized, uneven, disproportionate; crooked, askew, *colloq.* cockeyed. **one up** ahead, in the lead, at an advantage, on top, one step ahead.

-one /ōn/ *suffix Chem.* forming nouns denoting various compounds, esp. ketones (*acetone*). [Gk *-ōnē* fem. patronymic]

onefold /wúnfōld/ *adj.* consisting of only one member or element; simple.

Oneida /ōnídə/ *n. & adj.* ● *n.***1a** a N. American people native to New York state. **b** a member of this people. **2** the language of this people. ● *adj.* of or relating to this people or their language.

oneiric /ōnírik/ *adj.* of or relating to dreams or dreaming. [Gk *oneiros* dream]

oneiro- /ōnírō/ *comb. form* dream. [Gk *oneiros* dream]

oneiromancy /ōnírəmansee/ *n.* the interpretation of dreams.

oneness /wún-nis/ *n.* **1** the fact or state of being one; singleness. **2** uniqueness. **3** agreement; unity of opinion. **4** identity; sameness.

oner /wúnər/ *n. Brit. sl.* **1** one pound (of money). **2** a remarkable person or thing.

onerous /ónərəs, ōn-/ *adj.* **1** burdensome; causing or requiring trouble. **2** *Law* involving heavy obligations. □□ **onerously** *adv.* **onerousness** *n.* [ME f. OF *onereus* f. L *onerosus* f. *onus oneris* burden]

■ **1** see *burdensome* (BURDEN). □□ **onerously** see *severely* (SEVERE). **onerousness** see *severity* (SEVERE).

oneself /wunsélf/ *pron.* the reflexive and (in apposition) emphatic form of *one* (*kill oneself; one has to do it oneself*).

onetime /wúntīm/ *adj. & adv.* former.

ongoing /ón-gōing, áwn-/ *adj.* **1** continuing to exist or be operative, etc. **2** that is or are in progress (*ongoing discussions*). □□ **ongoingness** *n.*

■ developing, evolving, growing, successive, unfolding, progressing, progressive; continuing, continued, continuous, unbroken, uninterrupted, running.

onion /únyən/ *n.* **1** a liliaceous plant, *Allium cepa*, having a short stem and bearing greenish-white flowers. **2** the swollen bulb of this with many concentric skins used in cooking, pickling, etc. □ **know one's onions** *colloq.* be fully knowledgeable or experienced. **onion dome** a bulbous dome on a church, palace, etc. □□ **oniony** *adj.* [ME f. AF *union*, OF *oignon* ult. f. L *unio -onis*]

onionskin /únyənskin/ *n.* **1** the brown outermost skin or any outer skin of an onion. **2** a type of thin, smooth, translucent paper.

onkus /óngkəs/ *adj. Austral. colloq.* unpleasant; disorganized. [20th c.: orig. unkn.]

■ see HORRIBLE 2.

onlooker /ónlŏŏkər, áwn-/ *n.* a nonparticipating observer; a spectator. □□ **onlooking** *adj.*

■ spectator, observer, looker-on, eyewitness, witness, watcher, viewer; bystander, passerby.

only /ónlee/ *adv., adj., & conj.* ● *adv.* **1** solely, merely, exclusively; and no one or nothing more besides (*I only want to sit down; will only make matters worse; needed six only; is only a child*). **2** no longer ago than (*saw them only yesterday*). **3** not until (*arrives only on Tuesday*). **4** with no better result than (*hurried home only to find her gone*). ¶ In informal English *only* is usually placed between the subject and verb regardless of what it refers to (e.g., *I only want to talk to you*); in more formal English it is often placed more exactly, esp. to avoid ambiguity (e.g., *I want to talk only to you*). In speech, intonation usually serves to clarify the sense. ● *attrib.adj.* **1** existing alone of its or their kind (*their only son*). **2** best or alone worth knowing (*the only place to eat*). ● *conj. colloq.* **1** except that; but for the fact that (*I would go, only I feel ill*). **2** but then (as an extra consideration) (*he always makes promises, only he never keeps them*). □ **only-begotten** *literary*

begotten as the only child. **only too** extremely (*is only too willing*). [OE *ānlic*, *ǣnlic*, ME *onliche* (as ONE, -LY²)]

■ *adv.* **1** solely, just, exclusively, alone; merely, simply, barely, at best, at worst, at most, purely, not *or* no more than, not *or* no greater than. ● *attrib.adj.* sole, single, solitary, lone, one and only, exclusive, unique, nonpareil. ● *conj.* except (that), but, however, *archaic or poet.* save that. □ **only too** see *extremely* (EXTREME).

onomastic /ónəmástik/ *adj.* relating to names or nomenclature. [Gk *onomastikos* f. *onoma* name]

onomastics /ónəmástiks/ *n.pl.* (treated as *sing.*) the study of the origin and formation of (esp. personal) proper names.

onomatopoeia /ónəmátəpéeə, -maátə-/ *n.* **1** the formation of a word from a sound associated with what is named (e.g., *cuckoo, sizzle*). **2** the use of such words. □□ **onomatopoeic** *adj.* **onomatopoeically** *adv.* [LL f. Gk *onomatopoiia* word making f. *onoma -matos* name + *poieō* make]

Onondaga /aanəndáwgə, -day-, -daa-/ *n. & adj.* ● *n.***1a** a N. American people native to New York state. **b** a member of these people. **2** the language of these people. ● *adj.* of or relating to these people or their language.

onrush /ónrush, áwn-/ *n.* an onward rush.

■ see ONSET 1.

onset /ónset, áwn-/ *n.* **1** an attack. **2** a beginning, esp. an energetic or determined one.

■ **1** attack, assault, onrush, onslaught, charge, strike, hit, raid, storming, sally, sortie. **2** beginning, start, initiation, inauguration, launch, inception, dawn, origin, genesis, appearance, début, *formal* commencement, *rhet.* birth.

onshore /ónsháwr, áwn-/ *adj. & adv.* ● *adj.* **1** on the shore. **2** (of the wind) blowing from the sea toward the land. ● *adv.* ashore.

onside /ónsíd, áwn-/ *adj.* (of a player in a field or ice hockey game) in a lawful position; not offside.

onslaught /ónslawt, áwn-/ *n.* a fierce attack. [earlier *anslaight* f. MDu. *aenslag* f. *aen* on + *slag* blow, with assim. to obs. *slaught* slaughter]

■ see ATTACK *n.* 1.

onstage /ónstáyj/ *Theatr. adj. & adv.* on the stage; visible to the audience.

Ont. *abbr.* Ontario.

-ont /ont/ *comb. form Biol.* denoting an individual of a specified type (*symbiont*). [Gk *ōn ont-* being]

onto /óntoo, áwn-/ *prep. disp.* to a position or state on or in contact with (cf. *on to*). ¶ The form *onto* is still not fully accepted in the way that *into* is, although it is in wide use. It is, however, useful in distinguishing sense as between *we drove on to the beach* (i.e., in that direction) and *we drove onto the beach* (i.e., in contact with it).

ontogenesis /óntəjénisis/ *n.* the origin and development of an individual (cf. PHYLOGENESIS). □□ **ontogenetic** /-jinétik/ *adj.* **ontogenetically** /-jinétiklee/ *adv.* [formed as ONTOGENY + Gk *genesis* birth]

ontogeny /ontójənee/ *n.* = ONTOGENESIS. □□ **ontogenic** /-təjénik/ *adj.* **ontogenically** *adv.* [Gk *ōn ont-* being, pres. part. of *eimi* be + -GENY]

ontology /ontóləjee/ *n.* the branch of metaphysics dealing with the nature of being. □□ **ontological** /-təlójikəl/ *adj.* **ontologically** *adv.* **ontologist** *n.* [mod.L *ontologia* f. Gk *ōn ont-* being + -LOGY]

onus /ónəs/ *n.* (*pl.* **onuses**) a burden, duty, or responsibility. [L]

■ see BURDEN *n.* 1, 2.

onward /ónwərd, áwn-/ *adv. & adj.* ● *adv.* (also **onwards**) **1** further on. **2** toward the front. **3** with advancing motion. ● *adj.* directed onward.

■ *adv.* forward, ahead, in front, on, forth.

/.../ **pronunciation**	● **part of speech**
□ **phrases, idioms, and compounds**	
□□ **derivatives**	■ **synonym section**
cross-references appear in SMALL CAPITALS or *italics*	

● *adj.* forward, advancing, progressive, progressing.

onyx /óniks/ *n.* a semiprecious variety of agate with different colors in layers. □ **onyx marble** banded calcite, etc., used as a decorative material. [ME f. OF *oniche*, *onix* f. L f. Gk *onux* fingernail, onyx]

oo- /óə/ *comb. form Biol.* egg, ovum. [Gk *ōion* egg]

oocyte /óəsīt/ *n.* an immature ovum in an ovary.

oodles /óōd'lz/ *n.pl. colloq.* a very great amount. [19th-c. US: orig. unkn.]

■ see LOT *n.* 1.

oof /óōf/ *n. esp. Brit. sl.* money, cash. [Yiddish *ooftisch*, G *auf dem Tische* on the table (of money in gambling)]

■ see MONEY 1.

oofy /óōfee/ *adj. Brit. sl.* rich, wealthy. □□ **oofiness** *n.*

■ see RICH 1.

oogamous /ō-ógəməs/ *adj.* reproducing by the union of mobile male and immobile female cells. □□ **oogamy** *n.*

oogenesis /óəjénisis/ *n.* the production or development of an ovum.

ooh /óō/ *int.* expressing surprise, delight, pain, etc. [natural exclam.]

oolite /óəlīt/ *n.* **1** a sedimentary rock, usu. limestone, consisting of rounded grains made up of concentric layers. **2** = OOLITH. □□ **oolitic** /-lítik/ *adj.* [F *oölithe* (as OO-, -LITE)]

oolith /óəlith/ *n.* any of the rounded grains making up oolite.

oology /ō-óləjee/ *n.* the study or collecting of birds' eggs. □□ **oological** /óəlójikəl/ *adj.* **oologist** *n.*

oolong /óōlawng, -long/ *n.* a dark kind of cured China tea. [Chin. *wulong* black dragon]

oompah /óōmpaa/ *n. colloq.* the rhythmical sound of deep-toned brass instruments in a band. [imit.]

oomph /óōmf/ *n. sl.* **1** energy; enthusiasm. **2** attractiveness; esp. sexual appeal. [20th c.: orig. uncert.]

■ see VITALITY 1.

-oon /óōn/ *suffix* forming nouns, orig. from French words in stressed *-on* (*balloon*; *buffoon*). ¶ Replaced by *-on* in recent borrowings and those with unstressed *-on* (*baron*). [L *-o -onis*, sometimes via It. *-one*]

oops /óōps, ōōps/ *int. colloq.* expressing surprise or apology, esp. on making an obvious mistake. [natural exclam.]

oosperm /óəspərm/ *n.* a fertilized ovum.

ooze¹ /óōz/ *v. & n.* ● *v.* **1** *intr.* (of fluid) pass slowly through the pores of a body. **2** *intr.* trickle or leak slowly out. **3** *intr.* (of a substance) exude moisture. **4** *tr.* exude or exhibit (a feeling) liberally (*oozed sympathy*). ● *n.* **1** a sluggish flow or exudation. **2** an infusion of oak bark or other vegetable matter, used in tanning. □□ **oozy** *adj.* **oozily** *adv.* **ooziness** *n.* [orig. as noun (sense 2), f. OE *wōs* juice, sap]

■ *v.* exude; weep, seep, secrete, bleed, leak, drain, trickle; discharge.

ooze² /óōz/ *n.* **1** a deposit of wet mud or slime, esp. at the bottom of a river, lake, or estuary. **2** a bog or marsh; soft muddy ground. □□ **oozy** *adj.* [OE *wāse*]

■ **1** slime, muck, mud, mire, silt, sludge, sediment, slush, goo, *sl.* gunk, glop.

OP *abbr.* **1** *RC Ch.* Order of Preachers (Dominican). **2** observation post. **3** *Brit.* opposite prompt.

op. /op/ *abbr.* **1** *Mus.* opus. **2** operator.

o.p. *abbr.* **1** out of print. **2** overproof.

op- /op/ *prefix* assim. form of OB- before *p.*

opacify /ópásifī/ *v.tr.* & *intr.* (**-ies**, **-ied**) make or become opaque. □□ **opacifier** *n.*

opacity /ópásitee/ *n.* **1 a** the state of being opaque. **b** degree to which something is opaque. **2** obscurity of meaning. **3** obtuseness of understanding. [F *opacité* f. L *opacitas -tatis* (as OPAQUE)]

■ **1** opaqueness, darkness, murkiness, dimness, obscurity, impermeability, impenetrability. **2** opaqueness, obscurity, density, impenetrability, unintelligibility, unintelligibleness, indefiniteness, vagueness, reconditeness, abstruseness, ambiguity, equivocation, mystification. **3** opaqueness, stupidity, dullness, denseness, obtuseness, *colloq.* thickness.

opah /ópə/ *n.* a large rare deep-sea fish, *Lampris guttatus*, usu.

having a silver-blue back with white spots and crimson fins. Also called MOONFISH. [W. Afr. name]

opal /ópəl/ *n.* a quartzlike form of hydrated silica, usu. white or colorless and sometimes showing changing colors, often used as a gemstone. □ **opal glass** a semitranslucent white glass. [F *opale* or L *opalus* prob. ult. f. Skr. *upalas* precious stone]

opalescent /ópəlésənt/ *adj.* showing changing colors like an opal. □□ **opalesce** *v.intr.* **opalescence** /-səns/ *n.*

■ opaline, iridescent, lustrous; nacreous, pearly.

opaline /ópəlin, -leen, -līn/ *adj. & n.* ● *adj.* opallike; opalescent; iridescent. ● *n.* opal glass.

■ *adj.* see OPALESCENT.

opaque /ópáyk/ *adj. & n.* ● *adj.* (**opaquer**, **opaquest**) **1** not transmitting light. **2** impenetrable to sight. **3** obscure; not lucid. **4** obtuse; dull-witted. ● *n.* **1** an opaque thing or substance. **2** a substance for producing opaque areas on negatives. □□ **opaquely** *adv.* **opaqueness** *n.* [ME *opak* f. L *opacus*: spelling now assim. to F]

■ *adj.* **1, 2** dark, murky, dim, turbid, muddy, cloudy, obscure, obscured, obfuscated, black, impermeable, impenetrable, clouded, nontransparent, nontranslucent, hazy, blurred, blurry, smoky. **3** unclear, vague, indefinite, obscure, unfathomable, unplumbable, baffling, mystifying, ambiguous, equivocal, impenetrable, cryptic, enigmatic, puzzling, perplexing, mysterious, elusive, abstruse, arcane, recondite. **4** unintelligent, dense, dull, obtuse, stupid, dull-witted, stolid, thickheaded, blockheaded, dunderheaded, slow, doltish, backward, cloddish, *colloq.* thick.

op art /op/ *n. colloq.* = optical art. [abbr.]

op. cit. *abbr.* in the work already quoted. [L *opere citato*]

OPEC /ópek/ *abbr.* Organization of Petroleum Exporting Countries.

open /ópən/ *adj., v., & n.* ● *adj.* **1** not closed nor locked nor blocked up; allowing entrance or passage or access. **2 a** (of a room, field, or other area) having its door or gate in a position allowing access, or part of its confining boundary removed. **b** (of a container) not fastened nor sealed; in a position or with the lid, etc., in a position allowing access to the inside part. **3** unenclosed; unconfined; unobstructed (*the open road*; *open views*). **4 a** uncovered, bare, exposed (*open drain*; *open wound*). **b** *Sports* (of a goal or other object of attack) unprotected; vulnerable. **5** undisguised; public; manifest; not exclusive nor limited (*open scandal*; *open hostilities*). **6** expanded, unfolded, or spread out (*had the map open on the table*). **7** (of a fabric) not close; with gaps or intervals. **8 a** (of a person) frank and communicative. **b** (of the mind) accessible to new ideas; unprejudiced or undecided. **c** generous. **9 a** (of an exhibition, shop, etc.) accessible to visitors or customers; ready for business. **b** (of a meeting) admitting all, not restricted to members, etc. **10 a** (of a race, competition, scholarship, etc.) unrestricted as to who may compete. **b** (of a champion, scholar, etc.) having won such a contest. **11** (of government) conducted in an informative manner receptive to inquiry, criticism, etc., from the public. **12** (foll. by *to*) **a** willing to receive (*is open to offers*). **b** (of a choice, offer, or opportunity) still available (*there are three courses open to us*). **c** likely to suffer from or be affected by (*open to abuse*). **13 a** (of the mouth) with lips apart, esp. in surprise or incomprehension. **b** (of the ears or eyes) eagerly attentive. **14** *Mus.* **a** (of a string) allowed to vibrate along its whole length. **b** (of a pipe) unstopped at each end. **c** (of a note) sounded from an open string or pipe. **15** (of an electrical circuit) having a break in the conducting path. **16** (of the bowels) not constipated. **17** (of a return ticket) not restricted as to day of travel. **18** (of a boat) without a deck. **19** (of a river or harbor) free of ice. **20** (of the weather or winter) free of frost. **21** *Phonet.* **a** (of a vowel) produced with a relatively wide opening of the mouth. **b** (of a syllable) ending in a vowel. **22** (of a town, city, etc.) not defended even if attacked. ● *v.* **1** *tr.* & *intr.* make or become open or more open. **2 a** *tr.* change from a closed or fastened position so as to allow access (*opened the door*; *opened the* box). **b** *intr.* (of a door, lid, etc.) have its position changed to allow access (*the door opened slowly*). **3** *tr.* remove the sealing or fastening element of (a container) to get access to the contents (*opened the envelope*). **4** *intr.* (foll. by *into, on to*, etc.) (of a door, room, etc.) afford access as specified (*opened on to a large garden*). **5 a** *tr.* start or establish or set going (a business, activity, etc.). **b** *intr.* be initiated; make a start (*the session opens tomorrow; the story opens with a murder*). **c** *tr.* (of a counsel in a court of law) make a preliminary statement in (a case) before calling witnesses. **6** *tr.* **a** spread out or unfold (a map, newspaper, etc.). **b** (often *absol.*) refer to the contents of (a book). **7** *intr.* (often foll. by *with*) (of a person) begin speaking, writing, etc. (*he opened with a warning*). **8** *intr.* (of a prospect) come into view; be revealed. **9** *tr.* **a** reveal or communicate (one's feelings, intentions, etc.). **b** make available, provide. **10** *tr.* make (one's mind, heart, etc.) more sympathetic or enlightened. **11** *tr.* ceremonially declare (a building, etc.) to be completed and in use. **12** *tr.* break up (ground) with a plow, etc. **13** *tr.* cause evacuation of (the bowels). **14** *Naut.* **a** *tr.* get a view of by change of position. **b** *intr.* come into full view. ● *n.* **1** (prec. by *the*) **a** open space or country or air. **b** public notice or view; general attention (esp. *into the open*). **2** an open championship, competition, or scholarship. □ **be open with** speak frankly to. **keep open house** see HOUSE. **open air** (usu. prec. by *the*) a free or unenclosed space outdoors. **open-air** (*attrib.*) out of doors. **open-and-shut** (of an argument, case, etc.) straightforward and conclusive. **open-armed** cordial; warmly receptive. **open book** a person who is easily understood. **open door** free admission of foreign trade and immigrants. **open-door** *adj.* open, accessible, public. **open the door to** see DOOR. **open-ended** having no predetermined limit or boundary. **open a person's eyes** see EYE. **open-eyed 1** with the eyes open. **2** alert; watchful. **open-faced** having a frank or ingenuous expression. **open-hearted** frank and kindly. **open-heartedness** an openhearted quality. **open-hearth process** a process of steel manufacture, using a shallow reverberatory furnace. **open-heart surgery** surgery with the heart exposed and the blood made to bypass it. **open house 1** welcome or hospitality for all visitors. **2** time when real estate offered for sale is open to prospective buyers. **open ice** ice through which navigation is possible. **open letter** a letter, esp. of protest, addressed to an individual and published in a newspaper or journal. **open market** an unrestricted market with free competition of buyers and sellers. **open-minded** accessible to new ideas; unprejudiced. **open-mindedly** in an open-minded manner. **open-mindedness** the quality of being open-minded. **open-mouthed** with the mouth open, esp. in surprise. **open out 1** unfold; spread out. **2** develop, expand. **3** *Brit.* become communicative. **4** *Brit.* accelerate. **open-plan** (usu. *attrib.*) (of a house, office, etc.) having large undivided rooms. **open question** a matter on which differences of opinion are legitimate. **open-reel** (of a tape recorder) having reels of tape requiring individual threading, as distinct from a cassette. **open sandwich** a sandwich without a top slice of bread. **open sea** an expanse of sea away from land. **open season** the season when restrictions on the hunting of game, etc., are lifted. **open secret** a supposed secret that is known to many people. **open sesame** see SESAME. **open shop 1** a business, etc., where employees do not have to be members of a labor union (opp. *closed shop*). **2** this system. **open society** a society with wide dissemination of information and freedom of belief. **open-toed** (of a shoe) leaving the toes partly bare. **open up 1** unlock (premises). **2** make accessible. **3** reveal; bring to notice. **4** accelerate, esp. a motor vehicle. **5** begin shooting or sounding. **6** become communicative. **open verdict** esp. *Brit.* a verdict affirming that a crime has been committed but not specifying the criminal or (in case of violent death) the cause. **with open arms** see ARM[1]. □□ **openable** *adj.* **openness** *n.* [OE *open*]

■ *adj.* **1–4, 13, 20** ajar, gaping, agape; unfastened, unlocked, unbarred, unbolted, unlatched, unclosed; yawning, uncovered, revealed, unsealed, exposed, bare, vulnerable; unprotected, unsheltered, undefended, unfortified; unwrapped, unsealed, unfastened; clear, unobstructed, wide open, uncluttered, roomy, spacious, extensive, expansive; treeless, uncrowded, unfenced; unenclosed, unconfined; ice-free, navigable, unblocked, passable; attentive. **5** exposed, public, well-known, widely known, unconcealed, undisguised; evident, obvious, conspicuous, manifest, clear, unconcealed, unequivocal, plain, palpable, apparent, patent, downright, out-and-out, blatant, flagrant, glaring, brazen. **6** unfolded, extended, spread (out), outstretched, outspread, expanded. **7** open-weave, loose, loosely woven, rough, coarse. **8 a** unreserved, candid, frank, outspoken, communicative, straightforward, forthright, direct, honest, sincere, guileless, artless, fair. **b** receptive, open-minded, flexible, amenable, persuasible, persuadable, pliant, willing, responsive. **c** generous, charitable, unreserved, openhanded, munificent, magnanimous, bighearted, beneficent, unselfish, unstinting, humanitarian, altruistic, *poet.* bounteous. **9–11** free, accessible, public, available; obtainable; unrestricted, unobstructed, unencumbered, unimpeded, unhindered, unhampered, unregulated, unconditional, unqualified; unrestrained, unconstrained, uninhibited, unreserved; liberal. **12 b** available, accessible; unfilled, vacant; untaken. **c** liable, subject, susceptible, exposed, inclined, predisposed, disposed. **17** unscheduled, unbooked, unspoken for, unreserved, uncommitted, free, unpromised. ● *v.* **1–3** unlock, unbar, unlatch, unbolt, unfasten, open up; uncover, uncork, unseal; undo, untie, unwrap; pull out; unblock, clear, unobstruct, unclog, unstop. **4** (*open into* or *on to*) give access to, lead to, connect or communicate with. **5, 7** begin, start, get under way, *formal* commence; initiate, inaugurate, launch, put in or into operation, activate, get or set going, set in motion; establish, set up; *colloq.* get or start the ball rolling, get or put the show on the road, kick off. **6 a** expand, spread (out), stretch out, open out, unfurl, extend. **8** see APPEAR 1. **9 a** disclose, unveil, uncover, expose, display, show, exhibit, reveal, divulge, bring to light, communicate, bring out, explain, present, announce, release, publish, air, make known, advertise. **b** present, offer, furnish, provide, afford, yield, reveal, uncover, raise, contribute, introduce. □ **open-and-shut** see SIMPLE *adj.* 1. **open-armed** see CORDIAL *adj.* 2. **openhanded** philanthropic; see also BOUNTEOUS. **open-minded** catholic, unprejudiced, enlightened, undogmatic, *S.Afr.* verligte; see also LIBERAL *adj.* 3, 6. **open out 1** see OPEN *v.* 6a above. **open up 1** see OPEN *v.* 1–3 above. □□ **openness** see CANDOR.

opencast /ṓpənkast/ *adj. Brit.* (of a mine or mining) with removal of the surface layers and working from above, not from shafts.

opener /ṓpənər/ *n.* **1** a device for opening cans, bottles, etc. **2** *colloq.* the first item on a program, etc. □ **for openers** *colloq.* to start with.

openhanded /ṓpənhandid/ *adj.* generous. □□ **openhandedly** *adv.* **openhandedness** *n.*

opening /ṓpəniŋ/ *n. & adj.* ● *n.* **1** an aperture or gap, esp. allowing access. **2** a favorable situation or opportunity. **3** a beginning; an initial part. **4** *Chess* a recognized sequence of moves at the beginning of a game. **5** a counsel's preliminary statement of a case in a court of law. ● *adj.* initial; first. □ ■ *n.* **1** break, breach, rent, rift, cleft, crack, crevice, fissure, cranny, chink, pit, gap, split, slit, slot, aperture, hole, orifice, separation. **2** opportunity, chance, occasion, toehold, foothold, *colloq.* break; job, position, vacancy. **3** beginning, start, *formal* commencement;

/.../ **pronunciation**	● **part of speech**
□ **phrases, idioms, and compounds**	
□□ **derivatives**	■ **synonym section**
cross-references appear in SMALL CAPITALS or *italics*	

origin, outset, onset, inauguration, launch, send-off, initiation, presentation, début, *rhet.* birth; start-off, start-up. ● *adj.* initiatory, first; see also INITIAL *adj.*

openly /ṓpənlee/ *adv.* **1** frankly; honestly. **2** publicly; without concealment. [OE *openlīce* (as OPEN, -LY²)]
 ■ **1** frankly, honestly, unreservedly, plainly, forthrightly, candidly, directly, freely, outspokenly. **2** publicly, undisguisedly; brazenly, brashly, flagrantly, unabashedly, unashamedly, unreservedly, boldly, audaciously, flauntingly.

openwork /ṓpənwərk/ *n.* a pattern with intervening spaces in metal, leather, lace, etc.

opera¹ /ópərə, óprə/ *n.* **1 a** a dramatic work in one or more acts, set to music for singers (usu. in costume) and instrumentalists. **b** this as a genre. **2** a building for the performance of opera. □ **opera glasses** small binoculars for use at the opera or theater. **opera hat** a man's tall collapsible top hat. **opera house** a theater for the performance of opera. [It. f. L, = labor, work]
 ■ □ **opera glasses** see GLASS *n.* 3.

opera² *pl.* of OPUS.

operable /ópərəbəl/ *adj.* **1** that can be operated. **2** suitable for treatment by surgical operation. □□ **operability** /-bíli-tee/ *n.* [LL *operabilis* f. L (as OPERATE)]
 ■ **1** workable, practicable, serviceable, usable, functional, fit, operational, in working order or condition.

opera buffa /ópərə bṓofə, ṓprə, áwperaa bṓofaa/ *n.* (esp. Italian) comic opera, esp. with characters drawn from everyday life. [It.]

opéra comique /áwperaa kawmeék/ *n.* (esp. French) opera on a lighthearted theme, with spoken dialogue. [F]

operand /ópərand/ *n. Math.* the quantity, etc., on which an operation is to be done. [L *operandum* neut. gerundive of *operari*: see OPERATE]

opera seria /ópərə seéreeə, óprə/ *n.* (esp. 18th-c. Italian) opera on a serious, usu. classical or mythological theme. [It.]

operate /ópərayt/ *v.* **1** *tr.* manage; work; control; put or keep in a functional state. **2** *intr.* be in action; function. **3** *intr.* produce an effect; exercise influence (*the tax operates to our disadvantage*). **4** *intr.* (often foll. by *on*) **a** perform a surgical operation. **b** conduct a military or naval action. **c** be active in business, etc., esp. dealing in stocks and shares. **5** *intr.* (foll. by *on*) influence or affect (feelings, etc.). **6** *tr.* bring about; accomplish. □ **operating system** the basic software that enables the running of a computer program. **operating room** a room for surgical operations. [L *operari* to work f. *opus operis* work]
 ■ **1** manage, run, direct, conduct, work, control, carry on, ply, manipulate, handle; drive. **2** go, run, perform; work, function, serve, act. **6** produce, accomplish, bring about; effect, effectuate.

operatic /ópərátik/ *adj.* **1** of or relating to opera. **2** resembling or characteristic of opera. □□ **operatically** *adv.* [irreg. f. OPERA¹, after *dramatic*]

operatics /ópərátiks/ *n.pl.* the production and performance of operas.

operation /ópəráyshən/ *n.* **1 a** the action or process or method of working or operating. **b** the state of being active or functioning (*not yet in operation*). **c** the scope or range of effectiveness of a thing's activity. **2** an active process; a discharge of a function (*the operation of breathing*). **3** a piece of work, esp. one in a series (often in *pl.*: *begin operations*). **4** an act of surgery performed on a patient. **5 a** a strategic movement of troops, ships, etc., for military action. **b** preceding a code name (*Operation Desert Storm*). **6** a financial transaction. **7** *Math.* the subjection of a number or quantity or function to a process affecting its value or form, e.g., multiplication, differentiation. □ **operations research** = *operational research*. [ME f. OF f. L *operatio -onis* (as OPERATE)]
 ■ **1, 2** function, functioning, working, running, performance, action, motion, movement; manipulation, handling, direction, running, control, management; maneuvering. **3, 6** undertaking,

enterprise, venture, project, affair, deal, job, task, procedure, proceeding, (day-to-day) business, transaction. **5** a action, maneuver, mission, task, campaign, exercise.

operational /ópəráyshənəl/ *adj.* **1 a** of or used for operations. **b** engaged or involved in operations. **2** able or ready to function. □ **operational research** the application of scientific principles to business management, providing a quantitative basis for complex decisions. □□ **operationally** *adv.*
 ■ **2** see FUNCTIONAL 1.

operative /ópərətiv, óprə-/ *adj. & n.* ● *adj.* **1** in operation; having effect. **2** having the principal relevance (*"may" is the operative word*). **3** of or by surgery. **4** *Law* expressing an intent to perform a transaction. ● *n.* **1** a worker, esp. a skilled one. **2** an agent employed by a detective agency or secret service. □□ **operatively** *adv.* **operativeness** *n.* [LL *operativus* f. L (as OPERATE)]
 ■ *adj.* **1** functioning, working, in effect, in force, operating, operational, functional, effective. **2** significant, meaningful, important, telling, vital, critical, relevant; see also PERTINENT 1. ● *n.* **1** worker, hand, employee; craftsman, craftswoman, artisan, mechanic, machinist. **2** espionage or intelligence agent, counterespionage or counterintelligence agent, spy, counterspy, undercover agent or man, (FBI or CIA) agent, *colloq.* G-man; private detective, (private) investigator, P.I., *colloq.* private eye, eye, sleuth, sleuthhound, snoop, snooper, *sl.* (private) dick, gumshoe, shamus, peeper.

operator /ópəraytər/ *n.* **1** a person operating a machine, etc., esp. making connections of lines in a telephone exchange. **2** a person operating or engaging in business. **3** *colloq.* a person acting in a specified way (*a smooth operator*). **4** *Math.* a symbol or function denoting an operation (e.g., x, +). [LL f. L *operari* (as OPERATE)]
 ■ **1** driver; worker, operative, practitioner; switchboard. **2** businessman, businesswoman, business person, captain of industry, director, administrator, manager, supervisor, superintendent.

operculum /ōpérkyələm/ *n.* (*pl.* **opercula** /-lə/) **1** *Zool.* **a** a flaplike structure covering the gills in a fish. **b** a platelike structure closing the aperture of a gastropod mollusk's shell when the organism is retracted. **c** any of various other parts covering or closing an aperture, such as a flap over the nostrils in some birds. **2** *Bot.* a lidlike structure of the spore-containing capsule of mosses. □□ **opercular** *adj.* **operculate** /-lət/ *adj.* **operculi-** *comb. form.* [L f. *operire* cover]

operetta /ópərétə/ *n.* **1** a one-act or short opera. **2** a light opera. [It., dimin. of *opera*: see OPERA]

ophicleide /ófiklīd/ *n.* **1** an obsolete usu. bass brass wind instrument developed from the serpent. **2** a powerful organ reed stop. [F *ophicléide* f. Gk *ophis* serpent + *kleis kleidos* key]

ophidian /ōfídeeən/ *n. & adj.* ● *n.* any reptile of the suborder Serpentes (formerly Ophidia), including snakes. ● *adj.* **1** of or relating to this group. **2** snakelike. [mod.L *Ophidia* f. Gk *ophis* snake]

ophio- /ófeeō/ *comb. form* snake. [Gk *ophis* snake]

ophthalmia /of-thálmeeə, op-/ *n.* an inflammation of the eye, esp. conjunctivitis. [LL f. Gk f. *ophthalmos* eye]

ophthalmic /of-thálmik, op-/ *adj.* of or relating to the eye and its diseases. □ **ophthalmic optician** *Brit.* **1** ophthalmologist. **2** optometrist. [L *ophthalmicus* f. Gk *ophthalmikos* (as OPHTHALMIA)]

ophthalmo- /of-thálmō, op-/ *comb. form Optics* denoting the eye. [Gk *ophthalmos* eye]

ophthalmologist /óf-thalmóljist, -thə-, op-/ *n.* a medical doctor who specializes in ophthalmology.

ophthalmology /óf-thalmóljee, -thə-, op-/ *n.* the scientific study of the eye. □□ **ophthalmological** /-məlójikəl/ *adj.*

ophthalmoscope /of-thálməskōp, op-/ *n.* an instrument for inspecting the retina and other parts of the eye. □□ **ophthalmoscopic** /-skópik/ *adj.*

-opia /ṓpeeə/ *comb. form* denoting a visual disorder (*myopia*). [Gk f. *ōps* eye]

opiate *adj., n., & v.* ● *adj.* /ṓpeeət/ **1** containing opium. **2**

narcotic, soporific. ● *n.* /ṓpeeət/ **1** a drug containing opium, usu. to ease pain or induce sleep. **2** a thing which soothes or stupefies. ● *v.tr.* /ṓpeeayt/ **1** mix with opium. **2** stupefy. [med.L *opiatus, -um, opiare* f. L *opium*: see OPIUM]
■ *adj.* **2** see NARCOTIC *adj.* 1, 4. ● *n.* **1** see NARCOTIC *n.* **2** see SEDATIVE *n.*

opine /ōpín/ *v.tr.* (often foll. by *that* + clause) hold or express as an opinion. [L *opinari* think, believe]
■ see COMMENT *v.* 1.

opinion /əpínyən/ *n.* **1** a belief or assessment based on grounds short of proof. **2** a view held as probable. **3** (often foll. by *on*) what one thinks about a particular topic or question (*my opinion on capital punishment*). **4 a** a formal statement of professional advice (*will get a second opinion*). **b** *Law* a formal statement of reasons for a judgment given. **5** an estimation (*had a low opinion of it*). □ **be of the opinion that** believe or maintain that. **in one's opinion** according to one's view or belief. **a matter of opinion** a disputable point. **opinion poll** an assessment of public opinion by questioning a representative sample, as for forecasting the results of voting, etc. **public opinion** views generally prevalent, esp. on moral questions. [ME f. OF f. L *opinio -onis* (as OPINE)]
■ **1, 3** belief, judgment, thought, sentiment, (point of) view, viewpoint, conviction, persuasion, way of thinking, perception, idea, impression, notion, conception, theory, *idée reçue*. **5** evaluation, estimation, appraisal, impression.

opinionated /əpínyənaytid/ *adj.* conceitedly assertive or dogmatic in one's opinions. □□ **opinionatedly** *adv.* **opinionatedness** *n.* [obs. *opinionate* in the same sense f. OPINION]
■ stubborn, pigheaded, obstinate, doctrinaire, inflexible, dogmatic, cocksure, conceited, obdurate, dictatorial, dogged, mulish, bullheaded, overbearing; prejudiced, biased, bigoted, one-sided, jaundiced, colored, partial, partisan.

opium /ṓpeeəm/ *n.* **1** a reddish-brown heavy-scented addictive drug prepared from the juice of the opium poppy, used in medicine as an analgesic and narcotic. **2** anything regarded as soothing or stupefying. □ **opium den** a haunt of opium smokers. **opium poppy** a poppy, *Papaver somniferum*, native to Europe and E. Asia, with white, red, pink, or purple flowers. [ME f. L f. Gk *opion* poppy juice f. *opos* juice]

opossum /əpósəm/ *n.* **1 a** any mainly tree-living marsupial of the family Didelphidae, native to America, having a prehensile tail and hind feet with an opposable thumb. **b** (in full **water opossum**) an opossum, *Chironectes minimus*, suited to an aquatic habitat and having webbed hind feet. Also called YAPOK. **2** *Austral. & NZ* = POSSUM 2. [Virginian Ind. *āpassūm*]

opp. *abbr.* opposite.

opponent /əpṓnənt/ *n. & adj.* ● *n.* a person who opposes or belongs to an opposing side. ● *adj.* opposing; contrary; opposed. □ **opponent muscle** a muscle enabling the thumb to be placed front to front against a finger of the same hand. □□ **opponency** *n.* [L *opponere opponent-* (as OB-, *ponere* place)]
■ *n.* antagonist, adversary, disputant, contestant, competitor, contender, rival, enemy, esp. *poet. or formal* foe; (*opponents*) opposition, other side.

opportune /ópərtōōn, -tyōōn/ *adj.* **1** (of a time) well-chosen or especially favorable or appropriate (*an opportune moment*). **2** (of an action or event) well-timed; done or occurring at a favorable or useful time. □□ **opportunely** *adv.* **opportuneness** *n.* [ME f. OF *opportun -une* f. L *opportunus* (as OB-, *portus* harbor), orig. of the wind driving toward the harbor]
■ **1** favorable, advantageous, auspicious, good, appropriate, well-chosen, felicitous, happy, propitious, beneficial, helpful, fortunate, lucky, profitable. **2** timely, well-timed, seasonable, apt, appropriate, germane, pertinent, convenient, fitting, suitable.

opportunism /ópərtōōnizəm, -tyōō-/ *n.* **1** the adaptation of policy or judgment to circumstances or opportunity, esp. regardless of principle. **2** the seizing of opportunities when

they occur. □□ **opportunist** *n. & adj.* **opportunistic** *adj.* **opportunistically** *adv.* [OPPORTUNE after It. *opportunismo* and F *opportunisme* in political senses]
■ □□ **opportunistic** expedient, selfish, taking advantage, exploitive, exploitative, unprincipled, Machiavellian, opportunist.

opportunity /ópərtōōnitee, -tyōō-/ *n.* (*pl.* **-ies**) **1** a good chance; a favorable occasion. **2** a chance or opening offered by circumstances. **3** good fortune. □ **opportunity knocks** an opportunity occurs. [ME f. OF *opportunité* f. L *opportunitas -tatis* (as OPPORTUNE)]
■ **1, 2** chance, occasion, opening, possibility, moment, time, *colloq.* break.

opposable /əpṓzəbəl/ *adj.* **1** able to be opposed. **2** *Zool.* (of the thumb in primates) capable of facing and touching the other digits on the same hand.

oppose /əpṓz/ *v.tr.* (often *absol.*) **1** set oneself against; resist; argue against. **2** be hostile to. **3** take part in a game, sport, etc., against (another competitor or team). **4** (foll. by *to*) place in opposition or contrast. □ **as opposed to** in contrast with. □□ **opposer** *n.* [ME f. OF *opposer* f. L *opponere*: see OPPONENT]
■ **1–2** resist, counter, object to, counteract, defy, take a stand against, withstand, combat, contest, attack, counterattack, fight, grapple with, contend with; argue against, dispute, rebut, challenge. **3** meet, play; mark, pair with. **4** (*oppose to*) match *or* contrast with, offset *or* play off against. □ **as opposed to** as against, in contrast with; see also INSTEAD 1.

opposite /ópəzit/ *adj., n., adv., & prep.* ● *adj.* **1** (often foll. by *to*) having a position on the other or further side, facing or back to back. **2** (often foll. by *to, from*) **a** of a contrary kind; diametrically different. **b** being the other of a contrasted pair. **3** (of angles) between opposite sides of the intersection of two lines. **4** *Bot.* (of leaves, etc.) placed at the same height on the opposite sides of the stem, or placed straight in front of another organ. ● *n.* an opposite thing or person or term. ● *adv.* **1** in an opposite position (*the tree stands opposite*). **2** (of a leading theatrical, etc., part) in a complementary role to (another performer). ● *prep.* in a position opposite to (*opposite the house is a tree*). □ **opposite number** a person holding an equivalent position in another group or organization. **opposite prompt** *Brit.* the side of a theater stage usually to an actor's right. **the opposite sex** women in relation to men or vice versa. □□ **oppositely** *adv.* **oppositeness** *n.* [ME f. OF f. L *oppositus* past part. of *opponere*: see OPPONENT]
■ *adj.* **1** facing, vis-à-vis; back-to-back. **2 a** opposing, conflicting, contrary, contrasting, contradictory, antithetical, differing, different, divergent, diverse, antagonistic, inconsistent, irreconcilable. ● *n.* reverse, converse, contrary, antithesis. ● *adv.* **1** vis-à-vis, in front. ● *prep.* facing, in front of, vis-à-vis. □ **opposite number** see LIKE¹ *n.* 1.

opposition /ópəzíshən/ *n.* **1** resistance, antagonism. **2** the state of being hostile or in conflict or disagreement. **3** contrast or antithesis. **4 a** a group or party of opponents or competitors. **b** (**the Opposition**) the principal political party opposed to that in office. **5** the act of opposing or placing opposite. **6 a** a diametrically opposite position. **b** *Astrol. & Astron.* the position of two heavenly bodies when their longitude differs by 180°, as seen from the earth. □□ **oppositional** *adj.* [ME f. OF f. L *oppositio* (as OB-, POSITION)]
■ **1–3** hostility, antagonism, unfriendliness, resistance, counteraction, conflict, defiance, contrast, antipathy, adversity; disapproval, objection, criticism, abuse, flak. **4 a** competition, opponents, adversaries, competitors, antagonists, enemy, enemies, rivals, other side, esp. *poet. or formal* foe(s).

/. . ./ **pronunciation**   ● **part of speech**
□ **phrases, idioms, and compounds**
□□ **derivatives**   ■ **synonym section**
cross-references appear in SMALL CAPITALS or *italics*

oppress /əprés/ v.tr. **1** keep in subservience by coercion. **2** govern or treat harshly or with cruel injustice. **3** weigh down (with cares or unhappiness). □□ **oppressor** n. [ME f. OF oppresser f. med.L oppressare (as OB-, PRESS¹)]

■ **1, 2** crush, repress, put down, suppress, subjugate, tyrannize (over), subdue, overpower, enslave, persecute, maltreat, abuse, harry, harass, trample underfoot, ride roughshod over. **3** burden, afflict, trouble, weigh down, overload, encumber, wear (down), press, weary, overburden, overwhelm. □□ **oppressor** bully, tyrant, taskmaster, taskmistress, despot, autocrat, persecutor, slave driver, dictator, overlord, iron hand, scourge, tormentor, torturer, intimidator.

oppression /əpréshən/ n. **1** the act or an instance of oppressing; the state of being oppressed. **2** prolonged harsh or cruel treatment or control. **3** mental distress. [OF f. L oppressio (as OPPRESS)]

■ repression, suppression, subjugation, subjection, tyranny, despotism, enslavement; persecution, maltreatment, abuse, torment, torture, hardship, injury, pain, anguish; injustice.

oppressive /əprésiv/ adj. **1** oppressing; harsh or cruel. **2** difficult to endure. **3** (of weather) close and sultry. □□ **oppressively** adv. **oppressiveness** n. [F oppressif -ive f. med.L oppressivus (as OPPRESS)]

■ **1, 2** oppressing, burdensome, overpowering, overwhelming, onerous, heavy, cumbersome, exhausting, racking, unbearable, intolerable, agonizing, unendurable, harsh, cruel, brutal, severe, tyrannical, repressive; dispiriting, depressing, disheartening, discouraging, grievous, distressing, miserable, harrowing, wretched, literary or joc. dolorous. **3** suffocating, stifling, stuffy, close, airless, unventilated, uncomfortable; sultry, muggy.

opprobrious /əprṓbreeəs/ adj. (of language) severely scornful; abusive. □□ **opprobriously** adv. [ME f. LL opprobriosus (as OPPROBRIUM)]

■ see ABUSIVE 1, 2.

opprobrium /əprṓbreeəm/ n. **1** disgrace or bad reputation attaching to some act or conduct. **2** a cause of this. [L f. opprobrum (as OB-, probrum disgraceful act)]

■ **1** see DISGRACE n.

oppugn /əpyṓn/ v.tr. literary call into question; controvert. □□ **oppugner** n. [ME f. L oppugnare attack, besiege (as OB-, L pugnare fight)]

oppugnant /əpúgnənt/ adj. formal attacking; opposing. □□ **oppugnance** /-nəns/ n. **oppugnancy** n. **oppugnation** /-náyshən/ n.

opsonin /ópsənin/ n. an antibody that assists the action of phagocytes. □□ **opsonic** /opsónik/ adj. [Gk opsōnion victuals + -IN]

opt /opt/ v.intr. (usu. foll. by for, between) exercise an option; make a choice. □ **opt out** (often foll. by of) choose not to participate (opted out of the race). [F opter f. L optare choose, wish]

■ see CHOOSE 3.

optative /óptaytiv, óptətiv/ adj. & n. Gram. ● adj. expressing a wish. ● n. the optative mood. □ **optative mood** a set of verb forms expressing a wish, etc., distinct esp. in Sanskrit and Greek. □□ **optatively** adv. [F optatif -ive f. LL optativus (as OPT)]

optic /óptik/ adj. & n. ● adj. of or relating to the eye or vision (optic nerve). ● n. **1** a lens, etc., in an optical instrument. **2** archaic or joc. the eye. □ **optic axis 1** a line passing through the center of curvature of a lens or spherical mirror and parallel to the axis of symmetry. **2** the direction in a doubly refracting crystal for which no double refraction occurs. **optic lobe** the dorsal lobe in the brain from which the optic nerve arises. [F optique or med.L opticus f. Gk optikos f. optos seen]

optical /óptikəl/ adj. **1** of sight; visual. **2 a** of or concerning sight or light in relation to each other. **b** belonging to optics. **3** (esp. of a lens) constructed to assist sight or on the principles of optics. □ **optical activity** Chem. the property of rotating the plane of polarization of plane-polarized light. **optical art** a style of painting that gives the illusion of movement by the precise use of pattern and color. **optical character recognition** the identification of printed characters using photoelectric devices. **optical fiber** thin glass fiber through which light can be transmitted. **optical glass** a very pure kind of glass used for lenses, etc. **optical illusion 1** a thing having an appearance so resembling something else as to deceive the eye. **2** an instance of mental misapprehension caused by this. **optical microscope** a microscope using the direct perception of light (cf. electron microscope). □□ **optically** adv.

optician /optíshən/ n. **1** a maker or seller of optical instruments, esp. eyeglasses and contact lenses. **2** a person trained in the detection and correction of poor eyesight (see OPHTHALMOLOGIST, OPTOMETRIST). [F opticien f. med.L optica (as OPTIC)]

optics /óptiks/ n.pl. (treated as sing.) the scientific study of sight and the behavior of light, or of other radiation or particles (electron optics).

optima pl. of OPTIMUM.

optimal /óptiməl/ adj. best or most favorable, esp. under a particular set of circumstances. □□ **optimally** adv. [L optimus best]

■ see OPTIMUM adj.

optimism /óptimizəm/ n. **1** an inclination to hopefulness and confidence (opp. PESSIMISM). **2** Philos. **a** the doctrine, esp. as set forth by Leibniz, that this world is the best of all possible worlds. **b** the theory that good must ultimately prevail over evil in the universe. □□ **optimist** n. **optimistic** adj. **optimistically** adv. [F optimisme f. L OPTIMUM]

■ **1** positivity, positiveness, hopefulness, confidence, sanguineness, cheerfulness. □□ **optimist** see idealist (IDEALISM). **optimistic** sanguine, positive, cheerful, buoyant, bright, hopeful, expectant, confident, bullish, idealistic, Pollyannaish.

optimize /óptimiz/ v. **1** tr. make the best or most effective use of (a situation, an opportunity, etc.). **2** intr. be an optimist. □□ **optimization** n. [L optimus best]

optimum /óptiməm/ n. & adj. ● n. (pl. **optima** /-mə/ or **optimums**) **1 a** the most favorable conditions (for growth, reproduction, etc.). **b** the best or most favorable situation. **2** the best possible compromise between opposing tendencies. ● adj. = OPTIMAL. [L, neut. (as n.) of optimus best]

■ n. **1** best, finest, most favorable; ideal, perfection, model, paragon, exemplar. **2** lesser evil. ● adj. best, finest, most favorable, ideal, perfect, choicest, optimal; first-rate, first-class, sterling, prime, capital, excellent, exceptional, superlative; extraordinary, unique, peerless, unequaled, unexcelled, unrivaled, unsurpassed.

option /ópshən/ n. **1 a** the act or an instance of choosing; a choice. **b** a thing that is or may be chosen (those are the options). **2** the liberty of choosing; freedom of choice. **3** Stock Exch., etc., the right, obtained by payment, to buy, sell, etc., specified stocks, etc., at a specified price within a set time. □ **have no option but to** must. **keep** (or **leave**) **one's options open** not commit oneself. [F or f. L optio, stem of optare choose]

■ **1** choice, selection, alternative, recourse, opportunity, way out. **2** choice, privilege, election, opportunity, chance.

optional /ópshənəl/ adj. being an option only; not obligatory. □□ **optionality** /-álitee/ n. **optionally** adv.

■ voluntary, discretionary, discretional, elective, free, spontaneous, unforced, noncompulsory, nonmandatory, unmandatory, nonrequisite.

optometer /optómitər/ n. an instrument for testing the refractive power and visual range of the eye. □□ **optometric** /óptəmétrik/ adj. **optometry** n. [Gk optos seen + -METER]

optometrist /optómitrist/ n. a person who practices optometry.

optometry /optómitree/ n. the practice or profession of testing the eyes for defects in vision and prescribing corrective lenses or exercises.

optophone /óptəfōn/ *n.* an instrument converting light into sound, and so enabling the blind to read print, etc., by ear. [Gk *optos* seen + -PHONE]

opulent /ópyələnt/ *adj.* **1** ostentatiously rich; wealthy. **2** luxurious (*opulent surroundings*). **3** abundant; profuse. ◻◻ **opulence** /-ləns/ *n.* **opulently** *adv.* [L *opulens, opulent-* f. *opes* wealth]

■ **1** wealthy, affluent, rich, prosperous, well-to-do, well-off, comfortable, in clover, on velvet, in velvet, *colloq.* flush, well-heeled, made of money, on easy street, *sl.* loaded, rolling in it, in the chips. **2** see PLUSH *adj.* **3** abundant, copious, bountiful, plentiful, prolific, profuse, *poet.* plenteous.

opuntia /ōpúnsheeə, -shə/ *n.* any cactus of the genus *Opuntia,* with jointed cylindrical or elliptical stems and barbed bristles. Also called *prickly pear.* [L plant name f. *Opus -untis* in Locris in ancient Greece]

opus /ṓpəs/ *n.* (*pl.* **opera** /ópərə/ or **opuses**) **1** *Mus.* **a** a separate musical composition or set of compositions of any kind. **b** (also **op.**) used before a number given to a composer's work, usu. indicating the order of publication (*Beethoven, op. 15*). **2** any artistic work (cf. MAGNUM OPUS). ◻ **opus Dei** /dáyee/ *Eccl.* **1** liturgical worship regarded as man's primary duty to God. **2** (**Opus Dei**) a Roman Catholic organization of laymen and priests founded in Spain in 1928 with the aim of reestablishing Christian ideals in society. [L, = work]

■ work, composition, production, creation.

opuscule /ōpúskyōōl/ *n.* (also **opusculum** /əpúskyələm/) (*pl.* **opuscules** or **opuscula** /-lə/) a minor (esp. musical or literary) work. [F f. L *opusculum* dimin. of OPUS]

OR *abbr.* **1** operational research. **2** Oregon (in official postal use). **3** operating room.

or[1] /awr, ər/ *conj.* **1 a** introducing the second of two alternatives (*white or black*). **b** introducing all but the first, or only the last, of any number of alternatives (*white or gray or black*; *white, gray, or black*). **2** (often prec. by *either*) introducing the only remaining possibility or choice given (*take it or leave it*; *either come in or go out*). **3** (prec. by *whether*) introducing the second part of an indirect question or conditional clause (*ask him whether he was there or not*; *must go whether I like or dislike it*). **4** introducing a synonym or explanation of a preceding word, etc. (*suffered from vertigo or dizziness*). **5** introducing a significant afterthought (*he must know—or is he bluffing?*). **6** otherwise (*run or you'll be late*). **7** *poet.* each of two; either (*or in the heart or in the head*). ◻ **not A or B** not A, and also not B. **one or two** (or **two or three**, etc.) *colloq.* a few. **or else 1** otherwise (*do it now, or else you will have to do it tomorrow*). **2** *colloq.* expressing a warning or threat (*hand over the money or else*). **or rather** introducing a rephrasing or qualification of a preceding statement, etc. (*he was there, or rather I heard that he was*). **or so** (after a quantity or a number) or thereabouts (*send me ten or so*). [reduced form of obs. *other* conj. (which superseded OE *oththe* or), of uncert. orig.]

or[2] /awr/ *n. & adj. Heraldry* ● *n.* a gold or yellow color. ● *adj.* (usu. following noun) gold or yellow (*a crescent or*). [F f. L *aurum* gold]

-or[1] /ər/ *suffix* forming nouns denoting a person or thing performing the action of a verb, or an agent more generally (*actor; escalator; tailor*) (see also -ATOR, -ITOR). [L *-or, -ator,* etc., sometimes via AF *-eour, -our, -ëor, -ëur*]

-or[2] /ər/ *suffix* forming nouns denoting state or condition (*error; horror*). [L *-or -oris,* sometimes via (or after) OF *-or, -ur*]

-or[3] /ər/ *suffix* forming adjectives with comparative sense (*major; senior*). [AF *-our* f. L *-or*]

orache /áwrich, ór-/ *n.* (also **orach**) = SALTBUSH. [ME *arage* f. AF *arasche* f. L *atriplex* f. Gk *atraphaxus*]

oracle /áwrəkəl, ór-/ *n.* **1 a** a place at which advice or prophecy was sought from the gods in classical antiquity. **b** the usu. ambiguous or obscure response given at an oracle. **c** a prophet or prophetess at an oracle. **2 a** a person or thing regarded as an infallible guide to future action, etc. **b** a saying, etc., regarded as infallible guidance. **3** divine inspiration or revelation. [ME f. OF f. L *oraculum* f. *orare* speak]

■ **1 b** prophecy, augury, prediction, divination, advice, prognostication, answer, message. **c** prophet, sibyl, seer, soothsayer, augur, fortune-teller, diviner, prognosticator, Cassandra, Nostradamus. **2 a** authority, guru, mastermind, mentor, wizard.

oracular /awrákyələr/ *adj.* **1** of or concerning an oracle or oracles. **2** (esp. of advice, etc.) mysterious or ambiguous. **3** prophetic. ◻◻ **oracularity** /-láritee/ *n.* **oracularly** *adv.* [L (as ORACLE)]

■ **2** see AMBIGUOUS. **3** see PROPHETIC.

oracy /áwrəsee/ *n.* the ability to express oneself fluently in speech. [L *os oris* mouth, after *literacy*]

oral /áwrəl/ *adj. & n.* ● *adj.* **1** by word of mouth; spoken; not written (*the oral tradition*). **2** done or taken by the mouth (*oral contraceptive*). **3** of the mouth. **4** *Psychol.* of or concerning a supposed stage of infant emotional and sexual development, in which the mouth is of central interest. ● *n.* *colloq.* a spoken examination, test, etc. ◻ **oral sex** sexual activity in which the genitals of one partner are stimulated by the mouth of the other. **oral society** a society that has not reached the stage of literacy. ◻◻ **orally** *adv.* [LL *oralis* f. L *os oris* mouth]

■ *adj.* **1** spoken, said, verbal, uttered, voiced, vocal, vocalized, enunciated, pronounced, articulated, word-of-mouth, viva voce. ● *n.* viva voce, vivà.

Orange /áwrinj, ór-/ *adj.* of or relating to Orangemen or their activities. ◻◻ **Orangeism** *n.*

orange /áwrinj, ór-/ *n. & adj.* ● *n.* **1 a** a large roundish juicy citrus fruit with a bright reddish-yellow tough rind. **b** any of various trees or shrubs of the genus *Citrus,* esp. *C. sinensis* or *C. aurantium,* bearing fragrant white flowers and yielding this fruit. **2** a fruit or plant resembling this. **3 a** the reddish-yellow color of an orange. **b** orange pigment. ● *adj.* orange-colored; reddish-yellow. ◻ **orange blossom** the flowers of the orange tree, traditionally worn by the bride at a wedding. **orange flower water** a solution of neroli in water. **orange peel 1** the skin of an orange. **2** a rough surface resembling this. **orange pekoe** tea made from very small leaves. **orange stick** a thin stick, pointed at one end and usu. of orangewood, for manicuring the fingernails. [ME f. OF *orenge,* ult. f. Arab. *nāranj* f. Pers. *nārang*]

orangeade /áwrinjáyd, ór-/ *n.* a usu. carbonated nonalcoholic drink flavored with orange.

Orangeman /áwrinjmən, ór-/ *n.* (*pl.* **-men**) a member of a political society formed in 1795 to support Protestantism in Ireland. [after William of *Orange* (William III)]

orangery /áwrinjree, ór-/ *n.* (*pl.* **-ies**) a place, esp. a special structure, where orange trees are cultivated.

orangewood /áwrinjwŏŏd/ *n.* the wood of the orange tree.

orangutan /awrángətán, əráng-/ *n.* (also **orang-outang** /-táng/) a large red long-haired tree-living ape, *Pongo pygmaeus,* native to Borneo and Sumatra, with characteristic long arms and hooked hands and feet. [Malay *ōrang ūtan* wild man]

orate /awráyt, áwrayt/ *v.intr.* esp. *joc.* or *derog.* make a speech or speak, esp. pompously or at length. [back-form. f. ORATION]

oration /awráyshən, ōráy-/ *n.* **1** a formal speech, discourse, etc., esp. when ceremonial. **2** *Gram.* a way of speaking; language. [ME f. L *oratio* discourse, prayer f. *orare* speak, pray]

■ **1** speech, declaration, address, lecture, recitation, monologue, declamation, *literary* discourse, *sl.* spiel; valedictory, eulogy, homily, panegyric.

orator /áwrətər, ór-/ *n.* **1** a person making a speech. **2** an eloquent public speaker. ◻◻ **oratorial** /-táwreeəl/ *adj.* [ME f. AF *oratour,* OF *orateur* f. L *orator -oris* speaker, pleader (as ORATION)]

oratorio /áwrətáwreeō, ór-/ *n.* (*pl.* **-os**) a semidramatic work for orchestra and voices, esp. on a sacred theme, performed

---

/. . ./ **pronunciation** ● **part of speech**
◻ **phrases, idioms, and compounds**
◻◻ **derivatives** ■ **synonym section**
cross-references appear in SMALL CAPITALS or *italics*

without costume, scenery, or action. □□ **oratorial** adj. [It. f. eccl.L *oratorium*, orig. of musical services at church of Oratory of St. Philip Neri in Rome]

oratory /áwrətawree, ór-/ n. (pl. **-ies**) **1** the art or practice of formal speaking, esp. in public. **2** exaggerated, eloquent, or highly colored language. **3** a small chapel, esp. for private worship. **4** (**Oratory**) *RC Ch.* **a** a religious society of priests without vows founded in Rome in 1564 and providing plain preaching and popular services. **b** a branch of this in England, etc. □□ **oratorian** /-táwreeən/ adj. & n. **oratorical** /-táwrikəl/ adj. [senses 1 and 2 f. L *ars oratoria* art of speaking; senses 3 and 4 ME f. AF *oratorie*, OF *oratoire* f. eccl.L *oratorium*: both f. L *oratorius* f. *orare* pray, speak]

■ **1, 2** public speaking, speechmaking, eloquence, rhetoric, way with words, fluency, glibness, *colloq.* gift of (the) gab; grandiloquence, magniloquence, declamation.

orb /awrb/ n. & v. ● n. **1** a globe surmounted by a cross, esp. carried by a sovereign at a coronation. **2** a sphere; a globe. **3** *poet.* a heavenly body. **4** *poet.* an eyeball; an eye. ● v. **1** tr. enclose in (an orb); encircle. **2** intr. form or gather into an orb. [L *orbis* ring]

■ n. **2** sphere, ball, globe.

orbicular /awrbíkyələr/ adj. *formal* **1** circular and flat; disk-shaped; ring-shaped. **2** spherical; globular; rounded. **3** forming a complete whole. □□ **orbicularity** /-láritee/ n. **orbicularly** adv. [ME f. LL *orbicularis* f. L *orbiculus* dimin. of *orbis* ring]

orbiculate /awrbíkyəlit, -layt/ adj. *Bot.* (of a leaf, etc.) almost circular.

orbit /áwrbit/ n. & v. ● n. **1** a the curved, usu. closed course of a planet, satellite, etc. **b** (prec. by *in, into, out of*, etc.) the state of motion in an orbit. **c** one complete passage around an orbited body. **2** the path of an electron around an atomic nucleus. **3** a range or sphere of action. **4** a the eye socket. **b** the area around the eye of a bird or insect. ● v. (**orbited**, **orbiting**) **1** intr. **a** (of a satellite, etc.) go around in orbit. **b** fly in a circle. **2** tr. move in orbit around. **3** tr. put into orbit. □□ **orbiter** n. [L *orbita* course, track (in med.L eye cavity): fem. of *orbitus* circular f. *orbis* ring]

■ n. **1** a, c circuit, course, path, track, revolution, circle, round, cycle. ● v. **1, 2** revolve, turn; go around; circle, encircle.

orbital /áwrbitəl/ adj. & n. ● adj. **1** *Anat., Astron.,* & *Physics* of an orbit or orbits. **2** *Brit.* (of a road) passing around the outside of a town. ● n. *Physics* a state or function representing the possible motion of an electron around an atomic nucleus. □ **orbital sander** a sander having a circular and not oscillating motion.

orca /áwrkə/ n. **1** any of various whales, esp. the killer whale. **2** any other large sea creature. [F *orque* or L *orca* a kind of whale]

Orcadian /awrkáydeeən/ adj. & n. ● adj. of or relating to the Orkney Islands off the N. coast of Scotland. ● n. a native of the Orkney Islands. [L *Orcades* Orkney Islands]

orch. abbr. **1** orchestra. **2** orchestrated by.

orchard /áwrchərd/ n. a piece of land with fruit trees. □□ **orchardist** n. [OE *ortgeard* f. L *hortus* garden + YARD²]

orcharding /áwrchərding/ n. the cultivation of fruit trees.

orchardman /áwrchərdmən/ n. (pl. **-men**) a fruit grower.

orchestra /áwrkəstrə/ n. **1** a usu. large group of instrumentalists, esp. combining strings, woodwinds, brass, and percussion (*symphony orchestra*). **2 a** (in full **orchestra pit**) the part of a theater, opera house, etc., where the orchestra plays, usu. in front of the stage and on a lower level. **b** the main-floor seating area in a theater. **3** the semicircular space in front of an ancient Greek theater stage where the chorus danced and sang. □□ **orchestral** /-késtrəl/ adj. **orchestrally** adv. [L f. Gk *orkhēstra* f. *orkheomai* to dance (see sense 3)]

orchestrate /áwrkəstrayt/ v.tr. **1** arrange, score, or compose for orchestral performance. **2** combine, arrange, or build up (elements of a situation, etc.) for maximum effect. □□ **orchestration** /-tráyshən/ n. **orchestrator** n.

■ **1** see ARRANGE 6a. **2** see ARRANGE 1. □□ **orchestration**

see ARRANGEMENT 5, TACTICS 2a. **orchestrator** arranger; see also *tactician* (TACTICS).

orchid /áwrkid/ n. **1** any usu. epiphytic plant of the family Orchidaceae, bearing flowers in fantastic shapes and brilliant colors, usu. having one petal larger than the others and variously spurred, lobed, pouched, etc. **2** a flower of any of these plants. □□ **orchidaceous** /-dáyshəs/ adj. **orchidist** n. **orchidology** /-dóləjee/ n. [mod.L *Orchid(ac)eae* irreg. f. L *orchis*: see ORCHIS]

orchil /áwrkil, -chil / n. (also **archil** /áarkil, -chil /) **1** a red or violet dye from lichen, esp. from *Roccella tinctoria*, often used in litmus. **2** the tropical lichen yielding this. [ME f. OF *orcheil*, etc. perh. ult. f. L *herba urceolaris* a plant for polishing glass pitchers]

orchis /áwrkis/ n. **1** any orchid of the genus *Orchis*, with a tuberous root and an erect fleshy stem having a spike of usu. purple or red flowers. **2** any of various wild orchids. [L f. Gk *orkhis*, orig. = testicle (with ref. to the shape of its tuber)]

orchitis /awrkítis/ n. inflammation of the testicles. [mod.L f. Gk *orkhis* testicle]

orcinol /áwrsinawl, -ol/ n. (also **orcin** /áwrsin/) a crystalline substance, becoming red in air, extracted from any of several lichens and used to make dyes. [mod.L *orcina* f. It. *orcello* orchil]

ord. abbr. ordinary.

ordain /awrdáyn/ v.tr. **1** confer holy orders on; appoint to the Christian ministry (*ordained him priest; was ordained in 1970*). **2 a** (often foll. by *that* + clause) decree (*ordained that he should go*). **b** (of God, fate, etc.) destine; appoint (*has ordained us to die*). □□ **ordainer** n. **ordainment** n. [ME f. AF *ordeiner*, OF *ordein-* stressed stem of *ordener* f. L *ordinare* f. *ordo -inis* order]

■ **2 a** see DECREE v. **b** see DESTINE. □□ **ordainment** see *inauguration* (INAUGURATE).

ordeal /awrdeél/ n. **1** a painful or horrific experience; a severe trial. **2** *hist.* (in full **trial by ordeal**) an ancient esp. Germanic test of guilt or innocence by subjection of the accused to severe pain or torture, survival of which was taken as divine proof of innocence. [OE *ordāl, ordēl* f. Gmc: cf. DEAL¹]

■ **1** trial, test, tribulation, hardship, affliction, trouble, nightmare, misfortune, adversity, tragedy, disaster.

order /áwrdər/ n. & v. ● n. **1 a** the condition in which every part, unit, etc., is in its right place; tidiness (*restored some semblance of order*). **b** usu. specified sequence, succession, etc. (*alphabetical order; the order of events*). **2** (in *sing.* or *pl.*) an authoritative command, direction, instruction, etc. (*only obeying orders; gave orders for it to be done; the judge made an order*). **3** a state of peaceful harmony under a constituted authority (*order was restored; law and order*). **4** (in the UK; esp. in *pl.*) a social class, rank, etc., constituting a distinct group in society (*the lower orders; the order of baronets*). **5** a kind; a sort (*talents of a high order*). **6 a** a usu. written direction to a manufacturer, tradesman, waiter, etc., to supply something. **b** the quantity of goods, etc., supplied. **7** the constitution or nature of the world, society, etc. (*the moral order; the order of things*). **8** *Biol.* a taxonomic rank below a class and above a family. **9** (esp. **Order**) a fraternity of monks and friars, or formerly of knights, bound by a common rule of life (*the Franciscan order; the Order of Templars*). **10 a** any of the grades of the Christian ministry. **b** (in *pl.*) the status of a member of the clergy (*Anglican orders*). **11 a** any of the five classical styles of architecture (Doric, Ionic, Corinthian, Tuscan, and Composite) based on the proportions of columns, amount of decoration, etc. **b** any style or mode of architecture subject to uniform established proportions. **12** (in the UK; esp. **Order**) **a** a company of distinguished people instituted esp. by a sovereign to which appointments are made as an honor or reward (*Order of the Garter; Order of Merit*). **b** the insignia worn by members of an order. **13** *Math.* **a** a degree of complexity of a differential equation (*equation of the first order*). **b** the order of the highest derivative in the equation. **14** *Math.* **a** the size of a matrix. **b** the number of elements of a finite group. **15** *Eccl.* the stated form of divine service (*the order of confirmation*). **16** the principles of procedure, decorum, etc., accepted by a meeting, legislative assembly, etc., or enforced by its president. **17** *Mil.* **a** a style of dress and equipment (*review order*). **b** (prec. by *the*) the position of a company, etc., with arms ordered (see *order arms*). **18** a Masonic or similar fraternity. **19** any of the nine grades of angelic beings (seraphim, cherubim, thrones, dominations, principalities, powers, virtues, archangels, angels). **20** *Brit.* a pass admitting the bearer to a theater, museum, etc., free or at a reduced rate or as a privilege. ● *v.tr.* **1** (usu. foll. by *to* + infin., or *that* + clause) command; bid; prescribe (*ordered him to go*; *ordered that they should be sent*). **2** command or direct (a person) to a specified destination (*was ordered to Singapore*; *ordered them home*). **3** direct a manufacturer, waiter, tradesman, etc., to supply (*ordered a new suit*; *ordered dinner*). **4** put in order; regulate (*ordered her affairs*). **5** (of God, fate, etc.) ordain (*fate ordered it otherwise*). **6** command (a thing) done or (a person) dealt with (*ordered it settled*; *ordered him expelled*). □ **by order** according to the proper authority. **holy orders** the status of a member of the clergy, esp. the grades of bishop, priest, and deacon. **in bad** (or **good**, etc.) **order** not working (or working properly, etc.). **in order 1** one after another according to some principle. **2** ready or fit for use. **3** according to the rules (of procedure at a meeting, etc.). **in order that** with the intention; so that. **in order to** with the purpose of doing; with a view to. **keep order** enforce orderly behavior. **made to order 1** made according to individual requirements, measurements, etc. (opp. *ready-made*). **2** exactly what is wanted. **minor orders** *RC Ch. hist.* the grades of members of the clergy below that of deacon. **not in order** not working properly. **of** (or **in** or **on**) **the order of 1** approximately. **2** having the order of magnitude specified by (*of the order of one in a million*). **on order** (of goods, etc.) ordered but not yet received. **order about 1** dominate; command officiously. **2** send here and there. **order arms** *Mil.* hold a rifle with its butt on the ground close to one's right side. **order form** a printed form in which details are entered by a customer. **Order of the Garter** *Brit.* the highest order of knighthood. **order of the day 1** the prevailing state of things. **2** a principal topic of action or a procedure decided upon. **3** business set down for discussion; a program. **order of magnitude** a class in a system of classification determined by size, usu. by powers of 10. **out of order 1** not working properly. **2** not according to the rules (of a meeting, organization, etc.). **3** not in proper sequence. **take orders 1** accept commissions. **2** accept and carry out commands. **3** (also **take holy orders**) be ordained. □□ **orderer** *n.* [ME f. OF *ordre* f. L *ordo ordinis* row, array, degree, command, etc.]

■ *n.* **1** organization, uniformity, regularity, system, pattern, symmetry, harmony, tidiness, orderliness, neatness; shape, arrangement, grouping, disposition, form, structure, categorization, systematization, systemization, classification, codification, disposal, layout, array, sequence, setup. **2** command, direction, directive, instruction, commandment, diktat, dictate, mandate, edict, request, demand, ukase, decree, fiat, proclamation, pronouncement; rule, regulation, law, ordinance, statute, requirement. **3** calm, peace, peacefulness, tranquillity, quiet, serenity, law and order, discipline. **4** category, class, caste, level, kind, sort, rank, group, scale, position, status, degree. **5** style, kind, genre; see also SORT *n.* 1. **6** a purchase order, request, requisition, commission, instruction. **7** condition, state (of affairs), constitution, nature. **9, 18** brotherhood, fraternity, sisterhood, sorority, fellowship, sodality, association, organization, society, guild, sect, company, community, lodge, body. **16** procedure, proceeding(s), conduct, decorum; etiquette, protocol. ● *v.* **1, 2, 5, 6** direct, command, prescribe; instruct, charge, tell, require, enjoin, *archaic or literary* bid; demand, ordain; force, make. **3** requisition, ask for, send (away) for, call for, apply for, reserve, engage, commission, contract for. **4** organize, systematize, arrange, classify, categorize, codify, prioritize, rank, lay out, sort (out), straighten (out *or* up). □ **in order 1, 2**

neat, clean, tidy, shipshape, orderly, (well-)organized, ready, prepared, arranged. **3** fitting, suitable, appropriate, correct, right, apt, called for; required, demanded, needed. **in order that** so (that), with the aim *or* purpose *or* intention that, to the end that. **in order to** to, so as to, for the purpose of. **of** (or **in** or **on**) **the order of 1** roughly, somewhere near, something like, a matter of, say; see also NEARLY 1. **order about** see BOSS¹ *v.* 1. **out of order 1** out of commission, out of service, broken, in disrepair, nonfunctioning, nonfunctional, not working, broken-down, inoperative, out of kilter, down, *colloq.* haywire, bust(ed), shot, gone phut, *sl.* (gone) kaput, on the blink, out of whack, on the fritz. **2** unseemly, out of place, improper, uncalled-for, unsuitable, indecorous, *Brit. colloq.* not cricket, *Austral. & NZ sl.* over the fence. **3** disordered, nonsequential, out of sequence, nonalphabetical, disorganized, unorganized, in disorder, chaotic.

orderly /áwrd'rlee/ *adj. & n.* ● *adj.* **1** methodically arranged; regular. **2** obedient to discipline; well-behaved; not unruly. **3** *Mil.* **a** of or concerned with orders. **b** charged with the conveyance or execution of orders. ● *n.* (*pl.* **-ies**) **1** a hospital attendant with nonmedical duties, esp. cleaning, moving equipment, escorting patients, etc. **2** a soldier who carries orders for an officer, etc. □ **orderly officer** *Brit. Mil.* the officer of the day. **orderly room** *Brit. Mil.* a room in a barracks used for company business. □□ **orderliness** *n.*

■ *adj.* **1** in (good) order, (well-)organized, neat, shipshape, tidy, arranged, methodical, systematic, systematized, systemized, harmonious, symmetrical, regular, uniform. **2** well-behaved, disciplined, decorous, law-abiding, well-mannered, peaceable, tranquil, mannerly, polite, courteous, civil, civilized, nonviolent. ● *n.* assistant, adjutant, attendant, messenger.

ordinal /áwrd'nəl/ *n. & adj.* ● *n.* **1** (in full **ordinal number**) a number defining a thing's position in a series, e.g., "first," "second," "third," etc. (cf. CARDINAL). **2** *Eccl.* a service book, esp. one with the forms of service used at ordinations. ● *adj.* **1 a** of or relating to an ordinal number. **b** defining a thing's position in a series, etc. **2** *Biol.* of or concerning an order (see ORDER *n.* 8). [ME f. LL *ordinalis* & med.L *ordinale* neut. f. L (as ORDER)]

ordinance /áwrd'nəns/ *n.* **1** an authoritative order; a decree. **2** an enactment by a local authority. **3** a religious rite. **4** *archaic* = ORDONNANCE. [ME f. OF *ordenance* f. med.L *ordinantia* f. L *ordinare*: see ORDAIN]

■ **1** see DECREE *n.* 1. **2** see LAW 1a.

ordinand /áwrd'nənd/ *n. Eccl.* a candidate for ordination. [L *ordinandus*, gerundive of *ordinare* ORDAIN]

ordinary /áwrd'neree/ *adj. & n.* ● *adj.* **1 a** regular; normal; customary; usual (*in the ordinary course of events*). **b** boring; commonplace (*an ordinary man*). **2** (esp. of a judge) having immediate or ex officio jurisdiction. ● *n.* (*pl.* **-ies**) **1** a person, esp. a judge, having immediate or ex officio jurisdiction. **2** (**the Ordinary**) **a** an archbishop in a province. **b** a bishop in a diocese. **3** (usu. **Ordinary**) *RC Ch.* **a** those parts of a service, esp. the mass, that do not vary from day to day. **b** a rule or book laying down the order of divine service. **4** *Heraldry* a charge of the earliest, simplest, and commonest kind (esp. chief, pale, bend, fess, bar, chevron, cross, saltire). **5** (prec. by *the*) *colloq.* the customary or usual condition, course, or degree. **6** an early type of bicycle with one large and one very small wheel. **7** *Brit. hist.* **a** a public meal provided at a fixed time and price at an inn, etc. **b** an establishment providing this. □ **in ordinary** *Brit.* by permanent appointment (esp. to the royal household) (*physician in ordinary*). **in the ordinary way** if the circumstances are or were not exceptional. **ordinary seaman** a sailor of the lowest rank, that below able-bodied seaman. **out of the ordinary** unusual. □□ **ordinarily** /-áirəlee/ *adv.* **ordinariness** *n.* [ME f. L *ordinarius* orderly (as ORDER)]

■ *adj.* **1** usual, normal, expected, common, general, customary, routine, typical, habitual, accustomed, traditional, regular, standard, average, everyday, familiar, set; humdrum, boring, commonplace, conventional, modest, plain, simple, prosaic, homespun, run-of-the-mill, everyday, unpretentious, workaday, mediocre, fair, passable, so-so, undistinguished, unexceptional, unremarkable, uninspired, pedestrian, bourgeois, peasant, provincial, unrefined, *colloq.* common *or* garden variety. ● *n.* **5** standard, norm, average, status quo. □ **out of the ordinary** extraordinary, unusual, uncommon, strange, unfamiliar, different, unexpected, unconventional, curious, eccentric, peculiar, rare, exceptional, original, singular, unique, odd, bizarre, weird, offbeat, outlandish, striking, quaint, picturesque. □□ **ordinarily** usually, normally, as a rule, commonly, generally, in general, customarily, routinely, typically, habitually, by and large, for the most part.

ordinate /áwrd'nit/ *n. Math.* a straight line from any point drawn parallel to one coordinate axis and meeting the other, usually a coordinate measured parallel to the vertical (cf. ABSCISSA). [L *linea ordinata applicata* line applied parallel f. *ordinare*: see ORDAIN]

ordination /áwrd'náyshən/ *n.* **1 a** the act of conferring holy orders, esp. on a priest or deacon. **b** the admission of a priest, etc., to church ministry. **2** the arrangement of things, etc., in ranks; classification. **3** the act of decreeing or ordaining. [ME f. OF *ordination* or L *ordinatio* (as ORDAIN)]

■ **1** see INSTALLATION 1.

ordnance /áwrdnəns/ *n.* **1** mounted guns; cannon. **2** a branch of the armed forces dealing esp. with military stores and materials. □ **Ordnance Survey** *Brit.* (in the UK) an official survey organization, orig. under the Master of the Ordnance, preparing large-scale detailed maps of the whole country. [ME var. of ORDINANCE]

ordonnance /áwrdənəns/ *n.* the systematic arrangement, esp. of literary or architectural work. [F f. OF *ordenance*: see ORDINANCE]

Ordovician /áwrdəvíshən/ *adj. & n. Geol.* ● *adj.* of or relating to the second period of the Paleozoic era, with evidence of the first vertebrates and an abundance of marine invertebrates. ¶ Cf. Appendix VII. ● *n.* this period or system. [L *Ordovices* ancient British tribe in N. Wales]

ordure /áwrjər, -dyŏŏr/ *n.* **1** excrement; dung. **2** obscenity; filth; foul language. [ME f. OF f. *ord* foul f. L *horridus*: see HORRID]

■ **1** see MUCK *n.* 1, 2.

Ore. *abbr.* Oregon.

ore /awr/ *n.* a naturally occurring solid material from which metal or other valuable minerals may be extracted. [OE *ōra* unwrought metal, *ār* bronze, rel. to L *aes* crude metal, bronze]

öre /ŏ́rə/ *n.* (also **øre**) a Scandinavian monetary unit equal to one-hundredth of a krona or krone. [Swedish]

oread /áwreead/ *n.* (in Greek and Roman mythology) a mountain nymph. [ME f. L *oreas -ados* f. Gk *oreias* f. *oros* mountain]

orectic /awréktik/ *adj. Philos. & Med.* of or concerning desire or appetite. [Gk *orektikos* f. *oregō* stretch out]

Oreg. *abbr.* Oregon.

oregano /ərégənō, awrég-/ *n.* an aromatic herb, *Origanum vulgare*, the fresh or dried leaves of which are used as a flavoring in cooking. Also called **wild marjoram**. (cf. MARJORAM). [Sp., = ORIGAN]

organ /áwrgən/ *n.* **1 a** a usu. large musical instrument having pipes supplied with air from bellows, sounded by keys, and distributed into sets or stops that form partial organs, each with a separate keyboard (*choir organ*; *pedal organ*). **b** a smaller instrument without pipes, producing similar sounds electronically. **c** a smaller keyboard wind instrument with

metal reeds; a harmonium. **d** = *barrel organ*. **2 a** a usu. self-contained part of an organism having a special vital function (*vocal organs*; *digestive organs*). **b** esp. *joc.* the penis. **3 a** a medium of communication, esp. a newspaper, sectarian periodical, etc. **4** *archaic* a professionally trained singing voice. **5** *Phrenol. archaic* a region of the brain held to be the seat of a particular faculty. □ **organ-grinder** the player of a barrel organ. **organ loft** a gallery in a church or concert room for an organ. **organ of Corti** see CORTI. **organ pipe** any of the pipes on an organ. **organ screen** an ornamental screen usu. between the choir and the nave of a church, cathedral, etc., on which the organ is placed. **organ stop 1** a set of pipes of a similar tone in an organ. **2** the handle of the mechanism that brings it into action. [ME f. OE *organa* & OF *organe*, f. L *organum* f. Gk *organon* tool]

■ **2 a** device, instrument, implement, tool; member, part, element, unit, component, structure, process. **3** medium, vehicle, voice, mouthpiece, forum, publication; paper, magazine, newsletter, newspaper, annual, semiannual, quarterly, monthly, fortnightly, weekly, daily, journal, periodical.

organdy /áwrgəndee/ *n.* (also **organdie**) (*pl.* **-ies**) a fine translucent cotton muslin, usu. stiffened. [F *organdi*, of unkn. orig.]

organelle /áwrgənél/ *n. Biol.* any of various organized or specialized structures that form part of a cell. [mod.L *organella* dimin.; see ORGAN, -LE]

organic /awrgánik/ *adj.* **1 a** *Physiol.* of or relating to a bodily organ or organs. **b** *Med.* (of a disease) affecting the structure of an organ. **2** (of a plant or animal) having organs or an organized physical structure. **3** *Agriculture* produced or involving production without the use of chemical fertilizers, pesticides, etc. (*organic crop*; *organic farming*). **4** *Chem.* (of a compound, etc.) containing carbon (opp. INORGANIC). **5 a** structural; inherent. **b** constitutional; fundamental. **6** organized; systematic; coordinated (*an organic whole*). □ **organic chemistry** the chemistry of carbon compounds. **organic law** a law stating the formal constitution of a country. □□ **organically** *adv.* [F *organique* f. L *organicus* f. Gk *organikos* (as ORGAN)]

■ **2** living, natural, biological, biotic, animate, breathing. **5** basic, elementary, essential, innate, inborn, natural, native, ingrained, primary, fundamental, visceral, constitutional, inherent, structural, integral. **6** organized, systematic, coherent, coordinated, integrated, structured, methodical, orderly, consistent.

organism /áwrgənizəm/ *n.* **1** a living individual consisting of a single cell or of a group of interdependent parts sharing the life processes. **2 a** an individual live plant or animal. **b** the material structure of this. **3** a whole with interdependent parts compared to a living being. [F *organisme* (as ORGANIZE)]

■ living thing, structure, body, life-form; being, entity, creature.

organist /áwrgənist/ *n.* the player of an organ.

organization /áwrgənizáyshən/ *n.* **1** the act or an instance of organizing; the state of being organized. **2** an organized body, esp. a business, government department, charity, etc. **3** systematic arrangement; tidiness. □ **organization man** a man who subordinates his individuality and his personal life to the organization he serves. □□ **organizational** *adj.* **organizationally** *adv.*

■ **1** structuring, assembly, putting together, combination, coordination; systematization, classification, categorization, codification; structure, pattern, configuration, design, plan, scheme, order, system, organism, composition, arrangement, constitution, makeup, grouping, framework, format, form, shape. **2** body, institution, federation, confederacy, confederation, society, group, league, coalition, conglomerate, combine, consortium, syndicate, organism. **3** see ORDER *n.* 1.

organize /áwrgəniz/ *v.tr.* **1 a** give an orderly structure to; systematize. **b** bring the affairs of (another person or oneself) into order; make arrangements for (a person). **2** *Brit.*

a arrange for or initiate (a plan, etc.). **b** provide; take responsibility for (*organized some sandwiches*). **3** (often *absol.*) **a** enroll (new members) in a labor union, political party, etc. **b** form (a labor union or other political group). **4 a** form (different elements) into an organic whole. **b** form (an organic whole). **5** (esp. as **organized** *adj.*) make organic; make into a living being or tissue. □ **organized crime 1** an organization of people who carry out illegal activities for profit. **2** the people involved in this. □□ **organizable** *adj.* **organizer** *n.* [ME f. OF *organiser* f. med.L *organizare* f. L (as ORGAN)]

■ **1** structure, coordinate, systematize, systemize, order, arrange, sort (out), classify, categorize, codify, catalog, group, tabulate, pigeonhole, standardize. **2 a** form, found, set up, arrange for, establish, institute, start, begin, create, originate, initiate, put together, build, develop, pull together. **3b** see INSTITUTE *v.* 1, 2. **4** see STRUCTURE *v.*

organo- /áwrgənō/ *comb. form* **1** esp. *Biol.* organ. **2** *Chem.* organic. [Gk (as ORGAN)]

organoleptic /áwrgənōléptik, awrgánō-/ *adj.* affecting the organs of sense. [ORGANO- + Gk *lēptikos* disposed to take f. *lambanō* take]

organometallic /áwrgənōmitálik, awrgánō-/ *adj.* (of a compound) organic and containing a metal.

organon /áwrgənon/ *n.* (also **organum** /órgənəm/) an instrument of thought, esp. a means of reasoning or a system of logic. [Gk *organon* & L *organum* (as ORGAN): *Organon* was the title of Aristotle's logical writings, and *Novum* (new) *Organum* that of Bacon's]

organotherapy /áwrgənōthérəpee, awrgánō-/ *n.* the treatment of disease with extracts of organs.

organza /awrgánzə/ *n.* a thin stiff transparent silk or synthetic dress fabric. [prob. f. *Lorganza* (trade name)]

organzine /áwrgənzeen/ *n.* a silk thread in which the main twist is in a contrary direction to that of the strands. [F *organsin* f. It. *organzino*, of unkn. orig.]

orgasm /áwrgazəm/ *n.* & *v.* ● *n.* **1 a** the climax of sexual excitement, esp. during sexual intercourse. **b** an instance of this. **2** violent excitement; rage. ● *v.intr.* experience a sexual orgasm. □□ **orgasmic** /-gázmik/ *adj.* **orgasmically** *adv.* **orgastic** /-gástik/ *adj.* **orgastically** *adv.* [F *orgasme* or mod.L f. Gk *orgasmos* f. *orgaō* swell, be excited]

■ □□ **orgasmic** see ECSTATIC *adj.* 1, 2.

orgeat /awrzhát, áwrjat/ *n.* a cooling drink made from barley or almonds and orange flower water. [F f. Prov. *orjat* f. *ordi* barley f. L *hordeum*]

orgiastic /áwrjeeástik/ *adj.* of or resembling an orgy. □□ **orgiastically** *adv.* [Gk *orgiastikos* f. *orgiastēs* agent-noun f. *orgiazō* hold an orgy]

■ see EPICUREAN *adj.* 2.

orgulous /áwrgyələs/ *adj. archaic* haughty; splendid. [ME f. OF *orguillus* f. *orguill* pride f. Frank.]

orgy /áwrjee/ *n.* (*pl.* **-ies**) **1** a wild drunken festivity, esp. one at which indiscriminate sexual activity takes place. **2** excessive indulgence in an activity. **3** (usu. in *pl.*) *Gk & Rom. Hist.* secret rites used in the worship of esp. Bacchus, celebrated with dancing, drunkenness, singing, etc. [orig. pl., f. F *orgies* f. L *orgia* f. Gk *orgia* secret rites]

■ **1** bacchanalia, bacchanal, saturnalia, debauch, carousal, carouse, revel, party, *archaic* wassail, *colloq.* spree, bust, *sl.* binge, bender, jag, drunk, esp. *Brit. sl.* booze-up. **2** overindulgence, fling, *colloq.* spree, splurge, *sl.* bender.

oribi /áwribee, ór-/ *n.* (*pl.* same or **oribis**) a small S. African grazing antelope, *Ourebia ourebi*, having a reddish fawn back and white underparts. [prob. Khoisan]

oriel /áwreeəl/ *n.* **1** a large polygonal recess built out usu. from an upper story and supported from the ground or on corbels. **2** (in full **oriel window**) **a** any of the windows in an oriel. **b** the projecting window of an upper story. [ME f. OF *oriol* gallery, of unkn. orig.]

orient *n.*, *adj.*, & *v.* ● *n.* /áwreeənt/ **1** (**the Orient**) a *poet.* the east. **b** the countries E. of the Mediterranean, esp. E. Asia. **2** an orient pearl. ● *adj.* /áwreeənt/ **1** *poet.* oriental. **2**

(of precious stones and esp. the finest pearls coming orig. from the East) lustrous; sparkling; precious. **3** *archaic* **a** radiant. **b** (of the sun, daylight, etc.) rising. ● *v.* /áwree-ent/ **1** *tr.* **a** place or exactly determine the position of with the aid of a compass; settle or find the bearings of. **b** (often foll. by *toward*) bring (oneself, different elements, etc.) into a clearly understood position or relationship; direct. **2** *tr.* **a** place or build (a church, building, etc.) facing toward the East. **b** bury (a person) with the feet toward the East. **3** *intr.* turn eastward or in a specified direction. □ **orient oneself** determine how one stands in relation to one's surroundings. [ME f. OF *orient, orienter* f. L *oriens -entis* rising, sunrise, east, f. *oriri* rise]

■ *n.* **1** east. ● *adj.* **1** oriental, eastern. ● *v.* **1** adjust, adapt, acclimatize, habituate, accommodate, condition, accustom, familiarize, assess, orientate, acclimate. □ **orient oneself** feel one's way, get one's bearings, familiarize oneself, orientate oneself.

oriental /áwree-éntəl/ *adj.* & *n.* ● *adj.* **1** (often **Oriental**) **a** of or characteristic of Eastern civilization, etc. **b** of or concerning the East, esp. E. Asia. **2** (of a pearl, etc.) orient. ● *n.* (esp. **Oriental**) a native of the Orient. □□ **orientalism** *n.* **orientalist** *n.* **orientalize** *v.intr.* & *tr.* **orientally** *adv.* [ME f. OF *oriental* or L *orientalis* (as ORIENT)]

orientate /áwree-entayt/ *v.tr.* & *intr.* = ORIENT *v.* [prob. back-form. f. ORIENTATION]

orientation /áwree-entáyshən/ *n.* **1** the act or an instance of orienting; the state of being oriented. **2 a** a relative position. **b** a person's attitude or adjustment in relation to circumstances, esp. politically or psychologically. **3** an introduction to a subject or situation; a briefing. **4** the faculty by which birds, etc., find their way home from a distance. □ **orientation course** a course giving information to newcomers to a university, etc. □□ **orientational** *adj.* [app. f. ORIENT]

■ **1, 2** placement, bearings, attitude, alignment, adjustment, lie, placing, situation, layout, location, position, positioning, arrangement, setup. **3** introduction, training, induction, initiation, briefing, familiarization, assimilation, acclimatization, preparation, instruction.

orienteering /áwree-enteéring/ *n.* a competitive sport in which runners cross open country with a map, compass, etc. □□ **orienteer** *n.* & *v.intr.* [Sw. *orientering*]

orifice /áwrifis, ór-/ *n.* an opening, esp. the mouth of a cavity, a bodily aperture, etc. [F f. LL *orificium* f. *os oris* mouth + *facere* make]

■ see OPENING *n.* 1.

oriflamme /áwriflam, ór-/ *n.* **1** *hist.* the sacred scarlet silk banner of St. Denis given to early French kings by the abbot of St. Denis on setting out for war. **2** a standard, a principle, or an ideal as a rallying point in a struggle. **3** a bright conspicuous object, color, etc. [ME f. OF f. L *aurum* gold + *flamma* flame]

orig. *abbr.* **1** original. **2** originally.

origami /áwrigaámee/ *n.* the Japanese art of folding paper into decorative shapes and figures. [Jap. f. *ori* fold + *kami* paper]

origan /áwrigən, ór-/ *n.* (also **origanum** /ərígənəm/) any plant of the genus *Origanum*, esp. oregano. [(ME f. OF *origan*) f. L *origanum* f. Gk *origanon*]

origin /áwrijin, ór-/ *n.* **1** a beginning or starting point; a derivation; a source (*a word of Latin origin*). **2** (often in *pl.*) a person's ancestry (*what are his origins?*). **3** *Anat.* **a** a place at which a muscle is firmly attached. **b** a place where a nerve or blood vessel begins or branches from a main nerve or blood vessel. **4** *Math.* a fixed point from which coordinates are measured. [F *origine* or f. L *origo -ginis* f. *oriri* rise]

■ **1** source, root, derivation, rise, fountainhead, foundation, basis, base, wellspring, provenance,

---

provenience, *poet.* fount; creation, genesis, birth, birthplace, cradle, dawning, dawn, origination, start, beginning, outset, launch, launching, inception, inauguration, *formal* commencement. **2** (*origins*) parentage, ancestry, extraction, descent, lineage, pedigree, genealogy, stock, heritage.

original /əríjinəl/ *adj. & n.* ● *adj.* **1** existing from the beginning; innate. **2** novel; inventive; creative (*has an original mind*). **3** serving as a pattern; not derivative or imitative; firsthand (*in the original Greek; has an original Rembrandt*). ● *n.* **1** an original model, pattern, picture, etc., from which another is copied or translated (*kept the copy and destroyed the original*). **2** an eccentric or unusual person. **3 a** a garment specially designed for a fashion collection. **b** a copy of such a garment made to order. □ **original instrument** a musical instrument, or a copy of one, dating from the time the music played on it was composed. **original print** a print made directly from an artist's own woodcut, etching, etc., and printed under the artist's supervision. **original sin** the innate depravity of all humankind held to be a consequence of the Fall of Adam. □□ **originally** *adv.* [ME f. OF *original* or L *originalis* (as ORIGIN)]

■ *adj.* **1** initial, first, earliest, primary, beginning, starting, basic; native, innate, indigenous, autochthonous, aboriginal, primordial, primeval, primitive. **2** creative, novel, innovative, unique, imaginative, unusual, inventive, ingenious; fresh, underived, unprecedented, independent. **3** master, actual, primary, authentic, true, genuine, real, basic, firsthand; prototypic(al), archetypal, source. ● *n.* **1** prototype, archetype, source, model, pattern; master. **2** eccentric, nonconformist, individualist, *colloq.* case, card, character. □□ **originally** in *or* at *or* from the beginning, (at) first, from the first, initially, to begin with, at *or* from the outset, at *or* from the start, in the first place *or* instance, *colloq.* from the word go, from day one; creatively, unusually.

originality /ərijinálitee/ *n.* (*pl.* **-ies**) **1** the power of creating or thinking creatively. **2** newness or freshness (*this vase has originality*). **3** an original act, thing, trait, etc.

■ **1, 2** creativeness, creativity, inventiveness, ingenuity, innovativeness, innovation, novelty, newness, freshness, unorthodoxy, unconventionality, cleverness, daring, resourcefulness, independence, individuality, uniqueness, nonconformity. **3** innovation, novelty, invention.

originate /əríjinayt/ *v.* **1** *tr.* cause to begin; initiate. **2** *intr.* (usu. foll. by *from, in, with*) have as an origin; begin. □□ **origination** /-náyshən/ *n.* **originative** *adj.* **originator** *n.* [med. L *originare* (as ORIGIN)]

■ **1** create, bring about, engender, give birth to, *literary* beget; conceive, initiate, inaugurate, start, begin, introduce, launch, found, set up, institute, establish, invent, coin, devise, pioneer, design, contrive, concoct, mastermind, compose, organize, formulate, form, generate, produce, develop, evolve. **2** arise, rise, begin, start, come, spring, stem, flow, issue, emerge, emanate, proceed, grow, develop, evolve, derive, result. □□ **origination** emergence, initiation; see also ORIGIN 1.

orinasal /áwrináyzəl, or-/ *adj.* (esp. of French nasalized vowels) sounded with both the mouth and the nose. [L *os oris* mouth + NASAL]

O-ring /ṓ-ring/ *n.* a gasket in the form of a ring with a circular cross section.

oriole /áwreeōl/ *n.* **1** any Old World bird of the genus *Oriolus*, many of which have brightly colored plumage (see *golden oriole*). **2** any New World bird of the genus *Icterus*, with similar coloration. [med.L *oriolus* f. OF *oriol* f. L *aureolus* dimin. of *aureus* golden f. *aurum* gold]

Orion /əríən/ *n.* a brilliant constellation on the celestial equator visible from most parts of the earth. □ **Orion's belt** three bright stars in a short line across the middle of the constellation. **Orion's hound** Sirius. [ME f. L f. Gk *Ōriōn*, name of a legendary hunter]

orison /áwrizən, ór-/ *n.* (usu. in *pl.*) *archaic* a prayer. [ME f. AF *ureison*, OF *oreison* f. L (as ORATION)]

■ see PRAYER[1] 1a.

-orium /áwreeəm/ *suffix* forming nouns denoting a place for a particular function (*auditorium; crematorium*). [L, neut. of adjectives in *-orius*: see -ORY[1]]

Oriya /əwreéə/ *n.* **1** a native of the state of Orissa in India. **2** the Indo-European language of this people. [Hindi]

orle /awrl/ *n. Heraldry* a narrow band or border of charges near the edge of a shield. [F *o(u)rle* f. *ourler* to hem, ult. f. L *ora* edge]

Orlon /áwrlon/ *n. propr.* a synthetic fiber and fabric for textiles and knitwear. [invented word, after NYLON]

orlop /áwrlop/ *n.* the lowest deck of a ship with three or more decks. [ME f. MDu. *overloop* covering f. *overloopen* run over (as OVER-, LEAP)]

ormer /áwrmər/ *n.* an edible univalve mollusk, *Haliotis tuberculata*, having a flattened shell with a series of holes of increasing size along the outer margin. Also called **sea ear**. [Channel Islands F f. F *ormier* f. L *auris maris* ear of sea]

ormolu /áwrməloo/ *n.* **1** (often *attrib.*) **a** a gilded bronze or gold-colored alloy of copper, zinc, and tin used to decorate furniture, make ornaments, etc. **b** articles made of or decorated with these. **2** showy trash. [F *or moulu* powdered gold (for use in gilding)]

ornament *n. & v.* ● *n.* /áwrnəmənt/ **1 a** a thing used or serving to adorn, esp. a small trinket, vase, figure, etc. (*a mantelpiece crowded with ornaments; her only ornament was a brooch*). **b** a quality or person conferring adornment, grace, or honor (*an ornament to her profession*). **2** decoration added to embellish, esp. a building (*a tower rich in ornament*). **3** (in *pl.*) *Mus.* embellishments and decorations made to a melody. **4** (usu. in *pl.*) the accessories of worship, e.g., the altar, chalice, sacred vessels, etc. ● *v.tr.* /áwrnəment/ adorn; beautify. □□ **ornamentation** /-táyshən/ *n.* [ME f. AF *urnement*, OF *o(u)rnement* f. L *ornamentum* equipment f. *ornare* adorn]

■ *n.* **1, 2** enhancement, embellishment, adornment, decoration, ornamentation, gingerbread, trimming, garnish, garnishment, frill, embroidery, beautification, accessory; frippery; trinket, knickknack, furbelow, bauble, gewgaw. **3** (*ornaments*) ornamentation, grace notes. ● *v.* decorate, embellish, enhance, adorn, trim, garnish, embroider, elaborate, beautify, accessorize, deck (out), dress up.

ornamental /áwrnəmént'l/ *adj. & n.* ● *adj.* serving as an ornament; decorative. ● *n.* a thing considered to be ornamental, esp. a cultivated plant. □□ **ornamentalism** *n.* **ornamentalist** *n.* **ornamentally** *adv.*

■ *adj.* see FANCY *adj.* 1.

ornate /awrnáyt/ *adj.* **1** elaborately adorned; highly decorated. **2** (of literary style) convoluted; flowery. □□ **ornately** *adv.* **ornateness** *n.* [ME f. L *ornatus* past part. of *ornare* adorn]

■ elaborate, florid, overdone, labored, rococo, baroque, gingerbread, arabesque, fancy, lavish, rich, flowery, busy, convoluted, fussy, frilly, intricate; high-flown, euphuistic, bombastic, pompous, pretentious, affected, grandiose, fulsome, grandiloquent, flamboyant, *colloq.* highfalutin.

ornery /áwrnəree/ *adj. colloq.* **1** cantankerous; unpleasant. **2** of poor quality. □□ **orneriness** *n.* [var. of ORDINARY]

■ **1** see TESTY.

ornithic /awrníthik/ *adj.* of or relating to birds. [Gk *ornithikos* birdlike (as ORNITHO-)]

ornitho- /áwrnithō/ *comb. form* bird. [Gk f. *ornis ornithos* bird]

ornithology /áwrnithóləjee/ *n.* the scientific study of birds. □□ **ornithological** /-thəlójikəl/ *adj.* **ornithologically** *adv.* **ornithologist** *n.* [mod.L *ornithologia* f. Gk *ornithologos* treating of birds (as ORNITHO-, -LOGY)]

ornithorhynchus /áwrnithəríngkəs/ *n.* = PLATYPUS. [ORNITHO- + Gk *rhugkhos* bill]

oro- /áwrō/ *comb. form* mountain. [Gk *oros* mountain]

orogeny /awrójinee/ *n.* (also **orogenesis** /áwrōjénisis/) the process of the formation of mountains. □□ **orogenetic** /áwrōjinétik/ *adj.* **orogenic** /áwrəjénik/ *adj.*

orography /áwrógrəfee/ *n.* the branch of physical geography dealing with mountains. □□ **orographic** *adj.* **orographical** *adj.*

orotund /áwrətund/ *adj.* **1** (of the voice or phrasing) full and round; imposing. **2** (of writing, style, expression, etc.) pompous; pretentious. [L *ore rotundo* with rounded mouth]

orphan /áwrfən/ *n. & v.* ● *n.* (often *attrib.*) **1** a child bereaved of a parent or usu. both parents. **2** a young animal that has lost its mother. **3** a person or thing bereft of previous protection, support, advantages, etc. ● *v.tr.* bereave (a child) of its parents or a parent. □□ **orphanhood** *n.* **orphanize** *v.tr.* [ME f. LL *orphanus* f. Gk *orphanos* bereaved]

orphanage /áwrfənij/ *n.* **1** a usu. residential institution for the care and education of orphans. **2** orphanhood.

Orphean /awrféeən, áwrfeeən/ *adj.* like the music of Orpheus, a legendary Greek poet and lyre player; melodious; entrancing. [L *Orpheus* (adj.) f. Gk *Orpheios* f. *Orpheus*]

Orphic /áwrfik/ *adj.* **1** of or concerning Orpheus or the mysteries, doctrines, etc., associated with him; oracular; mysterious. **2** = ORPHEAN. □□ **Orphism** /-fizəm/ *n.* [L *Orphicus* f. Gk *Orphikos* f. *Orpheus*]

orphrey /áwrfree/ *n.* (*pl.* **-eys**) an ornamental stripe or border or separate piece of ornamental needlework, esp. on ecclesiastical vestments. [ME *orfreis* (taken as pl.) (gold) embroidery f. OF f. med.L *aurifrisium*, etc. f. L *aurum* gold + *Phrygius* Phrygian, also 'embroidered']

orpiment /áwrpimənt/ *n.* **1** a mineral form of arsenic trisulfide, formerly used as a dye and artist's pigment. Also called *yellow arsenic*. **2** (in full **red orpiment**) = REALGAR. [ME f. OF f. L *auripigmentum* f. *aurum* gold + *pigmentum* pigment]

orpine /áwrpin/ *n.* (also **orpin**) a succulent herbaceous purple-flowered plant, *Sedum telephium*. [ME f. OF *orpine*, prob. alt. of ORPIMENT, orig. of a yellow-flowered species of the same genus]

orra /áwrə, órə/ *adj. Sc.* **1** not matched; odd. **2** occasional; extra. [18th c.: orig. unkn.]

orrery /áwrəree, ór-/ *n.* (*pl.* **-ies**) a clockwork model of the solar system. [named after the fourth Earl of *Orrery* d. 1731, for whom one was made]

orris /áwris, ór-/ *n.* **1** any plant of the genus *Iris*, esp. *I. florentina*. **2** = ORRISROOT. □ **orris powder** powdered orrisroot. [16th c.: app. an unexpl. alt. of IRIS]

orrisroot /áwrisrōōt, -rŏŏt, ór-/ *n.* the fragrant rootstock of the orris, used in perfumery and formerly in medicine.

ortanique /áwrtəneék/ *n. Brit.* a citrus fruit produced by crossing an orange and a tangerine. [*orange* + *tangerine* + *unique*]

ortho- /áwrthō/ *comb. form* **1 a** straight, rectangular, upright. **b** right, correct. **2** *Chem.* **a** relating to two adjacent carbon atoms in a benzene ring. **b** relating to acids and salts (e.g., *orthophosphates*) giving *meta-* compounds on removal of water. [Gk *orthos* straight]

orthocephalic /áwrthōsifálik/ *adj.* having a head with a medium ratio of breadth to height.

orthochromatic /áwrthōkrōmátik/ *adj.* giving fairly correct relative intensity to colors in photography by being sensitive to all except red.

orthoclase /áwrthəklays, -klayz/ *n.* a common alkali feldspar usu. occurring as variously colored crystals, used in ceramics and glassmaking. [ORTHO- + Gk *klasis* breaking]

orthodontics /áwrthədóntiks/ *n.pl.* (treated as *sing.*) (also **orthodontia** /-dónshə/) the treatment of irregularities in the teeth and jaws. □□ **orthodontic** *adj.* **orthodontist** *n.* [ORTHO- + Gk *odous odont-* tooth]

orthodox /áwrthədoks/ *adj.* **1 a** holding correct or currently accepted opinions, esp. on religious doctrine, morals, etc. **b** not independent-minded; unoriginal; unheretical. **2** (of religious doctrine, standards of morality, etc.) generally accepted as right or true; authoritatively established; conventional. **3** (also **Orthodox**) (of Judaism) strictly keeping to traditional doctrine and ritual. □ **Orthodox Church** the Eastern Christian Church, separated from the Western Christian Church in the 11th c., having the Patriarch of

Constantinople as its head, and including the national churches of Russia, Romania, Greece, etc. □□ **orthodoxly** *adv.* [eccl. L *orthodoxus* f. Gk *orthodoxos* f. *doxa* opinion]

■ **1, 2** conformist, accepted, authoritative, authorized, recognized, received, official, standard, prevailing, prevalent, common, regular, popular, ordinary, doctrinal, unheretical, established, traditional, traditionalist, accustomed, conventional, customary, conservative, unoriginal.

orthodoxy /áwrthədoksee/ *n.* (*pl.* **-ies**) **1** the state of being orthodox. **2 a** the orthodox practice of Judaism. **b** the body of orthodox Jews. **3** esp. *Relig.* an authorized or generally accepted theory, doctrine, etc. [LL *orthodoxia* f. late Gk *orthodoxia* sound doctrine (as ORTHODOX)]

orthoepy /awrthŏ-ipee, áwrthōepee/ *n.* the study of the (correct) pronunciation of words. □□ **orthoepic** /-thŏépik/ *adj.* **orthoepist** *n.* [Gk *orthoepeia* correct speech (as ORTHO-, *epos* word)]

orthogenesis /áwrthōjénisis/ *n.* a theory of evolution that proposes that variations follow a defined direction and are not merely sporadic and fortuitous. □□ **orthogenetic** /-jənétik/ *adj.* **orthogenetically** *adv.*

orthognathous /awrthógnəthəs/ *adj.* (of mammals, including humans) having a jaw that does not project forward and a facial angle approaching a right angle. [ORTHO- + Gk *gnathos* jaw]

orthogonal /awrthógənəl/ *adj.* of or involving right angles. [F f. *orthogone* (as ORTHO-, -GON)]

orthography /awrthógrəfee/ *n.* (*pl.* **-ies**) **1 a** correct or conventional spelling. **b** spelling with reference to its correctness (*dreadful orthography*). **c** the study or science of spelling. **2 a** perspective projection used in maps and elevations in which the projection lines are parallel. **b** a map, etc., so projected. □□ **orthographer** *n.* **orthographic** /awrthəgráfik/ *adj.* **orthographical** *adj.* **orthographically** *adv.* [ME f. OF *ortografie* f. L *orthographia* f. Gk *orthographia* (as ORTHO-, -GRAPHY)]

orthopedics /áwrthəpeédiks/ *n.pl.* (treated as *sing.*) (*Brit.* **-paedics**) the branch of medicine dealing with the correction of deformities of bones or muscles, orig. in children. □□ **orthopedic** *adj.* **orthopedist** *n.* [F *orthopédie* (as ORTHO-, *pédie* f. Gk *paideia* rearing of children)]

orthopteran /awrthóptərən/ *n.* any insect of the order Orthoptera, with straight narrow forewings, and hind legs modified for jumping, etc., including grasshoppers and crickets. □□ **orthopterous** *adj.* [ORTHO- + Gk *pteros* wing]

orthoptic /awrthóptik/ *adj.* relating to the correct or normal use of the eyes. □□ **orthoptist** *n.* [ORTHO- + Gk *optikos* of sight: see OPTIC]

orthoptics /awrthóptiks/ *n. Med.* the study or treatment of irregularities of the eyes, esp. with reference to the eye muscles.

orthorhombic /áwrthōrómbik/ *adj. Crystallog.* (of a crystal) characterized by three mutually perpendicular axes that are unequal in length, as in topaz and talc.

orthotics /awrtháatiks/ *n.* **1** *Med.* the science of treating joint, bone, or muscle disorders with mechanical support, braces, etc. **2** devices, such as inserts for athletic shoes, used for such treatment.

orthotone /áwrthətōn/ *adj. & n.* ● *adj.* (of a word) having an independent stress pattern, not enclitic nor proclitic. ● *n.* a word of this kind.

ortolan /áwrt'lən/ *n.* (in full **ortolan bunting**) *Zool.* a small European bird, *Emberiza hortulana*, eaten as a delicacy. [F f. Prov., lit. gardener, f. L *hortulanus* f. *hortulus* dimin. of *hortus* garden]

Orwellian /awrwéleeən/ *adj.* of or characteristic of the writings of George Orwell (E. A. Blair), English writer d. 1950,

---

/ . . . / **pronunciation** ● **part of speech**
□ **phrases, idioms, and compounds**
□□ **derivatives** ■ **synonym section**
cross-references appear in SMALL CAPITALS or *italics*

esp. with reference to the totalitarian development of the state as depicted in *1984* and *Animal Farm*.

-ory[1] /áwree, əree/ *suffix* forming nouns denoting a place for a particular function (*dormitory*; *refectory*). □□ **-orial** /áwreeəl, óreeəl/ *suffix* forming adjectives. [L *-oria, -orium*, sometimes via ONF and AF *-orie*, OF *-oire*]

-ory[2] /əree/ *suffix* forming adjectives (and occasionally nouns) relating to or involving a verbal action (*accessory*; *compulsory*; *directory*). [L *-orius*, sometimes via AF *-ori(e)*, OF *-oir(e)*]

oryx /áwriks, ór-/ *n.* any large straight-horned antelope of the genus *Oryx*, native to Africa and Arabia. [ME f. L f. Gk *orux* stonemason's pickax, f. its pointed horns]

OS *abbr.* **1** old style. **2** ordinary seaman. **3** *oculus sinister* (left eye). **4** outsize. **5** out of stock.

Os *symb. Chem.* the element osmium.

Osage /ōsáyj, ṓ-/ *n. & adj.* ● *n.* **1 a** a N. American people native to Missouri. **b** a member of this people. **2** the language of this people. ● *adj.* of or relating to this people or their language. □ **Osage orange 1** a hardy thorny tree, *Maclura pomifera*, of the US, bearing inedible wrinkled orangelike fruit. **2** the durable orange-colored wood from this.

Oscan /óskən/ *n. & adj.* ● *n.* the ancient language of Campania in Italy, related to Latin and surviving only in inscriptions. ● *adj.* relating to or written in Oscan. [L *Oscus*]

Oscar /óskər/ *n.* any of the statuettes awarded by the Academy of Motion Picture Arts and Sciences for excellence in motion-picture acting, directing, etc. [the name *Oscar*]

oscillate /ósilayt/ *v.* **1** *intr. & tr.* **a** swing back and forth like a pendulum. **b** move back and forth between points. **2** *intr.* vacillate; vary between extremes of opinion, action, etc. **3** *intr. Physics* move with periodic regularity. **4** *intr. Electr.* (of a current) undergo high-frequency alternations as across a spark gap or in a valve-transmitter circuit. **5** *intr.* (of a radio receiver) radiate electromagnetic waves owing to faulty operation. □□ **oscillation** /-áyshən/ *n.* **oscillator** *n.* **oscillatory** /-ətáwree/ *adj.* [L *oscillare oscillat-* swing]
■ **1, 2** fluctuate, vibrate, waver, seesaw, swing, sway; vacillate, equivocate, shilly-shally, hum and haw.

oscillo- /əsílō/ *comb. form* oscillation, esp. of electric current.

oscillogram /əsíləgram/ *n.* a record obtained from an oscillograph.

oscillograph /əsíləgraf/ *n.* a device for recording oscillations. □□ **oscillographic** *adj.* **oscillography** /ósilógrəfee/ *n.*

oscilloscope /əsíləskōp/ *n.* a device for viewing oscillations by a display on the screen of a cathode-ray tube. □□ **oscilloscopic** /-skópik/ *adj.*

oscine /ósin, -īn/ *adj.* (also **oscinine** /ósineen/) of or relating to the suborder Oscines of passerine birds including many of the songbirds. [L *oscen -cinis* songbird (as OB-, *canere* sing)]

oscitation /ósitáyshən/ *n. formal* **1** yawning; drowsiness. **2** inattention; negligence. [L *oscitatio* f. *oscitare* gape f. *os* mouth + *citare* move]

oscula *pl.* of OSCULUM.

oscular /óskyələr/ *adj.* **1** of or relating to the mouth. **2** of or relating to kissing. [L *osculum* mouth, kiss, dimin. of *os* mouth]

osculate /óskyəlayt/ *v.* **1** *tr. Math.* (of a curve or surface) have contact of at least the second order with; have two branches with a common tangent, with each branch extending in both directions of the tangent. **2** *v.intr. & tr. joc.* kiss. **3** *intr. Biol.* (of a species, etc.) be related through an intermediate species; have common characteristics with another or with each other. □□ **osculant** *adj.* **osculation** /-láyshən/ *n.* **osculatory** /-lətáwree/ *adj.* [L *osculari* kiss (as OSCULAR)]

osculum /óskyələm/ *n.* (*pl.* **oscula** /-lə/) a mouthlike aperture, esp. of a sponge. [L: see OSCULAR]

-ose[1] /ōs/ *suffix* forming adjectives denoting possession of a quality (*grandiose*; *verbose*). □□ **-osely** *suffix* forming adverbs. **-oseness** *suffix* forming nouns (cf. -OSITY). [from or after L *-osus*]

-ose[2] /ōs/ *suffix Chem.* forming names of carbohydrates (*cellulose*; *sucrose*). [after GLUCOSE]

OSHA /óshə/ *abbr.* Occupational Safety and Health Administration.

osier /óžhər/ *n.* **1** any of various willows, esp. *Salix viminalis*, with long flexible shoots used in basketwork. **2** a shoot of a willow. [ME f. OF: cf. med.L *auseria* osier bed]

-osis /ósis/ *suffix* (*pl.* **-oses** /óseez/) denoting a process or condition (*apotheosis*; *metamorphosis*), esp. a pathological state (*acidosis*; *neurosis*; *thrombosis*). [L f. Gk *-ōsis* suffix of verbal nouns]

-osity /ósitee/ *suffix* forming nouns from adjectives in *-ose* (see -OSE[1]) and *-ous* (*verbosity*; *curiosity*). [F *-osité* or L *-ositas -ositatis*: cf. -ITY]

Osmanli /ozmánlee, os-/ *adj. & n.* = OTTOMAN. [Turk. f. *Osman* f. Arab. *'uṭmān* (see OTTOMAN) + *-li* adj. suffix]

osmic /ózmik/ *adj.* of or relating to odors or the sense of smell. □□ **osmically** *adv.* [Gk *osmē* smell, odor]

osmium /ózmeeəm/ *n. Chem.* a hard, bluish-white transition element, the heaviest known metal, occurring naturally in association with platinum and used in certain alloys. ¶ Symb.: **Os**. [Gk *osmē* smell (from the pungent smell of its tetroxide)]

osmosis /ozmósis, os-/ *n.* **1** *Biochem.* the passage of a solvent through a semipermeable partition into a more concentrated solution. **2** any process by which something is acquired by absorption. □□ **osmotic** /-mótik/ *adj.* **osmotically** /-mótikəlee/ *adv.* [orig. *osmose*, after F f. Gk *ōsmos* push]

osmund /ózmənd/ *n.* (also **osmunda** /ozmúndə/) any fern of the genus *Osmunda*, esp. the royal fern, having large divided fronds. [ME f. AF, of uncert. orig.]

osprey /óspray, -pree/ *n.* (*pl.* **-eys**) **1** a large bird of prey, *Pandion haliaetus*, with a brown back and white markings, feeding on fish. Also called **fish hawk**. **2** a plume on a woman's hat. [ME f. OF *ospres* app. ult. f. L *ossifraga* osprey f. *os* bone + *frangere* break]

OSS *abbr.* Office of Strategic Services.

ossein /óseein/ *n.* the collagen of bones. [L *osseus* (as OSSEOUS)]

osseous /óseeəs/ *adj.* **1** consisting of bone. **2** having a bony skeleton. **3** ossified. [L *osseus* f. *os ossis* bone]

ossicle /ósikəl/ *n.* **1** *Anat.* any small bone, esp. of the middle ear. **2** a small piece of bonelike substance. [L *ossiculum* dimin. (as OSSEOUS)]

ossify /ósifī/ *v.tr. & intr.* (**-ies, -ied**) **1** turn into bone; harden. **2** make or become rigid, callous, or unprogressive. □□ **ossific** /osífik/ *adj.* **ossification** /-fikáyshən/ *n.* [F *ossifier* f. L *os ossis* bone]
■ **1** see PETRIFY 2.

osso buco /áwsō bóōkō/ *n.* (also **osso bucco**) shank of veal stewed in wine with vegetables. [It., = marrowbone]

ossuary /óshōoeree, ósyōō-/ *n.* (*pl.* **-ies**) **1** a receptacle for the bones of the dead; a charnel house; a bone urn. **2** a cave in which ancient bones are found. [LL *ossuarium* irreg. f. *os ossis* bone]

osteitis /ósteeítis/ *n.* inflammation of the substance of a bone. [Gk *osteon* bone + -ITIS]

ostensible /osténsibəl/ *adj.* apparent but not necessarily real; professed (*his ostensible function was that of interpreter*). □□ **ostensibly** *adv.* [F f. med.L *ostensibilis* f. L *ostendere ostens-* stretch out to view (as OB-, *tendere* stretch)]
■ see APPARENT 2, *alleged* (ALLEGE). □□ **ostensibly** see *apparently* (APPARENT).

ostensive /osténsiv/ *adj.* **1** directly demonstrative. **2** (of a definition) indicating by direct demonstration that which is signified by a term. □□ **ostensively** *adv.* **ostensiveness** *n.* [LL *ostensivus* (as OSTENSIBLE)]
■ **1** see TANGIBLE 2.

ostensory /osténsəree/ *n.* (*pl.* **-ies**) *RC Ch.* a receptacle for displaying the host to the congregation; a monstrance. [med.L *ostensorium* (as OSTENSIBLE)]

ostentation /óstentáyshən/ *n.* **1** a pretentious and vulgar display, esp. of wealth and luxury. **2** the attempt or intention to attract notice; showing off. □□ **ostentatious** *adj.* **ostentatiously** *adv.* [ME f. OF f. L *ostentatio -onis* f. *ostentare* frequent. of *ostendere*: see OSTENSIBLE]

■ show, display, exhibition, exhibitionism, vanity, showing off, pretension, pretentiousness, flaunting, flashiness, flourish, flamboyance, parade, window dressing. □□ **ostentatious** showy, boastful, braggart, vain, flaunting, pretentious, grandiose, flamboyant, theatrical, *colloq.* flash, *literary* vaunting, vainglorious.

osteo- /ósteeō/ *comb. form* bone. [Gk *osteon*]

osteoarthritis /ósteeōaarthrítis/ *n.* a degenerative disease of joint cartilage, esp. in the elderly. □□ **osteoarthritic** /-thrítik/ *adj.*

osteogenesis /ósteeōjénisis/ *n.* the formation of bone. □□ **osteogenetic** /-jinétik/ *adj.*

osteology /ósteeóləjee/ *n.* the study of the structure and function of the skeleton and bony structures. □□ **osteological** /-teeəlójikəl/ *adj.* **osteologically** *adv.* **osteologist** *n.*

osteomalacia /ósteeōmáláyshə/ *n.* softening of the bones, often through a deficiency of vitamin D and calcium. □□ **osteomalacic** /-lásik/ *adj.* [mod.L (as OSTEO-, Gk *malakos* soft)]

osteomyelitis /ósteeōmī-ilítis/ *n.* inflammation of the bone or of bone marrow, usu. due to infection.

osteopathy /ósteeópəthee/ *n.* the treatment of disease through the manipulation of bones, esp. the spine, displacement of these being the supposed cause. □□ **osteopath** /ósteeəpath/ *n.* **osteopathic** *adj.*

osteoporosis /ósteeōpərósis/ *n.* a condition of brittle and fragile bones caused by loss of bony tissue, esp. as a result of hormonal changes, or deficiency of calcium or vitamin D. [OSTEO- + Gk *poros* passage, pore]

ostinato /óstinaáto/ *n.* (*pl.* **-os**) (often *attrib.*) *Mus.* a persistent phrase or rhythm repeated through all or part of a piece. [It., = OBSTINATE]

ostler /óslər/ *n. Brit. hist.* a stableman at an inn. [f. earlier HOSTLER, *hosteler* f. AF *hostiler*, OF (*h*)*ostelier* (as HOSTEL)] ■ see GROOM *n.* 1.

Ostmark /áwstmaark, óst-/ *n. hist.* the chief monetary unit of the former Democratic Republic of Germany. [G, = east mark: see MARK²]

Ostpolitik /áwstpawliteék/ *n. hist.* the foreign policy of many western European countries with reference to the former Communist bloc. [G f. *Ost* east + *Politik* politics]

ostracize /óstrəsīz/ *v.tr.* **1** exclude (a person) from a society, favor, common privileges, etc.; refuse to associate with. **2** (esp. in ancient Athens) banish (a powerful or unpopular citizen) for five or ten years by popular vote. □□ **ostracism** /-sizəm/ *n.* [Gk *ostrakizō* f. *ostrakon* shell, potsherd (used to write a name on in voting)]
■ **1** blackball, blacklist, banish, exile, boycott, isolate, segregate, exclude, snub, shun, avoid, keep at arm's length, send to Coventry, cut, cold-shoulder, give a person the cold shoulder, *Eccl.* excommunicate. **2** banish, exile.

ostrich /óstrich, áw-/ *n.* **1** a large African swift-running flightless bird, *Struthio camelus*, with long legs and two toes on each foot. **2** a person who refuses to accept facts (from the belief that ostriches bury their heads in the sand when pursued). □ **ostrich farm** a place that breeds ostriches for their eggs, meat, and feathers. **ostrich plume** a feather or bunch of feathers of an ostrich. [ME f. OF *ostric*(*h*)*e* f. L *avis* bird + LL *struthio* f. Gk *strouthiōn* ostrich f. *strouthos* sparrow, ostrich]

Ostrogoth /óstrəgoth/ *n. hist.* a member of the Eastern branch of the Goths, who conquered Italy in the 5th–6th c. □□ **Ostrogothic** /-góthik/ *adj.* [LL *Ostrogothi* (pl.) f. Gmc *austro-* (unrecorded) east + LL *Gothi* Goths: see GOTH]

OT *abbr.* Old Testament.

o.t. *abbr.* (also **O.T.**) **1** occupational therapist. **2** occupational therapy. **3** overtime.

-ot¹ /ət/ *suffix* forming nouns, orig. diminutives (*ballot*; *chariot*; *parrot*). [F]

-ot² /ət/ *suffix* forming nouns denoting persons (*patriot*), e.g., natives of a place (*Cypriot*). [F *-ote*, L *-ota*, Gk *-ōtēs*]

OTB *abbr.* off-track betting.

OTC *abbr.* **1** over-the-counter. **2** *Brit.* Officers' Training Corps.

other /úthər/ *adj.*, *n.* or *pron.*, & *adv.* ● *adj.* **1** not the same as one or some already mentioned or implied; separate in identity or distinct in kind (*other people*; *use other means*). **2 a** further; additional (*a few other examples*). **b** alternative of two (*open your other eye*) (cf. *every other*). **3** (prec. by *the*) that remains after all except the one or ones in question have been considered, eliminated, etc. (*must be in the other pocket*; *where are the other two?*; *the other three left*). **4** (foll. by *than*) apart from; excepting (*any person other than you*). ● *n.* or *pron.* (orig. an ellipt. use of the *adj.*, now with pl. in *-s*) **1** an additional, different, or extra person, thing, example, etc. (*some others have come*) (see also ANOTHER, *each other*). **2** (in *pl.*; prec. by *the*) the ones remaining (*where are the others?*). ● *adv.* (usu. foll. by *than*) *disp.* otherwise (*cannot react other than angrily*). ¶ In this sense *otherwise* is standard except in less formal use. □ **no other** *archaic* nothing else (*I can do no other*). **of all others** out of the·many possible or likely (*on this night of all others*). **on the other hand** see HAND. **the other day** (or **night** or **week**, etc.) a few days, etc., ago (*heard from him the other day*). **other-directed** governed by external circumstances and trends. **other half** *colloq.* one's wife or husband. **the other place** *Brit. joc.* Oxford University as regarded by Cambridge, and vice versa. **other ranks** *Brit.* soldiers other than commissioned officers. **other things being equal** if conditions are or were alike in all but the point in question. **the other woman** a married man's mistress. **the other world** see WORLD. **someone** (or **something** or **somehow**, etc.) **or other** some unspecified person, thing, manner, etc. [OE *ōther* f. Gmc]
■ *adj.* **2 a** see FURTHER *adj.* 2. **b** see ALTERNATIVE *adj.* 1. □ **on the other hand** see OTHERWISE *adv.* 1, 2.

otherness /úthərnis/ *n.* **1** the state of being different; diversity. **2** a thing or existence other than the thing mentioned and the thinking subject.

otherwhere /úthərhwáir, -wáir/ *adj.* *archaic* or *poet.* elsewhere.

otherwise /úthərwīz/ *adv.* & *adj.* ● *adv.* **1** else; or else; in the circumstances other than those considered, etc. (*bring your umbrella, otherwise you will get wet*). **2** in other respects (*he is somewhat unkempt, but otherwise very suitable*). **3** (often foll. by *than*) in a different way (*could not have acted otherwise*; *cannot react otherwise than angrily*). **4** as an alternative (*otherwise known as Jack*). ● *adj.* **1** (*predic.*) in a different state (*the matter is quite otherwise*). **2** *archaic* that would otherwise exist (*their otherwise dullness*). □ **and** (or **or**) **otherwise** the negation or opposite (of a specified thing) (*the merits or otherwise of the proposal*; *experiences pleasant and otherwise*). [OE *on ōthre wisan* (as OTHER, WISE²)]
■ *adv.* **1, 2** if not, (or) else; under *or* in other circumstances, in another situation, on the other hand; in other respects. **3** differently, in another manner *or* way, *disp.* other.

otherworldly /úthərwórldlee/ *adj.* **1** unworldly; impractical. **2** concerned with life after death, etc. □□ **otherworldliness** *n.*

otic /ótik, ótik/ *adj.* of or relating to the ear. [Gk *ōtikos* f. *ous ōtos* ear]

-otic /ótik/ *suffix* forming adjectives and nouns corresponding to nouns in *-osis*, meaning 'affected with or producing or resembling a condition in *-osis*' or 'a person affected with this' (*narcotic*; *neurotic*; *osmotic*). □□ **-otically** *suffix* forming adverbs. [from or after F *-otique* f. L f. Gk *-ōtikos* adj. suffix]

otiose /ósheeōs, ótee-/ *adj.* **1** serving no practical purpose; not required; functionless. **2** *archaic* indolent; futile. □□ **otiosely** *adv.* **otioseness** *n.* [L *otiosus* f. *otium* leisure]

otitis /ōtítis/ *n.* inflammation of the ear. [mod.L (as OTO-)]

oto- /ótō/ *comb. form* ear. [Gk *ōto-* f. *ous ōtos* ear]

otolaryngology /ótōláringgóləjee/ *n.* the study of diseases of

---

/.../ pronunciation	● part of speech
□ phrases, idioms, and compounds	
□□ derivatives	■ synonym section
cross-references appear in SMALL CAPITALS or *italics*	

the ear and throat. □□ **otolaryngological** /-gəlójikəl/ *adj.* **otolaryngologist** *n.*

otolith /ṓtəlith/ *n.* any of the small particles of calcium carbonate in the inner ear. □□ **otolithic** *adj.*

otology /ōtóləjee/ *n.* the study of the anatomy and diseases of the ear. □□ **otological** /ōtəlójikəl/ *adj.* **otologist** *n.*

otorhinolaryngology /ṓtōrīnōláringgólʹəjee/ *n.* the study of diseases of the ear, nose, and throat.

otoscope /ṓtəskōp/ *n.* an apparatus for examining the eardrum and the passage leading to it from the ear. □□ **otoscopic** /-skópik/ *adj.*

ottava rima /ōtáavə reémə/ *n.* a stanza of eight lines of 10 or 11 syllables, rhyming *abababcc*. [It., lit. eighth rhyme]

Ottawa /aátəwə, -waa, -waw/ *n.* & *adj.* ● *n.* **1 a** a N. American people native to Canada and the great Lakes region. **b** a member of this people. **2** the language of this people. ● *adj.* of or relating to this people or their language.

otter /ótər/ *n.* **1 a** any of several aquatic fish-eating mammals of the family Mustelidae, esp. of the genus *Lutra*, having strong claws and webbed feet. **b** its fur or pelt. **2** = *sea otter*. **3** a piece of board used to carry fishing bait in water. **4** *Brit.* a type of paravane, esp. as used on nonnaval craft. □ **otter board** a device for keeping the mouth of a trawl net open. **otter hound** (or **dog**) a dog of a breed used in otter hunting. [OE *otr, ot(t)or* f. Gmc]

otto var. of ATTAR.

Ottoman /ótəmən/ *adj.* & *n.* ● *adj. hist.* **1** of or concerning the dynasty of Osman or Othman I, the branch of the Turks to which he belonged, or the empire ruled by his descendants. **2** Turkish. ● *n.* (*pl.* **Ottomans**) an Ottoman person; a Turk. □ **the Ottoman Porte** see PORTE. [F f. Arab. *'uṭmānī* adj. of Othman (*'uṭmān*)]

ottoman /ótəmən/ *n.* (*pl.* **ottomans**) **1 a** an upholstered seat, usu. square and without a back or arms, sometimes a box with a padded top. **b** a footstool of similar design. **2 a** heavy silken fabric with a mixture of cotton or wool. [F *ottomane* fem. (as OTTOMAN)]

oubliette /ōblee-ét/ *n.* a secret dungeon with access only through a trapdoor. [F f. *oublier* forget]

ouch /owch/ *int.* expressing pain or annoyance. [imit.: cf. G *autsch*]

ought[1] /awt/ *v. aux.* (usu. foll. by *to* + infin.; present and past indicated by the following infin.) **1** expressing duty or rightness (*we ought to love our neighbors*). **2** expressing shortcoming (*it ought to have been done long ago*). **3** expressing advisability or prudence (*you ought to go for your own good*). **4** expressing esp. strong probability (*he ought to be there by now*). □ **ought not** the negative form of *ought* (*he ought not to have stolen it*). [OE *āhte*, past of *āgan* OWE] ▪ see MUST[1] *v.* 1, 3, 4.

ought[2] var. of AUGHT[2].

ought[3] var. of AUGHT[1].

oughtn't /áwt'nt/ *contr.* ought not.

Ouija /weéjə, -jee/ *n.* (in full **Ouija board**) *propr.* a board having letters or signs at its rim to which a planchette, movable pointer, or upturned glass points in answer to questions from attenders at a seance, etc. [F *oui* yes + G *ja* yes]

ounce[1] /owns/ *n.* **1 a** a unit of weight of one-sixteenth of a pound avoirdupois (approx. 28 grams). ¶ Abbr.: **oz. b** a unit of one-twelfth of a pound troy or apothecaries' measure, equal to 480 grains (approx. 31 grams). **2** a small quantity. □ **fluid ounce 1** a unit of capacity equal to one-sixteenth of a pint (approx. 0.034 liter). **2** *Brit.* a unit of capacity equal to one-twentieth of a pint (approx. 0.028 liter). [ME & OF *unce* f. L *uncia* twelfth part of pound or foot: cf. INCH[1]]

ounce[2] /owns/ *n.* a large Asian feline, *Panthera uncia*, with leopardlike markings on a cream-colored coat. Also called *mountain panther, snow leopard*. [ME f. OF *once* (earlier *lonce*) = L. *lonza* ult. f. L *lynx*: see LYNX]

our /owr, aar/ *poss.pron.* (*attrib.*) **1** of or belonging to us or ourselves (*our house; our own business*). **2** of or belonging to all people (*our children's future*). **3** (esp. as **Our**) of Us the king or queen, emperor or empress, etc. (*given under Our seal*). **4** of us, the editorial staff of a newspaper, etc. (*a foolish adventure in our view*). **5** *colloq.* indicating a relative, acquain-

tance, or colleague of the speaker (*our Barry works there*). □ **Our Father 1** the Lord's Prayer. **2** God. **Our Lady** the Virgin Mary. **Our Lord 1** Jesus Christ. **2** God. **Our Savior** Jesus Christ. [OE *ūre* orig. genit. pl. of 1st pers. pron. = of us, later treated as possessive adj.]

-our /ər/ *suffix Brit.* **1** var. of -OR[1] (*saviour*). **2** var. of -OR[2] (*ardour; colour; valour*).

ours /owrz, aars/ *poss.pron.* the one or ones belonging to or associated with us (*it is ours; ours are over there*). □ **of ours** of or belonging to us (*a friend of ours*).

ourself /owrsélf, aar-/ *pron. archaic* a word formerly used instead of *myself* by a sovereign, newspaper editorial staff, etc. (cf. OUR 3, 4).

ourselves /owrsélvz, aar-/ *pron.* **1 a** *emphat. form* of WE or US (*we ourselves did it; made it ourselves; for our friends and ourselves*). **b** *refl. form* of US (*are pleased with ourselves*). **2** in our normal state of body or mind (*not quite ourselves today*). □ **be ourselves** act in our normal unconstrained manner. **by ourselves** see *by oneself*.

-ous /əs/ *suffix* **1** forming adjectives meaning 'abounding in, characterized by, of the nature of' (*envious; glorious; mountainous; poisonous*). **2** *Chem.* denoting a state of lower valence than the corresponding word in -*ic* (*ferrous*). □□ **-ously** *suffix* forming adverbs. **-ousness** *suffix* forming nouns. [from or after AF *-ous*, OF *-eus*, f. L *-osus*]

ousel var. of OUZEL.

oust /owst/ *v.tr.* **1** (usu. foll. by *from*) drive out or expel, esp. by forcing oneself into the place of. **2** (usu. foll. by *of*) *Law* put (a person) out of possession; deprive. [AF *ouster*, OF *oster* take away, f. L *obstare* oppose, hinder (as OB-, *stare* stand)] ▪ **1** see EXPEL 1. **2** see DISPOSSESS 1.

ouster /ówstər/ *n.* **1** ejection as a result of physical action, judicial process, or political upheaval. **2** dismissal; expulsion.

out /owt/ *adv., prep., n., adj., int.,* & *v.* ● *adv.* **1** away from or not in or at a place, etc. (*keep him out; get out of here; my son is out in California*). **2** (forming part of phrasal verbs) **a** indicating dispersal away from a center, etc. (*hire out; share out; board out*). **b** indicating coming or bringing into the open for public attention, etc. (*call out; send out; shine out; stand out*). **c** indicating a need for attentiveness (*watch out; look out; listen out*). **3 a** not in one's house, office, etc. (*went out for a walk*). **b** no longer in prison. **4** to or at an end; completely (*tired out; die out; out of bananas; fight it out; typed it out*). **5** (of a fire, candle, etc.) not burning. **6** in error (*was 3% out in my calculations*). **7** *colloq.* unconscious (*she was out for five minutes*). **8 a** (of a tooth) extracted. **b** (of a joint, bone, etc.) dislocated (*put his shoulder out*). **9** (of a party, politician, etc.) not in office. **10** (of a jury) considering its verdict in secrecy. **11** (of workers) on strike. **12** (of a secret) revealed. **13** (of a flower) blooming, open. **14** (of a book) published. **15** (of a star) visible after dark. **16** unfashionable (*wide lapels are out*). **17** *Sports* (of a batter, baserunner, etc.) no longer taking part as such, having been tagged, struck out, caught, etc. **18 a** not worth considering; rejected (*that idea is out*). **b** not allowed. **19** *colloq.* (prec. by *superl.*) known to exist (*the best game out*). **20** (of a stain, mark, etc.) not visible; removed (*painted out the sign*). **21 a** (of time) not spent working (*took five minutes out*). **b** into the future (*let's look five years out*). **22** (of a rash, bruise, etc.) visible. **23** (of the tide) at the lowest point. **24** *Boxing* unable to rise from the floor (*out for the count*). **25** *archaic* (of a young upperclass woman) introduced into society. **26** (in a radio conversation, etc.) transmission ends (*over and out*). ● *prep.* **1** out of (*looked out the window*). **2** *archaic* outside; beyond the limits of. ● *n.* **1** *colloq.* a way of escape; an excuse. **2** (**the outs**) the political party out of office. **3** *Baseball* play in which a batter or baserunner is retired from an inning. ● *adj.* **1** esp. *Brit.* (of a match) played away. **2** (of an island) away from the mainland. ● *int.* a peremptory dismissal, reproach, etc. (*out, you scoundrel!*). ● *v.* **1** *tr.* **a** put out. **b** *colloq.* eject forcibly. **2** *intr.* come or go out; emerge (*murder will out*). **3** *tr. Boxing* knock out. **4** *tr. colloq.* expose the homosexuality of (esp. a prominent person). □ **at outs** at variance or enmity. **out and about** (of a person, esp. after an illness) engaging in normal activity. **out and away** by far. **out-and-out** adj. thorough; surpassing. ● adv. thoroughly; surpassingly. **out-box** a box, tray, basket, etc., usu. on a desk, for holding finished work, outgoing correspondence, etc. **out for** having one's interest or effort directed to; intent on. **out of 1** from within (*came out of the house*). **2** not within (*I was never out of the city*). **3** from among (*nine people out of ten; must choose out of these*). **4** beyond the range of (*is out of reach*). **5** without or so as to be without (*was swindled out of his money; out of breath; out of sugar*). **6** from (*get money out of him*). **7** owing to; because of (*asked out of curiosity*). **8** by the use of (material) (*what did you make it out of?*). **9** at a specified distance from (a town, port, etc.) (*seven miles out of Topeka*). **10** beyond (*something out of the ordinary*). **11** *Racing* (of an animal, esp. a horse) born of. **out of bounds** see BOUND². **out of the closet** see CLOSET. **out-of-date** see DATE¹. **out of doors** see DOOR. **out of drawing** see DRAWING. **out of hand** see HAND. **out of it 1** not included; forlorn. **2** *sl.* extremely drunk or otherwise disoriented. **out of order** see ORDER. **out of pocket** see POCKET. **out of the question** see QUESTION. **out of sorts** see SORT. **out of temper** see TEMPER. **out of this world** see WORLD. **out of the way** see WAY. **out to** keenly striving to do. **out to lunch** *colloq.* crazy; mad. **out with** an exhortation to expel or dismiss (an unwanted person). **out with it** say what you are thinking. [OE *ūt*, OHG *ūz*, rel. to Skr. *ud-*]

■ *adv.* **1** away, abroad, elsewhere, not (at) home, absent. **2a, b, 3a, 12** outside, outdoors, in *or* into the open air; in *or* into the open, to *or* into public notice, for all to see, out of the closet; revealed, exposed, visible, discernible, manifest, in sight, in view. **3 b** free, at liberty, at large, loose, unconfined. **4** completely, thoroughly, effectively, entirely. **5** extinguished, unlit; off, doused; exhausted, gone, finished, ended; over, completed; inoperative, nonfunctioning. **6** inaccurate, incorrect, wrong, at fault, in error, faulty, off, wide of the mark; short, minus, missing, in default, out of pocket. **7, 24** *colloq.* (out) cold, out for the count; see also INSENSIBLE 1. **8a** pulled, removed, taken out, extracted, gone. **8b** out of place, out of joint, dislocated. **11** striking, on strike. **13** open, blooming, in flower *or* bloom *or* blossom. **14** in print, published, issued, produced. **16** dated, outdated, outmoded, passé, old-fashioned, antiquated, old hat, *démodé*, obsolete, unfashionable. **18 a** see UNWELCOME. **b** unacceptable, forbidden, prohibited, not allowed. ● *n.* **1** excuse, escape, loophole, evasion, alibi, esp. *Brit. colloq.* get-out. ● *adj.* **2** outlying, distant, far-off; peripheral. □ **out and about** active, busy, back to normal, energetic, *colloq.* bustling. **out-and-out** *adj.* complete, unmitigated, unalloyed, undiluted, pure, utter, perfect, consummate, surpassing, outright, total, downright, unqualified, thorough, thoroughgoing, dyed-in-the-wool. **out for** interested in, intent *or* focused *or* bent on, aiming at *or* for, after, seeking, in search of, out to get. **out of it 1** left out, excluded, omitted; forlorn; see also ABANDONED 1a. **2** see DRUNK *adj.* 1. **out to** trying *or* aiming *or* keen *or* eager to. **out to lunch** see CRAZY 1.

out- /owt/ *prefix* added to verbs and nouns, meaning: **1** so as to surpass or exceed (*outdo; outnumber*). **2** external; separate (*outline; outhouse; outdoors*). **3** out of; away from; outward (*outspread; outgrowth*).

outact /owtákt/ *v.tr.* surpass in acting or performing.

outage /ówtij/ *n.* a period of time during which a power supply, etc., is not operating.

out-and-outer /ówtənówtər/ *n. sl.* **1** a thorough or supreme person or thing. **2** an extremist.

outback /ówtbak/ *n.* esp. *Austral.* the remote and usu. uninhabited inland districts. □□ **outbacker** *n.*

■ see BACKCOUNTRY.

outbalance /owtbálans/ *v.tr.* **1** count as more important than. **2** outweigh.

outbid /ówtbíd/ *v.tr.* (**-bidding;** *past* and *past part.* **-bid**) **1**

bid higher than (another person) at an auction. **2** surpass in exaggeration, etc.

outboard /ówtbawrd/ *adj., adv.,* & *n.* ● *adj.* **1** (of a motor) portable and attachable to the outside of the stern of a boat. **2** (of a boat) having an outboard motor. ● *adj.* & *adv.* on, toward, or near the outside of a ship, an aircraft, etc. ● *n.* **1** an outboard engine. **2** a boat with an outboard engine.

outbound /ówtbownd/ *adj.* outward bound.

outbrave /ówtbráyv/ *v.tr.* **1** outdo in bravery. **2** face defiantly.

outbreak /ówtbrayk/ *n.* **1** a usu. sudden eruption of war, disease, rebellion, etc. **2** an outcrop.

■ **1** see *eruption* (ERUPT).

outbreeding /ówtbreeding/ *n.* the theory or practice of breeding from animals not closely related. □□ **outbreed** *v.intr.* & *tr.* (*past* and *past part.* **-bred**).

outbuilding /ówtbilding/ *n.* a detached shed, barn, garage, etc., within the grounds of a main building.

outburst /ówtbərst/ *n.* **1** an explosion of anger, etc., expressed in words. **2** an act or instance of bursting out. **3** an outcrop.

■ **1, 2** eruption, explosion, blowup, flare-up, fulmination; upsurge, surge, outpouring, welling (forth), outflow(ing), rush, flood, effusion, effluence, efflux; fit, access, attack, spasm, paroxysm, seizure, tantrum.

outcast /ówtkast/ *n.* & *adj.* ● *n.* **1** a person cast out from or rejected by his or her home, country, society, etc. **2** a tramp or vagabond. ● *adj.* rejected; homeless; friendless.

■ *n.* **1** pariah, exile, reject, persona non grata, leper, untouchable; expatriate, refugee, displaced person, DP, evacuee.

outcaste *n.* & *v.* ● *n.* /ówtkast/ (also *attrib.*) **1** a person who has no caste, esp. in Hindu society. **2** a person who has lost his or her caste. ● *v.tr.* /ówtkást/ cause (a person) to lose his or her caste.

outclass /ówtklás/ *v.tr.* **1** belong to a higher class than. **2** defeat easily.

■ **2** see SURPASS 1.

outcome /ówtkum/ *n.* a result; a visible effect.

■ result, consequence, end (result *or* product), aftereffect, effect, upshot, sequel, development, outgrowth, aftermath, wake, follow-up, *Med.* sequela(e), *colloq.* bottom line, *sl.* payoff.

outcrop /ówtkrop/ *n.* & *v.* ● *n.* **1 a** the emergence of a stratum, vein, or rock, at the surface. **b** a stratum, etc., emerging. **2** a noticeable manifestation or occurrence. ● *v.intr.* (**-cropped, -cropping**) appear as an outcrop; crop out. ■ *n.* **1** see ROCK¹ 3a.

outcry /ówtkri/ *n.* (*pl.* **-ies**) **1** the act or an instance of crying out. **2** an uproar. **3** a noisy or prolonged public protest.

■ protest, protestation, decrial, complaint, indignation, uproar, vociferation, clamor, clamoring, commotion, outburst, noise, hullabaloo, howl, hoot, boo, hiss.

outdance /ówtdáns/ *v.tr.* surpass in dancing.

outdare /ówtdáir/ *v.tr.* **1** outdo in daring. **2** overcome by daring.

outdated /ówtdáytid/ *adj.* out of date; obsolete.

outdistance /ówtdístəns/ *v.tr.* leave (a competitor) behind completely.

outdo /ówtdoo/ *v.tr.* (*3rd sing. present* **-does;** *past* **-did;** *past part.* **-done**) exceed or excel in doing or performance; surpass.

■ exceed, surpass, excel, transcend, beat, outstrip, outshine, top, cap, trump, overcome, defeat, outweigh, overshadow, eclipse.

outdoor /ówtdawr/ *adj.* done, existing, or used out of doors. ■ alfresco, open-air; see also OUTSIDE *adj.* 1.

outdoors /owtdáwrz/ *adv.* & *n.* ● *adv.* in or into the open air; out of doors. ● *n.* the world outside buildings; the open air.

/.../ **pronunciation**	● **part of speech**
□ **phrases, idioms, and compounds**	
□□ **derivatives**	■ **synonym section**
cross-references appear in SMALL CAPITALS or *italics*	

■ *adv.* see OUTSIDE *adv.* 1–3.

outdoorsman /ówtdŏrzmən, -dáwrz-/ *n.* a person who spends much time in outdoor activities, as fishing, camping, etc.

outdoorsy /owtdŏrzee, -dáwrz-/ *adj.* **1** relating to or suitable for the outdoors. **2** having a fondness for the outdoors.

outer /ówtər/ *adj. & n.* ● *adj.* **1** outside; external (*pierced the outer layer*). **2** farther from the center or inside; relatively far out. **3** objective or physical, not subjective nor psychical. ● *n.* **1** *Brit.* **a** the division of a target furthest from the bull's-eye. **b** a shot that strikes this. **2** esp. *Brit.* an outer garment or part of one. **3** *Austral. sl.* the part of a racecourse outside the enclosure. **4** *Brit.* an outer container for transport or display. □ **the outer bar** see BAR[1]. **outer man** (or **woman**) personal appearance; dress. **outer planet** a planet with an orbit outside that of Mars: Jupiter, Saturn, Uranus, Neptune, or Pluto. **outer space** the universe beyond the earth's atmosphere. **the outer world** people outside one's own circle. [ME f. OUT, replacing UTTER[1]]

■ *adj.* **1** see EXTERNAL *adj.* 1a, 3;1b. **2** see OUTLYING.

outermost /ówtərmōst/ *adj.* furthest from the inside; the most far out.

■ see OUTLYING.

outerwear /ówtərwair/ *n.* clothes worn over other clothes, esp. for warmth, protection, etc.

outface /ówtfáys/ *v.tr.* disconcert or defeat by staring or by a display of confidence.

outfall /ówtfawl/ *n.* the mouth of a river, drain, etc., where it empties into the sea, etc.

■ see MOUTH *n.* 3.

outfield /ówtfeeld/ *n.* **1** the outer part of a playing area, esp. a baseball field. **2** outlying land. □□ **outfielder** *n.*

outfight /ówtfīt/ *v.tr.* fight better than; beat in a fight.

outfit /ówtfit/ *n. & v.* ● *n.* **1** a set of clothes worn or esp. designed to be worn together. **2** a complete set of equipment, etc., for a specific purpose. **3** *colloq.* a group of people regarded as a unit, organization, etc.; a team. ● *v.tr.* (also *refl.*) (**-fitted, -fitting**) provide with an outfit, esp. of clothes.

■ *n.* **1** suit, costume, ensemble, *colloq.* getup; garb, clothes, clothing, dress, *colloq.* togs, duds, threads, *formal* attire. **2** gear, rig, kit, equipment, equipage, apparatus, accoutrements, paraphernalia, trappings, tackle, tack, utensils. **3** firm, corporation, company, concern, business, organization, setup, (military) unit, team; party, set, group. ● *v.* fit (out *or* up), equip, kit (out *or* up), provision, stock, accoutre, rig (out *or* up), supply, furnish; dress, clothe, *formal* attire.

outfitter /ówtfitər/ *n.* **1** a business that supplies outdoor equipment, arranges tours, etc. **2** a supplier of men's clothing; a haberdasher.

outflank /ówtflángk/ *v.tr.* **1 a** extend one's flank beyond that of (an enemy). **b** outmaneuver (an enemy) in this way. **2** get the better of; confound (an opponent).

outflow /ówtflō/ *n.* **1** an outward flow. **2** the amount that flows out.

■ see OUTPOURING.

outfly /ówtflí/ *v.tr.* (**-flies;** *past* **-flew;** *past part.* **-flown**) **1** surpass in flying. **2** fly faster or farther than.

outfox /ówtfóks/ *v.tr. colloq.* outwit.

outgeneral /ówtjénərəl/ *v.tr.* **1** outdo in generalship. **2** get the better of by superior strategy or tactics.

outgo *v. & n.* ● *v.tr.* /ówtgṓ/ (*3rd sing. present* **-goes;** *past* **-went;** *past part.* **-gone**) *archaic* go faster than; surpass. ● *n.* /ówtgō/ (*pl.* esp. *Brit.* **-goes**) expenditure of money, effort, etc.

outgoing *adj. & n.* ● *adj.* /ówtgṓing/ **1** friendly; sociable; extrovert. **2** retiring from office. **3** going out or away. ● *n.* /ówtgṓing/ **1** the act or an instance of going out. **2** *Brit.* (in *pl.*) expenditure.

■ *adj.* **1** genial, friendly, amiable, cordial, warm, expansive, approachable, affable, accessible, amenable, easygoing, amicable, sociable, congenial, extrovert, familiar, informal, communicative. **2, 3** departing,

retiring, ex-, former, past, emeritus; leaving, withdrawing.

outgrow /ówtgrṓ/ *v.tr.* (*past* **-grew;** *past part.* **-grown**) **1** grow too big for (one's clothes). **2** leave behind (a childish habit, taste, ailment, etc.) as one matures. **3** grow faster or taller than (a person, plant, etc.). □ **outgrow one's strength** esp. *Brit.* become lanky and weak through too rapid growth.

outgrowth /ówtgrōth/ *n.* **1** something that grows out. **2** an offshoot; a natural product. **3** the process of growing out.

■ **1** see PROMINENCE 2. **2** see OFFSHOOT 2.

outguess /ówtgés/ *v.tr.* guess correctly what is intended by (another person).

outgun /ówtgún/ *v.tr.* (**-gunned, -gunning**) **1** surpass in military or other power or strength. **2** shoot better than.

outhouse /ówt-hows/ *n.* **1** a building, esp. a shed, lean-to, barn, etc., built next to or in the grounds of a house. **2** an outbuilding used as a toilet, usu. with no plumbing.

outing /ówting/ *n.* **1** a short holiday away from home, esp. of one day or part of a day; a pleasure trip; an excursion. **2** any brief journey from home. **3** an appearance in an athletic contest, race, etc. **4** *colloq.* the practice or policy of exposing the homosexuality of a prominent person. [OUT *v.* = put out, go out + -ING[1]]

■ **1, 2** jaunt, junket, excursion, trip, expedition, tour, ride, drive, *colloq.* spin.

outjockey /ówtjókee/ *v.tr.* (**-eys, -eyed**) outwit by adroitness or trickery.

outjump /ówtjúmp/ *v.tr.* surpass in jumping.

outlander /ówtlandər/ *n.* a foreigner, alien, or stranger.

■ see STRANGER 1.

outlandish /owtlándish/ *adj.* **1** looking or sounding foreign. **2** bizarre; strange; unfamiliar. □□ **outlandishly** *adv.* **outlandishness** *n.* [OE *ūtlendisc* f. *ūtland* foreign country f. OUT + LAND]

■ unfamiliar, strange, odd, queer, offbeat, peculiar, curious, exotic, foreign, alien, unknown, unheard-of, different, exceptional, extraordinary, quaint, eccentric, bizarre, outré, weird, fantastic, unusual, singular, unique, freakish, grotesque, barbarous, far-out, kinky, camp(y).

outlast /ówtlást/ *v.tr.* last longer than (a person, thing, or duration) (*outlasted its usefulness*).

■ survive, outlive; outwear; weather, endure; see also *sit out.*

outlaw /ówtlaw/ *n. & v.* ● *n.* **1** a fugitive from the law. **2** *hist.* a person deprived of the protection of the law. ● *v.tr.* **1** declare (a person) an outlaw. **2** make illegal; proscribe (a practice, etc.). □ **outlaw strike** *Brit.* = *wildcat strike.* □□ **outlawry** *n.* [OE *ūtlaga, ūtlagian* f. ON *útlagi* f. *útlagr* outlawed, rel. to OUT, LAW]

■ *n.* **1** criminal, gangster, robber, desperado, bandit, highwayman, brigand, picaroon, pirate, fugitive, renegade, *hist.* footpad. ● *v.* **2** forbid, disallow, ban, interdict, bar, exclude, prohibit, proscribe.

outlay /ówtlay/ *n.* what is spent on something.

■ expense, cost, expenditure, spending, disbursement, payment.

outlet /ówtlet, -lit/ *n.* **1** a means of exit or escape. **2** (usu. foll. by *for*) a means of expression (of a talent, emotion, etc.) (*find an outlet for tension*). **3** an agency, distributor, or market for goods (*a new retail outlet in China*). **4** *US* an electrical power receptacle. [ME f. OUT- + LET[1]]

■ **1** way out, exit, egress, loophole, relief, escape, escape hatch, vent, opening, release, safety valve, discharge. **3** retailer, boutique, booth, kiosk, stall, stand, agency, distributor, esp. *Brit.* hypermarket; see also MARKET *n.* 3, 4.

outlier /ówtlīər/ *n.* **1** (also *attrib.*) an outlying part or member. **2** *Geol.* a younger rock formation isolated in older rocks. **3** *Statistics* a result differing greatly from others in the same sample.

outline /ówtlin/ *n. & v.* ● *n.* **1** a rough draft of a diagram, plan, proposal, etc. **2 a** a précis of a proposed novel, article, etc. **b** a verbal description of essential parts only; a sum-

mary. **3** a sketch containing only contour lines. **4** (in *sing.* or *pl.*) **a** lines enclosing or indicating an object (*the outline of a shape under the blankets*). **b** a contour. **c** an external boundary. **5** (in *pl.*) the main features or general principles (*the outlines of a plan*). **6** the representation of a word in shorthand. ● *v.tr.* **1** draw or describe in outline. **2** mark the outline of. □ **in outline** sketched or represented as an outline.
  ▪ *n.* **1, 2** précis, synopsis, résumé, summary, digest, abstract, conspectus, survey, overview, recapitulation, review, (thumbnail) sketch, skeleton, (overall) plan, layout, framework, draft, scenario. **4** contour, periphery, boundary; footprint; profile, silhouette. ● *v.* trace, draft, sketch, rough out, profile, block (out), plan (out), lay out, define, delineate.

outlive /ówtlív/ *v.tr.* **1** live longer than (another person). **2** live beyond (a specified date or time). **3** live through (an experience).

outlook /ówtlŏŏk/ *n.* **1** the prospect for the future (*the outlook is bleak*). **2** one's mental attitude or point of view (*narrow in their outlook*). **3** what is seen on looking out.
  ▪ **1** prospect, forecast, expectation(s), promise, hope, potentiality; see also FORECAST *n.* **2** view, position, point of view, viewpoint, prospect, perspective, slant, angle, standpoint, attitude, opinion, philosophy, *Weltanschauung.* **3** see VIEW *n.* 2a.

outlying /ówtlī-ing/ *adj.* situated far from a center; remote.
  ▪ distant, far-off, far-flung, outer, outermost, out-of-the-way, remote, faraway, peripheral; furthest, farthest.

outmaneuver /ówtmənŏŏvər/ *v.tr.* (*Brit.* **-manoeuvre**) **1** use skill and cunning to secure an advantage over (a person). **2** outdo in maneuvering.
  ▪ **1** see OUTSMART.

outmatch /ówtmách/ *v.tr.* be more than a match for (an opponent, etc.); surpass.

outmeasure /ówtmézhər/ *v.tr.* exceed in quantity or extent.

outmoded /ówtmŏdid/ *adj.* **1** no longer in fashion. **2** obsolete. □□ **outmodedly** *adv.* **outmodedness** *n.*

outmost /ówtmŏst/ *adj.* **1** outermost; furthest. **2** uttermost. [ME, var. of *utmost* UTMOST.]

outnumber /ówtnúmbər/ *v.tr.* exceed in number.

outpace /ówtpáys/ *v.tr.* **1** go faster than. **2** outdo in a contest.

outpatient /ówtpayshənt/ *n.* a hospital patient whose treatment does not require overnight hospitalization.

outperform /ówtpərfáwrm/ *v.tr.* **1** perform better than. **2** surpass in a specified field or activity. □□ **outperformance** *n.*
  ▪ see SURPASS 1.

outplacement /ówtplaysmənt/ *n.* the act or process of finding new employment for workers who have been dismissed.

outplay /ówtpláy/ *v.tr.* surpass in playing; play better than.

outpoint /ówtpóynt/ *v.tr.* (in various sports, esp. boxing) score more points than.

outport /ówtpawrt/ *n.* **1** esp. *Brit.* a subsidiary port. **2** *Can.* a small remote fishing village.

outpost /ówtpŏst/ *n.* **1** a detachment set at a distance from the main body of an army, esp. to prevent surprise. **2** a distant branch or settlement. **3** the furthest territory of an (esp. the British) empire.
  ▪ **2** see SETTLEMENT 2.

outpouring /ówtpawring/ *n.* **1** (usu. in *pl.*) a copious spoken or written expression of emotion. **2** what is poured out.
  ▪ effusion, outflow, flow, outburst, flood, deluge, torrent, spate, emanation, spouting, spurt, gush, efflux, effluence, outrush, tide, cascade, cataract, debouchment.

output /ówtpŏŏt/ *n.* & *v.* ● *n.* **1** the product of a process, esp. of manufacture, or of mental or artistic work. **2** the quantity or amount of this. **3** the printout, results, etc., supplied by a computer. **4** the power, etc., delivered by an apparatus. **5** a place where energy, information, etc., leaves a system. ● *v.tr.* (**-putting**; *past* and *past part.* **-put** or **-putted**) **1** put or send out. **2** (of a computer) supply (results, etc.).
  ▪ *n.* **1, 2** production, result, outturn, turnout, yield, crop,

harvest; achievement; see also WORK *n.* 3. **3** printout, results, dump. ● *v.* **1** put *or* send out, produce, generate, create, manufacture, yield, achieve, deliver; print out, transmit.

outrage /ówt-rayj/ *n.* & *v.* ● *n.* **1** an extreme or shocking violation of others' rights, sentiments, etc. **2** a gross offense or indignity. **3** fierce anger or resentment (*a feeling of outrage*). ● *v.tr.* **1** subject to outrage. **2** injure, insult, etc., flagrantly. **3** shock and anger. [ME f. OF *outrage* f. *outrer* exceed f. *outre* f. L *ultra* beyond]
  ▪ *n.* **1** violation, violence, atrocity, inhumanity, barbarism, enormity, evil, barbarity, savagery, brutality, malignity, malefaction, wrongdoing, evildoing, maltreatment, abuse, cruelty, injury, harm, damage. **2** see INSULT *n.* **3** resentment, affront, bitterness, indignation, hurt, shock, anger, *literary* wrath, ire. ● *v.* **1** violate, desecrate, defile, do violence to, injure, harm, abuse, damage; rape, violate, ravage, assault, ravish, attack. **2, 3** offend, insult, injure, affront, vex, displease, distress, nettle, chafe, infuriate, anger, enrage, madden, make a person's blood boil, make a person's hackles rise, *colloq.* rile; see also SHOCK¹ *v.* 1.

outrageous /owt-ráyjəs/ *adj.* **1** immoderate. **2** shocking. **3** grossly cruel. **4** immoral; offensive. □□ **outrageously** *adv.* **outrageousness** *n.* [ME f. OF *outrageus* (as OUTRAGE)]
  ▪ **1, 2** excessive, extravagant, immoderate, fulsome, exorbitant, enormous, unreasonable, preposterous, shocking, outré, extreme, unwarranted, exaggerated, unconscionable, inordinate, intolerable, disgraceful, shameful, scandalous. **3** vicious, cruel, heinous, atrocious, barbaric, inhuman, abusive, beastly, horrible, horrid, horrendous, iniquitous, villainous, wicked, evil, egregious, flagrant, grievous, infamous, execrable, abominable, grisly, hideous, monstrous, vile, unthinkable, foul, unspeakable, appalling, *colloq.* awful. **4** indecent, offensive, immoral, rude, indelicate, obnoxious, profane, obscene, dirty, filthy, lewd, salacious, foul, smutty, scatological, pornographic, objectionable, repellent, repulsive, nauseating, nauseous, nasty, gross, revolting, shocking, repugnant, disgusting, perverted, depraved, dissolute, degenerate, dissipated, debauched, profligate; explicit, unrestrained; foulmouthed, insulting; unseemly, inappropriate, indecorous, improper, appalling, embarrassing.

outran *past* of OUTRUN.

outrange /ówt-ráynj/ *v.tr.* (of a gun or its user) have a longer range than.

outrank /ówt-rángk/ *v.tr.* **1** be superior in rank to. **2** take priority over.

outré /ŏŏtráy/ *adj.* **1** outside the bounds of what is usual or proper. **2** eccentric or indecorous. [F, past part. of *outrer*: see OUTRAGE]
  ▪ unconventional, unusual, extravagant, bizarre, weird, strange, odd, peculiar, grotesque, outlandish, freakish; outrageous; eccentric, indecorous.

outreach *v.* & *n.* ● *v.tr.* /ówt-reech/ **1** reach further than. **2** surpass. **3** *poet.* stretch out (one's arms, etc.). ● *n.* /ówt-reech/ **1 a** any organization's involvement with or influence in the community, esp. in the context of social welfare. **b** the extent of this. **2** the extent or length of reaching out (*an outreach of 38 feet*).

outride /ówt-ríd/ *v.tr.* (*past* **-rode**; *past part.* **-ridden**) **1** ride better, faster, or further than. **2** (of a ship) come safely through (a storm, etc.).

outrider /ówt-rídər/ *n.* **1** a mounted attendant riding ahead of, or with, a carriage, etc. **2** a motorcyclist acting as a guard in a similar manner. **3** a cowhand, etc., keeping cattle, etc., within bounds. □□ **outriding** *n.*

/.../ **pronunciation** ● **part of speech**
□ **phrases, idioms, and compounds**
□□ **derivatives** ▪ **synonym section**
cross-references appear in SMALL CAPITALS or *italics*

outrigged /ówt-rigd/ *adj.* (of a boat, etc.) having outriggers.

outrigger /ówt-rigər/ *n.* **1** a beam, spar, or framework, rigged out and projecting from or over a ship's side for various purposes. **2** a similar projecting beam, etc., in a building. **3** a log, etc., fixed parallel to a canoe to stabilize it. **4** esp. *Brit.* **a** an extension of the crossbar of a carriage, etc., to enable another horse to be harnessed outside the shafts. **b** a horse harnessed in this way. **5 a** an iron bracket bearing an oarlock attached horizontally to a boat's side to increase the leverage of the oar. **b** a boat fitted with these. [OUT- + RIG¹: perh. partly after obs. (*Naut.*) *outligger*]

outright *adv. & adj.* ● *adv.* /owt-rít/ **1** altogether; entirely (*proved outright*). **2** not gradually, nor by degrees, nor by installments (*bought it outright*). **3** without reservation; openly (*denied the charge outright*). ● *adj.* /ówt-rit/ **1** downright; direct; complete (*their resentment turned to outright anger*). **2** undisputed; clear (*the outright winner*). □□ **outrightness** *n.*

■ *adv.* **1, 3** completely, altogether, entirely, thoroughly, quite, absolutely, totally, in toto, utterly; exactly, precisely, baldly, starkly, consummately, purely, directly, unhesitatingly, explicitly, categorically, straightforwardly, plainly, openly, forthrightly, unequivocally, unambiguously, candidly; unrestrictedly, unqualifiedly, unreservedly, unconditionally; peremptorily, out of hand. **2** directly, at once, immediately, instantaneously, instantly, then and there, there and then, straight *or* right away, right off, on the spot. ● *adj.* **1** undisguised, unmitigated, utter, consummate, pure, out-and-out, all-out, sheer, absolute, complete, stark, bald, thorough, arrant, thoroughgoing, downright, direct, definite, unmistakable. **2** unqualified, undisputed, total, unreserved, unrestricted, full, complete, unconditional, unequivocal, clear, direct, definite, unmistakable.

outrival /ówt-rívəl/ *v.tr.* outdo as a rival.

outrode *past* of OUTRIDE.

outrun *v.tr.* /ówt-rún/ (**-running**; *past* **-ran**; *past part.* **-run**) **1 a** run faster or farther than. **b** escape from. **2** go beyond (a specified point or limit).

outrush /ówt-rush/ *n.* **1** a rushing out. **2** a violent overflow.

■ see OUTPOURING.

outsail /ówtsáyl/ *v.tr.* sail better or faster than.

outsat *past* and *past part.* of OUTSIT.

outsell /ówtsél/ *v.tr.* (*past* and *past part.* **-sold**) **1** sell more than. **2** be sold in greater quantities than.

outset /ówtset/ *n.* the start; the beginning. □ **at** (or **from**) **the outset** at or from the beginning.

■ beginning, start, inauguration, inception, *colloq.* kickoff, *formal* commencement. □ **at the outset** originally; see also *at first* (FIRST).

outshine /ówtshín/ *v.tr.* (*past* and *past part.* **-shone**) shine brighter than; surpass in ability, excellence, etc.

outshoot /ówtshoot/ *v.tr.* (*past* and *past part.* **-shot**) **1** shoot better or further than (another person). **2** attempt or score more goals, points, etc., than (another player or team).

outside *n., adj., adv., & prep.* ● *n.* /ówtsíd/ **1** the external side or surface; the outer parts (*painted blue on the outside*). **2** the external appearance; the outward aspect of a building, etc. **3** (of a roadway, etc.) the side or lane farthest from the center. **4** (also *attrib.*) all that is without; the world as distinct from the thinking subject (*learn about the outside world*; *viewed from the outside the problem is simple*). **5** a position on the outer side (*the gate opens from the outside*). **6** *colloq.* the highest computation (*it is a mile at the outside*). **7** an outside player in soccer, etc. **8** (in *pl.*) the outer sheets of a ream of paper. ● *adj.* /ówtsid/ **1** of or on or nearer the outside; outer. **2 a** not of or belonging to some circle or institution (*outside help*; *outside work*). **b** (of a broker) not a member of the stock exchange. **3** (of a chance, etc.) remote; very unlikely. **4** (of an estimate, etc.) the greatest or highest possible (*the outside price*). **5** (of a player in soccer, etc.) positioned nearest to the edge of the field. **6** *Baseball* (of a pitched ball) missing the strike zone by passing home plate on the side away from the batter. ● *adv.* /owtsíd/ **1** on or to the outside.

2 in or to the open air. **3** not within or enclosed or included. **4** *sl.* not in prison. ● *prep.* /ówtsíd/ (also *disp.* foll. by *of*) **1** not in; to or at the exterior of (*meet me outside the post office*). **2** external to; not included in; beyond the limits of (*outside the law*). **3** *colloq.* other than; apart from. □ **at the outside** (of an estimate, etc.) at the most. **get outside of** *sl.* eat or drink. **outside and in** outside and inside. **outside edge** (on an ice skate) each of the edges facing outward when both feet are together. **outside in** = inside out. **outside interest** a hobby; an interest not connected with one's work or normal way of life. **outside seat** a seat nearer the end of a row. **outside track** the outside lane of a sports track, etc., which is longer because of the curve.

■ *n.* **1** exterior, face, facing, shell, skin, case, casing, surface, front; façade. **2** aspect, appearance, look, demeanor, face, front, façade, *literary* mien; mask, disguise, false front, pretense. **4** the outside *or* external *or* outer *or* manifest *or* physical world, the world at large; externals. **6** extreme, limit, most, maximum, utmost, best, worst, longest. ● *adj.* **1** exterior, external, outer; outdoor. **2 a** foreign, alien, outward; unconnected, excluded, uninvolved, separate, different; private, home, cottage, secondary, peripheral; independent, freelance. **3** faint; see also SLENDER 2. **4** maximum, maximal, highest, best, worst, greatest, most, largest, longest, furthest, farthest. ● *adv.* **1-3** on the outside, externally; out, outdoors, out of doors. □ **at the outside** at (the) maximum, at the most, at top, at the limit.

outsider /ówtsídər/ *n.* **1 a** a nonmember of some circle, party, profession, etc. **b** an uninitiated person; a layman. **2** a person without special knowledge, breeding, etc., or not fit to mix with good society. **3** a competitor, applicant, etc., thought to have little chance of success.

■ **1, 2** nonmember, noninitiate, layman, laywoman, foreigner, alien, outlander, stranger; newcomer, guest, visitor, trespasser, interloper, intruder, squatter, invader, gatecrasher. **3** dark horse, *Austral. sl.* roughie.

outsit /ówtsít/ *v.tr.* (**-sitting**; *past* and *past part.* **-sat**) sit longer than (another person or thing).

outsize /ówtsiz/ *adj. & n.* ● *adj.* **1** unusually large. **2** (of garments, etc.) of an exceptionally large size. ● *n.* an exceptionally large person or thing, esp. a garment.

outskirts /ówtskərts/ *n.pl.* the outer border or fringe of a town, district, subject, etc.

■ periphery, edge, environs, vicinity, border(s), suburb(s), exurb(s), neighborhood, purlieus, fringe(s), vicinage, faubourg(s).

outsmart /ówtsmaárt/ *v.tr. colloq.* outwit; be cleverer than.

■ outwit, outthink, outmaneuver, outmanipulate, outplay, steal a march on, get the better *or* best of, trick, dupe, hoodwink, fool, pull a fast one on, take in, deceive, hoax, gull, make a fool of, make a monkey (out) of, *colloq.* outfox; swindle, cheat, defraud, *colloq.* slip *or* put one over on, bamboozle, *literary* cozen, *sl.* con.

outsold *past* and *past part.* of OUTSELL.

outspan /ówtspan/ *v. & n. S.Afr.* ● *v.* (**-spanned**, **-spanning**) **1** *tr.* (also *absol.*) unharness (animals) from a cart, plow, etc. **2** *intr.* make a rest stop during a wagon journey. ● *n.* a place for grazing or encampment. [S.Afr. Du. *uitspannen* unyoke]

outspend /ówtspénd/ *v.tr.* (*past* and *past part.* **-spent**) spend more than (one's resources or another person).

outspoken /ówtspókən/ *adj.* given to or involving plain speaking; frank in stating one's opinions. □□ **outspokenly** *adv.* **outspokenness** *n.*

■ candid, frank, open, free, direct, unreserved, straightforward, forthright, explicit, specific, plainspoken, plain-speaking, unequivocal, unceremonious, unambiguous, unsubtle, uninhibited, unshrinking, blunt, bold, brusque, brash, undiplomatic, tactless, crude.

outspread /ówtspréd/ *adj. & v.* ● *adj.*, spread out; fully ex-

tended or expanded. ● *v.tr.* & *intr.* (*past* and *past part.*
-spread) spread out; expand.

outstanding /ówtstánding/ *adj.* **1 a** conspicuous; eminent,
esp. because of excellence. **b** (usu. foll. by *at, in*) remarkable
in (a specified field). **2** (esp. of a debt) not yet settled (*$200
still outstanding*). □□ **outstandingly** *adv.*

■ **1** prominent, eminent, renowned, famous, famed,
unforgettable, memorable, celebrated, distinguished,
special, choice, noteworthy, notable, noted, important,
conspicuous, exceptional, excellent, superior, first-
class, first-rate, superb, remarkable, extraordinary,
marvelous, sensational, *colloq.* smashing, super.
2 unsettled, ongoing, unresolved, unpaid, due, owed,
owing, receivable, payable; remaining, leftover.

outstare /ówtstáir/ *v.tr.* **1** outdo in staring. **2** abash by staring.

outstation /ówtstáyshən/ *n.* **1** a branch of an organization,
enterprise, or business in a remote area or at a considerable
distance from headquarters. **2** esp. *Austral.* & *NZ* part of a
farming estate separate from the main estate.

outstay /ówtstáy/ *v.tr.* **1** stay beyond the limit of (one's welcome, invitation, etc.). **2** stay or endure longer than (another person, etc.).

outstep /ówtstép/ *v.tr.* (**-stepped, -stepping**) step outside
or beyond.

outstretch /ówtstréch/ *v.tr.* **1** (usu. as **outstretched** *adj.*)
reach out or stretch out (esp. one's hands or arms). **2** reach
or stretch further than.

outstrip /ówtstríp/ *v.tr.* (**-stripped, -stripping**) **1** pass in
running, etc. **2** surpass in competition or relative progress
or ability.

■ overcome, surpass, outdo, outperform, outshine,
outclass, better, beat, transcend, best, worst, exceed,
excel, outdistance, overtake, top, cap, put in the shade,
eclipse, overshadow.

outtake /ówt-tayk/ *n.* a length of film or tape rejected in editing.

outtalk /ówt-táwk/ *v.tr.* outdo or overcome in talking.

outthink /ówt-thíngk/ *v.tr.* (*past* and *past part.* **-thought**)
outwit; outdo in thinking.

outthrust *adj., v.,* & *n.* ● *adj.* /ówt-thrúst/ extended; projected (*ran forward with outthrust arms*). ● *v.tr.* /ówt-thrúst/
(*past* and *past part.* **-thrust**) thrust out. ● *n.* /ówt-thrúst/
1 the act or an instance of thrusting forcibly outward. **2** the
act or an instance of becoming prominent or noticeable.

outtop /ówt-tóp/ *v.tr.* (**-topped, -topping**) surmount, surpass in height, extent, etc.

outturn /ówt-tərn/ *n.* **1** the quantity produced. **2** the result
of a process or sequence of events.

outvalue /ówtvályōo/ *v.tr.* (**-values, -valued, -valuing**) be
of greater value than.

outvote /ówtvṓt/ *v.tr.* defeat by a majority of votes.

outwalk /ówt-wáwk/ *v.tr.* **1** outdo in walking. **2** walk beyond.

outward /ówt-wərd/ *adj., adv.,* & *n.* ● *adj.* **1** situated on or
directed toward the outside. **2** going out (*on the outward
voyage*). **3** bodily; external; apparent; superficial (*in all outward respects*). **4** *archaic* outer (*the outward man*). ● *adv.*
(also **outwards**) in an outward direction; toward the outside. ● *n.* the outward appearance of something; the exterior. □ **outward-bound 1** (of a ship, passenger, etc.) going
away from home. **2** (**Outward Bound**) a movement to provide adventure training and other outdoor activities. **outward form** appearance. **outward things** the world around
us. **to outward seeming** esp. *Brit.* apparently. □□ **outwardly** *adv.* [OE *ūtweard* (as OUT, -WARD)]

■ *adj.* **1, 3** external, exterior, outer, outside, outlying,
manifest, obvious, evident, apparent, visible,
observable; superficial, surface, extrinsic, skin-deep,
shallow, pretended, false, ostensible, formal, physical,
bodily, fleshly, carnal, mundane, worldly, secular,
temporal, terrestrial, material, nonspiritual.
● *adv.* outwards, outside, away, out, *archaic* without.
□□ **outwardly** externally, apparently, visibly,
superficially, ostensibly, evidently, seemingly, on the
surface, to all appearances, to outward seeming.

outwardness /ówt-wərdnis/ *n.* **1** external existence; objectivity. **2** an interest or belief in outward things; objectivity.

outwards var. of OUTWARD *adv.*

outwash /ówt-wosh, -wawsh/ *n.* the material carried from a
glacier by meltwater and deposited beyond the moraine.

outwatch /ówt-wóch/ *v.tr.* **1** watch more than or longer
than. **2** *archaic* keep awake beyond the end of (night, etc.).

outwear *v.* & *n.* ● *v.tr.* /ówt-wáir/ (*past* **-wore**; *past part.*
-worn) **1** exhaust; wear out; wear away. **2** live or last beyond the duration of. **3** (as **outworn** *adj.*) out of date; obsolete. ● *n. Brit.* /ówt-wair/ outer clothing.

■ **3** (**outworn**) see *out of date* (DATE¹).

outweigh /ówt-wáy/ *v.tr.* exceed in weight, value, importance, or influence.

■ overcome, outbalance, overbalance, tip the scales,
preponderate over, surpass, prevail over, override, take
precedence over, compensate for, (more than) make up
for.

outwent *past* of OUTGO.

outwit /ówt-wít/ *v.tr.* (**-witted, -witting**) be too clever or
crafty for; deceive by greater ingenuity.

■ see OUTSMART.

outwith /ówt-wíth/ *prep. Sc.* outside, beyond.

outwore *past* of OUTWEAR.

outwork /ówt-wərk/ *v.* & *n.* ● *v.* work harder, faster, or longer
than. ● *n.* **1** an advanced or detached part of a fortification.
2 *Brit.* work done outside the shop or factory that supplies
it. □□ **outworker** *n.* (in sense 2).

outworn *past part.* of OUTWEAR.

ouzel /ōozəl/ *n.* (also **ousel**) **1** = *ring ouzel* (see RING¹). **2** (in
full **water ouzel**) = DIPPER. **3** *archaic* a blackbird. [OE *ōsle*
blackbird, of unkn. orig.]

ouzo /ōozō/ *n.* (*pl.* **-os**) a Greek anise-flavored liqueur.
[mod.Gk]

ova *pl.* of OVUM.

oval /ṓvəl/ *adj.* & *n.* ● *adj.* **1** egg-shaped; ellipsoidal. **2** having
the outline of an egg; elliptical. ● *n.* **1** an egg-shaped or
elliptical closed curve. **2** any object with an oval outline. **3**
Austral. a field for Australian Rules football. □ **Oval Office**
the office of the US president in the White House. □□ **oval-
ity** /ōválitee/ *n.* **ovally** *adv.* **ovalness** *n.* [med.L *ovalis* (as
OVUM)]

■ *adj.* egg-shaped, ovoid, oviform, *Biol.* obovate, ovate;
elliptical, ellipsoid(al), *Geom.* oblate.

ovary /ṓvəree/ *n.* (*pl.* **-ies**) **1** each of the female reproductive
organs in which ova are produced. **2** the hollow base of the
carpel of a flower, containing one or more ovules. □□ **ovarian** /ōváireeən/ *adj.* **ovariectomy** /-ree-éktəmee/ *n.* (*pl.*
-ies) (in sense 1). **ovariotomy** /-reeótəmee/ *n.* (*pl.* **-ies**)
(in sense 1). **ovaritis** /-rítis/ *n.* (in sense 1). [mod.L *ovarium*
(as OVUM)]

ovate /ṓvayt/ *adj. Biol.* egg-shaped as a solid or in outline;
oval. [L *ovatus* (as OVUM)]

ovation /ōváyshən/ *n.* **1** an enthusiastic reception, esp. spontaneous and sustained applause. **2** *Rom. Antiq.* a lesser form
of triumph. □ **standing ovation** prolonged applause during
which the crowd or audience rise to their feet. □□ **ovational**
adj. [L *ovatio* f. *ovare* exult]

■ **1** applause, acclamation, acclaim, plaudits, cheers,
cheering, clapping, praise, *colloq.* (big) hand, *formal*
laudation.

oven /úvən/ *n.* **1** an enclosed compartment of brick, stone,
or metal for cooking food. **2** a chamber for heating or drying. **3** a small furnace or kiln used in chemistry, metallurgy,
etc. □ **oven-ready** esp. *Brit.* (of food) prepared before sale
so as to be ready for immediate cooking in the oven. [OE
ofen f. Gmc]

ovenbird /úvənbərd/ *n.* **1** an American warbler, *Seiurus au-
rocapillus*, noted for the oven-shaped nest it builds on or near

/.../ **pronunciation**	● **part of speech**
□ **phrases, idioms, and compounds**	
□□ **derivatives**	■ **synonym section**
cross-references appear in SMALL CAPITALS or *italics*	

the ground. **2** any Central or S. American bird of the family Furnariidae, many of which make domed nests.

ovenproof /úvənpr͞oof/ *adj.* suitable for use in an oven; heat-resistant.

ovenware /úvənwair/ *n.* dishes that can be used for cooking food in the oven.

over /ṓvər/ *adv., prep., n.,* & *adj.* • *adv.* expressing movement or position or state above or beyond something stated or implied: **1** outward and downward from a brink or from any erect position (*knocked the man over*). **2** so as to cover or touch a whole surface (*paint it over*). **3** so as to produce a fold, or reverse a position; with the effect of being upside down. **4 a** across a street or other space (*decided to cross over*; *came over from England*). **b** for a visit, etc. (*invited them over last night*). **5** with transference or change from one hand or part to another (*went over to the enemy*; *handed them over*). **6** with motion above something; so as to pass across something (*climb over*; *fly over*; *boil over*). **7 a** from beginning to end with repetition or detailed concentration (*think it over*; *did it six times over*). **b** again, once more. **8** in excess; more than is right or required (*left over*). **9** for or until a later time (*hold it over*). **10** at an end; settled (*the crisis is over*; *all is over between us*). **11** (in full **over to you**) (as *int.*) (in radio conversations, etc.) said to indicate that it is the other person's turn to speak. **12** (as *int.*) Cricket an umpire's call to change ends. • *prep.* **1** above, in, or to a position higher than; upon. **2** out and down from; down from the edge of (*fell over the cliff*). **3** so as to cover (*a hat over his eyes*). **4** above and across; so as to clear (*flew over the North Pole*; *a bridge over the Hudson*). **5** concerning; engaged with; as a result of; while occupied with (*laughed over a good joke*; *fell asleep over the newspaper*). **6 a** in superiority of; superior to; in charge of (*a victory over the enemy*; *reign over three kingdoms*). **b** in preference to. **7** divided by. **8 a** throughout; covering the extent of (*traveled over most of Africa*; *a blush spread over his face*). **b** so as to deal with completely (*went over the plans*). **9 a** for the duration of (*stay over Saturday night*). **b** at any point during the course of (*I'll do it over the weekend*). **10** beyond; more than (*bids of over $50*; *are you over 18?*). **11** transmitted by (*heard it over the radio*). **12** in comparison with (*gained 20% over last year*). **13** having recovered from (*am now over my cold*; *will get over it in time*). • *n.* Cricket **1** a sequence of balls (now usu. six), bowled from one end of the field. **2** play resulting from this (*a maiden over*). • *adj.* (see also OVER-). **1** upper, outer. **2** superior. **3** extra. □ **begin** (or **start**, etc.) **over** begin again. **get it over with** do or undergo something unpleasant, etc., so as to be rid of it. **not over** not very; not at all (*not over friendly*). **over again** once again; again from the beginning. **over against** in an opposite situation to; adjacent to, in contrast with. **over and above** in addition to; not to mention (*$100 over and above the asking price*). **over and over** so that the same thing or the same point comes up again and again (*said it over and over*; *rolled it over and over*). **over-the-counter 1** (of medicine) sold without a prescription. **2** (of stocks, etc.) not listed on or traded by an organized securities exchange. **over the fence** Austral. & NZ *sl.* unreasonable; unfair; indecent. **over one's head** see HEAD. **over the hill** see HILL. **over the moon** see MOON. **over-the-top** Brit. *colloq.* (esp. of behavior, dress, etc.) outrageous, excessive. **over the way** Brit. (in a street, etc.) facing or opposite. [OE *ofer* f. Gmc]

■ *adv.* **1** down, to the ground *or* floor. **4** across. **7 a** see THROUGH *adv.* **b** (once) again, once more, one more time. **8** remaining, as a remainder, as surplus, outstanding. **10** over and done with, done (with), finished, terminated, concluded, ended, past, settled, closed, at an end, over with. • *prep.* **1** above, on, upon, on top of, atop. **3, 4** across. **5** see ABOUT *prep.* 1, *in the middle of* (MIDDLE). **8, 9** for, during, in *or* over *or* during the course of, throughout; (all) through, (all) about, all over. **10** more than, greater than, upwards of, in excess of, (over) and above, (over and) beyond; exceeding. □ **over and above** on top of, not to mention; see also BESIDES *prep.* **over and over** see

repeatedly (REPEAT). **over the fence** see UNREASONABLE 1. **over-the-top** see UNREASONABLE 1, CAMP² *adj.* 1. **over the way** across the street, facing, opposite, on the other side.

over- /ṓvər/ *prefix* added to verbs, nouns, adjectives, and adverbs, meaning: **1** excessively; to an unwanted degree (*overheat*; *overdue*). **2** upper; outer; extra (*overcoat*; *overtime*). **3** 'over' in various senses (*overhang*; *overshadow*). **4** completely; utterly (*overawe*; *overjoyed*).

overabundant /ṓvərəbúndənt/ *adj.* in excessive quantity. □□ **overabound** /-əbównd/ *v.intr.* **overabundance** *n.* **overabundantly** *adv.*

overachieve /ṓvərəcheév/ *v.* **1** *intr.* do more than might be expected (esp. scholastically). **2** *tr.* achieve more than (an expected goal or objective, etc.). □□ **overachievement** *n.* **overachiever** *n.*

overact /ṓvərákt/ *v.tr.* & *intr.* act in an exaggerated manner.
■ see OVERDO 1.

overactive /ṓvəráktiv/ *adj.* excessively active. □□ **overactivity** /-tívitee/ *n.*
■ see HECTIC *adj.* 1.

overage¹ /ṓvəráyj/ *adj.* **1** having attained a certain age limit. **2** too old.

overage² /ṓvərij/ *n.* a surplus or excess, esp. an amount greater than estimated.
■ see SURPLUS *n.*

overall *adj., adv.,* & *n.* • *adj.* /ṓvərawl/ **1** from end to end (*overall length*). **2** total; inclusive of all (*overall cost*). • *adv.* /ṓvəráwl/ in all parts; taken as a whole (*overall, the performance was excellent*). • *n.* /ṓvərawl/ **1** (in *pl.*) protective trousers, dungarees, or a combination suit, worn by workmen, etc. **2** Brit. an outer garment worn to keep out dirt, wet, etc. **3** Brit. close-fitting trousers worn as part of army uniform. □□ **overalled** /ṓvərawld/ *adj.*
■ *adj.* **2** total, complete, comprehensive, all-inclusive, inclusive, whole, entire, all-embracing, blanket.

overambitious /ṓvərambíshəs/ *adj.* excessively ambitious. □□ **overambition** *n.* **overambitiously** *adv.*
■ see AMBITIOUS 1a.

overanxious /ṓvərángkshəs/ *adj.* excessively anxious. □□ **overanxiety** /-angzí-itee/ *n.* **overanxiously** *adv.*

overarch /ṓvəraárch/ *v.tr.* form an arch over.

overarching /ṓvəraárching/ *adj.* **1** forming an arch. **2** dominating or encompassing everything else.

overarm /ṓvəraarm/ *adj.* & *adv.* **1** thrown with the hand above the shoulder (*pitch it overarm*; *an overarm tennis serve*). **2** Swimming with one or both arms lifted out of the water during a stroke.

overate *past* of OVEREAT.

overawe /ṓvər-áw/ *v.tr.* **1** restrain by awe. **2** keep in awe.
■ overwhelm, intimidate, cow, daunt, awe, bully, hector, browbeat, dominate, domineer, frighten, scare, terrify, disconcert, discomfit, abash.

overbalance /ṓvərbáləns/ *v.* & *n.* • *v.* **1** *tr.* outweigh. **2** *intr.* fall over, capsize. **3** *tr.* esp. Brit. cause (a person or thing) to lose its balance and fall. • *n.* **1** an excess. **2** the amount of this.
■ *v.* **1** see OUTWEIGH.

overbear /ṓvərbáir/ *v.tr.* (*past* **-bore**; *past part.* **-borne**) **1** bear down; upset by weight, force, or emotional pressure. **2** put down or repress by power or authority. **3** surpass in importance, etc.; outweigh.

overbearing /ṓvərbéring/ *adj.* **1** domineering; masterful. **2** overpowerful; of critical import. □□ **overbearingly** *adv.* **overbearingness** *n.*
■ repressive, domineering, masterful, bullying, imperious, officious, high and mighty, high-handed, overweening, magisterial, lordly, authoritarian, willful, despotic, dogmatic, autocratic, tyrannical, dictatorial, peremptory, arbitrary, assertive, arrogant, cavalier, haughty, superior, supercilious, hoity-toity, *colloq.* bossy, pushy, highfalutin, snooty, snotty.
□□ **overbearingly** see *imperatively* (IMPERATIVE).

overbid *v.* & *n.* • *v.* /ṓvərbíd/ (**-bidding**; *past* and *past part.* **-bid**) **1** *tr.* make a higher bid than. **2** *tr.* (also *absol.*) Bridge

a bid more on (one's hand) than warranted. **b** overcall. ● *n.* /ṓvərbid/ a bid that is higher than another, or higher than is justified. □□ **overbidder** *n.*

overbite /ṓvərbīt/ *n.* a condition in which the teeth of the upper jaw project forward over those of the lower jaw.

overblouse /ṓvərblows, -blowz/ *n.* a garment like a blouse, but worn without tucking it into a skirt or slacks.

overblown /ṓvərblṓn/ *adj.* **1** excessively inflated or pretentious. **2** (of a flower or a woman's beauty, etc.) past its prime.
  ■ **1** see IMMODERATE.

overboard /ṓvərbáwrd/ *adv.* from on a ship into the water (*fall overboard*). □ **go overboard 1** be highly enthusiastic. **2** behave immoderately; go too far. **throw overboard** abandon; discard.

overbold /ṓvərbṓld/ *adj.* excessively bold.

overbook /ṓvərbŏŏk/ *v.tr.* (also *absol.*) make too many bookings for (an aircraft, hotel, etc.).

overboot /ṓvərbŏŏt/ *n.* a boot worn over another boot or shoe.

overbore *past* of OVERBEAR.

overborne *past part.* of OVERBEAR.

overbought *past* and *past part.* of OVERBUY.

overbuild /ṓvərbíld/ *v.tr.* (*past* and *past part.* **-built**) **1** build over or upon. **2** place too many buildings on (land, etc.).

overburden /ṓvərbə́rd'n/ *v.* & *n.* ● *v.tr.* burden (a person, thing, etc.) to excess. ● *n.* **1** rock, etc., that must be removed prior to mining the mineral deposit beneath it. **2** an excessive burden. □□ **overburdensome** *adj.*
  ■ *v.* see OVERLOAD *v.* ● *n.* **2** see OVERLOAD *n.*

overbusy /ṓvərbízee/ *adj.* excessively busy.

overbuy /ṓvərbí/ *v.tr.* & *intr.* (*past* and *past part.* **-bought**) buy (a commodity, etc.) in excess of immediate need.

overcall *v.* & *n.* ● *v.tr.* /ṓvərkáwl/ (also *absol.*) *Bridge* **1** make a higher bid than (a previous bid or opponent). **2** *Brit.* = OVERBID *v.* 2b. ● *n.* /ṓvərkawl/ an act or instance of overcalling.

overcame *past* of OVERCOME.

overcapacity /ṓvərkəpásitee/ *n.* a state of saturation or an excess of productive capacity.

overcapitalize /ṓvərkápit'līz/ *v.tr.* fix or estimate the capital of (a company, etc.) too high.

overcareful /ṓvərkáirfŏŏl/ *adj.* excessively careful. □□ **overcarefully** *adv.*

overcast /ṓvərkást/ *adj.*, *v.*, & *n.* ● *adj.* **1** (of the sky, weather, etc.) covered with cloud; dull and gloomy. **2** (in sewing) edged with stitching to prevent fraying. ● *v.tr.* (*past* and *past part.* **-cast**) **1** cover (the sky, etc.) with clouds or darkness. **2** stitch over (a raw edge, etc.) to prevent fraying. ● *n.* /ṓvərkast/ a cloud covering part of the sky.
  ■ *adj.* **1** cloudy, clouded, sunless, moonless, starless, murky, gray, lowering, dull, dark, darkened, dreary, somber, gloomy, dismal, threatening, menacing.

overcautious /ṓvərkáwshəs/ *adj.* excessively cautious. □□ **overcaution** *n.* **overcautiously** *adv.* **overcautiousness** *n.*

overcharge /ṓvərchaárj/ *v.* & *n.* ● *v.tr.* **1 a** charge too high a price to (a person) or for (a thing). **b** charge (a specified sum) beyond the right price. **2** put too much charge into (a battery, gun, etc.). **3** put exaggerated or excessive detail into (a description, picture, etc.). ● *n.* an excessive charge (of explosive, money, etc.).
  ■ *v.* **1** see FLEECE *v.* 1.

overcheck /ṓvərchek/ *n.* **1** a combination of two differentsized check patterns. **2** a cloth with this pattern.

overcloud /ṓvərklówd/ *v.tr.* **1** cover with cloud. **2** mar, spoil, or dim, esp. as the result of anxiety, etc. (*overclouded by uncertainties*). **3** make obscure.

overcoat /ṓvərkōt/ *n.* **1** a heavy coat, esp. one worn over indoor clothes for warmth outdoors in cold weather. **2** a protective coat of paint, etc.
  ■ **1** see COAT *n.* 1.

overcome /ṓvərkúm/ *v.* (*past* **-came**; *past part.* **-come**) **1** *tr.* prevail over; master; conquer. **2** *tr.* (as **overcome** *adj.*) **a** exhausted; made helpless. **b** (usu. foll. by *with*, *by*) affected

by (emotion, etc.). **3** *intr.* be victorious. [OE *ofercuman* (as OVER-, COME)]
  ■ **1** beat, defeat, conquer, overpower, subdue, worst, triumph over, win over, prevail over, overthrow, overwhelm, get the better *or* best of, whip, drub, rout, break, subjugate, suppress, crush, master, *colloq.* lick, best, *literary* vanquish. **2** (**overcome**) beaten, defeated, exhausted, overwhelmed, subdued, worsted, bested; affected, speechless, swept off one's feet, helpless, overpowered, moved, influenced, at a loss (for words), *colloq.* bowled over, flabbergasted.

overcompensate /ṓvərkómpensayt/ *v.* **1** *tr.* (usu. foll. by *for*) compensate excessively for (something). **2** *intr. Psychol.* strive for power, etc., in an exaggerated way, esp. to make allowance or amends for a real or fancied grievance, defect, handicap, etc. □□ **overcompensation** /-áyshən/ *n.* **overcompensatory** /-kəmpénsitawree/ *adj.*

overconfident /ṓvərkónfidənt/ *adj.* excessively confident. □□ **overconfidence** *n.* **overconfidently** *adv.*
  ■ brash, arrogant, cocksure, cocky, brazen, hubristic, swaggering, audacious, overbearing, *colloq.* pushy, *literary* vainglorious; reckless, heedless, foolhardy, thoughtless, shortsighted, hasty.

overcook /ṓvərkŏŏk/ *v.tr.* cook too much or for too long. □□ **overcooked** *adj.*
  ■ see BURN¹ *v.* 5.

overcritical /ṓvərkrítikəl/ *adj.* excessively critical; quick to find fault.
  ■ supercritical, hypercritical, captious, carping, niggling, caviling, querulous, faultfinding, finicky, fussy, hairsplitting, difficult, fastidious, harsh, severe, demanding, exacting, small, small-minded, picayune, *colloq.* picky, nitpicking, persnickety.

overcrop /ṓvərkróp/ *v.tr.* (**-cropped**, **-cropping**) exhaust (the land) by the continuous growing of crops.

overcrowd /ṓvərkrówd/ *v.tr.* (often as **overcrowded** *adj.*) fill (a space, object, etc.) beyond what is usual or comfortable. □□ **overcrowding** *n.*
  ■ see CRAM 1; (**overcrowded**) jammed, packed, crowded, congested.

overcurious /ṓvərkyŏŏreeəs/ *adj.* excessively curious. □□ **overcuriosity** /-reeósitee/ *n.* **overcuriously** *adv.*

overdelicate /ṓvərdélikət/ *adj.* excessively delicate. □□ **overdelicacy** *n.*

overdevelop /ṓvərdivéləp/ *v.tr.* **1** develop too much. **2** *Photog.* treat with developer for too long.

overdo /ṓvərdŏŏ/ *v.tr.* (*3rd sing. present* **-does**; *past* **-did**; *past part.* **-done**) **1** carry to excess; take too far; exaggerate (*I think you overdid the sarcasm*). **2** (esp. as **overdone** *adj.*) overcook. □ **overdo it** (or **things**) exhaust oneself. [OE *oferdōn* (as OVER-, DO¹)]
  ■ **1** take *or* carry to excess, take *or* carry to extremes, exaggerate, carry *or* take too far, not know when to stop, go overboard with, do to death; overindulge in. **2** see BURN¹ *v.* 5. □ **overdo it** (or **things**) overwork, do too much, overtax *or* overload *or* overburden oneself, exhaust oneself, bite off more than one can chew, burn the candle at both ends.

overdose /ṓvərdōs/ *n.* & *v.* ● *n.* an excessive dose (of a drug, etc.). ● *v.* **1** *tr.* give an excessive dose of (a drug, etc.) or to (a person). **2** *intr.* take an excessive dose (of a drug, etc.). **3** *sl.* (usu. foll. by *on*) have or experience an excessive amount of (*we overdosed on movies this weekend*) □□ **overdosage** /ṓvərdṓsij/ *n.*

overdraft /ṓvərdraft/ *n.* **1** a deficit in a bank account caused by drawing more money than is credited to it. **2** the amount of this.

overdraw /ṓvərdráw/ *v.* (*past* **-drew**; *past part.* **-drawn**) **1** *tr.* **a** draw a sum of money in excess of the amount credited

---

/.../ **pronunciation**	● **part of speech**
□ **phrases, idioms, and compounds**	
□□ **derivatives**	■ **synonym section**
cross-references appear in SMALL CAPITALS or *italics*	

to (one's bank account). **b** (as **overdrawn** *adj.*) having overdrawn one's account. **2** *intr.* overdraw one's account. **3** *tr.* exaggerate in describing or depicting. □□ **overdrawer** *n.* (in senses 1 & 2).

■ **3** see EXAGGERATE 1.

overdress *v. & n.* ● *v.* /ōvərdrés/ **1** *tr.* dress with too much display or formality. **2** *intr.* overdress oneself. ● *n.* /ōvərdres/ a dress worn over another dress or a blouse, etc.

overdrink /ōvərdríngk/ *v.intr. & refl.* (*past* **-drank**; *past part.* **-drunk**) drink too much, esp. of alcoholic beverages.

overdrive /ōvərdrīv/ *n.* **1 a** a mechanism in a motor vehicle providing a gear ratio higher than that of the usual gear. **b** an additional speed-increasing gear. **2** (usu. prec. by *in*, *into*) a state of high or excessive activity.

overdub *v. & n.* ● *v.tr.* /ōvərdúb/ (**-dubbed**, **-dubbing**) (also *absol.*) impose (additional sounds) on an existing recording. ● *n.* /ōvərdub/ the act or an instance of overdubbing.

overdue /ōvərdōō, -dyōō/ *adj.* **1** past the time when due or ready. **2** not yet paid, arrived, born, etc., although after the expected time. **3** (of a library book, etc.) retained longer than the period allowed.

■ late, tardy, behindhand, behind, unpunctual, belated, past due.

overeager /ōvəreéegər/ *adj.* excessively eager. □□ **overeagerly** *adv.* **overeagerness** *n.*

overeat /ōvəreét/ *v.intr. & refl.* (*past* **-ate**; *past part.* **-eaten**) eat too much.

■ gorge, surfeit, gormandize, stuff oneself, overindulge, guzzle, feast, make a pig of oneself, *sl.* binge, pig out.

overelaborate /ōvərilábərət/ *adj.* excessively elaborate. □□ **overelaborately** *adv.*

overemotional /ōvərimṓshənəl/ *adj.* excessively emotional. □□ **overemotionally** *adv.*

■ see SENTIMENTAL.

overemphasis /ōvərémfəsis/ *n.* excessive emphasis. □□ **overemphasize** /-fəsīz/ *v.tr. & intr.*

■ see *exaggeration* (EXAGGERATE). □□ **overemphasize** see EXAGGERATE 1.

overenthusiasm /ōvərinthōōzeeazəm, -thyōō-/ *n.* excessive enthusiasm. □□ **overenthusiastic** /-zeeástik/ *adj.* **overenthusiastically** *adv.*

overestimate *v. & n.* ● *v.tr.* (also *absol.*) /ōvəréstimayt/ form too high an estimate of (a person, ability, cost, etc.). ● *n.* /ōvəréstimit/ too high an estimate. □□ **overestimation** /-áyshən/ *n.*

■ *v.* see MISCALCULATE.

overexcite /ōvəriksít/ *v.tr.* excite excessively. □□ **overexcitement** *n.*

overexercise /ōvəréksərsīz/ *v. & n.* ● *v.tr.* use or exert (a part of the body, one's authority, etc.) too much. **2** *intr.* do too much exercise; overexert oneself. ● *n.* excessive exercise.

overexert /ōvərigzƏrt/ *v.tr. & refl.* exert too much. □□ **overexertion** /-zƏrshən/ *n.*

overexpose /ōvərikspṓz/ *v.tr.* (also *absol.*) **1** expose too much, esp. to the public eye. **2** *Photog.* expose (film) for too long a time. □□ **overexposure** /-spṓzhər/ *n.*

overextend /ōvərikstƏnd/ *v.tr.* **1** extend (a thing) too far. **2** (also *refl.*) take on (oneself) or impose on (another person) an excessive burden of work.

■ **1** see EXCEED 2. **2** see STRETCH *v.* 6.

overfalls /ōvərfawlz/ *n.* **1** a turbulent stretch of sea, etc., caused by a strong current or tide over a submarine ridge, or by a meeting of currents. **2** a place provided on a dam, weir, etc., for the overflow of surplus water.

overfamiliar /ōvərfəmílyər/ *adj.* excessively familiar.

overfatigue /ōvərfəteég/ *n.* excessive fatigue.

overfeed /ōvərfeéd/ *v.tr.* (*past* and *past part.* **-fed**) feed excessively.

■ see STUFF *v.* 5a.

overfill /ōvərfíl/ *v.tr. & intr.* fill to excess or to overflowing.

■ see SATE 2.

overfine /ōvərfín/ *adj.* excessively fine; too precise.

overfish /ōvərfísh/ *v.tr.* deplete (a stream, etc.) by too much fishing.

overflow *v. & n.* ● *v.* /ōvərflṓ/ **1** *tr.* **a** flow over (the brim, limits, etc.). **b** flow over the brim or limits of. **2** *intr.* **a** (of a receptacle, etc.) be so full that the contents overflow it (*until the cup was overflowing*). **b** (of contents) overflow a container. **3** *tr.* (of a crowd, etc.) extend beyond the limits of (a room, etc.). **4** *tr.* flood (a surface or area). **5** *intr.* (foll. by *with*) be full of. **6** *intr.* (of kindness, a harvest, etc.) be very abundant. ● *n.* /ōvərflṓ/ (also *attrib.*) **1** what overflows or is superfluous (*mop up the overflow*; *put the audience overflow in another room*). **2** an instance of overflowing (*overflow occurs when both systems are run together*). **3** (esp. in a bath or sink) an outlet for excess water, etc. **4** *Computing* the generation of a number having more digits than the assigned location. □ **overflow meeting** esp. *Brit.* a meeting for those who cannot be accommodated at the main gathering. [OE *oferflōwan* (as OVER-, FLOW)]

■ *v.* **1** see *run over* 1. **2** see *brim over*. **3** see FILL *v.* 2. **4** see FLOOD *v.* 1. **5** (*overflow with*) see TEEM[1] *v.* 2. **6** (*overflow with*) see ABOUND 2. ● *n.* **1** see EXCESS *n.* 1. **2** see FLOOD *n.* 1.

overfly /ōvərflí/ *v.tr.* (**-flies**; *past* **-flew**; *past part.* **-flown**) fly over or beyond (a place or territory). □□ **overflight** /ōvərflīt/ *n.*

overfold /ōvərfōld/ *n.* a series of strata folded so that the middle part is upside down.

overfond /ōvərfónd/ *adj.* (often foll. by *of*) having too great an affection or liking (for a person or thing) (*overfond of chocolate*; *an overfond parent*). □□ **overfondly** *adv.* **overfondness** *n.*

overfulfill /ōvərfōōlfíl/ *v.tr.* fulfill (a plan, quota, etc.) beyond expectation or before the appointed time. □□ **overfulfillment** *n.*

overfull /ōvərfōōl/ *adj.* filled excessively or to overflowing.

overgeneralize /ōvərjénərəlīz/ *v.* **1** *intr.* draw general conclusions from inadequate data, etc. **2** *intr.* argue more widely than is justified by the available evidence, by circumstances, etc. **3** *tr.* draw an overgeneral conclusion from (data, circumstances, etc.). □□ **overgeneralization** *n.*

overgenerous /ōvərjénərəs/ *adj.* excessively generous. □□ **overgenerously** *adv.*

overglaze /ōvərglayz/ *n. & adj.* ● *n.* **1** a second glaze applied to ceramic ware. **2** decoration on a glazed surface. ● *adj.* (of painting, etc.) done on a glazed surface.

overground /ōvərgrownd/ *adj.* **1** raised above the ground. **2** not underground.

overgrow /ōvərgrṓ/ *v.tr.* (*past* **-grew**; *past part.* **-grown**) **1** (as **overgrown** *adj.* /ōvərgrṓn/) **a** abnormally large (*an overgrown eggplant*). **b** wild; grown over with vegetation (*an overgrown pond*). **2** grow over, overspread, esp. so as to choke (*brambles have overgrown the pathway*). **3** esp. *Brit.* grow too big for (one's strength, etc.). □□ **overgrowth** *n.*

■ **1** (**overgrown**) **a** see ENORMOUS, TALL *adj.* 1. **b** covered, overrun, wild, overspread, luxuriant, weedy, abundant.

overhand /ōvərhand/ *adj. & adv.* **1** (in tennis, baseball, etc.) thrown or played with the hand above the shoulder; overarm. **2** *Swimming* = OVERARM. **3 a** with the palm of the hand downward or inward. **b** with the hand above the object held. □ **overhand knot** a simple knot made by forming a loop and passing the free end through it.

overhang *v. & n.* ● *v.* /ōvərháng/ (*past* and *past part.* **-hung**) **1** *tr. & intr.* project or hang over. **2** *tr.* menace; preoccupy; threaten. ● *n.* /ōvərhang/ **1** the overhanging part of a structure or rock formation. **2** the amount by which this projects.

■ *v.* **1** jut (out), beetle, bulge (out), project (out), protrude, stick out, loom (out), extend (out), impend, hang (out) over. **2** threaten, menace, imperil; preoccupy. ● *n.* ledge; projection, bulge, protrusion, extension.

overhaste /ōvərháyst/ *n.* excessive haste. □□ **overhasty** *adj.* **overhastily** *adv.*

■ □□ **overhasty** see PREMATURE 1.

overhaul *v. & n.* ● *v.tr.* /ōvərháwl/ **1 a** take to pieces in order to examine. **b** examine the condition of (and repair if necessary). **2** overtake. ● *n.* /ṓvərhawl/ a thorough examination, with repairs if necessary. [orig. Naut., = release (rope tackle) by slackening]

■ *v.* **1** strip (down), take to pieces *or* bits, take apart; renovate, refurbish, recondition, rebuild, restore, repair, service, adjust, patch (up), mend, fix (up). **2** overtake, pass, gain on *or* upon, draw ahead of, catch up (with), get ahead of, outstrip, outdistance, leave behind, lap. ● *n.* reconditioning, overhauling, refurbishing, rebuilding, renovation, servicing, service, repair, adjustment, mending, fixing (up); see EXAMINATION 1, 2.

overhead *adv., adj.,* & *n.* ● *adv.* /ṓvərhéd/ **1** above one's head. **2** in the sky or on the floor above. ● *adj.* /ṓvərhed/ **1** (of a driving mechanism, etc.) above the object driven. **2** (of expenses) arising from general operating costs, as distinct from particular business transactions. ● *n.* /ṓvərhed/ overhead expenses. □ **overhead projector** a device that projects an enlarged image of a transparency onto a surface above and behind the user.

■ *adv.* over *or* above one's head, (up) above, (up) in the air *or* sky, high up, on high, aloft, skyward. ● *adj.* **1** elevated, raised, upper. ● *n.* (basic *or* fixed *or* running) costs, operating cost(s), expense(s), outlay, disbursement(s), expenditure(s), maintenance.

overhear /ṓvərheer/ *v.tr.* (*past* and *past part.* **-heard**) (also *absol.*) hear as an eavesdropper or as an unperceived or unintentional listener.

overheat /ṓvərheet/ *v.* **1** *tr.* & *intr.* make or become too hot; heat to excess. **2** *tr.* (as **overheated** *adj.*) too passionate about a matter.

overindulge /ṓvərindúlj/ *v.tr.* & *intr.* indulge to excess. □□ **overindulgence** *n.* **overindulgent** *adj.*

■ see OVERDO 1. □□ **overindulgence** see EXCESS *n.* 4. **overindulgent** see DISSOLUTE.

overinsure /ṓvərinshŏŏr/ *v.tr.* insure (property, etc.) for more than its real value; insure excessively. □□ **overinsurance** *n.*

overissue /ṓvəríshŏŏ/ *v.* & *n.* ● *v.tr.* (**-issues, -issued, -issuing**) issue (notes, shares, etc.) beyond the authorized amount, or the ability to pay. ● *n.* the notes, shares, etc., or the amount so issued.

overjoyed /ṓvərjóyd/ *adj.* (often foll. by *at, to hear,* etc.) filled with great joy.

■ delighted, ecstatic, elated, happy, rapturous, euphoric, jubilant, thrilled, cock-a-hoop, transported, in seventh heaven, over the moon, *colloq.* tickled pink *or* to death, on cloud nine *or* seven.

overkill /ṓvərkil/ *n.* & *v.* ● *n.* **1** the amount by which destruction or the capacity for destruction exceeds what is necessary for victory or annihilation. **2** excess; excessive behavior. ● *v.tr.* & *intr.* kill or destroy to a greater extent than necessary.

overladen /ṓvərláyd'n/ *adj.* bearing or carrying too large a load.

overlaid *past* and *past part.* of OVERLAY[1].

overlain *past part.* of OVERLIE.

overland /ṓvərland, -lənd/ *adj., adv.,* & *v.* ● *adj.* & *adv.* also /ṓvərlánd/ **1** by land. **2** not by sea. ● *v. Austral.* **1** *tr.* drive (livestock) overland. **2** *intr.* go a long distance overland.

overlander /ṓvərlandər/ *n. Austral.* & *NZ* **1** a person who drives livestock overland. **2** *sl.* a tramp; a sundowner.

■ see TRAMP *n.* 1.

overlap *v.* & *n.* ● *v.* /ṓvərláp/ (**-lapped, -lapping**) **1** *tr.* (of part of an object) partly cover (another object). **2** *tr.* cover and extend beyond. **3** *intr.* (of two things) partly coincide; not be completely separate (*where psychology and philosophy overlap*). ● *n.* /ṓvərlap/ **1** an instance of overlapping. **2** the amount of this.

■ *v.* **1, 2** lap (over), overlie, overlay, imbricate. **3** coincide, correspond, intersect; see also MEET[1] *v.* 3. ● *n.* lap, flap, overlay; imbrication.

overlay[1] *v.* & *n.* ● *v.tr.* /ṓvərláy/ (*past* and *past part.* **-laid**) **1** lay over. **2** (foll. by *with*) cover the surface of (a thing)

with (a coating, etc.). **3** overlie. ● *n.* /ṓvərlay/ **1** a thing laid over another. **2** (in printing, map reading, etc.) a transparent sheet to be superimposed on another sheet. **3** *Computing* **a** the process of transferring a block of data, etc., to replace what is already stored. **b** a section so transferred. **4** a coverlet, small tablecloth, etc.

■ *v.* **1, 3** see OVERLAP *v.* 1, 2. **2** see SPREAD *v.* 4a. ● *n.* **1** see SKIN *n.* 4, OVERLAP *n.*

overlay[2] *past* of OVERLIE.

overleaf /ṓvərleef/ *adv.* on the other side of the leaf (of a book) (*see the diagram overleaf*).

overleap /ṓvərleep/ *v.tr.* (*past* and *past part.* **-leaped** or **-leapt**) **1** leap over; surmount. **2** omit; ignore. [OE *oferhlēapan* (as OVER, LEAP)]

overlie /ṓvərlí/ *v.tr.* (**-lying**; *past* **-lay**; *past part.* **-lain**) **1** lie on top of. **2** smother (a child, etc.) by lying on top.

■ **1** see OVERLAP *v.* 1, 2.

overload *v.* & *n.* ● *v.tr.* /ṓvərlṓd/ load excessively; force (a person, thing, etc.) beyond normal or reasonable capacity. ● *n.* /ṓvərlōd/ an excessive quantity; a demand, etc., that surpasses capability or capacity.

■ *v.* weigh down, burden, overburden, load (up), overtax, saddle, tax, strain, impede, handicap, oppress, encumber, overcharge, *literary* cumber. ● *n.* surcharge, overcharge, overburden, *literary* dead weight, oppression, handicap, tax, load, encumbrance, impediment, hindrance.

overlook *v.* & *n.* ● *v.tr.* /ṓvərlŏŏk/ **1** fail to notice; ignore; condone (an offense, etc.). **2** have a view from above; be higher than. **3** supervise; oversee. **4** bewitch with the evil eye. ● *n.* /ṓvərlŏŏk/ a commanding position or view. □□ **overlooker** *n.*

■ *v.* **1** miss, slip up on, omit, neglect, slight, disregard, fail to notice, ignore, pass over, leave out, forget, *colloq.* pass up; blink at, wink at, let go (by), let pass, let ride, turn a blind eye to, shut one's eyes to, pretend not to notice, take no notice of, disregard, forgive, pardon, excuse, permit, allow, forget about, write off, condone, make allowances for, gloss over. **2** command a view of, look over.

overlord /ṓvərlawrd/ *n.* & *v.* ● *n.* **1** a supreme lord. **2** a powerful authoritarian; a highly influential person (*the overlords of technology*). ● *v.* **1** rule as a tyrant. **2** domineer. □□ **overlordship** *n.*

overly /ṓvərlee/ *adv.* excessively; too.

■ excessively, too, exceedingly, immoderately, disproportionately, unduly, inordinately, extraordinarily, very, *colloq.* damned.

overlying *pres. part.* of OVERLIE.

overman *v.* & *n.* ● *v.tr.* /ṓvərmán/ (**-manned, -manning**) provide with too large a crew, staff, etc. ● *n.* /ṓvərman, -mən/ (*pl.* **-men**) esp. *Brit.* an overseer in a coal-mining operation.

overmantel /ṓvərmant'l/ *n.* ornamental shelves, etc., over a mantelpiece.

overmaster /ṓvərmástər/ *v.tr.* master completely; conquer. □□ **overmastering** *adj.* **overmastery** *n.*

overmatch /ṓvərmách/ *v.tr.* be more than a match for; defeat by superior strength, etc.

overmeasure /ṓvərmezhər/ *n.* an amount beyond what is proper or sufficient.

overmuch /ṓvərmúch/ *adv.* & *adj.* ● *adv.* to too great an extent; excessively. ● *adj.* excessive; superabundant.

overnice /ṓvərnís/ *adj.* excessively fussy, punctilious, particular, etc. □□ **overniceness** *n.* **overnicety** *n.*

■ see FINICKY 1.

overnight *adv.* & *adj.* ● *adv.* /ṓvərnít/ **1** for the duration of a night (*stay overnight*). **2** during the course of a night. **3** suddenly; immediately (*the situation changed overnight*).

/. . . / pronunciation	● part of speech
□ **phrases, idioms, and compounds**	
□□ **derivatives**	■ **synonym section**
cross-references appear in SMALL CAPITALS or *italics*	

● *adj.* /ṓvərnīt/ **1** for use overnight (*an overnight bag*). **2** done, etc., overnight (*an overnight stop*).

overnighter /ṓvərnītər/ *n.* **1** a person who stops at a place overnight. **2** an overnight bag.

overpaid *past* and *past part.* of OVERPAY.

overparticular /ṓvərpərtíkyələr, -pətík-/ *adj.* excessively particular or fussy.
■ see FINICKY 1.

overpass *n. & v.* ● *n.* /ṓvərpas/ a road or railroad line that passes over another by means of a bridge. ● *v.tr.* /ṓvərpás/ **1** pass over or across or beyond. **2** get to the end of; surmount. **3** (as **overpassed** or **overpast** *adj.*) that has gone by; past.

overpay /ṓvərpáy/ *v.tr.* (*past* and *past part.* **-paid**) recompense (a person, service, etc.) too highly. □□ **overpayment** *n.*

overpitch /ṓvərpích/ *v.tr.* *Brit.* exaggerate.

overplay /ṓvərpláy/ *v.tr.* play (a part) to excess; give undue importance to; overemphasize. □ **overplay one's hand 1** be unduly optimistic about one's capabilities. **2** spoil a good case by exaggerating its value.
■ see EXAGGERATE 1.

overplus /ṓvərplus/ *n.* a surplus; a superabundance. [ME, partial transl. of AF *surplus* or med.L *su(pe)rplus*]

overpopulated /ṓvərpópyəlaytid/ *adj.* having too large a population. □□ **overpopulation** /-láyshən/ *n.*
■ see *overcrowded* (OVERCROWD).

overpower /ṓvərpówr/ *v.tr.* **1** reduce to submission; subdue. **2** make (a thing) ineffective or imperceptible by greater intensity. **3** (of heat, emotion, etc.) be too intense for; overwhelm. □□ **overpowering** *adj.* **overpoweringly** *adv.*
■ **1** overcome, overwhelm, beat, conquer, defeat, crush, put down, worst, prevail, master, quell, subdue, subjugate, *colloq.* best, *literary* vanquish. **3** overcome, overwhelm, dumbfound, daze, stagger, amaze, stun, stupefy, nonplus, strike, *colloq.* floor. □□ **overpowering** overwhelming, irresistible, powerful, telling, compelling, unendurable, unbearable, oppressive.

overprice /ṓvərprís/ *v.tr.* price (a thing) too highly.

overprint *v. & n.* ● *v.tr.* /ṓvərprínt/ **1** print further matter on (a surface already printed, esp. a postage stamp). **2** print (further matter) in this way. **3** *Photog.* print (a positive) darker than was intended. **4** (also *absol.*) print too many copies of (a work). ● *n.* /ṓvərprint/ **1** the words, etc., overprinted. **2** an overprinted postage stamp.

overproduce /ṓvərprədṓs, -dyṓs/ *v.tr.* (usu. *absol.*) **1** produce more of (a commodity) than is wanted. **2** produce to an excessive degree. □□ **overproduction** /-dúkshən/ *n.*

overproof /ṓvərprṓf/ *adj.* containing more alcohol than proof spirit does.

overprotective /ṓvərprətéktiv/ *adj.* excessively protective, esp. of a person in one's charge.

overqualified /ṓvərkwólifīd/ *adj.* too highly qualified (esp. for a particular job, etc.).

overran *past* of OVERRUN.

overrate /ṓvəráyt/ *v.tr.* assess too highly.
■ overvalue, overestimate, make too much of, overprize.

overreach /ṓvəréech/ *v.tr.* circumvent; outwit; get the better of by cunning or artifice. □ **overreach oneself 1** strain oneself by reaching too far. **2** defeat one's object by going too far.

overreact /ṓvəreeákt/ *v.intr.* respond more forcibly, etc., than is justified. □□ **overreaction** /-ákshən/ *n.*
■ make too much of a thing, make a mountain out of a molehill, lose all *or* one's sense of proportion, go overboard, go too far.

overrefine /ṓvərifín/ *v.tr.* (also *absol.*) **1** refine too much. **2** make too subtle distinctions in (an argument, etc.).

override *v. & n.* ● *v.tr.* /ṓvəríd/ (*past* **-rode**; *past part.* **-ridden**) **1** (often as **overriding** *adj.*) have or claim precedence or superiority over (*an overriding consideration*). **2 a** intervene and make ineffective. **b** interrupt the action of (an automatic device), esp. to take manual control. **3 a** trample down or underfoot. **b** supersede arrogantly. **4** extend over, esp. (of a part of a fractured bone) overlap (another part). **5** ride over

(enemy country). **6** exhaust (a horse, etc.) by hard riding. ● *n.* /ṓvərīd/ **1** the action or process of suspending an automatic function. **2** a device for this.
■ *v.* **1** see OUTWEIGH; (**overriding**) dominant, dominating, predominant, prevailing, preponderant, primary, prime, overruling, principal, main, chief. **2 a** see REVERSE *v.* 2, 5.

overripe /ṓvəríp/ *adj.* (esp. of fruit, etc.) past its best; excessively ripe; full-blown.

overrode *past* of OVERRIDE.

overruff *Cards v. & n.* ● *v.tr.* /ṓvərúf/ (also *absol.*) overtrump. ● *n.* /ṓvəruf/ an instance of this.

overrule /ṓvərṓl/ *v.tr.* **1** set aside (a decision, argument, proposal, etc.) by exercising a superior authority. **2** annul a decision by or reject a proposal of (a person) in this way.

overrun *v. & n.* ● *v.tr.* /ṓvərún/ (**-running**; *past* **-ran**; *past part.* **-run**) **1** (of pests, weeds, etc.) swarm or spread over. **2** conquer or ravage (territory) by force. **3** (of time, expenditure, production, etc.) exceed (a fixed limit). **4** *Printing* carry over (a word, etc.) to the next line or page. **5** *Mech.* rotate faster than. **6** flood (land). ● *n.* /ṓvərun/ **1** an instance of overrunning. **2** the amount of this. **3** the movement of a vehicle at a speed greater than is imparted by the engine. [OE *oferyrnan* (as OVER-, RUN)]
■ *v.* **1, 2** invade, defeat, attack, ravage, destroy, overwhelm, conquer, harry, vandalize, plunder, scourge, sack, strip, pillage, storm, *colloq.* blitz, *literary* despoil.

oversaw *past* of OVERSEE.

overscrupulous /ṓvərskrṓpyələs/ *adj.* excessively scrupulous or particular.
■ see *pedantic* (PEDANT).

overseas *adv. & adj.* ● *adv.* /ṓvərseéz/ (also *Brit.* **oversea**) abroad (*was sent overseas for training; came back from overseas*). ● *adj.* /ṓvərseez/ (also *Brit.* **oversea**) **1** foreign; across or beyond the sea. **2** of or connected with movement or transport over the sea (*overseas postage rates*).
■ *adv.* see ABROAD 1. ● *adj.* **1** see EXTERNAL *adj.* 2.

oversee /ṓvərseé/ *v.tr.* (**-sees**; *past* **-saw**; *past part.* **-seen**) officially supervise (workers, work, etc.). [OE *oferseon* look at from above (as OVER-, SEE¹)]
■ direct, manage, watch (over), keep an eye on, administer, superintend, run, supervise; handle, control.

overseer /ṓvərseer, -seéər/ *n.* a person who supervises others, esp. workers. [OVERSEE]
■ superintendent, supervisor, manager, foreman, forewoman, chief, superior, straw boss, *colloq.* boss, super, *Brit. colloq.* gaffer, *sl.* honcho.

oversell /ṓvərsél/ *v.tr.* (*past* and *past part.* **-sold**) (also *absol.*) **1** sell more of (a commodity, etc.) than one can deliver. **2** exaggerate the merits of.
■ **2** see MAXIMIZE.

oversensitive /ṓvərsénsitiv/ *adj.* excessively sensitive; easily hurt by, or too quick to react to, outside influences. □□ **oversensitiveness** *n.* **oversensitivity** /-tívitee/ *n.*
■ see TOUCHY 1. □□ **oversensitivity** see SENSITIVITY.

overset /ṓvərsét/ *v.tr.* (**-setting**; *past* and *past part.* **-set**) **1** overturn; upset. **2** *Printing* set up (type) in excess of the available space.

oversew /ṓvərsṓ/ *v.tr.* (*past part.* **-sewn** or **-sewed**) **1** sew (two edges) with every stitch passing over the join. **2** join the sections of (a book) by a stitch of this type.

oversexed /ṓvərsékst/ *adj.* having unusually strong sexual desires.

overshadow /ṓvərshádō/ *v.tr.* **1** appear much more prominent or important than. **2 a** cast into the shade; shelter from the sun. **b** cast gloom over; mar; spoil. [OE *ofersceadwian* (as OVER-, SHADOW)]
■ **1** dominate, outshine, eclipse, dwarf, diminish, minimize, put in *or* throw into *or* leave in the shade, steal the limelight from, tower over *or* above, excel. **2 b** spoil, blight, ruin, mar, take (all) the pleasure from *or* out of, put a damper on, take the edge off, impair, take the enjoyment out of.

overshoe /ṓvərsho͞o/ *n.* a shoe of rubber, felt, etc., worn over another as protection from wet, cold, etc.

overshoot *v. & n.* ● *v.tr.* /ṓvərsho͞ot/ (*past* and *past part.* **-shot**) **1** pass or send beyond (a target or limit). **2** (of an aircraft) fly beyond or taxi too far along (the runway) when landing or taking off. ● *n.* /ṓvərsho͞ot/ **1** the act of overshooting. **2** the amount of this. □ **overshoot the mark** go beyond what is intended or proper; go too far. **overshoot wheel** a waterwheel operated by the weight of water falling into buckets attached to its periphery.

■ *v.* **1** see PASS[1] *v.* 4.

overside /ṓvərsíd/ *adv.* over the side of a ship (into a smaller boat, or into the sea).

oversight /ṓvərsit/ *n.* **1** a failure to notice something. **2** an inadvertent mistake. **3** supervision.

■ **1** carelessness, heedlessness, inadvertence, neglect, laxity, laxness, failure, dereliction. **2** error, mistake, slip, fault, omission, blunder. **3** supervision, superintendence, surveillance, management, direction, guidance, administration; charge, care, custody, keeping, hands, protection, auspices.

oversimplify /ṓvərsímplifi/ *v.tr.* (**-ies, -ied**) (also *absol.*) distort (a problem, etc.) by stating it in too simple terms. □□ **oversimplification** *n.*

oversize /ṓvərsiz/ *adj.* (also **-sized** /-sizd/) of more than the usual size.

■ see LARGE *adj.* 1, 2.

overskirt /ṓvərskərt/ *n.* an outer or second skirt.

overslaugh /ṓvərslaw/ *n. & v.* ● *n. Brit. Mil.* the passing over of one's turn of duty. ● *v.tr.* **1** *Brit. Mil.* pass over (one's duty) in consideration of another duty that takes precedence. **2** pass over in favor of another. **3** omit to consider. [Du. *overslag* (n.) f. *overslaan* omit (as OVER, *slaan* strike)]

oversleep /ṓvərsle͞ep/ *v.intr. & refl.* (*past* and *past part.* **-slept**) **1** continue sleeping beyond the intended time of waking. **2** sleep too long.

oversleeve /ṓvərsle͞ev/ *n.* a protective sleeve covering an ordinary sleeve.

oversold *past* and *past part.* of OVERSELL.

oversolicitous /ṓvərsəlísitəs/ *adj.* excessively worried, anxious, eager, etc. □□ **oversolicitude** /-sito͞od, -tyo͞od/ *n.*

oversoul /ṓvərsōl/ *n.* God as a spirit animating the universe and including all human souls.

overspecialize /ṓvərspéshəliz/ *v.intr.* concentrate too much on one aspect or area. □□ **overspecialization** *n.*

overspend /ṓvərspénd/ *v.* (*past* and *past part.* **-spent**) **1** *intr. & refl.* spend too much. **2** *tr.* spend more than (a specified amount).

overspill /ṓvərspil/ *n.* **1** what is spilled over or overflows. **2** *Brit.* the surplus population leaving a country or city to live elsewhere.

overspread /ṓvərspréd/ *v.tr.* (*past* and *past part.* **-spread**) **1** become spread or diffused over. **2** cover or occupy the surface of. **3** (as **overspread** *adj.*) (usu. foll. by *with*) covered (*high mountains overspread with trees*). [OE *ofersprǣdan* (as OVER-, SPREAD)]

■ **1** see SPREAD *v.* 4a. **2** see COVER *v.* 2.

overstaff /ṓvərstáf/ *v.tr.* provide with too large a staff.

overstate /ṓvərstáyt/ *v.tr.* **1** state (esp. a case or argument) too strongly. **2** exaggerate. □□ **overstatement** *n.*

■ exaggerate, magnify, hyperbolize, embroider, overstress, color, make (too) much of, overdraw, overemphasize, stretch, enlarge, inflate, blow up.

overstay /ṓvərstáy/ *v.tr.* stay longer than (one's welcome, a time limit, etc.).

oversteer /ṓvərste͞er/ *v. & n.* ● *v.intr.* (of a motor vehicle) have a tendency to turn more sharply than was intended. ● *n.* this tendency.

overstep /ṓvərstép/ *v.tr.* (**-stepped, -stepping**) **1** pass beyond (a boundary or mark). **2** violate (certain standards of behavior, etc.).

■ **1** exceed, transcend, surpass, go beyond; see also PASS[1] *v.* 4.

overstock /ṓvərstók/ *v. & n.* ● *v.tr.* stock excessively. ● *n.* stock that is in excess of need or demand.

■ see GLUT *v.* 2, 3.

overstrain /ṓvərstráyn/ *v.tr.* strain too much.

■ see OVERWORK *v.* 2–4.

overstress /ṓvərstrés/ *v. & n.* ● *v.tr.* stress too much. ● *n.* an excessive degree of stress.

■ *v.* see EXAGGERATE 1.

overstretch /ṓvərstréch/ *v.tr.* **1** stretch too much. **2** (esp. as **overstretched** *adj.*) make excessive demands on (resources, a person, etc.).

overstrung *adj.* **1** /ṓvərstrúng/ (of a person, disposition, etc.) intensely strained, highly strung. **2** /ṓvərstrung/ (of a piano) with strings in sets crossing each other obliquely.

overstudy /ṓvərstúdee/ *v.tr.* (**-ies, -ied**) **1** study beyond what is necessary or desirable. **2** (as **overstudied** *adj.*) excessively deliberate; affected.

■ **2** (**overstudied**) see AFFECTED 2.

overstuff /ṓvərstúf/ *v.tr.* **1** stuff more than is necessary. **2** (as **overstuffed** *adj.*) (of furniture) made soft and comfortable by thick upholstery.

■ **1** see CRAM 1.

oversubscribe /ṓvərsəbskríb/ *v.tr.* (usu. as **oversubscribed** *adj.*) subscribe for more than the amount available of (a commodity offered for sale, etc.) (*the offer was oversubscribed*).

oversubtle /ṓvərsút'l/ *adj.* excessively subtle; not plain or clear.

oversupply /ṓvərsəplí/ *v. & n.* ● *v.tr.* (**-ies, -ied**) supply with too much. ● *n.* an excessive supply.

■ *v.* see GLUT *v.* 2, 3. ● *n.* see SURPLUS *n.* 1.

oversusceptible /ṓvərsəséptibəl/ *adj.* too susceptible or vulnerable.

overt /ṓvə́rt, ṓvərt/ *adj.* unconcealed; done openly. □□ **overtly** *adv.* **overtness** *n.* [ME f. OF past part. of *ovrir* open f. L *aperire*]

■ apparent, evident, plain, clear, obvious, manifest, clear-cut, unconcealed, patent, open, visible, observable, public. □□ **overtly** (out) in the open, for all to see, in plain *or* full view, straight (out); see also OPENLY 2.

overtake /ṓvərtáyk/ *v.tr.* (*past* **-took;** *past part.* **-taken**) **1** (esp. *Brit.* also *absol.*) catch up with and pass in the same direction. **2** (of a storm, misfortune, etc.) come suddenly or unexpectedly upon. **3** become level with and exceed (a compared value, etc.).

■ **1, 3** catch (up *or* up with *or* up to), reach, draw level *or* even with, overhaul, move by *or* past, pass, leave behind, outstrip, outdistance. **2** come upon, seize, catch (unprepared), strike, hit, *poet.* befall.

overtask /ṓvərtásk/ *v.tr.* **1** give too heavy a task to. **2** be too heavy a task for.

overtax /ṓvərtáks/ *v.tr.* **1** make excessive demands on (a person's strength, etc.). **2** tax too heavily.

■ **1** see OVERLOAD *v.*

overthrow *v. & n.* ● *v.tr.* /ṓvərthrṓ/ (*past* **-threw;** *past part.* **-thrown**) **1** remove forcibly from power. **2** put an end to (an institution, etc.). **3** conquer; overcome. **4** knock down; upset. **5** *Baseball* **a** (of a fielder) throw beyond the intended place. **b** (of a pitcher) throw too vigorously. ● *n.* /ṓvərthrṓ/ **1** a defeat or downfall. **2** *Archit.* a panel of decorated wrought-iron work in an arch or gateway.

■ *v.* **1–3** defeat, beat, rout, conquer, overcome, overpower, master, bring down, end, depose, oust, overwhelm, unseat, unhorse, topple, overturn, dethrone, thrash, worst, *colloq.* best. ● *n.* **1** defeat, rout, conquest, deposing, ousting, unseating, toppling, overturn, overturning, downfall, end, ruin, fall, collapse, destruction, suppression, quashing, crushing, subjugation, ouster.

overthrust /ṓvərthrust/ *n. Geol.* the thrust of esp. lower strata on one side of a fault over those on the other side.

/. . ./ pronunciation	● **part of speech**
□ **phrases, idioms, and compounds**	
□□ **derivatives**	■ **synonym section**
cross-references appear in SMALL CAPITALS or *italics*	

overtime /ṓvərtīm/ *n. & adv.* ● *n.* **1** the time during which a person works at a job in addition to the regular hours. **2** payment for this. **3** *Sports* an additional period of play at the end of a game when the scores are equal. ● *adv.* in addition to regular hours.

overtire /ṓvərtír/ *v.tr. & refl.* exhaust or wear out (esp. an invalid, etc.).
■ see KILL[1] 3a.

overtone /ṓvərtōn/ *n.* **1** *Mus.* any of the tones above the lowest in a harmonic series. **2** a subtle or elusive quality or implication (*sinister overtones*). [OVER- + TONE, after G *Oberton*]
■ **2** undertone, connotation, hint, suggestion, innuendo, insinuation, intimation, indication, implication.

overtop /ṓvərtóp/ *v.tr.* (**-topped, -topping**) **1** be or become higher than. **2** surpass.

overtrain /ṓvərtráyn/ *v.tr. & intr.* subject to or undergo too much (esp. athletic) training with a consequent loss of proficiency.

overtrick /ṓvərtrik/ *n. Bridge* a trick taken in excess of one's contract.

overtrump /ṓvərtrúmp/ *v.tr.* (also *absol.*) play a higher trump than (another player).

overture /ṓvərchər, -choor/ *n.* **1** an orchestral piece opening an opera, etc. **2** a one-movement composition in this style. **3** (usu. in *pl.*) **a** an opening of negotiations. **b** a formal proposal or offer (esp. *make overtures to*). **4** the beginning of a poem, etc. [ME f. OF f. L *apertura* APERTURE]
■ **3** (*overtures*) approach, advance, offer, proposal, proposition, tender.

overturn *v. & n.* ● *v.* /ṓvərtɔ́rn/ **1** *tr.* cause to turn over; upset. **2** *tr.* reverse; subvert; abolish; invalidate. **3** *intr.* turn over; fall over. ● *n.* /ṓvərtərn/ a subversion, an act of upsetting.
■ *v.* **1, 3** turn over, tip over, capsize, upend, upset, tumble, subvert, turn upside down, turn topsy-turvy, invert; knock down *or* over; esp. *Brit.* turn turtle. **2** bring down, overthrow, throw over, upset, depose, unthrone, unseat, oust, eject; invalidate; see also ABOLISH. ● *n.* **3** subversion, overturning, overthrow, unseating, ousting, toppling, upsetting; fall, destruction, abolition, ruin, defeat, ouster.

overuse *v. & n.* ● *v.tr.* /ṓvəryōōz/ use too much. ● *n.* /ṓvəryōōs/ excessive use.

overvalue /ṓvərvályōō/ *v.tr.* (**-values, -valued, -valuing**) value too highly; have too high an opinion of.

overview /ṓvərvyōō/ *n.* a general survey.

overweening /ṓvərwéening/ *adj.* arrogant, presumptuous, conceited, self-confident. □□ **overweeningly** *adv.* **overweeningness** *n.*
■ see ARROGANT. □□ **overweeningness** see PRIDE *n.* 2.

overweight *adj., n., & v.* ● *adj.* /ṓvərwáyt/ beyond an allowed or suitable weight. ● *n.* /ṓvərwayt/ excessive or extra weight; preponderance. ● *v.tr.* /ṓvərwáyt/ (usu. foll. by *with*) load unduly.
■ *adj.* see FAT *adj.* 1.

overwhelm /ṓvərhwélm, -wélm/ *v.tr.* **1** overpower with emotion. **2** (usu. foll. by *with*) overpower with an excess of business, etc. **3** bring to sudden ruin or destruction; crush. **4** bury or drown beneath a huge mass; submerge utterly.
■ **1** overcome, overpower, stagger, astound, astonish, dumbfound, shock, stun, bewilder, confuse, confound, nonplus, surprise, take aback, *colloq.* bowl over, knock off one's feet *or* pins, knock a person's socks off, *joc.* discombobulate, *sl.* blow a person's mind. **2, 4** overpower, inundate, overcome, engulf, submerge, drown, flood; deluge, swamp, bury, immerse. **3** overpower, overcome, overtax, devastate, stagger, crush, defeat, destroy, subdue, suppress, quash, quell, conquer, beat, bring down, prostrate, weigh down, oppress.

overwhelming /ṓvərhwélming, -wél-/ *adj.* irresistible by force of numbers, influence, amount, etc. □□ **overwhelmingly** *adv.* **overwhelmingness** *n.*
■ overpowering, uncontrollable, irresistible, devastating, unendurable, unbearable, crushing, burdensome,

formidable; awesome, awe-inspiring, stupefying, astounding, astonishing, staggering, bewildering, shattering, prodigious, *colloq.* mind-boggling, *sl.* mind-blowing.

overwind *v. & n.* ● *v.tr.* /ṓvərwínd/ (*past* and *past part.* **-wound**) wind (a mechanism, esp. a watch) beyond the proper stopping point. ● *n.* /ṓvərwīnd/ an instance of this.

overwinter /ṓvərwíntər/ *v.* **1** *intr.* (usu. foll. by *at, in*) spend the winter. **2** *intr.* (of insects, fungi, etc.) live through the winter. **3** *tr.* keep (animals, plants, etc.) alive through the winter.

overwork /ṓvərwɔ́rk/ *v. & n.* ● *v.* **1** *intr.* work too hard. **2** *tr.* cause (another person) to work too hard. **3** *tr.* weary or exhaust with too much work. **4** *tr.* make excessive use of. ● *n.* excessive work.
■ *v.* **1** work too hard, do too much, overtax *or* overburden *or* overload oneself, exhaust oneself, overdo it, burn the candle at both ends, slave (away), burn the midnight oil. **2–4** overexert, overstrain, overburden, oppress, overtax, overload, overuse. ● *n.* overexertion, strain.

overwound *past* and *past part.* of OVERWIND.

overwrite /ṓvərrít/ *v.* (*past* **-wrote**; *past part.* **-written**) **1** *tr.* write on top of (other writing). **2** *tr. Computing* destroy (data) in (a file, etc.) by entering new data. **3** *intr.* (esp. as **overwritten** *adj.*) write too elaborately or too ornately. **4** *intr. & refl.* write too much; exhaust oneself by writing. **5** *tr.* write too much about. **6** *intr.* (esp. as **overwriting** *n.*) in shipping insurance, accept more risk than the premium income limits allow.

overwrought /ṓvərráwt/ *adj.* **1** overexcited; nervous; distraught. **2** overdone; too elaborate.
■ **1** tense, nervous, edgy, jumpy, fidgety, touchy, overexcited, on edge, overstimulated, frantic, frenetic, distracted, distraught, strung up *or* out, *colloq.* jittery, all of a dither, in a tizzy, keyed up, worked up, wound up, uptight. **2** overdone, ornate, elaborate, baroque, rococo, florid, flowery, fussy, ostentatious, busy, gaudy, garish.

overzealous /ṓvərzéləs/ *adj.* too zealous in one's attitude, behavior, etc.; excessively enthusiastic. □□ **overzeal** /-zéel/ *n.*
■ see AMBITIOUS *adj.* 1a.

ovi-[1] /ṓvee/ *comb. form* egg, ovum. [L *ovum* egg]

ovi-[2] /ṓvee/ *comb. form* sheep. [L *ovis* sheep]

ovibovine /ṓvibṓvin, -veen/ *adj. & n. Zool.* ● *adj.* having characteristics intermediate between a sheep and an ox. ● *n.* such an animal, e.g., a musk ox.

oviduct /ṓvidukt/ *n.* the tube through which an ovum passes from the ovary. □□ **oviducal** /-dōōkəl, -dyōō-/ *adj.* **oviductal** /-dúktəl/ *adj.*

oviform /ṓvifawrm/ *adj.* egg-shaped.
■ see OVAL *adj.*

ovine /ṓvin/ *adj.* of or like sheep. [LL *ovinus* f. L *ovis* sheep]

oviparous /ōvípərəs/ *adj. Zool.* producing young by means of eggs expelled from the body before they are hatched (cf. VIVIPAROUS). □□ **oviparity** /-páritee/ *n.* **oviparously** *adv.*

oviposit /ṓvipózit/ *v.intr.* lay an egg or eggs, esp. with an ovipositor. □□ **oviposition** /-pəzíshən/ *n.* [OVI-[1] + L *ponere posit-* to place]

ovipositor /ṓvipózitər/ *n.* a pointed tubular organ with which a female insect deposits her eggs. [mod.L f. OVI-[1] + L *positor* f. *ponere posit-* to place]

ovoid /ṓvoyd/ *adj. & n.* ● *adj.* **1** (of a solid or of a surface) egg-shaped. **2** oval, with one end more pointed than the other. ● *n.* an ovoid body or surface. [F *ovoïde* f. mod.L *ovoides* (as OVUM)]
■ *adj.* see OVAL *adj.*

ovolo /ṓvəlō/ *n.* (*pl.* **ovoli** /-lee/) *Archit.* a rounded convex molding. [It. dimin. of *ovo* egg f. L OVUM]

ovotestis /ṓvətéstis/ *n.* (*pl.* **-testes** /-teez/) *Zool.* an organ producing both ova and spermatozoa. [OVUM + TESTIS]

ovoviviparous /ṓvōvivípərəs/ *adj. Zool.* producing young by means of eggs hatched within the body (cf. OVIPAROUS, VI-

VIPAROUS). □□ **ovoviviparity** /-páritee/ *n.* [OVUM + VIVIPA-ROUS]

ovulate /óvyəlayt, óvyə-/ *v.intr.* produce ova or ovules, or discharge them from the ovary. □□ **ovulation** /-láyshən/ *n.* **ovulatory** /-lətáwree/ *adj.* [mod.L *ovulum* (as OVULE)]

ovule /aavyōōl, óvyōōl/ *n.* the part of the ovary of seed plants that contains the germ cell; an unfertilized seed. □□ **ovular** *adj.* [F f. med.L *ovulum,* dimin. of OVUM]

ovum /óvəm/ *n.* (*pl.* **ova** /óvə/) **1** a mature reproductive cell of female animals, produced by the ovary. **2** the egg cell of plants. [L, = egg]
■ **2** see SEED *n.* 1a.

ow /ow/ *int.* expressing sudden pain. [natural exclam.]

owe /ō/ *v.tr.* **1 a** be under obligation (to a person, etc.) to pay or repay (money, etc.) (*we owe you five dollars*; *owe more than I can pay*). **b** (*absol.*, usu. foll. by *for*) be in debt (*still owe for my car*). **2** (often foll. by *to*) be under obligation to render (gratitude, honor, etc.) (*owe grateful thanks to*). **3** (usu. foll. by *to*) be indebted to a person or thing for (*we owe to Newton the principle of gravitation*). □ **owe it to oneself** (often foll. by *to* + infin.) need (to do) something to protect one's own interests. [OE *āgan* (see OUGHT¹) f. Gmc]
■ be in debt to, be indebted to, be beholden to.

owing /ó-ing/ *predic.adj.* **1** owed; yet to be paid (*the balance owing*). **2** (foll. by *to*) **a** caused by; attributable to (*the cancellation was owing to ill health*). **b** (as *prep.*) because of (*trains are delayed owing to bad weather*).
■ **1** in arrears; see also OUTSTANDING 2. **2** (*owing to*) because of, on account of, thanks to; through, as a result of, caused by, attributable to.

owl /owl/ *n.* **1** any nocturnal bird of prey of the order Strigiformes, with large eyes and a hooked beak, including barn owls, great horned owls, etc. **2** *colloq.* a person compared to an owl, esp. in looking solemn or wise. □ **owl monkey** (*pl.* **-eys**) a douroucouli. □□ **owlish** *adj.* **owlishly** *adv.* **owlishness** *n.* (in sense 2). **owllike** *adj.* [OE *ūle* f. Gmc]

owlet /ówlit/ *n.* a small or young owl.

own /ōn/ *adj. & v.* ● *adj.* (prec. by possessive) **1 a** belonging to oneself or itself; not another's (*saw it with my own eyes*). **b** individual; peculiar; particular (*a charm all of its own*). **2** used to emphasize identity rather than possession (*cooks his own meals*). **3** (*absol.*) **a** private property (*is it your own?*). **b** kindred (*among my own*). ● *v.* **1** *tr.* have as property; possess. **2 a** *tr.* confess; admit as valid, true, etc. (*own their faults*; *owns he did not know*). **b** *intr.* (foll. by *to*) confess to (*owned to a prejudice*). **3** *tr.* acknowledge paternity, authorship, or possession of. □ **come into one's own 1** receive one's due. **2** achieve recognition. **get one's own back** (often foll. by *on*) *colloq.* get revenge. **hold one's own** maintain one's position; not be defeated or lose strength. **of one's own** belonging to oneself alone. **on one's own 1** alone. **2** independently, without help. **own brand** esp. *Brit.* (often *attrib.*) goods manufactured specially for a retailer and bearing the retailer's name. **own goal** *Brit.* **1** a goal scored (usu. by mistake) against the scorer's own side. **2** an act or initiative that has the unintended effect of harming one's own interests. **own up** (often foll. by *to*) confess frankly. □□ **-owned** *adj.* (in *comb.*). [OE *āgen, āgnian*: see OWE]
■ *adj.* **1 b** see INDIVIDUAL *adj.* 2–4. **3 a** see PRIVATE *adj.* 1.
● *v.* **1** see POSSESS 1. **2** see CONFESS 1a. **3** see ACKNOWLEDGE 1.

owner /ónər/ *n.* **1** a person who owns something. **2** *sl.* the captain of a ship. □ **owner-occupier** esp. *Brit.* a person who owns the house, etc., he or she lives in. □□ **ownerless** *adj.* **ownership** *n.*
■ **1** possessor, holder; proprietor, proprietress; see also USER 1.

ox /oks/ *n.* (*pl.* **oxen** /óksən/) **1** any bovine animal, esp. a large usu. horned domesticated ruminant used for draft, for supplying milk, and for eating as meat. **2** a castrated male of a domesticated species of cattle, *Bos taurus.* □ [OE *oxa* f. Gmc]
■ **1** (*oxen*) see CATTLE.

ox- var. of OXY-².

oxalic acid /oksálik/ *n. Chem.* a very poisonous and sour acid

found in sorrel and rhubarb leaves. ¶ Chem. formula: (COOH)₂. □□ **oxalate** /óksəlayt/ *n.* [F *oxalique* f. L *oxalis* f. Gk *oxalis* wood sorrel]

oxalis /óksəlis, oksál-/ *n.* any plant of the genus *Oxalis,* with trifoliate leaves and white or pink flowers. [L f. Gk f. *oxus* sour]

oxbow /óksbō/ *n.* **1** a U-shaped collar of an ox yoke. **2 a** a loop formed by a horseshoe bend in a river. **b** a lake formed when the river cuts across the narrow end of the loop.

Oxbridge /óksbrij/ *n. Brit.* **1** (also *attrib.*) Oxford and Cambridge universities regarded together, esp. in contrast to newer institutions. **2** (often *attrib.*) the characteristics of these universities. [portmanteau word f. *Ox*(ford) + (Cam)*bridge*]

oxen *pl.* of OX.

oxeye /óksī/ *n.* a plant with a flower like the eye of an ox. □ **oxeye daisy** *n.* a daisy, *Leucanthemum vulgare,* having flowers with white petals and a yellow center. □□ **oxeyed** *adj.*

Oxfam /óksfam/ *abbr.* Oxford Committee for Famine Relief.

oxford /óksfərd/ *n.* **1** a low-heeled shoe that laces over the instep. **2** a fabric of cotton or a cotton blend made in a basket weave, used for shirts and sportswear. [for *Oxford,* England]

Oxford Group /óksfərd/ *n.* a religious movement founded at Oxford, England, in 1921, with discussion of personal problems by groups.

Oxford movement /óksfərd/ *n.* an Anglican High Church movement started in Oxford, England, in 1833, advocating traditional forms of worship.

oxhide /óks-hīd/ *n.* **1** the hide of an ox. **2** leather made from this.

oxidant /óksidənt/ *n.* an oxidizing agent. □□ **oxidation** /-dáyshən/ *n.* **oxidational** *adj.* **oxidative** /-daytiv/ *adj.* [F, part. of *oxider* (as OXIDE)]

oxide /óksīd/ *n.* a binary compound of oxygen. [F f. *oxygène* OXYGEN + *-ide* after *acide* ACID]

oxidize /óksidīz/ *v.* **1** *intr. & tr.* combine or cause to combine with oxygen. **2** *tr. & intr.* cover (metal) or (of metal) become covered with a coating of oxide; make or become rusty. **3** *intr. & tr.* undergo or cause to undergo a loss of electrons. □ **oxidized silver** esp. *Brit.* a popular name for silver covered with a dark coat of silver sulfide. **oxidizing agent** *Chem.* a substance that brings about oxidation by being reduced and gaining electrons. □□ **oxidizable** *adj.* **oxidization** *n.* **oxidizer** *n.*

oxlip /ókslip/ *n.* **1** a woodland primula, *Primula elatior.* **2** (in general use) a natural hybrid between a primrose and a cowslip.

Oxon. /óksən/ *abbr.* **1** Oxfordshire. **2** of Oxford University or the diocese of Oxford. [abbr. of med.L *Oxoniensis* f. *Oxonia:* see OXONIAN]

Oxonian /oksóneeən/ *adj. & n.* ● *adj.* of or relating to Oxford or Oxford University. ● *n.* **1** a member of Oxford University. **2** a native or inhabitant of Oxford. [*Oxonia* Latinized name of *Ox*(en)ford]

oxpecker /ókspekər/ *n.* any African bird of the genus *Buphagus,* feeding on skin parasites living on animals.

oxtail /ókstayl/ *n.* the tail of an ox, often used in making soup.

oxter /ókstər/ *n. Sc. & No. of Engl.* the armpit. [OE *ōhsta, ōxta*]

oxtongue /ókstung/ *n.* **1** the tongue of an ox, esp. cooked as food. **2** any composite plant of the genus *Picris,* with bright yellow flowers.

oxy-¹ /óksee/ *comb. form* denoting sharpness (*oxytone*). [Gk *oxu-* f. *oxus* sharp]

oxy-² /óksee/ *comb. form* (also **ox-** /oks/) *Chem.* oxygen (*oxyacetylene*). [abbr.]

oxyacetylene /ókseeəsét'leen/ *adj.* of or using a mixture of oxygen and acetylene, esp. in cutting or welding metals (*oxyacetylene burner*).

oxyacid /óksijəd/ *n. Chem.* an acid containing oxygen.

oxygen /óksijən/ *n. Chem.* a colorless, tasteless, odorless gaseous element, occurring naturally in air, water, and most minerals and organic substances, and essential to plant and animal life. ¶ Symb.: **O**. □ **oxygen mask** a mask placed over the nose and mouth to supply oxygen for breathing. **oxygen tent** a tentlike enclosure supplying a patient with air rich in oxygen. □□ **oxygenous** /oksíjinəs/ *adj.* [F *oxygène* acidifying principle (as OXY-²): it was at first held to be the essential principle in the formation of acids]

oxygenate /óksijənayt/ *v.tr.* **1** supply, treat, or mix with oxygen; oxidize. **2** charge (blood) with oxygen by respiration. □□ **oxygenation** /-náyshən/ *n.* [F *oxygéner* (as OXYGEN)]

oxygenator /óksijənaytər/ *n.* an apparatus for oxygenating the blood.

oxygenize /óksijəniz/ *v.tr.* = OXYGENATE.

oxyhemoglobin /ókseeheémaglóbin/ *n. Biochem.* a bright red complex formed when hemoglobin combines with oxygen.

oxymoron /ókseemáwron/ *n. rhet.* a figure of speech in which apparently contradictory terms appear in conjunction (e.g., *faith unfaithful kept him falsely true*). [Gk *oxumōron* neut. of *oxumōros* pointedly foolish f. *oxus* sharp + *mōros* foolish]

oxytocin /óksitósin/ *n.* **1** a hormone released by the pituitary gland that causes increased contraction of the womb during labor and stimulates the ejection of milk into the ducts of the breasts. **2** a synthetic form of this used to induce labor, etc. [*oxytocic* accelerating parturition f. Gk *oxutokia* sudden delivery (as OXY-¹, *tokos* childbirth)]

oxytone /óksitōn/ *adj.* & *n.* ● *adj.* (esp. in ancient Greek) having an acute accent on the last syllable. ● *n.* a word of this kind. [Gk *oxutonos* (as OXY-¹, *tonos* tone)]

oy /oy/ *int.* calling attention or expressing alarm, etc. [var. of HOY¹]

oyer and terminer /óyər ənd términər/ *n.* **1** (in some US states) a high criminal court. **2** *hist.* a commission issued to judges on a circuit to hold courts. [ME f. AF *oyer et terminer* f. L *audire* hear + *et* and + *terminare* determine]

oyez /ō-yés, ō-yéz/ *int.* (also **oyes**) uttered, usu. three times, by a public crier or a court officer to command silence and attention. [ME f. AF, OF *oiez, oyez,* imper. pl. of *oïr* hear f. L *audire*]

oyster /óystər/ *n.* **1** any of various bivalve mollusks of the family Ostreidae or Aviculidae, esp. edible kinds. **2** an oyster-shaped morsel of meat in a fowl's back. **3** something regarded as containing all that one desires (*the world is my oyster*). **4** (in full **oyster white**) a white color with a gray tinge. □ **oyster bed** a part of the sea bottom where oysters breed or are bred. **oyster farm** an area of the seabed used for breeding oysters. **oyster plant 1** = SALSIFY. **2** a blue-flowered plant, *Mertensia maritima,* growing on beaches. [ME & OF *oistre* f. L *ostrea, ostreum* f. Gk *ostreon*]

Oz /oz/ *n. Austral. sl.* Australia. [abbr.]

oz. *abbr.* ounce(s). [It. f. *onza* ounce]

ozocerite /ōzōkərīt/ *n.* (also **ozokerite**) a waxlike fossil paraffin used for candles, insulation, etc. [G *Ozokerit* f. Gk *ozō* smell + *kēros* wax]

ozone /ōzōn/ *n.* **1** *Chem.* a colorless unstable gas with a pungent odor and powerful oxidizing properties, used for bleaching, etc. ¶ Chem. formula: O_3. **2** *colloq.* **a** invigorating air at the seaside, etc. **b** *Brit.* exhilarating influence. □ **ozone depletion** a reduction of ozone concentration in the stratosphere, caused by atmospheric pollution. **ozone-friendly** (of manufactured articles) containing chemicals that are not destructive to the ozone layer. **ozone hole** an area of the ozone layer in which depletion has occurred. **ozone layer** a layer of ozone in the stratosphere that absorbs most of the sun's ultraviolet radiation. □□ **ozonic** /ōzónik/ *adj.* **ozonize** *v.tr.* **ozonization** *n.* **ozonizer** *n.* [G *Ozon* f. Gk, neut. pres. part. of *ozō* smell]

Pp

P¹ /pee/ *n.* (also **p**) (*pl.* **Ps** or **P's**) the sixteenth letter of the alphabet.

P² *abbr.* (also **P.**) **1** (on road signs) parking. **2** *Chess* pawn. **3** *Physics* poise (unit).

P³ *symb. Chem.* the element phosphorus.

p *abbr.* (also **p.**) **1** page. **2** piano (softly). **3** pico-. **4** *Brit.* penny; pence.

PA *abbr.* **1** Pennsylvania (in official postal use). **2** public address (esp. *PA system*). **3** Press Association. **4** *Brit.* personal assistant.

Pa *symb. Chem.* the element protactinium.

pa /paa/ *n. colloq.* father. [abbr. of PAPA]

p.a. *abbr.* per annum.

PABA *abbr. Biochem.* PARA-AMINOBENZOIC ACID.

Pablum /páblǝm/ *n.* **1** *propr.* a bland cereal food for infants. **2** (**pablum**) simplistic or unimaginative writing, speech, or ideas.

pabulum /pábyǝlǝm/ *n.* **1** food, esp. for the mind (*mental pabulum*). **2** insipid or bland ideas, writings, etc. [L f. *pascere* feed]

PAC /pak/ *abbr. political action committee.*

paca /pákǝ/ *n.* any tailless rodent of the genus *Cuniculus*, esp. the spotted cavy of S. and Central America. [Sp. & Port., f. Tupi]

pace¹ /pays/ *n. & v.* ● *n.* **1 a** a single step in walking or running. **b** the distance covered in this (about 30 in. or 75 cm). **c** the distance between two successive stationary positions of the same foot in walking. **2** speed in walking or running. **3** *Theatr. & Mus.* speed or tempo in theatrical or musical performance (*played with great pace*). **4** a rate of progression. **5 a** a manner of walking or running; a gait. **b** any of various gaits, esp. of a trained horse, etc. (*rode at an ambling pace*). ● *v.* **1** *intr.* **a** walk (esp. repeatedly or methodically) with a slow or regular pace (*pacing up and down*). **b** (of a horse) = AMBLE. **2** *tr.* traverse by pacing. **3** *tr.* set the pace for (a rider, runner, etc.). **4** *tr.* (often foll. by *out*) measure (a distance) by pacing. □ **keep pace** (often foll. by *with*) advance at an equal rate (as). **put a person through his** (or **her**) **paces** test a person's qualities in action, etc. **set the pace** determine the speed, esp. by leading. **stand** (or **stay**) **the pace** be able to keep up with others. □□ **paced** *adj.* **pacer** *n.* [ME f. OF *pas* f. L *passus* f. *pandere* pass-stretch]

■ *n.* **1 a** footstep, step, stride, tread. **b** step, stride. **2** rate, tempo, speed, velocity, *colloq.* clip, *Austral. & NZ sl.* toe. ● *v.* **1 a** walk, stride, tread. **2** walk, stride, tread, traverse, perambulate. **4** measure, gauge, judge, rate, estimate, determine, reckon, figure, compute.

□ **keep pace** keep up, keep in step *or* stride, stay level; compare, contend, compete, vie; (*keep pace with*) rival.

pace² /paáchay, -kay, páysee/ *prep.* (in stating a contrary opinion) with due deference to (the person named). [L, ablat. of *pax* peace]

pacemaker /páysmaykǝr/ *n.* **1** a natural or artificial device for stimulating the heart muscle and determining the rate of its contractions. **2** a competitor who sets the pace in a race.

pacesetter /páys-setǝr/ *n.* a leader.

pacha var. of PASHA.

pachinko /pǝchíngkō/ *n.* a Japanese form of pinball. [Jap.]

pachisi /pǝcheézee/ *n.* a four-handed board game orig. from India historically using six cowries like dice. [Hindi, = of 25 (the highest throw)]

pachyderm /pákidǝrm/ *n.* any thick-skinned mammal, esp. an elephant or rhinoceros. □□ **pachydermatous** /-dérmǝtǝs/ *adj.* [F *pachyderme* f. Gk *pakhudermos* f. *pakhus* thick + *derma -matos* skin]

pachysandra /pakisándrǝ/ *n.* any low-growing evergreen plant of the genus *Pachysandra*, used as a ground cover.

pacific /pǝsífik/ *adj. & n.* ● *adj.* **1** characterized by or tending to peace; tranquil. **2** (**Pacific**) of or adjoining the Pacific. ● *n.* (**the Pacific**) the expanse of ocean between N. and S. America to the east and Asia to the west. □ **Pacific Time** the standard time used in the Pacific region of Canada and the US. □□ **pacifically** *adv.* [F *pacifique* or L *pacificus* f. *pax pacis* peace]

pacification /pásifikáyshǝn/ *n.* the act of pacifying or the process of being pacified. □□ **pacificatory** /pǝsífikǝtáwree/ *adj.* [F f. L *pacificatio -onis* (as PACIFY)]

pacifier /pásifīǝr/ *n.* **1** a person or thing that pacifies. **2** a rubber or plastic nipple for a baby to suck on.

pacifism /pásifizǝm/ *n.* the belief that war and violence are morally unjustified and that all disputes can be settled by peaceful means. □□ **pacifist** *n. & adj.* [F *pacifisme* f. *pacifier* PACIFY]

pacify /pásifī/ *v.tr.* (**-ies, -ied**) **1** appease (a person, anger, etc.). **2** bring (a country, etc.) to a state of peace. [ME f. OF *pacifier* or L *pacificare* (as PACIFIC)]

pack¹ /pak/ *n. & v.* ● *n.* **1 a** a collection of things wrapped up or tied together for carrying. **b** = BACKPACK. **2** a set of items packaged for use or disposal together. **3** usu. *derog.* a lot or set (of similar things or persons) (*a pack of lies; a pack of thieves*). **4** a set of playing cards. **5 a** a group of hounds esp. for foxhunting. **b** a group of wild animals, esp. wolves, hunting together. **6** an organized group of Cub Scouts or Brownies. **7** *Rugby* a team's forward. **8 a** a medicinal or cosmetic substance applied to the skin. **b** a hot or cold pad of absorbent material for treating a wound, etc. **9** = *pack ice*. **10** a quantity of fish, fruit, etc., packed in a season, etc. **11** *Med.* **a** the wrapping of a body or part of a body in a wet sheet, etc. **b** a sheet, etc., used for this. ● *v.* **1** *tr.* (often foll. by *up*) **a** fill (a suitcase, bag, etc.) with clothes and other items. **b** put (things) together in a bag or suitcase, esp. for traveling. **2** *intr. & tr.* come or put closely together; crowd or cram (*packed a lot into a few hours; passengers packed like sardines*). **3** *tr.* (in *passive*; often foll. by *with*) be filled (with); contain extensively (*the restaurant was packed; the book is packed with information*). **4** *tr.* fill (a hall, theater, etc.) with an audience, etc. **5** *tr.* cover (a thing) with something pressed tightly around. **6** *intr.* be suitable for packing. **7** *tr. colloq.* **a** carry (a gun, etc.). **b** be capable of delivering (a punch) with skill or force. **8** *intr.* (of animals, etc.) form a pack. □ **pack animal** an animal used for carrying packs. **pack drill** a military punishment of marching up and down carrying full equipment. **packed lunch** a lunch carried in a

---

/ . . / **pronunciation** ● **part of speech**
□ **phrases, idioms, and compounds**
□□ **derivatives** ■ **synonym section**
cross-references appear in SMALL CAPITALS or *italics*

bag, box, etc., esp. to work, school, etc. **packed out** *Brit. colloq.* full; crowded. **pack ice** an area of large crowded pieces of floating ice in the sea. **pack it in** (or **up**) *colloq.* end or stop it. **pack off** send (a person) away, esp. abruptly or promptly. **pack rat 1** a large hoarding rodent. **2** a person who hoards unneeded things. **pack up** *Brit. colloq.* **1** (esp. of a machine) stop functioning; break down. **2** retire from an activity, contest, etc. **send packing** *colloq.* dismiss (a person) summarily. □□ **packable** *adj.* [ME f. MDu., MLG *pak, pakken,* of unkn. orig.]

■ *n.* **1** parcel, package, packet, bundle, bale, load, backpack, knapsack, rucksack, haversack, kitbag, kit, duffel bag. **2** parcel, package, packet, bag, bale, load, lot, bunch. **3** group, collection, assembly, assemblage, congregation, gathering, crowd, number, throng, horde, mass, crew, gang, body, lot, load, band, company, party, set, flock, herd, drove, swarm, bevy, covey, circle, coterie, clique, *colloq.* mob. **4** deck, set, stack. **8** compress, poultice, compound. ● *v.* **1 a** fill. **b** bundle, crowd, cram, jam, squeeze; stuff, ram, press. **2** bundle, crowd, cram, jam, squeeze, press, ram, stuff, wedge. **3, 4** crowd, cram, jam, squeeze, stuff. □ **packed out** filled, full, loaded, crowded, stuffed, jammed, crammed, brimful, chockablock, chock-full, jam-packed, overloaded, overflowing, bursting, groaning, swollen, replete. **pack it in** (or **up**) stop (it), cease, end, finish, quit, give up, call it a day, *colloq.* chuck it (in), *sl.* cut it out. **pack off** dismiss, send off *or* away, bundle off *or* out, hustle off *or* out *or* away, get rid of, drive off *or* away, order off *or* away *or* out. **pack up 1** stop, break down, fail, give out, stall, die, *archaic or colloq.* give up the ghost, *colloq.* conk (out), have had it.

pack² /pak/ *v.tr.* select (a jury, etc.) or fill (a meeting) so as to secure a decision in one's favor. [prob. f. obs. verb *pact* f. PACT]

package /pákij/ *n. & v.* ● *n.* **1 a** a bundle of things packed. **b** a box, parcel, etc., in which things are packed. **2** (in full **package deal**) a set of proposals or items offered or agreed to as a whole. **3** *Computing* a piece of software suitable for various applications rather than one which is custom-built. **4** *colloq.* = *package tour.* ● *v.tr.* make up into or enclose in a package. □ **package store** a retail store selling alcoholic beverages in sealed containers. **package tour** (or *Brit.* **holiday**) a tour with all arrangements made at an inclusive price. □□ **packager** *n.* [PACK¹ + -AGE]

■ *n.* **1** packet, parcel, pack, box, container, case, carton, bundle. **2** combination, unit; proposals; deal, agreement, contract, arrangement, settlement, understanding, commitment, compact. ● *v.* wrap, pack, containerize, case, encase, enclose; include; combine, unite, couple, incorporate.

packaging /pákijing/ *n.* **1** a wrapping or container for goods. **2** the process of packing goods.

packer /pákər/ *n.* a person or thing that packs, esp. a dealer who processes and packs food for transportation and sale.

packet /pákit/ *n.* **1** a small package. **2** esp. *Brit. colloq.* a large sum of money won, lost, or spent. **3** (in full **packet boat**) *hist.* a mail boat or passenger ship. [PACK¹ + -ET¹]

■ **1** package, pack, box, container, case, carton. **2** load(s), lot(s), great deal, (small) fortune, mint, king's ransom, *colloq.* pile(s), tidy sum, *iron.* pretty penny, *sl.* bundle, *Brit. sl.* bomb.

packhorse /pák-hawrs/ *n.* a horse for carrying loads.

packing /páking/ *n.* **1** the act or process of packing. **2** material used as padding to pack esp. fragile articles. **3** material used to seal a joint or assist in lubricating an axle. □ **packing case** (also *US* **box**) a case (usu. wooden) or crate for packing goods in.

packthread /pákthred/ *n.* strong thread for sewing or tying up packs.

pact /pakt/ *n.* an agreement or a treaty. [ME f. OF *pact(e)* f. L *pactum,* neut. past part. of *pacisci* agree]

■ agreement, treaty, bargain, alliance, contract, compact, concord, covenant, concordat, entente, understanding, arrangement, deal.

pad¹ /pad/ *n. & v.* ● *n.* **1** a piece of soft material used to reduce friction or jarring, fill out hollows, hold or absorb liquid, etc. **2** a number of sheets of blank paper fastened together at one edge, for writing or drawing on. **3** the fleshy underpart of an animal's foot or of a human finger. **4** a soft guard for the limbs or joints protecting them from injury, esp. in sports. **5** a flat surface for helicopter takeoff or rocket launching. **6** *colloq.* an apartment or bedroom. **7** the floating leaf of a water lily. ● *v.tr.* (**padded, padding**) **1** provide with a pad or padding; stuff. **2 a** (foll. by *out*) lengthen or fill out (a book, etc.) with unnecessary material. **b** to increase fraudulently, as an expense account. □ **padded cell** a room with padded walls in a mental hospital. [prob. of LG or Du. orig.]

■ *n.* **1** cushion, pillow, wad, wadding, stuffing, padding, filling, filler. **2** writing pad, notepad, drawing pad, tablet, memo pad, jotter, *Brit.* block (of paper). **6** apartment, room(s), home, place, quarters, lodging(s), *Brit.* flat, bedsitter, digs. ● *v.* **1** cushion, wad, stuff, fill; upholster. **2** (*pad out*) expand, inflate, stretch, dilate, lengthen, protract, extend, blow up, flesh out, puff up, augment, spin out, amplify.

pad² /pad/ *v. & n.* ● *v.* (**padded, padding**) **1** *intr.* walk with a soft dull steady step. **2 a** *tr.* hike along (a road, etc.) on foot. **b** *intr.* travel on foot. ● *n.* the sound of soft steady steps. [LG *padden* tread, *pad* PATH]

padding /páding/ *n.* soft material used to pad or stuff with.

paddle¹ /pád'l/ *n. & v.* ● *n.* **1** a short broad-bladed oar used without an oarlock. **2** a paddle-shaped instrument. **3** *Zool.* a fin or flipper. **4** each of the boards fitted around the circumference of a paddle wheel or mill wheel. **5** esp. *Brit.* the action or a period of paddling. ● *v.* **1** *intr. & tr.* move on water or propel a boat by means of paddles. **2** *intr. & tr.* row gently. **3** *tr. colloq.* spank. □ **paddle wheel** a wheel for propelling a ship, with boards around the circumference so as to press backward against the water. □□ **paddler** *n.* [15th c.: orig. unkn.]

■ *n.* **1** oar, sweep, scull, blade. ● *v.* **1, 2** row, scull; propel, move. **3** spank, thrash, beat, whip, flog.

paddle² /pád'l/ *v. & n.* esp. *Brit.* ● *v.intr.* walk barefoot or dabble the feet or hands in shallow water. ● *n.* the action or a period of paddling. □□ **paddler** *n.* [prob. of LG or Du. orig.: cf. LG *paddeln* tramp about]

■ *v.* slosh; see also WADE *v.* 1.

paddleball /pád'lbawl/ *n.* a game played on an enclosed court with short-handled perforated paddles and a ball similar to a tennis ball.

paddleboat /pád'lbōt/ *n.* a boat propelled by a paddle wheel.

paddock /pádək/ *n.* **1** a small field, esp. for keeping horses in. **2** an enclosure adjoining a racecourse where horses or cars are assembled before a race. **3** *Austral. & NZ* a field; a plot of land. [app. var. of (now dial.) *parrock* (OE *pearruc*): see PARK]

Paddy /pádee/ *n.* (*pl.* **-ies**) *colloq.* often *offens.* **1** an Irishman. **2** (**paddy**) a policeman. □ **paddy wagon** *colloq.* a police van for transporting those under arrest. [nickname for the Irish name *Padraig* (= Patrick)]

paddy¹ /pádee/ *n.* (*pl.* **-ies**) **1** a field where rice is grown. **2** rice before threshing or in the husk. [Malay *pādī*]

paddy² /pádee/ *n.* (*pl.* **-ies**) *Brit. colloq.* a rage; a fit of temper. [PADDY]

■ rage, (fit of) temper, fit, tantrum, *sl.* rampage, *Brit. sl.* wax, bate.

pademelon /pádeemèllən/ *n.* any small wallaby of the genus *Thylogale,* inhabiting the coastal scrub of Australia. [corrupt. of an Aboriginal name]

padlock /pádlok/ *n. & v.* ● *n.* a detachable lock hanging by a pivoted hook on the object fastened. ● *v.tr.* secure with a padlock. [ME f. LOCK¹: first element unexpl.]

padouk /pədook/ *n.* **1** any timber tree of the genus *Pterocarpus,* esp. *P. indicus.* **2** the wood of this tree, resembling rosewood. [Burmese]

padre /paadray, -dree/ *n.* **1** a clergyman, esp. a priest. **2** a chaplain in any of the armed services. [It., Sp., & Port., = father, priest, f. L *pater patris* father]

paean /peéən/ n. a song of praise or triumph. [L f. Doric Gk *paian* hymn of thanksgiving to Apollo (under the name of *Paian*)]

paedo /pédō/ *Brit.* var. of PEDO-.

paella /pī-élə, paa-áyaa/ n. a Spanish dish of rice, saffron, chicken, seafood, etc., cooked and served in a large shallow pan. [Catalan f. OF *paele* f. L *patella* pan]

paeon /peéən/ n. a metrical foot of one long syllable and three short syllables in any order. □□ **paeonic** /pee-ónik/ adj. [L f. Gk *paiōn*, the Attic form of *paian* PAEAN]

pagan /páygən/ n. & adj. ● n. **1** a person not subscribing to any of the main religions of the world. **2** a person following a polytheistic or pantheistic religion. **3** a hedonist. ● adj. **1 a** of or relating to or associated with pagans. **b** irreligious. **2** identifying divinity or spirituality in nature; pantheistic. □□ **paganish** adj. **paganism** n. **paganize** v.tr. & intr. [ME f. L *paganus* villager, rustic f. *pagus* country district: in Christian L = civilian, heathen]
■ n. heathen, unbeliever, idolater, infidel. ● adj. **1** idolatrous, gentile; see also HEATHEN adj.

page¹ /payj/ n. & v. ● n. **1 a** a leaf of a book, periodical, etc. **b** each side of this. **c** what is written or printed on this. **2 a** an episode that might fill a page in written history, etc.; a record. **b** a memorable event. **3** *Computing* a section of computer memory of specified size, esp. one that can be readily transferred between main and auxiliary memories. ● v.tr. paginate. [F f. L *pagina* f. *pangere* fasten]
■ n. **1 a** leaf, sheet, folio. **b, c** side, verso, recto. **2** episode, phase, period, time, stage, point, era, epoch, age, record, event, chapter. ● v. paginate, number.

page² /payj/ n. & v. ● n. **1** a person employed to run errands, attend to a door, etc. **2** a boy employed as a personal attendant of a bride, etc. **3** *hist.* a boy in training for knighthood and attached to a knight's service. ● v.tr. **1** (in hotels, airports, etc.) summon by making an announcement or by sending a messenger. **2** summon by means of a pager. □ **page boy** n. = PAGE² n. 2. **2** a hairstyle with the hair reaching to the shoulder and rolled under at the ends. [ME f. OF, perh. f. It. *paggio* f. Gk *paidion*, dimin. of *pais paidos* boy]
■ n. **1, 2** attendant, page boy, servant, errand boy, messenger; bellman, bellboy, esp. *Brit. colloq.* buttons. ● v. summon (forth), send for *or* after, call, call for, call out, beep, buzz.

pageant /pájənt/ n. **1 a** an elaborate parade or spectacle. **b** a spectacular procession, or play performed in the open, illustrating historical events. **c** a tableau, etc., on a fixed stage or moving vehicle. **2** an empty or specious show. [ME *pagyn*, of unkn. orig.]
■ **1** spectacle, display, tableau, show, parade, procession, ceremony, ritual, event, affair, extravaganza, presentation, gala.

pageantry /pájəntree/ n. (pl. -ies) **1** elaborate or sumptuous show or display. **2** an instance of this.
■ **1** pomp, ceremony, display, magnificence, extravagance, showiness, show.

pager /páyjər/ n. a radio device with a beeper, activated from a central point to alert the person wearing it.

paginal /pájinəl/ adj. **1** of pages (of books, etc.). **2** corresponding page for page. □□ **paginary** adj. [LL *paginalis* (as PAGE¹)]

paginate /pájinayt/ v.tr. assign numbers to the pages of a book, etc. □□ **pagination** /-náyshən/ n. [F *paginer* f. L *pagina* PAGE¹]

pagoda /pəgódə/ n. **1** a Hindu or Buddhist temple or sacred building, esp. a many-tiered tower, in India and the Far East. **2** an ornamental imitation of this. □ **pagoda tree** any of various trees, esp. *Sophora japonica*, resembling a pagoda in shape. [Port. *pagode*, prob. ult. f. Pers. *butkada* idol temple]

pah /paa/ int. expressing disgust or contempt. [natural utterance]

Pahlavi /páaləvee/ n. (also **Pehlevi** /páyləvee/) the writing system of Persia from the 2nd c. BC to the advent of Islam in the 7th c. AD. [Pers. *pahlawī* f. *pahlav* f. *parthava* Parthia]

paid *past* and *past part.* of PAY¹.

pail /payl/ n. **1** a bucket. **2** an amount contained in this. □□ **pailful** n. (pl. -fuls). [OE *pægel* gill (cf. MDu. *pegel* gauge), assoc. with OF *paelle*: see PAELLA]

paillasse esp. *Brit.* var. of PALLIASSE.

paillette /pìyét, pəlét/ n. **1** a piece of bright metal used in enamel painting. **2** a spangle. [F, dimin. of *paille* f. L *palea* straw, chaff]

pain /payn/ n. & v. ● n. **1 a** the range of unpleasant bodily sensations produced by illness or by harmful physical contact, etc. **b** a particular kind or instance of this (often in *pl.*: *suffering from stomach pains*). **2** mental suffering or distress. **3** (in *pl.*) careful effort; trouble taken (*take pains*; *got nothing for my pains*). **4** (also **pain in the neck**, etc.) *colloq.* a troublesome person or thing; a nuisance. ● v.tr. **1** cause pain to. **2** (as **pained** adj.) expressing pain (*a pained expression*). □ **in pain** suffering pain. **on** (or **under**) **pain of** with (death, etc.) as the penalty. [ME f. OF *peine* f. L *poena* penalty]
■ n. **1** hurt, suffering, discomfort, distress, soreness, ache, aching, pang, spasm, smart, cramp. **2** anguish, agony, affliction, distress, grief, suffering, misery, wretchedness, despair, torment, tribulation, trial, torture, discomposure, ordeal, disquiet, *archaic or literary* woe, *literary* travail, dolor. **3** (*pains*) effort, trouble, exertion, toil, labor. **4** irritation, vexation, annoyance, bother, nuisance, pest, bore, *colloq.* headache, drag, *sl.* pain in the butt. ● v. **1** hurt, distress, grieve, wound, injure; trouble, depress, sadden, sorrow, cut (to the quick). **2** (**pained**) see HURT adj. □ **in pain** in agony *or* anguish *or* distress, agonized, hurt, wounded, tormented, sore, hurting, aching, suffering, racked (with pain), smarting, throbbing with pain, burning, stinging.

painful /páynfŏŏl/ adj. **1** causing bodily or mental pain or distress. **2** (esp. of part of the body) suffering pain. **3** causing trouble or difficulty; laborious (*a painful climb*). □□ **painfully** adv. **painfulness** n.
■ **1** hurting, grievous, hurtful, distressful, excruciating, torturous, agonizing, smarting, stinging, burning, piercing, stabbing, sharp; vexatious, annoying, harassing, irritating, irksome, galling, exasperating, unpleasant, afflictive, harrowing, worrisome, worrying, troubling, disquieting, disturbing, distressing, *disp.* aggravating. **2** hurting, grievous, hurtful, sore, excruciating, torturous, afflicted, agonizing, smarting, stinging, aching, achy, throbbing, burning, tender, sensitive, raw. **3** laborious, arduous, onerous, exacting, demanding, trying, troublesome. □□ **painfully** agonizingly, distressingly, disagreeably, unpleasantly, unfortunately, sadly, woefully, lamentably, ruefully, unhappily; laboriously.

painkiller /páynkilər/ n. a medicine or drug for alleviating pain. □□ **painkilling** adj.
■ anodyne, analgesic, anesthetic, sedative, palliative.

painless /páynlis/ adj. not causing or suffering pain. □□ **painlessly** adv. **painlessness** n.
■ trouble-free, easy, simple, comfortable, effortless, easy as pie, *colloq.* a piece of cake.

painstaking /páynztayking/ adj. careful, industrious, thorough. □□ **painstakingly** adv. **painstakingness** n.
■ see THOROUGH 2.

paint /paynt/ n. & v. ● n. **1** a coloring matter, esp. in liquid form for imparting color to a surface. **b** this as a dried film or coating (*the paint peeled off*). **2** cosmetic makeup, esp. rouge or nail polish. **3** = PINTO. ● v.tr. **1 a** cover the surface of (a wall, object, etc.) with paint. **b** apply paint of a specified color to (*paint the door green*). **2** depict (an object, scene, etc.) with paint; produce (a picture) by painting. **3** describe vividly as if by painting (*painted a gloomy picture of the future*).

/. . ./ **pronunciation**	● **part of speech**
□ **phrases, idioms, and compounds**	
□□ **derivatives**	■ **synonym section**
cross-references appear in SMALL CAPITALS or *italics*	

4 a apply liquid or cosmetic to (the face, skin, etc.). **b** apply (a liquid to the skin, etc.). □ **painted lady 1** an orange-red butterfly, esp. *Vanessa cardui*, with black and brown markings. **2** (also **painted woman**) PROSTITUTE 1a. **paint out** efface with paint. **paint shop** the part of a factory where goods are painted, esp. by spraying. **paint stick** a stick of water-soluble paint used like a crayon. **paint the town red** *colloq.* enjoy oneself flamboyantly; celebrate. □□ **paintable** *adj.* [ME f. *peint* past part. of OF *peindre* f. L *pingere pict-paint*]

■ *n.* **1** color, tint, dye, coloring, pigment, stain; coating, coat, surface; enamel. **2** makeup, cosmetics, maquillage, greasepaint, *colloq.* warpaint. ● *v.* **1** coat, brush, cover, daub, color, tint, dye, stain, decorate. **2** depict, portray, picture, show, represent, render, *archaic* limn. **3** depict, portray, picture, draw, characterize, describe. □ **paint the town red** make merry, carouse, revel, have a good time, go out on the town, step out, *colloq.* go on a spree, whoop it up, live it up, make whoopee.

paintbox /páyntboks/ *n.* a box holding dry paints for painting pictures.

paintbrush /páyntbrush/ *n.* a brush for applying paint.

painter[1] /páyntər/ *n.* a person who paints, esp. an artist or decorator. [ME f. OF *peintour* ult. f. L *pictor* (as PAINT)]

painter[2] /páyntər/ *n.* a rope attached to the bow of a boat for tying it to a pier, dock, etc. [ME, prob. f. OF *penteur* rope from a masthead: cf. G *Pentertakel* f. *pentern* fish the anchor]

painterly /páyntərlee/ *adj.* **1 a** using paint well; artistic. **b** characteristic of a painter or paintings. **2** (of a painting) lacking clearly defined outlines.

painting /páynting/ *n.* **1** the process or art of using paint. **2** a painted picture.

paintwork /páyntwərk/ *n.* **1** a painted surface or area in a building, etc. **2** the work of painting.

painty /páyntee/ *adj.* (**paintier, paintiest**) **1** of or covered in paint. **2** (of a picture, etc.) overcharged with paint.

pair /pair/ *n. & v.* ● *n.* **1** a set of two persons or things used together or regarded as a unit (*a pair of gloves; a pair of eyes*). **2** an article (e.g., scissors, pants, or pajamas) consisting of two joined or corresponding parts not used separately. **3 a** a romantically involved couple. **b** a mated couple of animals. **4** two horses harnessed side by side (*a coach and pair*). **5** the second member of a pair in relation to the first (*cannot find its pair*). **6** two playing cards of the same denomination. **7** either or both of two members of a legislative assembly on opposite sides absenting themselves from voting by mutual arrangement. ● *v.tr. & intr.* **1** (often foll. by *off* or *up*) arrange or be arranged in couples. **2 a** join or be joined in marriage. **b** (of animals) mate. **3** form a legislative pair. □ **in pairs** in twos. **pair production** *Physics* the conversion of a radiation quantum into an electron and a positron. **pair royal** *Cribbage* a set of three cards of the same denomination. [ME f. OF *paire* f. L *paria* neut. pl. of *par* equal]

■ *n.* **1** couple, twosome, two of a kind, set of two, duo, brace, tandem, twins, *Math.* dyad. **3** (courting *or* engaged *or* married) couple, twosome. **4** yoke, span. **5** twin, double, doublet. ● *v.* **1** match (up), pair off *or* up, team (up), put together, partner, twin, double, join, unite, yoke. **2 a** marry, *formal or literary* wed; join *or* be joined in wedlock *or* (holy) matrimony. **b** mate.

paisa /písaà/ *n.* (*pl.* **paise** /-sáy/) a coin and monetary unit of India, Pakistan, Nepal, and Bangladesh, equal to one hundredth of a rupee or taka. [Hindi]

Paisley /páyzlee/ *n.* (also **paisley**) (often *attrib.*) **1** a distinctive detailed pattern of curved feather-shaped figures. **2** a soft woolen garment or fabric having this pattern. [*Paisley* in Scotland]

Paiute /píyoot/ *n.* (also **Piute**) **1 a** a N. American people native to the southwestern US. **b** a member of this people. **2** the language of this people.

pajamas /pəjáaməz, -jám-/ *n.pl.* **1** a suit of loose pants and jacket for sleeping in. **2** loose pants tied at the waist, worn by both sexes in some Asian countries. **3** (**pajama**) (*attrib.*) designating parts of a suit of pajamas (*pajama top; pajama*

pants; *pajama bottoms*). [Urdu *pā(ē)jāma* f. Pers. *pae, pay* leg + Hindi *jāma* clothing]

pakeha /paákihaa/ *n.* *NZ* a white person as opposed to a Maori. [Maori]

Paki /páakee/ *n.* (*pl.* **Pakis**) *Brit. sl. offens.* a Pakistani, esp. an immigrant in Britain. [abbr.]

Pakistani /pákistánee, paákistaánee/ *n. & adj.* ● *n.* **1** a native or national of Pakistan. **2** a person of Pakistani descent. ● *adj.* of or relating to Pakistan. [Hindu]

pakora /pəkáwrə/ *n.* a piece of cauliflower, carrot, or other vegetable, coated in seasoned batter and deep-fried. [Hind.]

pal /pal/ *n. & v.* ● *n. colloq.* a friend or comrade. ● *v.intr.* (**palled, palling**) (usu. foll. by *up*) associate; form a friendship. [Romany = brother, friend, ult. f. Skr. *bhrātr* BROTHER]

■ *n.* friend, comrade, alter ego, crony, mate, companion, playmate, classmate, *colloq.* chum, sidekick, amigo, buddy. ● *v.* associate, be *or* become friendly *or* friends, be *or* get *or* become on friendly *or* intimate terms, make friends, go (around *or* about), fraternize, consort, keep company, knock about *or* around, hang about *or* around, *sl.* hang out.

palace /pális/ *n.* **1 a** the official residence of a president or sovereign. **b** esp. *Brit.* the official residence of an archbishop or bishop. **2** a mansion; a spacious building. □ **palace revolution** (or **coup**) the (usu. nonviolent) overthrow of a sovereign, government, etc. at the hands of senior officials. [ME f. OF *palais* f. L *Palatium* Palatine (hill) in Rome where the house of the emperor was situated]

■ **2** mansion, castle, stately home, manor (house), (country) estate, château, villa.

paladin /pálədin/ *n. hist.* **1** any of the twelve peers of Charlemagne's court, of whom the Count Palatine was the chief. **2** a knight errant; a champion. [F *paladin* f. It. *paladino* f. L *palatinus*: see PALATINE[1]]

palaeo- *comb. form Brit.* var. of PALEO-.

Palaeozoic *Brit.* var. of PALEOZOIC.

palaestra /pəléstrə/ *n.* (also **palestra**) *Gk & Rom. Antiq.* a wrestling school or gymnasium. [ME f. L *palaestra* f. Gk *palaistra* f. *palaiō* wrestle]

palais /paláy/ *n. Brit. colloq.* a public hall for dancing. [F *palais (de danse)* (dance) hall]

palanquin /pálənkeen/ *n.* (also **palankeen**) (in India and Asia) a covered litter for one passenger. [Port. *palanquim*: cf. Hindi *pālkī* f. Skr. *palyanka* bed, couch]

palatable /pálətəbəl/ *adj.* **1** pleasant to taste. **2** (of an idea, suggestion, etc.) acceptable, satisfactory. □□ **palatability** *n.* **palatableness** *n.* **palatably** *adv.*

palatal /pálət'l/ *adj. & n.* ● *adj.* **1** of the palate. **2** (of a sound) made by placing the surface of the tongue against the hard palate (e.g., *y* in *yes*). ● *n.* a palatal sound. □□ **palatalize** *v.tr.* **palatalization** *n.* **palatally** *adv.* [F (as PALATE)]

palate /pálət/ *n.* **1** a structure closing the upper part of the mouth cavity in vertebrates. **2** the sense of taste. **3** a mental taste or inclination; liking. [ME f. L *palatum*]

palatial /pəláyshəl/ *adj.* (of a building) like a palace, esp. spacious and magnificent. □□ **palatially** *adv.* [L (as PALACE)]

■ luxurious, deluxe, magnificent, splendid, stately, sumptuous, opulent, majestic, grand, elegant, swanky, *colloq.* posh, ritzy, classy.

palatinate /pəlát'nayt/ *n.* territory under the jurisdiction of a Count Palatine.

palatine[1] /pálətin/ *adj.* (also **Palatine**) *hist.* **1** (of an official or feudal lord) having local authority that elsewhere belongs only to a sovereign (*Count Palatine*). **2** (of a territory) subject to this authority. [ME f. F *palatin -ine* f. L *palatinus* of the PALACE]

palatine[2] /pálətin/ *adj. & n.* ● *adj.* of or connected with the palate. ● *n.* (in full **palatine bone**) each of two bones forming the hard palate. [F *palatin -ine* (as PALATE)]

palaver /pəlávər, -laávər/ *n. & v.* ● *n.* **1** fuss and bother, esp. prolonged. **2** profuse or idle talk. **3** cajolery. **4** *colloq.* a prolonged or tiresome business. **5** esp. *hist.* a parley between European traders and Africans or other indigenous peoples. ● *v.* **1** *intr.* talk profusely. **2** *tr.* flatter, wheedle. [Port. *palavra* word f. L (as PARABLE)]

■ *n.* **1** fuss, bother, trouble, red tape, commotion, bother, nonsense, *colloq.* song and dance, carrying-on. **2** chatter, babble, jabber, (empty *or* small) talk, blather, gossip, prating, prattle, *colloq.* natter, jaw, *Brit. colloq.* waffle, *sl.* hot air. **3** blarney, soft soap, weasel *or* honeyed words; see also *cajolery* (CAJOLE). **4** rigmarole, procedure, business, nuisance, to-do, *colloq.* performance. **5** parley, talk, conference, discussion, colloquy, conversation, confabulation, meeting, get-together, round table, powwow, *colloq.* confab, *sl.* chinwag. ● *v.* **1** chatter, babble, jabber, blather, gossip, prattle, prate, gabble, *colloq.* jaw, chitchat, natter, *Brit. colloq.* waffle, *sl.* chin-wag, *sl. derog.* yak, yakety-yak. **2** see CAJOLE.

pale[1] /payl/ *adj. & v.* ● *adj.* **1** (of a person or complexion) diminished in coloration; of a whitish or ashen appearance. **2 a** (of a color) faint; not dark or deep. **b** faintly colored. **3** of faint luster; dim. **4** lacking intensity, vigor, or strength (*pale imitation*). ● *v.* **1** *intr. & tr.* grow or make pale. **2** *intr.* (often foll. by *before, beside*) become feeble in comparison (with). □□ **palely** *adv.* **paleness** *n.* **palish** *adj.* [ME f. OF *pale, palir* f. L *pallidus* f. *pallēre* be pale]
■ *adj.* **1** colorless, white, wan, sallow, waxen, livid, ashen, ashy, pallid, bloodless, whitish, pasty, whey-faced, washed-out, anemic, blanched, drained, ghostly, ghastly, peaked, peaky, peakish, cadaverous. **2** faint, light, dim, washed-out, pastel. **3** see DIM *adj.* 1. **4** feeble, weak, flimsy, meager, enfeebled, ineffective, ineffectual, puny, insignificant, paltry, lame, poor, inadequate, half-hearted, tame, spiritless, empty, sterile, lifeless, uninspired, anemic, bloodless, *colloq.* half-baked. ● *v.* **1** blanch, dim, whiten. **2** diminish, lessen, fade (away), decrease, abate.

pale[2] /payl/ *n.* **1** a pointed piece of wood for fencing, etc.; a stake. **2** a boundary or enclosed area. **3** *Heraldry* a vertical stripe in the middle of a shield. □ **beyond the pale** outside the bounds of acceptable behavior. **in pale** *Heraldry* arranged vertically. [ME f. OF *pal* f. L *palus* stake]
■ **1** paling, palisade, picket, upright, post, stake. **2** boundary, limit(s), restriction, bounds, border(s), confines. □ **beyond the pale** improper, irregular, unseemly, unsuitable, indecent, unacceptable, inadmissible, forbidden, anathema, disallowed, prohibited, verboten, interdicted, taboo; unusual, bizarre, peculiar, outré, weird, abnormal, strange.

palea /páyleeə/ *n.* (*pl.* **paleae** /-lee-ee/) *Bot.* a chafflike bract, esp. in a flower of grasses. [L, = chaff]

paled /payld/ *adj.* having palings.

paleface /páylfays/ *n.* a white person.

paleo- /páyleeō/ *comb. form* ancient; old; of ancient (esp. prehistoric) times. [Gk *palaios* ancient]

paleobotany /páyleeōbót'nee/ *n.* the study of fossil plants.

Paleocene /páyleeəseén/ *adj. & n. Geol.* ● *adj.* of or relating to the earliest epoch of the Tertiary period with evidence of the emergence and development of mammals. ● *n.* this epoch or system. ¶ Cf. Appendix VII. [PALEO- + Gk *kainos* new]

paleoclimatology /páyleeōklímətóləjee/ *n.* (*Brit.* **palaeoclimatology**) the study of the climate in geologically past times.

paleogeography /páyleeōjeeógrəfee/ *n.* (*Brit.* **palaeogeography**) the study of the geographical features at periods in the geological past.

paleography /páyleeógrəfee/ *n.* (*Brit.* **palaeography**) the study of documents and writings from the past. □□ **paleographer** *n.* **paleographic** /-leeəgráfik/ *adj.* **paleographical** *adj.* **paleographically** *adv.* [F *paléographie* f. mod.L *paleographia* (as PALEO-, -GRAPHY)]

paleolithic /páyleeəlíthik/ *adj.* (*Brit.* **palaeolithic**) *Archaeol.* of or relating to the early part of the Stone Age. [PALEO- + Gk *lithos* stone]

paleomagnetism /páyleeōmágnitizəm/ *n.* (*Brit.* **palaeomagnetism**) the study of the magnetism remaining in rocks.

paleontology /páyleeontóləjee/ *n.* (*Brit.* **palaeontology**) the study of life in the geological past. □□ **paleontological** *adj.* **paleontologist** *n.* [PALEO- + Gk *onta* neut. pl. of *ōn* being, part. of *eimi* be + -LOGY]

Paleozoic /páyleeəzóik/ *adj. & n. Geol.* ● *adj.* of or relating to an era of geological time marked by the appearance of marine and terrestrial plants and animals, esp. invertebrates. ¶ Cf. Appendix VII. ● *n.* this era (cf. CENOZOIC, MESOZOIC). [PALEO- + Gk *zōē* life, *zōos* living]

Palestinian /pálistíneeən/ *adj. & n.* ● *adj.* of or relating to Palestine, a region (in ancient and modern times) and former British territory on the E. Mediterranean coast. ● *n.* **1** a native of Palestine in ancient or modern times. **2** an Arab, or a descendant of one, born or living in the area called Palestine.

palestra var. of PALAESTRA.

palette /pálit/ *n.* **1** a thin board or slab or other surface, usu. with a hole for the thumb, on which an artist holds and mixes colors. **2** the range of colors, etc., used by an artist. □ **palette knife 1** a thin steel blade with a handle for mixing colors or applying or removing paint. **2** *Brit.* a kitchen knife with a long blunt round-ended flexible blade. [F, dimin. of *pale* shovel f. L *pala* spade]

palfrey /páwlfree/ *n.* (*pl.* **-eys**) *archaic* a horse for ordinary riding, esp. for women. [ME f. OF *palefrei* f. med.L *palefredus*, LL *paraveredus* f. Gk *para* beside, extra, + L *veredus* light horse, of Gaulish orig.]

Pali /paálee/ *n.* an Indic language used in the canonical books of Buddhists. [Skr. *pāli-bhāsā* f. *pāli* canon + *bhāsā* language]

palimony /pálimōnee/ *n. colloq.* usu. court-ordered allowance made by one member of an unmarried couple to the other after separation. [PAL + ALIMONY]

palimpsest /pálimpsest/ *n.* **1** a piece of writing material or manuscript on which the original writing has been erased to make room for other writing. **2** a place, etc., showing layers of history, etc. **3** a monumental brass turned and re-engraved on the reverse side. [L *palimpsestus* f. Gk *palimpsēstos* f. *palin* again + *psēstos* rubbed smooth]

palindrome /pálindrōm/ *n.* a word or phrase that reads the same backward as forward (e.g., *rotator, nurses run*). □□ **palindromic** /-drómik, -drō/ *adj.* **palindromist** *n.* [Gk *palindromos* running back again f. *palin* again + *drom-* run]

paling /páyling/ *n.* **1** a fence of pales. **2** a pale.

palingenesis /pálinjénisis/ *n.* **1** *Biol.* the exact reproduction of ancestral characteristics in ontogenesis. **2** transmigration of souls. □□ **palingenetic** /-jənétik/ *adj.* [Gk *palin* again + *genesis* birth, GENESIS]

palinode /pálinōd/ *n.* **1** a poem in which the writer retracts a view or sentiment expressed in a former poem. **2** a recantation. [F *palinode* or LL *palinodia* f. Gk *palinōidia* f. *palin* again + *ōidē* song]

palisade /pálisáyd/ *n. & v.* ● *n.* **1 a** a fence of pales or iron railings. **b** a strong pointed wooden stake used in a close row for defense. **2** (in *pl.*) a line of high cliffs. ● *v.tr.* enclose or provide with a palisade. □ **palisade layer** *Bot.* a layer of elongated cells below the epidermis. [F *palissade* f. Prov. *palissada* f. *palissa* paling ult. f. L *palus* stake]

pall[1] /pawl/ *n.* **1** a cloth spread over a coffin, hearse, or tomb. **2** a shoulder band with pendants, worn as an ecclesiastical vestment and sign of authority. **3** a dark covering (*a pall of darkness; a pall of smoke*). **4** *Heraldry* a Y-shaped bearing charged with crosses representing the front of an ecclesiastical pall. [OE *pæll*, f. L *pallium* cloak]
■ **3** see MANTLE *n.* 2.

pall[2] /pawl/ *v.* **1** *intr.* (often foll. by *on*) become uninteresting (to). **2** *tr.* satiate; cloy. [ME, f. APPALL]
■ **1** (*pall on*) bore, tire, weary, jade, irk, irritate, sicken. **2** see SATE 2.

/ . . . / **pronunciation**   ● **part of speech**

□ **phrases, idioms, and compounds**

□□ **derivatives**   ■ **synonym section**

cross-references appear in SMALL CAPITALS or *italics*

---

palladia *pl.* of PALLADIUM².

Palladian /pəláydeeən/ *adj. Archit.* in the neoclassical style of Palladio. □□ **Palladianism** *n.* [A. *Palladio*, It. architect d. 1580]

palladium¹ /pəláydeeəm/ *n. Chem.* a white ductile metallic element occurring naturally in various ores and used in chemistry as a catalyst and for making jewelry. ¶ Symb.: **Pd**. [mod.L f. *Pallas*, an asteroid discovered (1803) just before the element, + -IUM; cf. CERIUM]

palladium² /pəláydeeəm/ *n.* (*pl.* **palladia** /-deeə/) a safeguard or source of protection. [ME f. L f. Gk *palladion* image of Pallas (Athene), a protecting deity]

pallbearer /páwlbairər/ *n.* a person helping to carry or officially escorting a coffin at a funeral.

pallet¹ /pálit/ *n.* **1** a straw mattress. **2** a mean or makeshift bed. [ME *pailet*, *paillet* f. AF *paillete* straw f. OF *paille* f. L *palea*]

pallet² /pálit/ *n.* **1** a flat wooden blade with a handle, used in ceramics to shape clay. **2** = PALETTE. **3** a portable platform for transporting and storing loads. **4** a projection in a timepiece transmitting motion from an escapement to a pendulum, etc. **5** a projection on a machine part, serving to change the mode of motion of a wheel. □□ **palletize** *v.tr.* (in sense 3). [F *palette*: see PALETTE]

pallia *pl.* of PALLIUM.

palliasse /palyás/ *n.* (also esp. *Brit.* **paillasse**) a straw mattress. [F *paillasse* f. It. *pagliaccio* ult. f. L *palea* straw]

palliate /páleeayt/ *v.tr.* **1** alleviate (disease) without curing it. **2** excuse; extenuate. □□ **palliation** /-áyshən/ *n.* **palliator** *n.* [LL *palliare* to cloak f. *pallium* cloak]

palliative /páleeətiv/ *n.* & *adj.* ● *n.* anything used to alleviate pain, anxiety, etc. ● *adj.* serving to alleviate. □□ **palliatively** *adv.* [F *palliatif -ive* or med.L *palliativus* (as PALLIATE)]

pallid /pálid/ *adj.* pale, esp. from illness. □□ **pallidity** /-líditee/ *n.* **pallidly** *adv.* **pallidness** *n.* [L *pallidus* PALE¹]

pallium /páleeəm/ *n.* (*pl.* **palliums** or **pallia** /-leeə/) **1** an ecclesiastical pall, esp. that sent by the Pope to an archbishop as symbol of authority. **2** *hist.* a man's large rectangular cloak, esp. as worn in antiquity. **3** *Zool.* the mantle of a mollusk or brachiopod. [L]

pall-mall /pélmél, pálmál, páwlmáwl/ *n. hist.* a game in which a ball was driven through an iron ring suspended in a long alley. [obs. F *pallemaille* f. It. *pallamaglio* f. *palla* ball + *maglio* mallet]

pallor /pálər/ *n.* pallidness; paleness. [L f. *pallēre* be pale]

pally /pálee/ *adj.* (**pallier**, **palliest**) *colloq.* like a pal; friendly.

palm¹ /paam, paw(l)m/ *n.* **1** any usu. tropical tree of the family Palmae, with no branches and a mass of large pinnate or fan-shaped leaves at the top. **2 a** the leaf of this tree as a symbol of victory. **b** a military decoration shaped like a palm leaf. **3 a** supreme excellence. **b** a prize for this. **4** a branch of various trees used instead of a palm in non-tropical countries, esp. in celebrating Palm Sunday. □ **palm oil** oil from the fruit of any of various palms. **Palm Sunday** the Sunday before Easter, celebrating Christ's entry into Jerusalem. **palm wine** an alcoholic drink made from fermented palm sap. □□ **palmaceous** /palmáyshəs, paa(l)-/ *adj.* [OE *palm(a)* f. Gmc f. L *palma* PALM², its leaf being likened to a spread hand]

palm² /paam, paw(l)m/ *n.* & *v.* ● *n.* **1** the inner surface of the hand between the wrist and fingers. **2** the part of a glove, etc., that covers this. **3** the palmate part of an antler. ● *v.tr.* **1** conceal in the hand. **2** *Basketball* to hold (the ball) in one hand. □ **in the palm of one's hand** under one's control or influence. **palm off 1** (often foll. by *on*) **a** impose or thrust fraudulently (on a person). **b** cause a person to accept unwillingly or unknowingly (*palmed my old typewriter off on him*). **2** (often foll. by *with*) cause (a person) to accept unwillingly or unknowingly (*palmed him off with my old typewriter*). □□ **palmar** /pálmər, paa(l)-/ *adj.* **palmed** *adj.* **palmful** *n.* (*pl.* **-fuls**). [ME *paume* f. OF *paume* f. L *palma*: later assim. to L]

palmate /pálmayt, paál-, paámayt/ *adj.* **1** shaped like an open hand. **2** having lobes, etc., like spread fingers. [L *palmatus* (as PALM²)]

palmer /paamər, paál-/ *n.* **1** *hist.* **a** a pilgrim returning from the Holy Land with a palm branch or leaf. **b** an itinerant monk under a vow of poverty. **2** a hairy artificial fly used in fishing. [ME f. AF *palmer*, OF *palmier* f. med.L *palmarius* pilgrim]

palmerworm /paamərwərm/ *n.* a destructive hairy caterpillar of a moth, *Dichomeris ligulella*, of the eastern US.

palmette /palmét/ *n. Archaeol.* an ornament of radiating petals like a palm leaf. [F, dimin. of *palme* PALM¹]

palmetto /palmétō/ *n.* (*pl.* **-os**) **1** a small palm tree, e.g., any of various fan palms of the genus *Sabal*. **2** palm fronds used in weaving. [Sp. *palmito*, dimin. of *palma* PALM¹, assim. to It. words in *-etto*]

palmiped /pálmiped/ *adj.* & *n.* (also **palmipede** /-peed/) ● *adj.* web-footed. ● *n.* a web-footed bird. [L *palmipes -pedis* (as PALM², *pes pedis* foot)]

palmistry /paámistree/ *n.* supposed divination from lines and other features on the palm of the hand. □□ **palmist** *n.* [ME (orig. *palmestry*) f. PALM²: second element unexpl.]

palmy /paámee/ *adj.* (**palmier**, **palmiest**) **1** of or like or abounding in palms. **2** triumphant; flourishing (*palmy days*).

palmyra /palmírə/ *n.* an Asian palm, *Borassus flabellifer*, with fan-shaped leaves used for matting, etc. [Port. *palmeira* palm tree, assim. to *Palmyra* in Syria]

palomino /páləmeénō/ *n.* (*pl.* **-os**) a golden or tan-colored horse with a light-colored mane and tail, orig. bred in the southwestern US. [Amer. Sp. f. Sp. *palomino* young pigeon f. *paloma* dove f. L *palumba*]

paloverde /pálōvərdee, -vərd/ *n.* a thorny tree of the genus *Cercidium* having greenish bark and yellow flowers, found in the southwestern US. [Amer. Sp., = green tree]

palp /palp/ *n.* (also **palpus** /pálpəs/) (*pl.* **palps** or **palpi** /-pī/) a segmented sensory organ at the mouth of an arthropod; a feeler. □□ **palpal** *adj.* [L *palpus* f. *palpare* feel]

palpable /pálpəbəl/ *adj.* **1** that can be touched or felt. **2** readily perceived by the senses or mind. □□ **palpability** *n.* **palpably** *adv.* [ME f. LL *palpabilis* (as PALPATE)]

palpate /pálpayt/ *v.tr.* examine (esp. medically) by touch. □□ **palpation** /-páyshən/ *n.* [L *palpare palpat-* touch gently]

palpebral /palpeébrəl, pálpibrəl/ *adj.* of or relating to the eyelids. [LL *palpebralis* f. L *palpebra* eyelid]

palpitate /pálpitayt/ *v.intr.* **1** pulsate; throb. **2** tremble. □□ **palpitant** *adj.* [L *palpitare* frequent. of *palpare* touch gently]

palpitation /pálpitáyshən/ *n.* **1** throbbing; trembling. **2** (often in *pl.*) increased activity of the heart due to exertion, agitation, or disease. [L *palpitatio* (as PALPITATE)]

palpus var. of PALP.

palsgrave /páwlzgrayv/ *n.* a Count Palatine. [Du. *paltsgrave* f. *palts* palatinate + *grave* count]

palstave /páwlstayv/ *n. Archaeol.* a type of chisel made of bronze, etc., shaped to fit into a split handle. [Da. *paalstav* f. ON *pálstavr* f. *páll* hoe (cf. L *palus* stake) + *stafr* STAFF¹]

palsy /páwlzee/ *n.* & *v.* ● *n.* (*pl.* **-ies**) **1** paralysis, esp. with involuntary tremors. **2 a** a condition of utter helplessness. **b** a cause of this. ● *v.tr.* (**-ies**, **-ied**) **1** affect with palsy. **2** render helpless. [ME *pa(r)lesi* f. OF *paralisie* ult. f. L *paralysis*: see PARALYSIS]

palter /páwltər/ *v.intr.* **1** haggle or equivocate. **2** trifle. □□ **palterer** *n.* [16th c.: orig. unkn.]

paltry /páwltree/ *adj.* (**paltrier**, **paltriest**) worthless; contemptible; trifling. □□ **paltriness** *n.* [16th c.: f. *paltry* trash app. f. *palt*, *pelt* rubbish + -RY (cf. *trumpery*): cf. LG *paltrig* ragged]

■ trifling, trivial, petty, small, insignificant, worthless, pitiful, pathetic, pitiable, puny, sorry, wretched, miserable, inconsequential, inconsiderable, unimportant, meager, mean, measly, beggarly, base, low, contemptible, *colloq.* piddling, piffling, two-bit, *Brit. colloq.* mingy, twopenny.

paludal /pəlŏŏd'l, pályə-/ *adj.* **1** of a marsh. **2** malarial. □□ **paludism** /pályədizəm/ *n.* (in sense 2). [L *palus -udis* marsh + -AL]

palynology /pálinóləjee/ *n.* the study of pollen, spores, etc., for rock dating and the study of past environments. □□ **palynological** /-nəlójikəl/ *adj.* **palynologist** *n.* [Gk *palunō* sprinkle + -LOGY]

pampas /pámpəs/ *n.pl.* large treeless plains in S. America. □ **pampas grass** a tall grass, *Cortaderia selloana*, from S. America, with silky flowering plumes. [Sp. f. Quechua *pampa* plain]

pamper /pámpər/ *v.tr.* **1** overindulge (a person, taste, etc.); cosset. **2** spoil (a person) with luxury. □□ **pamperer** *n.* [ME, prob. of LG or Du. orig.]
■ baby, coddle, cosset, (over)indulge, spoil, mollycoddle, pet.

pampero /pampáirō/ *n.* (*pl.* **-os**) a strong cold SW wind in S. America, blowing from the Andes to the Atlantic. [Sp. (as PAMPAS)]

pamphlet /pámflit/ *n. & v.* ● *n.* a small, usu. unbound booklet or leaflet containing information or a short treatise. ● *v.tr.* (**pamphleted, pamphleting**) distribute pamphlets to. [ME f. *Pamphilet*, the familiar name of the 12th-c. Latin love poem *Pamphilus seu de Amore*]
■ *n.* booklet, brochure, tract, leaflet, circular; handbill, bill, notice, bulletin, hand-out, flyer.

pamphleteer /pámfliteér/ *n. & v.* ● *n.* a writer of (esp. political) pamphlets. ● *v.intr.* write pamphlets.

pan[1] /pan/ *n. & v.* ● *n.* **1 a** a vessel of metal, earthenware, etc., usu. broad and shallow, used for cooking and other domestic purposes. **b** the contents of this. **2** a panlike vessel in which substances are heated, etc. **3** any similar shallow container such as the bowl of a pair of scales or that used for washing gravel, etc., to separate gold. **4** *Brit.* toilet bowl. **5** part of the lock that held the priming in old guns. **6** a hollow in the ground (*salt pan*). **7** a hard substratum of soil. **8** *sl.* the face. **9** a negative or unfavorable review. ● *v.* (**panned, panning**) **1** *tr. colloq.* criticize severely. **2 a** *tr.* (often foll. by *off, out*) wash (gold-bearing gravel) in a pan. **b** *intr.* search for gold by panning gravel. **c** *intr.* (foll. by *out*) (of gravel) yield gold. □ **pan out** (of an action, etc.) turn out well or in a specified way. □□ **panful** *n.* (*pl.* **-fuls**). **panlike** *adj.* [OE *panne*, perh. ult. f. L *patina* dish]
■ *n.* **1** saucepan, frying pan, pot, casserole, skillet. **4** bowl. **6** depression, indentation, concavity, cavity, hollow, pit, hole, crater. **8** face, façade, *literary* visage, mien, *sl.* kisser, mug. ● *v.* **1** criticize, censure, find fault with, put down, reject, flay, excoriate, roast, *colloq.* trash, *Brit. colloq.* slate, *sl.* knock. **2 a** wash, separate, sift. **b** see SEARCH *v.* 1, 3. □ **pan out** work out, turn out (well); result, come out, end (up), conclude, culminate, *formal* eventuate.

pan[2] /pan/ *v. & n.* ● *v.* (**panned, panning**) **1** *tr.* swing (a video or movie camera) horizontally to give a panoramic effect or to follow a moving object. **2** *intr.* (of a video or movie camera) be moved in this way. ● *n.* a panning movement. [abbr. of PANORAMA]

pan[3] /paan/ *n. Bot.* **1** a leaf of the betel. **2** this enclosing lime and areca-nut parings, chewed in India, etc. [Hindi f. Skr. *parna* feather, leaf]

pan- /pan/ *comb. form* **1** all; the whole of. **2** relating to the whole or all the parts of a continent, racial group, religion, etc. (*pan-American*; *pan-African*; *pan-Hellenic*; *pan-Anglican*). [Gk f. *pan* neut. of *pas* all]

panacea /pánəseéə/ *n.* a universal remedy. □□ **panacean** *adj.* [L f. Gk *panakeia* f. *panakēs* all-healing (as PAN-, *akos* remedy)]

panache /pənásh, -naásh/ *n.* **1** assertiveness or flamboyant confidence of style or manner. **2** *hist.* a tuft or plume of feathers, esp. as a headdress or on a helmet. [F f. It. *pennacchio* f. LL *pinnaculum* dimin. of *pinna* feather]
■ **1** flourish, dash, élan, éclat, chic, sophistication, savoir faire, savoir vivre, flamboyance, verve, style, vivacity, cultivation, flair, smartness, boldness, self-assurance, swagger, vigor, liveliness, spirit, brio, gusto, zest, animation, enthusiasm, energy.

panada /pənaádə/ *n.* **1** a thick paste of flour, etc., used as a sauce base or binder. **2** bread boiled to a pulp and flavored. [Sp. ult. f. L *panis* bread]

panama /pánəmaa/ *n.* a hat of strawlike material made from the leaves of a palmlike tropical plant. [*Panama* in Central America]

Panamanian /pánəmáyneeən/ *n. & adj.* ● *n.* **1** a native or national of the Republic of Panama in Central America. **2** a person of Panamanian descent. ● *adj.* of or relating to Panama.

panatella /pánətélə/ *n.* a long thin cigar. [Amer. Sp. *panatela*, = long thin biscuit f. It. *panatella* dimin. of *panata* (as PANADA)]

pancake /pánkayk/ *n. & v.* ● *n.* **1** a thin flat cake of batter usu. fried and turned in a pan or on a griddle. **2** a flat cake of makeup, etc. ● *v.* **1** *intr.* make a pancake landing. **2** *tr.* cause (an aircraft) to pancake. □ **flat as a pancake** completely flat. **pancake landing** an emergency landing by an aircraft with its landing gear still retracted, in which the pilot attempts to keep the aircraft in a horizontal position throughout. [ME f. PAN[1] + CAKE]

Panchen lama /paánchən laámə/ *n.* a Tibetan lama ranking next after the Dalai lama. [Tibetan *panchen* great learned one]

panchromatic /pánkrōmátik/ *adj. Photog.* (of film, etc.) sensitive to all visible colors of the spectrum.

pancreas /pángkreeəs/ *n.* a gland near the stomach supplying the duodenum with digestive fluid and secreting insulin into the blood. □□ **pancreatic** /-kreeátik/ *adj.* **pancreatitis** /-kreeətítis/ *n.* [mod.L f. Gk *pagkreas* (as PAN-, *kreas* -*atos* flesh)]

pancreatin /pánkreeətən, páng-/ *n.* a digestive extract containing pancreatic enzymes, prepared from animal pancreases.

panda /pándə/ *n.* **1** (also **giant panda**) a large bearlike mammal, *Ailuropoda melanoleuca*, native to China and Tibet, having characteristic black and white markings. **2** (also **red panda**) a Himalayan raccoon-like mammal, *Ailurus fulgens*, with reddish-brown fur and a long bushy tail. □ **panda car** *Brit.* a police patrol car (orig. white with black stripes on the doors). [Nepali name]

pandect /pándekt/ *n.* (usu. in *pl.*) **1** a complete body of laws. **2** *hist.* a compendium in 50 books of the Roman civil law made by order of Justinian in the 6th c. [F *pandecte* or L *pandecta pandectes* f. Gk *pandektēs* all-receiver (as PAN-, *dektēs* f. *dekhomai* receive)]

pandemic /pandémik/ *adj. & n.* ● *adj.* (of a disease) prevalent over a whole country or the world. ● *n.* a pandemic disease. [Gk *pandēmos* (as PAN-, *dēmos* people)]

pandemonium /pándimǒneeəm/ *n.* **1** uproar; utter confusion. **2** a scene of this. [mod.L (place of all demons in Milton's *Paradise Lost*) f. PAN- + Gk *daimōn* DEMON[1]]
■ bedlam, chaos, turmoil, disorder, tumult, frenzy, uproar, furor, confusion.

pander /pándər/ *v. & n.* ● *v.intr.* (foll. by *to*) gratify or indulge a person, a desire or weakness, etc. ● *n.* (*US* also **panderer**) **1** a go-between in illicit love affairs; a procurer. **2** a person who encourages licentiousness. [*Pandare*, a character in Boccaccio and in Chaucer's *Troilus and Criseyde*, f. L *Pandarus* f. Gk *Pandaros*]
■ *v.* (**pander to**) satisfy, gratify, humor, indulge, fulfill, bow to, yield to, truckle to, cater to. ● *n.* **1** pimp, procurer, solicitor, *archaic* whoremonger, *Brit. sl.* ponce.

pandit var. of PUNDIT 1.

Pandora's box /pandáwrəz/ *n.* a process that once activated will generate many unmanageable problems. [in Gk Mythol. the box from which the ills of humankind were released, hope alone remaining: f. Gk *Pandōra* all-gifted (as PAN-, *dōron* gift)]

pane /payn/ *n.* **1** a single sheet of glass in a window or door.

/.../ **pronunciation** ● **part of speech**
□ **phrases, idioms, and compounds**
□□ **derivatives** ■ **synonym section**
cross-references appear in SMALL CAPITALS or *italics*

2 a rectangular division of a checkered pattern, etc. **3** a sheet of postage stamps. [ME f. OF *pan* f. L *pannus* piece of cloth] ■ **1** panel, sheet, glass, windowpane, light, bull's-eye.

panegyric /pánijirik, -jírik/ *n.* a laudatory discourse; a eulogy. □□ **panegyrical** *adj.* [F *panégyrique* f. L *panegyricus* f. Gk *panēgurikos* of public assembly (as PAN-, *ēguris* = *agora* assembly)]

panegyrize /pánijiríz/ *v.tr.* speak or write in praise of; eulogize. □□ **panegyrist** /-jírist/ *n.* [Gk *panēgurizō* (as PANE-GYRIC)]
■ □□ **panegyrist** eulogizer, eulogist, encomiast; flatterer.

panel /pánəl/ *n. & v.* ● *n.* **1 a** a distinct, usu. rectangular, section of a surface (e.g., of a wall or door). **b** a control panel (see CONTROL *n.* 5). **c** = *instrument panel*. **2** a strip of material as part of a garment. **3** a group of people gathered to form a team in a broadcast game, for a discussion, etc. **4** *Brit. hist.* a list of medical practitioners registered in a district as accepting patients under the National Insurance Act. **5 a** a list of available jurors; a jury. **b** *Sc.* a person or persons accused of a crime. **6** a comic strip or one frame of a comic strip. ● *v.tr.* (**paneled** or **panelled**, **paneling** or **panelling**) **1** fit or provide with panels. **2** cover or decorate with panels. □ **panel game** a quiz show, etc., played by a panel. **panel heating** the heating of rooms by panels in the wall, etc., containing the sources of heat. **panel saw** a saw with small teeth for cutting thin wood for panels. **panel truck** a small enclosed delivery truck. [ME & OF, = piece of cloth, ult. f. L *pannus*: see PANE]

paneling /pánəling/ *n.* (also **panelling**) **1** paneled work. **2** wood for making panels.

panelist /pánəlist/ *n.* (also **panellist**) a member of a panel (esp. in broadcasting).

pang /pang/ *n.* (often in *pl.*) a sudden sharp pain or painful emotion. [16th c.: var. of earlier *prange* pinching f. Gmc]
■ pain, stab, ache, pinch, prick, twinge, stitch, spasm; qualm, hesitation, scruple, misgiving.

panga /pánggə/ *n.* a bladed African tool like a machete. [native name in E. Africa]

pangolin /pánggəlin, panggō-/ *n.* any scaly anteater of the genus *Manis*, native to Asia and Africa, having a small head with elongated snout and tongue, and a tapering tail. [Malay *peng-gōling* roller (from its habit of rolling itself up)]

panhandle /pánhand'l/ *n. & v.* ● *n.* a narrow strip of territory extending from one state into another. ● *v.tr. & intr. colloq.* beg for money in the street. □□ **panhandler** *n.*

panic¹ /pánik/ *n. & v.* ● *n.* **1 a** a sudden uncontrollable fear or alarm. **b** (*attrib.*) characterized or caused by panic (*panic buying*). **2** infectious apprehension or fright esp. in commercial dealings. ● *v.tr. & intr.* (**panicked**, **panicking**) (often foll. by *into*) affect or be affected with panic (*was panicked into buying*). □ **panic button** a button for summoning help in an emergency. **panic-monger** a person who fosters a panic. **panic stations** *Brit.* a state of emergency. **panic-stricken** (or **-struck**) affected with panic; very apprehensive. □□ **panicky** *adj.* [F *panique* f. mod.L *panicus* f. Gk *panikos* f. *Pan* a rural god causing terror]
■ *n.* terror, alarm, fear, fright, dread, horror, dismay, consternation, hysteria; anxiety, apprehension, apprehensiveness, nervousness. ● *v.* frighten, scare, alarm, terrify, unnerve; become terrified *or* alarmed *or* fearful *or* frightened, lose one's nerve, go to pieces, fall apart, *colloq.* chicken (out), *Brit. sl.* lose one's bottle. □ **panic-stricken** (or **-struck**) terrified, alarmed, horrified, aghast, terror-stricken *or* terror-struck, panicky, frenzied, in a frenzy, hysterical, beside oneself, fearful, afraid, scared (stiff), petrified, horror-struck *or* horror-stricken, frightened *or* scared out of one's wits, appalled, stunned, stupefied; perturbed, unnerved, nervous, distressed, upset, jumpy, worked up, in a cold sweat, *colloq.* in a flap *or* tizzy. □□ **panicky** see *panic-stricken* above.

panic² /pánik/ *n.* any grass of the genus *Panicum*, including various cereals. [OE f. L *panicum* f. *panus* thread on bobbin, millet ear f. Gk *pēnos* web]

panicle /pánikəl/ *n. Bot.* a loose branching cluster of flowers,

as in oats. □□ **panicled** *adj.* [L *paniculum* dimin. of *panus* thread]

panjandrum /panjándrəm/ *n.* **1** a mock title for an important person. **2** a pompous or pretentious official, etc. [app. invented in nonsense verse by S. Foote 1755]

panne /pan/ *n.* (in full **panne velvet**) a silk or rayon velvet fabric with a flattened pile. [F]

pannier /pányər/ *n.* **1** a basket, esp. one of a pair carried by a beast of burden. **2** each of a pair of bags or boxes on either side of the rear wheel of a bicycle or motorcycle. **3** *hist* also /panyáy/ **a** part of a skirt looped up around the hips. **b** a frame supporting this. [ME f. OF *panier* f. L *panarium* bread basket f. *panis* bread]

pannikin /pánikin/ *n.* **1** *Brit.* a small metal drinking cup. **2** *Brit.* the contents of this. **3** *Austral. sl.* the head (esp. *off one's pannikin*). □ **pannikin boss** *Austral. sl.* a minor overseer or foreman. [PAN¹ + -KIN, after *cannikin*]
■ **3** see HEAD *n.* 1; (*off one's pannikin*) see CRAZY 1.

panoply /pánəplee/ *n.* (*pl.* **-ies**) **1** a complete or magnificent array. **2** a complete suit of armor. □□ **panoplied** *adj.* [F *panoplie* or mod.L *panoplia* full armor f. Gk (as PAN-, *oplia* f. *hopla* arms)]

panoptic /panóptik/ *adj.* showing or seeing the whole at one view. [Gk *panoptos* seen by all, *panoptēs* all-seeing]

panorama /pánərámə, -raa-/ *n.* **1** an unbroken view of a surrounding region. **2** a complete survey or presentation of a subject, sequence of events, etc. **3** a picture or photograph containing a wide view. **4** a continuous passing scene. □□ **panoramic** *adj.* **panoramically** *adv.* [PAN- + Gk *horama* view f. *horaō* see]
■ **1, 3** see VIEW *n.* 2. **2** see VIEW *n.* 3. □□ **panoramic** sweeping, commanding, extensive, comprehensive, wide, overall, scenic, far-reaching, all-embracing, far-ranging, all-encompassing, inclusive, bird's-eye, general.

panpipes /pánpīps/ *n.pl.* a musical instrument orig. associated with the Greek rural god Pan, made of a series of short pipes graduated in length and fixed together with the mouthpieces in line.

pansy /pánzee/ *n.* (*pl.* **-ies**) **1** any garden plant of the genus *Viola*, with flowers of various rich colors. **2** *colloq. derog.* **a** an effeminate man. **b** a male homosexual. [F *pensée* thought, pansy f. *penser* think f. L *pensare* frequent. of *pendere* pensweigh]

pant /pant/ *v. & n.* ● *v.* **1** *intr.* breathe with short quick breaths. **2** *tr.* (often foll. by *out*) utter breathlessly. **3** *intr.* (often foll. by *for*) yearn or crave. **4** *intr.* (of the heart, etc.) throb violently. ● *n.* **1** a panting breath. **2** a throb. □□ **pantingly** *adv.* [ME f. OF *pantaisier* ult. f. Gk *phantasioō* cause to imagine (as FANTASY)]
■ *v.* **1, 2** gasp, huff, puff, blow, heave, wheeze. **3** (*pant for*) crave, hanker after, hunger *or* thirst for *or* after, yearn for, ache for, want, desire, covet, wish for, long *or* pine *or* sigh for, have one's heart set on, die for, be dying for, *colloq.* have a yen for.

pantalets /pántəléts/ *n.pl.* (also **pantalettes**) *hist.* long underpants worn by women and girls in the 19th c., with a frill at the bottom of each leg. [dimin. of PANTALOON]

pantaloon /pántəloʻon/ *n.* **1** (in *pl.*) *hist.* men's close-fitting breeches fastened below the calf or at the foot. **2** (**Pantaloon**) a character in Italian comedy wearing pantaloons. [F *pantalon* f. It. *pantalone*, a character in Italian comedy]

pantechnicon /pantéknikən/ *n. Brit.* a large van for transporting furniture. [PAN- + TECHNIC orig. as the name of a bazaar and then a furniture warehouse]

pantheism /pántheeizəm/ *n.* **1** the belief that God is identifiable with the forces of nature and with natural substances. **2** worship that admits or tolerates all gods. □□ **pantheist** *n.* **pantheistic** *adj.* **pantheistical** *adj.* **pantheistically** *adv.* [PAN- + Gk *theos* god]

pantheon /pántheeon, -ən/ *n.* **1** a building in which illustrious dead are buried or have memorials. **2** the deities of a people collectively. **3** a temple dedicated to all the gods, esp. the circular one at Rome. **4** a group of esteemed persons. [ME f. L f. Gk *pantheion* (as PAN-, *theion* holy f. *theos* god)]

panther /pánthər/ n. **1** a leopard, esp. with black fur. **2** a cougar. [ME f. OF *pantere* f. L *panthera* f. Gk *panthēr*]

pantie girdle /pánteegərd'l/ n. (also **panty girdle**) a woman's girdle with a crotch.

panties /pánteez/ n.pl. colloq. short-legged or legless underpants worn by women and girls. [dimin. of PANTS]

pantile /pántīl/ n. a roofing tile curved to form an S-shaped section, fitted to overlap. [PAN¹ + TILE]

panto /pántō/ n. (pl. **-os**) Brit. colloq. = PANTOMIME 2. [abbr.]

panto- /pántō/ comb. form all; universal. [Gk *pas pantos* all]

pantograph /pántəgraf/ n. **1** Art & Painting an instrument for copying a plan or drawing, etc., on a different scale by a system of jointed rods. **2** a jointed framework conveying a current to an electric vehicle from overhead wires. □□ **pantographic** adj. [PANTO- + Gk -*graphos* writing]

pantomime /pántəmīm/ n. & v. ● n. **1** the use of gestures and facial expression to convey meaning without speech, esp. in drama and dance. **2** Brit. a theatrical entertainment based on a fairy tale, with music, topical jokes, etc., usu. produced around Christmas. **3** colloq. an absurd or outrageous piece of behavior. v. to convey meaning without speech using only gestures. □□ **pantomimic** /-mímik/ adj. [F *pantomime* or L *pantomimus* f. Gk *pantomimos* (as PANTO-, MIME)]

pantothenic acid /pántəthénik/ n. a vitamin of the B complex, found in rice, bran, and many other foods, and essential for the oxidation of fats and carbohydrates. [Gk *pantothen* from every side]

pantry /pántree/ n. (pl. **-ies**) **1** a small room or cupboard in which dishes, silverware, table linen, etc., are kept. **2** a small room or cupboard in which groceries, etc., are kept. [ME f. AF *panetrie*, OF *paneterie* f. *panetier* baker ult. f. LL *panarius* bread seller f. L *panis* bread]

pantryman /pántreemən/ n. (pl. **-men**) a person who works in a pantry, esp. in a hotel or hospital.

pants /pants/ n.pl. **1** an outer garment reaching from the waist usu. to the ankles, divided into two parts to cover the legs. **2** Brit. underpants. □ **bore** (or **scare**, etc.) **the pants off** colloq. bore, scare, etc., to an intolerable degree. **wear the pants** be the dominant partner in a marriage. **with one's pants down** colloq. in an embarrassingly unprepared state. [abbr. of PANTALOON(S)]

■ **1** slacks, trousers, knickerbockers, flannels, bellbottoms, flares, (blue) jeans, denims, cords, dungarees, knickers, esp. Brit. trews, (Oxford) bags; Sc. breeks, colloq. breeches, propr. Levis, Austral. & S. Afr. sl. rammies. **2** underpants, underwear, trunks, briefs, boxer shorts, undershorts; knickers, drawers, Brit. camiknickers, colloq. panties, bloomers, hist. pantalets; underclothes, undergarments, lingerie, colloq. undies, underthings, Brit. colloq. smalls, joc. unmentionables.
□ **with one's pants down** see UNPREPARED.

pantsuit /pántsōōt/ n. (also **pants suit**) a woman's suit with pants and a jacket.

panty girdle var. of PANTIE GIRDLE.

panty hose /pánteehōz/ n. (usu. treated as pl.) usu. sheer one-piece garment combining panties and stockings. [PANTIES + HOSE]

panzer /pánzər, páants-/ n. **1** (in pl.) armored troops. **2** (attrib.) heavily armored (panzer division). [G, = coat of mail]

pap¹ /pap/ n. **1 a** a soft or semiliquid food for infants or invalids. **b** a mash or pulp. **2** light or trivial reading matter; nonsense. □□ **pappy** adj. [ME prob. f. MLG, MDu. *pappe*, prob. ult. f. L *pappare* eat]

pap² /pap/ n. archaic or dial. the nipple of a breast or something shaped like a nipple. [ME, of Scand. orig.: ult. imit. of sucking]

papa /paápə, pəpaá/ n. father (esp. as a child's word). [F f. LL f. Gk *papas*]

papacy /páypəsee/ n. (pl. **-ies**) **1** a pope's office or tenure. **2** the papal system. [ME f. med.L *papatia* f. *papa* pope]

Papago /paápəgō, pá-/ n. **1 a** a N. American people native to southwestern Arizona and adjoining parts of Mexico. **b** a member of this people. **2** the language of this people.

papain /pəpáyin, -pī-in/ n. an enzyme obtained from unripe papaya, used to tenderize meat and as a food supplement to aid digestion. [PAPAYA + -IN]

papal /páypəl/ adj. of or relating to a pope or to the papacy. □ **Papal States** hist. the temporal dominions belonging to the Pope, esp. in central Italy. □□ **papally** adv. [ME f. OF f. med.L *papalis* f. eccl.L *papa* POPE¹]

paparazzo /paápəraátsō/ n. (pl. **paparazzi** /-see/) a freelance photographer who pursues celebrities to get photographs of them. [It.]

papaverous /pəpávərəs/ adj. like or related to the poppy. □□ **papaveraceous** /-ráyshəs/ adj. [L *papaver* poppy]

papaw var. of PAWPAW.

papaya /pəpíə/ n. **1** an elongated melon-shaped fruit with edible orange flesh and small black seeds. **2** a tropical tree, *Carica papaya*, bearing this and producing a milky sap from which papain is obtained. [earlier form of PAWPAW]

paper /páypər/ n. & v. ● n. **1** a material manufactured in thin sheets from the pulp of wood or other fibrous substances, used for writing or drawing or printing on, or as wrapping material, etc. **2** (attrib.) **a** made of or using paper. **b** flimsy like paper. **3** = NEWSPAPER. **4 a** a document printed on paper. **b** (in pl.) documents attesting identity or credentials. **c** (in pl.) documents belonging to a person or relating to a matter. **5** Commerce **a** negotiable documents, e.g., bills of exchange. **b** (attrib.) recorded on paper though not existing (paper profits). **6 a** a set of questions to be answered at one session in an examination. **b** the written answers to these. **7** = WALLPAPER. **8** an essay or dissertation, esp. one read to a learned society or published in a learned journal. **9** a piece of paper, esp. as a wrapper, etc. **10** Theatr. sl. free tickets or the people admitted by them (the house is full of paper). ● v.tr. **1** apply paper to, esp. decorate (a wall, etc.) with wallpaper. **2** (foll. by over) **a** cover (a hole or blemish) with paper. **b** disguise or try to hide (a fault, etc.). **3** Theatr. sl. fill (a theater) by giving free passes. **4** distribute flyers, pamphlets, etc., as in a neighborhood. □ **on paper 1** in writing. **2** in theory; to judge from written or printed evidence. **paper clip** a clip of bent wire or of plastic for holding several sheets of paper together. **paper knife** a blunt knife for opening letters, etc. **paper mill** a mill in which paper is made. **paper money** money in the form of bills. **paper mulberry** a small Asiatic tree, *Broussonetia papyrifera*, of the mulberry family, whose bark is used for making paper and cloth. **paper nautilus** see NAUTILUS 2. **paper route** (Brit. **round**) **1** a job of regularly delivering newspapers. **2** a route taken doing this. **paper tape** Computing tape made of paper, esp. that on which data or instructions are represented by means of holes punched in it, for conveying to a processor, etc. **paper tiger** an apparently threatening, but ineffectual, person or thing. **paper trail** documentation of transactions, etc. □□ **paperer** n. **paperless** adj. [ME f. AF *papir*, = OF *papier* f. L *papyrus*: see PAPYRUS]

■ n. **3** newspaper, tabloid, daily, weekly, journal, gazette, publication, periodical, newsletter, organ, derog. rag, sheet. **4** document(s), instrument, form, certificate, deed; credential(s), identification; docket, file, dossier, record, archive. **5 a** see NOTE n. 6b. **8** article, composition, essay, assignment, report, thesis, study, tract, analysis, critique, exegesis, treatise, monograph, dissertation, disquisition. ● v. **1** wallpaper, line; decorate. **2** (paper over) cover up; see also COVER v. 1.
□ **on paper 1** in writing, on record, documented, in black and white. **2** see ideally (IDEAL).

paperback /páypərbak/ (US also **paperbound**) adj. & n. ● adj. (of a book) bound in stiff paper. ● n. a paperback book.

paperboy /páypərboy/ (fem. **papergirl** /-gərl/) n. a boy or girl who delivers or sells newspapers.

paperweight /páypərwayt/ n. a small heavy object for keeping loose papers in place.

paperwork /páypərwərk/ n. **1** routine clerical or administrative work. **2** documents, esp. for a particular purpose.

papery /páypəree/ adj. like paper in thinness or texture.

papier mâché /páypər məsháy, papyáy/ n. paper pulp used for molding into boxes, trays, etc. [F, = chewed paper]

papilionaceous /pəpíleeənáyshəs/ adj. (of a plant) with a corolla like a butterfly. [mod.L papilionaceus f. L papilio -onis butterfly]

papilla /pəpílə/ n. (pl. **papillae** /-pílee/) **1** a small nipplelike protuberance in a part or organ of the body. **2** Bot. a small fleshy projection on a plant. □□ **papillary** adj. **papillate** /pápilayt/ adj. **papillose** /pápilōs/ adj. [L, = nipple, dimin. of papula: see PAPULA]

papilloma /pápilṓmə/ n. (pl. **papillomas** or **papillomata** /-mətə/) a wartlike usu. benign tumor.

papillon /paapeeyṓN, pá-/ n. **1** a toy dog of a breed with ears suggesting the form of a butterfly. **2** this breed. [F, = butterfly, f. L papilio -onis]

papist /páypist/ n. & adj. often derog. ● n. **1** a Roman Catholic. **2** hist. an advocate of papal supremacy. ● adj. of or relating to Roman Catholics. □□ **papistic** adj. **papistical** adj. **papistry** n. [F papiste or mod.L papista f. eccl.L papa POPE[1]]

papoose /papṓs, pə-/ n. a young Native American child. [Algonquian]

pappus /pápəs/ n. (pl. **pappi** /-pī/) a group of hairs on the fruit of thistles, dandelions, etc. □□ **pappose** adj. [L f. Gk pappos]

paprika /pəpreékə, páprikə/ n. **1** Bot. a red pepper. **2** a condiment made from it. [Magyar]

Pap smear /pap/ (also **Pap test**) n. a test for cervical cancer, etc., done by a cervical smear. [abbr. of G. N. Papanicolaou, US scientist d. 1962]

papula /pápyələ/ n. (also **papule** /pápyōol/) (pl. **papulae** /-lee/) **1** a pimple. **2** a small fleshy projection on a plant. □□ **papular** adj. **papulose** adj. **papulous** adj. [L]

papyrology /pápiróləjee/ n. the study of ancient papyri. □□ **papyrological** /-rəlójikəl/ adj. **papyrologist** n.

papyrus /pəpírəs/ n. (pl. **papyri** /-rī/) **1** an aquatic plant, Cyperus papyrus, with dark green stems topped with fluffy inflorescences. **2 a** a writing material prepared in ancient Egypt from the pithy stem of this. **b** a document written on this. [ME f. L papyrus f. Gk papuros]

par[1] /paar/ n. & v. ● n. **1** the average or normal amount, degree, condition, etc. (be up to par). **2** equality; an equal status or footing (on a par with). **3** Golf the number of strokes a skilled player should normally require for a hole or course. **4** Stock Exch. the face value of stocks and shares, etc. (at par). **5** (in full **par of exchange**) the recognized value of one country's currency in terms of another's. ● v. Golf to score par. □ **above par** Stock Exch. at a premium. **at par** Stock Exch. at face value. **below par 1** less good than usual in health or other quality. **2** Stock Exch. at a discount. **par for the course** colloq. what is normal or expected in any given circumstances. [L (adj. & n.) = equal, equality]

■ **1** standard, normal, average, norm, expectation. **2** level; see also PARITY[1] 1. □ **below par 1** below average, substandard, inferior, second-rate, mediocre, middling, poor, inadequate, unsatisfactory, wanting, bad, wretched, miserable, awful, terrible, not up to standard or scratch, colloq. lousy, not up to snuff; ill, sickly, poorly, unhealthy, unwell, not (very) well, not oneself, not in good or the best shape, in bad shape, off form, off color, colloq. under the weather.

par[2] /paar/ n. Brit. esp. Journalism colloq. paragraph. [abbr.]

par. abbr. (also **para.**) paragraph.

par- /pər, par, paar/ prefix var. of PARA-[1] before a vowel or h; (paraldehyde; parody; parhelion).

para /párə/ n. colloq. **1** a paratrooper. **2** a paraprofessional. **3** Brit. a paragraph. [abbr.]

para-[1] /párə/ prefix (also **par-**) **1** beside (paramilitary). **2** beyond (paranormal). **3** Chem. **a** modification of (paraldehyde). **b** relating to diametrically opposite carbon atoms in a benzene ring (paradichlorobenzene). [from or after Gk para- f. para beside, past, beyond]

para-[2] /párə/ comb. form protect; ward off (parachute; parasol). [F f. It. f. L parare defend]

para-aminobenzoic acid /párə-əmeénōbenzṓik/ n. Biochem. a yellow crystalline compound, often used in suntan lotions and sunscreens to absorb ultraviolet light. ¶ Abbr.: **PABA**.

parabiosis /párəbiṓsis/ n. Biol. the natural or artificial joining of two individuals. □□ **parabiotic** /-biótik/ adj. [mod.L, formed as PARA-[1] + Gk biōsis mode of life f. bios life]

parable /párəbəl/ n. **1** a narrative of imagined events used to illustrate a moral or spiritual lesson. **2** an allegory. [ME f. OF parabole f. LL sense 'allegory, discourse' of L parabola comparison]

■ allegory, fable, lesson, morality tale.

parabola /pərábələ/ n. an open plane curve formed by the intersection of a cone with a plane parallel to its side, resembling the path of a projectile under the action of gravity. [mod.L f. Gk parabolē placing side by side, comparison (as PARA-[1], bolē a throw f. ballō)]

parabolic /párəbólik/ adj. **1** of or expressed in a parable. **2** of or like a parabola. □□ **parabolically** adv. [LL parabolicus f. Gk parabolikos (as PARABOLA)]

parabolical /párəbólikəl/ adj. = PARABOLIC 1.

paraboloid /párábəloyd/ n. **1** (in full **paraboloid of revolution**) a solid generated by the rotation of a parabola about its axis of symmetry. **2** a solid having two or more nonparallel parabolic cross sections. □□ **paraboloidal** adj.

paracetamol /párəsétəmawl, -mol, -seetə-/ n. Brit. ACET-AMINOPHEN. [para-acetylaminophenol]

parachronism /pərákrənizəm/ n. an error in chronology, esp. by assigning too late a date. [PARA-[1] + Gk khronos time, perh. after anachronism]

parachute /párəshōot/ n. & v. ● n. **1** a rectangular or umbrella-shaped canopy allowing a person or heavy object attached to it to descend slowly from a height, esp. from an aircraft, or to retard motion in other ways. **2** (attrib.) dropped or to be dropped by parachute (parachute drop). ● v.tr. & intr. convey or descend by parachute. [F (as PARA-[2], CHUTE[1])]

parachutist /párəshōotist/ n. **1** a person who uses a parachute. **2** (in pl.) parachute troops.

Paraclete /párəkleet/ n. the Holy Spirit as advocate or counselor. [ME f. OF paraclet f. LL paracletus f. Gk paraklētos called in aid (as PARA-[1], klētos f. kaleō call)]

parade /pəráyd/ n. & v. ● n. **1 a** a formal or ceremonial muster of troops for inspection. **b** = parade ground. **2 a** public procession. **3** ostentatious display (made a parade of their wealth). **4** Brit. a public square, promenade, or row of shops. ● v. **1** intr. assemble for parade. **2 a** tr. march through (streets, etc.) in procession. **b** intr. march ceremonially. **3** tr. display ostentatiously. □ **on parade 1** taking part in a parade. **2** on display. **parade ground** a place for the muster of troops. □□ **parader** n. [F, = show, f. Sp. parada and It. parata ult. f. L parare prepare, furnish]

■ n. **2** procession, march, train, file, promenade, cortège; column. **3** exhibition, display, show, spectacle, array, splash. **4** promenade, walkway, mall, esplanade, precinct; row. ● v. **2** march, pass in review, promenade, walk, file. **3** flaunt, show (off), brandish, wave, display, air, literary vaunt. □ **parade ground** parade, Anglo-Ind. maidan.

paradiddle /párədid'l/ n. a drum roll with alternate beating of sticks. [imit.]

paradigm /párədim/ n. **1** an example or pattern. **2** Gram. a representative set of the inflections of a noun, verb, etc. □□ **paradigmatic** /-digmátik/ adj. **paradigmatically** adv. [LL paradigma f. Gk paradeigma f. paradeiknumi show side by side (as PARA-[1], deiknumi show)]

paradise /párədis/ n. **1** (in some religions) heaven as the ultimate abode of the just. **2** a place or state of complete happiness. **3** (in full **earthly paradise**) the abode of Adam and Eve in the biblical account of the Creation; the garden of Eden. □□ **paradisaical** /-disáyikəl/ adj. **paradisal**

/párədisəl/ *adj.* **paradisiacal** /-disíəkəl/ *adj.* **paradisical** /-dísikəl/ *adj.* [ME f. OF *paradis* f. LL *paradisus* f. Gk *paradeisos* f. Avestan *pairidaēza* park]

■ **1** heaven, Zion, Elysium, Elysian Fields, happy hunting ground, the promised land, Valhalla. **2** heaven on earth, dreamland, seventh heaven, (Garden of) Eden, utopia, Shangri-la; bliss, happiness, rapture, heaven, delight, blessedness, ecstasy, joy, nirvana.

parados /párədos/ *n.* an elevation of earth behind a fortified place as a protection against attack from the rear, esp. a mound along the back of a trench. [F (as PARA-², *dos* back f. L *dorsum*)]

paradox /párədoks/ *n.* **1 a** a seemingly absurd or contradictory statement, even if actually well-founded. **b** a self-contradictory or essentially absurd statement. **2** a person or thing conflicting with a preconceived notion of what is reasonable or possible. **3** a paradoxical quality or character. [orig. = a statement contrary to accepted opinion, f. LL *paradoxum* f. Gk *paradoxon* neut. adj. (as PARA-¹, *doxa* opinion)]

■ contradiction, self-contradiction, incongruity, inconsistency, absurdity, ambiguity, enigma, puzzle, mystery, quandary, problem, *disp.* dilemma; *rhet.* oxymoron.

paradoxical /párədóksikəl/ *adj.* **1** of or like or involving paradox. **2** fond of paradox. □□ **paradoxically** *adv.*

■ **1** contradictory, self-contradictory, conflicting, impossible, improbable, incongruous, illogical, inconsistent, absurd, ambiguous, confusing, equivocal, enigmatic, puzzling, baffling, incomprehensible, bewildering, perplexing, mysterious, problematic.

paraffin /párəfin/ *n.* **1** (also **paraffin wax**) a waxy mixture of hydrocarbons used in candles, waterproofing, etc. **2** *Brit.* = KEROSENE. **3** *Chem.* = ALKANE. [G (1830) f. L *parum* little + *affinis* related, from the small affinity it has for other substances]

paragoge /párəgójee/ *n.* the addition of a letter or syllable to a word in some contexts or as a language develops (e.g., *t* in *peasant*). □□ **paragogic** /-gójik/ *adj.* [LL f. Gk *paragōgē* derivation (as PARA-¹, *agōgē* f. *agō* lead)]

paragon /párəgon, -gən/ *n.* **1 a** a model of excellence. **b** a supremely excellent person or thing. **2** (foll. by *of*) a model (of virtue, etc.). **3** a perfect diamond of 100 carats or more. [obs. F f. It. *paragone* touchstone, f. med.Gk *parakonē* whetstone]

■ **1, 2** epitome, archetype, model, prototype, quintessence, pattern, standard, exemplar, ideal, beau ideal, criterion.

paragraph /párəgraf/ *n. & v.* ● *n.* **1** a distinct section of a piece of writing, beginning on a new usu. indented line. **2** a symbol (usu. ¶) used to mark a new paragraph, and also as a reference mark. **3** a short item in a newspaper, usu. of only one paragraph. ● *v.tr.* arrange (a piece of writing) in paragraphs. □□ **paragraphic** /-gráfik/ *adj.* [F *paragraphe* or med.L *paragraphus* f. Gk *paragraphos* short stroke marking a break in sense (as PARA-¹, *graphō* write)]

parakeet /párəkeet/ *n.* any of various small usu. long-tailed parrots. [OF *paroquet*, It. *parrocchetto*, Sp. *periquito*, perh. ult. f. dimin. of *Pierre*, etc. Peter: cf. PARROT]

paralanguage /párəlanggwij/ *n.* elements or factors in communication that are ancillary to language proper, e.g., intonation and gesture.

paraldehyde /pəráldihid/ *n.* a cyclic polymer of acetaldehyde, used as a narcotic and sedative. [PARA-¹ + ALDEHYDE]

paralegal /párəleegəl/ *adj. & n.* ● *adj.* of or relating to auxiliary aspects of the law. ● *n.* a person trained in subsidiary legal matters. [PARA-¹ + LEGAL]

paralipomena /párəlipóminə/ *n. pl.* (also **-leipomena** /párəlī-/) **1** things omitted from a work and added as a supplement. **2** *Bibl.* the books of Chronicles in the Old Testament, containing particulars omitted from Kings. [ME f. eccl.L f. Gk *paraleipomena* f. *paraleipō* omit (as PARA-¹, *leipō* leave)]

paralipsis /párəlípsis/ *n.* (also **-leipsis** /-lípsis/) (*pl.* **-ses** /-seez/) *Rhet.* **1** the device of giving emphasis by professing to say little or nothing of a subject, as in *not to mention their unpaid debts of several million dollars.* **2** an instance of this. [LL f. Gk *paraleipsis* passing over (as PARA-¹, *leipsis* f. *leipō* leave)]

parallax /párəlaks/ *n.* **1** the apparent difference in the position or direction of an object caused when the observer's position is changed. **2** the angular amount of this. □□ **parallactic** /-láktik/ *adj.* [F *parallaxe* f. mod.L *parallaxis* f. Gk *parallaxis* change f. *parallassō* to alternate (as PARA-¹, *allassō* exchange f. *allos* other)]

parallel /párəlel/ *adj., n., & v.* ● *adj.* **1 a** (of lines or planes) side by side and having the same distance continuously between them. **b** (foll. by *to, with*) (of a line or plane) having this relation (to another). **2** (of circumstances, etc.) precisely similar, analogous, or corresponding. **3 a** (of processes, etc.) occurring or performed simultaneously. **b** *Computing* involving the simultaneous performance of operations. ● *n.* **1** a person or thing precisely analogous or equal to another. **2** a comparison (*drew a parallel between the two situations*). **3** (in full **parallel of latitude**) *Geog.* **a** each of the imaginary parallel circles of constant latitude on the earth's surface. **b** a corresponding line on a map (*the 49th parallel*). **4** *Printing* two parallel lines (‖) as a reference mark. ● *v.tr.* (**paralleled, paralleling**) **1** be parallel to; correspond to. **2** represent as similar; compare. **3** adduce as a parallel instance. □ **in parallel** (of electric circuits) arranged so as to join at common points at each end. **parallel bars** a pair of parallel rails on posts for gymnastics. □□ **parallelism** *n.* [F *parallèle* f. L *parallelus* f. Gk *parallēlos* (as PARA-¹, *allēlos* one another)]

■ *adj.* **2** similar, corresponding, congruent, analogous, analogical, correspondent, like, matching, homologous, coordinate, equivalent, proportional, proportionate, uniform, *archaic or literary* coequal. **3** contemporary, contemporaneous, simultaneous. ● *n.* **1** analog, match, homologue, equivalent, counterpart, equal, *archaic or literary* coequal. **2** analogy, parallelism, equivalence, correspondence, symmetry, equality, parity, correlation, *archaic or literary* coequality; see also COMPARISON 3. ● *v.* **1** correspond to or with, match, equate to or with, be likened to, correlate to or with, compare with or to, imitate, repeat, echo, iterate, reiterate, duplicate, follow, agree with; keep pace with, conform to or with, balance, set off, offset, be accompanied by, coincide with, *colloq.* jibe with. **2** match, equate, liken, compare, juxtapose, associate, correlate.

parallelepiped /párəlelləpípid, -pípid/ *n. Geom.* a solid body of which each face is a parallelogram. [Gk *parallēlepipedon* (as PARALLEL, *epipedon* plane surface)]

parallelogram /párəléləgram/ *n. Geom.* a four-sided plane rectilinear figure with opposite sides parallel. □ **parallelogram of forces** **1** a parallelogram illustrating the theorem that if two forces acting at a point are represented in magnitude and direction by two sides of a parallelogram meeting at that point, their resultant is represented by the diagonal drawn from that point. **2** this theorem. [F *parallélogramme* f. LL *parallelogrammum* f. Gk *parallēlogrammon* (as PARALLEL, *grammē* line)]

paralogism /pərálejizəm/ *n. Logic* **1** a fallacy. **2** illogical reasoning (esp. of which the reasoner is unconscious). □□ **paralogist** *n.* **paralogize** *v.intr.* [F *paralogisme* f. LL *paralogismus* f. Gk *paralogismos* f. *paralogizomai* reason falsely f. *paralogos* contrary to reason (as PARA-¹, *logos* reason)]

paralysis /pərálisis/ *n.* (*pl.* **paralyses** /-seez/) **1** impairment or loss of esp. the motor function of the nerves. **2** a state of utter powerlessness. [L f. Gk *paralusis* f. *paraluō* disable (as PARA-¹, *luō* loosen)]

paralytic /párəlítik/ *adj. & n.* ● *adj.* **1** affected by paralysis.

/. . ./ pronunciation	■ **part of speech**
□ **phrases, idioms, and compounds**	
□□ **derivatives**	■ **synonym section**
cross-references appear in SMALL CAPITALS or *italics*	

2 esp. *Brit. sl.* very drunk. ● *n.* a person affected by paralysis. □□ **paralytically** *adv.* [ME f. OF *paralytique* f. L *paralyticus* f. Gk *paralutikos* (as PARALYSIS)]

paralyze /párəlīz/ *v.tr.* (also *Brit.* **paralyse**) **1** affect with paralysis. **2** render powerless; cripple. □□ **paralyzation** *n.* **paralyzingly** *adv.* [F *paralyser* f. *paralysie*: cf. PALSY]

■ **2** disable, cripple, incapacitate; immobilize, inactivate, deactivate, transfix; halt, stop.

paramagnetic /párəmagnétik/ *adj.* (of a body or substance) tending to become weakly magnetized so as to lie parallel to a magnetic field force. □□ **paramagnetism** /-mágnitizəm/ *n.*

paramatta var. of PARRAMATTA.

paramecium /párəmée̯seeəm/ *n.* (also *Brit.* **paramoecium**) any freshwater protozoan of the genus *Paramecium,* of a characteristic slipper-like shape covered with cilia. [mod.L f. Gk *paramēkēs* oval (as PARA-¹, *mēkos* length)]

paramedic /párəmédik/ *n.* **1** a paramedical worker. **2** a person trained in emergency medical procedures.

paramedical /párəmédikəl/ *adj.* (of services, etc.) supplementing and supporting medical work.

parameter /pərámitər/ *n.* **1** *Math.* a quantity constant in the case considered but varying in different cases. **2 a** an (esp. measurable or quantifiable) characteristic or feature. **b** (loosely) a constant element or factor, esp. serving as a limit or boundary. □□ **parametric** /párəmétrik/ *adj.* **parametrize** *v.tr.* [mod.L f. Gk *para* beside + *metron* measure]

paramilitary /párəmíliteree/ *adj.* (of forces) ancillary to and similarly organized to military forces.

paramnesia /páramnee̱zhə/ *n. Psychol.* = DÉJÀ VU. [PARA-¹ + AMNESIA]

paramo /párəmō/, páar-/ *n.* (*pl.* **-os**) a high treeless plateau in tropical S. America. [Sp. & Port. f. L *paramus*]

paramoecium *Brit.* var. of PARAMECIUM.

paramount /párəmownt/ *adj.* **1** supreme; requiring first consideration; preeminent (*of paramount importance*). **2** in supreme authority. □□ **paramountcy** *n.* **paramountly** *adv.* [AF *paramont* f. OF *par* by + *amont* above: cf. AMOUNT]

■ **1** preeminent, chief, supreme, dominant, main, major, predominant, cardinal, first, prime, primary, principal, essential, vital, requisite, basic. **2** see SUPREME *adj* 1.

paramour /párəmŏŏr/ *n.* an illicit lover, esp. of a married person. [ME f. OF *par amour* by love]

■ lover, love, inamorato, inamorata, mistress, gigolo, concubine, kept woman, (the) other woman, *sl.* sugar daddy, *sl. derog.* fancy man *or* woman.

parang /párang/ *n.* a large heavy Malayan knife used for clearing vegetation, etc. [Malay]

paranoia /párənóyə/ *n.* **1** a personality disorder esp. characterized by delusions of persecution and self-importance. **2** an abnormal tendency to suspect and mistrust others. □□ **paranoiac** *adj. & n.* **paranoiacally** *adv.* **paranoic** /-nóyik, -nṓ-ik/ *adj.* **paranoically** *adv.* **paranoid** /-noyd/ *adj. & n.* [mod.L f. Gk f. *paranoos* distracted (as PARA-¹, *noos* mind)]

paranormal /párənórməl/ *adj.* beyond the scope of normal objective investigation or explanation. □□ **paranormally** *adv.*

parapet /párəpit/ *n.* **1** a low wall at the edge of a roof, balcony, etc., or along the sides of a bridge. **2** a defense of earth or stone to conceal and protect troops. □□ **parapeted** *adj.* [F *parapet* or It. *parapetto* breast-high wall (as PARA-², *petto* breast f. L *pectus*)]

paraph /párəf/ *n.* a flourish after a signature, orig. as a precaution against forgery. [ME f. F *paraphe* f. med.L *paraphus* for *paragraphus* PARAGRAPH]

paraphernalia /párəfərnáylyə/ *n.pl.* (also treated as *sing.*) miscellaneous belongings, items of equipment, accessories, etc. [orig. = property owned by a married woman, f. med.L *paraphernalia* f. LL *parapherna* f. Gk *parapherna* property apart from a dowry (as PARA-¹, *pherna* f. *phernē* dower)]

■ equipment, apparatus, accessories, outfit, kit, appliances, utensils, gear, rig, material(s), matériel, things, tackle, equipage, accoutrements, effects, chattels, possessions, belongings, appurtenances,

trappings, property, baggage, impedimenta, supplies, stuff, junk, esp. *Brit.* rubbish, *Brit. sl.* clobber.

paraphrase /párəfrayz/ *n. & v.* ● *n.* a free rendering or rewording of a passage. ● *v.tr.* express the meaning of (a passage) in other words. □□ **paraphrastic** /-frástik/ *adj.* [F *paraphrase* or L *paraphrasis* f. Gk *paraphrasis* f. *paraphrazō* (as PARA-¹ *phrazō* tell)]

■ *n.* rephrasing, rewording, restatement, rewriting, rewrite, rehash, rendition, rendering, version.

● *v.* rephrase, metaphrase, reword, restate, rewrite, rehash.

paraplegia /párəplée̯jə/ *n.* paralysis of the legs and part or the whole of the trunk. □□ **paraplegic** *adj. & n.* [mod.L f. Gk *paraplēgia* f. *paraplēssō* (as PARA-¹, *plēssō* strike)]

parapsychology /párəsikóləjee/ *n.* the study of mental phenomena outside the sphere of ordinary psychology (hypnosis, telepathy, etc.). □□ **parapsychological** /-sikəlójikəl/ *adj.* **parapsychologist** *n.*

paraquat /párəkwot/ *n.* a quick-acting herbicide, becoming inactive on contact with the soil. [PARA-¹ + QUATERNARY (from the position of the bond between the two parts of the molecule relative to quaternary nitrogen atom)]

parasailing /párəsayling/ *n.* a sport in which participants wearing open parachutes are towed behind a vehicle or motor boat to gain height, sometimes releasing for a conventional descent, usu. toward a predetermined target. □□ **parasailer** *n.* **parasailor** *n.*

paraselene /párəsilée̯nee/ *n.* (*pl.* **paraselenae** /-nee/) a bright spot, esp. an image of the moon, on a lunar halo. Also called *mock moon.* [mod.L (as PARA-¹, Gk *selēnē* moon)]

parasite /párəsīt/ *n.* **1** an organism living in or on another and benefiting at the expense of the other. **2** a person who lives off or exploits another or others. **3** *Philol.* an inorganic sound or letter developing from an adjacent one. □□ **parasitic** /-sítik/ *adj.* **parasitical** /-sítikəl/ *adj.* **parasitically** *adv.* **parasiticide** /-sítisīd/ *n.* **parasitism** /-sítizəm/ *n.* **parasitology** /-tóləjee/ *n.* **parasitologist** /-tóləjist/ *n.* [L *parasitus* f. Gk *parasitos* one who eats at another's table (as PARA-¹, *sitos* food)]

■ **2** leech, bloodsucker, hanger-on, sponger, sponge, cadger, scrounger, barnacle, *colloq.* moocher, *sl.* freeloader, *Austral. & NZ sl.* bludger.

parasitize /párəsitīz/ *v.tr.* infest as a parasite. □□ **parasitization** *n.*

parasol /párəsawl, -sol/ *n.* a light umbrella used to give shade from the sun. [F f. It. *parasole* (as PARA-², *sole* sun f. L *sol*)]

parasympathetic /párəsímpəthétik/ *adj. Anat.* relating to the part of the nervous system that consists of nerves leaving the lower end of the spinal cord and connecting with those in or near the viscera (cf. SYMPATHETIC 9). [PARA-¹ + SYMPATHETIC, because some of these nerves run alongside sympathetic nerves]

parasynthesis /párəsínthisis/ *n. Philol.* **1** a derivation from a compound, e.g., *black-eyed* from *black eye*(s) + *-ed.* **2** a word formed by adding both a prefix and a derivational ending. □□ **parasynthetic** /-thétik/ *adj.* [Gk *parasunthesis* (as PARA-¹, SYNTHESIS)]

parataxis /párətáksis/ *n. Gram.* the placing of clauses, etc., one after another, without words to indicate coordination or subordination, e.g., *Tell me, how are you?* □□ **paratactic** /-táktik/ *adj.* **paratactically** *adv.* [Gk *parataxis* (as PARA-¹, *taxis* arrangement f. *tassō* arrange)]

parathion /párəthíon/ *n.* a highly toxic agricultural insecticide. [PARA-¹ + THIO- + -ON]

parathyroid /párəthíroyd/ *n. & adj. Anat.* ● *n.* a gland next to the thyroid, secreting a hormone that regulates calcium levels in the body. ● *adj.* of or associated with this gland.

paratroop /párətrŏōp/ *n.* (*attrib.*) of or consisting of paratroops (*paratroop regiment*).

paratrooper /párətrŏōpər/ *n.* a member of a body of paratroops.

paratroops /párətrŏōps/ *n.pl.* troops equipped to be dropped by parachute from aircraft. [contr. of PARACHUTE + TROOP]

paratyphoid /párətífoyd/ *n. & adj.* ● *n.* a fever resembling typhoid but caused by various different though related bacteria. ● *adj.* of, relating to, or caused by this fever.

paravane /párəvayn/ *n.* a torpedo-shaped device towed at a depth regulated by its vanes or planes to cut the moorings of submerged mines.

par avion /paár avyáwN/ *adv.* by airmail. [F, = by airplane]

parboil /paárboyl/ *v.tr.* partly cook by boiling. [ME f. OF *parbo(u)illir* f. LL *perbullire* boil thoroughly (as PER-, *bullire* boil: confused with PART)]

parbuckle /paárbukəl/ *n.* & *v.* ● *n.* a rope arranged like a sling, for raising or lowering casks and cylindrical objects. ● *v.tr.* raise or lower with this. [earlier *parbunkle*, of unkn. orig.: assoc. with BUCKLE]

parcel /paársəl/ *n.* & *v.* ● *n.* **1 a** goods, etc., wrapped up in a single package. **b** a bundle of things wrapped up, usu. in paper. **2** a piece of land, esp. as part of a larger lot. **3** a quantity dealt with in one commercial transaction. **4** a group or collection of things, people, etc. **5** part. ● *v.tr.* (**parceled, parceling** or **parcelled, parcelling**) **1** (foll. by *out*) divide into portions **2** (foll. by *up*) wrap as a parcel. **3** cover (rope) with strips of canvas. □ **parcel post 1** a mail service dealing with parcels. **2** a postage rate for parcels. [ME f. OF *parcelle* ult. f. L *particula* (as PART)]
■ *n.* **1** package, packet, carton, box, container, case; bundle, lot, group, batch, collection, pack, set.
2 portion, plot, piece, section, tract, lot, plat. **3** set, group, number, quantity, assortment, lot, bunch, pack, bundle, collection, batch, assemblage. ● *v.* **1** (*parcel out*) apportion, allot, deal (out), dole (out), hand out, distribute, share (out), divide (out), *colloq.* divvy (up), *literary* mete (out). **2** (*parcel up*) see WRAP *v.* 1, BOX¹ *v.* 1.

parch /paarch/ *v.* **1** *tr.* & *intr.* make or become hot and dry. **2** *tr.* roast (peas, grain, etc.) slightly. [ME *perch, parche*, of unkn. orig.]
■ **1** dry (out *or* up), desiccate, dehydrate; scorch, sear, burn, bake, roast; shrivel (up), wither.

parched /paarcht/ *adj.* **1** hot and dry; dried out with heat. **2** *colloq.* thirsty.

Parcheesi /paarcheézee, pər-, -see/ *n. propr.* a board game, played with dice, similar to pachisi.

parchment /paárchmənt/ *n.* **1 a** an animal skin, esp. that of a sheep or goat, prepared as a writing or painting surface. **b** a manuscript written on this. **c** a diploma, esp. one written on this. **2** (in full **vegetable parchment**) high-grade paper made to resemble parchment. [ME f. OF *parchemin*, ult. a blend of LL *pergamina* writing material from Pergamum (in Asia Minor) with *Parthica pellis* Parthian skin (leather)]

parclose /paárklōz/ *n.* a screen or railing in a church, separating a side chapel. [ME f. OF *parclos -ose* past part. of *parclore* enclose]

pard /paard/ *n. archaic* or *poet.* a leopard. [ME f. OF f. L *pardus* f. Gk *pardos*]

pardner /paárdnər/ *n. US dial. colloq.* a partner or comrade. [corrupt.]

pardon /paárd'n/ *n., v.,* & *int.* ● *n.* **1** the act of excusing or forgiving an offense, error, etc. **2** (in full **full pardon**, *Brit.* **free pardon**) a remission of the legal consequences of a crime or conviction. **3** *RC Ch.* an indulgence. ● *v.tr.* **1** release from the consequences of an offense, error, etc. **2** forgive or excuse a person for (an offense, etc.). **3** make (esp. courteous) allowances for; excuse. ● *int.* (also **pardon me** or **I beg your pardon**) **1** a formula of apology or disagreement. **2** a request to repeat something said. □□ **pardonable** *adj.* **pardonably** *adv.* [ME f. OF *pardun, pardoner* f. med.L *perdonare* concede, remit (as PER-, *donare* give)]
■ *n.* **1** forgiveness, amnesty, remission, release, reprieve, absolution, excuse, excusal, allowance, overlooking, condonation, exoneration, *formal* exculpation.
● *v.* forgive, remit, release, reprieve, absolve, overlook, let off, excuse, condone, exonerate, *formal* exculpate.
● *int.* **1** excuse me, I'm sorry, I apologize, my apologies. **2** what (did you say)?, say (it) again, what (was that)?, eh? □□ **pardonable** see PERMISSIBLE.

pardoner /paárd'nər/ *n. hist.* a person licensed to sell papal pardons or indulgences. [ME f. AF (as PARDON)]

pare /pair/ *v.tr.* **1 a** trim (esp. fruit and vegetables) by cutting away the surface or edge. **b** (often foll. by *off, away*) cut off (the surface or edge). **2** (often foll. by *away, down*) diminish little by little. □□ **parer** *n.* [ME f. OF *parer* adorn, peel (fruit), f. L *parare* prepare]
■ **1 a** trim, peel, skin, shave; decorticate, excoriate. **b** trim *or* peel *or* shave off; excoriate. **2** reduce, diminish, decrease, cut (back *or* down), curtail, lower, lessen.

paregoric /párigáwrik, -gór-/ *n.* a camphorated tincture of opium used to reduce pain or relieve diarrhea. [LL *paregoricus* f. Gk *parēgorikos* soothing (as PARA-¹, *-agoros* speaking f. *agora* assembly)]

pareira /pəráirə/ *n.* a drug from the root of a Brazilian shrub, *Chondrodendron tomentosum*, used as a muscle relaxant in surgery, etc. [Port. *parreira* vine trained against a wall]

parenchyma /pəréngkimə/ *n.* **1** *Anat.* the functional part of an organ as distinguished from the connective and supporting tissue. **2** *Bot.* the cellular material, usu. soft and succulent, found esp. in the softer parts of leaves, pulp of fruits, bark and pith of stems, etc. □□ **parenchymal** *adj.* **parenchymatous** /-kímətəs/ *adj.* [Gk *paregkhuma* something poured in besides (as PARA-¹, *egkhuma* infusion f. *egkheō* pour in)]

parent /páirənt, pár-/ *n.* & *v.* ● *n.* **1** a person who has begotten or borne offspring; a father or mother. **2** a person who holds the position or exercises the functions of such a parent. **3** an ancestor. **4** an animal or plant from which others are derived. **5** a source or origin. **6** an initiating organization or enterprise. ● *v.tr.* (also *absol.*) be a parent of. □ **parent company** a company of which other companies are subsidiaries. **parent–teacher association** a local organization of parents and teachers for promoting closer relations and improving educational facilities at a school. □□ **parental** /pərént'l/ *adj.* **parentally** /pəréntəlee/ *adv.* **parenthood** *n.* [ME f. OF f. L *parens parentis* f. *parere* bring forth]
■ *n.* **1** father, mother, surrogate mother, progenitor, procreator, materfamilias, paterfamilias, *colloq.* old lady *or* woman, old man, *literary* begetter, *Brit. sl.* mater, pater. **2** adoptive parent *or* mother *or* father, foster parent, foster mother, foster father, stepparent, stepmother, stepfather, guardian. **5** source, origin, originator, wellspring, fountainhead, root.

parentage /páirəntij, pár-/ *n.* lineage; descent from or through parents (*their parentage is unknown*). [ME f. OF (as PARENT)]
■ lineage, ancestry, line, family, extraction, descent, origin, pedigree, stock, birth, strain, bloodline, heritage, roots.

parenteral /pəréntərəl/ *adj. Med.* administered or occurring elsewhere than in the alimentary canal. □□ **parenterally** *adv.* [PARA-¹ + Gk *enteron* intestine]

parenthesis /pərénthəsis/ *n.* (*pl.* **parentheses** /-seez/) **1 a** a word, clause, or sentence inserted as an explanation or afterthought into a passage which is grammatically complete without it, and usu. marked off by brackets or dashes or commas. **b** (in *pl.*) a pair of rounded brackets ( ) used for this. **2** an interlude or interval. □ **in parenthesis** as a parenthesis or afterthought. [LL f. Gk *parenthesis* f. *parentithēmi* put in beside]

parenthesize /pərénthəsiz/ *v.tr.* **1** (also *absol.*) insert as a parenthesis. **2** put into brackets or similar punctuation.

parenthetic /párənthétik/ *adj.* **1** of or by way of a parenthesis. **2** interposed. □□ **parenthetical** *adj.* **parenthetically** *adv.* [PARENTHESIS after *synthesis, synthetic*, etc.]

parenting /páirənting, pár-/ *n.* the occupation or concerns of parents.

/.../	pronunciation	●	part of speech
	□	phrases, idioms, and compounds	
	□□	derivatives	■ synonym section
	cross-references appear in SMALL CAPITALS or *italics*		

■ rearing, upbringing, raising, nurturing; parenthood.

parergon /pərɔ́rgən/ n. (pl. **parerga** /-gə/) **1** work subsidiary to one's main employment. **2** an ornamental accessory. [L f. Gk parergon (as PARA-[1], ergon work)]

paresis /pə́reesis, párisis/ n. (pl. **pareses** /-seez/) Med. partial paralysis. □□ **paretic** /pərétik/ adj. [mod.L f. Gk f. pariēmi let go (as PARA-[1], hiēmi let go)]

pareve /paárəvə, paárvə/ adj. made without milk or meat and thus suitable for kosher use.

par excellence /paár eksəlóns/ adv. as having special excellence; being the supreme example of its kind (the short story par excellence). [F, = by excellence]

parfait /paarfáy/ n. **1** a rich frozen custard of whipped cream, eggs, etc. **2** layers of ice cream, meringue, etc., served in a tall glass. [F parfait PERFECT adj.]

parget /paárjit/ v. & n. ● v.tr. (**pargeted**, **pargeting**) **1** plaster (a wall, etc.) esp. with an ornamental pattern. **2** roughcast. ● n. **1** plaster applied in this way; ornamental plasterwork. **2** roughcast. [ME f. OF pargeter, parjeter f. par all over + jeter throw]

parhelion /paarhéeleeən/ n. (pl. **parhelia** /-leeə/) a bright spot on the solar halo. Also called mock sun, sundog. □□ **parheliacal** /-hilíəkəl/ adj. **parhelic** adj. [L parelion f. Gk (as PARA-[1], hēlios sun)]

pariah /pəríə/ n. **1** a social outcast. **2** hist. a member of a low caste or of no caste in S. India. [Tamil paraiyar pl. of paraiyan hereditary drummer f. parai drum]

parietal /pəríətəl/ adj. **1** Anat. of the wall of the body or any of its cavities. **2** Bot. of the wall of a hollow structure, etc. **3** relating to residence and visitation rules in a college dormitory. □ **parietal bone** either of a pair of bones forming the central part of the sides and top of the skull. [F pariétal or LL parietalis f. L paries -etis wall]

pari-mutuel /párimyōōchōōəl/ n. **1** a form of betting in which those backing the first three places divide the losers' stakes (less the operator's commission). **2 a** a device showing the number and amount of bets staked on a race, to facilitate the division of the total among those backing the winner. **b** a system of betting based on this. [F, = mutual stake]

paring /páiring/ n. a strip or piece cut off.

pari passu /paáree pásōō, páree/ adv. **1** with equal speed. **2** simultaneously and equally. [L]

Paris commune see COMMUNE[1].

Paris green /páris/ n. a poisonous chemical used as a pigment and insecticide. [Paris in France]

parish /párish/ n. **1** an area having its own church and clergy. **2** a county in Louisiana. **3** Brit. (in full **civil parish**) a district constituted for purposes of local government. **4** the inhabitants of a parish. □ **parish clerk** an official performing various duties concerned with the church. **parish council** Brit. the administrative body in a civil parish. **parish register** a book recording christenings, marriages, and burials, at a parish church. [ME paroche, parosse f. OF paroche, paroisse f. eccl.L parochia, paroechia f. Gk paroikia sojourning f. paroikos (as PARA-[1], -oikos -dwelling f. oikeō dwell)]

parishioner /pəríshənər/ n. an inhabitant or member of a parish. [obs. parishen f. ME f. OF parossien, formed as PARISH]

Parisian /pəréezhən, -rízhən, -rízeeən/ adj. & n. ● adj. of or relating to Paris in France. ● n. **1** a native or inhabitant of Paris. **2** the kind of French spoken in Paris. [F parisien]

parison /párisən/ n. a rounded mass of glass formed by rolling immediately after taking it from the furnace. [F paraison f. parer prepare f. L parare]

parity[1] /páritee/ n. **1** equality or equal status, esp. as regards status or pay. **2** parallelism or analogy (parity of reasoning). **3** equivalence of one currency with another; being at par. **4 a** (of a number) the fact of being even or odd. **b** Computing mathematical parity used for error detection. **5** Physics (of a quantity) the fact of changing its sign or remaining unaltered under a given transformation of coordinates, etc. [F parité or LL paritas (as PAR[1])]

■ **1** equality, equivalence, consistency, uniformity, congruity, similitude, conformity, congruence.

2 analogy, parallelism, likeness, similarity, proportion, balance, correspondence.

parity[2] /páritee/ n. Med. **1** the fact or condition of having borne children. **2** the number of children previously borne. [formed as -PAROUS + -ITY]

park /paark/ n. & v. ● n. **1** a large public area in a town, used for recreation. **2** a large enclosed piece of ground, usu. with woodland and pasture, attached to a country house, etc. **3 a** a large area of land kept in its natural state for public recreational use. **b** esp. Brit. a large enclosed area of land used to accommodate wild animals in captivity (wildlife park). **4** esp. Brit. an area for motor vehicles, etc., to be left in (car park). **5** the gear position or function in an automatic transmission in which the gears are locked, preventing the vehicle's movement. **6** an area devoted to a specified purpose (industrial park). **7** a sports arena or stadium. ● v. **1** tr. (also absol.) leave (a vehicle) usu. temporarily, in a parking lot, by the side of the road, etc. **2** tr. colloq. deposit and leave, usu. temporarily. **3** intr. sl. engage in petting or kissing in a parked car. □ **parking lot** US an area for parking vehicles. **parking meter** a coin-operated meter that receives payment for vehicles parked in the street and indicates the time available. **parking ticket** a notice, usu. attached to a vehicle, of a penalty imposed for parking illegally. **park oneself** colloq. sit down. [ME f. OF parc f. med.L parricus of Gmc orig., rel. to pearruc: see PADDOCK]

■ n. **1–3** garden(s), green(s), common(s), preserve, reserve, parkland, woodland, estate, Anglo-Ind. maidan, archaic or literary greensward; playground. ● v. leave, store, colloq. stash, dump, sl. ditch; see also SET[1] v. 1, 3, 5.

parka /paárkə/ n. **1** a skin jacket with hood, worn by Eskimos. **2** a similar windproof fabric garment worn in cold weather. [Aleutian]

parkin /paárkin/ n. Brit. a cake or cookie made with oatmeal, ginger, and sugar syrup or molasses. [perh. f. the name Parkin, dimin. of Peter]

Parkinsonism /paárkinsənizəm/ n. = PARKINSON'S DISEASE.

Parkinson's disease /paárkinsənz/ n. a progressive disease of the nervous system with tremor, muscular rigidity, and emaciation. Also called PARKINSONISM. [J. Parkinson, Engl. surgeon d. 1824]

Parkinson's law /paárkinsənz/ n. the notion that work expands so as to fill the time available for its completion. [C. N. Parkinson, Engl. writer b. 1909]

parkland /paárkland/ n. open grassland with clumps of trees, etc.

parkway /paárkway/ n. **1** an open landscaped highway. **2** Brit. a railroad station with extensive parking facilities.

Parl. abbr. Brit. **1** Parliament. **2** Parliamentary.

parlance /paárləns/ n. a particular way of speaking, esp. as regards choice of words, idiom, etc. [OF f. parler speak, ult. f. L parabola (see PARABLE): in LL = 'speech']

■ way or manner of speaking, phrasing, phraseology, speech, wording, language, idiom, dialect, jargon, idiolect, colloq. lingo.

parlay /paárlay/ v. & n. ● v.tr. **1** use (money won on a bet) as a further stake. **2** increase in value by or as if by parlaying. ● n. **1** an act of parlaying. **2** a bet made by parlaying. [F paroli f. It. f. paro like f. L par equal]

parley /paárlee/ n. & v. ● n. (pl. **-eys**) a conference for debating points in a dispute, esp. a discussion of terms for an armistice, etc. ● v.intr. (**-leys**, **-leyed**) (often foll. by with) hold a parley. [perh. f. OF parlee, fem. past part. of parler speak: see PARLANCE]

■ n. conference, discussion, dialogue, negotiation, deliberation, meeting, colloquy, colloquium, confabulation, powwow, talk(s), colloq. huddle, confab, esp. hist. palaver. ● v. confer, discuss, deliberate, talk, negotiate, powwow.

parliament /paárləmənt/ n. **1** (**Parliament**) **a** (in the UK) the highest legislature, consisting of the Sovereign, the House of Lords, and the House of Commons. **b** the members of this legislature for a particular period, esp. between one dissolution and the next. **2** a similar legislature in other nations. [ME f. OF *parlement* speaking (as PARLANCE)]

■ **1 a** (**Parliament**) Houses of Parliament, Westminster; House of Lords, House of Commons, the Commons, the Lords, the House, *Brit.* another place. **2** legislature, council, congress, diet, assembly, Upper *or* Lower House, upper *or* lower chamber.

parliamentarian /paárləmentáireeən/ *n. & adj.* ● *n.* **1** a member of a parliament. **2** a person who is well-versed in parliamentary procedures. **3** *hist.* an adherent of Parliament in the English Civil War of the 17th c. ● *adj.* = PARLIA-MENTARY.

parliamentary /paárləméntəree, -tree/ *adj.* **1** of or relating to a parliament. **2** enacted or established by a parliament. **3** (of language) admissible in a parliament; polite.

■ **3** proper, polite, formal, ordered, orderly, acceptable.

parlor /paárlər/ *n.* (*Brit.* **parlour**) **1** a sitting room in a private house. **2** a room in a hotel, club, etc., for the private use of residents. **3** a store providing specified goods or services (*beauty parlor*; *ice cream parlor*). **4** a room or building equipped for milking cows. **5** (*attrib.*) *derog.* denoting support for esp. political views by those who do not try to practice them (*parlor socialist*). □ **parlor game** an indoor game, esp. a word game. [ME f. AF *parlur*, OF *parleor*, *parleur*: see PARLANCE]

■ **1, 2** living room, drawing room, sitting room, morning room, reception (room), lounge, *archaic* withdrawing room.

parlous /paárləs/ *adj. & adv.* ● *adj.* **1** dangerous or difficult. **2** *archaic* clever; cunning. ● *adv.* extremely. □□ **parlously** *adv.* **parlousness** *n.* [ME, = PERILOUS]

■ *adj.* **1** perilous, risky, precarious, uncertain, dangerous, hazardous, difficult, ticklish, awkward, chancy, *colloq.* iffy, *sl.* hairy.

Parma violet /paármə/ *n.* a variety of sweet violet with heavy scent and lavender-colored flowers. [*Parma* in Italy]

Parmesan /paármizaán, -zán, -zən/ *n.* a kind of hard dry cheese made orig. at Parma and used esp. in grated form. [F f. It. *parmegiano* of Parma in Italy]

Parnassian /paarnáseeən/ *adj. & n.* ● *adj.* **1** of Parnassus, a mountain in central Greece, in antiquity sacred to the Muses. **2** poetic. **3** of or relating to a group of French poets in the late 19th c., emphasizing strictness of form, named from the anthology *Le Parnasse contemporain* (1866). ● *n.* a member of this group.

parochial /pərṓkeeəl/ *adj.* **1** of or concerning a parish. **2** (of affairs, views, etc.) merely local, narrow or restricted in scope. □ **parochial school** a private elementary or high school maintained by a religious organization, esp. the Roman Catholic Church. □□ **parochialism** *n.* **parochiality** /-álitee/ *n.* **parochially** *adv.* [ME f. AF *parochiel*, OF *parochial* f. eccl.L *parochialis* (as PARISH)]

■ **1** regional, provincial, local. **2** narrow, insular, isolated, provincial, limited, restricted, narrow-minded, petty, shortsighted, hidebound, conservative, conventional, illiberal, bigoted, prejudiced, intolerant, one-sided, partial, biased, stubborn, opinionated, dogmatic, rigid, stiff, stiff-necked, immovable, intractable, unchangeable, unchanging, close-minded, unsophisticated, unworldly, uncultivated, uncultured.

parody /párədee/ *n. & v.* ● *n.* (*pl.* **-ies**) **1** a humorous exaggerated imitation of an author, literary work, style, etc. **2** a feeble imitation; a travesty. ● *v.tr.* (**-ies, -ied**) **1** compose a parody of. **2** mimic humorously. □□ **parodic** /pərṓdik/ *adj.* **parodist** *n.* [LL *parodia* or Gk *parōidia* burlesque poem (as PARA-[1], *ōidē* ode)]

■ *n.* **1** burlesque, lampoon, satire, caricature, mockery, *colloq.* takeoff, spoof, send-up; mimicry. **2** travesty, mockery, feeble *or* poor imitation; distortion, perversion, corruption, debasement. ● *v.* burlesque, lampoon, satirize, caricature, mock, mimic, ape, ridicule, deride, laugh at, poke fun at, guy, scoff at, sneer at, rib, tease, twit, roast, pillory, make a laughingstock (of), make sport of, make fun of, make a monkey (out) of, fleer, *colloq.* take off, spoof, send up.

parol /pərṓl/ *adj. & n. Law* ● *adj.* given orally. ● *n.* an oral declaration. [OF *parole* (as PAROLE)]

parole /pərṓl/ *n. & v.* ● *n.* **1 a** the release of a prisoner temporarily for a special purpose or completely before the fulfillment of a sentence, on the promise of good behavior. **b** such a promise. **2** a word of honor. ● *v.tr.* put (a prisoner) on parole. □ **on parole** released on the terms of parole. □□ **parolee** /-leé/ *n.* [F, = word: see PARLANCE]

paronomasia /párənōmáyzhə, -zheeə/ *n.* a play on words; a pun. [L f. Gk *paronomasia* (as PARA-[1], *onomasia* naming f. *onomazō* to name f. *onoma* a name)]

paronym /párənim/ *n.* **1** a word cognate with another. **2** a word formed from a foreign word. □□ **paronymous** /pəróniməs/ *adj.* [Gk *parōnumon*, neut. of *parōnumos* (as PARA-[1], *onuma* name)]

parotid /pərótid/ *adj. & n.* ● *adj.* situated near the ear. ● *n.* (in full **parotid gland**) a salivary gland in front of the ear. □ **parotid duct** a duct opening from the parotid gland into the mouth. [F *parotide* or L *parotis parotid-* f. Gk *parōtis -idos* (as PARA-[1], *ous ōtos* ear)]

parotitis /párətítis/ *n.* **1** inflammation of the parotid gland. **2** mumps. [PAROTID + -ITIS]

-parous /pərəs/ *comb. form* bearing offspring of a specified number or kind (*multiparous*; *viviparous*). [L *-parus* -bearing f. *parere* bring forth]

Parousia /paarōōseeə, pərṓōzeeə/ *n. Theol.* the supposed second coming of Christ. [Gk, = presence, coming]

paroxysm /párəksizəm/ *n.* **1** (often foll. by *of*) a sudden attack or outburst (of rage, laughter, etc.). **2** a fit of disease. □□ **paroxysmal** /-sízməl/ *adj.* [F *paroxysme* f. med.L *paroxysmus* f. Gk *paroxusmos* f. *paroxunō* exasperate (as PARA-[1], *oxunō* sharpen f. *oxus* sharp)]

■ attack, fit, convulsion, spasm, throe, seizure, spell, outburst, eruption, explosion, flare-up.

parpen /paárpən/ *n.* (also **perpend**) a stone passing through a wall from side to side, with two smooth vertical faces. [ME f. OF *parpain*, prob. ult. f. L *per* through + *pannus* piece of cloth, in Rmc 'piece of wall']

parquet /paárkáy/ *n. & v.* ● *n.* **1** a flooring of wooden blocks arranged in a pattern. **2** the main-floor seating area of a theater. ● *v.tr.* (**parqueted** /-káyd/; **parqueting** /-káying/) furnish (a room) with a parquet floor. □ **parquet circle** the rear seating area of a theater, esp. the section under the balcony. [F, = small compartment, floor, dimin. of *parc* PARK]

parquetry /paárkitree/ *n.* the use of wooden blocks to make floors or inlay for furniture.

parr /paar/ *n.* a young salmon with blue-gray fingerlike markings on its sides, younger than a smolt. [18th c.: orig. unkn.]

parramatta /párəmátə/ *n.* (also **paramatta**) a light dress fabric of wool and silk or cotton. [*Parramatta* in New South Wales, Australia]

parricide /párisid/ *n.* **1** the killing of a near relative, esp. of a parent. **2** an act of parricide. **3** a person who commits parricide. □□ **parricidal** /-síd'l/ *adj.* [F *parricide* or L *parricida* (= sense 3), *parricidium* (= sense 1), of uncert. orig., assoc. in L with *pater* father and *parens* parent]

parrot /párət/ *n. & v.* ● *n.* **1** any of various mainly tropical birds of the order Psittaciformes, with a short hooked bill, often having vivid plumage and able to mimic the human voice. **2** a person who mechanically repeats the words or actions of another. ● *v.tr.* (**parroted, parroting**) repeat mechanically. □ **parrot fish** any fish of the genus *Scarus*, with a mouth like a parrot's bill. [prob. f. obs. or dial. F *perrot* parrot, dimin. of *Pierre* Peter: cf. PARAKEET]

■ *n.* **2** imitator, mimic, *colloq.* copycat. ● *v.* imitate, mimic, ape; echo, repeat, reiterate.

parry /páree/ *v. & n.* ● *v.tr.* (**-ies, -ied**) **1** avert or ward off (a weapon or attack), esp. with a countermove. **2** deal skillfully with (an awkward question, etc.). ● *n.* (*pl.* **-ies**) an act of parrying. [prob. repr. F *parez* imper. of *parer* f. It. *parare* ward off]

parse /paars/ *v.tr.* **1** describe (a word in context) grammatically, stating its inflection, relation to the sentence, etc. **2** resolve (a sentence) into its component parts and describe them grammatically. □□ **parser** *n.* esp. *Computing.* [perh. f. ME *pars* parts of speech f. OF *pars*, pl. of *part* PART, infl. by L *pars* part]

parsec /paársek/ *n.* a unit of stellar distance, equal to about 3.25 light years (3.08 x 10^{16} meters), the distance at which the mean radius of the earth's orbit subtends an angle of one second of arc. [PARALLAX + SECOND^2]

Parsee /paársee/ *n.* **1** an adherent of Zoroastrianism. **2** a descendant of the Persians who fled to India from Muslim persecution in the 7th–8th c. **3** = PAHLAVI. □□ **Parseeism** *n.* [Pers. *pārsī* Persian f. *pārs* Persia]

parsimony /paársimōnee/ *n.* **1** carefulness in the use of money or other resources. **2** stinginess. □ **law of parsimony** the assertion that no more causes or forces should be assumed than are necessary to account for the facts. □□ **parsimonious** /-mŏneeəs/ *adj.* **parsimoniously** *adv.* **parsimoniousness** *n.* [ME f. L *parsimonia, parcimonia* f. *parcere* *pars-* spare]

parsley /paárslee/ *n.* a biennial herb, *Petroselinum crispum*, with white flowers and crinkly aromatic leaves, used for seasoning and garnishing food. □ **parsley fern** a fern, *Cryptogramma crispa*, with leaves like parsley. **parsley piert** a dwarf annual herb, *Aphanes arvensis*. [ME *percil, per(e)sil* f. OF *peresil*, and OE *petersilie* ult. f. L *petroselinum* f. Gk *petroselinon; parsley piert* prob. corrupt. of F *perce-pierre* pierce stone]

parsnip /paársnip/ *n.* **1** a biennial umbelliferous plant, *Pastinaca sativa*, with yellow flowers and a large pale yellow tapering root. **2** this root eaten as a vegetable. [ME *pas(se)nep* (with assim. to *nep* turnip) f. OF *pasnaie* f. L *pastinaca*]

parson /paársən/ *n.* **1** a rector. **2** any (esp. Protestant) member of the clergy. □ **parson's nose** the piece of fatty flesh at the rump of a fowl. □□ **parsonical** /-sónikəl/ *adj.* [ME *person(e), parson* f. OF *persone* f. L *persona* PERSON (in med.L rector)]

parsonage /paársənij/ *n.* a church house provided for a parson.

part /paart/ *n., v.,* & *adv.* ● *n.* **1** some but not all of a thing or number of things. **2** an essential member or constituent of anything (*part of the family; a large part of the job*). **3** a component of a machine, etc. (*spare parts; needs a new part*). **4 a** a portion of a human or animal body. **b** (in *pl.*) *colloq.* = *private parts.* **5** a division of a book, broadcast serial, etc., esp. as much as is issued or broadcast at one time. **6** each of several equal portions of a whole (*the recipe has 3 parts sugar to 2 parts flour*). **7 a** a portion allotted; a share. **b** a person's share in an action or enterprise (*will have no part in it*). **c** one's duty (*was not my part to interfere*). **8 a** a character assigned to an actor on stage. **b** the words spoken by an actor on stage. **c** a copy of these. **9** *Mus.* a melody or other constituent of harmony assigned to a particular voice or instrument. **10** each of the sides in an agreement or dispute. **11** (in *pl.*) a region or district (*am not from these parts*). **12** (in *pl.*) abilities (*a man of many parts*). **13** a dividing line in combed hair. ● *v.* **1** *tr.* & *intr.* divide or separate into parts (*the crowd parted to let them through*). **2** *intr.* **a** leave one another's company (*they parted the best of friends*). **b** (foll. by *from*) say goodbye to. **3** *tr.* cause to separate (*they fought hard and had to be parted*). **4** *intr.* (foll. by *with*) give up possession of; hand over. **5** *tr.* separate (the hair of the head on either side of the part) with a comb. ● *adv.* to some extent; partly (*is part iron and part wood; a lie that is part truth*). □ **for the most part** see MOST. **for one's part** as far as one is concerned. **in part** (or **parts**) to some extent; partly. **look the part** appear suitable for a role. **on the part of** on the behalf or initiative of (*no objection on my part*). **part and parcel** (usu. foll. by *of*) an essential part. **part company** see COMPANY. **part-exchange** *Brit. n.* a transaction in which goods

are given as part of the payment for other goods, with the balance in money. ● *v.tr.* give (goods) in such a transaction. **part of speech** *n.* each of the categories to which words are assigned in accordance with their grammatical and semantic functions (in English esp. noun, pronoun, adjective, adverb, verb, preposition, conjunction, and interjection). **part-song** a song with three or more voice parts, often without accompaniment, and harmonic rather than contrapuntal in character. **part time** less than the full time required by an activity. **part-time** *adj.* occupying or using only part of one's working time. **part-timer** a person employed in part-time work. **part-work** *Brit.* a publication appearing in several parts over a period of time. **play a part 1** be significant or contributory. **2** act deceitfully. **3** perform a theatrical role. **take part** (often foll. by *in*) assist or have a share (in). **take the part of 1** support; back up. **2** perform the role of. **three parts** three quarters. [ME f. OF f. L *pars partis* (n.), *partire, partiri* (v.)]

■ *n.* **1** some, a few, not all. **2** piece, portion, division, segment, section. **3** component, constituent, element, ingredient, unit. **4 a** member, organ, limb. **5** episode, installment, chapter. **6** portion, measure, unit, share. **7 a** allotment, share, percentage, participation, interest, parcel. **b** share, interest, participation, say, voice, influence. **c** role, function, duty, responsibility, share, business. **8 a** role, character. **b, c** lines, script, words. **10** side, interest, cause, faction, party. **11** (*parts*) neighborhood, quarter, section, district, region, area, corner, vicinity, vicinage, *colloq.* neck of the woods. **12** (*parts*) accomplishment(s), capability; see also TALENT 1. **13** *Brit.* parting. ● *v.* **1, 3** separate, divide, split (up); put *or* pull apart, *literary* put asunder. **2** separate, part company, split (up), go one's way, break up, say good-bye, *archaic or literary* bid good-bye *or* farewell; leave, depart, go (away *or* off). **4** (*part with*) give up, yield, relinquish, release, sacrifice, forgo, go without, renounce, forsake, let go, surrender. ● *adv.* see *in part* (PART) below. □ **in part** partly, partially, part, to some extent *or* degree, in some measure; relatively, comparatively, somewhat. **on the part of** on the behalf of; by; as regards, with regard to. **take part** participate, join in, be (a) party, play a part *or* role, be involved *or* associated, have *or* take a hand, have *or* take a share, contribute, assist. **take the part of 1** stand *or* stick up for, take the side of; see also SUPPORT *v.* 4, 6, 7.

partake /paartáyk/ *v.intr.* (*past* **partook** /-tŏŏk/; *past part.* **partaken** /-táykən/) **1** (foll. by *of, in*) take a share or part. **2** (foll. by *of*) eat or drink some or *colloq.* all (of a thing). **3** (foll. by *of*) have some (of a quality, etc.) (*their manner partook of insolence*). □□ **partakable** *adj.* **partaker** *n.* [16th c.: back-form. f. *partaker, partaking* = parttaker, etc.]

■ **1** share, participate, take (a) part, enter. **2** (*partake of*) receive, get, have (a share *or* portion *or* part *or* bit of); see also EAT 1a, DRINK *v.* 1. **3** (*partake of*) evoke, suggest, hint at, intimate, imply; have the *or* a quality of.

parterre /paartáir/ *n.* **1** a level space in a garden occupied by flower beds arranged formally. **2** *US* = *parquet circle.* [F, = *par terre* on the ground]

parthenogenesis /paárthinōjénisis/ *n. Biol.* reproduction by a female gamete without fertilization, esp. as a normal process in invertebrates and lower plants. □□ **parthenogenetic** /-jinétik/ *adj.* **parthenogenetically** *adv.* [mod.L f. Gk *parthenos* virgin + *genesis* as GENESIS]

Parthian shot /paártheeən/ *n.* a remark or glance, etc., reserved for the moment of departure. [*Parthia*, an ancient kingdom in W. Asia: from the custom of a retreating Parthian horseman firing a shot at the enemy]

partial /paárshəl/ *adj.* & *n.* ● *adj.* **1** not complete; forming only part (*a partial success*). **2** biased; unfair. **3** (foll. by *to*) having a liking for. ● *n.* **1** *Mus.* any of the component tones of a complex tone. **2** a denture for replacing one or several, but not all, of the teeth. □ **partial eclipse** an eclipse in which only part of the luminary is covered or darkened. **par-**

tial verdict a verdict finding a person guilty of part of a charge. □□ **partially** adv. **partialness** n. [ME f. OF parcial f. LL partialis (as PART)]

■ adj. **1** incomplete, fragmentary, imperfect; see also INCOMPLETE. **2** prejudiced, biased, partisan, inclined, influenced, one-sided, jaundiced, unfair, discriminatory. **3** (partial to) in favor of, predisposed to or toward, fond of, with a liking or taste or predilection or fondness or weakness or soft spot for. □□ **partially** partly, in part, to some extent or degree, to a limited extent or degree, to a certain extent or degree, not totally or wholly or entirely, restrictedly, incompletely, in some measure, relatively, comparatively, moderately, (up) to a point, somewhat.

partiality /paársheeálitee/ n. **1** bias; favoritism. **2** (foll. by for) fondness. [ME f. OF parcialité f. med.L partialitas (as PARTIAL)]

■ **1** prejudice, bias, inclination, favoritism, predilection, predisposition, leaning, preference. **2** preference, taste, relish, liking, fondness, appreciation, fancy, love, eye, weakness, soft spot, penchant; fetish.

participant /paartísipənt/ n. someone who or something that participates.

■ participator, partaker, sharer, party, contributor.

participate /paartísipayt/ v.intr. **1** (often foll. by in) take a part or share (in). **2** literary or formal (foll. by of) have a certain quality (the speech participated of wit). □□ **participation** /-páyshən/ n. **participator** n. **participatory** /-tísəpətáwree/ adj. [L participare f. particeps -cipis taking part, formed as PART + -cip- = cap- stem of capere take]

■ **1** take part, partake, have or take a hand, get or become involved; (participate in) engage in, share in, join in, enter into, be or become associated with, contribute to. □□ **participation** see VOICE n. 2c.

participle /paártisipəl/ n. Gram. a word formed from a verb (e.g., going, gone, being, been) and used in compound verb forms (e.g., is going, has been) or as an adjective (e.g., working woman, burned toast). □□ **participial** /-sípeeəl/ adj. **participially** /-sípeeəlee/ adv. [ME f. OF, by-form of participe f. L participium (as PARTICIPATE)]

particle /paártikəl/ n. **1** a minute portion of matter. **2** the least possible amount (not a particle of sense). **3** Gram. **a** a minor part of speech, esp. a short indeclinable one. **b** a common prefix or suffix such as in-, -ness. [ME f. L particula (as PART)]

■ **1** atom, molecule. **2** atom, molecule, scintilla, spark, mote, suggestion, hint, suspicion, gleam, bit, crumb, jot, tittle, whit, mite, speck, dot, spot, iota, grain, morsel, shred, sliver, scrap, colloq. smidgen.

particleboard /paártikəlbórd, -bawrd / n. a building material made in flat sheets from scrap wood bonded with adhesive.

parti-colored /paárteekúlərd/ adj. partly of one color, partly of another or others. [PARTY² + COLORED]

■ motley, variegated, pied, mottled.

particular /pərtíkyələr/ adj. & n. ● adj. **1** relating to or considered as one thing or person as distinct from others; individual (in this particular instance). **2** more than is usual; special; noteworthy (took particular trouble). **3** scrupulously exact; fastidious. **4** detailed (a full and particular account). **5** Logic (of a proposition) in which something is asserted of some but not all of a class (opp. UNIVERSAL adj. 2). ● n. **1** a detail; an item. **2** (in pl.) points of information; a detailed account. □ **in particular** especially; specifically. [ME f. OF particuler f. L particularis (as PARTICLE)]

■ adj. **1** certain, specific, special, peculiar, singular, single, isolated, individual, distinct, discrete, separate, definite, precise, express. **2** marked, special, especial, exceptional, remarkable, noteworthy, notable, outstanding, unusual. **3** fussy, meticulous, finicky, finical, fastidious, discriminating, selective, demanding, hypercritical, critical, colloq. persnickety, choosy, picky. **4** detailed, itemized, item-by-item, thorough, minute, precise, exact, exacting, painstaking, nice, rigorous, close, blow-by-blow. ● n. **1** detail, fine point, item, specific, element, fact, circumstance. **2** (particulars)

information, minutiae, details, facts, circumstances, account. □ **in particular** particularly, specifically, precisely, exactly, especially, specially.

particularism /pərtíkyələrízəm, pətík-/ n. **1** exclusive devotion to one party, sect, etc. **2** the principle of leaving political independence to each state in an empire or federation. **3** the theological doctrine of individual election or redemption. □□ **particularist** n. [F particularisme, mod.L particularismus, and G Partikularismus (as PARTICULAR)]

particularity /pərtíkyəláritee, pətík-/ n. **1** the quality of being individual or particular. **2** fullness or minuteness of detail in a description.

particularize /pərtíkyələrīz, pətík-/ v. tr. (also absol.) **1** name specifically or one by one. **2** specify (items). □□ **particularization** n. [F particulariser (as PARTICULAR)]

particularly /pərtíkyələrlee, pətík-/ adv. **1** especially; very. **2** specifically (they particularly asked for you). **3** in a particular or fastidious manner.

■ **1** especially, specially, exceptionally, peculiarly, singularly, distinctively, uniquely, unusually, uncommonly, notably, outstandingly, markedly, extraordinarily, very, extremely, strikingly, surprisingly, amazingly. **2** in particular, specifically, especially, principally, mainly, exceptionally, expressly, explicitly, notably, markedly; only, solely. **3** just so, neatly, tidily, systematically, perfectly, accurately; see also PRECISELY 1.

particulate /pərtíkyələyt, -lət, paar-/ adj. & n. ● adj. in the form of separate particles. ● n. matter in this form. [L particula PARTICLE]

parting /paárting/ n. **1** a leave-taking or departure (often attrib.: parting words). **2** Brit. = PART n. 13. **3** a division; an act of separating. □ **parting shot** = PARTHIAN SHOT.

■ **1** leave-taking, farewell, saying goodbye, departure, leaving, going (away), making one's adieus or adieux; valediction; (attrib.) closing, final, concluding, last, departing, farewell, valedictory; deathbed, dying. **3** splitting, dividing, breaking (up or apart); separation, split, division, breakup, rift, rupture, partition.

parti pris /paártee preé/ n. & adj. ● n. a preconceived view; a bias. ● adj. prejudiced; biased. [F, = side taken]

partisan /paártizən/ n. & adj. (also **partizan**) ● n. **1** a strong, esp. unreasoning, supporter of a party, cause, etc. **2** Mil. a guerrilla in wartime. ● adj. **1** of or characteristic of partisans. **2** loyal to a particular cause; biased. □□ **partisanship** n. [F f. It. dial. partigiano, etc. f. parte PART]

■ n. **1** devotee, follower, supporter, adherent, backer, champion, enthusiast, fan, zealot, fanatic, sl. rooter. **2** guerrilla, freedom fighter, underground or resistance fighter, irregular. ● adj. **1** guerrilla, freedom, underground, resistance, irregular. **2** one-sided, factional, biased, sectarian, opinionated, partial, bigoted, prejudiced, parochial, myopic, shortsighted, narrow, narrow-minded, limited, nearsighted, derog. tendentious; see also LOYAL.

partita /paarteéta/ n. (pl. **partite** /-tay/) Mus. **1** a suite. **2** an air with variations. [It., fem. past part. of partire divide, formed as PART]

partite /paártit/ adj. **1** divided (esp. in comb.: tripartite). **2** Bot. & Zool. divided to or nearly to the base. [L partitus past part. of partiri PART v.]

partition /paartíshən/ n. & v. ● n. **1** division into parts, esp. Polit. of a country with separate areas of government. **2** a structure dividing a space into two parts, esp. a light interior wall. ● v.tr. **1** divide into parts. **2** (foll. by off) separate (part of a room, etc.) with a partition. □□ **partitioned** adj. **partitioner** n. **partitionist** n. [ME f. OF f. L partitio -onis (as PARTITE)]

■ n. **1** separation, division, splitting (up), split-up,

breakup, segmentation. **2** (room) divider, (dividing) wall, barrier, screen, separator. • *v.* **1** divide (up), separate, cut up, subdivide, split (up). **2** (*partition off*) divide (off), separate (off), wall off, screen (off), fence off.

partitive /paártitiv/ *adj. & n. Gram.* • *adj.* (of a word, form, etc.) denoting part of a collective group or quantity. • *n.* a partitive word (e.g., *some*, *any*) or form. □ **partitive genitive** a genitive used to indicate a whole divided into or regarded in parts, expressed in English by *of* as in *most of us*. □□ **partitively** *adv.* [F *partitif -ive* or med.L *partitivus* (as PARTITE)]

partizan var. of PARTISAN.

partly /paártlee/ *adv.* **1** with respect to a part or parts. **2** to some extent.
■ **2** see *partially* (PARTIAL).

partner /paártnər/ *n. & v.* • *n.* **1** a person who shares or takes part with another or others, esp. in a business firm with shared risks and profits. **2** a companion in dancing. **3** a player (esp. one of two) on the same side in a game. **4** either member of a married couple, or of an unmarried couple living together. • *v.tr.* **1** be the partner of. **2** associate as partners. □□ **partnerless** *adj.* [ME, alt. of *parcener* joint heir, after PART]
■ *n.* **1** sharer, partaker, associate, colleague, participant, accomplice, accessory, confederate, comrade, ally, collaborator, companion, mate, helpmate, fellow, alter ego, friend, cohort, *colloq.* pal, sidekick, buddy, *Austral. colloq.* offsider. **3** teammate. **4** wife, husband, spouse, helpmate, consort, *colloq.* mate, other *or* better half, *sl.* Dutch; lover, live-in lover *or* partner, cohabitant, cohabitee, cohabitor; common-law husband *or* wife.

partnership /paártnərship/ *n.* **1** the state of being a partner or partners. **2** a joint business. **3** a pair or group of partners.

partook past of PARTAKE.

partridge /paártrij/ *n.* (*pl.* same or **partridges**) **1** any game bird of the genus *Perdix*, esp. *P. perdix* of Europe and Asia. **2** any other of various similar birds of Europe or N. America, including the snow partridge, ruffed grouse, and bobwhite. [ME *partrich*, etc. f. OF *perdriz*, etc. f. L *perdix -dicis*: for -*dge* cf. CABBAGE]

parturient /paartŏŏreeənt, -tyŏŏr-/ *adj.* about to give birth. [L *parturire* be in labor, incept. f. *parere* part- bring forth]

parturition /paártŏŏrishən, -tyŏŏ-, -chŏŏ-/ *n. Med.* the act of bringing forth young; childbirth. [LL *parturitio* (as PARTURIENT)]

party[1] /paártee/ *n. & v.* • *n.* (*pl.* **-ies**) **1** a social gathering, usu. of invited guests. **2** a body of persons engaged in an activity or traveling together (*fishing party*; *search party*). **3** a group of people united in a cause, opinion, etc., esp. an organized political group. **4** a person or persons forming one side in an agreement or dispute. **5** (foll. by *to*) *Law* an accessory (to an action). **6** *colloq.* a person. • *v.tr. & intr.* (**-ies, -ied**) entertain at or attend a party. □ **party line 1** the policy adopted by a political party. **2** a telephone line shared by two or more subscribers. **party pooper** *sl.* a person whose manner or behavior inhibits other people's enjoyment; a killjoy. **party wall** a wall common to two adjoining buildings or rooms. [ME f. OF *partie* ult. f. L *partire*: see PART]
■ *n.* **1** (social) gathering, celebration, fete, function, reception, soiree, festivity, festival, frolic, romp, carousal, carouse, saturnalia, bacchanalia, debauch, orgy, ball, dance, at home, levee, *colloq.* get-together, shindig, shindy, do, spree, bust, hop, *Austral. colloq.* shivoo, *Brit. colloq.* rave(-up), beanfeast, knees-up, *sl.* bash, blast, wingding. **2** group, company, band, body, corps, gang, crew, commando, team, squad, troop, platoon, detachment, detail, cadre, unit, *colloq.* bunch, outfit. **3** side, interest, faction, league, club, coalition, bloc, division, sect, denomination, clique, coterie, set, cabal, junta, adherents, confederacy, confederation, federation, conference, congress, lobby, caucus. **4** individual, person, litigant, plaintiff, defendant, side, part, interest, signer, signatory, cosignatory, participant; interested party. **5** participant, participator,

confederate, associate, ally, accomplice, accessory, abetter, supporter, backer, aid, helper, seconder.

party[2] /paártee/ *adj. Heraldry* divided into parts of different colors. [ME f. OF *parti* f. L (as PARTY[1])]

parvenu /paárvənŏŏ/ *n. & adj.* • *n.* (*fem.* **parvenue**) **1** a person who has recently gained wealth or position. **2** an upstart. • *adj.* **1** associated with or characteristic of such a person. **2** upstart. [F, past part. of *parvenir* arrive f. L *pervenire* (as PER-, *venire* come)]
■ *n.* upstart, arriviste, nouveau riche, adventurer, social climber; intruder. • *adj.* nouveau riche, upstart, social-climbing, status-seeking.

parvis /paárvis/ *n.* (also **parvise**) **1** an enclosed area in front of a cathedral, church, etc. **2** a room over a church porch. [ME f. OF *parvis* ult. f. LL *paradisus* PARADISE, a court in front of St. Peter's, Rome]

pas /paa/ *n.* (*pl.* same) a step in dancing, esp. in classical ballet. □ **pas de chat** /də shaá/ a leap in which each foot in turn is raised to the opposite knee. **pas de deux** /də dö/ a dance for two persons. **pas glissé** /gleesáy/ a gliding step. **pas seul** /söl/ a solo dance. [F, = step]

pascal /paskál, paaskaál/ *n.* **1** a standard unit of pressure, equal to one newton per square meter. **2** (**Pascal** or **PASCAL**) *Computing* a programming language esp. used in education. [B. *Pascal*, Fr. scientist d. 1662: sense 2 so named because he built a calculating machine]

paschal /paskəl/ *adj.* **1** of or relating to the Jewish Passover. **2** of or relating to Easter. □ **paschal lamb 1** a lamb sacrificed at Passover. **2** Christ. [ME f. OF *pascal* f. eccl.L *paschalis* f. *pascha* f. Gk *paskha* f. Aram. *pasḥa*, rel. to Heb. *pesaḥ* PASSOVER]

pash /pash/ *n.* esp. *Brit. sl.* a brief infatuation. [abbr. of PASSION]

pasha /paáshə/ *n.* (also **pacha**) *hist.* the title (placed after the name) of a Turkish officer of high rank, e.g., a military commander, the governor of a province, etc. [Turk. *paşa*, prob. = *başa* f. *baş* head, chief]

pashm /páshəm/ *n.* the underfur of some Tibetan animals, esp. that of goats as used for cashmere shawls.

Pashto /póshtō/ *n. & adj.* • *n.* the official language of Afghanistan, also spoken in areas of Pakistan. • *adj.* of or in this language. [Pashto]

paso doble /páso dóblay/ *n.* **1** a ballroom dance based on a quick march played at bullfights. **2** a quick style of marching. [Sp., = double step]

pasqueflower /páskflowər/ *n.* a ranunculaceous plant, genus *Anemone*, with bell-shaped purple flowers and fernlike foliage. Also called ANEMONE. [earlier *passe-flower* f. F *passefleur*: assim. to *pasque* = obs. *pasch* (as PASCHAL), Easter]

pasquinade /páskwináyd/ *n.* a lampoon or satire, orig. one displayed in a public place. [It. *pasquinata* f. *Pasquino*, a statue in Rome on which abusive Latin verses were annually posted]

pass[1] /pas/ *v. & n.* • *v.* (*past part.* **passed**) (see also PAST). **1** *intr.* (often foll. by *along, by, down, on,* etc.) move onward; proceed, esp. past some point of reference (*saw the procession passing*). **2** *tr.* **a** go past; leave (a thing, etc.) on one side or behind in proceeding. **b** overtake, esp. in a vehicle. **c** go across (a frontier, mountain range, etc.). **3** *intr. & tr.* be transferred or cause to be transferred from one person or place to another (*pass the butter*; *the estate passes to his son*). **4** *tr.* surpass; be too great for (*it passes my comprehension*). **5** *intr.* get through; effect a passage. **6** *intr.* **a** be accepted as adequate; go uncensured (*let the matter pass*). **b** (foll. by *as, for*) be accepted or currently known as. **c** (of a person with some African-American ancestry) be accepted as white. **7** *tr.* move; cause to go (*passed her hand over her face*; *passed a rope round it*). **8** **a** *tr.* (of a candidate in an examination) be successful. **b** *tr.* be successful in (an examination). **c** *tr.* (of an examiner) judge the performance of (a candidate) to be satisfactory. **9** **a** *tr.* (of a bill) be approved by (a parliamentary body or process). **b** *tr.* cause or allow (a bill) to proceed to further legislative processes. **c** *intr.* (of a bill or proposal) be approved. **10** *intr.* **a** occur; elapse (*the remark passed unnoticed*; *time passes slowly*). **b** happen; be done or said (*heard what passed between them*). **11 a** *intr.* circulate; be current. **b** *tr.* put into circulation (*was passing forged checks*). **12** *tr.* spend or use up (a certain time or period) (*passed the afternoon reading*). **13** *tr.* (also *absol.*) *Sports* send (the ball) to another player of one's own team. **14** *intr.* forgo one's turn or chance in a game, etc. **15** *intr.* (foll. by *to, into*) change from one form (to another). **16** *intr.* come to an end. **17** *tr.* discharge from the body as or with excreta. **18** *tr.* (foll. by *on, upon*) **a** utter (criticism) about. **b** pronounce (a judicial sentence) on. **19** *intr.* (often foll. by *on, upon*) adjudicate. **20** *tr.* not declare or pay (a dividend). **21** *tr.* cause (troops, etc.) to go by, esp. ceremonially. ● *n.* **1** an act or instance of passing. **2** *Brit.* **a** success in an examination. **b** the status of a university degree without honors. **3** written permission to pass into or out of a place, or to be absent from quarters. **4 a** a ticket or permit giving free entry or access, etc. **b** = *free pass*. **5** *Sports* a transference of the ball to another player on the same side. **6** *Baseball* a base on balls. **7** a thrust in fencing. **8** a juggling trick. **9** an act of passing the hands over anything, as in conjuring or hypnotism. **10** a critical position (*has come to a fine pass*). □ **in passing 1** by the way. **2** in the course of speech, conversation, etc. **make a pass at** *colloq.* make amorous or sexual advances to. **pass around 1** distribute. **2** send or give to each of a number in turn. **pass away 1** *euphem.* die. **2** cease to exist; come to an end. **pass the buck** *US colloq.* deny or shift responsibility. **pass by 1** go past. **2** disregard; omit. **passed pawn** *Chess* a pawn that has advanced beyond the pawns on the other side. **pass** (or **run**) **one's eye over** see EYE. **pass muster** see MUSTER. **pass off 1** (of feelings, etc.) disappear gradually. **2** (of proceedings) be carried through (in a specified way). **3** (foll. by *as*) misrepresent (a person or thing) as something else. **4** evade or lightly dismiss (an awkward remark, etc.). **pass on 1** proceed on one's way. **2** *euphem.* die. **3** transmit to the next person in a series. **pass out 1** become unconscious. **2** *Brit. Mil.* complete one's training as a cadet. **3** distribute. **pass over 1** omit, ignore, or disregard. **2** ignore the claims of (a person) to promotion or advancement. **3** *euphem.* die. **pass through** experience. **pass the time of day** see TIME. **pass up** *colloq.* refuse or neglect (an opportunity, etc.). **pass water** urinate. □□ **passer** *n.* [ME f. OF *passer* ult. f. L *passus* PACE¹]

■ *v.* **1** proceed, move (onwards), go (ahead), progress, extend, lie; run, flow, fly, roll, course, stream, drift, sweep. **2** proceed *or* move past, go by *or* past; overtake; cross, go across, traverse. **3, 11, 13** give, hand around *or* along *or* over, transfer, circulate, pass on *or* over, deliver, convey, lob, hurl, toss, throw, release. **4** surpass, exceed, outdo, transcend, go beyond, overshoot, outstrip, outrun, surmount, outdistance. **5** go *or* travel *or* voyage *or* make one's way past *or* through *or* by, progress, make headway, advance. **6 a** see STAND *v.* 9. **b** (*pass for* or *as*) be taken for, be mistaken for, be regarded as, be accepted as. **7** see PUT¹ *v.* 1. **8 a** qualify, pass muster, get *or* come through, succeed. **9 b** allow, permit, approve, sanction, enact, accept, authorize, endorse, carry, agree to, confirm. **10 a** go (by), expire, elapse; slip by *or* away, fly; crawl, creep, drag. **b** *formal* eventuate; see also OCCUR 1. **12** spend, devote, use (up), expend, employ, occupy, fill, while away; dissipate, waste, fritter away, kill. **14** decline, abstain, go *or* do without. **15** see RESOLVE *v.* 4, 6. **16** go away, disappear, vanish, evaporate, fade away, melt away, blow over, evanesce, cease (to exist), (come to an) end, die out, go by the board, terminate. **17** evacuate, void, eliminate, excrete. **18** utter, express, issue, declare, pronounce, deliver, set forth, offer. ● *n.* **1** maneuver, approach; passage, flight, flyby, transit. **2 a** see SUCCESS 1. **3** authorization, permit, license, approval, safe conduct, protection; permission, freedom, liberty, authority, sanction, clearance, go-ahead, *colloq.* green light, OK. **4 a** permit, ticket. **5** transfer, toss, throw, ball. **10** state (of affairs), condition, situation, stage, juncture, status, crux; predicament, crisis. □ **in passing** by the way,

incidentally, by the by, parenthetically, en passant. **make a pass at** court, pay court to, make advances to, *archaic* make love to. **pass around 1** see DISTRIBUTE 1. **2** see CIRCULATE 2a, b. **pass away 1** die, expire, perish, succumb, breathe one's last, *archaic or colloq.* give up the ghost, *colloq.* turn up one's toes, *euphem.* pass on *or* over, *sl.* go west, croak, kick the bucket, bite the dust. **2** vanish, disappear, go away, stop, cease, end. **pass off 1** camouflage, misrepresent, disguise, dress up, disimulate. **2** evaporate, disappear, evanesce. **3** come about, shape up, come to pass, be accomplished; see also *pan out*. **4** see DISMISS 4. **pass on 1** see PROCEED 1. **2** see *pass away* 1 above. **3** see PASS¹ *v.* 3, 11, 13 above. **pass out 1** faint, collapse, black out, drop, keel over, *colloq.* conk (out), *literary* swoon. **3** see DISTRIBUTE 1. **pass over 1** leave, let go (by), overlook, disregard, ignore, pay no heed to, omit, skip. **3** see *pass away* 1 above. **pass through** see UNDERGO. **pass up** reject, decline, refuse, waive, turn down, dismiss, spurn, renounce; deny (oneself); skip, give up, forgo, let go (by), abandon, forswear, forsake, let pass, ignore, pay no heed, disregard, omit, neglect. **pass water** see URINATE.

pass² /pas/ *n.* **1** a narrow passage through mountains. **2** a navigable channel, esp. at the mouth of a river. □ **sell the pass** *Brit.* betray a cause. [ME, var. of PACE¹, infl. by F *pas* and by PASS¹]

■ **1** defile, gorge, col, cut, canyon, notch, gap, gully, couloir; passage, opening, way, route, road.

passable /pásəbəl/ *adj.* **1** barely satisfactory; just adequate. **2** (of a road, pass, etc.) that can be passed. □□ **passableness** *n.* **passably** *adv.* [ME f. OF (as PASS¹)]

■ **1** satisfactory, acceptable, tolerable, all right, adequate, admissible, allowable, presentable, average, fair (enough), (fair to) middling, fairly good, not bad, unexceptional, sufficient, indifferent, so-so, *colloq.* OK. **2** traversable, navigable, negotiable, open, unobstructed, unblocked. □□ **passably** see FAIRLY 2, PRETTY *adv.*

passacaglia /paásəkaályə, pásəkályə/ *n. Mus.* an instrumental piece usu. with a ground bass. [It. f. Sp. *pasacalle* f. *pasar* pass + *calle* street: orig. often played in the streets]

passage¹ /pásij/ *n.* **1** the process or means of passing; transit. **2** = PASSAGEWAY. **3** the liberty or right to pass through. **4 a** the right of conveyance as a passenger by sea or air. **b** a journey by sea or air. **5** a transition from one state to another. **6 a** a short extract from a book, etc. **b** a section of a piece of music. **c** a detail or section of a painting. **7** the passing of a bill, etc., into law. **8** (in *pl.*) an interchange of words, etc. **9** *Anat.* a duct, etc., in the body. □ **passage of** (or **at**) **arms** a fight or dispute. **work one's passage** earn a right (orig. of passage) by working for it. [ME f. OF (as PASS¹)]

■ **1** movement, moving, going, transition, transit, traversal, traverse, progress, crossing, passing. **3** safe conduct, protection, permission, right of way, privilege, liberty, freedom, visa, authorization, allowance. **4** voyage, trip, journey, cruise, crossing, sail, run, travel, traveling. **5** transition, change, mutation, shift, conversion, progression, passing; progress, flow, march, advance. **6** extract, excerpt, selection, section, part, snippet, portion, text, paragraph, canto, stanza, verse, line, sentence, phrase; citation, quotation. **7** enactment, ratification, sanction, approval, acceptance, passing, adoption, endorsement, legitimatization, legitimization, legalization, legislation. **9** duct; aperture, hole, orifice, opening; entry, access, inlet; exit, outlet.

passage² /pásij/ *v.* **1** *intr.* (of a horse or rider) move sideways, by the pressure of the rein on the horse's neck and of the

---

/.../ pronunciation	● part of speech
□ phrases, idioms, and compounds	
□□ derivatives	■ synonym section
cross-references appear in SMALL CAPITALS or *italics*	

rider's leg on the opposite side. **2** *tr.* make (a horse) do this. [F *passager*, earlier *passéger* f. It. *passeggiare* to walk, pace f. *passeggio* walk f. L *passus* PACE¹]

passageway /pásijway/ *n.* a narrow way for passing along, esp. with walls on either side; a corridor.
■ corridor, hall, passage, hallway, lobby; way, route, avenue, course, channel; road, thoroughfare.

passant /pásənt/ *adj. Heraldry* (of an animal) walking and looking to the dexter side, with three paws on the ground and the right forepaw raised. [ME f. OF, part. of *passer* PASS¹]

passband /pásband/ *n.* a frequency band within which signals are transmitted by a filter without attenuation.

passbook /pásbŏok/ *n.* a book issued by a bank, etc., to an account holder for recording amounts deposited and withdrawn.

passé /pasáy/ *adj.* **1** behind the times; out-of-date. **2** past its prime. [F, past part. of *passer* PASS¹]
■ **1** old-fashioned, unfashionable, dated, out-of-date, behind the times, outmoded, obsolete, obsolescent, antiquated, archaic, démodé, quaint, antique, superseded, *colloq.* out, old hat.

passementerie /pasméntree/ *n.* a trimming of gold or silver lace, braid, beads, etc. [F f. *passement* gold lace, etc. f. *passer* PASS¹]

passenger /pásinjər/ *n.* **1** a traveler in or on a public or private conveyance (other than the driver, pilot, crew, etc.). **2** *colloq.* a member of a team, crew, etc., who does no effective work. **3** (*attrib.*) for the use of passengers (*passenger seat*). □ **passenger mile** one mile traveled by one passenger, as a unit of traffic. **passenger pigeon** an extinct wild migratory pigeon of N. America. [ME f. OF *passager* (adj.) passing (as PASSAGE¹): -*n*- as in *messenger*, etc.]
■ **1** rider, fare, traveler, voyager, commuter.

passe-partout /páspaartŏo/ *n.* **1** a master key. **2** a picture frame (esp. for mounted photographs) consisting of two pieces of glass or one piece of glass and a backing of cardboard, etc., stuck together at the edges with adhesive paper or tape. **3** adhesive tape or paper used for this. [F, = passes everywhere]
■ **1** skeleton key, passkey.

passerby /pásərbí/ *n.* (*pl.* **passersby**) a person who goes past, esp. by chance.

passerine /pásərin, -reen/ *n.* & *adj.* ● *n.* any perching bird of the order Passeriformes, having feet with three toes pointing forward and one pointing backward, including sparrows and most land birds. ● *adj.* **1** of or relating to this order. **2** of the size of a sparrow. [L *passer* sparrow]

passible /pásibəl/ *adj.* capable of feeling or suffering. □□ **passibility** *n.* [ME f. OF *passible* or LL *passibilis* f. L *pati* *pass*- suffer]

passim /pásim/ *adv.* (of allusions or references in a published work) to be found at various places throughout the text. [L f. *passus* scattered f. *pandere* spread]

passing /pásing/ *adj., adv., & n.* ● *adj.* **1** in senses of PASS *v.* **2** transient; fleeting (*a passing glance*). **3** cursory; incidental (*a passing reference*). ● *adv.* exceedingly; very. ● *n.* **1** in senses of PASS *v.* **2** *euphem.* the death of a person (*mourned his passing*). □ **passing note** *Mus.* a note not belonging to the harmony but interposed to secure a smooth transition. **passing shot** *Tennis* a shot aiming the ball beyond and out of reach of the other player. □□ **passingly** *adv.*
■ *adj.* **2** disappearing, vanishing, ephemeral, brief, going, fading (away), slipping away, short-lived, expiring, transient, transitory, temporary, momentary, fleeting, transitional, impermanent. **3** hasty, superficial, cursory, incidental, casual, quick, fleeting, brief, summary, abrupt, dismissive; glancing. ● *n.* **2** death, dying, demise, end, loss, expiry, expiration.

passion /páshən/ *n.* **1** strong barely controllable emotion. **2** an outburst of anger (*flew into a passion*). **3 a** intense sexual love. **b** a person arousing this. **4 a** strong enthusiasm (*has a passion for football*). **b** an object arousing this. **5** (**the Passion**) **a** *Relig.* the suffering of Christ during his last days. **b** a narrative of this from the Gospels. **c** a musical setting of any of these narratives. **6** *archaic* the suffering of any martyr. □ **passion fruit** the edible fruit of some species of passionflower, esp. *Passiflora edulis*: also called GRANADILLA. **passion play** a miracle play representing Christ's Passion. **Passion Sunday** *Eccl.* formerly the fifth Sunday in Lent, now used synonymously for Palm Sunday. **Passion Week** *Eccl.* formerly the week between the fifth Sunday in Lent and Palm Sunday, now used synonymously for Holy Week. □□ **passionless** *adj.* [ME f. OF f. LL *passio -onis* f. L *pati* *pass*- suffer]
■ **1, 3a, 4a** ardor, ardency, eagerness, intensity, fervor, fervency, fervidness, zeal, zealousness, avidity, avidness, zest, zestfulness, vivacity, vivaciousness, gusto, verve, emotion, feeling, animation, spirit, spiritedness, vigor, enthusiasm, zealotry, fanaticism, feverishness; infatuation, mania, obsession, craze, craving, lust, thirst, hunger, itch, yearning, longing, desire, love, affection, compulsion, fondness, predilection, keenness, fancy, fascination, partiality, liking, interest, weakness, *Brit. sl.* pash, *colloq.* yen, crush, *formal* concupiscence. **2** fit, outburst, frenzy, paroxysm, fury, furor. **3 b** love, heart's desire, beloved, idol, hero, heroine, obsession, infatuation, *colloq.* crush, heartthrob. **4 b** see ENTHUSIASM 2. **5 a** (**Passion**) pain, suffering, agony, martyrdom.

passional /páshənəl/ *adj. & n.* ● *adj.* of or marked by passion. ● *n.* a book of the sufferings of saints and martyrs.

passionate /páshənət/ *adj.* **1** dominated by or easily moved to strong feeling, esp. love or anger. **2** showing or caused by passion. □□ **passionately** *adv.* **passionateness** *n.* [ME f. med.L *passionatus* (as PASSION)]
■ ardent, eager, intense, fervid, zealous, avid, earnest, zestful, feverish, fanatic(al), vehement, impassioned, emotional, animated, spirited, enthusiastic, vigorous, invigorated, energetic, *literary* passional; quick-tempered, irascible, hotheaded, fiery, testy, huffy, huffish, peevish, peppery, choleric, touchy, bilious, snappish, volatile, cross, temperamental, irritable, quarrelsome, pugnacious, argumentative, contentious, belligerent, cranky, *literary* atrabilious; aroused, lustful, lecherous, erotic, sexual, amorous, sensual, hot, randy, sexy.

passionflower /páshənflowr, -flowər/ *n.* any climbing plant of the genus *Passiflora*, with a flower that was supposed to suggest the instruments of the Crucifixion.

Passiontide /páshəntid/ *n.* the last two weeks of Lent.

passivate /pásivayt/ *v.tr.* make (esp. metal) passive (see PASSIVE). □□ **passivation** /-váyshən/ *n.*

passive /pásiv/ *adj.* **1** suffering action; acted upon. **2** offering no opposition; submissive. **3 a** not active; inert. **b** (of a metal) abnormally unreactive. **4** *Gram.* designating the voice in which the subject undergoes the action of the verb (e.g., in *they were killed*). **5** (of a debt) incurring no interest payment. **6** collecting or distributing the sun's energy without use of machinery (*passive solar heating*). □ **passive obedience 1** surrender to another's will without cooperation. **2** compliance with commands irrespective of their nature. **passive resistance** a nonviolent refusal to cooperate. **passive smoking** the involuntary inhaling, esp. by a nonsmoker, of smoke from others' cigarettes, etc. □□ **passively** *adv.* **passiveness** *n.* **passivity** /-sívətee/ *n.* [ME f. OF *passif* -*ive* or L *passivus* (as PASSION)]
■ **2** submissive, repressed, deferential, yielding, compliant, complaisant, receptive, flexible, malleable, pliable, tractable, docile, subdued, lamblike, tame, gentle, meek, patient, unresisting, unassertive, forbearing, tolerant, resigned, long-suffering. **3 a** inactive, nonaggressive, inert, motionless, unresponsive, quiet, calm, tranquil, serene, placid, still, idle, unmoving, unmoved, impassive, untouched, cool, indifferent, phlegmatic, uninterested, uninvolved, dispassionate, apathetic, lifeless, listless, quiescent, unperturbed, unaffected, imperturbable, unshaken, *colloq.* laid-back.

passkey /páskee/ *n.* **1** a private key to a gate, etc., for special purposes. **2** a skeleton key or master key.

Passover /pásōvər/ *n.* **1** the Jewish spring festival commemorating the liberation of the Israelites from Egyptian bondage, held from the 14th to the 21st day of the seventh month of the Jewish year. **2** = *paschal lamb.* [*pass over* = pass without touching, with ref. to the exemption of the Israelites from the death of the firstborn (Exod. 12)]

passport /páspawrt/ *n.* **1** an official document issued by a government certifying the holder's identity and citizenship, and entitling the holder to travel under its protection to and from foreign countries. **2** (foll. by *to*) a thing that ensures admission or attainment (*a passport to success*). [F *passeport* (as PASS¹, PORT¹)]

password /pásword/ *n.* **1** a selected word or phrase securing recognition, admission, etc., when used by those to whom it is disclosed. **2** *Computing* a word or string of characters securing access to an account or file for those authorized.
■ watchword, open sesame, sign, countersign.

past /past/ *adj., n., prep.,* & *adv.* ● *adj.* **1** gone by in time and no longer existing (*in past years*; *the time is past*). **2** recently completed or gone by (*the past month*; *for some time past*). **3** relating to a former time (*past president*). **4** *Gram.* expressing a past action or state. ● *n.* **1** (prec. by *the*) a past time. **b** what has happened in past time (*cannot undo the past*). **2** a person's past life or career, esp. if discreditable (*a man with a past*). **3** a past tense or form. ● *prep.* **1** beyond in time or place (*is past two o'clock*; *ran past the house*). **2** beyond the range, duration, or compass of (*past belief*; *past endurance*). ● *adv.* so as to pass by (*hurried past*). □ **not put it past a person** believe it possible of a person. **past it** *colloq.* incompetent or unusable through age. **past master 1** a person who is especially adept or expert in an activity, subject, etc. **2** a person who has been a master in a guild, lodge, etc. **past perfect** = PLUPERFECT. [past part. of PASS¹ *v.*]
■ *adj.* **1** over, done, finished, (over and) done with, gone (and forgotten), dead (and buried *or* gone), defunct. **2** last, recent. **3** late, former, onetime, sometime, previous, prior, erstwhile, quondam, ex-, *archaic* whilom. ● *n.* **1** (*the past*) days *or* years *or* times gone by, old times, former times, the (good) old days, days of old, yesterday, yesteryear, *Sc.* (auld) lang syne, *archaic* olden times *or* days. **2** history, background, life, career, biography. ● *prep.* **1** beyond, across, over; after. **2** beyond, surpassing, exceeding. ● *adv.* on, by, along, away. □ **past it** see OLD 1, 4, STALE *adj.* 1.

pasta /paásta/ *n.* **1** a dried flour paste used in various shapes in cooking (e.g., lasagna, spaghetti). **2** a cooked dish made from this. [It., = PASTE]

paste /payst/ *n.* & *v.* ● *n.* **1** any moist fairly stiff mixture, esp. of powder and liquid. **2** a dough of flour with fat, water, etc., used in baking. **3** an adhesive of flour, water, etc., esp. for sticking paper and other light materials. **4** an easily spread preparation of ground meat, fish, etc. (*anchovy paste*). **5** a hard vitreous composition used in making imitation gems. **6** a mixture of clay, water, etc., used in making ceramic ware, esp. a mixture of low plasticity used in making porcelain. ● *v.tr.* **1** fasten or coat with paste. **2** *sl.* a beat soundly. **b** bomb or bombard heavily. □ **paste-up** a document prepared for copying, etc., by combining and pasting various sections on a backing. □□ **pasting** *n.* (esp. in sense 2 of *v.*). [ME f. OF f. LL *pasta* small square medicinal lozenge f. Gk *pastē* f. *pastos* sprinkled]

pasteboard /páystbawrd/ *n.* **1** a sheet of stiff material made by pasting together sheets of paper. **2** (*attrib.*) a flimsy; unsubstantial. **b** fake.

pastel /pastél/ *n.* **1** a crayon consisting of powdered pigments bound with a gum solution. **2** a work of art in pastel. **3** a light and subdued shade of a color. □□ **pastelist** *n.* **pastellist** *n.* [F *pastel* or It. *pastello,* dimin. of *pasta* PASTE]

pastern /pástərn/ *n.* **1** the part of a horse's foot between the fetlock and the hoof. **2** a corresponding part in other animals. [ME *pastron* f. OF *pasturon* f. *pasture* hobble ult. f. L *pastorius* of a shepherd: see PASTOR]

pasteurize /páschəriz, pástyə-/ *v.tr.* subject (milk, etc.) to the process of partial sterilization by heating. □□ **pasteurization** /-záyshən/ *n.* **pasteurizer** *n.* [L. *Pasteur,* Fr. chemist d. 1895]

pasticcio /pasteéchō, -cheeó/ *n.* (*pl.* **-os**) = PASTICHE. [It.: see PASTICHE]

pastiche /pasteésh/ *n.* **1** a medley, a picture or a musical composition, made up from or imitating various sources. **2** a literary or other work of art composed in the style of a well-known author. [F f. It. *pasticcio* ult. f. LL *pasta* PASTE]
■ **1** mixture, medley, blend, compound, composite, patchwork, olio, olla podrida, potpourri, motley, miscellany, mélange, pasticcio, gallimaufry, farrago, mishmash, hodgepodge, tangle, *colloq.* omnium gatherum, *derog.* mess. **2** parody, pasticcio, takeoff.

pastille /pasteél, -tíl/ *n.* **1** a small candy or medicated lozenge. **2** a small roll of aromatic paste burned as a fumigator, etc. [F f. L *pastillus* little loaf, lozenge f. *panis* loaf]

pastime /pástīm/ *n.* **1** a pleasant recreation or hobby. **2** a sport or game. [PASS¹ + TIME]
■ **1** hobby, avocation, recreation, diversion, distraction, amusement, entertainment, fun, play, relaxation, leisure, divertissement. **2** game, sport.

pastis /pasteés/ *n.* an aniseed-flavored liqueur. [F]

pastor /pástər/ *n.* **1** a priest or minister in charge of a church or a congregation. **2** a person exercising spiritual guidance. **3** a pink starling, *Sturnus roseus,* of Europe and Asia. □□ **pastorship** *n.* [ME f. AF & OF *pastour* f. L *pastor -oris* shepherd f. *pascere past-* feed, graze]
■ **1** vicar, clergyman, clergywoman, parson, minister, churchman, churchwoman, rector, canon, reverend, father, divine, ecclesiastic, priest, bishop.

pastoral /pástərəl/ *adj.* & *n.* ● *adj.* **1** of, relating to, or associated with shepherds or flocks and herds. **2** (of land) used for pasture. **3** (of a poem, picture, etc.) portraying country life, usu. in a romantic or idealized form. **4** of or appropriate to a pastor. ● *n.* **1** a pastoral poem, play, picture, etc. **2** a letter from a pastor (esp. a bishop) to the clergy or people. □ **pastoral staff** a bishop's crosier. **pastoral theology** that considering religious truth in relation to spiritual needs. □□ **pastoralism** *n.* **pastorality** /-álitee/ *n.* **pastorally** *adv.* [ME f. L *pastoralis* (as PASTOR)]
■ *adj.* **1** country, rural, rustic, provincial, farming, agricultural, agrarian; humble. **3** bucolic, idyllic, innocent, simple, tranquil, serene, quiet, restful, peaceful, peaceable, placid, pacific, harmonious, uncomplicated, arcadian. **4** clerical, ministerial, ecclesiastic(al), church(ly). ● *n.* **1** idyll, eclogue, pastorale.

pastorale /pástəraál, -rál, -raálee/ *n.* (*pl.* **pastorales** or **pastorali** /-lee/) **1** a slow instrumental composition in compound time, usu. with drone notes in the bass. **2** a simple musical play with a rural subject. [It. (as PASTORAL)]

pastorate /pástərət/ *n.* **1** the office or tenure of a pastor. **2** a body of pastors.

pastrami /pəstraámee/ *n.* seasoned smoked beef. [Yiddish]

pastry /páystree/ *n.* (*pl.* **-ies**) **1** a dough of flour, fat, and water baked and used as a base and covering for pies, etc. **2 a** food, made wholly or partly of this. **b** a piece or item of this food. [PASTE after OF *pastaierie*]

pasturage /páschərij/ *n.* **1** land for pasture. **2** the process of pasturing cattle, etc. [OF (as PASTURE)]

pasture /páschər/ *n.* & *v.* ● *n.* **1** land covered with grass, etc., suitable for grazing animals, esp. cattle or sheep. **2** herbage for animals. ● *v.* **1** *tr.* put (animals) to graze in a pasture. **2** *intr.* & *tr.* (of animals) graze. [ME f. OF f. LL *pastura* (as PASTOR)]
■ *n.* **1** meadow, meadowland, pasture land, pasturage, grassland, grass, range, *poet.* lea.

┌───┐
/ . . . / pronunciation   ● **part of speech**
□ **phrases, idioms, and compounds**
□□ **derivatives**   ■ **synonym section**
cross-references appear in SMALL CAPITALS or *italics*
└───┘

pasty[1] /pástee/ n. esp. Brit. (pl. **-ies**) a pastry case with a sweet or savory filling, baked without a dish to shape it. [ME f. OF pasté ult. f. LL pasta PASTE]

pasty[2] /páystee/ adj. (**pastier, pastiest**) **1** of or like or covered with paste. **2** unhealthily pale (esp. in complexion) (pasty-faced). □□ **pastily** adv. **pastiness** n.
 ■ **1** moist, damp, sticky, gummy, clammy, viscous, slimy. **2** wan, pallid, pasty-faced, sallow, pale, pale-faced, whey-faced, sickly, anemic.

Pat. abbr. Patent.

pat[1] /pat/ v. & n. ● v. (**patted, patting**) **1** tr. strike gently with the hand or a flat surface. **2** tr. flatten or mold by patting. **3** tr. strike gently with the inner surface of the hand, esp. as a sign of affection, sympathy, or congratulation. **4** intr. beat lightly. ● n. **1** a light stroke or tap, esp. with the hand in affection, etc. **2** the sound made by this. **3** a small mass (esp. of butter) formed by patting. □ **pat-a-cake** (also **patty-cake**) a child's game with the patting of hands (the first words of a nursery rhyme). **pat on the back** a gesture of approval or congratulation. **pat a person on the back** congratulate a person. [ME, prob. imit.]
 ■ v. **1** strike, tap, touch, dab. **3** pet, stroke, caress. ● n. **1, 2** tap, touch, dab; stroke, caress. **3** piece, patty, lump, cake, portion. □ **pat on the back** commendation, praise, compliment, flattery, encouragement, credit, reassurance, approval, endorsement, recognition. **pat a person on the back** congratulate, commend, praise, compliment, encourage, reassure.

pat[2] /pat/ adj. & adv. ● adj. **1** known thoroughly and ready for any occasion. **2** apposite or opportune, esp. unconvincingly so (gave a pat answer). ● adv. **1** in a pat manner. **2** appositely; opportunely. □ **have** (or **know**) **down pat** (Brit. **have off pat**) know or have memorized perfectly. **stand pat 1** stick stubbornly to one's opinion or decision. **2** Poker retain one's hand as dealt; not draw other cards. □□ **patly** adv. **patness** n. [16th c.: rel. to PAT[1]]
 ■ adj. **1** see READY adj. 1, 2. **2** apt, suitable, apposite, ready, appropriate, fitting, relevant; well-rehearsed; glib, slick. ● adv. **1** thoroughly, perfectly, exactly, precisely, faultlessly, flawlessly, just so or right, readily; off pat; slickly, glibly. **2** aptly, suitably, appositely, opportunely, appropriately, fittingly, relevantly.
 □ **have** (or **know**) **down pat** see KNOW 1a.

patagium /pətáyjeeəm/ n. (pl. **patagia** /-jeeə/) Zool. **1** the wing membrane of a bat or similar animal. **2** a scale covering the wing joint in moths and butterflies. [med.L use of L patagium f. Gk patageion gold edging]

patch /pach/ n. & v. ● n. **1** a piece of material or metal, etc., used to mend a hole or as reinforcement. **2** a pad worn to protect an injured eye. **3** a dressing, etc., put over a wound. **4** a large or irregular distinguishable area on a surface. **5** Brit. colloq. a period of time in terms of its characteristic quality (went through a bad patch). **6** a piece of ground. **7** Brit. colloq. an area assigned to or patrolled by an authorized person, esp. a police officer. **8** a number of plants growing in one place (brier patch). **9** a scrap or remnant. **10** a temporary electrical connection. **11** a temporary correction in a computer program. **12** hist. a small disk, etc., of black silk attached to the face, worn esp. by women in the 17th–18th c. for adornment. **13** Mil. a piece of cloth on a uniform as the badge of a unit. ● v.tr. **1** (often foll. by up) repair with a patch or patches; put a patch or patches on. **2** (of material) serve as a patch to. **3** (often foll. by up) put together, esp. hastily or in a makeshift way. **4** (foll. by up) settle (a quarrel, etc.) esp. hastily or temporarily. □ **not a patch on** Brit. colloq. greatly inferior to. **patch cord** an insulated lead with a plug at each end, for use with a patchboard. **patch panel** = PATCHBOARD. **patch pocket** one made of a piece of cloth sewn on a garment. **patch test** a test for allergy by applying to the skin patches containing allergenic substances. □□ **patcher** n. [ME pacche, patche, perh. var. of peche f. OF pieche dial. var. of piece PIECE]
 ■ n. **1** piece, scrap, reinforcement. **2** eye patch. **3** pad, bandage, dressing, plaster. **4** area, region, zone, stretch,

section, segment. **5** period, time, interval, spell, bit, stage, episode; experience. **6** plot, tract, ground, parcel, field, plat, lot. **7** responsibility, area, territory, round, beat, precinct, Law or joc. bailiwick, Brit. colloq. manor. **8** border, bed, garden. **9** piece, scrap, shred, snip, snippet, tatter. ● v. **1, 2** patch up or over, mend, repair, vamp, revamp, darn, sew (up), reinforce, cover. **3** patch up, fix (up), improvise, knock together or up, Naut. jury-rig, colloq. doctor. **4** (patch up) settle, set right or straight, straighten out, reconcile, resolve, heal.

patchboard /páchbawrd/ n. a board with electrical sockets linked to enable changeable permutations of connection.

patchouli /pəchŏolee, páchŏolee/ n. **1** a strongly scented E. Indian plant, Pogostemon cablin. **2** the perfume obtained from this. [a native name in Madras]

patchwork /páchwərk/ n. **1** sewn work using small pieces of cloth with different designs, forming a pattern. **2** a thing composed of various small pieces or fragments.
 ■ **2** pastiche, pasticcio, mixture, confusion, hodgepodge, gallimaufry, olio, olla podrida, mishmash, jumble, mosaic, mélange, medley, hash, mixed bag or bunch, potpourri.

patchy /páchee/ adj. (**patchier, patchiest**) **1** uneven in quality. **2** having or existing in patches. □□ **patchily** adv. **patchiness** n.

pate /payt/ n. colloq. or joc. **1** the top of the head **2** the head, esp. representing the seat of intellect. [ME: orig. unkn.]

pâté /paatáy, pa-/ n. a rich paste or spread of finely chopped and spiced meat or fish, etc. □ **pâté de foie gras** /də fwaa graá/ a paste of fatted goose liver. [F f. OF pasté (as PASTY[1])]

pâte /paat/ n. the paste of which porcelain is made. [F, = PASTE]

patella /pətélə/ n. (pl. **patellae** /-lee/) the kneecap. □□ **patellar** adj. **patellate** /-lət/ adj. [L, dimin. of patina: see PATEN]

paten /pátən/ n. **1** a shallow dish used for the bread at the Eucharist. **2** a thin circular plate of metal. [ME ult. f. OF patene or L patina, patena shallow dish f. Gk patanē a plate]

patent /pát'nt/ n., adj., & v. ● n. **1** a government authority to an individual or organization conferring a right or title, esp. the sole right to make or use or sell some invention. **2** a document granting this authority. **3** an invention or process protected by it. ● adj. **1** /páyt'nt/ obvious; plain. **2** conferred or protected by patent. **3 a** made and marketed under a patent; proprietary. **b** to which one has a proprietary claim. **4** such as might be patented; ingenious; well-contrived. **5** (of an opening, etc.) allowing free passage. ● v.tr. obtain a patent for (an invention). □ **letters patent** an open document from a sovereign or government conferring a patent or other right. **patent leather** leather with a glossy varnished surface. **patent medicine** medicine made and marketed under a patent and available without prescription. **patent office** an office from which patents are issued. □□ **patency** n. **patentable** adj. **patently** /páyt'ntlee, pát-/ adv. (in sense 1 of adj.). [ME f. OF patent and L patēre lie open]
 ■ n. **1, 2** letters patent, trade name, (registered) trademark, copyright, license, permit, charter, franchise, grant. **3** see INVENTION 2. ● adj. **1** obvious, clear, transparent, manifest, apparent, plain, evident, self-evident, unmistakable, unequivocal, explicit, palpable, tangible, physical, conspicuous, flagrant, blatant, prominent. **2, 3** protected, proprietary. **4** see INGENIOUS. □ **letters patent** see PATENT n. 1, 2 above.
 □□ **patently** see manifestly (MANIFEST[1]).

patentee /pát'ntée/ n. **1** a person who takes out or holds a patent. **2** a person for the time being entitled to the benefit of a patent.

patentor /pát'ntər/ n. a person or body that grants a patent.

pater /páytər/ n. Brit. sl. father. ¶ Now only in jocular or affected use. [L]

paterfamilias /páytərfəmíleeas, paá-, pátər-/ n. the male head of a family or household. [L, = father of the family]

paternal /pətérnəl/ adj. **1** of or like or appropriate to a father. **2** fatherly. **3** related through the father. **4** (of a government, etc.) limiting freedom and responsibility by well-meaning regulations. □□ **paternally** adv. [LL paternalis f. L paternus f. pater father]

■ **1, 2** fatherly, kindly, indulgent, solicitous, fond, concerned, devoted, loving; patriarchal. **3** patrilineal, patrimonial. **4** paternalistic.

paternalism /pətə́rnəlizəm/ n. the policy of governing in a paternal way, or behaving paternally to one's associates or subordinates. □□ **paternalist** n. **paternalistic** adj. **paternalistically** adv.

paternity /pətə́rnitee/ n. **1** fatherhood. **2** one's paternal origin. **3** the source or authorship of a thing. □ **paternity suit** a lawsuit held to determine whether a certain man is the father of a certain child. **paternity test** a blood test to determine whether a man may be or cannot be the father of a particular child. [ME f. OF paternité or LL paternitas]

■ **1** fatherhood, fathership. **2** parentage, descent, heritage, line, lineage, extraction, family, stock, strain, blood.

paternoster /páytərnóstər, paá-, pátər-/ n. **1 a** the Lord's Prayer, esp. in Latin. **b** a rosary bead indicating that this is to be said. **2** an elevator consisting of a series of linked doorless compartments moving continuously on a circular belt. [OE f. L pater noster our father]

path /path/ n. (pl. **paths** /paathz/) **1** a way or track laid or trodden down for walking. **2** the line along which a person or thing moves (flight path). **3** a course of action or conduct. **4** a sequence of movements or operations taken by a system. □□ **pathless** adj. [OE pæth f. WG]

■ **1** footpath, pathway, track, trail, walk, walkway, footway, pavement, sidewalk. **2** way, course, track, route, road, orbit, trajectory, circuit, Math. locus. **3** course, approach, channel, direction, procedure, process, way, avenue, means, method, technique, strategy, scheme, plan, scenario, game plan.

-path /path/ comb. form forming nouns denoting: **1** a practitioner of curative treatment (homoeopath; osteopath). **2** a person who suffers from a disease (psychopath). [back-form. f. -PATHY, or f. Gk -pathēs -sufferer (as PATHOS)]

Pathan /pətaán/ n. a member of a Pashto-speaking people inhabiting NW Pakistan and SE Afghanistan. [Hindi]

pathetic /pəthétik/ adj. **1** arousing pity or sadness or contempt. **2** colloq. miserably inadequate. **3** archaic of the emotions. □ **pathetic fallacy** the attribution of human feelings and responses to inanimate things, esp. in art and literature. □□ **pathetically** adv. [F pathétique f. LL patheticus f. Gk pathētikos (as PATHOS)]

■ **1** moving, stirring, affecting, affective, touching, emotional, emotive, poignant, tragic, heartrending, heartbreaking, pitiful, pitiable, piteous, plaintive, wretched, miserable, sorrowful, grievous, sad, doleful, mournful, woeful, literary lamentable, literary or joc. dolorous. **2** meager, paltry, feeble, inadequate, poor, petty, puny, sorry, colloq. piddling, measly, crummy. □ **pathetic fallacy** anthropomorphism.

pathfinder /páthfindər/ n. **1** a person who explores new territory, investigates a new subject, etc. **2** an aircraft or its pilot sent ahead to locate and mark the target area for bombing.

■ **1** pioneer, trailblazer.

patho- /páthō/ comb. form disease. [Gk pathos suffering: see PATHOS]

pathogen /páthəjən/ n. an agent causing disease. □□ **pathogenic** /-jenik/ adj. **pathogenous** /-thójənəs/ adj. [PATHO- + -GEN]

pathogenesis /páthəjénisis/ n. (also **pathogeny** /pəthójənee/) the manner of development of a disease. □□ **pathogenetic** /-jinétik/ adj.

pathological /páthəlójikəl/ adj. **1** of pathology. **2** of or caused by a physical or mental disorder (a pathological fear of spiders). □□ **pathologically** adv.

pathology /pəthóləjee/ n. **1** the science of bodily diseases. **2** the symptoms of a disease. □□ **pathologist** n. [F pathologie or mod.L pathologia (as PATHO-, -LOGY)]

pathos /páythos, -thaws, -thōs/ n. a quality in speech, writing, events, etc., that evokes pity or sadness. [Gk pathos suffering, rel. to paskhō suffer, penthos grief]

pathway /páthway/ n. **1** a path or its course. **2** Biochem., etc., a sequence of reactions undergone in a living organism.

-pathy /pəthee/ comb. form forming nouns denoting: **1** curative treatment (allopathy; homoeopathy). **2** feeling (telepathy). [Gk patheia suffering]

patience /páyshəns/ n. **1** calm endurance of hardship, provocation, pain, delay, etc. **2** tolerant perseverance or forbearance. **3** the capacity for calm self-possessed waiting. **4** esp. Brit. = SOLITAIRE 4. □ **have no patience with 1** be unable to tolerate. **2** be irritated by. [ME f. OF f. L patientia (as PATIENT)]

■ **1, 3** tolerance, forbearance, restraint, toleration, stoicism, fortitude, endurance, sufferance, submission, resignation, self-control, imperturbability, even temper, unflappability, composure, calmness, serenity, equanimity. **2** diligence, tenacity, doggedness, indefatigability, endurance, assiduity, perseverance, constancy, persistence, steadfastness, pertinacity, determination, resolve, resolution, firmness; forbearance.

patient /páyshənt/ adj. & n. ● adj. having or showing patience. ● n. a person receiving or registered to receive medical treatment. □□ **patiently** adv. [ME f. OF f. L patiens -entis pres. part. of pati suffer]

■ adj. resigned, submissive, stoical, long-suffering, compliant, acquiescent, passive, self-possessed, philosophical, serene; forbearing, tolerant, forgiving, accommodating; diligent, dogged, tenacious, persistent, assiduous, sedulous, steadfast, staunch, perseverant, unwavering, unswerving, constant, unfaltering, unfailing, untiring, tireless, indefatigable, pertinacious, determined, resolved, resolute, firm, unyielding. ● n. invalid, sufferer, case, client.

patina /pətéenə, pát'nə/ n. (pl. **patinas**) **1** a film, usu. green, formed on the surface of old bronze. **2** a similar film on other surfaces. **3** a gloss produced by age on woodwork. □□ **patinated** /pát'naytid/ adj. **patination** n. [It. f. L patina dish]

patio /páteeō/ n. (pl. **-os**) **1** a paved usu. roofless area adjoining and belonging to a house. **2** an inner court open to the sky esp. in a Spanish or Spanish-American house. [Sp.]

patisserie /pətísəree, paateesreé/ n. **1** a shop where pastries are made and sold. **2** pastries collectively. [F pâtisserie f. med.L pasticium pastry f. pasta PASTE]

patois /patwaá, pátwaa/ n. (pl. same, pronunc. /-waaz/) the dialect of the common people in a region, differing fundamentally from the literary language. [F, = rough speech, perh. f. OF patoier treat roughly f. patte paw]

■ dialect, vernacular.

patriarch /páytreeaark/ n. **1** the male head of a family or tribe. **2** (often in pl.) Bibl. any of those regarded as fathers of the human race, esp. Adam and his descendants, including Noah; Abraham, Isaac, and Jacob; or the sons of Jacob, founders of the tribes of Israel. **3** Eccl. **a** the title of a chief bishop, esp. those presiding over the Churches of Antioch, Alexandria, Constantinople, and (formerly) Rome; now also the title of the heads of certain autocephalous Orthodox Churches. **b** (in the Roman Catholic Church) a bishop ranking next above primates and metropolitans, and immediately below the pope. **c** the head of a Uniate community. **d** a high dignitary of the Mormon church. **4 a** the founder of an order, science, etc. **b** a venerable old man. **c** the oldest member of a group. □□ **patriarchal** /-aárkəl/ adj. **patriarchally** /-aárkəlee/ adv. [ME f. OF patriarche f. eccl.L patriarcha f. Gk patriarkhēs f. patria family f. patēr father + -arkhēs -ruler]

■ **4 a** (founding) father. **b** archaic graybeard.

patriarchate /páytreeaarkət, -kayt/ n. **1** the office, see, or residence of an ecclesiastical patriarch. **2** the rank of a tribal patriarch. [med.L *patriarchatus* (as PATRIARCH)]

patriarchy /páytreeaarkee/ n. (pl. **-ies**) a system of society, government, etc., ruled by a man or men and with descent through the male line. □□ **patriarchism** n. [med.L *patriarchia* f. Gk *patriarkhia* (as PATRIARCH)]

patrician /pətríshən/ n. & adj. ● n. **1** hist. a member of the ancient Roman nobility (cf. PLEBEIAN). **2** hist. a nobleman in some Italian republics. **3** an aristocrat. **4** a person of educated or refined tastes and upbringing. ● adj. **1** noble; aristocratic; well-bred. **2** hist. of the ancient Roman nobility. [ME f. OF *patricien* f. L *patricius* having a noble father f. *pater patris* father]

patriciate /pətrísheeət, -ayt/ n. **1** a patrician order; an aristocracy. **2** the rank of patrician. [L *patriciatus* (as PATRICIAN)]

patricide /pátrisīd/ n. = PARRICIDE (esp. with reference to the killing of one's father). □□ **patricidal** /-síd'l/ adj. [LL *patricida*, *patricidium*, alt. of L *parricida*, *parricidium* (see PARRICIDE) after *pater* father]

patrilineal /pátrilíneeəl/ adj. of or relating to, or based on kinship with, the father or descent through the male line. [L *pater patris* father + LINEAL]

patrimony /pátrimōnee/ n. (pl. **-ies**) **1** property inherited from one's father or ancestor. **2** a heritage. **3** the endowment of a church, etc. □□ **patrimonial** adj. [ME *patrimoigne* f. OF *patrimoine* f. L *patrimonium* f. *pater patris* father]

patriot /páytreeət, -ot/ n. a person who is devoted to and ready to support or defend his or her country. □□ **patriotic** /-reeótik/ adj. **patriotically** adv. **patriotism** n. [F *patriote* f. LL *patriota* f. Gk *patriōtēs* f. *patrios* of one's fathers f. *patēr patros* father]

■ nationalist, loyalist; flag-waver, jingo, jingoist, chauvinist.

patristic /pətrístik/ adj. of the early Christian writers or their work. □□ **patristics** n.pl. (usu. treated as sing.). [G *patristisch* f. L *pater patris* father]

patrol /pətrṓl/ n. & v. ● n. **1** the act of walking or traveling around an area, esp. at regular intervals, in order to protect or supervise it. **2** one or more persons or vehicles assigned or sent out on patrol, esp. a detachment of guards, police, etc. **3 a** a detachment of troops sent out to reconnoiter. **b** such reconnaissance. **4** a routine operational voyage of a ship or aircraft. **5** a routine monitoring of astronomical or other phenomena. **6** Brit. an official controlling traffic where children cross the road. **7** a unit of Boy or Girl Scouts. ● v. (**patrolled**, **patrolling**) **1** tr. carry out a patrol of. **2** intr. act as a patrol. □ **patrol car** a police car used in patrolling roads and streets. **patrol wagon** a police van for transporting prisoners. □□ **patroller** n. [F *patrouiller* paddle in mud f. *patte* paw: (n.) f. G *Patrolle* f. F *patrouille*]

■ n. **1** rounds, policing, patrolling, beat; protection, (safe)guarding, defense, watchfulness, vigilance, watch. **2** guard, sentry, sentinel, patrolman, archaic or hist. watchman, hist. watch; see also SQUAD. **6** Brit. colloq. lollipop man or lady or woman. ● v. **1** police, guard, protect, defend, watch over, stand or keep guard over, stand or keep watch over. **2** walk a beat, make or do the rounds, be on or stand or keep guard, be on or stand or keep watch, keep vigil. □ **patrol car** police car, squad car, prowl car, Brit. panda car. **patrol wagon** sl. Black Maria.

patrolman /pətrṓlmən/ n. (pl. **-men**) a police officer assigned to or patrolling a specific route.

■ police officer, Brit. (police) constable, PC.

patrology /pətróləjee/ n. (pl. **-ies**) **1** the study of the writings of the Fathers of the Church. **2** a collection of such writings. □□ **patrological** /pátrəlójikəl/ adj. **patrologist** n. [Gk *patēr patros* father]

patron /páytrən/ n. (fem. **patroness**) **1** a person who gives financial or other support to a person, cause, work of art, etc., esp. one who buys works of art. **2** a usu. regular customer of a store, etc. **3** Rom. Antiq. **a** the former owner of a freed slave. **b** the protector of a client. **4** Brit. a person who has the right of presenting a member of the clergy to a benefice. □ **patron saint** the protecting or guiding saint of a person, place, etc. [ME f. OF f. L *patronus* protector of clients, defender f. *pater patris* father]

■ **1** benefactor, philanthropist, Maecenas, protector, supporter, defender, advocate, champion, guardian (angel), sponsor, backer, promoter, sympathizer, friend (at court), colloq. booster, sl. angel. **2** customer, client, purchaser, buyer, patronizer, habitué, regular, frequenter.

patronage /pátrənij/ n. **1** the support, promotion, or encouragement given by a patron. **2** a patronizing or condescending manner. **3 a** the power to appoint others to government jobs. **b** the distribution of such jobs. **4** Rom. Antiq. the rights and duties or position of a patron. **5** Brit. the right of presenting a member of the clergy to a benefice, etc. **6** a customer's support for a store, etc. [ME f. OF (as PATRON)]

■ **1** sponsorship, support, backing, promotion, encouragement, boosting, aid, help, sympathy, financing, auspices, protection, guardianship, aegis. **2** condescension, disdain, scorn, patronizing, stooping, deigning, superiority, superciliousness, snobbishness. **6** trade, business, custom; trading, traffic.

patronize /páytrənīz, pát-/ v.tr. **1** treat condescendingly. **2** act as a patron toward (a person, cause, artist, etc.); support; encourage. **3** frequent (a store, etc.) as a customer. □□ **patronization** n. **patronizer** n. **patronizing** adj. **patronizingly** adv. [obs. F *patroniser* or med.L *patronizare* (as PATRON)]

■ **1** look down on or upon, scorn, look down one's nose at, talk down to; disdain, demean, put down, humiliate, treat de haut en bas. **2** sponsor, support, back, promote, encourage, aid, assist, help, fund, contribute or subscribe to, underwrite, foster, colloq. boost. **3** deal or trade with, do or transact business with, buy or purchase from, frequent, shop at, be a customer or client of, go to or attend regularly.

patronymic /pátrənímik/ n. & adj. ● n. a name derived from the name of a father or ancestor, e.g., Johnson, O'Brien, Ivanovich. ● adj. (of a name) so derived. [LL *patronymicus* f. Gk *patrōnumikos* f. *patrōnumos* f. *patēr patros* father + *onuma*, *onoma* name]

patroon /pətrṓn/ n. hist. a landowner with manorial privileges under the Dutch governments of New York and New Jersey. [Du., = PATRON]

patsy /pátsee/ n. (pl. **-ies**) sl. a person who is deceived, ridiculed, tricked, etc. [20th c.: orig. unkn.]

patten /pát'n/ n. hist. a shoe or clog with a raised sole or set on an iron ring, for walking in mud, etc. [ME f. OF *patin* f. *patte* paw]

patter[1] /pátər/ v. & n. ● v. **1** intr. make a rapid succession of taps, as of rain on a windowpane. **2** intr. run with quick short steps. **3** tr. cause (water, etc.) to patter. ● n. a rapid succession of taps, short light steps, etc. [PAT[1]]

■ v. **1** spatter, tap; beat, pelt. **2** tiptoe, scurry, scuttle, skip, trip, scamper. **3** spatter. ● n. spatter, pitterpatter, pit-a-pat, tapping, tattoo, drum, thrum, beat, beating, tap, rat-a-tat.

patter[2] /pátər/ n. & v. ● n. **1 a** the rapid speech used by a comedian or introduced into a song. **b** the words of a comic song. **2** the words used by a person selling or promoting a product; a sales pitch. **3** the special language or jargon of a profession, class, etc. **4** colloq. mere talk; chatter. ● v. **1** tr. repeat (prayers, etc.) in a rapid mechanical way. **2** intr. talk glibly or mechanically. [ME f. *pater* = PATERNOSTER]

■ n. **2** pitch, sales talk, colloq. line, sl. spiel. **3** see JARGON[1] 1, 2. **4** chatter, prattle, prate, babble, gabble, cackle, palaver, jabber, jabbering, small talk, gossip, blather, blether, gibberish, gibber, colloq. gab, natter, chitchat, sl. gas, hot air, sl. derog. (yackety-)yak. ● v. **1** jabber, gabble, babble. **2** chatter, prattle, prate, babble, gabble, cackle, palaver, jabber, rattle (on), blather, gibber, colloq. chitchat, natter (on), witter (on), gas, sl. derog. (yackety-)yak.

pattern /pátərn/ n. & v. ● n. **1** a repeated decorative design on wallpaper, cloth, a carpet, etc. **2** a regular or logical form, order, or arrangement of parts (*behavior pattern; the pattern of one's daily life*). **3** a model or design, e.g., of a garment, from which copies can be made. **4** an example of excellence; an ideal; a model (*a pattern of elegance*). **5** the prescribed flight path for an airplane taking off or esp. landing at an airport. **6** a wooden or metal figure from which a mold is made for a casting. **7** a sample (of cloth, wallpaper, etc.). **8** the marks made by shots, bombs, etc. on a target or target area. **9** a random combination of shapes or colors. ● *v.tr.* **1** (usu. foll. by *after, on*) model (a thing) on a design, etc. **2** decorate with a pattern. □ **pattern bombing** bombing over a large area, not on a single target. [ME *patron* (see PATRON): differentiated in sense and spelling since the 16th–17th c.]

■ *n.* **1** figure, motif, design, device; decoration, ornament. **2** system, order, arrangement, plan, theme; repetition, consistency, orderliness, regularity, sequence, cycle, habit. **3** model, original, blueprint, diagram, plan, layout, design, draft, guide, template, stencil, mold, matrix. **4** model, archetype, prototype, exemplar, paragon, ideal, standard, yardstick, criterion, gauge, measure. **7** sample, example, instance, specimen. **9** layout, configuration, formation, composition. ● *v.* **1** (*pattern after* or *on*) model on; see also IMITATE 1, 2. **2** decorate, figure, ornament; see also EMBELLISH 1.

patty /páttee/ *n.* (*pl.* **-ies**) **1** a small flat cake of ground meat, etc., sometimes breaded and fried. **2** esp. *Brit.* a little pie or pastry. [F *pâté* PASTY[1]]

pattypan /páteepan/ *n.* **1** a flattish summer squash having a scalloped edge. **2** a pan for baking a patty.

patulous /páchələs/ *adj.* **1** (of branches, etc.) spreading. **2** open; expanded. □□ **patulously** *adv.* **patulousness** *n.* [L *patulus* f. *patēre* be open]

paua /pówə/ *n.* **1** a large edible New Zealand shellfish of the genus *Haliotis.* **2** its ornamental shell. **3** a fishhook made from this. [Maori]

paucity /páwsitee/ *n.* smallness of number or quantity. [ME f. OF *paucité* or f. L *paucitas* f. *paucus* few]

Pauli exclusion principle /páwlee, pów-/ *n. Physics* the assertion that no two fermions can have the same quantum number. [W. *Pauli,* Austrian physicist d. 1958]

Pauline /páwlin, -leen/ *adj.* of or relating to St. Paul (*the Pauline epistles*). [ME f. med.L *Paulinus* f. L *Paulus* Paul]

paulownia /pawlṓneeə/ *n.* any Asian tree of the genus *Paulownia,* with fragrant purple flowers. [Anna *Paulovna,* Russian princess d. 1865]

paunch /pawnch/ *n.* **1** the belly or stomach, esp. when protruding. **2** a ruminant's first stomach; the rumen. □□ **paunchy** *adj.* (**paunchier, paunchiest**). **paunchiness** *n.* [ME f. AF *pa(u)nche,* ONF *panche* ult. f. L *pantex panticis* bowels]

■ *n.* **1** belly, potbelly, stomach, *colloq.* tummy, gut, *joc.* corporation, *sl.* beer belly.

pauper /páwpər/ *n.* **1** a person without means; a beggar. **2** a person dependent on private or organized charity. □□ **pauperdom** /-pərdəm/ *n.* **pauperism** /-rizəm/ *n.* **pauperize** *v.tr.* **pauperization** /-rizáysh'n/ *n.* [L, = poor]

■ **1** indigent, down-and-out, bankrupt, insolvent, *colloq.* have-not; beggar, mendicant.

pause /pawz/ *n. &v.* ● *n.* **1** an interval of inaction, esp. when due to hesitation; a temporary stop. **2** a break in speaking or reading; a silence. **3** *Mus.* a fermata. ● *v.* **1** *intr.* make a pause; wait. **2** *intr.* (usu. foll. by *upon*) linger over (a word, etc.). **3** *tr.* cause to hesitate or pause. □ **give pause to** cause (a person) to hesitate. [ME f. OF *pause* or L *pausa* f. Gk *pausis* f. *pauō* stop]

■ *n.* hesitation, interruption, delay, lull, lapse, moratorium, holdup, wait, break, rest, breathing space, interval, stop, discontinuity, lacuna, gap, hiatus, abeyance, discontinuation, discontinuance, *Mus.* fermata, *Prosody* caesura, *colloq.* letup, breather. ● *v.* **1, 3** delay, break, hesitate, wait, mark time, falter, rest, *colloq.* take a breather; interrupt, hold up, suspend, discontinue, intermit.

pavane /pəvaán, -ván/ *n.* (also **pavan**) *hist.* **1** a stately dance in elaborate clothing. **2** the music for this. [F *pavane* f. Sp. *pavana,* perh. f. *pavon* peacock]

pave /payv/ *v.tr.* **1** cover (a street, floor, etc.) with paving, etc. **2** cover or strew (a floor, etc.) as of asphalt or concrete. **2** esp. *Brit.* = SIDEWALK. **3** a roadway. **4** *Zool.* a pavement-like formation of close-set teeth, scales, etc. [ME f. OF f. L *pavimentum* f. *pavire* beat, ram]

■ **2** walk, footpath, footway, sidewalk. **3** road, roadway.

pavé /paváy, pávay/ *n.* **1** a paved street, road, or path. **2** a setting of jewels placed closely together. [F, past part. of *paver:* see PAVE]

pavement /páyvmənt/ *n.* **1** the hard, durable covering of a street, driveway, etc., as of asphalt or concrete. **2** esp. *Brit.* = SIDEWALK. **3** a roadway. **4** *Zool.* a pavement-like formation of close-set teeth, scales, etc. [ME f. OF f. L *pavimentum* f. *pavire* beat, ram]

■ **2** walk, footpath, footway, sidewalk. **3** road, roadway.

pavilion /pəvílyən/ *n. & v.* ● *n.* **1** a usu. open building at a fairground, park, etc., used for exhibits, refreshments, etc. **2** a decorative building in a garden. **3** a tent, esp. a large one at a show, fair, etc. **4** a building used for entertainments. **5** a temporary stand at an exhibition. **6** a detached building that is part of a connected set of buildings, as at a hospital. **7** the part of a cut gemstone below the girdle. ● *v.tr.* enclose in or provide with a pavilion. [ME f. OF *pavillon* f. L *papilio -onis* butterfly, tent]

pavior, paviour SEE PAVE.

pavlova /pavlṓvə/ *n.* esp. *Austral. & NZ* a meringue dessert served with cream and fruit. [A. *Pavlova,* Russ. ballerina d. 1931]

Pavlovian /pavlṓviən/ *adj.* of or relating to I. P. Pavlov, Russian physiologist d. 1936, or his work, esp. on conditioned reflexes.

paw /paw/ *n. & v.* ● *n.* **1** a foot of an animal having claws or nails. **2** *colloq.* a person's hand. ● *v.* **1** *tr.* strike or scrape with a paw or foot. **2** *intr.* scrape the ground with a paw or hoof. **3** *tr. colloq.* fondle awkwardly or indecently. [ME *pawe, powe* f. OF *poue,* etc. ult. f. Frank.]

pawky /páwkee/ *adj.* (**pawkier, pawkiest**) *Sc. & Brit. dial.* **1** dryly humorous. **2** shrewd. □□ **pawkily** *adv.* **pawkiness** *n.* [Sc. & North Engl. dial. *pawk* trick, of unkn. orig.]

pawl /pawl/ *n. & v.* ● *n.* **1** a lever with a catch for the teeth of a wheel or bar. **2** *Naut.* a short bar used to lock a capstan, windlass, etc., to prevent it from recoiling. ● *v.tr.* secure (a capstan, etc.) with a pawl. [perh. f. LG & Du. *pal,* rel. to *pal* fixed]

pawn[1] /pawn/ *n.* **1** *Chess* a piece of the smallest size and value. **2** a person used by others for their own purposes. [ME f. AF *poun,* OF *peon* f. med.L *pedo -onis* foot soldier f. L *pes pedis* foot: cf. PEON]

■ **2** tool, cat's-paw, puppet, instrument, dupe, *colloq.* dummy, stooge.

pawn[2] /pawn/ *v. & n.* ● *v.tr.* **1** deposit an object, esp. with a pawnbroker, as security for money lent. **2** pledge or wager (one's life, honor, word, etc.). ● *n.* **1** an object left as security for money, etc., lent. **2** anything or any person left with another as security, etc. [ME f. OF *pan, pand, pant,* pledge, security f. WG]

■ *v.* pledge, mortgage, hypothecate, deposit, *archaic* plight, gage, *colloq.* hock, *Brit. sl.* pop. ● *n.* collateral, guaranty, guarantee, pledge, surety, security, assurance, deposit; bond, bail.

pawnbroker /páwnbrōkər/ *n.* a person who lends money at interest on the security of personal property pawned. □□ **pawnbroking** *n.*

/.../ **pronunciation**	● **part of speech**	
□ **phrases, idioms, and compounds**		
□□ **derivatives**	■ **synonym section**	
cross-references appear in SMALL CAPITALS or *italics*		

Pawnee /pawnee, paa-/ *n*. **1 a** a N. American people native to Kansas and Nebraska. **b** a member of this people. **2** the language of this people.

pawnshop /páwnshop/ *n*. a shop where pawnbroking is conducted.

pawpaw /páwpaw/ *n*. (also **papaw**) a N. American tree, *Asimina triloba*, with purple flowers and edible fruit. [earlier *papay*(*a*) f. Sp. & Port. *papaya*, of Carib orig.]

pax /paks, paaks/ *n*. **1** the kiss of peace. **2** (as *int*.) *Brit. sl*. a call for a truce (used esp. by schoolchildren). **3** (also **Pax**) a historical period of peace, usu. enforced by a dominant military power (**Pax Romana**). [ME f. L, = peace]

pay[1] /pay/ *v*., *n*., & *adj*. ● *v.tr*. (*past* and *past part*. **paid** /payd/) **1** (also *absol*.) give (a person, etc.) what is due for services done, goods received, debts incurred, etc. (*paid him in full*; *I assure you I have paid*). **2 a** give (a usu. specified amount) for work done, a debt, a ransom, etc. (*they pay $6 an hour*). **b** (foll. by *to*) hand over the amount of (a debt, wages, recompense, etc.) to (*paid the money to the assistant*). **3 a** give, bestow, or express (attention, respect, a compliment, etc.) (*paid them no heed*). **b** make (a visit, a call, etc.) (*paid a visit to their uncle*). **4** (also *absol*.) (of a business, undertaking, attitude, etc.) be profitable or advantageous to (a person, etc.). **5** reward or punish (*can never pay you for what you have done for us*; *I shall pay you for that*). **6** (usu. as **paid** *adj*.) recompense (work, time, etc.) (*paid holiday*). **7** (usu. foll. by *out*, *away*) let out (a rope) by slackening it. ● *n*. wages; payment. ● *adj*. **1** requiring payment for (a service, etc.) **2** requiring payment of a coin for use (*pay phone*). □ **in the pay of** employed by. **paid vacation** an agreed period of time off from work for which wages are paid as normal. **pay back 1** repay. **2** punish or be revenged on. **pay dearly** (usu. foll. by *for*) **1** obtain at a high cost, great effort, etc. **2** suffer for a wrongdoing, etc. **pay dirt 1** *Mineral*. ground worth working for ore. **2** a financially promising situation. **pay for 1** hand over the price of. **2** bear the cost of. **3** suffer or be punished for (a fault, etc.). **pay in** pay (money) into a bank account. **paying guest** a boarder. **pay its** (or **one's**) **way** cover costs; not be indebted. **pay one's dues** earn status or respect from hard effort. **pay one's last respects** show respect toward a dead person by attending the funeral. **pay off 1** dismiss (workers) with a final payment. **2** *colloq*. yield good results; succeed. **3** pay (a debt) in full. **4** (of a ship) turn to leeward through the movement of the helm. **pay out 1** spend; hand out (money). **2** = *pay back*. **3** let out (a rope). **pay phone** a telephone usu. requiring a coin payment for use. **pay the piper 1** bear a cost or consequence. **2** (**pay the piper and call the tune**) pay for, and therefore have control over, a proceeding. **pay one's respects** make a polite visit. **pay through the nose** *colloq*. pay much more than a fair price. **pay up** pay the full amount, or the full amount of. **put paid to** esp. *Brit. colloq*. **1** deal effectively with (a person). **2** terminate (hopes, etc.). □□ **payee** /payee/ *n*. **payer** *n*. [ME f. OF *paie*, *payer* f. L *pacare* appease f. *pax pacis* peace]

■ *v*. **1** recompense, compensate, remunerate, reward, indemnify, repay, reimburse. **2** repay, refund, reimburse, pay off, pay out, pay up, satisfy, clear, remit, discharge, liquidate, settle, honor, meet; disburse, expend, spend, contribute, lay out, *colloq*. shell out, *sl*. fork over *or* out *or* up, cough up. **3** extend, bestow, transmit, pass on, give, deliver; make, do; express. **4** benefit, profit, avail, help, advantage; (*absol*.) be *or* prove profitable, be *or* prove worthwhile, yield a return, be advantageous, produce results, show a profit, pay off; see also SUCCEED 1b. **5** pay back *or* out, repay, settle (accounts) with, requite; take *or* get revenge on, avenge oneself on, hit *or* strike *or* get back at, even the score with, make a person pay for, punish, chastise, castigate, get even with. **7** (*pay out*) release, loosen, let out, slack *or* slacken off (on). ● *n*. remuneration, consideration, reward, money, wage(s), salary, fee, honorarium, remittance, allowance, stipend, income, take-home pay, *Brit. sl*. screw; payment,

compensation, recompense, defrayment, settlement, payoff, return; gain, profit; takings, take. □ **pay for 3** suffer for, answer for, make amends for, atone for, get one's (just) desserts for, be punished for. **pay in** see DEPOSIT *v*. 2. **pay off 1** see DISMISS 2. **2** see PAY[1] *v*. 4 above. **3** see PAY[1] *v*. 2 above. **pay back** see PAY[1] *v*. 5 above. **pay up** see PAY[1] *v*. 2 above. **put paid to 1** see *dispose of* 1a, c. **2** see END *v*. 1.

pay[2] /pay/ *v.tr*. (*past* and *past part*. **payed**) *Naut*. smear (a ship) with pitch, tar, etc., as waterproofing. [OF *peier* f. L *picare* f. *pix picis* PITCH[2]]

payable /páyəbəl/ *adj*. **1** that must be paid; due (*payable in April*). **2** that may be paid. **3** (of a mine, etc.) profitable.
■ **1** due, owed, owing, outstanding, unpaid, receivable, mature.

payback /páybak/ *n*. **1** a financial return; a reward. **2** the profit from an investment, etc., esp. one equal to the initial outlay. □ **payback period** the length of time required for an investment to pay for itself in terms of profits or savings.

payday /páyday/ *n*. a day on which salary or wages are paid.

payload /páylōd/ *n*. **1** the part of an aircraft's load from which revenue is derived, as paying passengers. **2 a** the explosive warhead carried by an aircraft or rocket. **b** the instruments, etc., carried by a spaceship.

paymaster /páymastər/ *n*. **1** an official who pays troops, workers, etc. **2** a person, organization, etc., to whom another owes duty or loyalty because of payment given. **3** (in full **Paymaster General**) *Brit*. the minister at the head of the Treasury department responsible for payments.

payment /páymənt/ *n*. **1** the act or an instance of paying. **2** an amount paid. **3** reward; recompense. [ME f. OF *paiement* (as PAY[1])]
■ **1** remuneration, compensation, settlement. **2** expenditure, disbursement, distribution, outlay, fee, contribution, charge, expense. **3** see PAY[1] *n*.

paynim /páynim/ *n*. *archaic* **1** a pagan. **2** a non-Christian, esp. a Muslim. [ME f. OF *pai*(*e*)*nime* f. eccl.L *paganismus* heathenism (as PAGAN)]

payoff /páyawf/ *n*. *sl*. **1** an act of payment. **2** a climax. **3** a final reckoning. **4** *colloq*. a bribe; bribery.

payola /payṓlə/ *n*. **1** a bribe offered in return for unofficial promotion of a product, etc., in the media. **2** the practice of such bribery. [PAY[1] + *-ola* as in *Victrola*, make of gramophone]

payroll /páyrōl/ *n*. a list of employees receiving regular pay.

Pb *symb. Chem*. the element lead. [L *plumbum*]

PBS *abbr*. Public Broadcasting Service.

PBX *abbr*. private branch exchange (private telephone switchboard).

PC *abbr*. **1** personal computer. **2** political correctness; politically correct. **3** Peace Corps. **4** (in the UK) police constable.
■ **1** (personal) computer, micro, microcomputer, work station. **4** see *police officer*.

p.c. *abbr*. **1** percent. **2** postcard.

PCB *abbr*. **1** *Computing* printed circuit board. **2** *Chem*. polychlorinated biphenyl, any of several toxic compounds containing two benzene molecules in which hydrogens have been replaced by chlorine atoms, formed as waste in industrial processes.

PCP *n*. **1** *sl*. an illicit hallucinogenic drug, phencyclidine hydrochloride (*p*henyl *cyclohexyl p*iperidine). **2** pneumocystis carinii pneumonia. **3** primary care physician.

pct. *abbr*. percent.

PD *abbr*. Police Department.

Pd *symb. Chem*. the element palladium.

pd. *abbr*. paid.

p.d.q. *abbr. colloq*. pretty damn quick.
■ see FAST[1] *adv*. 1.

PDT *abbr*. Pacific Daylight Time.

PE *abbr*. physical education.

p/e *abbr*. price/earnings (ratio).

pea /pee/ *n*. **1 a** a hardy climbing plant, *Pisum sativum*, with seeds growing in pods and used for food. **b** its seed. **2** any of several similar plants (*sweet pea*; *chickpea*). □ **pea brain** *colloq*. a stupid or dim-witted person. **pea green** bright green. **pea-souper** esp. *Brit. colloq.* a thick fog. [back-form. f. PEASE (taken as pl.: cf. CHERRY)]

■ □ **pea-souper** see FOG¹ *n.* 1.

peace /pees/ *n.* **1 a** quiet; tranquillity (*needs peace to work well*). **b** mental calm; serenity (*peace of mind*). **2 a** (often *attrib.*) freedom from or the cessation of war (*peace talks*). **b** (esp. **Peace**) a treaty of peace between two nations, etc., at war. **3** freedom from civil disorder. **4** *Eccl.* a ritual liturgical greeting. □ **at peace 1** in a state of friendliness. **2** serene. **3** *euphem.* dead. **hold one's peace** keep silent. **keep the peace** prevent, or refrain from, strife. **make one's peace** (often foll. by *with*) reestablish friendly relations. **make peace** bring about peace; reconcile. **the peace** (or *Brit.* **the queen's peace**) peace existing within a realm; civil order. **Peace Corps** a federal governmental organization sending people to work as volunteers in developing countries. **peace dividend** public money that becomes available when defense spending is reduced. **peace offering 1** a propitiatory or conciliatory gift. **2** *Bibl.* an offering presented as a thanksgiving to God. **peace pipe** a tobacco pipe smoked as a token of peace among some Native Americans. [ME f. AF *pes*, OF *pais* f. L *pax pacis*]

■ **1** serenity, tranquillity, calm, calmness, placidity, placidness, peace of mind, quiet, peacefulness, peaceableness, stillness. **2** harmony, accord, harmoniousness, concord, amity, peacefulness, peacetime; cease-fire, armistice, truce. □ **at peace 1** see FRIENDLY *adj.* 2. **2** see SERENE. **3** see DEAD 1.

peaceable /péesəbəl/ *adj.* **1** disposed to peace; unwarlike. **2** free from disturbance; peaceful. □□ **peaceableness** *n.* **peaceably** *adv.* [ME f. OF *peisible*, *plaisible* f. LL *placibilis* pleasing f. L *placēre* please]

■ **1** pacific, inoffensive, dovish, peace-loving, mild, nonviolent, peaceful, nonbelligerent, unwarlike, nonwarring, noncombative, temperate, agreeable, compatible, congenial, genial, friendly, amiable, amicable, cordial, civil. **2** see PEACEFUL 1.

peaceful /péesfool/ *adj.* **1** characterized by peace; tranquil. **2** not violating or infringing peace (*peaceful coexistence*). **3** belonging to a state of peace. □□ **peacefully** *adv.* **peacefulness** *n.*

■ **1** peaceable, serene, placid, calm, quiet, quiescent, gentle, restful, tranquil, untroubled, undisturbed, unruffled. **2** see PEACEABLE 1.

peacemaker /péesmaykər/ *n.* a person who brings about peace. □□ **peacemaking** *n. & adj.*

■ conciliator, pacifier, reconciler, propitiator, placater, pacificator, mediator, arbitrator, intermediator, intermediary, diplomat, appeaser, interceder, intercessor, go-between; referee, umpire, adjudicator; peacemonger.

peacetime /péestim/ *n.* a period when a country is not at war.

■ see PEACE 2.

peach¹ /peech/ *n.* **1 a** a round juicy fruit with downy cream or yellow skin flushed with red. **b** the tree, *Prunus persica*, bearing it. **2** the yellowish pink color of a peach. **3** *colloq.* **a** a person or thing of superlative quality. **b** often *offens.* an attractive young woman. □ **peach bloom** an oriental porcelain glaze of reddish pink, usu. with green markings. **peaches and cream** (of a complexion) creamy skin with downy pink cheeks. **peach Melba** see MELBA. □□ **peachy** *adj.* (**peachier, peachiest**). **peachiness** *n.* [ME f. OF *peche, pesche,* f. med.L *persica* f. L *persicum* (*malum*), lit. Persian apple]

■ **3 a** see BEAUTY 2a. **b** see BEAUTY 3. □ **peaches and cream** see FAIR¹ *adj.* 2. □□ **peachy** see FINE¹ *adj.* 2b.

peach² /peech/ *v.* **1** *intr.* (usu. foll. by *against, on*) *colloq.* turn informer; inform. **2** *tr.* inform against. [ME f. *appeach* f. AF *enpecher*, OF *empechier* IMPEACH]

■ see INFORM 2.

peachick /péechik/ *n.* a young peafowl. [formed as PEACOCK + CHICK¹]

peacoat /péecōt/ = PEA JACKET.

peacock /péekok/ *n.* **1** a male peafowl, having brilliant plum-

age and a tail (with eyelike markings) that can be expanded erect in display like a fan. **2** an ostentatious strutting person. □ **peacock blue** the lustrous greenish blue of a peacock's neck. **peacock butterfly** a butterfly, *Inachis io*, with eyelike markings on its wings. [ME *pecock* f. OE *pēa* f. L *pavo* + COCK¹]

■ **2** see BRAGGART *n.*

peafowl /péefowl/ *n.* **1** a peacock or peahen. **2** a pheasant of the genus *Pavo.*

peahen /péehen/ *n.* a female peafowl.

pea jacket /pée jakit/ *n.* a sailor's short double-breasted woolen overcoat. Also called PEACOAT. [prob. f. Du. *pijjakker* f. *pij* coat of coarse cloth + *jekker* jacket: assim. to JACKET]

peak¹ /peek/ *n. & v.* ● *n.* **1** a projecting usu. pointed part, esp.: **a** the pointed top of a mountain. **b** a mountain with a peak. **c** a stiff brim at the front of a cap. **d** a pointed beard. **e** the narrow part of a ship's hold at the bow or stern. **f** *Naut.* the upper outer corner of a sail extended by a gaff. **2 a** the highest point in a curve (*on the peak of the wave*). **b** the time of greatest success (in a career, etc.). **c** the highest point on a graph, etc. ● *v.intr.* reach the highest value, quality, etc. (*output peaked in September*). **3** = *widow's peak.* □ **peak hour** esp. *Brit.* the time of the most intense traffic, etc. **peak load** the maximum of electric power demand, etc. □□ **peaked** *adj.* **peakiness** *n.* [prob. back-form. f. *peaked* var. of dial. *picked* pointed (PICK²)]

■ *n.* **1 a, b** top, pinnacle, crest, ridge, tor, mountain top, summit; mountain, eminence, elevation, hill. **c** visor, brim. **d** goatee. **2** top, tip, apex, acme, culmination, pinnacle, apogee, zenith, high point, crown, *colloq.* tiptop; extreme, utmost, uttermost, perfection, ne plus ultra, consummation, climax. ● *v.* crest, culminate, (reach a) climax, reach a peak, top (out); come to a head. □ **peak hour** rush hour; prime time.

peak² /peek/ *v.intr.* **1** waste away. **2** (as **peaked** /péekid/ *adj.*) pale; sickly. [16th c.: orig. unkn.]

■ *adj.* **2** peakish, pinched, unhealthy, sickly, ailing, ill, unwell, infirm, unwholesome, pale, pallid, wan, waxen, anemic, pasty, sallow, whey-faced, ashen, washed-out, drained, emaciated, wasted, gaunt, hollow-eyed, haggard, drawn, weak, feeble, *Brit.* peaky.

peal /peel/ *n. & v.* ● *n.* **1 a** the loud ringing of a bell or bells, esp. a series of changes. **b** a set of bells. **2** a loud repeated sound, esp. of thunder, laughter, etc. ● *v.* **1** *intr.* sound forth in a peal. **2** *tr.* utter sonorously. **3** *tr.* ring (bells) in peals. [ME *pele* f. *apele* APPEAL]

■ *n.* ringing, ring, carillon, chime, toll, tolling, tinkle, tinkling, tintinnabulation; changes; clang, clangor, clamor, reverberation; knell; clap, crash, roar, rumble, thunder. ● *v.* ring, toll, chime, clang, reverberate, resonate, resound; knell; boom, crash, roar, roll, rumble, thunder.

pean /peen/ *n. Heraldry* fur represented as sable spotted with or. [16th c.: orig. unkn.]

peanut /péenut/ *n.* **1** a leguminous plant, *Arachis hypogaea*, bearing pods that ripen underground and contain seeds used as food and yielding oil. **2** the seed of this plant. **3** (in *pl.*) *colloq.* a paltry or trivial thing or amount, esp. of money. □ **peanut brittle** a confection made with peanuts and caramelized sugar. **peanut butter** a paste of ground roasted peanuts.

■ **1** earth-nut, monkey nut, groundnut. **3** (*peanuts*) see PITTANCE.

pear /pair/ *n.* **1** a yellowish or brownish green fleshy fruit, tapering toward the stalk. **2** any of various trees of the genus *Pyrus* bearing it, esp. *P. communis.* □ **pear drop** a small candy in the shape of a pear. [OE *pere, peru* ult. f. L *pirum*]

pearl¹ /pərl/ *n. & v.* ● *n.* **1 a** (often *attrib.*) a usu. white or bluish gray hard mass formed within the shell of a pearl oyster or other bivalve mollusk, highly prized as a gem for its luster (*pearl necklace*). **b** an imitation of this. **c** (in *pl.*) a necklace of pearls. **d** = *mother-of-pearl* (cf. *seed pearl*). **2 a** precious thing; the finest example. **3** anything resembling a pearl, e.g., a dewdrop, tear, etc. ● *v.* **1** *tr. poet.* **a** sprinkle with pearly drops. **b** make pearly in color, etc. **2** adorn with pearls. **3** *tr.* reduce (barley, etc.) to small rounded grains. **4** *intr.* fish for pearl oysters. **5** *intr. poet.* form pearl-like drops. □ **cast pearls before swine** offer a treasure to a person unable to appreciate it. **pearl ash** commercial potassium carbonate. **pearl barley** barley reduced to small round grains by grinding. **pearl bulb** *Brit.* a translucent electric light bulb. **pearl button** a button made of mother-of-pearl or an imitation of it. **pearl diver** a person who dives for pearl oysters. **pearl millet** any of several tall cereals of the genus *Pennisetum*. **pearl onion** a very small onion used in pickles. **pearl oyster** any of various marine bivalve mollusks of the genus *Pinctada*, bearing pearls. □□ **pearler** *n.* [ME f. OF *perle* prob. f. L *perna* leg (applied to leg-of-mutton-shaped bivalve)]

■ *n.* **2** gem, treasure, prize, flower, wonder, nonpareil.

pearl[2] /pərl/ *n. Brit.* = PICOT. [var. of PURL[1]]

pearled /pərld/ *adj.* **1** adorned with pearls. **2** formed into pearl-like drops or grains. **3** pearl colored.

pearlescent /pərlésənt/ *adj.* having or producing the appearance of mother-of-pearl.

pearlite /pərlīt/ *n.* a ferrite and cementite mixture occurring in iron and carbon steel.

pearlized /pórlīzd/ *adj.* treated so as to resemble mother-of-pearl.

pearly /pórlee/ *adj. & n.* ● *adj.* (**pearlier, pearliest**) **1** resembling a pearl; lustrous. **2** containing pearls or mother-of-pearl. **3** adorned with pearls. ● *n.* (*pl.* **-ies**) (in *pl.*) *Brit.* **1** pearly kings and queens. **2** a pearly king's or queen's clothes or pearl buttons. □ **Pearly Gates** *colloq.* the gates of Heaven. **pearly king** (or **queen**) *Brit.* a London coster-monger (or his wife) wearing clothes covered with pearl buttons. **pearly nautilus** see NAUTILUS. □□ **pearliness** *n.*

■ *adj.* **1, 2** nacreous, pearl-like, lustrous; mother-of-pearl.

peart /pərt/ *adj. dial.* lively; cheerful. [var. of PERT]

peasant /pézənt/ *n.* **1** esp. *colloq.* a rural person; a rustic. **2 a** a worker on the land, esp. a laborer or farmer. **b** *hist.* a member of an agricultural class dependent on subsistence farming. **3** *derog.* a boorish or unsophisticated person. □□ **peasantry** *n.* (*pl.* **-ies**). **peasanty** *adj.* [ME f. AF *paisant*, OF *païsent*, earlier *paisence* f. *païs* country ult. f. L *pagus* canton]

■ rustic, countryman, countrywoman, farmer, provincial, (farm) worker, (country) bumpkin, bucolic, yokel, boor, peon, fellah, oaf, lout, *archaic* swain, churl, clown, *colloq.* hick, hayseed, rube, *colloq. often derog.* hillbilly, *hist.* muzhik, serf, hind, *offens.* mean white, poor white (trash), cracker.

pease /peez/ *n.pl. archaic* peas. □ **pease pudding** esp. *Brit.* boiled split peas (served esp. with boiled ham). [OE *pise* pea, pl. *pisan*, f. LL *pisa* f. L *pisum* f. Gk *pison*: cf. PEA]

peashooter /peesho͞otər/ *n.* a small tube for blowing dried peas through as a toy.

peat /peet/ *n.* **1** vegetable matter decomposed in water and partly carbonized, used for fuel, in horticulture, etc. **2** a cut piece of this. □□ **peaty** *adj.* [ME f. AL *peta*, perh. f. Celt.: cf. PIECE]

peatbog /peetbawg, -bog/ *n.* a bog composed of peat.

peatmoss /peetmaws, -mos/ *n.* **1** a peatbog. **2** any of various mosses of the genus *Sphagnum*, which grow in damp conditions and form peat as they decay.

peau-de-soie /pṓdəswaá/ *n.* a smooth ribbed satiny fabric of silk or rayon. [F, = skin of silk]

pebble /pébəl/ *n.* **1** a small smooth stone worn by the action of water. **2 a** a type of colorless transparent rock crystal used for eyeglasses. **b** a lens of this. **c** (*attrib.*) *colloq.* (of a lens) very thick and convex. **3** an agate or other gem, esp. when found as a pebble in a stream, etc. **4** an irregular or grainy surface, as on paper, leather, etc. □ **pebble dash** esp. *Brit.* mortar with pebbles in it used as a coating for external walls.

□□ **pebbly** *adj.* [OE *papel-stān* pebble-stone, *þyppelrīpig* pebble-stream, of unkn. orig.]

■ □□ **pebbly** see STONY 1.

pec /pek/ *abbr.* pectoral (muscle).

pecan /pikáɑn, -kán, peékan/ *n.* **1** a pinkish brown smooth nut with an edible kernel. **2** a hickory, *Carya illinoensis*, of the southern US, producing this. [earlier *paccan*, of Algonquian orig.]

peccable /pékəbəl/ *adj.* liable to sin. □□ **peccability** *n.* [F, f. med.L *peccabilis* f. *peccare* sin]

peccadillo /pékədílō/ *n.* (*pl.* **-oes** or **-os**) a trifling offense; a venial sin. [Sp. *pecadillo*, dimin. of *pecado* sin f. L (as PECCANT)]

■ slip, error, lapse, mistake, infraction, violation, misdeed, shortcoming, misstep, blunder, faux pas, indiscretion, gaffe, botch, stumble, fault, petty sin, transgression, trespass, *colloq.* slipup, *sl.* goof.

peccant /pékənt/ *adj.* **1** sinning. **2** faulty. □□ **peccancy** *n.* [F *peccant* or L *peccare* sin]

peccary /pékəree/ *n.* (*pl.* **-ies**) any American wild pig of the family Tayassuidae, esp. *Tayassu tajacu* and *T. pecari*. [Carib *pakira*]

peccavi /pekaávee, -wee, -káyvī/ *int. & n.* ● *int.* expressing guilt. ● *n.* (*pl.* **peccavis**) a confession of guilt. [L, = I have sinned]

peck[1] /pek/ *v. & n.* ● *v.tr.* **1** strike or bite (something) with a beak. **2** kiss (esp. a person's cheek) hastily or perfunctorily. **3 a** make (a hole) by pecking. **b** (foll. by *out, off*) remove or pluck out by pecking. **4** *colloq.* (also *absol.*) eat (food) listlessly; nibble at. **5** mark with short strokes. ● *n.* **1 a** a stroke or bite with a beak. **b** a mark made by this. **2 a** a hasty or perfunctory kiss. **3** *Brit. sl.* food. □ **peck at 1** eat (food) listlessly; nibble. **2** carp at; nag. **3** strike (a thing) repeatedly with a beak. **pecking order** a social hierarchy, orig. as observed among hens. [ME prob. f. MLG *pekken*, of unkn. orig.]

■ *v.* **1** see TAP[2] *v.* 1, 2. **2** see KISS *v.* 1. **4** see *pick at* 1 (PICK[1]). ● *n.* **1** see TAP[2] *v.* 2. **2** see KISS *n.* 1. □ **peck at 1** see *pick at* 1 (PICK[1]). **2** see *pick on* 1 (PICK[1]).

peck[2] /pek/ *n.* **1** a measure of capacity for dry goods, equal to 2 gallons or 8 quarts. **2** a vessel used to contain this amount. □ **a peck of** a large number or amount of (troubles, dirt, etc.). [ME f. AF *pek*, of unkn. orig.]

pecker /pékər/ *n.* **1** a bird that pecks (*woodpecker*). **2** *coarse sl.* the penis. □ **keep your pecker up** *Brit. colloq.* remain cheerful.

peckish /pékish/ *adj. colloq.* **1** esp. *Brit.* hungry. **2** irritable.

■ **1** see HUNGRY 1.

pecorino /pékəreénō/ *n.* (*pl.* **-os**) an Italian cheese made from sheep's milk. [It. f. *pecorino* (adj.) of ewes f. *pecora* sheep]

pecten /péktin/ *n.* (*pl.* **pectens** or **pectines** /-tineez/) *Zool.* **1** a comblike structure of various kinds in animal bodies. **2** any bivalve mollusk of the genus *Pecten*. Also called SCALLOP. □□ **pectinate** /-nət/ *adj.* **pectinated** /-naytid/ *adj.* **pectination** /-tináyshən/ *n.* (all in sense 1). [L *pecten pectinis* comb]

pectin /péktin/ *n. Biochem.* any of various soluble gelatinous polysaccharides found in ripe fruits, etc., and used as a gelling agent in jams and jellies. □□ **pectic** *adj.* [Gk *pēktos* congealed f. *pēgnumi* make solid]

pectoral /péktərəl/ *adj. & n.* ● *adj.* **1** of or relating to the breast or chest; thoracic (*pectoral fin; pectoral muscle*). **2** worn on the chest (*pectoral cross*). ● *n.* **1** (esp. in *pl.*) a pectoral muscle. **2** a pectoral fin. **3** an ornamental breastplate esp. of a Jewish high priest. [ME f. OF f. L *pectorale* (n.), *pectoralis* (adj.) f. *pectus pectoris* breast, chest]

pectose /péktōs/ *n. Biochem.* an insoluble polysaccharide derivative found in unripe fruits and converted into pectin by ripening, heating, etc. [*pectic* (see PECTIN) + -OSE[2]]

peculate /pékyəlayt/ *v.tr. & intr.* embezzle (money). □□ **peculation** /-láyshən/ *n.* **peculator** *n.* [L *peculari* rel. to *peculium*: see PECULIAR]

■ see EMBEZZLE. □□ **peculator** see THIEF.

peculiar /pikyoͻ́lyər/ *adj. & n.* ● *adj.* **1** strange; odd; unusual (*a peculiar flavor; is a little peculiar*). **2 a** (usu. foll. by *to*) belonging exclusively (*a fashion peculiar to the time*). **b** belonging to the individual (*in their own peculiar way*). **3** particular; special (*a point of peculiar interest*). ● *n.* **1** a peculiar property, privilege, etc. **2** esp. *Brit.* a parish or church exempt from the jurisdiction of the diocese in which it lies. [ME f. L *peculiaris* of private property f. *peculium* f. *pecu* cattle]

■ *adj.* **1** odd, curious, strange, queer, bizarre, weird, unusual, abnormal, anomalous, aberrant, deviant, eccentric, uncommon, outlandish, exceptional, extraordinary, out of the ordinary, offbeat, unorthodox, atypical, idiosyncratic, unconventional, out of the way, quaint, unique, singular, *sui generis*, distinct, special, particular, quirky, funny, freakish, freaky, far-out, *colloq.* way-out, *Brit. colloq.* rum. **2 a** (*peculiar to*) typical of, characteristic of, characterized by, natural to, symptomatic of, appropriate to or for, distinctive of, restricted to, specific to, indicative of, denotative of, limited to, individual to, personal to, special to, unique to; local to, native to, indigenous to. **3** see PARTICULAR *adj.* 1.

peculiarity /pikyŏŏleeáritee/ *n.* (*pl.* -ies) **1 a** idiosyncrasy; oddity. **b** an instance of this. **2** a characteristic or habit (*meanness is his peculiarity*). **3** the state of being peculiar.

■ **1** idiosyncrasy, oddity, unusualness, eccentricity, abnormality, irregularity, quirk, kink. **2** feature, characteristic, habit, property, quality, trait, attribute, earmark, hallmark, mark, particularity, singularity, speciality, specialty.

peculiarly /pikyŏŏlyərlee/ *adv.* **1** more than usually; especially (*peculiarly annoying*). **2** oddly. **3** as regards oneself alone; individually (*does not affect him peculiarly*).

■ **1** see ESPECIALLY.

pecuniary /pikyŏŏnee-eree/ *adj.* **1** of, concerning, or consisting of, money (*pecuniary aid*; *pecuniary considerations*). **2** (of an offense) entailing a money penalty or fine. □□ **pecuniarily** *adv.* [L *pecuniarius* f. *pecunia* money f. *pecu* cattle]

■ **1** see FINANCIAL 1.

pedagogue /pédəgog, -gawg/ *n.* a schoolmaster or teacher, esp. a pedantic one. □□ **pedagogic** /-gójik, -gójik/ *adj.* **pedagogical** *adj.* **pedagogically** *adv.* **pedagogism** *n.* (also **pedagoguism**). [ME f. L *paedagogus* f. Gk *paidagōgos* f. *pais paidos* boy + *agōgos* guide]

■ see TEACHER. □□ **pedagogic** see *pedantic* (PEDANT). **pedagogical** see *educational* (EDUCATION).

pedagogy /pédəgŏjee, -gojee/ *n.* the science of teaching. □□ **pedagogics** /-gójiks, -gójiks/ *n.* [F *pédagogie* f. Gk *paidagōgia* (as PEDAGOGUE)]

pedal[1] /péd'l/ *n.* & *v.* ● *n.* **1** any of several types of foot-operated levers or controls for mechanisms, esp.: **a** either of a pair of levers for transmitting power to a bicycle or tricycle wheel, etc. **b** any of the foot-operated controls in a motor vehicle. **c** any of the foot-operated keys of an organ used for playing notes, or for drawing out several stops at once, etc. **d** each of the foot-levers on a piano, etc., for making the tone fuller or softer. **e** each of the foot-levers on a harp for altering the pitch of the strings. **2** (in full **pedal point**) a note sustained in one part, usu. the bass, through successive harmonies, some of which are independent of it. ● *v.* (**pedaled** or **pedalled**, **pedaling** or **pedalling**) **1** *intr.* operate a cycle, organ, etc., by using the pedals. **2** *tr.* work (a bicycle, etc.) with the pedals. □ **pedal pushers** women's and girls' calf-length pants. [F *pédale* f. It. *pedale* f. L (as PEDAL[2])]

pedal[2] /péd'l, pee-/ *adj. Zool.* of the foot or feet (esp. of a mollusk). [L *pedalis* f. *pes pedis* foot]

pedalo /péd'lō/ *n. Brit.* (*pl.* -os) a pedal-operated pleasure boat.

pedant /péd'nt/ *n.* **1** a person who insists on strict adherence to formal rules or literal meaning at the expense of a wider view. **2** a person who rates academic learning or technical knowledge above everything. **3** a person who is obsessed by a theory; a doctrinaire. □□ **pedantic** /pidántik/ *adj.* **pedan-**

tically *adv.* **pedantize** *v.intr.* & *tr.* **pedantry** *n.* (*pl.* -ies). [F *pédant* f. It. *pedante*: app. formed as PEDAGOGUE]

■ **1** see PURIST. □□ **pedantic** didactic, doctrinaire, donnish, pedantical, professorial, bookish, sententious, pompous, stuffy, stilted, stiff, dry, *archaic or derog.* pedagogic, *colloq.* preachy; perfectionist, scrupulous, overscrupulous, finicky, finicking, finical, fussy, punctilious, fastidious, meticulous, exact, hairsplitting, quibbling, *colloq.* nit picking. **pedantry** see LEGALISM.

pedate /pédayt/ *adj.* **1** *Zool.* having feet. **2** *Bot.* (of a leaf) having divisions like toes or a bird's claws. [L *pedatus* f. *pes pedis* foot]

peddle /péd'l/ *v.* **1** *tr.* **a** sell (goods), esp. in small quantities, as a peddler. **b** advocate or promote (ideas, a philosophy, a way of life, etc.). **2** *tr.* sell (drugs) illegally. **3** *intr.* engage in selling, esp. as a peddler. [back-form. f. PEDDLER]

■ sell, hawk, market, vend, huckster, *colloq.* push, *Brit. sl.* flog.

peddler /pédlər/ *n.* **1** a traveling seller of small items esp. carried in a pack, etc. **2** (usu. foll. by *of*) a dealer in gossip, influence, etc. **3** a person who sells drugs illegally. □□ **peddlery** *n.* [ME *pedlere* alt. of *pedder* f. *ped* pannier, of unkn. orig.]

■ **1** hawker, (door-to-door) salesman, cheapjack, vendor, huckster, seller, *Brit.* pedlar, *colloq.* drummer, *hist.* chapman. **3** dealer, pusher.

pederast /pédərast/ *n.* a man who performs pederasty.

pederasty /pédərastee/ *n.* anal intercourse esp. between a man and a boy. [mod.L *paederastia* f. Gk *paiderastia* f. *pais paidos* boy + *erastēs* lover]

pedestal /pédistəl/ *n.* & *v.* ● *n.* **1** a base supporting a column or pillar. **2** the stone, etc., base of a statue, etc. **3** either of the two supports of a desk or table, usu. containing drawers. ● *v.tr.* (**pedestaled**, **pedestaling** or **pedestalled**, **pedestalling**) set or support on a pedestal. □ **pedestal table** a table with a single central support. **put** (or **set**) **on a pedestal** regard as highly admirable, important, etc.; venerate. [F *piédestal* f. It. *piedestallo* f. *piè* foot f. L *pes pedis* + *di* of + *stallo* STALL[1]]

■ *n.* **1, 2** foundation, base, platform, stand, substructure, mounting, pier, foot, leg, support, plinth, dado, *Archit.* socle. □ **put on a pedestal** glorify, exalt, worship, deify, revere, idolize, dignify, venerate, apotheosize, ennoble, elevate, raise.

pedestrian /pidéstreeən/ *n.* & *adj.* ● *n.* (often *attrib.*) a person who is walking, esp. in a town (*pedestrian crossing*). ● *adj.* prosaic; dull; uninspired. □ **pedestrian crossing** a specified part of a road or street where pedestrians have right of way to cross. □□ **pedestrianism** *n.* **pedestrianize** *v.tr.* & *intr.* **pedestrianization** *n.* [F *pédestre* or L *pedester -tris*]

■ *n.* walker, stroller, rambler, footslogger. ● *adj.* boring, dull, banal, tiresome, commonplace, mundane, tedious, unimaginative, uninteresting, monotonous, run-of-the-mill, humdrum, stock, prosaic, insipid, dry, flat, jejune, colorless, dreary, pale, ordinary, hackneyed, trite, vapid, stale, uninspired, uninspiring, spiritless, lifeless, dead.

pediatrics /peedeeátriks/ *n.pl.* (treated as *sing.*) the branch of medicine dealing with children and their diseases. □□ **pediatric** *adj.* **pediatrician** /-deeətríshən/ *n.* [PEDO- + Gk *iatros* physician]

pedicab /pédeekab/ *n.* a pedal-operated rickshaw.

pedicel /pédisəl/ *n.* (also **pedicle** /pédikəl/) **1** a small (esp. subordinate) stalk-like structure in a plant or animal (cf. PEDUNCLE). **2** *Surgery* part of a graft left temporarily attached to its original site. □□ **pedicellate** /-sélət, -ayt/ *adj.* **pediculate** /pidíkyələt, -layt/ *adj.* [mod.L *pedicellus* & L *pediculus* dimin. of *pes pedis* foot]

/.../ pronunciation	● part of speech
□ phrases, idioms, and compounds	
□□ derivatives	■ synonym section
cross-references appear in SMALL CAPITALS or *italics*	

■ **1** see STEM¹ *n.* 2.

pedicular /pidíkyələr/ *adj.* (also **pediculous** /-ləs/) infested with lice. □□ **pediculosis** /-lṓsis/ *n.* [L *pedicularis, -losus* f. *pediculus* louse]

■ see LOUSY 1.

pedicure /pédikyŏor/ *n. & v.* ● *n.* **1** the care or treatment of the feet, esp. of the toenails. **2** a person practicing this, esp. professionally. ● *v.tr.* treat (the feet) by removing corns, etc. [F *pédicure* f. L *pes pedis* foot + *curare*: see CURE]

pedigree /pédigree/ *n.* **1** (often *attrib.*) a recorded line of descent of a person or esp. a pure-bred domestic or pet animal. **2** the derivation of a word. **3** a genealogical table. **4** *Brit. colloq.* the 'life history' of a person, thing, idea, etc. □□ **pedigreed** *adj.* [ME *pedegru*, etc. f. AF f. OF *pie de grue* (unrecorded) crane's foot, a mark denoting succession in pedigrees]

■ **1** (line of) descent, ancestry, genealogy, blood, bloodline, line, extraction, lineage, stock, heritage, family, derivation, birth, parentage, strain, roots. **2** etymology. **3** family tree.

pediment /pédimənt/ *n.* **1 a** the triangular front part of a building in Grecian style, surmounting esp. a portico of columns. **b** a similar part of a building in Roman or Renaissance style. **2** *Geol.* a broad flattish rock surface at the foot of a mountain slope. □□ **pedimental** /-mént'l/ *adj.* **pedimented** *adj.* [earlier *pedament, periment*, perh. corrupt. of PYRAMID]

pedlar var. of PEDDLER.

pedo- *comb. form* child. [Gk *paid- pais* = child]

pedology /pidóləjee/ *n.* the scientific study of soil, esp. its formation, nature, and classification. □□ **pedological** /péd-əlójikəl/ *adj.* **pedologist** *n.* [Russ. *pedologiya* f. Gk *pedon* ground]

pedometer /pidómitər/ *n.* an instrument for estimating the distance traveled on foot by recording the number of steps taken. [F *pédomètre* f. L *pes pedis* foot]

pedophile /péedəfíl, péd-/ *n.* a person who displays pedophilia.

pedophilia /péedəfíleeə, pédə-/ *n.* sexual desire directed toward children.

peduncle /pedúngkəl, péedung-/ *n.* **1** *Bot.* the stalk of a flower, fruit, or cluster, esp. a main stalk bearing a solitary flower or subordinate stalks (cf. PEDICEL). **2** *Zool.* a stalklike projection in an animal body. □□ **peduncular** /-kyələr/ *adj.* **pedunculate** /-kyələt/ *adj.* [mod.L *pedunculus* f. L *pes pedis* foot: see -UNCLE]

■ **1** see STEM¹ *n.* 2.

pee /pee/ *v. & n. colloq.* or *coarse* ● *v.* (**pees, peed**) **1** *intr.* urinate. **2** *tr.* pass (urine, blood, etc.) from the bladder. ● *n.* **1** urination. **2** urine. [initial letter of PISS]

■ *v.* **1** see URINATE. ● *n.* **2** see PIDDLE *n.*

peek /peek/ *v. & n.* ● *v.intr.* (usu. foll. by *in, out, at*) look quickly or slyly; peep. ● *n.* a quick or sly look. [ME *pike, pyke*, of unkn. orig.]

■ *v.* see PEEP¹ *v.* ● *n.* see PEEP¹ *n.*

peekaboo /péekəbŏo/ *adj. & n.* ● *adj.* **1** (of a garment, etc.) transparent or having a pattern of small holes. **2** (of a hairstyle) concealing one eye with the bangs or a wave. ● *n.* game of hiding and suddenly reappearing, played with a young child. [PEEK + BOO]

■ *adj.* **1** see *see-through.*

peel¹ /peel/ *v. & n.* ● *v.* **1** *tr.* **a** strip the skin, rind, bark, wrapping, etc., from (a fruit, vegetable, tree, etc.). **b** (usu. foll. by *off*) strip (skin, peel, wrapping, etc.) from a fruit, etc. **2** *intr.* **a** (of a tree, an animal's or person's body, a painted surface, etc.) become bare of bark, skin, paint, etc. **b** (often foll. by *off*) (of bark, a person's skin, paint, etc.) flake off. **3** *intr.* (often foll. by *off*) *colloq.* (of a person) strip for exercise, etc. **4** *tr. Croquet* send (another player's ball) through a wicket. ● *n.* the outer covering of a fruit, vegetable, shrimp, etc.; rind. □ **peel off 1** veer away and detach oneself from a group of marchers, a formation of aircraft, etc. **2** *colloq.* strip off one's clothes. □□ **peeler** *n.* (in sense 1 of *v.*). [earlier *pill, pele* (orig. = plunder) f. ME *pilien*, etc. f. OE *pilian* (unrecorded) f. L *pilare* f. *pilus* hair]

■ *v.* **1, 2** skin, strip (off), pare, flay, flake (off), descale, decorticate, excoriate; hull, bark, scale, shuck; *Med.* desquamate. **3** undress, disrobe, *colloq.* peel off; see also STRIP¹ *v.* 2. ● *n.* skin, rind, coating, peeling. □ **peel off 1** part (company), separate, veer *or* go away, split (up), deviate. **2** see STRIP¹ *v.* 2.

peel² /peel/ *n.* a shovel, esp. a baker's shovel for bringing loaves, etc., into or out of an oven. [ME & OF *pele* f. L *pala*, rel. to *pangere* fix]

peel³ /peel/ *n.* (also **pele**) *hist.* a small square tower built in the 16th c. in the border counties of England and Scotland for defense against raids. [ME *pel* stake, palisade, f. AF & OF *pel* f. L *palus* stake: cf. PALE²]

peeler /péelər/ *n. Brit. archaic sl.* or *dial.* a policeman. [Sir Robert *Peel*, Engl. statesman d. 1850]

peeling /péeling/ *n.* a strip of the outer skin of a vegetable, fruit, etc. (*potato peelings*).

■ peel, skin, rind.

peen /peen/ *n. & v.* ● *n.* the wedge-shaped or thin or curved end of a hammer head (opp. FACE *n.* 5a). ● *v.tr.* **1** hammer with a peen. **2** treat (sheet metal) with a stream of metal shot in order to shape it. [17th c.: also *pane*, app. f. F *panne* f. Du. *pen* f. L *pinna* point]

peep¹ /peep/ *v. & n.* ● *v.intr.* **1** (usu. foll. by *at, in, out, into*) look through a narrow opening; look furtively. **2** (usu. foll. by *out*) **a** (of daylight, a flower beginning to bloom, etc.) come slowly into view; emerge. **b** (of a quality, etc.) show itself unconsciously. ● *n.* **1** a furtive or peering glance. **2** the first appearance (*at peep of day*). □ **peeping Tom** a furtive voyeur. **peep show 1** a small exhibition of pictures, etc., viewed through a lens or hole set into a box, etc. **2** an erotic movie or picture viewed through a usu. coin-operated machine. **peep sight** the aperture backsight of some rifles. [ME: cf. PEEK, PEER¹]

■ *v.* **1** peer, peek, glimpse, look, squint, *Sc.* keek, *sl.* take *or* have a gander, *Brit. sl.* take *or* have a dekko. ● *n.* **1** look, glimpse, peek, glance, squint, *Sc.* keek, *colloq.* look-see, *sl.* take *or* have a dekko, *Brit. sl.* dekko.

peep² /peep/ *v. & n.* ● *v.intr.* make a shrill feeble sound as of young birds, mice, etc.; squeak; chirp. ● *n.* **1** such a sound; a cheep. **2** the slightest sound or utterance, esp. of protest, etc. [imit.: cf. CHEEP]

■ *v.* chirp, tweet, cheep, squeak, twitter, pipe, chirrup, chirr. ● *n.* **1** chirp, tweet, cheep, squeak, twitter, pipe, chirrup, chirr. **2** sound, complaint, outcry, protest, protestation, grumble, murmur.

peeper /péepər/ *n.* **1** a person who peeps. **2** *colloq.* an eye. **3** *NE US* any of several species of frogs with a high peeping cry.

■ **1** peeping Tom, voyeur; see also BUSYBODY 1.

peephole /péephōl/ *n.* a tiny hole in a solid door, fence, etc., to look through.

peepul /péepəl/ *n.* (also **pipal**) = BO-TREE. [Hindi *pīpal* f. Skr. *pippala*]

peer¹ /peer/ *v.intr.* **1** (usu. foll. by *into, at*, etc.) look keenly or with difficulty (*peered into the fog*). **2** appear; peep out. **3** *archaic* come into view. [var. of *pire*, LG *pīren*; perh. partly f. APPEAR]

■ **1** peep, peek, squint, look; see also EYE *v.* **2** peep through *or* out, break through, show, emerge; see also APPEAR 1, 2.

peer² /peer/ *n. & v.* ● *n.* **1** a person who is equal in ability, standing, rank, or value; a contemporary (*tried by a jury of his peers*). **2 a** (*fem.* **peeress**) a member of one of the degrees of the nobility in Britain, i.e. a duke, marquis, earl, viscount, or baron. **b** a noble of any country. ● *v.intr. & tr.* (usu. foll. by *with*) rank or cause to rank equally. □ **peer group** a group of people of the same age, status, interests, etc. **peer of the realm** (or **the United Kingdom**) any of the class of peers (in the UK) whose adult members may all sit in the House of Lords. □□ **peerless** *adj.* [ME f. AF & OF *pe(e)r, perer* f. LL *pariare* f. L *par* equal]

■ *n.* **1** equal, compeer, *archaic or literary* coequal; like, match; confrère, associate, colleague. **2** noble, nobleman, noblewoman, lord, lady, aristocrat; duke, duchess, marquess, marquis, marchioness, earl, countess, viscount, viscountess, baron, baroness; count; life peer. □□ **peerless** without equal, unequaled, matchless, unmatched, unrivaled, unique, incomparable, beyond compare, unparalleled, nonpareil, inimitable, unsurpassed, superior, superb, excellent, supreme, superlative, finest, best, sovereign, consummate, preeminent, paramount.

peerage /peèrij/ *n.* **1** peers as a class; the nobility. **2** the rank of peer or peeress (*was given a life peerage*). **3** a book containing a list of peers with their genealogy, etc.
■ **1** nobility, aristocracy.

peeve /peev/ *v. & n. colloq.* ● *v.tr.* (usu. as **peeved** *adj.*) annoy; vex; irritate. ● *n.* **1** a cause of annoyance. **2** vexation. [back-form. f. PEEVISH]
■ *v.* see IRRITATE 1; (**peeved**) see DISGRUNTLED.

peevish /peèvish/ *adj.* querulous; irritable. □□ **peevishly** *adv.* **peevishness** *n.* [ME, = foolish, mad, spiteful, etc., of unkn. orig.]
■ irritable, testy, touchy, fretful, ill-humored, waspish, petulant, crabbed, churlish, querulous, short-tempered, ill-natured, tetchy, cross, bad-tempered, ill-tempered, faultfinding, captious, carping, caviling, crusty, curmudgeonly, crotchety, cantankerous, grumpy, pettish, acrimonious, splenetic, bilious, cranky, *colloq.* grumpish.

peewit /peèwit/ *n.* (also **pewit**) **1** a lapwing. **2** its cry. [imit.]

peg /peg/ *n. & v.* ● *n.* **1 a** a usu. cylindrical pin or bolt of wood or metal, often tapered at one end, and used for holding esp. two things together. **b** such a peg attached to a wall, etc., and used for hanging garments, etc., on. **c** a peg driven into the ground and attached to a rope for holding up a tent. **d** a bung for stoppering a cask, etc. **e** each of several pegs used to tighten or loosen the strings of a violin, etc. **f** a small peg, matchstick, etc., stuck into holes in a board for calculating the scores at cribbage. **2** *Brit.* = clothespin. **3** *Brit.* a measure of spirits or wine. ● *v.tr.* (**pegged**, **pegging**) **1** (usu. foll. by *down, in, out,* etc.) fix (a thing) with a peg. **2** *Econ.* **a** stabilize (prices, wages, exchange rates, etc.). **b** prevent the price of (stock, etc.) from falling or rising by freely buying or selling at a given price. **3** mark (the score) with pegs on a cribbage board. **4** throw. □ **off the peg** esp. *Brit.* (of clothes) ready-made. **peg away** (often foll. by *at*) work consistently and esp. for a long period. **peg down** restrict (a person, etc.) to rules, a commitment, etc. **peg leg 1** an artificial leg. **2** a person with an artificial leg. **peg on** = *peg away*. **peg out 1** mark the boundaries of (land, etc.). **2** score the winning point at cribbage. **3** *Croquet* hit the peg with the ball as the final stroke in a game. **4** *Brit. sl.* die. **a peg to hang an idea**, etc., **on** a suitable occasion or pretext, etc., for it. **a round** (or **square**) **peg in a square** (or **round**) **hole** a misfit. **take a person down a peg or two** humble a person. [ME, prob. of LG or Du. orig.: cf. MDu. *pegge,* Du. dial. *peg,* LG *pigge*]
■ *n.* **1, 2** pin, dowel, rod, stick, bolt; thole(pin); clothespin, hook. ● *v.* **1** fasten, secure, make fast, fix, attach, pin. **2** stabilize, fix, attach, pin, set (by), control (by), limit (by), restrict, confine, freeze, bind, regulate, govern. **4** toss, throw, shy, flip, sling, cast. □ **off the peg** ready-made, ready-to-wear, stock. **peg away, peg on** (*peg away* or *on at*) work (away) at, persevere at or with, apply oneself to, persist at or with, keep at, stick to or with or at, stay with or at, carry on with or at, hammer (away) at, *colloq.* plug (away) at, beaver (away) at. **peg down** see TIE *v.* 3. **a round** (or **square**) **peg in a square** (or **round**) **hole** see MISFIT. **take a person down a peg or two** humble, diminish, lower, subdue, downgrade, mortify, humiliate, put down, abase, debase, devalue.

pegboard /pégbawrd/ *n.* a board having a regular pattern of small holes for pegs, used for commercial displays, games, etc.

pegmatite /pégmǝtit/ *n.* a coarsely crystalline type of granite. [Gk *pēgma -atos* thing joined together f. *pēgnumi* fasten]

peg top /pég top/ *n.* a pear-shaped spinning top with a metal

pin or peg forming the point, spun by the rapid uncoiling of a string wound around it.

Pehlevi var. of PAHLAVI.

PEI *abbr.* Prince Edward Island.

peignoir /paynwaár, pen-, páynwaar, pén-/ *n.* a woman's loose dressing gown. [F f. *peigner* to comb]
■ see WRAPPER 4.

pejorative /pijáwrǝtiv, -jór-, péjǝra-, peé-/ *adj. & n.* ● *adj.* (of a word, an expression, etc.) depreciatory. ● *n.* a depreciatory word. □□ **pejoratively** *adv.* [F *péjoratif -ive* f. LL *pejorare* make worse (*pejor*)]

pekan /pékǝn/ = FISHER 1.

peke /peek/ *n. colloq.* a Pekingese dog. [abbr.]

Pekingese /peékineéz, -eés/ *n. & adj.* (also **Pekinese**) ● *n.* (*pl.* same) **1 a** a lapdog of a short-legged breed with long hair and a snub nose. **b** this breed. **2** a citizen of Peking (Beijing) in China. **3** the form of the Chinese language used in Beijing. ● *adj.* of or concerning Beijing or its language or citizens.

pekoe /peéko/ *n.* a superior kind of black tea. [Chin. dial. *pek-ho* f. *pek* white + *ho* down, leaves being picked young with down on them]

pelage /pélij/ *n.* the fur, hair, wool, etc., of a mammal. [F f. *poil* hair]

Pelagian /piláyjeeǝn/ *adj. & n.* ● *adj.* of or concerning the monk Pelagius (4th–5th c.) or his theory denying the doctrine of original sin. ● *n.* a follower of Pelagius. □□ **Pelagianism** *n.* [eccl.L *Pelagianus* f. *Pelagius*]

pelagian /piláyjeeǝn/ *adj. & n.* ● *adj.* inhabiting the open sea. ● *n.* an inhabitant of the open sea. [L *pelagius* f. Gk *pelagios* of the sea (*pelagos*)]

pelagic /piláyik/ *adj.* **1** of or performed on the open sea (*pelagic whaling*). **2** (of marine life) belonging to the upper layers of the open sea. [L *pelagicus* f. Gk *pelagikos* (as PELAGIAN)]
■ **1** see MARINE *adj.* 1.

pelargonium /pélǝrgōneeǝm/ *n.* any plant of the genus *Pelargonium,* with red, pink, or white flowers and fragrant leaves. Also called GERANIUM. [mod.L f. Gk *pelargos* stork: cf. GERANIUM]

pele var. of PEEL[3].

pelf /pelf/ *n. derog.* or *joc.* money; wealth. [ME f. ONF f. OF *pelfre, peufre* spoils, of unkn. orig.: cf. PILFER]
■ see MONEY 1.

pelham /pélǝm/ *n.* a horse's bit combining a curb and a snaffle. [the surname *Pelham*]

pelican /pélikǝn/ *n.* any large gregarious waterfowl of the family Pelecanidae with a large bill and a pouch in the throat for storing fish. □ **pelican crossing** (in the UK) a pedestrian crossing with traffic lights operated by pedestrians. **pelican hook** a hinged hook with a sliding ring by which it can be quickly secured or released. [OE *pellican* & OF *pelican* f. LL *pelicanus* f. Gk *pelekan* prob. f. *pelekus* axe, with ref. to its bill]

pelisse /pileés/ *n. hist.* **1** a woman's cloak with armholes or sleeves, reaching to the ankles. **2** a fur-lined cloak, esp. as part of a hussar's uniform. [F f. med.L *pellicia* (*vestis*) (garment) of fur f. *pellis* skin]
■ see MANTLE *n.* 1.

pelite /peélit/ *n.* a rock composed of claylike sediment. [Gk *pēlos* clay, mud]

pellagra /pilágrǝ, -láygrǝ, -laá-/ *n.* a disease caused by deficiency of nicotinic acid, characterized by cracking of the skin and often resulting in insanity. □□ **pellagrous** *adj.* [It. f. *pelle* skin, after PODAGRA]

pellet /pélit/ *n. & v.* ● *n.* **1** a small compressed ball of paper, bread, etc. **2** a pill. **3 a** a small mass of bones, feathers, etc., regurgitated by a bird of prey. **b** a small hard piece of animal, usu. rodent, excreta. **4 a** a piece of small shot. **b** an imitation

---

/.../ **pronunciation**	● **part of speech**
□ **phrases, idioms, and compounds**	
□□ **derivatives**	■ **synonym section**
cross-references appear in SMALL CAPITALS or *italics*	

bullet for a toy gun. • *v.tr.* (**pelleted, pelleting**) **1** make into a pellet or pellets. **2** hit with (esp. paper) pellets. □□ **pelletize** *v.tr.* [ME f. OF *pelote* f. L *pila* ball]

▪ *n.* **2** see PILL 1a. **4** see SHOT¹ 3.

pellicle /pélikəl/ *n.* a thin skin, membrane, or film. □□ **pellicular** /-líkyōōlər/ *adj.* [F *pellicule* f. L *pellicula*, dimin. of *pellis* skin]

▪ see SKIN *n.* 4.

pellitory /pélitawree/ *n.* any of several wild plants, esp.: **1** (in full **pellitory of Spain**) a composite plant, *Anacyclus pyrethrum*, with a pungent flavored root, used as a local irritant, etc. **2** (in full **pellitory of the wall**) a low bushy plant, *Parietaria judaica*, with greenish flowers growing on or at the foot of walls. [(sense 1) alt. f. ME f. OF *peletre, peretre* f. L *pyrethrum* f. Gk *purethron* feverfew: (sense 2) ult. f. OF *paritaire* f. LL *parietaria* f. L *paries -etis* wall]

pell-mell /pélmél/ *adv., adj., & n.* • *adv.* **1** headlong; recklessly (*rushed pell-mell out of the room*). **2** in disorder or confusion (*stuffed the papers together pell-mell*). • *adj.* confused; tumultuous. • *n.* confusion; a mixture. [F *pêle-mêle*, OF *pesle mesle, mesle pesle*, etc., redupl. of *mesle* f. *mesler* mix]

▪ *adv.* **1** headlong, helter-skelter, recklessly, heedlessly, slam-bang, slapdash, feverishly, incautiously, wildly, impulsively, impetuously, hastily, hurriedly, hell for leather, precipitately, *Brit.* slap-bang. **2** confusedly, chaotically, in disorder; see also HELTER-SKELTER *adv.*
• *adj.* helter-skelter, feverish, confused, disordered, disorderly, disorganized, slapdash, wild, mad, chaotic, tumultuous, panicky, impulsive, reckless, precipitate, impetuous, hasty, hurried; see also TOPSY-TURVY *adj.* 2.
• *n.* confusion, disorder, chaos, tumult, pandemonium, turmoil, mêlée, uproar, furor, commotion, bedlam, brouhaha, hubbub, excitement; see also MIXTURE 2.

pellucid /pilōōsid/ *adj.* **1** (of water, light, etc.) transparent; clear. **2** (of style, speech, etc.) not confused; clear. **3** mentally clear. □□ **pellucidity** /-síditee/ *n.* **pellucidly** *adv.* [L *pellucidus* f. *perlucēre* (as PER-, *lucēre* shine)]

▪ **1** see TRANSPARENT 1. **2, 3** see CLEAR *adj.* 6.
□□ **pellucidity** see CLARITY.

pelmet /pélmit/ *n.* a narrow border of cloth, wood, etc., above esp. a window, concealing the curtain rail. [prob. f. F PALMETTE]

▪ valance, swag, lambrequin.

pelorus /piláwrəs/ *n.* a sighting device like a ship's compass for taking bearings. [perh. f. *Pelorus*, reputed name of Hannibal's pilot]

pelota /pilōtə/ *n.* **1** a Basque or Spanish game similar to jai alai played in a walled court with a ball and basket-like rackets attached to the hand. **2** the ball used in jai alai. [Sp., = ball, augment. of *pella* f. L *pila*]

pelt¹ /pelt/ *v. & n.* • *v.* **1** *tr.* (usu. foll. by *with*) **a** hurl many small missiles at. **b** strike repeatedly with missiles. **c** assail (a person, etc.) with insults, abuse, etc. **2** *intr.* (usu. foll. by *down*) (of rain, etc.) fall quickly and torrentially. **3** *intr.* run fast. **4** *intr.* (often foll. by *at*) fire repeatedly. • *n.* the act or an instance of pelting. □ **at full pelt** esp. *Brit.* as fast as possible. [16th c.: orig. unkn.]

▪ *v.* **1** bombard, shower, bomb, pepper, strafe, batter, shell, assail, assault, attack, pummel, pommel, belabor, pound. **2** (*pelt down*) come down in sheets *or* buckets, sheet down, pour (down), rain cats and dogs. **3** hurry, rush, run, shoot, scurry, *colloq.* scoot; see also DASH *v.* 1. • *n.* stroke, blow, hit, smack, slap, bang, thump, *colloq.* whack, thwack, *sl.* wallop, belt, whop; see also DASH *n.* 1. □ **at full pelt** see BREAKNECK.

pelt² /pelt/ *n.* **1** the undressed skin of a fur-bearing mammal. **2** the skin of a sheep, goat, etc., with short wool, or stripped ready for tanning. **3** *joc.* the human skin. □□ **peltry** *n.* [ME f. obs. *pellet* skin, dimin. of *pel* f. AF *pell*, OF *pel*, or back-form. f. *peltry*, AF *pelterie*, OF *peleterie* f. *peletier* furrier, ult. f. L *pellis* skin]

▪ **1, 2** skin, hide, coat, fur, fleece.

pelta /péltə/ *n.* (*pl.* **peltae** /-tee/) **1** a small light shield used by the ancient Greeks, Romans, etc. **2** *Bot.* a shieldlike structure. □□ **peltate** *adj.* [L f. Gk *peltē*]

pelvic /pélvik/ *adj.* of or relating to the pelvis. □ **pelvic girdle** the bony or cartilaginous structure in vertebrates to which the posterior limbs are attached.

pelvis /pélvis/ *n.* (*pl.* **pelvises** or **pelves** /-veez/) **1** a basin-shaped cavity at the lower end of the torso of most vertebrates, formed from the innominate bones with the sacrum and other vertebrae. **2** the basin-like cavity of the kidney. [L, = basin]

pemmican /pémikən/ *n.* **1** a cake of dried pounded meat mixed with melted fat, orig. made by Native Americans. **2** beef so treated and flavored with dried fruit, etc., for use by Arctic travelers, etc. [Cree *pimecan* f. *pime* fat]

pemphigus /pémfigəs/ *n. Med.* the formation of watery blisters or eruptions on the skin. □□ **pemphigoid** *adj.* **pemphigous** *adj.* [mod.L f. Gk *pemphix -igos* bubble]

PEN *abbr.* International Association of Poets, Playwrights, Editors, Essayists, and Novelists.

Pen. *abbr.* Peninsula.

pen¹ /pen/ *n. & v.* • *n.* **1** an instrument for writing or drawing with ink, orig. consisting of a shaft with a sharpened quill or metal nib, now more widely applied. **2 a** (usu. prec. by *the*) the occupation of writing. **b** a style of writing. **3** *Zool.* the internal feather-shaped cartilaginous shell of certain cuttlefish, esp. squid. • *v.tr.* (**penned, penning**) **1** write. **2** compose and write. □ **pen and ink** *n.* **1** the instruments of writing. **2** writing. **pen-and-ink** *adj.* drawn or written with ink. **pen-feather** a quill-feather of a bird's wing. **pen-friend** *Brit.* = *pen pal.* **pen name** a literary pseudonym. **pen pal** *colloq.* a friend communicated with by letter only. **put pen to paper** begin writing. [ME f. OF *penne* f. L *penna* feather]

▪ *n.* **1** fountain pen, ballpoint (pen), felt-tip, quill. • *v.* **1** write (down *or* out), jot down, make a note of, note, put on paper, commit to paper, commit to writing, put in writing, scribble, scrawl, scratch, *formal or joc.* indite. **2** draft, compose; see *draw up* 1. □ **pen and ink** (*n.*) **2** see WRITING 2.

pen² /pen/ *n. & v.* • *n.* **1** a small enclosure for cows, sheep, poultry, etc. **2** a place of confinement. **3** an enclosure for sheltering submarines. • *v.tr.* (**penned, penning**) (often foll. by *in, up*) enclose or shut in a pen. [OE *penn*, of unkn. orig.]

▪ *n.* **1** coop, enclosure, hutch, sty, pound, fold, stall, confine, corral. • *v.* **2** enclose, confine, coop up, shut up *or* in, impound, corral.

pen³ /pen/ *n.* a female swan. [16th c.: orig. unkn.]

pen⁴ /pen/ *n. sl.* = PENITENTIARY 1. [abbr.]

penal /péenəl/ *adj.* **1 a** of or concerning punishment or its infliction (*penal laws; a penal sentence; a penal colony*). **b** (of an offense) punishable, esp. by law. **2** extremely severe (*penal taxation*). □ **penal servitude** *hist.* imprisonment with compulsory labor. □□ **penally** *adv.* [ME f. OF *penal* or L *poenalis* f. *poena* PAIN]

▪ **1 a** correctional, punitive, disciplinary. **2** see HARSH 2.

penalize /péenəliz/ *v.tr.* **1** subject (a person) to a penalty or comparative disadvantage. **2** make or declare (an action) penal. □□ **penalization** *n.*

▪ **1** discipline, mulct, fine, impose a penalty on, *Law* amerce; see also PUNISH 1.

penalty /pénəltee/ *n.* (*pl.* **-ies**) **1 a** a punishment, esp. a fine, for a breach of law, contract, etc. **b** a fine paid. **2** a disadvantage, loss, etc., esp. as a result of one's own actions (*paid the penalty for his carelessness*). **3 a** a disadvantage imposed on a competitor or team in a game, etc., for a breach of the rules, etc. **b** (*attrib.*) awarded against a side incurring a penalty (*clipping penalty; penalty kick*). **4** *Bridge*, etc., points gained by opponents when a contract is not fulfilled. □ **penalty area** *Soccer* the area in front of the goal in which a foul by defenders involves the award of a penalty kick. **penalty box** *Ice Hockey* an area reserved for penalized players and some officials. **the penalty of** a disadvantage resulting from (a quality, etc.). **under** (or **on**) **penalty of** under the threat of (dismissal, etc.). [AF *penalte* (unrecorded), F *pénalité* f. med.L *penalitas* (as PENAL)]

▪ **1** punishment, discipline, penance, sentence; forfeit,

toll, exaction, fine, mulct, *Law* amercement. **2** price; loss, disadvantage, handicap; sacrifice. □ **under penalty of** on *or* under pain of, under threat of.

penance /pénəns/ *n. & v.* ● *n.* **1** an act of self-punishment as reparation for guilt. **2 a** (esp. in the RC and Orthodox Church) a sacrament including confession of and absolution for a sin. **b** a penalty imposed esp. by a priest, or undertaken voluntarily, for a sin. ● *v.tr.* impose a penance on. □ **do penance** perform a penance. [ME f. OF f. L *paenitentia* (as PENITENT)]

■ *n.* **1** (self-)punishment, penalty, repentance, penitence; reparation, atonement, regret, contrition. □ **do penance** pay, suffer; make amends *or* reparation(s), atone, wear sackcloth and ashes *or* a hair shirt.

penannular /penányələr/ *adj.* almost ringlike. [L *paene* almost + ANNULAR]

penates /pináyteez, pinaá-/ *n.pl.* (often **Penates**) (in Roman mythology) the household gods, esp. of the storeroom (see LARES). [L f. *penus* provision of food]

pence *Brit. pl.* of PENNY.

penchant /pénchənt/ *n.* an inclination or liking (*has a penchant for old films*). [F, pres. part. of *pencher* incline]

■ inclination, bent, proclivity, leaning, bias, predisposition, predilection, partiality, proneness, propensity, tendency, affinity, liking, preference, fondness, taste.

pencil /pénsil/ *n. & v.* ● *n.* **1** (often *attrib.*) **a** an instrument for writing or drawing, usu. consisting of a thin rod of graphite, etc., enclosed in a wooden cylinder (*a pencil sketch*). **b** a similar instrument with a metal or plastic cover and retractable lead. **c** a cosmetic in pencil form. **2** (*attrib.*) resembling a pencil in shape (*pencil skirt*). **3** *Optics* a set of rays meeting at a point. **4** *Geom.* a figure formed by a set of straight lines meeting at a point. **5** a draftsman's or artist's art or style. ● *v.tr.* (**penciled, penciling** or **pencilled, pencilling**) **1** tint or mark with or as if with a pencil. **2** (usu. foll. by *in*) **a** write, esp. tentatively or provisionally (*have penciled in the 29th for our meeting*). **b** (esp. as **penciled** *adj.*) fill (an area) with soft pencil strokes (*penciled in her eyebrows*). □ **pencil case** (or **box**) a container for pencils, etc. **pencil pusher** *colloq. derog.* a clerical worker or one who does considerable paperwork. **pencil pushing** *colloq. derog.* clerical work. □□ **penciler** or *Brit.* **penciller** *n.* [ME f. OF *pincel* ult. f. L *penicillum* paintbrush, dimin. of *peniculus* brush, dimin. of *penis* tail]

pendant /péndənt/ *n.* (also **pendent**) **1** a hanging jewel, etc., esp. one attached to a necklace, bracelet, etc. **2** a light fitting, ornament, etc., hanging from a ceiling. **3** *Naut.* **a** a short rope hanging from the head of a mast, etc., used for attaching tackles. **b** *Brit.* = PENNANT 1. **4** the shank and ring of a pocket watch by which it is suspended. **5** /péndənt, pɔ́ndən/ (usu. foll. by *to*) a match, companion, parallel, complement, etc. [ME f. OF f. *pendre* hang f. L *pendere*]

■ **1** ornament, luster, medallion, locket, eardrop, teardrop, drop. **5** SEE PARALLEL *n.* 1.

pendent /péndənt/ *adj.* (also **pendant**) **1 a** hanging. **b** overhanging. **2** undecided; pending. **3** *Gram.* (esp. of a sentence) incomplete; not having a finite verb (*pendent nominative*). □□ **pendency** *n.* [ME (as PENDANT)]

■ **1** SEE PENDULOUS 1.

pendente lite /pendéntee lítee/ *adv. Law* during the progress of a suit. [L]

pendentive /pendéntiv/ *n. Archit.* a curved triangle of vaulting formed by the intersection of a dome with its supporting arches. [F *pendentif -ive* (adj.) (as PENDANT)]

pending /pénding/ *adj. & prep.* ● *predic.adj.* **1** awaiting decision or settlement; undecided (*a settlement was pending*). **2** about to come into existence (*patent pending*). ● *prep.* **1** during (*pending these negotiations*). **2** until (*pending his return*). □ **pending-tray** esp. *Brit.* = *in-box*. [after F *pendant* (see PENDENT)]

■ *predic.adj.* **1** unsettled, undetermined, undecided, unconfirmed, unfinished, inconclusive, (up) in the air, in the balance, abeyant, on hold, deferred, *colloq.* on ice; see also ABEYANCE. **2** forthcoming, impending, in the offing, *archaic or dial.* nigh; see also IMMINENT. ● *prep.* **1** see THROUGHOUT *prep.* **2** awaiting, waiting (for), till, until.

pendragon /pendrágən/ *n. hist.* an ancient British or Welsh prince (often as a title). [Welsh, = chief war leader, f. *pen* head + *dragon* standard]

penduline /pénjəlin, péndə-, -dyə-/ *adj.* **1** (of a nest) suspended. **2** (of a bird) of a kind that builds such a nest. [F (as PENDULOUS)]

pendulous /pénjələs, péndə-, -dyə-/ *adj.* **1** (of ears, breasts, flowers, bird's nests, etc.) hanging down; drooping and esp. swinging. **2** oscillating. □□ **pendulously** *adv.* [L *pendulus* f. *pendēre* hang]

■ **1** pendent, hanging, drooping, sagging, dangling, suspended, pensile. **2** swinging, swaying, oscillating, oscillatory.

pendulum /pénjələm, péndə-, -dyə-/ *n.* a weight suspended so as to swing freely, esp. a rod with a weighted end regulating the movement of a clock's works. □ **swing of the pendulum** the tendency of public opinion to oscillate between extremes, esp. between political parties. [L neut. adj. (as PENDULOUS)]

peneplain /péeniplayn/ *n. Geol.* a fairly flat area of land produced by erosion. [L *paene* almost + PLAIN[1]]

penetralia /pénitráyleeə/ *n.pl.* **1** innermost shrines or recesses. **2** secret or hidden parts; mysteries. [L, neut. pl. of *penetralis* interior (as PENETRATE)]

■ **1** SEE RECESS *n.* 2.

penetrate /pénitrayt/ *v.* **1** *tr.* **a** find access into or through, esp. forcibly. **b** (usu. foll. by *with*) imbue (a person or thing) with; permeate. **2** *tr.* see into, find out, or discern (a person's mind, the truth, a meaning, etc.). **3** *tr.* see through (darkness, fog, etc.) (*could not penetrate the gloom*). **4** *intr.* be absorbed by the mind (*my hint did not penetrate*). **5** *tr.* (as **penetrating** *adj.*) **a** having or suggesting sensitivity or insight (*a penetrating remark*). **b** (of a voice, etc.) easily heard through or above other sounds; piercing. **c** (of a smell) sharp; pungent. **6** *tr.* (of a man) put the penis into the vagina of (a woman). **7** *intr.* (usu. foll. by *into, through, to*) make a way. □□ **penetrable** *adj.* **penetrability** *n.* **penetrant** *adj. & n.* **penetratingly** *adv.* **penetration** *n.* **penetrative** /-trətiv/ *adj.* **penetrator** *n.* [L *penetrare* place or enter within f. *penitus* interior]

■ **1 a** enter, go through *or* into, pass through *or* into, pierce, bore (into), lance, spear, probe, perforate; reach, get to, get at, touch, affect. **b** permeate, suffuse, pervade, filter through *or* into, seep through *or* into, percolate through, spread throughout, soak into, be absorbed by; see also CHARGE *v.* 9. **2** see into, understand, sense, become aware *or* conscious of, see (through), gain insight into, discern, uncover, discover, find (out), comprehend, grasp, work out, unravel, fathom, perceive, figure out, figure, *sl.* dig, *Brit. sl.* suss out. **4** sink in, be absorbed, be understood, register, get through, become clear, come across, be realized, *colloq.* soak in. **5** (**penetrating**) **a** incisive, trenchant, keen, searching, deep, acute, sharp, perceptive, perspicacious, percipient, quick, discriminating, intelligent, sensitive, clever, smart, discerning. **b** audible; piercing, shrill, strident, earsplitting, ear-shattering, pervasive. **c** pungent, harsh, sharp, biting, mordant, strong, stinging. □□ **penetration** perforation, incision; insight, keenness, perception, percipience, intelligence, perspicacity, perspicuity, perspicaciousness, perceptiveness, incisiveness, sensitivity, sentience, understanding, acuteness, discernment, discrimination, cleverness, shrewdness, wit, quick-wittedness; pungency; shrillness.

penguin /pénggwin/ *n.* any flightless sea bird of the family

/.../ **pronunciation**	● **part of speech**
□ **phrases, idioms, and compounds**	
□□ **derivatives**	■ **synonym section**
cross-references appear in SMALL CAPITALS or *italics*	

Spheniscidae of the southern hemisphere, with black upperparts and white underparts, and wings developed into scaly flippers for swimming underwater. [16th c., orig. = great auk: orig. unkn.]

penholder /pénhōldər/ n. **1** the esp. wooden shaft of a pen with a metal nib. **2** a rack for storing pens or nibs.

penicillate /pénisilit, -ayt/ adj. Biol. **1** having or forming a small tuft or tufts. **2** marked with streaks as of a pencil or brush. [L penicillum: see PENCIL]

penicillin /pénisílin/ n. any of various antibiotics produced naturally by molds of the genus Penicillium, or synthetically, and able to prevent the growth of certain disease-causing bacteria. [mod.L Penicillium genus name f. L penicillum: see PENCIL]

penile /peenil, -nəl/ adj. of or concerning the penis. [mod.L penilis]

penillion pl. of PENNILL.

peninsula /pənínsələ, -syələ/ n. a piece of land almost surrounded by water or projecting far into a sea or lake, etc. □□ **peninsular** adj. [L paeninsula f. paene almost + insula island]

■ see POINT n. 22.

penis /peenis/ n. (pl. **penises** or **penes** /-neez/) **1** the male organ of copulation and (in mammals) urination. **2** the male copulatory organ in lower vertebrates. [L, = tail, penis]

■ **1** phallus, archaic membrum virile, esp. joc. organ.

penitent /pénitənt/ adj. & n. ● adj. regretting and wishing to atone for sins, etc.; repentant. ● n. **1** a repentant sinner. **2** a person doing penance under the direction of a confessor. **3** (in pl.) various RC orders associated for mutual discipline, etc. □□ **penitence** n. **penitently** adv. [ME f. OF f. L paenitens f. paenitēre repent]

■ adj. regretful, repentant, remorseful, sorrowful, sorry, rueful, contrite, apologetic, shamefaced, self-reproachful, conscience-stricken. □□ **penitence** contrition, regret, repentance, regretfulness, compunction, remorse, shame, ruefulness, shamefacedness, self-reproach.

penitential /péniténshəl/ adj. of or concerning penitence or penance. □□ **penitentially** adv. [OF penitencial f. LL paenitentialis f. paenitentia penitence (as PENITENT)]

■ see SORRY 1, compensatory (COMPENSATE).

penitentiary /péniténshəree/ n. & adj. ● n. (pl. **-ies**) **1** a reformatory prison, esp. a state or federal prison. **2** an office in the papal court deciding questions of penance, dispensations, etc. ● adj. **1** of or concerning penance. **2** of or concerning reformatory treatment. **3** (of an offense) making a culprit liable to a prison sentence. [ME f. med.L paenitentiarius (adj. & n.) (as PENITENT)]

■ n. **1** see PRISON n. 1.

penknife /pén-nif/ n. a small folding knife, esp. for carrying in a pocket.

■ knife, pocketknife, jackknife; clasp knife.

penlight /pénlīt/ n. a pen-sized flashlight.

penman /pénmən/ n. (pl. **-men**) **1** a person who writes by hand with a specified skill (a good penman). **2** an author. □□ **penmanship** n.

■ **2** see AUTHOR n. 1, SCRIBE n. 4. □□ **penmanship** calligraphy, handwriting, script, writing, chirography.

Penn. abbr. (also **Penna.**) Pennsylvania.

pennant /pénənt/ n. **1** Naut. a tapering flag, esp. that flown at the masthead of a vessel in commission. **2** = PENDANT 3a. **3** = PENNON. **4 a** a flag denoting a sports championship, etc. **b** (by extension) a sports championship. [blend of PENDANT and PENNON]

■ **1, 3** flag, banner, pennon, streamer, banderole, gonfalon, ensign, colors, standard, labarum, jack, burgee, Rom.Antiq. vexillum.

penniless /pénilis/ adj. having no money; destitute. □□ **pennilessly** adv. **pennilessness** n.

■ see DESTITUTE 1.

pennill /pénil/ n. (pl. **penillion** /penílyən/) (usu. in pl.) an improvised stanza sung to a harp accompaniment at an eisteddfod, etc. [Welsh f. penn head]

pennon /pénən/ n. **1** a long narrow flag, triangular or swal-

low-tailed, esp. as the military ensign of lancer regiments. **2** Naut. a long pointed streamer on a ship. **3** a flag. □□ **pennoned** adj. [ME f. OF f. L penna feather]

■ see FLAG¹ n.

Pennsylvania Dutch /pénsilváynyə/ n. **1** a dialect of High German spoken by descendants of 17th–18th-c. German and Swiss immigrants to Pennsylvania, etc. **2** (as pl.) these settlers or their descendants.

Pennsylvanian /pénsilváynyən/ n. & adj. ● n. **1** a native or inhabitant of Pennsylvania. **2** (prec. by the) Geol. the upper Carboniferous period or system in N. America. ● adj. **1** of or relating to Pennsylvania. **2** Geol. of or relating to the upper Carboniferous period or system in N. America.

penny /pénee/ n. (pl. for separate coins **-ies**, Brit. for a sum of money **pence** /pens/) **1** (in the US, Canada, etc.) a one-cent coin. **2** a British coin and monetary unit equal to one hundredth of a pound. ¶ Abbr.: **p. 3** hist. a former British bronze coin and monetary unit equal to one two-hundred-and-fortieth of a pound. ¶ Abbr.: **d. 4** Bibl. a denarius. □ **in for a penny, in for a pound** an exhortation to total commitment to an undertaking. **like a bad penny** continually returning when unwanted. **pennies from heaven** unexpected benefits. **penny-a-liner** esp. Brit. a hack writer. **penny black** the first adhesive postage stamp (1840, value one penny). **penny dreadful** a cheap sensational adventure story or comic. **the penny drops** Brit. colloq. one begins to understand at last. **a penny for your thoughts** a request to a thoughtful person to confide in the speaker. **penny-pincher** a very frugal person. **penny-pinching** n. frugality; cheapness. ● adj. frugal. **penny whistle** a tin pipe with six holes giving different notes. **penny wise and pound foolish** frugal in small expenditures but wasteful of large amounts. **a pretty penny** a large sum of money. **two a penny** almost worthless though easily obtained. [OE penig, penning f. Gmc, perh. rel. to PAWN²]

■ □ **penny-pinching** (n.) miserliness, frugality, cheapness, stinginess. (adj.) see MEAN² 1. **penny wise and pound foolish** see WASTEFUL. **two a penny** see COMMON adj. 1.

-penny comb. form **1** /pénee/ denoting a size of nail (based on former price per hundred) (tenpenny nail). **2** /pəni/ Brit. forming attributive adjectives meaning 'costing . . . pence' (esp. in pre-decimal currency) (fivepenny).

pennyroyal /péneeróyəl/ n. **1** a European creeping mint, Mentha pulegium, cultivated for its supposed medicinal properties. **2** an aromatic N. American plant, Hedeoma pulegioides. [app. f. earlier puliol(e) ryall f. AF puliol, OF pouliol ult. f. L pulegium + real ROYAL]

pennyweight /péneewayt/ n. a unit of weight, 24 grains or one twentieth of an ounce troy.

pennywort /péneewərt, -wawrt/ n. any of several wild plants with rounded leaves, esp.: **1** (**wall pennywort**) Umbilicus rupestris, growing in crevices. **2** (**marsh** or **water pennywort**) Hydrocotyle vulgaris, growing in marshy places. [ME, f. PENNY + WORT]

pennyworth /péneewərth/ n. esp. Brit. (also **penn'orth** /pénərth/) **1** as much as can be bought for a penny. **2** a bargain of a specified kind (a bad pennyworth). □ **not a pennyworth** not the least bit.

Penobscot /pənóbskot, -skət/ n. **1 a** a N. American people native to Maine. **b** a member of this people. **2** the language of this people.

penology /peenóləjee/ n. the study of the punishment of crime and of prison management. □□ **penological** /-nəlójikəl/ adj. **penologist** n. [L poena penalty + -LOGY]

pensée /poNsáy/ n. a thought or reflection put into literary form; an aphorism. [F]

pensile /pénsil/ adj. **1** hanging down; pendulous. **2** (of a bird, etc.) building a pensile nest. [L pensilis f. pendēre pens- hang]

■ **1** see PENDULOUS 1.

pension¹ /pénshən/ n. & v. ● n. **1** a regular payment made by an employer, etc., after the retirement of an employee. **2** a similar payment made by a government to people above a specified age, to the disabled, etc. ● v.tr. **1** grant a pension to. **2** bribe with a pension. □ **pension off** dismiss with a

pension. □□ **pensionless** adj. [ME f. OF f. L pensio -onis payment f. pendere pens- pay]
■ n. **1** retirement income, superannuation, social security, colloq. golden handshake. **2** benefit, allowance, annuity, subsistence, allotment. □ **pension off** (cause to) retire, superannuate, shelve, put on the shelf; see also DISMISS 2.

pension² /paaNsyŎN/ n. a European, esp. French, boarding-house providing full or half board at a fixed rate. □ **en pension** /oN/ as a boarder. [F: see PENSION¹]

pensionable /pénshənəbəl/ adj. **1** entitled to a pension. **2** (of a service, job, etc.) entitling an employee to a pension. □□ **pensionability** n.

pensionary /pénshəneree/ adj. & n. ● adj. of or concerning a pension. ● n. (pl. **-ies**) **1** a pensioner. **2** a creature; a hireling. [med.L pensionarius (as PENSION¹)]

pensioner /pénshənər/ n. a recipient of a pension, esp. a retirement pension. [ME f. AF pensionner, OF pensionnier (as PENSION¹)]
■ veteran, senior citizen, retiree, golden-ager, oldster, Brit. old-age pensioner, retirer, OAP, colloq. oldie.

pensive /pénsiv/ adj. **1** deep in thought. **2** sorrowfully thoughtful. □□ **pensively** adv. **pensiveness** n. [ME f. OF pensif, -ive f. penser think f. L pensare frequent. of pendere pens- weigh]
■ **1** thoughtful, meditative, musing, cogitative, absorbed, contemplative, reflective, preoccupied, ruminative, daydreaming; in a trance, in a reverie, in a brown study. **2** brooding, sober, serious, grave; wistful.

penstemon /penstéemən, pénstəmən/ n. (also **pentstemon** /pentstéemən/) any American herbaceous plant of the genus Penstemon, with showy flowers and five stamens, one of which is sterile. [mod.L, irreg. f. PENTA- + Gk stēmōn warp, used for 'stamen']

penstock /pénstok/ n. **1** a sluice; a floodgate. **2** a channel for conveying water to a waterwheel, etc. [PEN² in sense 'mill dam' + STOCK]

pent /pent/ adj. (often foll. by in, up) closely confined; shut in (pent-up feelings). [past part. of pend var. of PEN² v.]
■ (pent-up) restrained, constrained, repressed, stifled, bottled up, held in, checked, held back, shut in, curbed, inhibited, restricted.

penta- /péntə/ comb. form **1** five. **2** Chem. (forming the names of compounds) containing five atoms or groups of a specified kind (pentachloride; pentoxide). [Gk f. pente five]

pentacle /péntəkəl/ n. a figure used as a symbol, esp. in magic, e.g., a pentagram. [med.L pentaculum (as PENTA-)]

pentad /péntad/ n. **1** the number five. **2** a group of five. [Gk pentas -ados f. pente five]

pentadactyl /péntədáktil/ adj. Zool. having five toes or fingers.

pentagon /péntəgon/ n. **1** a plane figure with five sides and angles. **2** (**the Pentagon**) **a** the pentagonal headquarters building of the US armed forces, located near Washington, D.C. **b** the US Department of Defense; the leaders of the US armed forces. □□ **pentagonal** /-tágənəl/ adj. [F pentagone or f. LL pentagonus f. Gk pentagōnon (as PENTA-, -GON)]

pentagram /péntəgram/ n. a five-pointed star formed by extending the sides of a pentagon both ways until they intersect, formerly used as a mystic symbol. [Gk pentagrammon (as PENTA-, -GRAM)]

pentagynous /pentájinəs/ adj. Bot. having five pistils.

pentahedron /péntəhéedrən/ n. a solid figure with five faces. □□ **pentahedral** adj.

pentamerous /pentámərəs/ adj. **1** Bot. having five parts in a flower whorl. **2** Zool. having five joints or parts.

pentameter /pentámitər/ n. **1** a verse of five feet, e.g., English iambic verse of ten syllables. **2** a form of Gk or Latin dactylic verse composed of two halves each of two feet and a long syllable, used in elegiac verse. [L f. Gk pentametros (as PENTA-, -METER)]

pentandrous /pentándrəs/ adj. Bot. having five stamens.

pentane /péntayn/ n. Chem. a hydrocarbon of the alkane series. ¶ Chem. formula: C_5H_{12}. [Gk pente five + ALKANE]

pentangle /péntanggəl/ n. = PENTAGRAM. [ME perh. f. med.L pentaculum PENTACLE, assim. to L angulus ANGLE¹]

pentaprism /péntəprizəm/ n. a five-sided prism with two silvered surfaces used in a viewfinder to obtain a constant deviation of all rays of light through 90°.

Pentateuch /péntətook, -took/ n. the first five books of the Old Testament, traditionally ascribed to Moses. □□ **pentateuchal** adj. [eccl.L pentateuchus f. eccl.Gk pentateukhos (as PENTA-, teukhos implement, book)]

pentathlon /pentáthlən, -laan/ n. an athletic event comprising five different events for each competitor. □□ **pentathlete** /-táthleet/ n. [Gk f. pente five + athlon contest]

pentatonic /péntətónik/ adj. Mus. **1** consisting of five notes. **2** relating to such a scale.

pentavalent /péntəváylənt/ adj. Chem. having a valence of five; quinquevalent.

Pentecost /péntikawst, -kost/ n. **1 a** Whitsunday. **b** a festival celebrating the descent of the Holy Spirit on Whitsunday, fifty days after Easter. **2 a** the Jewish harvest festival, on the fiftieth day after the second day of Passover (Lev. 23:15–16). **b** a synagogue ceremony on the anniversary of the giving of the Law on Mount Sinai. [OE pentecosten & OF pentecoste, f. eccl.L pentecoste f. Gk pentēkostē (hēmera) fiftieth (day)]

Pentecostal /péntikóst'l, -káwst'l/ adj. & n. ● adj. (also **pentecostal**) **1** of or relating to Pentecost. **2** of or designating Christian sects and individuals who emphasize the gifts of the Holy Spirit, are often fundamentalist in outlook, and express religious feelings by clapping, shouting, dancing, etc. ● n. a Pentecostalist. □□ **Pentecostalism** n. **Pentecostalist** adj. & n.

penthouse /pént-hows/ n. **1** a house or apartment on the roof or the top floor of a tall building. **2** a sloping roof, esp. of an outhouse built on to another building. **3** an awning; a canopy. [ME pentis f. OF apentis, -dis, f. med.L appendicium, in LL = appendage, f. L (as APPEND): infl. by HOUSE]

pentimento /péntiméntō/ n. (pl. **pentimenti** /-tee/) the phenomenon of earlier painting showing through a layer or layers of paint on a canvas. [It., = repentance]

pentobarbital /péntəbaárbitawl, -tal/ n. (also **pentobarbitone** /-tōn/) a narcotic and sedative barbiturate drug formerly used to relieve insomnia. [PENTA-, BARBITAL]

pentode /péntōd/ n. a thermionic valve having five electrodes. [Gk pente five + hodos way]

pentose /péntōs, -tōz/ n. Biochem. any monosaccharide containing five carbon atoms, including ribose. [PENTA- + -OSE²]

Pentothal /péntəthawl/ n. propr. an intravenous anesthetic, thiopental sodium.

pent-roof /péntroof, -roof/ n. a roof sloping in one direction only. [PENTHOUSE + ROOF]

pentstemon var. of PENSTEMON.

pentyl /péntil/ n. = AMYL. [PENTANE + -YL]

penult /pinúlt, peénult/ n. & adj. ● n. the last but one (esp. syllable). ● adj. last but one. [abbr. of L paenultimus (see PENULTIMATE) or of PENULTIMATE]

penultimate /pinúltimət/ adj. & n. ● adj. last but one. ● n. **1** the last but one. **2** the last syllable but one. [L paenultimus f. paene almost + ultimus last, after ultimate]

penumbra /pinúmbrə/ n. (pl. **penumbrae** /-bree/ or **penumbras**) **1 a** the partly shaded region around the shadow of an opaque body, esp. that around the total shadow of the moon or earth in an eclipse. **b** the less dark outer part of a sunspot. **2** a partial shadow. □□ **penumbral** adj. [mod.L f. L paene almost + UMBRA shadow]

penurious /pinŏŏreeəs, pinyŏŏr-/ adj. **1** poor; destitute. **2** stingy; grudging. **3** scanty. □□ **penuriously** adv. **penuriousness** n. [med.L penuriosus (as PENURY)]
■ **1** poor, poverty-stricken, destitute, impoverished, penniless, indigent, needy, impecunious, necessitous,

/ . . . / **pronunciation**   ● **part of speech**
□ **phrases, idioms, and compounds**
□□ **derivatives**   ■ **synonym section**
cross-references appear in SMALL CAPITALS or italics

beggarly, bankrupt, hard up, *sl.* stone-broke; see also BROKE. **2** stingy, penny-pinching, miserly, tight, tightfisted, closefisted, cheap, cheeseparing, niggardly, ungenerous, parsimonious, skinflinty, begrudging, grudging, near, close, costive, sordid, *Brit. colloq.* mingy.

penury /pényəree/ *n.* (*pl.* **-ies**) **1** destitution; poverty. **2** a lack; scarcity. [ME f. L *penuria*, perh. rel. to *paene* almost]
  ■ **1** see POVERTY 1.

peon /peéon, peéən/ *n.* **1** a Spanish American day laborer or farmworker. **2** an unskilled worker; drudge. **3** *hist.* a worker held in servitude in the southwestern US. **4** also *Brit.* /pyo͞on/ (in India) an office messenger, attendant, or orderly. **5** a bullfighter's assistant. □□ **peonage** *n.* [Port. *peão* & Sp. *peon* f. med.L *pedo -onis* walker f. L *pes pedis* foot: cf. PAWN¹]
  ■ **1–3** see PEASANT.

peony /peéənee/ *n.* (*pl.* **-ies**) any herbaceous plant of the genus *Paeonia*, with large globular red, pink, or white flowers, often double in cultivated varieties. [OE *peonie* f. L *peonia* f. Gk *paiōnia* f. *Paiōn*, physician of the gods]

people /peépəl/ *n.* & *v.* ● *n.* **1** (usu. as *pl.*) **a** persons composing a community, tribe, race, nation, etc. (*the American people*; *a warlike people*). **b** a group of persons of a usu. specified kind (*the chosen people*; *these people here*; *right-thinking people*). **2** (prec. by *the*; treated as *pl.*) **a** the mass of people in a country, etc., not having special rank or position. **b** these considered as an electorate (*the people will reject it*). **3** parents or other relatives. **4 a** subjects, armed followers, a retinue, etc. **b** a congregation of a parish priest, etc. **5** persons in general (*people do not like rudeness*). ● *v.tr.* (usu. foll. by *with*) **1** fill with people, animals, etc.; populate. **2** (esp. as **peopled** *adj.*) inhabit; occupy; fill (*thickly peopled*). [ME f. AF *poeple*, *people*, OF *pople*, *peuple*, f. L *populus*]
  ■ *n.* **1 a** race, community, clan, tribe, folk, nation, population, society. **2** masses, (general) public, hoi polloi, multitude, populace, common people, common man *or* woman, commoners, subjects, citizenry, plebeians, proletariat, rank and file, the crowd, commonalty, commonage, the rabble, silent majority, *colloq.* proles, plebs, *derog.* ragtag and bobtail, common herd; electorate, voters, voting public, grass roots; man in the street, everyman, *Brit.* Mr. *or* Mrs. Average, *colloq.* Joe Blow, John Q. Public. **3** parents, relations, relatives, kin, kinsmen, kinsfolk, family, kith and kin; ancestors, forebears. **4 b** flock, congregation. **5** persons, individuals, human beings; living souls, mortals, bodies. ● *v.* **1, 2** populate, colonize, settle, occupy, inhabit; fill.

pep /pep/ *n.* & *v. colloq.* ● *n.* vigor; go; spirit. ● *v.tr.* (**pepped**, **pepping**) (usu. foll. by *up*) fill with vigor. □ **pep pill** a pill containing a stimulant drug. **pep talk** a usu. short talk intended to enthuse, encourage, etc. [abbr. of PEPPER]
  ■ *n.* vigor, vim (and vigor), spirit, animation, go, vivacity, energy, verve, zest, fire, sprightliness, life, effervescence, sparkle, ebullience, dash, enthusiasm, brio, élan, zip, *colloq.* zing, get-up-and-go. ● *v.* (*pep up*) stimulate, invigorate, animate, enliven, vitalize, vivify, energize, exhilarate, quicken, arouse, breathe (some) life into, inspire, activate, fire, cheer up, spark, fire up, *colloq.* buck up. □ **pep pill** *sl.* upper.

peperino /pépəreénō/ *n.* a light porous (esp. brown) volcanic rock formed of small grains of sand, cinders, etc. [It. f. *pepere* pepper]

peperoni var. of PEPPERONI.

peplum /pépləm/ *n.* **1** a short flounce, ruffle, etc., at waist level, esp. of a blouse or jacket over a skirt. **2** *Gk Antiq.* a woman's outer garment. [L f. Gk *peplos*]
  ■ **1** see FLOUNCE² *n.*

pepo /peépō/ *n.* (*pl.* **-os**) any fleshy fruit of the melon, squash, or cucumber type, with numerous seeds and surrounded by a hard skin. [L, = pumpkin, f. Gk *pepōn* abbr. of *pepōn sikuos* ripe gourd]

pepper /pépər/ *n.* & *v.* ● *n.* **1 a** a hot aromatic condiment from the dried berries of certain plants used whole or

ground. **b** any climbing vine of the genus *Piper*, esp. *P. nigrum*, yielding these berries. **2** anything hot or pungent. **3 a** any plant of the genus *Capsicum*, esp. *C. annuum*. **b** the fruit of this used esp. as a vegetable or salad ingredient. **4** = CAYENNE. ● *v.tr.* **1** sprinkle or treat with or as if with pepper. **2 a** pelt with missiles. **b** hurl abuse, etc., at. **3** punish severely. □ **black pepper** the unripe ground or whole berries of *Piper nigrum* as a condiment. **green pepper** the unripe fruit of *Capsicum annuum*. **pepper mill** a device for grinding pepper by hand. **pepper pot 1** a W. Indian dish of meat, etc., stewed with cayenne pepper. **2** (also **Philadelphia pepper pot**) a thick soup containing tripe, meat, vegetables, and seasonings, esp. pepper. **red** (or **yellow**) **pepper** the ripe fruit of *Capsicum annuum*. **sweet pepper** a small *Capsicum* pepper with a relatively mild taste. **white pepper** the ripe or husked ground or whole berries of *Piper nigrum* as a condiment. [OE *piper*, *pipor* f. L *piper* f. Gk *peperi* f. Skr. *pippalī-* berry, peppercorn]
  ■ *v.* **1** sprinkle, scatter, dot, speckle, fleck, spot, spray, spatter, stipple, mottle. **2 a** see PELT¹ *v.* 1. **b** see ABUSE *v.* 2. **3** see PUNISH 1.

peppercorn /pépərkawrn/ *n.* **1** the dried berry of *Piper nigrum* as a condiment. **2** *Brit.* (in full **peppercorn rent**) a nominal rent.

peppermint /pépərmint/ *n.* **1 a** a mint plant, *Mentha piperita*, grown for the strong-flavored oil obtained from its leaves. **b** the oil from this. **2** a candy flavored with peppermint. **3** *Austral.* any of various eucalyptuses yielding oil with a similar flavor. □ **peppermint stick** a hard usu. cylindrical stick of peppermint-flavored candy. □□ **pepperminty** *adj.*

pepperoni /pépərṓnee/ *n.* (also **peperoni**) beef and pork sausage seasoned with pepper. [It. *peperone* chilli]

pepperwort /pépərwərt, -wawrt/ *n.* any cruciferous plant of the genus *Lepidium*, esp. garden cress.

peppery /pépəree/ *adj.* **1** of, like, or containing much pepper. **2** hot-tempered. **3** pungent; stinging. □□ **pepperiness** *n.*
  ■ **1** see SPICY 1. **2** see PASSIONATE. **3** see PUNGENT 1.

peppy /pépee/ *adj.* (**peppier**, **peppiest**) *colloq.* vigorous; energetic; bouncy. □□ **peppily** *adv.* **peppiness** *n.*
  ■ see ENERGETIC 1, 2.

pepsin /pépsin/ *n.* an enzyme contained in the gastric juice that hydrolyzes proteins. [G f. Gk *pepsis* digestion]

peptic /péptik/ *adj.* concerning or promoting digestion. □ **peptic glands** glands secreting gastric juice. **peptic ulcer** an ulcer in the stomach or duodenum. [Gk *peptikos* able to digest (as PEPTONE)]

peptide /péptid/ *n. Biochem.* any of a group of organic compounds consisting of two or more amino acids bonded in sequence. [G *Peptid*, back-form. (as POLYPEPTIDE)]

peptone /péptōn/ *n.* a protein fragment formed by hydrolysis in the process of digestion. □□ **peptonize** /-tənīz/ *v.tr.* [G *Pepton* f. Gk *peptos*, neut. *pepton* cooked]

Pequot /peékwot/ *n.* **1 a** a N. American people native to eastern Connecticut. **b** a member of this people. **2** the language of this people.

per /pər/ *prep.* & *adv.* ● *prep.* **1** for each; for every (*two cupcakes per child*; *five miles per hour*). **2** by means of; by; through (*per rail*). **3** (in full **as per**) in accordance with (*as per instructions*). **4** *Heraldry* in the direction of. ● *adv. colloq.* each; apiece. □ **as per usual** *colloq.* as usual. [L]

per- /pər/ *prefix* **1** forming verbs, nouns, and adjectives meaning: **a** through; all over (*perforate*; *perforation*; *pervade*). **b** completely; very (*perfervid*; *perturb*). **c** to destruction; to the bad (*pervert*; *perdition*). **2** *Chem.* having the maximum of some element in combination, esp.: **a** in the names of binary compounds in *-ide* (*peroxide*). **b** in the names of oxides, acids, etc., in *-ic* (*perchloric*; *permanganic*). **c** in the names of salts of these acids (*perchlorate*; *permanganate*). [L *per-* (as PER)]

peradventure /pərədvénchər, pér-/ *adv.* & *n. archaic* or *joc.* ● *adv.* perhaps. ● *n.* uncertainty; chance; conjecture; doubt (esp. *beyond* or *without peradventure*). [ME f. OF *per* or *par aventure* by chance (as PER, ADVENTURE)]
  ■ *adv.* see PERHAPS.

perambulate /pərámbyəlayt/ *v.* **1** *tr.* walk through, over, or about (streets, the country, etc.). **2** *intr.* walk from place to place. **3** *tr.* **a** travel through and inspect (territory). **b** formally establish the boundaries of (a parish, etc.) by walking round them. □□ **perambulation** /-láyshən/ *n.* **perambulatory** /-lətáwree/ *adj.* [L *perambulare perambulat-* (as PER-, *ambulare* walk)]

■ **1, 2** see WALK *v.* 1, 2. □□ **perambulation** see TOUR *n.* 1b.

perambulator /pərámbyəláytər/ *n. Brit. formal* = PRAM¹. [PERAMBULATE]

per annum /pər ánəm/ *adv.* for each year. [L]

■ see YEARLY *adv.*

percale /pərkáyl/ *n.* a closely woven cotton fabric like calico. [F, of uncert. orig.]

per capita /pər kápitə/ *adv.* & *adj.* (also **per caput** /kápoot/) for each person. [L, = by heads]

perceive /pərseev/ *v.tr.* **1** apprehend, esp. through the sight; observe. **2** (usu. foll. by *that, how,* etc., + clause) apprehend with the mind; understand. **3** regard mentally in a specified manner (*perceives the universe as infinite*). □□ **perceivable** *adj.* **perceiver** *n.* [ME f. OF *perçoivre,* f. L *percipere* (as PER-, *capere* take)]

■ **1** see, make out, discern, catch sight of, glimpse, spot, apprehend, take in, notice, note, discover, observe, mark, identify, distinguish, detect, *literary* espy, descry. **2** apprehend, understand, gather, comprehend, appreciate, grasp, feel, sense, deduce, infer, figure out, ascertain, determine, conclude, decipher, *colloq.* catch on, *sl.* dig. **3** regard, view, look on, consider, judge, believe, think, *formal* deem.

percent /pərsént/ *adv.* & *n.* (also **per cent**) ● *adv.* in every hundred. ● *n.* **1** percentage. **2** one part in every hundred (*half a percent*). **3** (in *pl.*) *Brit.* public securities yielding interest of so much percent (*three percents*).

percentage /pərséntij/ *n.* **1** a rate or proportion percent. **2** a proportion. **3** *colloq.* personal benefit or advantage.

■ **2** share, part, portion, proportion, interest, piece, commission, *colloq.* cut.

percentile /pərséntil/ *n. Statistics* one of 99 values of a variable dividing a population into 100 equal groups as regards the value of that variable.

percept /pérsept/ *n. Philos.* **1** an object of perception. **2** a mental concept resulting from perceiving, esp. by sight. [L *perceptum* perceived (thing), neut. past part. of *percipere* PERCEIVE, after *concept*]

perceptible /pərséptibəl/ *adj.* capable of being perceived by the senses or intellect. □□ **perceptibility** /-bílitee/ *n.* **perceptibly** *adv.* [OF *perceptible* or LL *perceptibilis* f. L (as PERCEIVE)]

■ discernible, detectable, observable, perceivable, noticeable, distinguishable, recognizable, apparent, evident, notable, obvious, patent, manifest, palpable, plain, clear, prominent, unmistakable.

perception /pərsépshən/ *n.* **1 a** the faculty of perceiving. **b** an instance of this. **2** (often foll. by *of*) **a** the intuitive recognition of a truth, aesthetic quality, etc. **b** an instance of this (*a sudden perception of the true position*). **3** *Philos.* the ability of the mind to refer sensory information to an external object as its cause. □□ **perceptional** *adj.* **perceptual** /-chōōəl/ *adj.* **perceptually** *adv.* [ME f. L *perceptio* (as PERCEIVE)]

■ **2** appreciation, recognition, grasp, awareness, consciousness, realization, apprehension, understanding, comprehension, knowledge; intuition, insight, feeling, sense, impression, idea, notion.

perceptive /pərséptiv/ *adj.* **1** capable of perceiving. **2** sensitive; discerning; observant (*a perceptive remark*). □□ **perceptively** *adv.* **perceptiveness** *n.* **perceptivity** /-septivitee/ *n.* [med.L *perceptivus* (as PERCEIVE)]

■ **2** astute, alert, attentive, quick, alive, quick-witted, intelligent, acute, sharp, sensitive, sensible, percipient, discerning, perspicacious, incisive, *colloq.* on the ball; see also OBSERVANT 1a.

perch¹ /pərch/ *n.* & *v.* ● *n.* **1** a usu. horizontal bar, branch, etc., used by a bird to rest on. **2** a usu. high or precarious

place for a person or thing to rest on. **3** esp. *Brit.* a measure of length, esp. for land, of 5½ yards (see also ROD, POLE). ● *v.intr.* & *tr.* (usu. foll. by *on*) settle or rest, or cause to settle or rest on or as if on a perch, etc. (*the bird perched on a branch; a town perched on a hill*). □ **knock a person off his or her perch 1** vanquish; destroy. **2** make less confident or secure. [ME f. OF *perche, percher* f. L *pertica* pole]

■ *n.* **2** spot, location, position, place, site, vantage point, perspective. ● *v.* roost, rest, sit, nest; place, put, set, situate, locate, position, site. □ **knock a person off his or her perch 1** destroy, defeat, disgrace; see also RUIN *v.* 1a. **2** see DEMORALIZE 1.

perch² /pərch/ *n.* (*pl.* same or **perches**) **1** any spiny-finned freshwater edible fish of the genus *Perca,* esp. *P. flavescens* of N. America or *P. fluviatilis* of Europe. **2** any fish of several similar or related species. [ME f. OF *perche* f. L *perca* f. Gk *perkē*]

perchance /pərcháns/ *adv.* **1** by chance. **2** possibly; maybe. [ME f. AF *par chance* f. *par* by, CHANCE]

■ **2** see MAYBE.

percher /pórchər/ *n.* any bird with feet adapted for perching; a passerine.

percheron /pórchəron, -shə-/ *n.* a powerful breed of draft horse. [F, orig. bred in le *Perche,* a district of N. France]

perchlorate /pərkláwrayt/ *n. Chem.* a salt or ester of perchloric acid.

perchloric acid /pərkláwrik/ *n. Chem.* a strong liquid acid containing heptavalent chlorine. [PER- + CHLORINE]

percipient /pərsípeeənt/ *adj.* & *n.* ● *adj.* **1** able to perceive; conscious. **2** discerning; observant. ● *n.* a person who perceives, esp. something outside the range of the senses. □□ **percipience** *n.* **percipiently** *adv.* [L (as PERCEIVE)]

■ *adj.* **2** see PERCEPTIVE. □□ **percipience** see INSIGHT.

percolate /pérkəlayt/ *v.* **1** *intr.* (often foll. by *through*) **a** (of liquid, etc.) filter or ooze gradually (esp. through a porous surface). **b** (of an idea, etc.) permeate gradually. **2** *tr.* prepare (coffee) by repeatedly passing boiling water through ground beans. **3** *tr.* ooze through; permeate. **4** *tr.* strain (a liquid, powder, etc.) through a fine mesh, etc. **5** *intr. colloq.* become livelier, more active, etc. □□ **percolation** /-láyshən/ *n.* [L *percolare* (as PER-, *colare* strain f. *colum* strainer)]

■ **1** seep, transfuse, leach, drip, drain, strain, filter, infuse, ooze, transude, filtrate, trickle, sink in. **3** suffuse, penetrate; see also PERMEATE.

percolator /pérkəlaytər/ *n.* a machine for making coffee by circulating boiling water through ground beans.

per contra /per kóntrə/ *adv.* on the opposite side (of an account, assessment, etc.); on the contrary. [It.]

percuss /pərkús/ *v.tr. Med.* tap (a part of the body) gently with a finger or an instrument as part of a diagnosis. [L *percutere percuss-* strike (as PER-, *cutere* = *quatere* shake)]

percussion /pərkúshən/ *n.* **1** *Mus.* **a** (often *attrib.*) the playing of music by striking instruments with sticks, etc. (*a percussion band*). **b** the section of such instruments in an orchestra or band (*asked the percussion to stay behind*). **2** *Med.* the act or an instance of percussing. **3** the forcible striking of one esp. solid body against another. □ **percussion cap** a small amount of explosive powder contained in metal or paper and exploded by striking, used esp. in toy guns and formerly in some firearms. □□ **percussionist** *n.* **percussive** *adj.* **percussively** *adv.* **percussiveness** *n.* [F *percussion* or L *percussio* (as PERCUSS)]

percutaneous /pérkyōōtáyneeəs/ *adj.* esp. *Med.* made or done through the skin. [L *per cutem* through the skin]

per diem /pər dee-em, díem/ *adv., adj.,* & *n.* ● *adv.* & *adj.* for each day. ● *n.* an allowance or payment for each day. [L]

perdition /pərdíshən/ *n.* eternal death; damnation. [ME f.

/.../ pronunciation	● part of speech
□ phrases, idioms, and compounds	
□□ derivatives	■ synonym section
cross-references appear in SMALL CAPITALS or *italics*	

OF *perdiciun* or eccl.L *perditio* f. L *perdere* destroy (as PER-, *dere dit-* = *dare* give)]

■ damnation, hell, hellfire, doom, ruin, condemnation, destruction, ruination, downfall.

perdurable /pərdŏŏrəbəl, -dyŏŏr-/ *adj. formal* permanent; eternal; durable. □□ **perdurability** /-bílitee/ *n.* **perdurably** *adv.* [ME f. OF f. LL *perdurabilis* (as PER-, DURABLE)]

père /pair/ *n.* (added to a surname to distinguish a father from a son) the father; senior (cf. FILS). [F, = father]

Père David's deer /páir daavéedz, dáyvidz/ *n.* a large slender-antlered deer, *Elaphurus davidianus.* [after Father A. David, Fr. missionary d. 1900]

peregrinate /périgrinayt/ *v.intr.* travel; journey, esp. extensively or at leisure. □□ **peregrination** /-náyshən/ *n.* **peregrinator** *n.* [L *peregrinari* (as PEREGRINE)]

■ see JOURNEY *v.* □□ **peregrination** see JOURNEY *n.* **peregrinator** see MIGRANT *n.*

peregrine /périgrin, -green/ *n. & adj.* ● *n.* (in full **peregrine falcon**) a widely distributed falcon, *Falco peregrinus,* much used for falconry. ● *adj.* **1** imported from abroad; foreign; outlandish. **2** inclined to wander. [L *peregrinus* f. *peregre* abroad f. *per* through + *ager* field]

peremptory /pərémptəree/ *adj.* **1** (of a statement or command) admitting no denial or refusal. **2** (of a person, a person's manner, etc.) dogmatic; imperious; dictatorial. **3** *Law* not open to appeal or challenge; final. **4** absolutely fixed; essential. □ **peremptory challenge** *Law* a defendant's objection to a proposed juror, made without needing to give a reason. □□ **peremptorily** *adv.* **peremptoriness** *n.* [AF *peremptorie,* OF *peremptoire* f. L *peremptorius* deadly, decisive, f. *perimere perempt-* destroy, cut off (as PER-, *emere* take, buy)]

■ **1** commanding, imperative, emphatic, positive, firm, insistent, compelling. **2** imperious, dogmatic, authoritative, tyrannical, despotic, dictatorial, autocratic, domineering, *colloq.* bossy. **3** decisive, final, preclusive, incontrovertible, irrefutable, categorical, unequivocal, unconditional, unreserved, flat, out-and-out, outright, unqualified, unmitigated, unchallengeable, esp. *Law* unappealable. **4** see IMPERATIVE 2.

perennial /pəréneeəl/ *adj. & n.* ● *adj.* **1** lasting through a year or several years. **2** (of a plant) lasting several years (cf. ANNUAL). **3** lasting a long time or for ever. **4** (of a stream) flowing through all seasons of the year. ● *n.* a perennial plant (*a herbaceous perennial*). □□ **perenniality** /-neeálitee/ *n.* **perennially** *adv.* [L *perennis* (as PER-, *annus* year)]

■ *adj.* **3** lasting, continuing, enduring, lifelong, persistent; endless, unending, ceaseless, unceasing, imperishable, undying, constant, perpetual, continual, everlasting, timeless, eternal, immortal, permanent, unfailing, never-failing, *rhet.* sempiternal.

perestroika /pérestróykə/ *n. hist.* (in the former Soviet Union) the policy or practice of restructuring or reforming the economic and political system. [Russ. *perestroika* = restructuring]

■ see REFORM *n.*

perfect *adj., v., & n.* ● *adj.* /pə́rfikt/ **1** complete; not deficient. **2 a** faultless (*a perfect diamond*). **b** blameless in morals or behavior. **3 a** very satisfactory (*a perfect evening*). **b** (often foll. by *for*) most appropriate; suitable. **4** exact; precise (*a perfect circle*). **5** entire; unqualified (*a perfect stranger*). **6** *Math.* (of a number) equal to the sum of its divisors. **7** *Gram.* (of a tense) denoting a completed action or event in the past, formed in English with *have* or *has* and the past participle, as in *they have eaten.* **8** *Mus.* (of pitch) absolute. **9** *Bot.* **a** (of a flower) having all four types of whorl. **b** (of a fungus) in the stage where the sexual spores occur. **10** (often foll. by *in*) thoroughly trained or skilled (*is perfect in geometry*). ● *v.tr.* /pərfékt/ **1** make perfect; improve. **2** carry through; complete. **3** complete (a sheet) by printing the other side. ● *n.* /pə́rfikt/ *Gram.* the perfect tense. □ **perfect binding** a form of bookbinding in which the leaves are attached to the spine by gluing rather than sewing. **perfect interval** *Mus.* a fourth or fifth as it would occur in a major

or minor scale starting on the lower note of the interval, or octave. **perfect pitch** = *absolute pitch* 1. □□ **perfecter** *n.* **perfectible** *adj.* **perfectibility** *n.* **perfectness** *n.* [ME and OF *parfit, perfet* f. L *perfectus* past part. of *perficere* complete (as PER-, *facere* do)]

■ *adj.* **1** complete, absolute, finished, (fully) realized, fulfilled, consummate, pure, entire, whole, perfected, best, ideal. **2 a** flawless, faultless, sublime, ideal, superb, supreme, superlative, preeminent, excellent, exquisite, unexcelled, unrivaled, unequaled, unmatched, matchless, incomparable, nonpareil, peerless, inimitable. **b** blameless, righteous, holy, faultless, flawless, spotless, pure, immaculate. **3 a** see DELIGHTFUL. **b** fitting, appropriate, (just) right, apt, suitable, correct, proper, made to order, *Brit. colloq.* spot on. **4** precise, exact, accurate, correct, unerring, true. **5** utter, entire, complete, thorough, out-and-out, unqualified, unalloyed, unmitigated, 24-karat; see also ABSOLUTE *adj.* 1. **10** expert, proficient, accomplished, experienced, practiced, skillful, skilled, gifted, talented, adept, deft, adroit, polished, professional, masterly, masterful. ● *v.* **1** refine, polish, cultivate, better, bring to perfection, *formal* ameliorate; see also IMPROVE 1a. **2** complete, finish, realize, fulfill, consummate, accomplish, achieve, effect, execute, carry out *or* through, bring to completion.

perfecta /pərféktə/ *n.* a form of betting in which the first two places in a race must be predicted in the correct order. [Amer. Sp. *quiniela perfecta* perfect quinella]

perfection /pərfékshən/ *n.* **1** the act or process of making perfect. **2** the state of being perfect; faultlessness; excellence. **3** a perfect person, thing, or example. **4** an accomplishment. **5** full development; completion. □ **to perfection** exactly; completely. [ME f. OF f. L *perfectio -onis* (as PERFECT)]

■ **1** refinement, enhancement; improvement, *formal* amelioration. **2** purity, flawlessness, faultlessness, sublimity, superiority, preeminence, transcendence; see also EXCELLENCE 1. **3** ideal, paragon, model, archetype, pattern, mold, standard, idealization, essence, quintessence, acme, pinnacle, summit. **4** accomplishment, attainment, achievement; endowment, talent, ability, aptitude, gift, skill, faculty, flair. **5** completion, completeness, fulfillment, realization, consummation; maturity, ripeness, fullness, readiness, mellowness. □ **to perfection** see *completely* (COMPLETE).

perfectionism /pərfékshənizəm/ *n.* **1** the uncompromising pursuit of excellence. **2** *Philos.* the belief that religious or moral perfection is attainable. □□ **perfectionist** *n. & adj.* [PERFECT]

■ **1** strictness, fastidiousness, rigorousness, stringency. □□ **perfectionist** (*n.*) purist, pedant, precisian, precisionist, stickler, *colloq.* fusspot, nitpicker. (*adj.*) meticulous, precise, punctilious, scrupulous, exacting, particular, demanding, fastidious, obsessive, *colloq.* picky, nitpicking; see also FUSSY 3.

perfective /pərféktiv/ *adj. & n. Gram.* ● *adj.* (of an aspect of a verb, etc.) expressing the completion of an action (opp. IMPERFECTIVE). ● *n.* the perfective aspect or form of a verb. [med.L *perfectivus* (as PERFECT)]

perfectly /pérfiktlee/ *adv.* **1** completely; absolutely (*I understand you perfectly*). **2** quite; completely (*is perfectly capable of doing it*). **3** in a perfect way. **4** very (*you know perfectly well*).

■ **1, 2** completely, entirely, absolutely, utterly, totally, wholly, consummately, thoroughly, quite, definitely, positively, unambiguously, unequivocally, unmistakably, explicitly, extremely, extraordinarily, remarkably; exactly, precisely, accurately. **3** superbly, superlatively, flawlessly, faultlessly, impeccably, inimitably, incomparably, sublimely, exquisitely, marvelously, admirably, wonderfully. **4** very, full, quite, *archaic* right, *colloq.* damned, *Brit. colloq.* jolly.

perfecto /pərféktō/ *n.* (*pl.* **-os**) a large thick cigar pointed at each end. [Sp., = perfect]

perfervid /pərfə́rvid/ *adj.* very fervid. □□ **perfervidly** *adv.* **perfervidness** *n.* [mod.L *perfervidus* (as PER-, FERVID)]
■ see *fanatical* (FANATIC).

perfidy /pə́rfidee/ *n.* breach of faith; treachery. □□ **perfidious** /-fídeeəs/ *adj.* **perfidiously** *adv.* [L *perfidia* f. *perfidus* treacherous (as PER-, *fidus* f. *fides* faith)]
■ perfidiousness, treachery, deceit, traitorousness, treason, disloyalty, faithlessness, falseness, falsity, unfaithfulness, infidelity, hypocrisy, betrayal. □□ **perfidious** treacherous, deceitful, traitorous, treasonous, treasonable, disloyal, faithless, false, unfaithful, untrue, insidious, hypocritical, corrupt, dishonest.

perfoliate /pərfṓleeət/ *adj.* (of a plant) having the stalk apparently passing through the leaf. [mod.L *perfoliatus* (as PER-, FOLIATE)]

perforate *v.* & *adj.* ● *v.* /pə́rfərayt/ **1** *tr.* make a hole or holes through; pierce. **2** *tr.* make a row of small holes in (paper, etc.) so that a part may be torn off easily. **3** *tr.* make an opening into; pass into or extend through. **4** *intr.* (usu. foll. by *into, through,* etc.) penetrate. ● *adj.* /pə́rfərət/ perforated. □□ **perforation** /-ráyshən/ *n.* **perforative** /pə́rfərətiv/ *adj.* **perforator** /pə́rfəraytər/ *n.* [L *perforare* (as PER-, *forare* pierce)]
■ *v.* **1** puncture, drill, bore; see also PIERCE 1a, b.
3, 4 enter, penetrate, pass into or through, go into; see also PENETRATE 1a.

perforce /pərfáwrs/ *adv. archaic* unavoidably; necessarily. [ME f. OF *par force* by FORCE¹]
■ see NECESSARILY.

perform /pərfáwrm/ *v.* **1** *tr.* (also *absol.*) carry into effect; be the agent of; do (a command, promise, task, etc.). **2** *tr.* (also *absol.*) go through; execute (a public function, play, piece of music, etc.). **3** *intr.* act in a play; play an instrument or sing, etc., (*likes performing*). **4** *intr.* (of a trained animal) execute tricks, etc., at a public show. **5** *intr.* operate; function. □□ **performable** *adj.* **performability** *n.* **performatory** *adj.* & *n.* (*pl.* **-ies**) **performer** *n.* **performing** *adj.* [ME f. AF *parfourmer* f. OF *parfournir* (assim. to *forme* FORM) f. *par* PER- + *fournir* FURNISH]
■ **1** carry out, complete, bring off or about, accomplish, do, fulfill; see also EFFECT *v.* 1, 2. **2** execute, discharge, dispatch, conduct, carry on, go through, do; present, stage, produce, put on, mount. **5** do, act, behave, operate, function, run, work, go, respond. □□ **performer** actor, actress, esp. *Brit.* artiste, thespian, trouper, player, entertainer, *formal* executant.

performance /pərfáwrməns/ *n.* **1** (usu. foll. by *of*) **a** the act or process of performing or carrying out. **b** the execution or fulfillment (of a duty, etc.). **2** a staging or production of a drama, piece of music, etc.) (*the afternoon performance*). **3** a person's achievement under test conditions, etc. (*put up a good performance*). **4** *colloq.* a fuss; a scene; a public exhibition (*made such a performance about leaving*). **5 a** the capabilities of a machine, esp. a car or aircraft. **b** (*attrib.*) of high capability (*a performance car*).
■ **1** execution, accomplishment, effectuation, discharge, dispatch, conduct, fulfillment, completion. **2** show, showing, play, production, staging, act; concert, *colloq.* gig. **4** scene, show, exhibition, display, act; see also FUSS *n.* 1, 2a. **5 a** capability, capabilities, power, capacity, potential.

performative /pərfáwrmətiv/ *adj.* & *n.* ● *adj.* **1** of or relating to performance. **2** denoting an utterance that effects an action by being spoken or written (e.g., *I bet, I apologize*). ● *n.* a performative utterance.

performing arts /pərfáwrming/ *n.pl.* the arts, such as drama, music, and dance, that require performance for their realization.

perfume /pə́rfyoom/ *n.* & *v.* ● *n.* **1** a sweet smell. **2** fluid containing the essence of flowers, etc.; scent. ● *v.tr.* /also pərfyoom/ (usu. as **perfumed** *adj.*) impart a sweet scent to; impregnate with a sweet smell. □□ **perfumy** *adj.* [F *parfum,*

parfumer f. obs. It. *parfumare, perfumare* (as PER-, *fumare* smoke, FUME): orig. of smoke from a burning substance]
■ *n.* **1** fragrance, aroma, odor, smell, bouquet, nose, redolence, balm. **2** eau de cologne, toilet water, fragrance, scent, balm, essence. ● *v.* scent; (**perfumed**) see FRAGRANT.

perfumer /pərfyṓomər/ *n.* a maker or seller of perfumes. □□ **perfumery** *n.* (*pl.* **-ies**).

perfunctory /pərfúngktəree/ *adj.* **1 a** done merely for the sake of getting through a duty. **b** done in a cursory or careless manner. **2** superficial; mechanical. □□ **perfunctorily** *adv.* **perfunctoriness** *n.* [LL *perfunctorius* careless f. L *perfungi perfunct-* (as PER-, *fungi* perform)]
■ routine, mechanical, automatic, robotlike, unthinking, superficial, dismissive, inattentive, uninvolved, apathetic, indifferent, unconcerned, removed, distant, dégagé, offhand, heedless, uninterested; hasty, hurried, fleeting, rushed, cursory; careless, slipshod, slovenly, negligent, sketchy.

perfuse /pərfyṓoz/ *v.tr.* **1** (often foll. by *with*) **a** sprinkle (with water, etc.). **b** cover or suffuse (with radiance, etc.). **2** pour or diffuse (water, etc.) through or over. **3** *Med.* cause a fluid to pass through (an organ, etc.). □□ **perfusion** /-fyṓozhən/ *n.* **perfusive** /-fyṓosiv/ *adj.* [L *perfundere perfus-* (as PER-, *fundere* pour)]

pergola /pə́rgələ/ *n.* an arbor or covered walk, formed of growing plants trained over a trellis. [It. f. L *pergula* projecting roof f. *pergere* proceed]

perhaps /pərháps/ *adv.* **1** it may be; possibly (*perhaps it is lost*). **2** introducing a polite request (*perhaps you would open the window?*). [PER + HAP]
■ **1** maybe, possibly, it is possible (that), conceivably, it may be, *archaic* mayhap, *archaic or joc.* peradventure, *archaic or poet.* perchance, *No. of Engl. dial.* happen.

peri /peéree/ *n.* (*pl.* **peris**) **1** (in Persian mythology) a fairy; a good (orig. evil) genius. **2** a beautiful or graceful being. [Pers. *pārī*]

peri- /péree/ *prefix* **1** around; about. **2** *Astron.* the point nearest to (*perigee; perihelion*). [Gk *peri* around, about]

perianth /péreeánth/ *n.* the outer part of a flower. [F *périanthe* f. mod.L *perianthium* (as PERI- + Gk *anthos* flower)]

periapt /péreeápt/ *n.* a thing worn as a charm; an amulet. [F *périapte* f. Gk *periapton* f. *haptō* fasten]
■ see TALISMAN.

pericardium /périkaárdeeəm/ *n.* (*pl.* **pericardia** /-deeə/) the membranous sac enclosing the heart. □□ **pericardiac** /-deeak/ *adj.* **pericardial** *adj.* **pericarditis** /-dítis/ *n.* [mod.L f. Gk *perikardion* (as PERI- + *kardia* heart)]

pericarp /périkaarp/ *n.* the part of a fruit formed from the wall of the ripened ovary. [F *péricarpe* f. Gk *perikarpion* pod, shell (as PERI-, *karpos* fruit)]

perichondrium /périkóndreeəm/ *n.* the membrane enveloping cartilage tissue (except at the joints). [PERI- + Gk *khondros* cartilage]

periclase /périklays/ *n.* a pale mineral consisting of magnesia. [mod.L *periclasia,* erron. f. Gk *peri* exceedingly + *klasis* breaking, from its perfect cleavage]

periclinal /périklínəl/ *adj. Geol.* (of a mound, etc.) sloping down in all directions from a central point. [Gk *periklinēs* sloping on all sides (as PERI-, CLINE)]

pericope /pəríkəpee/ *n.* a short passage or paragraph, esp. a portion of Scripture read in public worship. [LL f. Gk *perikopē* (as PERI-, *kopē* cutting f. *koptō* cut)]
■ see EXCERPT *n.*

pericranium /périkráyneeəm/ *n.* the membrane enveloping the skull. [mod.L f. Gk (as PERI-, *kranion* skull)]

peridot /péridot/ *n.* a green variety of olivine, used esp. as a semiprecious stone. [ME f. OF *peritot,* of unkn. orig.]

perigee /périjee/ *n.* the point in an orbit where the orbiting

---

/. . ./ **pronunciation**	● **part of speech**
□ **phrases, idioms, and compounds**	
□□ **derivatives**	■ **synonym section**
cross-references appear in SMALL CAPITALS or *italics*	

body is nearest the center of the body it is orbiting. (opp. APOGEE). □□ **perigean** /périjeʹeən/ *adj.* [F *périgée* f. mod.L f. Gk *perigeion* around the earth (as PERI-, *gē* earth)]

periglacial /périgláyshəl/ *adj.* of or relating to a region adjoining a glacier.

perigynous /pərijinəs/ *adj.* (of stamens) situated around the pistil or ovary. [mod.L *perigynus* (as PERI-, -GYNOUS)]

perihelion /périheʹelyən/ *n.* (*pl.* **perihelia** /-lyə/) the point of a planet's or comet's orbit nearest to the sun's center. [Graecized f. mod.L *perihelium* (as PERI-, Gk *hēlios* sun)]

peril /péril/ *n.* & *v.* ● *n.* serious and immediate danger. ● *v.tr.* (**periled, periling** or **perilled, perilling**) threaten; endanger. □ **at one's peril** at one's own risk. **in peril of** with great risk to (*in peril of your life*). [ME f. OF f. L *peric(u)lum*]
■ *n.* danger, threat, risk, jeopardy, exposure, vulnerability, susceptibility, insecurity. ● *v.* see ENDANGER.

perilous /périləs/ *adj.* **1** full of risk; dangerous; hazardous. **2** exposed to imminent risk of destruction, etc. □□ **perilously** *adv.* **perilousness** *n.* [ME f. OF *perillous* f. L *periculosus* f. *periculum*: see PERIL]
■ **1** risky, hazardous, unsafe; see also DANGEROUS. **2** vulnerable, susceptible, exposed, at risk, in danger, in jeopardy.

perilune /périlōōn/ *n.* the point in a body's lunar orbit where it is closest to the moon's center (opp. APOLUNE). [PERI- + L *luna* moon, after *perigee*]

perilymph /périlimf/ *n.* the fluid in the labyrinth of the ear.

perimeter /pərímitər/ *n.* **1 a** the circumference or outline of a closed figure. **b** the length of this. **2 a** the outer boundary of an enclosed area. **b** a defended boundary. **3** an instrument for measuring a field of vision. □□ **perimetric** /périmétrik/ *adj.* [F *périmètre* or f. L *perimetrus* f. Gk *perimetros* (as PERI-, *metros* f. *metron* measure)]
■ **2** boundary, border, borderline, margin, periphery, limit(s), bounds, ambit, circumference, edge, verge, fringe(s), *archaic* bourn.

perinatal /pérináyt'l/ *adj.* of or relating to the time immediately before and after birth.

perineum /périneʹeəm/ *n.* the region of the body between the anus and the scrotum or vulva. □□ **perineal** *adj.* [LL f. Gk *perinaion*]

period /péereeəd/ *n.* & *adj.* ● *n.* **1** a length or portion of time (*periods of rain*). **2** a distinct portion of history, a person's life, etc. (*the Federal period*; *Picasso's Blue Period*). **3** *Geol.* a time forming part of a geological era (*the Quaternary period*). **4 a** an interval between recurrences of an astronomical or other phenomenon. **b** the time taken by a planet to rotate about its axis. **5** the time allowed for a lesson in school. **6** an occurrence of menstruation. **7 a** a complete sentence, esp. one consisting of several clauses. **b** (in *pl.*) rhetorical language. **8 a** a punctuation mark (.) used at the end of a sentence or an abbreviation. **b** used at the end of a sentence, etc., to indicate finality, absoluteness, etc. (*we want the best, period*). **9 a** a set of figures repeated in a recurring decimal. **b** the smallest interval over which a function takes the same value. **10** *Chem.* a sequence of elements between two noble gases forming a row in the periodic table. **11** *Music* a discrete division of a musical composition, containing two or more phrases and ending in a cadence. ● *adj.* belonging to or characteristic of some past period (*period furniture*). □ **of the period** of the era under discussion (*the custom of the period*). **period piece** an object or work whose main interest lies in its historical, etc., associations. [ME f. OF *periode* f. L *periodus* f. Gk *periodos* (as PERI-, *odos = hodos* way)]
■ *n.* **1** interval, time, term, span, duration, spell, space, stretch, *colloq.* patch; while. **2** time, era, days, epoch, eon, age, years. **3** lesson, class, session.

periodate /pəríʹədayt/ *n. Chem.* a salt or ester of periodic acid.

periodic /péereeódik/ *adj.* **1** appearing or occurring at regular intervals. **2** of or concerning the period of a celestial body (*periodic motion*). **3** (of diction, etc.) expressed in periods (see PERIOD *n.* 7a). □ **periodic decimal** *Math.* a set of figures repeated in a recurring decimal. **periodic function**

Math. a function returning to the same value at regular intervals. **periodic table** an arrangement of elements in order of increasing atomic number and in which elements of similar chemical properties appear at regular intervals. □□ **periodicity** /-reeədísitee/ *n.* [F *périodique* or L *periodicus* f. Gk *periodikos* (as PERIOD)]
■ **1** periodical, regular, recurrent, cyclical, cyclic, repeated.

periodic acid /pərīódik/ *n. Chem.* a hygroscopic solid acid containing heptavalent iodine. [PER- + IODINE]

periodical /péereeódikəl/ *n.* & *adj.* ● *n.* a newspaper, magazine, etc., issued at regular intervals, usu. monthly or weekly. ● *adj.* **1** published at regular intervals. **2** periodic; occasional. □□ **periodically** *adv.*
■ *n.* magazine, journal, newspaper, paper, publication, newsletter, organ, serial, weekly, monthly, quarterly, yearbook, almanac. ● *adj.* **2** see PERIODIC.

periodization /péereeədīzáyshən/ *n.* the division of history into periods.

periodontics /péereeədóntiks/ *n.pl.* (treated as *sing.*) the branch of dentistry concerned with the structures surrounding and supporting the teeth. □□ **periodontal** *adj.* **periodontist** *n.* [PERI- + Gk *odous odont-* tooth]

periodontology /péereeədontóləjee/ *n.* = PERIODONTICS.

periosteum /péereeósteeəm/ *n.* (*pl.* **periostea** /-teeə/) a membrane enveloping the bones where no cartilage is present. □□ **periosteal** *adj.* **periostitis** /-stítis/ *n.* [mod.L f. Gk *periosteon* (as PERI-, *osteon* bone)]

peripatetic /péripətétik/ *adj.* & *n.* ● *adj.* **1** (of a teacher) working in more than one school or college, etc. **2** going from place to place; itinerant. **3** (**Peripatetic**) Aristotelian (from Aristotle's habit of walking in the Lyceum while teaching). ● *n.* a peripatetic person, esp. a teacher. □□ **peripatetically** *adv.* **peripateticism** *n.* [ME f. OF *peripatetique* or L *peripateticus* f. Gk *peripatētikos* f. *peripateō* (as PERI-, *pateō* walk)]
■ *adj.* **1, 2** see *traveling* (TRAVEL).

peripeteia /péripitéeə, -tíə/ *n.* a sudden change of fortune in a drama or in life. [Gk (as PERI-, *pet-* f. *piptō* fall)]

peripheral /pərífərəl/ *adj.* & *n.* ● *adj.* **1** of minor importance; marginal. **2** of the periphery; on the fringe. **3** *Anat.* near the surface of the body, with special reference to the circulation and nervous system. **4** (of equipment) used with a computer, etc., but not an integral part of it. ● *n.* a peripheral device or piece of equipment. □ **peripheral nervous system** *Anat.* the nervous system outside the brain and spinal cord. **peripheral vision 1** area seen around the outside of one's field of vision. **2** ability to perceive in this way (*contact lenses offered better peripheral vision than glasses*). □□ **peripherally** *adv.*
■ *adj.* **1** incidental, unimportant, marginal, minor, secondary, inessential, unessential, nonessential, unnecessary, superficial, tangential, irrelevant, beside the point; see also IMMATERIAL 1. **2** circumferential, external, perimetric, outside, outer, border.

periphery /pərífəree/ *n.* (*pl.* **-ies**) **1** the boundary of an area or surface. **2** an outer or surrounding region (*built on the periphery of the old town*). [LL *peripheria* f. Gk *periphereia* circumference (as PERI-, *phereia* f. *phero* bear)]
■ **1** perimeter, circumference, border, edge, rim, brim, boundary, margin. **2** see OUTSKIRTS.

periphrasis /pərífrəsis/ *n.* (*pl.* **periphrases** /-seez/) **1** a roundabout way of speaking; circumlocution. **2** a roundabout phrase. [L f. Gk f. *periphrazō* (as PERI-, *phrazō* declare)]

periphrastic /périfrástik/ *adj.* **1** of or involving periphrasis. **2** *Gram.* (of a case, tense, etc.) formed by combination of words rather than by inflection (e.g., *did go, of the people* rather than *went, the people's*). □□ **periphrastically** *adv.* [Gk *periphrastikos* (as PERIPHRASIS)]
■ **1** see RAMBLING 2.

peripteral /pəríptərəl/ *adj.* (of a temple) surrounded by a single row of columns. [Gk *peripteron* (as PERI-, Gk *pteron* wing)]

periscope /périskōp/ *n.* an apparatus with a tube and mirrors or prisms, by which an observer in a trench, submerged submarine, or at the rear of a crowd, etc., can see things otherwise out of sight.

periscopic /pèriskópik/ *adj.* of a periscope. □ **periscopic lens** a lens allowing distinct vision over a wide angle. □□ **periscopically** *adv.*

perish /pérish/ *v.* **1** *intr.* be destroyed; suffer death or ruin. **2** *Brit.* **a** *intr.* (esp. of rubber, a rubber object, etc.) lose its normal qualities; deteriorate; rot. **b** *tr.* cause to rot or deteriorate. **3** *Brit. tr.* (in *passive*) suffer from cold or exposure (*we were perished standing outside*). □ **perish the thought** an exclamation of horror against an unwelcome idea. □□ **perishless** *adj.* [ME f. OF *perir* f. L *perire* pass away (as PER-, *ire* go)]

■ **1** expire, lose one's life, be killed, be lost, meet one's death, be destroyed; see also DIE[1] 1. **2** deteriorate, rot, decay, disintegrate, weaken, fall apart, crumble, corrode. □ **perish the thought** God forbid.

perishable /périshəbəl/ *adj. & n.* ● *adj.* liable to perish; subject to decay. ● *n.* (a thing, esp. a foodstuff, subject to speedy decay. □□ **perishability** /-bílitee/ *n.* **perishableness** *n.*

perishing /périshing/ *adj. & adv. Brit. colloq.* ● *adj.* **1** confounded. **2** freezing cold; extremely chilly. ● *adv.* confoundedly. □□ **perishingly** *adv.*

■ *adj.* **1** infernal, confounded; see also FLAMING 3b, TIRESOME 2.

perisperm /périspərm/ *n.* a mass of nutritive material outside the embryo in some seeds. [PERI- + Gk *sperma* seed]

peristalsis /péristáwlsis, -stál-/ *n.* an involuntary muscular wavelike movement by which the contents of the alimentary canal, etc., are propelled along. □□ **peristaltic** *adj.* **peristaltically** *adv.* [mod.L f. Gk *peristellō* wrap around (as PERI-, *stellō* place)]

peristome /péristōm/ *n.* **1** *Bot.* a fringe of small teeth around the mouth of a capsule in mosses and certain fungi. **2** *Zool.* the parts surrounding the mouth of various invertebrates. [mod.L *peristoma* f. PERI- + Gk *stoma* mouth]

peristyle /péristil/ *n.* a row of columns surrounding a temple, court, cloister, etc.; a space surrounded by columns. [F *péristyle* f. L *peristylum* f. Gk *peristulon* (as PERI-, *stulos* pillar)]

peritoneum /périt'neéəm/ *n.* (*pl.* **peritoneums** or **peritonea** /-neéə/) the serous membrane lining the cavity of the abdomen. □□ **peritoneal** *adj.* [LL f. Gk *peritonaion* (as PERI-, *tonaion* f. *-tonos* stretched)]

peritonitis /périt'nítis/ *n.* an inflammatory disease of the peritoneum.

periwig /périwig/ *n.* esp. *hist.* a wig. □□ **periwigged** *adj.* [alt. of PERUKE, with *-wi-* for F *-u-* sound]

periwinkle[1] /périwingkəl/ *n.* **1** any plant of the genus *Vinca*, esp. an evergreen trailing plant with blue or white flowers. **2** a tropical shrub, *Catharanthus roseus*, native to Madagascar. [ME f. AF *pervenke*, OF *pervenche* f. LL *pervinca*, assim. to PERIWINKLE[2]]

periwinkle[2] /périwingkəl/ *n.* any edible marine gastropod mollusk of the genus *Littorina*; a winkle. [16th c.: orig. unkn.]

perjure /pərjər/ *v.refl. Law* **1** willfully tell an untruth when under oath. **2** (as **perjured** *adj.*) guilty of or involving perjury. □□ **perjurer** *n.* [ME f. OF *parjurer* f. L *perjurare* (as PER-, *jurare* swear)]

■ **1** see LIE[2] *v.* □□ **perjurer** see LIAR.

perjury /pərjəree/ *n.* (*pl.* **-ies**) *Law* **1** a breach of an oath, esp. the act of willfully telling an untruth when under oath. **2** the practice of this. □□ **perjurious** /-jŏŏreeəs/ *adj.* [ME f. AF *perjurie* f. OF *parjurie* f. L *perjurium* (as PERJURE)]

■ **2** lying, mendacity, mendaciousness, falsification, deception, untruthfulness, dishonesty, duplicity.

perk[1] /pərk/ *v. & adj.* ● *v.tr.* raise (one's head, etc.) briskly. ● *adj.* perky; pert. □ **perk up 1** recover confidence, courage, life, or zest. **2** restore confidence or courage or liveliness in (esp. another person). **3** freshen up. [ME, perh. f. var. of PERCH[1]]

■ *adj.* see PERKY 2, JAUNTY. □ **perk up 1** cheer up, become jaunty, brighten, liven up, quicken, revive,

colloq. buck up. **2** invigorate, revitalize, vitalize, revive, inspirit, *colloq.* pep up, buck up. **3** see SPRUCE[1] *v.*

perk[2] /pərk/ *n. colloq.* a perquisite. [abbr.]

■ see PERQUISITE.

perk[3] /pərk/ *v. colloq.* **1** *intr.* (of coffee) percolate, make a bubbling sound in the percolator. **2** *tr.* percolate (coffee). [abbr. of PERCOLATE]

perky /pərkee/ *adj.* (**perkier**, **perkiest**) **1** self-assertive; cocky; pert. **2** lively; cheerful. □□ **perkily** *adv.* **perkiness** *n.*

■ **1** see PERT 1. **2** lively, cheery, cheerful, jaunty, bouncy, bright, perk, vigorous, vitalized, spirited, energetic, zestful, sprightly, frisky, animated, vivacious, effervescent, bubbly, buoyant, gay, *colloq.* full of pep, peppy.

perlite /pərlit/ *n.* (also **pearlite**) a glassy type of vermiculite, expandable to a solid form by heating, used for insulation, etc. [F f. *perle* pearl]

perm /pərm/ *n. & v.* ● *n.* a permanent wave. ● *v.tr.* give a permanent wave to (a person or a person's hair). [abbr.]

permafrost /pərməfrawst, -frost/ *n.* subsoil that remains frozen throughout the year, as in polar regions. [PERMANENT + FROST]

permalloy /pərmáloy, pərmálóy/ *n.* an alloy of nickel and iron that is easily magnetized and demagnetized. [PERMEABLE + ALLOY]

permanent /pərmənənt/ *adj. & n.* ● *adj.* lasting, or intended to last or function, indefinitely (opp. TEMPORARY). ● *n.* = *permanent wave.* □ **permanent magnet** a magnet retaining its magnetic properties without continued excitation. **permanent press** a process applied to a fabric to make it wrinkle-free. **Permanent Secretary** (or **Under-secretary**, etc.) *Brit.* a senior grade in the Civil Service, often a permanent adviser to a minister. **permanent tooth** a tooth succeeding a milk tooth in a mammal, and lasting most of the mammal's life. **permanent wave** an artificial wave in the hair, intended to last for some time. **permanent way** *Brit.* the finished roadbed of a railroad. □□ **permanency** *n.* **permanentize** *v.tr.* **permanently** *adv.* [ME f. OF *permanent* or L *permanēre* (as PER-, *manēre* remain)]

■ unchanging, invariable, changeless, fixed, unchangeable, immutable, unalterable, inalterable, stable, persistent, lasting, long-lasting, enduring, indefinite, perennial; everlasting, eternal, unending, endless, perpetual, undying, imperishable, indestructible. □□ **permanence, permanency** fixedness, changelessness, unalterableness, immutability, unchangeableness, longevity, endurance, perenniality, persistence, dependability, reliability, stability, durability. **permanently** for ever, for good, once and for all, always, eternally, everlastingly, forevermore.

permanganate /pərmánggənayt/ *n. Chem.* any salt of permanganic acid, esp. potassium permanganate.

permanganic acid /pərmanggánik/ *n. Chem.* an acid containing heptavalent manganese. [PER- + *manganic*: see MANGANESE]

permeability /pérmeeəbílitee/ *n.* **1** the state or quality of being permeable. **2** a quantity measuring the influence of a substance on the magnetic flux in the region it occupies.

permeable /pərmeeəbəl/ *adj.* capable of being permeated. [L *permeabilis* (as PERMEATE)]

■ see POROUS 1, 2.

permeate /pərmeeayt/ *v.* **1** *tr.* penetrate throughout; pervade; saturate. **2** *intr.* (usu. foll. by *through*, *among*, etc.) diffuse itself. □□ **permeance** *n.* **permeant** *adj.* **permeation** /-áyshən/ *n.* **permeator** *n.* [L *permeare permeat-* (as PER-, *meare* pass, go)]

■ **1** imbue, penetrate, pervade, infiltrate, enter, spread

/.../ **pronunciation**	● **part of speech**
□ **phrases, idioms, and compounds**	
□□ **derivatives**	■ **synonym section**
cross-references appear in SMALL CAPITALS or *italics*	

through(out), saturate, seep through(out), percolate (through), soak through.

Permian /pérmeeən/ *adj.* & *n. Geol.* ● *adj.* of or relating to the last period of the Paleozoic era with evidence of the development of reptiles and amphibians, and deposits of sandstone. ¶ Cf. Appendix VII. ● *n.* this period or system. [*Perm* in Russia]

per mill /per míl/ *adv.* (also **per mil**) in every thousand. [L]

permissible /pərmísibəl/ *adj.* allowable. □□ **permissibility** *n.* **permissibly** *adv.* [ME f. F or f. med.L *permissibilis* (as PERMIT)]
 ■ allowable, admissible, acceptable, allowed, permitted, tolerable, legal, licit, lawful, legitimate, authorized, proper, (all) right, *colloq.* OK, kosher, legit; pardonable, excusable, venial.

permission /pərmíshən/ *n.* (often foll. by *to* + infin.) consent; authorization. [ME f. OF or f. L *permissio* (as PERMIT)]
 ■ consent, assent, leave, license, sanction, acceptance, authorization, approval, approbation, countenance, allowance, indulgence, *formal* permit.

permissive /pərmísiv/ *adj.* **1** tolerant; liberal, esp. in sexual matters (*the permissive society*). **2** giving permission. □□ **permissively** *adv.* **permissiveness** *n.* [ME f. OF (*-if -ive*) or med.L *permissivus* (as PERMIT)]
 ■ **1** indulgent, lenient, latitudinarian, lax, easygoing, liberal, tolerant, nonrestrictive, libertarian. **2** assenting, consenting, acquiescent; see also AGREEABLE 2.

permit *v.* & *n.* ● *v.* /pərmít/ (**permitted**, **permitting**) **1** *tr.* give permission or consent to; authorize (*permit me to say*). **2 a** *tr.* allow as possible; give an opportunity to (*permit the traffic to flow again*). **b** *intr.* give an opportunity (*circumstances permitting*). **3** *intr.* (foll. by *of*) admit; allow for. ● *n.* /pérmit/ **1 a** a document giving permission to act in a specified way (*was granted a work permit*). **b** a document, etc., that allows entry into a specified zone. **2** permission. □□ **permittee** /-pérmitee/ *n.* **permitter** *n.* [L *permittere* (as PER-, *mittere miss-* let go)]
 ■ *v.* **1** see AUTHORIZE 1, 2a. **2 a** enable, allow, entitle.
 ● *n.* **1** license, authorization, warrant; pass, passport, visa. **2** see PERMISSION.

permittivity /pérmitívitee/ *n. Electr.* a quantity measuring the ability of a substance to store electrical energy in an electric field.

permutate /pérmyŏŏtayt/ *v.tr.* change the order or arrangement of. [as PERMUTE, or back-form. f. PERMUTATION]

permutation /pérmyŏŏtáyshən/ *n.* **1 a** an ordered arrangement or grouping of a set of numbers, items, etc. **b** any one of the range of possible groupings. **2** any combination or selection of a specified number of things from a larger group. □□ **permutational** *adj.* [ME f. OF or f. L *permutatio* (as PERMUTE)]
 ■ **1** see VARIATION 1.

permute /pərmyŏŏt/ *v.tr.* alter the sequence or arrangement of. [ME f. L *permutare* (as PER-, *mutare* change)]
 ■ see TRANSFORM *v.*

pernicious /pərníshəs/ *adj.* destructive; ruinous; fatal. □ **pernicious anemia** see ANEMIA. □□ **perniciously** *adv.* **perniciousness** *n.* [L *perniciosus* f. *pernicies* ruin f. *nex necis* death]
 ■ see DESTRUCTIVE 1. □□ **perniciousness** see *virulence* (VIRULENT).

pernickety /pərníkitee/ *Brit.* var. of PERSNICKETY.

peroneal /pérəneéəl/ *adj. Anat.* relating to or near the fibula. [mod.L *peronaeus* peroneal muscle f. *perone* fibula f. Gk *peronē* pin, fibula]

perorate /pérərayt/ *v.intr.* **1** sum up and conclude a speech. **2** speak at length. [L *perorare perorat-* (as PER-, *orare* speak)]
 ■ **2** see RANT *v.* 2, 3.

peroration /pérəráyshən/ *n.* **1** the concluding part of a speech, forcefully summing up what has been said. **2** a long or overly rhetorical speech.

peroxidase /pəróksidays, -dayz/ *n. Biochem.* any of a class of enzymes found esp. in plants, which catalyze the oxidation of a substrate by hydrogen peroxide.

peroxide /pəróksid/ *n.* & *v.* ● *n. Chem.* **1 a** = *hydrogen peroxide*. **b** (often *attrib.*) a solution of hydrogen peroxide used

to bleach the hair or as an antiseptic. **2** a compound of oxygen with another element containing the greatest possible proportion of oxygen. **3** any salt or ester of hydrogen peroxide. ● *v.tr.* bleach (the hair) with peroxide. [PER- + OXIDE]

perpend var. of PARPEN.

perpendicular /pérpəndíkyələr/ *adj.* & *n.* ● *adj.* **1 a** at right angles to the plane of the horizon. **b** (usu. foll. by *to*) *Geom.* at right angles (to a given line, plane, or surface). **2** upright; vertical. **3** (of a slope, etc.) very steep. **4** (**Perpendicular**) *Archit.* of the third stage of English Gothic (15th–16th c.) with vertical tracery in large windows. **5** in a standing position. ● *n.* **1** a perpendicular line. **2** a plumb rule or a similar instrument. **3** (prec. by *the*) a perpendicular line or direction (*is out of the perpendicular*). □□ **perpendicularity** /-dikyŏŏláritee/ *n.* **perpendicularly** *adv.* [ME f. L *perpendicularis* f. *perpendiculum* plumb line f. PER- + *pendēre* hang]
 ■ *adj.* **1** (*perpendicular to*) at right angles to, at 90 degrees to. **2** erect, upright, vertical, plumb, straight (up and down). **3** precipitous, sheer; see also STEEP[1] *adj.* 1.

perpetrate /pérpitrayt/ *v.tr.* commit or perform (a crime, blunder, or anything outrageous). □□ **perpetration** /-tráyshən/ *n.* **perpetrator** *n.* [L *perpetrare perpetrat-* (as PER-, *patrare* effect)]
 ■ commit, execute, perform, carry out *or* through, effect, effectuate, accomplish, do; practice.

perpetual /pərpéchŏŏəl/ *adj.* **1** eternal; lasting for ever or indefinitely. **2** continuous; uninterrupted. **3** *colloq.* frequent; much repeated (*perpetual interruptions*). **4** (of an office, etc.) held for life (*perpetual secretary*). □ **perpetual calendar** a calendar which can be adjusted to show any combination of day, month, and year. **perpetual check** *Chess* the position of play when a draw is obtained by repeated checking of the king. **perpetual motion** the motion of a hypothetical machine which once set in motion would run forever unless subject to an external force or to wear. □□ **perpetualism** *n.* **perpetually** *adv.* [ME f. OF *perpetuel* f. L *perpetualis* f. *perpetuus* f. *perpes -etis* continuous]
 ■ **1** eternal, everlasting, never-ending, unending, perennial, ageless, timeless, long-lived, permanent, indefinite, unceasing, lasting, enduring; unvarying, unchanging, immutable, invariable, undeviating, *rhet.* sempiternal. **2** constant, uninterrupted, continuous, incessant, persistent, unremitting, unending, nonstop, endless, recurrent. **3** frequent, constant, numerous, many, countless, innumerable, *sl.* umpteen; repeated, continual.

perpetuate /pərpéchŏŏ-ayt/ *v.tr.* **1** make perpetual. **2** preserve from oblivion. □□ **perpetuance** *n.* **perpetuation** /-áyshən/ *n.* **perpetuator** *n.* [L *perpetuare* (as PERPETUAL)]
 ■ **2** continue, maintain, extend, keep (on *or* up), keep going, preserve, memorialize, immortalize, eternalize.

perpetuity /pérpitŏŏ-itee, -tyŏŏ-/ *n.* (*pl.* **-ies**) **1** the state or quality of being perpetual. **2** a perpetual annuity. **3** a perpetual possession or position. □ **in** (or **to** or **for**) **perpetuity** forever. [ME f. OF *perpetuité* f. L *perpetuitas -tatis* (as PERPETUAL)]
 ■ **1** permanence, constancy, timelessness, everlastingness, unendingness; eternity, infinity. □ **in** (or **to** or **for**) **perpetuity** for ever, for all time, till the end of time, till doomsday, forevermore, *colloq.* till the cows come home, till kingdom come.

perplex /pərpléks/ *v.tr.* **1** puzzle, bewilder, or disconcert (a person, a person's mind, etc.). **2** complicate or confuse (a matter). **3** (as **perplexed** *adj.*) *archaic* entangled; intertwined. □□ **perplexedly** /-pléksidlee/ *adv.* **perplexing** *adj.* **perplexingly** *adv.* [back-form. f. *perplexed* f. obs. *perplex* (adj.) f. OF *perplexe* or L *perplexus* (as PER-, *plexus* past part. of *plectere* plait)]
 ■ **1** confuse, bewilder, puzzle, mystify, distract, baffle, befuddle, confound, muddle, disconcert, stump, nonplus, stymie, stupefy, stun, daze, dumbfound, *archaic* wilder, *colloq.* throw, bamboozle, flabbergast, *joc.* discombobulate. **2** see COMPLICATE 1. **3** (**perplexed**) entangled, intertwined, intertwisted,

interwoven, ensnarled, knotty, tangled, twisted, entwined. □□ **perplexing** confusing, bewildering, puzzling, mystifying, baffling, disconcerting, enigmatic, paradoxical, incomprehensible, unfathomable, impenetrable, recondite, arcane; labyrinthine, complex, complicated, Byzantine, intricate, involved, convoluted, twisted, knotty, Gordian.

perplexity /pərpléksitee/ n. (pl. **-ies**) **1** bewilderment; the state of being perplexed. **2** a thing which perplexes. **3** the state of being complicated. **4** archaic an entangled state. [ME f. OF perplexité or LL perplexitas (as PERPLEX)]
■ **1** confusion, bewilderment, bafflement, befuddlement, puzzlement, bemusement, doubt, difficulty. **2** puzzle, enigma, mystery, problem, paradox, quandary, predicament, bind, colloq. catch-22, disp. dilemma. **3** intricacy, complexity, complicatedness, arcaneness, reconditeness, impenetrability, impenetrableness, involvement, unfathomability, obscurity, difficulty.

per pro. /pər pró/ abbr. through the agency of (used in signatures). ¶ The correct sequence is A per pro. B, where B is signing on behalf of A. [L per procurationem]

perquisite /pérkwizit/ n. **1** an extra profit or allowance additional to a main income, etc. **2** a customary extra right or privilege. **3** an incidental benefit attached to employment, etc. **4** a thing which has served its primary use and to which a subordinate or servant has a customary right. [ME f. med.L perquisitum f. L perquirere search diligently for (as PER-, quaerere seek)]
■ **1–3** consideration, emolument, bonus, added attraction or extra, reward, (fringe) benefit, extra, dividend, appanage, token (of appreciation), colloq. perk; right, privilege.

Perrier /péreeay/ n. propr. a carbonated natural mineral water. [the name of a spring at Vergèze, France, its source]

perron /péron/ n. an exterior staircase leading up to a main entrance to a church or other (usu. large) building. [ME f. OF ult. f. L petra stone]

perry /péree/ n. (pl. **-ies**) a drink like cider, made from the fermented juice of pears. [ME pereye, etc. f. OF peré, ult. f. L pirum pear]

per se /pər sáy/ adv. by or in itself; intrinsically. [L]

persecute /pérsikyōōt/ v.tr. **1** subject (a person, etc.) to hostility or ill-treatment, esp. on the grounds of political or religious belief. **2** harass; worry. **3** (often foll. by with) bombard (a person) with questions, etc. □□ **persecutor** n. **persecutory** adj. [ME f. OF persecuter back-form. f. persecuteur persecutor f. LL persecutor f. L persequi (as PER-, sequi secut- follow, pursue)]
■ **1** oppress, maltreat, ill-treat, abuse, molest, victimize, tyrannize, afflict, punish, martyr, torment, torture.
2 bother, annoy, pester, plague, hector, bully, badger, harry, harass, irritate, worry, vex, trouble, importune, hound, Austral. colloq. heavy.

persecution /pérsikyōōshən/ n. the act or an instance of persecuting; the state of being persecuted. □ **persecution complex** (or **mania**) an irrational obsessive fear that others are scheming against one.
■ oppression, maltreatment, ill-treatment, abuse, molestation, victimization, tyrannization, punishment, torment, torture; hectoring, bullying, badgering, harassment.

perseverance /pérsiveérəns/ n. **1** the steadfast pursuit of an objective. **2** (often foll. by in) constant persistence (in a belief, etc.). [ME f. OF f. L perseverantia (as PERSEVERE)]
■ **1** persistence, steadfastness, determination, resolution, resolve, decision, firmness, purposefulness, pertinacity, staying power, stamina, sedulousness, assiduity, tirelessness, indefatigability, endurance, diligence, devotion, tenacity, doggedness.

perseverate /pərsévərayt/ v.intr. **1** continue action, etc., for an unusually or excessively long time. **2** Psychol. tend to prolong or repeat a response after the original stimulus has ceased. □□ **perseveration** /-ráyshən/ n. [L perseverare (as PERSEVERE)]

■ **1** see PERSIST 1.

persevere /pérsiveér/ v.intr. (often foll. by in, at, with) continue steadfastly or determinedly; persist. [ME f. OF perseverer f. L perseverare persist f. perseverus very strict (as PER-, severus severe)]
■ persist, continue, be steadfast or staunch or constant, keep going, stand fast or firm, show determination, stop at nothing, go the distance, keep at it, stick to (it), colloq. stick at it, stick it out, hang on, soldier on, hang in (there); (persevere in or with or at) endure, carry on or through, keep at or on or up, see through, cling to, stick to, go on with, colloq. stick with or at.

Persian /pérzhən, -shən/ n. & adj. ● n. **1 a** a native or inhabitant of ancient or modern Persia (now Iran). **b** a person of Persian descent. **2** the language of ancient Persia or modern Iran. ¶ With modern reference the preferred terms are Iranian and Farsi. **3** (in full **Persian cat**) **a** a cat of a breed with long silky hair and a thick tail. **b** this breed. ● adj. of or relating to Persia or its people or language. □ **Persian carpet** (or **rug**) a carpet or rug of a traditional pattern made in Persia. **Persian lamb** the silky tightly curled fur of a young karakul, used in clothing. [ME f. OF persien f. med.L]

persiennes /pérzee-énz/ n.pl. window shutters, or outside blinds, with louvers. [F, fem. pl. of obs. persien Persian]

persiflage /pérsiflaazh/ n. light raillery; banter. [F persifler banter, formed as PER- + siffler whistle]
■ see RAILLERY.

persimmon /pərsimən/ n. **1** any usu. tropical evergreen tree of the genus Diospyros bearing edible tomato-like fruits. **2** the fruit of this. [corrupt. of an Algonquian word]

persist /pərsíst/ v.intr. **1** (often foll. by in) continue firmly or obstinately (in an opinion or a course of action) esp. despite obstacles, remonstrance, etc. **2** (of an institution, custom, phenomenon, etc.) continue in existence; survive. [L persistere (as PER-, sistere stand)]
■ **1** be persistent, insist, stand firm or fast, be steadfast or staunch; persevere; see also PERSEVERE. **2** remain, continue, endure, carry on, keep up or on, last, linger, stay; see also SURVIVE.

persistent /pərsístənt/ adj. **1** continuing obstinately; persisting. **2** enduring. **3** constantly repeated (persistent nagging). **4** Biol. (of horns, leaves, etc.) remaining instead of falling off in the normal manner. □□ **persistence** n. **persistency** n. **persistently** adv.
■ **1** persisting, persevering, tenacious, steadfast, firm, fast, fixed, staunch, resolute, resolved, determined, unfaltering, unswerving, undeviating, unflagging, tireless, untiring, indefatigable, dogged, unwavering, stubborn, obstinate, obdurate, inflexible, rigid. **2, 3** continuing, enduring, lasting, persisting; constant, continuous, continual, unending, interminable, unremitting, unrelenting, perpetual, incessant, unceasing, nonstop. □□ **persistence** perseverance, resolve, determination, resolution, steadfastness, tenacity, constancy, assiduity, stamina, tirelessness, indefatigability, patience, diligence, pertinacity, doggedness, stubbornness, obstinacy, obduracy; perseverance.

persnickety /pərsníkitee/ adj. colloq. (also **pernickety**) **1** fastidious. **2** precise or overprecise. **3** requiring tact or careful handling. [19th-c. Sc.: orig. unkn.]
■ **1** see FASTIDIOUS 1.

person /pérsən/ n. **1** an individual human being (a cheerful and forthright person). **2** the living body of a human being (hidden about your person). **3** Gram. any of three classes of personal pronouns, verb forms, etc.: the person speaking (**first person**); the person spoken to (**second person**); the person spoken of (**third person**). **4** (in comb.) used to replace -man in words referring to either sex (salesperson). **5**

/.../ **pronunciation**   ● **part of speech**
□ **phrases, idioms, and compounds**
□□ **derivatives**   ■ **synonym section**
cross-references appear in SMALL CAPITALS or italics

(in Christianity) God as Father, Son, or Holy Ghost (*three persons in one God*). **6** *Brit. euphem.* the genitals (*expose one's person*). **7** a character in a play or story. □ **in one's own person** oneself; as oneself. **in person** physically present. **person-to-person 1** between individuals. **2** (of a phone call) booked through the operator to a specified person. [ME f. OF *persone* f. L *persona* actor's mask, character in a play, human being]
■ **1** individual, human (being), being, (living) soul; *Brit. colloq.* bod; mortal, *archaic* wight; (*persons*) people. □ **in person** physically, personally, bodily, actually, in the flesh, in propria persona, *colloq.* large as life; oneself.

persona /pərsṓnə/ *n.* (*pl.* **personae** /-nee/) **1** an aspect of the personality as shown to or perceived by others (opp. ANIMA). **2** *Literary criticism* an author's assumed character in his or her writing. □ **persona grata** /graátə/ a person, esp. a diplomat, acceptable to certain others. **persona non grata** /non graátə, grátə/ a person not acceptable. [L (as PERSON)]
■ **1** face, front, façade, mask, guise, exterior, role, part, character, identity; self.

personable /pə́rsənəbəl/ *adj.* pleasing in appearance and behavior. □□ **personableness** *n.* **personably** *adv.*

personage /pə́rsənij/ *n.* **1** a person, esp. of rank or importance. **2** a character in a play, etc. [ME f. PERSON + -AGE, infl. by med.L *personagium* effigy & F *personnage*]
■ **1** celebrity, luminary, VIP, name, notable, somebody, personality, star, magnate, mogul, big noise, *colloq.* big shot, hot stuff, hotshot, *sl.* big wheel; see also BIGWIG.

personal /pə́rsənəl/ *adj.* **1** one's own; individual; private. **2** done or made in person (*made a personal appearance*; *my personal attention*). **3** directed to or concerning an individual (*a personal letter*). **4 a** referring (esp. in a hostile way) to an individual's private life or concerns (*making personal remarks*; *no need to be personal*). **b** close; intimate (*a personal friend*). **5** of the body and clothing (*personal hygiene*; *personal appearance*). **6** existing as a person, not as an abstraction or thing (*a personal God*). **7** *Gram.* of or denoting one of the three persons (*personal pronoun*). □ **personal column** (or **personals**) the part of a newspaper devoted to private advertisements or messages. **personal computer** a computer designed for use by a single individual. **personal equation 1** the allowance for an individual person's time of reaction in making observations, esp. in astronomy. **2** a bias or prejudice. **personal identification number** a number allocated to an individual, serving as a password esp. for an ATM, computer, etc. ¶ Abbr.: **PIN. personal organizer 1** a loose-leaf notebook with sections for various kinds of information, including a diary, etc. **2** a handheld microcomputer serving the same purpose. **personal pronoun** a pronoun replacing the subject, object, etc., of a clause, etc., e.g., *I, we, you, them, us.* **personal property** (or **estate**) *Law* all one's property except land and those interests in land that pass to one's heirs (cf. REAL¹ *adj.* 3). **personal service** individual service given to a customer. **personal stereo** a small portable audio cassette or CD player, often with radio, used with lightweight headphones. **personal touch** a way of treating a matter characteristic of or designed for an individual. [ME f. OF f. L *personalis* (as PERSON)]
■ **1** private, particular; see also INDIVIDUAL *adj.* 2–4. **2** physical, bodily, actual, live. **3** private, confidential, intimate; unofficial. **4 a** see FAMILIAR *adj.* 4. **b** see INTIMATE¹ *adj.* 1. □ **personal property** (or **estate**) *Law* personalty.

personality /pə́rsənálitee/ *n.* (*pl.* **-ies**) **1** the distinctive character or qualities of a person, often as distinct from others (*an attractive personality*). **2** a famous person; a celebrity (*a TV personality*). **3** a person who stands out from others by virtue of his or her character (*is a real personality*). **4** personal existence or identity; the condition of being a person. **5** (usu. in *pl.*) personal remarks. □ **have personality** have a lively character or noteworthy qualities. **personality cult** the extreme adulation of an individual. **personality trait** a set pattern of perceiving, relating to, and thinking about

one's environment. [ME f. OF *personalité* f. LL *personalitas -tatis* (as PERSONAL)]
■ **1** character, nature, temperament, disposition, makeup, persona; identity. **2** celebrity, luminary, star, superstar, name, somebody, headliner. **3** see CHARACTER *n.* 4.

personalize /pə́rsənəliz/ *v.tr.* **1** make personal, esp. by marking with one's name, etc. **2** personify. □□ **personalization** *n.*
■ **1** monogram, initial, individualize; sign, autograph. **2** humanize, personify, anthropomorphize.

personally /pə́rsənəlee/ *adv.* **1** in person (*see to it personally*). **2** for one's own part (*speaking personally*). **3** in the form of a person (*a god existing personally*). **4** in a personal manner (*took the criticism personally*). **5** as a person; on a personal level.
■ **1** in person, oneself. **2** in one's (own) view *or* opinion, for one's part, for oneself, as far as one is concerned, from one's own viewpoint, from where one stands, as one sees it, as for oneself. **3** in the flesh, bodily, physically; actually. **5** as an individual, as a person.

personalty /pə́rsənəltee/ *n.* (*pl.* **-ies**) *Law* one's personal property or estate (opp. REALTY). [AF *personalté* (as PERSONAL)]

personate /pə́rsənayt/ *v.tr.* **1** play the part of (a character in a drama, etc.; another type of person). **2** pretend to be (another person), esp. for fraudulent purposes; impersonate. □□ **personation** /-náyshən/ *n.* **personator** *n.* [LL *personare personat-* (as PERSON)]
■ see ACT *v.* 5a.

personhood /pə́rsənhoŏd/ *n.* the quality or condition of being an individual person.

personification /pərsónifikáyshən/ *n.* **1** the act of personifying. **2** (foll. by *of*) a person or thing viewed as a striking example of (a quality, etc.) (*the personification of ugliness*).
■ **2** see *embodiment* (EMBODY).

personify /pərsónifi/ *v.tr.* (**-ies, -ied**) **1** attribute a personal nature to (an abstraction or thing). **2** symbolize (a quality, etc.) by a figure in human form. **3** (usu. as **personified** *adj.*) embody (a quality) in one's own person; exemplify typically (*has always been kindness personified*). □□ **personifier** *n.* [F *personnifier* (as PERSON)]
■ **1** humanize, personalize, anthropomorphize. **3** embody, typify, exemplify, epitomize, be the embodiment of, manifest, represent, stand for, symbolize, incarnate.

personnel /pə́rsənél/ *n.* a body of employees, persons involved in a public undertaking, armed forces, etc. □ **personnel carrier** an armored vehicle for transporting troops, etc. **personnel department**, etc., the part of an organization concerned with the appointment, training, and welfare of employees. [F, orig. adj. = personal]
■ see STAFF¹ *n.* 2.

perspective /pərspéktiv/ *n. & adj.* ● *n.* **1 a** the art of drawing solid objects on a two-dimensional surface so as to give the right impression of relative positions, size, etc. **b** a picture drawn in this way. **2** the apparent relation between visible objects as to position, distance, etc. **3** a mental view of the relative importance of things (*keep the right perspective*). **4** a geographical or imaginary prospect. ● *adj.* of or in perspective. □ **in perspective 1** drawn or viewed according to the rules of perspective. **2** correctly regarded in terms of relative importance. □□ **perspectival** *adj.* **perspectively** *adv.* [ME f. med.L *perspectiva* (*ars* art) f. *perspicere perspect-* (as PER-, *specere spect-* look)]
■ *n.* **3** attitude, position, angle, approach, sentiment, outlook, lookout. **4** (point of) view, viewpoint, standpoint, prospect, vantage point, position, angle.

Perspex /pə́rspeks/ *n. Brit. propr.* = PLEXIGLAS. [L *perspicere* look through (as PER-, *specere* look)]

perspicacious /pə́rspikáyshəs/ *adj.* having mental penetration or discernment. □□ **perspicaciously** *adv.* **perspicaciousness** *n.* **perspicacity** /-kásitee/ *n.* [L *perspicax -acis* (as PERSPEX)]

■ see SHREWD. □□ **perspicaciousness**, **perspicacity** see INSIGHT.

perspicuous /pərspíkyŏŏəs/ *adj.* **1** easily understood; clearly expressed. **2** (of a person) expressing things clearly. □□ **perspicuity** /pə́rspikyŏŏ-itee/ *n.* **perspicuously** *adv.* **perspicuousness** *n.* [ME, = transparent f. L *perspicuus* (as PERSPECTIVE)]

■ see CLEAR *adj.* 6b. □□ **perspicuity**, **perspicuousness** see WISDOM 2, 3.

perspiration /pə́rspiráyshən/ *n.* **1** = SWEAT. **2** sweating. □□ **perspiratory** /pərspírətawree, pə́rspirə-/ *adj.* [F (as PERSPIRE)]

■ **1** sweat, dampness, wetness. **2** sweating, *Med.* diaphoresis.

perspire /pərspír/ *v.* **1** *intr.* sweat or exude perspiration, esp. as the result of heat, exercise, anxiety, etc. **2** *tr.* sweat or exude (fluid, etc.). [F *perspirer* f. L *perspirare* (as PER-, *spirare* breathe)]

■ sweat, glow.

persuade /pərswáyd/ *v.tr.* & *refl.* **1** (often foll. by *of*, or *that* + clause) cause (another person or oneself) to believe; convince (*persuaded them that it would be helpful*; *tried to persuade me of its value*). **2 a** (often foll. by *to* + infin.) induce (another person or oneself) (*persuaded us to join them*; *managed to persuade them at last*). **b** (foll. by *away from*, *down to*, etc.) lure, attract, entice, etc. (*persuaded them away from the pub*). □□ **persuadable** *adj.* **persuadability** *n.* **persuasible** *adj.* [L *persuadēre* (as PER-, *suadēre suas-* advise)]

■ **1** convince; bring around, win over, convert; assure. **2 a** induce, prevail (up)on, exhort, importune, prompt, sway. **b** see LURE *v.*

persuader /pərswáydər/ *n.* **1** a person who persuades. **2** *sl.* a gun or other weapon.

persuasion /pərswáyzhən/ *n.* **1** persuading (*yielded to persuasion*). **2** persuasiveness (*use all your persuasion*). **3** a belief or conviction (*my private persuasion*). **4** a religious belief, or the group or sect holding it (*of a different persuasion*). **5** *colloq.* any group or party (*the male persuasion*). [ME f. L *persuasio* (as PERSUADE)]

■ **1** inducement, influence, exhortation; see also *encouragement* (ENCOURAGE). **3** opinion, creed, faith, conviction, set of beliefs; see also BELIEF 1. **4** religion, (religious) conviction; sect, denomination, faction, school (of thought), affiliation, group. **5** see SET² 3.

persuasive /pərswáysiv, -ziv/ *adj.* able to persuade. □□ **persuasively** *adv.* **persuasiveness** *n.* [F *persuasif -ive* or med.L *persuasivus*, (as PERSUADE)]

■ convincing, influential, effective, productive, impressive, efficacious, cogent, weighty, compelling, forceful, valid, winning, authoritative.

PERT *abbr.* program evaluation and review technique.

pert /pərt/ *adj.* **1** saucy or impudent, esp. in speech or conduct. **2** (of clothes, etc.) neat and jaunty. **3** = PEART. □□ **pertly** *adv.* **pertness** *n.* [ME f. OF *apert* f. L *apertus* past part. of *aperire* open & f. OF *aspert* f. L *expertus* EXPERT]

■ **1** forward, brash, brazen, cheeky, insolent, impertinent, flippant, saucy, bold, presumptuous, impudent, disrespectful, out of line, audacious, rude, impolite, uncivil, ill-mannered, unmannerly, brassy, archaic malapert, *colloq.* fresh, flip, wise-guy, *sl.* smart-assed. **2** lively, neat, dapper, sprightly, brisk, cheerful, bright, perky; see also JAUNTY.

pert. *abbr.* pertaining.

pertain /pərtáyn/ *v.intr.* **1** (foll. by *to*) **a** relate or have reference to. **b** belong to as a part or appendage or accessory. **2** (usu. foll. by *to*) be appropriate to. [ME f. OF *partenir* f. L *pertinēre* (as PER-, *tenēre* hold)]

■ **1 a** (*pertain to*) concern, refer to, have reference or relation to, apply to, relate to, include, cover, affect, appertain to, bear on, have bearing on. **2** be appropriate to, be fitting for, befit, suit.

pertinacious /pə́rt'náyshəs/ *adj.* stubborn; persistent; obstinate (in a course of action, etc.). □□ **pertinaciously** *adv.* **pertinaciousness** *n.* **pertinacity** /-násitee/ *n.* [L *pertinax* (as PER-, *tenax* tenacious)]

■ see STUBBORN. □□ **pertinaciousness**, **pertinacity** see *obstinacy* (OBSTINATE).

pertinent /pə́rt'nənt/ *adj.* **1** (often foll. by *to*) relevant to the matter in hand; apposite. **2** to the point. □□ **pertinence** *n.* **pertinency** *n.* **pertinently** *adv.* [ME f. OF *pertinent* or L *pertinēre* (as PERTAIN)]

■ **1** fitting, suitable, apt, relevant, germane, apropos, apposite; see also APPROPRIATE *adj.* **2** see INCISIVE 2.

perturb /pərtə́rb/ *v.tr.* **1** throw into confusion or disorder. **2** disturb mentally; agitate. **3** *Physics* & *Math.* subject (a physical system, or a set of equations, or its solution) to a perturbation. □□ **perturbable** *adj.* **perturbative** /pərtə́rbətiv, pə́rtərbáytiv/ *adj.* **perturbingly** *adv.* [ME f. OF *pertourber* f. L (as PER-, *turbare* disturb)]

■ **1** see DISORDER *v.* **2** upset, disturb, fluster, ruffle, unsettle, disconcert, make uneasy, discomfit, vex, worry, agitate, shake up, alarm, disquiet, confuse, discompose, unnerve.

perturbation /pə́rtərbáyshən/ *n.* **1** the act or an instance of perturbing; the state of being perturbed. **2** a cause of disturbance or agitation. **3** *Physics* a slight alteration of a physical system, e.g., of the electrons in an atom, caused by a secondary influence. **4** *Astron.* a minor deviation in the course of a celestial body, caused by the attraction of a neighboring body.

■ **1** see FLUSTER *n.*

pertussis /pərtúsis/ *n.* whooping cough. [mod.L f. PER- + L *tussis* cough]

peruke /pərŏŏk/ *n. hist.* a wig. [F *perruque* f. It. *perrucca parrucca*, of unkn. orig.]

peruse /pərŏŏz/ *v.tr.* **1** (also *absol.*) read or study, esp. thoroughly or carefully. **2** examine (a person's face, etc.) carefully. □□ **perusal** *n.* **peruser** *n.* [ME, orig. = use up, prob. f. AL f. Rmc (as PER-, USE)]

■ read, study, scrutinize, examine, inspect, review, look over *or* through, go over *or* through; scan, run one's eye over; search, explore, survey, appraise. □□ **perusal** reading, scrutiny, check, examination, study, inspection, scanning, review.

Peruvian /pərŏŏveeən/ *n.* & *adj.* ● *n.* **1** a native or national of Peru. **2** a person of Peruvian descent. ● *adj.* of or relating to Peru. □ **Peruvian bark** the bark of the cinchona tree. [mod.L *Peruvia* Peru]

perv /pərv/ *n.* & *v.* (also **perve**) *sl.* ● *n.* **1** *Brit.* a sexual pervert. **2** *Austral.* an erotic gaze. ● *v.intr.* **1** *Brit.* act like a sexual pervert. **2** (foll. by *at*, *on*) *Austral.* gaze with erotic interest. [abbr.]

pervade /pərváyd/ *v.tr.* **1** spread throughout, permeate. **2** (of influences, etc.) become widespread among or in. **3** be rife among or through. □□ **pervasion** /-váyzhən/ *n.* [L *pervadere* (as PER-, *vadere vas-* go)]

■ **1, 2** see PERMEATE. **3** see INFEST.

pervasive /pərváysiv, -ziv/ *adj.* **1** pervading. **2** able to pervade. □□ **pervasively** *adv.* **pervasiveness** *n.*

■ **1** penetrating, pervading, permeating, omnipresent, general, inescapable, prevalent, universal, widespread, ubiquitous.

perve var. of PERV.

perverse /pərvə́rs/ *adj.* **1** (of a person or action) deliberately or stubbornly departing from what is reasonable or required. **2** persistent in error. **3** wayward; intractable; peevish. **4** perverted; wicked. **5** (of a verdict, etc.) against the weight of evidence or the judge's direction. □□ **perversely** *adv.* **perverseness** *n.* **perversity** *n.* (*pl.* -ies). [ME f. OF *pervers perverse* f. L *perversus* (as PERVERT)]

■ **2** wrong, wrongheaded, awry, contrary, wayward, incorrect, irregular, improper, contradictory. **3** stubborn, self-willed, wayward, wrongheaded, intractable, willful, obdurate, obstinate, pigheaded,

---

adamant, inflexible, unbending, refractory, unyielding; cantankerous, testy, curmudgeonly, churlish, crusty, crotchety, bad-tempered, awkward, petulant, captious, cross, cross-grained, peevish, waspish, snappish, bilious, splenetic, fractious, ill-tempered, quarrelsome, irascible, sullen, contentious, tetchy, touchy, obstreperous, crabby, crabbed, irritable, surly, cranky, *colloq.* grouchy. **4** see ROTTEN 2a.

perversion /pərvȯrzhən, -shən/ *n.* **1** an act of perverting; the state of being perverted. **2** a perverted form of an act or thing. **3 a** preference for an abnormal form of sexual activity. **b** such an activity. [ME f. L *perversio* (as PERVERT)]

▪ **1** deviation, diversion, misdirection, corruption, subversion, distortion, twisting, falsification, misrepresentation. **3 b** deviation, deviance, deviancy, abnormality, depravity, debauchery, *colloq.* kinkiness; unnatural act, vice, aberration.

pervert *v.* & *n.* ● *v.tr.* /pərvȯrt/ **1** turn (a person or thing) aside from its proper use or nature. **2** misapply or misconstrue (words, etc.). **3** lead astray (a person, a person's mind, etc.) from his or her opinion or conduct, or esp. religious belief. **4** (as **perverted** *adj.*) showing perversion. ● *n.* /pȯrvərt/ **1** a perverted person. **2** a person showing sexual perversion. □□ **perversive** /-vȯrsiv/ *adj.* **pervertedly** /-vȯrtidlee/ *adv.* **perverter** /-vȯrtər/ *n.* [ME f. OF *pervertir* or f. L *pervertere* (as PER-, *vertere vers-* turn): cf. CONVERT]

▪ *v.* **1, 2** deflect, divert, sidetrack, turn aside or away, subvert, misdirect, distort, twist, abuse, falsify, misapply, misconstrue, misrepresent, corrupt. **3** lead astray, degrade, corrupt, *archaic* demoralize. **4** (**perverted**) deviant, deviate, abnormal, amoral, unmoral, immoral, bad, depraved, unnatural, warped, twisted, profligate, dissolute, delinquent, degenerate, evil, wicked, malign, malicious, malevolent, evil-minded, sinful, iniquitous, base, foul, corrupt, unprincipled, *literary* malefic. ● *n.* **1** see WEIRDO. **2** deviant, degenerate, debauchee, deviate.

pervious /pȯrveeəs/ *adj.* **1** permeable. **2** (usu. foll. by *to*) **a** affording passage. **b** accessible (to reason, etc.). □□ **perviousness** *n.* [L *pervius* (as PER-, *vius* f. *via* way)]

▪ **1** see POROUS 1, 2. **2 b** see RECEPTIVE.

Pesach /páysaakh, pé-/ *n.* the Passover festival. [Heb. *Pesaḥ*]

peseta /pəsáytə/ *n.* the chief monetary unit of Spain, orig. a silver coin. [Sp., dimin. of *pesa* weight f. L *pensa* pl. of *pensum*: see POISE¹]

pesky /péskee/ *adj.* (**peskier, peskiest**) *colloq.* troublesome; annoying. □□ **peskily** *adv.* **peskiness** *n.* [18th c.: perh. f. PEST]

▪ see TROUBLESOME 2.

peso /páysō/ *n.* (*pl.* **-os**) **1** the chief monetary unit of several Latin American countries and of the Philippines. **2** a note or coin worth one peso. [Sp., = weight, f. L *pensum*: see POISE¹]

pessary /pésəree/ *n.* (*pl.* **-ies**) *Med.* **1** a device worn in the vagina to support the uterus or as a contraceptive. **2** a vaginal suppository. [ME f. LL *pessarium, pessulum* f. *pessum, pessus* f. Gk *pessos* oval stone]

pessimism /pésimizəm/ *n.* **1** a tendency to take the worst view or expect the worst outcome. **2** *Philos.* a belief that this world is as bad as it could be or that all things tend to evil (opp. OPTIMISM). □□ **pessimist** *n.* **pessimistic** *adj.* **pessimistically** *adv.* [L *pessimus* worst, after OPTIMISM]

▪ **1** defeatism, negativity, cynicism; discouragement, gloom, melancholy, despondency, hopelessness, despair. □□ **pessimist** see MISERY 3. **pessimistic** gloomy, negative, despairing, depressed, despondent, dejected, downhearted, heavyhearted, defeatist, glum, unhappy, cheerless, joyless, cynical, bleak, hopeless, forlorn.

pest /pest/ *n.* **1** a troublesome or annoying person or thing; a nuisance. **2** a destructive animal, esp. an insect which attacks crops, livestock, etc. **3** *archaic* a pestilence; a plague. [F *peste* or L *pestis* plague]

▪ **1** nuisance, annoyance, nag, irritant, bother, gadfly, bane, trial, vexation, curse, thorn in one's flesh or side,

colloq. pain (in the neck), *sl.* pain in the butt. **3** see PLAGUE *n.* 1.

pester /péstər/ *v.tr.* trouble or annoy, esp. with frequent or persistent requests. □□ **pesterer** *n.* [prob. f. *impester* f. F *empestrer* encumber: infl. by PEST]

▪ annoy, nag, irritate, irk, bother, get at or to, badger, plague, vex, fret, hector, harass, harry, heckle, nettle, chafe, pique, provoke, exasperate, bedevil, get or grate on a person's nerves, torment, persecute, chivy, *colloq.* drive a person up the wall, get under a person's skin, get in a person's hair, hassle, needle, give a person the needle, peeve, *sl.* bug; trouble, importune.

pesticide /péstisid/ *n.* a substance used for destroying insects or other organisms harmful to cultivated plants or to animals. □□ **pesticidal** /-síd'l/ *adj.*

pestiferous /pestífərəs/ *adj.* **1** noxious; pestilent. **2** harmful; pernicious; bearing moral contagion. [L *pestifer, -ferus* (as PEST)]

▪ pestilential; see also HARMFUL.

pestilence /péstiləns/ *n.* **1** a fatal epidemic disease, esp. bubonic plague. **2** something evil or destructive. [ME f. OF f. L *pestilentia* (as PESTILENT)]

▪ **1** plague, epidemic, pandemic, black death, *archaic* pest. **2** scourge, blight, curse, cancer, canker, bane, affliction.

pestilent /péstilənt/ *adj.* **1** destructive to life; deadly. **2** harmful or morally destructive. **3** *colloq.* troublesome; annoying. □□ **pestilently** *adv.* [L *pestilens, pestilentus* f. *pestis* plague]

pestilential /péstilénshəl/ *adj.* **1** of or relating to pestilence. **2** dangerous; troublesome; pestilent. □□ **pestilentially** *adv.* [ME f. med.L *pestilentialis* f. L *pestilentia* (as PESTILENT)]

▪ **2** see HARMFUL, TROUBLESOME 2.

pestle /pésəl/ *n.* & *v.* ● *n.* **1** a club-shaped instrument for pounding substances in a mortar. **2** an appliance for pounding, etc. ● *v.* **1** *tr.* pound with a pestle or in a similar manner. **2** *intr.* use a pestle. [ME f. OF *pestel* f. L *pistillum* f. *pinsare pist-* to pound]

pesto /péstō/ *n.* a sauce made of fresh chopped basil, garlic, olive oil, and Parmesan cheese, used for pasta, fish, etc. [It., f. *pestare* to pound]

Pet. *abbr.* Peter (New Testament).

pet¹ /pet/ *n., adj.,* & *v.* ● *n.* **1** a domestic or tamed animal kept for pleasure or companionship. **2** a darling; a favorite (often as a term of endearment). ● *attrib.adj.* **1** kept as a pet (*pet lamb*). **2** of or for pet animals (*pet food*). **3** often *joc.* favorite or particular (*pet aversion*). **4** expressing fondness or familiarity (*pet name*). ● *v.tr.* (**petted, petting**) **1** treat as a pet. **2** (also *absol.*) fondle, esp. erotically. □ **pet peeve** *colloq.* something especially annoying to an individual. □□ **petter** *n.* [16th-c. Sc. & No. of Engl. dial.: orig. unkn.]

▪ *n.* **2** darling, favorite, idol, apple of one's eye, *colloq.* fair-haired boy, *derog.* minion. ● *attrib.adj.* **1** tame, trained, domesticated; broken, housebroken, esp. *Brit.* house-trained. **3** favorite, favored, preferred, cherished, special, particular; prized, treasured, precious, dearest, adored, darling. ● *v.* **1** pamper, favor, baby, coddle, cosset, mollycoddle, spoil, indulge, dote on. **2** caress, fondle, stroke, pat; cuddle, snuggle, *colloq.* neck, smooch, canoodle, make out, *Austral.* & *NZ* smoodge.

pet² /pet/ *n.* a feeling of petty resentment or ill-humor (esp. *be in a pet*). [16th c.: orig. unkn.]

▪ (bad or ill) temper, fit of pique, sulk, (bad) mood, fume, esp. *Brit. sl.* wax.

peta- /pétə/ *comb. form* denoting a factor of 10^{15}. [perh. f. PENTA-]

petal /pét'l/ *n.* each of the parts of the corolla of a flower. □□ **petaline** /-lin, -lin/ *adj.* **petalled** *adj.* (also in *comb.*). **petallike** *adj.* **petaloid** *adj.* [mod.L *petalum*, in LL metal plate f. Gk *petalon* leaf f. *petalos* outspread]

petard /pitaard/ *n. hist.* **1** a small bomb used to blast down a door, etc. **2** a kind of firework. □ **hoist with** (or **by**) **one's own petard** affected oneself by one's schemes against others. [F *pétard* f. *péter* break wind]

petasus /pétəsəs/ *n.* an ancient Greek hat with a low crown and broad brim, esp. (in Greek mythology) as worn by Hermes. [L f. Gk *petasos*]

petaurist /pətáwrist/ *n.* any flying squirrel of the genus *Petaurista*, native to E. Asia. [Gk *petauristēs* performer on a springboard (*petauron*)]

petechia /piteékeeə/ *n.* (*pl.* **petechiae** /-kee-ee/) *Med.* a small red or purple spot as a result of bleeding into the skin. □□ **petechial** *adj.* [mod.L f. It. *petecchia* a freckle or spot on one's face]

peter[1] /peétər/ *v. & n.* ● *v.intr.* **1** (foll. by *out*) (orig. of a vein of ore, etc.) diminish; come to an end. **2** *Bridge* play an echo. ● *n. Bridge* an echo. [19th c.: orig. unkn.]
■ *v.* **1** (*peter out*) diminish, evaporate, wane, come to nothing, die out, disappear, fail, fade (out *or* away), dwindle, run out, give out, flag, melt away.

peter[2] /peétər/ *n. sl.* **1** a prison cell. **2** a safe. **3** *coarse sl.* penis. [perh. f. the name *Peter*]

peterman /peétərmən/ *n.* (*pl.* **-men**) (also **peteman**) *sl.* a safecracker.

Peter Pan /peétər pán/ *n.* a person who retains youthful features, or who is immature. [hero of J. M. Barrie's play of the same name (1904)]

Peter Principle /peétər/ *n. joc.* the principle that members of a hierarchy are promoted until they reach the level at which they are no longer competent. [L. J. *Peter*, its propounder, b. 1919]

petersham /peétərshəm/ *n.* thick corded silk ribbon used for belts, etc. [Lord *Petersham*, Engl. army officer d. 1851]

Peter's pence /peétərz/ *n.pl. RC Ch.* **1** *hist.* an annual tax of one penny, formerly paid to the papal see by English landowners. **2** (since 1860) a voluntary payment to the papal treasury. [St. *Peter*, as first pope]

petiole /péteeōl/ *n.* the slender stalk joining a leaf to a stem. □□ **petiolar** *adj.* **petiolate** /pétiəláyt/ *adj.* [F *pétiole* f. L *petiolus* little foot, stalk]

petit /pétee/ *adj. esp. Law* petty; small; of lesser importance. □ **petit jury** a jury of 12 persons who try the final issue of fact in civil or criminal cases and pronounce a verdict. [ME f. OF, = small, f. Rmc, perh. imit. of child's speech]

petit bourgeois /pétee boŏrzhwaa, boŏrzhwaá, pətée/ *n.* (*pl.* **petits bourgeois** *pronunc.* same) a member of the lower middle classes. [F]

petite /pəteét/ *adj. & n.* ● *adj.* (of a woman) of small and dainty build. ● *n.* a clothing size for petite women. □ **petite bourgeoisie** the lower middle classes. [F, fem. of PETIT]
■ delicate, dainty, diminutive, small, little, slight, tiny, small-boned, *Brit. colloq.* dinky.

petit four /pétee fáwr/ *n.* (*pl.* **petits fours** /fórz/) a very small fancy frosted cake. [F, = little oven]

petition /pətíshən/ *n. & v.* ● *n.* **1** a supplication or request. **2** a formal written request, esp. one signed by many people, appealing to authority in some cause. **3** *Law* an application to a court for a writ, etc. ● *v.* **1** *tr.* make or address a petition to (*petition the court*). **2** *intr.* (often foll. by *for, to*) appeal earnestly or humbly. □ **Petition of Right 1** *Brit. hist.* a parliamentary declaration of rights and liberties of the people assented to by Charles I in 1628. **2** *Brit. Law* a common-law remedy against the crown for the recovery of property. □□ **petitionable** *adj.* **petitionary** *adj.* **petitioner** *n.* [ME f. OF f. L *petitio -onis*]
■ *n.* **1** request, application, solicitation, suit, entreaty, supplication, plea, appeal. ● *v.* **1** request, ask, apply to, solicit, call upon. **2** supplicate, plead; (*petition for or to*) entreat, beseech, implore, importune, pray; see also APPEAL *v.* 1.

petitio principii /pitísheeō prinkípee-ee, -sípee-ī/ *n.* a logical fallacy in which a conclusion is taken for granted in the premise; begging the question. [L, = assuming a principle: see PETITION]

petit-maître /pəteemáytrə/ *n.* a dandy or fop. [F, = little master]

petit mal /pétee maál, mál/ *n.* a mild form of epilepsy with only momentary loss of consciousness (cf. GRAND MAL). [F, = little sickness]

petit point /pétee póynt, pətée pwáN/ *n.* **1** embroidery on canvas using small stitches. **2** tent stitch. [F, = little point]

Petrarchan /pitraárkən/ *adj.* denoting a sonnet of the kind used by the Italian poet Petrarch (d. 1374), with an octave rhyming *abbaabba*, and a sestet usu. rhyming *cdcdcd* or *cdecde.*

petrel /pétrəl/ *n.* any of various sea birds of the family Procellariidae or Hydrobatidae, usu. flying far from land. [17th c. (also *pitteral*), of uncert. orig.: later assoc. with St. Peter (Matt. 14:30)]

Petri dish /peetree/ *n.* a shallow covered dish used for the culture of bacteria, etc. [J. R. *Petri*, Ger. bacteriologist d. 1921]

petrifaction /pétrifákshən/ *n.* **1** the process of fossilization whereby organic matter is turned into a stony substance. **2** a petrified substance or mass. **3** a state of extreme fear or terror. [PETRIFY after *stupefaction*]

petrify /pétrifī/ *v.* (**-ies, -ied**) **1** *tr.* (also as **petrified** *adj.*) paralyze with fear, astonishment, etc. **2** *tr.* change (organic matter) into a stony substance. **3** *intr.* become like stone. **4** *tr.* deprive (the mind, a doctrine, etc.) of vitality; deaden. [F *pétrifier* f. med.L *petrificare* f. L *petra* rock f. Gk]
■ **1** frighten, scare, horrify, terrify, paralyze, numb, benumb; shock, dumbfound, strike dumb, stun, astonish, astound, amaze, confound, disconcert, stupefy, appall, *colloq.* flabbergast; (**petrified**) horrified, horror-struck, terrified, terror-stricken, panic-stricken, frightened, afraid, scared, paralyzed, numbed, benumbed, frozen; shocked, speechless, dumbfounded, dumbstruck, stunned, thunderstruck, astonished, astounded, stupefied, appalled, aghast, *colloq.* flabbergasted. **2** ossify, fossilize, turn to stone. **4** see DEADEN.

petro- /pétrō/ *comb. form* **1** rock. **2** petroleum (*petrochemistry*). [Gk *petros* stone or *petra* rock]

petrochemical /pétrōkémikəl/ *n. & adj.* ● *n.* a substance industrially obtained from petroleum or natural gas. ● *adj.* of or relating to petrochemistry or petrochemicals.

petrochemistry /pétrōkémistree/ *n.* **1** the chemistry of rocks. **2** the chemistry of petroleum.

petrodollar /pétrōdolər/ *n.* a notional unit of currency earned by a petroleum-exporting country.

petroglyph /pétrəglif/ *n.* a rock carving, esp. a prehistoric one. [PETRO- + Gk *glyphē* carving]

petrography /petrógrəfee/ *n.* the scientific description of the composition and formation of rocks. □□ **petrographer** *n.* **petrographic** /-rəgráfik/ *adj.* **petrographical** *adj.*

petrol /pétrəl/ *n. Brit.* **1** refined petroleum used as a fuel in motor vehicles, aircraft, etc.; gasoline. **2** (*attrib.*) concerned with the supply of petrol (*petrol pump*; *petrol station*). □ **petrol bomb** *Brit.* a simple bomb made of a petrol-filled bottle and a wick; Molotov cocktail. [F *pétrole* f. med.L *petroleum*: see PETROLEUM]

petrolatum /pétrəláytəm/ *n.* petroleum jelly. [mod.L f. PETROL + -*atum*]

petroleum /pətrṓleeəm/ *n.* a hydrocarbon oil found in the upper strata of the earth, refined for use as a fuel for heating and in internal combustion engines, for lighting, dry cleaning, etc. □ **petroleum ether** a volatile liquid distilled from petroleum, consisting of a mixture of hydrocarbons. **petroleum jelly** a translucent solid mixture of hydrocarbons used as a lubricant, ointment, etc. [med.L f. L *petra* rock f. Gk + L *oleum* oil]

petrolic /petrólik/ *adj.* of or relating to petrol or petroleum.

petrology /petróləjee/ *n.* the study of the origin, structure, composition, etc., of rocks. □□ **petrologic** /pétrəlójik/ *adj.* **petrological** *adj.* **petrologist** *n.*

petrous /pétrəs/ *adj.* **1** *Anat.* denoting the hard part of the

/.../ **pronunciation** ● **part of speech**
□ **phrases, idioms, and compounds**
□□ **derivatives** ■ **synonym section**
cross-references appear in SMALL CAPITALS or *italics*

temporal bone protecting the inner ear. **2** *Geol.* of, like, or relating to rock. [L *petrosus* f. L *petra* rock f. Gk]

petticoat /péteekŏt/ *n.* **1** a woman's or girl's skirted undergarment hanging from the waist or shoulders. **2** often *derog. sl.* **a** a woman or girl. **b** (in *pl.*) the female sex. **3** (*attrib.*) often *derog.* feminine; associated with women (*petticoat pedantry*). □□ **petticoated** *adj.* **petticoatless** *adj.* [ME f. *petty coat*]

pettifog /péteefawg, -fog/ *v.intr.* (**pettifogged, pettifogging**) **1** practice legal deception or trickery. **2** quibble or wrangle about petty points. [back-form. f. PETTIFOGGER]
■ **2** see QUIBBLE *v.*

pettifogger /péteefáwgər, -fóg-/ *n.* **1** a rascally lawyer; an inferior legal practitioner. **2** a petty practitioner in any activity. □□ **pettifoggery** *n.* **pettifogging** *adj.* [PETTY + *fogger* underhanded dealer, prob. f. *Fugger* family of German merchants in the 15th–16th c.]
■ □□ **pettifogging** see *legalistic* (LEGALISM).

pettish /pétish/ *adj.* peevish, petulant; easily put out. □□ **pettishly** *adv.* **pettishness** *n.* [PET² + -ISH¹]
■ see PETULANT.

petty /pétee/ *adj.* (**pettier, pettiest**) **1** unimportant; trivial. **2** mean; small-minded; contemptible. **3** minor; inferior; on a small scale (*petty princes*). **4** *Law* (of a crime) of lesser importance (*petty sessions*) (cf. COMMON, GRAND). □ **petty bourgeois** = PETIT BOURGEOIS. **petty bourgeoisie** = *petite bourgeoisie*. **petty cash** money from or for small items of receipt or expenditure. **petty officer** a naval NCO. **petty treason** see TREASON. □□ **pettily** *adv.* **pettiness** *n.* [ME *pety*, var. of PETIT]
■ **1** insignificant, unimportant, trivial, paltry, niggling, trifling, negligible, puny, inessential, nonessential, inconsequential, slight, nugatory, picayune, dinky, *colloq.* piddling. **2** mean, miserly, stingy, cheeseparing, grudging, small-minded, cheap, niggardly, parsimonious, ungenerous, tight, tightfisted, close, closefisted, picayune, *Brit. colloq.* mingy. **3** inferior, *colloq.* measly, small-time; see also MINOR *adj.*

petulant /péchələnt/ *adj.* peevishly impatient or irritable. □□ **petulance** *n.* **petulantly** *adv.* [F *pétulant* f. L *petulans* -*antis* f. *petere* seek]
■ peevish, pettish, impatient, ill-humored, testy, waspish, irascible, choleric, cross, captious, ill-tempered, bad-tempered, splenetic, moody, sour, bilious, crabby, crabbed, irritable, huffish, huffy, perverse, snappish, crotchety, cantankerous, curmudgeonly, grumpy, *colloq.* grouchy.

petunia /pitōōnyə, -tyōōn-/ *n.* **1** any plant of the genus *Petunia* with white, purple, red, etc., funnel-shaped flowers. **2** a dark violet or purple color. [mod.L f. F *petun* f. Guarani *petŷ* tobacco]

petuntse /pitōŏntsee/ *n.* a white variable feldspathic mineral used for making porcelain. [Chin. *baidunzi* f. *bai* white + *dun* stone + suffix -*zi*]

pew /pyōō/ *n. & v.* ● *n.* **1** (in a church) a long bench with a back; an enclosed compartment. **2** *Brit. colloq.* a seat (esp. *take a pew*). ● *v.tr.* furnish with pews. □□ **pewage** *n.* **pewless** *adj.* [ME *pywe, puwe* f. OF *puye* balcony f. L *podia* pl. of PODIUM]

pewit var. of PEEWIT.

pewter /pyōōtər/ *n.* **1** a gray alloy of tin with lead, copper, antimony, or various other metals. **2** utensils made of this. **3** *Brit. sl.* a tankard, etc., as a prize. □□ **pewterer** *n.* [ME f. OF *peutre, peualtre* f. Rmc, of unkn. orig.]

peyote /payōtee/ *n.* **1** any Mexican cactus of the genus *Lophophora*, esp. *L. williamsii* having no spines and button-like tops when dried. **2** a hallucinogenic drug containing mescaline prepared from this. [Amer. Sp. f. Nahuatl *peyotl*]

Pf. *abbr.* pfennig.

Pfc. *abbr.* (also **PFC**) Private First Class.

pfennig / fénig, pfénikh / *n.* a small German coin, worth one hundredth of a mark. [G, rel. to PENNY]

PG *abbr.* (of movies) classified as suitable for children subject to parental guidance.

pg. *abbr.* page.

PGA *abbr.* Professional Golfers' Association.

PG-13 *abbr.* (of a film) classified as suitable for children under age 13 subject to parental guidance.

pH /pee-áych/ *n. Chem.* a logarithm of the reciprocal of the hydrogen-ion concentration in moles per liter of a solution, giving a measure of its acidity or alkalinity. [G, f. *Potenz* power + *H* (symbol for hydrogen)]

phaeton /fáyit'n, fáyt'n/ *n.* **1** a light open four-wheeled carriage, usu. drawn by a pair of horses. **2** a vintage touring car. [F *phaéton* f. L *Phaethon* f. Gk *Phaethōn*, son of Helios the sun god who was allowed to drive the sun-chariot for a day, with disastrous results]

phage / fayj / *n.* = BACTERIOPHAGE. [abbr.]

phagocyte / fágəsit / *n.* a type of cell capable of engulfing and absorbing foreign matter, esp. a leukocyte ingesting bacteria in the body. □□ **phagocytic** /-sítik/ *adj.* [Gk *phag-* eat + -CYTE]

phagocytosis / fágəsitōsis / *n.* the ingestion of bacteria, etc., by phagocytes. □□ **phagocytize** *v.tr.* **phagocytose** *v.tr.*

-phagous / fəgəs / *comb. form* that eats (as specified) (*ichthyophagous*). [L -*phagus* f. Gk -*phagos* f. *phagein* eat]

-phagy / fəjee / *comb. form* the eating of (specified food) (*ichthyophagy*). [Gk -*phagia* (as -PHAGOUS)]

phalange / fálanj, fəlánj / *n.* **1** *Anat.* = PHALANX 4. **2** (**Phalange**) a right-wing activist Maronite party in Lebanon (cf. FALANGE). [F f. L *phalanx*: see PHALANX]

phalangeal / fəlánjeeəl / *adj. Anat.* of or relating to a phalanx.

phalanger / fəlánjər / *n.* any of various marsupials of the family Phalangeridae, including cuscuses and possums. [F f. Gk *phalaggion* spider's web, f. the webbed toes of its hind feet]

phalanx / fálangks / *n.* (*pl.* **phalanxes** or **phalanges** / fəlánjeez/) **1** *Gk Antiq.* a line of battle, esp. a body of Macedonian infantry drawn up in close order. **2** a set of people, etc., forming a compact mass, or banded for a common purpose. **3** a bone of the finger or toe. **4** *Bot.* a bundle of stamens united by filaments. [L f. Gk *phalagx -ggos*]

phalarope / fálərōp / *n.* any small wading or swimming bird of the subfamily Phalaropodidae, with a straight bill and lobed feet. [F f. mod.L *Phalaropus*, irreg. f. Gk *phalaris* coot + *pous podos* foot]

phalli *pl.* of PHALLUS.

phallic / fálik / *adj.* **1** of, relating to, or resembling a phallus. **2** *Psychol.* denoting the stage of male sexual development characterized by preoccupation with the genitals. □□ **phallically** *adv.* [F *phallique* & Gk *phallikos* (as PHALLUS)]

phallocentric / fálōséntrik / *adj.* centered on the phallus or on male attitudes. □□ **phallocentricity** /-sentrísitee/ *n.* **phallocentrism** /-trizəm/ *n.*

phallus / fáləs / *n.* (*pl.* **phalli** /-li/ or **phalluses**) **1** the (esp. erect) penis. **2** an image of this as a symbol of generative power in nature. □□ **phallicism** /-lisízəm/ *n.* **phallism** *n.* [LL f. Gk *phallos*]

phanariot / fənáreeət / *n. hist.* a member of a class of Greek officials in Constantinople under the Ottoman Empire. [mod.Gk *phanariōtēs* f. *Phanar* the part of the city where they lived f. Gk *phanarion* lighthouse (on the Golden Horn)]

phanerogam / fánərəgám / *n. Bot.* a plant that has stamens and pistils, a flowering plant (cf. CRYPTOGAM). □□ **phanerogamic** /-gámik/ *adj.* **phanerogamous** /-rógəməs/ *adj.* [F *phanérogame* f. Gk *phaneros* visible + *gamos* marriage]

phantasm / fántazəm / *n.* **1** an illusion; a phantom. **2** (usu. foll. by *of*) an illusory likeness. **3** a supposed vision of an absent (living or dead) person. □□ **phantasmal** /-tázm'l/ *adj.* **phantasmic** /-tázmik/ *adj.* [ME f. OF *fantasme* f. L f. Gk *phantasma* f. *phantazō* make visible f. *phainō* show]
■ **1** see ILLUSION 4. **3** see VISION *n.* 2. □□ **phantasmal** see INSUBSTANTIAL 2.

phantasmagoria / fántazməgáwreeə / *n.* **1** a shifting series of real or imaginary figures as seen in a dream. **2** an optical device for rapidly varying the size of images on a screen. □□ **phantasmagoric** /-gáwrik, -gór-/ *adj.* **phantasmagorical** *adj.* [prob. f. F *fantasmagorie* (as PHANTASM + fanciful ending)]
■ **1** see ILLUSION 4. □□ **phantasmagorical** see INSUBSTANTIAL 2.

phantom /fántəm/ n. & adj. ● n. **1** a ghost; an apparition; a specter. **2** a form without substance or reality; a mental illusion. **3** Med. a model of the whole or part of the body used to practice or demonstrate operative or therapeutic methods. ● adj. merely apparent; illusory. □ **phantom circuit** an arrangement of telegraph or other electrical wires equivalent to an extra circuit. **phantom limb** a continuing sensation of the presence of a limb which has been amputated. **phantom pregnancy** Med. the symptoms of pregnancy in a person not actually pregnant. [ME f. OF fantosme ult. f. Gk phantasma (as PHANTASM)]
■ n. **1** apparition, specter, ghost, spirit, phantasm, wraith, revenant, vision, eidolon, colloq. spook, literary shade. **2** figment (of the imagination), delusion, phantasm, chimera, hallucination, fancy, mirage; see also ILLUSION 3, 4. ● adj. see ILLUSORY.

phar. abbr. (also **pharm.** or **Pharm.**) **1** pharmaceutical. **2** pharmacist. **3** pharmacy.

Pharaoh /fáirō, fárō, fáyrō/ n. **1** the ruler of ancient Egypt. **2** the title of this ruler. □□ **Pharaonic** /fáirayónik/ adj. [OE f. eccl.L Pharao f. Gk Pharaō f. Heb. par'ōh f. Egypt. pr-'o great house]

Pharisee /fárisee/ (also **pharisee**) n. **1** a member of an ancient Jewish sect, distinguished by strict observance of the traditional and written law. **2** a person of the spirit or disposition attributed to the Pharisees in the New Testament; a self-righteous person; a hypocrite. □□ **Pharisaic** /fárisáyik/ adj. **Pharisaical** /fárisáyikəl/ adj. **Pharisaism** /fárisayizəm/ n. [OE fariseus & OF pharise f. eccl.L pharisaeus f. Gk Pharisaios f. Aram. p'rišayyā pl. f. Heb. pārûs separated]
■ **2** hypocrite, pretender, dissembler, humbug, fraud, whited sepulcher, pietist, charlatan, prig, colloq. goody, goody-goody. □□ **Pharisaic, Pharisaical** hypocritical, insincere, self-righteous, pretentious, sanctimonious, pietistical, priggish, pietistic, colloq. goody-goody, holier-than-thou, smarmy.

pharmaceutical /fáarməsõõtikəl/ adj. & n. ● adj. **1** of or engaged in pharmacy. **2** of the use or sale of medicinal drugs. ● n. a medicinal drug. □□ **pharmaceutically** adv. **pharmaceutics** n. [LL pharmaceuticus f. Gk pharmakeutikos f. pharmakeutēs druggist f. pharmakon drug]
■ n. see MEDICINE. □□ **pharmaceutics** pharmacy.

pharmacist /fáarməsist/ n. a person qualified to prepare and dispense drugs.
■ pharmacologist, druggist, Brit. chemist, archaic apothecary.

pharmacognosy /fáarməkógnəsee/ n. the science of drugs, esp. relating to medicinal products in their natural or unprepared state. [Gk pharmakon drug + gnōsis knowledge]

pharmacology /fáarməkóləjee/ n. the science of the action of drugs on the body. □□ **pharmacological** adj. **pharmacologically** adv. **pharmacologist** n. [mod.L pharmacologia f. Gk pharmakon drug]

pharmacopoeia /fáarməkəpeéə/ n. **1** a book, esp. one officially published, containing a list of drugs with directions for use. **2** a stock of drugs. □□ **pharmacopoeial** adj. [mod.L f. Gk pharmakopoiia f. pharmakopoios drug maker (as PHARMACOLOGY + -poios making)]

pharmacy /fáarməsee/ n. (pl. -ies) **1** the preparation and the (esp. medicinal) dispensing of drugs. **2** a drugstore; a dispensary. [ME f. OF farmacie f. med.L pharmacia f. Gk pharmakeia practice of the druggist f. pharmakeus f. pharmakon drug]
■ **1** pharmaceutics. **2** dispensary, druggist, drugstore; Brit. chemist, dispensing chemist, chemist's (shop), archaic apothecary.

pharos /fáiros/ n. a lighthouse or a beacon to guide sailors. [L f. Gk Pharos island off Alexandria where a famous lighthouse stood]

pharyngo- /fáringgō/ comb. form denoting the pharynx.

pharyngotomy /fáringgótəmee/ n. (pl. -ies) an incision into the pharynx.

pharynx /fáringks/ n. (pl. **pharynges** /fərínjeez/) a cavity, with enclosing muscles and mucous membrane, behind the nose and mouth, and connecting them to the esophagus.

□□ **pharyngal** /-rínggəl/ adj. **pharyngeal** /fərínjeeəl/, -jəl, fárinjeéəl/ adj. **pharyngitis** /-rinjítis/ n. [mod.L f. Gk pharugx -ggos]

phase /fayz/ n. & v. ● n. **1** a distinct period or stage in a process of change or development. **2** each of the aspects of the moon or a planet, according to the amount of its illumination, esp. the new moon, the first quarter, the last quarter, and the full moon. **3** Physics a stage in a periodically recurring sequence, esp. of alternating electric currents or light vibrations. **4** a difficult or unhappy period, esp. in adolescence. **5** a genetic or seasonal variety of an animal's coloration, etc. **6** Chem. a distinct and homogeneous form of matter separated by its surface from other forms. ● v.tr. carry out (a program, etc.) in phases or stages. □ **in phase** having the same phase at the same time. **out of phase** not in phase. **phase in** (or **out**) bring gradually into (or out of) use. **phase rule** Chem. a rule relating numbers of phases, constituents, and degrees of freedom. **three-phase** (of an electric generator, motor, etc.) designed to supply or use simultaneously three separate alternating currents of the same voltage, but with phases differing by a third of a period. □□ **phasic** adj. [F phase & f. earlier phasis f. Gk phasis appearance f. phainō phan- show]
■ n. **1** see STAGE n. 1. **2** stage, state, form, shape, aspect, appearance, look. **4** stage, step, spell, period. **5** variety, race, form; coat, plumage. □ **phase in** (gradually) introduce, usher in, work in, inject, insert, insinuate, include, incorporate. **phase out** ease off, wind up, put a stop to, (gradually) eliminate, remove, withdraw, discontinue, end.

phatic /fátik/ adj. (of speech, etc.) used to convey general sociability rather than to communicate a specific meaning, e.g., "How do you do?" [Gk phatos spoken f. phēmi phan-speak]

Ph.D. abbr. Doctor of Philosophy. [L philosophiae doctor]

pheasant /fézənt/ n. any of several long-tailed game birds of the family Phasianidae, orig. from Asia. □□ **pheasantry** n. (pl. -ies). [ME f. AF fesaunt f. OF faisan f. L phasianus f. Gk phasianos (bird) of the river Phasis in Asia Minor]

phenacetin /finásitin/ n. an acetyl derivative of phenol used to treat fever, etc. [PHENO- + ACETYL + -IN]

pheno- /feénō/ comb. form **1** Chem. derived from benzene (phenol; phenyl). **2** showing (phenocryst). [Gk phainō shine (with ref. to substances used for illumination), show]

phenobarbital /feénōbáarbitawl, -tal/ n. (Brit. **phenobarbitone** /-bitón/) a narcotic and sedative barbiturate drug used esp. to treat epilepsy.

phenocryst /feénəkrist/ n. a large or conspicuous crystal in porphyritic rock. [F phénocryste (as PHENO-, CRYSTAL)]

phenol /feénawl, -nol/ n. Chem. **1** the monohydroxyl derivative of benzene used in dilute form as an antiseptic and disinfectant. Also called CARBOLIC. ¶ Chem. formula: C_6H_5OH. **2** any hydroxyl derivative of an aromatic hydrocarbon. □□ **phenolic** /finólik/ adj. [F phénole f. phène benzene (formed as PHENO-)]

phenolphthalein /feénoltháyleen/ n. Chem. a white crystalline solid used in solution as an acid-base indicator and medicinally as a laxative. [PHENOL + phthal f. NAPHTHALENE + -IN]

phenomena pl. of PHENOMENON.

phenomenal /finómináal/ adj. **1** of the nature of a phenomenon. **2** extraordinary; remarkable; prodigious. **3** perceptible by, or perceptible only to, the senses. □□ **phenomenalize** v.tr. **phenomenally** adv.
■ **2** outstanding, remarkable, exceptional, extraordinary, unusual, freakish, rare, uncommon, singular, unorthodox, unprecedented, unheard-of, unparalleled, unbelievable, marvelous, wonderful, amazing, astonishing, astounding, staggering, prodigious,

---

/.../ **pronunciation**	● **part of speech**
□ **phrases, idioms, and compounds**	
□□ **derivatives**	■ **synonym section**
cross-references appear in SMALL CAPITALS or italics	

miraculous, fantastic, surprising, *colloq.* stunning, mind-boggling, incredible.

phenomenalism /finóminəlizəm/ *n. Philos.* **1** the doctrine that human knowledge is confined to the appearances presented to the senses. **2** the doctrine that appearances are the foundation of all our knowledge. □□ **phenomenalist** *n.* **phenomenalistic** *adj.*

phenomenology /finóminóləjee/ *n. Philos.* **1** the science of phenomena. **2** the description and classification of phenomena. □□ **phenomenological** /-nəlójikəl/ *adj.* **phenomenologically** *adv.*

phenomenon /finóminən/ *n.* (*pl.* **phenomena** /-nə/) **1** a fact or occurrence that appears or is perceived, esp. one of which the cause is in question. **2** a remarkable person or thing. **3** *Philos.* the object of a person's perception; what the senses or the mind notice. [LL f. Gk *phainomenon* neut. pres. part. of *phainomai* appear f. *phainō* show]
  ■ **1** event, happening, occurrence, incident, occasion, experience, fact. **2** wonder, curiosity, spectacle, sight, sensation, marvel, rarity, exception, miracle, standout, *Brit. colloq.* one-off. **3** *Philos.* percept.

phenotype /féenōtip/ *n. Biol.* a set of observable characteristics of an individual or group as determined by its genotype and environment. □□ **phenotypic** /-típik/ *adj.* **phenotypical** *adj.* **phenotypically** *adv.* [G *Phaenotypus* (as PHENO-, TYPE)]

phenyl /fénil, fee-/ *n. Chem.* the univalent radical formed from benzene by the removal of a hydrogen atom. [PHENO- + -YL]

phenylalanine /fénilálǝneen, fee-/ *n. Biochem.* an amino acid widely distributed in plant proteins and essential in the human diet. [PHENYL + *alanine* a simple amino acid]

phenylketonuria /fénilkeétōnŏŏreeǝ, -yŏŏr-, fee-/ *n.* an inherited inability to metabolize phenylalanine, ultimately leading to mental deficiency if untreated. [PHENYL + KETONE + -URIA]

pheromone /férǝmōn/ *n.* a chemical substance secreted and released by an animal for detection and response by another usu. of the same species. □□ **pheromonal** /-mŏn'l/ *adj.* [Gk *pherō* convey + HORMONE]

phew /fyŏŏ/ *int.* an expression of impatience, discomfort, relief, astonishment, or disgust. [imit. of puffing]

phi /fī/ *n.* the twenty-first letter of the Greek alphabet (Φ, φ).
  □ **Phi Beta Kappa 1** an intercollegiate honorary society to which distinguished scholars may be elected (from the initial letters of a Greek motto, = philosophy is the guide to life). **2** a member of this society. [Gk]

phial /fíǝl/ *n.* a small glass bottle, esp. for liquid medicine; vial. [ME f. OF *fiole* f. L *phiola phiala* f. Gk *phialē*, a broad flat vessel: cf. VIAL]

Phil. *abbr.* **1** Philharmonic. **2** Philippians (New Testament). **3** Philippines. **4** Philosophy.

phil- *comb. form* var. of PHILO-.

-phil *comb. form* var. of -PHILE.

philadelphus /filǝdélfǝs/ *n.* any highly-scented deciduous flowering shrub of the genus *Philadelphus*, esp. the mock orange. [mod.L f. Gk *philadelphon*]

philander /filándǝr/ *v.intr.* (often foll. by *with*) flirt or have casual affairs with women; womanize. □□ **philanderer** *n.* [*philander* (n.) used in Gk literature as the proper name of a lover, f. Gk *philandros* fond of men f. *anēr* male person: see PHIL-]
  ■ play about *or* around, flirt, womanize, carry on, dally, tease, toy, *colloq.* play the field, gallivant.
  □□ **philanderer** gallant, roué, rake, debauchee, Casanova, lothario, libertine, seducer, Don Juan, Romeo, womanizer, satyr, lecher, sport, *colloq.* stud; see also FLIRT *n.*

philanthrope /fílǝnthrōp/ *n.* = *philanthropist* (see PHILANTHROPY). [Gk *philanthrōpos* (as PHIL-, *anthrōpos* human being)]

philanthropic /filǝnthrópik/ *adj.* loving one's fellow people; benevolent. □□ **philanthropically** *adv.* [F *philanthropique* (as PHILANTHROPE)]
  ■ charitable, eleemosynary, generous, magnanimous,

munificent, benevolent, openhanded, ungrudging, unstinting, beneficent, humanitarian, altruistic, humane.

philanthropy /filánthrǝpee/ *n.* **1** a love of humankind. **2** practical benevolence, esp. charity on a large scale. □□ **philanthropism** *n.* **philanthropist** *n.* **philanthropize** *v.tr.* & *intr.* [LL *philanthropia* f. Gk *philanthrōpia* (as PHILANTHROPE)]
  ■ **1** see ALTRUISM. **2** generosity, benevolence, magnanimity, charitableness, public-spiritedness, bigheartedness, largesse, thoughtfulness, kindheartedness, beneficence, benignity, liberality, openhandedness; charity, patronage, *hist.* almsgiving.
  □□ **philanthropist** philanthrope, contributor, donor, benefactor, benefactress, patron, patroness, sponsor, Maecenas, Good Samaritan, humanitarian, altruist; Lady Bountiful.

philately /filát'lee/ *n.* the collection and study of postage stamps. □□ **philatelic** /fílǝtélik/ *adj.* **philatelically** *adv.* **philatelist** *n.* [F *philatélie* f. Gk *ateleia* exemption from payment f. *a-* not + *telos* toll, tax]

-phile /fil/ *comb. form* (also **-phil** /fil/) forming nouns and adjectives denoting fondness for what is specified (*bibliophile*; *Francophile*). [Gk *philos* dear, loving]

Philem. *abbr.* Philemon (New Testament).

philharmonic /fílhaarmónik/ *adj.* **1** fond of music. **2** used characteristically in the names of orchestras, choirs, etc. (*New York Philharmonic Orchestra*). [F *philharmonique* f. It. *filarmonico* (as PHIL-, HARMONIC)]

philhellene /fílhéleen/ *n.* (often *attrib.*) **1** a lover of Greece and Greek culture. **2** *hist.* a supporter of the cause of Greek independence. □□ **philhellenic** /-helénik/ *adj.* **philhellenism** /-hélinizǝm/ *n.* **philhellenist** /-hélinist/ *n.* [Gk *philellēn* (as PHIL-, HELLENE)]

-philia /fíleeǝ/ *comb. form* **1** denoting (esp. abnormal) fondness or love for what is specified (*necrophilia*). **2** denoting undue inclination (*hemophilia*). □□ **-philiac** /-leeak/ *comb. form* forming nouns and adjectives. **-philic** /-ik/ *comb. form* forming adjectives. **-philous** /-ǝs/ *comb. form* forming adjectives. [Gk f. *philos* loving]

philippic /filípik/ *n.* a bitter verbal attack or denunciation. [L *philippicus* f. Gk *philippikos* the name of Demosthenes' speeches against Philip II of Macedon and Cicero's against Mark Antony]
  ■ see TIRADE.

Philippine /filípeen/ *adj.* of or relating to the Philippine Islands or their people; Filipino. [*Philip* II of Spain]

Philistine /filisteen, -stīn, filístin, -teen/ *n.* & *adj.* ● *n.* **1** a member of a people opposing the Israelites in ancient Palestine. **2** (usu. **philistine**) a person who is hostile or indifferent to culture, or one whose interests or tastes are commonplace or material. ● *adj.* hostile or indifferent to culture; commonplace; prosaic. □□ **philistinism** /fílǝstinizǝm/ *n.* [ME f. F *Philistin* or LL *Philistinus* f. Gk *Philistinos = Palaistinos* f. Heb. *p^elištī*]
  ■ *n.* **2** vulgarian, ignoramus, Babbitt, materialist, barbarian, boor, yahoo, lowbrow, lout, oaf, clod, lubber, churl. ● *adj.* uncultured, uncultivated, unenlightened, unrefined, unread, unlettered, untaught, uneducated, untutored, unlearned, narrowminded, anti-intellectual, boorish, lowbrow, prosaic, commonplace, bourgeois, commercial, materialistic.

Phillips /fílips/ *n.* (usu. *attrib.*) *propr.* denoting a screw with a cross-shaped slot for turning, or a corresponding screwdriver. [H. M. *Phillips* d. 1935, original US manufacturer]

phillumenist /filŏŏmǝnist/ *n.* a collector of matchbooks or matchbox labels. □□ **phillumeny** *n.* [PHIL- + L *lumen* light]

Philly /fílee/ *n. sl.* Philadelphia. [abbr.]

philo- /fílō/ *comb. form* (also **phil-** before a vowel or *h*) denoting a liking for what is specified.

philodendron /filǝdéndrǝn/ *n.* (*pl.* **philodendrons** or **philodendra** /-drǝ/) any tropical American climbing plant of the genus *Philodendron*, with bright foliage. [PHILO- + Gk *dendron* tree]

philogynist /filójənist/ *n.* a person who likes or admires women. [PHILO- + Gk *gunē* woman]

philology /filóləjee/ *n.* **1** the science of language, esp. in its historical and comparative aspects. **2** the love of learning and literature. □□ **philologian** /-lələjeeən/ *n.* **philologist** *n.* **philological** /-ləlójikəl/ *adj.* **philologically** /-ləlójiklee/ *adv.* **philologize** *v.intr.* [F *philologie* f. L *philologia* love of learning f. Gk (as PHILO-, -LOGY)]

Philomel /fíləmel/ *n.* (also **philomel**, **Philomela** /fíləmeélə/) *poet.* the nightingale. [earlier *philomene* f. med.L *philomena* f. L *philomela* nightingale f. Gk *philomēla*: cap. with ref. to the myth of *Philomela*]

philoprogenitive /fílōprōjénitiv/ *adj.* **1** prolific. **2** loving one's offspring.

philosopher /filósəfər/ *n.* **1** a person engaged or learned in philosophy or a branch of it. **2** a person who lives by philosophy. **3** a person who shows philosophic calmness in trying circumstances. □ **philosophers'** (or **philosopher's**) **stone** the supreme object of alchemy, a substance supposed to change other metals into gold or silver. [ME f. AF *philosofre* var. of OF, *philosophe* f. L *philosophus* f. Gk *philosophos* (as PHILO-, *sophos* wise)]

philosophical /fíləsófikəl/ *adj.* (also **philosophic**) **1** of or according to philosophy. **2** skilled in or devoted to philosophy or learning; learned (*philosophical society*). **3** wise; serene; temperate. **4** calm in adverse circumstances. □□ **philosophically** *adv.* [LL *philosophicus* f. L *philosophia* (as PHILOSOPHY)]

■ **1, 2** rational, logical, reasoned, argued; see also LEARNED 2–4. **3, 4** detached, unconcerned, unemotional, unimpassioned, composed, thoughtful, reflective, meditative, cogitative, contemplative, judicious, sober, levelheaded, realistic, practical, pragmatical, pragmatic, down-to-earth, cool, calm, serene, placid, stoical, patient, unruffled, coolheaded, tranquil, unperturbed, even-tempered, temperate, moderate, equable, equanimous, imperturbable; see also WISE *adj.* 1.

philosophize /filósəfīz/ *v.* **1** *intr.* reason like a philosopher. **2** *intr.* moralize. **3** *intr.* speculate; theorize. **4** *tr.* render philosophic. □□ **philosophizer** *n.* [app. f. F *philosopher*]

philosophy /filósəfee/ *n.* (*pl.* **-ies**) **1** the use of reason and argument in seeking truth and knowledge of reality, esp. of the causes and nature of things and of the principles governing existence, the material universe, perception of physical phenomena, and human behavior. **2 a** a particular system or set of beliefs reached by this. **b** a personal rule of life. **3** advanced learning in general (*doctor of philosophy*). **4** serenity; calmness; conduct governed by a particular philosophy. [ME f. OF *filosofie* f. L *philosophia* wisdom f. Gk (as PHILO-, *sophos* wise)]

■ **1** metaphysics, epistemology, logic, rationalism, reason, thinking; argument. **2** viewpoint, (point of) view, outlook, opinion, attitude, feeling, sentiment, idea, notion, ideology, (set of) beliefs *or* values, tenets, credo, *Weltanschauung*, worldview. **4** composure, calmness, serenity, sangfroid, control, self-control, restraint, coolness, placidity, coolheadedness, equanimity, thoughtfulness, imperturbability, self-possession, aplomb, dispassion, patience, stoicism, resignation.

philter /fíltər/ *n.* (also **philtre**) a drink supposed to excite sexual love in the drinker. [F *philtre* f. L *philtrum* f. Gk *philtron* f. *phileō* to love]

-phily /filee/ *comb. form* = -PHILIA.

phimosis /fīmósis/ *n.* a constriction of the foreskin, making it difficult to retract. □□ **phimotic** /-mótik/ *adj.* [mod.L f. Gk, = muzzling]

phiz /fiz/ *n.* (also **phizog** /fízog/) *colloq.* **1** the face. **2** the expression on a face. [abbr. of *phiznomy* = PHYSIOGNOMY]

■ **1** see FACE *n.* 1. **2** see FACE *n.* 2a.

phlebitis /flibítis/ *n.* inflammation of the walls of a vein. □□ **phlebitic** /-bítik/ *adj.* [mod.L f. Gk f. *phleps phlebos* vein]

phlebotomy /flibótəmee/ *n.* **1** the surgical opening or puncture of a vein. **2** esp. *hist.* bloodletting as a medical treat-

ment. □□ **phlebotomist** *n.* **phlebotomize** *v.tr.* [ME f. OF *flebothomi* f. LL *phlebotomia* f. Gk f. *phleps phlebos* vein + -TOMY]

phlegm /flem/ *n.* **1** the thick viscous substance secreted by the mucous membranes of the respiratory passages, discharged by coughing. **2 a** coolness and calmness of disposition. **b** sluggishness or apathy (supposed to result from too much phlegm in the constitution). **3** *archaic* phlegm regarded as one of the four bodily humors. □□ **phlegmy** *adj.* [ME & OF *fleume* f. LL *phlegma* f. Gk *phlegma -atos* inflammation f. *phlegō* burn]

■ **2 a** see SANG-FROID. **b** see *sluggishness* (SLUGGISH).

phlegmatic /flegmátik/ *adj.* stolidly calm; unexcitable; unemotional. □□ **phlegmatically** *adv.*

■ stoical, stoic, unemotional, unexcitable, apathetic, uninvolved, unfeeling, uncaring, unresponsive, stolid, unmoved, insensitive, unaffected, insensible, indifferent, unconcerned, uninterested; self-possessed, self-controlled, controlled, restrained, composed, calm, tranquil, placid, coolheaded, equable, equanimous, cool, undisturbed, unperturbed, unruffled, imperturbable, even-tempered, philosophical; listless, indolent, inactive, passive.

phloem /flṓem/ *n. Bot.* the tissue conducting food material in plants (cf. XYLEM). [Gk *phloos* bark]

phlogiston /flōjíston/ *n.* a substance formerly supposed to exist in all combustible bodies, and to be released in combustion. [mod.L f. Gk *phlogizō* set on fire f. *phlox phlogos* flame]

phlox /floks/ *n.* any cultivated plant of the genus *Phlox*, with scented clusters of esp. white, blue, and red flowers. [L f. Gk *phlox*, the name of a plant (lit. flame)]

-phobe /fōb/ *comb. form* forming nouns and adjectives denoting a person having a fear or dislike of what is specified (*xenophobe*). [F f. L *-phobus* f. Gk *-phobos* f. *phobos* fear]

phobia /fṓbeeə/ *n.* an abnormal or morbid fear or aversion. □□ **phobic** *adj.* & *n.* [-PHOBIA used as a separate word]

■ fear, horror, terror, dread, hatred, detestation, abhorrence, loathing, execration, aversion, revulsion, repugnance, dislike, distaste, antipathy; nervousness, distrust, suspicion.

-phobia /fṓbeeə/ *comb. form* forming abstract nouns denoting a fear or dislike of what is specified (*agoraphobia*; *xenophobia*). □□ **-phobic** *comb. form* forming adjectives. [L f. Gk]

phoebe /feébee/ *n.* any American flycatcher of the genus *Sayornis*. [imit.: infl. by the name]

Phoenician /fəneéshən, fəní-/ *n.* & *adj.* ● *n.* a member of a Semitic people of ancient Phoenicia in S. Syria or of its colonies. ● *adj.* of or relating to Phoenicia. [ME f. OF *phenicien* f. L *Phoenicia* f. L *Phoenice* f. Gk *Phoinikē* Phoenicia]

phoenix /feéniks/ *n.* **1** a mythical bird, the only one of its kind, that after living for five or six centuries in the Arabian desert, burned itself on a funeral pyre and rose from the ashes with renewed youth to live through another cycle. **2 a** a unique person or thing. **b** a person or thing having recovered, esp. seemingly miraculously, from a disaster. [OE & OF *fenix* f. L *phoenix* f. Gk *phoinix* Phoenician, purple, phoenix]

phon /fon/ *n.* a unit of the perceived loudness of sounds. [Gk *phōnē* sound]

phonate /fṓnayt/ *v.intr.* utter a vocal sound. □□ **phonation** /-náyshən/ *n.* **phonatory** /fṓnətawree/ *adj.* [Gk *phōnē* voice]

phone¹ /fōn/ *n.* & *v.tr.* & *intr. colloq.* = TELEPHONE. □ **phone book** = *telephone directory.* **phone-in** *n.* a broadcast program during which the listeners or viewers telephone the studio, etc., and participate; call-in show. [abbr.]

phone² /fōn/ *n.* a simple vowel or consonant sound. [formed as PHONEME]

-phone /fōn/ *comb. form* forming nouns and adjectives mean-

/.../ pronunciation	● part of speech
□ phrases, idioms, and compounds	
□□ derivatives	■ synonym section
cross-references appear in SMALL CAPITALS or *italics*	

ing: **1** an instrument using or connected with sound (*telephone*; *xylophone*). **2** a person who uses a specified language (*anglophone*). [Gk *phōnē* voice, sound]

phoneme /fōneem/ *n.* any of the units of sound in a specified language that distinguish one word from another (e.g., *p*, *b*, *d*, *t* as in pad, pat, bad, bat, in English). □□ **phonemic** /-néemik/ *adj.* **phonemics** /-néemiks/ *n.* [F *phonème* f. Gk *phōnēma* sound, speech f. *phōneō* speak]

phonetic /fənétik/ *adj.* **1** representing vocal sounds. **2** (of a system of spelling, etc.) having a direct correspondence between symbols and sounds. **3** of or relating to phonetics. □□ **phonetically** *adv.* **phoneticism** /-nétəsizəm/ *n.* **phoneticist** /-nétəsist/ *n.* **phoneticize** /-nétəsiz/ *v.tr.* [mod.L *phoneticus* f. Gk *phōnētikos* f. *phōneō* speak]

phonetics /fənétiks/ *n.pl.* (usu. treated as *sing.*) **1** vocal sounds and their classification. **2** the study of these. □□ **phonetician** /fōnitíshən/ *n.*

phonetist /fōnitist/ *n.* an advocate of phonetic spelling.

phonic /fónik/ *adj.* & *n.* ● *adj.* of sound; acoustic; of vocal sounds. ● *n.* (in *pl.*) a method of teaching reading based on sounds. □□ **phonically** *adv.* [Gk *phōnē* voice]

phono- /fónō/ *comb. form* denoting sound. [Gk *phōnē* voice, sound]

phonogram /fónəgram/ *n.* a symbol representing a spoken sound.

phonograph /fónəgraf/ *n.* an instrument that reproduces recorded sound by a stylus that is in contact with a rotating grooved disk. ¶ Now more usually called a *record player.*

phonography /fənógrəfee/ *n.* **1** writing in esp. shorthand symbols, corresponding to the sounds of speech. **2** the recording of sounds by phonograph. □□ **phonographic** /fōnəgráfik/ *adj.*

phonology /fənóləjee/ *n.* the study of sounds in a language. □□ **phonological** /fōnəlójikəl/ *adj.* **phonologically** *adv.* **phonologist** /fənóləjist/ *n.*
■ phonemics; phonetics.

phonon /fónon/ *n. Physics* a quantum of sound or elastic vibrations. [Gk *phōnē* sound, after PHOTON]

phony /fónee/ *adj.* & *n.* (also **phoney**) *colloq.* ● *adj.* (**phonier**, **phoniest**) **1** sham; counterfeit. **2** fictitious; fraudulent. ● *n.* (*pl.* **-ies** or **-eys**) a phony person or thing. □□ **phonily** *adv.* **phoniness** *n.* [20th c.: orig. unkn.]
■ *adj.* unreal, fake, pretend, synthetic, artificial, factitious, false, fictitious, fraudulent, imitation, bogus, spurious, counterfeit, mock, ersatz, pseudo, sham; pretended, insincere, hypocritical, dissimulating, deceitful, dishonest, esp. *Brit. colloq.* pseud. ● *n.* fake, fraud, imitation, counterfeit, forgery, hoax, sham; trickster, faker, humbug, impostor, pretender, charlatan, mountebank, double-dealer, counterfeiter, quack, deceiver, *colloq.* con man, esp. *Brit. colloq.* pseud.

phooey /fóo-ee/ *int.* an expression of disgust or disbelief. [imit.]

-phore /fawr/ *comb. form* forming nouns meaning 'bearer' (*ctenophore*; *semaphore*). □□ **-phorous** /fərəs/ *comb. form* forming adjectives. [mod.L f. Gk *-phoros -phoron* bearing, bearer f. *pherō* bear]

phoresy /fáwrəsee/ *n. Biol.* an association in which one organism is carried by another, without being a parasite. □□ **phoretic** /fawrétik/ *adj.* [F *phorésie* f. Gk *phorēsis* being carried]

phosgene /fósjeen, fóz-/ *n.* a colorless poisonous gas (carbonyl chloride), formerly used in warfare. ¶ Chem. formula: $COCl_2$. [Gk *phōs* light + -GEN, with ref. to its orig. production by the action of sunlight on chlorine and carbon monoxide]

phosphatase /fósfətays, -tayz/ *n. Biochem.* any enzyme that catalyzes the synthesis or hydrolysis of an organic phosphate.

phosphate /fósfayt/ *n.* **1** any salt or ester of phosphoric acid, esp. used as a fertilizer. **2** a flavored effervescent drink containing a small amount of phosphate. □□ **phosphatic** /-fátik/ *adj.* [F f. *phosphore* PHOSPHORUS]

phosphene /fósfeen/ *n.* the sensation of rings of light produced by pressure on the eyeball due to irritation of the retina. [irreg. f. Gk *phōs* light + *phainō* show]

phosphide /fósfīd/ *n. Chem.* a binary compound of phosphorus with another element or group.

phosphine /fósfeen/ *n. Chem.* a colorless ill-smelling gas, phosphorus trihydride. ¶ Chem. formula: PH_3. □□ **phosphinic** /-fínik/ *adj.* [PHOSPHO- + -INE[4], after *amine*]

phosphite /fósfīt/ *n. Chem.* any salt or ester of phosphorous acid. [F (as PHOSPHO-)]

phospho- /fósfō/ *comb. form* denoting phosphorus. [abbr.]

phospholipid /fósfəlípid/ *n. Biochem.* any lipid consisting of a phosphate group and one or more fatty acids.

phosphor /fósfər/ *n.* **1** = PHOSPHORUS. **2** a synthetic fluorescent or phosphorescent substance esp. used in cathode-ray tubes. □ **phosphor bronze** a tough hard bronze alloy containing a small amount of phosphorus, used esp. for bearings. [G f. L *phosphorus* PHOSPHORUS]

phosphorate /fósfərayt/ *v.tr.* combine or impregnate with phosphorus.

phosphorescence /fósfərésəns/ *n.* **1** radiation similar to fluorescence but detectable after excitation ceases. **2** the emission of light without combustion or perceptible heat. □□ **phosphoresce** *v.intr.* **phosphorescent** *adj.*
■ **2** see GLOW *v.* 1. □□ **phosphoresce** see GLOW *v.* 1.

phosphorite /fósfərīt/ *n.* a noncrystalline form of apatite.

phosphorus /fósfərəs/ *n. Chem.* a nonmetallic element occurring naturally in various phosphate rocks and existing in allotropic forms, esp. as a poisonous whitish waxy substance burning slowly at ordinary temperatures and so appearing luminous in the dark, and a reddish form used in matches, fertilizers, etc. ¶ Symb.: P. □□ **phosphoric** /-fórik/ *adj.* **phosphorous** *adj.* [L, = morning star, f. Gk *phōsphoros* f. *phōs* light + *-phoros* -bringing]

phosphorylate /fósfərilayt, fosfáwr-/ *v.tr. Chem.* introduce a phosphate group into (an organic molecule, etc.). □□ **phosphorylation** /-láyshən/ *n.*

phot /fot, fōt/ *n.* a unit of illumination equal to one lumen per square centimeter. [Gk *phōs phōtos* light]

photic /fótik/ *adj.* **1** of or relating to light. **2** (of ocean layers) reached by sunlight.

photism /fótizəm/ *n.* a hallucinatory sensation or vision of light. [Gk *phōtismos* f. *phōtizō* shine f. *phōs phōtos* light]

photo /fótō/ *n.* & *v.* ● *n.* (*pl.* **-os**) = PHOTOGRAPH *n.* ● *v.tr.* (**-oes, -oed**) = PHOTOGRAPH *v.* □ **photo-call** *Brit.* = *photo opportunity.* **photo finish** a close finish of a race or contest, esp. one where the winner is only distinguishable on a photograph. **photo opportunity** (also **photo-op**) an occasion on which theatrical performers, famous personalities, etc., pose for photographers by arrangement. [abbr.]

photo- /fótō/ *comb. form* denoting: **1** light (*photosensitive*). **2** photography (*photocomposition*). [Gk *phōs phōtos* light, or as abbr. of PHOTOGRAPH]

photobiology /fótōbióləjee/ *n.* the study of the effects of light on living organisms.

photocell /fótōsel/ *n.* = photoelectric cell.

photochemistry /fótōkémistree/ *n.* the study of the chemical effects of light. □□ **photochemical** *adj.*

photocomposition /fótōkómpəzíshən/ *n. Printing* a typesetting process in which characters, etc., are projected onto a light-sensitive material such as photographic film.

photoconductivity /fótōkónduktívitee/ *n.* conductivity due to the action of light. □□ **photoconductive** /-dúktiv/ *adj.* **photoconductor** /-dúktər/ *n.*

photocopier /fótōkópeeər/ *n.* a machine for producing photocopies.

photocopy /fótōkópee/ *n.* & *v.* ● *n.* (*pl.* **-ies**) a photographic copy of printed or written material produced by a process involving the action of light on a specially prepared surface. ● *v.tr.* (**-ies, -ied**) make a photocopy of. □□ **photocopiable** *adj.*
■ copy, *propr.* Xerox, Photostat.

photodiode /fótōdíod/ *n.* a semiconductor diode responding electrically to illumination.

photoelectric /fótōiléktrik/ *adj.* marked by or using emissions of electrons from substances exposed to light. □ **pho-**

toelectric cell a device using this effect to generate current. □□ **photoelectricity** /-trísitee/ *n.*

photoelectron /fōtōiléktron/ *n.* an electron emitted from an atom by interaction with a photon, esp. one emitted from a solid surface by the action of light.

photoemission /fōtōimíshən/ *n.* the emission of electrons from a surface by the action of light incident on it. □□ **photoemitter** *n.*

photofinishing /fōtōfínishing/ *n.* the process of developing and printing photographic film.

photogenic /fōtəjénik/ *adj.* **1** (esp. of a person) having an appearance that looks pleasing in photographs. **2** *Biol.* producing or emitting light. □□ **photogenically** *adv.*

photogram /fōtəgram/ *n.* **1** a picture produced with photographic materials but without a camera. **2** *archaic* a photograph.

photogrammetry /fōtəgrámitree/ *n.* the use of photography for surveying. □□ **photogrammetrist** *n.*

photograph /fōtəgraf/ *n. & v.* ● *n.* a picture taken by means of the chemical action of light or other radiation on sensitive film. ● *v.tr.* (also *absol.*) take a photograph of (a person, etc.). □□ **photographable** *adj.* **photographer** /fətógrəfər/ *n.* **photographically** /-gráfiklee/ *adv.*

■ *n.* snapshot, print, picture, snap, photo, shot, *archaic* photogram, *colloq.* pic. ● *v.* take a picture of, shoot, film, take, snap; take a person's picture.
□□ **photographer** cameraman, cinematographer, paparazzo.

photographic /fōtəgráfik/ *adj.* **1** of, used in, or produced by photography. **2** having the accuracy of a photograph (*photographic likeness*).

■ **1** cinematic, filmic; pictorial. **2** vivid, natural, realistic, graphic, accurate, exact, precise, faithful, detailed, lifelike, true to life.

photography /fətógrəfee/ *n.* the taking and processing of photographs.

photogravure /fōtōgrəvyŏŏr/ *n.* **1** an image produced from a photographic negative transferred to a metal plate and etched in. **2** this process. [F (as PHOTO-, *gravure* engraving)]

photojournalism /fōtōjórnəlizəm/ *n.* the art or practice of relating news by photographs, with or without an accompanying text, esp. in magazines, etc. □□ **photojournalist** *n.*

photolithography /fōtōlithógrəfee/ *n.* (*Brit.* also **photolitho** /-líthō/) lithography using plates made photographically. □□ **photolithographer** *n.* **photolithographic** /-thəgráfik/ *adj.* **photolithographically** *adv.*

photolysis /fōtólisis/ *n.* decomposition or dissociation of molecules by the action of light. □□ **photolyze** /fōtəliz/ *v.tr. & intr.* **photolytic** /-təlítik/ *adj.*

photometer /fōtómitər/ *n.* an instrument for measuring light. □□ **photometric** /fōtōmétrik/ *adj.* **photometry** /-tómitree/ *n.*

photomicrograph /fōtōmíkrəgraf/ *n.* a photograph of an image produced by a microscope. □□ **photomicrography** /-krógrəfee/ *n.*

photon /fōton/ *n.* **1** a quantum of electromagnetic radiation energy, proportional to the frequency of radiation. **2** a unit of luminous intensity as measured at the retina. [Gk *phōs phōtos* light, after *electron*]

photonovel /fōtōnóvəl/ *n.* a novel told in a series of photographs with superimposed speech bubbles.

photo-offset /fōtō-áwfset, -óf-/ *n.* offset printing with plates made photographically.

photoperiod /fōtōpéereeəd/ *n.* the period of daily illumination which an organism receives. □□ **photoperiodic** /-eeódik/ *adj.*

photoperiodism /fōtōpéereeədizəm/ *n.* the response of an organism to changes in the lengths of the daily periods of light.

photophobia /fōtōfōbeeə/ *n.* an abnormal fear of or aversion to light. □□ **photophobic** *adj.*

photoreceptor /fōtōriséptər/ *n.* any living structure that responds to incident light.

photosensitive /fōtōsénsitiv/ *adj.* reacting chemically, electrically, etc., to light. □□ **photosensitivity** /-tívitee/ *n.*

photosetting /fōtōseting/ *n.* = PHOTOCOMPOSITION. □□ **photoset** *v.tr.* (*past* and *past part.* **-set**). **photosetter** *n.*

photosphere /fōtəsfeer/ *n.* the luminous envelope of a star from which its light and heat radiate. □□ **photospheric** /-sférik/ *adj.*

Photostat /fōtəstat/ *n. & v. propr.* ● *n.* **1** a type of machine for making photocopies. **2** a copy made by this means. ● *v.tr.* (**photostat**) (**-statted, -statting**) make a Photostat of. □□ **photostatic** /-státik/ *adj.*

■ *n.* **1** photocopier. **2** photocopy, copy, stat, *propr.* Xerox. ● *v.* photocopy, copy, xerox.

photosynthesis /fōtōsínthisis/ *n.* the process in which the energy of sunlight is used by organisms, esp. green plants, to synthesize carbohydrates from carbon dioxide and water. □□ **photosynthesize** *v.tr. & intr.* **photosynthetic** /-thétik/ *adj.* **photosynthetically** *adv.*

phototransistor /fōtōtranzístər/ *n.* a transistor that responds to incident light by generating and amplifying an electric current.

phototropism /fətótrəpizəm, fōtōtrōpizəm/ *n.* the tendency of a plant, etc., to bend or turn toward or away from a source of light. □□ **phototropic** /-trópik/ *adj.*

photovoltaic /fōtōvoltáyik, -vōl-/ *adj.* relating to the production of electric current at the junction of two substances exposed to light.

phrasal /fráyzəl/ *adj. Gram.* consisting of a phrase. □ **phrasal verb** an idiomatic phrase consisting of a verb and an adverb (e.g., *break down*), a verb and a preposition (e.g., *see to*), or a combination of both (e.g., *look down on*).

phrase /frayz/ *n. & v.* ● *n.* **1** a group of words forming a conceptual unit, but not a sentence. **2** an idiomatic or short pithy expression. **3** a manner or mode of expression (*a nice turn of phrase*). **4** *Mus.* a group of notes forming a distinct unit within a larger piece. ● *v.tr.* **1** express in words (*phrased the reply badly*). **2** (esp. when reading aloud or speaking) divide (sentences, etc.) into units so as to convey the meaning of the whole. **3** *Mus.* divide (music) into phrases, etc., in performance. □ **phrase book** a book for tourists, etc., listing useful expressions with their equivalents in a foreign language. □□ **phrasing** *n.* [earlier *phrasis* f. L f. Gk f. *phrazō* declare, tell]

■ *n.* **1** clause, word group, collocation, locution. **2** expression, idiom, idiomatic expression, proverb, motto, slogan, saying, catchphrase, adage, maxim, axiom, saw, colloquialism, cliché. **3** phraseology, wording, language, way *or* manner of speaking, style, choice of words, vocabulary. ● *v.* **1** express, word, put into words, put, frame, formulate, couch, put *or* set forth, verbalize, articulate, voice, utter, say, write.

phraseogram /fráyzeeəgram/ *n.* a written symbol representing a phrase, esp. in shorthand.

phraseology /fráyzeeóləjee/ *n.* (*pl.* **-ies**) **1** a choice or arrangement of words. **2** a mode of expression. □□ **phraseological** /-əlójikəl/ *adj.* [mod.L *phraseologia* f. Gk *phraseōn* genit. pl. of *phrasis* PHRASE]

■ wording, phrasing, expression, language, style, diction, usage, speech, delivery.

phreatic /freeátik/ *adj. Geol.* **1** (of water) situated underground in the zone of saturation; ground water. **2** (of a volcanic eruption or explosion) caused by the heating and expansion of underground water. [Gk *phrear phreatos* well]

phrenetic /frənétik/ *adj.* (also **frenetic**) **1** frantic. **2** fanatic. □□ **phrenetically** *adv.* [ME, var. of FRENETIC]

phrenic /frénik/ *adj. Anat.* of or relating to the diaphragm. [F *phrénique* f. Gk *phrēn phrenos* diaphragm, mind]

phrenology /frinóləjee/ *n. hist.* the study of the shape and size of the cranium as a supposed indication of character and mental faculties. □□ **phrenological** /-nəlójikəl/ *adj.* **phrenologist** *n.*

/.../ **pronunciation**	● **part of speech**
□ **phrases, idioms, and compounds**	
□□ **derivatives**	■ **synonym section**
cross-references appear in SMALL CAPITALS or *italics*	

Phrygian /fríjeeən/ *n.* & *adj.* ● *n.* **1** a native or inhabitant of ancient Phrygia in central Asia Minor. **2** the language of this people. ● *adj.* of or relating to Phrygia or its people or language. □ **Phrygian cap** (or **bonnet**) an ancient conical cap with the top bent forward, now identified with the liberty cap. **Phrygian mode** *Mus.* the mode represented by the natural diatonic scale E–E.

phthalic acid /thálik, fthál-/ *n. Chem.* one of three isomeric dicarboxylic acids derived from benzene. □□ **phthalate** /-layt/ *n.* [abbr. of *naphthalic*: see NAPHTHALENE]

phthisis /thísis, tí-/ *n.* any progressive wasting disease, esp. pulmonary tuberculosis. □□ **phthisic** /tízik, thíz-/ *adj.* **phthisical** *adj.* [L f. Gk f. *phthinō* to decay]

phut /fut/ *n.* esp. *Brit.* a dull abrupt sound as of an impact or explosion. □ **go phut** *colloq.* (esp. of a scheme or plan) collapse; break down. [perh. f. Hindi *phaṭnā* to burst]

phycology /fíkóləjee/ *n.* the study of algae. □□ **phycological** /-kəlójikəl/ *adj.* **phycologist** *n.* [Gk *phukos* seaweed + -LOGY]

phycomycete /fíkōmíseet, -mīseét/ *n.* any of various fungi that typically resemble algae. [Gk *phukos* seaweed + pl. of Gk *mukēs* mushroom]

phyla *pl.* of PHYLUM.

phylactery /filáktəree/ *n.* (*pl.* **-ies**) **1** a small leather box containing Hebrew texts on vellum, worn by Jewish men at morning prayer as a reminder to keep the law. **2** an amulet; a charm. [ME f. OF f. LL *phylacterium* f. Gk *phulaktērion* amulet f. *phulassō* guard]

phyletic /filétik/ *adj. Biol.* of or relating to the development of a species or other group. [Gk *phuletikos* f. *phuletēs* tribesman f. *phulē* tribe]

phyllo- /fílō/ *comb. form* leaf. [Gk *phullo-* f. *phullon* leaf]

phyllode /fílōd/ *n.* a flattened leafstalk resembling a leaf. [mod.L *phyllodium* f. Gk *phullōdēs* leaflike (as PHYLLO-)]

phyllophagous /filófəgəs/ *adj.* feeding on leaves.

phylloquinone /fílōkwinōn, -kwínōn/ *n.* one of the K vitamins, found in cabbage, spinach, and other leafy green vegetables, and essential for the blood clotting process. Also called *vitamin K₁*.

phyllostome /fíləstōm/ *n.* any bat of the family Phyllostomatidae having a nose leaf. [PHYLLO- + *stoma* mouth]

phyllotaxis /fílōtáksis/ *n.* (also **phyllotaxy** /-táksee/) the arrangement of leaves on an axis or stem. □□ **phyllotactic** *adj.*

phylloxera /filóksərə/ *n.* any plant louse of the genus *Phylloxera*, esp. of a species attacking vines. [mod.L f. Gk *phullon* leaf + *xēros* dry]

phylo- /fílō/ *comb. form Biol.* denoting a race or tribe. [Gk *phulon, phulē*]

phylogenesis /fílōjénisis/ *n.* (also **phylogeny** /fīlójənee/) **1** the evolutionary development of an organism or groups of organisms. **2** a history of this. □□ **phylogenetic** /-jinétik/ *adj.* **phylogenic** /-jénik/ *adj.*
■ see EVOLUTION.

phylum /fíləm/ *n.* (*pl.* **phyla** /-lə/) *Biol.* a taxonomic rank below kingdom comprising a class or classes and subordinate taxa. [mod.L f. Gk *phulon* race]

physic /fízik/ *n.* & *v.* esp. *archaic* ● *n.* **1 a** a medicine or drug. **b** a laxative; cathartic (*a dose of physic*). **2** the art of healing. **3** the medical profession. ● *v.tr.* (**physicked, physicking**) dose with physic. □ **physic garden** *Brit.* a garden for cultivating medicinal herbs, etc. [ME f. OF *fisique* medicine f. L *physica* f. Gk *phusikē* (*epistēmē*) (knowledge) of nature]
■ *n.* **1 a** see MEDICINE 2.

physical /fízikəl/ *adj.* & *n.* ● *adj.* **1** of or concerning the body (*physical exercise; physical education*). **2** of matter; material (*both mental and physical force*). **3 a** of, or according to, the laws of nature (*a physical impossibility*). **b** belonging to physics (*physical science*). **4** rough; violent. ● *n.* (in full **physical examination**) a medical examination to determine physical fitness. □ **physical chemistry** the application of physics to the study of chemical behavior. **physical geography** geography dealing with natural features. **physical jerks** *Brit. colloq.* physical exercises. **physical science** the sciences used in the study of inanimate natural objects, e.g., physics,

chemistry, astronomy, etc. **physical therapy** *n.* the treatment of disease, injury, deformity, etc., by physical methods including manipulation, massage, infrared heat treatment, remedial exercise, etc., not by drugs. □□ **physical therapist** *n.* **physicality** /-kálitee/ *n.* **physically** *adv.* **physicalness** *n.* [ME f. med.L *physicalis* f. L *physica* (as PHYSIC)]
■ *adj.* **1** bodily, corporal. **2** material, corporeal, tangible, palpable, real, actual, true, concrete, manifest, solid; fleshly, incarnate, carnal, animal, mortal, earthly, natural, somatic, worldly; non-spiritual.

physician /fizíshən/ *n.* **1 a** a person legally qualified to practice medicine and surgery. **b** a specialist in medical diagnosis and treatment. **c** any medical practitioner. **2** a healer (*work is the best physician*). [ME f. OF *fisicien* (as PHYSIC)]
■ **1** doctor, medical practitioner, general practitioner, GP, surgeon, *colloq.* doc, medico, medic, *sl.* quack, sawbones; specialist, diplomate, internist.

physicist /fízisist/ *n.* a person skilled or qualified in physics.

physico- /fíziko/ *comb. form* **1** physical (and). **2** of physics (and). [Gk *phusikos* (as PHYSIC)]

physicochemical /fízikōkémikəl/ *adj.* relating to physics and chemistry or to physical chemistry.

physics /fíziks/ *n.* the science dealing with the properties and interactions of matter and energy. [pl. of *physic* physical (thing), after L *physica*, Gk *phusika* natural things f. *phusis* nature]

physio- /fízeeō/ *comb. form* nature; what is natural. [Gk *phusis* nature]

physiocracy /fízeeókrəsee/ *n.* (*pl.* **-ies**) *hist.* **1** government according to the natural order, esp. as advocated by some 18th-c. economists. **2** a society based on this. □□ **physiocrat** /-zeeəkrát/ *n.* **physiocratic** *adj.* [F *physiocratie* (as PHYSIO-, -CRACY)]

physiognomy /fízeeógnəmee, -ónəmee/ *n.* (*pl.* **-ies**) **1 a** the cast or form of a person's features, expression, body, etc. **b** the art of supposedly judging character from facial characteristics, etc. **2** the external features of a landscape, etc. **3** a characteristic, esp. moral, aspect. □□ **physiognomic** /-ognómik, -ənómik/ *adj.* **physiognomical** *adj.* **physiognomically** *adv.* **physiognomist** *n.* [ME *fisnomie*, etc. f. OF *phisonomie* f. med.L *phisonomia* f. Gk *phusiognōmonia* judging of a man's nature (by his features) (as PHYSIO-, *gnōmōn* judge)]
■ **1 a** see FEATURE *n.* 2.

physiography /fízeeógrəfee/ *n.* the description of nature, of natural phenomena, or of a class of objects; physical geography. □□ **physiographer** *n.* **physiographic** /-zeeəgráfik/ *adj.* **physiographical** *adj.* **physiographically** *adv.* [F *physiographie* (as PHYSIO-, -GRAPHY)]

physiological /fízeeəlójikəl/ *adj.* (also **physiologic**) of or concerning physiology. □ **physiological salt solution** (or **saline**) a saline solution having a concentration about equal to that of body fluids. □□ **physiologically** *adv.*

physiology /fízeeóləjee/ *n.* **1** the science of the functions of living organisms and their parts. **2** these functions. □□ **physiologist** *n.* [F *physiologie* or L *physiologia* f. Gk *phusiologia* (as PHYSIO-, -LOGY)]

physiotherapy /fízeeōthérəpee/ = *physical therapy*.

physique /fizeek/ *n.* the bodily structure, development, and organization of an individual (*an athletic physique*). [F, orig. adj. (as PHYSIC)]
■ build, figure, body, frame, shape, form.

-phyte /fīt/ *comb. form* forming nouns denoting a vegetable or plantlike organism (*saprophyte; zoophyte*). □□ **-phytic** /fítik/ *comb. form* forming adjectives. [Gk *phuton* plant f. *phuō* come into being]

phyto- /fítō/ *comb. form* denoting a plant.

phytochemistry /fítōkémistree/ *n.* the chemistry of plant products. □□ **phytochemical** *adj.* **phytochemist** *n.*

phytochrome /fítəkrōm/ *n. Biochem.* a blue-green pigment found in many plants, and regulating various developmental processes according to the nature and timing of the light it absorbs. [PHYTO- + Gk *khrōma* color]

phytogenesis /fítōjénisis/ *n.* (also **phytogeny** /-tójinee/) the science of the origin or evolution of plants.

phytogeography /fītōjeeógrəfee/ *n.* the geographical distribution of plants.

phytopathology /fītōpəthóləjee/ *n.* the study of plant diseases.

phytophagous /fītófəgəs/ *adj.* feeding on plants.

phytoplankton /fītōplángktən/ *n.* plankton consisting of plants.

phytotomy /fītótəmee/ *n.* the dissection of plants.

phytotoxic /fītōtóksik/ *adj.* poisonous to plants.

phytotoxin /fītōtóksin/ *n.* **1** any toxin derived from a plant. **2** a substance poisonous or injurious to plants, esp. one produced by a parasite.

pi[1] /pī/ *n.* **1** the sixteenth letter of the Greek alphabet (Π, π). **2** (as π) the symbol of the ratio of the circumference of a circle to its diameter (approx. 3.14159). □ **pi-meson** = PION. [Gk: sense 2 f. Gk *periphereia* circumference]

pi[2] /pī/ *adj. Brit. sl.* pious. □ **pi jaw** a long moralizing lecture or reprimand. [abbr.]
■ see SANCTIMONIOUS.

pi[3] /pī/ *n. & v.* (also **pie**) ● *n.* **1** a confused mass of printers' type. **2** chaos. ● *v.tr.* (**pieing**) muddle up (type). [perh. transl. F PÂTÉ = PIE[1]]

piacular /pīákyələr/ *adj.* **1** expiatory. **2** needing expiation. [L *piacularis* f. *piaculum* expiation f. *piare* appease]
■ **1** see *compensatory* (COMPENSATE).

piaffe /pyáf/ *v.intr.* (of a horse, etc.) move as in a trot, but slower. [F *piaffer* to strut]

piaffer /pyáfər/ *n.* the action of piaffing.

pia mater /pīə máytər, peéə/ *n. Anat.* the delicate innermost membrane enveloping the brain and spinal cord (see MENINX). [med.L, = tender mother, transl. of Arab. *al-'umm al-rakīka*: cf. DURA MATER]

piani *pl.* of PIANO[2].

pianism /peéənizəm/ *n.* **1** the art or technique of piano playing. **2** the skill or style of a composer of piano music. □□ **pianistic** /-nístik/ *adj.* **pianistically** /-nístiklee/ *adv.*

pianissimo /peéənísimō/ *adj., adv., & n. Mus.* ● *adj.* performed very softly. ● *adv.* very softly. ● *n.* (*pl.* **-os** or **pianissimi** /-mee/) a passage to be performed very softly. [It., superl. of PIANO[2]]

pianist /peéənist, pee-án-/ *n.* the player of a piano. [F *pianiste* (as PIANO[1])]

piano[1] /peeáanō, pyánō/ *n.* (*pl.* **-os**) a large musical instrument played by pressing down keys on a keyboard and causing hammers to strike metal strings, the vibration from which is stopped by dampers when the keys are released. □ **piano accordion** an accordion with the melody played on a small vertical keyboard like that of a piano. **piano organ** a mechanical piano constructed like a barrel organ. **piano player 1** a pianist. **2** a contrivance for playing a piano automatically. [It., abbr. of PIANOFORTE]

piano[2] /pyáanō/ *adj., adv., & n.* ● *adj.* **1** *Mus.* performed softly. **2** subdued. ● *adv.* **1** *Mus.* softly. **2** in a subdued manner. ● *n.* (*pl.* **-os** or **piani** /-nee/) *Mus.* a piano passage. [It. f. L *planus* flat, (of sound) soft]

pianoforte /pyánófáwrt, -fáwrtee/ *n. Mus.* a piano. [It., earlier *piano e forte* soft and loud, expressing its gradation of tone]

Pianola /peéənólə/ *n. propr.* a kind of automatic piano; a player piano. **2** (**pianola**) *Bridge* an easy hand needing no skill. **3** (**pianola**) an easy task. [app. dimin. of PIANO[1]]

piano nobile /pyáanō nóbilay/ *n. Archit.* the main story of a large house. [It., = noble floor]

piassava /peéəsáavə/ *n.* **1** a stout fiber obtained from the leafstalks of various American and African palm trees. **2** any of these trees. [Port. f. Tupi *piaçába*]

piastre /peeástər/ *n.* (also **piaster**) a small coin and monetary unit of several Middle Eastern countries. [F *piastre* f. It. *piastra* (*d'argento*) plate (of silver), formed as PLASTER]

piazza *n.* /pee-áatsə, -saa/ **1** a public square or marketplace esp. in an Italian town. **2** /peeázə, -áazə/ *dial.* the veranda of a house. [It., formed as PLACE]
■ **1** see SQUARE *n.* 3a.

pibroch /peébrokh, -brawkh/ *n.* a series of esp. martial or

funerary variations on a theme for the bagpipes. [Gael. *piobaireachd* art of piping f. *piobair* piper f. *piob* f. E PIPE]

pic /pik/ *n. colloq.* a picture, esp. a movie. [abbr.]
■ see FILM *n.* 3a, b, PICTURE *n.* 1a.

pica[1] /pīkə/ *n. Printing* **1** a unit of type size (¹/₆ inch). **2** a size of letters in typewriting (10 per inch). [AL *pica* 15th-c. book of rules about church feasts, perh. formed as PIE[2]]

pica[2] /pīkə/ *n. Med.* the eating of substances other than normal food. [mod.L or med.L, = magpie]

picador /píkədawr/ *n.* a mounted man with a lance who goads the bull in a bullfight. [Sp. f. *picar* prick]

picaresque /píkərésk/ *adj.* (of a style of fiction) dealing with the episodic adventures of rogues, etc. [F f. Sp. *picaresco* f. *pícaro* rogue]

picaroon /píkəroōn/ *n.* **1 a** a rogue. **b** a thief. **2 a** a pirate. **b** a pirate ship. [Sp. *picarón* (as PICARESQUE)]
■ **1 a** see ROGUE *n.* 1. **b** see THIEF. **2 a** see PIRATE *n.* 1a.

picayune /píkəyoōn/ *n. & adj.* ● *n.* **1** *colloq.* a small coin of little value, esp. a 5-cent piece. **2** an insignificant person or thing. ● *adj.* **1** of little value; trivial. **2** mean; contemptible; petty. [F *picaillon* Piedmontese coin, cash, f. Prov. *picaioun*, of unkn. orig.]
■ *adj.* see PETTY 1, 2.

piccalilli /píkəlílee/ *n.* (*pl.* **piccalillis**) a pickle of chopped vegetables, mustard, and hot spices. [18th c.: perh. f. PICKLE + CHILI]

piccaninny var. of PICKANINNY.

piccolo /píkəlō/ *n. & adj.* ● *n.* (*pl.* **-os**) **1** a small flute sounding an octave higher than the ordinary one. **2** its player. ● *adj.* (esp. of a musical instrument) smaller or having a higher range than usual. [It., = small (flute)]

pick[1] /pik/ *v. & n.* ● *v.tr.* **1** (also *absol.*) choose carefully from a number of alternatives (*picked the pink one*; *picked a team*; *picked the right moment to intervene*). **2** detach or pluck (a flower, fruit, etc.) from a stem, tree, etc. **3 a** probe (the teeth, nose, ears, a pimple, etc.) with the finger, an instrument, etc., to remove unwanted matter. **b** clear (a bone, carcass, etc.) of scraps of meat, etc. **4** (also *absol.*) (of a person) eat (food, a meal, etc.) in small bits; nibble without appetite. **5** (also *absol.*) pluck the strings of (a banjo, etc.). **6** remove stalks, etc., from (esp. soft fruit) before cooking. **7 a** select (a route or path) carefully over difficult terrain by foot. **b** place (one's steps, etc.) carefully. **8** pull apart. **9** (of a bird) take up (grains, etc.) in the beak. **10** open (a lock) with an instrument other than the proper key. ● *n.* **1** the act or an instance of picking. **2 a** a selection or choice. **b** the right to select (*had first pick of the prizes*). **3** (usu. foll. by *of*) the best (*the pick of the bunch*). □ **pick and choose** select carefully or fastidiously. **pick at 1** eat (food) without interest; nibble. **2** = *pick on* 1 (PICK[1]). **pick a person's brains** extract ideas, information, etc., from a person for one's own use. **pick holes** (or **a hole**) **in 1** make holes in (material, etc.) by plucking, poking, etc. **2** find fault with (an idea, etc.). **pick-me-up 1** a restorative tonic, as for the nerves, etc. **2** a good experience, good news, etc., that cheers. **pick off 1** pluck (leaves, etc.) off. **2** shoot (people, etc.) one by one without haste. **3** eliminate (opposition, etc.) singly. **4** *Baseball* put out a base runner caught off base. **pick on 1** find fault with; nag at. **2** select, as for special attention. **pick out 1** take from a larger number (*picked him out from the others*). **2** distinguish from surrounding objects or at a distance (*can just pick out the church spire*). **3** play (a tune) by ear on the piano, etc. **4** (often foll. by *in*, *with*) **a** highlight (a painting, etc.) with touches of another color. **b** accentuate (decoration, a painting, etc.) with a contrasting color (*picked out the handles in red*). **5** make out (the meaning of a passage, etc.). **pick over** select the best from. **pick a person's pockets** steal the contents of a person's pockets. **pick a quarrel** (or **fight**) start an argument or a fight deliber-

/.../ **pronunciation** ● **part of speech**
□ **phrases, idioms, and compounds**
□□ **derivatives** ■ **synonym section**
cross-references appear in SMALL CAPITALS or *italics*

ately. **pick to pieces** = *take to pieces* (see PIECE). **pick up 1 a** grasp and raise (from the ground, etc.) (*picked up his hat*). **b** clean up; straighten up. **2** gain or acquire by chance or without effort (*picked up a cold*). **3 a** fetch (a person, animal, or thing) left in another person's charge. **b** stop for and take along with one, esp. in a vehicle (*pick me up on the corner*). **4** make the acquaintance of (a person) casually, esp. as a sexual overture. **5** (of one's health, the weather, stock prices, etc.) recover; prosper; improve. **6** (of an engine, etc.) recover speed; accelerate. **7** (of the police, etc.) take into custody; arrest. **8** detect by scrutiny or with a telescope, searchlight, radio, etc. (*picked up most of the mistakes*; *picked up a distress signal*). **9** (often foll. by *with*) form or renew a friendship. **10** accept the responsibility of paying (a bill, etc.). **11** (*refl.*) raise (oneself, etc.) after a fall, etc. **12** raise (the feet, etc.) clear of the ground. **13** *Golf* pick up one's ball, esp. when conceding a hole. **pick-your-own** (usu. *attrib.*) (of commercially grown fruit and vegetables) dug or picked by the customer at the place of production. **take one's pick** make a choice. □□ **pickable** *adj*. [ME, earlier *pike*, of unkn. orig.]

■ *v.* **1** select, choose, pick out, pick on, cull, sort out, single out, opt for, fix *or* decide upon, go for, elect, settle upon *or* on, screen out, sift out. **2** pluck, gather, collect, harvest, bring *or* take in, garner. **4** pick at, nibble, peck; snack. ● *n.* **2 a** selection, choice, option, preference. **3** choicest, best, crème de la crème, cream, finest, first. □ **pick at 1** nibble (at), peck at; play *or* toy *or* mess *or* fiddle with. **pick holes** (or **a hole**) **in 2** see CRITICIZE 1. **pick off 2, 3** shoot (down); kill; see also ELIMINATE 1. **pick on 1** bully, intimidate, abuse, browbeat, badger, harry, hector, tease, taunt, needle, torment, ride; criticize, carp at, find fault with, cavil at, quibble at, pick at, nag (at), niggle (at), harass, pester, annoy, irritate, bother. **2** see PICK *v.* 1 above. **pick out 1** see PICK *v.* 1 above. **2** discern, distinguish, make out, recognize, discriminate. **pick a quarrel** (or **fight**) start a quarrel *or* fight. **pick up 1 a** raise (up), lift (up), take up. **2** acquire, learn, become acquainted with, *colloq.* get the hang of; find, come by, get hold of, obtain; catch, come down with, contract, get, develop, fall ill with, *Brit.* go down with. **3** fetch; call for, give a lift *or* ride to, collect, come *or* go for. **4** meet, introduce oneself to, strike up an acquaintance with; make advances to; see also APPROACH *v.* 3. **5** improve, get better, make headway, recover, perk up, rally, (make) progress, move ahead, increase, prosper, make a comeback. **6** recover, revive, accelerate, speed up. **7** arrest, apprehend, detain, take into custody, collar, *colloq.* run in, pull in, bust, *sl.* pinch, nab, *Brit. sl.* nick.

pick² /pik/ *n.* & *v.* ● *n.* **1** a long-handled tool having a usu. curved iron bar pointed at one or both ends, used for breaking up hard ground, masonry, etc. **2** *colloq.* a plectrum. **3** any instrument for picking, such as a toothpick. ● *v.tr.* **1** break the surface of (the ground, etc.) with or as if with a pick. **2** make (holes, etc.) in this way. [ME, app. var. of PIKE²]

pickaback var. of PIGGYBACK.

pickaninny /píkəninee/ *n.* & *adj.* (also **piccaninny**) ● *n.* (*pl.* **-ies**) *offens.* a small African-American child. ● *adj. archaic* very small. [W.Ind. Negro f. Sp. *pequeño* or Port. *pequeno* little]

pickax /píkaks/ *n.* & *v.* (also **pickaxe**) ● *n.* = PICK² *n.* 1. ● *v.* **1** *tr.* break (the ground, etc.) with a pickaxe. **2** *intr.* work with a pickaxe. [ME *pikois* f. OF *picois*, rel. to PIKE²: assim. to AX]

picker /píkər/ *n.* **1** a person or thing that picks. **2** (often in *comb.*) a person who gathers or collects (*grape-picker*; *rag-picker*).

pickerel /píkərəl/ *n.* (*pl.* same or **pickerels**) **1** any of various species of N. American pike of the genus *Esox*. **2** = WALLEYE. **3** esp. *Brit.* a young pike. [ME, dimin. of PIKE¹]

picket /píkit/ *n.* & *v.* ● *n.* **1** a person or group of people outside a place of work, intending to persuade esp. workers not to enter during a strike, etc. **2** a pointed stake or peg

driven into the ground to form a fence or palisade, to tether a horse, etc. **3** (also **picquet, piquet**) *Mil.* **a** a small body of troops or a single soldier sent out to watch for the enemy, held in readiness, etc. **b** a party of sentries. **c** an outpost. **d** a camp guard on police duty in a garrison town, etc. ● *v.* (**picketed, picketing**) **1 a** *tr.* & *intr.* station or act as a picket. **b** *tr.* beset or guard (a factory, workers, etc.) with a picket or pickets. **2** *tr.* secure with stakes. **3** *tr.* tether (an animal). □ **picket line** a boundary established by workers on strike, esp. at the entrance to the place of work, which others are asked not to cross. □□ **picketer** *n.* [F *piquet* pointed stake f. *piquer* prick, f. *pic* PICK²]

■ *n.* **1** picketer, demonstrator, protester, striker. **2** stake, pale, post, peg, stanchion, upright, rod, palisade, paling. **3 a, b** guard, patrol, watch; sentry, sentinel, scout, observer, vedette, *archaic or hist.* watchman.
● *v.* **1** protest, demonstrate; blockade; see also STRIKE *v.* 17a. **2** enclose, shut in, wall in, fence (in), hem in, box in. **3** see TETHER *v.*

pickings /píkingz/ *n.pl.* **1** perquisites; pilferings (*rich pickings*). **2** remaining scraps; gleanings.
■ **1** see SPOIL *n.* 1. **2** see SCRAP *n.* 6a.

pickle /píkəl/ *n.* & *v.* ● *n.* **1 a** (often in *pl.*) vegetables, esp. cucumbers, preserved in brine, vinegar, mustard, etc., and used as a relish. **b** the brine, vinegar, etc., in which food is preserved. **2** *colloq.* a plight (*a fine pickle we are in!*). **3** *Brit. colloq.* a mischievous child. **4** an acid solution for cleaning metal, etc. ● *v.tr.* **1** preserve in pickle. **2** treat with pickle. **3** (as **pickled** *adj.*) *sl.* drunk. [ME *pekille, pykyl*, f. MDu., MLG *pekel*, of unkn. orig.]
■ *n.* **2** see PLIGHT¹. ● *v.* **3** (**pickled**) see DRUNK *adj.* 1.

pickler /píklər/ *n.* **1** a person who pickles vegetables, etc. **2** a vegetable suitable for pickling.

picklock /píklok/ *n.* **1** a person who picks locks. **2** an instrument for this.
■ **1** see THIEF.

pickpocket /píkpokit/ *n.* a person who steals from the pockets of others.
■ **1** see THIEF.

pickup /píkəp/ *n.* **1** *sl.* a person met casually, esp. for sexual purposes. **2** a small truck with an enclosed cab and open back. **3 a** the part of a record player carrying the stylus. **b** a detector of vibrations, etc. **4 a** the act of picking up. **b** something picked up. **5** the capacity for acceleration. **6** = *pick-me-up.*

Pickwickian /pikwíkeeən/ *adj.* **1** of or like Mr. Pickwick in Dickens's *Pickwick Papers*, esp. in being jovial, plump, etc. **2** (of words or their sense) misunderstood or misused, esp. to avoid offense.

picky /píkee/ *adj.* (**pickier, pickiest**) *colloq.* excessively fastidious; choosy. □□ **pickiness** *n.*
■ see FASTIDIOUS 1.

picnic /píknik/ *n.* & *v.* ● *n.* **1** an outing or excursion including a packed meal eaten out of doors. **2** any meal eaten out of doors or without preparation, tables, chairs, etc. **3** (usu. with *neg.*) *colloq.* something agreeable or easily accomplished, etc. (*it was no picnic organizing the meeting*). ● *v.intr.* (**picnicked, picnicking**) take part in a picnic. □□ **picnicker** *n.* **picnicky** *adj. colloq.* [F *pique-nique*, of unkn. orig.]
■ *n.* **2** garden party, barbecue, cookout. **3** child's play, *colloq.* pushover, cinch, piece of cake, breeze; see also BREEZE¹ *n.* 4; (*no picnic*) torture, agony, *colloq.* a pain in the neck, *sl.* pain in the butt; difficult, arduous, torturous, agonizing, painful, disagreeable, tough, hard, rough, unpleasant.

pico- /peékō, píkō/ *comb. form* denoting a factor of 10^{-12} (*picometer*). [Sp. *pico* beak, peak, little bit]

picot /peékō, peekó/ *n.* a small loop of twisted thread in a lace edging, etc. [F, dimin. of *pic* peak, point]

picotee /píkətee/ *n.* a type of carnation of which the flowers have light petals with darker edges. [F *picoté -ée* past part. of *picoter* prick (as PICOT)]

picquet var. of PICKET 3.

picric acid /píkrik/ *n.* a very bitter yellow compound used in dyeing and surgery and in explosives. □□ **picrate** /-rayt/ *n.* [Gk *pikros* bitter]

Pict /pikt/ *n.* a member of an ancient people of northern Britain. □□ **Pictish** *adj.* [ME f. LL *Picti* perh. f. *pingere pict-* paint, tattoo]

pictograph /píktəgraf/ *n.* (also **pictogram** /píktəgram/) **1 a** a pictorial symbol for a word or phrase. **b** an ancient record consisting of these. **2** a pictorial representation of statistics, etc., on a chart, graph, etc. □□ **pictographic** *adj.* **pictography** /-tógrəfee/ *n.* [L *pingere pict-* paint]

pictorial /piktáwreeəl/ *adj.* & *n.* ● *adj.* **1** of or expressed in a picture or pictures. **2** illustrated. **3** picturesque. ● *n.* a journal, postage stamp, etc., with a picture or pictures as the main feature. □□ **pictorially** *adv.* [LL *pictorius* f. L *pictor* painter (as PICTURE)]

■ *adj.* **3** see PICTURESQUE 1.

picture /píkchər/ *n.* & *v.* ● *n.* **1 a** (often *attrib.*) a painting, drawing, photograph, etc., esp. as a work of art (*picture frame*). **b** a portrait, esp. a photograph, of a person (*does not like to have her picture taken*). **c** a beautiful object (*her hat is a picture*). **2 a** a total visual or mental impression produced; a scene (*the picture looks bleak*). **b** a written or spoken description (*drew a vivid picture of moral decay*). **3 a** a movie. **b** (in *pl.*) a showing of movies at a movie theater (*went to the pictures*). **c** (in *pl.*) movies in general. **4** an image on a television screen. **5** *colloq.* **a** esp. *iron.* a person or thing exemplifying something (*he was the picture of innocence*). **b** a person or thing resembling another closely (*the picture of her aunt*). ● *v.tr.* **1** represent in a picture. **2** (also *refl.*; often foll. by *to*) imagine, esp. visually or vividly (*pictured it to herself*). **3** describe graphically. □ **get the picture** *colloq.* grasp the tendency or drift of circumstances, information, etc. **in the picture** fully informed or noticed. **out of the picture** uninvolved; inactive; irrelevant. **picture book** a book containing many illustrations, esp. one intended for small children. **picture card** a face card. **picture gallery** a place containing an exhibition or collection of pictures. **picture molding** (or **mold** or **rail**) **1** woodwork, etc., used for framing pictures. **2** a rail on a wall used for hanging pictures from. **picture postcard** a postcard with a picture on one side. **picture tube** the cathode-ray tube of a television set. **picture window** a very large window consisting of one pane of glass. **picture writing** a mode of recording events, etc., by pictorial symbols as in early hieroglyphics, etc. [ME f. L *pictura* f. *pingere pict-* paint]

■ *n.* **1 a** drawing, painting, portrait, depiction, representation, illustration, sketch, photograph, photo. **2** impression, idea, notion, understanding, image; see also SCENE 6. **3** movie, film, movies, *Brit. colloq.* flick, cinema, *colloq.* flicks. **5 a** model, prototype, epitome, essence, embodiment, incarnation, personification, perfect example. **b** image, (perfect *or* exact) likeness, double, duplicate, twin, (exact) replica, facsimile, dead ringer, *colloq.* spitting image. ● *v.* **1** depict, draw, portray, paint, represent, show, illustrate. **2** envision, envisage, visualize, imagine, fancy, conceive (of), see in the mind's eye, contemplate. □ **get the picture** get the gist *or* drift; see also UNDERSTAND 7. **in the picture** see INFORMED 1; (*put in the picture*) inform *or* advise fully, *colloq.* fill in. **out of the picture** see IRRELEVANT.

picturesque /píkchərésk/ *adj.* **1** (of landscape, etc.) beautiful or striking, as in a picture. **2** (of language, etc.) strikingly graphic; vivid. □□ **picturesquely** *adv.* **picturesqueness** *n.* [F *pittoresque* f. It. *pittoresco* f. *pittore* painter f. L (as PICTORIAL): assim. to PICTURE]

■ **1** beautiful, charming, idyllic, fetching, attractive, pretty, lovely, quaint, delightful, pleasing, scenic, interesting, striking. **2** colorful, graphic, realistic, vivid, striking.

piddle /píd'l/ *v.* & *n.* ● *v.intr.* **1** *colloq.* urinate (used esp. to or by children). **2** work or act in a trifling way. **3** (as **piddling** *adj.*) *colloq.* trivial; trifling. ● *n. colloq.* **1** urination. **2** urine (used esp. to or by children). □□ **piddler** *n.* [sense 1 prob. f. PISS + PUDDLE: sense 2 perh. f. PEDDLE]

■ *v.* **1** see URINATE. **3** (**piddling**) see TRIFLING. ● *n.* **2** urine, *colloq.* pee, esp. *Brit. sl.* wee.

piddock /pídək/ *n.* any rock-boring bivalve mollusk of the family Pholadidae, used for bait. [18th c.: orig. unkn.]

pidgin /píjin/ *n.* a simplified language containing vocabulary from two or more languages, used for communication between people not having a common language. □ **pidgin English** a pidgin in which the chief language is English, used orig. between Chinese and Europeans. [corrupt. of *business*]

pi-dog var. of PYE-DOG.

pie[1] /pī/ *n.* **1 a** a baked dish of fruit, meat, custard, etc., usu. with a top and base of pastry. **2** anything resembling a pie in form (*a mud pie*). □ **easy as pie** very easy. **pie chart** a circle divided into sections to represent relative quantities. **pie-eater** *Austral. sl.* a person of little account. **pie-eyed** *sl.* drunk. **pie in the sky** an unrealistic prospect of future happiness after present suffering; a misleading promise. [ME, perh. = PIE[2] f. miscellaneous contents compared to objects collected by a magpie]

■ **1** see TART[1] 2. □ **pie-eyed** see DRUNK *adj.* 1.

pie[2] /pī/ *n. archaic* **1** a magpie. **2** a pied animal. [ME f. OF f. L *pica*]

pie[3] /pī/ *n.* var. of PI.

pie[4] /pī/ *n. hist.* a former monetary unit of India equal to one twelfth of an anna. [Hind., etc. *pā'ī* f. Skr. *pad, padī* quarter]

piebald /píbawld/ *adj.* & *n.* ● *adj.* **1** (usu. of an animal, esp. a horse) having irregular patches of two colors, esp. black and white. **2** motley; mongrel. ● *n.* a piebald animal, esp. a horse.

■ *adj.* **1** see *dapple gray* 1. ● *n.* see DAPPLE *n.* 2.

piece /pees/ *n.* & *v.* ● *n.* **1 a** (often foll. by *of*) one of the distinct portions forming part of or broken off from a larger object; a bit; a part (*a piece of string*). **b** each of the parts of which a set or category is composed (*a five-piece band*; *a piece of furniture*). **2** a coin of specified value (*50-cent piece*). **3 a** a usu. short literary or musical composition or a picture. **b** a theatrical play. **4** an item, instance, or example (*a piece of news*). **5 a** any of the objects used to make moves in board games. **b** a chessman (strictly, other than a pawn). **6** a definite quantity in which a thing is sold. **7** (often foll. by *of*) an enclosed portion (of land, etc.). **8** *sl. derog.* a woman. **9** (foll. by *of*) *sl.* a financial share or investment in (*has a piece of the new production*). **10** *colloq.* a short distance. **11** *sl.* = PISTOL. ● *v.tr.* **1** (usu. foll. by *together*) form into a whole; put together; join (*finally pieced his story together*). **2** (usu. foll. by *out*) **a** eke out. **b** form (a theory, etc.) by combining parts, etc. **3** (usu. foll. by *up*) patch. **4** join (threads) in spinning. □ **break to pieces** break into fragments. **by the piece** (paid) according to the quantity of work done. **go to pieces** collapse emotionally; suffer a breakdown. **in one piece 1** unbroken. **2** unharmed. **in pieces** broken. **of a piece** (often foll. by *with*) uniform; consistent; in keeping. **piece goods** fabrics woven in standard lengths. **a piece of the action** *sl.* a share of the profits; a share in the excitement. **piece of ass** *sl. offens.* a person regarded as a sexual partner. **a piece of cake** see CAKE. **piece of eight** *hist.* a Spanish dollar, equivalent to 8 reals. **a piece of one's mind** a sharp rebuke or lecture. **piece of water** *Brit.* a small lake, etc. **piece of work 1** a thing made by working (cf. *nasty piece of work*). **2** a remarkable person or thing. **piece rates** a rate paid according to the amount produced. **piece work** work paid for by the amount produced. **say one's piece** give one's opinion or make a prepared statement. **take to pieces 1** break up or dismantle. **2** criticize harshly. □□ **piecer** *n.* (in sense 4 of *v.*). [ME f. AF *pece*, OF *piece* f. Rmc, prob. of Gaulish orig.: cf. PEAT]

■ *n.* **1 a** bit, morsel, scrap, chunk, hunk, sliver, lump, particle, fragment, shred, shard, wedge, slice; share, portion, part, segment, section, percentage, proportion;

serving, helping. **3** work, composition; (short) story, article, essay, poem; piece of music, opus, (musical) number, arrangement, tune, melody, song, air, jingle, ditty; production, play, drama, sketch, show. **4** item, instance; see also EXAMPLE *n.* 1. **5** man, token; chessman, checker, *Brit.* draughtsman, checkerman. **9** share, investment, interest, holding, percentage, stake, quota, portion. ● *v.* **1** (*piece together*) assemble, put together; join, fix, unite, mend; make sense of. **2** (*piece out*) **a** see SHARE¹ *v.* 1, 2, 5. □ **break to pieces** fall apart, disintegrate, crumble, shatter; see also BREAK¹ *v.* 1a. **go to pieces** collapse, be shattered, have a nervous breakdown, disintegrate, go out of *or* lose control, break down, *colloq.* crack up. **in one piece 2** see UNSCATHED. **in pieces** smashed, destroyed, ruined, shattered, broken. **of a piece** similar, alike, of the same sort *or* kind *or* type; uniform, consistent; in harmony, in agreement, harmonious, in keeping. **a piece of one's mind** scolding, rebuke, lecture, reprimand, tongue-lashing, telling-off, chiding, rap over *or* on the knuckles, esp. *Brit.* ticking-off, *colloq.* what for, dressing-down. **say one's piece** have one's say, give one's opinion, say what is on one's mind; vent one's spleen, *colloq.* get a load *or* thing off one's chest. **take to pieces 1** strip (down), dismantle, take apart. **2** see ATTACK *v.* 3.

pièce de résistance /pyés də rayzéestoNs/ *n.* (*pl.* **pièces de résistance** *pronunc.* same) **1** the most important or remarkable item. **2** the most substantial dish at a meal. [F]
  ■ **1** highlight, (special *or* main) feature, (special *or* main) attraction, specialty, *Brit.* speciality; masterpiece, chef-d'œuvre.

piecemeal /péesmeel/ *adv. & adj.* ● *adv.* piece by piece; gradually. ● *adj.* partial; gradual; unsystematic. [ME f. PIECE + -*meal* f. OE *mǣlum* (instr. dative pl. of *mǣl* MEAL¹)]
  ■ *adv.* piece by piece, little by little, inch by inch, bit by bit, inchmeal, gradually, by degrees, slowly; by fits and starts, fitfully, intermittently, sporadically, disjointedly. ● *adj.* partial, inchmeal, gradual; disjointed, fragmentary, sporadic, unsystematic.

piecrust /píkrust/ *n.* the baked pastry crust of a pie. □ **piecrust table** a table with an indented edge like a piecrust.

pied /pīd/ *adj.* particolored. □ **Pied Piper** a person enticing followers, esp. to their doom. [ME f. PIE², orig. of friars]
  ■ see *mottled* (MOTTLE).

pied-à-terre /pyáydaatáir/ *n.* (*pl.* **pieds-à-terre** *pronunc.* same) a usu. small apartment, house, etc., kept for occasional use. [F, lit. 'foot to earth']

piedmont /péedmont/ *n.* a gentle slope leading from the foot of mountains to a region of flat land. [It. *piemonte* mountain foot, name of a region at the foot of the Alps]

pie-dog var. of PYE-DOG.

pier /peer/ *n.* **1 a** a structure of iron or wood raised on piles and leading out to sea, a lake, etc., used as a promenade and landing place. **b** a breakwater; a mole. **2 a** a support of an arch or of the span of a bridge; a pillar. **b** solid masonry between windows, etc. □ **pier glass** a large mirror, used orig. to fill wall space between windows. [ME *per* f. AL *pera*, of unkn. orig.]
  ■ **1 a** wharf, landing place, jetty, quay. **2 a** pillar, column, support, pile, piling, post, upright; see also BUTTRESS *n.*

pierce /peers/ *v.* **1** *tr.* **a** (of a sharp instrument, etc.) penetrate the surface of. **b** (often foll. by *with*) prick with a sharp instrument, esp. to make a hole in. **c** make (a hole, etc.) (*pierced a hole in the belt*). **d** (of cold, grief, etc.) affect keenly or sharply. **e** (of a light, glance, sound, etc.) penetrate keenly or sharply. **2** (as **piercing** *adj.*) (of a glance, intuition, high noise, bright light, etc.) keen, sharp, or unpleasantly penetrating. **3** *tr.* force (a way, etc.) through or into (something) (*pierced their way through the jungle*). **4** *intr.* (usu. foll. by *through*, *into*) penetrate. □□ **piercer** *n.* **piercingly** *adv.* [ME f. OF *percer* f. L *pertundere* bore through (as PER-, *tundere tus-*thrust)]
  ■ **1 a, b** puncture, penetrate, thrust *or* poke into, lance,

spear, spit, run through *or* into, skewer, impale, fix, transfix; bore into *or* through, drill into *or* through, perforate, hole. **c** see PUNCH¹ *v.* 3. **d** touch, move, melt, stir, rouse, strike; pain, cut to the quick, wound. **2** (*piercing*) strident, shrill, harsh, earsplitting, high-pitched, loud, blaring; probing, searching, penetrating, sharp, keen; icy, frosty, frigid, chilling, freezing, cold, numbing, wintry, raw, bitter, fierce, biting, nipping, *colloq.* arctic, nippy; stabbing, shooting, excruciating, acute, sharp, severe, agonizing, fierce, intense, painful, racking. **4** (*pierce through* or *into*) see PENETRATE 1a.

pierogi /pərógee, pee-/ *n.* (also **pirogi**) (*pl.* **-gi** or **-gies**) small pastry envelopes filled with mashed potatoes, cabbage, or chopped meat. [Pol. pl. of *pieróg* dumpling]

Pierrot /péerō, pyeró/ *n. Theatr.* a French pantomime character dressed in a loose white clown's costume. [F, dimin. of *Pierre* Peter]
  ■ see FOOL¹ *n.* 2.

pietà /pyetáa/ *n.* a picture or sculpture of the Virgin Mary holding the dead body of Christ on her lap or in her arms. [It. f. L (as PIETY)]

pietas /píətaas/ *n.* respect due to an ancestor, a forerunner, etc. [L: see PIETY]

pietism /píətizəm/ *n.* **1 a** pious sentiment. **b** an exaggerated or affected piety. **2** (esp. as **Pietism**) *hist.* a movement for the revival of piety in the Lutheran Church in the 17th c. □□ **pietist** *n.* **pietistic** *adj.* **pietistical** *adj.* [G *Pietismus* (as PIETY)]
  ■ **1** see PIETY. □□ **pietistic, pietistical** see PIOUS 2.

piety /píətee/ *n.* (*pl.* **-ies**) **1** the quality of being pious. **2** a pious act. [ME f. OF *pieté* f. L *pietas -tatis* dutifulness (as PIOUS)]
  ■ **1** devotion, devotedness, respect, deference, dedication, dutifulness, loyalty, affection; piousness, reverence, veneration, devoutness, holiness, godliness, pietism, observance, religiousness, sanctity; sanctimoniousness, sanctimony.

piezoelectricity /pī-eezōilektrísitee, pee-áyzō-/ *n.* electric polarization in a substance resulting from the application of mechanical stress, esp. in certain crystals. □□ **piezoelectric** /-iléktrik/ *adj.* **piezoelectrically** *adv.* [Gk *piezō* press + ELECTRIC]

piezometer /pí-izómitər, peéi-/ *n.* an instrument for measuring the magnitude or direction of pressure.

piffle /pífəl/ *n. & v. colloq.* ● *n.* nonsense; empty speech. ● *v.intr.* talk or act feebly; trifle. □□ **piffler** *n.* [imit.]
  ■ *n.* see RUBBISH *n.* 3.

piffling /pífling/ *adj. colloq.* trivial; worthless.

pig /pig/ *n. & v.* ● *n.* **1 a** any omnivorous hoofed bristly mammal of the family Suidae, esp. a domesticated kind, *Sus scrofa.* **b** a young pig; a piglet. **c** (often in *comb.*) any similar animal (*guinea pig*). **2** the flesh of esp. a young or suckling pig as food (*roast pig*). **3** *colloq.* **a** a greedy, dirty, obstinate, sulky, or annoying person. **b** a person who eats too much or too fast. **c** an unpleasant, awkward, or difficult thing, task, etc. **4** an oblong mass of metal (esp. iron or lead) from a smelting furnace. **5** *sl. derog.* a policeman. **6** *sl. derog.* a sexist or racist person. ● *v.* (**pigged**, **pigging**) **1** *tr.* (also *absol.*) (of a sow) bring forth (piglets). **2** *tr. colloq.* eat (food) greedily. **3** *intr.* herd together or behave like pigs. □ **bleed like a pig** (or **stuck pig**) bleed copiously. **buy a pig in a poke** buy, accept, etc., something without knowing its value or esp. seeing it. **in a pig's eye** *colloq.* certainly not. **make a pig of oneself** overeat. **make a pig's ear of** *Brit. colloq.* make a mess of; bungle. **pig in the middle** esp. *Brit.* a person who is placed in an awkward situation between two others (after a ball game for three with one in the middle). **pig iron** crude iron from a smelting furnace. **Pig Island** *Austral. & NZ sl.* New Zealand. **pig it** live in a disorderly, untidy, or filthy fashion. **pig Latin** a jargon based on alternation of English sounds (e.g., "igpay atinlay" for *pig Latin*). **pig-meat** *Brit.* pork, ham, or bacon. **pig out** (often foll. by *on*) *sl.* eat gluttonously. **pigs might fly** esp. *Brit. iron.* an expression of disbelief. **pig's wash** = PIGSWILL. □□ **piggish**

adj. **piggishly** *adv.* **piggishness** *n.* **piglet** *n.* **piglike** *adj.* **pigling** *n.* [ME *pigge* f. OE *pigga* (unrecorded)]

■ *n.* **3 a** see GLUTTON 1, SLOB, STINKER. **5** see *police officer*. ● *v.* **2** see OVEREAT. □ **pig out** see OVEREAT. □□ **piggish** see GREEDY 1. **piggishness** see GREED.

pigeon[1] /píjin/ *n.* **1** any of several large usu. gray and white birds of the family Columbidae, esp. *Columba livia*, often domesticated and bred and trained to carry messages, etc.; a dove (cf. *rock pigeon*). **2** a person easily swindled; a simpleton. □ **pigeon breast** (or **chest**) a deformed human chest with a projecting breastbone. **pigeon breasted** (or **chested**) having a pigeon breast. **pigeon fancier** a person who keeps and breeds fancy pigeons. **pigeon fancying** this pursuit. **pigeon hawk** = MERLIN. **pigeon pair** *Brit.* **1** boy and girl twins. **2** a boy and girl as sole children. **pigeon's milk 1** a secretion from the esophagus with which pigeons feed their young. **2** esp. *Brit.* an imaginary article for which children are sent on a fool's errand. **pigeon-toed** (of a person) having the toes turned inward. □□ **pigeonry** *n.* (*pl.* **-ies**). [ME f. OF *pijon* f. LL *pipio -onis* (imit.)]

■ **2** see DUPE *n.*

pigeon[2] /píjin/ *n.* **1** = PIDGIN. **2** *colloq.* a particular concern, job, or business (*that's not my pigeon*).

pigeonhole /píjinhōl/ *n. & v.* ● *n.* **1** each of a set of compartments in a cabinet or on a wall for papers, letters, etc. **2** a small recess for a pigeon to nest in. ● *v.tr.* **1** deposit (a document) in a pigeonhole. **2** put (a matter) aside for future consideration or to forget it. **3** assign (a person or thing) to a preconceived category.

piggery /pígəree/ *n.* (*pl.* **-ies**) **1** a pig-breeding farm, etc. **2** = PIGSTY. **3** piggishness.

piggy /pígee/ *n. & adj.* ● *n.* (also **piggie**) *colloq.* **1** a little pig. **2 a** a child's word for a pig. **b** a child's word for a toe. **3** *Brit.* the game of tipcat. ● *adj.* (**piggier**, **piggiest**) **1** like a pig. **2** (of features, etc.) like those of a pig (*little piggy eyes*). □ **piggy bank** a pig-shaped box for coins. **piggy in the middle** = *pig in the middle*.

piggyback /pígeebak/ *n. & adv.* (also **pickaback** /píkəbak/) ● *n.* a ride on the back and shoulders of another person. ● *adv.* **1** on the back and shoulders of another person. **2 a** on the back or top of a larger object. **b** in addition to; along with. [16th c.: orig. unkn.]

pigheaded /píg-hédid/ *adj.* obstinate. □□ **pigheadedly** *adv.* **pigheadedness** *n.*

■ see OBSTINATE. □□ **pigheadedness** see *obstinacy* (OBSTINATE).

pigment /pígmənt/ *n. & v.* ● *n.* **1** coloring matter used as paint or dye, usu. as an insoluble suspension. **2** the natural coloring matter of animal or plant tissue, e.g., chlorophyll, hemoglobin. ● *v.tr.* color with or as if with pigment. □□ **pigmental** /-mént'l/ *adj.* **pigmentary** /-məntéree/ *adj.* [ME f. L *pigmentum* f. *pingere* paint]

■ *n.* see COLOR *n.* 3. ● *v.* see COLOR *v.* 1.

pigmentation /pígməntáyshən/ *n.* **1** the natural coloring of plants, animals, etc. **2** the excessive coloring of tissue by the deposition of pigment.

■ **1** see COLOR *n.* 3, 5a.

pigmy var. of PYGMY.

pignut /pígnut/ *n.* one of two species of hickory trees or their nuts.

pigpen /pígpen/ *n.* = PIGSTY.

pigskin /pígskin/ *n.* **1** the hide of a pig. **2** leather made from this. **3** a football.

pigsticking /pígstìking/ *n.* **1** the hunting of wild boar with a spear on horseback. **2** the butchering of pigs.

pigsty /pígstī/ *n.* (*pl.* **-ies**) **1** a pen or enclosure for a pig or pigs. **2** a filthy house, room, etc.

■ **2** see SHAMBLES 1.

pigswill /pígswil/ *n.* kitchen refuse and scraps fed to pigs.

■ see SWILL *n.* 2, 4.

pigtail /pígtayl/ *n.* **1** a braid or gathered hank of hair hanging from the back of the head, or either of a pair at the sides. **2** a thin twist of tobacco. □□ **pigtailed** *adj.*

■ **1** braid, plait. **2** chew, plug, twist, quid.

pigwash /pígwawsh, -wosh/ *n.* = PIGSWILL.

pigweed /pígweed/ *n.* any herb of the genus *Amaranthus*, grown for grain or fodder.

pika /peékə, píkə/ *n.* any small rabbit-like mammal of the genus *Ochotona*, with small ears and no tail. [Tungus *piika*]

pike[1] /pīk/ *n.* (*pl.* same) **1** a large voracious freshwater fish, *Esox lucius*, with a long narrow snout and sharp teeth. **2** any other fish of the family Esocidae. □ **pike perch** any of various pikelike perches of the genus *Lucioperca* or *Stizostedion*. [ME, = PIKE[2] (because of its pointed jaw)]

pike[2] /pīk/ *n. & v.* ● *n.* **1** *hist.* an infantry weapon with a pointed steel or iron head on a long wooden shaft. **2** *Northern Engl.* the peaked top of a hill, esp. in place names. ● *v.tr.* thrust through or kill with a pike. □ **pike on** *Brit. colloq.* withdraw timidly from. [OE *pīc* point, prick: sense 2 perh. f. ON]

■ *n.* **1** see LANCE *n.* 1.

pike[3] /pīk/ *n.* a turnpike. □□ **come down the pike** *colloq.* appear; occur. [abbr. of TURNPIKE]

■ see ROAD[1] 1.

pike[4] /pīk/ *n.* a jackknife position in diving or gymnastics. [20th c.: orig. unkn.]

piker /píkər/ *n.* a cautious, timid, or cheap person.

pikestaff /píkstaf/ *n.* **1** the wooden shaft of a pike. **2** a walking stick with a metal point. □ **plain as a pikestaff** quite plain or obvious (orig. *packstaff*, a smooth staff used by a peddler).

pilaf /pilaáf, peélaaf/ *n.* (also **pilaff; pilaw, pilau** /-láw, -lów/) a dish of spiced rice or wheat with meat, fish, vegetables, etc. [Turk. *pilâv*]

pilaster /pilástər/ *n.* a rectangular column, esp. one projecting from a wall. □□ **pilastered** *adj.* [F *pilastre* f. It. *pilastro* f. med.L *pilastrum* f. L *pila* pillar]

■ see PILLAR 1.

pilchard /pílchərd/ *n.* a small marine fish, *Sardinia pilchardus*, of the herring family (see SARDINE). [16th-c. *pilcher*, etc.: orig. unkn.]

pile[1] /pīl/ *n. & v.* ● *n.* **1** a heap of things laid or gathered upon one another (*a pile of leaves*). **2 a** a large imposing building (*a stately pile*). **b** a large group of tall buildings. **3** *colloq.* **a** a large quantity. **b** a large amount of money; a fortune (*made his pile*). **4 a** a series of plates of dissimilar metals laid one on another alternately to produce an electric current. **b** = *atomic pile*. **5** a funeral pyre. ● *v.* **1** *tr.* **a** (often foll. by *up, on*) heap up (*piled the plates on the table*). **b** (foll. by *with*) load (*piled the bed with coats*). **2** *intr.* (usu. foll. by *in, into, on, out of*, etc.) crowd hurriedly or tightly (*all piled into the car; piled out of the restaurant*). □ **pile arms** *hist.* place (usu. four) rifles with their butts on the ground and the muzzles together. **pile it on** *colloq.* exaggerate. **pile on the agony** *colloq.* exaggerate for effect or to gain sympathy, etc. **pile up 1** accumulate; heap up. **2** *colloq.* run (a ship) aground or cause (a vehicle, etc.) to crash. [ME f. OF f. L *pila* pillar, pier, mole]

■ *n.* **1** heap, mound, stack, accumulation, mass, mountain, collection, assemblage, batch, hoard, aggregation, congeries, agglomeration, amassment. **3 a** large *or* great amount, a lot, *colloq.* great *or* good deal; (*piles*) ocean(s), lots, masses, stack(s), *colloq.* oodles, tons, bags, heaps, loads. **b** money, fortune, wealth, wad, *sl.* bundle, loot; *colloq.* packet, tidy sum; see also MINT[2] *n.* 2. ● *v.* **1** stack (up), heap (up), mound; accumulate, pile up *or* with, stockpile, amass, collect, assemble, hoard, aggregate, cumulate; load (up). **2** (*pile in* or *into*) crowd in, pack in, jam in, crush in, cram into, jump in. □ **pile it on** see EXAGGERATE 1. **pile up 1** see PILE *v.* 1 above. **2** see CRASH[1] *v.* 3a.

pile[2] /pīl/ *n. & v.* ● *n.* **1** a heavy beam driven vertically into the bed of a river, soft ground, etc., to support the foundations of a superstructure. **2** a pointed stake or post. **3** *Heraldry* a wedge-shaped device. ● *v.tr.* **1** provide with

/.../ **pronunciation**	● **part of speech**
□ **phrases, idioms, and compounds**	
□□ **derivatives**	■ **synonym section**
cross-references appear in SMALL CAPITALS or *italics*	

piles. **2** drive (piles) into the ground, etc. □ **pile driver** a machine for driving piles into the ground. **pile dwelling** a dwelling built on piles, esp. in a lake. [OE *pīl* f. L *pilum* javelin]

pile³ /pil/ *n.* **1** the soft projecting surface on velvet, plush, etc., or esp. on a carpet; nap. **2** soft hair or down, or the wool of a sheep. [ME prob. f. AF *pyle, peile,* OF *poil* f. L *pilus* hair]
■ nap, shag, plush; fuzz, down, fleece.

pileated /pílee-aytəd/ *adj.* (of birds) having a crest on the top of the head. □ **pileated woodpecker** a black-and-white N. American woodpecker, *Dryocopus pileatus,* with a red crest.

piles /pilz/ *n.pl. colloq.* hemorrhoids. [ME prob. f. L *pila* ball, f. the globular form of external piles]

pileup /pílup/ *n.* **1** a collision of (esp. several) motor vehicles. **2** any mass or pile resulting from accumulation.

pileus /píleeəs/ *n.* (*pl.* **pilei** /-lee-ī/) the caplike part of a mushroom or other fungus. □□ **pileate** /-leeət/ *adj.* **pileated** /-leeaytid/ *adj.* [L, = felt cap]

pilewort /pílwərt, -wawrt/ *n.* the lesser celandine. [PILES, f. its reputed efficacy against piles]

pilfer /pílfər/ *v.tr.* (also *absol.*) steal (objects) esp. in small quantities. □□ **pilferage** /-fərij/ *n.* **pilferer** *n.* [ME f. AF & OF *pelfrer* pillage, of unkn. orig.: assoc. with archaic *pill* plunder: PELF]
■ steal, rob, plunder, thieve, filch, take, snatch, grab, *colloq.* walk off with, lift, swipe, rip off, *Brit. colloq.* snaffle, *formal or joc.* purloin, *sl.* hook, snitch, pinch, *Brit. sl.* nick; see also APPROPRIATE *v.* 1.

pilgrim /pílgrim/ *n.* & *v.* ● *n.* **1** a person who journeys to a sacred place for religious reasons. **2** a person regarded as journeying through life, etc. **3** a traveler. **4** (**Pilgrim**) one of the English Puritans who founded the colony of Plymouth, Massachusetts, in 1620. ● *v.intr.* (**pilgrimed, pilgriming**) wander like a pilgrim. □□ **pilgrimize** *v.intr.* [ME *pilegrim* f. Prov. *pelegrin* f. L *peregrinus* stranger: see PEREGRINE]
■ *n.* **1** hajji, *hist.* palmer.

pilgrimage /pílgrimij/ *n.* & *v.* ● *n.* **1** a pilgrim's journey (*go on a pilgrimage*). **2** life viewed as a journey. **3** any journey taken for nostalgic or sentimental reasons. ● *v.intr.* go on a pilgrimage. [ME f. Prov. *pilgrinatge* (as PILGRIM)]
■ *n.* **1** hajj, holy expedition. **3** expedition, journey, trek, voyage, tour, trip, excursion.

Pilipino /pílipeenō/ *n.* the national language of the Philippines. [Tagalog f. Sp. *Filipino*]

pill /pil/ *n.* **1 a** solid medicine formed into a ball or a flat disk for swallowing whole. **b** (usu. prec. by *the*) *colloq.* a contraceptive pill. **2** an unpleasant or painful necessity; a humiliation (*a bitter pill; must swallow the pill*). **3** *colloq.* or *joc.* a ball. **4** *sl.* a difficult or unpleasant person. □ **pill popper** *colloq.* a person who takes pills freely; a drug addict. **pill pusher** *colloq.* a drug pusher. **sweeten** (or **sugar**) **the pill** make an unpleasant necessity acceptable. [MDu., MLG *pille* prob. f. L *pilula* dimin. of *pila* ball]
■ **1 a** tablet, capsule, caplet, bolus, pellet, pilule; pastille, lozenge, troche. **2** see DISCOMFORT *n.* 1a, BURDEN *n.* 1, 2. **4** nuisance, bore, pest, *colloq.* pain (in the neck), crank, drag. □ **pill popper** see ADDICT *n.* 1. **sweeten the pill** ease the pain, lighten the load.

pillage /pílij/ *v.* & *n.* ● *v.tr.* (also *absol.*) plunder; sack (a place or a person). ● *n.* **1** the act or an instance of pillaging, esp. in war. **2** *hist.* goods plundered. □□ **pillager** *n.* [ME f. OF f. *piller* plunder]
■ *v.* plunder, raid, ravage, sack, rob, loot, ransack, rifle, maraud, vandalize, *literary* despoil. ● *n.* **1** plunder, despoliation, looting, robbery, sack, ransacking, brigandage, piracy, banditry, depredation, vandalization, destruction, *literary* despoiling, *rhet.* rapine. **2** plunder, loot, booty, spoils.

pillar /pílər/ *n.* **1 a** a usu. slender vertical structure of wood, metal, or esp. stone used as a support for a roof, etc. **b** a similar structure used for ornament. **c** a post supporting a structure. **2** a person regarded as a mainstay or support (*a pillar of the faith; a pillar of strength*). **3** an upright mass of air, water, rock, etc. (*pillar of salt*). **4** a solid mass of coal, etc., left to support the roof of a mine. □ **from pillar to**

post (driven, etc.) from one place to another; to and fro. **pillar-box** *Brit.* a public mailbox shaped like a pillar. **pillar-box red** *Brit.* a bright red color, as of pillar-boxes. **Pillars of Hercules 1** two rocks on either side of the Strait of Gibraltar. **2** the ultimate limit. □□ **pillared** *adj.* **pillaret** *n.* [ME & AF *piler,* OF *pilier* ult. f. L *pila* pillar]
■ **1** column, pilaster, pile, piling, pier, upright, post, shaft, prop. **2** mainstay, support(er), upholder, backbone, lynchpin; leader. □ **from pillar to post** to and fro, up and down, back and forth, *literary or dial.* hither and yon; all over (the place).

pillbox /pílboks/ *n.* **1** a small shallow cylindrical box for holding pills. **2** a hat of a similar shape. **3** *Mil.* a small partly underground enclosed concrete fort used as an outpost.

pillion /pílyən/ *n.* **1** esp. *Brit.* seating for a passenger behind a cyclist. **2** *hist.* **a** a woman's light saddle. **b** a cushion attached to the back of a saddle for a usu. female passenger. □ **ride pillion** esp. *Brit.* travel seated behind a motorcyclist, etc. [Gael. *pillean, pillin* dimin. of *pell* cushion f. L *pellis* skin]

pilliwinks /píliwingks/ *n. hist.* an instrument of torture used for squeezing the fingers. [ME *pyrwykes, pyrewinkes,* of unkn. orig.]

pillock /pílək/ *n. Brit. sl.* a stupid person; a fool. [16th c., = penis (var. of *pillicock*): 20th c. in sense defined]

pillory /píləree/ *n.* & *v.* ● *n.* (*pl.* **-ies**) *hist.* a wooden framework with holes for the head and hands, enabling the public to assault or ridicule a person so imprisoned. ● *v.tr.* (**-ies, -ied**) **1** expose (a person) to ridicule or public contempt. **2** *hist.* put in the pillory. [ME f. AL *pillorium* f. OF *pilori,* etc.: prob. f. Prov. *espilori* of uncert. orig.]
■ *v.* **1** see DENOUNCE 1, RIDICULE *v.*

pillow /pílō/ *n.* & *v.* ● *n.* **1 a** a usu. oblong support for the head, esp. in bed, with a cloth cover stuffed with feathers, down, foam rubber, etc. **b** any pillow-shaped block or support. **2** = *lace pillow.* ● *v.tr.* **1** rest (the head, etc.) on or as if on a pillow (*pillowed his head on his arms*). **2** serve as a pillow for (*moss pillowed her head*). □ **pillow fight** a mock fight with pillows, esp. by children. **pillow lace** lace made on a lace pillow. **pillow lava** lava forming rounded masses. **pillow talk** romantic or intimate conversation in bed. □□ **pillowy** *adj.* [OE *pyle, pylu,* ult. f. L *pulvinus* cushion]
■ *n.* **1** bolster, pad, cushion.

pillowcase /pílōkays/ *n.* a washable cotton, etc., cover for a pillow.

pillowslip /pílōslip/ *n.* = PILLOWCASE.

pillule var. of PILULE.

pillwort /pílwərt, -wawrt/ *n.* an aquatic fern, *Pilularia globulifera,* with small globular spore-producing bracts.

pilose /pílōs/ *adj.* (also **pilous** /-ləs/) covered with hair. □□ **pilosity** /pīlósitee/ *n.* [L *pilosus* f. *pilus* hair]

pilot /pílət/ *n.* & *v.* ● *n.* **1** a person who operates the flying controls of an aircraft. **2** a person qualified to take charge of a ship entering or leaving a harbor. **3** (usu. *attrib.*) an experimental undertaking or test, esp. in advance of a larger one (*a pilot project*). **4** a guide; a leader. **5** = *pilot light.* **6** *archaic* a steersman. ● *v.tr.* (**piloted, piloting**) **1** act as a pilot on (a ship) or of (an aircraft). **2** conduct, lead, or initiate as a pilot (*piloted the new scheme*). □ **pilot balloon** a small balloon used to track air currents, etc. **pilot bird** a rare dark-brown Australian babbler, *Pycnoptilus floccosus,* with a distinctive loud cry. **pilot chute** a small parachute used to bring the main one into operation. **pilot-cloth** thick blue woolen cloth for seamen's coats, etc. **pilot fish** a small fish, *Naucrates ductor,* said to act as a pilot leading a shark to food. **pilot light 1** a small gas burner kept alight to light another. **2** an electric indicator light or control light. **pilot officer** *Brit.* the lowest commissioned rank in the RAF. □□ **pilotage** *n.* **pilotless** *adj.* [F *pilote* f. med.L *pilotus, pedot(t)a* f. Gk *pēdon* oar]
■ *n.* **1** captain, aviator, aviatrix, airman, airwoman, *colloq.* flyer. **2, 6** steersman, helmsman, navigator, wheelsman. **3** see TRIAL 2a–c. **4** leader, cicerone, conductor; see also GUIDE *n.* 1–4. ● *v.* steer, navigate, drive; fly; conduct, guide, run, control, lead; initiate; see also DIRECT *v.* 1.

pilothouse /pílət-hows/ *n.* an enclosed area on a vessel for the helmsman, etc.

Pilsner /pílznər, píls-/ *n.* (also **Pilsener**) **1** a lager beer brewed or like that brewed at *Pilsen* (Plzeň) in the Czech Republic. **2** (usu. **pilsner**) a tall tapered glass used for serving beer, etc.

pilule /pílyōol/ *n.* (also **pillule**) a small pill. ▫▫ **pilular** /-yələr/ *adj.* **pilulous** *adj.* [F f. L *pilula*: see PILL]
▪ see PILL 1a.

Pima /péemə/ *n.* **1 a** a N. American people native to southern Arizona and adjoining parts of Mexico. **b** a member of this people. **2** the language of this people. ▫▫ **Piman** *adj.*

pimento /piméntō/ *n.* (*pl.* **-os**) **1** a small tropical tree, *Pimenta dioica*, native to Jamaica. **2** the unripe dried berries of this, usu. crushed for culinary use. Also called ALLSPICE. **3** = PIMIENTO. [Sp. *pimiento* (as PIMIENTO)]

pimiento /piméntō, pímyéntō/ *n.* (*pl.* **-os**) **1** = *sweet pepper* (see PEPPER). **2** a sweet red pepper used as a garnish, esp. in olives. [Sp. f. L *pigmentum* PIGMENT, in med.L = spice]

pimp /pimp/ *n.* & *v.* ● *n.* a man who lives off the earnings of a prostitute or a brothel; a pander; a ponce. ● *v.intr.* act as a pimp. [17th c.: orig. unkn.]
▪ *n.* procurer, pander, *archaic* whoremonger, whoremaster, *Brit. sl.* ponce, *sl. derog.* fancy man.
● *v.* procure.

pimpernel /pímpərnel/ *n.* any plant of the genus *Anagallis*, esp. = *scarlet pimpernel*. [ME f. OF *pimpernelle*, *piprenelle* ult. f. L *piper* PEPPER]

pimping /pímping/ *adj.* **1** small or insignificant. **2** esp. *dial.* sickly. [17th c.: orig. unkn.]

pimple /pímpəl/ *n.* **1** a small hard inflamed spot on the skin. **2** anything resembling a pimple, esp. in relative size. ▫▫ **pimpled** *adj.* **pimply** *adj.* [ME nasalized f. OE *piplian* break out in pustules]
▪ **1** spot, pustule, papula, blackhead, pock, *Med.* comedo, *colloq.* whitehead, *sl.* zit; boil, swelling, eruption, carbuncle, excrescence.

PIN /pin/ *n.* personal identification number (as issued by a bank, etc., to validate electronic transactions). [abbr.]

pin /pin/ *n.* & *v.* ● *n.* **1 a** a small thin pointed piece of esp. steel wire with a round or flattened head used (esp. in sewing) for holding things in place, attaching one thing to another, etc. **b** any of several types of pin (*safety pin*; *hairpin*). **c** a small brooch (*diamond pin*). **d** a badge fastened with a pin. **2** a peg of wood or metal for various purposes, e.g., one of the slender rods making up part of an electrical connector. **3** something of small value (*don't care a pin*). **4** (in *pl.*) *colloq.* legs (*quick on his pins*). **5** *Med.* a steel rod used to join the ends of fractured bones while they heal. **6** *Chess* a position in which a piece is pinned to another. **7** *Golf* a stick with a flag placed in a hole to mark its position. **8** *Mus.* a peg around which one string of a musical instrument is fastened. ● *v.tr.* (**pinned**, **pinning**) **1 a** (often foll. by *to*, *up*, *together*) fasten with a pin or pins (*pinned up the hem*; *pinned the fabrics together*). **b** transfix with a pin, lance, etc. **2** (usu. foll. by *on*) fix (blame, responsibility, etc.) on a person, etc., (*pinned the blame on his friend*). **3** (often foll. by *against*, *on*, etc.) seize and hold fast. **4** *Chess* prevent (an opposing piece) from moving except by exposing a more valuable piece to capture. **5** *US* show affection for a woman by giving her a fraternity pin. ▫ **on pins and needles** in an agitated state of suspense. **pin down 1** (often foll. by *to*) bind (a person, etc.) to a promise, arrangement, etc. **2** force (a person) to declare his or her intentions. **3** restrict the actions or movement of (an enemy, etc.). **4** specify (a thing) precisely (*could not pin down his reason for leaving*). **5** hold (a person, etc.) down by force. **pin one's faith** (or **hopes**, etc.) **on** rely implicitly on. **pin money 1** *hist.* an allowance to a woman for clothing, etc., from her husband. **2** a very small sum of money, esp. for spending on inessentials (*only works for pin money*). **pins and needles** a tingling sensation in a limb recovering from numbness. **pin-table** *Brit.* a pinball machine. **split pin** a metal cotter pin passed through a hole and held in place by its gaping split end. [OE *pinn* f. L *pinna* point, etc., assoc. with *penna* PEN[1]]

▪ *n.* **1a, b, 2** tack, nail, peg, dowel, bolt, thole, spike, rivet, stud; thumbtack, *Brit.* drawing pin, tintack. **1 c, d** brooch, clip, badge; tiepin, stickpin. **3** two figs, a fig, a rap, a stiver, *archaic* a groat, *sl.* a hoot, two hoots.
● *v.* **1** fasten, secure, tack, hold, staple, clip; attach, fix, affix, stick; see also TRANSFIX 1. **2** (*pin the blame on*) blame, hold responsible *or* accountable, point the finger at, accuse, lay at the door of. ▫ **on pins and needles** see TENSE[1] *adj.* 1. **pin down 1** keep, bind, hold, commit, oblige. **3** confine, hold (down), immobilize, tie down, constrain, restrict. **4** specify, pinpoint, name, identify, determine, put *or* lay one's finger on, home *or* zero in on. **pin one's faith on** see RELY. **pin money 2** pocket money, spending money; *colloq.* peanuts.

pina colada /péenə kəláádə/ *n.* (also **piña colada** /péenyə/) a drink made from pineapple juice, rum, and cream of coconut. [Sp., lit. 'strained pineapple']

pinafore /pínəfawr/ *n.* **1 a** *Brit.* an apron, esp. with a bib. **b** a woman's sleeveless, wraparound, washable covering for the clothes, tied at the back. **2** (in full **pinafore dress**) a collarless sleeveless dress worn over a blouse or sweater. [PIN + AFORE (because orig. pinned on the front of a dress)]

pinaster /pinástər/ *n.* = *cluster pine*. [L, = wild pine f. *pinus* pine + -ASTER]

piñata /peenyáatə/ *n.* a decorated container, often of papier mâché, filled with toys, candy, etc., that is used in a game in which it is suspended at a height and attempts are made to break it open with a stick while blindfolded. [Sp., lit., pot f. It. *pignatta* perh. f. *pigna* pinecone]

pinball /pínbawl/ *n.* a game in which small metal balls are shot across a board and score points by striking pins with lights, etc.

pince-nez /pánsnáy, píns-/ *n.* (*pl.* same) a pair of eyeglasses with a nose-clip instead of earpieces. [F, lit. = pinch-nose]

pincers /pínsərz/ *n.pl.* **1** (also **pair of pincers**) a gripping tool resembling scissors but with blunt usu. concave jaws to hold a nail, etc., for extraction. **2** the front claws of lobsters and some other crustaceans. ▫ **pincer movement** *Mil.* a movement by two wings of a military unit converging on the enemy. [ME *pinsers*, *pinsours* f. AF f. OF *pincier* PINCH]
▪ **1** pliers, nippers, tweezers.

pinch /pinch/ *v.* & *n.* ● *v.* **1** *tr.* **a** grip (esp. the skin of part of the body or of another person) tightly, esp. between finger and thumb (*pinched my finger in the door*; *stop pinching me*). **b** (often *absol.*) (of a shoe, garment, etc.) constrict (the flesh) painfully. **2** *tr.* (of cold, hunger, etc.) grip (a person) painfully (*she was pinched with cold*). **3** *tr. sl.* **a** steal; take without permission. **b** arrest (a person) (*pinched him for loitering*). **4** (as **pinched** *adj.*) (of the features) drawn, as with cold, hunger, worry, etc. **5 a** *tr.* (usu. foll. by *in*, *of*, *for*, etc.) stint (a person). **b** *intr.* be niggardly with money, food, etc. **6** *tr.* (usu. foll. by *out*, *back*, *down*) *Hort.* remove (leaves, buds, etc.) to encourage bushy growth. **7** *intr.* sail very close to the wind. ● *n.* **1** the act or an instance of pinching, etc., the flesh. **2** an amount that can be taken up with fingers and thumb (*a pinch of snuff*). **3** the stress or pain caused by poverty, cold, hunger, etc. **4** *sl.* **a** an arrest. **b** a theft. ▫ **at** (or **in**) **a pinch** in an emergency; if necessary. **feel the pinch** experience the effects of poverty. **pinch-hit 1** *Baseball* bat instead of another player. **2** fill in as a substitute, esp. at the last minute. **pinch hitter 1** a baseball player who bats instead of another. **2** a person acting as a substitute. [ME f. AF & ONF *pinchier* (unrecorded), OF *pincier*, ult. f. L *pungere punct-* prick]
▪ *v.* **1** squeeze, nip, tweak, compress, constrict, grip, crush. **3 a** steal, thieve, rob, take, shoplift, filch, pilfer, snatch, grab, *colloq.* lift, swipe, *formal or joc.* purloin, *sl.* knock off, *Brit. sl.* nick; see also APPROPRIATE *v.* 1. **b**

/ . . . / **pronunciation** ● **part of speech**
▫ **phrases, idioms, and compounds**
▫▫ **derivatives** ▪ **synonym section**
cross-references appear in SMALL CAPITALS or *italics*

arrest, apprehend, take into custody, collar, *colloq.* run in, bust, *sl.* nab, *Brit. sl.* nick. **4** (**pinched**) see DRAWN. **5 b** see STINT *v.* 1. ● *n.* **1** squeeze, nip, tweak, twinge. **2** see BIT[1] 1, DASH *n.* 7. **4 a** see ARREST *n.* 1. **b** see THEFT. □ **at** (or **in**) **a pinch** in a predicament *or* emergency *or* crisis *or* difficulty, in a ticklish *or* delicate situation, *colloq.* in a pickle *or* jam *or* scrape, in a crunch; if necessary *or* required *or* needed, if the worst comes to the worst, if all else fails, *faute de mieux*.
    pinch hitter 2 see SUBSTITUTE *n.* 1a.

pinchbeck /pínchbek/ *n. & adj.* ● *n.* an alloy of copper and zinc resembling gold and used in cheap jewelry, etc. ● *adj.* **1** counterfeit; sham. **2** cheap; tawdry. [C. *Pinchbeck*, Engl. watchmaker d. 1732]
    ■ *adj.* **1** see FAKE[1] *adj.* **2** see SHODDY *adj.* 1.

pinchpenny /pínchpenee/ *n.* (*pl.* **-ies**) (also *attrib.*) a miserly person.
    ■ see MISER.

pincushion /pínkŏōshən/ *n.* a small cushion for holding pins.

pine[1] /pīn/ *n.* **1** any evergreen tree of the genus *Pinus* native to northern temperate regions, with needle-shaped leaves growing in clusters. **2** the soft timber of this, often used to make furniture. Also called DEAL[2]. **3** (*attrib.*) made of pine. **4** = PINEAPPLE. □ **pine cone** the cone-shaped fruit of the pine tree. **pine marten** a weasel-like mammal, *Martes martes*, native to Europe and America, with a dark brown coat and white throat and stomach. **pine nut** the edible seed of various pine trees. □□ **pinery** *n.* (*pl.* **-ies**). [ME f. OE *pīn* & OF *pin* f. L *pinus*]

pine[2] /pīn/ *v.intr.* **1** (often foll. by *away*) decline or waste away, esp. from grief, disease, etc. **2** (usu. foll. by *for, after,* or *to* + infin.) long eagerly; yearn. [OE *pīnian*, rel. to obs. E *pine* punishment, f. Gmc f. med.L *pena*, L *poena*]
    ■ **2** see YEARN.

pineal /píneeəl, pī-/ *adj.* shaped like a pine cone. □ **pineal gland** (or **body**) a pea-sized conical mass of tissue behind the third ventricle of the brain, secreting a hormonelike substance in some mammals. [F *pinéal* f. L *pinea* pine cone: see PINE[1]]

pineapple /pínapəl/ *n.* **1** a tropical plant, *Ananas comosus*, with a spiral of sword-shaped leaves and a thick stem bearing a large fruit developed from many flowers. **2** the fruit of this, consisting of yellow flesh surrounded by a tough segmented skin and topped with a tuft of stiff leaves. □ **the rough end of the pineapple** *Austral. colloq.* a raw deal. [PINE[1], from the fruit's resemblance to a pine cone]

pinetum /pīneetəm/ *n.* (*pl.* **pineta** /-tə/) a plantation of pine trees or other conifers for scientific or ornamental purposes. [L f. *pinus* pine]

piney var. of PINY.

pinfold /pínfōld/ *n. & v.* ● *n.* **1** a pound for stray cattle, etc. **2** any place of confinement. ● *v.tr.* confine (cattle) in a pinfold. [OE *pundfald* (as POUND[3], FOLD[2])]

ping /ping/ *n. & v.* ● *n.* a single short high ringing sound. ● *v.intr.* **1** make a ping. **2** = KNOCK 5b. [imit.]

pinger /píngər/ *n.* **1** a device that transmits pings at short intervals for purposes of detection or measurement, etc. **2** a device to ring a bell.

pingo /pínggō/ *n.* (*pl.* **-os**) *Geol.* a dome-shaped mound found in permafrost areas. [Eskimo]

Ping-Pong /píngpong/ *n. propr.* = *table tennis.* [imit. f. the sound of a paddle striking a ball]

pinguid /pínggwid/ *adj.* fat, oily, or greasy. [L *pinguis* fat]
    ■ see OILY 1, 2.

pinhead /pínhed/ *n.* **1** the flattened head of a pin. **2** a very small thing. **3** *colloq.* a stupid or foolish person.
    ■ **3** see FOOL[1] *n.* 1.

pinheaded /pínhédid/ *adj. colloq.* stupid; foolish. □□ **pinheadedness** *n.*
    ■ see STUPID *adj.* 1, 5.

pinhole /pínhōl/ *n.* **1** a hole made by a pin. **2** a hole into which a peg fits. □ **pinhole camera** a camera with a pinhole aperture and no lens.
    ■ **1** see PRICK *n.* 2.

pinion[1] /pínyən/ *n. & v.* ● *n.* **1** the outer part of a bird's wing, usu. including the flight feathers. **2** *poet.* a wing; a flight feather. ● *v.tr.* **1** cut off the pinion of (a wing or bird) to prevent flight. **2 a** bind the arms of (a person). **b** (often foll. by *to*) bind (the arms, a person, etc.) esp. to a thing. [ME f. OF *pignon* ult. f. L *pinna*: see PIN]
    ■ *v.* **2** see TIE *v.* 1a.

pinion[2] /pínyən/ *n.* **1** a small toothed gear engaging with a larger one. **2** a toothed spindle engaging with a wheel. [F *pignon* alt. f. obs. *pignol* f. L *pinea* pine cone (as PINE[1])]

pink[1] /pingk/ *n. & adj.* ● *n.* **1** a pale red color (*decorated in pink*). **2 a** any cultivated plant of the genus *Dianthus*, with sweet-smelling white, pink, crimson, etc., flowers. **b** the flower of this plant. **3** (prec. by *the*) the most perfect condition, etc. (*the pink of health*). **4** (also **hunting pink**) **a** a foxhunter's red coat. **b** the cloth for this. **c** a foxhunter. ● *adj.* **1** (often in *comb.*) of a pale red color of any of various shades (*rose pink*; *salmon pink*). **2** *esp. derog.* tending to socialism. □ **in the pink** *colloq.* in very good health. **pink-collar** (usu. *attrib.*) (of a profession, etc.) traditionally held by women (cf. *white-collar, blue-collar* (see BLUE[1])). **pink elephants** *colloq.* hallucinations caused by alcoholism. **pink gin** *Brit.* gin flavored with angostura bitters. **pink slip** a notice of layoff or termination from one's job. □□ **pinkish** *adj.* **pinkly** *adv.* **pinkness** *n.* **pinky** *adj.* [perh. f. dial. *pink-eyed* having small eyes]
    ■ *adj.* **1** rosy, rose, rose-colored, pinkish, flesh-colored, flesh, salmon, carnation, magnolia, *poet.* incarnadine. **2** socialist, left, left-wing, bolshie, *colloq.* red. □ **in the pink** at one's best, healthy, (hale and) hearty, in the best of health, in top form, in good shape, *colloq.* in tiptop condition, in great shape.

pink[2] /pingk/ *v.tr.* **1** pierce slightly with a sword, etc. **2** cut a scalloped or zigzag edge on. **3** (often foll. by *out*) ornament (leather, etc.) with perforations. **4** adorn; deck. □ **pinking shears** (or **scissors**) a dressmaker's serrated shears for cutting a zigzag edge. [ME, perh. f. LG or Du.: cf. LG *pinken* strike, peck]
    ■ **1** perforate, puncture, prick, pierce. **2** serrate, notch, scallop.

pink[3] /pingk/ *Brit.* = KNOCK 5b.

pink[4] /pingk/ *n. hist.* a sailing ship, esp. with a narrow stern, orig. small and flatbottomed. [ME f. MDu. *pin(c)ke*, of unkn. orig.]

pinkeye /pingki/ *n.* acute conjunctivitis.

pinkie[1] /píngkee/ *n.* (also **pinky**) *esp. US & Sc.* the little finger. [cf. dial. *pink* small, half-shut (eye)]

pinkie[2] /píngkee/ *n.* (also **pinky**) *esp. Austral. sl.* cheap red wine.

Pinkster /píngkstər/ *n. regional* Whitsuntide. □ **pinkster flower** the pink azalea, *Rhododendron nudiflorum*. [Du., = Pentecost]

pinky[1] var. of PINKIE[1].

pinky[2] var. of PINKIE[2].

pinna /pínə/ *n.* (*pl.* **pinnae** /-nee/ or **pinnas**) **1** the auricle; the external part of the ear. **2** a primary division of a pinnate leaf. **3** a fin or finlike structure, feather, wing, etc. [L, = *penna* feather, wing, fin]

pinnace /pínis/ *n. Naut.* a warship's or other ship's small boat, usu. motor-driven, orig. schooner-rigged or eight-oared. [F *pinnace, pinasse* ult. f. L *pinus* PINE[1]]

pinnacle /pínəkəl/ *n. & v.* ● *n.* **1** the culmination or climax (of endeavor, success, etc.). **2** a natural peak. **3** a small ornamental turret usu. ending in a pyramid or cone, crowning a buttress, roof, etc. ● *v.tr.* **1** set on or as if on a pinnacle. **2** form the pinnacle of. **3** provide with pinnacles. [ME *pinacle* f. OF *pin(n)acle* f. LL *pinnaculum* f. *pinna* wing, point (as PIN, -CULE)]
    ■ *n.* **1** culmination, peak, apex, acme, summit, zenith, climax, crowning point, consummation, utmost, extreme. **2** peak, top, summit, tip, cap, crest, crown.
    ● *v.* **2** see TOP[1] *v.* 1.

pinnae *pl.* of PINNA.

pinnate /pínayt/ *adj.* **1** (of a compound leaf) having leaflets arranged on either side of the stem, usu. in pairs opposite each other. **2** having branches, tentacles, etc., on each side of an axis. ▫▫ **pinnated** adj. **pinnately** adv. **pinnation** /-náyshən/ n. [L *pinnatus* feathered (as PINNA)]

pinni- /pínee/ comb. form wing; fin. [L *pinna*]

pinniped /píniped/ adj. & n. ● adj. denoting any aquatic mammal with limbs ending in fins. ● n. a pinniped mammal. [L *pinna* fin + *pes ped-* foot]

pinnule /pínyōōl/ n. **1** the secondary division of a pinnate leaf. **2** a part or organ like a small wing or fin. ▫▫ **pinnular** adj. [L *pinnula* dimin. of *pinna* fin, wing]

pinny /pínee/ n. (pl. **-ies**) Brit. colloq. a pinafore. [abbr.]

pinochle /peénokəl/ n. **1** a card game with a double pack of 48 cards (nine to ace only). **2** the combination of queen of spades and jack of diamonds in this game. [19th c.: orig. unkn.]

pinole /pinōlee/ n. flour made from parched cornflour, esp. mixed with sweet flour made of mesquite beans, sugar, etc. [Amer. Sp. f. Aztec *pinolli*]

piñon /peenyŏn, pínyən/ n. **1** a pine, *Pinus cembra*, bearing edible seeds. **2** the seed of this, a type of pine nut. [Sp. f. L *pinea* pine cone]

pinpoint /pínpoynt/ n. & v. ● n. **1** the point of a pin. **2** something very small or sharp. **3** (attrib.) **a** very small. **b** precise; accurate. ● v.tr. locate with precision (*pinpointed the target*).
■ v. see LOCATE 1, 3.

pinprick /pínprik/ n. **1** a prick caused by a pin. **2** a trifling irritation.
■ **1** see PRICK n. 2.

pinstripe /pínstrip/ n. **1** a very narrow stripe in cloth. **2** a fabric or garment with this.

pint /pīnt/ n. **1** a measure of capacity for liquids, etc., one eighth of a gallon or 20 fluid oz. (0.568 liter). **2** esp. Brit. a colloq. a pint of beer. **b** a pint of a liquid, esp. milk. **3** Brit. a measure of shellfish, being the amount containable in a pint mug (*bought a pint of whelks*). ▫ **pint-pot** a mug, esp. of pewter, holding one pint, esp. of beer. **pint-sized** (also **pint-size**) colloq. very small, esp. of a person. [ME f. OF *pinte*, of unkn. orig.]
■ **2 a** see DRINK n. 2b. ▫ **pint-sized** see SMALL adj. 1.

pinta /píntə/ n. Brit. colloq. a pint of milk. [corrupt. of *pint of*]

pintail /píntayl/ n. a duck, esp. *Anas acuta*, or a grouse with a pointed tail.

pintle /pínt'l/ n. a pin or bolt, esp. one on which some other part turns. [OE *pintel* penis, of unkn. orig.: cf. OFris., etc., *pint*]
■ see PIVOT n. 1.

pinto /píntō/ adj. & n. ● adj. piebald. ● n. (pl. **-os**) a piebald horse. ▫ **pinto bean** a variety of bean with a mottled or spotted appearance, grown mainly in the southwestern US. [Sp., = mottled, ult. f. L *pictus* past part. of *pingere* paint]
■ adj. see DAPPLE gray. ▫ see DAPPLE n. 2.

pinup /pínup/ n. **1** a photograph of a movie star, etc., for display. **2** a person in such a photograph.

pinwheel /pínhweel/ n. **1** a fireworks device that whirls and emits colored fire. **2** a child's toy consisting of a stick with vanes that twirl in the wind.

pinworm /pínwərm/ n. a small parasitic nematode worm, *Enterobius vermicularis*, of which the female has a pointed tail.

piny /pínee/ adj. (also **piney**) of, like, or full of pines.

Pinyin /pínyín/ n. a system of romanized spelling for transliterating Chinese. [Chin. *pīnyīn*, lit. 'spell sound']

piolet /peeəláy/ n. a two-headed ice ax for mountaineering. [F]

pion /píon/ n. Physics a meson having a mass approximately 270 times that of an electron. Also called *pi-meson* (see PI¹). ▫▫ **pionic** /píónik/ adj. [PI¹ (the letter used as a symbol for the particle) + -ON]

pioneer /píəneér/ n. & v. ● n. **1** an initiator of a new enterprise, an inventor, etc. **2** an explorer or settler; a colonist. **3** Mil. a member of an infantry group preparing roads, terrain, etc., for the main body of troops. ● v. **1 a** tr. initiate or originate (an enterprise, etc.). **b** intr. act or prepare the way as a pioneer. **2** tr. Mil. open up (a road, etc.) as a pioneer. **3** tr. go before, lead, or conduct (another person or

persons). [F *pionnier* foot soldier, pioneer, OF *paonier*, *peon(n)ier* (as PEON)]
■ n. **1** initiator, groundbreaker, innovator, inventor, leader, trendsetter, pacemaker, pacesetter, trailblazer. **2** explorer, pathfinder, frontiersman, trailblazer, colonist, (early) settler; navigator, conquistador, conqueror.
● v. **1** create, originate, invent, initiate, take the first step in, introduce, institute, inaugurate, launch, establish, found, set up, develop, set or put in motion, open up; lay the groundwork or foundation, take the lead, lead or show the way, blaze the trail, be a prime mover. **3** see LEAD¹ v. 1.

pious /píəs/ adj. **1** devout; religious. **2** hypocritically virtuous; sanctimonious. **3** dutiful. ▫ **pious fraud** a deception intended to benefit those deceived, esp. religiously. ▫▫ **piously** adv. **piousness** n. [L *pius* dutiful, pious]
■ **1** devout, religious, reverent, reverential, God-fearing, godly, faithful, holy, dedicated, devoted, spiritual, moral, good, virtuous, saintly, angelic, seraphic, Christlike, godlike, archaic worshipful. **2** hypocritical, sanctimonious, pietistic, pietistical, self-righteous, pharisaic, colloq. goody-goody. **3** see DUTIFUL.

pip¹ /pip/ n. & v. ● n. **1** the seed of an apple, pear, orange, grape, etc. **2** an extraordinary person or thing. ● v.tr. (**pipped**, **pipping**) remove the pips from (fruit, etc.). ▫▫ **pipless** adj. [abbr. of PIPPIN]

pip² /pip/ n. Brit. a short high-pitched sound, usu. mechanically produced, esp. as a radio time signal. [imit.]

pip³ /pip/ n. **1** any of the spots on playing cards, dice, or dominos. **2** Brit. a star (1–3 according to rank) on the shoulder of an army officer's uniform. **3** a single blossom of a clustered head of flowers. **4** a diamond-shaped segment of the surface of a pineapple. **5** an image of an object on a radar screen. [16th c. *peep*, of unkn. orig.]

pip⁴ /pip/ n. **1** a disease of poultry, etc., causing thick mucus in the throat and white scale on the tongue. **2** esp. Brit. colloq. a fit of disgust or bad temper (esp. *give one the pip*). [ME f. MDu. *pippe*, MLG *pip* prob. ult. f. corrupt. of L *pituita* slime]

pip⁵ /pip/ v.tr. (**pipped**, **pipping**) Brit. colloq. **1** hit with a shot. **2** defeat. **3** blackball. ▫ **pip at the post** defeat at the last moment. **pip out** die. [PIP² or PIP¹]

pipa /pípə/ n. an aquatic S. American toad, *Pipa pipa*, having a flat body with long webbed feet, the female of which carries her eggs and tadpoles in pockets on her back. Also called SURINAM TOAD. [Surinam *pipál* (masc.), *pipá* (fem.)]

pipal var. of PEEPUL.

pipe /pīp/ n. & v. ● n. **1** a tube of metal, plastic, wood, etc., used to convey water, gas, etc. **2 a** (also **tobacco pipe**) a narrow wooden or clay, etc., tube with a bowl at one end containing burning tobacco, etc., the smoke from which is drawn into the mouth. **b** the quantity of tobacco held by this (*smoked a pipe*). **c** a hookah. **3** Mus. **a** a wind instrument consisting of a single tube. **b** any of the tubes by which sound is produced in an organ. **c** (in pl.) = BAGPIPE(S). **d** (in pl.) a set of pipes joined together, e.g., panpipes. **4** a tubal organ, vessel, etc., in an animal's body. **5** a high note or song, esp. of a bird. **6** a cylindrical vein of ore. **7** a cavity in cast metal. **8 a** a boatswain's whistle. **b** the sounding of this. **9** a cask for wine, esp. as a measure of two hogsheads, usu. equivalent to 105 gallons (about 477 liters). **10** colloq. (also in pl.) the voice, esp. in singing. ● v.tr. **1** (also absol.) play (a tune, etc.) on a pipe or pipes. **2 a** convey (oil, water, gas, etc.) by pipes. **b** provide with pipes. **3** transmit (music, a radio program, etc.) by wire or cable. **4** (usu. foll. by up, on, to, etc.) Naut. **a** summon (a crew) to a meal, work, etc. **b** signal the arrival of (an officer, etc.) on board. **5** utter in a shrill voice; whistle. **6 a** arrange (icing, etc.) in decorative lines or twists on a cake, etc. **b** ornament (a cake, etc.) with

---

/.../ pronunciation	● part of speech
▫ phrases, idioms, and compounds	
▫▫ derivatives	■ synonym section
cross-references appear in SMALL CAPITALS or *italics*	

piping. **7** trim (a dress, etc.) with piping. **8** lead or bring (a person, etc.) by the sound of a pipe. **9** propagate (pinks, etc.) by taking cuttings at the joint of a stem. □ **pipe away** give a signal for (a boat) to start. **pipe cleaner** a piece of flexible covered wire for cleaning a tobacco pipe. **pipe down 1** *colloq.* be quiet or less insistent. **2** *Naut.* dismiss from duty. **pipe organ** *Mus.* an organ using pipes instead of or as well as reeds. **pipe rack** a rack for holding tobacco pipes. **pipe up** begin to play, sing, speak, etc. **put that in your pipe and smoke it** *colloq.* a challenge to another to accept something frank or unwelcome. □□ **pipeful** *n.* (*pl.* **-fuls**). **pipeless** *adj.* **pipy** *adj.* [OE *pipe, pīpian* & OF *piper* f. Gmc ult. f. L *pipare* peep, chirp]

■ *n.* **1** tube, duct, hose, line, main, conduit, pipeline, channel. **2 a** brier, meerschaum, chibouk; hookah, narghile, calumet, hubble-bubble. ● *v.* **1** tootle, skirl, whistle. **2 a** transmit, deliver, channel, conduct, convey. **3** see BROADCAST *v.* 1a. □ **pipe down 1** be quiet, quiet down, make less noise, tone (it) down, hush (up), shush, *Brit.* quieten down, *colloq.* shut up, *sl.* shut your face *or* head *or* mouth *or* trap, *Brit. sl.* put a sock in it. **pipe up** speak (up), raise one's voice, make oneself heard.

pipe clay /pípí klay/ *n.* & *v.* ● *n.* a fine white clay used for tobacco pipes, whitening leather, etc. ● *v.tr.* (**pipe-clay**) **1** whiten (leather, etc.) with this. **2** put in order.

pipe dream /pípí dreem/ *n.* an unattainable or fanciful hope or scheme. [orig. as experienced when smoking an opium pipe]

■ see FANTASY *n.* 2.

pipefitter /pípfitər/ *n.* a person who installs and repairs pipes.

pipefitting /pípfiting/ *n.* **1** a coupling, elbow, etc., used as a connector in a pipe system. **2** the work of a pipefitter.

pipeline /pípplin/ *n.* **1** a long, usu. underground, pipe for conveying esp. oil. **2** a channel supplying goods, information, etc. □ **in the pipeline** awaiting completion or processing.

■ **1** pipe, tube, duct, hose, line, main, conduit, passage, channel. □ **in the pipeline** on the way, under way, in preparation, in the offing, ready, imminent, coming, *colloq.* in the works, cooking, in work.

pip emma /pip émə/ *adv.* & *n. Brit. colloq.* = P.M. [formerly signalers' names for letters PM]

piper /pípər/ *n.* **1 a** bagpipe player. **b** a person who plays a pipe, esp. an itinerant musician. [OE *pīpere* (as PIPE)]

piperidine /pipérideen, pī-/ *n. Chem.* a peppery-smelling liquid formed by the reduction of pyridine. [L *piper* pepper + -IDE + -INE⁴]

pipette /pípét/ *n.* & *v.* ● *n.* a slender tube for transferring or measuring small quantities of liquids esp. in chemistry. ● *v.tr.* transfer or measure (a liquid) using a pipette. [F, dimin. of *pipe* PIPE]

piping /pípíng/ *n.* & *adj.* ● *n.* **1** the act or an instance of piping, esp. whistling or singing. **2** a thin pipelike fold used to edge hems or frills on clothing, seams on upholstery, etc. **3** ornamental lines of icing, potato, etc., on a cake or other dish. **4** lengths of pipe, or a system of pipes, esp. in domestic use. ● *adj.* (of a noise) high; whistling. □ **piping hot** very or suitably hot (esp. as required of food, water, etc.).

■ *adj.* see SHRILL *adj.* □ **piping hot** see HOT *adj.* 1.

pipistrelle /pípistrél/ *n.* any bat of the genus *Pipistrellus*, native to temperate regions and feeding on insects. [F f. It. *pipistrello, vip-,* f. L *vespertilio* bat f. *vesper* evening]

pipit /pípit/ *n.* any of various birds of the family Motacillidae, esp. of the genus *Anthus*, found worldwide and having brown plumage often heavily streaked with a lighter color. [prob. imit.]

pipkin /pípkin/ *n.* a small earthenware pot or pan. [16th c.: orig. unkn.]

pippin /pípin/ *n.* **1 a** an apple grown from seed. **b** a red and yellow dessert apple. **2** *colloq.* an excellent person or thing; a beauty. [ME f. OF *pepin*, of unkn. orig.]

pipsqueak /pípskweek/ *n. colloq.* an insignificant or contemptible person or thing. [imit.]

piquant /peékənt, -kaant, peekaant/ *adj.* **1** agreeably pungent, sharp, or appetizing. **2** pleasantly stimulating, or dis-

quieting, to the mind. □□ **piquancy** *n.* **piquantly** *adv.* [F, pres. part. of *piquer* (as PIQUE¹)]

■ **1** see PUNGENT 1. **2** keen, acute, intense, incisive, sharp, stinging, pointed, piercing, penetrating, barbed, cutting, caustic, acid, acerbic, bitter, biting; see also *stimulating* (STIMULATE), WITTY. □□ **piquancy** see SPICE *n.* 3a.

pique¹ /peek/ *v.* & *n.* ● *v.tr.* (**piques, piqued, piquing**) **1** wound the pride of; irritate. **2** arouse (curiosity, interest, etc.). **3** (*refl.*; usu. foll. by *on*) pride or congratulate oneself. ● *n.* ill-feeling; enmity; resentment (*in a fit of pique*). [F *piquer* prick, irritate, f. Rmc]

■ *v.* **1** see IRRITATE 1. **2** see EXCITE 1a, b. ● *n.* see RESENTMENT.

pique² /peek/ *n.* & *v.* ● *n.* the winning of 30 points on cards and play in piquet before one's opponent scores anything. ● *v.* (**piques, piqued, piquing**) **1** *tr.* score a pique against. **2** *intr.* score a pique. [F *pic*, of unkn. orig.]

piqué /peekáy/ *n.* a stiff ribbed cotton or other fabric. [F, past part. of *piquer*: see PIQUE¹]

piquet¹ /pikáy, -két/ *n.* a game for two players with a pack of 32 cards (seven to ace only). [F, of unkn. orig.]

piquet² var. of PICKET 3.

piracy /pírəsee/ *n.* (*pl.* **-ies**) **1** the practice or an act of robbery of ships at sea. **2** a similar practice or act in other forms, esp. hijacking. **3** the infringement of copyright. [med.L *piratia* f. Gk *pirateia* (as PIRATE)]

■ **3** see PLAGIARISM 1.

piragua /piráagwə, -rág-/ *n.* **1** a long narrow canoe made from a single tree trunk; a pirogue. **2** a two-masted sailing barge. [Sp. f. Carib.: = dug-out]

piranha /piráanə, -ránə, -raányə, -rányə/ *n.* any of various freshwater predatory fish of the genera *Pygocentrus, Rooseveltiella*, or *Serrasalmus*, native to S. America and having sharp cutting teeth. [Port. f. Tupi, var. of *piraya* scissors]

pirate /pírət/ *n.* & *v.* ● *n.* **1 a** a person who commits piracy. **b** a ship used by pirates. **2** a person who infringes another's copyright or other business rights; a plagiarist. **3** (often *attrib.*) a person, organization, etc., that broadcasts without official authorization (*pirate radio station*). ● *v.tr.* **1** appropriate or reproduce (the work or ideas, etc., of another) without permission, for one's own benefit. **2** plunder. □□ **piratic** /-rátik/ *adj.* **piratical** *adj.* **piratically** *adv.* [ME f. L *pirata* f. Gk *peiratēs* f. *peiraō* attempt, assault]

■ *n.* **1 a** buccaneer, rover, corsair, freebooter, sea robber, picaroon, *hist.* filibuster, rapparee. **2** plagiarist, plagiarizer, infringer. ● *v.* **1** plagiarize, copy, reproduce, steal, appropriate, poach, *colloq.* lift, crib, *sl.* pinch. **2** see PLUNDER *v.* 2.

pirogue /pirŏg/ *n.* = PIRAGUA. [F, prob. f. Galibi]

pirouette /pírŏo-ét/ *n.* & *v.* ● *n.* a dancer's spin on one foot or the point of the toe. ● *v.intr.* perform a pirouette. [F, = spinning top]

■ *n.* spin, whirl, twirl, turn, revolution. ● *v.* spin, whirl, twirl, turn (around), revolve, pivot.

pis aller /peez aláy/ *n.* a course of action followed as a last resort. [F f. *pis* worse + *aller* go]

piscary /pískəree/ *n.* □ **common of piscary** the right of fishing in another's water in common with the owner and others. [ME f. med.L *piscaria* neut. pl. of L *piscarius* f. *piscis* fish]

piscatorial /pískətáwreeəl/ *adj.* = PISCATORY 1. □□ **piscatorially** *adv.*

piscatory /pískətawree/ *adj.* **1** of or concerning fishermen or fishing. **2** addicted to fishing. [L *piscatorius* f. *piscator* fisherman f. *piscis* fish]

■ **1** piscatorial, fishy, piscine, fishlike.

Pisces /píseez/ *n.* (*pl.* same) **1** a constellation, traditionally regarded as contained in the figure of fishes. **2 a** the twelfth sign of the zodiac (the Fishes). **b** a person born when the sun is in this sign. □□ **Piscean** /píseeən/ *n.* & *adj.* [ME f. L, pl. of *piscis* fish]

pisciculture /písikulchər/ *n.* the artificial rearing of fish. □□ **piscicultural** *adj.* **pisciculturist** *n.* [L *piscis* fish, after *agriculture*, etc.]

piscina /piséenə, -sínə/ *n.* (*pl.* **piscinae** /-nee/ or **piscinas**) **1** a basin near the altar in some churches for draining water from liturgical ablutions. **2** a fishpond. **3** *hist.* a Roman bathing pool. [L f. *piscis* fish]

piscine[1] /píseen, písin/ *adj.* of or concerning fish. [L *piscis* fish]

■ piscatory, piscatorial, *joc. or poet.* fishy.

piscine[2] /píseen/ *n.* a swimming pool. [F (as PISCINA)]

piscivorous /pisívərəs, pí-/ *adj.* fish-eating. [L *piscis* fish + -VOROUS]

pish /pish/ *int. & n.* ● *int.* an expression of contempt, impatience, or disgust. ● *n.* nonsense; rubbish. [imit.]

pisiform /písifawrm/ *adj.* pea-shaped. □ **pisiform bone** a small bone in the wrist in the upper row of the carpus. [mod.L *pisiformis* f. *pisum* pea]

pismire /písmir/ *n. dial.* an ant. [ME f. PISS (from smell of anthill) + obs. *mire* ant]

piss /pis/ *v. & n. coarse sl.* ¶ Usually considered a taboo word. ● *v.* **1** *intr.* urinate. **2** *tr.* **a** discharge (blood, etc.) when urinating. **b** wet with urine. **3** *tr.* (as **pissed** *adj.*) **a** esp. *Brit.* drunk. **b** angry; annoyed. ● *n.* **1** urine. **2** an act of urinating. □ **piss off 1** (often as **pissed off** *adj.*) annoy; depress. **2** *Brit.* go away. [ME f. OF *pisser* (imit.)]

pissoir /peeswaár/ *n.* a public urinal, esp. in Europe. [F]

■ see TOILET 1.

pistachio /pistásheeō, -staásheeō/ *n.* (*pl.* **-os**) **1** an evergreen tree, *Pistacia vera*, bearing small brownish green flowers and ovoid reddish fruit. **2** (in full **pistachio nut**) the edible pale green seed of this. **3** a pale green color. [It. *pistaccio* and Sp. *pistacho* f. L *pistacium* f. Gk *pistakion* f. Pers. *pistah*]

piste /peest/ *n.* a ski run of compacted snow. [F, = racetrack]

pistil /pístil/ *n.* the female organs of a flower, comprising the stigma, style, and ovary. □□ **pistillary** *adj.* **pistilliferous** /-lifərəs/ *adj.* **pistilline** /-lin/ *adj.* [F *pistile* or L *pistillum* PESTLE]

pistillate /pístilət, -layt/ *adj.* **1** having pistils. **2** having pistils but no stamens.

pistol /pístəl/ *n. & v.* ● *n.* **1** a small hand-held firearm. **2** anything of a similar shape. ● *v.tr.* (**pistoled, pistoling** or **pistolled, pistolling**) shoot with a pistol. □ **pistol grip** a handle shaped like a pistol butt. **pistol shot 1** the range of a pistol. **2** a shot fired from a pistol. **pistol-whip** (**-whipped, -whipping**) beat with a pistol. [obs. F f. G *Pistole* f. Czech *pišt'al*]

■ *n.* **1** gun, handgun, revolver, six-shooter, *colloq.* shooting iron, *sl.* piece, Saturday night special, gat, heater, shooter, rod, roscoe.

pistole /pistốl/ *n. hist.* a foreign (esp. Spanish) gold coin. [F *pistole* abbr. of *pistolet*, of uncert. orig.]

pistoleer /pístəleer/ *n.* a soldier armed with a pistol.

piston /pístən/ *n.* **1** a disk or short cylinder fitting closely within a tube in which it moves up and down against a liquid or gas, used in an internal combustion engine to impart motion, or in a pump to receive motion. **2** a sliding valve in a trumpet, etc. □ **piston ring** a ring on a piston sealing the gap between the piston and the cylinder wall. **piston rod** a rod or crankshaft attached to a piston to drive a wheel or to impart motion. [F f. It. *pistone* var. of *pestone* augment. of *pestello* PESTLE]

pit[1] /pit/ *n. & v.* ● *n.* **1 a** a usu. large deep hole in the ground. **b** a hole made in digging for industrial purposes, esp. for coal (*chalk pit; gravel pit*). **c** a covered hole as a trap for esp. wild animals. **2 a** an indentation left after smallpox, acne, etc. **b** a hollow in a plant or animal body or on any surface. **3** *Theatr.* **a** = *orchestra pit*. **b** usu. *hist.* seating behind the orchesta seats. **c** the people in the pit. **4 a** (**the pit** or **bottomless pit**) hell. **b** (**the pits**) *sl.* a wretched or the worst imaginable place, situation, person, etc. **5 a** an area at the side of a track where racing cars are serviced and refueled. **b** a sunken area in a workshop floor for access to a car's underside. **6** the part of the floor of an exchange allotted to special trading (*wheat pit*). **7** = COCKPIT. **8** *Brit. sl.* a bed. ● *v.* (**pitted, pitting**) **1** *tr.* (usu. foll. by *against*) **a** set (one's wits, strength, etc.) in opposition or rivalry. **b** set (a cock, dog, etc.) to fight, orig. in a pit, against another. **2** *tr.* (usu.

as **pitted** *adj.*) make pits, esp. scars, in. **3** *intr.* (of the flesh, etc.) retain the impression of a finger, etc., when touched. **4** *tr.* put (esp. vegetables, etc., for storage) into a pit. □ **dig a pit for** try to ensnare. **pit bull** (**terrier**) a strong, compact breed of American dog noted for its ferocity. **pit of the stomach 1** the floor of the stomach. **2** the depression below the bottom of the breastbone. **pit pony** *Brit. hist.* a pony kept underground for haulage in coal mines. **pit prop** a beam of wood used to support the roof of a coal mine. **pit saw** a large saw for use in a saw pit. **pit stop 1** a brief stop at the pit by a racing car for servicing or refueling. **2** *colloq.* **a** a stop, as during a long journey, for food, rest, etc. **b** the place where such a stop is made. **pit viper** any venomous snake of the family Crotalidae of the US and Asia with a pit between the eye and the nostril. [OE *pytt* ult. f. L *puteus* well]

■ *n.* **1** hole, shaft, cavity, mine, well, mine shaft, quarry, working, ditch, trench, trough; abyss, chasm, crater. **2** hollow, depression, dent, indentation, dimple, pockmark, pock. **4 a** (**the pit** or **bottomless pit**) see HELL 1. **b** (**the pits**) lowest of the low, rock bottom; the worst, awful, terrible, *sl.* lousy. **8** bed, *sl.* flop, esp. *Brit. sl.* doss, kip. ● *v.* **1** (*pit against*) match, set against; see also OPPOSE 1–3. **2** dent, pockmark, scar; (**pitted**) pockmarked, defaced, marred, marked. □ **dig a pit for** set a trap for; see also AMBUSH *v.*

pit[2] /pit/ *n. & v.* ● *n.* the stone of a fruit. ● *v.tr.* (**pitted, pitting**) remove pits from (fruit). [perh. Du., rel. to PITH]

■ *n.* see STONE *n.* 6a.

pita /peétə/ *n.* (also **pitta**) a flat, hollow, unleavened bread that can be split and filled with salad, etc. [mod.Gk, = a cake]

pit-a-pat /pítəpát/ *adv. & n.* (also **pitter-patter** /pítərpátər/) ● *adv.* **1** with a sound like quick light steps. **2** with a faltering sound (*heart went pit-a-pat*). ● *n.* such a sound. [imit.]

■ *n.* see PATTER[1] *n.*

pitch[1] /pich/ *v. & n.* ● *v.* **1** *tr.* (also *absol.*) erect and fix (a tent, camp, etc.). **2** *tr.* **a** throw; fling. **b** (in games) throw (an object) toward a mark. **3** *tr.* fix or plant (a thing) in a definite position. **4** *tr.* express in a particular style or at a particular level (*pitched his argument at the most basic level*). **5** *intr.* (often foll. by *against, into*, etc.) fall heavily, esp. headlong. **6** *intr.* (of a ship, aircraft, etc.) plunge in a longitudinal direction (cf. ROLL *v.* 8a). **7** *tr. Mus.* set at a particular pitch. **8** *intr.* (of a roof, etc.) slope downwards. **9** *intr.* (often foll. by *about*) move with a vigorous jogging motion, as in a train, carriage, etc. **10 a** *tr. Baseball* deliver (the ball) to the batter. **b** *intr. Baseball* play at the position of pitcher. **c** *tr. Cricket* cause (a bowled ball) to strike the ground at a specified point, etc. **d** *intr. Cricket* (of a bowled ball) strike the ground. **11** *tr. colloq.* tell (a yarn or a tale). **12** *tr. Golf* play (a ball) with a pitch shot. **13** *tr.* pave (a road) with stones. ● *n.* **1 a** *Brit.* the area of play in a field game. **b** *Cricket* the area between the creases. **2** height, degree, intensity, etc. (*the pitch of despair; nerves were strung to a pitch*). **3 a** the steepness of a slope, esp. of a roof, stratum, etc. **b** the degree of such a pitch. **4** *Mus.* **a** that quality of a sound which is governed by the rate of vibrations producing it; the degree of highness or lowness of a tone. **b** = *concert pitch*. **5** the pitching motion of a ship, etc. **6** the delivery of a baseball by a pitcher. **7** *colloq.* a salesman's advertising or selling approach. **8** *Brit.* a place where a street vendor sells wares, has a stall, etc. **9** (also **pitch shot**) *Golf* a high approach shot with a short run. **10** *Mech.* the distance between successive corresponding points or lines, e.g., between the teeth of a cogwheel, etc. **11** the height to which a falcon, etc., soars before swooping on its prey. **12** *Cricket* the act or mode of delivery in bowling, or the spot where the ball bounces. □ **pitch-and-toss** a gambling game in which coins are pitched at a

---

/.../ pronunciation	● part of speech
□ phrases, idioms, and compounds	
□□ derivatives	■ synonym section
cross-references appear in SMALL CAPITALS or *italics*	

mark and then tossed. **pitched battle 1** a vigorous argument, etc. **2** *Mil.* a battle planned beforehand and fought on chosen ground. **pitched roof** a sloping roof. **pitch in** *colloq.* **1** set to work vigorously. **2** assist; cooperate. **pitch into** *colloq.* **1** attack forcibly with blows, words, etc. **2** assail (food, work, etc.) vigorously. **pitch on** (or **upon**) *Brit. Brit.* happen to select. **pitch pipe** *Mus.* a small pipe blown to set the pitch for singing or tuning. [ME *pic(c)he*, perh. f. OE *picc(e)an* (unrecorded: cf. *picung* stigmata)]

■ *v.* **1** erect, raise, set *or* put up, position, fix, place. **2 a** toss, throw, cast, fling, hurl, sling, fire, launch, shoot, send, let fly, lob, *colloq.* chuck. **4** see DIRECT *v.* 4. **5** plunge, fall (headlong), dive, drop, plummet, (take a) nosedive. **6** toss about, lurch, plunge, go head over heels. **9** see LURCH[1] *v.* ● *n.* **1** playing field, field, ground; court. **2** see HEIGHT 7. **3** see SLANT *n.* 1. **8** see PATCH *n.* 6, 7. □ **pitched battle 1** see ARGUMENT 1. **pitch in 1** see *put one's shoulder to the wheel* (SHOULDER). **2** contribute, cooperate, help, assist, *colloq.* chip in. **pitch into 1** attack, lay into, assail, lash out at, abuse, rail against, tear into, *colloq.* jump down a person's throat, jump on; assault, set upon, belabor, *colloq.* light into, sail into, tear into. **pitch on** (or **upon**) decide on, select, pick, choose, opt for, elect for, name; *colloq.* light on; see also *hit on.*

pitch[2] /pich/ *n. & v.* ● *n.* **1** a sticky resinous black or dark brown substance obtained by distilling tar or turpentine, semiliquid when hot, hard when cold, and used for caulking the seams of ships, etc. **2** any of various bituminous substances including asphalt. ● *v.tr.* cover, coat, or smear with pitch. □ **pitch-black** (or **-dark**) very or completely dark. **pitch pine** any of various pine trees, esp. *Pinus rigida* or *P. palustris*, yielding much resin. [OE *pic* f. Gmc f. L *pix picis*]

■ *n.* tar, bitumen, asphalt. □ **pitch-black** (or **-dark**) black, dark, ebony, inky, coal-black, sooty, jet-black, raven, esp. *poet.* sable; unlit, unlighted, moonless, starless, *literary* stygian.

pitchblende /píchblend/ *n.* a mineral form of uranium oxide occurring in pitchlike masses and yielding radium. [G *Pechblende* (as PITCH[2], BLENDE)]

pitcher[1] /píchər/ *n.* **1** a large usu. earthenware or glass jug with a lip and a handle, for holding liquids. **2** a modified leaf in pitcher form. □ **pitcher plant** any of various plants, esp. of the family Nepenthaceae or Sarraceniaceae, with pitcher leaves that can hold liquids, trap insects, etc. □□ **pitcherful** *n.* (*pl.* **-fuls**). [ME f. OF *pichier*, *pechier*, f. Frank.]

■ **1** see JUG *n.* 1, 2.

pitcher[2] /píchər/ *n.* **1** a person or thing that pitches. **2** *Baseball* a player who delivers the ball to the batter. **3** a stone used for paving.

pitchfork /píchfawrk/ *n. & v.* ● *n.* a long-handled two-pronged fork for pitching hay, etc. ● *v.tr.* **1** throw with or as if with a pitchfork. **2** (usu. foll. by *into*) thrust (a person) forcibly into a position, office, etc. [in ME *pickfork*, prob. f. PICK[1] + FORK, assoc. with PITCH[1]]

pitchman /píchmən/ *n.* **1** a salesperson who uses overly aggressive selling tactics. **2** a person who delivers commercial messages on radio or television. **3** a person who sells small goods from a portable stand, as at a fair or on the street.

pitchstone /píchstōn/ *n.* obsidian, etc., resembling pitch.

pitchy /píchee/ *adj.* (**pitchier**, **pitchiest**) of, like, or dark as pitch.

piteous /píteeəs/ *adj.* deserving or causing pity; wretched. □□ **piteously** *adv.* **piteousness** *n.* [ME *pito(u)s*, etc., f. AF *pitous*, OF *pitos* f. Rmc (as PIETY)]

■ pitiable, pathetic, pitiful, plaintive, miserable, heartrending, poignant, distressing, grievous, heartbreaking, moving, painful, lamentable, deplorable, regrettable; wretched, mournful, sad, doleful, tearful, rueful, woeful, *literary or joc.* dolorous.

pitfall /pítfawl/ *n.* **1** an unsuspected snare, danger, or drawback. **2** a covered pit for trapping animals, etc.

■ **1** danger, peril, hazard, catch, difficulty, snag; snare, trap. **2** trap, pit.

pith /pith/ *n. & v.* ● *n.* **1** spongy white tissue lining the rind of an orange, lemon, etc. **2** the essential part; the quintessence (*came to the pith of his argument*). **3** *Bot.* the spongy cellular tissue in the stems and branches of dicotyledonous plants. **4 a** physical strength; vigor. **b** force; energy. **5** importance; weight. **6** *archaic* spinal cord. ● *v.tr.* **1** remove the pith or marrow from. **2** slaughter or immobilize (an animal) by severing the spinal cord. □ **pith helmet** a lightweight sun helmet made from the dried pith of the sola, etc. □□ **pithless** *adj.* [OE *pitha* f. WG]

■ *n.* **2** core, heart, kernel, nucleus, crux, focus, focal point, essence, meat, marrow, nub, point, spirit, substance, quintessence. **4** see VIGOR 1. **5** weight, burden, gravamen, gravity, force, moment, import, importance, significance, substance, depth, matter.

pithecanthrope /píthikánthrōp/ *n.* any prehistoric apelike human of the extinct genus *Pithecanthropus*, now considered to be part of the genus *Homo* (see also JAVA MAN). [Gk *pithēkos* ape + *anthrōpos* man]

pithos /píthos, pí-/ *n.* (*pl.* **pithoi** /-thoy/) *Archaeol.* a large storage jar. [Gk]

pithy /píthee/ *adj.* (**pithier**, **pithiest**) **1** (of style, speech, etc.) condensed, terse, and forceful. **2** of, like, or containing much pith. □□ **pithily** *adv.* **pithiness** *n.*

■ **1** see TERSE 1. □□ **pithiness** see BREVITY.

pitiable /píteeəbəl/ *adj.* **1** deserving or causing pity. **2** contemptible. □□ **pitiableness** *n.* **pitiably** *adv.* [ME f. OF *piteable, pitoiable* (as PITY)]

■ **1** see PITEOUS. **2** see CONTEMPTIBLE.

pitiful /pítifool/ *adj.* **1** causing pity. **2** contemptible. **3** *archaic* compassionate. □□ **pitifully** *adv.* **pitifulness** *n.*

■ **1** see PITEOUS. **2** beggarly, sorry, mean, contemptible; small, little, insignificant, trifling, pathetic.

pitiless /pítilis/ *adj.* showing no pity (*the pitiless heat of the desert*). □□ **pitilessly** *adv.* **pitilessness** *n.*

■ see MERCILESS. □□ **pitilessly** see ROUGHLY 1. **pitilessness** see *severity* (SEVERE).

pitman /pítmən/ *n.* **1** (*pl.* **-men**) a person who works in a pit, as a miner. **2** (*pl.* **-mans**) a connecting rod in machinery.

piton /peéton/ *n.* a peg or spike driven into a rock or crack to support a climber or a rope. [F, = eye-bolt]

Pitot tube /peétō, peétō/ *n.* a device consisting of an open-ended right-angled tube used to measure the speed or flow of a fluid. [H. *Pitot*, Fr. physicist d. 1771]

pitta var. of PITA.

pittance /pít'ns/ *n.* **1** a scanty or meager allowance, remuneration, etc. (*paid him a mere pittance*). **2** a small number or amount. **3** *hist.* a pious bequest to a religious house for extra food, etc. [ME f. OF *pitance* f. med.L *pi(e)tantia* f. L *pietas* PITY]

■ **2** *colloq.* peanuts, chicken feed, small potatoes.

pitter-patter var. of PIT-A-PAT.

pittosporum /pitóspərəm, pítōspáwrəm/ *n.* any evergreen shrub of the family Pittosporaceae, chiefly native to Australasia with many species having fragrant foliage. [Gk *pitta* PITCH[2] + *sporos* seed]

pituitary /pitōō-iteree, -tyōō-/ *n. & adj.* ● *n.* (*pl.* **-ies**) (also **pituitary gland** or **body**) a small ductless gland at the base of the brain secreting various hormones essential for growth and other bodily functions. ● *adj.* of or relating to this gland. [L *pituitarius* secreting phlegm f. *pituita* phlegm]

pity /pítee/ *n. & v.* ● *n.* (*pl.* **-ies**) **1** sorrow and compassion aroused by another's condition (*felt pity for the child*). **2** something to be regretted; grounds for regret (*what a pity!*). ● *v.tr.* (**-ies**, **-ied**) feel (often contemptuous) pity for (*they are to be pitied*; *I pity you if you think that*). □ **for pity's sake** an exclamation of urgent supplication, anger, etc. **more's the pity** so much the worse. **take pity on** feel or act compassionately toward. □□ **pitying** *adj.* **pityingly** *adv.* [ME f. OF *pité* f. L *pietas* (as PIETY)]

■ *n.* **1** sympathy, sorrow, compassion; commiseration, condolence. **2** (crying) shame; disgrace, sin, sacrilege, *colloq.* crime. ● *v.* sympathize with, feel for, commiserate with, feel sorry for, bleed for, weep for, be moved by, take pity on; have one's heart go out to. □ **for pity's sake** for Christ's *or* God's *or* goodness' *or* Heaven's sake.

pityriasis /pítiríəsis/ *n.* any of a group of skin diseases characterized by the shedding of branlike scales. [mod.L f. Gk *pituriasis* f. *pituron* bran]

più /pyōō/ *adv. Mus.* more (*più piano*). [It.]

Piute /píōōt, pīōōt/ *n.* = PAIUTE.

pivot /pívət/ *n. & v.* ● *n.* **1** a short shaft or pin on which something turns or oscillates. **2** a crucial or essential person, point, etc., in a scheme or enterprise. **3** *Mil.* the man or men about whom a body of troops wheels. ● *v.* (**pivoted, pivoting**) **1** *intr.* turn on or as if on a pivot. **2** *intr.* (foll. by *on, upon*) hinge on; depend on. **3** *tr.* provide with or attach by a pivot. □□ **pivotable** *adj.* **pivotability** *n.* **pivotal** *adj.* [F, of uncert. orig.]

■ *n.* **1** fulcrum, pintle, gudgeon, hinge, swivel, kingpin, spindle. **2** center, heart, focal point, hub, crux; see also KEYSTONE. ● *v.* **1** rotate, revolve, turn, spin, twirl, whirl, swivel. **2** hinge, depend, hang, be contingent, rely; (*pivot on*) revolve around; see also TURN *v.* 17.
□□ **pivotal** critical, central, focal, crucial, significant, important, essential, vital.

pix[1] /piks/ *n.pl. colloq.* pictures, esp. photographs. [abbr.: cf. PIC]

pix[2] var. of PYX.

pixel /píksəl/ *n. Electronics* any of the minute areas of uniform illumination of which an image on a display screen is composed. [abbr. of *picture element*: cf. PIX[1]]

pixie /píksee/ *n.* (also **pixy**) (*pl.* **-ies**) a being like a fairy; an elf. □ **pixie hat** (or **hood**) a child's hat with a pointed crown. [17th c.: orig. unkn.]

■ see IMP *n.* 2.

pixilated /píksilaytid/ *adj.* (also **pixillated**) **1** bewildered; crazy. **2** drunk. [var. of *pixie-led* (as PIXIE, LED)]

■ **1** see *in a daze* (DAZE). **2** see DRUNK *adj.* 1.

pizza /peétsə/ *n.* a flat round base of dough baked with a topping of tomatoes, cheese, onions, etc. [It., = pie]

pizzazz /pizáz/ *n.* (also **pizazz**) *sl.* verve; energy; liveliness; sparkle.

■ see VERVE.

pizzeria /peétsəreéə/ *n.* a place where pizzas are made or sold. [It. (as PIZZA)]

pizzicato /pítsikaátō/ *adv., adj., & n. Mus.* ● *adv.* plucking the strings of a violin, etc., with the finger. ● *adj.* (of a note, passage, etc.) performed pizzicato. ● *n.* (*pl.* **pizzicatos** or **pizzicati** /-tee/) a note, passage, etc., played pizzicato. [It., past part. of *pizzicare* twitch f. *pizzare* f. *pizza* edge]

pizzle /pízəl/ *n.* the penis of an animal, esp. a bull, formerly used as a whip. [LG *pesel*, dimin. of MLG *pēse*, MDu. *pēze*]

pk. *abbr.* **1** park. **2** peak. **3** peck(s). **4** pack.

pkg. *abbr.* (also **pkge.**) package.

pl. *abbr.* **1** plural. **2** place. **3** plate. **4** esp. *Mil.* platoon.

placable /plákəbəl, pláy-/ *adj.* easily placated; mild; forgiving. □□ **placability** *n.* **placably** *adv.* [ME f. OF *placable* or L *placabilis* f. *placare* appease]

placard /plákaard, -kərd/ *n. & v.* ● *n.* a printed or handwritten poster esp. for advertising. ● *v.tr.* **1** set up placards on (a wall, etc.). **2** advertise by placards. **3** display (a poster, etc.) as a placard. [ME f. OF *placquart* f. *plaquier* to plaster f. MDu. *placken*]

■ *n.* see POSTER.

placate /pláykayt, plák-/ *v.tr.* pacify; conciliate. □□ **placatingly** *adv.* **placation** /-áyshən/ *n.* **placatory** /-kətawree/ *adj.* [L *placare placat-*]

■ see CALM *v.* □□ **placation** conciliation, appeasement, propitiation, pacification. **placatory** see PROPITIATORY.

place /plays/ *n. & v.* ● *n.* **1 a** a particular portion of space. **b** a portion of space occupied by a person or thing (*it has changed its place*). **c** a proper or natural position (*he is out of his place; take your places*). **d** situation; circumstances (*put yourself in my place*). **2** a city, town, village, etc. (*was born in this place*). **3** a residence; a dwelling (*has a place in the country; come around to my place*). **4 a** a group of houses in a town, etc., esp. a square. **b** a country house with its sur-

roundings. **5** a person's rank or status (*know their place; a place in history*). **6** a space, esp. a seat, for a person (*two places in the coach*). **7** a building or area for a specific purpose (*place of worship; fireplace*). **8 a** a point reached in a book, etc. (*lost my place*). **b** a passage in a book. **9** a particular spot on a surface, esp. of the skin (*a sore place on his wrist*). **10 a** employment or office (*lost his place at the university*). **b** the duties or entitlements of office, etc. (*is his place to hire staff*). **11** a position as a member of a team, a student in a college, etc. **12 a** *US* the second finishing position, esp. in a horse race. **b** *Brit.* any of the first three or sometimes four positions in a race, esp. other than the winner (*backed it for a place*). **13** the position of a number in a series indicated in decimal or similar notation (*calculated to 5 decimal places*). ● *v.tr.* **1** put (a thing, etc.) in a particular place or state; arrange. **2** identify, classify, or remember correctly (*cannot place him*). **3** assign to a particular place; locate. **4 a** appoint (a person, esp. a member of the clergy) to a post. **b** find a job, clerical post, etc., for. **c** (usu. foll. by *with*) consign to a person's care, etc. (*placed her with her aunt*). **5** assign rank, importance, or worth to (*place him among the best teachers*). **6 a** dispose of (goods) to a customer. **b** make (an order for goods, etc.). **7** (often foll. by *in, on*, etc.) have (confidence, etc.). **8** invest (money). **9** *Brit.* state the position of (any of the first three or sometimes four runners) in a race. **10** *tr.* (as **placed** *adj.*) **a** *US* second in a race. **b** *Brit.* among the first three or sometimes four in a race. □ **all over the place** in disorder; chaotic. **give place to 1** make room for. **2** yield precedence to. **3** be succeeded by. **go places** *colloq.* be successful. **in place** in the right position; suitable. **in place of** in exchange for; instead of. **in places** at some places or in some parts, but not others. **keep a person in his** or **her place** suppress a person's esp. social pretensions. **out of place 1** in the wrong position. **2** unsuitable. **place bet 1** *US* a bet on a horse to come in second. **2** *Brit.* a bet on a horse to come first, second, third, or sometimes fourth in a race. **place card** a card marking a person's place at a table, etc. **place in the sun** a favorable situation, position, etc. **place mat** a small mat on a table underneath a person's plate. **place-name** the name of a geographic location, as a city, town, hill, lake, etc. **place setting** a set of plates, silverware, etc., for one person at a meal. **put oneself in another's place** imagine oneself in another's position. **put a person in his** or **her place** deflate or humiliate a person. **take place** occur, happen. **take one's place** go to one's correct position, be seated, etc. **take the place of** be substituted for; replace. □□ **placeless** *adj.* **placement** *n.* [ME f. OF f. L *platea* f. Gk *plateia* (*hodos*) broad (way)]

■ *n.* **1 a, b** location, site, position, point, spot, locus, area, locale, scene, setting. **d** position, situation, circumstances, condition. **2** locale, area, neighborhood, vicinity, district, section, quarter, region; city, town, village, hamlet. **3** home, house, flat, apartment, room(s), quarters, lodgings, residence, domicile, abode, *colloq.* pad, *Brit. colloq.* digs, diggings, *formal* dwelling (place). **5** status, station, standing, grade, rank, position, niche, slot, situation, state, *archaic or literary* estate. **6** seat, chair, position, spot. **10 a** position, job, post, appointment, situation, *colloq.* billet, berth; employment, occupation. **b** function, role, part, purpose, duty, obligation, task, responsibility, charge, burden, concern, mission. ● *v.* **1** put (out), position, dispose, arrange, order, set (out), lay, lodge, deposit, *colloq.* stick. **2** put one's finger on; recall, remember, recognize; see IDENTIFY 1, 2. **3** locate, station, post; see also SITUATE *v.* **4** see APPOINT 1. **5** class, classify, rank, group, categorize, bracket, grade; regard, view, see, consider; put, set, assign. □ **all over the place** see *chaotic* (CHAOS). **go places** succeed, become successful,

---

/.../ pronunciation	● part of speech
□ phrases, idioms, and compounds	
□□ derivatives	■ synonym section
cross-references appear in SMALL CAPITALS or *italics*	

get ahead, advance, prosper, thrive, flourish, go (*or* come) up in the world, make good, *colloq.* strike it rich. **in place** in situ, in position, ready, in order, *colloq.* all set; fitting, suitable, appropriate, right, proper, correct. **in place of** instead of, in lieu of, in exchange for. **out of place 2** unsuitable, inappropriate, wrong, improper, misplaced. **put a person in his** or **her place** deflate, humiliate, humble, mortify, bring down, squelch, take a person down a peg (or two), *colloq.* cut a person down to size. **take place** happen, go on, come about; arise, *disp.* transpire; see also OCCUR 1. **take the place of** see REPLACE 2. □□ **placement** arrangement, placing, position, distribution, array, disposition, deployment, positioning, stationing, organization, order, ordering, location, emplacement; employment, appointment, engagement.

placebo /pləséebō/ n. (*pl.* -os) **1 a** a pill, medicine, etc., prescribed more for psychological reasons than for any physiological effect. **b** a placebo used as a control in testing new drugs, etc. **2** *RC Ch.* the opening antiphon of the vespers for the dead. [L, = I shall be acceptable or pleasing f. *placēre* please, first word of Ps. 114:9]

placekick /pláyskik/ n. *Football* a kick made with the ball held on the ground or on a tee.

placenta /pləséntə/ n. (*pl.* **placentae** /-tee/ or **placentas**) **1** a flattened circular organ in the uterus of pregnant mammals nourishing and maintaining the fetus through the umbilical cord and expelled after birth. **2** (in flowers) part of the ovary wall carrying the ovules. □□ **placental** adj. [L f. Gk *plakous -ountos* flat cake f. the root of *plax plakos* flat plate]

placer /plásər/ n. a deposit of sand, gravel, etc., in the bed of a stream, etc., containing valuable minerals in particles. [Amer. Sp., rel. to *placel* sandbank f. *plaza* PLACE]

placet /pláyset/ n. esp. *Brit.* an affirmative vote in a church or university assembly. [L, = it pleases]

placid /plásid/ adj. **1** (of a person) not easily aroused or disturbed; peaceful. **2** mild; calm; serene. □□ **placidity** /pləsíditee/ n. **placidly** adv. **placidness** n. [F *placide* or L *placidus* f. *placēre* please]
  ■ see SERENE. □□ **placidity, placidness** see CALM n. 1.

placket /plákit/ n. **1** an opening or slit in a garment, for fastenings or access to a pocket. **2** the flap of fabric under this. [var. of PLACARD]

placoid /plákoyd/ adj. & n. ● adj. **1** (of a fish scale) consisting of a hard base embedded in the skin and a spiny backward projection (cf. CTENOID). **2** (of a fish) covered with these scales. ● n. a placoid fish, e.g., a shark. [Gk *plax plakos* flat plate]

plafond /plafóN/ n. **1 a** an ornately decorated ceiling. **b** such decoration. **2** an early form of contract bridge. [F f. *plat* flat + *fond* bottom]

plagal /pláygəl/ adj. *Mus.* (of a church mode) having sounds between the dominant and its octave (cf. AUTHENTIC). □ **plagal cadence** (or **close**) a cadence in which the chord of the subdominant immediately precedes that of the tonic. [med.L *plagalis* f. *plaga* plagal mode f. L *plagius* f. med. Gk *plagios* (in anc. Gk = oblique) f. Gk *plagos* side]

plage /plaazh/ n. **1** *Astron.* an unusually bright region on the sun. **2** a seaside beach, esp. at a fashionable resort. [F, = beach]

plagiarism /pláyjərizəm/ n. **1** the act or an instance of plagiarizing. **2** something plagiarized. □□ **plagiarist** n. **plagiaristic** adj.
  ■ **1** plagiary, piracy, theft, stealing, appropriation, thievery, usurpation, infringement, borrowing. **2** borrowing, *colloq.* crib.

plagiarize /pláyjəriz/ v.tr. (also *absol.*) **1** take and use (the thoughts, writings, inventions, etc., of another person) as one's own. **2** pass off the thoughts, etc., of (another person) as one's own. □□ **plagiarizer** n. [L *plagiarius* kidnapper f. *plagium* a kidnapping f. Gk *plagion*]
  ■ see PIRATE v. 1. □□ **plagiarizer** see PIRATE n. 2.

plagio- /pláyjeeō/ *comb. form* oblique. [Gk *plagios* oblique f. *plagos* side]

plagioclase /pláyjeeōkláys/ n. a series of feldspar minerals forming glassy crystals. [PLAGIO- + Gk *klasis* cleavage]

plague /playg/ n., v., & int. ● n. **1** a deadly contagious disease spreading rapidly over a wide area. **2** (foll. by *of*) an unusual infestation of a pest, etc. (*a plague of frogs*). **3 a** great trouble. **b** an affliction, esp. as regarded as divine punishment. **4** *colloq.* a nuisance. ● v.tr. (**plagues, plagued, plaguing**) **1** affect with plague. **2** *colloq.* pester or harass continually. ● int. *joc.* or *archaic* a curse, etc. (*a plague on it!*). □□ **plaguesome** adj. [ME f. L *plaga* stroke, wound prob. f. Gk *plaga, plēgē*]
  ■ n. **1** epidemic, pestilence, pandemic, *archaic* pest. **3** scourge, affliction, misfortune, curse, bane, calamity, evil, blight, adversity. **4** irritation, annoyance, nuisance, pest, vexation, bother, thorn in one's side *or* flesh, torment, *colloq.* pain (in the neck), headache, hassle, drag, *disp.* aggravation, *sl.* bitch, pain in the butt.
  ● v. **2** badger, harry, hound, pester, bother, harass, vex, nag, torment, torture, anguish, distress, chivy, pursue. ● int. curse; see also BOTHER int.

plaice /plays/ n. (*pl.* same) **1** a European flatfish, *Pleuronectes platessa*, having a brown back with orange spots and a white underside, much used for food. **2** (in full **American plaice**) a N. Atlantic fish, *Hippoglossoides platessoides*. [ME f. OF *plaïz* f. LL *platessa* app. f. Gk *platus* broad]

plaid /plad/ n. **1 a** (often *attrib.*) tartan usu. woolen twilled cloth (*a plaid skirt*). **b** any cloth with a tartan pattern. **2** a long piece of plaid worn over the shoulder as part of Highland Scottish costume. □□ **plaided** adj. [Gael. *plaide*, of unkn. orig.]
  ■ **1** tartan, checkered, checked.

plain¹ /playn/ adj., adv., & n. ● adj. **1** clear; evident (*is plain to see*). **2** readily understood; simple (*in plain words*). **3 a** (of food, sewing, decoration, etc.) uncomplicated; not elaborate; unembellished; simple. **b** without a decorative pattern. **4** (esp. of a woman or girl) not good-looking; homely. **5** outspoken; straightforward. **6** (of manners, dress, etc.) unsophisticated; homely (*a plain man*). **7** (of drawings, etc.) not colored. **8** not in code. ● adv. **1** clearly; unequivocally (*to speak plain, I don't approve*). **2** simply (*that is plain stupid*). ● n. **1** a level tract of esp. treeless country. **2** a basic knitting stitch made by putting the needle through the back of the stitch and passing the wool round the front of the needle (opp. PURL¹). □ **as plain as day** obvious. **be plain with** speak bluntly to. **plain card** neither a trump nor a face card. **plain chocolate** *Brit.* dark chocolate without added milk. **plain cook** *Brit.* a person competent in plain English cooking. **plain dealing** candor; straightforwardness. **plain sailing 1** sailing a straightforward course. **2** an uncomplicated situation or course of action. **plain service** *Eccl.* a church service without music. **plain suit** a suit that is not trumps. **plain text** a text not in cipher or code. **plain time** *Brit.* time not paid for at overtime rates. **plain weaving** weaving with the weft alternately over and under the warp. □□ **plainly** adv. **plainness** /pláyn-nis/ n. [ME f. OF *plain* (adj. & n.) f. L *planus* (adj.), *planum* (n.)]
  ■ adj. **1, 2** clear, evident, simple, distinct, crystal clear, lucid, vivid, transparent, apparent, obvious, patent, self-evident, manifest, unmistakable, unequivocal, unambiguous, understandable, intelligible, direct. **3** unadorned, undecorated, unembellished, unostentatious, unpretentious, uncomplicated, homely, basic, austere, stark, bare, unvarnished, featureless, Spartan; see also SIMPLE adj. 2. **4** unattractive, ordinary-looking, unlovely, ugly, homely. **5** open, honest, straightforward, forthright, plainspoken, direct, frank, candid, blunt, outspoken, unreserved, sincere, guileless, artless. ● adv. **1** see *clearly* (CLEAR). **2** see SIMPLY 2. ● n. **1** prairie, grassland, pasture, meadowland, pampas, llano, savannah, steppe, tundra, *S.Afr.* veld, *literary* champaign, *poet. or archaic* mead; heath, wold, moor, moorland; plateau, tableland, mesa. □ **plain dealing** see CANDOR.

plain² /playn/ v.intr. *archaic* or *poet.* **1** mourn. **2** complain. **3**

make a plaintive sound. [ME f. OF *plaindre* (stem *plaign-*) f. L *plangere planct-* lament]

plainchant /pláynchant/ *n.* = PLAINSONG.

plainclothesman /playnklṓzmən, klṓthz-, -man/ *n.* a police officer who wears civilian clothes while on duty.

plainsman /pláynzmən/ *n.* (*pl.* **-men**) a person who lives on a plain, esp. in N. America.

plainsong /pláynsawng, -song/ *n.* unaccompanied church music sung in unison in medieval modes and in free rhythm corresponding to the accentuation of the words (cf. GREGORIAN CHANT).

plaint /playnt/ *n.* **1** *Brit. Law* an accusation; a charge. **2** *literary* or *archaic* a complaint; a lamentation. [ME f. OF *plainte* fem. past part. of *plaindre*, and OF *plaint* f. L *planctus* (as PLAIN²)]
■ see GRIEVANCE.

plaintiff /pláyntif/ *n. Law* a person who brings a case against another into court (opp. DEFENDANT). [ME f. OF *plaintif* (adj.) (as PLAINTIVE)]
■ see LITIGANT *n.*

plaintive /pláyntiv/ *adj.* **1** expressing sorrow; mournful. **2** mournful-sounding. □□ **plaintively** *adv.* **plaintiveness** *n.* [ME f. OF (*-if, -ive*) f. *plainte* (as PLAINT)]
■ see PITEOUS.

plait /playt, plat/ *n. & v.* ● *n.* **1** = BRAID 2. **2** = PLEAT. ● *v.tr.* = BRAID 1. [ME f. OF *pleit* fold ult. f. L *plicare* fold]
■ *n.* **1** braid, pigtail, esp. *Brit.* queue. ● *v.* see BRAID *v.* 1.

plan /plan/ *n. & v.* ● *n.* **1 a** a formulated and esp. detailed method by which a thing is to be done; a design or scheme. **b** an intention or proposed proceeding (*my plan was to distract them; plan of campaign*). **2** a drawing or diagram made by projection on a horizontal plane, esp. showing a building or one floor of a building (cf. ELEVATION). **3** a large-scale detailed map of a town or district. **4 a** a table, etc., indicating times, places, etc., of intended proceedings. **b** a scheme or arrangement (*prepared the seating plan*). **5** an imaginary plane perpendicular to the line of vision and containing the objects shown in a picture. ● *v.* (**planned, planning**) **1** *tr.* (often foll. by *that* + clause or *to* + infin.) arrange (a procedure, etc.) beforehand; form a plan (*planned to catch the evening ferry*). **2** *tr.* **a** design (a building, new town, etc.). **b** make a plan of (an existing building, an area, etc.). **3** *tr.* (as **planned** *adj.*) in accordance with a plan (*his planned arrival*). **4** *intr.* make plans. □ **planning permission** *Brit.* formal permission for building development, etc., esp. from a local authority. **plan on** *colloq.* aim at doing; intend. □□ **planning** *n.* [F f. earlier *plant*, f. It. *pianta* plan of building: cf. PLANT]
■ *n.* **1 a** scheme, method, procedure, system, arrangement, program, project, formula, pattern; see also DESIGN *n.* 1a. **b** see INTENTION 1. **2** drawing, sketch, design, layout, blueprint, chart, map, diagram, arrangement, scheme. ● *v.* **1** intend, expect, aim, contrive, devise; envisage, envision, foresee, contemplate, propose; see also ARRANGE 2, 3. **2** see DESIGN *v.* 1. □ **plan on** see INTEND 1, 2.

planar /pláynər/ *adj. Math.* of, relating to, or in the form of a plane.

planarian /plənáireeən/ *n.* any flatworm of the class Turbellaria, usu. living in fresh water. [mod.L *Planaria* the genus name, fem. of L *planarius* lying flat]

planchet /plánchit/ *n.* a plain metal disk, esp. one from which a coin is made. [dimin. of *planch* slab of metal f. OF *planche*: see PLANK]

planchette /planshét/ *n.* a small usu. heart-shaped board on casters with a pencil that is supposedly caused to write spirit messages when a person's fingers rest lightly on it. [F, dimin. of *planche* PLANK]

Planck's constant /plangks/ *n.* (also **Planck constant**) a fundamental constant, equal to the energy of quanta of electromagnetic radiation divided by its frequency, with a value of 6.626 x 10⁻³⁴ joules. [M. *Planck*, Ger. physicist d. 1947]

plane¹ /playn/ *n., adj., & v.* ● *n.* **1 a** a flat surface on which a straight line joining any two points on it would wholly lie. **b** an imaginary flat surface through or joining, etc., material

objects. **2** a level surface. **3** *colloq.* = AIRPLANE. **4** a flat surface producing lift by the action of air or water over and under it (usu. in *comb.*: *hydroplane*). **5** (often foll. by *of*) a level of attainment, thought, knowledge, etc. **6** a flat thin object such as a tabletop. ● *adj.* **1** (of a surface, etc.) perfectly level. **2** (of an angle, figure, etc.) lying in a plane. ● *v.intr.* **1** (often foll. by *down*) travel or glide in an airplane. **2** (of a speedboat, etc.) skim over water. **3** soar. □ **plane chart** a chart on which meridians and parallels of latitude are represented by equidistant straight lines, used in plane sailing. **plane polarization** a process restricting the vibrations of electromagnetic radiation, esp. light, to one direction. **plane sailing 1** the practice of determining a ship's position on the theory that she is moving on a plane. **2** = *plain sailing* (see PLAIN¹). **plane table** a surveying instrument used for direct plotting in the field, with a circular drawing board and pivoted alidade. [L *planum* flat surface, neut. of *planus* PLAIN¹ (different. f. PLAIN¹ in 17th c.): adj. after F *plan, plane*]
■ *n.* **2** flat, level. **3** aircraft, airliner, jet (plane), airplane, *Brit.* aeroplane. **5** see DEGREE 10. ● *adj.* **1** flat, even, level, horizontal; smooth. ● *v.* **2** glide, skim, skate, slip, slide.

plane² /playn/ *n. & v.* ● *n.* **1** a tool consisting of a wooden or metal block with a projecting steel blade, used to smooth a wooden surface by paring shavings from it. **2** a similar tool for smoothing metal. ● *v.tr.* **1** smooth (wood, metal, etc.) with a plane. **2** (often foll. by *away, down*) pare (irregularities) with a plane. **3** *archaic* level (*plane the way*). [ME f. OF var. of *plaine* f. LL *plana* f. L *planus* PLAIN¹]

plane³ /playn/ *n.* (in full **plane tree**) any tree of the genus *Platanus* often growing to great heights, with maple-like leaves and bark which peels in uneven patches. [ME f. OF f. L *platanus* f. Gk *platanos* f. *platus* broad]

planet /plánit/ *n.* **1 a** a celestial body moving in an elliptical orbit around a star. **b** the earth. **2** esp. *Astrol. hist.* a celestial body distinguished from the fixed stars by having an apparent motion of its own (including the moon and sun), esp. with reference to its supposed influence on people and events. □□ **planetology** /-tólǝjee/ *n.* [ME f. OF *planete* f. LL *planeta, planetes* f. Gk *planētēs* wanderer, planet f. *planaomai* wander]

planetarium /plánitáireeəm/ *n.* (*pl.* **planetariums** or **planetaria** /-reeə/) **1** a domed building in which images of stars, planets, constellations, etc., are projected for public entertainment or education. **2** the device used for such projection. **3** = ORRERY. [mod.L (as PLANET)]

planetary /plániteree/ *adj.* **1** of or like planets (*planetary influence*). **2** terrestrial; mundane. **3** wandering; erratic. □ **planetary nebula** a ring-shaped nebula formed by an expanding shell of gas round a star. [LL *planetarius* (as PLANET)]
■ **3** see ERRATIC 2.

planetesimal /plánitésiməl/ *n.* any of a vast number of minute planets or planetary bodies. □ **planetesimal hypothesis** the theory that planets were formed by the accretion of planetesimals in a cold state. [PLANET, after *infinitesimal*]

planetoid /plánitoyd/ *n.* = ASTEROID.

plangent /plánjənt/ *adj.* **1** (of a sound) loud and reverberating. **2** (of a sound) plaintive; sad. □□ **plangency** *n.* [L *plangere plangent-* lament]

planimeter /plənímitər/ *n.* an instrument for mechanically measuring the area of a plane figure. □□ **planimetric** /plánimétrik/ *adj.* **planimetrical** *adj.* **planimetry** /-mətree/ *n.* [F *planimètre* f. L *planus* level]

planish /plánish/ *v.tr.* flatten (sheet metal, coining metal, etc.) with a smooth-faced hammer or between rollers. □□ **planisher** *n.* [ME f. OF *planir* smooth f. *plain* PLANE¹ adj.]

/. . ./ **pronunciation**   ● **part of speech**
□ **phrases, idioms, and compounds**
□□ **derivatives**   ■ **synonym section**
cross-references appear in SMALL CAPITALS or *italics*

planisphere /plánisfeer/ *n.* a map formed by the projection of a sphere or part of a sphere on a plane, esp. to show the appearance of the heavens at a specific time or place. □□ **planispheric** /-sférik/ *adj.* [ME f. med.L *planisphaerium* (as PLANE¹, SPHERE): infl. by F *planisphère*]

plank /plangk/ *n. & v.* ● *n.* **1** a long flat piece of timber used esp. in building, flooring, etc. **2** an item of a political or other program (cf. PLATFORM). ● *v.tr.* **1** provide, cover, or floor, with planks. **2** cook and serve (fish, steak, etc.) on a plank. **3** (usu. foll. by *down*; also *absol.*) *colloq.* **a** put (a thing, person, etc.) down roughly or violently. **b** pay (money) on the spot or abruptly (*planked down $5*). □ **plank bed** a bed of boards without a mattress, esp. in prison. **walk the plank** *hist.* (of a pirate's captive, etc.) be made to walk blindfold along a plank over the side of a ship to one's death in the sea. [ME f. ONF *planke*, OF *planche* f. LL *planca* board f. *plancus* flat-footed]

■ *n.* **1** board, timber, slab. ● *v.* **3** a slap, slam, dump, fling, toss, throw, sling.

planking /plángking/ *n.* planks as flooring, etc.

■ flooring, boarding.

plankton /plángktən/ *n.* the chiefly microscopic organisms drifting or floating in the sea or fresh water (see BENTHOS, NEKTON). □□ **planktonic** /-tónik/ *adj.* [G f. Gk *plagktos* wandering f. *plazomai* wander]

planner /plánər/ *n.* **1** a person who controls or plans the development of towns, designs buildings, etc. **2** a person who makes plans. **3** a list, table, booklet, etc., with information helpful in planning.

■ **2** see MASTERMIND *n.*

plano- /pláynō/ *comb. form* level; flat. [L *planus* flat]

plano-concave /pláynōkónkayv, -konkáyv/ *adj.* (of a lens, etc.) with one surface plane and the other concave.

plano-convex /pláynōkónveks, -konvéks/ *adj.* (of a lens, etc.) with one surface plane and the other convex.

planographic /pláynəgráfik/ *adj.* relating to or produced by a process in which printing is done from a plane surface. □□ **planography** /plənógrəfee/ *n.*

planometer /plənómitər/ *n.* a flat plate used as a gauge for plane surfaces in metalwork.

plant /plant/ *n. & v.* ● *n.* **1 a** any living organism of the kingdom Plantae, usu. containing chlorophyll enabling it to live wholly on inorganic substances and lacking specialized sense organs and the power of voluntary movement. **b** a small organism of this kind, as distinguished from a shrub or tree. **2 a** machinery, fixtures, etc., used in industrial processes. **b** a factory. **c** buildings, fixtures, equipment, etc., of an institution. **3 a** *colloq.* something, esp. incriminating or compromising, positioned or concealed so as to be discovered later. **b** *sl.* a spy or detective; hidden police officers. ● *v.tr.* **1** place (a seed, bulb, or growing thing) in the ground so that it may take root and flourish. **2** (often foll. by *in*, *on*, etc.) put or fix in position. **3** deposit (young fish, spawn, oysters, etc.) in a river or lake. **4** station (a person, etc.), esp. as a spy or source of information. **5** *refl.* take up a position (*planted myself by the door*). **6** cause (an idea, etc.) to be established esp. in another person's mind. **7** deliver (a blow, kiss, etc.) with a deliberate aim. **8 a** *colloq.* position or conceal (something incriminating or compromising) for later discovery. **b** *sl.* post or infiltrate (a person) as a spy. **9 a** settle or people (a colony, etc.). **b** found or establish (a city, community, etc.). **10** bury. □ **plant louse** a small insect that infests plants, esp. an aphid. **plant out** transfer (a plant) from a pot or frame to the open ground; set out (seedlings) at intervals. □□ **plantable** *adj.* **plantlet** *n.* **plantlike** *adj.* [OE *plante* & F *plante* f. L *planta* sprout, slip, cutting]

■ *n.* **2 a** machinery, apparatus; gear, fixtures; see also EQUIPMENT. **b** factory, mill, works, workshop. **3 b** spy, (undercover *or* secret) agent, informer, informant. ● *v.* **1** bed (out), sow, seed, set (out). **2** place, put, position, station, situate, set (out), *colloq.* stick. **6** implant, establish, root, fix, ingrain, lodge, sow, instill, insinuate, introduce, impress, imprint. **8 a** hide, conceal; see also SECRETE².

Plantagenet /plantájinit/ *adj. & n.* ● *adj.* of or relating to the kings of England from Henry II to Richard II (1154–1485). ● *n.* any of these kings. [f. L *planta genista* sprig of broom, worn as a distinctive mark, the origin of their surname]

plantain¹ /plántin/ *n.* any shrub of the genus *Plantago*, with broad flat leaves spread out close to the ground and seeds used as food for birds and as a mild laxative. □ **plantain lily** = HOSTA. [ME f. OF f. L *plantago -ginis* f. *planta* sole of the foot (from its broad prostrate leaves)]

plantain² /plántin/ *n.* **1** a banana plant, *Musa paradisiaca*, widely grown for its fruit. **2** the starchy fruit of this containing less sugar than a banana and chiefly used in cooking. [earlier *platan* f. Sp. *plá(n)tano* plane tree, prob. assim. f. Galibi *palatana*, etc.]

plantar /plántər/ *adj.* of or relating to the sole of the foot. [L *plantaris* f. *planta* sole]

plantation /plantáyshən/ *n.* **1** an estate on which cotton, tobacco, etc., is cultivated esp. by resident (formerly slave) labor. **2** an area planted with trees, etc., for cultivation. **3** *hist.* a colony; colonization. □ **plantation song** a song of the kind formerly sung by African-American slaves on American plantations. [ME f. OF *plantation* or L *plantatio* (as PLANT)]

planter /plántər/ *n.* **1** a person who cultivates the soil. **2** the manager or occupier of a coffee, cotton, tobacco, etc., plantation. **3** a large container for decorative plants. **4** a machine for planting seeds, etc.

■ **3** flowerpot, plant pot.

plantigrade /plántigrayd/ *adj. & n.* ● *adj.* (of an animal) walking on the soles of its feet. ● *n.* a plantigrade animal, e.g., humans or bears (cf. DIGITIGRADE). [F f. mod.L *plantigradus* f. L *planta* sole + *-gradus* -walking]

plaque /plak/ *n.* **1** an ornamental tablet of metal, porcelain, etc., esp. affixed to a building in commemoration. **2** a deposit on teeth where bacteria proliferate. **3** *Med.* **a** a patch or eruption of skin, etc., as a result of damage. **b** a fibrous lesion in atherosclerosis. **4** a small badge of rank in an honorary order. □□ **plaquette** /plakét/ *n.* [F f. Du. *plak* tablet f. *plakken* stick]

■ **1** tablet, medallion, plate, panel, marker, slab, plaquette. **4** badge, pin, patch, medallion, medal, insignia.

plash¹ /plash/ *n. & v.* ● *n.* **1** a splash; a plunge. **2 a** a marshy pool. **b** a puddle. ● *v.* **1** *intr. & tr.* splash. **2** *tr.* strike the surface of (water). □□ **plashy** *adj.* [OE *plæsc*, prob. imit.]

■ *v.* **1** see GURGLE *v.*, SPLASH *v.* 3.

plash² /plash/ *v.tr.* esp. *Brit.* **1** bend down and interweave (branches, twigs, etc.) to form a hedge. **2** make or renew (a hedge) in this way. [ME f. OF *pla(i)ssier* ult. f. L *plectere* plait: cf. PLEACH]

plasma /plázmə/ *n.* (also **plasm** /plázəm/) **1** the colorless fluid part of blood, lymph, or milk, in which corpuscles or fat globules are suspended. **2** = PROTOPLASM. **3** a gas of positive ions and free electrons with an approximately equal positive and negative charge. **4** a green variety of quartz used in mosaic and for other decorative purposes. □□ **plasmatic** /-mátik/ *adj.* **plasmic** *adj.* [LL, = mold f. Gk *plasma -atos* f. *plassō* to shape]

plasmodesma /plázmədézmə/ *n.* (*pl.* **plasmodesmata** /-mətə/) a narrow thread of cytoplasm that passes through cell walls and affords communication between plant cells. [PLASMA + Gk *desma* bond, fetter]

plasmodium /plazmṓdeeəm/ *n.* (*pl.* **plasmodia** /-deeə/) **1** any parasitic protozoan of the genus *Plasmodium*, including those causing malaria in man. **2** a form within the life cycle of various microorganisms including slime molds, usu. consisting of a mass of naked protoplasm containing many nuclei. □□ **plasmodial** *adj.* [mod.L f. PLASMA + *-odium*: see -ODE¹]

plasmolysis /plazmólisis/ *n.* contraction of the protoplast of a plant cell as a result of loss of water from the cell. [mod.L (as PLASMA, -LYSIS)]

plasmolyze /plázməlīz/ *v.intr. & tr.* (*Brit.* **plasmolyse**) undergo or subject to plasmolysis.

plaster /plástər/ *n. & v.* ● *n.* **1** a soft pliable mixture esp. of

lime putty with sand or Portland cement, etc., for spreading on walls, ceilings, etc., to form a smooth hard surface when dried. **2** *Brit.* = *sticking plaster* (see STICK²). **3** *hist.* a curative or protective substance spread on a bandage, etc., and applied to the body (*mustard plaster*). ● *v.tr.* **1** cover (a wall, etc.) with plaster or a similar substance. **2** (often foll. by *with*) coat thickly or to excess; bedaub (*plastered the bread with jam; the wall was plastered with slogans*). **3** stick or apply (a thing) thickly like plaster (*plastered glue all over it*). **4** (often foll. by *down*) make (esp. hair) smooth with water, gel, etc.; fix flat. **5** (as **plastered** *adj.*) *sl.* drunk. **6** apply a medical plaster or plaster cast to. **7** *sl.* bomb or shell heavily. □ **plaster cast 1** a bandage stiffened with plaster of Paris and applied to a broken limb, etc. **2** a statue or mold made of plaster. **plaster of Paris** fine white plaster made of gypsum and used for making plaster casts, etc. **plaster saint** *iron.* a person regarded as being without moral faults or human frailty. □□ **plasterer** *n.* **plastery** *adj.* [ME f. OE & OF *plastre* or F *plastrer* f. med.L *plastrum* f. L *emplastrum* f. Gk *emplastron*]
■ *v.* **2** smear, daub, bedaub, spread, coat, cover, overlay, smother. **3** smear, stick, daub, spread. **5** (**plastered**) see DRUNK *adj.* 1. **7** see SHELL *v.* 2.

plasterboard /plástərbawrd/ *n.* a type of board with a center filling of plaster, used to form or line the inner walls of houses, etc.

plastic /plástik/ *n. & adj.* ● *n.* **1** any of a number of synthetic polymeric substances that can be given any required shape. **2** (*attrib.*) made of plastic (*plastic bag*); made of cheap materials. **3** = *plastic money*. ● *adj.* **1 a** capable of being molded; pliant; supple. **b** susceptible; impressionable. **c** artificial; unsincere. **2** molding or giving form to clay, wax, etc. **3** *Biol.* exhibiting an adaptability to environmental changes. **4** (esp. in philosophy) formative; creative. □ **plastic arts** art forms involving modeling or molding, e.g., sculpture and ceramics, or art involving the representation of solid objects with three-dimensional effects. **plastic bomb** a bomb containing plastic explosive. **plastic explosive** a putty-like explosive capable of being molded by hand. **plastic money** *colloq.* a credit card, charge card, or other plastic card that can be used in place of money. **plastic surgeon** a qualified practitioner of plastic surgery. **plastic surgery** the process of reconstructing or repairing parts of the body by the transfer of tissue, either in the treatment of injury or for cosmetic reasons. □□ **plastically** *adv.* **plasticity** /-tísitee/ *n.* **plasticize** /-tisiz/ *v.tr.* **plasticization** /-tisizáyshən/ *n.* **plasticizer** *n.* **plasticky** *adj.* [F *plastique* or L *plasticus* f. Gk *plastikos* f. *plassō* mold]
■ *n.* **2** (*attrib.*) cheap, inferior, worthless, pinchbeck, shoddy, chintzy, gaudy, *colloq.* crummy. ● *adj.* **1 a** moldable, pliable, shapable, soft, waxy, malleable, workable, ductile, flexible, pliant, supple. **b** impressionable, receptive, open, persuadable *or* persuasible, susceptible, tractable, compliant, responsive, manageable; unformed, inexperienced. **4** see SEMINAL 4.

Plasticine /plástiseen/ *n. propr.* a soft plastic material used, esp. by children, for modeling. [PLASTIC + -INE⁴]

plastid /plástid/ *n.* any small organelle in the cytoplasm of a plant cell, containing pigment or food. [G f. Gk *plastos* shaped]

plastron /plástrən, -tron/ *n.* **1 a** a fencer's leather-covered breastplate. **b** a lancer's breast-covering of facings cloth. **2 a** an ornamental front on a woman's bodice. **b** a man's starched shirt front. **3 a** the ventral part of the shell of a tortoise or turtle. **b** the corresponding part in other animals. **4** *hist.* a steel breastplate. □□ **plastral** *adj.* [F f. It. *piastrone* augment. of *piastra* breastplate, f. L *emplastrum* PLASTER]

plat¹ /plat/ *n.* **1** a plot of land. **2** a plan of an area of land. [16th c.: collateral form of PLOT]
■ **1** see PLOT *n.* 1.

plat² /plat/ *n. & v.* ● *n.* = PLAIT *n.* 1. ● *v.tr.* (**platted, platting**) = PLAIT *v.*

platan /plátən/ *n.* = PLANE³. [ME f. L *platanus*: see PLANE³]

plat du jour /plaá də zhŏŏr/ *n.* a dish specially featured on a day's menu. [F, = dish of the day]

plate /playt/ *n. & v.* ● *n.* **1 a** a shallow vessel, usu. circular and of earthenware or china, from which food is eaten or served. **b** the contents of this (*ate a plate of sandwiches*). **2** a similar vessel usu. of metal or wood, used esp. for making a collection in a church, etc. **3** a main course of a meal, served on one plate. **4** food and service for one person (*a fundraiser with a $30 per plate dinner*). **5 a** (*collect.*) utensils of silver, gold, or other metal. **b** (*collect.*) objects of plated metal. **c** = PLATING. **6 a** a piece of metal with a name or inscription for affixing to a door, container, etc. **b** = *license plate*. **7** an illustration on special paper in a book. **8** a thin sheet of metal, glass, etc., coated with a sensitive film for photography. **9** a flat thin usu. rigid sheet of metal, etc., with an even surface and uniform thickness, often as part of a mechanism. **10 a** a smooth piece of metal, etc., for engraving. **b** an impression made from this. **11** *Brit.* **a** a silver or gold cup as a prize for a horse race, etc. **b** a race with this as a prize. **12 a** a thin piece of plastic material, molded to the shape of the mouth and gums, to which artificial teeth or another orthodontic appliance are attached. **b** *colloq.* a complete denture or orthodontic appliance. **13** *Geol.* each of several rigid sheets of rock thought to form the earth's outer crust. **14** *Biol.* a thin flat organic structure or formation. **15** a light shoe for a racehorse. **16** a stereotype, electrotype, or plastic cast of a page of composed movable types, or a metal or plastic copy of filmset matter, from which sheets are printed. **17** *Baseball* a flat five-sided piece of whitened rubber at which the batter stands and by stepping on which a runner scores. **18** the anode of a thermionic valve. **19** a horizontal timber laid along the top of a wall to support the ends of joists or rafters. ● *v.tr.* **1** apply a thin coat esp. of silver, gold, or tin to (another metal). **2** cover (esp. a ship) with plates of metal, esp. for protection. **3** make a plate of (type, etc.) for printing. □ **on a plate** *colloq.* available with little trouble to the recipient. **on one's plate** for one to deal with or consider. **plate armor** armor of metal plates, for a man, ship, etc. **plate glass** thick fine-quality glass for storefront windows, etc., orig. cast in plates. **plate mark** a hallmark. **plate rack** *Brit.* a rack in which plates are placed to drain. **plate tectonics** *Geol.* the study of the earth's surface based on the concept of moving plates (see sense 13 of *n.*) forming its structure. **plate tracery** *Archit.* tracery with perforations in otherwise continuous stone. □□ **plateful** *n.* (*pl.* **-fuls**). **plateless** *adj.* **plater** *n.* [ME f. OF f. med.L *plata* plate armor f. *platus* (adj.) ult. f. Gk *platus* flat]
■ *n.* **1 a** platter, dish, bowl, *archaic* charger, *hist.* trencher. **b** plateful, serving, portion, dish, platter. **6 a** see PLAQUE 1. **7** illustration, picture, print, vignette. **9** layer, leaf, sheet, pane, panel, lamina, slab. ● *v.* **1** cover, coat, overlay, face, laminate.

plateau /platṓ/ *n. & v.* ● *n.* (*pl.* **plateaux** /-tṓz/ or **plateaus**) **1** an area of fairly level high ground. **2** a state of little variation after an increase. ● *v.intr.* (**plateaus, plateaued**) (often foll. by *out*) reach a level or stable state after an increase. [F f. OF *platel* dimin. of *plat* flat surface]
■ *n.* **1** tableland, table, upland, plain. ● *v.* see LEVEL *v.* 1.

platelayer /pláytlayər/ *n. Brit.* a person employed in fixing and repairing railroad rails.

platelet /pláytlit/ *n.* a small colorless disk of protoplasm found in blood and involved in clotting.

platen /plát'n/ *n.* **1** a plate in a printing press which presses the paper against the type. **2** a cylindrical roller in a typewriter against which the paper is held. [OF *platine* a flat piece f. *plat* flat]

plateresque /plátərésk/ *adj.* richly ornamented in a style sug-

---

gesting silverware. [Sp. *plateresco* f. *platero* silversmith f. *plata* silver]

platform /plátfawrm/ *n.* **1** a raised level surface; a natural or artificial terrace. **2** a raised surface from which a speaker addresses an audience. **3** a raised elongated structure along the side of a track in a railroad, subway station, etc. **4** the floor area at the entrance to a bus. **5** a thick sole of a shoe. **6** the declared policy of a political party. □ **platform ticket** *Brit.* a ticket allowing a nontraveler access to a station platform. [F *plateforme* flat plan f. *plate* flat + *forme* FORM]
 ■ **2** stand, dais, stage, podium, rostrum. **6** policy, party line, principle(s), tenet(s), program, manifesto.

plating /pláyting/ *n.* **1** a coating of gold, silver, etc. **2** an act of plating.
 ■ **1** plate, coat, coating, layer, lamination.

platinic /plətínik/ *adj.* of or containing (esp. tetravalent) platinum.

platinize /plát'nīz/ *v.tr.* coat with platinum. □□ **platinization** *n.*

platinoid /plát'noyd/ *n.* an alloy of copper, zinc, nickel, and tungsten.

platinum /plát'nəm/ *n. Chem.* a ductile malleable silvery-white metallic element occurring naturally in nickel and copper ores, unaffected by simple acids and fusible only at a very high temperature, used in making jewelry and laboratory apparatus. ¶ Symb.: **Pt.** □ **platinum black** platinum in powder form like lampblack. **platinum blonde** (or **blond**) *adj.* silvery-blond. ● *n.* a person with esp. bleached or dyed silvery-blond hair. **platinum metal** any metallic element found with and resembling platinum, e.g., osmium, iridium, and palladium. [mod.L f. earlier *platina* f. Sp., dimin. of *plata* silver]

platitude /plátitōōd, -tyōōd/ *n.* **1** a trite or commonplace remark, esp. one solemnly delivered. **2** the use of platitudes; dullness; insipidity. □□ **platitudinize** /-tōōd'nīz, -tyōō-/ *v.intr.* **platitudinous** /-tōōdənəs/ *adj.* [F f. *plat* flat, after *certitude, multitudinous,* etc.]
 ■ **1** see CLICHÉ. □□ **platitudinous** see BANAL.

Platonic /plətónik/ *adj.* **1** of or associated with the Greek philosopher Plato (d. 347 BC) or his ideas. **2** (**platonic**) (of love or friendship) purely spiritual; not sexual. **3** (**platonic**) confined to words or theory; not leading to action; harmless. □ **Platonic solid** (or **body**) any of the five regular solids (tetrahedron, cube, octahedron, dodecahedron, icosahedron). □□ **Platonically** *adv.* [L *Platonicus* f. Gk *Platōnikos* f. *Platōn* Plato]
 ■ **2** (**platonic**) nonphysical, asexual, nonsexual, chaste, dispassionate, detached, spiritual, friendly.
 3 (**platonic**) see ABSTRACT *adj.* 1a.

Platonism /pláyt'nizəm/ *n.* the philosophy of Plato or his followers. □□ **Platonist** *n.*

platoon /plətōōn/ *n.* **1** *Mil.* a subdivision of a company, a tactical unit commanded by a lieutenant and usu. divided into three sections. **2** a group of persons acting together. [F *peloton* small ball, dimin. of *pelote*: see PELLET, -OON]
 ■ company, squad, squadron, group, patrol, team, cadre, body, formation, unit, *colloq.* outfit.

platter /plátər/ *n.* **1** a large flat dish or plate, esp. for food. **2** *colloq.* a phonograph record. □ **on a platter** = *on a plate* (see PLATE). [ME & AF *plater* f. AF *plat* PLATE]
 ■ **1** serving dish, server, plate, dish, salver, tray.

platy- /pláti, -tee/ *comb. form* broad; flat. [Gk *platu-* f. *platus* broad, flat]

platyhelminth /plátihélminth/ *n.* any invertebrate of the phylum Platyhelminthes, including flatworms, flukes, and tapeworms.

platypus /plátipəs/ *n.* an Australian aquatic egg-laying mammal, *Ornithorhynchus anatinus,* having a pliable ducklike bill, webbed feet, and sleek gray fur. Also called DUCKBILL.

platyrrhine /plátirin/ *adj. & n.* ● *adj.* (of primates) having nostrils far apart and directed forward or sideways (cf. CAT-ARRHINE). ● *n.* such an animal. [PLATY- + Gk *rhis rhin-* nose]

plaudit /pláwdit/ *n.* (usu. in *pl.*) **1** a round of applause. **2** an emphatic expression of approval. [shortened f. L *plaudite*

applaud, imper. pl. of *plaudere plaus-* applaud, said by Roman actors at the end of a play]
 ■ **1** see APPLAUSE 1. **2** see APPLAUSE 2.

plausible /pláwzibəl/ *adj.* **1** (of an argument, statement, etc.) seeming reasonable or probable. **2** (of a person) persuasive but deceptive. □□ **plausibility** /-bílitee/ *n.* **plausibly** *adv.* [L *plausibilis* (as PLAUDIT)]
 ■ **1** likely, believable, cogent, convincing, reasonable, feasible, credible, creditable, tenable, conceivable, thinkable, probable, imaginable, possible, admissible, compelling, sound, rational, logical, acceptable.
 2 specious, meretricious, misleading, deceitful, casuistic, sophistical, smooth; see also DECEPTIVE.

play /play/ *v. & n.* ● *v.* **1** *intr.* (often foll. by *with*) occupy or amuse oneself pleasantly with some recreation, game, exercise, etc. **2** *intr.* (foll. by *with*) act lightheartedly or flippantly (with feelings, etc.). **3** *tr.* **a** perform on or be able to perform on (a musical instrument). **b** perform (a piece of music, etc.). **c** cause (a record, record player, etc.) to produce sounds. **4 a** *intr.* (foll. by *in*) perform a role in (a drama, etc.). **b** *tr.* perform (a drama or role) on stage, or in a movie or broadcast. **c** *tr.* give a dramatic performance at (a particular theater or place). **5** *tr.* act in real life the part of (*play truant; play the fool*). **6** *tr.* (foll. by *on*) perform (a trick or joke, etc.) on (a person). **7** *tr.* (foll. by *for*) regard (a person) as (something specified) (*played me for a fool*). **8** *intr. colloq.* participate; cooperate; do what is wanted (*they won't play*). **9** *intr.* gamble. **10** *tr.* gamble on. **11** *tr.* **a** take part in (a game or recreation). **b** compete with (another player or team) in a game. **c** occupy (a specified position) in a team for a game. **d** (foll. by *in, on, at,* etc.) assign (a player) to a position. **12** *tr.* move (a piece) or display (a playing card) in one's turn in a game. **13** *tr.* (also *absol.*) strike or catch (a ball, etc.) or execute (a stroke) in a game. **14** *intr.* move about in a lively or unrestrained manner. **15** *intr.* (often foll. by *on*) a touch gently. **b** emit light, water, etc. (*fountains gently playing*). **16** *tr.* allow (a fish) to exhaust itself pulling against a line. **17** *intr.* (often foll. by *at*) **a** engage in a half-hearted way (in an activity). **b** pretend to be. **18** *intr.* (of a court, field, etc.) be conducive to play as specified (*the greens are playing fast*). **19** *intr. colloq.* act or behave (as specified) (*play fair*). **20** *tr.* (foll. by *in, out,* etc.) accompany (a person) with music (*were played out with bagpipes*). ● *n.* **1** recreation, amusement, esp. as the spontaneous activity of children and young animals. **2 a** the playing of a game. **b** the action or manner of this. **c** the status of the ball, etc., in a game as being available to be played according to the rules (*in play; out of play*). **3** a dramatic piece for the stage, etc. **4** activity or operation (*are in full play; brought into play*). **5 a** freedom of movement. **b** space or scope for this. **6** brisk, light, or fitful movement. **7** gambling. **8** an action or maneuver, esp. in or as in a game. □ **at play** engaged in recreation. **in play** for amusement; not seriously. **make play** *Brit.* act effectively. **make a play for** *colloq.* make a conspicuous attempt to acquire or attract. **make play with** use ostentatiously. **play along** pretend to cooperate. **play around** (or **about**) **1** behave irresponsibly. **2** philander. **play back** play (sounds recently recorded), esp. to monitor recording quality, etc. **play ball** see BALL[1]. **play by ear 1** perform (music) previously heard without having or having seen a score. **2** (also **play it by ear**) proceed instinctively or step by step according to results and circumstances. **play-by-play** *adj.* pertaining to a description, esp. of a sports event, with continuous commentary. ● *n.* such a description (*he called the play-by-play for the big game*). **play one's cards right** (or **well**) make good use of opportunities; act shrewdly. **play down** minimize the importance of. **played out** exhausted of energy or usefulness. **play false** act, or treat a (person), deceitfully or treacherously. **play fast and loose** act unreliably; ignore one's obligations. **play the field** see FIELD. **play for time** seek to gain time by delaying. **play the game** see GAME[1]. **play God** see GOD. **play havoc with** see HAVOC. **play hell with** see HELL. **play hooky** see HOOKY. **play into a person's hands** act so as unwittingly to give a person an advantage. **play it cool** *colloq.* **1** affect indifference. **2** be

relaxed or unemotional. **play the market** speculate in stocks, etc. **play off** (usu. foll. by *against*) **1** oppose (one person against another), esp. for one's own advantage. **2** play an extra match to decide a draw or tie. **play-off** *Sports* a game played to break a tie. **play on 1** continue to play. **2** take advantage of (a person's feelings, etc.). **play on words** a pun. **play possum** see POSSUM. **play safe** (or **for safety**) avoid risks. **play to the gallery** see GALLERY. **play up 1** make the most of; emphasize. **2** *Brit.* cause trouble; be irritating (*my rheumatism is playing up again*). **3** *Brit.* obstruct or annoy in this way (*played the teacher up*). **4** *Brit.* put all one's energy into a game. **5** *Brit.* behave mischievously. **play up to** flatter, esp. to win favor. **play with fire** take foolish risks. □□ **playable** *adj.* **playability** /pláyabílitee/ *n.* [OE *plega* (n.), *pleg(i)an* (v.), orig. = (to) exercise]
■ *v.* **1** amuse oneself, frolic, caper, sport, have fun, have a good time, enjoy oneself, disport (oneself). **2** see TOY *v.* 1. **3 a** perform upon or on. **c** operate; put or turn on. **4 a** perform, act; appear. **b** put on, perform; act, take the role or part of, appear as. **7** see TAKE *v.* 20. **8** participate, take part, join in, cooperate, play the game, play ball, play along. **9, 10** gamble, bet; see also SPECULATE 3. **11 a** take part in, join in, participate in, be occupied in or with, occupy oneself in or with, engage in; take up. **b** engage (with), contend with, compete with or against, challenge, vie with, pit oneself against, take on. **17 b** sham, feign, pretend, fake, dissemble; (*play at*) fake, feign, simulate, affect. **19** see BEHAVE 1a. ● *n.* **1** amusement, frivolity, entertainment, recreation, fun, pleasure, sport, merrymaking, revelry; tomfoolery, horseplay, skylarking. **3** drama, stage play, show, piece, production, entertainment. **4** see OPERATION 1, 2. **5** flexibility, looseness, freedom, leeway, margin, room, space, movement, motion, give. **8** move, action; see also MANEUVER *n.* 1, 3. □ **in play** in jest, in fun, jokingly, teasingly, playfully, tongue in cheek, for a laugh. **make a play for** see *go for* 4. **play along** (*play along with*) cooperate with, go along with; see also OBLIGE 3. **play around** or **about 1** fool around or about, monkey around, horse around, act up, mess around, misbehave, cause trouble; tease. **2** dally, flirt, be unfaithful; philander, womanize; *colloq.* fool around, run around, sleep around, play the field. **play by ear 2** improvise, ad lib; take it as it comes. **play down** belittle, minimize, diminish, make light of, de-emphasize, brush off, shrug off, laugh off, pooh-pooh. **played out** see *exhausted* (EXHAUST *v.* 2). **play for time** delay, procrastinate, stall, temporize, hesitate, drag one's feet or heels, hold back. **play on 2** trade on, exploit, take advantage of, use, make use of, misuse, abuse. **play up 1** stress, emphasize, underscore, underline, accentuate, call attention to, highlight, spotlight, dramatize, build up. **2** give or cause trouble, malfunction, *sl.* go on the blink. **play up to** curry favor with, toady to, ingratiate oneself with, truckle to, court, fawn on, *colloq.* soft-soap, butter up, suck up to, bootlick; see also FLATTER 1. **play with fire** undertake a risk or hazard or peril, run a risk, risk a thing or everything, imperil or endanger a thing, tempt fate, live dangerously, sail close to the wind.

playa /pláaya/ *n.* a flat dried-up area, esp. a desert basin from which water evaporates quickly. [Sp., = beach, f. LL *plagia*]

playact /pláyakt/ *v.* **1** *intr.* act in a play. **2** *intr.* behave affectedly or insincerely. **3** *tr.* act (a scene, part, etc.). □□ **playacting** *n.* **playactor** *n.*
■ **2** act, put on an act; see also SHAM *v.* 1. □□ **playacting** see MASQUERADE *n.* 1.

playback /pláybak/ *n.* an act or instance of replaying recorded audio or video from a tape, etc.

playbill /pláybil/ *n.* **1** a poster announcing a theatrical performance. **2** a theater program.

playboy /pláyboy/ *n.* an irresponsible pleasure-seeking man, esp. a wealthy one.
■ man about town, roué, rake, debauchee, womanizer; Don Juan, Casanova, lothario, lady-killer.

player /pláyər/ *n.* **1 a** a person taking part in a sport or game. **b** a gambler. **2** a person playing a musical instrument. **3** a person who plays a part on the stage; an actor. **4** = *record player*. □ **player piano** a piano fitted with an apparatus enabling it to be played automatically. [OE *plegere* (as PLAY)]
■ **1 a** contestant, participant, competitor, contender; athlete, sportswoman, sportsman. **b** gambler, bettor, gamester, speculator, *Brit.* punter. **2** musician, instrumentalist, performer. **3** actor, actress, performer, entertainer, trouper, thespian.

playfellow /pláyfelō/ *n.* a playmate.
■ see PLAYMATE.

playful /pláyfool/ *adj.* **1** fond of or inclined to play. **2** done in fun; humorous; jocular. □□ **playfully** *adv.* **playfulness** *n.*
■ **1** fun-loving, sportive, gamesome, frolicsome, puppyish, kittenish, *archaic* frolic, wanton. **2** humorous, jocular, jocose, teasing, humorous, tongue-in-cheek.

playgoer /pláygōər/ *n.* a person who goes often to the theater.

playground /pláygrownd/ *n.* an outdoor area set aside for children to play.

playgroup /pláygrōop/ *n.* a group of preschool children who play regularly together at a particular place under supervision.

playhouse /pláyhows/ *n.* **1** a theater. **2** a toy house for children to play in.
■ **1** see THEATER 1a.

playing card /pláying/ *n.* each of a set of usu. 52 rectangular pieces of card or other material with an identical pattern on one side and different values represented by numbers and symbols on the other, used to play various games.

playing field /pláying/ *n.* a field used for outdoor team games.
■ field, ground, esp. *Brit.* pitch.

playlet /pláylit/ *n.* a short play or dramatic piece.

playmate /pláymayt/ *n.* a child's companion in play.
■ playfellow, friend, *colloq.* pal, buddy; see also CHUM¹.

playpen /pláypen/ *n.* a portable enclosure for young children to play in.

plaything /pláything/ *n.* **1** a toy or other thing to play with. **2** a person treated as a toy.
■ **1** toy, game, gewgaw, *archaic* whim-wham. **2** pawn, puppet, toy, tool, cat's-paw, sport.

playtime /pláytim/ *n.* time for play or recreation.
■ break, rest period, recess.

playwright /pláyrīt/ *n.* a person who writes plays.
■ dramatist, dramaturge, scriptwriter, screenwriter, scenarist.

plaza /pláaza/ *n.* **1** a marketplace or open square (esp. in a town). **2** a public area beside an expressway with facilities such as restaurants or service stations. [Sp., = place]
■ see SQUARE *n.* 3a.

plc *Brit. abbr.* (also **PLC**) Public Limited Company.

plea /plee/ *n.* **1** an earnest appeal or entreaty. **2** *Law* a formal statement by or on behalf of a defendant. **3** an argument or excuse. □ **plea bargain** (or **bargaining**) an arrangement between prosecutor and defendant whereby the defendant pleads guilty to a lesser charge in the expectation of leniency. **plea-bargain** negotiate a plea bargain agreement. [ME & AF *ple, plai*, OF *plait, plaid* agreement, discussion f. L *placitum* a decree, neut. past part. of *placēre* to please]
■ **1** entreaty, appeal, petition, request, supplication, suit, cry, solicitation. **2** answer, defense, argument; case. **3** argument, explanation, justification; pretext; see also EXCUSE *n.* 1, 2.

pleach /pleech/ *v.tr.* entwine or interlace (esp. branches to form a hedge). [ME *pleche* f. OF (as PLASH²)]
■ see TWIST *v.* 2.

plead /pleed/ *v.* (*past* and *past part.* **pleaded** or **pled** /pled/)

/.../ **pronunciation**	● **part of speech**
□ **phrases, idioms, and compounds**	
□□ **derivatives**	■ **synonym section**
cross-references appear in SMALL CAPITALS or *italics*	

1 *intr.* (foll. by *with*) make an earnest appeal to. **2** *intr. Law* address a court of law as an advocate on behalf of a party. **3** *tr.* maintain (a cause) esp. in a court of law. **4** *tr. Law* declare to be one's state as regards guilt in or responsibility for a crime (*plead guilty*; *plead insanity*). **5** *tr.* offer or allege as an excuse (*pleaded forgetfulness*). **6** *intr.* make an appeal or entreaty. □ **plead** (or **take**) **the Fifth** refuse to incriminate oneself legally, in accordance with the Fifth Amendment to the Constitution. □□ **pleadable** *adj.* **pleader** *n.* **pleadingly** *adv.* [ME f. AF *pleder*, OF *plaidier* (as PLEA)]
■ **1** (*plead with*) request, entreat, appeal to, petition, apply to, implore, beseech, beg, importune, solicit, supplicate (to). **3** argue, maintain, put forward. **6** (*plead for*) appeal for, cry for, ask (for), seek, beg (for), pray for, request, supplicate for.

pleading /pléeding/ *n.* (usu. in *pl.*) a formal statement of the cause of an action or defense.
■ see *supplication* (SUPPLICATE).

pleasance /plézəns/ *n.* a secluded enclosure or part of a garden, esp. one attached to a large house. [ME f. OF *plaisance* (as PLEASANT)]

pleasant /plézənt/ *adj.* (**pleasanter, pleasantest**) pleasing to the mind, feelings, or senses. □□ **pleasantly** *adv.* **pleasantness** *n.* [ME f. OF *plaisant* (as PLEASE)]
■ pleasing, pleasurable, nice, enjoyable, satisfying, good, lovely, attractive, gratifying, delightful, charming, agreeable, acceptable, enjoyable, salubrious, savory, beautiful, esp. *literary* delectable; friendly, affable, amiable, amicable, sweet, companionable, engaging, winning, congenial, genial, likable, cordial, *Sc. & No. of Engl.* canny.

pleasantry /plézəntree/ *n.* (*pl.* **-ies**) **1** a pleasant or amusing remark, esp. made in casual conversation. **2** a humorous manner of speech. **3** jocularity. [F *plaisanterie* (as PLEASANT)]
■ **2, 3** see BANTER *n.*

please /pleez/ *v.* **1** *tr.* (also *absol.*) be agreeable to; make glad; give pleasure to (*the gift will please them; anxious to please*). **2** *tr.* (in *passive*) **a** (foll. by *to* + infin.) be glad or willing to (*am pleased to help*). **b** (often foll. by *about, at, with*) derive pleasure or satisfaction (from). **3** *tr.* (with *it* as subject; usu. foll. by *to* + infin.) be the inclination or wish of (*it did not please them to attend*). **4** *intr.* think fit; have the will or desire (*take as many as you please*). **5** *tr.* (short for **may it please you**) used in polite requests (*come in, please*). □ **if you please** if you are willing, esp. *iron.* to indicate unreasonableness (*then, if you please, we had to pay*). **pleased as Punch** see PUNCH[4]. **please oneself** do as one likes. □□ **pleased** *adj.* **pleasing** *adj.* **pleasingly** *adv.* [ME *plaise* f. OF *plaisir* f. L *placēre*]
■ **1** delight, gratify, humor, content, cheer, gladden, amuse, divert, interest, entertain. **2 a** (*be pleased*) be content, be glad, be willing, be happy, be delighted. **4** like, prefer, choose, desire, want, see fit, wish, will. □□ **pleased** happy, delighted, glad, gratified, satisfied, contented, thrilled.

pleasurable /plézhərəbəl/ *adj.* causing pleasure; agreeable. □□ **pleasurableness** *n.* **pleasurably** *adv.* [PLEASURE + -ABLE, after *comfortable*]
■ see PLEASANT.

pleasure /plézhər/ *n. & v.* ● *n.* **1** a feeling of satisfaction or joy. **2** enjoyment. **3** a source of pleasure or gratification (*painting was my chief pleasure*; *it is a pleasure to talk to them*). **4** *formal* a person's will or desire (*what is your pleasure?*). **5** sensual gratification or enjoyment (*a life of pleasure*). **6** (*attrib.*) done or used for pleasure (*pleasure ground*). ● *v.* **1** *tr.* give (esp. sexual) pleasure to. **2** *intr.* (often foll. by *in*) take pleasure. □ **take pleasure in** like doing. **with pleasure** gladly. [ME & OF *plesir, plaisir* PLEASE, used as a noun]
■ *n.* **1, 2** happiness, delight, joy; satisfaction, fulfillment, contentment, enjoyment, gratification. **3** comfort, solace; recreation, amusement, entertainment, diversion. **4** desire, wish, will, preference, inclination; discretion. **5** hedonism, debauchery, libertinism, indulgence, self-indulgence, self-gratification, profligacy, dissipation. ● *v.* **2** see REJOICE 1–3;

(*pleasure in*) ENJOY 1. □ **take pleasure in** see ENJOY 1. **with pleasure** gladly, willingly, happily, readily.

pleat /pleet/ *n. & v.* ● *n.* a fold or crease, esp. a flattened fold in cloth doubled upon itself. ● *v.tr.* make a pleat or pleats in. [ME, var. of PLAIT]

pleb /pleb/ *n. colloq.* usu. *derog.* an ordinary insignificant person. □□ **plebby** *adj.* [abbr. of PLEBEIAN]
■ see PLEBEIAN *n.*

plebe /pleeb/ *n.* a first-year student at a military academy.

plebeian /plibéeən/ *n. & adj.* ● *n.* a commoner, esp. in ancient Rome. ● *adj.* **1** of low birth; of the common people. **2** uncultured. **3** coarse; ignoble. □□ **plebeianism** *n.* [L *plebeius* f. *plebs plebis* the common people]
■ *n.* proletarian, common man *or* woman, commoner, *colloq.* usu. *derog.* pleb, prole. ● *adj.* **1** proletarian, working-class, blue-collar, lower-class, lowly, lowborn, mean, humble, *derog.* common. **2** unrefined, uncultured, uncultivated, lowbrow, unpolished, provincial, rustic, popular, commonplace, undistinguished. **3** uncouth, crass, coarse, vulgar, ignoble, brutish, barbaric, philistine.

plebiscite /plébisīt, -sit/ *n.* **1** the direct vote of all the electors of a nation, etc., on an important public question, e.g., a change in the constitution. **2** the public expression of a community's opinion, with or without binding force. **3** *Rom.Hist.* a law enacted by the plebeians' assembly. □□ **plebiscitary** /pləbísiteree, plebisít-/ *adj.* [F *plébiscite* f. L *plebiscitum* f. *plebs plebis* the common people + *scitum* decree f. *sciscere* vote for]
■ **2** popular vote *or* ballot, referendum, poll.

plectrum /pléktrəm/ *n.* (*pl.* **plectrums** or **plectra** /-trə/) **1** a thin flat piece of plastic or horn, etc., held in the hand and used to pluck a string, esp. of a guitar. **2** the corresponding mechanical part of a harpsichord, etc. [L f. Gk *plēktron* f. *plēssō* strike]

pled *past* of PLEAD.

pledge /plej/ *n. & v.* ● *n.* **1** a solemn promise or undertaking. **2** a thing given as security for the fulfillment of a contract, the payment of a debt, etc., and liable to forfeiture in the event of failure. **3** a thing put in pawn. **4** a thing given as a token of love, favor, or something to come. **5** the drinking of a person's health; a toast. **6** a solemn undertaking to abstain from alcohol (*sign the pledge*). **7** a person who has promised to join a fraternity or sorority. ● *v.tr.* **1 a** deposit as security. **b** pawn. **2** promise solemnly by the pledge of (one's honor, word, etc.). **3** (often *refl.*) bind by a solemn promise. **4** drink to the health of. □ **pledge one's troth** see TROTH. □□ **pledgeable** *adj.* **pledger** *n.* **pledgor** *n.* [ME *plege* f. OF *plege* f. LL *plebium* f. *plebire* assure]
■ *n.* **1** promise, oath, vow, word (of honor), covenant, bond, agreement, assurance, guaranty, guarantee. **2** gage, bond, guaranty, guarantee; collateral, security, earnest, surety. **5** salutation, toast, tribute, health. ● *v.* **1** deposit, pawn, *archaic* gage, *colloq.* hock. **2** swear, vow, promise, undertake, *archaic* plight, vouch. **3** see BIND *v.* 5. **4** salute, toast, drink to; drink a person's health.

pledgee /plejée/ *n.* a person to whom a pledge is given.

pledget /pléjit/ *n.* a small wad of lint, cotton, etc., used as a bandage or compress. [16th c.: orig. unkn.]

pleiad /pléeəd, pláy-/ *n.* a brilliant group of (usu. seven) persons or things. [named after PLEIADES]

Pleiades /pléeədeez, pláy-/ *n.pl.* a cluster of six visible stars in the constellation Taurus, usu. known as the Seven Sisters after seven sisters in Greek mythology. [ME f. L *Pleïas* f. Gk *Pleïas -ados*]

Pleistocene /plístəseen/ *adj. & n. Geol.* ● *adj.* of or relating to the first epoch of the Quaternary period marked by great fluctuations in temperature with glacial periods followed by interglacial periods. ● *n.* this epoch or system. Also called *Ice Age.* ¶ Cf. Appendix VII. [Gk *pleistos* most + *kainos* new]

plenary /pléenəree, plén-/ *adj.* **1** entire; unqualified; absolute (*plenary indulgence*). **2** (of an assembly) to be attended by all members. [LL *plenarius* f. *plenus* full]
■ **1** see FULL[1] *adj.* 3, 6.

plenipotentiary /plénipəténshəree, -shee-eree/ *n.* & *adj.*
● *n.* (*pl.* **-ies**) a person (esp. a diplomat) invested with the full power of independent action. ● *adj.* **1** having this power. **2** (of power) absolute. [med.L *plenipotentiarius* f. *plenus* full + *potentia* power]
■ *n.* see AMBASSADOR.

plenitude /plénitŏŏd, -tyŏŏd/ *n.* **1** fullness; completeness. **2** abundance. [ME f. OF f. LL *plenitudo* f. *plenus* full]
■ **2** see ABUNDANCE 1.

plenteous /plénteeəs/ *adj.* plentiful. □□ **plenteously** *adv.* **plenteousness** *n.* [ME f. OF *plentivous* f. *plentif -ive* f. *plenté* PLENTY: cf. *bounteous*]
■ see PLENTIFUL. □□ **plenteousness** see PLENTY *n.* 2.

plentiful /pléntifŏŏl/ *adj.* abundant; copious. □□ **plentifully** *adv.* **plentifulness** *n.*
■ ample, abundant, profuse, copious, lavish, bountiful, generous, fruitful, productive, bumper, luxuriant, thriving, prolific, *poet.* bounteous, plenteous.

plenty /pléntee/ *n.*, *adj.*, & *adv.* ● *n.* **1** (often foll. by *of*) a great or sufficient quantity or number (*we have plenty*; *plenty of time*). **2** abundance (*in great plenty*). ● *adj. colloq.* existing in an ample quantity. ● *adv. colloq.* fully; entirely (*it is plenty large enough*). [ME *plenteth, plente* f. OF *plentet* f. L *plenitas -tatis* f. *plenus* full]
■ *n.* **1** see LOT *n.* 1. **2** plentifulness, copiousness, abundance, wealth, profusion, lavishness, prodigality, bountifulness, *literary* plenitude, *poet.* plenteousness.

plenum /pléenəm, plénəm/ *n.* **1** a full assembly of people or a committee, etc. **2** *Physics* space filled with matter. [L, neut. of *plenus* full]

pleochroic /plee͞əkró͞ik/ *adj.* showing different colors when viewed in different directions. □□ **pleochroism** *n.* [Gk *pleiōn* more + -*khroos* f. *khrōs* color]

pleomorphism /plee͞əmáwrfizəm/ *n. Biol.*, *Chem.*, & *Mineral.* the occurrence of more than one distinct form. □□ **pleomorphic** *adj.* [Gk *pleiōn* more + *morphē* form]

pleonasm /plee͞ənazəm/ *n.* the use of more words than are needed to give the sense (e.g., *see with one's eyes*). □□ **pleonastic** /-nástik/ *adj.* **pleonastically** *adv.* [LL *pleonasmus* f. Gk *pleonasmos* f. *pleonazō* be superfluous]
■ see TAUTOLOGY. □□ **pleonastic** see REPETITIOUS.

plesiosaurus /plee͞seeəsáwrəs/ *n.* (also **plesiosaur** /-sawr/) any of a group of extinct marine reptiles with a broad flat body, short tail, long flexible neck, and large paddle-like limbs. [mod.L f. Gk *plēsios* near + *sauros* lizard]

plessor var. of PLEXOR.

plethora /pléthərə/ *n.* **1** an oversupply, glut, or excess. **2** *Med.* **a** an abnormal excess of red corpuscles in the blood. **b** an excess of any body fluid. □□ **plethoric** /plətháwrik, -thór-/ *adj.* **plethorically** *adv.* [LL f. Gk *plēthōrē* f. *plēthō* be full]
■ **1** see EXCESS *n.* 1.

pleura[1] /plŏŏrə/ *n.* (*pl.* **pleurae** /-ree/) **1** each of a pair of serous membranes lining the thorax and enveloping the lungs in mammals. **2** lateral extensions of the body wall in arthropods. □□ **pleural** *adj.* [med.L f. Gk, = side of the body, rib]

pleura[2] *pl.* of PLEURON.

pleurisy /plŏŏrisee/ *n.* inflammation of the pleura, marked by pain in the chest or side, fever, etc. □□ **pleuritic** /-rítik/ *adj.* [ME f. OF *pleurisie* f. LL *pleurisis* alt. f. L *pleuritis* f. Gk (as PLEURA[1])]

pleuro- /plŏŏrō/ *comb. form* **1** denoting the pleura. **2** denoting the side.

pleuron /plŏŏron/ *n.* (*pl.* **pleura** /-rə/) = PLEURA[1] 2. [Gk, = side of the body, rib]

pleuropneumonia /plŏŏrōnŏŏmónyə, -nyŏŏ-/ *n.* pneumonia complicated with pleurisy.

Plexiglas /pléksiglas/ *n. propr.* tough, clear thermoplastic used instead of glass. [formed as PLEXOR + GLASS]

plexor /pléksər/ *n.* (also **plessor** /plésər/) *Med.* a small hammer used to test reflexes and in percussing. [irreg. f. Gk *plēxis* percussion + -OR[1]]

plexus /pléksəs/ *n.* (*pl.* same or **plexuses**) **1** *Anat.* a network of nerves or vessels in an animal body (*gastric plexus*). **2** any

network or weblike formation. □□ **plexiform** *adj.* [L f. *plectere plex-* braid]
■ **2** see NETWORK *n.* 2.

pliable /plíəbəl/ *adj.* **1** bending easily; supple. **2** yielding; compliant. □□ **pliability** *n.* **pliableness** *n.* **pliably** *adv.* [F f. *plier* bend: see PLY[1]]
■ **1** flexible, pliant, elastic, plastic, malleable, workable, bendable, ductile, *colloq.* bendy; supple, lithe, limber. **2** tractable, adaptable, flexible, pliant, yielding, compliant, persuadable, persuasible, impressionable, susceptible, responsive, receptive, manageable.

pliant /plíənt/ *adj.* = PLIABLE 1. □□ **pliancy** *n.* **pliantly** *adv.* [ME f. OF (as PLIABLE)]

plicate /plíkayt/ *adj. Biol.* & *Geol.* folded; crumpled; corrugated. □□ **plicated** *adj.* [L *plicatus* past part. of *plicare* fold]

plication /plikáyshən/ *n.* **1** the act of folding. **2** a fold; a folded condition. [ME f. med.L *plicatio* or L *plicare* fold, after *complication*]

plié /plee-áy/ *n. Ballet* a bending of the knees with the feet on the ground. [F, past part. of *plier* bend: see PLY[1]]

pliers /plíərz/ *n.pl.* pincers with parallel flat usu. serrated surfaces for holding small objects, bending wire, etc. [(dial.) *ply* bend (as PLIABLE)]

plight[1] /plit/ *n.* a condition or state, esp. an unfortunate one. [ME & AF *plit* = OF *pleit* fold: see PLAIT: -*gh*- by confusion with PLIGHT[2]]
■ condition, state, circumstances, situation, case; difficulty, predicament, quandary, trouble, extremity; mess, bind, *colloq.* hole, jam, pickle, spot, scrape, fix, *disp.* dilemma.

plight[2] /plit/ *v.* & *n. archaic* ● *v.tr.* **1** pledge or promise solemnly (one's faith, loyalty, etc.). **2** (foll. by *to*) engage, esp. in marriage. ● *n.* an engagement or act of pledging. □ **plight one's troth** see TROTH. [orig. as noun, f. OE *pliht* danger f. Gmc]

plimsoll /plímsəl, -sōl/ *n.* (also **plimsole**) *Brit.* a kind of sneaker with a canvas upper. [prob. from the resemblance of the side of the sole to a PLIMSOLL LINE]

Plimsoll line /plímsəl, -sōl/ *n.* (also **Plimsoll mark**) a marking on a ship's side showing the limit of legal submersion under various conditions. [S. *Plimsoll*, Engl. politician d. 1898]

plinth /plinth/ *n.* **1** the lower square slab at the base of a column. **2** a base supporting a vase or statue, etc. [F *plinthe* or L *plinthus* f. Gk *plinthos* tile, brick, squared stone]
■ see PEDESTAL *n.*

Pliocene /plíəseen/ *adj.* & *n. Geol.* ● *adj.* of or relating to the last epoch of the Tertiary period with evidence of the extinction of many mammals, and the development of hominids. ● *n.* this epoch or system. ¶ Cf. Appendix VII. [Gk *pleiōn* more + *kainos* new]

plissé /pleesáy, pli-/ *adj.* & *n.* ● *adj.* (of cloth, etc.) treated so as to cause permanent puckering. ● *n.* material treated in this way. [F, past part. of *plisser* pleat]

PLO *abbr.* Palestine Liberation Organization.

plod /plod/ *v.* & *n.* ● *v.* (**plodded, plodding**) **1** *intr.* (often foll. by *along, on*, etc.) walk doggedly or laboriously; trudge. **2** *intr.* (often foll. by *at*) work slowly and steadily. **3** *tr.* tread or make (one's way) laboriously. ● *n.* the act or a spell of plodding. □□ **plodder** *n.* **ploddingly** *adv.* [16th c.: prob. imit.]
■ *v.* **1** trudge, tramp, lumber, labor, *colloq.* galumph. **2** labor, work, drudge, toil, slave (away), grind (away), grub (on *or* along), peg away (at), *colloq.* plug (along *or* away), *archaic* moil.

-ploid /ployd/ *comb. form Biol.* forming adjectives denoting the number of sets of chromosomes in a cell (*diploid*; *polyploid*). [after HAPLOID]

/. . ./ **pronunciation**	● **part of speech**
□ **phrases, idioms, and compounds**	
□□ **derivatives**	■ **synonym section**
cross-references appear in SMALL CAPITALS or *italics*	

ploidy /plóydee/ *n.* the number of sets of chromosomes in a cell. [after DIPLOIDY, *polyploidy*, etc.]

plonk[1] var. of PLUNK.

plonk[2] /plongk/ *n.* esp. *Brit. colloq.* cheap or inferior wine. [orig. Austral.: prob. corrupt. of *blanc* in F *vin blanc* white wine]

plonker /plóngkər/ *n. coarse Brit. sl.* a stupid person.

plonko /plóngkō/ *n.* (*pl.* -os) *Austral. sl.* an excessive drinker of cheap wine; an alcoholic.

plop /plop/ *n., v.,* & *adv.* • *n.* **1** a sound as of a smooth object dropping into water without a splash. **2** an act of falling with this sound. • *v.* (**plopped, plopping**) *intr.* & *tr.* fall or drop with a plop. • *adv.* with a plop. [19th c.: imit.]
■ *v.* see PLUMP[2] *v.* 1.

plosion /plốzhən/ *n. Phonet.* the sudden release of breath in the pronunciation of a stop consonant. [EXPLOSION]

plosive /plốsiv/ *adj.* & *n. Phonet.* • *adj.* pronounced with a sudden release of breath. • *n.* a plosive sound. [EXPLOSIVE]

plot /plot/ *n.* & *v.* • *n.* **1** a defined and usu. small piece of ground. **2** the interrelationship of the main events in a play, novel, movie, etc. **3** a conspiracy or secret plan, esp. to achieve an unlawful end. **4** a graph or diagram. **5** a graph showing the relation between two variables. • *v.* (**plotted, plotting**) *tr.* **1** make a plan or map of (an existing object, a place or thing to be laid out, constructed, etc.). **2** (also *absol.*) plan or contrive secretly (a crime, conspiracy, etc.). **3** mark (a point or course, etc.) on a chart or diagram. **4 a** mark out or allocate (points) on a graph. **b** make (a curve, etc.) by marking out a number of points. □□ **plotless** *adj.* **plotlessness** *n.* **plotter** *n.* [OE and f. OF *complot* secret plan: both of unkn. orig.]
■ *n.* **1** patch, tract, acreage, area, allotment, lot, plat. **2** story, story line, scenario. **3** scheme, plan, intrigue, machination, cabal, conspiracy, stratagem. **4** chart, diagram, graph; table, tabulation. • *v.* **1, 3** draw, plan, map (out); diagram, lay down, outline, represent, figure, chart; mark, indicate, designate, label. **2** scheme, plan, intrigue, machinate, cabal, collude, conspire, hatch, devise, design, arrange, organize, concoct, dream up, conceive, *colloq.* cook up.

plough esp. *Brit.* var. of **plow**. □ **the Plough** *Brit.* = *Big Dipper*. **Plough Monday** *Brit.* the first Monday after the Epiphany.

ploughman's lunch *Brit.* a meal of bread and cheese with pickle or salad.

plover /plúvər, plố-/ *n.* any plump-breasted shorebird of the family Charadriidae, including the lapwing, sandpiper, etc., usu. having a short bill. [ME & AF f. OF *plo(u)vier* ult. f. L *pluvia* rain]

plow /plow/ *n.* & *v.* (also *Brit.* **plough**) • *n.* **1** an implement with a cutting blade fixed in a frame drawn by a tractor or by horses, for cutting furrows in the soil and turning it up. **2** an implement resembling this and having a comparable function (*snowplow*). **3** plowed land. • *v.* **1** *tr.* (also *absol.*) turn up (the earth) with a plow, esp. before sowing. **2** *tr.* (foll. by *out, up, down,* etc.) turn or extract (roots, weeds, etc.) with a plow. **3 a** *tr.* furrow, or scratch (a surface) as if with a plow. **b** move through or break the surface of (water). **4** *tr.* produce (a furrow, line, or wake) in this way. **5** *intr.* (foll. by *through*) advance laboriously, esp. through work, a book, etc. **6** *intr.* (foll. by *through, into*) move like a plow steadily or violently. **7** (**plough**) *intr.* & *tr. Brit. colloq.* fail in an examination. □ **plow back 1** plow (grass, etc.) into the soil to enrich it. **2** reinvest (profits) in the business producing them. **put one's hand to the plow** undertake a task (Luke 9:62). □□ **plowable** *adj.* **plower** *n.* [OE *plōh* f. ON *plógr* f. Gmc]
■ *v.* **1** till, cultivate, furrow, harrow, rib. **5** see PROCEED 1. **6** drive, plunge, push, career, bulldoze, lunge, dive, lurch, hurtle, crash. **7** see FAIL *v.* 1, 2a.

plowman /plówmən/ *n.* (also *Brit.* **ploughman**) (*pl.* **-men**) a person who uses a plow.

plowshare /plówshair/ *n.* the cutting blade of a plow.

ploy /ploy/ *n. colloq.* a stratagem; a cunning maneuver to gain an advantage. [orig. Sc., 18th c.: orig. unkn.]

■ see STRATAGEM 1.

pluck /pluk/ *v.* & *n.* • *v.* **1** *tr.* (often foll. by *out, off,* etc.) remove by picking or pulling out or away. **2** *tr.* strip (a bird) of feathers. **3** *tr.* pull at; twitch. **4** *intr.* (foll. by *at*) tug or snatch at. **5** *tr.* sound (the string of a musical instrument) with the finger or plectrum, etc. **6** *tr.* plunder. **7** *tr.* swindle. • *n.* **1** courage; spirit. **2** an act of plucking; a twitch. **3** the heart, liver, and lungs of an animal as food. □ **pluck up** summon up (one's courage, spirits, etc.). □□ **plucker** *n.* **pluckless** *adj.* [OE *ploccian, pluccian,* f. Gmc]
■ *v.* **1** pick; snatch, grab, yank off, tear (off *or* away); (*pluck out*) remove, withdraw, draw out, extract, pull *or* take out. **3, 4** tug (at), pull (at), catch (at), clutch (at), jerk, twitch, snatch, *colloq.* yank. **6** see PLUNDER *v.* 2. **7** see SWINDLE *v.* • *n.* **1** courage, spirit, bravery, boldness, intrepidity, backbone, mettle, determination, gameness, resolve, resolution, steadfastness, hardiness, sturdiness, stoutheartedness, stoutness, fortitude, manfulness, nerve, *colloq.* gumption, guts, spunk, grit, sand, *sl.* moxie. □ **pluck up** see *summon up.*

plucky /plúkee/ *adj.* (**pluckier, pluckiest**) brave; spirited. □□ **pluckily** *adv.* **pluckiness** *n.*
■ see BRAVE *adj.* 1.

plug /plug/ *n.* & *v.* • *n.* **1** a piece of solid material fitting tightly into a hole, used to fill a gap or cavity or act as a wedge or stopper. **2 a** a device of metal pins in an insulated casing fitting into holes in a socket for making an electrical connection, esp. between an appliance and a power supply. **b** *colloq.* an electric socket. **3** = *spark plug* (see SPARK[1]). **4** *colloq.* a piece of (often free) publicity for an idea, product, etc. **5** a mass of solidified lava filling the neck of a volcano. **6** a cake or stick of tobacco; a piece of this for chewing. **7** = FIREPLUG. • *v.* (**plugged, plugging**) **1** *tr.* (often foll. by *up*) stop up (a hole, etc.) with a plug. **2** *tr. sl.* shoot or hit (a person, etc.). **3** *tr. colloq.* seek to popularize (an idea, product, etc.) by constant recommendation. **4** *intr. colloq.* (often foll. by *at*) work steadily away (at). □ **plug away (at)** work steadily (at). **plug in** connect electrically by inserting a plug in a socket. **plug-in** *adj.* able to be connected by means of a plug. **plug into** connect with, as by means of a plug. **plug-ugly** *sl. n.* (*pl.* **-ies**) a thug or ruffian. • *adj.* villainous-looking. □□ **plugger** *n.* [MDu. & MLG *plugge,* of unkn. orig.]
■ *n.* **1** stopper, stopple, bung, cork. **4** mention, promotion, recommendation, puff; advertisement, *colloq.* promo, *Brit. colloq.* advert; (*plugs*) publicity, *sl.* hype. **6** chew, twist, quid, pigtail. • *v.* **1** stop (up), close (up *or* off), seal (off *or up*), cork, stopper, stopple, bung, block (up *or* off), dam (up). **2** see SHOOT *v.* 1c. **3** publicize, mention, promote, beat the drum for, push, advertise, puff, commend, *colloq.* boost. **4** see PLOD *v.* 2. □ **plug-ugly** (*n.*) see THUG.

plugola /plugốlə/ *n. colloq.* **1** a bribe offered in return for incidental or surreptitious promotion of a person or product, esp. on radio or television. **2** the practice of such bribery. [PLUG + *-ola,* prob. after PAYOLA]

plum /plum/ *n.* **1 a** an oval fleshy fruit, usu. purple or yellow when ripe, with sweet pulp and a flattish pointed stone. **b** any deciduous tree of the genus *Prunus* bearing this. **2** a reddish-purple color. **3** a dried grape or raisin used in cooking. **4** *colloq.* the best of a collection; something especially prized (often *attrib.: a plum job*). □ **plum cake** esp. *Brit.* a cake containing raisins, currants, etc. **plum duff** *Brit.* a plain flour pudding with raisins or currants. **plum pudding** a rich boiled or steamed pudding with raisins, currants, spices, etc. [OE *plūme* f. med.L *pruna* f. L *prunum*]
■ **4** find, catch, coup, prize, treasure; (*attrib.*) prized, esteemed, favored, *often joc.* pet.

plumage /plōomij/ *n.* a bird's feathers. □□ **plumaged** *adj.* (usu. in *comb.*). [ME f. OF (as PLUME)]

plumb[1] /plum/ *n., adv., adj.,* & *v.* • *n.* a ball of lead or other heavy material, esp. one attached to the end of a line for finding the depth of water or determining the vertical on an upright surface. • *adv.* **1** exactly (*plumb in the center*). **2** vertically. **3** *sl.* quite; utterly (*plumb crazy*). • *adj.* **1** vertical.

2 downright; sheer (*plumb nonsense*). **3** *Cricket* (of the wicket) level; true. ● *v.tr.* **1 a** measure the depth of (water) with a plumb. **b** determine (a depth). **2** test (an upright surface) to determine the vertical. **3** reach or experience in extremes (*plumb the depths of fear*). **4** learn in detail the facts about (a matter). □ **out of plumb** not vertical. **plumb line** a line with a plumb attached. **plumb rule** a plumb line attached to a board for determining the vertical. [ME, prob. ult. f. L *plumbum* lead, assim. to OF *plomb* lead]

■ *n.* weight, bob, plummet, sinker. ● *adv.* **1** exactly, precisely, dead, right, directly, slap, *colloq.* (slam)bang. **2** vertically, perpendicularly, straight up and down. **3** see DOWNRIGHT *adv.* ● *adj.* **1** see PERPENDICULAR 2. **2** see ABSOLUTE *adj.* 1. ● *v.* **1** sound, fathom, probe; measure, gauge, test; determine. **3** reach, experience, go through, go into, explore, probe, delve into, penetrate; see also TASTE *v.* 4.

plumb² /plum/ *v.* **1** *tr.* provide (a building or room, etc.) with plumbing. **2** *tr.* (often foll. by *in*) fit as part of a plumbing system. **3** *intr.* work as a plumber. [back-form. f. PLUMBER]

plumbago /plumbáygō/ *n.* (*pl.* **-os**) **1** = GRAPHITE. **2** any plant of the genus *Plumbago*, with gray or blue flowers. Also called LEADWORT. [L f. *plumbum* LEAD²]

plumbeous /plúmbeeəs/ *adj.* **1** of or like lead. **2** lead-glazed. [L *plumbeus* f. *plumbum* LEAD²]

plumber /plúmər/ *n.* a person who fits and repairs the apparatus of a water supply system. [ME *plummer*, etc. f. OF *plommier* f. L *plumbarius* f. *plumbum* LEAD²]

plumbic /plúmbik/ *adj.* **1** *Chem.* containing lead esp. in its tetravalent form. **2** *Med.* due to the presence of lead. □□ **plumbism** *n.* (in sense 2). [L *plumbum* lead]

plumbing /plúming/ *n.* **1** the system or apparatus of water supply, heating, etc., in a building. **2** the work of a plumber. **3** *colloq.* any system of tubes, vessels, etc., that carry fluids.

plumbless /plúmlis/ *adj.* (of a depth of water, etc.) that cannot be plumbed.

plumbous /plúmbəs/ *n. Chem.* containing lead in its divalent form.

plume /ploom/ *n. & v.* ● *n.* **1** a feather, esp. a large one used for ornament. **2** an ornament of feathers, etc., attached to a helmet or hat or worn in the hair. **3** something resembling this (*a plume of smoke*). **4** *Zool.* a feather-like part or formation. ● *v.* **1** *tr.* decorate or provide with a plume or plumes. **2** *refl.* (foll. by *on, upon*) pride (oneself on esp. something trivial). **3** *tr.* (of a bird) preen (itself or its feathers). □□ **plumeless** *adj.* **plumelike** *adj.* **plumery** *n.* [ME f. OF f. L *pluma* down]

■ *v.* **3** see PREEN 1.

plummet /plúmit/ *n. & v.* ● *n.* **1** a plumb or plumb line. **2** a sounding line. **3** a weight attached to a fishing line to keep the float upright. ● *v.intr.* (**plummeted, plummeting**) fall or plunge rapidly. [ME f. OF *plommet* dimin. (as PLUMB¹)]

■ *v.* see PLUNGE *v.* 1b.

plummy /plúmee/ *adj.* (**plummier, plummiest**) **1** abounding in or rich in plums. **2** *colloq.* **a** (of a voice) sounding affectedly rich or deep in tone. **b** snobbish. **3** *colloq.* good; desirable.

■ **3** see DESIRABLE 1.

plumose /ploomōs/ *adj.* **1** feathered. **2** feather-like. [L *plumosus* (as PLUME)]

plump¹ /plump/ *adj. & v.* ● *adj.* (esp. of a person or animal or part of the body) having a full rounded shape; fleshy; filled out. ● *v.tr. & intr.* (often foll. by *up, out*) make or become plump; fatten. □□ **plumpish** *adj.* **plumply** *adv.* **plumpness** *n.* **plumpy** *adj.* [ME *plompe* f. MDu. *plomp* blunt, MLG *plump, plomp* shapeless, etc.]

■ *adj.* plump, chubby, stout, fleshy, full-bodied, portly, tubby, rotund, round, squat, chunky, buxom, corpulent, roly-poly, hippy, beefy, fat, overweight, pudgy, esp. *Brit.* podgy, *colloq.* well-covered, porky, *Austral. colloq.* poddy, *joc.* well-upholstered. ● *v.* puff up *or* out; fatten, fill out; see also PAD¹ *v.* 2.

plump² /plump/ *v., n., adv., & adj.* ● *v.* **1** *intr. & tr.* (often foll. by *down*) drop or fall abruptly (*plumped down on the*

chair; *plumped it on the floor*). **2** *intr.* (foll. by *for*) decide definitely in favor of (one of two or more possibilities). **3** *tr.* (often foll. by *out*) utter abruptly; blurt out. ● *n.* an abrupt plunge; a heavy fall. ● *adv. colloq.* **1** with a sudden or heavy fall. **2** directly; bluntly (*I told him plump*). ● *adj. colloq.* direct; unqualified (*answered with a plump 'no'*). [ME f. MLG *plumpen*, MDu. *plompen*: orig. imit.]

■ *v.* **1** drop, plummet, fall, plunge, dive, sink, collapse, flop (down); deposit, set *or* put (down), plonk, plop, dump. **2** (*plump for*) go for, opt for, choose, select, pick (out), settle on, pitch on; back, favor, side with, campaign for. **3** see BLURT. ● *n.* plunge, fall, drop, plonk, flop, thump, clunk, clump, thud, bump, clonk. ● *adv.* **2** abruptly, suddenly, directly, at once, unexpectedly, without warning, bang; see also STRAIGHT *adv.* 1. ● *adj.* direct, unequivocal, unqualified, unmistakable, unambiguous, definite, definitive, blunt, simple, plain, forthright, downright, straight.

plumule /ploomyool/ *n.* **1** the rudimentary shoot or stem of an embryo plant. **2** a down feather on a young bird. □□ **plumulaceous** /ploomyəláyshəs/ *adj.* (in sense 2). **plumular** *adj.* (in sense 1). [F *plumule* or L *plumula*, dimin. (as PLUME)]

plumy /ploomee/ *adj.* (**plumier, plumiest**) **1** plumelike; feathery. **2** adorned with plumes.

plunder /plúndər/ *v. & n.* ● *v.tr.* **1** rob (a place or person) forcibly of goods, e.g., as in war. **2** rob systematically. **3** (also *absol.*) steal or embezzle (goods). ● *n.* **1** the violent or dishonest acquisition of property. **2** property acquired by plundering. **3** *colloq.* profit; gain. □□ **plunderer** *n.* [LG *plündern* lit. 'rob of household goods' f. MHG *plunder* clothing, etc.]

■ *v.* **2** pillage, loot, rob, ravage, ransack, rifle (through), pirate, sack, strip, pluck, maraud, lay waste, *archaic or literary* spoil, *literary* despoil. **3** see STEAL *v.* 1. ● *n.* **1** pillage, looting, robbery, depredation, spoliation, ransacking, brigandage, piracy, banditry, *literary* despoliation, *rhet.* rapine. **2** booty, loot, spoils, takings, *Bibl. or archaic* prey, *hist.* pillage, *sl.* boodle, swag. **3** see PROFIT *n.* 2.

plunge /plunj/ *v. & n.* ● *v.* **1** (usu. foll. by *in, into*) **a** *tr.* thrust forcefully or abruptly. **b** *intr.* dive; propel oneself forcibly. **c** *intr. & tr.* enter or cause to enter a certain condition or embark on a certain course abruptly or impetuously (*they plunged into a lively discussion; the room was plunged into darkness*). **2** *tr.* immerse completely. **3** *intr.* **a** move suddenly and dramatically downward. **b** (foll. by *down, into*, etc.) move with a rush (*plunged down the stairs*). **c** diminish rapidly (*share prices have plunged*). **4** *intr.* (of a horse) start violently forward. **5** *intr.* (of a ship) pitch. **6** *intr. colloq.* gamble heavily; run into debt. ● *n.* a plunging action or movement; a dive. □ **plunging neckline** a low-cut neckline. **take the plunge** *colloq.* commit oneself to a (usu. risky) course of action. [ME f. OF *plungier* ult. f. L *plumbum* plummet]

■ *v.* **1 a** see THRUST *v.* 1. **b** descend, drop, plummet, fall (headlong); dive, pitch, nosedive, catapult *or* hurl oneself. **c** see LAUNCH¹ *v.* 1, 3, 4, 5. **2** submerge, sink; see also IMMERSE 1. **3 c** see DROP *v.* 8a. **5** see PITCH¹ *v.* 6. ● *n.* dive, nosedive, fall, pitch, drop, descent; submersion, immersion. □ **plunging neckline** décolletage, décolleté. **take the plunge** gamble, wager, bet, risk; jump in at the deep end, give it one's all, give it all one has, *colloq.* go for it, go all out, *sl.* go for broke.

plunger /plúnjər/ *n.* **1** a part of a mechanism that works with a plunging or thrusting movement. **2** a rubber cup on a handle for clearing blocked pipes by a plunging and sucking action. **3** *colloq.* a reckless gamble.

plunk /plungk/ *n. & v.* ● *n.* **1** the sound made by the sharply plucked string of a stringed instrument. **2** a heavy blow or

---

/. . ./ **pronunciation**	● **part of speech**
□ **phrases, idioms, and compounds**	
□□ **derivatives**	■ **synonym section**
cross-references appear in SMALL CAPITALS or *italics*	

thud. • *v.* **1** *intr.* & *tr.* sound or cause to sound with a plunk. **2** *tr.* hit abruptly. **3** *tr.* set down hurriedly or clumsily. **4** *tr.* (usu. foll. by *down*) set down firmly. [imit.]
■ *v.* **3, 4** see SET¹ 1, 3, 5.

pluperfect /plŏŏpɔ́rfikt/ *adj.* & *n.* Gram. • *adj.* (of a tense) denoting an action completed prior to some past point of time specified or implied, formed in English by *had* and the past participle, as: *he had gone by then*. • *n.* the pluperfect tense. [mod.L *plusperfectum* f. L *plus quam perfectum* more than perfect]

plural /plŏŏrɔl/ *adj.* & *n.* • *adj.* **1** more than one in number. **2** Gram. (of a word or form) denoting more than one, or (in languages without a dual number) more than two. • *n. Gram.* **1** a plural word or form. **2** the plural number. □□ **plurally** *adv.* [ME f. OF *plurel* f. L *pluralis* f. *plus pluris* more]

pluralism /plŏŏrɔlizɔm/ *n.* **1** holding more than one office, esp. an ecclesiastical office or benefice, at a time. **2** a form of society in which the members of minority groups maintain their independent cultural traditions. **3** *Philos.* a system that recognizes more than one ultimate principle (cf. MONISM 2). □□ **pluralist** *n.* **pluralistic** *adj.* **pluralistically** *adv.*

plurality /plŏŏrálitee/ *n.* (*pl.* **-ies**) **1** the state of being plural. **2** = PLURALISM 1. **3** a large or the greater number. **4** a majority that is not absolute. [ME f. OF *pluralité* f. LL *pluralitas* (as PLURAL)]

pluralize /plŏŏrɔliz/ *v.* **1** *tr.* & *intr.* make or become plural. **2** *tr.* express in the plural. **3** *intr.* hold more than one ecclesiastical office or benefice.

pluri- /plŏŏree/ *comb. form* several. [L *plus pluris* more, *plures* several]

plus /plus/ *prep., adj., n.,* & *conj.* • *prep.* **1** *Math.* with the addition of (*3 plus 4 equals 7*). ¶ Symbol: +. **2** (of temperature) above zero (*plus 2°C*). **3** *colloq.* with; having gained; newly possessing (*returned plus a new car*). • *adj.* **1** (after a number) at least (*fifteen plus*). **2** (after a grade, etc.) somewhat better than (*C plus*). **3** *Math.* positive. **4** having a positive electrical charge. **5** (*attrib.*) additional; extra (*plus business*). • *n.* **1** = *plus* sign. **2** *Math.* an additional or positive quantity. **3** an advantage (*experience is a definite plus*). • *conj. colloq. disp.* also; and furthermore (*they arrived late, plus they were hungry*). □ **plus fours** long wide men's knickers usu. worn for golf, etc. **plus sign** the symbol +, indicating addition or a positive value. [L, = more]
■ *prep.* **1** and, added to, increased by, with the addition of, with an increment of, (coupled) with, together with. • *adj.* **5** added, additional, supplementary, extra. • *n.* benefit, asset, advantage, addition, bonus, extra.

plush /plush/ *n.* & *adj.* • *n.* cloth of silk, cotton, etc., with a long soft nap. • *adj.* **1** made of plush. **2** plushy. □□ **plushly** *adv.* **plushness** *n.* [obs. F *pluche* contr. f. *peluche* f. OF *peluchier* f. It. *peluzzo* dimin. of *pelo* f. L *pilus* hair]
■ *adj.* **2** luxurious, costly, deluxe, palatial, lavish, rich, opulent, sumptuous, regal, elegant, swanky, *colloq.* ritzy, classy, posh, plushy, swank.

plushy /plúshee/ *adj.* (**plushier, plushiest**) *colloq.* stylish; luxurious. □□ **plushiness** *n.*
■ see STYLISH 1, LUXURIOUS 1.

plutarchy /plŏŏtaarkee/ *n.* (*pl.* **-ies**) plutocracy. [Gk *ploutos* wealth + *-arkhia* -rule]

Pluto /plŏŏtō/ *n.* the outermost known planet of the solar system. [L f. Gk *Ploutōn* god of the underworld]

plutocracy /plŏŏtókrɔsee/ *n.* (*pl.* **-ies**) **1 a** a government by the wealthy. **b** a nation governed in this way. **2** a wealthy élite or ruling class. □□ **plutocratic** /plŏŏtɔkrátik/ *adj.* **plutocratically** *adv.* [Gk *ploutokratia* f. *ploutos* wealth + -CRACY]

plutocrat /plŏŏtɔkrat/ *n.* **1** a member of a plutocracy or wealthy élite. **2** a wealthy and influential person.

pluton /plŏŏton/ *n. Geol.* a body of plutonic rock. [back-form. f. PLUTONIC]

Plutonian /plŏŏtṓneeɔn/ *adj.* **1** infernal. **2** of the infernal regions. [L *Plutonius* f. Gk *Ploutōnios* (as PLUTO)]

plutonic /plŏŏtónik/ *adj.* **1** *Geol.* (of rock) formed as igneous

rock by solidification below the surface of the earth. **2** (**Plutonic**) = PLUTONIAN. [formed as PLUTONIAN]

plutonium /plŏŏtṓneeɔm/ *n. Chem.* a dense silvery radioactive metallic transuranic element of the actinide series, used in some nuclear reactors and weapons. ¶ Symb.: **Pu**. [PLUTO (as the next planet beyond Neptune) + -IUM]

pluvial /plŏŏveeɔl/ *adj.* & *n.* • *adj.* **1** of rain; rainy. **2** *Geol.* caused by rain. • *n.* a period of prolonged rainfall. □□ **pluvious** *adj.* (in sense 1). [L *pluvialis* f. *pluvia* rain]

pluviometer /plŏŏveeómitɔr/ *n.* a rain gauge. □□ **pluviometric** /-veeɔmétrik/ *adj.* **pluviometrical** *adj.* **pluviometrically** *adv.* [L *pluvia* rain + -METER]

ply¹ /pli/ *n.* (*pl.* **-ies**) **1** a thickness or layer of certain materials, esp. wood or cloth (*three-ply*). **2** a strand of yarn or rope, etc. [ME f. F *pli* f. *plier, pleier* f. L *plicare* fold]
■ **1** layer, leaf, thickness, fold.

ply² /pli/ *v.* (**-ies, -ied**) **1** *tr.* use or wield vigorously (a tool, weapon, etc.). **2** *tr.* work steadily at (one's business or trade). **3** *tr.* (foll. by *with*) **a** supply (a person) continuously (with food, drink, etc.). **b** approach repeatedly (with questions, demands, etc.). **4 a** *intr.* (often foll. by *between*) (of a vehicle, etc.) travel regularly (to and fro between two points). **b** *tr.* work (a route) in this way. **5** *intr.* (of a taxi driver, boatman, etc.) attend regularly for custom (*ply for trade*). **6** *intr.* sail to windward. [ME *plye*, f. APPLY]

plywood /plíwŏŏd/ *n.* a strong thin board consisting of two or more layers glued and pressed together with the direction of the grain alternating.

PM *abbr.* **1** Postmaster. **2** postmortem. **3** Prime Minister.

Pm *symb. Chem.* the element promethium.

p.m. *abbr.* between noon and midnight. [L *post meridiem*]

PMS *abbr.* premenstrual syndrome.

pneumatic /nŏŏmátik, nyŏŏ-/ *adj.* & *n.* • *adj.* **1** of or relating to air or wind. **2** containing or operated by compressed air. **3** connected with or containing air cavities esp. in the bones of birds or in fish. □ **pneumatic drill** a drill driven by compressed air, for breaking up a hard surface. **pneumatic trough** a shallow container used in laboratories to collect gases in jars over the surface of water or mercury. □□ **pneumatically** *adv.* **pneumaticity** /nŏŏmɔtísitee, nyŏŏ-/ *n.* [F *pneumatique* or L *pneumaticus* f. Gk *pneumatikos* f. *pneuma* wind f. *pneō* breathe]

pneumatics /nŏŏmátiks, nyŏŏ-/ *n.pl.* (treated as *sing.*) the science of the mechanical properties of gases.

pneumato- /nŏŏmɔtō, nyŏŏ-/ *comb. form* denoting: **1** air. **2** breath. **3** spirit. [Gk f. *pneuma* (as PNEUMATIC)]

pneumatology /nŏŏmɔtólɔjee, nyŏŏ-/ *n.* **1** the branch of theology concerned with the Holy Ghost and other spiritual concepts. **2** *archaic* psychology. □□ **pneumatological** /-tɔlójikɔl/ *adj.*

pneumatophore /nŏŏmátɔfawr, nyŏŏ-, nŏŏmɔ-, nyóŏ-/ *n.* **1** the gaseous cavity of various hydrozoa, such as the Portuguese man-of-war. **2** an aerial root specialized for gaseous exchange found in various plants growing in swampy areas.

pneumo- /nŏŏmō, nyŏŏ-/ *comb. form* denoting the lungs. [abbr. of *pneumono-* f. Gk *pneumōn* lung]

pneumoconiosis /nŏŏmōkōneeósis, nyŏŏ-/ *n.* a lung disease caused by inhalation of dust or small particles. [PNEUMO- + Gk *konis* dust]

pneumogastric /nŏŏmōgástrik, nyŏŏ-/ *adj.* of or relating to the lungs and stomach.

pneumonectomy /nŏŏmɔnéktɔmee, nyŏŏ-/ *n.* (*pl.* **-ies**) *Surgery* the surgical removal of a lung or part of a lung.

pneumonia /nŏŏmṓnyɔ, nyŏŏ-/ *n.* a bacterial inflammation of one lung (**single pneumonia**) or both lungs (**double pneumonia**) causing the air sacs to fill with pus and become solid. □□ **pneumonic** /-mónik/ *adj.* [L f. Gk f. *pneumōn* lung]

pneumonitis /nŏŏmɔnítis, nyŏŏ-/ *n.* inflammation of the lungs usu. caused by a virus.

pneumothorax /nŏŏmōtháwraks, nyŏŏ-/ *n.* the presence of air or gas in the cavity between the lungs and the chest wall.

PNG *abbr.* Papua New Guinea.

PO *abbr.* **1** Post Office. **2** postal order. **3** Petty Officer.

Po *symb. Chem.* the element polonium.

po /pō/ n. (pl. **pos**) Brit. colloq. a chamber pot.

poach[1] /pōch/ v.tr. **1** cook (an egg) without its shell in or over boiling water. **2** cook (fish, etc.) by simmering in a small amount of liquid. □□ **poacher** n. [ME f. OF pochier f. poche POKE[2]]

poach[2] /pōch/ v. **1** tr. (also absol.) catch (game or fish) illegally. **2** intr. (often foll. by on) trespass or encroach (on another's property, ideas, etc.). **3** tr. appropriate illicitly or unfairly (a person, thing, idea, etc.) **4** tr. Tennis, etc., take (a shot) in one's partner's portion of the court. **5 a** tr. trample or cut up (turf) with hoofs. **b** intr. (of land) become sodden by being trampled. □□ **poacher** n. [earlier poche, perh. f. F pocher put in a pocket (as POACH[1])]

■ **3** see PIRATE v. 1.

pochard /pōchərd/ n. any duck of the genus Aythya, esp. A. ferina, the male of which has a bright reddish-brown head and neck and a gray breast. [16th c.: orig. unkn.]

pock /pok/ n. (also **pockmark**) **1** a small pus-filled spot on the skin, esp. caused by chickenpox or smallpox. **2** a mark resembling this. □ **pockmarked** bearing marks resembling or left by such spots. □□ **pocky** adj. [OE poc f. Gmc]

pocket /pókit/ n. & v. ● n. **1** a small bag sewn into or on clothing, for carrying small articles. **2** a pouchlike compartment in a suitcase, car door, etc. **3** one's financial resources (it is beyond my pocket). **4** an isolated group or area (a few pockets of resistance remain). **5 a** a cavity in the earth containing ore, esp. gold. **b** a cavity in rock, esp. filled with foreign matter. **6** a pouch at the corner or on the side of a billiard table into which balls are driven. **7** = air pocket. **8** (attrib.) **a** of a suitable size and shape for carrying in a pocket. **b** smaller than the usual size. **9** the area of a baseball mitt or glove around the center of the palm. ● v.tr. (**pocketed**, **pocketing**) **1** put into one's pocket. **2** appropriate, esp. dishonestly. **3** confine as in a pocket. **4** submit to (an injury or affront). **5** conceal or suppress (one's feelings). **6** Billiards, etc., drive (a ball) into a pocket. □ **in pocket 1** having gained in a transaction. **2** (of money) available. **in a person's pocket 1** under a person's control. **2** close to or intimate with a person. **out of pocket** having lost in a transaction. **out-of-pocket expenses** the actual outlay of cash incurred. **pocket battleship** hist. a warship armored and equipped like, but smaller than, a battleship. **pocket borough** Brit. hist. a borough in which the election of political representatives was controlled by one person or family. **pocket knife** a knife with a folding blade or blades, for carrying in the pocket. **pocket money** money for minor expenses. **pocket veto** executive veto of a legislative bill by allowing it to go unsigned. **put one's hand in one's pocket** spend or provide money. □□ **pocketable** adj. **pocketless** adj. **pockety** adj. (in sense 5 of n.). [ME f. AF poket(e) dimin. of poke POKE[2]]

■ n. **1** pouch, sack, bag. **3** see MEANS 2. **4** area, island, center, cluster, concentration, group. **5 b** pit, hollow, crater; see also CAVITY. **8 b** see SMALL adj. 1. ● v. **2** take, appropriate, keep; filch, embezzle, steal, thieve, pilfer, help oneself to, colloq. swipe, walk off or away with, rip off, lift, snaffle, formal or joc. purloin, sl. pinch, hook, snitch, Brit. sl. nick. **5** see SUPPRESS 2. □ **put one's hand in one's pocket** see PRESENT[2] v. 2.

pocketbook /pókitbook/ n. **1** a notebook. **2** a booklike case for papers or money carried in a pocket. **3** a purse or handbag. **4** a paperback or other small book. **5** economic resources.

■ **2** see WALLET. **3** see PURSE n. 1, 2.

pocketful /pókitfool/ n. (pl. **-fuls**) as much as a pocket will hold.

■ see WAD n. 3.

poco /pōkō/ adv. Mus. a little; somewhat (poco adagio). [It.]

pod /pod/ n. & v. ● n. **1** a long seed vessel esp. of a leguminous plant, e.g., a pea. **2** the cocoon of a silkworm. **3** the case surrounding grasshopper eggs. **4** a narrow-necked eel net. **5** a compartment suspended under an aircraft for equipment, etc. ● v. (**podded**, **podding**) **1** intr. bear or form pods. **2** tr. remove (peas, etc.) from pods. □ **in pod** colloq. pregnant. [back-form. f. dial. podware, podder field crops, of unkn. orig.]

■ n. **1** shell, hull, case, husk, skin, shuck.

podagra /pədágrə, pódəgrə/ n. Med. gout of the foot, esp. the big toe. □□ **podagral** adj. **podagric** adj. **podagrous** adj. [L f. Gk pous podos foot + agra seizure]

poddy /pódee/ adj., n., & v. colloq. ● adj. **1** Brit. corpulent; obese. **2** Austral. (of a calf, lamb, etc.) fed by hand. ● n. (pl. **-ies**) Austral. **1** an unbranded calf. **2** a calf fed by hand. ● v.tr. Austral. feed (a young animal) by hand. [E dial. word: f. POD + -Y[1]]

podgy Brit. var. of PUDGY.

podiatry /pədíətree/ n. Med. care and treatment of the foot. □□ **podiatrist** n. [Gk pous podos foot + iatros physician]

podium /pódeeəm/ n. (pl. **podiums** or **podia** /-deeə/) **1** a continuous projecting base or pedestal around a room or house, etc. **2** a raised platform around the arena of an amphitheater. **3** a platform or rostrum. [L f. Gk podion dimin. of pous pod- foot]

■ **2, 3** see PLATFORM 2.

podzol /pódzol, -zawl/ n. (also **podsol** /-sol, -sawl/) a soil with minerals leached from its surface layers into a lower stratum. □□ **podzolize** v.tr. & intr. [Russ. f. pod under, zola ashes]

poem /pōəm/ n. **1** a metrical composition, usu. concerned with feeling or imaginative description. **2** an elevated composition in verse or prose. **3** something with poetic qualities (a poem in stone). [F poème or L poema f. Gk poēma = poiēma f. poieō make]

■ **1** verse, lyric, rhyme, song, ode, ballad, sonnet, Gk Antiq. rhapsody, archaic poesy.

poesy /pōəzee, -see/ n. archaic **1** poetry. **2** the art or composition of poetry. [ME f. OF poesie ult. f. L poesis f. Gk poēsis = poiēsis making, poetry (as POEM)]

■ **1** poetry, verse, versification.

poet /pōit/ n. (fem. **poetess** /pōətis/) **1** a writer of poems. **2** a person possessing high powers of imagination or expression, etc. □ **poet laureate** a poet appointed to write poems for official state occasions. **Poets' Corner** part of Westminster Abbey in London where several poets are buried or commemorated. [ME f. OF poete f. L poeta f. Gk poētēs = poiētēs maker, poet (as POEM)]

■ **1** versifier, rhymester, lyricist, lyrist, rhymer, minstrel, poetaster, usu. derog. sonneteer, poet. bard.

poetaster /pōətastər/ n. a paltry or inferior poet. [mod.L (as POET): see -ASTER]

■ see POET.

poetic /pō-étik/ adj. (also **poetical** /-tikəl/) **1 a** of or like poetry or poets. **b** written in verse. **2** elevated or sublime in expression. □ **poetic justice** well-deserved unforeseen retribution or reward. **poetic license** a writer's or artist's transgression of established rules for effect. □□ **poetically** adv. [F poétique f. L poeticus f. Gk poētikos (as POET)]

■ **1 b** lyrical, lyric, metrical, rhapsodic. **2** elevated, artistic, fine, aesthetic, Parnassian; see SUBLIME adj. 1.

poeticize /pō-étisiz/ v.tr. make (a theme) poetic.

poetics /pō-étiks/ n. **1** the art of writing poetry. **2** the study of poetry and its techniques.

poetize /pōətīz/ v. **1** intr. play the poet. **2** intr. compose poetry. **3** tr. treat poetically. **4** tr. celebrate in poetry. [F poétiser (as POET)]

poetry /pōətree/ n. **1** the art or work of a poet. **2** poems collectively. **3** a poetic or tenderly pleasing quality. **4** anything compared to poetry. [ME f. med.L poetria f. L poeta POET, prob. after geometry]

■ **1, 2** verse, versification, archaic poesy.

po-faced /pō-fáyst/ adj. Brit. **1** solemn-faced; humorless. **2** smug. [20th c.: perh. f. PO, infl. by poker-faced]

■ **1** austere, dour, disapproving, severe, stern, grave,

/.../ **pronunciation**	● **part of speech**
□ **phrases, idioms, and compounds**	
□□ **derivatives**	■ **synonym section**
cross-references appear in SMALL CAPITALS or italics	

solemn, somber, humorless, grim, forbidding; expressionless, impassive, poker-faced.

pogo stick /pṓgō/ *n.* a toy consisting of a spring-loaded stick with rests for the feet, for jumping around on. [20th c.: orig. uncert.]

pogrom /pṓgrəm, pəgrúm, -gróm/ *n.* an organized massacre (orig. of Jews in Russia). [Russ., = devastation f. *gromit'* destroy]
- see MASSACRE *n.* 1.

poignant /póynyənt/ *adj.* **1** painfully sharp to the emotions or senses; deeply moving. **2** arousing sympathy. **3** sharp or pungent in taste or smell. **4** pleasantly piquant. **5** *archaic* (of words, etc.) sharp; severe. □□ **poignance** *n.* **poignancy** *n.* **poignantly** *adv.* [ME f. OF, pres. part. of *poindre* prick f. L *pungere*]
- **1, 2** distressing, upsetting, agonizing, grievous, painful, woeful, sad, sorrowful, heartrending, heartbreaking, excruciating, pathetic, pitiable, piteous, pitiful, moving, touching, stirring, emotional. **3** see PUNGENT 1. **5** keen, acute, intense, incisive, sharp, stinging, pointed, piercing, penetrating, barbed, cutting, caustic, acid, acerbic, bitter, biting, hurtful, mordant, sarcastic, sardonic, severe.

poikilotherm /póykiləthərm, póykilə-/ *n.* an organism that regulates its body temperature by behavioral means, such as basking or burrowing; a cold-blooded organism (cf. HOMEOTHERM). □□ **poikilothermal** *adj.* **poikilothermia** /-thə́rmeeə/ *n.* **poikilothermic** *adj.* **poikilothermy** *n.* [Gk *poikilos* multicolored, changeable + *thermē* heat]

poilu /pwaalṓ/ *n. hist.* a French private soldier, esp. as a nickname. [F, lit. hairy f. *poil* hair]

poinciana /póynseeánə/ *n.* any tropical tree of the genus *Poinciana*, with bright showy red flowers. [mod.L f. M. de *Poinci*, 17th-c. governor in the West Indies + *-ana* fem. suffix]

poinsettia /póynséteeə, -sétə/ *n.* a shrub, *Euphorbia pulcherrima*, with large showy scarlet or cream-colored bracts surrounding small yellow flowers. [mod.L f. J. R. *Poinsett*, Amer. diplomat d. 1851]

point /poynt/ *n. & v.* ● *n.* **1** the sharp or tapered end of a tool, weapon, pencil, etc. **2** a tip or extreme end. **3** that which in geometry has position but not magnitude, e.g., the intersection of two lines. **4** a particular place or position (*Bombay and points east*; *point of contact*). **5 a** a precise or particular moment (*at the point of death*). **b** the critical or decisive moment (*when it came to the point, he refused*). **6** a very small mark on a surface. **7 a** a dot or other punctuation mark, esp. = PERIOD. **b** a dot or small stroke used in Semitic languages to indicate vowels or distinguish consonants. **8** = *decimal point*. **9** a stage or degree in progress or increase (*abrupt to the point of rudeness*; *at that point we gave up*). **10** a level of temperature at which a change of state occurs (*freezing point*). **11** a single item; a detail or particular (*we differ on these points*; *it is a point of principle*). **12 a** a unit of scoring in games or of measuring value, etc. **b** an advantage or success in less quantifiable contexts such as an argument or discussion. **c** a unit of weight (2 mg) for diamonds. **d** a unit (of varying value) in quoting the price of stocks, etc. **e** a percentage point. **13 a** (usu. prec. by *the*) the significant or essential thing; what is actually intended or under discussion (*that was the point of the question*). **b** (usu. with *neg.* or *interrog.*; often foll. by *in*) sense or purpose; advantage or value (*saw no point in staying*). **c** (usu. prec. by *the*) a salient feature of a story, joke, remark, etc. (*don't see the point*). **14** a distinctive feature or characteristic (*it has its points*; *tact is not his good point*). **15** pungency; effectiveness (*their comments lacked point*). **16 a** each of 32 directions marked at equal distances round a compass. **b** the corresponding direction toward the horizon. **17** (usu. in *pl.*) *Brit.* a junction of two railroad lines, with a pair of linked tapering rails that can be moved laterally to allow a train to pass from one line to the other, = SWITCH *n.* 5. **18** *Brit.* = electrical outlet. **19** (usu. in *pl.*) each of a set of electrical contacts in the distributor of a motor vehicle. **20** *Cricket* **a** a fielder on the off side near the batsman. **b** this position. **21** the tip of the toe

in ballet. **22** a promontory. **23** the prong of a deer's antler. **24** the extremities of a dog, horse, etc. **25** *Printing* a unit of measurement for type bodies (in the US and UK 0.351 mm, in Europe 0.376 mm). **26** *Heraldry* any of nine particular positions on a shield used for specifying the position of charges, etc. **27** *Mil.* a small leading party of an advanced guard, or the lead soldier's position in a patrol unit. **28** *Naut.* a short piece of cord at the lower edge of a sail for tying up a reef. **29** the act or position of a dog in pointing. ● *v.* **1** (usu. foll. by *to, at*) **a** *tr.* direct or aim (a finger, weapon, etc.). **b** *intr.* direct attention in a certain direction (*pointed to the house across the road*). **2** *intr.* (foll. by *at, toward*) **a** aim or be directed to. **b** tend toward. **3** *intr.* (foll. by *to*) indicate; be evidence of (*it all points to murder*). **4** *tr.* give point or force to (words or actions). **5** *tr.* fill in or repair the joints of (brickwork) with smoothly finished mortar or cement. **6** *tr.* **a** punctuate. **b** insert points in (written Hebrew, etc.). **c** mark (Psalms, etc.) with signs for chanting. **7** *tr.* sharpen (a pencil, tool, etc.). **8** *tr.* (also *absol.*) (of a dog) indicate the presence of (game) by acting as pointer. □ **at all points** in every part or respect. **at the point of** (often foll. by verbal noun) on the verge of; about to do (the action specified). **beside the point** irrelevant or irrelevantly. **case in point** an instance that is relevant or (prec. by *the*) under consideration. **have a point** be correct or effective in one's contention. **in point** apposite; relevant. **in point of fact** see FACT. **make** (or **prove**) **a** (or **one's**) **point** establish a proposition; prove one's contention. **make a point of** (often foll. by verbal noun) insist on; treat or regard as essential. **nine points** nine tenths, i.e. nearly the whole (esp. *possession is nine points of the law*). **on** (or **upon**) **the point of** (foll. by verbal noun) about to do (the action specified). **point-blank** *adj.* **1 a** (of a shot) aimed or fired horizontally at a range very close to the target. **b** (of a distance or range) very close. **2** (of a remark, question, etc.) blunt; direct. ● *adv.* **1** at very close range. **2** directly, bluntly. **point-duty** *Brit.* the positioning of a police or traffic officer to control traffic. **point lace** thread lace made wholly with a needle. **point of honor** an action or circumstance that affects one's reputation. **point of no return** a point in a journey or enterprise at which it becomes essential or more practical to continue to the end. **point of order** a query in a debate, etc., as to whether correct procedure is being followed. **point-of-sale** (usu. *attrib.*) denoting advertising, etc., at the actual location at which goods are retailed. **point of view 1** a position from which a thing is viewed. **2** a particular way of considering a matter. **point out** (often foll. by *that* + clause) indicate; show; draw attention to. **point-to-point** a steeplechase over a marked course for horses used regularly in hunting. **point up** emphasize; show as important. **score points off** get the better of in an argument, etc. **take a person's point** esp. *Brit.* concede that a person has made a valid contention. **to the point** relevant or relevantly. **up to a point** to some extent but not completely. **win on points** *Boxing* win by scoring more points, not by a knockout. [ME f. OF *point*, *pointer* f. L *punctum* f. *pungere* *punct-* prick]
- *n.* **1** spike, spur, prong, sharp end. **2** tip, peak, apex, end. **4** place, site, position; location, locale, spot. **5 a** time, moment, instant, juncture. **6** dot, mark, speck, spot, fleck. **7, 8** dot, period, (full) stop, decimal point, esp. *Brit.* full point. **9** see STAGE *n.* 1. **11** detail, particular, item, element, aspect, facet, matter, issue, subject, question. **13 a** focus, essence, meat, pith, substance, heart, nucleus, crux, nub, core, bottom, details, *sl.* brass tacks, nitty-gritty. **b, c** purpose, intent, intention, aim, goal, object, objective, sense, thrust, drift, theme, import, implication, significance, meaning; application, applicability, relevancy, relevance, appropriateness; advantage, value. **14** attribute, characteristic, feature, aspect, trait, quality, property. **15** pungency, acuteness, sharpness, keenness; effectiveness. **22** promontory, projection, headland, cape, peninsula, bluff, ness. ● *v.* **1 a** direct, level, aim, train. **b** (*point to*) see INDICATE 1, 4. **3** (*point to*) see

SUGGEST 2. □ **at the point of** on the point of, on the verge *or* brink of, just about to. **beside the point** irrelevant, incidental, immaterial, unimportant, inconsequential. **have a point** have something. **make a point of** make an effort to, put *or* place emphasis on, go out of one's way to; emphasize, single out, stress, highlight; see also *insist on.* **point-blank** *adj.* **1 b** close, short, near. **2** direct, straight, blunt, flat, straightforward, abrupt, categorical, explicit, uncompromising, unmitigated, unalloyed, downright, outright, absolute, unreserved. ● *adv.* **2** directly, straightaway, right away, bluntly, flatly, abruptly, categorically, unqualifiedly, explicitly, uncompromisingly, unmitigatedly, outright, unreservedly, plainly, frankly, openly, candidly, straight, *colloq.* flat. **point of view 1** viewpoint, perspective, approach, position, angle, slant, orientation, outlook, stance, standpoint, vantage point. **2** opinion, view, belief, (way of) thinking, principle, doctrine, tenet. **point out** designate, call *or* direct *or* draw attention to, show, indicate, identify; bring up, mention, emphasize, stress, point up, single out. **point up** emphasize, stress, accentuate, underline, underscore, accent, spotlight. **to the point** relevant, pertinent, appropriate, fitting, apropos, germane, apt, applicable, apposite.

pointed /póyntid/ *adj.* **1** sharpened or tapering to a point. **2** (of a remark, etc.) having point; penetrating; cutting. **3** emphasized; made evident. □□ **pointedly** *adv.* **pointedness** *n.*
■ **1** sharp, barbed, spined, pointy, *Biol.* acuminate, *Bot.* & *Zool.* spiculate, mucronate. **2** piercing, cutting, sharp, pungent, keen, penetrating, trenchant, biting, barbed; see also INCISIVE 3. **3** see EXPLICIT 1.

pointer /póyntər/ *n.* **1** a thing that points, e.g., the index hand of a gauge, etc. **2** a rod for pointing to features on a map, chart, etc. **3** *colloq.* a hint, clue, or indication. **4 a** a dog of a breed that on scenting game stands rigid looking toward it. **b** this breed. **5** (in *pl.*) two stars in the Big Dipper in line with the pole star.
■ **1** indicator, arrow, hand; cursor. **3** tip, hint, clue, suggestion, recommendation, piece of advice.

pointillism /pwántilizəm, póyn-/ *n. Art* a technique of impressionist painting using tiny dots of various pure colors, which become blended in the viewer's eye. □□ **pointillist** *n.* & *adj.* **pointillistic** /-lístik/ *adj.* [F *pointillisme* f. *pointiller* mark with dots]

pointing /póynting/ *n.* **1** cement or mortar filling the joints of brickwork. **2** facing produced by this. **3** the process of producing this.

pointless /póyntlis/ *adj.* **1** without a point. **2** lacking force, purpose, or meaning. **3** (in games) without a point scored. □□ **pointlessly** *adv.* **pointlessness** *n.*
■ **2** purposeless, aimless, worthless, meaningless, futile, ineffectual, ineffective, unproductive, fruitless, useless, vain, senseless, absurd, silly, empty, hollow, *archaic* bootless.

pointsman /póyntsmən/ *n.* (*pl.* **-men**) *Brit.* **1** a railroad switchman. **2** a police officer or traffic warden on point-duty.

pointy /póyntee/ *adj.* (**pointier**, **pointiest**) having a noticeably sharp end; pointed.

poise[1] /poyz/ *n.* & *v.* ● *n.* **1** composure or self-possession of manner. **2** equilibrium; a stable state. **3** carriage (of the head, etc.). ● *v.* **1** *tr.* balance; hold suspended or supported. **2** *tr.* carry (one's head, etc., in a specified way). **3** *intr.* be balanced; hover in the air, etc. [ME f. OF *pois, peis, peser* ult. f. L *pensum* weight f. *pendere pens-* weigh]
■ *n.* **1** composure, control, self-possession, aplomb, assurance, dignity, equanimity, sangfroid, coolheadedness, imperturbability, presence of mind, coolness, calmness, serenity, *sl.* cool. **2** balance, equilibrium, equipoise, counterpoise. ● *v.* **1** balance, hold, steady, suspend; equilibrate. **3** balance, hover, hang, float.

poise[2] /poyz/ *n. Physics* a unit of dynamic viscosity, such that

a tangential force of one dyne per square centimeter causes a velocity change one centimeter per second between two parallel planes in a liquid separated by one centimeter. [J. L. M. *Poiseuille,* Fr. physician d. 1869]

poised /poyzd/ *adj.* **1** composed; self-assured. **2** (often foll. by *for,* or *to* + infin.) ready for action.
■ **1** composed, controlled, self-assured, self-possessed, self-confident, assured, dignified, coolheaded, imperturbable, unruffled, cool, reserved, calm, serene, *colloq.* unflappable, together. **2** ready, standing by, waiting, prepared, *colloq.* all set.

poison /póyzən/ *n.* & *v.* ● *n.* **1** a substance that when introduced into or absorbed by a living organism causes death or injury, esp. one that kills by rapid action even in a small quantity. **2** *colloq.* a harmful influence or principle, etc. **3** *Physics & Chem.* a substance that interferes with the normal progress of a nuclear reaction, chain reaction, catalytic reaction, etc. ● *v.tr.* **1** administer poison to (a person or animal). **2** kill or injure or infect with poison. **3** infect (air, water, etc.) with poison. **4** (esp. as **poisoned** *adj.*) treat (a weapon) with poison. **5** corrupt or pervert (a person or mind). **6** spoil or destroy (a person's pleasure, etc.). **7** render (land, etc.) foul and unfit for its purpose by a noxious application, etc. □ **poison gas** = GAS *n.* 4. **poison ivy** a N. American climbing plant, *Rhus toxicodendron,* secreting an irritant oil from its leaves. **poison oak** a bushy plant (genus *Rhus*) that secretes an irritant oil from its leaves. **poison-pen letter** an anonymous libelous or abusive letter. **poison sumac** a swamp shrub (genus *Rhus*) that secretes an irritant oil. □□ **poisoner** *n.* **poisonous** *adj.* **poisonously** *adv.* [ME f. OF *poison, poisoner* (as POTION)]
■ *n.* **1** toxin, venom, *archaic* virus, bane; mephitis, *archaic* miasma. **2** cancer, canker, virus, bad influence, blight, contagion. ● *v.* **3** defile, adulterate, envenom, infect, taint, pollute, contaminate, debase. **5** pervert, corrupt, vitiate, subvert, warp, degrade, deprave. **6** taint, destroy; see also SPOIL *v.* 1. □□ **poisonous** toxic, virulent, venomous, noxious, mephitic, pernicious, deleterious, lethal, deadly, fatal, mortal, *archaic* miasmic, *literary* nocuous; malicious, malevolent, malignant, corruptive, vicious, ugly, baleful, evil, foul.

Poisson distribution /pwaasṓN/ *n. Statistics* a discrete frequency distribution which gives the probability of events occurring in a fixed time. [S. D. *Poisson,* French mathematician d. 1840]

poke[1] /pōk/ *v.* & *n.* ● *v.* **1** (foll. by *in, up, down,* etc.) **a** *tr.* thrust or push with the hand, point of a stick, etc. **b** *intr.* be thrust forward. **2** *intr.* (foll. by *at,* etc.) make thrusts with a stick, etc. **3** *tr.* thrust the end of a finger, etc., against. **4** *tr.* (foll. by *in*) produce (a hole, etc., in a thing) by poking. **5** *tr.* thrust forward, esp. obtrusively. **6** *tr.* stir (a fire) with a poker. **7** *intr.* **a** (often foll. by *about, along, around*) move or act desultorily; putter. **b** (foll. by *about, into*) pry; search casually. **8** *tr. coarse sl.* have sexual intercourse with. **9** *tr.* (foll. by *up*) *colloq.* confine (esp. oneself) in a poky place. ● *n.* **1** the act or an instance of poking. **2** a thrust or nudge. **3** a punch; a jab. **4 a** a projecting brim or front of a woman's bonnet or hat. **b** (in full **poke bonnet**) a bonnet having this. □ **poke fun at** ridicule; tease. **poke** (or **stick**) **one's nose into** *colloq.* pry or intrude into (esp. a person's affairs). [ME f. MDu. and MLG *poken,* of unkn. orig.]
■ *v.* **1 a** jab, prod, dig (into), stab, push, elbow, butt, shove, stick; see also PUNCH *v.* 1. **7 a** see *mess about.* **b** (*poke about*) pry, nose (about *or* around), intrude; meddle, interfere; *colloq.* snoop (about); (*poke into*) dig into, tamper with, probe into, *colloq.* poke *or* stick one's nose into. **9** (*poke oneself up*) see HIDE[1] *v.* 2. ● *n.* **2** jab, prod, dig, stab, thrust, push, nudge, jog, shove; see also PUNCH *n.* 1. □ **poke fun at** tease, ridicule, mock,

make fun of, jeer at, chaff at, taunt, guy, gibe at, twit, make sport of, laugh at, *colloq.* rib, *Brit. colloq.* send up. **poke** (or **stick**) **one's nose into** pry *or* dig *or* probe into, meddle *or* interfere in, nose around, intrude on.

poke² /pōk/ *n. dial.* a bag or sack. □ **buy a pig in a poke** see PIG. [ME f. ONF *poke, poque* = OF *poche*: cf. POUCH]

poker¹ /pṓkər/ *n.* a stiff metal rod with a handle for stirring an open fire.

poker² /pṓkər/ *n.* a card game in which bluff is used as players bet on the value of their hands. □ **poker face 1** the impassive countenance appropriate to a poker player. **2** a person with this. **poker-faced** having a poker face. [19th c.: orig. unkn.: cf. G *pochen* to brag, *Pochspiel* bragging game]
■ □ **poker-faced** serious; see also WOODEN 3b, IMPASSIVE 1b.

pokeweed /pṓkweed/ *n.* a tall hardy American plant, *Phytolacca americana*, with spikes of cream flowers and purple berries that yield emetics and purgatives. [*poke*, Algonquian word + WEED]

pokey /pṓkee/ *n. sl.* prison. [perh. f. POKY]
■ see PRISON *n.* 1.

poky /pṓkee/ *adj.* (**pokier, pokiest**) **1** (of a room, etc.) small and cramped. **2** slow. □□ **pokily** *adv.* **pokiness** *n.* [POKE¹ (in colloq. sense 'confine') + -Y¹]

Polack /pṓlok, -lak/ *n. sl. offens.* a person of Polish origin. [F *Polaque* and G *Polack* f. Pol. *Polak*]

polar /pṓlər/ *adj.* **1 a** of or near a pole of the earth or a celestial body, or of the celestial sphere. **b** (of a species or variety) living in the north polar region. **2** having magnetic polarity. **3 a** (of a molecule) having a positive charge at one end and a negative charge at the other. **b** (of a compound) having electric charges. **4** *Geom.* of or relating to a pole. **5** directly opposite in character or tendency. **6** *colloq.* (esp. of weather) very cold. □ **polar bear** a white bear, *Ursus maritimus*, of the Arctic regions. **polar body** a small cell produced from an oocyte during the formation of an ovum, which does not develop further. **polar circle** each of the circles parallel to the equator at a distance of 23° 27′ from either pole. **polar coordinates** a system by which a point can be located with reference to two angles. **polar curve** a curve related in a particular way to a given curve and to a fixed point called a *pole*. **polar distance** the angular distance of a point on a sphere from the nearest pole. **polar star** = POLESTAR. □□ **polarly** *adv.* [F *polaire* or mod.L *polaris* (as POLE²)]
■ **5** opposite, opposed, antithetical, contrary, contradictory, antipodal. **6** frigid, glacial, freezing, frozen, numbing, wintry, chilling, chilly, *colloq.* Siberian, arctic, nippy, perishing; see also ICY 1.

polari- /pṓləri/ *comb. form* polar. [mod.L *polaris* (as POLAR)]

polarimeter /pṓlərímitər/ *n.* an instrument used to measure the polarization of light or the effect of a substance on the rotation of the plane of polarized light. □□ **polarimetric** /-métrik/ *adj.* **polarimetry** *n.*

polariscope /pōláriskōp/ *n.* = POLARIMETER. □□ **polariscopic** /-skópik/ *adj.*

polarity /pəláritee/ *n.* (*pl.* **-ies**) **1** the tendency of a lodestone, magnetized bar, etc., to point with its extremities to the magnetic poles of the earth. **2** the condition of having two poles with contrary qualities. **3** the state of having two opposite tendencies, opinions, etc. **4** the electrical condition of a body (positive or negative). **5** a magnetic attraction toward an object or person.

polarize /pṓləriz/ *v.* **1** *tr.* restrict the vibrations of (a transverse wave, esp. light) to one direction. **2** *tr.* give magnetic or electric polarity to (a substance or body). **3** *tr.* reduce the voltage of (an electric cell) by the action of electrolysis products. **4** *tr. & intr.* divide into two groups of opposing opinion, etc. □□ **polarizable** *adj.* **polarization** *n.* **polarizer** *n.*

polarography /pṓlərógrəfee/ *n. Chem.* the analysis by measurement of current-voltage relationships in electrolysis between mercury electrodes. □□ **polarographic** /-ərəgráfik/ *adj.*

Polaroid /pṓləroyd/ *n. propr.* **1** material in thin plastic sheets that produces a high degree of plane polarization in light passing through it. **2 a** a type of camera with internal pro-

cessing that produces a finished print rapidly after each exposure. **b** a print made with such a camera. **3** (in *pl.*) sunglasses with lenses made from Polaroid. [POLARI- + -OID]

polder /pṓldər/ *n.* a piece of low-lying land reclaimed from the sea or a river, esp. in the Netherlands. [MDu. *polre*, Du. *polder*]

Pole /pōl/ *n.* **1** a native or national of Poland. **2** a person of Polish descent. [G f. Pol. *Polanie*, lit. field dwellers f. *pole* field]

pole¹ /pōl/ *n. & v.* ● *n.* **1** a long slender rounded piece of wood or metal, esp. with the end placed in the ground as a support, etc. **2** a wooden shaft fitted to the front of a vehicle and attached to the yokes or collars of the draft animals. **3** = PERCH¹ 3. ● *v.tr.* **1** provide with poles. **2** push or propel (a small boat) with a pole. □ **pole position** the most favorable position at the start of a race (orig. next to the inside boundary fence). **pole vault** (or *Brit.* **jump**) *n.* the sport of vaulting over a high bar with the aid of a long flexible pole held in the hands and giving extra spring. ● *v.intr.* take part in this sport. **pole-vaulter** a person who pole vaults. **under bare poles** *Naut.* with no sail set. **up the pole** *Brit. sl.* **1** crazy; eccentric. **2** in difficulty. [OE *pāl* ult. f. L *palus* stake]
■ **1** rod, stick, staff, spar, shaft, mast, upright.

pole² /pōl/ *n.* **1** (in full **north pole, south pole**) **a** each of the two points in the celestial sphere about which the stars appear to revolve. **b** each of the extremities of the axis of rotation of the earth or another body. **c** see *magnetic pole.* ¶ The spelling is *North Pole* and *South Pole* when used as geographical designations. **2** each of the two opposite points on the surface of a magnet at which magnetic forces are strongest. **3** each of two terminals (positive and negative) of an electric cell or battery, etc. **4** each of two opposed principles or ideas. **5** *Geom.* each of two points in which the axis of a circle cuts the surface of a sphere. **6** a fixed point to which others are referred. **7** *Biol.* an extremity of the main axis of any spherical or oval organ. □ **be poles apart** differ greatly, esp. in nature or opinion. □□ **poleward** *adj.* **polewards** *adj. & adv.* [ME f. L *polus* f. Gk *polos* pivot, axis, sky]
■ **4** extremity, end, limit, extreme. □ **poles apart** (very *or* completely) different, as different as chalk and cheese, worlds apart, at opposite extremes, at opposite ends of the earth; irreconcilable.

poleax /pṓlaks/ *n. & v.* ● *n.* **1** a battleax. **2** a butcher's ax. ● *v.tr.* hit or kill with or as if with a poleax. [ME *pol(l)ax, -ex* f. MDu. *pol(l)aex*, MLG *pol(l)exe* (as POLL, AX)]

polecat /pṓlkat/ *n.* **1** *US* a skunk. **2** *Brit.* a small European brownish black fetid flesh-eating mammal, *Mustela putorius*, of the weasel family. [*pole* (unexplained) + CAT]

polemic /pəlémik/ *n. & adj.* ● *n.* **1** a controversial discussion. **2** *Polit.* a verbal or written attack, esp. on a political opponent. ● *adj.* (also **polemical**) involving dispute; controversial. □□ **polemically** *adv.* **polemicist** /-misist/ *n.* **polemicize** *v.tr.* **polemize** /pólimīz/ *v.tr.* [med.L *polemicus* f. Gk *polemikos* f. *polemos* war]
■ *n.* **1** see DEBATE *n.* 1. ● *adj.* see DEBATABLE.

polemics /pəlémiks/ *n.pl.* the art or practice of controversial discussion.

polenta /pəléntə, pō-/ *n.* mush made of cornmeal, etc. [It. f. L, = pearl barley]

polestar /pṓlstar/ *n.* **1** *Astron.* a star in Ursa Minor now about 1° distant from the celestial north pole. **2 a** a thing or principle serving as a guide. **b** a center of attraction.
■ **1** North star, lodestar. **2** see GUIDE *n.* 5.

police /pəlées/ *n. & v.* ● *n.* **1** (usu. prec. by *the*) the civil force of a government, responsible for maintaining public order. **2** (as *pl.*) the members of a police force (*several hundred police*). **3** a force with similar functions of enforcing regulations (*military police; transit police*). ● *v.tr.* **1** control (a country or area) by means of police. **2** provide with police. **3** keep order in; control; monitor. □ **police constable** see CONSTABLE. **police dog** a dog, esp. a German shepherd, used in police work. **police officer** a policeman or policewoman. **police state** a totalitarian country controlled by political police supervising the citizens' activities. **police**

station the office of a local police force. [F f. med.L *politia*

POLICY[1]

■ *n.* **1, 2** the (long arm of the) law, constabulary, *Brit.* boys in blue, *colloq.* law, *hist.* Bow Street runner, *sl.* fuzz, pigs, the Man; policemen, policewomen, police officers. ● *v.* **1** patrol, guard, watch, protect; see also CONTROL *v.* 1, 2. **3** enforce, regulate, administer, oversee, control, observe, supervise, monitor. □ **police officer** officer (of the law), policeman, policewoman, gendarme, lawman, patrolman, patrolwoman, busy, finger, jack, *Brit.* (police) constable, *Brit. colloq.* bobby, *sl.* cop, shamus, fuzz, copper, flatfoot, *Austral. sl.* demon, John Hop, walloper, *Brit. archaic sl. or dial.* peeler, *sl. derog.* pig.

policeman /pəleésmən/ *n.* (*pl.* **-men**; *fem.* **policewoman**, *pl.* **-women**) a member of a police force.
■ see *police officer.*

policy[1] /pólisee/ *n.* (*pl.* **-ies**) **1** a course or principle of action adopted or proposed by a government, party, business, or individual, etc. **2** prudent conduct; sagacity. [ME f. OF *policie* f. L *politia* f. Gk *politeia* citizenship f. *politēs* citizen f. *polis* city]
■ **1** course, approach, procedure, plan, design, scheme, action, strategy, tactic(s), principle(s), program, method, system, practice, game plan. **2** see *prudence* (PRUDENT).

policy[2] /pólisee/ *n.* (*pl.* **-ies**) **1** a contract of insurance. **2** a document containing this. [F *police* bill of lading, contract of insurance, f. Prov. *poliss*(*i*)*a* prob. f. med.L *apodissa*, *apodixa*, f. L *apodixis* f. Gk *apodeixis* evidence, proof (as APO-, *deiknumi* show)]

policyholder /póliseehőldər/ *n.* a person or body holding an insurance policy.

polio /pőleeō/ *n.* = POLIOMYELITIS. [abbr.]

poliomyelitis /pőleeōmí-ilítis/ *n. Med.* an infectious viral disease that affects the central nervous system and that can cause temporary or permanent paralysis. [mod.L f. Gk *polios* gray + *muelos* marrow]

Polish /pőlish/ *adj. & n.* ● *adj.* **1** of or relating to Poland. **2** of the Poles or their language. ● *n.* the language of Poland. □ **Polish notation** *Math.* a system of formula notation without brackets and punctuation. [POLE + -ISH[1]]

polish /pólish/ *v. & n.* ● *v.* **1** *tr. & intr.* make or become smooth or glossy esp. by rubbing. **2** (esp. as **polished** *adj.*) refine or improve; add finishing touches to. ● *n.* **1** a substance used for polishing. **2** smoothness or glossiness produced by friction. **3** the act or an instance of polishing. **4** refinement or elegance of manner, conduct, etc. □ **polish off 1** finish (esp. food) quickly. **2** *colloq.* kill; murder. **polish up** revise or improve (a skill, etc.). □□ **polishable** *adj.* **polisher** *n.* [ME f. OF *polir* f. L *polire polit-*]
■ *v.* **1** shine, brighten, burnish, buff, furbish, wax, clean, gloss. **2** (**polished**) accomplished, finished, masterful, masterly, virtuoso, outstanding; flawless, faultless, perfect, impeccable; refined, elegant, cultivated, graceful, debonair, sophisticated, urbane, soigné, courtly, genteel, cultured, civilized, well-bred, well-mannered, polite. ● *n.* **1** wax, beeswax, oil. **2** gloss, shine, luster, sheen, glossiness, smoothness, glaze, brilliance, sparkle, gleam. **4** see REFINEMENT 3. □ **polish off 1** dispose of, put away, eat up, gobble (up), consume, wolf (down), *joc.* demolish. **2** see MURDER *v.* 1. **polish up** refine, improve, perfect, cultivate, enhance, *formal* ameliorate; study, review, revise, *archaic* con, *colloq.* bone up (on), *Brit. colloq.* swot up (on).

politburo /pólitbyőōrō, pəlít-/ *n.* (*pl.* **-os**) the principal policy-making committee of a Communist party, esp. in the former USSR. [Rus. *politbyuro* f. *politicheskoe byuró* political bureau]

polite /pəlít/ *adj.* (**politer**, **politest**) **1** having good manners; courteous. **2** cultivated; cultured. **3** refined; elegant (*polite letters*). □□ **politely** *adv.* **politeness** *n.* [L *politus* (as POLISH)]
■ **1** civil, respectful, well-mannered, mannerly,

courteous, diplomatic, considerate, tactful, formal, proper, cordial. **2** see *polished* (POLISH).

politesse /pólités/ *n.* formal politeness. [F f. It. *politezza*, *pulitezza* f. *pulito* polite]
■ see ETIQUETTE 1.

politic /pólitik/ *adj. & v.* ● *adj.* **1** (of an action) judicious; expedient. **2** (of a person:) **a** prudent; sagacious. **b** scheming; sly. **3** political (now only in *body politic*). ● *v.intr.* (**politicked**, **politicking**) engage in politics. □□ **politicly** *adv.* [ME f. OF *politique* f. L *politicus* f. Gk *politikos* f. *politēs* citizen f. *polis* city]
■ *adj.* **1** see JUDICIOUS. **2 a** prudent, tactful, diplomatic, discreet, judicious, wise, sage, sagacious, sensible, percipient, discriminating, farsighted, perceptive. **b** ingenious, shrewd, crafty, canny, cunning, designing, scheming, clever, sly, wily, foxy, tricky, artful, machiavellian, evasive, *colloq.* shifty, cagey.

political /pəlítikəl/ *adj.* **1 a** of or concerning government, or public affairs generally. **b** of, relating to, or engaged in politics. **c** belonging to or forming part of a civil administration. **2** having an organized form of society or government. **3** taking or belonging to a side in politics or in controversial matters. **4** relating to or affecting interests of status or authority in an organization rather than matters of principle (*a political decision*). □ **political action committee** a permanent organization that collects and distributes funds for political purposes. ¶ Abbr.: **PAC. political asylum** see ASYLUM. **political correctness** avoidance of forms of expression and action that exclude or marginalize sexual, racial, and cultural minorities; advocacy of this. **political economist** a student of or expert in political economy. **political economy** the study of the economic aspects of government. **political geography** that dealing with boundaries and the possessions of nations. **politically correct** in conformance with political correctness. **political prisoner** a person imprisoned for political beliefs or actions. **political science** the study of systems of government. **political scientist** a specialist in political science. □□ **politically** *adv.* [L *politicus* (as POLITIC)]
■ **1** governmental, state, public, national; civic, civil; administrative, bureaucratic. **3** partisan, factional, factious; active, involved, committed, militant.

politician /pólitíshən/ *n.* **1** a person engaged in or concerned with politics, esp. as a practitioner. **2** a person skilled in politics. **3** *derog.* a person with self-interested political concerns.
■ **1** legislator, lawmaker, statesman, stateswoman; minister, senator, congressman, congresswoman, representative, Member of Parliament, MP, *Austral.* polly; public servant, administrator, official, bureaucrat, officeholder; *colloq.* politico; *sl.* pol.

politicize /pəlítisiz/ *v.* **1** *tr.* **a** give a political character to. **b** make politically aware. **2** *intr.* engage in or talk politics. □□ **politicization** *n.*

politico /pəlítikō/ *n.* (*pl.* **-os**) *colloq.* a politician or political enthusiast. [Sp. or It. (as POLITIC)]
■ see POLITICIAN.

politico- /pəlítikō/ *comb. form* **1** politically. **2** political and (*politico-social*). [Gk *politikos*: see POLITIC]

politics /pólitiks/ *n.pl.* **1** (treated as *sing.* or *pl.*) **a** the art and science of government. **b** public life and affairs as involving authority and government. **2** (usu. treated as *pl.*) **a** a particular set of ideas, principles, or commitments in politics (*what are their politics?*). **b** activities concerned with the acquisition or exercise of authority or government. **c** an organizational process or principle affecting authority, status, etc. (*the politics of the decision*).
■ **1** political science, government, statecraft, diplomacy, statesmanship; public affairs *or* life, civil affairs.

/.../ **pronunciation**	● **part of speech**
□ **phrases, idioms, and compounds**	
□□ **derivatives**	■ **synonym section**
cross-references appear in SMALL CAPITALS or *italics*	

2 a belief, conviction, persuasion; see also LEANING. **b** manipulation, machination, maneuvering, wirepulling; see also GOVERNMENT 1.

polity /pólitee/ *n.* (*pl.* **-ies**) **1** a form or process of civil government or constitution. **2** an organized society; a nation as a political entity. [L *politia* f. Gk *politeia* f. *politēs* citizen f. *polis* city]
■ **2** see NATION.

polka /pólkə, pókə/ *n. & v.* ● *n.* **1** a lively dance of Bohemian origin in duple time. **2** the music for this. ● *v.intr.* (**polkas**, **polkaed** /-kəd/ or **polka'd**, **polkaing** /-kəing/) dance the polka. □ **polka dot** a round dot as one of many forming a regular pattern on a textile fabric, etc. [F and G f. Czech *půlka* half-step f. *půl* half]

poll /pōl/ *n. & v.* ● *n.* **1 a** the process of voting at an election. **b** the counting of votes at an election. **c** the result of voting. **d** the number of votes recorded (*a heavy poll*). **e** (also **polls**) place for voting. **2** = GALLUP POLL, *opinion poll*. **3 a** a human head. **b** the part of this on which hair grows (*flaxen poll*). **4** a hornless animal, esp. one of a breed of hornless cattle. ● *v.* **1** *tr.* **a** take the vote or votes of. **b** (in *passive*) have one's vote taken. **c** (of a candidate) receive (so many votes). **d** give (a vote). **2** *tr.* record the opinion of (a person or group) in an opinion poll. **3** *intr.* give one's vote. **4** *tr.* cut off the top of (a tree or plant), esp. make a pollard of. **5** *tr.* (esp. as **polled** *adj.*) cut the horns off (cattle). **6** *tr. Computing* check the status of (a computer system) at intervals. □ **poll tax 1** *hist.* a tax levied on every adult. **2** *Brit.* = *community charge*. □□ **pollee** /pōleé/ *n.* (in sense 2 of *n.*). **pollster** *n.* [ME, perh. f. LG or Du.]
■ *n.* **1 c** voting, vote, return, tally, figures, ballot, count. **2** opinion poll, survey, canvass, census. **4** pollard. ● *v.* **1 a** ballot. **c** receive, get, win, register, tally. **2** canvass, ballot, sample, survey.

pollack /pólək/ *n.* (also **pollock**) a European marine fish, *Pollachius pollachius*, with a characteristic protruding lower jaw, used for food. [earlier (Sc.) *podlock*: orig. unkn.]

pollan /pólən/ *n.* a freshwater fish, *Coregonus pollan*, found in Irish lakes. [perh. f. Ir. *poll* deep water]

pollard /pólərd/ *n. & v.* ● *n.* **1** an animal that has lost or cast its horns; an ox, sheep, or goat of a hornless breed. **2** a tree whose branches have been cut off to encourage the growth of new young branches, esp. a riverside willow. **3 a** the bran sifted from flour. **b** a fine bran containing some flour. ● *v.tr.* make (a tree) a pollard. [POLL + -ARD]

pollen /pólən/ *n.* the fine dustlike grains discharged from the male part of a flower containing the gamete that fertilizes the female ovule. □ **pollen analysis** = PALYNOLOGY. **pollen count** an index of the amount of pollen in the air, published esp. for the benefit of those allergic to it. □□ **pollenless** *adj.* **pollinic** /pəlínik/ *adj.* [L *pollen pollinis* fine flour, dust]

pollex /póleks/ *n.* (*pl.* **pollices** /-liseez/) the innermost digit of a forelimb, usu. the thumb in primates. [L, = thumb or big toe]

pollie var. of POLLY².

pollinate /pólinayt/ *v.tr.* (also *absol.*) sprinkle (a stigma) with pollen. □□ **pollination** /-náyshən/ *n.* **pollinator** *n.*
■ see FERTILIZE 2.

polling /pōling/ *n.* the registering or casting of votes. □ **polling booth** a compartment in which a voter stands to mark a paper ballot or use a voting machine. **polling day** the day of a local or general election. **polling place** a building where voting takes place during an election.

pollinic see POLLEN.

polliniferous /pólinífərəs/ *adj.* bearing or producing pollen.

polliwog /póleewog/ *n.* (also **pollywog**) *dial.* a tadpole. [earlier *polwigge*, *polwygle* f. POLL¹ + WIGGLE]

pollock var. of POLLACK.

pollute /pəlóot/ *v.tr.* **1** contaminate or defile (the environment). **2** make foul or filthy. **3** destroy the purity or sanctity of. □□ **pollutant** *adj. & n.* **polluter** *n.* **pollution** *n.* [ME f. L *polluere pollut-*]
■ **1** defile, poison; see also CONTAMINATE 1. **2** foul, soil, taint, stain, dirty, grime, *poet.* befoul, sully; see also DIRTY *v.* **3** corrupt, desecrate, profane, defile, violate.

□□ **pollution** contamination, adulteration, dirtying; vitiation, corruption, debasement; see also SACRILEGE.

polly² /pólee/ *n.* (also **pollie**) (*pl.* **-ies**) *Austral.* a politician. [abbr.]

Pollyanna /póleeánə/ *n.* a cheerful optimist; an excessively cheerful person. □□ **Pollyannaish** *adj.* **Pollyannaism** *n.* [character in a novel (1913) by E. Porter]

pollywog var. of POLLIWOG.

polo /pōlō/ *n.* a game of Asian origin played on horseback with a long-handled mallet. □ **polo-neck** *Brit.* a high round turned-over collar; a turtleneck. **polo shirt** a pullover shirt, usu. of knit fabric, with a rounded neckband or a turnover collar. **polo stick** a mallet for playing polo. [Balti, = ball]

polonaise /pólənáyz, pō-/ *n. & adj.* ● *n.* **1** a dance of Polish origin in triple time. **2** the music for this. **3** *hist.* a woman's dress consisting of a bodice and a draped skirt open from the waist downward to show an underskirt. ● *adj.* cooked in a Polish style. [F, fem. of *polonais* Polish f. med.L *Polonia* Poland]

polonium /pəlōneeəm/ *n. Chem.* a rare radioactive metallic element, occurring naturally in uranium ores. ¶ Symb.: **Po**. [F & med.L f. med.L *Polonia* Poland (the discoverer's native country) + -IUM]

poltergeist /pōltərgist/ *n.* a noisy mischievous ghost, esp. one manifesting itself by physical damage. [G f. *poltern* create a disturbance + *Geist* GHOST]
■ see GHOST *n.* 1.

poltroon /poltrōōn/ *n.* a spiritless coward. □□ **poltroonery** *n.* [F *poltron* f. It. *poltrone* perh. f. *poltro* sluggard]
■ see COWARD *n.*

poly /pólee/ *n.* (*pl.* **polys**) esp. *Brit. colloq.* polytechnic. [abbr.]

poly-¹ /pólee/ *comb. form* denoting many or much. [Gk *polu-* f. *polus* much, *polloi* many]

poly-² /pólee/ *comb. form Chem.* polymerized (*polyunsaturated*). [POLYMER]

polyadelphous /póleeədélfəs/ *adj. Bot.* having numerous stamens grouped into three or more bundles.

polyamide /póleeámīd/ *n. Chem.* any of a class of condensation polymers produced from the interaction of an amino group of one molecule and a carboxylic acid group of another, and which includes many synthetic fibers such as nylon.

polyandry /póleeandree/ *n.* **1** polygamy in which a woman has more than one husband. **2** *Bot.* the state of having numerous stamens. □□ **polyandrous** /-ándrəs/ *adj.* [POLY-¹ + andry f. Gk *anēr andros* male]

polyanthus /póleeánthəs/ *n.* (*pl.* **polyanthuses**) **1** a hybridized primrose, *Primula polyantha*. **2** a narcissus, *Narcissus tazetta*, with small white or yellow flowers. [mod.L, formed as POLY-¹ + Gk *anthos* flower]

polycarbonate /póleekaárbənayt/ *n.* any of a class of polymers in which the units are linked through a carbonate group, mainly used as molding materials.

polychaete /pólikeet/ *n.* any aquatic annelid worm of the class Polychaeta, including lugworms and ragworms, having numerous bristles on the fleshy lobes of each body segment. □□ **polychaetan** /-keét'n/ *adj.* **polychaetous** /-keétəs/ *adj.*

polychromatic /póleekrōmátik/ *adj.* **1** many-colored. **2** (of radiation) containing more than one wavelength. □□ **polychromatism** /-krōmətizəm/ *n.*
■ **1** see *variegated* (VARIEGATE).

polychrome /póleekrōm/ *adj. & n.* ● *adj.* painted, printed, or decorated in many colors. ● *n.* **1** a work of art in several colors, esp. a colored statue. **2** varied coloring. □□ **polychromic** /-krōmik/ *adj.* **polychromous** /-krōməs/ *adj.* [F f. Gk *polukhrōmos* as POLY-¹, *khrōma* color]
■ *adj.* see *variegated* (VARIEGATE).

polychromy /póleekrōmee/ *n.* the art of painting in several colors, esp. as applied to ancient pottery, architecture, etc. [F *polychromie* (as POLYCHROME)]

polyclinic /póleeklinik/ *n.* a clinic devoted to various diseases; a general hospital.

polycrystalline /póleekríst'lin, -lin, -leen/ *adj.* (of a solid substance) consisting of many crystalline parts at various orientations, e.g., a metal casting.

polycyclic /póleesíklik, -sík-/ *adj. Chem.* having more than one ring of atoms in the molecule.

polydactyl /póleedáktil/ *adj. & n.* • *adj.* (of an animal) having more than five fingers or toes. • *n.* a polydactyl animal.

polyester /pólee-éstər/ *n.* any of a group of condensation polymers used to form synthetic fibers or to make resins.

polyethene /pólee-étheen/ *n. Chem.* = POLYETHYLENE.

polyethylene /pólee-éthileen/ *n. Chem.* a tough light thermoplastic polymer of ethylene, usu. translucent and flexible or opaque and rigid, used for packaging and insulating materials. Also called POLYETHENE, POLYTHENE.

polygamous /pəlígəməs/ *adj.* **1** having more than one wife or husband at the same time. **2** having more than one mate. **3** bearing some flowers with stamens only, some with pistils only, some with both, on the same or different plants. □□ **polygamic** /póligámik/ *adj.* **polygamist** /-gəmist/ *n.* **polygamously** *adv.* [Gk *polugamos* (as POLY-¹, -*gamos* marrying)]

polygamy /pəlígəmee/ *n.* the practice of having more than one spouse at a time.

polygene /póleejeen/ *n. Biol.* each of a group of independent genes that collectively affect a characteristic.

polygenesis /póleejénisis/ *n.* the (usu. postulated) origination of a race or species from several independent stocks. □□ **polygenetic** /-jinétik/ *adj.*

polygeny /pəlíjənee/ *n.* the theory that the human species originated from several independent pairs of ancestors. □□ **polygenism** *n.* **polygenist** *n.*

polyglot /póleeglot/ *adj. & n.* • *adj.* **1** of many languages. **2** (of a person) speaking or writing several languages. **3** (of a book, esp. the Bible) with the text translated into several languages. • *n.* **1** a polyglot person. **2** a polyglot book, esp. a Bible. □□ **polyglottal** *adj.* **polyglottic** *adj.* **polyglotism** *n.* **polyglottism** *n.* [F *polyglotte* f. Gk *poluglōttos* (as POLY-¹, *glōtta* tongue)]

polygon /póleegon/ *n.* a plane figure with many (usu. a minimum of three) sides and angles. □ **polygon of forces** a polygon that represents by the length and direction of its sides all the forces acting on a body or point. □□ **polygonal** /pəlígənəl/ *adj.* [LL *polygonum* f. Gk *polugōnon* (neut. *adj.*) (as POLY-¹ + -*gōnos* angled)]

polygonum /pəlígənəm/ *n.* any plant of the genus *Polygonum*, with small bell-shaped flowers. Also called KNOTGRASS, KNOTWEED. [mod.L f. Gk *polugonon*]

polygraph /póleegraf/ *n.* a machine designed to detect and record changes in physiological characteristics (e.g., rates of pulse and breathing), used esp. as a lie-detector.

polygyny /pəlíjinee/ *n.* polygamy in which a man has more than one wife. □□ **polygynous** /pəlíjinəs/ *adj.* [POLY-¹ + *gyny* f. Gk *gunē* woman]

polyhedron /póleeheédrən/ *n.* (*pl.* **polyhedra** /-drə/) a solid figure with many (usu. more than six) faces. □□ **polyhedral** *adj.* **polyhedric** *adj.* [Gk *poluedron* neut. of *poluedros* (as POLY-¹, *hedra* base)]

polyhistor /póleehístər/ *n.* = POLYMATH.

polymath /póleemath/ *n.* **1** a person of much or varied learning. **2** a great scholar. □□ **polymathic** /-máthik/ *adj.* **polymathy** /pəlímathee/ *n.* [Gk *polumathēs* (as POLY-¹, *math*-stem *manthanō* learn)]

■ see INTELLECTUAL *n.*

polymer /pólimər/ *n.* a compound composed of one or more large molecules that are formed from repeated units of smaller molecules. □□ **polymeric** /-mérik/ *adj.* **polymerism** *n.* **polymerize** *v.intr. & tr.* **polymerization** *n.* [G f. Gk *polumeros* having many parts (as POLY-¹, *meros* share)]

polymerous /pəlímərəs/ *adj. Biol.* having many parts.

polymorphism /póleemáwrfizəm/ *n.* **1 a** *Biol.* the existence of various different forms in the successive stages of the development of an organism. **b** = PLEOMORPHISM. **2** *Chem.* = ALLOTROPY. □□ **polymorphic** *adj.* **polymorphous** *adj.*

■ □□ **polymorphic, polymorphous** see PROTEAN 1.

Polynesian /póleenéezhən/ *adj. & n.* • *adj.* of or relating to Polynesia, a group of Pacific islands including New Zealand, Hawaii, Samoa, etc. • *n.* **1 a** a native of Polynesia. **b** a

person of Polynesian descent. **2** the family of languages including Maori, Hawaiian, and Samoan. [as POLY-¹ + Gk *nēsos* island]

polyneuritis /póleenŏorítis, nyŏo-/ *n.* any disorder that affects many of the peripheral nerves. □□ **polyneuritic** /-rítik/ *adj.*

polynomial /pólinṓmeeəl/ *n. & adj. Math.* • *n.* an expression of more than two algebraic terms, esp. the sum of several terms that contain different powers of the same variable(s). • *adj.* of or being a polynomial. [POLY-¹ after *multinomial*]

polynya /pəlínyə/ *n.* a stretch of open water surrounded by ice, esp. in the Arctic seas. [Russ. f. *pole* field]

polyp /pólip/ *n.* **1** *Zool.* an individual coelenterate. **2** *Med.* a small usu. benign growth protruding from a mucous membrane. [F *polype*, ult. f. Gk *pōlupos* cuttlefish, polyp (as POLY-¹, *pous podos* foot)]

polypary /póliperee/ *n.* (*pl.* **-ies**) the common stem or support of a colony of polyps. [mod.L *polyparium* (as POLYPUS)]

polypeptide /póleepéptid/ *n. Biochem.* a peptide formed by the combination of about ten or more amino acids. [G *Polypeptid* (as POLY-², PEPTONE)]

polyphagous /pəlífəgəs/ *adj. Zool.* able to feed on various kinds of food.

polyphase /pólifayz/ *adj. Electr.* (of a device or circuit) designed to supply or use simultaneously several alternating currents of the same voltage but with different phases.

polyphone /póleefōn/ *n. Phonet.* a symbol or letter that represents several different sounds.

polyphonic /póleefónik/ *adj.* **1** *Mus.* (of vocal music, etc.) in two or more relatively independent parts; contrapuntal. **2** *Phonet.* (of a letter, etc.) representing more than one sound. □□ **polyphonically** *adv.* [Gk *poluphōnos* (as POLY-¹, *phōnē* voice, sound)]

polyphony /pəlífənee/ *n.* (*pl.* **-ies**) **1** *Mus.* **a** polyphonic style in musical composition; counterpoint. **b** a composition written in this style. **2** *Philol.* the symbolization of different vocal sounds by the same letter or character. □□ **polyphonous** *adj.*

polyploid /póleeployd/ *n. & adj. Biol.* • *n.* a nucleus or organism that contains more than two sets of chromosomes. • *adj.* of or being a polyploid. □□ **polyploidy** *n.* [G (as POLY-¹, -PLOID)]

polypod /póleepod/ *adj. & n. Zool.* • *adj.* having many feet. • *n.* a polypod animal. [F *polypode* (adj.) f. Gk (as POLYP)]

polypody /póleepōdee/ *n.* (*pl.* **-ies**) any fern of the genus *Polypodium*, usu. found in woods growing on trees, walls, and stones. [ME f. L *polypodium* f. Gk *polupodion* (as POLYP)]

polypoid /póleepoyd/ *adj.* of or like a polyp. □□ **polypous** /-pəs/ *adj.*

polypropene /póleeprṓpeen/ *n.* = POLYPROPYLENE.

polypropylene /póleeprṓpileen/ *n. Chem.* any of various polymers of propylene including thermoplastic materials used for films, fibers, or molding materials. Also called POLYPROPENE.

polysaccharide /póleesákərid/ *n.* any of a group of carbohydrates whose molecules consist of long chains of monosaccharides.

polysemy /póleeseémee, pəlísəmee/ *n. Philol.* the existence of many meanings (of a word, etc.). □□ **polysemic** /-seémik/ *adj.* **polysemous** /-seéməs, -səməs/ *adj.* [POLY-¹ + Gk *sēma* sign]

polystyrene /póleestíreen/ *n.* a thermoplastic polymer of styrene, usu. hard and colorless or expanded with a gas to produce a lightweight rigid white substance, used for insulation and in packaging.

polysyllabic /póleesilábik/ *adj.* **1** (of a word) having many syllables. **2** characterized by the use of words of many syllables. □□ **polysyllabically** *adv.*

polysyllable /póleesiləbəl/ *n.* a polysyllabic word.

polytechnic /pòleetéknik/ *n. & adj.* ● *n.* an institution of higher education offering courses in many esp. vocational or technical subjects. ● *adj.* dealing with or devoted to various vocational or technical subjects. [F *polytechnique* f. Gk *polutekhnos* (as POLY-[1] *tekhnē* art)]
 ■ *adj.* see TECHNICAL 1.

polytetrafluoroethylene /pòlitétrəflōōrō-éthileen, -fláwr-/ *n. Chem.* a tough translucent polymer resistant to chemicals and used to coat cooking utensils, etc. ¶ Abbr.: PTFE. [POLY-[2] + TETRA- + FLUORO- + ETHYLENE]

polytheism /pòleethéeizəm/ *n.* the belief in or worship of more than one god. □□ **polytheist** *n.* **polytheistic** *adj.* [F *polythéisme* f. Gk *polutheos* of many gods (as POLY-[1], *theos* god)]

polythene /pòleetheen/ *n. Brit.* = POLYETHYLENE.

polytonality /pòleetōnálitee/ *n. Mus.* the simultaneous use of two or more keys in a composition. □□ **polytonal** /-tṓnəl/ *adj.*

polyunsaturated /pòleeunsáchəraytid/ *adj. Chem.* (of a compound, esp. a fat or oil molecule) containing several double or triple bonds and therefore capable of further reaction.

polyurethane /pòleeyōōrəthayn/ *n.* any polymer containing the urethane group, used in adhesives, paints, plastics, foams, etc.

polyvalent /pòleeváylənt/ *adj. Chem.* having a valence of more than two, or several valencies. □□ **polyvalence** *n.*

polyvinyl acetate /pòleevínil/ *n. Chem.* a soft plastic polymer used in paints and adhesives. ¶ Abbr.: PVA.

polyvinyl chloride /pòleevínil/ *n.* a tough transparent solid polymer of vinyl chloride, easily colored and used for a wide variety of products including pipes, flooring, etc. ¶ Abbr.: PVC.

polyzoan /pòleezṓən/ *n.* = BRYOZOAN.

pom /pom/ *n. Brit.* a Pomeranian dog. [abbr.]

pomace /púmis, póm-/ *n.* **1** the mass of crushed apples in cider making before or after the juice is pressed out. **2** the refuse of fish, etc., after the oil has been extracted, generally used as a fertilizer. [ME f. med.L *pomacium* cider f. L *pomum* apple]

pomade /pomáyd, -máad/ *n. & v.* ● *n.* scented dressing for the hair and the skin of the head. ● *v.tr.* anoint with pomade. [F *pommade* f. It. *pomata* f. med.L f. L *pomum* apple (from which it was orig. made)]

pomander /pṓmandər, pōmán-/ *n.* **1** a ball of mixed aromatic substances placed in a cupboard, etc., or *hist.* carried in a box, bag, etc., as a protection against infection. **2** a (usu. spherical) container for this. **3** a spiced orange, etc., similarly used. [earlier *pom(e)amber* f. AF f. OF *pome d'embre* f. med.L *pomum de ambra* apple of ambergris]

pomatum /pōmáytəm, pəmáat-/ *n. & v.tr.* = POMADE. [mod.L f. L *pomum* apple]

pome /pōm/ *n.* a firm-fleshed fruit in which the carpels from the central core enclose the seeds, e.g., the apple, pear, and quince. □□ **pomiferous** /pəmífərəs/ *adj.* [ME f. OF ult. f. *poma* pl. of L *pomum* fruit, apple]

pomegranate /pómigranit, pómgranit, púm-/ *n.* **1 a** an orange-sized fruit with a tough reddish outer skin and containing many seeds in a red pulp. **b** the tree bearing this fruit, *Punica granatum*, native to N. Africa and W. Asia. **2** an ornamental representation of a pomegranate. [ME f. OF *pome grenate* (as POME, L *granatum* having many seeds f. *granum* seed)]

pomelo /póməlō/ *n.* (*pl.* **-os**) **1** = SHADDOCK. **2** = GRAPEFRUIT. [19th c.: orig. unkn.]

Pomeranian /póməráyneeən/ *n.* **1** a small dog with long silky hair, a pointed muzzle, and pricked ears. **2** this breed. [*Pomerania* in Germany and Poland]

pomfret /pómfrit, púm-/ *n.* **1** any of various fish of the family Stromateidae of the Indian and Pacific Oceans. **2** a dark-colored deep-bodied marine fish, *Brama brama*, used as food. [app. f. Port. *pampo*]

pomiculture /pómikulchər/ *n.* fruit-growing. [L *pomum* fruit + CULTURE]

pommel /páməl, póm-/ *n. & v.* ● *n.* **1** a knob, esp. at the end of a sword hilt. **2** the upward projecting front part of a saddle. ● *v.tr.* (**pommeled, pommeling** or **pommelled, pommelling**) = PUMMEL. □ **pommel horse** a vaulting horse fitted with a pair of curved handgrips. [ME f. OF *pomel* f. Rmc *pomellum* (unrecorded), dimin. of L *pomum* fruit, apple]

pomology /pōmóləjee/ *n.* the science of fruit-growing. □□ **pomological** /-məlójikəl/ *adj.* **pomologist** *n.* [L *pomum* fruit + -LOGY]

pomp /pomp/ *n.* **1** a splendid display; splendor. **2** (often in *pl.*) vainglory (*the pomps and vanities of this wicked world*). [ME f. OF *pompe* f. L *pompa* f. Gk *pompē* procession, pomp f. *pempō* send]
 ■ **1** glory, grandeur, magnificence, splendor, show, pageantry, ceremony, spectacle, brilliance, ceremoniousness. **2** see VANITY 1, OSTENTATION.

pompadour /pómpədawr, -dōōr/ *n.* a woman's hairstyle with the hair in a high turned-back roll around the face. [f. Marquise de *Pompadour*, the mistress of Louis XV of France d. 1764]

pompano /pómpənō/ *n.* (*pl.* **-os**) any of various fish of the family Carangidae or Stromateidae of the Atlantic and Pacific Oceans, used as food. [Sp. *pámpano*]

pompom[1] /pómpom/ *n.* an automatic quick-firing gun esp. on a ship. [imit.]

pompom[2] /pómpom/ *n.* (also **pompon** /-pon/) **1** an ornamental ball or tuft of wool, silk, or ribbons, often worn on hats or clothing. **2** (often *attrib.*) (usu. **pompon**) a dahlia or chrysanthemum with small tightly-clustered petals. [F, of unkn. orig.]

pompous /pómpəs/ *adj.* **1** self-important, affectedly grand or solemn. **2** (of language) pretentious; unduly grand in style. **3** *archaic* magnificent; splendid. □□ **pomposity** /pompósitee/ *n.* (*pl.* **-ies**) **pompously** *adv.* **pompousness** *n.* [ME f. OF *pompeux* f. LL *pomposus* (as POMP)]
 ■ **1** self-important, vain, proud, arrogant, haughty, overbearing, conceited, egotistical, boastful, braggart, snobbish, magisterial, imperious, pontifical, stuffy, affected, high-hat, *colloq.* uppity, highfalutin, stuck-up, hoity-toity, la-di-da, *literary* vainglorious, *Brit. sl.* toffee-nosed. **2** bombastic, pretentious, ostentatious, showy, grandiose, flowery, inflated, grandiloquent, pedantic, fustian, orotund, ornate, embroidered, flatulent, turgid, high-flown, euphuistic, *colloq.* windy.

ponce /pons/ *n. & v. Brit. sl.* ● *n.* **1** a man who lives off a prostitute's earnings; a pimp. **2** *offens.* a homosexual; an effeminate man. ● *v.intr.* act as a ponce. □ **ponce about** move about effeminately or ineffectually. □□ **poncy** *adj.* (also **poncy**) (in sense 2 of *n.*). [perh. f. POUNCE[1]]
 ■ *n.* **1** see PIMP *n.* □□ **poncey** see EFFEMINATE.

poncho /pónchō/ *n.* (*pl.* **-os**) **1** a S. American cloak made of a blanket-like piece of cloth with a slit in the middle for the head. **2** a garment in this style, esp. one waterproof and worn as a raincoat. [S.Amer. Sp., f. Araucan]
 ■ see CLOAK *n.* 1.

pond /pond/ *n. & v.* ● *n.* **1** a fairly small body of still water formed naturally or by hollowing or embanking. **2** *joc.* the sea. ● *v.* **1** *tr.* hold back; dam up (a stream, etc.). **2** *intr.* form a pond. □ **pond life** animals (esp. invertebrates) that live in ponds. [ME var. of POUND[3]]
 ■ *n.* **1** pool, tarn, lake, *archaic or poet.* mere. **2** see SEA 1.

ponder /póndər/ *v.* **1** *tr.* weigh mentally; think over; consider. **2** *intr.* (usu. foll. by *on, over*) think; muse. [ME f. OF *ponderer* f. L *ponderare* f. *pondus -eris* weight]
 ■ brood over or upon, mull over, deliberate over, meditate upon or on, think over or on or about, ruminate over, chew over, reflect on or over, *literary* muse over or on; contemplate, consider, cogitate.

ponderable /póndərəbəl/ *adj.* having appreciable weight or significance. □□ **ponderability** /-bílitee/ *n.* [LL *ponderabilis* (as PONDER)]
 ■ see TANGIBLE 2.

ponderation /póndəráyshən/ *n. literary* the act or an instance of weighing, balancing, or considering. [L *ponderatio* (as PONDER)]

ponderosa /pŏndərōsə/ *n.* **1** a N. American pine tree, *Pinus ponderosa*. **2** the timber of this tree. [mod.L, fem. of L *ponderosus*: see PONDEROUS]

ponderous /pŏndərəs/ *adj.* **1** heavy; unwieldy. **2** laborious. **3** (of style, etc.) dull; tedious. □□ **ponderosity** /-rósitee/ *n.* **ponderously** *adv.* **ponderousness** *n.* [ME f. L *ponderosus* f. *pondus -eris* weight]

■ **1** weighty, unwieldy, heavy, cumbersome, cumbrous, elephantine. **2** tiresome, difficult; see also LABORIOUS 1. **3** labored, turgid, dull, pedestrian, stilted, inflated, wordy, verbose, prolix, pompous, grandiloquent, overdone, *colloq.* windy; see also TEDIOUS.

pondweed /pŏndweed/ *n.* any of various aquatic plants, esp. of the genus *Potamogeton*, growing in still or running water.

pone[1] /pōn/ *n. US dial.* **1** unleavened cornbread, esp. as made by Native Americans. **2** a fine light bread made with milk, eggs, etc. **3** a cake or loaf of this. [Algonquian, = bread]

pone[2] /pōnee/ *n.* the dealer's opponent in two-handed card games. [L, 2nd sing. imper. of *ponere* place]

pong /pong/ *n. & v. Brit. colloq.* ● *n.* an unpleasant smell. ● *v.intr.* stink. □□ **pongy** /póngee/ *adj.* (**pongier, pongiest**). [20th c.: orig. unkn.]

pongee /ponjeé, pun-, pónjee/ *n.* **1** a soft usu. unbleached type of Chinese silk fabric. **2** an imitation of this in cotton, etc. [perh. f. Chin. dial. *punchī* own loom, i.e., homemade]

pongid /pónjid/ *n. & adj.* ● *n.* any ape of the family Pongidae, including gorillas, chimpanzees, and orangutans. ● *adj.* of or relating to this family. [mod.L *Pongidae* f. *Pongo* the genus name: see PONGO 1]

pongo /pónggō/ *n.* (*pl.* **-os**) **1** an orangutan. **2** *Naut. sl.* a soldier. [Congolese *mpongo*, orig. of African apes]

poniard /pónyərd/ *n.* a small slim dagger. [F *poignard* f. OF *poignal* f. med.L *pugnale* f. L *pugnus* fist]

■ see DAGGER 1.

pons /ponz/ *n.* (*pl.* **pontes** /pónteez/) *Anat.* (in full **pons Varolii** /vərōleeī/) the part of the brain stem that links the medulla oblongata and the thalamus. □ **pons asinorum** /ásináwrəm/ any difficult proposition, orig. a rule of geometry from Euclid ('bridge of asses'). [L, = bridge: *Varolii* f. C. *Varoli*, It. anatomist d. 1575]

pont /pont/ *n. S.Afr.* a flat-bottomed ferryboat. [Du.]

pontes *pl.* of PONS.

pontifex /póntifeks/ *n.* (*pl.* **pontifices** /pontífiseez/) **1** = PONTIFF. **2** *Rom. Antiq.* a member of the principal college of priests in Rome. □ **Pontifex Maximus** the head of this. [L *pontifex -ficis* f. *pons pontis* bridge + *-fex* f. *facere* make]

pontiff /póntif/ *n. RC Ch.* (in full **sovereign** or **supreme pontiff**) the pope. [F *pontife* (as PONTIFEX)]

pontifical /pontífikəl/ *adj. & n.* ● *adj.* **1** *RC Ch.* of or befitting a pontiff; papal. **2** pompously dogmatic; with an attitude of infallibility. ● *n.* **1** an office book containing rites to be performed by bishops. **2** (in *pl.*) the vestments and insignia of a bishop, cardinal, or abbot. □ **Pontifical Mass** a high Mass, usu. celebrated by a cardinal, bishop, etc. □□ **pontifically** *adv.* [ME f. F *pontifical* or L *pontificalis* (as PONTIFEX)]

■ *adj.* **2** see DOGMATIC.

pontificate *v. & n.* ● *v.intr.* /pontífikayt/ **1 a** play the pontiff; pretend to be infallible. **b** be pompously dogmatic. **2** *RC Ch.* officiate as bishop, esp. at mass. ● *n.* /pontífikət/ **1** the office of pontifex, bishop, or pope. **2** the period of this. [L *pontificatus* (as PONTIFEX)]

■ *v.* **1** see PREACH 2, RANT *v.* 2, 3.

pontifices *pl.* of PONTIFEX.

pontoon[1] /pontōōn/ *n. & v.* ● *n.* **1** a flat-bottomed boat. **2 a** each of several boats, hollow metal cylinders, etc., used to support a temporary bridge. **b** a bridge so formed; a floating platform. **3** = CAISSON 1, 2. **4** a float for a seaplane. ● *v.tr.* cross (a river) by means of pontoons. [F *ponton* f. L *ponto -onis* f. *pons pontis* bridge]

■ *n.* **1** punt. **2 a** float.

pontoon[2] /pontōōn/ *n. Brit.* = BLACKJACK[1] 1. [prob. corrupt.]

pony /pónee/ *n.* (*pl.* **-ies**) **1** a horse of any small breed. **2** a small drinking glass. **3** (in *pl.*) *sl.* racehorses. **4** a literal translation of a foreign-language text, used by students. **5** *Brit. sl.* £25. □ **pony express** (also **Pony Express**) *US Hist.* an

express delivery system of the early 1860s that carried mail, etc., by relays of pony riders. [perh. f. *poulney* (unrecorded) f. F *poulenet* dimin. of *poulain* foal]

ponytail /póneetayl/ *n.* a person's hair drawn back, tied, and hanging down like a pony's tail.

pooch /pōōch/ *n. sl.* a dog. [20th c.: orig. unkn.]

poodle /pōōd'l/ *n.* **1 a** a dog of a breed with a curly coat that is usually clipped. **b** this breed. **2** *Brit.* a lackey or servile follower. [G *Pudel(hund)* f. LG *pud(d)eln* splash in water: cf. PUDDLE]

poof /pōōf, pŏŏf/ *n.* (also **poove** /pōōv/) *Brit. sl. derog.* **1** an effeminate man. **2** a male homosexual. □□ **poofy** /pōōfee/ *adj.* [19th c.: cf. PUFF in sense 'braggart']

pooh /pōō/ *int. & n.* (**poo**) ● *int.* expressing impatience or contempt. ● *n. sl.* **1** excrement. **2** an act of defecation. [imit.]

Pooh-Bah /pōōbaá/ *n.* (also **pooh-bah**) a holder of many offices at once. [a character in W. S. Gilbert's *The Mikado* (1885)]

pooh-pooh /pōōpōō/ *v.tr.* express contempt for; ridicule; dismiss (an idea, etc.) scornfully. [redupl. of POOH]

■ see BELITTLE, DISMISS 4.

pooka /pōōkə/ *n. Ir.* a hobgoblin. [Ir. *púca*]

pool[1] /pōōl/ *n. & v.* ● *n.* **1** a small body of still water, usu. of natural formation. **2** a small shallow body of any liquid. **3** = *swimming pool* (see SWIM). **4** a deep place in a river. ● *v.* **1** *tr.* form into a pool. **2** *intr.* (of blood) become static. [OE *pōl*, MLG, MDu. *pōl*, OHG *pfuol* f. WG]

■ *n.* **1** pond, lake, tarn, *archaic or poet.* mere.

pool[2] /pōōl/ *n. & v.* ● *n.* **1 a** (often *attrib.*) a common supply of persons, vehicles, commodities, etc., for sharing by a group of people (*a typing pool; a car pool*). **b** a group of persons sharing duties, etc. **2 a** the collective amount of players' stakes in gambling, etc. **b** a receptacle for this. **3 a** a joint commercial venture, esp. an arrangement between competing parties to fix prices and share business to eliminate competition. **b** the common funding for this. **4** any of several games similar to billiards played on a pool table with usu. 16 balls. **5** a group of contestants who compete against each other in a tournament for the right to advance to the next round. ● *v.tr.* **1** put (resources, etc.) into a common fund. **2** share (things) in common. **3** (of transport or organizations, etc.) share (traffic, receipts). **4** *Austral. sl.* **a** involve (a person) in a scheme, etc., often by deception. **b** implicate; inform on. [F *poule* (= hen) in same sense: assoc. with POOL[1]]

■ *n.* **2** a pot, jackpot, kitty, stakes, bank, purse. **3 a** syndicate, combine, cartel, trust, group, consortium. ● *v.* **1** combine, merge, consolidate, amalgamate.

poolroom /pōōlrōōm, -rŏŏm/ *n.* **1** a place for playing pool; pool hall. **2** a bookmaking establishment.

poon[1] /pōōn/ *n.* any E. Indian tree of the genus *Calophyllum*. □ **poon oil** an oil from the seeds of this tree, used in medicine and for lamps. [Sinh. *pūna*]

poon[2] /pōōn/ *n.* esp. *Austral. sl.* a simple or foolish person. [orig. unkn.]

poop[1] /pōōp/ *n. & v.* ● *n.* the stern of a ship; the aftermost and highest deck. ● *v.tr.* **1** (of a wave) break over the stern of (a ship). **2** (of a ship) receive (a wave) over the stern. [ME f. OF *pupe, pope* ult. f. L *puppis*]

poop[2] /pōōp/ *v.tr.* (esp. as **pooped** *adj.*) *colloq.* exhaust; tire out. [20th c.: orig. unkn.]

■ (**pooped**) see *exhausted* (EXHAUST).

poop[3] /pōōp/ *n. sl.* up to date or inside information; the low-down. [20th c.: orig. unkn.]

poop[4] /pōōp/ *n. & v. sl.* ● *n.* excrement. ● *v. intr.* defecate. [f. earlier 'break wind,' prob. f. ME *powpen* sound a horn]

poor /pŏŏr/ *adj.* **1** lacking adequate money or means to live comfortably. **2 a** (foll. by *in*) deficient in (a possession or

---

/.../	**pronunciation**	●	**part of speech**
□	**phrases, idioms, and compounds**		
□□	**derivatives**	■	**synonym section**
	cross-references appear in SMALL CAPITALS or *italics*		

quality) (*the poor in spirit*). **b** (of soil, ore, etc.) unproductive. **3 a** scanty; inadequate (*a poor crop*). **b** less good than is usual or expected (*poor visibility; is a poor driver; in poor health*). **c** paltry; inferior (*poor condition; came a poor third*). **4 a** deserving pity or sympathy; unfortunate (*you poor thing*). **b** with reference to a dead person (*as my poor father used to say*). **5** spiritless; despicable (*is a poor creature*). **6** often *iron.* or *joc.* humble; insignificant (*in my poor opinion*). □ **poor box** a collection box, esp. in church, for the relief of the poor. **poor boy** = *submarine sandwich.* **poor law** *hist.* a law relating to the support of paupers. **poor man's** an inferior or cheaper substitute for. **poor rate** *Brit. hist.* a rate or assessment for relief or support of the poor. **poor relation** an inferior or subordinate member of a family or any other group. **poor-spirited** timid; cowardly. **poor white** *offens.* a member of a socially inferior group of white people. **take a poor view of** regard with disfavor or pessimism. [ME & OF *pov(e)re, poure* f. L *pauper*]
■ **1** needy, destitute, indigent, penniless, poverty-stricken, impoverished, badly off, necessitous, low-income, impecunious, financially embarrassed, down-and-out, hard up, *colloq.* on one's uppers, *Brit. sl.* skint; see also BROKE. **2 a** (*poor in*) deficient *or* low in; lacking (in), wanting. **b** barren, unproductive, unfruitful, infertile, sterile; depleted, exhausted, impoverished, low-yielding. **3 a** low, skimpy, meager, scant, scanty, inadequate, insufficient, sparse. **b, c** bad, awful, inadequate, unsatisfactory, unacceptable, inefficient, amateurish, unprofessional, inferior, paltry, inconsequential, second-rate, third-rate, low-grade, shoddy, mediocre, defective, faulty, flawed, substandard, sorry, slipshod, below *or* under par, *colloq.* lousy. **4 a** unfortunate, unlucky, pathetic, luckless, pitiful, pitiable, ill-fated, miserable, wretched, hapless. **6** see INFERIOR *adj.* 1, 2. ■ **poor-spirited** see COWARDLY *adj.* **take a poor view of** see DISAPPROVE.

poorhouse /póorhows/ *n. hist.* = WORKHOUSE 1.

poorly /póorlee/ *adv. & adj.* ● *adv.* **1** scantily; defectively. **2** with no great success. **3** meanly; contemptibly. ● *predic.adj.* unwell.
■ *adv.* **1** defectively, scantily, skimpily, badly, inadequately, unsatisfactorily, incompetently, inexpertly, improperly, crudely, shoddily, unprofessionally, amateurishly, inefficiently.
● *predic.adj.* unwell, indisposed, ailing, sick, off-color, indisposed, *colloq.* under the weather; see also ILL *adj.*

poorness /póornis/ *n.* **1** defectiveness. **2** the lack of some good quality or constituent.

poove var. of POOF.

pop¹ /pop/ *n., v., & adv.* ● *n.* **1** a sudden sharp explosive sound as of a cork when drawn. **2** *colloq.* an effervescent soft drink. **3** = *pop fly.* ● *v.* (**popped, popping**) **1** *intr. & tr.* make or cause to make a pop. **2** *intr. & tr.* (foll. by *in, out, up, down,* etc.) go, move, come, or put unexpectedly or in a quick or hasty manner (*pop out to the store; pop in for a visit; pop it on your head*). **3 a** *intr. & tr.* burst, making a popping sound. **b** *tr.* heat (popcorn, etc.) until it pops. **4** *intr.* (often foll. by *at*) *colloq.* fire a gun (at birds, etc.). **5** *tr. Brit. sl.* pawn. **6** *tr. sl.* take or inject (a drug, etc.). **7** *intr.* (often foll. by *up*) (of a ball) rise up into the air. ● *adv.* with the sound of a pop (*heard it go pop*). □ **in pop** *Brit. sl.* in pawn. **pop-eyed** *colloq.* **1** having bulging eyes. **2** wide-eyed (with surprise, etc.). **pop fly** *Baseball* a high fly ball hit esp. to the infield. **pop off** *colloq.* **1** die. **2** quietly slip away (cf. sense 2 of *v.*). **pop one's clogs** *Brit. sl.* die. **pop the question** *colloq.* propose marriage. **pop-shop** *Brit. sl.* a pawnbroker's shop. **pop-up 1** (of a toaster, etc.) operating so as to move the object (toast when ready, etc.) quickly upward. **2** (of a book, greeting card, etc.) containing three-dimensional figures, illustrations, etc., that rise up when the page is turned. **3** = *pop fly.* **4** *Computing* (of a menu) able to be superimposed on the screen being worked on and suppressed rapidly. [ME: imit.]
■ *n.* **1** explosion, bang, report, crack, snap. **2** fizzy *or* carbonated drink, soda, *Brit.* mineral(s). ● *v.* **1, 3**

burst; explode, bang, go off. **2** nip, run; (*pop in* or *by*) visit, pay a visit, stop (by), call, come by, *colloq.* drop in *or* by. **4** open fire, shoot, *colloq.* blast. **5** pledge, *colloq.* hock; see also PAWN² *v.* □ **pop off 1** see DIE 1. **pop the question** propose, ask for a person's hand (in marriage).

pop² /pop/ *adj. & n. colloq.* ● *adj.* **1** in a popular or modern style. **2** performing popular music, etc. (*pop group; pop star*). ● *n.* **1** pop music. **2** a pop record or song (*top of the pops*). □ **pop art** art based on modern popular culture and the mass media, esp. as a critical comment on traditional fine art values. **pop culture** commercial culture based on popular taste. **pop festival** a festival at which popular music, etc., is performed. [abbr.]

pop³ /pop/ *n. esp. colloq.* father. [abbr. of POPPA]

pop. *abbr.* population.

popadam var. of POPPADAM.

popcorn /pópkawrn/ *n.* **1** corn which bursts open when heated. **2** these kernels when popped.

pope¹ /pōp/ *n.* **1** (as title usu. **Pope**) the head of the Roman Catholic Church (also called the Bishop of Rome). **2** the head of the Coptic Church and Orthodox patriarch of Alexandria. **3** = RUFF². **pope's nose** the tail of a cooked chicken, turkey, etc. □□ **popedom** *n.* **popeless** *adj.* [OE f. eccl.L *pāpa* bishop, pope f. eccl.Gk *papas* = Gk *pappas* father: cf. PAPA]

pope² /pōp/ *n.* a parish priest of the Orthodox Church in Russia, etc. [Russ. *pop* f. OSlav. *popŭ* f. WG f. eccl.Gk (as POPE¹)]

popery /pṓpəree/ *n. derog.* the papal system; the Roman Catholic Church.

popgun /pópgun/ *n.* **1** a child's toy gun which shoots a pellet, etc., by the compression of air with a piston. **2** *derog.* an inefficient firearm.

popinjay /pópinjay/ *n.* **1** a fop; a conceited person; a coxcomb. **2 a** *archaic* a parrot. **b** *hist.* a figure of a parrot on a pole as a mark to shoot at. [ME f. AF *papeiaye*, OF *papingay*, etc., f. Sp. *papagayo* f. Arab. *babaġā*: assim. to JAY]
■ **1** see DUDE 1.

popish /pópish/ *adj. derog.* Roman Catholic. □□ **popishly** *adv.*

poplar /póplər/ *n.* **1** any tree of the genus *Populus*, with a usu. rapidly growing trunk and tremulous leaves. **2** = *tulip tree.* [ME f. AF *popler*, OF *poplier* f. *pople* f. L *populus*]

poplin /póplin/ *n.* a plain woven fabric usu. of cotton, with a corded surface. [obs. F *papeline* perh. f. It. *papalina* (fem.) PAPAL, f. the papal town Avignon where it was made]

popliteal /póplíteeəl, -liteéəl/ *adj.* of the hollow at the back of the knee. [mod.L *popliteus* f. L *poples -itis* this hollow]

popover /pópōvər/ *n.* a light puffy hollow muffin made from an egg-rich batter.

poppa /pópə/ *n. colloq.* father (esp. as a child's word). [var. of PAPA]

poppadam /pópədəm/ *n.* (also **poppadom, popadam**) *Ind.* a thin, crisp, spiced bread eaten with curry, etc. [Tamil *pappaḍam*]

popper /pópər/ *n.* **1 a** a person or thing that pops. **b** a device or machine for making popcorn. **2** *colloq.* a small vial of amyl nitrite used for inhalation. **3** *Brit. colloq.* a snap fastener.

poppet /pópit/ *n.* **1** (also **poppet valve**) *Engin.* a mushroom-shaped valve, lifted bodily from its seat rather than hinged. **2** (in full **poppet head**) the head of a lathe. **3** a small square piece of wood fitted inside the gunwale or washstrake of a boat. **4** *Brit. colloq.* (esp. as a term of endearment) a small or dainty person. □ **poppet head** *Brit.* the frame at the top of a mine shaft supporting pulleys for the ropes used in hoisting. [ME *popet(te)*, ult. f. L *pup(p)a*: cf. PUPPET]
■ **4** see DEAR *n.*

popple /pópəl/ *v. & n.* ● *v.intr.* (of water) tumble or bubble, toss to and fro. ● *n.* the act or an instance of rolling, tossing, or rippling of water. □□ **popply** *adj.* [ME prob. f. MDu. *popelen* murmur, quiver, of imit. orig.]

poppy /pópee/ *n.* (*pl.* **-ies**) any plant of the genus *Papaver*, with showy often red flowers and a milky sap with narcotic properties. ▫▫ **poppied** *adj.* [OE *popig, papæg*, etc., f. med.L *papauum* f. L *papaver*]

poppycock /pópeekok/ *n. sl.* nonsense. [Du. dial. *pappekak*]

Popsicle /pópsikəl/ *n. propr.* a flavored ice confection on a stick.

populace /pópyələs/ *n.* **1** the common people. **2** *derog.* the rabble. [F f. It. *popolaccio* f. *popolo* people + *-accio* pejorative suffix]

■ **1** (common *or* ordinary) people, masses, commonalty, commonality, (general) public, commoners, multitude, hoi polloi, peasantry, proletariat, common folk, working class, rank and file. **2** rabble, riffraff, canaille, *colloq.* the great unwashed, *colloq. usu. derog.* the plebs, *usu. derog.* mob, *derog.* ragtag and bobtail.

popular /pópyələr/ *adj.* **1** liked or admired by many people or by a specified group (*popular teachers; a popular hero*). **2 a** of or carried on by the general public (*popular meetings*). **b** prevalent among the general public (*popular discontent*). **3** adapted to the understanding, taste, or means of the people (*popular science; popular medicine*). ▫ **popular front** a party or coalition representing left-wing elements. **popular music** songs, folk tunes, etc., appealing to popular tastes. ▫▫ **popularism** *n.* **popularity** /-láritee/ *n.* **popularly** *adv.* [ME f. AF *populer*, OF *populeir* or L *popularis* f. *populus* people]

■ **1** favorite, favored, well-received, well-liked; see also FASHIONABLE. **3** lay, nonprofessional; public, general, universal, average, everyday, ordinary, common. ▫▫ **popularity** acceptance, reputation; vogue, trend, stylishness, *colloq. often derog.* trendiness. **popularly** commonly, generally, ordinarily, usually, universally, widely, regularly, customarily, habitually.

popularize /pópyələrīz/ *v.tr.* **1** make popular. **2** cause (a person, principle, etc.) to be generally known or liked. **3** present (a technical subject, specialized vocabulary, etc.) in a popular or readily understandable form. ▫▫ **popularization** /-rəzayshən/ *n.* **popularizer** *n.*

populate /pópyəlayt/ *v.tr.* **1** inhabit; form the population of (a town, country, etc.). **2** supply with inhabitants; people (*a densely populated district*). [med.L *populare populat-* (as PEOPLE)]

■ **1** inhabit, reside in, live in, occupy, *literary* dwell in. **2** colonize, settle, people.

population /pópyəláyshən/ *n.* **1 a** the inhabitants of a place, country, etc., referred to collectively. **b** any specified group within this (*the Polish population of Chicago*). **2** the total number of any of these (*a population of eight million; the seal population*). **3** the act or process of supplying with inhabitants (*the population of forest areas*). **4** *Statistics* any finite or infinite collection of items under consideration. ▫ **population explosion** a sudden large increase of population. [LL *populatio* (as PEOPLE)]

■ **1 a** people, populace, inhabitants, residents, natives, citizenry, citizens, folk, *poet.* denizens. **3** colonization, settlement, settling, populating.

populist /pópyəlist/ *n. & adj.* ● *n.* a member or adherent of a political party seeking support mainly from the ordinary people. ● *adj.* of or relating to such a political party. ▫ **Populist Party** a US political party formed in 1891 that advocated the interests of labor and farmers, free coinage of silver, a graduated income tax, and government control of monopolies. ▫▫ **populism** *n.* **populistic** /-lístik/ *adj.* [L *populus* people]

populous /pópyələs/ *adj.* thickly inhabited. ▫▫ **populously** *adv.* **populousness** *n.* [ME f. LL *populosus* (as PEOPLE)]

■ crowded, heavily populated, teeming, thronged, jam-packed, packed.

porbeagle /páwrbeegəl/ *n.* a large shark, *Lamna nasus*, having a pointed snout. [18th-c. Corn. dial., of unkn. orig.]

porcelain /páwrsəlin, páwrslin/ *n.* **1** a hard vitrified translucent ceramic. **2** objects made of this. ▫ **porcelain clay** kaolin. **porcelain shell** cowrie. ▫▫ **porcellaneous** /páwrsəláyneeəs/ *adj.* **porcellanous** /porsélənəs/ *adj.* [F *porcelaine* cowrie, porcelain f. It. *porcellana* f. *porcella* dimin.

of *porca* sow (a cowrie being perh. likened to a sow's vulva) f. L *porca* fem. of *porcus* pig]

■ **2** see POTTERY 1.

porch /pawrch/ *n.* **1** a covered shelter for the entrance of a building. **2** a veranda. **3** (**the Porch**) = *the Stoa* (see STOA 2). ▫▫ **porched** *adj.* **porchless** *adj.* [ME f. OF *porche* f. L *porticus* (transl. Gk *stoa*) f. *porta* passage]

porcine /páwrsīn, -sin/ *adj.* of or like pigs. [F *porcin* or f. L *porcinus* f. *porcus* pig]

porcupine /páwrkyəpín/ *n.* **1** any rodent of the family Hystricidae native to Africa, Asia, and SE Europe, or the family Erethizontidae native to America, having defensive spines or quills. **2** (*attrib.*) denoting any of various animals or other organisms with spines. ▫ **porcupine fish** a marine fish, *Diodon hystrix*, covered with sharp spines and often distending itself into a spherical shape. ▫▫ **porcupinish** *adj.* **porcupiny** *adj.* [ME f. OF *porc espin* f. Prov. *porc espi(n)* ult. f. L *porcus* pig + *spina* thorn]

pore[1] /pawr/ *n. esp. Biol.* a minute opening in a surface through which gases, liquids, or fine solids may pass. [ME f. OF f. L *porus* f. Gk *poros* passage, pore]

■ opening, orifice, hole, aperture, vent, perforation, *Biol.* spiracle, *Bot.* stoma.

pore[2] /pawr/ *v.intr.* (foll. by *over*) **1** be absorbed in studying (a book, etc.). **2** meditate on, think intently about (a subject). [ME *pure*, etc. perh. f. OE *purian* (unrecorded): cf. PEER[1]]

■ (*pore over*) study, examine, scrutinize, peruse, read, go over; see also MEDITATE 2.

porgy /páwrgee/ *n.* (*pl.* **-ies**) any usu. marine fish of the family Sparidae, used as food. Also called *sea bream*. [18th c.: orig. uncert.: cf. Sp. & Port. *pargo*]

porifer /páwrifər/ *n.* any aquatic invertebrate of the phylum Porifera, including sponges. [mod.L *Porifera* f. L *porus* PORE[1] + *-fer* bearing]

pork /pawrk/ *n.* **1** the (esp. unsalted) flesh of a pig, used as food. **2** = *pork barrel* ▫ **pork barrel** *US colloq.* government funds as a source of political benefit. **pork pie** a pie of ground pork, etc., eaten cold. [ME *porc* f. OF *porc* f. L *porcus* pig]

porker /páwrkər/ *n.* **1** a pig raised for food. **2** a young fattened pig.

porkling /páwrkling/ *n.* a young or small pig.

porkpie hat /páwrkpī/ *n.* a hat with a flat crown and a brim turned up all around.

porky[1] /páwrkee/ *adj. & n.* ● *adj.* (**porkier, porkiest**) **1** *colloq.* fleshy; fat. **2** of or like pork. ● *n. Brit. rhyming sl.* a lie (short for *porky pie*).

■ *adj.* **1** see PLUMP[1] *adj.*

porky[2] /páwrkee/ *n.* (*pl.* **-ies**) *colloq.* a porcupine. [abbr.]

porn /pawrn/ *n. colloq.* pornography. [abbr.]

porno /páwrnō/ *n. & adj. colloq.* ● *n.* pornography. ● *adj.* pornographic. [abbr.]

pornography /pawrnógrəfee/ *n.* **1** the explicit description or exhibition of sexual activity in literature, films, etc., intended to stimulate erotic rather than aesthetic or emotional feelings. **2** literature, etc., characterized by this. ▫▫ **pornographer** *n.* **pornographic** /-nəgráfik/ *adj.* **pornographically** *adv.* [Gk *pornographos* writing of prostitutes f. *pornē* prostitute + *graphō* write]

■ **2** erotica, curiosa, *colloq.* porn, porno; smut, filth, dirt. ▫▫ **pornographic** obscene, lewd, offensive, indecent, prurient, smutty, blue, dirty, salacious, licentious, nasty, x-rated, *colloq.* porno, *euphem.* curious, adult.

porous /páwrəs/ *adj.* **1** full of pores. **2** letting through air, water, etc. **3** (of an argument, security system, etc.) leaky; admitting infiltration. ▫▫ **porosity** /porósitee/ *n.* **porously** *adv.* **porousness** *n.* [ME f. OF *poreux* f. med.L *porosus* f. L *porus* PORE[1]]

/. . . ./ **pronunciation**	● **part of speech**
▫ **phrases, idioms, and compounds**	
▫▫ **derivatives**	■ **synonym section**
cross-references appear in SMALL CAPITALS or *italics*	

■ **1, 2** spongy, spongelike; permeable, pervious, penetrable. **3** see DEFICIENT 2.

porphyria /pawrfíreeə/ *n.* any of a group of genetic disorders associated with abnormal metabolism of various pigments. [mod.L f. *porphyrin* purple substance excreted by porphyria patients f. Gk *porphura* purple]

porphyry /páwrfiree/ *n.* (*pl.* **-ies**) **1** a hard rock quarried in ancient Egypt, composed of crystals of white or red feldspar in a red matrix. **2** *Geol.* an igneous rock with large crystals scattered in a matrix of much smaller crystals. □□ **porphyritic** /-rítik/ *adj.* [ME ult. f. med.L *porphyreum* f. Gk *porphurītēs* f. *porphura* purple]

porpoise /páwrpəs/ *n.* any of various small toothed whales of the family Phocaenidae, esp. of the genus *Phocaena*, with a low triangular dorsal fin and a blunt rounded snout. [ME *porpays*, etc.; f. OF *po(u)rpois*, etc.; ult. f. L *porcus* pig + *piscis* fish]

porridge /páwrij, pór-/ *n.* **1** a dish consisting of oatmeal or another cereal boiled in water or milk. **2** *Brit. sl.* imprisonment. □□ **porridgy** *adj.* [16th c.: alt. of POTTAGE]

porringer /páwrinjər, pór-/ *n.* a small bowl, often with a handle, for soup, stew, etc. [earlier *pottinger* f. OF *potager* f. *potage* (see POTTAGE): -n- as in *messenger*, etc.]

port[1] /pawrt/ *n.* **1** a harbor. **2** a place of refuge. **3** a town or place possessing a harbor, esp. one where customs officers are stationed. □ **port of call** a place where a ship or a person stops on a journey. [OE f. L *portus* & ME prob. f. OF f. L *portus*]

■ harbor, haven; seaport.

port[2] /pawrt/ *n.* (in full **port wine**) a strong, sweet, dark red (occas. brown or white) fortified wine of Portugal. [shortened form of *Oporto*, city in Portugal from which port is shipped]

port[3] /pawrt/ *n. & v.* ● *n.* the left side (looking forward) of a ship, boat, or aircraft (cf. STARBOARD). ● *v.tr.* (also *absol.*) turn (the helm) to port. □ **port tack** see TACK[1] 4. **port watch** see WATCH *n.* 3b. [prob. orig. the side turned toward PORT[1]]

port[4] /pawrt/ *n.* **1 a** an opening in the side of a ship for entrance, loading, etc. **b** a porthole. **2** an aperture for the passage of steam, water, etc. **3** *Electr.* a socket or aperture in an electronic circuit, esp. in a computer network, where connections can be made with peripheral equipment. **4** an aperture in a wall, etc., for a gun to be fired through. **5** esp. *Sc.* a gate or gateway, esp. of a walled town. [ME & OF *porte* f. L *porta*]

port[5] /pawrt/ *v. & n.* ● *v.tr. Mil.* carry (a rifle, or other weapon) diagonally across and close to the body with the barrel, etc., near the left shoulder (esp. *port arms!*). ● *n.* **1** *Mil.* this position. **2** external deportment; carriage; bearing. [ME f. OF *port* ult. f. L *portare* carry]

portable /páwrtəbəl/ *adj. & n.* ● *adj.* easily movable; convenient for carrying (*portable TV*; *portable computer*). ● *n.* a portable object, e.g., a radio, typewriter, etc. (*decided to buy a portable*). □□ **portability** *n.* **portableness** *n.* **portably** *adv.* [ME f. OF *portable* or LL *portabilis* f. L *portare* carry]

■ *adj.* **1** transportable, manageable, handy, light, lightweight, compact.

portage /páwrtij, -taazh/ *n. & v.* ● *n.* **1** the carrying of boats or goods between two navigable waters. **2** a place at which this is necessary. **3 a** the act or an instance of carrying or transporting. **b** the cost of this. ● *v.tr.* convey (a boat or goods) between navigable waters. [ME f. OF f. *porter*: see PORT[5]]

portal[1] /páwrt'l/ *n.* a doorway or gate, etc., esp. a large and elaborate one. [ME f. OF f. med.L *portale* (neut. adj.): see PORTAL[2]]

portal[2] /páwrt'l/ *adj.* **1** of or relating to an aperture in an organ through which its associated vessels pass. **2** of or relating to the portal vein. □ **portal vein** a vein conveying blood to the liver from the spleen, stomach, pancreas, and intestines. [mod.L *portalis* f. L *porta* gate]

portamento /páwrtəméntō/ *n.* (*pl.* **portamenti** /-tee/) *Mus.* **1** the act or an instance of gliding from one note to another in singing, playing the violin, etc. **2** piano playing in a manner intermediate between legato and staccato. [It., = carrying]

portative /páwrtətiv/ *adj.* **1** serving to carry or support. **2** *Mus. hist.* (esp. of a small pipe organ) portable. [ME f. OF *portatif*, app. alt. of *portatil* f. med.L *portatilis* f. L *portare* carry]

portcullis /pawrtkúlis/ *n.* a strong heavy grating sliding up and down in vertical grooves, lowered to block a gateway in a fortress, etc. □□ **portcullised** *adj.* [ME f. OF *porte coleïce* sliding door f. *porte* door f. L *porta* + *col(e)ïce* fem. of *couleïs* sliding ult. f. L *colare* filter]

Porte /pawrt/ *n.* (in full **the Sublime** or **Ottoman Porte**) *hist.* the Ottoman court at Constantinople. [F (*la Sublime Porte* = the exalted gate), transl. of Turk. title of the central office of the Ottoman government]

porte cochère /pawrt kōsháir/ *n.* **1** a covered passage large enough for vehicles to pass through, usu. into a courtyard. **2** a roofed structure extending from the entrance of a building over a place where vehicles stop to discharge passengers. [F f. *porte* PORT[4] + *cochère* (fem. adj.) f. *coche* COACH]

portend /pawrténd/ *v.tr.* **1** foreshadow as an omen. **2** give warning of. [ME f. L *portendere* portent- f. por- PRO-[1] + *tendere* stretch]

■ see FORESHADOW, SPELL[1] 2b.

portent /páwrtent/ *n.* **1** an omen, a sign of something to come, esp. something of a momentous or calamitous nature. **2** a prodigy; a marvelous thing. [L *portentum* (as PORTEND)]

■ see OMEN *n.*

portentous /pawrténtəs/ *adj.* **1** like or serving as a portent. **2** pompously solemn. □□ **portentously** *adv.*

■ **1** ominous, threatening, fateful, menacing, foreboding, lowering, unpromising, unpropitious, ill-omened, inauspicious, ill-starred, ill-fated, *archaic* star-crossed. **2** solemn, dignified, stately, courtly, majestic, august, imperial.

porter[1] /páwrtər/ *n.* **1 a** a person employed to carry luggage, etc., at an airport, hotel, etc. **b** a hospital employee who moves equipment, trolleys, etc. **2** a dark brown bitter beer brewed from charred or browned malt (app. orig. made esp. for porters). **3** a sleeping-car attendant. **4** a cleaning person or maintenance worker, as in a hospital, etc. □□ **porterage** *n.* [ME f. OF *port(e)our* f. med.L *portator -oris* f. *portare* carry]

■ **1** a bearer, (baggage) carrier *or* attendant, redcap.

porter[2] /páwrtər/ *n. Brit.* a gatekeeper or doorkeeper, esp. of a large building. [ME & AF, OF *portier* f. LL *portarius* f. *porta* door]

■ doorkeeper, watchman, doorman, gatekeeper, concierge; caretaker, janitor.

porterhouse /páwrtərhows/ *n.* **1** *hist.* a house at which porter and other drinks were sold. **2** a house where steaks, chops, etc., were served. □ **porterhouse steak** a thick steak cut from the thick end of a sirloin.

portfire /páwrtfir/ *n.* a device for firing rockets, igniting explosives in mining, etc. [after F *porte-feu* f. *porter* carry + *feu* fire]

portfolio /pawrtfóleeō/ *n.* (*pl.* **-os**) **1** a case for keeping loose sheets of paper, drawings, etc. **2** a range of investments held by a person, a company, etc. **3** the office of a minister of state. **4** samples of an artist's work. [It. *portafogli* f. *portare* carry + *foglio* leaf f. L *folium*]

porthole /páwrt-hōl/ *n.* **1** an (esp. glassed-in) aperture in a ship's or aircraft's side for the admission of light. **2** *hist.* an aperture for pointing a cannon through.

portico /páwrtikō/ *n.* (*pl.* **-oes** or **-os**) a colonnade; a roof supported by columns at regular intervals usu. attached as a porch to a building. [It. f. L *porticus* PORCH]

■ porch, veranda, gallery, colonnade, stoa.

portière /pawrtyáir, -teér/ *n.* a curtain hung over a door or doorway. [F f. *porte* door f. L *porta*]

■ see DRAPERY.

portion /páwrshən/ *n. & v.* ● *n.* **1** a part or share. **2** the amount of food allotted to one person. **3** a specified or limited quantity. **4** one's destiny or lot. **5** a dowry. ● *v.tr.* **1** divide (a thing) into portions. **2** (foll. by *out*) distribute. **3** give a dowry to. **4** (foll. by *to*) assign (a thing) to (a person).

▫▫ **portionless** *adj.* (in sense 5 of *n.*). [ME f. OF *porcion portion* f. L *portio -onis*]

■ *n.* **1** share, allotment, quota, ration, apportionment, allowance, allocation, percentage, measure; segment, part, section, division, subdivision, parcel. **2** helping, serving; ration, share; piece. **4** see DESTINY 2. ● *v.* **1** partition, divide, split up, carve up, cut up, break up, section, *colloq.* divvy up. **2** (*portion out*) share out, allocate, ration, allot, dole out, deal (out), parcel out, distribute, administer, dispense, disperse. **4** see ASSIGN 1a.

Portland cement /páwrtlənd/ *n.* a cement manufactured from chalk and clay that when hard resembles Portland stone in color.

Portland stone /páwrtlənd/ *n.* a limestone from the Isle of Portland in Dorset, England, used in building.

portly /páwrtlee/ *adj.* (**portlier, portliest**) **1** corpulent; stout. **2** *archaic* of a stately appearance. ▫▫ **portliness** *n.* [PORT⁵ (in the sense 'bearing') + -LY¹]

■ **1** see STOUT *adj.* 1. ▫▫ **portliness** see FAT *n.* 3.

portmanteau /pawrtmántō, páwrtmantō/ *n.* (*pl.* **portmanteaus** or **portmanteaux** /-tōz, -tōz/) a leather trunk for clothes, etc., opening into two equal parts. □ **portmanteau word** a word blending the sounds and combining the meanings of two others, e.g., *motel* from *motor* and *hotel*. [F *portmanteau* f. *porter* carry f. L *portare* + *manteau* MANTLE]

portolano /páwrt'laánō/ *n.* (also **portolan** /páwrt'laan/) (*pl.* **portolanos** or **portolans**) *hist.* a book of sailing directions with charts, descriptions of harbors, etc. [It. *portolano* f. *porto* PORT¹]

portrait /páwrtrit, -trayt/ *n.* **1** a representation of a person or animal, esp. of the face, made by drawing, painting, photography, etc. **2** a verbal picture; a graphic description. **3** (in graphic design, etc.) a format in which the height of an illustration, etc., is greater than the width (cf. LANDSCAPE). [F, past part. of OF *portraire* PORTRAY]

■ **1** picture, likeness, vignette, image, representation, rendition, portrayal; sketch, drawing, painting. **2** description, profile, portrayal; account, characterization. **3** picture, spitting image; see also IMAGE *n.* 5.

portraitist /páwrtritist/ *n.* a person who takes or paints portraits.

portraiture /páwrtrichər/ *n.* **1** the art of painting or taking portraits. **2** graphic description. **3** a portrait. [ME f. OF (as PORTRAIT)]

portray /pawrtráy/ *v.tr.* **1** represent (an object) by a painting, carving, etc; make a likeness of. **2** describe graphically. **3** represent dramatically. ▫▫ **portrayable** *adj.* **portrayal** *n.* **portrayer** *n.* [ME f. OF *portraire* f. *por-* = PRO-¹ + *traire* draw f. L *trahere*]

■ **1, 2** represent, picture, show, depict, render, characterize, describe, delineate. **3** act *or* play (the part of), take the part *or* role of, represent. ▫▫ **portrayal** see PORTRAIT 1, 2, RENDERING 1a.

Port Salut /páwr səlōō/ *n.* a pale mild type of cheese. [after the Trappist monastery in France where it was first produced]

Portuguese /páwrchəgeéz, -geés/ *n.* & *adj.* ● *n.* (*pl.* same) **1 a** a native or national of Portugal. **b** a person of Portuguese descent. **2** the language of Portugal. ● *adj.* of or relating to Portugal or its people or language. □ **Portuguese man-of-war** a dangerous tropical or subtropical marine hydrozoan of the genus *Physalia* with a large crest and a poisonous sting. [Port. *portuguez* f. med.L *portugalensis*]

POS *abbr.* point-of-sale.

pose¹ /pōz/ *v.* & *n.* ● *v.* **1** *intr.* assume a certain attitude of body, esp. when being photographed or being painted for a portrait. **2** *intr.* (foll. by *as*) set oneself up as or pretend to be (another person, etc.) (*posing as a celebrity*). **3** *intr.* behave affectedly in order to impress others. **4** *tr.* put forward or present (a question, etc.). **5** *tr.* place (an artist's model, etc.) in a certain attitude or position. ● *n.* **1** an attitude of body or mind. **2** an attitude or pretense, esp. one assumed for effect (*his generosity is a mere pose*). [F *poser* (v.), *pose* (n.) f.

LL *pausare* PAUSE: some senses by confusion with L *ponere* place (cf. COMPOSE)]

■ *v.* **1** sit, model. **2** (*pose as*) impersonate, be disguised as, masquerade as, pretend *or* profess to be, pass for, imitate, mimic. **3** attitudinize, posture, put on airs; see also *show off*. **4** set, put (forward), ask, submit, broach, advance, present, raise. **5** see POSITION *v.* ● *n.* **1** position, posture, stance; see also ATTITUDE. **2** affectation, act, pretense, affectedness, display, façade, show; attitude.

pose² /pōz/ *v.tr.* puzzle (a person) with a question or problem. [obs. *appose* f. OF *aposer* var. of *oposer* OPPOSE]

poser /pōzər/ *n.* **1** a person who poses (see POSE¹ *v.* 3). **2** a puzzling question or problem.

■ **2** see PUZZLE *n.*

poseur /pōzőr/ *n.* (*fem.* **poseuse** /pōzőz/) a person who poses for effect or behaves affectedly. [F f. *poser* POSE¹]

posh /posh/ *adj.* & *adv. colloq.* ● *adj.* **1** elegant; stylish. **2** esp. *Brit.* of or associated with the upper classes (*spoke with a posh accent*). ● *adv.* esp. *Brit.* in a stylish or upper-class way (*talk posh; act posh*). ▫▫ **poshly** *adv.* **poshness** *n.* [20th c.: perh. f. sl. *posh* a dandy; *port out starboard home* (referring to the more comfortable accommodation on ships to and from Asia) is a later association and not the true origin]

■ *adj.* **1** smart, stylish, upmarket, high-class, deluxe, plush, luxurious, elegant, grand, swanky, *colloq.* classy, ritzy, top drawer, plushy, swank, tony, *sl.* snazzy. **2** upper-class, snobby, snobbish, *colloq.* upper-crust, esp. *Brit. colloq.* U.

posit /pózit/ *v.* & *n.* ● *v.tr.* (**posited, positing**) **1** assume as a fact; postulate. **2** put in place or position. ● *n. Philos.* a statement made on the assumption that it will prove valid. [L *ponere posit-* place]

■ *v.* **1** postulate, hypothesize, propound, put *or* set forth, put forward, advance, pose, predicate. **2** see POSITION *v.*

position /pəzíshən/ *n.* & *v.* ● *n.* **1** a place occupied by a person or thing. **2** the way in which a thing or its parts are placed or arranged (*sitting in an uncomfortable position*). **3** the proper place (*in position*). **4** the state of being advantageously placed (*jockeying for position*). **5** a person's mental attitude; a way of looking at a question (*changed their position on nuclear disarmament*). **6** a person's situation in relation to others (*puts one in an awkward position*). **7** rank or status; high social standing. **8** paid employment. **9** a place where troops, etc., are posted for strategical purposes (*the position was stormed*). **10** the configuration of chessmen, etc., during a game. **11** a specific pose in ballet, etc. (*hold first position*). **12** *Logic* **a** a proposition. **b** a statement of a proposition. ● *v.tr.* place in position. □ **in a position to** enabled by circumstances, resources, information, etc., to (do, state, etc.). **position paper** (in government, business, etc.) a written report of attitude or intentions. ▫▫ **positional** *adj.* **positionally** *adv.* **positioner** *n.* [ME f. OF *position* or L *positio -onis* (as POSIT)]

■ *n.* **1** spot, location, site, situation; whereabouts. **2** posture, attitude, stance, pose; disposition, arrangement, configuration. **3** see PLACE *n.* 1a, b. **5** viewpoint, point of view, outlook, attitude, stance, vantage, vantage point, stand, standpoint, opinion, way of thinking, angle, slant, inclination, leaning, bent, sentiment, feeling. **6** condition, state, situation; circumstances. **7** class, place, rank, standing, station, status. **8** job, occupation, situation, post, office, place, appointment, *colloq.* billet, berth. **12** hypothesis, thesis, tenet, principle, contention, assertion, predication, belief, proposition, postulate. ● *v.* put, place, lay, lie, situate, site, locate, establish, set, fix, settle, pose, posit, dispose, arrange.

/.../ **pronunciation**	● **part of speech**
□ **phrases, idioms, and compounds**	
▫▫ **derivatives**	■ **synonym section**
cross-references appear in SMALL CAPITALS or *italics*	

positive /pózitiv/ *adj. & n.* ● *adj.* **1** formally or explicitly stated; definite; unquestionable (*positive proof*). **2** (of a person) convinced, confident, or overconfident in his or her opinion (*positive that I was not there*). **3 a** absolute; not relative. **b** *Gram.* (of an adjective or adverb) expressing a simple quality without comparison (cf. COMPARATIVE, SUPERLATIVE). **4** *colloq.* downright; complete (*it would be a positive miracle*). **5 a** constructive; directional (*positive criticism*; *positive thinking*). **b** favorable; optimistic (*positive reaction*; *positive outlook*). **6** marked by the presence rather than absence of qualities or *Med.* symptoms (*the test was positive*). **7** esp. *Philos.* dealing only with matters of fact; practical (cf. POSITIVISM 1). **8** tending in a direction naturally or arbitrarily taken as that of increase or progress (*clockwise rotation is positive*). **9** greater than zero (*positive and negative integers*) (opp. NEGATIVE). **10** *Electr.* of, containing, or producing the kind of electrical charge produced by rubbing glass with silk; an absence of electrons. **11** (of a photographic image) showing lights and shades or colors true to the original (opp. NEGATIVE). ● *n.* a positive adjective, photograph, quantity, etc. ■ **positive feedback 1** a constructive response to an experiment, questionnaire, etc. **2** *Electronics* the return of part of an output signal to the input, tending to increase the amplification, etc. **positive geotropism** see GEOTROPISM. **positive pole** the north-seeking pole. **positive ray** *Physics* a canal ray. **positive sign** = *plus sign*. □□ **positively** *adv.* **positiveness** *n.* **positivity** /pózitívitee/ *n.* [ME f. OF *positif* -*ive* or L *positivus* (as POSIT)]

■ *adj.* **1** sure, certain, definite, unequivocal, categorical, absolute, unqualified, unambiguous, unmistakable, clear-cut, clear, firm, explicit, express, decisive, indisputable, indubitable, unquestionable, incontestable, undeniable, reliable, persuasive, convincing, irrefutable. **2** sure, certain, confident, convinced, satisfied, decided; overconfident, dogmatic, pontifical, opinionated, pigheaded, stubborn, obstinate, obdurate, arbitrary, overweening, arrogant, assertive. **4** complete, utter, downright, total, perfect, out-and-out, consummate, unmitigated, thorough, thoroughgoing, outright; see also ABSOLUTE *adj.* 1. **5 a** constructive, productive, useful, practical, functional, pragmatic; directional. **b** beneficial, favorable, complimentary, productive, supportive, constructive, reassuring, enthusiastic, affirmative; promising, encouraging, optimistic, cheerful, confident, *colloq.* bullish, upbeat. **6** affirmative, confirming. □□ **positively** definitely, absolutely, unquestionably, certainly, assuredly, undeniably, undoubtedly, surely, emphatically, unmistakably, categorically, indisputably, beyond *or* without a doubt, indubitably, beyond question; constructively; see also *utterly* (UTTER).

positivism /pózitivizəm/ *n.* **1** *Philos.* the philosophical system of Auguste Comte, recognizing only nonmetaphysical facts and observable phenomena, and rejecting metaphysics and theism. **2** a religious system founded on this. **3** = *logical positivism.* □□ **positivist** *n.* **positivistic** *adj.* **positivistically** /-vístiklee/ *adv.* [F *positivisme* (as POSITIVE)]

positron /pózitron/ *n.* *Physics* an elementary particle with a positive charge equal to the negative charge of an electron and having the same mass as an electron. [POSITIVE + -TRON]

posology /pəsóləjee, pō-/ *n.* the study of the dosage of medicines. □□ **posological** /pósəlójikəl/ *adj.* [F *posologie* f. Gk *posos* how much]

poss. *abbr.* **1** possession. **2** possessive. **3** possible. **4** possibly.

posse /pósee/ *n.* **1** a strong force or company or assemblage. **2** (in full **posse comitatus** /kómitáytəs/) **a** a body of constables, enforcers of the law, etc. **b** a body of men summoned by a sheriff, etc., to enforce the law. [med.L, = power f. L *posse* be able: *comitatus* = of the county]

possess /pəzés/ *v.tr.* **1** hold as property; own. **2** have a faculty, quality, etc. (*they possess a special value for us*). **3** (also *refl.*; foll. by *in*) maintain (oneself, one's soul, etc.) in a specified state (*possess oneself in patience*). **4 a** (of a demon, etc.) occupy; have power over (a person, etc.) (*possessed by the devil*). **b** (of an emotion, infatuation, etc.) dominate; be an

obsession of (*possessed by fear*). **5** have sexual intercourse with (esp. a woman). □ **be possessed of** own; have. **possess oneself of** take or get for one's own. **what possessed you?** an expression of incredulity. □□ **possessor** *n.* **possessory** *adj.* [OF *possesser* f. L *possidēre possess-* f. *potis* able + *sedēre* sit]

■ **1** be in possession of, be possessed of, have, own, enjoy, be blessed *or* endowed with. **2** have, hold, contain, embody, embrace, include. **3** see MAINTAIN 1, 2. **4 a** occupy, take over, take control of, have power over, bedevil, captivate, enchant, cast a spell on *or* over, enthrall; see also BEWITCH 2. **b** dominate, control, govern, influence, hold, consume, take control of, preoccupy, obsess, haunt, eat up. **5** see LAY¹ *v.* 16. □ **possess oneself of** acquire, achieve, get, win, obtain, procure, secure, take, seize, take *or* gain possession of.

possession /pəzéshən/ *n.* **1** the act or state of possessing or being possessed. **2 a** the thing possessed. **b** a foreign territory subject to a state or ruler. **3** the act or state of actual holding or occupancy. **4** *Law* power or control similar to lawful ownership but which may exist separately from it (*prosecuted for possession of narcotic drugs*). **5** (in *pl.*) property, wealth, subject territory, etc. **6** *Sports* temporary control, in team sports, of the ball, puck, etc., by a particular player. □ **in possession 1** (of a person) possessing. **2** (of a thing) possessed. **in possession of 1** having in one's possession. **2** maintaining control over (*in possession of one's wits*). **in the possession of** held or owned by. **take possession** (often foll. by *of*) become the owner or possessor (of a thing). □□ **possessionless** *adj.* [ME f. OF *possession* or L *possessio -onis* (as POSSESS)]

■ **1, 3** ownership, proprietorship; control, hold, tenure, keeping, care, custody, guardianship, protection; occupancy. **2 b** holding, territory, province, dominion, colony, protectorate. **5** (*possessions*) belongings, property, effects, chattels, assets, worldly goods, things. □ **take possession** (*take possession of*) seize, capture, take, get, conquer, occupy, acquire, win, possess oneself of, secure, obtain.

possessive /pəzésiv/ *adj. & n.* ● *adj.* **1** showing a desire to possess or retain what one already owns. **2** showing jealous and domineering tendencies toward another person. **3** *Gram.* indicating possession. ● *n.* (in full **possessive case**) *Gram.* the case of nouns and pronouns expressing possession. □ **possessive pronoun** each of the pronouns indicating possession (*my, your, his, their*, etc.) or the corresponding absolute forms (*mine, yours, his, theirs*, etc.). □□ **possessively** *adv.* **possessiveness** *n.* [L *possessivus* (as POSSESS), transl. Gk *ktētikē* (*ptōsis* case)]

■ *adj.* **1** greedy, selfish, ungenerous, stingy, niggardly, materialistic, covetous, acquisitive. **2** overprotective, controlling, domineering, overbearing; jealous.

posset /pósit/ *n. hist.* a drink made of hot milk curdled with ale, wine, etc., often flavored with spices, formerly much used as a remedy for colds, etc. [ME *poshote*: orig. unkn.]

possibility /pósibílitee/ *n.* (*pl.* **-ies**) **1** the state or fact of being possible, or an occurrence of this (*outside the range of possibility*; *saw no possibility of going away*). **2** a thing that may exist or happen (*there are three possibilities*). **3** (usu. in *pl.*) the capability of being used, improved, etc.; the potential of an object or situation (esp. *have possibilities*). [ME f. OF *possibilité* or LL *possibilitas -tatis* (as POSSIBLE)]

■ **1** conceivability, feasibility, plausibility, admissibility; likelihood, chance, prospect. **3** (*possibilities*) potentiality, potential, promise; capability, capacity.

possible /pósibəl/ *adj. & n.* ● *adj.* **1** capable of existing or happening; that may be managed, achieved, etc. (*came as early as possible*; *did as much as possible*). **2** that is likely to happen, etc. (*few thought their victory possible*). **3** acceptable; potential (*a possible way of doing it*). ● *n.* **1** a possible candidate, member of a team, etc. **2** (prec. by *the*) whatever is likely, manageable, etc. **3** the highest possible score, esp. in shooting, etc. [ME f. OF *possible* or L *possibilis* f. *posse* be able]

■ *adj.* **1** feasible, plausible, imaginable, conceivable, thinkable, credible, believable, tenable, admissible. **2** realizable, achievable, attainable, reachable, accomplishable; likely, probable.

possibly /pósiblee/ *adv.* **1** perhaps. **2** in accordance with possibility (*cannot possibly refuse*).

■ **1** maybe, perhaps, if possible, *archaic* mayhap, *archaic or joc.* peradventure, *archaic or poet.* perchance. **2** in any way, under any circumstances, at all, by any chance, ever.

possum /pósəm/ *n.* **1** *colloq.* = OPOSSUM 1. **2** *Austral. & NZ colloq.* a phalanger resembling an American opossum. □ **play possum 1** pretend to be asleep or unconscious when threatened. **2** feign ignorance. [abbr.]

post[1] /pōst/ *n. & v.* ● *n.* **1** a long stout piece of timber or metal set upright in the ground, etc.: **a** to support something, esp. in building. **b** to mark a position, boundary, etc. **c** to carry notices. **2** a pole, etc., marking the start or finish of a race. **3** a metal pin, as on a pierced earring. ● *v.tr.* **1** (often foll. by *up*) **a** attach (a paper, etc.) in a prominent place; stick up (*post no bills*). **b** announce or advertise by placard or in a published text. **2** publish the name of (a ship, etc.) as overdue or missing. **3** placard (a wall, etc.) with handbills, etc. **4** achieve (a score in a game, etc.). [OE f. L *postis*: in ME also f. OF, etc.]

■ *n.* **1** pole, stake, upright, column, pillar, pale, picket, shaft, pier, pylon, pile, piling, strut, shore, stanchion. ● *v.* **1 a** put *or* pin *or* tack *or* stick *or* hang up, affix. **b** advertise, announce, proclaim, publish, propagate, promulgate.

post[2] /pōst/ *n., v., & adv.* ● *n.* **1** esp. *Brit.* the official conveyance of packages, letters, etc.; the mail (*send it by post*). **2** esp. *Brit.* a single collection, dispatch, or delivery of the mail; the letters, etc., dispatched (*has the post arrived yet?*). **3** esp. *Brit.* a place where letters, etc., are dealt with; a post office or mailbox (*take it to the post*). **4** *hist.* **a** one of a series of couriers who carried mail on horseback between fixed stages. **b** a letter carrier; a mail cart. ● *v.* **1** *tr.* esp. *Brit.* put (a letter, etc.) in the mail. **2** *tr.* (esp. as **posted** *adj.*) supply a person with information (*keep me posted*). **3** *tr.* **a** enter (an item) in a ledger. **b** (often foll. by *up*) complete (a ledger) in this way. **c** carry (an entry) from an auxiliary book to a more formal one, or from one account to another. **4** *intr.* **a** travel with haste; hurry. **b** *hist.* travel with relays of horses. ● *adv.* express; with haste. □ **post chaise** *hist.* a fast carriage drawn by horses that were changed at regular intervals. **post exchange** *Mil.* a store at a military base, etc. **post-haste** with great speed. **Post Office 1** the public department or corporation responsible for postal services and (in some countries) telecommunication. **2** (**post office**) **a** a room or building where postal business is carried on. **b** a kissing game played esp. by children in which kisses are given for the pretended delivery of a letter. **post office box** a numbered box in a post office where letters are kept until called for. [F *poste* (fem.) f. It. *posta* ult. f. L *ponere posit-* place]

■ *n.* **1** postal service, mail. **2** collection, dispatch, delivery; letters, mail, correspondence. ● *v.* **1** send (off), dispatch, mail. **2** (*keep a person posted*) advise, brief, notify, *colloq.* fill in; see also INFORM 1. **3 a** record, enter, register, list. ● *adv.* see FAST[1] *adv.* 1.

post[3] /pōst/ *n. & v.* ● *n.* **1** a place where a soldier is stationed or which he patrols. **2** a place of duty. **3 a** a position taken up by a body of soldiers. **b** a force occupying this. **c** a fort. **4** a situation; paid employment. **5** = *trading post*. **6** *Naut. hist.* a commission as an officer in command of a vessel of 20 guns or more. ● *v.tr.* **1** place or station (soldiers, an employee, etc.). **2** esp. *Brit.* appoint to a post or command. □ **first post** *Brit.* the earliest of several bugle calls giving notice of the hour of retiring at night. **last post** *Brit.* the final such bugle call, also blown at military funerals, etc. [F *poste* (masc.) f. It. *posto* f. Rmc *postum* (unrecorded) f. L *ponere posit-* place]

■ *n.* **1** assignment, appointment, position, situation, job, place; employment, work. ● *v.* **1** place, put, station, position, situate, set, locate. **2** see APPOINT 1.

post- /pōst/ *prefix* after in time or order. [from or after L *post* (adv. & prep.)]

postage /pṓstij/ *n.* the amount charged for sending a letter, etc., by mail, usu. prepaid in the form of a stamp (*$5 for postage*). □ **postage meter** a machine for printing prepaid postage and a postmark. **postage stamp** an official stamp affixed to or imprinted on a letter, etc., indicating the amount of postage paid.

postal /pṓst'l/ *adj.* & *n.* ● *adj.* **1** of the post office or mail. **2** by mail. **postal code 1** = POSTCODE. **2** a Canadian system equivalent to a postcode postage meter or ZIP code. **postal order** *Brit.* a money order issued by the Post Office, payable to a specified person. **Postal Union** a union of the governments of various countries for the regulation of international postage. □□ **postally** *adv.* [F (*poste* POST[2])]

postbag /pṓstbag/ *n. Brit.* = MAILBAG.

postbox /pṓstboks/ *n. Brit.* a mailbox.

postcard /pṓstkaard/ *n.* a card, often with a photograph on one side, for sending a short message by mail without an envelope.

postclassical /pṓstklásikəl/ *adj.* (esp. of Greek and Roman literature) later than the classical period.

postcode /pṓstkōd/ *n. Brit., Austral., & NZ* a group of letters or letters and figures that are added to a mailing address to assist sorting.

postcoital /pṓstkṓit'l, -kō-eét'l/ *adj.* occurring or existing after sexual intercourse. □□ **postcoitally** *adv.*

postdate *v. & n.* ● *v.tr.* /pṓstdáyt/ affix or assign a date later than the actual one to (a document, event, etc.). ● *n.* /pṓstdayt/ such a date.

postdoctoral /pṓstdóktərəl/ *adj.* of or relating to research undertaken after the completion of doctoral research.

post entry /pṓst/ *n.* (*pl.* **-ies**) a late or subsequent entry, esp. in a race or in bookkeeping.

poster /pṓstər/ *n.* **1** a placard in a public place. **2** a large printed picture. **3** *Brit.* a billposter. □ **poster paint** a gummy opaque paint.

■ **1** placard, notice, bill; see also SIGN *n.* 4. **2** print, picture, reproduction.

poste restante /pōst restóNt/ *n. Brit.* **1** a direction on a letter to indicate that it should be kept at a specified post office until collected by the addressee. **2** general delivery; the department in a post office where such letters are kept. [F, = letter(s) remaining]

posterior /posteéreeər, pō-/ *adj.* & *n.* ● *adj.* **1** later; coming after in series, order, or time. **2** situated at the back. ● *n.* (in *sing.* or *pl.*) the buttocks. □□ **posteriority** /-áwritee, -ór-/ *n.* **posteriorly** *adv.* [L, compar. of *posterus* following f. *post* after]

■ *adj.* **1** later, ensuing, following, succeeding; see also SUBSEQUENT. **2** hind, rear, back, hinder, rearward. ● *n.* rump, seat, backside(s), *colloq.* bottom, *colloq. euphem.* derrière, *sl.* tush, *sl.* ass, butt, can, esp. *Brit. sl.* bum; see also BUTTOCK.

posterity /postéritee/ *n.* **1** all succeeding generations. **2** the descendants of a person. [ME f. OF *posterité* f. L *posteritas -tatis* f. *posterus*: see POSTERIOR]

■ **2** descendants, successors, heirs, children, offspring, issue, progeny.

postern /pṓstərn, pó-/ *n.* **1** a back door. **2** a side way or entrance. [ME f. OF *posterne, posterle*, f. LL *posterula* dimin. of *posterus*: see POSTERIOR]

postfix *n. & v.* ● *n.* /pṓstfiks/ a suffix. ● *v.tr.* /pṓstfíks/ append (letters) at the end of a word.

postglacial /pṓstgláyshəl/ *adj.* & *n.* ● *adj.* formed or occurring after a glacial period. ● *n.* a postglacial period or deposit.

postgraduate /pṓstgrájōoət/ *adj.* & *n.* ● *adj.* **1** (of a course of study) carried on after taking a high school or college degree. **2** of or relating to students following this course of study (*postgraduate fees*). ● *n.* a postgraduate student.

posthumous /póschəməs/ *adj.* **1** occurring after death. **2** (of a child) born after the death of its father. **3** (of a book, etc.) published after the author's death. □□ **posthumously** *adv.* [L *postumus* last (superl. f. *post* after): in LL *posth-* by assoc. with *humus* ground]

postiche /posteésh/ *n.* a hairpiece, worn as an adornment. [F, = false, f. It. *posticcio*]

postie /póstee/ *n. Brit. colloq.* a postman or postwoman. [abbr.]

postil /póstil/ *n. hist.* **1** a marginal note or comment, esp. on a text of Scripture. **2** a commentary. [ME f. OF *postille* f. med.L *postilla*, of uncert. orig.]

postilion /postílyən, pō-/ *n.* (also **postillion**) the rider on the near (left-hand side) horse drawing a coach, etc., when there is no coachman. [F *postillon* f. It. *postiglione* post boy f. *posta* POST²]

Postimpressionism /póstimpréshənizəm/ *n.* artistic aims and methods developed as a reaction against impressionism and intending to express the individual artist's conception of the objects represented rather than the ordinary observer's view. □□ **Postimpressionist** *n.* & *adj.* **Postimpressionistic** *adj.*

postindustrial /póstindústreeəl/ *adj.* relating to or characteristic of a society or economy that no longer relies on heavy industry.

postliminy /pōstlíminee/ *n.* **1** (in international law) the restoration to their former status of persons and things taken in war. **2** (in Roman law) the right of a banished person or captive to resume civic privileges on return from exile. [L *postliminium* (as POST-, *limen liminis* threshold)]

postlude /póstlōōd/ *n. Mus.* a concluding voluntary. [POST-, after PRELUDE]

postman /póstmən/ *n.* (*pl.* **-men**; *fem.* **postwoman**, *pl.* **-women**) a person who is employed to deliver and collect letters, etc. □ **postman's knock** *Brit.* = *post office* 2b.

postmark /póstmaark/ *n.* & *v.* ● *n.* an official mark stamped on a letter, esp. one giving the place, date, etc., of sending or arrival, and serving to cancel the stamp. ● *v.tr.* mark (an envelope, etc.) with this.

postmaster /póstmastər/ *n.* the person in charge of a post office. □ **postmaster general** the head of a country's postal service.

postmillennial /póstmiléneeəl/ *adj.* following the millennium.

postmillennialism /póstiméneeəlizəm/ *n.* the doctrine that a second Advent will follow the millennium. □□ **postmillennialist** *n.*

postmistress /póstmistris/ *n.* a woman in charge of a post office.

postmodern /póstmódərn/ *adj.* (in literature, architecture, the arts, etc.) denoting a movement reacting against modern tendencies, esp. by drawing attention to former conventions. □□ **postmodernism** *n.* **postmodernist** *n.* & *adj.*

postmortem /pōstmáwrtəm/ *n.*, *adv.*, & *adj.* ● *n.* **1** (in full **postmortem examination**) an examination made after death, esp. to determine its cause. **2** *colloq.* a discussion analysing the course and result of a game, election, etc. ● *adv.* & *adj.* after death. [L]
■ *n.* **1** autopsy, necropsy. **2** see ANALYSIS 1.

postnatal /póstnáyt'l/ *adj.* characteristic of or relating to the period after childbirth.

postnuptial /póstnúpshəl/ *adj.* after marriage.

post-obit *n.* & *adj.* ● *n.* /póstóbit/ esp. *Brit.* a bond given to a lender by a borrower to secure a sum for payment on the death of another person from whom the borrower expects to inherit. ● *adj.* /póstóbit/ taking effect after death. [L *post obitum* f. *post* after + *obitus* decease f. *obire* die]

postpaid /póstpáyd/ *adj.* on which postage has been paid.

postpartum /póstpaártəm/ *adj.* following parturition.

postpone /pōstpốn, pəspốn/ *v.tr.* cause or arrange (an event, etc.) to take place at a later time. □□ **postponable** *adj.* **postponement** *n.* **postponer** *n.* [L *postponere* (as POST-, *ponere posit-* place)]

■ delay, adjourn, defer, keep in abeyance, put off *or* aside *or* back, lay aside, suspend, shelve, table, *colloq.* put on the back burner, put *or* keep on ice. □□ **postponement** delay, adjournment, suspension, deferment, deferral; stay; moratorium.

postposition /póstpəzíshən/ *n.* **1** a word or particle, esp. an enclitic, placed after the word it modifies, e.g., *-ward* in *homeward* and *at* in *the books we looked at.* **2** the use of a postposition. □□ **postpositional** *adj.* & *n.* **postpositive** /póstpózitiv/ *adj.* & *n.* **postpositively** *adv.* [LL *postpositio* (as POSTPONE)]

postprandial /póstprándeeəl/ *adj. formal or joc.* after dinner or lunch. [POST- + L *prandium* a meal]

postscript /póstskript, pốskript/ *n.* **1** an additional paragraph or remark, usu. at the end of a letter after the signature and introduced by 'PS.' **2** any additional information, action, etc. [L *postscriptum* neut. past part. of *postscribere* (as POST-, *scribere* write)]
■ **2** see SUPPLEMENT *n.* 1, 2.

post-tax /póst-táks/ *adj.* = AFTER-TAX.

postulant /póschələnt/ *n.* a candidate, esp. for admission into a religious order. [F *postulant* or L *postulans -antis* (as POSTULATE)]

postulate *v.* & *n.* ● *v.tr.* /póschəlayt/ **1** (often foll. by *that* + clause) assume as a necessary condition, esp. as a basis for reasoning; take for granted. **2** claim. **3** (in ecclesiastical law) nominate or elect to a higher rank. ● *n.* /póschələt/ **1** a thing postulated. **2** a fundamental prerequisite or condition. **3** *Math.* an assumption used as a basis for mathematical reasoning. □□ **postulation** /-láyshən/ *n.* [L *postulare postulat-* demand]
■ *v.* **1** see PRESUME 1. **2** see PROPOUND. ● *n.* **1, 2** see PREMISE. □□ **postulation** see PRESUMPTION 2.

postulator /póschəlaytər/ *n.* **1** a person who postulates. **2** *RC Ch.* a person who presents a case for canonization or beatification.

posture /póschər/ *n.* & *v.* ● *n.* **1** the relative position of parts, esp. of the body (*in a reclining posture*). **2** carriage or bearing (*improved by good posture and balance*). **3** a mental or spiritual attitude or condition. **4** the condition or state (of affairs, etc.) (*in more diplomatic postures*). ● *v.* **1** *intr.* assume a mental or physical attitude, esp. for effect (*inclined to strut and posture*). **2** *tr.* pose (a person). □□ **postural** *adj.* **posturer** *n.* [F f. It. *postura* f. L *positura* f. *ponere posit-* place]
■ *n.* **1** pose, position, attitude, stance. **2** see CARRIAGE 6. **3** attitude, stance, position, feeling, sentiment, outlook, (point of) view, viewpoint, orientation, disposition, frame of mind, mood. **4** position, condition, situation, state, disposition, circumstance, status. ● *v.* **1** pose, attitudinize, put on airs, put on a show, do for effect, *colloq.* show off.

postwar /póstwáwr/ *adj.* occurring or existing after a war (esp. the most recent major war).

posy /pốzee/ *n.* (*pl.* **-ies**) **1** a small bunch of flowers. **2** *archaic* a short motto, line of verse, etc., inscribed within a ring. □ **posy-ring** a ring with this inscription. [alt. f. POESY]
■ **1** bouquet, nosegay, spray.

pot¹ /pot/ *n.* & *v.* ● *n.* **1** a vessel, usu. rounded, of ceramic ware or metal or glass for holding liquids or solids or for cooking in. **2 a** a coffeepot, flowerpot, teapot, etc. **b** = *chimney pot.* **c** = *lobster pot.* **3** a drinking vessel of pewter, etc. **4** the contents of a pot (*ate a whole pot of jam*). **5** the total amount of the bet in a game, etc. **6** *colloq.* a large sum (*pots of money*). **7** *Brit. sl.* a vessel given as a prize in an athletic contest, esp. a silver cup. **8** = POTBELLY. ● *v.tr.* (**potted**, **potting**) **1** place in a pot. **2** (usu. as **potted** *adj.*) preserve in a sealed pot (*potted shrimps*). **3** *Brit.* sit (a young child) on a chamber pot. **4** *Brit.* pocket (a ball) in billiards, etc. **5** shoot at, hit, or kill (an animal) with a potshot. **6** seize or secure. **7** *Brit.* abridge or epitomize (*in a potted version*; *potted wisdom*). □ **go to pot** *colloq.* deteriorate; be ruined. **potbound** (of a plant) having roots that fill the flowerpot, leaving no room to expand. **pot cheese** cottage cheese. **pot of gold** an imaginary reward; an ideal; a jackpot. **pot plant 1** a marijuana plant. **2** *Brit.* a plant grown in a flowerpot. **pot**

roast a piece of meat cooked slowly in a covered dish. **pot-roast** *v.tr.* cook (a piece of meat) in this way. **put a person's pot on** *Austral.* & *NZ sl.* inform on a person. □□ **potful** *n.* (*pl.* **-fuls**). [OE *pott*, corresp. to OFris., MDu., MLG *pot*, f. pop.L]

■ *n.* **1** pan, saucepan, cauldron, casserole, cooking pot, stewpan. **5** jackpot, bank, kitty, stakes, pool. **6** see LOT *n.* 1. ● *v.* **5** see SHOOT *v.* 1c. **6** see SECURE *v.* 3. **7** see ABRIDGE 1. □ **go to pot** see DETERIORATE. **pot-valor** Dutch courage.

pot[2] /pot/ *n. sl.* marijuana. [prob. f. Mex. Sp. *potiguaya*]

potable /pótəbəl/ *adj.* drinkable. □□ **potability** /-bílitee/ *n.* [F *potable* or LL *potabilis* f. L *potare* drink]

potage /pōtaazh/ *n.* thick soup. [F (as POTTAGE)]

potamic /pətámik, pō-/ *adj.* of rivers. □□ **potamology** /pótəmólijee/ *n.* [Gk *potamos* river]

potash /pótash/ *n.* an alkaline potassium compound, usu. potassium carbonate or hydroxide. [17th-c. *pot-ashes* f. Du. *pot-asschen* (as POT[1], ASH[1]): orig. obtained by leaching vegetable ashes and evaporating the solution in iron pots]

potassium /pətáseeəm/ *n. Chem.* a soft silvery white metallic element occurring naturally in seawater and various minerals, an essential element for living organisms, and forming many useful compounds used industrially. ¶ Symb.: **K**. □ **potassium chloride** a white crystalline solid used as a fertilizer and in photographic processing. **potassium cyanide** a highly toxic solid that can be hydrolyzed to give poisonous hydrogen cyanide gas: also called CYANIDE. **potassium iodide** a white crystalline solid used as an additive to table salt to prevent iodine deficiency. **potassium permanganate** a purple crystalline solid that is used in solution as an oxidizing agent and disinfectant. □□ **potassic** *adj.* [POTASH + -IUM]

potation /pōtáyshən/ *n.* **1** a drink. **2** the act or an instance of drinking. **3** (usu. in *pl.*) the act or an instance of tippling. □□ **potatory** /pōtətawree/ *adj.* [ME f. OF *potation* or L *potatio* f. *potare* drink]

■ **1** see DRINK *n.* 1a.

potato /pətáytō/ *n.* (*pl.* **-oes**) **1** a starchy plant tuber that is cooked and used for food. **2** the plant, *Solanum tuberosum*, bearing this. **3** = *sweet potato*. **4** *Brit. colloq.* a hole in (esp. the heel of) a sock or stocking. □ **potato chip** a thin slice of potato deep-fried, eaten as a snack food. [Sp. *patata* var. of Taino *batata*]

pot-au-feu /páwtōfő/ *n.* **1** the traditional French dish of boiled meat and vegetables. **2** the soup or broth from it. **3** a large cooking pot of the kind common in France. [F, = pot on the fire]

potbelly /pótbelee/ *n.* (*pl.* **-ies**) **1** a protruding stomach. **2** a person with this. **3** a small bulbous stove. □□ **potbellied** *adj.*

potboiler /pótboylər/ *n.* **1** a work of literature or art done merely to make the writer or artist a living. **2** a writer or artist who does this.

potch /poch/ *n.* an opal of inferior quality. [19th c.: orig. unkn.]

poteen /pōtéen, pə-/ *n.* (also **potheen** /-cheen/) *Ir.* alcohol made illicitly, usu. from potatoes. [Ir. *poitín* dimin. of *pota* POT[1]]

■ moonshine, home brew, *colloq.* hooch.

potent[1] /pót'nt/ *adj.* **1** powerful; strong. **2** (of a reason) cogent; forceful. **3** (of a male) capable of sexual erection or orgasm. **4** *literary* mighty. □□ **potence** *n.* **potency** *n.* **potently** *adv.* [L *potens -entis* pres. part. of *posse* be able]

■ **1** powerful, strong, mighty, vigorous, forceful, formidable, influential, *literary or archaic* puissant. **2** forceful, effective, convincing, cogent, persuasive, compelling, efficacious, sound, valid, impressive, weighty, authoritative, influential. **3** virile, masculine, manly.

potent[2] /pót'nt/ *adj.* & *n. Heraldry* ● *adj.* **1** with a crutch-head shape. **2** (of a fur) formed by a series of such shapes. ● *n.* this fur. [ME f. OF *potence* crutch f. L *potentia* power (as POTENT[1])]

potentate /pót'ntayt/ *n.* a monarch or ruler. [ME f. OF *potentat* or L *potentatus* dominion (as POTENT[2])]

■ see MONARCH 1, 2.

potential /pəténshəl/ *adj.* & *n.* ● *adj.* capable of coming into being or action; latent. ● *n.* **1** the capacity for use or development; possibility (*achieved its highest potential*). **2** usable resources. **3** *Physics* the quantity determining the energy of mass in a gravitational field or of charge in an electric field. □ **potential barrier** a region of high potential impeding the movement of particles, etc. **potential difference** the difference of electric potential between two points. **potential energy** a body's ability to do work by virtue of its position relative to others, stresses within itself, electric charge, etc. □□ **potentiality** /-sheeálitee/ *n.* **potentialize** *v.tr.* **potentially** *adv.* [ME f. OF *potencial* or LL *potentialis* f. *potentia* (as POTENT[1])]

■ *adj.* possible, likely, latent, implicit, implied, imminent, developing, budding, embryonic, dormant, quiescent, future, unrealized. ● *n.* **1** capacity, capability, possibility, aptitude, potency; (*have potential*) *colloq.* have what it takes, have the necessary. **2** see *the necessary* 2 (NECESSARY).

potentiate /pəténsheeayt/ *v.tr.* **1** make more powerful, esp. increase the effectiveness of (a drug). **2** make possible. [as POTENT[1] after SUBSTANTIATE]

potentilla /pót'ntílə/ *n.* any plant or shrub of the genus *Potentilla*; a cinquefoil. [med.L, dimin. of L *potens* POTENT[1]]

potentiometer /pəténsheeómitər/ *n.* an instrument for measuring or adjusting small electrical potentials. □□ **potentiometric** /-sheeəmétrik/ *adj.* **potentiometry** /-sheeómitree/ *n.*

pothead /póthed/ *n. sl.* a person who smokes marijuana frequently.

potheen var. of POTEEN.

pother /póthər/ *n.* & *v.* ● *n.* a noise; commotion; fuss. ● *v.* **1** *tr.* fluster; worry. **2** *intr.* make a fuss. [16th c.: orig. unkn.]

■ *n.* see FUSS *n.* 1, 2a.

potherb /pótərb, -hərb/ *n.* any herb grown in a kitchen garden or a pot.

pothole /pót-hōl/ *n.* & *v.* ● *n.* **1** *Geol.* a deep hole or system of caves and underground riverbeds formed by the erosion of rock esp. by the action of water. **2** a deep hole in the ground or a riverbed. **3** a hole in a road surface caused by wear, weather, or subsidence. ● *v.intr. Brit.* explore potholes. □□ **potholed** *adj.* **potholer** *n.* **potholing** *n.*

■ *n.* **2, 3** see HOLE *n.* 1.

potion /pōshən/ *n.* a liquid medicine, drug, poison, etc. [ME f. OF f. L *potio -onis* f. *potus* having drunk]

■ draft, brew, potation, *formal* beverage, *joc.* libation; philter, elixir, tonic, concoction; dose.

potlatch /pótlach/ *n.* (among Native Americans of the Pacific Northwest) a ceremonial festival of gift giving or destruction of the owner's property to display wealth. [Chinook f. Nootka *patlatsh* gift]

potluck /pótlək/ *n.* **1** whatever (hospitality, food, etc.) is available. **2** a meal to which each guest brings a dish to share.

potoroo /pótərōō/ *n. Austral.* any small marsupial of the genus *Potorus*, native to Australia and Tasmania; a rat kangaroo. [Aboriginal]

potpie /pótpī/ *n.* a pie of meat, vegetables, etc., with a crust baked in a pot or deep-dish pie plate.

potpourri /pōpōōrée/ *n.* **1** a mixture of dried petals and spices used to perfume a room, etc. **2** a musical or literary medley. [F, = rotten pot]

■ **2** mixture, medley, miscellany, assortment, olla podrida, gallimaufry, salmagundi, patchwork, collection, hodgepodge, mélange, pastiche, pasticcio.

potsherd /pótshərd/ *n.* a broken piece of pottery, esp. one found on an archaeological site.

■ shard, sherd.

potshot /pótshot/ *n.* **1** a random shot. **2** a shot aimed at an

/. . ./ **pronunciation**	● **part of speech**
□ **phrases, idioms, and compounds**	
□□ **derivatives**	■ **synonym section**
cross-references appear in SMALL CAPITALS or *italics*	

animal, etc., within easy reach. **3** a shot at a game bird, etc., merely to provide a meal.

pottage /pótij/ *n. archaic* soup; stew. [ME f. OF *potage* (as POT¹)]

potter¹ /pótər/ *n.* a maker of ceramic vessels. □ **potter's field** a burial place for paupers, strangers, etc. (after Matt. 27:7). **potter's wheel** a horizontal revolving disk to carry clay for making pots. [OE *pottere* (as POT¹)]

potter² /pótər/ *Brit.* var. of PUTTER³.

pottery /pótəree/ *n.* (*pl.* **-ies**) **1** vessels, etc., made of fired clay. **2** a potter's work. **3** a potter's workshop. [ME f. OF *poterie* f. *potier* POTTER²]

■ **1** earthenware, ceramics, terra cotta, crockery, stoneware, porcelain, china.

potting shed /póting/ *n.* a building in which plants are potted and tools, etc., are stored.

pottle /pót'l/ *n.* **1** *Brit.* a small carton for strawberries, etc. **2** *archaic* **a** a measure for liquids; a half gallon. **b** a pot, etc., containing this. [ME f. OF *potel* (as POT¹)]

potto /pótō/ *n.* (*pl.* **-os**) **1** a W. African lemurlike mammal, *Perodicticus potto.* **2** a kinkajou. [perh. f. Guinea dial.]

Pott's fracture /pots/ *n.* a fracture of the lower end of the fibula, usu. with dislocation of the ankle. [P. *Pott*, Engl. surgeon d. 1788]

potty¹ /pótee/ *adj.* (**pottier, pottiest**) *Brit. sl.* **1** foolish or crazy. **2** insignificant; trivial (esp. *potty little*). □□ **pottiness** *n.* [19th c.: orig. unkn.]

■ **1** see FOOLISH.

potty² /pótee/ *n.* (*pl.* **-ies**) *colloq.* a small pot for toilet-training a child.

pouch /powch/ *n. & v.* ● *n.* **1** a small bag or detachable outside pocket. **2** a baggy area of skin underneath the eyes, etc. **3 a** a pocketlike receptacle in which marsupials carry their young during lactation. **b** any of several similar structures in various animals, e.g., in the cheeks of rodents. **4** a soldier's ammunition bag. **5** a lockable bag for mail or dispatches. **6** *Bot.* a baglike cavity, esp. the seed vessel, in a plant. ● *v.tr.* **1** put or make into a pouch. **2** take possession of; pocket. **3** make (part of a dress, etc.) hang like a pouch. □□ **pouched** *adj.* **pouchy** *adj.* [ME f. ONF *pouche*: cf. POKE²]

■ *n.* **1** pocket, sack, bag, purse, *dial.* poke, *usu. hist.* reticule. ● *v.* **2** see POCKET *v.* 2.

pouffe /poof/ *n.* (also **pouf**) a large firm cushion used as a low seat or footstool. [F *pouf*; ult. imit.]

poularde /poolaárd/ *n.* (also **poulard**) a domestic hen that has been spayed and fattened for eating. [F *poularde* f. *poule* hen]

poult¹ /pōlt/ *n.* a young domestic fowl, turkey, pheasant, etc. [ME, contr. f. PULLET]

poult² /poolt/ *n.* (in full **poult-de-soie** /pōōdəswaá/) a fine corded silk or taffeta, usu. colored. [F, of unkn. orig.]

poulterer /pōltərər/ *n. Brit.* a dealer in poultry and usu. game. [ME *poulter* f. OF *pouletier* (as PULLET)]

poultice /pōltis/ *n. & v.* ● *n.* a soft medicated and usu. heated mass applied to the body and kept in place with muslin, etc., for relieving soreness and inflammation. ● *v.tr.* apply a poultice to. [orig. *pultes* (pl.) f. L *puls pultis* pottage, pap, etc.]

poultry /pōltree/ *n.* domestic fowls (ducks, geese, turkeys, chickens, etc.), esp. as a source of food. [ME f. OF *pouletrie* (as POULTERER)]

pounce¹ /powns/ *v. & n.* ● *v.intr.* **1** spring or swoop, esp. as in capturing prey. **2** (often foll. by *on, upon*) **a** make a sudden attack. **b** seize eagerly upon an object, remark, etc. (*pounced on what we said*). ● *n.* **1** the act or an instance of pouncing. **2** the claw or talon of a bird of prey. □□ **pouncer** *n.* [perh. f. PUNCHEON¹]

■ *v.* **1, 2a** spring, leap, swoop down (on *or* upon), jump; (*pounce on*) fall upon, take by surprise *or* unawares, attack, ambush, mug. **2 b** seize, leap, fasten, dive, sweep down. ● *n.* **1** spring, swoop, dive, sweep, leap, jump.

pounce² /powns/ *n. & v.* ● *n.* **1** a fine powder formerly used to prevent ink from spreading on unglazed paper. **2** pow-

dered charcoal, etc., dusted over a perforated pattern to transfer the design to the object beneath. ● *v.tr.* **1** dust with pounce. **2** transfer (a design, etc.) by use of pounce. **3** smooth (paper, etc.) with pounce or pumice. □□ **pouncer** *n.* [F *ponce, poncer* f. L *pumex* PUMICE]

pouncet box /pównsit/ *n. archaic* a small box with a perforated lid for perfumes, etc. [16th c.: perh. orig. erron. f. *pounced* (= perforated) *box*]

pound¹ /pownd/ *n.* **1** a unit of weight equal to 16 oz. avoirdupois (0.4536 kg), or 12 oz. troy (0.3732 kg). **2** (in full **pound sterling**) (*pl.* same or **pounds**) the chief monetary unit of the UK and several other countries. □ **pound cake** a rich cake orig. containing a pound (or equal weights) of each chief ingredient. **pound coin** (or **note**) a coin or note worth one pound sterling. **pound of flesh** any legitimate but crippling demand. **pound sign 1** the sign #. **2** the sign £, representing a pound. [OE *pund* ult. f. L *pondo* Roman pound weight of 12 ounces]

■ **2** sovereign, *Brit. sl.* nicker, oner, quid.

pound² /pownd/ *v. & n.* ● *v.* **1** *tr.* **a** crush or beat with repeated heavy blows. **b** pummel, esp. with the fists. **c** grind to a powder or pulp. **2** *intr.* (foll. by *at, on*) deliver heavy blows or gunfire. **3** *intr.* (foll. by *along*, etc.) make one's way heavily or clumsily. **4** *intr.* (of the heart) beat heavily. ● *n.* a heavy blow or thump; the sound of this. □ **pound into** instill (an attitude, behavior, etc.) forcefully (*pounded into me*). **pound out 1** produce with or as if with heavy blows. **2** remove (an attitude, behavior, etc.) forcefully (*pounded out of him*). □□ **pounder** *n.* [OE *pūnian*, rel. to Du. *puin*, LG *pün* rubbish]

■ *v.* **1 a, b** batter, pelt, hammer, pummel; thump, belabor, thrash, bludgeon, cudgel, strike, *colloq.* lambaste, give a person the works, work over, *sl.* paste, clobber, give a person a pasting; see also BEAT *v.* 1. **c** crush, grind, powder, pulverize, triturate, mash, pulp, *archaic* bray. **3** see TRAMP *v.* 1a. **4** beat, throb, hammer, thump, pulse, pulsate, palpitate. ● *n.* pounding, beat, beating, thump, thumping. □ **pound into** instill, din *or* drill *or* drub *or* hammer *or* beat into. **pound out 1** beat out, hammer out, produce. **2** remove, rid, expel, clear, empty, purge, beat out, hammer out, *usu. formal* cleanse.

pound³ /pownd/ *n. & v.* ● *n.* **1** an enclosure where stray animals or officially removed vehicles are kept until redeemed. **2** a place of confinement. ● *v.tr.* enclose (cattle, etc.) in a pound. □ **pound lock** a lock with two gates to confine water and often a side reservoir to maintain the water level. [ME f. OE *pund-* in *pundfald*: see PINFOLD]

■ **1** pen, compound, confine, yard; see also ENCLOSURE 2.

poundage /pówndij/ *n.* **1 a** weight in pounds. **b** a person's weight, esp. that which is regarded as excess. **2** *Brit.* a commission or fee of so much per pound sterling or weight. **3** *Brit.* a percentage of the total earnings of a business, paid as wages.

poundal /pównd'l/ *n. Physics* a unit of force equal to the force required to give a mass of one pound an acceleration of one foot per second per second. [POUND¹ + *-al* perh. after *quintal*]

pounder /pówndər/ *n.* (usu. in *comb.*) **1** a thing or person weighing a specified number of pounds (*a five-pounder*). **2** a gun carrying a shell of a specified number of pounds. **3** a thing worth, or a person possessing, so many pounds sterling.

pour /pawr/ *v.* **1** *intr. & tr.* (usu. foll. by *down, out, over*, etc.) flow or cause to flow esp. downwards in a stream or shower. **2** *tr.* dispense (a drink) by pouring. **3** *intr.* (of rain, or with *it* as subject) fall heavily. **4** *intr.* (usu. foll. by *in, out*, etc.) come or go in profusion or rapid succession (*the crowd poured out; letters poured in; poems poured from her fertile mind*). **5** *tr.* discharge or send freely (*poured forth arrows*). **6** *tr.* (often foll. by *out*) utter at length or in a rush (*poured out their story; poured scorn on my attempts*). □ **it never rains but it pours** misfortunes rarely come singly. **pour cold water on** see COLD. **pour oil on the waters** (or **on troubled wa-**

ters) calm a disagreement or disturbance, esp. with conciliatory words. □□ **pourable** *adj.* **pourer** *n.* [ME: orig. unkn.]
■ **1** flow, run, gush, rush, flood, stream, course, spout,
spurt, spew out *or* forth, cascade; discharge, let out, let
flow. **3** rain, teem down, fall, come down in buckets *or*
by the bucketful *or* in sheets, rain cats and dogs, pelt
down. **4** stream, swarm, crowd, throng, gush, teem,
issue (forth), go (forth), *archaic* sally forth.

pourboire /po͞orbwaár/ *n.* a gratuity or tip. [F, = *pour boire*
(money) for drinking]
■ see TIP³ *n.* 1.

pout¹ /powt/ *v. & n.* ● *v.* **1** *intr.* **a** push the lips forward as
an expression of displeasure or sulking. **b** (of the lips) be
pushed forward. **2** *tr.* push (the lips) forward in pouting.
● *n.* **1** such an action or expression. **2** (**the pouts**) a fit of
sulking. □□ **pouter** *n.* **poutingly** *adv.* **pouty** *adj.* [ME, perh.
f. OE *putian* (unrecorded) be inflated: cf. POUT²]
■ *v.* **1 a** make a moue, pull a long face, frown, lower,
knit one's brows; mope, brood, sulk. ● *n.* **1** moue,
(long) face, grimace, mouth, scowl, frown. **2** (**the
pouts**) sulk, huff, mood; the sulks.

pout² /powt/ *n.* **1** = BIB¹ 3. **2** = EELPOUT. **3** = BULLHEAD. [OE
-puta = *ǽlepūta* eelpout, f. WG]

pouter /pówtər/ *n.* **1** a person who pouts. **2** a kind of pigeon
able to inflate its crop considerably.

poverty /póvərtee/ *n.* **1** the state of being poor; want of the
necessities of life. **2** (often foll. by *of, in*) scarcity or lack. **3**
inferiority; poorness; meanness. **4** *Eccl.* renunciation of the
right to individual ownership of property esp. by a member
of a religious order. □ **poverty line** (also **level**) the minimum income level, as defined by a government standard,
needed to secure the necessities of life. **poverty-stricken**
extremely poor. [ME f. OF *poverte*, *poverté* f. L *paupertas*
-tatis f. *pauper* poor]
■ **1** want, penury, indigence, destitution, pauperism,
impecuniousness, neediness, beggary, narrow *or*
reduced circumstances, necessity, need. **2** scarcity,
scarceness, want, need, lack, insufficiency, shortage,
dearth, paucity, inadequacy. **3** see INFERIORITY.
□ **poverty-stricken** see POOR 1.

POW *abbr.* prisoner of war.

pow /pow/ *int.* expressing the sound of a blow or explosion.
[imit.]

powder /pówdər/ *n. & v.* ● *n.* **1** a substance in the form of
fine dry particles. **2** a medicine or cosmetic in this form. **3**
= GUNPOWDER. ● *v.tr.* **1 a** apply powder to. **b** sprinkle or
decorate with or as with powder. **2** (esp. as **powdered** *adj.*)
reduce to a fine powder (*powdered milk*). □ **keep one's
powder dry** be cautious and alert. **powder blue** pale blue.
powder flask (also **powder horn**) *hist.* a small case for
carrying gunpowder. **powder keg 1** a barrel of gunpowder.
2 a dangerous or volatile situation. **powder monkey** *hist.* a
boy employed on board ship to carry powder to the guns.
powder puff a soft pad for applying powder to the skin,
esp. the face. **powder-puff 1** designating an activity intended for or restricted to women. **2** lightweight; frivolous.
powder room a women's toilet in a public building. **take
a powder** *sl.* depart quickly. □□ **powdery** *adj.* [ME f. OF
poudre f. L *pulvis pulveris* dust]
■ *n.* **1** dust; talc. ● *v.* **1** dust; dredge, flour. **2** pulverize,
grind, crush, pound, granulate, levigate, triturate,
archaic bray. □ **keep one's powder dry** see *watch out*.
powder keg 2 time bomb, precipice; dynamite.
powder room toilet, lavatory, ladies' room, rest room,
bathroom, washroom, *Brit.* Ladies, (public)
conveniences, *Brit. colloq.* loo, *euphem.* comfort station,
Brit. euphem. cloakroom. **take a powder** abscond,
escape, vanish, disappear, *sl.* hightail it, take it on the
lam, *Brit. sl.* do a moonlight flit; see also RUN *v.* 2.

power /pówər/ *n. & v.* ● *n.* **1** the ability to do or act (*will do
all in my power; has the power to change color*). **2** a particular
faculty of body or mind (*lost the power of speech; powers of
persuasion*). **3 a** government, influence, or authority. **b** political or social ascendancy or control (*the party in power*). **4**
authorization; delegated authority (*power of attorney; police*

powers). **5** (often foll. by *over*) personal ascendancy. **6** an
influential person, group, or organization (*the press is a power
in the land*). **7 a** military strength. **b** a nation having international influence, esp. based on military strength (*the leading powers*). **8** vigor; energy. **9** an active property or function
(*has a high heating power*). **10** *colloq.* a large number or
amount (*has done me a power of good*). **11** the capacity for
exerting mechanical force or doing work (*horsepower*). **12**
mechanical or electrical energy as distinct from hand labor
(often *attrib.*: *power tools; power steering*). **13 a** a public supply of (esp. electrical) energy. **b** a particular source or form
of energy (*hydroelectric power*). **14** a mechanical force applied, e.g., by means of a lever. **15** *Physics* the rate of energy
output. **16** the product obtained when a number is multiplied by itself a certain number of times (*2 to the power of 3
= 8*). **17** the magnifying capacity of a lens. **18 a** a deity. **b**
(in *pl.*) the sixth order of the ninefold celestial hierarchy.
● *v.tr.* **1** supply with mechanical or electrical energy. **2** (foll.
by *up, down*) increase or decrease the power supplied to (a
device); switch on or off. □ **in the power of** under the control of. **power behind the throne** a person who asserts
authority or influence without having formal status. **power
block** a group of nations constituting an international political force. **power brakes** automotive brakes in which engine power supplements that provided by the driver's pressure on the brake pedal. **power cut** esp. *Brit.* = *power
failure.* **power dive** *n.* a steep dive of an aircraft with the
engines providing thrust. ● *v.intr.* perform a power dive.
power failure a temporary withdrawal or failure of an electric power supply. **power line** a conductor supplying electrical power, esp. one supported by pylons or poles. **power
of attorney** see ATTORNEY. **power pack 1** a unit for supplying power. **2** the equipment for converting an alternating
current (from an electrical outlet) to a direct current at a
different (usu. lower) voltage. **power plant 1** a facility producing esp. electrical power. **2** source of power, as an engine. **power play 1** tactics involving the concentration of
players at a particular point. **2** similar tactics in business,
politics, etc., involving a concentration of resources, effort,
etc. **3** *Ice Hockey* situation in which one team has an extra
skater owing to a penalty on the opposing team. **power
point** *Brit.* an electrical outlet. **power-sharing** a policy
agreed between parties or within a coalition to share responsibility for decision making and political action. **the
powers that be** those in authority. **power stroke** the stroke
of an internal-combustion engine, in which the piston is
moved downward by the expansion of gases. □□ **powered**
adj. (also in *comb.*). [ME & AF *poer*, etc., OF *poeir* ult. f. L
posse be able]
■ *n.* **2** capacity, capability, ability, potential, faculty,
competence, potentiality, energies; talent, skill, ability,
gift, aptitude, genius, knack. **3a, 5** control, dominance,
authority, mastery, rule, influence, government,
command, ascendancy, sovereignty, dominion, *archaic*
puissance; weight, sway, pull, *colloq.* clout, *sl.* drag.
4 authority, right, authorization, warrant; see also
LICENSE 2, PERMISSION. **8** strength, might, vigor, energy,
force, mightiness, potency, forcefulness, brawn,
muscle, *archaic* puissance. **10** see LOT *n.* 1. **13** energy;
electricity. **14** energy, momentum, impetus, drive,
force. **18 a** see GOD 1a. ● *v.* **2** see *turn on* 1, *turn off* 1.
□ **in the power of** under a person's thumb, at the
mercy of. **power behind the throne** kingmaker,
éminence grise, gray eminence. **power failure** power
outage, blackout, esp. *Brit.* power cut. **power point**
socket, outlet, *Brit.* point(s). **the powers that be**
establishment, government, administration, authorities.

powerboat /pówərbōt/ *n.* a powerful motorboat.

powerful /pówərfo͝ol/ *adj.* **1** having much power or strength.

/.../ **pronunciation**	● **part of speech**
□ **phrases, idioms, and compounds**	
□□ **derivatives**	■ **synonym section**
cross-references appear in SMALL CAPITALS or *italics*	

2 politically or socially influential. □□ **powerfully** adv. **powerfulness** n.

■ **1** potent, strong, mighty, vigorous, robust, energetic, sturdy, stalwart, tough, resilient, dynamic; intense, substantial, great, high. **2** influential, strong, compelling, forceful, potent, substantial, weighty, authoritative, effective, persuasive; important, impressive, effectual, formidable.

powerhouse /pówərhows/ n. **1** = power plant. **2** a person or thing of great energy.

powerless /pówərlis/ adj. **1** without power or strength. **2** (often foll. by to + infin.) wholly unable (powerless to help). □□ **powerlessly** adv. **powerlessness** n.

■ **1** helpless, ineffectual, ineffective, incapacitated, weak, feeble, debilitated. **2** (powerless to) unable or not able to, unfit or incompetent or unqualified to, incapable of.

powwow /pów-wow/ n. & v. ● n. a conference or meeting for discussion (orig. among Native Americans). ● v.tr. hold a powwow. [Algonquian powah, powwaw magician (lit. 'he dreams')]

■ n. see DISCUSSION 1, PALAVER n. 5. ● v. see CONFER 2.

pox /poks/ n. **1** any virus disease producing a rash of pimples that become pus-filled and leave pockmarks on healing. **2** colloq. = SYPHILIS. **3** a plant disease that causes pocklike spots. □ **a pox on** archaic an exclamation of anger or impatience with (a person). [alt. spelling of pocks pl. of POCK]

pozzolana /pótsəláanə/ n. (also **puzzolana**) a volcanic ash used for mortar or hydraulic cement. [It., f. pozz(u)olano (adj.) of Pozzuoli near Naples]

pp abbr. pianissimo.

pp. abbr. pages.

p.p. abbr. (also **pp**) per pro.

p.p.b. abbr. parts per billion.

ppd. abbr. **1** postpaid. **2** prepaid.

p.p.m. abbr. parts per million.

PPO abbr. preferred provider organization (see PREFER).

PPS abbr. **1** additional postscript. **2** Brit. Parliamentary Private Secretary.

PR abbr. **1** public relations. **2** Puerto Rico. **3** proportional representation.

Pr symb. Chem. the element praseodymium.

pr. abbr. pair.

practicable /práktikəbəl/ adj. **1** that can be done or used. **2** possible in practice. □□ **practicability** /-bílitee/ n. **practicableness** n. **practicably** adv. [F praticable f. pratiquer put into practice (as PRACTICAL)]

■ possible, feasible, workable, performable, doable, achievable, attainable, accomplishable, viable.

practical /práktikəl/ adj. & n. ● adj. **1** of or concerned with practice or use rather than theory. **2** suited to use or action; designed mainly to fulfill a function (practical shoes). **3** (of a person) inclined to action rather than speculation; able to make things function well. **4 a** that is such in effect though not nominally (for all practical purposes). **b** virtual (in practical control). **5** feasible; concerned with what is actually possible (practical politics). ● n. Brit. a practical examination or lesson. □ **practical joke** a humorous trick played on a person. □□ **practicality** /-kálitee/ n. (pl. **-ies**). **practicalness** n. [earlier practic f. obs. F practique or LL practicus f. Gk praktikos f. prassō do, act]

■ adj. **1** empirical, pragmatic, empiric, experimental, applied, field, hands-on. **2** pragmatic, functional, useful, usable, utilitarian, serviceable; appropriate, suitable, expedient; everyday, ordinary. **3** down-to-earth, pragmatic, hardheaded, realistic, businesslike, commonsensical, sensible, efficient, matter-of-fact, no-nonsense, colloq. hard-nosed. **4 b** virtual, effective, essential. □ **practical joke** see PRANK.

practically /práktiklee/ adv. **1** virtually; almost (practically nothing). **2** in a practical way.

■ **1** almost, (very) nearly, virtually, just about, more or less, archaic or rhet. wellnigh. **2** realistically, in fact, in reality; empirically, experimentally; sensibly, efficiently, matter-of-factly.

practice /práktis/ n. & v. ● n. **1** habitual action or perfor-

mance (the practice of teaching; makes a practice of saving). **2** a habit or custom (has been my regular practice). **3 a** repeated exercise in an activity requiring the development of skill (to sing well needs much practice). **b** a session of this (time for target practice). **4** action or execution as opposed to theory. **5** the professional work or business of a doctor, lawyer, etc. (has a practice in town). **6** an established method of legal procedure. **7** procedure generally, esp. of a specified kind (bad practice). ● v.tr. & intr. (also Brit. **practise**). **1** tr. perform habitually; carry out in action (practice the same method; practice what you preach). **2** tr. & (foll. by in, on) intr. do repeatedly as an exercise to improve a skill; exercise oneself in or on (an activity requiring skill) (had to practice in the art of speaking; practice your reading). **3** tr. (as **practiced** adj.) experienced, expert (a practiced liar; with a practiced hand). **4** tr. **a** pursue or be engaged in (a profession, religion, etc.). **b** (as **practicing** adj.) currently active or engaged in (a profession or activity) (a practicing Christian; a practicing lawyer). **5** intr. (foll. by on, upon) take advantage of; impose upon. **6** intr. archaic scheme; contrive (when first we practice to deceive). □ **in practice 1** when actually applied; in reality. **2** skillful because of recent exercise in a particular pursuit. **out of practice** lacking a former skill from lack of recent practice. **put into practice** actually apply (an idea, method, etc.). □□ **practicer** n. [ME f. OF pra(c)tiser or med.L practizare alt. f. practicare (as PRACTICAL)]

■ n. **2, 7** custom, habit, praxis, formal or joc. wont; routine, convention, tradition, rule, procedure, mode, style, way, modus operandi, m.o., technique. **3** exercise, discipline, drill, repetition, rehearsal, training, preparation; workout. **4** action, execution, operation, enactment, reality, actuality, fact, truth. ● v. **1** carry out, make a practice of, perform, do, act, put into practice. **2** exercise, work out, train, prepare, rehearse, study; run through, go through. **3** (**practiced**) accomplished, proficient, expert, skilled, experienced, capable, adept, seasoned, able, qualified, gifted, talented, skillful, masterful, consummate, well-trained, well-versed. **5** (practice on or upon) see IMPOSE 3. □ **in practice 1** practically, actually, in reality, realistically, in real life. **out of practice** unpracticed, unaccustomed, rusty; out of touch. **put into practice** see APPLY 3a.

practician /praktíshən/ n. a worker; a practitioner. [obs. F practicien f. practique f. med.L practica f. Gk praktikē fem. of praktikos: see PRACTICAL]

practise Brit. var. of PRACTICE v.

practitioner /praktíshənər/ n. a person practicing a profession, esp. medicine (general practitioner). [obs. practitian = PRACTICIAN]

prad /prad/ n. esp. Austral. sl. a horse. [by metathesis f. Du. paard f. LL paraveredus; see PALFREY]

prae- /pree/ prefix = PRE- (esp. in words regarded as Latin or relating to Roman antiquity). [L: see PRE-]

praecipe /preésipee, prés-/ n. **1** a writ demanding action or an explanation of inaction. **2** an order requesting a writ. [L (the first word of the writ), imper. of praecipere enjoin: see PRECEPT]

praecocial Brit. var. of PRECOCIAL.

praemunire /preémyŏŏnfree/ n. hist. a writ charging a sheriff to summon a person accused of asserting or maintaining papal jurisdiction in England. [med.L, = forewarn, for L praemonēre (as PRAE-, monēre warn): the words praemunire facias that you warn (a person to appear) occur in the writ]

praenomen /preenṓmen/ n. an ancient Roman's first or personal name (e.g., Marcus Tullius Cicero). [L f. prae before + nomen name]

praesidium var. of PRESIDIUM.

praetor /preétər/ n. (also **pretor**) Rom.Hist. each of two ancient Roman magistrates ranking below consul. □□ **praetorial** /-tóreeəl/ adj. **praetorship** n. [ME f. F préteur or L praetor (perh. as PRAE-, ire it- go)]

praetorian /preetáwreeən/ adj. & n. (also **pretorian**) Rom.Hist. ● adj. of or having the powers of a praetor. ● n. a man of praetorian rank. □ **praetorian guard** the bodyguard of the Roman emperor. [ME f. L *praetorianus* (as PRAETOR)]

pragmatic /pragmátik/ *adj.* **1** dealing with matters with regard to their practical requirements or consequences. **2** treating the facts of history with reference to their practical lessons. **3** *hist.* of or relating to the affairs of a state. **4** (also **pragmatical**) **a** concerning pragmatism. **b** meddlesome. **c** dogmatic. □ **pragmatic sanction** *hist.* an imperial or royal ordinance issued as a fundamental law, esp. regarding a question of royal succession. □□ **pragmaticality** /-tikálitee/ *n.* **pragmatically** *adv.* [LL *pragmaticus* f. Gk *pragmatikos* f. *pragma -matos* deed]
■ **1** see PRACTICAL 1–3.

pragmatics /pragmátiks/ *n.pl.* (usu. treated as *sing.*) the branch of linguistics dealing with language in use.

pragmatism /prágmətizəm/ *n.* **1** a pragmatic attitude or procedure. **2** a philosophy that evaluates assertions solely by their practical consequences and bearing on human interests. □□ **pragmatist** *n.* **pragmatistic** /-tístik/ *adj.* [Gk *pragma*: see PRAGMATIC]

pragmatize /prágmətīz/ *v.tr.* **1** represent as real. **2** rationalize (a myth).

prahu var. of PROA.

prairie /práiree/ *n.* a large area of usu. treeless grassland esp. in central N. America. □ **prairie chicken** a central N. American grouse, *Tympanuchus cupido*. **prairie dog** any central or western N. American rodent of the genus *Cynomys*, living in burrows and making a barking sound. **prairie oyster 1** a seasoned raw egg or egg yolk, often served in a drink as a cure for a hangover. **2** the cooked testis of a calf served as food. **prairie schooner** a covered wagon used by the 19th-c. pioneers in crossing the prairies. **prairie wolf** = COYOTE. [F f. OF *praerie* ult. f. L *pratum* meadow]
■ see PLAIN¹ *n.* 1.

praise /prayz/ *v. & n.* ● *v.tr.* **1** express warm approval or admiration of. **2** glorify (God) in words. ● *n.* the act or an instance of praising; commendation (*won high praise; were loud in their praises*). □ **praise be!** an exclamation of pious gratitude. **sing the praises of** commend (a person) highly. □□ **praiseful** *adj.* **praiser** *n.* [ME f. OF *preisier* price, prize, praise, f. LL *pretiare* f. L *pretium* price: cf. PRIZE¹]
■ *v.* **1** acclaim, laud, applaud, pay tribute to, compliment, commend, eulogize, extol, honor, sing the praises of, pay homage to, endorse. **2** worship, revere, reverence, exalt, glorify, venerate, hallow. ● *n.* acclaim, approval, approbation, applause, plaudits, acclamation, tribute, encomium, compliment, commendation, glory, *colloq.* kudos; honor, glorification, adoration, exaltation, worship, veneration, adulation, reverence. □ **sing the praises of** see PRAISE *v.* 1 above.

praiseworthy /práyzwərthee/ *adj.* worthy of praise; commendable. □□ **praiseworthily** *adv.* **praiseworthiness** *n.*
■ commendable, laudable, admirable, creditable, worthy, meritorious, deserving, exemplary.

Prakrit /praákrit/ *n.* any of the (*esp.* ancient or medieval) vernacular dialects of north and central India existing alongside or derived from Sanskrit. [Skr. *prākrta* unrefined: cf. SANSKRIT]

praline /praáleen, práy-/ *n.* any of several candies made with almonds, pecans, or other nuts and sugar. [F f. Marshal de Plessis-*Praslin*, Fr. soldier d. 1675, whose cook invented it]

pralltriller /praáltrilər/ *n.* a musical ornament consisting of one rapid alternation of the written note with the note immediately above it. [G f. *prallen* rebound + *Triller* TRILL]

pram¹ /pram/ *n. Brit.* a baby carriage. [abbr. of PERAMBULATOR]

pram² /praam/ *n.* (also **praam**) **1** a flat-bottomed gunboat or Baltic Sea cargo boat. **2** a Scandinavian ship's dinghy. [MDu. *prame, praem*, MLG *prām(e)*, f. OSlav. *pramŭ*]

prana /praánə/ *n.* **1** (in Hinduism) breath as a life-giving force. **2** the breath; breathing. [Skr.]

prance /prans/ *v. & n.* ● *v.intr.* **1** (of a horse) raise the forelegs and spring from the hind legs. **2** (often foll. by *about*) walk or behave in an arrogant manner. ● *n.* **1** the act of

prancing. **2** a prancing movement. □□ **prancer** *n.* [ME: orig. unkn.]
■ *v.* **1** curvet, capriole, caper, skip, frisk, jump, spring, bound. ● *n.* **2** see CAPER¹ *n.* 1.

prandial /prándeeəl/ *adj.* of a meal, usu. dinner. [L *prandium* meal]

prang /prang/ *v. & n. Brit. sl.* ● *v.tr.* **1** crash or damage (an aircraft or vehicle). **2** bomb (a target) successfully. ● *n.* the act or an instance of pranging. [imit.]
■ *v.* **1** crash, smash, bump, dent, damage. **2** see BOMB *v.* 1. ● *n.* see COLLISION 1.

prank /prangk/ *n.* a practical joke; a piece of mischief. □□ **prankful** *adj.* **prankish** *adj.* **pranksome** *adj.* [16th c.: orig. unkn.]
■ trick, practical joke, frolic, escapade, antic, caper, stunt, jape, *Austral.* goak; (*pranks*) mischief, *colloq.* lark, monkey business *or* tricks, shenanigans, monkeyshines.

prankster /prángkstər/ *n.* a person fond of playing pranks.
■ see JOKER 1.

prase /prayz/ *n.* a translucent leek-green type of quartz. [F f. L *prasius* f. Gk *prasios* (adj.) leek-green f. *prason* leek]

praseodymium /práyzeeōdímeeəm, práysee-/ *n. Chem.* a soft silvery metallic element of the lanthanide series, occurring naturally in various minerals and used in catalyst mixtures. ¶ Symb.: **Pr**. [G *Praseodym* f. Gk *prasios* (see PRASE) from its green salts, + G *Didym* DIDYMIUM]

prat /prat/ *n. Brit. sl.* **1** a silly or foolish person. **2** the buttocks. [16th-c. cant (in sense 2): orig. unkn.]
■ **1** see FOOL¹ *n.* 1. **2** see BUTTOCK.

prate /prayt/ *v. & n.* ● *v.* **1** *intr.* chatter; talk too much. **2** *intr.* talk foolishly or irrelevantly. **3** *tr.* tell or say in a prating manner. ● *n.* prating; idle talk. □□ **prater** *n.* **prating** *adj.* [ME f. MDu., MLG *praten*, prob. imit.]
■ *v.* see CHATTER *v.* 1. ● *n.* see CHATTER *n.* 1.

pratfall /prátfawl/ *n. sl.* **1** a fall on the buttocks. **2** a humiliating failure.

pratincole /prátingkōl/ *n.* any of various birds of the subfamily Glareolinae, inhabiting sandy and stony areas and feeding on insects. [mod.L *pratincola* f. L *pratum* meadow + *incola* inhabitant]

pratique /prateék/ *n.* a license to have dealings with a port, granted to a ship after quarantine or on showing a clean bill of health. [F, = practice, intercourse, f. It. *pratica* f. med.L *practica*: see PRACTICIAN]

prattle /prát'l/ *v. & n.* ● *v.intr. & tr.* chatter or say in a childish or inconsequential way. ● *n.* **1** childish chatter. **2** inconsequential talk. □□ **prattler** *n.* **prattling** *adj.* [MLG *pratelen* (as PRATE)]
■ *v.* prate, babble, blab, blather, gibber, jabber, palaver, tattle, twaddle, gabble, chatter, patter, drivel on, twitter, rattle on, go on (and on), run (on), *colloq.* natter, gas, gab, jaw, *sl.* shoot one's mouth off, *sl. derog.* yak, yackety-yak. ● *n.* prate, prating, talk, babble, blather, gibber, jabber, palaver, tattle, twaddle, chatter, gabble, patter, drivel, cackle, clack, *colloq.* gab, *sl. derog.* yackety-yak.

prau var. of PROA.

prawn /prawn/ *n. & v.* ● *n.* any of various marine crustaceans, resembling a shrimp but usu. larger. ● *v.intr.* fish for prawns. [ME *pra(y)ne*, of unkn. orig.]

praxis /práksis/ *n.* **1** accepted practice or custom. **2** the practicing of an art or skill. [med.L f. Gk, = doing, f. *prassō* do]
■ **1** see PRACTICE *n.* 2, 7.

pray /pray/ *v.* (often foll. by *for* or *to* + infin. or *that* + clause) **1** *intr.* (often foll. by *to*) say prayers (to God, etc.); make devout supplication. **2 a** *tr.* entreat; beseech. **b** *tr. & intr.* ask earnestly (*prayed to be released*). **3** *tr.* (as *imper.*) old-fashioned

─────────────────────────

/.../ pronunciation	● part of speech
□ phrases, idioms, and compounds	
□□ derivatives	■ synonym section
cross-references appear in SMALL CAPITALS or *italics*	

please (*pray tell me*). □ **praying mantis** see MANTIS. [ME f. OF *preier* f. LL *precare* f. L *precari* entreat]

■ **1** say one's prayers, offer a prayer. **2 a** beseech, ask, call upon *or* on, entreat, implore, appeal to, plead (with), beg, importune, solicit, petition, supplicate. **b** see ASK 2, BEG 2.

prayer¹ /prair/ *n.* **1 a** a solemn request or thanksgiving to God or an object of worship (*say a prayer*). **b** a formula or form of words used in praying (*the Lord's prayer*). **c** the act of praying (*be at prayer*). **d** a religious service consisting largely of prayers (*morning prayers*). **2 a** an entreaty to a person. **b** a thing entreated or prayed for. □ **not have a prayer** *colloq.* have no chance (of success, etc.). **prayer book** a book containing the forms of prayer in regular use. **prayer rug** (or **mat**) a small carpet knelt on by Muslims when praying. **prayer wheel** a revolving cylindrical box inscribed with or containing prayers, used esp. by Tibetan Buddhists. □□ **prayerless** *adj.* [ME f. OF *preiere* ult. f. L *precarius* obtained by entreaty f. *prex precis* prayer]

■ **1 a** invocation, intercession, *archaic* orison; see also LITANY 1. **c, d** devotion, praying, intercession, worship; (divine) service. **2 a** petition, supplication, request, entreaty, plea, suit, appeal, obsecration. □ **not have a prayer** have *or* stand no chance, not have *or* stand a chance, *colloq.* not have a hope (in hell), *Austral. & NZ colloq.* not have a Buckley's.

prayer² /práyǝr/ *n.* a person who prays.

prayerful /práirfŏŏl/ *adj.* **1** (of a person) given to praying; devout. **2** (of speech, actions, etc.) characterized by or expressive of prayer. □□ **prayerfully** *adv.* **prayerfulness** *n.*

pre- /pree/ *prefix* before (in time, place, order, degree, or importance). [from *or* after L *prae-* f. *prae* (adv. & prep.)]

preach /preech/ *v.* **1 a** *intr.* deliver a sermon or religious address. **b** *tr.* deliver (a sermon); proclaim or expound. **2** *intr.* give moral advice in an obtrusive way. **3** *tr.* advocate or inculcate (a quality or practice, etc.). □□ **preachable** *adj.* [ME f. OF *prechier* f. L *praedicare* proclaim, in eccl.L preach (as PRAE-, *dicare* declare)]

■ **1 a** deliver a sermon, sermonize, *colloq.* preachify. **b** teach, proclaim, evangelize, expound, propagate, explain; see also INTERPRET 1, 2. **2** moralize, sermonize, lecture, pontificate, *colloq.* preachify; see also RANT *v.* 2, 3. **3** urge, inculcate, advocate, instill, teach; see also CHAMPION *v.*

preacher /preéchǝr/ *n.* a person who preaches, esp. a minister of religion. [ME f. AF *prech(o)ur*, OF *prech(e)or* f. eccl.L *praedicator* (as PREACH)]

■ orator, rhetorician, speechmaker, *usu. derog.* rhetor; minister, clergyman, clergywoman, cleric, ecclesiastic, reverend, divine, *colloq.* tub-thumper.

preachify /preéchifī/ *v.intr.* (**-ies, -ied**) *colloq.* preach or moralize tediously.

preachment /preéchmǝnt/ *n.* usu. *derog.* preaching; sermonizing.

preachy /preéchee/ *adj.* (**preachier, preachiest**) *colloq.* inclined to preach or moralize. □□ **preachiness** *n.*

■ priggish, prescriptive; see also *pedantic* (PEDANT), PURITAN *adj.* 2.

preadolescent /preéad'lésǝnt/ *adj. & n.* ● *adj.* **1** (of a child) having nearly reached adolescence. **2** of or relating to the two or three years preceding adolescence. ● *n.* a preadolescent child. □□ **preadolescence** *n.*

preamble /preé-ámbǝl/ *n.* **1** a preliminary statement or introduction. **2** the introductory part of a constitution, statute, or deed, etc. □□ **preambular** /-ámbyŏŏlǝr/ *adj.* [ME f. OF *preambule* f. med.L *praeambulum* f. LL *praeambulus* (adj.) going before (as PRE-, AMBLE)]

■ **1** introduction, foreword, prologue, preface; proem, prolegomenon, exordium.

preamp /preé-ámp/ *n.* = PREAMPLIFIER. [abbr.]

preamplifier /preé-ámplifīǝr/ *n.* an electronic device that amplifies a very weak signal (e.g., from a microphone or pickup) and transmits it to a main amplifier. □□ **preamplified** *adj.*

prearrange /preéǝráynj/ *v.tr.* arrange beforehand. □□ **prearrangement** *n.*

■ see ARRANGE 2, 3. □□ **prearrangement** see PROVISION *n.* 1a.

preatomic /preéǝtómik/ *adj.* existing or occurring before the use of atomic weapons or energy.

prebend /prébǝnd/ *n. Eccl.* **1** the stipend of a canon or member of a chapter. **2** a portion of land or tithe from which this is drawn. □□ **prebendal** /pribénd'l, préban-/ *adj.* [ME f. OF *prebende* f. LL *praebenda* pension, neut.pl. gerundive of L *praebēre* grant f. *prae* forth + *habēre* hold]

prebendary /prébǝnderee/ *n.* (*pl.* **-ies**) **1** the holder of a prebend. **2** an honorary canon. □□ **prebendaryship** *n.* [ME f. med.L *praebendarius* (as PREBEND)]

Precambrian /preékámbreeǝn/ *adj. & n. Geol.* ● *adj.* of or relating to the earliest era of geological time from the formation of the earth to the first forms of life. ● *n.* this era.

precancer /preékánsǝr, -kántsǝr/ *n.* a precancerous state or condition.

precancerous /preékánsrǝs, -kántsǝr-/ *adj.* having the tendency to develop into a cancer. □□ **precancerously** *adv.*

precarious /prikáireeǝs/ *adj.* **1** uncertain; dependent on chance (*makes a precarious living*). **2** insecure; perilous (*precarious health*). □□ **precariously** *adv.* **precariousness** *n.* [L *precarius*: see PRAYER¹]

■ uncertain, unreliable, unsure, unpredictable, insecure, unstable, unsteady, unsettled, shaky, doubtful, dubious, questionable, delicate, (hanging) in the balance, hanging by a thread; perilous, risky, hazardous, treacherous, dangerous, difficult, problematic, chancy, esp. *Brit. colloq.* dodgy, *sl.* dicey, hairy.

precast /preékást/ *adj.* (of concrete) cast in its final shape before positioning.

precative /prékǝtiv/ *adj.* (also **precatory** /-tawree/) (of a word or form) expressing a wish or request. [LL *precativus* f. *precari* pray]

precaution /prikáwshǝn/ *n.* **1** an action taken beforehand to avoid risk or ensure a good result. **2** (in *pl.*) *colloq.* the use of contraceptives. **3** caution exercised beforehand; prudent foresight. □□ **precautionary** *adj.* [F *précaution* f. LL *praecautio -onis* f. L *praecavēre* (as PRAE-, *cavēre caut-* beware of)]

■ **1** preventive measure, safety measure, safeguard. **3** foresight, prudence, providence, forethought, caution, cautiousness, circumspection, care, attention, watchfulness, vigilance, alertness, wariness, chariness, apprehension, farsightedness, anticipation.

precede /priseéd/ *v.tr.* **1 a** (often as **preceding** *adj.*) come or go before in time, order, importance, etc. (*preceding generations; the preceding paragraph*). **b** walk, etc., in front of (*preceded by our guide*). **2** (foll. by *by*) cause to be preceded (*must precede this measure by milder ones*). [OF *preceder* f. L *praecedere* (as PRAE-, *cedere cess-* go)]

■ **1** come *or* go ahead *or* in advance of, lead, pave the way for, herald, usher in, introduce; foreshadow, antedate, predate; (**preceding**) foregoing, former, previous, prior, earlier, abovementioned, aforementioned, above, above-stated, above-named; *formal* prevenient.

precedence /présidǝns, priseéd'ns/ *n.* (also **precedency**) **1** priority in time, order, or importance, etc. **2** the right to precede others on formal occasions. □ **take precedence** (often foll. by *over, of*) have priority (over).

■ **1** preeminence, preference, privilege, primacy; see also PRIORITY.

precedent *n. & adj.* ● *n.* /présidǝnt/ a previous case or legal decision, etc., taken as a guide for subsequent cases or as a justification. ● *adj.* /priseéd'nt, présidǝnt/ preceding in time, order, importance, etc. □□ **precedently** /présidǝntlee/ *adv.* [ME f. OF (n. & adj.) (as PRECEDE)]

■ *n.* yardstick, criterion, standard, prototype, model, example, exemplar, pattern, paradigm, lead, guide.

precedented /présidentid/ *adj.* having or supported by a precedent.

precent /prisént/ v. **1** intr. act as a precentor. **2** tr. lead the singing of (a psalm, etc.). [back-form. f. PRECENTOR]

precentor /priséntər/ n. **1** a person who leads the singing or (in a synagogue) the prayers of a congregation. **2** Brit. a minor canon who administers the musical life of a cathedral. □□ **precentorship** n. [F précenteur or L praecentor f. praecinere (as PRAE-, canere sing)]

precept /préesept/ n. **1** a command; a rule of conduct. **2 a** moral instruction (example is better than precept). **b** a general or proverbial rule; a maxim. **3** Law a writ, order, or warrant. □□ **preceptive** /-séptiv/ adj. [ME f. L praeceptum neut. past part. of praecipere praecept- warn, instruct (as PRAE-, capere take)]

■ **1** rule, guide, principle, law, unwritten law, canon, guideline, dictate, code, injunction, commandment, instruction, directive, prescription, mandate, charge. **2 b** maxim, proverb, axiom, motto, slogan, saying, byword, aphorism, apothegm.

preceptor /priséptər/ n. a teacher or instructor. □□ **preceptorial** /préeseptawreeəl/ adj. **preceptorship** n. **preceptress** /-tris/ n. [L praeceptor (as PRECEPT)]

■ see INSTRUCTOR.

precess /preesés, préeses/ v. undergo or be subject to precession.

precession /priséshən/ n. the slow movement of the axis of a spinning body around another axis. □ **precession of the equinoxes 1** the slow retrograde motion of equinoctial points along the ecliptic. **2** the resulting earlier occurrence of equinoxes in each successive sidereal year. □□ **precessional** adj. [LL praecessio (as PRECEDE)]

pre-Christian /préekríschən/ adj. before Christ or the advent of Christianity.

precinct /préesingkt/ n. **1** an enclosed or specially designated area. **2** (in pl.) **a** the surrounding area or environs. **b** the boundaries. **3 a** a subdivision of a county, city, etc., for police or electoral purposes. **b** a police station in such a subdivision. **c** (in pl.) a neighborhood. [ME f. med.L praecinctum neut. past part. of praecingere encircle (as PRAE-, cingere gird)]

■ **2** (precincts) environs, suburbs; purlieus, outskirts; boundaries, borders, bounds, confines. **3 c** (precincts) area, territory, region, province, sphere, neighborhood, zone, sector, section, quarter, district, locale.

preciosity /présheeósitee/ n. overrefinement in art or language, esp. in the choice of words. [OF préciosité f. L pretiositas f. pretiosus (as PRECIOUS)]

precious /préshəs/ adj. & adv. ● adj. **1** of great value or worth. **2** beloved; much prized (precious memories). **3** affectedly refined, esp. in language or manner. **4** colloq. often iron. **a** considerable (a precious lot you know about it). **b** expressing contempt or disdain (you can keep your precious flowers). ● adv. colloq. extremely; very (tried precious hard; had precious little left). □ **precious metals** gold, silver, and platinum. **precious stone** a piece of mineral having great value esp. as used in jewelry. □□ **preciously** adv. **preciousness** n. [ME f. OF precios f. L pretiosus f. pretium price]

■ adj. **1** valuable, invaluable, costly, expensive, high-priced, priceless. **2** cherished, beloved, esteemed, valued, prized, choice, dear, dearest, adored, loved, revered, venerated, hallowed. **3** precise, overrefined, chichi, overnice, studied, artificial, affected, overdone, pretentious, euphuistic, Brit. usu. derog. twee. **4 a** colloq. iron. fat. ● adv. see VERY adv.

precipice /présipis/ n. **1** a vertical or steep face of a rock, cliff, mountain, etc. **2** a dangerous situation. [F précipice or L praecipitium falling headlong, precipice (as PRECIPITOUS)]

■ **1** escarpment, bluff, crag; see also CLIFF. **2** powder keg, time bomb; dynamite.

precipitant /prisípi'nt/ adj. & n. ● adj. = PRECIPITATE adj. ● n. Chem. a substance that causes another substance to precipitate. □□ **precipitance** n. **precipitancy** n. [obs. F précipitant pres. part. of précipiter (as PRECIPITATE)]

precipitate v., adj., & n. ● v.tr. /prisípitayt/ **1** hasten the occurrence of; cause to occur prematurely. **2** (foll. by into) send rapidly into a certain state or condition (were precipi-

tated into war). **3** throw down headlong. **4** Chem. cause (a substance) to be deposited in solid form from a solution. **5** Physics **a** cause (dust, etc.) to be deposited from the air on a surface. **b** condense (vapor) into drops and so deposit it. ● adj. /prisípitət/ **1** headlong; violently hurried (precipitate departure). **2** (of a person or act) hasty; rash; inconsiderate. ● n. /prisípitət/ **1** Chem. a substance precipitated from a solution. **2** Physics moisture condensed from vapor by cooling and depositing, e.g., rain or dew. □□ **precipitable** /-sípitəbəl/ adj. **precipitability** n. **precipitately** /-sípitətlee/ adv. **precipitateness** /-sípitətnəs/ n. **precipitator** n. [L praecipitare praecipitat- f. praeceps praecipitis headlong (as PRAE-, caput head)]

■ v. **1** accelerate, hasten, speed (up), advance, hurry, quicken, expedite, bring on or about, trigger, provoke, instigate, incite, facilitate, further, push forward. **2, 3** throw, catapult, hurl, fling, cast, launch, project. ● adj. **1** headlong, violent, hurried, rapid, swift, quick, speedy, meteoric, fast; sudden, abrupt, unannounced, unexpected, unanticipated. **2** rash, impetuous, hasty, careless, reckless, incautious, inconsiderate, injudicious, harum-scarum, foolhardy, impulsive, unrestrained; volatile, hotheaded.

precipitation /prisipitáyshən/ n. **1** the act of precipitating or the process of being precipitated. **2** rash haste. **3 a** rain or snow, etc., falling to the ground. **b** a quantity of this. [F précipitation or L praecipitatio (as PRECIPITATE)]

■ **2** see HASTE n. 2. **3 a** showers, drizzle, rain, rainfall; snow, snowfall, hail, sleet.

precipitous /prisípitəs/ adj. **1 a** of or like a precipice. **b** dangerously steep. **2** = PRECIPITATE adj. □□ **precipitously** adv. **precipitousness** n. [obs. F précipiteux f. L praeceps (as PRECIPITATE)]

■ **1** perpendicular, abrupt, steep, sheer, bluff, vertical.

précis /práysee/ n. & v. (pl. same /-seez/) a summary or abstract, esp. of a text or speech. ● v.tr. (**précises** /-seez/; **précised** /-seed/; **précising** /-seeing/) make a précis of. [F, = PRECISE (as n.)]

■ n. outline, summary, synopsis, aperçu, résumé, conspectus, survey, overview, abstract, abridgment, digest, compendium. ● v. see ABBREVIATE.

precise /prisís/ adj. **1 a** accurately expressed. **b** definite; exact. **2 a** punctilious; scrupulous in being exact, observing rules, etc. **b** often derog. rigid; fastidious. **3** identical; exact (at that precise moment). □□ **preciseness** n. [F précis -ise f. L praecidere praecis- cut short (as PRAE-, caedere cut)]

■ **1** correct, exact, definite, accurate, unerring, strict, meticulous, faithful, perfect, true, absolute, truthful, error-free. **2 a** punctilious, strict, meticulous, scrupulous, careful, conscientious, exact, particular, nice, exacting, critical, demanding. **b** fastidious, rigorous, rigid, puritanical, unbending, inflexible, unyielding, demanding, severe, finicky, finical, fussy, prim. **3** identical, very same; see also VERY adj. 1a.

precisely /prisíslee/ adv. **1** in a precise manner; exactly. **2** (as a reply) quite so; as you say.

■ **1** exactly, correctly, absolutely, punctiliously, minutely, carefully, meticulously, scrupulously, conscientiously, strictly; in all respects, in every way. **2** see ABSOLUTELY 6.

precisian /prisízhən/ n. a person who is rigidly precise or punctilious, esp. in religious observance. □□ **precisianism** n.

■ see PURIST. □□ **precisianism** see LEGALISM.

precision /prisízhən/ n. **1** the condition of being precise; accuracy. **2** the degree of refinement in measurement, etc. **3** (attrib.) marked by or adapted for precision (precision instruments; precision timing). □□ **precisionism** n. **precisionist** n. [F précision or L praecisio (as PRECISE)]

/. . ./ **pronunciation**	● **part of speech**
□ **phrases, idioms, and compounds**	
□□ **derivatives**	■ **synonym section**
cross-references appear in SMALL CAPITALS or italics	

■ **1** correctness, accuracy, exactness, exactitude, fidelity, faithfulness, preciseness, perfection, flawlessness, faultlessness, unerringness. **2** nicety, rigor, rigorousness, strictness, meticulousness, punctiliousness, scrupulousness; see also CARE *n.* 3.

preclassical /preeklásikəl/ *adj.* before a period regarded as classical, esp. in music and literature.

preclinical /preeklínikəl/ *adj.* **1** of or relating to the first, chiefly theoretical, stage of a medical or dental education. **2** (of a stage in a disease) before symptoms can be identified.

preclude /priklŏŏd/ *v.tr.* **1** (foll. by *from*) prevent; exclude (*precluded from taking part*). **2** make impossible; remove (*so as to preclude all doubt*). □□ **preclusion** /-klŏŏzhən/ *n.* **preclusive** /-klŏŏsiv/ *adj.* [L *praecludere praeclus-* (as PRAE-, *claudere* shut)]

■ **1** bar, prevent, stop, exclude, prohibit, debar, obstruct, impede, inhibit. **2** remove, forestall, rule out, obviate, avoid, get rid of.

precocial /prikóshəl/ *adj.* & *n.* (*Brit.* **praecocial**) ● *adj.* (esp. of a bird) having young that can feed themselves as soon as they are hatched. ● *n.* a precocial bird or animal. (cf. ALTRICIAL). [L *praecox -cocis* (as PRECOCIOUS)]

precocious /prikóshəs/ *adj.* **1** (of a person, esp. a child) prematurely developed in some faculty or characteristic. **2** (of an action, etc.) indicating such development. **3** (of a plant) flowering or fruiting early. □□ **precociously** *adv.* **precociousness** *n.* **precocity** /-kósitee/ *n.* [L *praecox -cocis* f. *praecoquere* ripen fully (as PRAE-, *coquere* cook)]

■ **1** advanced, forward, bright, gifted, intelligent, smart, quick.

precognition /preekogníshən/ *n.* (supposed) foreknowledge, esp. of a supernatural kind. □□ **precognitive** /-kógnitiv/ *adj.* [LL *praecognitio* (as PRE-, COGNITION)]

■ **1** see ANTICIPATION 1.

precoital /preekóit'l, -kō-eét'l/ *adj.* preceding sexual intercourse. □□ **precoitally** *adv.*

pre-Columbian /preekəlúmbeeən/ *adj.* before the arrival in America of Columbus.

preconceive /preekənseév/ *v.tr.* (esp. as **preconceived** *adj.*) form (an idea or opinion, etc.) beforehand; anticipate in thought.

■ (**preconceived**) prejudged, predetermined, prejudiced, biased, anticipatory.

preconception /preekənsépshən/ *n.* **1** a preconceived idea. **2** a prejudice.

■ prejudgment, presupposition, assumption, presumption, idée fixe, preconceived notion *or* idea; prejudice, bias.

preconcert /preekənsért/ *v.tr.* arrange or organize beforehand.

precondition /preekəndíshən/ *n.* & *v.* ● *n.* a prior condition, that must be fulfilled before other things can be done. ● *v.tr.* bring into a required condition beforehand.

■ *n.* prerequisite, stipulation, condition, essential, must, sine qua non, imperative, requirement, proviso, qualification.

preconize /preekəniz/ *v.tr.* **1** proclaim or commend publicly. **2** summon by name. **3** *RC Ch.* (of the pope) approve publicly the appointment of (a bishop, etc.). □□ **preconization** *n.* [ME f. med.L *praeconizare* f. L *praeco -onis* herald]

preconscious *adj.* & *n. Psychol.* ● *adj.* /preekónshəs/ **1** preceding consciousness. **2** of or associated with a part of the mind below the level of immediate conscious awareness, from which memories and emotions can be recalled. ● *n.* /preekónshəs/ this part of the mind. □□ **preconsciousness** *n.*

precook /preekŏŏk/ *v.tr.* cook in advance.

precool /preekŏŏl/ *v.tr.* cool in advance.

precursor /prikórsər, preekər-/ *n.* **1 a** a forerunner. **b** a person who precedes in office, etc. **2** a harbinger. **3** a substance from which another is formed by decay or chemical reaction, etc. [L *praecursor* f. *praecurrere praecurs-* (as PRAE-, *currere* run)]

■ **1** forerunner, predecessor, antecedent; progenitor,

foregoer. **2** harbinger, herald, forerunner, envoy, messenger.

precursory /prikórsəree/ *adj.* (also **precursive** /-siv/) **1** preliminary; introductory. **2** (foll. by *of*) serving as a harbinger of. [L *praecursorius* (as PRECURSOR)]

precut /preekút/ *v.tr.* (*past* and *past part.* **-cut**) cut in advance.

pred. *abbr.* predicate.

predacious /pridáyshəs/ *adj.* (also **predaceous**) **1** (of an animal) predatory. **2** relating to such animals (*predacious instincts*). □□ **predaciousness** *n.* **predacity** /-dásitee/ *n.* [L *praeda* booty: cf. *audacious*]

■ see PREDATORY 1, RAPACIOUS. □□ **predaciousness** see *rapacity* (RAPACIOUS).

predate /preedáyt/ *v.tr.* exist or occur at a date earlier than. ■ see PRECEDE.

predation /pridáyshən/ *n.* **1** (usu. in *pl.*) = DEPREDATION. **2** *Zool.* the natural preying of one animal on others. [L *praedatio -onis* taking of booty f. L *praeda* booty]

predator /prédətər/ *n.* **1** an animal naturally preying on others. **2** a predatory person, institution, etc. [L *praedator* plunderer f. *praedari* seize as plunder f. *praeda* booty (as PREDACIOUS)]

predatory /prédətawree/ *adj.* **1** (of an animal) preying naturally upon others. **2** (of a nation, state, or individual) plundering or exploiting others. □□ **predatorily** *adv.* **predatoriness** *n.* [L *praedatorius* (as PREDATOR)]

■ **1** predacious, carnivorous, preying, raptorial. **2** ravenous, piratical, vulturine, exploitative, parasitic, parasitical; see also RAPACIOUS.

predecease /preedisees/ *v.* & *n.* ● *v.tr.* die earlier than (another person). ● *n.* a death preceding that of another.

predecessor /prédisesər, preé-/ *n.* **1** a former holder of an office or position with respect to a later holder (*my immediate predecessor*). **2** an ancestor. **3** a thing to which another has succeeded (*the new plan will share the fate of its predecessor*). [ME f. OF *predecesseur* f. LL *praedecessor* (as PRAE-, *decessor* retiring officer, as DECEASE)]

■ **1, 3** forerunner, antecedent, precursor. **2** forebear, forefather, ancestor, antecedent.

predella /pridélə/ *n.* **1** an altar step, or raised shelf at the back of an altar. **2** a painting or sculpture on this, or any picture forming an appendage to a larger one, esp. beneath an altarpiece. [It., = stool]

predestinarian /preedéstináireeən/ *n.* & *adj.* ● *n.* a person who believes in predestination. ● *adj.* of or relating to predestination.

predestinate *v.* & *adj.* ● *v.tr.* /preedéstinayt/ = PREDESTINE. ● *adj.* /-déstinət/ predestined. [ME f. eccl.L *praedestinare praedestinat-* (as PRAE-, *destinare* establish)]

predestination /preedestináyshən/ *n. Theol.* (as a belief or doctrine) the divine foreordaining of all that will happen, esp. with regard to the salvation of some and not others. [ME f. eccl.L *praedestinatio* (as PREDESTINATE)]

■ destiny; doom, fate, lot, kismet, karma; foreordination; predetermination.

predestine /preedéstin/ *v.tr.* **1** determine beforehand. **2** ordain in advance by divine will or as if by fate. [ME f. OF *predestiner* or eccl.L *praedestinare* PREDESTINATE *v.*]

■ see DESTINE.

predetermine /preediter," -mín/ *v.tr.* **1** determine or decree beforehand. **2** predestine. □□ **predeterminable** *adj.* **predeterminate** /-nət/ *adj.* **predetermination** *n.* [LL *praedeterminare* (as PRAE-, DETERMINE)]

■ **1** fix, prearrange, preestablish, preplan, preset, set up; see also ARRANGE 2, 3. **2** fate, doom, destine, predestine, predestinate, predoom, ordain, foreordain, preordain; see also DESTINE. □□ **predetermination** see PREDESTINATION.

predial /preédeeəl/ *adj.* & *n. hist.* ● *adj.* **1 a** of land or farms. **b** rural; agrarian. **c** (of a slave, tenant, etc.) attached to farms or the land. **2** (of a tithe) consisting of agricultural produce. ● *n.* a predial slave. [med.L *praedialis* f. L *praedium* farm]

predicable /prédikəbəl/ *adj.* & *n.* ● *adj.* that may be predicated or affirmed. ● *n.* **1** a predicable thing. **2** (in *pl.*) *Logic* the five classes to which predicates belong: genus, species, difference, property, and accident. □□ **predicability** *n.* [med.L *praedicabilis* that may be affirmed (as PREDICATE)]

predicament /pridíkəmənt/ *n.* **1** a difficult, unpleasant, or embarrassing situation. **2** *Philos.* a category in (esp. Aristotelian) logic. [ME (in sense 2) f. LL *praedicamentum* thing predicated: see PREDICATE]
■ **1** quandary, difficulty, trial, imbroglio, emergency, crisis, impasse, bind, box, *colloq.* pickle, state, jam, fix, scrape, mess, spot, corner, hole, *disp.* dilemma.

predicant /prédikənt/ *adj.* & *n.* ● *adj. hist.* (of a religious order) engaged in preaching. ● *n. hist.* a predicant person, esp. a Dominican friar. [L *praedicans* part. of *praedicare* (as PREDICATE)]

predicate *v.* & *n.* ● *v.tr.* /prédikayt/ **1** assert or affirm as true or existent. **2** (foll. by *on*) found or base (a statement, etc.) on. ● *n.* /-kət/ **1** *Gram.* what is said about the subject of a sentence, etc. (e.g., *went home* in *John went home*). **2** *Logic* **a** what is predicated. **b** what is affirmed or denied of the subject by means of the copula (e.g., *mortal* in *all men are mortal*). □□ **predication** /-káyshən/ *n.* [L *praedicare praedicat-* proclaim (as PRAE-, *dicare* declare)]
■ *v.* **1** assume, propose, postulate, posit, assert, affirm, suppose, presuppose, surmise. **2** see BASE[1] *v.* 1.
□□ **predication** hypothesis, thesis, principle, contention, assertion, belief, proposition, postulate.

predicative /prédikaytiv/ *adj.* **1** *Gram.* (of an adjective or noun) forming or contained in the predicate, as *old* in *the dog is old* (but not in *the old dog*) and *house* in *there is a large house* (opp. ATTRIBUTIVE). **2** that predicates. □□ **predicatively** *adv.* [L *praedicativus* (as PREDICATE)]

predict /pridíkt/ *v.tr.* (often foll. by *that* + clause) make a statement about the future; foretell; prophesy. □□ **predictive** *adj.* **predictively** *adv.* **predictor** *n.* [L *praedicere praedict-* (as PRAE-, *dicere* say)]
■ foretell, prophesy, forecast, foresee, augur, prognosticate, presage, *formal* vaticinate, *literary* previse; intimate, hint, suggest.

predictable /pridíktəbəl/ *adj.* that can be predicted or is to be expected. □□ **predictability** *n.* **predictably** *adv.*
■ foreseeable, expected, anticipated, imaginable.

prediction /pridíkshən/ *n.* **1** the art of predicting or the process of being predicted. **2** a thing predicted; a forecast. [L *praedictio -onis* (as PREDICT)]
■ **2** see FORECAST *n.*

predigest /preedijést/ *v.tr.* **1** render (food) easily digestible before being eaten. **2** make (reading matter) easier to read or understand. □□ **predigestion** /-jéschən/ *n.*

predilection /préd'lékshən, prée-/ *n.* (often foll. by *for*) a preference or special liking. [F *prédilection* ult. f. L *praediligere praedilect-* prefer (as PRAE-, *diligere* select): see DILIGENT]
■ see LIKING 2.

predispose /preedispóz/ *v.tr.* **1** influence favorably in advance. **2** (foll. by *to*, or *to* + infin.) render liable or inclined beforehand. □□ **predisposition** /-pəzíshən/ *n.*
■ **1** see INCLINE *v.* 1. **2** see INCLINE *v.* 2.
□□ **predisposition** see INCLINATION 1.

prednisone /prédnizōn, -sōn/ *n.* a synthetic drug similar to cortisone, used to relieve rheumatic and allergic conditions and to treat leukemia. [perh. f. *pregnant* + *diene* + *cortisone*]

predominant /pridóminənt/ *adj.* **1** predominating. **2** being the strongest or main element. □□ **predominance** *n.* **predominantly** *adv.*
■ **1** dominant, predominating, controlling, sovereign, ruling, preeminent, preponderant, preponderating, ascendant, superior, supreme, transcendent. **2** main, primary, leading, chief, prevailing, prevalent; see also CHIEF *adj.* 2. □□ **predominance** superiority, influence, dominance, preeminence, preponderance, transcendence, transcendency, ascendancy, supremacy, power, hold, hegemony, mastery, control, dominion, sovereignty, authority.

predominate /pridóminayt/ *v.intr.* **1** (foll. by *over*) have or exert control. **2** be superior. **3** be the strongest or main element; preponderate (*a garden in which dahlias predominate*). [med.L *praedominari* (as PRAE-, DOMINATE)]
■ **1** control, rule, reign, get *or* have the upper hand, be in charge, hold sway; see also DOMINATE 1. **3** preponderate, dominate, obtain, prevail, be in the majority, stick out, stand out; be prevalent *or* widespread *or* current, be the order of the day.

predominately /pridóminətlee/ *adv.* = *predominantly* (see PREDOMINANT). [rare *predominate* (adj.) = PREDOMINANT]

predynastic /preedinástik/ *adj.* of or relating to a period before the normally recognized dynasties (esp. of ancient Egypt).

preecho /prée-ékō/ *n.* (*pl.* **-oes**) **1** a faint copy heard just before an actual sound in a recording, caused by the accidental transfer of signals. **2** a foreshadowing.

preeclampsia /preeiklámpseeə/ *n.* a condition of pregnancy characterized by high blood pressure and other symptoms associated with eclampsia. □□ **preeclamptic** *adj.* & *n.*

preelect /prée-ilékt/ *v.tr.* elect beforehand.

preelection /prée-ilékshən/ *n.* **1** an election held beforehand. **2** (*attrib.*) (esp. of an act or undertaking) done or given before an election.

preembryo /pree-émbreeō/ *n. Med.* a human embryo in the first fourteen days after fertilization. □□ **pre-embryonic** /-breeónik/ *adj.*

preemie /prée-mee/ *n. colloq.* an infant born prematurely.

preeminent /prée-éminənt/ *adj.* **1** surpassing others. **2** outstanding; distinguished in some quality. **3** principal; leading; predominant. □□ **preeminence** *n.* **preeminently** *adv.* [ME f. L *praeeminens* (as PRAE-, EMINENT)]
■ **2** peerless, excellent, distinguished, eminent, inimitable, superb, unequaled, matchless, incomparable, outstanding, unique, unrivaled, unsurpassed, supreme, superior. **3** see CHIEF *adj.* 2. □□ **preeminence** peerlessness, magnificence, excellence, distinction, eminence, inimitability, superiority, greatness. **preeminently** manifestly, eminently, notably, conspicuously, prominently, signally, uniquely, matchlessly, incomparably, outstandingly; primarily, principally, chiefly, mainly, mostly.

preempt /prée-émpt/ *v.* **1** *tr.* **a** forestall. **b** acquire or appropriate in advance. **2** *tr.* prevent (an attack) by disabling the enemy. **3** *tr.* obtain by preemption. **4** *tr.* take for oneself (esp. public land) so as to have the right of preemption. **5** *intr. Bridge* make a preemptive bid. □□ **preemptor** *n.* **preemptory** *adj.* [back-form. f. PREEMPTION]
■ **1 a** see ANTICIPATE 3. **b** appropriate, usurp, arrogate, take over, assume, take possession of, seize, acquire, take, possess, expropriate.

preemption /prée-émpshən/ *n.* **1 a** the purchase or appropriation by one person or party before the opportunity is offered to others. **b** the right to purchase (esp. public land) in this way. **2** prior appropriation or acquisition. [med.L *praeemptio* (as PRAE-, *emere empt-* buy)]

preemptive /prée-émptiv/ *adj.* **1** preempting; serving to preempt. **2** (of military action) intended to prevent attack by disabling the enemy (*a preemptive strike*). **3** *Bridge* (of a bid) intended to be high enough to discourage further bidding.

preen /preen/ *v.tr.* & *refl.* **1** (of a bird) straighten (the feathers or itself) with its beak. **2** (of a person) primp or admire (oneself, one's hair, clothes, etc.). **3** (often foll. by *on*) congratulate or pride (oneself). □ **preen gland** a gland situated at the base of a bird's tail and producing oil used in preening. □□ **preener** *n.* [ME, app. var. of earlier *prune* (perh. rel. to PRUNE[2]): assoc. with Sc. & dial. *preen* pierce, pin]
■ **1** plume, groom, prink, trim, clean. **2** primp, smarten, dress up, prettify, beautify, prink, spruce up, doll up,

---

/. . ./ **pronunciation**	● **part of speech**
□ **phrases, idioms, and compounds**	
□□ **derivatives**	■ **synonym section**
cross-references appear in SMALL CAPITALS or *italics*	

titivate, *Brit. colloq.* tart up. **3** (*preen oneself on*) see
PRIDE *v.*

preestablish /preéistáblish/ *v.tr.* establish beforehand.

preexist /preéigzíst/ *v.intr.* exist at an earlier time. □□ **preex-
istence** *n.* **preexistent** *adj.*

pref. *abbr.* **1** prefix. **2** preface. **3 a** preference. **b** preferred.

prefab /preéfáb/ *n. colloq.* a prefabricated building, esp. a
small house. [abbr.]

prefabricate /preéfábrikayt/ *v.tr.* **1** manufacture sections of
(a building, etc.) prior to their assembly on a site. **2** produce
in an artificially standardized way. □□ **prefabrication** /-bri-
káyshən/ *n.*

preface /préfəs/ *n. & v.* ● *n.* **1** an introduction to a book
stating its subject, scope, etc. **2** the preliminary part of a
speech. **3** *Eccl.* the introduction to the central part of a Eucharistic service. ● *v.tr.* **1** (foll. by *with*) introduce or begin
(a speech or event) (*prefaced my remarks with a warning*). **2**
provide (a book, etc.) with a preface. **3** (of an event, etc.)
lead up to (another). □□ **prefatorial** /-fətáwreeəl/ *adj.* **prefatory** /-fətawree/ *adj.* [ME f. OF f. med.L *praefatio* for L
praefatio f. *praefari* (as PRAE-, *fari* speak)]

■ *n.* **1, 2** introduction, foreword, prologue, preamble,
proem, prolegomenon, exordium. ● *v.* **1** prefix,
prologue, begin, open, start off; see also INTRODUCE 8.
3 see *lead up to* 1. □□ **prefatory** see INTRODUCTORY.

prefect /preéfekt/ *n.* **1** *Rom. Antiq.* a senior magistrate or
military commander. **2** a student monitor, as in a private
school. **3** the chief administrative officer of certain government departments, esp. in France. □□ **prefectoral**
/-féktərəl/ *adj.* **prefectorial** /-táwreeəl/ *adj.* [ME f. OF f. L
praefectus past part. of *praeficere* set in authority over (as
PRAE-, *facere* make)]

prefecture /preéfekchər/ *n.* **1** a district under the government of a prefect. **2** a prefect's office, tenure, or official residence. □□ **prefectural** /prifékchərəl/ *adj.* [F *préfecture* or L
praefectura (as PREFECT)]

prefer /prifár/ *v.tr.* (**preferred, preferring**) **1** (often foll. by
to, or *to* + infin.) choose; like better (*would prefer to stay*;
prefers coffee to tea). **2** submit (information, an accusation,
etc.) for consideration. **3** promote or advance (a person).
□ **preferred provider organization** a health insurance
plan that allows members to choose their own physicians,
etc. ¶ Abbr.: **PPO. preferred stock** stock whose entitlement to dividend takes priority over that of common stock.
[ME f. OF *preferer* f. L *praeferre* (as PRAE-, *ferre lat-* bear)]

■ **1** favor, like better, lean or incline toward, be inclined
toward, be partial to. **2** present, offer, propose, proffer,
advance, submit, tender, put forward, file, lodge, enter.
3 see PROMOTE 1.

preferable /préfərəbəl, *disp.* prifér-/ *adj.* **1** to be preferred. **2**
more desirable. □□ **preferably** *adv.*

■ preferred, better, best, advantageous, beneficial,
desirable, convenient, favorable, promising, propitious.
□□ **preferably** see RATHER 1.

preference /préfərəns, préfrəns/ *n.* **1** the act or an instance
of preferring or being preferred. **2** a thing preferred. **3 a** the
favoring of one person, etc., before others. **b** *Commerce* the
favoring of one country by admitting its products at a lower
import duty. **4** *Law* a prior right, esp. to the payment of
debts. □ **in preference to** as a thing preferred over (another). **preference shares** (or **stock**) *Brit.* = preferred stock
[F *préférence* f. med.L *praeferentia* (as PREFER)]

■ **1** partiality, proclivity, predilection, liking;
predisposition, bent, inclination, leaning. **2** favorite,
choice, selection, pick, desire, option. **3 a** see
FAVORITISM.

preferential /préfərénshəl/ *adj.* **1** of or involving preference
(*preferential treatment*). **2** giving or receiving a favor. **3** *Commerce* (of a tariff, etc.) favoring particular countries. **4** (of
voting) in which the voter puts candidates in order of preference. □□ **preferentially** *adv.* [as PREFERENCE, after *differential*]

■ **1** privileged, better, favored, superior, advantageous,
favorable; biased, prejudiced, partial.

preferment /prifármənt/ *n.* **1** act or state of being preferred.
2 promotion to office.

■ promotion, advance, rise, elevation.

prefigure /preéfígyər/ *v.tr.* **1** represent beforehand by a figure
or type. **2** imagine beforehand. □□ **prefiguration** *n.* **prefig-
urative** /-rətiv/ *adj.* **prefigurement** *n.* [ME f. eccl.L *prae-
figurare* (as PRAE-, FIGURE)]

prefix /preéfiks/ *n. & v.* ● *n.* **1** a verbal element placed at the
beginning of a word to adjust or qualify its meaning (e.g.,
ex-, *non-*, *re-*) or (in some languages) as an inflectional formative. **2** a title placed before a name (e.g., *Mr.*). ● *v.tr.*
(often foll. by *to*) **1** add as an introduction. **2** join (a word
or element) as a prefix. □□ **prefixation** *n.* **prefixion**
/-fíkshən/ *n.* [earlier as verb: ME f. OF *prefixer* (as PRE-,
FIX): (n.) f. L *praefixum*]

■ *v.* **1** see PREFACE *v.* 1.

preflight /preéflit/ *attrib.adj.* occurring or provided before an
aircraft flight.

preform /preéfáwrm/ *v.tr.* form beforehand. □□ **preforma-
tion** /-máyshən/ *n.*

preformative /preéfáwrmətiv/ *adj. & n.* ● *adj.* **1** forming
beforehand. **2** prefixed as the formative element of a word.
● *n.* a preformative syllable or letter.

prefrontal /preéfrúnt'l/ *adj.* **1** in front of the frontal bone of
the skull. **2** in the forepart of the frontal lobe of the brain.
□ **prefrontal lobotomy** the surgical cutting of the nerve fibers that connect the frontal lobes with the rest of the brain,
formerly used in psychosurgery.

preglacial /preégláyshəl/ *adj.* before a glacial period.

pregnable /prégnəbəl/ *adj.* able to be captured, etc.; not impregnable. [ME f. OF *prenable* takable: see IMPREGNABLE[1]]

pregnancy /prégnənsee/ *n.* (*pl.* **-ies**) the condition or an instance of being pregnant.

pregnant /prégnənt/ *adj.* **1** (of a woman or female animal)
having a child or young developing in the uterus. **2** full of
meaning; significant or suggestive (*a pregnant pause*). **3** (esp.
of a person's mind) imaginative; inventive. **4** (foll. by *with*)
full of; abundant in (*pregnant with danger*). □ **pregnant
construction** *Gram.* one in which more is implied than the
words express (e.g., *not have a chance* implying *of success*,
etc.). □□ **pregnantly** *adv.* (in sense 2). [ME f. F *prégnant* or
L *praegnans -antis*, earlier *praegnas* (prob. as PRAE-, (*g*)*nasci*
be born)]

■ **1** expectant, impregnate, *archaic* in a delicate or
interesting condition, enceinte, *literary* with child,
literary or Zool. gravid, *colloq.* in the family way, *Brit.
sl.* in the (pudding) club; (*be pregnant*) *colloq.* be
expecting, *sl.* have a bun in the oven. **2** charged,
fraught, loaded, weighty, significant, meaningful,
suggestive, expressive, pointed. **3** fertile, fecund,
fruitful, productive; see also IMAGINATIVE 1.
4 (*pregnant with*) see ABUNDANT 2.

preheat /preéheét/ *v.tr.* heat beforehand.

prehensile /preéhénsəl, -sil/ *adj. Zool.* (of a tail or limb) capable of grasping. □□ **prehensility** /-sílitee/ *n.* [F *préhensile*
f. L *prehendere prehens-* (as PRE-, *hendere* grasp)]

prehension /prihénshən/ *n.* **1** grasping; seizing. **2** mental apprehension. [L *prehensio* (as PREHENSILE)]

prehistoric /preéhistáwrik, -stór-/ *adj.* **1** of or relating to the
period before written records. **2** *colloq.* utterly out of date.
□□ **prehistorian** /-stáwreeən, -stór-/ *n.* **prehistorically**
adv. **prehistory** /-hístəree/ *n.* [F *préhistorique* (as PRE-, HIS-
TORIC)]

■ **1** primordial, primal, primeval, primitive, earliest,
early, antediluvian, ancient. **2** out of date, outdated,
old-fashioned, passé; see also ANTIQUATED.

prehuman /preéhyoomən/ *adj.* existing before the time of humans.

preignition /preéignishən/ *n.* the premature firing of the explosive mixture in an internal combustion engine.

prejudge /preéjúj/ *v.tr.* **1** form a premature judgment on (a
person, issue, etc.). **2** pass judgment on (a person) before a
trial or proper inquiry. □□ **prejudgment** *n.* **prejudication**
/-joodikáyshən/ *n.*

■ □□ **prejudgment** see PRECONCEPTION.

prejudice /préjədis/ *n. & v.* ● *n.* **1 a** a preconceived opinion. **b** (usu. foll. by *against, in favor of*) bias or partiality. **c** intolerance of or discrimination against a person or group, esp. on account of race, religion, or gender; bigotry (*racial prejudice*). **2** harm or injury that results or may result from some action or judgment (*to the prejudice of*). ● *v.tr.* **1** impair the validity or force of (a right, claim, statement, etc.). **2** (esp. as **prejudiced** *adj.*) cause (a person) to have a prejudice. □ **without prejudice** (often foll. by *to*) without detriment (to any existing right or claim). [ME f. OF *prejudice* f. L *praejudicium* (as PRAE-, *judicium* judgment)]

■ *n.* **1 a, b** preconception, prejudgment, preconceived notion; partiality, bias, leaning, warp, twist, predisposition, predilection; favoritism, partisanship, prepossession. **c** bigotry, bias, partisanship, discrimination, intolerance, inequality; racism, racialism, apartheid, sexism, (male) chauvinism, jim crowism. **2** see DETRIMENT. ● *v.* **1** bias, influence, warp, twist, distort, slant; color, jaundice, poison. **2** (**prejudiced**) predisposed, partial, prepossessed; unfair, one-sided, biased, jaundiced, opinionated, partisan, nonobjective, unobjective, bigoted, intolerant, narrow-minded, parochial, chauvinistic.

prejudicial /préjədíshəl/ *adj.* causing prejudice; detrimental. □□ **prejudicially** *adv.* [ME f. OF *prejudiciel* (as PREJUDICE)]

■ injurious, damaging, detrimental, harmful, unfavorable, inimical, deleterious, disadvantageous, counterproductive, pernicious.

prelacy /préləsee/ *n.* (*pl.* **-ies**) **1** church government by prelates. **2** (prec. by *the*) prelates collectively. **3** the office or rank of prelate. [ME f. AF *prelacie* f. med.L *prelatia* (as PRELATE)]

prelapsarian /preelapsáireeən/ *adj. Theol.* before the Fall of Adam and Eve.

prelate /prélət/ *n.* a high ecclesiastical dignitary, e.g., a bishop, abbot, etc. □□ **prelatic** /prilátik/ *adj.* **prelatical** *adj.* [ME f. OF *prelat* f. med.L *praelatus* past part.: see PREFER]

prelature /prélǝchǝr, -choor/ *n.* **1** the office of prelate. **2** (prec. by *the*) prelates collectively. [F *prélature* f. med.L *praelatura* (as PRELATE)]

prelim /preélim, prilím/ *n. colloq.* preliminary. [abbr.]

preliminary /prilíminəree/ *adj., n., & adv.* ● *adj.* introductory; preparatory. ● *n.* (*pl.* **-ies**) (usu. in *pl.*) **1 a** a preliminary action or arrangement (*dispense with the preliminaries*). **2 a** a preliminary trial or contest. **b** a preliminary examination. ● *adv.* (foll. by *to*) preparatory to; in advance of (*was completed preliminary to the main event*). □□ **preliminarily** *adv.* [mod.L *praeliminaris* or F *préliminaire* (as PRE-, L *limen liminis* threshold)]

■ *adj.* introductory, initial, opening, preparatory, prefatory, preceding, precursory, antecedent, initiatory, preambular, preludial; exploratory, premonitory; *Med.* prodromal, prodromic. ● *n.* **1** introduction, beginning, opening, preparation, prelude, overture, prologue. **2 a** trial, round; see also HEAT *n.* 6. ● *adv.* (*preliminary to*) in advance of, preparatory to, prior to, ahead of; see also BEFORE *prep.* 2.

preliterate /preélitǝrǝt/ *adj.* of or relating to a society or culture that has not developed the use of writing.

prelude /prélyood, práylood, pree-/ *n. & v.* ● *n.* (often foll. by *to*) **1** an action, event, or situation serving as an introduction. **2** the introductory part of a poem, etc. **3 a** an introductory piece of music, often preceding a fugue or forming the first piece of a suite or beginning an act of an opera. **b** a short piece of music of a similar type, esp. for the piano. ● *v.tr.* **1** serve as a prelude to. **2** introduce with a prelude. □□ **preludial** /priloodeeəl/ *adj.* [F *prélude* or med.L *praeludium* f. L *praeludere praelus-* (as PRAE-, *ludere* play)]

■ *n.* **1** see PRELIMINARY *n.* 1. **2** see FOREWORD.

premarital /preémárit'l/ *adj.* existing or (esp. of sexual relations) occurring before marriage. □□ **premaritally** *adv.*

premature /preemǝchoor, -tyoor, -toor/ *adj.* **1 a** occurring or done before the usual or proper time; too early (*a premature decision*). **b** too hasty (*must not be premature*). **2** (of a baby, esp. a viable one) born (esp. three or more weeks) before the end of the full term of gestation. □□ **prematurely** *adv.* **prematureness** *n.* **prematurity** /-choorətee/ *n.* [L *praematurus* very early (as PRAE-, MATURE)]

■ **1** untimely, unready, early, unseasonable, too soon, hasty, ill-timed, overhasty, impulsive. **2** preterm. □□ **prematurely** preterm, before one's or its time, ahead of time, too soon, too early, hastily, overhastily, at half cock, *archaic* untimely.

premaxillary /preemáksileree/ *adj.* in front of the upper jaw.

premed /preéméd/ *n. colloq.* a premedical course of study or student. [abbr.]

premedical /preémédikǝl/ *adj.* of or relating to preparation for a course of study in medicine.

premeditate /preéméditayt/ *v.tr.* (often as **premeditated** *adj.*) think out or plan (an action) beforehand (*premeditated murder*). □□ **premeditation** *n.* [L *praemeditari* (as PRAE-, MEDITATE)]

■ (**premeditated**) planned, conscious, intentional, intended, willful, deliberate, studied, purposive, aforethought, esp. *Law* prepense; contrived, preplanned, calculated, preconceived. □□ **premeditation** planning, preplanning, forethought, intent; criminal intent, mens rea.

premenstrual /preéménstrooǝl/ *adj.* of, occurring, or experienced before menstruation (*premenstrual tension*). □ **premenstrual syndrome** any of a complex of symptoms (including tension, fluid retention, etc.) experienced by some women in the days immediately preceding menstruation. □□ **premenstrually** *adv.*

premier /prǝmeér, -myeér, preémeer/ *n. & adj.* ● *n.* a prime minister or other head of government in certain countries. ● *adj.* **1** first in importance, order, or time. **2** of earliest creation; oldest. □□ **premiership** *n.* [ME f. OF = first, f. L (as PRIMARY)]

■ *n.* prime minister, PM, head of government, chief executive, president, chancellor. ● *adj.* **1** premiere, first, prime, primary, chief, principal, head, main, foremost, top-ranking, high-ranking, senior, leading, top, preeminent, ranking.

premiere or **première** /prǝmeér, -myáir/ *n., adj., & v.* ● *n.* the first performance or showing of a play or movie. ● *adj.* = PREMIER *adj.* 1 ● *v.tr.* give a première of. [F, fem. of *premier* (adj.) (as PREMIER)]

■ *n.* first night, opening (night). ● *v.* open, launch.

premillennial /preémiléneeǝl/ *adj.* existing or occurring before the millennium, esp. with reference to the supposed second coming of Christ. □□ **premillennialism** *n.* **premillennialist** *n.*

premise /prémis/ *n. & v.* ● *n.* **1** *Logic* (also esp. *Brit.* **premiss**) a previous statement from which another is inferred. **2** (in *pl.*) **a** a house or building with its grounds and appurtenances. **b** *Law* houses, land, etc., previously specified in a document, etc. ● *v.* **1** *tr.* say or write by way of introduction. **2** *tr. & intr.* assert or assume as a premise. □ **on the premises** in the building, etc., concerned. [ME f. OF *premisse* f. med.L *praemissa* (*propositio*) (proposition) set in front f. L *praemittere praemiss-* (as PRAE-, *mittere* send)]

■ *n.* **1** assumption, proposition, postulate, hypothesis, conjecture, assertion, supposition, thesis, presupposition, proposal, surmise, basis, ground(s); see also PRESUMPTION 2. ● *v.* **2** assume, propose, postulate, hypothesize, hypothecate, conjecture, posit, assert, suppose, presuppose, theorize, surmise, put or set forth, predicate, argue.

premiss esp. *Brit.* var. of PREMISE *n.* 1

premium /preémeeǝm/ *n.* **1** an amount to be paid for a con-

---

/.../ **pronunciation**	● **part of speech**
□ **phrases, idioms, and compounds**	
□□ **derivatives**	■ **synonym section**
cross-references appear in SMALL CAPITALS or *italics*	

tract of insurance. **2 a** a sum added to interest, wages, etc.; a bonus. **b** a sum added to ordinary charges. **3** a reward or prize. **4** (*attrib.*) (of a commodity) of best quality and therefore more expensive. **5** an item offered free or cheaply as an incentive to buy, sample, or subscribe to something. □ **at a premium 1** highly valued; above the usual or nominal price. **2** scarce and in demand. **put a premium on 1** provide or act as an incentive to. **2** attach special value to. [L *praemium* booty, reward (as PRAE-, *emere* buy, take)]
■ **2** extra, dividend, perquisite; see also BONUS 2. **3** see REWARD *n.* 1a. **4** see CHOICE *adj.* **5** incentive, inducement, stimulus, incitement, lure, bait, spur, goad, reward, *colloq.* freebie, come-on. □ **at a premium 1** costly, expensive, dear, high-priced, upmarket; valuable, precious, priceless; *Stock Exch.* above par. **2** scarce, rare, hard to come by, in short supply, thin on the ground.

premolar /preemṓlər/ *adj. & n.* ● *adj.* in front of a molar tooth. ● *n.* (in an adult human) each of eight teeth situated in pairs between each of the four canine teeth and each first molar.

premonition /prémənĭshən, pree-/ *n.* a forewarning; a presentiment. □□ **premonitor** /primónitər/ *n.* **premonitory** /primónitawree/ *adj.* [F *prémonition* or LL *praemonitio* f. L *praemonēre praemonit-* (as PRAE-, *monēre* warn)]
■ foreboding, presentiment, forewarning, suspicion, feeling, hunch, sneaking suspicion, *colloq.* funny feeling.

Premonstratensian /primónstrətənseeən/ *adj. & n. hist.* ● *adj.* of or relating to an order of regular canons founded at Prémontré in France in 1120, or of the corresponding order of nuns. ● *n.* a member of either of these orders. [med.L *Praemonstratensis* f. *Praemonstratus* the abbey of Prémontré (lit. = foreshown)]

premorse /preemáwrs/ *adj. Bot. & Zool.* with the end abruptly terminated. [L *praemordēre praemors-* bite off (as PRAE-, *mordēre* bite)]

prenatal /preenáyt'l/ *adj.* of or concerning the period before birth. □□ **prenatally** *adv.*

prentice /préntis/ *n. & v. archaic* ● *n.* = APPRENTICE. ● *v.tr.* (as **prenticed** *adj.*) apprenticed. □ **prentice hand** an inexperienced hand. □□ **prenticeship** *n.* [ME f. APPRENTICE]

prenuptial /preenúpshəl, -chəl/ *adj.* existing or occurring before marriage. □ **prenuptial contract** a contract between two persons intending to marry each other, setting out the terms and conditions of their marriage and usu. the division of property in the event of divorce.

preoccupation /preé-ókyəpáyshən/ *n.* **1** the state of being preoccupied. **2** a thing that engrosses or dominates the mind. [F *préoccupation* or L *praeoccupatio* (as PREOCCUPY)]
■ **2** see OBSESSION.

preoccupy /preé-ókyəpī/ *v.tr.* (**-ies, -ied**) **1** (of a thought, etc.) dominate or engross the mind of (a person) to the exclusion of other thoughts. **2** (as **preoccupied** *adj.*) otherwise engrossed; mentally distracted. **3** occupy beforehand. [PRE- + OCCUPY, after L *praeoccupare* seize beforehand]
■ **1** see OCCUPY 6. **2** (**preoccupied**) engrossed, rapt, thoughtful, pensive, absorbed, meditative, cogitative; distracted, abstracted, oblivious, unaware, wrapped up, immersed, distrait.

preocular /preé-ókyələr/ *adj.* in front of the eye.

preordain /preéawrdáyn/ *v.tr.* ordain or determine beforehand.
■ see DESTINE.

prep /prep/ *n. & v. colloq.* ● *n.* **1 a** a student in a preparatory school. **b** a preparatory school. **2** *Brit.* **a** the preparation of school work by a pupil. **b** the period when this is done. ● *v. intr.* attend a preparatory school. [abbr. of PREPARATION]
■ *n.* **2 a** homework.

prep. *abbr.* preposition.

prepackage /preépákij/ *v.tr.* (also **prepack** /-pák/) package (goods) on the site of production or before retail.

prepaid *past* and *past part.* of PREPAY.

preparation /prépəráyshən/ *n.* **1** the act or an instance of preparing; the process of being prepared. **2** (often in *pl.*) something done to make ready. **3** a specially prepared sub-

stance, esp. a food or medicine. **4** work done by students to prepare for a lesson. **5** *Mus.* the sounding of the discordant note in a chord in the preceding chord where it is not discordant, lessening the effect of the discord. [ME f. OF f. L *praeparatio -onis* (as PREPARE)]
■ **1** organization, planning; groundwork, spadework; training, education, teaching, instruction, tuition, briefing. **2** (*preparations*) plans, arrangements, provision(s), measures, program, schedule, itinerary. **3** substance, compound, concoction, mixture, product, material, composition.

preparative /pripárətiv, -páir-/ *adj. & n.* ● *adj.* preparatory. ● *n.* a preparatory act. □□ **preparatively** *adv.* [ME f. OF *preparatif -ive* f. med.L *praeparativus* (as PREPARE)]
■ *adj.* see INTRODUCTORY.

preparatory /pripárətawree, -páir-, prépərə-/ *adj. & adv.* ● *adj.* (often foll. by *to*) serving to prepare; introductory. ● *adv.* (often foll. by *to*) in a preparatory manner (*was packing preparatory to departure*). □ **preparatory school** a usu. private school preparing pupils for college. □□ **preparatorily** *adv.* [ME f. LL *praeparatorius* (as PREPARE)]
■ *adj.* preparative, preliminary, prefatory, initial; see also INTRODUCTORY. ● *adv.* (*preparatory to*) in preparation for, preceding; see also BEFORE *prep.* 1a, b, 2.

prepare /pripáir/ *v.* **1** *tr.* make or get ready for use, consideration, etc. **2** *tr.* make ready or assemble (food, a meal, etc.) for eating. **3 a** *tr.* make (a person or oneself) ready or disposed in some way (*prepares students for university; prepared them for a shock*). **b** *intr.* put oneself or things in readiness; get ready (*prepare to jump*). **4** *tr.* make (a chemical product, etc.) by a regular process; manufacture. **5** *tr. Mus.* lead up to (a discord). □ **be prepared** (often foll. by *for*, or *to* + infin.) be disposed or willing to. □□ **preparer** *n.* [ME f. F *préparer* or L *praeparare* (as PRAE-, *parare* make ready)]
■ **1** (get *or* make) ready, arrange, lay, set, (put in) order, organize, provide for, make provision(s) for, lay the groundwork for. **2** cook (up), make, do, whip up, *colloq.* fix. **3 a** (get *or* make) ready, prime, make fit, fit (out), equip, outfit, adapt; brace, steel; train, groom, brief. **4** process, produce, make, treat; manufacture, fabricate, put out, build, construct, assemble, put together, turn out, fashion, forge, mold.
□ **be prepared** be willing *or* disposed *or* predisposed *or* inclined *or* of a mind.

preparedness /pripáiridnis/ *n.* a state of readiness, esp. for war.
■ vigilance, alertness, readiness, fitness.

prepay /preépáy/ *v.tr.* (*past* and *past part.* **prepaid**) **1** pay (a charge) in advance. **2** pay postage on (a letter or package, etc.) before mailing. □□ **prepayable** *adj.* **prepayment** *n.*
■ □□ **prepayment** advance.

prepense /pripéns/ *adj.* (usu. placed after noun) esp. *Law* deliberate; intentional (*malice prepense*). □□ **prepensely** *adv.* [earlier *prepensed* past part. of obs. *prepense* (v.) alt. f. earlier *purpense* f. AF & OF *purpenser* (as PUR-, *penser*): see PENSIVE]

preplan /preéplán/ *v.tr.* (**preplanned, preplanning**) plan in advance.

preponderant /pripóndərənt/ *adj.* surpassing in influence, power, number, or importance; predominant; preponderating. □□ **preponderance** *n.* **preponderantly** *adv.*
■ see PREDOMINANT 1. □□ **preponderance** dominance, predominance, primacy, ascendancy, superiority, supremacy; majority, bulk, mass.

preponderate /pripóndərayt/ *v.intr.* (often foll. by *over*) **1 a** be greater in influence, quantity, or number. **b** predominate. **2 a** be of greater importance. **b** weigh more. [L *praeponderare* (as PRAE-, PONDER)]
■ **1** see PREDOMINATE 3. **2 a** (*preponderate over*) see OUTWEIGH.

preposition /prépəzíshən/ *n. Gram.* a word governing (and usu. preceding) a noun or pronoun and expressing a relation to another word or element, as in: "the man *on* the platform," "came *after* dinner," "what did you do it *for*?". □□ **prepositional** *adj.* **prepositionally** *adv.* [ME f. L *praepositio* f. *praeponere praeposit-* (as PRAE-, *ponere* place)]

prepositive /preepózitiv/ adj. Gram. (of a word, particle, etc.) that should be placed before or prefixed. [LL praepositivus (as PREPOSITION)]

prepossess /preepəzés/ v.tr. 1 (usu. in passive) (of an idea, feeling, etc.) take possession of (a person); imbue. 2 a prejudice (usu. favorably and spontaneously). b (as prepossessing adj.) attractive; appealing. □□ prepossession /-zéshən/ n.
  ■ 2 a see BIAS v. b (prepossessing) attractive, appealing, pleasing, engaging, charming, captivating, fascinating, winsome, winning, magnetic, alluring, bewitching, fetching, inviting, good-looking, handsome, lovely, beautiful. □□ prepossession see OBSESSION, PRECONCEPTION.

preposterous /pripóstərəs/ adj. 1 utterly absurd; outrageous. 2 contrary to nature, reason, or common sense. □□ preposterously adv. preposterousness n. [L praeposterus reversed, absurd (as PRAE-, posterus coming after)]
  ■ absurd, ridiculous, ludicrous, laughable, risible, senseless, mad, irrational, incredible, unbelievable, outrageous, extreme, outlandish, nonsensical, fatuous, mindless, colloq. moronic, insane, crazy, idiotic, imbecilic; weird, bizarre.

prepotent /pripót'nt/ adj. 1 greater than others in power, influence, etc. 2 dominant in transmitting hereditary qualities. □□ prepotence n. prepotency n. [ME f. L praepotens -entis, part. of praeposse (as PRAE-, posse be able)]

preppy /prépee/ n. & adj. (also preppie) US colloq. ● n. (pl. -ies) a person attending an expensive private school or who strives to look like such a person. ● adj. (preppier, preppiest) 1 like a preppy. 2 neat and fashionable. [PREP (SCHOOL) + -Y²]

preprandial /preeprándeeəl/ adj. formal or joc. before a meal, esp. dinner. [PRE- + L prandium a meal]

prepreference /preepréfərəns, -préfrəns/ adj. Brit. (of shares, claims, etc.) ranking before preference shares, etc.

preprint /preeprint/ n. a printed document issued in advance of general publication.

preprocessor /preeprósesər/ n. a computer program that modifies data to conform with the input requirements of another program.

prep school /prep/ n. = preparatory school. [abbr. of PREPARATORY]

prepubescence /preepyoōbésəns/ n. the time, esp. the last two or three years, before puberty. □□ prepubescent adj.
  ■ see CHILDHOOD.

prepublication /preepublikáyshən/ adj. & n. ● attrib.adj. produced or occurring before publication. ● n. publication in advance or beforehand.

prepuce /preepyoōs/ n. 1 = FORESKIN. 2 the fold of skin surrounding the clitoris. □□ preputial /preepyoōshəl/ adj. [ME f. L praeputium]

prequel /preekwəl/ n. a story, movie, etc., whose events or concerns precede those of an existing work. [PRE- + SEQUEL]

Pre-Raphaelite /preeráfeeəlit/ n. & adj. ● n. a member of a group of English 19th-c. artists, including Holman Hunt, Millais, and D. G. Rossetti, emulating the work of Italian artists before the time of Raphael. ● adj. 1 of or relating to the Pre-Raphaelites. 2 (pre-Raphaelite) (esp. of a woman) like a type painted by a Pre-Raphaelite (e.g., with long thick curly auburn hair). □ Pre-Raphaelite Brotherhood the chosen name of the Pre-Raphaelites. □□ pre-Raphaelitism n.

prerecord /preerikáwrd/ v.tr. record (esp. material for broadcasting) in advance.

prerequisite /preerékwizit/ adj. & n. ● adj. required as a precondition. ● n. a prerequisite thing.
  ■ adj. essential, necessary, requisite, imperative, indispensable, obligatory, required. ● n. precondition, requirement, requisite, condition, stipulation, sine qua non, proviso, necessity.

prerogative /prirógativ/ n. 1 a right or privilege exclusive to an individual or class. 2 (in full royal prerogative) Brit. the right of the sovereign, theoretically subject to no restriction. [ME f. OF prerogative or L praerogativa privilege (orig. to vote first) f. praerogativus asked first (as PRAE-, rogare ask)]
  ■ 1 privilege, right, liberty, power, due, advantage, license, authority.

Pres. abbr. President.

presage /présij/ n. & v. ● n. 1 an omen or portent. 2 a presentiment or foreboding. ● v.tr. (also prisáyj/ 1 portend; foreshadow. 2 give warning of (an event, etc.) by natural means. 3 (of a person) predict or have a presentiment of. □□ presageful adj. presager n. [ME f. F présage, présager f. L praesagium f. praesagire forebode (as PRAE-, sagire perceive keenly)]
  ■ n. 1 see OMEN n. 2 see FOREBODING. ● v. 1 see FORESHADOW. 2 see SPELL¹. 3 see PREDICT.

presbyopia /prézbeeŏpeeə, prés-/ n. farsightedness caused by loss of elasticity of the eye lens, occurring esp. in middle and old age. □□ presbyopic /-beeópik/ adj. [mod.L f. Gk presbus old man + ōps ōpos eye]
  ■ □□ presbyopic see FARSIGHTED 2.

presbyter /prézbitər/ n. 1 an elder in the early Christian Church. 2 (in episcopal churches) a minister of the second order; a priest. 3 (in the Presbyterian Church) an elder. □□ presbyteral /-bítərəl/ adj. presbyterate /-bítərət/ n. presbyterial /-téereeəl/ adj. presbytership n. [eccl.L f. Gk presbuteros elder, compar. of presbus old]

Presbyterian /prézbitéereeən/ adj. & n. ● adj. (of a church) governed by elders all of equal rank. ● n. 1 a member of a Presbyterian Church. 2 an adherent of the Presbyterian system. □□ Presbyterianism n. [eccl.L presbyterium (as PRESBYTERY)]

presbytery /prézbiteree/ n. (pl. -ies) 1 the eastern part of a chancel beyond the choir; the sanctuary. 2 a a body of presbyters. b a district represented by this. 3 the house of a Roman Catholic priest. [ME f. OF presbiterie f. eccl.L f. Gk presbuterion (as PRESBYTER)]

preschool /preeskoōl/ adj. of or relating to the time before a child is old enough to go to school. □□ preschooler n.

prescient /préshənt, -eeənt, pré-/ adj. having foreknowledge or foresight. □□ prescience n. presciently adv. [L praescire praescient- know beforehand (as PRAE-, scire know)]
  ■ clairvoyant; see also FARSIGHTED 1. □□ prescience clairvoyance, prevision, vision, foresight, foreknowledge.

prescind /prisínd/ v. 1 tr. (foll. by from) cut off (a part from a whole), esp. prematurely or abruptly. 2 intr. (foll. by from) leave out of consideration. 3 withdraw or turn away in thought. [L praescindere (as PRAE-, scindere cut)]

prescribe /priskríb/ v. 1 tr. a advise the use of (a medicine, etc.), esp. by an authorized prescription. b recommend, esp. as a benefit (prescribed a change of scenery). 2 tr. lay down or impose authoritatively. 3 intr. (foll. by to, for) assert a prescriptive right or claim. □□ prescriber n. [L praescribere praescript- direct in writing (as PRAE-, scribere write)]
  ■ 1 b see ADVISE 1, 2. 2 ordain, order, dictate, decree, enjoin, rule, set down, stipulate, specify, impose, lay down.

prescript /preeskript/ adj. & n. ● adj. prescribed. ● n. an ordinance, law, or command. [L praescriptum neut. past part.: see PRESCRIBE]

prescription /priskrípshən/ n. 1 the act or an instance of prescribing. 2 a a doctor's (usu. written) instruction for the preparation and use of a medicine. b the medicine prescribed. 3 (in full positive prescription) uninterrupted use or possession from time immemorial or for the period fixed by law as giving a title or right. 4 a an ancient custom viewed as authoritative. b a claim founded on long use. [ME f. OF f. L praescriptio -onis (as PRESCRIBE)]
  ■ 1 see INSTRUCTION 1. 2 a formula, recipe. b remedy, medication, medicine, drug, preparation, medicament.

/.../ pronunciation	● part of speech
□ phrases, idioms, and compounds	
□□ derivatives	■ synonym section
cross-references appear in SMALL CAPITALS or italics	

prescriptive /priskríptiv/ *adj.* **1** prescribing. **2** *Linguistics* concerned with or laying down rules of usage. **3** based on prescription (*prescriptive right*). **4** prescribed by custom. □□ **prescriptively** *adv.* **prescriptiveness** *n.* **prescriptivism** *n.* **prescriptivist** *n.* & *adj.* [LL *praescriptivus* (as PRESCRIBE)]
■ **1** dictatorial, constrictive, didactic, restrictive, dogmatic, authoritarian, overbearing, autocratic, imperious.

preselect /preesilékt/ *v.tr.* select in advance. □□ **preselection** *n.*

preselective /preesiléktiv/ *adj.* that can be selected or set in advance.

preselector /preesiléktər/ *n.* any of various devices for selecting a mechanical or electrical operation in advance of its execution.

presence /prézəns/ *n.* **1 a** the state or condition of being present (*your presence is requested*). **b** existence; location (*the presence of a hospital nearby*). **2** a place where a person is (*was admitted to their presence*). **3 a** a person's appearance or bearing, esp. when imposing (*an august presence*). **b** a person's force of personality (esp. *have presence*). **4** a person or thing that is present (*there was a presence in the room*). **5** representation for reasons of political influence (*maintained a presence*). □ **in the presence of** in front of; observed by. **presence of mind** calmness and self-command in sudden difficulty, etc. [ME f. OF f. L *praesentia* (as PRESENT¹)]
■ **1 a** attendance, company, companionship, society, fellowship, coming. **b** existence; location, situation. **3** bearing, carriage, deportment, air, aspect, aura, appearance, *literary* comportment; personality. **4** being, manifestation; spirit, wraith, specter. □ **presence of mind** self-possession, self-control, self-assurance, coolness, coolheadedness, composure, imperturbability, sangfroid, calm, equanimity, levelheadedness.

present¹ /prézənt/ *adj.* & *n.* ● *adj.* **1** (usu. *predic.*) being in the place in question (*was present at the trial*). **2 a** now existing, occurring, or being such (*during the present season*). **b** now being considered or discussed, etc. (*in the present case*). **3** *Gram.* expressing an action, etc., now going on or habitually performed (*present participle*; *present tense*). ● *n.* (prec. by *the*) **1** the time now passing (*no time like the present*). **2** *Gram.* the present tense. □ **at present** now. **by these presents** *Law* by this document (*know all men by these presents*). **for the present 1** just now. **2** as far as the present is concerned. **present company excepted** excluding those who are here now. **present-day** *adj.* of this time; modern. [ME f. OF f. L *praesens -entis* part. of *praeesse* be at hand (as PRAE-, *esse* be)]
■ *adj.* **2 a** current, contemporary, present-day, existing, existent. ● *n.* **1** (*the present*) the time being, right now, this moment; see also NOW *adv.* 1, 4. □ **at present** right *or* just now, currently, at this point, at this *or* the moment, presently, *colloq.* at this point *or* moment in time; see also NOW *adv.* 1, 4. **for the present 2** for the time being, for the nonce, for now, for a little while, for the moment; see also *temporarily* (TEMPORARY).
present-day see MODERN *adj.*

present² /prizént/ *v.* & *n.* ● *v.tr.* **1** introduce, offer, or exhibit, esp. for public attention or consideration. **2 a** (with a thing as object, usu. foll. by *to*) offer, give, or award as a gift (to a person), esp. formally or ceremonially. **b** (with a person as object, foll. by *with*) make available to; cause to have (*presented them with a new car*; *that presents us with a problem*). **3 a** (of a company, producer, etc.) put (a form of entertainment) before the public. **b** (of a performer, etc.) introduce or put before an audience. **4** introduce (a person) formally (*may I present my fiancée?*). **5** offer; give (compliments, etc.) (*may I present my card*; *present my regards to your family*). **6 a** (of a circumstance) reveal (some quality, etc.) (*this presents some difficulty*). **b** exhibit (an appearance, etc.) (*presented a tough exterior*). **7** (of an idea, etc.) offer or suggest itself. **8** deliver (a check, bill, etc.) for acceptance or payment. **9 a** (usu. foll. by *at*) aim (a weapon). **b** hold out (a weapon) in

a position for aiming. **10** (*refl.* or *absol.*) *Med.* (of a patient or illness, etc.) come forward for or undergo initial medical examination. **11** (*absol.*) *Med.* (of a part of a fetus) be directed toward the cervix at the time of delivery. **12** (foll. by *to*) *Law* bring formally under notice; submit (an offense, complaint, etc.). **13** (foll. by *to*) *Eccl.* recommend (a clergyman) to a bishop for institution to a benefice. ● *n.* the position of presenting arms in salute. □ **present arms** hold a rifle, etc., vertically in front of the body as a salute. **present oneself 1** appear. **2** come forward for examination, etc. □□ **presenter** *n.* (in sense 3 of *v.*). [ME f. OF *presenter* f. L *praesentare* (as PRESENT¹)]
■ *v.* **1** introduce, bring in *or* up, proffer, tender, produce, submit, set forth, put forward *or* up, offer, *formal* put forth; exhibit, display. **2** offer, give (out), award, bestow, grant, confer, turn *or* hand over; provide, furnish, supply; dispense, distribute, dole out, pass out, deal out, mete out. **3 a** give, stage, show, exhibit, put on, mount, produce. **b** introduce, host, give, offer, *Brit.* compère, *colloq.* emcee; announce. **4** introduce, make known, acquaint. **5** see VENTURE *v.* 3. **6 b** see EXHIBIT *v.* 1, 2a. □ **present oneself 1** see ARRIVE 1, APPEAR 2. **2** come *or* step forward, volunteer, offer oneself, put oneself forward.

present³ /prézənt/ *n.* a gift; a thing given or presented. □ **make a present of** give as a gift. [ME f. OF (as PRESENT¹), orig. in phr. *mettre une chose en present à quelqu'un* put a thing into the presence of a person]
■ gift, donation, offering, bounty, donative, *archaic* boon, propitiation, *Brit. colloq.* pressie.

presentable /prizéntəbəl/ *adj.* **1** of good appearance; fit to be presented to other people. **2** fit for presentation. □□ **presentability** /-bílitee/ *n.* **presentableness** *n.* **presentably** *adv.*
■ **1** decent, respectable; see also SMART *adj.* 2. **2** fit, fitting, suitable, acceptable, satisfactory, adequate, passable, tolerable, admissible, all right, allowable, up to par *or* standard, up to scratch, *colloq.* OK, up to snuff.

presentation /prézəntáyshən, preezen-/ *n.* **1 a** the act or an instance of presenting; the process of being presented. **b** a thing presented. **2** the manner or quality of presenting. **3** a demonstration or display of materials, information, etc.; a lecture. **4** an exhibition or theatrical performance. **5** a formal introduction. **6** the position of the fetus in relation to the cervix at the time of delivery. □□ **presentational** *adj.* **presentationally** *adv.* [ME f. OF f. LL *praesentatio -onis* (as PRESENT²)]
■ **1** bestowal, donation, conferral, conferment; handover, transfer, giving; see also ENDOWMENT 1. **2** delivery, *archaic* address; appearance; production. **3** see DEMONSTRATION 3, LECTURE *n.* 1. **4** performance, show, showing, play, production, staging.

presentationism /prézəntáyshənizəm, preezen-/ *n. Philos.* the doctrine that in perception the mind has immediate cognition of the object. □□ **presentationist** *n.*

presentative /prizéntətiv/ *adj.* **1** *Philos.* subject to direct cognition. **2** *hist.* (of a benefice) to which a patron has the right of presentation. [prob. f. med.L (as PRESENTATION)]

presentee /prézəntee, prizén-/ *n.* **1** the recipient of a present. **2** a person presented. [ME f. AF (as PRESENT²)]

presentient /preesénshənt, -sheeənt/ *adj.* (often foll. by *of*) having a presentiment. [L *praesentiens* (as PRAE-, SENTIENT)]

presentiment /prizéntimənt, -séntimənt/ *n.* a vague expectation; a foreboding (esp. of misfortune). [obs. F *présentiment* (as PRE-, SENTIMENT)]
■ see FOREBODING.

presently /prézəntlee/ *adv.* **1** soon; after a short time. **2** at the present time; now.
■ **1** soon, by and by, in a little while, shortly, after a short time, in due course, after a while *or* time, before long, in a moment *or* minute *or* while, in two shakes (of a lamb's tail), (at) any moment, (at) any moment now, momentarily, *archaic or literary* anon, *colloq.* in a jiffy. **2** see NOW *n.* 1, 4.

presentment /prizéntmənt/ *n.* **1** an act or a manner of presenting. **2** the presenting of a bill, note, etc., esp. for payment. **3** the act of presenting information, esp. a statement on oath by a jury of a fact known to them. [ME f. OF *presentement* (as PRESENT²)]

preservation /prézərváyshən/ *n.* **1** the act of preserving or process of being preserved. **2** a state of being well or badly preserved (*in an excellent state of preservation*). [ME f. OF f. med.L *praeservatio -onis* (as PRESERVE)]

■ **1** upkeep, maintenance, care, conservation; retention, perpetuation, continuation, safekeeping, safeguarding, protection.

preservationist /prézərváyshənist/ *n.* a supporter or advocate of preservation, esp. of wildlife or historic buildings.
■ conservationist, protectionist.

preservative /prizárvətiv/ *n. & adj.* ● *n.* a substance for preserving perishable foods, wood, etc. ● *adj.* tending to preserve. [ME f. OF *preservatif -ive* f. med.L *praeservativus -um* (as PRESERVE)]

preserve /prizárv/ *v. & n.* ● *v.tr.* **1 a** keep safe or free from harm, decay, etc. **b** keep alive (a name, memory, etc.). **2** maintain (a thing) in its existing state. **3** retain (a quality or condition). **4 a** treat or refrigerate (food) to prevent decomposition or fermentation. **b** prepare (fruit or vegetables) by boiling with sugar, canning, etc., for long-term storage. **5** keep (wildlife, a river, etc.) undisturbed for private use. ● *n.* (in *sing.* or *pl.*) **1** preserved fruit; jam. **2** a place where game or fish, etc., are preserved. **3** a sphere or area of activity regarded as a person's own. □ **well-preserved** showing little sign of aging. □□ **preservable** *adj.* **preserver** *n.* [ME f. OF *preserver* f. LL *praeservare* (as PRAE-, *servare* keep)]

■ *v.* **1 a** keep safe, protect, guard, safeguard, shield, shelter, defend, spare. **2** keep (up), conserve; see also MAINTAIN 4. **3** retain, keep, sustain, hold; see MAINTAIN 1, 2. **4 a** conserve, pickle, cure, smoke, kipper, salt, corn, marinate, can, freeze, freeze-dry, refrigerate, dry, irradiate. ● *n.* **1** conserve, jam, jelly, marmalade. **2** (wildlife) reserve, sanctuary, park. **3** see SPHERE *n.* 4a.

preset /preesét/ *v.tr.* (**-setting**; *past* and *past part.* **-set**) **1** set or fix (a device) in advance of its operation. **2** settle or decide beforehand.

preshrunk /preeshrúngk/ *adj.* (of a fabric or garment) treated so that it shrinks during manufacture and not in use.

preside /prizíd/ *v.intr.* **1** (often foll. by *at, over*) be in a position of authority, esp. as the chairperson or president. **2 a** exercise control or authority. **b** (foll. by *at*) play a featured instrument (*presided at the piano*). [F *présider* f. L *praesidēre* (as PRAE-, *sedēre* sit)]

■ **1** (*preside over* or *at*) chair, administer, officiate at; manage, handle, supervise, run, oversee, head (up), control, direct, administrate, regulate. **2 a** see CHAIR *v.*

presidency /prézidənsee/ *n.* (*pl.* **-ies**) **1** the office, term, or function of president. **2** the office of the President of the United States. **3** a Mormon administrative or governing body. [Sp. & Port. *presidencia*, It. *presidenza* f. med.L *praesidentia* (as PRESIDE)]

■ premiership, leadership, rule, command; *colloq.* driver's seat, saddle; administration.

president /prézidənt/ *n.* **1** the elected head of a republican government. **2** the head of a college, university, company, society, etc. **3** a person in charge of a meeting, council, etc. □□ **presidential** /-dénshəl/ *adj.* **presidentially** *adv.* **presidentship** *n.* [ME f. OF f. L (as PRESIDE)]

■ **1–2** chief, leader, principal, *colloq.* boss, *sl.* (big) cheese, (chief) honcho, Mr. Big, *Brit. sl.* guv'nor, guv. **2** *sl.* prez, prex, prexy; see also PRINCIPAL *n.* 2; *Brit.* director, managing director. **3** chair, chairman, chairwoman, chairperson.

presidium /prisídeeəm, -zídeeəm/ *n.* (also **praesidium**) a standing executive committee in a Communist country, esp. *hist.* in the former USSR. [Russ. *prezidium* f. L *praesidium* protection, etc. (as PRESIDE)]

pre-Socratic /preeəskrátik, -sṓ-/ *adj.* (of philosophy) of the time before Socrates.

press¹ /pres/ *v. & n.* ● *v.* **1** *tr.* apply steady force to (a thing in contact) (*pressed the two surfaces together*). **2** *tr.* **a** compress or apply pressure to a thing to flatten, shape, or smooth it, as by ironing (*got the curtains pressed*). **b** squeeze (a fruit, etc.) to extract its juice. **c** manufacture (a record, etc.) by molding under pressure. **3** *tr.* (foll. by *out of, from*, etc.) squeeze (juice, etc.). **4** *tr.* embrace or caress by squeezing (*pressed my hand*). **5** *intr.* (foll. by *on, against*, etc.) exert pressure. **6** *intr.* be urgent; demand immediate action (*time was pressing*). **7** *intr.* (foll. by *for*) make an insistent demand. **8** *intr.* (foll. by *up, round*, etc.) form a crowd. **9** *intr.* (foll. by *on, forward*, etc.) hasten insistently. **10** *tr.* (often in *passive*) (of an enemy, etc.) bear heavily on. **11** *tr.* (often foll. by *for*, or *to* + infin.) urge or entreat (*pressed me to stay; pressed me for an answer*). **12** *tr.* (foll. by *on, upon*) **a** put forward or urge (an opinion, claim, or course of action). **b** insist on the acceptance of (an offer, a gift, etc.). **13** *tr.* insist on (*did not press the point*). **14** *intr.* (foll. by *on*) produce a strong mental or moral impression; oppress; weigh heavily. **15** *intr. Sports* try too hard and so perform inadequately. **16** (in weightlifting) raise weight in a press. ● *n.* **1** the act or an instance of pressing (*give it a slight press*). **2 a** a device for compressing, flattening, shaping, extracting juice, etc. (*flower press; wine press*). **b** a machine that applies pressure to a workpiece by means of a tool, in order to punch shapes, bend it, etc. **3** = *printing press.* **4** (prec. by *the*) **a** the art or practice of printing. **b** newspapers, journalists, etc., generally or collectively (*read it in the press; pursued by the press*). **5** a notice or piece of publicity in newspapers, etc. (*got a good press*). **6** (**Press**) **a** a printing house or establishment. **b** a publishing company (*Yale University Press*). **7 a** crowding. **b** a crowd (of people, etc.). **8** the pressure of affairs. **9** a large usu. shelved cupboard for clothes, books, etc. **10** (in basketball) an aggressive close defense. **11** (in weightlifting) an exercise in which the weight is lifted so that the arms are fully extended, without moving the legs or feet. □ **at** (or **in**) **press** (or **the press**) being printed. **be pressed for** have barely enough (time, etc.). **full-court press** *Basketball* a defensive strategy in which the team with the ball is closely guarded the full length of the court. **go** (or **send**) **to press** go or send to be printed. **press agent** a person employed to attend to advertising and press publicity. **press box** a reporters' enclosure esp. at a sports event. **press the button 1** set machinery in motion. **2** *colloq.* take a decisive initial step. **press-button** *Brit. adj.* = *push button.* **press conference** an interview given to journalists to make an announcement or answer questions. **press gallery** a gallery for reporters esp. in a legislative assembly. **press-on** (of a material) that can be pressed or ironed on. **press release** an official statement issued to newspapers for information. **press-stud** *Brit.* = *snap fastener.* **press-up** = *push-up.* [ME f. OF *presser, presse* f. L *pressare* frequent. of *premere* press-]

■ *v.* **1** squeeze, compress, push; depress, press *or* push down. **2 a** iron, smooth, flatten, esp. *Brit hist.* put through a mangle. **b** squeeze, crush, compress, mash; cream, purée. **3** see EXPRESS¹ 4. **4** clasp, embrace, hug, hold (close *or* tight), take in one's arms, throw one's arms about *or* around, grip, clip. **5** exert pressure *or* force, jab, prod, dig, poke, nudge, depress. **7** (*press for*) cry out for, call for, insist on; see ASK 4a. **8** crowd, flock, gather, mill, swarm, throng, seethe, cluster, congregate, converge, huddle. **9** (*press on* or *forward*) see HURRY *v.* 1. **11** urge, pressure, pressurize, importune, beseech, ask, request, beg, entreat. **12 b** push, force; see also THRUST *v.* 2. **13** pursue; see also LABOR *v.* 3a. **14** (*press on*) see OPPRESS 3. ● *n.* **1** push, squeeze, nudge, shove, thrust. **4 b** (*the press*) the newspapers, the papers, Fleet Street, *joc.* the fourth estate; newspapermen, newsmen, reporters, ladies *or*

/.../ **pronunciation**	● **part of speech**
□ **phrases, idioms, and compounds**	
□□ **derivatives**	■ **synonym section**
cross-references appear in SMALL CAPITALS or *italics*	

gentlemen of the press, journalists, paparazzi, newshounds, *Austral. colloq.* journos. **5** review(s); see also NOTICE *n.* 4. **7 b** crowd, throng, swarm, cluster, huddle, pack, herd, host, mob, crush, *usu. derog.* horde. **8** pressure, stress; urgency, haste, hurry, (hustle and) bustle, hurly-burly. □ **be pressed for** (*be pressed for time*) be busy, be run or rushed off one's feet, *colloq.* be pushed (for time), be up to one's neck.

press² /pres/ *v. & n.* ● *v.tr.* **1** *hist.* force to serve in the army or navy; impress. **2** bring into use as a makeshift (*was pressed into service*). ● *n. hist.* compulsory enlistment esp. in the navy; impressment. [alt. f. obs. *prest* (v. & n.) f. OF *prest* loan, advance pay f. *prester* f. L *praestare* furnish (as PRAE-, *stare* stand)]

press-gang /présgang/ *n. & v.* ● *n.* **1** *hist.* a body of men employed to press men into service in the army or navy. **2** any group using similar coercive methods. ● *v.tr.* force into service.

pressing /présing/ *adj. & n.* ● *adj.* **1** urgent (*pressing business*). **2 a** urging strongly (*a pressing invitation*). **b** persistent; importunate (*since you are so pressing*). ● *n.* **1** a thing made by pressing, esp. a record, compact disc, etc. **2** a series of these made at one time. **3** the act or an instance of pressing a thing, esp. a record or grapes, etc. (*all at one pressing*). □□ **pressingly** *adv.*
■ *adj.* **1** urgent, compelling, pivotal, major, important, vital, high-priority, critical, portentous, momentous, significant, *colloq. disp.* crucial. **2 b** see INSISTENT 1.

pressman /présmən/ *n.* (*pl.* **-men**) **1** an operator of a printing press. **2** *Brit.* a journalist.
■ **2** see JOURNALIST.

pressmark /présmaark/ *n. Brit.* an assigned number or mark showing the location of a book, etc., in a library.

pressure /préshər/ *n. & v.* ● *n.* **1 a** the exertion of continuous force on or against a body by another in contact with it. **b** the force exerted. **c** the amount of this (expressed by the force on a unit area) (*atmospheric pressure*). **2** urgency; the need to meet a deadline, etc. (*work under pressure*). **3** affliction or difficulty (*under financial pressure*). **4** constraining influence (*if pressure is brought to bear*). ● *v.tr.* **1** apply pressure to. **2 a** coerce. **b** (often foll. by *into*) persuade (*was pressured into attending*). □ **pressure-cook** cook in a pressure cooker. **pressure cooker** an airtight pot for cooking quickly under steam pressure. **pressure gauge** a gauge showing the pressure of steam, etc. **pressure group** a group or association formed to promote a particular interest or cause by influencing public policy. **pressure point 1** a point where an artery can be pressed against a bone to inhibit bleeding. **2** a point on the skin sensitive to pressure. **3** a target for political pressure or influence. **pressure suit** an inflatable suit for flying at a high altitude. [ME f. L *pressura* (as PRESS¹)]
■ *n.* **1 a, b** force, compression, tension; weight, power, strength. **2, 3** stress, strain, constraint; urgency, demand(s); affliction, oppression, press, weight, burden, load; difficulty. **4** influence, power, sway; insistence, coercion, inducement, persuasion, *colloq.* arm-twisting. ● *v.* **1** bring pressure to bear on, apply pressure on or to, pressurize, *colloq.* lean on, twist a person's arm, turn the heat on, put the screws on; intimidate, constrain. **2 a** see FORCE¹ *v.* 1. **b** persuade, prevail upon or on, induce, get.

pressurize /préshəriz/ *v.tr.* **1** (esp. as **pressurized** *adj.*) maintain normal atmospheric pressure in (an aircraft cabin, etc.) at a high altitude. **2** raise to a high pressure. **3** pressure (a person). □ **pressurized-water reactor** *Brit.* a nuclear reactor in which the coolant is water at high pressure. □□ **pressurization** *n.*
■ **3** see PRESSURE *v.*

prestidigitator /préstidíjitaytər/ *n. formal* a magician. □□ **prestidigitation** /-táyshən/ *n.* [F *prestidigitateur* f. *preste* nimble (as PRESTO) + L *digitus* finger]
■ conjuror, illusionist. □□ **prestidigitation** see MAGIC *n.* 2.

prestige /presteézh/ *n.* **1** respect, reputation, or influence de-

rived from achievements, power, associations, etc. **2** (*attrib.*) having or conferring prestige. □□ **prestigeful** *adj.* [F, = illusion, glamour, f. LL *praestigium* (as PRESTIGIOUS)]
■ **1** status, respect, reputation, standing, rank, stature, influence, eminence, esteem, preeminence, distinction, renown, regard, fame, cachet, repute, glamour.

prestigious /presteéjəs, -stíj-/ *adj.* having or showing prestige. □□ **prestigiously** *adv.* **prestigiousness** *n.* [orig. = deceptive, f. L *praestigiosus* f. *praestigiae* juggler's tricks]
■ prestigeful, distinguished, august, dignified, illustrious, acclaimed, respected, celebrated, renowned, eminent, estimable, influential, impressive, preeminent, famous, famed, well-known, noted, notable, noteworthy, outstanding; (*attrib.*) prestige.

prestissimo /prestísimō/ *adv. & n. Mus.* ● *adv.* in a very quick tempo. ● *n.* (*pl.* **-os**) a movement or passage played in this way. [It., superl. (as PRESTO 1)]

presto /préstō/ *adv. & n.* ● *adv.* **1** *Mus.* in quick tempo. **2** (in a magician's formula in performing a trick) quickly. ● *n.* (*pl.* **-os**) *Mus.* a movement to be played in a quick tempo. [It. f. LL *praestus* f. L *praesto* ready]
■ *adv.* **1** see FAST¹ *adv.* 1.

prestressed /preéstrést/ *adj.* strengthened by stressing in advance, esp. of concrete by means of stretched rods or wires put in during manufacture.

presumably /prizoómables/ *adv.* as may reasonably be presumed.
■ probably, in all likelihood, (very or most) likely, in all probability, as likely as not.

presume /prizoóm/ *v.* **1** *tr.* (often foll. by *that* + clause) suppose to be true; take for granted. **2** *tr.* (often foll. by *to* + infin.) **a** take the liberty; be impudent enough (*presumed to question their authority*). **b** dare; venture (*may I presume to ask?*). **3** *intr.* be presumptuous; take liberties. **4** *intr.* (foll. by *on, upon*) take advantage of or make unscrupulous use of (a person's good nature, etc.). □□ **presumable** *adj.* **presumedly** /-zoómidlee/ *adv.* [ME f. OF *presumer* f. L *praesumere praesumpt-* anticipate, venture (as PRAE-, *sumere* take)]
■ **1** assume, take for granted, suppose, surmise, infer, presuppose, take it; postulate, posit. **2** take the liberty, be so presumptuous as, make so bold as, have the audacity or effrontery, go so far as; dare, venture. **4** (*presume on* or *upon*) take advantage of, abuse, misemploy, misuse, impose on or upon, take liberties with, *colloq.* put upon, *usu. derog.* exploit.

presuming /prizoóming/ *adj.* presumptuous. □□ **presumingly** *adv.* **presumingness** *n.*
■ see PRESUMPTIVE.

presumption /prizúmpshən/ *n.* **1** arrogance; presumptuous behavior. **2 a** the act of presuming a thing to be true. **b** a thing that is or may be presumed to be true; a belief based on reasonable evidence. **3** a ground for presuming (*a strong presumption against their being guilty*). **4** *Law* an inference from known facts. [ME f. OF *presumpcion* f. L *praesumptio -onis* (as PRESUME)]
■ **1** arrogance, effrontery, hubris, audacity, boldness, brazenness, impudence, impertinence, insolence, temerity, overconfidence, presumptuousness, forwardness, immodesty, cheek, cheekiness, *colloq.* nerve, *sl.* gall, chutzpah, brass, *Brit. sl.* brass neck. **2** assumption, supposition, presupposition, preconception, surmise, proposition, postulation; premise; belief, thought, feeling, conviction, inference, deduction, guess, theory, hypothesis, conjecture. **3** see ARGUMENT 2.

presumptive /prizúmptiv/ *adj.* **1** based on presumption or inference. **2** giving reasonable grounds for presumption (*presumptive evidence*). □□ **presumptively** *adv.* [F *présomptif -ive* f. LL *praesumptivus* (as PRESUME)]
■ **1** inferred, presumed, assumed, supposed, understood, predicted, predicated. **2** likely, reasonable, plausible, tenable, believable, credible, conceivable, acceptable, justifiable, sensible, rational, sound.

presumptuous /prizúmpchoōəs/ *adj.* unduly or overbearingly confident and presuming. □□ **presumptuously** *adv.*

presumptuousness *n.* [ME f. OF *presumptueux* f. LL *praesumptuosus, -tiosus* (as PRESUME)]
■ arrogant, proud, prideful, overconfident, overweening, forward, egotistical, presuming, audacious, bold, brazen, impertinent, insolent, cheeky, esp. *Brit. colloq.* uppish.

presuppose /preésəpóz/ *v.tr.* (often foll. by *that* + clause) **1** assume beforehand. **2** require as a precondition; imply. [ME f. OF *presupposer*, after med.L *praesupponere* (as PRE-, SUPPOSE)]
■ **1** see PRESUME 1. **2** see IMPLY 3, REQUIRE 1.

presupposition /preésúpəzíshən/ *n.* **1** the act or an instance of presupposing. **2** a thing assumed beforehand as the basis of argument, etc. [med.L *praesuppositio* (as PRAE-, *supponere* as SUPPOSE)]
■ **1** see PRESUMPTION 2. **2** see PREMISE *n.*

pretax /preétáks/ *adj.* (of income or profits) before the deduction of taxes.
■ gross.

preteen /preéteén/ *adj.* of or relating to a child just under the age of thirteen.

pretence esp. *Brit.* var. of PRETENSE.

pretend /priténd/ *v. & adj.* ● *v.* **1** *tr.* claim or assert falsely so as to deceive (*pretend knowledge*; *pretended that they were foreigners*). **2 a** *tr.* imagine to oneself in play (*pretended to be monsters*; *pretended it was night*). **b** *absol.* make pretense, esp. in imagination or play; make believe (*they're just pretending*). **3** *tr.* **a** profess, esp. falsely or extravagantly (*does not pretend to be a scholar*). **b** (as **pretended** *adj.*) falsely claim to be such (*a pretended friend*). **4** *intr.* (foll. by *to*) **a** lay claim to (a right or title, etc.). **b** profess to have (a quality, etc.). **5** *tr.* (foll. by *to*) aspire or presume; venture (*I cannot pretend to guess*). ● *adj. colloq.* pretended; in pretense (*pretend money*). [ME f. F *prétendre* or f. L (as PRAE-, *tendere tent-*, later *tens-* stretch)]
■ *v.* **1** see COUNTERFEIT *v.* 2, *make believe* (BELIEVE). **2 b** make believe, act, play, playact, put on an act; dissemble, sham. **3 a** profess, (lay) claim, make a pretense, purport; maintain, declare. **b** (**pretended**) self-styled, so-called, alleged, professed, ostensible, purported, sham, false, fake, feigned, bogus, counterfeit, spurious, pseudo, *colloq.* phony, pretend. **5** try, attempt, endeavor, venture, presume, aspire, undertake. ● *adj.* see PRETEND *v.* 3b above.

pretender /priténdər/ *n.* **1** a person who claims a throne or title, etc. **2** a person who pretends.
■ **1** claimant, aspirant, candidate, suitor, seeker.

pretense /preétens, priténs/ *n.* (also **pretence**) **1** pretending; make-believe. **2 a** a pretext or excuse (*on the slightest pretense*). **b** a false show of intentions or motives (*under the pretense of friendship*; *under false pretenses*). **3** (foll. by *to*) a claim, esp. a false or ambitious one (*has no pretense to any great talent*). **4 a** affectation; display. **b** pretentiousness; ostentation (*stripped of all pretense*). [ME f. AF *pretense* ult. f. med.L *pretensus* pretended (as PRETEND)]
■ **1** make-believe, fiction, pretending, fabrication, invention. **2 a** pretext, pretension, blind; see also EXCUSE *n.* 1, 2. **b** front, façade, appearance, show, cover, cloak, veil, mask; hoax, artifice, sham, pose, cover-up, masquerade, guise, ruse, dodge, blind. **3** claim; right, title. **4** affectation, display, ostentation, show, airs, pretentiousness, pretension, posturing; hypocrisy, fakery, humbuggery, humbug, deception, artifice, falseness.

pretension /priténshən/ *n.* **1** (often foll. by *to*) **a** an assertion of a claim. **b** a justifiable claim (*has no pretensions to the name*; *has some pretensions to be included*). **2** pretentiousness. [med.L *praetensio, -tio* (as PRETEND)]
■ **1 a** claim; aspiration(s), ambitiousness; see also AMBITION 2. **b** claim, right, title. **2** pretense, pretentiousness, ostentation, affectation, hypocrisy, show, artifice, falseness, fakery, *Austral. & NZ sl.* guiver.

pretentious /priténshəs/ *adj.* **1** making an excessive claim to great merit or importance. **2** ostentatious. □□ **pretentiously** *adv.* **pretentiousness** *n.* [F *prétentieux* (as PRETENSION)]
■ **1** pompous, self-aggrandizing, self-important, affected, *colloq.* highfalutin; snobbish, lofty, haughty, hoity-toity, *colloq.* high-hat, snotty, *Brit. sl.* toffee-nosed. **2** ostentatious, showy, superficial, grandiose, grandiloquent, extravagant, magniloquent; bombastic, inflated, high-flown, exaggerated, flowery, fustian, orotund, ornate, flatulent, turgid, euphuistic, *colloq.* windy.

preter- /preétər/ *comb. form* more than. [L *praeter* (adv. & prep.), = past, beyond]

preterit /prétərit/ *adj. & n.* (also **preterite**) *Gram.* ● *adj.* expressing a past action or state. ● *n.* a preterit tense or form. [ME f. OF *preterite* or L *praeteritus* past part. of *praeterire* pass (as PRETER-, *ire it-* go)]

preterm *adj.* /preétərm/ born or occurring prematurely.

pretermit /preétərmít/ *v.tr.* (**pretermitted, pretermitting**) *formal* **1** omit to mention (a fact, etc.). **2** omit to do or perform; neglect. **3** leave off (a custom or continuous action) for a time. □□ **pretermission** /-míshən/ *n.* [L *praetermittere* (as PRETER-, *mittere miss-* let go)]
■ **1, 2** see DISREGARD *v.* 1, NEGLECT *v.* 1, 2. □□ **pretermission** see DISREGARD *n.*, NEGLECT *n.*

preternatural /preétərnáchərəl/ *adj.* outside the ordinary course of nature; supernatural. □□ **preternaturalism** *n.* **preternaturally** *adv.*
■ see SUPERNATURAL *adj.* □□ **preternaturalism** see MYSTIQUE 1.

pretext /preétekst/ *n.* **1** an ostensible or alleged reason or intention. **2** an excuse offered. □ **on** (or **under**) **the pretext** (foll. by *of*, or *that* + clause) professing as one's object or intention. [L *praetextus* outward display f. *praetexere praetext-* (as PRAE-, *texere* weave)]
■ pretense, guise; rationalization, explanation; see also EXCUSE *n.* 1, 2.

pretor var. of PRAETOR.

pretorian var. of PRAETORIAN.

prettify /prítifī/ *v.tr.* (**-ies, -ied**) make (a thing or person) pretty esp. in an affected way. □□ **prettification** *n.* **prettifier** *n.*
■ see PREEN 2.

pretty /prítee/ *adj., n., v., & adv.* ● *adj.* (**prettier, prettiest**) **1** attractive in a delicate way without being truly beautiful or handsome (*a pretty child*; *a pretty dress*; *a pretty tune*). **2** fine or good of its kind (*a pretty wit*). **3** *iron.* considerable; fine (*a pretty penny*; *a pretty mess you have made*). ● *adv. colloq.* fairly; moderately; considerably (*am pretty well*; *find it pretty difficult*). ● *n.* (*pl.* **-ies**) a pretty person (esp. as a form of address to a child). ● *v.tr.* (**-ies, -ied**) (often foll. by *up*) make pretty or attractive. □ **pretty much** (or **nearly** or **well**) *colloq.* almost; very nearly. **pretty-pretty** *Brit.* too pretty. **sitting pretty** *colloq.* in a favorable or advantageous position. □□ **prettily** *adv.* **prettiness** *n.* **prettyish** *adj.* [OE *prættig* f. WG]
■ *adj.* **1** comely, attractive, good-looking, nice-looking, appealing, lovely, fair, fetching, charming, winsome, esp. *No. of Engl.* bonny, *colloq.* cute; sweet, melodic, melodious, dulcet, musical, harmonious, mellifluous, euphonious, *colloq.* easy on the eye(s) or ear(s). **2** see FINE[1] *adj.* 2. ● *adv.* rather, quite, fairly, moderately, reasonably, tolerably, somewhat; considerably, very, extremely, unbelievably, incredibly. □ **pretty much** (or **nearly** or **well**) see ALMOST.

pretzel /prétsəl/ *n.* a crisp or chewy knot-shaped or stick-shaped bread, usu. salted. [G]

prevail /priváyl/ *v.intr.* **1** (often foll. by *against, over*) be victorious or gain mastery. **2** be the more usual or predominant. **3** exist or occur in general use or experience; be cur-

---

/.../ **pronunciation**	● **part of speech**
□ **phrases, idioms, and compounds**	
□□ **derivatives**	■ **synonym section**
cross-references appear in SMALL CAPITALS or *italics*	

rent. **4** (foll. by *on, upon*) persuade. **5** (as **prevailing** *adj.*) predominant; generally current or accepted (*prevailing opinion*). □ **prevailing wind** the wind that most frequently occurs at a place. □□ **prevailingly** *adv.* [ME f. L *praevalēre* (as PRAE-, *valēre* have power), infl. by AVAIL]

■ **1** win (out), succeed, triumph, gain *or* achieve victory, prove superior, gain mastery *or* control. **2, 3** predominate, preponderate, dominate; be prevalent *or* widespread *or* current, be the order of the day, hold sway. **4** (*prevail on* or *upon*) persuade, induce, sway, convince, prompt. **5** (**prevailing**) dominant, predominant, prevalent, common(est), usual, customary, universal, general, accepted, popular, shared.

prevalent /prévələnt/ *adj.* **1** generally existing or occurring. **2** predominant. □□ **prevalence** *n.* **prevalently** *adv.* [as PRE-VAIL]

■ **1** current, general, universal, catholic, common, frequent, ubiquitous, pervasive, omnipresent, extensive, widespread, established. **2** prevailing, dominant, governing, ruling; see also PREDOMINANT 1. □□ **prevalence** frequency, commonness, currency, universality, ubiquitousness, ubiquity, pervasiveness, omnipresence, extensiveness, popularity; predominance; primacy.

prevaricate /privárikayt/ *v.intr.* **1** speak or act evasively or misleadingly. **2** quibble; equivocate. □□ **prevarication** /-rikáyshən/ *n.* **prevaricator** *n.* [L *praevaricari* walk crookedly, practice collusion, in eccl.L transgress (as PRAE-, *varicari* straddle f. *varus* bent, knock-kneed)]

■ see EQUIVOCATE. □□ **prevarication** see EVASION 2, FLANNEL *n.* 3.

prevenient /privéenyənt/ *adj. formal* preceding something else. [L *praeveniens* pres. part of *praevenire* (as PREVENT)]

prevent /privént/ *v.tr.* **1** (often foll. by *from* + verbal noun) stop from happening or doing something; hinder; make impossible (*the weather prevented me from going*). **2** *archaic* go or arrive before; precede. □□ **preventable** *adj.* (also **preventible**). **preventability** *n.* **preventer** *n.* **prevention** /-vénshən/ *n.* [ME = anticipate, f. L *praevenire praevent*-come before, hinder (as PRAE-, *venire* come)]

■ **1** stop, put a stop to, arrest, (bring to a) halt; hinder, impede, curb, restrain, hamper, obstruct, inhibit, delay, retard, slow, thwart, foil, frustrate, check, block, balk, control; preclude, forestall, avert, avoid, ward *or* fend *or* stave off; prohibit, ban, bar, forbid, interdict, taboo, debar. **2** see PRECEDE. □□ **prevention** preclusion, avoidance, prohibition, forbiddance, interdiction; obstruction, hindrance; stopping, arrest, halt; restraint, retardation, control.

preventative /privéntətiv/ *adj. & n.* = PREVENTIVE. □□ **preventatively** *adv.*

preventive /privéntiv/ *adj. & n.* ● *adj.* serving to prevent, esp. preventing disease, breakdown, etc. (*preventive medicine*; *preventive maintenance*). ● *n.* a preventive agent, measure, drug, etc. □□ **preventively** *adv.*

■ *adj.* preventative, inhibitive, inhibitory, restrictive, preclusive, interdictory; prophylactic, precautionary; protective; counteractive. ● *n.* preventative, inhibitor, hindrance, curb, block, barrier, obstacle; prophylactic, protection, shield, safeguard, prevention, countermeasure.

preview /préevyoo/ *n. & v.* ● *n.* **1** the act of seeing in advance. **2 a** the showing of a movie, play, exhibition, etc., before it is seen by the general public. **b** (also **prevue**) an advance promotional sample of a movie; trailer. ● *v.tr.* see or show in advance.

■ *n.* **2 a** advance showing, private viewing.

previous /préeveeəs/ *adj. & adv.* ● *adj.* **1** (often foll. by *to*) coming before in time or order. **2** done or acting hastily. ● *adv.* (foll. by *to*) before (*had called previous to writing*). □ **previous question** *Parl.* a motion concerning the vote on a main question. □□ **previously** *adv.* **previousness** *n.* [L *praevius* (as PRAE-, *via* way)]

■ *adj.* **1** former, prior, past, earlier, sometime, erstwhile,

archaic whilom; above, preceding, antecedent, anterior, aforementioned, aforesaid, above-mentioned, above-named, aforestated, *formal* prevenient. **2** see PREMATURE 1. ● *adv.* (*previous to*) previously to, prior to, in advance of; see also BEFORE *prep.* 1a, b, 2. □□ **previously** before, once, formerly, earlier, at one time, then, beforehand, hitherto, thitherto, *formal* heretofore, theretofore; in the past, in days gone by, in days of old, in days *or* times past, in the old days, some time ago, a while ago, once upon a time, *archaic* in olden days *or* times, *literary* in days of yore.

previse /privíz/ *v.tr. literary* foresee or forecast (an event, etc.). □□ **prevision** /-vízhən/ *n.* **previsional** *adj.* [L *praevidēre praevis*- (as PRAE-, *vidēre* see)]

■ □□ **prevision** clairvoyance, foresight, vision, foreknowledge, prescience.

prevue var. of PREVIEW *n.* 2b.

prewar /préewáwr/ *adj.* existing or occurring before a war (esp. the most recent major war).

prex /preks/ *n.* (also **prexy**) *sl.* a president (esp. of a college). [abbr.]

prey /pray/ *n. & v.* ● *n.* **1** an animal that is hunted or killed by another for food. **2** (often foll. by *to*) a person or thing that is influenced by or vulnerable to (something undesirable) (*became a prey to morbid fears*). **3** *Bibl.* or *archaic* plunder, booty, etc. ● *v.intr.* (foll. by *on, upon*) **1** seek or take as prey. **2** make a victim of. **3** (of a disease, emotion, etc.) exert a harmful influence (*fear preyed on his mind*). □ **beast** (or **bird**) **of prey** an animal (or bird) that hunts animals for food. □□ **preyer** *n.* [ME f. OF *preie* f. L *praeda* booty]

■ *n.* **1** quarry, kill; victim; game. **2** victim, target, objective; dupe, *Brit.* mug, *colloq.* mark, *sl.* fall guy, pushover. ● *v.* (*prey on* or *upon*) **1** live off, feed on *or* upon, eat, consume, devour; stalk, pursue, hunt. **2** victimize, go after, exploit, use, take advantage of, intimidate, bully. **3** oppress, weigh on *or* upon, burden, depress, strain, vex, worry, gnaw (at), plague, trouble, torment.

priapic /príápik/ *adj.* phallic. [*Priapos* (as PRIAPISM) + -IC]

priapism /príəpizəm/ *n.* **1** lewdness; licentiousness. **2** *Med.* persistent erection of the penis. [F *priapisme* f. LL *priapismus* f. Gk *priapismos* f. *priapizō* be lewd f. *Priapos* god of procreation]

price /pris/ *n. & v.* ● *n.* **1 a** the amount of money or goods for which a thing is bought or sold. **b** value or worth (*a pearl of great price*; *beyond price*). **2** what is or must be given, done, sacrificed, etc., to obtain or achieve something. **3** the odds in betting (*starting price*). **4** a sum of money offered or given as a reward, esp. for the capture or killing of a person. ● *v.tr.* **1** fix or find the price of (a thing for sale). **2** estimate the value of. □ **above** (or **beyond** or **without**) **price** so valuable that no price can be stated. **at any price** no matter what the cost, sacrifice, etc. (*peace at any price*). **at a price** at a high cost. **price-fixing** (also **price fixing**) the maintaining of prices at a certain level by agreement between competing sellers. **price on a person's head** a reward for a person's capture or death. **price oneself out of the market** lose to one's competitors by charging more than customers are willing to pay. **price tag 1** the label on an item showing its price. **2** the cost of an enterprise or undertaking. **price war** fierce competition among traders cutting prices. **set a price on** declare the price of. **what price . . .?** (often foll. by verbal noun) *colloq.* **1** *iron.* the expected or much boasted . . . proves disappointing (*what price your friendship now?*). **2** *Brit.* what is the chance of . . . ? (*what price your finishing the course?*). □□ **priced** *adj.* (also in *comb.*). **pricer** *n.* [(n.) ME f. OF *pris* f. L *pretium*: (v.) var. of *prise* = PRIZE¹]

■ *n.* **1 a** charge, cost, expense, expenditure, outlay, payment, amount, figure, fee, *sl.* damage. **b** value, worth; appraisal, valuation, evaluation. **2** sacrifice, toll, penalty, cost; see also LOSS 2, 3. **4** reward, bounty, premium, prize, payment, bonus, *poet.* guerdon. ● *v.* value, evaluate, rate, cost. □ **above price** see PRICELESS 1.

priceless /príslis/ *adj.* **1** invaluable; beyond price. **2** *colloq.*

very amusing or absurd. □□ **pricelessly** *adv.* **pricelessness** *n.*

■ **1** costly, dear, expensive, high-priced, valuable, invaluable, precious, above *or* beyond *or* without price. **2** hilarious, (screamingly) funny, sidesplitting, *colloq.* hysterical; absurd, ridiculous, droll, comical.

pricey /príseε/ *adj.* (also **pricy**) (**pricier**, **priciest**) *colloq.* expensive. □□ **priciness** *n.*

■ costly, dear, expensive; overpriced, exorbitant, outrageous, excessive.

prick /prik/ *v. & n.* ● *v.* **1** *tr.* pierce slightly; make a small hole in. **2** *tr.* (foll. by *off, out*) mark (esp. a pattern) with small holes or dots. **3** *tr.* trouble mentally (*my conscience is pricking me*). **4** *intr.* feel a pricking sensation. **5** *tr.* (foll. by *at, into,* etc.) make a thrust as if to prick. **6** *tr.* (foll. by *in, off, out*) plant (seedlings, etc.) in small holes pricked in the earth. **7** *tr. Brit. archaic* mark off (a name in a list, esp. to select a sheriff) by pricking. **8** *tr. archaic* spur or urge on (a horse, etc.). ● *n.* **1** the act or an instance of pricking. **2** a small hole or mark made by pricking. **3** a pain caused as by pricking. **4** a mental pain (*felt the pricks of conscience*). **5** *coarse sl.* **a** the penis. **b** *derog.* (as a term of contempt) a contemptible or mean-spirited person. ¶ Usually considered a taboo use. **6** *archaic* a goad for oxen. □ **kick against the pricks** *Brit.* persist in futile resistance. **prick up one's ears 1** (of a dog, etc.) make the ears erect when on the alert. **2** (of a person) become suddenly attentive. [OE *prician* (v.), *pricca* (n.)]

■ *v.* **1, 2** puncture, pierce, punch, perforate, penetrate. **3** see TROUBLE *v.* 1, 3. **4** smart, sting, stab, tingle, tickle, prickle, pinch, hurt. ● *n.* **2** pinhole, pinprick; hole, perforation, mark; see also LEAK *n.* 1a. **3** sting, pinch, twinge, prickle, tingle, smart. **4** see PANG.

pricker /príkər/ *n.* **1** one that pricks, as an animal or plant. **2** a small thorn or other sharp pointed outgrowth.

pricket /príkit/ *n.* **1** a male fallow deer in its second year, having straight unbranched horns. **2** a spike for holding a candle. [ME f. AL *prikettus -um,* dimin. of PRICK]

prickle /príkəl/ *n. & v.* ● *n.* **1 a** a small thorn. **b** *Bot.* a thornlike process developed from the epidermis of a plant. **2** a hard pointed spine of a hedgehog, etc. **3** a prickling sensation. ● *v.tr. & intr.* affect or be affected with a sensation as of pricking. [OE *pricel* PRICK: (v.) also dimin. of PRICK]

■ *n.* **1, 2** spine, bristle, barb, thorn, needle, spike. **3** prickliness, itch, itchiness, sting, tingling, prick, tingle. ● *v.* tingle, sting, itch, smart; jab, prick.

prickly /príklee/ *adj.* (**pricklier, prickliest**) **1** (esp. in the names of plants and animals) having prickles. **2 a** (of a person) ready to take offense. **b** (of a topic, argument, etc.) full of contentious or complicated points; thorny. **3** tingling. □ **prickly heat** an itchy inflammation of the skin, causing a tingling sensation and common in hot countries. **prickly pear 1** any cactus of the genus *Opuntia,* native to arid regions of America, bearing barbed bristles and large pear-shaped prickly fruits. **2** its fruit. **prickly poppy** a tropical poppylike plant, *Argemone mexicana,* with prickly leaves and yellow flowers. □□ **prickliness** *n.*

■ **1** bristly, thorny, brambly, spiny, barbed, briery, spiky, *Biol.* setose, *Bot.* spinous, spinose, aculeate, spiculate, *Bot. & Zool.* setaceous. **2 a** touchy, irritable, petulant, cantankerous, testy, peevish, fractious, spiky, short-tempered, quick-tempered, flammable, cranky. **b** nettlesome, thorny, ticklish, touchy, troublesome, intricate, complicated, complex, knotty, hard, difficult, contentious. **3** tingling, tingly, stinging, pricking, prickling, itchy, scratchy.

pricy var. of PRICEY.

pride /prīd/ *n. & v.* ● *n.* **1 a** a feeling of elation or satisfaction at achievements, qualities, or possessions, etc., that do one credit. **b** an object of this feeling. **2** a high or overbearing opinion of one's worth or importance. **3** a proper sense of what befits one's position; self-respect. **4** a group or company (of animals, esp. lions). **5** the best condition; the prime. ● *v.refl.* (foll. by *on, upon*) be proud of. □ **my, his,** etc., **pride and joy** a thing of which one is very proud.

pride of the morning a mist or shower at sunrise, supposedly indicating a fine day to come. **pride of place** the most important or prominent position. **take pride** (or **a pride**) **in 1** be proud of. **2** maintain in good condition or appearance. □□ **prideful** *adj.* **pridefully** *adv.* **prideless** *adj.* [OE *prýtu, prýte, prýde* f. *prūd* PROUD]

■ *n.* **1 b** boast, prize, pride and joy, treasure, jewel, gem, delight, joy, darling, ideal. **2** self-satisfaction, conceit, proudness, egotism, egocentricity, self-importance, haughtiness, hauteur, vanity, hubris, arrogance, overconfidence, overweeningness, self-admiration, self-love, smugness. **3** honor, self-esteem, self-respect, amour propre, dignity; credit. **5** see PRIME[1] *n.* 1. ● *v.* (*pride oneself on*) be proud of, take pride in, plume oneself on, preen oneself on, delight in, revel in, celebrate, glory in. □ **my, his,** etc., **pride and joy** see PRIDE *n.* 1b above. **take (a) pride in 1** see PRIZE[1] *v.* **2** see CHERISH 1.

prie-dieu /preedyó/ *n.* (*pl.* **prie-dieux** *pronunc.* same) a kneeling desk for prayer. [F, = pray God]

priest /preest/ *n.* **1** an ordained minister of the Roman Catholic or Orthodox Church, or of the Anglican Church (above a deacon and below a bishop), authorized to perform certain rites and administer certain sacraments. **2** an official minister of a non-Christian religion. □□ **priestless** *adj.* **priestlike** *adj.* **priestling** *n.* [OE *prēost,* ult. f. eccl.L *presbyter:* see PRESBYTER]

■ **1** clergyman, clergywoman, ecclesiastic, cleric, churchman, reverend, vicar, divine, man of the cloth, man of God, confessor, minister, servant of God, father, holy man, padre.

priestess /preestis/ *n.* a female priest of a non-Christian religion.

priesthood /preest-hŏod/ *n.* (usu. prec. by *the*) **1** the office or position of a priest. **2** priests in general.

■ see MINISTRY 1, 2.

priestly /preestlee/ *adj.* of or associated with priests. □□ **priestliness** *n.* [OE *prēostlic* (as PRIEST)]

■ clerical, ecclesiastical, pastoral, hieratic, sacerdotal, ministerial.

prig /prig/ *n.* a self-righteously correct or moralistic person. □□ **priggery** *n.* **priggish** *adj.* **priggishly** *adv.* **priggishness** *n.* [16th-c. cant, = tinker: orig. unkn.]

■ prude, purist, pedant, puritan, moralist, (Mrs.) Grundy, precisionist, precisian, conformist, *colloq.* stuffed shirt, goody-goody. □□ **priggish** prim, demure, prudish, prissy, puristic, moralistic, pedantic, straitlaced, stiff-necked, puritanical, old-maidish, (Mrs.) Grundyish, punctilious, formal, strict, overnice, *colloq.* goody-goody, schoolmarmish, stuffy, uptight.

prim /prim/ *adj. & v.* ● *adj.* (**primmer, primmest**) **1** (of a person or manner) stiffly formal and precise. **2** (of a woman or girl) demure. **3** prudish. ● *v.tr.* (**primmed, primming**) **1** form (the face, lips, etc.) into a prim expression. **2** make prim. □□ **primly** *adv.* **primness** *n.* [17th c.: prob. orig. cant f. OF *prin prime* excellent f. L *primus* first]

■ *adj.* **1** see FORMAL *adj.* 4. **2** see RESERVED. **3** see *prudish* (PRUDE). □□ **primness** see *prudery* (PRUDE).

prima ballerina /preemə/ *n.* the chief female dancer in a ballet or ballet company. [It.]

■ see LEAD[1] *n.* 6.

primacy /prímasee/ *n.* (*pl.* **-ies**) **1** preeminence. **2** the office of an ecclesiastical primate. [ME f. OF *primatie* or med.L *primatia* (as PRIMATE)]

■ **1** see SUPERIORITY.

prima donna /preemə/ *n.* (*pl.* **prima donnas**) **1** the chief female singer in an opera or opera company. **2** a temperamentally self-important person. □□ **prima donna-ish** *adj.* [It.]

/.../ **pronunciation**	● **part of speech**
□ **phrases, idioms, and compounds**	
□□ **derivatives**	■ **synonym section**
cross-references appear in SMALL CAPITALS or *italics*	

■ diva; see also LEAD¹ *n.* 6.

prima facie /príma fáyshee, -shee-ee, shə, préemə/ *adv.* & *adj.* ● *adv.* at first sight; from a first impression (*seems prima facie to be guilty*). ● *adj.* (of evidence) based on the first impression (*can see a prima facie reason for it*). [ME f. L, fem. ablat. of *primus* first, *facies* FACE]

primal /prímal/ *adj.* **1** primitive; primeval. **2** chief; fundamental. □□ **primally** *adv.* [med.L *primalis* f. L *primus* first] ■ **1** see PRIMITIVE *adj.* 1. **2** see FUNDAMENTAL *adj.*

primary /prímeree, -məree/ *adj.* & *n.* ● *adj.* **1 a** of the first importance; chief (*that is our primary concern*). **b** fundamental; basic. **2** earliest; original; first in a series. **3** of the first rank in a series; not derived (*the primary meaning of a word*). **4** designating any of the colors red, green, and blue, or for pigments red, blue, and yellow, from which all other colors can be obtained by mixing. **5** (of a battery or cell) generating electricity by irreversible chemical reaction. **6** (of education) for young children, esp. below the age of 11. **7** (**Primary**) *Geol.* of the lowest series of strata. **8** *Biol.* belonging to the first stage of development. **9** (of an industry or source of production) concerned with obtaining or using raw materials. ● *n.* (*pl.* **-ies**) **1** a thing that is primary. **2** (in full **primary election**) a preliminary election to appoint delegates to a party convention or to select the candidates for a principal election. **3** = *primary planet.* **4** (**Primary**) *Geol.* the Primary period. **5** = *primary feather.* **6** = *primary coil.* □ **primary coil** a coil to which current is supplied in a transformer. **primary feather** a large flight feather of a bird's wing. **primary industry** industry (such as mining, forestry, agriculture, etc.) that provides raw materials for conversion into commodities and products for the consumer. **primary planet** a planet that directly orbits the sun (cf. *secondary planet*). **primary school** a school where young children are taught, esp. the first three elementary grades and kindergarten. □□ **primarily** /prímérilee/ [ME f. L *primarius* f. *primus* first]
■ *adj.* **1 a** first, prime, principal, chief, main, leading, preeminent, predominant; cardinal. **b** fundamental, basic, essential, rudimentary, elemental, first, primitive. **2** earliest, first, original, initial, primitive, primeval, germinal, beginning. □ **primary school** see *elementary school.* □□ **primarily** principally, mainly, chiefly, at bottom, first of all, preeminently, basically, essentially, fundamentally, mostly, predominantly, generally.

primate /prímayt/ *n.* **1** any animal of the order Primates, the highest order of mammals, including tarsiers, lemurs, apes, monkeys, and human beings. **2** an archbishop. □□ **primatial** /-máyshəl/ *adj.* **primatology** /-mətóləjee/ *n.* (in sense 1). [ME f. OF *primat* f. L *primas -atis* (adj.) of the first rank f. *primus* first, in med.L = primate]

primavera¹ /preémavaíra/ *n.* **1** a Central American tree, *Cybistax donnellsmithii*, bearing yellow blooms. **2** the hard light-colored timber from this. [Sp., = spring (the season) f. L *primus* first + *ver* SPRING]

primavera² /preémavaíra/ *adj.* (of pasta, seafood, etc.) made with or containing an assortment of sliced vegetables. [It. *primavera* spring, springtime]

prime¹ /prim/ *adj.* & *n.* ● *adj.* **1** chief; most important (*the prime agent; the prime motive*). **2** (esp. of beef) first-rate; excellent. **3** primary; fundamental. **4** *Math.* ● **a** (of a number) divisible only by itself and 1 (e.g., 2, 3, 5, 7, 11). **b** (of numbers) having no common factor but 1. ● *n.* **1** the state of the highest perfection of something (*in the prime of life*). **2** (prec. by *the*; foll. by *of*) the best part. **3** the beginning or first age of anything. **4** *Eccl.* **a** the second canonical hour of prayer, appointed for the first hour of the day (i.e., 6 a.m.). **b** the office of this. **c** *archaic* this time. **5** a prime number. **6** *Printing* a symbol (′) added to a letter, etc., as a distinguishing mark, or to a figure as a symbol for minutes or feet. **7** the first of eight parrying positions in fencing. **8** *Mus.* tonic. □ **prime cost** the direct cost of a commodity in terms of materials, labor, etc. **prime meridian 1** the meridian from which longitude is reckoned, esp. that passing through Greenwich. **2** the corresponding line on a map. **prime minister** the head of an elected parliamentary government;

the principal minister of a nation or sovereign. **prime mover 1** an initial natural or mechanical source of motive power. **2** the author of a fruitful idea. **prime rate** the lowest rate at which money can be borrowed commercially. **prime time** the time at which a radio or television audience is expected to consist of the greatest number of people. **prime vertical** the great circle of the heavens passing through the zenith and the E. and W. points of the horizon. □□ **primeness** *n.* [(n.) OE *prīm* f. L *prima* (*hora*) first (hour), & MF f. OF *prime*: (adj.) ME f. OF f. L *primus* first]
■ *adj.* **1** see MAIN¹ *adj.* 1. **2** first-rate, first-class, excellent, choice, select, superior, preeminent, leading, unparalleled, matchless, peerless, noteworthy, outstanding, admirable, worthy, exceptional. **3** primary, original, fundamental, basic, elemental, elementary, primitive. ● *n.* **1** best years, heyday; springtime, *poet.* springtide; pinnacle, acme, peak, zenith. **3** see BEGINNING. □ **prime minister** see PREMIER *n.* **prime mover 2** see AUTHOR *n.* 2.

prime² /prim/ *v.tr.* **1** prepare (a thing) for use or action. **2** prepare (a gun) for firing or (an explosive) for detonation. **3 a** pour (liquid) into a pump to prepare it for working. **b** inject fuel into (the cylinder or carburetor of an internal-combustion engine). **4** prepare (wood, etc.) for painting by applying a substance that prevents paint from being absorbed. **5** equip (a person) with information, etc. **6** ply (a person) with food or drink in preparation for something. [16th c.: orig. unkn.]
■ **1** see PREPARE 1, 3a. **5** educate, teach, instruct, coach, train, tutor, drill; inform, brief, apprise.

primer¹ /prímər/ *n.* **1** a substance used to prime wood, etc. **2** a cap, cylinder, etc., used to ignite the powder of a cartridge, etc.

primer² /prímər, prímər/ *n.* **1** an elementary textbook for teaching children to read. **2** an introductory book. [ME f. AF f. med.L *primarius -arium* f. L *primus* first]
■ see TEXT 6.

primeval /primeévəl/ *adj.* **1** of or relating to the earliest age of the world. **2** ancient; primitive. □□ **primevally** *adv.* [L *primaevus* f. *primus* first + *aevum* age]
■ **1** see PREHISTORIC 1. **2** see ANCIENT¹ *adj.*

priming¹ /príming/ *n.* **1** a mixture used by painters for a preparatory coat. **2** a preparation of sugar added to beer. **3 a** gunpowder placed in the pan of a firearm. **b** a train of powder connecting the fuse with the charge in blasting, etc.

priming² /príming/ *n.* an acceleration of the tides taking place from the neap to the spring tides. [*prime* (v.) f. PRIME¹ + -ING¹]

primipara /primípərə/ *n.* (*pl.* **primiparae** /-ree/) a woman who is bearing a child for the first time. □□ **primiparous** *adj.* [mod.L fem. f. *primus* first + *-parus* f. *parere* bring forth]

primitive /prímitiv/ *adj.* & *n.* ● *adj.* **1** early; ancient; at an early stage of civilization (*primitive humans*). **2** undeveloped; crude; simple (*primitive methods*). **3** original; primary. **4** *Gram.* & *Philol.* (of words or language) radical; not derivative. **5** *Math.* (of a line, figure, etc.) from which another is derived, from which some construction begins, etc. **6** (of a color) primary. **7** *Geol.* of the earliest period. **8** *Biol.* appearing in the earliest or a very early stage of growth or evolution. ● *n.* **1 a** a painter of the period before the Renaissance. **b** a modern imitator of such. **c** an untutored painter with a direct naïve style. **d** a picture by such a painter. **2** a primitive word, line, etc. □□ **primitively** *adv.* **primitiveness** *n.* [ME f. OF *primitif -ive* or L *primitivus* first of its kind f. *primitus* in the first place f. *primus* first]
■ *adj.* **1** antediluvian, ancient, aboriginal, early, primordial, primal, primeval, pristine, prehistoric, *archaic* olden. **2** crude, rude, raw, barbaric, uncultured, barbarian, coarse, rough, uncivilized, savage, uncultivated, unsophisticated, uncouth; simple, basic, naïve, undeveloped, unrefined, unpolished, untutored, untaught, untrained, unschooled, childlike. **3** germinal, first; see also ORIGINAL *adj.* 1. **7, 8** lower, early; primordial, ancestral, unspecialized, undeveloped.

primitivism /prímitivizəm/ *n.* **1** primitive behavior. **2** belief in the superiority of what is primitive. **3** the practice of primitive art. □□ **primitivist** *n.* & *adj.*

primo /préemō/ *n.* (*pl.* **-os**) **1** *Mus.* the leading or upper part in a duet, etc. **2** *colloq.* first-rate; excellent.

primogenitor /prímōjénitər/ *n.* **1** the earliest ancestor of a people, etc. **2** an ancestor. [var. of *progenitor*, after PRIMOGENITURE]
■ see ANCESTOR 1.

primogeniture /prímōjénichər/ *n.* **1** the fact or condition of being the firstborn child. **2** (in full **right of primogeniture**) the right of succession belonging to the firstborn, esp. the feudal rule by which the whole real estate of an intestate passes to the eldest son. □□ **primogenital** *adj.* **primogenitary** *adj.* [med.L *primogenitura* f. L *primo* first + *genitura* f. *gignere genit-* beget]

primordial /prímáwrdeeəl/ *adj.* **1** existing at or from the beginning; primeval. **2** original; fundamental. □□ **primordiality** /-mawrdeeálitee/ *n.* **primordially** *adv.* [ME f. LL *primordialis* (as PRIMORDIUM)]
■ **1** see PREHISTORIC 1. **2** see ORIGINAL *adj.* 1.

primordium /prīmáwrdeeəm/ *n.* (*pl.* **primordia** /-deeə/) *Biol.* an organ or tissue in the early stages of development. [L, neut. of *primordius* original f. *primus* first + *ordiri* begin]

primp /primp/ *v.tr.* **1** make (the hair, one's clothes, etc.) neat or overly tidy. **2** *refl.* groom (oneself) painstakingly. [dial. var. of PRIM]
■ **1** groom, tidy, preen, prink, *colloq.* gussy up, *sl.* dude up. **2** (*primp oneself*) preen *or* prink *or* prettify *or* plume oneself, spruce oneself (up), deck *or* fig oneself out, trick oneself out *or* up, smarten oneself (up), smarten up, doll (oneself) up, get (oneself) dolled up, dress (oneself) up, put on one's best bib and tucker, *colloq.* titivate oneself, esp. *Brit. colloq.* tart oneself up.

primrose /prímrōz/ *n.* **1 a** any plant of the genus *Primula*, esp. *P. vulgaris*, bearing pale yellow flowers. **b** the flower of this. **2** a pale yellow color. □ **primrose path** the pursuit of pleasure, esp. with disastrous consequences (with ref. to Shakesp. *Hamlet* I. iii. 50). [ME *primerose*, corresp. to OF *primerose* and med.L *prima rosa*, lit. first rose: reason for the name unkn.]

primula /prímyələ/ *n.* any plant of the genus *Primula*, bearing primrose-like flowers in a wide variety of colors during the spring, including primroses, cowslips, and polyanthuses. [med.L, fem. of *primulus* dimin. of *primus* first]

primum mobile /prímōōm mṓbilee, préemōōm mṓbilay/ *n.* **1** the central or most important source of motion or action. **2** *Astron.* in the medieval version of the Ptolemaic system, an outer sphere supposed to move around the earth in 24 hours carrying the inner spheres with it. [med.L, = first moving thing]

Primus /príməs/ *n. Brit. propr.* a brand of portable stove burning oil for cooking, etc. [L (as PRIMUS)]

primus /príməs/ *n.* the presiding bishop of the Scottish Episcopal Church. [L, = first]

primus inter pares /préemōōs íntər paáres, príməs íntər páireez/ *n.* a first among equals; the senior or representative member of a group. [L]

prince /prins/ *n.* (as a title usu. **Prince**) **1** a male member of a royal family other than a reigning king. **2** (in full **prince of the blood**) a son or grandson of a British monarch. **3** a ruler of a small nation, actually or nominally subject to a king or emperor. **4** (as an English rendering of foreign titles) a noble usu. ranking next below a duke. **5** (as a courtesy title in some connections) a duke, marquess, or earl. **6** (often foll. by *of*) the chief or greatest (*the prince of novelists*). □ **Prince Charming** an idealized young hero or lover. **prince consort 1** the husband of a reigning female sovereign who is himself a prince. **2** the title conferred on him. **Prince of Darkness** Satan. **Prince of Peace** Christ. **Prince of Wales** the heir apparent to the British throne, as a title conferred by the monarch. **Prince Regent** a prince who acts as regent. **prince royal** the eldest son of a reigning monarch. **prince's-feather** a tall plant, *Amaranthus hypochondriacus*, with feathery spikes of small red flowers. □□ **princedom** *n.* **princelet** *n.* **princelike** *adj.* **princeship**

n. [ME f. OF f. L *princeps principis* first, chief, sovereign f. *primus* first + *capere* take]
■ □ **Prince of Darkness** see DEVIL *n.* 1, 2. **Prince of Peace** see SAVIOR 2. □□ **princelike** see PRINCELY 1a.

princeling /prínsling/ *n.* a young or insignificant prince.

princely /prínslee/ *adj.* (**princelier, princeliest**) **1 a** of or worthy of a prince. **b** held by a prince. **2 a** sumptuous; generous; splendid. **b** (of a sum of money) substantial. □□ **princeliness** *n.*
■ **1 a** royal, noble, regal, sovereign, majestic, imperial. **2** lavish, bountiful, generous, liberal, ample; magnificent, splendid, luxurious, majestic, sumptuous, swanky, plush, posh, *colloq.* ritzy, plushy, swank; substantial, considerable, huge, enormous, large.

princess /prínses/ *n.* (as a title usu. **Princess**) **1** the wife of a prince. **2** a female member of a royal family other than a reigning queen. **3** (in full **princess of the blood**) a daughter or granddaughter of a British monarch. **4** a preeminent woman or thing personified as a woman. □ **Princess Regent 1** a princess who acts as regent. **2** the wife of a Prince Regent. **Princess Royal** a monarch's eldest daughter, as a title conferred by the monarch. [ME f. OF *princesse* (as PRINCE)]

principal /prínsipəl/ *adj.* & *n.* ● *adj.* **1** (usu. *attrib.*) first in rank or importance; chief (*the principal town of the district*). **2** main; leading (*a principal cause of my success*). **3** (of money) constituting the original sum invested or lent. ● *n.* **1** a head, ruler, or superior. **2** the head of an elementary, middle, or high school. **3** the leading performer in a concert, play, etc. **4** a capital sum as distinguished from interest or income. **5** a person for whom another acts as agent, etc. **6** (in the UK) a civil servant of the grade below Secretary. **7** the person actually responsible for a crime. **8** a person for whom another is surety. **9** each of the combatants in a duel. **10** a main rafter or girder providing support for other members in a framed structure. **11** an organ stop sounding an octave above the diapason. **12** *Mus.* the leading player in each section of an orchestra. □ **principal boy** (or **girl**) *Brit.* an actress who takes the leading male (or female) part in a pantomime. **principal clause** *Gram.* a clause to which another clause is subordinate. **principal parts** *Gram.* the parts of a verb from which all other parts can be deduced. □□ **principalship** *n.* [ME f. OF f. L *principalis* first, original (as PRINCE)]
■ *adj.* **1, 2** chief, primary, prime, paramount, main, first, foremost, prominent, leading, key, preeminent, predominant, dominant, prevailing; leading, starring, important. **3** capital, original, basic, initial. ● *n.* **1** director, head, president, chief, employer, chief executive, ruler, superior, manager, manageress, superintendent, overseer, supervisor, *colloq.* boss. **2** dean, director, headmaster, headmistress, master, mistress, provost, rector, chancellor, vice-chancellor, president, *sl.* prex(y). **3** star, lead, leading lady *or* man, leading role, main part. **4** capital, capital funds, resources, investment, reserves, assets.

principality /prínsipálitee/ *n.* (*pl.* **-ies**) **1** a nation ruled by a prince. **2** the government of a prince. **3** (in *pl.*) the fifth order of the ninefold celestial hierarchy. **4** (**the Principality**) *Brit.* Wales. [ME f. OF *principalité* f. LL *principalitas -tatis* (as PRINCIPAL)]

principally /prínsiplee/ *adv.* for the most part; chiefly.
■ chiefly, mainly, first (and foremost), primarily, above all, in the main, mostly, for the most part, largely, predominantly, on the whole, at bottom, in essence, essentially, basically, fundamentally; especially, particularly.

principate /prínsipayt/ *n.* **1** a nation ruled by a prince. **2**

/.../ **pronunciation**	● **part of speech**
□ **phrases, idioms, and compounds**	
□□ **derivatives**	■ **synonym section**
cross-references appear in SMALL CAPITALS or *italics*	

supreme office or authority. **3** *Rom. Hist.* the rule of the early emperors during which some republican forms were retained. [ME f. OF *principat* or L *principatus* first place]

principle /prínsipəl/ *n.* **1** a fundamental truth or law as the basis of reasoning or action (*arguing from first principles*; *moral principles*). **2 a** a personal code of conduct (*a person of high principle*). **b** (in *pl.*) such rules of conduct (*has no principles*). **3** a general law in physics, etc. (*the uncertainty principle*). **4** a law of nature forming the basis for the construction or working of a machine, etc. **5** a fundamental source; a primary element (*held water to be the first principle of all things*). **6** *Chem.* a constituent of a substance, esp. one giving rise to some quality, etc. □ **in principle** as regards fundamentals but not necessarily in detail. **on principle** on the basis of a moral attitude (*I refuse on principle*). [ME f. OF *principe* f. L *principium* source, (in pl.) foundations (as PRINCE)]

■ **1** truth, given, precept, tenet, fundamental, law, rule, dictum, canon, doctrine, teaching, dogma, proposition, (basic) assumption, postulate, axiom, maxim, standard, criterion, model. **2** honor, uprightness, honesty, morality, morals, probity, integrity, conscience; (*principles*) philosophy, attitude, (point of) view, viewpoint, sentiment, belief, credo, creed, notion, ethics; sense of right and wrong. **5** see ORIGIN 1. □ **in principle** in theory, theoretically, ideally; fundamentally, at bottom, in essence, essentially.

principled /prínsipəld/ *adj.* based on or having (esp. praiseworthy) principles of behavior.

■ moral, righteous, right-minded, virtuous, noble, high-minded, ethical, honorable, proper, correct, right, just, upright, honest, scrupulous.

prink /pringk/ *v.* **1** *tr.* (usu. *refl.*) PRIMP. **2** (of a bird) preen. **3** *intr.* dress oneself up. [16th c.: prob. f. *prank* dress, adorn, rel. to MLG *prank* pomp, Du. *pronk* finery]

■ **1, 3** see PREEN 2. **2** see PREEN 1.

print /print/ *n., v.,* & *adj.* ● *n.* **1** an indentation or mark on a surface left by the pressure of a thing in contact with it (*fingerprint*; *footprint*). **2 a** printed lettering or writing (*large print*). **b** words in printed form. **c** a printed publication, esp. a newspaper. **d** the quantity of a book, etc., printed at one time. **e** the state of being printed. **3** a picture or design printed from a block or plate. **4 a** *Photog.* a picture produced on paper from a negative. **b** a copy of a motion picture suitable for showing. **5** a printed cotton fabric. ● *v.tr.* **1 a** produce or reproduce (a book, picture, etc.) by applying inked types, blocks, or plates, to paper, vellum, etc. **b** (of an author, publisher, or editor) cause (a book or manuscript, etc.) to be produced or reproduced in this way. **2** express or publish in print. **3 a** (often foll. by *on, in*) impress or stamp (a mark or figure on a surface). **b** (often foll. by *with*) impress or stamp (a soft surface, e.g., of butter or wax, with a seal, die, etc.). **4** (often *absol.*) write (words or letters) without joining, in imitation of typography. **5** (often foll. by *off, out*) *Photog.* produce (a picture) by the transmission of light through a negative. **6** (usu. foll. by *out*) (of a computer, etc.) produce output in printed form. **7** mark (a textile fabric) with a decorative design in colors. **8** (foll. by *on*) impress (an idea, scene, etc., on the mind or memory). **9** transfer (a colored or plain design) from paper, etc., to the unglazed or glazed surface of ceramic ware. ● *adj.* of, for, or concerning printed publications. □ **appear in print** have one's work published. **in print 1** (of a book, etc.) available from the publisher. **2** in printed form. **out of print** no longer available from the publisher. **printed circuit** an electric circuit with thin strips of conductive material on a flat insulating sheet, usu. made by a process like printing. □□ **printable** *adj.* **printability** /príntəbílitee/ *n.* **printless** *adj.* (in sense 1 of *n.*). [ME f. OF *priente, preinte,* fem. past part. of *preindre* press f. L *premere*]

■ *n.* **1** indentation, impression; see also MARK¹ *n.* 1. **2 a, b** text, printed matter; see also TYPE *n.* 6. **3** reproduction, copy, replica, facsimile; picture, illustration; design, pattern, motif. **4 a** see PHOTOGRAPH

n. ● *v.* **1, 2** publish, issue, run off, put out. **3** see STAMP *v.* 2.

printer /príntər/ *n.* **1** a person who prints books, magazines, advertising matter, etc. **2** the owner of a printing business. **3** a device that prints, esp. as part of a computer system. □ **printer's devil** one who runs errands in a printer's office. **printer's mark** a device used as a printer's trademark. **printer's pie** = PI² *n.*

printery /príntəree/ *n.* (*pl.* **-ies**) a printer's office or works.

printhead /prínt-hed/ *n.* the component in a printer (see PRINTER 3) that assembles and prints the characters on the paper.

printing /prínting/ *n.* **1** the production of printed books, etc. **2** a single impression of a book. **3** printed letters or writing imitating them. □ **printing press** a machine for printing from types or plates, etc.

■ **2** see IMPRESSION 5.

printmaker /príntmaykər/ *n.* a person who makes a print. □□ **printmaking** *n.*

printout /príntowt/ *n.* computer output in printed form.

printworks /príntwərks/ *n.* a factory where fabrics are printed.

prior /príər/ *adj., adv.,* & *n.* ● *adj.* **1** earlier. **2** (often foll. by *to*) coming before in time, order, or importance. ● *adv.* (foll. by *to*) before (*decided prior to their arrival*). ● *n.* **1** the superior officer of a religious house or order. **2** (in an abbey) the officer next under the abbot. □□ **priorate** /-rət/ *n.* **prioress** /príəris/ *n.* **priorship** *n.* [L, = former, elder, compar. of OL *pri* = L *prae* before]

■ *adj.* **1** former, previous, earlier; see also FOREGOING. ● *adv.* (*prior to*) previous to, previously to; see also BEFORE *prep.* 2.

priority /priáwritee, -ór-/ *n.* (*pl.* **-ies**) **1** the fact or condition of being earlier or antecedent. **2** precedence in rank, etc. **3** an interest having prior claim to consideration. □□ **prioritize** *v.tr.* **prioritization** *n.* [ME f. OF *priorité* f. med.L *prioritas -tatis* f. L *prior* (as PRIOR)]

■ **2** precedence, precedency, preference; primacy, urgency, predominance, preeminence, rank, superiority, prerogative, right, seniority, importance, weight.

priory /príəree/ *n.* (*pl.* **-ies**) a monastery governed by a prior or a convent governed by a prioress. [ME f. AF *priorie,* med.L *prioria* (as PRIOR)]

prise esp. *Brit.* var. of PRIZE³.

prism /prízəm/ *n.* **1** a solid geometric figure whose two ends are similar, equal, and parallel rectilinear figures, and whose sides are parallelograms. **2** a transparent body in this form, usu. triangular with refracting surfaces at an acute angle with each other, which separates white light into a spectrum of colors. □□ **prismal** /prízməl/ *adj.* [LL *prisma* f. Gk *prisma prismatos* thing sawn f. *prizō* to saw]

prismatic /prizmátik/ *adj.* **1** of, like, or using a prism. **2 a** (of colors) distributed by or as if by a transparent prism. **b** (of light) displayed in the form of a spectrum. □□ **prismatically** *adv.* [F *prismatique* f. Gk *prisma* (as PRISM)]

prismoid /prízmoyd/ *n.* a body like a prism, with similar but unequal parallel polygonal ends. □□ **prismoidal** *adj.*

prison /prízən/ *n.* & *v.* ● *n.* **1** a place in which a person is kept in captivity, esp. a building to which persons are legally committed while awaiting trial or for punishment; a jail. **2** custody; confinement (*in prison*). ● *v.tr. poet.* (**prisoned, prisoning**) put in prison. □ **prison camp 1** a camp for prisoners of war or political prisoners. **2** a minimum-security prison. [ME f. OF *prisun, -on* f. L *prensio -onis* f. *prehensio* f. *prehendere prehens-* lay hold of]

■ *n.* **1** jail, lockup, penal institution, guardhouse, penitentiary, brig, calaboose, correctional facility, *archaic* bridewell, house of correction, bagnio, *hist.* bastille, roundhouse, *sl.* clink, can, cooler, jug, stir, slammer, big house, pokey, pen, hoosegow, slam, *Brit. sl.* glasshouse, nick, quod, choky. **2** confinement, detention, custody; (*in prison*) see *behind bars* (BAR¹). ● *v.* see IMPRISON 1.

prisoner /príznər/ *n.* **1** a person kept in prison. **2** *Brit.* (in full

prisoner at the bar) a person in custody on a criminal charge and on trial. **3** a person or thing confined by illness, another's grasp, etc. **4** (in full **prisoner of war**) a person who has been captured in war. □ **political prisoner** a person confined for political reasons. **prisoner's base** a game played by two teams of children, each occupying a distinct base or home. **take prisoner** seize and hold as a prisoner. [ME f. AF *prisoner*, OF *prisonier* (as PRISON)]
■ **1** convict, inmate, internee, detainee, jailbird, *sl.* con, yardbird, esp. *Brit. sl.* (old) lag.

prissy /prísee/ *adj.* (**prissier, prissiest**) prim; prudish. □□ **prissily** *adv.* **prissiness** *n.* [perh. f. PRIM + SISSY]
■ precious, overnice, straitlaced, old-maidish, prim (and proper), prudish, *colloq.* schoolmarmish.

pristine /prísteen, pristeén/ *adj.* **1** in its original condition; unspoiled. **2** *disp.* spotless; fresh as if new. **3** ancient; primitive. [L *pristinus* former]
■ **1** uncorrupted, pure, unsullied, undefiled, virginal, virgin, chaste, untouched, unspoiled, unpolluted, untarnished, immaculate, natural. **2** spotless, clean, gleaming, shiny, polished, unspotted, spick-and-span; immaculate, fresh, as new; mint. **3** ancient, original, primal, basic, primeval, primitive, primordial, earliest, first, initial.

prithee /príthee/ *int. archaic* pray; please. [= *I pray thee*]

privacy /prívǝsee/ *n.* **1 a** the state of being private and undisturbed. **b** a person's right to this. **2** freedom from intrusion or public attention. **3** avoidance of publicity.
■ **1** seclusion, retirement, solitude, isolation, reclusion, solitariness, reclusiveness, separation; monasticism. **3** secretiveness, confidentiality; see also SECRECY.

private /prívǝt/ *adj. & n.* ● *adj.* **1** belonging to an individual; one's own; personal (*private property*). **2** confidential; not to be disclosed to others (*private talks*). **3** kept or removed from public knowledge or observation. **4 a** not open to the public. **b** for an individual's exclusive use (*private room*). **5** (of a place) secluded; affording privacy. **6** (of a person) not holding public office or an official position. **7** (of education) conducted outside the government system. **8** (of a person) retiring; reserved; unsociable. **9** (of a company) not having publicly traded shares. ● *n.* **1** a soldier with a rank below corporal. **2** (in *pl.*) *colloq.* the genitals. □ **in private** privately; in private company or life. **private bill** a legislative bill affecting an individual or corporation only. **private detective** a detective engaged privately, outside an official police force. **private enterprise 1** a business or businesses not under government control. **2** individual initiative. **private eye** *colloq.* a private detective. **private first class** a soldier ranking above an ordinary private but below a corporal. **private house** the dwelling house of a private person, as distinct from a shop, office, or public building. **private investigator** private detective. **private law** the body of laws relating to individual persons and private property. **private life** life as a private person, not as an official, public performer, etc. **private parts** the genitals. **private practice 1** *US* an independent practice, esp. of law, medicine, or counseling services. **2** *Brit.* medical practice that is not part of the National Health Service. **private press** a printing establishment operated by a private person or group not primarily for profit and usu. on a small scale. **private school 1** *US* a school not supported mainly by the government. **2** *Brit.* a school supported wholly by the payment of fees. **private secretary** a secretary dealing with the personal and confidential concerns of a business executive. **private sector** the part of the economy free of direct government control. **private war 1** a feud between persons or families disregarding the law of murder, etc. **2** hostilities against members of another nation without the sanction of one's own government. **private wrong** an offense against an individual but not against society as a whole. □□ **privately** *adv.* [ME f. L *privatus*, orig. past part. of *privare* deprive]
■ *adj.* **1** personal, individual, one's own, *archaic* proper. **2** (top) secret, confidential, clandestine, hidden, concealed, covert, surreptitious, *colloq.* hush-hush; unofficial. **3, 5** hidden, secluded, concealed, secret;

undisclosed, sneaking, undeclared, unspoken. **4** restrictive, restricted, exclusive, special, reserved. **8** solitary, seclusive, reclusive, withdrawn, retiring, reticent, ungregarious, nongregarious, unsocial, unsociable, antisocial, reserved, uncommunicative, hermitic(al), hermitlike, eremitic(al); sequestered, secluded, retired. ● *n.* **1** infantryman, foot soldier, poilu, enlisted man, GI, *Brit. colloq.* Tommy. **2** (*privates*) genitals, private parts, sexual *or* sex organs, genitalia, pudenda, *euphem.* one's person. □ **in private** in secret, secretly, privately, sub rosa, personally, in confidence, confidentially, behind closed doors, in camera, off the record; clandestinely, secretively, sneakily, sneakingly, surreptitiously, furtively, covertly, on the sly, on the quiet, *colloq.* on the q.t. **private detective** see DETECTIVE *n.* **private eye** see DETECTIVE *n.* **private parts** see PRIVATE *n.* 2 above. **private soldier** see PRIVATE *n.* 1 above.

privateer /prívǝteé'er/ *n.* **1** an armed vessel owned and officered by private individuals holding a government commission and authorized for war service. **2 a** a commander of such a vessel. **b** (in *pl.*) its crew. □□ **privateering** *n.* [PRIVATE, after *volunteer*]

privateersman /prívǝteé'erzmǝn/ *n.* (*pl.* **-men**) = PRIVATEER 2.

privation /prívaýshǝn/ *n.* **1** lack of the comforts or necessities of life (*suffered many privations*). **2** (often foll. by *of*) loss or absence (of a quality). [ME f. L *privatio* (as PRIVATE)]
■ **1** deprivation, hardship, indigence, poverty, penury, destitution, pauperism, beggary, neediness, necessity, need, want; distress, misery. **2** see LACK *n.*, LOSS 1.

privative /prívǝtiv/ *adj.* **1** consisting in or marked by the loss or removal or absence of some quality or attribute. **2** (of a term) denoting the privation or absence of a quality, etc. **3** *Gram.* (of a particle, etc.) expressing privation, as Gk *a-* = 'not.' □□ **privatively** *adv.* [F *privatif -ive* or L *privativus* (as PRIVATION)]

privatize /prívǝtiz/ *v.tr.* make private, esp. transfer (a business, etc.) to private as distinct from government control or ownership. □□ **privatization** *n.*

privet /prívit/ *n.* any deciduous or evergreen shrub of the genus *Ligustrum*, esp. *L. vulgare* bearing small white flowers and black berries, and much used for hedges. [16th c.: orig. unkn.]

privilege /prívilij, prívlij/ *n. & v.* ● *n.* **1 a** a right, advantage, or immunity, belonging to a person, class, or office. **b** the freedom of members of a legislative assembly when speaking at its meetings. **2** a special benefit or honor (*it is a privilege to meet you*). **3** a monopoly or patent granted to an individual, corporation, etc. **4** *Stock Exch.* an option to buy or sell. ● *v.tr.* **1** invest with a privilege. **2** (foll. by *to* + infin.) allow (a person) as a privilege (to do something). **3** (often foll. by *from*) exempt (a person from a liability, etc.). [ME f. OF *privilege* f. L *privilegium* bill or law affecting an individual, f. *privus* private + *lex legis* law]
■ *n.* **1 a** benefit, advantage, right, prerogative, concession, freedom, liberty, franchise; permission, consent, leave, authorization, sanction, authority, license, allowance, indulgence; immunity, exemption, dispensation. **2** honor, pleasure; see also HONOR *n.* 5. ● *v.* **3** see EXEMPT *v.*

privileged /prívilijd, prívlijd/ *adj.* **1 a** invested with or enjoying a certain privilege or privileges; honored; favored. **b** exempt from standard regulations or procedures. **c** powerful; affluent. **2** (of information, etc.) confidential; restricted.
■ **1** favored, élite, special, honored, advantaged. **b** protected, immune; licensed, authorized, chartered. **c** wealthy, rich, affluent, advantaged, well-off, *colloq.* comfortable, well-heeled; powerful, empowered, well-

/.../ **pronunciation**	● **part of speech**
□ **phrases, idioms, and compounds**	
□□ **derivatives**	■ **synonym section**
cross-references appear in SMALL CAPITALS or *italics*	

connected. **2** confidential, secret, private, restricted, off-the-record, *archaic* privy, *colloq.* hush-hush.

privity /prívitee/ *n.* (*pl.* **-ies**) **1** *Law* a relation between two parties that is recognized by law, e.g., that of blood, lease, or service. **2** (often foll. by *to*) the state of being privy (to plans, etc.). [ME f. OF *priveté* f. med.L *privitas -tatis* f. L *privus* private]

privy /privee/ *adj. & n.* ● *adj.* **1** (foll. by *to*) sharing in the secret of (a person's plans, etc.). **2** *archaic* hidden; secret. ● *n.* (*pl.* **-ies**) **1** a toilet, esp. an outhouse. **2** *Law* a person having a part or interest in any action, matter, or thing. □ **Privy Council 1** (in the UK) a body of advisers appointed by the sovereign (now chiefly on an honorary basis and including present and former government ministers, etc.). **2** usu. *hist.* a sovereign's or governor-general's private counselors. **privy counselor** (or **councilor**) a private adviser, esp. a member of a Privy Council. **privy purse** *Brit.* **1** an allowance from the public revenue for the monarch's private expenses. **2** the keeper of this. **privy seal** (in the UK) a seal formerly affixed to documents that are afterward to pass the Great Seal or that do not require it. □□ **privily** *adv.* [ME f. OF *privé* f. L *privatus* PRIVATE]

■ *adj.* **1** (*privy to*) aware of, in on, sharing (in), cognizant of, apprised of, informed *or* advised about *or* of, *colloq.* wise to, *sl.* hip to. **2** see SECRET *adj.* 1. ● *n.* **1** bathroom, lavatory, toilet, outhouse, latrine, *sl.* can, john, head, *Brit.* convenience, water closet, WC, *Brit. colloq.* loo, lav, *Brit. sl.* bog, esp. *Austral. sl.* dyke, *Austral. & NZ sl.* dunny.

prize[1] /priz/ *n. & v.* ● *n.* **1** something that can be won in a competition, lottery, etc. **2** a reward given as a symbol of victory or superiority. **3** something striven for or worth striving for (*missed all the great prizes of life*). **4** (*attrib.*) **a** to which a prize is awarded (*a prize bull; a prize poem*). **b** supremely excellent or outstanding of its kind. ● *v.tr.* value highly (*a much prized possession*). □ **prize money** money offered as a prize. **prize ring 1** an enclosed area (now usu. a square) for prizefighting. **2** the practice of prizefighting. [(n.) ME, var. of PRICE: (v.) ME f. OF *pris-* stem of *preisier* PRAISE]

■ *n.* **2** reward, award, trophy, premium; honor, accolade, *poet.* guerdon; winnings, jackpot. **4 b** (*attrib.*) choice, excellent, winning, champion, outstanding, select, superior, superlative, first-rate, first-class. ● *v.* value, treasure, esteem, cherish, appreciate, rate highly, hold dear.

prize[2] /priz/ *n. & v.* ● *n.* **1** a ship or property captured in naval warfare. **2** a find or windfall. ● *v.tr.* make a prize of. [ME f. OF *prize* taking, booty, fem. past part. of *prendre* f. L *prehendere prehens-* seize: later identified with PRIZE[1]]

■ *n.* **1** loot, booty, spoil(s), trophy, plunder, pickings. **2** find, gain, haul, take; see also WINDFALL.

prize[3] /priz/ *v. & n.* (also **prise**) ● *v.tr.* force open or out by leverage (*prized up the lid; prized the box open*). ● *n.* leverage; purchase. [ME & OF *prise* levering instrument (as PRIZE[1])]
■ *v.* see FORCE[1] *v.* 2.

prizefight /prízfit/ *n.* a boxing match fought for prize money. □□ **prizefighter** *n.*

■ see BOUT 2a. □□ **prizefighter** see PUGILIST.

prizeman /prízmən/ *n. Brit.* (*pl.* **-men**) a winner of a prize, esp. a specified academic one.

prizewinner /prízwinər/ *n.* a winner of a prize. □□ **prizewinning** *adj.*
■ see WINNER 1.

pro[1] /prō/ *n. & adj. colloq.* ● *n.* (*pl.* **pros**) a professional. ● *adj.* professional. □ **pro-am** involving professionals and amateurs. [abbr.]

■ *n.* see PROFESSIONAL *n.* ● *adj.* see PROFESSIONAL *adj.*

pro[2] /prō/ *adj., n., & prep.* ● *adj.* (of an argument or reason) for; in favor. ● *n.* (*pl.* **pros**) a reason or argument for or in favor. ● *prep.* in favor of. □ **pro bono** pertaining to a service, esp. legal work, for which no fee is charged. **pro-choice** in favor of the right to legal abortion. **pro-life** opposed to the right to legal abortion. **pros and cons** reasons or considerations for and against a proposition, etc. [L, = for, on behalf of]

■ *adj. & prep.* see *in favor* (FAVOR), FOR *prep.* 2. ● *n.* see ADVANTAGE *n.* 1, 3.

pro-[1] /prō/ *prefix* **1** favoring or supporting (*pro-government*). **2** acting as a substitute or deputy for (*proconsul*). **3** forward (*produce*). **4** forward and downward (*prostrate*). **5** onward (*proceed; progress*). **6** in front of (*protect*). [L *pro* in front (of), for, on behalf of, instead of, on account of]

pro-[2] /prō/ *prefix* before in time, place, order, etc. (*problem; proboscis; prophet*). [Gk *pro* before]

proa /prṓə/ *n.* (also **prau, prahu** /praá-ōō/) a Malay boat, esp. with a large triangular sail and a canoe-like outrigger. [Malay *prāŭ, prāhŭ*]

proactive /prō-áktiv/ *adj.* **1** (of a person, policy, etc.) creating or controlling a situation by taking the initiative. **2** of or relating to mental conditioning or a habit, etc., which has been learned. □□ **proaction** /-ákshən/ *n.* **proactively** *adv.* **proactivity** /-tívitee/ *n.* [PRO-[2], after REACTIVE]

prob. *abbr.* **1** probable. **2** probably. **3** problem.

probabilism /próbəbəlizəm/ *n.* **1** *Philos.* the doctrine that probability is the basis for belief and action since certainty is impossible. **2** *RC Ch.* an ethical theory that it is allowable to follow any one of many conflicting opinions even though an opposing one may be more probable.

probabilistic /próbəbəlístik/ *adj.* **1** relating to or established by probabilism. **2** based on or subject to probability.

probability /próbəbilitee/ *n.* (*pl.* **-ies**) **1** the state or condition of being probable. **2** the likelihood of something happening. **3** a probable or most probable event (*the probability is that they will come*). **4** *Math.* the extent to which an event is likely to occur, measured by the ratio of the favorable cases to the whole number of cases possible. □ **in all probability** most probably. [F *probabilité* or L *probabilitas* (as PROBABLE)]

■ **2, 3** likelihood, likeliness, odds, (good) chance, (strong *or* distinct) possibility, good prospect. □ **in all probability** (most *or* very) probably, almost certainly, (most *or* very) likely, in all likelihood, as likely as not, presumably.

probable /próbəbəl/ *adj. & n.* ● *adj.* **1** (often foll. by *that* + clause) that may be expected to happen or prove true; likely (*the probable explanation; it is probable that they forgot*). **2** statistically likely but not proven. ● *n.* a probable candidate, member of a team, etc. □ **probable cause** *Law* a reasonable ground for suspicion that a usu. criminal charge is justified; used esp. in cases in which a police search has been made without a search warrant. □□ **probably** *adv.* [ME f. OF f. L *probabilis* f. *probare* prove]

■ *adj.* **1** (most) likely, possible, plausible, feasible, believable, credible, conceivable, tenable, expected, *disp.* anticipated. □□ **probably** (very) likely, in all likelihood, in all probability; presumably, as likely as not.

proband /próband/ *n.* a person forming the starting point for the genetic study of a family, etc. [L *probandus*, gerundive of *probare* test]

probang /próbang/ *n. Surgery* a flexible rod with a sponge or ball, etc., at the end for introducing medications into or removing obstructions from the throat. [17th c. (named *provang* by its inventor): orig. unkn., perh. alt. after *probe*]

probate /próbayt/ *n. & v.* ● *n.* **1** the official proving of a will. **2** a verified copy of a will. ● *v.tr.* **1** establish the validity of (a will). **2** to put (a criminal offender) on probation. [ME f. L *probatum* neut. past part. of *probare* PROVE]

probation /prəbáyshən/ *n.* **1** *Law* a system of suspending the sentence of a criminal offender subject to a period of good behavior under supervision. **2** a process or period of testing the character or abilities of a person in a certain role, esp. of a new employee. **3** a moral trial or discipline. □ **on probation** undergoing probation, esp. legal supervision. **probation officer** an official supervising offenders on probation. □□ **probational** *adj.* **probationary** *adj.* [ME f. OF *probation* or L *probatio* (as PROVE)]

probationer /prəbáyshənər/ *n.* **1** a person on probation, e.g., a newly appointed nurse, teacher, etc. **2** a criminal offender on probation. □□ **probationership** *n.*

probative /prṓbətiv/ *adj.* affording proof; evidential. [L *probativus* (as PROVE)]
- see DEMONSTRATIVE *adj.* 2.

probe /prōb/ *n. & v.* ● *n.* **1** a penetrating investigation. **2** any small device, esp. an electrode, for measuring, testing, etc. **3** a blunt surgical instrument usu. of metal for exploring a wound, etc. **4** (in full **space probe**) an unmanned exploratory spacecraft transmitting information about its environment. ● *v.* **1** *tr.* examine or inquire into closely. **2** *tr.* explore (a wound or part of the body) with a probe. **3** *tr.* penetrate with or as with a sharp instrument, esp. in order to explore. **4** *intr.* make an investigation with or as with a probe (*the detective probed into her past life*). □□ **probeable** *adj.* **prober** *n.* **probingly** *adv.* [LL *proba* proof, in med.L = examination, f. L *probare* test]
- *n.* **1** investigation, examination, exploration, scrutiny, search, study, inquiry. ● *v.* **1** explore, examine, scrutinize, investigate, search (into), look into, go into, study; dig into, delve into, poke into. **3** explore, examine; plumb, poke, prod, dig.

probit /prṓbit/ *n. Statistics* a unit of probability based on deviation from the mean of a standard distribution. [*probability unit*]

probity /prṓbitee, prób-/ *n.* uprightness; honesty. [F *probité* or L *probitas* f. *probus* good]
- integrity, uprightness, honesty, morality, rectitude, virtue, goodness, decency, righteousness, rightmindedness, sincerity, trustworthiness, honor, equity, justness, justice, fairness.

problem /próbləm/ *n.* **1** a doubtful or difficult matter requiring a solution (*how to prevent it is a problem; the problem of ventilation*). **2** something hard to understand, accomplish, or deal with. **3** (*attrib.*) **a** causing problems; difficult to deal with (*problem child*). **b** (of a play, novel, etc.) in which a social or other problem is treated. **4 a** *Physics & Math.* an inquiry starting from given conditions to investigate or demonstrate a fact, result, or law. **b** *Geom.* a proposition in which something has to be constructed (cf. THEOREM). **5 a** (in various games, esp. chess) an arrangement of men, cards, etc., in which the solver has to achieve a specified result. **b** a puzzle or question for solution. [ME f. OF *probleme* or L *problema* f. Gk *problēma -matos* f. *proballō* (as PRO-², *ballō* throw)]
- **1, 2** difficulty, trouble, complication, knot, question, Gordian knot, hornet's nest, *colloq.* can of worms, proposition, hard *or* tough nut to crack, *Brit.* facer, *disp.* dilemma. **3 a** (*attrib.*) unruly, unmanageable, intractable, uncontrollable, difficult, ungovernable, refractory, incorrigible, obstreperous, delinquent, maladjusted, disturbed. **5 b** puzzle, conundrum, poser, riddle, question, enigma, puzzler.

problematic /próbləmátik/ *adj.* (also **problematical**) **1** difficult; posing a problem. **2** doubtful or questionable. **3** *Logic* enunciating or supporting what is possible but not necessarily true. □□ **problematically** *adv.* [F *problématique* or LL *problematicus* f. Gk *problēmatikos* (as PROBLEM)]
- **1** see DIFFICULT 1. **2** uncertain, questionable, doubtful, debatable, disputable, moot, controversial, tricky, touchy, sensitive, delicate.

proboscidean /prŏbəsídeeən, prōbósideeən/ *adj. & n.* (also **proboscidian**) ● *adj.* **1** having a proboscis. **2** of or like a proboscis. **3** of the mammalian order Proboscidea, including elephants and their extinct relatives. ● *n.* a mammal of this order. [mod.L *Proboscidea* (as PROBOSCIS)]

proboscis /prōbósis/ *n.* **1** the long flexible trunk or snout of some mammals, e.g., an elephant or tapir. **2** the elongated mouth parts of some insects. **3** the sucking organ in some worms. **4** *joc.* the human nose. □ **proboscis monkey** a monkey, *Nasalis larvatus*, native to Borneo, the male of which has a large pendulous nose. □□ **proboscidiferous** /-sidífərəs/ *adj.* **proboscidiform** /-sídifawrm/ *adj.* [L *proboscis -cidis* f. Gk *proboskis* f. *boskō* feed)]

procaine /prṓkayn/ *n.* (also **procain**) a synthetic compound used as a local anesthetic. [PRO-¹ + COCAINE]

procaryote var. of PROKARYOTE.

procedure /prəseejər/ *n.* **1** a way of proceeding, esp. a mode of conducting business or a legal action. **2** a mode of performing a task. **3** a series of actions conducted in a certain order or manner. **4** a proceeding. **5** *Computing* = SUBROUTINE. □□ **procedural** *adj.* **procedurally** *adv.* [F *procédure* (as PROCEED)]
- **1–3** conduct, course, action, course of action, process, methodology, form, system, approach, strategy, plan (of action), scheme, modus operandi; routine, drill, practice, method, *colloq.* MO (= 'modus operandi'), SOP (= 'standard operating procedure'). **4** see PROCEEDING 1.

proceed /prōseéd, prə-/ *v.intr.* **1** (often foll. by *to*) go forward or on further; make one's way. **2** (often foll. by *with*, or *to* + infin.) continue; go on with an activity (*proceeded with their work; proceeded to tell the whole story*). **3** (of an action) be carried on or continued (*the case will now proceed*). **4** adopt a course of action (*how shall we proceed?*). **5** go on to say. **6** (foll. by *against*) start a lawsuit (against a person). **7** (often foll. by *from*) come forth or originate (*shouts proceeded from the bedroom*). [ME f. OF *proceder* f. L *procedere process-* (as PRO-¹, *cedere* go)]
- **1** go *or* move on *or* ahead *or* forward, advance, progress, move along, push *or* press on *or* onward(s), forge ahead, make one's way. **2** continue; pass on, go on; see also *carry on* 1. **4** go on, continue; see also START *v.* 1, 2. **7** result, arise, come (forth), stem, spring, develop, issue, derive, descend, emerge, grow, originate, begin, start.

proceeding /prōseeding, prə-/ *n.* **1** an action or piece of conduct. **2** (in *pl.*) (in full **legal proceedings**) a legal action; a lawsuit. **3** (in *pl.*) a published report of discussions or a conference. **4** (in *pl.*) business, actions, or events in progress (*the proceedings were enlivened by a dog running onto the field*).
- **1** measure, act, (course of) action, move, step, undertaking, deed, procedure, process, operation, transaction, maneuver, feat, accomplishment. **2 legal proceedings** suit, lawsuit, action, case, process, cause, trial; litigation. **3** (*proceedings*) transactions, procès-verbal, report(s); minutes, record(s), annals, account(s), archives. **4** (*proceedings*) affairs, dealings, business; events, goings-on, doings; celebration(s); performance(s).

proceeds /prṓseedz/ *n.pl.* money produced by a transaction or other undertaking. [pl. of obs. *proceed* (n.) f. PROCEED]
- profit(s), gain, yield; income, takings, receipts, return(s), gate, take.

process¹ /próses, prṓ-/ *n. & v.* ● *n.* **1** a course of action or proceeding, esp. a series of stages in manufacture or some other operation. **2** the progress or course of something (*in process of construction*). **3** a natural or involuntary operation or series of changes (*the process of growing old*). **4** a legal action; a summons or writ. **5** *Anat., Zool., & Bot.* a natural appendage or outgrowth on an organism. ● *v.tr.* **1** handle or deal with by a particular process. **2** treat (food, esp. to prevent decay) (*processed cheese*). **3** *Computing* operate on (data) by means of a program. □ **in process of time** as time goes on. **process server** a person who serves legal summonses or writs. □□ **processable** *adj.* [ME f. OF *proces* f. L *processus* (as PROCEED)]
- *n.* **1** proceeding, operation, system, method, approach, technique; course of action; see also PROCEDURE 1–3. **2** course, progress; midst, middle. **3** see OPERATION 1, 2. **4** see ACTION *n.* 8, WARRANT *n.* 2. ● *v.* **1** handle, take care of, deal with, manage, look after; prepare, make or get ready; answer. **2** treat, prepare.

process² /prəsés/ *v.intr.* walk in procession. [back-form. f. PROCESSION]

procession /prəséshən/ *n.* **1** a number of people or vehicles,

---

/.../ **pronunciation**	● **part of speech**
□ **phrases, idioms, and compounds**	
□□ **derivatives**	■ **synonym section**
cross-references appear in SMALL CAPITALS or *italics*	

etc., moving forward in orderly succession, esp. at a ceremony, demonstration, or festivity. **2** the movement of such a group (*go in procession*). **3** a regular succession of things; a sequence. **4** *Theol.* the emanation of the Holy Spirit. □□ **processionist** *n.* [ME f. OF f. L *processio -onis* (as PROCEED)]
■ **1** parade, march, cortege, column, line, file, train, cavalcade, motorcade. **3** succession, cycle, sequence, string, train, chain, series, course, run, progression.

processional /prəséshənəl/ *adj.* & *n.* ● *adj.* **1** of processions. **2** used, carried, or sung in processions. ● *n. Eccl.* a book of processional hymns, etc. [med.L *processionalis* (adj.), *-ale* (n.) (as PROCESSION)]

processor /prósesər, prṓ-/ *n.* a machine that processes things, esp.: **1** = *central processor*. **2** = *food processor*.

procès-verbal /prōsáy-verbaál/ *n.* (*pl.* **procès-verbaux** /-bố/) a written report of proceedings; minutes. [F]

prochronism /prṓkrənizəm/ *n.* the action of referring an event, etc., to an earlier date than the true one. [PRO-² + Gk *khronos* time]
■ see ANACHRONISM 1.

proclaim /prōkláym, prə-/ *v.tr.* **1** (often foll. by *that* + clause) announce or declare publicly or officially. **2** declare (a person) to be (a king, traitor, etc.). **3** reveal as being (*an accent that proclaims you a Southerner*). □□ **proclaimer** *n.* **proclamation** /prṓkləmáyshən/ *n.* **proclamatory** /-klámətawree/ *adj.* [ME *proclame* f. L *proclamare* cry out (as PRO-¹, CLAIM)]
■ **1** announce, declare, pronounce, make known, bruit (about), trumpet, publish, advertise, broadcast, promulgate, herald; profess, assert. **2** brand, accuse of being, stigmatize as, pronounce, characterize as, declare, announce, decree. □□ **proclamation** announcement, declaration, publication, promulgation, statement, advertisement, manifesto, notification.

proclitic /prōklítik/ *adj.* & *n. Gram.* ● *adj.* (of a monosyllable) closely attached in pronunciation to a following word and having itself no accent. ● *n.* such a word, e.g., *at* in *at home.* □□ **proclitically** *adv.* [mod.L *procliticus* f. Gk *proklinō* lean forward, after LL *encliticus*: see ENCLITIC]

proclivity /prōklívitee/ *n.* (*pl.* **-ies**) a tendency or inclination. [L *proclivitas* f. *proclivis* inclined (as PRO-¹, *clivus* slope)]
■ see TENDENCY.

proconsul /prōkónsəl/ *n.* **1** *Rom.Hist.* a governor of a province, in the later republic usu. an ex-consul. **2** a governor of a modern colony, etc. **3** a deputy consul. □□ **proconsular** /-kónsələr/ *adj.* **proconsulate** /-kónsələt/ *n.* **proconsulship** *n.* [ME f. L, earlier *pro consule* (one acting) for the consul]

procrastinate /prōkrástinayt/ *v.* **1** *intr.* defer action; delay, esp. intentionally. **2** *tr.* defer or delay, esp. intentionally or habitually. □□ **procrastination** /-náyshən/ *n.* **procrastinative** /-nətiv/ *adj.* **procrastinator** *n.* **procrastinatory** /-nətawree/ *adj.* [L *procrastinare procrastinat-* (as PRO-¹, *crastinus* of tomorrow f. *cras* tomorrow)]
■ **1** temporize, play for time, dally, delay, stall, take one's time, dillydally; hesitate, pause, waver, vacillate, dawdle, shilly-shally, dither, be undecided.

procreate /prṓkreeayt/ *v.tr.* (often *absol.*) bring (offspring) into existence by the natural process of reproduction. □□ **procreant** /prṓkreeənt/ *adj.* **procreative** *adj.* **procreation** *n.* **procreator** *n.* [L *procreare procreat-* (as PRO-¹, *creare* create)]
■ see REPRODUCE 3. □□ **procreant**, **procreative** reproductive, sexual, progenitive, propagative. **procreation** see GENERATION 6. **procreator** see PARENT *n.* 1, 5.

Procrustean /prōkrústeeən/ *adj.* seeking to enforce uniformity by forceful or ruthless methods. [Gk *Prokroustēs*, lit. stretcher, f. *prokrouō* beat out: the name of a legendary robber who fitted victims to a bed by stretching them or cutting off parts of them]

proctology /prōktóləjee/ *n.* the branch of medicine concerned with the anus and rectum. □□ **proctological** /-təlójikəl/ *adj.* **proctologist** *n.* [Gk *prōktos* anus + -LOGY]

proctor /prṓktər/ *n.* **1** a supervisor of students in an exami-

nation, etc. **2** *Brit.* an officer (usu. one of two) at certain universities, appointed annually and having mainly disciplinary functions. **3** *Brit. Law* a person managing causes in a court (now chiefly ecclesiastical) that administers civil or canon law. □□ **proctorial** /-táwreeəl/ *adj.* **proctorship** *n.* [ME, syncopation of PROCURATOR]

proctoscope /prṓktəskōp/ *n.* a medical instrument for inspecting the rectum. [Gk *prōktos* anus + -SCOPE]

procumbent /prōkúmbənt/ *adj.* **1** lying on the face; prostrate. **2** *Bot.* growing along the ground. [L *procumbere* fall forward (as PRO-¹, *cumbere* lay oneself)]
■ **1** see PROSTRATE *adj.* 1. **2** creeping, low-growing, prostrate, *Bot.* repent, *Bot.* & *Zool.* decumbent.

procuration /prṓkyŏōráyshən/ *n.* **1** the action of procuring, obtaining, or bringing about. **2** the function or an authorized action of an attorney. [ME f. OF *procuration* or L *procuratio* (as PROCURE)]

procurator /prṓkyŏōraytər/ *n.* **1** an agent or proxy, esp. one who has power of attorney. **2** *Rom.Hist.* a treasury officer in an imperial province. □□ **procuratorial** /-rətáwreeəl/ *adj.* **procuratorship** *n.* [ME f. OF *procurateur* or L *procurator* administrator, finance agent (as PROCURE)]

procure /prōkyŏōr, prə-/ *v.tr.* **1** obtain, esp. by care or effort; acquire (*managed to procure a copy*). **2** bring about (*procured their dismissal*). **3** (also *absol.*) obtain (people) for prostitution. □□ **procurable** *adj.* **procural** *n.* **procurement** *n.* [ME f. OF *procurer* f. L *procurare* take care of, manage (as PRO-¹, *curare* see to)]
■ **1** obtain, acquire, get, come by, secure, get *or* lay one's hands on, get (a) hold of, pick up, appropriate, requisition; buy, purchase. **2** accomplish, contrive, effect, cause, produce; see also *bring about.* **3** pander, pimp.

procurer /prōkyŏōrər, prə-/ *n.* a person who obtains people for prostitution. [ME f. AF *procurour*, OF *procureur* f. L *procurator*: see PROCURATOR]
■ pander, *archaic* whoremaster, whoremonger; madam, procuress, bawd, *sl.* hustler; see also PIMP *n.*

prod /prod/ *v.* & *n.* ● *v.* (**prodded**, **prodding**) **1** *tr.* poke with the finger or a pointed object. **2** *tr.* stimulate or goad to action. **3** *intr.* (foll. by *at*) make a prodding motion. ● *n.* **1** a poke or thrust. **2** a stimulus to action. **3** a pointed instrument. □□ **prodder** *n.* [16th c.: perh. imit.]
■ *v.* **1** jab, dig, poke, nudge, thrust, job, elbow. **2** spur, urge, impel, push, prompt, rouse, stir, incite, move, motivate, provoke, encourage, stimulate; incite, goad, pester, harass, hector, badger, plague, nag. ● *n.* **1** jab, dig, poke, nudge, thrust, job, push. **2** stimulus, push, shove, prompt; see also SPUR *n.* 2.

prodigal /pródigəl/ *adj.* & *n.* ● *adj.* **1** recklessly wasteful. **2** (foll. by *of*) lavish. ● *n.* **1** a prodigal person. **2** (in full **prodigal son**) a repentant wastrel, returned wanderer, etc. (Luke 15:11–32). □□ **prodigality** /-gálitee/ *n.* **prodigally** *adv.* [med.L *prodigalis* f. L *prodigus* lavish]
■ *adj.* **1** wasteful, extravagant, spendthrift, profligate, immoderate, intemperate, wanton, improvident, reckless. **2** generous, bountiful, copious, profuse, excessive, lavish, liberal, luxuriant, abundant, abounding, rich, plentiful, *poet.* bounteous, plenteous. ● *n.* **1** wastrel, spendthrift, squanderer, waster, big spender; see also PROFLIGATE *n.* □□ **prodigality** wastefulness, extravagance, excessiveness, immoderation, intemperateness, wantonness, recklessness, profligacy, improvidence, dissipation, squandering; lavishness, luxuriousness, luxuriance, abundance, bounty, bountifulness, copiousness, profusion, profuseness, sumptuousness, richness, plentifulness, *poet.* bounteousness, plenteousness.

prodigious /prədíjəs/ *adj.* **1** marvelous or amazing. **2** enormous. **3** abnormal. □□ **prodigiously** *adv.* **prodigiousness** *n.* [L *prodigiosus* (as PRODIGY)]
■ **1** amazing, astonishing, astounding, startling, extraordinary, exceptional, marvelous, wonderful, incredible, phenomenal, spectacular, sensational, unusual, staggering, remarkable, noteworthy, notable,

colloq. fabulous, fantastic, mind-boggling, *poet.* wondrous. **2** vast, immeasurable, colossal, enormous, tremendous, huge, massive, immense; giant, gigantic, mammoth, monumental, stupendous, titanic, gargantuan, leviathan, monstrous, *sl.* humongous. **3** see ABNORMAL.

prodigy /pródijee/ *n.* (*pl.* **-ies**) **1** a person endowed with exceptional qualities or abilities, esp. a precocious child. **2** a marvelous thing, esp. one out of the ordinary course of nature. **3** (foll. by *of*) a wonderful example (of a quality). [L *prodigium* portent]
■ **1** genius, mastermind, mental giant, wizard, virtuoso, *colloq.* brain, wunderkind, Einstein, whiz kid, whiz, walking dictionary *or* encyclopedia. **2** marvel, phenomenon, sensation, miracle; see also WONDER *n.* 2.

prodrome /pródrōm/ *n.* **1** a preliminary book or treatise. **2** *Med.* a premonitory symptom. □□ **prodromal** /-drómǝl/ *adj.* **prodromic** /pródrómik/ *adj.* [F f. mod.L f. Gk *prodromos* precursor (as PRO-², *dromos* running)]
■ □□ **prodromal, prodromic** see PRELIMINARY *adj.*

produce *v. & n.* ● *v.tr.* /prǝdōōs, -dyōōs/ **1** bring forward for consideration, inspection, or use (*will produce evidence*). **2** manufacture (goods) from raw materials, etc. **3** bear or yield (offspring, fruit, a harvest, etc.). **4** bring into existence. **5** cause or bring about (a reaction, sensation, etc.). **6** *Geom.* extend or continue (a line). **7 a** bring (a play, performer, book, etc.) before the public. **b** supervise the production of (a movie, broadcast, etc.). ● *n.* /pródōs, -dyōōs, prō-/ **1 a** what is produced, esp. agricultural products. **b** fruits and vegetables collectively. **2** (often foll. by *of*) a result (of labor, efforts, etc.). **3** a yield, esp. in the assay of ore. **4** offspring (esp. of a female animal). □□ **producible** /-sib'l/ *adj.* **producibility** *n.* [ME f. L *producere* (as PRO-¹, *ducere duct-* lead)]
■ *v.* **1** bring forward *or* out, introduce, present, offer, show, exhibit, display; disclose, reveal, bring to light. **2** make, manufacture, fabricate, turn out, put *or* bring out; construct, assemble, put together, compose. **3** put out *or* forth, generate; see also BEAR¹ 3. **4, 5** give rise to, cause, bring forth, spark off, initiate, occasion, bring about, prompt, evoke, *literary* beget; create, generate, give birth to. ● *n.* **1** goods, merchandise, products, commodities, stock, staples, wares. **2** see RESULT *n.*

producer /prǝdōōsǝr, -dyōō-/ *n.* **1 a** *Econ.* a person who produces goods or commodities. **b** a person who or thing which produces something or someone. **2 a** a person generally responsible for the production of a movie, play, or radio or television program (apart from the direction of the acting). **b** *Brit.* the director of a play or broadcast program. **3** an organism that produces its own food from inorganic compounds. □ **producer gas** a combustible gas formed by passing air, or air and steam, through red-hot carbon.
■ **1** maker, manufacturer, fabricator, processor; creator, grower. **2 a** promoter, impresario, administrator, manager, stage manager, showman. **b** director, regisseur.

product /pródukt/ *n.* **1** a thing or substance produced by natural process or manufacture. **2** a result (*the product of their labors*). **3** *Math.* a quantity obtained by multiplying quantities together. [ME f. L *productum*, neut. past part. of *producere* PRODUCE]
■ **1** artifact, commodity; (*products*) see PRODUCE *n.* 1. **2** result, consequence, outcome, issue, effect, yield, upshot.

production /prǝdúkshǝn/ *n.* **1** the act or an instance of producing; the process of being produced. **2** the process of being manufactured, esp. in large quantities (*go into production*). **3** a total yield. **4** a thing produced, esp. a literary or artistic work, a movie, broadcast, play, etc. □ **production line** a systematized sequence of mechanical or manual operations involved in producing a commodity. □□ **productional** *adj.* [ME f. OF f. L *productio -onis* (as PRODUCT)]
■ **1** manufacture, manufacturing, making, fabrication, preparation, creation, development; formation, assembly, building, construction. **4** product; show, performance; work, opus; play, movie.

productive /prǝdúktiv/ *adj.* **1** of or engaged in the production of goods. **2 a** producing much (*productive soil*; *a productive writer*). **b** (of the mind) inventive; creative. **3** *Econ.* producing commodities of exchangeable value (*productive labor*). **4** (foll. by *of*) producing or giving rise to (*productive of great annoyance*). □□ **productively** *adv.* **productiveness** *n.* [F *productif -ive* or LL *productivus* (as PRODUCT)]
■ **2 a** fruitful, fertile, rich, fecund, plentiful, abundant, bountiful, prolific, dynamic, *poet.* bounteous, plenteous. **b** imaginative, creative, inventive, resourceful, generative, ingenious, fertile, vigorous.

productivity /próduktívitee, prŏ-/ *n.* **1** the capacity to produce. **2** the quality or state of being productive. **3** the effectiveness of productive effort, esp. in industry. **4** production per unit of effort.
■ **3** efficiency, productiveness.

proem /prŏim/ *n.* **1** a preface or preamble to a book or speech. **2** a beginning or prelude. □□ **proemial** /prŏeémeeǝl/ *adj.* [ME f. OF *proeme* or L *prooemium* f. Gk *prooimion* prelude (as PRO-², *oimē* song)]
■ **1** see PREAMBLE. **2** see PRELIMINARY *n.* 1.

Prof. *abbr.* Professor.

prof /prof/ *n. colloq.* a professor. [abbr.]

profane /prŏfáyn, prǝ-/ *adj. & v.* ● *adj.* **1** not belonging to what is sacred or biblical; secular. **2 a** irreverent; blasphemous. **b** vulgar; obscene. **3** (of a rite, etc.) heathen; pagan. **4** not initiated into religious rites or any esoteric knowledge. ● *v.tr.* **1** treat (a sacred thing) with irreverence or disregard. **2** violate or pollute (something entitled to respect). □□ **profanation** /prófǝnáyshǝn/ *n.* **profanely** *adv.* **profaneness** *n.* **profaner** *n.* [ME *prophane* f. OF *prophane* or med.L *prophanus* f. L *profanus* before (i.e. outside) the temple, not sacred (as PRO-¹, *fanum* temple)]
■ *adj.* **1** nonreligious, laic, lay, nonclerical, secular, temporal; unsanctified, unconsecrated, unhallowed. **2 a** irreverent, sacrilegious, blasphemous, idolatrous, irreligious, unbelieving, disbelieving, impious, godless, ungodly, unholy, disrespectful; bad, taboo; *Judaism* tref, not kosher. **b** impure, unclean, dirty, filthy, smutty, foul, foulmouthed, obscene, vulgar, coarse, uncouth, rude, low, bawdy, ribald, scurrilous, immodest, improper, indecent, unmentionable, indecorous, indelicate, common, off-color, *colloq. joc.* naughty. **3** see HEATHEN *adj.* ● *v.* **1** debase, contaminate, pollute, taint, vitiate, degrade, defile, desecrate, violate, pervert, corrupt, prostitute.

profanity /prŏfánitee, prǝ-/ *n.* (*pl.* **-ies**) **1** a profane act. **2** profane language; blasphemy. [LL *profanitas* (as PROFANE)]
■ **1** see SACRILEGE. **2** blasphemy, obscenity, cursing, swearing, foul *or* bad language.

profess /prǝfés, prō-/ *v.* **1** *tr.* claim openly to have (a quality or feeling). **2** *tr.* (foll. by *to* + infin.) pretend. **3** *tr.* (often foll. by *that* + clause; also *refl.*) declare (*profess ignorance*; *professed herself satisfied*). **4** *tr.* affirm one's faith in or allegiance to. **5** *tr.* receive into a religious order under vows. **6** *tr.* have as one's profession or business. **7 a** *tr.* teach (a subject) as a professor. **b** *intr.* perform the duties of a professor. [ME f. L *profitēri profess-* declare publicly (as PRO-¹, *fatēri* confess)]
■ **2** (*profess to*) pretend to, lay claim to, purport to, claim to, make a pretense of. **3** assert, claim, asseverate, state, affirm, confirm, confess, declare, maintain, set forth, put forward, pronounce, announce, *archaic* vow, *formal* aver.

professed /prǝfést, prō-/ *adj.* **1** self-acknowledged (*a professed Christian*). **2** alleged; ostensible. **3** claiming to be duly qualified. **4** (of a monk or nun) having taken the vows of a religious order. □□ **professedly** /-fésidlee/ *adv.* (in senses 1, 2).

■ **1** sworn, acknowledged, confirmed, self-acknowledged, certified, declared. **2** supposed, ostensible, apparent, alleged, purported, so-called. **3** see SELF-STYLED.

profession /prəféshən/ *n.* **1** a vocation or calling, esp. one that involves some branch of advanced learning or science (*the medical profession*). **2** a body of people engaged in a profession. **3** a declaration or avowal. **4** a declaration of belief in a religion. **5 a** the declaration or vows made on entering a religious order. **b** the ceremony or fact of being professed in a religious order. □ **the oldest profession** prostitution. □□ **professionless** *adj.* [ME f. OF f. L *professio -onis* (as PROFESS)]

■ **1** occupation, calling, work, field, vocation, employment, métier, trade, business, craft, line, sphere, specialty, job, position. **3** confession, affirmation, statement, assertion, asseveration, declaration, testimony, averment, announcement; admission, avowal.

professional /prəféshənəl/ *adj. & n.* ● *adj.* **1** of or belonging to or connected with a profession. **2 a** having or showing the skill of a professional; competent. **b** worthy of a professional (*professional conduct*). **3** engaged in a specified activity as one's main paid occupation (cf. AMATEUR) (*a professional boxer*). **4** *derog.* engaged in a specified activity regarded with disfavor (*a professional agitator*). ● *n.* a professional person. □□ **professionally** *adv.*

■ *adj.* **2** trained, practiced, veteran, experienced, qualified, licensed, official, seasoned; competent, able, skilled, skillful, expert, masterful, masterly, efficient, adept, proficient, polished, finished, thorough, authoritative, businesslike. ● *n.* master, expert, specialist, authority, proficient, adept, *colloq.* maven, esp. *Brit. colloq.* dab hand.

professionalism /prəféshənəlizəm/ *n.* the qualities or typical features of a profession or of professionals, esp. competence, skill, etc. □□ **professionalize** *v.tr.*

professor /prəfésər/ *n.* **1 a** (often as a title) a university academic of the highest rank. **b** a university teacher. **c** a teacher of some specific art, sport, or skill. **2** a person who professes a religion. □□ **professorate** /-rət/ *n.* **professorial** /prófisáwreeəl/ *adj.* **professorially** *adv.* **professoriate** /-fisáwreeət/ *n.* **professorship** *n.* [ME f. OF *professeur* or L *professor* (as PROFESS)]

■ **1** see TEACHER. □□ **professorship** see CHAIR *n* 2a, b.

proffer /prófər/ *v. & n.* ● *v.tr.* (esp. as **proffered** *adj.*) offer (a gift, services, a hand, etc.). ● *n.* an offer or proposal. [ME f. AF & OF *proffrir* (as PRO-¹, *offrir* OFFER)]

■ *v.* see OFFER *v.* 1, 3, 5. ● *n.* see OFFER *n.*

proficient /prəfishənt/ *adj. & n.* ● *adj.* (often foll. by *in, at*) adept; expert. ● *n.* a person who is proficient. □□ **proficiency** /-shənsee/ *n.* **proficiently** *adv.* [L *proficiens proficient-* (as PROFIT)]

■ *adj.* skillful, skilled, adept, expert, experienced, practiced, well-versed, trained, professional, qualified, capable, able, accomplished, dexterous, competent, knowledgeable. □□ **proficiency** skill, adeptness, expertise, expertness, know-how, skillfulness, aptitude, capability, ability, competence, competency.

profile /prófil/ *n. & v.* ● *n.* **1 a** an outline (esp. of a human face) as seen from one side. **b** a representation of this. **2 a** a short biographical or character sketch. **b** a report, esp. one written by a teacher on a pupil's academic and social progress. **3** *Statistics* a representation by a graph or chart of information (esp. on certain characteristics) recorded in a quantified form. **4** a characteristic personal manner or attitude. **5** a vertical cross section of a structure. **6** a flat outline piece of scenery on stage. ● *v.tr.* **1** represent in profile. **2** give a profile to. **3** write a profile about. □ **in profile** as seen from one side. **keep a low profile** remain inconspicuous. □□ **profiler** *n.* **profilist** *n.* [obs. It. *profilo, profilare* (as PRO-¹, *filare* spin f. L *filare* f. *filum* thread)]

■ *n.* **1** outline, contour, silhouette, side view. **2 a** biography, (biographical or thumbnail or character) sketch, portrait, vignette. **3** picture, idea, impression, notion, understanding; see also CHART *n.* 2. **4** see

CHARACTERISTIC *n.* ● *v.* **1** describe, draw, sketch, characterize, portray, paint, depict, style. **3** describe, detail, give an account of; outline, sketch. □ **keep a low profile** keep low *or* down, soft-pedal; see also *dummy up.*

profit /prófit/ *n. & v.* ● *n.* **1** an advantage or benefit. **2** financial gain; excess of returns over expenditures. ● *v.* (**profited, profiting**) **1** *tr.* (also *absol.*) be beneficial to. **2** *intr.* obtain an advantage or benefit (*profited by the experience*). **3** *intr.* make a profit. □ **at a profit** with financial gain. **profit and loss** a statement on which gains are credited and losses debited so as to show the net profit or loss at any time. **profit margin** the profit remaining in a business after costs have been deducted. **profit sharing** the sharing of profits esp. between employer and employees. **profit taking** the sale of shares, etc., at a time when profit will accrue. □□ **profitless** *adj.* [ME f. OF f. L *profectus* progress, profit f. *proficere profect-* advance (as PRO-¹, *facere* do)]

■ *n.* **1** advantage, avail, good, benefit, gain, value, interest, use, usefulness, *archaic* behoof. **2** net profit *or* income, net, return(s), gain, yield, payback, revenue, proceeds, surplus, take, *sl.* cleanup. ● *v.* **1** advance, further, be of profit *or* advantage to, benefit, promote, aid, help, be advantageous *or* beneficial to, serve, avail. **2** (*profit from* or *by*) take advantage of, turn to advantage *or* account, exploit, utilize, make (good) use of, make capital (out) of, capitalize on, maximize, make the most of, *colloq.* cash in on. **3** profiteer, make a killing, *colloq.* make a packet, rake it in, *sl.* clean up, make a bundle.

profitable /prófitəbəl/ *adj.* **1** yielding profit; lucrative. **2** beneficial; useful. □□ **profitability** /-bílitee/ *n.* **profitableness** *n.* **profitably** *adv.* [ME f. OF (as PROFIT)]

■ **1** productive, lucrative, fruitful, well-paid, cost-effective, gainful, remunerative, moneymaking, rewarding, payable, rentable, *colloq.* juicy, *Brit. colloq.* jammy. **2** beneficial, helpful, useful, utilitarian, valuable, worthwhile, advantageous, productive, rewarding, serviceable.

profiteer /prófiteer/ *v. & n.* ● *v.intr.* make or seek to make excessive profits, esp. illegally or in black market conditions. ● *n.* a person who profiteers.

■ *v.* see PROFIT *v.* 3. ● *n.* racketeer, exploiter, extortionist, extortioner, black marketer, bloodsucker.

profiterole /prəfitərōl/ *n.* a small hollow pastry usu. filled with cream and covered with chocolate sauce. [F, dimin. of *profit* PROFIT]

profligate /prófligət/ *adj. & n.* ● *adj.* **1** licentious; dissolute. **2** recklessly extravagant. ● *n.* a profligate person. □□ **profligacy** /-gəsee/ *n.* **profligately** *adv.* [L *profligatus* dissolute, past part. of *profligare* overthrow, ruin (as PRO-¹, *fligere* strike down)]

■ *adj.* **1** dissolute, degenerate, loose, licentious, depraved, debauched, immoral, unprincipled, shameless, dissipative, corrupt, promiscuous, lascivious, libertine, wanton, unrestrained, sybaritic. **2** extravagant, prodigal, wasteful, reckless, improvident, spendthrift, immoderate, excessive. ● *n.* debauchee, degenerate, reprobate, libertine, wanton, sybarite, voluptuary, sensualist; prodigal, spendthrift, wastrel, waster, squanderer. □□ **profligacy** debauchery, immorality, dissipation, dissoluteness, degeneracy, licentiousness, depravity, corruption, promiscuity, lasciviousness, lewdness, libertinism, wantonness, unrestraint, sybaritism, voluptuousness; prodigality, extravagance, wastefulness, recklessness, lavishness, improvidence.

pro forma /prō fáwrmə/ *adv., adj., & n.* ● *adv. & adj.* as or being a matter of form; for the sake of form. ● *n.* (in full **pro-forma invoice**) an invoice sent in advance of goods supplied. [L]

■ *adj.* see FORMAL *adj.* 1, 2, 7.

profound /prəfównd, prō-/ *adj. & n.* ● *adj.* (**profounder, profoundest**) **1 a** having or showing great knowledge or insight (*a profound treatise*). **b** demanding deep study or thought (*profound doctrines*). **2** (of a state or quality) deep;

intense; unqualified (*a profound sleep*; *profound indifference*).
3 at or extending to a great depth (*profound crevasses*). **4**
coming from a great depth (*a profound sigh*). **5** (of a disease)
deep-seated. ● *n.* (prec. by *the*) *poet.* the vast depth (of the
ocean, soul, etc.). □□ **profoundly** *adv.* **profoundness** *n.*
profundity /-fúnditee/ *n.* (*pl.* **-ies**). [ME f. AF & OF *pro-
fund, profond* f. L *profundus* deep (as PRO-¹, *fundus* bottom)]
■ *adj.* **1 a** learned, scholarly, intellectual, erudite,
discerning, astute, sagacious, sage, wise, penetrating,
insightful, analytical, knowledgeable, informed, well-
informed, well-read. **b** deep, unfathomable, abstruse,
recondite, arcane, esoteric, intricate, knotty, involved,
tricky, inscrutable, obscure, subtle. **2** deep, great,
intense; keen, acute, extreme, overpowering,
overwhelming; utter, complete, unqualified, total,
perfect, absolute, thorough, thoroughgoing, out-and-
out, downright, consummate. **3** see DEEP *adj.* 1.
● *n.* (*the profound*) see DEEP *n.* 1, *depths* (DEPTH 5).
□□ **profoundly** deeply, greatly, very, extremely, keenly,
acutely, intensely, *colloq.* terribly, awfully.
profoundness, **profundity** depth, intensity,
abstruseness, reconditeness, arcaneness, intricacy,
subtlety, complexity, complicatedness, difficulty,
inscrutability, involvement, involvedness; erudition,
discernment, scholarship, scholarliness, sagacity,
wisdom, astuteness, insightfulness, knowledgeableness,
knowledgeability.

profuse /prəfyóōs, prō-/ *adj.* **1** (often foll. by *in*, *of*) lavish;
extravagant (*was profuse in her generosity*). **2** (of a thing) exuberantly plentiful; abundant (*profuse bleeding*; *a profuse variety*). □□ **profusely** *adv.* **profuseness** *n.* **profusion**
/-fyóōzhən/ *n.* [ME f. L *profusus* past part. of *profundere pro-
fus-* (as PRO-¹, *fundere fus-* pour)]
■ **1** generous, lavish, extravagant, unsparing, unselfish,
unstinting, exuberant, magnanimous, ungrudging,
liberal, bountiful, *poet.* bounteous. **2** abundant, ample,
plentiful, copious, prolific, superabundant, lush,
overflowing, productive, fruitful, rich; excessive,
considerable. □□ **profuseness**, **profusion** abundance,
bounty, plenty, plentifulness, copiousness,
superabundance, wealth, plethora; superfluity, glut,
surplus, oversupply, surfeit, *poet.* plenteousness.

progenitive /prōjénitiv/ *adj.* capable of or connected with the
production of offspring.
■ reproductive, procreative, procreant, propagative;
sexual.

progenitor /prōjénitər/ *n.* **1** the ancestor of a person, animal,
or plant. **2** a political or intellectual predecessor. **3** the origin
of a copy. □□ **progenitorial** /-táwreeəl/ *adj.* **progenitor-
ship** *n.* [ME f. OF *progeniteur* f. L *progenitor -oris* f. *progignere
progenit-* (as PRO-¹, *gignere* beget)]
■ **1** see ANCESTOR 1. **2** predecessor, forerunner, precursor,
antecedent, foregoer. **3** origin, original, prototype,
archetype, source, originator, pattern.

progeny /prójinee/ *n.* **1** the offspring of a person or other
organism. **2** a descendant or descendants. **3** an outcome or
issue. [ME f. OF *progenie* f. L *progenies* f. *progignere* (as PRO-
GENITOR)]
■ **1** offspring, children, young, sons and daughters, *derog.*
spawn; see also ISSUE *n.* 5. **2** descendants, posterity,
heirs, scions, successors; see also SUCCESSION 2c. **3** see
OUTCOME.

progesterone /prōjéstərōn/ *n.* a steroid hormone released
by the corpus luteum which stimulates the preparation of
the uterus for pregnancy (see also PROGESTOGEN). [*proges*tin
(as PRO-², GESTATION) + luteo*sterone* f. CORPUS LUTEUM + STE-
ROL]

progestogen /prōjéstəjin/ *n.* **1** any of a group of steroid hormones (including progesterone) that maintain pregnancy
and prevent further ovulation during it. **2** a similar hormone
produced synthetically.

proglottid /prōglótid/ *n.* (also **proglottis**) (*pl.* **proglottides**
/-glótideez/) each segment in the strobile of a tapeworm
that contains a complete reproductive system. [mod.L f. Gk

proglōssis (as PRO-², *glōssis* f. *glōssa*, *glōtta* tongue), from its
shape]

prognathous /prognáythəs, prógnəthəs/ *adj.* **1** having a projecting jaw. **2** (of a jaw) projecting. □□ **prognathic** /prog-
náthik/ *adj.* **prognathism** *n.* [PRO-² + Gk *gnathos* jaw]

prognosis /prognōsis/ *n.* (*pl.* **prognoses** /-seez/) **1** a forecast; a prognostication. **2** a forecast of the course of a disease. [LL f. Gk *prognōsis* (as PRO-², *gignōskō* know)]
■ **1** forecast, prognostication, prediction, prophecy,
projection.

prognostic /prognóstik/ *n.* & *adj.* ● *n.* **1** (often foll. by *of*)
an advance indication or omen, esp. of the course of a disease, etc. **2** a prediction; a forecast. ● *adj.* foretelling; predictive (*prognostic of a good result*). □□ **prognostically** *adv.*
[ME f. OF *pronostique* f. L *prognosticum* f. Gk *prognōstikon*
neut. of *prognōstikos* (as PROGNOSIS)]
■ *n.* **1** see INDICATION 1b, OMEN *n.* **2** see FORECAST *n.*
● *adj.* see PROPHETIC.

prognosticate /prognóstikayt/ *v.tr.* **1** (often foll. by *that* +
clause) foretell; foresee; prophesy. **2** (of a thing) betoken;
indicate (future events, etc.). □□ **prognosticable** /-kəbəl/
adj. **prognostication** *n.* **prognosticative** /-kətiv/ *adj.*
prognosticator *n.* **prognosticatory** /-kətawree/ *adj.*
[med.L *prognosticare* (as PROGNOSTIC)]
■ **1** predict, foretell, prophesy, forecast, foresee, presage,
divine. **2** betoken, augur, herald, forebode, foreshadow,
foretoken, portend, harbinger, signal, indicate.

program /prṓgram, -grəm/ *n.* & *v.* (*Brit.* **programme**) ● *n.*
1 a usu. printed list of a series of events, performers, etc.,
at a public function, etc. **2** a radio or television broadcast.
3 a plan of future events (*the program is dinner and an early
night*). **4** a course or series of studies, lectures, etc.; a syllabus. **5** a series of coded instructions to control the operation
of a computer or other machine. ● *v.tr.* (**programmed**,
programming; also **programed**, **programing**) **1** make a
program or definite plan of. **2** express (a problem) or instruct (a computer) by means of a program. □ **program
music** a piece of music intended to tell a story, evoke
images, etc. □□ **programmable** *adj.* **programmability**
/-graməbílitee/ *n.* **programmatic** /-grəmátik/ *adj.* **pro-
grammatically** /-grəmátiklee/ *adv.* **programmer** *n.* **pro-
gramer** *n.* [LL *programma* f. Gk *programma -atos* f. *pro-
graphō* write publicly (as PRO-², *graphō* write)]
■ *n.* **1, 3** schedule, agenda, list, outline, calendar; plan,
order of the day. **2** broadcast, production, show,
presentation, telecast. **4** course, curriculum, syllabus;
timetable, schedule. ● *v.* **1** prearrange, plan, lay out,
map (out), set up, schedule, slate.

progress *n.* & *v.* ● *n.* /prógres/ **1** forward or onward movement toward a destination. **2** advance or development toward completion, betterment, etc.; improvement (*has made
little progress this term*; *the progress of civilization*). **3** *Brit.* archaic a state journey or official tour, esp. by royalty. ● *v.*
/prəgrés/ **1** *intr.* move or be moved forward or onward; continue (*the argument is progressing*). **2** *intr.* /prəgrés/ advance
or develop toward completion, improvement, etc. (*science
progresses*). **3** *tr.* cause (work, etc.) to make regular progress.
□ **in progress** in the course of developing; going on. **progress report** an account of progress made. [ME f. L *pro-
gressus* f. *progredi* (as PRO-¹, *gradi* walk)]
■ *n.* **1** forward *or* onward movement *or* motion,
progression, advancement; headway, moving. **2**
advancement, advance, promotion, development,
spread, furtherance, improvement, betterment,
evolution, maturation; elevation, rise; growth,
expansion, extension. ● *v.* **1** advance, move *or* go
(forward *or* onward *or* on), proceed, continue, go *or*
forge ahead, go *or* move along, make one's *or* its way,
make headway. **2** advance, improve, get better,

/ . . . / **pronunciation**   ● **part of speech**
□ **phrases, idioms, and compounds**
□□ **derivatives**   ■ **synonym section**
cross-references appear in SMALL CAPITALS or *italics*

develop, grow, expand, increase, evolve, mature, spread; rise, move up. □ **in progress** under way, ongoing, going on, taking place, at work, in operation, in the pipeline, awaiting completion, *colloq.* in the works.

progression /prəgréshən/ *n.* **1** the act or an instance of progressing (*a mode of progression*). **2** a succession; a series. **3** *Math.* **a** = *arithmetic progression.* **b** = *geometric progression.* **c** = *harmonic progression.* **4** *Mus.* passing from one note or chord to another. □□ **progressional** *adj.* [ME f. OF *progression* or L *progressio* (as PROGRESS)]

■ **1** forward movement, advance, advancement, progress, development; ascension, rise, elevation. **2** order, sequence, succession, train, chain, concatenation, course, flow; series, set.

progressionist /prəgréshənist/ *n.* **1** an advocate of or believer in esp. political or social progress. **2** a person who believes in the theory of gradual progression to higher forms of life.

progressive /prəgrésiv/ *adj.* & *n.* ● *adj.* **1** moving forward (*progressive motion*). **2** proceeding step-by-step; cumulative (*progressive drug use*). **3 a** (of a political party, government, etc.) favoring or implementing rapid progress or social reform. **b** modern; efficient (*this is a progressive company*). **4** (of disease, violence, etc.) increasing in severity or extent. **5** (of taxation) at rates increasing with the sum taxed. **6** (of a card game, dance, etc.) with periodic changes of partners. **7** *Gram.* (of an aspect) expressing an action in progress, e.g., *am writing, was writing.* **8** (of education) informal and without strict discipline, stressing individual needs. ● *n.* (also **Progressive**) an advocate of progressive political policies. □□ **progressively** *adv.* **progressiveness** *n.* **progressivism** *n.* **progressivist** *n.* & *adj.* [F *progressif -ive* or med.L *progressivus* (as PROGRESS)]

■ *adj.* **2, 4** continuing, developing, increasing, growing, ongoing; cumulative, step-by-step, gradual. **3 a** forward-looking, advanced, reform, reformist, progressivist, left-wing, radical, liberal, avant-garde, dynamic. **b** forward-looking, advanced, modern, new, go-ahead, enterprising, *colloq.* go; see also CAPABLE 1. **8** liberal, individualistic; open, informal. ● *n.* reformist, reformer, revisionist; leftist, left-winger; see also LIBERAL *n.*

prohibit /prōhíbit/ *v.tr.* (**prohibited, prohibiting**) (often foll. by *from* + verbal noun) **1** formally forbid, esp. by authority. **2** prevent; make impossible (*his accident prohibits him from playing football*). □ **prohibited degrees** degrees of blood relationship within which marriage is forbidden. □□ **prohibiter** *n.* **prohibitor** *n.* [ME f. L *prohibēre* (as PRO-¹, *habēre* hold)]

■ **1** forbid, bar, ban, disallow, interdict, outlaw, taboo, debar. **2** prevent, stop, obstruct, block, impede, hinder, hamper, inhibit, restrain; preclude, rule out.

prohibition /prōhibíshən, prōibíshən/ *n.* **1** the act or an instance of forbidding; a state of being forbidden. **2** *Law* an edict or order that forbids. **3** (usu. **Prohibition**) the period (1920–33) in the US when the manufacture and sale of alcoholic beverages was prohibited by law. □□ **prohibitionary** *adj.* **prohibitionist** *n.* [ME f. OF *prohibition* or L *prohibitio* (as PROHIBIT)]

■ **1** forbiddance, banning, disallowance, interdiction, outlawry, debarment, proscription; bar, interdict, injunction, embargo, ban.

prohibitive /prōhíbitiv/ *adj.* **1** prohibiting. **2** (of prices, taxes, etc.) so high as to prevent purchase, use, abuse, etc. (*published at a prohibitive price*). □□ **prohibitively** *adv.* **prohibitiveness** *n.* **prohibitory** *adj.* [F *prohibitif -ive* or L *prohibitivus* (as PROHIBIT)]

■ **1** suppressive, repressive, restrictive, prohibitory; inhibitory, restraining, obstructive. **2** excessive, high, extortionate, exorbitant, outrageous, outlandish, insupportable, scandalous, *colloq.* criminal.

project *n.* & *v.* ● *n.* /prójekt/ **1** a plan; a scheme. **2** a planned undertaking. **3** a usu. long-term task undertaken by a student or group of students to be submitted for grading. **4**

(often *pl.*) a housing development, esp. for low-income residents. ● *v.* /prəjékt/ **1** *tr.* plan or contrive (a course of action, scheme, etc.). **2** *intr.* protrude; jut out. **3** *tr.* throw; cast; impel. **4** *tr.* extrapolate (results, etc.) to a future time; forecast (*I project that we will produce two million next year*). **5** *tr.* cause (light, shadow, images, etc.) to fall on a surface, screen, etc. **6** *tr.* cause (a sound, esp. the voice) to be heard at a distance. **7** *tr.* (often *refl.* or *absol.*) express or promote (oneself or an image) forcefully or effectively. **8** *tr. Geom.* **a** draw straight lines from a center or parallel lines through every point of (a given figure) to produce a corresponding figure on a surface or a line by intersecting it. **b** draw (such lines). **c** produce (such a corresponding figure). **9** *tr.* make a projection of (the earth, sky, etc.). **10** *tr. Psychol.* **a** (also *absol.*) attribute (an emotion, etc.) to an external object or person, esp. unconsciously. **b** (*refl.*) project (oneself) into another's feelings, the future, etc. [ME f. L *projectum* neut. past part. of *projicere* (as PRO-¹, *jacĕre* throw)]

■ *n.* **1** proposal, idea, plan, scheme, program, design. **2** activity, enterprise, program, undertaking, venture, assignment; contract, engagement. ● *v.* **1** plan, scheme, propose, present, outline, devise, think up, contemplate, contrive, invent, work up *or* out, design, draft, draw up, delineate, describe, put forward, *formal* put forth. **2** jut out, stick out, protrude, overhang, stand out, bulge (out), extend (out), poke out, beetle (out). **3** cast, hurl, fling, toss, launch, propel, impel, lob, discharge, *colloq.* chuck; see also THROW *v.* 1, 2. **4** extrapolate; estimate, reckon, calculate, predict; see also FORECAST *v.* **5** reflect, transmit, cast, throw, shed, let fall, scatter, spread. **7** see COMMUNICATE 1a; (*project oneself*) carry on, conduct oneself, present oneself, express oneself, put oneself across; see also BEHAVE 1a. **10 a** see ATTRIBUTE *v.*

projectile /prəjéktəl, -tíl/ *n.* & *adj.* ● *n.* **1** a missile, esp. fired by a rocket. **2** a bullet, shell, etc., fired from a gun. **3** any object thrown as a weapon. ● *adj.* **1** capable of being projected by force, esp. from a gun. **2** projecting or impelling. [mod.L *projectilis* (adj.), *-ile* (n.) (as PROJECT)]

■ *n.* **1, 2** missile, brickbat; shell, bullet, cartridge, shot, rocket.

projection /prəjékshən/ *n.* **1** the act or an instance of projecting; the process of being projected. **2** a thing that projects or obtrudes. **3** the presentation of an image, etc., on a surface or screen. **4 a** a forecast or estimate based on present trends (*a projection of next year's profits*). **b** this process. **5 a** a mental image or preoccupation viewed as an objective reality. **b** the unconscious transfer of one's own impressions or feelings to external objects or persons. **6** *Geom.* the act or an instance of projecting a figure. **7** the representation on a plane surface of any part of the surface of the earth or a celestial sphere (*Mercator projection*). □□ **projectionist** *n.* (in sense 3). [L *projectio* (as PROJECT)]

■ **2** protrusion, protuberance, bulge, extension, overhang, ledge, *Engin.* flange; prominence, spur, outcrop, jut, crag. **4** estimate, forecast, prediction, prognostication, calculation, reckoning; forecasting, planning, estimation; extrapolation. **5 b** transference, ascription; see also *attribution* (ATTRIBUTE).

projective /prəjéktiv/ *adj.* **1** *Geom.* **a** relating to or derived by projection. **b** (of a property of a figure) unchanged by projection. **2** *Psychol.* mentally projecting or projected (*a projective imagination*). □ **projective geometry** the study of the projective properties of geometric figures. □□ **projectively** *adv.*

projector /prəjéktər/ *n.* **1 a** an apparatus containing a source of light and a system of lenses for projecting slides or movies onto a screen. **b** an apparatus for projecting rays of light. **2** a person who forms or promotes a project. **3** *archaic* a promoter of speculative companies.

prokaryote /prōkáreeōt/ *n.* (also **procaryote**) an organism in which the chromosomes are not separated from the cytoplasm by a membrane; a bacterium (cf. EUKARYOTE). □□ **prokaryotic** /-reeótik/ *adj.* [PRO-² + KARYO- + *-ote* as in ZYGOTE]

prolactin /prōláktin/ *n.* a hormone released from the anterior pituitary gland that stimulates milk production after childbirth. [PRO-¹ + LACTATION]

prolapse /prōláps/ *n. & v.* ● *n.* (also **prolapsus** /-lápsəs/) **1** the forward or downward displacement of a part or organ. **2** the prolapsed part or organ, esp. the womb or rectum. ● *v.intr.* undergo prolapse. [L *prolabi prolaps-* (as PRO-¹, *labi* slip)]

prolate /prōlayt/ *adj. Geom.* (of a spheroid) lengthened in the direction of a polar diameter (cf. OBLATE²). [L *prolatus* past part. of *proferre* prolong (as PRO-¹, *ferre* carry)]

prolative /prōláytiv/ *adj. Gram.* serving to continue or complete a predication, e.g., *go* (prolative infinitive) in *you may go.*

prole /prōl/ *adj. & n. derog. colloq.* ● *adj.* proletarian. ● *n.* a proletarian. [abbr.]
■ *adj.* see PLEBEIAN *adj.* 1. ● *n.* see PLEBEIAN *n.*

proleg /prōleg/ *n.* a fleshy abdominal limb of a caterpillar or other larva. [PRO-¹ + LEG]

prolegomenon /prōligóminon, -nən/ *n.* (*pl.* **prolegomena**) (usu. in *pl.*) an introduction or preface to a book, etc., esp. when critical or discursive. □□ **prolegomenary** *adj.* **prolegomenous** *adj.* [L f. Gk, neut. passive pres. part. of *prolegō* (as PRO-², *legō* say)]
■ see PREFACE *n.* 1, 2.

prolepsis /prōlépsis/ *n.* (*pl.* **prolepses** /-seez/) **1** the anticipation and answering of possible objections in rhetorical speech. **2** anticipation. **3** the representation of a thing as existing before it actually does or did so, as in *he was a dead man when he entered.* **4** *Gram.* the anticipatory use of adjectives, as in *paint the town red.* □□ **proleptic** *adj.* [LL f. Gk *prolēpsis* f. *prolambanō* anticipate (as PRO-², *lambanō* take)]

proletarian /prōlitáireeən/ *adj. & n.* ● *adj.* of or concerning the proletariat. ● *n.* a member of the proletariat. □□ **proletarianism** *n.* **proletarianize** *v.tr.* [L *proletarius* one who served the state not with property but with offspring (*proles*)]
■ *adj.* see PLEBEIAN *adj.* 1. ● *n.* see PLEBEIAN *n.* 3.

proletariat /prōlitáireeət/ *n.* (also **proletariate**) **1 a** *Econ.* wage earners collectively, esp. those without capital and dependent on selling their labor. **b** esp. *derog.* the lowest class of the community, esp. when considered as uncultured. **2** *Rom.Hist.* the lowest class of citizens. [F *prolétariat* (as PROLETARIAN)]
■ **1 b** see PEOPLE *n.* 2.

pro-life /prōlíf/ *adj.* in favor of preserving life, esp. in opposing abortion.

proliferate /prəlífərayt/ *v.* **1** *intr.* reproduce; increase rapidly in numbers; grow by multiplication. **2** *tr.* produce (cells, etc.) rapidly. □□ **proliferation** /-fəráyshən/ *n.* **proliferative** /-rətiv/ *adj.* [back-form. f. *proliferation* f. F *prolifération* f. *prolifère* (as PROLIFEROUS)]
■ **1** grow, increase, multiply, mushroom, snowball, flourish, *literary* burgeon; breed, reproduce. □□ **proliferation** growth, increase, escalation, multiplication, expansion, spread, buildup, rise.

proliferous /prəlífərəs/ *adj.* **1** (of a plant) producing many leaf or flower buds; growing luxuriantly. **2** growing or multiplying by budding. **3** spreading by proliferation. [L *proles* offspring + -FEROUS]

prolific /prəlífik/ *adj.* **1** producing many offspring or much output. **2** (often foll. by *of*) abundantly productive. **3** (often foll. by *in*) abounding; copious. □□ **prolificacy** *n.* **prolifically** *adv.* **prolificness** *n.* [med.L *prolificus* (as PROLIFEROUS)]
■ **1** productive, creative, fertile, fecund, fruitful, proliferative, proliferous. **3** abundant, copious, profuse, plentiful, bountiful, *poet.* bounteous, plenteous; lush, rich; rife.

prolix /prōliks, prōliks/ *adj.* (of speech, writing, etc.) lengthy; tedious. □□ **prolixity** /-liksitee/ *n.* **prolixly** *adv.* [ME f. OF *prolixe* or L *prolixus* poured forth, extended (as PRO-¹, *liquēre* be liquid)]
■ see LENGTHY 2. □□ **prolixity** see RHETORIC 2.

prolocutor /prōlókyətər/ *n.* **1** *Eccl.* the chairperson esp. of

the lower house of convocation of either province of the Church of England. **2** a spokesperson. □□ **prolocutorship** *n.* [ME f. L f. *prolocui prolocut-* (as PRO-¹, *loqui* speak)]

prologize /prōlawgiz, -logiz/ *v.intr.* (also **prologuize**) write or speak a prologue. [med.L *prologizare* f. Gk *prologizō* speak prologue (as PROLOGUE)]

prologue /prōlawg, -log/ *n. & v.* (also **prolog**) ● *n.* **1 a** a preliminary speech, poem, etc., esp. introducing a play (cf. EPILOGUE). **b** the actor speaking the prologue. **2** (usu. foll. by *to*) any act or event serving as an introduction. ● *v.tr.* (**prologues, prologued, prologuing**) introduce with or provide with a prologue. [ME *prolog* f. OF *prologue* f. L *prologus* f. Gk *prologos* (as PRO-², *logos* speech)]
■ *n.* **1 a** see FOREWORD. **2** see PRELIMINARY *n.* 1.

prolong /prəláwng, -lóng/ *v.tr.* **1** extend (an action, condition, etc.) in time or space. **2** lengthen the pronunciation of (a syllable, etc.). **3** (as **prolonged** *adj.*) lengthy, esp. tediously so. □□ **prolongation** *n.* **prolongedly** /-idli/ *adv.* **prolonger** *n.* [ME f. OF *prolonger* & f. LL *prolongare* (as PRO-¹, *longus* long)]
■ **1** extend, lengthen, elongate, stretch (out), draw *or* drag out, drag (on), keep up, string out, protract, continue. **3** (**prolonged**) see LENGTHY 2.

prolusion /prəloōzhən/ *n. formal* **1** a preliminary essay or article. **2** a first attempt. □□ **prolusory** /-loōsəree, -zə-/ *adj.* [L *prolusio* f. *proludere prolus-* practice beforehand (as PRO-¹, *ludere lus-* play)]

prom /prom/ *n. colloq.* **1** a school or college formal dance. **2** *Brit.* = PROMENADE *n.* 4a. **3** *Brit.* = *promenade concert.* [abbr.]

promenade /prómənáyd, -naád/ *n. & v.* ● *n.* **1** a walk, or sometimes a ride or drive, taken esp. for display, social intercourse, etc. **2** a school or university ball or dance. **3** a march of dancers in country dancing, etc. **4 a** *Brit.* a paved public walk along the sea front at a resort. **b** any paved public walk. ● *v.* **1** *intr.* make a promenade. **2** *tr.* lead (a person, etc.) about a place esp. for display. **3** *tr.* make a promenade through (a place). □ **promenade concert** *Brit.* a concert at which the audience, or part of it, can stand, sit on the floor, or move about. **promenade deck** an upper deck on a passenger ship where passengers may promenade. [F f. *se promener* walk, refl. of *promener* take for a walk]
■ *n.* **1** walk, stroll, saunter, ramble, turn, constitutional, airing; ride, drive. **4** walk, esplanade, parade. ● *v.* **1** walk, stroll, saunter, amble, ramble, perambulate, take a walk *or* stroll. **2** parade, display, flaunt, show (off), make an exhibit *or* a spectacle of, advertise.

promethazine /prōméthəzeen/ *n.* an antihistamine drug used to treat allergies, motion sickness, etc. [PROPYL + dimethylamine + phenothiazine]

Promethean /prəmeétheeən/ *adj.* daring or inventive like Prometheus, who in Greek myth was punished for stealing fire from the gods and giving it to the human race along with other skills.

promethium /prəmeétheeəm/ *n. Chem.* a radioactive metallic element of the lanthanide series occurring in nuclear waste material. ¶ Symb.: **Pm**. [*Prometheus*: see PROMETHEAN]

prominence /próminəns/ *n.* **1** the state of being prominent. **2** a prominent thing, esp. a jutting outcrop, mountain, etc. **3** *Astron.* a stream of incandescent gas projecting above the sun's chromosphere. [obs.F f. L *prominentia* jutting out (as PROMINENT)]
■ **1** celebrity, eminence, fame, distinction, notability, reputation, preeminence, standing, position, rank, prestige, renown, repute, importance, weight, influence, account, name, consequence. **2** hill, hillock, rise, hummock, outcrop, spur, tor, peak, arête, spine, ridge, jut, pinnacle, crag; headland, point, promontory; protuberance, projection, protrusion, extrusion, outshoot, outgrowth, bulge.

/.../ **pronunciation**	● **part of speech**
□ **phrases, idioms, and compounds**	
□□ **derivatives**	■ **synonym section**
cross-references appear in SMALL CAPITALS or *italics*	

prominent /próm`inənt/ *adj.* **1** jutting out; projecting. **2** conspicuous. **3** distinguished; important. □□ **prominency** *n.* **prominently** *adv.* [L *prominēre* jut out: cf. EMINENT]
■ **1** protuberant, protruding, protrusive, projecting; jutting; bulging, raised, elevated. **2** conspicuous, noticeable, pronounced, obvious, evident, recognizable, discernible, distinguishable, identifiable, eye-catching, striking, outstanding. **3** eminent, preeminent, distinguished, notable, noteworthy, noted, well-known, famed, illustrious, famous, celebrated, renowned, acclaimed, honored, esteemed, honorable, respected, well-thought-of, prestigious, reputable, creditable; significant, important.

promiscuous /prəmískyŏŏəs/ *adj.* **1 a** (of a person) having frequent and diverse sexual relationships, esp. transient ones. **b** (of sexual relationships) of this kind. **2** of mixed and indiscriminate composition or kinds; indiscriminate (*promiscuous hospitality*). **3** *colloq.* carelessly irregular; casual. □□ **promiscuity** /prómiskyŏŏitee/ *n.* **promiscuously** *adv.* **promiscuousness** *n.* [L *promiscuus* (as PRO-¹, *miscēre* mix)]
■ **1 a** lax, loose, wanton, wild, uninhibited, unrestrained, uncontrolled, unbridled, uncurbed, immoderate, abandoned, libertine, licentious, dissipated, dissolute, depraved, profligate, debauched, fast, sluttish, *sl.* trashy, cheap. **2, 3** indiscriminate, undiscriminating; mixed, miscellaneous, heterogeneous, random; careless, cursory, haphazard, unsystematic, indifferent, disregardful, slipshod, slovenly, sloppy, irresponsible, unthinking, thoughtless, unconsidered.

promise /prómis/ *n. & v.* ● *n.* **1** an assurance that one will or will not undertake a certain action, behavior, etc. (*a promise of help*; *gave a promise to be generous*). **2** a sign or signs of future achievements, good results, etc. (*a writer of great promise*). ● *v.tr.* **1** (usu. foll. by *to* + infin., or *that* + clause; also *absol.*) make (a person) a promise, esp. to do, give, or procure (a thing) (*I promise you a fair hearing*; *they promise not to be late*; *promised that he would be there*; *cannot positively promise*). **2 a** afford expectations of (*the discussions promise future problems*; *promises to be a good cook*). **b** (foll. by *to* + infin.) seem likely to (*is promising to rain*). **3** *colloq.* assure; confirm (*I promise you, it will not be easy*). **4** (usu. in *passive*) *esp. archaic* betroth (*she is promised to another*). □ **the promised land 1** *Bibl.* Canaan (Gen. 12:7, etc.). **2** any desired place, esp. heaven. **promise oneself** look forward to (a pleasant time, etc.). **promise well** (or **ill**, etc.) hold out good (or bad, etc.) prospects. □□ **promisee** /-séé/ *n.* esp. *Law.* **promiser** *n.* **promisor** *n.* esp. *Law.* [ME f. L *promissum* neut. past part. of *promittere* put forth, promise (as PRO-¹, *mittere* send)]
■ *n.* **1** assurance, word (of honor), pledge, vow, oath, bond, guarantee; undertaking, engagement, commitment; agreement, contract, covenant, compact. **2** potential, capability, capacity, aptitude; expectation, likelihood, probability; see also ABILITY. ● *v.* **1** give one's word (of honor), pledge, swear, vow, take an oath, undertake, commit oneself, guarantee, cross one's heart (and hope to die). **2 a** give (an or every) indication of, hint at, suggest, foretell, augur, indicate, betoken, bespeak, be evidence of. **b** (*promise to*) show signs of, look like, seem or appear likely to, bid fair to. **3** assure, swear, confirm. **4** engage, betroth, *literary* affiance. □ **the promised land 2** see HEAVEN 2. **promise well** bode well, augur well, prospect well, have good prospects, look good or rosy.

promising /prómising/ *adj.* likely to turn out well; hopeful; full of promise (*a promising start*). □□ **promisingly** *adv.*
■ hopeful, encouraging, favorable, auspicious, positive, rosy, optimistic, propitious, cheering, reassuring, heartening.

promissory /prómisawree/ *adj.* **1** conveying or implying a promise. **2** (often foll. by *of*) full of promise. □ **promissory note** a signed document containing a written promise to pay a stated sum to a specified person or the bearer at a specified date or on demand. [med.L *promissorius* f. L *promissor* (as PROMISE)]

■ □ **promissory note** letter of credit, (bank) draft, demand note, *Econ.* bill of exchange.

promo /prómō/ *n. & adj. colloq.* ● *n.* (*pl.* **-os**) **1** publicity blurb or advertisement. **2** a trailer for a television program. ● *adj.* promotional. [abbr.]

promontory /próməntawree/ *n.* (*pl.* **-ies**) **1** a point of high land jutting out into the sea, etc.; a headland. **2** *Anat.* a prominence or protuberance in the body. [med.L *promontorium* alt. (after *mons montis* mountain) f. L *promunturium* (perh. f. PRO-¹, *mons*)]
■ **1** see POINT *n.* 22.

promote /prəmōt/ *v.tr.* **1** (often foll. by *to*) advance or raise (a person) to a higher office, rank, grade, etc. (*was promoted to captain*). **2** help forward; encourage; support actively (a cause, process, desired result, etc.) (*promoted women's suffrage*). **3** publicize and sell (a product). **4** attempt to ensure the passing of (a legislative act). **5** *Chess* raise (a pawn) to the rank of queen, etc., when it reaches the opponent's end of the board. □□ **promotable** *adj.* **promotability** *n.* **promotion** /-mōshən/ *n.* **promotional** *adj.* **promotive** *adj.* [ME f. L *promovēre promot-* (as PRO-¹, *movēre* move)]
■ **1** advance, move up, prefer, raise, upgrade, elevate; create. **2** help, further, encourage, assist, advance, support, forward, advantage, abet, aid, foster, nurture, develop, inspirit, strengthen, stimulate, inspire, *colloq.* boost; endorse, sponsor, espouse, commend, advocate, champion, speak for, side with, call attention to. **3** advertise, publicize, push, market, beat the drum for, tout, ballyhoo, *colloq.* plug, *sl.* hype. □□ **promotion** furtherance, advancement, encouragement, support, development, improvement, stimulation; advance, rise, preferment, elevation; espousal, commendation, advocacy, championship; advertising, marketing, publicity, advertisement, public relations, propaganda, puffery, *sl.* (media) hype.

promoter /prəmōtər/ *n.* **1** a person who promotes. **2** a person who finances, organizes, etc., a sporting event, theatrical production, etc. **3** a person who promotes the formation of a company, project, etc. **4** *Chem.* an additive that increases the activity of a catalyst. [earlier *promotour* f. AF f. med.L *promotor* (as PROMOTE)]
■ **2** see *backer* (BACK).

prompt /prompt/ *adj., adv., v., & n.* ● *adj.* **1 a** acting with alacrity; ready. **b** made, done, etc., readily or at once (*a prompt reply*). **2 a** (of a payment) made quickly or immediately. **b** (of goods) for immediate delivery and payment. ● *adv.* punctually. ● *v.tr.* **1** (usu. foll. by *to*, or *to* + infin.) incite; urge (*prompted them to action*). **2 a** (also *absol.*) supply a forgotten word, sentence, etc., to (an actor, reciter, etc.). **b** assist (a hesitating speaker) with a suggestion. **3** give rise to; inspire (a feeling, thought, action, etc.). ● *n.* **1 a** an act of prompting. **b** a thing said to help the memory of an actor, etc. **c** = PROMPTER 2. **d** *Computing* an indication or sign on a computer screen to show that the system is waiting for input. **2** the time limit for the payment of an account, stated on a prompt note. □ **prompt side** the side of the stage where the prompter sits, usu. to the actor's right in the US, or left in the UK. □□ **prompting** *n.* **promptitude** *n.* **promptly** *adv.* **promptness** *n.* [ME f. OF *prompt* or L *promptus* past part. of *promere prompt-* produce (as PRO-¹, *emere* take)]
■ *adj.* **1 a** alert, eager, ready, quick, expeditious, ready and willing, disposed, predisposed, unhesitating, keen, avid. **b** quick, ready, immediate, instantaneous, unhesitating, rapid, fast, swift, speedy, punctual, timely, instant, summary, brisk. ● *adv.* on the dot, *Austral. & NZ colloq.* on the knocker, see also SHARP *adv.* 1. ● *v.* **1** urge, egg (on), prod, nudge, spur, incite, induce, impel, provoke, rouse, arouse, encourage, work or stir or fire up, move, motivate. **2** cue, remind, feed lines to. **3** bring about, inspire, occasion, give rise to, elicit, evoke, provoke, call forth, stimulate, awaken. ● *n.* **1 a** reminder, cue, hint, stimulus, refresher, suggestion. □□ **promptly** quickly, at once, straight away, directly, right away, immediately, without delay or hesitation,

unhesitatingly, swiftly, speedily, readily, instantly, instantaneously, punctually, expeditiously, momentarily; by return (of post).

prompter /prómptər/ *n.* **1** a person who prompts. **2** *Theatr.* a person seated out of sight of the audience who prompts the actors.

promulgate /prómʌlgayt/ *v.tr.* **1** make known to the public; disseminate; promote (a cause, etc.). **2** proclaim (a decree, news, etc.). □□ **promulgation** /-gáyshən/ *n.* **promulgator** *n.* [L *promulgare* (as PRO-¹, *mulgēre* milk, cause to come forth)]

■ see PROMOTE 3, PROCLAIM 1. □□ **promulgation** see *proclamation* (PROCLAIM).

promulge /prōmúlj/ *v.tr. archaic* = PROMULGATE. [PROMULGATE]

pronaos /prōnáyos/ *n.* (*pl.* **pronaoi** /-náyoy/) *Gk Antiq.* the space in front of the body of a temple, enclosed by a portico and projecting side walls. [L f. Gk *pronaos* hall of a temple (as PRO-², NAOS)]

pronate /prṓnayt/ *v.tr.* put (the hand, forearm, etc.) into a prone position (with the palm downwards) (cf. SUPINATE). □□ **pronation** /-náyshən/ *n.* [back-form. f. *pronation* (as PRONE)]

pronator /prōnáytər/ *n. Anat.* any muscle producing or assisting in pronation.

prone /prōn/ *adj.* **1 a** lying face downward (cf. SUPINE). **b** lying flat; prostrate. **c** having the front part downwards, esp. the palm of the hand. **2** (usu. foll. by *to*, or *to* + infin.) disposed or liable, esp. to a bad action, condition, etc. (*is prone to bite his nails*). **3** (usu. in *comb.*) more than usually likely to suffer (*accident-prone*). **4** *archaic* with a downward slope or direction. □□ **pronely** *adv.* **proneness** /prṓn-nis/ *n.* [ME f. L *pronus* f. *pro* forward]

■ **1 a, b** face down *or* downward; prostrate, reclining, recumbent, horizontal, procumbent, *Bot. & Zool.* decumbent. **2** inclined, apt, disposed, predisposed, of a mind, subject, given, tending, leaning, *disp.* liable.

prong /prong/ *n. & v.* ● *n.* each of two or more projecting pointed parts at the end of a fork, etc. ● *v.tr.* **1** pierce or stab with a fork. **2** turn up (soil) with a fork. □□ **pronged** *adj.* (also in *comb.*). [ME (also *prang*), perh. rel. to MLG *prange* pinching instrument]

■ *n.* tine.

pronominal /prōnóminəl/ *adj.* of, concerning, or being, a pronoun. □□ **pronominalize** *v.tr.* **pronominally** *adv.* [LL *pronominalis* f. L *pronomen* (as PRO-¹, *nomen, nominis* noun)]

pronoun /prṓnown/ *n.* a word used instead of and to indicate a noun already mentioned or known, esp. to avoid repetition (e.g., *we, their, this, ourselves*). [PRO-¹, + NOUN, after F *pronom*, L *pronomen* (as PRO-¹, *nomen* name)]

pronounce /prənówns/ *v.* **1** *tr.* (also *absol.*) utter or speak (words, sounds, etc.) in a certain way. **2** *tr.* **a** utter or deliver (a judgment, sentence, curse, etc.) formally or solemnly. **b** proclaim or announce officially (*I pronounce you husband and wife*). **3** *tr.* state or declare, as being one's opinion (*the apples were pronounced excellent*). **4** *intr.* (usu. foll. by *on, for, against, in favor of*) pass judgment; give one's opinion (*pronounced for the defendant*). □□ **pronounceable** /-nównsəbəl/ *adj.* **pronouncement** *n.* **pronouncer** *n.* [ME f. OF *pronuncier* f. L *pronuntiare* (as PRO-¹, *nuntiare* announce f. *nuntius* messenger)]

■ **1** utter, say, voice, express, articulate, enunciate, vocalize; put into words. **2 a** see PASS¹ *v.* 18. **b** declare, proclaim, announce, assert, say to be, decree. **3** declare, judge, adjudge, proclaim; accuse of being, stigmatize as, characterize as. □□ **pronouncement** statement, assertion, announcement, proclamation, declaration, avowal, affirmation, asseveration, averment, promulgation; opinion, judgment; decree, edict, dictum, order, ordinance.

pronounced /prənównst/ *adj.* **1** (of a word, sound, etc.) uttered. **2** strongly marked; decided (*a pronounced flavor; a pronounced limp*). □□ **pronouncedly** /-nównsidlee/ *adv.*

■ **2** definite, distinct, unmistakable, marked, strong, clear, plain, well-defined, decided, conspicuous,

noticeable, recognizable, identifiable, obvious, striking, prominent, notable.

pronto /próntō/ *adv. colloq.* promptly; quickly. [Sp. f. L (as PROMPT)]

■ see *quickly* (QUICK).

pronunciation /prənúnseeáyshən/ *n.* **1** the way in which a word is pronounced, esp. with reference to a standard. **2** the act or an instance of pronouncing. **3** a person's way of pronouncing words, etc. [ME f. OF *prononciation* or L *pronuntiatio* (as PRONOUNCE)]

■ **1, 3** enunciation, articulation, elocution, diction, speech, speech pattern, manner of speaking, delivery, accent.

proof /prōōf/ *n., adj., & v.* ● *n.* **1** facts, evidence, argument, etc., establishing or helping to establish a fact (*proof of their honesty; no proof that he was there*). **2** *Law* the spoken or written evidence in a trial. **3** a demonstration or act of proving (*not capable of proof; in proof of my assertion*). **4** a test or trial (*put them to the proof; the proof of the pudding is in the eating*). **5** the standard of strength of distilled alcoholic spirits. **6** *Printing* a trial impression taken from type or film, used for making corrections before final printing. **7** the stages in the resolution of a mathematical or philosophical problem. **8** each of a limited number of impressions from an engraved plate before the ordinary issue is printed and usu. (in full **proof before letters**) before an inscription or signature is added. **9** a photographic print made for selection, etc. **10** a newly struck coin struck from a polished die esp. for collectors, etc. ● *adj.* **1** impervious to penetration, ill effects, etc. (*proof against the harshest weather*). **2** (*in comb.*) able to withstand damage or destruction by a specified agent (*soundproof; childproof*). **3** being of proof alcoholic strength. **4** (of armor) of tried strength. ● *v.tr.* **1** proofread **2** make (something) proof, esp. make (fabric) waterproof. **3** make a proof of (a printed work, engraving, etc.). □ **proof positive** absolutely certain proof. **proof-of-purchase** a sales receipt, product label, etc., that serves as proof that a product has been purchased. **proof sheet** a sheet of printer's proof. **proof spirit** a mixture of alcohol and water having proof strength. □□ **proofless** *adj.* [ME *prōf* *prōve*, earlier *prēf*, etc., f. OF *proeve, prueve* f. LL *proba* f. L *probare* (see PROVE; adj. and sometimes v. formed app. by ellipsis f. phr. *of proof* = proved to be impenetrable]

■ *n.* **1** evidence, documentation, facts, data, certification, testimony, ammunition. **3** verification, corroboration, confirmation, validation, authentication, ratification, substantiation. **4** test, trial; measure; standard, touchstone, criterion. ● *adj.* **1** protected, resistant; impervious, impenetrable, impregnable.

proofread /prṓōfreed/ *v.tr.* (*past* and *past part.* -**read** /-red/) read (esp. printer's proofs) and mark any errors. □□ **proofreader** *n.* **proofreading** *n.*

prop¹ /prop/ *n. & v.* ● *n.* **1** a rigid support, esp. one not an integral part of the thing supported. **2** a person who supplies support, assistance, comfort, etc. **3** *Rugby* a forward at either end of the front row of a scrum. ● *v.* (**propped, propping**) *tr.* (often foll. by *against, up*, etc.) support with or as if with a prop (*propped him against the wall; propped it up with a brick*). [ME prob. f. MDu. *proppe*: cf. MLG, MDu. *proppen* (v.)]

■ *n.* **1** support, brace, stay, buttress, mainstay, upright, vertical, shore, post, pier. **2** see SUPPORT *n.* 2. ● *v.* (*prop up*) support, brace, hold (up), buttress, stay, bolster, uphold, sustain, shore up; lean, stand, rest.

prop² /prop/ *n. Theatr. colloq.* **1** = PROPERTY 3. **2** (in *pl.*) a property man or mistress. [abbr.]

prop³ /prop/ *n. colloq.* an aircraft propeller. [abbr.]

prop. *abbr.* **1** proper; properly. **2** property. **3** proprietary. **4** proprietor. **5** proposition.

/. . ./ **pronunciation** ● **part of speech**

□ **phrases, idioms, and compounds**

□□ **derivatives** ■ **synonym section**

cross-references appear in SMALL CAPITALS or *italics*

---

propaedeutic /prŏpidŏŏtik, -dyŏŏ-/ *adj. & n.* ● *adj.* serving as an introduction to higher study; introductory. ● *n.* (esp. in *pl.*) preliminary learning; a propaedeutic subject, study, etc. □□ **propaedeutical** *adj.* [PRO-² + Gk *paideutikos* of teaching, after Gk *propaideuō* teach beforehand]

propaganda /própəgándə/ *n.* **1 a** an organized program of publicity, selected information, etc., used to propagate a doctrine, practice, etc. **b** usu. *derog.* the information, doctrines, etc., propagated in this way. **2** (**Propaganda**) *RC Ch.* a committee of cardinals responsible for foreign missions. [It. f. mod.L *congregatio de propaganda fide* congregation for propagation of the faith]

■ **1 b** advertising, promotion, publicity; ballyhoo, puffery, *sl.* PR, hype; agitprop, disinformation, newspeak, rumors, lies.

propagandist /própəgándist/ *n.* a member or agent of a propaganda organization; a person who spreads propaganda. □□ **propagandism** *n.* **propagandistic** *adj.* **propagandistically** *adv.* **propagandize** *v.intr. & tr.*

propagate /própəgayt/ **1** *tr.* **a** breed specimens of (a plant, animal, etc.) by natural processes from the parent stock. **b** (*refl.* or *absol.*) (of a plant, animal, etc.) reproduce itself. **2 a** *tr.* disseminate; spread (a statement, belief, theory, etc.). **b** *intr.* grow more widespread or numerous; spread. **3** *tr.* hand down (a quality, etc.) from one generation to another. **4** *tr.* extend the operation of; transmit (a vibration, earthquake, etc.). □□ **propagation** /-gáyshən/ *n.* **propagative** *adj.* [L *propagare propagat-* multiply plants from layers, f. *propago* (as PRO-¹, *pangere* fix, layer)]

■ **1 b** breed, generate, reproduce, multiply, proliferate, procreate. **2 a** publicize, disseminate, dispense, distribute, spread, publish, broadcast, circulate, promulgate, transmit, disperse, propagandize; proclaim, make known, bruit about, noise abroad. **b** multiply, increase, spread, grow, develop.

propagator /própəgaytər/ *n.* **1** a person or thing that propagates. **2** a small box that can be heated, used for germinating seeds or raising seedlings.

propane /prŏpayn/ *n.* a gaseous hydrocarbon of the alkane series used as bottled fuel. ¶ Chem. formula: C_3H_8. [PROPIONIC (ACID) + -ANE¹]

propanoic acid /prŏpənŏik/ *n. Chem.* = PROPIONIC ACID. [PROPANE + -IC]

propanone /prŏpənōn/ *n. Chem. Brit.* = ACETONE. [PROPANE + -ONE]

propel /prəpél/ *v.tr.* (**propelled, propelling**) **1** drive or push forward. **2** urge on; encourage. [ME, = expel, f. L *propellere* (as PRO-¹, *pellere puls-* drive)]

■ **1** drive, impel, move, actuate, set in motion, get moving, push *or* thrust forward, launch. **2** see SPUR *v.*

propellant /prəpélənt/ *n. & adj.* (also **propellent**) ● *n.* **1** a thing that propels. **2** an explosive that fires bullets, etc., from a firearm. **3** a substance used as a reagent in a rocket engine, etc., to provide thrust. ● *adj.* propelling; capable of driving or pushing forward.

propeller /prəpélər/ *n.* **1** a person or thing that propels. **2** a revolving shaft with blades, esp. for propelling a ship or aircraft (cf. *screw propeller*, see SCREW 6). □ **propeller shaft** a shaft transmitting power from an engine to a propeller or to the driven wheels of a motor vehicle. **propeller turbine** a turbo-propeller.

propene /prŏpeen/ *n. Chem.* = PROPYLENE. [PROPANE + ALKENE]

propensity /prəpénsitee/ *n.* (*pl.* **-ies**) an inclination or tendency (*has a propensity for wandering*). [*propense* f. L *propensus* inclined, past part. of *propendēre* (as PRO-¹, *pendēre* hang)]

■ see TENDENCY.

proper /própər/ *adj., adv., & n.* ● *adj.* **1 a** accurate; correct (*in the proper sense of the word; gave him the proper amount*). **b** fit; suitable; right (*at the proper time; do it the proper way*). **2** decent; respectable, esp. excessively so (*not quite proper*). **3** (usu. foll. by *to*) belonging or relating exclusively or distinctively; particular; special (*with the respect proper to them*). **4** (usu. placed after noun) strictly so called; real; genuine (*this is the crypt, not the cathedral proper*). **5** esp. *Brit. colloq.*

thorough; complete (*had a proper row about it*). **6** (usu. placed after noun) *Heraldry* in the natural, not conventional, colors (*a peacock proper*). **7** *dial.* (of a person) handsome; comely. **8** (usu. with possessive pronoun) own (*with my proper eyes*). ● *adv. Brit. dial.* or *colloq.* **1** completely; very (*felt proper daft*). **2** (with reference to speech) in a genteel manner (*learn to talk proper*). ● *n. Eccl.* the part of a service that varies with the season or feast. □ **proper fraction** a fraction that is less than unity, with the numerator less than the denominator. **proper motion** *Astron.* the part of the apparent motion of a fixed star, etc., that is due to its actual movement in space relative to the sun. **proper noun** (or **name**) *Gram.* a name used for an individual person, place, animal, country, title, etc., and spelled with a capital letter, e.g., Jane, London, Everest. **proper psalms** (or **lessons**, etc.) *Eccl.* psalms or lessons, etc., appointed for a particular day. □□ **properness** *n.* [ME f. OF *propre* f. L *proprius* one's own, special]

■ *adj.* **1 a** correct, accurate, exact, right, precise, orthodox, formal, accepted, established. **b** fitting, suitable, suited, correct, right, appropriate, apt, fit, apposite, *archaic* meet. **2** decorous, dignified, genteel, decent, seemly, correct, comme il faut; gentlemanly, ladylike, polite, refined, punctilious, respectable, formal. **3** belonging, relating, own, individual, separate, distinct, correct, specific, special, particular, respective; characteristic, distinctive, peculiar, singular, unique; see also DUE *adj.* 2, 3. **4** see REAL¹ *adj.* 2. **5** complete, perfect, utter, thorough, thoroughgoing, out-and-out, unmitigated, absolute. **7** see BEAUTIFUL 1. **8** (very) own, personal, individual; private. ● *adv.* **2** genteelly, nicely, well, politely, respectably, correctly, fittingly.

properly /própərlee/ *adv.* **1** fittingly; suitably (*do it properly*). **2** accurately; correctly (*properly speaking*). **3** rightly (*he very properly refused*). **4** with decency; respectably (*behave properly*). **5** esp. *Brit. colloq.* thoroughly (*they were properly ashamed*).

■ **1** fittingly, duly, appropriately, well, suitably, rightly, correctly, aptly. **2** correctly, accurately, precisely, exactly, strictly, technically. **4** politely, decently, decorously, nicely, respectably, courteously, with decorum, genteelly, fittingly, correctly, well, becomingly. **5** see *thoroughly* (THOROUGH).

propertied /própərteed/ *adj.* having property, esp. land.

property /própərtee/ *n.* (*pl.* **-ies**) **1 a** something owned; a possession, esp. a house, land, etc. **b** *Law* the right to possession, use, etc. **c** possessions collectively, esp. real estate (*has money in property*). **2** an attribute, quality, or characteristic (*has the property of dissolving grease*). **3** a movable object used on a theater stage, in a movie, etc. **4** *Logic* a quality common to a whole class but not necessary to distinguish it from others. □ **common property** a thing known by most people. **property man** (or **mistress**) a man (or woman) in charge of theatrical properties. **property tax** a tax levied directly on property. [ME through AF f. OF *propriété* f. L *proprietas -tatis* (as PROPER)]

■ **1 c** land, acreage, ground(s), real estate, realty; see also ESTATE 3. **2** characteristic, attribute, quality, feature, trait, mark, hallmark.

prophase /prŏfayz/ *n. Biol.* the phase in cell division in which chromosomes contract and each becomes visible as two chromatids. [PRO-² + PHASE]

prophecy /prófisee/ *n.* (*pl.* **-ies**) **1 a** a prophetic utterance, esp. Biblical. **b** a prediction of future events (*a prophecy of massive inflation*). **2** the faculty, function, or practice of prophesying (*the gift of prophecy*). [ME f. OF *profecie* f. LL *prophetia* f. Gk *prophēteia* (as PROPHET)]

■ **1 b** see FORECAST *n.* **2** prediction, fortune-telling, divination, soothsaying, augury, prognostication, crystal gazing, *formal* vaticination.

prophesy /prófisi/ *v.* (**-ies, -ied**) **1** *tr.* (usu. foll. by *that, who,* etc.) foretell (an event, etc.). **2** *intr.* speak as a prophet; foretell future events. **3** *intr. archaic* expound the Scriptures. □□ **prophesier** /-siər/ *n.* [ME f. OF *profecier* (as PROPHECY)]

■ **1** predict, foretell, forecast, forewarn, prognosticate, *formal* vaticinate; augur, presage, foreshadow, portend, bode, harbinger, herald, promise.

prophet /prófit/ n. (*fem.* **prophetess** /-tis/) **1** a teacher or interpreter of the supposed will of God, esp. any of the Old Testament or Hebrew prophets. **2 a** a person who foretells events. **b** a person who advocates and speaks innovatively for a cause (*a prophet of the new order*). **3** (**the Prophet**) **a** Muhammad. **b** Joseph Smith, founder of the Mormons, or one of his successors. **c** (in *pl.*) the prophetic writings of the Old Testament. **4** *Brit. colloq.* a tipster. □□ **prophethood** n. **prophetism** n. **prophetship** n. [ME f. OF *prophete* f. L *propheta*, *prophetes* f. Gk *prophētēs* spokesman (as PRO-², *phētēs* speaker f. *phēmi* speak)]

■ **2 a** prophesier, oracle, forecaster, seer, soothsayer, clairvoyant, prognosticator, fortune-teller, palmist, augur, diviner, haruspex; sibyl, *formal* vaticinator; (*prophet of doom*) Cassandra, Calamity Jane. **b** see ADVOCATE n. 1. **4** tipster, tout, touter.

prophetic /prəfétik/ adj. **1** (often foll. by *of*) containing a prediction; predicting. **2** of or concerning a prophet. □□ **prophetical** adj. **prophetically** adv. **propheticism** /-sizəm/ n. [F *prophétique* or LL *propheticus* f. Gk *prophētikos* (as PROPHET)]

■ **1** prophetical, predictive, prognostic, divinatory, oracular, inspired, prescient, sibylline, apocalyptic, revelatory, fateful, *formal* vatic.

prophylactic /prófiláktik, próf-/ adj. & n. ● adj. tending to prevent disease. ● n. **1** a preventive medicine or course of action. **2** a condom. [F *prophylactique* or Gk *prophulaktikos* f. *prophulassō* (as PRO-², *phulassō* guard)]

■ adj. see PREVENTIVE adj. ● n. **1** see PREVENTIVE n. **2** condom, sheath, *colloq.* rubber, *Brit. esp. colloq.* French letter.

prophylaxis /prófiláksis, próf-/ n. (*pl.* **prophylaxes** /-seez/) preventive treatment against disease. [mod.L f. PRO-² + Gk *phulaxis* act of guarding]

propinquity /prəpíngkwitee/ n. **1** nearness in space; proximity. **2** close kinship. **3** similarity. [ME f. OF *propinquité* or L *propinquitas* f. *propinquus* near f. *prope* near to]

■ **1** see PROXIMITY. **3** see LIKENESS 1.

propionic acid /prōpeeónik/ n. a colorless sharp-smelling liquid carboxylic acid used for inhibiting the growth of mold in bread. ¶ Chem. formula: C_2H_5COOH. Also called PRO-PANOIC ACID. □□ **propionate** /prōpeeənayt/ n. [F *propionique*, formed as PRO-² + Gk *piōn* fat, as being the first in the series of 'true' fatty acids]

propitiate /prōpísheeayt/ v.tr. appease (an offended person, etc.). □□ **propitiator** n. [L *propitiare* (as PROPITIOUS)]

■ make amends to, placate, answer, compensate; see also HUMOR v. □□ **propitiator** see PEACEMAKER.

propitiation /prōpísheeáyshən/ n. **1** appeasement. **2** *Bibl.* atonement, esp. Christ's. **3** *archaic* a gift, etc., meant to propitiate. [ME f. LL *propitiatio* (as PROPITIATE)]

■ **1, 2** see ATONEMENT.

propitiatory /prōpísheeətawree, -píshə-/ adj. serving or intended to propitiate (*a propitiatory smile*). □□ **propitiatorily** adv. [ME f. LL *propitiatorius* (as PROPITIATE)]

■ conciliatory, pacifying, appeasing, expiatory, placative, pacificatory, placatory, propitiative.

propitious /prəpíshəs/ adj. **1** (of an omen, etc.) favorable. **2** (often foll. by *for, to*) (of the weather, an occasion, etc.) suitable. **3** well-disposed (*the fates were propitious*). □□ **propitiously** adv. **propitiousness** n. [ME f. OF *propicieus* or L *propitius*]

■ **1** favorable, auspicious, promising, advantageous, lucky, fortunate, happy, providential, bright, encouraging, rosy. **2** suitable, apt, fitting, timely, well-timed; fair, favorable, auspicious, benign; see also OPPORTUNE 1a, 3. **3** see FAVORABLE 1a, 3.

propjet /própjet/ n. a jet airplane powered by turboprops.

propolis /própəlis/ n. a red or brown resinous substance collected by bees from buds for use in constructing hives. [L f. Gk *propolis* suburb, bee glue, f. PRO-² + *polis* city]

proponent /prəpónənt/ n. & adj. ● n. a person advocating a

motion, theory, or proposal. ● adj. proposing or advocating a theory, etc. [L *proponere* (as PROPOUND)]

■ n. proposer, promoter, supporter, upholder, backer, subscriber, patron, espouser, adherent, enthusiast, champion, friend, partisan, defender, advocate, exponent, pleader, apologist, spokesman, spokeswoman, spokesperson.

proportion /prəpáwrshən/ n. & v. ● n. **1 a** a comparative part or share (*a large proportion of the profits*). **b** a comparative ratio (*the proportion of births to deaths*). **2** the correct or pleasing relation of things or parts of a thing (*the house has fine proportions*; *exaggerated out of all proportion*). **3** (in *pl.*) dimensions; size (*large proportions*). **4** *Math.* **a** an equality of ratios between two pairs of quantities, e.g., 3:5 and 9:15. **b** a set of such quantities. **c** *Math.* = *rule of three*; see also *direct proportion*, *inverse proportion*. ● v.tr. (usu. foll. by *to*) make (a thing, etc.) proportionate (*must proportion the punishment to the crime*). □ **in proportion 1** by the same factor. **2** without exaggerating (importance, etc.) (*must get the facts in proportion*). □□ **proportioned** adj. (also in *comb.*). **proportionless** adj. **proportionment** n. [ME f. OF *proportion* or L *proportio* (as PRO-¹, PORTION)]

■ n. **1 a** portion, division, share, part, percentage, quota, ration, *colloq.* cut. **b** ratio, relation, relationship, comparison, correlation. **2** balance, agreement, concord, harmony, symmetry, congruity, correspondence, correlation, arrangement. **3** (*proportions*) size, magnitude, dimensions, measurements, extent; volume, capacity, mass, bulk, expanse, scope, range. ● v. adjust, modify, regulate, change, modulate, poise, balance, shape, fit, match, conform.

proportionable /prəpáwrshənəbəl/ adj. = PROPORTIONAL. □□ **proportionably** adv.

proportional /prəpáwrshənəl/ adj. & n. ● adj. in due proportion; comparable (*a proportional increase in the expense*; *resentment proportional to his injuries*). ● n. *Math.* each of the terms of a proportion. □ **proportional representation** an electoral system in which all parties gain seats in proportion to the number of votes cast for them. □□ **proportionality** /-nálitee/ n. **proportionally** adv.

■ adj. proportionate, proportioned, comparable, analogous, analogical, relative, related, correlated, corresponding, compatible, harmonious, consistent, commensurate, in accordance with; balanced, symmetrical.

proportionate /prəpáwrshənət/ adj. = PROPORTIONAL. □□ **proportionately** adv.

proposal /prəpózəl/ n. **1 a** the act or an instance of proposing something. **b** a course of action, etc., so proposed (*the proposal was never carried out*). **2** an offer of marriage.

■ **1** offer, presentation, bid, tender, motion, overture, proposition, program, project, suggestion, recommendation, *literary* proffer; plan, scheme, draft, layout.

propose /prəpóz/ v. **1** tr. (also *absol.*) put forward for consideration or as a plan. **2** tr. (usu. foll. by *to* + infin., or verbal noun) intend; purpose (*propose to open a restaurant*). **3** intr. (usu. foll. by *to*) make an offer of marriage. **4** tr. nominate (a person) as a member of a society, for an office, etc. **5** tr. offer (a person's health, a person, etc.) as a subject for a toast. □□ **proposer** n. [ME f. OF *proposer* f. L *proponere* (as PROPOUND)]

■ **1** offer, tender, proffer; submit, advance, set forth, put forward, propound, recommend, suggest, come up with; *Brit.* table. **2** mean, intend, plan, resolve, have a mind, expect, aim; purpose. **3** ask for a person's hand (in marriage), *colloq.* pop the question. **4** see NOMINATE.

proposition /própəzíshən/ n. & v. ● n. **1** a statement or assertion. **2** a scheme proposed; a proposal. **3** *Logic* a statement consisting of subject and predicate that is subject to proof or disproof. **4** *colloq.* a problem, opponent, prospect, etc., that is to be dealt with (*a difficult proposition*). **5** *Math.* a formal statement of a theorem or problem, often including the demonstration. **6 a** an enterprise, etc., with regard to its likelihood of commercial, etc., success. **b** a person regarded similarly. **7** *colloq.* a sexual proposal. ● *v.tr. colloq.* make a proposal (esp. of sexual intercourse) to. □ **not a proposition** unlikely to succeed. □□ **propositional** *adj.* [ME f. OF *proposition* or L *propositio* (as PROPOUND)]

■ *n.* **1** see STATEMENT 1–3. **2** see SCHEME *n.* 1a. **4** see PROBLEM 1, 2. ● *v.* accost, solicit, make advances *or* overtures to, make a proposition to, *colloq.* make a pass at.

propound /prəpównd/ *v.tr.* **1** offer for consideration; propose. **2** *esp. Brit. Law* produce (a will, etc.) before the proper authority so as to establish its legality. □□ **propounder** *n.* [earlier *propoune, propone* f. L *proponere* (as PRO-¹, *ponere posit-* place): cf. *compound, expound*]

■ **1** put forward, set forth, propose, offer, proffer, suggest, submit, *Brit.* table.

proprietary /prəpríəteree/ *adj.* **1 a** of, holding, or concerning property (*the proprietary classes*). **b** of or relating to a proprietor (*proprietary rights*). **2** held in private ownership. □ **proprietary medicine** any of several drugs, medicines, etc., produced by private companies under brand names. □ **proprietary name** (or **term**) a name of a product, etc., registered by its owner as a trademark and not usable by another without permission. [LL *proprietarius* (as PROPERTY)]

proprietor /prəpríətər/ *n.* (*fem.* **proprietress**) **1** a holder of property. **2** the owner of a business, etc., esp. of a hotel. □□ **proprietorial** /-táwreeəl/ *adj.* **proprietorially** /-táwreeəlee/ *adv.* **proprietorship** *n.*

■ **1** owner, landowner, landlady, landlord, landholder, property owner. **2** owner, landlord, landlady, innkeeper, hotelkeeper, hotelier, manager.

propriety /prəprí-itee/ *n.* (*pl.* **-ies**) **1** fitness; rightness (*doubt the propriety of refusing him*). **2** correctness of behavior or morals (*highest standards of propriety*). **3** (in *pl.*) the details or rules of correct conduct (*must observe the proprieties*). [ME, = ownership, peculiarity f. OF *propriété* PROPERTY]

■ **1** correctness, properness, rightness, appropriateness, fitness, seemliness, decorum; advisability, wisdom. **2** decorum, politeness, courtesy, politesse, refinement, sedateness, dignity, decency, breeding, respectability, gentility, grace, mannerliness. **3** (*proprieties*) protocol, good *or* proper form, punctilio, etiquette, social graces, civilities, formality *or* formalities, social convention(s) *or* niceties, convenances, tradition.

proprioceptive /prṓpreeəséptiv/ *adj.* relating to stimuli produced and perceived within an organism, esp. relating to the position and movement of the body. [L *proprius* own + RECEPTIVE]

proptosis /proptṓsis/ *n. Med.* protrusion or displacement, esp. of an eye. [LL f. Gk *proptōsis* (as PRO-², *piptō* fall)]

propulsion /prəpúlshən/ *n.* **1** the act or an instance of driving or pushing forward. **2** an impelling influence. □□ **propulsive** /-púlsiv/ *adj.* [med.L *propulsio* f. L *propellere* (as PROPEL)]

■ **2** drive, impulse, impetus, thrust, power, driving force, momentum, push.

propyl /prṓpil/ *n. Chem.* the univalent radical of propane. ¶ *Chem.* formula: C_3H_7. [PROPIONIC (ACID) + -YL]

propyla *pl.* of PROPYLON.

propylaeum /prṓpilée-əm, prṓ-/ *n.* (*pl.* **propylaea** /-lée-ə/) **1** the entrance to a temple. **2** (**the Propylaeum**) the entrance to the Acropolis at Athens. [L f. Gk *propulaion* (as PRO-², *pulē* gate)]

propylene /prṓpəleen/ *n. Chem.* a gaseous hydrocarbon of the alkene series used in the manufacture of chemicals. ¶ *Chem.* formula: C_3H_6.

propylon /prṓpəlon, prṓ-/ *n.* (*pl.* **propylons** or **propyla** /-lə/) = PROPYLAEUM. [L f. Gk *propulon* (as PRO-², *pulē* gate)]

pro rata /prō ráytə, raʹatə/ *adj.* & *adv.* ● *adj.* proportional. ● *adv.* proportionally. [L, = according to the rate]

prorate /próráyt/ *v.tr.* allocate or distribute pro rata. □□ **proration** *n.*

prorogue /prōrṓg/ *v.* (**prorogues, prorogued, proroguing**) **1** *tr.* discontinue the meetings of (a parliament, etc.) without dissolving it. **2** *intr.* (of a parliament, etc.) be prorogued. □□ **prorogation** /prṓrəgáyshən/ *n.* [ME *proroge* f. OF *proroger, -guer* f. L *prorogare* prolong (as PRO-¹, *rogare* ask)]

■ **1** see SUSPEND 2.

pros- /pros/ *prefix* **1** to; toward. **2** in addition. [Gk f. *pros* (prep.)]

prosaic /prōzáyik/ *adj.* **1** like prose; lacking poetic beauty. **2** unromantic; dull; commonplace (*took a prosaic view of life*). □□ **prosaically** *adv.* **prosaicness** *n.* [F *prosaïque* or LL *prosaicus* (as PROSE)]

■ **2** dull, banal, tedious, prosy, commonplace, pedestrian, flat, routine, everyday, ordinary, common, workaday, mediocre, undistinguished, bland, characterless, plain, trite, tired, lifeless, dead, dry, jejune, boring, tiresome, hackneyed, unimaginative, unpoetic, unromantic, uninspiring, uninspired, insipid, uninteresting, humdrum, monotonous, run-of-the-mill, *colloq.* ho-hum, moldy.

prosaist /prṓzayist/ *n.* **1** a prose writer. **2** a prosaic person. □□ **prosaism** *n.* [F *prosaïste* f. L *prosa* PROSE]

proscenium /prəséeneeəm/ *n.* (*pl.* **prosceniums** or **proscenia** /-neeə/) **1** the part of the stage in front of the drop or curtain, usu. with the enclosing arch. **2** the stage of an ancient theater. [L f. Gk *proskēnion* (as PRO-², *skēnē* stage)]

prosciutto /prōshóōtō/ *n.* (*pl.* **-os**) specially cured ham, usu. sliced thin and used as an hors d'oeuvre. [It.]

proscribe /prəskríb/ *v.tr.* **1** banish; exile (*proscribed from the club*). **2** put (a person) outside the protection of the law. **3** reject or denounce (a practice, etc.) as dangerous, etc. □□ **proscription** /-skrípshən/ *n.* **proscriptive** /-skríptiv/ *adj.* [L *proscribere* (as PRO-¹, *scribere* write)]

■ **1** see EXPEL 1–3. **3** see FORBID 2. □□ **proscription** see PROHIBITION.

prose /prōz/ *n.* & *v.* ● *n.* **1** the ordinary form of the written or spoken language (opp. POETRY, VERSE) (*Milton's prose works*). **2** a passage of prose, esp. for translation into a foreign language. **3** a tedious speech or conversation. **4** a plain matter-of-fact quality (*the prose of existence*). **5** *Eccl.* = SEQUENCE 8. ● *v.* **1** *intr.* (usu. foll. by *about, away,* etc.) talk tediously (*was prosing away about his dog*). **2** *tr.* turn (a poem, etc.) into prose. **3** *tr.* write prose. □ **prose idyll** a short description in prose of a picturesque, esp. rustic, incident, character, etc. **prose poem** (or **poetry**) a piece of imaginative poetic writing in prose. □□ **proser** *n.* [ME f. OF f. L *prosa* (*oratio*) straightforward (discourse), fem. of *prosus*, earlier *prorsus* direct]

■ *v.* **1** see SPOUT *v.* 2. **2** prosify.

prosector /prōséktər/ *n.* a person who dissects dead bodies in preparation for an anatomical lecture, etc. [LL = anatomist, f. *prosecare prosect-* (as PRO-¹, *secare* cut), perh. after F *prosecteur*]

prosecute /prósikyōōt/ *v.tr.* **1** (also *absol.*) **a** institute legal proceedings against (a person). **b** institute a prosecution with reference to (a claim, crime, etc.) (*decided not to prosecute*). **2** follow up; pursue (an inquiry, studies, etc.). **3** carry on (a trade, pursuit, etc.). □□ **prosecutable** *adj.* [ME f. L *prosequi prosecut-* (as PRO-¹, *sequi* follow)]

■ **1 a** arraign, indict, charge, put on trial, bring to trial, try, take to court, sue, bring suit *or* action against, put in the dock. **2** pursue, follow up *or* through, see *or* carry through, persist with, go on with. **3** carry on *or* out, perform, do, conduct, follow, engage in, practice, continue.

prosecution /prósikyōōshən/ *n.* **1 a** the institution and carrying on of a criminal charge in a court. **b** the carrying on of legal proceedings against a person. **c** the prosecuting party in a court case (*the prosecution denied this*). **2** the act or an instance of prosecuting (*met her in the prosecution of his hobby*). [OF *prosecution* or LL *prosecutio* (as PROSECUTE)]

■ **2** see EXECUTION 2.

prosecutor /prósikyo͞otər/ n. (also **prosecuting attorney**) a person who prosecutes, esp. in a criminal court. □□ **prosecutorial** /-táwreeəl/ adj.

proselyte /prósilit/ n. & v. ● n. **1** a person converted, esp. recently, from one opinion, creed, party, etc., to another. **2** a convert to Judaism. ● v.tr. = PROSELYTIZE. □□ **proselytism** /-səlitízəm/ n. [ME f. LL proselytus f. Gk prosēluthos stranger, convert (as PROS-, stem ēluth- of erkhomai come)]
■ n. convert, neophyte.

proselytize /prósilitīz/ v.tr. (also absol.) convert (a person or people) from one belief, etc., to another, esp. habitually. □□ **proselytizer** n.
■ □□ **proselytizer** see MISSIONARY n.

prosenchyma /proséngkimə/ n. a plant tissue of elongated cells with interpenetrating tapering ends, occurring esp. in vascular tissue. □□ **prosenchymal** adj. **prosenchymatous** /-kímətəs/ adj. [Gk pros toward + egkhuma infusion, after parenchyma]

prosify /prózifī/ v. (-ies, -ied) **1** tr. turn into prose. **2** tr. make prosaic. **3** intr. write prose.

prosit /prózit/ int. an expression used in drinking a person's health. [G f. L, = may it benefit]

prosody /prósədee/ n. **1** the theory and practice of versification; the laws of meter. **2** the study of speech rhythms. □□ **prosodic** /prəsódik/ adj. **prosodist** n. [ME f. L prosodia accent f. Gk prosōidia (as PROS-, ODE)]

prosopography /prósəpógrəfee/ n. (pl. -ies) **1** a description of a person's appearance, personality, social and family connections, career, etc. **2** the study of such descriptions, esp. in Roman history. □□ **prosopographer** n. **prosopographic** /-pəgráfik/ adj. **prosopographical** adj. [mod.L prosopographia f. Gk prosōpon face, person]
■ **1** see RÉSUMÉ 2, PROFILE n. 2a.

prosopopoeia /prósəpəpee͞ə/ n. the rhetorical introduction of a pretended speaker or the personification of an abstract thing. [L f. Gk prosōpopoiia f. prosōpon person + poieō make]

prospect /próspekt/ n. & v. ● n. **1 a** (often in pl.) an expectation, esp. of success in a career, etc. (his prospects were brilliant; offers a gloomy prospect; no prospect of success). **b** something one has to look forward to (don't relish the prospect of meeting him). **2** an extensive view of landscape, etc. (a striking prospect). **3** a mental picture (a new prospect in his mind). **4 a** a place likely to yield mineral deposits. **b** a sample of ore for testing. **c** the resulting yield. **5** a possible or probable customer, subscriber, etc. ● v. **1** intr. (usu. foll. by for) **a** explore a region for gold, etc. **b** look out for or search for something. **2** tr. **a** explore (a region) for gold, etc. **b** work (a mine) experimentally. **c** (of a mine) promise a specified yield. □ **in prospect 1** in sight; within view. **2** within the range of expectation, likely. **prospect well** (or **ill**, etc.) (of a mine) promise well (or ill, etc.). □□ **prospectless** adj.

prospector /próspektər/ n. [ME f. L prospectus: see PROSPECTUS]
■ n. **1 a** (prospects) expectation(s); future, outlook, chances, hopes, possibilities, opportunities. **2** view, scene, panorama, landscape, vista, sight, spectacle.
● v. **1** (prospect for) search for, look for, seek, quest after or for, pursue, hunt (for), try to find, be after.
□ **in prospect** in or within sight or view, in the offing, on the horizon, in store, in the wind, projected, likely, probable, possible, on the table.

prospective /prəspéktiv/ adj. **1** concerned with or applying to the future (implies a prospective obligation) (cf. RETROSPECTIVE). **2** some day to be; expected; future (prospective bridegroom). □□ **prospectively** adv. **prospectiveness** n. [obs. F prospectif -ive or LL prospectivus (as PROSPECTUS)]
■ **2** expected, future, forthcoming, coming, approaching, imminent, nearing, pending, impending, destined, incipient, -to-be, disp. anticipated.

prospectus /prəspéktəs/ n. a printed document advertising or describing a school, commercial enterprise, forthcoming book, etc. [L, = prospect f. prospicere (as PRO-¹, specere look)]
■ brochure, pamphlet, booklet, leaflet; catalog.

prosper /próspər/ v. **1** intr. succeed; thrive (nothing he touches

prospers). **2** tr. make successful (Heaven prosper him). [ME f. OF prosperer or L prosperare (as PROSPEROUS)]
■ **1** flourish, thrive, succeed, progress, get ahead, grow, develop, literary fare well; profit, gain, become wealthy, grow rich, make a fortune, make good, colloq. make it, make a pile.

prosperity /prospéritee/ n. a state of being prosperous; wealth or success.
■ success, (good) fortune, wealth, riches, affluence, money, plenty, prosperousness, opulence, bounty, literary weal.

prosperous /próspərəs/ adj. **1** successful; rich (a prosperous merchant). **2** flourishing; thriving (a prosperous enterprise). **3** auspicious (a prosperous wind). □□ **prosperously** adv. **prosperousness** n. [ME f. obs. F prospereus f. L prosper(us)]
■ **1** rich, wealthy, moneyed, affluent, well-to-do, well-off, colloq. well-heeled, flush, sl. loaded; successful, fortunate, halcyon; (be prosperous) be in clover, be on velvet, colloq. be rolling (in it or money), be in the money or bucks, be on easy street. **2** thriving, flourishing, booming, prospering, thrifty; see also SUCCESSFUL. **3** see BENIGN 2, 3.

prostaglandin /próstəglándin/ n. any of a group of hormonelike substances causing contraction of the muscles in mammalian (esp. uterine) tissues, etc. [G f. PROSTATE + GLAND¹ + -IN]

prostate /próstayt/ n. (in full **prostate gland**) a gland surrounding the neck of the bladder in male mammals and releasing a fluid forming part of the semen. □□ **prostatic** /-státik/ adj. [F f. mod.L prostata f. Gk prostatēs one that stands before (as PRO-², statos standing)]

prosthesis /prósthéesis/ n. (pl. **prostheses** /-seez/) **1** an artificial part supplied to replace a missing body part, e.g., a false breast, leg, tooth, etc. **2** Gram. the addition of a letter or syllable at the beginning of a word, e.g., be- in beloved. □□ **prosthetic** /-thétik/ adj. **prosthetically** adv. [LL f. Gk prosthesis f. prostithēmi (as PROS-, tithēmi place)]

prosthetics /prósthétiks/ n.pl. (usu. treated as sing.) the branch of medicine or dentistry supplying and fitting prostheses.

prostitute /próstito͞ot, -tyo͞ot/ n. & v. ● n. **1 a** a woman who engages in sexual activity for payment. **b** (usu. **male prostitute**) a man or boy who engages in sexual activity, esp. with homosexual men, for payment. **2** a person who debases himself or herself for personal gain. ● v.tr. **1** (esp. refl.) make a prostitute of (esp. oneself). **2** a misuse (one's talents, skills, etc.) for money. **b** offer (oneself, one's honor, etc.) for unworthy ends, esp. for money. □□ **prostitution** /-to͞oshən/ n. **prostitutor** n. [L prostituere prostitut- offer for sale (as PRO-¹, statuere set up, place)]
■ n. **1 a** whore, call girl, streetwalker, slut, trollop, drab, fille de joie, lady of the night, lady of easy virtue, fallen or loose woman, archaic cocotte, wench, trull, woman of the streets, harlot, archaic or rhet. strumpet, derog. scarlet woman, literary hetaera, courtesan, doxy, sl. tart, hustler, working girl, pro, moll, floozy, hooker, Austral. sl. chromo. **b** catamite, gigolo; Brit. rent-boy. ● v. **2 a** misuse, devalue, abuse, corrupt, misemploy, misapply, pervert. **b** degrade, demean, lower, cheapen, debase, defile, discredit, shame, disgrace; see also PROFANE v.
□□ **prostitution** whoredom, archaic harlotry, colloq. or joc. the oldest profession; degradation, debasement, profanation, defilement, desecration, misuse, abuse, devaluation, lowering, corruption.

prostrate /próstrayt/ adj. & v. ● adj. **1 a** lying face downwards, esp. in submission. **b** lying horizontally. **2** overcome, esp. by grief, exhaustion, etc. (prostrate with self-pity). **3** Bot. growing along the ground. ● v.tr. **1** lay (a person, etc.) flat on the ground. **2** (refl.) throw (oneself) down in submission, etc. **3** (of fatigue, illness, etc.) overcome; reduce to extreme physical weakness. □□ **prostration** /prostráyshən/ *n.* [ME f. L *prostratus* past part. of *prosternere* (as PRO-¹, *sternere* stratlay flat)]

■ *adj.* **1** prone, horizontal, stretched out, procumbent, recumbent. **2** overwhelmed, overcome, overpowered, crushed, brought *or* laid low, paralyzed, brought down, humbled, helpless, powerless, impotent, defenseless, disarmed; exhausted, drained, fatigued, spent, worn-out, wearied, weary, tired (out). **3** *Bot.* procumbent, repent, *Bot. & Zool.* decumbent. ● *v.* **1** see LAY¹ *v.* 1. **2** (*prostrate oneself*) throw oneself down, lie down, kowtow, bow (down), bow and scrape, grovel, kneel, fall to *or* on one's knees, submit. **3** overwhelm, overcome, overpower, crush, lay *or* bring low, paralyze, bring down, make helpless, *colloq.* floor; exhaust, fatigue, weary, wear down *or* out, tire (out). □□ **prostration** submission, servility; weariness, exhaustion, tiredness, weakness, debility, feebleness, enervation, lassitude, paralysis; despair, misery, desolation, desperation, dejection, depression, despondency, wretchedness, unhappiness, grief, woefulness, *archaic or literary* woe.

prosy /prṓzee/ *adj.* (**prosier, prosiest**) tedious; commonplace; dull (*prosy talk*). □□ **prosily** *adv.* **prosiness** *n.*
■ see TEDIOUS.

Prot. *abbr.* Protestant.

protactinium /prṓtaktíneeəm/ *n. Chem.* a radioactive metallic element whose chief isotope yields actinium by decay. ¶ Symb.: **Pa**. [G (as PROTO-, ACTINIUM)]

protagonist /prōtágənist/ *n.* **1** the chief person in a drama, story, etc. **2** the leading person in a contest, etc.; a principal performer. **3** (usu. foll. by *of, for*) *disp.* an advocate or champion of a cause, course of action, etc. (*a protagonist of women's rights*). [Gk *prōtagōnistēs* (as PROTO-, *agōnistēs* actor)]
■ **1, 2** hero, heroine; principal, lead, leading role, title role; (*be the protagonist*) play first fiddle, take the lead. **3** leader, supporter, advocate, prime mover, moving spirit, champion, standard-bearer, exponent.

protamine /prṓtəmeen, protámin/ *n.* any of a group of proteins found in association with chromosomal DNA in the sperm of birds and fish. [PROTO- + AMINE]

protasis /prṓtəsis/ *n.* (*pl.* **protases** /-seez/) the clause expressing the condition in a conditional sentence. □□ **protatic** /prōtátik/ *adj.* [L, f. Gk *protasis* proposition (as PRO-², *teinō* stretch)]

protea /prṓteeə/ *n.* any shrub of the genus *Protea* native to S. Africa, with conelike flower heads. [mod.L f. PROTEUS, with ref. to the many species]

protean /prṓteeən, -teeán/ *adj.* **1** variable; taking many forms. **2** (of an artist, writer, etc.) versatile. [after *Proteus*: see PROTEUS]
■ **1** variable, ever-changing, multiform, changeable, polymorphous, polymorphic, *literary* mutable. **2** see VERSATILE 1.

protease /prṓteeays/ *n.* any enzyme able to hydrolyze proteins and peptides by proteolysis. [PROTEIN + -ASE]

protect /prətékt/ *v.tr.* **1** (often foll. by *from, against*) keep (a person, thing, etc.) safe; defend; guard (*goggles protected her eyes from dust; guards protected the military base*). **2** *Econ.* shield (domestic industry) from competition by imposing import duties on foreign goods. **3** cover; provide funds to meet (a bill, bank draft, etc.). [L *protegere protect-* (as PRO-¹, *tegere* cover)]
■ **1** defend, guard, safeguard, keep safe, shield, cover, screen; care for, preserve, keep, shelter, watch over, take care of, conserve.

protection /prətékshən/ *n.* **1 a** the act or an instance of protecting. **b** the state of being protected; defense (*affords protection against the weather*). **c** a thing, person, or animal that provides protection (*bought a dog as protection*). **2** (also **protectionism**) *Econ.* the theory or practice of protecting domestic industries. **3** *colloq.* **a** immunity from molestation obtained by payment to organized criminals, etc., under threat of violence. **b** (in full **protection money**) payment, as

bribes, made to police, etc., for overlooking criminal activities. **c** (in full **protection money**) the money so paid, esp. on a regular basis. **4** = *safe-conduct.* **5** *archaic* the keeping of a woman as a mistress. □□ **protectionist** *n.* [ME f. OF *protection* or LL *protectio* (as PROTECT)]
■ **1 a** care, guardianship, custody, charge, safekeeping. **b, c** defense, screen, shield, barrier, aegis, guard, bulwark, buffer, shelter, refuge, haven, sanctuary, tower; security, safety, immunity, preservation. **3 b** see BLACKMAIL *n.* 1.

protective /prətéktiv/ *adj. & n.* ● *adj.* **1** protecting; intended or intending to protect. **2** (of a person) tending to protect in a possessive way. ● *n. Brit.* something that protects, esp. a condom. □ **protective coloring** coloring disguising or camouflaging a plant or animal. **protective custody** the detention of a person for his or her own protection. □□ **protectively** *adv.* **protectiveness** *n.*
■ *adj.* **1** protecting, preservative, defensive. **2** overprotective, possessive; jealous.

protector /prətéktər/ *n.* (*fem.* **protectress** /-tris/) **1 a** a person who protects. **b** a guardian or patron. **2** *hist.* a regent in charge of a kingdom during the minority, absence, etc., of the sovereign. **3** (often in *comb.*) a thing or device that protects. **4** (**Protector**) (in full **Lord Protector of the Commonwealth**) *Brit. hist.* the title of Oliver Cromwell 1653–58 and his son Richard Cromwell 1658–59. □□ **protectoral** *adj.* **protectorship** *n.* [ME f. OF *protecteur* f. LL *protector* (as PROTECT)]
■ **1** defender, guardian (angel), champion, knight in shining armor, bodyguard, esp. *Brit. sl.* minder; patron.

protectorate /prətéktərət/ *n.* **1 a** a nation that is controlled and protected by another. **b** such a relation of one nation to another. **2** *hist.* **a** the office of the protector of a kingdom or nation. **b** the period of this, esp. in England under the Cromwells 1653–59.

protégé /prṓtizhay, prṓtizháy/ *n.* (*fem.* **protégée** *pronunc.* same) a person under the protection, patronage, tutelage, etc., of another. [F, past part. of *protéger* f. L *protegere* PROTECT]
■ ward, charge, dependent, foster child, fosterling; student, pupil.

protein /prṓteen/ *n.* any of a group of organic compounds composed of one or more chains of amino acids and forming an essential part of all living organisms. □□ **proteinaceous** /-teenáyshəs/ *adj.* **proteinic** /-teénik/ *adj.* **proteinous** /-teénəs/ *adj.* [F *protéine*, G *Protein* f. Gk *prōteios* primary]

pro tem /prō tém/ *adj. & adv. colloq.* = PRO TEMPORE. [abbr.]

pro tempore /prō témpəree/ *adj. & adv.* for the time being. [L]
■ *adj.* see TEMPORARY *adj.* ● *adv.* see *temporarily* (TEMPORARY).

proteolysis /prṓteeólisis/ *n.* the splitting of proteins or peptides by the action of enzymes esp. during the process of digestion. □□ **proteolytic** /-teeəlítik/ *adj.* [mod.L f. PROTEIN + -LYSIS]

Proterozoic /prṓtərəzṓik, prṓ-/ *adj. & n. Geol.* ● *adj.* of or relating to the later part of the Precambrian era, characterized by the oldest forms of life. ● *n.* this time. [Gk *proteros* former + *zōē* life, *zōos* living]

protest *n. & v.* ● *n.* /prṓtest/ **1** a statement of dissent or disapproval; a remonstrance (*made a protest*). **2** (often *attrib.*) a usu. public demonstration of objection to government, etc., policy (*marched in protest; protest demonstration*). **3** a solemn declaration. **4** *Law* a written declaration, usu. by a notary public, that a bill has been presented and payment or acceptance refused. ● *v.* /prətést, prō-/ **1** *intr.* (usu. foll. by *against, at, about,* etc.) make a protest against an action, proposal, etc. **2** *tr.* (often foll. by *that* + clause; also *absol.*) affirm (one's innocence, etc.) solemnly, esp. in reply to an accusation, etc. **3** *tr. Law* write or obtain a protest in regard to (a bill). **4** *tr.* object to (a decision, etc.). □ **under protest** unwillingly. □□ **protester** *n.* **protestingly** *adv.* **protestor** *n.* [ME f. OF *protest* (n.), *protester* (v.), f. L *protestari* (as PRO-¹, *testari* assert f. *testis* witness)]
■ *n.* **1** remonstrance, objection, complaint, outcry,

clamor, grumble, squawk, fuss, grievance, protestation, demur, demurral, expostulation, *Law* demurrer, *colloq.* gripe, grouse, *sl.* beef. **3** see ASSERTION 1, 2.
● *v.* **1** object, complain, grumble, dissent, demur, demonstrate, expostulate, remonstrate, declaim, rebel, make a fuss, make *or* kick up a fuss, *colloq.* gripe, grouse, *sl.* beef, squeal; (*protest at* or *against* or *about*) kick, take issue with. **2** assert, declare, asseverate, affirm, announce, profess, insist on, *archaic or rhet.* avouch, *formal* aver. □ **under protest** unwillingly, reluctantly, involuntarily, begrudgingly, grudgingly, without good grace, against one's better judgment; under duress.

Protestant /prótistǝnt/ *n. & adj.* ● *n.* **1** a member or follower of any of the western Christian Churches that are separate from the Roman Catholic Church in accordance with the principles of the Reformation. **2** (**protestant**) /also prǝtéstǝnt/ a protesting person. ● *adj.* **1** of or relating to any of the Protestant Churches or their members, etc. **2** (**protestant**) /also prǝtéstǝnt/ protesting. □□ **Protestantism** *n.* **Protestantize** *v.tr. & intr.* [mod.L *protestans*, part. of L *protestari* (see PROTEST)]

protestation /prótistáyshǝn, prṓte-/ *n.* **1** a strong affirmation. **2** a protest. [ME f. OF *protestation* or LL *protestatio* (as PROTEST)]
■ **1** see ASSERTION 1, 2. **2** see PROTEST *n.* 1.

Proteus /prṓteeǝs, -tyṓōs/ *n.* **1** a changing or inconstant person or thing. **2** (**proteus**) any bacterium of the genus *Proteus*, usu. found in the intestines and feces of animals. [L f. Gk *Prōteus* a sea god able to take various forms at will]

prothalamium /prṓthǝláymeeǝm/ *n.* (also **prothalamion** /-meeǝn/) (*pl.* **prothalamia** /-meeǝ/) a song or poem to celebrate a forthcoming wedding. [title of a poem by Spenser, after *epithalamium*]

prothallium /prṓtháleeǝm/ *n.* (*pl.* **prothallia** /-eeǝ/) *Bot.* the gametophyte of certain plants, esp. a fern. [mod.L f. PRO-2 + Gk *thallion* dimin. of *thallos*: see PROTHALLUS]

prothallus /prṓthálǝs/ *n.* (*pl.* **prothalli** /-lī/) = PROTHALLIUM [mod.L f. PRO-2 + Gk *thallos* green shoot]

prothesis /próthisis/ *n.* (*pl.* **protheses** /-seez/) *Gram.* = PROSTHESIS 2. □□ **prothetic** /prǝthétik/ *adj.* [Gk f. *protithēmi* (as PRO-2, *tithēmi* place)]

prothonotary /prṓthaánǝteree, prṓthǝnṓtǝree/ *n.* a chief clerk in some law courts, orig. in the Byzantine court.

protist /prṓtist/ *n.* any usu. unicellular organism of the kingdom Protista, with both plant and animal characteristics, including bacteria, algae, and protozoa. □□ **protistology** /-tistólǝjee/ *n.* [mod.L *Protista* f. Gk *prōtista* neut. pl. superl. f. *prōtos* first]

protium /prṓteeǝm, -sheeǝm/ *n.* the ordinary isotope of hydrogen as distinct from heavy hydrogen (cf. DEUTERIUM, TRITIUM). [mod.L f. PRO-2 + -IUM]

proto- /prṓtō/ *comb. form* **1** original; primitive (*protoGermanic*; *protoSlavic*). **2** first; original (*protomartyr*; *protophyte*). [Gk *prōto-* f. *prōtos* first]

protocol /prṓtǝkawl, -kol/ *n. & v.* ● *n.* **1 a** official, esp. diplomatic, formality and etiquette observed on governmental or military occasions, etc. **b** the rules, formalities, etc., of any procedure, group, etc. **2** the original draft of a diplomatic document, esp. of the terms of a treaty agreed to in conference and signed by the parties. **3** a formal statement of a transaction. **4** the official formulae at the beginning and end of a charter, papal bull, etc. **5** a plan or record of experimental observation, medical treatment, etc. **6** *Computing* a set of rules governing the electronic transmission of data between computers. ● *v.* (**protocolled**, **protocolling**) **1** *intr.* draw up a protocol or protocols. **2** *tr.* record in a protocol. [orig. Sc. *prothocoll* f. OF *prothocole* f. med.L *protocollum* f. Gk *protokollon* flyleaf (as PROTO-, *kolla* glue)]
■ *n.* **1** rule(s) *or* code(s) *or* standard(s) of behavior, conventions, customs, formality, form, etiquette, politesse, manners, practice, usage. **2** draft, outline.

protolanguage /prṓtōlanggwij/ *n.* a language from which other languages are believed to have been derived.

protomartyr /prṓtōmaártǝr/ *n.* the first martyr in any cause, esp. the first Christian martyr, St. Stephen.

proton /prṓton/ *n. Physics* a stable elementary particle with a positive electric charge, equal in magnitude to that of an electron, and occurring in all atomic nuclei. □□ **protonic** /prǝtónik/ *adj.* [Gk, neut. of *prōtos* first]

protonotary /prǝtaánǝteree, prṓtǝnṓtǝree/ *n.* (*pl.* **-ies**) var. of PROTHONOTARY. □ **Protonotary Apostolic** (or **Apostolical**) a member of the college of prelates who register papal acts, direct the canonization of saints, etc. [med.L *protonotarius* f. late Gk *protonotarios* (as PROTO-, NOTARY)]

protophyte /prṓtǝfīt/ *n.* a unicellular plant bearing gametes.

protoplasm /prṓtǝplazǝm/ *n.* the material comprising the living part of a cell, consisting of a nucleus embedded in membrane-enclosed cytoplasm. □□ **protoplasmal** /-plazmǝl/ *adj.* **protoplasmatic** /-mátik/ *adj.* **protoplasmic** *adj.* [Gk *protoplasma* (as PROTO-, PLASMA)]

protoplast /prṓtǝplast/ *n.* the protoplasm of one cell. □□ **protoplastic** *adj.* [F *protoplaste* or LL *protoplastus* f. Gk *protoplastos* (as PROTO-, *plassō* mold)]

prototherian /prṓtōtheéreeǝn/ *n. & adj.* ● *n.* any mammal of the subclass Prototheria, including monotremes. ● *adj.* of or relating to this subclass. [PROTO- + Gk *thēr* wild beast]

prototype /prṓtǝtip/ *n.* **1** an original thing or person of which or whom copies, imitations, improved forms, representations, etc., are made. **2** a trial model or preliminary version of a vehicle, machine, etc. **3** a thing or person representative of a type; an exemplar. □□ **prototypal** *adj.* **prototypic** /-típik/ *adj.* **prototypical**. **prototypically** *adv.* [F *prototype* or LL *prototypus* f. Gk *prototupos* (as PROTO-, TYPE)]
■ **1** model, archetype, pattern, exemplar, first, original, source; master. **3** example, instance, illustration, sample, pattern, norm, paragon, epitome, exemplar, model, standard.

protozoan /prṓtǝzṓǝn/ *n. & adj.* ● *n.* (also **protozoon** /-zṓon/) (*pl.* **protozoa** /-zṓǝ/ or **protozoans**) any usu. unicellular and microscopic organism of the subkingdom Protozoa, including amoebas and ciliates. ● *adj.* (also **protozoic** /-zṓ-ik/) of or relating to this phylum. □□ **protozoal** *adj.* [mod.L (as PROTO-, Gk *zōion* animal)]

protract /prṓträkt, prǝ-/ *v.tr.* **1** prolong or lengthen in space or esp. time (*protracted their stay for some weeks*). **b** (as **protracted** *adj.*) of excessive length or duration (*a protracted illness*). **2** draw (a plan, etc.) to scale. □□ **protractedly** *adv.* **protractedness** *n.* [L *protrahere protract-* (as PRO-1, *trahere* draw)]
■ **1 a** see LENGTHEN 1. **b** (**protracted**) long, long-drawn-out, interminable, prolonged, overlong, never-ending, extended, stretched out, marathon, endless, everlasting, long-winded.

protractile /prṓträktil, -til, prǝ-/ *adj.* (of a part of the body, etc.) capable of being protruded or extended.

protraction /prṓträkshǝn, prǝ-/ *n.* **1** the act or an instance of protracting; the state of being protracted. **2** a drawing to scale. **3** the action of a protractor muscle. [F *protraction* or LL *protractio* (as PROTRACT)]

protractor /prṓträktǝr, prǝ-/ *n.* **1** an instrument for measuring angles, usu. in the form of a graduated semicircle. **2** a muscle serving to extend a limb, etc.

protrude /prṓtrōōd/ *v.* **1** *intr.* extend beyond or above a surface; project. **2** *tr.* thrust or cause to thrust forth. □□ **protrudent** *adj.* **protrusible** /-sǝbǝl, -zǝ-/ *adj.* **protrusion** /-trṓōzhǝn/ *n.* **protrusive** *adj.* [L *protrudere* (as PRO-1, *trudere trus-* thrust)]
■ **1** stick out, jut (out), project, extend, poke out, stand out, thrust out *or* forward; bulge, balloon, bag (out), belly (out); pop, goggle. □□ **protrusion** projection, protuberance, prominence, swelling, excrescence, outgrowth, tumescence, bump, lump, knob, bulge.

/.../ **pronunciation** ● **part of speech**
□ **phrases, idioms, and compounds**
□□ **derivatives** ■ **synonym section**
cross-references appear in SMALL CAPITALS or *italics*

protrusile /prətrŏosil, -sĭl/ adj. (of a limb, etc.) capable of being thrust forward. [PRO-¹ + extrusile: see EXTRUDE]

protuberant /prŏtŏobərənt, -tyŏo-, prə-/ adj. bulging out; prominent (protuberant eyes). □□ **protuberance** n. [LL protuberare (as PRO-¹, tuber bump)]

■ protrusive, protruding, bulging, gibbous, bulbous; extrusive, excrescent, extruding, projecting, overhanging; prominent; undeniable.

proud /prowd/ adj. 1 feeling greatly honored or pleased (am proud to know him; proud of his friendship). 2 a (often foll. by of) valuing oneself, one's possessions, etc., highly, or esp. too highly; haughty; arrogant (proud of his ancient name). b (often in comb.) having a proper pride; satisfied (proud of a job well done). 3 a (of an occasion, etc.) justly arousing pride (a proud day for us; a proud sight). b (of an action, etc.) showing pride (a proud wave of the hand). 4 (of a thing) imposing; splendid. 5 Brit. slightly projecting from a surface, etc. (the nail stood proud of the plank). 6 (of flesh) overgrown around a healing wound. 7 Brit. (of water) swollen in flood. □ **do proud** colloq. 1 treat (a person) with lavish generosity or honor (they did us proud on our anniversary). 2 (refl.) act honorably or worthily. □□ **proudly** adv. **proudness** n. [OE prūt, prūd f. OF prud, prod oblique case of pruz, etc., valiant, ult. f. LL prode f. L prodesse be of value (as PRO-¹, esse be)]

■ 1 pleased, well-pleased, satisfied, contented, glad, happy, delighted, elated; honored, gratified. 2 a conceited, self-satisfied, self-important, vain, prideful, self-centered, complacent, haughty, smug, arrogant, boastful, braggart, literary vainglorious. 3 lofty, dignified, lordly, noble, great, respected, honored, honorable, glorious, august, illustrious, estimable, creditable, distinguished, noteworthy. 4 stately, majestic, magnificent, splendid, grand, impressive, imposing, great.

Prov. abbr. 1 Proverbs (Old Testament). 2 Province. 3 Provençal.

prove /prŏov/ v. (past part. **proved** or **proven**) 1 tr. (often foll. by that + clause) demonstrate the truth of by evidence or argument. 2 intr. a (usu. foll. by to + infin.) be found (it proved to be untrue). b emerge incontrovertibly as (will prove the winner). 3 tr. Math. test the accuracy of (a calculation). 4 tr. establish the genuineness and validity of (a will). 5 intr. (of dough) rise in breadmaking. 6 tr. = PROOF 3. 7 tr. subject (a gun, etc.) to a testing process. 8 tr. archaic test the qualities of; try. □ **prove oneself** show one's abilities, courage, etc. □□ **provable** adj. **provability** /prŏovəbĭlitee/ n. **provably** adv. [ME f. OF prover f. L probare test, approve, demonstrate f. probus good]

■ 1 verify, authenticate, confirm, make good, corroborate, demonstrate, show, validate, establish, substantiate, certify; support, sustain, back (up), uphold. 2 turn out, be found, be shown, be established; end up, emerge (as), result. 8 examine, check, analyze; try; see also TEST¹ v. 1.

provenance /próvinəns/ n. 1 the place of origin or history, esp. of a work of art, etc. 2 origin. [F f. provenir f. L provenire (as PRO-¹, venire come)]

■ see ORIGIN 1.

Provençal /prŏvonsaál, próv-/ adj. & n. ● adj. 1 of or concerning the language, inhabitants, landscape, etc., of Provence, a former province of SE France. 2 (also **Provençale**) cooked with garlic and tomato and usu. onions, olive oil, and herbs. ● n. 1 a native of Provence. 2 the language of Provence. [F (as PROVINCIAL f. provincia as L colloq. name for southern Gaul under Roman rule)]

provender /próvindər/ n. 1 animal fodder. 2 joc. food for human beings. [ME f. OF provendre, provende ult. f. L praebenda (see PREBEND)]

■ 1 fodder, forage, feed. 2 provisions, food, supplies, victuals, foodstuffs, nourishment, sustenance, groceries, edibles, colloq. grub, eats, formal aliment, formal or joc. comestibles, sl. nosh.

provenience /prəvéenyəns, -véeneeəns/ n. = PROVENANCE. [L provenire f. venire come]

proverb /próvərb/ n. 1 a short pithy saying in general use,

held to embody a general truth. 2 a person or thing that is notorious (he is a proverb for inaccuracy). 3 (**Proverbs** or **Book of Proverbs**) a didactic poetic Old Testament book of maxims attributed to Solomon and others. [ME f. OF proverbe or L proverbium (as PRO-¹, verbum word)]

■ 1 saying, maxim, aphorism, saw, adage, apothegm, axiom, dictum, gnome.

proverbial /prəvárbeeəl/ adj. 1 (esp. of a specific characteristic, etc.) as well-known as a proverb; notorious (his proverbial honesty). 2 of or referred to in a proverb (the proverbial ill wind). □□ **proverbiality** /-beeálitee/ n. **proverbially** adv. [ME f. L proverbialis (as PROVERB)]

■ 1 acknowledged, axiomatic, time-honored, notorious; see also well-known 1. 2 axiomatic, aphoristic, epigrammatic, apothegmatic, gnomic; well-known, celebrated, notorious.

provide /prəvĭd/ v. 1 tr. supply; furnish (provided them with food; provided food for them; provided a chance for escape). 2 intr. a (usu. foll. by for, against) make due preparation (provided for any eventuality; provided against invasion). b (usu. foll. by for) prepare for the maintenance of a person, etc. 3 tr. (also refl.) equip with necessities. 4 tr. (usu. foll. by that) stipulate in a will, statute, etc. [ME f. L providēre (as PRO-¹, vidēre vis- see)]

■ 1 supply, furnish, equip, outfit, fix up with, provision; produce, yield, afford, lend, give, present, offer, accord. 2 a make provision(s), arrange, cater, prepare, make or get ready, plan, take precautions, take measures; (provide for) anticipate. b (provide for) look after, care for, support, take care of, take under one's wing, minister to, attend (to). 4 stipulate, lay down, require, demand, specify, state.

provided /prəvĭdid/ adj. & conj. ● adj. supplied; furnished. ● conj. (often foll. by that) on the condition or understanding (that).

■ conj. providing (that), on (the) condition (that), if (only), only if, as long as, with the proviso that, with or on the understanding (that).

providence /próvidəns/ n. 1 the protective care of God or nature. 2 (**Providence**) God in this aspect. 3 timely care or preparation; foresight; thrift. □ **special providence** a particular instance of God's providence. [ME f. OF providence or L providentia (as PROVIDE)]

■ 1 protection, care, concern, beneficence, direction, control, divine intervention, guidance. 3 foresight, forethought, preparation, anticipation, farsightedness, discretion, prudence, care; thrift, frugality, husbandry, thriftiness, conservation, economy.

provident /próvidənt, -dent/ adj. having or showing foresight; thrifty. □ **Provident Society** Brit. = Friendly Society. □□ **providently** adv. [ME f. L (as PROVIDE)]

■ farsighted, longheaded, farseeing, thoughtful, anticipatory, wise, shrewd, sagacious, sage, judicious; frugal, economical, thrifty; canny, prudent.

providential /próvidénshəl/ adj. 1 of or by divine foresight or interposition. 2 opportune; lucky. □□ **providentially** adv. [PROVIDENCE + -IAL, after evidential, etc.]

■ 2 fortunate, lucky, blessed, felicitous, happy, opportune, timely.

provider /prəvĭdər/ n. 1 a person or thing that provides. 2 the breadwinner of a family, etc.

■ 1 see DONOR.

providing /prəvĭding/ conj. = PROVIDED conj.

province /próvins/ n. 1 a principal administrative division of some countries. 2 (**the provinces**) the whole of a country outside major cities, esp. regarded as uncultured, unsophisticated, etc. 3 a sphere of action; business (outside my province as a teacher). 4 a branch of learning, etc. (in the province of aesthetics). 5 Eccl. a district under an archbishop or a metropolitan. 6 Rom. Hist. a territory outside Italy under a Roman governor. [ME f. OF f. L provincia charge, province]

■ 1 territory, state, zone, region, area, district, domain, county. 2 (**the provinces**) (the) outlying districts, the countryside, the hinterland, the backwoods, colloq. the sticks, sl. the boonies, the boondocks; see also

BACKCOUNTRY. **3** sphere *or* area (of responsibility), responsibility, concern, function, charge, business, field, *joc.* bailiwick. **4** see BRANCH *n.* 2, 3, FIELD *n.* 8.

provincial /prəvínshəl/ *adj. & n.* • *adj.* **1 a** of or concerning a province. **b** of or concerning the provinces. **2** unsophisticated or uncultured in manner, speech, opinion, etc. • *n.* **1** an inhabitant of a province or the provinces. **2** an unsophisticated or uncultured person. **3** *Eccl.* the head or chief of a province or of a religious order in a province. □□ **provinciality** /-sheeálitee/ *n.* **provincialize** *v.tr.* **provincially** *adv.* [ME f. OF f. L *provincialis* (as PROVINCE)]

■ *adj.* **1** see LOCAL *adj.* 1–3. **2** uncultured, uncultivated, unsophisticated, limited, uninformed, naïve, innocent, ingenuous, unpolished, unrefined, homespun, rustic, rural, rude, country, parochial, insular, narrowminded, small-town, *colloq.* hick. ■ *n.* **2** rustic, (country) bumpkin, yokel, *Brit.* out-of-towner, *colloq.* hick, hayseed, *often derog.* country cousin.

provincialism /prəvínshəlizəm/ *n.* **1** provincial manners, fashion, mode of thought, etc., esp. regarded as restricting or narrow. **2** a word or phrase peculiar to a provincial region. **3** concern for one's local area rather than one's country. □□ **provincialist** *n.*

■ **1** narrow-mindedness, insularity, parochialism, narrowness, benightedness; unsophisticatedness, simplicity, naïveté, ingenuousness, innocence, inexperience. **2** localism, regionalism.

provision /prəvízhən/ *n. & v.* • *n.* **1 a** the act or an instance of providing (*made no provision for his future*). **b** something provided (*a provision of bread*). **2** (in *pl.*) food, drink, etc., esp. for an expedition. **3 a** a legal or formal statement providing for something. **b** a clause of this. • *v.tr.* supply (an expedition, etc.) with provisions. □□ **provisioner** *n.* **provisionless** *adj.* **provisionment** *n.* [ME f. OF f. L *provisio -onis* (as PROVIDE)]

■ *n.* **1 a** preparation(s), prearrangement, arrangement(s), plan(s); equipment; see also STEP *n.* 3. **2** (*provisions*) supplies, stores, stock(s); food, foodstuffs, eatables, edibles, victuals, rations, groceries, staples, *formal* viands, *formal or joc.* comestibles, *joc.* provender, *Austral. colloq.* tucker. **3 b** clause, term, stipulation, proviso, condition, restriction, qualification, demand, requirement. • *v.* stock, victual; see also EQUIP.

provisional /prəvízhənəl/ *adj. & n.* • *adj.* **1** providing for immediate needs only; temporary. **2** (**Provisional**) designating the unofficial wing of the Irish Republican Army (IRA), advocating terrorism. • *n.* (**Provisional**) a member of the Provisional wing of the IRA. □□ **provisionality** /-álitee/ *n.* **provisionally** *adv.* **provisionalness** *n.*

■ *adj.* **1** temporary, interim, transitional, stopgap, pro tempore, *colloq.* pro tem; conditional, contingent.

proviso /prəvízō/ *n.* (*pl.* **-os**) **1** a stipulation. **2** a clause of stipulation or limitation in a document. [L, neut. ablat. past part. of *providēre* PROVIDE, in med.L phr. *proviso quod* it being provided that]

■ see CONDITION *n.* 1.

provisory /prəvízəree/ *adj.* **1** conditional; having a proviso. **2** making provision (*provisory care*). □□ **provisorily** *adv.* [F *provisoire* or med.L *provisorius* (as PROVISOR)]

■ **1** conditional, contingent.

Provo /prōvō/ *n.* (*pl.* **-os**) *colloq.* a member of the Provisional IRA. [abbr.]

provocation /próvəkáyshən/ *n.* **1** the act or an instance of provoking; a state of being provoked (*did it under severe provocation*). **2** a cause of annoyance. **3** *Law* an action, insult, etc., held to be likely to provoke physical retaliation. [ME f. OF *provocation* or L *provocatio* (as PROVOKE)]

■ **1** incitement, instigation. **2** insult, offense, taunt, irritation; ground(s), reason, cause, justification, stimulus, incentive, motivation, motive, inducement.

provocative /prəvókətiv/ *adj. & n.* • *adj.* **1** (usu. foll. by *of*) tending to provoke, esp. anger or sexual desire. **2** intentionally annoying. • *n.* a provocative thing. □□ **provocatively** *adv.* **provocativeness** *n.* [ME f. obs. F *provocatif -ive* f. LL *provocativus* (as PROVOKE)]

■ *adj.* **1** alluring, seductive, stimulating, suggestive, erotic, arousing, exciting, outrageous, sexy. **2** irritating, annoying, galling, irksome, nettlesome, exasperating, infuriating, maddening.

provoke /prəvók/ *v.tr.* **1 a** (often foll. by *to*, or *to* + infin.) rouse or incite (*provoked him to fury*). **b** (often as **provoking** *adj.*) annoy; irritate; exasperate. **2** call forth; instigate (provdignation, an inquiry, a storm, etc.). **3** (usu. foll. by *into* + verbal noun) irritate or stimulate (a person) (*the itch provoked him into scratching*). **4** tempt; allure. **5** cause; give rise to (*will provoke discussion*). □□ **provokable** *adj.* **provokingly** *adv.* [ME f. OF *provoquer* f. L *provocare* (as PRO-¹, *vocare* call)]

■ **1 a** rouse, stir, stimulate, incite, move, motivate, prompt, induce, encourage, push, impel, drive, spur (on), goad, force, compel. **b** irritate, annoy, irk, pester, vex, pique, anger, enrage, madden, incense, infuriate, gall, rile, nettle, harass, hector, plague, badger, exasperate, get on one's nerves, try one's patience, frustrate, upset, disturb, perturb, distress, outrage, offend, insult, affront; (**provoking**) see TRYING. **2** start, incite, instigate, produce, foment, kindle, work up, call forth. **4** see TEMPT 2. **5** see CAUSE *v.* 1.

provolone /prōvəlónee/ *n.* a medium hard Italian cheese, often with a mild smoked flavor.

provost /próvōst, próvəst/ *n.* **1** a high administrative officer in a university. **2** *Brit.* the head of some colleges, esp. at Oxford or Cambridge. **3** *Eccl.* **a** the head of a chapter in a cathedral. **b** *hist.* the head of a religious community. **4** *Sc.* the head of a municipal corporation or burgh. **5** the Protestant minister of the principal church of a town, etc., in Germany, etc. **6** = *provost marshal*. □ **provost guard** /prōvō/ a body of soldiers under a provost marshal. **provost marshal** /prōvō/ **1** the head of military police within a military command, as on a military base. **2** the master-at-arms of a ship in which a court-martial is to be held. □□ **provostship** *n.* [ME f. OE *profost* & AF *provost, prevost* f. med.L *propositus* for *praepositus* past part. of *praeponere* set over]

prow /prow/ *n.* **1** the bow of a ship adjoining the stem. **2** a pointed or projecting front part. [F *proue* f. Prov. *proa* or It. dial. *prua* f. L *prora* f. Gk *prōira*]

■ **1** bow(s).

prowess /prówis/ *n.* **1** skill; expertise. **2** valor; gallantry. [ME f. OF *proesce* f. *prou* valiant]

■ **1** expertise, ability, skill, skillfulness, aptitude, adroitness, dexterity, dexterousness, adeptness, facility, mastery, know-how, capability, proficiency, competence. **2** bravery, valor, courage, boldness, daring, intrepidity, dauntlessness, mettle, stoutheartedness, lionheartedness, fearlessness, gallantry, fortitude, *archaic or joc.* doughtiness.

prowl /prowl/ *v. & n.* • *v.* **1** *tr.* roam (a place) in search or as if in search of prey, plunder, etc. **2** *intr.* (often foll. by *about, around*) move about like a hunter. • *n.* the act or an instance of prowling. □ **on the prowl** in search of something, esp. sexual contact, etc. **prowl car** a police squad car. □□ **prowler** *n.* [ME *prolle* f. unkn. orig.]

■ *v.* **1** scour, scavenge, range over, rove, roam, patrol, cruise. **2** lurk, sneak, skulk, steal, slink, creep; lie in wait. □ **on the prowl** searching, hunting, tracking, stalking, cruising. **prowl car** patrol car, squad car, *Brit.* panda car.

prox. *abbr.* proximo.

proxemics /prokseémiks/ *n. Sociol.* the study of socially conditioned spatial factors in ordinary human relations. [PROXIMITY + *-emics*: cf. *phonemics*]

proximal /próksiməl/ *adj.* situated toward the center of the body or point of attachment. □□ **proximally** *adv.* [L *proximus* nearest]

/. . ./ **pronunciation**	● **part of speech**
□ **phrases, idioms, and compounds**	
□□ **derivatives**	■ **synonym section**
cross-references appear in SMALL CAPITALS or *italics*	

proximate /próksimət/ *adj.* **1** nearest or next before or after (in place, order, time, causation, thought process, etc.). **2** approximate. □□ **proximately** *adv.* [L *proximatus* past part. of *proximare* draw near (as PROXIMAL)]
■ **1** see IMMEDIATE 2. **2** see APPROXIMATE *adj.* 1.

proximity /proksímitee/ *n.* nearness in space, time, etc. (*sat in close proximity to them*). □ **proximity fuse** (or **fuze**) an electronic device causing a projectile to explode when near its target. **proximity of blood** kinship. [ME f. F *proximité* or L *proximitas* (as PROXIMAL)]
■ nearness, closeness, adjacency, contiguity, contiguousness, propinquity.

proximo /próksimō/ *adj.* *Commerce archaic* of next month (*the third proximo*). [L *proximo mense* in the next month]

proxy /próksee/ *n.* (*pl.* **-ies**) (also *attrib.*) **1** the authorization given to a substitute or deputy (*a proxy vote*; *was married by proxy*). **2** a person authorized to act as a substitute, etc. **3 a** a document giving the power to act as a proxy, esp. in voting. **b** a vote given by this. [ME f. obs. *procuracy* f. med.L *procuratia* (as PROCURATION)]
■ **2** substitute, deputy, agent, delegate, surrogate, representative, factor.

prude /proōd/ *n.* a person having or affecting an attitude of extreme propriety or modesty, esp. in sexual matters. □□ **prudery** /proōdəree/ *n.* (*pl.* **-ies**). **prudish** *adj.* **prudishly** *adv.* **prudishness** *n.* [F, back-form. f. *prudefemme* fem. of *prud'homme* good man and true f. *prou* worthy]
■ prig, puritan, (Mrs.) Grundy, *colloq.* goody-goody. □□ **prudery**, **prudishness** priggishness, puritanicalness, puritanism, Grundyism, primness, stuffiness, old-maidishness. **prudish** priggish, puritanical, old-maidish, prissy, prim, straitlaced, stiff, overnice, proper, demure, formal, moralistic, stiff-necked, *colloq.* goody-goody, schoolmarmish, uptight.

prudent /proōd'nt/ *adj.* **1** (of a person or conduct) careful to avoid undesired consequences; circumspect. **2** discreet. □□ **prudence** *n.* **prudently** *adv.* [ME f. OF *prudent* or L *prudens* = *providens* PROVIDENT]
■ **1** careful, cautious, circumspect, watchful, wise, sage, sagacious, sensible, reasonable, canny, shrewd. **2** discreet, politic, judicious, discriminating; see also TACTFUL. □□ **prudence** discretion, wisdom, sagacity, discrimination, common sense, providence, canniness, presence of mind, awareness, care, tact, carefulness, caution, cautiousness, circumspection; foresightedness, forethought, foresight, farsightedness.

prudential /proōdénshəl/ *adj.* & *n.* ● *adj.* of, involving, or marked by prudence (*prudential motives*). ● *n.* (in *pl.*) **1** prudential considerations or matters. **2** minor administrative or financial matters. □□ **prudentialism** *n.* **prudentialist** *n.* **prudentially** *adv.* [PRUDENT + -IAL, after *evidential*, etc.]
■ *adj.* see PRUDENT.

pruinose /proōinōs/ *adj.* esp. *Bot.* covered with white powdery granules; frosted in appearance. [L *pruinosus* f. *pruina* hoarfrost]

prune[1] /proōn/ *n.* **1** a dried plum. **2** *colloq.* a stupid or disliked person. [ME f. OF ult. f. L *prunum* f. Gk *prou(m)non* plum]

prune[2] /proōn/ *v.tr.* **1 a** (often foll. by *down*) trim (a tree, etc.) by cutting away dead or overgrown branches, etc. **b** (usu. foll. by *off*, *away*) lop (branches, etc.) from a tree. **2** reduce (costs, etc.) (*must try to prune expenses*). **3 a** (often foll. by *of*) clear (a book, etc.) of superfluous matter. **b** remove (superfluous matter). □ **pruning hook** a long-handled hooked cutting tool used for pruning. □□ **pruner** *n.* [ME *prouyne* f. OF *pro(o)ignier* ult. f. L *rotundus* ROUND]
■ **1 a** trim (down), clip, cut back, pare (down). **b** lop (off), chop (off), cut (off), clip, shear, snip (off). **2** see CUT *v.* 6.

prunella[1] /proōnélə/ *n.* any plant of the genus *Prunella*, esp. *P. vulgaris*, bearing pink, purple, or white flower spikes, and formerly thought to cure quinsy. Also called SELF-HEAL. [mod.L, = quinsy: earlier *brunella* dimin. of med.L *brunus* brown]

prunella[2] /proōnélə/ *n.* a strong silk or worsted fabric used formerly for academic gowns, the uppers of women's shoes, etc. [perh. f. F *prunelle*, of uncert. orig.]

prurient /proōreeənt/ *adj.* **1** having an unhealthy obsession with sexual matters. **2** encouraging such an obsession. □□ **prurience** *n.* **pruriency** *n.* **pruriently** *adv.* [L *prurire* itch, be wanton]
■ **1** voyeuristic, lubricious, salacious. **2** dirty, lewd, filthy, pornographic, smutty, obscene, foul, scurrilous, vile, gross, lurid, blue, bawdy, ribald, titillating, suggestive, coarse, vulgar, rude, low, crude.

prurigo /proōrígō/ *n.* a skin disease marked by severe itching. □□ **pruriginous** /proōríjinəs/ *adj.* [L *prurigo -ginis* f. *prurire* to itch]

pruritus /proōrítəs/ *n.* severe itching of the skin. □□ **pruritic** /-rítik/ *adj.* [L, = itching (as PRURIGO)]

Prussian /prúshən/ *adj.* & *n.* ● *adj.* of or relating to Prussia, a former German kingdom, or relating to its rigidly militaristic tradition. ● *n.* a native of Prussia. □ **Old Prussian** the language spoken in Prussia until the 17th c. **Prussian blue** a deep blue pigment, ferric ferrocyanide, used in painting and dyeing.

prussic /prúsik/ *adj.* of or obtained from Prussian blue. □ **prussic acid** hydrocyanic acid. [F *prussique* f. *Prusse* Prussia]

pry[1] /prī/ *v.intr.* (**pries**, **pried**) **1** (usu. foll. by *into*) inquire presumptuously (into a person's private affairs, etc.). **2** (usu. foll. by *into*, *about*, etc.) look or peer inquisitively. □□ **prying** *adj.* **pryingly** *adv.* [ME *prie*, of unkn. orig.]
■ intrude, meddle, interfere, be nosy, nose about *or* around, poke about *or* around, ferret about, peer, peek, *colloq.* snoop; (*pry into*) *colloq.* poke *or* stick one's nose in *or* into, *Austral.* & *NZ sl.* stickybeak.

pry[2] /prī/ *v.tr.* (**pries**, **pried**) (often foll. by *out of*, *open*, etc.) = PRIZE[3]. [back-form. f. PRIZE]

PS *abbr.* **1** postscript. **2** *Brit.* Police Sergeant. **3** private secretary. **4** prompt side.

Ps. *abbr.* (*pl.* **Pss.**) Psalm, Psalms (Old Testament).

psalm /saam/ *n.* **1 a** (also **Psalm**) any of the sacred songs contained in the Book of Psalms. **b** (**the Psalms** or **the Book of Psalms**) the book of the Old Testament containing the Psalms. **2** a sacred song or hymn. □□ **psalmic** *adj.* [OE (*p*)*sealm* f. LL *psalmus* f. Gk *psalmos* song sung to a harp f. *psallō* pluck]

psalmist /saámist/ *n.* **1** the author or composer of a psalm. **2** (**the Psalmist**) David or the author of any of the Psalms. [LL *psalmista* (as PSALM)]

psalmody /saámədee, sál-/ *n.* **1** the practice or art of singing psalms, hymns, etc., esp. in public worship. **2 a** the arrangement of psalms for singing. **b** the psalms so arranged. □□ **psalmodic** /salmódik/ *adj.* **psalmodist** *n.* **psalmodize** *v.intr.* [ME f. LL *psalmodia* f. Gk *psalmōidia* singing to a harp (as PSALM, *ōidē* song)]

psalter /sáwltər/ *n.* **1 a** the Book of Psalms. **b** a version of this (*the English Psalter*). **2** a copy of the Psalms, esp. for liturgical use. [ME f. AF *sauter*, OF *sautier*, & OE (*p*)*saltere* f. LL *psalterium* f. Gk *psaltērion* stringed instrument (*psallō* pluck), in eccl.L Book of Psalms]

psalterium /sawlteéreeəm/ *n.* the third stomach of a ruminant, the omasum. [L (see PSALTER): named from its booklike form]

psaltery /sáwltəree/ *n.* (*pl.* **-ies**) an ancient and medieval instrument like a dulcimer but played by plucking the strings with the fingers or a plectrum. [ME f. OF *sauterie*, etc., f. L (as PSALTER)]

p's and q's *n.* □ **mind one's p's and q's 1** attend to one's own conduct and manners. **2** attend to one's own accuracy in work.

PSAT *abbr.* Preliminary Scholastic Assessment Test.

psephology /sefóləjee/ *n.* the statistical study of elections, voting, etc. □□ **psephological** /-əlójikəl/ *adj.* **psephologically** *adv.* **psephologist** *n.* [Gk *psēphos* pebble, vote + -LOGY]

pseud /soōd/ *adj.* & *n.* *Brit. colloq.* ● *adj.* intellectually or socially pretentious; not genuine. ● *n.* such a person; a poseur. [abbr. of PSEUDO]

pseud- var. of PSEUDO-.

pseud. *abbr.* pseudonym.

pseudepigrapha /sŏodipígrəfə/ *n.pl.* **1** Jewish writings ascribed to various Old Testament prophets, etc., but written during or just before the early Christian period. **2** spurious writings. □□ **pseudepigraphal** *adj.* **pseudepigraphic** /-gráfik/ *adj.* **pseudepigraphical** *adj.* [neut. pl. of Gk *pseudepigraphos* with false title (as PSEUDO-, EPIGRAPH)]

pseudo /sŏodō/ *adj.* & *n.* ● *adj.* **1** sham; spurious. **2** insincere. ● *n.* Brit. (*pl.* **-os**) a pretentious or insincere person. [see PSEUDO-]
■ *adj.* **1** see SPURIOUS. **2** see INSINCERE.

pseudo- /sŏodō/ *comb. form* (also **pseud-** before a vowel) **1** supposed or purporting to be but not really so; false; not genuine (*pseudointellectual*; *pseudepigrapha*). **2** resembling or imitating (often in technical applications) (*pseudomalaria*). [Gk f. *pseudēs* false, *pseudos* falsehood]

pseudocarp /sŏodōkaarp/ *n.* a fruit formed from parts other than the ovary, e.g., the strawberry or fig. Also called **accessory fruit.** [PSEUDO- + Gk *karpos* fruit]

pseudomorph /sŏodəmawrf/ *n.* **1** a crystal, etc., consisting of one mineral with the form characteristic of another. **2** a false form. □□ **pseudomorphic** /-máwrfik/ *adj.* **pseudomorphism.** **pseudomorphous** /-máwrfəs/ *adj.* [PSEUDO- + Gk *morphē* form]

pseudonym /sŏodənim/ *n.* a fictitious name, esp. one assumed by an author. [F *pseudonyme* f. Gk *pseudōnymos* (as PSEUDO-, *-ōnumos* f. *onoma* name)]
■ nom de plume, nom de guerre, alias, pen name, stage name, incognito.

pseudonymous /sŏodóniməs/ *adj.* writing or written under a false name. □□ **pseudonymity** /sŏodənímitee/ *n.* **pseudonymously** *adv.*

pseudopod /sŏodōpod/ *n.* = PSEUDOPODIUM. [mod.L (as PSEUDOPODIUM)]

pseudopodium /sŏodōpŏdeeəm/ *n.* (*pl.* **pseudopodia** /-deeə/) (in amoeboid cells) a temporary protrusion of protoplasm for movement, feeding, etc. [mod.L (as PSEUDO-, PODIUM)]

pseudoscience /sŏodōsiəns/ *n.* a pretended or spurious science. □□ **pseudoscientific** /-siəntifik/ *adj.*

psf. *abbr.* (also **p.s.f.**) pounds per square foot.

pshaw /shaw, pshaw/ *int. archaic* an expression of contempt or impatience. [imit.]

psi /sī, psī/ *n.* **1** the twenty-third letter of the Greek alphabet (Ψ, ψ). **2** supposed parapsychological faculties, phenomena, etc., regarded collectively. [Gk]

p.s.i. *abbr.* pounds per square inch.

psilocybin /síləsíbin/ *n.* a hallucinogenic alkaloid found in Mexican mushrooms of the genus *Psilocybe*. [*Psilocybe* f. Gk *psilos* bald + *kubē* head]

psilosis /sīlōsis/ *n.* = SPRUE[2]. [Gk *psilōsis* f. *psilos* bare]

psittacine /sítəsīn/ *adj.* of or relating to parrots; parrot-like. [L *psittacinus* f. *psittacus* f. Gk *psittakos* parrot]

psittacosis /sítəkósis/ *n.* a contagious viral disease of birds transmissible (esp. from parrots) to human beings as a form of pneumonia. [mod.L f. L *psittacus* (as PSITTACINE) + -OSIS]

psoas /sóəs/ *n.* either of two muscles used in flexing the hip joint. [Gk, accus. pl. of *psoa*, taken as sing.]

psoriasis /səríəsis/ *n.* a skin disease marked by red scaly patches. □□ **psoriatic** /sáwreeátik/ *adj.* [mod.L f. Gk *psōriasis* f. *psōriaō* have an itch f. *psōra* itch]

psst /pst/ *int.* (also **pst**) a whispered exclamation seeking to attract a person's attention surreptitiously. [imit.]

PST *abbr.* Pacific Standard Time.

psych /sīk/ *v.tr. colloq.* (also **psyche**) **1** (usu. foll. by *up*; often *refl.*) prepare (oneself or another person) mentally for an ordeal, etc. **2 a** (usu. foll. by *out*) analyze (a person's motivation, etc.) for one's own advantage (*can't psych him out*). **b** subject to psychoanalysis. **3** (often foll. by *out*) influence a person psychologically, esp. negatively; intimidate; frighten. [abbr.]
■ **1** set; see also PREPARE 1, 3a. **3** see DISTURB 2.

psych. /sīk/ (also **psychol.**) *abbr.* **1** psychological. **2** psychology.

psyche /síkee/ *n.* **1** the soul; the spirit. **2** the mind. **3** var. of PSYCH. [L f. Gk *psukhē* breath, life, soul]
■ **1** soul, spirit, life force, anima, (inner) self, subconscious, unconscious, inner man *or* woman. **2** mind, intellect.

psychedelia /síkideéleeə, -deélyə/ *n.pl.* **1** psychedelic articles, esp. posters, paintings, etc. **2** psychedelic drugs.

psychedelic /síkidélik/ *adj.* & *n.* ● *adj.* **1 a** expanding the mind's awareness, etc., esp. through the use of hallucinogenic drugs. **b** (of an experience) hallucinatory; bizarre. **c** (of a drug) producing hallucinations. **2** *colloq.* **a** producing an effect resembling that of a psychedelic drug; having vivid colors or designs, etc. **b** (of colors, patterns, etc.) bright, bold and often abstract. ● *n.* a hallucinogenic drug. □□ **psychedelically** *adv.* [irreg. f. Gk (as PSYCHE, *dēlos* clear, manifest)]

psychiatry /síkíətree/ *n.* the study and treatment of mental disease. □□ **psychiatric** /-keeátrik/ *adj.* **psychiatrical** *adj.* **psychiatrically** *adv.* **psychiatrist** /-kíətrist/ *n.* [as PSYCHE + *iatreia* healing f. *iatros* healer]
■ □□ **psychiatrist** see *therapist* (THERAPY).

psychic /síkik/ *adj.* & *n.* ● *adj.* **1 a** (of a person) considered to have occult powers, such as telepathy, clairvoyance, etc. **b** (of a faculty, phenomenon, etc.) inexplicable by natural laws. **2** of the soul or mind. **3** *Bridge* (of a bid) made on the basis of a hand not usually considered strong enough to support it. ● *n.* **1** a person considered to have psychic powers; a medium. **2** *Bridge* a psychic bid. **3** (in *pl.*) the study of psychic phenomena. [Gk *psukhikos* (as PSYCHE)]
■ *adj.* **1 a** telepathic, clairvoyant; see also PROPHETIC. **b** psychical, extrasensory, supernatural, occult, magical, telepathic, telekinetic, preternatural, spiritualistic, unearthly, extramundane, supermundane, metaphysical. **2** psychical, mental, spiritual, psychological, intellectual. ● *n.* **1** medium, spiritualist, clairvoyant, mind reader, telepathist; seer, seeress, crystal gazer, soothsayer, fortune-teller, prophet, prophetess, sibyl.

psychical /síkikəl/ *adj.* **1** concerning psychic phenomena or faculties (*psychical research*). **2** of the soul or mind. □□ **psychically** *adv.* **psychicism** /-kisizəm/ *n.* **psychicist** /-kisist/ *n.*
■ **1** see PSYCHIC *adj.* 1b. **2** see SPIRITUAL *adj.* 1, 4.

psycho /síkō/ *n.* & *adj. colloq.* ● *n.* (*pl.* **-os**) a psychopath. ● *adj.* psychopathic. [abbr.]
■ *n.* see PSYCHOTIC *n.*

psycho- /síkō/ *comb. form* relating to the mind or psychology. [Gk *psukho-* (as PSYCHE)]

psychoactive /síkō-áktiv/ *adj.* affecting the mind.

psychoanalysis /síkōənálisis/ *n.* a therapeutic method of treating mental disorders by investigating the interaction of conscious and unconscious elements in the mind and bringing repressed fears and conflicts into the conscious mind. □□ **psychoanalyze** /-ánəliz/ *v.tr.* **psychoanalyst** /-ánəlist/ *n.* **psychoanalytic** /-anəlítik/ *adj.* **psychoanalytical** *adj.* **psychoanalytically** *adv.*
■ see THERAPY 2b. □□ **psychoanalyst** see *therapist* (THERAPY).

psychobabble /síkōbabəl/ *n. colloq. derog.* jargon used in popular psychology. □□ **psychobabbler** *n.*

psychodrama /síkōdraamə, -drámə/ *n.* **1** a form of psychotherapy in which patients act out events from their past. **2** a play or movie, etc., in which psychological elements are the main interest.

psychodynamics /síkōdínámiks/ *n.pl.* (treated as *sing.*) the study of the activity of and the interrelation between the various parts of an individual's personality or psyche. □□ **psychodynamic** *adj.* **psychodynamically** *adv.*

/. . ./ **pronunciation**	● **part of speech**
□ **phrases, idioms, and compounds**	
□□ **derivatives**	■ **synonym section**
cross-references appear in SMALL CAPITALS or *italics*	

psychogenesis /sīkōjénisis/ *n.* the study of the origin of the mind's development.

psychokinesis /sīkōkineesis/ *n.* the movement of objects supposedly by mental effort without the action of natural forces.

psycholinguistics /sīkōlinggwístiks/ *n.pl.* (treated as *sing.*) the study of the psychological aspects of language and language acquisition. □□ **psycholinguist** /-línggwist/ *n.* **psycholinguistic** *adj.*

psychological /sīkəlójikəl/ *adj.* **1** of, relating to, or arising in the mind. **2** of or relating to psychology. **3** *colloq.* (of an ailment, etc.) having a basis in the mind; imaginary (*her cold is psychological*). □ **psychological block** a mental inability or inhibition caused by emotional factors. **psychological moment** the most appropriate time for achieving a particular effect or purpose. **psychological warfare** a campaign directed at reducing an opponent's morale. □□ **psychologically** *adv.*
 ■ **1** mental, nonphysical, psychosomatic, intellectual, psychical, psychic, subconscious, unconscious, subliminal. **3** see IMAGINARY.

psychology /sīkóləjee/ *n.* (*pl.* **-ies**) **1** the scientific study of the human mind and its functions, esp. those affecting behavior in a given context. **2** a treatise on or theory of this. **3 a** the mental characteristics or attitude of a person or group. **b** the mental factors governing a situation or activity (*the psychology of crime*). □□ **psychologist** *n.* **psychologize** *v.tr.* & *intr.* [mod.L *psychologia* (as PSYCHO-, -LOGY)]
 ■ **3 a** (mental) makeup, constitution, attitude, behavior, thought processes, thinking, psyche, nature, feeling(s), emotion(s), rationale, reasoning.

psychometrics /sīkōmétriks/ *n.pl.* (treated as *sing.*) the science of measuring mental capacities and processes.

psychometry /sīkómitree/ *n.* **1** the supposed divination of facts about events, people, etc., from inanimate objects associated with them. **2** the measurement of mental abilities. □□ **psychometric** /-kəmétrik/ *adj.* **psychometrically** *adv.* **psychometrist** *n.*

psychomotor /sīkōmốtər/ *adj.* concerning the study of movement resulting from mental activity.

psychoneurosis /sīkōnŏŏrṓsis, -nyŏŏ-/ *n.* neurosis, esp. with the indirect expression of emotions. □□ **psychoneurotic** /-nŏŏrótik, -nyŏŏ-/ *adj.*

psychopath /sīkəpath/ *n.* **1** a person suffering from chronic mental disorder esp. with abnormal or violent social behavior. **2** a mentally or emotionally unstable person. □□ **psychopathic** /-páthik/ *adj.* **psychopathically** *adv.*
 ■ see PSYCHOTIC *n.* □□ **psychopathic** see PSYCHOTIC *adj.*

psychopathology /sīkōpəthóləjee/ *n.* **1** the scientific study of mental disorders. **2** a mentally or behaviorally disordered state. □□ **psychopathological** /-pathəlójikəl/ *adj.*

psychopathy /sīkópəthee/ *n.* psychopathic or psychologically abnormal behavior.

psychophysics /sīkōfíziks/ *n.* the science of the relation between the mind and the body. □□ **psychophysical** *adj.*

psychophysiology /sīkōfízeeóləjee/ *n.* the branch of physiology dealing with mental phenomena. □□ **psychophysiological** /-zeeəlójikəl/ *adj.*

psychosexual /sīkōséksŏŏəl/ *adj.* of or involving the psychological aspects of the sexual impulse. □□ **psychosexually** *adv.*

psychosis /sīkṓsis/ *n.* (*pl.* **psychoses** /-seez/) a severe mental derangement, esp. when resulting in delusions and loss of or defective contact with external reality. [Gk *psukhōsis* f. *psukhoō* give life to (as PSYCHE)]
 ■ see *insanity* (INSANE).

psychosocial /sīkōsṓshəl/ *adj.* of or involving the influence of social factors or human interactive behavior. □□ **psychosocially** *adv.*

psychosomatic /sīkōsəmátik/ *adj.* **1** (of an illness, etc.) caused or aggravated by mental conflict, stress, etc. **2** of the mind and body together. □□ **psychosomatically** *adv.*

psychosurgery /sīkōsórjəree/ *n.* brain surgery as a means of treating mental disorder. □□ **psychosurgical** *adj.*

psychotherapy /sīkōthérəpee/ *n.* the treatment of mental disorder by psychological means. □□ **psychotherapeutic** /-pyṓōtik/ *adj.* **psychotherapist** *n.*
 ■ see THERAPY 2b. □□ **psychotherapist** see *therapist* (THERAPY).

psychotic /sīkótik/ *adj.* & *n.* ● *adj.* of or characterized by a psychosis. ● *n.* a person suffering from a psychosis. □□ **psychotically** *adv.*
 ■ *adj.* mad, insane, psychopathic, deranged, demented, lunatic, unbalanced, (mentally) ill *or* sick, disturbed, of unsound mind, certifiable, unhinged, *colloq.* schizo, mental. *sl.* nuts, off one's rocker, lost (his or her) marbles, stark raving mad. ● *n.* mental patient, madman, madwoman, maniac, lunatic, psychopath, *colloq.* schizo, mental.

psychotropic /sīkōtrṓpik, -trṓp-/ *n.* (of a drug) acting on the mind. [PSYCHO- + Gk *tropē* turning: see TROPIC]

psychrometer /sīkrómitər/ *n.* a thermometer consisting of a dry bulb and a wet bulb for measuring atmospheric humidity. [Gk *psukhros* cold + -METER]

PT *abbr.* **1** physical therapy. **2** physical training.

Pt *symb. Chem.* the element platinum.

pt. *abbr.* **1** part. **2** pint. **3** point. **4** port.

PTA *abbr.* Parent-Teacher Association.

ptarmigan /taármigən/ *n.* any of various grouses of the genus *Lagopus*, esp. *L. mutus*, with black or gray plumage in the summer and white in the winter. [Gael. *tàrmachan*: p- after Gk words in *pt*-]

PT boat *n.* a military patrol boat armed with torpedoes, etc. [*P*atrol *T*orpedo]

pteridology /téridóləjee/ *n.* the study of ferns. □□ **pteridological** /-dəlójikəl/ *adj.* **pteridologist** *n.* [Gk *pteris -idos* fern + -LOGY]

pteridophyte /tərídəfīt, téra'dō-/ *n.* any flowerless plant of the division Pteridophyta, including ferns, club mosses, and horsetails. [Gk *pteris -idos* fern + *phuton* plant]

ptero- /térō/ *comb. form* wing. [Gk *pteron* wing]

pterodactyl /térədáktil/ *n.* a large extinct flying birdlike reptile with a long slender head and neck.

pteropod /térəpod/ *n.* a marine gastropod with the middle part of its foot expanded into a pair of winglike lobes. [PTERO- + Gk *pous podos* foot]

pterosaur /térəsawr/ *n.* any of a group of extinct flying reptiles with large bat-like wings, including pterodactyls. [PTERO- + Gk *saura* lizard]

pteroylglutamic acid /térō-ilglōōtámik/ *n.* = FOLIC ACID. [*pter*oic acid + -YL + GLUTAMIC (ACID)]

pterygoid process /térigoyd/ *adj.* each of a pair of processes from the sphenoid bone in the skull. [Gk *pterux -ugos* wing]

PTFE *abbr.* polytetrafluoroethylene.

ptisan /tízən, tizán/ *n.* a nourishing drink, esp. barley water. [ME & OF *tizanne*, etc., f. L *ptisana* f. Gk *ptisanē* peeled barley]

PTO *abbr.* **1** Parent-Teacher Organization. **2** please turn over. **3** power takeoff.

Ptolemaic /tólimáyik/ *adj. hist.* **1** of or relating to Ptolemy, a 2nd-c. Alexandrian astronomer, or his theories. **2** of or relating to the Ptolemies, Macedonian rulers of Egypt from the death of Alexander the Great (323 BC) to the death of Cleopatra (30 BC). □ **Ptolemaic system** the theory that the earth is the stationary center of the universe (cf. COPERNICAN SYSTEM). [L *Ptolemaeus* f. Gk *Ptolemaios*]

ptomaine /tṓmayn/ *n.* any of various amine compounds, some toxic, in putrefying animal and vegetable matter. □ **ptomaine poisoning** food poisoning. [F *ptomaïne* f. It. *ptomaina* irreg. f. Gk *ptōma* corpse]

ptosis /tṓsis/ *n.* a drooping of the upper eyelid due to paralysis, etc. □□ **ptotic** /tótik/ *adj.* [Gk *ptōsis* f. *piptō* fall]

Pty. *abbr. Austral., NZ, & S.Afr.* proprietary.

ptyalin /tíəlin/ *n.* an enzyme that hydrolyzes certain carbohydrates and is found in the saliva of humans and some other animals. [Gk *ptualon* spittle]

Pu *symb. Chem.* the element plutonium.

pub /pub/ *n. colloq.* **1** a tavern or bar. **2** *Brit.* a public house. **3** *Austral.* a hotel. □ **pub-crawl** esp. *Brit. colloq.* a drinking tour of several pubs. [abbr.]

■ **1** bar room, bar, saloon, inn, taproom, *Austral. & NZ* hotel, *Brit.* public house, beerhouse, *archaic or literary* hostelry, *Brit. colloq.* local, boozer, public, *hist.* alehouse, *sl.* watering hole, joint, *Austral. sl.* rub-a-dub(-dub), rubbity(-dub).

pub. *abbr.* (also **publ.**) **1** public. **2** publication. **3** published. **4** publisher. **5** publishing.

puberty /pyōōbərtee/ *n.* the period during which adolescents reach sexual maturity and become capable of reproduction. □ **age of puberty** the age at which puberty begins. □□ **pubertal** *adj.* [ME f. F *puberté* or L *pubertas* f. *puber* adult]
■ pubescence, sexual maturity, adolescence, teens, young manhood, young womanhood, the awkward age.

pubes[1] /pyōōbeez/ *n.* (*pl.* same) **1** the lower part of the abdomen at the front of the pelvis, covered with hair from puberty. **2** the hair appearing on the pubic region.[L]

pubes[2] *pl.* of PUBIS.

pubescence /pyōōbésəns/ *n.* **1** the time when puberty begins. **2** *Bot.* soft down on the leaves and stems of plants. **3** *Zool.* soft down on various parts of animals, esp. insects. □□ **pubescent** *adj.* [F *pubescence* or med.L *pubescentia* f. L *pubescere* reach puberty]
■ **1** see PUBERTY. □□ **pubescent** see ADOLESCENT *adj.*

pubic /pyōōbik/ *adj.* of or relating to the pubes or pubis.

pubis /pyōōbis/ *n.* (*pl.* **pubes** /-beez/) either of a pair of bones forming the two sides of the pelvis. [L *os pubis* bone of the PUBES]

public /públik/ *adj. & n.* ● *adj.* **1** of or concerning the people as a whole (*a public holiday; the public interest*). **2** open to or shared by all the people (*public library; public meeting*). **3** done or existing openly (*made his views public; a public protest*). **4 a** (of a service, funds, etc.) provided by or concerning local or central government (*public money; public records; public expenditure*). **b** (of a person) in government (*had a distinguished public career*). **5** well-known; famous (*a public figure*). **6** *Brit.* of, for, or acting for, a university (*public examination*). ● *n.* **1** (as *sing.* or *pl.*) the community in general, or members of the community. **2** a section of the community having a particular interest or some special connection (*the reading public; my public demands my loyalty*). **3** *Brit. colloq.* **a** = *public bar*. **b** = *public house*. □ **go public** become a public company or corporation. **in public** openly; publicly. **in the public domain** belonging to the public as a whole, esp. not subject to copyright. **in the public eye** famous or notorious. **make public** publicize; make known; publish. **public act** an act of legislation affecting the public as a whole. **public-address system** loudspeakers, microphones, amplifiers, etc., used in addressing large audiences. **public bar** *Brit.* the least expensive bar in a public house. **public bill** a bill of legislation affecting the public as a whole. **public company** *Brit.* a company that sells shares to all buyers on the open market. **public corporation** a large corporation whose shares are sold or traded publicly. **public defender** an attorney who provides legal representation at public expense for defendants who cannot afford their own attorney. **public enemy** a notorious wanted criminal. **public figure** a famous person. **public health** the provision of adequate sanitation, drainage, etc., by government. **public house** *Brit.* an inn providing alcoholic drinks for consumption on the premises. **public land** land owned by the government and usu. open for use by the public. **public law 1** the law of relations between individuals and the government. **2** = *public act*. **public lending right** (in the UK) the right of authors to payment when their books, etc., are lent by public libraries. **public libel** a published libel. **public nuisance 1** an illegal act against the public generally. **2** *colloq.* an obnoxious person. **public opinion** views, esp. moral, prevalent among the general public. **public ownership** the government ownership of the means of production, distribution, and exchange. **public prosecutor** a law officer conducting criminal proceedings on behalf of the state or in the public interest. **Public Record Office** an institution keeping official archives, esp. birth, marriage, and death certificates, for public inspection. **public relations** the professional maintenance of a favorable public

image, esp. by a company, famous person, etc. **public school 1** *US, Austral., & Sc.*, etc., a free, government-supported school. **2** *Brit.* a private tuition-paying secondary school, esp. for boarders. **public sector** that part of an economy, industry, etc., that is controlled by the government. **public servant** a government official. **public spirit** a willingness to engage in community action. **public television** television funded by government appropriation and private donations rather than by advertising. **public transportation** buses, trains, etc., charging set fares and running on fixed routes, esp. when government-owned. **public utility** an organization supplying water, gas, etc., to the community. **public works** building operations, etc., done by or for the government on behalf of the community. **public wrong** an offense against society as a whole. □□ **publicly** *adv.* [ME f. OF *public* or L *publicus* f. *pubes* adult]
■ *adj.* **1** communal, community, common, general, collective, universal, popular, national, civil, civic, societal. **2** accessible, open, free, unrestricted, nonexclusive, communal. **3** open, known, manifest, visible, viewable, conspicuous, exposed, overt; projected, acknowledged, admitted. **4 a** government, state, national, federal, civic, civil. **5** well-known, prominent, eminent, celebrated, famous, renowned, notable; influential, illustrious. ● *n.* **1** community, people (at large *or* in general), citizenry, citizens, nation, populace, population, society, voters; plebeians, proletariat, rank and file, commonalty, masses, multitude, hoi polloi, man *or* woman in the street, John Q. Public, *Brit.* Mr. *or* Mrs. Average. **2** sector, segment, group, crowd; see also WORLD 7. □ **in public** publicly, openly, in the open, *coram populo*; see also *on the level* (LEVEL), ABOVEBOARD. **in the public eye** see *well-known* 1, NOTORIOUS. **make public** see PUBLISH. **public figure** see CELEBRITY 1. **public house 1** see PUB 2. **public nuisance 2** see PEST 1. **public servant** see OFFICER *n.* 1, 3, 4. **public-spirited** see CHARITABLE 1. **public-spiritedness** see ALTRUISM.

publican /públikən/ *n.* **1 a** *Brit.* the keeper of a public house. **b** *Austral.* the keeper of a hotel. **2** *Rom.Hist. & Bibl.* a tax collector. [ME f. OF *publicain* f. L *publicanus* f. *publicum* public revenue (as PUBLIC)]

publication /públikáyshən/ *n.* **1 a** the preparation and issuing of a book, newspaper, engraving, music, etc., to the public. **b** a book, etc., so issued. **2** the act or an instance of making something publicly known. [ME f. OF f. L *publicatio -onis* (as PUBLISH)]
■ **1 b** book, booklet, pamphlet, brochure, leaflet, periodical, magazine, journal, newsletter, newspaper, paper. **2** dissemination, promulgation, publicizing, publishing, proclamation, reporting, announcement, advertisement, pronouncement, revelation, declaration, appearance.

publicist /públisist/ *n.* **1** a publicity agent or public relations manager. **2** a journalist, esp. concerned with current affairs. **3** *archaic* a writer or other person skilled in international law. □□ **publicism** *n.* **publicistic** /-sístik/ *adj.* [F *publiciste* f. L (*jus*) *publicum* public law]

publicity /publísitee/ *n.* **1 a** the professional exploitation of a product, company, person, etc., by advertising or popularizing. **b** material or information used for this. **2** public exposure; notoriety. □ **publicity agent** a person employed to produce or heighten public exposure. [F *publicité* (as PUBLIC)]
■ **1 a** advertising, public relations, marketing, promotion; see also ADVERTISEMENT 2. **b** see ADVERTISEMENT 1. **2** see ATTENTION *n.* 1c.

publicize /públisīz/ *v.tr.* advertise; make publicly known.
■ promote, advertise, push, give publicity to, *colloq.* beat

/ . . . / **pronunciation**   ● **part of speech**
□ **phrases, idioms, and compounds**
□□ **derivatives**   ■ **synonym section**
cross-references appear in SMALL CAPITALS or *italics*

the drum for, plug, tout, *sl.* hype; make public *or* known, air, broadcast, circulate, announce, put out, release; disclose, reveal, expose.

publish /públish/ *v.tr.* **1** (also *absol.*) (of an author, publisher, etc.) prepare and issue (a book, newspaper, etc.) for public sale. **2** make generally known. **3** announce (an edict, etc.) formally; read (marriage banns). **4** *Law* communicate (a libel, etc.) to a third party. □□ **publishable** *adj.* [ME *puplise*, etc., f. OF *puplier, publier* f. L *publicare* (as PUBLIC)]
■ **2** make public, put out, broadcast, circulate, release, spread (about *or* around), advertise, make known, let a thing be known, tell, announce, publicize, report, proclaim, promulgate, bruit about, noise about; reveal, divulge, disclose.

publisher /públishər/ *n.* **1** a person or esp. a company that produces and distributes copies of a book, newspaper, etc., for sale. **2** the owner or chief executive of a publishing company. **3** a person or thing that publishes.

puce /pyōōs/ *adj. & n.* dark red or purplish brown. [F, = flea(-color) f. L *pulex -icis*]

puck[1] /puk/ *n.* a rubber disk used in ice hockey. [19th c.: orig. unkn.]

puck[2] /puk/ *n.* **1** a mischievous or evil sprite. **2** a mischievous child. □□ **puckish** *adj.* **puckishly** *adv.* **puckishness** *n.* **pucklike** *adj.* [OE *pūca*: cf. Welsh *pwca*, Ir. *púca*]
■ **1** see IMP *n.* 2. **2** see IMP *n.* 1. □□ **puckish** see MISCHIEVOUS 1, 2.

pucka var. of PUKKA.

pucker /púkər/ *v. & n.* ● *v.tr. & intr.* (often foll. by *up*) gather or cause to gather into wrinkles, folds, or bulges (*puckered her eyebrows; this seam is puckered up*). ● *n.* such a wrinkle, bulge, fold, etc. □□ **puckery** *adj.* [prob. frequent., formed as POKE[2], POCKET (cf. PURSE)]
■ *v.* gather, draw together, compress, purse, crinkle, ruck, ruffle, furrow, wrinkle, crease, screw up, tighten, contract, squeeze. ● *n.* gather, tuck, pleat, ruffle, ruck, wrinkle, fold, crinkle.

pud /pŏŏd/ *n. Brit. colloq.* = PUDDING. [abbr.]

pudding /pŏŏding/ *n.* **1 a** any of various dessert dishes, usu. containing flavoring, sugar, milk, etc. (*chocolate pudding; rice pudding*). **b** *Brit.* a savory dish containing flour, suet, etc. (*steak and kidney pudding*). **c** *Brit.* the dessert course of a meal. **d** the intestines of a pig, etc., stuffed with oatmeal, spices, blood, etc. **2** *colloq.* a person or thing resembling a pudding. **3** *Naut.* (also **puddening** /pŏŏd'ning/) esp. *Brit.* a pad or fender to prevent chafing between vessels, etc., esp. while being towed. □ **in the pudding club** *Brit. sl.* pregnant. **pudding face** *Brit. colloq.* a large fat face. **pudding head** *colloq.* a stupid person. **pudding stone** a conglomerate rock consisting of rounded pebbles in a siliceous matrix. □□ **puddinglike** *adj.* [ME *poding* f. OF *boudin* black pudding ult. f. L *botellus* sausage: see BOWEL]
■ **1 a, c** see SWEET *n.* 2.

puddle /púd'l/ *n. & v.* ● *n.* **1** a small pool, esp. of rainwater on a road, etc. **2** clay and sand mixed with water and used as a watertight covering for embankments, etc. **3** a circular patch of disturbed water made by the blade of an oar at each stroke. ● *v.* **1** *tr.* **a** knead (clay and sand) into puddle. **b** line (a canal, etc.) with puddle. **c** to coat the roots of (a plant) with mud to reduce water loss during transplantation. **2** *intr.* make puddle from clay, etc. **3** *tr.* stir (molten iron) to produce wrought iron by expelling carbon. **4** *intr.* **a** wade or wallow in mud or shallow water. **b** busy oneself in an untidy way. **5** *tr.* make (water, etc.) muddy. **6** *tr.* work (mixed water and clay) to separate gold or opal. **7** to be covered with puddles (*the field puddled*). □ **puddle jumper** *sl.* a small, light plane for short distances or commercial routes. □□ **puddler** *n.* **puddly** *adj.* [ME *podel, puddel*, dimin. of OE *pudd* ditch]

pudency /pyōōd'nsee/ *n. literary* modesty; shame. [LL *pudentia* (as PUDENDUM)]

pudendum /pyōōdéndəm/ *n.* (*pl.* **pudenda** /-də/) (usu. in *pl.*) the genitals, esp. of a woman. □□ **pudendal** *adj.* **pudic** /pyōōdik/ *adj.* [L *pudenda* (*membra* parts), neut. pl. of gerundive of *pudēre* be ashamed]

pudgy /pújee/ *adj.* (**pudgier, pudgiest**) *colloq.* (esp. of a person) plump; slightly overweight. □□ **pudge** *n.* **pudgily** *adv.* **pudginess** *n.* [f. *podge* a short fat person]
■ see PLUMP[1] *adj.*

pueblo /pwéblō/ *n.* (*pl.* **-os**) **1** (**Pueblo**) a member of a Native American people of the southwestern US. **2** a Native American settlement of the southwestern US, esp. one consisting of multistoried adobe houses built by the Pueblo people. [Sp., = people, f. L *populus*]

puerile /pyōōəril, pyōōril, -ríl/ *adj.* **1** trivial; childish; immature. **2** of or like a child. □□ **puerilely** *adv.* **puerility** /-ríl-itee/ *n.* (*pl.* **-ies**). [F *puéril* or L *puerilis* f. *puer* boy]
■ **1** childish, immature, babyish, infantile, juvenile, adolescent, sophomoric; trivial, ridiculous, shallow, inconsequential, insignificant. **2** childish, childlike, boyish, girlish, youthful, juvenile, infantile, babyish.

puerperal /pyōō-árpərəl/ *adj.* of or caused by childbirth. □ **puerperal fever** fever following childbirth and caused by uterine infection. [L *puerperus* f. *puer* child + *-parus* bearing]

Puerto Rican /pwértō réekən, páwrtə/ *n. & adj.* ● *n.* **1** a native of Puerto Rico, an island of the West Indies. **2** a person of Puerto Rican descent. ● *adj.* of or relating to Puerto Rico or its inhabitants.

puff /puf/ *n. & v.* ● *n.* **1 a** a short quick blast of breath or wind. **b** the sound of this; a similar sound. **c** a small quantity of vapor, smoke, etc., emitted in one blast; an inhalation or exhalation from a cigarette, pipe, etc. (*went up in a puff of smoke; took a puff from his cigarette*). **2** a light pastry containing jam, cream, etc. **3** a gathered mass of material in a dress, etc. (*puff sleeve*). **4** a protuberant roll of hair. **5 a** an extravagantly enthusiastic review of a book, etc., esp. in a newspaper. **b** *Brit.* an advertisement for goods, etc., esp. in a newspaper. **6** = *powder puff.* **7** an eiderdown. **8** *Brit. colloq.* one's life (*in all my puff*). ● *v.* **1** *intr.* emit a puff of air or breath; blow with short blasts. **2** *intr.* (usu. foll. by *away, out*, etc.) (of a person smoking, a steam engine, etc.) emit or move with puffs (*puffing away at his cigar; a train puffed out of the station*). **3** *tr.* esp. *Brit.* (usu. in *passive*; often foll. by *out*) put out of breath (*arrived somewhat puffed; completely puffed him out*). **4** *intr.* breathe hard; pant. **5** *tr.* utter pantingly ("*No more,*" *he puffed*). **6** *intr. & tr.* (usu. foll. by *up, out*) become or cause to become inflated; swell (*his eye was inflamed and puffed up*). **7** *tr.* (usu. foll. by *out, up, away*) blow or emit (dust, smoke, a light object, etc.) with a puff. **8** *tr.* smoke (a pipe, etc.) in puffs. **9** *tr.* (usu. as **puffed up** *adj.*) elate; make proud or boastful. **10** *tr.* advertise or promote (goods, a book, etc.) with exaggerated or false praise. □ **puff adder** a large venomous African viper, *Bitis arietans*, which inflates the upper part of its body and hisses when excited. **puff pastry** light flaky pastry. **puff-puff** *Brit.* a childish word for a steam engine or train. **puff up** = sense 9 of *v.* [ME *puf, puffe*, perh. f. OE, imit. of the sound of breath]
■ *n.* **1** blow, breath, wind, whiff, gust, blast; draw, pull, *sl.* drag. **5 b** advertisement, notice, *colloq.* plug, *Brit. colloq.* advert. **7** eiderdown, duvet, coverlet, bedspread, quilt, comforter. **8** life, existence, lifetime, lifespan, time, duration, days. ● *v.* **1** blow (out), exhale, breathe (out). **2** (*puff at or on*) draw on, pull at *or* on, smoke, drag on. **3** (*puffed out*) see EXHAUSTED (EXHAUST *v.* 2). **4** huff, pant, gasp, wheeze, blow, breathe. **6** inflate, distend, bloat, swell (up *or* out), stretch, balloon, expand, pump up. **7** see EXHALE 1. **9** (**puffed up**) see PROUD 2a. **10** publicize, advertise, promote, push, trumpet, blow up, ballyhoo, extol, commend, praise, *colloq.* plug, beat the drum for.

puffball /púfbawl/ *n.* any fungus of the genus *Lycoperdon* and related genera producing a ball-shaped spore-bearing structure that releases its contents in a powdery cloud when broken.

puffer /púfər/ *n.* **1** a person or thing that puffs. **2** any tropical fish of the family *Tetraodontidae*, able to inflate itself into a spherical form: also called *globe fish.* **3** = *puff-puff.* □□ **puffery** *n.*

puffin /púfin/ *n.* any of various seabirds of the family Alcidae native to the N. Atlantic and N. Pacific, esp. *Fratercula arctica*, having a large head with a brightly colored triangular bill and black and white plumage. [ME *poffin, pophyn*, of unkn. orig.]

puffy /púfee/ *adj.* (**puffier, puffiest**) **1** swollen, esp. of the face, etc. **2** fat. **3** gusty. **4** short-winded. □□ **puffily** *adv.* **puffiness** *n.*
■ **1** see SWELL *v.* 6.

pug[1] /pug/ *n.* **1** (in full **pugdog**) **a** a dwarf breed of dog like a bulldog with a broad flat nose and deeply wrinkled face. **b** a dog of this breed. **2** *Brit.* a small locomotive for shunting, etc. □ **pug nose** a short squat or snub nose. **pug-nosed** having such a nose. □□ **puggish** *adj.* **puggy** *adj.* [16th c.: perh. f. LG or Du.]

pug[2] /pug/ *n. & v.* ● *n.* loam or clay mixed and prepared for making bricks, pottery, etc. ● *v.tr.* (**pugged, pugging**) **1** prepare (clay) thus. **2** pack (esp. the space under the floor to deaden sound) with pug, sawdust, etc. □ **pug mill** a mill for preparing pug. □□ **pugging** *n.* [19th c.: orig. unkn.]

pug[3] /pug/ *n. sl.* a boxer. [abbr. of PUGILIST]
■ see PUGILIST.

pug[4] /pug/ *n. & v.* ● *n.* the footprint of an animal. ● *v.tr.* (**pugged, pugging**) track by pugs. [Hindi *pag* footprint]

puggaree /púgəree/ *n.* **1** an E. Indian turban. **2** a thin muslin scarf tied around a sun helmet, etc., and shielding the neck. [Hindi *pagrī* turban]

pugilist /pyốojilist/ *n.* a boxer, esp. a professional. □□ **pugilism** *n.* **pugilistic** *adj.* [L *pugil* boxer]
■ boxer, prizefighter, fighter, battler, combatant, *colloq.* bruiser, slugger, *sl.* pug. □□ **pugilism** boxing, prizefighting, fisticuffs.

pugnacious /pugnáyshəs/ *adj.* quarrelsome; disposed to fight. □□ **pugnaciously** *adv.* **pugnaciousness** *n.* **pugnacity** /-násitee/ *n.* [L *pugnax -acis* f. *pugnare* fight f. *pugnus* fist]
■ aggressive, belligerent, combative, quarrelsome, bellicose, antagonistic, argumentative, hostile, litigious, contentious, disputatious, disagreeable, hot-tempered, unfriendly, curmudgeonly, short-tempered.

puisne /pyốonee/ *adj. Brit. Law* denoting a judge of a superior court inferior in rank to chief justices. [OF f. *puis* f. L *postea* afterwards + *né* born f. L *natus*: cf. PUNY]

puissance /pwísəns, pyōō-ís-, pyōō-is-/ *n. literary* great power, might, or influence. [ME (in sense 2) f. OF (as PUISSANT)]
■ **2** see POWER *n.* 3a, 5, 8.

puissant /pwísənt, pyōō-ís-/ *adj. literary* or *archaic* having great power or influence; mighty. □□ **puissantly** *adv.* [ME f. OF f. L *posse* be able: cf. POTENT[1]]
■ see POWERFUL.

puke /pyōōk/ *v. & n. sl.* ● *v.tr. & intr.* vomit. □□ **pukey** *adj.* [16th c.: prob. imit.]

pukka /púkə/ *adj.* (also **pukkah, pucka**) *Anglo-Ind.* **1** genuine. **2** of good quality; reliable (*did a pukka job*). **3** of full weight. [Hindi *pakkā* cooked, ripe, substantial]
■ **1** see GENUINE. **2** good-quality, well-made; see also RELIABLE.

pulchritude /púlkritōōd, -tyōōd/ *n. literary* beauty. □□ **pulchritudinous** /-tōōdinəs, -tyōōd-/ *adj.* [ME f. L *pulchritudo -dinis* f. *pulcher -chri* beautiful]
■ see BEAUTY 1.

pule /pyōōl/ *v.intr.* cry querulously or weakly; whine; whimper. [16th c.: prob. imit.: cf. F *piauler*]
■ see CRY *v.* 2a.

Pulitzer prize /pōolitsər, pyōō-/ *n.* each of a group of annual awards for achievements in American journalism, literature, and music. [J. *Pulitzer*, Amer. newspaper publisher d. 1911]

pull /pōol/ *v. & n.* ● *v.* **1** *tr.* exert force upon (a thing) tending to move it to oneself or the origin of the force (*stop pulling my hair*). **2** *tr.* cause to move in this way (*pulled it nearer; pulled me into the room*). **3** *intr.* exert a pulling force (*the horse pulls well; the engine will not pull*). **4** *tr.* extract (a cork or tooth) by pulling. **5** *tr.* damage (a muscle, etc.) by abnormal strain. **6 a** *tr.* move (a boat) by pulling on the oars. **b** *intr.* (of a boat, etc.) be caused to move, esp. in a specified direction. **7** *intr.* (often foll. by *up*) proceed with effort (up a

hill, etc.). **8** *tr.* (foll. by *on*) bring out (a weapon) for use against (a person). **9 a** *tr.* check the speed of (a horse), esp. so as to make it lose the race. **b** *intr.* (of a horse) strain against the bit. **10** *tr.* attract or secure (custom or support). **11** *tr.* draw (liquor) from a barrel, etc. **12** *intr.* (foll. by *at*) tear or pluck at. **13** *intr.* (often foll. by *on, at*) inhale deeply; draw or suck (on a pipe, etc.). **14** *tr.* (often foll. by *up*) remove (a plant) by the root. **15** *tr.* **a** *Baseball* hit (a ball) to the left (for a right-handed batter) or to the right (for a left-handed batter). **b** *Golf* strike (the ball) widely to the left (or right for a left-handed swing). **16** *tr.* print (a proof, etc.). **17** *tr. colloq.* achieve or accomplish (esp. something illicit). **18** *tr.* to stretch repeatedly, as candy. ● *n.* **1** the act of pulling. **2** the force exerted by this. **3** a means of exerting influence; an advantage. **4** something that attracts or draws attention. **5** a deep draft of esp. liquor. **6** a prolonged effort, e.g., in going up a hill. **7** a handle, etc., for applying a pull. **8** a spell of rowing. **9** a printer's rough proof. **10** *Golf* a pulling stroke. **11** a suck at a cigarette. □ **pull apart** (or **to pieces**) = *take to pieces* (see PIECE). **pull away** withdraw; move away; move ahead. **pull back** retreat or cause to retreat. **pull down 1** demolish (esp. a building). **2** humiliate. **3** *colloq.* earn (a sum of money) as income, etc. **pull a face** esp. *Brit.* assume a distinctive or specified (e.g., sad or angry) expression. **pull a fast one** see FAST[1]. **pull in 1** arrive, esp. at a destination. **b** to restrain; tighten. **2** (of a bus, train, etc.) arrive to take passengers. **3** earn or acquire. **4** *colloq.* arrest. **pull-in** *n. Brit.* a roadside café or other stopping place. **pull a person's leg** deceive a person playfully. **pull off 1** remove by pulling. **2** succeed in achieving or winning. **pull oneself together** recover control of oneself. **pull the other one** *colloq.* expressing disbelief (with ref. to *pull a person's leg*). **pull out 1** take out by pulling. **2** depart. **3** withdraw from an undertaking. **4** (of a bus, train, etc.) leave with its passengers. **5 a** (of a vehicle) move out from the side of the road, or from its normal position to overtake. **b** (of an airplane) resume level flight from a dive. **pull over** (of a vehicle) move to the side of or off the road. **pull the plug on** *colloq.* withdraw support. **pull one's punches** avoid using one's full force. **pull rank** take unfair advantage of one's seniority. **pull strings** exert (esp. clandestine) influence. **pull the strings** be the real actuator of what another does. **pull-tab** (of a can) having a ring or tab for pulling to break its seal. **pull through** recover or cause to recover from an illness. **pull together** work in harmony. **pull up 1** stop or cause to stop moving. **2** pull out of the ground. **3** draw closer to or even with, as in a race. **4** check oneself. **pull one's weight** do one's fair share of work. □□ **puller** *n.* [OE (ā)*pullian*, perh. rel. to LG *pūlen*, MDu. *polen* to shell]
■ *v.* **1** jerk, pull at, pluck, tug, *colloq.* yank; wrench. **2** draw, haul, drag, lug, tow, trail; see also TUG *v.* 1. **4** see EXTRACT *v.* 1. **5** tear, stretch, strain, rip, wrench, sprain, *archaic or rhet.* rend. **10** attract, draw, pull in; secure, get, obtain; lure, entice, allure. **12** see PLUCK *v.* 3, 4. **13** draw, drag, puff, suck; see also INHALE. **14** pull out, pluck (out), extract, uproot, pick (up *or* out), withdraw, tear *or* rip out *or* up, take out, remove, dig up *or* out, *literary* deracinate. **17** see *pull off* 2 below. ● *n.* **1** see TUG *n.* 1. **2, 4** magnetism, appeal, pulling power, seductiveness, seduction; attraction, draw, lure. **3** influence, authority, weight, leverage, *colloq.* clout. **5** see DRAFT *n.* 5. **7** lever, grip; see also HANDLE *n.* 1. **11** puff, draw, inhalation, *sl.* drag. □ **pull away** withdraw, draw *or* drive *or* go *or* move away. **pull back** withdraw, draw back, back off *or* away, recoil, shrink (away *or* back), shy away, flinch, jump back, start, (beat a) retreat, take flight, flee, turn tail. **pull down 1** raze, level, destroy, wreck; see also DEMOLISH 1a. **2** lower, humiliate, debase, reduce, degrade, dishonor, disgrace,

---

/. . ./ **pronunciation**	● **part of speech**

□ **phrases, idioms, and compounds**

□□ **derivatives**   ■ **synonym section**

cross-references appear in SMALL CAPITALS or *italics*

discredit. **3** earn, draw, receive, get, be paid, take home, clear, pocket, net, bring in, pull in. **pull in 1** draw up *or* in *or* over; see also ARRIVE 1. **3** see EARN 1, ACQUIRE 1. **4** arrest, apprehend, take into custody, collar, *colloq.* bust, *sl.* pinch, nab, *Brit. sl.* lag, nick. **pull a person's leg** tease, chaff, rib, twit, make fun of, *colloq.* have on, rag; see also *poke fun at* (POKE¹). **pull off 1** detach, rip *or* tear off, wrench off *or* away; see also SEPARATE *v.* 1. **2** bring off, accomplish, do, complete, succeed in, carry out, manage, perform. **pull oneself together** get a grip (on oneself), *colloq.* buck up, *sl.* snap out of it; recover, get over it, recuperate. **pull the other one** see *go on!* (GO¹). **pull out 1** uproot, extract, withdraw, pull; pull up, take out; see also PULL *v.* 14 above. **2, 4** see LEAVE¹ *v.* 1b, 3, 4. **3** withdraw, give up; retreat, beat a retreat, draw back, run away *or* off, *colloq.* cry off, *sl.* beat it, *Brit. sl.* do a bunk. **pull rank** pull strings, pull wires, *colloq.* throw one's weight around. **pull strings** use *or* exert influence, use connections, pull wires. **pull the strings** be in control *or* command, be behind it all, be in the driving seat, hold the reins; see also DOMINATE. **pull through** recover, improve, get better, get over it; live, survive. **pull together** cooperate, agree, *colloq.* jell; see also *get along* 1. **pull up 1** see STOP *v.* 3. **2** see PULL *v.* 14 above. **4** stop, control oneself, check oneself, get a grip on *or* of oneself, get (a) hold on *or* of oneself, pull oneself together, (re)gain control of oneself, snap out of it. **pull one's weight** do one's fair share, perform, *colloq.* do one's bit, deliver the goods.

pullet /poōlit/ *n.* a young hen, esp. one less than one year old. [ME f. OF *poulet* dimin. of *poule* ult. fem. of L *pullus* chicken]

pulley /poōlee/ *n.* & *v.* ● *n.* (*pl.* **-eys**) **1** a grooved wheel or set of wheels for a rope, etc., to pass over, set in a block and used for changing the direction of a force. **2** a wheel or drum fixed on a shaft and turned by a belt, used esp. to increase speed or power. ● *v.tr.* (**-eys, -eyed**) **1** hoist or work with a pulley. **2** provide with a pulley. [ME f. OF *polie* prob. ult. f. med. Gk *polidion* (unrecorded) pivot, dimin. of *polos* POLE²]

■ *v.* **1** hoist, pull *or* lift up, haul up, elevate, raise, heave up, uplift, winch.

Pullman /poōlmən/ *n.* **1** a railroad car affording special comfort, esp. one with sleeping berths. **2** (in full **Pullman trunk** or **case**) a large suitcase. [G. M. *Pullman*, Amer. designer d. 1897]

pullover /poōlōvər/ *n.* a knitted garment put on over the head and covering the top half of the body.

pullulate /púlyəlayt/ *v.intr.* **1** (of a seed, shoot, etc.) bud, sprout; germinate. **2** (esp. of an animal) swarm; throng; breed prolifically. **3** develop; spring up; come to life. **4** (foll. by *with*) abound. □□ **pullulant** *adj.* **pullulation** /-láyshən/ *n.* [L *pullulare* sprout f. *pullulus* dimin. of *pullus* young of an animal]

pulmonary /poōlməneree, púl-/ *adj.* **1** of or relating to the lungs. **2** having lungs or lunglike organs. **3** affected with or susceptible to lung disease. □ **pulmonary artery** the artery conveying blood from the heart to the lungs. **pulmonary vein** the vein carrying oxygenated blood from the lungs to the heart. □□ **pulmonate** /-nayt, -nət/ *adj.* [L *pulmonarius* f. *pulmo -onis* lung]

pulmonic /poōlmónik, pul-/ *adj.* = PULMONARY 1. [F *pulmonique* or f. mod.L *pulmonicus* f. L *pulmo* (as PULMONARY)]

pulp /pulp/ *n.* & *v.* ● *n.* **1** the soft fleshy part of fruit, etc. **2** any soft thick wet mass. **3** a soft shapeless mass derived from rags, wood, etc., used in papermaking. **4** (often *attrib.*) poor quality (often sensational) writing orig. printed on rough paper (*pulp fiction*). **5** vascular tissue filling the interior cavity and root canals of a tooth. **6** *Mining* pulverized ore mixed with water. ● *v.* **1** *tr.* reduce to pulp. **2** *tr.* withdraw (a publication) from the market, usu. recycling the paper. **3** *tr.* remove pulp from. **4** *intr.* become pulp. □□ **pulper** *n.* **pulpless** *adj.* **pulpy** *adj.* **pulpiness** *n.* [L *pulpa*]

■ *n.* **1** marrow, flesh, soft part. **2** mush, paste, mash, pap,

pomace, mass. **4** (*attrib.*) bad, poor quality, shoddy, rubbishy, cheap; sensational, lurid. ● *v.* **1** mash, squash, pulverize, triturate, grind down, levigate.

pulpit /poōlpit, púl-/ *n.* **1** a raised enclosed platform in a church, etc., from which the preacher delivers a sermon. **2** (prec. by *the*) preachers or preaching collectively. [ME f. L *pulpitum* scaffold, platform]

■ **2** see MINISTRY 1, 2.

pulpwood /púlpwoŏd/ *n.* timber suitable for making pulp.

pulque /poōlkay, poōlkee, poōl-/ *n.* a Mexican fermented drink made from the sap of the maguey. □ **pulque brandy** a strong intoxicant made from pulque. [17th c.: Amer. Sp., of unkn. orig.]

pulsar /púlsaar/ *n. Astron.* a cosmic source of regular and rapid pulses of radiation usu. at radio frequencies, e.g., a rotating neutron star. [*pulsating* star, after *quasar*]

pulsate /púlsayt/ *v.intr.* **1** expand and contract rhythmically; throb. **2** vibrate; quiver; thrill. □□ **pulsation** /-sáyshən/ *n.* **pulsator** *n.* **pulsatory** /púlsətawree/ *adj.* [L *pulsare* frequent. of *pellere puls-* drive, beat]

■ beat, pulse, throb, pound, thrum, drum, thump, thud, reverberate, hammer, palpitate, vibrate, oscillate, quiver, thrill.

pulsatile /púlsətil, -til/ *adj.* **1** of or having the property of pulsation. **2** (of a musical instrument) played by percussion. [med.L *pulsatilis* (as PULSATE)]

pulse¹ /puls/ *n.* & *v.* ● *n.* **1 a** a rhythmical throbbing of the arteries as blood is propelled through them, esp. as felt in the wrists, temples, etc. **b** each successive beat of the arteries or heart. **c** (in full **pulse rate**) the number of such beats in a specified period of time, esp. one minute. **2** a throb or thrill of life or emotion. **3** a latent feeling. **4** a single vibration of sound, electric current, light, etc., esp. as a signal. **5** a musical beat. **6** any regular or recurrent rhythm, e.g., of the stroke of oars. ● *v.intr.* **1** pulsate. **2** (foll. by *out, in,* etc.) transmit, etc., by rhythmical beats. **pulse modulation** a type of modulation in which pulses are varied to represent a signal. □□ **pulseless** *adj.* [ME f. OF *pous* f. L *pulsus* f. *pellere puls-* drive, beat]

■ *n.* **2** see THRILL *n.* 2. **5, 6** beat, beating, throb, throbbing, pulsation, pounding, drumming, reverberation, hammering, palpitation, vibration; rhythm. ● *v.* **1** see PULSATE.

pulse² /puls/ *n.* (as *sing.* or *pl.*) **1** the edible seeds of various leguminous plants, e.g., chickpeas, lentils, beans, etc. **2** the plant or plants producing this. [ME f. OF *pols* f. L *puls pultis* porridge of meal, etc.]

pulsimeter /pulsímitər/ *n.* an instrument for measuring the rate or force of a pulse.

pulverize /púlvərīz/ *v.* **1** *tr.* reduce to fine particles. **2** *intr.* be reduced to dust. **3** *colloq. tr.* **a** demolish. **b** defeat utterly. □□ **pulverizable** *adj.* **pulverization** *n.* **pulverizer** *n.* [ME f. LL *pulverizare* f. *pulvis pulveris* dust]

■ **1, 2** powder, comminute, grind, crush, mill, granulate, crumble, break up, pound, triturate, levigate, *archaic* bray. **3** devastate, destroy, demolish, crush, smash, shatter, ruin, wreck, annihilate; see also BEAT *v.* 3a.

pulverulent /pulvéryələnt, -vérə-/ *adj.* **1** consisting of fine particles; powdery. **2** likely to crumble. [L *pulverulentus* (as PULVERIZE)]

puma /pyōomə, poō-/ *n.* a large American wild cat, *Felis concolor*, usu. with a plain tawny coat. Also called COUGAR, PANTHER, *mountain lion*. [Sp. f. Quechua]

pumice /púmis/ *n.* & *v.* ● *n.* (in full **pumice stone**) **1** a light porous volcanic rock often used as an abrasive in cleaning or polishing substances. **2** a piece of this used for removing callused skin, etc. ● *v.tr.* rub or clean with a pumice. □□ **pumiceous** /pyōomíshəs/ *adj.* [ME f. OF *pomis* f. L *pumex pumicis* (dial. *pom*-): cf. POUNCE²]

pummel /púməl/ *v.tr.* (**pummeled** or **pummelled, pummeling** or **pummelling**) strike repeatedly, esp. with the fist. [alt. f. POMMEL]

■ see BEAT *v.* 1, 2a.

pump¹ /pump/ *n.* & *v.* ● *n.* **1** a machine, usu. with rotary action or the reciprocal action of a piston, for raising or

moving liquids, compressing gases, inflating tires, etc. **2** a physiological or electromagnetic process or mechanism having a similar purpose. **3** an instance of pumping; a stroke of a pump. ● *v.* **1** *tr.* (often foll. by *in, out, into, up,* etc.) raise or remove (liquid, gas, etc.) with a pump. **2** *tr.* (often foll. by *up*) fill (a tire, etc.) with air. **3** *tr.* **a** remove (water, etc.) with a pump. **b** (foll. by *out*) remove liquid from (a place, well, etc.) with a pump. **4** *intr.* work a pump. **5** *tr.* (often foll. by *out*) cause to move, pour forth, etc., as if by pumping. **6** *tr.* question (a person) persistently to obtain information. **7** *tr.* **a** move vigorously up and down. **b** shake (a person's hand) effusively. **8** *tr.* (usu. foll. by *up*) arouse; excite. **pump iron** (also **pump up**) *colloq.* exercise with weights. [ME *pumpe, pompe* (orig. Naut.): prob. imit.]
■ *v.* **1, 3a, 5** send, deliver, push; (*pump out*) drive or force out, draw off *or* out, siphon (out *or* off), drain, tap, extract, withdraw. **2** (*pump up*) see INFLATE 1. **3 b** (*pump out*) pump dry *or* empty, empty, drain, bail out. **6** interrogate, question, examine, cross-examine, quiz, probe, grill, give a person the third degree. **8** (*pump up*) arouse, excite, inspire, stimulate, animate, inspirit, electrify, galvanize, energize, motivate, *colloq.* enthuse.

pump² /pump/ *n.* **1** a usu. medium-heeled slip-on women's dress shoe. **2** a slip-on men's patent leather shoe for formal wear. [16th c.: orig. unkn.]

pumpernickel /púmpərnikəl/ *n.* German-style dark, coarse rye bread. [G, earlier = lout, bumpkin, of uncert. orig.]

pumpkin /púmpkin, púng-/ *n.* **1** the rounded orange edible gourd of a vine (*Cucurbita pepa*). **2** *Brit.* **a** any of various plants of the genus *Cucurbita*, esp. *C. maxima*, with large lobed leaves and tendrils. **b** the large rounded yellow fruit of this with a thick rind and edible flesh. [alt. f. earlier *pompon, pumpion* f. obs. F *po(m)pon* f. L *pepo -onis* f. Gk *pepōn* large melon: see PEPO]

pun¹ /pun/ *n. & v.* ● *n.* the humorous use of a word to suggest different meanings, or of words of the same sound and different meanings. ● *v.intr.* (**punned, punning**) (foll. by *on*) make a pun or puns with (words). □□ **punningly** *adv.* [17th c.: perh. f. obs. *pundigrion*, a fanciful formation]
■ *n.* play on words, quibble, double entendre, innuendo, equivoque, paronomasia; wordplay; quip, witticism, bon mot.

pun² /pun/ *v.tr.* (**punned, punning**) *Brit.* consolidate (earth or rubble) by pounding or ramming. □□ **punner** *n.* [dial. var. of POUND²]

puna /póonə/ *n.* **1** a high plateau in the Peruvian Andes. **2** = *mountain sickness.* [Quechua, in sense 1]

punch¹ /punch/ *v. & n.* ● *v.tr.* **1** strike bluntly, esp. with a closed fist. **2** prod or poke with a blunt object. **3 a** pierce a hole in (metal, paper, a ticket, etc.) as or with a punch. **b** pierce (a hole) by punching. **4** drive (cattle) by prodding with a stick, etc. ● *n.* **1** a blow with a fist. **2** the ability to deliver this. **3** *colloq.* vigor; momentum; effective force. □ **punch** (or **punched**) **card** (or **tape**) a card or paper tape perforated according to a code, for conveying instructions or data to a data processor, etc. **punch-drunk** stupefied from or as though from a series of heavy blows. **punching bag** a usu. suspended stuffed or inflated bag used for punching as a form of exercise or training. **punch in** (or **out**) record the time of one's arrival at (or departure from) work by punching a time clock. **punch line** words giving the point of a joke or story. **punch-up** *Brit. colloq.* a fistfight; a brawl. □□ **puncher** *n.* [ME, var. of POUNCE¹]
■ *v.* **1** hit, clip, jab, smack, box, strike, clout, thump, cuff, poke, slug, *archaic or literary* smite, *colloq.* whack, sock, thwack, bop, *Austral. & NZ colloq.* dong, *sl.* wallop, biff, belt. **2** see POKE¹ *v.* 1a. **3** a puncture, perforate, penetrate, go through, rupture. **b** pierce, prick. ● *n.* **1** clip, jab, smack, blow, box, cuff, thump, uppercut, clout, hit, poke, slug, *colloq.* sock, whack, thwack, bop, *sl.* wallop, belt, biff, haymaker. **3** effect, impact, effectiveness, force, momentum, impetus, forcefulness, power, vitality, gusto, vigor, life, vim, zest, zip, *colloq.* zing, *sl.* oomph.

punch² /punch/ *n.* **1** any of various devices or machines for punching holes in materials (e.g., paper, leather, metal, plaster). **2** a tool or machine for impressing a design or stamping a die on a material. [perh. an abbr. of PUNCHEON¹, or f. PUNCH¹]
■ **1** awl, auger, bodkin, perforator.

punch³ /punch/ *n.* a drink of fruit juices, sometimes mixed with wine or liquor, served cold or hot. □ **punch bowl 1** a bowl in which punch is mixed and served. **2** esp. *Brit.* a deep round hollow in a hill. [17th c.: orig. unkn.]

punch⁴ /punch/ *n.* **1** (**Punch**) a humpbacked, hook-nosed figure in a puppet show called *Punch and Judy*. **2** (in full **Suffolk punch**) a short-legged thickset draft horse. □ **as pleased as Punch** showing great pleasure. [abbr. of PUNCHINELLO]

puncheon¹ /púnchən/ *n.* **1** a short post, esp. one supporting a roof in a coal mine. **2** = PUNCH². **3** a heavy timber finished on one side only, used in flooring, etc. [ME f. OF *poinson, po(i)nchon,* ult. f. L *pungere punct-* prick]

puncheon² /púnchən/ *n.* a large cask for liquids, etc., holding from 72 to 120 gallons. [ME f. OF *poinson, po(i)nchon,* of unkn. orig. (prob. not the same as in PUNCHEON¹)]

Punchinello /púnchinélō/ *n.* (*pl.* **-os**) **1** the chief character in a traditional Italian puppet show. **2** a short stout person of comical appearance. [Neapolitan dial. *Polecenella*, It. *Pulcinella*, perh. dimin. of *pollecena*, young turkey-cock with a hooked beak f. *pulcino* chicken ult. f. L *pullus*]

punchy /púnchee/ *adj.* (**punchier, punchiest**) **1** having punch or vigor; forceful. **2** = *punch-drunk.* □□ **punchily** *adv.* **punchiness** *n.*
■ see FORCEFUL.

punctate /púngktayt/ *adj. Biol.* marked or studded with points, dots, spots, etc. □□ **punctation** /-táyshən/ *n.* [L *punctum* (as POINT)]

punctilio /pungktíleeō/ *n.* (*pl.* **-os**) **1** a delicate point of ceremony or honor. **2** the etiquette of such points. **3** petty formality. [It. *puntiglio* & Sp. *puntillo* dimin. of *punto* POINT]
■ **2** see ETIQUETTE 1, see FORMALITY 2, 4.

punctilious /pungktíleeəs/ *adj.* **1** attentive to formality or etiquette. **2** precise in behavior. □□ **punctiliously** *adv.* **punctiliousness** *n.* [F *pointilleux* f. *pointille* f. It. (as PUNCTILIO)]
■ **1** see FORMAL *adj.* 4. **2** see PRECISE 2. □□ **punctiliously** see PRECISELY 1. **punctiliousness** see PRECISION 2.

punctual /púngkchooəl/ *adj.* **1** observant of the appointed time. **2** neither early nor late. **3** *Geom.* of a point. □□ **punctuality** /-álitee/ *n.* **punctually** *adv.* [ME f. med.L *punctualis* f. L *punctum* POINT]
■ **1, 2** on time, timely, prompt; on target.

punctuate /púngkchooayt/ *v.tr.* **1** insert punctuation marks in. **2** interrupt at intervals (*punctuated his tale with heavy sighs*). **3** emphasize. [med.L *punctuare punctuat-* (as PUNCTUAL)]
■ **2** interrupt, break; intersperse, interlard, pepper, sprinkle, besprinkle, dot.

punctuation /púngkchoo-áyshən/ *n.* **1** the system or arrangement of marks used to punctuate a written passage. **2** the practice or skill of punctuating. □ **punctuation mark** any of the marks (e.g., period and comma) used in writing to separate sentences and phrases, etc., and to clarify meaning. [med.L *punctuatio* (as PUNCTUATE)]

puncture /púngkchər/ *n. & v.* ● *n.* **1** a pierced hole, esp. the accidental piercing of a pneumatic tire. **2** a hole made in this way. ● *v.* **1** *tr.* make a puncture in. **2** *intr.* become punctured. **3** *tr.* prick or pierce. **4** *tr.* cause (hopes, confidence, etc.) to collapse; dash; deflate. [ME f. L *punctura* f. *pungere punct-* prick]
■ *n.* **1** perforation, holing, piercing; prick. **2** see LEAK *n.* 1a. ● *v.* **1, 3** hole, pierce, penetrate, go through, prick, nick. **4** deflate, disillusion, discourage, dash, destroy, ruin.

pundit /púndit/ n. **1** (also **pandit**) a Hindu learned in Sanskrit and in the philosophy, religion, and jurisprudence of India. **2** often *iron.* **a** a learned expert or teacher. **b** a critic. □□ **punditry** n. [Hind. *paṇḍit* f. Skr. *paṇḍita* learned]

■ **2** see EXPERT n.

pungent /púnjənt/ adj. **1** having a sharp or strong taste or smell. **2** (of remarks) penetrating; biting; caustic. **3** *Biol.* having a sharp point. □□ **pungency** n. **pungently** adv. [L *pungent-* pres. part. of *pungere* prick]

■ **1** spicy, hot, sharp, strong, penetrating, aromatic, seasoned, peppery, piquant, tangy, flavorful, tasty, *literary* sapid. **2** sharp, biting, penetrating, stinging, caustic, severe, astringent, stern, acrid, harsh, acid, acrimonious, bitter, cutting, keen, barbed, trenchant, scathing, incisive, mordant, sarcastic.

Punic /pyóonik/ adj. & n. ● adj. **1** of or relating to ancient Carthage in N. Africa. **2** treacherous. ● n. the language of Carthage, related to Phoenician. □ **Punic faith** treachery. [L *Punicus, Poenicus* f. *Poenus* f. Gk *Phoinix* Phoenician]

punish /púnish/ v.tr. **1** cause (an offender) to suffer for an offense. **2** inflict a penalty for (an offense). **3** *colloq.* inflict severe blows on (an opponent). **4 a** tax severely; subject to severe treatment. **b** abuse or treat improperly. □□ **punishable** adj. **punisher** n. **punishing** adj. (in sense 4a). **punishingly** adv. [ME f. OF *punir* f. L *punire = poenire* f. *poena* penalty]

■ **1** penalize, chastise, castigate, discipline, chasten, amerce, scold, rebuke, take to task, reprove, drop on, admonish, correct, trounce, teach a person a lesson, rap a person's knuckles, give a person a slap on the wrist, call on the carpet, make a person pay for, *Bibl.* visit, *colloq.* throw the book at, dress down, give it to a person, give a person hell, lay into; tar and feather; flog, beat, scourge, spank, whip, warm *or* tan a person's hide, cane, birch, bastinado. **3** rough up, knock about *or* around, thrash, trounce, batter, beat up; see also BEAT v. 1. **4** abuse, maltreat, mistreat, hurt, harm, injure, damage. □□ **punishing** grueling, hard, arduous, strenuous, exhausting, tiring, taxing, demanding, burdensome, backbreaking, torturous.

punishment /púnishmənt/ n. **1** the act or an instance of punishing; the condition of being punished. **2** the loss or suffering inflicted in this. **3** *colloq.* severe treatment or suffering. [ME f. AF & OF *punissement* f. *punir*]

■ **1, 2** chastisement, castigation, discipline, scolding, rebuke, reproof, admonishment, admonition, correction, sentencing, punitive measures; penance, penalty, sentence; (just) deserts, *colloq.* comeuppance; stick; flogging, beating, whipping, scourging, spanking, caning, birching. **3** injury, harm, damage, abuse, maltreatment, suffering, torture; beating, thrashing, battering; pounding; *colloq.* stick.

punitive /pyóonitiv/ adj. (also **punitory** /-tawree/) **1** inflicting or intended to inflict punishment. **2** (of taxation, etc.) extremely severe. □ **punitive damages** *Law* additional compensation awarded by a court to a plaintiff in a suit as punishment to the defendant. □□ **punitively** adv. [F *punitif -ive* or med.L *punitivus* (as PUNISHMENT)]

■ **1** chastening, castigatory, disciplinary, retributive, correctional. **2** see HARSH 2.

Punjabi /póonjaábee/ n. & adj. ● n. (pl. **Punjabis**) **1** a native of the Punjab in India. **2** the language of this people. ● adj. of or relating to the Punjab. [Hindi *pañjābī*]

punk /pungk/ n. & adj. ● n. **1 a** a worthless person or thing (often as a general term of abuse). **b** nonsense. **2 a** (in full **punk rock**) a loud fast-moving form of rock music with crude and aggressive effects. **b** (in full **punk rocker**) a devotee of this. **3** a hoodlum or ruffian. **4** a young male homosexual partner. **5** an inexperienced person; a novice. **6** soft crumbly wood used as tinder. **7** a spongy fungal substance, esp. as used as a fuse. ● adj. **1** worthless; poor in quality. **2** denoting punk rock and its associations. **3** (of wood) rotten; decayed. □□ **punky** adj. [18th c.: orig. unkn.: cf. SPUNK]

■ n. **1 a** see WRETCH 2. **b** see NONSENSE. **3** ruffian,

hooligan, delinquent, tough, thug, vandal, yahoo, barbarian, *sl.* mug; see also HOODLUM. **5** see NOVICE.
● adj. **1** inferior, unimportant, bad, poor, *colloq.* lousy, awful, *sl.* rotten; see also WORTHLESS.

punkah /púngkə/ n. **1** (in India) a fan usu. made from the leaf of the palmyra. **2** a large swinging cloth fan hung from the ceiling and worked by a cord or electrically. [Hindi *pankhā* fan f. Skr. *pakṣaka* f. *pakṣa* wing]

punnet /púnit/ n. *Brit.* a small light basket or container for fruit or vegetables. [19th c.: perh. dimin. of dial. *pun* POUND¹]

punster /púnstər/ n. a person who makes puns, esp. habitually.

punt¹ /punt/ n. & v. ● n. a long narrow flat-bottomed boat, square at both ends, used mainly on rivers and propelled by a long pole. ● v. **1** *tr.* propel (a punt) with a pole. **2** *intr.* & *tr.* travel or convey in a punt. □□ **punter** n. [ME f. MLG *punte, punto* & MDu. *ponte* ferryboat f. L *ponto* Gaulish transport vessel]

punt² /punt/ v. & n. ● v.tr. kick (a ball, as in football or rugby) after it has dropped from the hands and before it reaches the ground. ● n. such a kick. □□ **punter** n. [prob. f. dial. *punt* push forcibly: cf. BUNT¹]

punt³ /punt/ v. & n. ● v.intr. **1** (in some card games) lay a stake against the bank. **2** *Brit. colloq.* **a** bet on a horse, etc. **b** speculate in shares, etc. ● n. **1** esp. *Brit.* a bet. **2** a point in faro. **3** a person who plays against the bank in faro. [F *ponter* f. *ponte* player against the bank f. Sp. *punto* POINT]

■ v. **2 a** bet, wager, gamble, speculate, lay a bet *or* wager. ● n. **1** wager, stake; see also BET n. 1, 2.

punt⁴ /poont/ n. the chief monetary unit of the Republic of Ireland. [Ir., = pound]

punter /púntər/ n. **1** one who punts, esp. one who punts a ball. **2** *Brit.* a person who gambles or lays a bet. **3** *Brit.* **a** *colloq.* a customer or client; a member of an audience. **b** *colloq.* a participant in any activity; a person. **c** *sl.* a prostitute's client. **4** a point in faro.

■ **2** better, gambler, gamester, player, speculator, punt. **3 a** customer, buyer, shopper, client; patron. **b** fellow, chap, person, individual, man in the street, woman in the street; *colloq.* guy, *sl.* geezer, *Brit. sl.* bloke. **c** *sl.* john.

puny /pyóonee/ adj. (**punier, puniest**) **1** undersized. **2** weak; feeble. **3** petty. □□ **punily** adv. **puniness** n. [phonetic spelling of PUISNE]

■ **1, 2** small, little, diminutive, tiny, minute, undersized, stunted, dwarf, midget, pygmy; weak, feeble, frail, sickly, weakly, underfed, undernourished. **3** insignificant, petty, unimportant, inconsequential, paltry, trivial, trifling, minor, negligible, nugatory, small, little, worthless, useless, *colloq.* piddling.

pup /pup/ n. & v. ● n. **1** a young dog. **2** a young wolf, rat, seal, etc. **3** esp. *Brit.* an unpleasant or arrogant young man. ● v.tr. (**pupped, pupping**) (also *absol.*) bring forth (pups). □ **in pup** (of a dog, wolf, etc.) pregnant. **pup tent** a small two-person tent, usu. made of two pieces fastened together. **sell a person a pup** *Brit.* swindle a person, esp. by selling something worthless. [back-form. f. PUPPY as if a dimin. in -Y²]

■ n. **1** puppy, whelp. **3** puppy, whelp, upstart, whippersnapper, cub, *archaic* jackanapes.

pupa /pyóopə/ n. (pl. **pupae** /-pee/) an insect in the stage of development between larva and imago. □□ **pupal** adj. [mod.L f. L *pupa* girl, doll]

pupate /pyóopayt/ v.intr. become a pupa. □□ **pupation** n.

pupil¹ /pyóopəl/ n. a person who is taught by another, esp. a student in relation to a teacher. □□ **pupilage** n. (also **pupillage**). **pupillary** adj. [ME, orig. = orphan, ward f. OF *pupille* or L *pupillus, -illa,* dimin. of *pupus* boy, *pupa* girl]

■ student, learner, schoolchild, schoolgirl, schoolboy; disciple, apprentice.

pupil² /pyóopəl/ n. the dark circular opening in the center of the iris of the eye, varying in size to regulate the passage of light to the retina. □□ **pupillar** adj. (also **pupilar**). **pupillary** adj. (also **pupilary**). [OF *pupille* or L *pupilla,* dimin.

of *pūpa* doll (as PUPIL¹): so called from the tiny images visible in the eye]

pupiparous /pyŏŏpípərəs/ *adj. Entomol.* bringing forth young which are already in a pupal state. [mod.L *pupipara* neut. pl. of *pupiparus* (as PUPA, *parere* bring forth)]

puppet /púpit/ *n.* **1** a small figure representing a human being or animal and moved by various means as entertainment. **2** a person whose actions are controlled by another. □ **puppet state** a country that is nominally independent but actually under the control of another power. □□ **puppetry** *n.* [later form of POPPET]
  ■ **2** figurehead, cat's-paw, pawn, dupe, tool, instrument, *colloq.* yes-man, stooge.

puppeteer /púpite̊er/ *n.* a person who works puppets.

puppy /púpee/ *n.* (*pl.* -ies) **1** a young dog. **2** a conceited or arrogant young man. □ **puppy fat** *Brit.* temporary fatness of a child or adolescent. **puppy love** romantic attachment or affection between adolescents. □□ **puppyhood** *n.* **puppyish** *adj.* [ME perh. f. OF *po(u)pee* doll, plaything, toy f. Rmc (as POPPET)]
  ■ **2** see PUP *n.* 3.

pur- /pər/ *prefix* = PRO-¹ (*purchase*; *pursue*). [AF f. OF *por-*, *pur-*, *pour-* f. L *por-*, *pro-*]

Purana /pŏŏraánə/ *n.* any of a class of Sanskrit sacred writings on Hindu mythology, folklore, etc. □□ **Puranic** *adj.* [Skr. *purāna* ancient legend, ancient, f. *purā* formerly]

purblind /pə́rblind/ *adj.* **1** partly blind. **2** obtuse; dim-witted. □□ **purblindness** *n.* [ME *pur(e) blind* f. PURE orig. in sense 'utterly,' with assim. to PUR-]
  ■ **1** partially sighted, visually handicapped. **2** see DIM *adj.* 3.

purchase /pə́rchis/ *v. & n.* ● *v.tr.* **1** acquire by payment; buy. **2** obtain or achieve at some cost. **3** *Naut.* haul up (an anchor, etc.) by means of a pulley, lever, etc. ● *n.* **1** the act or an instance of buying. **2** something bought. **3** *Law* the acquisition of property by one's personal action and not by inheritance. **4 a** a firm hold on a thing to move it or to prevent it from slipping; leverage. **b** a device or tackle for moving heavy objects. **5** the annual rent or return from land. □□ **purchasable** *adj.* **purchaser** *n.* [ME f. AF *purchacer*, OF *pourchacier* seek to obtain (as PUR-, CHASE¹)]
  ■ *v.* **1** buy, acquire, procure, obtain, get, secure, pay for. **2** win, gain, achieve, realize, attain, obtain. ● *n.* **1** acquisition, buying, purchasing, procurement. **2** acquisition, *colloq.* buy. **4 a** grip, hold, support, toehold, foothold, grasp, footing; leverage; position, advantage, edge.

purdah /pə́rdə/ *n. Ind.* **1** a system in certain Muslim and Hindu societies of screening women from strangers by means of a veil or curtain. **2** a curtain in a house, used for this purpose. [Urdu & Pers. *pardah* veil, curtain]

pure /pyŏŏr/ *adj.* **1** unmixed; unadulterated (*pure white*; *pure alcohol*). **2** of unmixed origin or descent (*pure-blooded*). **3** chaste. **4** morally or sexually undefiled; not corrupt. **5** conforming absolutely to a standard of quality; faultless. **6** guiltless. **7** sincere. **8** mere; simple; nothing but; sheer (*it was pure malice*). **9** (of a sound) not discordant; perfectly in tune. **10** (of a subject of study) dealing with abstract concepts and not practical application. **11 a** (of a vowel) not joined with another in a diphthong. **b** (of a consonant) not accompanied by another. □ **pure science** a science depending on deductions from demonstrated truths (e.g., mathematics or logic), or one studied without practical applications. □□ **pureness** *n.* [ME f. OF *pur* pure f. L *purus*]
  ■ **1, 2** unmixed, unadulterated, uncontaminated, clear, unalloyed, entire, true, perfect; 24-karat, sterling, solid. **3, 4** chaste, virginal, virgin, intact, maidenly, vestal, immaculate, undefiled, uncorrupted, wholesome, unpolluted, spotless, unblemished, untainted, unsullied; virtuous, good, modest, moral, correct, proper, sinless, impeccable, honorable, (highly) principled, righteous, upright, honest, high-minded, pious, worthy, ethical. **5** faultless, flawless, correct, errorless, perfect. **6** guiltless, innocent, above suspicion, above reproach, blameless. **7** see SINCERE.

8 sheer, utter, absolute, unqualified, complete, total, perfect, thorough, outright, downright, out-and-out, mere, unalloyed, simple, unmitigated, nothing but. **10** abstract, conceptual, theoretical, hypothetical, conjectural, speculative, notional, philosophical, academic.

purebred /pyŏŏrbred/ *adj. & n.* ● *adj.* belonging to a recognized breed of unmixed lineage. ● *n.* a purebred animal.

purée /pyŏŏráy, pyŏŏe̊e/ *n. & v.* ● *n.* a pulp of vegetables or fruit, etc., reduced to a smooth, creamy substance. ● *v.tr.* (**purées, puréed**) make a purée of. [F]

purely /pyŏŏrlee/ *adv.* **1** in a pure manner. **2** merely; solely; exclusively.
  ■ **2** see *merely* (MERE¹).

purfle /pə́rfəl/ *n. & v.* ● *n.* **1** an ornamental border, esp. on a violin, etc. **2** *archaic* the ornamental or embroidered edge of a garment. ● *v.tr.* **1** decorate with a purfle. **2** (often foll. by *with*) ornament (the edge of a building). **3** beautify. □□ **purfling** *n.* [ME f. OF *porfil, porfiler* ult. f. L *filum* thread]

purgation /pərgáyshən/ *n.* **1** purification. **2** purging of the bowels. **3** spiritual cleansing, esp. (*RC Ch.*) of a soul in purgatory. **4** *hist.* the cleansing of oneself from accusation or suspicion by an oath or ordeal. [ME f. OF *purgation* or L *purgatio* (as PURGE)]

purgative /pə́rgətiv/ *adj. & n.* ● *adj.* **1** serving to purify. **2** strongly laxative. ● *n.* **1** a purgative thing. **2** a laxative. [ME f. OF *purgatif -ive* or LL *purgativus* (as PURGE)]
  ■ *adj.* **1** cathartic, depurative, purifying. **2** laxative, cathartic, aperient, evacuant. ● *n.* **1** purifier, depurative, purge. **2** laxative, cathartic, aperient, purge, depurative.

purgatory /pə́rgətawree/ *n. & adj.* ● *n.* (*pl.* -ies) **1** the condition or supposed place of spiritual cleansing, esp. (*RC Ch.*) of those dying in the grace of God but having to expiate venial sins, etc. **2** a place or state of temporary suffering or expiation. ● *adj.* purifying. □□ **purgatorial** /-táwreeəl/ *adj.* [ME f. AF *purgatorie*, OF *-oire* f. med.L *purgatorium*, neut. of LL *purgatorius* (as PURGE)]

purge /pərj/ *v. & n.* ● *v.tr.* **1** (often foll. by *of*, *from*) make physically or spiritually clean. **2** remove by a cleansing or erasing (as of computer files) process. **3 a** rid (an organization, party, etc.) of persons regarded as undesirable. **b** remove (a person regarded as undesirable) from an organization, party, etc., often violently or by force. **4 a** empty (the bowels). **b** empty the bowels of. **5** *Law* atone for or wipe out (an offense, esp. contempt of court). ● *n.* **1 a** the act or an instance of purging. **b** the removal, often in a forcible or violent manner, of people regarded as undesirable from an organization, party, etc. **2** a purgative. □□ **purger** *n.* [ME f. OF *purg(i)er* f. L *purgare* purify f. *purus* pure]
  ■ *v.* **1** purify, cleanse, make clean, scour (out), depurate, wash (out), *usu. formal* cleanse; clear, exonerate, absolve, *formal* exculpate. **3 a** rid, free from, clear. **b** eject, expel, eliminate, get rid of, dismiss, clear out *or* away, sweep away *or* out, oust, remove, rout out, weed out, root out. **4 a** see EMPTY *v.* 1. **5** see ATONE.
  ● *n.* **1** cleansing, purification; ousting, ouster, removal, ejection, expulsion, elimination. **2** see PURGATIVE *n.* 2.

purify /pyŏŏrifi̊/ *v.tr.* (**-ies, -ied**) **1** (often foll. by *of*, *from*) cleanse or make pure. **2** make ceremonially clean. **3** clear of extraneous elements. □□ **purification** /-fikáshən/ *n.* **purificatory** /-rífəkətawree/ *adj.* **purifier** *n.* [ME f. OF *purifier* f. L *purificare* (as PURE)]
  ■ **1** clean, clarify, refine, wash, sanitize, depurate, decontaminate, freshen, disinfect, *usu. formal* cleanse.

Purim /pŏŏrim, pŏŏre̊em/ *n.* a Jewish spring festival commemorating the defeat of Haman's plot to massacre the Jews (Esth. 9). [Heb., pl. of *pūr*, perh. = LOT *n.* 2]

purine /pyŏŏreen/ *n. Chem.* an organic nitrogenous base

/.../	pronunciation	●	part of speech
□	phrases, idioms, and compounds		
□□	derivatives	■	synonym section

cross-references appear in SMALL CAPITALS or *italics*

forming uric acid on oxidation. **2** any of a group of derivatives with purine-like structure, including the nucleotide constituents adenine and guanine. [G *Purin* L *purus* pure + *uricum* uric acid + -*in* -INE⁴]

purist /pyŏŏrist/ *n.* a stickler for or advocate of scrupulous purity, esp. in language or art. □□ **purism** *n.* **puristic** *adj.* [F *puriste* f. *pur* PURE]

■ pedant, precisionist, formalist, stickler, prescriptivist, *colloq.* diehard.

puritan /pyŏŏrit'n/ *n.* & *adj.* ● *n.* **1** (**Puritan**) *hist.* a member of a group of English Protestants who regarded the Reformation of the Church under Elizabeth as incomplete and sought to simplify and regulate forms of worship. **2** a purist member of any party. **3** a person practicing or affecting extreme strictness in religion or morals. ● *adj.* **1** *hist.* of or relating to the Puritans. **2** scrupulous and austere in religion or morals. □□ **puritanism** *n.* [LL *puritas* (as PURITY) after earlier *Catharan* (as CATHAR)]

■ *n.* **3** moralist, pietist, purist, precisian; religionist, fanatic, zealot, *Austral. sl.* wowser; see also PRIG. ● *adj.* **2** prudish, puritanical, prim, proper, straitlaced, ascetic, austere, moralistic, pietistic, intolerant, disapproving, bigoted, narrow-minded, stuffy, stiff-necked, rigid, uncompromising, hard-line, stern, severe, strict, *colloq.* uptight.

puritanical /pyŏŏritánikəl/ *adj.* often *derog.* practicing or affecting strict religious or moral behavior. □□ **puritanically** *adv.*

■ see PURITAN *adj.*

purity /pyŏŏritee/ *n.* **1** pureness; cleanness. **2** freedom from physical or moral pollution. [ME f. OF *pureté*, with assim. to LL *puritas -tatis* f. L *purus* pure]

■ **1** pureness, cleanness, cleanliness, clarity; healthfulness, wholesomeness, salubrity. **2** pureness, faultlessness, correctness, flawlessness, perfection, spotlessness; chastity, chasteness, virginity, virtuousness, virtue, modesty, morality, propriety, honesty, integrity, rectitude, properness, innocence, guilelessness, blamelessness, sinlessness.

purl¹ /pərl/ *n.* & *v.* ● *n.* **1** a knitting stitch made by putting the needle through the front of the previous stitch and passing the yarn around the back of the needle. **2** a cord of twisted gold or silver wire for bordering. **3** a chain of minute loops; a picot. **4** the ornamental edges of lace, ribbon, etc. ● *v.tr.* (also *absol.*) knit with a purl stitch. [orig. *pyrle, pirle* f. Sc. *pirl* twist: the knitting sense may be f. a different word]

purl² /pərl/ *v.* & *n.* ● *v.intr.* (of a brook, etc.) flow with a swirling motion and babbling sound. ● *n.* this motion or sound. [16th c.: prob. imit.: cf. Norw. *purla* bubble up]

■ *v.* see GURGLE *v.* ● *n.* see GURGLE *n.*

purler /pérlər/ *n. Brit. colloq.* a headlong fall. [*purl* upset, rel. to PURL¹]

purlieu /pérlyōō/ *n.* (*pl.* **purlieus**) **1** a person's bounds or limits. **2** a person's usual haunts. **3** *Brit. hist.* a tract on the border of a forest, esp. one earlier included in it and still partly subject to forest laws. **4** (in *pl.*) the outskirts; an outlying region. [ME *purlew*, prob. alt. after F *lieu* place f. AF *purale(e)*, OF *pouralee* a going around to settle the boundaries f. *po(u)raler* traverse]

■ **2** see TERRITORY 3. **4** (*purlieus*) see OUTSKIRTS.

purlin /pérlin/ *n.* a horizontal beam along the length of a roof, resting on principals and supporting the common rafters or boards. [ME: orig. uncert.]

purloin /pərlóyn/ *v.tr. literary* steal; pilfer. □□ **purloiner** *n.* [ME f. AF *purloigner* put away, do away with (as PUR-, *loign* far f. L *longe*)]

■ see PILFER. □□ **purloiner** see THIEF.

purple /pérpəl/ *n.*, *adj.*, & *v.* ● *n.* **1** a color intermediate between red and blue. **2** (in full **Tyrian purple**) a crimson dye obtained from some mollusks. **3** a purple robe, esp. as the dress of an emperor or senior magistrate. **4** the scarlet official dress of a cardinal. **5** (prec. by *the*) a position of rank, authority, or privilege. ● *adj.* of a purple color. ● *v.tr.* & *intr.* make or become purple. □ **born in (or to) the purple** **1** born into a reigning family. **2** belonging to the most priv-

ileged class. **Purple Heart** a US military decoration for those wounded in action. **purple passage** (or **prose** or **patch**) an overly ornate or elaborate passage, esp. in a literary composition. □□ **purpleness** *n.* **purplish** *adj.* **purply** *adj.* [OE alt. f. *purpure purpuran* f. L *purpura* (as PURPURA)]

purport *v.* & *n.* ● *v.tr.* /pərpáwrt/ **1** profess; be intended to seem (*purports to be the royal seal*). **2** (often foll. by *that* + clause) (of a document or speech) have as its meaning; state. ● *n.* /pérpawrt/ **1** the ostensible meaning of something. **2** the sense or tenor (of a document or statement). □□ **purportedly** /-páwrtidlee/ *adv.* [ME f. AF & OF *purport, porport* f. *purporter* f. med.L *proportare* (as PRO-¹, *portare* carry)]

■ *v.* **1** profess, pretend, (lay) claim, make a pretense. ● *n.* see MEANING *n.* 1, 2. □□ **purportedly** see *seemingly* (SEEMING¹).

purpose /pérpəs/ *n.* & *v.* ● *n.* **1** an object to be attained; a thing intended. **2** the intention to act. **3** resolution; determination. **4** the reason for which something is done or made. ● *v.tr.* have as one's purpose; design; intend. □ **on purpose** intentionally. **purpose-built** (or **-made**) esp. *Brit.* built or made for a specific purpose. **to no purpose** with no result or effect. **to the purpose 1** relevant. **2** useful. [ME f. OF *porpos, purpos* f. L *proponere* (as PROPOUND)]

■ *n.* **1** object, intention, intent, end, goal, ambition, objective, target, aim; rationale, reason, motive, motivation. **2** intent, intention, scheme, plan, design. **3** resolution, firmness, determination, persistence, drive, single-mindedness, deliberation, deliberateness, purposefulness, steadfastness, tenacity, doggedness, will, resolve, resoluteness, perseverance. **4** use, practicality, avail, effect, utility, usefulness; advantage, profit, gain, good, benefit; raison d'être. ● *v.* plan, intend, design, resolve, mean, aim, contemplate, have in mind *or* view, have a mind, propose. □ **on purpose** purposely, intentionally, deliberately, willfully, by design, consciously, knowingly, designedly, wittingly. **to the purpose 1** see RELEVANT. **2** see USEFUL.

purposeful /pérpəsfŏŏl/ *adj.* **1** having or indicating purpose. **2** intentional. **3** resolute. □□ **purposefully** *adv.* **purposefulness** *n.*

■ **2** intentional, intended, planned, deliberate, willful, intended. **3** resolved, settled, determined, resolute, decided, sure, certain, positive, definite, staunch, steadfast, persistent, strong-willed, dogged, tenacious, pertinacious, purposive, unfailing, unfaltering, firm, fixed.

purposeless /pérpəslis/ *adj.* having no aim or plan. □□ **purposelessly** *adv.* **purposelessness** *n.*

■ aimless, undirected, directionless; erratic, haphazard; pointless, meaningless, senseless.

purposely /pérpəslee/ *adv.* on purpose; intentionally.

■ see *on purpose* (PURPOSE).

purposive /pérpəsiv, pərpŏ́-/ *adj.* **1** having or serving a purpose. **2** done with a purpose. **3** (of a person or conduct) having purpose or resolution; purposeful. □□ **purposively** *adv.* **purposiveness** *n.*

■ **3** see RESOLUTE.

purpura /pérpyŏŏrə/ *n.* **1** a disease characterized by purple or livid spots on the skin, due to internal bleeding from small blood vessels. **2** any mollusk of the genus *Purpura*, some of which yield a purple dye. □□ **purpuric** /-pyŏŏrik/ *adj.* [L f. Gk *porphura* purple]

purpure /púrpyŏŏr/ *n.* & *adj. Heraldry* purple. [OE *purpure* & OF *purpre* L *purpura* (as PURPURA)]

purpurin /pérpyŏŏrin/ *n.* a red dye occurring naturally in madder roots, or manufactured synthetically.

purr /pər/ *v.* & *n.* ● *v.* **1** *intr.* (of a cat) make a low vibratory sound expressing contentment. **2** *intr.* (of machinery, etc.) make a similar sound. **3** *intr.* (of a person) express pleasure. **4** *tr.* utter or express (words or contentment) in this way. ● *n.* a purring sound. [imit.]

■ *v.* **2** see HUM¹ *v.* 1. ● *n.* see HUM¹ *n.*

purse /pərs/ *n.* & *v.* ● *n.* **1** a small pouch of leather, etc., for carrying money on the person. **2** a small bag for carrying personal effects, esp. one carried by a woman. **3** a receptacle resembling a purse in form or purpose. **4** money; funds. **5** a sum collected as a present or given as a prize in a contest. ● *v.* **1** *tr.* (often foll. by *up*) pucker or contract (the lips). **2** *intr.* become contracted and wrinkled. □ **hold the purse strings** have control of expenditure. **the public purse** the national treasury. [OE *purs* f. med.L *bursa, byrsa* purse f. Gk *bursa* hide, leather]

■ *n.* **1** pouch, bag, moneybag, wallet, pocketbook, *dial.* poke. **2** bag, handbag, pocketbook. **4** money, wealth, resources, funds, finances, capital, revenue, income, means, cash, riches, pocket. **5** prize, reward, award, present, gift. ● *v.* **1** pucker (up), contract, wrinkle, compress, press together.

purser /pərsər/ *n.* an officer on a ship who keeps the accounts, esp. the head steward in a passenger vessel. □□ **pursership** *n.*

purslane /pərslin, -layn/ *n.* any of various plants of the genus *Portulaca*, esp. *P. oleracea*, with green or golden leaves, used as a salad vegetable and herb. [ME f. OF *porcelaine* (cf. PORCELAIN) alt. f. L *porcil(l)aca, portulaca*]

pursuance /pərsōōəns/ *n.* (foll. by *of*) the carrying out or observance (of a plan, idea, etc.).

■ see EXECUTION 2.

pursuant /pərsōōənt/ *adj.* & *adv.* ● *adj.* pursuing. ● *adv.* (foll. by *to*) conforming to or in accordance with. □□ **pursuantly** *adv.* [ME, = prosecuting, f. OF *po(u)rsuiant* part. of *po(u)rsu(iv)ir* (as PURSUE): assim. to AF *pursuer* and PURSUE]

pursue /pərsōō/ *v.* (**pursues, pursued, pursuing**) **1** *tr.* follow with intent to overtake or capture or do harm to. **2** *tr.* continue or proceed along (a route or course of action). **3** *tr.* follow or engage in (study or other activity). **4** *tr.* proceed in compliance with (a plan, etc.). **5** *tr.* seek after; aim at. **6** *tr.* continue to investigate or discuss (a topic). **7** *tr.* seek the attention or acquaintance of (a person) persistently. **8** *tr.* (of misfortune, etc.) persistently assail. **9** *tr.* persistently attend; stick to. **10** *intr.* go in pursuit. □□ **pursuable** *adj.* **pursuer** *n.* [ME f. AF *pursiver, -suer* = OF *porsivre*, etc. ult. f. L *prosequi* follow after]

■ **1** follow, chase, go *or* run after, hunt (after *or* for), trail, track, run down, dog, stalk, shadow, *colloq.* tail. **2, 9** follow (on with), keep to; carry on with, continue, push, devote *or* dedicate oneself to, undertake, practice, persist *or* persevere in, maintain, proceed with, adhere to, stay with, apply oneself to, *colloq.* stick with, plug at. **3** follow, take; see also ENGAGE 8. **5** aspire to, aim at *or* for, work for *or* toward, try *or* strive for, seek, search for, go in search of, quest after *or* for, be intent on, be bent upon *or* on. **7** go after, woo, pay court to, court, pay suit *or* court to, set one's cap at; follow, hound; see also CHASE¹ *v.* 1, 4.

pursuit /pərsōōt/ *n.* **1** the act or an instance of pursuing. **2** an occupation or activity pursued. □ **in pursuit of** pursuing. [ME f. OF *poursuite* (as PUR-, SUIT)]

■ **1** hunt, tracking, stalking, chase; pursuance. **2** work, line (of work), activity, field, area, business, profession, trade, vocation, calling, career, lifework, *colloq.* avocation; hobby, pastime, interest.

pursuivant /pərswivənt/ *n.* **1** *Brit.* an officer of the College of Arms ranking below a herald. **2** a follower or attendant. [ME f. OF *pursivant* pres. part. of *pursivre* (as PURSUE)]

pursy /pərsee/ *adj.* **1** short-winded. **2** corpulent. □□ **pursiness** *n.* [ME, earlier *pursive* f. AF *porsif* f. OF *polsif* f. *polser* breathe with difficulty f. L *pulsare* (as PULSATE)]

purulent /pyŏŏrələnt, pyŏŏryə-/ *adj.* **1** consisting of or containing pus. **2** discharging pus. □□ **purulence** *n.* **purulency** *n.* **purulently** *adv.* [F *purulent* or L *purulentus* (as PUS)]

purvey /pərváy/ *v.* **1** *tr.* provide or supply (articles of food) as one's business. **2** *intr.* (often foll. by *for*) **a** make provision. **b** act as supplier. □□ **purveyor** *n.* [ME f. AF *purveier*, OF *porveïr* f. L *providēre* PROVIDE]

■ see SUPPLY¹ *v.* 1, 2.

purveyance /pərváyəns/ *n.* **1** the act of purveying. **2** *Brit. hist.* the right of the sovereign to provisions, etc., at a fixed price. [ME f. OF *porveance* f. L *providentia* PROVIDENCE]

■ **1** see SUPPLY¹ *n.* 1.

purview /pərvyōō/ *n.* **1** the scope or range of a document, scheme, etc. **2** the range of physical or mental vision. [ME f. AF *purveü*, OF *porveü* past part. of *porveïr* (as PURVEY)]

■ **2** see HORIZON.

pus /pus/ *n.* a thick yellowish or greenish liquid produced from infected tissue. [L *pus puris*]

■ see DISCHARGE *n.* 5.

push /pŏŏsh/ *v.* & *n.* ● *v.* **1** *tr.* exert a force on (a thing) to move it away from oneself or from the origin of the force. **2** *tr.* cause to move in this direction. **3** *intr.* exert such a force (*do not push against the door*). **4** *tr.* press; depress (*push the button for service*). **5** *intr.* & *tr.* **a** thrust forward or upward. **b** project or cause to project (*pushes out new roots; the cape pushes out into the sea*). **6** *intr.* move forward by force or persistence. **7** *tr.* make (one's way) by pushing. **8** *intr.* exert oneself, esp. to surpass others. **9** *tr.* (often foll. by *to, into*, or *to* + infin.) urge or impel. **10** *tr.* tax the abilities or tolerance of; press (a person) hard. **11** *tr.* pursue (a claim, etc.). **12** *tr.* promote the use or sale or adoption of, e.g., by advertising. **13** *intr.* (foll. by *for*) demand persistently (*pushed hard for reform*). **14** *tr. colloq.* sell (a drug) illegally. **15** *tr. colloq.* to approach, esp. in age (*pushing thirty*). ● *n.* **1** the act or an instance of pushing; a shove or thrust. **2** the force exerted in this. **3** a vigorous effort. **4** a military attack in force. **5** enterprise; determination to succeed. **6** the use of influence to advance a person. **7** the pressure of affairs. **8** a crisis. **9** (prec. by *the*) *Brit. colloq.* dismissal, esp. from employment. **10** *Austral. sl.* a group of people with a common interest; a clique. □ **be pushed for** *colloq.* have very little of (esp. time). **if (or when) push comes to shove** when a problem must be faced; in a crisis. **push along** (often in *imper.*) *Brit. colloq.* depart; leave. **push around** *colloq.* bully. **push-bike** *Brit. colloq.* a bicycle worked by pedals. **push button 1** a button to be pushed esp. to operate an electrical device. **2** (*attrib.*) operated in this way. **push one's luck** take undue risks. **2** act presumptuously. **push off 1 a** set off; depart. **b** push with an oar, etc., to get a boat out into a river, etc. **2** esp. *Brit.* (often in *imper.*) *colloq.* go away. **push-pull** *Electr.* consisting of two valves, etc., operated alternately. **push start** *n.* the starting of a motor vehicle by pushing it to turn the engine. ● *v.tr.* start (a vehicle) in this way. **push through** get (a scheme, proposal, etc.) completed or accepted quickly. **push-up** an exercise in which the body, extended and prone, is raised upwards by pushing down with the hands until the arms are straight. [ME f. OF *pousser, pou(l)ser* f. L *pulsare* (as PULSATE)]

■ *v.* **1** thrust, shove, drive, move, get moving, propel; press. **4** press, depress. **5 b** see PROJECT *v.* 2. **6** (*push on or forward*) move onward *or* ahead *or* forward, continue, proceed, advance, press on *or* onward. **7** shove, thrust, elbow, shoulder, force, jostle. **9** urge, encourage, press, induce, persuade, prod, spur, goad, rouse, prompt, incite, move, motivate, stimulate; impel, compel, force, dragoon, coerce, constrain; badger, hound, pester, plague, nag. **10** see TAX *v.* 3. **11** see PURSUE 2, 9. **12** promote, publicize, advertise, propagandize, puff, *colloq.* boost, plug, *sl.* ballyhoo, hype. **13** (*push for*) see *insist on*. **14** see PEDDLE. ● *n.* **1** shove, thrust, nudge; press. **2** drive, thrust; see also FORCE¹ *n.* 1. **3** see ATTEMPT *n.* **4** campaign, attack, assault, advance, offensive, charge, onslaught, foray, sortie, invasion, incursion, raid, sally, blitzkrieg, strike, *colloq.* blitz. **5** enterprise, ambition, initiative, resourcefulness, determination, energy, dynamism, drive, vigor, spirit, zip, zeal, verve, *colloq.* get-up-and-go, zing, gumption, go. **6** see PULL *n.* 3. **8** crisis, turning point, critical time *or* moment. **9** (*the push*) see *dismissal* (DISMISS). □ **push around** intimidate, bully, domineer, tyrannize, torment. **push off 2** leave, go away, take off, *colloq.* light out, skedaddle, scram, make oneself scarce, *sl.* hit the road; see also *beat it*. **push through** force through, press through, railroad through; see also EXPEDITE 1.

pushcart /pŏŏshkaart/ *n.* a handcart or barrow, esp. one used by a street vendor.

pushchair /pŏŏshchair/ *n. Brit.* = STROLLER.

pusher /pŏŏshər/ *n.* **1** *colloq.* an illegal seller of drugs. **2** *colloq.* a pushing or pushy person. **3** a child's utensil for pushing food onto a spoon, etc.

pushful /pŏŏshfŏŏl/ *adj.* esp. *Brit.* pushy; arrogantly self-assertive. □□ **pushfully** *adv.*

pushing /pŏŏshing/ *adj.* **1** pushy; aggressively ambitious. **2** *colloq.* having nearly reached (a specified age). □□ **pushingly** *adv.*

■ **1** see PUSHY. **2** see ALMOST.

pushover /pŏŏshōvər/ *n. colloq.* **1** something that is easily done. **2** a person who can easily be overcome, persuaded, etc.

■ **1** walkover, child's play, *colloq.* piece of cake, picnic, cinch, *sl.* snap, duck soup *Austral. sl.* snack; see also BREEZE[1] *n.* 4. **2** putty in a person's hands, *colloq.* soft touch, *sl.* (easy) mark, sucker, sap, patsy, *Brit. sl.* mug.

pushrod /pŏŏshrod/ *n.* a rod operated by cams that opens and closes the valves in an internal combustion engine.

Pushtu /pŭshtŏŏ/ *n. & adj.* = PASHTO. [Pers. *puštū*]

pushy /pŏŏshee/ *adj.* (**pushier, pushiest**) *colloq.* **1** excessively or unpleasantly self-assertive. **2** selfishly determined to succeed. □□ **pushily** *adv.* **pushiness** *n.*

■ forward, self-assertive, assertive, self-seeking, forceful, aggressive, domineering, overbearing, ambitious, bumptious, brassy, brazen, impertinent, insolent, pushing, pushful, presumptuous, officious, loud, cocky, brash, bold, *colloq.* bossy, go-getting.

pusillanimous /pyŏŏsilániməs/ *adj.* lacking courage; timid. □□ **pusillanimity** /-lənímitee/ *n.* **pusillanimously** *adv.* [eccl.L *pusillanimis* f. *pusillus* very small + *animus* mind]

■ see TIMID. □□ **pusillanimity** see COWARDICE.

puss /pŏŏs/ *n. colloq.* **1** a cat (esp. as a form of address). **2** a girl. **3** *Brit.* a hare. [prob. f. MLG *pūs*, Du. *poes*, of unkn. orig.]

pussy /pŏŏsee/ *n.* (*pl.* **-ies**) **1** (also **pussycat**) *colloq.* a cat. **2** *coarse sl.* the vulva. ¶ Usually considered a taboo use. □ **pussy willow** any of various willows, esp. *Salix discolor*, with furry catkins.

pussyfoot /pŏŏseefŏŏt/ *v.intr.* **1** move stealthily or warily. **2** act cautiously or noncommittally. □□ **pussyfooter** *n.*

■ **1** sneak, creep, slink, prowl, steal, tiptoe. **2** beat about the bush, hem *or* hum and haw, equivocate, be evasive, tergiversate, evade the issue, sidestep, prevaricate, shilly-shally, dither, hesitate; sit on the fence.

pustulate *v. & adj.* ● *v.tr. & intr.* /pŭschəlayt/ form into pustules. ● *adj.* /-chələt/ of or relating to a pustule or pustules. □□ **pustulation** /-láyshən/ *n.* [LL *pustulare* f. *pustula*: see PUSTULE]

pustule /pŭschŏŏl/ *n.* a pimple containing pus. □□ **pustular** *adj.* **pustulous** *adj.* [ME f. OF *pustule* or L *pustula*]

■ see PIMPLE.

put[1] /pŏŏt/ *v., n., & adj.* ● *v.* (**putting**; *past* and *past part.* **put**) **1** *tr.* move to or cause to be in a specified place or position (*put it in your pocket*; *put the children to bed*; *put your signature here*). **2** *tr.* bring into a specified condition, relation, or state (*puts me in great difficulty*; *an accident put the car out of action*). **3** *tr.* **a** (often foll. by *on*) impose or assign (*where do you put the blame?*). **b** (foll. by *on, to*) impose or enforce the existence of (*put a stop to it*). **4** *tr.* **a** cause (a person) to go or be, habitually or temporarily (*put them at their ease*; *put them on the right track*). **b** *refl.* imagine (oneself) in a specified situation (*put yourself in my shoes*). **5** *tr.* (foll. by *for*) substitute (one thing for another). **6** *tr.* express (a thought or idea) in a specified way (*to put it mildly*). **7** *tr.* (foll. by *at*) estimate (an amount, etc., at a specified amount) (*put the cost at $50*). **8** *tr.* (foll. by *into*) express or translate in (words, or another language). **9** *tr.* (foll. by *into*) invest

(money in an asset, e.g., land). **10** *tr.* (foll. by *on*) stake (money) on (a horse, etc.). **11** *tr.* (foll. by *to*) apply or devote to a use or purpose (*put it to good use*). **12** *tr.* (foll. by *to*) submit for consideration or attention (*let me put it to you another way*; *shall now put it to a vote*). **13** *tr.* (foll. by *to*) subject (a person) to (death, suffering, etc.). **14** *tr.* throw (esp. a shot or weight) as an athletic sport or exercise. **15** *tr.* (foll. by *to*) couple (an animal) with (another of the opposite sex) for breeding. **16** *intr.* (foll. by *back, off, out*, etc.) (of a ship, etc.) proceed or follow a course in a specified direction. ● *n.* **1** a throw of the shot or weight. **2** *Stock Exch.* the option of selling stock or a commodity at a fixed price at a given date. ● *adj.* stationary; fixed (*stay put*). □ **put about 1** spread (information, rumor, etc.). **2** *Naut.* turn around; put (a ship) on the opposite tack. **3** *Brit.* trouble; distress. **put across 1** make acceptable or effective. **2** express in an understandable way. **3** (often in **put it** (or **one**) **across**) achieve by deceit. **put aside 1** = *put by*. **2** set aside; ignore. **put away 1** put (a thing) back in the place where it is normally kept. **2** set (money, etc.) aside for future use. **3 a** confine or imprison. **b** commit to a mental institution. **4** consume (food and drink), esp. in large quantities. **5** put (an old or sick animal) to death. **put back 1** restore to its proper or former place. **2** change (a planned event) to a later date or time. **put a bold**, etc., **face on it** see FACE. **put by** lay (money, etc.) aside for future use. **put down 1** suppress by force or authority. **2** *colloq.* snub or humiliate. **3** record or enter in writing. **4** enter the name of (a person) on a list, esp. as a member or subscriber. **5** (foll. by *as, for*) account, reckon, or categorize. **6** (foll. by *to*) attribute (*put it down to bad planning*). **7** put (an old or sick animal) to death. **8** preserve or store (eggs, etc.) for future use. **9** pay (a specified sum) as a deposit. **10** put (a baby) to bed. **11** land (an aircraft). **12** stop to let (passengers) get off. **put-down** *colloq.* an act or instance of snubbing or humiliating (someone). **put an end to** see END. **put one's finger on** identify, esp. a problem or difficulty. **put one's foot down** see FOOT. **put one's foot in it** see FOOT. **put forth 1** (of a plant) send out (buds or leaves). **2** *formal* submit or put into circulation. **put forward** suggest or propose. **put in 1 a** enter or submit (a claim, etc.). **b** (foll. by *for*) submit a claim for (a specified thing). **2** (foll. by *for*) be a candidate for (an appointment, election, etc.). **3** spend (time). **4** perform (a spell of work) as part of a whole. **5** interpose (a remark, blow, etc.). **6** insert as an addition. **put in an appearance** see APPEARANCE. **put a person in mind of** see MIND. **put it to a person** (often foll. by *that* + clause) challenge a person to deny it. **put one's mind to** see MIND. **put off 1 a** postpone. **b** postpone an engagement with (a person). **2** (often foll. by *with*) evade (a person) with an excuse, etc. **3** hinder or dissuade. **put on 1** clothe oneself with. **2** cause (an electrical device, light, etc.) to function. **3** cause (esp. transport) to be available; provide. **4** stage (a play, show, etc.). **5 a** pretend to be affected by (an emotion). **b** assume; take on (a character or appearance). **c** (**put it on**) exaggerate one's feelings, etc. **6** increase one's weight by (a specified amount). **7** (foll. by *to*) make aware of or put in touch with (*put us on to their new accountant*). **8** *colloq.* tease; play a trick on. **put-on** *n. colloq.* a deception or hoax. **put out 1 a** (often as **put out** *adj.*) disconcert or annoy. **b** (often *refl.*) inconvenience (*don't put yourself out*). **2** extinguish (a fire or light). **3** *Baseball* cause (a batter or runner) to be out. **4** dislocate (a joint). **5** exert (strength, etc.). **6** allocate (work) to be done off the premises. **7** blind (a person's eyes). **8** issue; publish. **9** *coarse sl.* engage in sexual intercourse. **put out of its**, etc., **misery** see MISERY. **put over 1** make acceptable or effective. **2** express in an understandable way. **3** postpone. **4** achieve by deceit. **put one over** (usu. foll. by *on*) get the better of; outsmart; trick. **put a sock in it** see SOCK[1]. **put store by** see STORE. **put through 1** carry out or complete (a task or transaction). **2** (often foll. by *to*) connect (a person) by telephone to another. **put to flight** see FLIGHT[2]. **put together 1** assemble (a whole) from parts. **2** combine (parts) to form a whole. **put under** render unconscious by anesthetic, etc. **put up 1** build or erect. **2** to can; preserve (food) for later

use. **3** take or provide accommodation for (*friends put me up for the night*). **4** engage in (a fight, struggle, etc.) as a form of resistance. **5** present (a proposal). **6 a** present oneself for election. **b** propose for election. **7** provide (money) as a backer in an enterprise. **8** display (a notice). **9** publish (banns). **10** offer for sale or competition. **11** esp. *Brit.* raise (a price, etc.). **put-up** *adj.* fraudulently presented or devised. **put upon** *colloq.* make unfair or excessive demands on; take advantage of (a person). **put a person up to** (usu. foll. by verbal noun) instigate a person in (*put them up to stealing the money*). **put up with** endure; tolerate; submit to. **put the wind up** see WIND[1]. **put a person wise** see WISE. **put words into a person's mouth** see MOUTH. □□ **putter** *n.* [ME f. an unrecorded OE form *putian*, of unkn. orig.]
■ *v.* **1** place, position, situate, set, lay, station, stand, deposit, rest, settle. **3 a** place, assign, attribute, lay, pin, attach, fix; impose, raise, levy, exact. **4 b** imagine, consider, regard, picture, envisage. **5** exchange, substitute, change, swap, switch. **6, 8** express, word, phrase; say, utter; translate. **7** see GAUGE *v.* 3. **10** bet, gamble, wager, stake, chance, risk, hazard. **12** (*put to*) present, set before; refer to; see also SUBMIT 2. **13** (*put to*) subject to, cause to undergo *or* suffer, consign to, send to. **14** throw, heave, toss, fling, cast, pitch, bowl, lob, shy, shoot, catapult. ● *n.* **1** see THROW *n.* 1.
□ **put about 1** broadcast, publish, make known, publicize, announce, spread about *or* around. **2** turn, turn around, turn about. **put across 2** make clear, get across, make understood, explain, spell out, convey, communicate. **put aside 1** see *put by* below. **2** set aside, disregard, ignore, pay no heed to, push aside, shrug off. **put away 1** return, replace, put back; store. **2** see *put by* below. **3 a** jail, incarcerate, send up, *Brit.* send down, *sl.* jug; confine; see also IMPRISON 1. **b** commit, institutionalize. **4** consume, devour, gorge, gormandize, polish off, dispose of, eat up, wolf (down), *joc.* demolish. **put back 1** return, replace, restore, put away. **2** see POSTPONE. **put by** lay aside *or* by, set aside; put away *or* aside; save, store, hoard, stow *or* squirrel away, cache, bank, *sl.* salt away. **put down 1** suppress, quash, quell, put an end to, topple, crush, overthrow, subdue, check. **2** abash, humiliate, crush, silence, mortify, lower, take a person down a peg or two, shame; snub, deflate, slight, reject, dismiss, ignore; belittle, diminish, disparage, deprecate, depreciate, criticize. **3, 4** record, register, write down, set down, enter, list; log, note (down), jot down, make a note *or* notation of; enroll. **5** take, reckon, account, count, categorize, regard, assess. **6** ascribe, assign, attribute, impute. **7** destroy, put to death, put to sleep, put out of its misery, do away with. **12** let off, drop off. **put-down** snub, disparaging remark, slight, insult, criticism, *colloq.* dig. **put forth 1** grow, produce, send out *or* forth. **2** propose, offer, set forth, advance, suggest, put forward; promulgate, issue, publish, make known, make public, send out, put into circulation, air, announce. **put forward** propose, present, tender, recommend, suggest, offer, set forth, submit, proffer, propound, *formal* put forth. **put in 1 a** see SUBMIT 2. **b** (*put in for*) seek, apply for, pursue, file for, request, ask for, petition for. **3** devote, pass; see also SPEND 2a. **4** do, perform, effect, carry out. **5, 6** see INSERT *v.* **put off 1 a** postpone, delay, defer, put back, stay, hold off, shelve, put *or* set aside, table, put over. **3** see DETER. **put on 1** don, get dressed in, change *or* slip into. **2** turn on, switch on. **3** see PROVIDE 1. **4** stage, mount, produce, present; perform. **5 a** assume, take on, pretend, affect, feign, make a show of. **c** (**put it on**) see EXAGGERATE 1. **6** gain. **8** tease, mock, *colloq.* kid, pull (a person's) leg, rib, rag, *Brit.* have on. **put-on** deception, hoax, trick, jest, (practical) joke, prank, pretense, *colloq.* spoof, leg-pull. **put out 1 a** annoy, vex, irritate, exasperate, irk, perturb, disconcert, offend. **b** inconvenience, discommode, disturb, trouble, bother; impose upon *or* on, give trouble, create

difficulties for, *colloq.* put on the spot. **2** turn off; snuff out, extinguish, blow out, douse, quench, smother. **5** exert, expend, use. **8** publish, issue, broadcast, make public, circulate, spread, make known, release. **put over 2** put *or* get across, convey, communicate, make clear, set forth, relate. **3** see *put off* 1 above. **put one over** (*put one over on*) fool, mislead, pull a person's leg, pull the wool over a person's eyes, trick, hoodwink; see also DECEIVE 1. **put through 1** carry out *or* through, execute, (put into) effect, bring off, accomplish, complete, finish, conclude, pull off. **2** connect, hook up. **put together** see ASSEMBLE 3. **put up 1** erect, build, construct, raise, set up, put together, fabricate. **3** accommodate, lodge, board, house, take in, quarter, *Mil.* billet. **5** see PRESENT[2] *v.* 1. **7** contribute, pledge, give, supply, donate, advance, pay, offer. **8** see DISPLAY *v.* 1. **10** see OFFER 4. **put-up** (*put-up job*) see DECEIT 2. **put upon** see IMPOSE 3, TROUBLE 1, 3. **put a person up to** incite to, urge to, spur to, encourage to, prompt to, instigate in. **put up with** tolerate, take, stand (for), stomach, accept, bear, endure, swallow, submit to, esp. *Brit. colloq.* stick, *literary* brook.

put[2] var. of PUTT.

putative /pyōōtǝtiv/ *adj.* reputed; supposed (*his putative father*). □□ **putatively** *adv.* [ME f. OF *putatif -ive* or LL *putativus* f. L *putare* think]
■ see *supposed* (SUPPOSE 6).

putlog /pútlawg/, -log/ *n.* (also **putlock** /-lok/) a short horizontal timber projecting from a wall, on which scaffold floorboards rest. [17th c.: orig. uncert.]

put-put /pútpút/ *n. & v.* ● *n.* **1** the rapid intermittent sound of a small gasoline engine. **2** *colloq.* a small boat using such an engine. ● *v.intr.* (**put-putted, put-putting**) make this sound. [imit.]

putrefy /pyōōtrifī/ *v.* (**-ies, -ied**) **1** *intr. & tr.* become or make putrid; go bad. **2** *intr.* fester; suppurate. **3** *intr.* become morally corrupt. □□ **putrefacient** /-fáyshǝnt/ *adj.* **putrefaction** /-fákshǝn/ *n.* **putrefactive** /-fáktiv/ *adj.* [ME f. L *putrefacere* f. *puter putris* rotten]
■ **1** rot, decompose, decay, molder, go bad, deteriorate, go off. **2** suppurate, fester, decompose; see also ROT *v.* 1a.

putrescent /pyōōtrésǝnt/ *adj.* **1** in the process of rotting. **2** of or accompanying this process. □□ **putrescence** *n.* [L *putrescere* incept. of *putrēre* (as PUTRID)]
■ see ROTTEN 1. □□ **putrescence** see ROT *n.* 1.

putrid /pyōōtrid/ *adj.* **1** decomposed; rotten. **2** foul; noxious. **3** corrupt. **4** *sl.* of poor quality; contemptible; very unpleasant. □□ **putridity** /-tríditee/*n.* **putridly** *adv.* **putridness** *n.* [L *putridus* f. *putrēre* to rot f. *puter putris* rotten]
■ **1** rotten, rotting, decomposed, decomposing, decayed, decaying, moldy, putrefacient, putrescent. **2** fetid, rank, noxious; see also FOUL *adj.* 1, 4a. **3** tainted, corrupt; see also DEGENERATE *adj.* **4** see AWFUL 1a, b.

putsch /pōōch/ *n.* an attempt at political revolution; a violent uprising. [Swiss G, = thrust, blow]
■ see UPRISING.

putt /put/ *v. & n.* (also *Brit.* **put**) ● *v.tr.* (**putted, putting**) strike (a golf ball) gently to get it into or nearer to a hole on a putting green. ● *n.* a putting stroke. □ **putting green** (in golf) the area of close-cropped grass around a hole. [differentiated f. PUT[1]]

puttee /pútee/ *n.* **1** a long strip of cloth wound spirally around the leg from ankle to knee for protection and support. **2** a leather legging. [Hindi *paṭṭī* band, bandage]

putter[1] /pútǝr/ *n.* **1** a golf club used in putting. **2** a golfer who putts.

putter[2] /pútǝr/ *n. & v.* = PUT-PUT. [imit.]

/.../ **pronunciation**	● **part of speech**
□ **phrases, idioms, and compounds**	
□□ **derivatives**	■ **synonym section**
cross-references appear in SMALL CAPITALS or *italics*	

putter³ /pútər/ v. (also *Brit.* **potter**) **1** *intr.* **a** (often foll. by *about, around*) work or occupy oneself in a desultory but pleasant manner (*likes puttering around in the garden*). **b** (often foll. by *at, in*) dabble in a subject or occupation. **2** *intr.* go slowly; dawdle; loiter. **3** *tr.* (foll. by *away*) fritter away (one's time, etc.). □□ **putterer** n. [var. sp. of *potter*, a frequent. of dial. *pote* push f. OE *potian*]
  ■ **1 a** see MESS ABOUT. **b** dabble, tinker, experiment. **2** amble, saunter, stroll, dawdle, wander, loiter, *sl.* mosey. **3** (*putter away*) fritter (away), squander; see also WASTE v. 1.

putto /póotō/ n. (pl. **putti** /-tee/) a representation of a naked child (esp. a cherub or a cupid) in (esp. Renaissance) art. [It., = boy, f. L *putus*]

putty /pútee/ n. & v. ● n. (pl. **-ies**) **1** a cement made from whiting and raw linseed oil, used for fixing panes of glass, filling holes in woodwork, etc. **2** a fine white mortar of lime and water, used in pointing brickwork, etc. **3** a polishing powder usu. made from tin oxide, used in jewelry work. ● v.tr. (**-ies, -ied**) cover, fix, join, or fill up with putty. □ **putty in a person's hands** someone who is overcompliant, or easily influenced. [F *potée*, lit. potful]

putz /puts/ n. & v. ● n. **1** *coarse sl.* the penis. **2** *sl.* a simpleminded foolish person. ● v.intr. *sl.* (usu. foll. by *around*) move (about) or occupy oneself in an aimless or idle manner. [Yiddish *puts* ornament]

puzzle /púzəl/ n. & v. ● n. **1** a difficult or confusing problem; an enigma. **2** a problem or toy designed to test knowledge or ingenuity. ● v. **1** *tr.* confound or disconcert mentally. **2** *intr.* (usu. foll. by *over*, etc.) be perplexed (about). **3** *tr.* (usu. as **puzzling** adj.) require much thought to comprehend (*a puzzling situation*). **4** *tr.* (foll. by *out*) solve or understand by hard thought. □□ **puzzlement** n. **puzzlingly** adv. [16th c.: orig. unkn.]
  ■ n. **1** enigma, problem, question, paradox, poser, mystery. **2** poser, riddle, conundrum, *colloq.* brainteaser, *Brit. colloq.* brain-twister. ● v. **1** baffle, bewilder, confuse, confound, mystify, perplex, nonplus, stump, *archaic* wilder, *colloq.* flummox. **2** be confused *or* baffled *or* bewildered *or* perplexed; (*puzzle over*) study, ponder (over), mull over, contemplate, meditate on *or* upon *or* over, consider, reflect on *or* over, think about *or* over, *literary* muse over *or* on. **3** (*puzzling*) mystifying, enigmatic, bewildering, baffling, perplexing, confusing, ambiguous, contradictory; abstruse, obscure. **4** (*puzzle out*) solve, decipher, crack, unravel, work out, figure out, think through, sort out.

puzzler /púzlər/ n. a difficult question or problem.
  ■ see PROBLEM 1, 2, 5b.

puzzolana var. of POZZOLANA.

PVA abbr. polyvinyl acetate.

PVC abbr. polyvinyl chloride.

Pvt. abbr. private.

p.w. abbr. per week.

PWA abbr. person with AIDS.

PX abbr. post exchange.

pyaemia *Brit.* var. of PYEMIA.

pycnic var. of PYKNIC.

pye-dog /pídawg, -dog/ n. (also **pie-dog, pi-dog**) a vagrant mongrel, esp. in Asia. [Anglo-Ind. *pye, paë,* Hindi *pāhī* outsider + DOG]

pyelitis /pɪəlítis/ n. inflammation of the renal pelvis. [Gk *puelos* trough, basin + -ITIS]

pyemia /pɪeémeeə/ n. blood poisoning caused by the spread of pus-forming bacteria in the bloodstream from a source of infection. □□ **pyemic** adj. [mod.L f. Gk *puon* pus + *haima* blood]

pygmy /pígmee/ n. (also **pigmy**) (pl. **-ies**) **1** a member of a small people of equatorial Africa and parts of SE Asia. **2** a very small person, animal, or thing. **3** an insignificant person. **4** (*attrib.*) **a** of or relating to pygmies. **b** (of a person, animal, etc.) dwarf. □□ **pygmaean** /pigmeéən, pígmee-/ adj. (also **pygmean**) [ME f. L *pygmaeus* f. Gk *pugmaios* dwarf f. *pugmē* the length from elbow to knuckles, fist]
  ■ **2** dwarf, midget, runt. **4 b** see UNDERSIZED.

pyjamas esp. *Brit.* var. of PAJAMAS.

pyknic /píknik/ adj. & n. (also **pycnic**) *Anthropol.* ● adj. characterized by a thick neck, large abdomen, and relatively short limbs. ● n. a person of this body type. [Gk *puknos* thick]
  ■ adj. see STOCKY.

pylon /pílon/ n. **1** a tall structure erected as a support (esp. for electric power cables) or boundary or decoration. **2** a gateway, esp. of an ancient Egyptian temple. **3** a structure marking a path for aircraft. **4** a structure supporting an aircraft engine. [Gk *pulōn* f. *pulē* gate]

pylorus /pɪláwrəs, pi-/ n. (pl. **pylori** /-rī/) *Anat.* the opening from the stomach into the duodenum. □□ **pyloric** /-láwrik/ adj. [LL f. Gk *pulōros, pulouros* gatekeeper f. *pulē* gate + *ouros* warder]

pyorrhea /píreéə/ n. **1** a disease of periodontal tissue causing shrinkage of the gums and loosening of the teeth. **2** any discharge of pus. [Gk *puo-* f. *puon* pus + *rhoia* flux f. *rheō* flow]

pyracantha /pírəkánthə/ n. any evergreen thorny shrub of the genus *Pyracantha*, having white flowers and bright red or yellow berries. [L f. Gk *purakantha*]

pyramid /pírəmid/ n. & v. ● n. **1 a** a monumental structure, usu. of stone, with a square base and sloping sides meeting centrally at an apex, esp. an ancient Egyptian royal tomb. **b** a similar structure, esp. a Mayan temple of this type. **2** a solid of this type with a base of three or more sides. **3** a pyramid-shaped thing or pile of things. ● v. **1** *tr.* to build or shape into a pyramid. **2** *intr.* to speculate, as in the stock market, using paper profits as a margin for further stock acquisitions. □ **pyramid selling** a system of selling goods in which rights are sold to an increasing number of distributors at successively lower levels. □□ **pyramidal** /-rámid'l/ adj. **pyramidally** adv. **pyramidic** /-mídik/ adj. (also **pyramidical**). **pyramidically** adv. **pyramidwise** adj. [ME f. L *pyramis* f. Gk *puramis -idos*]

pyre /pir/ n. a heap of combustible material, esp. a funeral pile for burning a corpse. [L *pyra* f. Gk *pura* f. *pur* fire]

pyrethrin /pɪreéthrin, -réth-/ n. any of several active constituents of pyrethrum flowers used in the manufacture of insecticides.

pyrethrum /pɪreéthrəm, -réth-/ n. **1** any of several aromatic chrysanthemums of the genus *Chrysanthemum*. **2** an insecticide made from the dried flowers of these plants. [L f. Gk *purethron* feverfew]

pyretic /pɪrétik/ adj. of, for, or producing fever. [mod.L *pyreticus* f. Gk *puretos* fever]
  ■ pyrogenic; see also FEVERISH 1.

Pyrex /píreks/ n. propr. a hard heat-resistant type of glass, often used for cookware. [invented word]

pyrexia /pɪrékseeə/ n. *Med.* = FEVER. □□ **pyrexial** adj. **pyrexic** adj. **pyrexical** adj. [mod.L f. Gk *purexis* f. *puressō* be feverish f. *pur* fire]

pyridine /pírədeen/ n. *Chem.* a colorless volatile odorous liquid, formerly obtained from coal tar, used as a solvent and in chemical manufacture. ¶ Chem. formula: C_5H_5N. [Gk *pur* fire + -ID⁴ + -INE⁴]

pyridoxine /pírídókseen, -sin/ n. a vitamin of the B complex found in yeast, and important in the body's use of unsaturated fatty acids. Also called *vitamin B_6*. [PYRIDINE + OX- + -INE⁴]

pyrimidine /pɪrímideen, pi-/ n. **1** *Chem.* an organic nitrogenous base. **2** any of a group of derivatives with similar structure, including the nucleotide constituents uracil, thymine, and cytosine. [G *Pyrimidin* f. *Pyridin* (as PYRIDINE, IMIDE)]

pyrite /pírit/ n. = PYRITES. [F *pyrite* or L (as PYRITES)]

pyrites /pɪríteez, pírīts/ n. (in full **iron pyrites**) a yellow lustrous form of iron disulfide. □□ **pyritic** /-ritik/ adj. **pyritiferous** /-ritifərəs/ adj. **pyritize** /pírítīz/ v.tr. **pyritous** /pírítəs/ adj. [L f. Gk *puritēs* of fire (*pur*)]

pyro /pírō/ n. *colloq.* a pyromaniac.

pyro- /pírō/ *comb. form* **1** denoting fire. **2** *Chem.* denoting a new substance formed from another by elimination of water (*pyrophosphate*). **3** *Mineral.* denoting a mineral, etc., showing some property or change under the action of heat, or having a fiery red or yellow color. [Gk *puro-* f. *pur* fire]

pyroclastic /pīrōklástik/ *adj.* (of rocks, etc.) formed as the result of a volcanic eruption. □□ **pyroclast** *n.*

pyroelectric /pīrōiléktrik/ *adj.* having the property of becoming electrically charged when heated. □□ **pyroelectricity** /-trísitee/ *n.*

pyrogallol /pīrōgálawl, -ol, -gáwl-/ *n.* a weak acid used as a developer in photography, etc.

pyrogenic /pīrōjénik/ *adj.* (also **pyrogenous** /pīrójinəs/) **1 a** producing heat, esp. in the body. **b** producing fever. **2** produced by combustion or volcanic processes.

pyrography /pīrógrəfee/ *n.* **1** a technique for forming designs on wood, etc., by burning. **2** a design made with this technique.

pyroligneous /pīrōlígneeəs/ *adj.* produced by the action of fire or heat on wood.

pyrolysis /pīróləsis/ *n.* chemical decomposition brought about by heat. □□ **pyrolytic** /pírəlítik/ *adj.*

pyrolyze /pírəliz/ *v.tr.* decompose by pyrolysis. [PYROLYSIS after *analyze*]

pyromania /pírōmáyneeə/ *n.* an obsessive desire to set fire to things. □□ **pyromaniac** *n.*
■ □□ **pyromaniac** arsonist, *Brit.* fire-raiser.

pyrometer /pīrómitər/ *n.* an instrument for measuring high temperatures, esp. in furnaces and kilns. □□ **pyrometric** /-rəmétrik/ *adj.* **pyrometrically** *adv.* **pyrometry** /-rómitree/ *n.*

pyrope /pírōp/ *n.* a deep red variety of garnet. [ME f. OF *pirope* f. L *pyropus* f. Gk *purōpos* gold-bronze, lit. fiery-eyed, f. *pur* fire + *ōps* eye]

pyrophoric /pīrōfáwrik, -fór-/ *adj.* (of a substance) liable to ignite spontaneously on exposure to air. [mod.L *pyrophorus* f. Gk *purophoros* fire-bearing f. *pur* fire + *pherō* bear]

pyrosis /pīrósis/ *n. Med.* a burning sensation in the lower part of the chest, combined with the return of gastric acid to the mouth. Also called **heartburn.** [mod.L f. Gk *purōsis* f. *puroō* set on fire f. *pur* fire]

pyrotechnic /pīrōtéknik/ *adj.* **1** of or relating to fireworks. **2** (of wit, etc.) brilliant or sensational. □□ **pyrotechnical** *adj.* **pyrotechnist** *n.* **pyrotechny** *n.* [PYRO- + Gk *tekhnē* art]

pyrotechnics /pīrōtékniks/ *n.pl.* **1** the art of making fireworks. **2** a display of fireworks. **3** any brilliant display.
■ **3** see *virtuosity* (VIRTUOSO).

pyroxene /pīrókseen/ *n.* any of a group of minerals commonly found as components of igneous rocks, composed of silicates of calcium, magnesium, and iron. [PYRO- + Gk *xenos* stranger (because supposed to be alien to igneous rocks)]

pyroxylin /pīróksilin/ *n.* a form of nitrocellulose, soluble in ether and alcohol, used as a basis for lacquers, artificial leather, etc. [F *pyroxyline* (as PYRO-, Gk *xulon* wood)]

pyrrhic[1] /pírik/ *adj.* (of a victory) won at too great a cost to be of use to the victor. [*Pyrrhus* of Epirus, who defeated the Romans at Asculum in 279 BC, but sustained heavy losses]
■ see HOLLOW *adj.* 4.

pyrrhic[2] /pírik/ *n. & adj.* ● *n.* a metrical foot of two short or unaccented syllables. ● *adj.* written in or based on pyrrhics. [L *pyrrhichius* f. Gk *purrhikhios* (*pous*) pyrrhic (foot)]

Pyrrhonism /pírənizəm/ *n.* **1** the philosophy of Pyrrho of Elis (*c.*300 BC), maintaining that certainty of knowledge is unattainable. **2** skepticism; philosophical doubt. □□ **Pyrrhonist** *n.* [Gk *Purrhōn* Pyrrho]
■ **2** see *skepticism* (SKEPTIC). □□ **Pyrrhonist** see SKEPTIC 1.

pyruvate /pīróōvayt/ *n. Biochem.* any salt or ester of pyruvic acid.

pyruvic acid /pīróōvik/ *n.* an organic acid occurring as an intermediate in many stages of metabolism. [as PYRO- + L *uva* grape]

Pythagorean /pīthágəreéən/ *adj. & n.* ● *adj.* of or relating to the Greek philosopher Pythagoras (6th c. BC) or his philosophy, esp. regarding the transmigration of souls. ● *n.* a follower of Pythagoras.

Pythagorean theorem /pīthágəreéən/ *n.* the theorem attributed to Pythagoras (see PYTHAGOREAN) that the square of the hypotenuse of a right triangle is equal to the sum of the squares of the other two sides.

Pythian /pítheeən/ *adj.* of or relating to Delphi (in central Greece) or its ancient oracle of Apollo. [L *Pythius* f. Gk *Puthios* f. *Puthō,* an older name of Delphi]

python /píthon, -thən/ *n.* any constricting snake of the family Pythonidae, esp. of the genus *Python,* found throughout the tropics in the Old World. □□ **pythonic** /-thónik/ *adj.* [L f. Gk *Puthōn* a huge serpent or monster killed by Apollo]

pythoness /píthənis, píth-/ *n.* **1** the Pythian priestess. **2** a witch. [ME f. OF *phitonise* f. med.L *phitonissa* f. LL *pythonissa* fem. of *pytho* f. Gk *puthōn* soothsaying demon: cf. PYTHON]

pyuria /pīyóōreeə/ *n. Med.* the presence of pus in urine. [Gk *puon* pus + -URIA]

pyx /piks/ *n.* (also **pix**) **1** *Eccl.* the vessel in which the consecrated bread of the Eucharist is kept. **2** a box at a mint in which specimen coins are deposited to be tested by weight and assayed. [ME f. L (as PYXIS)]

pyxidium /piksídeeəm/ *n.* (*pl.* **pyxidia** /-deeə/) *Bot.* a seedcapsule with a top that comes off like the lid of a box. [mod.L f. Gk *puxidion,* dimin. of *puxis:* see PYXIS]

pyxis /píksis/ *n.* (*pl.* **pyxides** /-sideez/) **1** a small box or casket. **2** = PYXIDIUM. [ME f. L f. Gk *puxis* f. *puxos* BOX[3]]

/.../ **pronunciation**	● **part of speech**
□ **phrases, idioms, and compounds**	
□□ **derivatives**	■ **synonym section**
cross-references appear in SMALL CAPITALS or *italics*	

Q¹ /kyōō/ n. (also **q**) (pl. **Qs** or **Q's**) the seventeenth letter of the alphabet.

Q² abbr. (also **Q.**) **1** question. **2** esp. Brit. Queen, Queen's.

qadi /káadi, káydi/ n. (also **kadi**) (pl. **-is**) a judge in a Muslim country. [Arab. ḳāḍī f. ḳaḍā to judge]

qb abbr. quarterback.

QED abbr. QUOD ERAT DEMONSTRANDUM.

Q fever /kyōō/ n. a mild febrile disease caused by rickettsias. [Q = query]

qibla var. of KIBLAH.

Qld. abbr. Queensland.

QM abbr. quartermaster.

qr. abbr. quarter(s).

Q-ship /kyōōship/ n. an armed vessel disguised as a merchant ship used as a decoy to lure submarines into attack range. [Q = query]

QSO abbr. quasi-stellar object; quasar.

qt. abbr. quart(s).

q.t. n. colloq. quiet (esp. on the q.t.). [abbr.]
■ (on the q.t.) see secretly (SECRET).

Q-tip /kyōōtip/ n. propr. a swab consisting of a thin stick with cotton affixed to each end.

qty. abbr. quantity.

qu. abbr. **1** query. **2** question.

qua /kwaa/ conj. in the capacity of; as being (Napoleon qua general). [L, ablat. fem. sing. of qui who (rel. pron.)]

quack¹ /kwak/ v. & n. ● n. the harsh sound made by ducks. ● v.intr. **1** utter this sound. **2** colloq. talk loudly and foolishly. [imit.: cf. Du. kwakken, G quacken croak, quack]

quack² /kwak/ n. **1 a** an unqualified practitioner of medicine. **b** (attrib.) of or characteristic of unskilled medical practice (quack cure). **2 a** a charlatan. **b** (attrib.) of or characteristic of a charlatan; fraudulent; sham. **3** sl. any doctor or medical officer. □□ **quackery** n. **quackish** adj. [abbr. of quacksalver f. Du. (prob. f. obs. quacken prattle + salf SALVE¹)]
■ **2 a** charlatan, impostor, pretender, faker, fraud, colloq. phony. **b** (attrib.) fake, fraudulent, sham, counterfeit, colloq. phony. **3** see DOCTOR n. 1a.

quad¹ /kwod/ n. colloq. a quadrangle. [abbr.]

quad² /kwod/ n. colloq. = QUADRUPLET 1. [abbr.]

quad³ /kwod/ n. Printing a piece of blank metal type used in spacing. [abbr. of earlier QUADRAT]

quad⁴ /kwod/ n. & adj. ● n. quadraphony. ● adj. quadraphonic. [abbr.]

quadragenarian /kwódrəjináireeən/ n. & adj. ● n. a person from 40 to 49 years old. ● adj. of this age. [LL quadragenarius f. quadrageni distrib. of quadraginta forty]

Quadragesima /kwódrəjésimə/ n. the first Sunday in Lent. [LL, fem. of L quadragesimus fortieth f. quadraginta forty, Lent having 40 days]

quadragesimal /kwódrəjésimal/ adj. **1** (of a fast, esp. in Lent) lasting forty days. **2** Lenten.

quadrangle /kwódranggəl/ n. **1** a four-sided plane figure, esp. a square or rectangle. **2 a** a four-sided yard or courtyard, esp. enclosed by buildings, as in some colleges. **b** such a courtyard with the buildings around it. **3** the land area represented on one map sheet as published by the U.S. Geological Survey. □□ **quadrangular** /-ránggyələr/ adj. [ME f. OF f. LL quadrangulum square, neut. of quadrangulus (as QUADRI-, ANGLE¹)]

■ **2** colloq. quad; see also AREAWAY, SQUARE n. 3a.

quadrant /kwódrənt/ n. **1** a quarter of a circle's circumference. **2** a plane figure enclosed by two radii of a circle at right angles and the arc cut off by them. **3** a quarter of a sphere, etc. **4 a** a thing, esp. a graduated strip of metal, shaped like a quarter circle. **b** an instrument graduated (esp. through an arc of 90°) for taking angular measurements. □□ **quadrantal** /-dránt'l/ adj. [ME f. L quadrans -antis quarter f. quattuor four]

quadraphonic /kwódrəfónik/ adj. (also **quadrophonic** or **quadriphonic**) (of sound reproduction) using four transmission channels. □□ **quadraphonically** adv. **quadraphonics** n.pl. **quadraphony** /-rófənee/ n. [QUADRI- + STEREOPHONIC]

quadrat /kwódrət/ n. **1** Ecol. a small area marked out for study. **2** = QUAD³. [var. of QUADRATE]

quadrate adj., n., & v. ● adj. /kwódrət/ esp. Anat. & Zool. square or rectangular (quadrate bone; quadrate muscle). ● n. /kwódrət/ **1** a quadrate bone or muscle. **2** a rectangular object. ● v. /kwodráyt/ **1** tr. make square. **2** intr. & tr. (often foll. by with) conform or make conform. [ME f. L quadrare quadrat- make square f. quattuor four]

quadratic /kwódrátik/ adj. & n. Math. ● adj. **1** involving the second and no higher power of an unknown quantity or variable (quadratic equation). **2** square. ● n. **1** a quadratic equation. **2** (in pl.) the branch of algebra dealing with these. [F quadratique or mod.L quadraticus (as QUADRATE)]

quadrature /kwódrəchər/ n. **1** Math. the process of constructing a square with an area equal to that of a figure bounded by a curve, e.g., a circle. **2** Astron. **a** each of two points at which the moon is 90° from the sun as viewed from earth. **b** the position of a heavenly body in relation to another 90° away. [F quadrature or L quadratura (as QUADRATE)]

quadrennial /kwodréneeəl/ adj. **1** lasting four years. **2** recurring every four years. □□ **quadrennially** adv. [as QUADRENNIUM]

quadrennium /kwodréneeəm/ n. (pl. **quadrenniums** or **quadrennia** /-eeə/) a period of four years. [L quadriennium (as QUADRI-, annus year)]

quadri- /kwódree/ (also **quadr-** or **quadru-**) comb. form denoting four. [L f. quattuor four]

quadric /kwódrik/ adj. & n. Geom. ● adj. (of a surface) described by an equation of the second degree. ● n. a quadric surface. [L quadra square]

quadriceps /kwódriseps/ n. Anat. a four-part muscle at the front of the thigh. [mod.L (as QUADRI-, BICEPS)]

quadrifid /kwódrifid/ adj. Bot. having four divisions or lobes. [L quadrifidus (as QUADRI-, findere fid- cleave)]

quadrilateral /kwódrilátərəl/ adj. & n. ● adj. having four sides. ● n. a four-sided figure. [LL quadrilaterus (as QUADRI-, latus lateris side)]

quadrille¹ /kwodríl/ n. **1** a square dance containing usu. five figures. **2** the music for this. [F f. Sp. cuadrilla troop, company f. cuadra square or It. quadriglia f. quadra square]

quadrille² /kwodríl/ n. a card game for four players with forty cards, fashionable in the 18th c. [F, perh. f. Sp. cuartillo f. cuarto fourth, assim. to QUADRILLE¹]

quadrillion /kwodrílyən/ n. (pl. same or **quadrillions**) a thousand raised to the fifth (or esp. *Brit.* the eighth) power (10^{15} and 10^{24} respectively). [F (as QUADRI-, MILLION)]

quadrinomial /kwódrinŏmeeəl/ *n. & adj. Math.* ● *n.* an expression of four algebraic terms. ● *adj.* of or being a quadrinomial. [QUADRI- + Gk *nomos* part, portion]

quadripartite /kwódripaártīt/ *adj.* **1** consisting of four parts. **2** shared by or involving four parties.

quadriplegia /kwódripleéjeeə, -jə/ *n. Med.* paralysis of all four limbs. □□ **quadriplegic** *adj. & n.* [mod.L (as QUADRI-, Gk *plēgē* blow, strike)]

quadrivalent /kwódriváylənt/ *adj. Chem.* having a valence of four.

quadrivium /kwodríveeəm/ *n. hist.* the medieval university studies of arithmetic, geometry, astronomy, and music. [L, = the place where four roads meet (as QUADRI-, *via* road)]

quadroon /kwodroón/ *n.* a person of one-quarter black ancestry. [Sp. *cuarterón* f. *cuarto* fourth, assim. to QUADRI-]

quadrophonic var. of QUADRAPHONIC.

quadru- var. of QUADRI-.

quadrumanous /kwodroómənəs/ *adj.* (of primates other than humans) four-handed, i.e. with opposable digits on all four limbs. [mod.L *quadrumana* neut. pl. of *quadrumanus* (as QUADRI-, L *manus* hand)]

quadruped /kwódrəped/ *n. & adj.* ● *n.* a four-footed animal, esp. a four-footed mammal. ● *adj.* four-footed. □□ **quadrupedal** /-roópid'l/ *adj.* [F *quadrupède* or L *quadrupes -pedis* f. *quadru-* var. of QUADRI- + L *pes ped-* foot]

quadruple /kwodroópəl, -drúp-, kwódroópəl/ *adj., n., & v.* ● *adj.* **1** fourfold. **2 a** having four parts. **b** involving four participants (*quadruple alliance*). **3** being four times as many or as much. **4** (of time in music) having four beats in a bar. ● *n.* a fourfold number or amount. ● *v.tr. & intr.* multiply by four; increase fourfold. □□ **quadruply** *adv.* [F f. L *quadruplus* (as QUADRI-, *-plus* as in *duplus* DUPLE)]

quadruplet /kwodroóplit, -drúp-, kwódroóplit/ *n.* **1** each of four children born at one birth. **2** a set of four things working together. **3** *Mus.* a group of four notes to be performed in the time of three. [QUADRUPLE, after *triplet*]

quadruplicate *adj. & v.* ● *adj.* /kwodroóplikət/ **1** fourfold. **2** of which four copies are made. ● *v.tr.* /-kayt/ **1** multiply by four. **2** make four identical copies of. □ **in quadruplicate** in four identical copies. □□ **quadruplication** /-káyshən/ *n.* [L *quadruplicare* f. *quadruplex -plicis* fourfold: cf. QUADRUPED, DUPLEX]

quadruplicity /kwódroóplísitee/ *n.* the state of being fourfold. [L *quadruplex -plicis* (see QUADRUPLICATE), after *duplicity*]

quaestor /kwéstər, kwée-/ *n.* either of two ancient Roman magistrates with mainly financial responsibilities. □□ **quaestorial** /-stáwreeəl/ *adj.* **quaestorship** *n.* [ME f. L f. *quaerere quaesit-* seek]

quaff /kwof, kwaf, kwawf/ *v. literary* **1** *tr. & intr.* drink deeply. **2** *tr.* drain (a cup, etc.) in long drafts. □□ **quaffable** *adj.* **quaffer** *n.* [16th c.: perh. imit.]
■ **1** see DRINK *v.* 1. **2** drink up *or* down, drain, swallow, finish.

quag /kwag, kwog/ *n.* a marshy or boggy place. □□ **quaggy** *adj.* [rel. to dial. *quag* (v.) = shake: prob. imit.]

quagga /kwágə/ *n.* an extinct zebralike mammal, *Equus quagga*, formerly native to S. Africa, with yellowish-brown stripes on the head, neck, and forebody. [Xhosa-Kaffir *iqwara*]

quagmire /kwágmīr, kwóg-/ *n.* **1** a soft boggy or marshy area that gives way underfoot. **2** a hazardous or awkward situation. [QUAG + MIRE]
■ **1** see MARSH. **2** see MORASS 1.

quahog /kwáwhawg, -hog, kwŏ-, kŏ-/ *n.* (also **quahaug**) an edible clam, *Marcenaria* (formerly *Venus*) *mercinaria*, of the Atlantic coast of N. America. [Narragansett Indian]

quaich /kwaykh/ *n.* (also **quaigh**) *Sc.* a kind of drinking cup, usu. of wood and with two handles. [Gael. *cuach* cup, prob. f. L *caucus*]

quail[1] /kwayl/ *n.* (*pl.* same or **quails**) **1** any small migratory Old World bird of the genus *Coturnix*, with a short tail and related to the partridge. **2** any small migratory New World bird of the genus *Colinus*, esp. the bobwhite. [ME f. OF *quaille* f. med.L *coacula* (prob. imit.)]

quail[2] /kwayl/ *v.intr.* flinch; be apprehensive with fear. [ME, of unkn. orig.]
■ see FLINCH[1] *v.*

quaint /kwaynt/ *adj.* **1** piquantly or attractively unfamiliar or old-fashioned. **2** unusual; odd. □□ **quaintly** *adv.* **quaintness** *n.* [earlier senses 'wise, cunning': ME f. OF *cointe* f. L *cognitus* past part. of *cognoscere* ascertain]
■ **1** old-fashioned, outmoded, antiquated, outdated, antique; picturesque, sweet, bijou, *esp. Brit.* twee, *colloq.* cute. **2** curious, odd, strange, bizarre, peculiar, unusual, queer, uncommon, singular, eccentric, whimsical, offbeat, fanciful, outlandish, unconventional, fantastic.

quake /kwayk/ *v. & n.* ● *v.intr.* **1** shake; tremble. **2** (of a person) shake or shudder (*was quaking with fear*). ● *n.* **1** *colloq.* an earthquake. **2** an act of quaking. □ **quaking grass** any grass of the genus *Briza*, having slender stalks and trembling in the wind: also called *dodder-grass*. □□ **quaky** *adj.* (**quakier, quakiest**). [OE *cwacian*]
■ *v.* **1, 2** tremble, shake, quiver, shudder; vibrate. ● *n.* **1** earthquake, tremor. **2** shiver, tremble, shudder; see also SHAKE *n.* 1, 2.

Quaker /kwáykər/ *n.* a member of the Society of Friends, a Christian movement devoted to peaceful principles and eschewing formal doctrine, sacraments, and ordained ministers. □□ **Quakerish** *adj.* **Quakerism** *n.* [QUAKE + -ER[1]]
■ Friend.

qualification /kwólifikáyshən/ *n.* **1** the act or an instance of qualifying. **2** (often in *pl.*) a quality, skill, or accomplishment fitting a person for a position or purpose. **3 a** a circumstance, condition, etc., that modifies or limits (*the statement had many qualifications*). **b** a thing that detracts from completeness or absoluteness (*their relief had one qualification*). **4** a condition that must be fulfilled before a right can be acquired, etc. **5** an attribution of a quality (*the qualification of our policy as opportunist is unfair*). □□ **qualificatory** /-lífikətawree/ *adj.* [F *qualification* or med.L *qualificatio* (as QUALIFY)]
■ **2** (*qualifications*) ability, aptitude, competence, capacity, proficiency, skill(s), knowledge, *colloq.* know-how. **3 a** limitation, restriction, modification, reservation, caveat, condition, stipulation, proviso; prerequisite, requirement. **b** see DRAWBACK.

qualify /kwólifī/ *v.* (**-ies, -ied**) **1** *tr.* make competent or fit for a position or purpose. **2** *tr.* make legally entitled. **3** *intr.* (foll. by *for* or *as*) (of a person) satisfy the conditions or requirements for (a position, award, competition, etc.). **4** *tr.* add reservations to; modify or make less absolute (a statement or assertion). **5** *tr. Gram.* (of a word, esp. an adjective) attribute a quality to another word, esp. a noun. **6** *tr.* moderate; mitigate; make less severe or extreme. **7** *tr.* alter the strength or flavor of. **8** *tr.* (foll. by *as*) attribute a specified quality to; describe as (*the idea was qualified as absurd*). **9** *tr.* (as **qualifying** *adj.*) serving to determine those that qualify (*qualifying examination*). **10** (as **qualified** *adj.*) **a** having the qualifications necessary for a particular office or function. **b** dependent on other factors; not definite (*a qualified "yes"*). □□ **qualifiable** *adj.* **qualifier** *n.* [F *qualifier* f. med.L *qualificare* f. L *qualis* such as]
■ **1** equip, fit, ready, prepare, condition, make eligible. **2** certify. **3** be eligible, meet the requirements, have the qualifications, be fit *or* equipped *or* ready *or* prepared, *colloq.* make the grade. **4** modulate; restrict, limit; see also MODIFY 1. **6** temper, moderate; see also MITIGATE. **8** see DESCRIBE 1b. **10** (**qualified**) **a** experienced, practiced, knowledgeable, competent, able, suitable, capable, fit, fitted, trained, proficient, accomplished,

---

/ . . . / **pronunciation**   ● **part of speech**
□ **phrases, idioms, and compounds**
□□ **derivatives**   ■ **synonym section**
cross-references appear in SMALL CAPITALS or *italics*

expert, talented, adept, skillful, skilled, well-informed.
b contingent, conditional, restricted, modified, limited,
provisional. □□ **qualifier** see HEAT *n.* 6.

qualitative /kwólitaytiv/ *adj.* concerned with or depending
on quality (*led to a qualitative change in society*). □ **qualitative analysis** *Chem.* detection of the constituents, as elements, functional groups, etc., present in a substance (opp.
quantitative analysis). □□ **qualitatively** *adv.* [LL *qualitativus*
(as QUALITY)]

quality /kwólitee/ *n.* (*pl.* **-ies**) **1** the degree of excellence of
a thing (*of good quality; poor in quality*). **2 a** general excellence (*their work has quality*). **b** (*attrib.*) of high quality (*a
quality product*). **3** a distinctive attribute or faculty; a characteristic trait. **4** the relative nature or kind or character of
a thing. **5** the distinctive timbre of a voice or sound. **6** *archaic*
high social standing (*people of quality*). **7** *Logic* the property
of a proposition's being affirmative or negative. □ **quality
control** a system of maintaining standards in manufactured
products by testing a sample of the output against the specification. [ME f. OF *qualité* f. L *qualitas -tatis* f. *qualis* of what
kind]

■ **1** grade, caliber, rank, value, worth. **2 a** see
EXCELLENCE 1. **b** see *first-rate adj.* **3** property, attribute,
feature characteristic, mark, faculty, distinction, trait.
6 eminence, prominence, importance, superiority,
distinction, standing, dignity, nobility.

qualm /kwaam, kwawm/ *n.* **1** a misgiving; an uneasy doubt
esp. about one's own conduct. **2** a scruple of conscience. **3**
a momentary faint or sick feeling. □□ **qualmish** *adj.* [16th
c.: orig. uncert.]

■ **1** second thought(s), doubt, uncertainty, misgiving,
hesitation, uneasiness, reluctance, disinclination,
queasiness, sinking feeling, apprehension,
apprehensiveness, worry, concern, *colloq.* funny feeling.
2 scruple, compunction, twinge, pang.

quandary /kwóndəree, -dree/ *n.* (*pl.* **-ies**) **1** a state of perplexity. **2** a difficult situation; a practical dilemma. [16th c.:
orig. uncert.]

■ confusion; predicament, difficulty, plight; see also
DILEMMA.

quant /kwont/ *n. & v. Brit.* ● *n.* a punting pole with a prong
at the bottom to prevent it sinking into the mud, as used by
Norfolk (England) bargemen, etc. ● *v.tr.* (also *absol.*) propel (a boat) with a quant. [15th c.: perh. f. L *contus* f. Gk
kontos boat pole]

quanta *pl.* of QUANTUM.

quantal /kwónt'l/ *adj.* **1** composed of discrete units; varying
in steps, not continuously. **2** of or relating to a quantum or
quantum theory. □□ **quantally** *adv.* [L *quantus* how much]

quantic /kwóntik/ *n. Math.* a rational integral homogeneous
function of two or more variables.

quantify /kwóntifī/ *v.tr.* (**-ies, -ied**) **1** determine the quantity of. **2** measure or express as a quantity. **3** *Logic* define
the application of (a term or proposition) by the use of *all,
some*, etc., e.g., "for all *x* if *x* is A then *x* is B." □□ **quantifiable** *adj.* **quantifiability** *n.* **quantification** /-fikáyshən/
n. **quantifier** *n.* [med.L *quantificare* (as QUANTAL)]

■ **1** see COUNT¹ *v.* 1, CALCULATE 1.

quantitative /kwóntitaytiv/ *adj.* **1 a** concerned with quantity. **b** measured or measurable by quantity. **2** of or based
on the quantity of syllables. □ **quantitative analysis** *Chem.*
measurement of the amounts of the constituents of a substance (opp. *qualitative analysis*). □□ **quantitatively** *adv.*
[med.L *quantitativus* (as QUANTITY)]

quantitive /kwóntitiv/ *adj.* = QUANTITATIVE. □□ **quantitively**
adv.

quantity /kwóntitee/ *n.* (*pl.* **-ies**) **1** the property of things
that is measurable. **2** the size or extent or weight or amount
or number. **3** a specified or considerable portion or number
or amount (*buys in quantity; the quantity of heat in a body*).
4 (in *pl.*) large amounts or numbers; an abundance (*quantities of food; is found in quantities on the shore*). **5** the length
or shortness of vowel sounds or syllables. **6** *Math.* **a** a value,
component, etc., that may be expressed in numbers. **b** the
figure or symbol representing this. □ **quantity theory** the

hypothesis that prices correspond to changes in the monetary supply. [ME f. OF *quantité* f. L *quantitas -tatis* f. *quantus*
how much]

■ **2** amount, extent, volume; sum, number, total; weight,
measure. **3** see BULK *n.* 1a, AMOUNT *n.* 1. **4** see LOT *n.* 1.

quantize /kwóntīz/ *v.tr.* **1** form into quanta. **2** apply quantum mechanics to. □□ **quantization** *n.*

quantum /kwóntəm/ *n.* (*pl.* **quanta** /-tə/) **1** *Physics* **a** a discrete quantity of energy proportional in magnitude to the
frequency of radiation it represents. **b** an analogous discrete
amount of any other physical quantity. **2 a** a required or
allowed amount. **b** a share or portion. □ **quantum jump**
(or **leap**) **1** a sudden large increase or advance. **2** *Physics* an
abrupt transition in an atom or molecule from one quantum
state to another. **quantum mechanics** (or **theory**) *Physics*
a system or theory using the assumption that energy exists
in discrete units. **quantum number** *Physics* any integer or
half odd integer that defines the magnitude of various discrete states of a particle or system. [L, neut. of *quantus* how
much]

quaquaversal /kwáykwəvɔ́rsəl/ *adj. Geol.* pointing in every
direction. [LL *quaquaversus* f. *quaqua* wheresoever + *versus*
toward]

quarantine /kwáwrənteen, kwór-/ *n. & v.* ● *n.* **1** isolation
imposed on persons or animals that have arrived from elsewhere or been exposed to, and might spread, infectious or
contagious disease. **2** the period of this isolation. ● *v.tr.*
impose such isolation on; put in quarantine. [It. *quarantina*
forty days f. *quaranta* forty]

quark¹ /kwaawrk, kwaark/ *n. Physics* any of several postulated
components of elementary particles. [invented word, assoc.
with "Three quarks for Muster Mark" in Joyce's *Finnegans
Wake* (1939)]

quark² /kwawrk, kwaark/ *n.* a type of European lowfat curd
cheese. [G]

quarrel¹ /kwáwrəl, kwór-/ *n. & v.* ● *n.* **1** a usu. verbal contention or altercation between individuals or with others. **2**
a rupture of friendly relations. **3** an occasion of complaint
against a person, a person's actions, etc. ● *v.intr.* (**quar-
reled** or **quarrelled, quarreling** or **quarrelling**) **1** (often
foll. by *with*) take exception; find fault. **2** fall out; have a
dispute; break off friendly relations. □□ **quarreler** *n.* **quar-
reller** *n.* [ME f. OF *querele* f. L *querel(l)a* complaint f. *queri*
complain]

■ *n.* **1** dispute, argument, disagreement, debate,
controversy, difference (of opinion), contention,
wrangle, tiff, squabble, altercation, fight, falling out,
colloq. set-to, row, scrap *colloq.* spat, *esp. Brit. colloq.*
barney. **2** see RIFT *n.* 3. **3** complaint, objection, grudge,
colloq. gripe, *sl.* beef. ● *v.* **1** see OBJECT *v.*, OPPOSE 1–3.
2 argue, disagree, dispute, altercate, have an
altercation, differ, wrangle, bicker, be at odds *or*
loggerheads, clash, squabble, feud, fight, fall out, *colloq.*
scrap.

quarrel² /kwáwrəl, kwór-/ *n.* **1** *hist.* a short heavy square-
headed arrow or bolt used in a crossbow or arbalest. **2** =
QUARRY³ [ME f. OF *quar(r)el* ult. f. LL *quadrus* square]

quarrelsome /kwáwrəlsəm, kwór-/ *adj.* given to or characterized by quarreling. □□ **quarrelsomely** *adv.* **quarrel-
someness** *n.*

■ argumentative, querulous, contrary, combative,
antagonistic, pugnacious, bellicose, belligerent,
contentious, disputatious; irascible, cross, choleric,
curmudgeonly, irritable, disagreeable, peevish, cranky,
colloq. grouchy.

quarry¹ /kwáwree, kwór-/ *n. & v.* ● *n.* (*pl.* **-ies**) **1** an excavation made by taking stone, etc., for building, etc. **2** a place
from which stone, etc., may be extracted. **3** a source of information, knowledge, etc. ● *v.* (**-ies, -ied**) **1** *tr.* extract
(stone) from a quarry. **2** *tr.* extract (facts, etc.) laboriously
from books, etc. **3** *intr.* laboriously search documents, etc.
[ME f. med.L *quare(r)ia* f. OF *quarriere* f. L *quadrum* square]

■ *n.* **2** working. See MINE² *n.* 2. ● *v.* **2** mine, extract,
obtain, get, cull. **3** see SCRUTINIZE.

quarry² /kwáwree, kwór-/ *n.* (*pl.* **-ies**) **1** the object of pursuit

by a bird of prey, hounds, hunters, etc. **2** an intended victim or prey. [ME f. AF f. OF *cuiree*, *couree* (assim. to *cuir* leather and *curer* disembowel) ult. f. L *cor* heart: orig. = parts of deer placed on hide and given to hounds]
■ prey, game, victim; prize, object, target.

quarry[3] /kwáwree, kwór-/ *n.* (*pl.* **-ies**) **1** (also **quarrel**) a diamond-shaped pane of glass as used in lattice windows. **2** (in full **quarry tile**) an unglazed floor tile. [a later form of QUARREL[2] in the same sense]

quarryman /kwáwreemən, kwór-/ *n.* a worker in a quarry.

quart /kwawrt/ *n.* **1** a liquid measure equal to a quarter of a gallon; two pints (.95 liter). **2** a vessel containing this amount. **3** a unit of dry measure, equivalent to one-thirty-second of a bushel (1.1 liter). **4** /kaart/ (also **quarte**) the fourth of eight parrying positions in fencing. [ME f. OF *quarte* f. L *quarta* fem. of *quartus* fourth f. *quattuor* four]

quartan /kwáwrt'n/ *adj.* (of a fever, etc.) recurring every fourth day. [ME f. OF *quartaine* f. L (*febris* fever) *quartana* f. *quartus* fourth]

quarte var. of QUART 4.

quarter /kwáwrtər/ *n.* & *v.* ● *n.* **1** each of four equal parts into which a thing is or might be divided. **2** a period of three months. **3** a point of time 15 minutes before or after any hour. **4** a school term, usu. 10–12 weeks. **5 a** 25 cents. **b** a coin of this denomination. **6** a part of a town, esp. as occupied by a particular class or group (*residential quarter*). **7 a** a point of the compass. **b** a region at such a point. **8** the direction, district, or source of supply, etc. (*help from any quarter*; *came from all quarters*). **9** (in *pl.*) **a** lodgings; an abode. **b** *Mil.* the living accommodation of troops, etc. **10 a** one fourth of a lunar month. **b** the moon's position between the first and second (**first quarter**) or third and fourth (**last quarter**) of these. **11 a** each of the four parts into which an animal's or bird's carcass is divided, each including a leg or wing. **b** (in *pl.*) *hist.* the four parts into which a traitor, etc., was cut after execution. **c** (in *pl.*) *Brit.* = HINDQUARTERS. **12** mercy offered or granted to an enemy in battle, etc., on condition of surrender. **13 a** *Brit.* a grain measure equivalent to 8 bushels. **b** one-fourth of a hundredweight (25 lb. or *Brit.* 28 lb.). **14** *Heraldry* **a** each of four divisions on a shield. **b** a charge occupying this, placed in chief. **15** either side of a ship abaft the beam. **16** *Sports* each of four equal periods into which a game is divided, as in football or basketball. ● *v.tr.* **1** divide into quarters. **2** *hist.* divide (the body of an executed person) in this way. **3 a** put (troops, etc.) into quarters. **b** station or lodge in a specified place. **4** (foll. by *on*) impose (a person) on another as a lodger. **5** cut (a log) into quarters, and these into planks so as to show the grain well. **6** range or traverse (the ground) in every direction. **7** *Heraldry* **a** place or bear (charges or coats of arms) on the four quarters of a shield's surface. **b** add (another's coat) to one's hereditary arms. **c** (foll. by *with*) place in alternate quarters with. **d** divide (a shield) into four or more parts by vertical and horizontal lines. □ **quarter binding** the type of bookbinding in which the spine is bound in one material (usu. leather) and the sides in another. **quarter day** *Brit.* one of four days on which quarterly payments are due, tenancies begin and end, etc. **quarter hour 1** a period of 15 minutes. **2** = sense 3 of *n.* **quarter note** *Mus.* a note with a duration of one quarter of a whole note. **quarter sessions** *hist.* (in the UK) a court of limited criminal and civil jurisdiction and of appeal, usu. held quarterly. **quarter tone** *Mus.* half a semitone. [ME f. AF *quarter*, OF *quartier* f. L *quartarius* fourth part (of a measure) f. *quartus* fourth]

■ *n.* **6** area, region, district, zone, section, division, territory, neighborhood, locality, locale. **8** source, place, location, point, spot, area; direction. **9** (*quarters*) **a** living quarters, lodging(s), accommodation(s), rooms, residence, habitation, domicile, home, house, abode, *colloq.* pad, *Brit. colloq.* digs, diggings, *formal* dwelling (place). **b** billet, barracks, cantonment. **12** mercy, compassion, mercifulness, clemency, leniency, favor,

humanity, pity. ● *v.* **3** billet, lodge, accommodate, house, board, shelter, put up; post, station.

quarterage /kwáwrtərij/ *n.* **1** a quarterly payment. **2** a quarter's wages, allowance, pension, etc.

quarterback /kwáwrtərbak/ *n.* & *v.* *Football* ● *n.* a player who directs offensive play. ● *v.* **1** *intr.* to play at this position. **2** *tr.* to direct the action of, as a quarterback.

quarterdeck /kwáwrtərdek/ *n.* **1** part of a ship's upper deck near the stern, usu. reserved for officers. **2** the officers of a ship or the navy.

quarterfinal /kwáwrtərfín'l/ *adj.* & *n.* *Sports* ● *adj.* relating to a match or round immediately preceding a semifinal. ● *n.* a quarterfinal match, round, or contest.

quartering /kwáwrtəring/ *n.* & *adj.* ● *n.* **1** (in *pl.*) the coats of arms marshaled on a shield to denote the alliances of a family with others. **2** the provision of quarters for soldiers. **3** the act or an instance of dividing, esp. into four equal parts. **4** timber sawn into lengths, used for high-quality floorboards, etc. ● *adj.* (of the wind, waves, etc.) coming from abaft the beam of a ship.

quarterly /kwáwrtərlee/ *adj.*, *adv.*, & *n.* ● *adj.* **1** produced, payable, or occurring once every quarter of a year. **2** (of a shield) quartered. ● *adv.* **1** once every quarter of a year. **2** in the four, or in two diagonally opposite, quarters of a shield. ● *n.* (*pl.* **-ies**) a quarterly review or magazine.

quartermaster /kwáwrtərmastər/ *n.* **1** an army officer in charge of quartering, rations, etc. **2** a naval petty officer in charge of steering, signals, etc. □ **Quartermaster General** the head of the army branch in charge of quartering, etc.

quartern /kwáwrtərn/ *n.* *Brit. archaic* a quarter of a pint. □ **quartern loaf** a four-pound loaf. [ME, = quarter f. AF *quartrun*, OF *quart(e)ron* f. QUART fourth or *quartier* QUARTER]

quarterstaff /kwáwrtərstaf/ *n.* *hist.* a stout pole 6–8 feet long, formerly used as a weapon.

quartet /kwawrtét/ *n.* (also **quartette**) **1** *Mus.* **a** a composition for four voices or instruments. **b** the performers of such a piece. **2** any group of four. [It. *quartetto* f. *quarto* fourth f. L *quartus*]

quartic /kwáwrtik/ *adj.* & *n.* *Math.* ● *adj.* involving the fourth and no higher power of an unknown quantity or variable. ● *n.* a quartic equation. [L *quartus* fourth]

quartile /kwáwrtil, -til/ *adj.* & *n.* ● *adj.* *Astrol.* relating to the aspect of two celestial bodies 90° apart. ● *n.* **1** a quartile aspect. **2** *Statistics* one of three values of a variable dividing a population into four equal groups as regards the value of that variable. [med.L *quartilis* f. L *quartus* fourth]

quarto /kwáwrtō/ *n.* (*pl.* **-os**) *Printing* **1** the size given by folding a (usu. specified) sheet of paper twice. **2** a book consisting of sheets folded in this way. ¶ Abbr.: **4to**. □ **quarto paper** paper folded in this way and cut into sheets. [L (*in*) *quarto* (in) the fourth (of a sheet), ablat. of *quartus* fourth]

quartz /kwawrts/ *n.* a mineral form of silica that crystallizes as hexagonal prisms. □ **quartz clock** a clock operated by vibrations of an electrically driven quartz crystal. **quartz lamp** a quartz tube containing mercury vapor and used as a light source. [G *Quarz* f. WSlav. *kwardy*]

quartzite /kwáwrtsit/ *n.* a metamorphic rock consisting mainly of quartz.

quasar /kwáyzaar, -zər, -saar, -sər/ *n.* *Astron.* any of a class of starlike celestial objects having a spectrum with a large red shift. [*quasi-stellar*]

quash /kwosh/ *v.tr.* **1** annul; reject as not valid, esp. by a legal procedure. **2** suppress; crush (a rebellion, etc.). [ME f. OF *quasser*, *casser* annul f. LL *cassare* f. *cassus* null, void or f. L *cassare* frequent. of *quatere* shake]

■ **1** annul, nullify, void, declare *or* render null and void, invalidate, revoke, set aside, rescind, cancel, reject, throw out, reverse, overthrow, discharge, overrule,

---

/. . ./ **pronunciation**	● **part of speech**
□ **phrases, idioms, and compounds**	
□□ **derivatives**	■ **synonym section**
cross-references appear in SMALL CAPITALS or *italics*	

overturn, *Law* vacate. **2** suppress, subdue, quell, put down, squelch, stamp on, repress, overthrow, crush, overwhelm, put an end to.

quasi /kwáyzī, kwaázee/ *adj.* resembling; seemingly. [L, = as if, almost]

quasi- /kwáyzī, kwaázee/ *comb. form* **1** seemingly; apparently but not really (*quasi-scientific*). **2** being partly or almost (*quasi-independent*). [L *quasi* as if, almost]
■ **1** pseudo-; seemingly; see also *apparently* (APPARENT). **2** partly, to some extent; virtually; see also ALMOST.

quassia /kwóshə/ *n.* **1** an evergreen tree, *Quassia amara*, native to S. America. **2** the wood, bark, or root of this tree, yielding a bitter medicinal tonic and insecticide. [G. *Quassi*, 18th-c. Surinam slave, who discovered its medicinal properties]

quatercentenary /kwótərsenténəree, -sént'neree/ *n. & adj.*
● *n.* (*pl.* **-ies**) **1** a four-hundredth anniversary. **2** a festival marking this. ● *adj.* of this anniversary. [L *quater* four times + CENTENARY]

quaternary /kwótərneree, kwətə́rnəree/ *adj. & n.* ● *adj.* **1** having four parts. **2** (**Quaternary**) *Geol.* of or relating to the most recent period in the Cenozoic era with evidence of many species of present-day plants and animals (cf. PLEISTOCENE, HOLOCENE). ¶ Cf. Appendix VII. ● *n.* (*pl.* **-ies**) **1** a set of four things. **2** (**Quaternary**) *Geol.* the Quaternary period or system. [ME f. L *quaternarius* f. *quaterni* distrib. of *quattuor* four]

quaternion /kwətə́rneeən/ *n.* **1** a set of four. **2** *Math.* a complex number of the form $w + xi + yj + zk$, where w, x, y, z are real numbers and i, j, k are imaginary units that satisfy certain conditions. [ME f. LL *quaternio -onis* (as QUATERNARY)]

quatorze /kətáwrz/ *n.* a set of four aces, kings, queens, or jacks, in one hand at piquet, scoring fourteen. [F *quatorze* fourteen f. L *quattuordecim*]

quatrain /kwótrayn/ *n.* a stanza of four lines, usu. with alternate rhymes. [F f. *quatre* four f. L *quattuor*]

quatrefoil /kátərfoyl, kátrə-/ *n.* a four-pointed or four-leafed figure, esp. as an ornament in architectural tracery, resembling a flower or clover leaf. [ME f. AF f. *quatre* four: see FOIL²]

quattrocento /kwátrōchéntō/ *n.* the style of Italian art of the 15th c. □□ **quattrocentist** *n.* [It., = 400 used with reference to the years 1400–99]

quaver /kwáyvər/ *v. & n.* ● *v.* **1** *intr.* **a** (esp. of a voice or musical sound) vibrate; shake; tremble. **b** use trills or shakes in singing. **2** *tr.* **a** sing (a note or song) with quavering. **b** (often foll. by *out*) say in a trembling voice. ● *n.* **1** *Mus.* = eighth note. **2** a trill in singing. **3** a tremble in speech. □□ **quaveringly** *adv.* [ME f. *quave*, perh. f. OE *cwafian* (unrecorded: cf. *cwacian* QUAKE)]
■ *v.* **1 a** tremble, quiver, shake, shiver, vibrate, waver, shudder, oscillate, flutter. ● *n.* **3** trembling, tremble, quiver, tremor, shaking, vibration, wavering, fluctuation, oscillation.

quavery /kwáyvəree/ *adj.* (of a voice, etc.) tremulous. □□ **quaveriness** *n.*

quay /kee, kay/ *n.* a solid, stationary, artificial landing place lying alongside or projecting into water for loading and unloading ships. □□ **quayage** *n.* [ME *key(e)*, *kay* f. OF *kay* f. Gaulish *caio* f. OCelt.]
■ see LANDING 1c.

quayside /keéesīd, káy-/ *n.* the land forming or near a quay.

Que. *abbr.* Quebec.

quean /kween/ *n. archaic* an impudent or ill-behaved girl or woman. [OE *cwene* woman: cf. QUEEN]
■ hussy, minx, vixen.

queasy /kweézee/ *adj.* (**-ier**, **-iest**) **1 a** (of a person) feeling nausea. **b** (of a person's stomach) easily upset; weak of digestion. **2** (of the conscience, etc.) overscrupulous; tender. **3** (of a feeling, thought, etc.) uncomfortable; uneasy. □□ **queasily** *adv.* **queasiness** *n.* [ME *queysy*, *coisy* perh. f. AF & OF, rel. to OF *coisir* hurt]
■ **1 a** sick, nauseous, nauseated, ill, bilious, queer,

groggy. **3** uncomfortable, uneasy, nervous, apprehensive.

Quechua /kéchwə, -waa/ *n.* **1** a member of a central Peruvian native people. **2** a S. American native language widely spoken in Peru and neighboring countries. □□ **Quechuan** *adj.* [Sp. f. Quechua]

queen /kween/ *n. & v.* ● *n.* **1** (as a title usu. **Queen**) a female sovereign, etc., esp. the hereditary ruler of an independent nation. **2** (in full **queen consort**) a king's wife. **3** a woman, country, or thing preeminent or supreme in a specified area or of its kind (*tennis queen; the queen of roses*). **4** the fertile female among ants, bees, etc. **5** the most powerful piece in chess. **6** a playing card with a picture of a queen. **7** *sl.* a male homosexual, esp. an effeminate one. **8 a** an honored female, e.g., the Virgin Mary (*Queen of Heaven*). **b** an ancient goddess (*Venus, queen of love*). **9** a mock sovereign on some occasion (*beauty queen; queen of the May*). **10** a person's sweetheart, wife, or mistress. **11** (**the Queen**) (in the UK) the national anthem when there is a female sovereign. ● *v.* **1** *tr.* make (a woman) queen. **2** *tr. Chess* convert (a pawn) into a queen when it reaches the opponent's side of the board. **3** *intr.* to act like a queen, esp. to act imperiously or flamboyantly. **Queen Anne's lace** a widely cultivated orig. Eurasian herb, *Dancus carota*, with a whitish taproot; wild carrot. **queen bee 1** the fertile female in a hive. **2** the chief or controlling woman in an organization or social group. **queen dowager** the widow of a king. **queen mother** the dowager who is mother of the sovereign. **queen post** one of two upright timbers between the tie beam and principal rafters of a roof truss. **queen's bishop, knight**, etc. *Chess* (of pieces which exist in pairs) the piece starting on the queen's side of the board. **the Queen's English** see ENGLISH. **queen-size** (or **-sized**) of an extra-large size, between full-size and king-size. **queen's pawn** *Chess* the pawn in front of the queen at the beginning of a game. □□ **queendom** *n.* **queenhood** *n.* **queenless** *adj.* **queenlike** *adj.* **queenship** *n.* [OE *cwēn* f. Gmc; cf. QUEAN]
■ *n.* **1** sovereign, monarch, ruler; empress. **2** queen consort. **3** star; ideal, epitome, paragon, nonpareil. **10** see SWEETHEART 1.

queenie /kweénee/ *n. sl.* = QUEEN *n.* 7.

queenly /kweénlee/ *adj.* (**queenlier, queenliest**) **1** fit for or appropriate to a queen. **2** majestic; queenlike. □□ **queenliness** *n.*
■ see ROYAL *adj.* 5.

Queensberry Rules /kweénzberee, -bəree/ *n.pl.* the standard rules, esp. of boxing. [the 8th Marquis of *Queensberry*, Engl. nobleman d. 1900, who supervised the preparation of boxing laws in 1867]

queer /kweer/ *adj., n., & v.* ● *adj.* **1** strange; odd; eccentric. **2** shady; suspect; of questionable character. **3 a** esp. *Brit.* slightly ill; giddy; faint. **b** *Brit. sl.* drunk. **4** *derog. sl.* homosexual. **5** *colloq.* (of a person or behavior) crazy; unbalanced; slightly mad. **6** *sl.* counterfeit. ● *n. derog. sl.* a homosexual. ● *v.tr. sl.* spoil; put out of order. □ **in Queer Street** *Brit. sl.* in a difficulty; in debt, trouble, or disrepute. **queer a person's pitch** *Brit.* spoil a person's chances, esp. secretly or maliciously. □□ **queerish** *adj.* **queerly** *adv.* **queerness** *n.* [perh. f. G *quer* oblique (as THWART)]
■ *adj.* **1** odd, strange, peculiar, eccentric, funny, curious, uncommon, unconventional, unorthodox, atypical, singular, exceptional, anomalous, extraordinary, unusual, bizarre, uncanny, unnatural, freakish, remarkable, offbeat, irregular, unparalleled, incongruous, outlandish, outré, fey, quaint, absurd, *colloq.* weird. **2** questionable, dubious, shady, suspect, doubtful, puzzling, mysterious, *sl.* fishy. **3 a** (slightly) ill, queasy, sick, unwell, off-color, out of sorts, poorly, faint, dizzy, giddy, light-headed, *colloq.* under the weather. ● *v.* ruin, spoil, bungle, mess up, botch, muff, wreck, make a mess of, *colloq.* make a hash of, muck up, fluff, *sl.* blow, screw up, louse up, goof up, gum up the works, throw a monkey wrench into, *Brit. sl.* cock up.

quell /kwel/ *v.tr.* **1** crush or put down (a rebellion, etc.). **b**

reduce (rebels, etc.) to submission. **2** suppress or alleviate (fear, anger, etc.). □□ **queller** n. (also in *comb.*). [OE *cwellan* kill f. Gmc]

■ **1** suppress, put down, repress, subdue, quash, overcome, crush, squelch, overwhelm, defeat. **2** restrain, control, hold in check, hold back; moderate, mollify, soothe, assuage, alleviate, mitigate, allay, quiet, calm, *Brit.* quieten; pacify, tranquilize, compose; see also SUPPRESS 2.

quench /kwench/ v.tr. **1** satisfy (thirst) by drinking. **2** extinguish (a fire or light, etc.). **3** cool, esp. with water (heat, a heated thing). **4** esp. *Metallurgy* cool (a hot substance) in cold water, air, oil, etc. **5 a** stifle or suppress (desire, etc.). **b** *Physics & Electronics* inhibit or prevent (oscillation, luminescence, etc.) by counteractive means. □□ **quenchable** adj. **quencher** n. **quenchless** adj. [ME f. OE *-cwencan* causative f. *-cwincan* be extinguished]

■ **1** satisfy, slake, sate, satiate, allay, appease, assuage, gratify. **2** put out, extinguish, douse, smother, snuff out. **5 a** stifle, suppress, squelch, quell, repress, overcome, subdue; kill, destroy, get rid of.

quenelle /kənél/ n. a poached seasoned dumpling of minced fish or meat. [F, of unkn. orig.]

querist /kwéerist/ n. *literary* a person who asks questions; a questioner. [L *quaerere* ask]

quern /kwərn/ n. **1** a hand mill for grinding grain. **2** a small hand mill for pepper, etc. □ **quern stone** a millstone. [OE *cweorn(e)* f. Gmc]

■ mill, grinder, crusher, roller.

querulous /kwérələs, kwéryə-/ adj. complaining; peevish. □□ **querulously** adj. **querulousness** n. [LL *querulosus* or L *querulus* f. *queri* complain]

■ complaining, critical, hypercritical, finicky, finical, fussy, overparticular, censorious, *colloq.* persnickety; petulant, peevish, testy, carping, touchy, irritable, irascible, fractious, perverse, quarrelsome, ill-natured, ill-humored, cantankerous, curmudgeonly, crusty, crotchety, fretful, bad-tempered, ill-tempered, waspish, crabby, cross, splenetic, choleric, grumpy.

query /kwéeree/ n. & v. ● n. (*pl.* **-ies**) **1** a question, esp. expressing doubt or objection. **2** a question mark, or the word *query* spoken or written to question accuracy or as a mark of interrogation. ● v. (**-ies, -ied**) **1** tr. (often foll. by *whether, if,* etc. + clause) ask or inquire. **2** tr. call (a thing) in question in speech or writing. **3** tr. dispute the accuracy of. [Anglicized form of *quaere* f. L *quaerere* ask, after INQUIRY]

■ n. **1** question, inquiry, *Brit.* enquiry; doubt, uncertainty, reservation, problem. ● v. **1** ask (about), inquire (about), *Brit.* enquire (about). **3** challenge, doubt, dispute, take issue with, question, contest.

quest /kwest/ n. & v. ● n. **1** a search or the act of seeking. **2** the thing sought, esp. the object of a medieval knight's pursuit. ● v. **1** intr. (often foll. by *about*) **a** (often foll. by *after, for*) go around in search of something. **b** (of a dog, etc.) search around for game. **2** tr. *poet.* search for; seek out. □ **in quest of** seeking. □□ **quester** n. **questingly** adv. [ME f. OF *queste, quester* ult. f. L *quaerere quaest-* seek]

■ n. **1** search, pursuit, exploration, expedition, voyage (of discovery); chase, hunt. ● v. **1 a** (*quest (about) after* or *for*) seek (after or for), search after or for, seek out, hunt (for), pursue, look for.

question /kwéschən/ n. & v. ● n. **1** a sentence worded or expressed so as to seek information. **2 a** doubt about or objection to a thing's truth, credibility, advisability, etc. (*allowed it without question*). **b** the raising of such doubt, etc. **3** a matter to be discussed or decided or voted on. **4** a problem requiring an answer or solution. **5** (foll. by *of*) a matter or concern depending on conditions (*it's a question of money*). ● v.tr. **1** ask questions of; interrogate. **2** subject (a person) to examination. **3** throw doubt upon; raise objections to. **4** seek information from the study of (phenomena, facts). □ **be a question of time** be certain to happen sooner or later. **beyond all question** undoubtedly. **call in** (or **into**) **question** make a matter of dispute; query. **come into question** be discussed; become of practical importance. **in question**

1 that is being discussed or referred to (*the person in question*). **2** in dispute (*that was never in question*). **is not the question** is irrelevant. **out of the question** too impracticable, etc., to be worth discussing; impossible. **put the question** require supporters and opponents of a proposal to record their votes, divide a meeting. **question mark** a punctuation mark (?) indicating a question. **question time** *Brit. Parl.* a period during parliamentary proceedings when MPs may question ministers. **without question** see *beyond all question* above. □□ **questioner** n. **questioningly** adv. **questionless** adj. [ME f. AF *questiun*, OF *question, questionner* f. L *quaestio -onis* f. *quaerere quaest-* seek]

■ n. **2** query, demur, objection; see also DOUBT n. 1. **3, 5** issue, point, concern; see also MATTER n. 7. **4** problem, difficulty, doubt, uncertainty, query. ● v. **1** ask, interrogate, query, interview, sound out, quiz, pump, grill, give a person the third degree. **3** call in or into question, doubt, query, mistrust, distrust, cast doubt upon, dispute, suspect, have one's doubts about. □ **beyond all question** beyond (the shadow of) a doubt, without question, without a doubt, indubitably, undoubtedly, definitely, certainly, assuredly. **call in** or **into question** question, doubt, query, challenge, dispute, harbor or entertain or have doubts or suspicions about, suspect, cast doubt or suspicion on. **in question 1** under discussion or consideration, at issue. **2** questionable, debatable, in dispute, disputable, at issue, in doubt, doubtful, open to debate. **out of the question** unthinkable, impossible, absurd, ridiculous, preposterous, inconceivable, beyond consideration.

questionable /kwéschənəbəl/ adj. **1** doubtful as regards truth or quality. **2** not clearly in accordance with honesty, honor, wisdom, etc. □□ **questionability** /-əbílitee/ n. **questionableness** n. **questionably** adv.

■ **1** doubtful, dubious, debatable, moot, disputable, borderline, ambiguous, open to question, in dispute, problematic(al), uncertain, arguable, unsure. **2** suspect, shady; see also QUEER adj. 2.

questionary /kwéschəneree/ n. (*pl.* **-ies**) = QUESTIONNAIRE. [med.L *quaestionarium* or F (as QUESTIONNAIRE)]

questionnaire /kwéschənáir/ n. **1** a formulated series of questions, esp. for statistical study. **2** a document containing these. [F f. *questionner* QUESTION + *-aire* -ARY[1]]

quetzal /kétsaal, -sál/ n. **1** any of various brightly colored birds of the family Trogonidae, esp. the Central and S. American *Pharomachrus mocinno*, the male of which has long green tail coverts. **2** the chief monetary unit of Guatemala. [Sp. f. Aztec f. *quetzalli* the bird's tail feather]

queue /kyōo/ n. & v. ● n. **1** esp. *Brit.* a line or sequence of persons, vehicles, etc., awaiting their turn to be attended to or to proceed. **2** a pigtail or braid of hair. **3** *Computing* a sequence of jobs or processes waiting to be acted upon. ● v.intr. (**queues, queued, queuing** or **queueing**) esp. *Brit.* (often foll. by *up*) (of persons, etc.) form a line; take one's place in a line. □ **queue-jump** *Brit.* push forward out of turn in a line. [F f. L *cauda* tail]

■ n. **1** line, row, file, column, string, *Brit. colloq.* crocodile; train, cortège, procession, succession, chain; tail. **2** pigtail, ponytail, horse tail; braid, plait. ● v. line up, get in or into line, form a line or queue.

quibble /kwíbəl/ n. & v. ● n. **1** a petty objection; a trivial point of criticism. **2** a play on words; a pun. **3** an evasion; an insubstantial argument which relies on an ambiguity, etc. ● v.intr. use quibbles. □□ **quibbler** n. **quibbling** adj. **quibblingly** adv. [dimin. of obs. *quib* prob. f. L *quibus* dative & ablat. pl. of *qui* who (familiar from use in legal documents)]

■ n. **1** cavil, nicety, quiddity; trifle. **2** see PUN[1] n. **3** evasion, sophism, quip, equivocation. ● v. **1** equivocate, split hairs, evade the issue, be evasive, palter, chop logic, cavil, pettifog, find fault, *colloq.* nitpick.

quiche /keesh/ *n.* an unsweetened custard pie with a savory filling. □ **quiche Lorraine** a quiche made with ham or bacon and usu. Swiss or Gruyère cheese. [F]

quick /kwik/ *adj., adv.,* & *n.* ● *adj.* **1** taking only a short time (*a quick worker*; *a quick visit*). **2 a** arriving after a short time; prompt (*quick action*; *quick results*). **b** (of an action, occurrence, etc.) sudden; hasty; abrupt. **3** with only a short interval (*in quick succession*). **4** lively; intelligent. **5 a** acute; alert (*has a quick ear*). **b** agile; nimble; energetic. **6** (of a temper) easily roused. **7** *archaic* living; alive (*the quick and the dead*). ● *adv.* **1** quickly; at a rapid rate. **2** (as *int.*) come, go, etc., quickly. ● *n.* **1** the soft flesh below the nails, or the skin, or a sore. **2** the seat of feeling or emotion (*cut to the quick*). □ **be quick** act quickly. **quick-and-dirty** hurriedly made or done. **quick-fire 1** (of repartee, etc.) rapid. **2** firing shots in quick succession. **quick fix** an expedient but inadequate repair or solution. **quick march** *Mil.* **1** a march in quick time. **2** the command to begin this. **quick-tempered** quick to lose one's temper; irascible. **quick step** *Mil.* a step used in quick time (cf. QUICKSTEP). **quick study** one who learns rapidly. **quick time** *Mil.* marching at about 120 paces per minute. **quick with child** *archaic* at a stage of pregnancy when movements of the fetus have been felt. □□ **quickly** *adv.* **quickness** *n.* [OE *cwic(u)* alive f. Gmc]
■ *adj.* **1** rapid, fast, speedy, swift, *poet.* or *literary* fleet; expeditious, express, high-speed. **2 a** immediate, timely, instantaneous; see also PROMPT *adj.* 1b. **b** sudden, precipitate, hasty, brisk, short, abrupt, hurried, perfunctory, summary, brief. **4** lively, vivacious, animated; intelligent, bright, adept, adroit, dexterous, apt, able, astute, clever, shrewd, smart, ingenious, perceptive, perspicacious, discerning, far-sighted, responsive, nimble-witted, quick-witted. **5** alert, keen, sharp, acute; agile, nimble, energetic, spry, light. **6** short, excitable, touchy, testy, impatient. **7** see ALIVE 1. ● *adv.* **1** see *quickly* below. ● *n.* **2** see CORE *n.* 2a. □ **quick-tempered** excitable, impulsive, temperamental, hot-tempered, waspish, choleric, splenetic, impatient, short-tempered, touchy, irascible, irritable, snappish, abrupt, short, quarrelsome, testy, volatile, hot-blooded, bad-tempered, ill-tempered, churlish, highly strung, high-strung. □□ **quickly** quick, rapidly, swiftly, speedily, fast, in a trice *or* wink *or* twinkle, in the twinkling of an eye, in a flash, in two shakes (of a lamb's *or* dog's tail); posthaste, *tout de suite,* on the double, with all speed, quick, *archaic or joc.* instanter, *colloq.* lickety-split, PDQ, like a shot, *literary* apace; instantly, promptly, hastily, at once, instantaneously, unhesitatingly, spontaneously, immediately, straight away, right away, (right) now, here and now, then and there, there and then, on the spot, this (very) minute *or* second *or* instant, directly, forthwith, shortly, without delay *or* hesitation, without more ado, (very) soon, hurriedly, momentarily, *colloq.* pronto, in a jiffy.

quicken /kwíkən/ *v.* **1** *tr.* & *intr.* make or become quicker; accelerate. **2** *tr.* give life or vigor to; rouse; animate; stimulate. **3** *intr.* **a** (of a woman) reach a stage in pregnancy when movements of the fetus can be felt. **b** (of a fetus) begin to show signs of life. **4** *tr. archaic* kindle; make (a fire) burn brighter. **5** *intr.* come to life.
■ **1** accelerate, hasten, speed up, expedite, hurry, rush. **2** stimulate, arouse, kindle, spark, invigorate, excite, animate, vitalize, vivify, galvanize, enliven, awaken, energize, rouse. **4** see KINDLE 1.

quickie /kwíkee/ *n. colloq.* **1** a thing done or made quickly or hastily. **2** a drink taken quickly. **3** hasty act of sexual intercourse.

quicklime /kwíklim/ *n.* = LIME[1] *n.* 1.

quicksand /kwiksand/ *n.* **1** loose wet sand that sucks in anything placed or falling into it. **2** a bed of this.

quickset /kwíkset/ *adj.* & *n. Brit.* ● *adj.* (of a hedge) formed of cuttings of plants, esp. hawthorn set in the ground to grow. ● *n.* **1** such cuttings. **2** a hedge formed in this way.

quicksilver /kwiksilvər/ *n.* & *v.* ● *n.* **1** mercury. **2** mobility of temperament or mood. ● *v.tr.* coat (mirror glass) with an amalgam of tin.

quickstep /kwíkstep/ *n.* & *v.* ● *n.* a fast foxtrot (cf. *quick step*). ● *v.intr.* (**-stepped, -stepping**) dance the quickstep.

quick-witted /kwíkwítid/ *adj.* quick to grasp a situation, make repartee, etc. □□ **quick-wittedness** *n.*
■ quick, acute, sharp, clever, smart, nimble-witted, alert, keen, astute, perceptive, perspicacious, bright, intelligent.

quid[1] /kwid/ *n.* (*pl.* same) *Brit. sl.* one pound sterling. □ **not the full quid** *Austral. sl.* mentally deficient. **quids in** *sl.* in a position of profit. [prob. f. *quid* the nature of a thing f. L *quid* what, something]

quid[2] /kwid/ *n.* a lump of tobacco for chewing. [dial. var. of CUD]
■ plug, chew, twist, pigtail.

quiddity /kwíditee/ *n.* (*pl.* **-ies**) **1** *Philos.* the essence of a person or thing; what makes a thing what it is. **2** a quibble; a trivial objection. [med.L *quidditas* f. L *quid* what]

quidnunc /kwídnungk/ *n. archaic* a newsmonger; a person given to gossip. [L *quid* what + *nunc* now]
■ see GOSSIP *n.* 3.

quid pro quo /kwíd prō kwố/ *n.* **1** a thing given as compensation. **2** return made (for a gift, favor, etc.). [L, = something for something]
■ return, recompense, compensation, payment, requital, (just) desserts, *poet.* guerdon.

quiescent /kwiésənt, kwee-/ *adj.* **1** motionless; inert. **2** silent; dormant. □□ **quiescence** *n.* **quiescency** *n.* **quiescently** *adv.* [L *quiescere* f. *quies* QUIET]
■ **1** see INERT 1. **2** see QUIET *adj.* 1.

quiet /kwíət/ *adj., n.,* & *v.* ● *adj.* (**quieter, quietest**) **1** with little or no sound or motion. **2 a** of gentle or peaceful disposition. **b** shy; reticent; reserved. **3** (of a color, piece of clothing, etc.) unobtrusive; not showy. **4** not overt; private; disguised (*quiet resentment*). **5** undisturbed; uninterrupted; free or far from vigorous action (*a quiet time for prayer*). **6** informal; simple (*just a quiet wedding*). **7** enjoyed in quiet (*a quiet smoke*). **8** tranquil; not anxious or remorseful. ● *n.* **1** silence; stillness. **2** an undisturbed state; tranquillity. **3** a state of being free from urgent tasks or agitation (*a period of quiet*). **4** a peaceful state of affairs (*could do with some quiet*). ● *v.* **1** *tr.* soothe; make quiet. **2** *intr.* (often foll. by *down*) become quiet or calm. □ **be quiet** (esp. in *imper.*) cease talking, etc. **keep quiet 1** refrain from making a noise. **2** (often foll. by *about*) suppress or refrain from disclosing information, etc. **on the quiet** unobtrusively; secretly. □□ **quietly** *adv.* **quietness** *n.* [ME f. AF *quiete*, OF *quiet(e)*, *quieté* f. L *quietus* past part. of *quiescere*: see QUIESCENT]
■ *adj.* **1** silent, soundless, noiseless, hushed, quiescent; still, smooth, motionless, unmoving, at rest; inactive. **2 a** see GENTLE 1. **b** see SHY[1] *adj.* 1. **3** see UNOBTRUSIVE. **4** see PRIVATE *adj.* 2. **5** see PEACEFUL 1. **6** see MODEST 5. **8** serene, peaceful, unperturbed, calm, tranquil, placid, pacific, restful, unagitated, temperate, unexcited. ● *n.* **1** silence, stillness, still, soundlessness, noiselessness, hush, quietness, quietude. **2** calmness, serenity, tranquillity, peace; see also CALM *n.* 1. **3, 4** ease, rest, repose; see also PEACE 1. ● *v.* see CALM *v.* □ **be quiet** see HUSH *int.*, *wrap up* 3. **keep quiet 2** see HIDE[1] *v.* 3. **on the quiet** see *secretly* (SECRET).
□□ **quietly** silently, soundlessly, noiselessly, inaudibly, softly, in hushed tones, in whispers; peacefully, calmly, serenely, peaceably, meekly, mildly; unobtrusively; privately, secretly, in private.

quieten /kwíət'n/ *v.tr.* & *intr. Brit.* (often foll. by *down*) make or become quiet.
■ (*quieten down*) quiet (down), hush, calm (down), lull, soothe, still, silence.

quietism /kwíətizəm/ *n.* **1** a passive attitude toward life, with devotional contemplation and abandonment of the will, as a form of religious mysticism. **2** the principle of nonresistance. □□ **quietist** *n.* & *adj.* **quietistic** *adj.* [It. *quietismo* (as QUIET)]

quietude /kwí-itōōd, -tyōōd/ *n.* a state of quiet.
■ see QUIET *n.* 1.

quietus /kwī-eétəs/ *n.* **1** something which quiets or represses. **2** discharge or release from life; death; final riddance. [med.L *quietus est* he is quit (QUIET) used as a form of acquittal]

quiff /kwif/ *n. Brit.* **1** a man's tuft of hair, brushed upward over the forehead. **2** a curl plastered down on the forehead. [20th c.: orig. unkn.]

quill /kwil/ *n.* & *v.* ● *n.* **1** a large feather in a wing or tail. **2** the hollow stem of this. **3** (in full **quill pen**) a pen made of a quill. **4** (usu. in *pl.*) the spines of a porcupine. **5** a musical pipe made of a hollow stem. ● *v.tr.* form into cylindrical quill-like folds; goffer. □ **quill coverts** the feathers covering the base of quill feathers. [ME prob. f. (M)LG *quiele*]

quilt¹ /kwilt/ *n.* & *v.* ● *n.* **1** a bedcovering made of padding enclosed between layers of cloth, etc., and kept in place by patterned stitching. **2** a bedspread of similar design (*patchwork quilt*). ● *v.tr.* **1** cover or line with padded material. **2** make or join together (pieces of cloth with padding between) after the manner of a quilt. **3** sew up (a coin, letter, etc.) between two layers of a garment, etc. **4** compile (a literary work) out of extracts or borrowed ideas. □□ **quilter** *n.* **quilting** *n.* [ME f. OF *coilte*, *cuilte* f. L *culcita* mattress, cushion]
■ *n.* **1** duvet, *Brit.* continental quilt. **2** bedspread, eiderdown, counterpane, coverlet, bedcover, cover, comforter, throw.

quilt² /kwilt/ *v.tr. Austral. sl.* thrash; clout. [perh. f. QUILT¹]
■ see BEAT *v.* 1.

quim /kwim/ *n. coarse sl.* the female genitals. [18th c.: orig. unkn.]

quinacrine /kwínəkreen, -krin/ *n.* an antimalarial drug derived from acridine. [*quinine* + *acridine*]

quinary /kwínəree/ *adj.* **1** of the number five. **2** having five parts. [L *quinarius* f. *quini* distrib. of *quinque* five]

quinate /kwínayt/ *adj. Bot.* (of a leaf) having five leaflets. [L *quini* (as QUINARY)]

quince /kwins/ *n.* **1** a hard acidic pear-shaped fruit used chiefly in preserves. **2** any shrub or small tree of the genus *Cydonia*, esp. *C. oblonga*, bearing this fruit. [ME, orig. collect. pl. of obs. *quoyn*, *coyn*, f. OF *cooin* f. L *cotoneum* var. of *cydoneum* (apple) of *Cydonia* in Crete]

quincentenary /kwínsenténəree, -sént'neree/ *n.* & *adj.* ● *n.* (*pl.* **-ies**) **1** a five-hundredth anniversary. **2** a festival marking this. ● *adj.* of this anniversary. □□ **quincentennial** /-téneeəl/ *adj.* & *n.* [irreg. f. L *quinque* five + CENTENARY]

quincunx /kwínkungks/ *n.* **1** five objects set so that four are at the corners of a square or rectangle and the fifth is as at its center, e.g., the five on dice or cards. **2** this arrangement, esp. in planting trees. □□ **quincuncial** /-kúnshəl/ *adj.* **quincuncially** *adv.* [L, = five-twelfths f. *quinque* five, *uncia* twelfth]

quinella /kwinélə/ *n.* a form of betting in which the bettor must select the first two place winners in a race, not necessarily in the correct order. [Amer. Sp. *quiniela*]

quinine /kwínīn, kwín-/ *n.* **1** an alkaloid found esp. in cinchona bark. **2** a bitter drug containing this, used as a tonic and to reduce fever. □ **quinine water** a carbonated beverage flavored with quinine. [*quina* cinchona bark f. Sp. *quina* f. Quechua *kina* bark]

quinol /kwínol/ *n.* = HYDROQUINONE.

quinoline /kwínəleen, -lin/ *n. Chem.* an oily amine obtained from the distillation of coal tar or by synthesis and used in the preparation of drugs, etc.

quinone /kwínōn, kwinón/ *n. Chem.* **1** a yellow crystalline derivative of benzene with the hydrogen atoms on opposite carbon atoms replaced by two of oxygen. **2** any in a class of similar compounds.

quinquagenarian /kwíngkwəjináireeən/ *n.* & *adj.* ● *n.* a person from 50 to 59 years old. ● *adj.* of or relating to this age. [L *quinquagenarius* f. *quinquageni* distrib. of *quinquaginta* fifty]

Quinquagesima /kwíngkwəjésimə/ *n.* (in full **Quinquagesima Sunday**) the Sunday before the beginning of Lent. [med.L, fem. of L *quinquagesimus* fiftieth f. *quinquaginta* fifty, after QUADRAGESIMA]

quinque- /kwíngkwee/ *comb. form* five. [L f. *quinque* five]

quinquennial /kwinkwéneeəl/ *adj.* **1** lasting five years. **2** recurring every five years. □□ **quinquennially** *adv.* [L *quinquennis* (as QUINQUENNIUM)]

quinquennium /kwinkwéneeəm/ *n.* (*pl.* **quinquenniums** or **quinquennia** / -neeə/) a period of five years. [L f. *quinque* five + *annus* year]

quinquevalent /kwíngkwəváylənt/ *adj.* having a valence of five.

quinsy /kwínzee/ *n.* an inflammation of the throat, esp. an abscess in the region around the tonsils. □□ **quinsied** *adj.* [ME f. OF *quinencie* f. med.L *quinancia* f. Gk *kunagkhē* f. *kun-* dog + *agkhō* throttle]

quint /kwint/ *n.* **1** a sequence of five cards in the same suit in piquet, etc. **2** *colloq.* a quintuplet. □ **quint major** a quint headed by an ace. [F *quinte* f. L *quinta* fem. of *quintus* fifth f. *quinque* five]

quintain /kwínt'n/ *n. hist.* **1** a post set up as a target in tilting, and often provided with a sandbag to swing round and strike an unsuccessful tilter. **2** the medieval military exercise of tilting at such a mark. [ME f. OF *quintaine* perh. ult. f. L *quintana* camp market f. *quintus* (*manipulus*) fifth (maniple)]

quintal /kwínt'l/ *n.* **1** a weight of about 100 lb. **2** (in the UK) a weight of 112 lb. (a hundredweight). **3** a weight of 100 kg. [ME f. OF *quintal*, med.L *quintale* f. Arab. *ḳinṭār*]

quintan /kwínt'n/ *adj.* (of a fever, etc.) recurring every fifth day. [L *quintana* f. *quintus* fifth]

quinte /kaNt/ *n.* the fifth of eight parrying positions in fencing. [F: see QUINT]

quintessence /kwintésəns/ *n.* **1** the most essential part of any substance; a refined extract. **2** (usu. foll. by *of*) the purest and most perfect, or most typical, form, manifestation, or embodiment of some quality or class. **3** (in ancient philosophy) a fifth substance (beside the four elements) forming heavenly bodies and pervading all things. □□ **quintessential** /kwíntisénshəl/ *adj.* **quintessentially** *adv.* [ME (in sense 3) f. F f. med.L *quinta essentia* fifth ESSENCE]
■ **1** essence, heart, core, quiddity, pith, marrow, nub, *Philos.* haecceity. **2** epitome, embodiment, incarnation, personification, model, prototype, exemplar, ideal, beau ideal, paragon, pinnacle.

quintet /kwintét/ *n.* (also **quintette**) **1** *Mus.* **a** a composition for five voices or instruments. **b** the performers of such a piece. **2** any group of five. [F *quintette* f. It. *quintetto* f. *quinto* fifth f. L *quintus*]

quintillion /kwintílyən/ *n.* (*pl.* same or **quintillions**) a thousand raised to the sixth (or esp. *Brit.* the tenth) power (10^{18} and 10^{30} respectively). □□ **quintillionth** *adj.* & *n.* [L *quintus* fifth + MILLION]

quintuple /kwintōōpəl, -tyōō-, -túpəl, kwíntəpəl/ *adj., n.,* & *v.* ● *adj.* **1** fivefold; consisting of five parts. **2** involving five parties. **3** (of time in music) having five beats in a bar. ● *n.* a fivefold number or amount. ● *v.tr.* & *intr.* multiply by five; increase fivefold. □□ **quintuply** *adv.* [F *quintuple* f. L *quintus* fifth, after QUADRUPLE]

quintuplet /kwintúplit, -tōō-, -tyōō-, kwíntə-/ *n.* **1** each of five children born at one birth. **2** a set of five things working together. **3** *Mus.* a group of five notes to be performed in the time of three or four. [QUINTUPLE, after QUADRUPLET, TRIPLET]

quintuplicate *adj.* & *v.* ● *adj.* /kwintōōplikət, -tyōō-/ **1** fivefold. **2** of which five copies are made. ● *v.tr.* & *intr.* /-kayt/ multiply by five. □ **in quintuplicate 1** in five identical copies. **2** in groups of five. [F *quintuple* f. L *quintus* fifth, after QUADRUPLICATE]

/.../ **pronunciation**	● **part of speech**
□ **phrases, idioms, and compounds**	
□□ **derivatives**	■ **synonym section**
cross-references appear in SMALL CAPITALS or *italics*	

quip /kwip/ *n. & v.* ● *n.* **1** a clever saying; an epigram; a sarcastic remark, etc. **2** a quibble; an equivocation. ● *v.intr.* (**quipped, quipping**) make quips. □□ **quipster** *n.* [abbr. of obs. *quippy* perh. f. L *quippe* forsooth]

■ *n.* **1** bon mot, witticism, sally, aphorism, epigram, apothegm; jest, joke, gag, *colloq.* one-liner, crack, wisecrack, wheeze, chestnut. **2** quibble, equivocation, evasion, sophism. ● *v.* see JOKE *v.* 1.

quipu /keepoo, kwee-/ *n.* the ancient Peruvians' substitute for writing by variously knotting threads of various colors. [Quechua, = knot]

quire /kwir/ *n.* **1** four sheets of paper, etc., folded to form eight leaves, as often in medieval manuscripts. **2** any collection of leaves one within another in a manuscript or book. **3** 25 (also 24) sheets of paper. □ **in quires** unbound; in sheets. [ME f. OF *qua(i)er* ult. f. L *quaterni* set of four (as QUATERNARY)]

quirk /kwərk/ *n.* **1** a peculiarity of behavior. **2** a trick of fate; a freak. **3** a flourish in writing. **4** (often *attrib.*) *Archit.* a hollow in a molding. □□ **quirkish** *adj.* **quirky** *adj.* (**quirkier, quirkiest**). **quirkily** *adv.* **quirkiness** *n.* [16th c.: orig. unkn.]

■ **1** peculiarity, caprice, vagary, whim, idiosyncrasy, oddity, eccentricity, fancy, aberration, kink, characteristic. **2** trick, twist; oddity, aberration; fluke, accident.

quirt /kwərt/ *n. & v.* ● *n.* a short-handled riding whip with a braided leather lash. ● *v.tr.* strike with this. [Sp. *cuerda* CORD]

quisling /kwízling/ *n.* **1** a person cooperating with an occupying enemy; a collaborator or fifth columnist. **2** a traitor. □□ **quislingite** *adj. & n.* [V. *Quisling*, renegade Norwegian Army officer d. 1945]

■ see TRAITOR.

quit /kwit/ *v. & adj.* ● *v.tr.* (**quitting**; *past* and *past part.* **quit** or **quitted**) **1** (also *absol.*) give up; let go; abandon (a task, etc.). **2** cease; stop (*quit grumbling*). **3 a** leave or depart from (a place, person, employment, etc.). **b** (*absol.*) (of a tenant) leave occupied premises (esp. *notice to quit*). **4** (*refl.*) acquit; behave (*quit oneself well*). ● *predic.adj.* (foll. by *of*) rid (*glad to be quit of the problem*). □ **quit hold of** loose. [ME f. OF *quitte, quitter* f. med.L *quittus* f. L *quietus* QUIET]

■ *v.* **1** let go, resign, give up, relinquish, leave, renounce, retire from, withdraw from, abandon, forsake. **2** cease, stop, discontinue, leave off, *literary* desist from. **3 a** depart from, go (away) from, get away from, flee; see also LEAVE[1] *v.* 1b, 3, 4. **b** leave, move, move out. **4** see BEHAVE 1a. ● *predic.adj.* free, clear, discharged, rid, released, exempt; (*be* or *get quit of*) wash one's hands of, get rid of, be done with, get a thing off one's hands. □ **quit hold of** see LOOSE *v.* 1.

quitch /kwich/ *n.* (in full **quitch grass**) = COUCH[2]. [OE *cwice*, perh. rel. to QUICK]

quite /kwit/ *adv.* **1** completely; entirely; wholly; to the utmost extent; in the fullest sense. **2** somewhat; rather; to some extent. **3** (often foll. by *so*) said to indicate agreement. **4** absolutely; definitely; very much. □ **quite another** (or **other**) very different (*that's quite another matter*). **quite a few** *colloq.* a fairly large number of. **quite something** a remarkable thing. [ME f. obs. *quite* (adj.) = QUIT]

■ **1** completely, very, totally, utterly, entirely, fully, wholly, absolutely, perfectly, altogether, thoroughly. **2** rather, fairly, moderately, somewhat, relatively, to some or a certain extent, to some or a certain degree. **3** (*quite so*) see ABSOLUTELY 6. **4** very much, totally, entirely, wholly, altogether; really, actually, truly, definitely, positively, undoubtedly, indubitably, absolutely, unequivocally, certainly, unreservedly, absolutely. □ **quite another** (*quite another matter*) a (completely) different kettle of fish, something else (altogether), *colloq.* a whole new ball game. **quite a few** quite a lot, a fair number or few, a good number or few.

quits /kwits/ *predic.adj.* on even terms by retaliation or repayment (*then we'll be quits*). □ **call it** (or *Brit.* **cry**) **quits** acknowledge that things are now even; agree not to proceed

further in a quarrel, etc. [perh. colloq. abbr. of med.L *quittus*: see QUIT]

■ (*be quits*) be even or square or equal with.

quittance /kwít'ns/ *n.* **1** (foll. by *from*) a release. **2** an acknowledgment of payment; a receipt. [ME f. OF *quitance* f. *quiter* QUIT]

quitter /kwítər/ *n.* **1** a person who gives up easily. **2** a shirker.

quiver[1] /kwívər/ *v. & n.* ● *v.* **1** *intr.* tremble or vibrate with a slight rapid motion, esp.: **a** (usu. foll. by *with*) as the result of emotion (*quiver with anger*). **b** (usu. foll. by *in*) as the result of air currents, etc. (*quiver in the breeze*). **2** *tr.* (of a bird) make (its wings) quiver. ● *n.* a quivering motion or sound. □□ **quiveringly** *adv.* **quivery** *adj.* [ME f. obs. *quiver* nimble: cf. QUAVER]

■ *v.* **1** shake, tremble, vibrate, shiver, quaver; shudder, tremor, oscillate. ● *n.* tremble, quaver, shudder, spasm, shake, tremor, shiver.

quiver[2] /kwívər/ *n.* a case for holding arrows. □ **have an arrow** (or **shaft**) **left in one's quiver** not be resourceless. [ME f. OF *quivre* f. WG (cf. OE *cocor*)]

quiverful /kwívərfool/ *n.* (*pl.* **-fuls**) esp. *Brit.* **1** as much as a quiver can hold. **2** many children of one parent (Ps. 127:5). [QUIVER[2]]

qui vive /kee veev/ *n.* □ **on the qui vive** on the alert; watching for something to happen. [F, = lit. '(long) live who?', i.e., on whose side are you?, as a sentry's challenge]

■ □ **on the qui vive** see *on the alert* (ALERT).

quixotic /kwiksótik/ *adj.* **1** extravagantly and romantically chivalrous; regardless of material interests in comparison with honor or devotion. **2** visionary; pursuing lofty but unattainable ideals. **3** *derog.* ridiculously impractical; preposterous; foolhardy. □□ **quixotically** *adv.* **quixotism** /kwíksətizəm/ *n.* **quixotry** /kwíksətree/ *n.* [Don *Quixote*, hero of Cervantes' romance f. Sp. *quixote* thigh armor]

■ **1** romantic, chivalrous, gallant; sentimental. **2** idealistic, visionary, utopian, impractical, unpractical, unrealistic, romantic, heady, fantastic(al), starry-eyed. **3** absurd, mad, foolhardy, reckless, wild, preposterous, ridiculous; impracticable, unrealizable, impractical; chimerical, fanciful, dreamlike.

quiz[1] /kwiz/ *n. & v.* ● *n.* (*pl.* **quizzes**) **1 a** a quick or informal test. **b** an interrogation, examination, or questionnaire. **2** (also **quiz show**) a test of knowledge, esp. between individuals or teams as a form of entertainment. ● *v.tr.* (**quizzed, quizzing**) examine by questioning. □ [19th-c. dial.: orig. unkn.]

■ *n.* **1** examination, test, exam; interrogation, questioning; questionnaire, questionary. ● *v.* question, interrogate, ask, examine, interview, ask the opinion of, grill, pump.

quiz[2] /kwiz/ *v. & n. archaic Brit.* ● *v.tr.* (**quizzed, quizzing**) **1** look curiously at; observe the ways or oddities of; survey through an eyeglass. **2** make fun of; regard mockingly. ● *n.* (*pl.* **quizzes**) **1** a hoax; a practical joke. **2 a** an odd or eccentric person; a person of ridiculous appearance. **b** a person given to quizzing. □□ **quizzer** *n.* [18th c.: orig. unkn.]

quizzical /kwízikəl/ *adj.* **1** expressing or done with mild or amused perplexity. **2** strange; comical. □□ **quizzicality** /-kálitee/ *n.* **quizzically** *adv.* **quizzicalness** *n.*

■ **1** perplexed, bemused, puzzled, inquiring, questioning. **2** curious, queer, comical, strange; see ODD *adj.* 1.

quod /kwod/ *n. Brit. sl.* prison. [17th c.: orig. unkn.]

■ see PRISON *n.* 1.

quod erat demonstrandum /kwod érət démənstrándəm, éraat démōnstraándoōm/ (esp. at the conclusion of a proof, etc.) which was the thing to be proved. ¶ Abbr.: **QED**. [L]

quodlibet /kwódlibet/ *n.* **1** *hist.* **a** a topic for philosophical or theological discussion. **b** an exercise on this. **2** a whimsical medley of well-known tunes. □□ **quodlibetarian** /-bitáyreeən/ *n.* **quodlibetical** /-likétikəl/ *adj.* **quodlibetically** *adv.* [ME f. L f. *quod* what + *libet* it pleases one]

quod vide /kwod veéday, vídee/ which see (in cross-references, etc.). ¶ Abbr.: **q.v.** [L]

quoin /koyn, kwoin/ *n. & v.* ● *n.* **1** an external angle of a building. **2** a stone or brick forming an angle; a cornerstone.

3 a wedge used for locking type in a chase. **4** a wedge for raising the level of a gun, keeping the barrel from rolling, etc. ● *v.tr.* secure or raise with quoins. □□ **quoining** *n.* [var. of COIN]

quoit /koyt, kwoit/ *n. & v.* ● *n.* **1** a heavy flattish sharp-edged iron ring thrown to encircle an iron peg or to land as near as possible to the peg. **2** (in *pl.*) a game consisting of aiming and throwing these. **3** a ring of rope, rubber, etc., for use in a similar game. **4** *Brit.* **a** the flat stone of a dolmen. **b** the dolmen itself. ● *v.tr.* fling like a quoit. [ME: orig. unkn.]
■ *n.* **1, 3** ring, hoop.

quokka /kwókǝ/ *n.* a small Australian short-tailed wallaby, *Setonix brachyurus.* [Aboriginal name]

quondam /kwóndǝm, -dam/ *predic.adj.* that once was; sometime; former. [L (adv.), = formerly]
■ see FORMER[1] 1.

Quonset hut /kwónsit/ *n. propr.* a prefabricated metal building with a semicylindrical corrugated roof. [*Quonset* Point, Rhode Island, where it was first made]

quorate /kwáwrǝt, -rayt/ *adj. Brit.* (of a meeting) attended by a quorum. [QUORUM]

quorum /kwáwrǝm/ *n.* the fixed minimum number of members that must be present to make the proceedings of an assembly or society legally valid. [L, = of whom (we wish that you be two, three, etc.), in the wording of commissions]

quota /kwótǝ/ *n.* **1** the share that an individual person, group, or company is bound to contribute to or entitled to receive from a total. **2** a quantity of goods, etc., which under official controls must be manufactured, exported, imported, etc. **3** the number of immigrants allowed to enter a country annually, students allowed to enroll in a course, etc. [med.L *quota* (*pars*) how great (a part), fem. of *quotus* f. *quot* how many]
■ **1** apportionment, portion, allotment, allocation, allowance, ration, share, part, proportion, percentage, *colloq.* cut.

quotable /kwótǝbǝl/ *adj.* worth, or suitable for, quoting. □□ **quotability** *n.*

quotation /kwótáyshǝn/ *n.* **1** the act or an instance of quoting or being quoted. **2** a passage or remark quoted. **3** *Mus.* a short passage or tune taken from one piece of music to another. **4** *Stock Exch.* an amount stated as the current price of stocks or commodities. **5** a contractor's estimate. □ **quotation mark** each of a set of punctuation marks, single

(' ') or double (" "), used to mark the beginning and end of a quoted passage, a book title, etc., or words regarded as slang or jargon. [med.L *quotatio* (as QUOTE)]
■ **2** passage, citation, reference, extract, excerpt, selection, sound bite, *colloq.* quote. **4** (market) price, charge, rate, cost, *colloq.* quote; value. □ **quotation mark** *Brit.* inverted comma; (*quotation marks*) *colloq.* quotes.

quote /kwōt/ *v. & n.* ● *v.tr.* **1** cite or appeal to (an author, book, etc.) in confirmation of some view. **2** repeat a statement by (another person) or copy out a passage from (*don't quote me*). **3** (often *absol.*) **a** repeat or copy out (a passage) usu. with an indication that it is borrowed. **b** (foll. by *from*) cite (an author, book, etc.). **4** (foll. by *as*) cite (an author, etc.) as proof, evidence, etc. **5 a** enclose (words) in quotation marks. **b** (as *int.*) (in dictation, reading aloud, etc.) indicate the presence of opening quotation marks (*he said, quote, "I shall stay"*). **6** (often foll. by *at*) state the price of (a commodity, bet, etc.) (*quoted at 200 to 1*). **7** *Stock Exch.* regularly list the price of. ● *n. colloq.* **1** a passage quoted. **2 a** a price quoted. **b** a contractor's estimate. **3** (usu. in *pl.*) quotation marks. [ME, earlier 'mark with numbers,' f. med.L *quotare* f. *quot* how many, or as QUOTA]
■ *v.* **1** cite; appeal to, refer to. **3** cite, recite, repeat; extract, excerpt. **4** instance, name, identify, denominate, pinpoint. ● *n.* **1** see QUOTATION 2. **2** see QUOTATION 4. **3** (*quotes*) see *quotation mark.*

quoth /kwōth/ *v.tr.* (only in 1st and 3rd person) *archaic* said. [OE *cwæth* past of *cwethan* say f. Gmc]

quotidian /kwotídeeǝn/ *adj. & n.* ● *adj.* **1** daily; of every day. **2** commonplace; trivial. ● *n.* (in full **quotidian fever**) a fever recurring every day. [ME f. OF *cotidien* & L *cotidianus* f. *cotidie* daily]
■ *adj.* **1** diurnal, daily, everyday, *Physiol.* circadian.

quotient /kwóshǝnt/ *n.* a result obtained by dividing one quantity by another. [ME f. L *quotiens* how many times f. *quot* how many, by confusion with -ENT]

Qur'an var. of KORAN.

q.v. *abbr.* quod vide.

qwerty /kwɜ́rtee/ *attrib.adj.* denoting the standard keyboard on English-language typewriters, word processors, etc., with *q, w, e, r, t,* and *y* as the first keys on the top row of letters.

qy. *abbr.* query.

R¹ /aar/ *n.* (also **r**) (*pl.* **Rs** or **R's**) the eighteenth letter of the alphabet. □ **the r months** the months with *r* in their names (September to April) as the season for oysters.

R² *abbr.* (also **R.**) **1** river. **2** *Brit. Regina (Elizabeth R).* **3** *Brit. Rex.* **4** (also ®) registered as a trademark. **5** (in names of societies, etc.) Royal. **6** *Chess* rook. **7** ratio. **8** rand. **9** regiment. **10** *Electr.* resistance. **11** radius. **12** roentgen. **13** (of movies) classified as prohibited to people under a certain age (as 17) unless accompanied by a parent or guardian.

r. *abbr.* (also **r**) **1** right. **2** run(s). **4** radius.

RA *abbr.* **1** regular army. **2** rear admiral. **3 a** (in the UK) Royal Academy. **b** (in the UK) royal academician. **4** *Astron.* right ascension.

Ra *symb. Chem.* the element radium.

rabbet /rábit/ *n. & v.* ● *n.* a step-shaped channel, etc., cut along the edge or face or projecting angle of a length of wood, etc., usu. to receive the edge or tongue of another piece. ● *v.tr.* **1** join or fix with a rabbet. **2** make a rabbet in. □ **rabbet plane** a plane for cutting a groove along an edge. [ME f. OF *rab(b)at* abatement, recess f. *rabattre* REBATE]

rabbi /rábi/ *n.* (*pl.* **rabbis**) **1** a Jewish scholar or teacher, esp. of the law. **2** a person appointed as a Jewish religious leader. □□ **rabbinate** /rábinət/ *n.* [ME & OE f. eccl.L f. Gk *rhabbi* f. Heb. *rabbî* my master f. *rab* master + pronominal suffix]

rabbinical /rəbínikəl/ *adj.* of or relating to rabbis, or to Jewish law or teaching. □□ **rabbinically** *adv.*

rabbit /rábit/ *n. & v.* ● *n.* **1 a** any of various burrowing gregarious plant-eating mammals of the family Leporidae, esp. the eastern cottontail, *Sylvilagus floridanus*, with long ears and a short tail, varying in color from brown in the wild to black and white, and kept as a pet or for meat. **b** a hare. **c** the fur of the rabbit. **2** *Brit. colloq.* a poor performer in any sport or game. ● *v.intr.* **1** hunt rabbits. **2** (often foll. by *on, away*) *Brit. colloq.* talk excessively or pointlessly; chatter (*rabbiting on about his school*). □ **rabbit ears** a television antenna consisting of two movable rods, usu. on top of the set. **rabbit punch** a short chop with the edge of the hand to the nape of the neck. **rabbit's foot** the foot of a rabbit, carried to bring luck. **rabbit warren** an area in which rabbits have their burrows, or are kept for meat, etc. □□ **rabbity** *adj.* [ME perh. f. OF: cf. F dial. *rabotte*, Walloon *robète*, Flem. *robbe*]

▪ *v.* **2** see CHATTER *v.* 1.

rabble¹ /rábəl/ *n.* **1** a disorderly crowd; a mob. **2** a contemptible or inferior set of people. **3** (prec. by *the*) the lower or disorderly classes of the populace. □ **rabble-rouser** a person who stirs up the rabble or a crowd of people in agitation for social or political change. **rabble-rousing** *adj.* tending to arouse the emotions of a crowd. ● *n.* the act or process of doing this. [ME: orig. uncert.]

▪ **1** mob, crowd, horde, throng, swarm, gang. **2** vermin, trash, dregs (of society), *colloq.* scum. **3** (*the rabble*) populace, people (at large), masses, proletariat, hoi polloi, commoners, peasantry, commonalty, rank and file, lower classes, working class, *colloq.* great unwashed, *colloq. derog.* proles, *usu. derog.* ragtag and bobtail, riff-raff, canaille, plebs, mob. □ **rabble-rouser** agitator, demagogue, inciter, firebrand, incendiary, troublemaker, agent provocateur, revolutionary, insurrectionist, hell-raiser.

rabble² /rábəl/ *n.* an iron bar with a bent end for stirring molten metal, etc. [F *râble* f. med.L *rotabulum*, L *rutabulum* fire shovel f. *ruere rut-* rake up]

Rabelaisian /rábəláyzeeən, -zhən/ *adj. & n.* ● *adj.* **1** of or like Rabelais or his writings. **2** marked by exuberant imagination and language, coarse humor, and satire. ● *n.* an admirer or student of Rabelais. [F. *Rabelais*, Fr. satirist d. 1553]

▪ *adj.* **2** see BAWDY *adj.*, SATIRICAL.

rabid /rábid/ *adj.* **1** furious; violent (*rabid hatred*). **2** unreasoning; headstrong; fanatical (*a rabid anarchist*). **3** affected with rabies; mad. **4** of or connected with rabies. □□ **rabidity** /rəbíditee/ *n.* **rabidly** *adv.* **rabidness** *n.* [L *rabidus* f. *rabere* rave]

▪ **1** raging, furious; see also VIOLENT 2a. **2** unreasonable, unreasoning, extreme, fanatical, headstrong. **3** crazed, frenzied, maniacal, wild, mad, raving, berserk.

rabies /ráybeez/ *n.* a contagious and fatal viral disease, esp. of dogs, cats, raccoons, etc., transmissible through the saliva to humans, etc., and causing madness and convulsions; hydrophobia. [L f. *rabere* rave]

raccoon /rakoon/ *n.* (also **racoon**) **1** any grayish-brown furry N. American nocturnal flesh-eating mammal of the genus *Procyon*, with a bushy, ringed tail and masklike band across the eyes. **2** the fur of the raccoon. [Algonquian dial.]

race¹ /rays/ *n. & v.* ● *n.* **1** a contest of speed between runners, horses, vehicles, ships, etc. **2** (in *pl.*) a series of these for horses, dogs, etc., at a fixed time on a regular course. **3** a contest between persons to be first to achieve something. **4 a** a strong or rapid current flowing through a narrow channel in the sea or a river (*a tide race*). **b** the channel of a stream, etc. (*a millrace*). **5** each of two grooved rings in a ball bearing or roller bearing. **6** *Austral.* a fenced passageway for drafting sheep, etc. **7** (in weaving) the channel along which the shuttle moves. **8** *archaic* **a** the course of the sun or moon. **b** the course of life (*has run his race*). ● *v.* **1** *intr.* take part in a race. **2** *tr.* have a race with. **3** *tr.* try to surpass in speed. **4** *intr.* (foll. by *with*) compete in speed with. **5** *tr.* cause (a horse, car, etc.) to race. **6 a** *intr.* move swiftly; go at full or (of an engine, propeller, the pulse, etc.) excessive speed. **b** *tr.* cause (a person or thing) to do this (*raced the bill through the House*). **7** *intr.* (usu. as **racing** *adj.*) follow or take part in horse racing (*a racing man*). □ **out of the race** (of a person, etc., in contention for something) having no chance. **race car** a car built for racing on a prepared track. [ME, = running, f. ON *rás*]

▪ *n.* **1** competition, contest. **2** (*races*) race meeting, meeting, meet; *Brit. colloq.* the dogs. **4 b** sluice, flume, chute, watercourse, course, channel, bed, raceway. ● *v.* **6 a** speed, hurry, hasten, dash, sprint, fly, rush, scramble, step lively, *colloq.* tear, rip, zip, step on the gas, step on it, hop to it, get a move on, *Brit* hare, *sl.* get a wiggle on. **b** rush, push, press, drive; urge, egg.

race² /rays/ *n.* **1** each of the major divisions of humankind, having distinct physical characteristics. **2** a tribe, nation, etc., regarded as of a distinct ethnic stock. **3** the fact or concept of division into races (*discrimination based on race*). **4** a genus, species, breed, or variety of animals, plants, or microorganisms. **5** a group of persons, animals, or plants connected by common descent. **6** any great division of living creatures (*the feathered race*; *the four-footed race*). **7** descent; kindred (*of noble race*; *separate in language and race*). **8** a class of persons, etc., with some common feature (*the race of poets*). □ **race relations** relations between members of different races usu. in the same country. **race riot** an outbreak of violence due to racial antagonism. [F f. It. *razza*, of unkn. orig.]

■ **1, 2** stock, tribe, nation, people, folk, clan, family. **7** blood, descent, breed, kin, kindred, family, stock, line, lineage. **8** see CLASS *n.* 1.

race³ /rays/ *n.* a ginger root. [OF *rais, raiz* f. L *radix radicis* root]

racecourse /ráyskawrs/ *n.* a ground or track for esp. horse racing.

■ racetrack, raceway.

racegoer /ráysgōǝr/ *n.* a person who frequents horse races.

racehorse /ráys-hors/ *n.* a horse bred or kept for racing.

racemate /rayseémayt, rása-/ *n.* *Chem.* a racemic mixture.

raceme /rayseém, rǝ-/ *n.* *Bot.* a flower cluster with the separate flowers attached by short equal stalks at equal distances along a central stem (cf. CYME). [L *racemus* grape bunch]

racemic /rayseémik, -sém-, rǝ-/ *adj.* *Chem.* composed of equal numbers of dextrorotatory and levorotatory molecules of a compound. □□ **racemize** /rásimīz/ *v.tr.* & *intr.* [RACEME + -IC, orig. of tartaric acid in grape juice]

racemose /rásimōs/ *adj.* **1** *Bot.* in the form of a raceme. **2** *Anat.* (of a gland, etc.) clustered. [L *racemosus* (as RACEME)]

racer /ráysǝr/ *n.* **1** a horse, yacht, bicycle, etc., of a kind used for racing. **2** a circular horizontal rail along which the traversing platform of a heavy gun moves. **3** a person or thing that races.

racetrack /ráystrak/ *n.* **1** = RACECOURSE. **2** a track for automobile racing.

raceway /ráysway/ *n.* **1** a track or channel along which something runs, esp.: **a** esp. *Brit.* a channel for water. **b** a groove in which ball bearings run. **c** a pipe or tubing enclosing electrical wires. **2 a** a track for trotting, pacing, or harness racing. **b** = RACETRACK.

■ **1 a** see RACE¹ *n.* 4b.

rachis /ráykis/ *n.* (*pl.* **rachises** or **rachides** /rákideez, ráy-/) **1** *Bot.* **a** a stem of grass, etc., bearing flower stalks at short intervals. **b** the axis of a compound leaf or frond. **2** *Anat.* the vertebral column or the cord from which it develops. **3** *Zool.* a feather shaft, esp. the part bearing the barbs. □□ **rachidial** /rǝkídeeǝl/ *adj.* [mod.L f. Gk *rhakhis* spine: the E pl. *-ides* is erron.]

rachitis /rǝkítis/ *n.* rickets. □□ **rachitic** /-kítik/ *adj.* [mod.L f. Gk *rhakhitis* (as RACHIS)]

racial /ráyshǝl/ *adj.* **1** of or concerning race (*racial diversities*; *racial minority*). **2** on the grounds of or connected with difference in race (*racial discrimination*; *racial tension*). □□ **racially** *adv.*

■ **1** ethnic, genetic, ethnological, tribal; national.

racialism /ráyshǝlizǝm/ *n.* = RACISM 1. □□ **racialist** *n.* & *adj.*

racism /ráysizǝm/ *n.* **1 a** a belief in the superiority of a particular race; prejudice based on this. **b** antagonism toward other races, esp. as a result of this. **2** the theory that human abilities, etc., are determined by race. □□ **racist** *n.* & *adj.*

■ **1** racialism, apartheid, jim crowism, chauvinism, bigotry. □□ **racist** (*n.*) see SUPREMACIST *n.* (*adj.*) racialist, prejudiced, chauvinistic, bigoted.

rack¹ /rak/ *n.* & *v.* ● *n.* **1 a** a framework usu. with rails, bars, hooks, etc., for holding or storing things. **b** a frame for holding animal fodder. **2** a cogged or toothed bar or rail engaging with a wheel or pinion, etc., or using pegs to adjust the position of something. **3 a** *hist.* an instrument of torture stretching the victim's joints by the turning of rollers to which the wrists and ankles were tied. **b** a cause of suffering or anguish. ● *v.tr.* **1** (of disease or pain) inflict suffering on. **2** *hist.* torture (a person) on the rack. **3** place in or on a rack. **4** shake violently. **5** injure by straining. **6** *Brit.* oppress (tenants) by exacting excessive rent. **7** exhaust (the land) by excessive use. □ **on the rack** in distress or under strain. **rack one's brains** make a great mental effort (*racked my brains*

for something to say). **rack railway** = *cog railway*. **rack rent** *n.* **1** a high rent, annually equalling the full value of the property to which it relates. **2** an extortionate rent. **rack-rent** *v.tr.* exact this from (a tenant) or for (land). **rack-renter** a tenant paying or a landlord exacting an extortionate rent. **rack up** accumulate or achieve (a score, etc.). **rack wheel** a cogwheel. [ME *rakke* f. MDu., MLG *rak, rek*, prob. f. *recken* stretch]

■ *n.* **1** framework, frame, trestle, holder, support; stand, scaffold. **3 b** torment, torture, agony, anguish, pain, misery, distress, affliction, scourge. ● *v.* **1** distress, torment, torture, agonize, oppress, pain, persecute, anguish, beleaguer, plague, gnaw at, harrow. **4** see SHAKE *v.* 1, 2, 5. **5** strain, wrench, tear, pull, sprain, esp. *Brit.* rick. □ **on the rack** in distress, under stress *or* pressure *or* strain, *colloq.* stressed out; see also *worried* (WORRY *v.* 4).

rack² /rak/ *n.* destruction (esp. *rack and ruin*). [var. of WRACK, WRECK]

■ see DESTRUCTION 1.

rack³ /rak/ *n.* a joint of lamb, etc., including the front ribs. [perh. f. RACK¹]

rack⁴ /rak/ *v.tr.* (often foll. by *off*) draw off (wine, beer, etc.) from the lees. [ME f. Prov. *arracar* f. *raca* stems and husks of grapes, dregs]

rack⁵ /rak/ *n.* & *v.* ● *n.* driving clouds. ● *v.intr.* (of clouds) be driven before the wind. [ME, prob. of Scand. orig.: cf. Norw. and Sw. dial. *rak* wreckage, etc. f. *reka* drive]

rack⁶ /rak/ *n.* & *v.* ● *n.* a horse's gait between a trot and a canter. ● *v.intr.* progress in this way.

racket¹ /rákit/ *n.* (also **racquet**) **1** a hand-held implement with a round or oval frame strung with catgut, nylon, etc., used in tennis, squash, etc. **2** (in *pl.*) a ball game for two or four persons played with rackets in a plain four-walled court. **3** a snowshoe resembling a tennis racket. □ **rackettail** a S. American hummingbird, *Loddigesia mirabilis*, with a racket-shaped tail. [F *racquette* f. It. *racchetta* f. Arab. *rāḥa* palm of the hand]

racket² /rákit/ *n.* **1 a** a disturbance; an uproar; a din. **b** social excitement; gaiety. **2** *sl.* **a** a scheme for obtaining money or attaining other ends by fraudulent and often violent means. **b** a dodge; a sly game. **3** *colloq.* an activity; a way of life; a line of business (*starting up a new racket*). □□ **rackety** *adj.* [16th c.: perh. imit.]

■ **1 a** noise, din, uproar, disturbance, clamor, hubbub, hullabaloo, ballyhoo, fuss, ado, commotion, to-do, hue and cry, outcry, brouhaha, tumult, babel, *colloq.* row, rumpus, *joc.* alarums and excursions. **b** see GAIETY 2. **2** trick, dodge, scheme, swindle, stratagem, artifice, game, ruse, fraud, *Austral. colloq.* lurk, *sl.* gyp, con, scam *Brit. sl.* ramp. **3** business, line (of business), profession, occupation, trade, vocation, calling, job, employment.

racketeer /rákiteér/ *n.* a person who operates a dishonest or illegal business, as gambling, extortion, etc. □□ **racketeering** *n.*

■ gangster, *sl.* mobster; see also *swindler* (SWINDLE).

racon /ráykon/ *n.* a radar beacon that can be identified and located by its response to a radar signal from a ship, etc. [radar + beacon]

raconteur /rákontőr/ *n.* (*fem.* **raconteuse** /-tőz/) a teller of interesting anecdotes. [F f. *raconter* relate, RECOUNT]

■ storyteller, anecdotalist, anecdotist, taleteller; chronicler, narrator, *Austral. sl.* magsman.

racoon var. of RACCOON.

racquet var. of RACKET¹.

racquetball /rákǝtbawl/ *n.* a game played with rackets and a rubber ball on an enclosed, four-walled court.

racy /ráysee/ *adj.* (**racier**, **raciest**) **1** lively and vigorous in

/.../ **pronunciation**	● **part of speech**
□ **phrases, idioms, and compounds**	
□□ **derivatives**	■ **synonym section**
cross-references appear in SMALL CAPITALS or *italics*	

style. **2** risqué, suggestive. **3** having characteristic qualities in a high degree (*a racy flavor*). □□ **racily** *adv.* **raciness** *n.* [RACE² + -Y¹]

■ **1** fresh, lively, vigorous, bouncy, animated, spirited, sprightly, vivacious, energetic, dynamic, zestful, stimulating, *colloq.* peppy. **2** risqué, suggestive, ribald, bawdy, naughty, lusty, earthy, gross, salty, immodest, indelicate, improper, indecent, blue, smutty, lewd, salacious, vulgar, dirty, filthy, pornographic, obscene, rude, crude, coarse, spicy, off-color, *colloq.* raunchy. **3** strong, sharp, spicy, piquant, tasty, flavorful, pungent, savory, zesty, tangy.

rad¹ /rad/ *n.* (*pl.* same) radian. [abbr.]

rad² /rad/ *n. & adj.* ● *n. sl.* a political radical. *adj. sl.* wonderful; terrific. [abbr.]

rad³ /rad/ *n. Physics* a unit of absorbed dose of ionizing radiation, corresponding to the absorption of 0.01 joule per kilogram of absorbing material. [*radiation absorbed dose*]

radar /ráydaar/ *n.* **1** a system for detecting the direction, range, or presence of aircraft, ships, and other (usu. moving) objects, by sending out pulses of high-frequency electromagnetic waves. **2** the apparatus used for this. □ **radar trap** the use of radar to detect vehicles exceeding a speed limit. [*radio detecting and ranging*]

raddle /rád'l/ *n. & v.* (also **ruddle**) ● *n.* red ocher (often used to mark sheep). ● *v.tr.* **1** color with raddle or too much rouge. **2** (as **raddled** *adj.*) worn out; untidy, unkempt. [rel. to obs. *rud* red]

■ *v.* **2** (**raddled**) see DILAPIDATED, UNTIDY.

radial /ráydeeəl/ *adj. & n.* ● *adj.* **1** of, concerning, or in rays. **2 a** arranged like rays or radii; having the position or direction of a radius. **b** having spokes or radiating lines. **c** acting or moving along lines diverging from a center. **3** *Anat.* relating to the radius (*radial artery*). **4** (of a vehicle tire) having the core fabric layers arranged radially at right angles to the circumference and the tread strengthened. ● *n.* **1** *Anat.* the radial nerve or artery. **2** a radial tire. □ **radial engine** an engine having cylinders arranged along radii. **radial symmetry** symmetry occurring about any number of lines or planes passing through the center of an organism, etc. **radial velocity** esp. *Astron.* the speed of motion along a radial line, esp. between a star, etc., and an observer. □□ **radially** *adv.* [med.L *radialis* (as RADIUS)]

radian /ráydeeən/ *n. Geom.* a unit of angle, equal to an angle at the center of a circle, the arc of which is equal in length to the radius. [RADIUS + -AN]

radiant /ráydeeənt/ *adj. & n.* ● *adj.* **1** emitting rays of light. **2** (of eyes or looks) beaming with joy or hope or love. **3** (of beauty) splendid or dazzling. **4** (of light) issuing in rays. **5** operating radially. **6** extending radially; radiating. ● *n.* **1** the point or object from which light or heat radiates, esp. in an electric or gas heater. **2** *Astron.* a radiant point. □ **radiant heat** heat transmitted by radiation, not by conduction or convection. **radiant point 1** a point from which rays or radii proceed. **2** *Astron.* the apparent focal point of a meteor shower. □□ **radiance** *n.* **radiancy** *n.* **radiantly** *adv.* [ME f. L *radiare* (as RADIUS)]

■ *adj.* **1** shining, bright, beaming, burning, blazing, brilliant, luminous, resplendent, splendid, lustrous, gleaming, glowing, shimmering, incandescent, sparkling, dazzling, glittering, scintillating, twinkling, *literary* effulgent, refulgent. **2** happy, overjoyed, ecstatic, rapturous, delighted, joyful, blissful, glad, joyous, gay, jubilant, elated, rhapsodic, exultant, exhilarated, *colloq.* beatific, *poet.* blithe, blithesome; warm, lovely. **3** see *dazzling* (DAZZLE). □□ **radiance, radiancy** splendor, brightness, brilliance, resplendence, luminosity, luminousness, dazzle, sparkle, coruscation, scintillation, twinkle, incandescence, glow, luster, shimmer, *literary* effulgence, refulgence; warmth, gladness, joy, pleasure, happiness, cheerfulness, delight.

radiate *v. & adj.* ● *v.* /ráydeeayt/ **1** *intr.* **a** emit rays of light, heat, or other electromagnetic waves. **b** (of light or heat) be emitted in rays. **2** *tr.* emit (light, heat, or sound) from a

center. **3** *tr.* transmit or demonstrate (life, love, joy, etc.) (*radiates happiness*). **4** *intr. & tr.* diverge or cause to diverge or spread from a center. **5** *tr.* (as **radiated** *adj.*) with parts arranged in rays. ● *adj.* /ráydeeət/ having divergent rays or parts radially arranged. □□ **radiately** *adv.* **radiative** /-ətiv/ *adj.* [L *radiare radiat-* (as RADIUS)]

■ *v.* **1 a** shine, burn, blaze, gleam, glow, shimmer, glisten, sparkle, glitter, coruscate, scintillate, twinkle. **2** emanate, shed, send out, emit, give off *or* out. **3** transmit, give out, disseminate, disperse, spread, diffuse. **4** diverge, fan out, spread out, extend, unfurl.

radiation /ráydeeáyshən/ *n.* **1** the act or an instance of radiating; the process of being radiated. **2** *Physics* **a** the emission of energy as electromagnetic waves or as moving particles. **b** the energy transmitted in this way, esp. invisibly. **3** (in full **radiation therapy**) treatment of cancer and other diseases using radiation, such as X rays or ultraviolet light. □ **radiation chemistry** the study of the chemical effects of radiation on matter. **radiation sickness** sickness caused by exposure to radiation, such as X rays or gamma rays. □□ **radiational** *adj.* **radiationally** *adv.* [L *radiatio* (as RADIATE)]

■ **1** emission, emanation, diffusion, dispersal.

radiator /ráydeeaytər/ *n.* **1** a person or thing that radiates. **2 a** a device for heating a room, etc., consisting of a metal case through which hot water or steam circulates. **b** a usu. portable oil or electric heater resembling this. **3** an engine-cooling device in a motor vehicle or aircraft with a large surface for cooling circulating water. □ **radiator grille** a grille at the front of a motor vehicle allowing air to circulate to the radiator.

radical /rádikəl/ *adj. & n.* ● *adj.* **1** of the root or roots; fundamental (*a radical error*). **2** far-reaching; thorough; going to the root (*radical change*). **3 a** advocating thorough reform; holding extreme political views; left-wing; revolutionary. **b** (of a measure, etc.) advanced by or according to principles of this kind. **4** forming the basis; primary (*the radical idea*). **5** *Math.* of the root of a number or quantity. **6** (of surgery, etc.) seeking to ensure the removal of all diseased tissue. **7** of the roots of words. **8** *Mus.* belonging to the root of a chord. **9** *Bot.* of, or springing direct from, the root. **10** *hist.* belonging to an extreme section of the liberal party. **11** *US hist.* seeking extreme anti-South action at the time of the Civil War. ● *n.* **1** a person holding radical views or belonging to a radical party. **2** *Chem.* **a** a free radical. **b** an element or atom or a group of these normally forming part of a compound and remaining unaltered during the compound's ordinary chemical changes. **3** the root of a word. **4** a fundamental principle; a basis. **5** *Math.* **a** a quantity forming or expressed as the root of another. **b** a radical sign. □ **radical sign** √ , ∛ , etc., indicating the square, cube, etc., root of the number following. □□ **radicalism** *n.* **radicalize** *v.tr. & intr.* **radicalization** *n.* **radically** *adv.* **radicalness** *n.* [ME f. LL *radicalis* f. L *radix radicis* root]

■ *adj.* **1** basic, fundamental, elementary, inherent, constitutional, elemental, essential, cardinal, deep, deep-seated, deep-rooted, structural, profound, underlying, organic, natural. **2** far-reaching, thorough, thoroughgoing, complete, entire, total, exhaustive, sweeping, all-inclusive, comprehensive, all-embracing, out-and-out, drastic. **3** extremist, revolutionary, fanatical, militant, extreme; left-wing, leftist, socialist, communist, Bolshevik, *colloq.* red, esp. *derog.* pink. **4** see PRIMARY *adj.* 1b. ● *n.* **1** extremist, revolutionary, fanatic, zealot, militant; leftist, left-winger, communist, red, Bolshevik, Bolshevist, *colloq.* red. **4** see BASIS 1, 2.

radicchio /rədeékeeō/ *n.* (*pl.* **-os**) a variety of chicory with dark red leaves. [It., = chicory]

radices *pl.* of RADIX.

radicle /rádikəl/ *n.* **1** the part of a plant embryo that develops into the primary root; a rootlet. **2** a rootlike subdivision of a nerve or vein. □□ **radicular** /rədíkyŏólər/ *adj.* [L *radicula* (as RADIX)]

■ **1** see ROOT¹ *n.* 1a.

radii *pl.* of RADIUS.

radio /ráydeeō/ *n. & v.* ● *n.* (*pl.* **-os**) **1** (often *attrib.*) **a** the

transmission and reception of sound messages, etc., by electromagnetic waves of radio frequency. **b** an apparatus for receiving, broadcasting, or transmitting radio signals. **c** a message sent or received by radio. **2 a** sound broadcasting in general (*prefers the radio*). **b** a broadcasting station, channel, or organization (*Armed Forces Radio*). ● *v.* (**-oed**) **1** *tr.* **a** send (a message) by radio. **b** send a message to (a person) by radio. **2** *intr.* communicate or broadcast by radio. □ **radio astronomy** the branch of astronomy concerned with the radio-frequency range of the electromagnetic spectrum. **radio car** an automobile, esp. a taxicab or police vehicle, equipped with a two-way radio. **radio fix** the position of an aircraft, ship, etc., found by radio. **radio frequency** the frequency band of telecommunication, ranging from 10^4 to 10^{11} or 10^{12} Hz. **radio galaxy** a galaxy emitting radiation in the radio-frequency range of the electromagnetic spectrum. **radio ham** see HAM. **radio star** a small star, etc., emitting strong radio waves. **radio telescope** a directional aerial system for collecting and analyzing radiation in the radio-frequency range from stars, etc. [short for *radiotelegraphy*, etc.]
■ *n.* **1 b** receiver, transistor (radio), esp. *Brit.* wireless (set), *sl.* boom box, ghetto blaster. ● *v.* **1 a** send, transmit, broadcast, air; announce, present. **b** contact, get through to, communicate with.

radio- /ráydeeō/ *comb. form* **1** denoting radio or broadcasting. **2 a** connected with radioactivity. **b** denoting artificially prepared radioisotopes of elements (*radiocesium*). **3** connected with rays or radiation. **4** *Anat.* belonging to the radius in conjunction with some other part (*radiocarpal*). [RADIUS + -O- or f. RADIO]

radioactive /ráydeeō-áktiv/ *adj.* of or exhibiting radioactivity. □□ **radioactively** *adv.*

radioactivity /ráydeeō-aktívitee/ *n.* the spontaneous disintegration of atomic nucleii, with the emission of usu. penetrating radiation or particles.

radiobiology /ráydeeōbīóləjee/ *n.* the biology concerned with the effects of radiation on organisms and the application in biology of radiological techniques. □□ **radiobiological** /-biəlójikəl/ *adj.* **radiobiologically** *adv.* **radiobiologist** *n.*

radiocarbon /ráydeeōkáarbən/ *n.* a radioactive isotope of carbon. □ **radiocarbon dating** = *carbon dating*.

radiochemistry /ráydeeōkémistree/ *n.* the chemistry of radioactive materials. □□ **radiochemical** *adj.* **radiochemist** *n.*

radioelement /ráydeeō-élimənt/ *n.* a natural or artificial radioactive element or isotope.

radiogenic /ráydeeōjénik/ *adj.* **1** produced by radioactivity. **2** suitable for broadcasting by radio. □□ **radiogenically** *adv.*

radiogoniometer /ráydeeōgōneeómitər/ *n.* an instrument for finding direction using radio waves.

radiogram /ráydeeōgram/ *n.* **1** a picture obtained by X rays, gamma rays, etc. **2** a radiotelegram. [RADIO- + -GRAM]
■ **2** see TELEGRAM.

radiograph /ráydeeōgráf/ *n.* & *v.* ● *n.* **1** an instrument recording the intensity of radiation. **2** = RADIOGRAM 2. ● *v.tr.* obtain a picture of by X ray, gamma ray, etc. □□ **radiographer** /-deeógrəfər/ *n.* **radiographic** *adj.* **radiographically** *adv.* **radiography** /-deeógrəfee/ *n.*

radioimmunology /ráydeeō-ímyənóləjee/ *n.* the application of radiological techniques in immunology.

radioisotope /ráydeeō-īsətōp/ *n.* a radioactive isotope. □□ **radioisotopic** /-tópik/ *adj.* **radioisotopically** *adv.*

radiolarian /ráydeeōláireeən/ *n.* any marine protozoan of the order Radiolaria, having a siliceous skeleton and radiating pseudopodia. [mod.L *radiolaria* f. L *radiolus* dimin. of RADIUS]

radiology /ráydeeóləjee/ *n.* the scientific study of X rays and other high-energy radiation, esp. as used in medicine. □□ **radiologic** /-deeəlójik/ *adj.* **radiological** /-deeəlójikəl/ *adj.* **radiologist** *n.*

radiometer /ráydeeómitər/ *n.* an instrument for measuring the intensity or force of radiation. □□ **radiometry** *n.*

radiometric /ráydeeōmétrik/ *adj.* of or relating to the mea-

surement of radioactivity. □ **radiometric dating** a method of dating geological specimens by determining the relative proportions of the isotopes of a radioactive element present in a sample.

radionics /ráydeeóniks/ *n.pl.* (usu. treated as *sing.*) the study and interpretation of radiation believed to be emitted from substances, esp. as a form of diagnosis. [RADIO- + -*onics*, after ELECTRONICS]

radionuclide /ráydeeōnŏŏklid, -nyŏŏ-/ *n.* a radioactive nuclide.

radiopaque /ráydeeōpáyk/ *adj.* opaque to X rays or similar radiation. □□ **radiopacity** /-pásitee/ *n.* [RADIO- + OPAQUE]

radiophonic /ráydeeōfónik/ *adj.* of or relating to synthetic sound, esp. music, produced electronically.

radioscopy /ráydeeóskəpee/ *n.* the examination by X rays, etc., of objects opaque to light. □□ **radioscopic** /-deeəskópik/ *adj.*

radiosonde /ráydeeōsond/ *n.* a miniature radio transmitter broadcasting information about pressure, temperature, etc., from various levels of the atmosphere, carried esp. by balloon. [RADIO- + G *Sonde* probe]

radiotelegram /ráydeeōtéligram/ *n.* a telegram sent by radio, usu. from a ship to land.

radiotelegraphy /ráydeeōtilégrəfee/ = *wireless telegraphy*. □□ **radiotelegraph** /-téligraaf/ *n.*

radiotelephony /ráydeeōtiléfənee/ *n.* telephony using radio transmission. □□ **radiotelephone** /-télifōn/ *n.* **radiotelephonic** /-telifónik/ *adj.*

radiotelex /ráydeeōtéleks/ *n.* a telex sent usu. from a ship to land.

radiotherapy /ráydeeōthérəpee/ *n.* radiation therapy (see RADIATION). □□ **radiotherapeutic** /-pyŏŏtik/ *adj.* **radiotherapist** *n.*

radish /rádish/ *n.* **1** a cruciferous plant, *Raphanus sativus*, with a fleshy pungent root. **2** this root, eaten esp. raw in salads, etc. [OE *rædic* f. L *radix radicis* root]

radium /ráydeeəm/ *n. Chem.* a radioactive metallic element orig. obtained from pitchblende, etc., used esp. in luminous materials and in radiotherapy. ¶ Symb.: **Ra**. □ **radium therapy** the treatment of disease by the use of radium. [L *radius* ray]

radius /ráydeeəs/ *n.* & *v.* ● *n.* (*pl.* **radii** /-dee-ī/ or **radiuses**) **1** *Math.* **a** a straight line from the center to the circumference of a circle or sphere. **b** a radial line from the focus to any point of a curve. **c** the length of the radius of a circle, etc. **2** a usu. specified distance from a center in all directions (*within a radius of 20 miles*; *has a large radius of action*). **3 a** the thicker and shorter of the two bones in the human forearm (cf. ULNA). **b** the corresponding bone in a vertebrate's foreleg or a bird's wing. **4** any of the five armlike structures of a starfish. **5 a** any of a set of lines diverging from a point like the radii of a circle. **b** an object of this kind, e.g., a spoke. **6 a** the outer rim of a composite flower head, e.g., a daisy. **b** a radiating branch of an umbel. ● *v.tr.* give a rounded form to (an edge, etc.). □ **radius vector** *Math.* a variable line drawn from a fixed point to an orbit or other curve, or to any point as an indication of the latter's position. [L, = staff, spoke, ray]
■ *n.* **2** see RANGE *n.* 1a–c.

radix /ráydiks/ *n.* (*pl.* **radices** /-diseez/ or **radixes**) **1** *Math.* a number or symbol used as the basis of a numeration scale (e.g., ten in the decimal system). **2** (usu. foll. by *of*) a source or origin. [L, = root]

radome /ráydōm/ *n.* a dome or other structure, transparent to radio waves, protecting radar equipment, esp. on the outer surface of an aircraft. [radar + *dome*]

radon /ráydon/ *n. Chem.* a gaseous radioactive inert element arising from the disintegration of radium, and used in radiotherapy. ¶ Symb.: **Rn**. [RADIUM after *argon*, etc.]

/. . ./ **pronunciation**	● **part of speech**
□ **phrases, idioms, and compounds**	
□□ **derivatives**	■ **synonym section**
cross-references appear in SMALL CAPITALS or *italics*	

radula /rájōōlə/ n. (pl. **radulae** /-lee/ or **radulas**) a filelike structure in mollusks for scraping off food particles and drawing them into the mouth. □□ **radular** adj. [L, = scraper f. radere scrape]

RAF abbr. (in the UK) Royal Air Force.

Rafferty's rules /ráfərteez/ n. Austral. & NZ colloq. no rules at all, esp. in boxing. [E dial. corrupt. of refractory]

raffia /ráfeeə/ n. (also **raphia**) **1** a palm tree, Raphia ruffia, native to Madagascar, having very long leaves. **2** the fiber from its leaves used for making hats, baskets, etc., and for tying plants, etc. [Malagasy]

raffinate /ráfinayt/ n. Chem. a refined liquid oil produced by solvent extraction of impurities. [F raffiner + -ATE[1]]

raffish /ráfish/ adj. **1** disreputable; rakish. **2** tawdry. □□ **raffishly** adv. **raffishness** n. [as RAFT[2] + -ISH[1]]
 ■ **1** see RAKISH[1]. **2** see GAUDY[1].

raffle[1] /ráfəl/ n. & v. ● n. a fund-raising lottery with goods as prizes. ● v.tr. (often foll. by off) dispose of by means of a raffle. [ME, a kind of dice game, f. OF raf(f)le, of unkn. orig.]
 ■ n. lottery, draw.

raffle[2] /ráfəl/ n. **1** rubbish; refuse. **2** debris. [ME, perh. f. OF ne rifle, ne rafle nothing at all]

raft[1] /raft/ n. & v. ● n. **1** a flat floating structure of logs or other materials for conveying persons or things. **2** a lifeboat or small (often inflatable) boat, esp. for use in emergencies. **3** a floating accumulation of trees, ice, etc. ● v. **1** tr. transport as or on a raft. **2** tr. cross (water) on a raft. **3** tr. form into a raft. **4** intr. (often foll. by across) work a raft (across water, etc.). [ME f. ON raptr RAFTER[1]]

raft[2] /raft/ n. colloq. **1** a large collection. **2** (foll. by of) a crowd. [raff rubbish, perh. of Scand. orig.]
 ■ see HEAP n. 1, 2.

rafter[1] /ráftər/ n. each of the sloping beams forming the framework of a roof. □□ **raftered** adj. [OE ræfter, rel. to RAFT[1]]
 ■ see BEAM n. 1.

rafter[2] /ráftər/ n. **1** a person who builds rafts. **2** a person who travels by raft.

raftsman /ráftsmən/ n. (pl. **-men**) a worker on a raft.

rag[1] /rag/ n. **1 a** a torn, frayed, or worn piece of woven material. **b** one of the irregular scraps to which cloth, etc., is reduced by wear and tear. **2 a** (in pl.) old or worn clothes. **b** (usu. in pl.) colloq. a garment of any kind. **3** (collect.) scraps of cloth used as material for paper, stuffing, etc. **4** derog. **a** a newspaper. **b** a flag, handkerchief, curtain, etc. **5** (usu. with neg.) the smallest scrap of cloth, etc. (not a rag to cover him). **6** an odd scrap; an irregular piece. **7** a jagged projection, esp. on metal. □ **in rags 1** much torn. **2** in old torn clothes. **rag-and-bone man** Brit. an itinerant dealer in old clothes, furniture, etc. **rag book** Brit. = cloth book. **rag doll** a stuffed doll made of cloth. **rag paper** paper made from cotton or linen pulp. **rags to riches** poverty to affluence. **rag trade** colloq. the business of designing, making, and selling clothes. [ME, prob. back-form. f. RAGGED]
 ■ **2 b** (rags) clothes, clothing, dress, garments, formal attire, sl. duds. **4 a** paper, newspaper, periodical, magazine, publication, journal, daily, tabloid. **6** shred, scrap, fragment, bit, piece, esp. Brit. dial. clout. □ **in rags 1** in tatters, torn; see also TATTERED. **rag trade** garment industry, clothing business, fashion industry.

rag[2] /rag/ n. & v. ● n. Brit. **1** a fund-raising program of stunts, parades, and entertainment organized by students. **2** colloq. a prank. **3 a** a rowdy celebration. **b** a noisy disorderly scene. ● v. (**ragged, ragging**) **1** tr. tease; play rough jokes on. **2** tr. scold; reprove severely. **3** intr. Brit. engage in rough play; be noisy and riotous. [18th c.: orig. unkn.: cf. BALLYRAG]
 ■ n. **2** see PRANK. **3 b** see TUMULT 1, 2. ● v. **1** tease, taunt, twit, ridicule, mock, make fun of, joke, poke fun at, pull a person's leg, rally, colloq. kid; see also TORMENT v. 2. **2** see SCOLD v. 1.

rag[3] /rag/ n. **1** a large, coarse roofing slate. **2** any of various kinds of hard, coarse, sedimentary stone that break into thick slabs. [ME: orig. unkn., but assoc. with RAG[1]]

rag[4] /rag/ n. Mus. a ragtime composition or tune. [perh. f. RAGGED: see RAGTIME]

raga /raágə/ n. (also **rag** /raag/) Ind. Mus. **1** a pattern of notes used as a basis for improvisation. **2** a piece using a particular raga. [Skr., = color, musical tone]

ragamuffin /rágəmufin/ n. a person in ragged dirty clothes, esp. a child. [prob. based on RAG[1]: cf. 14th-c. ragamoffyn the name of a demon]
 ■ (street) urchin, waif, gamin, stray, guttersnipe, offens. street arab.

ragbag /rágbag/ n. **1** a bag in which scraps of fabric, etc., are kept for use. **2** a miscellaneous collection.

rage /rayj/ n. & v. ● n. **1** fierce or violent anger. **2** a fit of this (flew into a rage). **3** the violent action of a natural force (the rage of the storm). **4** (foll. by for) **a** a vehement desire or passion. **b** a widespread temporary enthusiasm or fashion. **5** poet. poetic, prophetic, or martial enthusiasm or ardor. **6** sl. a lively frolic. ● v.intr. **1** be full of anger. **2** (often foll. by at, against) speak furiously or madly; rave. **3** (of wind, battle, fever, etc.) be violent; be at its height; continue unchecked. **4** Austral. sl. seek enjoyment; go on a spree. □ **all the rage** popular; fashionable. [ME f. OF rager ult. f. L RABIES]
 ■ n. **1** fury, literary wrath, ire; see also ANGER n. **2** fury, frenzy, hysterics, tantrum, fit, temper. **3** violence, fury, strength; see also FORCE[1] n. **1. 4 a** see THIRST n. 2. **b** fashion, craze, vogue, mode, fad, trend. ● v. **1, 2** rant, rave, rant and rave, rail; storm, be beside oneself (with anger or fury), fulminate, fume, foam at the mouth, stew, smolder, seethe, simmer. □ **all the rage** popular; the last word, the dernier cri; see also FASHIONABLE.

ragged /rágid/ adj. **1 a** (of clothes, etc.) torn; frayed. **b** (of a place) dilapidated. **2** rough; shaggy; hanging in tufts. **3** (of a person) in ragged clothes. **4** with a broken or jagged outline or surface. **5** faulty; imperfect. **6 a** lacking finish, smoothness, or uniformity (ragged rhymes). **b** (of a sound) harsh, discordant. **7** exhausted (feel ragged). □ **ragged robin** a pink-flowered campion, Lychnis flos-cuculi, with tattered petals. □□ **raggedly** adv. **raggedness** n. **raggedy** adj. [ME f. ON roggvathr tufted]
 ■ **1a, 3** rough, shaggy, tattered, scraggy, torn, rent, ripped, frayed, worn (out), threadbare, patched, colloq. tatty; unkempt, shabby, seedy, down at (the) heel or heels. **1 b** run-down, battered, broken-down, neglected, deteriorated, dilapidated, colloq. beat-up. **4** rough, uneven, irregular, jagged; serrated, zigzag, notched, ridged. **5** faulty, imperfect, uneven, bad, poor, shabby, patchy, shoddy. **6 a** see ROUGH adj. 10. **b** rough, harsh, discordant, grating, rasping, hoarse, scratchy, croaking. **7** (run ragged) wear out, exhaust, weary; see also TIRE[1] 1.

raggle-taggle /rágəltagəl/ adj. (also **wraggle-taggle**) ragged; rambling; straggling. [app. fanciful var. of RAGTAG]

raglan /ráglən/ n. (often attrib.) an overcoat without shoulder seams, the sleeves running up to the neck. □ **raglan sleeve** a sleeve of this kind. [Lord Raglan, Brit. commander d. 1855]

ragman /rágmən/ n. = RAGPICKER.

ragout /ragōō/ n. & v. ● n. meat in small pieces stewed with vegetables and highly seasoned. ● v.tr. cook (food) in this way. [F ragoût f. ragoûter revive the taste of]
 ■ n. see STEW[1] n. 1. ● v. see STEW[1] v. 1.

ragpicker /rágpikər/ n. a collector and seller of rags.
 ■ scrap dealer, Brit. rag-and-bone man, knacker.

ragstone /rágstōn/ n. = RAG[3] 2.

ragtag /rágtag/ n. & adj. ● n. (in full **ragtag and bobtail**) derog. the rabble or common people. ● adj. motley. [earlier tag-rag, tag and rag, f. RAG[1] + TAG[1]]
 ■ (**ragtag and bobtail**) see RABBLE[1] 3.

ragtime /rágtim/ n. & adj. ● n. music characterized by a syncopated melodic line and regularly accented accompaniment, evolved by African-American musicians in the 1890s and played esp. on the piano. ● adj. sl. disorderly, disreputable, inferior (a ragtime army). [prob. f. RAG[4]]

raguly /rágyəlee/ *adj. Heraldry* like a row of sawn-off branches. [perh. f. RAGGED after *nebuly*]

ragweed /rágweed/ *n.* any plant of the genus *Ambrosia*, esp. *A. trifida*, with allergenic pollen.

ragwort /rágwərt, -wawrt/ *n.* any yellow-flowered ragged-leaved plant of the genus *Senecio*.

rah /raa/ *int. colloq.* an expression of encouragement, approval, etc., esp. to a team or a player. [shortening of HURRAH]

raid /rayd/ *n. & v.* ● *n.* **1** a rapid surprise attack, esp.: **a** by troops, aircraft, etc., in warfare. **b** to commit a crime or do harm. **2** a surprise attack by police, etc., to arrest suspected persons or seize illicit goods. **3** *Stock Exch.* an attempt to lower prices by the concerted selling of shares. **4** (foll. by *on, upon*) a forceful or insistent attempt to make a person or thing provide something. ● *v.tr.* **1** make a raid on (a person, place, or thing). **2** plunder; deplete. □□ **raider** *n.* [ME, Sc. form of OE *rād* ROAD¹]

■ *n.* **1** (surprise) attack, incursion, invasion, onset, onslaught, sortie, sally, *colloq.* blitz. **2** *colloq.* bust. ● *v.* **1** attack, invade, assault, storm, set upon, descend upon, swoop down on *or* upon, pounce upon. **2** sack, plunder, pillage, forage, loot, ransack, rifle, maraud, *colloq.* bust; deplete, strip.

rail¹ /rayl/ *n. & v.* ● *n.* **1** a level or sloping bar or series of bars: **a** used to hang things on. **b** running along the top of a set of banisters. **c** forming part of a fence or barrier as protection against contact, falling over, etc. **2** a steel bar or continuous line of bars laid on the ground, usu. as one of a pair forming a railroad track. **3** (often *attrib.*) a railroad (*send it by rail; rail fares*). **4** (in *pl.*) the inside boundary fence of a racecourse. **5** a horizontal piece in the frame of a paneled door, etc. (cf. STILE²). ● *v.tr.* **1** furnish with a rail or rails. **2** (usu. foll. by *in, off*) enclose with rails (*a small space was railed off*). **3** convey (goods) by rail. □ **off the rails** disorganized; out of order; deranged. □ **over the rails** over the side of a ship. **rail fence** a fence made of posts and rails. □□ **railage** *n.* **railless** *adj.* [ME f. OF *reille* iron rod f. L *regula* RULE]

■ *n.* **1** bar, rod; railing, banisters, balustrade; fence, barrier. **3** (*by rail*) by train, by railroad, *Brit.* by railway. □ **off the rails** see *chaotic* (CHAOS), MAD *adj.* 1.

rail² /rayl/ *v.intr.* (often foll. by *at, against*) complain using abusive language; rant. □□ **railer** *n.* **railing** *n. & adj.* [ME f. F *railler* f. Prov. *ralhar* jest, ult. f. L *rugire* bellow]

■ (*rail at or against*) rant at, fulminate against, rage at, rant and rave at; revile, attack, berate, scold, upbraid, criticize, have a go at, censure, decry, condemn, denounce, *colloq.* go on at.

rail³ /rayl/ *n.* any bird of the family Rallidae, often inhabiting marshes, esp. the Virginia rail and corn crake. [ME f. ONF *raille* f. Rmc, perh. imit.]

railcar /ráylkaar/ *n.* **1** any railroad car. **2** a railroad vehicle consisting of a single powered car.

railhead /ráylhed/ *n.* **1** the furthest point reached by a railroad under construction. **2** the point on a railroad at which road transport of goods begins.

railing /ráyling/ *n.* **1** (usu. in *pl.*) a fence or barrier made of rails. **2** the material for these.

■ **1** see FENCE *n.* 1.

raillery /ráyləree/ *n.* (*pl.* **-ies**) **1** good-humored ridicule; rallying. **2** an instance of this. [F *raillerie* (as RAIL²)]

■ **1** banter, badinage, persiflage, repartee, frivolity, joking, jesting, chaffing, teasing, ridicule, *colloq.* kidding.

railroad /ráylrōd/ *n. & v.* ● *n.* **1** a track or set of tracks made of steel rails upon which goods trucks and passenger trains run. **2** such a system worked by a single company (*B & O Railroad*). **3** the organization and personnel required for its working. **4** a similar set of tracks for other vehicles, etc. □ **railroad yard** the area where rolling stock is kept and made up into trains. ● *v.tr.* **1** (often foll. by *to, into, through,* etc.) rush or coerce (a person or thing) (*railroaded me into going too*). **2** send (a person) to prison by means of false evidence. **3** transport by railroad.

■ *v.* **1** force, urge, compel, coerce, intimidate, push, press, pressurize, pressure, drive, stampede, bully, hector, tyrannize, dragoon, browbeat, *colloq.* bulldoze.

railway /ráylway/ *n.* esp. *Brit.* = RAILROAD

railwayman /ráylwaymən/ *n.* (*pl.* **-men**) *Brit.* a railroad employee.

raiment /ráymənt/ *n. archaic* clothing. [ME f. obs. *arrayment* (as ARRAY)]

■ see CLOTHES.

rain /rayn/ *n. & v.* ● *n.* **1 a** the condensed moisture of the atmosphere falling visibly in separate drops. **b** the fall of such drops. **2** (in *pl.*) **a** rainfalls. **b** (prec. by *the*) the rainy season in tropical countries. **3 a** falling liquid or solid particles or objects. **b** the rainlike descent of these. **c** a large or overwhelming quantity (*a rain of congratulations*). ● *v.* **1** *intr.* (prec. by *it* as subject) rain falls (*it is raining; if it rains*). **2 a** *intr.* fall in showers or like rain (*tears rained down their cheeks; blows rain upon him*). **b** *tr.* (prec. by *it* as subject) send in large quantities (*it rained blood; it is raining invitations*). **3** *tr.* send down like rain; lavishly bestow (*rained benefits on us; rained blows upon him*). **4** *intr.* (of the sky, the clouds, etc.) send down rain. □ **rain cats and dogs** see CAT. **rain check** a ticket given for later use when a sports or other outdoor event is interrupted or postponed by rain. **2** a promise that an offer will be maintained though deferred. **rain cloud** a cloud bringing rain. **rain date** a date on which an event postponed by rain is held. **rain forest** luxuriant tropical forest with heavy rainfall. **rain gauge** an instrument measuring rainfall. **rain out** (esp. in *passive*) cause (an event, etc.) to be terminated or canceled because of rain. **rain or shine** whether it rains or not. **rain shadow** a region shielded from rain by mountains, etc. □□ **rainless** *adj.* **raintight** *adj.* [OE *regn, rēn, regnian* f. Gmc]

■ *n.* **1** precipitation, drizzle, mizzle. **3 c** flood, torrent, shower, volley, stream, outpouring, deluge. ● *v.* **1** pour (down), drizzle, spit, mizzle. **2 a** trickle, shower, pour, run, fall, spatter, splash, sprinkle; come down, descend. **3** bestow, lavish; pour down, hail.

rainbird /ráynbərd/ *n.* any of several birds said to foretell rain by their cry, esp. the black-billed and yellow-billed cuckoos.

rainbow /ráynbō/ *n. & adj.* ● *n.* **1** an arch of colors (conventionally red, orange, yellow, green, blue, indigo, violet) formed in the sky (or across a waterfall, etc.) opposite the sun by reflection, twofold refraction, and dispersion of the sun's rays in falling rain or in spray or mist. **2** a similar effect formed by the moon's rays. ● *adj.* many-colored. □ **rainbow trout** a large trout, *Salmo gairdneri*, orig. of the Pacific coast of N. America. **secondary rainbow** an additional arch with the colors in reverse order formed inside or outside a rainbow by twofold reflection and twofold refraction. [OE *regnboga* (as RAIN, BOW¹)]

raincoat /ráynkōt/ *n.* a waterproof or water-resistant coat.

■ slicker, trench coat, *Brit.* mackintosh, *Brit. colloq.* mac.

raindrop /ráyndrop/ *n.* a single drop of rain. [OE *regndropa*]

rainfall /ráynfawl/ *n.* **1** a fall of rain. **2** the quantity of rain falling within a given area in a given time.

■ **1** shower, cloudburst, downpour, rainstorm, deluge, monsoon; see also PRECIPITATION 3a. **2** precipitation.

rainmaking /ráynmayking/ *n.* the action of attempting to increase rainfall by artificial means.

rainproof /ráynprōof/ *adj.* (esp. of a building, garment, etc.) resistant to rainwater.

rainstorm /ráynstawrm/ *n.* a storm with heavy rain.

■ shower, cloudburst, downpour, deluge, monsoon, thundershower, thunderstorm.

rainwater /ráynwawtər, -wotər/ *n.* water obtained from collected rain, as distinct from a well, etc.

rainy /ráynee/ *adj.* (**rainier, rainiest**) **1** (of weather, a climate, day, region, etc.) in or on which rain is falling or much

---

/.../ pronunciation	● part of speech
□ phrases, idioms, and compounds	
□□ derivatives	■ synonym section
cross-references appear in SMALL CAPITALS or *italics*	

rain usually falls. **2** (of cloud, wind, etc.) laden with or bringing rain. □ **rainy day** a time of special need in the future. □□ **rainily** adv. **raininess** n. [OE *rēnig* (as RAIN)]
■ **1** see WET adj. 2.

raise /rayz/ v. & n. ● v.tr. **1** put or take into a higher position. **2** (often foll. by *up*) cause to rise or stand up or be vertical; set upright. **3** increase the amount or value or strength of (*raised their prices*). **4** (often foll. by *up*) construct or build up. **5** levy or collect or bring together (*raise money*; *raise an army*). **6** cause to be heard or considered (*raise a shout*; *raise an objection*). **7** set going or bring into being; arouse (*raise a protest*; *raise hopes*). **8** bring up; educate. **9** breed or grow (*raise one's own vegetables*). **10** promote to a higher rank. **11** (foll. by *to*) *Math.* multiply a quantity to a specified power. **12** cause (bread) to rise with yeast. **13** *Cards* a bet more than (another player). **b** increase (a stake). **c** *Bridge* make a bid contracting for more tricks in the same suit as (one's partner); increase (a bid) in this way. **14** abandon or force an enemy to abandon (a siege or blockade). **15** remove (a barrier or embargo). **16** cause (a ghost, etc.) to appear (opp. LAY¹ 6b). **17** *colloq.* find (a person, etc., wanted). **18** establish contact with (a person, etc.) by radio or telephone. **19** (usu. as **raised** *adj.*) *Brit.* cause (pastry, etc.) to stand without support (*a raised pie*). **20** *Naut.* come in sight of (land, a ship, etc.). **21** make a nap on (cloth). **22** extract from the earth. ● n. **1** *Cards* an increase in a stake or bid (cf. sense 13 of v.). **2** an increase in salary. □ **raise Cain** see CAIN. **raised beach** *Geol.* a beach lying above water level owing to changes since its formation. **raise the devil** *colloq.* make a disturbance. **raise a dust** *Brit.* **1** cause turmoil. **2** obscure the truth. **raise one's eyebrows** see EYEBROW. **raise one's eyes** see EYE. **raise from the dead** restore to life. **raise one's glass to** drink the health or good fortune of. **raise one's hand to** make as if to strike (a person). **raise one's hat** (often foll. by *to*) raise it momentarily as a gesture of courtesy or respect. **raise hell** *colloq.* make a disturbance. **raise a laugh** esp. *Brit.* cause others to laugh. **raise a person's spirits** give him or her new courage or cheerfulness. **raise one's voice** speak, esp. louder and in anger. **raise the wind** *Brit.* procure money for a purpose. □□ **raisable** *adj.* [ME f. ON *reisa*, rel. to REAR²]
■ v. **1** lift (up), elevate, upraise, take up; hoist, pull up, haul up. **3** increase, advance, put up, run up, *colloq.* jack (up). **4** erect, put up, construct, build, put together, assemble, frame, run up, produce, create. **5** assemble, gather, bring or gather together, muster, amass, mobilize, round up, rally, collect, convene, recruit, put together, *colloq.* pull together; levy. **6** introduce, broach, bring up, bring or put forward, present, suggest, mention, moot, set forth; utter, express, let out. **7** occasion, put or set in motion, institute, prompt, initiate, engender, stir up, instigate, inspire, give rise to, bring about, arouse, originate; rouse, buoy, lift, uplift, cheer, invigorate, stimulate, animate, vivify, *colloq.* boost; foster, nurture, heighten, quicken, encourage, develop. **8** bring up, nurture, rear; parent; see also EDUCATE 1, 2. **9** farm, grow, cultivate, plant, nurture, harvest, propagate; breed. **10** see PROMOTE 1. **15** remove, lift, abandon, discontinue, (bring to an) end, terminate. ● n. **2** see INCREASE n. 3. □ **raise from the dead** revive, resurrect, resuscitate; reanimate, recall. **raise one's glass to** see TOAST v. 4. **raise hell** make a disturbance, raise Cain, *Brit.* raise a dust, *colloq.* raise the devil; see also STORM v. 1.

raisin /ráyzən/ n. a partially dried grape. □□ **raisiny** *adj.* [ME f. OF ult. f. L *racemus* grape bunch]

raison d'être /ráyzon détrə/ n. (pl. **raisons d'être** *pronunc.* same) a purpose or reason that accounts for or justifies or originally caused a thing's existence. [F, = reason for being]
■ purpose, reason, function, role.

raj /raaj/ n. (prec. by *the*) *hist.* British sovereignty in India. [Hindi *rāj* reign]

raja /ráajə/ n. (also **rajah**) *hist.* **1** an Indian king or prince. **2** a petty dignitary or noble in India. **3** a Malay or Javanese chief. □□ **rajaship** n. [Hindi *rājā* f. Skr. *rājan* king]

Rajput /ráajpōōt/ n. (also **Rajpoot**) a member of a Hindu soldier caste claiming Kshatriya descent. [Hindi *rājpūt* f. Skr. *rājan* king + *putrá* son]

rake¹ /rayk/ n. & v. ● n. **1 a** an implement consisting of a pole with a crossbar toothed like a comb at the end, or with several tines held together by a crosspiece, for drawing together hay, etc., or smoothing loose soil or gravel. **b** a wheeled implement for the same purpose. **2** a similar implement used for other purposes, e.g., by a croupier drawing in money at a gaming table. ● v. **1** tr. (usu. foll. by *out*, *together*, *up*, etc.) collect or gather or remove with or as with a rake. **2** tr. make tidy or smooth with a rake (*raked it level*). **3** intr. use a rake. **4** tr. & intr. search with or as with a rake; search thoroughly; ransack. **5** tr. **a** direct gunfire along a (line) from end to end. **b** sweep with the eyes. **c** (of a window, etc.) have a commanding view of. **6** tr. scratch or scrape. □ **rake in** *colloq.* amass (profits, etc.). **rake it in** *colloq.* make much money. **rake-off** *colloq.* a commission or share, esp. in a disreputable deal. **rake up** (or **over**) revive the memory of (past quarrels, grievances, etc.). □□ **raker** n. [OE *raca*, *racu* f. Gmc, partly f. ON *raka* scrape, rake]
■ v. **1** (*rake together*) gather, collect, draw or drag together; (*rake out*) sift (out), remove, take out, clear (out), clean; (*rake up*) scrape up, pick up, dig up, dredge up, find, unearth. **2** see SMOOTH v. 1. **4** (*rake through*) search, probe, ransack, scour, comb, rummage through, pick through or over, go through, rifle (through). **6** scrape, scratch, grate, graze, rasp. □ **rake in** amass, collect, gather (up or in), pull in, accumulate. **rake it in** coin money, make money (hand over fist), become wealthy. **rake-off** commission, share, *colloq.* cut, kickback, *sl.* piece. **rake up** revive, resuscitate, resurrect, raise, bring up, recall, go over; dredge up, unearth, dig up.

rake² /rayk/ n. a dissolute man of fashion. □ **rake's progress** esp. *Brit.* a progressive deterioration, esp. through self-indulgence (the title of a series of engravings by Hogarth 1735). [short for archaic *rakehell* in the same sense]
■ debauchee, voluptuary, roué, libertine, profligate, prodigal, lothario, womanizer, lecher, playboy, ladies' man, lady-killer, Don Juan, Casanova, *sl.* wolf; young blood, fop, man about town; see also DANDY n.

rake³ /rayk/ v. & n. ● v. **1** tr. & intr. set or be set at a sloping angle. **2** intr. **a** (of a mast or funnel) incline from the perpendicular toward the stern. **b** (of a ship or its bow or stern) project at the upper part of the bow or stern beyond the keel. ● n. **1** a raking position or build. **2** the amount by which a thing rakes. **3** the slope of the stage or the auditorium in a theater. **4** the slope of a seat back, etc. **5** the angle of the edge or face of a cutting tool. [17th c.: prob. rel. to G *ragen* project, of unkn. orig.]

raki /raakeé, rákee, raáakee, -kə/ n. (pl. **rakis**) any of various liquors made in E. Europe and the Middle East. [Turk. *raqi*]

rakish¹ /ráykish/ adj. of or like a rake (see RAKE²); dashing; jaunty. □□ **rakishly** adv. **rakishness** n.
■ dashing, jaunty, dapper, spruce, debonair, raffish, smart, flashy, chic, fashionable, elegant, dandyish, foppish, *colloq.* sharp.

rakish² /ráykish/ adj. (of a ship) smart and fast looking, seemingly built for speed and therefore open to suspicion of piracy. [RAKE³, assoc. with RAKE²]

raku /raákōō/ n. a kind of Japanese earthenware, usu. lead-glazed. [Jap., lit. enjoyment]

rale /raal/ n. an abnormal rattling sound heard in the auscultation of unhealthy lungs. [F f. *râler* to rattle]

rall. /ral/ adv. & adj. & n. = RALLENTANDO. [abbr.]

rallentando /ráləntándō, raáləntaándō/ adv., adj., & n. *Mus.* ● adv. & adj. with a gradual decrease of speed. ● n. (pl. **-os** or **rallentandi** /-dee/) a passage to be performed in this way. [It.]

ralline /rálin, -in/ adj. of the bird-family Rallidae (see RAIL³). [mod.L *rallus* RAIL³]

rally¹ /rálee/ v. & n. ● v. (**-ies, -ied**) **1** tr. & intr. (often foll. by *round*, *behind*, *to*) bring or come together as support or for concentrated action. **2** *tr.* & *intr.* bring or come together again after a rout or dispersion. **3 a** *intr.* renew a conflict. **b** *tr.* cause to do this. **4 a** *tr.* revive (courage, etc.) by an effort of will. **b** *tr.* rouse (a person or animal) to fresh energy. **c** *intr.* pull oneself together. **5** *intr.* recover after illness or prostration or fear; regain health or consciousness; revive. **6** *intr.* (of share prices, etc.) increase after a fall. ● *n.* (*pl.* **-ies**) **1** an act of reassembling forces or renewing conflict; a reunion for fresh effort. **2** a recovery of energy after or in the middle of exhaustion or illness. **3** a mass meeting of supporters or persons having a common interest. **4** a competition for motor vehicles, usu. over public roads. **5** (in tennis, etc.) an extended exchange of strokes between players. □ **rally-cross** *Brit.* motor racing over roads and cross-country. □□ **rallier** *n.* [F *rallier* (as RE-, ALLY[1])]

■ *v.* **1, 2** (*rally round*) bring or call together, round up, marshal, mobilize, summon, gather, muster; get together, assemble, convene, group, congregate, come together; regroup, reform. **4 a** mobilize, summon, muster, marshal; revive. **b** see ROUSE 2a. **5** revive, recover, improve, get better, take a turn for the better, recuperate, perk up, pick up, make a comeback, come to. ● *n.* **1** see GATHERING. **2** recovery, improvement, revival, turn for the better, recuperation. **3** gathering, (mass) meeting, convocation, convention, assemblage, assembly.

rally² /rálee/ *v.tr.* (**-ies, -ied**) subject to good-humored ridicule. [F *railler*: see RAIL²]

RAM /ram/ *abbr.* **1** *Computing* random-access memory; internally stored software or data that is directly accessible, not requiring sequential search or reading. **2** (in the UK) Royal Academy of Music.

ram /ram/ *n.* & *v.* ● *n.* **1** an uncastrated male sheep. **2** (**the Ram**) the zodiacal sign or constellation Aries. **3** *hist.* **a** = *battering ram* (see BATTER¹). **b** a beak projecting from the bow of a battleship, for piercing the sides of other ships. **c** a battleship with such a beak. **4** the falling weight of a pile-driving machine. **5 a** a hydraulic water-raising or lifting machine. **b** the piston of a hydrostatic press. **c** the plunger of a force pump. **6** *Austral. sl.* an accomplice in petty crime. ● *v.tr.* (**rammed, ramming**) **1** force or squeeze into place by pressure. **2** (usu. foll. by *down, in, into*) beat down or drive in by heavy blows. **3** (of a ship, vehicle, etc.) strike violently; crash against. **4** (foll. by *against, at, on, into*) dash or violently impel. □ **ram home** stress forcefully (an argument, lesson, etc.). □□ **rammer** *n.* [OE *ram(m)*, perh. rel. to ON *rammr* strong]

■ *n.* **6** see ACCOMPLICE. ● *v.* **1** jam, force, drive, cram, crowd, pack, compress, stuff, squeeze, thrust. **2** pound, hammer, beat, tamp, bash, bang. **3** butt, bump, strike, hit, collide with, dash against, crash into, slam into.

□ **ram home** see STRESS *v.* 1.

Ramadan /rámədan, ramədaán/ *n.* (also **Ramadhan**) the ninth month of the Muslim year, during which strict fasting is observed from sunrise to sunset. [Arab. *ramaḍān* f. *ramaḍa* be hot; reason for name uncert.]

ramal /ráyməl/ *adj. Bot.* of or proceeding from a branch. [L *ramus* branch]

Raman effect /raámən/ *n.* the change of frequency in the scattering of radiation in a medium, used in spectroscopic analysis. [Sir C. V. *Raman*, Ind. physicist d. 1970]

ramble /rámbəl/ *v.* & *n.* ● *v.intr.* **1** walk for pleasure, with or without a definite route. **2** wander in discourse; talk or write disconnectedly. ● *n.* a walk taken for pleasure. [prob. f. MDu. *rammelen* (of an animal) wander about in sexual excitement, frequent. of *rammen* copulate with, rel. to RAM]

■ *v.* **1** amble, meander, wander, stroll, saunter, walk, perambulate, range, rove, hike, trek, *sl.* mosey. **2** wander, digress, maunder, get off the point, lose the thread; (*ramble on*) babble, chatter, gibber, rattle on, *colloq.* go on (and on), *Brit. colloq.* witter on. ● *n.* stroll, amble, saunter, walk, promenade, constitutional, turn, tour, hike, trek.

rambler /rámblər/ *n.* **1** a person who rambles. **2** a straggling or climbing rose (*crimson rambler*).

■ **1** walker, hiker, backpacker.

rambling /rámbling/ *adj.* **1** peripatetic; wandering. **2** disconnected; desultory; incoherent. **3** (of a house, street, etc.) irregularly arranged. **4** (of a plant) straggling; climbing. □□ **ramblingly** *adv.*

■ **1** roving, wandering, traveling, peripatetic, itinerant, wayfaring, migratory, nomadic. **2** discursive, roundabout, circuitous, tortuous, incoherent, diffuse, disconnected, disjointed, disorganized, unorganized, desultory, illogical, maundering, aimless, confused, muddled, jumbled, unintelligible, inarticulate, periphrastic, circumlocutory, circumlocutional, circumlocutionary, wordy, verbose, prolix. **3** straggling, irregular, sprawling, spread out, straggly.

rambunctious /rambúngkshəs/ *adj. colloq.* **1** uncontrollably exuberant. **2** unruly. □□ **rambunctiously** *adv.* **rambunctiousness** *n.* [19th c.: orig. unkn.]

■ see BOISTEROUS 1.

rambutan /rambóōt'n/ *n.* **1** a red, plum-sized prickly fruit. **2** an East Indian tree, *Nephelium lappaceum*, that bears this. [Malay *rambūtan* f. *rambut* hair, in allusion to its spines]

ramekin /rámikin/ *n.* (also **ramequin**) **1** a small dish for baking and serving an individual portion of food. **2** food served in such a dish, esp. a small quantity of cheese baked with bread crumbs, eggs, etc. [F *ramequin*, of LG or Du. orig.]

ramie /rámee, ráy-/ *n.* **1** any of various tall East Asian plants of the genus *Boehmeria*, esp. *B. nivea*. **2** a strong fiber obtained from this, woven into cloth. [Malay *rāmī*]

ramification /rámifikáyshən/ *n.* **1** the act or an instance of ramifying; the state of being ramified. **2** a subdivision of a complex structure or process comparable to a tree's branches. **3** a consequence, esp. when complex or unwelcome. [F f. *ramifier*: see RAMIFY]

■ **2** branch, extension, outgrowth, subdivision, offshoot. **3** consequence, result, effect, upshot, implication.

ramify /rámifī/ *v.* (**-ies, -ied**) **1** *intr.* form branches or subdivisions or offshoots; branch out. **2** *tr.* (usu. in *passive*) cause to branch out; arrange in a branching manner. [F *ramifier* f. med.L *ramificare* f. L *ramus* branch]

■ **1** see BRANCH *v.* 2.

ramjet /rámjet/ *n.* a type of jet engine in which air is drawn in and compressed by the forward motion of the engine.

rammer see RAM.

ramose /rámōs, ráy-/ *adj.* branched; branching. [L *ramosus* f. *ramus* branch]

ramp¹ /ramp/ *n.* & *v.* ● *n.* **1** a slope or inclined plane, esp. for joining two levels of ground, floor, etc. **2** (in full **boarding ramp**) movable stairs for entering or leaving an aircraft. **3** an upward bend in a staircase railing. **4** *Brit.* a transverse ridge in a road to control the speed of vehicles. ● *v.* **1** *tr.* furnish or build with a ramp. **2** *intr.* **a** assume or be in a threatening posture. **b** (often foll. by *about*) storm; rage; rush. **c** *Heraldry* be rampant. **3** *intr. Archit.* (of a wall) ascend or descend to a different level. [ME (as verb in heraldic sense) f. F *rampe* f. OF *ramper* creep, crawl]

■ *n.* **1** slope, grade, gradient, incline; rise, acclivity; dip, declivity. ● *v.* **2 b** see STORM *v.* 2.

ramp² /ramp/ *n.* & *v. Brit. sl.* ● *n.* a swindle or racket, esp. one conducted by the levying of exorbitant prices. ● *v.* **1** *intr.* engage in a ramp. **2** *tr.* subject (a person, etc.) to a ramp. [16th c.: orig. unkn.]

rampage *v.* & *n.* ● *v.intr.* /rámpáyj/ **1** (often foll. by *about*) rush wildly or violently about. **2** rage; storm. ● *n.* /rámpayj/ wild or violent behavior. □ **on the rampage** rampaging. □□ **rampageous** *adj.* **rampager** *n.* [18th c., perh. f. RAMP¹]

■ *v.* **1** career, charge, storm, ramp (about); see TEAR¹ *v.* 5. **2** storm, rant, rave, run amok, ramp (about); see also RAGE *v.* ● *n.* recklessness, riotousness, frenzy,

---

/.../ **pronunciation**	● **part of speech**
□ **phrases, idioms, and compounds**	
□□ **derivatives**	■ **synonym section**

cross-references appear in SMALL CAPITALS or *italics*

fury, outburst, rage, furor, esp. *Brit.* furore. □ **on the rampage** (*go on the rampage*) go berserk, run amok, run wild, go out of control, *sl.* flip one's lid.

rampant /rámpənt/ *adj.* **1** (placed after noun) *Heraldry* (of an animal) standing on its left hind foot with its forepaws in the air (*lion rampant*). **2** unchecked, flourishing excessively (*rampant violence*). **3** violent or extravagant in action or opinion (*rampant theorists*). **4** rank; luxuriant. □□ **rampancy** *n.* **rampantly** *adv.* [ME f. OF, part. of *ramper*: see RAMP¹]
■ **2** unchecked, unrestrained, uncontrolled, unbridled, uncontrollable, unbounded, abounding, flourishing, rife, widespread, pandemic, prevalent; indiscriminate. **3** violent, wild, frenzied; see also FURIOUS 3. **4** rank, luxuriant; see PROFUSE 2.

rampart /rámpaart/ *n. & v.* ● *n.* **1 a** a defensive wall with a broad top and usu. a stone parapet. **b** a walkway on top of such a wall. **2** a defense or protection. ● *v.tr.* fortify or protect with or as with a rampart. [F *rempart, rempar* f. *remparer* fortify f. *emparer* take possession of, ult. f. L *ante* before + *parare* prepare]
■ *n.* **1 a** defense, fortification, bulwark, barricade, wall; earthwork, parados. **2** defense, protection, shelter, cover, guard, shield, barrier, buffer.

rampion /rámpeeən/ *n.* **1** a bellflower, *Campanula rapunculus*, with white tuberous roots used as a salad. **2** any of various plants of the genus *Phyteuma*, with clusters of hornlike buds and flowers. [ult. f. med.L *rapuncium, rapontium*, prob. f. L *rapum* RAPE²]

ramrod /rámrod/ *n.* **1** a rod for ramming down the charge of a muzzleloading firearm. **2** a thing that is very straight or rigid.

ramshackle /rámshakəl/ *adj.* (usu. of a house or vehicle) tumbledown; rickety. [earlier *ramshackled* past part. of obs. *ransackle* RANSACK]
■ dilapidated, tumbledown, crumbling, broken-down, rickety, jerry-built, decrepit, flimsy, shaky, unstable, tottering, insubstantial, ruined, run-down, neglected, derelict.

ramsons /rámzɒnz, -sɒnz/ *n.* (usu. treated as *sing.*) **1** a broad-leaved garlic, *Allium ursinum*, with elongate pungent-smelling bulbous roots. **2** the root of this, eaten as a relish. [OE *hramsan* pl. of *hramsa* wild garlic, later taken as sing.]

ran *past* of RUN.

ranch /ranch/ *n. & v.* ● *n.* **1 a** a cattle-breeding establishment, esp. in the western US and Canada. **b** a farm where other animals are bred (*mink ranch*). **2** (in full **ranch house**) a single-story or split-level house. ● *v.intr.* farm on a ranch. [Sp. *rancho* group of persons eating together]
■ **1** see SPREAD *n.* 12.

rancher /ránchər/ *n.* a person who farms on a ranch.

ranchero /rancháirō/ *n.* (*pl.* **-os**) a person who farms or works on a ranch, esp. in Mexico. [Sp. (as RANCH)]

rancid /ránsid/ *adj.* smelling or tasting like rank stale fat. □□ **rancidity** /-síditee/ *n.* **rancidness** *n.* [L *rancidus* stinking]
■ stinking, foul-smelling, fetid, ill-smelling, evil-smelling, mephitic, smelly, rank, malodorous, fusty, *archaic* miasmal, miasmatic, miasmic, *literary* noisome; rotten, decayed, bad, high, gamy, putrid, off, stale.

rancor /rángkər/ *n.* (*Brit.* **rancour**) inveterate bitterness; malignant hate; spitefulness. □□ **rancorous** *adj.* **rancorously** *adv.* [ME f. OF f. LL *rancor -oris* (as RANCID)]
■ hatred, antipathy, spitefulness, resentment, resentfulness, antagonism, hostility, malignity, bitterness, malevolence, venomousness, vindictiveness, vengefulness, acrimony, animus, ill feeling, animosity, enmity, bad feeling, hate, spite, malice, venom, spleen. □□ **rancorous** hateful, spiteful, resentful, hostile, bitter, malevolent, malicious, venomous, vindictive, vengeful, splenetic, acrimonious.

rand¹ /rand, raant/ *n.* **1** the chief monetary unit of South Africa. **2** *S.Afr.* a ridge of high ground on either side of a river. [Afrik., = edge, rel. to RAND²: sense 1 f. *the Rand*, gold-field district near Johannesburg]

rand² /rand/ *n.* a levelling strip of leather between the heel and sides of a shoe or boot. [OE f. Gmc]

R & B *abbr.* (also **R. & B.**) rhythm and blues.

R & D *abbr.* (also **R. & D.**) research and development.

random /rándəm/ *adj.* **1** made, done, etc., without method or conscious choice (*random selection*). **2** *Statistics* **a** with equal chances for each item. **b** given by a random process. **3** (of masonry) with stones of irregular size and shape. □ **at random** without aim or purpose or principle. **random-access** *Computing* (of a memory or file) having all parts directly accessible, so that it need not be read sequentially. **random error** *Statistics* an error in measurement caused by factors that vary from one measurement to another. □□ **randomize** *v.tr.* **randomization** *n.* **randomly** *adv.* **randomness** *n.* [ME f. OF *randon* great speed f. *randir* gallop]
■ **1** haphazard, chance, fortuitous, aleatory, aleatoric, arbitrary, casual, indiscriminate, nonspecific, unspecific, unspecified, unordered, unorganized, undirected, unpremeditated, unplanned, accidental, uncalculated, unsystematic, adventitious, incidental, hit-or-miss. □ **at random** randomly, haphazardly, by chance, arbitrarily, casually, erratically, indiscriminately, unsystematically, adventitiously, unpremeditatedly.

R and R *abbr.* (also **R. and R.**) **1** rescue and resuscitation. **2** rest and recreation (or recuperation or relaxation). **3** rock and roll.
■ **2** see LEISURE 2.

randy /rándee/ *adj.* (**randier, randiest**) **1** esp. *Brit.* lustful; eager for sexual gratification. **2** *Sc.* loud-tongued; boisterous; lusty. □□ **randily** *adv.* **randiness** *n.* [perh. f. obs. *rand* f. obs. Du. *randen, ranten* RANT]
■ **1** aroused, lustful, lecherous, sexy, libidinous, hot, *formal* concupiscent, *sl.* horny.

ranee var. of RANI.

rang *past* of RING².

range /raynj/ *n. & v.* ● *n.* **1 a** the region between limits of variation, esp. as representing a scope of effective operation (*a voice of astonishing range*; *the whole range of politics*). **b** such limits. **c** a limited scale or series (*the range of the thermometer readings is about 10 degrees*). **d** a series representing variety or choice; a selection. **2** the area included in or concerned with something. **3 a** the distance attainable by a gun or projectile (*the enemy is out of range*). **b** the distance between a gun or projectile and its objective. **4** a row, series, line, or tier, esp. of mountains or buildings. **5 a** an open or enclosed area with targets for shooting. **b** a testing ground for military equipment. **6** a cooking stove with one or more ovens and a set of burners on the top surface. **7** the area over which a thing, esp. a plant or animal, is distributed (*gives the ranges of all species*). **8** the distance that can be covered by a vehicle or aircraft without refueling. **9** the distance between a camera and the subject to be photographed. **10** the extent of time covered by a forecast, etc. **11 a** a large area of open land for grazing or hunting. **b** a tract over which one wanders. **12** lie; direction (*the range of the strata is east and west*). ● *v.* **1** *intr.* **a** reach; lie spread out; extend; be found or occur over a specified district; vary between limits (*ages ranging from twenty to sixty*). **b** run in a line (*ranges north and south*). **2** *tr.* (usu. in *passive* or *refl.*) place or arrange in a row or ranks or in a specified situation or order or company (*ranged their troops*; *ranged themselves with the majority party*; *trees ranged in ascending order of height*). **3** *intr.* rove; wander (*ranged through the woods*; *his thoughts range over past, present, and future*). **4** *tr.* traverse in all directions (*ranging the woods*). **5** *Brit. Printing* **a** *tr.* make (type) lie flush at the ends of successive lines. **b** *intr.* (of type) lie flush. **6** *intr.* **a** (often foll. by *with*) be level. **b** (foll. by *with, among*) rank; find one's right place (*ranges with the great writers*). **7** *intr.* **a** (of a gun) send a projectile over a specified distance (*ranges over a mile*). **b** (of a projectile) cover a specified distance. **c** obtain the range of a target by adjustment after firing past it or short of it. □ **range finder** an instrument for estimating the distance of an object, esp. one to be shot at or photographed.

range pole *Surveying* a pole or rod for setting a straight line. [ME f. OF *range* row, rank f. *ranger* f. *rang* RANK¹]

■ *n.* **1 a–c** scope, sweep, reach, limit, round, extent, span, area, radius, distance, compass, latitude, stretch, sphere, orbit. **d** assortment, series, collection, lot, spread, selection, choice, number, variety, kind, sort, scale, gamut, register. **2** see AREA 4. **4** row, tier, rank, line, file, series, string, chain. **6** stove, cooking stove, *Brit.* cooker. **7** distribution, dispersal, spread. ● *v.* **1 a** vary, fluctuate; run the gamut, extend, reach, stretch, run, go. **2** line up, rank, order, align, array, arrange; organize, categorize, catalog, classify, sort, class, group, bracket, file, index, grade. **3** roam, rove; see also WANDER *v.* 1. **4** cover, traverse, travel over *or* across, go *or* pass over; extend over. **6 b** see RANK¹ *v.* 1.

ranger /ráynjər/ *n.* **1** a keeper of a national or royal park or forest. **2** a member of a body of armed men, esp.: **a** a mounted soldier. **b** a commando. **3** a wanderer. □□ **rangership** *n.*

rangy /ráynjee/ *adj.* (**rangier, rangiest**) **1** (of a person) tall and slim. **2** hilly; mountainous.

■ **1** see LANKY.

rani /raˊanee/ *n.* (also **ranee**) *hist.* a raja's wife or widow; a Hindu queen. [Hindi *rānī* = Skr. *rājñī* fem. of *rājan* king]

rank¹ /rangk/ *n.* & *v.* ● *n.* **1 a** a position in a hierarchy; a grade of advancement. **b** a distinct social class; a grade of dignity or achievement (*people of all ranks*; *in the top rank of performers*). **c** high social position (*persons of rank*). **d** a place in a scale. **2** a row or line. **3** a single line of soldiers drawn up abreast. **4** *Brit.* a place where taxis stand to await customers. **5** order; array. **6** *Chess* a row of squares across the board (cf. FILE²). ● *v.* **1** *intr.* have rank or place (*ranks next to the chief of staff*). **2** *tr.* classify; give a certain grade to. **3** *tr.* arrange (esp. soldiers) in a rank or ranks. **4 a** *tr.* take precedence of (a person) in respect to rank; outrank. **b** *intr.* have the senior position among the members of a hierarchy, etc. □ **break rank** fail to remain in line. **close ranks** maintain solidarity. **keep rank** remain in line. **other ranks** *Brit.* soldiers other than commissioned officers. **pull rank** use one's superior rank to gain advantage, coerce another, etc. **rank and file** ordinary undistinguished people (orig. = *the ranks*). **the ranks** the common soldiers, i.e., privates and corporals. **rise from the ranks 1** (of a private or a non-commissioned officer) receive a commission. **2** (of a self-made man or woman) advance by one's own exertions. [OF *ranc, renc,* f. Gmc, rel. to RING¹]

■ *n.* **1 a** position, place, level, echelon, grade. **b** class, social class, caste; status, standing; situation, circumstances, position, grade, level. **c** nobility, title, high birth, aristocracy, dignity, prestige, prominence, (blue) blood; weight, authority, power, superiority, seniority, influence, eminence. **2** line, row, string, file, column, tier. ● *v.* **1** have (one's) place, rate, count, stand, have standing *or* value. **2** grade, rate, classify, class, categorize. **3** arrange, array, align, range, organize, order, dispose, sort. □ **rank and file** see PEOPLE *n.* 2. **rise from the ranks** pull oneself up by one's bootstraps.

rank² /rangk/ *adj.* **1** too luxuriant; choked with or apt to produce weeds or excessive foliage. **2 a** foul-smelling; offensive. **b** loathsome; indecent; corrupt. **3** flagrant; virulent; gross; complete; unmistakable; strongly marked (*rank outsider*). □□ **rankly** *adv.* **rankness** *n.* [OE *ranc* f. Gmc]

■ **1** lush, luxuriant, abundant, flourishing, profuse, prolific, dense, superabundant, exuberant, fertile. **2 a** offensive, loathsome, disgusting, vile, horrible, gross, foul, foul-smelling, smelly, rancid, stinking, reeky, reeking, mephitic, fetid, noxious, rotten, putrid, musty, stale, *archaic* miasmic, miasmal, miasmatic, *literary* noisome. **b** corrupt, foul, low, base, gross; offensive, loathsome, disgusting, indecent, shocking, lurid, outrageous. **3** gross, downright, utter, complete, sheer, absolute, out-and-out, blatant, flagrant, virulent; unmistakable.

ranker /rángkər/ *n.* esp. *Brit.* **1** a soldier in the ranks. **2** a commissioned officer who has been in the ranks.

ranking /rángking/ *n.* & *adj.* ● *n.* ordering by rank; classification. ● *adj.* having a high rank or position.

■ *n.* rating; see also SCALE³ *n.* 1. ● *adj.* see CHIEF *adj.* 1.

rankle /rángkəl/ *v.intr.* **1** (of envy, disappointment, etc., or their cause) cause persistent annoyance or resentment. **2** *archaic* (of a wound, sore, etc.) fester; continue to be painful. [ME (in sense 2) f. OF *rancler* f. *rancle, draoncle* festering sore f. med.L *dranculus, dracunculus* dimin. of *draco* serpent]

■ **1** grate, hurt, chafe, smolder, fester; (*rankle with*) irk, vex, plague, nettle, torment, pain, anger, exasperate, get (to), upset. **2** fester, suppurate; see also SMART *v.*

ransack /ránsak/ *v.tr.* **1** pillage or plunder (a house, country, etc.). **2** thoroughly search (a place, a receptacle, a person's pockets, one's conscience, etc.) fester; continue to be painful. □□ **ransacker** *n.* [ME f. ON *rannsaka* f. *rann* house + *-saka* f. *sœkja* seek]

■ **1** rob, plunder, pillage, sack, loot, strip, ravage, maraud, lay waste, *archaic or literary* spoil, *literary* despoil. **2** search, examine, go through *or* over, comb, rake *or* rummage *or* rifle through, scour, scrutinize, turn inside out.

ransom /ránsəm/ *n.* & *v.* ● *n.* **1** a sum of money or other payment demanded or paid for the release of a prisoner. **2** the liberation of a prisoner in return for this. ● *v.tr.* **1** buy the freedom or restoration of; redeem. **2** hold to ransom. **3** release for a ransom. □□ **ransomer** *n.* (in sense 1 of *v.*). [ME f. OF *ransoun(er)* f. L *redemptio -onis* REDEMPTION]

■ *n.* **1** payment, payout, *sl.* payoff. **2** release, liberation, freedom; rescue, deliverance. ● *v.* **1, 3** redeem, rescue, release, deliver, free, liberate. **2** hold hostage; see also KIDNAP.

rant /rant/ *v.* & *n.* ● *v.* **1** *intr.* use bombastic language. **2** *tr.* & *intr.* declaim; recite theatrically. **3** *tr.* & *intr.* preach noisily. **4** *intr.* (often foll. by *about, on*) speak vehemently or intemperately. ● *n.* **1** a piece of ranting; a tirade. **2** empty turgid talk. □□ **ranter** *n.* **rantingly** *adv.* [Du. *ranten* rave]

■ *v.* **2, 3** declaim, hold forth, expound, expatiate, perorate, pontificate, trumpet, preach, lecture, deliver a tirade *or* diatribe. **4** vociferate, bluster, rave, rant and rave, bellow, rage. ● *n.* **1** tirade, philippic, verbal attack, diatribe, harangue, declamation, onslaught, screed, stream of abuse. **2** bluster, flatulence, rhetoric, bombast, pomposity, turgidity, theatrics.

ranunculaceous /rənúngkyəláyshəs/ *adj.* of or relating to the family Ranunculaceae of flowering plants, including clematis and delphiniums.

ranunculus /rənúngkyələs/ *n.* (*pl.* **ranunculuses** or **ranunculi** /-lī/) any plant of the genus *Ranunculus*, usu. having bowl-shaped flowers with many stamens and carpels, esp. buttercups. [L, orig. dimin. of *rana* frog]

rap¹ /rap/ *n.* & *v.* ● *n.* **1** a smart, slight blow. **2** a knock; a sharp tapping sound. **3** *sl.* blame; censure; punishment. **4** *sl.* a conversation. **5 a** a rhyming monologue recited rhythmically to prerecorded music. **b** (in full **rap music**) a style of pop music with a pronounced beat and words recited rather than sung. ● *v.* (**rapped, rapping**) **1** *tr.* strike smartly. **2** *intr.* knock; make a sharp tapping sound (*rapped on the table*). **3** *tr.* criticize adversely. **4** *intr. sl.* talk. □ **beat the rap** escape punishment. **rap on** (or **over**) **the knuckles** ● *n.* a reprimand or reproof. ● *v.* reprimand; reprove. **rap out 1** *Brit.* utter (an oath, order, pun, etc.) abruptly or on the spur of the moment. **2** *Spiritualism* express (a message or word) by raps. **take the rap** suffer the consequences, esp. for a crime, etc., committed by another. □□ **rapper** *n.* [ME, prob. imit.]

■ *n.* **1** hit, blow, crack, stroke, cuff, punch, thump, clout, slug, *colloq.* whack, thwack, sock, *sl.* belt, biff. **2** see TAP² *n.* **3** censure; responsibility; punishment, sentence;

---

see also BLAME *n.* 2. **4** conversation, discussion, chat, confabulation, talk, dialogue, colloquy, bull session, *colloq.* confab, *literary* discourse, *sl.* chin-wag. ● *v.* **1** see STRIKE *v.* 1. **2** knock, tap, hammer. **3** criticize, scold, reprimand, rap on the knuckles, esp. *Brit. colloq.* tick off, slate, *sl.* knock; see also REBUKE *v.* **4** converse, talk, chat, gossip, *colloq.* gab, *sl.* chew the fat *or* rag. □ **beat the rap** get off, *sl.* walk. **rap on** (or **over**) **the knuckles** (*n.*) see REPRIMAND *n.* (*v.*) see RAP¹ *v.* 3 above. **take the rap** suffer the consequences, accept responsibility, take what is coming to one.

rap² /rap/ *n.* a small amount, the least bit (*don't care a rap*). [Ir. *ropaire* Irish counterfeit coin]

rapacious /rəpáyshəs/ *adj.* grasping; extortionate; predatory. □□ **rapaciously** *adv.* **rapaciousness** *n.* **rapacity** /rəpásitee/ *n.* [L *rapax -acis* f. *rapere* snatch]
■ greedy, covetous, grasping, avaricious, acquisitive, predatory, preying, predacious, ravenous, wolfish, wolflike, lupine, vulturine, extortionate. □□ **rapacity** predaciousness, rapaciousness; greed, greediness, cupidity, avarice, covetousness, acquisitiveness.

rape¹ /rayp/ *n.* & *v.* ● *n.* **1 a** the act of forcing another person to have sexual intercourse. **b** forcible sodomy. **2** (often foll. by *of*) violent assault; forcible interference; violation. **3** esp. *hist.* carrying off (esp. of a woman) by force. **4** an instance of rape. ● *v.tr.* **1** commit rape on (a person, usu. a woman). **2** violate; assault; pillage. **3** esp. *hist.* take by force. [ME f. AF *rap(er)* f. L *rapere* seize]
■ *n.* **1** ravishment, violation, sexual assault. **2** violation, pillage, depredation, ravagement, ravaging, plundering, sack, sacking, looting, ransacking, defloration, deflowering, defilement, *literary* despoliation, despoilment. **3** abduction, kidnapping, seizure, capture. ● *v.* **1** violate, ravish, sexually assault. **2** violate, assault, pillage, deflower, defile, ravage, plunder, sack, loot, *literary* despoil. **3** see ABDUCT.

rape² /rayp/ *n.* a plant, *Brassica napus*, grown as food for livestock and for its seed, from which oil is made. Also called COLZA, COLE. [ME f. L *rapum*, *rapa* turnip]

rape³ /rayp/ *n. hist.* (in the UK) any of the six ancient divisions of Sussex. [OE, var. of *rāp* ROPE, with ref. to the fencing off of land]

rape⁴ /rayp/ *n.* **1** the refuse of grapes after wine making, used in making vinegar. **2** a vessel used in vinegar making. [F *râpe*, med.L *raspa*]

rapeseed /ráypseed/ *n.* the seed of the rape plant. □ **rapeseed oil** an oil made from rapeseed and used as a lubricant and in foodstuffs.

raphia var. of RAFFIA.

raphide /ráyfīd/ *n.* a needle-shaped crystal of an irritant substance such as oxalic acid formed in a plant. [back-form. f. *raphides* pl. of *raphis* f. Gk *rhaphis -idos* needle]

rapid /rápid/ *adj.* & *n.* ● *adj.* **1** quick; swift. **2** acting or completed in a short time. **3** (of a slope) descending steeply. **4** *Photog.* fast. ● *n.* (usu. in *pl.*) a steep descent in a riverbed, with a swift current. □ **rapid eye movement** a type of jerky movement of the eyes during periods of dreaming. **rapid-fire** (*attrib.*) fired, asked, etc., in quick succession. □□ **rapidity** /rəpíditee/ *n.* **rapidly** *adv.* **rapidness** *n.* [L *rapidus* f. *rapere* seize]
■ *adj.* **1, 2** quick, fast, swift, speedy, high-speed, brisk, expeditious, prompt, express, lightning, *literary* volant, *poet. or literary* fleet; hurried, hasty, precipitate, instantaneous, instant, sudden. □□ **rapidity** quickness, swiftness, speed, speediness, briskness, expeditiousness, promptness, promptitude, alacrity, dispatch; suddenness, hastiness, *archaic or literary* celerity. **rapidly** quickly, quick, fast, swiftly, speedily, briskly, expeditiously, like a shot, at the speed of light, at full speed, in a flash *or* twinkle, double-quick, like a bat out of hell, at a gallop, *colloq.* like (greased) lightning, like mad *or* crazy, lickety-split, before you can say Jack Robinson, in two shakes of a lamb's tail, *joc.* in (less than) no time, *sl.* like blazes; promptly,

without delay, at once, straightaway, right away, *archaic or joc.* instanter.

rapier /ráypeeər, ráypyər/ *n.* a light slender sword used for thrusting. [prob. f. Du. *rapier* or LG *rappir*, f. F *rapière*, of unkn. orig.]

rapine /rápin, -in/ *n. rhet.* plundering; robbery. [ME f. OF or f. L *rapina* f. *rapere* seize]
■ see PILLAGE *n.* 1.

rapist /ráypist/ *n.* a person who commits rape.

rapparee /ráparee/ *n. hist.* a 17th-c. Irish irregular soldier or freebooter. [Ir. *rapaire* short pike]

rappee /rapee/ *n.* a coarse kind of snuff. [F (*tabac*) *râpé* rasped (tobacco)]

rappel /rapél/ *n.* & *v.* (**rappelled**, **rappelling**; or **rappeled**, **rappeling**) ● *n.* technique or act of controlled descent from a height, as a steep rockface, by using a doubled rope coiled around the body and fixed at a higher point, with which one slides downward gradually. ● *v. intr.* make a descent in this way. [F, = recall, f. *rappeler* (as RE-, APPEAL)]

rapport /rapáwr/ *n.* **1** relationship or communication, esp. when useful and harmonious (*in rapport with*; *establish a rapport*). **2** *Spiritualism* communication through a medium. [F f. *rapporter* (as RE-, AP-, *porter* f. L *portare* carry)]
■ **1** empathy, relationship, affinity, accord, bond, (mutual) understanding.

rapporteur /rápawrtŏr/ *n.* a person who prepares an account of the proceedings of a committee, etc., for a higher body. [F (as RAPPORT)]

rapprochement /raprōshmón/ *n.* the resumption of harmonious relations, esp. between nations. [F f. *rapprocher* (as RE-, APPROACH)]
■ understanding, settlement; détente; see also *reconciliation* (RECONCILE).

rapscallion /rapskályən/ *n. archaic* or *joc.* rascal; scamp; rogue. [earlier *rascallion*, perh. f. RASCAL]
■ see RASCAL.

rapt /rapt/ *adj.* **1** fully absorbed or intent; enraptured (*listen with rapt attention*). **2** carried away with joyous feeling or lofty thought. **3** carried away bodily. □□ **raptly** *adv.* **raptness** *n.* [ME f. L *raptus* past part. of *rapere* seize]
■ **1** enraptured, entranced, fascinated, spellbound, engrossed, enthralled, bewitched, absorbed, transported, captivated. **2** elated, happy, blissful, overjoyed, rapturous, joyous, joyful, beatific, ecstatic; uplifted, elevated.

raptor /ráptər/ *n.* any bird of prey, e.g., an owl, falcon, or eagle. [L, = ravisher, plunderer f. *rapere* rapt- seize]

raptorial /raptáwreeəl/ *adj.* & *n.* ● *adj.* (of a bird or animal) adapted for seizing prey; predatory. ● *n.* **1** = RAPTOR. **2** a predatory animal. [L *raptor*: see RAPTOR]
■ *adj.* see PREDATORY 1.

rapture /rápchər/ *n.* **1** ecstatic delight; mental transport. **b** (in *pl.*) great pleasure or enthusiasm or the expression of it. **2** *archaic* the act of transporting a person from one place to another. **3** a mystical experience in which the soul gains a knowledge of divine things. □ **go into** (or **be in**) **raptures** be enthusiastic; talk enthusiastically. □□ **rapturous** *adj.* **rapturously** *adv.* **rapturousness** *n.* [obs. F *rapture* or med.L *raptura* (as RAPT)]
■ **1 a** ecstasy, delight, joy, joyfulness, joyousness, pleasure, exaltation, elation, thrill, enchantment, euphoria, ecstasy. □ **go into raptures** wax lyrical; see also GUSH *v.* 2. □□ **rapturous** ecstatic, delighted, joyful, joyous, elated, thrilled, euphoric, overjoyed, rhapsodic.

rara avis /ráirə áyvis, ráarə áavis/ *n.* (*pl.* **rarae aves** /-ree -veez/) a rarity; a kind of person or thing rarely encountered. [L, = rare bird]
■ see RARITY 2.

rare¹ /rair/ *adj.* (**rarer**, **rarest**) **1** seldom done or found or occurring; uncommon; unusual; few and far between. **2** esp. *Brit.* exceptionally good (*had a rare time*). **3** of less than the usual density, with only loosely packed substance (*the rare atmosphere of the mountaintops*). □ **rare bird** = RARA AVIS. **rare earth 1** a lanthanide element. **2** an oxide of such an element. **rare gas** *Brit.* = *noble gas.* □□ **rareness** *n.* [ME f. L *rarus*]

■ **1** uncommon, unfamiliar, unusual, exceptional, out of the ordinary, extraordinary, atypical; scarce, infrequent, few and far between, sparse, scanty, limited, thin on the ground; unparalleled, choice, recherché, unique, singular.

rare² /rair/ *adj.* (**rarer, rarest**) (of meat) cooked lightly, so as to be still red inside. [var. of obs. *rear* half-cooked (of eggs), f. OE *hrēr*]

■ underdone, undercooked.

rarebit /ráirbit/ *n.* = *Welsh rabbit.* [RARE¹ + BIT¹]

raree-show /ráireeshō/ *n.* **1** a show or spectacle. **2** a show carried about in a box; a peep show. [app. = *rare show* as pronounced by Savoyard showmen]

rarefy /ráirifī/ *v.* (**-ies, -ied**) (esp. as **rarefied** *adj.*) **1** *tr.* & *intr.* make or become less dense or solid (*rarefied air*). **2** *tr.* purify or refine (a person's nature, etc.). **3** *tr.* **a** make (an idea, etc.) subtle. **b** (as **rarefied** *adj.*) refined; subtle; elevated; exalted; select. □□ **rarefaction** /-fákshən/ *n.* **rarefactive** *adj.* **rarefication** /-fikáyshən/ *n.* [ME f. OF *rarefier* or med.L *rarificare* f. L *rarefacere* f. *rarus* rare + *facere* make]

■ **1** (**rarefied**) thin, diluted, insubstantial, sparse, tenuous, scant, scanty. **3 b** (**rarefied**) cliquish, exclusive, private, select; esoteric.

rarely /ráirlee/ *adv.* **1** seldom; not often. **2** in an unusual degree; exceptionally. **3** exceptionally well.

■ **1** seldom, infrequently, on rare occasions, hardly (ever), scarcely (ever), almost never, once in a blue moon. **3** see *admirably* (ADMIRABLE).

raring /ráiring/ *adj.* (foll. by *to* + infin.) *colloq.* enthusiastic, eager (*raring to go*). [part. of rare, dial. var. of ROAR OR REAR²]

rarity /ráiritee/ *n.* (*pl.* **-ies**) **1** rareness. **2** an uncommon thing, esp. one valued for being rare. [F *rareté* or L *raritas* (as RARE¹)]

■ **1** unusualness, uncommonness, rareness, uniqueness, scarcity, sparseness, scantiness, infrequency. **2** curiosity, oddity, curio, collector's item, find, treasure, conversation piece; rare bird, rara avis, *Brit. colloq.* one-off.

rascal /ráskəl/ *n.* often *joc.* a dishonest or mischievous person, esp. a child. □□ **rascaldom** *n.* **rascalism** *n.* **rascality** /-kálitee/ *n.* (*pl.* **-ies**). **rascally** *adj.* [ME f. OF *rascaille* rabble, prob. ult. f. L *radere ras-* scrape]

■ imp, devil, mischief-maker, scalawag, rogue, knave, good-for-nothing, ne'er-do-well, wastrel, scapegrace, *archaic or joc.* rapscallion, *colloq.* vagabond, scamp.

rase var. of RAZE.

rash¹ /rash/ *adj.* reckless; impetuous; hasty; acting or done without due consideration. □□ **rashly** *adv.* **rashness** *n.* [ME, prob. f. OE *ræsc* (unrecorded) f. Gmc]

■ reckless, impetuous, impulsive, unthinking, thoughtless, foolhardy, unconsidered, ill-considered, ill-advised, injudicious, imprudent, indiscreet, precipitate, hasty, careless, heedless, wild, madcap, harebrained, hotheaded.

rash² /rash/ *n.* **1** an eruption of the skin in spots or patches. **2** (usu. foll. by *of*) a sudden widespread phenomenon, esp. of something unwelcome (*a rash of strikes*). [18th c.: prob. rel. to OF *ra(s)che* eruptive sores, = It. *raschia* itch]

■ **1** eruption, redness, efflorescence; see also INFLAMMATION 2. **2** profusion, outbreak, series, succession, spate, wave, flood, deluge, plague, epidemic.

rasher /ráshər/ *n.* a thin slice of bacon or ham. [16th c.: orig. unkn.]

rasp /rasp/ *n.* & *v.* ● *n.* **1** a coarse kind of file having separate teeth. **2** a rough grating sound. ● *v.* **1** *tr.* **a** scrape with a rasp. **b** scrape roughly. **c** (foll. by *off, away*) remove by scraping. **2 a** *intr.* make a grating sound. **b** *tr.* say gratingly or hoarsely. **3** *tr.* grate upon (a person or a person's feelings); irritate. □□ **raspingly** *adv.* **raspy** *adj.* [ME f. OF *raspe(r)* ult. f. WG]

■ *n.* **1** file, grater, rasper. **2** grating, scrape, scraping, scratch, scratching, grinding, stridulation. ● *v.* **1**

scrape, abrade, grate, file. **2** croak, grate; see also JAR² *v.* 1, 2. **3** jar (upon), grate upon *or* against, wear on; get on a person's nerves, nettle, irk, annoy, vex; see also IRRITATE 1.

raspberry /rázberee/ *n.* (*pl.* **-ies**) **1 a** a bramble, *Rubus idaeus*, having usu. red berries consisting of numerous drupels on a conical receptacle. **b** this berry. **2** any of various red colors. **3** *colloq.* **a** a sound made with the lips expressing dislike, derision, or disapproval (orig. *raspberry tart*, rhyming sl. = *fart*). **b** a show of strong disapproval (*got a raspberry from the audience*). [16th-c. *rasp* (now dial.) f. obs. *raspis*, of unkn. orig., + BERRY]

rasper /ráspər/ *n.* **1** a person or thing that rasps. **2** *Hunting Brit.* a high difficult fence.

Rasta /raástə, rást-/ *n.* & *adj.* = RASTAFARIAN. [abbr.]

Rastafarian /raástəfaáreeən, rástəfáir-/ *n.* & *adj.* ● *n.* a member of a sect of Jamaican origin regarding blacks as a chosen people and the former Emperor Haile Selassie of Ethiopia (d. 1975, entitled *Ras Tafari*) as God. ● *adj.* of or relating to this sect. □□ **Rastafarianism** *n.*

raster /rástər/ *n.* a pattern of scanning lines for a cathode-ray tube picture. [G, = screen, f. L *rastrum* rake f. *radere* ras-scrape]

rat /rat/ *n.* & *v.* ● *n.* **1 a** any of several rodents of the genus *Rattus* (*brown rat*). **b** any similar rodent (*muskrat; water rat*). **2** a deserter from a party, cause, difficult situation, etc.; a turncoat (from the superstition that rats desert a sinking ship). **3** *colloq.* an unpleasant person. **4** a worker who refuses to join a strike, or a strikebreaker. **5** (in *pl.*) *sl.* an exclamation of contempt, annoyance, etc. ● *v.intr.* (**ratted, ratting**) **1** (of a person or dog) hunt or kill rats. **2** *colloq.* desert a cause, party, etc. **3** *colloq.* (foll. by *on*) **a** betray; let down. **b** inform on. □ **rat kangaroo** *Austral.* any of various small ratlike marsupials of the family Potoroidae, having kangaroo-like hind limbs for jumping. **rat race** a fiercely competitive struggle for position, power, etc. **rat-tail** shaped like a rat's tail (*rat-tail file*) [OE *ret* & OF *rat*]

■ *n.* **2** see *deserter* (DESERT¹). **3** see WRETCH 2. **5** (*rats*) damn, blast, esp. *Brit.* bother, *colloq.* hell, drat, shoot, esp. *Brit. colloq.* botheration, *euphem.* sugar, *sl.* tarnation. ● *v.* **2** see DESERT¹ *v.* 2, 4. **3 a** see BETRAY 2. **b** see INFORM 2.

ratable /ráytəbəl/ *adj.* (also **rateable**) **1** *Brit.* liable to payment of rates. **2** able to be rated or estimated. □ **ratable value** the value formerly ascribed to a building for the assessment of local rates. □□ **ratability** /-bílitee/ *n.* **ratably** *adv.*

ratafia /rátəfeéə/ *n.* **1** a liqueur flavored with almonds or kernels of peach, apricot, or cherry. **2** a kind of cookie similarly flavored. [F, perh. rel. to TAFIA]

ratan var. of RATTAN.

rataplan /rátəplán/ *n.* & *v.* ● *n.* a drumming sound. ● *v.* (**rataplanned, rataplanning**) **1** *tr.* play (a tune) on or as on a drum. **2** *intr.* make a rataplan. [F: imit.]

rat-a-tat /rátətát/ *n.* (also **rat-a-tat-tat**) a rapping or knocking sound. [imit.]

ratatouille /rátətoō-ee, raátaa-/ *n.* a vegetable dish made of stewed eggplant, onions, tomatoes, zucchini, and peppers. [F dial.]

ratbag /rátbag/ *n. Austral. sl.* an unpleasant or disgusting person.

ratch /rach/ *n.* **1** a ratchet. **2** a ratchet wheel. [perh. f. G *Ratsche*: cf. RATCHET]

ratchet /ráchit/ *n.* & *v.* ● *n.* **1** a set of teeth on the edge of a bar or wheel in which a device engages to ensure motion in one direction only. **2** (in full **ratchet wheel**) a wheel with a rim so toothed. ● *v.* **1** *tr.* **a** provide with a ratchet. **b** make into a ratchet. **2** *tr.* & *intr.* move as under the control of a ratchet. □ **ratchet up** (or **down**) move steadily or by

---

/. . . / **pronunciation**	● **part of speech**
□ **phrases, idioms, and compounds**	
□□ **derivatives**	■ **synonym section**
cross-references appear in SMALL CAPITALS or *italics*	

degrees (*health costs continue to ratchet up*). [F *rochet* blunt lance-head, bobbin, ratchet, etc., prob. ult. f. Gmc]

rate[1] /rayt/ *n. & v.* ● *n.* **1** a stated numerical proportion between two sets of things (the second usu. expressed as unity), esp. as a measure of amount or degree (*moving at a rate of 50 miles per hour*) or as the basis of calculating an amount or value (*rate of taxation*). **2** a fixed or appropriate charge or cost or value; a measure of this (*postal rates; the rate for the job*). **3** rapidity of movement or change (*traveling at a great rate; prices increasing at a dreadful rate*). **4** class or rank (*first-rate*). **5** *Brit.* **a** an assessment levied by local authorities on the assessed value of buildings and land owned or leased. **b** (in *pl.*) the amount payable by this. ● *v.* **1** *tr.* **a** estimate the worth or value of (*I do not rate him very highly; how do you rate your chances of winning the race?*). **b** assign a fixed value to (a coin or metal) in relation to a monetary standard. **c** assign a value to (work, the power of a machine, etc.). **2** *tr.* consider; regard as (*I rate them among my benefactors*). **3** *intr.* (foll. by *as*) rank or be rated. **4** *tr. Brit.* **a** subject to the payment of a local rate. **b** value for the purpose of assessing rates. **5** *tr.* be worthy of, deserve. **6** *tr. Naut.* place in a specified class (cf. RATING[1]). □ **at any rate** in any case; whatever happens. **at this** (or **that**) **rate** if this example is typical or this assumption is true. [ME f. OF f. med.L *rata* f. L *pro rata parte* or *portione* according to the proportional share f. *ratus* past part. of *rēri* reckon]
■ *n.* **1** scale, proportion; measure, level. **2** charge, price, fee, tariff, figure, amount; toll. **3** pace, gait, speed, velocity, *colloq.* clip. **4** rank, grade, place, position, class, rating, worth, value. ● *v.* **1 a** rank, grade, class, position, place; evaluate, estimate, calculate, compute, count, reckon, judge, gauge, assess, appraise, measure. **2** see CONSIDER 6. **3** count, be placed; see also RANK[1] *v.* 1. **5** merit, be entitled to, deserve, be worthy of, have a claim to. □ **at any rate** in any case, in any event, anyway, at all events, anyhow, under *or* in any circumstances, regardless, notwithstanding, whatever (else) happens.

rate[2] /rayt/ *v.tr.* scold angrily. [ME: orig. unkn.]
■ berate, reprimand, rebuke, reproach, reprove, take to task, upbraid, censure, *colloq.* bawl out, dress down, chew out; see also SCOLD *v.* 1.

rate[3] var. of RET.

rateable var. of RATABLE.

ratel /ráyt'l, raá-/ *n.* an African and Indian nocturnal flesh-eating burrowing mammal, *Mellivora capensis.* Also called *honey badger.* [Afrik., of unkn. orig.]

ratepayer /ráytpayər/ *n.* **1** a customer of a utility company, etc. **2** *Brit.* a person liable to local tax (see **rate** *n.* 5).

ratfink /rátfingk/ *n. sl.* = FINK.

rathe /rayth/ *adj. poet.* coming, blooming, etc., early in the year or day. [OE *hræth, hræd* f. Gmc]

rather /ráthər/ *adv.* **1** (often foll. by *than*) by preference; for choice (*would rather not go; would rather stay than go*). **2** (usu. foll. by *than*) more truly; as a more likely alternative (*is stupid rather than honest*). **3** more precisely (*a book, or rather, a pamphlet*). **4** slightly; to some extent; somewhat (*became rather drunk; I rather think you know him*). **5** /raathér/ *Brit.* (as an emphatic response) indeed; assuredly (*Did you like it? —Rather!*). □ **had** (or **would**) **rather** prefer to. [ME f. OE *hrathor,* compar. of *hræthe* (adv.) f. *hræth* (adj.): see RATHE]
■ **1** preferably, sooner, more readily *or* willingly, by choice. **4** quite, somewhat, fairly, moderately, to a certain extent *or* degree, to some extent, slightly, *colloq.* sort of, kind of, pretty. □ **had** (or **would**) **rather** had sooner, would sooner, prefer *or* choose to.

rathskeller /raátskelər, rát-, ráth-/ *n.* a beer hall or restaurant in a basement. [G, = (restaurant in) town-hall cellar]

ratify /rátifī/ *v.tr.* (**-ies, -ied**) confirm or accept (an agreement made in one's name) by formal consent, signature, etc. □□ **ratifiable** *adj.* **ratification** /-fikáyshən/ *n.* **ratifier** *n.* [ME f. OF *ratifier* f. med.L *ratificare* (as RATE[1])]
■ confirm, approve, sanction, endorse, support, corroborate, uphold, back (up), certify, affirm; sign.

rating[1] /ráyting/ *n.* **1** the act or an instance of placing in a

rank or class or assigning a value to. **2** the estimated standing of a person as regards credit, etc. **3** *Naut.* **a** *Brit.* a non-commissioned sailor. **b** a person's position or class on a ship's books. **4** *Brit.* an amount fixed as a local tax rate. **5** the relative popularity of a broadcast program as determined by the estimated size of the audience. **6** *Naut.* any of the classes into which racing yachts are distributed by tonnage.
■ **1** see SCALE[3] *n.* 1.

rating[2] /ráyting/ *n.* an angry reprimand.

ratio /ráysheeō, ráyshō/ *n.* (*pl.* **-os**) the quantitative relation between two similar magnitudes determined by the number of times one contains the other integrally or fractionally (*in the ratio of three to two; the ratios 1:5 and 20:100 are the same*). [L (as RATE[1])]
■ proportion, correlation, relation.

ratiocinate /rásheeósinayt/ *v.intr. literary* go through logical processes of reasoning, esp. using syllogisms. □□ **ratiocination** /-ōsináyshən, -ósináyshən/ *n.* **ratiocinative** *adj.* **ratiocinator** *n.* [L *ratiocinari* (as RATIO)]
■ see REASON *v.* 1. □□ **ratiocination** see *reasoning* (REASON). **ratiocinative** see RATIONAL 1.

ration /ráshən, ráy-/ *n. & v.* ● *n.* **1** a fixed official allowance of food, clothing, etc., in a time of shortage. **2** (foll. by *of*) a single portion of provisions, fuel, clothing, etc. **3** (usu. in *pl.*) a fixed daily allowance of food, esp. in the armed forces (and formerly of forage for animals). **4** (in *pl.*) provisions. ● *v.tr.* **1** limit (persons or provisions) to a fixed ration. **2** (usu. foll. by *out*) distribute (food, etc.) in fixed quantities. [F f. It. *razione* or Sp. *ración* f. L *ratio -onis* reckoning, RATIO]
■ *n.* **1** allowance, share, quota, allotment, allocation, portion, helping, percentage, measure, apportionment. **4** (*rations*) supplies, provisions, food, victuals, edibles, commons, *formal* viands, *formal or joc.* comestibles, *joc.* provender. ● *v.* **1** budget, restrict, confine, control, limit. **2** (*ration out*) allot, apportion, dole (out), give out, distribute, deal out, parcel out, measure out, admeasure, hand out, distribute, share out, dispense, *literary* mete out.

rational /ráshənəl/ *adj.* **1** of or based on reasoning or reason. **2** sensible, sane, moderate; not foolish nor absurd nor extreme. **3** endowed with reason or reasoning. **4** rejecting what is unreasonable or cannot be tested by reason in religion or custom. **5** *Math.* (of a quantity or ratio) expressible as a ratio of whole numbers. □□ **rationality** /-nálitee/ *n.* **rationally** *adv.* [ME f. L *rationalis* (as RATION)]
■ **1** reasoned, logical, practical, pragmatic, *literary* ratiocinative. **2** sensible, commonsense, commonsensical, practical, pragmatic, down-to-earth, reasonable, well-balanced, sane, sound, normal, clear-headed, clear-eyed, sober, moderate, measured. **3** discriminating, intelligent, thinking, enlightened, prudent, wise, knowledgeable, informed.

rationale /ráshənál/ *n.* **1** (often foll. by *for*) the fundamental reason or logical basis of anything. **2** a reasoned exposition; a statement of reasons. [mod.L, neut. of L *rationalis:* see RATIONAL]
■ reason, basis, ground(s), reasoning, philosophy, principle, theory, thinking, raison d'être; explanation, exposition.

rationalism /ráshənəlizəm/ *n.* **1** *Philos.* the theory that reason is the foundation of certainty in knowledge (opp. *empiricism* (see EMPIRIC), SENSATIONALISM). **2** *Theol.* the practice of treating reason as the ultimate authority in religion. **3** a belief in reason rather than religion as a guiding principle in life. □□ **rationalist** *n.* **rationalistic** *adj.* **rationalistically** *adv.*

rationalize /ráshənəlīz/ *v.* **1 a** *tr.* offer or subconsciously adopt a rational but specious explanation of (one's behavior or attitude). **b** *intr.* explain one's behavior or attitude in this way. **2** *tr.* make logical and consistent. **3** *tr.* make (a business, etc.) more efficient by reorganizing it to reduce or eliminate waste of labor, time, or materials. **4** *tr.* (often foll. by *away*) explain or explain away rationally. **5** *tr. Math.* eliminate irrational quantities from (an equation, etc.). **6**

intr. be or act as a rationalist. □□ **rationalization** *n.* **rationalizer** *n.*

■ **1a, 4** make acceptable *or* reasonable, make excuses for, account for, justify, excuse, reason away, explain (away). **2** think through, reason out; apply logic to, *literary* ratiocinate. **3** reorganize, realign, remodel, streamline, make efficient, simplify.

ratite /rátit/ *adj.* & *n.* ● *adj.* (of a bird) having a keelless breastbone, and unable to fly (opp. CARINATE). ● *n.* a flightless bird, e.g., an ostrich, emu, cassowary, or moa. [L *ratis* raft]

ratline /rátlin/ *n.* (also **ratlin**) (usu. in *pl.*) any of the small lines fastened across a sailing ship's shrouds like ladder rungs. [ME: orig. unkn.]

ratoon /rətŏŏn/ *n.* & *v.* ● *n.* a new shoot springing from a root of sugarcane, etc., after cropping. ● *v.intr.* send up ratoons. [Sp. *retoño* sprout]

ratsbane /rátsbayn/ *n.* anything poisonous to rats, esp. a plant.

rattail /rát-tayl/ *n.* **1** the grenadier fish. **2** a horse with a hairless tail. **3** such a tail.

rattan /rətán/ *n.* (also **ratan**) **1** any East Indian climbing palm of the genus *Calamus*, etc., with long, thin, jointed pliable stems. **2** a piece of rattan stem used as a walking stick, etc. [earlier *rot(t)ang* f. Malay *rōtan* prob. f. *raut* pare]

ratter /rátər/ *n.* **1** a dog or other animal that hunts rats. **2** *Brit. sl.* a person who betrays a cause, party, friend, etc.

rattle /rát'l/ *v.* & *n.* ● *v.* **1 a** *intr.* give out a rapid succession of short, sharp, hard sounds. **b** *tr.* make (a cup and saucer, window, etc.) do this. **c** *intr.* cause such sounds by shaking something (*rattled at the door*). **2 a** *intr.* move with a rattling noise. **b** *intr.* drive a vehicle or ride or run briskly. **c** *tr.* esp. *Brit.* cause to move quickly (*the bill was rattled through Parliament*). **3 a** *tr.* (usu. foll. by *off*) say or recite rapidly. **b** *intr.* (usu. foll. by *on*) talk in a lively thoughtless way. **4** *tr. colloq.* disconcert; alarm; fluster; make nervous; frighten. ● *n.* **1** a rattling sound. **2** an instrument or plaything made to rattle, esp. in order to amuse babies or to give an alarm. **3** the set of horny rings in a rattlesnake's tail. **4** a plant with seeds that rattle in their cases when ripe (*red rattle; yellow rattle*). **5** uproar; bustle; noisy gaiety; racket. **6 a** a noisy flow of words. **b** empty chatter; trivial talk. **7** *archaic* a lively or thoughtless incessant talker. □ **rattle the saber** threaten war. □□ **rattly** *adj.* [ME, prob. f. MDu. & LG *ratelen* (imit.)]

■ *v.* **1** clatter, jangle. **1b, 2a** shake, vibrate, joggle, jiggle; jounce, bounce, bump, jolt; clank. **2 b** speed, hurtle, race, rush. **c** race, rush, speed, expedite, push, press, drive. **3 a** (*rattle off*) recite, list, utter, reel off, run through, enumerate, call off. **b** chatter, babble, jabber, gibber, prate, prattle, blabber, blather, ramble, maunder, *colloq.* natter. **4** unnerve, disconcert, discomfit, disturb, perturb, shake, discompose, discountenance, upset, agitate, alarm, fluster, put off, *colloq.* faze, throw. ● *n.* **1** clatter, crackle, crackling; rale. **2** sistrum, noisemaker. **5** see RACKET² 1a. **6** see BABBLE *n.* 1. **7** see BLABBER *n.*

rattler /rátlər/ *n.* **1** a thing that rattles, esp. an old or rickety vehicle. **2** *colloq.* a rattlesnake. **3** *Brit. sl.* a remarkably good specimen of anything. **4** *colloq.* a fast freight train.

■ **1** see RATTLETRAP *n.*

rattlesnake /rát'lsnayk/ *n.* any of various poisonous American snakes of the family Viperidae, esp. of the genus *Crotalus* or *Sistrurus*, with a rattling structure of horny rings in its tail.

rattletrap /rát'ltrap/ *n.* & *adj. colloq.* ● *n.* a rickety old vehicle, etc. ● *adj.* rickety.

■ *n.* rattler, bone shaker, wreck, *colloq.* jalopy, heap, (old) crock, tin lizzie *sl.* flivver, *Brit. sl.* (old) banger.

rattling /rátling/ *adj.* & *adv.* ● *adj.* **1** that rattles. **2** brisk; vigorous (*a rattling pace*). ● *adv.* remarkably (*a rattling good story*).

■ *adj.* **2** see BRISK *adj.* 1. ● *adv.* see EXCEEDINGLY 1.

ratty /rátee/ *adj.* (**rattier, rattiest**) **1** relating to or infested with rats. **2** *Brit. colloq.* irritable or angry. **3** *colloq.* **a** shabby; wretched; nasty. **b** unkempt; seedy; dirty. □□ **rattily** *adv.* **rattiness** *n.*

■ **2** irritable, cross, testy, touchy, crabby, crabbed, angry, short-tempered, impatient, disagreeable. **3 a** see NASTY 1, 5a, b. **b** dirty, greasy, straggly, unkempt, matted; see also SEEDY 3.

raucous /ráwkəs/ *adj.* harsh sounding; loud and hoarse. □□ **raucously** *adv.* **raucousness** *n.* [L *raucus*]

■ harsh, rasping, rough, husky, hoarse, grating, scratchy, discordant, dissonant, jarring, strident, shrill, noisy, loud, earsplitting, piercing, penetrating.

raunchy /ráwnchee/ *adj.* (**raunchier, raunchiest**) *colloq.* **1** coarse; earthy; boisterous; sexually provocative. **2** slovenly; grubby. □□ **raunchily** *adv.* **raunchiness** *n.* [20th c.: orig. unkn.]

■ **1** see BAWDY *adj.*

ravage /rávij/ *v.* & *n.* ● *v.tr.* & *intr.* devastate; plunder. ● *n.* **1** the act or an instance of ravaging; devastation; damage. **2** (usu. in *pl.*) foll. by *of*) destructive effect (*survived the ravages of winter*). □□ **ravager** *n.* [F *ravage(r)* alt. f. *ravine* rush of water]

■ *v.* lay waste, devastate, ruin, destroy, demolish, raze, wreck, wreak havoc on; pillage, plunder, ransack, sack, loot, rape, maraud, *literary* despoil. ● *n.* **1** destruction, damage, depredation(s), ruin, devastation. **2** (*ravages*) ill effects, scars; see also DEPREDATION.

rave¹ /rayv/ *v.* & *n.* ● *v.* **1** *intr.* talk wildly or furiously in or as in delirium. **2** *intr.* (usu. foll. by *about, of, over*) speak with rapturous admiration; go into raptures. **3** *tr.* bring into a specified state by raving (*raved himself hoarse*). **4** *tr.* utter with ravings (*raved their grief*). **5** *intr.* (of the sea, wind, etc.) howl; roar. **6** *tr.* & *intr. Brit. colloq.* enjoy oneself freely (esp. *rave it up*). ● *n.* **1** (usu. *attrib.*) *colloq.* a highly enthusiastic review of a film, play, etc. (*a rave review*). **2** *Brit. sl.* **a** an infatuation. **b** a temporary fashion or craze. **3** (also **rave-up**) *Brit. colloq.* a lively party. **4** *Brit.* the sound of the wind, etc., raving. **5** a dance party, often involving drug use. [ME, prob. f. ONF *raver*, rel. to (M)LG *reven* be senseless, rave]

■ *v.* **1** rant, rant and rave, rage, storm, fulminate, roar, thunder, bellow, shout; fume, seethe. **2** (*rave about*) praise, sing the praises of, rhapsodize over *or* about, applaud, gush over, go into raptures about, be thrilled about, eulogize, extol, laud, *colloq.* go on about. **5** howl, rage, roar. **6** see *enjoy oneself.* ● *n.* **1** enthusiastic reception, tribute, testimonial, encomium, bouquet, plaudit, accolade.

rave² /rayv/ *n.* **1** a rail of a cart. **2** (in *pl.*) a permanent or removable framework added to the sides of a cart to increase its capacity. [var. of dial. *rathe* (15th c., of unkn. orig.)]

ravel /rávəl/ *v.* & *n.* ● *v.* **1** *tr.* & *intr.* entangle or become entangled or knotted. **2** *tr.* confuse or complicate (a question or problem). **3** *intr.* fray out. **4** *tr.* (often foll. by *out*) disentangle; unravel; distinguish the separate threads or subdivisions of. ● *n.* **1** a tangle or knot. **2** a complication. **3** a frayed or loose end. [prob. f. Du. *ravelen* tangle, fray out, unweave]

■ *v.* **1** see TANGLE¹ *v.* 1. **2** see COMPLICATE 1. **3** see FRAY¹. **4** see FREE *v.* 3, SEPARATE *v.* 6a. ● *n.* **1** see TANGLE¹ *n.* 1. **2** see TANGLE¹ *n.* 2.

ravelin /rávlin/ *n. hist.* an outwork of fortifications, with two faces forming a salient angle. [F f. obs. It. *ravellino*, of unkn. orig.]

raveling /rávəling/ *n.* a thread from fabric that is frayed or unraveled.

raven¹ /ráyvən/ *n.* & *adj.* ● *n.* a large glossy blue-black crow, *Corvus corax*, feeding chiefly on carrion, etc., having a hoarse cry. ● *adj.* glossy black (*raven tresses*). [OE *hræfn* f. Gmc]

■ *adj.* see BLACK *adj.* 1.

raven² /rávən/ *v.* **1** *intr.* **a** plunder. **b** (foll. by *after*) seek prey or booty. **c** (foll. by *about*) go plundering. **d** prowl for prey

┌───┐
│ /.../ **pronunciation**   ● **part of speech**   │
│   │
│ □ **phrases, idioms, and compounds**   │
│   │
│ □□ **derivatives**   ■ **synonym section**   │
│   │
│ **cross-references** appear in SMALL CAPITALS or *italics* │
└───┘

(*ravening beast*). **2 a** *tr.* devour voraciously. **b** *intr.* (usu. foll. by *for*) have a ravenous appetite. **c** *intr.* (often foll. by *on*) feed voraciously. [OF *raviner* ravage ult. f. L *rapina* RAPINE]

ravenous /rávənəs/ *adj.* **1** very hungry; famished. **2** (of hunger, eagerness, etc., or of an animal) voracious. **3** rapacious. □□ **ravenously** *adv.* **ravenousness** *n.* [ME f. OF *ravineus* (as RAVEN²)]

■ **1** hungry, famished, starving, starved. **2** insatiable, eager; see also VORACIOUS. **3** see RAPACIOUS.

ravin /rávin/ *n. poet.* or *rhet.* **1** robbery; plundering. **2** the seizing and devouring of prey. **3** prey. [ME f. OF *ravine* f. L *rapina* RAPINE]

ravine /rəveén/ *n.* a deep narrow gorge or cleft. □□ **ravined** *adj.* [F (as RAVIN)]

■ gorge, canyon, pass, cleft, defile, chine, gully, valley, gulch, arroyo, flume, coulée, gap, couloir, *Brit.* gill, *S.Afr.* kloof, donga, *Sc.* linn.

raving /ráyving/ *n., adj., & adv.* ● *n.* (usu. in *pl.*) wild or delirious talk. ● *adj.* **1** delirious; frenzied. **2** remarkable; intensive (*a raving beauty*) ● *adv.* intensively; wildly (*raving mad*). □□ **ravingly** *adv.*

■ *n.* (*ravings*) ranting, bombast, grandiloquence, magniloquence, rhetoric, bluster, blustering, babbling, hyperbole, fustian; delirium. ● *adj.* **1** mad, insane, raging, crazed, irrational, manic, maniacal, frantic, frenzied, delirious, hysterical, *colloq.* crazy. **2** real, outstanding, rare, phenomenal, great, extraordinary, remarkable, *colloq.* stunning. ● *adv.* completely, totally, absolutely.

ravioli /ráveeólee/ *n.* small pasta envelopes containing cheese, ground meat, etc. [It.]

ravish /rávish/ *v.tr.* **1** commit rape on (a woman). **2** enrapture; fill with delight. **3** *archaic* **a** carry off (a person or thing) by force. **b** (of death, circumstances, etc.) take from life or from sight. □□ **ravisher** *n.* **ravishment** *n.* [ME f. OF *ravir* ult. f. L *rapere* seize]

■ **1** rape; see also VIOLATE 4. **2** enrapture, delight, captivate, enthrall, fascinate, charm, entrance, spellbind, bewitch, transport. **3 a** carry off, seize, *poet.* rape; see also ABDUCT.

ravishing /rávishing/ *adj.* entrancing; delightful; very beautiful. □□ **ravishingly** *adv.*

■ dazzling, beautiful, gorgeous, striking, radiant, charming, alluring, attractive, entrancing, delightful, captivating, enthralling, bewitching, *colloq.* stunning.

raw /raw/ *adj. & n.* ● *adj.* **1** (of food) uncooked. **2** in the natural state; not processed or manufactured (*raw sewage*). **3** (of alcoholic spirit) undiluted. **4** (of statistics, etc.) not analyzed or processed. **5** (of a person) inexperienced; untrained; new to an activity (*raw recruits*). **6 a** stripped of skin; having the flesh exposed. **b** sensitive to the touch from having the flesh exposed. **c** sensitive to emotional pain, etc. **7** (of the atmosphere, day, etc.) chilly and damp. **8 a** crude in artistic quality; lacking finish. **b** unmitigated; brutal. **9** (of the edge of cloth) without hem or selvage. **10** (of silk) as reeled from cocoons. **11** (of grain) unmalted. ● *n.* a raw place on a person's or horse's body. □ **come the raw prawn** (foll. by *with*) *Austral. sl.* attempt to deceive (someone). **in the raw 1** in its natural state without mitigation (*life in the raw*). **2** naked. **raw deal** harsh or unfair treatment. **raw material** that from which the process of manufacture makes products. **raw sienna** a brownish-yellow ferruginous earth used as a pigment. **raw umber** umber in its natural state, dark yellow in color. **touch on the raw** *Brit.* upset (a person) on a sensitive matter. □□ **rawish** *adj.* **rawly** *adv.* **rawness** *n.* [OE *hrēaw* f. Gmc]

■ *adj.* **1** uncooked, fresh. **2** unprocessed, untreated, unrefined, unfinished, natural, crude. **5** new, inexperienced, unseasoned, immature, green, untried, fresh, untrained, unskilled, untested. **6a, b** exposed, unprotected, uncovered, open; sore, tender, inflamed, painful, sensitive. **6 c** sensitive, tender, susceptible. **7** chilly, chilling, cold, damp, freezing, biting, stinging, sharp, keen, piercing, penetrating, icy, bitter, *colloq.* nippy, *literary* chill. **8 a** see CRUDE *adj.* 1b. **b** brutal,

frank, candid, blunt, direct, unvarnished, unmollified, unmitigated, unembellished, realistic, honest, plain, unreserved, unrestrained, uninhibited, straightforward. **in the raw 2** naked, stark naked, undressed, unclothed, nude, in the nude, *colloq.* in the buff, in the altogether, *joc.* in one's birthday suit, *Brit. sl.* starkers.

rawboned /ráwbōnd/ *adj.* gaunt and bony.

■ gaunt, lean, gangling, thin, skinny, spare, meager, scrawny, underfed, bony, emaciated, half-starved, hollow-cheeked.

rawhide /ráwhīd/ *n.* **1** untanned hide. **2** a rope or whip of this.

■ **2** see WHIP *n.*

ray¹ /ray/ *n. & v.* ● *n.* **1** a single line or narrow beam of light from a small or distant source. **2** a straight line in which radiation travels to a given point. **3** (in *pl.*) radiation of a specified type (*gamma rays*; *X rays*). **4** a trace or beginning of an enlightening or cheering influence (*a ray of hope*). **5 a** any of a set of radiating lines or parts or things. **b** any of a set of straight lines passing through one point. **6** the marginal portion of a composite flower, e.g., a daisy. **7 a** a radial division of a starfish. **b** each of a set of bones, etc., supporting a fish's fin. ● *v.* **1** (foll. by *forth, out*) (of light, thought, emotion, etc.) issue in or as if in rays. **2** *intr. & tr.* radiate. □ **ray gun** (esp. in science fiction) a gun causing injury or damage by the emission of rays. □□ **rayed** *adj.* **rayless** *adj.* **raylet** *n.* [ME f. OF *rai* f. L *radius*: see RADIUS]

■ *n.* **1** beam, shaft, streak, gleam, flash. **4** glimmer, trace, spark, scintilla, flicker. ● *v.* **1** see BEAM *v.* 2a. **2** see RADIATE *v.*

ray² /ray/ *n.* a large cartilaginous fish of the order Batoidea, with a broad flat body, winglike pectoral fins, and a long slender tail, used as food. [ME f. OF *raie* f. L *raia*]

rayon /ráyon/ *n.* any of various textile fibers or fabrics made from cellulose. [arbitrary f. RAY¹]

raze /rayz/ *v.tr.* (also *Brit.* **rase**) **1** completely destroy; tear down (esp. *raze to the ground*). **2** erase; scratch out (esp. in abstract senses). [ME *rase* = wound slightly f. OF *raser* shave close ult. f. L *radere ras-* scrape]

■ **1** tear *or* pull *or* bring *or* knock *or* throw down, demolish, destroy, level, flatten, bulldoze.

razor /ráyzər/ *n. & v.* ● *n.* an instrument with a sharp blade used in cutting hair, esp. from the skin. ● *v.tr.* **1** use a razor on. **2** shave; cut down close. □ **razor clam** any of various bivalve mollusks of the family Solenidae, with a thin, elongated shell. **razor's edge 1** a keen edge. **2** a sharp mountain ridge. **3** a critical situation (*found themselves on the razor's edge*). **4** a sharp line of division. **razor wire** wire with sharpened projections, often coiled atop walls for security. [ME f. OF *rasor* (as RAZE)]

razorback /ráyzərbak/ *n.* an animal with a sharp ridged back, esp. a wild hog of the southern US.

razorbill /ráyzərbil/ *n.* a black and white auk, *Alca torda*, with a sharp-edged bill.

razz /raz/ *n. & v. sl.* ● *n.* = RASPBERRY 3. ● *v.tr.* tease; ridicule. [*razzberry*, corrupt. of RASPBERRY]

■ *v.* see RIDICULE *v.*

razzle-dazzle /rázəldázəl/ *n.* (also **razzle**) *sl.* **1 a** glamorous excitement; bustle. **b** a spree. **2** extravagant publicity. [redupl. of DAZZLE]

■ **1 a** see GLITTER *n.* 2, FLURRY *n.* 3. **2** *sl.* (media) hype.

razzmatazz /rázmətáz/ *n.* (also **razzamatazz** /rázəmə-/) *colloq.* **1** = RAZZLE-DAZZLE. **2** insincere actions; double-talk. [prob. alt. f. RAZZLE-DAZZLE]

■ **2** see MOONSHINE 1.

Rb *symb. Chem.* the element rubidium.

RC *abbr.* **1** Roman Catholic. **2** reinforced concrete.

RCAF *abbr.* Royal Canadian Air Force.

RCMP *abbr.* Royal Canadian Mounted Police.

RCN *abbr.* Royal Canadian Navy.

RD *abbr.* Rural Delivery.

Rd. *abbr.* Road (in names).

RDA *abbr.* **1** recommended daily allowance. **2** recommended dietary allowance.

RDF *abbr.* radio direction finder.

Re *symb. Chem.* the element rhenium.

re[1] /ray, ree/ *prep.* **1** in the matter of (as the first word in a heading, esp. of a legal document). **2** *colloq.* about; concerning. [L, ablat. of *res* thing]

■ see CONCERNING.

re[2] /ray/ *n. Mus.* **1** (in tonic sol-fa) the second note of a major scale. **2** the note D in the fixed-do system. [ME *re* f. L *resonare*: see GAMUT]

re- /ree, ri, re/ *prefix* **1** attachable to almost any verb or its derivative; meaning: **a** once more; afresh; anew (*readjust*; *renumber*). **b** back; with return to a previous state (*reassemble*; *reverse*). ¶ A hyphen is sometimes used when the word begins with *e* (*re-enact*), or to distinguish the compound from a more familiar one-word form (*re-form* = form again). **2** (also **red-** before a vowel, as in *redolent*) in verbs and verbal derivatives denoting: **a** in return; mutually (*react*; *resemble*). **b** opposition (*repel*; *resist*). **c** behind or after (*relic*; *remain*). **d** retirement or secrecy (*recluse*; *reticence*). **e** off; away; down (*recede*; *relegate*; *repress*). **f** frequentative or intensive force (*redouble*; *refine*; *resplendent*). **g** negative force (*recant*; *reveal*). [L *re-*, *red-*, again, back, etc.]

reabsorb /reéəbsáwrb, -záwrb/ *v.tr.* absorb again. □□ **reabsorption** /-absáwrpshən, -zawrp-/ *n.*

reaccept /reéəksépt/ *v.tr.* accept again. □□ **reacceptance** *n.*

reaccustom /reéəkústəm/ *v.tr.* accustom again.

reach /reech/ *v. & n.* ● *v.* **1** *intr. & tr.* (often foll. by *out*) stretch out; extend. **2** *intr.* stretch out a limb, the hand, etc.; make a reaching motion or effort. **3** *intr.* (often foll. by *for*) make a motion or effort to touch or get hold of, or to attain (*reached for his pipe*). **4** *tr.* get as far as; arrive at (*reached Lincoln at lunchtime*; *your letter reached me today*). **5** *tr.* get to or attain (a specified point) on a scale (*the temperature reached 90°; the number of applications reached 100*). **6** *intr.* (foll. by *to*) attain to; be adequate for (*my income will not reach to it*). **7** *tr.* succeed in achieving; attain (*have reached an agreement*). **8** *tr.* make contact with the hand, etc., or by telephone, etc. (*was out all day and could not be reached*). **9** *tr.* succeed in influencing or having the required effect on (*could not manage to reach their audience*). **10** *tr.* hand; pass (*reach that book for me*). **11** *tr.* take with an outstretched hand. **12** *intr. Naut.* sail with the wind abeam or abaft the beam. ● *n.* **1** the extent to which a hand, etc., can be reached out, influence exerted, motion carried out, or mental powers used (*it is beyond my reach*). **2** an act of reaching out. **3** a continuous extent, esp. a stretch of river between two bends, or the part of a canal between locks. **4** *Naut.* a distance traversed in reaching. **5** a pole connecting the rear axle, as of a wagon, to the bolster or bar at the front. □ **out of reach** not able to be reached or attained. **reach-me-down** *Brit.* = hand-me-down. □□ **reachable** *adj.* **reacher** *n.* [OE *ræcan* f. WG]

■ *v.* **1, 2** (*reach out*) hold out, extend, stretch (out), stick out, thrust out, outstretch, *poet.* outreach. **4** arrive at, get to, come to, get as far as, end up at *or* in, land at *or* in, *colloq.* make it to, make. **5** come *or* go *or* get up to, amount to, attain, climb to, rise to, run to; live to. **7** attain, achieve, accomplish, get *or* come to, get *or* come as far as. **8** contact, get, get in touch with, communicate with, establish *or* make contact with, get through to, get (a) hold of. **9** get through *or* across to, register with, communicate with, influence, sway, move, stir, carry weight with. **10** convey, hand, hand (over), pass (over). ● *n.* **1** range, extent, ambit, scope, orbit, compass; control, influence; capability, capacity.

reacquaint /reéəkwáynt/ *v.tr. & refl.* (usu. foll. by *with*) make (a person or oneself) acquainted again. □□ **reacquaintance** *n.*

reacquire /reéəkwír/ *v.tr.* acquire anew. □□ **reacquisition** /reé-akwizíshən/ *n.*

react /reeákt/ *v.* **1** *intr.* (foll. by *to*) respond to a stimulus; undergo a change or show behavior due to some influence (*how did they react to the news?*). **2** *intr.* (often foll. by *against*) be actuated by repulsion to; tend in a reverse or contrary direction. **3** *intr.* (often foll. by *upon*) produce a reciprocal or responsive effect; act upon the agent (*they react upon each*

other). **4** *intr.* (foll. by *with*) *Chem. & Physics* (of a substance or particle) be the cause of activity or interaction with another (*nitrous oxide reacts with the metal*). **5** *tr.* (foll. by *with*) *Chem.* cause (a substance) to react with another. **6** *intr. Mil.* make a counterattack. **7** *intr. Stock Exch.* (of shares) fall after rising. [RE- + ACT or med.L *reagere react-* (as RE-, L *agere* do, act)]

■ **1** respond; act, behave, conduct oneself; retaliate, reciprocate.

re-act /reé-ákt/ *v.tr.* act (a part) again.

reactance /reeáktəns/ *n. Electr.* a component of impedance in an AC circuit, due to capacitance or inductance or both.

reactant /reeáktənt/ *n. Chem.* a substance that takes part in, and undergoes change during, a reaction.

reaction /reeákshən/ *n.* **1** the act or an instance of reacting; a responsive or reciprocal action. **2 a** a responsive feeling (*what was your reaction to the news?*). **b** an immediate or first impression. **3** the occurrence of a (physical or emotional) condition after a period of its opposite. **4** a bodily response to an external stimulus, e.g., a drug. **5** a tendency to oppose change or to advocate return to a former system, esp. in politics. **6** the interaction of substances undergoing chemical change. **7** propulsion by emitting a jet of particles, etc., in the direction opposite to that of the intended motion. □□ **reactionist** *n. & adj.* [REACT + -ION or med.L *reactio* (as RE-, ACTION)]

■ **1** reply, answer; reciprocation; see also RESPONSE 1. **2** see RESPONSE 2. **3** counteraction, counterbalance, compensation.

reactionary /reeákshəneree/ *adj. & n.* ● *adj.* tending to oppose (esp. political) change and advocate return to a former system. ● *n.* (*pl.* **-ies**) a reactionary person.

■ *adj.* ultraconservative, conservative, rightist, right-wing, blimpish, traditionalist, traditional, conventional, old-fashioned. ● *n.* ultraconservative, conservative, rightist, Tory, right-winger, (Colonel) Blimp, traditionalist.

reactivate /reeáktivayt/ *v.tr.* restore to a state of activity; bring into action again. □□ **reactivation** /-váyshən/ *n.*

■ see REVIVE 2.

reactive /reeáktiv/ *adj.* **1** showing reaction. **2** of or relating to reactance. □□ **reactivity** /-tívitee/ *n.*

■ **1** see RESPONSIVE.

reactor /reeáktər/ *n.* **1** a person or thing that reacts. **2** (in full **nuclear reactor**) an apparatus or structure in which a controlled nuclear chain reaction releases energy. **3** *Electr.* a component used to provide reactance, esp. an inductor. **4** an apparatus for the chemical reaction of substances. **5** *Med.* a person who has a reaction to a drug, etc.

read /reed/ *v. & n.* ● *v.* (*past* and *past part.* **read** /red/) **1** *tr.* (also *absol.*) reproduce mentally or (often foll. by *aloud, out, off*, etc.) vocally the written or printed words of (a book, author, etc.) by following the symbols with the eyes or fingers. **2** *tr.* convert or be able to convert into the intended words or meaning (written or other symbols or the things expressed in this way). **3** *tr.* interpret mentally. **4** *tr.* deduce or declare an (esp. accurate) interpretation of (*read the expression on my face*). **5** *tr.* (often foll. by *that* + clause) find (a thing) recorded or stated in print, etc. (*I read somewhere that you are leaving*). **6** *tr.* interpret (a statement or action) in a certain sense (*my silence is not to be read as consent*). **7** *tr.* (often foll. by *into*) assume as intended or deducible from a writer's words; find (implications) (*you read too much into my letter*). **8** *tr.* bring into a specified state by reading (*read myself to sleep*). **9** *tr.* (of a meter or other recording instrument) show (a specified figure, etc.) (*the thermometer reads 20°*). **10** *intr.* convey meaning in a specified manner when read (*it reads persuasively*). **11** *intr.* sound or affect a hearer or reader as specified when read (*the book reads like a par-*

readable | real

ody). **12 a** *tr.* esp. *Brit.* study by reading (esp. a subject at university). **b** *intr.* carry out a course of study by reading (*is reading for the bar*). **13** *tr.* (as **read** /red/ *adj.*) versed in a subject (esp. literature) by reading (*a well-read person; was widely read in law*). **14** *tr.* **a** (of a computer) copy or transfer (data). **b** (foll. by *in, out*) enter or extract (data) in an electronic storage device. **15** *tr.* **a** understand or interpret (a person) by hearing words or seeing signs, gestures, etc. **b** interpret (cards, a person's hand, etc.) as a fortune teller. **c** interpret (the sky) as an astrologer or meteorologist. **16** *tr. Printing* check the correctness of and emend (a proof). **17** *tr.* (of an editor or text) give as the word or words probably used or intended by an author. ● *n.* **1** esp. *Brit.* a period of reading. **2** *colloq.* a book, etc., as regards its readability (*is a really good read*). □ **read a person like a book** understand a person's motives, etc. **read between the lines** look for or find hidden meaning (in a document, etc.). **read lips** determine what is being said by a person who cannot be heard by studying the movements of the speaker's lips. **read-only** *Computing* (of a memory) able to be read at high speed but not capable of being changed by program instructions. **read out 1** read aloud. **2** expel from a political party, etc. **read up** make a special study of (a subject). **read-write** *Computing* capable of reading existing data and accepting alterations or further input (cf. *read-only*). [OE *rǣdan* advise, consider, discern f. Gmc]

■ *v.* **1** peruse, study, look over, pore over; (*read out or aloud*) see *read out* 1 below. **2** understand, know, be familiar with, comprehend; translate, decode. **3, 6** see INTERPRET 1, 2; 4. **7** assign, impute, infer, assume, presume, conclude, find. **11** come over *or* across, appear; see also SOUND¹ *v.* 3. **12 a** study, take, major in. **13** (*adj.*) see KNOWLEDGEABLE. □ **read out 1** recite, read *or* say aloud, quote, read. **2** see EXPEL 2, 3. **read up** see STUDY *v.* 1, 3.

readable /réedəbəl/ *adj.* **1** able to be read; legible. **2** interesting or pleasant to read. □□ **readability** /-bílitee/ *n.* **readableness** *n.* **readably** *adv.*

■ **1** legible, decipherable, distinct; intelligible, comprehensible, understandable, easy to understand, easily understood, plain. **2** entertaining, easy to read, enjoyable, pleasurable, absorbing, interesting, engaging, stimulating.

readapt /réeədápt/ *v.intr.* & *tr.* become or cause to become adapted anew. □□ **readaptation** /rée-adaptáyshən/ *n.*

readdress /réeədrés/ *v.tr.* **1** change the address of (a letter or parcel). **2** address (a problem, etc.) anew. **3** speak or write to anew.

reader /réedər/ *n.* **1** a person who reads or is reading. **2** a book of extracts for learning, esp. a language. **3** a device for producing an image that can be read from microfilm, etc. **4** *Brit.* a university lecturer of the highest grade below professor. **5** a publisher's employee who reports on submitted manuscripts. **6** a printer's proof-corrector. **7** a person appointed to read aloud, esp. parts of a service in a church. [OE (as READ)]

readership /réedərship/ *n.* **1** the readers of a newspaper, etc. **2** the number or extent of these.

readily /rédlee/ *adv.* **1** without showing reluctance; willingly. **2 a** without difficulty. **b** without delay.

■ **1** willingly, eagerly, ungrudgingly, unhesitatingly, freely, gladly, happily, cheerfully. **2 a** effortlessly, smoothly, without difficulty; see also EASILY 1. **b** promptly, quickly, speedily, swiftly, at once, without delay, in no time, immediately, instantly, instantaneously, straightaway, right away, at *or* on short notice, *archaic or joc.* instanter, *colloq* pronto, *literary* apace.

reading /réeding/ *n.* **1 a** the act or an instance of reading or perusing (*the reading of the will*). **b** matter to be read (*have plenty of reading with me*). **c** the specified quality of this (*it made exciting reading*). **2** (in *comb.*) used for reading (*reading lamp; reading room*). **3** literary knowledge (*a person of wide reading*). **4** an entertainment at which a play, poems, etc., are read (*poetry reading*). **5** a figure, etc., shown by a meter

or other recording instrument. **6** an interpretation or view taken (*what is your reading of the facts?*). **7** an interpretation made (of drama, music, etc.). **8** each of the successive occasions on which a bill must be presented to a legislature for acceptance (see also *first reading, second reading, third reading*). **9** the version of a text, or the particular wording, conjectured or given by an editor, etc. □ [OE (as READ)]

■ **1 a** see *perusal* (PERUSE), RECITAL 1, 3. **6, 7** see *interpretation* (INTERPRET).

readjust /réeəjúst/ *v.tr.* adjust again or to a former state. □□ **readjustment** *n.*

readmit /réeədmít/ *v.tr.* (**readmitted, readmitting**) admit again. □□ **readmission** /-admíshən/ *n.*

readopt /réeədópt/ *v.tr.* adopt again. □□ **readoption** *n.*

readout /réedowt/ *n.* **1** display of information, as on a gauge, etc. **2** the information displayed.

ready /rédee/ *adj., adv., n.,* & *v.* ● *adj.* (**readier, readiest**) (usu. *predic.*) **1** with preparations complete (*dinner is ready*). **2** in a fit state (*are you ready to go?*). **3** willing, inclined, or resolved (*he is always ready to complain; I am ready for anything; a ready accomplice*). **4** within reach; easily secured (*a ready source of income*). **5** fit for immediate use (*was ready to hand*). **6** immediate; unqualified (*found ready acceptance*). **7** prompt; quick; facile (*is always ready with excuses; has a ready wit*). **8** (foll. by *to* + infin.) about to do something (*a bud just ready to burst*). **9** provided beforehand. ● *adv.* esp. *Brit.* **1** beforehand. **2** so as not to require doing when the time comes for use (*the boxes are ready packed*). ● *n.* (*pl.* **-ies**) *Brit. sl.* **1** (prec. by *the*) = *ready money*. **2** (in *pl.*) paper currency. ● *v.tr.* (**-ies, -ied**) make ready; prepare. □ **at the ready** ready for action. **make ready** prepare. **ready-made** (or **-to-wear**) **1** (esp. of clothes) made in a standard size, not to measure. **2** already available; convenient (*a ready-made excuse*). **ready-mix** (or **-mixed**) (of concrete, paint, food, etc.) having some or all of the constituents already mixed together. **ready money 1** available cash. **2** payment on the spot. **ready reckoner** a book or table listing standard numerical calculations as used esp. in commerce. **ready, steady** (or **get set**), **go** the usual formula for starting a race. □□ **readiness** *n.* [ME *rædi(g), re(a)di,* f. OE *rǣde* f. Gmc]

■ *adj.* **1, 2** prepared, (all) set, in readiness, primed, ripe, fit; *colloq.* psyched (up). **3** apt, likely, inclined, disposed, given, prone; willing, pleased, content; prepared, resolved; consenting, agreeable, acquiescent, eager, keen, *colloq.* game. **4** on *or* at *or* to hand, handy, available, accessible, at one's fingertips, at the ready, close at hand, convenient, within reach. **6** see IMMEDIATE 1. **7** prompt, rapid, quick, speedy, swift; (*of the mind*) clever, keen, sharp, agile, bright, intelligent, perceptive; (*of wit*) facile, fluent, glib. **8** about, likely, apt, *disp.* liable; (*ready to*) on the verge of, subject to, in danger of, on the brink of, on the point of, close to. ● *v.* make *or* get ready, set, equip, *colloq.* psych up; see also PREPARE 1, 3a. □ **at the ready** in position, poised, on deck, *colloq.* on tap; see also READY *adj.* 4 above. **make ready** see PREPARE 1, 3a. **ready-made 1** finished, off-the-rack, esp. *Brit.* off-the-peg, stock. **2** convenient, serviceable, usable, handy, useful, suitable, adaptable; see also STALE¹ *adj.* 2. **ready money 1** see CASH¹ *n.* 1. □□ **readiness** willingness, eagerness, enthusiasm, keenness; promptness, quickness, speediness; facility, ease, skill, proficiency.

reaffirm /réeəfŕrm/ *v.tr.* affirm again. □□ **reaffirmation** /-afərmáyshən/ *n.*

■ see RENEW 4.

reafforest /réeəfáwrist, -fór-/ *v.tr. Brit.* = REFOREST. □□ **reafforestation** /-stáyshən/ *n.*

reagent /ree-áyjənt/ *n. Chem.* **1** a substance used to cause a reaction, esp. to detect another substance. **2** a reactive substance or force. [RE- + AGENT: cf. REACT]

real¹ /reel/ *adj.* & *adv.* ● *adj.* **1** actually existing as a thing or occurring in fact. **2** genuine; rightly so called; not artificial or merely apparent. **3** *Law* consisting of or relating to immovable property such as land or houses (*real estate*) (cf. *personal property*). **4** appraised by purchasing power; ad-

justed for changes in the value of money (*real value*; *income in real terms*). **5** *Philos.* having an absolute and necessary and not merely contingent existence. **6** *Math.* (of a quantity) having no imaginary part (see IMAGINARY 2). **7** *Optics* (of an image, etc.) such that light actually passes through it. ● *adv. colloq.* really, very. □ **for real** *colloq.* as a serious or actual concern; in earnest. **real ale** *Brit.* beer regarded as brewed in a traditional way, with secondary fermentation in the cask. **real estate** property, esp. land and buildings. **real estate agent** a person whose business is the sale or lease of buildings and land on behalf of others. **real life** that lived by actual people, as distinct from fiction, drama, etc. **real live** (*attrib.*) often *joc.* actual; not pretended or simulated (*a real live burglar*). **the real McCoy** see MCCOY. **real money 1** current coin or notes; cash. **2** large amount of money. **real tennis** *Brit.* the original form of tennis played on an indoor court. **the real thing** (of an object or emotion) genuine; not inferior. **real time** the actual time during which a process or event occurs. **real-time** (*attrib.*) *Computing* (of a system) in which the response time is of the order of milliseconds, e.g., in an airline booking system. □□ **realness** *n.* [AF = OF *reel*, LL *realis* f. L *res* thing]
■ *adj.* **1** genuine, actual, true, existent, authentic, natural; material, physical, tangible, palpable, corporeal. **2** genuine, true, actual, proper, authentic, verified, verifiable, legitimate, bona fide, official; sincere, heartfelt, unfeigned, unaffected, earnest, honest, truthful; intrinsic. ● *adv.* see REALLY 2. □ **for real** see *in earnest* (EARNEST¹). **real money** see CASH¹ *n.* 1.

real² /rayaál/ *n. hist.* a former coin and monetary unit of various Spanish-speaking countries. [Sp., noun use of *real* (adj.) (as ROYAL)]

realgar /reeálgər/ *n.* a mineral of arsenic sulfide used as a pigment and in fireworks. [ME f. med.L f. Arab. *rahj al-ğār* dust of the cave]

realign /reeəlín/ *v.tr.* **1** align again. **2** regroup in politics, etc. □□ **realignment** *n.*
■ □□ **realignment** see *shake-up.*

realism /reeəlizəm/ *n.* **1** the practice of regarding things in their true nature and dealing with them as they are. **2** fidelity to nature in representation; the showing of life, etc., as it is in fact. **3** *Philos.* **a** the doctrine that universals or abstract concepts have an objective existence (opp. NOMINALISM). **b** the belief that matter as an object of perception has real existence. □□ **realist** *n.*

realistic /reeəlístik/ *adj.* **1** regarding things as they are; following a policy of realism. **2** based on facts rather than ideals. □□ **realistically** *adv.*
■ **1** natural, lifelike, true to life, naturalistic, vivid, graphic; factual. **2** practical, matter-of-fact, down-to-earth, pragmatic, sensible, reasonable, levelheaded, rational, sane, hardheaded, businesslike, no-nonsense, unromantic, unsentimental, tough, tough-minded, hard-boiled, *colloq.* hard-nosed.

reality /reeálitee/ *n.* (*pl.* **-ies**) **1** what is real or existent or underlies appearances. **2** (foll. by *of*) the real nature of (a thing). **3** real existence; the state of being real. **4** resemblance to an original (*the model was impressive in its reality*). □ **in reality** in fact. [med.L *realitas* or F *réalité* (as REAL¹)]
■ **1** actuality, fact, truth, genuineness, authenticity. **2** see NATURE 1, 7. □ **in reality** see *in fact* 1 (FACT).

realize /reeəliz/ *v.tr.* **1** (often foll. by *that* + clause) (also *absol.*) be fully aware of; conceive as real. **2** (also *absol.*) understand clearly. **3** present as real; make realistic; give apparent reality to (*the story was powerfully realized on stage*). **4** convert into actuality; achieve (*realized a childhood dream*). **5 a** convert into money. **b** acquire (profit). **c** be sold for (a specified price). **6** *Mus.* reconstruct (a part) in full from a figured bass. □□ **realizable** *adj.* **realizability** /-əbílitee/ *n.* **realization** *n.* **realizer** *n.*
■ **1** be *or* become aware (of), appreciate, be conscious *or* appreciative (of); see also KNOW *v.* 1b. **2** understand, comprehend, grasp, perceive, discern, recognize, see, *colloq.* catch on to, cotton on to, *Brit* twig. **4** make real, effect, bring about, make happen, make a reality,

produce, actualize, accomplish, achieve, fulfill, materialize, effectuate. **5 b** acquire, return, gain, clear, make, earn, bring *or* take in, net, produce, get.
□□ **realization 1** conception, understanding, comprehension, apprehension, awareness, appreciation, perception, recognition, cognizance; actualization, consummation, accomplishment, achievement, establishment, fulfillment, materialization, effectuation.

reallocate /ree-áləkayt/ *v.tr.* allocate again or differently. □□ **reallocation** /-káyshən/ *n.*

reallot /reeəlót/ *v.tr.* (**reallotted, reallotting**) allot again or differently. □□ **reallotment** *n.*

really /reeəlee, reélee/ *adv.* **1** in reality; in fact. **2** positively; assuredly (*really useful*). **3** (as a strong affirmative) indeed; I assure you. **4** an expression of mild protest or surprise. **5** (in *interrog.*) (expressing disbelief) is that so? (*They're musicians. — Really?*).
■ **1** in reality, in actuality, in (point of) fact, genuinely, actually, truly, honestly, as a matter of fact, indeed, definitely; in effect. **2** positively, assuredly, unqualifiedly, categorically, unquestionably, undeniably; very, extremely, exceptionally, remarkably, unusually, uncommonly, extraordinarily, exceedingly, *Sc.* & *US* real. **3** indeed, absolutely; see also DEFINITELY *adv.* 2. **5** well, I declare; well blow me down, well I never, you don't say so, is that so, go on, *archaic* go to, *colloq.* well I'm damned, *sl.* I'll be blowed, no kidding, come on, no bull.

realm /relm/ *n.* **1** *formal* esp. *Law* a kingdom. **2** a sphere or domain (*the realm of imagination*). [ME f. OF *realme, reaume*, f. L *regimen -minis* (see REGIMEN): infl. by OF *reiel* ROYAL]
■ **1** domain, kingdom, empire, principality, palatinate, duchy. **2** sphere, limits, domain, confines, bounds; territory, area.

realpolitik /rayaálpōliteék/ *n.* politics based on realities and material needs, rather than on morals or ideals. [G]

realtor /reeáltər/ *n.* a real estate agent, esp. (**Realtor**) a member of the National Association of Realtors.

realty /reeəltee/ *n.* *Law* real estate (opp. PERSONALTY).
■ see PROPERTY 1c.

ream¹ /reem/ *n.* **1** twenty quires or 500 (formerly 480) sheets of paper (or a larger number, to allow for waste). **2** (in *pl.*) a large quantity of paper or writing (*wrote reams about it*). [ME *rēm, rīm* f. OF *raime*, etc., ult. f. Arab. *rizma* bundle]

ream² /reem/ *v.tr.* **1** widen (a hole in metal, etc.) with a borer. **2** turn over the edge of (a cartridge case, etc.). **3** *Naut.* open (a seam) for caulking. **4** squeeze the juice from (fruit). □□ **reamer** *n.* [19th c.: orig. uncert.]
■ **1** widen, broaden, extend, drill out, bore out, open up.

reanimate /ree-ánimayt/ *v.tr.* **1** restore to life. **2** restore to activity or liveliness. □□ **reanimation** /-máyshən/ *n.*
■ **1** see RESURRECT 4. **2** see REJUVENATE. □□ **reanimation** see REVIVAL 1, 3;4a.

reap /reep/ *v.tr.* **1** cut or gather (a crop, esp. grain) as a harvest. **2** harvest the crop of (a field, etc.). **3** receive as the consequence of one's own or others' actions. [OE *ripan, reopan*, of unkn. orig.]
■ **1** harvest, garner, glean, gather (in), take in. **3** receive, bring in, gain, procure, acquire, get, obtain, take in.

reaper /reépər/ *n.* **1** a person who reaps. **2** a machine for reaping. □ **the reaper** (or **grim reaper**) death personified.

reappear /reeəpeér/ *v.intr.* appear again or as previously. □□ **reappearance** *n.*
■ see RETURN *v.* 1. □□ **reappearance** see RETURN *n.* 1.

reapply /reeəplí/ *v.tr.* & *intr.* (**-ies, -ied**) apply again, esp. submit a further application (for a position, etc.). □□ **reapplication** /ree-aplikáyshən/ *n.*

/. . ./ **pronunciation**	● **part of speech**
□ **phrases, idioms, and compounds**	
□□ **derivatives**	■ **synonym section**
cross-references appear in SMALL CAPITALS or *italics*	

reappoint /rēəpóynt/ *v.tr.* appoint again to a position previously held. □□ **reappointment** *n.*

reapportion /rēəpáwrshən/ *v.tr.* apportion again or differently. □□ **reapportionment** *n.*

reappraise /rēəpráyz/ *v.tr.* appraise or assess again. □□ **reappraisal** *n.*

rear[1] /reer/ *n. & adj.* ● *n.* **1** the back part of anything. **2** the space behind, or position at the back of, anything (*a large house with a terrace at the rear*). **3** the hindmost part of an army or fleet. **4** *colloq.* the buttocks. ● *adj.* at the back. □ **bring up the rear** come last. **in the rear** behind; at the back. **rear admiral** a naval officer ranking below vice admiral. **rear guard 1** a body of troops detached to protect the rear, esp. in retreats. **2** a defensive or conservative element in an organization, etc. **rearguard action 1** *Mil.* an engagement undertaken by a rear guard. **2** a defensive stand in argument, etc., esp. when losing. **rearview mirror** a mirror fixed inside the windshield of a motor vehicle enabling the driver to see traffic, etc., behind. [prob. f. (*in the*) REARWARD or *rear guard*]

■ *n.* **1** back, back end, end, hind part, tail (end), *Naut.* stern. **2** (*at or in the rear*) see BEHIND *prep.* 1a, b. **4** seat, hindquarters, posterior, rump, buttocks, rear end, *colloq.* bottom, behind, backside, *sl.* tush, *Brit. sl.* bum. ● *adj.* back, end, rearmost. □ **in the rear** see BEHIND *prep.* 1a, b.

rear[2] /reer/ *v.* **1** *tr.* **a** bring up and educate (children). **b** breed and care for (animals). **c** cultivate (crops). **2** *intr.* (of a horse, etc.) raise itself on its hind legs. **3** *tr.* **a** set upright. **b** build. **c** hold upward (*rear one's head*). **4** *intr.* extend to a great height. □□ **rearer** *n.* [OE *rǣran* f. Gmc]

■ **1 a** raise, bring up, nurture; cultivate, educate, train. **b** breed, raise; care for, look after, tend. **c** see CULTIVATE 2a. **3 b** erect, raise, build, put up, construct, fabricate. **c** raise, lift, put up, upraise, uplift, hold up.

rearm /rēé-aárm/ *v.tr.* (also *absol.*) arm again, esp. with improved weapons. □□ **rearmament** *n.*

rearmost /reermōst/ *adj.* furthest back.

■ see LAST[1] *adj.* 1, 5.

rearrange /rēəráynj/ *v.tr.* arrange again in a different way. □□ **rearrangement** *n.*

■ arrange, adjust, alter, reposition, shuffle, reshuffle, scramble, change, sort out; see also TIDY *v.*

rearrest /rēərést/ *v. & n.* ● *v.tr.* arrest again. ● *n.* an instance of rearresting or being rearrested.

rearward /reerwərd/ *n., adj., & adv.* ● *n.* rear, esp. in prepositional phrases (*to the rearward of*; *in the rearward*). ● *adj.* to the rear. ● *adv.* (also **rearwards**) toward the rear. [AF *rerewarde* = *rear guard*]

■ see BACKWARD.

reascend /rēəsénd/ *v.tr. & intr.* ascend again or to a former position. □□ **reascension** /-sénshən/ *n.*

reason /rēézən/ *n. & v.* ● *n.* **1** a motive, cause, or justification (*has good reasons for doing this*; *there is no reason to be angry*). **2** a fact adduced or serving as this (*I can give you my reasons*). **3** the intellectual faculty by which conclusions are drawn from premises. **4** sanity (*has lost his reason*). **5** *Logic* a premise of a syllogism, esp. a minor premise when given after the conclusion. **6** a faculty transcending the understanding and providing a priori principles; intuition. **7** sense; sensible conduct; what is right or practical or practicable; moderation. ● *v.* **1** *intr.* form or try to reach conclusions by connected thought. **2** *intr.* (foll. by *with*) use an argument (with a person) by way of persuasion. **3** *tr.* (foll. by *that* + clause) conclude or assert in argument. **4** *tr.* (foll. by *why, whether, what* + clause) discuss; ask oneself. **5** *tr.* (foll. by *into, out of*) persuade or move by argument (*I reasoned them out of their fears*). **6** *tr.* (foll. by *out*) think or work out (consequences, etc.). **7** *tr.* (often as **reasoned** *adj.*) express in logical or argumentative form. **8** *tr.* embody reason in (an amendment, etc.). □ **by reason of** owing to. **in** (or **within**) **reason** within the bounds of sense or moderation. **it stands to reason** (often foll. by *that* + clause) it is evident or logical. **listen to reason** be persuaded to act sensibly. **see reason** acknowledge the force of an argument. **with reason**

justifiably. □□ **reasoner** *n.* **reasoning** *n.* **reasonless** *adj.* [ME f. OF *reisun, res(o)un, raisoner*, ult. f. L *ratio -onis* f. *rēri rat-* consider]

■ *n.* **1, 2** cause, motive, purpose, aim, intention, objective, goal; justification, argument, case, explanation, rationale, ground(s), pretext, basis, defense; excuse, rationalization. **3** reasoning, logic, rationality, thought; mind, intellect, intelligence. **4** see SANITY 1. **6** judgment, insight, perspicacity, percipience, understanding; see also INTUITION. **7** common sense; moderation; see also SENSE *n.* 4, 5. ● *v.* **1** think rationally *or* logically, use (one's) judgment *or* common sense, think it through, use one's head, put two and two together, *literary* ratiocinate. **2** (*reason with*) argue with, remonstrate with, debate with, discuss with, talk with, plead with, prevail (up)on. **3, 6** argue, assert; conclude, calculate, reckon, estimate, figure (out), work out, deduce, think out *or* through. **7** (**reasoned**) see LOGICAL 2, 3. □ **by reason of** because of, on account of, owing to, by virtue of, as a result of, *disp.* due to. **in** (or **within**) **reason** reasonable, sensible, justifiable, rational, fitting, proper, acceptable. **with reason** see WELL[1] *adv.* 7. □□ **reasoning** thinking, logic, rationality, thought, analysis, rationalization; reasons, arguments, rationale, explanation, explication, *Logic* premises, *literary* ratiocination.

reasonable /rēézənəbəl/ *adj.* **1** having sound judgment; moderate; ready to listen to reason. **2** in accordance with reason; not absurd. **3 a** within the limits of reason; not greatly less or more than might be expected. **b** inexpensive; not extortionate. **c** tolerable; fair. **4** *archaic* endowed with the faculty of reason. □□ **reasonableness** *n.* **reasonably** *adv.* [ME f. OF *raisonable* (as REASON) after L *rationabilis*]

■ **1** sensible, rational, sane, logical, sober, moderate, sound, judicious, wise, intelligent. **2** tenable, reasoned, well-thought-out, logical, well-grounded, justifiable, justified, valid, sensible. **3 a, c** appropriate, suitable, moderate, tolerable, acceptable, within reason, average, normal; equitable, fair. **b** see INEXPENSIVE.

reassemble /rēəsémbəl/ *v.intr. & tr.* assemble again or into a former state. □□ **reassembly** *n.*

reassert /rēəsárt/ *v.tr.* assert again. □□ **reassertion** /-sárshən/ *n.*

■ see RENEW 4.

reassess /rēəsés/ *v.tr.* assess again, esp. differently. □□ **reassessment** *n.*

■ see REVIEW *v.* 2, 5. □□ **reassessment** see REVIEW *n.* 3.

reassign /rēəsín/ *v.tr.* assign again or differently. □□ **reassignment** *n.*

reassume /rēəsōōm/ *v.tr.* take on oneself or undertake again. □□ **reassumption** /-súmpshən/ *n.*

reassure /rēəshōōr/ *v.tr.* **1** restore confidence to; dispel the apprehensions of. **2** confirm in an opinion or impression. □□ **reassurance** *n.* **reassurer** *n.* **reassuring** *adj.* **reassuringly** *adv.*

■ **1** comfort, encourage, hearten, buoy (up), bolster, cheer, uplift, inspirit, support, restore confidence to, set *or* put a person's mind at rest, set *or* put at ease.

reattach /rēətách/ *v.tr.* attach again or in a former position. □□ **reattachment** *n.*

reattain /rēətáyn/ *v.tr.* attain again. □□ **reattainment** *n.*

reattempt /rēətémpt/ *v.tr.* attempt again, esp. after failure.

Réaumur /ráyōmyōōr/ *adj.* expressed in or related to the scale of temperature at which water freezes at 0° and boils at 80° under standard conditions. □ **Réaumur scale** this scale. [R. de *Réaumur*, Fr. physicist d. 1757]

reave /reev/ *v.* (*past* and *past part.* **reaved** or **reft** /reft/) *archaic* **1** *tr.* **a** (foll. by *of*) forcibly deprive of. **b** (foll. by *away, from*) take by force or carry off. **2** *intr.* make raids; plunder; = REIVE. [OE *rēafian* f. Gmc: cf. ROB]

reawaken /rēəwáykən/ *v.tr. & intr.* awaken again.

■ see REVIVE.

rebarbative /reebaárbətiv/ *adj.* *literary* repellent; unattractive. [F *rébarbatif -ive* f. *barbe* beard]

rebate[1] /reébayt/ *n. & v.* ● *n.* **1** a partial refund of money

paid. **2** a deduction from a sum to be paid; a discount. ● *v.tr.* pay back as a rebate. □□ **rebatable** *adj.* **rebater** *n.* [earlier = diminish: ME f. OF *rabattre* (as RE-, ABATE)]
■ *n.* discount, reduction, deduction, allowance, markdown, refund, repayment. ● *v.* refund, give back, pay back; see also REPAY 1, 3.

rebate[2] /reébayt/ *n. & v.tr.* = RABBET. [respelling of RABBET, after REBATE[1]]

rebec /reébek/ *n.* (also **rebeck**) *Mus.* a medieval usu. three-stringed instrument played with a bow. [F *rebec* var. of OF *rebebe rubebe* f. Arab. *rabāb*]

rebel *n., adj., & v.* ● *n.* /rébəl/ **1** a person who fights against, resists, or refuses allegiance to, the established government. **2** a person or thing that resists authority or control. ● *adj.* /rébəl/ (*attrib.*) **1** of or concerning rebels. **3** in rebellion. ● *v.intr.* /ribél/ (**rebelled, rebelling**) (usu. foll. by *against*) **1** act as a rebel; revolt. **2** feel or display repugnance. [ME f. OF *rebelle, rebeller* f. L *rebellis* (as RE-, *bellum* war)]
■ *n.* revolutionary, revolutionist, insurgent, insurrectionist, mutineer, resister, resistance fighter, freedom fighter, guerrilla; heretic, nonconformist, dissenter, recusant. ● *adj.* **1** see REBELLIOUS 1. ● *v.* **1** revolt, mutiny, rise up, dissent; (*rebel against*) defy, flout, challenge, disobey.

rebellion /ribélyən/ *n.* open resistance to authority, esp. (an) organized armed resistance to an established government. [ME f. OF f. L *rebellio -onis* (as REBEL)]
■ uprising, revolution, mutiny, insurrection, revolt, insurgence, insurgency; insubordination, disobedience, defiance, resistance, rebelliousness, contumacy.

rebellious /ribélyəs/ *adj.* **1** tending to rebel; insubordinate. **2** in rebellion. **3** defying lawful authority. **4** (of a thing) unmanageable; refractory. □□ **rebelliously** *adv.* **rebelliousness** *n.* [ME f. REBELLION + -OUS or f. earlier *rebellous* + -IOUS]
■ **1** rebel, insubordinate, defiant, mutinous, revolutionary, contumacious, insurgent, insurrectionary, seditious; unmanageable, disobedient, difficult, refractory, incorrigible, ungovernable, unruly, stubborn, obstinate, recalcitrant. **4** unmanageable, difficult, refractory.

rebid /reébíd/ *v. & n.* ● *v.* (**rebidding**; *past* and *past part.* **rebid**) *Cards* **1** *intr.* bid again. **2** *tr.* bid (a suit) again at a higher level. ● *n.* **1** the act of rebidding. **2** a bid made in this way.

rebind /reébínd/ *v.tr.* (*past* and *past part.* **rebound**) bind (esp. a book) again or differently.

rebirth /reébórth/ *n.* **1** a new incarnation. **2** spiritual enlightenment. **3** a revival (*the rebirth of learning*). □□ **reborn** /reébáwrn/ *adj.*
■ **1** see REINCARNATION. **2** see *illumination* (ILLUMINATE). **3** renaissance, renascence, revival, renewal, reawakening, resurgence, resurrection, regeneration, rejuvenation, restoration.

reboot /reébóōt/ *v.tr.* (often *absol.*) *Computing* start (a system) again.

rebore *v. & n.* ● *v.tr.* /reébáwr/ make a new boring in, esp. widen the bore of (the cylinder in an internal-combustion engine). ● *n.* /reébawr/ **1** the process of doing this. **2** a rebored engine.

rebound[1] *v. & n.* ● *v.intr.* /ribównd/ **1** spring back after action or impact. **2** (foll. by *upon*) (of an action) have an adverse effect upon (the doer). ● *n.* /reébownd/ **1** the act or an instance of rebounding; recoil. **2** a reaction after a strong emotion. □ **on the rebound** while still recovering from an emotional shock, esp. rejection by a lover. □□ **rebounder** *n.* [ME f. OF *rebonder, rebondir* (as RE-, BOUND[1])]
■ *v.* **1** spring back, bounce, recoil, ricochet, resile. ● *n.* **1** bounce, recoil, ricochet, return, comeback. **2** see BACKLASH 1.

rebound[2] /reébównd/ *past* and *past part.* of REBIND.

rebroadcast /reébráwdkast/ *v. & n.* ● *v.tr.* (*past* **rebroadcast** or **rebroadcasted**; *past part.* **rebroadcast**) broadcast again. ● *n.* a repeat broadcast.

■ repeat, rerun.

rebuff /ribúf/ *n. & v.* ● *n.* **1** a rejection of one who makes advances, proffers help or sympathy, shows interest or curiosity, makes a request, etc. **2** a repulse; a snub. ● *v.tr.* give a rebuff to. [obs. F *rebuffe(r)* f. It. *ribuffo, ribuffare, rabbuffo, rabbuffare* (as RE-, *buffo* puff)]
■ *n.* rejection, discouragement, snub, repulse, refusal, dismissal, brush-off, repudiation, slight, cut, *colloq.* put-down. ● *v.* reject, snub, repel, drive away, spurn, repulse, refuse, dismiss, repudiate, slight, ignore, give a person the cold shoulder, cut (dead), brush off, give a person the brush-off, *colloq.* put down, freeze out.

rebuild /reébíld/ *v.tr.* (*past* and *past part.* **rebuilt**) build again or differently.
■ see RESTORE 1.

rebuke /ribyóōk/ *v. & n.* ● *v.tr.* reprove sharply; subject to protest or censure. ● *n.* **1** the act of rebuking. **2** the process of being rebuked. **3** a reproof. □□ **rebuker** *n.* **rebukingly** *adv.* [ME f. AF & ONF *rebuker* (as RE-, OF *buchier* beat, orig. cut down wood f. *busche* log)]
■ *v.* scold, reproach, admonish, reprove, reprimand, lecture, censure, reprehend, berate, castigate, criticize, take to task, upbraid, have a go at, revile, give a piece of one's mind, haul or rake over the coals, *archaic or literary* chide, *colloq.* dress down, bawl out, give a person hell *or* what for, tell off, call on the carpet, chew out, *Brit. colloq.* tick off, wig, give a person a wigging, see also CASTIGATE. ● *n.* censure, reprehension, castigation, criticism, upbraiding, revilement; scolding, reproach, admonition, reproof, lecture, tongue-lashing, *colloq.* dressing-down, *Brit.* wigging; see also REPRIMAND *n.*

rebury /reébéree/ *v.tr.* (**-ies, -ied**) bury again. □□ **reburial** *n.*

rebus /reébəs/ *n.* **1** an enigmatic representation of a word (esp. a name), by pictures, etc., suggesting its parts. **2** *Heraldry* a device suggesting the name of its bearer. [F *rébus* f. L *rebus*, ablat. pl. of *res* thing]

rebut /ribút/ *v.tr.* (**rebutted, rebutting**) **1** refute or disprove (evidence or a charge). **2** force or turn back; check. □□ **rebutment** *n.* **rebuttable** *adj.* **rebuttal** *n.* [ME f. AF *rebuter,* OF *rebo(u)ter* (as RE-, BUTT[1])]
■ **1** refute, deny, disprove, confute, invalidate, negate, discredit, belie, contradict, controvert, puncture, expose, destroy, shoot down, knock the bottom out of. **2** force back, turn back; see also CHECK[1] *v.* 2a. □□ **rebuttal** counterargument, riposte, retaliation, denial, refutation, contradiction, confutation, negation, rejection; retort, response, rejoinder.

rebutter /ribútər/ *n.* **1** a refutation. **2** *Law* a defendant's reply to the plaintiff's surrejoinder. [AF *rebuter* (as REBUT)]
■ see ANSWER *n.* 1.

rec. *abbr.* **1** receipt. **2** record. **3** recreation.

recalcitrant /rikálsitrənt/ *adj. & n.* ● *adj.* **1** obstinately disobedient. **2** objecting to restraint. ● *n.* a recalcitrant person. □□ **recalcitrance** *n.* **recalcitrantly** *adv.* [L *recalcitrare* (as RE-, *calcitrare* kick out with the heels f. *calx calcis* heel)]
■ *adj.* **1** stubborn, disobedient, obstinate, willful, defiant, refractory, headstrong, perverse, contrary, contumacious, mutinous, rebellious, fractious, unruly, unmanageable, ungovernable, uncontrollable, wayward, insubordinate. **2** intractable, unsubmissive, unyielding, unbending, immovable, inflexible, firm.

recalculate /reékálkyəlayt/ *v.tr.* calculate again. □□ **recalculation** /-láyshən/ *n.*

recalesce /reékəléss/ *v.intr.* grow hot again (esp. of iron allowed to cool from white heat, whose temperature rises at a certain point for a short time). □□ **recalescence** *n.* [L *recalescere* (as RE-, *calescere* grow hot)]

recall /rikáwl/ *v. & n.* ● *v.tr.* **1** summon to return from a place or from a different occupation, inattention, a digression, etc. **2** recollect; remember. **3** bring back to memory; serve as a reminder of. **4** revoke or annul (an action or decision). **5** cancel or suspend the appointment of (an official sent overseas, etc.). **6** revive; resuscitate. **7** take back (a gift). ● *n.* /also reĕkawl/ **1** the act or an instance of recalling, esp. a summons to come back. **2** the act of remembering. **3** the ability to remember. **4** the possibility of recalling, esp. in the sense of revoking (*beyond recall*). **5** removal of an elected official from office. **6** a request from a manufacturer that consumers return a product for repair, replacement, etc. □□ **recallable** *adj.*

■ *v.* **1** call back, summon (back); rally, rouse. **2** remember, recollect, call to mind; think back to, reminisce over *or* about. **4** rescind, suspend, annul, nullify, retract, withdraw, revoke, recant, take back; see also CANCEL *v.* 1a, 4. **6** see REVIVE 2. ● *n.* **1** withdrawal, retraction, return; summons. **2, 3** memory, recollection; remembrance, reminiscence. **4** withdrawal, recantation, cancellation, revocation, annulment, nullification, rescission, retraction, repeal. **5** see *dismissal* (DISMISS).

recant /rikánt/ *v.* **1** *tr.* withdraw and renounce (a former belief or statement) as erroneous or heretical. **2** *intr.* disavow a former opinion, esp. with a public confession of error. □□ **recantation** /reĕkantáyshən/ *n.* **recanter** *n.* [L *recantare* revoke (as RE-, *cantare* sing, chant)]

■ **1** recall, forswear, deny, rescind, repudiate, disavow, disclaim, withdraw, revoke, retract, forsake, abandon, renounce, abjure, take back, reverse, renege. **2** apostatize; see also RENEGE 1a.

recap /reĕkap/ *v. & n. colloq.* ● *v.tr. & intr.* (**recapped, recapping**) recapitulate. ● *n.* recapitulation. [abbr.]

■ *v.* see RECAPITULATE. ● *n.* see RÉSUMÉ 1.

recapitalize /reĕkápitəliz/ *v.tr.* capitalize (shares, etc.) again. □□ **recapitalization** *n.*

recapitulate /reĕkəpíchəlayt/ *v.tr.* **1** go briefly through again; summarize. **2** go over the main points or headings of. □□ **recapitulative** /-ətiv/ *adj.* **recapitulatory** /-lətáwree/ *adj.* [L *recapitulare* (as RE-, *capitulum* CHAPTER)]

■ summarize, sum up; repeat, go over (again), reiterate, restate, review, *colloq.* recap; recount, enumerate, recite, relate, list.

recapitulation /reĕkəpíchəláyshən/ *n.* **1** the act or an instance of recapitulating. **2** *Biol.* the reappearance in embryos of successive type-forms in the evolutionary line of development. **3** *Mus.* part of a movement, esp. in sonata form, in which themes from the exposition are restated. [ME f. OF *recapitulation* or LL *recapitulatio* (as RECAPITULATE)]

■ **1** see RÉSUMÉ 1.

recapture /reĕkápchər/ *v. & n.* ● *v.tr.* **1** capture again; recover by capture. **2** reexperience (a past emotion, etc.). ● *n.* the act or an instance of recapturing.

■ *v.* **1** see RECOVER *v.* 1. **2** relive, reexperience, retrieve, recall.

recast /reĕkást/ *v. & n.* ● *v.tr.* (*past* and *past part.* **recast**) **1** put into a new form. **2** improve the arrangement of. **3** change the cast of (a play, etc.). ● *n.* **1** the act or an instance of recasting. **2** a recast form.

■ *v.* **1, 2** see MODIFY 2.

recce /rékee/ *n. & v. esp. Brit. colloq.* ● *n.* a reconnaissance. ● *v.tr. & intr.* (**recced, recceing**) reconnoiter. [abbr.]

■ *n.* see RECONNAISSANCE. ● *v.* see RECONNOITER *v.*

recd. *abbr.* received.

recede[1] /riseĕd/ *v.intr.* **1** go or shrink back or further off. **2** be left at an increasing distance by an observer's motion. **3** slope backward (*a receding chin*). **4** decline in force or value. **5** (foll. by *from*) withdraw from (an engagement, opinion, etc.). **6** (of a man's hair) cease to grow at the front, sides, etc. [ME f. L *recedere* (as RE-, *cedere cess-* go)]

■ **1** ebb, subside, fall *or* go *or* move back, shrink back, abate, withdraw, retreat. **4** diminish, lessen, dwindle, shrink, wane, fade, become less likely; see also DECLINE *v.* 1, 7. **5** see WITHDRAW 5.

recede[2] /reĕseĕd/ *v.tr.* cede back to a former owner.

receipt /riseĕt/ *n. & v.* ● *n.* **1** the act or an instance of receiving or being received into one's possession (*will pay on receipt of the goods*). **2** a written acknowledgment of this, esp. of the payment of money. **3** (usu. in *pl.*) an amount of money, etc., received. **4** *archaic* a recipe. ● *v.tr.* place a written or printed receipt on (a bill). [ME *receit(e)* f. AF & ONF *receite*, OF *reçoite*, *recete* f. med.L *recepta* fem. past part. of L *recipere* RECEIVE: *-p-* inserted after L]

■ *n.* **1** delivery, acceptance; arrival, appearance. **2** sales slip, ticket, stub, proof of purchase, voucher, esp. *Brit.* counterfoil. **3** (*receipts*) income, proceeds, gate, takings, return, take.

receive /riseĕv/ *v.tr.* **1** take or accept (something offered or given) into one's hands or possession. **2** acquire; be provided with or given (*have received no news; will receive a small fee*). **3** accept delivery of (something sent). **4** have conferred or inflicted on one (*received many honors; received a heavy blow to the head*). **5 a** stand the force or weight of. **b** bear up against; encounter with opposition. **6** consent to hear (a confession or oath) or consider (a petition). **7** (also *absol.*) accept or have dealings with (stolen property knowing of the theft). **8** admit; consent or prove able to hold; provide accommodation for (*received many visitors*). **9** (of a receptacle) be able to hold (a specified amount or contents). **10** greet or welcome, esp. in a specified manner (*how did they receive your offer?*). **11** entertain as a guest, etc. **12** admit to membership of a society, organization, etc. **13** be marked more or less permanently with (an impression, etc.). **14** convert (broadcast signals) into sound or pictures. **15 a** *Tennis* be the player to whom the server serves (the ball). **b** *Football* be the player or team to whom the ball is kicked or thrown. **16** (often as **received** *adj.*) give credit to; accept as authoritative or true (*received opinion*). **17** eat or drink (the Eucharistic bread and wine). □ **be at** (or **on**) **the receiving end** *colloq.* bear the brunt of something unpleasant. **Received Pronunciation** (or **Received Standard**) the form of spoken English based on educated speech in southern England. □□ **receivable** *adj.* [ME f. OF *receivre*, *reçoivre* f. L *recipere recept-* (as RE-, *capere* take)]

■ **1, 2** get, obtain, come by, be provided with, collect, take (into one's possession), accept, be given, acquire, come into, inherit, gain; hear, learn, ascertain, be told, be informed *or* notified of, find out, pick up; see also EARN 1. **4** (*of honors*) accept, collect, earn, win; (*of a blow, etc.*) experience, undergo, endure, suffer, bear, sustain, be subjected to, meet with. **8, 12** show in, let in; see also ADMIT 3, ACCOMMODATE 1. **9** see HOLD[1] *v.* 2. **10** greet, meet, welcome; respond to, react to. **11** see ENTERTAIN 2a. **16** (**received**) see ORTHODOX.

receiver /riseĕvər/ *n.* **1** a person or thing that receives. **2** the part of a machine or instrument that receives sound, signals, etc. (esp. the part of a telephone that contains the earpiece). **3** esp. *Brit.* (in full **official receiver**) a person appointed by a court to administer the property of a bankrupt or insane person, or property under litigation. **4** a radio or television receiving apparatus. **5** a person who receives stolen goods. **6** *Chem.* a vessel for collecting the products of distillation, chromatography, etc. **7 a** *Baseball* = CATCHER 2. **b** *Football* offensive player eligible to catch a forward pass.

■ **1** see RECIPIENT *n.* **4** see RADIO *n.*, TELEVISION 2.

receivership /riseĕvərship/ *n.* **1** the office of official receiver. **2** the state of being dealt with by a receiver (esp. *in receivership*).

recension /risénshən/ *n.* **1** the revision of a text. **2** a particular form or version of a text resulting from such revision. [L *recensio* f. *recensēre* revise (as RE-, *censēre* review)]

recent /reĕsənt/ *adj. & n.* ● *adj.* **1** not long past; that happened, appeared, began to exist, or existed lately. **2** not long established; lately begun; modern. **3** (**Recent**) *Geol.* = HOLOCENE. ● *n.* *Geol.* = HOLOCENE. □□ **recency** *n.* **recently** *adv.* **recentness** *n.* [L *recens recentis* or F *récent*]

■ *adj.* **2** new, current, modern, up-to-date.

receptacle /riséptəkəl/ *n.* **1** a containing vessel, place, or space. **2** *Bot.* **a** the common base of floral organs. **b** the part of a leaf or thallus in some algae where the reproductive organs are situated. [ME f. OF *receptacle* or L *receptaculum* (as RECEPTION)]

■ **1** container, holder, repository; box, tin, can, case, casket, chest, vessel, bag, basket.

reception /risépshən/ *n.* **1** the act or an instance of receiving or the process of being received, esp. of a person into a place or group. **2** the manner in which a person or thing is received (*got a cool reception*). **3** a social occasion for receiving guests, esp. after a wedding. **4** a formal or ceremonious welcome. **5** (also **reception desk**) a place where guests or clients, etc., report on arrival at a hotel, office, etc. **6 a** the receiving of broadcast signals. **b** the quality of this (*we have excellent reception*). □ **reception room** a room available or suitable for receiving company or visitors. [ME f. OF *reception* or L *receptio* (as RECEIVE)]

■ **2** welcome, greeting, treatment; reaction, response. **3** party, social (event), function, *archaic* levee, *colloq.* do.

□ **reception room** see PARLOR.

receptionist /risépshənist/ *n.* a person employed in a hotel, office, etc., to receive guests, clients, etc.

receptive /riséptiv/ *adj.* **1** able or quick to receive impressions or ideas. **2** concerned with receiving stimuli, etc. □□ **receptively** *adv.* **receptiveness** *n.* **receptivity** /réeseptívitee/ *n.* [F *réceptif -ive* or med.L *receptivus* (as RECEPTIVE)]

■ **1** open, responsive, impressionable, susceptive, amenable, recipient, sensitive, willing, tractable, flexible, pliant; quick, sharp, alert, perceptive, astute, bright.

receptor /riséptər/ *n.* (often *attrib.*) *Biol.* **1** an organ able to respond to an external stimulus such as light, heat, or a drug, and transmit a signal to a sensory nerve. **2** a region of a cell, tissue, etc., that responds to a molecule or other substance. [OF *receptour* or L *receptor* (as RECEPTIVE)]

recess /réeses, risés/ *n.* & *v.* ● *n.* **1** a space set back in a wall; a niche. **2** (often in *pl.*) a remote or secret place (*the innermost recesses*). **3** a temporary cessation from work, esp. of Congress, a court of law, or during a school day. **4** *Anat.* a fold or indentation in an organ. **5** *Geog.* a receding part of a mountain chain, etc. ● *v.* **1** *tr.* make a recess in. **2** *tr.* place in a recess; set back. **3 a** *intr.* take a recess; adjourn. **b** *tr.* order a temporary cessation from the work of (a court, etc.). [L *recessus* (as RECEDE)]

■ *n.* **1** alcove, niche, nook, cranny, bay, hollow. **2** (*recesses*) innermost reaches, corners, secret places, depths, penetralia. **3** respite, rest, interlude, break, intermission, breathing space, pause, cessation, *colloq.* breather; holiday, vacation. ● *v.* **3 a** take a break, break, stop, rest, pause, adjourn, *colloq.* take a breather.

recession /riséshən/ *n.* **1** a temporary decline in economic activity or prosperity. **2** a receding or withdrawal from a place or point. **3** a receding part of an object; a recess. □□ **recessionary** *adj.* [L *recessio* (as RECESS)]

■ **1** (economic) downturn, slump, decline, dip, depression, setback.

recessional /riséshənəl/ *adj.* & *n.* ● *adj.* sung while the clergy and choir withdraw after a service. ● *n.* a recessional hymn.

recessive /risésiv/ *adj.* **1** tending to recede. **2** *Phonet.* (of an accent) falling near the beginning of a word. **3** *Genetics* (of an inherited characteristic) appearing in offspring only when not masked by a dominant characteristic inherited from one parent. □□ **recessively** *adv.* **recessiveness** *n.* [RECESS after *excessive*]

recharge *v.* & *n.* ● *v.tr.* /réecháarj/ **1** charge again. **2** reload. ● *n.* /réecháarj/ **1** a renewed charge. **2** material, etc., used for this. □□ **rechargeable** *adj.*

réchauffé /ráyshōfáy/ *n.* **1** a warmed-up dish. **2** a rehash. [F past part. of *réchauffer* (as RE-, CHAFE)]

recheck *v.* & *n.* ● *v.tr.* & *intr.* /réechék/ check again. ● *n.* /réechek/ a second or further check or inspection.

recherché /rəsháirsháy/ *adj.* **1** carefully sought out; rare or exotic. **2** far-fetched; obscure. [F, past part. of *rechercher* (as RE-, *chercher* seek)]

■ **1** see RARE[1] **1. 2** see *far-fetched*.

rechristen /réekrísən/ *v.tr.* **1** christen again. **2** give a new name to.

recidivist /risídivist/ *n.* a person who relapses into crime. □□ **recidivism** *n.* **recidivistic** *adj.* [F *récidiviste* f. *récidiver* f. med.L *recidivare* f. L *recidivus* f. *recidere* (as RE-, *cadere* fall)]

recipe /résipee/ *n.* **1** a statement of the ingredients and procedure required for preparing cooked food. **2** an expedient; a device for achieving something. **3** a medical prescription. [2nd sing. imper. (as used in prescriptions) of L *recipere* take, RECEIVE]

■ **1** formula, *archaic* receipt. **2** expedient; plan, procedure, method, approach, technique, way, means, system, program, modus operandi.

recipient /risípeeənt/ *n.* & *adj.* ● *n.* a person who receives something. ● *adj.* **1** receiving. **2** receptive. □□ **recipiency** *n.* [F *récipient* f. It. *recipiente* or L *recipiens* f. *recipere* RECEIVE]

■ *n.* receiver, beneficiary, heir, heiress, legatee. ● *adj.* **2** see RECEPTIVE.

reciprocal /risíprəkəl/ *adj.* & *n.* ● *adj.* **1** in return (*offered a reciprocal greeting*). **2** mutual (*their feelings are reciprocal*). **3** *Gram.* (of a pronoun) expressing mutual action or relation (as in *each other*). **4** inversely correspondent; complementary (*natural kindness matched by a reciprocal severity*). ● *n.* *Math.* an expression or function so related to another that their product is one ($^1/_2$ is the reciprocal of 2). □□ **reciprocality** /-kálitee/ *n.* **reciprocally** *adv.* [L *reciprocus* ult. f. *re-* back + *pro* forward]

■ *adj.* **2** mutual; common, shared, joint. **4** complementary, correlative, matching, corresponding, correspondent.

reciprocate /risíprəkayt/ *v.* **1** *tr.* return or requite (affection, etc.). **2** *intr.* (foll. by *with*) offer or give something in return (*reciprocated with an invitation to lunch*). **3** *tr.* give and receive mutually; interchange. **4 a** *intr.* (of a part of a machine) move backward and forward. **b** *tr.* cause to do this. □ **reciprocating engine** an engine using a piston or pistons moving up and down in cylinders. □□ **reciprocation** /-káyshən/ *n.* **reciprocator** *n.* [L *reciprocare reciprocat-* (as RECIPROCAL)]

■ **1** repay, requite, return, match, equal. **2** see RESPOND *v.* 2. **3** exchange, interchange; swap, trade.

reciprocity /résiprósitee/ *n.* **1** the condition of being reciprocal. **2** mutual action. **3** give and take, esp. the interchange of privileges between countries and organizations. [F *réciprocité* f. *réciproque* f. L *reciprocus* (as RECIPROCATE)]

■ **3** see *give and take*.

recirculate /réesórkyəlayt/ *v.tr.* & *intr.* circulate again, esp. make available for reuse. □□ **recirculation** /-láyshən/ *n.*

recital /risít'l/ *n.* **1** the act or an instance of reciting or being recited. **2** the performance of a program of music by a solo instrumentalist or singer or by a small group. **3** (foll. by *of*) a detailed account of (connected things or facts); a narrative. **4** *Law* the part of a legal document that states the facts. □□ **recitalist** *n.*

■ **1, 3** narration, recitation, description, relation, reading, telling, recounting; report, account, narrative, version, recapitulation, *colloq.* recap. **2** concert, performance; *colloq.* gig.

recitation /résitáyshən/ *n.* **1** the act or an instance of reciting. **2** a thing recited. [OF *recitation* or L *recitatio* (as RECITE)]

■ see RECITAL 1, 3.

recitative /résitəteév/ *n.* **1** musical declamation of the kind usual in the narrative and dialogue parts of opera and oratorio. **2** the words or part given in this form. [It. *recitativo* (as RECITE)]

recite /risít/ *v.* **1** *tr.* repeat aloud or declaim (a poem or passage) from memory, esp. before an audience. **2** *intr.* give a recitation. **3** *tr.* mention in order; enumerate. □□ **reciter** *n.* [ME f. OF *reciter* or L *recitare* (as RE-, CITE)]

■ **1** repeat, quote, say aloud, read out *or* aloud, declaim.

/.../ **pronunciation**	● **part of speech**
□ **phrases, idioms, and compounds**	
□□ **derivatives**	■ **synonym section**
cross-references appear in SMALL CAPITALS or *italics*	

2 declaim, hold forth, speak, esp. *joc. or derog.* orate.
3 enumerate, spell out, detail, chronicle, list, recount, relate, report, repeat.

reck /rek/ *v. archaic* or *poet.* (only in *neg.* or *interrog.*) **1** *tr.* (foll. by *of*) pay heed to; take account of; care about. **2** *tr.* pay heed to. **3** *intr.* (usu. with *it* as subject) be of importance (*it recks little*). [OE *reccan*, rel. to OHG *ruohhen*]

reckless /réklis/ *adj.* disregarding the consequences or danger, etc.; lacking caution; rash. □□ **recklessly** *adv.* **recklessness** *n.* [OE *recceléas* (as RECK)]

■ careless, rash, thoughtless, incautious, heedless, foolhardy, imprudent, unwise, injudicious, impulsive, irresponsible, negligent, unmindful, foolish, devil-may-care, wild, madcap, mad, harebrained, wildcat.

reckon /rékən/ *v.* **1** *tr.* count or compute by calculation. **2** *tr.* (foll. by *in*) count in or include in computation. **3** *tr.* (often foll. by *as* or *to be*) consider or regard (*reckon him wise; reckon them to be beyond hope*). **4** *tr.* **a** (foll. by *that* + clause) conclude after calculation; be of the considered opinion. **b** *colloq.* (foll. by *to* + infin.) expect (*reckons to finish by Friday*). **5** *intr.* make calculations; add up an account or sum. **6** *intr.* (foll. by *on, upon*) rely on, count on, or base plans on. **7** *intr.* (foll. by *with*) **a** take into account. **b** settle accounts with. **8** *US dial.* think; suppose (*I reckon I'll just stay home tonight*). □ **reckon up 1** count up; find the total of. **2** settle accounts. **to be reckoned with** of considerable importance; not to be ignored. [OE (*ge)recenian* f. WG]

■ **1** calculate, compute; add (up), figure (up), tally (up), sum up, total (up), work out *or* up, reckon up. **2** include, count, number, enumerate, list, name, enter. **3** consider, account, judge, look upon, regard, view, think of, hold, gauge, estimate, appraise, *formal* deem. **4 a** suppose, think, assume, presume, guess, imagine, consider, conclude, be of the opinion. **b** see EXPECT 1a, 2. **6** (*reckon on*) count on, rely on, depend on, trust in, take for granted, bank on. **7** (*reckon with*) **a** take into account *or* consideration, consider, account for, remember, bear in mind, allow for. **b** reckon up with, settle (accounts) with, sort it out with; see also *attend to* (ATTEND 4). □ **reckon up 1** see RECKON 1 above. **2** see RECKON 7b above. **to be reckoned with** see IMPORTANT 1.

reckoner /rékənər/ *n.* = *ready reckoner*.

reckoning /rékəning/ *n.* **1** the act or an instance of counting or calculating. **2** a consideration or opinion. **3 a** the settlement of an account. **b** an account. □ **day of reckoning** the time when something must be atoned for or avenged.

■ **1** counting, calculating, calculation, computation, enumeration. **2** see OPINION 1, 3. **3 a** payment, settlement, return, *sl.* payoff. **b** bill, account, invoice, *colloq.* tab. □ **day of reckoning** judgment day, day of atonement, day of judgment; retribution, final account(ing) *or* settlement, doom.

reclaim /rikláym/ *v. & n.* ● *v.tr.* **1** seek the return of (one's property). **2** claim in return or as a rebate, etc. **3** bring under cultivation, esp. from a state of being under water. **4 a** win back or away from vice or error or a waste condition; reform. **b** tame; civilize. ● *n.* the act or an instance of reclaiming; the process of being reclaimed. □□ **reclaimable** *adj.* **reclaimer** *n.* **reclamation** /rékləmáyshən/ *n.* [ME f. OF *reclamer reclaim-* f. L *reclamare* cry out against (as RE-, *clamare* shout)]

■ *v.* **1, 3** take back, recover, redeem, salvage, save, regain, retrieve; regenerate, rejuvenate, restore. **4 a** reform; win back, rescue; see also SAVE¹ *v.* 1. **b** tame, civilize, enlighten, refine, improve.

reclassify /reéklásifī/ *v.tr.* (**-ies, -ied**) classify again or differently. □□ **reclassification** /-fikáyshən/ *n.*

reclinate /réklinayt/ *adj. Bot.* bending downward. [L *reclinatus*, past part. of *reclinare* (as RECLINE)]

recline /riklín/ *v.* **1** *intr.* assume or be in a horizontal or leaning position, esp. in resting. **2** *tr.* cause to recline or move from the vertical. □□ **reclinable** *adj.* [ME f. OE *recliner* or L *reclinare* bend back, recline (as RE-, *clinare* bend)]

■ **1** lie down, lie back, lean back, stretch out, rest, repose, lounge.

recliner /riklínər/ *n.* **1** a comfortable chair for reclining in. **2** a person who reclines.

reclothe /reéklṓth/ *v.tr.* clothe again or differently.

recluse /riklṓōs, riklṓōs/ *n. & adj.* ● *n.* a person given to or living in seclusion or isolation, esp. as a religious discipline; a hermit. ● *adj.* favoring seclusion; solitary. □□ **reclusion** /riklṓōzhən/ *n.* **reclusive** *adj.* [ME f. OF *reclus recluse* past part. of *reclure* f. L *recludere reclus-* (as RE-, *claudere* shut)]

■ *n.* hermit, anchorite, anchoress, eremite; loner, lone wolf. ● *adj.* see *reclusive* below. □□ **reclusive** recluse, seclusive, solitary, lone, secluded, isolated, eremitic(al), hermitic, anchoritic, monastic, cloistered, sequestered, retiring.

recognition /rékəgníshən/ *n.* the act or an instance of recognizing or being recognized. □□ **recognitory** /rikógnitáwree, -tree/ *adj.* [L *recognitio* (as RECOGNIZE)]

■ identification, detection; acknowledgment, acceptance, awareness, perception, admission; honor.

recognizance /rikógnizəns, -kónə-/ *n.* **1** a bond by which a person undertakes before a court, etc., to observe some condition, e.g., to appear when summoned. **2** a sum pledged as surety for this. [ME f. OF *recon(n)issance* (as RE-, COGNIZANCE)]

recognizant /rikógnizənt/ *adj.* (usu. foll. by *of*) **1** showing recognition (of a favor, etc.). **2** conscious or showing consciousness (of something).

recognize /rékəgnīz/ *v.tr.* **1** identify (a person or thing) as already known; know again. **2** realize or discover the nature of. **3** (foll. by *that*) realize or admit. **4** acknowledge the existence, validity, character, or claims of. **5** show appreciation of; reward. **6** (foll. by *as, for*) treat or acknowledge. **7** (of a chairperson, etc.) allow (a person) to speak in a debate, etc. □□ **recognizable** *adj.* **recognizability** /-əbílitee/ *n.* **recognizably** *adv.* **recognizer** *n.* [OF *recon(n)iss-* stem of *reconnaistre* f. L *recognoscere recognit-* (as RE-, *cognoscere* learn)]

■ **1** identify, detect, place, recall, remember, recollect, know (again). **2** realize, perceive, understand, be *or* become aware of, discover, know, appreciate, be conscious *or* appreciative (of). **3** acknowledge, realize, see, admit, accept, own, concede, allow, grant, appreciate. **4** acknowledge, approve, sanction, validate, ratify, endorse; see also SUPPORT *v.* 5. **5** honor, give recognition to, salute, show gratitude *or* appreciation of, reward, distinguish, pay respect to, pay homage to. **6** acknowledge, treat, accept.

recoil /rikóyl/ *v. & n.* ● *v.intr.* **1** suddenly move or spring back in fear, horror, or disgust. **2** shrink mentally in this way. **3** rebound after an impact. **4** (foll. by *on, upon*) have an adverse reactive effect on (the originator). **5** (of a gun) be driven backward by its discharge. **6** retreat under an enemy's attack. **7** *Physics* (of an atom, etc.) move backward by the conservation of momentum on emission of a particle. ● *n.* /also reékoyl/ **1** the act or an instance of recoiling. **2** the sensation of recoiling. [ME f. OF *reculer* (as RE-, L *culus* buttocks)]

■ *v.* **1, 2** jerk *or* jump *or* spring back, start, flinch, wince, shrink, blench, balk, shy away; (*recoil from*) see AVOID. **3** rebound, bounce *or* spring back, resile, kick back, ricochet. **6** see RETREAT *v.* 1a. ● *n.* **1** flinch, wince, shrinking, start; kick, rebound, comeback, return; backlash.

recollect /rékəlékt/ *v.tr.* **1** remember. **2** succeed in remembering; call to mind. [L *recolligere recollect-* (as RE-, COLLECT¹)]

■ **1** recall, remember, retain; call to mind. **2** see REMEMBER 2a.

re-collect /reékəlékt/ *v.tr.* **1** collect again. **2** (*refl.*) recover control of (oneself).

recollection /rékəlékshən/ *n.* **1** the act or power of recollecting. **2** a thing recollected. **3 a** a person's memory (*to the best of my recollection*). **b** the time over which memory extends (*happened within my recollection*). □□ **recollective** *adj.* [F *recollection* or med.L *recollectio* (as RECOLLECT)]

■ **2** memory, remembrance; reminiscence.

recolonize /reékóləniz/ *v.tr.* colonize again. □□ **recoloniza-tion** *n.*

recolor /reékúlər/ *v.tr.* color again or differently.

recombinant /reekómbinənt/ *adj.* & *n. Biol.* ● *adj.* (of a gene, etc.) formed by recombination. ● *n.* a recombinant organism or cell. □ **recombinant DNA** DNA that has been recombined using constituents from different sources.

recombination /reékombináyshən/ *n. Biol.* the rearrangement, esp. by crossing over in chromosomes, of nucleic acid molecules forming a new sequence of the constituent nucleotides.

recombine /reékəmbín/ *v.tr.* & *intr.* combine again or differently.

recommence /reékəméns/ *v.tr.* & *intr.* begin again. □□ **recommencement** *n.*

■ see RENEW 3.

recommend /rékəménd/ *v.tr.* **1 a** suggest as fit for some purpose or use. **b** suggest (a person) as suitable for a particular position. **2** (often foll. by *that* + clause or *to* + infin.) advise as a course of action, etc. (*I recommend that you stay where you are*). **3** (of qualities, conduct, etc.) make acceptable or desirable. **4** *Brit.* (foll. by *to*) commend or entrust (to a person or a person's care). □□ **recommendable** *adj.* **recommendation** *n.* **recommendatory** /-dətawree/ *adj.* **recommender** *n.* [ME (in sense 4) f. med.L *recommendare* (as RE-, COMMEND)]

■ **1 a** see SUGGEST 1. **b** endorse, propose, commend, support, promote, vouch for, second, back, push, favor, approve, stand up for. **2** counsel, advise, urge, exhort; suggest, advocate. **3** favor, make attractive *or* interesting *or* acceptable, back, support; see also ADVOCATE *v.* **4** see ENTRUST 1. □□ **recommendation** counsel, advice, exhortation, direction, encouragement, suggestion, advocacy, proposal; endorsement, commendation, blessing, approval, approbation, support, good word.

recommit /reékəmít/ *v.tr.* (**recommitted, recommitting**) **1** commit again. **2** return (a bill, etc.) to a committee for further consideration. □□ **recommitment** *n.* **recommittal** *n.*

recompense /rékəmpens/ *v.* & *n.* ● *v.tr.* **1** make amends to (a person) or for (a loss, etc.). **2** requite; reward or punish (a person or action). ● *n.* **1** a reward; requital. **2** retribution; satisfaction given for an injury. [ME f. OF *recompense(r)* f. LL *recompensare* (as RE-, COMPENSATE)]

■ *v.* **1** see COMPENSATE 1, 2. **2** see REQUITE. ● *n.* **1** see *requital* (REQUITE). **2** see RETRIBUTION.

recompose /reékəmpóz/ *v.tr.* compose again or differently.

reconcile /rékənsil/ *v.tr.* **1** make friendly again after an estrangement. **2** (usu. in *refl.* or *passive*; foll. by *to*) make acquiescent or contentedly submissive to (something disagreeable or unwelcome) (*was reconciled to failure*). **3** settle (a quarrel, etc.). **4 a** harmonize; make compatible. **b** show the compatibility of by argument or in practice (*cannot reconcile your views with the facts*). □□ **reconcilable** *adj.* **reconcilability** /-siləbílitee/ *n.* **reconcilement** *n.* **reconciler** *n.* **reconciliation** /-sileeáyshən/ *n.* **reconciliatory** /-sileeətáwree/ *adj.* [ME f. OF *reconcilier* or L *reconciliare* (as RE-, *conciliare* CONCILIATE)]

■ **1** get *or* bring (back) together, unite, reunite, settle *or* resolve differences between, restore harmony between, make peace between, placate. **2** (*be reconciled*) see RESIGN 4a. **3** sort out, smooth over; see also SETTLE[1] 5–7, 8b. □□ **reconciliation** conciliation, appeasement, propitiation, pacification, placation, rapprochement, reconcilement, understanding, détente, reunion; compromise, settlement, agreement.

recondite /rékəndit, rikón-/ *adj.* **1** (of a subject or knowledge) abstruse; out of the way; little known. **2** (of an author or style) dealing in abstruse knowledge or allusions; obscure. □□ **reconditely** *adv.* **reconditeness** *n.* [L *reconditus* (as RE-, *conditus* past part. of *condere* hide)]

■ **1** abstruse, arcane, obscure, little known, esoteric, deep, profound, incomprehensible, unfathomable,

impenetrable, undecipherable, opaque, dark, inexplicable, enigmatic.

recondition /reékəndíshən/ *v.tr.* **1** overhaul; refit; renovate. **2** make usable again. □□ **reconditioner** *n.*

■ see OVERHAUL *v.* 1.

reconfigure /reékənfígyər/ *v.tr.* configure again or differently. □□ **reconfiguration** *n.*

reconfirm /reékənfárm/ *v.tr.* confirm, establish, or ratify anew. □□ **reconfirmation** /-konfərmáyshən/ *n.*

■ see RENEW 4.

reconnaissance /rikónisəns/ *n.* **1** a survey of a region, esp. a military examination to locate an enemy or ascertain strategic features. **2** a preliminary survey or inspection. [F (earlier *-oissance*) f. stem of *reconnaître* (as RECONNOITER)]

■ reconnoiter, survey, examination, patrol, exploration, investigation, inspection, scrutiny, esp. *Brit. colloq.* recce.

reconnect /reékənékt/ *v.tr.* connect again. □□ **reconnection** /-nékshən/ *n.*

reconnoiter /reékənóytər, rékə-/ *v.* & *n.* ● *v.* **1** *tr.* make a reconnaissance of (an area, enemy position, etc.). **2** *intr.* make a reconnaissance. ● *n.* a reconnaissance. [obs. F *reconnoître* f. L *recognoscere* RECOGNIZE]

■ *v.* **1** survey, examine, scout (out), scan, explore, investigate, inspect, scrutinize, check out, check up (on), *Brit. colloq.* recce. ● *n.* see RECONNAISSANCE.

reconquer /reékóngkər/ *v.tr.* conquer again. □□ **reconquest** *n.*

reconsider /reékənsídər/ *v.tr.* & *intr.* consider again, esp. for a possible change of decision. □□ **reconsideration** *n.*

■ see REVIEW *v.* 2, 5. □□ **reconsideration** see REVIEW *n.* 3.

reconsign /reékənsín/ *v.tr.* consign again or differently. □□ **reconsignment** *n.*

reconsolidate /reékənsólidayt/ *v.tr.* & *intr.* consolidate again. □□ **reconsolidation** /-dáyshən/ *n.*

reconstitute /reékónstitoōt, -tyoōt/ *v.tr.* **1** build up again from parts; reconstruct. **2** reorganize. **3** restore the previous constitution of (dried food, etc.) by adding water. □□ **reconstitution** /-toōshən/ *n.*

reconstruct /reékənstrúkt/ *v.tr.* **1** build or form again. **2 a** form a mental or visual impression of (past events) by assembling the evidence for them. **b** reenact (a crime). **3** reorganize. □□ **reconstructable** *adj.* (also **reconstructible**). **reconstruction** /-strúkshən/ *n.* **reconstructive** *adj.* **reconstructor** *n.*

■ **1** see RESTORE 1. **3** see MODIFY 2. □□ **reconstruction** see RESTORATION 1a.

reconvene /reékənveén/ *v.tr.* & *intr.* convene again, esp. (of a meeting, etc.) after a pause in proceedings.

reconvert /reékənvárt/ *v.tr.* convert back to a former state. □□ **reconversion** /-várzhən/ *n.*

■ □□ **reconversion** see RESTORATION 1a.

record *n.* & *v.* ● *n.* /rékərd/ **1 a** a piece of evidence or information constituting an (esp. official) account of something that has occurred, been said, etc. **b** a document preserving this. **2** the state of being set down or preserved in writing or some other permanent form (*is a matter of record*). **3 a** (in full **phonograph record**) a thin plastic disk carrying recorded sound in grooves on each surface, for reproduction by a record player. **b** a trace made on this or some other medium, e.g., magnetic tape. **4 a** an official report of the proceedings and judgment in a court of justice. **b** a copy of the pleadings, etc., constituting a case to be decided by a court (see also *court of record*). **5 a** the facts known about a person's past (*has an honorable record of service*). **b** a list of a person's previous criminal convictions. **6** the best performance (esp. in sport) or most remarkable event of its kind on record (often *attrib.*: *a record attempt*). **7** an object serving

/.../ **pronunciation**   ● **part of speech**

□ **phrases, idioms, and compounds**

□□ **derivatives**   ■ **synonym section**

cross-references appear in SMALL CAPITALS or *italics*

as a memorial of a person or thing; a portrait. **8** *Computing* a number of related items of information which are handled as a unit. ● *v.tr.* /rikáwrd/ **1** set down in writing or some other permanent form for later reference, esp. as an official record. **2** convert (sound, a broadcast, etc.) into permanent form for later reproduction. **3** establish or constitute a historical or other record of. □ **break** (or **beat**) **the record** outdo all previous performances, etc. **for the record** as an official statement, etc. **go on record** state one's opinion or judgment openly or officially, so that it is recorded. **have a record** be known as a criminal. **a matter of record** a thing established as a fact by being recorded. **off the record** as an unofficial or confidential statement, etc. **on record** officially recorded; publicly known. **put** (or **get** or **set**, etc.) **the record straight** correct a misapprehension. **record player** an apparatus for reproducing sound from phonograph records. □□ **recordable** *adj.* [ME f. OF *record* remembrance, *recorder* record, f. L *recordari* remember (as RE-, *cor cordis* heart)]

■ *n.* **1** (*record* or *records*) documentation, data, information, evidence; report, document, archive(s), log, journal, memorandum, note, minute(s), annals, chronicle, diary, register, list, catalog *or* catalogue. **3 a** disk, album, release, LP, forty-five, single, *colloq.* platter. **5** history, reputation, track record, past, background, life; accomplishment(s), résumé, deed(s). **6** (best) performance; (*attrib.*) record-breaking. **7** see MEMENTO, PORTRAIT 1. ● *v.* **1** write (down), transcribe, document, register, note, make a note of, take down, put *or* set down, log, chronicle, report, itemize, list, enumerate, catalog. □ **off the record** confidential, unofficial, secret, private, between you and me; unofficially, privately, confidentially, not for publication, in (strict) confidence, sub rosa. **on record** see *well-known* 2 (WELL[1]). **record player** phonograph, gramophone.

recorder /rikáwrdər/ *n.* **1** an apparatus for recording, esp. a tape recorder. **2 a** a keeper of records. **b** a person who makes an official record. **3** *Brit.* **a** a barrister or solicitor of at least ten years' standing, appointed to serve as a part-time judge. **b** *hist.* a judge in certain courts. **4** *Mus.* a woodwind instrument like a flute but blown through the end and having a more hollow tone. □□ **recordership** *n.* (in sense 3). [ME f. AF *recordour*, OF *recordeur* & f. RECORD (in obs. sense 'practice a tune')]

recording /rikáwrding/ *n.* **1** the process by which audio or video signals are recorded for later reproduction. **2** material or a program recorded. □ **recording engineer** specialist who controls the recording of a record album, television show, etc.

■ **2** CD, compact disc; see also RECORD *n.* 3a, TAPE *n.* 4.

recordist /rikáwrdist/ *n.* **1** a person who records sound, esp. for a motion picture. **2** = *recording engineer*.

recount[1] /rikównt/ *v.tr.* **1** narrate. **2** tell in detail. [ONF & AF *reconter* (as RE-, COUNT[1])]

■ **1** relate, narrate, tell, recite, communicate, impart, unfold. **2** particularize, review, detail, describe, enumerate, specify, itemize, go over.

recount[2] *v. & n.* ● *v.* /reekównt/ *tr.* count again. ● *n.* /reekownt/ a recounting, esp. of votes in an election.

recoup /rikŏop/ *v.tr.* **1** recover or regain (a loss). **2** compensate or reimburse for a loss. **3** *Law* deduct or keep back (part of a sum due). □ **recoup oneself** recover a loss. □□ **recoupable** *adj.* **recoupment** *n.* [F *recouper* (as RE-, *couper* cut)]

■ **1** regain, make good, make up (for), repay, recover, redeem. **2** recompense, reimburse, compensate, repay, refund, pay back, remunerate.

recourse /reekawrs, rikáwrs/ *n.* **1** resorting to a possible source of help. **2** a person or thing resorted to. □ **have recourse to** turn to (a person or thing) for help. **without recourse** a formula used by the endorser of a bill, etc., to disclaim responsibility for payment. [ME f. OF *recours* f. L *recursus* (as RE-, COURSE)]

■ resort, access; backup, reserve, refuge, alternative, remedy.

recover /rikúvər/ *v. & n.* ● *v.* **1** *tr.* regain possession or use or control of, reclaim. **2** *intr.* return to health or consciousness or to a normal state or position (*have recovered from my illness; the country never recovered from the war*). **3** *tr.* obtain or secure (compensation, etc.) by legal process. **4** *tr.* retrieve or make up for (a loss, setback, etc.). **5** *refl.* regain composure or consciousness or control of one's limbs. **6** *tr.* retrieve (reusable substances) from industrial waste. ● *n.* the recovery of a normal position in fencing, etc. □□ **recoverable** *adj.* **recoverability** /-vərəbílitee/ *n.* **recoverer** *n.* [ME f. AF *recoverer*, OF *recovrer* f. L *recuperare* RECUPERATE]

■ *v.* **1** reclaim, retrieve, regain, get *or* take *or* win back (again), repossess, retake, recapture, bring back; save, salvage, rescue, restore. **2** get well *or* better, recuperate, convalesce, return to health, regain one's strength *or* health, be on the mend, improve, revive, rally, take a turn for the better, pull through, get over it; survive, live. **4** retrieve, make up (for), recoup, redeem, make good. **5** (*recover oneself*) see *pull oneself together*.

re-cover /reekúvər/ *v.tr.* **1** cover again. **2** provide (a chair, etc.) with a new cover.

recovery /rikúvəree/ *n.* (*pl.* **-ies**) **1** the act or an instance of recovering; the process of being recovered. **2** *Golf* a stroke bringing the ball out of a bunker, etc. [ME f. AF *recoverie*, OF *reco(u)vree* (as RECOVER)]

■ **1** recuperation, convalescence, improvement, rally, turn for the better, comeback; revival, advance, gain, advancement, *formal* amelioration; retrieval, repossession, retaking, reclamation, recapture, redemption, salvage, delivery, deliverance, rescue, return.

recreant /rékreeənt/ *adj. & n. literary* ● *adj.* **1** craven; cowardly. **2** apostate. ● *n.* **1** a coward. **2** an apostate. □□ **recreancy** *n.* **recreantly** *adv.* [ME f. OF, part. of *recroire* f. med.L (*se*) *recredere* yield in trial by combat (as RE-, *credere* entrust)]

■ *adj.* **1** see COWARDLY *adj.* **2** see DISLOYAL.

re-create /reekree-áyt/ *v.tr.* create over again. □□ **re-creation** *n.*

■ see REPRODUCE 1, 2.

recreation /rékree-áyshən/ *n.* **1** the process or means of refreshing or entertaining oneself. **2** a pleasurable activity. □□ **recreational** *adj.* **recreative** /rékreeáytiv/ *adj.* [ME f. OF f. L *recreatio -onis* f. *recreare* create again, renew]

■ entertainment, amusement, enjoyment, diversion, distraction, fun and games, leisure, relaxation, sport, play, R and R; leisure activity, pastime, hobby.

recriminate /rikríminayt/ *v.intr.* make mutual or counter accusations. □□ **recrimination** /-náyshən/ *n.* **recriminative** /-nətiv/ *adj.* **recriminatory** /-nətawree/ *adj.* [med.L *recriminare* (as RE-, *criminare* accuse f. *crimen* CRIME)]

■ □□ **recrimination** counteraccusation, countercharge, retaliation, counterattack, reprisal.

recross /reekráws, -krós/ *v.tr. & intr.* cross or pass over again.

recrudesce /reekrŏodés/ *v.intr.* (of a disease or difficulty, etc.) break out again, esp. after a dormant period. □□ **recrudescence** *n.* **recrudescent** *adj.* [back-form. f. *recrudescent*, -ence f. L *recrudescere* (as RE-, *crudus* raw)]

recruit /rikrŏot/ *n. & v.* ● *n.* **1** a serviceman or servicewoman newly enlisted and not yet fully trained. **2** a new member of a society or organization. **3** a beginner. ● *v.* **1** *tr.* enlist (a person) as a recruit. **2** *tr.* form (an army, etc.) by enlisting recruits. **3** *intr.* get or seek recruits. **4** *tr.* replenish or reinvigorate (numbers, strength, etc.). □□ **recruitable** *adj.* **recruiter** *n.* **recruitment** *n.* [earlier = reinforcement, f. obs. F dial. *recrute* ult. f. F *recroître* increase again f. L *recrescere*]

■ *n.* **1, 2** conscript, trainee, apprentice, draftee, *sl.* rookie; initiate, new boy, newcomer, freshman. **3** beginner, novice, neophyte, greenhorn, tyro, tenderfoot, fledgling, learner. ● *v.* **1** induct, enlist, enroll. **2** muster, raise, form; see also MOBILIZE. **4** replenish, restock, refill, fill *or* top up, reinvigorate.

recrystallize /reekrístəlīz/ *v.tr. & intr.* crystallize again. □□ **recrystallization** *n.*

recta pl. of RECTUM.

rectal /réktəl/ adj. of or by means of the rectum. □□ **rectally** adv.

rectangle /réktanggəl/ n. a plane figure with four straight sides and four right angles, esp. one with the adjacent sides unequal. [F *rectangle* or med.L *rectangulum* f. LL *rectiangulum* f. L *rectus* straight + *angulus* ANGLE¹]

rectangular /rektánggyələr/ adj. **1 a** shaped like a rectangle. **b** having the base or sides or section shaped like a rectangle. **2 a** placed at right angles. **b** having parts or lines placed at right angles. □ **rectangular coordinates** coordinates measured along axes at right angles. **rectangular hyperbola** a hyperbola with rectangular asymptotes. □□ **rectangularity** /-láritee/ n. **rectangularly** adv.

recti pl. of RECTUS.

rectifier /réktifiər/ n. **1** a person or thing that rectifies. **2** Electr. an electrical device that allows a current to flow preferentially in one direction by converting an alternating current into a direct one.

rectify /réktifī/ v.tr. (**-ies, -ied**) **1** adjust or make right; correct; amend. **2** purify or refine, esp. by repeated distillation. **3** find a straight line equal in length to (a curve). **4** convert (alternating current) to direct current. □□ **rectifiable** adj. **rectification** /-fikáyshən/ n. [ME f. OF *rectifier* f. med.L *rectificare* f. L *rectus* right]

■ **1** correct, redress, amend, put or set right, cure, repair, remedy, improve, emend, square, reconcile, adjust, *formal* ameliorate. **2** see REFINE 1.

rectilinear /réktilíneeər/ adj. (also **rectilineal** /-eeəl/) **1** bounded or characterized by straight lines. **2** in or forming a straight line. □□ **rectilinearity** /-neeáritee/ n. **rectilinearly** adv. [LL *rectilineus* f. L *rectus* straight + *linea* LINE¹]

rectitude /réktitōōd, -tyōōd/ n. **1** moral uprightness. **2** righteousness. **3** correctness. [ME f. OF *rectitude* or LL *rectitudo* f. L *rectus* right]

■ propriety, correctness, morality, uprightness, probity, virtue, decency, goodness, honesty, integrity, incorruptibility, righteousness, principle, good character, respectability.

recto /réktō/ n. (pl. **-os**) **1** the right-hand page of an open book. **2** the front of a printed leaf of paper or manuscript (opp. VERSO). [L *recto* (*folio*) on the right (leaf)]

rector /réktər/ n. **1** (in the Church of England) the incumbent of a parish where all tithes formerly passed to the incumbent (cf. VICAR). **2** RC Ch., Episcopal Ch. a priest in charge of a church or religious institution. **3 a** the head of some schools, universities, and colleges. **b** (in Scotland) an elected representative of students on a university's governing body. □□ **rectorate** /-rət/ n. **rectorial** /-táwreeəl/ adj. **rectorship** n. [ME f. OF *rectour* or L *rector* ruler f. *regere rect-* rule]

■ **1, 2** see CLERGYMAN. **3 a** see PRINCIPAL n. 2.

rectory /réktəree/ n. (pl. **-ies**) **1** a rector's house. **2** (in the Church of England) a rector's benefice. [AF & OF *rectorie* or med.L *rectoria* (as RECTOR)]

rectrix /réktriks/ n. (pl. **rectrices** /-triseez/) a bird's strong tail feather that directs flight. [L, fem. of *rector* ruler: see RECTOR]

rectum /réktəm/ n. (pl. **rectums** or **recta** /-tə/) the final section of the large intestine, terminating at the anus. [L *rectum* (*intestinum*) straight (intestine)]

rectus /réktəs/ n. (pl. **recti** /-tī/) Anat. a straight muscle. [L, = straight]

recumbent /rikúmbənt/ adj. lying down; reclining. □□ **recumbency** n. **recumbently** adv. [L *recumbere* recline (as RE-, *cumbere* lie)]

■ reclining, horizontal, reposing, supine, prone, prostrate, procumbent.

recuperate /rikōōpərayt/ v. **1** intr. recover from illness, exhaustion, loss, etc. **2** tr. regain (health, something lost, etc.). □□ **recuperable** adj. **recuperation** /-ráyshən/ n. **recuperative** /-rətiv/ adj. **recuperator** n. [L *recuperare* recuperat- recover]

■ **1** improve, recover, convalesce, get better, rally, revive, regain one's health or strength. **2** see RECOVER v. 1.

recur /rikər/ v.intr. (**recurred, recurring**) **1** occur again; be repeated. **2** (of a thought, idea, etc.) come back to one's mind. **3** (foll. by *to*) go back in thought or speech. □ **recurring decimal** = *repeating decimal*. [L *recurrere recurs-* (as RE-, *currere* run)]

■ **1** return, happen or occur again, reoccur, be repeated, repeat itself, come (back) again, reappear.

recurrent /rikərənt, -kúr-/ adj. **1** recurring; happening repeatedly. **2** (of a nerve, vein, branch, etc.) turning back so as to reverse direction. □□ **recurrence** n. **recurrently** adv.

■ **1** repeated, recurring, frequent, periodic, regular, repetitive, repetitious, persistent.

recursion /rikərzhən/ n. **1** the act or an instance of returning. **2** Math. the repeated application of a procedure or definition to a previous result to obtain a series of values. □ **recursion formula** Math. an expression giving successive terms of a series, etc. □□ **recursive** adj. [LL *recursio* (as RECUR)]

recurve /rikərv/ v.tr. & intr. bend backward. □□ **recurvate** /-vayt, -vət/ adj. **recurvature** n. [L *recurvare recurvat-* (as RE-, *curvare* bend)]

recusant /rékyəzənt, rikyōō-/ n. & adj. ● n. a person who refuses submission to an authority or compliance with a regulation, esp. Brit. hist. a Roman Catholic who refused to attend services of the Church of England. ● adj. of or being a recusant. □□ **recusance** n. **recusancy** n. [L *recusare* refuse]

■ n. see REBEL n.

recycle /reesíkəl/ v.tr. return (material) to a previous stage of a cyclic process, esp. convert (waste) to reusable material. □□ **recyclable** adj.

■ reuse, reclaim.

red /red/ adj. & n. ● adj. **1** of or near the color seen at the least-refracted end of the visible spectrum, of shades ranging from that of blood to pink or deep orange. **2** flushed in the face with shame, anger, etc. **3** (of the eyes) bloodshot or red-rimmed with weeping. **4** (of the hair) reddish-brown; orange; tawny. **5** involving or having to do with bloodshed, burning, violence, or revolution. **6** colloq. communist or socialist. **7** (**Red**) (formerly) Soviet or Russian (*the Red Army*). **8** (of wine) made from dark grapes and colored by their skins. ● n. **1** a red color or pigment. **2** red clothes or material (*dressed in red*). **3** colloq. a communist or socialist. **4 a** a red ball, piece, etc., in a game or sport. **b** the player using such pieces. **5** the debit side of an account (*in the red*). **6** a red light. □ **red admiral** a butterfly, *Vanessa atalanta*, with red bands on each pair of wings. **red alert 1** Mil. an alert sounded or given when an enemy attack appears imminent. **2** the signal for this. **red-blooded** virile; vigorous. **red-bloodedness** vigor, spirit. **red carpet** privileged treatment of an eminent visitor. **red cedar** an American juniper, *Juniperus virginiana*. **red cell** (or **corpuscle**) an erythrocyte. **red cent** the lowest-value (orig. copper) coin; a trivial sum (*not worth a red cent*). **Red Crescent** an organization like the Red Cross in Muslim countries. **red cross 1** St George's cross, the national emblem of England. **2** the Christian side in the crusades. **Red Cross 1** an international organization (originally medical) bringing relief to victims of war or natural disaster. **2** the emblem of this organization. **red deer** a deer, *Cervus elaphus*, of Europe and Asia, with a rich redbrown summer coat turning dull brown in winter. **red duster** Brit. colloq. = *red ensign*. **red dwarf** an old, relatively cool star. **red ensign** see ENSIGN. **red-eye 1** = RUDD. **2** latenight or overnight flight. **3** sl. cheap whiskey. **red-faced** embarrassed, ashamed. **red flag 1** the symbol of socialist revolution. **2** a warning of danger. **red fox** a fox, *Vulpes vulpes*, having a characteristic deep red or fawn coat. **red giant** a relatively cool giant star. **red grouse** a subspecies of the willow ptarmigan, native to Britain and noted for its

---

/. . ./ **pronunciation**	● **part of speech**
□ **phrases, idioms, and compounds**	
□□ **derivatives**	■ **synonym section**
cross-references appear in SMALL CAPITALS or *italics*	

lack of white winter plumage. **Red Guard** *hist.* a member of a militant youth movement in China (1966–76). **red gum 1** a teething rash in children. **2 a** a reddish resin. **b** any of various kinds of eucalyptus yielding this. **red-handed** in or just after the act of committing a crime, doing wrong, etc. (*caught them red-handed*). **red hat 1** a cardinal's hat. **2** the symbol of a cardinal's office. **red-headed 1** (of a person) having red hair. **2** (of birds, etc.) having a red head (*red-headed woodpecker*). **red heat 1** the temperature or state of something so hot as to emit red light. **2** great excitement. **red herring 1** dried smoked herring. **2** a misleading clue or distraction (so called from the practice of using the scent of red herring in training hounds). **red hot 1** *colloq.* a hot dog. **2** a small, red candy with a strong cinnamon flavor. **red-hot 1** heated until red. **2** highly exciting. **3** (of news) fresh; completely new. **4** intensely excited. **5** enraged. **red-hot poker** any plant of the genus *Kniphofia*, with spikes of usually red or yellow flowers. **Red Indian** *offens.* esp. *Brit.* = REDSKIN. **red lead** a red form of lead oxide used as a pigment. **red-letter day** a day that is pleasantly noteworthy or memorable (orig. a festival marked in red on the calendar). **red light 1** a signal to stop on a road, railroad, etc. **2** a warning or refusal. **red-light district** a district containing many brothels. **red man** *offens.* = REDSKIN. **red maple** a tree, *Acer rubram*, of eastern and central N. America, with reddish flowers and red leaves in the autumn. **red meat** meat that is red when raw (e.g., beef or lamb). **red mullet** a marine fish, *Mullus surmuletus*, valued as food. **red oak** any of several oak trees, as *Quercus rubra* or *Q. Borealis*, of eastern N. America. **red pepper 1** cayenne pepper. **2** the ripe fruit of the capsicum plant, *Capsicum annuum*. **red pine** a pine tree, *Pinus resinosa*, of eastern N. America. **red roan** see ROAN¹. **red rose** *Brit. Hist.* the emblem of Lancashire or the Lancastrians. **red spider** = *spider mite*. **red squirrel** a N. American squirrel, *Tamiasciurus hudsonicus*, with reddish fur. **red tape** excessive bureaucracy or adherence to formalities, esp. in public business. **red water 1** a bacterial disease of calves, a symptom of which is the passing of reddish urine. **2** a mass of water made red by pigmented plankton, esp. *Gonyanlax tamarensis*. □□ **reddish** *adj.* **reddy** *adj.* **redly** *adv.* **redness** *n.* [OE *rēad* f. Gmc]

■ *adj.* **1** crimson, scarlet, vermilion, burgundy, cherry, maroon, cardinal, russet, wine, ruby; *Bot.* & *Zool.* testaceous, *Heraldry* gules, *Heraldry or literary* sanguine; see also ROSY 1. **2** blushing, red-faced, red in the face, shamefaced, discountenanced, embarrassed, abashed. **4** orange, ginger, sandy, strawberry blonde, tawny, chestnut, copper, auburn, foxy, reddish-brown. **6** see LEFT¹ *adj.* 3. ● *n.* **1** see RED *adj.* 1 above. **3** see *left-winger* (LEFT¹). **5** (*in the red*) see DEBT. □ **red-blooded** see TOUGH *adj.* 2. **red-bloodedness** see VIGOR 1. **red-eye 3** see LIQUOR *n.* 1. **red-faced** see ASHAMED 1. **red-handed** in the (very) act, in flagrante (delicto), *colloq.* with one's hand in the till. **red herring 2** see *misinformation* (MISINFORM). **red-hot** *adj.* **1** see HOT *adj.* 1. **2** see EXCITING. **3** see *brand-new*. **4** see HOT *adj.* 5a. **5** see FURIOUS 1, 2. **red light 2** see WARNING 1, REFUSAL 1. **red tape** see BUREAUCRACY. □□ **reddish** see ROSY 1. **redness** see FLUSH¹ *n.* 1.

redact /ridákt/ *v.tr.* put into literary form; edit for publication. □□ **redactor** *n.* [L *redigere redact-* (as RE-, *agere* bring)]
■ see EDIT *v.* 1. □□ **redactor** see EDITOR 1.

redaction /ridákshən/ *n.* **1** preparation for publication. **2** revision; editing; rearrangement. **3** a new edition. □□ **redactional** *adj.* [F *rédaction* f. LL *redactio* (as REDACT)]
■ **2** see REVISION 1.

redan /ridán/ *n.* a fieldwork with two faces forming a salient angle. [F f. *redent* notching (as RE-, *dent* tooth)]

redbreast /rédbrest/ *n. colloq.* a robin, esp. the N. American robin, *Turdus migratorius*.

redbrick /rédbrik/ *adj.* esp. *Brit.* (of a university) founded relatively recently.

redbud /rédbud/ *n.* any American tree of the genus *Cercis*, with pale pink flowers.

redcap /rédkap/ *n.* **1** a baggage porter. **2** *Brit.* a member of the military police.

redcoat /rédkōt/ *n. hist.* a British soldier (so called from the scarlet uniform of most regiments).

redd /red/ *v.tr.* (*past* and *past part.* **redd**) *dial.* **1** clear up. **2** arrange; tidy; compose; settle. [ME: cf. MLG, MDu. *redden*]

redden /réd'n/ *v.tr.* & *intr.* make or become red.
■ go red; see also FLUSH¹ *v.* 1a.

reddle /réd'l/ *n.* red ocher; ruddle. [var. of RUDDLE]

rede /reed/ *n.* & *v.* esp. *Brit. archaic* ● *n.* advice, counsel. ● *v.tr.* **1** advise. **2** read (a riddle or dream). [OE *rǣd* f. Gmc, rel. to READ (of which the verb is a ME var. retained for archaic senses)]

redecorate /reedékərayt/ *v.tr.* decorate again or differently. □□ **redecoration** /-ráyshən/ *n.*
■ see DECORATE 2.

redeem /rideém/ *v.tr.* **1** buy back; recover by expenditure of effort or by a stipulated payment. **2** make a single payment to discharge (a regular charge or obligation). **3** convert (tokens or bonds, etc.) into goods or cash. **4** (of God or Christ) deliver from sin and damnation. **5** make up for; be a compensating factor in (*has one redeeming feature*). **6** (foll. by *from*) save from (a defect). **7** *refl.* save (oneself) from blame. **8** purchase the freedom of (a person). **9** save (a person's life) by ransom. **10** save or rescue or reclaim. **11** fulfill (a promise). □□ **redeemable** *adj.* [ME f. OF *redimer* or L *redimere redempt-* (as RE-, *emere* buy)]
■ **1** reclaim, recover, regain, repossess, retrieve, get back, buy back, repurchase. **2** see PAY¹ *v.* 2. **3** exchange, convert, cash (in), collect on, trade in. **4** save, rescue, absolve, deliver (from evil). **5** reinstate, restore to favor, rehabilitate, make amends for; make up for, atone for, redress, compensate for, offset, make restitution for. **8** ransom, reclaim, deliver, free, liberate, set free, emancipate, release. **9, 10** see RECLAIM *v.* 1, 3. **11** perform, fulfill, keep, make good, discharge, satisfy, abide by, keep faith with, be faithful to, hold to, carry out, see through.

redeemer /rideémər/ *n.* a person who redeems. □ **the Redeemer** Christ.
■ see SAVIOR 1.

redefine /reedifín/ *v.tr.* define again or differently. □□ **redefinition** /-definíshən/ *n.*

redemption /ridémpshən/ *n.* **1** the act or an instance of redeeming; the process of being redeemed. **2** man's deliverance from sin and damnation. **3** a thing that redeems. □□ **redemptive** *adj.* [ME f. OF f. L *redemptio* (as REDEEM)]
■ **1** see RECOVERY. □□ **redemptive** redeeming, compensating, compensatory, qualifying, extenuating, extenuatory.

redeploy /reediplóy/ *v.tr.* send (troops, workers, etc.) to a new place or task. □□ **redeployment** *n.*

redesign /reedizín/ *v.tr.* design again or differently.
■ see MODIFY 2.

redetermine /reeditərmin/ *v.tr.* determine again or differently. □□ **redetermination** *n.*

redevelop /reedivéləp/ *v.tr.* develop anew (esp. an urban area, with new buildings). □□ **redeveloper** *n.* **redevelopment** *n.*

redfish /rédfish/ *n.* **1** a bright red food fish, *Sebastes marinus*, of the N. Atlantic; a rosefish. **2** *Brit.* a male salmon in the spawning season.

redhead /rédhed/ *n.* a person with red hair.

redial /reedíəl, -díl/ *v.tr.* & *intr.* dial again.

redid *past* of REDO.

redingote /rédinggōt/ *n.* a woman's long coat with a cutaway front and a contrasting piece on the front. [F f. E *riding coat*]

redintegrate /ridíntigrayt/ *v.tr.* **1** restore to wholeness or unity. **2** renew or reestablish in a united or perfect state. □□ **redintegration** /-gráyshən/ *n.* **redintegrative** /-grətiv/ *adj.* [ME f. L *redintegrare* (as RE-, INTEGRATE)]

redirect /reedirékt, -di-/ *v.tr.* direct again, esp. change the address of (a letter). □□ **redirection** *n.*

■ see DIVERT 1a.

rediscover /re͞ediskúvər/ *v.tr.* discover again. □□ **rediscovery** *n.* (*pl.* **-ies**).

redissolve /re͞edizólv/ *v.tr.* & *intr.* dissolve again. □□ **redissolution** /-disəlo͞oshən/ *n.*

redistribute /re͞edistríbyo͞ot/ *v.tr.* distribute again or differently. □□ **redistribution** /-byo͞oshən/ *n.* **redistributive** /-tríbyo͞otiv/ *adj.*

redivide /re͞edivíd/ *v.tr.* divide again or differently. □□ **redivision** /-vízhən/ *n.*

redivivus /rédivívəs, -ve͞evəs/ *adj.* (placed after noun) come back to life. [L (as RE-, *vivus* living)]

redneck /rédnek/ *n.* often *derog.* a working-class, politically conservative or reactionary white person, esp. in the rural southern US.

redo /re͞edo͞o/ *v.tr.* (*3rd sing. present* **redoes**; *past* **redid**; *past part.* **redone**) **1** do again or differently. **2** redecorate.

redolent /rédʼlənt/ *adj.* **1** (foll. by *of, with*) strongly reminiscent or suggestive or mentally associated. **2** fragrant. **3** having a strong smell; odorous. □□ **redolence** *n.* **redolently** *adv.* [ME f. OF *redolent* or L *redolēre* (as RE-, *olēre* smell)]

■ **1** (*redolent with* or *of*) reminiscent of, suggestive of, evocative of, remindful of, similar to, comparable with *or* to. **2** fragrant, sweet-smelling, aromatic, perfumed, scented, odoriferous, ambrosial, sweet-scented. **3** odorous, aromatic, smelly.

redouble /re͞edúbəl/ *v.* & *n.* ● *v.* **1** *tr.* & *intr.* make or grow greater or more intense or numerous; intensify; increase. **2** *intr. Bridge* double again a bid already doubled by an opponent. ● *n. Bridge* the redoubling of a bid. [F *redoubler* (as RE-, DOUBLE)]

redoubt /ridówt/ *n. Mil.* an outwork or fieldwork usu. square or polygonal and without flanking defenses. [F *redoute* f. obs. It. *ridotta* f. med.L *reductus* refuge f. past part. of L *reducere* withdraw (see REDUCE): -*b*- after DOUBT (cf. REDOUBTABLE)]

redoubtable /ridówtəbəl/ *adj.* formidable, esp. as an opponent. □□ **redoubtably** *adv.* [ME f. OF *redoutable* f. *redouter* fear (as RE-, DOUBT)]

redound /ridównd/ *v.intr.* **1** (foll. by *to*) (of an action, etc.) make a great contribution to (one's credit or advantage, etc.). **2** (foll. by *upon, on*) come as the final result to; come back or recoil upon. [ME, orig. = overflow, f. OF *redonder* f. L *redundare* surge (as RE-, *unda* wave)]

redox /re͞edoks/ *n. Chem.* (often *attrib.*) oxidation and reduction. [*reduction* + *oxidation*]

redpoll /rédpōl/ *n.* any of several small finches with a red patch on the forehead.

redraft /re͞edráft/ *v.tr.* draft (a writing or document) again.

redraw /re͞edráw/ *v.tr.* (*past* **redrew**; *past part.* **redrawn**) draw again or differently.

redress /ridrés/ *v.* & *n.* ● *v.tr.* **1** remedy or rectify (a wrong or grievance, etc.). **2** readjust; set straight again. ● *n.* also /re͞edres/ **1** reparation for a wrong. **2** (foll. by *of*) the act or process of redressing (a grievance, etc.). □ **redress the balance** restore equality. □□ **redressable** *adj.* **redressal** *n.* **redresser** *n.* (also **redressor**). [ME f. OF *redresse(r)*, *redrecier* (as RE-, DRESS)]

re-dress /re͞edrés/ *v.tr.* & *intr.* dress again or differently.

redshank /rédshangk/ *n.* either of two sandpipers, *Tringa totanus* and *T. erythropus*, with bright red legs.

redshift /rédshift/ *n. Astron.* the displacement of the spectrum to longer wavelengths in the light coming from distant galaxies, etc., in recession.

redskin /rédskin/ *n. colloq. offens.* a Native American.

redstart /rédstaart/ *n.* **1** any European red-tailed songbird of the genus *Phoenicurus*. **2** any of various similar American warblers of the family Parulidae. [RED + OE *steort* tail]

reduce /rido͞os, -dyo͞os/ *v.* **1** *tr.* & *intr.* make or become smaller or less. **2** *tr.* (foll. by *to*) bring by force or necessity (to some undesirable state or action) (*reduced them to tears*; *were reduced to begging*). **3** *tr.* convert to another (esp. simpler) form (*reduced it to a powder*). **4** *tr.* convert (a fraction) to the form with the lowest terms. **5** *tr.* (foll. by *to*) bring or simplify or adapt by classification or analysis (*the dispute may*

be reduced to three issues). **6** *tr.* make lower in status or rank. **7** *tr.* lower the price of. **8** *intr.* lessen one's weight or size. **9** *tr.* weaken (*is in a very reduced state*). **10** *tr.* impoverish. **11** *tr.* subdue; bring back to obedience. **12** *Chem. intr.* & *tr.* **a** combine or cause to combine with hydrogen. **b** undergo or cause to undergo addition of electrons. **13** *tr. Chem.* convert (oxide, etc.) to metal. **14** *tr.* **a** (in surgery) restore (a dislocated, etc., part) to its proper position. **b** remedy (a dislocation, etc.) in this way. **15** *tr. Photog.* make (a negative or print) less dense. **16** *tr. Cookery* boil off excess liquid from. □ **reduced circumstances** poverty after relative prosperity. **reduce to the ranks** demote (an NCO) to the rank of private. **reducing agent** *Chem.* a substance that brings about reduction by oxidation and losing electrons. □□ **reducer** *n.* **reducible** *adj.* **reducibility** *n.* [ME in sense 'restore to original or proper position,' f. L *reducere* *reduct-* (as RE-, *ducere* bring)]

■ **1** decrease, diminish, abate, lessen; ease (up on), let up (on), moderate, tone down, slacken up (on); cut (back), cut down, shorten, crop, trim, compress. **2** (*reduce to*) bring to, force to, push *or* drive to. **3** turn, convert; break down *or* up; see also CHANGE *v.* 1. **6** demote, degrade, lower, downgrade, reduce to the ranks, relegate, *colloq.* bust, *Mil.* break, *Naut.* disrate. **7** cut, decrease, bring down, lower, drop, mark down, slash, *colloq.* knock down. **8** lose *or* shed weight, slim (down), diet, trim down, slenderize. **9** see WEAKEN 1. **10** see RUIN *v.* 1a. **11** see SUBDUE 1. **14** a set, adjust, reset. **16** boil down, distill; see also CONCENTRATE *v.* 3. □ **reduced circumstances** see POVERTY 1. **reduce to the ranks** see REDUCE 6 above.

reductio ad absurdum /ridúkte͞eō ad absórdəm/ *n.* a method of proving the falsity of a premise by showing that the logical consequence is absurd; an instance of this. [L, = reduction to the absurd]

reduction /ridúkshən/ *n.* **1** the act or an instance of reducing; the process of being reduced. **2** an amount by which prices, etc., are reduced. **3** a reduced copy of a picture, etc. **4** an arrangement of an orchestral score for piano, etc. □□ **reductive** *adj.* [ME f. OF *reduction* or L *reductio* (as REDUCE)]

reductionism /ridúkshənizəm/ *n.* **1** the tendency to or principle of analyzing complex things into simple constituents. **2** often *derog.* the doctrine that a system can be fully understood in terms of its isolated parts, or an idea in terms of simple concepts. □□ **reductionist** *n.* **reductionistic** /-nístik/ *adj.*

redundant /ridúndənt/ *adj.* **1** superfluous; not needed. **2** that can be omitted without any loss of significance. **3** *Brit.* (of a person) no longer needed for work and therefore unemployed. **4** *Engin.* & *Computing* (of a component) not needed but included in case of failure in another component. □□ **redundancy** *n.* (*pl.* **-ies**). **redundantly** *adv.* [L *redundare* *redundant-* (as REDOUND)]

■ **1** superfluous, unnecessary, surplus, inessential, unessential, nonessential, unneeded, unwanted, de trop. **3** see UNEMPLOYED 1.

reduplicate /rido͞oplikayt, -dyo͞o-/ *v.tr.* **1** make double. **2** repeat. **3** repeat (a letter or syllable or word) exactly or with a slight change (e.g., hurly-burly, go-go). □□ **reduplication** /-káyshən/ *n.* **reduplicative** /-kətiv/ *adj.* [LL *reduplicare* (as RE-, DUPLICATE)]

redwing /rédwing/ *n.* a thrush, *Turdus iliacus*, with red underwings showing in flight. □ **redwing** (also **red-winged**) **blackbird** a N. American blackbird, *Agelaius phoeniceus*, the male of which is marked with scarlet wing patches.

redwood /rédwo͞od/ *n.* **1** an exceptionally large Californian conifer, *Sequoia sempervirens*, yielding red wood. **2** any tree yielding red wood.

/.../ pronunciation	● part of speech
□ phrases, idioms, and compounds	
□□ derivatives	■ synonym section
cross-references appear in SMALL CAPITALS or *italics*	

reebok var of RHEBOK.

reecho /reé-ékō/ *v.intr.* & *tr.* (**-oes, -oed**) **1** echo. **2** echo repeatedly; resound.

reed¹ /reed/ *n.* & *v.* ● *n.* **1 a** any of various water or marsh plants with a firm stem, esp. of the genus *Phragmites*. **b** a tall straight stalk of this. **2** (*collect.*) reeds growing in a mass or used as material esp. for thatching. **3** *Brit.* wheat straw prepared for thatching. **4** a pipe of reed or straw. **5 a** the vibrating part of the mouthpiece of some wind instruments, e.g., the oboe and clarinet, made of reed or other material and producing the sound. **b** (esp. in *pl.*) a reed instrument. **6** a weaver's comblike implement for separating the threads of the warp and correctly positioning the weft. **7** (in *pl.*) a set of semicylindrical adjacent moldings like reeds laid together. ● *v.tr.* **1** thatch with reed. **2** make (straw) into reed. **3** fit (a musical instrument) with a reed. **4** decorate with a molding of reeds. **reed organ** a harmonium, etc., with the sound produced by metal reeds. **reed pipe 1** a wind instrument with sound produced by a reed. **2** a pipe-organ pipe with a reed. **reed stop** a reeded organ stop. [OE *hrēod* f. WG]

reed² /reed/ *n. Brit.* the abomasum. [OE *rēada*]

reedbuck /reédbuk/ *n.* an antelope, *Redunca redunca*, native to W. Africa.

reeded /reédid/ *adj. Mus.* (of an instrument) having a vibrating reed.

reeding /reéding/ *n. Archit.* a small semicylindrical molding or ornamentation (cf. REED¹ *n.* 7).

reedit /ree-édit/ *v.tr.* edit again or differently. □□ **reedition** /reéidíshən/ *n.*

reeducate /ree-édjəkayt/ *v.tr.* educate again, esp. to change a person's views or beliefs. □□ **reeducation** /-káyshən/ *n.*

reedy /reédee/ *adj.* (**reedier, reediest**) **1** full of reeds. **2** like a reed, esp. in weakness or slenderness. **3** (of a voice) like a reed instrument in tone; not full. □□ **reediness** *n.*

reef¹ /reef/ *n.* **1** a ridge of rock or coral, etc., at or near the surface of the sea. **2 a** a lode of ore. **b** the bedrock surrounding this. [earlier *riff(e)* f. MDu., MLG *rif, ref,* f. ON *rif* RIB]

reef² /reef/ *n.* & *v. Naut.* ● *n.* each of several strips across a sail, for taking it in or rolling it up to reduce the surface area in a high wind. ● *v.tr.* **1** take in a reef or reefs of (a sail). **2** shorten (a topmast or a bowsprit). □ **reef knot** a double knot made symmetrically to hold securely and cast off easily. [ME *riff, refe* f. Du. *reef, rif* f. ON *rif* RIB, in the same sense: cf. REEF¹]

reefer /reéfər/ *n.* **1** *sl.* a marijuana cigarette. **2** a thick close-fitting double-breasted jacket. [REEF² (in sense 1, = a thing rolled) + -ER¹]

reek /reek/ *v.* & *n.* ● *v.intr.* (often foll. by *of*) **1** smell strongly and unpleasantly. **2** have unpleasant or suspicious associations (*this reeks of corruption*). **3** give off smoke or fumes. ● *n.* **1** a foul or stale smell. **2** esp. *Sc.* smoke. **3** vapor; a visible exhalation (esp. from a chimney). □□ **reeky** *adj.* [OE *rēocan* (v.), *rēc* (n.), f. Gmc]

■ *v.* **1** stink, smell, smell to high heaven, *Brit. colloq.* pong, hum. **2** (*reek of*) be redolent of, suggest, smell of, smack of, savor of, imply. **3** smoke, steam, give off smoke, fume. ● *n.* **1** stink, stench, fetor, mephitis, odor, smell, *archaic* miasma, *Brit. colloq.* hum, pong. **2, 3** fumes, smoke, steam, vapor, cloud, mist, exhalation.

reel /reel/ *n.* & *v.* ● *n.* **1** a cylindrical device on which thread, silk, yarn, paper, film, wire, etc., are wound. **2** a quantity of thread, etc., wound on a reel. **3** a device for winding and unwinding a line as required, esp. in fishing. **4** a revolving part in various machines. **5 a** a lively folk or Scottish dance, of two or more couples facing each other. **b** a piece of music for this. ● *v.* **1** *tr.* wind (thread, a fishing line, etc.) on a reel. **2** *tr.* (foll. by *in, up*) draw (fish, etc.) in or up by the use of a reel. **3** *intr.* stand or walk or run unsteadily. **4** *intr.* be shaken mentally or physically. **5** *intr.* rock from side to side, or swing violently. **6** *intr.* dance a reel. □ **reel off** say or recite very rapidly and without apparent effort. □□ **reeler** *n.* [OE *hrēol*, of unkn. orig.]

■ *v.* **3** stagger, totter, waver, stumble, lurch, falter, flounder. **5** roll, rock, sway, pitch, swing, lurch. □ **reel off** list, recite, rattle off, enumerate, review, itemize, read off, call off, run through, run over.

reelect /reéilékt/ *v.tr.* elect again, esp. to a further term of office. □□ **reelection** /-ílékshən/ *n.*

reembark /reéimbaárk/ *v.intr.* & *tr.* go or put on board ship again. □□ **reembarkation** *n.*

reemerge /reéimárj/ *v.intr.* emerge again; come back out. □□ **reemergence** *n.* **reemergent** *adj.*

reemphasize /ree-émfəsīz/ *v.tr.* place renewed emphasis on. □□ **reemphasis** /-émfəsis/ *n.*

reemploy /reéimplóy/ *v.tr.* employ again. □□ **reemployment** *n.*

reenact /reéinákt/ *v.tr.* act out (a past event). □□ **reenactment** *n.*

reenlist /reéinlíst/ *v.intr.* enlist again, esp. in the armed services. □□ **reenlister** *n.*

reenter /ree-éntər/ *v.tr.* & *intr.* enter again; go back in. □□ **reentrance** /-éntrəns/ *n.*

reentrant /ree-éntrənt/ *adj.* & *n.* ● *adj.* **1** esp. *Fortification* (of an angle) pointing inward (opp. SALIENT). **2** *Geom.* reflex. ● *n.* a reentrant angle.

reentry /ree-éntree/ *n.* (*pl.* **-ies**) **1** the act of entering again, esp. (of a spacecraft, missile, etc.) reentering the earth's atmosphere. **2** *Law* an act of retaking or repossession.

reequip /reéikwíp/ *v.tr.* & *intr.* (**-equipped, -equipping**) provide or be provided with new equipment.

reerect /reéirékt/ *v.tr.* erect again.

reestablish /reéistáblish/ *v.tr.* establish again or anew. □□ **reestablishment** *n.*

reevaluate /reéiványōō-ayt/ *v.tr.* evaluate again or differently. □□ **reevaluation** /-áyshən/ *n.*

reeve¹ /reev/ *n.* **1** *hist.* **a** the chief administrator of a town or district. **b** *Brit.* an official supervising a landowner's estate. **c** any of various minor local officials. **2** *Can.* the president of a village or town council. [OE (*ge*)*rēfa, girǣfa*]

reeve² /reev/ *v.tr.* (*past* **rove** /rōv/ or **reeved**) *Naut.* **1** (usu. foll. by *through*) thread (a rope or rod, etc.) through a ring or other aperture. **2** pass a rope through (a block, etc.). **3** fasten (a rope or block) in this way. [prob. f. Du. *rēven* REEF²]

reeve³ /reev/ *n.* a female ruff (see RUFF¹). [17th c.: orig. unkn.]

reexamine /reéigzámin/ *v.tr.* examine again or further (esp. a witness after cross-examination). □□ **reexamination** /-náyshən/ *n.*

reexport *v.* & *n.* ● *v.tr.* /reéikspáwrt/ export again (esp. imported goods after further processing or manufacture). ● *n.* /ree-ékspawrt/ **1** the process of reexporting. **2** something reexported. □□ **reexportation** *n.* **reexporter** *n.*

ref /ref/ *n. colloq.* a referee in sports. [abbr.]

ref. *abbr.* **1** reference. **2** refer to.

reface /reéfáys/ *v.tr.* put a new facing on (a building).

refashion /reéfáshən/ *v.tr.* fashion again or differently.

refection /rifékshən/ *n. literary* **1** refreshment by food or drink (*we took refection*). **2** a light meal. [ME f. OF f. L *refectio -onis* f. *reficere* (as REFECTORY)]

refectory /riféktəree/ *n.* (*pl.* **-ies**) a room used for communal meals, esp. in a monastery or college. □ **refectory table** a long narrow table. [LL *refectorium* f. L *reficere* refresh (as RE-, *facere* make)]

refer /rifər/ *v.* (**referred, referring**) (usu. foll. by *to*) **1** *tr.* trace or ascribe (to a person or thing as a cause or source) (*referred their success to their popularity*). **2** *tr.* consider as belonging (to a certain date or place or class). **3** *tr.* send on or direct (a person, or a question for decision) (*the matter was referred to arbitration; referred him to her previous answer*). **4** *intr.* make an appeal or have recourse to (some authority or source of information) (*referred to his notes*). **5** *tr.* send (a person) to a medical specialist, etc. **6** *tr.* (foll. by *back to*) send (a proposal, etc.) back to (a lower body, court, etc.). **7** *intr.* (foll. by *to*) (of a person speaking) make an allusion or direct the hearer's attention (*decided not to refer to our other problems*). **8** *intr.* (foll. by *to*) (of a statement, etc.) have a particular relation; be directed (*this paragraph refers to the events of last year*). **9** *tr.* (foll. by *to*) interpret (a statement) as being directed to (a particular context, etc.). **10** *tr.* fail (a candidate in an examination). □□ **referable** /riférəbəl, réfər-/ *adj.* **referrer** *n.* [ME f. OF *referer* f. L *referre* carry back (as RE-, *ferre* bring)]

■ **1** see ATTRIBUTE *v.* **3** hand over, pass on *or* over, send on, assign, commit; direct, point. **4** (*refer to*) look at, study, check, consult, resort to, have recourse to, turn to, appeal to, confer with; talk to, ask, inquire of, apply to. **7, 8** (*refer to*) allude to, make reference to, mention, make mention of, touch on, bring up, speak of, talk *or* write about, turn *or* call *or* direct attention to, indicate, point to, specify, pick out, single out, quote, cite, *literary* advert to.

referee /réfəree/ *n.* & *v.* ● *n.* **1** an umpire, esp. in sports, such as football, boxing, etc. **2** a person whose opinion or judgment is sought in some connection, or who is referred to for a decision in a dispute, etc. **3** *Brit.* a person willing to testify to the character of an applicant for employment, etc. ● *v.* (**referees, refereed**) **1** *intr.* act as referee. **2** *tr.* be the referee of (a game, etc.).

reference /réfərəns, réfrəns/ *n.* & *v.* ● *n.* **1** the referring of a matter for decision or settlement or consideration to some authority. **2** the scope given to this authority. **3** (foll. by *to*) **a** a relation or respect or correspondence (*success seems to have little reference to merit*). **b** an allusion (*made no reference to our problems*). **c** a direction to a book, etc., (or a passage in it) where information may be found. **d** a book or passage so cited. **4 a** the act of looking up a passage, etc., or looking in a book for information. **b** the act of referring to a person, etc., for information. **5 a** a written testimonial supporting an applicant for employment, etc. **b** a person giving this. ● *v.tr.* provide (a book, etc.) with references to authorities. □ **reference book** a book intended to be consulted for information on individual matters rather than read continuously. **reference library** a library in which the books are for consultation not loan. **with** (or **in**) **reference to** regarding; as regards; about. **without reference to** not taking account of. □□ **referential** /réfərénshəl/ *adj.*

■ *n.* **1** referral, *Law* appeal. **3 a** regard, concern, connection, respect, relation, correspondence, relevance, pertinence. **b** allusion, mention, remark; hint, intimation, innuendo, insinuation. **c** direction, indication, specification, quotation, citation, note, notation. **5 a** endorsement, recommendation, testimonial. **b** referee.

referendum /réfəréndəm/ *n.* (*pl.* **referendums** or **referenda** /-də/) **1** the process of referring a political question to the electorate for a direct decision by general vote. **2** a vote taken by referendum. [L, gerund or neut. gerundive of *referre*: see REFER]

referent /réfərənt/ *n.* the idea or thing that a word, etc., symbolizes. [L *referens* (as REFERENDUM)]

referral /rifərəl/ *n.* the referring of an individual to an expert or specialist for advice, esp. the directing of a patient by a GP to a medical specialist.

refill *v.* & *n.* ● *v.tr.* /reefíl/ **1** fill again. **2** provide a new filling for. ● *n.* /réefil/ **1** a new filling. **2** the material for this. □□ **refillable** *adj.*

refine /rifín/ *v.* **1** *tr.* free from impurities or defects; purify; clarify. **2** *tr.* & *intr.* make or become more polished or elegant or cultured. **3** *tr.* & *intr.* make or become more subtle or delicate in thought, feelings, etc. □□ **refinable** *adj.* [RE- + FINE¹ *v.*]

■ **1** clear, clarify, decontaminate, *usu. formal* cleanse; see also PURIFY. **2** cultivate, civilize, polish, improve, elevate, perfect. **3** hone, sharpen, concentrate, focus, subtilize; see also ENHANCE.

refined /rifínd/ *adj.* **1** characterized by polish or elegance or subtlety. **2** purified; clarified.

■ **1** cultivated, cultured, civilized, polished, sophisticated, urbane, elegant, well-bred, genteel, courtly, ladylike, gentlemanly, polite, courteous, mannerly, well-

mannered, gracious, dignified, elevated; subtle, discriminating, discerning, sensitive, fastidious, nice, precise, exacting, educated, advanced. **2** purified, clarified, pure, clean, *usu. formal* cleansed; filtered, distilled.

refinement /rifínmənt/ *n.* **1** the act of refining or the process of being refined. **2** fineness of feeling or taste. **3** polish or elegance in behavior or manner. **4** an added development or improvement (*a car with several refinements*). **5** a piece of subtle reasoning. **6** a fine distinction. **7** a subtle or ingenious example or display (*all the refinements of reasoning*). [REFINE + -MENT, after F *raffinement*]

■ **1** improvement, betterment, enhancement, development, perfection; purification, clarification, cleaning, filtration, distillation, *usu. formal* cleansing. **2** fineness, delicacy, discrimination, discernment, sensitivity, finesse. **3** culture, polish, elegance, sophistication, urbanity, urbaneness, breeding, cultivation, gentility, propriety, courtliness, civility, politeness, tact, diplomacy, finesse, suavity, suaveness, good taste. **4** see IMPROVEMENT 1, 2. **6** subtlety, nicety, nuance, distinction, detail, fine point, minutia.

refiner /rifínər/ *n.* a person or firm whose business is to refine crude oil, metal, sugar, etc.

refinery /rifínəree/ *n.* (*pl.* **-ies**) a place where oil, etc., is refined.

refit *v.* & *n.* ● *v.tr.* & *intr.* /reefít/ (**refitted, refitting**) make or become fit or serviceable again (esp. of a ship undergoing renewal and repairs). ● *n.* /réefit/ the act or an instance of refitting; the process of being refitted. □□ **refitment** *n.*

refl. *abbr.* **1** reflex. **2** reflexive.

reflate /reefláyt/ *v.tr.* cause reflation of (a currency or economy, etc.). [RE- after *inflate, deflate*]

reflation /reefláyshən/ *n.* the inflation of a financial system to restore its previous condition after deflation. □□ **reflationary** *adj.* [RE- after *inflation, deflation*]

reflect /riflékt/ *v.* **1** *tr.* **a** (of a surface or body) throw back (heat, light, sound, etc.). **b** cause to rebound (*reflected light*). **2** *tr.* (of a mirror) show an image of; reproduce to the eye or mind. **3** *tr.* correspond in appearance or effect to; have as a cause or source (*their behavior reflects a wish to succeed*). **4** *tr.* **a** (of an action, result, etc.) show or bring (credit, discredit, etc.). **b** (*absol.*; usu. foll. by *on, upon*) bring discredit on. **5 a** *intr.* (often foll. by *on, upon*) meditate on; think about. **b** *tr.* (foll. by *that, how,* etc., + clause) consider; remind oneself. **6** *intr. Brit.* (usu. foll. by *upon, on*) make disparaging remarks. □ **reflecting telescope** = REFLECTOR. [ME f. OF *reflecter* or L *reflectere* (as RE-, *flectere flex-* bend)]

■ **1** mirror, send *or* throw back, return; echo. **3** show, demonstrate, exhibit, illustrate, exemplify, reveal, lay bare, expose, display, disclose, bring to light, uncover, point to, indicate, suggest, evidence. **4 a** bring, attract, cast, throw. **5 a** (*reflect on* or *upon*) think about *or* over *or* on, contemplate, consider, ponder about *or* over *or* on, deliberate on *or* over, ruminate *or* meditate about *or* on *or* over, cogitate about *or* on *or* over, mull over, *literary* muse about *or* on. **b** remind oneself, remember; see also CONSIDER 1.

reflection /riflékshən/ *n.* (also *Brit.* **reflexion**) **1** the act or an instance of reflecting; the process of being reflected. **2 a** reflected light, heat, or color. **b** a reflected image. **3** meditation; reconsideration (*on reflection*). **4** (often foll. by *on*) discredit or a thing bringing discredit. **5** (often foll. by *on, upon*) an idea arising in the mind; a comment or apothegm. **6** (usu. foll. by *of*) a consequence; evidence (*a reflection of how she feels*). □ **angle of reflection** *Physics* the angle made by a reflected ray with a perpendicular to the reflecting surface. □□ **reflectional** *adj.* [ME f. OF *reflexion* or LL *reflexio* (as REFLECT), with assim. to *reflect*]

■ **1** image, echo. **3** thought, thinking, meditation, consideration, cogitation, rumination, deliberation, pondering, cerebration; reconsideration, second thoughts. **4** see DISCREDIT *n.* 1. **5** see THOUGHT[1] 4, COMMENT *n.* 1. **6** result, consequence; sign, token, symbol, mark; evidence, testimony, testament, proof, substantiation, corroboration.

reflective /rifléktiv/ *adj.* **1** (of a surface, etc.) giving a reflection or image. **2** (of mental faculties) concerned in reflection or thought. **3** (of a person or mood, etc.) thoughtful; given to meditation. □□ **reflectively** *adv.* **reflectiveness** *n.*
■ **3** thoughtful, pensive, contemplative, meditative, cogitative, ruminative, deliberative.

reflector /rifléktər/ *n.* **1** a piece of glass or metal, etc., for reflecting light in a required direction, e.g., a red one on the back of a motor vehicle or bicycle. **2 a** a telescope, etc., using a mirror to produce images. **b** the mirror itself.

reflet /rəfláy/ *n.* luster or iridescence, esp. on pottery. [F f. It. *riflesso* reflection, REFLEX]

reflex /réefleks/ *adj. & n.* ● *adj.* **1** (of an action) independent of the will, as an automatic response to the stimulation of a nerve (e.g., a sneeze). **2** (of an angle) exceeding 180°. **3** bent backward. **4** (of light) reflected. **5** (of a thought, etc.) introspective; directed back upon itself or its own operations. **6** (of an effect or influence) reactive; coming back upon its author or source. ● *n.* **1** a reflex action. **2** a sign or secondary manifestation (*law is a reflex of public opinion*). **3** reflected light or a reflected image. **4** a word formed by development from an earlier stage of a language. □ **reflex arc** *Anat.* the sequence of nerves involved in a reflex action. **reflex camera** a camera with a ground-glass focusing screen on which the image is formed by a combination of lens and mirror, enabling the scene to be correctly composed and focused. □□ **reflexly** *adv.* [L *reflexus* (as REFLECT)]

reflexible /rifléksibəl/ *adj.* capable of being reflected. □□ **reflexibility** /-bílitee/ *n.*

reflexion var. of REFLECTION.

reflexive /rifléksiv/ *adj. & n. Gram.* ● *adj.* **1** (of a word or form) referring back to the subject of a sentence (esp. of a pronoun, e.g., *myself*). **2** (of a verb) having a reflexive pronoun as its object (as in *to wash oneself*). ● *n.* a reflexive word or form, esp. a pronoun. □□ **reflexively** *adv.* **reflexiveness** *n.* **reflexivity** /-sívitee/ *n.*

reflexology /réefleksólajee/ *n.* **1** a system of massage through reflex points on the feet, hands, and head, used to relieve tension and treat illness. **2** *Psychol.* the scientific study of reflexes. □□ **reflexologist** *n.*

refluent /réflōōənt/ *adj.* flowing back (*refluent tide*). □□ **refluence** *n.* [ME f. L *refluere* (as RE-, *fluere* flow)]

reflux /réefluks/ *n. & v.* ● *n.* **1** a backward flow. **2** *Chem.* a method of boiling a liquid so that any vapor is liquefied and returned to the boiler. ● *v.tr. & intr. Chem.* boil or be boiled under reflux.

refocus /réefókəs/ *v.tr.* (**refocused, refocusing** or **refocussed, refocussing**) adjust the focus of (esp. a lens).

reforest /réefáwrist, fór-/ *v.tr.* replant former forest land with trees. □□ **reforestation** /-stáyshən/ *n.*

reforge /réefáwrj/ *v.tr.* forge again or differently.

reform /rifáwrm/ *v., n., & adj.* ● *v.* **1** *tr. & intr.* make or become better by the removal of faults and errors. **2** *tr.* abolish or cure (an abuse or malpractice). **3** *tr.* correct (a legal document). **4** *tr. Chem.* convert (a straight-chain hydrocarbon) by catalytic reaction to a branched-chain form for use as gasoline. ● *n.* **1** the removal of faults or abuses, esp. of a moral or political or social kind. **2** an improvement made or suggested. ● *adj.* of or relating to reform. □ **Reformed Church** a church that has accepted the principles of the Reformation, esp. a Calvinist church (as distinct from Lutheran). **Reform Judaism** a simplified and rationalized form of Judaism. **reform school** an institution to which young offenders are sent to be reformed. □□ **reformable** *adj.* [ME f. OF *reformer* or L *reformare* (as RE-, FORM)]
■ *v.* **1** improve, better, emend, rectify, correct, mend, repair, fix, remedy, revise, revolutionize, rehabilitate, remodel, refashion, renovate, reorganize, rebuild,

formal ameliorate, *literary* meliorate; mend one's ways, turn over a new leaf, go straight. **2** see ABOLISH. ● *n.* **1** improvement, betterment, emendation, rectification, correction, rehabilitation, modification, reorganization, renovation, *formal* amelioration, *literary* melioration; change.

re-form /réefáwrm/ *v.tr. & intr.* form again.

reformat /réefáwrmat/ *v.tr.* (**reformatted, reformatting**) format anew.

reformation /réfərmáyshən/ *n.* the act of reforming or process of being reformed, esp. a radical change for the better in political or religious or social affairs. □ **the Reformation** *hist.* a 16th-c. movement for the reform of abuses in the Roman Church ending in the establishment of the Reformed and Protestant churches. □□ **Reformational** *adj.* [ME f. OF *reformation* or L *reformatio* (as REFORM)]

re-formation /réefawrmáyshən/ *n.* the process or an instance of forming or being formed again.

reformative /rifáwrmətiv/ *adj.* tending or intended to produce reform. [OF *reformatif -ive* or med.L *reformativus* (as REFORM)]

reformatory /rifáwrmətawree/ *n. & adj.* ● *n.* (*pl.* **-ies**) = *reform school.* ● *adj.* reformative.

reformer /rifáwrmər/ *n.* a person who advocates or brings about (esp. political or social) reform.

reformism /rifáwrmizəm/ *n.* a policy of reform rather than abolition or revolution. □□ **reformist** *n.*
■ gradualism, Fabianism, *often derog.* revisionism.

reformulate /réefáwrmyəlayt/ *v.tr.* formulate again or differently. □□ **reformulation** /-láyshən/ *n.*

refract /rifrákt/ *v.tr.* **1** (of water, air, glass, etc.) deflect (a ray of light, etc.) at a certain angle when it enters obliquely from another medium. **2** determine the refractive condition of (the eye). [L *refringere refract-* (as RE-, *frangere* break)]

refraction /rifrákshən/ *n.* the process by which or the extent to which light is refracted. □ **angle of refraction** the angle made by a refracted ray with the perpendicular to the refracting surface. [F *réfraction* or LL *refractio* (as REFRACT)]

refractive /rifráktiv/ *adj.* of or involving refraction. □ **refractive index** = *index of refraction.*

refractometer /réefraktómitər/ *n.* an instrument for measuring an index of refraction. □□ **refractometric** /-təmétrik/ *adj.* **refractometry** *n.*

refractor /rifráktər/ *n.* **1** a refracting medium or lens. **2** a telescope using a lens to produce an image.

refractory /rifráktəree/ *adj. & n.* ● *adj.* **1** stubborn; unmanageable, rebellious. **2 a** (of a wound, disease, etc.) not yielding to treatment. **b** (of a person, etc.) resistant to infection. **3** (of a substance) hard to fuse or work. ● *n.* (*pl.* **-ies**) a substance especially resistant to heat, corrosion, etc. □□ **refractorily** *adv.* **refractoriness** *n.* [alt. of obs. *refractary* f. L *refractarius* (as REFRACT)]

refrain[1] /rifráyn/ *v.intr.* (foll. by *from*) avoid doing (an action); forbear; desist (*refrain from smoking*). □□ **refrainment** *n.* [ME f. OF *refrener* f. L *refrenare* (as RE-, *frenum* bridle)]
■ (*refrain from*) keep from, abstain from, avoid, *literary* forbear from, eschew; stop, cease, give up, discontinue, leave off, renounce, quit, *literary* desist from, *sl.* stow.

refrain[2] /rifráyn/ *n.* **1** a recurring phrase or number of lines, esp. at the ends of stanzas. **2** the music accompanying this. [ME f. OF *refrain* (earlier *refrait*) ult. f. L *refringere* (as RE-, *frangere* break), because the refrain 'broke' the sequence]
■ **1** chorus, burden, reprise, tag.

refrangible /rifránjibəl/ *adj.* that can be refracted. □□ **refrangibility** *n.* [mod.L *refrangibilis* f. *refrangere* = L *refringere*: see REFRACT]

refreeze /réefréez/ *v.tr. & intr.* (*past* **refroze**; *past part.* **refrozen**) freeze again.

refresh /rifrésh/ *v.tr.* **1 a** (of food, rest, amusement, etc.) give fresh spirit or vigor to. **b** (esp. *refl.*) revive with food, rest, etc. (*refreshed myself with a short sleep*). **2** revive or stimulate (the memory), esp. by consulting the source of one's information. **3** make cool. **4** restore to a certain condition, esp. by provision of fresh supplies, equipment, etc.; replenish. **5** *Computing* **a** restore an image to the screen. **b** replace an image with one that displays more recent information. [ME f. OF *refreschi(e)r* f. *fres fresche* FRESH]

■ **1** enliven, renew, revive, freshen (up), resuscitate, bring back to life, breathe new life into, invigorate, vitalize, energize, brace, fortify, exhilarate, revitalize, reinvigorate, reanimate. **2** revive, renew, stimulate, jog, activate, prod. **4** renew, restock, restore, replenish; fix up, repair, redo, revamp, overhaul, spruce up, recondition, renovate, refurbish, refurnish.

refresher /rifréshər/ *n.* **1** something that refreshes, esp. a drink. **2** *Brit. Law* an extra fee payable to counsel in a prolonged case. □ **refresher course** a course reviewing or updating previous studies.

refreshing /rifréshing/ *adj.* **1** serving to refresh. **2** welcome or stimulating because sincere or untypical (*refreshing innocence*). □□ **refreshingly** *adv.*

■ **1** invigorating, stimulating, bracing, exhilarating, tonic, rejuvenating, enlivening, revitalizing, restorative; cool, thirst-quenching.

refreshment /rifréshmənt/ *n.* **1** the act of refreshing or the process of being refreshed in mind or body. **2** (usu. in *pl.*) food or drink that refreshes. **3** something that refreshes or stimulates the mind. [ME f. OF *refreschement* (as REFRESH)]

■ **1** stimulation, invigoration, exhilaration, rejuvenation, enlivenment, restoration, renewal, resuscitation. **2** (*refreshments*) food, drink(s), edibles, eatables, snack(s), tidbit(s), *colloq.* grub, eats, *sl.* chow, nosh. **3** stimulation, restorative; see also TONIC *n.*

refrigerant /rifríjərənt/ *n. & adj.* ● *n.* **1** a substance used for refrigeration. **2** *Med.* a substance that cools or allays fever. ● *adj.* cooling. [F *réfrigérant* or L *refrigerant-* (as REFRIGERATE)]

refrigerate /rifríjərayt/ *v.* **1** *tr. & intr.* make or become cool or cold. **2** *tr.* subject (food, etc.) to cold in order to freeze or preserve it. □□ **refrigeration** /-ráyshən/ *n.* **refrigerative** /-rətiv/ *adj.* [L *refrigerare* (as RE-, *frigus frigoris* cold)]

■ cool, chill, keep cool or cold or chilled, ice, freeze.

refrigerator /rifríjəraytər/ *n.* a cabinet or room in which food, etc., is kept cold.

refrigeratory /rifríjərətawree/ *adj. & n.* ● *adj.* serving to cool. ● *n.* (*pl.* **-ies**) *hist.* a cold-water vessel attached to a still for condensing vapor. [mod.L *refrigeratorium* (n.), L *refrigeratorius* (adj.) (as REFRIGERATE)]

refringent /rifrínjənt/ *adj. Physics* refracting. □□ **refringence** *n.* **refringency** *n.* [L *refringere*: see REFRACT]

refroze *past* of REFREEZE.

refrozen *past part.* of REFREEZE.

reft *past part.* of REAVE.

refuel /reéfyóoəl/ *v.* **1** *intr.* replenish a fuel supply. **2** *tr.* supply with more fuel.

refuge /réfyōoj/ *n.* **1** a shelter from pursuit or danger or trouble. **2** a person or place, etc., offering this. **3 a** a person, thing, or course resorted to in difficulties. **b** a pretext; an excuse. **4** a traffic island. [ME f. OF f. L *refugium* (as RE-, *fugere* flee)]

■ **1, 2** sanctuary, shelter, haven, asylum, protection, cover, retreat, harbor, security; safe house, stronghold, citadel, hideaway, *colloq.* hidey-hole, hideout, esp. *Brit.* bolt-hole. **3 a** resort, recourse. **b** excuse, pretext, ruse, trick, stratagem, subterfuge, dodge, evasion, expedient.

refugee /réfyōojeé/ *n.* a person taking refuge, esp. in a foreign country from war or persecution or natural disaster. [F *réfugié* past part. of (*se*) *réfugier* (as REFUGE)]

■ fugitive, runaway, escapee, displaced person, DP, exile, émigré.

refulgent /rifúljənt/ *adj. literary* shining; gloriously bright. □□ **refulgence** *n.* **refulgently** *adv.* [L *refulgēre* (as RE-, *fulgēre* shine)]

refund[1] *v. & n.* ● *v.* /rifúnd/ *tr.* (also *absol.*) **1** pay back (money or expenses). **2** reimburse (a person). ● *n.* /reéfund/ **1** an act of refunding. **2** a sum refunded; a repayment. □□ **refundable** *adj.* **refunder** *n.* [ME in sense 'pour back,' f. OF *refonder* or L *refundere* (as RE-, *fundere* pour), later assoc. with FUND]

refund[2] /reéfúnd/ *v.tr.* fund (a debt, etc.) again.

refurbish /rifúrbish/ *v.tr.* **1** brighten up. **2** restore and redecorate. □□ **refurbishment** *n.*

■ **2** restore, refurnish, redecorate, clean (up), polish, renew, renovate, spruce up, remodel, refit, overhaul, repair, recondition, revamp, rebuild, *colloq.* do up.

refurnish /reéfúrnish/ *v.tr.* furnish again or differently.

refusal /rifyóōzəl/ *n.* **1** the act or an instance of refusing; the state of being refused. **2** (in full **first refusal**) the right or privilege of deciding to take or leave a thing before it is offered to others.

■ **1** denial, rejection, rebuff. **2** option, choice, pick, selection, preference.

refuse[1] /rifyóoz/ *v.* **1** *tr.* withhold acceptance of or consent to (*refuse an offer*; *refuse orders*). **2** *tr.* (often foll. by *to* + infin.) indicate unwillingness (*I refuse to go*; *the car refuses to start*; *I refuse!*). **3** *tr.* (often with double object) not grant (a request) made by (a person) (*refused me a day off*; *I could not refuse them*). **4** *tr.* (also *absol.*) (of a horse) be unwilling to jump (a fence, etc.). □□ **refusable** *adj.* **refuser** *n.* [ME f. OF *refuser* prob. ult. f. L *recusare* (see RECUSANT) after *refutare* REFUTE]

■ **1** decline, reject, spurn, repudiate, turn down, rebuff, give the thumbs down, *colloq.* pass by or up. **3** deny, deprive (of); reject, turn down, decline.

refuse[2] /réfyōōs/ *n.* items rejected as worthless; waste. [ME, perh. f. OF *refusé* past part. (as REFUSE)]

■ rubbish, sweepings, waste, litter, dirt, dross, garbage, trash, debris, junk, *Austral. or dial.* mullock.

refusenik /rifyóōznik/ *n. hist.* a Jew refused permission to emigrate to Israel from the former Soviet Union. [REFUSE[1] + -NIK]

refute /rifyóot/ *v.tr.* **1** prove the falsity or error of (a statement, etc., or the person advancing it). **2** rebut or repel by argument. **3** *disp.* deny or contradict (without argument). ¶ Often confused in this sense with *repudiate*. □□ **refutable** *adj.* **refutal** *n.* **refutation** /réfyōōtáyshən/ *n.* **refuter** *n.* [L *refutare* (as RE-: cf. CONFUTE)]

■ **1, 2** rebut, confute. **3** deny, contradict, reject, repudiate.

reg /reg/ *n. colloq.* regulation. [abbr.]

regain /rigáyn/ *v.tr.* obtain possession or use of after loss (*regain consciousness*). [F *regagner* (as RE-, GAIN)]

regal /reégəl/ *adj.* **1** royal; of or by a monarch or monarchs. **2** fit for a monarch; magnificent. □□ **regally** *adv.* [ME f. OF *regal* or L *regalis* f. *rex regis* king]

■ **1** royal, kingly, queenly, princely, sovereign, imperial, stately. **2** majestic, splendid, magnificent, grand, resplendent, palatial, exalted; see also ROYAL *adj.* 6.

regale /rigáyl/ *v.tr.* **1** entertain lavishly with feasting. **2** (foll. by *with*) entertain or divert with (talk, etc.). **3** (of beauty, flowers, etc.) give delight to. □□ **regalement** *n.* [F *régaler* f. OF *gale* pleasure]

■ **1** entertain, feast, wine and dine, indulge, feed, treat, banquet. **2** entertain, amuse, delight, divert, indulge, please, gratify, captivate, fascinate, entrance, enchant, spellbind, bewitch, charm, enrapture.

regalia /rigáylyə/ *n.pl.* **1** the insignia of royalty used at coronations. **2** the insignia of an order or of civic dignity. **3** any distinctive or elaborate clothes, accoutrements, etc.; trappings; finery. [med.L, = royal privileges, f. L neut. pl. of *regalis* REGAL]

■ **1, 2** decorations, insignia, emblems, badges; see also SYMBOL *n.* **3** accoutrements, apparatus, gear, paraphernalia, trappings, tackle, appurtenances, equipment, equipage; finery.

regalism /reégəlizəm/ *n.* the doctrine of a sovereign's ecclesiastical supremacy.

regality /rigálitee/ *n.* (*pl.* **-ies**) **1** the state of being a king or

---

/.../ **pronunciation**	● **part of speech**
□ **phrases, idioms, and compounds**	
□□ **derivatives**	■ **synonym section**
cross-references appear in SMALL CAPITALS or *italics*	

queen. **2** an attribute of sovereign power. **3** a royal privilege. [ME f. OF *regalité* or med.L *regalitas* (as REGAL)]

regard /rigaárd/ *v. & n.* ● *v.tr.* **1** gaze on steadily (usu. in a specified way) (*regarded them suspiciously*). **2** give heed to; take into account; let one's course be affected by. **3** look upon or contemplate mentally in a specified way (*I regard them kindly*; *I regard it as an insult*). **4** (of a thing) have relation to; have some connection with. ● *n.* **1** a gaze; a steady or significant look. **2** (foll. by *to, for*) attention or care. **3** (foll. by *for*) esteem; kindly feeling; respectful opinion. **4 a** a respect; a point attended to (*in this regard*). **b** (usu. foll. by *to*) reference; connection, relevance. **5** (in *pl.*) an expression of friendliness in a letter, etc.; compliments (*sent my best regards*). □ **as regards** about; concerning; in respect of. **in** (or **with**) **regard to** as concerns; in respect of. [ME f. OF *regard* f. *regarder* (as RE-, *garder* GUARD)]

■ *v.* **1** view, look at *or* upon *or* on, observe, watch, eye, gaze at *or* upon, contemplate, stare at. **2** pay heed *or* attention to, esteem, account, take into account, allow for, take into consideration, consider, take note of, notice, have regard for *or* to. **3** consider, perceive, view, look upon *or* on, see, treat, think of, judge, rate, *formal* deem; (*regard highly*) respect, esteem, value, admire. **4** concern, relate to, be relevant to, pertain to, refer to, affect, have (a) bearing on, bear on *or* upon, involve, have *or* be to do with. ● *n.* **1** see GAZE *n.* **2** care, concern, heed, attention, thought, notice. **3** respect, consideration, concern, thought, sympathy, feeling, reverence, veneration, deference, honor, esteem, high opinion, approval, approbation, appreciation, admiration, affection, fondness. **4 a** point, particular, respect, aspect, detail, matter. **b** reference, relevance, relevancy, association, pertinence, application, bearing, connection, link, tie-in. **5** (*regards*) best wishes, good wishes, compliments, greetings, respects, salutations, attentions, remembrances, *archaic* devoirs. □ **as regards** see CONCERNING. **in** (or **with**) **regard to** with reference to, in relation to, as concerns, in respect of; see also CONCERNING.

regardant /rigaárd'nt/ *adj.* Heraldry (of a beast, etc.) looking backward. [AF & OF (as REGARD)]

regardful /rigaárdfŏŏl/ *adj.* (foll. by *of*) mindful of; paying attention to.

regarding /rigaárding/ *prep.* about; concerning; in respect of.

■ concerning, about; respecting, with regard to, with respect to, in respect of, with reference to, in *or* on the matter of, pertaining to, on the subject of, apropos, *archaic or Sc. or US* anent, *colloq.* in re.

regardless /rigaárdlis/ *adj. & adv.* ● *adj.* (foll. by *of*) without regard or consideration for (*regardless of the expense*). ● *adv.* without paying attention (*carried on regardless*). □□ **regardlessly** *adv.* **regardlessness** *n.*

■ *adj.* (*regardless of*) despite, notwithstanding, in spite of, heedless of, irrespective of, *dial. or joc.* irregardless of. ● *adv.* nevertheless, no matter what, in any event, in any case, anyway, anyhow, irrespectively, *dial. or joc.* irregardless.

regather /reegáthər/ *v.tr. & intr.* **1** gather or collect again. **2** meet again.

regatta /rigaátə, -gátə/ *n.* a sporting event consisting of a series of boat or yacht races. [It. (Venetian)]

regd. *abbr.* registered.

regency /reéjənsee/ *n.* (*pl.* **-ies**) **1** the office of regent. **2** a commission acting as regent. **3 a** the period of office of a regent or regency commission. **b** (**Regency**) a particular period of a regency, esp. (in Britain) from 1811 to 1820, and (in France) from 1715 to 1723 (often *attrib.*: *Regency costume*). [ME f. med.L *regentia* (as REGENT)]

regenerate *v. & adj.* ● *v.* /rijénərayt/ **1** *tr. & intr.* bring or come into renewed existence; generate again. **2** *tr.* improve the moral condition of. **3** *tr.* impart new, more vigorous, and spiritually greater life to (a person or institution, etc.). **4** *intr.* reform oneself. **5** *tr.* invest with a new and higher spiritual nature. **6** *intr. & tr. Biol.* regrow or cause (new tissue) to regrow to replace lost or injured tissue. **7** *tr. & intr. Chem.*

restore or be restored to an initial state of reaction or process. ● *adj.* /rijénərət/ **1** spiritually born again. **2** reformed. □□ **regeneration** /-jenəráyshən/ *n.* **regenerative** /-rətiv/ *adj.* **regeneratively** *adv.* **regenerator** *n.* [L *regenerare* (as RE-, GENERATE)]

regent /reéjənt/ *n. & adj.* ● *n.* **1** a person appointed to administer a kingdom because the monarch is a minor or is absent or incapacitated. **2** a member of the governing body of a state university. ● *adj.* (placed after noun) acting as regent (*prince regent*). □ **regent bird** an Australian bower bird, *Sericulus chrysocephalus*. [ME f. OF *regent* or L *regere* rule]

regerminate /reéjərminayt/ *v.tr. & intr.* germinate again. □□ **regermination** /-jərmináyshən/ *n.*

reggae /régay/ *n.* a W. Indian style of music with a strongly accented subsidiary beat. [W.Ind.]

regicide /réjisīd/ *n.* **1** a person who kills or takes part in killing a king. **2** the act of killing a king. □□ **regicidal** *adj.* [L *rex regis* king + -CIDE]

regild /reégild/ *v.tr.* gild again, esp. to renew faded or worn gilding.

regime /rayzheém/ *n.* (also **régime**) **1 a** a method or system of government. **b** *derog.* a particular government. **2** a prevailing order or system of things. **3** the conditions under which a scientific or industrial process occurs. **4** = REGIMEN 1. [F *régime* (as REGIMEN)]

■ **1** government, rule, administration, leadership, system, *archaic* regimen, regiment. **2** see ORDER *n.* 1.

regimen /réjimen/ *n.* **1** esp. *Med.* a prescribed course of exercise, way of life, and diet. **2** *archaic* a system of government. [L f. *regere* rule]

■ **1** see DIET¹ *n.* 2. **2** see REGIME 1.

regiment *n. & v.* ● *n.* /réjimənt/ **1 a** a permanent unit of an army usu. commanded by a colonel and divided into several companies or troops or batteries and often into two battalions. **b** an operational unit of artillery, etc. **2** (usu. foll. by *of*) a large array or number. **3** *archaic* rule; government. ● *v.tr.* /réjiment/ **1** organize (esp. oppressively) in groups or according to a system. **2** form into a regiment or regiments. □□ **regimentation** *n.* **regimentation** *n.* [ME (in sense 3) f. OF f. LL *regimentum* (as REGIMEN)]

■ *n.* **2** see LOT *n.* 1. ● *v.* **1** discipline, order, organize, systematize, lick *or* knock *or* whip into shape, regulate, control. □□ **regimented** see UNIFORM *adj.* 1, 2.

regimental /réjiment'l/ *adj. & n.* ● *adj.* of or relating to a regiment. ● *n.* (in *pl.*) military uniform, esp. of a particular regiment. □□ **regimentally** *adv.*

Regina /rijínə/ *n. Brit. Law* the reigning queen (following a name or in the titles of lawsuits, e.g., *Regina v. Jones*, the Crown versus Jones). [L, = queen f. *rex regis* king]

region /reéjən/ *n.* **1** an area of land, or division of the earth's surface, having definable boundaries or characteristics (*a mountainous region*; *the region between the river and the sea*). **2** an administrative district, esp. in Scotland. **3** a part of the body around or near some organ, etc. (*the lumbar region*). **4** a sphere or realm (*the region of metaphysics*). **5 a** a separate part of the world or universe. **b** a layer of the atmosphere or the sea according to its height or depth. □ **in the region of** approximately. □□ **regional** *adj.* **regionalism** *n.* **regionalist** *n. & adj.* **regionalize** *v.tr.* **regionally** *adv.* [ME f. OF f. L *regio -onis* direction, district f. *regere* direct]

■ **1** see AREA 2. **2** district, zone, division, locality, sector, precinct, state, province, quarter, department, ward, constituency, county, parish, borough. **4** sphere, domain, realm, province, field, ambit, jurisdiction. □ **in the region of** see *approximately* (APPROXIMATE). □□ **regional** see LOCAL *adj.* 1–3. **regionalism** localism, provincialism, parochialism; insularity, narrowness, narrow-mindedness.

regisseur /ráyzheesőr/ *n.* the director of a theatrical production, esp. a ballet. [F *régisseur* stage manager]

register /réjistər/ *n. & v.* ● *n.* **1** an official list, e.g., of births, marriages, and deaths; of shipping; of professionally qualified persons; or of qualified voters in a constituency. **2** a book in which items are recorded for reference. **3** a device recording speed, force, etc. **4** (in electronic devices) a location in a store of data, used for a specific purpose and with quick access time. **5 a** the range of a voice or instrument. **b** a part of this range (*lower register*). **6** an adjustable plate for widening or narrowing an opening and regulating a draft, esp. in a fire grate. **7 a** a set of organ pipes. **b** a sliding device controlling this. **8** = *cash register* (see CASH¹). **9** *Linguistics* each of several forms of a language (colloquial, formal, literary, etc.) usually used in particular circumstances. **10** *Printing* the exact correspondence of the position of printed matter on the two sides of a leaf. **11** *Printing & Photog.* the correspondence of the position of color components in a printed positive. ● *v.* **1** *tr.* set down (a name, fact, etc.) formally; record in writing. **2** *tr.* make a mental note of; notice. **3** *tr.* enter or cause to be entered in a particular register. **4** *tr.* entrust (a letter, etc.) to a post office for transmission by registered mail. **5** *intr.* & *refl.* put one's name on a register, esp. as an eligible voter or as a guest in a register kept by a hotel, etc. **6** *tr.* (of an instrument) record automatically; indicate. **7 a** *tr.* express (an emotion) facially or by gesture (*registered surprise*). **b** *intr.* (of an emotion) show in a person's face or gestures. **8** *intr.* make an impression on a person's mind (*did not register at all*). **9** *intr.* & *tr.* *Printing* correspond or cause to correspond exactly in position. **10** *tr.* make known formally or publicly; cause (an opinion, grievance, etc.) to be recorded or noted (*I wish to register my disapproval*). □ **registered mail** mail recorded at the post office and guaranteed against loss, damage, etc., during transmission. **registered nurse** a nurse with a state certificate of competence. □□ **registrable** *adj.* [ME & OF *registre, registre* or med.L *regestrum, registrum*, alt. of *regestum* f. LL *regesta* things recorded (as RE-, L *gerere gest-* carry)]

■ *n.* **1** record, roll, catalog, annal(s), archive, calendar, chronicle, schedule, program, directory, file, index, inventory, list, listing. ● *v.* **1** record, write *or* take *or* put *or* set down, list, enter, catalog, log, index, chronicle, note, make *or* take note of. **2** see NOTICE *v.* **5** check in, sign in, log in; sign on *or* up, enroll. **6** record, indicate, mark, measure, point to, exhibit, show. **7 a** show, display, express, indicate, manifest, reveal, betray, reflect. **8** sink in, make an impression, penetrate; (*register with*) dawn on, occur to. **10** make known, transmit, communicate, record.

registrar /réjistraár/ *n.* **1** an official responsible for keeping a register or official records. **2** the chief administrative officer in a university. **3** *Brit.* a middle-ranking hospital doctor undergoing training as a specialist; resident. **4** (in the UK) the judicial and administrative officer of the High Court, etc. □□ **registrarship** *n.* [med.L *registrarius* f. *registrum* REGISTER]

registration /réjistráyshən/ *n.* **1** the act or an instance of registering; the process of being registered. **2** a certificate, etc., that attests to the registering (of a person, vehicle, etc.). [obs. F *régistration* or med.L *registratio* (as REGISTRAR)]

registry /réjistree/ *n.* (*pl.* -ies) **1** a place or office where registers or records are kept. **2** registration. [obs. *registery* f. med.L *registerium* (as REGISTER)]

regius professor /réejeeəs/ *n. Brit.* the holder of a chair founded by a sovereign (esp. one at Oxford or Cambridge instituted by Henry VIII) or filled by Crown appointment. [L, = royal, f. *rex regis* king]

reglaze /reégláyz/ *v.tr.* glaze (a window, etc.) again.

reglet /réglit/ *n.* **1** *Archit.* a narrow strip separating moldings. **2** *Printing* a thin strip of wood or metal separating type. [F *réglet* dimin. of *règle* (as RULE)]

regnal /régnəl/ *adj.* of a reign. □ **regnal year** a year reckoned from the date or anniversary of a sovereign's accession. [AL *regnalis* (as REIGN)]

regnant /régnənt/ *adj.* **1** reigning (*queen regnant*). **2** (of things, qualities, etc.) predominant, prevalent. [L *regnare* REIGN]

regolith /régəlith/ *n. Geol.* unconsolidated solid material covering the bedrock of a planet. [erron. f. Gk *rhēgos* rug, blanket + -LITH]

regorge /rigáwrj/ *v.* **1** *tr.* bring up or expel again after swallowing. **2** *intr.* gush or flow back from a pit, channel, etc. [F *regorger* or RE- + GORGE]

regrade /reégráyd/ *v.tr.* grade again or differently.

regress *v.* & *n.* ● *v.* /rigrés/ **1** *intr.* move backward, esp. (in abstract senses) return to a former state. **2** *intr.* & *tr. Psychol.* return or cause to return mentally to a former stage of life, esp. through hypnosis or mental illness. ● *n.* /reégres/ **1** the act or an instance of going back. **2** reasoning from effect to cause. [ME (as n.) f. L *regressus* f. *regredi regress-* (as RE-, *gradi* step)]

regression /rigréshən/ *n.* **1** a backward movement, esp. a return to a former state. **2** a relapse or reversion. **3** *Psychol.* a return to an earlier stage of development, esp. through hypnosis or mental illness. **4** *Statistics* a measure of the relation between the mean value of one variable (e.g., output) and corresponding values of other variables (e.g., time and cost). [L *regressio* (as REGRESS)]

regressive /rigrésiv/ *adj.* **1** regressing; characterized by regression. **2** (of a tax) proportionally greater on lower incomes. □□ **regressively** *adv.* **regressiveness** *n.*

regret /rigrét/ *v.* & *n.* ● *v.tr.* (**regretted, regretting**) **1** (often foll. by *that* + clause) feel or express sorrow or repentance or distress over (an action or loss, etc.) (*I regret that I forgot; regretted your absence*). **2** (often foll. by *to* + infin. or *that* + clause) acknowledge with sorrow or remorse (*I regret to say that you are wrong; regretted he would not be attending*). ● *n.* **1** a feeling of sorrow, repentance, disappointment, etc., over an action or loss, etc. **2** (often in *pl.*) an (esp. polite or formal) expression of disappointment or sorrow at an occurrence, inability to comply, etc. (*refused with many regrets; heard with regret of her death*). □ **give** (or **send**) **one's regrets** formally decline an invitation. [ME f. OF *regreter* bewail]

■ *v.* rue, mourn, lament, bemoan, bewail; be *or* feel sorry for, repent, feel remorse for, be *or* feel upset about. ● *n.* **1** repentance, guilt, sorrow, disappointment, contrition, remorse, regretfulness, ruefulness, grief, sadness, mournfulness, *archaic* rue, *archaic or literary* woe, *literary* dolor; (*regrets*) qualms, second thoughts. □ **give** (or **send**) **one's regrets** refuse, decline, say no, give the thumbs down.

regretful /rigrétfool/ *adj.* feeling or showing regret. □□ **regretfully** *adv.* **regretfulness** *n.*

■ sorry, sorrowful, rueful, mournful, sad, repentant, guilty, disappointed, contrite, remorseful, penitent. □□ **regretfully** see *sadly* (SAD).

regrettable /rigrétəbəl/ *adj.* (of events or conduct) undesirable; unwelcome; deserving censure. □□ **regrettably** *adv.*

■ undesirable, unwelcome, lamentable, woeful, sad, distressing, upsetting, unhappy, unfortunate, unlucky; deplorable, reprehensible, wrong, shameful, *colloq.* terrible, awful.

regroup /reégroōp/ *v.tr.* & *intr.* group or arrange again or differently. □□ **regroupment** *n.*

regrow /reégrő/ *v.intr.* & *tr.* grow again, esp. after an interval. □□ **regrowth** *n.*

Regt. *abbr.* Regiment.

regulable /régyələbəl/ *adj.* able to be regulated.

regular /régyələr/ *adj.* & *n.* ● *adj.* **1** conforming to a rule or principle; systematic. **2 a** (of a structure or arrangement) harmonious; symmetrical (*regular features*). **b** (of a surface, line, etc.) smooth; level; uniform. **3** acting or done or recurring uniformly or calculably in time or manner; habitual; constant; orderly. **4** conforming to a standard of etiquette or procedure; correct; according to convention. **5** properly constituted or qualified; not defective or amateur; pursuing an occupation as one's main pursuit (*cooks as well as a regular cook; has no regular profession*). **6** *Gram.* (of a noun, verb, etc.) following the normal type of inflection. **7** *colloq.* complete; thorough; absolute (*a regular hero*). **8** *Geom.* **a** (of a figure) having all sides and all angles equal. **b** (of a solid) bounded by a number of equal figures. **9** *Eccl.* (placed be-

---

/ . . . / **pronunciation**   ● **part of speech**
□ **phrases, idioms, and compounds**
□□ **derivatives**   ■ **synonym section**
cross-references appear in SMALL CAPITALS or *italics*

fore or after noun) **a** bound by religious rule. **b** belonging to a religious or monastic order (*canon regular*). **10** (of forces or troops, etc.) relating to or constituting a permanent professional body (*regular soldiers*; *regular police force*). **11** (of a person) defecating or menstruating at predictable times. **12** *Bot.* (of a flower) having radial symmetry. **13** *colloq.* likable; normal; reliable (esp. as *regular guy*). ● *n.* **1** a regular soldier. **2** *colloq.* a regular customer, visitor, etc. **3** *Eccl.* one of the regular clergy. **4** *colloq.* a person permanently employed. □ **keep regular hours** do the same thing, esp. going to bed and getting up, at the same time each day. □□ **regularity** /-láritee/ *n.* **regularize** *v.tr.* **regularization** *n.* **regularly** *adv.* [ME *reguler, regular* f. OF *reguler* f. L *regularis* f. *regula* RULE]

■ *adj.* **1** scheduled, systematic, ordered, steady, consistent, uniform, logical. **2 a** symmetrical, uniform, even, harmonious, well-proportioned, classic. **b** even, smooth, level, straight, uniform, uninterrupted, unvarying, continuous, flat, plane, plumb. **3** routine, customary, accustomed, wonted, normal, usual, time-honored, habitual, constant, expected, familiar, standard, predictable; periodic, rhythmic(al), cyclic(al); dependable, methodical, well-regulated, well-ordered, orderly. **4** proper, correct, legal, official, bona fide, legitimate, established, recognized, orthodox, approved, *colloq.* kosher. **5** permanent, career; see also PROFESSIONAL *adj.* **7** complete, utter, out-and-out, thoroughgoing, unmitigated, unalloyed, unqualified, consummate, perfect, thorough, absolute; acknowledged, real, genuine. **8 a** even-sided, equal-sided, equilateral, equal-angled, equiangular. **13** estimable, fine, good, likable, amiable, easygoing, nice, popular, pleasant, acceptable, accepted; reliable, dependable; normal. ● *n.* **2** fixture, habitué, (steady) customer, patron, client, frequenter. □□ **regularity** consistency, constancy, uniformity, evenness, sameness, symmetry, balance, harmony, harmoniousness, orderliness, order, stability, predictability, routine, reliability, dependability, steadiness, invariability.

regulate /régyəlayt/ *v.tr.* **1** control by rule. **2** subject to restrictions. **3** adapt to requirements. **4** alter the speed of (a machine or clock) so that it may work accurately. □□ **regulative** /-lətiv/ *adj.* **regulator** *n.* **regulatory** /-lətáwree/ *adj.* [LL *regulare regulat-* f. L *regula* RULE]

■ **1** control, monitor; govern, run, operate, administer, handle, guide, steer, conduct, direct, oversee, manage. **2** see RESTRICT. **4** adjust, modify, modulate, control, balance, set, fix.

regulation /régyəláyshən/ *n.* **1** the act or an instance of regulating; the process of being regulated. **2** a prescribed rule; an authoritative direction. **3** (*attrib.*) in accordance with regulations; of the correct type, etc. (*the regulation speed*; *a regulation tie*). **b** *colloq.* usual (*the regulation soup*).

■ **1** adjustment, modification, modulation, control; see also DISCIPLINE *n.* 1a. **2** rule, ruling, law, edict, order, ordinance, statute, decree, directive, dictate, pronouncement, fiat. **3** (*attrib.*)**a** standard, accepted, official, required, prescribed, proper, correct, right. **b** see USUAL.

regulus /régyələs/ *n.* (*pl.* **reguluses** or **reguli** /-lī/) *Chem.* **1** the purer or metallic part of a mineral that separates by sinking on reduction. **2** an impure metallic product formed during the smelting of various ores. □□ **reguline** /-līn/ *adj.* [L, dimin. of *rex regis* king: orig. of a metallic form of antimony, so called because of its readiness to combine with gold]

regurgitate /rigə́rjitayt/ *v.* **1** *tr.* bring (swallowed food) up again to the mouth. **2** *tr.* cast or pour out again (*required by the exam to regurgitate facts*). **3** *intr.* be brought up again; gush back. □□ **regurgitation** /-táyshən/ *n.* [med.L *regurgitare* (as RE-, L *gurges gurgitis* whirlpool)]

■ **1** vomit, disgorge, spew up, *colloq.* throw up, *sl.* puke, barf, heave, toss one's cookies, upchuck. **2** reiterate, repeat, restate.

rehab /ree̊hab/ *n. colloq.* rehabilitation. [abbr.]

rehabilitate /ree̊həbílitayt/ *v.tr.* **1** restore to effectiveness or normal life by training, etc., esp. after imprisonment or illness. **2** restore to former privileges or reputation or a proper condition. □□ **rehabilitation** /-táyshən/ *n.* **rehabilitative** *adj.* [med.L *rehabilitare* (as RE-, HABILITATE)]

■ **1** restore, reestablish, reeducate, reintegrate, reorient, reform, straighten out. **2** reinstate; renew, renovate, refurbish, restore, fix (up), repair, reconstruct, rebuild; change, transform.

rehandle /ree̊hánd'l/ *v.tr.* **1** handle again. **2** give a new form or arrangement to.

rehang /ree̊háng/ *v.tr.* (*past* and *past part.* **rehung**) hang (esp. a picture or a curtain) again or differently.

rehash *v. & n.* ● *v.tr.* /ree̊hásh/ put (old material) into a new form without significant change or improvement. ● *n.* /ree̊hash/ **1** material rehashed. **2** the act or an instance of rehashing.

■ *v.* rework, go over again, restate, redo, rearrange, reshuffle, reuse. ● *n.* **2** reworking, restatement, rearrangement, reshuffle, reuse, rewording.

rehear /ree̊heér/ *v.tr.* (*past* and *past part.* **reheard** /ree̊hérd/) hear again.

rehearsal /rihɔ́rsəl/ *n.* **1** the act or an instance of rehearsing. **2** a trial performance or practice of a play, recital, etc.

■ **1** relation, recital, telling, description, enumeration, listing, account, narration, repetition, repeat. **2** practice, run-through, read-through, *colloq.* dry run.

rehearse /rihɔ́rs/ *v.* **1** *tr.* practice (a play, recital, etc.) for later public performance. **2** *intr.* hold a rehearsal. **3** *tr.* train (a person) by rehearsal. **4** *tr.* recite or say over. **5** *tr.* give a list of; enumerate. □□ **rehearser** *n.* [ME f. AF *rehearser*, OF *reherc(i)er*, perh. formed as RE- + *hercer* to harrow f. *herse* harrow: see HEARSE]

■ **1** practice, run through *or* over, go through *or* over. **3** see TRAIN *v.* 1a. **4** repeat, relate, recite, tell, describe, recount, review, go through *or* over, say over, recapitulate, *colloq.* recap. **5** see LIST¹ *v.* 1, ENUMERATE 1.

reheat *v. & n.* ● *v.tr.* /ree̊heét/ heat again. ● *n.* /ree̊heet/ the process of using the hot exhaust to burn extra fuel in a jet engine and produce extra power. □□ **reheater** *n.*

reheel /ree̊heél/ *v.tr.* fit (a shoe, etc.) with a new heel.

rehoboam /ree̊həbóəm/ *n.* a wine bottle of about six times the standard size. [*Rehoboam* King of Israel (1 Kings 11–14)]

rehouse /ree̊hówz/ *v.tr.* provide with new housing.

rehung *past* and *past part.* of REHANG.

rehydrate /ree̊hidráyt/ *v.* **1** *intr.* absorb water again after dehydration. **2** *tr.* add water to (esp. food) again to restore to a palatable state. □□ **rehydratable** *adj.* **rehydration** /-dráyshən/ *n.*

Reich /rīkh/ *n.* the former German state, esp. the Third Reich. □ **First Reich** the Holy Roman Empire, 962–1806. **Second Reich** the German Empire 1871–1918. **Third Reich** the Nazi regime, 1933–45. ¶ Only *Third Reich* is normal historical terminology. [G, = empire]

Reichstag /ríkhstaag/ *n. hist.* **1** the main legislature of the German state under the Second and Third Reichs. **2** the building in which this met. [G]

reify /ree̊ifī/ *v.tr.* (**-ies, -ied**) convert (a person, abstraction, etc.) into a thing; materialize. □□ **reification** /-fikáyshən/ *n.* **reificatory** /-ifikətáwree/ *adj.* [L *res* thing + -FY]

reign /rayn/ *v. & n.* ● *v.intr.* **1** hold royal office; be king or queen. **2** have power or predominance; prevail; hold sway (*confusion reigns*). **3** (as **reigning** *adj.*) (of a winner, champion, etc.) currently holding the title, etc. ● *n.* **1** sovereignty, rule. **2** the period during which a sovereign rules. [ME f. OF *reigne* kingdom f. L *regnare* f. *rex regis* king]

■ *v.* rule, command, govern, wear the crown, wield the scepter, occupy the throne, be king *or* queen. **2** prevail, be prevalent, predominate, hold sway, obtain, be rampant; win (out), prove superior, gain mastery *or* control, triumph, succeed; *colloq.* run the show, rule the roost, *sl.* call the shots. ● *n.* **1** rule, sovereignty, ascendancy, power, hegemony, command, jurisdiction, leadership, government, direction, control, domination, mastery.

reignite /reeignít/ *v.tr.* & *intr.* ignite again.

reimburse /reeimbôrs/ *v.tr.* **1** repay (a person who has expended money). **2** repay (a person's expenses). □□ **reimbursable** *adj.* **reimbursement** *n.* **reimburser** *n.* [RE- + obs. *imburse* put in a purse f. med.L *imbursare* (as IM-, PURSE)]

■ **1** repay, recompense, pay back, compensate, remunerate, indemnify.

reimport *v.* & *n.* ● *v.tr.* /reeimpáwrt/ import (goods processed from exported materials). ● *n.* /reé-impawrt/ **1** the act or an instance of reimporting. **2** a reimported item. □□ **reimportation** *n.*

reimpose /reeimpóz/ *v.tr.* impose again, esp. after a lapse. □□ **reimposition** /-pəzíshən/ *n.*

rein /rayn/ *n.* & *v.* ● *n.* (in *sing.* or *pl.*) **1** a long narrow strap with each end attached to the bit, used to guide or check a horse, etc., in riding or driving. **2** a similar device used to restrain a young child. **3** (a means of) control or guidance; a curb; a restraint. ● *v.tr.* **1** check or manage with reins. **2** (foll. by *up*, *back*) pull up or back with reins. **3** (foll. by *in*) hold in as with reins; restrain. **4** govern; restrain; control. □ **draw rein 1** stop one's horse. **2** pull up. **3** abandon an effort. **give free rein to** remove constraints from; allow full scope to. **keep a tight rein on** allow little freedom to. □□ **reinless** *adj.* [ME f. OF *rene*, *reigne*, earlier *resne*, ult. f. L *retinēre* RETAIN]

■ *n.* **3** check, curb, control, restraint, constraint, limitation, harness, bridle, brake, leash; (*hold the reins*) be in control *or* command; be at the tiller *or* helm; see also DOMINATE 1. ● *v.* **3, 4** (*rein in*) (keep under or in) check, curb, (keep *or* hold in) control, restrain, govern, limit, harness, bridle, restrict, hold in *or* back. □ **draw rein 3** see *give up* 1. **give free rein to** see INDULGE. **keep a tight rein on** see RESTRAIN 1.

reincarnation /reeinkaarnáyshən/ *n.* (in some beliefs) the rebirth of a soul in a new body. □□ **reincarnate** /-kaárnayt/ *v.tr.* **reincarnate** /-kaárnət/ *adj.*

■ rebirth, transmigration, metempsychosis. □□ **reincarnate** (*adj.*) reincarnated, reborn, redivivus.

reincorporate /reeinkáwrpərayt/ *v.tr.* incorporate afresh. □□ **reincorporation** /-ráyshən/ *n.*

reindeer /ráyndeer/ *n.* (*pl.* same or **reindeers**) a subarctic deer, *Rangifer tarandus*, of which both sexes have large antlers, used domestically for drawing sleds and as a source of milk, flesh, and hide. □ **reindeer moss** an arctic lichen, *Cladonia rangiferina*, with short branched stems growing in clumps. [ME f. ON *hreindýri* f. *hreinn* reindeer + *dýr* DEER]

reinfect /reeinfékt/ *v.tr.* infect again. □□ **reinfection** /reein-fékshən/ *n.*

reinforce /reeinfáwrs/ *v.tr.* strengthen or support, esp. with additional personnel or material or by an increase of numbers or quantity or size, etc. □ **reinforced concrete** concrete with metal bars or wire, etc., embedded to increase its tensile strength. □□ **reinforcer** *n.* [earlier *renforce* f. F *renforcer*]

■ strengthen, buttress, bolster, support, fortify, prop (up), shore up, brace, hold up, *archaic* stay.

reinforcement /reeinfáwrsmənt/ *n.* **1** the act or an instance of reinforcing; the process of being reinforced. **2** a thing that reinforces. **3** (in *pl.*) reinforcing personnel or equipment, etc.

■ **2** buttress, support, prop, brace, stay, bolster, reinforcer, strengthener. **3** (*reinforcements*) reserves, auxiliaries; help, aid, backup, support.

reinsert /reeinsôrt/ *v.tr.* insert again. □□ **reinsertion** /-sérshən/ *n.*

reinstate /reeinstáyt/ *v.tr.* **1** replace in a former position. **2** restore (a person, etc.) to former privileges. □□ **reinstatement** *n.*

reinsure /reeinshóōr/ *v.tr.* & *intr.* insure again (esp. of an insurer securing the risk by transferring some or all of it to another insurer). □□ **reinsurance** *n.* **reinsurer** *n.*

reintegrate /reé-íntigrayt/ *v.tr.* **1** esp. *Brit.* = REDINTEGRATE. **2** integrate back into society. □□ **reintegration** /-gráyshən/ *n.*

reinter /reeintər/ *v.tr.* inter (a corpse) again. □□ **reinterment** *n.*

reinterpret /reéintôrprit/ *v.tr.* interpret again or differently. □□ **reinterpretation** *n.*

reintroduce /reéintrədŏōs, -dyŏōs/ *v.tr.* introduce again. □□ **reintroduction** /-dúkshən/ *n.*

reinvest /reéinvést/ *v.tr.* invest again (esp. money in other property, etc.). □□ **reinvestment** *n.*

reinvigorate /reéinvígərayt/ *v.tr.* impart fresh vigor to. □□ **reinvigoration** /-ráyshən/ *n.*

reissue *v.* & *n.* ● *v.tr.* /reé-ishŏō/ (**reissues, reissued, reissuing**) issue again or in a different form. ● *n.* /reeishŏō/ a new issue, esp. of a previously published book.

REIT /reet/ *abbr.* real estate investment trust.

reiterate /reé-ítərayt/ *v.tr.* say or do again or repeatedly. □□ **reiteration** /-ráyshən/ *n.* **reiterative** /-raytiv, -rətiv/ *adj.* [L *reiterare* (as RE-, ITERATE)]

■ repeat, restate, iterate; labor, belabor, harp on about, dwell on.

reive /reev/ *v.intr.* esp. *Sc.* make raids; plunder. □□ **reiver** *n.* [var. of REAVE]

reject *v.* & *n.* ● *v.tr.* /rijékt/ **1** put aside or send back as not to be used or done or complied with, etc. **2** refuse to accept or believe in. **3** rebuff or snub (a person). **4** (of a body or digestive system) cast up again; vomit; evacuate. **5** *Med.* show an immune response to (a transplanted organ or tissue) so that it fails to survive. ● *n.* /reéjekt/ a thing or person rejected as unfit or below standard. □□ **rejectable** /rijéktəbəl/ *adj.* **rejecter** /rijéktər/ *n.* (also **rejector**) **rejection** /-jékshən/ *n.* **rejective** *adj.* [ME f. L *rejicere reject-* (as RE-, *jacere* throw)]

■ *v.* **1** decline, refuse, disallow, spurn, veto, turn down, say no to, give the thumbs down, set *or* put aside, sweep aside; throw away *or* out, discard, disown, jettison, eliminate, scrap, junk, scratch. **2** see DISMISS 4, RENOUNCE 1. **3** rebuff, shun, brush aside, snub, refuse, repel, repulse, spurn, turn down, give a person the cold shoulder, turn one's back on, ignore, give a person the brush-off; jilt, throw over, *colloq.* drop, chuck. ● *n.* second, irregular, discard, castoff; (*rejects*) defective *or* imperfect merchandise *or* goods. □□ **rejection** refusal, denial, repudiation, renunciation, rebuff, turndown.

rejigger /reéjigər/ *v.tr.* rearrange or alter, esp. in an unethical way.

rejoice /rijóys/ *v.* **1** *intr.* feel great joy. **2** *intr.* (foll. by *that* + clause or *to* + infin.) be glad. **3** *intr.* (foll. by *in*, *at*) take delight. **4** *intr.* celebrate some event. **5** *tr.* cause joy to. □□ **rejoicer** *n.* **rejoicingly** *adv.* [ME f. OF *rejoir rejoiss-* (as RE-, JOY)]

■ **1–3** delight, exult, glory, revel, be happy *or* delighted *or* overjoyed, be tickled. **4** exult; jump for joy, celebrate, revel, glory, delight.

rejoin[1] /reéjoyn/ *v.* **1** *tr.* & *intr.* join together again; reunite. **2** *tr.* join (a companion, etc.) again.

rejoin[2] /rijóyn/ *v.* **1** *tr.* say in answer; retort. **2** *intr.* *Law* reply to a charge or pleading in a lawsuit. [ME f. OF *rejoindre rejoign-* (as RE-, JOIN)]

rejoinder /rijóyndər/ *n.* **1** what is said in reply. **2** a retort. **3** *Law* a reply by rejoining. [AF *rejoinder* (unrecorded: as RE-JOIN[2])]

rejuvenate /rijŏōvinayt/ *v.tr.* make young or as if young again. □□ **rejuvenation** /-náyshən/ *n.* **rejuvenator** *n.* [RE- + L *juvenis* young]

■ restore, refresh, reinvigorate, revitalize, revivify, renew, reanimate, regenerate, recharge, breathe new life into.

rejuvenesce /rijŏōvinés/ *v.* **1** *intr.* become young again. **2**

/.../ pronunciation	● part of speech
□ phrases, idioms, and compounds	
□□ derivatives	■ synonym section
cross-references appear in SMALL CAPITALS or *italics*	

Biol. **a** *intr.* (of cells) gain fresh vitality. **b** *tr.* impart fresh vitality to (cells). □□ **rejuvenescent** *adj.* **rejuvenescence** *n.* [LL *rejuvenescere* (as RE-, L *juvenis* young)]

rekindle /reekínd'l/ *v.tr.* & *intr.* kindle again.

-rel /rəl/ *suffix* with diminutive or derogatory force (*cockerel*; *scoundrel*). [from or after OF *-erel* (*le*)]

rel. *abbr.* **1** relating. **2** relative. **3** released. **4** religion. **5** religious.

relabel /reeláybəl/ *v.tr.* (**relabeled, relabeling**; esp. *Brit.* **relabelled, relabelling**) label (esp. a commodity) again or differently.

relapse /riláps/ *v.* & *n.* ● *v.intr.* (usu. foll. by *into*) fall back or sink again (into a worse state after an improvement). ● *n.* /also reélaps/ the act or an instance of relapsing, esp. a deterioration in a patient's condition after a partial recovery. □ **relapsing fever** a bacterial infectious disease with recurrent periods of fever. □□ **relapser** *n.* [L *relabi relaps-* (as RE-, *labi* slip)]

■ *v.* fall back, decline, deteriorate, weaken, degenerate, fail, fade, sink again *or* back (down), sicken, worsen, get *or* become worse, slip back, regress; backslide, lapse, retrogress; (*relapse into*) get back into, go back *or* return *or* revert to. ● *n.* decline, deterioration, weakening, degeneration, fading, sinking, worsening; backsliding, falling *or* going back, lapse, return, reversion, regression, retrogression.

relate /riláyt/ *v.* **1** *tr.* narrate or recount (incidents, a story, etc.). **2** *tr.* (in *passive*; often foll. by *to*) be connected by blood or marriage. **3** *tr.* (usu. foll. by *to, with*) bring into relation (with one another); establish a connection between (*cannot relate your opinion to my own experience*). **4** *intr.* (foll. by *to*) have reference to; concern (*see only what relates to themselves*). **5** *intr.* (foll. by *to*) **a** bring oneself into relation to; associate with. **b** feel emotionally or sympathetically involved or connected; respond (*they relate well to one another*). □□ **relatable** *adj.* [L *referre relat-* bring back: see REFER]

■ **1** narrate, recount, tell, report, describe, recite, detail, set forth, communicate, impart, delineate, give an account of. **3** associate, connect, link, tie, correlate, coordinate. **4** (*relate to*) apply to, concern, coordinate with, respect, regard, have a bearing on, have reference to, have to do *or* be with, pertain to, refer to, appertain to, belong with *or* to. **5 b** (*relate to*) understand, empathize *or* sympathize with, comprehend, identify with, be in rapport *or* en rapport with, be tuned in to.

related /riláytid/ *adj.* **1** connected by blood or marriage. **2** having (mutual) relation; associated; connected. □□ **relatedness** *n.*

■ **1** kin, akin; kindred, consanguineous, cognate, agnate. **2** associated, affiliated, connected, linked, coupled, affiliate; allied, correlated, coordinated, interconnected, interrelated, interdependent.

relater /riláytər/ *n.* (also **relator**) a person who relates something, esp. a story; a narrator.

relation /riláyshən/ *n.* **1 a** what one person or thing has to do with another. **b** the way in which one person stands or is related to another. **c** the existence or effect of a connection, correspondence, contrast, or feeling prevailing between persons or things, esp. when qualified in some way (*bears no relation to the facts; enjoyed good relations for many years*). **2** a relative; a kinsman or kinswoman. **3** (in *pl.*) **a** (foll. by *with*) dealings (with others). **b** sexual intercourse. **4** = RELATIONSHIP. **5 a** narration (*his relation of the events*). **b** a narrative. **6** *Law* the laying of information. □ **in relation to** as regards. [ME f. OF *relation* or L *relatio* (as RELATE)]

■ **1 a, c** relationship, connection, interrelation, interrelationship, association, link, tie, tie-in, interconnection, interdependence, correspondence, kinship; pertinence. **b** see LINK¹ *n.* 2b. **2** relative, kinsman, kinswoman, blood relative, in-law, member of the family. **3** (*relations*) **a** dealings, intercourse, link(s), association(s), liaison, relationship, truck, doings. **b** sexual intercourse, coitus, sex; *Law* carnal knowledge, knowledge. **5 a** narration, telling, recounting, description, reporting, recital, recitation,

delineation, portrayal, recapitulation. **b** narrative, description, recital, delineation, portrayal, story, report. □ **in relation to** as regards, concerning, about, regarding, respecting, pertaining to, with regard to, with respect to, referring to, in *or* with reference to, in the matter of, on the subject of, vis-à-vis, apropos, *archaic or Sc. or US* anent, *colloq.* re.

relational /riláyshənəl/ *adj.* **1** of, belonging to, or characterized by relation. **2** having relation. □ **relational database** *Computing* a database structured to recognize the relation of stored items of information.

relationship /riláyshənship/ *n.* **1** the fact or state of being related. **2** *colloq.* **a** a connection or association (*enjoyed a good working relationship*). **b** an emotional (esp. sexual) association between two people. **3** a condition or character due to being related. **4** kinship.

■ **1, 2a** see ASSOCIATION 4. **2b** see *love affair*. **3** see AFFINITY 2–4.

relative /rélətiv/ *adj.* & *n.* ● *adj.* **1** considered or having significance in relation to something else (*relative velocity*). **2** (also foll. by *to*) existing or quantifiable only in terms of individual perception or consideration; not absolute nor independent (*truth is relative to your perspective; it's all relative, though, isn't it?*). **3** (foll. by *to*) proportioned to (something else) (*growth is relative to input*). **4** implying comparison or contextual relation (*"heat" is a relative word*). **5** comparative; compared one with another (*their relative advantages*). **6** having mutual relations; corresponding in some way; related to each other. **7** (foll. by *to*) having reference or relating (*the facts relative to the issue*). **8** involving a different but corresponding idea (*the concepts of husband and wife are relative to each other*). **9** *Gram.* **a** (of a word, esp. a pronoun) referring to an expressed or implied antecedent and attaching a subordinate clause to it, e.g., *which, who.* **b** (of a clause) attached to an antecedent by a relative word. **10** *Mus.* (of major and minor keys) having the same key signature. **11** (of a service rank) corresponding in grade to another in a different service. **12** pertinent; relevant; related to the subject (*need more relative proof*). ● *n.* **1** a person connected by blood or marriage. **2** a species related to another by common origin (*the apes, the human species' closest relatives*). **3** *Gram.* a relative word, esp. a pronoun. **4** *Philos.* a relative thing or term. □ **relative atomic mass** esp. *Brit.* = *atomic weight.* **relative density** = *specific gravity.* **relative molecular mass** esp. *Brit.* = *molecular weight.* □□ **relatival** /-tívəl/ *adj.* (in sense 3 of *n.*). **relatively** *adv.* **relativeness** *n.* [ME f. *relatif -ive* or LL *relativus* having reference or relation (as RELATE)]

■ *adj.* **2** (*relative to*) dependent on, contingent on, reliant on, subject to, conditioned by, subordinate to, provisional on. **3** proportionate, proportional; (*relative to*) commensurate to *or* with. **4** comparative, contextual. **5** comparative, related; see also PROPORTIONAL *adj.* **6** related, allied, affiliated, associated, correlated, corresponding. **7** (*relative to*) related *or* connected to, connected with, associated with, allied *or* affiliated to, interconnected with, interrelated to, pertinent *or* relevant *or* germane *or* applicable *or* appurtenant to. **8** see LIKE¹ *adj.* 1a. **12** pertinent, relevant, germane, related, appurtenant; see also APPLICABLE. ● *n.* **1** see RELATION 2. □□ **relatively** more or less, somewhat, comparatively, rather, to some degree, to some extent.

relativism /rélətivizəm/ *n.* the doctrine that knowledge is relative, not absolute. □□ **relativist** *n.*

relativistic /rélətivístik/ *adj.* *Physics* (of phenomena, etc.) accurately described only by the theory of relativity. □□ **relativistically** *adv.*

relativity /rélətívitee/ *n.* **1** the fact or state of being relative. **2** *Physics* **a** (**special theory of relativity** or **special relativity**) a theory based on the principle that all motion is relative and that light has constant velocity, regarding spacetime as a four-dimensional continuum, and modifying previous conceptions of geometry. **b** (**general theory of rel-**

ativity or **general relativity**) a theory extending this to gravitation and accelerated motion.

relator /riláytər/ n. **1** var. of RELATER. **2** Law a person who makes a relation (see RELATION 6). [L (as RELATE)]

relax /riláks/ v. **1 a** tr. & intr. (of the body, a muscle, etc.) make or become less stiff or rigid (his frown relaxed into a smile). **b** tr. & intr. make or become loose or slack; diminish in force or tension (relaxed my grip). **c** tr. & intr. (also as int.) make or become less tense or anxious. **2** tr. & intr. make or become less formal or strict (rules were relaxed). **3** tr. reduce or abate (one's attention, efforts, etc.). **4** intr. cease work or effort. **5** tr. (as **relaxed** adj.) at ease; unperturbed. □□ **relaxedly** adv. **relaxedness** n. **relaxer** n. [ME f. L relaxare (as RE-, LAX)]

■ **1 a, b** loosen, ease, slacken, release; let go. **c** calm or quiet or cool down, stay calm or cool, ease off or up, take it easy, unwind, sl. cool it, chill, chill out. **2** modify, tone down, moderate, modulate, lighten, check, temper, curb; lighten up (on). **3** reduce, diminish, decrease, lessen, weaken, ease, moderate, ease up on, slacken; abate, remit. **4** ease up, slow down, let up, rest, take it easy, unwind, colloq. put one's feet up, sl. cool it. **5** (**relaxed**) easygoing, nonchalant, calm, peaceful, tranquil, serene, mellow, at ease, composed, cool, collected, pacific, carefree, insouciant, unperturbed, free and easy, happy-go-lucky; sl. laid back.

relaxant /riláksənt/ n. & adj. ● n. a drug, etc., that relaxes and reduces tension. ● adj. causing relaxation.

relaxation /reélaksáyshən/ n. **1** the act of relaxing or state of being relaxed. **2** recreation or rest, esp. after a period of work. **3** a partial remission or relaxing of a penalty, duty, etc. **4** a lessening of severity, precision, etc. **5** Physics the restoration of equilibrium following disturbance. [L relaxatio (as RELAX)]

■ **2** recreation, rest, repose, leisure, amusement, entertainment, fun, pleasure, diversion, R and R. **3, 4** mitigation, moderation, slackening, weakening, easing (up or off), alleviation, letting up, diminution, lessening, abatement, remission, colloq. letup.

relay[1] /reélay/ n. & v. ● n. **1** a fresh set of people or horses substituted for tired ones. **2** a gang of workers, supply of material, etc., deployed on the same basis (operated in relays). **3** = relay race. **4** a device activating changes in an electric circuit, etc., in response to other changes affecting itself. **5 a** a device to receive, reinforce, and transmit a telegraph message, a broadcast program, etc. **b** a relayed message or transmission. ● v.tr. /also riláy/ **1** receive (a message, broadcast, etc.) and transmit it to others. **2 a** arrange in relays. **b** provide with or replace by relays. □ **relay race** a race between teams of which each member in turn covers part of the distance. [ME f. OF relai (n.), relayer (v.) (as RE-, laier ult. f. L laxare): cf. RELAX]

relay[2] /reélay/ v.tr. (past and past part. **relaid**) lay again or differently.

relearn /reélərn/ v.tr. learn again.

release /rileés/ v. & n. ● v.tr. **1** (often foll. by from) set free; liberate; unfasten. **2** allow to move from a fixed position. **3 a** make (information, a recording, etc.) publicly or generally available. **b** issue (a film, etc.) for general exhibition. **4** Law **a** remit (a debt). **b** surrender (a right). **c** make over (property or money) to another. ● n. **1** deliverance or liberation from a restriction, duty, or difficulty. **2** a handle or catch that releases part of a mechanism. **3** a document or item of information made available for publication (press release). **4 a** a film or record, etc., that is released. **b** the act or an instance of releasing or the process of being released in this way. **5** Law **a** the act of releasing (property, money, or a right) to another. **b** a document effecting this. □□ **releasable** adj. **releasee** /-seé/ n. (in sense 4 of v.). **releaser** n. **releasor** n. (in sense 4 of v.). [ME f. OF reles (n.), relesser (v.), relaiss(i)er f. L relaxare: see RELAX]

■ v. **1** let go, (set) free, liberate, (let) loose, set or turn loose, unloose, untie, unfasten, unchain, unfetter, unshackle, deliver, let out, discharge, emancipate, hist.

manumit, literary disenthrall. **3** issue, publish, make available, put out, pass out, hand out, come out with, circulate, distribute, disseminate; launch. ● n. **1** freeing, releasing, liberating, loosing, unloosing, delivering, emancipating, freedom, liberation, deliverance, discharge, emancipation, hist. manumission, manumitting. **3** press release, announcement, notice, story, report.

relegate /réligayt/ v.tr. **1** consign or dismiss to an inferior or less important position; demote. **2** transfer (a sports team) to a lower division of a league, etc. **3** banish or send into exile. **4** (foll. by to) **a** transfer (a matter) for decision or implementation. **b** refer (a person) for information. □□ **relegable** /-ligəbəl/ adj. **relegation** /-gáyshən/ n. [L relegare relegat- (as RE-, legare send)]

■ **1** demote; see also DOWNGRADE v. 1. **3** see BANISH 1. **4 a** assign, commit, hand over, transfer, pass on, send on. **b** refer, pass on, hand over, send on, direct, point.

relent /rilént/ v.intr. **1** abandon a harsh intention. **2** yield to compassion. **3** relax one's severity; become less stern. [ME f. med.L relentare (unrecorded), formed as RE- + L lentāre bend f. lentus flexible]

■ relax, soften, yield, give way, give ground, compromise, capitulate, be merciful, show pity or compassion or mercy, melt, succumb, come around.

relentless /riléntlis/ adj. **1** unrelenting; insistent and uncompromising. **2** continuous; oppressively constant (the pressure was relentless). □□ **relentlessly** adv. **relentlessness** n.

■ **1** unyielding, inexorable, unstoppable, unrelenting, dogged, implacable, inflexible, unbending, unrelieved, stiff-necked, rigid, obstinate, adamant, obdurate, intransigent, determined, unswerving, undeviating, intractable, persevering, steely, tough, unsparing, uncompromising, pitiless, unforgiving, ruthless, merciless, cruel, unmerciful, remorseless; unmoved. **2** nonstop, persistent, incessant, unrelenting, unremitting, unstoppable, perpetual, unflagging, unrelieved, unabated, unbroken, continual, continuous, ceaseless, constant, unceasing, steady.

relet /reélét/ v.tr. (**-letting**; past and past part. **-let**) esp. Brit. let (a property) for a further period or to a new tenant.

relevant /rélivənt/ adj. (often foll. by to) bearing on or having reference to the matter in hand. □□ **relevance** n. **relevancy** n. **relevantly** adv. [med.L relevans, part. of L relevare RELIEVE]

■ pertinent, appropriate, apt, related, relative, significant, applicable, germane, apposite; to the point. □□ **relevance, relevancy** appropriateness, aptness, pertinence, connection, tie-in, relation, significance, applicability, application.

reliable /rilíəbəl/ adj. **1** that may be relied on. **2** of sound and consistent character or quality. □□ **reliability** /-bílitee/ n. **reliableness** n. **reliably** adv.

■ dependable, trustworthy, trusted, sound, safe, infallible, archaic or joc. trusty; honest, responsible, principled, conscientious, honorable, unfailing, reputable; credible, believable.

reliance /rilíəns/ n. **1** (foll. by in, on) trust, confidence (put full reliance in you). **2** a thing relied upon. □□ **reliant** adj.

■ **1** (reliance in or on) confidence in, trust in, faith in, belief in, dependence on.

relic /rélik/ n. **1** an object interesting because of its age or association. **2** a part of a deceased holy person's body or belongings kept as an object of reverence. **3** a surviving custom or belief, etc., from a past age. **4** a memento or souvenir. **5** (in pl.) what has survived destruction or wasting or use. **6** (in pl.) the dead body or remains of a person. [ME relike, relique, etc. f. OF relique f. L reliquiae: see RELIQUIAE]

/.../ pronunciation	● part of speech
□ phrases, idioms, and compounds	
□□ derivatives	■ synonym section
cross-references appear in SMALL CAPITALS or italics	

■ **4** memento, souvenir, keepsake, remembrance, token, reminder, trophy. **5** (*relics*) remains, traces, remnants, fragments, pieces; embers, wreckage, rubble, debris, ruins. **6** see CORPSE.

relict /rélikt/ *n.* **1 a** a geological or other object surviving in its primitive form. **b** an animal or plant known to have existed in the same form in previous geological ages. **2** (foll. by *of*) *archaic* a widow. [L *relinquere relict-* leave behind (as RE-, *linquere* leave): sense 2 f. OF *relicte* f. L *relicta*]

relief /rileéf/ *n.* **1 a** the alleviation of or deliverance from pain, distress, anxiety, etc. **b** the feeling accompanying such deliverance. **2** a feature, etc., that diversifies monotony or relaxes tension. **3** assistance (esp. financial) given to those in special need or difficulty (*rent relief*). **4 a** the replacing of a person or persons on duty by another or others. **b** a person or persons replacing others in this way. **5** *Brit.* (usu. *attrib.*) a thing supplementing another in some service, esp. an extra vehicle providing public transport at peak times. **6 a** a method of molding or carving or stamping in which the design stands out from the surface, with projections proportioned and more (**high relief**) or less (**low** or **bas-relief**) closely approximating those of the objects depicted. **b** a piece of sculpture, etc., in relief. **c** a representation of relief given by an arrangement of line or color or shading. **7** vividness; distinctness (*brings the facts out in sharp relief*). **8** (foll. by *of*) the reinforcement (esp. the raising of a siege) of a place. **9** esp. *Law* the redress of a hardship or grievance. ◻ **relief map 1** a map indicating hills and valleys by shading, etc., rather than by contour lines alone. **2** a map model showing elevations and depressions, usu. on an exaggerated relative scale. **relief printing** = LETTERPRESS 2. [ME f AF *relef*, OF *relief* (in sense 6 F *relief* f. It. *rilievo*) f. *relever*: see RELIEVE]

■ **1 a** easing, abatement, deliverance, alleviation, release, remission, assuagement, liberation, freedom. **b** see EASE *n.* 2a. **3** aid, help, support, assistance, succor, benefit, reinforcement, backing; subsidy. **4 a** see SUBSTITUTE *n.* 1a, CHANGE *n.* 4. **b** substitute, surrogate, replacement, stand-in, double, alternate, esp. *Brit. colloq.* locum, esp. *Theatr.* understudy. **7** vividness, distinctness, sharpness, focus, precision, clarity. **9** redress, reparation, (legal) remedy, litigation.

relieve /rileév/ *v.tr.* **1** bring or provide aid or assistance to. **2** alleviate or reduce (pain, suffering, etc.). **3** mitigate the tedium or monotony of. **4** bring military support for (a besieged place). **5** release (a person) from a duty by acting as or providing a substitute. **6** (foll. by *of*) take (a burden or responsibility) away from (a person). **7** bring into relief; cause to appear solid or detached. ◻ **relieve one's feelings** *Brit.* use strong language or vigorous behavior when annoyed. **relieve oneself** urinate or defecate. ◻◻ **relievable** *adj.* **reliever** *n.* [ME f. OF *relever* f. L *relevare* (as RE-, *levis* light)]

■ **1** see ASSIST *v.* 1. **2** alleviate, ease, reduce, lessen, diminish, mitigate, palliate, soften, soothe. **3** see MITIGATE. **4** help, aid, assist, support, succor, rescue, save. **5** stand in for, replace, substitute for, take over for *or* from, spell, *colloq.* sub for. **6** (*relieve of*) disburden of, free of, rid of, liberate from, disencumber of, unburden of, rescue from, save from, release from. ◻ **relieve oneself** see URINATE.

relieved /rileévd/ *predic.adj.* freed from anxiety or distress (*am very relieved to hear it*). ◻◻ **relievedly** *adv.*

relievo /rileévō/ *n.* (*pl.* **-os**) (also **rilievo** /reelyáyvō/ *pl.* **-vi** /-vee/) = RELIEF 6. [It. *rilievo* RELIEF 6]

relight /reélít/ *v.tr.* light (a fire, etc.) again.

religio- /rilíjeeō/ *comb. form* **1** religion. **2** religious.

religion /rilíjən/ *n.* **1** the belief in a superhuman controlling power, esp. in a personal God or gods entitled to obedience and worship. **2** the expression of this in worship. **3** a particular system of faith and worship. **4** life under monastic vows (*the way of religion*). **5** a thing that one is devoted to (*football is their religion*). ◻ **freedom of religion** the right to follow whatever religion one chooses. ◻◻ **religionless** *adj.* [ME f.

AF *religiun*, OF *religion* f. L *religio -onis* obligation, bond, reverence]

■ **1, 3, 5** creed, belief, faith.

religionism /rilíjənizəm/ *n.* excessive religious zeal. ◻◻ **religionist** *n.*

religiose /rilíjeeōs/ *adj.* excessively religious. [L *religiosus* (as RELIGIOUS)]

religiosity /rilíjeeósitee/ *n.* the condition of being religious or religiose. [ME f. L *religiositas* (as RELIGIOUS)]

religious /rilíjəs/ *adj.* & *n.* ● *adj.* **1** devoted to religion; pious; devout. **2** of or concerned with religion. **3** of or belonging to a monastic order. **4** scrupulous; conscientious (*a religious attention to detail*). ● *n.* (*pl.* same) a person bound by monastic vows. ◻◻ **religiously** *adv.* **religiousness** *n.* [ME f. AF *religius*, OF *religious* f. L *religiosus* (as RELIGION)]

■ *adj.* **1** devout, churchgoing, pious, God-fearing, holy, spiritual. **2** see SPIRITUAL *adj.* 2. **4** scrupulous, exact, precise, conscientious, rigorous, strict, fastidious, meticulous, faithful, punctilious.

reline /reélín/ *v.tr.* renew the lining of (a garment, etc.).

relinquish /rilíngkwish/ *v.tr.* **1** surrender or resign (a right or possession). **2** give up or cease from (a habit, plan, belief, etc.). **3** relax hold of (an object held). ◻◻ **relinquishment** *n.* [ME f. OF *relinquir* f. L *relinquere* (as RE-, *linquere* leave)]

■ **1, 2** yield, cede, waive; give up, abandon, drop, forsake, forswear, desert, abdicate, resign, renounce, let go of, surrender; cease from. **3** release, free; see also *let go* 2 (LET¹).

reliquary /rélikweree/ *n.* (*pl.* **-ies**) esp. *Relig.* a receptacle for relics. [F *reliquaire* (as RELIC)]

reliquiae /rilíkweeī, -ee/ *n.pl.* **1** remains. **2** *Geol.* fossil remains of animals or plants. [L f. *reliquus* remaining, formed as RE- + *linquere liq-* leave]

relish /rélish/ *n.* & *v.* ● *n.* **1** (often foll. by *for*) **a** great liking or enjoyment. **b** keen or pleasurable longing (*had no relish for traveling*). **2 a** an appetizing flavor. **b** an attractive quality (*fishing loses its relish in winter*). **3** a condiment eaten with plainer food to add flavor, as chopped sweet pickle, etc. **4** (foll. by *of*) a distinctive taste or tinge. ● *v.tr.* **1 a** get pleasure out of; enjoy greatly. **b** look forward to, anticipate with pleasure (*did not relish what lay before her*). **2** add relish to. ◻◻ **relishable** *adj.* [alt. (with assim. to -ISH²) of obs. *reles* f. OF *reles, relais* remainder f. *relaisser*: see RELEASE]

■ *n.* **1 a** enjoyment, pleasure, delight, liking, appreciation, fondness, eagerness, avidity, partiality, preference, *archaic* gusto. **b** taste, zest, fancy; see also APPETITE 2. **2 a** see TANG¹ 1. **b** see APPEAL *n.* 4. **3** sauce, condiment, dressing, seasoning, flavoring. ● *v.* **1 a** enjoy, delight in, take pleasure in, fancy, be partial to, appreciate, savor. **b** look forward to, eagerly await. **2** season, garnish.

relive /reélív/ *v.tr.* live (an experience, etc.) over again, esp. in the imagination.

reload /reélōd/ *v.tr.* (also *absol.*) load (esp. a gun or a camera, etc.) again.

relocate /reélōkayt/ *v.* **1** *tr.* locate in a new place. **2** *tr.* & *intr.* move to a new place (esp. to live or work). ◻◻ **relocation** /-káyshən/ *n.*

reluctant /rilúktənt/ *adj.* (often foll. by *to* + infin.) unwilling or disinclined (*most reluctant to agree*). ◻◻ **reluctance** *n.* **reluctantly** *adv.* [L *reluctari* (as RE-, *luctari* struggle)]

■ unwilling, disinclined, unenthusiastic, hesitant; indisposed, loath; averse, opposed. ◻◻ **reluctance** unwillingness, disinclination, aversion, dislike, disrelish, distaste, hesitancy.

rely /rilí/ *v.intr.* (**-ies, -ied**) (foll. by *on, upon*) **1** depend on with confidence or assurance (*am relying on your judgment*). **2** be dependent on (*relies on her for everything*). [ME (earlier senses 'rally, be a vassal of') f. OF *relier* bind together f. L *religare* (as RE-, *ligare* bind)]

■ (*rely on* or *upon*) depend on *or* upon, count on *or* upon, trust in, swear by, bank on *or* upon, bet on, have confidence in, be sure *or* certain of; lean on *or* upon.

REM /rem/ *abbr.* rapid eye movement.

rem /rem/ *n.* (*pl.* same) a unit of effective absorbed dose of ionizing radiation in human tissue, equivalent to one roentgen of X rays. [roentgen *equivalent* man]

remade *past* and *past part.* of REMAKE.

remain /rimáyn/ *v.intr.* **1 a** be left over after others or other parts have been removed or used or dealt with. **b** (of a period of time) be still to elapse. **2** be in the same place or condition during further time; continue to exist or stay; be left behind (*remained at home*; *it will remain cold*). **3** (foll. by compl.) continue to be (*remained calm*; *remains president*). **4** (as **remaining** *adj.*) left behind; not having been used or dealt with. [ME f. OF *remain-* stressed stem of *remanoir* or f. OF *remaindre* ult. f. L *remanēre* (as RE-, *manēre* stay)]

■ **1** stay behind; be left (behind *or* over). **2** linger, wait, *archaic or literary* tarry, *colloq.* stay put; see also STAY¹ *v.* 1. **3** stay, continue to be *or* as, carry on as, persist as. **4** (**remaining**) left (over), extant, outstanding, leftover, surviving, residual, remanent; unused, uneaten, unconsumed.

remainder /rimáyndər/ *n. & v.* ● *n.* **1** a part remaining or left over. **2** remaining persons or things. **3** a number left after division or subtraction. **4** the copies of a book left unsold when demand has fallen. **5** *Law* an interest in an estate that becomes effective in possession only when a prior interest (devised at the same time) ends. ● *v.tr.* dispose of (a remainder of books) at a reduced price. [ME (in sense 5) f. AF, = OF *remaindre*: see REMAIN]

■ *n.* **1, 2** rest, balance, residue, residuum; remains, leftovers, remnants; excess, overage, surplus.

remains /rimáynz/ *n.pl.* **1** what remains after other parts have been removed or used, etc. **2 a** traces of former animal or plant life (*fossil remains*). **b** relics of antiquity, esp. of buildings (*Roman remains*). **3** a person's body after death. **4** an author's (esp. unpublished) works left after death.

■ **1** vestiges, relics, remnants, leavings, crumbs, leftovers, scraps, reliquiae; odds and ends. **2** see RELIC 5. **3** body, corpse, carcass, esp. *Med.* cadaver, *archaic* corse, *sl.* stiff.

remake *v. & n.* ● *v.tr.* /reemáyk/ (*past* and *past part.* **remade**) make again or differently. ● *n.* /reémayk/ a thing that has been remade, esp. a movie.

reman /reemán/ *v.tr.* (**remanned, remanning**) **1** equip (troops, etc.) with new personnel. **2** make courageous again.

remand /rimánd/ *v. & n.* ● *v.tr.* **1** return (a prisoner) to custody, esp. to allow further inquiries to be made. **2** return (a case) to a lower court for reconsideration. ● *n.* a recommittal to custody. □ **on remand** in custody pending trial. [ME f. LL *remandare* (as RE-, *mandare* commit)]

remanent /rémənənt/ *adj.* **1** remaining; residual. **2** (of magnetism) remaining after the magnetizing field has been removed. □□ **remanence** *n.* [ME f. L *remanēre* REMAIN]

remark /rimaark/ *v. & n.* ● *v.* **1** *tr.* (often foll. by *that* + clause) **a** say by way of comment. **b** take notice of; regard with attention. **2** *intr.* (usu. foll. by *on, upon*) make a comment. ● *n.* **1** a written or spoken comment; anything said. **2 a** the act of noticing or observing (*worthy of remark*). **b** the act of commenting (*let it pass without remark*). [F *remarque, remarquer* (as RE-, MARK¹)]

■ *v.* **1 a** comment, say, observe, reflect, mention, declare, state, assert. **b** note, notice, observe, perceive, regard, look at, take notice *or* note of. **2** comment (on *or* upon), reflect (on *or* upon), deliberate (over); (*remark on or upon*) discuss, talk about *or* over, chat about, review, examine. ● *n.* **1** see COMMENT *n.* 1. **2 a** see COMMENT *n.* 2a.

remarkable /rimaarkəbəl/ *adj.* **1** worth notice; exceptional; extraordinary. **2** striking; conspicuous. □□ **remarkableness** *n.* **remarkably** *adv.* [F *remarquable* (as REMARK)]

■ **1** extraordinary, unusual, singular, exceptional, outstanding, noteworthy, signal, notable, distinguished, uncommon, incredible, unbelievable, impressive, phenomenal, astonishing, astounding; strange, different, odd, peculiar, *colloq.* gee-whiz, *sl.* dynamite. **2** striking, conspicuous, distinctive, curious, special, wonderful, marvelous, out of the ordinary, unique,

significant, outstanding, rare, memorable, unforgettable, not to be forgotten.

remarry /reemáree/ *v.intr. & tr.* (**-ies, -ied**) marry again. □□ **remarriage** *n.*

remaster /reemástər/ *v.tr.* make a new master of (a recording), esp. to improve the sound quality.

rematch /reemach/ *n.* a return match or game.

remeasure /reeméZHər/ *v.tr.* measure again. □□ **remeasurement** *n.*

remedial /rimeedeeəl/ *adj.* **1** affording or intended as a remedy (*remedial therapy*). **2** (of teaching) for those in need of improvement in a particular discipline (*remedial math*; *remedial reading*). □□ **remedially** *adv.* [LL *remedialis* f. L *remedium* (as REMEDY)]

remedy /rémidee/ *n. & v.* ● *n.* (*pl.* **-ies**) (often foll. by *for, against*) **1** a medicine or treatment (for a disease, etc.). **2** a means of counteracting or removing anything undesirable. **3** redress; legal or other reparation. **4** the margin within which coins as minted may differ from the standard fineness and weight. ● *v.tr.* (**-ies, -ied**) **1** rectify; make good. **2** heal; cure (a person, diseased part, etc.) □□ **remediable** /rimeedeeəbəl/ *adj.* [ME f. AF *remedie*, OF *remede* or L *remedium* (as RE-, *medēri* heal)]

■ *n.* **1** cure, treatment, therapy, antidote, medicament, medicine, prescription, drug, pharmaceutical, cure-all, panacea, nostrum, restorative, *archaic* specific. **2** cure, antidote, cure-all, panacea, nostrum, countermeasure, answer, solution. **3** redress, legal remedy, reparation. ● *v.* **1** correct, rectify, reform, improve, redress, repair, make good, put *or* set right, straighten out, *formal* ameliorate. **2** cure, treat, heal, mend, restore, relieve, soothe, control, ease.

remember /rimémbər/ *v.tr.* **1** keep in the memory; not forget. **2 a** (also *absol.*) bring back into one's thoughts, call to mind (knowledge or experience, etc.). **b** (often foll. by *to* + infin. or *that* + clause) have in mind (a duty, commitment, etc.) (*will you remember to lock the door?*). **3** think of or acknowledge (a person) in some connection, esp. in making a gift, etc. **4** (foll. by *to*) convey greetings from (one person) to (another) (*remember me to your mother*). **5** mention (in prayer). □ **remember oneself** recover one's manners or intentions after a lapse. □□ **rememberer** *n.* [ME f. OF *remembrer* f. LL *rememorari* (as RE-, L *memor* mindful)]

■ **1** retain, keep *or* bear in mind, recall, call to mind; think back to. **2 a** call to mind; recall, recollect, reminisce over *or* about, think back on *or* to, *literary* muse on *or* about. **b** mind; not forget. **3** think of, acknowledge, tip, reward, remunerate, recompense, requite.

remembrance /rimémbrəns/ *n.* **1** the act of remembering or process of being remembered. **2** a memory or recollection. **3** a keepsake or souvenir. **4** (in *pl.*) greetings conveyed through a third person. □ **Remembrance Day 1** *Brit.* = *Remembrance Sunday.* **2** (in Canada) Nov. 11, observed in memory of those who died in World Wars I and II; Armistice Day. **Remembrance Sunday** (in the UK) the Remembrance Day holiday, observed on the Sunday nearest Nov. 11. [ME f. OF (as REMEMBER)]

■ **1** memory, recollection, retention; reminiscing. **2** memory, recollection, reminiscence, thought. **3** memento, reminder, souvenir, keepsake, token, relic, trophy. **4** (*remembrances*) greetings, regards, best wishes.

remex /reemeks/ *n.* (*pl.* **remiges** /rémijeez/) a primary or secondary feather in a bird's wing. [L, = rower, f. *remus* oar]

remind /rimínd/ *v.tr.* **1** (foll. by *of*) cause (a person) to remember or think of. **2** (foll. by *to* + infin. or *that* + clause)

/.../	**pronunciation**	● **part of speech**
	□ **phrases, idioms, and compounds**	
	□□ **derivatives**	■ **synonym section**
	cross-references appear in SMALL CAPITALS or *italics*	

1271

cause (a person) to remember (a commitment, etc.) (*remind them to pay their bills*).
■ **1** (*remind of*) cause to remember, put in mind of, make a person think of, take *or* carry back to. **2** prompt, encourage, urge; jog a person's memory.

reminder /rimíndər/ *n.* **1 a** a thing that reminds, esp. a letter or bill. **b** a means of reminding; an aide-mémoire. **2** (often foll. by *of*) a memento or souvenir.
■ **1 b** mnemonic, aide-mémoire; cue, prompt. **2** memento, souvenir, keepsake, remembrance, relic, trophy, token.

remindful /rimíndfŏŏl/ *adj.* (often foll. by *of*) acting as a reminder; reviving the memory.

reminisce /réminís/ *v.intr.* (often foll. by *about*) indulge in reminiscence. □□ **reminiscer** *n.* [back-form. f. REMINISCENCE]
■ remember, recollect, think back, look back, turn *or* cast one's mind *or* thoughts back, hark back, take a trip down memory lane.

reminiscence /réminísəns/ *n.* **1** the act of remembering things past; the recovery of knowledge by mental effort. **2 a** a past fact or experience that is remembered. **b** the process of narrating this. **3** (in *pl.*) a collection in literary form of incidents and experiences that a person remembers. **4** *Philos.* (esp. in Platonism) the theory of the recovery of things known to the soul in previous existences. **5** a characteristic of one thing reminding or suggestive of another. □□ **reminiscential** /-nisénshəl/ *adj.* [LL *reminiscentia* f. L *reminisci* remember]
■ **1, 2** recollection, memory, remembrance; thought. **3** (*reminiscences*) memories, reflections, memoirs.

reminiscent /réminísənt/ *adj.* **1** (foll. by *of*) tending to remind one of or suggest. **2** concerned with reminiscence. **3** (of a person) given to reminiscing. □□ **reminiscently** *adv.*
■ **1** (*reminiscent of*) redolent of, evocative of, suggestive of, similar to, comparable with *or* to.

remise /rimeéz/ *v. & n.* ● *v.intr.* **1** *Law* surrender or make over (a right or property). **2** *Fencing* make a remise. ● *n.* *Fencing* a second thrust made after the first has failed. [F f. *remis, remise* past part. of *remettre* put back: cf. REMIT]

remiss /rimís/ *adj.* careless of duty; lax; negligent. □□ **remissly** *adv.* **remissness** *n.* [ME f. L *remissus* past part. of *remittere* slacken: see REMIT]
■ slack, careless, negligent, neglectful, heedless, unheeding, inattentive, unmindful, thoughtless, forgetful, unthinking, lax, indolent, lazy, dilatory.

remissible /rimísibəl/ *adj.* that may be remitted. [F *rémissible* or LL *remissibilis* (as REMIT)]

remission /rimíshən/ *n.* **1** (often foll. by *of*) forgiveness (of sins, etc.). **2** the remitting of a debt or penalty, etc. **3** a diminution of force, effect, or degree (esp. of disease or pain). **4** *Brit.* the reduction of a prison sentence on account of good behavior. □□ **remissive** /-mísiv/ *adj.* [ME f. OF *remission* or L *remissio* (as REMIT)]
■ **1** forgiveness, deliverance, absolution; exoneration, *formal* exculpation. **3** diminution, abatement, decrease, lessening, subsidence, alleviation, mitigation, assuagement, ebbing, easing.

remit *v. & n.* ● *v.* /rimít/ (**remitted, remitting**) **1** *tr.* cancel or refrain from exacting or inflicting (a debt or punishment, etc.). **2** *intr. & tr.* abate or slacken; cease or cease from partly or entirely. **3** *tr.* send (money, etc.) in payment. **4** *tr.* cause to be conveyed by mail. **5** *tr.* **a** (foll. by *to*) refer (a matter for decision, etc.) to some authority. **b** *Law* send back (a case) to a lower court. **6** *tr.* **a** (often foll. by *to*) postpone or defer. **b** (foll. by *in, into*) send or put back into a previous state. **7** *tr.* *Theol.* (usu. of God) pardon (sins, etc.). ● *n.* /reémit, rimít/ **1** the terms of reference of a committee, etc. **2** an item remitted for consideration. □□ **remittable** /-mítəbəl/ *adj.* **remittal** *n.* **remittee** /reemiteé/ *n.* **remitter** *n.* [ME f. L *remittere remiss-* (as RE-, *mittere* send)]
■ *v.* **2** subside, ebb, dwindle, ease up *or* off, fall off; assuage; abate, diminish, slacken, decrease, reduce, lessen, alleviate, ease, mitigate. **3** see PAY¹ *v.* 2. **5 a** see REFER 3. **6 a** see POSTPONE.

remittance /rimít'ns/ *n.* **1** money sent, esp. by mail, for goods or services or as an allowance. **2** the act of sending money. □ **remittance man** *hist.* an emigrant subsisting on remittances from home.
■ **1** see PAY¹ *n.*

remittent /rimít'nt/ *adj.* (of a fever) that abates at intervals. [L *remittere* (as REMIT)]

remix *v. & n.* ● *v.tr.* /reémíks/ mix again. ● *n.* /reémiks/ a sound recording that has been remixed.

remnant /rémnənt/ *n.* **1** a small remaining quantity. **2** a piece of cloth, etc., left when the greater part has been used or sold. **3** (foll. by *of*) a surviving trace (*a remnant of the empire*). [ME (earlier *remenant*) f. OF *remenant* f. *remenoir* REMAIN]
■ **1** leftover, vestige, trace, scrap, fragment, relic, remains. **2** scrap, shred, fragment, end, bit, piece. **3** trace, relic, vestige; see also MEMENTO.

remodel /reémód'l/ *v.tr.* (**remodeled, remodeling**; esp. *Brit.* **remodelled, remodelling**) **1** model again or differently. **2** reconstruct.

remodify /reémódifī/ *v.tr.* (**-ies, -ied**) modify again. □□ **remodification** /-fikáyshən/ *n.*

remold *v. & n.* (*Brit.* **remould**) ● *v.tr.* /reémṓld/ **1** mold again; refashion. **2** reform the tread of (a tire). ● *n.* *Brit.* /reémṓld/ a remolded tire.

remonetize /reémónitiz, -mún-/ *v.tr.* restore (a metal, etc.) to its former position as legal tender. □□ **remonetization** *n.*

remonstrance /rimónstrəns/ *n.* **1** the act or an instance of remonstrating. **2** an expostulation or protest. [ME f. obs. F *remonstrance* or med.L *remonstrantia* (as REMONSTRATE)]

remonstrate /rémonstráyt, rimón-/ *v.* **1** *intr.* (foll. by *with*) make a protest; argue forcibly (*remonstrated with them over the delays*). **2** *tr.* (often foll. by *that* + clause) urge protestingly. □□ **remonstrant** /rimónstrənt/ *adj.* **remonstration** /rémənstráyshən/ *n.* **remonstrative** /rimónstrətiv/ *adj.* **remonstrator** *n.* [med.L *remonstrare* (as RE-, *monstrare* show)]

remontant /rimóntənt/ *adj. & n.* ● *adj.* blooming more than once a year. ● *n.* a remontant rose. [F f. *remonter* REMOUNT]

remora /rémərə, rimáwrə/ *n.* *Zool.* any of various marine fish of the family Echeneidae, which attach themselves by modified suckerlike fins to other fish and to ships. [L, = hindrance (as RE-, *mora* delay, from the former belief that the fish slowed ships down)]

remorse /rimáwrs/ *n.* **1** deep regret for a wrong committed. **2** compunction; a compassionate reluctance to inflict pain (esp. in *without remorse*). [ME f. OF *remors* f. med.L *remorsus* f. L *remordēre remors-* vex (as RE-, *mordēre* bite)]
■ regret, repentance, ruefulness, pangs *or* prickings of conscience, contrition, contriteness, penitence, compunction, guilt, self-reproach, shame, uneasiness of mind.

remorseful /rimáwrsfŏŏl/ *adj.* filled with repentance. □□ **remorsefully** *adv.*
■ regretful, repentant, rueful, sorry, apologetic, guilty, conscience-stricken, contrite, penitent, guilt-ridden, shamefaced, shameful, ashamed, *colloq.* bad.

remorseless /rimáwrslis/ *adj.* **1** without compassion or compunction. **2** relentless; unabating. □□ **remorselessly** *adv.* **remorselessness** *n.*
■ **1** cruel, heartless, callous, harsh, hard-hearted, stonyhearted, merciless, unmerciful, pitiless, ruthless. **2** relentless, unrelenting, unremitting, unabating, unstoppable, inexorable, implacable.

remortgage /reémáwrgij/ *v. & n.* ● *v.tr.* (also *absol.*) mortgage again; revise the terms of an existing mortgage on (a property). ● *n.* a different or altered mortgage.

remote /rimṓt/ *adj.* (**remoter, remotest**) **1** far away in place or time. **2** out of the way; situated away from the main centers of population, society, etc. **3** distantly related (*a remote ancestor*). **4** slight; faint (esp. in *not the remotest chance, idea*, etc.). **5** (of a person) aloof; not friendly. **6** (foll. by *from*) widely different; separate by nature (*ideas remote from the subject*). □ **remote control** control of a machine or apparatus from a distance by means of signals transmitted from a radio or electronic device. **remote-controlled** (of a machine, etc.) controlled at a distance. □□ **remotely** adv. **remoteness** n. [ME f. L remotus (as REMOVE)]

■ **1** distant, faraway, far-off, removed, outlying, inaccessible. **2** lonely, isolated, secluded, out-of-the-way, sequestered, godforsaken; sl. in the sticks, in the boondocks. **3** far-removed, distant; early, ancient. **4** slight, faint; small, meager, slim, slender, poor, inconsiderable, negligible, improbable, unlikely, implausible. **5** aloof, detached, withdrawn, standoffish, reserved, preoccupied, abstracted, indifferent. **6** (remote from) unrelated to, irrelevant to, unconnected to, outside.

remould Brit. var. of REMOLD.

remount v. & n. ● v. /reémównt/ **1 a** tr. mount (a horse, etc.) again. **b** intr. get on horseback again. **2** tr. get on to or ascend (a ladder, hill, etc.) again. **3** tr. provide (a person) with a fresh horse, etc. **4** tr. put (a picture) on a fresh mount. ● n. /reémownt/ **1** a fresh horse for a rider. **2** a supply of fresh horses for a regiment.

removal /rimoóvəl/ n. **1** the act or an instance of removing; the process of being removed. **2** Brit. the transfer of furniture and other contents on moving to another house. **3 a** dismissal from an office or post; deposition. **b** (an act of) murder.

■ **1** removing, taking away, elimination, eradication. **2** move, moving (house). **3 a** dismissal, transfer, transferral, discharge, throwing out, deposition, unseating, dethroning, dethronement, displacement, expulsion, ousting, riddance, purge, departure, move, ouster, colloq. sacking, sl. firing. **b** extermination, murder, elimination, killing, assassination, execution, liquidation, eradication, colloq. doing away with, sl. bumping off, doing in, rubbing out, wasting.

remove /rimoóv/ v. & n. ● v. **1** tr. take off or away from the place or position occupied; detach (remove the top carefully). **2** tr. a move or take to another place; change the situation of (will you remove the dishes?). **b** get rid of; eliminate (will remove all doubts). **3** tr. cause to be no longer present or available; take away (all privileges were removed). **4** tr. (often foll. by from) dismiss (from office). **5** tr. colloq. kill; assassinate. **6** tr. (in passive; foll. by from) distant or remote in condition (the country is not far removed from anarchy). **7** tr. (as **removed** adj.) (esp. of cousins) separated by a specified number of steps of descent (a first cousin twice removed = a grandchild of a first cousin). **8** formal **a** intr. (usu. foll. by from, to) change one's home or place of residence. **b** tr. conduct the removal of. ● n. **1** esp. Brit. a degree of remoteness; a distance. **2** a stage in a gradation; a degree (is several removes from what I expected). **3** Brit. a form or division in some schools. □□ **removable** adj. **removability** /-moóvəbílitee/ n. **remover** n. (esp. in sense 8b of v.). [ME f. OF removeir f. L removēre remot- (as RE-, movēre move)]

■ v. **1** take off, shed, strip or peel off, discard, literary doff; take out, unfasten, detach, disconnect, separate, undo. **2 a** take away, get rid of, carry away or off, shift; see also CONFISCATE. **b** obliterate, eradicate, eliminate, get rid of; wipe or rub out, erase, efface; wipe or rub off, take off, delete, expunge. **4** discharge, dismiss, displace, expel, oust, turn out, get rid of, purge, depose, unseat, kick out, colloq. sack, sl. fire. **5** murder, assassinate, kill, execute, eliminate, liquidate, dispose of, get rid of, colloq. do away with, sl. wipe out, do in, bump off, rub out, waste. **8 a** see MOVE v. 7. **b** relocate, move, transfer, shift. ● n. **1** see DISTANCE n. 2. **2** degree, level; see also STAGE n. 1.

remunerate /rimyoónərayt/ v.tr. **1** reward; pay for services rendered. **2** serve as or provide recompense for (toil, etc.) or to (a person). □□ **remuneration** /-ráyshən/ n. **remunerative** /-rətiv, -raytiv/ adj. **remuneratory** /-rətawree/ adj. [L remunerari (as RE-, munus muneris gift)]

■ □□ **remuneration** payment, compensation, salary, wages, earnings, emolument, income, pay, stipend, consideration, reward; recompense, repayment, reimbursement, restitution, reparation, damages, indemnity, indemnification; redress.

Renaissance /rénəsaáns, -zaáns, esp. Brit. rináysəns/ n. **1** the revival of art and literature under the influence of classical models in the 14th–16th c. **2** the period of this. **3** the culture and style of art, architecture, etc., developed during this era. **4** (**renaissance**) any similar revival. [F renaissance (as RE-, F naissance birth f. L nascentia or F naître naiss- be born f. Rmc: cf. NASCENT]

■ **4** (**renaissance**) renascence, rebirth, revival, reawakening, renewal, resurgence, regeneration, rejuvenation, new dawn, new birth.

renal /reénəl/ adj. of or concerning the kidneys. [F rénal f. LL renalis f. L renes kidneys]

rename /reénáym/ v.tr. name again; give a new name to.

renascence /rinásəns, rináy-/ n. **1** rebirth; renewal. **2** = RENAISSANCE. [RENASCENT]

renascent /rinásənt, rináy-/ adj. springing up anew; being reborn. [L renasci (as RE-, nasci be born)]

rencontre /renkóntər/ n. archaic = RENCOUNTER. [F (as REN-COUNTER)]

rencounter /renkówntər/ n. & v. ● n. **1** an encounter; a chance meeting. **2** a battle, skirmish, or duel. ● v.tr. encounter; meet by chance. [F rencontre(r) (as RE-, ENCOUNTER)]

rend /rend/ v. (past and past part. **rent** /rent/) archaic or rhet. **1** tr. (foll. by off, from, away, etc.; also absol.) tear or wrench forcibly. **2** tr. & intr. split or divide in pieces or into factions (a country rent by civil war). **3** tr. cause emotional pain to (the heart, etc.). □ **rend the air** sound piercingly. **rend one's garments** (or **hair**) display extreme grief or rage. [OE rendan, rel. to MLG rende]

■ **1** see WRENCH v. 1a. **2** split, tear or rip (to pieces or apart), divide, separate, shred, slice, archaic or poet. rive, literary cleave, tear or rip asunder; lacerate. **3** pain, distress, pierce, stab, wound, lacerate, afflict, torment, wring, hurt, archaic or literary smite. □ **rend one's garments** (or **hair**) tear one's hair out; see also FRET¹ v. 1a.

render /réndər/ v.tr. **1** cause to be or become; make (rendered us helpless). **2** give or pay (money, service, etc.), esp. in return or as a thing due (render thanks; rendered good for evil). **3** (often foll. by to) **a** give (assistance) (rendered aid to the injured man). **b** show (obedience, etc.). **c** do (a service, etc.). **4 a** submit; send in; present (an account, reason, etc.). **b** Law (of a judge or jury) deliver formally (a judgment or verdict). **5 a** represent or portray artistically, musically, etc. **b** act (a role); represent (a character, idea, etc.) (the dramatist's conception was well rendered). **c** Mus. perform; execute. **6** translate (rendered the poem into French). **7** (often foll. by down) melt down (fat, etc.) esp. to clarify; extract by melting. **8** cover (stone or brick) with a coat of plaster. **9** archaic **a** give back; hand over; deliver; give up; surrender (render unto Caesar the things that are Caesar's). **b** show (obedience). □□ **renderer** n. [ME f. OF rendre ult. f. L reddere reddit- (as RE-, dare give)]

■ **1** make, cause to be or become. **2** give (back), pay (back), reciprocate, return, repay; see also OFFER v. 3, 5. **3 a** give, offer, extend, proffer; see also PROVIDE 1. **c** do, perform, provide, offer, carry out, fulfill. **4 a** submit, deliver, hand in, present, offer, proffer, furnish, provide, tender. **b** deliver, return, hand down. **5 a** depict, represent, reproduce, portray, create, produce, do, execute, make. **b** see ACT v. 5a. **c** see PERFORM 2. **6** translate, put, interpret; transcribe, convert; restate, reword, rephrase. **7** melt (down); clarify, purify, clean; extract. **9 a** give up or back, yield (up), surrender, relinquish, cede, deliver, hand over, tender, offer, proffer, present, furnish, provide.

rendering /réndəring/ n. **1 a** the act or an instance of performing music, drama, etc.; an interpretation or perfor-

---

/.../ **pronunciation**	● **part of speech**
□ **phrases, idioms, and compounds**	
□□ **derivatives**	■ **synonym section**
cross-references appear in SMALL CAPITALS or italics	

mance (*an excellent rendering of the part*). **b** a translation. **2 a** the act or an instance of plastering stone, brick, etc. **b** this coating. **3** the act or an instance of giving, yielding, or surrendering.
  ▪ **1 a** interpretation, conception, construction, understanding, concept, reading, performance, depiction, delineation, portrayal, rendition, representation, version, reading. **b** translation, interpretation.

rendezvous /róndayvŏŏ, -də-/ *n. & v.* ● *n.* (*pl.* same /-vŏŏz/) **1** an agreed or regular meeting place. **2** a meeting by arrangement. **3** a place appointed for assembling troops, ships, etc. ● *v.intr.* (**rendezvouses** /-vŏŏz/; **rendezvoused** /-vŏŏd/; **rendezvousing** /-vŏŏing/) meet at a rendezvous. [F *rendez-vous* present yourselves f. *rendre*: see RENDER]

rendition /rendíshən/ *n.* (often foll. by *of*) **1** an interpretation or rendering of a dramatic role, piece of music, etc. **2** a visual representation. [obs. F f. *rendre* RENDER]
  ▪ **1** performance, interpretation, conception, concept, understanding, construction, reading, rendering, depiction, portrayal, delineation, representation, version. **2** representation, picture, version, execution, depiction, portrayal, delineation.

renegade /rénigayd/ *n., adj., & v.* ● *n.* **1** a person who deserts a party or principles. **2** an apostate; a person who abandons one religion for another. ● *adj.* traitorous, heretical. ● *v.intr.* be a renegade. [Sp. *renegado* f. med.L *renegatus* (as RE-, L *negare* deny)]
  ▪ *n.* **1** deserter, turncoat, heretic, defector, traitor, apostate, *archaic* renegado. **2** see DISSIDENT *n.*
  ● *adj.* traitorous, treacherous, perfidious, treasonous, apostate, heretical, disloyal.

renegado /rénigáydŏ, -gáa-/ *n.* (*pl.* **-os**) *archaic* = RENEGADE. [Sp. (as RENEGADE)]

renege /riníg, -nég, -néeg/ *v.* **1** *intr.* **a** go back on one's word; change one's mind; recant. **b** (foll. by *on*) go back on (a promise or undertaking or contract). **2** *tr.* deny; renounce; abandon (a person, faith, etc.). **3** *intr. Cards* revoke. □□ **reneger** *n.* [med.L *renegare* (as RE-, L *negare* deny)]
  ▪ **1 a** back out, default, go back on one's word, change one's mind, break one's word, break one's promise, recant. **b** (*renege on*) back out of, default on, welsh on; see also *go back on* (BACK). **2** deny, recant, renounce, abjure; see also ABANDON *v.* 2a.

renegotiate /réenigŏsheeayt/ *v.tr.* (also *absol.*) negotiate again or on different terms. □□ **renegotiable** /-sheeəbəl, -shəbəl/ *adj.* **renegotiation** /-sheeáyshən/ *n.*

renew /rinŏŏ, -nyŏŏ/ *v.tr.* **1** revive; regenerate; make new again; restore to the original state. **2** reinforce; resupply; replace. **3** repeat or reestablish; resume after an interruption (*renewed our acquaintance; a renewed attack*). **4** get, begin, make, say, give, etc., anew. **5** (also *absol.*) grant or be granted a continuation of or continued validity of (a license, subscription, lease, etc.). **6** recover (one's youth, strength, etc.). □□ **renewable** *adj.* **renewability** /-nyŏŏəbílitee/ *n.* **renewal** *n.* **renewer** *n.*
  ▪ **1** revive, regenerate, refresh, rejuvenate, revitalize, reinvigorate, resuscitate; restore, revamp, redo, refurbish, refurnish, renovate, refit, overhaul, recondition, modernize, redecorate, *colloq.* do over. **2** reinforce, resupply, restock, replenish, fill or top up, refill; replace. **3** resume, resurrect, pick or take up (again), recommence, restart, return to, reopen, reestablish. **4** repeat, reiterate, reaffirm, confirm, reconfirm, restate, reassert.

reniform /rénifawrm, rée-/ *adj.* esp. *Med.* kidney-shaped. [L *ren* kidney + -FORM]

rennet /rénit/ *n.* **1** curdled milk found in the stomach of an unweaned calf, used in curdling milk for cheese, junket, etc. **2** a preparation made from the stomach membrane of a calf or from certain fungi, used for the same purpose. [ME, prob. f. an OE form *rynet* (unrecorded), rel. to RUN]

rennin /rénin/ *n. Biochem.* an enzyme secreted into the stomach of unweaned mammals causing the clotting of milk. [RENNET + -IN]

renominate /réenómminayt/ *v.tr.* nominate for a further term of office. □□ **renomination** /-náyshən/ *n.*

renounce /rinówns/ *v.* **1** *tr.* consent formally to abandon; surrender; give up (a claim, right, possession, etc.). **2** *tr.* repudiate; refuse to recognize any longer (*renouncing their father's authority*). **3** *tr.* a decline further association or disclaim relationship with (*renounced my former friends*). **b** withdraw from; discontinue; forsake. **4** *intr. Law* refuse or resign a right or position esp. as an heir or trustee. **5** *intr. Cards* follow with a card of another suit when having no card of the suit led (cf. REVOKE). □ **renounce the world** abandon society or material affairs. □□ **renounceable** *adj.* **renouncement** *n.* **renouncer** *n.* [ME f. OF *renoncer* f. L *renuntiare* (as RE-, *nuntiare* announce)]
  ▪ **1** give up, forswear, surrender, abjure, abandon, desert, deny, forgo, abstain from, forsake, reject, repudiate, spurn, throw off or out, *colloq.* swear off, *literary* eschew. **2, 3** repudiate, reject, spurn, disown, scorn, abandon, discard, turn one's back on; see also SPURN *v.* □ **renounce the world** retreat, withdraw, turn one's back on the world, become a hermit, cloister or seclude or sequester oneself, hide away or out, shut or cut oneself off.

renovate /rénəvayt/ *v.tr.* **1** restore to good condition; repair. **2** make new again. □□ **renovation** /-váyshən/ *n.* **renovative** *adj.* **renovator** *n.* [L *renovare* (as RE-, *novus* new)]
  ▪ **1** redecorate, modernize, refurbish, refurnish, refit, recondition, restore, repair, revamp, overhaul, remodel, *colloq.* do over, do up. **2** see RENEW 1.

renown /rinówn/ *n.* fame; high distinction; celebrity (*a city of great renown*). [ME f. AF *ren(o)un*, OF *renon, renom* f. *renomer* make famous (as RE-, L *nominare* NOMINATE)]
  ▪ fame, celebrity, prestige, repute, glory, distinction, acclaim, prominence, eminence, note, éclat, luster, illustriousness; stardom.

renowned /rinównd/ *adj.* famous; celebrated.
  ▪ famous, famed, celebrated, distinguished, acclaimed, prominent, eminent, well-known, noted, notable, illustrious.

rent[1] /rent/ *n. & v.* ● *n.* **1** a tenant's periodical payment to an owner or landlord for the use of land or premises. **2** payment for the use of a service, equipment, etc. ● *v.* **1** *tr.* (often foll. by *from*) take, occupy, or use at a rent (*rented a boat from the marina*). **2** *tr.* (often foll. by *out*) let or hire (a thing) for rent. **3** *intr.* (foll. by *for, at*) be let or hired out at a specified rate (*the room rents for $300 per month*). □ **for rent** available to be rented. **rent-a-** (in *comb.*) denoting availability for hire (*rent-a-car*). **rent-free** with exemption from rent. **rent-roll** the register of a landlord's properties, with the rents due from them; the sum of one's income from rent. [ME f. OF *rente* f. Rmc (as RENDER)]
  ▪ *n.* **2** rental, hire, charge, lease; fee, cost, price, rate.
  ● *v.* **2, 3** let (out), lease, hire (out), charter.

rent[2] /rent/ *n.* **1** a large tear in a garment, etc. **2** an opening in clouds, etc. **3** a cleft, fissure, or gorge. [obs. *rent* var. of REND]
  ▪ **1** tear, rip, split, gash, slash, hole, slit. **3** cleft, fissure; see also GORGE *n.* 1.

rent[3] *past* and *past part.* of REND.

rentable /réntəbəl/ *adj.* **1** available or suitable for renting. **2** giving an adequate ratio of profit to capital. □□ **rentability** /-bílitee/ *n.*

rental /rént'l/ *n.* **1** the amount paid or received as rent. **2** the act of renting. **3** an income from rents. **4** a rented house, etc. [ME f. AF *rental* or AL *rentale* (as RENT[1])]

renter /réntər/ *n.* **1** a person who rents. **2** *Cinematog.* (in the UK) a person who distributes motion pictures. **3** *Brit. sl.* a male prostitute.

rentier /róntyay/ *n.* a person living on dividends from property, investments, etc. [F f. *rente* dividend]

renumber /réenúmbər/ *v.tr.* change the number or numbers given or allocated to.

renunciation /rinúnseeáyshən/ *n.* **1** the act or an instance of renouncing or giving up. **2** self-denial. **3** a document expressing renunciation. □□ **renunciant** /rinúnseeənt/ *n.* &

adj. **renunciative** /-seeətiv/ *adj.* **renunciatory** /-seeə-tawree, -shətawree/ *adj.* [ME f. OF *renonciation* or LL *renuntiatio* (as RENOUNCE)]

renvoi /renvóy/ *n. Law* the act or an instance of referring a case, dispute, etc., to a different jurisdiction. [F f. *renvoyer* send back]

reoccupy /ree-ókyəpī/ *v.tr.* (**-ies, -ied**) occupy again. □□ **reoccupation** /-páyshən/ *n.*

reoccur /ree-ə́kər/ *v.intr.* (**reoccurred, reoccurring**) occur again or habitually. □□ **reoccurrence** /-kúrəns/ *n.*

reopen /ree-ópən/ *v.tr. & intr.* open again.

reorder /ree-áwrdər/ *v. & n.* ● *v.tr.* order again. ● *n.* a renewed or repeated order for goods.

reorganize /ree-áwrgənīz/ *v.tr.* organize differently. □□ **reorganization** /-záyshən/ *n.* **reorganizer** *n.*

reorient /ree-áwree-ent, -óree-ent/ *v.tr.* **1** give a new direction to (ideas, etc.); redirect (a thing). **2** help (a person) find his or her bearings again. **3** change the outlook of (a person). **4** (*refl.*, often foll. by *to*) adjust oneself to or come to terms with something.

reorientate /ree-áwreeəntayt, -óreeən-/ *v.tr.* = REORIENT. □□ **reorientation** /-táyshən/ *n.*

Rep. *abbr.* **1** Representative (in Congress, state legislature, etc.). **2** Republican. **3** Republic.

rep[1] /rep/ *n. colloq.* a representative, esp. a salesperson. [abbr.]

rep[2] /rep/ *n. colloq.* **1** repertory. **2** a repertory theater or company. [abbr.]

rep[3] /rep/ *n.* (also **repp**) a textile fabric with a corded surface, used in curtains and upholstery. [F *reps*, of unkn. orig.]

rep[4] /rep/ *n. sl.* reputation. [abbr.]

repack /reepák/ *v.tr.* pack again.

repackage /reepákij/ *v.tr.* **1** package again or differently. **2** present in a new form. □□ **repackaging** *n.*

repaginate /reepájinayt/ *v.tr.* paginate again; renumber the pages of. □□ **repagination** /-náyshən/ *n.*

repaid *past* and *past part.* of REPAY.

repaint *v. & n.* ● *v.tr.* /reepáynt/ **1** paint again or differently. **2** restore the paint or coloring of. ● *n.* /reepaynt/ **1** the act of repainting. **2** esp. *Brit.* a repainted thing, esp. a golf ball.

repair[1] /ripáir/ *v. & n.* ● *v.tr.* **1** restore to good condition after damage or wear. **2** renovate or mend by replacing or fixing parts or by compensating for loss or exhaustion. **3** set right or make amends for (loss, wrong, error, etc.). ● *n.* **1** the act or an instance of restoring to sound condition (*in need of repair*; *closed during repair*). **2** the result of this (*the repair is hardly visible*). **3** good or relative condition for working or using (*must be kept in repair*; *in good repair*). □□ **repairable** *adj.* **repairer** *n.* [ME f. OF *reparer* f. L *reparare* (as RE-, *parare* make ready)]

■ *v.* **1, 2** put *or* set right, restore, fix (up), service, put (back) in *or* into working order, renovate, mend, patch (up), vamp, revamp, adjust. ● *n.* **1** restoration, fixing (up), servicing, adjustment, renovation, revamping. **2** mend; patch, darn. **3** form, condition, fettle, working order, shape, *Brit. colloq.* nick.

repair[2] /ripáir/ *v. & n.* ● *v.intr.* (foll. by *to*) resort; have recourse; go often or in great numbers or for a specific purpose (*repaired to Spain*). ● *n. archaic* **1** resort (*have repair to*). **2** a place of frequent resort. **3** popularity (*a place of great repair*). [ME f. OF *repaire(r)* f. LL *repatriare* REPATRIATE]

repairman /ripáirmən/ *n.* (*pl.* **-men**) a person who repairs machinery, etc.

repand /ripánd/ *adj. Bot.* with an undulating margin; wavy. [L *repandus* (as RE-, *pandus* bent)]

repaper /reepáypər/ *v.tr.* paper (a wall, etc.) again.

reparable /répərəbəl, ripáirəbəl/ *adj.* (of a loss, etc.) that can be made good. □□ **reparability** *n.* **reparably** *adv.* [F f. L *reparabilis* (as REPAIR[1])]

reparation /répəráyshən/ *n.* **1** the act or an instance of making amends. **2 a** compensation. **b** (esp. in *pl.*) compensation for war damage paid by the defeated nation, etc. **3** the act or an instance of repairing or being repaired. □□ **reparative** /ripáirətiv/ *adj.* [ME f. OF f. LL *reparatio -onis* (as REPAIR[1])]

repartee /répaartee, -táy/ *n.* **1** the practice or faculty of making witty retorts; sharpness or wit in quick reply. **2 a** a witty

retort. **b** witty retorts collectively. [F *repartie* fem. past part. of *repartir* start again, reply promptly (as RE-, *partir* PART)]

■ **2b** banter, badinage, patter, raillery, persiflage, wordplay.

repartition /reepaartíshən/ *v.tr.* partition again.

repass /reepás/ *v.tr. & intr.* pass again, esp. on the way back. [ME f. OF *repasser*]

repast /ripást/ *n.* **1** a meal, esp. of a specified kind (*a light repast*). **2** food and drink supplied for or eaten at a meal. [ME f. OF *repaistre* f. LL *repascere repast-* feed]

repatriate /reepáytreeayt/ *v. & n.* ● *v.* **1** *tr.* restore (a person) to his or her native land. **2** *intr.* return to one's own native land. ● *n.* a person who has been repatriated. □□ **repatriation** /-áyshən/ *n.* [LL *repatriare* (as RE-, L *patria* native land)]

repay /reepáy/ *v.* (*past* and *past part.* **repaid**) **1** *tr.* pay back (money). **2** *tr.* return (a blow, visit, etc.). **3** *tr.* make repayment to (a person). **4** *tr.* make return for; requite (a service, action, etc.) (*must repay their kindness*; *the book repays close study*). **5** *tr.* (often foll. by *for*) give in recompense. **6** *intr.* make repayment. □□ **repayable** *adj.* **repayment** *n.* [OF *repaier* (as RE-, PAY[1])]

■ **1** pay back, refund, square, give back, return. **2** return, pay back, reciprocate. **3** pay back, refund, recompense, compensate, reward, reimburse, settle up with, indemnify. **4** requite, reciprocate; return the compliment to, return the favor to. **5** pay back, recompense; see also PAY[1] v. 5.

repeal /ripeel/ *v. & n.* ● *v.tr.* revoke, rescind, or annul (a law, act of Congress, etc.). ● *n.* the act or an instance of repealing. □□ **repealable** *adj.* [ME f. AF *repeler*, OF *rapeler* (as RE-, APPEAL)]

■ *v.* revoke, recall, rescind, reverse, cancel, annul, nullify, invalidate, void, set aside, abolish, abrogate, *Law* vacate. ● *n.* revocation, recall, rescission, rescindment, reversal, cancellation, annulment, nullification, invalidation, voiding, abolition, abrogation.

repeat /ripeet/ *v. & n.* ● *v.* **1** *tr.* say or do over again. **2** *tr.* recite, rehearse, report, or reproduce (something from memory) (*repeated a poem*). **3** *tr.* imitate (an action, etc.). **4 a** *intr.* recur; appear again, perhaps several times (*a repeating pattern*). **b** *refl.* recur in the same or a similar form (*history repeats itself*). **5** *tr.* used for emphasis (*am not, repeat not, going*). **6** *tr.* (of food) be tasted intermittently for some time after being swallowed as a result of belching or indigestion. **7** *intr.* (of a watch, etc.) strike the last quarter, etc., over again when required. **8** *intr.* (of a firearm) fire several shots without reloading. **9** *intr.* illegally vote more than once in an election. ● *n.* **1 a** the act or an instance of repeating. **b** a thing repeated (often *attrib.*: *repeat performance*). **2** a repeated broadcast. **3** *Mus.* **a** a passage intended to be repeated. **b** a mark indicating this. **4** a pattern repeated in wallpaper, etc. **5** *Commerce* **a** a consignment similar to a previous one. **b** an order given for this; a reorder. □ **repeating decimal** a decimal fraction in which the same figures repeat indefinitely. **repeat oneself** say or do the same thing over again. □□ **repeatable** *adj.* **repeatability** /-peetəbílitee/ *n.* **repeatedly** *adv.* [ME f. OF *repeter* f. L *repetere* (as RE-, *petere* seek)]

■ *v.* **1** say again, reiterate, restate, retell, recapitulate, *colloq.* recap; echo; do again. **2** recite, quote, rehearse, report, reproduce, replicate, duplicate. **3** imitate, copy, duplicate, replicate, ape, mimic, parrot, monkey, emulate, simulate, impersonate, do an impression of. **4** see RECUR. **b** reproduce, replicate, duplicate. ● *n.* **1** a repetition; duplication, replication, reproduction; duplicate, copy, replica. **2** rerun, rebroadcast.

□□ **repeatedly** again and again, over again, over and again, over and over, frequently, often, time and (time) again, time after time, recurrently, repetitively, repetitiously.

repeater /ripeétər/ *n.* **1** a person or thing that repeats. **2** a firearm that fires several shots without reloading. **3** a watch or clock that repeats its last strike when required. **4** a device for the automatic retransmission or amplification of an electrically transmitted message. **5** a signal lamp indicating the state of another that is invisible.

repêchage /répishaázh/ *n.* (in rowing, etc.) an extra contest in which the runners-up in the eliminating heats compete for a place in the final. [F *repêcher* fish out, rescue]

repel /ripél/ *v.tr.* (**repelled, repelling**) **1** drive back; ward off; repulse. **2** refuse admission or approach or acceptance to (*repel an assailant*). **3** be repulsive or distasteful to. □□ **repeller** *n.* [ME f. L *repellere* (as RE-, *pellere puls-* drive)]
  ■ **1** repulse, reject, fend off, ward off, hold off, rebuff, resist, withstand, drive back *or* away *or* off; hold *or* keep at bay, keep at arm's length. **3** revolt, repulse, offend, disgust, sicken, nauseate, turn a person's stomach, make a person's skin crawl, *colloq.* give a person the creeps, turn off.

repellent /ripélənt/ *adj. & n.* ● *adj.* **1** that repels. **2** disgusting; repulsive. ● *n.* a substance that repels esp. insects, etc. □□ **repellence** *n.* **repellency** *n.* **repellently** *adv.* [L *repellere* (as REPEL)]
  ■ *adj.* repulsive, repelling, revolting, disgusting, nauseating, nauseous, stomach-turning, sickening, offensive, loathsome, repugnant, distasteful, disagreeable, obnoxious, off-putting.

repent[1] /ripént/ *v.* **1** *intr.* (often foll. by *of*) feel deep sorrow about one's actions, etc. **2** *tr.* (also *absol.*) wish one had not done; regret (one's wrong, omission, etc.); resolve not to continue (a wrongdoing, etc.). **3** *refl.* (often foll. by *of*) *archaic* feel regret or penitence about (*now I repent me*). □□ **repentance** *n.* **repentant** *adj.* **repenter** *n.* [ME f. OF *repentir* (as RE-, *pentir* ult. f. L *paenitēre*)]
  ■ regret, feel contrition, lament, bemoan, bewail, be sorry, rue, feel remorse, feel remorseful *or* penitent, show penitence. □□ **repentant** regretful, contrite, rueful, remorseful, apologetic, sorry, ashamed, penitent.

repent[2] /reépənt/ *adj. Bot.* creeping, esp. growing along the ground or just under the surface. [L *repere* creep]

repeople /reepeépəl/ *v.tr.* people again; increase the population of.

repercussion /reepərkúshən, répər-/ *n.* **1** (often foll. by *of*) an indirect effect or reaction following an event or action (*consider the repercussions of moving*). **2** the recoil after impact. **3** an echo or reverberation. □□ **repercussive** /-kúsiv/ *adj.* [ME f. OF *repercussion* or L *repercussio* (as RE-, PERCUSSION)]
  ■ **1** effect, consequence, aftereffect, result; outcome, conclusion, upshot. **3** reverberation, echo, echoing, reverberating, reecho, reechoing, resonating, ring; roll, boom, peal.

repertoire /répərtwaar/ *n.* **1** a stock of pieces, etc., that a company or a performer knows or is prepared to give. **2** a stock of regularly performed pieces, regularly used techniques, etc. (*went through his repertoire of excuses*). [F *répertoire* f. LL (as REPERTORY)]
  ■ **1** repertory, stock.

repertory /répərtawree/ *n.* (*pl.* **-ies**) **1** = REPERTOIRE. **2** the theatrical performance of various plays for short periods by one company. **3 a** a repertory company. **b** repertory theaters regarded collectively. **4** a store or collection, esp. of information, instances, etc. □ **repertory company** a theatrical company that performs plays from a repertoire. [LL *repertorium* f. L *reperire repert-* find]
  ■ **4** repertoire, store, reservoir, collection, hoard, stock, supply, stockpile.

repetend /répitend/ *n.* **1** the recurring figures of a decimal. **2** the recurring word or phrase; a refrain. [L *repetendum* (as REPEAT)]

répétiteur /repétitŏr/ *n.* **1** a tutor or coach of musicians, esp.

opera singers. **2** a person who supervises ballet rehearsals, etc. [F]

repetition /répitíshən/ *n.* **1 a** the act or an instance of repeating or being repeated. **b** the thing repeated. **2** a copy or replica. **3** a piece to be learned by heart. **4** the ability of a musical instrument to repeat a note quickly. □□ **repetitional** *adj.* **repetitionary** *adj.* [F *répétition* or L *repetitio* (as REPEAT)]
  ■ **1** reiteration, duplication, tautology, repeating, duplicating, recapitulation, replication, rereading, retelling, recital, rerunning, echoing; repeat, rehearsal, restatement, rerun, echo. **2** see COPY *n.* 1.

repetitious /répitíshəs/ *adj.* characterized by repetition, esp. when unnecessary or tiresome. □□ **repetitiously** *adv.* **repetitiousness** *n.*
  ■ tiresome, tedious, boring, redundant, prolix, long-winded, wordy, tautological, pleonastic, *colloq.* windy.

repetitive /ripétitiv/ *adj.* characterized by, or consisting of, repetition; monotonous. □ **repetitive strain injury** injury arising from the continued repeated use of particular muscles, esp. during keyboarding, etc. □□ **repetitively** *adv.* **repetitiveness** *n.*
  ■ repetitious, prolix, long-winded, wordy, tautological, pleonastic, *colloq.* windy; repeated, redundant; monotonous, humdrum, boring, tiresome, tedious.

rephrase /reéfráyz/ *v.tr.* express in an alternative way.
  ■ reword, reformulate.

repine /ripín/ *v.intr.* (often foll. by *at*, *against*, *for*) fret; be discontented. [RE- + PINE[2], after *repent*]

repique /ripeék/ *n. & v.* ● *n.* (in piquet) the winning of 30 points on cards alone before beginning to play. ● *v.* (**repiques, repiqued, repiquing**) **1** *intr.* score repique. **2** *tr.* score repique against (another person). [F *repic* (as RE-, PIQUE[2])]

replace /ripláys/ *v.tr.* **1** put back in place. **2** take the place of; succeed; be substituted for. **3** find or provide a substitute for; renew. **4** (often foll. by *with*, *by*) fill up the place of. **5** (in *passive*, often foll. by *by*) be succeeded or have one's place filled by another; be superseded. □□ **replaceable** *adj.* **replacer** *n.*
  ■ **1** restore, return, put back. **2** take the place of, supplant, succeed, supersede, take over from, substitute for; be substituted for, be put in place of. **3** change, renew. **4** see SUBSTITUTE *v.* **5** (*be replaced by*) be succeeded *or* superseded *or* supplanted *or* followed by.

replacement /ripláysmənt/ *n.* **1** the act or an instance of replacing or being replaced. **2** a person or thing that takes the place of another.
  ■ see SUBSTITUTE *n.* 1a.

replan /reéplán/ *v.tr.* (**replanned, replanning**) plan again or differently.

replant /reéplánt/ *v.tr.* **1** transfer (a plant, etc.) to a larger pot, a new site, etc. **2** plant (ground) again; provide with new plants.

replay *v. & n.* ● *v.tr.* /reépláy/ play (a match, recording, etc.) again. ● *n.* /reéplay/ the act or an instance of replaying a match, a recording, or a recorded incident in a game, etc.

replenish /riplénish/ *v.tr.* **1** (often foll. by *with*) fill up again. **2** renew (a supply, etc.). **3** (as **replenished** *adj.*) filled; fully stored or stocked; full. □□ **replenisher** *n.* **replenishment** *n.* [ME f. OF *replenir* (as RE-, *plenir* f. *plein* full f. L *plenus*)]
  ■ **1, 2** restock, refill, replace, fill *or* top up, reinforce; renew.

replete /ripleét/ *adj.* (often foll. by *with*) **1** filled or well-supplied with. **2** stuffed; gorged; sated. □□ **repleteness** *n.* **repletion** *n.* [ME f. OF *replet replete* or L *repletus* past part. of *replēre* (as RE-, *plēre plet-* fill)]
  ■ **1** well-supplied *or* -provided *or* -stocked, chock-full, crammed *or* jammed, brimful, chockablock, overflowing, brimming, bursting, teeming, loaded, overloaded, full, stuffed, *colloq.* jam-packed, gorged, lousy; filled up. **2** stuffed, gorged, sated, satisfied, full, *archaic* satiated; filled up.

replevin /riplévən/ *n. Law* **1** the provisional restoration or recovery of distrained goods pending the outcome of trial and judgment. **2** a writ granting this. **3** the action arising from this process. [ME f. AF f. OF *replevir* (as REPLEVY)]

replevy /riplévee/ *v.tr.* (**-ies, -ied**) *Law* recover by replevin. [OF *replevir* recover f. Gmc]

replica /réplikə/ *n.* **1** a duplicate of a work made by the original artist. **2 a** a facsimile; an exact copy. **b** (of a person) an exact likeness; a double. **3** a copy or model, esp. on a smaller scale. [It. f. *replicare* REPLY]

■ **2 a** copy, duplicate, facsimile, reproduction, replication; carbon copy, photocopy, duplication. **b** twin, clone, (dead) ringer, double, doppelgänger, exact *or* perfect likeness, *colloq.* picture, spitting image. **3** see MODEL *n.* 1, 3.

replicate *v., adj., & n.* ● *v.tr.* /réplikayt/ **1** repeat (an experiment, etc.). **2** make a replica of. **3** fold back. ● *adj.* /-kət/ *Bot.* folded back on itself. ● *n.* /-kət/ *Mus.* a tone one or more octaves above *or* below the given tone. □□ **replicable** /-kəbəl/ *adj.* (in sense 1 of *v.*). **replicability** /-bílitee/ *n.* (in sense 1 of *v.*). **replicative** /-kətiv/ *adj.* [L *replicare* (as RE-, *plicare* fold)]

replication /réplikáyshən/ *n.* **1** a reply or response, esp. a reply to an answer. **2** *Law* the plaintiff's reply to the defendant's plea. **3 a** the act or an instance of copying. **b** a copy. **c** the process by which genetic material or a living organism gives rise to a copy of itself. [ME f. OF *replicacion* f. L *replicatio -onis* (as REPLICATE)]

reply /riplí/ *v. & n.* ● *v.* (**-ies, -ied**) **1** *intr.* (often foll. by *to*) make an answer; respond in word or action. **2** *tr.* say in answer (*he replied, "Suit yourself"*). ● *n.* (*pl.* **-ies**) **1** the act of replying (*what did they say in reply?*). **2** what is replied; a response. **3** *Law* = REPLICATION. □ **reply paid 1** *hist.* (of a telegram) with the cost of a reply prepaid by the sender. **2** (of an envelope, etc.) for which the addressee undertakes to pay postage; postpaid. □□ **replier** *n.* [ME f. OF *replier* f. L (as REPLICATE)]

■ *v.* **1** answer, respond; counter, answer back, riposte, come back. **2** answer, respond, retort, rejoin, return, fling *or* hurl (back), come back. ● *n.* **1** response, reaction, answer, explanation, explication. **2** answer, response, rejoinder, retort, riposte, reaction, *sl.* comeback.

repolish /reepólish/ *v.tr.* polish again.

repopulate /reepópyəlayt/ *v.tr.* populate again or increase the population of. □□ **repopulation** /-láyshən/ *n.*

report /ripáwrt/ *v. & n.* ● *v.* **1** *tr.* **a** bring back or give an account of. **b** state as fact or news; narrate or describe or repeat, esp. as an eyewitness or hearer, etc. **c** relate as spoken by another. **2** *tr.* make an official or formal statement about. **3** *tr.* (often foll. by *to*) name or specify (an offender or offense) (*will report you for insubordination; reported them to the police*). **4** *intr.* (often foll. by *to*) present oneself as having returned or arrived (*report to the manager on arrival*). **5** *tr.* (also *absol.*) take down word for word or summarize or write a description of for publication. **6** *intr.* make or draw up or send in a report. **7** *intr.* (often foll. by *to*) be responsible (to a superior, supervisor, etc.) (*reports directly to the managing director*). **8** *tr.* (often foll. by *out*) (of a committee, etc.) send back (a bill, etc.), with comments and recommendations, to a legislature, etc. **9** *intr.* (often foll. by *of*) give a report to convey that one is well, badly, etc., impressed (*reports well of the prospects*). **10** *intr.* (usu. foll. by *on*) investigate or scrutinize for a journalistic report; act as a reporter. ● *n.* **1** an account given or opinion formally expressed after investigation or consideration. **2** a description, summary, or reproduction of an event or speech or legal case, esp. for newspaper publication or broadcast. **3** common talk; rumor. **4** the way a person or thing is spoken of (*I hear a good report of you*). **5** a periodical statement on (esp. a student's) work, conduct, etc. **6** the sound of an explosion. □ **report back** deliver a report to the person, organization, etc., for whom one acts, etc. **report card** an official report issued by a school showing a student's grades, progress, etc. **reported speech** the speaker's words with the changes of per-

son, tense, etc., usual in reports, e.g., *he said that he would go* (opp. *direct speech*). □□ **reportable** *adj.* **reportedly** *adv.* [ME f. OF *reporter* f. L *reportare* (as RE-, *portare* bring)]

■ *v.* **1 a, b** relate, recount, describe, narrate, tell of, detail, give an account of, communicate, set forth; document. **c** relate, recount, recite, communicate, give an account of. **2** publish, promulgate, publicize, put out, announce, set forth, reveal, disclose, divulge, circulate, make public, broadcast. **4** present *or* announce oneself, make oneself known. **10** (*report on*) investigate, cover, examine, explore, look into, inquire into, check into *or* on, check up on, research, study, probe, scrutinize, check out, *Brit. sl.* suss out. ● *n.* **1** see ACCOUNT *n.* 1. **2** description, story, article, piece, statement, dispatch, communication, communiqué, announcement, narrative, record, *colloq.* write-up. **3** piece of gossip *or* hearsay; see also RUMOR *n.* 1. **5** assessment, evaluation, appraisal, record (of achievement). **6** explosion, bang, boom, shot, gunshot, crack, blast, detonation.

reportage /ripáwrtij, répawrtaázh/ *n.* **1** the describing of events, esp. the reporting of news, etc., for the press and for broadcasting. **2** the typical style of this. **3** factual presentation in a book, etc. [REPORT, after F]

reporter /ripáwrtər/ *n.* **1** a person employed to report news, etc., for newspapers or broadcasts. **2** a person who reports.

■ **1** journalist, newspaperman, newsman, correspondent, columnist, newswriter, gentleman *or* lady of the press, newshound, newshawk, *Brit.* pressman, *colloq.* stringer, *Austral. colloq.* journo, *joc.* gentleman *or* lady of the fourth estate.

reportorial /rípawrtáwreeəl/ *adj.* **1** of newspaper reporters. **2** relating to or characteristic of a report. □□ **reportorially** *adv.* [REPORTER, after *editorial*]

repose¹ /ripóz/ *n. & v.* ● *n.* **1** the cessation of activity or excitement or toil. **2** sleep. **3** a peaceful or quiescent state; stillness; tranquillity. **4** *Art* a restful effect; harmonious combination. **5** composure or ease of manner. ● *v.* **1** *intr. & refl.* lie down in rest (*reposed on a sofa*). **2** *tr.* (often foll. by *on*) lay (one's head, etc.) to rest (on a pillow, etc.). **3** *intr.* (often foll. by *in, on*) lie, be lying or laid, esp. in sleep or death. **4** *tr.* give rest to; refresh with rest. **5** *intr.* esp. *Brit.* (foll. by *on, upon*) be supported or based on. **6** *intr.* (foll. by *on*) (of memory, etc.) dwell on. □□ **reposal** *n.* **reposeful** *adj.* **reposefully** *adv.* **reposefulness** *n.* [ME f. OF *repos(er)* f. LL *repausare* (as RE-, *pausare* PAUSE)]

■ *n.* **1** inactivity, quiet, peace (and quiet); breathing space, break, breather, interval, intermission. **2** see SLEEP *n.* 2. **3** calm, tranquillity, quiet, stillness, still, restfulness, peace, relaxation. **5** composure, calmness, calm, serenity, equanimity, poise, self-possession. ● *v.* **1, 2** see LIE¹ *v.* 1, REST¹ *v.* 1. **3** see REST¹ *v.* 2. **5** rest, be supported or based.

repose² /ripóz/ *v.tr.* (foll. by *in*) place (trust, etc.) in. □□ **reposal** *n.* [RE- + POSE¹ after L *reponere reposit-*]

reposition /reepəzíshən/ *v.* **1** *tr.* move or place in a different position. **2** *intr.* adjust or alter one's position.

repository /ripózitawree/ *n.* (*pl.* **-ies**) **1** a place where things are stored or may be found, esp. a warehouse or museum. **2** a receptacle. **3** (often foll. by *of*) **a** a book, person, etc., regarded as a store of information, etc. **b** the recipient of confidences or secrets. [obs. F *repositoire* or L *repositorium* (as REPOSE²)]

■ **3a** mine, storehouse, treasure trove.

repossess /reepəzés/ *v.tr.* regain possession of (esp. property or goods on which repayment of a debt is in arrears). □□ **repossession** *n.* **repossessor** *n.*

repot /reepót/ *v.tr.* (**repotted, repotting**) put (a plant) in another, esp. larger, pot.

/. . ./ **pronunciation**	● **part of speech**
□ **phrases, idioms, and compounds**	
□□ **derivatives**	■ **synonym section**
cross-references appear in SMALL CAPITALS or *italics*	

repoussé /rəpōōsáy/ *adj. & n.* ● *adj.* hammered into relief from the reverse side. ● *n.* ornamental metalwork fashioned in this way. [F, past part. of *repousser* (as RE-, *pousser* PUSH)]

repp var. of REP³.

repped /rept/ *adj.* having a surface like rep.

repr. *abbr.* **1** represent, represented, etc. **2** reprint, reprinted, etc.

reprehend /réprihénd/ *v.tr.* rebuke; blame; find fault with. □□ **reprehension** *n.* [ME f. L *reprehendere* (as RE-, *prehendere* seize)]

reprehensible /réprihénsibəl/ *adj.* deserving censure or rebuke; blameworthy. □□ **reprehensibility** *n.* **reprehensibly** *adv.* [LL *reprehensibilis* (as REPREHEND)]

represent /réprizént/ *v.tr.* **1** stand for or correspond to (*the comment does not represent all our views*). **2** (often in *passive*) be a specimen or example of; exemplify (*all types of people were represented in the audience*). **3** act as an embodiment of; symbolize (*the eagle represents the United States*; *numbers are represented by letters*). **4** call up in the mind by description or portrayal or imagination; place a likeness of before the mind or senses. **5** serve or be meant as a likeness of. **6 a** state by way of expostulation or persuasion (*represented the rashness of it*). **b** (foll. by *to*) try to bring (the facts influencing conduct) home to (*represented the risks to his client*). **7 a** (often foll. by *as, to be*) describe or depict as; declare or make out (*represented them as martyrs*; *not what you represent it to be*). **b** (often *refl.*; usu. foll by *as*) portray; assume the guise of; pose as (*represents himself as an honest broker*). **8** (foll. by *that +* clause) allege. **9** show, or play the part of, on stage. **10** fill the place of; be a substitute or deputy for; be entitled to act or speak for (*the president was represented by the secretary of state*). **11** be elected as a member of Congress, a legislature, etc., by (*represents a rural constituency*). □□ **representable** *adj.* **representativity** /-əbílitee/ *n.* [ME f. OF *representer* or f. L *repraesentare* (as RE-, PRESENT²)]

▪ **1** stand for, typify, exemplify, embody, illustrate, epitomize; correspond to, fit, match. **2** see EXEMPLIFY. **3** see SYMBOLIZE. **4** evoke, capture; see also CHARACTERIZE 1, 2. **5** show, present, display, exhibit; see also SYMBOLIZE. **6 a** argue, urge, plead, affirm, set forth. **7 a** present, depict, describe, delineate, show, characterize, define, sketch, note, picture, portray, draw, paint, report; declare, make out, pretend, assert, state, allege. **b** (*represent oneself as*) present oneself as, depict oneself as, put *or* set oneself forth as, masquerade as, take (on) *or* assume the guise of, take (on) the role *or* part of, impersonate, pretend to be, pose as. **8** see ALLEGE. **9** present, show, stage, produce, put on, mount, do, play, perform; see also ACT *v.* 5a. **10** substitute for, stand (in) for, deputize for, replace, act for *or* on behalf of, take the place of, be substituted for, be put in place of.

representation /réprizentáyshən/ *n.* **1** the act or an instance of representing or being represented. **2** a thing (esp. a painting, etc.) that represents another. **3** (esp. in *pl.*) a statement made by way of allegation or to convey opinion. [ME f. OF *representation* or L *repraesentatio* (as REPRESENT)]

▪ **2** reproduction, replica; image, portrait, likeness, picture, model, figure, figurine, statue, statuette, bust, head, effigy; depiction, portrayal, manifestation. **3** allegation, deposition, statement; declaration, account, exposition, assertion.

representational /réprizentáyshənəl/ *adj.* of representation. □ **representational art** art seeking to portray the physical appearance of a subject. □□ **representationalism** *n.* **representationalist** *adj. & n.*

representationism /réprizentáyshənizəm/ *n.* the doctrine that perceived objects are only a representation of real external objects. □□ **representationist** *n.*

representative /réprizéntətiv/ *adj. & n.* ● *adj.* **1** typical of a class or category. **2** containing typical specimens of all or many classes (*a representative sample*). **3 a** consisting of elected deputies, etc. **b** based on the representation of a nation, etc., by such deputies (*representative government*). **4** (foll. by *of*) serving as a portrayal or symbol of (*representative*

of their attitude to work). **5** that presents or can present ideas to the mind (*imagination is a representative faculty*). **6** (of art) representational. ● *n.* **1** (foll. by *of*) a sample, specimen, or typical embodiment or analog of. **2 a** the agent of a person or society. **b** a salesperson. **3** a delegate; a substitute. **4** a deputy in a representative assembly. □□ **representatively** *adv.* **representativeness** *n.* [ME f. OF *representatif -ive* or med.L *repraesentativus* (as REPRESENT)]

▪ *adj.* **1, 2** typical, characteristic, illustrative, exemplary; archetypal, paradigmatic. **3 b** elected, chosen, democratic, popular. **4** (*representative of*) typical of, characteristic of, illustrative of, symbolic of, emblematic of, in character with *or* of, like, indicative of; symptomatic of. ● *n.* **1** see SPECIMEN, embodiment (EMBODY). **2 a** see AGENT 1a. **b** salesman *or* saleswoman, traveling salesman, *colloq.* rep. **3** delegate, substitute, deputy, ambassador, spokesman, spokeswoman, proxy, envoy, emissary; missionary, *RC Ch.* (papal) nuncio, *archaic* legate. **4** member of Congress, congressman, congresswoman, member of Parliament, MP; councilor.

repress /riprés/ *v.tr.* **1 a** check; restrain; keep under; quell. **b** suppress; prevent from sounding, rioting, or bursting out. **2** *Psychol.* actively exclude (an unwelcome thought) from conscious awareness. **3** (usu. as **repressed** *adj.*) subject (a person) to the suppression of his or her thoughts or impulses. □□ **represser** *n.* **repressible** *adj.* **repression** /-préshən/ *n.* **repressive** *adj.* **repressively** *adv.* **repressiveness** *n.* **repressor** *n.* [ME f. L *reprimere* (as RE-, *premere* PRESS¹)]

▪ **1** suppress, put down, (keep in) check, curb, muzzle, quash, stifle, squelch, (keep under) control, contain, restrain, constrain, limit, keep back *or* in, quell, hold back *or* in, subdue, inhibit; deter, frustrate, discourage, disallow. **2** inhibit, suppress, stifle, control, keep under control, restrain, keep back *or* in, hold back *or* in; discourage, disallow. **3** (**repressed**) see PENT.

□□ **repression** restraint, suppression, subjugation, checking, squelching, control, inhibition, stifling, frustration, frustrating, deterrence, deterring.

repressive tyrannical, oppressive, dictatorial, despotic, brutal, suppressive, authoritarian, totalitarian.

reprice /réeprís/ *v.tr.* price again or differently.

reprieve /ripréev/ *v. & n.* ● *v.tr.* **1** remit, commute, or postpone the execution of (a condemned person). **2** give respite to. ● *n.* **1 a** the act or an instance of reprieving or being reprieved. **b** a warrant for this. **2** respite; a respite or temporary escape. [ME as past part. *repryed* f. AF & OF *repris* past part. of *reprendre* (as RE-, *prendre* f. L *prehendere* take): 16th-c. *-v-* unexpl.]

▪ *v.* remit, let off, spare, pardon; *Law* commute; respite, postpone. ● *n.* **1a, 2** respite, stay (of execution), postponement, delay, suspension, extension; amnesty, pardon.

reprimand /réprimand/ *n. & v.* ● *n.* (often foll. by *for*) an official or sharp rebuke (for a fault, etc.). ● *v.tr.* administer this to. [F *réprimande(r)* f. Sp. *reprimenda* f. L *reprimenda* neut. pl. gerundive of *reprimere* REPRESS]

▪ *n.* scolding, reproof, rebuke, admonition, upbraiding, castigation, reproach, lecture, tongue-lashing, rap on the knuckles, *colloq.* dressing-down, slap on the wrist, bawling out, talking-to, esp. *Brit.* telling-off, ticking-off. ● *v.* scold, reprove, rebuke, admonish, upbraid, castigate, reproach, berate, lecture, censure, criticize, find fault with, attack, flay, flay alive, reprehend, read a person the riot act, give a person a rap on the knuckles, take to task, haul over the coals, give a person a piece of one's mind, *archaic or literary* chide, *colloq.* bawl out, dress down, give a person a dressing-down, give a person a slap on the wrist, tell off, call on the carpet, *colloq.* tell a person a thing or two, give a person a piece of one's mind, chew out.

reprint *v. & n.* ● *v.tr.* /réeprínt/ print again. ● *n.* /réeprínt/ **1** the act or an instance of reprinting a book, etc. **2** the book, etc., reprinted. **3** the quantity reprinted. □□ **reprinter** *n.*

reprisal /ripríz-əl/ n. **1** (an act of) retaliation. **2** hist. the forcible seizure of a foreign subject or his or her goods as an act of retaliation. [ME (in sense 2) f. AF reprisaille f. med.L reprisalia f. repraehensalia (as REPREHEND)]
■ **1** retaliation, requital; revenge, retribution, vengeance, repayment, getting even.

reprise /ripreéz/ n. **1** a repeated passage in music. **2** a repeated item in a musical program. [F, fem. past part. of reprendre (see REPRIEVE)]

repro /reéprō/ n. (pl. -os) (often attrib.) **1** a reproduction or copy. **2** (also **reproduction proof**) a proof, usu. on glossy paper, that can be used as photographic copy for a printing plate. [abbr.]

reproach /ripróch/ v. & n. ● v.tr. **1** express disapproval to (a person) for a fault, etc. **2** scold; rebuke; censure. **3** archaic rebuke (an offense). ● n. **1** a rebuke or censure (heaped reproaches on them). **2** (often foll. by to) a thing that brings disgrace or discredit (their behavior is a reproach to us all). **3** a disgraced or discredited state (live in reproach and ignominy). **4** (in pl.) RC Ch. a set of antiphons and responses for Good Friday representing the reproaches of Christ to his people. □ **above** (or **beyond**) **reproach** perfect. □□ **reproachable** adj. **reproacher** n. **reproachingly** adv. [ME f. OF reproche(r) f. Rmc (as RE-, L prope near)]

reproachful /ripróchfŏŏl/ adj. full of or expressing reproach. □□ **reproachfully** adv. **reproachfulness** n.
■ faultfinding, critical, censorious, disapproving, disparaging, upbraiding, reproving, scolding, admonitory, condemnatory, hypercritical.

reprobate /réprəbayt/ n., adj., & v. ● n. **1** an unprincipled person; a person of highly immoral character. **2** a person who is condemned by God. ● adj. **1** immoral. **2** hardened in sin. ● v.tr. **1** express or feel disapproval of; censure. **2** (of God) condemn; exclude from salvation. □□ **reprobation** /-báyshən/ n. [ME f. L reprobare reprobat- disapprove (as RE-, probare approve)]
■ n. **1** scoundrel, blackguard, miscreant, rake, profligate, roué, wastrel, degenerate, unprincipled person, evil-doer, debauchee, libertine, good-for-nothing, ne'er-do-well, cur, knave, scalawag, archaic or joc. rapscallion, colloq. scamp, often joc. rascal. ● adj. **1, 2** unprincipled, immoral, amoral, abandoned, depraved, despicable, dissolute, low, base, mean, debased, cursed, degenerate, profligate, shameful, shameless, vile, evil, wicked, villainous, sinful, irredeemable, iniquitous, reprehensible, colloq. accursed, damned.

reprocess /reépróses, -prō-/ v.tr. process again or differently.

reproduce /reéprədóōs, -dyóōs/ v. **1** tr. produce a copy or representation of. **2** tr. cause to be seen or heard, etc., again (tried to reproduce the sound exactly). **3** intr. produce further members of the same species by natural means. **4** refl. produce offspring (reproduced itself several times). **5** intr. give a specified quality or result when copied (reproduces badly in black and white). **6** tr. Biol. form afresh (a lost part, etc., of the body). □□ **reproducer** n. **reproducible** adj. **reproducibility** /-əbílitee/ n. **reproducibly** adv.
■ **1, 2** duplicate, copy, replicate, recreate, repeat, simulate; imitate. **3** breed, multiply, propagate, procreate, spawn, proliferate. **5** duplicate, copy, photocopy, propr. Xerox.

reproduction /reéprədúkshən/ n. **1** the act or an instance of reproducing. **2** a copy of a work of art, esp. a print or photograph of a painting. **3** (attrib.) (of furniture, etc.) made in imitation of a certain style or of an earlier period. □□ **reproductive** adj. **reproductively** adv. **reproductiveness** n.
■ **1** duplication, copying, printing; propagation, breeding, spawning, proliferation, production. **2** print, imitation, copy, facsimile, replica; photograph. **3** see IMITATION adj.

reprogram /reéprógram/ v.tr. (**reprogrammed, reprogramming**) program (esp. a computer) again or differently. □□ **reprogrammable** /-prógraməbəl, -prógrám-/ adj.

reprography /riprógrəfee/ n. the science and practice of copying documents by photography, xerography, etc. □□ re-

prographer n. **reprographic** /reéprəgráfik/ adj. **reprographically** adv. [REPRODUCE + -GRAPHY]

reproof[1] /riprŏŏf/ n. **1** blame (a glance of reproof). **2** a rebuke; words expressing blame. [ME f. OF reprove f. reprover REPROVE]
■ **1** see BLAME n. 1. **2** see REBUKE n.

reproof[2] /reéprŏŏf/ v.tr. **1** esp. Brit. render (a coat, etc.) waterproof again. **2** make a fresh proof of (printed matter, etc.).

reprove /riprŏŏv/ v.tr. rebuke (a person, a person's conduct, etc.). □□ **reprovable** adj. **reprover** n. **reprovingly** adv. [ME f. OF reprover f. LL reprobare disapprove: see REPROBATE]
■ see REPRIMAND v.

reptant /réptənt/ adj. (of a plant or animal) creeping. [L reptare reptant- frequent. of repere crawl]

reptile /réptil/ n. & adj. ● n. **1** any cold-blooded scaly animal of the class Reptilia, including snakes, lizards, crocodiles, turtles, tortoises, etc. **2** a mean, groveling, or repulsive person. ● adj. **1** (of an animal) creeping. **2** mean; groveling. □□ **reptilian** /-tíleeən, -tílyən/ adj. & n. [ME f. LL reptilis f. L repere rept- crawl]

republic /ripúblik/ n. **1** a nation in which supreme power is held by the people or their elected representatives or by an elected or nominated president, not by a monarch, etc. **2** a society with equality between its members (the literary republic). [F république f. L respublica f. res concern + publicus PUBLIC]

republican /ripúblikən/ adj. & n. ● adj. **1** of or constituted as a republic. **2** characteristic of a republic. **3** advocating or supporting republican government. ● n. **1** a person advocating or supporting republican government. **2** (**Republican**) a member or supporter of the Republican Party. **3** an advocate of a united Ireland. □ **Republican party** one of the two main US political parties, favoring a lesser degree of central power (cf. Democratic party). □□ **republicanism** n.

republish /reépúblish/ v.tr. (also absol.) publish again or in a new edition, etc. □□ **republication** /-likáyshən/ n.

repudiate /ripyŏŏdeeayt/ v.tr. **1 a** disown; disavow; reject. **b** refuse dealings with. **c** deny. **2** refuse to recognize or obey (authority or a treaty). **3** refuse to discharge (an obligation or debt). **4** (esp. of the ancients or non-Christians) divorce (one's spouse). □□ **repudiable** adj. **repudiation** /-áyshən/ n. **repudiator** n. [L repudiare f. repudium divorce]
■ **1 a** disown, disavow, reject, scorn, renounce, retract, rescind, reverse, abandon, abrogate, forswear, forgo, deny, discard. **2** see DISOBEY.

repugnance /ripúgnəns/ n. (also **repugnancy**) **1** (usu. foll. by to, against) antipathy; aversion. **2** (usu. foll. by of, between, to, with) inconsistency or incompatibility of ideas, statements, etc. [ME (in sense 2) f. F répugnance or L repugnantia f. repugnare oppose (as RE-, pugnare fight)]

repugnant /ripúgnənt/ adj. **1** (often foll. by to) extremely distasteful. **2** (often foll. by to) contradictory. **3** (often foll. by with) incompatible. **4** poet. refractory; resisting. □□ **repugnantly** adv. [ME f. F répugnant or L (as REPUGNANCE)]
■ **1** repulsive, abhorrent, disgusting, off-putting, offensive, repellent, revolting, vile, abominable, loathsome, foul, distasteful, unpalatable, unsavory, execrable, intolerable, obnoxious, nauseating, nauseous, sickening, unpleasant, objectionable, literary noisome. **2** see CONTRADICTORY. **3** see INCOMPATIBLE 1, 3.

repulse /ripúls/ v. & n. ● v.tr. **1** drive back (an attack or attacking enemy) by force of arms. **2 a** rebuff (friendly advances or their maker). **b** refuse (a request or offer or its maker). **3** be repulsive to; repel. **4** foil in controversy. ● n.

/. . ./ **pronunciation**	● **part of speech**
□ **phrases, idioms, and compounds**	
□□ **derivatives**	■ **synonym section**
cross-references appear in SMALL CAPITALS or italics	

1 the act or an instance of repulsing or being repulsed. **2** a rebuff. [L *repellere repuls-* drive back (as REPEL)]
■ *v.* **1** repel, drive back, ward off, fight *or* beat off, check. **2 a** see REBUFF *v.* **b** see REFUSE¹ 1. **3** see REPEL 3. ● *n.* rejection, rebuff, refusal, denial, snub, cold shoulder, spurning.

repulsion /ripúlshən/ *n.* **1** aversion; disgust. **2** esp. *Physics* the force by which bodies tend to repel each other or increase their mutual distance (opp. ATTRACTION). [LL *repulsio* (as REPEL)]

repulsive /ripúlsiv/ *adj.* **1** causing aversion or loathing; loathsome; disgusting. **2** *Physics* exerting repulsion. **3** *archaic* (of behavior, etc.) cold; unsympathetic. □□ **repulsively** *adv.* **repulsiveness** *n.* [F *répulsif -ive* or f. REPULSE]
■ **1** disgusting, revolting, abhorrent, loathsome, repugnant, repellent, offensive, obnoxious, objectionable, unsavory, distasteful, nasty, unpleasant, displeasing, disagreeable, ugly, off-putting, sickening, nauseating, nauseous, vile, foul, odious, hideous, horrible, horrid, abominable, execrable, *sl.* gross.

repurchase /ree'pərchis/ *v.* & *n.* ● *v.tr.* purchase again. ● *n.* the act or an instance of purchasing again.

repurify /ree'pyoorifi/ *v.tr.* (-ies, -ied) purify again. □□ **repurification** /-fikáyshən/ *n.*

reputable /répyətəbəl/ *adj.* of good repute; respectable. □□ **reputably** *adv.* [obs. F or f. med.L *reputabilis* (as REPUTE)]
■ respectable, honorable, well-thought-of, estimable, esteemed, respected, trustworthy, trusted, honest, reliable, dependable, principled, virtuous, good, worthy.

reputation /répyətáyshən/ *n.* **1** what is generally said or believed about a person's or thing's character or standing (*has a reputation for dishonesty*). **2** the state of being well thought of; distinction; respectability (*have my reputation to think of*). **3** (foll. by *of, for* + verbal noun) credit or discredit (*has the reputation of driving hard bargains*). [ME f. L *reputatio* (as REPUTE)]
■ **1** name. **2** repute, name, standing, stature, position, status. **3** see HONOR *v.* 1, DISCREDIT *v.* 1.

repute /ripyoot/ *n.* & *v.* ● *n.* reputation (*known by repute*). ● *v.tr.* **1** (as **reputed** *adj.*) (often foll. by *to* + infin.) be generally considered or reckoned (*is reputed to be the best*). **2** (as **reputed** *adj.*) passing as being, but probably not being (*his reputed father*). □ **house of ill repute** a brothel. □□ **reputedly** *adv.* [ME f. OF *reputer* or L *reputare* (as RE-, *putare* think)]
■ *v.* **1** (**reputed**) rumored, said, held, regarded, viewed, looked on *or* upon, judged, considered, thought, believed, *formal* deemed; alleged, purported. **2** (**reputed**) see *supposed* (SUPPOSE 6).

request /rikwést/ *n.* & *v.* ● *n.* **1** the act or an instance of asking for something; a petition (*came at his request*). **2** a thing asked for. **3** the state of being sought after; demand (*in great request*). **4** a letter, etc., asking for a particular recording, etc., to be played on a radio program, often with a personal message. ● *v.tr.* **1** ask to be given or allowed or favored with (*request a hearing*; *requests your presence*). **2** (foll. by *to* + infin.) ask a person to do something (*requested her to answer*). **3** (foll. by *that* + clause) ask that. □ **by** (or **on**) **request** in response to an expressed wish. □□ **requester** *n.* [ME f. OF *requeste(r)* ult. f. L *requaerere* (as REQUIRE)]
■ *n.* **1, 2** solicitation, entreaty, plea, petition, application, requisition, call, demand. **3** (*in request*) see *in demand* (DEMAND). ● *v.* **1** ask for, seek, plead for, apply for, put in for, requisition, call for, demand, insist on, solicit, beg, entreat, beseech. **2** ask, call on, require, appeal to, beg, entreat, beseech, importune.

requiem /rékweeəm, rée'kwee-/ *n.* **1** (**Requiem**) (also *attrib.*) *RC Ch., Anglican Ch.* a Mass for the repose of the souls of the dead. **2** *Mus.* the musical setting for this. [ME f. accus. of L *requies* rest, the initial word of the mass]

requiescat /rékwee-éskat, -kaat/ *n.* a wish or prayer for the repose of a dead person. [L, = may he or she rest (in peace)]

require /rikwír/ *v.tr.* **1** need; depend on for success or fulfillment (*the work requires much patience*). **2** lay down as an imperative (*did all that was required by law*). **3** command; instruct (a person, etc.). **4** order; insist on (an action or measure). **5** (often foll. by *of, from,* or *that* + clause) demand (of or from a person) as a right. **6** wish to have (*is there anything else you require?*). □□ **requirer** *n.* **requirement** *n.* [ME f. OF *requere* ult. f. L *requirere* (as RE-, *quaerere* seek)]
■ **1** need, necessitate, demand, ask *or* call for, cry out for; rely *or* depend on. **2** see DECREE *v.* **3** order, command, ask (for), call (for), instruct, coerce, force, compel, make; insist, demand. **6** need, want, desire, lack, be lacking, be missing, be short of. □□ **requirement** requisite, prerequisite, demand, precondition, condition, qualification, stipulation, sine qua non, provision, proviso, necessity, essential, desideratum, must; need, want, demand, wish.

requisite /rékwizit/ *adj.* & *n.* ● *adj.* required by circumstances; necessary to success, etc. ● *n.* (often foll. by *for*) a thing needed (for some purpose). □□ **requisitely** *adv.* [ME f. L *requisitus* past part. (as REQUIRE)]

requisition /rékwizíshən/ *n.* & *v.* ● *n.* **1** an official order laying claim to the use of property or materials. **2** a formal written demand that some duty should be performed. **3** being called or put into service. ● *v.tr.* demand the use or supply of, esp. by requisition order. □□ **requisitioner** *n.* **requisitionist** *n.* [F *réquisition* or L *requisitio* (as REQUIRE)]
■ *n.* **2** see ORDER *n.* 2. ● *v.* request, order, demand, call for, mandate; seize, appropriate, confiscate, take possession of, take (over), occupy; expropriate.

requite /rikwít/ *v.tr.* **1** make return for (a service). **2** (often foll. by *with*) reward or avenge (a favor or injury). **3** (often foll. by *for*) make return to (a person). **4** (often foll. by *for, with*) repay with good or evil (*requite like for like*; *requite hate with love*). □□ **requital** *n.* [RE- + *quite* var. of QUIT]
■ **1** reciprocate, return, match, equal, complement. **2** reward, repay, reciprocate, recompense; avenge, revenge, pay back for, give tit for tat for. **3** repay, reward, recompense, pay back, compensate. □□ **requital** repayment, return, payment, quid pro quo; recompense, remuneration; revenge, retribution, vengeance; retaliation.

reran *past of* RERUN.

reread /rée-reed/ *v.* & *n.* ● *v.tr.* (*past* and *past part.* **reread** /-réd/) read again. ● *n.* an instance of reading again. □□ **rereadable** *adj.*

reredos /rérədos, rírə-/ *n. Eccl.* an ornamental screen covering the wall at the back of an altar. [ME f. AF f. OF *areredos* f. *arere* behind + *dos* back: cf. ARREARS]

rerelease /rée-rilée's/ *v.* & *n.* ● *v.tr.* release (a recording, motion picture, etc.) again. ● *n.* a rereleased recording, motion picture, etc.

reroute /rée-root, -rówt/ *v.tr.* send or carry by a different route.

rerun *v.* & *n.* ● *v.tr.* /rée-rún/ (**rerunning**; *past* **reran**; *past part.* **rerun**) run (a race, television program, etc.) again. ● *n.* /rée-run/ **1** the act or an instance of rerunning. **2** a television program, etc., shown again.

Res. *abbr.* Reservation.

resale /rée'sáyl/ *n.* the sale of a thing previously bought. □□ **resalable** *adj.*

reschedule /rée-skéjool/ *v.tr.* alter the schedule of; replan.

rescind /risínd/ *v.tr.* abrogate; revoke; cancel. □□ **rescindable** *adj.* **rescindment** *n.* **rescission** /-sízhən/ *n.* [L *rescindere resciss-* (as RE-, *scindere* cut)]

rescript /rée'skrípt/ *n.* **1** a Roman emperor's written reply to an appeal for guidance, esp. on a legal point. **2** *RC Ch.* the Pope's decision on a question of doctrine or papal law. **3** an official edict or announcement. **4 a** the act or an instance of rewriting. **b** the thing rewritten. [L *rescriptum*, neut. past part. of *rescribere rescript-* (as RE-, *scribere* write)]

rescue /réskyoo/ *v.* & *n.* ● *v.tr.* (**rescues, rescued, rescuing**) **1** (often foll. by *from*) save or set free or bring away from attack, custody, danger, or harm. **2** *Law* **a** unlawfully liberate (a person). **b** forcibly recover (property). ● *n.* the act or an instance of rescuing or being rescued; deliverance. □□ **rescuable** *adj.* **rescuer** *n.* [ME *rescowe* f. OF *rescoure* f. Rmc, formed as RE- + L *excutere* (as EX-¹, *quatere* shake)]

■ *v.* **1** save, deliver, (set) free, liberate, let go, release, (let) loose. ● *n.* freeing, liberation, release, liberating; deliverance, saving.

reseal /reeséel/ *v.tr.* seal again. □□ **resealable** *adj.*

research /risórch, reésərch/ *n. & v.* ● *n.* **1 a** the systematic investigation into and study of materials, sources, etc., in order to establish facts and reach new conclusions. **b** (usu. in *pl.*) an endeavor to discover new or collate old facts, etc., by the scientific study of a subject or by a course of critical investigation. **2** (*attrib.*) engaged in or intended for research (*research assistant*). ● *v.* **1** *tr.* do research into or for. **2** *intr.* make researches. □ **research and development** (in industry, etc.) work directed toward the innovation, introduction, and improvement of products and processes. □□ **researchable** *adj.* **researcher** *n.* [obs. F *recherche* (as RE-, SEARCH)]

■ *n.* **1** investigation(s), investigating(s), exploration(s), delving(s), digging(s), examination(s), inspection(s), probing(s), experimentation(s); analysis, analyses, inquiry; fact-finding, scrutiny. ● *v.* investigate, explore, delve (into), dig (into), inquire (into), study, inspect, check (into), check up (on), probe, experiment (with); scrutinize, examine, check out.

reseat /reéséet/ *v.tr.* **1** (also *refl.*) seat (oneself, a person, etc.) again. **2** provide with a fresh seat or seats.

resect /risékt/ *v.tr. Surgery* **1** cut out part of (a lung, etc.). **2** pare down (bone, cartilage, etc.). □□ **resection** *n.* **resectional** *adj.* **resectionist** *n.* [L *resecare resect-* (as RE-, *secare* cut)]

reseda /riseédə/ *n.* **1** any plant of the genus *Reseda*, with sweet-scented flowers, e.g., a mignonette. **2** /also réz-/ the pale green color of mignonette flowers. [L, perh. f. imper. of *resedare* assuage, with ref. to its supposed curative powers]

reselect /reesilékt/ *v.tr.* select again or differently. □□ **reselection** *n.*

resell /reésél/ *v.tr.* (*past* and *past part.* **resold**) sell (an object, etc.) after buying it.

resemblance /rizémbləns/ *n.* (often foll. by *to, between, of*) a likeness or similarity. □□ **resemblant** *adj.* [ME f. AF (as RESEMBLE)]

■ likeness, similarity; correspondence, congruity, coincidence, conformity, accord, agreement, equivalence, analogy, comparableness, comparability, comparison.

resemble /rizémbəl/ *v.tr.* be like; have a similarity to, or features in common with, or the same appearance as. □□ **resembler** *n.* [ME f. OF *resembler* (as RE-, *sembler* f. L *similare* f. *similis* like)]

■ be or seem or look or sound or taste like, be similar to, bear (a) resemblance to, approximate (to), smack of, correspond to, have (all) the hallmarks or earmarks of, take after, *colloq.* favor.

resent /rizént/ *v.tr.* show or feel indignation at; be aggrieved by (a circumstance, action, or person) (*we resent being patronized*). [obs. F *resentir* (as RE-, L *sentire* feel)]

■ feel embittered or bitter about, feel envious or jealous of, begrudge, have hard feelings about, be displeased or disgruntled at, be angry about.

resentful /rizéntfŏŏl/ *adj.* feeling resentment. □□ **resentfully** *adv.* **resentfulness** *n.*

■ embittered, bitter, acrimonious, envious, jealous, begrudging, indignant, displeased, disgruntled, dissatisfied, unsatisfied, unhappy, peeved, irritated, irked, annoyed, provoked, riled, angry, piqued, irate, furious, incensed, upset, worked up, agitated, antagonistic, hostile.

resentment /rizéntmənt/ *n.* (often foll. by *at, of*) indignant or bitter feelings; anger. [It. *risentimento* or F *ressentiment* (as RESENT)]

■ bitterness, acrimony, rancor, envy, jealousy, indignation, displeasure, dissatisfaction, unhappiness, irritation, annoyance, pique, anger, fury, ill will,

malice, antagonism, hostility, animosity, enmity, antipathy, hate, *literary* ire.

reserpine /risórpeen, -pin, résərpeen, -pin/ *n.* an alkaloid obtained from plants of the genus *Rauwolfia*, used as a tranquilizer and in the treatment of hypertension. [G *Reserpin* f. mod.L *Rauwolfia* (f. L. *Rauwolf*, Ger. botanist d. 1596) *serpentina*]

reservation /rézərváyshən/ *n.* **1** the act or an instance of reserving or being reserved. **2** a booking (of a room, berth, seat, etc.). **3** the thing booked, e.g., a room in a hotel. **4** an express or tacit limitation or exception to an agreement, etc. (*had reservations about the plan*). **5** an area of land reserved for a particular group, as a tract designated by the federal government for use by Native Americans. **6** *Brit.* a strip of land between the lanes of a divided highway. **7 a** a right or interest retained in an estate being conveyed. **b** the clause reserving this. **8** *Eccl.* **a** the practice of retaining for some purpose a portion of the Eucharistic elements (esp. the bread) after celebration. **b** *RC Ch.* the power of absolution reserved to a superior. **c** *RC Ch.* the right reserved to the pope of nomination to a vacant benefice. [ME f. OF *reservation* or LL *reservatio* (as RESERVE)]

■ *n.* **1, 2** booking, order, arrangement. **4** qualm, scruple; objection, *Law* demurrer; condition, proviso, provision; hesitancy, reticence, reluctance, hesitation; (*without reservation*) without reserve or demur or exception or limitation or qualification or restraint. **6** sanctuary, reserve.

reserve /rizórv/ *v. & n.* ● *v.tr.* **1** postpone; put aside; keep back for a later occasion or special use. **2** order to be specially retained or allocated for a particular person or at a particular time. **3** retain or secure, esp. by formal or legal stipulation (*reserve the right to*). **4** postpone delivery of (judgment, etc.) (*reserved my comments until the end*). ● *n.* **1 a** a thing reserved for future use; an extra stock or amount (*a great reserve of strength; huge energy reserves*). **2** a limitation, qualification, or exception attached to something (*accept your offer without reserve*). **3 a** a self-restraint; reticence; lack of cordiality (*difficult to overcome his reserve*). **b** (in artistic or literary expression) absence from exaggeration or ill-proportioned effects. **4** a company's profit added to capital. **5** (in *sing.* or *pl.*) assets kept readily available as cash or at a central bank, or as gold or foreign exchange (*reserve currency*). **6** (in *sing.* or *pl.*) **a** troops withheld from action to reinforce or protect others. **b** forces in addition to the regular army, navy, air force, etc., but available in an emergency. **7** a member of the military reserve. **8** an extra player chosen to be a possible substitute on a team. **9** a place reserved for special use, esp. as a habitat for a native tribe or for wildlife (*game reserve; nature reserve*). **10** the intentional suppression of the truth (*exercised a certain amount of reserve*). **11** (in the decoration of ceramics or textiles) an area that still has the original color of the material or the color of the background. □ **in reserve** unused and available if required. **reserve price** the lowest acceptable price stipulated for an item sold at an auction. **with all** (or **all proper**) **reserve** esp. *Brit.* without endorsing. **without reserve** without limits or restraints; freely. □□ **reservable** *adj.* **reserver** *n.* [ME f. OF *reserver* f. L *reservare* (as RE-, *servare* keep)]

■ *v.* **1, 4** keep or hold back, withhold, save, set or put aside, keep to or for oneself, hold over, postpone, delay, put off, defer; retain, conserve, preserve. **2** order, hold, keep, book, save, put or set aside, secure. **3** see RETAIN 1. ● *n.* **1** store, stock, stockpile, supply, reservoir, fund; hoard, cache. **2** see RESERVATION 4. **3** reticence, (self-)restraint, (self-)control, taciturnity, formality, coolness, aloofness, guardedness, standoffishness, remoteness, detachment. **6** backup; (*reserves*) auxiliaries, reinforcements. **9** reservation, sanctuary, conservation area, national park; preserve. □ **in reserve** ready, on hand, available, on call, accessible, in readiness, in store, *colloq.* on tap.

re-serve /reésárv/ *v.tr. & intr.* serve again.

reserved /rizárvd/ *adj.* **1** reticent; slow to reveal emotion or opinions; uncommunicative. **2 a** set apart; destined for some use or fate. **b** (often foll. by *for, to*) left by fate for; falling first or only to. □□ **reservedly** /-vidlee/ *adv.* **reservedness** *n.*

■ **1** reticent, restrained, silent, taciturn, uncommunicative, unforthcoming, closemouthed, unresponsive, undemonstrative, unemotional, cool, formal, aloof, guarded, standoffish, unsocial, antisocial, distant, remote, detached, retiring, withdrawn, demure, rigid, icy, frigid, ice-cold.

reservist /rizárvist/ *n.* a member of the reserve forces.

reservoir /rézərvwaar/ *n.* **1 a** large natural or artificial lake used as a source of water supply. **2 a** any natural or artificial receptacle esp. for or of fluid. **b** a place where fluid, etc., collects. **3** a part of a machine, etc., holding fluid. **4** (usu. foll. by *of*) a reserve or supply esp. of information. [F *réservoir* f. *réserver* RESERVE]

reset /reéset/ *v.tr.* (**resetting**; *past* and *past part.* **reset**) set (a broken bone, gems, a mechanical device, etc.) again or differently. □□ **resettable** *adj.* **resettability** /-sétəbílitee/ *n.*

resettle /reését'l/ *v.tr. & intr.* settle again. □□ **resettlement** *n.*

reshape /reésháyp/ *v.tr.* shape or form again or differently.

reshuffle /reéshúfəl/ *v. & n.* ● *v.tr.* **1** shuffle (cards) again. **2** interchange the posts of (government ministers, etc.). ● *n.* the act or an instance of reshuffling.

reside /rizíd/ *v.intr.* **1** (often foll. by *at, in, abroad,* etc.) (of a person) have one's home; dwell permanently. **2** (of power, a right, etc.) rest or be vested in. **3** (of an incumbent official) be in residence. **4** (foll. by *in*) (of a quality) be present or inherent in. [ME, prob. back-form. f. RESIDENT infl. by F *résider* or L *residēre* (as RE-, *sedēre* sit)]

residence /rézidəns/ *n.* **1** the act or an instance of residing. **2 a** the place where a person resides; an abode. **b** a mansion; the official house of a government minister, etc. **c** a house, esp. one of considerable pretension (*returned to their Beverly Hills residence*). □ **in residence** dwelling at a specified place, esp. for the performance of duties or work. [ME f. OF *residence* or med.L *residentia* f. L *residēre*: see RESIDE]

■ **1** residency, stay, sojourn, visit, stop, stopoff, layover, stopover; tenancy, occupancy. **2 a** abode, home, domicile, residency, place, house, habitation, *formal* dwelling (place). **b** see SEAT *n.* 10. **c** villa, mansion, manor (house), stately home, estate, château, hall. □ **in residence** see RESIDENT *adj.* 1.

residency /rézidənsee/ *n.* (*pl.* **-ies**) **1** = RESIDENCE 1, 2a. **2** a period of specialized medical training; the position of a resident. **3** *Brit. hist.* the official residence of the governor-general's representative or other government agent at an Indian native court; the territory supervised by this official. **4** *Brit.* a musician's regular engagement at a club, etc. **5** esp. *Brit.* a group or organization of intelligence agents in a foreign country. **6** *attrib.* based on or related to residence (*residency requirement for in-state tuition*).

resident /rézidənt/ *n. & adj.* ● *n.* **1** (often foll. by *of*) **a** a permanent inhabitant (of a town or neighborhood). **b** a bird belonging to a species that does not migrate. **2** *Brit.* a guest in a hotel, etc., staying overnight. **3** *hist.* a British government agent in any semi-independent nation, esp. the governor-general's agent at an Indian native court. **4** a medical graduate engaged in specialized practice under supervision in a hospital. **5** *Brit.* an intelligence agent in a foreign country. ● *adj.* **1** residing; in residence. **2 a** having quarters on the premises of one's work, etc. (*resident housekeeper; resident doctor*). **b** working regularly in a particular place. **3** located in; inherent (*powers of feeling are resident in the nerves*). **4** (of birds, etc.) nonmigratory. □□ **residentship** *n.* (in sense 3 of *n.*). [ME f. OF *resident* or L: see RESIDE]

■ *n.* **1 a** dweller, inhabitant, citizen, local, *poet.* denizen; householder, homeowner; tenant, occupant. ● *adj.* **1**

in residence, residing, living, staying, dwelling, *archaic* abiding. **3** situated *or* located *or* positioned, lodged *or* placed, found; see also INHERENT 1.

residential /rézidénshəl/ *adj.* **1** suitable for or occupied by private houses (*residential area*). **2** used as a residence (*residential hotel*). **3** based on or connected with residence (*the residential qualification for voters; a residential course of study*). □□ **residentially** *adv.*

residentiary /rézidénshee-eree, -shəree/ *adj. & n.* ● *adj.* of, subject to, or requiring, official residence. ● *n.* (*pl.* **-ies**) an ecclesiastic who must officially reside in a place. [med.L *residentiarius* (as RESIDENCE)]

residua *pl.* of RESIDUUM.

residual /rizíjōōəl/ *adj. & n.* ● *adj.* **1** remaining; left as a residue or residuum. **2** *Math.* resulting from subtraction. **3** (in calculation) still unaccounted for or not eliminated. ● *n.* **1** a quantity left over or *Math.* resulting from subtraction. **2** an error in calculation not accounted for or eliminated. □□ **residually** *adv.*

■ *adj.* **1** remaining, leftover, surplus, spare, extra, residuary. ● *n.* **1** see DIFFERENCE *n.* 4b.

residuary /rizíjōōeree/ *adj.* **1** of the residue of an estate (*residuary bequest*). **2** of or being a residuum; residual; still remaining.

residue /rézidōō, -dyōō/ *n.* **1** what is left over or remains; a remainder; the rest. **2** *Law* what remains of an estate after the payment of charges, debts, and bequests. **3** esp. *Chem.* a residuum. [ME f. OF *residu* f. L *residuum*: see RESIDUUM]

■ **1** remainder, leftovers, remains, rest, surplus, excess, dregs, residuum.

residuum /rizíjōōəm/ *n.* (*pl.* **residua** /-jōōə/) **1** *Chem.* a substance left after combustion or evaporation. **2** a remainder or residue. [L, neut. of *residuus* remaining f. *residēre*: see RESIDE]

resign /rizín/ *v.* **1** *intr.* **a** (often foll. by *from*) give up office, one's employment, etc. (*resigned from the faculty*). **b** (often foll. by *as*) retire (*resigned as chief executive*). **2** *tr.* give up (office, one's employment, etc.); surrender; hand over (a right, charge, task, etc.). **3** *tr.* give up hope, etc.). **4** *refl.* (usu. foll. by *to*) **a** reconcile (oneself, one's mind, etc.) to the inevitable (*have resigned myself to the idea*). **b** surrender (oneself to another's guidance). **5** *intr. Chess,* etc., discontinue play and admit defeat. □□ **resigner** *n.* [ME f. OF *resigner* f. L *resignare* unseal, cancel (as RE-, *signare* sign, seal)]

■ **1 a** leave, go, give notice, demit. **b** retire, stop *or* give up work(ing), quit, give up, stop. **2** surrender, hand over, yield up, abdicate, let go (of), release, deliver up, turn over; see also QUIT *v.* 1. **3** see RELINQUISH 1, 2. **4 a** (*resign oneself*) reconcile oneself *or* one's mind, be *or* become resigned *or* reconciled, accommodate oneself, adjust (oneself), adapt (oneself), acclimatize (oneself), acclimate (oneself), submit (oneself). **b** surrender, abandon, give up, hand over, yield up, deliver up, turn over.

re-sign /reésín/ *v.tr. & intr.* sign again.

resignation /rézignáyshən/ *n.* **1** the act or an instance of resigning, esp. from one's job or office. **2** the document, etc., conveying this intention. **3** the state of being resigned; the uncomplaining endurance of a sorrow or difficulty. [ME f. OF f. med.L *resignatio* (as RESIGN)]

■ **1** notice; abdication, abandonment, resigning, demission, renunciation, forgoing, relinquishment, surrender, yielding up. **3** reconciliation, reconcilement, adjustment, adaptation, acclimatization, submission, acceptance, compliance, abandonment, acquiescence; endurance, tolerance.

resigned /rizínd/ *adj.* (often foll. by *to*) having resigned oneself; submissive, acquiescent. □□ **resignedly** /-zínidlee/ *adv.* **resignedness** *n.*

resile /rizíl/ *v.intr.* **1** (of something stretched or compressed) recoil to resume a former size and shape; spring back. **2** have or show resilience or recuperative power. **3** (usu. foll. by *from*) withdraw from a course of action. [obs. F *resilir* or L *resilire* (as RE-, *salire* jump)]

resilient /rizílyənt/ *adj.* **1** (of a substance, etc.) recoiling;

springing back; resuming its original shape after bending, stretching, compression, etc. **2** (of a person) readily recovering from shock, depression, etc.; buoyant. □□ **resilience** *n.* **resiliency** *n.* **resiliently** *adv.* [L *resiliens resilient-* (as RESILE)]

■ **1** see ELASTIC *adj.* 1, 2. **2** see BUOYANT 2. □□ **resilience** bounce, elasticity, springiness, spring, flexibility, suppleness; buoyancy.

resin /rézin/ *n. & v.* ● *n.* **1** an adhesive flammable substance insoluble in water, secreted by some plants, and often extracted by incision, esp. from fir and pine (cf. GUM¹). **2** (in full **synthetic resin**) a solid or liquid organic compound made by polymerization, etc., and used in plastics, etc. ● *v.tr.* rub or treat with resin. □□ **resinate** /-nət/ *n.* **resinate** /-nayt/ *v.tr.* **resinoid** *adj. & n.* **resinous** *adj.* [ME *resyn, rosyn* f. L *resina* & med.L *rosina, rosinum*]

resist /rizíst/ *v. & n.* ● *v.* **1** *tr.* withstand the action or effect of; repel. **2** *tr.* stop the course or progress of; prevent from reaching, penetrating, etc. **3** *tr.* abstain from (pleasure, temptation, etc.). **4** *tr.* strive against; try to impede; refuse to comply with (*resist arrest*). **5** *intr.* offer opposition; refuse to comply. ● *n.* a protective coating of a resistant substance, applied esp. to parts of a fabric that are not to take dye or to parts of pottery that are not to take glaze or luster. □ **cannot** (or **could not,** etc.) **resist 1** (foll. by verbal noun) feel obliged or strongly inclined to (*cannot resist teasing me about it*). **2** is certain to be amused, attracted, etc., by (*can't resist children's clothes*). □□ **resistant** *adj.* **resister** *n.* **resistible** *adj.* **resistibility** *n.* [ME f. OF *resister* or L *resistere* (as RE-, *sistere* stop, redupl. of *stare* stand)]

■ *v.* **1, 2** withstand, hold out against, be proof against, keep *or* hold at bay, hold the line against, countervail against, counteract, stand up to *or* against; weather, endure, outlast; stop, hinder, repel, thwart, impede, block, obstruct, restrain, check, control, curb. **3** refuse, turn down, decline, forgo, abstain from, reject, dismiss; see also AVOID 1. **4** strive *or* struggle against, combat, fight (against), battle against, oppose, defy, counteract, countervail against. **5** see BATTLE *v.* 1, PROTEST *v.* 1. □ **cannot** (or **could not,** etc.) **resist** see LOVE *v.* 2–4. □□ **resistant** recalcitrant, defiant, stubborn, obstinate, intransigent, rebellious, immovable, intractable, refractory, willful, ungovernable, unmanageable, unruly, uncooperative; impenetrable; (*resistant to*) impervious to, proof against, unaffected by; opposed to, averse to, defiant of.

resistance /rizístəns/ *n.* **1** the act or an instance of resisting; refusal to comply. **2** the power of resisting (*showed resistance to wear and tear*). **3** *Biol.* the ability to withstand adverse conditions. **4** the impeding, slowing, or stopping effect exerted by one material thing on another. **5** *Physics* **a** the property of hindering the conduction of electricity, heat, etc. **b** the measure of this in a body. ¶ Symb.: R. **6** a resistor. **7** (in full **resistance movement**) a secret organization resisting authority, esp. in an occupied country. [ME f. F *résistance, résistence* f. LL *resistentia* (as RESIST)]

■ **1** opposition, defiance, obstruction, intransigence, rebelliousness, recalcitrance, stubbornness; refusal. **3** resilience, hardiness, endurance; immunity, insusceptibility, unsusceptibility; (*resistance to*) defenses against. **4** see OBSTRUCTION 3. **7** see UNDERGROUND *n.* 2.

resistive /rizístiv/ *adj.* **1** able to resist. **2** *Electr.* of or concerning resistance.

resistivity /réezistivitee/ *n. Electr.* a measure of the resisting power of a specified material to the flow of an electric current.

resistless /rizístlis/ *adj. archaic poet.* **1** irresistible; relentless. **2** unresisting. □□ **resistlessly** *adv.*

resistor /rizístər/ *n. Electr.* a device having resistance to the passage of an electrical current.

resold *past* and *past part.* of RESELL.

resoluble /rizólyəbəl/ *adj.* **1** that can be resolved. **2** (foll. by *into*) analyzable. [F *résoluble* or L *resolubilis* (as RESOLVE, after *soluble*)]

resolute /rézəlōōt/ *adj.* (of a person or a person's mind or

action) determined; decided; firm of purpose; not vacillating. □□ **resolutely** *adv.* **resoluteness** *n.* [L *resolutus* past part. of *resolvere* (see RESOLVE)]

■ resolved, determined, purposeful, stubborn, adamant, set, decided, dogged, persevering, persistent, pertinacious, tenacious, single-minded, dedicated, devoted, bold, purposive, deliberate, inflexible; steadfast, firm, unwavering, unshakable, unshaken, unfaltering, unhesitating, unswerving, undeviating, unchanging, changeless, unchangeable, immutable, unalterable.

resolution /rézəlōōshən/ *n.* **1** a resolute temper or character; boldness and firmness of purpose. **2** a thing resolved on; an intention (*New Year's resolutions*). **3 a** a formal expression of opinion or intention by a legislative body or public meeting. **b** the formulation of this (*passed a resolution*). **4** (usu. foll. by *of*) the act or an instance of solving doubt or a problem or question (*toward a resolution of the difficulty*). **5 a** separation into components; decomposition. **b** the replacing of a single force, etc., by two or more jointly equivalent to it. **6** (foll. by *into*) analysis; conversion into another form. **7** *Mus.* the act or an instance of causing discord to pass into concord. **8** *Physics*, etc., the smallest interval measurable by a scientific instrument; the resolving power. **9** *Med.* the disappearance of inflammation, etc., without suppuration. **10** *Prosody* the substitution of two short syllables for one long. [ME f. L *resolutio* (as RESOLVE)]

■ **1** resolve, resoluteness, determination, purpose, purposefulness, steadfastness, firmness, decidedness, decision, staunchness, doggedness, stubbornness, obstinacy, perseverance, persistence, pertinacity, boldness, tenacity, single-mindedness, dedication, devotion, constancy, devoutness, deliberation, deliberateness, inflexibility, unshakability, fixedness, changelessness, unchangeability, immutability, unalterability. **2** commitment, pledge, promise, word of honor, oath, vow, undertaking, obligation; intention. **3** proposal, proposition, plan; motion, resolve; verdict, judgment, decision, ruling, decree, settlement, conclusion, *Law* determination. **4** answer, answering, solution, solving, unraveling, disentanglement, sorting out. **6** analysis, assay, breakdown, division. **8** acutance, sharpness, precision, accuracy, exactness, exactitude, fineness, discrimination, detailing, distinguishability, resolving power.

resolutive /rézəlōōtiv/ *adj. Med.* having the power or ability to dissolve. [med.L *resolutivus* (as RESOLVE)]

resolve /rizólv/ *v. & n.* ● *v.* **1** *intr.* make up one's mind; decide firmly (*resolve to do better*). **2** *tr.* (of circumstances, etc.) cause (a person) to do this (*events resolved him to leave*). **3** *tr.* (foll. by *that* + clause) (of an assembly or meeting) pass a resolution by vote (*the committee resolved that immediate action should be taken*). **4** *intr. & tr.* (often foll. by *into*) separate or cause to separate into constituent parts; disintegrate; analyze; dissolve. **5** *tr.* (of optical or photographic equipment) separate or distinguish between closely adjacent objects. **6** *tr. & intr.* (foll. by *into*) convert or be converted. **7** *tr. & intr.* (foll. by *into*) reduce by mental analysis into. **8** *tr.* solve; explain; clear up; settle (doubt, argument, etc.). **9** *tr. & intr. Mus.* convert or be converted into concord. **10** *tr. Med.* remove (inflammation, etc.) without suppuration. **11** *tr. Prosody* replace (a long syllable) by two short syllables. **12** *tr. Mech.* replace (a force, etc.) by two or more jointly equivalent to it. ● *n.* **1 a** a firm mental decision or intention; a resolution (*made a resolve not to go*). **b** a formal resolution by a legislative body or public meeting. **2** resoluteness; steadfastness. □ **resolving power** an instrument's ability to distinguish very small or very close objects. □□ **resolvable**

/.../ **pronunciation**	● **part of speech**
□ **phrases, idioms, and compounds**	
□□ **derivatives**	■ **synonym section**
cross-references appear in SMALL CAPITALS or *italics*	

adj. **resolvability** /-zólvəbílitee/ *n.* **resolver** *n.* [ME f. L *resolvere resolut-* (as RE-, SOLVE)]
- *v.* **1** determine, decide, make up one's mind, agree, undertake, conclude. **2** see CAUSE *v.* 2. **3** decide, vote, move; see also RULE *v.* 3. **4, 6** (*resolve into*) change into, convert into, alter into, transform into, transmute into, metamorphose into, dissolve (into), break down (into), liquefy (into), disintegrate (into), reduce to or into; become, be converted into; analyze into. **7** see ANALYZE 2b. **8** explain, work out, figure out, solve, settle, clear up, answer. ● *n.* **1 a** see RESOLUTION 2. **b** see RESOLUTION 3. **2** see RESOLUTION 1. □ **resolving power** see RESOLUTION 8.

resolved /rizólvd/ *adj.* resolute; determined. □□ **resolvedly** /-zólvidlee/ *adv.* **resolvedness** *n.*

resolvent /rizólvənt/ *adj.* & *n.* esp. *Med.* ● *adj.* (of a drug, application, substance, etc.) effecting the resolution of a tumor, etc. ● *n.* such a drug, etc.

resonance /rézənəns/ *n.* **1** the reinforcement or prolongation of sound by reflection or synchronous vibration. **2** *Mech.* a condition in which an object or system is subjected to an oscillating force having a frequency close to its own natural frequency. **3** *Chem.* the property of a molecule having a structure best represented by two or more forms rather than a single structural formula. **4** *Physics* a short-lived elementary particle that is an excited state of a more stable particle. [OF f. L *resonantia* echo (as RESONANT)]

resonant /rézənənt/ *adj.* **1** (of sound) echoing; resounding; continuing to sound; reinforced or prolonged by reflection or synchronous vibration. **2** (of a body, room, etc.) tending to reinforce or prolong sounds esp. by synchronous vibration. **3** (often foll. by *with*) (of a place) resounding. **4** of or relating to resonance. □□ **resonantly** *adv.* [F *résonnant* or L *resonare resonant-* (as RE-, *sonare* sound)]
- **1** vibrating, vibrant, (re)echoing, reverberating, reverberant, ringing, resounding; booming, thundering, thunderous, loud.

resonate /rézənayt/ *v.intr.* produce or show resonance; resound. [L *resonare resonat-* (as RESONANT)]

resonator /rézənaytər/ *n.* *Mus.* **1** an instrument responding to a single note and used for detecting it in combinations. **2** an appliance for giving resonance to sound or other vibrations.

resorb /risáwrb, -záwrb/ *v.tr.* absorb again. □□ **resorbence** *n.* **resorbent** *adj.* [L *resorbēre resorpt-* (as RE-, *sorbēre* absorb)]
- reabsorb. □□ **resorbence** reabsorption, resorption. **resorbent** resorptive.

resorcin /rizáwrsin/ *n.* = RESORCINOL. [RESIN + ORCIN]

resorcinol /rizáwrsinawl, -nol/ *n.* *Chem.* a crystalline organic compound usu. made by synthesis and used in the production of dyes, drugs, resins, etc.

resorption /rizáwrpshən/ *n.* **1** the act or an instance of resorbing; the state of being resorbed. **2** the absorption of tissue within the body. □□ **resorptive** /-zórptiv/ *adj.* [RESORB after *absorption*]

resort /rizáwrt/ *n.* & *v.* ● *n.* **1** a place frequented esp. for vacations or for a specified purpose or quality (*seaside resort; health resort*). **2 a** a thing to which one has recourse; an expedient or measure (*a taxi was our best resort*). **b** (foll. by *to*) recourse to; use of (*to resort to violence*). **3** a tendency to frequent or be frequented (*places of great resort*). ● *v.intr.* **1** (foll. by *to*) turn to as an expedient (*resorted to threats*). **2** (foll. by *to*) go often or in large numbers to. □ **in the** (or **as a**) **last resort** when all else has failed. □□ **resorter** *n.* [ME f. OF *resortir* (as RE-, *sortir* come or go out)]
- *n.* **2 a** alternative, remedy, resource, recourse, backup, reserve, refuge. ● *v.* (*resort to*) **1** have recourse to, turn to, look to, fall back on, repair to, take to. **2** frequent, patronize, visit, go to, haunt, *sl.* hang out in.

re-sort /ree-sáwrt/ *v.tr.* sort again or differently.

resound /rizównd/ *v.* **1** intr. (often foll. by *with*) (of a place) ring or echo (*the hall resounded with laughter*). **2** intr. (of a voice, instrument, sound, etc.) produce echoes; go on sounding; fill the place with sound. **3** intr. **a** (of fame, a reputation, etc.) be much talked of. **b** (foll. by *through*) pro-

duce a sensation (*the call resounded through Europe*). **4** tr. (often foll. by *of*) proclaim or repeat loudly (the praises) of a person or thing (*resounded the praises of Greece*). **5** tr. (of a place) reecho (a sound). [ME f. RE- + SOUND¹ *v.*, after OF *resoner* or L *resonare*: see RESONANT]
- **1, 2** resonate, (re)echo, reverberate, ring, boom, pulsate; ring out, boom out, thunder (out).

resounding /rizównding/ *adj.* **1** in senses of RESOUND. **2** unmistakable; emphatic (*was a resounding success*). □□ **resoundingly** *adv.*

resource /réesawrs, -zawrs, risáwrs, -záwrs/ *n.* **1** an expedient or device (*escape was their only resource*). **2** (usu. in *pl.*) **a** the means available to achieve an end, fulfill a function, etc. **b** a stock or supply that can be drawn on. **c** available assets. **3** (in *pl.*) a country's collective wealth or means of defense. **4** *Brit.* a leisure occupation (*reading is a pleasant resource*). **5 a** (often in *pl.*) skill in devising expedients (*a person of great resource*). **b** practical ingenuity; quick wit (*full of resource*). **6** *archaic* the possibility of aid (*lost without resource*). □ **one's own resources** one's own abilities, ingenuity, etc. □□ **resourceful** *adj.* **resourcefully** *adv.* **resourcefulness** *n.* **resourceless** *n.* [F *ressource, ressource,* fem. past part. of OF dial. *resourdre* (as RE-, L *surgere* rise)]
- **1** expedient, device, means, measure, contrivance; see also RESORT *n.* 2 a, c (*resources*) see ASSET 2a, MEANS 2. **b** (*resources*) see STOCK *n.* 1, 2. **3** (*resources*) prosperity, wealth, riches; stockpile, stocks, reserves. **5 a** initiative, ingenuity, talent, inventiveness, originality, imagination, imaginativeness, cleverness, capability, resourcefulness, aptitude, flair, strength, quality, *colloq.* gumption, guts. □□ **resourceful** ingenious, inventive, imaginative, clever, enterprising, creative, skillful, smart, slick.

respect /rispékt/ *n.* & *v.* ● *n.* **1** deferential esteem felt or shown toward a person or quality. **2 a** (foll. by *of, for*) heed or regard. **b** (foll. by *to*) attention to or consideration of (*without respect to the results*). **3** an aspect, detail, particular, etc. (*correct except in this one respect*). **4** reference, relation (*a morality that has no respect to religion*). **5** (in *pl.*) a person's polite messages or attentions (*give my respects to your mother*). ● *v.tr.* **1** regard with deference, esteem, or honor. **2 a** avoid interfering with, harming, degrading, insulting, injuring, or interrupting. **b** treat with consideration. **c** refrain from offending, corrupting, or tempting (a person, a person's feelings, etc.). □ **in respect of** *Brit.* = *with respect to.* **in respect that** because. **with all due respect** a mollifying formula preceding an expression of one's disagreement with another's views. **with respect to** regarding; in reference to; as concerns. □□ **respecter** *n.* [ME f. OF *respect* or L *respectus* f. *respicere* (as RE-, *specere* look at) or f. *respectare* frequent. of *respicere*]
- *n.* **1** admiration, esteem, regard; consideration, appreciation, deference, reverence, veneration, courtesy, politeness, civility, attentiveness. **2** see REGARD *n.* 2. **3** detail, point, aspect, particular, characteristic, feature, quality, trait, matter, attribute, property, element. **4** reference, regard, relation, connection, comparison, bearing. **5** (*respects*) regards, good or best wishes, greetings, compliments, salutations, *archaic* devoirs. ● *v.* **1** admire, esteem, honor, appreciate, value, defer to, pay homage to, think highly or well of, much of, look up to, revere, reverence, venerate. **2 b, c** heed, obey, be considerate or polite or courteous to; show consideration or regard for, pay attention to, attend to, defer to.

respectability /rispéktəbílitee/ *n.* **1** the state of being respectable. **2** those who are respectable.

respectable /rispéktəbəl/ *adj.* **1** deserving or enjoying respect (*an intellectually respectable hypothesis; a respectable elder statesman*). **2 a** (of people) of good social standing or reputation (*comes from a respectable middle-class family*). **b** characteristic of or associated with people of such status or character (*a respectable neighborhood; a respectable profession*). **3 a** honest and decent in character or conduct. **b** characterized by (a sense of) convention or propriety; socially acceptable (*respectable behavior*; *a respectable publication*). **c** *derog.* highly conventional; prim. **4 a** commendable; meritorious (*an entirely respectable ambition*). **b** comparatively good or competent; passable; tolerable (*a respectable effort*; *speaks respectable French*). **5** reasonably good in condition or appearance; presentable. **6** appreciable in number, size, amount, etc. (*earns a very respectable salary*). **7** accepted or tolerated on account of prevalence (*materialism has become respectable again*). □□ **respectably** *adv.*

■ **1** estimable, worthy, respected, creditable; good, great, eminent; tenable, solid, sound, credible. **2** genteel, good, proper; dignified, worthy, estimable. **3 a, b** dignified, moral, decent, upright, straight, honest; seemly, proper, genteel, demure, refined; reputable, unimpeachable, law-abiding, aboveboard. **c** see SQUARE *adj.* 12. **4 a** laudable, commendable, creditable, meritorious, exemplary, worthy, praiseworthy, good, estimable, admirable. **b** decent, tolerable, passable, competent, fair, fairly good, not bad. **5** see SMART *adj.* 2. **6** moderate, appreciable, goodly, reasonable, fair, not inconsiderable, considerable, tolerable, satisfactory, sizable, good-sized, substantial, not insignificant, significant, *colloq.* tidy.

respectful /rispéktfŏol/ *adj.* showing deference (*stood at a respectful distance*). □□ **respectfully** *adv.* **respectfulness** *n.*

■ courteous, polite, well-mannered, well-behaved, mannerly, civil, cordial, gentlemanly, ladylike, gracious, obliging, accommodating, considerate, thoughtful.

respecting /rispékting/ *prep.* with reference or regard to; concerning.

respective /rispéktiv/ *adj.* concerning or appropriate to each of several individually; proper to each (*go to your respective places*). [F *respectif -ive* f. med.L *respectivus* (as RESPECT)]

■ separate, individual, personal, own, particular, several, pertinent, specific, special, relevant, corresponding.

respectively /rispéktivlee/ *adv.* for each separately or in turn, and in the order mentioned (*she and I gave $10 and $1, respectively*).

■ separately, individually, singly, severally.

respell /réespél/ *v.tr.* spell again or differently, esp. phonetically.

respirable /réspərəbəl, rispírə-/ *adj.* (of air, gas, etc.) able or fit to be breathed. [F *respirable* or LL *respirabilis* (as RESPIRE)]

respirate /réspirayt/ *v.tr.* subject to artificial respiration. [back-form. f. RESPIRATION]

respiration /réspiráyshən/ *n.* **1 a** the act or an instance of breathing. **b** a single inspiration or expiration; a breath. **2** *Biol.* in living organisms, the process involving the release of energy and carbon dioxide from the oxidation of complex organic substances. [ME f. F *respiration* or L *respiratio* (as RESPIRE)]

respirator /réspiraytər/ *n.* **1** an apparatus worn over the face to prevent poison gas, cold air, dust particles, etc., from being inhaled. **2** *Med.* an apparatus for maintaining artificial respiration.

respire /rispír/ *v.* **1** *intr.* breathe air. **2** *intr.* inhale and exhale air. **3** *intr.* (of a plant) carry out respiration. **4** *tr.* breathe (air, etc.). **5** *intr.* breathe again; take a breath. **6** *intr.* get rest or respite; recover hope or spirit. □□ **respiratory** /réspərətawree, rispírə-/ *adj.* [ME f. OF *respirer* or f. L *respirare* (as RE-, *spirare* breathe)]

respite /réspit/ *n. & v.* ● *n.* **1** an interval of rest or relief. **2** a delay permitted before the discharge of an obligation or the suffering of a penalty. ● *v.tr.* **1** grant respite to; reprieve (a condemned person). **2** postpone the execution or exaction of (a sentence, obligation, etc.). **3** give temporary relief from (pain or care) or to (a sufferer). [ME f. OF *respit* f. L *respectus* RESPECT]

■ *n.* **1** rest; interval, intermission, break, breather, interruption. **2** reprieve, stay, postponement, extension; pause, delay, hiatus. ● *v.* **1** reprieve, let off; see also SPARE *v.* 2. **2** see POSTPONE.

resplendent /rispléndənt/ *adj.* brilliant; dazzlingly or gloriously bright. □□ **resplendence** *n.* **resplendency** *n.* re-

splendently *adv.* [ME f. L *resplendēre* (as RE-, *splendēre* glitter)]

respond /rispónd/ *v. & n.* ● *v.* **1** *intr.* answer; give a reply. **2** *intr.* act or behave in an answering or corresponding manner. **3** *intr.* (usu. foll. by *to*) show sensitiveness to by behavior or change (*does not respond to kindness*). **4** *intr.* (of a congregation) make answers to a priest, etc. **5** *intr.* *Bridge* make a bid on the basis of a partner's preceding bid. **6** *tr.* say (something) in answer. ● *n.* **1** *Archit.* a half pillar or half pier attached to a wall to support an arch, esp. at the end of an arcade. **2** *Eccl.* a responsory; a response to a versicle. □□ **respondence** *n.* **respondency** *n.* **responder** *n.* [ME f. OF *respondre* answer ult. f. L *respondēre respons-* answer (as RE-, *spondēre* pledge)]

■ *v.* **1** answer (back), reply, (make a) retort, riposte, comeback; counter. **2** react, reciprocate; behave, conduct oneself, act; retaliate. **3** be responsive, react, be affected *or* moved *or* touched. **6** answer, reply, return, rejoin, retort, fling *or* hurl (back), comeback.

respondent /rispóndənt/ *n. & adj.* ● *n.* **1** a defendant, esp. in an appeal or divorce case. **2** a person who makes an answer or defends an argument, etc. ● *adj.* **1** giving answers. **2** (foll. by *to*) responsive. **3** in the position of defendant.

response /rispóns/ *n.* **1** an answer given in word or act; a reply. **2** a feeling, movement, change, etc., caused by a stimulus or influence. **3** (often in *pl.*) *Eccl.* any part of the liturgy said or sung in answer to the priest; a responsory. **4** *Bridge* a bid made in responding. [ME f. OF *respons(e)* or L *responsum* neut. past part. of *respondēre* RESPOND]

■ **1** answer, reply, retort, rejoinder, reaction, *sl.* comeback; reaction, feedback. **2** reaction, effect; result, consequence, outcome, upshot.

responsibility /rispónsibílitee/ *n.* (*pl.* **-ies**) **1 a** (often foll. by *for*, *of*) the state or fact of being responsible (*refuses all responsibility for it*; *will take the responsibility of doing it*). **b** authority; the ability to act independently and make decisions (*a job with more responsibility*). **2** the person or thing for which one is responsible (*the food is my responsibility*). □ **on one's own responsibility** without authorization.

■ **1 a** accountability, liability, chargeability, answerability, obligation; blame, guilt, culpability; see also *responsibleness* (RESPONSIBLE). **b** see POWER *n.* 3a, 5, INDEPENDENCE. **2** charge, duty, onus, burden, job, task, trust.

responsible /rispónsibəl/ *adj.* **1** (often foll. by *to*, *for*) liable to be called to account (to a person or for a thing). **2** morally accountable for one's actions; capable of rational conduct. **3** of good credit, position, or repute; respectable; evidently trustworthy. **4** (often foll. by *for*) being the primary cause (*a short circuit was responsible for the power failure*). **5** (of a ruler or government) not autocratic. **6** involving responsibility (*a responsible job*). □□ **responsibleness** *n.* **responsibly** *adv.* [obs. F f. L *respondēre*: see RESPOND]

■ **1, 2** accountable, answerable, liable, chargeable, (legally *or* statutorily) bound. **3** reliable, respectable, reputable, trustworthy, dependable, stable, creditable, accountable, ethical, honest. **4** guilty, to blame, at fault, culpable. **5** democratic, representative, popular; elected, chosen. **6** authoritative, important, top, leading, decision-making. □□ **responsibleness** responsibility; dependability, respectability, reputability, reliability, trustworthiness, stability, creditability; accountability.

responsive /rispónsiv/ *adj.* **1** (often foll. by *to*) responding readily (to some influence). **2** sympathetic; impressionable. **3 a** answering. **b** by way of answer. **4** (of a liturgy, etc.) using responses. □□ **responsively** *adv.* **responsiveness** *n.* [F *responsif -ive* or LL *responsivus* (as RESPOND)]

■ **1, 2** alert, alive, (wide-)awake, reactive,

communicative, sharp, keen, receptive, sensitive, open, sympathetic, impressionable.

responsory /rispónsəree/ *n.* (*pl.* **-ies**) an anthem said or sung by a soloist and choir after a lesson. [ME f. LL *responsorium* (as RESPOND)]

respray *v. & n.* ● *v.tr.* /reespráy/ spray again (esp. to change the color of the paint on a vehicle, etc.). ● *n.* /réespray/ the act or an instance of respraying.

rest[1] /rest/ *v. & n.* ● *v.* **1** *intr.* cease, abstain, or be relieved from exertion, action, movement, or employment; be tranquil. **2** *intr.* be still or asleep, esp. to refresh oneself or recover strength. **3** *tr.* give relief or repose to; allow to rest (*a chair to rest my legs*). **4** *intr.* (foll. by *on, upon, against*) lie on; be supported by; be spread out on; be propped against. **5** *intr.* (foll. by *on, upon*) depend; be based; rely. **6** *intr.* (foll. by *on, upon*) (of a look) light upon or be steadily directed on. **7** *tr.* (foll. by *on, upon*) place for support or foundation. **8** *intr.* (of a problem or subject) be left without further investigation or discussion (*let the matter rest*). **9** *intr.* **a** lie in death. **b** (foll. by *in*) lie buried in (a churchyard, etc.). **10** *tr.* (as **rested** *adj.*) refreshed or reinvigorated by resting. **11** *intr.* conclude the calling of witnesses in a court case (*the prosecution rests*). **12** *intr.* (of land) lie fallow. **13** *intr.* (foll. by *in*) repose trust in (*am content to rest in God*). ● *n.* **1** repose or sleep, esp. in bed at night (*get a good night's rest*). **2** freedom from or the cessation of exertion, worry, activity, etc. (*give the subject a rest*). **3** a period of resting (*take a 15-minute rest*). **4** a support or prop for holding or steadying something. **5** *Mus.* **a** an interval of silence of a specified duration. **b** the sign denoting this. **6** a place of resting or abiding, esp. a lodging place or shelter for travelers. **7** a pause in elocution. **8** a caesura in verse. □ **at rest** not moving; not agitated or troubled; dead. **lay to rest** inter (a corpse). **rest area** = *rest stop*. **rest one's case** conclude one's argument, etc. **rest** (or **God rest**) **his** (or **her**) **soul** may God grant his (or her) soul repose. **rest home** a place where old or frail people can be cared for. **rest mass** *Physics* the mass of a body when at rest. **rest on one's laurels** see LAUREL. **rest on one's oars** see OAR. **rest room** a public toilet in a restaurant, store, office building, etc. **rest stop** an area along a highway for travelers to stop for rest, refreshment, etc. **rest up** rest oneself thoroughly. **set** (or **put**) **to** (or **at**) **rest** settle or relieve (a question, a person's mind, etc.). □□ **rester** *n.* [OE *ræst, rest* (n.), *ræstan, restan* (v.)]

■ *v.* **1** relax, repose, take a rest, take one's ease, unwind, take it easy, *Austral.* spell, *colloq.* put one's feet up; loll, languish, laze about, be idle, idle about, lounge (about). **2** (go to) sleep, doze, take a rest, (take one's) repose, lie down, go *or* take to one's bed, (take a) nap, *colloq.* snooze, catch *or* get some shut-eye, hit the sack *or* hay, get *or* catch forty winks, *Brit. sl.* kip, doss down. **4** see LIE *v.* 1; (*resting on* or *upon* or *against*) supported by, spread out on, spread *or* extended over, propped (up) against, overlying. **5** (*rest on* or *upon*) see DEPEND 1. **8** drop, cease, end, stop, lie. **10** (**rested**) see REFRESH 1. ● *n.* **1** repose, sleep, nap, doze, siesta, esp. *Brit.* lie-down, *colloq.* snooze, *poet. rhet.* slumber; shut-eye. **2** relaxation, ease, breathing space, respite, time off *or* out, leisure; see also BREAK[1] *n.* 2. **3** intermission, interval, interlude, entr'acte, rest period, cessation, break, recess, *colloq.* breather, *Austral. & NZ colloq.* smoko; holiday, vacation. **4** prop, holder, trestle; see also SUPPORT *n.* 2. **6** see SHELTER *n.* 2a. □ **at rest** see CALM *adj.* 1, DEAD *adj.* 1. **rest room** see TOILET. **set** (or **put**) **to** (or **at**) **rest** see SETTLE[1] 5–7, 8b.

rest[2] /rest/ *n. & v.* ● *n.* (prec. by *the*) **1** the remaining part or parts; the others; the remainder of some quantity or number (*finish what you can and leave the rest*). **2** *Brit. Econ.* the reserve fund, esp. of the Bank of England. **3** *hist.* a rally in tennis. ● *v.intr.* **1** remain in a specified state (*rest assured*). **2** (foll. by *with*) be left in the hands or charge of (*the final arrangements rest with you*). □ **and all the rest** (or **the rest of it**) and all else that might be mentioned; et cetera. **for the rest** as regards anything else. [ME f. OF *reste rester* f. L *restare* (as RE-, *stare* stand)]

■ *n.* **1** remainder, balance; remains, remnants, leftovers, residue, residuum, excess, surplus, overage. ● *v.* **1** (continue to) be, remain, keep on being. **2** reside, be situated, be lodged, lie, be placed, be found, remain. □ **and all the rest** (or **the rest of it**) et cetera, and so on (and so forth), and so forth, and the like.

restart *v. & n.* ● *v.tr. & intr.* /reestáart/ begin again. ● *n.* /réestaart/ a new beginning.

restate /reestáyt/ *v.tr.* express again or differently, esp. more clearly or convincingly. □□ **restatement** *n.*

restaurant /réstərənt, -raant, réstraant/ *n.* public premises where meals or refreshments may be had. □ **restaurant car** *Brit.* a dining car on a train. [F f. *restaurer* RESTORE]

restaurateur /réstərətőr/ *n.* a restaurant owner or manager. [F (as RESTAURANT)]

restful /réstfŏŏl/ *adj.* **1** favorable to quiet or repose. **2** free from disturbing influences. **3** soothing. □□ **restfully** *adv.* **restfulness** *n.*

■ **1** tranquil, calm, peaceful, quiet, still, serene, pacific; relaxed, reposeful. **3** relaxing, soothing, comforting, tranquilizing, sedative, calming, sleep-inducing, hypnotic, soporific, somnolent.

restharrow /rést-harō/ *n.* any tough-rooted plant of the genus *Ononis*, native to Europe and the Mediterranean. [obs. *rest* (v.) = ARREST (in sense 'stop') + HARROW]

restitution /réstitŏŏshən, -tyŏŏ-/ *n.* **1** (often foll. by *of*) the act or an instance of restoring a thing to its proper owner. **2** reparation for an injury (esp. *make restitution*). **3** esp. *Theol.* the restoration of a thing to its original state. **4** the resumption of an original shape or position because of elasticity. □□ **restitutive** /réstitŏŏtiv, -tyŏŏ-/ *adj.* [ME f. OF *restitution* or L *restitutio* f. *restituere restitut-* restore (as RE-, *statuere* establish)]

■ **1** restoration, return, recovery, replacement, replacing, restoring; reinstatement, reestablishment. **2** amends, compensation, redress, remuneration, reparation, requital, indemnification, indemnity.

restive /réstiv/ *adj.* **1** fidgety; restless. **2** (of a horse) refusing to advance; stubbornly standing still or moving backward or sideways; refractory. **3** (of a person) unmanageable; rejecting control. □□ **restively** *adv.* **restiveness** *n.* [ME f. OF *restif -ive* f. Rmc (as REST[2])]

■ **1** see RESTLESS 2, 3. **2** see DISOBEDIENT. **3** see UNGOVERNABLE.

restless /réstlis/ *adj.* **1** finding or affording no rest. **2** uneasy; agitated. **3** constantly in motion, fidgeting, etc. □□ **restlessly** *adv.* **restlessness** *n.* [OE *restlēas* (as REST, -LESS)]

■ **1** sleepless, wakeful; see also UNSETTLED 1. **2** restive, uneasy, edgy, on edge, on tenterhooks, nervous, excitable, highly strung, high-strung, worked up, agitated, jumpy, skittish, fretful, apprehensive, jittery, uptight, *colloq.* antsy, *Austral. sl.* toey; (*be restless*) champ at the bit, *colloq.* have itchy feet, have ants in one's pants. **3** fidgety, jumpy, restive, skittish, *colloq.* antsy; (*be restless*) *colloq.* have ants in one's pants, have itchy feet.

restock /reestók/ *v.tr.* (also *absol.*) stock again or differently.

restoration /réstəráyshən/ *n.* **1 a** the act or an instance of restoring (a building, etc.) or of being restored. **b** = RESTITUTION 1. **2** a model or drawing representing the supposed original form of an extinct animal, ruined building, etc. **3 a** the reestablishment of a monarch, etc. **b** the period of this. **4** (**Restoration**) *hist.* **a** (prec. by *the*) the reestablishment of Charles II as king of England in 1660. **b** (often *attrib.*) the literary period following this (*Restoration comedy*). [17th-c. alt. (after RESTORE) of *restauration*, ME f. OF *restauration* or LL *restauratio* (as RESTORE)]

■ **1 a** renovation, refurbishment, repair, reconstruction, reconversion; resurrection. **3 a** reestablishment, rehabilitation, reinstatement.

restorative /ristáwrətiv, -stór-/ *adj. & n.* ● *adj.* tending to restore health or strength. ● *n.* a restorative medicine, food, etc. (*needs a restorative*). □□ **restoratively** *adv.* [ME var. of obs. *restaurative* f. OF *restauratif -ive* (as RESTORE)]

■ analeptic, tonic.

restore /ristáwr/ *v.tr.* **1** bring back or attempt to bring back to the original state by rebuilding, repairing, repainting, emending, etc. **2** bring back to health, etc.; cure. **3** give back to the original owner, etc.; make restitution of. **4** reinstate; bring back to dignity or right. **5** replace; put back; bring back to a former condition. **6** make a representation of the supposed original state of (a ruin, extinct animal, etc.). **7** reinstate by conjecture (missing words in a text, missing pieces, etc.). □□ **restorable** *adj.* **restorer** *n.* [ME f. OF *restorer* f. L *restaurare*]

■ **1** renovate, refurbish, make good, repair, reconstruct, rebuild; resurrect; mend, fix, touch (up). **2** make better, cure; see also HEAL 2. **3** give *or* hand *or* put *or* bring *or* pay back, return, replace, make good, make restitution of; repay. **4** reinstate, rehabilitate, reestablish, bring back. **5** replace, put back, reestablish, bring back.

restrain /ristráyn/ *v.tr.* **1** (often *refl.*, usu. foll. by *from*) check or hold in; keep in check or under control or within bounds. **2** repress; keep down. **3** confine; imprison. □□ **restrainable** *adj.* **restrainer** *n.* [ME f. OF *restrei(g)n-* stem of *restreindre* f. L *restringere restrict-* (as RE-, *stringere* tie)]

■ **1** (keep under *or* in) control, (keep *or* hold in) check, hold (back *or* in), curb, govern; limit, restrict, inhibit, regulate, curtail, hinder, interfere with, hamper, handicap. **2** keep down, stifle; see also REPRESS 2. **3** (place under) arrest, confine, imprison, incarcerate, detain, lock up, jail, shut up.

re-strain /réestráyn/ *v.tr.* strain again.

restrainedly /ristráynidlee/ *adv.* with self-restraint.

restraint /ristráynt/ *n.* **1** the act or an instance of restraining or being restrained. **2** a stoppage; a check; a controlling agency or influence. **3 a** self-control; avoidance of excess or exaggeration. **b** austerity of literary expression. **4** reserve of manner. **5** confinement, esp. because of insanity. **6** something that restrains or holds in check; bondage; shackles. □ **in restraint of** in order to restrain. **restraint of trade** action seeking to interfere with free-market conditions. [ME f. OF *restreinte* fem. past part. of *restreindre*: see RESTRAIN]

■ **2** control, check, curb, rein, bridle, restriction, constraint, limit, limitation, stoppage, curtailment, delimitation, bound. **3a, 4** control, reserve, self-control, self-possession, poise, equanimity, self-discipline, self-restraint. **5** duress, captivity, *archaic* durance; see also *imprisonment* (IMPRISON). **6** bondage, bonds, fetters, shackles, handcuffs, bilboes, pinions, manacles, straitjacket, *colloq.* cuffs, *sl.* bracelets.

restrict /ristríkt/ *v.tr.* (often foll. by *to*, *within*) **1** confine; bound; limit (*restricted parking*; *restricted them to five days a week*). **2** subject to limitation. **3** withhold from general circulation or disclosure. □□ **restrictedly** *adv.* **restrictedness** *n.* [L *restringere*: see RESTRAIN]

■ **1, 2** limit, confine, bound, circumscribe, delimit, mark off, demarcate, regulate, restrain, crib, impede.

restriction /ristríkshən/ *n.* **1** the act or an instance of restricting; the state of being restricted. **2** a thing that restricts. **3** a limitation placed on action. □□ **restrictionist** *adj.* & *n.* [ME f. OF *restriction* or L *restrictio* (as RESTRICT)]

■ **2** see RESTRAINT 2. **3** condition, provision, proviso, qualification; see also *stipulation* (STIPULATE¹).

restrictive /ristríktiv/ *adj.* imposing restrictions. □ **restrictive clause** *Gram.* a relative clause, usu. without surrounding commas. □□ **restrictively** *adv.* **restrictiveness** *n.* [ME f. OF *restrictif -ive* or med.L *restrictivus* (as RESTRICT)]

restring /réestríng/ *v.tr.* (*past* and *past part.* **restrung**) **1** fit (a musical instrument) with new strings. **2** thread (beads, etc.) on a new string.

restructure /réestrúkchər/ *v.tr.* give a new structure to; rebuild; rearrange.

restudy /réestúdee/ *v.tr.* (**-ies, -ied**) study again.

restyle /réestíl/ *v.tr.* **1** reshape; remake in a new style. **2** give a new designation to (a person or thing).

result /rizúlt/ *n.* & *v.* ● *n.* **1** a consequence, issue, or outcome of something. **2** a satisfactory outcome; a favorable result (*gets results*). **3** a quantity, formula, etc., obtained by cal-

culation. **4** (in *pl.*) a list of scores or winners, etc., in an examination or sporting event. ● *v.intr.* **1** (often foll. by *from*) arise as the actual consequence or follow as a logical consequence (from conditions, causes, etc.). **2** (often foll. by *in*) have a specified end or outcome (*resulted in a large profit*). □ **without result** in vain; fruitless. □□ **resultful** *adj.* **resultless** *adj.* [ME f. med.L *resultare* f. L (as RE-, *saltare* frequent. of *salire* jump)]

■ *n.* **1** consequence, effect, development; issue, fruit, conclusion, upshot, end (result), denouement. ● *v.* **1** develop, emerge, follow, happen, occur, come (about), come to pass, arise, evolve, be produced. **2** end, conclude, culminate, terminate, finish up. □ **without result** see *in vain* (VAIN), FRUITLESS 2.

resultant /rizúlt'nt/ *adj.* & *n.* ● *adj.* resulting, esp. as the total outcome of more or less opposed forces. ● *n.* *Math.* a vector equivalent to two or more acting in different directions at the same point.

resume /rizóóm/ *v.* & *n.* ● *v.* **1** *tr.* & *intr.* begin again or continue after an interruption. **2** *tr.* & *intr.* begin to speak, work, or use again; recommence. **3** *tr.* get back; take back; recover; reoccupy (*resume one's seat*). ● *n.* = RÉSUMÉ. □□ **resumable** *adj.* [ME f. OF *resumer* or L *resumere resumpt-* (as RE-, *sumere* take)]

■ *v.* **1** see CONTINUE 2, *carry on* 1. **2** recommence, restart, pick *or* take up (again), reopen, resurrect. **3** take back, reoccupy; see also RECOVER *v.* 1.

résumé /rézóómay/ *n.* (also **resumé, resume**) **1** a summary, esp. of a person's employment history. **2** a curriculum vitae. [F past part. of *résumer* (as RESUME)]

■ **1** summary, digest, abstract, synopsis, précis, outline, recapitulation, epitome, recap. **2** curriculum vitae, work *or* job history, biography, career description, prosopography.

resumption /rizúmpshən/ *n.* the act or an instance of resuming (*ready for the resumption of negotiations*). □□ **resumptive** *adj.* [ME f. OF *resumption* or LL *resumptio* (as RESUME)]

resupinate /risóópinayt, -nət/ *adj.* (of a leaf, etc.) upside down. [L *resupinatus* past part. of *resupinare* bend back: see SUPINE]

resurface /réesórfis/ *v.* **1** *tr.* lay a new surface on (a road, etc.). **2** *intr.* rise or arise again; turn up again.

resurgent /risórjənt/ *adj.* **1** rising or arising again. **2** tending to rise again. □□ **resurgence** *n.* [L *resurgere resurrect-* (as RE-, *surgere* rise)]

■ renascent, on the rise; see also *on the increase* (INCREASE). □□ **resurgence** renaissance, renascence, rebirth, revival, reawakening, renewal, return, resurrection, regeneration, rejuvenation.

resurrect /rézərékt/ *v.* **1** *tr.* *colloq.* revive the practice, use, or memory of. **2** *tr.* take from the grave; exhume. **3** *tr.* dig up. **4** *tr.* & *intr.* raise or rise from the dead. [back-form. f. RESURRECTION]

■ **1** revive, bring back, reintroduce, restore, renew, resuscitate. **2, 3** see DIG *v.* 4. **4** restore to life, raise (from the dead), resuscitate, breathe new life into, reanimate, reincarnate, regenerate; reawaken, rise.

resurrection /rézərékshən/ *n.* **1** the act or an instance of rising from the dead. **2** (**Resurrection**) **a** Christ's rising from the dead. **b** the rising of the dead at the Last Judgment. **3** a revival after disuse, inactivity, or decay. **4** exhumation. **5** the unearthing of a lost or forgotten thing; restoration to vogue or memory. □ **resurrection plant** any of various plants, including club mosses of the genus *Selaginella* and the Rose of Jericho, unfolding when moistened after being dried. □□ **resurrectional** *adj.* [ME f. OF f. LL *resurrectio -onis* (as RESURGENT)]

resurvey *v.* & *n.* ● *v.tr.* /réesərváy/ survey again; reconsider. ● *n.* /réesórvay/ the act or an instance of resurveying.

resuscitate /risúsitayt/ *v.tr.* & *intr.* **1** revive from unconsciousness or apparent death. **2** return or restore to vogue, vigor, or vividness. □□ **resuscitation** /-táyshən/ *n.* **resuscitative** *adj.* **resuscitator** *n.* [L *resuscitare* (as RE-, *suscitare* raise)]

ret /ret/ *v.* (also **rate** /rayt/) (**retted, retting**) **1** *tr.* soften (flax, hemp, etc.) by soaking or by exposure to moisture. **2** *intr.* (often as **retted** *adj.*) (of hay, etc.) be spoiled by wet or rot. [ME, rel. to ROT]

ret. *abbr.* **1** retired. **2** returned.

retable /ritáybəl, reétay-, rétə-/ *n.* **1** a frame enclosing decorated panels above the back of an altar. **2** a shelf. [F *rétable*, *retable* f. Sp. *retablo* f. med.L *retrotabulum* rear table (as RETRO-, TABLE)]

retail /reétayl/ *n., adj., adv.,* & *v.* ● *n.* the sale of goods in relatively small quantities to the public, and usu. not for resale (cf. WHOLESALE). ● *adj.* & *adv.* by retail; at a retail price (*do you buy wholesale or retail?*). ● *v.* /also ritáyl/ **1** *tr.* sell (goods) in retail trade. **2** *intr.* (often foll. by *at, for*) (of goods) be sold in this way (esp. for a specified price) (*retails at $4.95*). **3** *tr.* recount; relate details of. □ **retail price index** an index of the variation in the prices of retail goods. □□ **retailer** *n.* [ME f. OF *retaille* a piece cut off f. *retaillier* (as RE-, TAIL²)]

retain /ritáyn/ *v.tr.* **1 a** keep possession of; not lose; continue to have, practice, or recognize. **b** not abolish, discard, nor alter. **2** keep in one's memory. **3 a** keep in place; hold fixed. **b** hold (water, etc.). **4** secure the services of (a person, esp. an attorney) with a preliminary payment. □ **retaining fee** a fee paid to secure a person, service, etc. **retaining wall** a wall supporting and confining a mass of earth or water. □□ **retainable** *adj.* **retainability** /-taynəbílitee/ *n.* **retainment** *n.* [ME f. AF *retei(g)n-* f. stem of OF *retenir* ult. f. L *retinēre retent-* (as RE-, *tenēre* hold)]

■ **1** keep (possession of), hold on to, save, reserve, preserve, *colloq.* hang on to. **2** remember, keep in mind, memorize, impress on the memory. **3 a** see FIX *v.* 1. **b** hold (back), contain, absorb, soak up. **4** secure, engage, hire, employ, commission, take on.
□ **retaining fee** *Law* retainer.

retainer /ritáynər/ *n.* **1** a person or thing that retains. **2** *Law* a fee for retaining an attorney, etc. **3 a** *hist.* a dependent or follower of a person of rank. **b** *joc.* an old and faithful friend or servant (esp. *old retainer*). **4** *Brit.* a reduced rent paid to retain accommodation during a period of nonoccupancy.

retake *v.* & *n.* ● *v.tr.* (*past* **retook**; *past part.* **retaken**) **1** take again. **2** recapture. ● *n.* /reétayk/ **1 a** the act or an instance of retaking. **b** a thing retaken, e.g., an examination. **2 a** the act or an instance of filming a scene or recording music, etc., again. **b** the scene or recording obtained in this way.

retaliate /ritáleeayt/ *v.* **1** *intr.* repay an injury, insult, etc., in kind; attack in return; make reprisals. **2** *tr.* **a** (usu. foll. by *upon*) cast (an accusation) back upon a person. **b** repay (an injury or insult) in kind. □□ **retaliation** /-áyshən/ *n.* **retaliative** /-táleeətiv/ *adj.* **retaliator** *n.* **retaliatory** /-táleeətáwree/ *adj.* [L *retaliare* (as RE-, *talis* such)]

■ **1** counter, strike back, take revenge, wreak vengeance, revenge oneself, reciprocate, settle a score, give tit for tat, take an eye for an eye (and a tooth for a tooth), give as good as one gets, *colloq.* get one's own back. **2 b** avenge, revenge, repay, requite, pay back (in kind); (*retaliate against*) give a person a taste of his *or* her own medicine, get even with, strike back at, take revenge on, wreak vengeance *or* revenge on, settle a score with, get back at.

retard /ritáard/ *v.* & *n.* ● *v.tr.* **1** make slow or late. **2** delay the progress, development, arrival, or accomplishment of. ● *n.* **1** retardation. **2** /reétard/ *sl. derog.* a person with a mental handicap. □□ **retardant** *adj.* & *n.* **retardation** /reétaardáyshən/ *n.* **retardative** /-ətiv/ *adj.* **retardatory** /-ətáwree/ *adj.* **retarder** *n.* **retardment** *n.* [F *retarder* f. L *retardare* (as RE-, *tardus* slow)]

■ *v.* slow (down *or* up), hold up *or* back, delay; set back, hinder, impede, keep back, thwart, balk, block, restrict,

hold in check, frustrate, interfere with. ● *n.* **1** see DELAY *n.* 1, 2.

retardate /ritaárdayt/ *adj.* & *n.* ● *adj.* mentally retarded. ● *n.* a mentally retarded person. [L *retardare*: see RETARD]

retarded /ritaárdid/ *adj.* backward in mental or physical development.

retch /rech/ *v.* & *n.* ● *v.intr.* make a motion of vomiting esp. involuntarily and without effect. ● *n.* such a motion or the sound of it. [var. of (now dial.) *reach* f. OE *hrǣcan* spit, ON *hrækja* f. Gmc, of imit. orig.]

retd. *abbr.* **1** retired. **2** returned.

rete /reétee/ *n.* (*pl.* **retia** /-teeə, -sheeə, -shə/) *Anat.* an elaborate network or plexus of blood vessels and nerve cells. [L *rete* net]

reteach /reéteech/ *v.tr.* (*past* and *past part.* **retaught**) teach again or differently.

retell /reétél/ *v.tr.* (*past* and *past part.* **retold**) tell again or in a different version.

retention /riténshən/ *n.* **1 a** the act or an instance of retaining; the state of being retained. **b** the ability to retain things experienced or learned; memory. **2** *Med.* the failure to evacuate urine or another secretion. [ME f. OF *retention* or L *retentio* (as RETAIN)]

retentive /riténtiv/ *adj.* **1** (often foll. by *of*) tending to retain (moisture, etc.). **2** (of memory or a person) not forgetful. **3** *Surgery* (of a ligature, etc.) serving to keep something in place. □□ **retentively** *adv.* **retentiveness** *n.* [ME f. OF *retentif -ive* or med.L *retentivus* (as RETAIN)]

retexture /reétékschər/ *v.tr.* treat (material, a garment, etc.) so as to restore its original texture.

rethink *v.* & *n.* ● *v.tr.* /reéthíngk/ (*past* and *past part.* **rethought**) think about (something) again, esp. with a view to making changes. ● *n.* /reéthingk/ a reassessment; a period of rethinking.

retia *pl.* of RETE.

retiarius /reéshee-áireeəs/ *n.* (*pl.* **retiarii** /-áireeī, -áiree-ee/) a Roman gladiator using a net to trap his opponent. [L f. *rete* net]

reticence /rétisəns/ *n.* **1** the avoidance of saying all one knows or feels, or of saying more than is necessary; reserve in speech. **2** a disposition to silence; taciturnity. **3** the act or an instance of holding back some fact. **4** abstinence from overemphasis in art. □□ **reticent** *adj.* **reticently** *adv.* [L *reticentia* f. *reticēre* (as RE-, *tacēre* be silent)]

■ **1, 2** see RESERVE *n.* 3. □□ **reticent** quiet, shy, timid, retiring, reserved; taciturn, silent, unresponsive, tightlipped, unforthcoming.

reticle /rétikəl/ *n.* a network of fine threads or lines in the focal plane of an optical instrument to help accurate observation. [L *reticulum*: see RETICULUM]

reticula *pl.* of RETICULUM.

reticulate *v.* & *adj.* ● *v.tr.* & *intr.* /ritíkyəlayt/ **1** divide or be divided in fact or appearance into a network. **2** arrange or be arranged in small squares or with intersecting lines. ● *adj.* /-yələt, -layt/ reticulated. □□ **reticulately** *adv.* **reticulation** /-láyshən/ *n.* [L *reticulatus* reticulated (as RETICULUM)]

reticule /rétikyōol/ *n.* **1** = RETICLE. **2** usu. *hist.* a woman's netted or other bag, esp. with a drawstring, carried or worn to serve the purpose of a pocket. [F *réticule* f. L (as RETICULUM)]

reticulum /ritíkyələm/ *n.* (*pl.* **reticula** /-lə/) **1** a netlike structure; a fine network, esp. of membranes, etc., in living organisms. **2** a ruminant's second stomach. □□ **reticular** *adj.* **reticulose** *adj.* [L, dimin. of *rete* net]

retie /reétí/ *v.tr.* (**retying**) tie again.

retiform /reétifawrm, réti-/ *adj.* netlike; reticulated. [L *rete* net + -FORM]

retina /rét'nə/ *n.* (*pl.* **retinas, retinae** /-nee/) a layer at the back of the eyeball sensitive to light, and triggering nerve impulses via the optic nerve to the brain where the visual image is formed. □□ **retinal** *adj.* [ME f. med.L f. L *rete* net]

retinitis /rét'nítis/ *n.* inflammation of the retina.

retinol /rét'nawl, -nol/ *n.* a vitamin found in green and yellow vegetables, egg yolk, and fish-liver oil, essential for growth and vision in dim light. Also called *vitamin A*. [RETINA + -OL[1]]

retinue /rét'nōō, -yōō/ *n.* a body of attendants accompanying an important person. [ME f. OF *retenue* fem. past part. of *retenir* RETAIN]

■ entourage, escort, convoy, cortège, company, train, suite.

retire /ritír/ *v.* **1 a** *intr.* leave office or employment, esp. because of age (*retire from the army; retire on a pension*). **b** *tr.* cause (a person) to retire from work. **2** *intr.* withdraw; go away; retreat. **3** *intr.* seek seclusion or shelter. **4** *intr.* go to bed. **5** *tr.* withdraw (troops). **6** *intr. & tr. Baseball* (of a batter or side) put out. **7** *tr. Econ.* withdraw (a bill or note) from circulation or currency. □ **retire from the world** become a recluse. **retire into oneself** become uncommunicative or unsociable. □□ **retiree** *n.* **retirer** *n.* [F *retirer* (as RE-, *tirer* draw)]

■ **1 a** stop *or* give up work(ing), leave one's employment, go on a pension, *colloq.* be put on the shelf, take a golden handshake. **b** pension off, superannuate, put out to grass *or* pasture, *colloq.* give a person a golden handshake. **2, 3** withdraw, retreat, hibernate, seclude *or* sequester *or* cloister oneself; go off *or* away, take off; rusticate. **4** go to bed *or* sleep, go *or* take to one's bed, withdraw, call it a day, lie down, *colloq.* hit the hay *or* sack, turn in, *Brit. sl.* kip (down). **5** retreat, remove; see also WITHDRAW 3. □ **retire from the world** see *renounce the world*. **retire into oneself** see WITHDRAW 5. □□ **retiree, retirer** see PENSIONER.

retired /ritírd/ *adj.* **1 a** having retired from employment (*a retired teacher*). **b** *Brit.* relating to a retired person (*received retired pay*). **2** withdrawn from society or observation; secluded (*lives a retired life*). □□ **retiredness** *n.*

retirement /ritírmənt/ *n.* **1 a** the act or an instance of retiring. **b** the condition of having retired. **2 a** seclusion or privacy. **b** a secluded place. **3** income, esp. pension, on which a retired person lives.

retiring /ritíring/ *adj.* shy; fond of seclusion. □□ **retiringly** *adv.*

■ shy, bashful, coy, demure, modest, diffident, timid, unassuming, humble, self-effacing, timorous, meek, reticent, reserved, unsocial, unsociable, aloof, removed, standoffish, distant, reclusive, eremitic(al).

retold *past* and *past part.* of RETELL.

retook *past* of RETAKE.

retool /reetōōl/ *v.tr.* equip (a factory, etc.) with new tools.

retorsion /ritáwrshən/ *n.* (also **retortion**) retaliation by one nation on another, as for unfair trade, etc.

retort[1] /ritáwrt/ *n. & v.* ● *n.* **1** an incisive or witty or angry reply. **2** the turning of a charge or argument against its originator. **3** a retaliation. ● *v.* **1 a** *tr.* say by way of a retort. **b** *intr.* make a retort. **2** *tr.* repay (an insult or attack) in kind. **3** *tr.* (often foll. by *on, upon*) return (mischief, a charge, sarcasm, etc.) to its originator. **4** *tr.* (often foll. by *against*) make (an argument) tell against its user. **5** *tr.* (as **retorted** *adj.*) recurved; twisted or bent backward. [L *retorquēre retort-* (as RE-, *torquēre* twist)]

■ *n.* **1, 3** response, reply, rejoinder, answer; retaliation, riposte, quip, sally, gibe, barb, *colloq.* wisecrack, put-down, *sl.* comeback. ● *v.* **1** fling *or* hurl (back), rejoin, return; answer back, counter, respond, answer, reply, come back (with); riposte. **2** avenge, revenge, requite, repay, pay back, retaliate.

retort[2] /ritáwrt, reétawrt/ *n. & v.* ● *n.* **1** a vessel usu. of glass with a long recurved neck used in distilling liquids. **2** a vessel for heating mercury for purification, coal to generate gas, or iron and carbon to make steel. ● *v.tr.* purify (mercury) by heating in a retort. [F *retorte* f. med.L *retorta* fem. past part. of *retorquēre*: see RETORT[1]]

retortion /ritáwrshən/ *n.* **1** the act or an instance of bending back; the condition of being bent back. **2** = RETORSION. [RETORT[1], perh. after *contortion*]

retouch /reétúch/ *v. & n.* ● *v.tr.* improve or repair (a composition, picture, photographic negative or print, etc.) by fresh touches or alterations. ● *n.* the act or an instance of

retouching. □□ **retoucher** *n.* [prob. f. F *retoucher* (as RE-, TOUCH)]

■ *v.* touch up, correct; restore, repair, recondition, refresh, adjust, improve, finish, titivate, put the finishing touches on, add *or* give (the) finishing touches to.

retrace /reetráys/ *v.tr.* **1** go back over (one's steps, etc.). **2** trace back to a source or beginning. **3** recall the course of in one's memory. [F *retracer* (as RE-, TRACE[1])]

retract /ritrákt/ *v.* **1** *tr.* (also *absol.*) withdraw or revoke (a statement or undertaking). **2 a** *tr. & intr.* (esp. with ref. to part of the body) draw or be drawn back or in. **b** *tr.* draw (an undercarriage, etc.) into the body of an aircraft. □□ **retractable** *adj.* **retraction** *n.* **retractive** *adj.* [L *retrahere* or (in sense 1) *retractare* (as RE-, *trahere tract-* draw)]

■ **1** take back, withdraw, rescind, revoke, repeal, deny, disavow, recant, renounce, abjure, cancel, forswear, repudiate, disclaim, disown, reverse. **2 a** withdraw, pull *or* draw *or* take back.

retractile /ritráktil, -tíl/ *adj.* capable of being retracted. □□ **retractility** /-tílitee/ *n.* [RETRACT, after *contractile*]

retractor /ritráktər/ *n.* **1** a muscle used for retracting. **2** a device for retracting.

retrain /reetráyn/ *v.tr. & intr.* train again or further, esp. for new work.

retral /reétrəl, rét-/ *adj. Biol.* posterior; at the back. [RETRO- + -AL]

retranslate /reétranzláyt, -trans-, reetránzlayt, -tráns-/ *v.tr.* translate again, esp. back into the original language. □□ **retranslation** *n.*

retransmit /reétranzmít, -trans-/ *v.tr.* (**retransmitted, retransmitting**) transmit (esp. radio signals or broadcast programs) back again or to a further distance. □□ **retransmission** /-míshən/ *n.*

retread *v. & n.* ● *v.tr.* /reetréd/ (*past* **retrod**; *past part.* **retrodden**) **1** tread (a path, etc.) again. **2** put a fresh tread on (a tire). ● *n.* /reétred/ a retreaded tire.

retreat /ritreét/ *v. & n.* ● *v.* **1 a** *intr.* (esp. of military forces) go back, retire; relinquish a position. **b** *tr.* cause to retreat; move back. **2** *intr.* (esp. of features) recede; slope back. ● *n.* **1 a** the act or an instance of retreating. **b** *Mil.* a signal for this. **2** withdrawal into privacy or security. **3** a place of shelter or seclusion. **4** a period of seclusion for prayer and meditation. **5** *Mil.* a bugle call at sunset, signaling the lowering of the flag. **6** a place for the reception of the elderly or others in need of care. [ME f. OF *retret* (n.), *retraiter* (v.) f. L *trahere*: see RETRACT]

■ *v.* **1 a** decamp, fall *or* go back, give *or* lose ground, flee, take flight, run (away), turn tail, depart, retire, move back, recoil. **b** withdraw, pull *or* draw *or* move back, pull out, retire, evacuate. **2** see RECEDE 1. ● *n.* **1 a** decampment, retirement, withdrawal, falling back, evacuation, rout, flight. **2** retirement, seclusion, withdrawal, rustication, separation, escape, departure. **3** sanctuary, refuge, shelter, den, haven, asylum, hideaway, hiding place, *colloq.* sanctum, hideout. **6** old people's home, nursing home, home, rest home.

retrench /ritrénch/ *v.* **1 a** *tr.* reduce the amount of (costs). **b** *intr.* cut down expenses; introduce economies. **2** *tr.* shorten or abridge. □□ **retrenchment** *n.* [obs. F *retrencher* (as RE-, TRENCH)]

retrial /reétríəl/ *n.* a second or further (judicial) trial.

retribution /rétribyōōshən/ *n.* requital usu. for evil done; vengeance. □□ **retributive** /ritríbyətiv/ *adj.* **retributory** /ritríbyətawree/ *adj.* [ME f. LL *retributio* (as RE-, *tribuere tribut-* assign)]

■ vengeance, revenge, reprisal, retaliation, requital, recompense, redress, punishment; justice.

retrieve /ritreév/ *v. & n.* ● *v.tr.* **1 a** regain possession of. **b**

/.../	**pronunciation**	●	**part of speech**
□	**phrases, idioms, and compounds**		
□□	**derivatives**	■	**synonym section**
	cross-references appear in SMALL CAPITALS *or italics*		

recover by investigation or effort of memory. **2 a** restore to knowledge or recall to mind. **b** obtain (information stored in a computer, etc.). **3** (of a dog) find and bring in (killed or wounded game, etc.). **4** (foll. by *from*) recover or rescue (esp. from a bad state). **5** restore to a flourishing state; revive. **6** repair or set right (a loss or error, etc.) (*managed to retrieve the situation*). ● *n.* the possibility of recovery (*beyond retrieve*). □□ **retrievable** *adj.* **retrieval** *n.* [ME f. OF *retroeve-* stressed stem of *retrover* (as RE-, *trover* find)]

■ *v.* **1 a** reclaim, regain; see also RECOVER *v.* 1. **2 a** recall, remember, call to mind, summon back, recollect. **3** bring *or* get (back *or* in), fetch, come back with. **4** see DELIVER 2. **5** see REVIVE 2. **6** recoup, make up, recover, cover, redeem, get back, regain, be repaid *or* reimbursed for; repair, set right.

retriever /ritréevər/ *n.* **1 a** a dog of a breed used for retrieving game. **b** this breed. **2** a person who retrieves something.

retro /rétrō/ *adj.* & *n. sl.* ● *adj.* **1** reviving or harking back to the past. **2** retroactive. ● *n.* a retro fashion or style.

retro- /rétrō/ *comb. form* **1** denoting action back or in return (*retroact*; *retroflex*). **2** *Anat.* & *Med.* denoting location behind. [L *retro* backward]

retroact /rétrō-ákt/ *v.intr.* **1** operate in a backward direction. **2** have a retrospective effect. **3** react. □□ **retroaction** *n.*

retroactive /rétrō-áktiv/ *adj.* (esp. of legislation) having retrospective effect. □□ **retroactively** *adv.* **retroactivity** /-tívitee/ *n.*

retrocede /rétrōseéd/ *v.* **1** *intr.* move back; recede. **2** *tr.* cede back again. □□ **retrocedence** *n.* **retrocedent** *adj.* **retrocession** /-séshən/ *n.* **retrocessive** /-sésiv/ *adj.* [L *retrocedere* (as RETRO-, *cedere cess-* go)]

retrochoir /rétrōkwīr/ *n.* the part of a cathedral or large church behind the high altar. [med.L *retrochorus* (as RETRO-, CHOIR)]

retrod *past of* RETREAD.

retrodden *past part. of* RETREAD.

retrofit /rétrōfit/ *v.tr.* (**-fitted, -fitting**) modify (machinery, vehicles, etc.) to incorporate changes and developments introduced after manufacture. [RETROACTIVE + REFIT]

retroflex /rétrəfleks/ *adj.* (also **retroflexed**) **1** *Anat.*, *Med.*, & *Bot.* turned backward. **2** *Phonet.* pronounced with the tip of the tongue curled up toward the hard palate. □□ **retroflexion** /-flékshən/ *n.* [L *retroflectere retroflex-* (as RETRO-, *flectere* bend)]

retrogradation /rétrōgrədáyshən/ *n. Astron.* **1** the apparent backward motion of a planet in the zodiac. **2** the apparent motion of a celestial body from east to west. **3** backward movement of the lunar nodes on the ecliptic. [LL *retrogradatio* (as RETRO-, GRADATION)]

retrograde /rétrəgrayd/ *adj.*, *n.*, & *v.* ● *adj.* **1** directed backward; retreating. **2** reverting esp. to an inferior state; declining. **3** inverse; reversed (*in retrograde order*). **4** *Astron.* in or showing retrogradation. ● *n.* a degenerate person. ● *v.intr.* **1** move backward; recede; retire. **2** decline; revert. **3** *Astron.* show retrogradation. □□ **retrogradely** *adv.* [ME f. L *retrogradus* (as RETRO-, *gradus* step, *gradi* walk)]

retrogress /rétrəgrés/ *v.intr.* **1** go back; move backward. **2** deteriorate. □□ **retrogressive** *adj.* [RETRO-, after PROGRESS *v.*]

retrogression /rétrəgréshən/ *n.* **1** backward or reversed movement. **2** a return to a less advanced state; a reversal of development; a decline or deterioration. **3** *Astron.* = RETROGRADATION. □□ **retrogressive** /-grésiv/ *adj.* **retrogressively** *adv.* [RETRO-, after *progression*]

retroject /rétrōjekt/ *v.tr.* throw back (usu. opp. PROJECT). [RETRO-, after PROJECT *v.*]

retro-rocket /rétrō-rokít/ *n.* an auxiliary rocket for slowing down a spacecraft, etc., e.g., when reentering the earth's atmosphere.

retrorse /ritráwrs/ *adj. Biol.* turned back or down. □□ **retrorsely** *adv.* [L *retrorsus* = *retroversus* (as RETRO-, *versus* past part. of *vertere* turn)]

retrospect /rétrəspekt/ *n.* **1** (foll. by *to*) regard or reference to precedent or authority, or to previous conditions. **2** a

survey of past time or events. □ **in retrospect** when looked back on. [RETRO-, after PROSPECT *n.*]

■ **2** review, survey, reexamination, reconsideration, reassessment. □ **in retrospect** with hindsight, on reconsideration.

retrospection /rétrəspékshən/ *n.* **1** the action of looking back esp. into the past. **2** an indulgence or engagement in retrospect. [prob. f. *retrospect* (v.) (as RETROSPECT)]

retrospective /rétrəspéktiv/ *adj.* & *n.* ● *adj.* **1** looking back on or dealing with the past. **2** (of an exhibition, recital, etc.) showing an artist's development over his or her lifetime. **3** esp. *Brit.* (of a statute, etc.) applying to the past as well as the future; retroactive. **4** (of a view) lying to the rear. ● *n.* a retrospective exhibition, recital, etc. □□ **retrospectively** *adv.*

retrosternal /rétrōstárnəl/ *adj. Anat.* & *Med.* behind the breastbone.

retroussé /retrōōsáy/ *adj.* (of the nose) turned up at the tip. [F, past part. of *retrousser* tuck up (as RE-, TRUSS)]

retrovert /rétrōvərt/ *v.tr.* **1** turn backward. **2** *Med.* (as **retroverted** *adj.*) (of the womb) having a backward inclination. □□ **retroversion** /-vórzhən, -shən/ *n.* [LL *retrovertere* (as RETRO-, *vertere vers-* turn)]

retrovirus /rétrōvírəs/ *n. Biol.* any of a group of RNA viruses that form DNA during the replication of their RNA. [mod.L f. initial letters of *reverse transcriptase* + VIRUS]

retry /reétrí/ *v.tr.* (**-ies, -ied**) try (a defendant or lawsuit) a second or further time. □□ **retrial** *n.*

retsina /retseénə/ *n.* a Greek wine flavored with resin. [mod. Gk]

retune /reétoōn, -tyoōn/ *v.tr.* **1** tune (a musical instrument) again or differently. **2** tune (a radio, etc.) to a different frequency.

returf /reétárf/ *v.tr.* provide with new turf.

return /ritárn/ *v.* & *n.* ● *v.* **1** *intr.* come or go back. **2** *tr.* bring or put or send back to the person or place, etc., where originally belonging or obtained (*returned the fish to the river*; *have you returned my scissors?*). **3** *tr.* pay back or reciprocate; give in response (*decided not to return the compliment*). **4** *tr.* yield (a profit). **5** *tr.* say in reply; retort. **6** *tr.* (in tennis, etc.) hit or send (the ball) back after receiving it. **7** *tr.* state or mention or describe officially, esp. in answer to a writ or formal demand. **8** *tr.* elect, esp. reelect, to political office, etc. **9** *tr. Cards* **a** lead (a suit) previously led or bid by a partner. **b** lead (a suit or card) after taking a trick. **10** *tr. Archit.* continue (a wall, etc.) in a changed direction, esp. at right angles. ● *n.* **1** the act or an instance of coming or going back. **2 a** the act or an instance of giving or sending or putting or paying back. **b** a thing given or sent back. **3** a key on a computer or typewriter to start a new line. **4** (in *sing.* or *pl.*) **a** the proceeds or profit of an undertaking. **b** the acquisition of these. **5** a formal report or statement compiled or submitted by order (*an income-tax return*). **6** (in full **return match** or **game**) a second match, etc., between the same opponents. **7** esp. *Brit. Electr.* a conductor bringing a current back to its source. **8** a response or reply. **9** (in *pl.*) a report on votes counted in an election (*early returns from the third district*). **10** *Archit.* a part receding from the line of the front, e.g., the side of a house or of a window opening. □ **in return** as an exchange or reciprocal action. **many happy returns (of the day)** a greeting on a birthday, etc. **return ticket 1** a ticket for the returning portion of a trip. **2** *Brit.* a round-trip ticket. □□ **returnable** *adj.* **returner** *n.* **returnless** *adj.* [ME f. OF *returner* (as RE-, TURN)]

■ *v.* **1** come back, reappear, resurface, turn up again, make *or* put in an appearance again, *colloq.* show up again; recur, reoccur, crop up again, pop up again; go back, revert, turn back. **2** replace, restore, put *or* give *or* bring *or* carry *or* take back. **3** pay back, reciprocate, requite, repay. **4** earn, gain; see also YIELD *v.* 1. **5** see REPLY *v.* 2. **7** deliver, give, turn in, state, offer, proffer, report. **8** elect, reelect. ● *n.* **1** homecoming; recurrence, reappearance, repetition, renewal, recrudescence, resurfacing, reemergence; comeback. **2 a** replacement, replacing, restoration, restoring, restitution, reciprocation, repayment, recompense, reimbursement, compensation, payment, reparation, indemnity, indemnification, consideration, amends, redress, requital. **4 a** yield, earnings, profit, gain, income, revenue, proceeds, takings. **5** report, statement, record. □ **in return** in exchange, again; see also BACK *adv.* 2b.

returnable /ritə́rnəbəl/ *adj. & n.* ● *adj.* **1** intended to be returned, as an empty beverage container. **2** required by law to be returned, as a court writ. ● *n.* an empty beverage container, especially a bottle or can, that can be returned for a refund of the deposit paid at purchase.

returnee /ritərneé/ *n.* a person who returns home from abroad, esp. after war service.

retuse /ritōōs, -tyōōs/ *adj. esp. Bot.* having a broad end with a central depression. [L *retundere retus-* (as RE-, *tundere* beat)]

retying *pres. part.* of RETIE.

retype /reétíp/ *v.tr.* type again, esp. to correct errors.

reunify /reéyōōnifí/ *v.tr.* (**-ies, -ied**) restore (esp. separated territories) to a political unity. □□ **reunification** /-fikáyshən/ *n.*

reunion /reéyōónyən/ *n.* **1 a** the act or an instance of reuniting. **b** the condition of being reunited. **2** a social gathering esp. of people formerly associated. [F *réunion* or AL *reunio* f. L *reunire* unite (as RE-, UNION)]

reunite /reéyōōnít/ *v.tr. & intr.* bring or come back together.

reupholster /reéəphṓlstər, -əpṓl-/ *v.tr.* upholster anew. □□ **reupholstery** *n.*

reuse *v. & n.* ● *v.tr.* /reéyōóz/ use again or more than once. ● *n.* /reéyōós/ a second or further use. □□ **reusable** /-yōózəbəl/ *adj.*

reutilize /reéyōót'líz/ *v.tr.* utilize again or for a different purpose. □□ **reutilization** /-záyshən/ *n.*

Rev. *abbr.* **1** Reverend. **2** Revelation (New Testament).

rev /rev/ *n. & v. colloq.* ● *n.* (in *pl.*) the number of revolutions of an engine per minute; RPMs (*running at 3,000 revs*). ● *v.* (**revved, revving**) **1** *intr.* (of an engine) revolve; turn over. **2** *tr.* (also *absol.*; often foll. by *up*) cause (an engine) to run quickly. [abbr.]

revaccinate /reéváksinayt/ *v.tr.* vaccinate again. □□ **revaccination** /-náyshən/ *n.*

revalue /reévályōó/ *v.tr.* (**revalues, revalued, revaluing**) *Econ.* give a different value to, esp. give a higher value to, (a currency) in relation to other currencies or gold (opp. DEVALUE). □□ **revaluation** /-vályōōáyshən/ *n.*

revamp /reévámp/ *v.tr.* **1** renovate; revise; improve. **2** patch up. [RE- + VAMP[1]]
■ overhaul, redo, recondition, renovate, repair, fix, refit, refurbish, restore, *colloq.* do up; revise, improve; see also REPAIR[1] *v.*

revanchism /riváncḥizəm/ *n. Polit.* a policy of seeking to retaliate, esp. to recover lost territory. □□ **revanchist** *n. & adj.* [F *revanche* (as REVENGE)]

revarnish /reévaárnish/ *v.tr.* varnish again.

reveal[1] /riveél/ *v.tr.* **1** display or show; allow to appear. **2** (often as **revealing** *adj.*) disclose; divulge; betray (*revealed his plans; a revealing remark*). **3** *tr.* (in *refl.* or *passive*) come to sight or knowledge. **4** *Relig.* (esp. of God) make known by inspiration or supernatural means. □□ **revealed religion** a religion based on divine revelation (opp. *natural religion*). □□ **revealable** *adj.* **revealer** *n.* **revealingly** *adv.* [ME f. OF *reveler* or L *revelare* (as RE-, *velum* veil)]
■ **1** expose, display, show, present, exhibit, unveil, uncover, lay bare. **2** divulge, disclose, make known, communicate, give vent to, air, ventilate, let out, give away, let slip, betray, leak, *colloq.* let on.

reveal[2] /riveél/ *n.* an internal side surface of an opening or recess, esp. of a doorway or a window aperture. [obs. *revale* (v.) lower f. OF *revaler* f. *avaler* (as RE-, VAIL)]

reveille /révəlee/ *n.* a military wake-up call sounded in the morning on a bugle or drums, etc. [F *réveillez* imper. pl. of *réveiller* awaken (as RE-, *veiller* f. L *vigilare* keep watch)]

revel /révəl/ *v. & n.* ● *v.* (**reveled, reveling** or **revelled, revelling**) **1** *intr.* have a good time; be extravagantly festive.

2 *intr.* (foll. by *in*) take keen delight in. **3** *tr.* (foll. by *away*) throw away (money or time) in revelry. ● *n.* (in *sing.* or *pl.*) the act or an instance of reveling. □□ **reveler** *n.* **revelry** *n.* (*pl.* **-ies**). [ME f. OF *reveler* riot f. L *rebellare* REBEL *v.*]
■ *v.* **1** make merry, celebrate, rollick, roister, cut loose, (go on a) spree, carouse, *colloq.* live it up, whoop it up, make whoopee, paint the town red, party. **2** (*revel in*) (take) delight in, take pleasure in, rejoice in, luxuriate in, bask in, wallow in, lap up, glory in, savor, relish. ● *n.* party, celebration, debauch, romp, fling, carnival, jamboree, bacchanal, saturnalia, *colloq.* spree, *sl.* ball; festival, fête, gala. □□ **revelry** merrymaking, fun, reveling, gaiety, festivity, jollity, mirth, celebrations, high jinks, *colloq.* spree, *sl.* ball.

revelation /révəláyshən/ *n.* **1 a** the act or an instance of revealing, esp. the supposed disclosure of knowledge to humankind by a divine or supernatural agency. **b** knowledge disclosed in this way. **2** a striking disclosure (*it was a revelation to me*). **3** (**Revelation** or *colloq.* **Revelations**) (in full **the Revelation of St. John the Divine**) the last book of the New Testament, describing visions of heaven. □□ **revelational** *adj.* [ME f. OF *revelation* or LL *revelatio* (as REVEAL[1])]
■ **2** admission, confession; declaration, announcement, pronouncement, proclamation, statement; leak, discovery, unveiling, disclosure, exposé.

revelationist /révəláyshənist/ *n.* a believer in divine revelation.

revelatory /révələtawree, rəvélə-/ *adj.* serving to reveal, esp. something significant. [L *revelare*: see REVEAL[1]]

revenant /révənənt/ *n.* a person who has returned, esp. supposedly from the dead. [F, pres. part. of *revenir*: see REVENUE]

revenge /rivénj/ *n. & v.* ● *n.* **1** retaliation for an offense or injury. **2** an act of retaliation. **3** the desire for this; a vindictive feeling. **4** (in games) a chance to win after an earlier defeat. ● *v.* **1** *tr.* (in *refl.* or *passive*; often foll. by *on, upon*) inflict retaliation for an offense. **2** *tr.* take revenge for (an offense). **3** *tr.* avenge (a person). **4** *intr.* take vengeance. □□ **revenger** *n.* [ME f. OF *revenger, revencher* f. LL *revindicare* (as RE-, *vindicare* lay claim to)]
■ *n.* **1** vengeance, retaliation, reprisal, retribution, repayment, satisfaction, payback. **2** see BACKLASH 1. **3** vengeance, spitefulness, vindictiveness; see also RANCOR. ● *v.* **1** settle a score *or* an old score with, get even with, even the score, punish, *colloq.* get. **2** avenge, get even for, take revenge for, make reprisal for, right, exact retribution *or* payment *or* repayment for. **4** settle a score *or* an old score, get even, give tit for tat, take an eye for an eye (and a tooth for a tooth), give a person a taste of his *or* her own medicine, *colloq.* get one's own back, give a person his *or* her comeuppance.

revengeful /rivénjfŏŏl/ *adj.* eager for revenge. □□ **revengefully** *adv.* **revengefulness** *n.*

revenue /révənōō, -nyōō/ *n.* **1 a** income, esp. of a large amount, from any source. **b** (in *pl.*) items constituting this. **2** a government's annual income from which public expenses are met. **3** the department of the civil service collecting this. □ **revenue tariff** a tax imposed to raise revenue, rather than to affect trade. [ME f. OF *revenu(e)* past part. of *revenir* f. L *revenire* return (as RE-, *venire* come)]
■ **1** income, proceeds, receipts, return(s), yield, profit(s), gain, gate, gate money, take.

reverb /rivə́rb, reévərb/ *v. & n.* ● *v.* reverberate. ● *n. Mus. colloq.* **1** reverberation. **2** a device to produce this. [abbr.]

reverberate /rivə́rbərayt/ *v.* **1 a** *intr.* (of sound, light, or heat) be returned or echoed or reflected repeatedly. **b** *tr.* return (a sound, etc.) in this way. **2** *intr.* (of a story, rumor, etc.) be heard much or repeatedly. □ **reverberatory fur-**

nace a furnace constructed to throw heat back on to the substance exposed to it. □□ **reverberant** *adj.* **reverberantly** *adv.* **reverberation** /-ráyshən/ *n.* **reverberative** /-rətiv/ *adj.* **reverberator** *n.* **reverberatory** /-rətawree/ *adj.* [L *reverberare* (as RE-, *verberare* lash f. *verbera* (pl.) scourge)]

revere /riveér/ *v.tr.* hold in deep and usu. affectionate or religious respect; venerate. [F *révérer* or L *reverēri* (as RE-, *verēri* fear)]
■ adore, reverence, venerate, glorify, esteem, admire, respect, honor, worship, idolize, enshrine, sanctify.

reverence /révərəns, révrəns/ *n.* & *v.* ● *n.* **1 a** the act of revering or the state of being revered (*hold in reverence*; *feel reverence for*). **b** the capacity for revering (*lacks reverence*). **2** (also /revəráans/) *archaic* a gesture showing that one reveres; a bow or curtsy. **3** (**Reverence**) a title used of or to some members of the clergy. ● *v.tr.* regard or treat with reverence. [ME f. OF f. L *reverentia* (as REVERE)]
■ *n.* **1 a** honor, respect, esteem, admiration, veneration, idolization, awe; glorification, beatification, sanctification, worship, adoration, homage, obeisance, deference. ● *v.* see REVERE.

reverend /révərənd, révrənd/ *adj.* & *n.* ● *adj.* (esp. as the title of a clergyman) deserving reverence. ● *n. colloq.* a clergyman. □ **Most Reverend** the title of an archbishop, bishop, cardinal, etc. **Reverend Mother** the title of the Mother Superior of a convent. **Right Reverend** the title of a bishop. **Very Reverend** *Brit.* the title of a dean, etc. [ME f. OF *reverend* or L *reverendus* gerundive of *reverēri*: see REVERE]

reverent /révərənt, révrənt/ *adj.* feeling or showing reverence. □□ **reverently** *adv.* [ME f. L *reverens* (as REVERE)]

reverential /révərénshəl/ *n.* of the nature of, due to, or characterized by reverence. □□ **reverentially** *adv.* [med.L *reverentialis* (as REVERE)]

reverie /révəree/ *n.* **1** a fit of abstracted musing (*was lost in a reverie*). **2** *archaic* a fantastic notion or theory; a delusion. **3** *Mus.* an instrumental piece suggesting a dreamy or musing state. [obs. F *resverie* f. OF *reverie* rejoicing, revelry f. *rever* be delirious f. unkn. orig.]
■ **1** daydream, brown study; see also FANTASY *n.* 2.

revers /riveér/ *n.* (*pl.* same /-veérz/) **1** the turned-back edge of a garment revealing the undersurface. **2** the material on this surface. [F, = REVERSE]

reverse /rivárs/ *v.*, *adj.*, & *n.* ● *v.* **1** *tr.* turn the other way around or up or inside out. **2** *tr.* change to the opposite character or effect (*reversed the decision*). **3** *intr.* & *tr.* travel or cause to travel backward. **4** *tr.* make (an engine, etc.) work in a contrary direction. **5** *tr.* revoke or annul (a decree, act, etc.). **6** *intr.* (of a dancer, esp. in a waltz) revolve in the opposite direction. ● *adj.* **1** placed or turned in an opposite direction or position. **2** opposite or contrary in character or order; inverted. ● *n.* **1** the opposite or contrary (*the reverse is the case*; *is the reverse of the truth*). **2** the contrary of the usual manner. **3** an occurrence of misfortune; a disaster, esp. a defeat in battle (*suffered a reverse*). **4** reverse gear or motion. **5** the reverse side of something. **6 a** the side of a coin or medal, etc., bearing the secondary design. **b** this design (cf. OBVERSE). **7** the verso of a book leaf. □ **reverse arms** hold a rifle with the butt upward. **reverse the charges** make the recipient of a telephone call responsible for payment. **reverse fault** *Geol.* a fault in which the overlying side of a mass of rock is displaced upward in relation to the underlying side. **reverse gear** a gear used to make a vehicle, etc., travel backward. **reversing light** *Brit.* = *backup light*. □□ **reversal** *n.* **reversely** *adv.* **reverser** *n.* **reversible** *adj.* **reversibility** *n.* **reversibly** *adv.* [ME f. OF *revers* (n.), *reverser* (v.), f. L *revertere revers-* (as RE-, *vertere* turn)]
■ *v.* **1** invert, overturn, turn upside down, turn over, upend; transpose, switch. **2, 5** overturn, overthrow, quash, override, annul, nullify, revoke, annul, negate, declare null and void, disaffirm, invalidate, cancel, repeal, rescind, overrule, countermand, undo, *Law* vacate; renounce, recant, take back. **3** back up, go backward, backtrack, *Naut.* make sternway; move

backward. ● *adj.* **1** opposite, contrary, inverse, converse; inverted, upside-down, mirror, reversed, backward. ● *n.* **1** opposite, contrary, converse, antithesis. **3** misfortune, reversal, vicissitude, setback, disappointment, mishap, misadventure, disaster, catastrophe, debacle, rout, defeat, *colloq.* washout. **5** back, rear, wrong side, verso, underside, underneath; *colloq.* flip side. □□ **reversal** turnabout, turnaround, U-turn, change, volte-face, switch, about-face, *Brit.* about-turn; annulment, nullification, cancellation, revocation, repeal, rescission; see also REVERSE *n.* 3 above.

reversion /rivárzhən/ *n.* **1 a** the legal right (esp. of the original owner, or his or her heirs) to possess or succeed to property on the death of the present possessor. **b** property to which a person has such a right. **2** *Biol.* a return to ancestral type. **3** a return to a previous state, habit, etc. **4** a sum payable on a person's death, esp. by way of life insurance. □□ **reversional** *adj.* **reversionary** *adj.* [ME f. OF *reversion* or L *reversio* (as REVERSE)]

revert /rivárt/ *v.* **1** *intr.* (foll. by *to*) return to a former state, practice, opinion, etc. **2** *intr.* (of property, an office, etc.) return by reversion. **3** *intr.* fall back into a wild state. **4** *tr.* turn (one's eyes or steps) back. □□ **reverter** *n.* (in sense 2). [ME f. OF *revertir* or L *revertere* (as REVERSE)]
■ **1** (*revert to*) return to, come or go back to, take or pick up again, lapse (back) into, backslide into, relapse into.

revertible /rivártibəl/ *adj.* (of property) subject to reversion.

revet /rivét/ *v.tr.* (**revetted, revetting**) face (a rampart, wall, etc.) with masonry, esp. in fortification. [F *revêtir* f. OF *revestir* f. LL *revestire* (as RE-, *vestire* clothe f. *vestis*)]

revetment /rivétmənt/ *n.* a retaining wall or facing. [F *revêtement* (as REVET)]

review /rivyóō/ *n.* & *v.* ● *n.* **1** a general survey or assessment of a subject or thing. **2** a retrospect or survey of the past. **3** revision or reconsideration (*is under review*). **4** a display and formal inspection of troops, etc. **5** a published account or criticism of a book, play, etc. **6** a periodical publication with critical articles on current events, the arts, etc. **7** a second view. ● *v.tr.* **1** survey or look back on. **2** reconsider or revise. **3** hold a review of (troops, etc.). **4** write a review of (a book, play, etc.). **5** view again. □□ **reviewable** *adj.* **reviewal** *n.* **reviewer** *n.* [obs. F *reveue* f. *revoir* (as RE-, *voir* see)]
■ *n.* **1** survey, assessment, examination, study, inspection, analysis, consideration, scrutiny. **3** reexamination, reconsideration, reassessment, revaluation, revision, reappraisal. **4** inspection, parade, procession, array, march-past; flyover, flyby, esp. *Brit.* flypast. **5** criticism, critique, review article, *compte rendu*, assessment, judgment, evaluation, commentary, study, comment, notice. **6** see PERIODICAL *n.* ● *v.* **1** survey, examine, regard, look at *or* over, study, look back on, consider, weigh, inspect, scrutinize. **2, 5** reexamine, revise, go over again, look at *or* over again; reassess, reconsider. **4** criticize, critique, give one's opinion of, comment on *or* upon, discuss, judge.

revile /rivíl/ *v.* **1** *tr.* abuse; criticize abusively. **2** *intr.* talk abusively; rail. □□ **revilement** *n.* **reviler** *n.* **reviling** *n.* [ME f. OF *reviler* (as RE-, VILE)]

revise /rivíz/ *v.* & *n.* ● *v.tr.* **1** examine or reexamine and improve or amend (esp. written or printed matter). **2** consider and alter (an opinion, etc.). **3** (also *absol.*) *Brit.* read again (work learned or done) to improve one's knowledge, esp. for an examination. ● *n. Printing* a proof sheet including corrections made in an earlier proof. □ **Revised Standard Version** a revision in 1946–52 of the Authorized Version of the Bible. **Revised Version** a revision in 1881–85 of the Authorized Version of the Bible. □□ **revisable** *adj.* **revisal** *n.* **reviser** *n.* **revisory** *adj.* [F *réviser* look at, or L *revisere* (as RE-, *visere* intensive of *vidēre vis-* see)]
■ *v.* **1** edit, emend, improve, correct; revamp, rework, reexamine, overhaul, update; rewrite, reinterpret. **2** alter, change, amend, modify, adjust; see also *think better of.* **3** go over again; reread, practice, *archaic* con, *Brit. colloq.* swot up on; see also STUDY *v.* 2, 4.

revision /rivízhən/ n. **1** the act or an instance of revising; the process of being revised. **2** a revised edition or form. □□ **revisionary** adj. [OF revision or LL revisio (as REVISE)]

■ **1** editing, revising, redaction, emendation, improvement, correction, modification, revamping, reworking, overhaul, overhauling, updating, update; rewriting, reinterpretation. **2** rewrite, revised or new edition, revised or new version.

revisionism /rivízhənizəm/ n. often derog. **1** a policy of revision or modification, esp. of Marxism on evolutionary socialist (rather than revolutionary) or pluralist principles. **2** any departure from or modification of accepted doctrine, theory, view of history, etc. □□ **revisionist** n. & adj.

revisit /reévízit/ v.tr. visit again.

revitalize /reévít'liz/ v.tr. imbue with new life and vitality. □□ **revitalization** /-záyshən/ n.

revival /rivívəl/ n. **1** the act or an instance of reviving; the process of being revived. **2** a new production of an old play, etc. **3** a revived use of an old practice, custom, etc. **4 a** a reawakening of religious fervor. **b** one or a series of evangelistic meetings to promote this. **5** restoration to bodily or mental vigor or to life or consciousness.

■ **1, 3** resurrection, resuscitation, renewal, restoration, return, reanimation, revitalization, resurfacing; comeback. **4 a** rebirth, renascence, reanimation, resurgence, awakening, reawakening. **5** recovery, improvement, advance; increase, upsurge, upturn, upswing, rise, escalation, colloq. boost.

revivalism /rivívəlizəm/ n. belief in or the promotion of a revival, esp. of religious fervor. □□ **revivalist** n. **revivalistic** /-lístik/ adj.

revive /rivív/ v.intr. & tr. **1** come or bring back to consciousness or life or strength. **2** come or bring back to existence, use, notice, etc. □□ **revivable** adj. [ME f. OF revivre or LL revivere (as RE-, L vivere live)]

■ **1** (re)awaken, wake (up), waken; come around, recover, gain consciousness; bring around, resuscitate; revivify, revitalize. **2** reawaken, resume, reopen; stir up again, renew, bring back, reactivate, resurrect, recall, reestablish, revitalize, breathe new life into, reinvigorate.

reviver /rivívər/ n. **1** a person or thing that revives. **2** Brit. colloq. a stimulating drink. **3** Brit. a preparation used for restoring faded colors, etc.

revivify /rivívifi/ v.tr. (**-ies, -ied**) restore to animation, activity, vigor, or life. □□ **revivification** /-fikáyshən/ n. [F revivifier or LL revivificare (as RE-, VIVIFY)]

revoke /rivók/ v. & n. ● v. **1** tr. rescind, withdraw, or cancel (a decree or promise, etc.). **2** intr. Cards fail to follow suit when able to do so; renege. ● n. Cards the act of revoking. □□ **revocable** /révəkəbəl/ adj. **revocability** /révəkəbílitee/ n. **revocation** /révəkáyshən/ n. **revocatory** /révəkətawree/ adj. **revoker** n. [ME f. OF revoquer or L revocare (as RE-, vocare call)]

■ v. **1** cancel, invalidate, annul, declare null and void, void, nullify, negate, rescind, repeal, recall, quash, veto, abrogate, abolish; withdraw, take back, retract.

revolt /rivólt/ v. & n. ● v. **1** intr. **a** rise in rebellion against authority. **b** (as **revolted** adj.) having revolted. **2 a** tr. (often in passive) affect with strong disgust; nauseate (was revolted by the thought of it). **b** intr. (often foll. by at, against) feel strong disgust. ● n. **1** an act of rebelling. **2** a state of insurrection (in revolt). **3** a sense of loathing. **4** a mood of protest or defiance. [F révolter f. It. rivoltare ult. f. L revolvere (as REVOLVE)]

■ v. **1** a rebel, rise (up), mutiny, take up arms, kick over the traces; protest. **2 a** repel, offend, disgust, repulse, nauseate, sicken, shock, horrify. ● n. **1** rebellion, revolution, uprising, mutiny, insurrection, coup d'état, putsch, takeover.

revolting /rivólting/ adj. disgusting; horrible. □□ **revoltingly** adv.

■ sickening, nauseating, nauseous, loathsome, abhorrent, nasty, obnoxious, repulsive, offensive, objectionable, disagreeable, unpleasant, repellent, disgusting, foul,

horrid, horrible, vile, abominable, appalling, Brit. off-putting; stomach-turning, vomit-provoking, colloq. beastly, icky, sl. gross, rotten, yucky, Brit. colloq. sickmaking.

revolute /révəlōōt/ adj. Bot., etc., having a rolled-back edge. [L revolutus past part. of revolvere: see REVOLVE]

revolution /révəlōōshən/ n. **1 a** the forcible overthrow of a government or social order, in favor of a new system. **b** (in Marxism) the replacement of one ruling class by another; the class struggle that is expected to lead to political change and the triumph of communism. **2** any fundamental change or reversal of conditions. **3** the act or an instance of revolving. **4 a** motion in orbit or a circular course or around an axis or center; rotation. **b** the single completion of an orbit or rotation. **c** the time taken for this. **5** a cyclic recurrence. □ **revolution counter** Brit. = TACHOMETER 2. □□ **revolutionism** n. **revolutionist** n. [ME f. OF revolution or LL revolutio (as REVOLVE)]

■ **1 a** revolt, rebellion, coup, mutiny, coup d'état, uprising, insurgency, insurrection, putsch, takeover, overthrow; counterrevolution. **2** upheaval, cataclysm, transformation, (radical or major) change, sea change, reversal, metamorphosis. **3, 4** rotation, turn, gyration; wheel, whirl, pirouette, spin; orbit, circle, circuit, lap, round. **5** cycle, phase, period; see also TURN n. 1.

revolutionary /révəlōōshəneree/ adj. & n. ● adj. **1** involving great and often violent change or innovation. **2** of or causing political revolution. **3** (**Revolutionary**) of or relating to a particular revolution, esp. the American Revolution. ● n. (pl. **-ies**) an instigator or supporter of political revolution.

■ adj. **1** novel, innovative, creative, new, different, original, avant-garde. **2** mutinous, rebellious, insurgent, insurrectionist, insurrectionary, radical, seditious, subversive; rebel. ● n. rebel, mutineer, insurgent, insurrectionist, insurrectionary, revolutionist, sansculotte, radical, anarchist, extremist, Jacobin.

revolutionize /révəlōōshəniz/ v.tr. introduce fundamental change to.

revolve /rivólv/ v. **1** intr. & tr. turn or cause to turn around, esp. on an axis; rotate. **2** intr. move in a circular orbit. **3** tr. ponder (a problem, etc.) in the mind. □ **revolve on** esp. Brit. depend on. **revolving credit** credit that is automatically renewed as debts are paid off. **revolving door** a door with usu. four partitions turning around a central axis. □□ **revolvable** adj. [ME f. L revolvere (as RE-, volvere roll)]

■ **1, 2** spin (around), turn (around), whirl (around), twirl (around), swivel (around); pivot, rotate, gyrate, reel, wheel, go around, circle, orbit, cycle. **3** turn over (in one's mind), ponder, weigh, consider, meditate upon or on, think about, reflect upon or on, ruminate over or on, chew over, contemplate. □ **revolve on** turn or depend or pivot or rely on.

revolver /rivólvər/ n. a pistol with revolving chambers enabling several shots to be fired without reloading.

■ pistol, gun, firearm, handgun, side arm, colloq. shooting iron, sl. gat, rod, piece.

revue /rivyōō/ n. a theatrical entertainment of a series of short usu. satirical sketches and songs. [F, = REVIEW n.]

revulsion /rivúlshən/ n. **1** abhorrence; a sense of loathing. **2** a sudden violent change of feeling. **3** a sudden reaction in taste, fortune, trade, etc. **4** Med. counterirritation; the treatment of one disordered organ, etc., by acting upon another. [F revulsion or L revulsio (as RE-, vellere vuls- pull)]

■ **1** loathing, detestation, disgust, repugnance, abomination, abhorrence, aversion, hatred, antipathy, odium.

revulsive /rivúlsiv/ adj. & n. Med. ● adj. producing revulsion. ● n. a revulsive substance.

reward /riwáwrd/ n. & v. ● n. **1 a** a return or recompense

/. . ./ **pronunciation**	● **part of speech**
□ **phrases, idioms, and compounds**	
□□ **derivatives**	■ **synonym section**
cross-references appear in SMALL CAPITALS or italics	

for service or merit. **b** requital for good or evil; retribution. **2** a sum offered for the detection of a criminal, the restoration of lost property, etc. ● *v.tr.* give a reward to (a person) or for (a service, etc.). □□ **rewardless** *adj.* [ME f. AF, ONF *reward* = OF *reguard* REGARD]

■ *n.* **1 a** prize, award, tribute, honor, award, return, recompense, compensation, payment, pay, requital, *poet.* guerdon. **b** requital, retribution; (just) deserts. **2** see BOUNTY 2. ● *v.* recompense, compensate, pay, repay, remunerate, requite.

rewarding /riwáwrding/ *adj.* (of an activity, etc.) well worth doing; providing satisfaction. □□ **rewardingly** *adv.*
■ satisfying, gratifying, worthwhile, enriching, fruitful, profitable, advantageous, productive, gainful.

rewash /reéwáwsh, -wósh/ *v.tr.* wash again.

reweigh /reéwáy/ *v.tr.* weigh again.

rewind /reéwínd/ *v. & n.* ● *v.tr.* (*past* and *past part.* **rewound**) wind (a film or tape, etc.) back to the beginning. ● *n.* **1** function on a tape deck, camera, etc., to rewind (tape, film, etc.). **2** the button that activates this function. □□ **rewinder** *n.*

rewire /reéwír/ *v.tr.* provide (a building, etc.) with new wiring. □□ **rewirable** *adj.*

reword /reéwórd/ *v.tr.* change the wording of.
■ paraphrase, rephrase, put into different words *or* terms, put another way, express differently, rewrite, reformulate.

rework /reéwórk/ *v.tr.* revise; refashion; remake.

rewound *past* and *past part.* of REWIND.

rewrap /reéráp/ *v.tr.* (**rewrapped, rewrapping**) wrap again or differently.

rewrite *v. & n.* ● *v.tr.* /reérít/ (*past* **rewrote**; *past part.* **rewritten**) write again or differently. ● *n.* /reérít/ **1** the act or an instance of rewriting. **2** a thing rewritten.

Rex /reks/ *n.* the reigning king (following a name or in the titles of lawsuits, e.g., *Rex v. Jones*, the Crown versus Jones). [L]

Reye's syndrome /ríz, ráz/ *n. Med.* an acute, often fatal brain disease of children that usually follows a viral infection such as influenza or chicken pox and that is associated with the use of aspirin. [for Australian pediatrician Ralph D.K. Reye]

Reynard /ráynərd, -naard, rénərd/ *n.* a fox (esp. as a proper name in stories). [ME f. OF *Renart* name of a fox in the *Roman de Renart*]

Reynolds number /rénəldz/ *n. Physics* a quantity indicating the degree of turbulence of flow past an obstacle, etc. [O. *Reynolds*, Engl. physicist d. 1912]

Rf *symb. Chem.* the element rutherfordium.

r.f. *abbr.* (also **RF**) radio frequency.

RFC *abbr.* Reconstruction Finance Corporation.

RFD *abbr.* rural free delivery.

Rh[1] *symb. Chem.* the element rhodium.

Rh[2] see RH FACTOR.

r.h. *abbr.* right hand.

rhabdomancy /rábdəmansee/ *n.* the use of a divining rod, esp. for discovering subterranean water or mineral ore. [Gk *rhabdomanteia* f. *rhabdos* rod: see -MANCY]

Rhadamanthine /rádəmánthin, -thín/ *adj.* stern and incorruptible in judgment. [*Rhadamanthus* f. L f. Gk *Rhadamanthos*, name of a judge in the underworld]

Rhaeto-Romance /reétōrōmáns/ *adj. & n.* (also **Rhaeto-Romanic** /-mánik/) ● *adj.* of or in any of the Romance dialects of SE Switzerland and Tyrol, esp. Romansh and Ladin. ● *n.* any of these dialects. [L *Rhaetus* of Rhaetia in the Alps + ROMANIC]

rhapsode /rápsōd/ *n.* a reciter of epic poems, esp. of Homer in ancient Greece. [Gk *rhapsōidos* f. *rhaptō* stitch + *ōidē* song, ODE]

rhapsodist /rápsədist/ *n.* a person who rhapsodizes.

rhapsodize /rápsədīz/ *v.intr.* talk or write rhapsodies.

rhapsody /rápsədee/ *n.* (*pl.* **-ies**) **1** an enthusiastic, ecstatic, or extravagant utterance or composition. **2** *Mus.* a piece of music in one extended movement, usu. emotional in character. **3** *Gk Antiq.* an epic poem, or part of it, of a length

for one recitation. □□ **rhapsodic** /rapsódik/ *adj.* **rhapsodical** *adj.* (in senses 1, 2). [L *rhapsodia* f. Gk *rhapsōidia* (as RHAPSODE)]
■ □□ **rhapsodic, rhapsodical** ecstatic, enthusiastic, elated, overjoyed, effusive, rapturous, thrilled, blissful, transported, orgasmic, intoxicated, euphoric, delighted; walking on air, in seventh heaven, *colloq.* on top of the world.

rhatany /rát'nee/ *n.* (*pl.* **-ies**) **1** either of two American shrubs, *Krameria trianda* and *K. argentea*, having an astringent root when dried. **2** the root of either of these. [mod.L *rhatania* f. Port. *ratanha*, Sp. *ratania*, f. Quechua *rataña*]

rhea /reéə/ *n.* any of several S. American flightless birds of the family Rheidae, like but smaller than an ostrich. [mod.L genus name f. L f. Gk *Rhea* mother of Zeus]

rhebok /reébok/ *n.* (also esp. *Brit.* **reebok**) a small S. African antelope, *Pelea capreolus*, with sharp horns. [Du., = roebuck]

Rhenish /rénish/ *adj. & n.* ● *adj.* of the Rhine River and the regions adjoining it. ● *n.* wine from this area. [ME *rynis, rynisch*, etc., f. AF *reneis*, OF *r(a)inois* f. L *Rhenanus* f. *Rhenus* Rhine]

rhenium /reéneeəm/ *n. Chem.* a rare metallic element of the manganese group, occurring naturally in molybdenum ores and used in the manufacture of superconducting alloys. ¶ Symb.: **Re**. [mod.L f. L *Rhenus* Rhine]

rheology /reeóləjee/ *n.* the science dealing with the flow and deformation of matter. □□ **rheological** /-əlójikəl/ *adj.* **rheologist** *n.* [Gk *rheos* stream + -LOGY]

rheostat /reéəstat/ *n. Electr.* an instrument used to control a current by varying the resistance. □□ **rheostatic** /-státik/ *adj.* [Gk *rheos* stream + -STAT]

rhesus /reésəs/ *n.* (in full **rhesus monkey**) a small catarrhine monkey, *Macaca mulatta*, common in N. India. □ **rhesus baby** an infant with a hemolytic disorder caused by the incompatibility of its own Rh-positive blood with its mother's Rh-negative blood. **rhesus factor** = RH FACTOR. [mod.L, arbitrary use of L *Rhesus* f. Gk *Rhēsos*, mythical King of Thrace]

rhetor /reétər/ *n.* **1** an ancient Greek or Roman teacher or professor of rhetoric. **2** usu. *derog.* an orator. [ME f. LL *rethor* f. L *rhetor* f. Gk *rhētōr*]

rhetoric /rétərik/ *n.* **1** the art of effective or persuasive speaking or writing. **2** language designed to persuade or impress (often with an implication of insincerity or exaggeration, etc.). [ME f. OF *rethorique* f. L *rhetorica, -ice* f. Gk *rhētorikē* (*tekhnē*) (art) of rhetoric (as RHETOR)]
■ **1** eloquence, expressiveness, elocution, way with words, *colloq.* gift of (the) gab. **2** bombast, bluster, fustian, rodomontade, grandiloquence, magniloquence, oratory, wordiness, verbosity, prolixity, longwindedness, turgidity, flatulence, puffery, *colloq.* windiness, *sl.* hot air.

rhetorical /ritáwrikəl -tór-/ *adj.* **1 a** expressed with a view to persuasive or impressive effect; artificial or extravagant in language. **b** (of a question) assuming a preferred answer. **2** of the nature of rhetoric. **3 a** of or relating to the art of rhetoric. **b** given to rhetoric; oratorical. □ **rhetorical question** a question asked not for information but to produce an effect, e.g., *who cares?* for *nobody cares.* □□ **rhetorically** *adv.* [ME f. L *rhetoricus* f. Gk *rhētorikos* (as RHETOR)]
■ **1 a** pretentious, bombastic, flamboyant, extravagant, florid, fustian, high-flown, inflated, grandiose, euphuistic, turgid, grandiloquent, magniloquent, long-winded, orotund, wordy, prolix, *colloq.* windy, highfalutin. **b** artificial, contrived, for effect, unanswerable, not literal. **2, 3** oratorical, stylistic, linguistic, poetic, expressive.

rhetorician /rétəríshən/ *n.* **1** an orator. **2** a teacher of or expert in rhetoric. **3** a rhetorical speaker or writer. [ME f. OF *rethoricien* (as RHETORICAL)]

rheum /rōōm/ *n.* a watery discharge from a mucous membrane, esp. of the eyes or nose. □□ **rheumy** *adj.* [ME f. OF *reume* ult. f. Gk *rheuma -atos* stream f. *rheō* flow]

rheumatic /roomátik/ *adj. & n.* ● *adj.* **1** of, relating to, or suffering from rheumatism. **2** producing or produced by rheumatism. ● *n.* a person suffering from rheumatism. □ **rheumatic fever** a noninfectious fever with inflammation and pain in the joints. □□ **rheumatically** *adv.* **rheumaticky** *adj. colloq.* [ME f. OF *reumatique* or L *rheumaticus* f. Gk *rheumatikos* (as RHEUM)]

rheumatism /róŏmətizəm/ *n.* any disease marked by inflammation and pain in the joints, muscles, or fibrous tissue, esp. rheumatoid arthritis. [F *rhumatisme* or L *rheumatismus* f. Gk *rheumatismos* f. *rheumatizō* f. *rheuma* stream]

rheumatoid /róŏmətoyd/ *adj.* having the character of rheumatism. □ **rheumatoid arthritis** a chronic progressive disease causing inflammation and stiffening of the joints.

rheumatology /róŏmətóləjee/ *n.* the study of rheumatic diseases. □□ **rheumatological** /-təlójikəl/ *adj.* **rheumatologist** *n.*

Rh factor *Physiol.* an antigen occurring on the red blood cells of most humans and some other primates (as in the rhesus monkey, in which it was first observed).

rhinal /rínəl/ *adj. Anat.* of a nostril or the nose. [Gk *rhis rhin-*: see RHINO-]

rhinestone /rínstōn/ *n.* an imitation diamond or other precious stone. [*Rhine,* river and region in Germany + STONE]

rhinitis /rinítis/ *n.* inflammation of the mucous membrane of the nose. [Gk *rhis rhinos* nose]

rhino[1] /rínō/ *n.* (*pl.* same or **-os**) *colloq.* a rhinoceros. [abbr.]

rhino[2] /rínō/ *n. Brit. sl.* money. [17th c.: orig. unkn.]

rhino- /rínō/ *comb. form Anat.* the nose. [Gk *rhis rhinos* nostril, nose]

rhinoceros /rinósərəs/ *n.* (*pl.* same or **rhinoceroses**) any of various large thick-skinned plant-eating ungulates of the family Rhinocerotidae of Africa and S. Asia, with one horn or in some cases two horns on the nose and plated or folded skin. □ **rhinoceros bird** = OXPECKER. **rhinoceros horn** a mass of keratinized fibers, reputed to have medicinal or aphrodisiac powers. □□ **rhinocerotic** /rinósərótik/ *adj.* [ME f. L f. Gk *rhinokerōs* (as RHINO-, *keras* horn)]

rhinopharyngeal /rínōfarinjeeəl, -jəl, -fərínjeeəl/ *adj.* of or relating to the nose and pharynx.

rhinoplasty /rínōplastee/ *n.* plastic surgery of the nose. □□ **rhinoplastic** *adj.*

rhizo- /rízō/ *comb. form Bot.* a root. [Gk *rhiza* root]

rhizocarp /rízōkaarp/ *n.* a plant with a perennial root but stems that wither. [RHIZO- + Gk *karpos* fruit]

rhizoid /rízoyd/ *adj. & n. Bot.* ● *adj.* rootlike. ● *n.* a root hair or filament in mosses, ferns, etc.

rhizome /rízōm/ *n.* an underground rootlike stem bearing both roots and shoots. [Gk *rhizōma* f. *rhizoō* take root (as RHIZO-)]

rhizopod /rízōpod, -zə-/ *n.* any protozoa of the class Rhizopodea, forming rootlike pseudopodia.

rho /rō/ *n.* the seventeenth letter of the Greek alphabet (P, ρ). [Gk]

rhodamine /ródəmeen, -min/ *n. Chem.* any of various red synthetic dyes used to color textiles. [RHODO- + AMINE]

Rhode Island Red /rōd/ *n.* an orig. American breed of domestic fowl with brownish-red plumage.

Rhodes scholarship /rōdz/ *n.* any of several scholarships awarded annually and tenable at Oxford University by students from certain Commonwealth countries, South Africa, the United States, and Germany. □□ **Rhodes scholar** *n.* [Cecil *Rhodes,* Brit. statesman d. 1902, who founded them]

rhodium /ródeeəm/ *n. Chem.* a hard white metallic element of the platinum group, occurring naturally in platinum ores and used in making alloys and plating jewelry. ¶ Symb.: **Rh.** [Gk *rhodon* rose (from the color of the solution of its salts)]

rhodo- /ródō/ *comb. form esp. Mineral. & Chem.* rose-colored. [Gk *rhodon* rose]

rhodochrosite /ródōkrōsīt/ *n.* a mineral form of manganese carbonate occurring in rose-red crystals. [Gk *rhodokhrous* rose-colored]

rhododendron /ródədéndrən/ *n.* any evergreen shrub of the genus *Rhododendron,* with large clusters of trumpet-shaped flowers. [L, = oleander, f. Gk (as RHODO-, *dendron* tree)]

rhodopsin /ródópsin/ *n.* a light-sensitive pigment in the retina. Also called *visual purple.* [Gk *rhodon* rose + *opsis* sight]

rhodora /rədáwrə/ *n.* a N. American pink-flowered shrub, *Rhodora canadense.* [mod.L f. L plant-name f. Gk *rhodon* rose]

rhomb /rom/ *n.* = RHOMBUS. □□ **rhombic** *adj.* [F *rhombe* or L *rhombus*]

rhombi *pl.* of RHOMBUS.

rhombohedron /rómbəhéedrən/ *n.* (*pl.* **-hedrons** or **-hedra** /-drə/) **1** a solid bounded by six equal rhombuses. **2** a crystal in this form. □□ **rhombohedral** *adj.* [RHOMBUS, after *polyhedron,* etc.]

rhomboid /rómboyd/ *adj. & n.* ● *adj.* (also **rhomboidal** /-bóyd'l/) having or nearly having the shape of a rhombus. ● *n.* a quadrilateral of which only the opposite sides and angles are equal. [F *rhomboïde* or LL *rhomboides* f. Gk *rhomboeidēs* (as RHOMB)]

rhomboideus /rombóydeeəs/ *n.* (*pl.* **rhomboidei** /-dee-ī/) *Anat.* a muscle connecting the scapula to the vertebrae. [mod.L *rhomboideus* RHOMBOID]

rhombus /rómbəs/ *n.* (*pl.* **rhombuses** or **rhombi** /-bī/) *Geom.* a parallelogram with oblique angles and equal sides. [L f. Gk *rhombos*]

rhubarb /róŏbaarb/ *n.* **1 a** any of various plants of the genus *Rheum,* esp. *R. rhaponticum,* producing long fleshy dark-red leafstalks used cooked as food. **b** the leafstalks of this. **2 a** a root of a Chinese and Tibetan plant of the genus *Rheum.* **b** a purgative made from this. **3 a** *Brit. colloq.* a murmurous conversation or noise, esp. the repetition of the word "rhubarb" by crowd actors. **b** *sl.* nonsense; worthless stuff. **4** *sl.* a heated dispute. [ME f. OF *r(e)ubarbe,* shortening of med.L *r(h)eubarbarum,* alt. (by assoc. with Gk *rhēon* rhubarb) of *rhabarbarum* foreign 'rha,' ult. f. Gk *rha* + *barbaros* foreign]

rhumb /rum/ *n. Naut.* **1** any of the 32 points of the compass. **2** the angle between two successive compass points. **3** (in full **rhumb line**) **a** a line cutting all meridians at the same angle. **b** the line followed by a ship sailing in a fixed direction. [F *rumb* prob. f. Du. *ruim* room, assoc. with L *rhombus:* see RHOMBUS]

rhumba var. of RUMBA.

rhyme /rīm/ *n. & v.* ● *n.* **1** identity of sound between words or the endings of words, esp. in verse. **2** (in *sing.* or *pl.*) verse having rhymes. **3 a** the use of rhyme. **b** a poem having rhymes. **4** a word providing a rhyme. ● *v.* **1** *intr.* **a** (of words or lines) produce a rhyme. **b** (foll. by *with*) act as a rhyme (with another). **2** *intr.* make or write rhymes; versify. **3** *tr.* put or make (a story, etc.) into rhyme. **4** *tr.* (foll. by *with*) treat (a word) as rhyming with another. □ **rhyme or reason** sense; logic. **rhyming slang** slang that replaces words by rhyming words or phrases, e.g., *stairs* by *apples and pears,* often with the rhyming element omitted (as in TITFER). □□ **rhymeless** *adj.* **rhymer** *n.* **rhymist** *n.* [ME *rime* f. OF *rime* f. med.L *rithmus, rythmus* f. L f. Gk *rhuthmos* RHYTHM] ■ □ **rhyme or reason** (common) sense, logic, meaning, wisdom, rationality, rationale.

rhymester /rímstər/ *n.* a writer of (esp. simple or inferior) rhymes.

rhyolite /ríəlit/ *n.* a fine-grained volcanic rock of granitic composition. [G *Rhyolit* f. Gk *rhuax* lava stream + *lithos* stone]

rhythm /ríthəm/ *n.* **1** a measured flow of words and phrases in verse or prose determined by various relations of long and short or accented and unaccented syllables. **2** the aspect of musical composition concerned with periodical accent and the duration of notes. **3** *Physiol.* movement with a regular succession of strong and weak elements. **4** a regularly recurring sequence of events. **5** *Art* a harmonious correlation of parts. □ **rhythm and blues** popular music with a blues theme and a strong rhythm. **rhythm method** birth control

---

/ . . . / **pronunciation**	● **part of speech**
□ **phrases, idioms, and compounds**	
□□ **derivatives**	■ **synonym section**
cross-references appear in SMALL CAPITALS or *italics*	

by avoiding sexual intercourse when ovulation is likely to occur. **rhythm section** the part of a dance band or jazz band mainly supplying rhythm, usu. consisting of piano, bass, and drums. □□ **rhythmless** adj. [F *rhythme* or L *rhythmus* f. Gk *rhuthmos*, rel. to *rhēo* flow]

■ **1, 2** accent, measure, meter, stress, stress pattern, arsis; rhythmic pattern, tempo, beat, lilt; pulse, time, *Mus.* downbeat. **4** see CYCLE *n.* 1a.

rhythmic /ríthmik/ adj. (also **rhythmical**) **1** relating to or characterized by rhythm. **2** regularly occurring. □□ **rhythmically** adv. [F *rhythmique* or L *rhythmicus* (as RHYTHM)]

■ measured, cadenced, regular, steady, paced, even.

rhythmicity /rithmísitee/ n. **1** rhythmical quality or character. **2** the capacity for maintaining a rhythm.

RI abbr. Rhode Island (also in official postal use).

ria /rée∂/ n. *Geog.* a long narrow inlet formed by the partial submergence of a river valley. [Sp. *ría* estuary]

rial /reeáwl, -aál/ n. (also **riyal**) the monetary unit of several Middle Eastern countries. [Pers. f. Arab. *riyal* f. Sp. *real* ROYAL]

rib /rib/ n. & v. ● n. **1** each of the curved bones articulated in pairs to the spine and protecting the thoracic cavity and its organs. **2** a joint of meat from this part of an animal. **3** a ridge or long, raised piece often of stronger or thicker material across a surface or through a structure serving to support or strengthen it. **4** any of a ship's transverse curved timbers forming the framework of the hull. **5** *Knitting* a combination of plain and purl stitches producing a ribbed somewhat elastic fabric. **6** each of the hinged rods supporting the fabric of an umbrella. **7** a vein of a leaf or an insect's wing. **8** *Aeron.* a structural member in an airfoil. ● v.tr. (**ribbed**, **ribbing**) **1** provide with ribs; act as the ribs of. **2** colloq. make fun of; tease. **3** mark with ridges. □ **rib cage** the wall of bones formed by the ribs around the chest. □□ **ribless** adj. [OE *rib, ribb* f. Gmc]

ribald /ríbəld/ adj. & n. ● adj. (of language or its user) coarsely or disrespectfully humorous; scurrilous. ● n. a user of ribald language. [ME (earlier sense 'low-born retainer') f. OF *ribau(l)d* f. *riber* pursue licentious pleasures f. Gmc]

ribaldry /ríbəldree/ n. ribald talk or behavior.

■ vulgarity, immodesty, impudicity, indelicacy, indecency, coarseness, bawdiness, wantonness, raciness, shamelessness, rakishness, dissoluteness, lubricity, lasciviousness, looseness, scurrilousness, lewdness, salaciousness, licentiousness, grossness, offensiveness, rankness, rudeness, smuttiness, smut, dirt, filth, foulness, obscenity, *colloq. joc.* naughtiness.

riband /ríbənd/ n. a ribbon. [ME f. OF *riban*, prob. f. a Gmc compound of BAND¹]

ribbed /ribd/ adj. having ribs or riblike markings.

ribbing /ríbing/ n. **1** ribs or a riblike structure. **2** colloq. the act or an instance of teasing.

ribbon /ríbən/ n. **1 a** a narrow strip or band of fabric, used esp. for trimming or decoration. **b** material in this form. **2** a ribbon of a special color, etc., worn to indicate some honor or membership of a sports team, etc. **3** a long, narrow strip of anything, e.g., impregnated material forming the inking agent in a typewriter. **4** (in pl.) ragged strips (*torn to ribbons*). □ **ribbon worm** a nemertean. □□ **ribboned** adj. [var. of RIBAND]

ribbonfish /ríbənfish/ n. any of various long slender flat fishes of the family Trachypteridae.

riboflavin /ríbōfláyvin/ n. a vitamin of the B complex, found in liver, milk, and eggs, essential for energy production. Also called *vitamin B₂*. [RIBOSE + L *flavus* yellow]

ribonucleic acid /ríbənōōkleéik, -kláyik, -nyōō-/ n. a nucleic acid yielding ribose on hydrolysis, present in living cells, esp. in ribosomes where it is involved in protein synthesis. ¶ Abbr.: **RNA**. [RIBOSE + NUCLEIC ACID]

ribose /ríbōs/ n. a sugar found in many nucleosides and in several vitamins and enzymes. [G, alt. f. *Arabinose* a related sugar]

ribosome /ríbəsōm/ n. *Biochem.* each of the minute particles consisting of RNA and associated proteins found in the cy-

toplasm of living cells, concerned with the synthesis of proteins. □□ **ribosomal** adj. [RIBONUCLEIC (ACID) + -SOME³]

ribwort /ríbwərt, -wawrt/ n. a kind of plantain with long, narrow ribbed leaves (see PLANTAIN¹).

rice /rīs/ n. & v. n. **1** a swamp grass, *Oryza sativa*, cultivated in marshes, esp. in Asia. **2** the grains of this, used as cereal food. ● v.tr. sieve (cooked potatoes, etc.) into thin strings. □ **rice paper** edible paper made from the pith of an Asian tree and used for painting and in cookery. □□ **ricer** n. [ME *rys* f. OF *ris* f. It. *riso*, ult. f. Gk *oruza*, of oriental orig.]

ricercar /reéchərkaár/ n. (also **ricercare** /-kaáre/) an elaborate contrapuntal instrumental composition in fugal or canonic style, esp. of the 16th–18th c. [It., = seek out]

rich /rich/ adj. & n. ● adj. **1** having much wealth. **2** (often foll. by *in, with*) splendid; costly; elaborate (*rich tapestries*; *rich with lace*). **3** valuable (*rich offerings*). **4** copious; abundant; ample (*a rich harvest*; *a rich supply of ideas*). **5** (often foll. by *in, with*) (of soil or a region, etc.) abounding in natural resources or means of production; fertile (*rich in nutrients*; *rich with vines*). **6** (of food or diet) containing much fat or spice, etc. **7** (of the fuel-air mixture in an internal-combustion engine) containing a high proportion of fuel. **8** (of color or sound or smell) mellow and deep; strong and full. **9 a** (of an incident or assertion, etc.) highly amusing or ludicrous; outrageous. **b** (of humor) earthy. ● n. (**the rich**) (used with a pl. v.) wealthy persons, collectively (*the rich get richer*). □□ **richen** v.intr. & tr. **richness** n. [OE *rīce* f. Gmc f. Celt., rel. to L *rex* king: reinforced in ME f. OF *riche* rich, powerful, of Gmc orig.]

■ **1** adj. wealthy, affluent, prosperous, well-to-do, well-off, well provided for, opulent, moneyed, in clover, on velvet, *colloq.* flush, on easy street, rolling in it *or* money *or* wealth, in the money, well-heeled, *sl.* in the chips, loaded. **2** costly, expensive, dear, valuable, invaluable, precious, priceless; lavish, sumptuous, lush, luxurious, palatial, elaborate, splendid, exquisite, superb, elegant. **3** valuable, precious, invaluable, priceless, costly, high-priced, beyond *or* without price. **4** productive, plentiful, abundant, ample, bountiful, fruitful, fertile, fecund, copious, prolific, profitable, potent. **5** abundant, overflowing, fertile, fecund, productive, copious, abounding, well-supplied, well-stocked, rife, replete, profuse. **6** fatty, fat, fattening, heavy, creamy; spicy. **8** intense, dark, deep, warm, vibrant, strong; mellow, mellifluous, resonant, sonorous, full; aromatic, savory, fragrant, redolent, pungent, strong; ambrosial. **9 a** hilarious, comic(al), sidesplitting; ridiculous, preposterous, ludicrous, laughable, funny, absurd, nonsensical; outrageous, outlandish. **b** earthy; see also COARSE 2.

riches /ríchiz/ n.pl. abundant means; valuable possessions. [ME *richesse* f. OF *richeise* f. *riche* RICH, taken as pl.]

■ wealth, affluence, opulence, plenty, prosperity, abundance, fortune, means, resources, *derog. or joc.* pelf.

richly /ríchlee/ adv. **1** in a rich way. **2** fully; thoroughly (*richly deserves success*).

■ **1** sumptuously, lavishly, luxuriously, splendidly, elaborately, exquisitely, elegantly, superbly. **2** well, thoroughly, amply, fully; condignly; see also WHOLLY 1.

Richter scale /ríktər/ n. a scale of 0 to 10 for representing the strength of an earthquake. [C. F. *Richter*, Amer. seismologist d. 1985]

ricin /rísin, rís-/ n. a toxic substance obtained from castor beans and causing gastroenteritis, jaundice, and heart failure. [mod.L *ricinus communis* castor oil]

rick¹ /rik/ n. & v. **1** (also **hayrick**) a stack of hay, wheat, etc., built into a regular shape and usu. thatched. ● v.tr. form into a rick or ricks. [OE *hrēac*, of unkn. orig.]

rick² /rik/ n. & v. Brit. (also **wrick**) ● n. a slight sprain or strain. ● v.tr. sprain or strain slightly. [ME *wricke* f. MLG *wricken* move about, sprain]

rickets /ríkits/ n. (treated as *sing.* or *pl.*) a disease of children with softening of the bones (esp. the spine) and bowlegs, caused by a deficiency of vitamin D. [17th c.: orig. uncert., but assoc. by medical writers with Gk *rhakhitis* RACHITIS]

rickettsia /rikétseeə/ *n.* a parasitic microorganism of the genus *Rickettsia* causing typhus and other febrile diseases. □□ **rickettsial** *adj.* [mod.L f. H. T. *Ricketts*, Amer. pathologist d. 1910]

rickety /ríkitee/ *adj.* **1 a** insecure or shaky in construction; likely to collapse. **b** feeble. **2 a** suffering from rickets. **b** resembling or of the nature of rickets. □□ **ricketiness** *n.* [RICKETS + -Y¹]

■ **1 a** wobbly, unsteady, shaky, tottering, teetering, precarious, insecure. **b** broken-down, decrepit, ramshackle, flimsy, frail, dilapidated, in (a state of) disrepair; feeble.

rickey /ríkee/ *n.* (*pl.* **-eys**) a drink made with liquor (esp. gin), lime juice, etc. [20th c.: prob. f. the surname *Rickey*]

rickrack /ríkrak/ *n.* (also esp. *Brit.* **ricrac**) a zigzag braided trimming, esp. for garments. [redupl. of RACK¹]

ricksha /ríkshaw/ *n.* (also **rickshaw**) a light two-wheeled hooded vehicle drawn by one or more persons. [abbr. of *jinricksha, jinrikshaw* f. Jap. *jinrikisha* f. *jin* person + *riki* power + *sha* vehicle]

ricochet /ríkəshay, rikəsháy/ *n. & v.* ● *n.* **1** the action of a projectile, esp. a shell or bullet, in rebounding off a surface. **2** a hit made after this. ● *v.intr.* (**ricocheted** /-shayd/; **ricocheting** /-shaying/) (of a projectile) rebound one or more times from a surface. [F, of unkn. orig.]

ricotta /rikótə, -káwtaa/ *n.* a soft Italian cheese resembling cottage cheese. [It., = recooked, f. L *recoquere* (as RE-, *coquere* cook)]

ricrac esp. *Brit.* var. of RICKRACK.

rictus /ríktəs/ *n. Anat. & Zool.* the expanse or gape of a mouth or beak. □□ **rictal** *adj.* [L, = open mouth f. *ringi rict-* to gape]

rid /rid/ *v.tr.* (**ridding**; *past* and *past part.* **rid** or *archaic* **ridded**) (foll. by *of*) make (a person or place) free of something unwanted. □ **be** (or **get**) **rid of** be freed or relieved of (something unwanted); dispose of. [ME, earlier = 'clear (land, etc.).' f. ON *rythja*]

■ (*rid of*) deliver from, relieve of, free from or of, rescue from, save from. □ **be** (or **get**) **rid of** be freed or relieved of, send away, banish, exile, expel, eject, eliminate, reject, dismiss, shake off, *colloq.* unload; dispose of, throw out, discard, junk, dispense with; throw away.

riddance /rídəns/ *n.* the act of getting rid of something. □ **good riddance** welcome relief from an unwanted person or thing.

ridden *past part.* of RIDE.

riddle¹ /ríd'l/ *n. & v.* ● *n.* **1** a question or statement testing ingenuity in divining its answer or meaning. **2** a puzzling fact or thing or person. ● *v.* **1** *intr.* speak in or propound riddles. **2** *tr.* solve or explain (a riddle). □□ **riddler** *n.* [OE *rǣdels, rǣdelse* opinion, riddle, rel. to READ]

■ *n.* conundrum, puzzle, poser, problem, brainteaser, esp. *Brit. colloq.* brain-twister; koan; enigma, mystery. ● *v.* **2** see DECIPHER 2.

riddle² /ríd'l/ *v. & n.* ● *v.tr.* (usu. foll. by *with*) **1** make many holes in, esp. with gunshot. **2** (in *passive*) fill; spread through; permeate (*was riddled with errors*). **3** pass through a riddle. ● *n.* a coarse sieve. [OE *hriddel*, earlier *hrīder*: cf. *hrīdrian* sift]

■ *v.* **1** perforate, pepper, puncture, pierce, honeycomb. **2** fill, infest, pervade, permeate, spread through, infect. ● *n.* sieve, colander, sifter.

riddling /rídling/ *adj.* expressed in riddles; puzzling. □□ **riddlingly** *adv.*

ride /rid/ *v. & n.* ● *v.* (*past* **rode** /rōd/; *past part.* **ridden** /ríd'n/) **1** *tr.* travel or be carried on (a bicycle, etc.) or in (a vehicle). **2** *intr.* (often foll. by *on, in*) travel or be conveyed (on a bicycle or in a vehicle). **3** *tr.* sit on and control or be carried by (a horse, etc.). **4** *intr.* (often foll. by *on*) be carried (on a horse, etc.). **5** *tr.* be carried or supported by (*the ship rides the waves*). **6** *tr.* **a** traverse on horseback, etc., going over or through (*ride 50 miles; rode the prairie*). **b** compete

or take part in on horseback, etc. (*rode a good race*). **7** *intr.* **a** lie at anchor; float buoyantly. **b** (of the moon) seem to float. **8** *intr.* (foll. by *in, on*) rest in or on while moving. **9** *tr.* yield to (a blow) so as to reduce its impact. **10** *tr.* give a ride to; cause to ride (*rode the child on his back*). **11** *tr.* (of a rider) cause (a horse, etc.) to move forward (*rode their horses at the fence*). **12** *tr.* **a** (in *passive*; foll. by *by, with*) be oppressed or dominated by; be infested with (*was ridden with guilt*). **b** (as **ridden** *adj.*) infested or afflicted (usu. in *comb.*: *a rat-ridden cellar*). **13** *intr.* (of a thing normally level or even) project or overlap. **14** *tr. colloq.* mount (a sexual partner) in copulation. **15** *tr.* annoy or seek to annoy. ● *n.* **1** an act or period of travel in a vehicle. **2** a spell of riding on a horse, bicycle, person's back, etc. **3** esp. *Brit.* a path (esp. through woods) for riding on. **4** the quality of sensations when riding (*gives a bumpy ride*). □ **let a thing ride** leave it alone; let it take its natural course. **ride again** reappear, esp. unexpectedly and reinvigorated. **ride down** overtake or trample on horseback. **ride herd on** see HERD. **ride high** be elated or successful. **ride out** come safely through (a storm, etc., or a danger or difficulty). **ride roughshod over** see ROUGHSHOD. **ride shotgun 1** *hist.* carry a shotgun while riding on top of a stage coach as a guard. **2** guard or keep watch (over someone or something), esp. in transit. **3** ride in the front passenger seat of a vehicle. **ride up** (of a garment, carpet, etc.) work or move out of its proper position. **take for a ride 1** *colloq.* hoax or deceive. **2** *sl.* abduct in order to murder. □□ **ridable** *adj.* [OE *rīdan*]

■ *v.* **1** see DRIVE *v.* 3a, b. **2, 8** sit, travel, journey, go, proceed; be borne or carried or conveyed. **7** float, lie, rest, sit. **9** yield to, take, go or roll or stay with. **12 a** (*be ridden by* or *with*) be oppressed or plagued by or with, be dominated or tyrannized or terrorized by, be tormented or nagged or pestered by or with. **b** (**ridden**) afflicted, infested, infected. **14** mount, cover, mate or couple or copulate with. ● *n.* **1** drive, journey, trip, excursion, tour, jaunt, outing, *colloq.* spin. □ **let a thing ride** leave it, leave it alone, let it be. **ride high** fly (high); see also ACHIEVE 3, BOOM² *v.* **ride out** see through, spend, pass; see also ENDURE 1. **take for a ride 1** hoax, delude, swindle, trick, deceive, defraud, humbug, gull, take in, cheat, *colloq.* bamboozle. **2** (kidnap and) murder or kill or execute, *sl.* do in, bump off, (snatch and) rub out, waste.

rider /rídər/ *n.* **1** a person who rides (esp. a horse). **2 a** additional clause amending or supplementing a document. **b** an addition or amendment to a legislative bill. **c** a corollary. **d** *Brit.* a recommendation, etc., added to a judicial verdict. **3** *Math.* a problem arising as a corollary of a theorem, etc. **4** a piece in a machine, etc., that surmounts or bridges or works on or over others. **5** (in *pl.*) an additional set of timbers or iron plates strengthening a ship's frame. □□ **riderless** *adj.* [OE *rīdere* (as RIDE)]

ridge /rij/ *n. & v.* ● *n.* **1** the line of the junction of two surfaces sloping upward toward each other (*the ridge of a roof*). **2** a long, narrow hilltop, mountain range, or watershed. **3** any narrow elevation across a surface. **4** *Meteorol.* an elongated region of high barometric pressure. **5** *Agriculture* a raised strip of arable land, usu. one of a set separated by furrows. **6** *Hort.* a raised hotbed for melons, etc. ● *v.* **1** *tr.* mark with ridges. **2** *tr. Agriculture* break up (land) into ridges. **3** *tr. Hort.* plant (cucumbers, etc.) in ridges. **4** *tr. & intr.* gather into ridges. □□ **ridgy** *adj.* [OE *hrycg* f. Gmc]

■ *n.* **1** line, strip, top edge, angle; crest, peak. **2** mountain range, arête; watershed; see also PROMINENCE 2.

ridgepole /ríjpōl/ *n.* **1** the horizontal pole of a long tent. **2** a beam along the ridge of a roof.

ridgeway /ríjway/ *n. Brit.* a road or track along a ridge.

ridicule /rídikyōōl/ *n. & v.* ● *n.* subjection to derision or

/. . ./ **pronunciation**	● **part of speech**
□ **phrases, idioms, and compounds**	
□□ **derivatives**	■ **synonym section**
cross-references appear in SMALL CAPITALS or *italics*	

mockery. • *v.tr.* make fun of; subject to ridicule; laugh at. [F or f. L *ridiculum* neut. of *ridiculus* laughable f. *ridēre* laugh]

■ *n.* derision, deriding, jeering, taunting, mockery, mocking, gibing, raillery, *Austral.* mullock, *colloq.* ribbing, *sl.* joshing, razzing. • *v.* deride, jeer at, taunt, tease, mock, gibe at, guy, chaff, laugh at, caricature, poke fun at, make fun *or* sport of, lampoon, burlesque, travesty, parody, make a laughingstock of, *colloq.* rib, roast, *Brit. colloq.* send up, *sl.* josh, razz, rag.

ridiculous /rɪdíkyələs/ *adj.* **1** deserving or inviting ridicule. **2** unreasonable; absurd. □□ **ridiculously** *adv.* **ridiculousness** *n.* [L *ridiculosus* (as RIDICULE)]

■ absurd, laughable, comical, funny, humorous, ludicrous, farcical, droll, amusing, hilarious, sidesplitting, risible; unreasonable, ludicrous, preposterous, silly, nonsensical, foolish, stupid, outlandish, bizarre, grotesque, queer, zany, wild, far-out, *colloq.* crazy, insane.

riding[1] /rídɪŋ/ *n.* **1** in senses of RIDE *v.* **2** the practice or skill of riders of horses. **3** = RIDE *n.* 3. □ **riding light** esp. *Brit.* = *anchor light.* **riding school** an establishment teaching skills in horsemanship.

riding[2] /rídɪŋ/ *n.* **1** each of three former administrative divisions (**East Riding, North Riding, West Riding**) of Yorkshire, England. **2** an electoral division of Canada. [OE *thriding* (unrecorded) f. ON *thrithjungr* third part f. *thrithi* THIRD: th- was lost owing to the preceding -*t* or -*th* of *east*, etc.]

Riesling /rēezlɪŋ, rēes-/ *n.* **1** a kind of dry white wine produced in Europe, California, etc. **2** the variety of grape from which this is produced. [G]

rife /rif/ *predic.adj.* **1** of common occurrence; widespread. **2** (foll. by *with*) abounding in; teeming with. □□ **rifeness** *n.* [OE *rȳfe* prob. f. ON *rífr* acceptable f. *reifa* enrich, *reifr* cheerful]

riff /rif/ *n. & v.* • *n.* a short repeated phrase in jazz, etc. • *v.intr.* play riffs. [20th c.: abbr. of RIFFLE *n.*]

riffle /rífəl/ *v. & n.* • *v.* **1 tr.** a turn (pages) in quick succession. **b** shuffle (playing cards), esp. by flexing and combining the two halves of a pack. **2** *intr.* (often foll. by *through*) leaf quickly (through pages). • *n.* **1** the act or an instance of riffling. **2** (in gold panning) a groove or slat set in a trough or sluice to catch gold particles. **3 a** a shallow part of a stream where the water flows brokenly. **b** a patch of waves or ripples on water. [perh. var. of RUFFLE]

riff-raff /rífraf/ *n.* (often prec. by *the*) rabble; disreputable or undesirable persons. [ME *riff and raff* f. OF *rif et raf*]

■ rabble, hoi polloi, canaille; *colloq.* scum, *derog.* ragtag and bobtail; (*the riff-raff*) the dregs (of society *or* humanity), *colloq.* the great unwashed.

rifle[1] /rífəl/ *n. & v.* • *n.* **1** a gun with a long, rifled barrel, esp. one fired from shoulder level. **2** (in *pl.*) riflemen. • *v.tr.* make spiral grooves in (a gun or its barrel or bore) to make a bullet spin. □ **rifle range** a place for rifle practice. [OF *rifler* graze, scratch f. Gmc]

rifle[2] /rífəl/ *v.tr. &* (foll. by *through*) *intr.* **1** search and rob, esp. of all that can be found. **2** carry off as booty. [ME f. OF *rifler* graze, scratch, plunder f. ODu. *riffelen*]

■ **1** rob, ransack, plunder, pillage, loot, *literary* despoil; (*rifle through*) see RANSACK 2.

riflebird /rífəlbərd/ *n.* any dark green Australian bird of paradise of the genus *Ptiloris.*

rifleman /rífəlmən/ *n.* (*pl.* **-men**) **1** a soldier armed with a rifle. **2** a person skilled in shooting a rifle.

rifling /ríflɪŋ/ *n.* the arrangement of grooves on the inside of a gun's barrel.

rift /rift/ *n. & v.* • *n.* **1 a** a crack or split in an object. **b** an opening in a cloud, etc. **2** a cleft or fissure in earth or rock. **3** a disagreement; a breach in friendly relations. • *v.tr.* tear or burst apart. □ **rift valley** a steep-sided valley formed by subsidence of the earth's crust between nearly parallel faults. □□ **riftless** *adj.* **rifty** *adj.* [ME, of Scand. orig.]

■ *n.* **1** split, tear, rent, opening, hole, crack, chink, cleavage. **2** fissure, crevice, cleft, gulf, gap; see also CRACK *n.* 3, CREVASSE. **3** disagreement, schism, conflict,

difference; breach, separation, break, split, disruption, discord, breakup, division, alienation; gulf, gap, distance.

rig[1] /rig/ *v. & n.* • *v.tr.* (**rigged, rigging**) **1 a** provide (a sailing ship) with sails, rigging, etc. **b** prepare ready for sailing. **2** (often foll. by *out, up*) fit with clothes or other equipment. **3** (foll. by *up*) set up hastily or as a makeshift. **4** assemble and adjust the parts of (an aircraft). • *n.* **1** the arrangement of masts, sails, rigging, etc., of a sailing ship. **2** equipment for a special purpose, e.g., a radio transmitter. **3** a truck, esp. a tractor-trailer. **4** esp. *Brit.* a person's or thing's look as determined by clothing, equipment, etc., esp. uniform. □ **in full rig** esp. *Brit. colloq.* smartly or ceremonially dressed. **rig-out** *Brit. colloq.* an outfit of clothes. □□ **rigged** *adj.* (also in *comb.*). [ME, perh. of Scand. orig.: cf. Norw. *rigga* bind or wrap up]

■ *v.* **2** equip, set up, outfit, supply, provision, accoutre, caparison, esp. *Brit.* kit out; (*rig out* or *up*) fit out *or* up. • *n.* **2** equipment, equipage, gear, tackle, apparatus, outfit, accoutrements, paraphernalia, kit, *colloq.* things, stuff. □ **in full rig** (*be in full rig*) be in full fig, *colloq.* be (all) togged up, *joc.* wear *or* be in one's Sunday best, be dressed up to the nines, be dressed to kill, esp. *Brit.* be (all) kitted out. **rig-out** outfit, *colloq.* getup, togs, costume; see also ENSEMBLE 2, DRESS *n.* 2.

rig[2] /rig/ *v. & n.* • *v.tr.* (**rigged, rigging**) manage or conduct fraudulently (*they rigged the election*). • *n.* **1** a trick or dodge. **2** a way of swindling. □ **rig the market** cause an artificial rise or fall in prices. □□ **rigger** *n.* [19th c.: orig. unkn.]

■ *v.* falsify, manipulate, juggle with, tamper with, fake, *colloq.* doctor, fix, cook, *sl.* fiddle (with).

rigadoon /rígədoon/ *n.* **1** a lively dance in duple or quadruple time for two persons. **2** the music for this. [F *rigodon, rigaudon,* perh. f. its inventor *Rigaud*]

rigger /rígər/ *n.* **1** a person who rigs or who arranges rigging. **2** (of a rowboat) = OUTRIGGER 5a. **3** a ship rigged in a specified way. **4** a worker on an oil rig.

rigging /rígɪŋ/ *n.* **1** a ship's spars, ropes, etc., supporting and controlling the sails. **2** the ropes and wires supporting the structure of an airship or biplane.

right /rīt/ *adj., n., v., adv., & int.* • *adj.* **1** (of conduct, etc.) just; morally or socially correct (*it is only right to tell you; I want to do the right thing*). **2** true; correct; not mistaken (*the right time; you were right about the weather*). **3** less wrong or not wrong (*which is the right way to town?*). **4** more or most suitable or preferable (*the right person for the job; along the right lines*). **5** in a sound or normal condition; physically or mentally healthy; satisfactory (*the engine doesn't sound right*). **6 a** on or toward the side of the human body that corresponds to the position of east if one regards oneself as facing north. **b** on or toward that part of an object that is analogous to a person's right side or (with opposite sense) that is nearer to a spectator's right hand. **7** (of a side of fabric, etc.) meant for display or use (*turn it right side up*). **8** esp. *Brit. colloq.* or *archaic* real; properly so called (*made a right mess of it; a right royal welcome*). • *n.* **1** that which is morally or socially correct or just; fair treatment (often in *pl.: the rights and wrongs of the case*). **2** (often foll. by *to,* or *to* + infin.) a justification or fair claim (*has no right to speak like that*). **3** a thing one may legally or morally claim; the state of being entitled to a privilege or immunity or authority to act (*a right of reply; human rights*). **4** the right-hand part or region or direction. **5** *Boxing* **a** the right hand. **b** a blow with this. **6** (often **Right**) *Polit.* **a** a group or section favoring conservatism (orig. the more conservative section of a continental legislature, seated on the president's right). **b** such conservatives collectively. **7** the side of a stage which is to the right of a person facing the audience. **8** (esp. in marching) the right foot. **9** the right wing of an army. • *v.tr.* **1** (often *refl.*) restore to a proper or straight or vertical position. **2 a** correct (mistakes, etc.); set in order. **b** avenge (a wrong or a wronged person); make reparation for or to. **c** vindicate; justify; rehabilitate. • *adv.* **1** straight (*go right on*). **2** *colloq.* immediately; without delay (*I'll be right back; do it right now*). **3 a** (foll. by *to, around, through,* etc.) all the way (*sank right* to the bottom; *ran right around the block*). **b** (foll. by *off*, *out*, etc.) completely (*came right off its hinges*; *am right out of butter*). **4** exactly; quite (*right in the middle*). **5** justly; properly; correctly; truly; satisfactorily (*did not act right*; *not holding it right*; *if I remember right*). **6** on or to the right side. **7** *archaic* very; to the full (*am right glad to hear it*; *dined right royally*). ● *int. colloq.* expressing agreement or assent. □ **as right as rain** perfectly sound and healthy. **at right angles** placed to form a right angle. **by right** (or **rights**) if right were done. **do right by** act dutifully toward (a person). **in one's own right** through one's own position or effort, etc. **in the right** having justice or truth on one's side. **in one's right mind** sane; competent to think and act. **of** (or **as of**) **right** having legal or moral, etc., entitlement. **on the right side of 1** in the favor of (a person, etc.). **2** somewhat less than (a specified age). **put** (or **set**) **right 1** restore to order, health, etc. **2** correct the mistaken impression, etc., of (a person). **put** (or **set**) **to rights** make correct or well ordered. **right about face 1** a right turn continued to face the rear. **2** a reversal of policy. **3** a hasty retreat. **right and left** (or **right, left, and center**) on all sides. **right angle** an angle of 90°, made by lines meeting with equal angles on either side. **right-angled 1** containing or making a right angle. **2** involving right angles; not oblique. **right arm** one's most reliable helper. **right ascension** see ASCENSION. **right away** (or **off**) immediately. **right bank** the bank of a river on the right facing downstream. **right field** *Baseball* the part of the outfield to the right of center field from the perspective of home plate. **right hand 1** = *right-hand man*. **2** the most important position next to a person (*stand at God's right hand*). **right-hand** *adj.* **1** on or toward the right side of a person or thing (*right-hand drive*). **2** done with the right hand (*right-hand blow*). **3** (of a screw) = *right-handed* 4b. **right-handed 1** using the right hand by preference as more serviceable than the left. **2** (of a tool, etc.) made to be used with the right hand. **3** (of a blow) struck with the right hand. **4 a** turning to the right; toward the right. **b** (of a screw) advanced by turning to the right (clockwise). **right-hander 1** a right-handed person. **2** a right-handed blow. **right-hand man** an indispensable or chief assistant. **right-minded** (or **-thinking**) having sound views and principles. **right of search** *Naut.* see SEARCH. **right of way 1** a right established by usage to pass over another's ground. **2** a path subject to such a right. **3** the right of one vehicle to proceed before another. **right on!** *colloq.* an expression of strong approval or encouragement. **Right Reverend** see REVEREND. **right sphere** *Astron.* see SPHERE. **right-to-die** pertaining to the avoidance of using artificial life support in case of severe illness or injury. **right-to-know** pertaining to laws that make government or company records available to individuals. **right-to-life** pertaining to the movement opposing abortion. **right-to-work** pertaining to legislation outlawing obligatory union membership. **right turn** a turn that brings one's front to face as one's right side did before. **right whale** any large-headed whale of the family Balaenidae, rich in whalebone and easily captured. **right wing 1** the right side of a soccer, etc., team on the field. **2** the conservative section of a political party or system. **right-wing** *adj.* conservative or reactionary. **right-winger** a person on the right wing. **right you are!** *colloq.* an exclamation of assent. **she's** (or **she'll be**) **right** *Austral. colloq.* that will be all right. **too right** esp. *Brit. sl.* an expression of agreement. **within one's rights** not exceeding one's authority or entitlement. □□ **rightable** *adj.* **righter** *n.* **rightish** *adj.* **rightless** *adj.* **rightlessness** *n.* **rightness** *n.* [OE *riht* (adj.), *rihtan* (v.), *rihte* (adv.)]

■ *adj.* **1** just, moral, good, proper, sound, correct, legal, lawful, licit, honest, upright, righteous, virtuous, ethical, fair, true, honorable, right-minded, principled, open, aboveboard. **2** true, correct, not mistaken, accurate, exact, precise, perfect, valid, *colloq.* on the button, *Brit. colloq.* bang on. **4** fitting, suitable, proper, perfect, preferred, preferable, promising, advantageous, beneficial; (of time) favorable, propitious, convenient, auspicious, strategic. **5** sound, sane, normal, rational,

lucid, healthy; satisfactory, *colloq.* OK. **6 b** right-hand, dextral, esp. *Heraldry* dexter. **7** upper, front; (*right side*) face, surface, top, outside. **8** utter, complete, perfect, unmitigated, out-and-out, thorough, thoroughgoing, pure, absolute, real, *colloq.* proper. ● *n.* **1** justice, reason, truth, fairness, equity, good, goodness, integrity, virtue, virtuousness, honesty, honorableness, morality, propriety, rectitude, right-mindedness, nobility, uprightness. **2** see CAUSE *n.* 1c. **3** privilege, prerogative, license, power, claim, freedom, liberty; (*right to*) title to. **6** right wing, conservatives; *Brit.* Conservatives, Tories. ● *v.* **1** straighten (out), straighten up, set upright. **2 a** righten, put or set right, make right, put or set to rights, correct, straighten out, sort out, repair, fix; redress, amend, rectify. **b** avenge, get even for, requite, make up for; see also REVENGE *v.* 2. **c** vindicate, rehabilitate; see also JUSTIFY 1, 2, 4. ● *adv.* **2** directly, straightaway, right away or off, forthwith, unhesitatingly, immediately, promptly, at once, instantly, without hesitation, without delay, quickly, swiftly, speedily, *archaic* straight, *colloq.* pronto, straight off; just. **4** exactly, quite, precisely, just; see also SLAP *adv.* **5** correctly, accurately, justly, truly, properly, precisely, well, sensibly, fittingly, suitably, aptly, satisfactorily, advantageously, profitably, favorably, opportunely. ● *int.* certainly, definitely, absolutely, *colloq.* OK, sure, sure thing, *sl.* you got it. □ **as right as rain** fine; see also OK¹ *adj.* **by right(s)** to be just or fair, in fairness. **in the right** right, just, justified; see also RIGHTEOUS. **in one's right mind** see SANE 1. **put** (or **set**) **right** straighten out; see also STRAIGHTEN. **put** (or **set**) **to rights** straighten out; see also STRAIGHTEN. **right away** (or **off**) immediately, forthwith; see also *at once* 1 (ONCE). **right-minded** (or **-thinking**) see CONSCIENTIOUS. **right on!** excellent, *sl.* ace, first-rate; see also DIVINE *adj.* 2b, FABULOUS 2. **right wing 2** right, conservatives, *Brit.* Conservatives, Tories. **right-wing** rightist, right-wing, reactionary, conservative, *Brit.* Conservative, Tory. **right-winger** rightist, conservative, *Brit.* Conservative, Tory; see also REACTIONARY *n.* **right you are!** see ABSOLUTELY 6.

righten /rít'n/ *v.tr.* esp. *Brit.* make right or correct.
■ see RIGHT *v.* 2a.

righteous /ríchəs/ *adj.* **1** (of a person or conduct) morally right; virtuous; law-abiding. **2** *sl.* perfectly wonderful; fine and genuine (*she executed some righteous ski jumps*). □□ **righteously** *adv.* **righteousness** *n.* [OE *rihtwīs* (as RIGHT *n.* + -WISE or RIGHT *adj.* + WISE²), assim. to *bounteous*, etc.]
■ moral, just, virtuous, upstanding, upright, good, honest, ethical, honorable, fair, reputable, trustworthy; right, correct, justifiable, justified, appropriate, condign, fitting, apt.

rightful /rítfŏŏl/ *adj.* **1 a** (of a person) legitimately entitled to (a position, etc.) (*the rightful heir*). **b** (of status or property, etc.) that one is entitled to. **2** (of an action, etc.) equitable; fair. □□ **rightfully** *adv.* **rightfulness** *n.* [OE *rihtful* (as RIGHT *n.*)]
■ **1** legal, lawful, legitimate, licit, correct, proper, true, right; de jure; bona fide, valid, authorized. **2** see EQUITABLE.

rightism /rítizəm/ *n. Polit.* the principles or policy of the right. □□ **rightist** *n.* & *adj.*

rightly /rítlee/ *adv.* justly; properly; correctly; justifiably.

rightmost /rítmōst/ *adj.* furthest to the right.

righto /rító/ *int. Brit. colloq.* expressing agreement or assent.

rightward /rítwərd/ *adv.* & *adj.* ● *adv.* (also **rightwards** /-wərdz/) toward the right. ● *adj.* going toward or facing the right.

rigid /ríjid/ *adj.* **1** not flexible; that cannot be bent (*a rigid*

/.../ **pronunciation**	● **part of speech**
□ **phrases, idioms, and compounds**	
□□ **derivatives**	■ **synonym section**
cross-references appear in SMALL CAPITALS or *italics*	

frame). **2** (of a person, conduct, etc.) **a** inflexible; unbending; harsh (*a rigid disciplinarian; rigid economy*). **b** strict; precise; punctilious. □□ **rigidity** /rəjíditee/ *n.* **rigidly** *adv.* **rigidness** *n.* [F *rigide* or L *rigidus* f. *rigēre* be stiff]

■ **1** stiff, inflexible, unbending, inelastic, unbendable, firm, hard, strong. **2 a** inflexible, unyielding, undeviating, unbending, firm, unwavering, unswerving, strong, uncompromising, iron, unrelenting, intransigent, stringent, severe, strict, rigorous, stern, harsh, austere, hard; obstinate, stubborn, pigheaded, immovable, adamant, adamantine, fixed, obdurate, willful, headstrong, dogged, persevering, determined, resolute, steadfast, resolved, tenacious, relentless, unrelenting, uncompromising, unadaptable, mulish. **b** exact, precise, demanding, strict, hard-and-fast, literal, nice, close, thorough, scrupulous, careful, conscientious, painstaking, meticulous, punctilious, exacting, straitlaced.

rigidify /rijídifī/ *v.tr.* & *intr.* (**-ies, -ied**) make or become rigid.

rigmarole /rígmərōl/ (also **rigamarole** /rígə-/ *n.* **1** a lengthy and complicated procedure. **2 a** a rambling or meaningless account or tale. **b** such talk. [orig. *ragman roll* = a catalog, of unkn. orig.]

■ **1** ceremony, ritual, procedure; bother, *colloq.* hassle. **2b** mumbo-jumbo, gobbledegook, waffle, balderdash, rubbish, nonsense, bunkum, *sl.* bunk.

rigor¹ /rígər/ *n. Med.* **1** a sudden feeling of cold with shivering accompanied by a rise in temperature, preceding a fever, etc. **2** rigidity of the body caused by shock or poisoning, etc. [ME f. L f. *rigēre* be stiff]

rigor² /rígər/ *n.* (*Brit.* **rigour**) **1 a** severity; strictness; harshness. **b** (often in *pl.*) severity of weather or climate; extremity of cold. **c** (in *pl.*) harsh measures or conditions. **2** logical exactitude. **3** strict enforcement of rules, etc. (*the utmost rigor of the law*). **4** austerity of life; puritanical discipline. [ME f. OF *rigor* f. L *rigor* (as RIGOR¹)]

■ **1 a** strictness, harshness; see also *severity* (SEVERE). **b** inclemency, inhospitableness; bitterness, cold. **c** (*rigors*) austerities, asceticism; see also HARDSHIP. **3** strictness, rigidity, precision, preciseness, literalness, exactness, meticulousness, stringency, inflexibility. **4** harshness, severity, hardship, austerity, sternness, strictness, asceticism, discipline, rigidity, stringency.

rigor mortis /rígər máwrtis/ *n.* stiffening of the body after death. [L, = stiffness of death]

rigorous /rígərəs/ *adj.* **1** characterized by or showing rigor; strict, severe. **2** strictly exact or accurate. **3** (of the weather) cold, severe. □□ **rigorously** *adv.* **rigorousness** *n.* [OF *rigorous* or LL *rigorosus* (as RIGOR¹)]

rigour *Brit.* var. of RIGOR².

Rig-Veda /rigváydə, -véedə/ *n.* the oldest and principal of the Hindu Vedas (see VEDA). [Skr. *ṛigvēda* f. *ṛic* praise + *vēda* VEDA]

rile /rīl/ *v.tr.* **1** *colloq.* anger; irritate. **2** make (water) turbulent or muddy. [var. of ROIL]

Riley /rílee/ *n.* □ **the life of Riley** *colloq.* a carefree existence. [20th c.: orig. unkn.]

rilievo var. of RELIEVO.

rill /ril/ *n.* **1** a small stream. **2** a shallow channel cut in the surface of soil or rocks by running water. **3** (also **rille**) *Astron.* a cleft or narrow valley on the moon's surface. [LG *ril*, *rille*]

rim /rim/ *n.* & *v.* ● *n.* **1 a** a raised edge or border. **b** a margin or verge, esp. of something circular. **2** the part of a pair of spectacles surrounding the lenses. **3** the outer edge of a wheel, on which the tire is fitted. **4** a boundary line (*the rim of the horizon*). ● *v.tr.* (**rimmed, rimming**) **1 a** provide with a rim. **b** be a rim for or to. **2** edge; border. □□ **rimless** *adj.* **rimmed** *adj.* (also in *comb.*). [OE *rima* edge: cf. ON *rimi* ridge (the only known cognate)]

■ *n.* **1 a** edge, brim, lip, border, perimeter. **b** margin, verge; see also EDGE *n.* 1.

rime¹ /rīm/ *n.* & *v.* ● *n.* **1** frost, esp. formed from cloud or fog. **2** *poet.* hoarfrost. ● *v.tr.* cover with rime. [OE *hrīm*]

rime² *archaic* var. of RHYME.

rimose /rímōs, rimōs/ *adj.* (also **rimous** /-məs/) esp. *Bot.* full of chinks or fissures. [L *rimosus* f. *rima* chink]

rimy /rímee/ *adj.* (**rimier, rimiest**) frosty; covered with frost.

rind /rīnd/ *n.* & *v.* ● *n.* **1** the tough outer layer or covering of fruit and vegetables, cheese, bacon, etc. **2** the bark of a tree or plant. ● *v.tr.* strip the bark from. □□ **rinded** *adj.* (also in *comb.*). **rindless** *adj.* [OE *rind(e)*]

■ *n.* **1** peel, skin, husk, pod, hull, shell; see also CASE² *n.* 1, 3.

rinderpest /ríndərpest/ *n.* a virulent infectious disease of ruminants (esp. cattle). [G f. *Rinder* cattle + *Pest* PEST]

ring¹ /ring/ *n.* & *v.* ● *n.* **1** a circular band, usu. of precious metal, worn on a finger as an ornament or a token of marriage or betrothal. **2** a circular band of any material. **3** the rim of a cylindrical or circular object, or a line or band around it. **4** a mark or part having the form of a circular band (*had rings around his eyes; smoke rings*). **5** = *annual ring*. **6 a** an enclosure for a circus performance, betting at races, the showing of cattle, etc. **b** (prec. by *the*) bookmakers collectively. **c** a roped enclosure for boxing or wrestling. **7 a** a group of people or things arranged in a circle. **b** such an arrangement. **8** a combination of traders, bookmakers, spies, politicians, etc., acting together usu. illicitly for the control of operations or profit. **9** a circular or spiral course. **10** *Brit.* = *gas ring*. **11** *Astron.* **a** a thin band or disk of particles, etc., around a planet. **b** a halo around the moon. **12** *Archaeol.* a circular prehistoric earthwork usu. of a bank and ditch. **13** *Chem.* a group of atoms each bonded to two others in a closed sequence. **14** *Math.* a set of elements with two binary operations, addition and multiplication, the second being distributive over the first and associative. ● *v.tr.* **1** make or draw a circle around. **2** (often foll. by *around, about, in*) encircle or hem in (game or cattle). **3** put a ring through the nose of (a pig, bull, etc.). **4** cut (fruit, vegetables, etc.) into rings. □ **ring binder** a loose-leaf binder with ring-shaped clasps that can be opened to pass through holes in the paper. **ring circuit** *Brit.* an electrical circuit serving a number of power points with one fuse in the supply to the circuit. **ringed plover** either of two small plovers, *Charadrius hiaticula* and *C. dubius*. **ring finger** the finger next to the little finger, esp. of the left hand, on which the wedding ring is usu. worn. **ring-necked** *Zool.* having a band or bands of color around the neck. **ring ouzel** a thrush, *Turdus torquatus*, with a white crescent across its breast. **ring-pull** *Brit.* = *pull-tab*. **ring road** esp. *Brit.* a bypass encircling a town. **ring-tailed 1** (of monkeys, lemurs, raccoons, etc.) having a tail ringed in alternate colors. **2** with the tail curled at the end. **run** (or **make**) **rings around** *colloq.* outclass or outwit (another person). □□ **ringed** *adj.* (also in *comb.*). **ringless** *adj.* [OE *hring* f. Gmc]

■ *n.* **2** circle, necklace, bracelet, armlet, crown, coronet, tiara, diadem, *hist.* torque; bandeau, fillet, loop, band, circlet, belt, girdle, *literary* cincture; hoop, quoit; halo, aureole, nimbus; wreath, garland; *Anat.* cingulum. **6 a** enclosure, rink, arena, bullring, *Rom. Antiq.* circus. **8** organization, group, circle, team, crew; cartel, bloc, gang, band, pack, cell, coterie, set, clan, clique, junta, camarilla, cabal, faction, *colloq.* mob; fraternity, brotherhood, sisterhood, guild, (secret) society, league, alliance, federation, confederacy, confederation, combination, coalition, union. **9** see COIL¹ *n.*, SPIRAL *n.* ● *v.* **1** encircle, circle, loop, circumscribe, *literary* gird. **2** encircle, surround, hem in, *literary* compass. □ **run** (or **make**) **rings around** outclass, outwit, baffle, nonplus; see also MYSTIFY.

ring² /ring/ *v.* & *n.* ● *v.* (*past* **rang** /rang/; *past part.* **rung** /rung/) **1** *intr.* (often foll. by *out*, etc.) give a clear resonant or vibrating sound of or as of a bell (*a shot rang out; a ringing laugh; the telephone rang*). **2** *tr.* **a** make (esp. a bell) ring. **b** (*absol.*) call for service or attention by ringing a bell (*you rang, madam?*). **3** *tr.* (also *absol.*; often foll. by *up*) esp. *Brit.* call by telephone (*will ring you on Monday; did you ring?*). **4** *intr.* (usu. foll. by *with, to*) (of a place) resound or be permeated with a sound, or an attribute, e.g., fame (*the theater* rang with applause). **5** intr. (of the ears) be filled with a sensation of ringing. **6** tr. **a** sound (a peal, etc.) on bells. **b** (of a bell) sound (the hour, etc.). **7** tr. (foll. by in, out) usher in or out with bell-ringing (ring in the month of May; rang out the Old Year). **8** intr. (of sentiments, etc.) convey a specified impression (words rang hollow). ● n. **1** a ringing sound or tone. **2 a** the act of ringing a bell. **b** the sound caused by this. **3** colloq. a telephone call (give me a ring). **4** a specified feeling conveyed by an utterance (had a melancholy ring). **5** a set of, esp. church, bells. □ **ring back** esp. Brit. make a return telephone call to (a person who has telephoned earlier). **ring a bell** see BELL¹. **ring the changes (on)** see CHANGE. **ring down** (or up) **the curtain 1** cause the curtain to be lowered or raised. **2** (foll. by on) mark the end or the beginning of (an enterprise, etc.). **ring in 1** Brit. report or make contact by telephone. **2** Austral. & NZ sl. substitute fraudulently. **ring in one's ears** (or heart, etc.) linger in the memory. **ring off** Brit. end a telephone call by replacing the receiver. **ring true** (or false) convey an impression of truth or falsehood. **ring up 1** record (an amount, etc.) on a cash register. **2** Brit. call by telephone. □□ **ringed** adj. (also in comb.). **ringer** n. **ringing** adj. **ringingly** adv. [OE hringan]

■ v. **1** peal, chime (out), toll, knell, dong, archaic knoll; sound, resound, echo, reecho, reverberate, resonate; clang, jangle; tinkle, jingle. **3** telephone call, esp. Brit. ring up; colloq. phone, give a person a ring, Brit. colloq. get a person on the blower, sl. buzz, give a person a buzz. **4** resound, echo, reecho; see also ROLL v. 11. **6 b** toll, sound; see also CHIME¹ v. 1. ● n. **1** ringing, clang, clanging, jangle, jangling, tinkle, tinkling, jingle, jingling. **2 b** ringing, peal, pealing, chime, chiming, toll, tolling, knell, sounding, archaic knoll. **3** (telephone or phone) call, sl. buzz. **4** see UNDERCURRENT 2. □ **ring up the curtain 2** see LAUNCH¹ v. 1, 3, 4. **ring in 1** report, make contact, get in touch, call in. **ring off** hang up. **ring up 2** call, telephone, colloq. phone; see also BUZZ v. 2b.

ringbark /ríngbaark/ v.tr. cut a ring in the bark of (a tree) to kill it or retard its growth and thereby improve fruit production; girdle.

ringbolt /ríngbōlt/ n. a bolt with a ring attached for fitting a rope to, etc.

ringdove /ríngduv/ n. **1** = wood pigeon. **2** the collared dove.

ringer /ríngər/ n. sl. **1 a** an athlete or horse entered in a competition by fraudulent means, esp. as a substitute. **b** a person's double, esp. an impostor. **2** Austral. the fastest shearer in a sheep-shearing shed. **3** a person who rings, esp. a bell ringer. □ **be a ringer** (or **dead ringer**) **for** resemble (a person) exactly. [RING² + -ER¹]

ringhals /ríng-hals/ n. a large venomous snake, Hemachatus hemachatus, of Southern Africa, with a white ring or two across the neck. [Afrik. rinkhals f. ring RING¹ + hals neck]

ringleader /ríngleedər/ n. a leading instigator, esp. in an illicit or illegal activity.

ringlet /ríngit/ n. **1** a curly lock of hair, esp. a long one. **2** a butterfly, Aphantopus hyperantus, with spots on its wings. **3** Astron. one of the thin rings within the major rings of Saturn. □□ **ringleted** adj. **ringlety** adj.

ringmaster /ríngmastər/ n. the person directing a circus performance.

ringside /ríngsid/ n. (often attrib.) **1** the area immediately beside a boxing ring or circus ring, etc. **2** an advantageous position from which to observe or monitor something. □□ **ringsider** n.

ringster /ríngstər/ n. a person who participates in a political or commercial ring (see RING¹ n. 8).

ringtail /ríngtayl/ n. **1** a ring-tailed opossum, lemur, or phalanger. **2** a golden eagle up to its third year. **3** a female northern harrier.

ringworm /ríngwərm/ n. any of various fungous infections of the skin causing circular inflamed patches, esp. on a child's scalp.

rink /ringk/ n. **1** an area of natural or artificial ice for skating or playing ice hockey, etc. **2** an enclosed area for roller-

skating. **3** a building containing either of these. **4** a strip of the green used for playing a match of lawn bowling. **5** a team in lawn bowling or curling. [ME (orig. Sc.), = jousting ground: perh. orig. f. OF renc RANK¹]

rinse /rins/ v. & n. ● v.tr. (often foll. by through, out) **1** wash with clean water. **2** apply liquid to. **3** wash lightly. **4** put (clothes, etc.) through clean water to remove soap or detergent. **5** (foll. by out, away) clear (impurities) by rinsing. **6** treat (hair) with a rinse. ● n. **1** the act or an instance of rinsing (give it a rinse). **2** a solution for cleansing the mouth. **3** a dye for the temporary tinting of hair (a blue rinse). □□ **rinser** n. [ME f. OF rincer, raincier, of unkn. orig.]

■ v. **1** wash, clean, usu. formal cleanse; see also FLUSH¹ v. 3a. **5** (rinse out or away) wash out or away or off, clear (out), clean out, swill out or away, flush out. **6** highlight; see also TINT v. ● n. **1** rinsing, wash, washing, cleaning, ablution, flushing, usu. formal cleansing. **3** tint, dye.

riot /ríət/ n. & v. ● n. **1 a** a disturbance of the peace by a crowd; an occurrence of public disorder. **b** (attrib.) involved in suppressing riots (riot police; riot shield). **2** uncontrolled revelry; noisy behavior. **3** (foll. by of) a lavish display or enjoyment (a riot of emotion; a riot of color and sound). **4** colloq. a very amusing thing or person. ● v.intr. **1** make or engage in a riot. **2** live wantonly; revel. □ **read the Riot Act** put a firm stop to insubordination, etc.; give a severe warning (from the name of a former act partly read out to disperse rioters). **run riot 1** throw off all restraint. **2** (of plants) grow or spread uncontrolled. □□ **rioter** n. **riotless** adj. [ME f. OF riote, rioter, rihoter, of unkn. orig.]

■ n. **1** a disturbance, uproar, tumult, fracas, fray, affray, mêlée, donnybrook, brawl, commotion, to-do, colloq. row, ruction, rumpus, imbroglio, ruckus, Brit. colloq. punch-up. **4** funny man or woman, comedian, comedienne; sl. gas; see also LAUGH n. 2. ● v. **1** rebel, revolt, create or cause a disturbance, brawl, fight, rampage, go on the rampage, run riot, storm, go on a rampage. **2** see REVEL v. 1.

riotous /ríətəs/ adj. **1** marked by or involving rioting. **2** characterized by wanton conduct. **3** wildly profuse. □□ **riotously** adv. **riotousness** n. [ME f. OF (as RIOT)]

■ **1** tumultuous, wild, noisy, uncontrollable, unmanageable, chaotic, disorderly, lawless, turbulent, violent, brawling, obstreperous, uncontrolled. **2** rowdy, boisterous, unruly, uproarious, rollicking, roisterous, wild, unrestrained, uninhibited, colloq. no-holds-barred, rambunctious, esp. Brit. colloq. rumbustious. **3** extravagant, wild; see also PROFUSE 2.

RIP abbr. may he or she or they rest in peace. [L requiescat (pl. requiescant) in pace]

rip¹ /rip/ v. & n. ● v.tr. & intr. (**ripped, ripping**) **1** tr. tear or cut (a thing) quickly or forcibly away or apart (ripped out the lining; ripped the book up). **2** tr. **a** make (a hole, etc.) by ripping. **b** make a long tear or cut in. **3** intr. come violently apart; split. **4** intr. rush along. ● n. **1** a long tear or cut. **2** an act of ripping. □ **let rip** colloq. **1** act or proceed without restraint. **2** speak violently. **3** not check the speed of or interfere with (a person or thing). **rip cord** a cord for releasing a parachute from its pack. **rip into** attack (a person) verbally. **rip off** colloq. defraud; steal. **rip-off** n. colloq. **1** a fraud or swindle. **2** financial exploitation. [ME: orig. unkn.]

■ v. **1** tear, cut, archaic or rhet. rend; see also SLIT v. **2** tear, slash, slit, cut open, gash. **3** see SPLIT v. 1a. ● n. **1** tear, rent, split, slash, gash, cut. □ **rip into** see ATTACK v. 3. **rip off** defraud, rob, cheat, swindle, trick, fleece, dupe, deceive, rook, colloq. bamboozle, sl. con, bilk, skin, gyp; steal, snatch, pilfer, filch, take, colloq. lift, swipe, formal or joc. purloin, sl. pinch, Brit. sl. nick. **rip-off 1** swindle, confidence trick, cheat, fraud,

---

/.../ **pronunciation**	● **part of speech**
□ **phrases, idioms, and compounds**	
□□ **derivatives**	■ **synonym section**
cross-references appear in SMALL CAPITALS or italics	

deception; embezzlement, *Law* defalcation, *sl.* con, con job *or* trick. **2** overcharging, exploitation, *colloq.* daylight robbery.

rip[2] /rip/ *n.* a stretch of rough water in the sea or in a river, caused by the meeting of currents. □ **rip current 1** a strong surface current from the shore. **2** a state of conflicting psychological forces. [18th c.: perh. rel. to RIP[1]]

rip[3] /rip/ *n.* **1** a dissolute person. **2** a rascal. **3** a worthless horse. [perh. f. *rep,* abbr. of REPROBATE]

riparian /rīpáireeən/ *adj.* & *n.* esp. *Law* ● *adj.* of or on a riverbank (*riparian rights*). ● *n.* an owner of property on a riverbank. [L *riparius* f. *ripa* bank]

ripe /rīp/ *adj.* **1** (of grain, fruit, cheese, etc.) ready to be reaped or picked or eaten. **2** mature; fully developed (*ripe in judgment; a ripe beauty*). **3** (of a person's age) advanced. **4** (often foll. by *for*) fit or ready (*when the time is ripe; land ripe for development*). **5** (of the complexion, etc.) red and full like ripe fruit. □□ **ripely** *adv.* **ripeness** *n.* [OE *rīpe* f. WG]

■ **1** mature, matured, seasoned, fully grown, (well-) ripened, mellow, ready, (fully) aged. **2** mature, seasoned, sage, wise, sophisticated, informed, qualified, ready, experienced, prepared, veteran; full-grown; ripened, matured, mellow, seasoned, aged. **3** advanced, mature, adult. **4** right, ideal, apt, proper, suitable, suitably advanced, ready, prepared, fit.

ripen /rīpən/ *v.tr.* & *intr.* make or become ripe.

■ mature, develop; age, season, come to maturity; bring to maturity.

ripieno /ripyáynō/ *n.* (*pl.* **-os** or **ripieni** /-nee/) *Mus.* a body of accompanying instruments in baroque concerto music. [It. (as RE-, *pieno* full)]

riposte /ripóst/ *n.* & *v.* ● *n.* **1** a quick sharp reply or retort. **2** a quick return thrust in fencing. ● *v.intr.* deliver a riposte. [F *ri(s)poste, ri(s)poster* f. It. *risposta* RESPONSE]

ripper /rípər/ *n.* **1** a person or thing that rips. **2** a murderer who rips the victims' bodies.

ripping /ríping/ *adj.* *Brit.* *archaic sl.* very enjoyable (*a ripping good yarn*). □□ **rippingly** *adv.*

■ fine, splendid, marvelous, excellent, exciting, thrilling, stirring.

ripple[1] /rípəl/ *n.* & *v.* ● *n.* **1** a ruffling of the water's surface; a small wave or series of waves. **2 a** a gentle lively sound that rises and falls, e.g., of laughter or applause. **b** a brief wave of emotion, excitement, etc. (*the new recruit caused a ripple of interest in the company*). **3** a wavy appearance in hair, material, etc. **4** *Electr.* a slight variation in the strength of a current, etc. **5** ice cream with added syrup giving a colored ripple effect (*raspberry ripple*). **6** a riffle in a stream. ● *v.* **1 a** *intr.* form ripples; flow in ripples. **b** *tr.* cause to do this. **2** *intr.* show or sound like ripples. □□ **ripplet** *n.* **ripply** *adj.* [17th c.: orig. unkn.]

■ *n.* **1** wavelet, wave, ruffle, ruffling, undulation, purling, riffle. **2 b** flurry, flutter, wave, disturbance, stir. ● *v.* **1** ruffle, undulate, purl. **2** see GURGLE *v.*

ripple[2] /rípəl/ *n.* & *v.* ● *n.* a toothed implement used to remove seeds from flax. ● *v.tr.* treat with a ripple. [corresp. to MDu. & MLG repel(en), OHG *riffila, rifilon*]

riprap /ríprap/ *n.* a collection of loose stone as a foundation for a structure. [redupl. of RAP[1]]

rip-roaring /rípráwring/ *adj.* **1** wildly noisy or boisterous. **2** excellent, first-rate. □□ **rip-roaringly** *adv.*

ripsaw /rípsaw/ *n.* a coarse saw for sawing wood along the grain.

ripsnorter /rípsnawrtər/ *n.* *colloq.* an energetic, remarkable, or excellent person or thing. □□ **ripsnorting** *adj.* **ripsnortingly** *adv.*

riptide /ríptīd/ *n.* = rip current (see RIP[2]).

rise /rīz/ *v.* & *n.* ● *v.intr.* (*past* **rose** /rōz/; *past part.* **risen** /rízən/) **1** move from a lower position to a higher one; come or go up. **2** grow, project, expand, or incline upwards; become higher. **3** (of the sun, moon, or stars) appear above the horizon. **4 a** get up from lying or sitting or kneeling (*rose to their feet; rose from the table*). **b** get out of bed, esp. in the morning (*do you rise early?*). **5** recover a standing or vertical position; become erect (*rose to my full height*). **6** *Brit.* (of a

meeting, etc.) cease to sit for business; adjourn (*Parliament rises next week; the court will rise*). **7** reach a higher position or level or amount (*the flood has risen; prices are rising*). **8** develop greater intensity, strength, volume, or pitch (*the color rose in her cheeks; the wind is rising; their voices rose with excitement*). **9** make progress; reach a higher social position (*rose from the ranks*). **10 a** come to the surface of liquid (*bubbles rose from the bottom; waited for the fish to rise*). **b** (of a person) react to provocation (*rise to the bait*). **11** become or be visible above the surroundings, etc., stand prominently (*mountains rose to our right*). **12 a** (of buildings, etc.) undergo construction from the foundations (*office buildings were rising all around*). **b** (of a tree, etc.) grow to a (usu. specified) height. **13** come to life again (*rise from the ashes; risen from the dead*). **14** (of dough) swell by the action of yeast, etc. **15** (often foll. by *up*) cease to be quiet or submissive; rebel (*rise in arms*). **16** originate; have as its source (*the river rises in the mountains*). **17** (of wind) start to blow. **18** (of a person's spirits) become cheerful. **19** (of a barometer) show a higher atmospheric pressure. **20** (of a horse) rear (*rose on its hind legs*). **21** (of a bump, blister, etc.) form. ● *n.* **1** an act or manner or amount of rising. **2** an upward slope or hill or movement (*a rise in the road; the house stood on a rise; the rise and fall of the waves*). **3** an increase in sound or pitch. **4 a** an increase in amount, extent, etc. (*a rise in unemployment*). **b** *Brit.* an increase in salary, wages, etc. **5** an increase in status or power. **6** social, commercial, or political advancement; upward progress. **7** the movement of fish to the surface. **8** origin. **9 a** the vertical height of a step, arch, incline, etc. **b** = RISER 2. □ **get** (or **take**) **a rise out of** *colloq.* provoke an emotional reaction from (a person), esp. by teasing. **on the rise** on the increase. **rise above 1** be superior to (petty feelings, etc.). **2** show dignity or strength in the face of (difficulty, poor conditions, etc.). **rise and shine** (usu. as *imper.*) *colloq.* get out of bed; wake up. **rise in the world** attain a higher social position. **rise to** develop powers equal to (an occasion). [OE *rīsan* f. Gmc]

■ *v.* **1** lift, climb, soar, mount, esp. *archaic & poet.* arise; fly, take flight, take wing, take to the air, take off. **2** slant *or* incline *or* slope (upwards), ascend, climb, go uphill, *colloq.* surface. **3** ascend, come up, appear, come out. **4a, 5, 20** get up, stand (up), esp. *archaic & poet.* arise; get to one's feet; rear (up). **4 b** get up, awaken, waken, wake up, start *or* begin the day, *colloq.* turn out, esp. *archaic & poet.* arise. **6** see DISSOLVE *v.* 3b. **7** swell, flood, increase, grow, wax; increase, go up, climb, escalate, ascend, snowball; see also *go up* (GO[1]). **8** see DEEPEN. **9** advance, improve a person's lot *or* position, progress, get ahead, go somewhere, succeed, make something of oneself, be promoted, prosper, thrive, make good, *colloq.* get somewhere, make it, make the grade, go places. **10 a** ascend, climb, come *or* go *or* move up, mount, lift, surface. **b** (*rise to*) react to, respond to, succumb to, be tempted by. **11** see *stand out*. **12 a** ascend, be elevated, climb, lift, go up, mount, esp. *archaic & poet.* arise. **13** come back, return, resurface, arise, turn up again, reappear, be resurrected; see also RESURRECT 4. **15** rebel, revolt, mutiny, kick over the traces, take up arms. **16** start, begin, originate, arise, be produced, be generated, be created, spring up, be engendered; grow, occur, happen, take place. **18** lift, improve, get better. ● *n.* **1** ascent, ascension, elevation, flight, climb, takeoff. **2** ascent, hill, hillock, knoll, eminence, prominence, elevation, upland, highland, (upward) slope *or* incline, acclivity, upgrade. **3** increase, intensification, amplification, buildup, strengthening, raising, heightening. **4 a** see INCREASE *n.* 1, 2. **b** raise; increase, increment, gain, addition. **5, 6** see PROGRESS *n.* 2. **8** see ORIGIN 1. □ **get** (or **take**) **a rise out of** provoke, stimulate, incite, instigate, foment, goad, encourage, press, push, shake up, waken, awaken, move, motivate, activate, agitate, stir (up), inflame, impassion. **on the rise** see *on the increase* (INCREASE). **rise above** see TRANSCEND 2. **rise in the world** see PROGRESS *v.* **rise** to come *or* measure up to, meet, be equal to, prove adequate to.

riser /rízər/ *n.* **1** a person who rises, esp. from bed (*an early riser*). **2** a vertical section between the treads of a staircase. **3** a vertical pipe for the flow of liquid or gas.

rishi /ríshee/ *n.* (*pl.* **rishis**) a Hindu sage or saint. [Skr. *ṛṣi*]

risible /rízibəl/ *adj.* **1** laughable; ludicrous. **2** inclined to laugh. **3** *Anat.* relating to laughter (*risible nerves*). □□ **risibility** *n.* **risibly** *adv.* [LL *risibilis* f. L *rīdēre ris-* laugh]

rising /rízing/ *adj.* & *n.* ● *adj.* **1** going up; getting higher. **2** increasing (*rising costs*). **3** advancing to maturity or high standing (*the rising generation*; *a rising young lawyer*). **4** approaching a higher level, grade, etc. (*rising seniors*) or a specified age (*the rising fives*). **5** (of ground) sloping upward. ● *n.* a revolt or insurrection; uprising. □ **rising damp** *Brit.* moisture absorbed from the ground into a wall.

risk /risk/ *n.* & *v.* ● *n.* **1** a chance or possibility of danger, loss, injury, or other adverse consequences (*a health risk*; *a risk of fire*). **2** a person or thing causing a risk or regarded in relation to risk (*is a poor risk*). ● *v.tr.* **1** expose to risk. **2** accept the chance of (*could not risk getting wet*). **3** venture on. □ **at risk** exposed to danger. **at one's (own) risk** accepting responsibility or liability. **at the risk of** with the possibility of (an adverse consequence). **put at risk** expose to danger. **risk capital** = *venture capital*. **risk one's neck** put one's own life in danger. **run a** (or **the**) **risk** (often foll. by *of*) expose oneself to danger or loss, etc. **take** (or **run**) **a risk** chance the possibility of danger, etc. [F *risque*, *risquer* f. It. *risco* danger, *riscare* run into danger]

■ *n.* **1** danger, peril; hazard, chance. **2** danger, gamble, hazard, liability; threat, menace. ● *v.* **1** endanger, imperil, hazard, jeopardize. **2** chance. □ **at risk in** danger, in jeopardy; in peril. **put at risk** see ENDANGER.

risky /rískee/ *adj.* (**riskier**, **riskiest**) **1** involving risk. **2** *Brit.* = RISQUÉ. □□ **riskily** *adv.* **riskiness** *n.*

■ **1** dangerous, perilous, hazardous, chancy, touch and go, precarious, *colloq.* iffy, esp. *Brit. colloq.* dodgy, *sl.* dicey.

Risorgimento /risáwrjiméntō/ *n. hist.* a movement for the unification and independence of Italy (achieved in 1870). [It., = resurrection]

risotto /risáwtō, -sótō, -záwtō/ *n.* (*pl.* **-os**) an Italian dish of rice cooked in stock with meat, onions, etc. [It.]

risqué /riskáy/ *adj.* (of a story, etc.) slightly indecent or liable to shock. [F, past part. of *risquer* RISK]

■ risky, indelicate, unrefined, indecorous, indecent, improper, broad, naughty, spicy, salty, racy, bawdy, suggestive, blue, ribald, daring, off-color.

rissole /risōl, rísōl/ *n.* a pastry filled with a mixture of meat or fish and spices, usu. deep-fried. [F f. OF *ruissole*, *roussole* ult. f. LL *russeolus* reddish f. L *russus* red]

rit. /rit/ *abbr. Mus.* ritardando.

ritardando /réetardándō/ *adv.* & *n. Mus.* (*pl.* **-os** or **ritardandi** /-dee/) = RALLENTANDO. [It.]

rite /rīt/ *n.* **1** a religious or solemn observance or act (*burial rites*). **2** an action or procedure required or usual in this. **3** a body of customary observances characteristic of a church or a part of it (*the Latin rite*). □ **rite of passage** (often in *pl.*) a ritual or event marking a stage of a person's advance through life, e.g., marriage. □□ **riteless** *adj.* [ME f. OF *rit*, *rite* or L *ritus* (esp. religious) usage]

■ **1** observance, solemnity. **2** ceremony, ritual, ceremonial, observance, formality, custom, convention, practice, routine, procedure, solemnity.

ritenuto /réetənóotō/ *adv.* & *n. Mus.* ● *adv.* with immediate reduction of speed. ● *n.* (*pl.* **-os** or **ritenuti** /-tee/) a passage played in this way. [It.]

ritornello /réetawrnélō/ *n. Mus.* (*pl.* **-os** or **ritornelli** /-lee/) a short instrumental refrain, interlude, etc., in a vocal work. [It., dimin. of *ritorno* RETURN]

ritual /ríchōōəl/ *n.* & *adj.* ● *n.* **1** a prescribed order of performing rites. **2** a procedure regularly followed. ● *adj.* of or done as a ritual or rites (*ritual murder*). □□ **ritualize** *v.tr.* & *intr.* **ritualization** *n.* **ritually** *adv.* [L *ritualis* (as RITE)]

■ *n.* **1** routine, practice, procedure, protocol. **2** see

RITE 2. ● *adj.* ceremonial, ceremonious, sacramental; procedural, formal, conventional, customary, habitual, routine, prescribed, usual, automatic.

ritualism /ríchōōəlizəm/ *n.* the regular or excessive practice of ritual. □□ **ritualist** *n.* **ritualistic** *adj.* **ritualistically** *adv.*

ritzy /rítsee/ *adj.* (**ritzier**, **ritziest**) *colloq.* **1** high-class; luxurious. **2** ostentatiously smart. □□ **ritzily** *adv.* **ritziness** *n.* [*Ritz*, the name of luxury hotels f. C. *Ritz*, Swiss hotel owner d. 1918]

riv. *abbr.* river.

rival /rívəl/ *n.* & *v.* ● *n.* **1** a person competing with another for the same objective. **2** a person or thing that equals another in quality. **3** (*attrib.*) being a rival or rivals (*a rival firm*). ● *v.tr.* **1** be the rival of or comparable to. **2** seem or claim to be as good as. [L *rivalis*, orig. = using the same stream, f. *rivus* stream]

■ *n.* **1** competitor, opponent, contender, challenger, antagonist, adversary; opposition. **2** match, equal; see also EQUIVALENT *n.* **1**. ● *v.* **1**, **2** compete with, contend with, challenge, compare with, equal, measure up to, match, be a match for, vie with, oppose.

rivalry /rívəlree/ *n.* (*pl.* **-ies**) the state or an instance of being rivals; competition.

■ competition, conflict, struggle, controversy; competitiveness, contention, vying, feuding, strife, dissension, discord.

rive /rīv/ *v.* (*past* **rived**; *past part.* **riven** /rívən/) *archaic* or *poet.* **1** *tr.* split or tear apart violently. **2** *a tr.* split (wood or stone). **b** *intr.* be split. [ME f. ON *rífa*]

river /rívər/ *n.* **1** a copious natural stream of water flowing in a channel to the sea or a lake, etc. **2** a copious flow (*a river of lava*; *rivers of blood*). **3** (*attrib.*) (in the names of animals, plants, etc.) living in or associated with the river. □ **river blindness** = ONCHOCERCIASIS. **sell down the river** *colloq.* betray or let down. □□ **rivered** *adj.* (also in *comb.*). **riverless** *adj.* [ME f. AF *river*, *rivere*, OF *riviere* river or riverbank ult. f. L *riparius* f. *ripa* bank]

■ **1** watercourse, tributary, stream, waterway, creek, *dial.* kill. **2** stream, flood, torrent, quantity, cataract, cascade. □ **sell down the river** see BETRAY 2.

riverine /rívərīn, -reen/ *adj.* of or on a river or riverbank; riparian.

riverside /rívərsīd/ *n.* the ground along a riverbank.

rivet /rívit/ *n.* & *v.* ● *n.* a nail or bolt for holding together metal plates, etc., its headless end being beaten out or pressed down when in place. ● *v.tr.* **1 a** join or fasten with rivets. **b** beat out or press down the end of (a nail or bolt). **c** fix; make immovable. **2 a** (foll. by *on*, *upon*) direct intently (one's eyes or attention, etc.). **b** (esp. as **riveting** *adj.*) engross (a person or the attention). □□ **riveter** *n.* [ME f. OF f. *river* clench, of unkn. orig.]

■ *v.* **1 c** fix, make secure; see also ANCHOR *v.* 1, 2. **2 a** see FIX *v.* 5a, b. **b** (**riveting**) spellbinding, engrossing, hypnotic, hypnotizing, transfixing, fascinating, enthralling, gripping, captivating, absorbing.

riviera /ríveeáirə/ *n.* (often **Riviera**) a coastal region with a subtropical climate, vegetation, etc., esp. that of SE France and NW Italy. [It., = seashore]

rivière /reevyáir/ *n.* a gem necklace, esp. of more than one string. [F, = RIVER]

rivulet /rívyəəlit/ *n.* a small stream. [obs. *riveret* f. F, dimin. of *rivière* RIVER, perh. after It. *rivoletto* dimin. of *rivolo* dimin. of *rivo* f. L *rivus* stream]

■ see STREAM *n.* 1.

riyal var. of RIAL.

rm. *abbr.* room.

r.m.s. *abbr. Math.* root-mean-square.

RN *abbr.* **1** registered nurse. **2** (in the UK) Royal Navy.

/.../ **pronunciation**	● **part of speech**
□ **phrases, idioms, and compounds**	
□□ **derivatives**	■ **synonym section**
cross-references appear in SMALL CAPITALS or *italics*	

Rn *symb. Chem.* the element radon.

RNA *abbr.* ribonucleic acid.

roach[1] /rōch/ *n.* (*pl.* same) a small freshwater fish, esp. *Rutilus rutilus*, allied to the carp. [ME f. OF *roc(h)e*, of unkn. orig.]

roach[2] /rōch/ *n.* **1** *colloq.* a cockroach. **2** *sl.* the butt of a marijuana cigarette. [abbr.]

roach[3] /rōch/ *n. Naut.* an upward curve in the foot of a sail. [18th c.: orig. unkn.]

road[1] /rōd/ *n.* **1 a** a path or way with a specially prepared surface, used by vehicles, pedestrians, etc. **b** the part of this used by vehicles (*don't step in the road*). **2 a** one's way or route (*our road took us through unexplored territory*). **b** a method or means of accomplishing something. **3** an underground passage in a mine. **4** a railroad. **5** (usu. in *pl.*) a partly sheltered piece of water near the shore in which ships can ride at anchor. □ **by road** using transport along roads. **get out of the** (or *my*, etc.) **road** esp. *Brit. colloq.* cease to obstruct a person. **in the** (or *my*, etc.) **road** esp. *Brit. colloq.* obstructing a person or thing. **one for the road** *colloq.* a final (esp. alcoholic) drink before departure. **on the road** traveling, esp. as a firm's representative, itinerant performer, or vagrant. **road hog** *colloq.* a reckless or inconsiderate motorist. **road manager** the organizer and supervisor of a musicians' tour. **road map** a map showing the roads of a country or area. **road metal** *Brit.* broken stone used in road making or for railroad ballast. **road show 1 a** a performance given by a touring company, esp. a group of pop musicians. **b** a company giving such performances. **2** a radio or television program done on location. **road sign** a sign giving information or instructions to road users. **road test** a test of the performance of a vehicle on the road. **the road to** the way of getting to or achieving (*the road to Miami; the road to ruin*). **rule of the road** the custom or law regulating which side of the road is to be taken by vehicles (also riders or ships) meeting or passing each other. **take the road** set out. □□ **roadless** *adj.* [OE *rād* f. *rīdan* RIDE]

■ **1** thoroughfare, way, byway, roadway, avenue, boulevard, street, lane, alley, alleyway; highway, high road, pike, parkway, autobahn, autostrada, autoroute, superhighway, turnpike, expressway, freeway, thruway, *Brit.* motorway, carriageway. **2 a** way, route; see also PATH 2. **b** way, means, approach, route, procedure, technique, method, course. **4** railway, railroad. □ **take the road** see *set forth* 1 (SET[1]).

road[2] /rōd/ *v.tr.* (also *absol.*) (of a dog) follow and pursue (a game bird) by the scent of its trail. [19th c.: orig. unkn.]

roadbed /rōdbed/ *n.* **1** the foundation structure of a railroad. **2** the material laid down to form a road. **3** the part of a road on which vehicles travel.

roadblock /rōdblok/ *n.* a barrier or barricade on a road, esp. one set up by the authorities to stop and examine traffic.

roadhouse /rōdhows/ *n.* an inn or club on a major road.

roadie /rōdee/ *n. colloq.* an assistant employed by a touring band of musicians to erect and maintain equipment.

roadrunner /rōdrunər/ *n.* a bird of Mexican and US deserts, *Geococcyx californianus*, related to the cuckoo, known as a poor flier but a fast runner.

roadside /rōdsīd/ *n.* the strip of land beside a road.

roadstead /rōdsted/ *n.* = ROAD[1] 5. [ROAD[1] + *stead* in obs. sense 'place']

roadster /rōdstər/ *n.* **1** an open car without rear seats. **2** a horse or bicycle for use on the road.

roadway /rōdway/ *n.* **1** a road. **2** = ROAD[1] 1b. **3** the part of a bridge or railroad used for traffic.

■ **1** see ROAD[1] 1.

roadwork /rōdwərk/ *n.* **1** the construction or repair of roads, or other work involving digging up a road surface. **2** athletic exercise or training involving running on roads.

roadworthy /rōdwərthee/ *adj.* **1** fit to be used on the road. **2** (of a person) fit to travel. □□ **roadworthiness** *n.*

roam /rōm/ *v. & n.* ● *v.* **1** *intr.* ramble; wander. **2** *tr.* travel unsystematically over, through, or about. ● *n.* an act of roaming; a ramble. □□ **roamer** *n.* [ME: orig. unkn.]

■ *v.* wander, rove (around), range, drift, meander, ramble; walk *or* stroll *or* amble *or* saunter *or* perambulate (around *or* about), travel *or* voyage (around *or* about), archaic *or joc.* peregrinate, *formal* circumambulate, *sl.* mosey (around *or* about).

roan[1] /rōn/ *adj. & n.* ● *adj.* (of an animal, esp. a horse or cow) having a coat of which the prevailing color is thickly interspersed with hairs of another color, esp. bay or sorrel or chestnut mixed with white or gray. ● *n.* a roan animal. □ **blue roan** *adj.* black mixed with white. ● *n.* a blue roan animal. **red roan** *adj.* bay mixed with white or gray. ● *n.* a red roan animal. **strawberry roan** *adj.* chestnut mixed with white or gray. ● *n.* a strawberry roan animal. [OF, of unkn. orig.]

roan[2] /rōn/ *n.* soft sheepskin leather used in bookbinding as a substitute for morocco. [ME, perh. f. *Roan*, old name of *Rouen* in N. France]

roar /rawr/ *n. & v.* ● *n.* **1** a loud, deep, hoarse sound, as made by a lion, a person in pain or rage or excitement, thunder, a loud engine, etc. **2** a loud laugh. ● *v.* **1** *intr.* **a** utter or make a roar. **b** utter loud laughter. **c** (of a horse) make a loud noise in breathing as a symptom of disease. **2** *intr.* travel in a vehicle at high speed, esp. with the engine roaring. **3** *tr.* (often foll. by *out*) say, sing, or utter (words, an oath, etc.) in a loud tone. □□ **roarer** *n.* [OE *rārian* f. imit. orig.]

■ *n.* **1** roaring, bellow, thunder, rumble, boom; howl, squall, cry, yell, yowl, clamor, outcry. **2** guffaw, howl, hoot. ● *v.* **1 b** laugh, guffaw, howl, howl with laughter, hoot. **3** bellow, thunder, bawl (out), cry (out), yell, bark, bay, snarl, growl.

roaring /ráwring/ *adj.* in senses of ROAR *v.* □ **roaring drunk** very drunk and noisy. **roaring forties** stormy ocean tracts between lat. 40° and 50° S. **roaring trade** (or **business**) esp. *Brit.* very brisk trade or business. **roaring twenties** the decade of the 1920s (with ref. to its postwar buoyancy). □□ **roaringly** *adv.*

■ see THUNDEROUS.

roast /rōst/ *v., adj., & n.* ● *v.* **1** *tr.* **a** cook (food, esp. meat) in an oven or by exposure to open heat. **b** heat (coffee beans) before grinding. **2** *tr.* heat (the ore of metal) in a furnace. **3** *tr.* **a** expose (a torture victim) to fire or great heat. **b** *tr. & refl.* expose (oneself or part of oneself) to warmth. **4** *tr.* criticize severely; denounce. **5** *intr.* undergo roasting. ● *attrib.adj.* (of meat or a potato, chestnut, etc.) roasted. ● *n.* **1 a** roast meat. **b** a dish of this. **c** a piece of meat for roasting. **2** the process of roasting. **3** a party where roasted food is eaten. **4** a banquet to honor a person at which the honoree is subjected to good-natured ridicule. [ME f. OF *rost, rostir*, f. Gmc]

■ *v.* **3 b** warm, toast, cook. **4** see CRITICIZE 1, TAUNT *v.*

roaster /rōstər/ *n.* **1** a person or thing that roasts. **2 a** an oven or dish for roasting food in. **b** an ore-roasting furnace. **c** a coffee-roasting apparatus. **3** something fit for roasting, e.g., a fowl, a potato, etc.

roasting /rōsting/ *adj. & n.* ● *adj.* very hot. ● *n.* **1** in senses of ROAST *v.* **2** a severe criticism or denunciation.

■ *adj.* see HOT *adj.* 1. ● *n.* **2** see REPRIMAND *n.*

rob /rob/ *v.tr.* (**robbed, robbing**) (often foll. by *of*) **1** take unlawfully from, esp. by force or threat of force (*robbed the safe; robbed her of her jewels*). **2** deprive of what is due or normal (*was robbed of my sleep*). **3** (*absol.*) commit robbery. **4** *colloq.* cheat; swindle. □ **rob Peter to pay Paul** take away from one to give to another; discharge one debt by incurring another. [ME f. OF *rob(b)er* f. Gmc: cf. REAVE]

■ **1** loot, rifle, ransack, plunder, raid, pillage, sack; burgle, burglarize; hold up, mug, *colloq.* stick up, *sl.* roll; (*rob of*) strip of, *colloq.* do out of. **2** deny, refuse; (*rob of*) deprive of, strip of. **4** cheat, swindle, defraud, fleece, mulct, rook, *colloq.* rip off, diddle, *sl.* bilk, gyp.

robber /róbər/ *n.* a person who commits robbery. □ **robber baron 1** a plundering feudal lord. **2** an unscrupulous plutocrat. [ME f. AF & OF (as ROB)]

■ thief, pickpocket, sneak thief, shoplifter; housebreaker, burglar, cat burglar; bandit, brigand, highwayman; pirate, freebooter, buccaneer, corsair; mugger, holdup man, *sl.* stickup man; safe breaker, safecracker, *sl.* cracksman.

robbery /róbəree/ *n.* (*pl.* **-ies**) **1 a** the act or process of robbing, esp. with force or threat of force. **b** an instance of this. **2** excessive financial demand or cost (*set us back $20—it was sheer robbery*). [ME f. OF *roberie* (as ROB)]

■ **1 a** robbing, thieving, theft, stealing, thievery, pilfering, *sl.* pinching, *Brit. sl.* nicking; plunder, sack, looting, plundering, sacking, ransacking, depredation, pillage, pillaging; breaking and entering; burglary, larceny; mugging; *colloq.* ripping off. **b** theft, burglary, looting, sacking, ransacking, depredation; *sl.* heist; holdup, mugging, *colloq.* stickup. **2** overcharging, exploitation, *colloq.* ripoff.

robe /rōb/ *n.* & *v.* ● *n.* **1** a long, loose outer garment. **2** a loose, usu. belted garment worn over nightwear, while resting, or after bathing. **3** a baby's outer garment, esp. at a christening. **4** (often in *pl.*) a long outer garment worn as an indication of the wearer's rank, office, profession, etc.; a gown or vestment. **5** a blanket or wrap of fur. ● *v.* **1** *tr.* clothe (a person) in a robe; dress. **2** *intr.* put on one's robes or vestments. [ME f. OF f. Gmc (as ROB, orig. sense 'booty')]

■ *n.* **1** cloak, wrapper, mantle, cape, wrap, poncho. **2** bathrobe, dressing gown, lounging robe, housecoat, kimono, peignoir. **4** (*robes*) costume, uniform, garb, vestments, livery, garments, accoutrements, regalia, finery, trappings, equipage, *archaic* habit, raiment, *colloq.* gear, *formal* attire, apparel, *poet.* vesture. ● *v.* **1** see DRESS *v.* 1a. **2** enrobe, dress, get dressed up, dress oneself up; dress up.

robin /róbin/ *n.* **1** a red-breasted thrush, *Turdus migratorius.* **2** (also **robin redbreast**) a small brown European bird, *Erithacus rubecula,* the adult of which has a red throat and breast. **3** a bird similar in appearance, etc., to either of these. □ **Robin Hood** (with ref. to the legend of the medieval forest outlaw) a person who acts illegally or unfavorably toward the rich for the benefit of the poor. [ME f. OF, familiar var. of the name *Robert*]

robinia /rəbíneeə/ *n.* any N. American tree or shrub of the genus *Robinia,* e.g., a locust tree or false acacia. [mod.L. f. J. *Robin,* 17th-c. French gardener]

roborant /róbərənt/ *adj.* & *n. Med.* ● *adj.* strengthening. ● *n.* a strengthening drug. [L *roborare* f. *robur -oris* strength]

■ *adj.* see TONIC *adj.* ● *n.* see TONIC *n.*

robot /rōbot/ *n.* **1** a machine with a human appearance or functioning like a human. **2** a machine capable of carrying out a complex series of actions automatically. **3** a person who works mechanically and efficiently but insensitively. **4** *S.Afr.* an automatic traffic signal. □ **robot bomb** a pilotless aircraft with an explosive warhead. □□ **robotic** /-bótik/ *adj.* **robotize** *v.tr.* [Czech (in K. Čapek's play *R.U.R.* (*Rossum's Universal Robots*) 1920), f. *robota* forced labor]

■ **1, 2** mechanical man *or* monster, android, automaton. **3** automaton; drudge.

robotics /rōbótiks/ *n.pl.* the study of robots; the art or science of their design and operation.

robust /rōbúst/ *adj.* (**robuster, robustest**) **1** (of a person, animal, or thing) strong and sturdy, esp. in physique or construction. **2** (of exercise, discipline, etc.) vigorous; requiring strength. **3** (of intellect or mental attitude) straightforward, not given to nor confused by subtleties. **4** (of a statement, reply, etc.) bold; firm; unyielding. **5** (of wine, etc.) full-bodied. □□ **robustly** *adv.* **robustness** *n.* [F *robuste* or L *robustus* firm and hard f. *robus, robur* oak, strength]

■ **1** sound, sturdy, strong; healthy, fit, hale (and hearty), hardy, hearty, stout, tough, strapping, brawny, sinewy, muscular, powerful, athletic, vigorous; in fine fettle, husky. **2** see SEVERE 1, 5. **3** see SOLID *adj.* 6a, SIMPLE *adj.* 6. **4** see FIRM[1] *adj.* 2a, b **5** strong, flavorful, full-bodied, *literary* sapid.

roc /rok/ *n.* a gigantic bird of Eastern legend. [Sp. *rocho* ult. f. Arab *ruk*]

rocaille /rōkí/ *n.* **1** an 18th-c. style of ornamentation based

on rock and shell motifs. **2** a rococo style. [F f. *roc* (as ROCK[1])]

rocambole /rókəmbōl/ *n.* an alliaceous plant, *Allium scorodoprasum,* with a garliclike bulb used for seasoning. [F f. G *Rockenbolle*]

roche moutonnée /rawsh mŏŏtawnáy/ *n. Geol.* a small, bare outcrop of rock shaped by glacial erosion. [F, = fleecy rock]

rochet /róchit/ *n.* a vestment resembling a surplice, used chiefly by bishops and abbots. [ME f. OF, dimin. f. Gmc]

rock[1] /rok/ *n.* **1 a** the hard material of the earth's crust, exposed on the surface or underlying the soil. **b** a similar material on other planets. **2** *Geol.* any natural material, hard or soft (e.g., clay), consisting of one or more minerals. **3 a** a mass of rock projecting and forming a hill, cliff, reef, etc. **b** (**the Rock**) Gibraltar. **4** a large detached stone. **5** a stone of any size. **6** a firm and dependable support or protection. **7** esp. *Brit.* a source of danger or destruction. **8** *Brit.* a hard usu. cylindrical stick of candy made from sugar with flavoring, esp. of peppermint. **9** (in *pl.*) *sl.* money. **10** *sl.* a precious stone, esp. a diamond. **11** *sl.* a solid form of cocaine. **12** (in *pl.*) *coarse sl.* the testicles. □ **between a rock and a hard place** forced to choose between two unpleasant or difficult alternatives. **get one's rocks off** *coarse sl.* **1** achieve sexual satisfaction. **2** obtain enjoyment. **on the rocks** *colloq.* **1** short of money. **2** broken down. **3** (of a drink) served over ice cubes. **rock bed** a base of rock or a rocky bottom. **rock-bottom** (of prices, etc.) the very lowest. **rock bottom** the very lowest level. **rockbound** (of a coast) rocky and inaccessible. **rock candy** sugar crystallized in large masses onto a string or stick, eaten as candy. **rock crystal** transparent colorless quartz usu. in hexagonal prisms. **rock dove** a wild dove, *Columba livia,* frequenting rocks, supposed ancestor of the domestic pigeon. **rock face** a vertical surface of natural rock. **rock garden** a garden in which interesting stones and rocks are a chief feature. **rock pigeon** = *rock dove.* **rock plant** any plant growing on or among rocks. **rock rabbit** any of several species of hyrax; pika. **rock salt** common salt as a solid mineral. **rock wool** inorganic material made into matted fiber, esp. for insulation or soundproofing. □□ **rockless** *adj.* **rocklet** *n.* **rocklike** *adj.* [ME f. OF *ro(c)que, roche,* med.L *rocca,* of unkn. orig.]

■ **3 a** tor, crag, outcrop, outcropping; see also CLIFF. **4** stone, pebble, *Austral. sl.* goolie; boulder. **6** pillar *or* tower of strength, mainstay, backbone, *sl.* brick. □ **on the rocks 1** see DESTITUTE 1. **2** in ruins, ruined, broken-down, beyond repair, in tatters *or* shreds, in pieces, *colloq.* in (a) shambles; destroyed, shattered, in disarray. **3** with ice, on ice.

rock[2] /rok/ *v.* & *n.* ● *v.* **1** *tr.* move gently to and fro in or as if in a cradle; set or maintain such motion (*rock him to sleep; the ship was rocked by the waves*). **2** *intr.* be or continue in such motion (*sat rocking in his chair; the ship was rocking on the waves*). **3 a** *intr.* sway from side to side; shake; oscillate; reel (*the house rocks*). **b** *tr.* cause to do this (*an earthquake rocked the house*). **4** *tr.* distress; perturb. **5** *intr.* dance to or play rock music. ● *n.* **1** a rocking movement (*gave the chair a rock*). **2** a spell of rocking (*had a rock in his chair*). **3 a** = *rock and roll.* **b** any of a variety of types of modern popular music with a rocking or swinging beat, derived from rock and roll. □ **rock and** (or **rock 'n'**) **roll** a type of popular dance music originating in the 1950s, characterized by a heavy beat and simple melodies, often with a blues element. **rock and** (or **rock 'n'**) **roller** a devotee of rock and roll. **rock the boat** *colloq.* disturb the equilibrium of a situation. **rocking chair** a chair mounted on rockers or springs for gently rocking in. **rocking horse** a model of a horse on rockers or springs for a child to rock on. **rocking stone** a poised boulder easily rocked. [OE *roccian,* prob. f. Gmc]

■ *v.* **1** sway, swing, move to and fro, move back and

/.../ **pronunciation**	● **part of speech**
□ **phrases, idioms, and compounds**	
□□ **derivatives**	■ **synonym section**
cross-references appear in SMALL CAPITALS or *italics*	

forth, move backward and forward; lull. **2, 3a** toss; roll, reel, lurch, swing, sway, shake, oscillate; wobble. **3 b** sway, roll, swing, move, shake, shudder, rattle. **4** astound, astonish, shock, distress, surprise, jar, stagger, amaze, stun, dumbfound, daze, stupefy, overwhelm, disconcert, unnerve, disturb, perturb, *colloq.* throw, rattle, shake, shake up.

rockabilly /rókəbilee/ *n.* a type of popular music combining elements of rock and roll and hillbilly music. [blend of *rock and roll* and *hillbilly*]

rocker /rókər/ *n.* **1** a person or thing that rocks. **2** a curved bar or similar support, on which something can rock. **3** a rocking chair. **4 a** a young devotee of rock music, characteristically associated with leather clothing and motorcycles. **b** a performer of rock music. **5** an ice skate with a highly curved blade. **6** a switch constructed on a pivot mechanism operating between the "on" and "off" positions. **7** any rocking device forming part of a mechanism. □ **off one's rocker** *sl.* crazy.

■ □ **off one's rocker** see CRAZY 1.

rockery /rókəree/ *n.* (*pl.* **-ies**) a rock garden.

rocket[1] /rókit/ *n. & v.* ● *n.* **1** a cylindrical projectile that can be propelled to a great height or distance by combustion of its contents, used esp. as a firework or signal. **2** an engine using a similar principle but not dependent on air intake for its operation. **3** a rocket-propelled missile, spacecraft, etc. **4** *Brit. sl.* a severe reprimand. ● *v.* **1** *tr.* bombard with rockets. **2** *intr.* **a** move rapidly upward or away. **b** increase rapidly (*prices rocketed*). [F *roquette* f. It. *rochetto* dimin. of *rocca* ROCK[2], with ref. to its cylindrical shape]

■ *n.* **4** see *tongue-lashing*. ● *v.* **2 a** see SPEED *v.* **b** skyrocket, shoot up, climb, soar, spiral (upward), *colloq.* go through the roof.

rocket[2] /rókit/ *n.* **1** (also **sweet rocket**) any of various fast-growing plants, esp. of the genus *Hesperis* or *Sisymbrium*. **2** a cruciferous annual plant, *Eruca sativa*, grown for salad. □ **wall rocket** a yellow-flowered weed, *Diplotaxis muralis*, emitting a foul smell when crushed. **yellow rocket** winter cress. [F *roquette* f. It. *rochetta, ruchetta* dimin. of *ruca* f. L *eruca* downy-stemmed plant]

rocketeer /rókiteér/ *n.* **1** a discharger of rockets. **2** a rocket expert or enthusiast.

rocketry /rókitree/ *n.* the science or practice of rocket propulsion.

rockfall /rókfawl/ *n.* **1** a descent of loose rocks. **2** a mass of fallen rock.

rockfish /rókfish/ *n.* **1** any of various fishes that live among rocks. **2** = *striped bass.*

rockhopper /rók-hopər/ *n.* a small penguin, *Eudyptes crestatus,* of the Antarctic and New Zealand, with a crest of feathers on the forehead.

rockling /rókling/ *n.* any of various small marine fish of the cod family, esp. of the genus *Ciliata* and *Rhinomenus,* found in pools among rocks.

rockrose /rókrōz/ *n.* any plant of the genus *Cistus, Helianthum,* etc., with roselike flowers.

rockshaft /rókshaft/ *n.* a shaft that oscillates about an axis without making complete revolutions.

rocky[1] /rókee/ *adj. & n.* ● *adj.* (**rockier, rockiest**) **1** of or like rock. **2** full of or abounding in rock or rocks (*a rocky shore*). **3 a** firm as a rock; determined; steadfast. **b** unfeeling; cold; hard. ● *n.* (**the Rockies**) the Rocky Mountains in western N. America. □□ **rockiness** *n.*

■ *adj.* **1, 2** stony, pebbly, shingly, shingled; boulder-strewn, craggy; hard, bumpy, uncomfortable. **3 a** stony, adamant, adamantine, firm, unyielding, rocklike, tough, unbending, flinty, firm, solid, steadfast, steady, unfaltering, staunch, unflinching, determined, resolute, unwavering, unchanging, unvarying, reliable, dependable, sure, certain. **b** stony, flinty, unfeeling, unsympathetic, unemotional, emotionless, impassive, cold, cool, apathetic, indifferent, uncaring, detached, callous, thick-skinned, tough, hard.

rocky[2] /rókee/ *adj.* (**rockier, rockiest**) *colloq.* unsteady; tottering. □□ **rockily** *adv.* **rockiness** *n.* [ROCK[2]]

■ unstable, unsteady, tottering, teetering, shaky, rickety, unsure, uncertain, weak, flimsy, wobbly, vacillating, dubious, doubtful, questionable, *colloq.* iffy.

rococo /rəkókō/ *adj. & n.* ● *adj.* **1** of a late baroque style of decoration prevalent in 18th-c. continental Europe, with asymmetrical patterns involving scrollwork, shell motifs, etc. **2** (of literature, music, architecture, and the decorative arts) highly ornamented; florid. ● *n.* the rococo style. [F, joc. alt. f. ROCAILLE]

■ *adj.* **2** see ORNATE.

rod /rod/ *n.* **1** a slender straight bar, esp. of wood or metal. **2** this as a symbol of office. **3 a** a stick or bundle of twigs used in caning or flogging. **b** (prec. by *the*) the use of this; punishment; chastisement. **4 a** = *fishing rod.* **b** an angler using a rod. **5 a** a slender straight round stick growing as a shoot on a tree. **b** this when cut. **6** (as a measure) a perch or square perch (see PERCH[1]). **7** *sl.* = *hot rod.* **8** *sl.* a pistol or revolver. **9** *Anat.* any of numerous rod-shaped structures in the eye, detecting dim light. □□ **rodless** *adj.* **rodlet** *n.* **rodlike** *adj.* [OE *rodd,* prob. rel. to ON *rudda* club]

■ **1** bar, pole, baton, wand, staff, stick. **2** see STAFF[1] *n.* 1a, b. **3 a** cane, birch, birch rod, switch. **b** (*the rod*) (corporal) punishment, chastisement, castigation, discipline, chastening, correction; birching, caning.

rode[1] *past* of RIDE.

rode[2] /rōd/ *v.intr.* **1** (of wildfowl) fly landward in the evening. **2** (of woodcock) fly in the evening during the breeding season. [18th c.: orig. unkn.]

rodent /rṓd'nt/ *n. & adj.* ● *n.* any mammal of the order Rodentia with strong incisors and no canine teeth, e.g., rat, mouse, squirrel, beaver, porcupine. ● *adj.* **1** of the order Rodentia. **2** gnawing (esp. *Med.* of slow-growing ulcers). □□ **rodential** /-dénshəl/ *adj.* [L *rodere ros-* gnaw]

rodenticide /rədéntisid/ *n.* a poison used to kill rodents.

rodeo /rṓdiō, rōdáyō/ *n.* (*pl.* **-os**) **1** an exhibition or entertainment involving cowboys' skills in handling animals. **2** an exhibition of other skills, e.g., in motorcycling. **3 a** a roundup of cattle on a ranch for branding, etc. **b** an enclosure for this. [Sp. f. *rodear* go round ult. f. L *rotare* ROTATE[1]]

rodomontade /ródəmontáyd, -táad, rōdə-/ *n., adj., & v.* ● *n.* **1** boastful or bragging talk or behavior. **2** an instance of this. ● *adj.* boastful or bragging. ● *v.intr.* brag; talk boastfully. [F f. obs. It. *rodomontada* f. F *rodomont* & It. *rodomonte* f. the name of a boastful character in the *Orlando* epics]

■ *n.* **1** see BRAVADO. **2** see BOAST *n.* 1.

roe[1] /rō/ *n.* **1** (also **hard roe**) the mass of eggs in a female fish's ovary. **2** (also **soft roe**) the milt of a male fish. □□ **roed** *adj.* (also in *comb.*). [ME *row(e),* rough, f. MLG, MDu. *roge(n),* OHG *rogo, rogan,* ON *hrogn*]

roe[2] /rō/ *n.* (*pl.* same or **roes**) (also **roe deer**) a small European and Asian deer, *Capreolus capreolus.* [OE *rā(ha)*]

roebuck /rṓbuk/ *n.* (*pl.* same or **roebucks**) a male roe deer.

roentgen /réntgən, -jən, rúnt-/ *n.* a unit of ionizing radiation, the amount producing one electrostatic unit of positive or negative ionic charge in one cubic centimeter of air under standard conditions. □ **roentgen rays** X rays. [W. C. *Röntgen,* Ger. physicist d. 1923, discoverer of X rays]

roentgenography /réntgənógrəfee, -jə-, rúnt-/ *n.* photography using X rays.

roentgenology /réntgənóləjee, -jə-, rúnt-/ *n.* = RADIOLOGY.

rogation /rōgáyshən/ *n.* (usu. in *pl.*) *Eccl.* a solemn supplication, esp. for the harvest, consisting of the litany of the saints chanted on the three days before Ascension Day. □ **Rogation Days** the three days before Ascension Day. **Rogation Sunday** the Sunday preceding these. □□ **rogational** *adj.* [ME f. L *rogatio* f. *rogare* ask]

roger /rójər/ *int. & v.* ● *int.* **1** your message has been received and understood (used in radio communication, etc.). **2** *sl.* I agree. ● *v. Brit. coarse sl.* **1** *intr.* have sexual intercourse. **2** *tr.* have sexual intercourse with (a woman). [the name *Roger,* code for *R*]

■ *v.* see *make love* (LOVE).

rogue /rōg/ *n. & v.* ● *n.* **1** a dishonest or unprincipled person. **2** *joc.* a mischievous person, esp. a child. **3** (usu. *attrib.*) **a** a

wild animal driven away or living apart from the herd and of fierce temper (*rogue elephant*). **b** a stray, irresponsible, or undisciplined person or thing (*rogue trader*). **4** an inferior or defective specimen among many acceptable ones. ● *v.tr.* remove rogues (sense 4 of *n.*) from. □ **rogues' gallery** a collection of photographs of known criminals, etc., used for identification of suspects. [16th-c. cant word: orig. unkn.]
■ *n.* **1** trickster, swindler, cheat, cad, ne'er-do-well, wastrel, good-for-nothing, miscreant, scoundrel, blackguard, knave, scapegrace, cur, villain, wretch, charlatan, mountebank, rip, *archaic or joc.* rapscallion, *colloq.* scamp, rat, son of a gun, *colloq. or joc.* bounder, *Brit. colloq.* blighter, *often joc.* rascal, *sl.* louse, stinker, bastard, son of a bitch, SOB *or s.o.b.*, *Austral. sl.* illywhacker, esp. *Brit. sl.* rotter. **2** see RASCAL. **3** (*attrib.*)**a** undisciplined, uncontrollable, ungovernable, unmanageable, disobedient, fractious, self-willed, unruly, intractable, unrestrained, wild, lawless, strong-willed, headstrong, refractory, contumacious, recalcitrant, cross-grained, rampageous.

roguery /rṓgəree/ *n.* (*pl.* **-ies**) conduct or an action characteristic of rogues.
■ see DEVILRY.

roguish /rṓgish/ *adj.* **1** playfully mischievous. **2** characteristic of rogues. □□ **roguishly** *adv.* **roguishness** *n.*
■ **1** see MISCHIEVOUS 1, 2. **2** see WICKED 1.

roil /royl/ *v.tr.* **1** make (a liquid) turbid by agitating it. **2** = RILE 1. [perh. f. OF *ruiler* mix mortar f. LL *regulare* regulate]
■ **1** see AGITATE 3.

roister /róystər/ *v.intr.* (esp. as **roistering** *adj.*) revel noisily; be uproarious. □□ **roisterer** *n.* **roistering** *n.* **roisterous** *adj.* [obs. *roister* roisterer f. F *rustre* ruffian var. of *ruste* f. L *rusticus* RUSTIC]
■ see REVEL *v.* 1.

role /rōl/ *n.* (also **rôle**) **1** an actor's part in a play, motion picture, etc. **2** a person's or thing's characteristic or expected function (*the role of the tape recorder in language learning*). □ **role model** a person looked to by others as an example in a particular role. **role-playing** an exercise in which participants act the part of another character, used in psychology, language teaching, etc. [F *rôle* and obs. F *roule, rolle*, = ROLL *n.*]
■ **1** part, character. **2** function, place, part, job; duty, task, responsibility.

roll /rōl/ *v. & n.* ● *v.* **1 a** *intr.* move or go in some direction by turning over and over on an axis or by a rotary movement (*the ball rolled under the table; a barrel started rolling*). **b** *tr.* cause to do this (*rolled the barrel into the cellar*). **2** *tr.* make revolve between two surfaces (*rolled the clay between his palms*). **3 a** *intr.* (foll. by *along, by*, etc.) move or advance on or (of time, etc.) as if on wheels, etc. (*the bus rolled past; the years rolled by*). **b** *tr.* cause to do this (*rolled the dessert cart to our table*). **c** *intr.* (of a person) be conveyed in a vehicle (*the farmer rolled by on his tractor*). **4 a** *tr.* turn over and over on itself to form a more or less cylindrical or spherical shape (*rolled a newspaper*). **b** *tr.* make by forming material into a cylinder or ball (*rolled a cigarette; rolled a huge snowball*). **c** *tr.* accumulate into a mass (*rolled the dough into a ball*). **d** *intr.* (foll. by *into*) make a specified shape of itself (*the caterpillar rolled into a ball*). **5** *tr.* flatten or form by passing a roller, etc., over or by passing between rollers (*roll the lawn; roll pastry*). **6** *intr. & tr.* change or cause to change direction by rotatory movement (*his eyes rolled; he rolled his eyes*). **7** *intr.* **a** wallow, turn about in a fluid or a loose medium (*the dog rolled in the dust*). **b** (of a horse, etc.) lie on its back and kick about, esp. in an attempt to dislodge its rider. **8** *intr.* **a** (of a moving ship, aircraft, or vehicle) sway to and fro on an axis parallel to the direction of motion. **b** walk with an unsteady swaying gait (*they rolled out of the bar*). **9 a** *intr.* undulate; show or go with an undulating surface or motion (*rolling hills; rolling mist; the waves roll in*). **b** *tr.* carry or propel with such motion (*the river rolls its waters to the sea*). **10 a** *intr.* (of machinery) start functioning or moving (*the cameras rolled; the train began to roll*). **b** *tr.* cause (machinery) to do this. **11** *intr. & tr.* sound or utter with a vibratory or trilling

effect (*words rolled off his tongue; thunder rolled in the distance; he rolls his* rs). **12** *sl.* **a** *tr.* overturn (a car, etc.). **b** *intr.* (of a car, etc.) overturn. **13** *tr.* throw (dice). **14** *tr. sl.* rob (esp. a helpless victim). ● *n.* **1** a rolling motion or gait; rotation; spin; undulation (*the roll of the hills*). **2 a** a spell of rolling (*a roll in the mud*). **b** a gymnastic exercise in which the body is rolled into a tucked position and turned in a forward or backward circle. **c** (esp. **a roll in the hay**) *colloq.* an act of sexual intercourse or erotic fondling. **3** the continuous rhythmic sound of thunder or a drum. **4** *Aeron.* a complete revolution of an aircraft about its longitudinal axis. **5 a** a cylinder formed by turning flexible material over and over on itself without folding (*a roll of carpet; a roll of wallpaper*). **b** esp. *Brit.* a filled cake or pastry of similar form (*fig roll; sausage roll*). **6 a** a small portion of bread individually baked. **b** this with a specified filling (*ham roll*). **7** a more or less cylindrical or semicylindrical straight or curved mass of something (*rolls of fat; a roll of hair*). **8 a** an official list or register (*the electoral roll*). **b** the total numbers on this (*the schools' rolls have fallen*). **c** a document, esp. an official record, in scroll form. **9** a cylinder or roller, esp. to shape metal in a rolling mill. **10** *Archit.* **a** a molding of convex section. **b** a spiral scroll of an Ionic capital. **11** *colloq.* money, esp. as bills rolled together. □ **be rolling in** *colloq.* have plenty of (esp. money). **on a roll** *sl.* experiencing a bout of success or progress; engaged in a period of intense activity. **roll back** cause (esp. prices) to decrease. **roll bar** an overhead metal bar strengthening the frame of a vehicle (esp. in racing) and protecting the occupants if the vehicle overturns. **roll call** a process of calling out a list of names to establish who is present. **rolled gold** gold in the form of a thin coating applied to a baser metal by rolling. **rolled into one** combined in one person or thing. **rolled oats** oats that have been husked and crushed. **roll in 1** arrive in great numbers or quantity. **2** wallow; luxuriate in. **rolling drunk** swaying or staggering from drunkenness. **rolling mill** a machine or factory for rolling metal into shape. **rolling pin** a cylinder for rolling out pastry, dough, etc. **rolling stock 1** the locomotives, cars, or other vehicles, used on a railroad. **2** the road vehicles of a company. **rolling stone** a person who is unwilling to settle for long in one place. **roll neck** *Brit.* = TURTLENECK. **roll of honor** esp. *Brit.* = honor roll. **roll on** *v.tr.* **1** put on or apply by rolling. **2** (in *imper.*) *Brit. colloq.* (of a time, in eager expectation) come quickly (*roll on Friday!*). **roll-on** (*attrib.*) (of deodorant, etc.) applied by means of a rotating ball in the neck of the container. ● *n.* *Brit.* a light elastic corset. **roll-on roll-off** (of a ship, a method of transport, etc.) in which vehicles are driven directly on at the start of the voyage and off at the end of it. **roll out** unroll; spread out. **roll over 1** esp. *Brit.* send (a person) sprawling or rolling. **2 a** *Econ.* finance the repayment of (maturing stock, etc.) by an issue of new stock. **b** reinvest funds in a similar financial instrument (*we decided to roll over the CDs*). **roll-top desk** a desk with a flexible cover sliding in curved grooves. **roll up 1** *colloq.* arrive in a vehicle; appear on the scene. **2** make into or form a roll. **3** *Mil.* drive the flank of (an enemy line) back and around so that the line is shortened or surrounded. **roll with the punches** withstand adversity, difficulties, etc. **roll up one's sleeves** see SLEEVE. **roll-your-own** a hand-rolled cigarette. □□ **rollable** *adj.* [ME f. OF *rol(l)er, rouler, ro(u)lle* f. L *rotulus* dimin. of *rota* wheel]
■ *v.* **1** wheel *or* trundle along, spin along; rotate, cycle, turn, turn over (and over), turn round (and round); go around, orbit, tumble, somersault, roll over; see also SPIN *v.* 3 **a** bowl, be carried *or* conveyed, cruise, coast; float (by *or* past), sail (by *or* past), fly (by *or* past), flit *or* glide *or* slide by *or* past; pass, go, flow, slip by *or* past, move on; expire, elapse, disappear, vanish,

evaporate. **b** wheel, trundle. **5** roll out, flatten, level (off *or* out), smooth (out), even (out). **7 a** see WALLOW *v.* 1. **8 b** see STAGGER *v.* 1a. **9 a** undulate, billow, rise and fall; see also WAVE *v.* 2. **11** rumble, reverberate, resound, echo, reecho, boom, peal, resonate. **12** see OVERTURN *v.* 1, 3. **14** see ROB 1. ● *n.* **1** rolling, billowing, wave, billow, undulation, pitching, rocking, tossing; rotation, spin, toss, whirl, twirl. **3** rumble, reverberation, boom, echo, clap, crash, roar; tattoo, rataplan, rub-a-dub. **5 a** reel, spool, cylinder, scroll. **6 a** bun, bagel, *Brit.* bread-roll, bap. **8 a** list, register, record, directory, listing, catalog. **11** wad, bankroll, *sl.* bundle. □ **roll in 1** arrive, come in, pour in, flow in, turn up, *colloq.* show up. **2** luxuriate in, revel in, wallow in, savor, bask in, delight in, take pleasure in, indulge in, rejoice in, relish. **roll out** unroll, unfurl, spread (out), unfold, uncoil, uncurl, unwind, open (out). **roll up 1** see ARRIVE 1. **2** furl, coil, curl, wind up; see also WIND² *v.* 4.

rollaway /rṓləway/ *adj.* (of a bed, etc.) that can be removed on wheels or casters.

roller /rṓlər/ *n.* **1 a** a hard revolving cylinder for smoothing the ground, spreading ink or paint, crushing or stamping, rolling up cloth on, etc., used alone or as a rotating part of a machine. **b** a cylinder for diminishing friction when moving a heavy object. **2** a small cylinder on which hair is rolled for setting. **3** a long, swelling wave. **4** (also **roller bandage**) a long surgical bandage rolled up for convenient application. **5** a kind of tumbler pigeon. **6 a** any brilliantly plumaged bird of the family Coraciidae, with characteristic tumbling display-flight. **b** a breed of canary with a trilling song. □ **roller bearing** a bearing like a ball bearing but with small cylinders instead of balls. **roller coaster** *n.* an amusement ride consisting of an elevated track with open-car trains that rise and plunge steeply. **roller-coaster** *adj.* that goes up and down, or changes, suddenly and repeatedly. ● *v.intr.* (or **roller-coast**) go up and down or change in this way. **roller skate** see SKATE¹. **roller towel** a towel with the ends joined, hung on a roller.

■ **1 a** drum, cylinder; calender; wringer, esp. *Brit. hist.* mangle; windlass. **3** see WAVE *n.* 1, 2.

Rollerblade /rṓlərblayd/ *n. & v.* ● *n.propr.* (usu. *pl.*) roller skates with wheels arranged in a straight line, used like ice skates; in-line skates. *v.intr.* use Rollerblades.

rollick /rólik/ *v. & n.* ● *v.intr.* (esp. as **rollicking** *adj.*) be jovial or exuberant; indulge in high spirits; revel. ● *n.* **1** exuberant gaiety. **2** a spree or escapade. [19th-c., prob. dial.: perh. f. ROMP + FROLIC]

■ *v.* see REVEL *v.* 1.

rollover /rṓlōvər/ *n.* **1** *Econ.* the extension or transfer of a debt or other financial relationship. **2** *colloq.* the overturning of a vehicle, etc.

roly-poly /rṓleepṓlee/ *n. & adj.* ● *n.* (*pl.* **-ies**) *Brit.* (also **roly-poly pudding**) a sweet pastry dough covered with jam, etc., formed into a roll, and boiled, steamed, or baked. ● *adj.* (usu. of a child) pudgy; plump. [prob. formed on ROLL]

■ *adj.* see PLUMP¹ *adj.*

ROM /rom/ *n.* *Computing* a memory not capable of being changed by program instruction. [*read-only memory*]

Rom /rōm/ *n.* (*pl.* **Roma** /rṓmə/) a male gypsy. [Romany, = man, husband]

Rom. *abbr.* Romans (New Testament).

rom. *abbr.* roman (type).

Romaic /rōmáyik/ *n. & adj.* ● *n.* the vernacular language of modern Greece. ● *adj.* of or relating to this language. [Gk *Rhōmaikos* Roman (used esp. of the Eastern Empire)]

romaine /rōmáyn/ *n.* a cos lettuce. [F, fem. of *romain* (as ROMAN)]

romaji /rṓməjee/ *n.* a system of romanized spelling used to transliterate Japanese. [Jap.]

Roman /rṓmən/ *adj. & n.* ● *adj.* **1 a** of ancient Rome or its territory or people. **b** *archaic* of its language. **2** of medieval or modern Rome. **3** of papal Rome, esp. = ROMAN CATHOLIC. **4** of a kind ascribed to the early Romans (*Roman vir-*

tue). **5** surviving from a period of Roman rule (*Roman road*). **6** (**roman**) (of type) of a plain upright kind used in ordinary print. **7** (of the alphabet, etc.) based on the ancient Roman system with letters A–Z. ● *n.* **1 a** a citizen of the ancient Roman Republic or Empire. **b** a soldier of the Roman Empire. **2** a citizen of modern Rome. **3** = ROMAN CATHOLIC. **4** (**roman**) roman type. **5** (in *pl.*) the Christians of ancient Rome. □ **Roman candle** a firework discharging a series of flaming colored balls and sparks. **Roman Empire** *hist.* that established by Augustus in 27 BC and divided by Theodosius in AD 395 into the Western or Latin and Eastern or Greek Empire. **Roman holiday** enjoyment derived from others' discomfiture. **Roman law** the law-code developed by the ancient Romans and forming the basis of many modern codes. **Roman nose** one with a high bridge; an aquiline nose. **Roman numeral** any of the Roman letters representing numbers: I = 1, V = 5, X = 10, L = 50, C = 100, D = 500, M = 1000. [ME f. OF *Romain* (n. & adj.) f. L *Romanus* f. *Roma* Rome]

roman à clef /rōmáanaakláy/ *n.* (*pl.* **romans à clef** *pronunc.* same) a novel in which real persons or events appear with invented names. [F, = novel with a key]

Roman Catholic /rṓmən/ *adj. & n.* ● *adj.* of the part of the Christian Church acknowledging the pope as its head. ● *n.* a member of this Church. □□ **Roman Catholicism** *n.* [17th-c. transl. L (*Ecclesia*) *Romana Catholica* (*et Apostolica*), app. orig. as a conciliatory term: see ROMAN, CATHOLIC]

■ *n.* Catholic, Romanist.

romance /rōmáns/ *n., adj., & v.* ● *n.* /also *disp.* rṓmans/ **1** an atmosphere or tendency characterized by a sense of remoteness from or idealization of everyday life. **2 a** a prevailing sense of wonder or mystery surrounding the mutual attraction in a love affair. **b** sentimental or idealized love. **c** a love affair. **3 a** a literary genre with romantic love or highly imaginative unrealistic episodes forming the central theme. **b** a work of this genre. **4** a medieval tale, usu. in verse, of some hero of chivalry, of the kind common in the Romance languages. **5 a** exaggeration or picturesque falsehood. **b** an instance of this. **6** (**Romance**) the languages descended from Latin regarded collectively. **7** *Mus.* a short informal piece. ● *adj.* (**Romance**) of any of the languages descended from Latin (French, Italian, Spanish, etc.). ● *v.* **1** *intr.* exaggerate or distort the truth, esp. fantastically. **2** *tr.* court; woo; court the favor of, esp. by flattery. [ME f. OF *romanz, -ans, -ance*, ult. f. L *Romanicus* ROMANIC]

■ *n.* **1** fantasy, mystery, nostalgia; glamour, color, colorfulness, exoticism. **2 a** mystery, intrigue, excitement, fascination, wonder, sentiment. **c** (love) affair, amour, *affaire*, liaison, relationship, dalliance, *archaic* intrigue. **3 a** fantasy, melodrama, Gothic, Gothic horror. **b** love story, idyll; mystery (story), thriller, horror story, ghost story, fantasy, melodrama, Gothic novel *or* tale, fairy story *or* tale, epic, legend. **5 a** fantasy, fiction, imagination; see also *exaggeration* (EXAGGERATE). **b** tall story, tall tale, fantasy, fabrication, fairy story *or* tale; exaggeration, concoction, flight of fancy, fiction. **6** Romanic. ● *v.* **1** exaggerate, *colloq.* lay it on thick, lay it on with a trowel, pile it on. **2** court, woo, chase, pursue, *archaic* make love to; pander to, flatter, curry favor with, toady (up) to, *colloq.* butter up, soft-soap.

romancer /rōmánsər/ *n.* **1** a writer of romances, esp. in the medieval period. **2** a liar who resorts to fantasy.

Romanesque /rṓmənésk/ *n. & adj.* ● *n.* a style of architecture prevalent in Europe *c.* 900–1200, with massive vaulting and round arches (cf. NORMAN). ● *adj.* of the Romanesque style of architecture. [F f. *roman* ROMANCE]

roman-fleuve /rṓmoNflŏv/ *n.* (*pl.* **romans-fleuves** *pronunc.* same) **1** a novel featuring the leisurely description of the lives of members of a family, etc. **2** a sequence of self-contained novels. [F, = river novel]

Romanian /rōmáyneeən/ *n. & adj.* (also **Rumanian** /roo-/) ● *n.* **1 a** a native or national of Romania in E. Europe. **b** a person of Romanian descent. **2** the language of Romania. ● *adj.* of or relating to Romania or its people or language.

Romanic /rōmánik/ *n. & adj.* ● *n.* = ROMANCE *n.* 6. ● *adj.* **1 a** of or relating to Romance. **b** Romance-speaking. **2** descended from the ancient Romans or inheriting aspects of their social or political life. [L *Romanicus* (as ROMAN)]

Romanism /rṓmənizəm/ *n.* often *offens.* Roman Catholicism.

Romanist /rṓmənist/ *n.* **1** a student of Roman history or law or of the Romance languages. **2 a** a supporter of Roman Catholicism. **b** a Roman Catholic. [mod.L *Romanista* (as ROMAN)]

romanize /rṓmənīz/ *v.tr.* **1** make Roman or Roman Catholic in character. **2** put into the Roman alphabet or into roman type. ◻◻ **romanization** *n.*

Romano /rōmáanō/ *n.* a strong-tasting hard cheese, orig. made in Italy. [It.,= ROMAN]

Romano- /rōmáanō/ *comb. form* Roman; Roman and (*Romano-British*).

Romansh /rōmánsh, -máansh/ *n. & adj.* (also **Rumansh** /roo-/) ● *n.* the Rhaeto-Romanic dialects, esp. as spoken in the Swiss canton of Grisons. ● *adj.* of these dialects. [Romansh *Ruman(t)sch, Roman(t)sch* f. med.L *romanice* (adv.) (as ROMANCE)]

romantic /rōmántik/ *adj. & n.* ● *adj.* **1** of, characterized by, or suggestive of an idealized, sentimental, or fantastic view of reality; remote from experience (*a romantic picture*; *a romantic setting*). **2** inclined toward or suggestive of romance in love (*a romantic woman*; *a romantic evening*; *romantic words*). **3** (of a person) imaginative; visionary; idealistic. **4 a** (of style in art, music, etc.) concerned more with feeling and emotion than with form and aesthetic qualities; preferring grandeur or picturesqueness to finish and proportion. **b** (also **Romantic**) of or relating to the 18th–19th-c. romantic movement or style in the European arts. **5** (of a project, etc.) unpractical; fantastic. ● *n.* **1** a romantic person. **2** a romanticist. ◻◻ **romantically** *adv.* [*romant* tale of chivalry, etc., f. OF f. *romanz* ROMANCE]

■ *adj.* **1** imaginary, imagined, fictitious, fictional, ideal, idealized, fancied, fabulous, made-up, dreamed-up, fantasized, fanciful, fairy-tale, mythical, idyllic, utopian, illusory; picturesque, exotic, glamorous; sentimental, mawkish, maudlin, saccharine, mushy, sloppy, esp. *Brit. colloq.* soppy, sugary. **2** sentimental, emotional; see also TENDER[1] 5. **3** see IMAGINATIVE 2, *idealistic* (IDEALISM). **5** impractical, visionary, unpractical, unrealistic, ideal, abstract, quixotic, chimerical, absurd, extravagant, wild, mad, *sl.* crackpot. ● *n.* **1** Don Quixote, visionary, idealist; sentimentalist; see also DREAMER.

romanticism /rōmántisizəm/ *n.* (also **Romanticism**) adherence to a romantic style in art, music, etc.

romanticist /rōmántisist/ *n.* (also **Romanticist**) a writer or artist of the romantic school.

romanticize /rōmántisīz/ *v.* **1** *tr.* **a** make or render romantic or unreal (*a romanticized account of war*). **b** describe or portray in a romantic fashion. **2** *intr.* indulge in romantic thoughts or actions. ◻◻ **romanticization** *n.*

■ **1** see IDEALIZE. **2** see FANTASIZE 1.

Romany /rómənee, rṓ-/ *n. & adj.* ● *n.* (*pl.* **-ies**) **1** a Gypsy. **2** the Indo-European language of the Gypsies. ● *adj.* **1** of or concerning Gypsies. **2** of the Romany language. [Romany *Romani* fem. and pl. of *Romano* (adj.) (ROM)]

Romeo /rṓmeeō/ *n.* (*pl.* **-os**) a passionate male lover or seducer. [the hero of Shakesp. *Romeo and Juliet*]

■ see GALLANT *n.* 1.

Romish /rṓmish/ *adj.* usu. *derog.* Roman Catholic.

romneya /rómneeə/ *n.* any shrub of the genus *Romneya*, bearing poppylike flowers. [T. *Romney* Robinson, Brit. astronomer d. 1882]

romp /romp/ *v. & n.* ● *v.intr.* **1** play about roughly and energetically. **2** (foll. by *along, past,* etc.) *colloq.* proceed without effort. ● *n.* a spell of romping or boisterous play. ◻ **romp in** (or **home**) *Brit. colloq.* finish as the easy winner. ◻◻ **rompingly** *adv.* **rompy** *adj.* (**rompier, rompiest**). [perh. var. of RAMP[1]]

■ *v.* **1** see FROLIC *v.* **2** sail, skip, coast, sweep. ● *n.* see FROLIC *n.* 1, 3, 5.

romper /rómpər/ *n.* (usu. in *pl.*) (also esp. *Brit.* **romper suit**) a one-piece garment, esp. for a child, that covers the trunk and has short pants.

ronde /rond/ *n.* **1** a dance in which the dancers move in a circle. **2** a course of talk, activity, etc. [F, fem. of *rond* ROUND *adj.*]

rondeau /róndō, rondṓ/ *n.* (*pl.* **rondeaux** *pronunc.* same or /-dōz/) a poem of ten or thirteen lines with only two rhymes throughout and with the opening words used twice as a refrain. [F, earlier *rondel*: see RONDEL]

rondel /rónd'l, rondél/ *n.* a rondeau, esp. one of special form. [ME f. OF f. *rond* ROUND: cf. ROUNDEL]

rondo /róndō/ *n.* (*pl.* **-os**) *Mus.* a form with a recurring leading theme, often found in the final movement of a sonata or concerto, etc. [It. f. F *rondeau*: see RONDEAU]

ronin /rṓnin/ *n. hist.* (in feudal Japan) a lordless wandering samurai; an outlaw. [Jap.]

röntgen, etc., var. of ROENTGEN, etc.

roo /rōō/ *n.* (also **'roo**) *Austral. colloq.* a kangaroo. [abbr.]

rood /rōōd/ *n.* **1** a crucifix, esp. one raised on a screen or beam at the entrance to the chancel. **2** a quarter of an acre. ◻ **rood loft** a gallery on top of a rood screen. **rood screen** a wooden or stone carved screen separating nave and chancel. [OE *rōd*]

■ **1** crucifix, cross.

roof /rōōf, roof/ *n. & v.* ● *n.* (*pl.* **roofs** or *disp.* **rooves** /rōōvz, roovz/) **1 a** the upper covering of a building, usu. supported by its walls. **b** the top of a covered vehicle. **c** the top inner surface of an oven, refrigerator, etc. **2** the overhead rock in a cave or mine, etc. **3** the branches or the sky, etc., overhead. **4** (of prices, etc.) the upper limit or ceiling. ● *v.tr.* **1** (often foll. by *in, over*) cover with or as with a roof. **2** be the roof of. ◻ **go through the roof** *colloq.* (of prices, etc.) reach extreme or unexpected heights. **hit** (or **go through** or **raise**) **the roof** *colloq.* become very angry. **raise the roof 1** create a noisy racket. **2** protest noisily. **roof garden 1** a garden on the flat roof of a building. **2** a rooftop restaurant. **roof of the mouth** the palate. **a roof over one's head** somewhere to live. **roof rack** a framework for carrying luggage, etc. on the roof of a vehicle. **under one roof** in the same building. **under a person's roof** in a person's house (esp. with ref. to hospitality). ◻◻ **roofed** *adj.* (also in *comb.*). **roofless** *adj.* [OE *hrōf*]

roofage /rōōfij, roof-/ *n.* esp. *Brit.* the expanse of a roof or roofs.

roofer /rōōfər, roof-/ *n.* a person who constructs or repairs roofs.

roofing /rōōfing, roof-/ *n.* **1** material for constructing a roof. **2** the process of constructing a roof or roofs.

roofscape /rōōfskayp, roof-/ *n.* esp. *Brit.* a scene or view of roofs.

rooftop /rōōftop, roof-/ *n.* **1** the outer surface of a roof. **2** (esp. in *pl.*) the level of a roof.

rooftree /rōōftree, roof-/ *n.* a roof's ridgepole.

rooinek /róynek, rṓo-ee-/ *n. S.Afr. sl. offens.* a British or English-speaking South African. [Afrik., = red-neck]

rook[1] /rook/ *n. & v.* ● *n.* **1** a black European and Asiatic bird, *Corvus frugilegus*, of the crow family, nesting in colonies in treetops. **2** a sharper, esp. at dice or cards; a person who lives off inexperienced gamblers, etc. ● *v.tr.* **1** charge (a customer) extortionately. **2** win money from (a person) at cards, etc., esp. by swindling. [OE *hrōc*]

■ *v.* **1** see FLEECE *v.* 1. **2** see SWINDLE *v.* 1.

rook[2] /rook/ *n.* a chess piece with its top in the shape of a battlement; castle. [ME f. OF *roc(k)* ult. f. Arab. *rukk*, orig. sense uncert.]

rookery /rŏŏkəree/ *n.* (*pl.* **-ies**) **1 a** a colony of rooks. **b** a clump of trees having rooks' nests. **2** a colony of seabirds (esp. penguins) or seals.

/.../ **pronunciation**	● **part of speech**
◻ **phrases, idioms, and compounds**	
◻◻ **derivatives**	■ **synonym section**
cross-references appear in SMALL CAPITALS or *italics*	

rookie /róokee/ *n. sl.* **1** a new recruit, esp. in the army or police. **2** member of a sports team in his or her first season. [corrupt. of *recruit*, after ROOK¹]

■ **1** see RECRUIT *n.* 1, 2.

room /room, room/ *n. & v.* ● *n.* **1 a** space that is or might be occupied by something; capaciousness or ability to accommodate contents (*it takes up too much room; there is plenty of room; we have no room here for idlers*). **b** space in or on (*schoolroom*). **2 a** a part of a building enclosed by walls or partitions, floor, and ceiling. **b** (in *pl.*) a set of these occupied by a person or family; apartments, etc. **c** persons present in a room (*the room fell silent*). **3** (in *comb.*) a room or area for a specified purpose (*reading room*). **4** (foll. by *for*, or *to* + infin.) opportunity or scope (*room to improve things; no room for dispute*). ● *v.intr.* have a room or rooms; lodge; board. □ **make room** (often foll. by *for*) clear a space (for a person or thing) by removal of others; make way; yield place. **not** (or **no**) **room to swing a cat** a very confined space. **rooming house** a house with rented rooms for lodging. **room service** (in a hotel, etc.) service of food or drink taken to a guest's room. □□ **-roomed** *adj.* (in *comb.*). **roomful** *n.* (*pl.* **-fuls**). [OE *rūm* f. Gmc]

■ *n.* **1 a, b** see SPACE *n.* 1c. **2 a** see CELL 1. **b** (*rooms*) quarters, lodgings, apartments; see also PLACE *n.* 3. **4** allowance, latitude, leeway, margin; see also OCCASION *n.* 3, SCOPE¹. ● *v.* lodge; board; live, reside, stay, *archaic* abide, *literary* dwell. □ **rooming house** lodging house, boarding house; see also HOTEL 1.

roomer /róomər, róomər/ *n.* a renter of a room in another's house.

■ see GUEST *n.* 2.

roomette /roomét, roo-/ *n.* **1** a private single compartment in a railroad sleeping car. **2** a small bedroom, etc., for rent.

roomie /róomee, room-/ *n. colloq.* a roommate.

roommate /róom-mayt, room-/ *n.* a person occupying the same room, apartment, etc., as another.

roomy /róomee, roo-/ *adj.* (**roomier**, **roomiest**) having much room; spacious. □□ **roomily** *adv.* **roominess** *n.*

■ spacious, capacious, commodious, large, sizable, big, ample.

roost /roost/ *n. & v.* ● *n.* **1** a branch or other support on which a bird perches, esp. a place where birds regularly settle to sleep. **2** a place offering temporary sleeping accommodation. ● *v.* **1** *intr.* **a** (of a bird) settle for rest or sleep. **b** (of a person) stay for the night. **2** *tr.* provide with a sleeping place. □ **come home to roost** (of a scheme, etc.) recoil unfavorably upon the originator. **rule the roost** hold a position of control; be in charge (esp. of others). [OE *hrōst*]

■ *n.* **1** perch. ● *v.* **1** perch, sit, rest, sleep; *sl.* crash; nest.

rooster /róostər/ *n.* esp. a male domestic fowl; cock.

root¹ /root, root/ *n. & v.* ● *n.* **1 a** the part of a plant normally below the ground, attaching it to the earth and conveying nourishment to it from the soil. **b** (in *pl.*) such a part divided into branches or fibers. **c** the corresponding organ of an epiphyte; the part attaching ivy to its support. **d** the permanent underground stock of a plant. **e** any small plant with a root for transplanting. **2 a** any plant, e.g., a turnip or carrot, with an edible root. **b** such a root. **3** (in *pl.*) the sources of or reasons for one's long-standing emotional attachment to a place, community, etc. **4 a** the embedded part of a bodily organ or structure, e.g., hair, tooth, nail, etc. **b** the part of a thing attaching it to a greater or more fundamental whole. **c** (in *pl.*) the base of a mountain, etc. **5 a** the basic cause, source, or origin (*love of money is the root of all evil; has its roots in the distant past*). **b** (*attrib.*) (of an idea, etc.) from which the rest originated. **6** the basis of something, its means of continuance or growth (*has its root(s) in selfishness; has no root in the nature of things*). **7** the essential substance or nature of something (*get to the root of things*). **8** *Math.* **a** a number or quantity that when multiplied by itself a usu. specified number of times gives a specified number or quantity (*the cube root of eight is two*). **b** a square root. **c** a value of an unknown quantity satisfying a given equation. **9** *Philol.* any ultimate unanalyzable element of language; a basis, not

necessarily surviving as a word in itself, on which words are made by the addition of prefixes or suffixes or by other modification. **10** *Mus.* the fundamental note of a chord. **11** *Bibl.* a scion, an offshoot (*there shall be a root of Jesse*). ● *v.* **1 a** *intr.* take root or grow roots. **b** *tr.* cause to do this (*take care to root them firmly*). **2** *tr.* **a** fix firmly; establish (*fear rooted him to the spot*). **b** (as **rooted** *adj.*) firmly established (*her affection was deeply rooted; rooted objection to*). **3** *tr.* (usu. foll. by *out*, *up*) drag or dig up by the roots. □ **pull up by the roots 1** uproot. **2** eradicate; destroy. **put down roots 1** begin to draw nourishment from the soil. **2** become settled or established. **root and branch** thorough(ly), radical(ly). **root beer** a carbonated drink made from an extract of roots. **root canal** *Dentistry* surgery to remove the diseased nerve of a tooth. **root-mean-square** *Math.* the square root of the arithmetic mean of the squares of a set of values. **root out** find and get rid of. **root sign** *Math.* = *radical sign.* **strike at the root** (or **roots**) of set about destroying. **take root 1** begin to grow and draw nourishment from the soil. **2** become fixed or established. □□ **rootage** *n.* **rootedness** *n.* **rootless** *adj.* **rootlet** *n.* **rootlike** *adj.* **rooty** *adj.* [OE *rōt* f. ON *rót*, rel. to WORT & L *radix*: see RADIX]

■ *n.* **1 a** rootstock, taproot, rootlet, tuber, radicle, rhizome, rhizomorph. **b** (*roots*) rootstock, rhizome. **3** (*roots*) origins; heritage; family; antecedents, ancestors, predecessors; birthplace, native land *or* country, native soil. **5a, 6** base, basis, foundation, source, seat, cause, fountainhead, origin, wellspring, *poet.* fount. **7** see ESSENCE 1. ● *v.* **1 b** plant, embed, bed (out), set (out), sow, fix. **2 b** (**rooted**) established, set, fixed, fast, firm, deep-rooted, deep-seated, entrenched, ingrained, engrained, (firmly) embedded, implanted, instilled; inbred, inherent, intrinsic, fundamental, basic, *colloq. disp.* chronic. □ **pull up by the roots 1** see UPROOT 1. **2** see UPROOT 3. **put down roots 2** see SETTLE¹ 1, 2a, b. **root and branch** thorough(ly), radical(ly), complete(ly), utter(ly), entire(ly), total(ly). **root out** find, uncover, discover, dig up *or* out, unearth, turn up, bring to light; eradicate, eliminate, destroy, exterminate. **take root 1** germinate, sprout, strike, grow, develop, thrive, flourish, *literary* burgeon. **2** become set *or* established *or* settled, catch on, take hold.

root² /root, root/ *v.* **1 a** *intr.* (of an animal, esp. a pig) turn up the ground with the snout, beak, etc., in search of food. **b** *tr.* (foll. by *up*) turn up (the ground) by rooting. **2 a** *intr.* (foll. by *around*, *in*, etc.) rummage. **b** *tr.* (foll. by *out* or *up*) find or extract by rummaging. **3** *intr.* (foll. by *for*) *sl.* encourage by applause or support. □□ **rooter** *n.* (in sense 3). [earlier *wroot* f. OE *wrōtan* & ON *róta*: rel. to OE *wrōt* snout]

■ **2** forage, dig, nose, poke, ferret, burrow, rummage, delve, search; (*root about, in, etc.*) ransack. **3** (*root for*) cheer (for), applaud (for); support, encourage, urge on, *colloq.* boost.

rootstock /róotstok, root-/ *n.* **1** a rhizome. **2** a plant into which a graft is inserted. **3** a primary form from which offshoots have arisen.

rooves see ROOF.

rope /rōp/ *n. & v.* ● *n.* **1 a** stout cord made by twisting together strands of hemp, sisal, flax, cotton, nylon, wire, or similar material. **b** a piece of this. **c** a lasso. **2** (foll. by *of*) a quantity of onions, garlic bulbs, pearls, etc., strung together. **3** (in *pl.*, prec. by *the*) **a** the conditions in some sphere of action (*know the ropes; show a person the ropes*). **b** the ropes enclosing a boxing or wrestling ring, etc. **4** (prec. by *the*) **a** a noose or halter for hanging a person. **b** execution by hanging. ● *v.* **1** *tr.* fasten, secure, or catch with rope. **2** *tr.* (usu. foll. by *off*, *in*) enclose (a space) with rope. **3** *Mountaineering* **a** *tr.* connect (a party) with a rope; attach (a person) to a rope. **b** (*absol.*) put on a rope. **c** *intr.* (foll. by *down*, *up*) climb down or up using a rope. □ **give a person plenty of rope** (or **enough rope to hang himself** or **herself**) give a person enough freedom of action to bring about his or her own downfall. **on the rope** *Mountaineering* roped together. **on the ropes 1** *Boxing* forced against the ropes by the oppo-

nent's attack. **2** near defeat. **rope in** persuade to take part. **rope into** persuade to take part in (*was roped into doing the laundry*). **rope ladder** two long ropes connected by short crosspieces, used as a ladder. **rope molding** a molding cut spirally in imitation of rope strands. **rope of sand** esp. *Brit.* delusive security. **rope's end** *hist.* a short piece of rope used to flog (formerly, esp. a sailor) with. **rope yarn 1** material obtained by unpicking rope strands, or used for making them. **2** a piece of this. **3** *Brit.* a mere trifle. [OE *rāp* f. Gmc]
■ *n.* **1 a** see CABLE *n.* 1. **2** see STRING *n.* 6. **3 a** (*the ropes*) the routine, the procedure, *colloq.* the score. ● *v.* **1** tie, bind, lash, hitch, fasten, secure, tether. □ **rope in** attract, draw (in), tempt, entice, lure, persuade.

ropemanship /rṓpmənship/ *n.* skill in ropewalking or climbing with ropes.

ropewalk /rṓpwawk/ *n.* a long stretch of ground or building where ropes are made.

ropewalker /rṓpwawkər/ *n.* a performer on a tightrope. □ **ropewalking** the action of performing on a tightrope.

ropeway /rṓpway/ *n.* a cable railroad; tramway.

roping /rṓping/ *n.* a set or arrangement of ropes.

ropy /rṓpee/ *adj.* (also **ropey**) (**ropier**, **ropiest**) **1** (of wine, bread, etc.) forming viscous or gelatinous threads. **2** like a rope. **3** *Brit. colloq.* **a** poor in quality. **b** unwell. □□ **ropily** *adv.* **ropiness** *n.*
■ **1** viscous, viscid, glutinous, mucilaginous, gluey, gummy; stringy, thready, fibrous, filamentous. **3 a** inadequate, inferior, deficient, indifferent, mediocre, substandard, unsatisfactory, poor. **b** see ILL *adj.* 1.

roque /rōk/ *n.* croquet played on a hard court surrounded by a bank. [alt. form of ROQUET]

Roquefort /rókfərt/ *n. propr.* **1** a soft blue cheese made from sheep's milk. **2** a salad dressing made of this. [*Roquefort* in S. France]

roquet /rōkáy/ *v. & n. Croquet* ● *v.* (**roqueted**, **roqueting**) **1** *tr.* **a** cause one's ball to strike (another ball). **b** (of a ball) strike (another). **2** *intr.* strike another ball thus. ● *n.* an instance of roqueting. [app. arbitr. f. CROQUET *v.*, orig. used in the same sense]

rorqual /ráwrkwəl/ *n.* any of various whales of the family Balaenopteridae, esp. *Balaenoptera musculus*, having a dorsal fin. Also called FINBACK, *fin whale.* [F f. Norw. *røyrkval* f. OIcel. *reythr* the specific name + *hvalr* WHALE[1]]

Rorschach test /ráwrshaak/ *n. Psychol.* a type of personality test in which a standard set of inkblot designs is presented one by one to the subject, who is asked to describe what they suggest or resemble. [H. *Rorschach*, Swiss psychiatrist d. 1922]

rort /rawrt/ *n. Austral. sl.* **1** a trick; a fraud; a dishonest practice. **2** a wild party. [back-form. f. RORTY]
■ **1** see FRAUD 2. **2** see JAMBOREE.

rorty /ráwrtee/ *adj.* (**rortier**, **rortiest**) *Brit. sl.* **1** splendid; boisterous; rowdy (*had a rorty time*). **2** coarse; earthy. [19th c.: orig. unkn.]

rosace /rṓzays/ *n.* **1** esp. *Brit.* a rose window. **2** a rose-shaped ornament or design; rosette. [F f. L *rosaceus*: see ROSACEOUS]

rosaceous /rōzáyshəs/ *adj. Bot.* of the large plant family Rosaceae, which includes the rose. [L *rosaceus* f. *rosa* rose]

rosaniline /rōzánilin, -lin/ *n.* **1 a** an organic base derived from aniline. **b** a red dye obtained from this. **2** fuchsin. [ROSE[1] + ANILINE]

rosarian /rəzáireeən/ *n.* a person who cultivates roses, esp. professionally. [L *rosarium* ROSARY]

rosarium /rəzáireeəm/ *n.* a rose garden. [L (as ROSARY)]

rosary /rṓzəree/ *n.* (*pl.* **-ies**) **1** *RC Ch.* **a** a form of devotion in which prayers are said while counting them on a special string of beads. **b** a string of 55 (or 165) beads for keeping count in this. **c** a book containing this devotion. **2** a similar string of beads used in other religions. **3** a rose garden or rose bed. [ME f. L *rosarium* rose garden, neut. of *rosarius* (as ROSE[1])]

roscoe /róskō/ *n. sl.* a gun, esp. a pistol or revolver. [the name *Roscoe*]
■ see PISTOL *n.*

rose[1] /rōz/ *n., adj., & v.* ● *n.* **1** any prickly bush or shrub of

the genus *Rosa*, bearing usu. fragrant flowers generally of a red, pink, yellow, or white color. **2** this flower. **3** any flowering plant resembling this (*rose of Sharon*; *rockrose*). **4 a** a light crimson color; pink. **b** (usu. in *pl.*) a rosy complexion (*roses in her cheeks*). **5 a** a representation of the flower in heraldry or decoration (esp. as the national emblem of England). **b** a rose-shaped design, e.g., on a compass card, etc. **6** the sprinkling nozzle of a watering can or hose. **7** an ornamental through which the shaft of a doorknob passes. **8 a** a rose diamond. **b** a rose window. **9** (in *pl.*) used in various phrases to express favorable circumstances, ease, success, etc. (*roses all the way*; *everything's roses*). **10** an excellent person or thing, esp. a beautiful woman (*English rose*; *rose between two thorns*). ● *adj.* = *rose-colored* 1. ● *v.tr.* (esp. as **rosed** *adj.*) make (one's face, cheeks, etc.) rosy. □ **rose apple 1** a tropical tree of the genus *Syzygium*, cultivated for its foliage and fragrant fruit. **2** this fruit. **rose chafer** a destructive beetle, *Macrodactylus subspinosis*, frequenting roses, fruit trees, etc. **rose-colored 1** of a rose color. **2** optimistic; sanguine; cheerful (*takes rose-colored views*). **rose comb** a flat fleshy comb of a fowl. **rose-cut** cut as a rose diamond. **rose diamond** a hemispherical diamond with the curved part cut in triangular facets. **rose geranium** a pink-flowered, sweet-scented pelargonium, *Pelargonium graveolus.* **rose hip** = HIP[2]. **rose madder** a pale pink pigment. **rose mallow** = HIBISCUS. **rose of Jericho** a resurrection plant, *Anastatica hierochuntica.* **rose of Sharon 1 a** a species of hypericum, *Hypericum calycinum*, with dense foliage and golden-yellow flowers: also called AARON'S BEARD. **b** a shrub, *Hibiscus syriacus*, of the mallow family, with rose, lavender, or white flowers. **2** *Bibl.* a flowering plant of unknown identity. **rose-pink** pink like a rose; rose-colored. **rose-red** *adj.* red like a rose, rose-colored. ● *n.* this color. **rose-tinted** = *rose-colored.* **rose water** perfume made from roses. **rose window** a circular window, usu. with roselike or spokelike tracery. **see** (or **look**) **through rose-colored** (or **-tinted**) **glasses** regard (circumstances, etc.) with unfounded favor or optimism. **under the rose** = SUB ROSA. **Wars of the Roses** *hist.* the 15th-c. civil wars in England between Yorkists with a white rose as an emblem and Lancastrians with a red rose. □□ **roseless** *adj.* **roselike** *adj.* [ME f. OE *rōse* f. L *rosa*]

rose[2] *past of* RISE.

rosé /rōzáy/ *n.* any light pink wine, colored by only brief contact with red grape skins. [F, = pink]

roseate /rṓzeeət, -ayt/ *adj.* **1** = *rose-colored* (see ROSE[1]). **2** having a partly pink plumage (*roseate spoonbill*; *roseate tern*). [L *roseus* rosy (as ROSE[1])]

rosebay /rṓzbay/ *n.* an oleander, rhododendron, or, esp. *Brit.*, willow herb.

rosebud /rṓzbud/ *n.* a bud of a rose.

rosefish /rṓzfish/ *n.* = REDFISH 1.

rosella /rəzélə/ *n.* **1** any brightly colored Australian parakeet of the genus *Platycercus*. **2** *Austral.* an easily shorn sheep. [corrupt. of *Rosehill*, NSW, where the bird was first found]

rosemaling /rṓzəmaaling/ *n.* the art of painting wooden furniture, etc., with flower motifs. [Norw., = rose painting]

rosemary /rṓzmairee, -məree/ *n.* an evergreen fragrant shrub, *Rosmarinus officinalis*, with leaves used as a culinary herb, in perfumery, etc., and taken as an emblem of remembrance. [ME, earlier *rosmarine* ult. f. L *ros marinus* f. *ros* dew + *marinus* MARINE, with assim. to ROSE[1] and *Mary* name of the Virgin]

roseola /rōzeeólə, rōzéeələ/ *n.* **1** a rosy rash in measles and similar diseases. **2** a mild febrile disease of infants. □□ **roseolar** *adj.* **roseolous** *adj.* [mod. var. of RUBEOLA f. L *roseus* rose-colored]

rosery /rṓzəree/ *n.* (*pl.* **-ies**) *Brit.* a rose garden.

Rosetta stone /rōzétə/ *n.* a key to previously unattainable

/.../ pronunciation	● part of speech
□ phrases, idioms, and compounds	
□□ derivatives	■ synonym section
cross-references appear in SMALL CAPITALS or *italics*	

understanding. [a stone found near *Rosetta* in Egypt, with a trilingual inscription of the 2nd c. BC in Egyptian hieroglyphs, demotic, and Greek, important in the decipherment of hieroglyphs]

rosette /rōzét/ *n.* **1** a rose-shaped ornament made usu. of ribbon and worn esp. as the badge of a contest official, etc., or as an award or the symbol of an award in a competition. **2** *Archit.* **a** a carved or molded ornament resembling or representing a rose. **b** a rose window. **3** an object or symbol or arrangement of parts resembling a rose. **4** *Biol.* **a** a roselike cluster of parts. **b** markings resembling a rose. **5** esp. *Brit.* a rose diamond. □□ **rosetted** *adj.* [F dimin. of *rose* ROSE¹]

rosewood /rōzwŏŏd/ *n.* any of several fragrant close-grained woods used in making furniture.

Rosh Hashanah /ráwsh həsháwnə, -shaa-, haashaanáa, rōsh/ *n.* (also **Rosh Hashana**) the Jewish New Year. [Heb., = beginning (lit. "head") of the year]

Roshi /rōshee/ *n.* (*pl.* **Roshis**) the spiritual leader of a community of Zen Buddhist monks. [Jap.]

Rosicrucian /rōzikrōōshən, rōzi-/ *n. & adj.* ● *n.* **1** *hist.* a member of a 17th–18th-c. society devoted to the study of metaphysical and mystical lore (said to have been founded in 1484 by Christian Rosenkreuz). **2** a member of any of several later organizations deriving from this. ● *adj.* of or relating to the Rosicrucians. □□ **Rosicrucianism** *n.* [mod.L *rosa crucis* (or *crux*), as Latinization of G *Rosenkreuz*]

rosin /rózin/ *n. & v.* ● *n.* resin, esp. the solid residue after distillation of oil of turpentine from crude turpentine. ● *v.tr.* (**rosined, rosining**) **1** rub (esp. the bow of a violin, etc.) with rosin. **2** smear or seal up with rosin. □□ **rosiny** *adj.* [ME, alt. f. RESIN]

rosolio /rəzólyō/ *n.* (also **rosoglio**) (*pl.* **-os**) a sweet cordial of liquor, sugar, and flavoring, esp. rose petals and cloves. [It., f. mod.L *ros solis* dew of the sun]

roster /róstər/ *n. & v.* ● *n.* **1** a list or plan showing turns of duty or leave for individuals or groups esp. of a military force. **2** *Sports* a list of players, esp. one showing batting order in baseball. ● *v.tr.* place on a roster. [Du. *rooster* list, orig. gridiron f. *roosten* ROAST, with ref. to its parallel lines]
■ *n.* list, docket, esp. *Brit.* rota.

rostra *pl.* of ROSTRUM.

rostral /róstrəl/ *adj.* **1** *Zool. & Bot.* of or on the rostrum. **2** *Anat.* **a** nearer the hypophysial area in the early embryo. **b** nearer the region of the nose and mouth in postembryonic life. **3** (of a column, etc.) adorned with the rams of ancient warships or with representations of these. □□ **rostrally** *adv.*

rostrated /róstraytid/ *adj.* **1** *Zool. & Bot.* having or ending in a rostrum. **2** = ROSTRAL 3. [L *rostratus* (as ROSTRUM)]

rostrum /róstrəm/ *n.* (*pl.* **rostra** /-strə/ or **rostrums**) **1 a** a platform for public speaking. **b** a conductor's platform facing the orchestra. **c** a similar platform for other purposes, e.g., for supporting a movie or television camera. **2** *Zool. & Bot.* a beak, stiff snout, or beaklike part, esp. of an insect or arachnid. **3** *Rom. Antiq.* the beaklike projection of a warship. □□ (all in sense 2) **rostrate** /-trayt/ *adj.* **rostriferous** /-trífərəs/ *adj.* **rostriform** *adj.* [L, = beak f. *rodere* rosgnaw: orig. *rostra* (pl., in sense 1a) in the Roman forum adorned with beaks of captured galleys]
■ **1 a** platform, stage, dais, podium, stand.

rosy /rōzee/ *adj.* (**rosier, rosiest**) **1** colored like a pink or red rose (esp. of the complexion as indicating good health, of a blush, wine, the sky, light, etc.). **2** optimistic; hopeful; cheerful (*a rosy future; a rosy attitude to life*). □□ **rosily** *adv.* **rosiness** *n.*
■ **1** pink, rose-colored, red, roseate, reddish, pinkish, cherry, cerise, ruddy, flushed, glowing, blushing, ruby, rubicund, florid, rose-red. **2** optimistic, promising, favorable, auspicious, hopeful, encouraging, sunny, bright, cheerful.

rot /rot/ *v., n., & int.* ● *v.* (**rotted, rotting**) **1** *intr.* **a** (of animal or vegetable matter) lose its original form by the chemical action of bacteria, fungi, etc.; decay. **b** (foll. by *off, away*) crumble or drop from a stem, etc., through decomposition. **2** *intr.* **a** (of society, institutions, etc.) gradually perish from lack of activity, participation, or use. **b** (of a

prisoner, etc.) waste away (*left to rot in prison*); (of a person) languish. **3** *tr.* cause to rot; make rotten. **4** *tr. Brit. sl.* tease; abuse; denigrate. **5** *intr. Brit. sl.* joke. ● *n.* **1** the process or state of rotting. **2** *sl.* nonsense; an absurd or foolish statement, argument, or proposal. **3** *Brit.* a sudden series of (usu. unaccountable) failures; a rapid decline in standards, etc. (*a rot set in; we must try to stop the rot*). **4** (often prec. by *the*) a virulent liver disease of sheep. ● *int.* expressing incredulity or ridicule. [OE *rotian* (v.): (n.) ME, perh. f. Scand.: cf. Icel., Norw. *rot*]
■ *v.* **1** decay, decompose, fester, molder (away); spoil, go bad *or* off, be tainted, mold. **b** corrode, disintegrate, deteriorate, crumble *or* go *or* fall to pieces. **2 a** degenerate, decay, decline, atrophy, waste away, wither, disintegrate, crumble, fall apart, deteriorate. **b** waste away, wither away, molder (away), degenerate, decay; languish, die, decline, deteriorate, atrophy. **4** see TEASE *v.* ● *n.* **1** decay, decomposition, putrefaction, putrescence, blight, corrosion, disintegration, deterioration; corruption. **2** (stuff and) nonsense, balderdash, rubbish, bunkum, twaddle, drivel, claptrap, moonshine, trash *colloq.* hogwash, malarkey, esp. *Brit.* tosh, *sl.* tommyrot, bosh, bull, eyewash, bunk, baloney, poppycock, bull, *Brit. sl.* codswallop. ● *int.* see *go on!* (GO¹), FIDDLESTICK.

rota /rōtə/ *n.* **1** esp. *Brit.* a list of persons acting, or duties to be done, in rotation; a roster. **2** (**Rota**) *RC Ch.* the supreme ecclesiastical and secular court. [L, = wheel]
■ **1** roster.

Rotarian /rōtáireeən/ *n. & adj.* ● *n.* a member of a Rotary club. ● *adj.* of Rotarians or Rotary club. [ROTARY + -AN]

rotary /rōtəree/ *adj. & n.* ● *adj.* acting by rotation (*rotary drill; rotary pump*). ● *n.* (*pl.* **-ies**) **1** a rotary machine. **2** a traffic circle. **3** (**Rotary**) (in full **Rotary International**) a world-wide charitable society of business people, orig. named from members entertaining in rotation. □ **Rotary Club** a local branch of Rotary. **rotary-wing** (of an aircraft) deriving lift from rotary airfoils. [med.L *rotarius* (as ROTA)]
■ *adj.* rotating, rotatory, revolving, spinning.
■ *n.* **2** traffic circle, *Brit.* roundabout.

rotate¹ /rōtayt/ *v.tr. & tr.* **1** *intr. & tr.* move around an axis or center, revolve. **2 a** *tr.* take or arrange in rotation. **b** *intr.* act or take place in rotation (*the chairmanship will rotate*). □□ **rotatable** *adj.* **rotative** /rōtaytiv/ *adj.* **rotatory** /rōtətawree/ *adj.* [L *rotare* f. *rota* wheel]
■ **1** revolve, go around, gyrate, pirouette, whirl, twirl, pivot, reel; turn, spin, whirl *or* twirl around, wheel around. **2** change, alternate, interchange, switch, swap; exchange; trade places, take turns.

rotate² /rōtayt/ *adj. Bot.* wheel-shaped. [formed as ROTA]

rotation /rōtáyshən/ *n.* **1** the act or an instance of rotating or being rotated. **2** a recurrence; a recurrent series or period; a regular succession of various members of a group in office, etc. **3** a system of growing different crops in regular order to avoid exhausting the soil. □□ **rotational** *adj.* **rotationally** *adv.* [L *rotatio*]
■ **1** see REVOLUTION 3, 4.

rotator /rōtaytər/ *n.* **1** a machine or device for causing something to rotate. **2** *Anat.* a muscle that rotates a limb, etc. **3** a revolving apparatus or part. [L (as ROTATE¹)]

ROTC /rótsee/ *abbr.* Reserve Officers Training Corps.

rote /rōt/ *n.* (usu. prec. by *by*) mechanical or habitual repetition (with ref. to acquiring knowledge). [ME: orig. unkn.]
■ routine, ritual; (*by rote*) by heart, from memory; unthinkingly, automatically, mechanically.

rotenone /rót'nōn/ *n.* a toxic crystalline substance obtained from the roots of derris and other plants, used as an insecticide. [Jap. *rotenon* f. *roten* derris]

rotgut /rótgut/ *n.* inferior whiskey.

rotifer /rótifər/ *n.* any minute aquatic animal of the phylum Rotifera, with rotatory organs used in swimming and feeding. [mod.L *rotiferus* f. L *rota* wheel + -*fer* bearing]

rotisserie /rōtísəree/ *n.* **1** a cooking appliance with a rotating spit for roasting and barbecuing meat. **2** esp. *Brit.* a restaurant, etc., where meat is roasted or barbecued. [F *rôtisserie* (as ROAST)]

rotogravure /rṓtəgrəvyŏor/ *n.* **1** a printing system using a rotary press with intaglio cylinders, usu. running at high speed. **2** a sheet, etc., printed with this system. [G *Rotogravur* (name of a company) assim. to PHOTOGRAVURE]

rotor /rṓtər/ *n.* **1** a rotary part of a machine, esp. in the distributor of an internal-combustion engine. **2** a set of radiating airfoils around a hub on a helicopter, providing lift when rotated. [irreg. for ROTATOR]

rototiller /rṓtətilər/ *n.* a machine with a rotating blade for breaking up or tilling the soil. □□ **rototill** *v.tr.* [propr., ROTARY + TILL³]

rotten /rót'n/ *adj.* (**rottener, rottenest**) **1** rotting or rotted; falling to pieces or liable to break or tear from age or use. **2 a** morally, socially, or politically corrupt. **b** despicable; contemptible. **3** *sl.* **a** disagreeable; unpleasant (*had a rotten time*). **b** (of a plan, etc.) ill-advised, unsatisfactory (*a rotten idea*). **c** disagreeably ill (*feel rotten today*). □ **rotten borough** *hist.* (before 1832) an English borough able to elect an MP though having very few voters. □□ **rottenly** *adv.* **rottenness** *n.* [ME f. ON *rotinn*, rel. to ROT, RET]

■ **1** rotted, decayed, decomposed, rotting, decomposing, putrid, putrescent, putrescing, moldy, moldering, spoiled, mildewy, tainted, festering, bad, off; corroded, deteriorating, disintegrating, crumbling, crumbly, friable; falling to pieces. **2 a** immoral, corrupt, dishonest, deceitful, venal, shameless, degenerate, villainous, heinous, iniquitous, evil, wicked, vile, debased, base, perverted, depraved, unscrupulous, unprincipled, amoral, warped, *sl.* bent. **b** base, despicable, wretched, miserable, horrific, nasty, contemptible, low-down, dirty rotten, mean, low, filthy. **3 a** disagreeable, unpleasant, *colloq.* vile, awful, terrible, horrible, lousy, *sl.* stinking. **b** see UNSATISFACTORY. **c** ill, unwell, off-color, sick.

rottenstone /rót'nstōn/ *n.* decomposed siliceous limestone used as a powder for polishing metals.

rotter /rótər/ *n.* esp. *Brit. sl.* an objectionable, unpleasant, or reprehensible person. [ROT]

■ see WRETCH 2.

Rottweiler /rótwīlər/ *n.* **1** a dog of a tall black-and-tan breed. **2** this breed. [G f. *Rottweil* in SW Germany]

rotund /rōtúnd/ *adj.* **1 a** circular; round. **b** (of a person) large and plump, pudgy. **2** (of speech, literary style, etc.) sonorous, grandiloquent. □□ **rotundity** *n.* **rotundly** *adv.* [L *rotundus* f. *rotare* ROTATE¹]

■ **1 a** round(ed), circular, globular, spherical, *formal* orbicular. **b** chubby, plump, portly, tubby, heavy, fleshy, corpulent, stout, fat, obese, overweight, roly-poly, *Brit.*, podgy, *colloq.* pudgy, *Austral. colloq.* poddy. **2** orotund; grandiloquent, imposing, grand; full, full-toned, deep, resonant, reverberant, reverberating, sonorous, rich, round, mellow; see also POMPOUS 2.

rotunda /rōtúndə/ *n.* **1** a building with a circular ground plan, esp. one with a dome. **2** a circular hall or room. [earlier *rotonda* f. It. *rotonda* (*camera*) round (chamber), fem. of *rotondo* round (as ROTUND)]

rouble var. of RUBLE.

roué /rŏŏ-áy/ *n.* a debauchee, esp. an elderly one; a rake. [F, past part. of *rouer* break on wheel, = one deserving this]

■ playboy, womanizer, rake, lecher, lothario, Don Juan, Casanova, libertine, debauchee, flirt, lady-killer, *sl.* wolf, dirty old man.

rouge /rŏŏzh/ *n. & v.* ● *n.* **1** a red powder or cream used for coloring the cheeks. **2** powdered ferric oxide, etc., as a polishing agent, esp. for metal. ● *v.* **1** *tr.* color with rouge. **2** *intr.* **a** apply rouge to one's cheeks. **b** become red; blush. □ **rouge et noir** /rŏŏzhaynwaár/ a gambling game using a table with red and black marks, on which players place stakes. [F, = red, f. L *rubeus*, rel. to RED]

rough /ruf/ *adj., adv., n., & v.* ● *adj.* **1 a** having an uneven or irregular surface, not smooth or level or polished. **b** *Tennis* applied to the side of a racket from which the twisted gut projects. **2** (of ground, country, etc.) having many bumps,

obstacles, etc. **3 a** hairy; shaggy. **b** (of cloth) coarse in texture. **4 a** (of a person or behavior) not mild nor quiet nor gentle; boisterous; unrestrained (*rough manners*; *rough play*). **b** (of language, etc.) coarse; indelicate. **c** (of wine, etc.) sharp or harsh in taste. **d** (of a sound, the voice, etc.) harsh; discordant; gruff; hoarse. **5** (of the sea, weather, etc.) violent; stormy. **6** disorderly; riotous (*a rough part of town*). **7** harsh; insensitive; inconsiderate (*rough words*; *rough treatment*). **8 a** unpleasant; severe; demanding (*had a rough time*). **b** esp. *Brit.* unfortunate; unreasonable; undeserved (*had rough luck*). **c** (foll. by *on*) hard or unfair toward. **9** lacking finish, elaboration, comfort, etc. (*rough accommodations*; *a rough welcome*). **10** incomplete; rudimentary (*a rough attempt*). **11 a** inexact; approximate; preliminary (*a rough estimate*; *a rough sketch*). **b** (of stationery, etc.) esp. *Brit.* for use in writing rough notes, etc. **12** esp. *Brit. colloq.* **a** ill; unwell (*am feeling rough*). **b** depressed; dejected. ● *adv.* in a rough manner (*the land should be plowed rough*; *play rough*). ● *n.* **1** (usu. prec. by *the*) a hard part or aspect of life; hardship (*take the rough with the smooth*). **2** rough ground (*over rough and smooth*). **3** esp. *Brit.* a rough or violent person (*met a bunch of roughs*). **4** *Golf* rough ground off the fairway between tee and green. **5** an unfinished or provisional or natural state (*have written it in rough*; *shaped from the rough*); a rough draft or sketch. **6** esp. *Brit.* (prec. by *the*) the general way or tendency (*is true in the rough*). ● *v.tr.* **1** (foll. by *up*) ruffle (feathers, hair, etc.) by rubbing against the grain. **2 a** (foll. by *out*) shape or plan roughly. **b** (foll. by *in*) sketch roughly. **3** give the first shaping to (a gun, lens, etc.). □ **rough-and-ready** rough or crude but effective; not elaborate or over-particular. **rough-and-tumble** *adj.* irregular; scrambling; disorderly. ● *n.* a haphazard fight; a scuffle. **rough breathing** see BREATHING. **rough coat** a first coat of plaster applied to a surface. **rough copy 1** esp. *Brit.* = *rough draft*. **2** a copy of a picture, etc. showing only the essential features. **rough deal** hard or unfair treatment. **rough diamond 1** an uncut diamond. **2** (also **diamond in the rough**) a person of good nature but rough manners. **rough draft** a first or original draft (of a story, report, document, etc.). **rough-dry** (**-dries, -dried**) (of clothes) dry without ironing. **the rough edge** (or **side**) **of one's tongue** severe or harsh words. **rough-handle** treat or handle roughly. **rough-hew** (*past part.* **-hewed** or **-hewn**) shape out roughly; give crude form to. **rough-hewn** uncouth; unrefined. **rough it** do without basic comforts. **rough justice** *Brit.* **1** treatment that is approximately fair. **2** treatment that is not at all fair. **rough passage 1** a crossing over rough sea. **2** a difficult time or experience. **rough ride** a difficult time or experience. **rough stuff** *colloq.* boisterous or violent behavior. **rough tongue** *Brit.* a habit of rudeness in speaking. **rough trade** *sl.* a tough or sadistic element among male homosexuals. **rough up** *sl.* treat (a person) with violence; attack violently. **rough work** esp. *Brit.* **1** preliminary or provisional work. **2** *colloq.* violence. **3** a task requiring the use of force. **sleep rough** *Brit.* sleep outdoors, or not in a proper bed. □□ **roughness** *n.* [OE *rūh* f. WG]

■ *adj.* **1** uneven, irregular, coarse, jagged, rugged, bumpy, lumpy. **2** uneven, rugged, broken; see also BUMPY 1. **3 a** see HAIRY 1. **b** see COARSE 1a. **4 a** brusque, bluff, curt, short, abrupt, unpleasant, churlish, discourteous, impolite, ungracious, surly, disrespectful, rude, uncouth, loutish, unrefined, uncivil, uncivilized, uncultured, vulgar, unladylike, ungentlemanly, coarse, ill-mannered, ill-bred; boisterous, unrestrained. **b** see COARSE 2. **d** harsh, grating, cacophonous, discordant, jarring, strident, raucous; rasping, gruff, husky, hoarse; unmusical, esp. *Mus.* inharmonious. **5** agitated, turbulent, choppy,

stormy, storm-tossed, tempestuous, violent, roiled.
6 tough, rough-and-tumble, roughneck; rowdy,
disorderly, riotous. **7** harsh, insensitive, inconsiderate,
violent, unfeeling, unjust, severe, cruel, tough, hard,
brutal, extreme, ungentle. **8 a** hard, tough, severe,
demanding, difficult, arduous, laborious, unpleasant.
b unfair, unjust, bad, tough; unlucky, unfortunate,
unreasonable, undeserved. **9** see RUDE 2. **10** unfinished,
incomplete, uncompleted, imperfect, undeveloped,
unworked, unwrought, unprocessed, unrefined,
unpolished, raw; rudimentary, rough-and-ready, rough-
hewn, *colloq.* sketchy. **11 a** crude, general, estimated,
approximate, inexact, cursory, quick, sketchy, vague,
colloq. ballpark; preliminary, roughcast, shapeless,
formless, unformed. **12 a** see ROTTEN 3c. **b** see
MELANCHOLY adj. ● *adv.* violently, savagely, brutally,
brutishly; see also ROUGHLY 1. ● *n.* **3** rowdy, tough,
hooligan, hoodlum, ruffian, thug, brawler, yahoo,
Austral. larrikin, esp. *Sc. & Austral.* roughie, *colloq.*
roughneck, *sl.* hood, goon, mug, *Brit. sl.* yob. **5** sketch,
(rough) draft, rough copy, mock-up, outline. ● *v.* **2**
sketch, draft, mock up, outline, mark out; trace (out),
block out. □ **rough-and-tumble** (*adj.*) see IRREGULAR
adj. 4, DISORDERLY 1. (*n.*) see BRAWL *n.* **rough draft 1**
rough, esp. *Brit.* rough copy; see also DRAFT *n.* 1.
rough passage rough ride, hard time; see also ORDEAL.
rough ride rough passage, hard time; see also ORDEAL.
rough up beat (up), thrash, attack, batter, assault,
knock about, *colloq.* lambaste. **rough work 2** see
VIOLENCE 1.

roughage /rúfij/ *n.* **1** coarse material with a high fiber content, the part of food that stimulates digestion. **2** coarse fodder. [ROUGH + -AGE 3]

roughcast /rúfkast/ *n., adj.,* & *v.* ● *n.* plaster of lime and
gravel, used on outside walls. ● *adj.* **1** (of a wall, etc.) coated
with roughcast. **2** (of a plan, etc.) roughly formed; preliminary. ● *v.tr.* (*past* and *past part.* **-cast**) **1** coat (a wall) with
roughcast. **2** prepare (a plan, essay, etc.) in outline.
■ *adj.* **2** see ROUGH *adj.* 10, 11a.

roughen /rúfən/ *v.tr.* & *intr.* make or become rough.

roughish /rúfish/ *adj.* somewhat rough.

roughhouse /rúfhows/ *n.* & *v. sl.* ● *n.* a disturbance or row;
boisterous play. ● *v.* **1** *tr.* handle (a person) roughly. **2** *intr.*
make a disturbance; act violently.
■ *n.* boisterousness, rowdiness, rowdyism, violence,
brawling, disorderliness, disorderly conduct,
ruffianism; see also FRACAS. ● *v.* **2** see BRAWL *v.*

roughly /rúflee/ *adv.* **1** in a rough manner. **2** approximately
(*roughly 20 people attended*). □ **roughly speaking** in an approximate sense (*it is, roughly speaking, a square*).
■ **1** harshly, unkindly, severely, sternly,
unsympathetically, brutally, violently, savagely,
inhumanly, mercilessly, unmercifully, ruthlessly,
pitilessly, cruelly, heartlessly; clumsily, rudely, crudely,
awkwardly, primitively, inexpertly, amateurishly,
maladroitly, heavy-handedly, ineptly, inefficiently,
unskillfully. **2** around, around about, about, nearly;
see also *approximately* (APPROXIMATE).

roughneck /rúfnek/ *n. colloq.* **1** a rough or rowdy person. **2**
a worker on a drill rig.
■ **1** see ROUGH *n.* 3.

roughrider /rúfrīdər/ *n.* **1** a person who breaks in or can ride
unbroken horses. **2** (**Rough Rider**) a member of the cavalry
unit in which Theodore Roosevelt fought during the Spanish-American War.

roughshod /rúfshod/ *adj.* (of a horse) having shoes with nail
heads projecting to prevent slipping. □ **ride roughshod
over** treat inconsiderately or arrogantly.

roulade /roolaád/ *n.* **1** a dish cooked or served in the shape
of a roll, esp. a rolled piece of meat with a filling. **2** a florid
passage of runs, etc., in solo vocal music, usu. sung to one
syllable. [F f. *rouler* to roll]

rouleau /roolō/ *n.* (*pl.* **rouleaux** or **rouleaus** /-lōz/) **1** a cylindrical packet of coins. **2** a coil or roll of ribbon, etc., esp.
as trimming. [F f. *rôle* ROLL *n.*]

roulette /roolét/ *n.* **1** a gambling game using a table in which
a ball is dropped on to a revolving wheel with numbered
compartments, players betting on the number at which the
ball comes to rest. **2** *Math.* a curve generated by a point on
a curve rolling on another. **3 a** a revolving toothed wheel
used in engraving. **b** a similar wheel for making perforations
between postage stamps in a sheet. □□ **rouletted** *adj.* (in
sense 3b). [F, dimin. of *rouelle* f. LL *rotella* dimin. of L *rota*
wheel]

round /rownd/ *adj., n., adv., prep.,* & *v.* ● *adj.* **1** shaped like
or approximately like a circle, sphere, or cylinder; having a
convex or circular outline or surface; curved; not angular. **2**
done with or involving circular motion. **3 a** entire; continuous; complete (*a round dozen*); fully expressed or developed; all together; not broken or defective or scanty. **b** (of
a sum of money) considerable. **4** genuine; candid; outspoken; (of a statement, etc.) categorical; unmistakable. **5** (usu.
attrib.) (of a number) expressed for convenience or as an
estimate in fewer significant numerals or with a fraction removed (*spent $297.32, or in round figures $300*). **6 a** (of a
style) flowing. **b** (of a voice) not harsh. **7** *Phonet.* (of a vowel)
pronounced with rounded lips. ● *n.* **1** a round object or
form. **2 a** a revolving motion; a circular or recurring course
(*the earth in its yearly round*). **b** a regular recurring series of
activities or functions (*one's daily round; a continuous round
of pleasure*). **c** a recurring succession or series of meetings
for discussion, etc. (*a new round of talks on disarmament*). **3
a** esp. *Brit.* a fixed route on which things are regularly delivered (*milk round*). **b** a route or sequence by which people
or things are regularly supervised or inspected (*a watchman's
round; a doctor's rounds*). **4** an allowance of something distributed or measured out, esp.: **a** a single provision of
drinks, etc., to each member of a group. **b** ammunition to
fire one shot; the act of firing this. **5 a** esp. *Brit.* a slice across
a loaf of bread. **b** esp. *Brit.* a sandwich made from whole
slices of bread. **c** a thick disk of beef cut from the haunch
as a joint. **6** each of a set or series, a sequence of actions by
each member of a group in turn, esp. **a** one spell of play in
a game, etc. **b** one stage in a competition. **7** *Golf* the playing
of all the holes in a course once. **8** *Archery* a fixed number
of arrows shot from a fixed distance. **9** (**the round**) a form
of sculpture in which the figure stands clear of any ground
(cf. RELIEF 6a). **10** *Mus.* a canon for three or more unaccompanied voices singing at the same pitch or in octaves.
11 (in *pl.*) *Brit. Mil.* **a** a watch that goes around inspecting
sentries. **b** a circuit made by this. **12** a rung of a ladder. **13**
(foll. by *of*) the circumference, bounds, or extent of (*in all
the round of Nature*). ● *adv.* = AROUND *adv.* 5-12. ● *prep.*
= AROUND *prep.* 5-12. ● *v.* **1 a** *tr.* give a round shape to. **b**
intr. assume a round shape. **2** *tr.* double or pass around (a
corner, cape, etc.). **3** *tr.* express (a number) in a less exact
but more convenient form (also foll. by *down* when the number is decreased and *up* when it is increased). **4** *tr.* pronounce (a vowel) with rounded lips. □ **in the round 1** with
all features shown; all things considered. **2** *Theatr.* with the
audience around at least three sides of the stage. **3** (of sculpture) with all sides shown; not in relief. **make the round
of** go around. **make one's rounds** take a customary route
for inspection, etc. **make the rounds** (of news, etc.) be
passed on from person to person, etc. **round about 1** in a
ring (about); all around; on all sides (of). **2** with a change
to an opposite position. **3** approximately (*cost round about
$50*). **round and round** several times around. **round
brackets** *Brit.* = *parentheses* (see PARENTHESIS). **round
dance 1** a dance in which couples move in circles around
the ballroom. **2** a dance in which the dancers form one large
circle. **round down** see sense 3 of *v.* **round off** (or **out**) **1**
bring to a complete or symmetrical or well-ordered state. **2**
smooth out; blunt the corners or angles of. **round out** =
round off 1. **round peg in a square hole** = *square peg in a
round hole* (see PEG). **round robin 1** a petition, esp. with
signatures written in a circle to conceal the order of writing.
2 a tournament in which each competitor plays in turn
against every other. **round-shouldered** with shoulders
bent forward so that the back is rounded. **Round Table** (in

allusion to that at which King Arthur and his knights sat so that none should have precedence) **1** an international charitable association that holds discussions, debates, etc., and undertakes community service. **2** (**round table**) an assembly for discussion, esp. at a conference (often *attrib.*: *round-table talks*). **round trip** a trip to one or more places and back again (esp. by a circular route). **round up** collect or bring together, esp. by going around (see also sense 3 of *v.*). □□ **roundish** *adj.* **roundness** *n.* [ME f. OF *ro(u)nd-* stem of *ro(o)nt, reont* f. L *rotundus* ROTUND]

■ *adj.* **1** circular, disk-shaped, discoid, disklike; ring-shaped, annular, hoop-shaped, hooplike; spherical, ball-shaped, ball-like, globular, spheroid, spheroidal, globe-shaped, globelike, orb-shaped, orblike, *formal* orbicular; curved, curvilinear, rounded, arched. **2** circular, roundabout, circuitous, twisting, spiraling. **3 a** exact, precise, complete, entire, full, continuous. **b** see CONSIDERABLE 1, 2. **4** plain, honest, straightforward, direct, unvarnished, outspoken, candid, genuine, truthful, frank, open, blunt, *colloq.* upfront; categorical, unmistakable. **5** approximate, rough, *colloq.* ballpark; rounded off. **6 a** see FLUENT 1a. **b** rounded, mellow, full, vibrant, reverberant, reverberating, sonorous, rich, mellifluous. ● *n.* **1** circle, disk; ring, hoop, esp. *Math. & Biol.* annulus; ball, sphere, globe, orb, bead. **2 a** see CYCLE *n.* 1a. **c** cycle, series, sequence, succession, bout, spell. **3** circuit, course; beat, tour, turn; see also ROUTE *n.* **4 b** bullet(s), cartridge(s), shell(s), shot(s). **6** heat, stage, level, turn, game, bout. **13** circumference, bounds, extent, scope, compass; see also RANGE *n.* 1a–c. ● *v.* **2** turn, go around; orbit, go around. □ **make the round of** go around, look in on; see also VISIT *v.* 1. **round about 1** see AROUND *adv.* 1, *prep.* 2. **3** see *approximately* (APPROXIMATE). **round off** *or* **out 1** complete, close, end, bring to an end *or* a close, finish. **round up** gather, assemble, muster, draw *or* get *or* bring together, pull together, collect, herd, marshal, corral, wrangle.

roundabout /równdəbowt/ *n. & adj.* ● *n.* **1** *Brit.* = *traffic circle.* **2** *Brit.* = MERRY-GO-ROUND 1. ● *adj.* circuitous; circumlocutory; indirect.

■ *adj.* circuitous, circular, indirect, long; circumlocutory, devious, evasive, oblique.

roundel /równd'l/ *n.* **1** a small disk, esp. a decorative medallion. **2** *Brit.* a circular identifying mark painted on military aircraft, e.g., the red, white, and blue of the RAF. **3** a poem, esp. a modified rondeau, of eleven lines in three stanzas. [ME f. OF *rondel(le)* (as ROUND)]

roundelay /równdilay/ *n.* a short simple song with a refrain. [F *rondelet* (as RONDEL), with assim. to LAY³ or *virelay*]

rounder /równdər/ *n. Brit.* **1** (in *pl.*; treated as *sing.*) a baseball-like game with a bat and ball in which players after hitting the ball run through a round of bases. **2** a complete run of a player through all the bases as a unit of scoring in rounders.

Roundhead /równhed/ *n. hist.* a member of the Parliamentary party in the English Civil War. [f. their custom of wearing the hair cut short]

roundhouse /równdhows/ *n.* **1** a circular repair shed for railroad locomotives, built around a turntable. **2** *sl.* **a** a blow given with a wide sweep of the arm. **b** *Baseball* a pitch made with a sweeping sidearm motion. **3** *hist.* a prison; a place of detention. **4** *Naut.* a cabin or set of cabins on the after part of the quarterdeck, esp. on a sailing ship.

roundly /równdlee/ *adv.* **1** bluntly; in plain language; severely (*was roundly criticized*; *told them roundly that he refused*). **2** in a thoroughgoing manner (*go roundly to work*). **3** in a circular way (*swells out roundly*).

roundsman /równdzmən/ *n.* (*pl.* **-men**) **1** *Brit.* a person on a regular route delivering and taking orders for milk, bread, etc. **2** a police officer in charge of a patrol. **3** *Austral.* a journalist covering a specified subject (*political roundsman*).

roundup /równdup/ *n.* **1** a systematic rounding up of people or things. **2** a summary; a résumé of facts or events.

■ **1** gathering, assembly, rally, collection, herding, corralling, wrangling. **2** summary, synopsis, digest, outline, recapitulation, review, survey, *colloq.* recap.

roundworm /równdwərm/ *n.* a worm, esp. a nematode, with a rounded body.

roup¹ /rowp/ *n. & v. Sc. & No. of Engl.* ● *n.* an auction. ● *v.tr.* sell by auction. [ME 'to shout,' of Scand. orig.]

roup² /ro͞op/ *n.* an infectious poultry disease, esp. of the respiratory tract. □□ **roupy** *adj.* [16th c.: orig. unkn.]

rouse /rowz/ *v.* **1 a** *tr.* (often foll. by *from, out of*) bring out of sleep; wake. **b** *intr.* (often foll. by *up*) cease to sleep; wake up. **2** (often foll. by *up*) **a** *tr.* stir up; make active or excited; startle out of inactivity or confidence or carelessness (*roused them from their complacency*; *was roused to protest*). **b** *intr.* become active. **3** *tr.* provoke to anger (*is terrible when roused*). **4** *tr.* evoke (feelings). **5** *tr.* (usu. foll. by *in, out, up*) *Naut.* haul vigorously. **6** *tr.* startle (game) from a lair or cover. **7** *tr.* stir (liquid, esp. beer while brewing). □ **rouse oneself** esp. *Brit.* overcome one's indolence. □□ **rousable** *adj.* **rouser** *n.* [orig. as a hawking and hunting term, so prob. f. AF: orig. unkn.]

■ **1** arouse; waken, awaken, wake (up), get up; esp. *archaic & poet.* arise. **2 a** stir (up), arouse, stimulate, inspirit, animate, invigorate, prod, prompt, electrify, galvanize, move, excite, fire. **b** see STIR¹ *v.* 2c, 3. **3** provoke, stir (up), goad, incite, work up, fire up. **4** see EVOKE 2. □ **rouse oneself** see STIR¹ *v.* 2c.

rousing /rówzing/ *adj.* **1** exciting; stirring (*a rousing cheer*; *a rousing song*). **2** (of a fire) blazing strongly. □□ **rousingly** *adv.*

■ **1** stimulating, inspiriting, animating, enlivening, energizing, inspiring, invigorating, vitalizing, electrifying, exciting, stirring.

roust /rowst/ *v.tr.* **1** (often foll. by *up, out*) **a** rouse; stir up. **b** root out. **2** *sl.* jostle; harass; rough up. □ **roust around** esp. *Brit.* rummage. [perh. alt. of ROUSE]

roustabout /rówstəbowt/ *n.* **1** a laborer on an oil rig. **2** an unskilled or casual laborer. **3** a dock laborer or deckhand. **4** a circus laborer.

rout¹ /rowt/ *n. & v.* ● *n.* **1 a** a disorderly retreat of defeated troops. **b** a heavy defeat. **2 a** an assemblage or company, esp. of revelers or rioters. **b** *Law* an assemblage of three or more persons who have made a move toward committing an illegal act. **3** riot; tumult; disturbance; clamor; fuss. **4** *Brit. archaic* a large evening party or reception. ● *v.tr.* put to rout. □ **put to rout** put to flight; defeat utterly. [ME f. AF *rute*, OF *route* ult. f. L *ruptus* broken]

■ *n.* **1 a** dispersal, withdrawal; see also RETREAT *n.* 1a. **b** defeat, trouncing, overthrow, subjugation, *literary* vanquishment; debacle, conquest, thrashing, beating, *colloq.* licking, *sl.* shellacking. ● *v.* defeat, win out over, trounce, overthrow, bring down, subjugate, subdue, suppress, conquer, overwhelm, overpower, put to rout *or* flight, worst, beat, crush, destroy, put down, *colloq.* best, lick, wipe the floor with, walk (all) over, *literary* vanquish, *sl.* clobber, *sl.* shellack, skunk.

rout² /rowt/ *v.* **1** *intr. & tr.* = ROOT². **2** *tr.* cut a groove, or any pattern not extending to the edges, in (a wooden or metal surface). □ **rout out** force or fetch out of bed or from a house or a hiding place. [var. of ROOT²]

route /ro͞ot, rowt/ *n. & v.* ● *n.* **1** a way or course taken (esp. regularly) in getting from a starting point to a destination. **2** a round traveled in delivering, selling, or collecting goods. **3** *Mil. archaic* marching orders. ● *v.tr.* send or forward or direct to be sent by a particular route. □ **route march** a training march for troops. [ME f. OF *r(o)ute* road ult. f. L *ruptus* broken]

■ *n.* **1** way, itinerary, course, direction, path, road, avenue. ● *v.* direct, send; see also FORWARD *v.* 1.

/.../ **pronunciation**	● **part of speech**
□ **phrases, idioms, and compounds**	
□□ **derivatives**	■ **synonym section**
cross-references appear in SMALL CAPITALS or *italics*	

routeman /rówtmən/ *n.* a delivery person working on an assigned route.

router /rówtər/ *n.* any of various tools used in routing, including a two-handled plane used in carpentry, a power machine for routing, etc.

routine /roōteén/ *n., adj.,* & *v.* ● *n.* **1** a regular course or procedure, an unvarying performance of certain acts. **2** a set sequence in a performance, esp. a dance, comedy act, etc. **3** *Computing* a sequence of instructions for performing a task. ● *adj.* **1** performed as part of a routine; unvarying; mechanical (*routine duties; a routine job shelling peas*). **2** of a customary or standard kind. ● *v.tr.* organize according to a routine. □□ **routinely** *adv.* [F (as ROUTE)]

■ *n.* **1** procedure, way, method; pattern, practice, drill, formula; ways, customs; program, schedule, plan. **2** act, performance, number, part, *sl.* shtick. ● *adj.* **1** accustomed; regular, ordinary, run-of-the-mill, everyday, unvarying, unchanging, unvaried; programmed, assigned, designated, scheduled; boring, tedious, tiresome, unimaginative, uninteresting; hackneyed, trite, stereotypic(al), clichéd; monotonous, uneventful, automatic, mechanical, perfunctory. **2** customary, habitual, familiar, standard, conventional, usual. ● *v.* routinize.

routinism /roōteénizəm/ *n.* the prevalence of routine. □□ **routinist** *n.* & *adj.*

routinize /roōteéniz, roót'niz/ *v.tr.* subject to a routine; make into a matter of routine. □□ **routinization** *n.*

roux /roō/ *n.* (*pl.* same) a cooked mixture of fat (esp. butter) and flour used in making sauces, etc. [F, = browned (butter): see RUSSET]

rove[1] /rōv/ *v.* & *n.* ● *v.* **1** *intr.* wander without a settled destination; roam; ramble. **2** *intr.* (of eyes) look in changing directions. **3** *tr.* wander over or through. ● *n.* an act of roving (*on the rove*). □ **rove beetle** any long-bodied beetle of the family Staphylinidae, usu. found in decaying animal and vegetable matter. **roving commission** authority given to a person or persons conducting an inquiry to travel as may be necessary. **roving eye** a tendency to ogle or toward infidelity. [ME, orig. a term in archery = shoot at a casual mark with the range not determined, perh. f. dial. *rave* stray, prob. of Scand. orig.]

rove[2] *past* of REEVE[2].

rove[3] /rōv/ *n.* & *v.* ● *n.* a sliver of cotton, wool, etc., drawn out and slightly twisted. ● *v.tr.* form into roves. [18th c.: orig. unkn.]

rove[4] /rōv/ *n.* a small metal plate or ring for a rivet to pass through and be clenched over, esp. in boat building. [ON *ró*, with excrescent *v*]

rover[1] /rōvər/ *n.* **1** a roving person; a wanderer. **2** *Croquet* **a** a ball that has passed through all the wickets but has not yet struck the last peg. **b** a player whose ball is a rover. **3** *Archery* **a** a mark chosen at undetermined range. **b** a mark for long-distance shooting.

■ **1** wanderer, bird of passage, itinerant, traveler, rolling stone, nomad, gypsy, wayfarer, sojourner, drifter, tramp, gadabout, vagabond, vagrant, hobo, *sl.* bum.

rover[2] /rōvər/ *n.* a sea robber, a pirate. [ME f. MLG, MDu. *rōver* f. *rōven* rob, rel. to REAVE]

rover[3] /rōvər/ *n.* a person or machine that makes roves of fiber.

row[1] /rō/ *n.* **1** a number of persons or things in a more or less straight line. **2** a line of seats across a theater, etc. (*in the front row*). **3** a street with a continuous line of houses along one or each side. **4** a line of plants in a field or garden. **5** a horizontal line of entries in a table, etc. □ **a hard** (or **tough**) **row to hoe** a difficult task. **in a row 1** forming a row. **2** *colloq.* in succession (*two Sundays in a row*). **row house** any of a row of houses joined by common sidewalls. [ME *raw, row,* f. OE f. Gmc]

■ **1, 4** line, file, column, rank, string. **2** see TIER. □ **in a row 2** consecutively, one after the other; see also *in succession* (SUCCESSION).

row[2] /rō/ *v.* & *n.* ● *v.* **1** *tr.* propel (a boat) with oars. **2** *tr.*

convey (a passenger) in a boat in this way. **3** *intr.* propel a boat in this way. **4** *tr.* make (a stroke) or achieve (a rate of striking) in rowing. **5** *tr.* compete in (a race) by rowing. **6** *tr.* row a race with. ● *n.* **1** a spell of rowing. **2** an excursion in a rowboat. □ **row down** esp. *Brit.* overtake in a rowing, esp. bumping, race. **rowing boat** *Brit.* = ROWBOAT. **rowing machine** a device for exercising the muscles used in rowing. **row out** exhaust by rowing (*the crew were completely rowed out at the finish*). **row over** esp. *Brit.* complete the course of a boat race with little effort, owing to the absence or inferiority of competitors. □□ **rower** *n.* [OE *rōwan* f. Gmc, rel. to RUDDER, L *remus* oar]

row[3] /row/ *n.* & *v. colloq.* ● *n.* **1** a loud noise or commotion. **2** a fierce quarrel or dispute. **3 a** a severe reprimand. **b** the condition of being reprimanded (*shall get into a row*). ● *v.* **1** *intr.* make or engage in a row. **2** *tr.* reprimand. □ **make** (or **kick up**) **a row 1** raise a noise. **2** make a vigorous protest. [18th-c. sl.: orig. unkn.]

■ *n.* **1** commotion, disturbance, clamor, hubbub, racket, din, tumult, uproar, brouhaha, fuss, stir, turmoil, hullabaloo, ruckus, *colloq.* rumpus. **2** altercation, argument, dispute, quarrel, disagreement, squabble, tiff, conflict, fracas, falling-out, *colloq.* shouting match, scrap, *US colloq.* spat. ● *v.* **1** dispute, quarrel, argue, disagree, wrangle, cross swords, have words, bicker, tiff, fall out. **2** see REPRIMAND *v.* □ **make** (or **kick up**) **a row 2** see PROTEST *v.* 1.

rowan /rōən, rów-/ *n.* **1** the mountain ash. **2** a similar tree, *Sorbus americana,* native to N. America. **3** (also **rowanberry**) the scarlet berry of either of these trees. [Scand., corresp. to Norw. *rogn, raun,* Icel. *reynir*]

rowboat /rōbōt/ *n.* a small boat propelled by oars.

rowdy /rówdee/ *adj.* & *n.* ● *adj.* (**rowdier, rowdiest**) noisy and disorderly. ● *n.* (*pl.* **-ies**) a rowdy person. □□ **rowdily** *adv.* **rowdiness** *n.* **rowdyism** *n.* [19th-c. US, orig. = lawless backwoodsman: orig. unkn.]

■ *adj.* boisterous, uproarious, disorderly, noisy, loud, obstreperous, unruly. ● *n.* ruffian, tough, hooligan, yahoo, brawler, lout, hoodlum, hood. □□ **rowdyism** rowdiness, ruffianism, hooliganism, roughhouse, barbarism, troublemaking, brawling, unruliness, boisterousness.

rowel /rówəl/ *n.* & *v.* ● *n.* **1** a spiked revolving disk at the end of a spur. **2** a circular piece of leather, etc., with a hole in the center inserted under a horse's skin to promote drainage of an infection. ● *v.tr.* **1** urge with a rowel. **2** insert a rowel in. [ME f. OF *roel(e)* f. LL *rotella* dimin. of L *rota* wheel]

rowen /rówən/ *n.* (in *sing.* or *pl.*) a season's second growth of hay or grass; an aftermath. [ME f. OF *regain* (as GAIN)]

rowlock /rōlok, also rōlək, rúlək/ *n. Brit.* = OARLOCK.

royal /róyəl/ *adj.* & *n.* ● *adj.* **1** of or suited to or worthy of a king or queen. **2** in the service or under the patronage of a king or queen. **3** belonging to the king or queen (*the royal hands; the royal anger*). **4** of the family of a king or queen. **5** kingly; majestic; stately; splendid. **6** on a great scale; of exceptional size or quality; first-rate (*gave us royal entertainment; had a royal time*). ● *n.* **1** *colloq.* a member of the royal family. **2** a royal sail or mast. **3** a royal stag. **4** a size of paper, about 620 × 500 mm (25 × 20 in.). □ **Royal Air Force** the British air force. **royal assent** see ASSENT. **royal blue** a deep vivid blue. **royal family** the family to which a sovereign belongs. **royal fern** a fern, *Osmunda regalis,* with huge spreading fronds. **royal flush** see FLUSH[3]. **royal jelly** a substance secreted by honeybee workers and fed by them to future queen bees. **Royal Marine** a British marine (see MARINE *n.* 2). **royal mast** a mast above a topgallant mast. **Royal Navy** the British navy. **royal plural** *Brit.* the first person plural "we" used by a single person. **royal road to** *Brit.* way of attaining without trouble. **royal sail** a sail above a topgallant sail. **Royal Society** (in full **Royal Society of London**) a society founded in 1662 to promote scientific discussion. **royal stag** esp. *Brit.* a stag with a head of 12 or more points. **royal standard** a banner bearing royal heraldic arms. **royal tennis** = *court tennis.* □□ **royally** *adv.* [ME f. OF *roial* f. L *regalis* REGAL]

■ *adj.* **1, 3** see SOVEREIGN *adj.* **4. 5** stately, queenly, kingly, queenlike, kinglike, regal, imperial, sovereign, princely; see also MAJESTIC. **6** grand, splendid, stately, impressive, august, imposing, superior, superb, magnificent, majestic; first-rate.

royalist /róyəlist/ *n.* **1 a** a supporter of monarchy. **b** *hist.* a supporter of the royal side in the English Civil War. **2** *hist.* a loyalist in the American Revolution. □□ **royalism** *n.*

royalty /róyəltee/ *n.* (*pl.* **-ies**) **1** the office or dignity or power of a king or queen; sovereignty. **2 a** royal persons. **b** a member of a royal family. **3** a sum paid to a patentee for the use of a patent or to an author, etc., for each copy of a book, etc., sold or for each public performance of a work. **4 a** a royal right (now esp. over minerals) granted by the sovereign to an individual or corporation. **b** a payment made by a producer of minerals, oil, or natural gas to the owner of the site or of the mineral rights over it. [ME f. OF *roialté* (as ROYAL)]

■ **1** see *sovereignty* (SOVEREIGN). **3** percentage, commission, share, payment, compensation.

rozzer /rózər/ *n.* Brit. *sl.* a policeman. [19th c.: orig. unkn.]

■ see *police officer.*

RP *abbr.* Brit. received pronunciation.

r.p.m. *abbr.* revolutions per minute.

rps *abbr.* (also **r.p.s.**) revolutions per second.

RR *abbr.* **1** railroad. **2** rural route.

RS *abbr.* (in the UK) Royal Society.

Rs. *abbr.* rupee(s).

RSA *abbr.* Republic of South Africa.

RSFSR *abbr. hist.* Russian Soviet Federated Socialist Republic.

RSV *abbr.* Revised Standard Version (of the Bible).

RSVP *abbr.* (in an invitation, etc.) please answer. [F *répondez s'il vous plaît*]

RT *abbr.* **1** radio telegraphy. **2** radio telephony.

rt. *abbr.* right.

rte. *abbr.* route.

Rt. Hon. *abbr.* Right Honorable.

Rt. Revd. *abbr.* (also **Rt. Rev.**) Right Reverend.

Ru *symb. Chem.* the element ruthenium.

rub[1] /rub/ *v. & n.* ● *v.* (**rubbed, rubbing**) **1** *tr.* move one's hand or another object with firm pressure over the surface of. **2** *tr.* (usu. foll. by *against, in, on, over*) apply (one's hand, etc.) in this way. **3** *tr.* clean or polish or make dry or bare by rubbing. **4** *tr.* (often foll. by *over*) apply (polish, ointment, etc.) by rubbing. **5** *tr.* (foll. by *in, into, through*) use rubbing to make (a substance) go into or through something. **6** *tr.* (often foll. by *together*) move or slide (objects) against each other. **7** *intr.* (foll. by *against, on*) move with contact or friction. **8** *tr.* chafe or make sore by rubbing. **9** *intr.* (of cloth, skin, etc.) become frayed or worn or sore or bare with friction. **10** *tr.* reproduce the design of (a sepulchral brass or stone, etc.) by rubbing paper laid on it with heelball or colored chalk, etc. **11** *tr.* (foll. by *to*) reduce to powder, etc., by rubbing. ● *n.* **1** a spell or an instance of rubbing (*give it a rub*). **2 a** an impediment or difficulty (*there's the rub*). **b** an inequality of the ground impeding or diverting a bowl in lawn bowling; the diversion or hindering of a bowl by this. □ **rub along** Brit. *colloq.* cope or manage without undue difficulty. **rub away** remove by rubbing. **rub elbows with** associate or come into contract with (another person), esp. socially. **rub one's hands** esp. Brit. rub one's hands together usu. in sign of keen satisfaction, or for warmth. **rub it in** (or **rub a person's nose in it**) emphasize or repeat an embarrassing fact, etc. **rub noses** rub one's nose against another's in greeting. **rub off 1** (usu. foll. by *on*) be transferred by contact; be transmitted (*some of his attitudes have rubbed off on me*). **2** remove by rubbing. **rub of** (or **on**) **the green** Golf an accidental interference with the course or position of a ball. **rub on** Brit. *colloq.* = *rub along.* **rub out 1** erase with an eraser. **2** *sl.* kill; eliminate. **rub shoulders with** = *rub elbows with.* **rub up** Brit. **1** polish (a tarnished object). **2** brush up (a subject or one's memory). **3** mix (pig-

ment, etc.) into paste by rubbing. **rub-up** *n.* Brit. the act or an instance of rubbing up. **rub the wrong way** irritate or repel as by stroking a cat against the lie of its fur. [ME *rubben*, perh. f. LG *rubben*, of unkn. orig.]

■ *v.* **1** massage, knead, smooth, stroke. **3** scour, scrub, clean; wipe, polish, shine, buff, burnish. **4** apply, smooth, smear, spread, put. **5** (*rub in* or *into* or *through*) smooth in or into, spread in or into or through. **8** see CHAFE *v.* 1. **9** wear (down), chafe, abrade, erode; see also FRAY[1]. ● *n.* **1** wipe, stroke, rubbing, rubdown, massage. **2 a** hindrance, obstacle, impediment, difficulty, problem, trouble; catch, hitch, snag. □ **rub away** see ERODE. **rub elbows with** associate with, socialize with, hobnob with, mix with, fraternize with, keep company with, consort with, Brit. **rub shoulders with**, *colloq.* run or pal or chum around with. **rub it in** (or **rub a person's nose in it**) keep going on about it, make an issue of it, harp on it, dwell on it. **rub off 1** be passed on or along, be transferred, be transmitted or communicated or imparted; (*rub off on*) affect. **2** erase, remove, delete, eliminate, eradicate. **rub out 1** erase, efface, remove, *colloq.* scrub. **2** see KILL *v.* 1a. **rub up 2** brush up, refresh; see also STUDY *v.* 1, 3. **rub the wrong way** annoy, irritate, irk, provoke, anger, stroke a person (*or* a person's hair) the wrong way, *colloq.* get under a person's skin, peeve, *sl.* bug.

rub[2] /rub/ *n.* = RUBBER[2]. [abbr.]

rub-a-dub / rúbədub/ *n. & v.* ● *n.* **1** the rolling sound of a drum. **2** (also **rub-a-dub-dub**) Austral. *rhyming sl.* a pub. ● *v.intr.* (**rub-a-dubbed, rub-a-dubbing**) make this sound. [imit.]

rubato /rōōbaátō/ *adj. & n.* Mus. ● *n.* (*pl.* **-os** or **rubati** /-tee/) the temporary disregarding of strict tempo. ● *adj.* performed with a flexible tempo. [It., = robbed]

rubber[1] /rúbər/ *n.* **1** a tough elastic polymeric substance made from the latex of plants or synthetically. **2** esp. Brit. a piece of this or another substance for erasing pencil or ink marks. **3** *colloq.* a condom. **4** (in *pl.*) galoshes. **5** a person who rubs; a masseur or masseuse. **6 a** an implement used for rubbing. **b** part of a machine operating by rubbing. □ **rubber band** a loop of rubber for holding papers, etc., together. **rubber plant 1** an evergreen plant, *Ficus elastica*, with dark-green shiny leaves, often cultivated as a houseplant. **2** (also **rubber tree**) any of various tropical trees yielding latex, esp. *Hevea brasiliensis.* **rubber stamp 1** a device for inking and imprinting on a surface. **2 a** a person who mechanically copies or agrees to others' actions. **b** an indication of such agreement. **rubber-stamp** *v.tr.* **1** use a rubber stamp. **2** approve automatically without proper consideration. □□ **rubbery** *adj.* **rubberiness** *n.* [RUB[1] + -ER[1], from its early use to rub out pencil marks]

■ □□ **rubbery** see YIELDING 2. **rubberiness** see *elasticity* (ELASTIC).

rubber[2] /rúbər/ *n.* **1** a match of three or five successive games between the same sides or persons at whist, bridge, tennis, etc. **2** (prec. by *the*) **a** the act of winning two games in a rubber. **b** a third game when each side has won one. [orig. unkn.: used as a term in lawn bowling from *c.* 1600]

rubberize /rúbəriz/ *v.tr.* treat or coat with rubber.

rubberneck /rúbərnek/ *n. & v. colloq.* ● *n.* a person, esp. a tourist, who stares inquisitively or stupidly. ● *v.intr.* act in this way.

■ *n.* tourist, sightseer, rubbernecker, out-of-towner.

● *v.* gape, stare, goggle, gawk.

rubbing /rúbing/ *n.* **1** in senses of RUB[1] *v.* **2** an impression or copy made by rubbing (see RUB[1] *v.* 10). □ **rubbing alcohol** an isopropyl alcohol solution for external application.

■ **1** see FRICTION 1.

rubbish /rúbish/ *n. & v.* ● *n.* esp. Brit. **1** waste material;

/.../ **pronunciation**	● **part of speech**
□ **phrases, idioms, and compounds**	
□□ **derivatives**	■ **synonym section**
cross-references appear in SMALL CAPITALS or *italics*

debris; refuse; litter. **2** worthless material or articles; junk. **3** (often as *int.*) absurd ideas or suggestions; nonsense. ● *v.tr. Brit. colloq.* **1** criticize severely. **2** reject as worthless. □□ **rubbishy** *adj.* [ME f. AF *rubbous*, etc., perh. f. RUBBLE] ■ *n.* **1** refuse, waste, litter, garbage, dross, sweepings, offal; debris, detritus, trash, *Austral. or dial.* mullock, *sl.* dreck. **2** junk, rejects, dregs, lees, scraps, fragments, leftovers, remnants, leavings, trash. **3** (stuff and) nonsense, balderdash, moonshine, gibberish, bunkum, garbage, trash, *colloq.* gobbledegook, flapdoodle, piffle, malarkey, hogwash, esp. *Brit. colloq.* tosh, gammon, *sl.* tommy-rot, twaddle, rot, bosh, hooey, bunk, baloney, poppycock, eyewash, bilgewater, bull, hokum, *Brit. sl.* codswallop, cobblers. ● *v.* **1** criticize, attack, bad-mouth, *colloq.* pan, jump on, *colloq.* trash, *sl.* clobber.

rubble /rúbəl/ *n.* **1** waste or rough fragments of stone or brick, etc. **2** pieces of undressed stone used, esp. as fill, for walls. **3** *Geol.* loose angular stones, etc., as the covering of some rocks. **4** water-worn stones. □□ **rubbly** *adj.* [ME *robyl*, *rubel*, of uncert. orig.: cf. OF *robe* spoils] ■ **1** debris.

rube /rōōb/ *n. colloq.* a country bumpkin. [abbr. of the name *Reuben*] ■ see PEASANT.

Rube Goldberg /rōōb góldbərg/ *adj.* unnecessarily or comically complex in design. [for US cartoonist (1883–1970) noted for such drawings]

rubella /rōōbélə/ *n. Med.* an acute infectious viral disease with a red rash; German measles. [mod.L, neut. pl. of L *rubellus* reddish]

rubellite /rōōbəlit/ *n.* a red variety of tourmaline. [L *rubellus* reddish]

rubeola /rōōbeeólə, -beeélə/ *n. Med.* measles. [med.L f. L *rubeus* red]

Rubicon /rōōbikon/ *n.* a boundary which once crossed betokens irrevocable commitment; a point of no return. [the ancient name of a stream forming the boundary of Julius Caesar's province and crossed by him in 49 BC as the start of a war with Pompey]

rubicund /rōōbikund/ *adj.* (of a face, complexion, or person in these respects) ruddy; high-colored. □□ **rubicundity** /-kúnditee/ *n.* [F *rubicond* or L *rubicundus* f. *rubēre* be red] ■ see ROSY 1.

rubidium /rōōbídeeəm/ *n. Chem.* a soft silvery element occurring naturally in various minerals and as the radioactive isotope rubidium-87. ¶ Symb.: **Rb**. [L *rubidus* red (with ref. to its spectral lines)]

rubify /rōōbifi/ *v.tr.* (**-ies, -ied**) **1** make red. **2** *Med.* (of a counterirritant) stimulate (the skin, etc.) to redness. □□ **rubefacient** /-fáyshənt/ *adj. & n.* **rubefaction** /-fákshən/ *n.* [ME f. OF *rubifier*, *rubefier* f. med.L *rubificare* f. L *rubefacere* f. *rubeus* red]

rubiginous /rōōbíjinəs/ *adj. formal* rust-colored. [L *rubiginis* rust]

ruble /rōōbəl/ *n.* (also **rouble**) the chief monetary unit of Russia, the USSR (*hist.*), and some other former republics of the USSR. [F f. Russ. *rubl'*]

rubric /rōōbrik/ *n.* **1** a direction for the conduct of divine service inserted in a liturgical book. **2** a heading or passage in red or special lettering. **3** explanatory words. **4** an established custom. □□ **rubrical** *adj.* [ME f. OF *rubrique*, *rubrice* or L *rubrica* (*terra*) red (earth or ocher) as writing material, rel. to *rubeus* red]

rubricate /rōōbrikayt/ *v.tr.* **1** mark with red; print or write in red. **2** provide with rubrics. □□ **rubrication** /-káyshən/ *n.* **rubricator** *n.* [L *rubricare* f. *rubrica*: see RUBRIC]

ruby /rōōbee/ *n., adj., & v.* ● *n.* (*pl.* **-ies**) **1** a rare precious stone consisting of corundum with a color varying from deep crimson or purple to pale rose. **2** a glowing, purple-tinged red color. ● *adj.* of this color. ● *v.tr.* (**-ies, -ied**) dye or tinge ruby color. □ **ruby anniversary** the fortieth anniversary of a wedding. **ruby glass** glass colored with oxides of copper, iron, lead, tin, etc. **ruby-throated hummingbird** a hummingbird of eastern N. America, *Archilochus colubris*, the male of which has a bright red throat. [ME

f. OF *rubi* f. med.L *rubinus* (*lapis*) red (stone), rel. to L *rubeus* red]

ruche /rōōsh/ *n.* a frill or gathering of lace, etc., as a trimming. □□ **ruched** *adj.* **ruching** *n.* [F f. med.L *rusca* tree bark, of Celt. orig.] ■ see RUFFLE *n.* 1.

ruck[1] /ruk/ *n.* **1** (prec. by *the*) the main body of competitors not likely to overtake the leaders. **2** an undistinguished crowd of persons or things. [ME, = stack of fuel, heap, rick: app. Scand., = Norw. *ruka* in the same senses]

ruck[2] /ruk/ *v. & n.* ● *v.tr. & intr.* (often foll. by *up*) make or become creased or wrinkled. ● *n.* a crease or wrinkle. [ON *hrukka*] ■ *v.* see PUCKER *v.* ● *n.* see PUCKER *n.*

rucksack /rúksak, rōōk-/ = BACKPACK *n.* [G f. *rucken* dial. var. of *Rücken* back + *Sack* SACK[1]] ■ pack, backpack, knapsack, haversack.

ruckus /rúkəs/ *n.* esp. a fracas or commotion. [cf. RUCTION, RUMPUS] ■ see ROW[3] *n.* 1.

ruction /rúkshən/ *n. colloq.* **1** a disturbance or tumult. **2** (in *pl.*) unpleasant arguments or reactions. [19th c.: orig. unkn.] ■ **1** see DISTURBANCE 2. **2** (*ructions*) see TROUBLE *n.* 5, 6.

rudbeckia /rudbékeeə/ *n.* a composite garden plant of the genus *Rudbeckia*, native to N. America. [mod.L f. O. *Rudbeck*, Sw. botanist d. 1740]

rudd /rud/ *n.* (*pl.* same) a red-finned freshwater fish, *Scardinius erythrophthalmus*, of the carp family. [app. rel. to *rud* red color f. OE *rudu*, rel. to RED]

rudder /rúdər/ *n.* **1 a** a flat piece hinged vertically to the stern of a ship for steering. **b** a vertical airfoil pivoted from the horizontal stabilizer of an aircraft, for controlling its horizontal movement. **2** a guiding principle, etc. □□ **rudderless** *adj.* [OE *rōther* f. WG *rōthra-* f. the stem of ROW[2]]

ruddle var. of RADDLE.

ruddock /rúdək/ *n. dial.* the robin redbreast. [OE *rudduc* (as RUDDLE)]

ruddy /rúdee/ *adj. & v.* ● *adj.* (**ruddier, ruddiest**) **1 a** (of a person or complexion) freshly or healthily red. **b** (of health, youth, etc.) marked by this. **2** reddish. **3** *Brit. colloq.* bloody; damnable. ● *v.tr. & intr.* (**-ies, -ied**) make or grow ruddy. □□ **ruddily** *adv.* **ruddiness** *n.* [OE *rudig* (as RUDD)] ■ *adj.* 1a, 2 see ROSY 1.

rude /rōōd/ *adj.* **1** (of a person, remark, etc.) impolite or offensive. **2** roughly made or done; lacking subtlety or accuracy (*a rude shelter*). **3** primitive or uneducated (*rude chaos; rude simplicity*). **4** abrupt; sudden; startling; violent (*a rude awakening; a rude reminder*). **5** *colloq.* indecent; lewd (*a rude joke*). **6** esp. *Brit.* vigorous or hearty (*rude health*). □ **be rude to** speak impolitely to; insult. □□ **rudely** *adv.* **rudeness** *n.* **rudery** *n.* **rudish** *adj.* [ME f. OF f. L *rudis* unwrought] ■ **1** impolite, impertinent, impudent, discourteous, unmannerly, ungentlemanly, unladylike, ungallant, ungracious, unceremonious; insulting, insolent, offensive, saucy, bold, disrespectful, uncivil, flippant, brusque, curt, gruff, tactless, outrageous, *colloq.* fresh; ill-mannered, bad-mannered, ill-bred, uncouth, rough, boorish, churlish, oafish, loutish. **2** crude, rough, clumsy, awkward, unskillful, unskilled, artless, inartistic, imperfect, unpolished, inaccurate, raw, inelegant, makeshift, homespun, primitive, unfinished, simple, basic, bare. **3** primitive, uneducated, coarse, unrefined, unpolished; uncivilized, uncultured; plain, unsophisticated. **4** sudden, startling, violent; see also ABRUPT 1. **5** naughty, unrefined, ribald, bawdy, indecent, indelicate, vulgar, obscene, dirty, filthy, lubricious, lewd, gross, smutty, taboo, pornographic. **6** see VIGOROUS 2.

ruderal /rōōdərəl/ *adj. & n.* ● *adj.* (of a plant) growing on or in rubbish or rubble. ● *n.* a ruderal plant. [mod.L *ruderalis* f. L *rudera* pl. of *rudus* rubble]

rudiment /rōōdimənt/ *n.* **1** (in *pl.*) the elements or first principles of a subject. **2** (in *pl.*) an imperfect beginning of something undeveloped or yet to develop. **3** a part or organ imperfectly developed as being vestigial or having no function (e.g., the breast in males). [F *rudiment* or L *rudimentum* (as RUDE, after *elementum* ELEMENT)]

■ **1** (*rudiments*) basics, elements, essentials, fundamentals, first principles.

rudimentary /ro͞odiméntəree/ *adj.* **1** involving basic principles; fundamental. **2** incompletely developed; vestigial. □□ **rudimentarily** /-mentáirəlee, -méntərilee/ *adv.* **rudimentariness** /-méntəreenis, -méntreenis/ *n.*

■ **1** basic, essential, elementary, fundamental, primary, introductory, first, elemental, primal. **3** unshaped, unfinished, imperfect, primitive, undeveloped; primordial, immature, embryonic; seminal, vestigial.

rue[1] /ro͞o/ *v. & n.* ● *v.tr.* (**rues, rued, ruing**) repent of; bitterly feel the consequences of; wish to be undone or nonexistent (esp. *rue the day*). ● *n. archaic* **1** repentance; dejection at some occurrence. **2** compassion or pity. [OE *hrēow, hrēowan*]

■ *v.* see REGRET *v.* ● *n.* **1** see REGRET *n.*

rue[2] /ro͞o/ *n.* a perennial evergreen shrub, *Ruta graveolens*, with bitter strong-scented leaves formerly used in medicine. [ME f. OF f. L *ruta* f. Gk *rhutē*]

rueful /ro͞ofo͞ol/ *adj.* expressing sorrow, genuine or humorously affected. □□ **ruefully** *adv.* **ruefulness** *n.* [ME, f. RUE[1]]

■ see REGRETFUL. □□ **ruefully** see *sadly* (SAD). **ruefulness** see REGRET *n.*

rufescent /ro͞ofésənt/ *adj. Zool.*, etc., reddish. □□ **rufescence** *n.* [L *rufescere* f. *rufus* reddish]

ruff[1] /ruf/ *n.* **1** a projecting starched frill worn around the neck, esp. in the 16th c. **2** a projecting or conspicuously colored ring of feathers or hair around a bird's or animal's neck. **3** a domestic pigeon like a jacobin. **4** (*fem.* **reeve** /reev/) a wading bird, *Philomachus pugnax*, of which the male has a ruff and ear tufts in the breeding season. □□ **rufflike** *adj.* [perh. f. *ruff* = ROUGH]

■ **1** see RUFFLE *n.* 1.

ruff[2] /ruf/ *n.* (also **ruffe**) any of various fish, esp. a perchlike freshwater fish, *Gymnocephalus cernua*, found in European lakes and rivers. [ME, prob. f. ROUGH]

ruff[3] /ruf/ *v. & n.* ● *v.intr. & tr.* trump at cards. ● *n.* an act of ruffing. [orig. the name of a card game: f. OF *roffle, rouffle*, = It. *ronfa* (perh. alt. of *trionfo* TRUMP[1])]

ruffian /rúfeeən/ *n.* a violent, lawless person. □□ **ruffianism** *n.* **ruffianly** *adv.* [F *ruf(f)ian* f. It. *ruffiano*, perh. f. dial. *rofia* scurf]

■ see THUG.

ruffle /rúfəl/ *v. & n.* ● *v.* **1** *tr.* disturb the smoothness or tranquillity of. **2** *tr.* upset the calmness of (a person). **3** *tr.* gather (lace, etc.) into a ruffle. **4** *tr.* (often foll. by *up*) (of a bird) erect (its feathers) in anger, display, etc. **5** *intr.* undergo ruffling. **6** *intr.* lose smoothness or calmness. ● *n.* **1** an ornamental gathered or goffered frill of lace, etc., worn at the opening of a garment esp. around the wrist, breast, or neck. **2** perturbation; bustle. **3** a rippling effect on water. **4** the ruff of a bird, etc. (see RUFF[1] 2). **5** *Mil.* a vibrating drumbeat. [ME: orig. unkn.]

■ *v.* **1** see DISTURB 1. **2** agitate, disconcert, confuse, discompose, discomfit, upset, disturb, stir up, perturb, unsettle, disorient, unnerve, fluster, affect, bother, put out, vex, shake up, trouble, worry, *colloq.* rattle, throw, *joc.* discombobulate, *sl.* get (a person) all shook up; (*ruffled*) unstrung. **6** see FRET[1] *v.* 1a. ● *n.* **1** trimming, flounce, frill, ruff, ruche, ruching. **2** perturbation, bustle, flurry; see also STIR[1] *n.* 2. **3** ripple, disturbance, undulation, riffle.

rufous /ro͞ofəs/ *adj.* (esp. of animals) reddish-brown. [L *rufus* red, reddish]

rug /rug/ *n.* **1** a floor covering of shaggy material or thick pile. **2** esp. *Brit.* a thick woolen coverlet or wrap. □ **pull the rug (out) from under** deprive of support; weaken; unsettle. [prob. f. Scand.: cf. Norw. dial. *rugga* coverlet, Sw. *rugg* ruffled hair: rel. to RAG[1]]

rugby /rúgbee/ *n.* (also **Rugby football**) a team game played with an oval ball that may be kicked, carried, and passed from hand to hand. [*Rugby* School in S. England, where it was first played]

rugged /rúgid/ *adj.* **1** (of ground or terrain) having a rough uneven surface. **2** (of features) strongly marked; irregular in outline. **3 a** unpolished; lacking gentleness or refinement (*rugged grandeur*). **b** harsh in sound. **c** austere; unbending (*rugged honesty*). **d** involving hardship (*a rugged life*). **4** (esp. of a machine) robust; sturdy. □□ **ruggedly** *adv.* **ruggedness** *n.* [ME, prob. f. Scand.: cf. RUG, and Sw. *rugga*, roughen]

■ **1** rough, uneven, broken, irregular, bumpy, jagged. **2** craggy, strong; irregular. **3 a** rude, uncouth, uncultured, uncivilized, unrefined, unpolished, crude, ungraceful, churlish. **b** see STRIDENT. **c** austere, unbending; see also DOUR. **d** tough, rough, severe, hard, harsh, difficult, arduous, Spartan, austere, rigorous, onerous, stern, demanding, burdensome. **4** hardy, durable, strong, sturdy, hale, robust, tough, vigorous, hard, stalwart.

rugger /rúgər/ *n. Brit. colloq.* rugby.

rugose /ro͞ogōs/ *adj.* esp. *Biol.* wrinkled; corrugated. □□ **rugosely** *adv.* **rugosity** /-gósitee/ *n.* [L *rugosus* f. *ruga* wrinkle]

ruin /ro͞oin/ *n. & v.* ● *n.* **1** a destroyed or wrecked state (*after centuries of neglect, the palace fell to ruin*). **2 a** a person's or thing's downfall or elimination (*the ruin of my hopes*). **b** *archaic* a woman's loss of chastity by seduction or rape; dishonor resulting from this. **3 a** the complete loss of one's property or position (*bring to ruin*). **b** a person who has suffered ruin. **4** (in *sing.* or *pl.*) the remains of a building, etc., that has suffered ruin (*an old ruin; ancient ruins*). **5** a cause of ruin; a destructive thing or influence (*will be the ruin of us*). ● *v.* **1** *tr.* a bring to ruin (*your extravagance has ruined me*). **b** utterly impair or wreck (*the rain ruined my hat*). **c** *archaic* seduce and abandon (a woman). **2** *tr.* (esp. as **ruined** *adj.*) reduce to ruins. **3** *intr. poet.* fall headlong or with a crash. □ **in ruins 1** in a state of ruin. **2** completely wrecked (*their hopes were in ruins*). [ME f. OF *ruine* f. L *ruina* f. *ruere* fall]

■ *n.* **1** see DESTRUCTION 1. **2 a** downfall, destruction, collapse, fall, devastation, undoing, breakdown, breakup, debacle, disintegration, ruination, dissolution, wiping out, failure, decay, end, defeat, overthrow; elimination, liquidation. **b** degradation, dishonor, debasement, defilement; seduction, violation, defloration. **3 a** bankruptcy, penury, insolvency; see also DOWNFALL. **4** wreck; (*ruins*) debris, fragments, rubble, remains. **5** nemesis, curse, end, bane. ● *v.* **1** bring to ruin, undo, reduce to nothing, crush, *archaic or literary* reduce to naught; pauperize, impoverish, reduce to penury *or* poverty *or* destitution. **b** spoil, damage, mess up, make a mess of, mar, destroy, wreck, damage, harm, hurt, impair, *Austral.* euchre; poison, put the kibosh on, botch, *sl.* louse up, screw up, *Brit. sl.* scupper; disfigure, uglify. **c** violate, deflower, ravish, seduce, lead astray, defile, debase, *archaic* dishonor. **2** destroy, devastate, demolish, annihilate, wipe out, lay waste, raze, wreck, flatten, reduce to nothing, pulverize. □ **in ruins 1** see DILAPIDATED. **2** see UNDONE 3.

ruination /ro͞oináyshən/ *n.* **1** the act of bringing to ruin. **2** the act of ruining or the state of being ruined. [obs. *ruinate* (as RUIN)]

■ see RUIN *n.* 2a.

ruinous /ro͞oinəs/ *adj.* **1** bringing ruin; disastrous (*at ruinous expense*). **2** in ruins; dilapidated. □□ **ruinously** *adv.* **ruinousness** *n.* [ME f. L *ruinosus* (as RUIN)]

■ **1** disastrous, destructive, catastrophic, calamitous, deleterious, pernicious, crippling, baleful, fatal, noxious, harmful, injurious, nasty, baneful. **2** see DILAPIDATED.

/. . ./ **pronunciation**	● **part of speech**
□ **phrases, idioms, and compounds**	
□□ **derivatives**	■ **synonym section**
cross-references appear in SMALL CAPITALS or *italics*	

rule /rool/ n. & v. ● n. **1** a principle to which an action conforms or is required to conform. **2** a prevailing custom or standard; the normal state of things. **3** government or dominion (*under British rule*; *the rule of law*). **4** a graduated straight measure used in carpentry, etc.; a ruler. **5** *Printing* **a** a thin strip of metal for separating headings, columns, etc. **b** a thin line or dash. **6** a code of discipline of a religious order. **7** *Law* an order made by a judge or court with reference to a particular case only. ● v. **1** tr. exercise decisive influence over; keep under control. **2** tr. & (often foll. by *over*) intr. have sovereign control of (*rules over a vast kingdom*). **3** tr. (often foll. by *that* + clause) pronounce authoritatively (*was ruled out of order*). **4** tr. **a** make parallel lines across (paper). **b** make (a straight line) with a ruler, etc. **5** intr. (of prices or goods, etc., in regard to price or quality, etc.) have a specified general level; be for the most part (*the market ruled high*). **6** tr. (in *passive*; foll. by *by*) consent to follow (advice, etc.); be guided by. □ **as a rule** usually; more often than not. **by rule** in a regulation manner; mechanically. **rule of the road** see ROAD¹. **rule of three** a method of finding a number in the same ratio to one given as exists between two others given. **rule of thumb** a rule for general guidance, based on experience or practice rather than theory. **rule out** exclude; pronounce irrelevant or ineligible. **rule the roost** (or *Brit.* **roast**) be in control. **run the rule over** *Brit.* examine cursorily for correctness or adequacy. □□ **ruleless** adj. [ME f. OF *reule, reuler* f. LL *regulare* f. L *regula* straight stick]

■ n. **1** regulation, order, law, ordinance, ruling, decree, statute, principle, direction, guide, guideline, precept, ukase. **2** fact, standard, benchmark, custom, practice, form, routine, convention, policy, way things are. **3** dominion, authority, government, control, sovereignty, sway, command, ascendancy, direction, oversight, supervision, mastery. ● v. **1** direct, guide, manage, control, lead, head (up), preside over, superintend, oversee, supervise, regulate, govern, run. **2** run, control; govern, be in control (of *or* over), be in charge (of), be in command (of), reign (over), be in power (over), hold sway (over); wield the scepter, wear the crown. **3** decide, resolve, judge, decree, find, declare, pronounce; hand down a judgment *or* decision, *formal* deem. □ **as a rule** generally, usually, normally, customarily, for the most part, mostly, ordinarily, mainly, in the main, chiefly, on the whole, commonly, more often than not. **by rule** mechanically, automatically; unthinkingly. **rule out** ban, bar, prohibit, exclude, eliminate, forbid, preclude, proscribe, dismiss, disregard. **rule the roost** (or *Brit.* **roast**) see DOMINATE 1.

ruler /roolər/ n. **1** a person exercising government or dominion. **2** a straight usu. graduated strip or cylinder of wood, metal, etc., used to draw lines or measure distance. □□ **rulership** n.

■ **1** see LEADER 1. **2** rule, measure.

ruling /rooling/ n. & adj. ● n. an authoritative decision or announcement. ● adj. dominant; prevailing; currently in force (*ruling prices*). □ **ruling passion** a motive that habitually directs one's actions.

■ n. see DECISION 2, 3. ● adj. prevalent, dominating; see also DOMINANT adj.

rum¹ /rum/ n. **1** a spirit distilled from sugarcane residues or molasses. **2** *colloq.* intoxicating liquor in general (*the demon rum*). □ **rum baba** see BABA. [17th c.: perh. abbr. of contemporary forms *rumbullion, rumbustion*, of unkn. orig.]

rum² /rum/ adj. *Brit. colloq.* **1** odd; strange; queer. **2** difficult; dangerous. □ **rum go** (or **do** or **start**) *colloq.* a surprising occurrence or unforeseen turn of affairs. □□ **rumly** adv. **rumness** n. [16th-c. cant, orig. = fine, spirited, perh. var. of ROM]

■ **1** see STRANGE 1.

Rumanian var. of ROMANIAN.

Rumansh var. of ROMANSH.

rumba /rúmbə, room-/ n. & v. (also **rhumba**) ● n. **1** Cuban dance. **2 a** a ballroom dance imitative of this. **b** the music

for it. ● v.tr. (**rumbas, rumbaed** /-bəd/, **rumbaing** /-bə-ing/) dance the rumba. [Amer. Sp.]

rumble /rúmbəl/ v. & n. ● v. **1** intr. make a continuous deep resonant sound as of distant thunder. **2** intr. (foll. by *along, by, past*, etc.) (of a person or vehicle) move with a rumbling noise. **3** intr. engage in a street fight, esp. as part of a gang. **4** tr. (often foll. by *out*) utter or say with a rumbling sound. **5** tr. *Brit. sl.* find out about (esp. something illicit). ● n. **1** a rumbling sound. **2** sl. a street fight between gangs. □ **rumble seat** an uncovered folding seat in the rear of an automobile. **rumble strip** a closely-spaced series of ridges built into a roadway as a warning to drivers. □□ **rumbler** n. [ME *romble*, prob. f. MDu. *rommelen, rummelen* (imit.)]

■ v. **1** see THUNDER v. 2. **4** see DISCOVER 1a, b. ● n. **1** see THUNDER n. 1, 2. **2** see FIGHT n. 1a.

rumbustious /rumbúschəs/ adj. esp. *Brit. colloq.* boisterous, noisy, uproarious. □□ **rumbustiously** adv. **rumbustiousness** n. [prob. var. of *robustious* boisterous, ROBUST]

■ see BOISTEROUS 1.

rumen /roomen/ n. (pl. **rumina** /-minə/ or **rumens**) the first stomach of a ruminant, in which food, esp. cellulose, is partly digested by bacteria. [L *rumen ruminis* throat]

ruminant /roominənt/ n. & adj. ● n. an animal that chews the cud regurgitated from its rumen. ● adj. **1** of or belonging to ruminants. **2** contemplative; given to or engaged in meditation. [L *ruminari ruminant-* (as RUMEN)]

ruminate /roominayt/ v. **1** tr. & (foll. by *over, on*, etc.) intr. meditate, ponder. **2** intr. (of ruminants) chew the cud. □□ **rumination** /-náyshən/ n. **ruminative** /-nətiv/ adj. **ruminatively** adv. **ruminator** n.

■ **1** (*ruminate over, on*) see PONDER.

rummage /rúmij/ v. & n. ● v. **1** tr. & (foll. by *in, through, among*) intr. search, esp. *untidily and unsystematically*. **2** tr. (foll. by *out, up*) find among other things. **3** tr. (foll. by *about*) disarrange; make untidy in searching. ● n. **1** an instance of rummaging. **2** things found by rummaging; a miscellaneous accumulation. □ **rummage sale** a sale of miscellaneous usu. secondhand articles, esp. for charity. □□ **rummager** n. [earlier as noun in obs. sense 'arranging of casks, etc., in a hold': OF *arrumage* f. *arrumer* stow (as AD-, *run* ship's hold f. MDu. *ruim* ROOM)]

■ v. **1** search, comb, scour, *colloq.* turn inside out, turn upside down, *Austral & NZ colloq.* fossick about *or* around; (*rummage in, through, among*) search in *or* through *or* among, hunt in *or* through *or* among, comb through, scour through, scrabble about in, sift through. **2** (*rummage out* or *up*) search out, hunt out *or* up; see also LOCATE 1, 3. ● n. **2** jumble, miscellanea, knickknacks, bits and pieces, odds and ends.

rummer /rúmər/ n. a large drinking glass. [rel. to Du. *roemer*, LG *römer* f. *roemen* praise, boast]

rummy¹ /rúmee/ n. any of various card games in which the players try to form sets and sequences of cards. [20th c.: orig. unkn.]

rummy² /rúmee/ n. & adj. ● n. sl. a drunkard or sot. ● adj. *Brit. colloq.* = RUM².

rumor /roomər/ n. & v. (*Brit.* **rumour**) ● n. **1** general talk or hearsay of doubtful accuracy. **2** (often foll. by *of*, or *that* + clause) a current but unverified statement or assertion (*heard a rumor that you are leaving*). ● v.tr. (usu. in *passive*) report by way of rumor (*it is rumored that you are leaving; you are rumored to be leaving*). [ME f. OF *rumur, rumor* f. L *rumor -oris* noise]

■ n. **1** gossip, hearsay, chat, tittle-tattle, *colloq.* chitchat, scuttlebutt, *sl.* poop. **2** a piece of gossip *or* hearsay, see also WORD n. 7. ● v. bruit about *or* abroad, noise (abroad), intimate, breathe, suggest, whisper, leak, reveal, make known, put about, say, report, tell.

rump /rump/ n. **1** the hind part of a mammal, esp. the buttocks. **2 a** a small or contemptible remnant of a parliament or similar body. **b** (**the Rump**) *hist.* the remnant of the English Long Parliament 1648–53 or after its restoration in 1659. □ **rump roast** a cut of beef from the rump. □□ **rumpless** adj. [ME, prob. f. Scand.]

rumple /rúmpəl/ *v.tr.* & *intr.* make or become creased or ruf-fled. ▢▢ **rumply** *adj.* [obs. *rumple* (n.) f. MDu. *rompel* f. *rompe* wrinkle]

■ wrinkle, crumple, crush, crease, crinkle, ruffle, scrunch (up), pucker.

rumpus /rúmpəs/ *n. colloq.* a disturbance, brawl, row, or up-roar. ▢ **rumpus room** a room, usu. in the basement of a house, for games and play. [18th c.: prob. fanciful]

■ commotion, disturbance, fuss, confusion, uproar, tumult, to-do, brouhaha, stir, *literary* pother; affray, fracas, melee, brawl, *colloq.* row, *sl.* roughhouse.

run /run/ *v.* & *n.* ● *v.* (**running**; *past* **ran** /ran/; *past part.* **run**) **1** *intr.* go with quick steps on alternate feet, never hav-ing both or all feet on the ground at the same time. **2** *intr.* flee; abscond. **3** *intr.* go or travel hurriedly, briefly, etc. **4** *intr.* **a** advance by or as by rolling or on wheels, or smoothly or easily. **b** be in action or operation (*left the engine running*). **5** *intr.* be current or operative; have duration (*the lease runs for 99 years*). **6** *intr.* (of a bus, train, etc.) travel or be trav-eling on its route (*the train is running late*). **7** *intr.* (of a play, exhibition, etc.) be staged or presented (*is now running at the Apollo*). **8** *intr.* extend; have a course or order or tendency (*the road runs by the coast; prices are running high*). **9 a** *intr.* compete in a race. **b** *intr.* finish a race in a specified position. **c** *tr.* compete in (a race). **10** *intr.* (often foll. by *for*) seek election (*ran for president*). **11 a** *intr.* (of a liquid, etc., or its container) flow or be wet; drip. **b** *tr.* flow with (a specified liquid) (*after the massacre, the rivers ran blood*). **12** *tr.* **a** cause (water, etc.) to flow. **b** fill (a bath) with water. **13** *intr.* spread rapidly or beyond the proper place (*ink ran over the table; a shiver ran down my spine*). **14** *intr. Cricket* (of a batsman) run from one wicket to the other in scoring a run. **15** *tr.* traverse or make one's way through or over (a course, race, or dis-tance). **16** *tr.* perform (an errand). **17** *tr.* publish (an article, etc.) in a newspaper or magazine. **18 a** *tr.* cause (a machine or vehicle, etc.) to operate. **b** *intr.* (of a mechanism or com-ponent, etc.) move or work freely. **19** *tr.* direct or manage (a business, household, etc.). **20** *tr. Brit.* own and use (a vehicle) regularly. **21** *tr.* take (a person) for a journey in a vehicle (*shall I run you to the post office?*). **22** *tr.* cause to run or go in a specified way (*ran the car into a tree*). **23** *tr.* enter (a horse, etc.) for a race. **24** *tr.* smuggle (guns, etc.). **25** *tr.* chase or hunt. **26** *tr.* allow (an account) to accumulate for a time before paying. **27** *intr. Naut.* (of a ship, etc.) go straight and fast. **28** *intr.* (of salmon) go upriver from the sea. **29** *intr.* (of a color in a fabric) spread from the dyed parts. **30 a** *intr.* (of a thought, the eye, the memory, etc.) pass in a transitory or cursory way (*ideas ran through my mind*). **b** *tr.* cause (one's eye) to look cursorily (*ran my eye down the page*). **c** *tr.* pass (a hand, etc.) rapidly over (*ran his fingers down her spine*). **31** *intr.* (of hosiery) unravel along a line from the point of a snag. **32** *intr.* (of a candle) gutter. **33** *intr.* (of an orifice, esp. the eyes or nose) exude liquid matter. **34** *tr.* sew (fabric) loosely or hastily with running stitches; baste. **35** *tr.* turn (cattle, etc.) out to graze. ● *n.* **1** an act or spell of running. **2** a short trip or excursion, esp. for pleasure. **3** a distance traveled. **4** a general tendency of development or movement. **5** a rapid motion. **6** a regular route. **7 a** a continuous or long stretch or spell or course (*a 50-foot run of wiring; had a run of bad luck*). **b** a series or sequence, esp. of cards in a specified suit. **8** (often foll. by *on*) **a** a high general demand (for a commodity, currency, etc.) (*a run on the dollar*). **b** a sudden demand for repayment by a large number of customers of (a bank). **9** a quantity produced in one period of production (*a print run*). **10** a general or average type or class (*not typical of the general run*). **11 a** *Baseball* a point scored by a base runner upon touching home plate safely. **b** *Cricket* a point scored by the batsmen each running to the other's wicket, or an equivalent point awarded for some other reason. **12** (foll. by *of*) free use of or access to (*had the run of the house*). **13 a** an animal's reg-ular track. **b** an enclosure for domestic animals or fowls. **c** a range of pasture. **14** a line of unraveled stitches, esp. from the point of a snag (in hosiery). **15** *Mus.* a rapid scale pas-

sage. **16** a class or line of goods. **17** a batch or drove of animals born or reared together. **18** a shoal of fish in motion. **19** a trough for water to run in. **20** a small stream or brook. **21 a** a single journey, esp. by an aircraft. **b** (of an aircraft) a flight on a straight and even course at a constant speed before or while dropping bombs. **c** an offensive military op-eration. **22** a slope used for skiing or tobogganing, etc. **23** (**the runs**) *colloq.* an attack of diarrhea. ▢ **at a** (or **the**) **run** running. **on the run 1** escaping; running away. **2** hurrying about from place to place. **run about 1** bustle; hurry from one person or place to another. **2** (esp. of children) play or wander without restraint. **run across 1** happen to meet. **2** (foll. by *to*) make a brief journey or a flying visit (to a place). **run afoul of** collide or become entangled with (another vessel, etc.). **run after 1** pursue with attentions; seek the society of. **2** give much time to (a pursuit, etc.). **3** pursue at a run. **run against 1** oppose, as in an election. **2** esp. *Brit.* happen to meet. **run along** *colloq.* depart. **run around 1** *Brit.* take from place to place by car, etc. **2** deceive or evade repeatedly. **3** (foll. by *with*) *sl.* engage in sexual rela-tions (esp. casually or illicitly). **run at** attack by charging or rushing. **run away 1** get away by running; flee; abscond. **2** elope. **3** (of a horse) bolt. **run away with 1** carry off (a person, stolen property, etc.). **2** win (a prize) easily. **3** accept (a notion) hastily. **4** (of expense, etc.) consume (money, etc.). **5** (of a horse) bolt with (a rider, a carriage or its oc-cupants). **run a blockade** see BLOCKADE. **run down 1** knock down or collide with. **2** reduce the strength or num-bers of (resources). **3** (of an unwound clock, etc.) stop. **4** (of a person or a person's health) become feeble from over-work or underfeeding. **5** discover after a search. **6** disparage. **run-down 1** decayed after prosperity. **2** enfeebled through overwork, etc. **run dry** cease to flow; be exhausted. **run for it** seek safety by fleeing. **a run** (or **a good run**) **for one's money 1** vigorous competition. **2** pleasure or reward de-rived from an activity. **run the gauntlet** see GAUNTLET[2]. **run a person hard** (or **close**) press a person severely in a race or competition, or in comparative merit. **run high 1** (of the sea) have a strong current with a high tide. **2** (of feelings) be strong. **run in 1** *colloq.* arrest. **2** (of a combatant) rush to close quarters. **3** incur (a debt). **4** *Brit.* run (a new engine or vehicle) carefully in the early stages. **run-in** *n.* **1** the ap-proach to an action or event. **2** a quarrel. **run in the family** (of a trait) be common in the members of a family. **run into 1** collide with. **2** encounter. **3** reach as many as (a specified figure). **4** fall into (a practice, absurdity, etc.). **5** be contin-uous or coalesce with. **run into the ground** *colloq.* bring (a person, vehicle, etc.) to exhaustion, disrepair, etc. **run its course** follow its natural progress; be left to itself. **run low** (or **short**) become depleted; have too little (*our money ran short; we ran short of gas*). **run off 1** flee. **2** produce (copies, etc.) on a machine. **3** decide (a race or other contest) after a series of heats or in the event of a tie. **4** flow or cause to flow away. **5** write or recite fluently. **6** digress suddenly. **run off at the mouth** *sl.* talk incessantly. **run off one's feet** very busy. **run-of-the-mill** ordinary; undistinguished. **run on 1** (of written characters) be joined together. **2** continue in operation. **3** elapse. **4** speak volubly. **5** talk incessantly. **6** *Printing* continue on the same line as the preceding matter. **run** (or **pass**) **one's eye over** see EYE. **run out 1** come to an end; become used up. **2** (foll. by *of*) exhaust one's stock of. **3** escape from a containing vessel. **4** expel; drive out (*they ran him out of town*). **run out on** *colloq.* desert (a person). **run over 1** overflow; extend beyond. **2** study or repeat quickly. **3** (of a vehicle or its driver) pass over; knock down or crush. **4** touch (the notes of a piano, etc.) in quick suc-cession. **5** (often foll. by *to*) go quickly by a brief journey or for a quick visit. **run ragged** exhaust (a person). **run rings**

/. . ./ **pronunciation**	● **part of speech**
▢ **phrases, idioms, and compounds**	
▢▢ **derivatives**	■ **synonym section**
cross-references appear in SMALL CAPITALS or *italics*	

around see RING¹. **run riot** see RIOT. **run a** (or **the**) **risk** see RISK. **run the show** *colloq.* dominate in an undertaking, etc. **run a temperature** be feverish. **run through 1** examine or rehearse briefly. **2** peruse. **3** deal successively with. **4** consume (an estate, etc.) by reckless or quick spending. **5** traverse. **6** pervade. **7** pierce with a sword, etc. **8** draw a line through (written words). **run-through** *n.* **1** a rehearsal. **2** a brief survey. **run to 1** have the money or ability for. **2** reach (an amount or number). **3** (of a person) show a tendency to (*runs to fat*). **4** be enough for (some expense or undertaking). **b** have the resources or capacity for. **5** fall into (ruin). **run to earth** (or **ground**) **1** *Hunting* chase to its lair. **2** discover after a long search. **run to meet** anticipate (one's troubles, etc.). **run to seed** see SEED. **run up 1** accumulate (a debt, etc.) quickly. **2** build or make hurriedly. **3** raise (a flag). **4** grow quickly. **5** rise in price. **6** (foll. by *to*) amount to. **7** force (a rival bidder) to bid higher. **8** add up (a column of figures). **9** (foll. by *to*) go quickly by a brief journey or for a quick visit. **run-up** *n.* **1** esp. *Brit.* the period preceding an important event. **2** *Golf* a low approach shot. **run up against** meet with (a difficulty or difficulties). **run upon** (of a person's thoughts, etc.) be engrossed by; dwell upon. **run wild** grow or stray unchecked or undisciplined or untrained. □□ **runnable** *adj.* [OE *rinnan*]

■ *v.* **1, 3** sprint, race, scamper, scurry, scud, dart, bolt, dash, flit, tear, scuttle, zip, whiz, gallop, lope, esp. *Brit.* hare, *colloq.* scoot; rush, hurry, hasten, scramble, hustle, *archaic or poet.* hie; step lively, put on some speed, hotfoot (it), *colloq.* step on it, get a move on, leg it, get cracking, stir one's stumps, step on the gas, *sl.* hoof it, hop (to) it, get a wiggle on. **2** run away *or* off, flee, escape, take flight, take to one's heels, bolt, decamp, abscond, beat a hasty retreat, make off *or* away, (make a) run for it, make a getaway, take off, take French leave, *colloq.* clear out, show a clean pair of heels, scram, skedaddle, skip (out), *sl.* cut and run, beat it, take a powder, go on the lam, vamoose, skiddoo, *Austral. sl.* go through, *Brit. sl.* scarper, do a bunk. **4 a** see ADVANCE *v.* 1, 2. **b** see WORK *v.* 5. **5** be current *or* operative, last, be in effect, be in force, be effective *or* valid, have force *or* effect. **7** play, show, be on, be presented *or* screened. **8** extend, stretch, reach; amount, total up, mount up. **9 a** compete, take part; participate. **b** finish, come (in). **10** compete, be a candidate, vie, fight, stand; contend. **11a, 13** flow, pour, stream, flood, gush, spill, dribble, drip, spurt, trickle, seep, cascade, spout; issue, pass, move. **15** go, cover, sprint, race. **16** perform, do, fulfill, carry out. **17** print, publish, reproduce, issue, put out, release, carry. **18 b** operate, perform, function, work, tick, go. **19** operate, manage, direct, supervise, oversee, conduct, superintend, control, handle, manipulate, head, lead, regulate, take care of, look after, administer, be in charge of, coordinate; keep, maintain. **21** convey, transport, give (a person) a lift, drive, take, bring. **22** drive, steer, pilot; guide, navigate. **23** enter, put in, put down, register; enroll, enlist. **24** smuggle, bootleg, deal *or* traffic in. **25** see CHASE¹ *v.* 1, 4. **29** spread, flow, diffuse. **30 a** pass, meander, flow, float, drift, flit, fly, race. ● *n.* **1** sprint, dash, race, jog, trot. **2** trip, outing, excursion, jaunt, junket; *colloq.* spin, joyride. **3** way, journey; see also DISTANCE *n.* 2. **6** route, circuit, round; beat. **7 a** period, spate, spell, stretch, course, interval, time. **b** series, sequence, string, succession. **8 a** demand, call, request. **10** type, category, class, kind, sort. **12** freedom, liberty, free use of *or* access to. **13 b** pen, enclosure. **c** paddock, field; pound; see also PASTURE *n.* **15** roulade. **16** class, range; see also LINE¹ *n.* 22. **20** stream, brook, runnel, rill, rivulet, creek, *N. of Engl.* beck, *Sc.* burn, *dial.* kill. **21 a** journey, flight, crossing, passage. **22** trail, track, path, slope. **23** (**the runs**) see DIARRHEA. □ **on the run 1** on the loose, fleeing, escaping, in flight, running away, *sl.* on the lam. **2** running *or* hurrying about, on the move, hastily,

in haste, hurriedly, at speed, in a rush *or* a hurry, *colloq.* on the go. **run about 1** bustle, hurry; see also SCURRY *v.* **run across 1** meet (up with), run into *or* against, come across, find, stumble (up)on, hit (up)on, chance (up)on, happen (up)on, *colloq.* bump into. **run after 1** chase, pursue, go after, court, woo, set one's cap at. **run against 2** see *run across* above. **run along** go away, leave, *sl.* get lost; see also DEPART 1. **run around 3** philander, be unfaithful, *colloq.* gallivant, sleep around, play the field. **run away 1** see RUN *v.* 2 above. **run away with 1** see STEAL *v.* 1, ABDUCT. **run down 1** run over, knock over *or* down, collide with, strike, hit, smash *or* crash into, *sl.* slam into. **3** stop (working), play itself out; burn out, fail; see also PETER¹ *v.* **4** weaken, tire, become weary *or* exhausted *or* worn out *or* feeble, be out of shape *or* condition *or* below par. **5** trace, track *or* hunt (down), find, discover; see also LOCATE 1, 3. **6** criticize, decry, defame, vilify, disparage, deprecate, depreciate, denigrate, *colloq.* pan, *sl.* knock. **run-down 1** ramshackle, dilapidated, tumbledown, decrepit, rickety, broken-down. **2** weary, exhausted, debilitated, weak, worn out, peaked, fatigued, enervated, tired, drained, enfeebled, spent, burnt-out, *Brit. sl.* knackered; out of shape *or* condition, below par, in bad shape; unhealthy, sickly, ill. **run** (or **a good run**) **for one's money 2** return, satisfaction, reward, recompense, compensation, profit. **run in 1** arrest, take into custody, apprehend, take *or* bring in, pinch, collar, *colloq.* pull in, bust, *sl.* nab, *Brit. sl.* nick. **run-in 2** disagreement, argument, dispute, altercation, quarrel, confrontation, contretemps. **run into 1** see COLLIDE 1. **2** see *run across* above. **run off 1** see RUN *v.* 2 above. **2** duplicate, print, turn out, produce, make, do, churn out. **6** see DIGRESS. **run off one's feet** see BUSY *adj.* 1, 3. **run-of-the-mill** see ORDINARY *adj.* **run on 3** see ELAPSE. **run out 1** be exhausted, end, finish, go, be used up, peter out; expire, terminate, come to a close *or* end, draw to a close *or* end, cease. **2** (*run out of*) use up, consume, eat up, exhaust, be out of. **run out on** desert, abandon, leave high and dry, forsake, leave in the lurch, leave holding the baby. **run over 1** overflow, spill (over), brim over, slosh over, pour over; extend *or* reach *or* spread *or* stretch over *or* beyond, exceed, go beyond, overreach, overshoot. **2** rehearse, run through, repeat, practice, review, go over, study, learn. **3** see *run down* 1 above. **run the show** be in charge, *colloq.* be boss; see also *call the shots.* **run through 1** see *run over* 2 above. **2** peruse, scan, go over, look over, flip *or* leaf *or* thumb through, look at, skim (through), browse through, dip into, review. **4** squander, consume, use up, waste, fritter away, exhaust, spend, dissipate, throw away, *sl.* blow. **7** pierce, stab, transfix, stick, spit. **run-through 1** rehearsal, practice, trial, test. **2** see SURVEY *n.* **run to 2** see REACH *v.* 5. **3** see TEND¹ 1. **run to earth 2** see *run down* 5 above. **run up 1** accumulate. **2** see *knock up* 1. **5** see SOAR 2. **6** (*run up to*) see AMOUNT *v.* 1. **8** see ADD 2. **run up against** see ENCOUNTER *v.* 3. **run upon** see *dwell on.* **run wild** wander, run, rove, roam, meander, drift; see also *on the rampage* (RAMPAGE).

runabout /rúnəbowt/ *n.* a light car, boat, or aircraft.

runaround /rúnərownd/ *n.* (esp. in phr. **give a person the runaround**) deceit or evasion.

runaway /rúnəway/ *n.* **1** a fugitive. **2** an animal or vehicle that is running out of control. **3** (*attrib.*) **a** that is running away or out of control (*runaway inflation; had a runaway success*). **b** done or performed after running away (*a runaway wedding*).

■ **1** fugitive, escapee, refugee, deserter, truant, absconder. **3 a** (*attrib.*) wild, uncontrolled, unchecked, rampant, unsuppressed; driverless, riderless; overwhelming; see also *out-and-out*.

runcible spoon /rúnsibəl/ *n.* a fork curved like a spoon, with three broad prongs, one edged. [nonsense word used by E.

Lear, Engl. humorist d. 1888, perh. after *rouncival* large pea]

runcinate /rúnsinayt, -nət/ *adj. Bot.* (of a leaf) saw-toothed, with lobes pointing toward the base. [mod.L *runcinatus* f. L *runcina* PLANE² (formerly taken to mean saw)]

rundown /rúndown/ *n.* **1** *Baseball* a play in which a base runner is caught between two bases and is chased by fielders who try to tag the runner out. **2** a summary or brief analysis.
■ **2** runthrough, synopsis, summary, survey, précis, résumé, (thumbnail) sketch, outline, rough idea, review, recapitulation.

rune /rōōn/ *n.* **1** any of the letters of the earliest Germanic alphabet used by Scandinavians and Anglo-Saxons from about the 3rd c. and formed by modifying Roman or Greek characters to suit carving. **2** a similar mark of mysterious or magic significance. **3** a Finnish poem or a division of it. □ **rune-staff 1** a magic wand inscribed with runes. **2** a runic calendar. □□ **runic** *adj.* [ON *rún* (only in pl. *rúnar*) magic sign, rel. to OE *rūn*]

rung¹ /rung/ *n.* **1** each of the horizontal supports of a ladder. **2** a strengthening crosspiece in the structure of a chair, etc. □□ **runged** *adj.* **rungless** *adj.* [OE *hrung*]

rung² *past part.* of RING².

runlet /rúnlit/ *n.* a small stream.

runnel /rúnəl/ *n.* **1** a brook or rill. **2** a gutter. [later form (assim. to RUN) of *rinel* f. OE *rynel* (as RUN)]

runner /rúnər/ *n.* **1** a person, horse, etc. that runs, esp. in a race. **2 a** a creeping plant stem that can take root. **b** a twining plant. **3** a rod or groove or blade on which a thing slides. **4** a sliding ring on a rod, etc. **5** a messenger, scout, collector, or agent for a bank, etc.; a tout. **6** *hist.* a police officer. **7** a running bird. **8 a** a smuggler. **b** = *blockade-runner.* **9** a revolving millstone. **10** *Naut.* a rope in a single block with one end around a tackle block and the other having a hook. **11** (in full **runner bean**) esp. *Brit.* a twining bean plant, *Phaseolus coccineus*, with red flowers and long green seed pods. Also called *scarlet runner.* **12** each of the long pieces on the underside of a sled, etc., that forms the contact in sliding. **13** a roller for moving a heavy article. **14** a long, narrow ornamental cloth or rug. □ **do a runner** *Brit. sl.* leave hastily; flee. **runner-up** (*pl.* **runners-up** or **runner-ups**) the competitor or team taking second place.
■ **1** sprinter, racer, jogger; *colloq.* miler. **2 b** creeper, twining plant. **5** messenger, courier, errand boy, errand girl, messenger boy, messenger girl, page, dispatch bearer, dispatch rider, *sl.* gofer; scout; collector, agent, tout. **6** see *police officer.* □ **do a runner** see FLEE 1.

running /rúning/ *n. & adj.* ● *n.* **1** the action of runners in a race, etc. **2** the way a race, etc., proceeds. **3** management; control; operation ● *adj.* **1** continuing on an essentially continuous basis though changing in detail (*a running battle*). **2** consecutive; one after another (*three days running*). **3** done with a run (*a running jump*). □ **in** (or **out of**) **the running** (of a competitor) with a good (or poor) chance of winning. **make** (or **take up**) **the running** take the lead; set the pace. **running account** esp. *Brit.* a current account. **running board** a footboard on either side of a vehicle. **running commentary** an oral description of events as they occur. **running fire** successive shots from a line of troops, etc. **running gear** the moving or running parts of a machine, esp. the wheels and suspension of a vehicle. **running hand** writing in which the pen, etc., is not lifted after each letter. **running head** (or **headline**) a heading printed at the top of a number of consecutive pages of a book, etc. **running knot** a knot that slips along the rope, etc., and changes the size of a noose. **running light 1** any of the navigational lights displayed by a ship, aircraft, etc., during hours of darkness. **2** *Brit.* lights on a motor vehicle that remain illuminated while the vehicle is running. **running mate 1** a candidate for a secondary position in an election. **2** a horse entered in a race in order to set the pace for another horse from the same stable which is intended to win. **running repairs** minor or temporary repairs, etc., to machinery while in use. **running rope** a rope that is freely movable

through a pulley, etc. **running sore** a suppurating sore. **running stitch 1** a line of small nonoverlapping stitches for gathering, etc. **2** one of these stitches. **running water** water flowing in a stream or from a tap, etc. **take a running jump** (esp. as *int.*) *Brit. sl.* go away.
■ *n.* **3** see OPERATION 1, 2. ● *adj.* **1** continuous, ongoing, perpetual, sustained, constant, uninterrupted, ceaseless, unceasing. **2** see SUCCESSIVE. □ **make** (or **take up**) **the running** take the lead, set the pace; see also LEAD¹ *v.* 5.

runny /rúnee/ *adj.* (**runnier, runniest**) **1** tending to run or flow. **2** excessively fluid.

runoff /rúnawf/ *n.* **1** an additional competition, election, race, etc., after a tie. **2** an amount of rainfall that is carried off an area by streams and rivers.

runt /runt/ *n.* **1** a small piglet, puppy, etc., esp. the smallest in a litter. **2** a weakling; an undersized person. **3** esp. *Brit.* a large domestic pigeon. □□ **runty** *adj.* [16th c.: orig. unkn.]
■ **2** dwarf, pygmy, midget; see also WEAKLING.

runway /rúnway/ *n.* **1** a specially prepared surface along which aircraft take off and land. **2** a trail to an animals' watering place. **3** an incline down which logs are slid. **4** a narrow walkway extending out from a stage into an auditorium. **5** a passageway along which football players, etc., run to enter the field.

rupee /rōōpée, rōōpee/ *n.* the chief monetary unit of India, Pakistan, Sri Lanka, Nepal, Mauritius, and the Seychelles. [Hind. *rūpiyah* f. Skr. *rūpya* wrought silver]

rupiah /rōōpéeə/ *n.* the chief monetary unit of Indonesia. [as RUPEE]

rupture /rúpchər/ *n. & v.* ● *n.* **1** the act or an instance of breaking; a breach. **2** a breach of harmonious relations; a disagreement and parting. **3** *Med.* an abdominal hernia. ● *v.* **1** *tr.* break or burst (a cell or membrane, etc.). **2** *tr.* sever (a connection). **3** *intr.* undergo a rupture. **4** *tr. & intr.* affect with or suffer a hernia. □□ **rupturable** *adj.* [ME f. OF *rupture* or L *ruptura* f. *rumpere rupt-* break]
■ *n.* **1, 2** breakup, breach, disagreement, schism, breaking up, severance, division, separation, parting; break, breaking, rift, split, splitting; fissure, cleavage, bursting. ● *v.* **1** break, split. **2** sever, break, breach, *archaic or literary* sunder. **3** divide, separate.

rural /rōōrəl/ *adj.* **1** in, of, or suggesting the country (opp. URBAN); pastoral or agricultural (*in rural seclusion; a rural constituency*). **2** often *derog.* characteristic of country people; rustic; plain; simple. □ **rural dean** see DEAN¹. **rural free delivery** (also **rural delivery service**) postal delivery to mailboxes in rural areas. □□ **ruralism** *n.* **ruralist** *n.* **rurality** /-rálitee/ *n.* **ruralize** *v.* **ruralization** *n.* **rurally** *adv.* [ME f. OF *rural* or LL *ruralis* f. *rus ruris* the country]
■ **1** country, pastoral, countrified, sylvan, bucolic, rustic, arcadian, exurban, ruralist; agricultural, agrarian. **2** see RUSTIC *adj.* 2.

Ruritanian /rōōritáyneeən/ *adj.* relating to or characteristic of romantic adventure or its setting. [*Ruritania*, an imaginary setting in SE Europe in the novels of Anthony Hope (d. 1933)]

ruse /rōōz/ *n.* a stratagem or trick. [ME f. OF f. *ruser* drive back, perh. ult. f. L *rursus* backward: cf. RUSH¹]
■ trick, device, deception, maneuver, dodge, pretense, subterfuge, stratagem, wile, artifice, imposture, expedient, *colloq.* ploy.

rush¹ /rush/ *v. & n.* ● *v.* **1** *intr.* go, move, or act precipitately or with great speed. **2** *tr.* move or transport with great haste (*was rushed to the hospital*). **3** (foll. by *at*) **a** move suddenly and quickly toward. **b** begin impetuously. **4** *tr.* perform or deal with hurriedly (*don't rush your dinner; the bill was rushed through Congress*). **5** *tr.* force (a person) to act hastily. **6** *tr.* attack or capture by sudden assault. **7** *tr. Brit.*

/.../ pronunciation	● **part of speech**
□ **phrases, idioms, and compounds**	
□□ **derivatives**	■ **synonym section**
cross-references appear in SMALL CAPITALS or *italics*	

sl. overcharge (a customer). **8** *tr.* pay attentions to (a person) with a view to securing acceptance of a proposal. **9** *tr.* pass (an obstacle) with a rapid dash. **10** *intr.* flow, fall, spread, or roll impetuously or fast (*felt the blood rush to my face*; *the river rushes past*). **11** *tr.* & *intr.* *Football* advance the ball in a running play or plays. ● *n.* **1** an act of rushing; a violent advance or attack. **2** a period of great activity; a commotion. **3** (*attrib.*) done with great haste or speed (*a rush job*). **4** a sudden migration of large numbers. **5** a surge of emotion, excitement, etc. **6** (foll. by *on, for*) a sudden, strong demand for a commodity. **7** (in *pl.*) *colloq.* the first prints of a film after a period of shooting. **8** *Football* **a** the act of carrying the ball. **b** an attempt by a defensive player or players to reach the passer or kicker. □ **rush one's fences** *Brit.* act with undue haste. **rush hour** a time each day when traffic is at its heaviest. □□ **rusher** *n.* **rushingly** *adv.* [ME f. AF *russher,* = OF *ruser, russer:* see RUSE]

■ *v.* **1** hurry (up), hasten, run, race, bustle, make haste, dash, speed, scurry, jump, sprint, scuttle, hustle, scramble, hotfoot (it), go like a bat out of hell, shake a leg, *colloq.* scoot, move (it), step on it, make it snappy, get moving, get cracking, look alive *or* lively, hightail (it), step on the gas, *sl.* get a wiggle on. **3 a** run, race, dash, jump; see also TEAR[1] *v.* 5. **4** hurry, race, push. **6** attack, assault, charge, storm, *colloq.* blitz. **7** see FLEECE *v.* 1. **10** see SURGE *v.* 1. ● *n.* **1** hurry, haste, (hustle and) bustle; surge, charge, advance; see also ATTACK *n.* 1. **2** fuss, excitement, flurry, commotion, ferment, to-do, *literary* pother. **3** (*attrib.*) hasty, speedy, urgent, pressing, high-priority, top-priority, emergency. **5** surge, sensation, thrill.

rush² /rush/ *n.* **1 a** any marsh or waterside plant of the family Juncaceae, with naked slender tapering pith-filled stems (properly leaves) formerly used for strewing floors and still used for making chair bottoms and plaiting baskets, etc. **b** a stem of this. **c** (*collect.*) rushes as a material. **2** *archaic* a thing of no value (*not worth a rush*). □ **rush candle** a candle made by dipping the pith of a rush in tallow. □□ **rushlike** *adv.* **rushy** *adj.* [OE *rysc, rysce,* corresp. to MLG, MHG *rusch*]

rushlight /rushlīt/ *n. Brit.* a rush candle.

rusk /rusk/ *n.* a slice of bread rebaked usu. as a light biscuit, esp. as food for babies. [Sp. or Port. *rosca* twist, coil, roll of bread]

russet /rúsit/ *adj.* & *n.* ● *adj.* **1** reddish-brown. **2** *archaic* rustic; homely; simple. ● *n.* **1** a reddish-brown color. **2** a kind of rough-skinned, russet-colored apple. **3** *hist.* a coarse, homespun reddish-brown or gray cloth used for simple clothing. **4** a baking potato, esp. one from Idaho. □□ **russety** *adj.* [ME f. AF f. OF *rosset, rousset,* dimin. of *roux* red f. Prov. *ros,* It. *rosso* f. L *russus* red]

Russia leather /rúshə/ *n.* a durable bookbinding leather from skins impregnated with birch-bark oil. [*Russia* in E. Europe]

Russian /rúshən/ *n.* & *adj.* ● *n.* **1 a** a native or national of Russia or the former Soviet Union. **b** a person of Russian descent. **2** the language of Russia and the official language of the former Soviet Union. ● *adj.* **1** of or relating to Russia. **2** of or in Russian. □ **Russian boot** a boot that loosely encloses the calf. **Russian olive** = OLEASTER. **Russian roulette 1** an act of daring in which one (usu. with others in turn) squeezes the trigger of a revolver held to one's head with one chamber loaded, having first spun the chamber. **2** a potentially dangerous enterprise. □□ **Russianize** *v.tr.* **Russianization** *n.* **Russianness** *n.* [med.L *Russianus*]

Russify /rúsifī/ *v.tr.* (**-ies, -ied**) make Russian in character. □□ **Russification** *n.*

Russki /rúskee, róos-, róŏs-/ *n.* (also **Russky**) (*pl.* **Russkis** or **-ies**) *often offens.* a Russian or (formerly) a Soviet citizen. [RUSSIAN after Russ. surnames ending in *-ski*]

Russo- /rúsō/ *comb. form* Russian; Russian and.

Russophile /rúsəfīl/ *n.* a person who is fond of Russia or the Russians.

rust /rust/ *n.* & *v.* ● *n.* **1 a** a reddish or yellowish-brown

coating formed on iron or steel by oxidation, esp. as a result of moisture. **b** a similar coating on other metals. **2 a** any of various plant diseases with rust-colored spots caused by fungi of the order Uredinales. **b** the fungus causing this. **3** an impaired state due to disuse or inactivity. ● *v.* **1** *tr.* & *intr.* affect or be affected with rust; undergo oxidation. **2** *intr.* (of bracken, etc.) become rust-colored. **3** *intr.* (of a plant) be attacked by rust. **4** *intr.* lose quality or efficiency by disuse or inactivity. □□ **rustless** *adj.* [OE *rūst* f. Gmc]

rustic /rústik/ *adj.* & *n.* ● *adj.* **1** having the characteristics of or associations with the country or country life. **2** unsophisticated; simple; unrefined. **3** of rude or country workmanship. **4** made of untrimmed branches or rough lumber (*a rustic bench*). **5** (of lettering) freely formed. **6** *Archit.* with rough-hewn or roughened surface or with sunk joints. ● *n.* a person from or living in the country, esp. a simple, unsophisticated one. □□ **rustically** *adv.* **rusticity** /-tísitee/ *n.* [ME f. L *rusticus* f. *rus* the country]

■ *adj.* **1** see RURAL 1. **2** peasant, plain, simple, uncomplicated, unsophisticated, naive, ingenuous, guileless, artless, unrefined, unpolished, countrified, uncultivated, uncultured, crude, rough, unmannerly, cloddish, lumpen, boorish, oafish, loutish, *colloq. often derog.* hillbilly. ● *n.* peasant, ryot, bumpkin, yokel, countryman, countrywoman, country boy *or* girl, *archaic* villain, *colloq.* hick, hayseed, *colloq. often derog.* hillbilly, *Austral.* & *NZ colloq.* bushy, *often derog.* country cousin, *sl.* clodhopper, clod, .

rusticate /rústikayt/ *v.* **1** *intr.* retire to or live in the country. **2** *tr.* make rural. **3** *tr. Brit.* dismiss (a student) temporarily from a university. □□ **rustication** /-káyshən/ *n.* [L *rusticari* live in the country (as RUSTIC)]

rustle /rúsəl/ *v.* & *n.* ● *v.* **1** *intr.* & *tr.* make or cause to make a gentle sound as of dry leaves blown in a breeze. **2** *intr.* (often foll. by *along,* etc.) move with a rustling sound. **3** *tr.* (also *absol.*) steal (cattle or horses). **4** *intr. colloq.* hustle. ● *n.* a rustling sound or movement. □ **rustle up** *colloq.* produce quickly when needed. □□ **rustler** *n.* (esp. in sense 3 of *v.*). [ME *rustel,* etc. (imit.): cf. obs. Flem. *ruysselen,* Du. *ritselen*]

■ *v.* **1** whisper, swish. ● *n.* whisper, whispering, rustling, swish, swishing, *literary* susurration.

rustproof /rústproof/ *adj.* & *v.* ● *adj.* (of a metal) not susceptible to corrosion by rust. ● *v.tr.* make rustproof.

rusty /rústee/ *adj.* (**rustier, rustiest**) **1** rusted or affected by rust. **2** stiff with age or disuse. **3** (of knowledge, etc.) faded or impaired by neglect (*my French is a bit rusty*). **4** rust-colored. **5** (of black clothes) discolored by age. **6 a** of antiquated appearance. **b** antiquated or behind the times. **7** (of a voice) croaking or creaking. □□ **rustily** *adv.* **rustiness** *n.* [OE *rūstig* (as RUST)]

rut¹ /rut/ *n.* & *v.* ● *n.* **1** a deep track made by the passage of wheels. **2** an established (esp. tedious) mode of practice or procedure. ● *v.tr.* (**rutted, rutting**) mark with ruts. □ **in a rut** following a fixed (esp. tedious or dreary) pattern of behavior that is difficult to change. □□ **rutty** *adj.* [prob. f. OF *rote* (as ROUTE)]

■ **1** groove, furrow, track. **2** routine, groove, grind, treadmill, dead end.

rut² /rut/ *n.* & *v.* ● *n.* the periodic sexual excitement of a male deer, goat, sheep, etc. ● *v.intr.* (**rutted, rutting**) be affected with rut. □□ **ruttish** *adj.* [ME f. OF *rut, ruit* f. L *rugitus* f. *rugire* roar]

rutabaga /róotəbáygə/ *n.* a large yellow-fleshed turnip, *Brassica napus,* orig. from Sweden. Also called *swede.* [Sw. dial. *rotabagge*]

ruthenium /rōōthéeneeəm/ *n. Chem.* a rare hard white metallic transition element, occurring naturally in platinum ores, and used as a chemical catalyst and in certain alloys. ¶ Symb.: **Ru.** [med.L *Ruthenia* Russia (from its discovery in ores from the Urals)]

rutherfordium /rúthərfáwrdeeəm/ *n. Chem.* an artificially made transuranic metallic element produced by bombarding an isotope of Californium. ¶ Symb.: **Rf.** [E. *Rutherford,* Engl. physicist d. 1937]

ruthless /roŏthlis/ *adj.* having no pity nor compassion. □□ **ruthlessly** *adv.* **ruthlessness** *n.* [ME, f. *ruth* compassion f. RUE¹]
- pitiless, unpitying, cruel, unsympathetic, merciless, unmerciful, harsh, fierce, remorseless, uncompassionate, vicious, savage, ferocious, hardhearted, callous, unfeeling, tough, severe, heartless, inhuman, brutal, brutish, unrelenting, relentless, mean.

rutile /roŏteel, -tīl/ *n.* a mineral form of titanium dioxide. [F *rutile* or G *Rutil* f. L *rutilus* reddish]

RV *abbr.* **1** Revised Version (of the Bible). **2** recreational vehicle.

-ry /ree/ *suffix* = -ERY (*infantry*; *rivalry*). [shortened f. -ERY, or by analogy]

rye /rī/ *n.* **1 a** a cereal plant, *Secale cereale*, with spikes bearing florets which yield wheatlike grains. **b** the grain of this used for bread and fodder. **2** (in full **rye whiskey**) whiskey distilled from fermented rye. [OE *ryge* f. Gmc]

ryegrass /rīgras/ *n.* any forage or lawn grass of the genus *Lolium*, esp. *L. perenne* or *L. multiflorum*. [obs. *ray grass*, of unkn. orig.]

ryokan /reeōkaán/ *n.* a traditional Japanese inn. [Jap.]

ryot /rī́ət/ *n.* (in India) a peasant. [Urdu *raʿīyat* f. Arab. *raʿīya* flock, subjects f. *raʿā* to pasture]

/.../	pronunciation	●	part of speech
□	phrases, idioms, and compounds		
□□	derivatives	■	synonym section
cross-references appear in SMALL CAPITALS or *italics*			

Ss

S¹ /es/ *n.* (also **s**) (*pl.* **Ss** or **S's** /ésiz/) **1** the nineteenth letter of the alphabet. **2** an S-shaped object or curve.

S² *abbr.* (also **S.**) **1** Saint. **2** siemens. **3** society. **4** south, southern.

S³ *symb. Chem.* the element sulfur.

s. *abbr.* **1** second(s). **2** shilling(s). **3** singular. **4** son. **5** succeeded. [sense 2 orig. f. L *solidus*: see SOLIDUS]

-s' /s; z after a vowel sound or voiced consonant/ *suffix* denoting the possessive case of plural nouns and sometimes of singular nouns ending in *s* (*the boys' shoes*; *Charles' book*). [as -'s¹]

's- /s, z/ *prefix archaic* (esp. in oaths) God's (*'sblood*; *'struth*). [abbr.]

's /s; z after a vowel sound or voiced consonant/ *abbr.* **1** is; has (*he's*; *it's*; *John's*; *Charles's*). **2** us (*let's*). **3** *colloq.* does (*what's he say?*).

-s¹ /s; z after a vowel sound or voiced consonant, e.g., *ways, bags*/ *suffix* denoting the plurals of nouns (cf. -ES¹). [OE *-as* pl. ending]

-s² /s; z after a vowel sound or voiced consonant, e.g., *ties, begs*/ *suffix* forming the 3rd person sing. present of verbs (cf. -ES²). [OE dial., prob. f. OE 2nd person sing. present ending *-es, -as*]

-s³ /s; z after a vowel sound or voiced consonant, e.g., *besides*/ *suffix* **1** forming adverbs (*afterwards*; *besides*; *mornings*). **2** forming possessive pronouns (*hers*; *ours*). [formed as -'s¹]

-s⁴ /s; z after a vowel sound or voiced consonant/ *suffix* forming nicknames or pet names (*Fats*; *Cutes*). [after -s¹]

-'s¹ /s; z after a vowel sound or voiced consonant/ *suffix* denoting the possessive case of singular nouns and of plural nouns not ending in -s (*John's book*; *the book's cover*; *the children's shoes*). [OE genit. sing. ending]

-'s² /s; z after a vowel sound or voiced consonant/ *suffix* denoting the plural of a letter or symbol (*S's*; *8's*). [as -s¹]

SA *abbr.* **1** Salvation Army. **2** sex appeal. **3 a** South Africa. **b** South America. **c** South Australia. **4** *hist.* Sturmabteilung (the paramilitary force of the Nazi party).

sabadilla /sábədílə, -deéə/ *n.* **1** a Mexican plant, *Schoenocaulon officinale*, with seeds yielding veratrine. **2** a preparation of these seeds, used in medicine and agriculture. [Sp. *cebadilla* dimin. of *cebada* barley]

Sabaoth /sábay-oth, sábee-, səbáy-ōth/ *n.pl. Bibl.* heavenly hosts (see HOST¹ 2) (*Lord of Sabaoth*). [ME f. LL f. Gk *Sabaōth* f. Heb. *ṣᵉbāōt* pl. of *ṣābā* host (of heaven)]

Sabbatarian /sábətáireeən/ *n. & adj.* ● *n.* **1** a strict Sabbath-keeping Jew. **2** a Christian who favors observing Sunday strictly as the Sabbath. **3** a Christian who observes Saturday as the Sabbath. ● *adj.* relating to or holding the tenets of Sabbatarians. □□ **Sabbatarianism** *n.* [LL *sabbatarius* f. L *sabbatum*: see SABBATH]

Sabbath /sábəth/ *n.* **1** (in full **Sabbath day**) a day of rest and religious observance kept by Christians on Sunday, Jews on Saturday, and Muslims on Friday. **2** a period of rest. [OE *sabat*, L *sabbatum*, & OF *sabbat*, f. Gk *sabbaton* f. Heb. *šabbāt* f. *šābat* to rest]

sabbatical /səbátikəl/ *adj. & n.* ● *adj.* **1** of or appropriate to the Sabbath. **2** (of leave) granted at intervals to a university teacher for study or travel, orig. every seventh year. ● *n.* a period of sabbatical leave. □ **sabbatical year 1** *Bibl.* every seventh year, prescribed by the Mosaic law to be observed as a "sabbath," during which the land was allowed to rest. **2** a year's sabbatical leave. □□ **sabbatically** *adv.* [LL *sabbaticus* f. Gk *sabbatikos* of the sabbath]

■ *n.* see LEAVE² 2.

saber /sáybər/ *n. & v.* (*Brit.* **sabre**) ● *n.* **1** a cavalry sword with a curved blade. **2** a cavalry soldier and horse. **3** a light fencing sword with a tapering blade. ● *v.tr.* cut down or wound with a saber. □ **saber rattling** a display or threat of military force. **saber-toothed** designating any of various extinct mammals having long, saber-shaped upper canines. [F, earlier *sable* f. G *Sabel*, *Säbel*, *Schabel* f. Pol. *szabla* or Magyar *szablya*]

■ *n.* **1, 3** see BLADE 6.

Sabian /sáybeeən/ *adj. & n.* ● *adj.* of a sect classed in the Koran with Muslims, Jews, and Christians, as believers in the true God. ● *n.* a member of this sect. [Arab. *ṣābī*]

Sabine /sáybīn/ *adj. & n.* ● *adj.* of or relating to a people of the central Apennines in ancient Italy. ● *n.* a member of this people. [L *Sabinus*]

Sabin vaccine /sáybin/ *n.* an oral vaccine giving immunity against poliomyelitis. [A. B. *Sabin*, US virologist b. 1906]

sable¹ /sáybəl/ *n.* **1 a** a small, brown-furred, flesh-eating mammal, *Martes zibellina*, of N. Europe and parts of N. Asia, related to the marten. **b** its skin or fur. **2** a fine paintbrush made of sable fur. [ME f. OF f. med.L *sabelum* f. Slav.]

sable² /sáybəl/ *n. & adj.* ● *n.* **1** esp. *poet.* black. **2** (in *pl.*) mourning garments. **3** (in full **sable antelope**) a large stout-horned African antelope, *Hippotragus niger*, the males of which are mostly black in old age. ● *adj.* **1** (usu. placed after noun) *Heraldry* black. **2** esp. *poet.* dark, gloomy. □□ **sabled** *adj.* **sably** *adv.* [ME f. OF (in *Heraldry*): gen. taken to be identical with SABLE¹, although sable fur is dark brown]

■ *n.* **2** (*sables*) see MOURNING 2. ● *adj.* **2** see *pitch-black* (PITCH²).

sabot /sabṓ, sábō/ *n.* **1** a kind of simple shoe hollowed out from a block of wood. **2** a wooden-soled shoe. □□ **saboted** /sábōd/ *adj.* [F, blend of *savate* shoe + *botte* boot]

sabotage /sábətaazh/ *n. & v.* ● *n.* deliberate damage to productive capacity, esp. as a political act. ● *v.tr.* **1** commit sabotage on. **2** destroy; spoil; make useless (*sabotaged my plans*). [F f. *saboter* make a noise with sabots, bungle, willfully destroy: see SABOT]

■ *n.* destruction, damage, wrecking, impairment; subversion, treachery, treason. ● *v.* damage, incapacitate, disable, cripple; destroy, wreck, spoil, ruin, disrupt; subvert, undermine; gum up *or* screw up the works, *Brit.* queer a person's pitch.

saboteur /sábətȫr/ *n.* a person who commits sabotage. [F]

■ see SUBVERSIVE *n.*

sabra /saábrə/ *n.* a Jew born in Israel. [mod. Heb. *sābrāh* opuntia fruit]

sabre *Brit.* var. of SABER.

SAC /sak/ Strategic Air Command. [abbr.]

Sac /sak, sawk/ *n.* SAUK.

sac /sak/ *n.* **1** a baglike cavity, enclosed by a membrane, in an animal or plant. **2** the distended membrane surrounding a hernia, cyst, tumor, etc. [F *sac* or L *saccus* SACK¹]

saccade /sakaád/ *n.* a brief rapid movement of the eye between fixation points. □□ **saccadic** /səkaádik/ *adj.* [F, = violent pull, f. OF *saquer, sachier* pull]

saccate /sákayt/ *adj. Bot.* **1** dilated into a bag. **2** contained in a sac.

saccharide /sákərid/ *n. Chem.* = SUGAR *n.* 2. [mod.L *saccharum* sugar + -IDE]

saccharimeter /sákərímitər/ *n.* any instrument, esp. a polarimeter, for measuring the sugar content of a solution. [F *saccharimètre* (as SACCHARIDE)]

saccharin /sákərin/ *n.* a very sweet substance used as a non-fattening substitute for sugar. [G (as SACCHARIDE) + -IN]

saccharine /sákərin, -reen, -rin/ *adj.* **1** sugary. **2** of, containing, or like sugar. **3** unpleasantly overpolite, sentimental, etc.

■ **3** see SENTIMENTAL.

saccharo- /sákərō/ *comb. form* sugar; sugar and. [Gk *sakkharon* sugar]

saccharogenic /sákərōjénik/ *adj.* producing sugar.

saccharometer /sákərómitər/ *n.* any instrument, esp. a hydrometer, for measuring the sugar content of a solution.

saccharose /sákərōs/ *n.* sucrose. [mod.L *saccharum* sugar + -OSE²]

sacciform /sáksifawrm/ *adj.* sac-shaped. [L *saccus* sac + -FORM]

saccule /sákyōōl/ *n.* a small sac or cyst. □□ **saccular** *adj.* [L *sacculus* (as SAC)]

sacerdotal /sásərdōtəl, sák-/ *adj.* **1** of priests or the priestly office; priestly. **2** (of a doctrine, etc.) ascribing sacrificial functions and supernatural powers to ordained priests; claiming excessive authority for the priesthood. □□ **sacerdotalism** *n.* **sacerdotalist** *n.* **sacerdotally** *adv.* [ME f. OF *sacerdotal* or L *sacerdotalis* f. *sacerdos -dotis* priest]

■ **1** see PRIESTLY.

sachem /sáychəm/ *n.* **1** the supreme leader of some Native American tribes. **2** *sl.* a political leader. [Narragansett, = SAGAMORE]

sachet /sasháy/ *n.* **1** a small bag or packet containing a small portion of a substance, esp. shampoo. **2** a small perfumed bag. **3 a** dry perfume for laying among clothes, etc. **b** a packet of this. [F, dimin. of *sac* f. L *saccus*]

sack¹ /sak/ *n. & v.* ● *n.* **1 a** a large, strong bag, usu. made of burlap, paper, or plastic, for storing or conveying goods. **b** (usu. foll. by *of*) this with its contents (*a sack of potatoes*). **c** a quantity contained in a sack. **2** (prec. by *the*) *colloq.* dismissal from employment. **3** (prec. by *the*) *sl.* bed. **4 a** a woman's short, loose dress with a sacklike appearance. **b** *archaic* or *hist.* a woman's loose gown, or a silk train attached to the shoulders of this. **5** a man's or woman's loose-hanging coat not shaped to the back. ● *v.tr.* **1** put into a sack or sacks. **2** *colloq.* dismiss from employment. □ **sack race** a race between competitors in sacks up to the waist or neck. □□ **sackful** *n.* (*pl.* **-fuls**). **sacklike** *adj.* [OE *sacc* f. L *saccus* f. Gk *sakkos*, of Semitic orig.]

■ *n.* **1** bag, pouch, *dial.* poke. **2** one's marching orders, *colloq.* one's walking papers, the boot, the push, *colloq.* the bounce. ● *v.* **2** dismiss, discharge, lay off, axe, make *or* declare redundant, give a person his *or* her marching orders, *colloq.* give a person his *or* her walking papers, give a person the sack *or* boot *or* push, *colloq.* bounce, *Austral. colloq.* tramp, *sl.* fire.

sack² /sak/ *v. & n.* ● *v.tr.* **1** plunder and destroy (a captured town, etc.). **2** steal valuables from (a place). ● *n.* the sacking of a captured place. [orig. as noun, f. F *sac* in phr. *mettre à sac* put to sack, f. It. *sacco* SACK¹]

sack³ /sak/ *n. hist.* a white wine formerly imported into Britain from Spain and the Canary Islands (*sherry sack*). [16th-c. *wyne seck*, f. F *vin sec* dry wine]

sackbut /sákbut/ *n.* an early form of trombone. [F *saquebute,* earlier *saqueboute* hook for pulling a man off a horse f. *saquer* pull, *boute* (as BUTT¹)]

sackcloth /sák-klawth, -kloth/ *n.* **1** a coarse fabric of flax or hemp. **2** clothing made of this, formerly worn as a penance or in mourning (esp. *sackcloth and ashes*).

■ **2** see MOURNING 2.

sacking /sáking/ *n.* material for making sacks; sackcloth.

sacra *pl.* of SACRUM.

sacral /sáykrəl, sa-/ *adj.* **1** *Anat.* of or relating to the sacrum. **2** *Anthropol.* of or for sacred rites. [E or L *sacrum*: see SACRUM]

sacrament /sákrəmənt/ *n.* **1** a religious ceremony or act of the Christian churches regarded as an outward and visible sign of inward and spiritual grace: applied by the Eastern, pre-Reformation Western, and Roman Catholic churches to the seven rites of baptism, confirmation, the Eucharist, penance, extreme unction, ordination, and matrimony, but restricted by most Protestants to baptism and the Eucharist. **2** a thing of mysterious and sacred significance; a sacred influence, symbol, etc. **3** (also **Blessed** or **Holy Sacrament**) (prec. by *the*) **a** the Eucharist. **b** the consecrated elements, esp. the bread or Host. **4** an oath or solemn engagement taken. [ME f. OF *sacrement* f. L *sacramentum* solemn oath, etc., f. *sacrare* hallow f. *sacer* SACRED, used in Christian L as transl. of Gk *mustērion* MYSTERY¹]

■ **3** see EUCHARIST.

sacramental /sákrəmént'l/ *adj. & n.* ● *adj.* **1** of or of the nature of a sacrament or the sacrament. **2** (of a doctrine, etc.) attaching great importance to the sacraments. ● *n.* an observance analogous to but not reckoned among the sacraments, e.g., the use of holy water or the sign of the cross. □□ **sacramentalism** *n.* **sacramentalist** *n.* **sacramentality** /-tálitee/ *n.* **sacramentally** *adv.* [ME f. F *sacramental* or LL *sacramentalis* (as SACRAMENT)]

■ *adj.* **1** see SACRED 1b–c, 2a.

sacrarium /səkráireeəm/ *n.* (*pl.* **sacraria** /-reeə/) **1** the sanctuary of a church. **2** *RC Ch.* a piscina. **3** *Rom. Antiq.* a shrine; the room (in a house) containing the penates. [L f. *sacer sacri* holy]

sacred /sáykrid/ *adj.* **1 a** (often foll. by *to*) exclusively dedicated or appropriated (to a god or to some religious purpose). **b** made holy by religious association. **c** connected with religion; used for a religious purpose (*sacred music*). **2 a** safeguarded or required by religion, reverence, or tradition. **b** sacrosanct. **3** (of writings, etc.) embodying the laws or doctrines of a religion. □ **Sacred College** *RC Ch.* the body of cardinals. **sacred cow** *colloq.* an idea or institution unreasonably held to be above criticism (with ref. to the Hindus' respect for the cow as a holy animal). **Sacred Heart** *RC Ch.* the heart of Christ as an object of devotion. **sacred number** a number associated with religious symbolism, e.g., 7. □□ **sacredly** *adv.* **sacredness** *n.* [ME, past part. of obs. *sacre* consecrate f. OF *sacrer* f. L *sacrare* f. *sacer sacri* holy]

■ **1 a** dedicated, consecrated. **b** hallowed, holy, blessed, sanctified, revered, divine, venerable, venerated, *poet.* blest. **c** religious, spiritual; church, chapel, ecclesiastical; priestly, hieratic. **2 a** ritual, ceremonial, solemn, sacramental, liturgical, votive. **b** inviolable, inviolate, untouchable, protected, sacrosanct.

sacrifice /sákrifīs/ *n. & v.* ● *n.* **1 a** the act of giving up something valued for the sake of something else more important or worthy. **b** a thing given up in this way. **c** the loss entailed in this. **2 a** the slaughter of an animal or person or the surrender of a possession as an offering to a deity. **b** an animal, person, or thing offered in this way. **3** an act of prayer, thanksgiving, or penitence as propitiation. **4** *Theol.* **a** Christ's offering of himself in the Crucifixion. **b** the Eucharist as either a propitiatory offering of the body and blood of Christ or an act of thanksgiving. **5** (in games) a loss incurred deliberately to avoid a greater loss or to obtain a compensating advantage. ● *v.* **1** *tr.* give up (a thing) as a sacrifice. **2** *tr.* (foll. by *to*) devote or give over to. **3** *tr.* (also *absol.*) offer or kill as a sacrifice. □□ **sacrificial** /-físhəl/ *adj.* **sacrificially** /-físhəlee/ *adv.* [ME f. OF f. L *sacrificium* f. *sacrificus* (as SACRED)]

/.../ **pronunciation**	● **part of speech**
□ **phrases, idioms, and compounds**	
□□ **derivatives**	■ **synonym section**
cross-references appear in SMALL CAPITALS or *italics*	

■ *n.* **1 a** forfeiture, forgoing, giving up, relinquishment, loss. **b** loss, forfeit; see also OFFERING. **2 a** immolation; surrender, forfeiture, forgoing, giving up, yielding up, offering (up). **b** (burnt) offering, holocaust, hecatomb; donation, gift, *Relig.* oblation. ● *v.* **1** give up, forgo, forfeit, relinquish, surrender, let go (of), lose, yield, renounce, forswear; cease, stop, refrain from, *literary* desist from, forbear (from). **2** devote to, give over *or* up to, offer up to, yield up to. **3** immolate, offer (up), yield (up), give up. □□ **sacrificial** sacrificed, immolated, surrendered; atoning, expiatory, propitiatory, conciliatory.

sacrilege /sákrilij/ *n.* the violation or misuse of what is regarded as sacred. □□ **sacrilegious** /-líjəs/ *adj.* **sacrilegiously** *adv.* [ME f. OF f. L *sacrilegium* f. *sacrilegus* stealer of sacred things, f. *sacer sacri* sacred + *legere* take possession of]

■ desecration, profanation, debasement, violation, prostitution, dishonoring, vitiation, defilement, fouling, contamination, misuse, abuse, perversion, impiety, heresy, violation, profanity, blasphemy, irreverence, *poet.* befouling; outrage; impiousness, disrespect, maltreatment. □□ **sacrilegious** profane, impious, heretical, blasphemous, irreverent, disrespectful.

sacristan /sákristən/ *n.* **1** a person in charge of a sacristy and its contents. **2** *archaic* the sexton of a parish church. [ME f. med.L *sacristanus* (as SACRED)]

sacristy /sákristee/ *n.* (*pl.* **-ies**) a room in a church where the vestments, sacred vessels, etc., are kept and the celebrant can prepare for a service. [F *sacristie* or It. *sacrestia* or med.L *sacristia* (as SACRED)]

sacro- /sákrō, sáy-/ *comb. form* denoting the sacrum (*sacroiliac*).

sacroiliac /sákrōíleeak, sákrō-/ *adj. & n.* ● *adj.* of or relating to the juncture of the sacrum and the ilium bones of the pelvis ● *n.* the sacroiliac region.

sacrosanct /sákrōsangkt/ *adj.* (of a person, place, law, etc.) most sacred; inviolable. □□ **sacrosanctity** /-sángktitee/ *n.* [L *sacrosanctus* f. *sacro* ablat. of *sacrum* sacred rite (see SACRED) + *sanctus* (as SAINT)]

■ see SACRED 2b.

sacrum /sáykrəm, sák-/ *n.* (*pl.* **sacra** /-krə/ *or* **sacrums**) *Anat.* a triangular bone formed from fused vertebrae and situated between the two hipbones of the pelvis. [L *os sacrum* transl. Gk *hieron osteon* sacred bone (from its sacrificial use)]

SAD *abbr.* seasonal affective disorder.

sad /sad/ *adj.* (**sadder, saddest**) **1** unhappy; feeling sorrow or regret. **2** causing or suggesting sorrow (*a sad story*). **3** regrettable. **4** shameful; deplorable (*is in a sad state*). **5** (of a color) dull; neutral-tinted. **6** (of dough, etc.) *Brit.* heavy, having failed to rise. □ **sad sack** *colloq.* a very inept person, esp. a soldier. □□ **sadly** *adv.* **sadness** *n.* [OE *sæd* f. Gmc, rel. to L *satis*]

■ **1** unhappy, melancholy, downcast, dejected, depressed, low, sorrowful, gloomy, morose, glum, lugubrious, mournful, heartsick, crestfallen, chapfallen, disheartened, downhearted, blue, despondent, brokenhearted, heartbroken, woebegone, miserable, wretched. **2** depressing, gloomy, disheartening, dreary, dismal, funereal, somber, lugubrious, saddening, tearful, heartbreaking, bleak, distressing, dispiriting, calamitous. **3** see REGRETTABLE. **4** unfortunate, unsatisfactory, awful, bad, shabby, dirty, shameful, lamentable, miserable, sorry, wretched, pathetic, pitiful, pitiable, deplorable, terrible, *colloq.* lousy, *sl.* rotten. □□ **sadly** unhappily, gloomily, morosely, mournfully, despondently, miserably, wretchedly, dejectedly, dismally, somberly, lugubriously; unfortunately, alas, unluckily, lamentably, regrettably, deplorably, sad to relate. **sadness** unhappiness, misery, sorrow, dispiritedness, grief, depression, dejection, dejectedness, sorrowfulness, despondency, melancholy, gloom, gloominess, *literary* dolor.

sadden /sád'n/ *v.tr. & intr.* make or become sad.

■ depress, deject, sorrow, dishearten, distress, dispirit, discourage, grieve.

saddle /sád'l/ *n. & v.* ● *n.* **1** a seat of leather, etc., usu. raised at the front and rear, fastened on a horse, etc., for riding. **2** a seat for the rider of a bicycle, etc. **3** a cut of meat consisting of the two loins. **4** a ridge rising to a summit at each end. **5** the part of a draft horse's harness to which the shafts are attached. **6** a part of an animal's back resembling a saddle in shape or marking. **7** the rear part of a male fowl's back. **8** a support for a cable or wire on top of a suspension bridge, pier, or telegraph pole. **9** a fireclay bar for supporting ceramic ware in a kiln. ● *v.tr.* **1** put a saddle on (a horse, etc.). **2 a** (foll. by *with*) burden (a person) with a task, responsibility, etc. **b** (foll. by *on, upon*) impose (a burden) on a person. □ **in the saddle 1** mounted. **2** in office or control.

saddle horse a horse for riding. **saddle shoes** laced shoes with yokes that contrast in color with the rest of the upper.

saddle sore 1 a chafe from riding on a saddle. **2** a sore on a horse from the chafing of a saddle. **saddle stitch** a stitch of thread or a wire staple passed through the center of a magazine or booklet. □□ **saddleless** *adj.* [OE *sadol, sadul* f. Gmc]

■ *v.* **2** see BURDEN *v.* □ **saddle horse** see HACK² *n.* 1.

saddleback /sád'lbak/ *n.* **1** *Archit.* a tower-roof with two opposite gables. **2** a hill with a concave upper outline. **3** a black pig with a white stripe across the back. **4** any of various birds with a saddle-like marking esp. a New Zealand bird, *Philesturnus carunculatus.* □□ **saddlebacked** *adj.*

saddlebag /sád'lbag/ *n.* **1** each of a pair of bags laid across a horse, etc., behind the saddle. **2** a bag attached behind the saddle of a bicycle or motorcycle.

saddlebow /sád'lbō/ *n.* the arched front or rear of a saddle.

saddlecloth /sád'lklawth/ *n.* a cloth laid on a horse's back under the saddle.

saddler /sádlər/ *n.* a maker of or dealer in saddles and other equipment for horses.

saddlery /sádləree/ *n.* (*pl.* **-ies**) **1** the saddles and other equipment of a saddler. **2** a saddler's business or premises.

■ **1** see TACK².

saddletree /sád'ltree/ *n.* the frame of a saddle.

Sadducee /sájəsee, sádyə-/ *n.* a member of a Jewish sect or party of the time of Christ that denied the resurrection of the dead, the existence of spirits, and the obligation of the traditional oral law (cf. PHARISEE, ESSENE). □□ **Sadducean** /-seéən/ *adj.* [OE *sadducēas* f. LL *Sadducaeus* f. Gk *Saddoukaios* f. Heb. *ṣᵊdûḳî*, prob. = descendant of Zadok (2 Sam. 8:17)]

sadhu /saádoō/ *n.* (in India) a holy man, sage, or ascetic. [Skr., = holy man]

sadism /sáydizəm, sád-/ *n.* **1** a form of sexual perversion characterized by the enjoyment of inflicting pain or suffering on others (cf. MASOCHISM). **2** *colloq.* the enjoyment of cruelty to others. □□ **sadist** *n.* **sadistic** /sədístik/ *adj.* **sadistically** *adv.* [F *sadisme* f. Count or Marquis de *Sade*, Fr. writer d. 1814]

■ **2** see *brutality* (BRUTAL). □□ **sadist** brute, beast, savage, monster, devil. **sadistic** cruel, monstrous, brutal, brutish, beastly, ruthless, merciless, perverse, algolagnic.

sadomasochism /sáydōmásəkizəm, sádō-/ *n.* the combination of sadism and masochism in one person. □□ **sadomasochist** *n.* **sadomasochistic** /-kístik/ *adj.*

safari /səfáaree/ *n.* (*pl.* **safaris**) **1** a hunting or scientific expedition, esp. in E. Africa (*go on safari*). **2** a sightseeing trip to see African animals in their natural habitat. □ **safari park** an enclosed area where lions, etc., are kept in the open and through which visitors may drive. **safari suit** a lightweight suit usu. with short sleeves and four pleated pockets in the jacket. [Swahili f. Arab. *safara* to travel]

safe /sayf/ *adj. & n.* ● *adj.* **1 a** free of danger or injury. **b** (often foll. by *from*) out of or not exposed to danger (*safe from their enemies*). **2** affording security or not involving danger or risk (*put it in a safe place*). **3** reliable; certain; that can be counted on (*a safe catch; a safe method; is safe to win*). **4** prevented from escaping or doing harm (*have got him safe behind bars*). **5** (also **safe and sound**) uninjured; with no

harm done. **6** cautious and unenterprising; consistently moderate. ● *n.* **1** a strong, lockable cabinet, etc., for valuables. **2** esp. *Brit.* = meat safe. □ **on the safe side** with a margin of security against risks. **safe bet** a bet that is certain to succeed. **safe-conduct 1** a privilege of immunity from arrest or harm, esp. on a particular occasion. **2** a document securing this. **safe-deposit box** a secured box (esp. in a bank vault) for storing valuables. **safe house** a place of refuge or rendezvous for spies, etc. **safe period** the time during and near the menstrual period when conception is least likely. **safe sex** sexual activity in which precautions are taken to reduce the risk of spreading sexually transmitted diseases, esp. AIDS. □□ **safely** *adv.* **safeness** *n.* [ME f. AF *saf*, OF *sauf* f. L *salvus* uninjured: (n.) orig. *save* f. SAVE[1]]
■ *adj.* **1 a** see HARMLESS 1. **2** secure, protected, secured, sheltered, shielded; see also IMPREGNABLE[1]. **3** certain, sure, secure, sound, risk-free, riskless, reliable, dependable, solid, tried and tested *or* true. **5** unharmed, whole, uninjured, unhurt, sound, secure, out of harm's way, all right, *colloq.* OK. **6** cautious, conservative, moderate, tame; see also STEADY *adj.* 4, MODERATE *adj.* 1. ● *n.* **1** strongbox, safe-deposit box; coffer, chest. □ **on the safe side** secure, safe; see also SOUND[2] *adj.* 4. **safe house** see REFUGE 1, 2.

safecracker /sáyfkrakər/ *n.* a person who breaks open and robs safes.

safeguard /sáyfgaard/ *n.* & *v.* ● *n.* **1** a proviso, stipulation, quality, or circumstance that tends to prevent something undesirable. **2** a safe conduct. ● *v.tr.* guard or protect (rights, etc.) by a precaution or stipulation. [ME f. AF *salve garde*, OF *sauve garde* (as SAFE, GUARD)]
■ *n.* **1** precaution, preventive measure, safety measure, countermeasure, preventive, preventative. ● *v.* protect, defend, conserve, save, keep, care for, look after, shield, keep safe, guard.

safekeeping /sáyfkeeping/ *n.* preservation in a safe place.
■ safety, preservation; see also PROTECTION 1a.

safelight /sáyflīt/ *n.* *Photog.* a filtered light for use in a darkroom.

safety /sáyftee/ *n.* (*pl.* **-ies**) **1** the condition of being safe; freedom from danger or risks. **2** (*attrib.*) **a** designating any of various devices for preventing injury from machinery (*safety bar*; *safety lock*). **b** designating items of protective clothing (*safety helmet*). □ **safety belt 1** = *seat belt*. **2** any belt or strap securing a person to prevent injury. **safety catch** a contrivance for locking a gun trigger or preventing the accidental operation of machinery. **safety curtain** a fireproof curtain that can be lowered to cut off the auditorium in a theater from the stage. **safety-deposit box** = *safe-deposit box*. **safety factor** (or **factor of safety**) **1** the ratio of a material's strength to an expected strain. **2** a margin of security against risks. **safety film** a cinematographic film on a slow-burning or nonflammable base. **safety first** a motto advising caution. **safety fuse 1** a fuse (see FUSE[2]) containing a slow-burning composition for firing detonators from a distance. **2** *Electr.* a protective fuse (see FUSE[1]). **safety glass** glass that will not splinter when broken. **safety lamp** a miner's lamp so protected as not to ignite firedamp. **safety match** a match igniting only on a specially prepared surface. **safety net** a net placed to catch an acrobat, etc., in case of a fall. **safety pin** a pin with a point that is bent back to the head and is held in a guard when closed. **safety razor** a razor with a guard to reduce the risk of cutting the skin. **safety valve 1** (in a steam boiler) a valve opening automatically to relieve excessive pressure. **2** a means of giving harmless vent to excitement, etc. [ME *sauvete* f. OF *sauveté* f. med.L *salvitas -tatis* f. L *salvus* (as SAFE)]
■ **1** safeness, protection, shelter, security; aegis, cover, refuge, sanctuary; safekeeping.

safflower /sáflowr/ *n.* **1 a** a thistlelike plant, *Carthamus tinctorius*, yielding a red dye. **b** its dried petals. **2** a dye made from these, used in rouge, etc. □ **safflower oil** oil expressed from safflower seeds, used for food, paints, medicines, etc. [Du. *saffloer* or G *Safflor* f. OF *saffleur* f. obs. It. *saffiore*, of unkn. orig.]

saffron /sáfrən/ *n.* & *adj.* ● *n.* **1** a bright yellow-orange food coloring and flavoring made from the dried stigmas of the crocus, *Crocus sativus*. **2** the color of this. ● *adj.* saffroncolored. □□ **saffrony** *adj.* [ME f. OF *safran* f. Arab. *za'farān*]

safranine /sáfrəneen, -nin/ *n.* (also **safranin** /-nin/) any of a large group of mainly red dyes used in biological staining, etc. [F *safranine* (as SAFFRON): orig. of dye from saffron]

sag /sag/ *v.* & *n.* ● *v.intr.* (**sagged**, **sagging**) **1** sink or subside under weight or pressure, esp. unevenly. **2** have a downward bulge or curve in the middle. **3 a** fall in price. **b** (of a price) fall. **4** (of a ship) drift from its course, esp. to leeward. ● *n.* **1 a** the amount that a rope, etc., sags. **b** the distance from the middle of its curve to a straight line between its supports. **2** a sinking condition; subsidence. **3** a fall in price. **4** *Naut.* a tendency to leeward. □□ **saggy** *adj.* [ME f. MLG *sacken*, Du. *zakken* subside]
■ *v.* **1, 2** droop, sink, subside, slump, bend, dip; swag, bag. **3 a** drop, go *or* come down, fall, decrease, lessen. **b** drop, go *or* come down, fall, decline, slide, slip, weaken, slump, descend, diminish. ● *n.* **2** sagging, drop, droop, sinking, sinkage, subsidence, dip. **3** reduction, fall, decrease, drop, decline, slide, weakening, slump, flagging, faltering.

saga /saagə/ *n.* **1** a long story of heroic achievement, esp. a medieval Icelandic or Norwegian prose narrative. **2** a series of connected books giving the history of a family, etc. **3** a long, involved story. [ON, = narrative, rel. to SAW[3]]
■ **1** legend, epic, romance; *Edda*.

sagacious /səgáyshəs/ *adj.* **1** mentally penetrating; gifted with discernment; having practical wisdom. **2** acuteminded; shrewd. **3** (of a saying, plan, etc.) showing wisdom. **4** (of an animal) exceptionally intelligent; seeming to reason or deliberate. □□ **sagaciously** *adv.* **sagacity** /səgásitee/ *n.* [L *sagax sagacis*]
■ see ASTUTE 1. □□ **sagacity** see *astuteness* (ASTUTE).

sagamore /ságəmawr/ *n.* = SACHEM 1. [Penobscot *sagamo*]

sage[1] /sayj/ *n.* **1** an aromatic herb, *Salvia officinalis*, with dull grayish-green leaves. **2** its leaves used in cookery. **3** any plant of the genus *Salvia*. □ **sage green** the color of sage leaves. □□ **sagy** *adj.* [ME f. OF *sauge* f. L *salvia* healing plant f. *salvus* safe]

sage[2] /sayj/ *n.* & *adj.* ● *n.* **1** often *iron.* a profoundly wise person. **2** any of the ancients traditionally regarded as the wisest of their time. ● *adj.* **1** profoundly wise, esp. from experience. **2** of or indicating profound wisdom. **3** often *iron.* wise-looking; solemn-faced. □□ **sagely** *adv.* **sageness** *n.* **sageship** *n.* [ME f. OF ult. f. L *sapere* be wise]
■ *n.* **1** philosopher, wise man, guru, pundit, oracle, savant, expert, authority, elder, doyen *or* doyenne, Solomon. ● *adj.* **1** sensible, judicious, wise, prudent, commonsensical; commonsense. **2** wise, sagacious, perspicacious, profound, discerning, shrewd, intelligent, acute, penetrating.

sagebrush /sáyjbrush/ *n.* **1** a growth of shrubby aromatic plants of the genus *Artemisia*, esp. *A. tridentata*, found in some semiarid regions of western N. America. **2** this plant.

sagger /ságər/ *n.* (also **saggar**) a protective fireclay box enclosing ceramic ware while it is being fired. [prob. contr. of SAFEGUARD]

sagittal /sájit'l/ *adj.* *Anat.* **1** of or relating to the suture between the parietal bones of the skull. **2** in the same plane as this, or in a parallel plane. [F f. med.L *sagittalis* f. *sagitta* arrow]

Sagittarius /sájitáireeəs/ *n.* **1** a constellation, traditionally regarded as contained in the figure of an archer. **2 a** the ninth sign of the zodiac (the Archer). **b** a person born when the sun is in this sign. □□ **Sagittarian** *adj.* & *n.* [ME f. L, = archer, f. *sagitta* arrow]

/.../ **pronunciation**   ● **part of speech**
□ **phrases, idioms, and compounds**
□□ **derivatives**   ■ **synonym section**
cross-references appear in SMALL CAPITALS or *italics*

sagittate /sájitayt/ *adj. Bot.* & *Zool.* shaped like an arrow-head.

sago /sáygō/ *n.* (*pl.* **-os**) **1** a kind of starch, made from the powdered pith of the sago palm and used in puddings, etc. **2** (in full **sago palm**) any of several tropical palms and cy-cads, esp. *Cycas circinalis* and *Metroxylon sagu*, from which sago is made. [Malay *sāgū* (orig. through Port.)]

saguaro /səgwaárō, səwaárō/ *n.* (*pl.* **-os**) a giant cactus, *Carnegiea gigantea*, of the SW United States and Mexico. [Mex. Sp.]

sahib /saab, saáhib/ *n.* **1** *hist.* (in India) a form of address, often placed after the name, to European men. **2** *colloq.* a gentleman (*pukka sahib*). [Urdu f. Arab. *ṣāḥib* friend, lord]

said *past* and *past part.* of SAY.

saiga /síɡə, sáy-/ *n.* an antelope, *Saiga tatarica*, of the Asian steppes. [Russ.]

sail /sayl/ *n.* & *v.* ● *n.* **1** a piece of material (orig. canvas, now usu. nylon, etc.) extended on rigging to catch the wind and propel a boat or ship. **2** a ship's sails collectively. **3 a** a voyage or excursion in a sailing ship. **b** a voyage of specified duration. **4** a ship, esp. as discerned from its sails. **5** (*collect.*) ships in a squadron or company (*a fleet of twenty sail*). **6** (in *pl.*) *Naut.* esp. *Brit.* **a** *sl.* a maker or repairer of sails. **b** *hist.* a chief petty officer in charge of rigging. **7** a wind-catching apparatus, viz. a set of boards, attached to the arm of a windmill. **8 a** the dorsal fin of a sailfish. **b** the tentacle of a nautilus. **c** the float of a Portuguese man-of-war. ● *v.* **1** *intr.* travel on water by the use of sails or engine power. **2** *tr.* **a** navigate (a ship, etc.). **b** travel on (a sea). **3** *tr.* set (a toy boat) afloat. **4** *intr.* glide or move smoothly or in a stately manner. **5** *intr.* (often foll. by *through*) *colloq.* succeed easily (*sailed through the exams*). □ **sail arm** the arm of a windmill. **sail close to** (or **near**) **the wind 1** sail as nearly against the wind as possible. **2** *colloq.* come close to indecency or dishonesty; risk overstepping the mark. **sailing boat** *Brit.* = SAILBOAT. **sailing orders** instructions to a captain regarding departure, destination, etc. **sail into** *colloq.* attack physically or verbally with force. **take in sail** (or **the sails**) **1** furl the sail or sails of a vessel. **2** esp. *Brit.* moderate one's ambitions. **trim sails** cut expenses, etc. **under sail** with sails set. □□ **sailable** *adj.* **sailed** *adj.* (also in *comb.*). **sailless** *adj.* [OE *segel* f. Gmc]

■ *n.* **3** voyage, journey, trip, cruise; excursion. ● *v.* **1** go sailing *or* boating *or* yachting, cruise, set sail, put (out) to sea, travel. **2 a** navigate, pilot, steer. **4** drift, flow, waft, sweep, coast, float, scud, glide, slide, slip, skim; plane. **5** *colloq.* romp. □□ **sail close to** (or **near**) **the wind 2** take risks, play with fire, take one's life in one's hands, stick one's neck out, *colloq.* skate on thin ice; *sl.* go for broke.

sailboard /sáylbawrd/ *n.* a board with a mast and sail, used in windsurfing. □□ **sailboarder** *n.* **sailboarding** *n.*

sailboat /sáylbōt/ *n.* a boat driven by sails.

■ see BOAT *n.*

sailcloth /sáylklawth, -kloth/ *n.* **1** canvas for sails, upholstery, tents, etc. **2** a canvaslike dress material.

sailer /sáylər/ *n.* a ship of specified sailing power (*a good sailer*).

sailfish /sáylfish/ *n.* **1** any fish of the genus *Istiophorus*, with a large dorsal fin. **2** a basking shark.

sailor /sáylər/ *n.* **1** a seaman or mariner, esp. one below the rank of officer. **2** a person considered as liable or not liable to seasickness (*a good sailor*). □ **sailor hat 1** a straw hat with a straight narrow brim and flat top. **2** a hat with a turned-up brim in imitation of a sailor's. □□ **sailoring** *n.* **sailorless** *adj.* **sailorly** *adj.* [var. of SAILER]

■ **1** seaman, seafarer, seafaring man *or* woman, seagoing man *or* woman, mariner, (old) salt, sea dog, bluejacket, jack-tar, *colloq.* tar, *sl.* shellback, gob; yachtsman, yachtswoman.

sailplane /sáylplayn/ *n.* a glider designed for sustained flight.

sainfoin /sáynfoyn, sán-/ *n.* a leguminous plant, *Onobrychis viciifolia*, grown for fodder and having pink flowers. [obs. F *saintfoin* f. mod.L *sanum foenum* wholesome hay (because of its medicinal properties)]

saint /saynt/ *n.* & *v.* ● *n.* (*abbr.* **St.** or **S.**; *pl.* **Sts.** or **SS.**) **1** a holy or (in some churches) a canonized person regarded as having a place in heaven. **2** (**Saint** or **St.**) the title of a saint or archangel, hence the name of a church, etc. (*St. Paul's*) or (often with the loss of the apostrophe) the name of a town, etc. (*St. Andrews*). **3** a very virtuous person; a person of great real or affected holiness (*would try the patience of a saint*). **4** a member of the company of heaven (*with all the angels and saints*). **5** (*Bibl., archaic,* and used by Puritans, Mormons, etc.) one of God's chosen people; a member of the Christian Church or one's own branch of it. ● *v.tr.* **1** canonize; admit to the calendar of saints. **2** call or regard as a saint. **3** (as **sainted** *adj.*) sacred; of a saintly life; worthy to be regarded as a saint. □ **saint's day** a church festival in memory of a saint. □□ **saintdom** *n.* **sainthood** *n.* **saintlike** *adj.* **saintship** *n.* [ME f. OF *seint, saint* f. L *sanctus* holy, past part. of *sancire* consecrate]

■ *v.* **3** (**sainted**) see SAINTLY. □□ **saintlike** see HOLY 1, 2.

St. Andrew's cross /ándrōōz/ *n.* an X-shaped cross.

St. Anthony cross /ánthənee/ *n.* (also **St. Anthony's cross** /ánthəneez/) a T-shaped cross.

St. Anthony's fire /ánthəneez/ *n.* erysipelas or ergotism.

St. Bernard /bərnaárd/ *n.* (in full **St. Bernard dog**) **1** a very large dog of a breed orig. kept to rescue travelers by the monks of the Hospice on the Great St. Bernard pass in the Alps. **2** this breed.

St. Elmo's fire /élmōz/ *n.* a luminous electrical discharge sometimes seen on a ship or aircraft during a storm.

St. George's cross /jáwrjiz/ *n.* a +-shaped cross, red on a white background.

St. John's-wort /jónzwərt/ *n.* any yellow-flowered plant of the genus *Hypericum*, esp. *H. androsaemum*.

St. Luke's summer /lōōks/ *n. Brit.* a period of fine weather expected about Oct. 18.

saintly /sáyntlee/ *adj.* (**saintlier, saintliest**) very holy or virtuous. □□ **saintliness** *n.*

■ holy, blessed, beatific, godly, sainted, angelic, seraphic, pure, righteous, virtuous, blameless, *poet.* blest.

St. Martin's summer /maárt'nz/ *n. Brit.* a period of fine weather expected about Nov. 11.

saintpaulia /səntpáwleeə/ *n.* any plant of the genus *Saintpaulia*, esp. the African violet. [Baron W. von *Saint Paul*, Ger. soldier d. 1910, its discoverer]

St. Vitus's dance /vítəsiz, vítəs/ *n.* = *Sydenham's chorea* (see CHOREA).

saith /seth, sáyith/ *archaic 3rd sing. present* of SAY.

saithe /sayth/ *n. Sc.* a codlike fish, *Pollachius virens*, with skin that soils fingers like wet coal. Also called COALFISH, *coley*, POLLOCK. [ON *seithr*]

sake[1] /sayk/ *n.* □ **for Christ's** (or **God's** or **goodness'** or **Heaven's** or **Pete's**, etc.) **sake** an expression of urgency, impatience, supplication, anger, etc. **for old times' sake** in memory of former times. **for the sake of** (or **for a person's sake**) **1** out of consideration for; in the interest of; because of; owing to (*for my own sake as well as yours*). **2** in order to please, honor, get, or keep (*for the sake of uniformity*). [OE *sacu* contention, charge, fault, sake f. Gmc]

■ □ **for Christ's** (or **God's** or **goodness'** or **Heaven's** or **Pete's**, etc.) **sake** see GOD *int.* **for the sake of** out of consideration for, in the interest of, because of, owing to, for the benefit *or* well-being *or* good of. **for a person's sake** on a person's behalf *or* account.

sake[2] /saákee, -ke/ *n.* a Japanese alcoholic drink made from rice. [Jap.]

saker /sáykər/ *n.* **1** a large falcon, *Falco cherrug*, used in falconry, esp. the larger female bird. **2** *hist.* an old form of cannon. [ME f. OF *sacre* (in both senses), f. Arab. *ṣakr*]

saki /saákee/ *n.* (*pl.* **sakis**) any monkey of the genus *Pithecia* or *Chiropotes*, native to S. America, having coarse fur and a long nonprehensile tail. [F f. Tupi *çahy*]

Sakta var. of SHAKTA.

Sakti var. of SHAKTI.

sal /sál/ *n. Pharm.* salt.

salaam /səlaám/ *n.* & *v.* ● *n.* **1** the esp. Islamic salutation denoting 'peace.' **2** (in India) an obeisance, with or without the salutation, consisting of a low bow of the head and body with the right palm on the forehead. **3** (in *pl.*) respectful compliments. ● *v.* **1** *tr.* make a salaam to (a person). **2** *intr.* make a salaam. [Arab. *salām*]

■ *n.* **2** see BOW² *n.* ● *v.* **2** see BOW² *v.* 1.

salable /sáylǝbǝl/ *adj.* (also **saleable**) fit to be sold; finding purchasers. □□ **salability** /-bílitee/ *n.*

■ popular, sought-after, commercial, marketable.

salacious /sǝláyshǝs/ *adj.* **1** lustful; lecherous. **2** (of writings, pictures, talk, etc.) tending to cause sexual desire. □□ **salaciously** *adv.* **salaciousness** *n.* **salacity** /sǝlásitee/ *n.* [L *salax salacis* f. *salire* leap]

■ **1** see LECHEROUS. **2** see EROTIC. □□ **salaciousness** see RIBALDRY.

salad /sálǝd/ *n.* **1** a cold dish of various mixtures of raw or cooked vegetables or herbs, usu. seasoned with oil, vinegar, etc. **2** a vegetable or herb suitable for eating raw. □ **salad cream** *Brit.* creamy salad dressing. **salad days** a period of youthful inexperience. **salad dressing** a mixture of oil, vinegar, etc., used in a salad. [ME f. OF *salade* f. Prov. *salada* ult. f. L *sal* salt]

■ □ **salad days** see YOUTH 1.

salade var. of SALLET.

salamander /sálǝmandǝr/ *n.* **1** *Zool.* any tailed newtlike amphibian of the order Urodela, esp. the genus *Salamandra*, once thought able to endure fire. **2** a mythical lizardlike creature credited with this property. **3** a portable cooking device, esp. one with burners. **4** an elemental spirit living in fire. **5** a red-hot iron used for lighting pipes, gunpowder, etc. **6** a metal plate heated and placed over food to brown it. □□ **salamandrian** /-mándreeǝn/ *adj.* **salamandrine** /-mándrin/ *adj.* **salamandroid** /-mándroyd/ *adj.* & *n.* (in sense 1). [ME f. OF *salamandre* f. L *salamandra* f. Gk *salamandra*]

salami /sǝlaámee/ *n.* (*pl.* **salamis**) a highly seasoned orig. Italian sausage often flavored with garlic. [It., pl. of *salame*, f. LL *salare* (unrecorded) to salt]

sal ammoniac /sál ǝmṓneeak/ *n.* ammonium chloride, a white crystalline salt. [L *sal ammoniacus* 'salt of Ammon,' associated with the Roman temple of Ammon in N. Africa]

salariat /sǝláireeǝt/ *n.* the salaried class. [F f. *salaire* (see SALARY), after *prolétariat*]

salary /sálǝree/ *n.* & *v.* ● *n.* (*pl.* **-ies**) a fixed regular payment, usu. monthly or quarterly, made by an employer to an employee, esp. a professional or white-collar worker (cf. WAGE *n.* 1). ● *v.tr.* (**-ies, -ied**) (usu. as **salaried** *adj.*) pay a salary to. [ME f. AF *salarie*, OF *salaire* f. L *salarium* orig. soldier's salt-money f. *sal* salt]

■ *n.* income, pay, earnings, emolument, compensation; wage(s).

sale /sayl/ *n.* **1** the exchange of a commodity for money, etc.; an act or instance of selling. **2** the amount sold (*the sales were enormous*). **3** the rapid disposal of goods at reduced prices for a period, esp. at the end of a season, etc. **4 a** an event at which goods are sold. **b** a public auction. □ **for** (or **up for**) **sale** offered for purchase. **on sale** available for purchase, esp. at a reduced price. **sales department**, etc., the section of a firm concerned with selling as opposed to manufacturing or dispatching goods. **sales talk** persuasive talk to promote the sale of goods or the acceptance of an idea, etc. **sales tax** a tax on sales or on the receipts from sales. [OE *sala* f. ON]

■ **1** selling, vending, marketing, trafficking, trading, traffic, trade; exchange, transaction.□ **for** (or **up for**) **sale** on the market, on offer, on the block.

saleable var. of SALABLE.

salep /sálǝp/ *n.* a starchy preparation of the dried tubers of various orchids, used in cookery and formerly medicinally. [F f. Turk. *sālep* f. Arab. (*kuṣa-'l-*) *ta'lab* fox, fox's testicles]

saleratus /sálǝráytǝs/ *n.* an ingredient of baking powder consisting mainly of potassium or sodium bicarbonate; baking soda. [mod.L *sal aeratus* aerated salt]

saleroom /sáylrōōm, -rŏŏm/ *n.* esp. *Brit.* a salesroom.

salesclerk /sáylzklǝrk/ *n.* a salesperson in a retail store.

salesgirl /sáylzgǝrl/ *n.* a saleswoman.

■ salesperson, cashier, (sales)clerk, *Brit.* shop assistant.

Salesian /sǝléezhǝn, -shǝn/ *n.* & *adj.* ● *n.* a member of an educational religious order within the RC Church. ● *adj.* of or relating to this order. [St. François de *Sales*, Fr. RC bishop d. 1622]

saleslady /sáylzlaydee/ *n.* (*pl.* **-ies**) a saleswoman.

■ salesperson, cashier, (sales)clerk, *Brit.* shop assistant.

salesman /sáylzmǝn/ *n.* (*pl.* **-men**; *fem.* **saleswoman**, *pl.* **-women**) a person employed to sell goods or services in a store or on a route, etc., or as an agent between the producer and retailer.

■ salesperson, cashier, (sales)clerk, *Brit.* shop assistant.

salesmanship /sáylzmǝnship/ *n.* **1** skill in selling. **2** the techniques used in selling.

salesperson /sáylzpǝrsǝn/ *n.* a salesman or saleswoman (used as a neutral alternative).

■ salesman, saleswoman, saleslady, salesgirl, (sales)clerk, *Brit.* shop assistant.

salesroom /sáylzrōōm, -rŏŏm/ *n.* a room for the display and purchase of items, esp. at an auction.

Salian /sáyleeǝn, -yǝn/ *adj.* & *n.* ● *adj.* of or relating to the Salii, a 4th-c. Frankish people living near the Ijssel River, from which the Merovingians were descended. ● *n.* a member of this people. [LL *Salii*]

Salic /sálik, sáy-/ *adj.* = SALIAN. □ **Salic law** *hist.* **1** a law excluding females from dynastic succession, esp. as the alleged fundamental law of the French monarchy. **2** a Frankish law book extant in Merovingian and Carolingian times. [F *Salique* or med.L *Salicus* f. *Salii* (as SALIAN)]

salicet /sálisit/ *n.* an organ stop like a salicional but one octave higher. [as SALICIONAL]

salicin /sálisin/ *n.* (also **salicine** /-seen/) a bitter crystalline glucoside with analgesic properties, obtained from poplar and willow bark. [F *salicine* f. L *salix -icis* willow]

salicional /sálíshǝnǝl/ *n.* an organ stop with a soft reedy tone like that of a willow pipe. [G f. L *salix* as SALICIN]

salicylic acid /sálisílik/ *n.* a bitter chemical used as a fungicide and in the manufacture of aspirin and dyestuffs. □□ **salicylate** /sǝlísilayt/ *n.* [*salicyl* its radical f. F *salicyle* (as SALICIN)]

salient /sáylyǝnt/ *adj.* & *n.* ● *adj.* **1** jutting out; prominent; conspicuous; most noticeable. **2** (of an angle, esp. in fortification) pointing outward (opp. REENTRANT). **3** *Heraldry* (of a lion, etc.) standing on its hind legs with the forepaws raised. **4** *archaic* **a** leaping or dancing. **b** (of water, etc.) jetting forth. ● *n.* a salient angle or part of a work in fortification; an outward bulge in a line of military attack or defense. □ **salient point** *archaic* the initial stage, origin, or first beginning. □□ **salience** *n.* **saliency** *n.* **saliently** *adv.* [L *salire* leap]

■ *adj.* **1** conspicuous, outstanding, pronounced, noticeable, prominent, significant, important, marked, striking, remarkable, distinguishing, distinctive, eminent, noteworthy, notable, principal, chief, primary, *disp.* unique.

salientian /sáylee-énshǝn/ *adj.* & *n.* = ANURAN. [mod.L *Salientia* (as SALIENT)]

saliferous /sǝlífǝrǝs/ *adj.* *Geol.* (of rock, etc.) containing much salt. [L *sal* salt + -FEROUS]

salina /sǝlínǝ, -leé-/ *n.* a salt lake. [Sp. f. med.L, = salt pit (as SALINE)]

saline /sáyleen, -lín/ *adj.* & *n.* ● *adj.* **1** (of natural waters, springs, etc.) impregnated with or containing salt or salts. **2** (of food or drink, etc.) tasting of salt. **3** of chemical salts. **4** of the nature of a salt. **5** (of medicine) containing a salt or salts of alkaline metals or magnesium. ● *n.* **1** a salt lake, spring, marsh, etc. **2** a salt pan or saltworks. **3** a saline substance, esp. a medicine. **4** a solution of salt in water. □□ **sa-**

/.../ **pronunciation**	● **part of speech**
□ **phrases, idioms, and compounds**	
□□ **derivatives**	■ **synonym section**
cross-references appear in SMALL CAPITALS or *italics*	

linity /səlínitee/ *n.* **salinization** /sálinizáyshən/ *n.* **salinometer** /sálinómitər/ *n.* [ME f. L *sal* salt]
■ *adj.* **1, 2** see SALT *adj.*

saliva /səlívə/ *n.* liquid secreted into the mouth by glands to provide moisture and facilitate chewing and swallowing. □ **saliva test** a scientific test requiring a saliva sample. □□ **salivary** /sáliveree/ *adj.* [ME f. L]
■ see SPIT¹ *n.*

salivate /sálivayt/ *v.* **1** *intr.* secrete or discharge saliva esp. in excess or in greedy anticipation. **2** *tr.* produce an unusual secretion of saliva in (a person) usu. with mercury. □□ **salivation** /-váyshən/ *n.* [L *salivare* (as SALIVA)]
■ **1** see SLAVER² *v.*

Salk vaccine /sawlk/ *n.* a vaccine developed against polio. [J. E. *Salk*, Amer. scientist b. 1914]

sallet /sálit/ *n.* (also **salade** /səláad/) *hist.* a light helmet with an outward-curving rear part. [F *salade* ult. f. L *caelare* engrave f. *caelum* chisel]

sallow¹ /sálō/ *adj.* & *v.* ● *adj.* (**sallower, sallowest**) (of the skin or complexion, or of a person) of a sickly yellow or pale brown. ● *v.tr.* & *intr.* make or become sallow. □□ **sallowish** *adj.* **sallowness** *n.* [OE *salo* dusky f. Gmc]
■ *adj.* see PALE¹ *adj.* 1.

sallow² /sálō/ *n. Brit.* **1** a willow tree, esp. one of a low-growing or shrubby kind. **2** the wood or a shoot of this. □□ **sallowy** *adj.* [OE *salh salg-* f. Gmc, rel. to OHG *salaha*, ON *selja*, L *salix*]

sally¹ /sálee/ *n.* & *v.* (*pl.* **-ies**) ● *n.* **1** a sudden charge from a fortification upon its besiegers; a sortie. **2** a going forth; an excursion. **3** a witticism; a piece of banter; a lively remark, esp. by way of attack upon a person or thing or of a diversion in argument. **4** a sudden start into activity; an outburst. **5** *archaic* an escapade. ● *v.intr.* (**-ies, -ied**) **1** (usu. foll. by *out, forth*) go for a walk, set out on a journey, etc. **2** (usu. foll. by *out*) make a military sally. **3** *archaic* issue or come out suddenly. □ **sally port** an opening in a fortification for making a sally from. [F *saillie* fem. past part. of *saillir* issue f. OF *salir* f. L *salire* leap]
■ *n.* **1** see CHARGE *n.* 4a. **3** see WITTICISM. ● *v.* **1** (*sally forth*) see *set forth* 1 (SET¹). **3** see ISSUE *v.* 1.

sally² /sálee/ *n. Brit.* (*pl.* **-ies**) **1** the part of a bell rope prepared with inwoven wool for holding. **2 a** the first movement of a bell when set for ringing. **b** the bell's position when set. □ **sally hole** the hole through which the bell rope passes. [perh. f. SALLY¹ in sense 'leaping motion']

Sally Lunn /sálee lún/ *n.* a sweet, light teacake, usu. served hot. [perh. f. the name of a woman selling them at Bath *c.*1800]

salmagundi /sálməgúndee/ *n.* (*pl.* **salmagundis**) **1** a dish of chopped meat, anchovies, eggs, onions, etc., and seasoning, usu. served as a salad. **2** a general mixture; a miscellaneous collection of articles, subjects, qualities, etc. [F *salmigondis* of unkn. orig.]
■ **2** see MIXTURE 2.

Salmanazar /sálmənázər/ *n.* a wine bottle of about 12 times the standard size. [*Shalmaneser* king of Assyria (2 Kings 17-18)]

salmi /sálmee/ *n.* (*pl.* **salmis**) a ragout or casserole esp. of partly roasted gamebirds. [F, abbr. formed as SALMAGUNDI]

salmon /sámən/ *n.* & *adj.* ● *n.* (*pl.* same or (esp. of types) **salmons**) **1** any anadromous fish of the family Salmonidae, esp. of the genus *Salmo*, much prized for its (often smoked) pink flesh. **2** *Austral.* & *NZ* the barramundi or a similar fish. ● *adj.* salmon pink. □ **salmon pink** the color of salmon flesh. **salmon trout** a large, silver-colored trout, *Salmo trutta.* □□ **salmonoid** *adj.* & *n.* (in sense 1). **salmony** *adj.* [ME f. AF *sa(u)moun*, OF *saumon* f. L *salmo -onis*]
■ *adj.* see PINK¹ *adj.* 1.

salmonella /sálmənélə/ *n.* (*pl.* **salmonellae** /-lee/) **1** any bacterium of the genus *Salmonella*, esp. any of various serotypes causing food poisoning. **2** food poisoning caused by infection with salmonellae. □□ **salmonellosis** /-lōsis/ *n.* [mod.L f. D. E. *Salmon*, Amer. veterinary surgeon d. 1914]

salon /səlón, saláwN/ *n.* **1** the reception room of a large or fashionable house. **2** a room or establishment where a hair-

dresser, beautician, etc., conducts business. **3** *hist.* a meeting of eminent people in the reception room of a (esp. Parisian) lady of fashion. **4** (**Salon**) an annual exhibition in Paris of the work of living artists. □ **salon music** light music often played by a small orchestra. [F: see SALOON]
■ **1** see LOUNGE *n.* 1.

saloon /səlōōn/ *n.* **1** a drinking establishment; bar; tavern. **2** (in full **saloon car**) *Brit.* an automobile with a closed body and no partition behind the driver; sedan. **3** a public room on a ship. **4** esp. *Brit.* **a** a large room or hall, esp. in a hotel or public building. **b** a public room or gallery for a specified purpose (*billiard saloon; shooting saloon*). **5** (in full **saloon bar**) *Brit.* the more comfortable room in a bar. **6** (in full **saloon car**) *Brit.* a luxurious railroad car serving as a lounge, etc. □ **saloon deck** a deck for passengers using the saloon. **saloon keeper** a bartender, manager, or owner of a bar. [F *salon* f. It. *salone* augment. of *sala* hall]
■ **1, 5** see BAR¹ *n.* 4b, c. **2** sedan.

salpiglossis /sálpiglósis/ *n.* any solanaceous plant of the genus *Salpiglossis*, cultivated for its funnel-shaped flowers. [mod.L, irreg. f. Gk *salpigx* trumpet + *glōssa* tongue]

salping- /sálping/ *comb. form Med.* denoting the Fallopian tubes. [Gk *salpigx salpiggos*, lit. 'trumpet']

salpingectomy /sálpinjéktəmee/ *n.* (*pl.* **-ies**) *Med.* the surgical removal of the Fallopian tubes.

salpingitis /sálpinjítis/ *n. Med.* inflammation of the Fallopian tubes.

salsa /sáalsə/ *n.* **1** a kind of dance music of Latin American origin, incorporating jazz and rock elements. **2** a dance performed to this music. **3** a spicy sauce made from tomatoes, chilies, onions, etc., often served as a dip or condiment. [Sp. (as SAUCE)]

salsify /sálsifee, -fī/ *n.* (*pl.* **-ies**) **1** a European plant, *Tragopogon porrifolius*, with long cylindrical fleshy roots. **2** this root used as a vegetable. □ **black salsify** scorzonera. [F *salsifis* f. obs. It. *salsefica*, of unkn. orig.]

SALT /sawlt/ *abbr.* Strategic Arms Limitation Talks (or Treaty).

salt /sawlt/ *n., adj.,* & *v.* ● *n.* **1** (also **common salt**) sodium chloride; the substance that gives seawater its characteristic taste, got in crystalline form by mining from strata consisting of it or by the evaporation of seawater, and used for seasoning or preserving food, or for other purposes. **2** a chemical compound formed from the reaction of an acid with a base, with all or part of the hydrogen of the acid replaced by a metal or metallike radical. **3** sting; piquancy; pungency; wit (*added salt to the conversation*). **4** (in *sing.* or *pl.*) **a** a substance resembling salt in taste, form, etc. (*bath salts; Epsom salts; smelling salts*). **b** (esp. in *pl.*) this type of substance used as a laxative. **5** a marsh, esp. one flooded by the tide, often used as a pasture or for collecting water for salt making. **6** (also **old salt**) an experienced sailor. **7** (in *pl.*) an exceptional rush of seawater up river. ● *adj.* **1** impregnated with, containing, or tasting of salt; cured or preserved or seasoned with salt. **2** (of a plant) growing in the sea or in salt marshes. **3** (of tears, etc.) bitter. **4** (of wit) pungent. ● *v.tr.* **1** cure or preserve with salt or brine. **2** season with salt. **3** make (a narrative, etc.) piquant. **4** sprinkle (the ground, etc.) with salt, esp. in order to melt snow, etc. **5** treat with a solution of salt or mixture of salts. □ **eat salt with** *Brit.* be a guest of. **not made of salt** *Brit.* not disconcerted by wet weather. **put salt on the tail of** capture (with ref. to jocular directions given to children for catching a bird). **salt an account** *Brit. sl.* set an extremely high or low price for articles. **salt-and-pepper** (of materials, etc., and esp. of hair) with light and dark colors mixed together. **salt away** (or **down**) *sl.* lay away or stash money, etc.; save. **salt the books** *sl.* show receipts as larger than they really have been. **salt dome** a mass of salt forced up into sedimentary rocks. **salt glaze** a hard stoneware glaze produced by throwing salt into a hot kiln containing the ware. **salt grass** grass growing in salt meadows or in alkaline regions. **salt horse** *Naut. sl.* **1** salted beef. **2** a naval officer with general duties. **salt lake** a lake of salt water. **salt lick 1** a place where animals go to lick salt from the ground. **2** this salt. **salt marsh** = sense 5 of *n.* **salt meadow** a meadow subject to flooding with salt water. **salt mine** a mine yielding rock salt. **salt a mine** *sl.* introduce extraneous ore, material, etc., to make the source seem rich. **the salt of the earth** a person or people of great worthiness, reliability, honesty, etc.; those whose qualities are a model for the rest (Matt. 5:13). **salt pan** a vessel, or a depression near the sea, used for getting salt by evaporation. **salt spoon** a small spoon usu. with a short handle and a roundish deep bowl for serving table salt. **salt water 1** sea water. **2** *sl.* tears. **salt well** a bored well yielding brine. **take with a grain of salt** regard as exaggerated; be incredulous about; believe only part of. **worth one's salt** efficient; capable. □□ **saltish** *adj.* **saltless** *adj.* **saltly** *adv.* **saltness** *n.* [OE *s(e)alt s(e)altan,* OS, ON, Goth. *salt,* OHG *salz* f. Gmc]

■ **1** sodium chloride; sea salt, rock salt, table salt. **3** sting, piquancy, spice, spiciness, zest, zestiness, pungency, vigor, vitality, liveliness, pepper, poignancy, bite, seasoning, zip, *colloq.* pep, zing, punch; wit, Attic salt *or* wit. **6** see SAILOR. ● *adj.* **1** salty, saline, brackish, briny; pickled, kippered, soused; corned, cured. ● *v.* **1** cure, preserve, corn; pickle, souse. **2** season, flavor. **3** see SPICE *v.* 2. □ **salt away** (or **down**) save (up), hoard, put *or* lay away, put *or* lay *or* set aside, squirrel (away), store up, stockpile, amass, accumulate, pile up, *archaic* set by, *colloq.* stash away. **salt the books** *colloq.* cook the books. **take with a grain of salt** see DISTRUST *v.* **worth one's salt** see CAPABLE 1.

saltarello /sáltərélō, sáwl-/ *n.* (*pl.* **-os** or **saltarelli** /-lee/) an Italian and Spanish dance for one or two persons, with sudden skips. [It. *salterello,* Sp. *saltarelo,* rel. to It. *saltare* and Sp. *saltar* leap, dance f. L *saltare* (as SALTATION)]

saltation /saltáyshən, sawl-/ *n.* **1** the act or an instance of leaping or dancing; a jump. **2** a sudden transition or movement. □□ **saltatory** /sáltətawree, -sáwl-/ *adj.* **saltatorial** /-tətáwreeəl/ *adj.* [L *saltatio* f. *saltare* frequent. of *salire* salt-leap]

saltbush /sáwltbŏŏsh/ *n.* an edible plant, *Atriplex hortensis,* with red, yellow, or green leaves sometimes used as a substitute for spinach or sorrel. Also called ORACHE.

saltcellar /sáwltselər/ *n.* **1** a vessel holding salt for table use. **2** *Brit. colloq.* an unusually deep hollow above the collarbone, esp. found in women. [SALT + obs. *saler* f. AF f. OF *salier* salt-box f. L (as SALARY), assim. to CELLAR]

■ **1** cruet, saltshaker.

salter /sáwltər/ *n.* **1** a manufacturer or dealer in salt. **2** a worker at a saltworks. **3** a person who salts fish, etc. **4** = DRYSALTER. [OE *sealtere* (as SALT)]

saltern /sáwltərn/ *n.* **1** a saltworks. **2** a set of pools for the natural evaporation of seawater. [OE *sealtærn* (as SALT, *ærn* building)]

saltigrade /sáltigrayd, sáwl-/ *adj. & n. Zool.* ● *adj.* (of arthropods) moving by leaping or jumping. ● *n.* a saltigrade arthropod, e.g., a jumping spider, beach flea, etc. [mod.L *Saltigradae* f. L *saltus* leap f. *salire* salt- + *-gradus* walking]

saltine /sawltéen/ *n.* a lightly salted, square, flat cracker.

salting /sáwlting/ *n. Brit.* **1** in senses of SALT *v.* **2** (esp. in *pl.*) *Geol.* a salt marsh; a marsh overflowed by the sea.

saltire /sáwlteer, -tīr, sál-/ *n. Heraldry* an ordinary formed by a bend and a bend sinister crossing like a St Andrew's cross. □ **in saltire** arranged in this way. □□ **saltirewise** *adv.* [ME f. OF *sau(l)toir* etc., stirrup cord, stile, saltire, f. med.L *saltatorium* (as SALTATION)]

saltpeter /sáwltpeetər/ *n.* (*Brit.* **saltpetre**) potassium nitrate, a white crystalline salty substance used in preserving meat and as a constituent of gunpowder. [ME f. OF *salpetre* f. med.L *salpetra* prob. for *sal petrae* (unrecorded) salt of rock (i.e. found as an incrustation): assim. to SALT]

saltshaker /sáwltshaykər/ *n.* a container of salt for sprinkling on food.

saltus /sáltəs, sáw-/ *n. literary* a sudden transition; a breach of continuity. [L, = leap]

saltwater /sáwltwawtər/ *adj.* **1** of or living in the sea. **2** pertaining to or made with salt water.

saltworks /sáwltwərks/ *n.* a place where salt is produced.

saltwort /sáwltwərt, -wawrt/ *n.* any plant of the genus *Salsola;* glasswort.

salty /sáwltee/ *adj.* (**saltier, saltiest**) **1** tasting of, containing, or preserved with salt. **2** racy, risqué. □□ **saltiness** *n.*

■ **2** see RACY 2.

salubrious /səlŏŏbreeəs/ *adj.* **1** health-giving; healthy. **2** (of surroundings, etc.) pleasant; agreeable. □□ **salubriously** *adv.* **salubriousness** *n.* **salubrity** *n.* [L *salubris* f. *salus* health]

■ **1** see WHOLESOME 1. **2** see PLEASANT.

saluki /səlŏŏkee/ *n.* (*pl.* **salukis**) **1** a tall, swift, slender dog of a silky-coated breed with large ears and a fringed tail and feet. **2** this breed. [Arab. *salūkī*]

salutary /sályəteree/ *adj.* **1** producing good effects; beneficial. **2** *archaic* health-giving. [ME f. F *salutaire* or L *salutaris* f. *salus -utis* health]

■ see BENEFICIAL.

salutation /sályətáyshən/ *n.* **1** a sign or expression of greeting or recognition of another's arrival or departure. **2** (usu. in *pl.*) words spoken or written to inquire about another's health or well-being. □□ **salutational** *adj.* [ME f. OF *salutation* or L *salutatio* (as SALUTE)]

■ **1** greeting, glad hand.

salutatory /səlŏŏtətawree/ *adj. & n.* ● *adj.* of salutation. ● *n.* (*pl.* **-ies**) an oration, esp. as given by a member of a graduating class, often the second-ranking member. □□ **salutatorian** /-táwreeən/ *n.* (in sense of *n.*). [L *salutatorius* (as SALUTE)]

salute /səlŏŏt/ *n. & v.* ● *n.* **1** a gesture of respect, homage, or courteous recognition, esp. made to or by a person when arriving or departing. **2 a** *Mil. & Naut.* a prescribed or specified movement of the hand or of weapons or flags as a sign of respect or recognition. **b** (prec. by *the*) the attitude taken by an individual soldier, sailor, policeman, etc., in saluting. **3** the discharge of a gun or guns as a formal or ceremonial sign of respect or celebration. **4** *Fencing* the formal performance of certain guards, etc., by fencers before engaging. ● *v.* **1 a** *tr.* make a salute to. **b** *intr.* (often foll. by *to*) perform a salute. **2** *tr.* greet; make a salutation to. **3** *tr.* (foll. by *with*) receive or greet with (a smile, etc.). **4** *tr. archaic* hail as (king, etc.). □ **take the salute 1** (of the highest officer present) acknowledge it by gesture as meant for him. **2** receive ceremonial salutes by members of a procession. □□ **saluter** *n.* [ME f. L *salutare* f. *salus -utis* health]

■ *n.* **1** greeting, salutation. ● *v.* **2** greet, hail, accost; address. **4** hail as, acclaim, recognize *or* acknowledge as.

salvage /sálvij/ *n. & v.* ● *n.* **1** the rescue of a ship, its cargo, or other property, from loss at sea, destruction by fire, etc. **2** the property, etc., saved in this way. **3 a** the saving and utilization of waste paper, scrap material, etc. **b** the materials salvaged. **4** payment made or due to a person who has saved a ship or its cargo. ● *v.tr.* **1** save from a wreck, fire, etc. **2** retrieve or preserve (something favorable) in adverse circumstances (*tried to salvage some dignity*). □□ **salvageable** *adj.* **salvager** *n.* [F f. med.L *salvagium* f. L *salvare* SAVE[1]]

■ *n.* **1** recovery, rescue, retrieval, deliverance, reclamation, salvation. **3 a** reclamation, recycling, reuse, reutilization. ● *v.* **1** save, recover, rescue, deliver, retrieve, salve, reclaim. **2** preserve, retain, save, retrieve; see also RECOVER *v.* 1.

salvation /salváyshən/ *n.* **1** the act of saving or being saved; preservation from loss, calamity, etc. **2** deliverance from sin and its consequences and admission to heaven, brought about by Christ. **3** a religious conversion. **4** a person or thing that saves (*was the salvation of*). □ **Salvation Army** a worldwide evangelical group organized on quasi-military lines for the revival of Christianity and helping the poor. □□ **salvationism** *n.* **salvationist** *n.* (both nouns esp. with ref. to the

Salvation Army). [ME f. OF *sauvacion, salvacion,* f. eccl.L *salvatio -onis* f. *salvare* SAVE[1], transl. Gk *sōtēria*]

■ **1** see SALVAGE *n.* 1. **2** redemption, deliverance. **4** see SAVIOR 1.

salve[1] /sav, saav/ *n. & v.* ● *n.* **1** a healing ointment. **2** (often foll. by *for*) a thing that is soothing or consoling for wounded feelings, an uneasy conscience, etc. **3** *archaic* a thing that explains away a discrepancy or palliates a fault. ● *v.tr.* **1** soothe (pride, self-love, conscience, etc.). **2** *archaic* anoint (a wound, etc.). **3** *archaic* smooth over; make good; vindicate; harmonize. [OE *s(e)alf(e), s(e)alfian* f. Gmc; senses 1 and 3 of v. partly f. L *salvare* SAVE[1]]

■ *n.* **1** balm, ointment, unguent, lotion; dressing; embrocation, liniment. **2** balm, palliative, opiate, narcotic, relief. ● *v.* **1** relieve, ease, alleviate, assuage, palliate, soothe, mollify, comfort, appease. **3** see *sort out* 4.

salve[2] /salv/ *v.tr.* **1** save (a ship or its cargo) from loss at sea. **2** save (property) from fire. □□ **salvable** *adj.* [back-form. f. SALVAGE]

■ see SALVAGE *v.* 1.

salver /sálvər/ *n.* a tray usu. of gold, silver, brass, or electroplate, on which drinks, letters, etc., are offered. [F *salve* tray for presenting food to the king f. Sp. *salva* assaying of food f. *salvar* SAVE: assoc. with *platter*]

■ see PLATTER.

Salve Regina /saálvay rəjéenə/ *n.* **1** a Roman Catholic hymn or prayer said or sung to the Virgin Mary. **2** the music for this. [f. the opening words *salve regina* hail (holy) queen]

salvia /sálveeə/ *n.* any plant of the genus *Salvia,* esp. *S. splendens* with red or blue flowers. [L, = SAGE[1]]

salvo[1] /sálvō/ *n.* (*pl.* -**oes** or -**os**) **1** the simultaneous firing of artillery or other guns, esp. as a salute or in a seafight. **2** a number of bombs released from aircraft at the same moment. **3** a round or volley of applause. [earlier *salve* f. F f. It. *salva* salutation (as SAVE[1])]

■ **1, 2** see VOLLEY *n.* 1. **3** see APPLAUSE 1.

salvo[2] /sálvō/ *n.* (*pl.* -**os**) **1** a saving clause; a reservation (*with an express salvo of their rights*). **2** a tacit reservation. **3** a quibbling evasion; a bad excuse. **4** an expedient for saving reputation or soothing pride or conscience. [L, ablat. of *salvus* SAFE as used in *salvo jure* without prejudice to the rights of (a person)]

sal volatile /sál vōlát'lee/ *n.* ammonium carbonate, esp. in the form of a flavored solution in alcohol used as smelling salts. [mod.L, = volatile salt]

salvor /sálvər/ *n.* a person or ship making or assisting in salvage. [SALVE[2]]

SAM *abbr.* surface-to-air missile.

Sam. *abbr.* Samuel (Old Testament).

samadhi /səmaádee/ *n. Buddhism & Hinduism* **1** a state of concentration induced by meditation. **2** a state into which a perfected holy man is said to pass at his apparent death. [Skr. *samādhi* contemplation]

samara /sámərə, səmáirə, səmaá-/ *n. Bot.* a winged seed from the sycamore, ash, etc. [mod.L f. L, = elm-seed]

Samaritan /səmárit'n/ *n. & adj.* ● *n.* **1** (in full **good Samaritan**) a charitable or helpful person (with ref. to Luke 10:33, etc.). **2** a native of Samaria in West Jordan. **3** the language of this people. ● *adj.* of Samaria or the Samaritans. □□ **Samaritanism** *n.* [LL *Samaritanus* f. Gk *Samareitēs* f. *Samareia* Samaria]

samarium /səmáireeəm/ *n. Chem.* a soft, silvery metallic element of the lanthanide series, occurring naturally in monazite, etc., and used in making ferromagnetic alloys. ¶ Symb.: **Sm.** [*samarskite* the mineral in which its spectrum was first observed, f. *Samarski* name of a 19th-c. Russ. official]

samba /sámbə, saám-/ *n. & v.* ● *n.* **1** a Brazilian dance of African origin. **2** a ballroom dance imitative of this. **3** the music for this. ● *v.intr.* (**sambas, sambaed** /-bəd/, **sambaing** /-bə-ing/) dance the samba. [Port., of Afr. orig.]

sambar /sámbər, saám-/ *n.* (also **samba, sambhar**) either of two large deer, *Cervus unicolor* or *C. equinus,* native to S. Asia. [Hindi *sā(m)bar*]

Sam Browne /sam brówn/ *n.* (in full **Sam Browne belt**) an army officer's belt and the shoulder strap supporting it. [Sir *Sam*uel J. *Browne,* Brit. military commander d. 1901]

same /saym/ *adj., pron., & adv.* ● *adj.* **1** (often prec. by *the*) identical; not different; unchanged (*everyone was looking in the same direction; the same car was used in another crime; saying the same thing over and over*). **2** unvarying; uniform; monotonous (*the same old story*). **3** (usu. prec. by *this, these, that, those*) (of a person or thing) previously alluded to; just mentioned; aforesaid (*this same man was later my husband*). ● *pron.* (prec. by *the*) **1** the same person or thing (*the others asked for the same*). **2** *Law* or *archaic* the person or thing just mentioned (*detected the youth breaking in and apprehended the same*). ● *adv.* (usu. prec. by *the*) similarly; in the same way (*we all feel the same; I want to go, the same as you do*). □ **all** (or **just**) **the same 1** emphatically the same. **2** in spite of changed conditions, adverse circumstances, etc. (*but you should offer, all the same*). **at the same time 1** simultaneously. **2** notwithstanding; in spite of circumstances, etc. **be all** (or **just**) **the same to** an expression of indifference or impartiality (*it's all the same to me what we do*). **by the same token** see TOKEN. **same here** *colloq.* the same applies to me. **the same to you!** may you do, have, find, etc., the same thing; likewise. **the very same** emphatically the same. □□ **sameness** *n.* [ME f. ON *sami, sama,* with Gmc cognates]

■ *adj.* **1** identical, exactly or just the same; selfsame, very; unchanged, unaltered. **2** unchanging, changeless, unchanged, unmodified, unaltered, constant, uniform, unvaried, unvarying, monotonous. **3** aforesaid, aforementioned, aforestated, abovementioned, abovestated, above-named. ● *pron.* **2** see SAME *adj.* 3 above. ● *adv.* (*the same*) similarly, in the same way; see also ALIKE *adv.* □ **all** (or **just**) **the same 2** at the same time, nevertheless, nonetheless, even so, yet, but, anyway, anyhow, in any case, in any event, at any rate, regardless, notwithstanding, still, for all that, *colloq.* still and all; that (having been) said, having said that, when all is said and done. **at the same time 1** see *at once* 2 (ONCE). **2** see NOTWITHSTANDING *adv., conj.* □□ **sameness** see UNIFORMITY.

samey /sáymee/ *adj.* (**samier, samiest**) *Brit. colloq.* lacking in variety; monotonous. □□ **sameyness** *n.*

Samhain /saáwin/ *n. Brit.* Nov. 1, celebrated by the Celts as a festival marking the beginning of winter. [Ir. *Samhain*]

samisen /sámisen/ *n.* a long three-stringed Japanese guitar, played with a plectrum. [Jap. f. Chin. *san-hsien* f. *san* three + *hsien* string]

samite /sámīt, sáy-/ *n. hist.* a rich medieval dress fabric of silk occas. interwoven with gold. [ME f. OF *samit* f. med.L *examitum* f. med. Gk *hexamiton* f. Gk *hexa-* six + *mitos* thread]

samizdat /saámizdáat, səmyizdáat/ *n.* a system of clandestine publication of banned literature in the former USSR. [Russ., = self-publishing house]

Samnite /sámnīt/ *n. & adj.* ● *n.* **1** a member of a people of ancient Italy often at war with republican Rome. **2** the language of this people. ● *adj.* of this people or their language. [ME f. L *Samnites* (pl.), rel. to *Sabinus* SABINE]

Samoan /səmṓən/ *n. & adj.* ● *n.* **1** a native of Samoa, a group of islands in the Pacific. **2** the language of this people. ● *adj.* of or relating to Samoa or its people or language. [*Samoa*]

samovar /sáməvaar/ *n.* a Russian urn for making tea, with an internal heating tube to keep water at boiling point. [Russ., = self-boiler]

Samoyed /sáməyed, səmóyed/ *n.* **1** a member of a people of northern Siberia. **2** the language of this people. **3** (also **samoyed**) **a** a dog of a white Arctic breed. **b** this breed. [Russ. *samoed*]

Samoyedic /sáməyédik/ *n. & adj.* ● *n.* the language of the Samoyeds. ● *adj.* of or relating to the Samoyeds.

samp /samp/ *n.* **1** coarsely ground corn. **2** porridge made of this. [Algonquian *nasamp* softened by water]

sampan /sámpan/ *n.* a small boat usu. with a stern oar or stern oars, used in the Far East. [Chin. *san-ban* f. *san* three + *ban* board]

samphire /sámfīr/ *n.* **1** an umbelliferous maritime rock plant, *Crithmum maritimum*, with aromatic fleshy leaves used in pickles. **2** the glasswort. [earlier *samp(i)ere* f. F (*herbe de*) *Saint Pierre* St Peter('s herb)]

sample /sámpəl/ *n. & v.* ● *n.* **1** (also *attrib.*) a small part or quantity intended to show what the whole is like. **2** a small amount of fabric, food, or other commodity, esp. given to a prospective customer. **3** a specimen, esp. one taken for scientific testing or analysis. **4** an illustrative or typical example. ● *v.tr.* **1** take or give samples of. **2** try the qualities of. **3** get a representative experience of. [ME f. AF *assample*, OF *essample* EXAMPLE]

■ *n.* **1** specimen, example, representative, representation, illustration, sampling, crosssection, sampler; (*attrib.*) specimen, representative, illustrative, trial, test. **2** swatch; bite, nibble, taste. **3** specimen, *Biol.* section. **4** see ILLUSTRATION 2. ● *v.* test, taste, experience; see also TRY *v.* 3.

sampler[1] /sámplər/ *n.* a piece of embroidery worked in various stitches as a specimen of proficiency (often displayed on a wall, etc.). [OF *essamplaire* (as EXEMPLAR)]

sampler[2] /sámplər/ *n.* **1** a person who samples. **2** a collection of representative items, etc.

■ **2** see SAMPLE *n.* 1.

sampling /sámpling/ *n.* a technique in electronic music involving digitally encoding a piece of sound and reusing it as part of a composition or recording.

samsara /səmsaárə/ *n. Ind. Philos.* the endless cycle of death and rebirth to which life in the material world is bound. □□ **samsaric** *adj.* [Skr. *saṃsāra* a wandering through]

samskara /səmskaárə/ *n. Ind. Philos.* **1** a purificatory ceremony or rite marking an event in one's life. **2** a mental impression, instinct, or memory. [Skr. *saṃskāra* a making perfect, preparation]

Samson /sámsən/ *n.* a person of great strength or resembling Samson in some respect. □ **samson post 1** a strong pillar passing through the hold of a ship or between decks. **2** a post in a whaler to which a harpoon rope is attached. [LL f. Gk *Sampsōn* f. Heb. *šimšôn* (Judg. 13–16)]

samurai /sámŏōri, sáa-/ *n.* (*pl.* same) **1** a Japanese army officer. **2** *hist.* a military retainer; a member of a military caste in Japan. [Jap.]

sanative /sánətiv/ *adj.* **1** healing; curative. **2** of or tending to physical or moral health. [ME f. OF *sanatif* or LL *sanativus* f. L *sanare* cure]

■ **1** see MEDICINAL *adj.*

sanatorium /sánətáwreeəm/ *n.* (*pl.* **sanatoriums** or **sanatoria** /-reeə/) **1** an establishment for the treatment of invalids, esp. of convalescents and the chronically sick. **2** *Brit.* a room or building for sick people in a school, etc. [mod.L (as SANATIVE)]

■ **1** rest home, convalescent home, nursing home, sanitarium, *Brit.* health farm. **2** infirmary, sickroom, sick bay.

sanctify /sángktifī/ *v.tr.* (**-ies, -ied**) **1** consecrate; set apart or observe as holy. **2** purify or free from sin. **3** make legitimate or binding by religious sanction; justify; give the color of morality or innocence to. **4** make productive of or conducive to holiness. □□ **sanctification** /-fikáyshən/ *n.* **sanctifier** *n.* [ME f. OF *saintifier* f. eccl.L *sanctificare* f. L *sanctus* holy]

■ **1** consecrate, hallow, make sacred *or* holy; glorify, exalt. **2** purify, cleanse; see also PURGE *v.* 1. **3** confirm, sanction, ratify, justify, legitimate, legitimatize, legitimize, legalize, license, canonize.

sanctimonious /sángktimōneeəs/ *adj.* making a show of sanctity or piety. □□ **sanctimoniously** *adv.* **sanctimoniousness** *n.* **sanctimony** /sángktimōnee/ *n.* [L *sanctimonia* sanctity (as SAINT)]

■ hypocritical, self-righteous, canting, pharisaical, pietistic, unctuous, *colloq.* holier-than-thou, goody-goody, smarmy.

sanction /sángkshən/ *n. & v.* ● *n.* **1** approval or encouragement given to an action, etc., by custom or tradition; express permission. **2** confirmation or ratification of a law, etc. **3 a** a penalty for disobeying a law or rule, or a reward for obeying it. **b** a clause containing this. **4** *Ethics* a consideration operating to enforce obedience to any rule of conduct. **5** (esp. in *pl.*) military or esp. economic action by a nation to coerce another to conform to an international agreement or norms of conduct. **6** *Law hist.* a law or decree. ● *v.tr.* **1** authorize, countenance, or agree to (an action, etc.). **2** ratify; attach a penalty or reward to; make binding. □□ **sanctionable** *adj.* [F f. L *sanctio -onis* f. *sancire sanct-* make sacred]

■ *n.* **1** agreement, concurrence, acceptance, affirmation, assent, acquiescence, compliance, approval, permission, OK, encouragement, support, advocacy, backing, sponsorship, favor, countenance. **2** confirmation, ratification, authorization, legalization, legitimatization, legitimation, legitimization, validation, license, certification, approval, permission, imprimatur, seal *or* stamp (of approval), signet. **3 a** see PENALTY 1, REWARD *n.* 1a. ● *v.* **1** authorize, countenance, agree to, approve, permit, allow, subscribe to, commission, consent to, support, encourage, advocate, back, sponsor, favor, approbate. **2** confirm, ratify, second, authorize, legalize, legitimatize, legitimize, legitimate, validate, license, certify, notarize.

sanctitude /sángktitōōd, -tyōōd/ *n. archaic* saintliness. [ME f. L *sanctitudo* (as SAINT)]

■ see SANCTITY 1.

sanctity /sángktitee/ *n.* (*pl.* **-ies**) **1** holiness of life; saintliness. **2** sacredness; the state of being hallowed. **3** inviolability. **4** (in *pl.*) sacred obligations, feelings, etc. [ME f. OF *sain(c)tité* or L *sanctitas* (as SAINT)]

■ **1** piety, holiness, saintliness, divinity, grace, sacredness, godliness, *archaic* sanctitude. **2** sacredness, holiness. **3** unassailability, inviolability, indomitability.

sanctuary /sángkchōōeree/ *n.* (*pl.* **-ies**) **1** a holy place; a church, temple, etc. **2 a** the inmost recess or holiest part of a temple, etc. **b** the part of the chancel containing the high altar. **3** a place where birds, wild animals, etc., are bred and protected. **4** a place of refuge, esp. for political refugees. **5 a** immunity from arrest. **b** the right to offer this. **6** *hist.* a sacred place where a fugitive from the law or a debtor was secured by medieval church law against arrest or violence. □ **take sanctuary** resort to a place of refuge. [ME f. AF *sanctuarie*, OF *sanctuaire* f. L *sanctuarium* (as SAINT)]

■ **1** sanctum, shrine, chapel, temple, church, house of worship, house of God, holy place; synagogue, mosque, pagoda. **3** reserve, preserve, conservation area, national park. **4** asylum, refuge, retreat, shelter. **5 a** asylum, refuge, protection, shelter, safety. □ **take sanctuary** seek asylum.

sanctum /sángktəm/ *n.* (*pl.* **sanctums**) **1** a holy place. **2** *colloq.* a person's private room, study, or den. □ **sanctum sanctorum** /sangktórəm/ **1** the holy of holies in the Jewish temple. **2** = sense 2 of *n.* **3** an inner retreat. **4** an esoteric doctrine, etc. [L, neut. of *sanctus* holy, past part. of *sancire* consecrate: *sanctorum* genit. pl. in transl. of Heb. *ḳōdeš haḳḳ°ḏāšīm* holy of holies]

■ **1** sanctuary, holy place, shrine, chapel, temple. **2** sanctum sanctorum, den, study, retreat; hiding place, hideaway, cubby(hole), *colloq.* hideout.

Sanctus /sángktəs, saángktōōs/ *n.* (also **sanctus**) **1** the prayer or hymn beginning "Holy, holy, holy" said or sung at the end of the Eucharistic preface. **2** the music for this. □ **Sanctus bell** a handbell or the bell in the turret at the junction of the nave and the chancel, rung at the Sanctus or at the elevation of the Eucharist. [ME f. L, = holy]

sand /sand/ *n. & v.* ● *n.* **1** a loose granular substance resulting from the wearing down of esp. siliceous rocks and found on the seashore, riverbeds, deserts, etc. **2** (in *pl.*) grains of

/.../ **pronunciation**	● **part of speech**
□ **phrases, idioms, and compounds**	
□□ **derivatives**	■ **synonym section**
cross-references appear in SMALL CAPITALS or *italics*	

sand. **3** (in *pl.*) an expanse or tracts of sand. **4** a light yellow-brown color like that of sand. **5** (in *pl.*) a sandbank. **6** *colloq.* firmness of purpose; grit. ● *v.tr.* **1** smooth or polish with sandpaper or sand. **2** sprinkle or overlay with, or bury under, sand. **3** adulterate (sugar, etc.) with sand. □ **sand crack 1** a fissure in a horse's hoof. **2** a crack in the human foot from walking on hot sand. **3** esp. *Brit.* a crack in brick due to imperfect mixing. **sand dollar** any of various round, flat sea urchins, esp. of the order Clypeasteroida. **sand dune** (or **hill**) a mound or ridge of sand formed by the wind. **sand fly 1** any small fly of the genus *Simulium*. **2** any biting fly of the genus *Phlebotomus* transmitting the viral disease leishmaniasis. **sand flea** a chigoe or a beach flea. **sand-groper** *Austral.* **1** a gold-rush pioneer. **2** *joc.* a Western Australian. **sand hill** a dune. **sand hopper** any of various small jumping crustaceans of the order Amphipoda, burrowing on the seashore; a beach flea. **sand lance** any eellike fish of the family Ammodytidae or Hypotychidae: also called LAUNCE. **sand martin** = *bank swallow.* **the sands are running out** the allotted time is nearly at an end. **sand yacht** esp. *Brit.* = *land yacht.* □□ **sander** *n.* **sandlike** *adj.* [OE *sand* f. Gmc] ■ *n.* **6** see GRIT *n.* ● *v.* **1** see SMOOTH *v.* 1. □ **sand bar** see SHALLOW *n.*

sandal[1] /sándˀl/ *n.* & *v.* ● *n.* **1** a light shoe with an openwork upper or no upper, attached to the foot usu. by straps. **2** a strap for fastening a low shoe, passing over the instep or around the ankle. ● *v.tr.* **1** (esp. as **sandaled** *adj.*) put sandals on (a person, a person's feet). **2** fasten or provide (a shoe) with a sandal. [ME f. L *sandalium* f. Gk *sandalion* dimin. of *sandalon* wooden shoe, prob. of Asiatic orig.]

sandal[2] /sándˀl/ *n.* = SANDALWOOD. □ **sandal tree** any tree yielding sandalwood, esp. the white sandalwood, *Santalum album*, of India. [ME f. med.L *sandalum*, ult. f. Skr. *candana*]

sandalwood /sándˀlwŏŏd/ *n.* **1** the scented wood of a sandal tree. **2** a perfume derived from this. **3** any tree from which such is derived. □ **red sandalwood** the red wood from either of two SE Asian trees, *Adenanthera pavonina* and *Pterocarpus santalinus*, used as lumber and to produce a red dye. **sandalwood oil** a yellow aromatic oil made from the sandal tree.

sandarac /sándərak/ *n.* (also **sandarach**) **1** the gummy resin of a N. African conifer, *Tetraclinis articulata*, used in making varnish. **2** *Brit.* = REALGAR. [L *sandaraca* f. Gk *sandarakē*, of Asiatic orig.]

sandbag /sándbag/ *n.* & *v.* ● *n.* a bag filled with sand for use: **1** (in fortification) for making temporary defenses or for the protection of a building, etc., against blast and splinters or floodwaters. **2** as ballast esp. for a boat or balloon. **3** as a weapon to inflict a heavy blow without leaving a mark. **4** to stop a draft from a window or door. ● *v.tr.* (**-bagged**, **-bagging**) **1** barricade or defend. **2** place sandbags against (a window, chink, etc.). **3** fell with a blow from a sandbag. **4** coerce by harsh means. □□ **sandbagger** *n.*

sandbank /sándbangk/ *n.* a deposit of sand forming a shallow place in the sea or a river. ■ see SHALLOW *n.*

sandbar /sándbaar/ *n.* a sandbank at the mouth of a river or on the coast.

sandblast /sándblast/ *v.* & *n.* ● *v.tr.* roughen, treat, or clean with a jet of sand driven by compressed air or steam. ● *n.* this jet. □□ **sandblaster** *n.*

sandbox /sándboks/ *n.* **1** a box of sand, esp. one for children to play in. **2** *hist.* a device for sprinkling sand to dry ink.

sandcastle /sándkasəl/ *n.* a shape like a castle made in sand, usu. by a child on the seashore.

sanderling /sándərling/ *n.* a small wading bird, *Calidris alba*, of the sandpiper family. [perh. f. an OE form *sandyrthling* (unrecorded, as SAND + *yrthling* plowman, also the name of a bird)]

sandhi /sándee, saán-/ *n.* *Gram.* the process whereby the form of a word changes as a result of its position in an utterance (e.g., the change from *a* to *an* before a vowel). [Skr. *saṃdhi* putting together]

sandhog /sándhawg, -hog/ *n.* a person who works underwater laying foundations, constructing tunnels, etc.

sandiver /sándivər/ *n.* liquid scum formed in glass making. [ME app. f. F *suin de verre* exhalation of glass f. *suer* to sweat]

sandlot /sándlot/ *n.* a vacant lot or a piece of unoccupied sandy land used for children's games.

sandman /sándman/ *n.* the personification of tiredness causing children's eyes to smart toward bedtime.

sandpaper /sándpaypər/ *n.* & *v.* ● *n.* paper with sand or another abrasive stuck to it for smoothing or polishing. ● *v.tr.* smooth with sandpaper.

sandpiper /sándpipər/ *n.* any of various wading birds of the family Scolopacidae, frequenting coastal areas.

sandpit /sándpit/ *n.* **1** a pit from which sand is excavated. **2** *Brit.* a children's sandbox.

sandsoap /sándsōp/ *n.* heavy-duty gritty soap.

sandstone /sándstōn/ *n.* **1** any clastic rock containing particles visible to the naked eye. **2** a sedimentary rock of consolidated sand commonly red, yellow, brown, gray, or white.

sandstorm /sándstawrm/ *n.* a desert storm of wind with clouds of sand. ■ see STORM *n.* 1.

sandwich /sándwich, sán-/ *n.* & *v.* ● *n.* **1** two or more slices of bread with a filling of meat, cheese, etc., between them. **2** *Brit.* a cake of two or more layers with jam or cream between (*bake a sponge sandwich*). ● *v.tr.* **1** put (a thing, statement, etc.) between two of another character. **2** squeeze in between others (*sat sandwiched in the middle*). □ **sandwich board** two hinged advertisement boards made to hang from the shoulders. **sandwich man** (*pl.* **men**) a person hired to walk the streets displaying sandwich boards. [4th Earl of *Sandwich*, Engl. nobleman d. 1792, said to have eaten food in this form so as not to leave the gaming table]

sandwort /sándwərt, -wawrt/ *n.* any low-growing plant of the genus *Arenaria*, usu. bearing small white flowers.

sandy /sándee/ *adj.* (**sandier**, **sandiest**) **1** having the texture of sand. **2** having much sand. **3 a** (of hair) yellowish-red. **b** (of a person) having sandy hair. □ **sandy blight** *Austral.* conjunctivitis with sandlike grains in the eye; trachoma. □□ **sandiness** *n.* **sandyish** *adj.* [OE *sandig* (as SAND)] ■ **1** gritty, grainy, granular. **3 a** see RED *adj.* 4.

sane /sayn/ *adj.* **1** of sound mind; not mad. **2** (of views, etc.) moderate; sensible. □□ **sanely** *adv.* **saneness** *n.* [L *sanus* healthy] ■ **1** normal, of sound mind, rational, compos (mentis), *colloq.* right in the head, all there. **2** sound, well-balanced, right-minded, levelheaded, reasonable, moderate, sensible, judicious.

sang past of SING.

sangaree /sánggəree/ *n.* **1** a cold drink of wine diluted and spiced. **2** sangria. [Sp. *sangría* SANGRIA]

sang-froid /saaNfrwaá/ *n.* composure, coolness, etc., in danger or under agitating circumstances. [F, = cold blood] ■ cold-bloodedness, coolness, coolheadedness, indifference, composure, phlegm, self-possession, self-control, poise, imperturbability, equanimity, *colloq.* unflappability, *sl.* cool.

sangrail /sanggráyl/ *n.* = GRAIL. [ME f. OF *saint graal* (as SAINT, GRAIL)]

sangria /sanggreeə/ *n.* a sweet Spanish drink of iced red wine with lemonade, fruit, spices, etc. [Sp., = bleeding:]

sanguinary /sánggwəneree/ *adj.* **1** accompanied by or delighting in bloodshed. **2** bloody; bloodthirsty. **3** (of laws) inflicting death freely. □□ **sanguinarily** /-nérəlee/ *adv.* **sanguinariness** *n.* [L *sanguinarius* f. *sanguis -inis* blood] ■ **1** bloodthirsty, gory; slaughterous, murderous, homicidal; brutal, brutish, savage, barbarous. **2** bloody, bloodthirsty, sanguineous, *archaic* sanguine.

sanguine /sánggwin/ *adj.* & *n.* ● *adj.* **1** optimistic; confident. **2** (of the complexion) florid; bright; ruddy. **3** *hist.* of a ruddy complexion with a courageous and hopeful amorous disposition. **4** *hist.* of the temperament in which blood predominates over the other humors. **5** *Heraldry* or *literary* blood red. **6** *archaic* bloody; bloodthirsty. ● *n.* **1** a blood-red color. **2** a crayon of chalk colored red or flesh with iron oxide.

□□ **sanguinely** adv. **sanguineness** n. (both in sense 1 of n.). [ME f. OF sanguin -ine blood-red f. L sanguineus (as SANGUINARY)]

■ adj. **1** optimistic, rosy, confident, hopeful. **2** florid, bright, ruddy; see also ROSY 1. **6** bloody, bloodthirsty; see also GORY.

sanguineous /sanggwíneeəs/ adj. **1** sanguinary. **2** Med. of or relating to blood. **3** blood-red. **4** full-blooded; plethoric. [L sanguineus (as SANGUINE)]

■ **1** sanguinary, bloody.

Sanhedrin /sanhédrin, -heé-, saan-/ n. (also **Sanhedrim** /-drim/) the highest court of justice and the supreme council in ancient Jerusalem with 71 members. [late Heb. sanhedrîn f. Gk sunedrion (as SYN-, hedra seat)]

sanicle /sánikəl/ n. any umbelliferous plant of the genus Sanicula, esp. S. europaea, formerly believed to have healing properties. [ME ult. f. med.L sanicula perh. f. L sanus healthy]

sanify /sánifî/ v.tr. (-ies, -ied) esp. Brit. make healthy; improve the sanitary state of. [L sanus healthy]

sanitarium /sánitáireeəm/ n. (pl. **sanitariums** or **sanitaria** /-reeə/) **1** an establishment for the restoration of health; sanatorium. **2** a health resort. [pseudo-L f. L sanitas health]

sanitary /sániteree/ adj. **1** of the conditions that affect health, esp. with regard to dirt and infection. **2** hygienic; free from or designed to kill germs, infection, etc. □ **sanitary engineer** a person dealing with systems needed to maintain public health. **sanitary napkin** (Brit. **towel**) an absorbent pad used during menstruation. **sanitary ware** porcelain for bathrooms, etc. □□ **sanitarian** /-áireeən/ n. & adj. **sanitarily** adv. **sanitariness** n. [F sanitaire f. L sanitas: see SANITY]

■ **2** clean, sterile, hygienic, antiseptic, disinfected, aseptic, germ-free, bacteria-free.

sanitation /sánitáyshən/ n. **1** sanitary conditions. **2** the maintenance or improving of these. **3** the disposal of sewage and refuse from houses, etc. □□ **sanitate** /sánitayt/ v.tr. & intr. **sanitationist** n. [irreg. f. SANITARY]

sanitize /sánitîz/ v.tr. **1** make sanitary; disinfect. **2** render (information, etc.) more acceptable by removing improper or disturbing material. □□ **sanitizer** n.

■ **1** see DISINFECT. □□ **sanitizer** see DISINFECTANT n.

sanity /sánitee/ n. **1 a** the state of being sane. **b** mental health. **2** the tendency to avoid extreme views. [ME f. L sanitas (as SANE)]

■ **1** saneness, reason, mental health or soundness, normality, rationality, stability, balance. **2** see SENSE n. 4, 5, STABILITY.

sank past of SINK.

sannyasi /sunyaásee/ n. (also **sanyasi**) (pl. same) a Hindu religious mendicant. [Hindi & Urdu sannyāsī f. Skr. saṃnyāsin laying aside f. saṃ together, ni down, as throw]

sans /sanz, soN/ prep. archaic or joc. without. [ME f. OF san(z), sen(s) ult. f. L sine, infl. by L absentia in the absence of]

sansculotte /sánzkyoōlót, -koō-, saaNkʏláwt/ n. **1** hist. a lower-class Parisian republican in the French Revolution. **2** an extreme republican or revolutionary. □□ **sansculottism** n. [F, lit. = without knee breeches]

■ **2** see REVOLUTIONARY n.

Sanskrit /sánskrit/ n. & adj. ● n. the ancient and sacred language of the Hindus in India. ● adj. of or in this language. □□ **Sanskritic** /-skrítik/ adj. **Sanskritist** n. [Skr. saṃskṛta composed, elaborated, f. saṃ together, kṛ make, -ta past part. ending]

sans serif /sansérif/ n. & adj. (also **sanserif**) Printing ● n. a form of type without serifs. ● adj. without serifs. [app. f. SANS + SERIF]

Santa Claus /sántə klawz/ n. (also colloq. **Santa**) a legendary person said to bring children presents on the night before Christmas. [orig. US f. Du. dial. Sante Klaas St. Nicholas]

santolina /sántəleénə/ n. any aromatic shrub of the genus Santolina, with finely divided leaves and small usu. yellow flowers. [mod.L, var. of SANTONICA]

santonica /santónikə/ n. **1** a shrubby wormwood plant, Artemisia cina, yielding santonin. **2** the dried flower heads of this used as an anthelmintic. [L f. Santones an Aquitanian tribe]

santonin /sántənin/ n. a toxic drug extracted from santonica and other plants of the genus Artemisia, used as an anthelmintic. [SANTONICA + -IN]

sanyasi var. of SANNYASI.

sap[1] /sap/ n. & v. ● n. **1** the vital juice circulating in plants. **2** vigour; vitality. **3** = SAPWOOD. ● v.tr. (**sapped, sapping**) **1** drain or dry (wood) of sap. **2** exhaust the vigor of (my energy had been sapped by disappointment). **3** remove the sapwood from (a log). □ **sap green** n. **1** the pigment made from buckthorn berries. **2** the color of this. ● adj. of this color. □□ **sapful** adj. **sapless** adj. [OE sæp prob. f. Gmc]

■ n. **1** (vital) juice or fluid. **2** vigor, vitality, lifeblood, poet. ichor; see also LIFE 8. ● v. **2** bleed, drain, draw, rob, milk.

sap[2] /sap/ n. & v. ● n. **1** a tunnel or trench to conceal assailants' approach to a fortified place; a covered siege trench. **2** an insidious or slow undermining of a belief, resolution, etc. ● v. (**sapped, sapping**) **1** intr. **a** dig a sap or saps. **b** approach by a sap. **2** tr. undermine; make insecure by removing the foundations. **3** tr. weaken or destroy insidiously. [ult. f. It. zappa spade, spadework, in part through F sappe sap(p)er, prob. of Arab. orig.]

■ v. **2** see UNDERCUT v. 4. **3** weaken, devitalize, deplete, drain, erode, enervate, debilitate; destroy, cripple, wreck; see also UNDERMINE 1, 2.

sap[3] /sap/ n. sl. a foolish person. [abbr. of sapskull f. SAP[1] = sapwood + SKULL]

■ fool, nincompoop, ninny, dunce, ass, simpleton, ignoramus, noddy, noodle, colloq. idiot, nitwit, dimwit, chump, Brit. sl. muggins, esp. Brit. sl. twit; dupe, gull, colloq. pushover, sl. sucker, fall guy, (easy) mark, sl. patsy, schnook.

sapanwood var. of SAPPANWOOD.

sapid /sápid/ adj. literary **1** having (esp. an agreeable) flavor; savory; palatable; not insipid. **2** literary (of talk, writing, etc.) not vapid or uninteresting. □□ **sapidity** /səpíditee/ n. [L sapidus f. sapere taste]

■ **1** see TASTY.

sapient /sáypeeənt/ adj. literary **1** wise. **2** aping wisdom; of fancied sagacity. □□ **sapience** n. **sapiently** adv. [ME f. OF sapient or L part. stem of sapere be wise]

■ **1** see WISE adj. 1. □□ **sapience** see WISDOM 2, 3.

sapiential /sáypee-énshəl/ adj. literary of or relating to wisdom. [ME f. F sapiential or eccl.L sapientialis f. L sapientia wisdom]

sapling /sápling/ n. **1** a young tree. **2** a youth. **3** a greyhound in its first year.

sapodilla /sápədíllə, -deéyə/ n. a large evergreen tropical American tree, Manilkara zapota, with edible fruit and durable wood, and sap from which chicle is obtained. □ **sapodilla plum** the fruit of this tree. [Sp. zapotillo dimin. of zapote f. Aztec tzápotl]

saponaceous /sápənáyshəs/ adj. **1** of, like, or containing soap; soapy. **2** joc. unctuous; flattering. [mod.L saponaceus f. L sapo -onis soap]

■ **2** see OILY 3.

saponify /səpónifî/ v. (-ies, -ied) **1** tr. turn (fat or oil) into soap by reaction with an alkali. **2** tr. convert (an ester) to an acid and alcohol. **3** intr. become saponified. □□ **saponifiable** adj. **saponification** /-fikáyshən/ n. [F saponifier (as SAPONACEOUS)]

saponin /sápənin/ n. any of a group of plant glycosides, esp. those derived from the bark of the tree Quillaja saponaria, that foam when shaken with water and are used in detergents and fire extinguishers. [F saponine f. L sapo -onis soap]

sapor /sáypər, -pawr/ n. **1** a quality perceptible by taste, e.g., sweetness. **2** the distinctive taste of a substance. **3** the sensation of taste. [ME f. L *sapere* taste]

■ **1, 2** see FLAVOR *n.* 1.

sappanwood /səpánwŏŏd, sápən-/ *n.* (also **sapanwood**) the heartwood of an E. Indian tree, *Caesalpinia sappan*, formerly used as a source of red dye. [Du. *sapan* f. Malay *sapang*, of S. Indian orig.]

sapper /sápər/ *n.* **1** a person who digs saps. **2** a military demolitions expert.

Sapphic /sáfik/ *adj. & n.* ● *adj.* **1** of or relating to Sappho, poetess of Lesbos *c.*600 BC, or her poetry. **2** lesbian. ● *n.* (in *pl.*) (**sapphics**) verse in a meter associated with Sappho. [F *sa(p)phique* f. L *Sapphicus* f. Gk *Sapphikos* f. *Sapphō*]

■ *adj.* **2** lesbian, homosexual, *colloq.* gay.

sapphire /sáfīr/ *n. & adj.* ● *n.* **1** a transparent blue precious stone consisting of corundum. **2** precious transparent corundum of any color. **3** the bright blue of a sapphire. **4** a hummingbird with bright blue coloring. ● *adj.* of sapphire blue. □ **sapphire anniversary** a 45th wedding anniversary. □□ **sapphirine** /sáfirīn, -rín, -rīn/ *adj.* [ME f. OF *safir* f. L *sapphirus* f. Gk *sappheiros* prob. = lapis lazuli]

sappy /sápee/ *adj.* (**sappier, sappiest**) **1** full of sap. **2** young and vigorous. **3** overly emotional or sentimental. □□ **sappily** *adv.* **sappiness** *n.*

sapro- /sáprō/ *comb. form Biol.* rotten, putrefying. [Gk *sapros* putrid]

saprogenic /sáprəjénik/ *adj.* causing or produced by putrefaction.

saprophagous /saprófəgəs/ *adj.* feeding on decaying matter.

saprophile /sáprəfīl/ *n.* a bacterium inhabiting putrid matter. □□ **saprophilous** /-prófiləs/ *adj.*

saprophyte /sáprəfīt/ *n.* any plant or microorganism living on dead or decayed organic matter. □□ **saprophytic** /-fítik/ *adj.*

sapwood /sápwŏŏd/ *n.* the soft outer layers of recently formed wood between the heartwood and the bark.

saraband /sárəband/ *n.* **1** a stately old Spanish dance. **2** music for this or in its rhythm, usu. in triple time often with a long note on the second beat of the bar. [F *sarabande* f. Sp. & It. *zarabanda*]

Saracen /sárəsən/ *n. & adj. hist.* ● *n.* **1** an Arab or Muslim at the time of the Crusades. **2** a nomad of the Syrian and Arabian desert. ● *adj.* of the Saracens. □ **Saracen corn** *Brit. archaic* buckwheat. **Saracen's head** the head of a Saracen or Turk as a heraldic charge or inn sign. □□ **Saracenic** /sárəsénik/ *adj.* [ME f. OF *sar(r)azin, sar(r)acin* f. LL *Saracenus* f. late Gk *Sarakēnos* perh. f. Arab. *šarḳī* eastern]

sarangi /səránggee/ *n.* (*pl.* **sarangis**) an E. Indian stringed instrument played with a bow. [Hindi *sāraṅgī*]

sarape var. of SERAPE.

sarcasm /sáarkazəm/ *n.* **1** a bitter or wounding remark. **2** a taunt, esp. one ironically worded. **3** language consisting of such remarks. **4** the use of or the faculty of using this. □□ **sarcastic** /-kástik/ *adj.* **sarcastically** *adv.* [F *sarcasme* or f. LL *sarcasmus* f. late Gk *sarkasmos* f. Gk *sarkazō* tear flesh, in late Gk gnash the teeth, speak bitterly f. *sarx sarkos* flesh]

■ **1, 2** see TAUNT *n.*, DIG *n.* 3. **3** irony, contumely, satire. **4** irony, scorn, derision, ridicule, venom; sharpness, edge, trenchancy, mordancy. □□ **sarcastic** scornful, derisive, derisory, mocking, ridiculing, satiric(al), ironic, sardonic, scathing, caustic, cutting, trenchant, incisive, biting, acerbic, acid, acidic, acidulous, venomous, poisonous, *Brit. sl.* sarky.

sarcenet /sáarsənit/ *n.* (also **sarsenet**) a fine, soft, silk material used esp. for linings. [ME f. AF *sarzinett* perh. dimin. of *sarzin* SARACEN after OF *drap sarrasinois* Saracen cloth]

sarcoma /saarkṓmə/ *n.* (*pl.* **sarcomas** or **sarcomata** /-mətə/) a malignant tumor of connective or other non-epithelial tissue. □□ **sarcomatosis** /-mətósis/ *n.* **sarcomatous** *adj.* [mod.L f. Gk *sarkōma* f. *sarkoō* become fleshy f. *sarx sarkos* flesh]

■ see TUMOR.

sarcophagus /saarkófəgəs/ *n.* (*pl.* **sarcophagi** /-gī, -jī/) a stone coffin, esp. one adorned with a sculpture or inscription. [L f. Gk *sarkophagos* flesh-consuming (as SARCOMA, -*phagos* -eating)]

■ coffin, casket.

sarcoplasm /sáarkəplazəm/ *n. Anat.* the cytoplasm in which muscle fibrils are embedded. [Gk *sarx sarkos* flesh + PLASMA]

sarcous /sáarkəs/ *adj.* consisting of flesh or muscle. [Gk *sarx sarkos* flesh]

sard /saard/ *n.* a yellow or orange-red cornelian. [ME f. F *sarde* or L *sarda* = LL *sardius* f. Gk *sardios* prob. f. *Sardō* Sardinia]

sardelle /saardél/ *n.* any of several fish resembling the sardine. [It. *sardella* dimin. of *sarda* f. L (as SARDINE[1])]

sardine[1] /saardeén/ *n.* a young pilchard or similar young or small herringlike marine fish. □ **like sardines** crowded close together (as sardines are in tins). [ME f. OF *sardine* = It. *sardina* f. L f. *sarda* f. Gk, perh. f. *Sardō* Sardinia]

sardine[2] /sáardin/ *n.* a precious stone mentioned in Rev. 4:3. [ME f. LL *sardinus* f. Gk *sardinos* var. of *sardios* SARD]

sardius /sáardeeəs/ *n. Bibl.*, etc., a precious stone. [ME f. LL f. Gk *sardios* sard]

sardonic /saardónik/ *adj.* **1** grimly jocular. **2** (of laughter, etc.) bitterly mocking or cynical. □□ **sardonically** *adv.* **sardonicism** /-nisizəm/ *n.* [F *sardonique*, earlier *sardonien* f. L *sardonius* f. Gk *sardonios* of Sardinia, alt. of *sardanios* Homeric epithet of bitter or scornful laughter]

■ **1** ironic, cynical, sarcastic; see also INCISIVE 3. **2** derisive, derisory, mocking, cynical, sarcastic, ironic.

sardonyx /saardóniks, sáard'n-/ *n.* onyx in which white layers alternate with sard. [ME f. L f. Gk *sardonux* (prob. as SARD, ONYX)]

saree var. of SARI.

sargasso /saargásō/ *n.* (also **sargassum**) (*pl.* **-os** or **-oes** or **sargassa**) any seaweed of the genus *Sargassum*, with berrylike air vessels, found floating in islandlike masses, esp. in the Sargasso Sea of the N. Atlantic. Also called GULFWEED. [Port. *sargaço*, of unkn. orig.]

sarge /saarj/ *n. sl.* sergeant. [abbr.]

sari /sáaree/ *n.* (also **saree**) (*pl.* **saris** or **sarees**) a length of cotton or silk draped around the body, traditionally worn as a main garment by women of India. [Hindi *sāṛ(h)ī*]

sark /saark/ *n. Sc. & No. of Engl.* a shirt or chemise. [ME *serk* f. ON *serkr* f. Gmc]

sarking /sáarking/ *n. Brit.* boarding between the rafters and the roof. [SARK + -ING[1]]

sarky /sáarkee/ *adj.* (**sarkier, sarkiest**) *Brit. sl.* sarcastic. □□ **sarkily** *adv.* **sarkiness** *n.* [abbr.]

sarmentose /sáarməntōs/ *adj.* (also **sarmentous** /-méntəs/) *Bot.* having long, thin trailing shoots. [L *sarmentosus* f. *sarmenta* (pl.) twigs, brushwood, f. *sarpere* to prune]

sarong /səráwng, -róng/ *n.* **1** a Malay and Javanese garment consisting of a long strip of (often striped) cloth worn by both sexes tucked around the waist or under the armpits. **2** a woman's garment resembling this. [Malay, lit. 'sheath']

saros /sáaros, -aws/ *n. Astron.* a period of about 18 years between repetitions of eclipses. [Gk f. Babylonian *šār(u)* 3,600 (years)]

sarrusophone /sərōŏsəfōn/ *n.* a metal wind instrument played with a double reed like an oboe. [*Sarrus*, 19th-c. Fr. inventor]

sarsaparilla /sáspərílə, sáars-/ *n.* **1** a preparation of the dried roots of various plants, esp. smilax, used to flavor some drinks and medicines and formerly as a tonic. **2** any of the plants yielding this. [Sp. *zarzaparilla* f. *zarza* bramble, prob. + dimin. of *parra* vine]

sarsen /sáarsən/ *n. Geol.* a sandstone boulder carried by ice during a glacial period. [prob. var. of SARACEN]

sarsenet var. of SARCENET.

sartorial /saartáwreeəl/ *adj.* **1** of a tailor or tailoring. **2** of men's clothes. □□ **sartorially** *adv.* [L *sartor* tailor f. *sarcire sart-* patch]

sartorius /saartáwreeəs/ *n. Anat.* the long, narrow muscle running across the front of each thigh. [mod.L f. L *sartor* tailor (the muscle being used in adopting a tailor's cross-legged posture)]

Sarum use /sáirəm/ *n. Eccl.* the order of divine service used in the diocese of Salisbury before the Reformation. [med.L *Sarum* Salisbury, perh. f. L *Sarisburia*]

s.a.s.e. *abbr.* self-addressed stamped envelope.

sash[1] /sash/ *n.* a long strip or loop of cloth, etc., worn over one shoulder usu. as part of a uniform or insignia, or worn around the waist, usu. by a woman or child. □□ **sashed** *adj.* [earlier *shash* f. Arab. *šāš* muslin, turban]
■ see BELT *n.* 1.

sash[2] /sash/ *n.* **1** a frame holding the glass in a window and usu. made to slide up and down in the grooves of a window aperture. **2** esp. *Brit.* the glazed sliding pane of a greenhouse, etc. □ **sash cord** a strong cord attaching the sash weights to a sash. **sash weight** a weight attached to each end of a sash to balance it at any height. **sash window** a window with one or two sashes of which one or each can be slid vertically over the other to make an opening. □□ **sashed** *adj.* [*sashes* corrupt. of CHASSIS, mistaken for pl.]

sashay /sasháy/ *v.intr. colloq.* walk or move ostentatiously, casually, or diagonally. [corrupt. of CHASSÉ]
■ see SWAGGER *v.* 1.

sashimi /saasheemee/ *n.* a Japanese dish of garnished raw fish in thin slices. [Jap.]

sasin /sásin, sáy-/ *n.* = *black buck.* [Nepali]

Sask. *abbr.* Saskatchewan.

Sasquatch /sáskwoch, -kwach/ *n.* a supposed yetilike animal of NW America. Also called *Bigfoot.* [Amer. Indian]

sass /sas/ *n. & v. colloq.* ● *n.* impudence; disrespectful mannerism or speech. ● *v.tr.* be impudent to. [var. of SAUCE]
■ *n.* see SAUCE *n.* 3.

sassaby /sásəbee/ *n.* (*pl.* **-ies**) a S. African antelope, *Damaliscus lunatus*, similar to the hartebeest. [Setswana *tsessébe*, *-ábi*]

sassafras /sásəfras/ *n.* **1** a small tree, *Sassafras albidum*, native to N. America, with aromatic leaves and bark. **2** a preparation of oil extracted from the leaves or bark of this tree, used medicinally or in perfumery. [Sp. *sasafrás* or Port. *sassafraz*, of unkn. orig.]

Sassanian /sasáyneeən/ *n. & adj.* (also **Sassanid** /sásənid/) ● *n.* a member of a Persian dynasty ruling 211-651. ● *adj.* of or relating to this dynasty. [*Sasan*, founder of the dynasty]

Sassenach /sásənakh, -nak/ *n. & adj. Sc. & Ir.* usu. *derog.* ● *n.* an English person. ● *adj.* English. [Gael. *Sasunnoch*, Ir. *Sasanach* f. L *Saxones* Saxons]

sassy /sásee/ *adj.* (**sassier, sassiest**) *colloq.* = SAUCY. □□ **sassily** *adv.* **sassiness** *n.* [var. of SAUCY]

sastrugi /sastroōgee/ *n.pl.* wavelike irregularities on the surface of hard polar snow, caused by winds. [Russ. *zastrugi* small ridges]

SAT *abbr. propr.* **1** Scholastic Assessment Test. **2** (formerly) Scholastic Aptitude Test.

Sat. *abbr.* Saturday.

sat *past* and *past part.* of SIT.

Satan /sáyt'n/ *n.* the Devil; Lucifer. [OE f. LL f. Gk f. Heb. *śāṭān* lit. 'adversary' f. *śāṭan* oppose, plot against]
■ see DEVIL *n.* 1, 2.

satanic /sətánik, say-/ *adj.* **1** of, like, or befitting Satan. **2** diabolical; hellish. □□ **satanically** *adv.*
■ diabolic, fiendish, devilish, Mephistophelian, demonic, demoniac(al), infernal, cacodemonic, ghoulish; hellish, diabolical, evil, wicked, iniquitous, corrupt, depraved, perverted, perverse, godless, ungodly, impious, unholy, sinister, dark, black, immoral, amoral; dire, monstrous, heinous, atrocious, hideous, horrible, horrendous, horrid, horrifying, loathsome, vile, abhorrent, unspeakable, damnable, despicable, abominable.

Satanism /sáyt'nizəm/ *n.* **1** the worship of Satan, with a travesty of Christian forms. **2** the pursuit of evil for its own sake. **3** deliberate wickedness. □□ **Satanist** *n.* **Satanize** *v.tr.*

Satanology /sáyt'nóləjee/ *n.* **1** beliefs concerning the Devil. **2** a history or collection of these.

satay /saatay/ *n.* (also **satai, saté**) an Indonesian and Malaysian dish consisting of small pieces of meat grilled on a skewer and usu. served with spiced peanut sauce. [Malayan *satai sate*, Indonesian *sate*]

SATB *abbr. Mus.* soprano, alto, tenor, and bass (as a combination of voices).

satchel /sáchəl/ *n.* a small bag usu. of leather and hung from the shoulder with a strap, for carrying books, etc., esp. to and from school. [ME f. OF *sachel* f. L *saccellus* (as SACK[1])]
■ see BAG *n.* 1, 2a.

sate /sayt/ *v.tr.* **1** gratify (desire, or a desirous person) to the full. **2** cloy; surfeit; weary with overabundance (*sated with pleasure*). □□ **sateless** *adj. poet.* [prob. f. dial. *sade*, OE *sadian* (as SAD), assim. to SATIATE]
■ **1** satiate, slake, satisfy, gratify, content, quench. **2** satiate, stuff, glut, gorge, cloy, surfeit, overfill, overstuff, pall, overindulge, saturate, deluge, flood, suffocate; weary, exhaust, bore, tire, jade.

sateen /sateen/ *n.* cotton fabric woven like satin with a glossy surface. [*satin* after *velveteen*]

satellite /sát'lit/ *n. & adj.* ● *n.* **1** a celestial body orbiting the earth or another planet. **2** an artificial body placed in orbit around the earth or another planet. **3** a follower; a hanger-on. **4** an underling; a member of an important person's staff or retinue. ● *adj.* **1** transmitted by satellite (*satellite communications; satellite television*). **2** dependent; secondary (*networks of small satellite computers*). □ **satellite dish** a concave dish-shaped antenna for receiving broadcasting signals transmitted by satellite. □□ **satellitic** /-lítik/ *adj.* **satellitism** *n.* [F *satellite* or L *satelles satellitis* attendant]
■ *n.* **1** moon, planet. **2** sputnik, spacecraft, rocket. **3** follower, disciple, shadow, hanger-on, parasite, sycophant, *derog.* minion. **4** underling, *derog.* minion; aide-de-camp, assistant, attendant, acolyte, aide, *hist.* retainer. ● *adj.* **2** secondary, dependent, minor, subsidiary, ancillary.

sati var. of SUTTEE.

satiate /sáysheeayt/ *adj. & v.* ● *adj. archaic* satiated. ● *v.tr.* = SATE. □□ **satiable** /-shəbəl/ *adj. archaic.* **satiation** /-áyshən/ *n.* [L *satiatus* past part. of *satiare* f. *satis* enough]

satiety /səti-itee/ *n.* **1** the state of being glutted or satiated. **2** the feeling of having too much of something. **3** (foll. by *of*) a cloyed dislike of. □ **to satiety** to an extent beyond what is desired. [obs. F *sacieté* f. L *satietas -tatis* f. *satis* enough]
■ **1** surfeit, glut, superabundance, overindulgence, saturation, excess, superfluity. **3** excess, surfeit; see also DISGUST *n.* 2.

satin /sát'n/ *n., adj., & v.* ● *n.* a fabric of silk or various synthetic fibers, with a glossy surface on one side produced by a twill weave with the weft threads almost hidden. ● *adj.* smooth as satin. ● *v.tr.* give a glossy surface to (paper). □ **satin finish 1** a polish given to silver, etc., with a metallic brush. **2** any effect resembling satin in texture produced on materials in various ways. **satin paper** fine glossy writing paper. **satin spar** a fibrous variety of gypsum. **satin stitch** a long, straight embroidery stitch, giving the appearance of satin. **satin white** a white pigment of calcium sulfate and alumina. □□ **satinized** *adj.* **satiny** *adj.* [ME f. OF f. Arab. *zaytūnī* of *Tseutung* in China]
■ □□ **satiny** see SILKY 1.

satinet /sát'nét/ *n.* (also **satinette**) a satinlike fabric made partly or wholly of cotton or synthetic fiber.

satinflower /sát'nflowr/ *n.* **1** any plant of the genus *Clarkia*, with pink or lavender flowers. **2** = HONESTY 3.

satinwood /sát'nwood/ *n.* **1 a** (in full **Ceylon satinwood**) a tree, *Chloroxylon swietenia*, native to central and southern India and Ceylon (Sri Lanka). **b** (in full **West Indian satinwood**) a tree, *Fagara flava*, native to the West Indies, Bermuda, the Bahamas, and southern Florida. **2** the yellow, glossy wood of either of these trees.

satire /sátir/ *n.* **1** the use of ridicule, irony, sarcasm, etc., to

/.../ **pronunciation**	● **part of speech**
□ **phrases, idioms, and compounds**	
□□ **derivatives**	■ **synonym section**
cross-references appear in SMALL CAPITALS or *italics*	

expose folly or vice or to lampoon an individual. **2** a work or composition in prose or verse using satire. **3** this branch of literature. **4** a thing that brings ridicule upon something else. **5** *Rom. Antiq.* a poetic medley, esp. a poem ridiculing prevalent vices or follies. [F *satire* or L *satira* later form of *satura* medley]

■ **1** ridicule, irony, sarcasm, mockery, caricature, *colloq.* spoofing. **2** burlesque, lampoon, parody, pasquinade, caricature, *colloq.* takeoff, spoof, send-up.

satiric /sətírik/ *adj.* **1** of satire or satires. **2** containing satire (*wrote a satiric review*). **3** writing satire (*a satiric poet*). [F *satirique* or LL *satiricus* (as SATIRE)]

■ see SATIRICAL.

satirical /sətírikəl/ *adj.* **1** = SATIRIC. **2** given to the use of satire in speech or writing or to cynical observation of others; sarcastic; humorously critical. □□ **satirically** *adv.*

■ **2** satiric, ironic, sarcastic, mocking, irreverent, derisive, scornful, flippant, ridiculing, chaffing, teasing, *colloq.* spoofing.

satirist /sátərist/ *n.* **1** a writer of satires. **2** a satirical person.

■ see WIT¹ 3.

satirize /sátiriz/ *v.tr.* **1** assail or ridicule with satire. **2** write a satire upon. **3** describe satirically. □□ **satirization** *n.* [F *satiriser* (as SATIRE)]

■ **1** poke fun at, ridicule, make fun *or* sport of, pillory, deride, mock. **2, 3** lampoon, burlesque, parody, caricature, travesty, *colloq.* send up; mimic, imitate, *colloq.* take off.

satisfaction /sátisfákshən/ *n.* **1** the act or an instance of satisfying; the state of being satisfied (*heard this with great satisfaction*). **2** a thing that satisfies desire or gratifies feeling (*is a great satisfaction to me*). **3** a thing that settles an obligation or pays a debt. **4 a** (foll. by *for*) atonement; compensation (*demanded satisfaction*). **b** *Theol.* Christ's atonement for the sins of mankind. □ **to one's satisfaction** so that one is satisfied. [ME f. OF f. L *satisfactio -onis* (as SATISFY)]

■ **1** gratification, comfort, delight, joy, pleasure, happiness, fulfillment, contentment, enjoyment. **2** comfort, delight, joy, pleasure. **4** a payment, requital, repayment, reparation, compensation, remuneration, recompense, restitution, indemnity, indemnification, damages; redress, atonement, expiation, amends, retribution.

satisfactory /sátisfáktəree/ *adj.* **1** adequate; causing or giving satisfaction (*was a satisfactory pupil*). **2** satisfying expectations or needs; leaving no room for complaint (*a satisfactory result*). □□ **satisfactorily** *adv.* **satisfactoriness** *n.* [F *satisfactoire* or med.L *satisfactorius* (as SATISFY)]

■ adequate, sufficient, acceptable, passable, good enough, fair, *colloq.* OK, *Austral. & NZ sl.* jake; all right, not bad, *colloq.* all-right.

satisfy /sátisfi/ *v.* (**-ies, -ied**) **1** *tr.* **a** meet the expectations or desires of; comply with (a demand). **b** be accepted by (a person, his or her taste) as adequate; be equal to (a preconception, etc.). **2** *tr.* put an end to (an appetite or want) by supplying what was required. **3** *tr.* rid (a person) of an appetite or want in a similar way. **4** *intr.* give satisfaction; leave nothing to be desired. **5** *tr.* pay (a debt or creditor). **6** *tr.* adequately meet, fulfill, or comply with (conditions, obligations, etc.) (*has satisfied all the legal conditions*). **7** *tr.* (often foll. by *of, that*) provide with adequate information or proof; convince (*satisfied the others that they were right; satisfy the court of their innocence*). **8** *tr.* *Math.* (of a quantity) make (an equation) true. **9** *tr.* (in *passive*) **a** (foll. by *with*) contented or pleased with. **b** (foll. by *to*) demand no more than or consider it enough to do. □ **satisfy oneself** (often foll. by *that* + clause) be certain in one's own mind. □□ **satisfiable** *adj.* **satisfiability** /-fìəbílitee/ *n.* **satisfiedly** *adv.* **satisfying** *adj.* **satisfyingly** *adv.* [ME f. OF *satisfier* f. L *satisfacere* *satisfact-* f. *satis* enough]

■ **1a, 6** meet, comply with; see also FULFILL 4, 5. **1 b** gratify, please, fulfill, comfort, content; placate, appease, pacify. **2, 3** slake, quench, sate, satiate; meet, fulfill, provide for, look after, serve, answer, gratify, indulge. **4** see SUIT *v.* 2. **5** pay, repay, make good,

settle, liquidate. **7** convince, persuade, assure; reassure, content; put a person's mind at rest. **9** (*be satisfied*) be contented *or* pleased *or* happy. □□ **satisfying** gratifying, satisfactory, fulfilling, filling, satiating; comforting, pleasing, pacifying, pleasurable.

satori /sətáwree/ *n.* *Buddhism* sudden enlightenment. [Jap.]

satrap /sátrap, sáy-/ *n.* **1** a provincial governor in the ancient Persian empire. **2** a subordinate ruler, colonial governor, etc. [ME f. OF *satrape* or L *satrapa* f. Gk *satrapēs* f. OPers. *xšathra-pāvan* country protector]

satrapy /sátrəpee, sáy-/ *n.* (*pl.* **-s**) a province ruled over by a satrap.

satsuma /satsŏŏmə, sátsŏŏmə/ *n.* **1** a variety of tangerine orig. grown in Japan. **2** (**Satsuma**) (in full **Satsuma ware**) cream-colored Japanese pottery. [*Satsuma* a province in Japan]

saturate /sáchərayt/ *v.tr.* **1** fill with moisture; soak thoroughly. **2** (often foll. by *with*) fill to capacity. **3** cause (a substance, solution, vapor, metal, or air) to absorb, hold, or combine with the greatest possible amount of another substance, or of moisture, magnetism, electricity, etc. **4** cause (a substance) to combine with the maximum amount of another substance. **5** supply (a market) beyond the point at which the demand for a product is satisfied. **6** (foll. by *with, in*) imbue with or steep in (learning, tradition, prejudice, etc.). **7** overwhelm (enemy defenses, a target area, etc.) by concentrated bombing. **8** (as **saturated** *adj.*) **a** (of color) full; rich; free from an admixture of white. **b** (of fat molecules) containing the greatest number of hydrogen atoms. □□ **saturate** /-rət/ *adj.* *literary.* **saturable** /-rəbəl/ *adj.* **saturant** /-rənt/ *n.* & *adj.* [L *saturare* f. *satur* full]

■ **1** soak, drench, waterlog. **2** steep, fill; see also IMPREGNATE *v.* 1, 2. **5** flood, glut; overload; see also SWAMP *v.* **6** (*saturate with* or *in*) imbue *or* suffuse *or* impregnate *or* permeate with, steep in.

saturation /sáchəráyshən/ *n.* the act or an instance of saturating; the state of being saturated. □ **saturation point** the stage beyond which no more can be absorbed or accepted.

■ see GLUT *n.*

Saturday /sátərday, -dee/ *n.* & *adv.* ● *n.* the seventh day of the week, following Friday. ● *adv.* *colloq.* **1** on Saturday. **2** (**Saturdays**) on Saturdays; each Saturday. □ **Saturday-night special** *sl.* any inexpensive handgun that is easy to obtain and conceal. [OE *Sætern(es) dæg* transl. of L *Saturni dies* day of Saturn]

Saturn /sátərn/ *n.* **1 a** the sixth planet from the sun, with a system of broad flat rings circling it, and the most distant of the five planets known in the ancient world. **b** *Astrol.* Saturn as a supposed astrological influence on those born under its sign, characterized by coldness and gloominess. **2** *Alchemy* the metal lead. □□ **Saturnian** /satərneeən/ *adj.* [L *Saturnus*, Roman god of agriculture, identified with Kronos, father of Zeus, perh. f. Etruscan]

saturnalia /sátərnáylees/ *n.* (*pl.* same or **saturnalias**) **1** (usu. **Saturnalia**) *Rom. Hist.* the festival of Saturn in December, characterized by unrestrained merrymaking for all, the predecessor of Christmas. **2** (as *sing.* or *pl.*) a scene of wild revelry or tumult; an orgy. □□ **saturnalian** *adj.* [L, neut. pl. of *Saturnalis* (as SATURN)]

■ **2** see ORGY 1. □□ **saturnalian** see EPICUREAN *adj.* 2.

saturnic /sətárnik/ *adj.* *Med.* affected with lead poisoning. □□ **saturnism** /sátərnizəm/ [SATURN 2]

saturniid /satárneeid/ *n.* any large moth of the family Saturniidae, including emperor moths. [mod.L]

saturnine /sátərnin/ *adj.* **1 a** of a sluggish gloomy temperament. **b** (of looks, etc.) dark and brooding. **2** *archaic* **a** of the metal lead. **b** *Med.* of or affected by lead poisoning. □□ **saturninely** *adv.* [ME f. OF *saturnin* f. med.L *Saturninus* (as SATURN)]

■ **1 a** see GLOOMY 2.

satyagraha /sutyaágrəhə/ *n.* *Ind.* **1** *hist.* a policy of passive resistance to British rule advocated by Gandhi. **2** passive resistance as a policy. [Skr. f. *satya* truth + *āgraha* obstinacy]

satyr /sáytər, sát-/ *n.* **1** (in Greek mythology) one of a class of Greek woodland gods with a horse's ears and tail, or (in

1340

Roman representations) with a goat's ears, tail, legs, and budding horns. **2** a lustful or sensual man. **3** = SATYRID. [ME f. OF *satyre* or L *satyrus* f. Gk *saturos*]

satyriasis /sáytiríəsis, sát-/ *n. Med.* excessive sexual desire in men. [LL f. Gk *saturiasis* (as SATYR)]

satyric /sətírik/ *adj.* (in Greek mythology) of or relating to satyrs. □ **satyric drama** a kind of ancient Greek comic play with a chorus of satyrs. [L *satyricus* f. Gk *saturikos* (as SATYR)]

satyrid /sáytərid, sát-, sətírid/ *n.* any butterfly of the family Satyridae, with distinctive eyelike markings on the wings. [mod.L *Satyridae* f. the genus *Satyrus* (as SATYR)]

sauce /saws/ *n. & v.* ● *n.* **1** any of various liquid or semisolid preparations taken as a relish with food; the liquid constituent of a dish (*mint sauce; tomato sauce; chicken in a lemon sauce*). **2** something adding piquancy or excitement. **3** esp. *Brit. colloq.* impudence; impertinence. **4** stewed fruit, etc., eaten as dessert or used as a garnish. ● *v.tr.* **1** *colloq.* be impudent to. **2** *archaic* **a** season with sauce or condiments. **b** add excitement to. □ **sauce for the goose** what is appropriate in one case (by implication is appropriate in others). □□ **sauceless** *adj.* [ME f. OF ult. f. L *salsus* f. *salere sals-* to salt f. *sal* salt]

■ *n.* **1** gravy, condiment, relish, dressing. **2** see SPICE *n.* 3a. **3** impertinence, sauciness, impudence, audacity, insolence, brazenness, pertness, disrespect, disrespectfulness, cheek, cheekiness, *colloq.* lip, *colloq.* brass, nerve, crust, sassiness, back talk, sass, esp. *Brit. colloq.* backchat, *sl.* gall. ● *v.* **2 b** see ENLIVEN 1.

sauceboat /sáwsbōt/ *n.* a kind of small pitcher or dish used for serving sauces, etc.

saucepan /sáwspan/ *n.* a usu. metal cooking pan, usu. round with a lid and a long handle at the side, used for boiling, stewing, etc., on top of a stove. □□ **saucepanful** *n.* (*pl.* **-fuls**).

■ see PAN¹ *n.* 1.

saucer /sáwsər/ *n.* **1** a shallow circular dish used for standing a cup on and to catch drips. **2** any similar dish used to stand a plant pot, etc., on. □□ **saucerful** *n.* (*pl.* **-fuls**). **saucerless** *adj.* [ME, = condiment dish, f. OF *saussier(e)* sauceboat, prob. f. LL *salsarium* (as SAUCE)]

saucy /sáwsee/ *adj.* (**saucier, sauciest**) **1** impudent; flippant. **2** *colloq.* smart-looking (*a saucy hat*). **3** *colloq.* smutty; suggestive. □□ **saucily** *adv.* **sauciness** *n.* [earlier sense 'savory,' f. SAUCE]

■ **1** see IMPUDENT 1, 2. **2** jaunty, *colloq.* swish, natty, *sl.* snazzy. **3** see BAWDY *adj.* □□ **sauciness** see *impudence* (IMPUDENT).

Saudi /sówdee, sáw-/ *n. & adj.* (also **Saudi Arabian**) ● *n.* (*pl.* **Saudis**) **1 a** a native or national of Saudi Arabia. **b** a person of Saudi descent. **2** a member of the dynasty founded by King Saud. ● *adj.* of or relating to Saudi Arabia or the Saudi dynasty. [A. Ibn-*Saud*, Arab. king d. 1953]

sauerkraut /sówərkrowt/ *n.* a German dish of chopped pickled cabbage. [G f. *sauer* SOUR + *Kraut* vegetable]

sauger /sáwgər/ *n.* a small N. American pike perch. [19th c.: orig. unkn.]

Sauk /sawk/ *n.* (also **Sak**) **1 a** a N. American people native to Wisconsin. **b** a member of this people. **2** the language of this people.

sauna /sáwnə, sow-/ *n.* **1** a Finnish-style steam bath. **2** a building used for this. [Finn.]

saunter /sáwntər/ *v. & n.* ● *v.intr.* **1** walk slowly; amble; stroll. **2** proceed without hurry or effort. ● *n.* **1** a leisurely ramble. **2** a slow gait. □□ **saunterer** *n.* [ME, = muse: orig. unkn.]

■ *v.* walk, stroll, amble, ramble, wander, traipse, *sl.* mosey. ● *n.* **1** walk, ramble, stroll, amble, wander, traipse, *sl.* mosey. **2** see WALK *n.* 1, 2b.

saurian /sáwreeən/ *adj.* of or like a lizard. [mod.L *Sauria* f. Gk *saura* lizard]

sauropod /sáwrōpod/ *n.* any of a group of plant-eating dinosaurs with a long neck and tail, and four thick limbs. [Gk *saura* lizard + *pous pod-* foot]

saury /sáwree/ *n.* (*pl.* **-ies**) a long-beaked marine fish, *Scom-*

beresox saurus, of temperate waters. [perh. f. LL f. Gk *sauros* horse mackerel]

sausage /sáwsij/ *n.* **1 a** ground pork, beef, or other meat seasoned and often mixed with other ingredients, encased in cylindrical form in a skin, for cooking and eating hot or cold. **b** a length of this. **2** a sausage-shaped object. □ **not a sausage** *Brit. colloq.* nothing at all. **sausage dog** *Brit. colloq.* a dachshund. **sausage machine 1** a sausage-making machine. **2** *Brit.* a relentlessly uniform process. [ME f. ONF *saussiche* f. med.L *salsicia* f. *salsus*: see SAUCE]

sauté /sōtáy, saw-/ *adj., n.,* & *v.* ● *adj.* quickly cooked or browned in a little hot fat. ● *n.* food cooked in this way. ● *v.tr.* (**sautéed** or **sautéd**) cook in this way. [F, past part. of *sauter* jump]

Sauternes /sōtɔ́rn, saw-/ *n.* **1** a sweet white wine from Sauternes in the Bordeaux region of France. **2** (usu. **sauterne**) a type of semisweet white wine.

savage /sávij/ *adj., n.,* & *v.* ● *adj.* **1** fierce; cruel (*savage persecution; a savage blow*). **2** wild; primitive (*savage tribes; a savage animal*). **3** *archaic* (of scenery, etc.) uncultivated (*a savage scene*). **4** *colloq.* angry; bad-tempered (*in a savage mood*). **5** *Heraldry* (of the human figure) naked. ● *n.* **1** *Anthropol. derog.* a member of a primitive tribe. **2** a cruel or barbarous person. ● *v.tr.* **1** (esp. of a dog, wolf, etc.) attack and bite or trample. **2** (of a critic, etc.) attack fiercely. □□ **savagedom** *n.* **savagely** *adv.* **savageness** *n.* **savagery** *n.* (*pl.* **-ies**). [ME f. OF *sauvage* wild f. L *silvaticus* f. *silva* a wood]

■ *adj.* **1** vicious, ferocious, fierce, beastly, bestial, brutish, bloodthirsty, brutal, cruel, ruthless, pitiless, merciless, harsh, bloody, unmerciful, barbarous, barbaric, murderous, demonic, demoniac, sadistic, *poet. or rhet.* fell. **2** primitive, uncivilized, bestial, inhuman, barbaric, barbarous, rude, wild; untamed, undomesticated, feral, unbroken. **4** angry, bad-tempered; see also NASTY 3. ● *n.* **1** wild man *or* woman. **2** see BEAST 2a. ● *v.* **2** see ATTACK *v.* 3.

savanna /səvánə/ *n.* (also **savannah**) a grassy plain in tropical and subtropical regions, with few or no trees. [Sp. *zavana* perh. f. Carib orig.]

■ see PLAIN¹ *n.*

savant /savaánt, sávənt/ *n.* (*fem.* **savante**) a learned person, esp. a distinguished scientist, etc. [F, part. of *savoir* know (as SAPIENT)]

■ see SCHOLAR 1.

savate /səvaát/ *n.* a form of boxing in which feet and fists are used. [F, orig. a kind of shoe: cf. SABOT]

save¹ /sayv/ *v. & n.* ● *v.* **1** *tr.* (often foll. by *from*) rescue, preserve, protect, or deliver from danger, harm, discredit, etc. (*saved my life; saved me from drowning*). **2** *tr.* (often foll. by *up*) keep for future use; reserve; refrain from spending (*saved up $150 for a new bike; likes to save plastic bags*). **3** *tr.* (often *refl.*) **a** relieve (another person or oneself) from spending (money, time, trouble, etc.); prevent exposure to (annoyance, etc.) (*saved myself $50; a word processor saves time*). **b** obviate the need or likelihood of (*soaking saves scrubbing*). **4** *tr.* preserve from damnation; convert (*saved her soul*). **5** *tr.* & *refl.* husband or preserve (one's strength, health, etc.) (*saving himself for the last lap; save your energy*). **6** *intr.* (often foll. by *up*) save money for future use. **7** *tr.* **a** avoid losing (a game, match, etc.). **b** prevent an opponent from scoring (a goal, etc.). **c** stop (a ball, etc.) from entering the goal. ● *n.* **1** *Ice hockey, soccer,* etc., the act of preventing an opponent's scoring, etc. **2** *Bridge* a sacrifice bid to prevent unnecessary losses. □ **save-all** *n.* a device to prevent waste. **2** *hist.* a pan with a spike for burning up candle ends. **save appearances** present a prosperous, respectable, etc., appearance. **save-as-you-earn** *Brit.* a method of saving by regular deduction from earnings at source. **save face** see

---

/.../ **pronunciation**   ● **part of speech**
□ **phrases, idioms, and compounds**
□□ **derivatives**   ■ **synonym section**
cross-references appear in SMALL CAPITALS or *italics*

FACE. **save one's breath** not waste time speaking to no effect. **save the day** find or provide a solution to difficulty or disaster. **save one's skin** (or **neck** or **bacon**) avoid loss, injury, or death; escape from danger. **save the tide** get in or out (of port, etc.) while it lasts. **save the trouble** avoid useless or pointless effort. □□ **savable** *adj.* (also **saveable**). [ME f. AF *sa(u)ver*, OF *salver, sauver* f. LL *salvare* f. L *salvus* SAFE]

■ *v.* **1** (come to a person's) rescue, deliver; (set) free, liberate, release, redeem, bail out; recover, salvage, retrieve; keep, preserve, guard, safeguard, protect, conserve, shelter, shield. **2** lay *or* put *or* set aside, lay *or* put by, lay *or* put away, keep; retain, reserve, preserve, conserve. **3 a** obviate, preclude, spare, prevent. **b** obviate, prevent, stop; see also PRECLUDE 2. **4** see REDEEM 4. **5** see CONSERVE *v.* 1. **6** scrimp, scrape; see also ECONOMIZE 1. □ **save the day** come to the rescue.

save[2] /sayv/ *prep. & conj. archaic* or *poet.* ● *prep.* except; but (*all save him*). ● *conj.* (often foll. by *for*) unless; but; except (*happy save for one want; is well save that he has a cold*). [ME f. OF *sauf sauve* f. L *salvo, salva*, ablat. sing. of *salvus* SAFE]

saveloy /sávəloy/ *n. Brit.* a seasoned red pork sausage, dried and smoked, and sold ready to eat. [corrupt. of F *cervelas, -at*, f. It. *cervellata* (*cervello* brain)]

saver /sáyvər/ *n.* **1** a person who saves, esp. money. **2** (often in *comb.*) a device for economical use (of time, etc.) (*found the short cut a time-saver*). **3** *Racing sl.* a hedging bet.

savin /sávin/ *n.* (also **savine**) **1** a bushy juniper, *Juniperus sabina*, usu. spreading horizontally, and yielding oil formerly used in the treatment of amenorrhea. **2** = *red cedar*. [OE f. OF *savine* f. L *sabina* (*herba*) Sabine (herb)]

saving /sáyving/ *adj., n., & prep.* ● *adj.* (often in *comb.*) making economical use of (*labor-saving*). ● *n.* **1** anything that is saved. **2** an economy (*a saving in expenses*). **3** (usu. in *pl.*) money saved. ● *prep.* **1** with the exception of; except (*all saving that one*). **2** without offense to (*saving your presence*). □ **saving clause** *Law* a clause containing a stipulation of exemption, etc. **saving grace 1** the redeeming grace of God. **2** a redeeming quality or characteristic. **savings account** a bank account that earns interest and from which withdrawals are usu. made in person. **savings and loan association** an institution, usu. owned by depositors and regulated by state or federal government, that accepts funds for savings accounts and lends funds for mortgages. **savings bank** a bank receiving deposits at interest and returning the profits to the depositors. [ME f. SAVE[1]: prep. prob. f. SAVE[2] after *touching*]

■ *n.* **3** (*savings*) cache, nest egg; see also HOARD *n.*
□ **saving grace 2** redeeming quality, good point; see also VIRTUE 4.

savior /sávyər/ *n.* (esp. *Brit.* **saviour**) **1** a person who saves or delivers from danger, destruction, etc. (*the savior of the nation*). **2** (**Savior**) (prec. by *the*, *our*) Christ. [ME f. OF *sauvēour* f. eccl.L *salvator -oris* (transl. Gk *sōtēr*) f. LL *salvare* SAVE[1]]

■ **1** rescuer, salvation, Good Samaritan, liberator, redeemer, deliverer, emancipator, champion, knight in shining armor. **2** (*the* or *our Savior*) Christ, the Redeemer, Jesus, (the) Messiah, The Lamb (of God), Our Lord, the Son of God, the King of Kings, the Prince of Peace.

savoir faire /sávwaar fáir/ *n.* the ability to act suitably in any situation; tact. [F, = know how to do]

■ tact, tactfulness, discretion; sophistication, finesse, urbanity, knowledgeability, diplomacy, smoothness, polish, suavity, suaveness, poise, grace, style, skill, adroitness, knowledge, *sl.* savvy.

savoir vivre /véevrə/ *n.* knowledge of the world and the ways of society; ability to conduct oneself well; sophistication. [F, = know how to live]

■ knowledge; breeding, upbringing, polish; see also *sophistication* (SOPHISTICATE).

savor /sáyvər/ *n. & v.* (*Brit.* **savour**) ● *n.* **1** a characteristic taste, flavor, relish, etc. **2** a quality suggestive of or containing a small amount of another. **3** *archaic* a characteristic

smell. ● *v.* **1** *tr.* **a** appreciate and enjoy the taste of (food). **b** enjoy or appreciate (an experience, etc.). **2** *intr.* (foll. by *of*) **a** suggest by taste, smell, etc. (*savors of mushrooms*). **b** imply or suggest a specified quality (*savors of impertinence*). □□ **savorless** *adj.* [ME f. OF f. L *sapor -oris* f. *sapere* to taste]

■ *n.* **1** taste, flavor, zest, tang, piquancy. **2** hint, suggestion, redolence, smack, breath, trace, quality, soupçon, dash. **3** odor, scent, fragrance, smell, perfume, redolence, bouquet, breath. ● *v.* **1** enjoy, relish, appreciate; smack one's lips over; indulge in, bask in, revel in, delight in, value, cherish, luxuriate in. **2 b** (*savor of*) see SUGGEST 2.

savory[1] /sáyvəree/ *n.* (*pl.* **-ies**) any herb of the genus *Satureia*, esp. *S. hortensis* and *S. montana*, used esp. in cookery. [ME *saverey*, perh. f. OE *sætherie* f. L *satureia*]

savory[2] /sáyvəree/ *adj. & n.* (*Brit.* **savoury**) ● *adj.* **1** having an appetizing taste or smell. **2** (of food) salty or piquant, not sweet (*a savory omelette*). **3** pleasant; acceptable. ● *n.* (*pl.* **-ies**) *Brit.* a savory dish served as an appetizer or at the end of dinner. □□ **savorily** *adv.* **savoriness** *n.* [ME f. OF *savoré* past part. (as SAVOR)]

■ *adj.* **1** palatable, delicious, tasty, toothsome, appetizing, flavorful, flavorous, flavorsome, ambrosial, *colloq.* luscious, *literary* delectable. **3** acceptable, pleasant, honest, proper, decent, reputable, respectable, honorable, creditable, upright, decorous, seemly, wholesome. ● *n.* appetizer, hors-d'œuvre, starter.

savour *Brit.* var. of SAVOR.

savoury *Brit.* var. of SAVORY[2].

savoy /səvóy/ *n.* a hardy variety of cabbage with wrinkled leaves. [*Savoy* in SE France]

Savoyard[1] /səvóyaard, sávoyaárd/ *n. & adj.* ● *n.* a native of Savoy in SE France. ● *adj.* of or relating to Savoy or its people, etc. [F f. *Savoie* Savoy]

Savoyard[2] /səvóyaard, sávoyaárd/ *n.* a devotee or performer of Gilbert and Sullivan operas. [*Savoy* Theatre in London, built for their presentation]

savvy /sávee/ *v., n., & adj. sl.* ● *v.intr. & tr.* (**-ies, -ied**) know. ● *n.* knowingness; shrewdness; understanding. ● *adj.* (**savvier, savviest**) knowing; wise. [orig. Creole & Pidgin E after Sp. *sabe usted* you know]

■ *n.* see UNDERSTANDING *n.* 1. ● *adj.* see INTELLIGENT 2.

saw[1] /saw/ *n. & v.* ● *n.* **1 a** a hand tool having a toothed blade used to cut esp. wood with a to-and-fro movement. **b** any of several mechanical power-driven devices with a toothed rotating disk or moving band, for cutting. **2** *Zool.*, etc., a serrated organ or part. ● *v.* (*past part.* **sawed** or **sawn** /sawn/) **1** *tr.* **a** cut (wood, etc.) with a saw. **b** make (boards, etc.) with a saw. **2** *intr.* use a saw. **3 a** *intr.* move to and fro with a motion as of a saw or person sawing (*sawing away on his violin*). **b** *tr.* divide (the air, etc.) with gesticulations. □ **saw-edged** with a jagged edge like a saw. **sawed-off** (or **sawn-off**) **1** (of a gun) having part of the barrel sawed off to make it easier to handle and give a wider field of fire. **2** *colloq.* (of a person) short. **saw pit** a pit in which the lower of two men working a pit saw stands. **saw set** a tool for wrenching saw teeth in alternate directions to allow the saw to work freely. **saw-whet owl** a small N. American owl, *Aegolius acadicus*, noted for its harsh cry. □□ **sawlike** *adj.* [OE *saga* f. Gmc]

saw[2] *past* of SEE[1].

saw[3] /saw/ *n.* a proverb; a maxim (*that's just an old saw*). [OE *sagu* f. Gmc, rel. to SAY: cf. SAGA]

■ proverb, maxim, saying, aphorism, apothegm, axiom, adage, epigram, gnome, byword, slogan, motto, dictum.

sawbones /sáwbōnz/ *n. sl.* a doctor or surgeon.

■ see DOCTOR *n.* 1a.

sawbuck /sáwbuk/ *n.* **1** a sawhorse. **2** *sl.* a $10 bill.

sawdust /sáwdust/ *n.* powdery particles of wood produced in sawing.

sawfish /sáwfish/ *n.* any large marine fish of the family Pristidae, with a toothed flat snout used as a weapon.

sawfly /sáwflī/ *n.* (*pl.* **-flies**) any insect of the superfamily

Tenthredinoidea, with a serrated ovipositor, the larvae of which are injurious to plants.

sawhorse /sáwhawrs/ *n.* a rack supporting wood for sawing.

sawmill /sáwmil/ *n.* a factory in which wood is sawed mechanically into planks or boards.

sawn *past part.* of SAW¹.

sawtooth /sáwtŏŏth/ *adj.* **1** (also **sawtoothed** /-tŏŏtht/) (esp. of a roof, wave, etc.) shaped like the teeth of a saw with one steep and one slanting side. **2** (of a wave form) showing a slow linear rise and rapid linear fall.

sawyer /sáwyər/ *n.* **1** a person who saws lumber professionally. **2** an uprooted tree held fast by one end in a river. **3** *NZ* a large wingless horned grasshopper whose grubs bore in wood. [ME, earlier *sawer*, f. SAW¹]

sax¹ /saks/ *n. colloq.* **1** a saxophone. **2** esp. *Brit.* a saxophone player. □□ **saxist** *n.* [abbr.]

sax² /saks/ *n.* (also **zax** /zaks/) a slater's chopper, with a point for making nail holes. [OE *seax* knife f. Gmc]

saxatile /sáksətil, -til/ *adj.* living or growing on or among rocks. [F *saxatile* or L *saxatilis* f. *saxum* rock]

saxhorn /sáks-hawrn/ *n.* any of a series of different-sized brass wind instruments with valves and a funnel-shaped mouthpiece, used mainly in military and brass bands. [*Sax*, name of its Belgian inventors, + HORN]

saxicoline /saksíkəlin/ *adj.* (also **saxicolous**) *Biol.* = SAXATILE. [mod.L *saxicolus* f. *saxum* rock + *colere* inhabit]

saxifrage /sáksifrij, -frayj/ *n.* any plant of the genus *Saxifraga*, growing on rocky or stony ground and usu. bearing small white, yellow, or red flowers. [ME f. OF *saxifrage* or LL *saxifraga* (*herba*) f. L *saxum* rock + *frangere* break]

Saxon /sáksən/ *n. & adj.* ● *n.* **1** *hist.* **a** a member of the Germanic people that conquered parts of England in 5th–6th c. **b** (usu. **Old Saxon**) the language of the Saxons. **2** = ANGLO-SAXON. **3** a native of modern Saxony in Germany. **4** the Germanic (as opposed to Latin or Romance) elements of English. ● *adj.* **1** *hist.* of or concerning the Saxons. **2** belonging to or originating from the Saxon language or Old English. **3** of or concerning modern Saxony or Saxons. □ **Saxon architecture** the form of Romanesque architecture preceding the Norman in England. **Saxon blue** a solution of indigo in sulfuric acid as a dye. □□ **Saxondom** *n.* **Saxonism** *n.* **Saxonist** *n.* **Saxonize** /-nīz/ *v.tr. & intr.* [ME f. OF f. LL *Saxo -onis* f. Gk *Saxones* (pl.) f. WG: cf. OE *Seaxan, Seaxe* (pl.)]

saxony /sáksənee/ *n.* **1** a fine kind of wool. **2** cloth made from this. [*Saxony* in Germany f. LL *Saxonia* (as SAXON)]

saxophone /sáksəfōn/ *n.* **1** a keyed brass reed instrument in several sizes and registers, used esp. in jazz and dance music. **2** a saxophone player. □□ **saxophonic** /-fónik/ *adj.* **saxophonist** /-sófənist, -səfōnist/ *n.* [*Sax* (as SAXHORN) + -PHONE]

say /say/ *v. & n.* ● *v.* (*3rd sing. present* **says** /sez/; *past and past part.* **said** /sed/) **1** *tr.* (often foll. by *that* + clause) **a** utter (specified words) in a speaking voice; remark (*said "Damn!"; said that he was satisfied*). **b** put into words; express (*that was well said; cannot say what I feel*). **2** *tr.* (often foll. by *that* + clause) **a** state; promise or prophesy (*says that there will be war*). **b** have specified wording; indicate (*says here that he was killed; the clock says ten to six*). **3** *tr.* (in passive; usu. foll. by *to* + infin.) be asserted or described (*is said to be 93 years old*). **4** *tr.* (foll. by *to* + infin.) *colloq.* tell a person to do something (*he said to bring the car*). **5** *tr.* convey (information) (*spoke for an hour but said little*). **6** *tr.* put forward as an argument or excuse (*much to be said in favor of it; what have you to say for yourself?*). **7** *tr.* (often *absol.*) form and give an opinion or decision as to (*who did it I cannot say; please say which you prefer*). **8** *tr.* select, assume, or take as an example or (a specified number, etc.) as near enough (*shall we say this one?; paid, say, $*). **9** *tr.* a speak the words of (prayers, Mass, a grace, etc.). **b** repeat (a lesson, etc.); recite (*can't say his tables*). **10** *tr. Art,* etc., convey (inner meaning or intention) (*what is the director saying in this film?*). **11** *intr.* **a** speak; talk. **b** (in *imper.*) *poet.* tell me (*what is your name, say!*). **12** *tr.* (**the said**) *Law* or *joc.* the previously mentioned (*the said witness*). **13** *intr.* (as *int.*) an ex-

clamation of surprise, to attract attention, etc. ● *n.* **1 a** an opportunity for stating one's opinion, etc. (*let him have his say*). **b** a stated opinion. **2** a share in a decision (*had no say in the matter*). □ **how say you?** *Law* how do you find? (addressed to the jury requesting its verdict). **I,** etc., **cannot** (or **could not**) **say** I, etc., do not know. **I'll say** *colloq.* yes indeed. **I say!** *Brit.* an exclamation expressing surprise, drawing attention, etc. **it is said** the rumor is that. **not to say** and indeed; or possibly even (*his language was rude, not to say offensive*). **said he** (or **I,** etc.) *colloq.* or *poet.* he, etc., said. **say for oneself** say by way of conversation, oratory, etc. **say much** (or **something**) **for** indicate the high quality of. **say no** refuse or disagree. **say out** esp. *Brit.* express fully or candidly. **says I** (or **he,** etc.) esp. *Brit. colloq.* I, he, etc., said (used in reporting conversation). **say-so 1** the power of decision. **2** mere assertion (*cannot proceed merely on his say-so*). **say something** make a short speech. **says you!** *colloq.* I disagree. **say when** *colloq.* indicate when enough drink or food has been given. **say the word 1** indicate that you agree or give permission. **2** give the order, etc. **say yes** agree. **that is to say 1** in other words, more explicitly. **2** or at least. **they say** it is rumored. **to say nothing of** = *not to mention* (see MENTION). **what do** (or **would**) **you say to?** would you like? **when all is said and done** after all; in the long run. **you can say that again!** (or **you said it!**) *colloq.* I agree emphatically. **you don't say so** *colloq.* an expression of amazement or disbelief. □□ **sayable** *adj.* **sayer** *n.* [OE *secgan* f. Gmc]

■ *v.* **1 a** remark, state, affirm, declare, utter, maintain, hold, assert, claim, asseverate, announce, *formal* aver. **b** tell, put, express, verbalize, communicate, explain, reveal, impart. **2 a** state; promise, prophesy, predict, prognosticate, foretell. **3** (*be said*) be described, be mentioned, be asserted, be suggested *or* hinted. **4** order *or* require *or* command a person, *archaic or literary* bid a person. **5** see COMMUNICATE 1a. **6** reply, respond, answer; see also STATE *v.* 1. **7** guess, estimate, conjecture, venture, imagine, believe, think, judge, decide; tell. **8** suppose, assume; for example, for instance, e.g.; approximately, about, roughly, circa, nearly. **9 a** deliver, utter, speak. **10** signify, denote, symbolize, communicate, indicate, convey, suggest, imply, mean, get across. **11 a** speak, talk, chat, declaim; see also SPEAK 1. **12** (*the said*) the aforementioned, the aforesaid; see also *preceding* (PRECEDE). ● *n.* **1 a** turn, chance, opportunity, moment. **2** voice, authority, influence, power, weight, sway, *colloq.* clout. □ I, etc., **cannot** (or **could not**) **say** I, etc., do not know, *colloq.* I, etc., have no idea; see also *ask me another.* **I'll say** see ABSOLUTELY 6. **it is said** it is alleged *or* reported *or* rumored *or* whispered *or* bruited about *or* put about *or* noised (abroad), they say, the rumor is, rumor has it. **say no** see DIFFER 2; (*say no to*) see REFUSE¹ 1. **say out** see EXPRESS¹ 1, 2. **say-so 1** authority, say; word; authorization. **say yes** see CONSENT *v.* **that is to say 1** see NAMELY. **they say** see *it is said* above. **when all is said and done** see *eventually* (EVENTUAL). **you can say that again!** (or **you said it!**) see ABSOLUTELY 6. **you don't say so** well, I declare; well I never.

saying /sáying/ *n.* **1** the act or an instance of saying. **2** a maxim, proverb, adage, etc. □ **as the saying goes** (or **is**) an expression used in introducing a proverb, cliché, etc. **go without saying** be too well known or obvious to need mention. **there is no saying** it is impossible to know.

■ **2** see MAXIM.

SBA *abbr.* Small Business Administration.

Sb *symb. Chem.* the element antimony. [L *stibium*]

SbE *abbr.* south by east.

/.../ pronunciation	● part of speech
□ phrases, idioms, and compounds	
□□ derivatives	■ synonym section
cross-references appear in SMALL CAPITALS or *italics*	

SBN *abbr.* Standard Book Number (cf. ISBN).

SbW *abbr.* south by west.

SC *abbr.* **1** South Carolina (also in official postal use). **2** *Brit.* special constable.

Sc *symb. Chem.* the element scandium.

sc. *abbr.* scilicet.

■ see NAMELY.

s.c. *abbr.* small capitals.

scab /skab/ *n. & v.* ● *n.* **1** a dry rough crust formed over a cut, sore, etc., in healing. **2** (often *attrib.*) *colloq. derog.* a person who refuses to strike or join a trade union, or who tries to break a strike by working. **3** the mange or a similar skin disease, esp. in animals. **4** a fungus plant disease causing scablike roughness. **5** a dislikeable person. ● *v.intr.* (**scabbed**, **scabbing**) **1** act as a scab. **2** (of a wound, etc.) form a scab; heal over. □□ **scabbed** *adj.* **scabby** *adj.* (**scabbier**, **scabbiest**). **scabbiness** *n.* **scablike** *adj.* [ME f. ON *skabbr* (unrecorded), corresp. to OE *sceabb*]

■ *n.* **2** strikebreaker, *Brit. derog.* blackleg.

scabbard /skábbərd/ *n.* **1** *hist.* a sheath for a sword, bayonet, etc. **2** a sheath for a revolver, etc. □ **scabbard fish** any of various silvery-white marine fish shaped like a sword scabbard, esp. *Lepidopus caudatus.* [ME *sca(u)berc*, etc., f. AF prob. f. Frank.]

scabies /skáybeez/ *n.* a contagious skin disease causing severe itching (cf. ITCH). [ME f. L *scabere* scratch]

scabious /skáybeeəs/ *n. & adj.* ● *n.* any plant of the genus *Scabiosa, Knautia,* etc., with pink, white, or esp. blue pincushion-shaped flowers. ● *adj.* affected with mange; scabby. [ME f. med.L *scabiosa* (*herba*) formerly regarded as a cure for skin disease: see SCABIES]

scabrous /skábrəs, skáy-/ *adj.* **1** having a rough surface; bearing short stiff hairs, scales, etc.; scurfy. **2** (of a subject, situation, etc.) requiring tactful treatment; hard to handle with decency. **3 a** indecent; salacious. **b** behaving licentiously. □□ **scabrously** *adv.* **scabrousness** *n.* [F *scabreux* or LL *scabrosus* f. L *scaber* rough]

■ **2** see DELICATE 3a. **3 a** see INDECENT 1. **b** see LEWD 1.

scad /skad/ *n.* any fish of the family Carangidae native to tropical and subtropical seas, usu. having an elongated body and very large spiky scales. [17th c.: orig. unkn.]

scads /skadz/ *n.pl. colloq.* large quantities. [19th c.: orig. unkn.]

■ see LOT *n.* 1.

scaffold /skáfəld, -fōld/ *n. & v.* ● *n.* **1 a** *hist.* a raised wooden platform used for the execution of criminals. **b** a similar platform used for drying tobacco, etc. **2** = SCAFFOLDING. **3** (prec. by *the*) death by execution. ● *v.tr.* attach scaffolding to (a building). □□ **scaffolder** *n.* [ME f. AF f. OF (*e*)*schaffaut*, earlier *escadafaut*: cf. CATAFALQUE]

scaffolding /skáfəlding, -fōlding/ *n.* **1 a** a temporary structure formed of poles, planks, etc., erected by workers and used by them while building or repairing a house, etc. **b** materials used for this. **2** a temporary conceptual framework used for constructing theories, etc.

■ **2** see FRAME *n.* 6a.

scagliola /skalyṓlə/ *n.* imitation stone or plaster mixed with glue. [It. *scagliuola* dimin. of *scaglia* SCALE[1]]

scalable /skáyləbəl/ *adj.* **1** capable of being scaled or climbed. **2** *Computing* (of a font) capable of being used in a range of sizes. □□ **scalability** /-bílitee/ *n.*

scalar /skáylər/ *adj. & n. Math. & Physics* ● *adj.* (of a quantity) having only magnitude, not direction. ● *n.* a scalar quantity (cf. VECTOR). [L *scalaris* f. *scala* ladder; see SCALE[3]]

scalawag /skáləwag/ *n.* (also **scallywag**) **1** a scamp; a rascal. **2** *US hist.* a white Southerner who supported Reconstructionists usu. for personal profit. [19th-c. US sl.: orig unknown.]

■ **1** see RASCAL.

scald[1] /skawld/ *v. & n.* ● *v.tr.* **1** burn (the skin, etc.) with hot liquid or steam. **2** heat (esp. milk) to near boiling point. **3** (usu. foll. by *out*) clean (a pan, etc.) by rinsing with boiling water. **4** treat (poultry, etc.) with boiling water to remove feathers, etc. ● *n.* **1** a burn, etc., caused by scalding. **2** a skin disease caused esp. by air pollution, etc., affecting the

fruits of some plants. □ **scalded cream** *Brit.* a dessert made from milk scalded and allowed to stand. **scalding tears** hot bitter tears of grief, etc. □□ **scalder** *n.* [ME f. AF, ONF *escalder,* OF *eschalder* f. LL *excaldare* (as EX-[1], L *calidus* hot)]

scald[2] var. of SKALD.

scale[1] /skayl/ *n. & v.* ● *n.* **1** each of the small, thin, bony or horny overlapping plates protecting the skin of fish and reptiles. **2** something resembling a fish scale, esp.: **a** a pod or husk. **b** a flake of skin; a scab. **c** a rudimentary leaf, feather, or bract. **d** each of the structures covering the wings of butterflies and moths. **e** *Bot.* a layer of a bulb. **3 a** a flake formed on the surface of rusty iron. **b** a thick, white deposit formed in a kettle, boiler, etc., by the action of heat on water. **4** plaque formed on teeth. ● *v.* **1** *tr.* remove scale or scales from (fish, nuts, iron, etc.). **2** *tr.* remove plaque from (teeth) by scraping. **3** *intr.* **a** (of skin, metal, etc.) form, come off in, or drop, scales. **b** (usu. foll. by *off*) (of scales) come off. □ **scale armor** *hist.* armor formed of metal scales attached to leather, etc. **scale bug** = *scale insect.* **scale fern** any of various spleenworts, esp. *Asplenium ceterach.* **scale insect** any of various insects, esp. of the family Coccidae, clinging to plants and secreting a shieldlike scale as covering. **scales fall from a person's eyes** a person is no longer deceived (cf. Acts 9:18). **scale-winged** lepidopterous. □□ **scaled** *adj.* (also in *comb.*). **scaleless** *adj.* **scaler** *n.* [ME f. OF *escale* f. Gmc, rel. to SCALE[2]]

■ *n.* **1** plate, lamina, lamella, scute, scutum. **2 a** pod, husk, shell, skin, case, shuck. **c** squama. **4** tartar, plaque. □ **scales fall from a person's eyes** be undeceived.

scale[2] /skayl/ *n. & v.* ● *n.* **1 a** (often in *pl.*) a weighing machine or device (*bathroom scales*). **b** (also **scalepan**) each of the dishes on a simple scale balance. **2** (**the Scales**) the zodiacal sign or constellation Libra. ● *v.tr.* (of something weighed) show (a specified weight) in the scales. □ **pair of scales** a simple balance. **throw into the scale** cause to be a factor in a contest, debate, etc. **tip** (or **turn**) **the scales 1** (usu. foll. by *at*) outweigh the opposite scalepan (at a specified weight); weigh. **2** (of a motive, circumstance, etc.) be decisive. [ME f. ON *skál* bowl f. Gmc]

■ *n.* **1 a** see BALANCE *n.* 1.

scale[3] /skayl/ *n. & v.* ● *n.* **1** a series of degrees; a graded classification system (*pay fees according to a prescribed scale; high on the social scale; seven points on the Richter scale*). **2 a** (often *attrib.*) *Geog. & Archit.* a ratio of size in a map, model, picture, etc. (*on a scale of one inch to the mile; a scale model*). **b** relative dimensions or degree (*generosity on a grand scale*). **3** *Mus.* an arrangement of all the notes in any system of music in ascending or descending order (*chromatic scale; major scale*). **4 a** a set of marks on a line used in measuring, reducing, enlarging, etc. **b** a rule determining the distances between these. **c** a piece of metal, apparatus, etc., on which these are marked. **5** (in full **scale of notation**) *Math.* the ratio between units in a numerical system (*decimal scale*). ● *v.* **1** *tr.* **a** (also *absol.*) climb (a wall, height, etc.) esp. with a ladder. **b** climb (the social scale, heights of ambition, etc.). **2** *tr.* represent in proportional dimensions; reduce to a common scale. **3** *intr.* (of quantities, etc.) have a common scale; be commensurable. □ **economies of scale** proportionate savings gained by using larger quantities. **in scale** (of drawing, etc.) in proportion to the surroundings, etc. **play** (or **sing**) **scales** *Mus.* perform the notes of a scale as an exercise for the fingers or voice. **scale down** make smaller in proportion; reduce in size. **scale up** make larger in proportion; increase in size. **to scale** with a uniform reduction or enlargement. □□ **scaler** *n.* [(n.) ME (= ladder): (v.) ME f. OF *escaler* or med.L *scalare* f. L *scala* f. *scandere* climb]

■ *n.* **1** ranking, graduation, hierarchy, range, classification. **2 a** proportion, ratio. ● *v.* **1** climb, ascend, mount, clamber up, go up. **2** regulate, prorate, standardize. □ **scale down** decrease, reduce, diminish. **scale up** see ENLARGE 1, 3.

scalene /skáyleen/ *adj. & n.* ● *adj.* (esp. of a triangle) having sides unequal in length. ● *n.* **1** (in full **scalene muscle**) = SCALENUS. **2** a scalene triangle. □ **scalene cone** (or **cylin-**

der) a cone (or cylinder) with the axis not perpendicular to the base. [LL *scalenus* f. Gk *skalēnos* unequal, rel. to *skolios* bent]

scalenus /skəleˈenəs/ *n.* (*pl.* **scaleni** /-nī/) any of several muscles extending from the neck to the first and second ribs. [mod.L: see SCALENE]

scallion /skályən/ *n.* a shallot or spring onion; any long-necked onion with a small bulb. [ME f. AF *scal(o)un* = OF *escalo(i)gne* ult. f. L *Ascalonia* (*caepa*) (onion) of *Ascalon* in anc. Palestine]

scallop /skáləp, skól-/ *n.* & *v.* (also **scollop** /skól-/) • *n.* **1** any of various bivalve mollusks of the family Pectinidae, esp. of the genus *Chlamys* or *Pecten*, much prized as food. **2** (in full **scallop shell**) **a** a single valve from the shell of a scallop, with grooves and ridges radiating from the middle of the hinge and edged with small rounded lobes, often used for cooking or serving food. **b** *hist.* a representation of this shell worn as a pilgrim's badge. **3** (in *pl.*) an ornamental edging cut in material in imitation of a scallop edge. **4** a small pan or dish shaped like a scallop shell and used for baking or serving food. • *v.tr.* (**scalloped, scalloping**) **1** cook in a scallop. **2** ornament (an edge or material) with scallops or scalloping. □□ **scalloper** *n.* **scalloping** *n.* (in sense 3 of *n.*). [ME f. OF *escalope* prob. f. Gmc]
■ *v.* **2** pink, serrate, notch.

scallywag var. of SCALAWAG.

scalp /skalp/ *n.* & *v.* • *n.* **1** the skin covering the top of the head, with the hair, etc., attached. **2 a** *hist.* the scalp of an enemy cut or torn away as a trophy by a Native American. **b** a trophy or symbol of triumph, conquest, etc. **3** *Sc.* a bare rock projecting above water, etc. • *v.tr.* **1** *hist.* take the scalp of (an enemy). **2** criticize savagely. **3** defeat; humiliate. **4** *colloq.* resell (shares, tickets, etc.) at a high or quick profit. □□ **scalper** *n.* **scalpless** *adj.* [ME, prob. of Scand. orig.]

scalpel /skálpəl/ *n.* a surgeon's small sharp knife shaped for holding like a pen. [F *scalpel* or L *scalpellum* dimin. of *scalprum* chisel f. *scalpere* scratch]

scaly /skáylee/ *adj.* (**scalier, scaliest**) covered in or having many scales. □□ **scaliness** *n.*
■ imbricated, lamellar, laminar, lamellate, scutate; squamous, squamose, scurfy, *Med.* furfuraceous.

scam /skam/ *n. sl.* **1** a trick or swindle; a fraud. **2** esp. *Brit.* a story or rumor. [20th c.: orig. unkn.]
■ **1** see TRICK *n.* 1.

scammony /skámənee/ *n.* (*pl.* **-ies**) an Asian plant, *Convolvulus scammonia*, bearing white or pink flowers, the dried roots of which are used as a purgative. [ME f. OF *scamonee*, *escamonie* or L *scammonia* f. Gk *skammōnia*]

scamp¹ /skamp/ *n. colloq.* a rascal; a rogue. □□ **scampish** *adj.* [*scamp* rob on highway, prob. f. MDu. *schampen* decamp f. OF *esc(h)amper* (as EX-¹, L *campus* field)]
■ see RASCAL. □□ **scampish** see WICKED 3.

scamp² /skamp/ *v.tr.* do (work, etc.) in a perfunctory or inadequate way. [perh. formed as SCAMP¹: cf. SKIMP]

scamper /skámpər/ *v.* & *n.* • *v.intr.* (usu. foll. by *about*, *through*) run and skip impulsively or playfully. • *n.* the act or an instance of scampering. [prob. formed as SCAMP¹]
■ *v.* see SCURRY *v.*

scampi /skámpee/ *n.pl.* **1** large shrimp. **2** (often treated as *sing.*) a dish of these sautéed in garlic butter. [It.]

scan /skan/ *v.* & *n.* • *v.* (**scanned, scanning**) **1** *tr.* look at intently or quickly (*scanned the horizon; rapidly scanned the speech for errors*). **2** *intr.* (of a verse, etc.) be metrically correct; be capable of being recited, etc., metrically (*this line doesn't scan*). **3** *tr.* **a** examine all parts of (a surface, etc.) to detect radioactivity, etc. **b** cause (a particular region) to be traversed by a radar, etc., beam. **4** *tr.* resolve (a picture) into its elements of light and shade in a prearranged pattern for the purposes, esp. of television transmission. **5** *tr.* test the meter of (a line of verse, etc.) by reading with the emphasis on its rhythm, or by examining the number of feet, etc. **6** *tr.* **a** make a scan of (the body or part of it). **b** examine (a patient, etc.) with a scanner. • *n.* **1** the act or an instance of scanning. **2** an image obtained by scanning or with a scanner. □□ **scannable** *adj.* [ME f. L *scandere* climb: in LL =

scan verses (from the raising of one's foot in marking rhythm)]
■ *v.* **1** glance at *or* through, look at *or* over, pass *or* run one's eye over, skim, read over, peruse, flick *or* flip through, thumb *or* leaf through. • *n.* **1** look, survey, inspection, examination, overview. **2** see IMAGE *n.* 3, 4.

scandal /skánd'l/ *n.* **1 a** a thing or a person causing general public outrage or indignation. **b** the outrage, etc., so caused, esp. as a subject of common talk. **c** malicious gossip or backbiting. **2** *Law* a public affront, esp. an irrelevant abusive statement in court. □ **scandal sheet** *derog.* a newspaper, etc., giving prominence to esp. malicious gossip. □□ **scandalous** *adj.* **scandalously** *adv.* **scandalousness** *n.* [ME f. OF *scandale* f. eccl.L *scandalum* f. Gk *skandalon* snare, stumbling block]
■ **1 a** disgrace, embarrassment, dishonor, discredit; defilement, stigma; blemish, spot, smirch, black mark, blot (on one's escutcheon), skeleton in the cupboard. **b** shame, sin, outrage, disgrace; discredit, damage, ignominy, obloquy, dishonor, degradation, disrepute, infamy. **c** slander, libel, calumny, abuse, dirt, defamation; gossip, rumor, backbiting. □ **scandalous** shocking, disgraceful, ignominious, improper, indecorous, unseemly, infamous, outrageous, shameful, immodest, dishonorable, disreputable, sordid, despicable, wicked, sinful, iniquitous, profligate, immoral, atrocious, heinous, disgusting, taboo, unmentionable, unspeakable; defamatory, libelous, slanderous, calumnious, calumniatory, aspersive, abusive, injurious, scurrilous.

scandalize /skándəlīz/ *v.tr.* offend the moral feelings, sensibilities, etc., of; shock. [ME in sense 'make a scandal of' f. F *scandaliser* or eccl.L *scandaliso* f. Gk *skandalizō* (as SCANDAL)]
■ appall, shock, outrage, affront, offend, horrify, upset, disturb.

scandalmonger /skánd'lmənggər, -monggər/ *n.* a person who spreads malicious scandal.
■ see GOSSIP *n.* 3.

Scandinavian /skándináyveeən/ *n.* & *adj.* • *n.* **1 a** a native or inhabitant of Scandinavia (Denmark, Norway, Sweden, and sometimes Finland and Iceland). **b** a person of Scandinavian descent. **2** the family of languages of Scandinavia. • *adj.* of or relating to Scandinavia or its people or languages. [L *Scandinavia*]

scandium /skándeeəm/ *n.* *Chem.* a rare, soft, silver-white metallic element occurring naturally in lanthanide ores. ¶ Symb.: **Sc**. [mod.L f. *Scandia* Scandinavia (source of the minerals containing it)]

scannable see SCAN.

scanner /skánər/ *n.* **1 a** a device for scanning or systematically examining all the parts of something. **b** a device for monitoring several radio frequencies, esp. police or emergency frequencies. **2** a machine for measuring the intensity of radiation, ultrasound reflections, etc., from the body as a diagnostic aid. **3** a person who scans or examines critically. **4** a person who scans verse.

scansion /skánshən/ *n.* **1** the metrical scanning of verse. **2** the way a verse, etc., scans. [L *scansio* (LL of meter) f. *scandere scans-* climb]
■ **1** prosody. **2** rhythm, meter.

scant /skant/ *adj.* & *v.* • *adj.* barely sufficient; deficient (*with scant regard for the truth; scant of breath*). • *v.tr.* *archaic* provide (a supply, material, a person, etc.) grudgingly; skimp; stint. □□ **scantly** *adv.* **scantness** *n.* [ME f. ON *skamt* neut. of *skammr* short]
■ *adj.* see INSUFFICIENT.

scantling /skántling/ *n.* **1 a** a timber beam of small cross section. **b** a size to which a stone or timber is to be cut. **2** a

---

/.../ **pronunciation**	● **part of speech**
□ **phrases, idioms, and compounds**	
□□ **derivatives**	■ **synonym section**
cross-references appear in SMALL CAPITALS or *italics*	

set of standard dimensions for parts of a structure, esp. in shipbuilding. **3** (usu. foll. by *of*) *archaic* **a** a specimen or sample. **b** one's necessary supply; a modicum or small amount. [alt. after -LING¹ f. obs. *scantlon* f. OF *escantillon* sample]

scanty /skántee/ *adj.* (**scantier**, **scantiest**) **1** of small extent or amount. **2** barely sufficient. □□ **scantily** *adv.* **scantiness** *n.* [obs. *scant* scanty supply f. ON *skamt* neut. adj.: see SCANT]

■ scant, sparse, scarce, meager, slight, skimpy, minimal, small, little; barely adequate *or* sufficient, limited, insufficient, restricted, *colloq.* measly; short, in short supply, thin on the ground.

scape /skayp/ *n.* **1** a long flower stalk coming directly from the root. **2** the base of an insect's antenna. [L *scapus* f. Gk *skapos*, rel. to SCEPTER]

-scape /skayp/ *comb. form* forming nouns denoting a view or a representation of a view (*moonscape*; *seascape*). [after LANDSCAPE]

scapegoat /skáypgōt/ *n. & v.* ● *n.* **1** a person bearing the blame for the sins, shortcomings, etc., of others, esp. as an expedient. **2** *Bibl.* a goat sent into the wilderness after the Jewish chief priest had symbolically laid the sins of the people upon it (Lev. 16). ● *v.tr.* make a scapegoat of. □□ **scapegoater** *n.* [*scape* (archaic, = escape) + GOAT, = the goat that escapes]

■ *n.* **1** victim, cat's-paw, whipping boy, straw man, *Brit.* Aunt Sally, *sl.* fall guy. ● *v.* see ACCUSE 2.

scapegrace /skáypgrays/ *n.* a rascal; a scamp, esp. a young person or child. [*scape* (as SCAPEGOAT) + GRACE = one who escapes the grace of God]

■ see RASCAL.

scaphoid /skáfoyd/ *adj. & n. Anat.* = NAVICULAR. [mod.L *scaphoides* f. Gk *skaphoeidēs* f. *skaphos* boat]

scapula /skápyələ/ *n.* (*pl.* **scapulae** /-lee/ or **scapulas**) the shoulder blade. [LL, sing. of L *scapulae*]

scapular /skápyələr/ *adj. & n.* ● *adj.* of or relating to the shoulder or shoulder blade. ● *n.* **1 a** a monastic short cloak covering the shoulders. **b** a symbol of affiliation to an ecclesiastical order, consisting of two strips of cloth hanging down the breast and back and joined across the shoulders. **2** a bandage for or over the shoulders. **3** a scapular feather. □ **scapular feather** a feather growing near the insertion of the wing. [(adj.) f. SCAPULA: (n.) f. LL *scapulare* (as SCAPULA)]

scapulary /skápyəleree/ *n.* (*pl.* **-ies**) **1** = SCAPULAR *n.* 1. **2** = SCAPULAR *n.* 3. [ME f. OF *eschapeloyre* f. med.L *scapelorium*, *scapularium* (as SCAPULA)]

scar¹ /skaar/ *n. & v.* ● *n.* **1** a usu. permanent mark on the skin left after the healing of a wound, burn, or sore. **2** the lasting effect of grief, etc., on a person's character or disposition. **3** a mark left by damage, etc. (*the table bore many scars*). **4** a mark left on the stem, etc., of a plant by the fall of a leaf, etc. ● *v.* (**scarred**, **scarring**) **1** *tr.* (esp. as **scarred** *adj.*) mark with a scar or scars (*was scarred for life*). **2** *intr.* heal over; form a scar. **3** *tr.* form a scar on. □□ **scarless** *adj.* [ME f. OF *eschar(r)e* f. LL *eschara* f. Gk *eskhara* scab]

■ *n.* **1** blemish, mark, disfigurement, cicatrice. ● *v.* **1** blemish, mark, disfigure, mar, wound, injure, damage.

scar² /skaar/ *n.* (also esp. *Brit.* **scaur** /skawr/) a steep craggy outcrop of a mountain or cliff. [ME f. ON *sker* low reef in the sea]

scarab /skárəb/ *n.* **1 a** the sacred dung beetle of ancient Egypt. **b** = SCARABAEID. **2** an ancient Egyptian gem cut in the form of a beetle and engraved with symbols on its flat side, used as a signet, etc. [L *scarabaeus* f. Gk *skarabeios*]

scarabaeid /skárəbéeid/ *n.* any beetle of the family Scarabaeidae, including the dung beetle, cockchafer, etc. [mod.L *Scarabaeidae* (as SCARAB)]

scaramouch /skárəmōōsh/ *n. archaic* a boastful coward; a braggart. [It. *Scaramuccia* stock character in Italian farce f. *scaramuccia* = SKIRMISH, infl. by F form *Scaramouche*]

■ see BRAGGART *n.*

scarce /skairs/ *adj. & adv.* ● *adj.* **1** (usu. *predic.*) (esp. of food, money, etc.) insufficient for the demand; scanty. **2**

hard to find; rare. ● *adv. archaic* or *literary* scarcely. □ **make oneself scarce** *colloq.* keep out of the way; surreptitiously disappear. □□ **scarceness** *n.* [ME f. AF & ONF (e)*scars*, OF *eschars* f. L *excerpere*: see EXCERPT]

■ *adj.* **1** scanty, scant, insufficient, inadequate, deficient, meager, wanting, lacking. **2** at a premium, in short supply, hard to find *or* come by; rare, unusual, few and far between, thin on the ground, seldom met with. ● *adv.* see HARDLY 1, 2. □ **make oneself scarce** see BOLT¹ *v.* 4a.

scarcely /skáirslee/ *adv.* **1** hardly; barely; only just (*I scarcely know her*). **2** surely not (*he can scarcely have said so*). **3** a mild or apologetic or ironical substitute for "not" (*I scarcely expected to be insulted*).

■ **1** hardly, barely; only just, not quite, almost not. **2** surely *or* certainly *or* definitely not, not at all, not in the least, by no means, on no account, under no circumstances, nowise, noway. **3** see HARDLY 1, 2.

scarcity /skáirsitee/ *n.* (*pl.* **-ies**) (often foll. by *of*) a lack or inadequacy, esp. of food.

■ lack, want, need, paucity, dearth, insufficiency, shortage, inadequacy.

scare /skair/ *v. & n.* ● *v.* **1** *tr.* frighten, esp. suddenly (*his expression scared us*). **2** *tr.* (as **scared** *adj.*) (usu. foll. by *of*, or *to* + infin.) frightened; terrified (*scared of his own shadow*). **3** *tr.* (usu. foll. by *away*, *off*, *up*, etc.) drive away by frightening. **4** *intr.* become scared (*they don't scare easily*). ● *n.* **1** a sudden attack of fright (*gave me a scare*). **2** a general, esp. baseless, fear of war, invasion, epidemic, etc. (*a measles scare*). **3** a financial panic causing share selling, etc. □ **scaredy-cat** /skáirdeekat/ *colloq.* a timid person. **scare up** (or **out**) **1** frighten (game, etc.) out of cover. **2** *colloq.* manage to find; discover (*see if we can scare up a meal*). □□ **scarer** *n.* [ME *skerre* f. ON *skirra* frighten f. *skjarr* timid]

■ *v.* **1** frighten, alarm, startle, shock, give a person a shock *or* a fright, terrify, terrorize, horrify, make a person's hair stand on end, *colloq.* scarify, scare the pants off, scare the life *or* the living daylights *or* the hell out of, scare out of one's wits, make a person's flesh creep *or* crawl, give a person goose bumps *or* goose pimples, *sl.* spook. **2** (**scared**) alarmed, afraid, shocked, terrified, horrified, startled, frightened, *colloq.* scared out of one's wits, *sl.* spooked. **3** (*scare off*) see SHOO *v.* **4** frighten, shock, *sl.* spook. ● *n.* **1** fright, shock, surprise, start. □ **scaredy-cat** see COWARD *n.* **scare up** (or **out**) **2** scrape together *or* up, find, dig up, discover, get, come by, gather, collect, *colloq.* raise.

scarecrow /skáirkrō/ *n.* **1** a human figure dressed in old clothes and set up in a field to scare birds away. **2** *colloq.* a badly dressed, grotesque-looking, or very thin person. **3** *archaic* an object of baseless fear.

scarehead /skárhed/ *n.* a shockingly large or sensational newspaper headline.

scaremonger /skáirmunggər, -monggər/ *n.* a person who spreads frightening reports or rumors. □□ **scaremongering** *n.*

scarf¹ /skaarf/ *n.* (*pl.* **scarfs** or **scarves** /skaarvz/) a square, triangular, or esp. long narrow strip of material worn around the neck, over the shoulders, or tied around the head for warmth or ornament. □□ **scarfed** *adj.* [prob. alt. of *scarp* (infl. by SCARF²) f. ONF *escarpe* = OF *escherpe* sash]

■ see MUFFLER 1.

scarf² /skaarf/ *v. & n.* ● *v.tr.* **1** join the ends of (pieces of esp. lumber, metal, or leather) by beveling or notching them to fit and then bolting, brazing, or sewing them together. **2** cut the blubber of (a whale). ● *n.* **1** a joint made by scarfing. **2** a cut on a whale made by scarfing. [ME (earlier as noun) prob. f. OF *escarf* (unrecorded) perh. f. ON]

scarf³ /skaarf/ *v. tr. & intr.* (often foll. by *up* or *down*) eat, esp. quickly, voraciously, greedily, etc.

scarfpin /skáarfpin/ *n.* = TIEPIN.

scarfskin /skaarfskin/ *n.* the outermost layer of the skin constantly scaling off, esp. that at the base of the nails.

scarifier /skárif īər, skáir-/ *n.* **1** a thing or person that scarifies.

2 a machine with prongs for loosening soil without turning it. **3** a spiked road-breaking machine.

scarify[1] /skárifī, skáir-/ v.tr. (**-ies, -ied**) **1 a** make superficial incisions in. **b** cut off skin from. **2** hurt by severe criticism, etc. **3** loosen (soil) with a scarifier. □□ **scarification** /-fikáyshən/ n. [ME f. F scarifier f. LL scarificare f. L scarifare f. Gk skariphaomai f. skariphos stylus]

scarify[2] /skáirifī/ v.tr. & intr. (**-ies, -ied**) colloq. scare; terrify.

scarious /skáireeəs/ adj. (of a part of a plant, etc.) having a dry membranous appearance; thin and brittle. [F scarieux or mod.L scariosus]

scarlatina /skaárlətéenə/ n. = scarlet fever. [mod.L f. It. scarlattina (febbre fever) dimin. of scarlatto SCARLET]

scarlet /skáarlit/ n. & adj. ● n. **1** a brilliant red color tinged with orange. **2** clothes or material of this color (dressed in scarlet). ● adj. of a scarlet color. □ **scarlet fever** an infectious bacterial fever, affecting esp. children, with a scarlet rash. **scarlet hat** RC Ch. a cardinal's hat as a symbol of rank. **scarlet pimpernel** a small annual wild plant, Anagallis arvensis, with small, esp. scarlet, flowers closing in rainy or cloudy weather: also called poor man's weather-glass. **scarlet rash** = ROSEOLA 1. **scarlet runner 1** a runner bean. **2** a scarlet-flowered climber bearing this bean. **scarlet woman** derog. a notoriously promiscuous woman; a prostitute. [ME f. OF escarlate: ult. orig. unkn.]

scaroid /skároyd, skáir-/ n. & adj. ● n. any colorful marine fish of the family Scaridae, native to tropical and temperate seas, including the scarus. ● adj. of or relating to this family.

scarp /skaarp/ n. & v. ● n. **1** the inner wall or slope of a ditch in a fortification (cf. COUNTERSCARP). **2** a steep slope. ● v.tr. **1** make (a slope) perpendicular or steep. **2** provide (a ditch) with a steep scarp and counterscarp. **3** (as scarped adj.) (of a hillside, etc.) steep; precipitous. [It. scarpa]
■ n. **2** see SLOPE n. 1–3. ● v. **3** (scarped) see STEEP[1] adj. 1.

scarper /skaárpər/ v.intr. Brit. sl. run away; escape. [prob. f. It. scappare escape, infl. by rhyming sl. Scapa Flow = go]
■ see RUN v. 2.

scarus /skáirəs/ n. any fish of the genus Scarus, with brightly colored scales, and teeth fused to form a parrotlike beak used for eating coral. Also called parrot-fish. [L f. Gk skaros]

scarves pl. of SCARF[1].

scary /skáiree/ adj. (**scarier, scariest**) colloq. scaring; frightening. □□ **scarily** adv.
■ frightening, scaring, eerie, terrifying, hair-raising, unnerving, bloodcurdling, horrifying, spine-chilling, horrendous, horrid, horrible, colloq. creepy, crawly, spooky.

scat[1] /skat/ v. & int. colloq. ● v.intr. (**scatted, scatting**) depart quickly. ● int. go! [perh. abbr. of SCATTER]
■ int. see SHOO int.

scat[2] /skat/ n. & v. ● n. improvised jazz singing using sounds imitating instruments, instead of words. ● v.intr. (**scatted, scatting**) sing scat. [prob. imit.]
■ n. improvisation, extemporization. ● v. see IMPROVISE 1.

scathe /skayth/ v. & n. ● v.tr. **1** poet. injure esp. by blasting or withering. **2** (as scathing adj.) witheringly scornful (scathing sarcasm). **3** (with neg.) do the least harm to (shall not be scathed) (cf. UNSCATHED). ● n. (usu. with neg.) archaic harm; injury (without scathe). □□ **scatheless** predic.adj.
scathingly adv. [(v.) ME f. ON skatha = OE sceathian: (n.) OE f. ON skathi = OE sceatha malefactor, injury, f. Gmc]
■ v. **2** (scathing) searing, withering, scornful, damaging, harmful, severe, harsh, nasty, biting, acrid, acrimonious, mordant, incisive, cutting, virulent, vitriolic, acid, burning, fierce, savage, ferocious, colloq. scorching. □□ **scatheless** see UNSCATHED.

scatology /skatóləjee, skə-/ n. **1 a** a morbid interest in excrement. **b** a preoccupation with obscene literature, esp. that concerned with the excretory functions. **c** such literature. **2** the study of fossilized dung. **3** the study of excrement for esp. diagnosis. □□ **scatological** /-təlójikəl/ adj. [Gk skōr skatos dung + -LOGY]
■ **1 a** coprophilia. □□ **scatological** see FOUL adj. 5.

scatophagous /skatófəgəs/ adj. feeding on dung. [as SCATOLOGY + Gk -phagos -eating]

scatter /skátər/ v. & n. ● v. **1** tr. **a** throw here and there; strew (scattered gravel on the road). **b** cover by scattering (scattered the road with gravel). **2** tr. & intr. **a** move or cause to move in flight, etc.; disperse (scattered to safety at the sound). **b** disperse or cause (hopes, clouds, etc.) to disperse. **3** tr. (as scattered adj.) not clustered together; wide apart; sporadic (scattered villages). **4** tr. Physics deflect or diffuse (light, particles, etc.). **5 a** intr. (of esp. a shotgun) fire a charge of shot diffusely. **b** tr. fire (a charge) in this way. ● n. (also **scattering**) **1** the act or an instance of scattering. **2** a small amount scattered. **3** the extent of distribution of esp. shot. □ **scatter cushions** (or **rugs**, etc.) cushions, rugs, etc., placed here and there for effect. □□ **scatterer** n. [ME, prob. var. of SHATTER]
■ v. **1 a** shower, sprinkle, strew, spread. **b** shower, sprinkle, besprinkle, strew, bestrew, litter; blanket. **2** dispel, diffuse, dissipate, go off, disappear; see also DISPERSE 1, 2a. **3** (scattered) see DIFFUSE adj. 1, SPORADIC. ● n. **2** (scattering) smattering, sprinkling, bit; suggestion, hint, soupçon, suspicion; see also TOUCH n. 3.

scatterbrain /skátərbrayn/ n. a person given to silly or disorganized thought with lack of concentration. □□ **scatterbrained** adj.
■ □□ **scatterbrained** dazed, woolgathering, dizzy, colloq. dopey, Brit. colloq. scatty, sl. dippy.

scattershot /skátərshot/ n. & adj. firing at random.

scatty /skátee/ adj. (**scattier, scattiest**) Brit. colloq. scatterbrained; disorganized. □□ **scattily** adv. **scattiness** n. [abbr.]

scaup /skawp/ n. any diving duck of the genus Aythya. [scaup Sc. var. of scalp mussel bed, which it frequents]

scaur var. of SCAR[2].

scavenge /skávinj/ v. **1** tr. & intr. (usu. foll. by for) search for and collect (discarded items). **2** tr. remove unwanted products from (an internal-combustion engine cylinder, etc.). **3** feed on carrion, refuse, etc. [back-form. f. SCAVENGER]

scavenger /skávinjər/ n. **1** a person who seeks and collects discarded items. **2** an animal, esp. a beetle, feeding on carrion, refuse, etc. **3** Brit. archaic a person employed to clean the streets, etc. □□ **scavengery** n. [ME scavager f. AF scawager f. scawage f. ONF escauwer inspect f. Flem. scauwen, rel. to SHOW: for -n- cf. MESSENGER]

scazon /skáyzən, skáz-/ n. Prosody a Greek or Latin meter of limping character, esp. a trimeter of two iambuses and a spondee or trochee. [L f. Gk skazōn f. skazō limp]

Sc.D. abbr. Doctor of Science. [L scientiae doctor]

scena /sháynaa/ n. Mus. **1** an elaborate dramatic solo, usu. including recitative. **2** a scene or part of an opera. [It. f. L: see SCENE]

scenario /sinárreeō, -naáreeō/ n. (pl. **-os**) **1** an outline of the plot of a play, film, opera, etc., with details of the scenes, situations, etc. **2** a postulated sequence of future events. □□ **scenarist** n. (in sense 1). [It. (as SCENA)]
■ **1** synopsis, plot (summary), schema, sequence of events; scheme, framework, structure.

scend /send/ n. & v. Naut. ● n. **1** the impulse given by a wave or waves (scend of the sea). **2** a plunge of a vessel. ● v.intr. (of a vessel) plunge or pitch owing to the impulse of a wave. [alt. f. SEND or DESCEND]

scene /seen/ n. **1** a place in which events in real life, drama, or fiction occur; the locality of an event, etc. (the scene was set in India; the scene of the disaster). **2 a** an incident in real life, fiction, etc. (distressing scenes occurred). **b** a description or representation of an incident, etc. (scenes of clerical life). **3** a public incident displaying emotion, temper, etc., esp.

/.../ **pronunciation**	● **part of speech**
□ **phrases, idioms, and compounds**	
□□ **derivatives**	■ **synonym section**
cross-references appear in SMALL CAPITALS or italics	

when embarrassing to others (*made a scene in the restaurant*). **4 a** a continuous portion of a play in a fixed setting and usu. without a change of personnel; a subdivision of an act. **b** a similar section of a film, book, etc. **5 a** any of the pieces of scenery used in a play. **b** these collectively. **6** a landscape or a view (*a desolate scene*). **7** *colloq.* **a** an area of action or interest (*not my scene*). **b** a way of life; a milieu (*well-known on the jazz scene*). **8** *archaic* the stage of a theater. □ **behind the scenes 1** *Theatr.* among the actors, scenery, etc., offstage. **2** unknown to the public; secret(ly). **behind-the-scenes** (*attrib.*) secret, using secret information (*a behind-the-scenes investigation*). **change of scene** a variation of surroundings. **come on the scene** arrive. **make the scene** participate or make an appearance in a particular activity or at a particular site (*make the theater scene in Greenwich Village*). **quit the scene** die; leave. **scene dock** a space for storing scenery near the stage. **set the scene 1** describe the location of events. **2** give preliminary information. [L *scena* f. Gk *skēnē* tent, stage]

■ **1** location, site, place, area, locale, spot, locality, setting. **2 a** see INCIDENT *n.* 1. **3** commotion, upset, brouhaha, disturbance, furor, tantrum, argument, altercation, episode, incident, *colloq.* row. **4 b** episode, part, chapter, section, segment. **5 a** *Theatr.* flat. **b** scenery, *Theatr.* mise en scène. **6** view, sight, landscape, panorama, vista, picture, prospect. **7 a** see SPECIALTY 1. **b** see SPHERE *n.* 4. □ **behind the scenes 2** secret(ly), private(ly), clandestine(ly), confidential(ly), surreptitious(ly), *colloq.* on the q.t. **behind-the-scenes** see SECRET *adj.* 1, 2. **come on the scene** see ARRIVE 1. **quit the scene** see DIE¹ 1, LEAVE¹ *v.* 1b, 3, 4.

scenery /séenəree/ *n.* **1** the general appearance of the natural features of a landscape, esp. when picturesque. **2** *Theatr.* the painted representations of landscape, rooms, etc., used as the background in a play, etc. □ **change of scenery** = change of scene (see SCENE). [earlier *scenary* f. It. SCENARIO: assim. to -ERY]

■ **1** see LANDSCAPE *n.* **2** see SET² 18.

sceneshifter /séenshiftər/ *n.* a person who moves scenery in a theater. □□ **sceneshifting** *n.*

scenic /séenik/ *adj.* **1 a** picturesque; impressive or beautiful (*took the scenic route*). **b** of or concerning natural scenery (*flatness is the main scenic feature*). **2** (of a picture, etc.) representing an incident. **3** *Theatr.* of or on the stage (*scenic performances*). □□ **scenically** *adv.* [L *scenicus* f. Gk *skēnikos* of the stage (as SCENE)]

■ **1 a** picturesque, pretty, beautiful, impressive, grand, striking, spectacular, breathtaking, awesome, awe-inspiring.

scent /sent/ *n. & v.* ● *n.* **1** a distinctive, esp. pleasant, smell (*the scent of hay*). **2 a** a scent trail left by an animal perceptible to hounds, etc. **b** clues, etc., that can be followed like a scent trail (*lost the scent in Paris*). **c** the power of detecting or distinguishing smells, etc., or of discovering things (*some dogs have little scent; the scent for talent*). **3** *Brit.* = PERFUME 2. **4** a trail laid in a paper chase. ● *v.* **1** *tr.* **a** discern by scent (*the dog scented game*). **b** sense the presence of (*scent treachery*). **2** *tr.* make fragrant or foul-smelling. **3** *tr.* (as **scented** *adj.*) having esp. a pleasant smell (*scented soap*). **4** *intr.* exercise the sense of smell (*goes scenting about*). **5** *tr.* apply the sense of smell to (*scented the air*). □ **false scent 1** a scent trail laid to deceive. **2** false clues, etc., intended to deflect pursuers. **on the scent** having a clue. **put** (or **throw**) **off the scent** deceive by false clues, etc. **scent bag** a bag of aniseed, etc., used to lay a trail in drag hunting. **scent gland** (or **organ**) a gland in some animals secreting musk, civet, etc. **scent out** discover by smelling or searching. □□ **scentless** *adj.* [ME *sent* f. OF *sentir* perceive, smell, f. L *sentire*; -c- (17th c.) unexpl.]

■ *n.* **1** fragrance, aroma, perfume, redolence, smell, odor, bouquet, whiff. **2 a** trail, spoor, track, smell. ● *v.* **1 a** smell, sniff (out). **b** discern, perceive, detect, distinguish, recognize, sense, smell, sniff. **3** (**scented**) see FRAGRANT. **5** perfume. □ **false scent 2** see

misinformation (MISINFORM). **scent out** smell *or* sniff out, detect; see also DISCOVER 1a, b.

scepsis *Brit.* var. OF SKEPSIS.

scepter /séptər/ *n.* (*Brit.* **sceptre**) **1** a staff borne esp. at a coronation as a symbol of sovereignty. **2** royal or imperial authority. □□ **sceptered** *adj.* [ME f. OF (*s*)*ceptre* f. L *sceptrum* f. Gk *skēptron* f. *skēptō* lean on]

■ **1** see STAFF¹ *n.* 1a, b.

sceptic *Brit.* var. of SKEPTIC.

sceptical *Brit.* var. of SKEPTICAL.

sceptre *Brit.* var. of SCEPTER.

sch. *abbr.* **1** scholar. **2** school. **3** schooner.

schadenfreude /shaád'nfroydə/ *n.* the malicious enjoyment of another's misfortunes. [G f. *Schaden* harm + *Freude* joy]

schappe /shaápə/ *n.* fabric or yarn made from waste silk. [G, = waste silk]

schedule /skéjool, -oōəl/ *n. & v.* ● *n.* **1 a** a list or plan of intended events, times, etc. **b** a plan of work (*not on my schedule for next week*). **2** a list of rates or prices. **3** a timetable. **4** a tabulated inventory, etc., esp. as an appendix to a document. ● *v.tr.* **1** include in a schedule. **2** make a schedule of. **3** *Brit.* include (a building) in a list for preservation or protection. □□ **scheduler** *n.* [ME f. OF *cedule* f. LL *schedula* slip of paper, dimin. of *scheda* f. Gk *skhedē* papyrus leaf]

■ *n.* **1** program, timetable, plan; calendar, agenda, outline, list, timetable, listing. **2** list, index. ● *v.* **1, 2** program, organize, plan, arrange, book, time, appoint, assign, allot; list, record, register; outline, slate.

scheelite /shéelit/ *n.* *Mineral.* calcium tungstate in its mineral crystalline form. [K. W. *Scheele*, Sw. chemist d. 1786]

schema /skéemə/ *n.* (*pl.* **schemata** /-mətə/ or **schemas**) **1** a synopsis, outline, or diagram. **2** a proposed arrangement. **3** *Logic* a syllogistic figure. **4** (in Kantian philosophy) a conception of what is common to all members of a class; a general type or essential form. [Gk *skhēma -atos* form, figure]

■ **1, 2** see OUTLINE *n.* 1, 2.

schematic /skimátik, skee-/ *adj. & n.* ● *adj.* **1** of or concerning a scheme or schema. **2** representing objects by symbols, etc. ● *n.* a schematic diagram, esp. of an electronic circuit. □□ **schematically** *adv.*

■ *adj.* **2** diagrammatical, representational; symbolic. ● *n.* diagram, schema; layout, design, plan, pattern, configuration.

schematism /skéemətizəm/ *n.* a schematic arrangement or presentation. [mod.L *schematismus* f. Gk *skhēmatismos* (as SCHEMATIZE)]

schematize /skéemətiz/ *v.tr.* **1** put in a schematic form; arrange. **2** represent by a scheme or schema. □□ **schematization** *n.*

scheme /skeem/ *n. & v.* ● *n.* **1 a** a systematic plan or arrangement for work, action, etc. **b** a proposed or operational systematic arrangement (*a color scheme*). **2** an artful or deceitful plot. **3** a timetable, outline, syllabus, etc. ● *v.* **1** *intr.* (often foll. by *for*, or to + infin.) plan esp. secretly or deceitfully; intrigue. **2** *tr.* plan to bring about, esp. artfully or deceitfully (*schemed their downfall*). □□ **schemer** *n.* [L *schema* f. Gk (as SCHEMA)]

■ *n.* **1 a** plan, design, program, system, course (of action), schema, projection, draft, outline, game plan. **b** pattern, arrangement, layout, design, blueprint, chart, map, schematic, order, organization, schema. **2** plot, plan, maneuver, strategy, stratagem, tactic, machination, subterfuge, trick, device, dodge, wile, ruse, intrigue, *colloq.* ploy, *sl.* racket; (*schemes*) games, scheming. ● *v.* **1** plan, plot, conspire, maneuver, intrigue with, machinate, connive. **2** plan, plot, devise, contrive, concoct, *colloq.* cook up.

scheming /skéeming/ *adj. & n.* ● *adj.* artful, cunning, or deceitful. ● *n.* plots; intrigues. □□ **schemingly** *adv.*

■ *adj.* conniving, plotting, crafty, cunning, artful, sly, wily, devious, machiavellian, intriguing, nefarious, treacherous, slick, calculating, tricky, foxy, slippery, underhand(ed), duplicitous, deceitful.

schemozzle var. of SHEMOZZLE.

scherzando /skairtsaándō/ *adv., adj.,* & *n. Mus.* ● *adv.* & *adj.* in a playful manner. ● *n.* (*pl.* **scherzandos** or **scherzandi** /-dee/) a passage played in this way. [It., gerund of *scherzare* to jest (as SCHERZO)]

scherzo /skáirtsō/ *n.* (*pl.* **-os**) *Mus.* a vigorous, light, or playful composition, usu. as a movement in a symphony, sonata, etc. [It., lit. 'jest']

schilling /shíling/ *n.* **1** the chief monetary unit of Austria. **2** a coin equal to the value of one schilling. [G (as SHILLING)]

schipperke /skípərkee, shíp / *n.* **1** a small, black, tailless dog of a breed with a ruff of fur around its neck. **2** this breed. [Du. dial., = little boatman, f. its use as a watchdog on barges]

schism /sízəm, skíz-/ *n.* **1 a** the division of a group into opposing sections or parties. **b** any of the sections so formed. **2 a** the separation of a church into two churches or the secession of a group owing to doctrinal, disciplinary, etc., differences. **b** the offense of causing or promoting such a separation. [ME f. OF *s(c)isme* f. eccl.L *schisma* f. Gk *skhisma -atos* cleft f. *skhizō* to split]
■ **1 a** split, rift, break, breach; division, rupture, separation; disunion. **b** faction, cabal, splinter group, clique, wing, camarilla, camp, set, sect, coterie, circle.

schismatic /sizmátik, skiz-/ *adj.* & *n.* (also **schismatical**) ● *adj.* inclining to, concerning, or guilty of, schism. ● *n.* **1** a holder of schismatic opinions. **2** a member of a schismatic faction or a seceded branch of a church. □□ **schismatically** *adv.* [ME f. OF *scismatique* f. eccl.L *schismaticus* f. eccl.Gk *skhismatikos* (as SCHISM)]
■ *adj.* separatist, divisive, dissident, heretical; breakaway. ● *n.* **1** separatist, dissident, dissenter, heretic; see also INFIDEL *n.*

schist /shist/ *n.* a foliated metamorphic rock composed of layers of different minerals and splitting into thin irregular plates. □□ **schistose** *adj.* [F *schiste* f. L *schistos* f. Gk *skhistos* split (as SCHISM)]

schistosome /shístəsōm/ *n.* = BILHARZIA 1. [Gk *skhistos* divided (as SCHISM) + *sōma* body]

schistosomiasis /shístəsōmíəsis/ *n.* = BILHARZIASIS. [mod.L *Schistosoma* (the genus-name, as SCHISTOSOME)]

schizanthus /skizánthəs/ *n.* any plant of the genus *Schizanthus,* with showy flowers in various colors, and finely divided leaves. [mod.L f. Gk *skhizō* to split + *anthos* flower]

schizo /skítsō/ *adj.* & *n. colloq.* ● *adj.* schizophrenic. ● *n.* (*pl.* **-os**) a schizophrenic. [abbr.]

schizocarp /skízəkaarp, skítsə-/ *n. Bot.* any of a group of dry fruits that split into single-seeded parts when ripe. □□ **schizocarpic** /-kaárpik/ *adj.* **schizocarpous** /-kaárpəs/ *adj.* [Gk *skhizō* to split + *karpos* fruit]

schizoid /skítsoyd/ *adj.* & *n.* ● *adj.* (of a person or personality, etc.) tending to or resembling schizophrenia or a schizophrenic, but usu. without delusions. ● *n.* a schizoid person.

schizomycete /skítsōmíseet, -míseet/ *n.* a former name for a bacterium. [Gk *skhizō* to split + *mukēs -ētos* mushroom]

schizophrenia /skítsəfréeneeə, -fréneeə/ *n.* a mental disease marked by a breakdown in the relation between thoughts, feelings, and actions, frequently accompanied by delusions and retreat from social life. □□ **schizophrenic** /-frénik/ *adj.* & *n.* [mod.L f. Gk *skhizō* to split + *phrēn* mind]

schizothymia /skítsōthímeeə, skíz-/ *n. Psychol.* an introvert condition with a tendency to schizophrenia. □□ **schizothymic** *adj.* [mod.L (as SCHIZOPHRENIA + Gk *thumos* temper)]

schlemiel /shləmeél/ *n. colloq.* a foolish or unlucky person. [Yiddish *shlumiel*]
■ see LOSER.

schlep /shlep/ *v.* & *n.* (also **schlepp**) *colloq.* ● *v.* (**schlepped**, **schlepping**) **1** *tr.* carry; drag. **2** *intr.* go or work tediously or effortfully. ● *n.* (also **schlepper**) a person or thing that is tedious, awkward, or slow. [Yiddish *shlepn* f. G *schleppen* drag]
■ *v.* **1** see CARRY *v.* 1, 2. ● *n.* see STRUGGLE *n.* 1, 3.

schlieren /shleérən/ *n.* **1** a visually discernible area or stratum of different density in a transparent medium. **2** *Geol.*

an irregular streak of mineral in igneous rock. [G, pl. of *Schliere* streak]

schlock /shlok/ *n. colloq.* inferior goods; trash. [Yiddish *shlak* a blow]

schmaltz /shmaalts/ *n. colloq.* sentimentality, esp. in music, drama, etc. □□ **schmaltzy** *adj.* (**schmaltzier, schmaltziest**). [Yiddish f. G *Schmalz* dripping, lard]
■ see *sentimentality* (SENTIMENTAL). □□ **schmaltzy** see SENTIMENTAL.

schmuck /shmuk/ *n. sl.* a foolish or contemptible person. [Yiddish]
■ see FOOL[1] *n.* 1.

schnapps /shnaaps, shnaps/ *n.* any of various spirits drunk in N. Europe. [G, = dram of liquor f. LG & Du. *snaps* mouthful (as SNAP)]

schnauzer /shnówzər, shnówtsər/ *n.* **1** a dog of a German breed with a close wiry coat and heavy whiskers around the muzzle. **2** this breed. [G f. *Schnauze* muzzle, SNOUT]

schnitzel /shnítsəl/ *n.* a cutlet of veal. □ **Wiener** /veénər/(or **Vienna** /vee-énə/) **schnitzel** a breaded, fried, and garnished schnitzel. [G, = slice]

schnook /shnook/ *n. sl.* a dupe; a sucker; a simpleton. [perh. f. G *Schnucke* a small sheep or Yiddish *shnuk* snout.]

schnorkel var. of SNORKEL.

schnorrer /shnawrər/ *n. sl.* a beggar or scrounger; a layabout. [Yiddish f. G *Schnurrer*]

scholar /skólər/ *n.* **1** a learned person, esp. in language, literature, etc.; an academic. **2** the holder of a scholarship. **3 a** a person with specified academic ability (*is a poor scholar*). **b** a person who learns (*am a scholar of life*). **4** *archaic colloq.* a person able to read and write. **5** *archaic* a schoolboy or schoolgirl. □ **scholar's mate** see MATE[2]. □□ **scholarly** *adj.* **scholarliness** *n.* [ME f. OE *scol(i)ere* & OF *escol(i)er* f. LL *scholaris* f. L *schola* SCHOOL[1]]
■ **1** authority, expert, pundit, savant, intellectual, longhair, *colloq.* highbrow, egghead, brain; bookman; man of letters; academic, professor, teacher, *archaic or derog.* pedagogue. **3 a** student, pupil, learner. **5** pupil, student, schoolboy, schoolgirl. □□ **scholarly** learned, erudite, lettered, scholastic, intellectual, academic, brainy, *colloq.* highbrow.

scholarship /skólərship/ *n.* **1 a** academic achievement; learning of a high level. **b** the methods and standards characteristic of a good scholar (*shows great scholarship*). **2** payment from the funds of a school, university, local government, etc., to maintain a student in full-time education, awarded on the basis of scholarly achievement.
■ **1 a** learning, erudition, knowledge, know-how, expertise. **2** grant, endowment, award, fellowship, *Brit.* exhibition, bursarship, bursary.

scholastic /skəlástik/ *adj.* & *n.* ● *adj.* **1** of or concerning universities, schools, education, teachers, etc. **2** pedantic; formal (*shows scholastic precision*). **3** *Philos. hist.* of, resembling, or concerning the schoolmen, esp. in dealing with logical subtleties. ● *n.* **1** a student. **2** *Philos. hist.* a schoolman. **3** a theologian of scholastic tendencies. **4** *RC Ch.* a member of any of several religious orders, who is between the novitiate and the priesthood. □□ **scholastically** *adv.* **scholasticism** /-tisizəm/ *n.* [L *scholasticus* f. Gk *skholastikos* studious f. *skholazō* be at leisure, formed as SCHOOL[1]]
■ *adj.* **1** ACADEMIC *adj.* 1.

scholiast /skóleeast/ *n. hist.* an ancient or medieval scholar, esp. a grammarian, who annotated ancient literary texts. □□ **scholiastic** *adj.* [med.Gk *skholiastēs* f. *skholiazō* write scholia: see SCHOLIUM]

scholium /skóleeəm/ *n.* (*pl.* **scholia** /-leeə/) a marginal note or explanatory comment, esp. by an ancient grammarian on a classical text. [mod.L f. Gk *skholion* f. *skholē* disputation: see SCHOOL[1]]

/. . ./ **pronunciation**	● **part of speech**
□ **phrases, idioms, and compounds**	
□□ **derivatives**	■ **synonym section**
cross-references appear in SMALL CAPITALS or *italics*	

■ see NOTE *n*. 2, 5.

school[1] /skŏŏl/ *n. & v.* ● *n.* **1 a** an institution for educating or giving instruction at any level including college or university, or esp *Brit.* for children under 19 years. **b** (*attrib.*) associated with or for use in school (*a school bag; school dinners*). **2 a** the buildings used by such an institution. **b** the pupils, staff, etc., of a school. **c** the time during which teaching is done, or the teaching itself (*no school today*). **3 a** a branch of study with separate examinations at a university; a department or faculty (*the history school*). **b** *Brit.* the hall in which university examinations are held. **c** (in *pl.*) *Brit.* such examinations. **4 a** the disciples, imitators, or followers of a philosopher, artist, etc., (*the school of Epicurus*). **b** a group of artists, etc., whose works share distinctive characteristics. **c** a group of people sharing a cause, principle, method, etc. (*school of thought*). **5** *Brit.* a group of gamblers or of persons drinking together (*a poker school*). **6** *colloq.* instructive or disciplinary circumstances, occupation, etc. (*the school of adversity; learned in a hard school*). **7** *hist.* a medieval lecture room. **8** *Mus.* (usu. foll. by *of*) a handbook or book of instruction (*school of counterpoint*). **9** (in *pl.*; prec. by *the*) *hist.* medieval universities, their teachers, disputations, etc. ● *v.tr.* **1** send to school; provide for the education of. **2** (often foll. by *to*) discipline; train; control. **3** (as **schooled** *adj.*) (foll. by *in*) educated or trained (*schooled in humility*). □ **go to school 1** begin one's education. **2** attend lessons. **leave school 1** finish one's education. **2** terminate one's education before the completion of one's course of study, etc. **of the old school** according to former and esp. better tradition (*a gentleman of the old school*). **school age** the age range in which children normally attend school. **school board** a board or authority for local education. **school days** the time of being at school, esp. in retrospect. **school of hard knocks** experience gained from hard work, tough circumstances, etc. **school ship** a training ship. **school year** = *academic year*. [ME f. OE *scōl, scolu*, & f. OF *escole* ult. f. L *schola* school f. Gk *skholē* leisure, disputation, philosophy, lecture place]

■ *n.* **1a, 2a, b** (educational) institution; institute, college, university, seminary. **4a** followers, devotees, adherents, votaries, disciples. **b** set, circle, group, coterie, clique, sect. **c** see PERSUASION 4. ● *v.* **1** see EDUCATE 1, 2. **2** discipline, control; train, teach, mold, shape, form. **3** (**schooled**) educated, drilled, indoctrinated, instructed, tutored, trained, disciplined, coached, prepared, primed, equipped.

school[2] /skŏŏl/ *n. & v.* ● *n.* (often foll. by *of*) a shoal of fish, porpoises, whales, etc. ● *v.intr.* form schools. [ME f. MLG, MDu. *schōle* f. WG]

schoolable /skŏŏləbəl/ *adj.* liable by age, etc., to compulsory education.

schoolboy /skŏŏlboy/ *n.* a boy attending school.
■ pupil, student.

schoolchild /skŏŏlchīld/ *n.* a child attending school.
■ pupil, student.

schoolfellow /skŏŏlfelō/ *n.* esp. *Brit.* = SCHOOLMATE.

schoolgirl /skŏŏlgərl/ *n.* a girl attending school.
■ pupil, student.

schoolhouse /skŏŏlhows/ *n.* **1** a building used as a school. **2** *Brit.* a dwelling house adjoining a school.

schoolie /skŏŏlee/ *n. Austral. sl. & dial.* a schoolteacher.
■ see TEACHER.

schooling /skŏŏling/ *n.* **1** education, esp. at school. **2** training or discipline, esp. of an animal.
■ **1** education, teaching, instruction, tutelage, tuition, guidance, training, preparation, indoctrination.

schoolman /skŏŏlmən/ *n.* (*pl.* **-men**) **1** *hist.* a teacher in a medieval European university. **2** *RC Ch. hist.* a theologian seeking to deal with religious doctrines by the rules of Aristotelian logic. **3** a person involved in academic pursuits.

schoolmarm /skŏŏlmaarm/ *n. colloq.* (also **schoolma'am** /-mäm/) a female schoolteacher, esp. in a rural school, characterized by priggishness and strict displine. □□ **schoolmarmish** *adj.*

■ □□ **schoolmarmish** prim, straitlaced, fussy, punctilious, *colloq.* schoolmistressy.

schoolmaster /skŏŏlmastər/ *n.* a head or assistant male teacher. □□ **schoolmasterly** *adj.*
■ see TEACHER.

schoolmastering /skŏŏlmastəring/ *n.* teaching as a profession.

schoolmate /skŏŏlmayt/ *n.* a past or esp. present member of the same school.

schoolmistress /skŏŏlmistris/ *n.* a head or assistant female teacher.
■ see TEACHER.

schoolmistressy /skŏŏlmistrisee/ *adj. colloq.* prim and fussy.
■ see SCHOOL.MARM.

schoolroom /skŏŏlrōŏm, -rŏŏm/ *n.* a room used for lessons in a school.

schoolteacher /skŏŏlteechər/ *n.* a person who teaches in a school. □□ **schoolteaching** *n.*
■ see TEACHER.

schooltime /skŏŏltīm/ *n.* **1** lesson time at school or at home. **2** school days.

schooner /skŏŏnər/ *n.* **1** a fore-and-aft rigged ship with two or more masts, the foremast being smaller than the other masts. **2 a** *Brit.* a measure or glass for esp. sherry. **b** *US & Austral.* a very tall beer glass. **3** *US hist.* = *prairie schooner.* [18th c.: orig. uncert.]

schorl /shorl/ *n.* black tourmaline. [G *Schörl*]

schottische /shótish, shoteésh/ *n.* **1** a kind of slow polka. **2** the music for this. [G *der schottische Tanz* the Scottish dance]

Schottky effect /shótkee/ *n. Electronics* the increase in thermionic emission from a solid surface due to the presence of an external electric field. [W. *Schottky*, Ger. physicist d. 1976]

Schrödinger equation /shrŏdingər, shráy-/ *n. Physics* a differential equation used in quantum mechanics for the wave function of a particle. [E. *Schrödinger*, Austrian physicist d. 1961]

schuss /shŏŏs/ *n. & v.* ● *n.* a straight downhill run on skis. ● *v.intr.* make a schuss. [G, lit. 'shot']

schwa /shwaa/ *n.* (also **sheva** /shəvaa/) *Phonet.* **1** the indistinct unstressed vowel sound as in *a* moment *ago.* **2** the symbol /ə/ representing this in the International Phonetic Alphabet. [G f. Heb. *š'wā*, app. f. *šaw'* emptiness]

sciagraphy *Brit.* var. of SKIAGRAPHY.

sciamachy /siáməkee/ *n. formal* **1** fighting with shadows. **2** imaginary or futile combat. [Gk *skiamakhia* (as SKIAGRAPHY, *-makhia* -fighting)]

sciatic /siátik/ *adj.* **1** of the hip. **2** of or affecting the sciatic nerve. **3** suffering from or liable to sciatica. □ **sciatic nerve** the largest nerve in the human body, running from the pelvis to the thigh. □□ **sciatically** *adv.* [F *sciatique* f. LL *sciaticus* f. L *ischiadicus* f. Gk *iskhiadikos* subject to sciatica f. *iskhion* hip joint]

sciatica /siátikə/ *n.* neuralgia of the hip and thigh; a pain in the sciatic nerve. [ME f. LL *sciatica* (*passio*) fem. of *sciaticus*: see SCIATIC]

science /sīəns/ *n.* **1** a branch of knowledge conducted on objective principles involving the systematized observation of and experiment with phenomena, esp. concerned with the material and functions of the physical universe (see also *natural science*). **2 a** systematic and formulated knowledge, esp. of a specified type or on a specified subject (*political science*). **b** the pursuit or principles of this. **3** an organized body of knowledge on a subject (*the science of philology*). **4** skillful technique rather than strength or natural ability. **5** *archaic* knowledge of any kind. □ **science fiction** fiction based on imagined future scientific discoveries or environmental changes, frequently dealing with space travel, life on other planets, etc. **science park** an area devoted to scientific research or the development of science-based industries. [ME f. OF f. L *scientia* f. *scire* know]

■ **3** body of knowledge *or* information, discipline, branch, field, area, subject, realm, sphere. **4** skill, art, technique, method, system.

scienter /siéntər/ *adv. Law* intentionally; knowingly. [L f. *scire* know]

sciential /siénshəl/ *adj.* concerning or having knowledge. [LL *scientialis* (as SCIENCE)]

scientific /síəntífik/ *adj.* **1 a** (of an investigation, etc.) according to rules laid down in exact science for performing observations and testing the soundness of conclusions. **b** systematic; accurate. **2** used in, engaged in, or relating to (esp. natural) science (*scientific discoveries*; *scientific terminology*). **3** assisted by expert knowledge. □□ **scientifically** *adv.* [F *scientifique* or LL *scientificus* (as SCIENCE)]
■ **1 b** (well-)organized, (well-)regulated, controlled, (well-)ordered, orderly, systematic, methodical, precise, accurate, meticulous, thorough. **3** see PROFESSIONAL *adj.*

scientism /síəntizəm/ *n.* **1 a** a method or doctrine regarded as characteristic of scientists. **b** the use or practice of this. **2** *often derog.* an excessive belief in or application of scientific method. □□ **scientistic** /-tístik/ *adj.*

scientist /síəntist/ *n.* **1** a person with expert knowledge of a (usu. physical or natural) science. **2** a person using scientific methods.

Scientology /síəntólajee/ *n.* a religious system based on self-improvement and promotion through grades of esp. self-knowledge. □□ **Scientologist** *n.* [L *scientia* knowledge + -LOGY]

sci-fi /sífí/ *n.* (often *attrib.*) *colloq.* science fiction. [abbr.: cf. HI-FI]

scilicet /skéeliket, síliset/ *adv.* to wit; that is to say; namely (introducing a word to be supplied or an explanation of an ambiguity). [ME f. L, = *scire licet* one is permitted to know]
■ see NAMELY.

scilla /sílə/ *n.* any liliaceous plant of the genus *Scilla*, related to the bluebell, usu. bearing small blue star-shaped or bell-shaped flowers and having long, glossy, straplike leaves. [L f. Gk *skilla*]

scimitar /símitər, -taar/ *n.* an Oriental curved sword usu. broadening toward the point. [F *cimeterre*, It. *scimitarra*, etc., of unkn. orig.]

scintigram /síntigram/ *n.* an image of an internal part of the body, produced by scintigraphy.

scintigraphy /sintígrəfee/ *n.* the use of a radioisotope and a scintillation counter to get an image or record of a bodily organ, etc. [SCINTILLATION + -GRAPHY]

scintilla /sintílə/ *n.* **1** a trace. **2** a spark. [L]
■ **1** see TRACE¹ *n.* 1b. **2** see SPARK¹ *n.* 2.

scintillate /síntilayt/ *v.intr.* **1** (esp. as **scintillating** *adj.*) talk cleverly or wittily; be brilliant. **2** sparkle; twinkle; emit sparks. **3** *Physics* fluoresce momentarily when struck by a charged particle, etc. □□ **scintillant** *adj.* **scintillatingly** *adv.* [L *scintillare* (as SCINTILLA)]
■ **1** (scintillating) witty, clever; see also BRILLIANT *adj.* 2. **2** see TWINKLE *v.*

scintillation /síntiláyshən/ *n.* **1** the process or state of scintillating. **2** the twinkling of a star. **3** a flash produced in a material by an ionizing particle, etc. □ **scintillation counter** a device for detecting and recording scintillation.
■ **1, 2** see TWINKLE *n.*

scintiscan /síntiskan/ *n.* an image or other record showing the distribution of radioactive traces in parts of the body, used in the detection and diagnosis of various diseases. [SCINTILLATION + SCAN]

sciolist /síəlist/ *n.* a superficial pretender to knowledge. □□ **sciolism** *n.* **sciolistic** *adj.* [LL *sciolus* smatterer f. L *scire* know]

scion /síən/ *n.* **1** (also **cion**) a shoot of a plant, etc., esp. one cut for grafting or planting. **2** a descendant; a younger member of (esp. a noble) family. [ME f. OF *ciun, cion, sion* shoot, twig, of unkn. orig.]
■ **1** see SHOOT *n.* **2** see DESCENDANT.

scire facias /síree fáysheeas, skée're faákee-aas/ *n. Law* a writ to enforce or annul a judgment, patent, etc. [L, = let (him) know]

scirocco var. of SIROCCO.

scirrhus /sírəs, skír-/ *n.* (*pl.* **scirrhi** /-rī/) a carcinoma which is hard to the touch. □□ **scirrhoid** *adj.* **scirrhosity** /sirósitee/ *n.* **scirrhous** *adj.* [mod.L f. Gk *skir(r)os* f. *skiros* hard]

scissel /skísəl/ *n.* waste clippings, etc., of metal produced during coin manufacture. [F *cisaille* f. *cisailler* clip with shears]

scissile /sísil, -īl/ *adj.* able to be cut or divided. [L *scissilis* f. *scindere sciss-* cut]
■ see SEPARABLE.

scission /sízhən, sísh-/ *n.* **1** the act or an instance of cutting; the state of being cut. **2** a division or split. [ME f. OF *scission* or LL *scissio* (as SCISSILE)]
■ see SEPARATION.

scissor /sízər/ *v.tr.* **1** (usu. foll. by *off, up, into,* etc.) cut with scissors. **2** (usu. foll. by *out*) clip out (a newspaper cutting, etc.).

scissors /sízərz/ *n.pl.* **1** (also **pair of scissors** *sing.*) an instrument for cutting fabric, paper, hair, etc., having two pivoted blades with finger and thumb holes in the handles, operating by closing on the material to be cut. **2** (treated as *sing.*) **a** a method of high jump with a forward and backward movement of the legs. **b** a hold in wrestling in which the opponent's body or esp. head is gripped between the legs. □ **scissor-bill** = SKIMMER 4. **scissors and paste** a method of compiling a book, article, etc., from extracts from others or without independent research. □□ **scissorwise** *adv.* [ME *sisoures* f. OF *cisoires* f. LL *cisoria* pl. of *cisorium* cutting instrument (as CHISEL): assoc. with L *scindere sciss-* cut]
■ **1** see SNIP *n.* 4.

sciurine /síyŏorin/ *adj.* **1** of or relating to the family Sciuridae, including squirrels and chipmunks. **2** squirrellike. □□ **sciuroid** *adj.* [L *sciurus* f. Gk *skiouros* squirrel f. *skia* shadow + *oura* tail]

sclera /skléerə/ *n.* the white of the eye; a white membrane coating the eyeball. □□ **scleral** *adj.* **scleritis** /skleerítis/ *n.* **sclerotomy** /-rótəmee/ *n.* (*pl.* **-ies**). [mod.L f. fem. of Gk *sklēros* hard]

sclerenchyma /skleeréngkimə/ *n.* the woody tissue found in a plant, formed from lignified cells and usu. providing support. [mod.L f. Gk *sklēros* hard + *egkhuma* infusion, after *parenchyma*]

scleroid /skléeroyd/ *adj. Bot. & Zool.* having a hard texture; hardened. [Gk *sklēros* hard]

scleroma /sklərómə/ *n.* (*pl.* **scleromata** /-mətə/) an abnormal patch of hardened skin or mucous membrane. [mod.L f. Gk *sklērōma* (as SCLEROSIS)]

sclerometer /sklərómitər/ *n.* an instrument for determining the hardness of materials. [Gk *sklēros* hard + -METER]

sclerophyll /skléerəfil/ *n.* any woody plant with leathery leaves retaining water. □□ **sclerophyllous** /-rófiləs/ *adj.* [Gk *sklēros* hard + *phullon* leaf]

scleroprotein /skléerōprōteen/ *n. Biochem.* any insoluble structural protein. [Gk *sklēros* hard + PROTEIN]

sclerosed /skléerōst, -rōzd/ *adj.* affected by sclerosis.

sclerosis /sklərósis/ *n.* **1** an abnormal hardening of body tissue (see also ARTERIOSCLEROSIS, ATHEROSCLEROSIS). **2** (in full **multiple** or **disseminated sclerosis**) a chronic and progressive disease of the nervous system resulting in symptoms including paralysis and speech defects. **3** *Bot.* the hardening of a cell wall with lignified matter. [ME f. med.L f. Gk *sklērōsis* f. *sklēroō* harden]

sclerotic /sklərótik/ *adj. & n.* ● *adj.* **1** of or having sclerosis. **2** of or relating to the sclera. ● *n.* = SCLERA. □□ **sclerotitis** /-rətítis/ *n.* [med.L *sclerotica* (as SCLEROSIS)]

sclerous /skléerəs/ *adj. Physiol.* hardened; bony. [Gk *sklēros* hard]

scoff¹ /skof/ *v. & n.* ● *v.intr.* (usu. foll. by *at*) speak derisively, esp. of serious subjects; mock; be scornful. ● *n.* **1** mocking words; a taunt. **2** an object of ridicule. □□ **scoffer**

/.../ **pronunciation**   ● **part of speech**
□ **phrases, idioms, and compounds**
□□ **derivatives**   ■ **synonym section**
cross-references appear in SMALL CAPITALS or *italics*

n. **scoffingly** *adv.* [perh. f. Scand.: cf. early mod. Da. *skuf*, *skof* jest, mockery]

■ *v.* mock, chaff, tease, sneer (at), poke fun (at), jeer (at), hiss, *colloq.* kid; (*scoff at*) deride, belittle, dismiss, disparage, make light of, twit, ridicule, lampoon, esp. *Brit.* rag, *colloq.* spoof, rib.

scoff[2] /skof/ *v. & n. colloq.* ● *v.tr. & intr.* eat greedily. ● *n.* food; a meal. [(n.) f. Afrik. *schoff* repr. Du. *schoft* quarter of a day (hence, meal): (v.) orig. var. of dial. *scaff*, assoc. with the noun]

■ *v.* devour, put away, wolf (down), bolt, gulp (down), ingurgitate; gorge oneself (on), stuff oneself (with), gobble (up *or* down), guzzle. ● *n.* food, victuals, edibles, provisions, *colloq.* grub, eats, *sl.* nosh, chow.

scold /skōld/ *v. & n.* ● *v.* **1** *tr.* rebuke (esp. a child, employee, or inferior). **2** *intr.* find fault noisily; complain; rail. ● *n.* *archaic* a nagging or grumbling woman. □□ **scolder** *n.* **scolding** *n.* [ME (earlier as noun), prob. f. ON *skáld* SKALD]

■ *v.* **1** reprimand, reprove, upbraid, criticize, censure, find fault with, rebuke, reproach, lecture, berate, rate, castigate, take to task, rap (on) the knuckles, give a person a piece of one's mind, give a person a tongue-lashing, haul over the coals, rip *or* tear into, *archaic or literary* chide, *colloq.* bawl out, dress down, give a person hell *or* what for, jump on, jump down a person's throat, give a person a (good) talking-to, tell off, call a person on the carpet, light *or* lace *or* sail into, chew out. **2** find fault, complain, rail, lecture, *archaic or literary* chide. ● *n.* nag, shrew, termagant, virago, fishwife, harridan, hellcat, fury, tigress, Xanthippe, *archaic* beldam, *colloq.* battleaxe.

scolex /skṓleks/ *n.* (*pl.* **scoleces** /-leeseez/ or **scolices** /-liseez/) the head of a larval or adult tapeworm. [mod.L f. Gk *skṓlēx* worm]

scoliosis /skōleeṓsis, skól-/ *n.* an abnormal lateral curvature of the spine. □□ **scoliotic** /-liótik/ *adj.* [mod.L f. Gk f. *skolios* bent]

scollop var. of SCALLOP.

scolopendrium /skóləpéndreeəm/ *n.* any of various ferns, esp. hart's tongue. [mod.L f. Gk *skolopendrion* f. *skolopendra* millipede (because of the supposed resemblance)]

scomber /skómbər/ *n.* any marine fish of the family Scombridae, including mackerels, tunas, and bonitos. □□ **scombrid** *n.* **scombroid** *adj. & n.* [L f. Gk *skombros*]

sconce[1] /skons/ *n.* **1** a flat candlestick with a handle. **2** a bracket candlestick to hang on a wall. [ME f. OF *esconse* lantern or med.L *sconsa* f. L *absconsa* fem. past part. of *abscondere* hide: see ABSCOND]

sconce[2] /skons/ *n.* **1** a small fort or earthwork usu. defending a ford, pass, etc. **2** *archaic* a shelter or screen. [Du. *schans* brushwood f. MHG *schanze*]

scone /skon, skōn/ *n.* a small sweet or savory cake of flour, shortening, and milk, baked quickly in an oven. [orig. Sc., perh. f. MDu. *schoon(broot)*, MLG *schon(brot)* fine (bread)]

scoop /skōop/ *n. & v.* ● *n.* **1** any of various objects resembling a spoon, esp.: **a** a short-handled deep shovel used for transferring grain, sugar, coal, coins, etc. **b** a large long-handled ladle used for transferring liquids. **c** the excavating part of a digging machine, etc. **d** *Med.* a long-handled spoonlike instrument used for scraping parts of the body, etc. **e** an instrument used for serving portions of mashed potato, ice cream, etc. **2** a quantity taken up by a scoop. **3** a movement of or resembling scooping. **4** a piece of news published by a newspaper, etc., in advance of its rivals. **5** a large profit made quickly or by anticipating one's competitors. **6** *Mus.* a singer's exaggerated portamento. **7** a scooped-out hollow, etc. ● *v.tr.* **1** (usu. foll. by *out*) hollow out with or as if with a scoop. **2** (usu. foll. by *up*) lift with or as if with a scoop. **3** forestall (a rival newspaper, reporter, etc.) with a scoop. **4** secure (a large profit, etc.), esp. suddenly. □ **scoop neck** the rounded low-cut neck of a garment. **scoop net** a net used for sweeping a river bottom, or for catching bait. □□ **scooper** *n.* **scoopful** *n.* (*pl.* **-fuls**). [ME f. MDu., MLG *schōpe* bucket, etc., rel. to SHAPE]

■ *n.* **1 b** ladle, dipper, spoon, bailer. **c** bucket. **5** killing.

● *v.* **1** (*scoop out*) gouge out, spoon out, hollow out, cut, dig out, excavate. **2** (*scoop up*) pick up, gather (up), sweep up, take up *or* in.

scoot /skōot/ *v. & n. colloq.* ● *v.intr.* run or dart away, esp. quickly. ● *n.* the act or an instance of scooting. [19th-c. US (earlier *scout*): orig. unkn.]

■ *v.* see SCURRY *v.*

scooter /skṓotər/ *n. & v.* ● *n.* **1** a child's toy consisting of a footboard mounted on two wheels and a long steering handle, propelled by resting one foot on the footboard and pushing the other against the ground. **2** (in full **motor scooter**) a light two-wheeled open motor vehicle with a shieldlike protective front. **3** a sailboat able to travel on either water or ice. ● *v.intr.* travel or ride on a scooter. □□ **scooterist** *n.*

scopa /skṓpə/ *n.* (*pl.* **scopae** /-pee/) a small brushlike tuft of hairs, esp. on the leg of a bee for collecting pollen. [sing. of L *scopae* = twigs, broom]

scope[1] /skōp/ *n.* **1 a** the extent to which it is possible to range; the opportunity for action, etc. (*this is beyond the scope of our research*). **b** the sweep or reach of mental activity, observation, or outlook (*an intellect limited in its scope*). **2** *Naut.* the length of cable extended when a ship rides at anchor. **3** *archaic* a purpose, end, or intention. [It. *scopo* aim f. Gk *skopos* target f. *skeptomai* look at]

■ **1** space, room, leeway, elbowroom, freedom, opportunity; range, reach, extent, compass, orbit, span, breadth, expanse, capacity, stretch, latitude, spread; sphere, field, area.

scope[2] /skōp/ *n. colloq.* a telescope, microscope, or other device ending in *-scope*. [abbr.]

-scope /skōp/ *comb. form* forming nouns denoting: **1** a device looked at or through (*kaleidoscope; telescope*). **2** an instrument for observing or showing (*gyroscope; oscilloscope*). □□ **-scopic** /skópik/ *comb. form* forming adjectives. [from or after mod.L *-scopium* f. Gk *skopeō* look at]

scopolamine /skəpóləmeen, -min/ *n.* = HYOSCINE. [*Scopolia* genus name of the plants yielding it, f. G. A. *Scopoli*, It. naturalist d. 1788 + AMINE]

scopula /skópyələ/ *n.* (*pl.* **scopulae** /-lee/) any of various small brushlike structures, esp. on the legs of spiders. [LL, dimin. of L *scopa*: see SCOPA]

-scopy /skəpee/ *comb. form* indicating viewing or observation, usu. with an instrument ending in *-scope* (*microscopy*).

scorbutic /skawrbyṓotik/ *adj. & n.* ● *adj.* relating to, resembling, or affected with scurvy. ● *n.* a person affected with scurvy. □□ **scorbutically** *adv.* [mod.L *scorbuticus* f. med.L *scorbutus* scurvy, perh. f. MLG *schorbūk* f. *schoren* break + *būk* belly]

scorch /skawrch/ *v. & n.* ● *v.* **1** *tr.* **a** burn the surface of with flame or heat so as to discolor, parch, injure, or hurt. **b** affect with the sensation of burning. **2** *intr.* become discolored, etc., with heat. **3** *tr.* (as **scorching** *adj.*) *colloq.* **a** (of the weather) very hot. **b** (of criticism, etc.) stringent; harsh. **4** *intr. colloq.* (of a motorist, etc.) go at excessive speed. ● *n.* **1** a mark made by scorching. **2** *colloq.* a spell of fast driving, etc. □ **scorched earth policy** the burning of crops, etc., and the removing or destroying of anything that might be of use to an occupying enemy force. □□ **scorchingly** *adv.* [ME, perh. rel. to *skorkle* in the same sense]

■ *v.* **1, 2** sear, burn, roast; singe, char, blacken. **3** (**scorching**) **a** hot, torrid, boiling, roasting, sweltering, searing, parching, shriveling, tropical, hellish, sizzling, broiling. **b** stringent, critical, caustic, scathing, mordant, vituperative, harsh, acrimonious, bitter. **4** see SPEED *v.* 1.

scorcher /skáwrchər/ *n.* **1** a person or thing that scorches. **2** *colloq.* a very hot day. **b** *Brit.* a fine specimen.

score /skawr/ *n. & v.* ● *n.* **1 a** the number of points, goals, runs, etc., made by a player, side, etc., in some games. **b** the total number of points, etc., at the end of a game (*the score was five to one*). **c** the act of gaining, esp. a goal (*an exciting score there!*). **2** (*pl.* same or **scores**) twenty or a set of twenty. **3** (in *pl.*) a great many (*scores of people arrived*). **4 a** a reason or motive (*rejected on the score of absurdity*). **b**

topic; subject (*no worries on that score*). **5** *Mus.* **a** a usu. printed copy of a composition showing all the vocal and instrumental parts arranged one below the other. **b** the music composed for a film or play, esp. for a musical. **6** *colloq.* **a** a piece of good fortune. **b** the act or an instance of scoring off another person. **7** *colloq.* the state of affairs; the present situation (*asked what the score was*). **8** a notch, line, etc., cut or scratched into a surface. **9 a** an amount due for payment. **b** a running account kept by marks against a customer's name. **10** *Naut.* a groove in a block or deadeye to hold a rope. ● *v.* **1** *tr.* **a** win or gain (a goal, run, points, etc., or success, etc.) (*scored six runs in the third inning*). **b** count for a score of (points in a game, etc.) (*a bull's-eye scores the most points*). **c** allot a score to (a competitor, etc.). **d** make a record of (a point, etc.). **2** *intr.* **a** make a score in a game (*failed to score*). **b** keep the tally of points, runs, etc., in a game. **3** *tr.* mark with notches, incisions, lines, etc.; slash; furrow (*scored his name on the desk*). **4** *intr.* secure an advantage by luck, cunning, etc. (*that is where he scores*). **5** *tr.* *Mus.* **a** orchestrate (a piece of music). **b** (usu. foll. by *for*) arrange for an instrument or instruments. **c** write the music for (a film, musical, etc.). **d** write out in a score. **6** *tr.* **a** (usu. foll. by *up*) mark (a total owed, etc.) in a score (see sense 9b of *n.*). **b** (usu. foll. by *against, to*) enter (an item of debt to a customer). **7** *intr.* *sl.* **a** obtain drugs illegally. **b** make a sexual conquest. **8** *tr.* (usu. foll. by *against, to*) mentally record (an offense, etc.). **9** *tr.* criticize (a person) severely. □ **keep score** (or **the score**) register the score as it is made. **know the score** *colloq.* be aware of the essential facts. **on the score of** *Brit.* for the reason that; because of. **on that score** so far as that is concerned. **score off** (or **score points off**) esp *Brit.* *colloq.* humiliate, esp. verbally in repartee, etc. **score out** draw a line through (words, etc.). **score points with** make a favorable impression on. **settle a** (or **the**) **score** retaliate; commit an act of vengeance. □□ **scorer** *n.* **scoring** *n.* *Mus.* [(n.) f. OE: sense 5 f. the line or bar drawn through all staves: (v.) partly f. ON *skora* f. ON *skor* notch, tally, twenty, f. Gmc: see SHEAR]
■ *n.* **1 a, b** number, tally, sum (total), total. **3** (*scores*) a great many, dozens, hundreds, (tens *or* hundreds of) thousands, millions, droves, hordes, multitudes, herds, legions, lots, masses, shoals, bevies, swarms, flocks, armies, crowds, throngs. **4 a** ground(s), basis, account, rationale, cause, reason, motive. **b** see SUBJECT *n.* 1a. **5 a** music, accompaniment; vocal score, *Mus.* full score. **7** state of affairs *or* things *or* play, situation, news, status quo, word, intelligence, latest, *sl.* poop. **8** nick, groove, scratch, line, mark, stroke, notch, cut. **9 b** see TALLY *n.* 1. ● *v.* **1 a** see GAIN *v.* 1. **d** record, notch up; see also TALLY *v.* 2. **2 b** keep the tally, keep (the) score. **3** mark, line, incise, scratch, nick, notch, cut, groove, furrow, scrape, gouge, slash, *archaic* scotch. **4** succeed, be successful, triumph, win, make an impression, have an impact, make a hit. **5 c** write, orchestrate; see also COMPOSE *v.* 1a. **6 b** charge, chalk up, put on account, *Brit.* put on the slate. □ **keep score** (or **the score**) score, keep the tally. **know the score** be in the picture, *colloq.* be in the know, be switched-on.

scoreboard /skáwrbawrd/ *n.* a large board for publicly displaying the score in a game or match.

scorecard /skáwrkaard/ *n.* a card prepared for entering scores on and usu. for indicating players by name, number, etc.

scoria /skáwreeə/ *n.* (*pl.* **scoriae** /-ree-ee/) **1** cellular lava, or fragments of it. **2** the slag or dross of metals. □□ **scoriaceous** /-reeáyshəs/ *adj.* [L f. Gk *skōria* refuse f. *skōr* dung]

scorify /skáwrifī/ *v.tr.* (**-ies, -ied**) **1** reduce to dross. **2** assay (precious metal) by treating a portion of its ore fused with lead and borax. □□ **scorification** /-fikáyshən/ *n.* **scorifier** *n.*

scorn /skawrn/ *n.* & *v.* ● *n.* **1** disdain; contempt; derision. **2** an object of contempt, etc. (*the scorn of all onlookers*). ● *v.tr.* **1** hold in contempt or disdain. **2** (often foll. by *to* + infin.) abstain from or refuse to do as unworthy (*scorns lying*; *scorns*

to lie). □ **think scorn of** *Brit.* despise. □□ **scorner** *n.* [ME f. OF *esc*(*h*)*arn*(*ir*) ult. f. Gmc: cf. OS *skern* MOCKERY]
■ *n.* **1** contumely, contempt, contemptuousness, disdain, deprecation, mockery, derision, derisiveness, sneering, ridicule, scoffing, jeering, taunting; dismissal. ● *v.* **1** reject, rebuff, disown, disavow, disregard, ignore, shun, snub, flout, treat with contempt, hold in contempt, have no use for, disdain, spurn, mock, deride, despise, curl one's lip at, sneer at, scoff at, jeer at, make fun of, laugh at, ridicule, look down on *or* upon, look down one's nose at, thumb one's nose at, pooh-pooh, *colloq.* turn up one's nose at, put down, *literary* contemn, *sl.* cock a snook at. **2** (*scorn to*) see REFRAIN[1].

scornful /skáwrnfŏŏl/ *adj.* (often foll. by *of*) full of scorn; contemptuous. □□ **scornfully** *adv.* **scornfulness** *n.*
■ contemptuous, disdainful, disparaging, derisory, derisive, snide, contumelious, deprecative, supercilious, mocking, sneering, scoffing, haughty, high-handed, superior, *colloq.* snooty, snotty.

Scorpio /skáwrpeeō/ *n.* (*pl.* **-os**) **1** a constellation, traditionally regarded as contained in the figure of a scorpion. **2 a** the eighth sign of the zodiac (the Scorpion). **b** a person born when the sun is in this sign. □□ **Scorpian** *adj.* & *n.* [ME f. L (as SCORPION)]

scorpioid /skáwrpeeoyd/ *adj.* & *n.* ● *adj.* **1** *Zool.* of, relating to, or resembling a scorpion; of the scorpion order. **2** *Bot.* (of an inflorescence) curled up at the end, and uncurling as the flowers develop. ● *n.* this type of inflorescence. [Gk *skorpioeidēs* (as SCORPIO)]

scorpion /skáwrpeeən/ *n.* **1** an arachnid of the order Scorpionida, with lobsterlike pincers and a jointed tail that can be bent over to inflict a poisoned sting on prey held in its pincers. **2** (in full **false scorpion**) a similar arachnid of the order Pseudoscorpionida, smaller and without a tail. **3** (**the Scorpion**) the zodiacal sign or constellation Scorpio. **4** *Bibl.* a whip with metal points (1 Kings 12:11). □ **scorpion fish** any of various marine fish of the family Scorpaenidae, with venomous spines on the head and gills. **scorpion fly** any insect of the order Mecoptera, esp. of the family Panorpidae, the males of which have a swollen abdomen curved upward like a scorpion's sting. **scorpion grass** = *forget-me-not*. [ME f. OF f. L *scorpio* -*onis* f. *scorpius* f. Gk *skorpios*]

scorzonera /skáwrzəneérə/ *n.* **1** a composite plant, *Scorzonera hispanica*, with long, tapering purple-brown roots. **2** the root used as a vegetable. [It. f. *scorzone* venomous snake ult. f. med.L *curtio*]

Scot /skot/ *n.* **1 a** a native of Scotland. **b** a person of Scottish descent. **2** *hist.* a member of a Gaelic people that migrated from Ireland to Scotland around the 6th c. [OE *Scottas* (pl.) f. LL *Scottus*]

scot /skot/ *n.* *hist.* a payment corresponding to a modern tax, rate, etc. □ **scot-free** unharmed; unpunished; safe. [ME f. ON *skot* & f. OF *escot*, of Gmc orig.: cf. SHOT[1]]
■ see TAX *n.* 1.

Scotch /skoch/ *adj.* & *n.* ● *adj.* **1** var. of SCOTTISH or SCOTS. **2** Scotch whiskey. ● *n.* **1** var. of SCOTTISH or SCOTS. **2** Scotch whiskey. □ **Scotch broth** a soup made from beef or mutton with pearl barley, etc. **Scotch egg** a hard-boiled egg enclosed in sausage meat and fried. **Scotch mist 1** a thick drizzly mist common in the Highlands of Scotland. **2** *Brit.* a retort made to a person implying that he or she has imagined or failed to understand something. **Scotch pebble** agate, jasper, cairngorm, etc., found in Scotland. **Scotch pine** a pine tree, *Pinus sylvestris*, native to Europe and Asia. **Scotch terrier** = *Scottish terrier*. **Scotch whiskey** whiskey distilled in Scotland, esp. from malted barley. ¶ *Scots* or *Scottish* is generally preferred in Scotland, except in the special compounds given above. [contr. of SCOTTISH]
■ *n.* **2** see WHISKEY.

/.../ **pronunciation**	● **part of speech**
□ **phrases, idioms, and compounds**	
□□ **derivatives**	■ **synonym section**
cross-references appear in SMALL CAPITALS or *italics*	

scotch[1] /skoch/ *v. & n.* ● *v.tr.* **1** put an end to; frustrate (*injury scotched his attempt*). **2** *archaic* **a** wound without killing; slightly disable. **b** make incisions in; score. ● *n.* **1** *archaic* a slash. **2** a line on the ground for hopscotch. [ME: orig. unkn.]

scotch[2] /skoch/ *n. & v.* ● *n.* a wedge or block placed against a wheel, etc., to prevent its slipping. ● *v.tr.* hold back (a wheel, barrel, etc.) with a scotch. [17th c.: perh. = *scatch* stilt f. OF *escache*]

Scotchman /skóchmən/ *n.* (*pl.* **-men**; *fem.* **Scotchwoman**, *pl.* **-women**) = SCOTSMAN. ¶ *Scotsman*, etc., are generally preferred in Scotland.

scoter /skṓtər/ *n.* (*pl.* same or **scoters**) a large marine duck of the genus *Melanitta*. [17th c.: orig. unkn.]

scotia /skṓshə/ *n.* a concave molding, esp. at the base of a column. [L f. Gk *skotia* f. *skotos* darkness, with ref. to the shadow produced]

Scoticism var. of SCOTTICISM.

Scoticize var. of SCOTTICIZE.

Scotland Yard /skótlənd/ *n.* **1** the headquarters of the London Metropolitan Police. **2** its Criminal Investigation Department. [*Great* and *New Scotland Yard*, streets where it was successively situated until 1967]

scotoma /skətṓmə/ *n.* (*pl.* **scotomata** /-mətə/) a partial loss of vision or blind spot in an otherwise normal visual field. [LL f. Gk *skotōma* f. *skotoō* darken f. *skotos* darkness]

Scots /skots/ *adj. & n.* esp. *Sc.* ● *adj.* **1** = SCOTTISH *adj.* **2** in the dialect, accent, etc., of (esp. Lowlands) Scotland. ● *n.* **1** = SCOTTISH *n.* **2** the form of English spoken in (esp. Lowlands) Scotland. [ME orig. *Scottis*, north. var. of SCOTTISH]

Scotsman /skótsmən/ *n.* (*pl.* **-men**; *fem.* **Scotswoman**, *pl.* **-women**) **1** a native of Scotland. **2** a person of Scottish descent.

Scotticism /skótisizəm/ *n.* (also **Scoticism**) a Scottish phrase, word, or idiom. [LL *Scot*(*t*)*icus*]

Scotticize /skótisiz/ *v.* (also **Scoticize**) **1** *tr.* imbue with or model on Scottish ways, etc. **2** *intr.* imitate the Scottish in idiom or habits.

Scottie /skótee/ *n. colloq.* **1** (also **Scottie dog**) a Scottish terrier. **2** a Scot.

Scottish /skótish/ *adj. & n.* ● *adj.* of or relating to Scotland or its inhabitants. ● *n.* (prec. by *the*; treated as *pl.*) the people of Scotland (see also SCOTS). □ **Scottish terrier 1** a small terrier of a rough-haired short-legged breed. **2** this breed. □□ **Scottishness** *n.*

scoundrel /skówndrəl/ *n.* an unscrupulous villain; a rogue. □□ **scoundreldom** *n.* **scoundrelism** *n.* **scoundrelly** *adj.* [16th c.: orig. unkn.]
■ villain, rogue, wretch, good-for-nothing, scapegrace, blackguard, cur, cad, knave, *colloq.* scamp, heel, *colloq. or joc.* bounder, *often joc.* rascal, *sl.* louse, *Austral. sl.* dingo, esp. *Brit. sl.* rotter.

scour[1] /skowr/ *v. & n.* ● *v.tr.* **1 a** cleanse or brighten by rubbing, esp. with soap, chemicals, sand, etc. **b** (usu. foll. by *away*, *off*, etc.) clear (rust, stains, reputation, etc.) by rubbing, hard work, etc. (*scoured the slur from his name*). **2** (of water, or a person with water) clear out (a pipe, channel, etc.) by flushing through. **3** *hist.* purge (the bowels) drastically. ● *n.* **1** the act or an instance of scouring; the state of being scoured, esp. by a swift water current (*the scour of the tide*). **2** diarrhea in cattle. **3** a substance used for scouring. □ **scouring rush** any of various horsetail plants with a rough siliceous coating used for polishing wood, etc. □□ **scourer** *n.* [ME f. MDu., MLG *schüren* f. F *escurer* f. LL *excurare* clean (off) (as EX-[1], CURE)]
■ *v.* **1** scrub, clean, wash, rub, polish, burnish, buff, shine, *usu. formal* cleanse. **b** clear; (*scour away*, *off*, etc.) scrub *or* clean *or* wash off, scrub *or* clean *or* wash *or* rub away.

scour[2] /skowr/ *v.* **1** *tr.* hasten over (an area, etc.) searching thoroughly (*scoured the streets for him*; *scoured the pages of the newspaper*). **2** *intr.* range hastily, esp. in search or pursuit. [ME: orig. unkn.]
■ **1** rake, comb, search, hunt through.

scourge /skərj/ *n. & v.* ● *n.* **1** a whip used for punishment, esp. of people. **2** a person or thing seen as punishing, esp. on a large scale (*the scourge of famine*; *Genghis Khan, the scourge of Asia*). ● *v.tr.* **1** whip. **2** punish; afflict; oppress. □□ **scourger** *n.* [ME f. OF *escorge* (n.), *escorgier* (v.) (ult. as EX-[1], L *corrigia* thong, whip)]
■ *n.* **1** whip, lash, quirt, horsewhip, *hist.* cat-o'-nine-tails, knout. **2** curse, misfortune, bane, evil, affliction, plague, torment, misery, *archaic or literary* woe. ● *v.* **1** whip, flog, beat, lash, belt, flagellate, *colloq.* whale. **2** punish, castigate, chastise, discipline, afflict, oppress, torment.

Scouse /skows/ *n. & adj. colloq.* ● *n.* **1** the dialect of Liverpool. **2** (also **Scouser** /skówsə/) a native of Liverpool. **3** (**scouse**) = LOBSCOUSE. ● *adj.* of or relating to Liverpool. [abbr. of LOBSCOUSE]

scout[1] /skowt/ *n. & v.* ● *n.* **1** a person, esp. a soldier, sent out to get information about the enemy's position, strength, etc. **2** the act of seeking (esp. military) information (*on the scout*). **3** = *talent scout.* **4** (**Scout**) a Boy Scout or Girl Scout. **5** esp. *Brit.* a domestic worker at a college, esp. at Oxford University. **6** esp. *Brit. colloq.* a person; a fellow. **7** a ship or aircraft designed for reconnoitring, esp. a small fast aircraft. ● *v.* **1** *intr.* act as a scout. **2** *intr.* (foll. by *about*, *around*) make a search. **3** *tr.* (often foll. by *out*) *colloq.* explore to get information about (territory, etc.). □□ **scouter** *n.* **scouting** *n.* [ME f. OF *escouter* listen, earlier *ascolter* ult. f. L *auscultare*]
■ *n.* **6** person, *colloq.* fellow; see also GUY[1] *n.* 1. ● *v.* **1** spy, reconnoiter. **2, 3** search *or* look (about *or* around) (for), hunt (about *or* around) (for), cast around *or* about (for), check (about *or* around) (for); reconnoiter, investigate, explore.

scout[2] /skowt/ *v.tr.* reject (an idea, etc.) with scorn. [Scand.: cf. ON *skúta*, *skúti* taunt]

Scouter /skówtər/ *n.* an adult member of the Boy Scouts.

scoutmaster /skówtmastər/ *n.* a person in charge of a group of Scouts.

scow /skow/ *n.* a flat-bottomed boat used as a lighter, etc. [Du. *schouw* ferry boat]

scowl /skowl/ *n. & v.* ● *n.* a severe frown producing a sullen, bad-tempered, or threatening look on a person's face. ● *v.intr.* make a scowl. □□ **scowler** *n.* [ME, prob. f. Scand.: cf. Da. *skule* look down or sidelong]
■ *n.* frown, grimace, glare, glower, lower, *colloq.* dirty look. ● *v.* glower, frown, grimace, glare, look daggers, lower.

scr. *abbr.* scruple(s) (of weight).

scrabble /skrábəl/ *v. & n.* ● *v.intr.* (often foll. by *about*, *at*) scratch or grope to find or collect or hold on to something. ● *n.* **1** an act of scrabbling. **2** (**Scrabble**) *propr.* a game in which players build up words from letter blocks on a board. [MDu. *schrabbelen* frequent. of *schrabben* SCRAPE]

scrag /skrag/ *n. & v. Brit.* ● *n.* **1** (also **scrag end**) the inferior end of a neck of mutton. **2** a skinny person or animal. **3** *colloq.* a person's neck. ● *v.tr.* (**scragged**, **scragging**) *sl.* **1** strangle, hang. **2** seize roughly by the neck. **3** handle roughly; beat up. [perh. alt. f. dial. *crag* neck, rel. to MDu. *crāghe*, MLG *krage*]

scraggly /skráglee/ *adj.* sparse and irregular.

scraggy /skrágee/ *adj.* (**scraggier**, **scraggiest**) thin and bony. □□ **scraggily** *adv.* **scragginess** *n.*
■ see THIN *adj.* 4.

scram /skram/ *v.intr.* (**scrammed**, **scramming**) (esp. in *imper.*) *colloq.* go away. [20th c.: perh. f. SCRAMBLE]
■ see *beat it.*

scramble /skrámbəl/ *v. & n.* ● *v.* **1** *intr.* make one's way over rough ground, rocks, etc., by clambering, crawling, etc. **2** *intr.* (foll. by *for*, *at*) struggle with competitors (for a thing or share of it). **3** *intr.* move with difficulty or awkwardly. **4** *tr.* **a** mix together indiscriminately. **b** jumble or muddle. **5** *tr.* cook (eggs) by heating them when broken and well mixed, often with butter, milk, etc. **6** *tr.* change the speech frequency of (a broadcast transmission or telephone conversation) so as to make it unintelligible without a corresponding decoding device. **7** *intr.* move hastily. **8** *tr. colloq.* execute (an action, etc.) awkwardly and inefficiently. **9** *intr.* (of fighter aircraft or their pilots) take off quickly in an emergency or for action. ● *n.* **1** an act of scrambling. **2** a difficult climb or walk. **3** (foll. by *for*) an eager struggle or competition. **4** *Brit.* a motorcycle race over rough ground. **5** an emergency takeoff by fighter aircraft. □ **scrambled eggs** *colloq.* gold braid on a military officer's cap. [16th c. (imit.): cf. dial. synonyms *scamble*, *cramble*]

■ *v.* **1** climb, clamber, crawl, scrabble, struggle. **2** jostle, tussle, struggle, wrestle, grapple, fight, battle. **3** struggle, flounder, blunder. **4** mix up, confuse, shuffle, jumble (up), intermingle, mingle, *literary* commingle. **7** rush, hurry, scamper, run, hasten, race, scurry, scuttle, dash, hotfoot (it), hustle, *colloq.* scoot, skedaddle, hightail. **8** see *knock up* 1. ● *n.* **1** scrabble, scrimmage, struggle, tussle. **2** struggle, pull, climb. **3** (*scramble for*) competition *or* contest for, race *or* rush for, commotion *or* riot *or* free-for-all over.

scrambler /skrámblər/ *n.* a device for scrambling telephone conversations.

scran /skran/ *n. Brit. sl.* **1** food; eatables. **2** remains of food. □ **bad scran** *Ir.* bad luck. [18th c.: orig. unkn.]

scrap¹ /skrap/ *n. & v.* ● *n.* **1** a small detached piece; a fragment or remnant. **2** rubbish or waste material. **3** an extract or cutting from something written or printed. **4** discarded metal for reprocessing (often *attrib.*: *scrap metal*). **5** (with *neg.*) the smallest piece or amount (*not a scrap of food left*). **6** (in *pl.*) **a** odds and ends. **b** bits of uneaten food. **7** (in *sing* or *pl.*) a residuum of melted fat or of fish with the oil expressed. ● *v.tr.* (**scrapped, scrapping**) discard as useless. □ **scrap heap 1** a pile of scrap materials. **2** a state of uselessness. **scrap merchant** a dealer in scrap. [ME f. ON *skrap*, rel. to *skrapa* SCRAPE]

■ *n.* **1** bit, piece, shred, remnant; see also FRAGMENT *n.* **2** waste, debris, junk; see also RUBBISH *n.* 1. **3** extract, cutting, excerpt, clipping. **5** mite, bit, shred, morsel, piece, fragment, particle, sliver, snippet, snip, crumb, whit, iota, jot, tittle, drop, grain, speck, molecule, atom, trace, scintilla, vestige, trace, *Austral. colloq.* skerrick. **6** (*scraps*) **a** remnants, leavings, remains; see also *odds and ends*. **b** leftovers, leavings, scrapings, crumbs. ● *v.* discard, throw away, reject, abandon, give up, consign to the scrap heap, get rid of, dispose of, dispense with, junk.

scrap² /skrap/ *n. & v. colloq.* ● *n.* a fight or rough quarrel, esp. a spontaneous one. ● *v.tr.* (**scrapped, scrapping**) (often foll. by *with*) have a scrap. □□ **scrapper** *n.* [perh. f. SCRAPE]

■ *n.* fight, brawl, fracas, fray, affray, scuffle, Donnybrook, battle (royal), ruckus, *colloq.* rumpus, dustup; dispute, argument, quarrel, disagreement, wrangle, squabble, tiff, *colloq.* row, set-to, spat. ● *v.* fight, brawl, scuffle, battle; row, wrangle, spar, argue, disagree, squabble, bicker.

scrapbook /skrápbŏok/ *n.* a book of blank pages for sticking cuttings, drawings, etc., in.
■ album, portfolio, collection.

scrape /skrayp/ *v. & n.* ● *v.* **1 a** move a hard or sharp edge across (a surface), esp. to make something smooth. **b** apply (a hard or sharp edge) in this way. **2** *tr.* (foll. by *away*, *off*, etc.) remove (a stain, projection, etc.) by scraping. **3** *tr.* **a** rub (a surface) harshly against another. **b** scratch or damage by scraping. **4** *tr.* make (a hollow) by scraping. **5 a** *tr.* draw or move with a sound of, or resembling, scraping. **b** *intr.* emit or produce such a sound. **c** *tr.* produce such a sound from. **6** *intr.* (often foll. by *along, by, through,* etc.) move or pass along while almost touching close or surrounding features, obstacles, etc. (*the car scraped through the narrow lane*). **7** *tr.* just manage to achieve (a living, an examination pass, etc.). **8** *intr.* (often foll. by *by, through*) **a** barely manage. **b** pass an examination, etc., with difficulty. **9** *tr.* (foll. by *together, up*) contrive to bring or provide; amass with difficulty. **10** *intr.* be economical. **11** *intr.* draw back a foot in making a clumsy bow. **12** *tr.* clear (a ship's bottom)

of barnacles, etc. **13** *tr.* completely clear (a plate) of food. **14** *tr. Brit.* (foll. by *back*) draw (the hair) tightly back off the forehead. ● *n.* **1** the act or sound of scraping. **2** a scraped place (on the skin, etc.). **3** *Brit.* a thinly applied layer of butter, etc., on bread. **4** the scraping of a foot in bowing. **5** *colloq.* an awkward predicament, esp. resulting from an escapade. □ **scrape acquaintance with** esp. *Brit.* contrive to get to know (a person). **scrape the barrel** *colloq.* be reduced to one's last resources. [ME f. ON *skrapa* or MDu. *schrapen*]

■ *v.* **2** (*scrape away, off,* etc.) rub off *or* away, scour off *or* away, scrub off *or* away, clean off *or* away, scratch off *or* away. **3 b** graze, scratch, abrade, bark, scuff, bruise, damage, injure. **4** gouge out, dig out; see also SCOOP *v.* 1. **6** squeeze. **7** eke out, manage. **8 a** get by, cope, (barely) manage, survive, scratch along. **b** just *or* barely pass, *colloq.* squeak by *or* through. **9** gather, garner, glean, get together, save (up), get hold of, marshal, amass, muster, aggregate, compile, accumulate, pile up, assemble; scratch together *or* up, rake together, dredge up. **10** skimp, scrimp, save, stint, be frugal *or* stingy *or* parsimonious *or* thrifty, pinch, economize. ● *n.* **2** abrasion, bruise, scratch, graze, scuff; injury. **5** predicament, difficulty, quandary, plight, pretty kettle of fish, muddle, mess, tight spot *or* place *or* corner, tough spot, *colloq.* pickle, fix, *disp.* dilemma. □ **scrape acquaintance with** see CULTIVATE 3b.

scraper /skráypər/ *n.* a device used for scraping, esp. for removing dirt, etc., from a surface.

scraperboard /skráypərbawrd/ *n.* = SCRATCHBOARD.

scrapie /skráypee, skráp-/ *n.* a viral disease of sheep involving the central nervous system and characterized by lack of coordination causing affected animals to rub against trees, etc., for support.

scraping /skráyping/ *n.* **1** in senses of SCRAPE *v. & n.* **2** (esp. in *pl.*) a fragment produced by this.
■ **1** see FRICTION 1, *groveling* (GROVEL). **2** see SHRED *n.* 1, SCRAP¹ *n.* 6b.

scrappy /skrápee/ *adj.* (**scrappier, scrappiest**) **1** consisting of scraps. **2** incomplete; carelessly arranged or put together. **3 a** quick to engage in fighting; argumentative. **b** (of a fighter) wiry and aggressive. □□ **scrappily** *adv.* **scrappiness** *n.*
■ **2** see INCOMPLETE.

scrapyard /skrápyaard/ *n.* a place where (esp. metal) scrap is collected.

scratch /skrach/ *v., n., & adj.* ● *v.* **1** *tr.* score or mark the surface of with a sharp or pointed object. **2** *tr.* **a** make a long, narrow superficial wound in (the skin). **b** cause (a person or part of the body) to be scratched (*scratched himself on the table*). **3** *tr.* (also *absol.*) scrape without marking, esp. with the hand to relieve itching (*stood there scratching*). **4** *tr.* make or form by scratching. **5** *tr.* scribble; write hurriedly or awkwardly (*scratched a quick reply; scratched a large A*). **6** *tr.* (foll. by *together, up,* etc.) obtain (a thing) by scratching or with difficulty. **7** *tr.* (foll. by *out, off, through*) cancel or strike (out) with a pencil, etc. **8** *tr.* (also *absol.*) withdraw (a competitor, candidate, etc.) from a race or competition. **9** *intr.* (often foll. by *about, around,* etc.) **a** scratch the ground, etc., in search. **b** look around haphazardly (*they were scratching about for evidence*). ● *n.* **1** a mark or wound made by scratching. **2** a sound of scratching. **3** a spell of scratching oneself. **4** *colloq.* a superficial wound. **5** a line from which competitors in a race (esp. those not receiving a handicap) start. **6** (in *pl.*) a disease of horses in which the pastern appears scratched. **7** *sl.* money. ● *attrib.adj.* **1** collected by chance. **2** collected or made from whatever is available; heterogeneous (*a scratch crew*). **3** with no handicap given (*a scratch race*). □ **from scratch 1** from the beginning. **2** without help

---

or advantage. **3** (of baked goods, etc.) without premixed ingredients. **scratch along** make a living, etc., with difficulty. **scratch one's head** be perplexed. **scratch my back and I will scratch yours 1** do me a favor and I will return it. **2** used in reference to mutual aid or flattery. **scratch pad 1** a pad of paper for scribbling. **2** *Computing* a small fast memory for the temporary storage of data. **scratch the surface** deal with a matter only superficially. **up to scratch** up to the required standard. □□ **scratcher** *n.* [ME, prob. f. synonymous ME *scrat* & *cratch*, both of uncert. orig.: cf. MLG *kratsen*, OHG *krazzōn*]

■ *v.* **1** score, mar, mark, gouge, claw. **2** gash, abrade, graze, scuff, bruise; damage, injure. **3** scrape, chafe, rub. **5** scribble, scrawl; see also WRITE 3, 4. **7** obliterate, cross out, delete, strike out *or* off, expunge. **8** withdraw, take out, eliminate, remove. **9 b** cast about *or* around, look around, search. ● *n.* **1** gouge; gash, abrasion, scrape, graze, scuff, bruise, injury, wound. **4** scrape, graze, scuff, bruise. **7** see MONEY 1.

● *attrib.adj.* **2** random, haphazard, casual, makeshift, extempore, stopgap; heterogeneous, composite, motley. □ **from scratch 1** from the start *or* beginning *or* outset, *colloq.* from the word go. **scratch along** see SCRAPE *v.* 8a. **up to scratch** up to standard *or* par, adequate, sufficient, good enough, competent, satisfactory, *colloq.* up to snuff.

scratchboard /skráchbawrd/ *n.* cardboard or board with a blackened surface which can be scraped off for making white-line drawings.

scratchy /skráchee/ *adj.* (**scratchier, scratchiest**) **1** tending to make scratches or a scratching noise. **2** (esp. of a garment) tending to cause itchiness. **3** (of a drawing, etc.) done in scratches or carelessly. □□ **scratchily** *adv.* **scratchiness** *n.*

■ **1** rough, hoarse, raw, grating, raspy; jagged, jaggy. **2** itchy, irritating, prickly. **3** see SKETCHY.

scrawl /skrawl/ *v.* & *n.* ● *v.* **1** *tr.* & *intr.* write in a hurried untidy way. **2** *tr.* (foll. by *out*) cross out by scrawling over. ● *n.* **1** a piece of hurried writing. **2** a scrawled note. □□ **scrawly** *adj.* [perh. f. obs. *scrawl* sprawl, alt. of CRAWL]

■ *v.* **1** scribble; scratch. ● *n.* **1** scribble, squiggle. □□ **scrawly** see SKETCHY.

scrawny /skráwnee/ *adj.* (**scrawnier, scrawniest**) lean; scraggy. □□ **scrawniness** *n.* [var. of dial. *scranny*: cf. archaic *scrannel* (of sound) weak, feeble]

■ bony, skinny, spare, reedy, lean, lank(y), scraggy, gaunt, raw-boned, angular, emaciated, cadaverous; *colloq.* anorexic.

scream /skreem/ *n.* & *v.* ● *n.* **1** a loud, high-pitched, piercing cry expressing fear, pain, extreme fright, etc. **2** the act of emitting a scream. **3** *colloq.* an irresistibly funny occurrence or person. ● *v.* **1** *intr.* emit a scream. **2** *tr.* speak or sing (words, etc.) in a screaming tone. **3** *intr.* make or move with a shrill sound like a scream. **4** *intr.* laugh uncontrollably. **5** *intr.* be blatantly obvious or conspicuous. **6** *intr. colloq.* turn informer. [OE or MDu.]

■ *n.* **1** shriek, screech, squeal, yowl, wail, caterwaul, howl, cry. **3** *colloq.* card, riot, hoot. ● *v.* **1, 2** shriek, screech, squeal, yowl, wail, caterwaul, howl, cry. **4** laugh, roar, howl, guffaw, *colloq.* hoot. **5** glare, stick out like a sore thumb, stick out a mile. **6** see INFORM 2.

screamer /skréemər/ *n.* **1** a person or thing that screams. **2** any S. American gooselike bird of the family Anhimidae, frequenting marshland and having a characteristic shrill cry. **3** *colloq.* a tale that raises screams of laughter. **4** *colloq.* a sensational headline.

scree /skree/ *n.* (in *sing.* or *pl.*) **1** small loose stones. **2** a mountain slope covered with these. [prob. back-form. f. *screes* (pl.) ult. f. ON *skritha* landslip, rel. to *skrítha* glide]

screech /skreech/ *n.* & *v.* ● *n.* a harsh, high-pitched scream. ● *v.tr.* & *intr.* utter with or make a screech. □ **screech owl** any owl that screeches instead of hooting, esp. a barn owl or a small American owl, *Otus asio.* □□ **screecher** *n.*

screechy *adj.* (**screechier, screechiest**). [16th-c. var. of ME *scritch* (imit.)]

■ *n.* see SCREAM *n.* 1. ● *v.* see SCREAM *v.* 1, 2. □□ **screechy** see SHRILL *adj.*

screed /skreed/ *n.* **1** a long usu. tiresome piece of writing or speech. **2 a** a strip of plaster or other material placed on a surface as a guide to thickness. **b** a leveled layer of material (e.g., concrete) applied to a floor or other surface. [ME, prob. var. of SHRED]

■ **1** see LECTURE *n.* 2.

screen /skreen/ *n.* & *v.* ● *n.* **1** a fixed or movable upright partition for separating, concealing, or sheltering from drafts or excessive heat or light. **2** a thing used as a shelter, esp. from observation. **3 a** a measure adopted for concealment. **b** the protection afforded by this (*under the screen of night*). **4 a** a blank usu. white or silver surface on which a photographic image is projected. **b** (prec. by *the*) movies or the motion-picture industry. **5** the surface of a cathode-ray tube or similar electronic device, esp. of a television, computer monitor, etc., on which images appear. **6** = WINDSCREEN. **7** a frame with fine wire netting to keep out flies, mosquitoes, etc. **8** *Physics* a body intercepting light, heat, electric or magnetic induction, etc., in a physical apparatus. **9** *Photog.* a piece of ground glass in a camera for focusing. **10** a large sieve or riddle, esp. for sorting grain, coal, etc., into sizes. **11** a system of checking for the presence or absence of a disease, ability, attribute, etc. **12** *Printing* a transparent, finely ruled plate or film used in half-tone reproduction. **13** *Mil.* a body of troops, ships, etc., detached to warn of the presence of an enemy force. ● *v.tr.* **1** (often foll. by *from*) **a** afford shelter to; hide partly or completely. **b** protect from detection, censure, etc. **2** (foll. by *off*) shut off or hide behind a screen. **3 a** show (a film, etc.) on a screen. **b** broadcast (a television program). **4** prevent from causing, or protect from, electrical interference. **5 a** test (a person or group) for the presence or absence of a disease. **b** check on (a person) for the presence or absence of a quality, esp. reliability or loyalty. **6** pass (grain, coal, etc.) through a screen. □ **screen printing** a process like stenciling with ink forced through a prepared sheet of fine material (orig. silk). **screen test** an audition for a part in a motion picture. □□ **screenable** *adj.* **screener** *n.* [ME f. ONF *escren, escran:* cf. OHG *skrank* barrier]

■ *n.* **1** partition, divider, wall, shield. **2** shelter, shield, cover; see also VEIL *n.* 4. **3 b** protection, shelter, cover, concealment; camouflage, curtain, shroud, cloak. **4 b** cinema (industry), silver screen, movies. **10** sieve, strainer, filter, riddle, colander. **11** scan, survey; see also CHECK[1] *n.* 1 ● *v.* **1** shield, shelter, protect, guard, hide, conceal, cover, mask, veil. **2** partition (off), separate, divide, wall off, shut off. **3 b** see BROADCAST *v.* 1a. **5 b** check (on *or* out), test, evaluate, examine, investigate, inspect, look over, vet.

screening /skréening/ *n.* **1** the act of a person or thing that screens, as of applicants for employment. **2** the showing of a motion picture.

screenings /skréeningz/ *n.pl.* refuse separated by sifting.

screenplay /skréenplay/ *n.* the script of a motion picture or television show, etc., with acting instructions, scene directions, etc.

■ see SCRIPT *n.* 4.

screenwriter /skréenritər/ *n.* a person who writes a screenplay.

■ see DRAMATIST.

screw /skrōō/ *n.* & *v.* ● *n.* **1** a thin cylinder or cone with a spiral ridge or thread running around the outside (**male screw**) or the inside (**female screw**). **2** (in full **wood screw**) a metal male screw with a slotted head and a sharp point for fastening things, esp. in carpentry, by being rotated to form a thread in wood, etc. **3** (in full **screw bolt**) a metal male screw with a blunt end on which a nut is threaded to bolt things together. **4** a wooden or metal straight screw used to exert pressure. **5** (in *sing.* or *pl.*) an instrument of torture acting in this way. **6** (in full **screw propeller**) a form of propeller with twisted blades acting like a screw on

the water or air. **7** one turn of a screw. **8** (foll. by *of*) *Brit.* a small twisted-up paper (filled with sugar, tobacco, etc.). **9** *Brit.* (in billiards, etc.) an oblique curling motion of the ball. **10** *sl.* a prison warden or guard. **11** *Brit. sl.* an amount of salary or wages. **12** *coarse sl.* **a** an act of sexual intercourse. **b** a partner in this. ¶ Usually considered a taboo use. **13** *Brit. sl.* a mean or miserly person. **14** *Brit. sl.* a worn-out horse. ● *v.* **1** *tr.* fasten or tighten with a screw or screws. **2** *tr.* turn (a screw). **3** *intr.* twist or turn around like a screw. **4** *Brit. intr.* (of a ball, etc.) swerve. **5** *tr.* **a** put psychological, etc., pressure on to achieve an end. **b** oppress. **6** *tr.* (foll. by *out of*) extort (consent, money, etc.) from (a person). **7** *tr.* (also *absol.*) *coarse sl.* have sexual intercourse with. ¶ Usually considered a taboo use. **8** *intr.* (of a rolling ball, or of a person, etc.) take a curling course; swerve. **9** *intr.* (often foll. by *up*) make tenser or more efficient. □ **have one's head screwed on the right way** *colloq.* have common sense. **have a screw loose** *colloq.* be slightly crazy. **put the screws on** *colloq.* exert pressure on, esp. to extort or intimidate. **screw cap** = *screw top*. **screw coupling** a female screw with threads at both ends for joining lengths of pipes or rods. **screw eye** a screw with a loop for passing cord, etc., through instead of a slotted head. **screw hook** a hook to hang things on, with a screw point for fastening it. **screw jack** a vehicle jack (see JACK¹) worked by a screw device. **screw pine** any plant of the genus *Pandanus*, with its leaves arranged spirally and resembling those of a pineapple. **screw plate** a steel plate with threaded holes for making male screws. **screw tap** a tool for making female screws. **screw top** (also (with hyphen) *attrib.*) a cap or lid that can be screwed on to a bottle, jar, etc. **screw up 1** contract or contort (one's face, etc.). **2** contract and crush into a tight mass (a piece of paper, etc.). **3** summon up (one's courage, etc.). **4** *sl.* **a** bungle or mismanage. **b** spoil or ruin (an event, opportunity, etc.). **screw-up** *n. sl.* a bungle, muddle, or mess. **screw valve** a stopcock opened and shut by a screw. □□ **screwable** *adj.* **screwer** *n.* [ME f. OF *escroue* female screw, nut, f. L *scrofa* sow]
■ *n.* **3** bolt. **7** twist, turn, rotation, revolution, wind, coil. ● *v.* **2, 3** twist, turn, rotate. **5 a** see INDUCE 1. **b** see OPPRESS 1, 2. **6** (*screw out of*) extort *or* force from. **8** see SWERVE *v.* **9** see TIGHTEN. □ **have a screw loose** be crazy, be as mad as a hatter *or* March hare, have bats in the belfry. **put the screws on** pressure, influence, force, constrain, press, coerce, compel, apply pressure to, bring pressure to bear on *or* upon, pressurize, *colloq.* twist a person's arm, put the squeeze on. **screw up 1** contract, contort, twist. **2** crumple. **3** raise, stretch, strain, summon (up), call up, call upon, tap, draw on *or* upon. **4** ruin, spoil, destroy, make a mess of, botch, bungle, muddle, mismanage, mishandle, *colloq.* make a hash of, *sl.* louse up, *Brit. sl.* scupper.

screwball /skróobawl/ *n. & adj. sl.* ● *n.* **1** *Baseball* a pitch thrown with spin opposite that of a curveball. **2** a crazy or eccentric person. ● *adj.* crazy.
■ *n.* see MADMAN. ● *adj.* see CRAZY 1.

screwdriver /skróodrīvǝr/ *n.* a tool with a shaped tip to fit into the head of a screw to turn it.

screwed /skrood/ *adj.* **1** twisted. **2** *sl.* a ruined; rendered ineffective. **b** esp. *Brit.* drunk.

screwy /skróo-ee/ *adj.* (**screwier, screwiest**) *sl.* **1** crazy or eccentric. **2** absurd. □□ **screwiness** *n.*
■ **1** see CRAZY 1. **2** see ABSURD.

scribble¹ /skríbǝl/ *v. & n.* ● *v.* **1** *tr. & intr.* write carelessly or hurriedly. **2** *intr. often derog.* be an author or writer. **3** *intr. & tr.* draw carelessly or meaninglessly. ● *n.* **1** a scrawl. **2** a hasty note, etc. **3** careless handwriting. □□ **scribbler** *n.* **scribbly** *adj.* [ME f. med.L *scribillare* dimin. of L *scribere* write]
■ *v.* **1, 3** scrawl, scratch. □□ **scribbler** see WRITER 1.

scribble² /skríbǝl/ *v.tr.* card (wool, cotton, etc.) coarsely. [prob. f. LG: cf. G *schrubbeln* (in the same sense), frequent. f. LG *schrubben*: see SCRUB¹]

scribe /skrīb/ *n. & v.* ● *n.* **1** a person who writes out documents, esp. an ancient or medieval copyist of manuscripts.

2 *Bibl.* an ancient Jewish record keeper or professional theologian and jurist. **3** (in full **scribe awl**) a pointed instrument for making marks on wood, bricks, etc., to guide a saw, or in sign writing. **4** *colloq.* a writer, esp. a journalist. ● *v.tr.* mark (wood, etc.) with a scribe (see sense 3 of *n.*). □□ **scribal** *adj.* **scriber** *n.* [(n.) ME f. L *scriba* f. *scribere* write: (v.) perh. f. DESCRIBE]
■ *n.* **1** copyist, copier, transcriber, *hist.* scrivener; amanuensis, clerk, secretary. **4** writer, author, penman, wordsmith, hack, esp. *Brit.* penny-a-liner, *often derog.* scribbler; columnist, journalist, gentleman *or* lady of the press, newspaperman, newspaperwoman, reporter, *Austral. colloq.* journo, *joc.* member of the fourth estate. ● *v.* inscribe, incise, etch, engrave, mark, scratch, score, grave, scrimshaw, carve; chase, enchase.

scrim /skrim/ *n.* open-weave fabric for lining or upholstery, etc. [18th c.: orig. unkn.]

scrimmage /skrímij/ *n. & v.* ● *n.* **1** a rough or confused struggle; a brawl. **2** *Football* a single play from the snap of the ball till the ball is dead. **3** *Sports* a practice game. ● *v.* **1** *intr.* engage in a scrimmage. **2** *tr. Sports* have a practice game (with). □□ **scrimmager** *n.* [var. of SKIRMISH]
■ *n.* **1** skirmish, scuffle, fray, affray, disturbance, brouhaha, melee, riot, brawl, struggle, scramble, tussle, fracas, donnybrook, battle, fight, free-for-all, ruckus, *colloq.* row, rumpus, set-to, dustup, scrap, *Brit. sl.* (bit of) bovver. ● *v.* see BRAWL *v.*

scrimp /skrimp/ *v.* **1** *intr.* be sparing or parsimonious. **2** *tr.* use sparingly. □□ **scrimpy** *adj.* [18th c., orig. Sc.: perh. rel. to SHRIMP]
■ **1** see ECONOMIZE 1. □□ **scrimpy** see MEAGER 1.

scrimshank /skrímshangk/ *v.intr. Brit. sl.* esp. *Mil.* shirk duty. □□ **scrimshanker** *n.* [19th c.: orig. unkn.]

scrimshaw /skrímshaw/ *v. & n.* ● *v.tr.* (also *absol.*) adorn (shells, ivory, etc.) with carved or colored designs (as sailors' pastime at sea). ● *n.* work or a piece of work of this kind. [19th c.: perh. f. a surname]
■ *v.* see SCRIBE *v.*

scrip /skrip/ *n.* **1** a provisional certificate of money subscribed to a bank or company, etc., entitling the holder to a formal certificate and dividends. **2** (*collect.*) such certificates. **3** an extra share or shares instead of a dividend. [abbr. of *subscription receipt*]

script /skript/ *n. & v.* ● *n.* **1** handwriting as distinct from print; written characters. **2** type imitating handwriting. **3** an alphabet or system of writing (*the Russian script*). **4** the text of a play, film, or broadcast. **5** an examinee's set of written answers. **6** *Law* an original document as distinct from a copy. ● *v.tr.* write a script for (a motion picture, etc.). [ME, = thing written, f. OF *escri(p)t* f. L *scriptum*, neut. past part. of *scribere* write]
■ *n.* **1** handwriting, (cursive) writing, calligraphy. **4** manuscript, text, book, play, screenplay, libretto.

scriptorium /skriptáwreeǝm/ *n.* (*pl.* **scriptoria** /-reeǝ/ or **scriptoriums**) a room set apart for writing, esp. in a monastery. □□ **scriptorial** *adj.* [med.L (as SCRIPT)]

scriptural /skrípchǝrǝl/ *adj.* **1** of or relating to a scripture, esp. the Bible. **2** having the authority of a scripture. □□ **scripturally** *adv.* [LL *scripturalis* f. L *scriptura*: see SCRIPTURE]

scripture /skrípchǝr/ *n.* **1** sacred writings. **2** (**Scripture** or **the Scriptures**) **a** the Bible as a collection of sacred writings in Christianity. **b** the sacred writings of any other religion. [ME f. L *scriptura* (as SCRIPT)]
■ **1** sacred writings, holy writ. **2** (**Scripture** *or* the **Scriptures**) **a** the Bible, the good book, holy writ *or* Scripture, the word (of God), Gospel(s). **b** Shastra; Koran; Granth; Upanishads; Sutra.

/.../ **pronunciation**	● **part of speech**
□ **phrases, idioms, and compounds**	
□□ **derivatives**	■ **synonym section**
cross-references appear in SMALL CAPITALS or *italics*	

scriptwriter /skríptrítər/ *n.* a person who writes a script for a motion picture, broadcast, etc. □□ **scriptwriting** *n.*
■ see DRAMATIST.

scrivener /skrívənər, skrívnər/ *n. hist.* **1** a copyist or drafter of documents. **2** a notary. **3** a broker. **4** a moneylender. [ME f. obs. *scrivein* f. OF *escrivein* ult. f. L (as SCRIBE)]
■ **1** see SCRIBE *n.* 1. **3** see BROKER 1.

scrobiculate /skrōbíkyələt, -layt/ *adj. Bot.* & *Zool.* pitted; furrowed. [L *scrobiculus* f. *scrobis* trench]

scrod /skrod/ *n.* a young cod or haddock, esp. as food. [19th c.: perh. rel. to SHRED]

scrofula /skrófyələ/ *n. archaic* a disease with glandular swellings, prob. a form of tuberculosis. Also called *king's evil*. □□ **scrofulous** *adj.* [ME f. med.L (sing.) f. LL *scrofulae* (pl.) scrofulous swelling, dimin. of L *scrofa* a sow]

scroll /skrōl/ *n.* & *v.* ● *n.* **1** a roll of parchment or paper esp. with writing on it. **2** a book in the ancient roll form. **3** an ornamental design or carving imitating a roll of parchment. ● *v.* **1** *tr.* (often foll. by *down, up*) move (a display on a computer screen) in order to view new material. **2** *tr.* inscribe in or like a scroll. **3** *intr.* curl up like paper. □ **scroll saw** a saw for cutting along curved lines in ornamental work. [ME *scrowle* alt. f. *rowle* ROLL, perh. after *scrow* (in the same sense), formed as ESCROW]
● *n.* **3** coil, spiral, whorl.

scrolled /skrōld/ *adj.* having a scroll ornament.

scrollwork /skrōlwərk/ decoration of spiral lines, esp. as cut by a scroll saw.

Scrooge /skrōōj/ *n.* a mean or miserly person. [a character in Dickens's *Christmas Carol*]
■ see MISER.

scrotum /skrōtəm/ *n.* (*pl.* **scrota** /-tə/ or **scrotums**) a pouch of skin containing the testicles. □□ **scrotal** *adj.* **scrotitis** /-títis/ *n.* [L]

scrounge /skrownj/ *v.* & *n. colloq.* ● *v.* **1** *tr.* (also *absol.*) obtain (things) illicitly or by cadging. **2** *intr.* search about to find something at no cost. ● *n.* an act of scrounging. □ **on the scrounge** engaged in scrounging. **scrounge around** forage or search haphazardly (*we scrounged around for loose change*). □□ **scrounger** *n.* [var. of dial. *scrunge* steal]
■ *v.* **1** cadge, beg, sponge, *sl.* bum. **2** sponge, *sl.* freeload. □□ **scrounger** cadger, parasite, sponger, *sl.* freeloader.

scrub[1] /skrub/ *v.* & *n.* ● *v.* (**scrubbed, scrubbing**) **1** *tr.* rub hard so as to clean, esp. with a hard brush. **2** *intr.* use a brush in this way. **3** *intr.* (often foll. by *up*) (of a surgeon, etc.) thoroughly clean the hands and arms by scrubbing, before operating. **4** *tr. colloq.* scrap or cancel (a plan, order, etc.). **5** *tr.* use water to remove impurities from (gas, etc.). ● *n.* the act or an instance of scrubbing; the process of being scrubbed. □ **scrub** (also **scrubbing**) **brush** a hard brush for scrubbing floors. [ME prob. f. MLG, MDu. *schrobben, schrubben*]
■ *v.* **1, 2** scour, rub, scrape, clean, *usu. formal* cleanse. **4** cancel, scrap, call off, abort, drop, terminate, give up, end, abandon, stop, cease, discontinue, do away with.

scrub[2] /skrub/ *n.* **1 a** vegetation consisting mainly of brushwood or stunted forest growth. **b** an area of land covered with this. **2** (of livestock) of inferior breed or physique (often *attrib.*: *scrub horse*). **3** a small or dwarf variety (often *attrib.*: *scrub pine*). **4** *Sports colloq.* a team or player not of the first class. □ **scrub typhus** a rickettsial disease of the W. Pacific transmitted by mites. □□ **scrubby** *adj.* [ME, var. of SHRUB[1]]

scrubber /skrúbər/ *n.* an apparatus using water or a solution for purifying gases, etc.

scruff[1] /skruf/ *n.* the back of the neck as used to grasp and lift or drag an animal or person by (esp. *scruff of the neck*). [alt. of *scuff*, perh. f. ON *skoft* hair]

scruff[2] /skruf/ *n. Brit. colloq.* an untidy or scruffy person. [orig. = SCURF, later 'worthless thing,' or back-form. f. SCRUFFY]

scruffy /skrúfee/ *adj.* (**scruffier, scruffiest**) *colloq.* shabby; slovenly; untidy. □□ **scruffily** *adv.* **scruffiness** *n.* [*scruff* var. of SCURF + -Y[1]]
■ see SHABBY 1, 2.

scrum /skrum/ *n.* **1** *Rugby* an arrangement of the forwards of each team in two opposing groups, each with arms interlocked and heads down, with the ball thrown in between them to restart play. **2** *Brit. colloq.* a milling crowd. □ **scrum half** a halfback who puts the ball into the scrum. [abbr. of SCRUMMAGE]

scrummage /skrúmij/ *n. Rugby* = SCRUM 1. [as SCRIMMAGE]

scrummy /skrúmee/ *adj. Brit. colloq.* excellent; enjoyable; delicious. [SCRUMPTIOUS + -Y[1]]

scrumptious /skrúmpshəs/ *adj. colloq.* **1** delicious. **2** pleasing; delightful. □□ **scrumptiously** *adv.* **scrumptiousness** *n.* [19th c.: orig. unkn.]
■ **1** see DELICIOUS.

scrunch /skrunch/ *v.* & *n.* ● *v.tr.* & *intr.* **1** (usu. foll. by *up*) make or become crushed or crumpled. **2** make or cause to make a crunching sound. ● *n.* the act or an instance of scrunching. [var. of CRUNCH]
■ *v.* **1** see RUMPLE. **2** see MUNCH.

scrunchie /skrúnchee/ *n.* a hair band of elastic enclosed by crumpled fabric, used for ponytails, etc.

scruple /skrōōpəl/ *n.* & *v.* ● *n.* **1** (in *sing.* or *pl.*) **a** a regard to the morality or propriety of an action. **b** a feeling of doubt or hesitation caused by this. **2** *Brit. hist.* an apothecaries' weight of 20 grains. **3** *archaic* a very small quantity. ● *v.intr.* **1** (foll. by *to* + infin.; usu. with *neg.*) be reluctant because of scruples (*did not scruple to stop their allowance*). **2** feel or be influenced by scruples. [F *scrupule* or L *scrupulus* f. *scrupus* rough pebble, anxiety]
■ *n.* **1** qualm, misgiving, doubt, twinge of conscience. ● *v.* **1** (*scruple to*) balk at, have (any) scruples about, hesitate to, have any doubts *or* compunction about, shrink from *or* at, have (any) misgivings *or* qualms about *or* over, think twice about, be loath *or* reluctant to. **2** hesitate, think twice, pause, falter, vacillate, demur, waver.

scrupulous /skrōōpyələs/ *adj.* **1** conscientious or thorough even in small matters. **2** careful to avoid doing wrong. **3** punctilious; overattentive to details. □□ **scrupulosity** /-lósitee/ *n.* **scrupulously** *adv.* **scrupulousness** *n.* [ME f. F *scrupuleux* or L *scrupulosus* (as SCRUPLE)]
■ **1, 3** careful, cautious, meticulous, exacting, precise, nice, strict, rigid, rigorous, severe, critical, fastidious, neat, conscientious, painstaking, thorough; finicky, finical, fussy, punctilious. **2** ethical, honorable, upstanding, moral, righteous, principled, high-minded, just.

scrutineer /skrōōt'neer/ *n. Brit.* a person who scrutinizes or examines something, esp. the conduct and result of a ballot.

scrutinize /skrōōt'niz/ *v.tr.* look closely at; examine with close scrutiny. □□ **scrutinizer** *n.*
■ examine, analyze, dissect, investigate, probe, study, inspect, sift, go over *or* through, check.

scrutiny /skrōōt'nee/ *n.* (*pl.* **-ies**) **1** a critical gaze. **2** a close investigation or examination of details. **3** an official examination of ballot papers to check their validity or accuracy of counting. [ME f. L *scrutinium* f. *scrutari* search f. *scruta* rubbish: orig. of rag-collectors]
■ **2** examination, analysis, investigation, probing, study, inspection, sifting, inquiry, exploration; probe, check.

scry /skri/ *v.intr.* (**-ies, -ied**) divine by crystal gazing. □□ **scryer** *n.* [shortening f. DESCRY]

scuba /skōōbə/ *n.* (*pl.* **scubas**) an aqualung. □ **scuba diving** swimming underwater using a scuba, esp. as a sport. □□ **scuba dive** *v.intr.* **scuba diver** *n.* [acronym f. self-contained underwater breathing apparatus]

scud /skud/ *v.* & *n.* ● *v.intr.* (**scudded, scudding**) **1** fly or run straight, fast, and lightly; skim along. **2** *Naut.* run before the wind. ● *n.* **1** a spell of scudding. **2** a scudding motion. **3** vapory driving clouds. **4** a driving shower; a gust. **5** wind-blown spray. **6** (**Scud**) a type of long-range surface-to-surface guided missile originally developed in the former Soviet Union. [perh. alt. of SCUT, as if to race like a hare]
■ *v.* **1** fly, skim, race, speed, shoot, *colloq.* scoot.

scuff /skuf/ *v.* & *n.* ● *v.* **1** *tr.* graze or brush against. **2** *tr.*

mark or wear down (shoes) in this way. **3** *intr.* walk with dragging feet; shuffle. ● *n.* a mark of scuffing. [imit.]

■ *v.* **2** see SCRAPE *v.* 3b. **3** shuffle, stumble, drag one's feet. ● *n.* see SCRAPE *n.* 2.

scuffle /skúfəl/ *n. & v.* ● *n.* a confused struggle or disorderly fight at close quarters. ● *v.intr.* engage in a scuffle. [prob. f. Scand.: cf. Sw. *skuffa* to push, rel. to SHOVE]

■ *n.* see FIGHT *n.* 1a. ● *v.* see FIGHT *v.* 1a.

sculduggery var. of SKULDUGGERY.

scull /skul/ *n. & v.* ● *n.* **1** either of a pair of small oars used by a single rower. **2** an oar placed over the stern of a boat to propel it, usu. by a twisting motion. **3** (in *pl.*) a race between boats with single pairs of oars. **4** a racing boat propelled by sculls. ● *v.tr.* propel (a boat) with sculls. [ME: orig. unkn.]

■ *n.* **1, 2** oar, paddle, sweep. ● *v.* see PADDLE¹ *v.* 1, 2.

sculler /skúlər/ *n.* **1** a user of sculls. **2** a boat intended for sculling.

■ **1** see OAR 2.

scullery /skúləree/ *n.* (*pl.* **-ies**) a small kitchen or room at the back of a house for washing dishes, etc. [ME f. AF *squillerie*, OF *escuelerie* f. *escuele* dish f. L *scutella* salver dimin. of *scutra* wooden platter]

■ see KITCHEN.

scullion /skúlyən/ *n. archaic* **1** a cook's boy. **2** a person who washes dishes, etc. [ME: orig. unkn.]

■ see SERVANT.

sculpin /skúlpin/ *n.* any of numerous fish of the family Cottidae, native to nontropical regions, having large spiny heads. [perh. f. obs. *scorpene* f. L *scorpaena* f. Gk *skorpaina* a fish]

sculpt /skulpt/ *v.tr. & intr.* (also **sculp**) sculpture. [F *sculpter* f. *sculpteur* SCULPTOR: now regarded as an abbr.]

■ see SCULPTURE *v.*

sculptor /skúlptər/ *n.* (*fem.* **sculptress** /-tris/) an artist who makes sculptures. [L (as SCULPTURE)]

sculpture /skúlpchər/ *n. & v.* ● *n.* **1** the art of making forms, often representational, in the round or in relief by chiseling stone, carving wood, modeling clay, casting metal, etc. **2** a work or works of sculpture. **3** *Zool. & Bot.* raised or sunken markings on a shell, etc. ● *v.* **1** *tr.* represent in or adorn with sculpture. **2** *intr.* practice sculpture. □□ **sculptural** *adj.* **sculpturally** *adv.* **sculpturesque** *adj.* [ME f. L *sculptura* f. *sculpere sculpt-* carve]

■ *n.* **2** statue, statuette, relief; (*sculptures*) marbles. ● *v.* **1** sculpt, model, chisel, carve, cast, form, fashion.

scum /skum/ *n. & v.* ● *n.* **1** a layer of dirt, froth, or impurities, etc., forming at the top of liquid, esp. in boiling or fermentation. **2** (foll. by *of*) the most worthless part of something. **3** *colloq.* a worthless person or group. ● *v.* (**scummed, scumming**) **1** *tr.* remove scum from; skim. **2** *tr.* be or form a scum on. **3** *intr.* (of a liquid) develop scum. □□ **scummy** *adj.* (**scummier, scummiest**) *adj.* [ME f. MLG, MDu. *schum*, OHG *scūm* f. Gmc]

■ *n.* **1** see DIRT 1. **3** see RIFF-RAFF. □□ **scummy** see FILTHY *adj.* 1.

scumbag /skúmbag/ *n. sl.* a worthless despicable person.

■ see WRETCH 2.

scumble /skúmbəl/ *v. & n.* ● *v.tr.* **1** modify (a painting) by applying a thin opaque coat of paint to give a softer or duller effect. **2** modify (a drawing) similarly with light penciling, etc. ● *n.* **1** material used in scumbling. **2** the effect produced by scumbling. [perh. frequent. of SCUM *v.tr.*]

scunner /skúnər/ *v. & n. Sc.* ● *v.intr. & tr.* feel disgust; nauseate. ● *n.* **1** a strong dislike (esp. *take a scunner at or against*). **2** an object of loathing. [14th c.: orig. uncert.]

scup /skup/ *n.* an E. American fish, *Stenostomus chrysops*, a kind of porgy. [Narragansett *mishcup* thick-scaled f. *mishe* large + *cuppi* scale]

scupper¹ /skúpər/ *n.* a hole at the edge of a boat's deck to allow water to run off. [ME (perh. f. AF) f. OF *escopir* f. Rmc *skuppire* (unrecorded) to spit: orig. imit.]

scupper² /skúpər/ *v.tr. Brit. sl.* **1** sink (a ship or its crew). **2** defeat or ruin (a plan, etc.). **3** kill. [19th c.: orig. unkn.]

scurf /skərf/ *n.* **1** flakes on the surface of the skin, cast off as fresh skin develops below, esp. those of the head; dandruff. **2** any scaly matter on a surface. □□ **scurfy** *adj.* [OE, prob. f. ON & earlier OE *sceorf*, rel. to *sceorfan* gnaw, *sceorfian* cut to shreds]

■ scaliness, flakiness, scales, flakes, particles, laminae; dandruff. □□ **scurfy** see SCALY.

scurrilous /skáriləs, skúr-/ *adj.* **1** (of a person or language) grossly or indecently abusive. **2** given to or expressed with low humor. □□ **scurrility** /-rílitee/ *n.* (*pl.* **-ies**). **scurrilously** *adv.* **scurrilousness** *n.* [F *scurrile* or L *scurrilus* f. *scurra* buffoon]

■ **1** foulmouthed, gross, indecent, vulgar, obscene, licentious, foul, coarse, scabrous, low, vile; nasty, vituperative, defamatory, derogatory, disparaging, vilifying, calumnious, malign, aspersive, opprobrious, offensive, abusive, insulting. **2** see COARSE 2.

scurry /skóree, skúree/ *v. & n.* ● *v.intr.* (**-ies, -ied**) run or move hurriedly, esp. with short quick steps; scamper. ● *n.* (*pl.* **-ies**) **1** the act or sound of scurrying. **2** bustle; haste. **3** a flurry of rain or snow. [abbr. of *hurry-scurry* redupl. of HURRY]

■ *v.* dash, scramble, dart, fly, race, sprint, scamper, scuttle, hurry, hasten, speed, hustle, rush, tear, zoom, zip, bolt, rip, scud, *colloq.* scoot. ● *n.* **2** haste, rush, hustle, bustle; see also FLURRY *n.* 3.

scurvy /skúrvee/ *n. & adj.* ● *n.* a disease caused by a deficiency of vitamin C, characterized by swollen bleeding gums and the opening of previously healed wounds, esp. formerly affecting sailors. ● *adj.* (**scurvier, scurviest**) paltry; low; mean; dishonorable; contemptible. □ **scurvy grass** any cresslike seaside plant of the genus *Cochlearia*, orig. taken as a cure for scurvy. □□ **scurvied** *adj.* **scurvily** *adv.* [SCURF + -Y¹: noun sense by assoc. with F *scorbut* (cf. SCORBUTIC)]

■ *adj.* low, paltry, miserable, contemptible, vile, base, despicable, rotten, sorry, bad, ignoble, dishonorable, mean, worthless, shabby.

scut /skut/ *n.* a short tail, esp. of a hare, rabbit, or deer. [ME: orig. unkn.: cf. obs. *scut* short, shorten]

■ see TAIL¹ *n.* 1.

scuta *pl.* of SCUTUM.

scutage /skyōōtij/ *n. hist.* money paid by a feudal landowner instead of personal service. [ME f. med.L *scutagium* f. L *scutum* shield]

scutch /skuch/ *v.tr.* dress (fibrous material, esp. retted flax) by beating. □□ **scutcher** *n.* [OF *escouche, escoucher* (dial.), *escousser*, ult. f. L *excutere excuss-* (as EX-¹, *quatere* shake)]

scutcheon /skúchən/ *n.* **1** = ESCUTCHEON. **2** an ornamented brass, etc., plate around or over a keyhole. **3** a plate for a name or inscription. [ME f. ESCUTCHEON]

scute /skyōōt/ *n. Zool.* = SCUTUM. [L (as SCUTUM)]

scutellum /skyōōtéləm/ *n.* (*pl.* **scutella** /-lə/) *Bot. & Zool.* a scale, plate, or any shieldlike formation on a plant, insect, bird, etc., esp. one of the horny scales on a bird's foot. □□ **scutellate** /skyōōtélit, skyōōtəlayt/ *adj.* **scutellation** /skyōōtəláyshən/ *n.* [mod.L dimin. of L *scutum* shield]

scutter /skútər/ *v. & n. v.intr. Brit. colloq.* scurry. ● *n.* the act or an instance of scuttering. [perh. alt. of SCUTTLE²]

scuttle¹ /skút'l/ *n.* **1** a receptacle for carrying and holding a small supply of coal. **2** *Brit.* the part of an automobile between the windshield and the hood. [ME f. ON *skutill*, OHG *scuzzila* f. L *scutella* dish]

■ **1** bucket, pail.

scuttle² /skút'l/ *v. & n.* ● *v.intr.* **1** scurry; hurry along. **2** run away; flee from danger or difficulty. ● *n.* **1** a hurried gait. **2** a precipitate flight or departure. [cf. dial. *scuddle* frequent. of SCUD]

■ *v.* **1** see SCURRY *v.*

scuttle³ /skút'l/ *n. & v.* ● *n.* a hole with a lid in a ship's deck

or side. ● *v.tr.* let water into (a ship) to sink it, esp. by opening the seacocks. [ME, perh. f. obs. F *escoutille* f. Sp. *escotilla* hatchway dimin. of *escota* cutting out cloth]
■ *v.* sink, *Brit. sl.* scupper.

scuttlebutt /skút'lbut/ *n.* **1** a water cask on the deck of a ship, for drinking from. **2** *colloq.* rumor; gossip.
■ **2** see RUMOR *n.* 1.

scutum /skyŏōtəm/ *n.* (*pl.* **scuta** /-tə/) each of the shieldlike plates or scales forming the bony covering of a crocodile, sturgeon, turtle, armadillo, etc. □□ **scutal** *adj.* **scutate** *adj.* [L, = oblong shield]
■ see SCALE[1] *n.* 1.

scuzzy /skúzee/ *adj. sl.* abhorrent or disgusting. [prob. f. DISGUSTING]

Scylla and Charybdis /sílə ənd kəríbdis/ *n.pl.* two dangers such that avoidance of one increases the risk from the other. [the names of a sea monster and whirlpool in Gk mythology]

scyphozoan /sífəzṓən/ *n.* & *adj.* ● *n.* any marine jellyfish of the class Scyphozoa, with tentacles bearing stinging cells. ● *adj.* of or relating to this class. [as SCYPHUS + Gk *zōion* animal]

scyphus /sífəs/ *n.* (*pl.* **scyphi** /-fī/) **1** *Gk Antiq.* a footless drinking cup with two handles below the level of the rim. **2** *Bot.* a cup-shaped part as in a narcissus flower or in lichens. □□ **scyphose** *adj.* [mod.L f. Gk *skuphos*]

scythe /sith/ *n.* & *v.* ● *n.* a mowing and reaping implement with a long curved blade swung over the ground by a long pole with two short handles projecting from it. ● *v.tr.* cut with a scythe. [OE *sīthe* f. Gmc]
■ *v.* see MOW[1].

Scythian /sítheeən, -thee-/ *adj.* & *n.* ● *adj.* of or relating to ancient Scythia, a region north of the Black Sea. ● *n.* **1** an inhabitant of Scythia. **2** the language of this region. [L *Scythia* f. Gk *Skuthia* Scythia]

SD *abbr.* South Dakota (in official postal use).

S.Dak. *abbr.* South Dakota.

SDI *abbr.* strategic defense initiative.

SE *abbr.* **1** southeast. **2** southeastern. **3** Standard English.

Se *symb. Chem.* the element selenium.

se- /sə, see/ *prefix* apart, without (*seclude*; *secure*). [L f. OL *se* (prep. & adv.)]

sea /see/ *n.* **1** the expanse of salt water that covers most of the earth's surface and surrounds its landmasses. **2** any part of this as opposed to land or fresh water. **3** a particular (usu. named) tract of salt water partly or wholly enclosed by land (*the North Sea*; *the Dead Sea*). **4** a large inland lake (*the Sea of Galilee*). **5** the waves of the sea, esp. with reference to their local motion or state (*a choppy sea*). **6** (foll. by *of*) a vast quantity or expanse (*a sea of troubles*; *a sea of faces*). **7** (*attrib.*) living or used in, on, or near the sea (often prefixed to the name of a marine animal, plant, etc., having a superficial resemblance to what it is named after) (*sea lettuce*). □ **at sea 1** in a ship on the sea. **2** (also **all at sea**) perplexed; confused. **by sea** in a ship or ships. **go to sea** become a sailor. **on the sea 1** in a ship at sea. **2** situated on the coast. **put** (or **put out**) **to sea** leave land or port. **sea anchor** a device such as a heavy bag dragged in the water to retard the drifting of a ship. **sea anemone** any of various coelenterates of the order Actiniaria having a polypoid body bearing a ring of tentacles around the mouth. **sea angel** an angelfish. **sea bass** any of various marine fishes like the bass, esp. *Centropristis striatus*. **sea bream** = PORGY. **sea breeze** a breeze blowing toward the land from the sea, esp. during the day (cf. *land breeze*). **sea buckthorn** a maritime shrub, *Hippophaë rhamnoides* with orange berries. **sea change** a notable or unexpected transformation (with ref. to Shakesp. *Tempest* I. ii. 403). **sea chest** a sailor's storage chest. **sea coal** *archaic* mineral coal, as distinct from charcoal, etc. **sea cow 1** a sirenian. **2** a walrus. **sea cucumber** a holothurian, esp. a bêche-de-mer. **sea dog** an old or experienced sailor. **sea eagle** any fish-eating eagle esp. of the genus *Haliaëtus*. **sea elephant** = *elephant seal*. **sea fan** any colonial coral of the order Gorgonacea supported by a fanlike horny skeleton. **sea gooseberry** any marine animal of the phylum Ctenophora, with an ovoid body bearing numerous cilia.

sea green bluish green (as of the sea). **sea hare** any of various marine mollusks of the order Anaspidea, having an internal shell and long extensions from its foot. **sea holly** a spiny-leaved blue-flowered evergreen plant, *Eryngium maritimum*. **sea horse 1** any of various small upright marine fish of the family Syngnathidae, esp. *Hippocampus hippocampus*, having a body suggestive of the head and neck of a horse. **2** a mythical creature with a horse's head and fish's tail. **sea island cotton** a fine-quality long-stapled cotton grown on islands off the southern US. **sea kale** a cruciferous maritime plant, *Crambe maritima*, having coarsely-toothed leaves and used as a vegetable. **sea lavender** any maritime plant of the genus *Limonium*, with small brightly colored funnel-shaped flowers. **sea legs** the ability to keep one's balance and avoid seasickness when at sea. **sea level** the mean level of the sea's surface, used in reckoning the height of hills, etc., and as a barometric standard. **sea lily** any of various sessile echinoderms, esp. of the class Crinoidea, with long jointed stalks and featherlike arms for trapping food. **sea lion** any large, eared seal of the Pacific, esp. of the genus *Zalophus* or *Otaria*. **sea loch** = LOCH 2. **sea mile** = *nautical mile*. **sea mouse** any iridescent marine annelid of the genus *Aphrodite*. **sea onion** = SQUILL 2. **sea otter** a Pacific otter, *Enhydra lutris*, using a stone balanced on its abdomen to crack bivalve mollusks. **sea pink** a maritime plant, *Armeria maritima*, with bright pink flowers: also called THRIFT. **sea purse** the egg case of a skate or shark. **sea room** clear space at sea for a ship to turn or maneuver in. **sea salt** salt produced by evaporating sea water. **Sea Scout** a member of a maritime scouting association. **sea serpent** (or **snake**) **1** a snake of the family Hydrophidae, living in the sea. **2** an enormous legendary serpentlike sea monster. **sea squirt** any marine tunicate of the class Ascidiacea, consisting of a baglike structure with apertures for the flow of water. **sea trout** = *salmon trout*. **sea urchin** a small marine echinoderm of the class Echinoidea, with a spherical or flattened spiny shell. [OE *sæ* f. Gmc]
■ **1** ocean, high sea(s), blue water, *archaic or poet.* main, *colloq.* the drink, *joc.* pond, *poet.* deep, *Brit. sl.* briny. **5** see WAVE *n.* 1, 2. **6** plethora, quantity, abundance, surfeit, profusion, flood, multitude, spate, legion, mass, mountain, *colloq.* lot, heap, pile, load. □ **at sea 2** confused, disoriented, bewildered, perplexed, baffled, mystified, lost; at sixes and sevens, adrift. **sea change** transformation, watershed, landmark, turning point, crossroads. **sea dog** see SAILOR.

seabed /seebed/ *n.* the ground under the sea; the ocean floor.

seabird /seebərd/ *n.* seabird a bird frequenting the sea or the land near the sea.

seaboard /seebawrd/ *n.* **1** the seashore or coastal region. **2** the line of a coast.
■ see COAST *n.*

seaborgium /seebáwrgeeəm/ *n.* an artificially produced chemical element, atomic number 106. ¶ Symb.: **Sg**. [for US chemist Glenn T. Seaborg (b. 1912)]

seaborne /seebawrn/ *adj.* transported by sea.

seacoast /seekōst/ *n.* the land adjacent to the sea.
■ see COAST *n.*

seacock /seekok/ *n.* a valve below a ship's waterline for letting water in or out.
■ see TAP[1] *n.* 1.

seafarer /seefairər/ *n.* **1** a sailor. **2** a traveler by sea.
■ **1** see SAILOR.

seafaring /seefairing/ *adj.* & *n.* traveling by sea, esp. regularly.
■ *adj.* maritime, nautical, naval, marine.

seafood /seefŏod/ *n.* edible sea fish or shellfish.

seafront /seefrənt/ *n.* the part of a coastal town directly facing the sea.

seagirt /seegərt/ *adj. literary* surrounded by sea.

seagoing /seegōing/ *adj.* **1** (of ships) fit for crossing the sea. **2** (of a person) seafaring.
■ **2** seafaring, oceangoing.

seagull /seegul/ *n.* = GULL[1].

seal[1] /seel/ *n.* & *v.* ● *n.* **1** a piece of wax, lead, paper, etc.,

with a stamped design, attached to a document as a guarantee of authenticity. **2** a similar material attached to a receptacle, envelope, etc., affording security by having to be broken to allow access to the contents. **3** an engraved piece of metal, gemstone, etc., for stamping a design on a seal. **4 a** a substance or device used to close an aperture or act as a fastening. **b** an amount of water standing in the trap of a drain to prevent foul air from rising. **5** an act or gesture or event regarded as a confirmation or guarantee (*gave her seal of approval to the venture*). **6** a significant or prophetic mark (*has the seal of death in his face*). **7** a decorative adhesive stamp. **8** esp. *Eccl.* a vow of secrecy; an obligation to silence. ● *v.tr.* **1** close securely or hermetically. **2** stamp or fasten with a seal. **3** fix a seal to. **4** certify as correct with a seal or stamp. **5** (often foll. by *up*) confine or fasten securely. **6** settle or decide (*their fate is sealed*). **7** (foll. by *off*) put barriers around (an area) to prevent entry and exit, esp. as a security measure. **8** apply a nonporous coating to (a surface) to make it impervious. □ **one's lips are sealed** one is obliged to keep a secret. **sealed-beam** (*attrib.*) designating a vehicle headlight with a sealed unit consisting of the light source, reflector, and lens. **sealed book** see BOOK. **sealed orders** orders for procedure not to be opened before a specified time. **sealing wax** a mixture of shellac and rosin with turpentine and pigment, softened by heating and used to make seals. **seal ring** a finger ring with a seal. **set one's seal to** (or **on**) authorize or confirm. □□ **sealable** *adj.* [ME f. AF *seal*, OF *seel* f. L *sigillum* dimin. of *signum* SIGN]
 ■ *n.* **5** authentication, confirmation, verification, validation, affirmation, attestation, ratification, corroboration, assurance, guarantee, guaranty, endorsement, substantiation, notification. **6** see SIGN *n.* 1. ● *v.* **1** seal up, close up, zip up, plug (up), stop (up), lock, bolt, secure, batten down, make airtight *or* waterproof; cork. **4** authenticate, confirm, verify, validate, affirm, attest, ratify, corroborate, guarantee, endorse. **7** close off, shut off, barricade, block.

seal² /seel/ *n. & v.* ● *n.* any fish-eating amphibious sea mammal of the family Phocidae or Otariidae, with flippers and webbed feet. ● *v.intr.* hunt for seals. [OE *seolh seol-* f. Gmc]

sealant /seelənt/ *n.* material for sealing, esp. to make something airtight or watertight.

sealer /seelər/ *n.* a ship or person engaged in hunting seals.

sealery /seeləree/ *n.* (*pl.* **-ies**) a place for hunting seals.

sealskin /seelskin/ *n.* **1** the skin or prepared fur of a seal. **2** (often *attrib.*) a garment made from this.

Sealyham /seeleeəm, esp. *Brit.* -leeəm/ *n.* (in full **Sealyham terrier**) **1** a terrier of a wire-haired, short-legged breed. **2** this breed. [*Sealyham* in S. Wales]

seam /seem/ *n. & v.* ● *n.* **1 a** a line where two edges join, esp. of two pieces of cloth, etc., turned back and stitched together, or of boards fitted edge to edge. **2** a fissure between parallel edges. **3** a wrinkle or scar. **4** a stratum of coal, etc. ● *v.tr.* **1** join with a seam. **2** (esp. as **seamed** *adj.*) mark or score with or as with a seam. □ **bursting at the seams** full to overflowing. □□ **seamer** *n.* **seamless** *adj.* [OE *seam* f. Gmc]
 ■ *n.* **1** junction, juncture, join, joint, commissure. **3** wrinkle, scar, cicatrice. **4** lode, vein, stratum, bed, layer. □ **bursting at the seams** see FULL¹ *adj.* 1.

seaman /seemən/ *n.* (*pl.* **-men**) **1** a sailor, esp. one below the rank of officer. **2** a person regarded in terms of skill in navigation (*a poor seaman*). □□ **seamanlike** *adj.* **seamanly** *adj.* [OE *sǣman* (as SEA, MAN)]
 ■ **1** see SAILOR. **2** see NAVIGATOR.

seamanship /seemənship/ *n.* skill in managing a ship or boat.
 ■ see NAVIGATION.

seamstress /seemstris/ *n.* (also **sempstress** /semp-/) a woman who sews, esp. professionally. [OE *sēamestre* fem. f. *sēamere* tailor, formed as SEAM + -STER + -ESS¹]
 ■ see DRESSMAKER.

seamy /seemee/ *adj.* (**seamier**, **seamiest**) **1** marked with or showing seams. **2** unpleasant; disreputable (esp. *the seamy side*). □□ **seaminess** *n.*
 ■ **2** sordid, nasty, dark, disreputable, unpleasant,

shameful, unwholesome, unpalatable, unsavory, distasteful, unseemly, squalid, low, depraved, degenerate, degraded, foul, vile, odious, abhorrent, contemptible, scurvy, rotten, unattractive, ugly, repulsive, repellent.

Seanad /shánəth/ *n.* the upper house of Parliament in the Republic of Ireland. [Ir., = senate]

seance /sáyons/ *n.* (also **séance**) a meeting at which spiritualists attempt to make contact with the dead. [F *séance* f. OF *seoir* f. L *sedēre* sit]

seaplane /seeplayn/ *n.* an aircraft designed to take off from and land and float on water.

seaport /seepawrt/ *n.* a town with a harbor for seagoing ships.
 ■ port, harbor, haven.

seaquake /seekwayk/ *n.* an earthquake under the sea.

sear /seer/ *v. & adj.* ● *v.tr.* **1 a** scorch, esp. with a hot iron; cauterize; brand. **b** (as **searing** *adj.*) scorching; burning (*searing pain*). **2** cause pain or great anguish to. **3** brown (meat) quickly at a high temperature so that it will retain its juices in cooking. **4** make (one's conscience, feelings, etc.) callous. **5** *archaic* blast; wither. ● *adj.* var. of SERE². [OE *sēar* (adj.), *sēarian* (v.), f. Gmc]
 ■ *v.* **1 a** see SCORCH *v.* 1, 2. **b** (**searing**) see *scorching* (SCORCH *v.* 3). ● *adj.* withered, shriveled (up), dry, parched.

search /sərch/ *v. & n.* ● *v.* **1** *tr.* look through or go over thoroughly to find something. **2** *tr.* examine or feel over (a person) to find anything concealed. **3** *tr.* **a** probe or penetrate into. **b** examine or question (one's mind, conscience, etc.) thoroughly. **4** *intr.* (often foll. by *for*) make a search or investigation. **5** *intr.* (as **searching** *adj.*) (of an examination) thorough; leaving no loopholes. **6** *tr.* (foll. by *out*) look probingly for; seek out. ● *n.* **1** an act of searching. **2** an investigation. □ **in search of** trying to find. **right of search** a belligerent's right to stop a neutral vessel and search it for prohibited goods. **search me!** *colloq.* I do not know. **search party** a group of people organized to look for a lost person or thing. **search warrant** an official authorization to enter and search a building. □□ **searchable** *adj.* **searcher** *n.* **searchingly** *adv.* [ME f. AF *sercher*, OF *cerchier* f. LL *circare* go round (as CIRCUS)]
 ■ *v.* **1, 3** search through, examine, scrutinize, check, comb (through), explore, go through, investigate, inspect, look at *or* into, probe, scour, sift through, hunt *or* rummage through, plow through; probe, penetrate, pry into; inquire of. **2** see FRISK *v.* 2. **4** look (about *or* around), cast about, seek. **5** (**searching**) see THOROUGH 2. **6** seek (out), scout out, look for, hunt for; track down, uncover, pinpoint. ● *n.* **1** hunt, pursuit; see also QUEST *n.* **2** analysis, investigation, exploration, examination, scrutiny, probe, study, perusal, sifting, inspection, scouring, inquiry. □ **search me!** see *ask me another.* □□ **searchingly** penetratingly, piercingly, intently, deeply.

searchlight /sərchlit/ *n.* **1** a powerful outdoor electric light with a concentrated beam that can be turned in any direction. **2** the light or beam from this.
 ■ spotlight, arc light, spot; beam, ray, shaft.

seascape /seeskayp/ *n.* a picture or view of the sea.
 ■ see VIEW *n.* 2.

seashell /seeshel/ *n.* the shell of a saltwater mollusk.

seashore /seeshawr/ *n.* **1** land close to or bordering on the sea. **2** *Law* the area between high and low water marks.
 ■ **1** see COAST *n.*

seasick /seesik/ *adj.* suffering from sickness or nausea from the motion of a ship at sea. □□ **seasickness** *n.*
 ■ see SICK¹ *adj.* 1. □□ **seasickness** *mal de mer.*

seaside /seesid/ *n.* the seacoast, esp. as a holiday resort.

/.../ **pronunciation**	● **part of speech**
□ **phrases, idioms, and compounds**	
□□ **derivatives**	■ **synonym section**
cross-references appear in SMALL CAPITALS or *italics*	

■ see COAST *n.*

season /se/ezən/ *n. & v.* ● *n.* **1** each of the four divisions of the year (spring, summer, autumn, and winter) associated with a type of weather and a stage of vegetation. **2** a time of year characterized by climatic or other features (*the dry season*). **3 a** the time of year when a plant is mature or flowering, etc. **b** the time of year when an animal breeds or is hunted. **4** a proper or suitable time. **5** a time when something is plentiful or active or in vogue. **6** (usu. prec. by *the*) = *high season.* **7** the time of year regularly devoted to an activity (*the football season*). **8** the time of year dedicated to social life generally (*went up to their cottage for the season*). **9** a period of indefinite or varying length. **10** *Brit. colloq.* = *season ticket.* ● *v.* **1** *tr.* flavor (food) with salt, herbs, etc. **2** *tr.* enhance with wit, excitement, etc. **3** *tr.* temper or moderate. **4** *tr. & intr.* **a** make or become suitable or in the desired condition, esp. by exposure to the air or weather; mature. **b** (usu. as **seasoned** *adj.*) make or become experienced or accustomed (*seasoned soldiers*). □ **in season 1** (of foodstuff) available in plenty and in good condition. **2** (of an animal) in heat. **3** timely. **season ticket** a ticket entitling the holder to any number of journeys, admittances, etc., in a given period. □□ **seasoner** *n.* [ME f. OF *seson* f. L *satio -onis* (in Rmc sense 'seed time') f. *serere sat-* sow]

■ *n.* **1–3, 5** time, period. ● *v.* **1** spice, salt, flavor, *colloq.* pep up. **2** see ENLIVEN 1. **3** see MODERATE *v.* 1. **4 a** ripen, mature, age, condition, mellow. **b** (**seasoned**) experienced, long-standing, practiced, well-versed, habituated, acclimatized, accustomed, familiarized, prepared, established, veteran, tempered, hardened, toughened, inured, acclimated. □ **in season 1** ripe, ready, edible; seasoned, seasonable; available, plentiful. **3** see TIMELY.

seasonable /se/ezənəbəl/ *adj.* **1** suitable to or usual in the season. **2** opportune. **3** meeting the needs of the occasion. □□ **seasonableness** *n.* **seasonably** *adv.*

■ **1** appropriate, suitable, apt, opportune, timely, fitting, well-timed, proper, fit. **2, 3** appropriate, suitable, apt, opportune, timely, fitting, well-timed, proper, fit, propitious, welcome, well-suited, providential, happy, lucky, fortunate, convenient, auspicious, favorable, advantageous, expedient.

seasonal /se/ezənəl/ *adj.* of, depending on, or varying with the season. □ **seasonal affective disorder** a depressive state associated with late autumn and winter and thought to be caused by a lack of light. □□ **seasonality** /-nálitee/ *n.* **seasonally** *adv.*

■ see INTERMITTENT.

seasoning /se/ezəning/ *n.* condiments added to food.

■ spice, flavoring, zest, relish, sauce; condiments.

seat /seet/ *n. & v.* ● *n.* **1** a thing made or used for sitting on; a chair, stool, saddle, etc. **2** the buttocks. **3** the part of a garment covering the buttocks. **4** the part of a chair, etc., on which the sitter's weight directly rests. **5** a place for one person in a theater, vehicle, etc. **6** the occupation of a seat. **7** *Polit.* the right to occupy a seat, esp. as a member of Congress, etc. **8** the part of a machine that supports or guides another part. **9** a site or location of something specified (*a seat of learning; the seat of the emotions*). **10** a country mansion, esp. with large grounds. **11** the manner of sitting on a horse, etc. ● *v.tr.* **1** cause to sit. **2 a** provide sitting accommodation for (*the theater seats 500*). **b** provide with seats. **3** (as **seated** *adj.*) sitting. **4** put or fit in position. □ **be seated** sit down. **by the seat of one's pants** *colloq.* by instinct rather than logic or knowledge. **seat belt** a belt securing a person in the seat of a car, aircraft, etc. **take a** (or **one's**) **seat** sit down. □□ **seatless** *adj.* [ME f. ON *sæti* (=OE *gesete* f. Gmc)]

■ *n.* **1** place, chair; bench, sofa, settee, settle, stool, throne, saddle. **2** bottom, buttocks, posterior(s), rump, hindquarters, *colloq.* behind, backside, rear, *colloq. euphem.* derrière, *joc.* fundament, *sl.* tush, butt, tail; *Brit. sl.* bum. **7** place, position; incumbency. **9** focus, base, center, heart, hub, site, location, capital, cradle, headquarters, fountainhead. **10** (country) house,

abode, residence, home, domicile, estate, mansion. ● *v.* **2** hold, accommodate, contain, have room or capacity or space for, sit, have seats or seating for. **3** (**seated**) sitting (down); sedentary. **4** locate, position, site, fit.

-seater /se/etər/ *n.* (in *comb.*) having a specified number of seats (*a 16-seater bus*).

seating /se/eting/ *n.* **1** seats collectively. **2** sitting accommodation.

■ accommodation, capacity, space, room.

SEATO /se/etō/ *abbr.* Southeast Asia Treaty Organization.

seawall /se/ewawl/ *n.* a wall or embankment erected to prevent encroachment by the sea.

seaward /se/ewərd/ *adv., adj., & n.* ● *adv.* (also **seawards** /-wərdz/) toward the sea. ● *adj.* going or facing toward the sea. ● *n.* such a direction or position.

seawater /se/ewawtər/ *n.* water in or taken from the sea.

seaway /se/eway/ *n.* **1** an inland waterway open to seagoing ships. **2** a ship's progress. **3** a ship's path across the sea.

seaweed /se/eweed/ *n.* any of various algae growing in the sea or on the rocks on a shore.

seaworthy /se/ewərthee/ *adj.* (esp. of a ship) fit to put to sea. □□ **seaworthiness** *n.*

■ see NAVIGABLE 2, 3.

sebaceous /sibáyshəs/ *adj.* fatty; of or relating to tallow or fat. □ **sebaceous gland** (or **follicle** or **duct**) a gland, etc., secreting or conveying oily matter to lubricate the skin and hair. [L *sebaceus* f. *sebum* tallow]

■ see FAT *adj.* 4.

seborrhea /sébəree/ə/ *n.* excessive discharge of sebum from the sebaceous glands. □□ **seborrheic** *adj.* [SEBUM after *gonorrhea,* etc.]

sebum /se/ebəm/ *n.* the oily secretion of the sebaceous glands. [mod.L f. L *sebum* grease]

SEC *abbr.* Securities and Exchange Commission.

Sec. *abbr.* secretary.

sec[1] *abbr.* secant.

sec[2] /sek/ *n. colloq.* (in phrases) a second (of time). [abbr.]

■ see SECOND[2].

sec[3] /sek/ *adj.* (of wine) dry. [F f. L *siccus*]

sec. *abbr.* second(s).

secant /se/ekant, -kənt/ *adj. & n. Math.* ● *adj.* cutting (*secant line*). ● *n.* **1** a line cutting a curve at one or more points. **2** the ratio of the hypotenuse to the shorter side adjacent to an acute angle (in a right triangle). ¶ Abbr.: **sec.** [F *sécant(e)* f. L *secare secant-* cut]

secateurs /sékətərz/ *n.pl.* esp. *Brit.* a pair of pruning shears for use with one hand. [F *sécateur* cutter, irreg. f. L *secare* cut]

secco /sékō/ *n.* the technique of painting on dry plaster with pigments mixed in water. [It., = dry, f. L *siccus*]

secede /sise/ed/ *v.intr.* (usu. foll. by *from*) withdraw formally from membership of a political federation or a religious body. □□ **seceder** *n.* [L *secedere secess-* (as SE-, *cedere* go)]

■ withdraw, resign, retire, apostatize, break away, disaffiliate, defect, drop or pull out; (*secede from*) withdraw or resign or retire from, abandon, quit, leave, forsake, break with, break away from, drop or pull out of, turn one's back to or on, separate from, wash one's hands of, have nothing further to do with.

secession /sise/shən/ *n.* **1** the act or an instance of seceding. **2** (**Secession**) *hist.* the withdrawal of eleven southern states from the US Union in 1860–61, leading to the Civil War. □□ **secessional** *adj.* **secessionism** *n.* **secessionist** *n.* [F *sécession* or L *secessio* (as SECEDE)]

■ **1** withdrawal, seceding, defection, break, breaking, disaffiliation, retirement, separation, splitting off or away, apostasy.

seclude /sikloOd/ *v.tr.* (also *refl.*) **1** keep (a person or place) retired or away from company. **2** (esp. as **secluded** *adj.*) hide or screen from view. [ME f. L *secludere seclus-* (as SE-, *claudere* shut)]

■ **1** see SEGREGATE[1] 1. **2** (**secluded**) private, separated, isolated, lonely, cloistered, sequestered, segregated, detached, solitary, eremitic, monastic; off the beaten track, out-of-the-way, remote, faraway, far-off.

seclusion /siklŏŏzhən/ n. **1** a secluded state; retirement; privacy. **2** a secluded place. □□ **seclusionist** n. **seclusive** /-klŏŏsiv/ adj. [med.L seclusio (as SECLUDE)]

■ **1** privacy, retirement, separation, isolation, loneliness, solitude. **2** see RETREAT n. 3.

second[1] /sékənd/ n., adj., & v. ● n. **1** the position in a sequence corresponding to that of the number 2 in the sequence 1–2. **2** something occupying this position. **3** the second person, etc., in a race or competition. **4** Mus. **a** an interval or chord spanning two consecutive notes in the diatonic scale (e.g., C to D). **b** a note separated from another by this interval. **5** = second gear. **6** another person or thing in addition to one previously mentioned or considered (the police officer was then joined by a second). **7** (in pl.) **a** goods of a second or inferior quality. **b** coarse flour, or bread made from it. **8** (in pl.) colloq. **a** a second helping of food at a meal. **b** the second course of a meal. **9** an attendant assisting a combatant in a duel, boxing match, etc. **10** esp. Brit. **a** a place in the second class of an examination. **b** a person having this. ● adj. **1** that is the second; next after first. **2** additional; further; other besides one previously mentioned or considered (ate a second cupcake). **3** subordinate in position or importance, etc.; inferior. **4** Mus. performing a lower or subordinate part (second violins). **5** such as to be comparable to; closely reminiscent of (a second Callas). ● v.tr. **1** supplement; support; back up. **2** formally support or endorse (a nomination or resolution, etc., or its proposer). □ **at second hand** by hearsay, not direct observation, etc. **in the second place** as a second consideration, etc. **on second thought** after (brief) reconsideration. **Second Advent** a supposed return of Christ to earth. **second ballot** a deciding ballot between candidates coming first (without an absolute majority) and second in a previous ballot. **second best** a less adequate or desirable alternative. **second-best** adj. next after best. **second cause** Logic a cause that is itself caused. **second chamber** the upper house of a bicameral parliament. **second class** the second-best group or category, esp. of hotel or train accommodation or of postal services. **second-class** adj. **1** of or belonging to the second class. **2** inferior in quality, status, etc. (second-class citizens). ● adv. by second-class post, train, etc. (traveled second-class). **Second Coming** Theol. the second advent of Christ on earth. **second cousin** see COUSIN. **second-degree** Med. denoting burns that cause blistering but not permanent scars. **second fiddle** see FIDDLE. **second floor 1** the floor above the ground floor. **2** Brit., etc., the floor two levels above the ground floor. **second gear** the second (and next to lowest) in a sequence of gears. **second-generation** denoting the offspring of a first generation, esp. of immigrants. **second-guess** colloq. **1** anticipate or predict by guesswork. **2** judge or criticize with hindsight. **second honeymoon** a vacation like a honeymoon, taken by a couple after some years of marriage. **second in command** the officer next in rank to the commanding or chief officer. **second lieutenant** in the US, the lowest-ranked commissioned officer of the army, air force, or marines. **second nature** (often foll. by to) an acquired tendency that has become instinctive (is second nature to him). **second officer** an assistant mate on a merchant ship. **second person** Gram. see PERSON. **second-rate** of mediocre quality; inferior. **second-rater** a person or thing that is second-rate. **second reading** a second presentation of a bill to a legislative assembly, in the UK to approve its general principles and in the US to debate committee reports. **second self** a close friend or associate. **second sight** the supposed power of being able to perceive future or distant events. **second string** an alternative available in case of need. **second teeth** the teeth that replace the milk teeth in a mammal. **second thoughts** a new opinion or resolution reached after further consideration. **second to none** surpassed by no other. **second wind 1** recovery of the power of normal breathing during exercise after initial breathlessness. **2** renewed energy to continue an effort. □□ **seconder**

n. (esp. in sense 2 of v.). [ME f. OF f. L secundus f. sequi follow]

■ n. **7 a** (seconds) rejects, defective or imperfect merchandise or goods. ● adj. **2** additional, further, other, subsequent, later, following, next, more recent. **3** subordinate, next; inferior, second-best. **5** duplicate; reincarnate, reborn, redivivus. ● v. **1** supplement, support, back up, aid, help, assist, approve of, subscribe to, espouse, sponsor, patronize, favor, encourage, go along with. **2** support, back, endorse, approve, go along with.

second[2] /sékənd/ n. **1** a sixtieth of a minute of time or angular distance. ¶ Symb.: ("). **2** the SI unit of time, based on the natural periodicity of the cesium atom. ¶ Abbr.: **s**. **3** colloq. a very short time (wait a second). □ **second hand** a hand in some watches and clocks, recording seconds. [F f. med.L secunda (minuta) secondary (minute)]

■ **3** moment, instant, flash, minute, split second, colloq. sec, jiffy, jiff, tick, Brit. colloq. (half a) mo; (in a second) in a twinkle or a twinkling or the twinkle of an eye, in two shakes (of a lamb's tail).

second[3] /sikónd/ v.tr. Brit. transfer (a military officer or other official or worker) temporarily to other employment or to another position. □□ **secondment** n. [F en second in the second rank (of officers)]

■ transfer, move, shift, relocate.

secondary /sékəndèree/ adj. & n. ● adj. **1** coming after or next below what is primary. **2** derived from or depending on or supplementing what is primary. **3** (of education, a school, etc.) for those who have had primary education, usu. from 11 to 18 years. **4** Electr. **a** (of a cell or battery) having a reversible chemical reaction and therefore able to store energy. **b** denoting a device using electromagnetic induction, esp. a transformer. ● n. (pl. -ies) **1** a secondary thing. **2** a secondary device or current. □ **secondary color** the result of mixing two primary colors. **secondary feather** a feather growing from the second joint of a bird's wing. **secondary planet** a satellite of a planet (cf. primary planet). **secondary sexual characteristics** those distinctive of one sex but not directly related to reproduction. □□ **secondarily** adv. **secondariness** n. [ME f. L secundarius (as SECOND[1])]

■ adj. **1** subsidiary, ancillary, subordinate, inferior, minor, unimportant, inessential, unessential, nonessential, noncritical. **2** derivative, derived, indirect, secondhand, unoriginal.

seconde /səkónd/ n. Fencing the second of eight parrying positions. [F, fem. of second SECOND[1]]

secondhand /sékəndhánd/ adj. & adv. ● adj. **1 a** (of goods) having had a previous owner; not new. **b** (of a store, etc.) where such goods can be bought. **2** (of information, etc.) accepted on another's authority and not from original investigation. ● adv. **1** on a secondhand basis. **2** at second hand; not directly.

■ adj. **1 a** used, old, worn, colloq. hand-me-down.

secondly /sékəndlee/ adv. **1** furthermore; in the second place. **2** as a second item.

secondo /sikóndō/ n. (pl. **secondi** /-dee/) Mus. the second or lower part in a duet, etc. [It.]

secrecy /séekrisee/ n. **1** the keeping of secrets as a fact, habit, or faculty. **2** a state in which all information is withheld (was done in great secrecy). □ **sworn to secrecy** having promised to keep a secret. [ME f. secretie f. obs. secre (adj.) or SECRET adj.]

■ mystery, concealment, confidentiality, stealth, secretiveness, surreptitiousness, privacy, furtiveness, covertness, clandestineness.

secret /séekrit/ adj. & n. ● adj. **1** kept or meant to be kept private, unknown, or hidden from all or all but a few. **2** acting or operating secretly. **3** fond of, prone to, or able to preserve secrecy. **4** (of a place) hidden, completely secluded. ● *n.* **1** a thing kept or meant to be kept secret. **2** a thing known only to a few. **3** a mystery. **4** a valid but not commonly known or recognized method of achieving or maintaining something (*what's their secret?*; *correct breathing is the secret of good health*). **5** *RC Ch.* a prayer concluding the offertory of the mass. □ **in secret** secretly. **in** (or **in on**) **the secret** among the number of those who know it. **keep a secret** not reveal it. **secret agent** a spy acting for a country. **secret ballot** a ballot in which votes are cast in secret. **secret police** a police force operating in secret for political purposes. **secret service 1** a government department concerned with espionage. **2** (**Secret Service**) a branch of the US Treasury Department charged with apprehending counterfeitors and with protecting the president and certain other officials and their families. **secret society** a society whose members are sworn to secrecy about it. □□ **secretly** *adv.* [ME f. OF f. L *secretus* (adj.) separate, set apart f. *secernere secret-* (as SE-, *cernere* sift)]

■ *adj.* **1** concealed, hidden, private, shrouded, under wraps, confidential, classified, quiet, undercover, *colloq.* hush-hush; unpublishable, unpublished; cryptographic, encrypted, encoded. **2** confidential, private, undercover, *colloq.* hush-hush. **3** private, clandestine, covert, secretive, arcane, mysterious, cryptic, *colloq.* hush-hush. **4** concealed, hidden, covert, secluded. ● *n.* **1, 2** private or confidential matter or affair. **3** see MYSTERY[1] 1. □ **in secret** see *secretly* below. **in** (or **in on**) **the secret** in the picture, *colloq.* in the know. □□ **secretly** surreptitiously, quietly, privately, covertly, furtively, under cover, by stealth, stealthily, mysteriously, clandestinely, in secret, confidentially, on the sly, slyly, sub rosa, *colloq.* on the q.t.

secretaire /sékritáir/ *n.* an escritoire. [F (as SECRETARY)]

secretariat /sékrìtáireeət/ *n.* **1** a permanent administrative office or department, esp. a governmental one. **2** its members or premises. **3** the office of secretary. [F *secrétariat* f. med.L *secretariatus* (as SECRETARY)]

secretary /sékriteree/ *n.* (*pl.* **-ies**) **1** a person employed by an individual or in an office, etc., to assist with correspondence, keep records, make appointments, etc. **2** an official appointed by a society, etc., to conduct its correspondence, keep its records, etc. **3** (in the UK) the principal assistant of a government minister, ambassador, etc. □ **secretary bird** a long-legged, snake-eating African bird, *Sagittarius serpentarius*, with a crest likened to a quill pen stuck over a writer's ear. **secretary-general** the principal administrator of certain organizations, as the United Nations. **secretary of state 1** (in the US) the chief government official responsible for foreign affairs. **2** (in the UK) the head of a major government department. □□ **secretarial** /-táireeəl/ *adj.* **secretaryship** *n.* [ME f. LL *secretarius* (as SECRET)]

■ □□ **secretarial** see CLERICAL 2.

secrete[1] /sikreet/ *v.tr. Biol.* (of a cell, organ, etc.) produce by secretion. □□ **secretor** *n.* **secretory** /seekrətáwree/ *adj.* [back-form. f. SECRETION]

■ excrete, pass, generate, release, ooze, exude, discharge, leak, drip, drop, dribble, trickle, emit, give off, emanate, emit, extravasate.

secrete[2] /sikreet/ *v.tr.* conceal; put into hiding. [obs. *secret* (v.) f. SECRET]

■ hide, conceal, cache, bury, *colloq.* stash away.

secretion /sikreeshən/ *n.* **1** *Biol.* **a** a process by which substances are produced and discharged from a cell for a function in the organism or for excretion. **b** the secreted substance. **2** the act or an instance of concealing (*the secretion of stolen goods*). [F *sécrétion* or L *secretio* separation (as SECRET)]

■ **1 a** secreting, release, oozing, seeping, seepage, discharge, discharging, leak, leaking, leakage, drip, dripping, drop, dropping, dribbling, trickling, trickle, running, drain, draining, emission, emitting, giving off, exudation, transudation, excretion, excreting, emanation, emanating, generation, extravasation. **b** discharge, excreta. **2** concealment, hiding.

secretive /seekritiv, səkree-/ *adj.* inclined to make or keep secrets; uncommunicative. □□ **secretively** *adv.* **secretiveness** *n.* [back-form. f. *secretiveness* after F *secrétivité* (as SECRET)]

■ cryptic, mysterious, enigmatic; conspiratorial, furtive; reticent, silent, closemouthed, taciturn, uncommunicative, reserved, tight-lipped, close, *colloq.* mum.

sect /sekt/ *n.* **1 a** a body of people subscribing to religious doctrines usu. different from those of an established church from which they have separated. **b** usu. *derog.* a nonconformist or other church. **c** a party or faction in a religious body. **d** a religious denomination. **2** the followers of a particular philosopher or philosophy, or school of thought in politics, etc. [ME f. OF *secte* or L *secta* f. the stem of *sequi secut-* follow]

■ **1** religious group *or* denomination *or* body *or* cult, persuasion. **2** school (of thought), faction, set, clique, cabal, *colloq. usu. derog.* ism.

sect. *abbr.* section.

sectarian /sektáireeən/ *adj.* & *n.* ● *adj.* **1** of or concerning a sect. **2** bigoted or narrow-minded in following the doctrines of one's sect. ● *n.* **1** a member of a sect. **2** a bigot. □□ **sectarianism** *n.* **sectarianize** *v.tr.* [SECTARY]

■ *adj.* **1** partisan, factional, cliquish, *usu. derog.* clannish. **2** parochial, narrow, narrow-minded, limited, insular, provincial, rigid, fanatic(al), prejudicial, prejudiced, bigoted, partial, dogmatic, doctrinaire. ● *n.* **1** adherent, member, sectary, votary, cultist, partisan. **2** dogmatist, fanatic, bigot, zealot, extremist.

sectary /séktəree/ *n.* (*pl.* **-ies**) a member of a religious or political sect. [med.L *sectarius* adherent (as SECT)]

■ see SECTARIAN *n.* 1.

section /sékshən/ *n.* & *v.* ● *n.* **1** a part cut off or separated from something. **2** each of the parts into which a thing is divided (actually or conceptually) or divisible or out of which a structure can be fitted together. **3** a distinct group or subdivision of a larger body of people (*the wind section of an orchestra*). **4** a subdivision of a book, document, statute, etc. **5 a** an area of land. **b** one square mile of land. **c** a particular district of a town (*residential section*). **6** a subdivision of an army platoon. **7** esp. *Surgery* a separation by cutting. **8** *Biol.* a thin slice of tissue, etc., cut off for microscopic examination. **9 a** the cutting of a solid by or along a plane. **b** the resulting figure or the area of this. **10** a representation of the internal structure of something as if cut across along a vertical or horizontal plane. **11** *Biol.* a group, esp. a subgenus. ● *v.tr.* **1** arrange in or divide into sections. **2** *Brit.* cause (a person) to be compulsorily committed to a psychiatric hospital in accordance with a section of a mental health act. **3** *Biol.* cut into thin slices for microscopic examination. □ **section mark** the sign (§) used as a reference mark to indicate the start of a section of a book, etc. [F *section* or L *sectio* f. *secare sect-* cut]

■ *n.* **1** part, fraction, segment, portion, slice, sample, division. **2** part, segment, portion, fraction, division, slice; sample, cross section; stage, stretch, lap. **3** part, division, department, branch, sector, group, segment, portion, subdivision, component, element. **4** part, subdivision; paragraph; chapter. **5 c** district, quarter; see also ZONE *n.* 8 sample, slice, cross section. ● *v.* **1** cut (up), divide (up), segment, split, *literary* cleave.

sectional /sékshənəl/ *adj.* **1 a** relating to a section, esp. of a community. **b** partisan. **2** made in sections as, e.g., some furniture (*a sectional sofa*). **3** local rather than general. □□ **sectionalism** *n.* **sectionalist** *n.* & *adj.* **sectionalize** *v.tr.* **sectionally** *adv.*

sector /séktər/ *n.* **1** a distinct part or branch of an enterprise, or of society, the economy, etc. **2** *Mil.* a subdivision of an area for military operations, controlled by one commander or headquarters. **3** the plane figure enclosed by two radii of a circle, ellipse, etc., and the arc between them. **4** a mathematical instrument consisting of two arms hinged at one end and marked with sines, tangents, etc., for making diagrams, etc. □□ **sectoral** *adj.* [LL, techn. use of L *sector* cutter (as SECTION)]

■ **1** see SECTION *n.* 3.

sectorial /sektáwreeəl/ *adj.* **1** of or like a sector or sectors. **2** = CARNASSIAL.

secular /sékyələr/ *adj.* & *n.* ● *adj.* **1** concerned with the affairs of this world; not spiritual nor sacred. **2** (of education, etc.) not concerned with religion nor religious belief. **3 a** not ecclesiastical nor monastic. **b** (of clergy) not bound by a religious rule. **4** occurring once in an age or century. **5** lasting for or occurring over an indefinitely long time. ● *n.* a secular priest. □ **secular variation** *Astron.* variation compensated over a long period of time. □□ **secularism** *n.* **secularist** *n.* **secularity** /-láirətee/ *n.* **secularize** *v.tr.* **secularization** *n.* **secularly** *adv.* [ME (in senses 1–3 f. OF *seculer*) f. L *saecularis* f. *saeculum* generation, age]

■ *adj.* **1** worldly, terrestrial, mundane, temporal, material, lay, laic(al), nonclerical, nonecclesiastic(al), nonspiritual, nonreligious.

secund /seékund, sikúnd/ *adj.* *Bot.* arranged on one side only (as the flowers of lily of the valley). □□ **secundly** *adv.* [L *secundus* (as SECOND¹)]

secure /sikyŏor/ *adj.* & *v.* ● *adj.* **1** untroubled by danger or fear. **2** safe against attack; impregnable. **3** reliable; certain not to fail (*the plan is secure*). **4** fixed or fastened so as not to give way or get loose or be lost (*made the door secure*). **5 a** (foll. by *of*) certain to achieve (*secure of victory*). **b** (foll. by *against*, *from*) safe; protected (*secure against attack*). ● *v.tr.* **1** make secure or safe; fortify. **2** fasten, close, or confine securely. **3** succeed in obtaining or achieving (*have secured front seats*). **4** guarantee against loss (*a loan secured by property*). **5** compress (a blood vessel) to prevent bleeding. □□ **securable** *adj.* **securely** *adv.* **securement** *n.* [L *securus* (as SE-, *cura* care)]

■ *adj.* **1** untroubled, unthreatened, protected, sheltered, safe, shielded, unexposed, immune, snug, cozy. **2** safe, sheltered, shielded, protected, unexposed; impregnable. **3** reliable, safe, good, solid, healthy. **4** firm, steady, stable, fixed, fast, immovable, closed, shut, fastened, locked (up), tight, sound, solid, sturdy, strong; moored, anchored. **5 a** sure, certain, assured. **b** safe, sheltered, shielded, protected. ● *v.* **1** see FORTIFY 1. **2** fasten, close, make fast, fix, affix, attach, anchor; confine. **3** obtain, get (hold of), come by, acquire, procure, win, gain, get possession of, take possession of. **4** guarantee, underwrite.

security /sikyŏoritee/ *n.* (*pl.* **-ies**) **1** a secure condition or feeling. **2** a thing that guards or guarantees. **3 a** the safety of a nation, company, etc., against espionage, theft, or other danger. **b** an organization for ensuring this. **4** a thing deposited or pledged as a guarantee of the fulfillment of an undertaking or the payment of a loan, to be forfeited in case of default. **5** (often in *pl.*) a certificate attesting credit or the ownership of stock, bonds, etc. □ **on security of** using as a guarantee. **security blanket 1** an official sanction on information in the interest of security. **2** a blanket or other familiar object given as a comfort to a child. **Security Council** a permanent body of the United Nations seeking to maintain peace and security. **security guard** a person employed to protect the security of buildings, vehicles, etc. **security risk** a person whose presence may threaten security. [ME f. OF *securité* or L *securitas* (as SECURE)]

■ **1** confidence, certainty, assurance, conviction, safety, protection, fastness. **2** refuge, sanctuary, asylum, shelter. **3 a** safeguarding, guarding, safekeeping, protection. **4** guarantee, collateral, deposit, gage, pledge, insurance.

secy. *abbr.* secretary.

sedan /sidán/ *n.* **1** (in full **sedan chair**) an enclosed chair for conveying one person, carried between horizontal poles by two porters, common in the 17th–18th c. **2** an enclosed automobile for four or more people. [perh. alt. f. It. dial., ult. f. L *sella* saddle f. *sedēre* sit]

■ **1** see LITTER *n.* 4, 5. **2** passenger car, *Brit.* saloon (car).

sedate¹ /sidáyt/ *adj.* tranquil and dignified; equable; serious.

□□ **sedately** *adv.* **sedateness** *n.* [L *sedatus* past part. of *sedare* settle f. *sedēre* sit]

■ composed, serene, peaceful, calm, tranquil, cool, collected, even-tempered, equable, detached, imperturbable, unruffled, undisturbed, unperturbed, controlled, placid, grave, serious, sober, solemn, *colloq.* unflappable; dignified, decorous, formal, stiff, staid, proper, straitlaced, prudish, fussy, prim, conventional, old-fashioned.

sedate² /sidáyt/ *v.tr.* put under sedation. [back-form. f. SEDATION]

sedation /sidáyshən/ *n.* a state of rest or sleep, esp. produced by a sedative drug. [F *sédation* or L *sedatio* (as SEDATE¹)]

sedative /sédətiv/ *n.* & *adj.* ● *n.* a drug, influence, etc., that tends to calm or soothe. ● *adj.* calming; soothing; inducing sleep. [ME f. OF *sedatif* or med.L *sedativus* (as SEDATE¹)]

■ *n.* narcotic, tranquilizer, opiate, sleeping pill, soporific, calmative, anodyne, depressant, hypnotic, barbiturate, *Med.* lenitive, *sl.* downer, Mickey Finn; knockout drops. ● *adj.* narcotic, tranquilizing, relaxing, soothing, calming, opiate, soporific, sleep-inducing, calmative, anodyne, lenitive, depressing, hypnotic.

sedentary /séd'nteree/ *adj.* **1** sitting (*a sedentary posture*). **2** (of work, etc.) characterized by much sitting and little physical exercise. **3** (of a person) spending much time seated. **4** *Zool.* not migratory, free-swimming, etc. □□ **sedentarily** /-táirəlee/ *adv.* **sedentariness** *n.* [F *sédentaire* or L *sedentarius* f. *sedēre* sit]

■ **1** seated, sitting. **2, 3** stationary, immobile, unmoving, housebound, deskbound; seated, sitting.

Seder /sáydər/ *n.* the ritual for the first night or first two nights of the Passover. [Heb. *sēder* order]

sedge /sej/ *n.* **1** any grasslike plant of the genus *Carex* with triangular stems, usu. growing in wet areas. **2** an expanse of this plant. □□ **sedgy** *adj.* [OE *secg* f. Gmc]

sedile /sidílee/ *n.* (*pl.* **sedilia** /-díleeə/) (usu. in *pl.*) *Eccl.* each of usu. three stone seats for priests in the south wall of a chancel, often canopied and decorated. [L, = seat f. *sedēre* sit]

sediment /sédimənt/ *n.* **1** matter that settles to the bottom of a liquid; dregs. **2** *Geol.* matter that is carried by water or wind and deposited on the surface of the land, and may in time become consolidated into rock. □□ **sedimentary** /-méntəree/ *adj.* **sedimentation** /-táyshən/ *n.* [F *sédiment* or L *sedimentum* (as SEDILE)]

■ **1** lees, dregs, deposit, grounds, remains, residue, residuum, *Chem.* precipitate.

sedition /sidíshən/ *n.* **1** conduct or speech inciting to rebellion or a breach of public order. **2** agitation against the authority of a government. □□ **seditious** *adj.* **seditiously** *adv.* [ME f. OF *sedition* or L *seditio* f. *sed-* = SE- + *ire it-* go]

■ **1** agitation, rabble-rousing, insubordination; fomentation, incitement, instigation, stirring *or* whipping up. **2** agitation, mutiny, insurrection, uprising, insurgency, insurgence, rebellion; treason, treachery. □□ **seditious** rebellious, mutinous, riotous, revolutionary, insurgent, insurrectionist, insurrectionary, refractory, subversive, dissenting, insubordinate, treacherous, dissident, disloyal, turncoat, unfaithful; inflammatory, rabble-rousing, unruly, restive, factious.

seduce /sidóos, -dyóos/ *v.tr.* **1** tempt or entice into sexual activity or into wrongdoing. **2** coax or lead astray; tempt (*seduced by the smell of coffee*). □□ **seducer** *n.* **seducible** *adj.* [L *seducere seduct-* (as SE-, *ducere* lead)]

■ **1** defile, debauch, deflower, violate, ravish; vamp; dishonor, ruin, corrupt, lead astray. **2** lure, entice, attract, allure, enthrall, bewitch, tempt, mislead, beguile, inveigle, deceive, decoy, lead astray, draw on,

---

/.../ **pronunciation**	● **part of speech**
□ **phrases, idioms, and compounds**	
□□ **derivatives**	■ **synonym section**
cross-references appear in SMALL CAPITALS or *italics*	

charm, captivate, blandish, entrap, ensnare, trap, *colloq.* sweet-talk. □□ **seducer** rake, libertine, roué, debauchee, debaucher, lothario, lecher, Casanova, playboy, Don Juan, philanderer, tempter, ravisher, ladies' man, *colloq.* lady-killer, *sl.* wolf; see also SEDUCTRESS.

seduction /sidúkshən/ *n.* **1** the act or an instance of seducing; the process of being seduced. **2** something that tempts or allures. [F *séduction* or L *seductio* (as SEDUCE)]
  ■ see *enticement* (ENTICE).

seductive /sidúktiv/ *adj.* tending to seduce; alluring; enticing. □□ **seductively** *adv.* **seductiveness** *n.* [SEDUCTION after *inductive*, etc.]
  ■ alluring, attractive, tempting, enticing, inviting, seducing, enchanting, entrancing, bewitching, fascinating, captivating, beguiling, provocative, tantalizing, irresistible, winning, winsome, appealing, prepossessing, ravishing, sexy; siren; flirtatious, coquettish.

seductress /sidúktris/ *n.* a female seducer. [obs. *seductor* male seducer (as SEDUCE)]
  ■ temptress, siren, femme fatale, enchantress, Circe, coquette, Jezebel, *colloq.* vamp.

sedulous /séjələs/ *adj.* **1** persevering; diligent; assiduous. **2** (of an action, etc.) deliberately and consciously continued; painstaking. □□ **sedulity** /sidóōlitee, -dyōō-/ *n.* **sedulously** *adv.* **sedulousness** *n.* [L *sedulus* zealous]
  ■ **1** see DILIGENT. **2** see CAREFUL 1, 3. □□ **sedulity** see *exertion* (EXERT). **sedulously** see HARD *adv.* 1. **sedulousness** see *exertion* (EXERT).

sedum /séedəm/ *n.* any plant of the genus *Sedum*, with fleshy leaves and star-shaped yellow, pink, or white flowers, e.g., stonecrop. [L, = houseleek]

see¹ /see/ *v.* (*past* **saw** /saw/; *past part.* **seen** /seen/) **1** *tr.* discern by use of the eyes; observe; look at (*can you see that spider?*; *saw him fall over*). **2** *intr.* have or use the power of discerning objects with the eyes (*sees best at night*). **3** *tr.* discern mentally; understand (*I see what you mean*; *could not see the joke*). **4** *tr.* watch; be a spectator of (a motion picture, game, etc.). **5** *tr.* ascertain or establish by inquiry or research or reflection (*I will see if the door is open*). **6** *tr.* consider; deduce from observation (*I see that you are a brave man*). **7** *tr.* contemplate; foresee mentally (*we saw that no good would come of it*; *can see myself doing this job indefinitely*). **8** *tr.* look at for information (usu. in *imper.* as a direction in or to a book: *see page 15*). **9** *tr.* meet or be near and recognize (*I saw your mother in town*). **10** *tr.* **a** meet socially (*sees her sister most weeks*). **b** meet regularly as a boyfriend or girlfriend; court (*is still seeing that tall man*). **11** *tr.* give an interview to (*the doctor will see you now*). **12** *tr.* visit to consult (*went to see the doctor*). **13** *tr.* find out or learn, esp. from a visual source (*I see the match has been canceled*). **14 a** *intr.* reflect; consider further; wait until one knows more (*we shall have to see*). **b** *tr.* (foll. by *whether* or *if* + clause) consider; decide (on). **15** *tr.* interpret or have an opinion of (*I see things differently now*). **16** *tr.* experience; have presented to one's attention (*I never thought I would see this day*). **17** *tr.* recognize as acceptable; foresee (*do you see your daughter marrying this man?*). **18** *tr.* observe without interfering (*stood by and saw them squander my money*). **19** *tr.* (usu. foll. by *in*) find attractive or interesting (*can't think what she sees in him*). **20** *intr.* (usu. foll. by *to*, or *that* + infin.) make provision for; ensure; attend to (*shall see to your request immediately*; *see that he gets home safely*) (cf. *see to it*). **21** *tr.* escort or conduct (to a place, etc.) (*saw them home*). **22** *tr.* be a witness of (an event, etc.) (*see the New Year in*). **23** *tr.* supervise (an action, etc.) (*will stay and see the doors locked*). **24** *tr.* **a** (in gambling, esp. poker) equal (a bet). **b** equal the bet of (a player), esp. to see the player's cards. □ **as far as I can see** to the best of my understanding or belief. **as I see it** in my opinion. **do you see?** do you understand? **has seen better days** has declined from former prosperity, good condition, etc. **I'll be seeing you** *colloq.* an expression on parting. **I see** I understand (referring to an explanation, etc.). **let me see** an appeal for time to think before speaking, etc. **see about 1** attend to. **2**

consider; look into. **see after 1** take care of. **2** = *see about*. **see the back of** esp. *Brit. colloq.* be rid of (an unwanted person or thing). **see a person damned first** esp. *Brit. colloq.* refuse categorically and with hostility to do what a person wants. **see eye to eye** see EYE. **see fit** see FIT¹. **see here!** = *look here* (LOOK *int.*). **see into** investigate. **see life** gain experience of the world, often by enjoying oneself. **see the light 1** realize one's mistakes, etc. **2** suddenly see the way to proceed. **3** undergo religious conversion. **see the light of day** (usu. with *neg.*) come into existence. **see off 1** be present at the departure of (a person) (*saw them off at the airport*). **2** *Brit. colloq.* ward off; get the better of (*managed to see off an investigation into their working methods*). **see out 1** accompany out of a building, etc. **2** finish (a project, etc.) completely. **3** *Brit.* remain awake, alive, etc., until the end of (a period). **4** *Brit.* last longer than; outlive. **see over** *Brit.* inspect; tour and examine. **see reason** see REASON. **see red** become suddenly enraged. **see a person right** *Brit.* make sure that a person is rewarded, safe, etc. **see service** see SERVICE. **see stars** *colloq.* see lights before one's eyes as a result of a blow on the head. **see things** have hallucinations or false imaginings. **see through 1** not be deceived by; detect the true nature of. **2** penetrate visually. **see-through** *adj.* (esp. of clothing) translucent. **see a person through** support a person during a difficult time; assist financially. **see a thing through** persist with it until it is completed. **see to** = *see about*. **see to it** (foll. by *that* + clause) ensure (*see to it that I am not disturbed*) (cf. sense 20 of *v.*). **see one's way clear to** feel able or entitled to. **see the world** see WORLD. **see you** (or **see you later**) *colloq.* an expression on parting. **we shall see 1** let us await the outcome. **2** a formula for declining to act at once. **will see about it** a formula for declining to act at once. **you see 1** you understand. **2** you will understand when I explain. □□ **seeable** *adj.* [OE *sēon* f. Gmc]

  ■ **1** perceive, note, notice, mark, spot, watch, witness, discern, distinguish, observe, sight, catch sight of, spy, make out, view, glimpse, catch a glimpse of, *literary* behold, espy, descry, *sl.* get a load of. **3** understand, comprehend, apprehend, perceive, appreciate, fathom, grasp, take in, realize, know, be aware *or* conscious of, get the idea *or* meaning of, *colloq.* get, *sl.* dig, get the drift of, get the hang of. **4** attend, watch, look at, observe, view. **5** determine, ascertain, establish, find out, discover, learn; investigate, study, probe, look into, make inquiries, inquire about. **6** see PERCEIVE 2. **7, 17** contemplate, foresee, foretell, imagine, envisage, envision, visualize, picture, conceive (of). **10 a** socialize with, spend time with, keep company with, consort with, associate with. **b** court, woo, *colloq.* go out with, go steady with, date. **11** receive, meet (with), talk *or* speak to *or* with, have a word with, sit down with, (give an) interview (to); welcome, greet. **12** confer with, consult (with), talk *or* speak to *or* with, have a word with, visit, sit down with. **13** see LEARN 5. **14 a** think, reflect, decide, consider, make up one's mind; wait (and see). **b** think (about), decide (on), consider, mull over, ponder on *or* over, contemplate, reflect (on), meditate (on *or* over *or* about), ruminate (on *or* over), brood over. **15** see TAKE *v.* 18. **16** see MEET¹ *v.* 8, EXPERIENCE *v.* 1. **18** see WATCH *v.* 2b. **19** see LIKE² *v.* 1. **20** see to it, attend to, make provision for; ensure, assure, make sure *or* certain, mind. **21** accompany, escort, show, lead, conduct, usher, take, convoy, bring, walk, drive. □ **as I see it** see *to my mind* (MIND). **I'll be seeing you** see GOOD-BYE *int.* **I see** I comprehend, I understand, *colloq.* I get it, I get the drift, *Brit.* I twig. **see about 1** see to, attend to, look after, take care *or* charge of, look to, organize, manage, do, undertake, sort out. **2** consider, give some thought to, pay attention *or* heed to; investigate, study, probe, look into, make inquiries about, inquire about. **see after 1** take care of, look after; keep safe. **see the back of** see *be rid of* (RID). **see into** see INVESTIGATE. **see the light of day** see OCCUR 1. **see off 1** say *or* wave good-bye, wave (off), *archaic or literary* bid adieu *or* bon voyage. **see out 2** see COMPLETE *v.* 1. **3** last out *or* through, wait out, live through; endure. **see red** see *blow up* 6 (BLOW¹). **see through 1** penetrate, detect, perceive, *colloq.* be *or* get wise to. **see-through** sheer, diaphanous, gauzy, transparent, translucent, gossamer, filmy, peekaboo. **see a person through** help, aid, guide, shepherd, assist, support; finance, pay a person's way, sponsor; last. **see a thing through** persevere *or* persist with; *colloq.* stick (out). **see you** (or **see you later**) see GOOD-BYE *int.*

see² /see/ *n.* **1** the area under the authority of a bishop or archbishop, a diocese (*the see of Norwich*). **2** the office or jurisdiction of a bishop or archbishop (*fill a vacant see*). □ **See of Rome** the papacy, the Holy See. [ME f. AF *se(d)* ult. f. L *sedes* seat f. *sedēre* sit]

seed /seed/ *n. & v.* ● *n.* **1 a** a flowering plant's unit of reproduction (esp. in the form of grain) capable of developing into another such plant. **b** seeds collectively, esp. as collected for sowing (*is full of seed; to be kept for seed*). **2 a** semen. **b** milt. **3** (foll. by *of*) prime cause; beginning; germ (*seeds of doubt*). **4** *archaic* offspring; progeny; descendants (*the seed of Abraham*). **5** *Sports* a seeded player. **6** a small seedlike container for the application of radium, etc. **7** a seed crystal. ● *v.* **1** *tr.* **a** place seeds in. **b** sprinkle with or as with seed. **2** *intr.* sow seeds. **3** *intr.* produce or drop seed. **4** *tr.* remove seeds from (fruit, etc.). **5** *tr.* place a crystal or crystalline substance in (a solution, etc.) to cause crystallization or condensation (in a cloud to produce rain). **6** *tr. Sports* **a** assign to (a strong competitor in a knockout competition) a position in an ordered list so that strong competitors do not meet each other in early rounds (*is seeded seventh*). **b** arrange (the order of play) in this way. **7** *intr.* go to seed. □ **go** (or **run**) **to seed 1** cease flowering as seed develops. **2** become degenerate; unkempt; ineffective, etc. **raise up seed** *archaic* beget children. **seed coat** the outer integument of a seed. **seed corn 1** good quality corn kept for seed. **2** *Brit.* assets reused for future profit or benefit. **seed crystal** a crystal used to initiate crystallization. **seed leaf** a cotyledon. **seed money** money allocated to initiate a project. **seed pearl** a very small pearl. **seed plot** a place of development. **seed potato** a potato kept for seed. **seed vessel** a pericarp. □□ **seedless** *adj.* [OE *sǣd* f. Gmc, rel. to SOW¹]

■ *n.* **1** grain, spore, kernel, pit, bulb, ovum, ovule, germ, *Biol.* egg. **2** semen, spermatozoa, sperm; milt, (soft) roe. **3** germ, beginning, root, origin, cause; reason, basis, source; grounds. **4** offspring, children, progeny, young, descendants, heirs, successors, *Law* issue. ● *v.* **1** sow, plant. **4** stone, pit. □ **go** (or **run**) **to seed 2** become dilapidated *or* worn out *or* shabby *or* seedy *or* run down, decay, decline, degenerate, deteriorate, go to rack and ruin, *colloq.* go downhill, go to pot. **raise up seed** see REPRODUCE 3.

seedbed /seedbed/ *n.* **1** a bed of fine soil in which to sow seeds. **2** a place of development.

seedcake /seedkayk/ *n.* cake containing whole seeds esp. of sesame or caraway as flavoring.

seedeater /seedeetər/ *n.* a bird (esp. a finch) living mainly on seeds.

seeder /seedər/ *n.* **1** a person or thing that seeds. **2** a machine for sowing seed, esp. a drill. **3** an apparatus for seeding raisins, etc. **4** *Brit.* a spawning fish.

seedling /seedling/ *n.* a young plant, esp. one raised from seed and not from a cutting, etc.

seedsman /seedzmən/ *n.* (*pl.* -**men**) a dealer in seeds.

seedtime /seedtim/ *n.* the sowing season.

seedy /seedee/ *adj.* (**seedier, seediest**) **1** full of seed. **2** going to seed. **3** shabby looking; in worn clothes. **4** *colloq.* unwell. □□ **seedily** *adv.* **seediness** *n.*

■ **3** shabby, dilapidated, worn (out), mangy, grubby, scruffy, *colloq.* tatty; run-down, broken-down, decaying, squalid, sleazy, *colloq.* ratty. **4** unwell, out of sorts, poorly, *colloq.* under the weather; ailing, ill, sickly.

seeing /seeing/ *conj. & v.* ● *conj.* (usu. foll. by *that* + clause)

considering that; inasmuch as; because (*seeing that you do not know it yourself*). ● *n. Astron.* the quality of observed images as determined by atmospheric conditions.

■ *conj.* in view of (the fact that), whereas, in the light of, inasmuch as, since, considering that, because, in light of.

seek /seek/ *v.* (*past* and *past part.* **sought** /sawt/) **1** *tr.* make a search or inquiry for. **b** *intr.* (foll. by *for, after*) make a search or inquiry. **2** *tr.* **a** try or want to find or get. **b** ask for; request (*sought help from him; seeks my aid*). **3** *tr.* (foll. by *to* + infin.) endeavor or try. **4** *tr.* make for or resort to (a place or person, for advice, health, etc.) (*sought his bed; sought a fortune-teller; sought the shore*). **5** *tr. archaic* aim at; attempt. **6** *intr.* (foll. by *to*) *archaic* resort. □ **seek dead** an order to a retriever to find killed game. **seek out 1** search for and find. **2** single out for companionship, etc. **sought-after** much in demand; generally desired or courted. **to seek** (or **much to seek** or **far to seek**) esp. *Brit.* deficient, lacking, or not yet found (*the reason is not far to seek; an efficient leader is yet to seek*). □□ **seeker** *n.* (also in *comb.*). [OE *sēcan* f. Gmc]

■ **1a, 2a** look for, be after, search for, hunt (for), quest for *or* after, pursue. **2 b** ask for, request, beg, solicit, invite; demand. **3** attempt, try, endeavor, undertake, hope, aim, aspire. **4** see *take* to 5. **5** attempt, aim at, contrive, plot. □ **seek out 1** see DISCOVER 1a, b. **to seek** (or **much to seek** or **far to seek**) see ELUSIVE 1.

seel /seel/ *v.tr.* **1** *Falconry* sew shut a falcon's eyelids during its training. **2** *archaic* close (a person's eyes). [obs. *sile* f. F *ciller, siller,* or med.L *ciliare* f. L *cilium* eyelid]

seem /seem/ *v.intr.* **1** give the impression or sensation of being (*seems ridiculous; seems certain to win*). **2** (foll. by *to* + infin.) appear or be perceived or ascertained (*he seems to be breathing; they seem to have left*). □ **can't seem to** *colloq.* seem unable to. **do not seem to** *colloq.* somehow do not (*I do not seem to like him*). **it seems** (or **would seem**) (often foll. by *that* + clause) it appears to be true or the fact (in a hesitant, guarded, or ironical statement). [ME f. ON *sǣma* honor f. *sǿmr* fitting]

■ **1** appear, look; sound, feel, have (all) the hallmarks *or* earmarks of, give every indication *or* appearance of (being). **2** appear, look; see also FEEL *v.* 7. □ **it seems** (or **would seem**) it appears, it would appear.

seeming¹ /seeming/ *adj.* **1** apparent but perhaps not real (*with seeming sincerity*). **2** apparent only; ostensible (*the seeming and the real; seeming virtuous*). □□ **seemingly** *adv.*

■ **1** see APPARENT 2, OUTWARD 1, 3. **2** apparent; ostensible, superficial, surface, assumed, feigned, pretended, false, so-called, specious, alleged, purported, professed. □ **seemingly** evidently; apparently, outwardly, ostensibly, superficially, falsely, allegedly, speciously, on the face of it, purportedly, professedly.

seeming² /seeming/ *n. literary* **1** appearance; aspect. **2** deceptive appearance.

seemly /seemlee/ *adj.* (**seemlier, seemliest**) conforming to propriety or good taste; decorous; suitable. □□ **seemliness** *n.* [ME f. ON *sǿmiligr* (as SEEM)]

■ proper, fitting, appropriate, becoming, suitable, fit, befitting, apt, right, apropos, apposite, *archaic* meet; *comme il faut*; decent, decorous, dignified, genteel, gentlemanly, ladylike, diplomatic, discreet, prudent, sensible, reasonable, politic.

seen *past part.* of SEE¹.

seep /seep/ *v. & n.* ● *v.intr.* ooze out; percolate slowly. ● *n.* a place where petroleum, etc. oozes slowly out of the ground. [perh. dial. form of OE *sipian* to soak]

■ *v.* see OOZE¹ *v.*

/. . ./ **pronunciation**	● **part of speech**
□ **phrases, idioms, and compounds**	
□□ **derivatives**	■ **synonym section**
cross-references appear in SMALL CAPITALS or *italics*	

seepage /séepij/ *n.* **1** the act of seeping. **2** the quantity that seeps out.
- ■ see LEAK *n.* 1b, c.

seer[1] /séeər, seer/ *n.* **1** a person who sees. **2** a prophet; a person who sees visions; a person of supposed supernatural insight esp. as regards the future. [ME f. SEE[1]]
- ■ **2** soothsayer, fortune-teller, oracle, augur, prophesier, clairvoyant, psychic, crystal gazer, *usu. derog. or joc.* stargazer, *formal* vaticinator; sibyl, prophetess; prophet.

seer[2] /seer/ *n.* an E. Indian (varying) measure of weight (about two pounds) or liquid measure (about one quart). [Hindi *ser*]

seersucker /séersukər/ *n.* material of linen, cotton, etc., with a puckered surface. [Pers. *šir o šakar*, lit. 'milk and sugar']

seesaw /séesaw/ *n., v., adj., & adv.* ● *n.* **1 a** a device consisting of a long plank balanced on a central support for children to sit on at each end and move up and down by pushing the ground with their feet. **b** a game played on this. **2** an up-and-down or to-and-fro motion. **3** a contest in which the advantage repeatedly changes from one side to the other. ● *v.intr.* **1** play on a seesaw. **2** move up and down as on a seesaw. **3** vacillate in policy, emotion, etc. ● *adj. & adv.* with up-and-down or backward-and-forward motion (*seesaw motion*). □ **go seesaw** vacillate or alternate. [redupl. of SAW[1]]
- ■ *v.* **3** teeter, totter, waver, vary, vacillate, oscillate, alternate, fluctuate, swing, switch. □ **go seesaw** vacillate, alternate; see also OSCILLATE.

seethe /seeth/ *v.* **1** *intr.* boil; bubble over. **2** *intr.* be very agitated, esp. with anger (*seething with discontent; I was seething inwardly*). **3** *tr. & intr. archaic* cook by boiling. □□ **seethingly** *adv.* [OE *sēothan* f. Gmc]
- ■ **1** boil, simmer, foam, bubble (over). **2** foam at the mouth, fume, burn with anger, rage, rant (and rave), be furious *or* incensed *or* livid, get hot under the collar, get up steam, *colloq.* take on, get red in the face, get (all) steamed up; simmer, smolder.

segment /ségmənt/ *n. & v.* ● *n.* **1** each of several parts into which a thing is or can be divided or marked off. **2** *Geom.* a part of a figure cut off by a line or plane intersecting it, esp.: **a** the part of a circle enclosed between an arc and a chord. **b** the part of a line included between two points. **c** the part of a sphere cut off by any plane not passing through the center. **3** the smallest distinct part of a spoken utterance. **4** *Zool.* each of the longitudinal sections of the body of certain animals (e.g., worms). ● *v. /usu.* -mént/ **1** *intr. & tr.* divide into segments. **2** *intr. Biol.* (of a cell) undergo cleavage or divide into many cells. □□ **segmental** /-mént'l/ *adj.* **segmentalize** /-mént'liz/ *v.tr.* **segmentalization** *n.* **segmentally** /-mént'lee/ *adv.* **segmentary** /ségməntairee/ *adj.* **segmentation** /-táyshən/ *n.* [L *segmentum* f. *secare* cut]
- ■ *n.* **1** section, part, division, portion, piece, fraction, fragment, slice, wedge; component, element. ● *v.* divide, separate, part, split, subdivide, fragment, *literary* cleave; partition, section.

sego /séegō/ *n.* (*pl.* **-os**) (in full **sego lily**) a N. American plant, *Calochortus nuttallii*, with green and white bell-shaped flowers. [Paiute]

segregate[1] /ségrigayt/ *v.* **1** *tr.* put apart from the rest; isolate. **2** *tr.* enforce racial segregation on (persons) or in (a community, etc.). **3** *intr.* separate from a mass and collect together. **4** *intr. Biol.* (of alleles) separate into dominant and recessive groups. □□ **segregable** /-gəbəl/ *adj.* **segregative** *adj.* [L *segregare* (as SE-, *grex gregis* flock)]
- ■ **1** partition, seclude, sequester, set apart, compartmentalize, exclude, isolate, ostracize. **3** separate, segment; see also COLLECT[1] *v.* 1.

segregate[2] /ségrigət, -gayt/ *adj.* **1** *Zool.* simple or solitary; not compound. **2** *archaic* set apart; separate. [L *segregatus* past part. (as SEGREGATE[1])]

segregation /ségrigáyshən/ *n.* **1** enforced separation of racial groups in a community, etc. **2** the act or an instance of segregating; the state of being segregated. □□ **segregational** *adj.* **segregationist** *n. & adj.* [LL *segregatio* (as SEGREGATE[1])]
- ■ **1** jim crowism, apartheid. **2** separation, segmentation,

partition, seclusion, isolation, sequestration, setting apart, compartmentalization, exclusion; ostracism.

segue /ségway/ *v. & n.* esp. *Mus.* ● *v.intr.* (**segues, segued, segueing**) (usu. foll. by *into*) go on without a pause. ● *n.* an uninterrupted transition from one song or melody to another. [It., = follows]

seguidilla /ségidílyə, -déeyə/ *n.* **1** a Spanish dance in triple time. **2** the music for this. [Sp. f. *seguida* following f. *seguir* follow]

sei /say/ *n.* a small rorqual, *Balaenoptera borealis*. [Norw. *sejhval* sei whale]

seicento /saychéntō/ *n.* the style of Italian art and literature of the 17th c. □□ **seicentist** *n.* **seicentoist** *n.* [It., = 600, used with ref. to the years 1600–99]

seiche /saysh/ *n.* a fluctuation in the water level of a lake, etc., usu. caused by changes in barometric pressure. [Swiss F]

Seidlitz powders /sédlits/ *n.* a laxative medicine of two powders mixed separately with water and then poured together to effervesce. [named with ref. to the mineral water of *Seidlitz* in Bohemia]

seif /seef, sayf/ *n.* (in full **seif dune**) a sand dune in the form of a long narrow ridge. [Arab. *saif* sword (from its shape)]

seigneur /saynyőr/ *n.* (also **seignior** /sáynyawr/) a feudal lord; the lord of a manor. □ **grand seigneur** /groN/ a person of high rank or noble presence. □□ **seigneurial** *adj.* **seigniorial** /-nyáwreeəl/ *adj.* [ME f. OF *seigneur, seignor* f. L SENIOR]

seigniorage /sáynyərij/ *n.* (also **seignorage**) **1 a** a profit made by issuing currency, esp. by issuing coins rated above their intrinsic value. **b** *hist.* a sovereign's right to a percentage on bullion brought to a mint for coining. **2** *hist.* something claimed by a sovereign or feudal superior as a prerogative. [ME f. OF *seignorage, seigneurage* (as SEIGNEUR)]

seigniory /sáynyəree/ *n.* (*pl.* **-ies**) **1** lordship; sovereign authority. **2** (also **seigneury**) a seigneur's domain. [ME f. OF *seignorie* (as SEIGNEUR)]

seine /sayn/ *n. & v.* ● *n.* a fishing net for encircling fish, with floats at the top and weights at the bottom edge, and usu. hauled ashore. ● *v.intr. & tr.* fish or catch with a seine. □□ **seiner** *n.* [ME f. OF *saïne*, & OE *segne* f. WG f. L *sagena* f. Gk *sagēnē*]

seise var. of SEIZE 9.

seisin /séezin/ *n.* (also **seizin**) *Law* **1** possession of land by freehold. **2** the act of taking such possession. **3** what is so held. [ME f. AF *sesine*, OF *seisine, saisine* (as SEIZE)]

seismic /sízmik/ *adj.* of or relating to an earthquake or earthquakes. □□ **seismal** *adj.* **seismical** *adj.* **seismically** *adv.* [Gk *seismos* earthquake f. *seiō* shake]

seismo- /sízmō/ *comb. form* earthquake. [Gk *seismos*]

seismogram /sízməgram/ *n.* a record given by a seismograph.

seismograph /sízməgraf/ *n.* an instrument that records the force, direction, etc., of earthquakes. □□ **seismographic** *adj.* **seismographical** *adj.*

seismology /sízmóləjee/ *n.* the scientific study and recording of earthquakes and related phenomena. □□ **seismological** /-məlójikəl/ *adj.* **seismologically** /-lójiklee/ *adv.* **seismologist** *n.*

seize /seez/ *v.* **1** *tr.* take hold of forcibly or suddenly. **2** *tr.* take possession of forcibly (*seized the fortress; seized power*). **3** *tr.* **a** take possession of (contraband goods, documents, etc.) by warrant or legal right; confiscate; impound. **b** arrest or apprehend (a person); take prisoner. **4** *tr.* affect suddenly (*panic seized us; was seized by apoplexy; was seized with remorse*). **5** *tr.* take advantage of (an opportunity). **6** *tr.* comprehend quickly or clearly. **7** *intr.* (usu. foll. by *on, upon*) **a** take hold forcibly or suddenly. **b** take advantage eagerly (*seized on a pretext*). **8** *intr.* (usu. foll. by *up*) (of a moving part in a machine) become stuck or jammed from undue heat, friction, etc. **9** *tr.* (also seise) (usu. foll. by *of*) *Law* put in possession of. **10** *tr. Naut.* fasten or attach by binding with turns of yarn, etc. □ **seized** (or **seised**) **of 1** possessing legally. **2** aware or informed of. □□ **seizable** *adj.* **seizer** *n.* [ME f. OF *seizir, saisir* give seisin f. Frank. f. L *sacire* f. Gmc]

■ **1** grab, grasp, clutch, grip, snatch. **2** capture, take, appropriate, commandeer; see also GRAB v. 2. **3 a** confiscate, take (away), capture, take possession of, impound. **b** capture, catch, arrest, take into custody, apprehend, round up, collar, pick up, *colloq.* bust, *sl.* pinch, nab, *Brit. sl.* nick. **4** catch, transfix, stop, hold, possess, take possession of, afflict, beset, visit. **5** take advantage of, make the most of, make good use of, exploit. **6** see REALIZE 2. **8** jam, stop, lock (up), stick, freeze (up). □ **seized of 2** see AWARE 1.

seizin var. of SEISIN.

seizing /seézing/ n. *Naut.* a cord or cords used for seizing (see SEIZE 10).

seizure /seézhər/ n. **1** the act or an instance of seizing; the state of being seized. **2** a sudden attack of apoplexy, etc.; a stroke.

■ **1** seizing, confiscating, confiscation, impounding, capture, taking, possession; annexation, appropriation, commandeering, usurpation. **2** spasm, attack, fit, paroxysm, convulsion, *Med.* ictus; stroke.

sejant /seéjənt/ adj. (placed after noun) *Heraldry* (of an animal) sitting upright on its haunches. [properly *seiant* f. OF var. of *seant* sitting f. *seoir* f. L *sedēre* sit]

Sekt /zekt/ n. a German sparkling white wine. [G]

selachian /siláykeeən/ n. & adj. ● n. any fish of the subclass Selachii, including sharks and dogfish. ● adj. of or relating to this subclass. [mod.L *Selachii* f. Gk *selakhos* shark]

seladang /səláadaang/ n. a Malayan gaur. [Malay]

selah /seélə, sélə/ int. often used at the end of a verse in Psalms and Habakkuk, supposed to be a musical direction. [Heb. *se'lāh*]

seldom /séldəm/ adv. & adj. ● adv. rarely; not often. ● adj. rare; uncommon. [OE *seldan* f. Gmc]

■ *adv.* rarely, infrequently, not often, hardly ever, very occasionally. ● *adj.* see RARE 1.

select /silékt/ v. & adj. ● v.tr. choose, esp. as the best or most suitable. ● adj. **1** chosen for excellence or suitability; choice. **2** (of a society, etc.) exclusive; cautious in admitting members. □ **select committee** see COMMITTEE. □□ **selectable** adj. **selectness** n. [L *seligere select-* (as SE-, *legere* choose)]

■ *v.* choose, pick, show (a) preference for, prefer, opt for, single out, handpick. ● *adj.* **1** selected, chosen, handpicked, choice, special, preferred, favored, favorite, exceptional, excellent, first-rate, first-class, superior, supreme, prime, best, finest, *colloq.* tiptop. **2** privileged, elite, closed; see also EXCLUSIVE *adj.* 3, 4.

selectee /siléktee/ n. one drafted for service in the armed forces.

selection /silékshən/ n. **1** the act or an instance of selecting; the state of being selected. **2** a selected person or thing. **3** things from which a choice may be made. **4** *Biol.* the process in which environmental and genetic influences determine which types of organism thrive better than others, regarded as a factor in evolution. □□ **selectional** adj. **selectionally** adv. [L *selectio* (as SELECT)]

■ **1** selecting, choosing, picking, singling out; electing, voting; election. **2** choice, pick, preference, option. **3** assortment, variety, collection, range, batch, number, set, series, group.

selective /siléktiv/ adj. **1** using or characterized by selection. **2** able to select, esp. (of a radio receiver) able to respond to a chosen frequency without interference from others. □ **selective service** service in the armed forces under conscription. □□ **selectively** adv. **selectiveness** n. **selectivity** /silektívitee, sél-, seél-/ n.

■ **1** particular, discerning, discriminative, discriminating, discriminatory, exacting, demanding, *colloq.* choosy, picky.

selector /siléktər/ n. **1** a person who selects, esp. one who selects a representative team in a sport. **2** a device that selects, esp. a device in a vehicle that selects the required gear.

selenite /sélinīt/ n. a form of gypsum occurring as transparent crystals or thin plates. □□ **selenitic** /-nítik/ adj. [L *selenites* f. Gk *selēnītēs lithos* moonstone f. *selēnē* moon]

selenium /sileéneeəm/ n. *Chem.* a nonmetallic element occurring naturally in various metallic sulfide ores and characterized by the variation of its electrical resistivity with intensity of illumination. ¶ Symb.: **Se**. □ **selenium cell** a piece of this used as a photoelectric device. □□ **selenate** /sélinayt/ n. **selenic** /sileénik/ adj. **selenious** adj. [mod.L f. Gk *selēnē* moon + -IUM]

seleno- /sileénō/ comb. form moon. [Gk *selēnē* moon]

selenography /seélinógrəfee/ n. the study or mapping of the moon. □□ **selenographer** n. **selenographic** /-nəgráfik/ adj.

selenology /seélinóləjee/ n. the scientific study of the moon. □□ **selenologist** n.

self /self/ n. & adj. ● n. (pl. **selves** /selvz/) **1** a person's or thing's own individuality or essence (*showed his true self*). **2** a person or thing as the object of introspection or reflexive action (*the consciousness of self*). **3 a** one's own interests or pleasure (*cares for nothing but self*). **b** concentration on these (*self is a bad guide to happiness*). **4** *Commerce* or *colloq.* myself, yourself, himself, etc. (*check drawn to self; ticket admitting self and friend*). **5** used in phrases equivalent to *myself, yourself, himself*, etc. (*his very self; your good selves*). **6** (pl. **selfs**) a flower of uniform color, or of the natural wild color. ● adj. **1** of the same color as the rest or throughout. **2** (of a flower) of the natural wild color. **3** (of color) uniform, the same throughout. □ **one's better self** one's nobler impulses. **one's former** (or **old**) **self** oneself as one formerly was. [OE f. Gmc]

■ *n.* **1** see IDENTITY 1.

self- /self/ comb. form expressing reflexive action: **1** of or directed toward oneself or itself (*self-respect; self-cleaning*). **2** by oneself or itself, esp. without external agency (*self-evident*). **3** on, in, for, or relating to oneself or itself (*self-absorbed; self-confident*).

self-abandon /sélfəbándən/ n. (also **self-abandonment**) the abandonment of oneself, esp. to passion or an impulse. □□ **self-abandoned** adj.

self-abasement /sélfəbáysmənt/ n. the abasement of oneself; self-humiliation; cringing.

■ see HUMILITY 1.

self-abhorrence /sélfəbháwrəns, -hór-/ n. the abhorrence of oneself; self-hatred.

self-abnegation /sélfábnigáyshən/ n. the abnegation of oneself, one's interests, needs, etc.; self-sacrifice.

self-absorption /sélfəbsáwrpshən, -záwrp-/ n. **1** absorption in oneself. **2** *Physics* the absorption, by a body, of radiation emitted within it. □□ **self-absorbed** /-sáwrbd, -záwrbd/ adj.

■ □□ **self-absorbed** see *egoistic* (EGOISM).

self-abuse /sélfəbyoós/ n. **1** the reviling or abuse of oneself. **2** masturbation.

■ **1** self-deprecation, self-hatred; masochism. **2** see *masturbation* (MASTURBATE).

self-accusation /sélfákyoózáyshən/ n. the accusing of oneself. □□ **self-accusatory** /-əkyoózətáwree/ adj.

self-acting /sélfákting/ adj. acting without external influence or control; automatic. □□ **self-action** /-ákshən/ n. **self-activity** /-aktívitee/ n.

■ see AUTOMATIC *adj.* 1.

self-addressed /sélfədrést/ adj. (of an envelope, etc.) having one's own address on for return communication.

self-adhesive /sélfədheésiv/ adj. (of an envelope, label, etc.) adhesive, esp. without being moistened.

self-adjusting /sélfəjústing/ adj. (of machinery, etc.) adjusting itself. □□ **self-adjustment** n.

self-admiration /sélfádməráyshən/ n. the admiration of oneself; pride; conceit.

■ see CONCEIT 1.

self-advancement /sélfədvánsmənt/ n. the advancement of oneself.

self-advertisement /sélfádvərtízmənt, -ədvórtiz-/ n. the

/. . ./ **pronunciation**	● **part of speech**
□ **phrases, idioms, and compounds**	
□□ **derivatives**	■ **synonym section**
cross-references appear in SMALL CAPITALS or *italics*	

advertising or promotion of oneself. □□ **self-advertiser** /-ádvərtizər/ *n.*

self-affirmation /sélfáfərmáyshən/ *n. Psychol.* the recognition and assertion of the existence of the conscious self.

self-aggrandizement /sélfəgrándizmənt/ *n.* the act or process of enriching oneself or making oneself powerful. □□ **self-aggrandizing** /-gránd izing/ *adj.*

self-analysis /sélfənálisis/ *n. Psychol.* the analysis of oneself, one's motives, character, etc. □□ **self-analyzing** /-ánelizing/ *adj.*

self-appointed /sélfəpóyntid/ *adj.* designated so by oneself; not authorized by another (*a self-appointed guardian*).
■ see SELF-STYLED.

self-appreciation /sélfəpreesheeáyshən/ *n.* a good opinion of oneself; conceit.

self-approbation /sélfáprəbáyshən/ *n.* = SELF-APPRECIATION.

self-approval /sélfəproovəl/ *n.* = SELF-APPRECIATION.

self-assembly /sélfəsémblee/ *n.* (often *attrib.*) construction (of furniture, etc.) from materials sold in kit form.

self-assertion /sélfəsŕshən/ *n.* the aggressive promotion of oneself, one's views, etc. □□ **self-asserting** *adj.* **self-assertive** *adj.* **self-assertiveness** *n.*
■ see *arrogance* (ARROGANT). □□ **self-assertive** see ARROGANT.

self-assurance /sélfəshoorəns/ *n.* confidence in one's own abilities, etc. □□ **self-assured** *adj.* **self-assuredly** *adv.*
■ confidence, self-confidence, self-respect, self-esteem, assurance, poise, aplomb, self-reliance, self-sufficiency. □□ **self-assured** confident, self-confident, assured, poised, self-reliant, secure, positive, definite, assertive, independent; sure of oneself; self-collected.

self-aware /sélfəwáir/ *adj.* conscious of one's character, feelings, motives, etc. □□ **self-awareness** *n.*

self-begotten /sélfbigót'n/ *adj.* produced by oneself or itself; not made externally.

self-betrayal /sélfbitráyəl/ *n.* **1** the betrayal of oneself. **2** the inadvertent revelation of one's true thoughts, etc.

self-binder /sélfbíndər/ *n.* a reaping machine with an automatic mechanism for binding the sheaves.

self-born /sélfbáwrn/ *adj.* produced by itself or oneself; not made externally.

self-catering /sélfkáytəring/ *adj. Brit.* (esp. of a vacation or vacation premises) providing rented accommodations but without food.

self-censorship /sélfsénsərship/ *n.* the censoring of oneself.

self-centered /sélfséntərd/ *adj.* preoccupied with one's own personality or affairs. □□ **self-centeredly** *adv.* **self-centeredness** *n.*
■ see SELFISH. □□ **self-centeredness** see SELF-ESTEEM 2.

self-cleaning /sélfkleening/ *adj.* (esp. of an oven) cleaning itself when heated, etc.

self-closing /sélfklozing/ *adj.* (of a door, etc.) closing automatically.

self-cocking /sélfkóking/ *adj.* (of a gun) with the hammer raised by the trigger, not by hand.

self-collected /sélfkəléktid/ *adj.* composed; serene; self-assured.

self-colored /sélfkúlərd/ *adj.* **1 a** having the same color throughout (*buttons and belt are self-colored*). **b** (of material) natural; undyed. **2 a** (of a flower) of uniform color. **b** having its color unchanged by cultivation or hybridization.

self-command /sélfkəmánd/ *n.* = SELF-CONTROL.

self-communion /sélfkəmyoonyən/ *n.* meditation upon one's own character, conduct, etc.

self-conceit /sélfkənseét/ *n.* = SELF-SATISFACTION. □□ **self-conceited** *adj.*

self-condemnation /sélfkóndemnáyshən/ *n.* **1** the blaming of oneself. **2** the inadvertent revelation of one's own sin, crime, etc. □□ **self-condemned** /-kəndémd/ *adj.*
■ **1** self-reproach, self-accusation.

self-confessed /sélfkənfést/ *adj.* openly admitting oneself to be (*a self-confessed thief*).

self-confidence /sélfkónfidəns/ *n.* = SELF-ASSURANCE. □□ **self-confident** *adj.* **self-confidently** *adv.*

self-congratulation /sélfkəngráchəláyshən, -gráj-, -kəng-/

n. = SELF-SATISFACTION. □□ **self-congratulatory** /-kəngrátyoolətáwree/ *adj.*

self-conquest /sélfkóngkwest/ *n.* the overcoming of one's worst characteristics, etc.

self-conscious /sélfkónshəs/ *adj.* **1** socially inept through embarrassment or shyness. **2** *Philos.* having knowledge of one's own existence; self-contemplating. □□ **self-consciously** *adv.* **self-consciousness** *n.*
■ **1** embarrassed, coy, diffident, shy, self-effacing, sheepish, shrinking, retiring, unsure, apprehensive, reserved, insecure, affected, awkward, nervous, uncomfortable, hesitant, timid, timorous.

self-consistent /sélfkənsístənt/ *adj.* (of parts of the same whole, etc.) consistent; not conflicting. □□ **self-consistency** *n.*

self-constituted /sélfkónstitootid -tyoo-/ *adj.* (of a person, group, etc.) assuming a function without authorization or right; self-appointed.

self-contained /sélfkəntáynd/ *adj.* **1** (of a person) uncommunicative or reserved; independent, self-possessed. **2** *Brit.* (esp. of living-accommodation) complete in itself. □□ **self-containment** *n.*
■ **1** uncommunicative, reserved, distant, aloof, withdrawn, reticent, standoffish; self-possessed, unemotional, self-controlled, self-collected, composed, serene, peaceful, calm, tranquil, cool, collected, even-tempered, detached, imperturbable, unruffled, undisturbed, unperturbed, controlled, placid, grave, serious, sober, solemn, *colloq.* unflappable; in control. **2** whole, entire, complete.

self-contempt /sélfkəntémpt/ *n.* contempt for oneself. □□ **self-contemptuous** *adj.*

self-content /sélfkəntént/ *n.* satisfaction with oneself, one's life, achievements, etc. □□ **self-contented** *adj.*

self-contradiction /sélfkóntrədíkshən/ *n.* internal inconsistency. □□ **self-contradictory** *adj.*
■ see PARADOX. □□ **self-contradictory** see PARADOXICAL.

self-control /sélfkəntról/ *n.* the power of controlling one's external reactions, emotions, etc.; equanimity. □□ **self-controlled** *adj.*
■ self-discipline, self-restraint, restraint, forbearance, self-denial, control, willpower, strength (of character *or* of mind *or* of will), mettle, fortitude, moral fiber, self-possession, determination, resoluteness, resolve, will; poise, balance, equilibrium, levelheadedness, calmness, tranquillity, serenity, placidity, imperturbability, coolheadedness, coolness, patience, composure, aplomb, dignity, equanimity, forbearance, even temper.

self-convicted /sélfkənvíktid/ *adj.* = *self-condemned* (see SELF-CONDEMNATION).

self-correcting /sélfkərékting/ *adj.* correcting oneself or itself without external help.

self-created /sélfkreeáytid/ *adj.* created by oneself or itself. □□ **self-creation** /-áyshən/ *n.*

self-critical /sélfkrítikəl/ *adj.* critical of oneself, one's abilities, etc. □□ **self-criticism** /-tisizəm/ *n.*

self-deception /sélfdisépshən/ *n.* deceiving oneself esp. concerning one's true feelings, etc. □□ **self-deceit** /-diseét/ *n.* **self-deceiver** /-diseévər/ *n.* **self-deceiving** /-diseéving/ *adj.* **self-deceptive** *adj.*

self-defeating /sélfdifeéting/ *adj.* (of an attempt, action, etc.) doomed to failure because of internal inconsistencies, etc.

self-defense /sélfdiféns/ *n.* **1** an aggressive act, speech, etc., intended as defense (*had to hit him in self-defense*). **2** (usu. **the noble art of self-defense**) boxing. □□ **self-defensive** *adj.*

self-delight /sélfdilít/ *n.* delight in oneself or one's existence.

self-delusion /sélfdiloozhən/ *n.* the act or an instance of deluding oneself.

self-denial /sélfdiníəl/ *n.* the negation of one's interests, needs, or wishes, esp. in favor of those of others; self-control; forbearance. □ **self-denying ordinance** *hist.* a resolution of the Long Parliament 1645 depriving members of Parliament of civil and military office. □□ **self-denying** *adj.*

■ self-sacrifice, self-abnegation, renunciation, selflessness, altruism, unselfishness, magnanimity, self-mortification, asceticism, privation, renunciation, temperance, sobriety, moderation, abstemiousness, abstinence, abstention, self-deprivation, refusal, giving up, desisting, *colloq.* swearing off; see also SELF-CONTROL.

self-dependence /sélfdipéndəns/ *adj.* dependence only on oneself or itself; independence. □□ **self-dependent** *adj.*

self-deprecation /sélfdéprikáyshən/ *n.* the act of disparaging or belittling oneself. □□ **self-deprecating** /-kayting/ *adj.* **self-deprecatingly** *adv.*

self-despair /sélfdispáir/ *n.* despair with oneself.

self-destroying /sélfdistróying/ *adj.* destroying oneself or itself.

self-destruct /sélfdistrúkt/ *v. & adj.* ● *v.intr.* (of a spacecraft, bomb, etc.) explode or disintegrate automatically, esp. when preset to do so. ● *attrib.adj.* enabling a thing to self-destruct (*a self-destruct device*).

self-destruction /sélfdistrúkshən/ *n.* **1** the process or an act of destroying oneself or itself. **2** the process or an act of self-destructing. □□ **self-destructive** *adj.* **self-destructively** *adv.*

self-determination /sélfditərmináyshən/ *n.* **1** a nation's right to determine its own allegiance, government, etc. **2** the ability to act with free will, as opposed to fatalism, etc. □□ **self-determined** /-términd/ *adj.* **self-determining** /-términing/ *adj.*

■ **1** see SELF-GOVERNMENT.

self-development /sélfdivéləpmənt/ *n.* the development of oneself, one's abilities, etc.

self-devotion /sélfdivóshən/ *n.* the devotion of oneself to a person or cause.

self-discipline /sélfdísiplin/ *n.* the act of or ability to apply oneself, control one's feelings, etc.; self-control. □□ **self-disciplined** *adj.*

■ see SELF-CONTROL.

self-discovery /sélfdiskúvəree/ *n.* the process of acquiring insight into oneself, one's character, desires, etc.

self-disgust /sélfdisgúst/ *n.* disgust with oneself.

self-doubt /sélfdówt/ *n.* lack of confidence in oneself, one's abilities, etc.

self-drive /sélfdrív/ *adj. Brit.* (of a rented vehicle) driven by the renter.

self-educated /sélféjəkaytid/ *adj.* educated by oneself by reading, etc., without formal instruction. □□ **self-education** /-káyshən/ *n.*

self-effacing /sélfifáysing/ *adj.* retiring; modest; timid. □□ **self-effacement** *n.* **self-effacingly** *adv.*

■ see RETIRING. □□ **self-effacement** see HUMILITY 1.

self-elective /sélfiléktiv/ *adj. Brit.* (of a committee, etc.) proceeding esp. by coopting members, etc.

self-employed /sélfimplóyd/ *adj.* working for oneself, as a freelance or owner of a business, etc.; not employed by an employer. □□ **self-employment** *n.*

self-esteem /sélfistéem/ *n.* **1** a good opinion of oneself; self-confidence. **2** an unduly high regard for oneself; conceit.

■ **1** see SELF-ASSURANCE. **2** conceit, vanity, egoism, narcissism, self-centeredness, egotism, self-approbation, self-satisfaction, self-admiration, self-love, self-adulation, self-idolatry, smugness, self-importance, self-regard, *amour propre.*

self-evident /sélfévidənt/ *adj.* obvious; without the need of evidence or further explanation. □□ **self-evidence** *n.* **self-evidently** *adv.*

■ evident, obvious, patent, clear, incontrovertible, definite, distinct, clear-cut, apparent, unmistakable, undeniable, inescapable, incontestable, plain, axiomatic, proverbial, manifest, true, palpable, tangible; express.

self-examination /sélfigzáminayshən/ *n.* **1** the study of one's own conduct, reasons, etc. **2** the examining of one's body for signs of illness, etc.

self-executing /sélféksikyōōting/ *adj. Law* (of a law, legal clause, etc.) not needing legislation, etc., to be enforced; automatic.

self-existent /sélfigzístənt/ *adj.* existing without prior cause; independent.

self-explanatory /sélfiksplánətawree/ *adj.* easily understood; not needing explanation.

■ see OBVIOUS.

self-expression /sélfikspréshən/ *n.* the expression of one's feelings, thoughts, etc., esp. in writing, painting, music, etc. □□ **self-expressive** *adj.*

self-faced /sélf-fáyst/ *adj.* (of stone) unhewn; undressed.

self-feeder /sélf-féedər/ *n.* **1** a furnace, machine, etc., that renews its own fuel or material automatically. **2** a device for supplying food to farm animals automatically. □□ **self-feeding** *adj.*

self-fertile /sélf-fért'l/ *adj.* (of a plant, etc.) self-fertilizing. □□ **self-fertility** /-tílitee/ *n.*

self-fertilization /sélf-fərt'lizáyshən/ *n.* the fertilization of plants by their own pollen, not from others. □□ **self-fertilized** /-fárt'lizd/ *adj.* **self-fertilizing** /-fárt'lizing/ *adj.*

self-financing /sélf-fínansing, -fənán-/ *adj.* that finances itself, esp. (of a project or undertaking) that pays for its own implementation or continuation. □□ **self-finance** *v.tr.*

self-flattery /sélf-flátəree/ *n.* = SELF-APPRECIATION. □□ **self-flattering** *adj.*

self-forgetful /sélf-fərgétfōōl/ *adj.* unselfish. □□ **self-forgetfulness** *n.*

self-fulfilling /sélf-fōōlfiling/ *adj.* (of a prophecy, forecast, etc.) bound to come true as a result of actions brought about by its being made.

self-fulfillment /sélf-fōōlfílmənt/ *n.* the fulfillment of one's own hopes and ambitions.

self-generating /sélfjénərayting/ *adj.* generated by itself or oneself, not externally.

self-glorification /sélfgláwrifikáyshən/ *n.* the proclamation of oneself, one's abilities, etc.; self-satisfaction.

self-government /sélfgúvərnmənt/ *n.* **1** (esp. of a former colony, etc.) government by its own people. **2** = SELF-CONTROL. □□ **self-governed** *adj.* **self-governing** *adj.*

■ **1** self-rule, independence, self-determination, home rule, autonomy, freedom.

self-gratification /sélfgrátifikáyshən/ *n.* **1** gratification or pleasing of oneself. **2** self-indulgence; dissipation. **3** masturbation. □□ **self-gratifying** *adj.*

■ **1, 2** see INDULGENCE 1, DISSIPATION 1. **3** see *masturbation* (MASTURBATE). □□ **self-gratifying** see SELF-INDULGENT.

self-hate /sélfháyt/ *n.* = SELF-HATRED.

self-hatred /sélfháytrid/ *n.* hatred of oneself, esp. of one's actual self when contrasted with one's imagined self.

self-heal /sélfhéel/ *n.* any of several plants, esp. *Prunella vulgaris,* believed to have healing properties.

self-help /sélfhélp/ *n.* **1** the theory that individuals should provide for their own support and improvement in society. **2** the act or faculty of providing for or improving oneself.

selfhood /sélfhōōd/ *n.* personality, separate and conscious existence.

self-image /sélfímij/ *n.* one's own idea or picture of oneself, esp. in relation to others.

self-importance /sélfimpáwrt'ns/ *n.* a high opinion of oneself; pompousness. □□ **self-important** *adj.* **self-importantly** *adv.*

■ see *arrogance* (ARROGANT), VANITY 1. □□ **self-important** conceited, self-centered, self-seeking, self-absorbed, vain, egotistic(al), self-satisfied, smug, pompous, arrogant, overweening, overbearing, self-glorifying, self-engrossed, presumptuous, snobbish, haughty, *colloq.* snooty, snotty, swollen-headed, bigheaded, stuck-up, *literary* vainglorious.

/. . ./ **pronunciation**	● **part of speech**
□ **phrases, idioms, and compounds**	
□□ **derivatives**	■ **synonym section**
cross-references appear in SMALL CAPITALS or *italics*	

self-imposed /sélfimpṓzd/ *adj.* (of a task or condition, etc.) imposed on and by oneself, not externally (*self-imposed exile*).

self-improvement /sélfimprŏŏvmənt/ *n.* the improvement of one's own position or disposition by one's own efforts.

self-induced /sélfindŏŏst, -dyŏŏst/ *adj.* **1** induced by oneself or itself. **2** *Electr.* produced by self-induction.

self-inductance /sélfindúktəns/ *n. Electr.* the property of an electric circuit that causes an electromotive force to be generated in it by a change in the current flowing through it (cf. *mutual inductance*).

self-induction /sélfindúkshən/ *n. Electr.* the production of an electromotive force in a circuit when the current in that circuit is varied. □□ **self-inductive** *adj.*

self-indulgent /sélfindúljənt/ *adj.* indulging or tending to indulge oneself in pleasure, idleness, etc. □□ **self-indulgence** *n.* **self-indulgently** *adv.*

■ self-gratifying, selfish, extravagant, intemperate, overindulgent, immoderate, hedonistic, sybaritic, epicurean, pleasure-seeking; dissolute, dissipated, licentious, profligate, sensual; gluttonous, greedy, gormandizing.

self-inflicted /sélfinflíktid/ *adj.* (esp. of a wound, damage, etc.) inflicted by and on oneself, not externally.

self-interest /sélfíntrist, -tərist/ *n.* one's personal interest or advantage. □□ **self-interested** *adj.*

■ □□ **self-interested** see SELFISH.

selfish /sélfish/ *adj.* **1** deficient in consideration for others; concerned chiefly with one's own personal profit or pleasure; actuated by self-interest. **2** (of a motive, etc.) appealing to self-interest. □□ **selfishly** *adv.* **selfishness** *n.*

■ inconsiderate, thoughtless, ungenerous, illiberal, grudging, uncharitable; self-indulgent, self-aggrandizing, self-seeking, self-loving, self-centered, self-absorbed, self-interested, self-serving, egotistic(al), egoistic(al); greedy, acquisitive, covetous, grasping, avaricious, mercenary.

self-justification /sélfjústifikáyshən/ *n.* the justification or excusing of oneself, one's actions, etc.

self-knowledge /sélfnólij/ *n.* the understanding of oneself, one's motives, etc.

selfless /sélflis/ *adj.* disregarding oneself or one's own interests; unselfish. □□ **selflessly** *adv.* **selflessness** *n.*

■ unselfish, charitable, self-denying, generous, altruistic, ungrudging, magnanimous, considerate, thoughtful; self-sacrificing.

self-loading /sélflṓding/ *adj.* (esp. of a gun) loading itself. □□ **self-loader** *n.*

self-locking /sélflóking/ *adj.* locking itself.

self-love /sélflúv/ *n.* **1** selfishness; self-indulgence. **2** *Philos.* regard for one's own well-being and happiness.

■ **1** selfishness, self-regard, self-indulgence, selfness; see also CONCEIT 1.

self-made /sélfmáyd/ *adj.* **1** successful or rich by one's own effort. **2** made by oneself.

■ **1** independent, self-reliant, entrepreneurial, self-sufficient.

self-mastery /sélfmástəree/ *n.* = SELF-CONTROL.

selfmate /sélfmayt/ *n. Chess* checkmate in which a player forces the opponent to achieve checkmate.

self-mocking /sélfmóking/ *adj.* mocking oneself or itself.

self-motion /sélfmṓshən/ *n.* motion caused by oneself or itself, not externally. □□ **self-moving** /-mṓoving/ *adj.*

self-motivated /sélfmṓtivaytid/ *adj.* acting on one's own initiative without external pressure. □□ **self-motivation** /-váyshən/ *n.*

self-murder /sélfmə́rdər/ *n.* = SUICIDE. □□ **self-murderer** *n.*

self-neglect /sélfniglékt/ *n.* neglect of oneself.

selfness /sélfnis/ *n.* **1** individuality; personality; essence. **2** selfishness or self-regard.

self-opinionated /sélfəpínyənaytid/ *adj.* **1** stubbornly adhering to one's own opinions. **2** arrogant. □□ **self-opinion** *n.*

self-perpetuating /sélfpərpéchŏŏ-ayting/ *adj.* perpetuating itself or oneself without external agency. □□ **self-perpetuation** /-áyshən/ *n.*

self-pity /sélfpítee/ *n.* extreme sorrow for one's own troubles, etc. □□ **self-pitying** *adj.* **self-pityingly** *adv.*

self-pollination /sélfpólináyshən/ *n.* the pollination of a flower by pollen from the same plant. □□ **self-pollinated** *adj.* **self-pollinating** *adj.* **self-pollinator** *n.*

self-portrait /sélfpáwrtrit/ *n.* a portrait or description of an artist, writer, etc., by himself or herself.

self-possessed /sélfpəzést/ *adj.* habitually exercising self-control; composed. □□ **self-possession** /-zéshən/ *n.*

■ composed, cool, serene, placid, collected, self-assured, peaceful, calm, tranquil, even-tempered, detached, imperturbable, unruffled, undisturbed, unperturbed, (self-)controlled, dignified, refined, *colloq.* unflappable.

self-praise /sélfpráyz/ *n.* boasting; self-glorification.

self-preservation /sélfprézərváyshən/ *n.* **1** the preservation of one's own life, safety, etc. **2** this as a basic instinct of human beings and animals.

self-proclaimed /sélfprəkláymd/ *adj.* proclaimed by oneself or itself to be such.

self-propagating /sélfprópəgayting/ *adj.* (esp. of a plant) able to propagate itself.

self-propelled /sélfprəpéld/ *adj.* (esp. of a motor vehicle, etc.) moving or able to move without external propulsion. □□ **self-propelling** *adj.*

self-protection /sélfprətékshən/ *n.* protecting oneself or itself. □□ **self-protective** *adj.*

self-raising /sélfráyzing/ *adj. Brit.* = SELF-RISING.

self-realization /sélfréeəlizáyshən/ *n.* **1** the development of one's faculties, abilities, etc. **2** this as an ethical principle.

self-recording /sélfrikáwrding/ *adj.* (of a scientific instrument, etc.) automatically recording its measurements.

self-regard /sélfrigaárd/ *n.* **1** a proper regard for oneself. **2 a** selfishness. **b** conceit.

■ **1** see SELF-RESPECT. **2 b** see SELF-ESTEEM 2.

self-registering /sélfréjistəring/ *adj.* (of a scientific instrument, etc.) automatically registering its measurements.

self-regulating /sélfrégyəlayting/ *adj.* regulating oneself or itself without intervention. □□ **self-regulation** /-láyshən/ *n.* **self-regulatory** /-lətawree/ *adj.*

■ see AUTOMATIC *adj.* 1.

self-reliance /sélfrilíəns/ *n.* reliance on one's own resources, etc.; independence. □□ **self-reliant** *adj.* **self-reliantly** *adv.*

■ see INDEPENDENCE. □□ **self-reliant** see INDEPENDENT *adj.* 2a, 3.

self-renewal /sélfrinŏŏəl, -nyŏŏ-/ *n.* the act or process of renewing oneself or itself.

self-renunciation /sélfrinúnseeáyshən/ *n.* **1** = SELF-SACRIFICE. **2** unselfishness.

self-reproach /sélfriprṓch/ *n.* reproach or blame directed at oneself. □□ **self-reproachful** *adj.*

■ self-condemnation, self-accusation. □□ **self-reproachful** see PENITENT *adj.*

self-respect /sélfrispékt/ *n.* respect for oneself; a feeling that one is behaving with honor, dignity, etc. □□ **self-respecting** *adj.*

■ honor, dignity, integrity, self-regard, self-esteem, pride, *amour propre*, morale.

self-restraint /sélfristráynt/ *n.* = SELF-CONTROL. □□ **self-restrained** *adj.*

self-revealing /sélfrivéeling/ *adj.* revealing one's character, motives, etc., esp. inadvertently. □□ **self-revelation** /-révəláyshən/ *n.*

self-righteous /sélfríchəs/ *adj.* excessively conscious of or insistent on one's rectitude, correctness, etc. □□ **self-righteously** *adv.* **self-righteousness** *n.*

■ Pharisaic(al), sanctimonious, pietistic, hypocritical, complacent, smug, self-satisfied, priggish, superior, canting, *colloq.* holier-than-thou, goody-goody, *Brit. sl.* pi.

self-righting /sélfríting/ *adj.* (of a boat) righting itself when capsized.

self-rising /sélfrízing/ *adj.* (of flour) having a raising agent already added.

self-rule /sélfrŏŏl/ *n.* = SELF-GOVERNMENT 1.

self-sacrifice /sélfsákrifīs/ *n.* the negation of one's own interests, wishes, etc., in favor of those of others. □□ **self-sac-rificing** *adj.*

■ see SELF-DENIAL. □□ **self-sacrificing** see SELFLESS.

selfsame /sélfsaym/ *attrib.adj.* (prec. by *the*) the very same (*the selfsame village*).

■ see SAME *adj.* 1.

self-satisfaction /sélfsátisfákshən/ *n.* excessive and unwarranted satisfaction with oneself, one's achievements, etc.; complacency. □□ **self-satisfied** /-sátisfīd/ *adj.* **self-satisfiedly** /-fīdlee/ *adv.*

■ see SELF-ESTEEM 2. □□ **self-satisfied** see SMUG.

self-sealing /sélfseéling/ *adj.* **1** (of a pneumatic tire, fuel tank, etc.) automatically able to seal small punctures. **2** (of an envelope) self-adhesive.

self-seeking /sélfseéking/ *adj.* & *n.* seeking one's own welfare before that of others. □□ **self-seeker** *n.*

■ see SELFISH.

self-selection /sélfsilékshən/ *n.* the act of selecting oneself or itself. □□ **self-selecting** *adj.*

self-service /sélfsórvis/ *adj.* & *n.* ● *adj.* (often *attrib.*) **1** (of a store, restaurant, gas station, etc.) where customers serve themselves and pay at a checkout counter, etc. **2** (of a machine) serving goods after the insertion of coins. ● *n. colloq.* a self-service store, gas station, etc.

self-serving /sélfsórving/ *adj.* = SELF-SEEKING.

self-slaughter /sélfsláwtər/ *n.* = SUICIDE.

self-sown /sélfsón/ *adj.* grown from seed scattered naturally.

self-starter /sélfstaártər/ *n.* **1** an electric appliance for starting a motor vehicle engine without the use of a crank. **2** an ambitious person who needs no external motivation.

self-sterile /sélfstéril, -il/ *adj. Biol.* not being self-fertile. □□ **self-sterility** /-stərilitee/ *n.*

self-styled /sélfstīld/ *adj.* called so by oneself; would-be; pretended (*a self-styled artist*).

■ would-be, *soi-disant*, professed, self-appointed, self-proclaimed, so-called, quasi-.

self-sufficient /sélfsəfíshənt/ *adj.* **1 a** needing nothing; independent. **b** (of a person, nation, etc.) able to supply one's needs for a commodity, esp. food, from one's own resources. **2** content with one's own opinion; arrogant. □□ **self-sufficiency** *n.* **self-sufficiently** *adv.* **self-sufficing** /-səfísing/ *adj.*

■ **1** independent, self-reliant, self-supporting, self-sustaining. **2** see SELF-CONTAINED 1, ARROGANT.

self-suggestion /sélfsəgjés-chən, -səjés-/ *n.* = AUTOSUGGESTION.

self-supporting /sélfsəpáwrting/ *adj.* **1** capable of maintaining oneself or itself financially. **2** staying up or standing without external aid. □□ **self-support** *n.*

■ **1** see SELF-SUFFICIENT 1.

self-surrender /sélfsəréndər/ *n.* the surrender of oneself or one's will, etc., to an influence, emotion, or other person.

self-sustaining /sélfsəstáyning/ *adj.* sustaining oneself or itself. □□ **self-sustained** *adj.*

■ see SELF-SUFFICIENT 1. □□ **self-sustained** see UNATTACHED 1.

self-taught /sélftáwt/ *adj.* educated or trained by oneself, not externally.

self-torture /sélftáwrchər/ *n.* the inflicting of pain, esp. mental, on oneself.

self-willed /sélfwíld/ *adj.* obstinately pursuing one's own wishes. □□ **self-will** *n.*

■ headstrong, determined, refractory, stubborn, obstinate, bullish, mulish, pigheaded, willful, ungovernable, uncontrollable, unruly, unmanageable, intractable, contrary, intransigent, uncooperative, contumacious, recalcitrant, stiff-necked, vexatious, restive, difficult, incorrigible, disobedient.

self-winding /sélfwínding/ *adj.* (of a watch, etc.) having an automatic winding apparatus.

self-worth /sélfwórth/ *n.* = SELF-ESTEEM 1.

Seljuk /séljóok/ *n.* & *adj.* ● *n.* a member of any of the Turkish dynasties (11th–13th c.) of central and western Asia preceding Ottoman rule. ● *adj.* of or relating to the Seljuks.

□□ **Seljukian** /-jóokeeən/ *adj.* & *n.* [Turk. *seljūq* (name of their reputed ancestor)]

sell /sel/ *v.* & *n.* ● *v.* (*past* and *past part.* **sold** /sōld/) **1** *tr.* make over or dispose of in exchange for money. **2** *tr.* keep a stock of for sale or be a dealer in (*do you sell candles?*). **3** *intr.* (of goods) be purchased (*will never sell; these are selling well*). **4** *intr.* (foll. by *at, for*) have a specified price (*sells at $5*). **5** *tr.* betray for money or other reward (*sell one's country*). **6** *tr.* offer dishonorably for money or other consideration; make a matter of corrupt bargaining (*sell justice; sell oneself; sell one's honor*). **7** *tr.* **a** advertise or publish the merits of. **b** give (a person) information on the value of something; inspire (a person) with a desire to buy or acquire or agree to something. **8** *tr.* cause to be sold (*the author's name alone will sell many copies*). **9** *tr. Brit. sl.* disappoint by not keeping an engagement, etc., by failing in some way, or by trickery (*sold again!*). ● *n. colloq.* **1** a manner of selling (*soft sell*). **2** a deception or disappointment. □ **sell-by date** the latest recommended date of sale marked on the packaging of esp. perishable food. **sell down the river** see RIVER. **sell the** (or **a**) **dummy** see DUMMY. **selling point** an advantageous feature. **selling race** a horse race after which the winning horse must be auctioned. **sell one's life dear** (or **dearly**) esp. *Brit.* do great injury before being killed. **sell off** sell the remainder of (goods) at reduced prices. **sell out 1 a** sell all one's stock-in-trade, one's shares in a company, etc. **b** sell (all or some of one's stock, shares, etc.). **2 a** betray. **b** be treacherous or disloyal. **sell the pass** see PASS². **sell a pup** see PUP. **sell short** disparage; underestimate. **sell up** *Brit.* **1** sell one's business, house, etc. **2** sell the goods of (a debtor). **sold on** *colloq.* enthusiastic about. □□ **sellable** *adj.* [OE *sellan* f. Gmc]

■ *v.* **1** *Law* vend, esp. *Brit. sl.* flog. **2** market, deal in, merchandise, trade in, traffic in, peddle, vend, hawk, handle, retail, carry, stock, offer, esp. *Brit. sl.* flog; *colloq.* push. **3** go, be sold, move. **7** advertise, push; see also PROMOTE 3. □ **sell out 2** inform against, give away, *colloq.* rat on, tell on, sell down the river, blow the whistle on, esp. *Brit. sl.* shop; see also BETRAY 2. **sell short a** see DISPARAGE 1, UNDERESTIMATE *v.* **sold on** enthusiastic *or* persuaded *or* convinced about, won over by.

seller /sélər/ *n.* **1** a person who sells. **2** a commodity that sells well or badly. □ **seller's** (or **sellers'**) **market** an economic position in which goods are scarce and expensive.

■ **1** dealer, vendor, merchant, retailer, shopkeeper, peddler, hawker, monger; salesperson, salesman, saleswoman, saleslady, clerk, salesclerk, shopgirl, *Brit.* shop assistant; sales agent, representative, commercial salesman, door-to-door salesman *colloq.* rep, drummer.

sellout /sélowt/ *n. n.* **1** a commercial success, esp. the selling of all tickets for a show. **2** a betrayal.

■ **2** see *betrayal* (BETRAY).

seltzer /séltsər/ *n.* (in full **seltzer water**) **1** medicinal mineral water from Nieder-Selters in Germany. **2** an artificial substitute for this; soda water. [G *Selterser* (adj.) f. *Selters*]

■ soda (water), mineral water, tonic water.

selvage /sélvij/ *n.* (also **selvedge**) **1 a** an edging that prevents cloth from unraveling (either an edge along the warp or a specially woven edging). **b** a border of different material or finish intended to be removed or hidden. **2** *Geol.* an alteration zone at the edge of a rock mass. **3** the edge plate of a lock with an opening for the bolt. [ME f. SELF + EDGE, after Du. *selfegghe*]

selves *pl.* of SELF.

semanteme /símánteem/ *n. Linguistics* a fundamental element expressing an image or idea. [F *sémantème* (as SEMANTIC)]

semantic /símántik/ *adj.* relating to meaning in language;

/.../ **pronunciation**	● **part of speech**
□ **phrases, idioms, and compounds**	
□□ **derivatives**	■ **synonym section**
cross-references appear in SMALL CAPITALS or *italics*	

relating to the connotations of words. □□ **semantically** *adv.*
[F *sémantique* f. Gk *sēmantikos* significant f. *sēmainō* signify
f. *sēma* sign]

semantics /simántiks/ *n.pl.* (usu. treated as *sing.*) the branch
of linguistics concerned with meaning. □□ **semantician**
/-tíshən/ *n.* **semanticist** /-tisist/ *n.*

semaphore /sémǝfawr/ *n. & v.* ● *n.* **1** *Mil.*, etc., a system of
sending messages by holding the arms or two flags in certain
positions according to an alphabetic code. **2** a signaling apparatus consisting of a post with a movable arm or arms,
lanterns, etc., for use (esp. on railroads) by day or night.
● *v.intr. & tr.* signal or send by semaphore. □□ **semaphoric**
adj. **semaphorically** /-fáwriklee/ *adv.* [F *sémaphore*, irreg.
f. Gk *sēma* sign + *-phoros* -PHORE]

semasiology /simáyseeólǝjee/ *n.* semantics. □□ **semasiolog-
ical** /-seeǝlójikǝl/ *adj.* [G *Semasiologie* f. Gk *sēmasia* meaning
f. *sēmainō* signify]

sematic /simátik/ *adj. Zool.* (of coloring, markings, etc.) significant; serving to warn off enemies or attract attention.
[Gk *sēma sēmatos* sign]

semblable /sémblǝbǝl/ *n. & adj.* ● *n.* a counterpart or equal.
● *adj. archaic* having the semblance of something; seeming.
[ME f. OF (as SEMBLANCE)]

semblance /sémblǝns/ *n.* **1** the outward or superficial appearance of something (*put on a semblance of anger*). **2** resemblance. [ME f. OF f. *sembler* f. L *similare, simulare* SIM-
ULATE]

■ **1** appearance, image, bearing, aspect, air, look,
exterior, mask, façade, front, face, show, veneer, guise,
pretense, cloak, impression, affectation, *literary* mien.
2 see RESEMBLANCE.

semé /sǝmáy/ *adj.* (also **semée**) *Heraldry* covered with small
bearings of indefinite number (e.g., stars, fleurs-de-lis) arranged all over the field. [F, past part. of *semer* to sow]

sememe /sémeem, seé-/ *n. Linguistics* the unit of meaning
carried by a morpheme. [as SEMANTIC]

semen /seémǝn/ *n.* the reproductive fluid of male animals,
containing spermatozoa in suspension. [ME f. L *semen sem-
inis* seed f. *serere* to sow]

semester /siméstǝr/ *n.* **1** half of the academic year in an educational institution, usu. an 18-week period. **2** a half-year
course or term in (esp. German) universities. [G f. L *semes-
tris* six-monthly f. *sex* six + *mensis* month]

■ term, session.

semi /sémī, sémee/ *n.* (*pl.* **semis**) *colloq.* **1** a semitrailer; tractor-trailer. **2** *Brit.* a semidetached house. **3** a semifinal.
[abbr.]

semi- /sémee, sémī/ *prefix* **1** half (*semicircle*). **2** partly; in some
degree or particular (*semiofficial*; *semidetached*). **3** almost (*a
semismile*). **4** occurring or appearing twice in a specified period (*semiannual*). [F, It., etc., or L, corresp. to Gk HEMI-,
Skr. *sāmi*]

■ **1** demi-, hemi-.

semiannual /sémeeányooǝl, sémī-/ *adj.* occurring, published, etc., twice a year. □□ **semiannually** *adv.*

semiautomatic /sémeeáwtǝmátik, sémī-/ *adj.* **1** partially automatic. **2** (of a firearm) having a mechanism for continuous
loading but not for continuous firing.

semibasement /sémeebáysmǝnt, sémī-/ *n.* a story partly below ground level.

semibold /sémeebóld, sémī-/ *adj. Printing* printed in a type
darker than normal but not as dark as bold.

semibreve /sémeebrev, -breev, sémī-/ *n.* esp *Brit. Mus.* =
whole note.

semicircle /sémeesǝrkǝl, sémī-/ *n.* **1** half of a circle or of its
circumference. **2** a set of objects ranged in, or an object
forming, a semicircle. [L *semicirculus* (as SEMI-, CIRCLE)]

semicircular /sémeesórkyǝlǝr, sémī-/ *adj.* **1** forming or
shaped like a semicircle. **2** arranged as or in a semicircle.
□ **semicircular canal** one of three fluid-filled channels in
the ear giving information to the brain to help maintain balance. [LL *semicircularis* (as SEMICIRCLE)]

semicivilized /sémeesívilizd, sémī-/ *adj.* partially civilized.

semicolon /sémikólǝn/ *n.* a punctuation mark (;) of intermediate value between a comma and a period.

semiconducting /sémeekǝndúkting, sémī-/ *adj.* having the
properties of a semiconductor.

semiconductor /sémeekǝndúktǝr, sémī-/ *n.* a solid substance that is a nonconductor when pure or at a low temperature but has a conductivity between that of insulators
and that of most metals when containing a suitable impurity
or at a higher temperature and is used in integrated circuits,
transistors, diodes, etc.

semiconscious /sémeekónshǝs, sémī-/ *adj.* partly or imperfectly conscious.

semicylinder /sémeesílindǝr, sémī-/ *n.* half of a cylinder cut
longitudinally. □□ **semicylindrical** /-líndrikǝl/ *adj.*

semidemisemiquaver /sémeedémeesémeekwayvǝr/ *n. Brit.
Mus.* = *sixty-fourth note.* [SEMI- + DEMISEMIQUAVER]

semideponent /sémeedipónǝnt, sémī-/ *adj. Gram.* (of a
Latin verb) having active forms in present tenses and passive
forms with active sense in perfect tenses.

semidetached /sémeeditácht, sémī-/ *adj. & n.* ● *adj.* (of a
house) joined to another by a party wall on one side only.
● *n.* a semidetached house.

semidiameter /sémeedīámitǝr, sémī-/ *n.* half of a diameter;
radius. [LL (as SEMI-, DIAMETER)]

semidocumentary /sémeedókyǝméntǝree, sémī-/ *adj. & n.*
● *adj.* (of a motion picture) having a factual background and
a fictitious story. ● *n.* (*pl.* **-ies**) a semidocumentary motion
picture.

semidome /sémeedóm, sémī-/ *n.* **1** a halfdome formed by
vertical section. **2** a part of a structure more or less resembling a dome.

semidouble /sémeedúbǝl, sémī-/ *adj.* (of a flower) intermediate between single and double in having only the outer
stamens converted to petals.

semifinal /sémeefínǝl, sémī-/ *n.* a match or round immediately preceding the final.

semifinalist /sémeefínǝlist, sémī-/ *n.* a competitor in a semifinal.

semifinished /sémeefínisht, sémī-/ *adj.* prepared for the final stage of manufacture.

semifitted /sémeefítid, sémī-/ *adj.* (of a garment) shaped to
the body but not closely fitted.

semifluid /sémeeflóoid, sémī-/ *adj. & n.* ● *adj.* of a consistency between solid and liquid. ● *n.* a semifluid substance.

semi-infinite /sémee-ínfinit, sémī-/ *adj. Math.* limited in one
direction and stretching to infinity in the other.

semi-invalid /sémee-ínvǝlid, sémī-/ *n.* a person somewhat
enfeebled or partially disabled.

semiliquid /sémeelíkwid, sémī-/ *adj. & n.* = SEMIFLUID.

semilunar /sémeelóonǝr, sémī-/ *adj.* shaped like a half moon
or crescent. □ **semilunar bone** a bone of this shape in the
carpus. **semilunar cartilage** a cartilage of this shape in the
knee. **semilunar valve** a valve of this shape in the heart.
[mod.L *semilunaris* (as SEMI-, LUNAR)]

semimetal /sémeemét'l, sémī-/ *n.* a substance with some of
the properties of metals. [mod.L *semimetallum* (as SEMI-,
METAL)]

semimonthly /sémeemúnthlee, sémī-/ *adj. & adv.* ● *adj.* occurring, published, etc., twice a month. ● *adv.* twice a
month.

seminal /séminǝl/ *adj.* **1** of or relating to seed, semen, or
reproduction. **2** germinal. **3** rudimentary; undeveloped. **4**
(of ideas, etc.) providing the basis for future development.
□ **seminal fluid** semen. □□ **seminally** *adv.* [ME f. OF *seminal* or L *seminalis* (as SEMEN)]

■ **2, 3** embryonic, germinal, rudimentary, potential,
inchoate, unformed, undeveloped, incipient. **4** original,
basic, creative, plastic, primary, prime, formative,
innovative, new, unprecedented, landmark, important,
influential.

seminar /séminaar/ *n.* **1** a small class at a university, etc., for
discussion and research. **2** a short intensive course of study.
3 a conference of specialists. [G (as SEMINARY)]

■ **1** class; workshop. **2** course, lecture series. **3** see
CONFERENCE 2.

seminary /sémineree/ *n.* (*pl.* **-ies**) **1** a training college for
priests, rabbis, etc. **2** a place of education or development.

□□ **seminarian** /-náireeən/ *n.* **seminarist** *n.* [ME f. L *seminarium* seed plot, neut. of *seminarius* (adj.) (as SEMEN)]

■ **2** academy, school, institute, institution, college, university.

seminiferous /sémeenífərəs, sémī-/ *adj.* **1** bearing seed. **2** conveying semen. [L *semin-* f. SEMEN + -FEROUS]

Seminole /sémənōl/ *n.* **1 a** a N. American people native to Florida. **b** a member of this people. **2** the language of this people.

semiofficial /sémeeəfíshəl, sémī-/ *adj.* **1** partly official; rather less than official. **2** (of communications to newspapers, etc.) made by an official with the stipulation that the source should not be revealed. □□ **semiofficially** *adv.*

semiology /seémeeóləjee, sémee-/ *n.* (also **semeiology**) = SEMIOTICS. □□ **semiological** /-meeəlójikəl/ *adj.* **semiologist** *n.* [Gk *sēmeion* sign f. *sēma* mark]

semiopaque /sémeeōpáyk, sémī-/ *adj.* not fully transparent.

semiotics /seémeeótiks, sém-/ *n.* (also **semeiotics**) **1** the study of signs and symbols in various fields, esp. language. **2** *Med.* symptomatology. □□ **semiotic** *adj.* **semiotical** *adj.* **semiotically** *adv.* **semiotician** /-tíshən/ *n.* [Gk *sēmeiōtikos* of signs (as SEMIOLOGY)]

semipermanent /sémeepórmənənt, sémī-/ *adj.* rather less than permanent.

semipermeable /sémeepórmeeəbəl, sémī-/ *adj.* (of a membrane, etc.) allowing small molecules, but not large ones, to pass through.

semiplume /sémeeplŏŏm, sémī-/ *n.* a feather with a firm stem and a downy web.

semiprecious /sémeepréshəs, sémī-/ *adj.* (of a gem) less valuable than a precious stone.

semipro /sémeeprŏ, sémī-/ *adj.* & *n.* (*pl.* **-os**) *colloq.* = SEMIPROFESSIONAL.

semiprofessional /sémeeprəféshənəl, sémī-/ *adj.* & *n.* ● *adj.* **1** receiving payment for an activity but not relying on it for a living. **2** involving semiprofessionals. ● *n.* a semiprofessional musician, sportsman, etc.

semiquaver /sémeekwayvər, sémī-/ *n.* esp. *Brit. Mus.* = *sixteenth note.*

semirigid /sémeeríjid, sémī-/ *adj.* (of an airship) having a stiffened keel attached to a flexible gas container.

semiskilled /sémeeskíld, sémī-/ *adj.* (of work or a worker) having or needing some training but less than for a skilled worker.

semiskimmed /sémeeskímd, sémī-/ *adj.* (of milk) from which some cream has been skimmed.

semismile /sémeesmíl, sémī-/ *n.* an expression that is not quite a smile.

semisolid /sémeesólid, sémī-/ *adj.* viscous; semifluid.

■ see STIFF *adj.* 1, 2.

semisweet /sémeeswéet, sémī-/ *adj.* (of cookies, chocolate, etc.) slightly sweetened.

semisynthetic /sémeesinthétik, sémī-/ *adj. Chem.* (of a substance) that is prepared synthetically but derives from a naturally occurring material.

Semite /sémīt/ *n.* a member of any of the peoples supposed to be descended from Shem, son of Noah (Gen. 10:21 ff.), including esp. the Jews, Arabs, Assyrians, and Phoenicians. □□ **Semitism** /sémitizəm/ *n.* **Semitist** /sémitist/ *n.* **Semitize** /-tīz/ *v.tr.* **Semitization** *n.* [mod.L *Semita* f. LL f. Gk *Sēm* Shem]

Semitic /simítik/ *adj.* **1** of or relating to the Semites, esp. the Jews. **2** of or relating to the languages of the family including Hebrew and Arabic. [mod.L *Semiticus* (as SEMITE)]

semitone /sémeetōn, sémī-/ *n. Mus.* the smallest interval used in classical European music; half a tone.

semitrailer /sémeetráylər, sémī-/ *n.* a trailer having wheels at the back but supported at the front by a towing vehicle.

semitransparent /sémeetránzpárənt, sémī-, -páir/ *adj.* partially or imperfectly transparent.

■ translucent, semiopaque.

semitropics /sémeetrópiks, sémī-/ *n.pl.* = SUBTROPICS. □□ **semitropical** *adj.*

semivowel /sémeevowəl/ *n.* **1** a sound intermediate between a vowel and a consonant (e.g., *w*, *y*). **2** a letter representing this. [after L *semivocalis*]

semiweekly /sémeeweéklee, sémī-/ *adj.* & *adv.* ● *adj.* occurring; published, etc., twice a week. ● *adv.* twice a week.

semmit /sémit/ *n. Sc.* an undershirt. [ME: orig. unkn.]

semolina /séməleénə/ *n.* **1** the hard grains left after the milling of flour, used in puddings, etc., and in pasta. **2** a pudding, etc., made of this. [It. *semolino* dimin. of *semola* bran f. L *simila* flour]

sempiternal /sémpitórnəl/ *adj. rhet.* eternal; everlasting. □□ **sempiternally** *adv.* **sempiternity** *n.* [ME f. OF *sempiternel* f. LL *sempiternalis* f. L *sempiternus* f. *semper* always + *aeternus* eternal]

■ see EVERLASTING *adj.* 1.

semplice /sémplichay/ *adv. Mus.* in a simple style of performance. [It., = SIMPLE]

sempre /sémpray/ *adv. Mus.* throughout; always (*sempre forte*). [It.]

sempstress var. of SEAMSTRESS.

Semtex /sémteks/ *n. propr.* a highly malleable, odorless plastic explosive. [prob. f. *Semtín*, a village in the Czech Republic near the place of production]

sen. *abbr.* **1 a** senator. **b** senate. **2** senior.

senarius /sináreeəs/ *n.* (*pl.* **senarii** /-ee-ī/) *Prosody* a verse of six feet, esp. an iambic trimeter. [L: see SENARY]

senary /seénoree, sén-/ *adj.* of six, by sixes. [L *senarius* f. *seni* distrib. of *sex* six]

senate /sénit/ *n.* **1** a legislative body, esp. the upper and smaller assembly in the US, France, and other countries, in the states of the US, etc. **2** the governing body of a university or college. **3** *Rom.Hist.* the state council of the republic and empire sharing legislative power with the popular assemblies, administration with the magistrates, and judicial power with the knights. [ME f. OF *senat* f. L *senatus* f. *senex* old man]

■ **1** see CHAMBER *n.* 1b, c.

senator /sénətər/ *n.* **1** a member of a senate. **2** (in Scotland) a Lord of Session. □□ **senatorial** /-táwreeəl/ *adj.* **senatorship** *n.* [ME f. OF *senateur* f. L *senator -oris* (as SENATE)]

■ **1** see POLITICIAN.

send /send/ *v.* (*past* and *past part.* **sent** /sent/) **1** *tr.* **a** order or cause to go or be conveyed (*send a message to headquarters*; *sent me a book*; *sends goods all over the world*). **b** propel; cause to move (*send a bullet*; *sent him flying*). **c** cause to go or become (*send into raptures*; *send to sleep*). **d** dismiss with or without force (*sent her away*; *sent him about his business*). **2** *intr.* send a message or letter (*he sent to warn me*). **3** *tr.* (of God, providence, etc.) grant or bestow or inflict; bring about; cause to be (*send rain*; *send a judgment*; *send her victorious!*). **4** *tr. sl.* affect emotionally; put into ecstasy. **5** *tr.* (freq. foll. by *forth* or *off*) emit or give out (light, heat, odor, etc.); utter or produce (sound) (*send a voice, cry, etc.*) to carry, or travel. □ **send away for** send an order to a dealer for (goods). **send down** *Brit.* **1** expel from a university. **2** sentence to imprisonment. **send for 1** summon. **2** order by mail. **send in 1** cause to go in. **2** submit (an entry, etc.) for a competition, etc. **send off 1** get (a letter, parcel, etc.) dispatched. **2** attend the departure of (a person) as a sign of respect, etc. **3** *Sports* (of a referee) order (a player) to leave the field and take no further part in the game. **send-off** *n.* a demonstration of goodwill, etc., at the departure of a person, the start of a project, etc. **send off for** esp. *Brit.* = *send away for.* **send on** transmit to a further destination or in advance of one's own arrival. **send a person to Coventry** refuse to deal with a person. **send up 1** cause to go up. **2** transmit to a higher authority. **3** *colloq.* satirize or ridicule, esp. by mimicking. **4** sentence to imprisonment. **send-up** *n. colloq.* a satire or parody. **send word** send information. □□ **sendable** *adj.* **sender** *n.* [OE *sendan* f. Gmc]

/.../ pronunciation	● **part of speech**
□ **phrases, idioms, and compounds**	
□□ **derivatives**	■ **synonym section**
cross-references appear in SMALL CAPITALS or *italics*	

■ **1 a** communicate, transmit, convey, deliver, consign, address to, mail, post, fax, remit, ship, forward; broadcast, telecast, televise, radio, telegraph. **b** release, discharge, shoot, propel, fire, fling, project, hurl; cast, throw, toss, let fly, *colloq.* sling, chuck. **d** dismiss, dispatch, commission, charge, depute, delegate, assign. **3** see BESTOW, INFLICT. **4** delight, please, charm, enrapture, stir, thrill, move, electrify, *colloq.* turn on, *sl.* blow a person's mind. **5** emit, radiate, discharge, pour out *or* forth, give out *or* off, exude, emanate; produce, yield, generate, propagate; utter, let out, issue. □ **send down 2** imprison, incarcerate, jail, send up, *Brit.* gaol. **send for** call for, summon; order, request, ask for. **send in 2** see SUBMIT *v.* **send off 3** dismiss, discharge, expel, send away, *colloq.* send packing, give a person his *or* her walking papers; order off, give a person his *or* her marching orders. *Soccer* show a person the red card. **send on** see FORWARD *v.* 1b. **send up 3** lampoon, satirize, burlesque, ridicule, parody, make fun of, *colloq.* take off, spoof. **4** see *send down* above. **send-up** see PARODY *n.* 1.

sendal /séndʹl/ *n. hist.* **1** a thin, rich, silk material. **2** a garment of this. [ME f. OF *cendal*, ult. f. Gk *sindōn*]

Seneca /sénikə/ *n.* **1 a** a N. American people native to western New York. **b** a member of this people. **2** the language of this people. □□ **Senecan** *adj.*

senecio /sinéesheeō/ *n.* any composite plant of the genus *Senecio,* including many cultivated species as well as groundsel and ragwort. [L *senecio* old man, groundsel, with ref. to the hairy fruits]

senesce /sinés/ *v.intr.* grow old. □□ **senescence** *n.* **senescent** *adj.* [L *senescere* f. *senex* old]

■ □□ **senescence** see AGE *n.* 3. **senescent** see ELDERLY *adj.*

seneschal /sénishəl/ *n.* the steward or majordomo of a medieval estate [ME f. OF f. med.L *seniscalus* f. Gmc, = old servant]

■ **1** see SERVANT. **2** see JUDGE *n.* 1.

senhor /saynyáwr/ *n.* a title used of or to a Portuguese or Brazilian man. [Port. f. L *senior*: see SENIOR]

senhora /saynyáwrə/ *n.* a title used of or to a Portuguese or a Brazilian married woman. [Port., fem. of SENHOR]

senhorita /sáynyəréetə/ *n.* a title used of or to a Portuguese or Brazilian unmarried woman. [Port., dimin. of SENHORA]

senile /séenīl/ *adj. & n.* ● *adj.* **1** of or characteristic of old age (*senile apathy; senile decay*). **2** having the weaknesses or diseases of old age. ● *n.* a senile person. □ **senile dementia** a severe form of mental deterioration in old age, characterized by loss of memory and disorientation, and most often due to Alzheimer's disease. □□ **senility** /sinílitee/ *n.* [F *sénile* or L *senilis* f. *senex* old man]

■ *adj.* **2** senescent, decrepit, declining, failing, geriatric, in one's dotage, doddering, in one's second childhood, *colloq.* past it; simple, feeble-minded, *colloq.* dotty; forgetful. □□ **senility** old age, senescence; dotage, second childhood; decrepitude, decline; senile dementia, Alzheimer's disease.

senior /séenyər/ *adj. & n.* ● *adj.* **1** (often foll. by *to*) more or most advanced in age or standing. **2** of high or highest position. **3** (placed after a person's name) senior to another of the same name. **4** of the final year at a university, high school, etc. ● *n.* **1** a person of advanced age or comparatively long service, etc. **2** one's elder, or one's superior in length of service, membership, etc. (*is my senior*). **3** a senior student. □ **senior citizen** an elderly person, esp. a retiree. **senior college** a college in which the last two years' work for a bachelor's degree is done. **senior officer** an officer to whom a junior is responsible. □□ **seniority** /séenyáwritee, -yor-/ *n.* [ME f. L, = older, older man, compar. of *senex senis* old man, old]

■ *adj.* **1–3** elder, older, *Brit.* major; (higher-)ranking, superior; chief. ● **senior citizen** elderly person, retired person, (old-age) pensioner, retirer, retiree, goldenager, *Brit.* OAP, geriatric. □□ **seniority** see STATUS 2.

senna /sénə/ *n.* **1** a cassia tree. **2** a laxative prepared from the dried pod of this. [med.L *sena* f. Arab. *sanā*]

sennet[1] /sénit/ *n. hist.* a signal call on a trumpet or cornet (in the stage directions of Elizabethan plays). [perh. var. of SIGNET]

sennet[2] var. of SENNIT.

sennight /sénit/ *n. archaic* a week. [OE *seofon nihta* seven nights]

sennit /sénit/ *n.* **1** *hist.* plaited straw, palm leaves, etc., used for making hats. **2** *Naut.* braided cordage made in flat or round or square form from 3 to 9 cords. [17th c.: orig. unkn.]

señor /senyáwr/ *n.* (*pl.* **señores** /-rez/) a title used of or to a Spanish-speaking man. [Sp. f. L *senior*: see SENIOR]

señora /senyáwrə/ *n.* a title used of or to a Spanish-speaking married woman. [Sp., fem. of SEÑOR]

señorita /sényəréetə/ *n.* a title used of or to a Spanish-speaking unmarried woman. [Sp., dimin. of SEÑORA]

sensate /sénsayt/ *adj.* perceived by the senses. [LL *sensatus* having senses (as SENSE)]

sensation /sensáyshən/ *n.* **1** the consciousness of perceiving or seeming to perceive some state or condition of one's body or its parts or senses or of one's mind or its emotions; an instance of such consciousness (*lost all sensation in my left arm; had a sensation of giddiness; a sensation of pride; in search of a new sensation*). **2 a** a stirring of emotions or intense interest esp. among a large group of people (*the news caused a sensation*). **b** a person, event, etc., causing such interest. **3** the sensational use of literary, etc., material. [med.L *sensatio* f. L *sensus* SENSE]

■ **1** feeling, sense, impression, awareness, perception, experience; foreboding, presentiment, prescience; (sneaking) suspicion, hunch, conjecture. **2 a** commotion, stir, thrill, furor, storm; excitement. **b** success, sellout, *colloq.* hit, showstopper, riot, *sl.* blockbuster.

sensational /sensáyshənəl/ *adj.* **1** causing or intended to cause great public excitement, etc. **2** of or causing sensation. □□ **sensationalize** *v.tr.* **sensationally** *adv.*

■ **1** exciting, stimulating, electrifying, galvanizing, shocking, hair-raising, spine-tingling, thrilling, stirring, breathtaking, stupendous, amazing, astonishing, astounding, staggering, mind-boggling, unbelievable, incredible, spectacular, far-out, *sl.* mind-blowing; good, great, marvelous, wonderful, superior, superb, matchless, peerless, unequaled, nonpareil, extraordinary, terrific, phenomenal, splendid, *colloq.* fabulous, fantastic, super, smashing; lurid, vivid, overdone, overdrawn, extreme, melodramatic, exaggerated, dramatic, extravagant.

sensationalism /sensáyshənəlizəm/ *n.* **1** the use of or interest in the sensational in literature, political agitation, etc. **2** *Philos.* the theory that ideas are derived solely from sensation (opp. RATIONALISM). □□ **sensationalist** *n. & adj.* **sensationalistic** /-lístik/ *adj.*

■ □□ **sensationalistic** see *melodramatic* (MELODRAMA).

sense /sens/ *n. & v.* ● *n.* **1 a** any of the special bodily faculties by which sensation is roused (*has keen senses; has a dull sense of smell*). **b** sensitiveness of all or any of these. **2** the ability to perceive or feel or to be conscious of the presence or properties of things. **3** (foll. by *of*) consciousness; intuitive awareness (*sense of having done well; sense of one's own importance*). **4** (often foll. by *of*) **a** quick or accurate appreciation, understanding, or instinct regarding a specified matter (*sense of the ridiculous; road sense; the moral sense*). **b** the habit of basing one's conduct on such instinct. **5** practical wisdom or judgment; common sense; conformity to these (*has plenty of sense; what is the sense of talking like that?; has more sense than to do that*). **6 a** a meaning; the way in which a word, etc., is to be understood (*the sense of the word is clear; I mean that in the literal sense*). **b** intelligibility or coherence or possession of a meaning. **7** the prevailing opinion among a number of people. **8** (in *pl.*) a person's sanity or normal state of mind (*taken leave of his senses*). **9** *Math.,* etc., **a** a direction of movement. **b** that which distinguishes

a pair of entities which differ only in that each is the reverse of the other. ● *v.tr.* **1** perceive by a sense or senses. **2** be vaguely aware of. **3** realize. **4** (of a machine, etc.) detect. **5** understand. □ **bring a person to his** or **her senses 1** cure a person of folly. **2** restore a person to consciousness. **come to one's senses 1** regain consciousness. **2** become sensible after acting foolishly. **the five senses** sight, hearing, smell, taste, and touch. **in a** (or **one**) **sense** if the statement is understood in a particular way (*what you say is true in a sense*). **in one's senses** sane. **make sense** be intelligible or practicable. **make sense of** show or find the meaning of. **man of sense** a sagacious man. **out of one's senses** in or into a state of madness (*is out of her senses; frightened him out of his senses*). **sense-datum** (*pl.* **-data**) *Philos.* an element of experience received through the senses. **sense of direction** the ability to know without guidance the direction in which one is or should be moving. **sense of humor** see HUMOR. **sense organ** a bodily organ conveying external stimuli to the sensory system. **take leave of one's senses** go mad. **take the sense of the meeting** ascertain the prevailing opinion. **under a sense of wrong** feeling wronged. [ME f. L *sensus* faculty of feeling, thought, meaning, f. *sentire sens-* feel]
■ *n.* **1** faculty; sight, vision, hearing, taste, smell, touch. **2, 3** see UNDERSTANDING *n.* 1. **4, 5** common sense, intelligence, perception, quick-wittedness, quickness, (mother) wit, judgment, reason, sanity, wisdom, sagacity, discrimination, discernment, brains, *Brit. colloq.* nous. **6** meaning; intelligibility, coherence, drift, gist, import, purport, nuance, significance, message, substance. **7** consensus. **8** (*senses*) see SANITY 1. ● *v.* feel, perceive, detect, realize, divine, intuit, have a hunch *or* feeling, have *or* get the impression, suspect; see also UNDERSTAND 1, 2. □ **bring a person to his** or **her senses 1** see ENLIGHTEN 1a. **2** see WAKE[1] *v.* 1. **come to one's senses 1** see AWAKE *v.* 1. **in a** (or **one sense**) in a way, in a manner of speaking. **make sense** see *add up* 3. **take leave of one's senses** go mad, go out of one's head, go insane, *sl.* flip one's lid, lose one's marbles.

senseless /sénslis/ *adj.* **1** unconscious. **2** wildly foolish. **3** without meaning or purpose. **4** incapable of sensation. □□ **senselessly** *adv.* **senselessness** *n.*
■ **1, 4** insensible, unconscious, (knocked) out (cold), stunned, insensate, comatose; unfeeling, benumbed, anesthetized, dead, deadened, insentient. **2, 3** pointless, purposeless, ridiculous, ludicrous, unintelligent, illogical, irrational, incongruous, meaningless, absurd, wild, mad, demented, insane, asinine, nonsensical, simpleminded, fatuous, stupid, foolish, silly, dizzy, halfwitted, mindless, brainless, witless, empty-headed, harebrained, muddleheaded, *colloq.* crazy, dotty, imbecilic, imbecile, idiotic, moronic, pea-brained, birdbrained, esp. *Brit. colloq.* daft, *sl.* daffy, nutty, nuts, cuckoo, screwy, batty, wacky, dippy. □□ **senselessness** see FOLLY 1, *emptiness* (EMPTY).

sensibility /sénsibílitee/ *n.* (*pl.* **-ies**) **1** capacity to feel (*little finger lost its sensibility*). **2 a** openness to emotional impressions; susceptibility; sensitiveness (*sensibility to kindness*). **b** an exceptional or excessive degree of this (*sense and sensibility*). **3** (in *pl.*) emotional capacities or feelings. [ME f. LL *sensibilitas* (as SENSIBLE)]
■ **1** see FEELING *n.* 1. **2 a** responsiveness, responsivity, openness, susceptibility, sensitivity, sensitiveness. **3** (*sensibilities*) feelings, emotions, sentiments, susceptibilities.

sensible /sénsibəl/ *adj.* **1** having or showing wisdom or common sense; reasonable; judicious (*a sensible person; a sensible compromise*). **2** perceptible by the senses (*sensible phenomena*). **b** great enough to be perceived; appreciable (*a sensible difference*). **3** (of clothing, etc.) practical and functional. **4** (foll. by *of*) aware; not unmindful (*was sensible of his peril*). □ **sensible horizon** see HORIZON 1b. □□ **sensibleness** *n.* **sensibly** *adv.* [ME f. OF *sensible* or L *sensibilis* (as SENSE)]

■ **1, 3** reasonable, realistic, logical, commonsensical, rational, reasoned, sound, practical, prudent, judicious, discreet, intelligent, sage, wise, sane; down-to-earth, practical; well-thought-out; functional. **2** perceivable, perceptible, detectable, evident, discernible, recognizable, ascertainable, apprehensible, cognizable, manifest, palpable, physical, tangible, corporeal, material, visible, observable, seeable, *archaic* substantive; appreciable, significant, considerable, substantial, noticeable. **4** (*sensible of*) aware of, acquainted with, cognizant of, sensitive to, alive to, mindful of, understanding of, in touch with, observant of, awake to, alert to, *colloq.* wise to, *sl.* hip to.

sensitive /sénsitiv/ *adj.* & *n.* ● *adj.* **1** (often foll. by *to*) very open to or acutely affected by external stimuli or mental impressions; having sensibility. **2** (of a person) easily offended or emotionally hurt. **3** (often foll. by *to*) (of an instrument, etc.) responsive to or recording slight changes. **4** (often foll. by *to*) **a** (of photographic materials) prepared so as to respond (esp. rapidly) to the action of light. **b** (of any material) readily affected by or responsive to external action. **5** (of a topic, etc.) subject to restriction of discussion to prevent embarrassment, ensure security, etc. **6** (of a market) liable to quick changes of price. ● *n.* a person who is sensitive (esp. to supposed occult influences). □ **sensitive plant 1** a plant whose leaves curve downward and leaflets fold together when touched, esp. mimosa. **2** a sensitive person. □□ **sensitively** *adv.* **sensitiveness** *n.* [ME, = sensory, f. OF *sensitif -ive* or med.L *sensitivus*, irreg. f. L *sentire sens-* feel]
■ *adj.* **1** delicate, tender, sore, susceptible. **2** touchy, susceptible, susceptive, reactive, responsive, attuned, impressionable, emotional, thin-skinned, tender, vulnerable, supersensitive, hypersensitive, testy, irascible, quarrelsome, irritable, volatile, excitable, temperamental, petulant, hot-tempered, quick-tempered. **3, 4, 6** finely tuned, delicate, responsive, subtle, acute, reactive, receptive. **5** see DELICATE 3a.

sensitivity /sénsitívitee/ *n.* the quality or degree of being sensitive.
■ sensibility, sensitiveness, delicacy, touchiness, oversensitivity, hypersensitivity, supersensitivity; soreness, irritability; awareness, consciousness, acuteness, perception, understanding, intuition, feeling, sense, receptivity, receptiveness, appreciation, appreciativeness, susceptibility, susceptibleness, susceptivity, susceptiveness; compassion, concern, sympathy, tenderness, tenderheartedness, kindheartedness, kindliness, warmth.

sensitize /sénsitīz/ *v.tr.* **1** make sensitive. **2** *Photog.* make sensitive to light. **3** make (an organism, etc.) abnormally sensitive to a foreign substance. □□ **sensitization** *n.* **sensitizer** *n.*

sensitometer /sénsitómitər/ *n. Photog.* a device for measuring sensitivity to light.

sensor /sénsər/ *n.* a device giving a signal for the detection or measurement of a physical property to which it responds. [SENSORY, after MOTOR]
■ probe, feeler.

sensorium /sensáwreeəm/ *n.* (*pl.* **sensoria** /-reeə/ or **sensoriums**) **1** the seat of sensation, the brain, brain and spinal cord, or gray matter of these. **2** *Biol.* the whole sensory apparatus including the nerve system. □□ **sensorial** *adj.* **sensorially** *adv.* [LL f. L *sentire sens-* feel]

sensory /sénsəree/ *adj.* of sensation or the senses. □□ **sensorily** *adv.* [as SENSORIUM]

sensual /sénshōōəl/ *adj.* **1 a** of or depending on the senses only and not on the intellect or spirit; carnal; fleshly (*sensual pleasures*). **b** given to the pursuit of sensual pleasures or the

---

/.../ **pronunciation**	● **part of speech**
□ **phrases, idioms, and compounds**	
□□ **derivatives**	■ **synonym section**
cross-references appear in SMALL CAPITALS or *italics*	

gratification of the appetites; self-indulgent sexually or in regard to food and drink; voluptuous; licentious. **c** indicative of a sensual nature (*sensual lips*). **2** of sense or sensation; sensory. **3** *Philos.* of, according to, or holding the doctrine of, sensationalism. □□ **sensualism** *n.* **sensualist** *n.* **sensualize** *v.tr.* **sensually** *adv.* [ME f. LL *sensualis* (as SENSE)]

■ **1** physical, appetitive, voluptuous, carnal, bodily, fleshly; erotic, sexual, lustful, unchaste, abandoned, dissolute, profligate, dissipated, licentious, lewd, lascivious, lubricious, goatish, lecherous, libidinous, salacious, prurient, rakish, wanton, debauched, loose, dirty, randy. □□ **sensualist** lecher, profligate, wanton, debauchee, roué, rake, Romeo, Don Juan, Casanova, lothario, libertine; voluptuary, hedonist, sybarite, bon viveur, bon vivant, epicure, epicurean, gourmet, gourmand, gastronome, pleasure seeker.

sensuality /sénshoo-álitee/ *n.* gratification of the senses, self-indulgence. [ME f. F *sensualité* f. LL *sensualitas* (as SENSUAL)]
■ eroticism, sexuality, physicality, carnality.

sensum /sénsəm/ *n.* (*pl.* **sensa** /-sə/) *Philos.* a sense-datum. [mod.L, neut. past part. of L *sentire* feel]

sensuous /sénshooəs/ *adj.* **1** of or derived from or affecting the senses, esp. aesthetically rather than sensually; aesthetically pleasing. **2** readily affected by the senses. □□ **sensuously** *adv.* **sensuousness** *n.* [L *sensus* sense]
■ **1** sensory, sensorial; sumptuous, luxurious, rich, affective, intense. **2** responsive, receptive; see also SENSITIVE *adj.* 2

sent *past* and *past part.* of SEND.

sentence /séntəns/ *n.* & *v.* ● *n.* **1 a** a set of words complete in itself as the expression of a thought, containing or implying a subject and predicate, and conveying a statement, question, exclamation, or command. **b** a piece of writing or speech between two full stops or equivalent pauses, often including several grammatical sentences (e.g., *I went; he came*). **2 a** a decision of a court of law, esp. the punishment allotted to a person convicted in a criminal trial. **b** the declaration of this. **3** *Logic* a series of signs or symbols expressing a proposition in an artificial or logical language. ● *v.tr.* **1** declare the sentence of (a convicted criminal, etc.). **2** (foll. by *to*) declare (such a person) to be condemned to a specified punishment. □ **under sentence of** having been condemned to (*under sentence of death*). [ME f. OF f. L *sententia* opinion f. *sentire* be of opinion]
■ *n.* **2** judgment, decision, ruling, verdict, decree, determination; punishment.

sentential /senténshəl/ *adj.* *Gram.* & *Logic* of a sentence. [L *sententialis* (as SENTENCE)]

sententious /senténshəs/ *adj.* **1** (of a person) fond of pompous moralizing. **2** (of a style) affectedly formal. **3** aphoristic; pithy; given to the use of maxims, affecting a concise impressive style. □□ **sententiously** *adv.* **sententiousness** *n.* [L *sententiosus* (as SENTENCE)]
■ **1** see *pedantic* (PEDANT). **2** see POMPOUS 2. **3** see *epigrammatic* (EPIGRAM).

sentient /sénshənt/ *adj.* having the power of perception by the senses. □□ **sentience** *n.* **sentiency** *n.* **sentiently** *adv.* [L *sentire* feel]

sentiment /séntimənt/ *n.* **1** a mental feeling (*the sentiment of pity*). **2 a** the sum of what one feels on some subject. **b** a verbal expression of this. **3** the expression of a view or desire esp. as formulated for a toast (*concluded his speech with a sentiment*). **4** an opinion as distinguished from the words meant to convey it (*the sentiment is good though the words are injudicious*). **5** a view or tendency based on or colored with emotion (*animated by noble sentiments*). **6** such views collectively, esp. as an influence (*sentiment unchecked by reason is a bad guide*). **7** the tendency to be swayed by feeling rather than by reason. **8 a** mawkish tenderness. **b** the display of this. **9** an emotional feeling conveyed in literature or art. [ME f. OF *sentement* f. med.L *sentimentum* f. L *sentire* feel]
■ **1, 9** attitude, feeling, sensibility, emotion. **2, 5** thought; (*sentiments*) view, outlook, opinion, belief, position, judgment. **4** thought. **8** sentimentality, sentimentalism.

sentimental /séntimént'l/ *adj.* **1** of or characterized by sen-

timent. **2** showing or affected by emotion rather than reason. **3** appealing to sentiment. □ **sentimental value** the value of a thing to a particular person because of its associations. □□ **sentimentalism** *n.* **sentimentalist** *n.* **sentimentality** /-tálitee/ *n.* **sentimentalize** *v.intr.* & *tr.* **sentimentalization** *n.* **sentimentally** *adv.*

■ emotional; sympathetic, compassionate, tender, warmhearted, tenderhearted; romantic, nostalgic, maudlin, mawkish, overemotional, tearful, sickening, nauseating, simpering, sweet, saccharine, sickly, mushy, gushy, *colloq.* weepy, sloppy, slushy, lovey-dovey, corny, icky, *colloq.* soppy, schmaltzy, *sl.* gooey, drippy, yucky. □□ **sentimentality** romanticism, nostalgia, pathos, emotionalism, mawkishness, overemotionalism, tenderness, tearfulness, sweetness, sickliness, mushiness, gushiness, *colloq.* sloppiness, weepiness, corniness, corn, soppiness, schmaltz, schmaltziness, *sl.* gooeyness, slushiness, drippiness, ickiness, yuckiness.

sentinel /séntinəl/ *n.* & *v.* ● *n.* a sentry or lookout. ● *v.tr.* (**sentineled, sentineling**) **1** station sentinels at or in. **2** *poet.* keep guard over or in. [F *sentinelle* f. It. *sentinella*, of unkn. orig.]
■ *n.* sentry, guard, watchman, watch, lookout, patrol, *Mil.* picket.

sentry /séntree/ *n.* (*pl.* -**ies**) a soldier, etc., stationed to keep guard. □ **sentry box** a wooden cabin intended to shelter a standing sentry. [perh. f. obs. *centrinel*, var. of SENTINEL]
■ see GUARD *n.* 2.

sepal /seépəl/ *n.* *Bot.* each of the divisions or leaves of the calyx. [F *sépale*, mod.L *sepalum*, perh. formed as SEPARATE + PETAL]

separable /sépərəbəl/ *adj.* **1** able to be separated. **2** *Gram.* (of a prefix, or a verb in respect of a prefix) written as a separate word in some collocations. □□ **separability** *n.* **separableness** *n.* **separably** *adv.* [F *séparable* or L *separabilis* (as SEPARATE)]
■ **1** distinguishable; segregable, detachable, divisible, severable, removable, fissile, scissile.

separate *adj., n.,* & *v.* ● *adj.* /sépərət, séprət/ (often foll. by *from*) forming a unit that is or may be regarded as apart or by itself; physically disconnected, distinct, or individual (*living in separate rooms; the two questions are essentially separate*). ● *n.* /sépərət, séprət/ **1** (in *pl.*) separate articles of clothing suitable for wearing together in various combinations. **2** an offprint. ● *v.* /sépərayt/ **1** *tr.* make separate; sever; disunite. **2** *tr.* prevent union or contact of. **3** *intr.* go different ways; disperse. **4** *intr.* cease to live together as a married couple. **5** *intr.* (foll. by *from*) secede. **6** *tr.* **a** divide or sort (milk, ore, fruit, light, etc.) into constituent parts or sizes. **b** (often foll. by *out*) extract or remove (an ingredient, waste product, etc.) by such a process for use or rejection. **7** *tr.* discharge or dismiss, esp. from an armed service, etc. □□ **separately** *adv.* **separateness** *n.* **separative** /-rətiv/ *adj.* **separatory** /-rətawree/ *adj.* [L *separare separat-* (as SE-, *parare* make ready)]

■ *adj.* divided, separated, disjoined, disconnected, detached, isolated, discrete, distinct, individual, independent, solitary, different; unrelated, other; withdrawn, solitary, alone; shut *or* closed off *or* away, apart, removed, cloistered, secluded, sequestered. ● *v.* **1** sever, disjoin, pull *or* take *or* break apart, take *or* break to pieces, split *or* divide *or* break (up), split *or* break (off *or* away), disconnect, disengage, part, partition, uncouple, disarticulate, disassemble, unhook, detach, disunite, unyoke, disentangle, unravel. **3, 4** disperse, split (up), break up, part (company), divide (up), disband, divorce; fork, bifurcate, diverge, branch. **5** see SECEDE. **6 a** distinguish, discriminate, analyze, sort (out), break down, classify, segregate, single out, sequester, type, codify, organize, split up; group, collate. □□ **separately** individually, independently, singly, one by one, one at a time, personally, alone, severally.

separation /sépəráyshən/ *n.* **1** the act or an instance of sep-

arating; the state of being separated. **2** (in full **judicial separation** or **legal separation**) an arrangement by which a husband and wife remain married but live apart. **3** any of three or more monochrome reproductions of a colored picture that can combine to reproduce the full color of the original. □ **separation order** a court order for judicial separation. [ME f. OF f. L *separatio -onis* (as SEPARATE)]
■ **1, 2** partition, division, split, schism; dissociation, disassociation, severance; disintegration, shattering, breakup, fragmentation, disunion, dismemberment, taking *or* keeping apart, segregation, disjunction, fission, scission, rupture, fracture, break; rift, split, split-up, estrangement.

separatist /sépərətist, séprə-/ *n.* a person who favors separation, esp. for political or ecclesiastical independence (opp. UNIONIST 2). □□ **separatism** *n.*

separator /sépəraytər/ *n.* a machine for separating, e.g., cream from milk.

Sephardi /sifaárdee/ *n.* (*pl.* **Sephardim** /-dim/) a Jew of Spanish or Portuguese descent (cf. ASHKENAZI). □□ **Sephardic** *adj.* [LHeb., f. s^e*p̄ārad*, a country mentioned in Obad. 20 and taken to be Spain]

sepia /seépeeə/ *n.* **1** a dark reddish-brown color. **2 a** a brown pigment prepared from a black fluid secreted by cuttlefish, used in monochrome drawing and in watercolors. **b** a brown tint used in photography. **3** a drawing done in sepia. **4** the fluid secreted by cuttlefish. [L f. Gk *sēpia* cuttlefish]

sepoy /seépoy/ *n. hist.* a native Indian soldier under European, esp. British, discipline. [Urdu & Pers. *sipāhī* soldier f. *sipāh* army]

seppuku /sépo͞oko͞o, sepo͞ok-/ *n.* hara-kiri. [Jap.]

sepsis /sépsis/ *n.* **1** the state of being septic. **2** blood poisoning. [mod.L f. Gk *sēpsis* f. *sēpō* make rotten]

Sept. *abbr.* **1** September. **2** Septuagint.

sept /sept/ *n.* a clan, esp. in Ireland. [prob. alt. of SECT]
■ see TRIBE.

sept- var. of SEPTI-.

septa *pl.* of SEPTUM.

septal[1] /séptəl/ *adj.* **1** of a septum or septa. **2** *Archaeol.* (of a stone or slab) separating compartments in a burial chamber. [SEPTUM]

septal[2] /séptəl/ *adj.* of a sept or septs.

septate /séptayt/ *adj. Bot., Zool., & Anat.* having a septum or septa; partitioned. □□ **septation** /-táyshən/ *n.*

septcentenary /séptsentónaree/ *n. & adj.* ● *n.* (*pl.* **-ies**) **1** a seven-hundredth anniversary. **2** a festival marking this. ● *adj.* of or concerning a septcentenary.

September /septémbər/ *n.* the ninth month of the year. [ME f. L *September* f. *septem* seven: orig. the seventh month of the Roman year]

septenarius /séptináireeəs/ *n.* (*pl.* **septenarii** /-ree-i/) *Prosody* a verse of seven feet, esp. a trochaic or iambic tetrameter catalectic. [L f. *septeni* distributive of *septem* seven]

septenary /séptəneree/ *adj. & n.* ● *adj.* of seven, by sevens, on the basis of seven. ● *n.* (*pl.* **-ies**) **1** a group or set of seven (esp. years). **2** a septenarius. [L *septenarius* (as SEPTENARIUS)]

septenate /séptinayt/ *adj. Bot.* **1** growing in sevens. **2** having seven divisions. [L *septeni* (as SEPTENARIUS)]

septennial /septéneeəl/ *adj.* **1** lasting for seven years. **2** recurring every seven years. [LL *septennis* f. L *septem* seven + *annus* year]

septennium /septéneeəm/ *n.* (*pl.* **septenniums** or **septennia** /-neeə/) a period of seven years.

septet /septét/ *n.* (also **septette**) **1** *Mus.* **a** a composition for seven performers. **b** the performers of such a composition. **2** any group of seven. [G *Septett* f. L *septem* seven]

septfoil /sétfoyl/ *n.* **1** a seven-lobed ornamental figure. **2** *archaic* tormentil. [LL *septifolium* after CINQUEFOIL, TREFOIL]

septi- /séptee/ *comb. form* (also **sept-** before a vowel) seven. [L f. *septem* seven]

septic /séptik/ *adj.* contaminated with bacteria from a festering wound, etc.; putrefying. □ **septic tank** a tank in which the organic matter in sewage is disintegrated through bac-

terial activity. □□ **septically** *adv.* **septicity** /-tísitee/ *n.* [L *septicus* f. Gk *sēptikos* f. *sēpō* make rotten]
■ see *ulcerous* (ULCER).

septicemia /séptiseémeeə/ *n.* blood poisoning. □□ **septicemic** *adj.* [mod.L f. Gk *sēptikos* + *haima* blood]

septillion /septílyən/ *n.* (*pl.* same) a thousand raised to the eighth (or formerly, esp. *Brit.*, the fourteenth) power (10^{24} and 10^{42}, respectively). [F f. *sept* seven, after *billion*, etc.]

septimal /séptiməl/ *adj.* of the number seven. [L *septimus* seventh f. *septem* seven]

septime /sépteem/ *n. Fencing* the seventh of the eight parrying positions. [L *septimus* (as SEPTIMAL)]

septivalent /septiváylənt/ *adj.* (also **septavalent**) *Chem.* having a valence of seven.

septuagenarian /sépcho͞oəjináireeən, -to͞o-, -tyo͞o-/ *n. & adj.* ● *n.* a person from 70 to 79 years old. ● *adj.* of this age. [L *septuagenarius* f. *septuageni* distributive of *septuaginta* seventy]

Septuagesima /sépto͞oəjésimə, -cho͞o-, -tyo͞o-/ *n.* (in full **Septuagesima Sunday**) the Sunday before Sexagesima. [ME f. L, = seventieth (day), formed as SEPTUAGINT, perh. after QUINQUAGESIMA or with ref. to the period of 70 days from Septuagesima to the Saturday after Easter]

Septuagint /sépto͞oəjint, -tyo͞o-/ *n.* a Greek version of the Old Testament including the Apocrypha, said to have been made about 270 BC by seventy-two translators. [L *septuaginta* seventy]

septum /séptəm/ *n.* (*pl.* **septa** /-tə/) *Anat., Bot., & Zool.* a partition such as that between the nostrils or the chambers of a poppy fruit or of a shell. [L *s(a)eptum* f. *saepire* saept-enclose f. *saepes* hedge]

septuple /sépto͞opəl, -tyo͞o-, -túpəl, sépto͞opəl/ *adj., n., & v.* ● *adj.* **1** sevenfold, having seven parts. **2** being seven times as many or as much. ● *n.* a sevenfold number or amount. ● *v.tr. & intr.* multiply by seven. [LL *septuplus* f. L *septem* seven]

septuplet /sépto͞oplit, -to͞o-, -tyo͞o-/ *n.* **1** one of seven children born at one birth. **2** *Mus.* a group of seven notes to be played in the time of four or six. [as SEPTUPLE, after TRIPLET, etc.]

sepulchral /sipúlkrəl/ *adj.* **1** of a tomb or interment (*sepulchral mound*; *sepulchral customs*). **2** suggestive of the tomb; funereal; gloomy; dismal (*sepulchral look*). □□ **sepulchrally** *adv.* [F *sépulchral* or L *sepulchralis* (as SEPULCHER)]
■ **2** see FUNEREAL.

sepulcher /sépəlkər/ *n. & v.* (also **sepulchre**) ● *n.* a tomb esp. cut in rock or built of stone or brick, a burial vault or cave. ● *v.tr.* **1** lay in a sepulcher. **2** serve as a sepulcher for. □ **the Holy Sepulchre** the tomb in which Christ was laid. **whited sepulcher** a hypocrite (with ref. to Matt. 23:27). [ME f. OF f. L *sepulc(h)rum* f. *sepelire* sepult- bury]
■ *n.* tomb, mausoleum, burial vault, grave, crypt, pyramid, burial place.

sepulture /sépəlchər/ *n. literary* the act or an instance of burying or putting in the grave. [ME f. OF f. L *sepultura* (as SEPULCHER)]
■ see BURIAL 1.

seq. *abbr.* (*pl.* **seqq.**) the following. [L *sequens*, etc.]

sequacious /sikwáyshəs/ *adj.* **1** (of reasoning or a reasoner) not inconsequent; coherent. **2** *archaic* inclined to follow; lacking independence or originality; servile. □□ **sequaciously** *adv.* **sequacity** /sikwásitee/ *n.* [L *sequax* f. *sequi* follow]

sequel /seékwəl/ *n.* **1** what follows (esp. as a result). **2** a novel, motion picture, etc., that continues the story of an earlier one. □ **in the sequel** *Brit.* as things developed afterward. [ME f. OF *sequelle* or L *sequel(l)a* f. *sequi* follow]
■ upshot, issue, result, consequence, development; follow-up, supplement.

sequela /sikwélə/ *n.* (*pl.* **sequelae** /-ee/) *Med.* (esp. in *pl.*)

/.../ **pronunciation**	● **part of speech**
□ **phrases, idioms, and compounds**	
□□ **derivatives**	■ **synonym section**
cross-references appear in SMALL CAPITALS or *italics*	

a morbid condition or symptom following a disease. [L f. *sequi* follow]

sequence /séekwəns/ *n. & v.* ● *n.* **1** succession; coming after or next. **2** order of succession (*shall follow the sequence of events*; *give the facts in historical sequence*). **3** a set of things belonging next to one another on some principle of order; a series without gaps. **4** a part of a motion picture, etc., dealing with one scene or topic. **5** a set of poems on one theme. **6** a set of three or more playing cards next to one another in value. **7** *Mus.* repetition of a phrase or melody at a higher or lower pitch. **8** *Eccl.* a hymn said or sung after the gradual or alleluia that precedes the gospel. **9** succession without implication of causality (opp. CONSEQUENCE). ● *v.tr.* **1** arrange in a definite order. **2** *Biochem.* ascertain the sequence of monomers in (esp. a polypeptide or nucleic acid). □ **sequence of tenses** *Gram.* the dependence of the tense of a subordinate verb on the tense of the principal verb, according to certain rules (e.g., *I think you are*, *thought you were*, *wrong*). [ME f. LL *sequentia* f. L *sequens* pres. part. of *sequi* follow]

■ *n.* **1–3** succession, progression, chronology, order, series, chain, string, course, cycle, arrangement, organization, train, line, set, run, concatenation; system.

sequencer /séekwənsər/ *n.* a programmable device for storing sequences of musical notes, chords, etc., and transmitting them when required to an electronic musical instrument.

sequent /séekwənt/ *adj.* **1** following as a sequence or consequence. **2** consecutive. □□ **sequently** *adv.* [OF *sequent* or L *sequens* (as SEQUENCE)]

sequential /sikwénshəl/ *adj.* forming a sequence or consequence or sequela. □□ **sequentiality** /-sheeálitee/ *n.* **sequentially** *adv.* [SEQUENCE, after CONSEQUENTIAL]

■ successive, ordered, orderly, serial, progressive, organized, systematic, continuous.

sequester /sikwéstər/ *v.tr.* **1** (esp. as **sequestered** *adj.*) seclude; isolate; set apart (*sequester oneself from the world*; *a sequestered life*; *a sequestered jury*). **2** = SEQUESTRATE. **3** *Chem.* bind (a metal ion) so that it cannot react. [ME f. OF *sequestrer* or LL *sequestrare* commit for safe keeping f. L *sequester* trustee]

■ **1** see ISOLATE 1.

sequestrate /sikwéstrayt/ *v.tr.* **1** confiscate; appropriate. **2** *Law* take temporary possession of (a debtor's estate, etc.). **3** *Eccl.* apply (the income of a benefice) to clearing the incumbent's debts or accumulating a fund for the next incumbent. □□ **sequestrable** /-trəbəl/ *adj.* **sequestration** /séekwistráyshən/ *n.* **sequestrator** /séekwistraytər/ *n.* [LL *sequestrare* (as SEQUESTER)]

■ **1** see CONFISCATE. □□ **sequestration** see FORFEIT *n.* 4.

sequestrum /sikwéstrəm/ *n.* (*pl.* **sequestra** /-trə/) a piece of dead bone or other tissue detached from the surrounding parts. □□ **sequestral** *adj.* **sequestrotomy** /séekwistrótəmee/ *n.* (*pl.* **-ies**). [mod.L, neut. of L *sequester* standing apart]

sequin /séekwin/ *n.* **1** a circular spangle for attaching to clothing as an ornament. **2** *hist.* a Venetian gold coin. □□ **sequined** *adj.* (also **sequinned**). [F f. It. *zecchino* f. *zecca* a mint f. Arab. *sikka* die]

sequoia /sikwóyə/ *n.* a Californian evergreen coniferous tree, *Sequoia sempervirens*, of very great height. [mod.L genus name, f. *Sequoiah*, the name of a Cherokee]

sera *pl.* of SERUM.

serac /serák/ *n.* one of the tower-shaped masses into which a glacier is divided at steep points by crevasses crossing it. [Swiss F *sérac*, orig. the name of a compact white cheese]

seraglio /sərályō, raal-/ *n.* (*pl.* **-os**) **1** a harem. **2** *hist.* a Turkish palace, esp. that of the sultan with government offices, etc., at Constantinople. [It. *serraglio* f. Turk. f. Pers. *sarāy* palace: cf. SERAI]

serai /serí/ *n.* a caravansary. [Turk. f. Pers. (as SERAGLIO)]

serape /səráapee/ *n.* (also **sarape** /sa-/, **zarape** /za-/) a shawl or blanket worn as a cloak by Spanish Americans. [Mexican Sp.]

■ see WRAP *n.* 1.

seraph /sérəf/ *n.* (*pl.* **seraphim** /-fim/ or **seraphs**) an angelic being, one of the highest order of the ninefold celestial hierarchy gifted esp. with love and associated with light, ardor, and purity. [back-form. f. *seraphim* (cf. CHERUB) (pl.) f. LL f. Gk *seraphim* f. Heb. *s'rāpīm*]

seraphic /səráfik/ *adj.* **1** of or like the seraphim. **2** ecstatically adoring, fervent, or serene. □□ **seraphically** *adv.* [med.L *seraphicus* f. LL (as SERAPH)]

■ angelic, celestial, divine, heavenly, blissful, sublime, empyrean, elysian, ethereal, holy, saintly, godly.

Serb /sərb/ *n. & adj.* ● *n.* **1** a native of Serbia in the former Yugoslavia. **2** a person of Serbian descent. ● *adj.* = SERBIAN. [Serbian *Srb*]

Serbian /sə́rbeeən/ *n. & adj.* ● *n.* **1** the dialect of the Serbs (cf. SERBO-CROAT). **2** = SERB. ● *adj.* of or relating to the Serbs or their dialect.

Serbo- /sə́rbō/ *comb. form* Serbian.

Serbo-Croat /sə́rbōkrōat/ *n. & adj.* (also **Serbo-Croatian** /-krō-áyshən/) ● *n.* the main official language of the former Yugoslavia, combining Serbian and Croatian dialects. ● *adj.* of or relating to this language.

sere[1] /seer/ *n.* a catch of a gunlock holding the hammer at half or full cock. [prob. f. OF *serre* lock, bolt, grasp, f. *serrer* (see SERRIED)]

sere[2] /seer/ *adj.* (also **sear**) *literary* (esp. of a plant, etc.) withered; dried up. [see SEAR]

sere[3] /seer/ *n. Ecol.* a sequence of animal or plant communities. [L *serere* join in a SERIES]

serein /sərán/ *n.* a fine rain falling in tropical climates from a cloudless sky. [F f. OF *serain* ult. f. L *serum* evening f. *serus* late]

serenade /sérənáyd/ *n. & v.* ● *n.* **1** a piece of music sung or played at night, esp. by a lover under his lady's window, or suitable for this. **2** = SERENATA. ● *v.tr.* sing or play a serenade to. □□ **serenader** *n.* [F *sérénade* f. It. *serenata* f. *sereno* SERENE]

serenata /sérənáatə/ *n. Mus.* **1** a cantata with a pastoral subject. **2** a simple form of suite for orchestra or wind band. [It. (as SERENADE)]

serendipity /sérəndípitee/ *n.* the faculty of making happy and unexpected discoveries by accident. □□ **serendipitous** *adj.* **serendipitously** *adv.* [coined by Horace Walpole (1754) after *The Three Princes of Serendip* (Sri Lanka), a fairy tale]

■ see LUCK 3. □□ **serendipitous** see ACCIDENTAL *adj.* 1. **serendipitously** see *at random* (RANDOM).

serene /sireén/ *adj. & n.* ● *adj.* (**serener**, **serenest**) **1 a** (of the sky, the air, etc.) clear and calm. **b** (of the sea, etc.) unruffled. **2** placid; tranquil; unperturbed. ● *n. poet.* a serene expanse of sky, sea, etc. □ **all serene** *Brit. sl.* all right. **Serene Highness** a title used in addressing and referring to members of some European royal families (*His Serene Highness*; *Their Serene Highnesses*; *Your Serene Highness*). □□ **serenely** *adv.* **sereneness** *n.* [L *serenus*]

■ *adj.* peaceful, tranquil, calm, pacific, peaceable, restful, halcyon, idyllic, bucolic, pastoral, undisturbed, unruffled, imperturbable, unperturbed, untroubled, quiet, still; cool, collected, placid, composed, self-possessed, poised, unexcitable, even-tempered, temperate, nonchalant, easygoing, coolheaded, easy, *colloq.* unflappable.

serenity /sirénitee/ *n.* (*pl.* **-ies**) **1** tranquillity; being serene. **2** (**Serenity**) a title used in addressing and referring to a reigning prince or similar dignitary (*your Serenity*). [F *sérénité* or L *serenitas* (as SERENE)]

■ **1** peacefulness, peace, tranquillity, calm, calmness, restfulness, quiet, stillness; peaceableness, unexcitability, composure, self-possession, poise, aplomb, even-temperedness, nonchalance, coolheadedness, placidity, *colloq.* unflappability.

serf /sərf/ *n. hist.* **1** a laborer not allowed to leave the land on which he worked; a villein. **2** an oppressed person; a drudge. □□ **serfage** *n.* **serfdom** *n.* **serfhood** *n.* [OF f. L *servus* slave]

■ **1** *hist.* vassal, villein. **2** see MENIAL *n.* 1. □□ **serfdom** see SLAVERY 1.

serge /sərj/ n. a durable twilled worsted, etc., fabric. [ME f. OF *sarge*, *serge* ult. f. L *serica* (*lana*): see SILK]

sergeant /sáarjənt/ n. **1** a noncommissioned army, marine, or air force officer next below warrant officer. **2** a police officer ranking below captain. **sergeant-at-arms** (pl. **sergeants-at-arms**) an official of a court or city or legislature, with ceremonial duties. **Sergeant Baker** *Austral.* a large brightly colored marine fish, *Aulopus purpurissatus.* **sergeant fish** a marine fish, *Rachycentron canadum*, with lateral stripes suggesting a chevron. **sergeant major 1** *Mil.* the highest-ranking noncommissioned officer. **2** a black-striped damselfish of the tropical western Atlantic. □□ **sergeancy** n. (pl. **-ies**). **sergeantship** n. [ME f. OF *sergent* f. L *serviens* *-entis* servant f. *servire* SERVE]

sergt. abbr. sergeant.

serial /séereeəl/ n. & adj. ● n. **1** a story, play, motion picture, etc., that is published, broadcast, or shown in regular installments. **2** a periodical. ● adj. **1** of or in or forming a series. **2** (of a story, etc.) in the form of a serial. **3** *Mus.* using transformations of a fixed series of notes (see SERIES). **4** (of a publication) appearing in successive parts published usu. at regular intervals; periodical. □ **serial killer** a person who murders continually with no apparent motive. **serial number** a number showing the position of an item in a series. **serial rights** the right to publish a story or book as a serial. □□ **seriality** /-reeálitee/ n. **serially** adv. [SERIES + -AL]
■ n. **1** see PERIODICAL n. ● adj. **1** see SEQUENTIAL.

serialist /séereeəlist/ n. a composer or advocate of serial music. □□ **serialism** n.

serialize /séereeəlīz/ v.tr. **1** publish or produce in installments. **2** arrange in a series. **3** *Mus.* compose according to a serial technique. □□ **serialization** n.

seriate adj. & v. ● adj. /séereeət/ in the form of a series; in orderly sequence. ● v.tr. /séereeayt/ arrange in a seriate manner. □□ **seriation** /-reeáyshən/ n.

seriatim /séeree-áytim, sér-/ adv. point by point; taking one subject, etc., after another in regular order (*consider seriatim*). [med.L f. L *series*, after LITERATIM, etc.]
■ see *singly* (SINGLE).

Seric /séerik/ adj. archaic Chinese. [L *sericus*; see SILK]

sericeous /siríshəs/ adj. *Bot. & Zool.* covered with silky hairs. [LL *sericeus* silken]
■ see SILKY 1.

sericulture /sérikulchər/ n. **1** silkworm breeding. **2** the production of raw silk. □□ **sericultural** adj. **sericulturist** n. [F *sériciculture* f. LL *sericum*: see SILK, CULTURE]

seriema /séree-eémə/ n. (also **cariama** /káreeaámə/) *Zool.* any S. American bird of the family Cariamidae, having a long neck and legs and a crest above the bill. [mod.L f. Tupi *siriema*, etc., crested]

series /séereez/ n. (pl. same) **1** a number of things of which each is similar to the preceding or in which each successive pair are similarly related; a sequence, succession, order, row, or set. **2** a set of successive games between the same teams. **3** a set of programs with the same actors, etc., or on related subjects but each complete in itself. **4** a set of lectures by the same speaker or on the same subject. **5 a** a set of successive issues of a periodical, of articles on one subject or by one writer, etc., esp. when numbered separately from a preceding or following set (*second series*). **b** a set of independent books in a common format or under a common title or supervised by a common general editor. **6** *Philately* a set of stamps, coins, etc., of different denominations but issued at one time, in one reign, etc. **7** *Geol.* **a** a set of strata with a common characteristic. **b** the rocks deposited during a specific epoch. **8** *Mus.* = *tone row.* **9** *Electr.* **a** a set of circuits or components arranged so that the current passes through each successively. **b** a set of batteries, etc., having the positive electrode of each connected with the negative electrode of the next. **10** *Chem.* a set of elements with common properties or of compounds related in composition or structure. **11** *Math.* a set of quantities constituting a progression or having the several values determined by a common relation. □ **arithmetical** (or **geometrical**) **series** a series in arithmetical (or geometrical) progression. **in series**

1 in ordered succession. **2** *Electr.* (of a set of circuits or components) arranged so that the current passes through each successively. [L, = row, chain f. *serere* join, connect]
■ **1** see SEQUENCE n. **2–6** see SET² 1, 2.

serif /sérif/ n. a slight projection finishing off a stroke of a letter as in T contrasted with T (cf. SANS SERIF). □□ **seriffed** adj. [perh. f. Du. *schreef* dash, line f. Gmc]

serigraphy /sərígrəfee/ n. the art or process of printing designs by means of a silk screen. □□ **serigraph** /sérigraf/ n. **serigrapher** /sərígrəfər/ n. [irreg. f. L *sericum* SILK]

serin /sérin/ n. any small yellow Mediterranean finch of the genus *Serinus*, esp. the wild canary *S. serinus.* [F, of uncert. orig.]

seringa /sərínggə/ n. **1** = SYRINGA. **2** any of various rubber trees of the genus *Hevea*, native to Brazil. [F (as SYRINGA)]

seriocomic /séeree-ōkómik/ adj. combining the serious and the comic; jocular in intention but simulating seriousness or vice versa. □□ **seriocomically** adv.

serious /séereeəs/ adj. **1** thoughtful; earnest; sober; sedate; responsible; not reckless nor given to trifling (*has a serious air*; *a serious young person*). **2** important, demanding consideration (*this is a serious matter*). **3** not slight or negligible (*a serious injury*; *a serious offense*). **4** sincere; in earnest; not ironic nor joking (*are you serious?*). **5** (of music and literature) not merely for amusement (opp. LIGHT² 5a). **6** not perfunctory (*serious thought*). **7** not to be trifled with (*a serious opponent*). **8** concerned with religion or ethics (*serious subjects*). □□ **seriousness** n. [ME f. OF *serieux* or LL *seriosus* f. L *serius*]
■ **1** grave, solemn, earnest, unsmiling, poker-faced, straight-faced, sedate, sober, pensive, thoughtful; responsible; humorless, somber, grim, dour, severe. **2, 3, 7** grave, important, vital, weighty, significant, momentous, crucial, consequential, life-and-death, urgent, pressing; acute, critical, life-threatening, bad, dangerous, nasty, perilous, alarming, severe, precarious. **4** sincere, straightforward, genuine, (in) earnest, honest.

seriously /séereeəslee/ adv. **1** in a serious manner (esp. introducing a sentence, implying that irony, etc., is now to cease). **2** to a serious extent. **3** *colloq.* (as an intensifier) very; really; substantially (*seriously rich*).
■ **1** soberly, earnestly, without a doubt, at face value; really, honestly, sincerely, truly, candidly, openly, joking aside *or* apart. **2** gravely, badly, severely, critically, grievously, dangerously, acutely. **3** see VERY adv.

serjeant /sáarjənt/ n. *Brit.* (in full **serjeant-at-law**, pl. **serjeants-at-law**) *hist.* a barrister of the highest rank. [var. of SERGEANT]

sermon /sérmən/ n. **1** a spoken or written discourse on a religious or moral subject, esp. a discourse based on a text or passage of Scripture and delivered in a service by way of religious instruction or exhortation. **2** a piece of admonition or reproof; a lecture. **3** a moral reflection suggested by natural objects, etc. (*sermons in stones*). □ **Sermon on the Mount** the discourse of Christ recorded in Matt. 5–7. [ME f. AF *sermun*, OF *sermon* f. L *sermo -onis* discourse, talk]
■ **1** homily, address, exhortation, lecture, speech, talk, *literary* discourse. **2** lecture, lesson, reprimand, reproach, admonition, reproof, rebuke, remonstration, remonstrance, scolding, harangue, *colloq.* talking-to, dressing-down, esp. *Brit.* telling-off, ticking-off.

sermonette /sérmənét/ n. a short sermon.

sermonize /sérmənīz/ v. **1** tr. deliver a moral lecture to. **2** intr. deliver a moral lecture. □□ **sermonizer** n.
■ see LECTURE v. 1, 2.

serology /seeróləjee/ n. the scientific study of blood sera and their effects. □□ **serological** /-rəlójikəl/ adj. **serologist** n.

/.../ pronunciation	● part of speech
□ phrases, idioms, and compounds	
□□ derivatives	■ synonym section
cross-references appear in SMALL CAPITALS or *italics*	

serosa /sərṓsə/ n. a serous membrane. [mod.L, fem. of med.L serosus SEROUS]

serotine /sérətin, -tīn/ n. a chestnut-colored European bat, *Eptesicus serotinus*. [F *sérotine* f. L *serotinus* late, of the evening, f. *serus* late]

serotonin /sérətŏnin/ n. Biol. a compound present in blood serum, which constricts the blood vessels and acts as a neurotransmitter. [SERUM + TONIC + -IN]

serous /séərəs/ adj. of or like or producing serum; watery. □ **serous gland** (or **membrane**) a gland or membrane with a serous secretion. □□ **serosity** /-rósitee/ n. [F *séreux* or med.L *serosus* (as SERUM)]

serpent /sə́rpənt/ n. **1** usu. *literary* **a** a snake, esp. of a large kind. **b** a scaly limbless reptile. **2** a sly or treacherous person, esp. one who exploits a position of trust to betray it. **3** *Mus.* an old bass wind instrument made from leather-covered wood, roughly in the form of an S. **4** (**the Serpent**) *Bibl.* Satan (see Gen. 3, Rev. 20). [ME f. OF f. L *serpens -entis* part. of *serpere* creep]
∎ **1 a** snake, ophidian. **2** see SNAKE n. 2.

serpentine /sə́rpəntin/ adj., n., & v. ● adj. **1** of or like a serpent. **2** coiling; tortuous; sinuous; meandering; writhing (*the serpentine windings of the stream*). **3** cunning; subtle; treacherous. ● n. **1** a soft rock mainly of hydrated magnesium silicate, usu. dark green and sometimes mottled or spotted like a serpent's skin, taking a high polish and used as a decorative material. **2** *Skating* a figure of three circles in a line. ● v.intr. move sinuously; meander. □ **serpentine verse** a metrical line beginning and ending with the same word. [ME f. OF *serpentin* f. LL *serpentinus* (as SERPENT)]
∎ adj. **2** twisting, winding, tortuous, coiling, writhing, snaking, snakelike, sinuous, anfractuous, roundabout, meandering, indirect, devious, crooked, labyrinthine, vermicular, vermiculate, complex, complicated, Byzantine. **3** evil, bad, diabolic(al), satanic, Mephistophelean, reptilian, devilish, wily, cunning, treacherous, conniving, sneaky, shrewd, artful, crafty, subtle, slick, sly, insidious, tricky, scheming, plotting, furtive, machiavellian, *colloq.* shifty; snakelike, vermicular.

serpiginous /sərpíjinəs/ adj. (of a skin disease, etc.) creeping from one part to another. [med.L *serpigo -ginis* ringworm f. L *serpere* creep]

serpula /sə́rpyələ/ n. (*pl.* **serpulae** /-lee/) any of various marine worms of the family Serpulidae, living in intricately twisted shell-like tubes. [LL, = small serpent, f. L *serpere* creep]

serra /sérə/ n. (*pl.* **serrae** /-ree/) a serrated organ, structure, or edge. [L, = saw]

serradilla /sérədílə/ n. (*pl.* **serradillae** /-lee/) a clover, *Ornithopus sativus*, grown as fodder. [Port., dimin. of *serrado* serrated]

serran /sérən/ n. any marine fish of the family Serranidae. [mod.L *serranus* f. L *serra* saw]

serrate v. & adj. ● v.tr. /səráyt/ (usu. as **serrated** adj.) provide with a sawlike edge. ● adj. /sérayt/ esp. *Anat.*, *Bot.*, & *Zool.* notched like a saw. □□ **serration** /-ráyshən/ n. [LL *serrare serrat-* f. L *serra* saw]
∎ v. (**serrated**) sawlike, sawtooth(ed), crenellated, toothed, notched, zigzag, jagged, serrate, esp. *Anat.*, *Bot.*, & *Zool.* serrulate, *Bot.* & *Zool.* crenate(d), *Zool.* denticulate. □□ **serration** tooth, spike, point, prong; notch.

serried /séreed/ adj. (of ranks of soldiers, rows of trees, etc.) pressed together; without gaps; close. [past part. of *serry* press close prob. f. F *serré* past part. of *serrer* close ult. f. L *sera* lock, or past part. of obs. *serr* f. OF *serrer*]
∎ ranked, tiered, ranged, assembled, packed, close, tight, compacted, compact.

serrulate /séryələt, -layt, sérə-/ adj. esp. *Anat.*, *Bot.*, & *Zool.* finely serrate; with a series of small notches. □□ **serrulation** /-láyshən/ n. [mod.L *serrulatus* f. L *serrula* dimin. of *serra* saw]

serum /séərəm/ n. (*pl.* **sera** /-rə/ or **serums**) **1 a** an amber-colored liquid that separates from a clot when blood coag-ulates. **b** whey. **2** *Med.* blood serum (usu. from a nonhuman mammal) as an antitoxin or therapeutic agent, esp. in inoculation. **3** a watery fluid in animal bodies. □ **serum sickness** a reaction to an injection of serum, characterized by skin eruption, fever, etc. [L, = whey]

serval /sə́rvəl/ n. a tawny, black-spotted, long-legged African feline, *Felis serval*. [F f. Port. *cerval* deerlike f. *cervo* deer f. L *cervus*]

servant /sə́rvənt/ n. **1** a person who has undertaken (usu. in return for stipulated pay) to carry out the orders of an individual or corporate employer, esp. a person employed in a house on domestic duties or as a personal attendant. **2** a devoted follower; a person willing to serve another (*a servant of Jesus Christ*). □ **your humble servant** *archaic* a formula preceding a signature or expressing ironical courtesy. **your obedient servant** a formula preceding a signature, now used only in certain (esp. *Brit.*) formal letters. [ME f. OF (as SERVE)]
∎ **1** domestic, help, menial, lackey, drudge, amah, factotum, *archaic* servitor, esp. *Brit. colloq.* dogsbody, *joc.* retainer; maid, housemaid, maidservant, chambermaid, lady's maid, boy, page, valet, man, gentleman's gentleman, manservant, *hist.* parlormaid; housekeeper, majordomo, steward, seneschal, butler, houseman, handyman, houseboy, servingman, footman, chauffeur, driver, coachman, postilion, attendant, groom, *Brit.* boots; governess, nurse, nursemaid, nanny, ayah, au pair (girl); cook, chef, waiter, waitress, stewardess, sommelier, *archaic* scullion; cleaning man, cleaning woman *or* lady, charwoman, charlady, cleaner, *Brit. colloq.* char, daily.

serve /sərv/ v. & n. ● v. **1** tr. do a service for (a person, community, etc.). **2** tr. (also *absol.*) be a servant to. **3** intr. carry out duties (*served on six committees*). **4** intr. **a** (foll. by *in*) be employed in (an organization, esp. the armed forces, or a place, esp. a foreign country) (*served in the air force*). **b** be a member of the armed forces. **5 a** tr. be useful to or serviceable for; meet the needs of; do what is required for (*serve a purpose*; *one packet serves him for a week*). **b** intr. meet requirements; perform a function (*a sofa serving as a bed*). **c** intr. (foll. by *to* + infin.) avail; suffice (*his attempt served only to postpone the inevitable*; *it serves to show the folly of such action*). **d** tr. (of the memory) to prove reliable; to assist or prompt (*if memory serves*). **6** tr. go through a due period of (office, apprenticeship, a prison sentence, etc.). **7** tr. set out or present (food) for those about to eat it (*asparagus served with butter*; *dinner was then served*). **8** intr. (act as a waiter. **9** tr. **a** attend to (a customer in a store). **b** (foll. by *with*) supply with (goods) (*was serving a customer with apples*; *served the town with gas*). **10** tr. treat or act toward (a person) in a specified way (*has served me shamefully*; *you may serve me as you will*). **11** tr. **a** (often foll. by *on*) deliver (a writ, etc.) to the person concerned in a legally formal manner (*served a warrant on him*). **b** (foll. by *with*) deliver a writ, etc., to (a person) in this way (*served her with a summons*). **12** tr. *Tennis*, etc. **a** (also *absol.*) deliver (a ball, etc.) to begin or resume play. **b** produce (a fault, etc.) by doing this. **13** tr. *Mil.* keep (a gun, battery, etc.) firing. **14** tr. (of an animal, esp. a stallion, etc., hired for the purpose) copulate with (a female). **15** tr. distribute (*served out the ammunition*; *served the rations around*). **16** tr. render obedience to (a deity, etc.). **17** *Eccl.* **a** intr. act as a server. **b** tr. act as a server at (a service). **18** tr. (of a tide) be suitable for a ship to leave harbor, etc. **19** tr. *Naut.* bind (a rope, etc.) with thin cord to strengthen it. **20** tr. *Brit.* play (a trick, etc.) on. ● n. **1** *Tennis*, etc. **a** the act or an instance of serving. **b** a manner of serving. **c** a person's turn to serve. **2** *Austral. sl.* a reprimand. □ **it will serve** it will be adequate. **serve one's needs** (or **need**) be adequate. **serve out** *Brit.* retaliate on. **serve the purpose of** take the place of; be used as. **serve a person right** be a person's deserved punishment or misfortune. **serve one's time 1** esp. *Brit.* hold office for the normal period. **2** (also **serve time**) undergo imprisonment, apprenticeship, etc. **serve one's** (or **the**) **turn** be adequate.

serve up offer for acceptance. [ME f. OF *servir* f. L *servire* f. *servus* slave]

■ *v.* **1, 2, 9a** attend (to *or* on), wait on *or* upon, minister to, look after, assist, help, be of assistance *or* help to, be at a person's service, oblige, accommodate, gratify; fight for; be obedient to. **3, 4** see WORK *v.* 2a. **5 a–c** fulfill, carry out, perform, discharge, work, do, suffice, be used *or* of use *or* useful, function, act, fill the bill, be serviceable, be available, answer, be sufficient *or* adequate *or* suitable, suit, be advantageous *or* of advantage (to), avail. **d** not fail, not play tricks (on), work *or* function (for), be accurate *or* correct. **6** go through, complete; survive. **7, 8, 15** distribute, deal out, dole out, give out, present, set out, provide, supply, offer, pass out *or* about *or* around, make available, dish up *or* out; wait. **9 b** see SUPPLY¹ *v.* 1, 2. **10** see TREAT *v.* 1. **11 a** deliver, hand over *or* out, give, present. **b** (*serve with*) deliver *or* give to, present with, hand over *or* out to. **16** see WORSHIP *v.* **18** be convenient *or* opportune *or* favorable *or* right. □ **serve up** see PROPOSE 1.

server /sɔ́rvər/ *n.* **1** a person who serves. **2** *Eccl.* a person assisting the celebrant at a service, esp. the Eucharist.

servery /sɔ́rvəree/ *n. Brit.* (*pl.* **-ies**) a room from which meals, etc., are served and in which utensils are kept.

service¹ /sɔ́rvis/ *n. & v.* ● *n.* **1** the act of helping or doing work for another or for a community, etc. **2** work done in this way. **3** assistance or benefit given to someone. **4** the provision or system of supplying a public need, e.g., transport, or (*Brit.*) (often in *pl.*) the supply of water, gas, electricity, telephone, etc. **5 a** the fact or status of being a servant. **b** employment or a position as a servant. **6** a state or period of employment doing work for an individual or organization (*resigned after 15 years' service*). **7 a** a public department or organization employing officials working for the government (*civil service*; *secret service*). **b** employment in this. **8** (in *pl.*) the armed forces. **9** (*attrib.*) of the kind issued to the armed forces (*a service revolver*). **10 a** a ceremony of worship according to prescribed forms. **b** a form of liturgy for this. **11 a** the provision of what is necessary for the installation and maintenance of a machine, etc., or operation. **b** a periodic routine maintenance of a motor vehicle, etc. **12** assistance or advice given to customers after the sale of goods. **13 a** the act or process of serving food, drinks, etc. **b** an extra charge nominally made for this. **14** a set of dishes, plates, etc., used for serving meals (*a dinner service*). **15** *Tennis*, etc. **a** the act or an instance of serving. **b** a person's turn to serve. **c** the manner or quality of serving. **d** (in full **service game**) a game in which a particular player serves. ● *v.tr.* **1** provide service or services for, esp. maintain. **2** maintain or repair (a car, machine, etc.). **3** pay interest on (a debt). **4** supply with a service. □ **at a person's service** ready to serve or assist a person. **be of service** be available to assist. **in service 1** employed as a servant. **2** available for use. **on active service** serving in the armed forces in wartime. **out of service** not available for use. **see service 1** have experience of service, esp. in the armed forces. **2** (of a thing) be much used. **service area 1** an area beside a major road for the supply of gasoline, refreshments, etc. **2** the area served by a broadcasting station. **service book** a book of authorized forms of worship of a church. **service charge** an additional charge for service in a restaurant, hotel, etc. **service dress** *Brit.* ordinary military, etc., uniform. **service industry** one providing services not goods. **service line** (in tennis, etc.) a line marking the limit of the area into which the ball must be served. **service road** a road parallel to a main road, serving houses, stores, etc. **service station** an establishment beside a road selling gasoline and oil, etc., to motorists and often able to carry out maintenance. **take service with** *Brit.* become a servant to. [ME f. OF *service* or L *servitium* f. *servus* slave]

■ *n.* **1–3, 12** help, assistance, aid, backing, support; use, usefulness, utility, benefit, advantage; serving, care, attention; advice. **4** see SYSTEM 1, SUPPLY¹ *n.* 1. **5, 6** employment, employ; assignment, post, position, appointment. **8** (*services*) army, navy, air force, marines; forces, troops, armed forces *or* services, military; militia. **10** rite, ceremony, ritual, worship; liturgy. **11** maintenance, overhaul, servicing, checking, repair, mending. **15** serve. ● *v.* **1, 2** see MAINTAIN 4. □ **out of service** see DEFUNCT 1, 2.

service² /sɔ́rvis/ *n.* (in full **service tree**) a European tree of the genus *Sorbus*, esp. *S. domestica* with toothed leaves, cream-colored flowers, and small round or pear-shaped fruit eaten when overripe. [earlier *serves*, pl. of obs. *serve* f. OE *syrfe* f. Gmc *surbhjōn* ult. f. L *sorbus*]

serviceable /sɔ́rvisəbəl/ *adj.* **1** useful or usable. **2** able to render service. **3** durable; capable of withstanding difficult conditions. **4** suited for ordinary use rather than ornamental. □□ **serviceability** *n.* **serviceableness** *n.* **serviceably** *adv.* [ME f. OF *servisable* (as SERVICE¹)]

■ **1, 2** workable, working, functional, functioning, usable, useful, operative. **3** hardwearing, durable, long-lasting, tough, wear-resistant. **4** practical, functional, utilitarian.

serviceberry /sɔ́rvisberee/ *n.* **1** the fruit of the service tree. **2 a** any American shrub of the genus *Amelanchier*. **b** the edible fruit of this.

serviceman /sɔ́rvismən/ *n.* (*pl.* **-men**) **1** a man serving in the armed forces. **2** a man providing service or maintenance.

■ **1** see SOLDIER *n.*

servicewoman /sɔ́rviswo͞omən/ *n.* (*pl.* **-women**) a woman serving in the armed forces.

■ see SOLDIER *n.*

serviette /sɔ́rvee-ét/ *n.* esp. *Brit.* a napkin for use at table. [ME f. OF f. *servir* SERVE]

servile /sɔ́rvil/ *adj.* **1** of or being or like a slave or slaves. **2** slavish; fawning; completely dependent. □□ **servilely** *adv.* **servility** /-vílitee/ *n.* [ME f. L *servilis* f. *servus* slave]

■ **2** submissive, subservient, menial, craven, acquiescent, abject, cringing, slavish, mean, fawning, deferential, ingratiating, groveling, obsequious, toadying, toadyish, sycophantish, sycophantic, wheedling, unctuous, slimy, flattering, timeserving, *colloq.* smarmy, bootlicking, creepytoadying, toadyism, sycophancy, truckling, wheedling, unctuousness, sliminess, flattery, *colloq.* smarminess, bootlicking.

serving /sɔ́rving/ *n.* a quantity of food served to one person.

■ see PORTION *n.* 2.

servitor /sɔ́rvitər/ *n.* **1** *archaic* **a** a servant. **b** an attendant. **2** *hist.* an Oxford undergraduate performing menial duties in exchange for assistance from college funds. □□ **servitorship** *n.* [ME f. OF f. LL (as SERVE)]

■ **1** see SERVANT.

servitude /sɔ́rvito͞od, -tyo͞od/ *n.* **1** slavery. **2** subjection (esp. involuntary); bondage. **3** *Law* the subjection of property to an easement. [ME f. OF f. L *servitudo -inis* f. *servus* slave]

■ **1, 2** bondage, slavery, serfdom, subjugation, enslavement, subjection, *hist.* vassalage, *literary* thrall, thralldom.

servo /sɔ́rvō/ *n.* (*pl.* **-os**) **1** (in full **servomechanism**) a powered mechanism producing motion or forces at a higher level of energy than the input level, e.g., in the brakes and steering of large motor vehicles, esp. where feedback is employed to make the control automatic. **2** (in full **servomotor**) the motive element in a servomechanism. **3** (in *comb.*) of or involving a servomechanism (*servo-assisted*). [L *servus* slave]

sesame /séssəmee/ *n. Bot.* **1** an E. Indian herbaceous plant, *Sesamum indicum*, with seeds used as food and yielding an edible oil. **2** its seeds. □ **open sesame** a means of acquiring or achieving what is normally unattainable (from the magic words used in the *Arabian Nights' Entertainments*). [L *sesamum* f. Gk *sēsamon*, *sēsamē*]

/.../ **pronunciation**	● **part of speech**
□ **phrases, idioms, and compounds**	
□□ **derivatives**	■ **synonym section**
cross-references appear in SMALL CAPITALS *or italics*	

sesamoid /sésəmoyd/ *adj. & n.* ● *adj.* shaped like a sesame seed; nodular (esp. of small independent bones developed in tendons passing over an angular structure such as the kneecap and the navicular bone). ● *n.* a sesamoid bone.

sesqui- /séskwee/ *comb. form* **1** denoting one and a half. **2** *Chem.* (of a compound) in which there are three equivalents of a named element or radical to two others. [L (as SEMI-, -*que* and)]

sesquicentenary /séskwisenténəree/ *n.* (*pl.* -**ies**) = SESQUI-CENTENNIAL.

sesquicentennial /séskwisenténeeəl/ *n. & adj.* ● *n.* a one-hundred-and-fiftieth anniversary. ● *adj.* of or relating to a sesquicentennial.

sessile /sésil, -əl/ *adj.* **1** *Bot. & Zool.* (of a flower, leaf, eye, etc.) attached directly by its base without a stalk or peduncle. **2** fixed in one position; immobile. □ **sessile oak** = DUR-MAST. [L *sessilis* f. *sedēre sess-* sit]

session /séshən/ *n.* **1** the process of assembly of a deliberative or judicial body to conduct its business. **2** a single meeting for this purpose. **3** a period during which such meetings are regularly held. **4 a** an academic year. **b** the period during which a school, etc., has classes. **5** a period devoted to an activity (*poker session; recording session*). **6** the governing body of a Presbyterian church. □ **in session** assembled for business; not on vacation. □□ **sessional** *adj.* [ME f. OF *session* or L *sessio -onis* (as SESSILE)]

■ **1, 2** sitting, seating, assembly, conference, meeting, hearing. **3, 5** see TIME *n.* 4, 6. **4 b** term, semester, trimester.

sesterce /séstərs/ *n.* (also **sestertius** /sestərshəs/) (*pl.* **ses-terces** /séstərseez/ or **sestertii** /-stərshee-ī/) an ancient Roman coin and monetary unit equal to one quarter of a denarius. [L *sestertius* (*nummus* coin) = $2^1/_2$ f. *semis* half + *tertius* third]

sestet /sestét/ *n.* **1** the last six lines of a sonnet. **2** a sextet. [It. *sestetto* f. *sesto* f. L *sextus* a sixth]

sestina /sesteénə/ *n.* a form of rhymed or unrhymed poem with six stanzas of six lines and a final triplet, all stanzas having the same six words at the line ends in six different sequences. [It. (as SESTET)]

set¹ /set/ *v.* (**setting**; *past* and *past part.* **set**) **1** *tr.* put, lay, or stand (a thing) in a certain position or location (*set it on the table; set it upright*). **2** *tr.* (foll. by *to*) apply (one thing) to (another) (*set pen to paper*). **3** *tr.* **a** fix ready or in position. **b** dispose suitably for use, action, or display. **4** *tr.* **a** adjust the hands of (a clock or watch) to show the right time. **b** adjust (an alarm clock) to sound at the required time. **5** *tr.* **a** fix, arrange, or mount. **b** insert (a jewel) in a ring, framework, etc. **6** *tr.* make (a device) ready to operate. **7** *tr.* lay (a table) for a meal. **8** *tr.* arrange (the hair) while damp so that it dries in the required style. **9** *tr.* (foll. by *with*) ornament or provide (a surface, esp. a precious item) (*gold set with gems*). **10** *tr.* bring by placing or arranging or other means into a specified state; cause to be (*set things in motion; set it on fire*). **11** *intr. & tr.* harden or solidify (*the jelly is set; the cement has set*). **12** *intr.* (of the sun, moon, etc.) appear to move toward and below the earth's horizon (as the earth rotates). **13** *tr.* represent (a story, play, scene, etc.) as happening in a certain time or place. **14** *tr.* **a** (foll. by *to* + infin.) cause or instruct (a person) to perform a specified activity (*set them to work*). **b** (foll. by pres. part.) start (a person or thing) doing something (*set him chatting; set the ball rolling*). **15** *tr.* present or impose as work to be done or a matter to be dealt with (*set them an essay*). **16** *tr.* exhibit as a type or model (*set a good example*). **17** *tr.* initiate; take the lead in (*set the fashion; set the pace*). **18** *tr.* establish (a record, etc.). **19** *tr.* determine or decide (*the itinerary is set*). **20** *tr.* appoint or establish (*set them in authority*). **21** *tr.* join, attach, or fasten. **22** *tr.* **a** put parts of (a broken or dislocated bone, limb, etc.) into the correct position for healing. **b** deal with (a fracture or dislocation) in this way. **23** *tr.* (in full **set to music**) provide (words, etc.) with music for singing. **24** *tr.* (often foll. by *up*) *Printing* **a** arrange or produce (type or film, etc.) as required. **b** arrange the type or film, etc., for (a book, etc.). **25** *intr.* (of a tide, current, etc.) have a certain

motion or direction. **26** *intr.* (of a face) assume a hard expression. **27** *tr.* **a** cause (a hen) to sit on eggs. **b** place (eggs) for a hen to sit on. **28** *tr.* put (a seed, plant, etc.) in the ground to grow. **29** *tr.* give the teeth of (a saw) an alternate outward inclination. **30** *tr.* esp. start (a fire). **31** *intr.* (of eyes, etc.) become motionless. **32** *intr.* feel or show a certain tendency (*opinion is setting against it*). **33** *intr.* **a** (of blossom) form into fruit. **b** (of fruit) develop from blossom. **c** (of a tree) develop fruit. **34** *intr.* (in full **set to partner**) (of a dancer) take a position facing one's partner. **35** *intr.* (of a hunting dog) take a rigid attitude indicating the presence of game. **36** *intr. dial.* or *sl.* sit. **37** sink a nail head, esp. with a nail set. □ **set about 1** begin or take steps toward. **2** *Brit. colloq.* attack. **set a person** (or **thing**) **against** (**another**) **1** consider or reckon (a person or thing) as a counterbalance or compensation for. **2** cause to oppose. **set apart** separate; reserve; differentiate. **set aside** see ASIDE. **set back 1** place further back in place or time. **2** impede or reverse the progress of. **3** *colloq.* cost (a person) a specified amount. **set by** save for future use. **set down 1** record in writing. **2** land an aircraft (*we were forced to set down just outside of Atlanta*). **3** (foll. by *to*) attribute to. **4** (foll. by *as*) explain or describe to oneself as. **set eyes on** see EYE. **set one's face against** see FACE. **set foot on** (or **in**) see FOOT. **set forth 1** begin a journey. **2** make known; expound. **set forward** begin to advance. **set free** release. **set one's hand to** see HAND. **set one's heart** (or **hopes**) **on** want or hope for eagerly. **set in 1** (of weather, a condition, etc.) begin (and seem likely to continue); become established. **2** insert (esp. a sleeve, etc., into a garment). **set in motion** put under way; implement the initial actions (of a plan, project, etc.) **set little by** consider to be of little value. **set a person's mind at rest** see MIND. **set much by** consider to be of much value. **set off 1** begin a journey. **2** detonate (a bomb, etc.). **3** initiate; stimulate. **4** cause (a person) to start laughing, talking, etc. **5** serve as an adornment or foil to; enhance. **6** (foll. by *against*) use as a compensating item. **set on** (or **upon**) **1** attack violently. **2** cause or urge to attack. **set out 1** begin a journey. **2** (foll. by *to* + infin.) aim or intend. **3** demonstrate, arrange, or exhibit. **4** mark out. **5** declare. **set the pace** determine the rate of speed, proficiency, etc. for others to follow. **set sail 1** hoist the sails. **2** begin a voyage. **set the scene** see SCENE. **set one's sights on** have an object or goal. **set the stage** see STAGE. **set store by** (or **on**) see STORE. **set one's teeth 1** clench them. **2** summon one's resolve. **set to** begin doing something vigorously, esp. fighting, arguing, or eating. **set-to** *n.* (*pl.* **-tos**) *colloq.* a fight or argument. **set up 1** place in position or view. **2** organize or start (a business, etc.). **3** establish in some capacity. **4** supply the needs of. **5** begin making (a loud sound). **6** cause or make arrangements for (a condition or situation). **7** prepare (a task, etc., for another). **8** restore or enhance the health of (a person). **9** establish (a record). **10** propound (a theory). **11** *colloq.* put (a person) in a dangerous or vulnerable position. **set oneself up as** make pretensions to being. [OE *settan* f. Gmc]

■ **1, 3, 5** set down, place, put, situate, locate, site, plant, position, station, stand, lay, install, insert, lodge, mount, park, deposit, plump, drop, plunk (down); prepare, set up, concoct; arrange, fix, dispose, set out. **2** put, apply, place, lay, bring. **4, 6** adjust, regulate, turn, synchronize, fix, calibrate, coordinate. **7** arrange, lay, spread; prepare. **9** see ORNAMENT *v.* **11** stiffen, harden, freeze; gel, congeal, solidify, clot, coagulate, thicken, cake, *colloq.* jell. **12** go down, sink, decline. **13** see SITUATE *v.* **14 a** see CAUSE *v.* 2. **b** see INITIATE *v.* 1. **15** see ASSIGN *v.* 1a. **17** see INITIATE *v.* 1. **18–20** lay down, appoint, impose, stipulate, define, designate, specify, determine, decide, establish, introduce, set up; indicate, set *or* mark off, delineate; fix. **21, 22** see ATTACH 1, MEND *v.* 1. **26** stiffen, harden, freeze. **28** sow, plant. □ **set about 1** get *or* make ready, start, begin, get to work on, get under way, undertake, launch into, tackle, address oneself to, enter upon, *colloq.* get cracking on. **2** assail, assault, set on *or* upon, beat up, mug, *colloq.* lay into; see also ATTACK *v.* 1. **set a person** or **thing against (another)** 1 compare with, rate against, balance against, weigh (up) against, juxtapose with, contrast with. 2 antagonize, set at odds with, alienate *or* divide *or* disunite from. **set apart** distinguish, separate, differentiate; reserve, put *or* set aside, store, earmark, put away, lay away, save, keep back, *archaic* set by. **set back** 2 put back, hinder, slow, hold up, retard, delay, impede, obstruct, thwart, frustrate, inhibit, *archaic or literary* stay. **set down** 1 write (down), put in writing, put down, record, register, mark *or* jot down, make a note of, note, list. 2 land, make a landing, touch down. 3 ascribe, assign, attribute, impute. **set forth** 1 set out *or* off, begin, start (out), get under way, go, embark, put out, sally forth, depart, leave, *formal* put forth. 2 make known, expound, express, voice, propose, propound, state, offer, submit, suggest, broach, move; set out, present, declare, describe, state, articulate, enunciate. **set free** see RELEASE *v.* 1. **set one's heart on** see WANT *v.* 1a. **set in** 1 begin, start, get under way, become established, arrive, come, settle in. **set off** 1 see *set forth* 1 above. 2 ignite, kindle, detonate, explode, blow up, light, touch off, trigger, trip. 3 see INITIATE *v.* 1. 4 start off *or* up, get going. 5 dramatize, enhance, highlight, throw into relief, show (off), display. **set on** (or **upon**) 1 attack, assault, pounce on *or* upon, fall on *or* upon, fly at; ambush, beat up, set about, mug. **set out** 1 see *set forth* 1 above. 2 (*set out to*) see AIM *v.* 1, 4. 3 put out, lay out, arrange, dispose; display, exhibit, demonstrate. 5 see DECLARE 1, 2. **set-to** see FIGHT *n.* 1a, ARGUMENT 1. **set up** 1 build, put up, erect, assemble, construct, raise, elevate, put together, arrange, prepare. 2, 3 start, begin, initiate, organize, establish, found. 4 finance, fund, invest in, back, subsidize; supply. 6 see ORGANIZE 2b. 7 see PREPARE *v.* 1. 9 see SET¹ 18–20 above. 10 see *set forth* 2 above. 11 trap, entrap, *sl.* frame.

set² /set/ *n.* 1 a number of things or persons that belong together or resemble one another or are usually found together. 2 a collection or group. 3 a section of society consorting together or having similar interests, etc. 4 a collection of implements, vessels, etc., regarded collectively and needed for a specified purpose (*croquet set; tea set; a set of teeth*). 5 a piece of electric or electronic apparatus, esp. a radio or television receiver. 6 (in tennis, etc.) a group of games counting as a unit toward a match for the player or side that wins a defined number or proportion of the games. 7 *Math. & Logic* a collection of distinct entities, individually specified or satisfying specified conditions, forming a unit. 8 a group of pupils or students having the same average ability. 9 a a slip, shoot, bulb, etc., for planting. b a young fruit just set. 10 a a habitual posture or conformation; the way the head, etc., is carried or a dress, etc., flows. b (also **dead set**) a setter's pointing in the presence of game. 11 the way, drift, or tendency (of a current, public opinion, state of mind, etc.) (*the set of public feeling is against it*). 12 the way in which a machine, device, etc., is set or adjusted. 13 esp. *Austral. & NZ colloq.* a grudge. 14 a the alternate outward deflection of the teeth of a saw. b the amount of this. 15 the last coat of plaster on a wall. 16 *Printing* a the amount of spacing in type controlling the distance between letters. b the width of a piece of type. 17 a warp or bend or displacement caused by continued pressure or a continued position. 18 a setting, including stage furniture, etc., for a play or motion picture, etc. 19 a sequence of songs or pieces performed in jazz or popular music. 20 the setting of the hair when damp. 21 (also **sett**) a badger's burrow. 22 (also **sett**) a granite paving block. 23 a predisposition or expectation influencing a response. 24 a number of people making up a square dance. □ **make a dead set at** *Brit.* 1 make a determined attack on. 2 seek to win the affections of. **set point** *Tennis*, etc. 1 the state of a game when one side needs only one more point to win the set. 2 this point. **set theory** the branch of mathematics concerned with the manipula-

tion of sets. [sense 1 (and related senses) f. OF *sette* f. L *secta* SECT: other senses f. SET¹]

■ **1, 2, 7** collection, group, combination, number, grouping, assortment, selection, arrangement, series, unit; order, ordering, succession, array, disposition. **3** clique, coterie, company, circle, ring, crowd, faction, sect, gang, cabal, fraternity, league, lobby; see also GROUP *n.* 1, 3. **4, 5** kit, outfit, rig; equipment, apparatus, deck, console, system, machine, gadget; service, canteen. **8** *Brit.* stream, class. **10 a** drape, hang; carriage, bearing, gait; see also POSTURE *n.* 1. **18** setting, scene, mounting, scenery, *mise en scène*. **19** sequence, cycle, series.

set³ /set/ *adj.* 1 in senses of SET¹. 2 prescribed or determined in advance. 3 fixed; unchanging; unmoving. 4 (of a phrase or speech, etc.) having invariable or predetermined wording; not extempore. 5 prepared for action. 6 (foll. by *on, upon*) determined to acquire or achieve, etc. 7 (of a book, etc.) specified for reading in preparation for an examination. 8 (of a meal) served according to a fixed menu. □ **set fair** *Brit.* (of the weather) fine without a sign of breaking. **set piece** 1 a formal or elaborate arrangement, esp. in art or literature. 2 fireworks arranged on scaffolding, etc. **set screw** a screw for adjusting or clamping parts of a machine. **set square** a right-angled triangular plate for drawing lines, esp. at 90°, 45°, 60°, or 30°. [past part. of SET¹]

■ **2–4, 7, 8** fixed, established, determined, predetermined, arranged, prearranged, prescribed, decided, defined, scheduled; customary, usual, normal, regular, agreed, conventional, habitual, routine, standard, wonted; definite, firm, unvarying, unchanging, rigid, strict, settled; stereotyped, trite, hackneyed, traditional, unchanged, unvaried, invariable. **5** prepared, ready, fit, primed, ripe, equipped. **6** see INTENT *adj.* 1a.

seta /seeta/ *n.* (*pl.* **setae** /-tee/) *Bot. & Zool.* stiff hair; bristle. □□ **setaceous** /-táyshəs/ *adj.* [L, = bristle]

■ hair, bristle, whisker. □□ **setaceous** see PRICKLY 1.

setback /sétbak/ *n.* 1 a reversal or arrest of progress. 2 a relapse. 3 the recession of the upper part of a building from the lower part. 4 the automatic lowering of the temperature on a thermostat.

■ **1** hindrance, hitch, check, reverse, reversal, impediment, block, obstruction, defeat, holdup, delay, check, obstacle, hiccup, snag. **2** see RELAPSE *n.*

setiferous /sitífərəs/ *adj.* (also **setigerous** /sitíjərəs/) *Biol.* having bristles. [L *seta* bristle, *setiger* bristly + -FEROUS, -GEROUS]

■ see PRICKLY 1, HAIRY 1.

setoff /sétawf/ *n.* 1 a thing set off against another. 2 a thing of which the amount or effect may be deducted from that of another or opposite tendency. 3 a counterbalance. 4 a counterclaim. 5 a thing that embellishes; an adornment to something. 6 *Printing* = OFFSET 7.

seton /seet'n/ *n.* *Surgery* a skein of cotton, etc., passed below the skin and left with the ends protruding to promote drainage, etc. [ME f. med.L *seto, seta* silk, app. f. L *seta* bristle]

setose /seetōs/ *adj.* *Biol.* bristly. [L *seta* bristle]

■ see PRICKLY 1, HAIRY 1.

Setswana var. of TSWANA (and the preferred form for the language).

sett var. of SET² 21, 22.

settee /setee/ *n.* a seat (usu. upholstered), with a back and usu. arms, for more than one person. [18th c.: perh. a fanciful var. of SETTLE²]

■ see SEAT *n.* 1.

setter /sétər/ *n.* 1 a a dog of a large, long-haired breed trained to stand rigid when scenting game (see SET¹ 35). b this breed. 2 a person or thing that sets.

/.../ **pronunciation**	● **part of speech**
□ **phrases, idioms, and compounds**	
□□ **derivatives**	■ **synonym section**
cross-references appear in SMALL CAPITALS or *italics*	

setting /séting/ *n*. **1** the position or manner in which a thing is set. **2** the immediate surroundings (of a house, etc.). **3** the surroundings of any object regarded as its framework; the environment of a thing. **4** the place and time, scenery, etc., of a story, drama, etc. **5** a frame in which a jewel is set. **6** the music to which words of a poem, song, etc., are set. **7** a set of cutlery and other accessories for one person at a table. **8** the way in which or level at which a machine is set to operate.
  ■ **1–3** scenery, background, backdrop, locale, location, surroundings, situation, habitat, home, environs, environment, milieu, frame, context, site, placement, mounting; (stage) set, scene, *mise en scène*.

settle¹ /sét'l/ *v*. **1** *tr. & intr.* (often foll. by *down*) establish or become established in a more or less permanent abode or way of life. **2** *intr. & tr.* (often foll. by *down*) **a** cease or cause to cease from wandering, disturbance, movement, etc. **b** adopt a regular or secure style of life. **c** (foll. by *to*) apply oneself (to work, an activity, a way of life, etc.) (*settled down to writing letters*). **3 a** *intr.* sit or come down to stay for some time. **b** *tr.* cause to do this. **4** *tr. & intr.* bring to or attain fixity, certainty, composure, or quietness. **5** *tr.* determine or decide or agree upon (*shall we settle a date?*). **6** *tr.* **a** resolve (a dispute, etc.). **b** deal with (a matter) finally. **7** *tr.* terminate (a lawsuit) by mutual agreement. **8** *intr.* **a** (foll. by *for*) accept or agree to (esp. an alternative not one's first choice). **b** (foll. by *on*) decide on. **9** *tr.* (also *absol.*) pay (a debt, an account, etc.). **10** *intr.* (as **settled** *adj.*) not likely to change for a time (*settled weather*). **11** *tr.* **a** aid the digestion of (food). **b** remedy the disordered state of (nerves, the stomach, etc.). **12** *tr.* **a** colonize. **b** establish colonists in. **13** *intr.* subside; fall to the bottom or on to a surface (*the foundations have settled*; *wait till the sediment settles*; *the dust will settle*). **14** *intr.* (of a ship) begin to sink. **15** *tr.* get rid of the obstruction of (a person) by argument or conflict or killing. □ **settle one's affairs** make any necessary arrangements (e.g., write a will) when death is near. **settle in** become established in a place. **settle up 1** (also *absol.*) pay (an account, debt, etc.). **2** finally arrange (a matter). **settle with 1** pay all or part of an amount due to (a creditor). **2** get revenge on. □□ **settleable** *adj*. [OE *setlan* (as SETTLE²) f. Gmc]
  ■ **1, 2a, b** (*intr.*) take up residence, go, come, move, make one's home, set up home *or* house, put down roots, locate, *archaic* abide, *literary* dwell. **2 c** see APPLY 5. **3** light, alight, land, come down, sit down, put down, set down, (come to) rest, descend, perch. **4** calm down, subside, quiet (down), *Brit*. quieten (down); calm, soothe, tranquilize, relax; arrange, order, dispose, organize, straighten out, put in *or* into order, compose, sort out, classify, coordinate, resolve, set to rights; clarify, clear. **5–7, 8b** decide (on), establish, appoint, set, confirm, affirm, make sure *or* certain (of), determine, agree (upon *or* on), pick, choose, select; decide, reconcile, resolve, put an end to, clear up, patch up, negotiate, mediate, adjust. **8 a** see CONSENT *v*. **9** pay, square, dispose of, clear, defray, balance, liquidate, discharge; settle up. **12** populate, people, colonize, plant. **13** subside, sink, decline, fall; gravitate, precipitate (out). □ **settle up** see SETTLE¹ 9 above.

settle² /sét'l/ *n*. a bench with a high back and arms and often with a box fitted below the seat. [OE *setl* place to sit f. Gmc]

settlement /sét'lmənt/ *n*. **1** the act or an instance of settling; the process of being settled. **2 a** the colonization of a region. **b** a place or area occupied by settlers. **c** a small village. **3 a** a political or financial, etc., agreement. **b** an arrangement ending a dispute. **4 a** the terms on which property is given to a person. **b** a deed stating these. **c** the amount or property given. **5** the process of settling an account. **6** subsidence of a wall, house, soil, etc.
  ■ **1** settling, decision, conclusion, confirmation, affirmation, establishment, setting, stabilization, determination, agreement, choice, selection. **2 a** colonization, settling, populating, *hist*. plantation. **b, c** colony, outpost, post, camp, community, encampment,

hist. plantation; village, hamlet. **3** agreement, rapprochement, resolution, adjustment, elimination, reconciliation, working out, accommodation, arbitration, arrangement. **5** payment, defrayal, discharge, liquidation, satisfaction, settling, clearance, settling up. **6** see SAG *n*. 2.

settler /sétlər/ *n*. a person who goes to settle in a new country or place; an early colonist.
  ■ colonist, colonizer, frontiersman, pioneer, immigrant, *hist*. homesteader.

settlor /sétlər/ *n. Law* a person who makes a settlement esp. of a property.

setup /sétup/ *n*. **1** an arrangement or organization. **2** the manner or structure or position of this. **3** *colloq*. a trick or conspiracy, esp. to make an innocent person appear guilty. **4** the glass, ice, mixers, etc., for preparing alcoholic drinks.
  ■ **1, 2** arrangement, system, organization, layout, regime, structure, makeup, composition, framework; conditions, circumstances. **3** trick, trap, ambush, *sl*. frame, put-up job, frame-up; conspiracy.

seven /sévən/ *n. & adj.* ● *n*. **1** one more than six, or three less than ten; the sum of four units and three units. **2** a symbol for this (7, vii, VII). **3** a size, etc., denoted by seven. **4** a set or team of seven individuals. **5** the time of seven o'clock (*is it seven yet?*). **6** a card with seven pips. ● *adj*. that amount to seven. □ **the seven deadly sins** the sins of pride, covetousness, lust, anger, gluttony, envy, and sloth. **the seven seas** the oceans of the world: the Arctic, Antarctic, N. Pacific, S. Pacific, N. Atlantic, S. Atlantic, and Indian Oceans. **the seven wonders of the world** see WONDER. **seven-year itch** a supposed tendency to infidelity after seven years of marriage. [OE *seofon* f. Gmc]

sevenfold /sévənfōld/ *adj. & adv.* **1** seven times as much or as many. **2** consisting of seven parts.

seventeen /sévəntéen/ *n. & adj.* ● *n*. **1** one more than sixteen, or seven more than ten. **2** a symbol for this (17, xvii, XVII). **3** a size, etc., denoted by seventeen. ● *adj*. that amount to seventeen. □□ **seventeenth** *adj. & n*. [OE *seofontīene*]

seventh /sévənth/ *n. & adj.* ● *n*. **1** the position in a sequence corresponding to the number 7 in the sequence 1–7. **2** something occupying this position. **3** one of seven equal parts of a thing. **4** *Mus.* **a** an interval or chord spanning seven consecutive notes in the diatonic scale (e.g., C to B). **b** a note separated from another by this interval. ● *adj*. that is the seventh. □ **in seventh heaven** see HEAVEN. **Seventh-Day Adventists** a staunchly protestant branch of the Adventists with beliefs based rigidly on faith and the Scriptures and the imminent return of Christ to earth, and observing the sabbath on Saturday. □□ **seventhly** *adv*.

seventy /sévəntee/ *n. & adj.* ● *n*. (*pl*. **-ies**) **1** the product of seven and ten. **2** a symbol for this (70, lxx, LXX). **3** (in *pl*.) the numbers from 70 to 79, esp. the years of a century or of a person's life. ● *adj*. that amount to seventy. □ **seventy-first, -second**, etc., the ordinal numbers between seventieth and eightieth. **seventy-one, -two**, etc., the cardinal numbers between seventy and eighty. □□ **seventieth** *adj. & n*. **seventyfold** *adj. & adv*. [OE *-seofontig*]

sever /sévər/ *v*. **1** *tr. & intr.* (often foll. by *from*) divide, break, or make separate, esp. by cutting. **2** *tr. & intr.* break off or away; separate; part; divide (*severed our friendship*). **3** *tr.* end the employment contract of (a person). □□ **severable** *adj*. [ME f. AF *severer*, OF *sevrer* ult. f. L *separare* SEPARATE *v*.]
  ■ **1** cut (off *or* apart *or* in two), lop *or* chop *or* hack (off), hew *or* shear off, slice (off), dock, bob, dissever, split, break, separate, divide, disjoin, detach, disconnect, *literary* cleave. **2** separate, part, divide, disunite; dissolve, break off *or* up, terminate, end, cease, stop, discontinue, suspend, abandon, put an end to.

several /sévrəl/ *adj. & n.* ● *adj. & n.* more than two but not many. ● *adj*. **1** separate or respective; distinct (*all went their several ways*). **2** *Law* applied or regarded separately (opp. JOINT). □□ **severally** *adv*. [ME f. AF f. AL *separalis* f. L *separ* SEPARATE *adj.*]
  ■ *adj. & n.* some, a few, not too many, not very many, a

handful *or* a sprinkling *or* a number (of). ● *adj.* **1** separate, various, sundry, diverse, different, respective, individual, distinct, disparate, particular, specific, discrete, dissimilar, *archaic or literary* divers.

severalty /sévrəltee/ *n.* **1** separateness. **2** the individual or unshared tenure of an estate, etc. (esp. *in severalty*). [ME f. AF *severalte* (as SEVERAL)]

severance /sévərəns, sévrəns/ *n.* **1** the act or an instance of severing. **2** a severed state. □ **severance pay** an amount paid to an employee on the early termination of a contract. ■ see SEPARATION.

severe /siveér/ *adj.* **1** rigorous, strict, and harsh in attitude or treatment (*a severe critic; severe discipline*). **2** serious; critical (*a severe shortage*). **3** vehement or forceful (*a severe storm*). **4** extreme (in an unpleasant quality) (*a severe winter; severe cold*). **5** arduous or exacting; making great demands on energy, skill, etc. (*severe competition*). **6** unadorned; plain in style (*severe dress*). □□ **severely** *adv.* **severity** /-véritee/ *n.* [F *sévère* or L *severus*]

■ **1, 5** strict, harsh, rigorous, austere, hard, stony, stonyhearted, hard-hearted, flinty, inexorable, oppressive, unbending, rigid, uncompromising, relentless, unyielding, obdurate, pitiless, merciless, unsympathetic, unfeeling, cruel, brutal, mean, savage, inhuman, beastly, ruthless; despotic, dictatorial, tyrannical, autocratic; demanding, exacting, arduous, exigent, taxing; painstaking, fastidious; stringent, punishing, punitive, burdensome, tough, onerous, grievous, painful, draconian; stern, forbidding, dour, glowering, grave, grim, stiff, straitlaced, serious, unsmiling, sober, cold, frigid, aloof. **2** serious, dangerous, critical, grave, terrible, dreadful, life-threatening, acute, dire, *colloq.* awful; mortal, fatal, terminal. **3, 4** harsh, bitter, cold, extreme, intense, fierce, inclement, keen, violent, vehement, forceful, stormy, turbulent; wicked. **6** stark, bare, plain, austere, Spartan, ascetic, primitive, simple, crude, sparse, spare, monastic, modest, unadorned, unembellished, unembroidered. □□ **severely** acutely, seriously, badly, dangerously, dreadfully, critically; strictly, harshly, rigorously, austerely, oppressively, relentlessly, mercilessly, cruelly, brutally, savagely, inhumanly, tyrannically; sternly, forbiddingly, dourly, gloweringly, gravely, grimly, unsmilingly, soberly, coldly, coolly; stringently, punitively, onerously, grievously, painfully, mortally, fatally, terminally; starkly, plainly, barely, modestly, ascetically, monastically, primitively, simply, crudely, sparsely, sparely. **severity** strictness, harshness, rigor, rigorousness, austerity, hardness, flintiness, inexorability, inexorableness, stringency, oppression, oppressiveness, rigidity, inflexibility, relentlessness, obduracy, obdurateness, pitilessness, mercilessness, cold-bloodedness, abusiveness, cruelty, brutality, meanness, savagery, inhumanity, beastliness, ruthlessness, despotism, tyranny; fastidiousness, exigency; coldness, aloofness, sternness, gravity, grimness, frigidity, solemnity; dangerousness, acuteness, seriousness, ferocity, fierceness, virulence, violence, intensity, extremeness; punitiveness, punishment, onerousness, grievousness, painfulness, burdensomeness; inclemency, storminess, fury, furiousness, tempestuousness; plainness, starkness, asceticism, bareness, modesty, simplicity, primitiveness, spareness, sparseness, monasticism, crudeness.

severy /sévəree/ *n.* (*pl.* **-ies**) *Archit.* a space or compartment in a vaulted ceiling. [ME f. OF *civoire* (as CIBORIUM)]

Seville orange /səvíl/ *n.* a bitter orange used for marmalade. [*Seville* in Spain]

Sèvres /sévrə/ *n.* fine porcelain, often with elaborate decoration, made at Sèvres in the suburbs of Paris.

sew /sō/ *v.tr.* (*past part.* **sewn** /sōn/ or **sewed**) **1** (also *absol.*) fasten, join, etc., by making stitches with a needle and thread or a sewing machine. **2** make (a garment, etc.) by sewing. **3** (often foll. by *on, in,* etc.) attach by sewing (*shall*

I sew on your buttons?). □ **sew up 1** join or enclose by sewing. **2** *colloq.* (esp. in *passive*) satisfactorily arrange or finish dealing with (a project, etc.). **3** obtain exclusive use of. □□ **sewer** *n.* [OE *si(o)wan*]

■ **1, 3** sew up, stitch, darn, mend, repair; sew on, attach, fasten; tack, baste, hem. □ **sew up 1** see SEW above. **2** see CLINCH *v.* 1.

sewage /sóoij/ (also **sewerage** /sóoᵊrij/) *n.* waste matter, esp. excremental, conveyed in sewers. ■ see MUCK *n.* 1, 2.

sewer /sóoᵊr/ *n.* a conduit, usu. underground, for carrying off drainage water and sewage. □ **sewer rat** the common brown rat. [ME f. AF *sever(e)*, ONF *se(u)wiere* channel to carry off the overflow from a fishpond, ult. f. L *ex-* out of + *aqua* water] ■ see DRAIN *n.* 1a.

sewerage /sóoᵊrij/ *n.* **1** a system of or drainage by sewers. **2** SEWAGE.

sewing /sóing/ *n.* a piece of material or work to be sewn.

sewing machine /sóing/ *n.* a machine for sewing or stitching.

sewn *past part.* of SEW.

sex /seks/ *n.,* *adj.,* & *v.* ● *n.* **1** either of the main divisions (male and female) into which living things are placed on the basis of their reproductive functions. **2** the fact of belonging to one of these. **3** males or females collectively. **4** sexual instincts, desires, etc., or their manifestation. **5** *colloq.* sexual intercourse. ● *adj.* **1** of or relating to sex (*sex education*). **2** arising from a difference or consciousness of sex (*sex antagonism; sex urge*). ● *v.tr.* **1** determine the sex of. **2** (as **sexed** *adj.*) **a** having a sexual appetite (*highly sexed*). **b** having sexual characteristics. □ **sex act** (usu. prec. by *the*) the (or an) act of sexual intercourse. **sex appeal** sexual attractiveness. **sex change** an apparent change of sex by surgical means and hormone treatment. **sex chromosome** a chromosome concerned in determining the sex of an organism, which in most animals are of two kinds, the X-chromosome and the Y-chromosome. **sex hormone** a hormone affecting sexual development or behavior. **sex kitten** *colloq.* a young woman who asserts her sex appeal. **sex life** a person's activity related to sexual instincts. **sex-linked** *Genetics* carried on or by a sex chromosome. **sex maniac** *colloq.* a person needing or seeking excessive gratification of the sexual instincts. **sex object** a person regarded mainly in terms of sexual attractiveness. **sex-starved** lacking sexual gratification. **sex symbol** a person widely noted for sex appeal. □□ **sexer** *n.* [ME f. OF *sexe* or L *sexus*]

■ **1, 2** gender. **5** see *sexual intercourse*. ● *adj.* see SEXUAL 1. □ **sex maniac** nymphomaniac, satyr, *colloq.* nympho; see also PLAYBOY.

sexagenarian /séksəjináireeən/ *n.* & *adj.* ● *n.* a person from 60 to 69 years old. ● *adj.* of this age. [L *sexagenarius* f. *sexageni* distrib. of *sexaginta* sixty]

Sexagesima /séksəjésimə/ *n.* the Sunday before Quinquagesima. [ME f. eccl.L, = sixtieth (day), prob. named loosely as preceding QUINQUAGESIMA]

sexagesimal /séksəjésimal/ *adj.* & *n.* ● *adj.* **1** of sixtieths. **2** of sixty. **3** reckoning or reckoned by sixtieths. ● *n.* (in full **sexagesimal fraction**) a fraction with a denominator equal to a power of 60 as in the divisions of the degree and hour. □□ **sexagesimally** *adv.* [L *sexagesimus* (as SEXAGESIMA)]

sexcentenary /séksenténəree/ *n.* & *adj.* ● *n.* (*pl.* **-ies**) **1** a six-hundredth anniversary. **2** a celebration of this. ● *adj.* **1** of or relating to a sexcentenary. **2** occurring every six hundred years.

sexennial /sekséneeəl/ *adj.* **1** lasting six years. **2** recurring every six years. [SEXI- + L *annus* year]

sexfoil /séksfoyl/ *n.* a six-lobed ornamental figure. [SEXI-, after CINQUEFOIL, TREFOIL]

/.../ **pronunciation**	● **part of speech**
□ **phrases, idioms, and compounds**	
□□ **derivatives**	■ **synonym section**
cross-references appear in SMALL CAPITALS or *italics*	

sexi- /séksee/ *comb. form* (also **sex-** before a vowel) six. [L *sex* six]

sexism /séksizəm/ *n.* prejudice or discrimination, esp. against women, on the grounds of sex. □□ **sexist** *adj. & n.*
■ see PREJUDICE *n.* 1c.

sexivalent /séksiváylənt/ *adj. Chem.* esp. *Brit.* = HEXAVA-LENT.

sexless /sékslis/ *adj.* **1** *Biol.* neither male nor female. **2** lacking in sexual desire or attractiveness. □□ **sexlessly** *adv.* **sexlessness** *n.*
■ **1** see NEUTER *adj.* 2, 3.

sexology /seksólǝjee/ *n.* the study of sexual life or relationships, esp. in human beings. □□ **sexological** /séksǝlójikǝl/ *adj.* **sexologist** *n.*

sexpartite /sekspaártīt/ *adj.* divided into six parts.

sexploitation /séksploytáyshǝn/ *n. colloq.* the exploitation of sex, esp. commercially.

sexpot /sékspot/ *n. colloq.* a sexy person (esp. a woman).
■ see TEMPTER 1.

sext /sekst/ *n. Eccl.* **1** the canonical hour of prayer appointed for the sixth daytime hour (i.e., noon). **2** the office of sext. [ME f. L *sexta hora* sixth hour f. *sextus* sixth]

sextant /sékstǝnt/ *n.* an instrument with a graduated arc of 60° used in navigation and surveying for measuring the angular distance of objects by means of mirrors. [L *sextans -ntis* sixth part f. *sextus* sixth]

sextet /sekstét/ *n.* (also **sextette**) **1** *Mus.* a composition for six voices or instruments. **2** the performers of such a piece. **3** any group of six. [alt. of SESTET after L *sex* six]

sextillion /sekstílyǝn/ *n.* (*pl.* same or **sextillions**) a thousand raised to the seventh (or formerly, esp. *Brit.*, the twelfth) power (10²¹ and 10³⁶, respectively) (cf. BILLION). □□ **sextillionth** [F f. L *sex* six, after *septillion*, etc.]

sexto /sékstō/ *n.* (*pl.* **-os**) **1** a size of book or page in which each leaf is one-sixth that of a printing sheet. **2** a book or sheet of this size. [L *sextus* sixth, as QUARTO]

sextodecimo /sékstōdésimō/ *n.* (*pl.* **-os**) **1** a size of book or page in which each leaf is one-sixteenth that of a printing sheet. **2** a book or sheet of this size. [L *sextus decimus* 16th (as QUARTO)]

sexton /sékstǝn/ *n.* a person who looks after a church and churchyard, often acting as bell ringer and gravedigger. □ **sexton beetle** any beetle of the genus *Necrophorus*, burying carrion to serve as a nidus for its eggs. [ME *segerstane*, etc., f. AF, OF *segerstein, secrestein* f. med.L *sacristanus* SAC-RISTAN]

sextuple /sekstōopǝl, -tyōo-, -túpǝl, sékstōopǝl/ *adj., n., & v.* ● *adj.* **1** sixfold. **2** having six parts. **3** being six times as many or much. ● *n.* a sixfold number or amount. ● *v.tr. & intr.* multiply by six; increase sixfold. □□ **sextuply** *adv.* [med.L *sextuplus*, irreg. f. L *sex* six, after LL *quintuplus* QUINTUPLE]

sextuplet /sekstúplit, -tōo-, -tyōo-, sékstōo-, tyōo-/ *n.* **1** each of six children born at one birth. **2** *Mus.* a group of six notes to be played in the time of four. [SEXTUPLE, after *triplet*, etc.]

sexual /sékshōoǝl/ *adj.* **1** of or relating to sex, or to the sexes or the relations between them. **2** *Bot.* (of classification) based on the distinction of sexes in plants. **3** *Biol.* having a sex. □ **sexual intercourse** the insertion of a man's erect penis into a woman's vagina, usu. followed by the ejaculation of semen. □□ **sexuality** /-álitee/ *n.* **sexually** *adv.* [LL *sexualis* (as SEX)]
■ **1** sex, reproductive, genital, procreative, procreant, progenitive, propagative; erotic, carnal, fleshly, voluptuous, libidinous, earthy, bodily, physical, lustful, animal, sexy. □ **sexual intercourse** sexual intercourse, mating, copulation, sexual relations, (sexual) union, intimacy, lovemaking, making love, coupling, *Law* carnal knowledge, *Med.* coitus, coition, *colloq.* going to bed.

sexy /séksee/ *adj.* (**sexier, sexiest**) **1** sexually attractive or stimulating. **2** sexually aroused. **3** concerned with or engrossed in sex. **4** *sl.* exciting great interest; appealing. □□ **sexily** *adv.* **sexiness** *n.*
■ **1** erotic, arousing, exciting, sensual, sensuous, seductive, suggestive, provocative, inviting, alluring,

flirtatious, appealing, fascinating, striking, tempting, captivating, enchanting, *colloq.* come-hither; bedroom. **2** randy, (sexually) aroused, lustful, lecherous, libidinous, hot, *formal* concupiscent, *sl.* horny. **3** blue, dirty, pornographic, obscene, filthy, smutty, lewd, foul, lascivious, indecent, explicit, gross, vulgar, rude, coarse, risqué, titillating, bawdy, ribald, lusty, immodest, indelicate, suggestive, unseemly, improper, indecorous, naughty, shameless, off-color, *colloq.* raunchy.

sez /sez/ *sl.* says (*sez you*). [phonetic repr.]

SF *abbr.* science fiction.

sf *abbr. Mus.* sforzando.

sforzando /sfawrtsaándō/ *adj., adv., & n.* (also **sforzato** /-saátō/) ● *adj. & adv. Mus.* with sudden emphasis. ● *n.* (*pl.* **-os** or **sforzandi** /-dee/) **1** a note or group of notes especially emphasized. **2** an increase in emphasis and loudness. [It., verbal noun and past part. of *sforzare* use force]

sfumato /sfōōmaátō/ *adj. & n. Painting* ● *adj.* with indistinct outlines. ● *n.* the technique of allowing tones and colors to shade gradually into one another. [It., past part. of *sfumare* shade off f. *s-* = EX-¹ + *fumare* smoke]

sfz *abbr. Mus.* sforzando.

SG *abbr.* **1** senior grade. **2** *Law* solicitor general. **3** specific gravity.

Sg *abbr.* SEABORGIUM.

sgd. *abbr.* signed.

sgraffito /sgraafeétō/ *n.* (*pl.* **sgraffiti** /-tee/) a form of decoration made by scratching through wet plaster on a wall or through slip on ceramic ware, showing a different-colored undersurface. [It., past part. of *sgraffire* scratch f. *s-* = EX-¹ + *graffio* scratch]

Sgt. (also **SGT**) *abbr.* Sergeant.

sh *int.* calling for silence. [var. of HUSH]

sh. *abbr. Brit. hist.* shilling(s).

shabby /shábee/ *adj.* (**shabbier, shabbiest**) **1** in bad repair or condition; faded and worn; dingy; dilapidated. **2** dressed in old or worn clothes. **3** of poor quality. **4** contemptible; dishonorable (*a shabby trick*). □□ **shabbily** *adv.* **shabbiness** *n.* **shabbyish** *adj.* [*shab* scab f. OE *sceabb* f. ON, rel. to SCAB]
■ **1, 2** worn (out), dingy, faded, threadbare, tattered, frayed, raggedy, ragged, scruffy, dilapidated, dirty, bedraggled, mangy, run-down, seedy, the worse for wear, down-at-the-heels *or* down at heel, grubby, *colloq.* tatty, tacky; tumbledown, broken-down, shattered, battered, run-down, ramshackle, neglected, squalid, slummy, *colloq.* beat-up, crummy. **3** see POOR 3b, c. **4** unpleasant, nasty, disagreeable, mean, contemptible, demeaning, grudging, ungenerous, impolite, rude, unfriendly, unhelpful, shoddy, ungentlemanly, unladylike, dishonorable, unworthy, scurvy; stingy, niggardly, contemptible, low, lowly, base, mean-spirited, despicable, vile, uncouth, discreditable, disreputable, infamous, abominable, ignoble, atrocious, ignominious, odious, detestable, opprobrious, *sl.* rotten.

shack /shak/ *n. & v.* ● *n.* a roughly built hut or cabin. ● *v.intr.* (foll. by *up*) *sl.* cohabit, esp. as lovers. [perh. f. Mex. *jacal*, Aztec *xacatli* wooden hut]
■ *n.* hut, hovel, shanty, cabin, lean-to. ● *v.* (*shack up*) live together, cohabit, *colloq.* live in sin.

shackle /shákǝl/ *n. & v.* ● *n.* **1** a metal loop or link, closed by a bolt, to connect chains, etc. **2** a fetter enclosing the ankle or wrist. **3** (usu. in *pl.*) a restraint or impediment. ● *v.tr.* fetter; impede; restrain. □ **shackle bolt 1** a bolt for closing a shackle. **2** a bolt with a shackle at its end. [OE *sc(e)acul* fetter, corresp. to LG *shäkel* link, coupling, ON *skökull* wagon pole f. Gmc]
■ *n.* **2** fetter(s), leg iron, chain, irons, gyve(s), ball and chain, manacle, handcuff, trammel(s), *colloq.* cuffs, *hist.* bilboes, *sl.* bracelets, *Brit. sl.* darbies. **3** (*shackles*) restriction, restraint, trammels, deterrent, impediment, check, obstacle, obstruction, barrier, hindrance, bar, encumbrance. ● *v.* chain, fetter, manacle, handcuff, bind, tie, trammel, secure, truss, pinion, tether;

restrain, impede, hold back, check, deter, hinder, discourage, hobble, handicap, restrict, curb, rein, bridle, control, inhibit, limit.

shad /shad/ *n.* (*pl.* same or **shads**) *Zool.* any deep-bodied edible marine fish of the genus *Alosa*, spawning in fresh water. [OE *sceadd*, of unkn. orig.]

shaddock /shádək/ *n. Bot.* **1** the largest citrus fruit, with a thick yellow skin and bitter pulp. Also called POMELO. **2** the tree, *Citrus grandis*, bearing these. [Capt. *Shaddock*, who introduced it to the W. Indies in the 17th c.]

shade /shayd/ *n. & v.* ● *n.* **1** comparative darkness (and usu. coolness) caused by shelter from direct light and heat. **2** a place or area sheltered from the sun. **3** a darker part of a picture, etc. **4** a color, esp. with regard to its depth or as distinguished from one nearly like it. **5** comparative obscurity. **6** a slight amount (*am a shade better today*). **7** a translucent cover for a lamp, etc. **8** a screen excluding or moderating light. **9** an eye shield. **10** (in *pl.*) *colloq.* sunglasses. **11** a slightly differing variety (*all shades of opinion*). **12** *literary* **a** a ghost. **b** (in *pl.*) Hades. **13** (in *pl.*; foll. by *of*) suggesting reminiscence or unfavorable comparison (*shades of Dr Johnson!*). ● *v.* **1** *tr.* screen from light. **2** *tr.* cover, moderate, or exclude the light of. **3** *tr.* darken, esp. with parallel pencil lines to represent shadow, etc. **4** *intr. & tr.* (often foll. by *away*, *off*, *into*) (cause to) pass or change by degrees; border on. □ **in the shade** in comparative obscurity. **put in** (or **into**) **the shade** eclipse; surpass; appear superior. □□ **shadeless** *adj.* [OE *sc(e)adu* f. Gmc]

■ *n.* **1, 2, 5** shadow, shadiness, dimness, duskiness, semidarkness, gloominess, murkiness, dusk, gloom, murk, darkness, obscurity. **4** tint, tinge, tone, color, hue; intensity. **6** hint, intimation, tinge, suggestion, modicum, sprinkling, soupçon, trace, suspicion, undertone, overtone, touch, speck, dash, nuance, atom, grain, scintilla, iota, jot, tittle, *colloq.* tad; fraction, hair's breadth, bit, *colloq.* smidgen, whisker. **7, 8** lampshade; blind, window blind, curtain, venetian blind; screen, cover, covering, protection, veil, awning, canopy, shield, shelter, umbrella, parasol, sunshade. **10** (*shades*) sunglasses, *propr.* Polaroids. **11** variation, variety, difference, nuance, degree, modulation. **12 a** ghost, specter, apparition, phantom, phantasm, spirit, wraith, vision, *colloq.* spook. ● *v.* **1, 2** screen, protect, shield, shelter, cover; dim, shadow, veil, blot out, cloud, conceal, hide, obscure, shroud; mask, camouflage, disguise. **3** darken, opaque, black out, blacken; shadow, hatch. **4** see MERGE, BORDER *v.* 3.
□ **put in** (or **into**) **the shade** overshadow, exceed, surpass, outstrip, outclass, eclipse, outshine, better, beat, put to shame, outplay, outperform, outdo, *colloq.* run rings *or* circles around, show up.

shading /sháyding/ *n.* **1** the representation of light and shade, e.g., by penciled lines, on a map or drawing. **2** the graduation of tones from light to dark to create a sense of depth.

shadoof /shədoof/ *n.* a pole with a bucket and counterbalance used esp. in Egypt for raising water. [Egypt. Arab. *šādūf*]

shadow /shádō/ *n. & v.* ● *n.* **1** shade or a patch of shade. **2** a dark figure projected by a body intercepting rays of light, often regarded as an appendage. **3** an inseparable attendant or companion. **4** a person secretly following another. **5** the slightest trace (*not the shadow of a doubt*). **6** a weak or insubstantial remnant or thing (*a shadow of his former self*). **7** (*attrib.*) *Brit.* denoting members of a political party in opposition holding responsibilities parallel to those of the government (*shadow minister*; *shadow cabinet*). **8** the shaded part of a picture. **9** a substance used to color the eyelids. **10** gloom or sadness. ● *v.tr.* **1** cast a shadow over. **2** secretly follow and watch the movements of. □ **shadow box** a shallow case, usu. with a glass front panel or door, used to display and protect items. □□ **shadower** *n.* **shadowless** *adj.* [repr. OE *scead(u)we*, oblique case of *sceadu* SHADE]

■ *n.* **1** shade, darkness, gloom, dimness, dusk, obscurity. **3** companion, alter ego, other half, comrade, crony, second self, *fidus Achates*, mate, *colloq.* sidekick, chum,

(bosom) pal, (bosom) buddy. **4** *colloq.* tail. **5** hint, intimation, suggestion, suspicion, trace, vestige; remnant. **10** see GLOOM *n.* 2. ● *v.* **2** follow, trail, track, dog, stalk, pursue, trace, tail, *colloq.* keep tabs on.

shadowbox /shádōboks/ *v. intr.* box against an imaginary opponent as a form of training. □□ **shadowboxing** *n.*

shadowgraph /shádōgraf/ *n.* **1** an image or photograph made by means of X rays; = RADIOGRAM 2. **2** a picture formed by a shadow cast on a lighted surface. **3** an image formed by light refracted differently by different densities of a fluid.

shadowy /shádōee/ *adj.* **1** like or having a shadow. **2** full of shadows. **3** vague; indistinct. **4 a** unreal; imaginary. **b** spectral; ghostly. □□ **shadowiness** *n.*

■ **1, 2** dark, shady, bowery, leafy, shaded, gloomy, dusky, dim, *literary* bosky. **3** vague, dim, dark, obscure, faint, indistinct, indefinite, hazy, ill-defined, unclear, indeterminate. **4 a** illusory, dreamlike, imaginary, visionary, chimerical, hallucinatory, unreal, unsubstantial, fleeting, impalpable, transitory, ethereal, immaterial. **b** spectral, ghostly, phantom, phantasmal, wraithlike, phantasmagoric(al).

shady /sháydee/ *adj.* (**shadier**, **shadiest**) **1** giving shade. **2** situated in shade. **3** (of a person or behavior) disreputable; of doubtful honesty. □□ **shadily** *adv.* **shadiness** *n.*

■ **3** questionable, doubtful, uncertain, unreliable, suspicious, suspect, dubious, disreputable, devious, tricky, slippery, underhand(ed), unethical, unscrupulous, dishonorable, dishonest, *colloq.* shifty, crooked, dodgy, *sl.* fishy, bent.

shaft /shaft/ *n. & v.* ● *n.* **1 a** an arrow or spear. **b** the long slender stem of these. **2** a remark intended to hurt or provoke (*a shaft of malice*; *shafts of wit*). **3** (foll. by *of*) **a** a ray (of light). **b** a bolt (of lightning). **4** the stem or handle of a tool, implement, etc. **5** a column, esp. between the base and capital. **6** a long narrow space, usu. vertical, for access to a mine, a lift in a building, for ventilation, etc. **7** a long and narrow part supporting or connecting or driving a part or parts of greater thickness, etc. **8** each of the pair of poles between which a horse is harnessed to a vehicle. **9** the central stem of a feather. **10** *Mech.* a large axle or revolving bar transferring force by belts or cogs. **11** *colloq.* harsh or unfair treatment. ● *v.tr.* **1** *colloq.* treat unfairly. **2** *coarse sl.* (of a man) copulate with. [OE *scæft*, *sceaft* f. Gmc]

■ *n.* **1 a** arrow, spear; see also LANCE *n.* **2** thrust, barb, sting, dart, gibe, taunt, rebuff, affront, slap in the face, *colloq.* put-down. **3** beam, ray, gleam, streak, *Optics* pencil; bolt, flash, fulmination, *archaic* levin. **4** pole, rod, staff, stick, stem, shank, handle, helve. **5** pillar, column, post, stanchion, upright. **6** mine shaft, tunnel, adit, well, pit; air shaft, duct, vent, flue; passage, entrance, access.

shafting /sháfting/ *n. Mech.* **1** a system of connected shafts for transmitting motion. **2** material from which shafts are cut.

shag[1] /shag/ *n.* **1** a rough growth or mass of hair, etc. **2** a coarse kind of cut tobacco. **3** a cormorant, esp. the crested cormorant, *Phalacrocorax aristotelis*. **4 a** a thick, shaggy carpet pile. **b** the carpet itself. [OE *sceacga*, rel. to ON *skegg* beard, OE *sceaga* coppice]

■ **1** see PILE[3].

shag[2] /shag/ *v. & n. Brit. coarse sl.* ¶ Usually considered a taboo word. ● *v.tr.* (**shagged**, **shagging**) **1** have sexual intercourse with. **2** (usu. in *passive*; often foll. by *out*) exhaust; tire out. ● *n.* (an act of) sexual intercourse. [18th c.: orig. unkn.]

shag[3] /shag/ *v.tr.* (**shagged**, **shagging**) **1** pursue; chase after. **2** *Baseball* catch and return (fly balls) during practice.

shaggy /shágee/ *adj.* (**shaggier**, **shaggiest**) **1** hairy; rough-

---

/.../ **pronunciation**	● **part of speech**	
□ **phrases, idioms, and compounds**		
□□ **derivatives**	■ **synonym section**	
cross-references appear in SMALL CAPITALS or *italics*		

haired. **2** unkempt. **3** (of the hair) coarse and abundant. **4** *Biol.* having a hairlike covering. □ **shaggy-dog story** a long rambling story amusing only by its being inconsequential. □□ **shaggily** *adv.* **shagginess** *n.*

■ **1, 2** hairy, woolly, unkempt, unshorn, uncut, hirsute, disheveled, matted, untidy.

shagreen /shəgreén/ *n.* **1** a kind of untanned leather with a rough, granulated surface. **2** a sharkskin rough with natural denticles, used for rasping and polishing. [var. of CHAGRIN in the sense 'rough skin']

shah /shaa/ *n. hist.* a title of the former monarch of Iran. □□ **shahdom** *n.* [Pers. *šāh* f. OPers. *kšāytiya* king]
■ see SOVEREIGN *n.*

shaikh var. of SHEIKH.

shake /shayk/ *v. & n.* ● *v.* (*past* **shook** /shŏŏk/; *past part.* **shaken** /sháykən/) **1** *tr. & intr.* move forcefully or quickly up and down or to and fro. **2 a** *intr.* tremble or vibrate markedly. **b** *tr.* cause to do this. **3** *tr.* **a** agitate or shock. **b** *colloq.* upset the composure of. **4** *tr.* weaken or impair; make less convincing or firm or courageous (*shook his confidence*). **5** *intr.* (of a voice, note, etc.) make tremulous or rapidly alternating sounds; trill (*his voice shook with emotion*). **6** *tr.* brandish; make a threatening gesture with (one's fist, a stick, etc.). **7** *intr. colloq.* shake hands (*they shook on the deal*). **8** *tr. colloq.* = *shake off.* ● *n.* **1** the act or an instance of shaking; the process of being shaken. **2** a jerk or shock. **3** (in *pl.*; prec. by *the*) a fit of or tendency to trembling or shivering. **4** *Mus.* a trill. **5** = *milk shake.* **6** a shingle made by splitting sections from a log. □ **in two shakes (of a lamb's or dog's tail)** very quickly. **no great shakes** *colloq.* not very good or significant. **shake a person by the hand** = *shake hands.* **shake down 1** settle or cause to fall by shaking. **2** settle down. **3** become established; get into harmony with circumstances, surroundings, etc. **4** *sl.* extort money from. **shake the dust off one's feet** depart indignantly or disdainfully. **shake hands** (often foll. by *with*) clasp right hands at meeting or parting, in reconciliation or congratulation, or over a concluded bargain. **shake one's head** move one's head from side to side in refusal, denial, disapproval, or concern. **shake in one's shoes** (or **boots**) tremble with apprehension. **shake a leg 1** begin dancing. **2** make a start. **shake off 1** get rid of (something unwanted). **2** manage to evade (a person who is following or pestering one). **shake out 1** empty by shaking. **2** spread or open (a sail, flag, etc.) by shaking. **shake up 1** mix (ingredients) by shaking. **2** restore to shape by shaking. **3** disturb or make uncomfortable. **4** rouse from lethargy, apathy, conventionality, etc. **shake-up** *n.* an upheaval or drastic reorganization. □□ **shakable** *adj.* (also **shakeable**). [OE *sc(e)acan* f. Gmc]

■ *v.* **1, 2, 5** quiver, quake, shudder, rattle, waver, wobble, tremble, shiver; wriggle, squirm, shimmy, twitch, joggle, jiggle, rock, sway, swing, roll, bump, grind, vibrate, oscillate, pulsate, gyrate, *colloq.* waggle, wiggle. **3** agitate, stir (up), mix (up); upset, distress, frighten, scare, shock, disturb, unnerve, unsettle, disconcert, discomfit, worry, fluster, disquiet, confound, confuse, perplex, puzzle, *colloq.* rattle, get to, throw. **4** weaken, undermine, impair, harm, damage, discourage; disenchant, disappoint, disaffect. **6** wave, brandish, flourish; display, show (off). ● *n.* **1** rattle, quiver, quake, shudder, waver, wobble, tremble, shiver, wiggle, wriggle, twitch, joggle, jiggle, sway, swing, roll, gyration. **2** agitation, shaking, stirring (up), jolt, jar, shock, jounce; see also JERK *n.* 1, 2. **3** (*the shakes*) trembling, tremors, delirium tremens, d.t.('s), the horrors, *colloq.* the jitters, the jimjams, the jumps, the willies, *sl.* the heebie-jeebies. □ **in two shakes** see SOON 1. **no great shakes** see UNDISTINGUISHED. **shake down 2** settle down; break in, condition, test, prove, *colloq.* debug. **4** blackmail, extort *or* extract *or* squeeze *or* wrest money from, squeeze, threaten. **shake a leg 2** see RUSH[1] *v.* 1. **shake off** get rid of, discard, dislodge, drop; brush off, elude, evade, lose, throw off, rid oneself of, give a person the slip, *colloq.* shake. **shake up 3** see DISTURB 2a. **4** see ROUSE 2a. **shake-up**

reorganization, rearrangement, overhaul, revamp, restructuring, rehabilitation, realignment; upheaval.

shakedown /sháykdown/ *n.* **1** a makeshift bed. **2** *sl.* a swindle; a piece of extortion. **3** (*attrib.*) *colloq.* denoting a voyage, flight, etc., to test a new ship or aircraft and its crew.
■ **3** (*attrib.*) see MAIDEN 5.

shaken *past part.* of SHAKE.

shakeout /sháykowt/ *n.* **1** a rapid devaluation of securities, etc., sold in a stock exchange, etc. **2** a decline in the number of companies, services, products, etc., esp. as a result of competitive pressures.

shaker /sháykər/ *n.* **1** a person or thing that shakes. **2** a container for shaking together the ingredients of cocktails, etc. **3** (**Shaker**) a member of an American religious sect living simply, in celibate mixed communities. □□ **Shakeress** *n.* (in sense 3). **Shakerism** *n.* (in sense 3). [ME, f. SHAKE: sense 3 from religious dances]

Shakespearean /shaykspe͞ereeən/ *adj. & n.* (also **Shakespearian**) ● *adj.* **1** of or relating to William Shakespeare, English dramatist d. 1616. **2** in the style of Shakespeare. ● *n.* a student of Shakespeare's works, etc.

shako /sháykō/ *n.* (*pl.* **-os**) a cylindrical peaked military hat with a plume. [F *schako* f. Magyar *csákó* (*süveg*) peaked (cap) f. *csák* peak f. G *Zacken* spike]

Shakta /shaákta/ *n.* (also **Sakta**) a member of a Hindu sect worshiping the Shakti. [Skr. *śākta* relating to power or to the SHAKTI]

Shakti /shúkti/ *n.* (also **Sakti**) (in Hinduism) the female principle, esp. when personified as the wife of a god. [Skr. *śaktí* power, divine energy]

shakuhachi /shaákōōha͞achee/ *n.* (*pl.* **shakuhachis**) a Japanese bamboo flute. [Jap. f. *shaku* a measure of length + *hachi* eight (tenths)]

shaky /sháykee/ *adj.* (**shakier**, **shakiest**) **1** unsteady; apt to shake; trembling. **2** unsound; infirm (*a shaky hand*). **3** unreliable; wavering (*a shaky promise*; *got off to a shaky start*). □□ **shakily** *adv.* **shakiness** *n.*

■ uncertain, wobbly, unstable, precarious, unsound, rickety, insecure, flimsy, weak, feeble, infirm, unsteady, tottering, teetering, unsupported, unsubstantiated, undependable, unreliable, wavering, tenuous, untrustworthy, dubious, questionable, doubtful, *colloq.* rocky, iffy, esp. *Brit.* dodgy; dilapidated, unsound, ramshackle, on its last legs, decrepit, falling down *or* apart, unsubstantial, insubstantial.

shale /shayl/ *n.* soft, finely stratified rock that splits easily, consisting of consolidated mud or clay. □ **shale oil** oil obtained from bituminous shale. □□ **shaly** *adj.* [prob. f. G *Schale* f. OE *sc(e)alu* rel. to ON *skál* (see SCALE[2])]

shall /shal, shəl/ *v.aux.* (*3rd sing. present* **shall**; *archaic 2nd sing. present* **shalt** as below; *past* **should** /shŏŏd, shəd/) (foll. by infin. without *to*, or *absol.*; present and past only in use) **1** (in the 1st person) expressing the future tense (*I shall return soon*) or (with *shall* stressed) emphatic intention (*I shall have a party*). **2** (in the 2nd and 3rd persons) expressing a strong assertion or command rather than a wish (cf. WILL[1]) (*you shall not catch me again*; *they shall go to the party*). ¶ **For the other persons in senses 1, 2 see WILL[1]. 3** expressing a command or duty (*thou shalt not steal*; *they shall obey*). **4** (in 2nd-person questions) expressing an inquiry, esp. to avoid the form of a request (cf. WILL[1]) (*shall you go to France?*). □ **shall I?** do you want me to? [OE *sceal* f. Gmc]

shallot /shálət, shəlót/ *n.* an onionlike plant, *Allium ascalonicum*, with a cluster of small bulbs. [*eschalot* f. F *eschalotte* alt. of OF *escaloigne*: see SCALLION]

shallow /shálō/ *adj., n., & v.* ● *adj.* **1** of little depth. **2** superficial; trivial (*a shallow mind*). ● *n.* (often in *pl.*) a shallow place. ● *v.intr. & tr.* become or make shallow. □□ **shallowly** *adv.* **shallowness** *n.* [ME, prob. rel. to *schald*, OE *sceald* SHOAL[2]]

■ *adj.* surface, skin-deep, superficial, thin; empty, flimsy, trivial, unimportant, slight, frivolous, idle, foolish. ● *n.* shoal, sandbar, sandbank, bank, shelf.

shalom /shaalṓm/ *n. & int.* a Jewish salutation at meeting or parting. [Heb. *šālôm* peace]

shalt /shalt/ *archaic 2nd person sing.* of SHALL.
sham /sham/ *v., n.,* & *adj.* ● *v.* (**shammed, shamming**) **1** *intr.* feign; pretend. **2** *tr.* **a** pretend to be. **b** simulate (*is shamming sleep*). ● *n.* **1** imposture; pretense. **2** a person or thing pretending or pretended to be what he or she or it is not. ● *adj.* pretended; counterfeit. □□ **shammer** *n.* [perh. north. dial. var. of SHAME]
■ *v.* **1** feign, pretend, fake, dissemble. **2** simulate, feign, fake, affect, dissemble, make a pretense of. ● *n.* fake, fraud, counterfeit, imitation, hoax, humbug, pretense, forgery, copy, imposture, ersatz, charlatan, *colloq.* phony, *Brit. colloq.* pseud. ● *adj.* fake, fraudulent, counterfeit, imitation, paste, simulated, pretend(ed), false, make-believe, fictitious, made-up, bogus, spurious, mock, ersatz, artificial, synthetic, pseudo, *colloq.* phony.

shaman /shaámən, sháy-/ *n.* a witch doctor or priest claiming to communicate with and receive healing powers from gods, etc. □□ **shamanism** *n.* **shamanist** *n.* & *adj.* **shamanistic** /-nístik/ *adj.* [G *Schamane* & Russ. *shaman* f. Tungusian *samán*]
■ see SORCERER. □□ **shamanism** see *sorcery* (SORCERER). **shamanistic** see MAGIC *adj.* 1.

shamble /shámbəl/ *v.* & *n.* ● *v.intr.* walk or run with a shuffling or awkward gait. ● *n.* a shambling gait. [prob. f. dial. *shamble* (adj.) ungainly, perh. f. *shamble legs* with ref. to straddling trestles: see SHAMBLES]
■ *v.* shuffle, scrape along; see also HOBBLE *v.* 1. ● *n.* see SHUFFLE *n.* 1.

shambles /shámbəlz/ *n.pl.* (usu. treated as *sing.*) **1** *colloq.* a mess or muddle (*the room was a shambles*). **2** a butcher's slaughterhouse. **3** a scene of carnage. [pl. of *shamble* stool, stall f. OE *sc(e)amul* f. WG f. L *scamellum* dimin. of *scamnum* bench]
■ **1** chaos, devastation, mess, disaster, pigsty, muddle, pigpen.

shame /shaym/ *n.* & *v.* ● *n.* **1** a feeling of distress or humiliation caused by consciousness of the guilt or folly of oneself or an associate. **2** a capacity for experiencing this feeling, esp. as imposing a restraint on behavior (*has no sense of shame*). **3** a state of disgrace, discredit, or intense regret. **4 a** a person or thing that brings disgrace, etc. **b** a thing or action that is wrong or regrettable. ● *v.tr.* **1** bring shame on; make ashamed; put to shame. **2** (foll. by *into, out of*) force by shame (*was shamed into confessing*). □ **for shame!** a reproof to a person for not showing shame. **put to shame** disgrace or humiliate by revealing superior qualities, etc. **shame on you!** you should be ashamed. **what a shame!** how unfortunate! [OE *sc(e)amu*]
■ *n.* **1** embarrassment, humiliation, mortification, chagrin, ignominy, shamefacedness, loss of face, abashment, guilt. **2** humility, modesty, (sense of) decency *or* decorum *or* propriety, respectability, decorousness; diffidence, shyness, coyness, prudishness, timidity, shamefacedness. **3, 4** disgrace, ignominy, dishonor, disrepute, degradation, opprobrium, vilification, calumniation, infamy, obloquy, odium, contempt, scandal, denigration, loss of face, defamation, discredit, disesteem, disfavor, derogation, disparagement; pity, calamity, disaster, catastrophe; outrage. ● *v.* **1** embarrass, humiliate, mortify, humble, chagrin, disconcert, discountenance, put down, bring down, abash, chasten, take a person down a peg or two; disgrace, dishonor, degrade, debase, defame, discredit, stigmatize; blacken, stain, taint, besmirch, tarnish. **2** coerce, force, drive; embarrass, humiliate. □ **put to shame** surpass, eclipse, outclass, overshadow, put in the shade, outdo, outstrip, outshine, show up. **what a shame!** (what a) pity, how unfortunate.

shamefaced /sháymfàyst/ *adj.* **1** showing shame. **2** bashful; diffident. □□ **shamefacedly** /-fáystlee, -fáysidlee/ *adv.* **shamefacedness** *n.* [16th-c. alt. of *shamefast*, by assim. to FACE]
■ **1** ashamed, shamed, abashed, embarrassed,

humiliated, dishonored, mortified, humbled, chastened, chagrined, uncomfortable, discomfited, remorseful, red-faced, sheepish. **2** bashful, shy, modest, self-effacing, diffident, timid, meek, coy, sheepish, timorous.

shameful /sháymfŏol/ *adj.* **1** that causes or is worthy of shame. **2** disgraceful; scandalous. □□ **shamefully** *adv.* **shamefulness** *n.* [OE *sc(e)amful* (as SHAME, -FUL)]
■ disgraceful, dishonorable, base, low, mean, vile, degrading, indecent, inglorious, deplorable, discreditable, corrupt, disreputable, infamous, ignominious, humiliating, embarrassing, mortifying, humbling, chastening, discomfiting, shaming, blameworthy, scandalous, outrageous, unprincipled.

shameless /sháymlis/ *adj.* **1** having or showing no sense of shame. **2** impudent. □□ **shamelessly** *adv.* **shamelessness** *n.* [OE *sc(e)amlēas* (as SHAME, -LESS)]
■ wild, flagrant, unreserved, uncontrolled, immodest, wanton, indecorous, indecent, rude, improper, forward, bold, unblushing, audacious, brazen, brash, unabashed, unashamed, impudent, shocking, outrageous.

shammy /shámee/ *n.* (*pl.* **-ies**) (in full **shammy leather**) *colloq.* = CHAMOIS 2. [repr. corrupted pronunc.]

shampoo /shampŏo/ *n.* & *v.* ● *n.* **1** liquid or cream used to lather and wash the hair. **2** a similar substance for washing a car or carpet, etc. **3** an act or instance of cleaning with shampoo. ● *v.tr.* (**shampoos, shampooed**) wash with shampoo. [Hind. *chhāmpo*, imper. of *chhāmpnā* to press]
■ *n.* **3** see WASH *n.* 1. ● *v.* see WASH *v.* 1, 3.

shamrock /shámrok/ *n.* any of various plants with trifoliate leaves, esp. *Trifolium repens* or *Medicago lupulina*, used as the national emblem of Ireland. [Ir. *seamróg* trefoil, dimin. of *seamar* clover + *og* young]

shamus /sháyməs/ *n. sl.* a detective. [20th c.: orig. uncert.]
■ see SLEUTH *n.*

shandy /shándee/ *n.* (*pl.* **-ies**) **1** a mixture of beer with lemonade. **2** (also **shandygaff**) a mixture of beer with ginger beer. [19th c.: orig. unkn.]

shanghai /shanghí/ *v.* & *n.* ● *v.tr.* (**shanghais, shanghaied, shanghaiing**) **1** force (a person) to be a sailor on a ship by using drugs or other trickery. **2** *colloq.* put into detention or an awkward situation by trickery. **3** *Austral.* & *NZ* shoot with a catapult. ● *n.* (*pl.* **shanghais**) *Austral.* & *NZ* a catapult. [*Shanghai* in China]

Shangri-la /shánggrilaá/ *n.* an imaginary paradise on earth. [the name of a hidden Tibetan valley in J. Hilton's *Lost Horizon* (1933)]
■ see PARADISE 2.

shank /shangk/ *n.* & *v.* ● *n.* **1 a** the leg. **b** the lower part of the leg; the leg from knee to ankle. **c** the shinbone. **2** the lower part of an animal's foreleg, esp. as a cut of meat. **3** a shaft or stem. **4 a** the long narrow part of a tool, etc., joining the handle to the working end. **b** the stem of a key, spoon, anchor, etc. **c** the straight part of a nail or fishhook. **5** the narrow middle of the sole of a shoe. ● *v. Golf* hit the ball with the shaft of the club. □ **shanks's mare** (or **pony**) one's own legs as a means of conveyance. □□ **shanked** *adj.* (also in *comb.*). [OE *sceanca* f. WG]
■ **1** see LEG *n.* 1, 3. **2** see LEG *n.* 2. **3** see SHAFT *n.* 4, 7. **4 a** see TANG¹ 3.

shanny /shánee/ *n.* (*pl.* **-ies**) a long-bodied, olive-green European marine fish, *Blennius pholis*. [19th c.: orig. unkn.: cf. 18th-c. *shan*]

shan't /shant/ *contr.* shall not.

shantung /shantúng/ *n.* soft undressed Chinese silk, usu. undyed. [*Shantung*, Chinese province]

shanty¹ /shántee/ *n.* (*pl.* **-ies**) **1** a hut or cabin. **2** a crudely built shack. □ **shanty town** a poor or depressed area of a

/.../ **pronunciation**	● **part of speech**
□ **phrases, idioms, and compounds**	
□□ **derivatives**	■ **synonym section**
cross-references appear in SMALL CAPITALS or *italics*	

town, consisting of shanties. [19th c., orig. N.Amer.: perh. f. Can.F *chantier*]

■ **1** see HUT *n*. **2** see SHACK *n*. □ **shanty town** see SLUM *n*. 1.

shanty[2] /shántee/ *n*. (*pl*. **-ies**) var. of CHANTEY.

SHAPE /shayp/ *abbr*. Supreme Headquarters Allied Powers Europe.

shape /shayp/ *n*. & *v*. ● *n*. **1** the total effect produced by the outlines of a thing. **2** the external form or appearance of a person or thing. **3** a specific form or guise. **4** a description or sort or way (*not on offer in any shape or form*). **5** a definite or proper arrangement (*must get our ideas into shape*). **6 a** condition, as qualified in some way (*in good shape; in poor shape*). **b** (when unqualified) good condition (*back in shape*). **7** a person or thing as seen, esp. indistinctly or in the imagination (*a shape emerged from the mist*). **8** a mold or pattern. **9** *Brit*. a jelly, etc., shaped in a mold. **10** a piece of material, paper, etc., made or cut in a particular form. ● *v*. **1** *tr*. give a certain shape or form to; fashion; create. **2** *tr*. (foll. by *to*) adapt or make conform. **3** *intr*. give signs of a future shape or development. **4** *tr*. frame mentally; imagine. **5** *intr*. assume or develop into a shape. **6** *tr*. direct (one's life, course, etc.). □ **lick** (or **knock** or **whip**) **into shape** make presentable or efficient. **shape up 1** take a (specified) form. **2** show promise; make good progress. **shape up well** be promising. □□ **shapable** *adj*. (also **shapeable**). **shaped** *adj*. (also in *comb*.). **shaper** *n*. [OE *gesceap* creation f. Gmc]

■ *n*. **1, 2** appearance, form, pattern, configuration, structure, aspect, figure, build, body, physique; line(s), profile, silhouette, outline, contour(s). **3** guise, disguise, form, appearance, likeness, image. **4** see DESCRIPTION 2. **5** see ORDER *n*. 1. **6** state, condition, fettle, status, (state of) health, order, trim. ● *v*. **1** form, fashion, mold, cast, make, create, model, sculpture, sculpt; cut, carve, hew, hack, trim; word, express, embody in words, put, formulate. **2** change, modify, remodel, accommodate, fit, adapt, adjust. **3** see *turn out* 9. **4** see IMAGINE 1. **6** determine, control, govern, affect, regulate, condition, influence, decree, frame, define, direct. □ **shape up 1** take form, take shape, develop, evolve, proceed. **2** improve, (make) progress, go *or* move *or* come along, show improvement *or* promise.

shapeless /sháyplis/ *adj*. lacking definite or attractive shape. □□ **shapelessly** *adv*. **shapelessness** *n*.

■ amorphous, formless, nebulous, unformed, indefinite, unstructured, vague; unshapely, deformed, misshapen, distorted, twisted, bent, battered, baggy.

shapely /sháyplee/ *adj*. (**shapelier**, **shapeliest**) **1** well formed or proportioned. **2** of elegant or pleasing shape or appearance. □□ **shapeliness** *n*.

■ comely, well-proportioned, graceful, neat, well turned out, good-looking, pleasing, attractive, *colloq*. curvy, curvaceous; voluptuous, sexy.

shard /shaard/ *n*. **1** a broken piece of pottery or glass, etc. **2** = POTSHERD. **3** a fragment of volcanic rock. **4** the elytron of a beetle. [OE *sceard*: sense 3 f. *shard-borne* (Shakesp.) = born in a shard (dial., = cow-dung), wrongly taken as 'borne on shards']

■ **1** see FRAGMENT *n*.

share[1] /shair/ *n*. & *v*. ● *n*. **1** a portion that a person receives from or gives to a common amount. **2 a** a part contributed by an individual to an enterprise or commitment. **b** a part received by an individual from this (*got a large share of the credit*). **3** part-proprietorship of property held by joint owners, esp. any of the equal parts into which a company's capital is divided entitling its owner to a proportion of the profits. ● *v*. **1** *tr*. get or have or give a share of. **2** *tr*. use or benefit from jointly with others. **3** *intr*. have a share; be a sharer (*shall I share with you?*). **4** *intr*. (foll. by *in*) participate. **5** *tr*. *Brit*. (often foll. by *out*) **a** divide and distribute. **b** give away part of. □ **share and share alike** make an equal division. □□ **shareable** *adj*. (also **sharable**). **sharer** *n*. [ME f. OE *scearu* division, rel. to SHEAR]

■ *n*. portion, allotment, division, apportionment,

allocation, ration, appropriation, dispensation, allowance, part, due, percentage, interest, dividend, quota, helping, serving, *colloq*. cut. **2, 3** interest, piece, part, stake, equity, slice. ● *v*. **1, 2, 5** share out, divide up, allot, apportion, allocate, ration, appropriate, share in, split, partition, parcel *or* deal *or* dole out, pay out, *colloq*. divvy (up). **4** (*share in*) see PARTICIPATE.

share[2] /shair/ *n*. = PLOWSHARE. [OE *scear, scær* f. Gmc]

sharecropper /sháirkropər/ *n*. a tenant farmer who gives a part of each crop as rent. □□ **sharecrop** *v.tr*. & *intr*. (**-cropped**, **-cropping**).

shareholder /sháirhōldər/ *n*. an owner of shares in a company.

shareware /sháirwair/ *n*. *Computing* software that is developed for sharing free of charge with other computer users rather than for sale.

shari'ah /shaaree-aa / *n*. the Muslim code of religious law. [Arab. *šarī'a*]

sharif /shəree'ef/ *n*. (also **shereef**, **sherif**) **1** a descendant of Muhammad through his daughter Fatima, entitled to wear a green turban or veil. **2** a Muslim leader. [Arab. *šarīf* noble f. *šarafa* be exalted]

shark[1] /shaark/ *n*. any of various large, usu. voracious marine fish with a long body and prominent dorsal fin. [16th c.: orig. unkn.]

shark[2] /shaark/ *n*. *colloq*. a person who unscrupulously exploits or swindles others. [16th c.: orig. perh. f. G *Schurke* worthless rogue: infl. by SHARK[1]]

■ see *swindler* (SWINDLE).

sharkskin /sháarkskin/ *n*. **1** the skin of a shark. **2** a smooth, dull-surfaced fabric.

sharp /shaarp/ *adj., n., adv.*, & *v*. ● *adj*. **1** having an edge or point able to cut or pierce. **2** tapering to a point or edge. **3** abrupt; steep; angular (*a sharp fall; a sharp turn*). **4** well-defined, clean-cut. **5 a** severe or intense (*has a sharp temper*). **b** (of food, etc.) pungent; keen (*a sharp appetite*). **c** (of a frost) severe; hard. **6** (of a voice or sound) shrill and piercing. **7** (of sand, etc.) composed of angular grains. **8** (of words, etc.) harsh or acrimonious (*had a sharp tongue*). **9** (of a person) acute; quick to perceive or comprehend. **10** quick to take advantage; artful; unscrupulous; dishonest. **11** vigorous or brisk. **12** *Mus*. **a** above the normal pitch. **b** (of a key) having a sharp or sharps in the signature. **c** (C, F, etc., **sharp**) a semitone higher than C, F, etc. **13** *colloq*. stylish or flashy with regard to dress. ● *n*. **1** *Mus*. **a** a note raised a semitone above natural pitch. **b** the sign (♯) indicating this. **2** *colloq*. a swindler or cheat. **3** a fine sewing needle. ● *adv*. **1** punctually (*at nine o'clock sharp*). **2** suddenly; abruptly; promptly (*pulled up sharp*). **3** at a sharp angle. **4** *Mus*. above the true pitch (*sings sharp*). ● *v*. **1** *intr*. *archaic* cheat or swindle at cards, etc. **2** *tr*. *Mus*. make sharp. □ **sharp end** esp. *Brit*. *colloq*. **1** the bow of a ship. **2** the scene of direct action or decision. **sharp-eyed** having good sight; observant. **sharp practice** dishonest or barely honest dealings. **sharp-set 1** set with a sharp edge. **2** hungry. **sharp-witted** keenly perceptive or intelligent. □□ **sharply** *adv*. **sharpness** *n*. [OE *sc(e)arp* f. Gmc]

■ *adj*. **1, 2** acute, keen; razor-sharp, knife-edged, sharpened; pointed. **3** abrupt, sudden, steep, precipitous, sheer, vertical, marked, angular, tight. **4** see DEFINITE 2. **5 a, c** hard, poignant, severe, cutting, intense, sudden, piercing, extreme, keen, acute, fierce. **b** hot, spicy, pungent, piquant, tangy, sour, tart. **6** high-pitched, shrill, penetrating, piercing, strident, harsh, earsplitting, loud. **8** acid, acidulous, acerbic, harsh, vitriolic, acrimonious, cutting, piquant, biting, bitter, unkind, strict, hurtful, spiteful, virulent, sarcastic, sardonic, trenchant, severe, scathing, malicious, nasty, malignant, venomous, poisonous. **9** acute, keen, keen-witted, keen-minded, sharp-witted, shrewd, intelligent, smart, alert, bright, quick, agile, astute, clever, on the qui vive, penetrating, observant. **10** clever, shrewd, artful, crafty, sly, cunning, foxy, calculating, unscrupulous, dishonest, sneaky, *Brit*. *sl*. fly. **11** see VIGOROUS 1, 3, 4, BRISK *adj*. 1. **13** chic, dapper, spruce, stylish, smart, fashionable, *colloq.* snappy, natty, classy, nifty, swanky. ● *adv.* **1** precisely, exactly, punctually, on the dot, *sl.* on the button, on the nose. **2** sharply, abruptly, promptly; see also *suddenly* (SUDDEN). □ **sharp-eyed** keen-sighted, eagle-eyed, hawk-eyed, lynx-eyed; watchful, observant, alert. **sharp-witted** see INTELLIGENT 2. □□ **sharply** severely, sternly, harshly, cuttingly, acerbically, peremptorily, angrily, strictly, firmly; suddenly, quickly, abruptly, precipitously, precipitately; acutely, distinctly, definitely, definitively.

sharpen /sháárpən/ *v.tr. & intr.* make or become sharp. □□ **sharpener** *n.*
■ hone, grind, strop, whet; put an edge on.

sharper /sháárpər/ *n.* a swindler, esp. at cards.
■ see *swindler* (SWINDLE).

sharpish /sháárpish/ *adj. & adv. colloq.* ● *adj.* fairly sharp. ● *adv.* **1** fairly sharply. **2** quite quickly.

sharpshooter /sháárpshōōtər/ *n.* a skilled marksman. □□ **sharpshooting** *n. & adj.*

shashlik /sháashlik/ *n.* (in Asia and E. Europe) a kebab of mutton and garnishings. [Russ. *shashlyk*, ult. f. Turk. *šiš* spit, skewer: cf. SHISH KEBAB]

Shasta /shástə/ *n.* (in full **Shasta daisy**) a European plant, *Chrysanthemum maximum*, with large daisylike flowers. [*Shasta* in California]

Shastra /sháastrə/ *n.* Hindu sacred writings. [Hindi *śāstr*, Skr. *śāstra*]

shatter /shátər/ *v.* **1** *tr. & intr.* break suddenly in pieces. **2** *tr.* severely damage or utterly destroy (*shattered hopes*). **3** *tr.* greatly upset or discompose. **4** *tr.* (usu. as **shattered** *adj.*) exhaust. □□ **shatterer** *n.* **shattering** *adj.* **shatteringly** *adv.* **shatter-proof** *adj.* [ME, rel. to SCATTER]
■ **1** disintegrate, burst, pulverize, shiver, smash, demolish, break (to smithereens), splinter, fragment, fracture, dash to pieces, disrupt. **2** destroy, ruin, devastate, wreck, dash, crush, demolish, torpedo, undermine, disrupt, blast. **3** upset, disturb, perturb, trouble, discompose, unnerve, overcome, overwhelm, crush, devastate, depress, deject, rattle, shake (up), unsettle, agitate, confound, confuse, stupefy, daze, stun, paralyze, *colloq.* throw. **4** (**shattered**) see *exhausted* (EXHAUST *v.* 2). □□ **shattering** see OVERWHELMING.

shave /shayv/ *v. & n.* ● *v.tr.* (*past part.* **shaved** or (as *adj.*) **shaven**) **1** remove (bristles or hair) from the face, etc., with a razor. **2** (also *absol.*) remove bristles or hair with a razor from the face, etc., of (a person) or (a part of the body). **3** a reduce by a small amount. **b** take (a small amount) away from. **4** cut thin slices from the surface of (wood, etc.) to shape it. **5** pass close to without touching; miss narrowly. ● *n.* **1** an act of shaving or the process of being shaved. **2** a close approach without contact. **3** a narrow miss or escape; = *close shave* (see CLOSE¹). **4** a tool for shaving wood, etc. [OE *sc(e)afan* (sense 4 of noun f. OE *sceafa*) f. Gmc]
■ *v.* **3** trim, clip, crop; pare; snip off. **4** pare (down *or* away), scrape, plane, whittle, shave off, trim.

shaveling /sháyvling/ *n.* **1** *archaic* a shaven person. **2** *often offens.* a head-shaven monk, friar, or priest. **3** *colloq.* a young boy.

shaven see SHAVE.

shaver /sháyvər/ *n.* **1** a person or thing that shaves. **2** an electric razor. **3** *colloq.* a young lad.
■ **3** see LAD 1.

Shavian /sháyveeən/ *adj. & n.* ● *adj.* of or in the manner of G. B. Shaw, Irish-born dramatist d. 1950, or his ideas. ● *n.* an admirer of Shaw. [*Shavius*, Latinized form of *Shaw*]

shaving /sháyving/ *n.* **1** a thin strip cut off the surface of wood, etc. **2** (*attrib.*) used in shaving the face (*shaving cream*).
■ **1** see SLIVER *n.*

Shavuoth /shəvōōōs, sháavōō-áwt/ *n.* (also **Shavuot**) the Jewish Pentecost. [Heb. *šāḇû'ôt*, = weeks, with ref. to the weeks between Passover and Pentecost]

shaw /shaw/ *n.* **1** a small wooded area; thicket. **2** esp. *Brit.* the stalks and leaves of potatoes, turnips, etc. [perh. = SHOW *n.*]

shawl /shawl/ *n.* a piece of fabric, usu. rectangular and often folded into a triangle, worn over the shoulders or head or wrapped around a baby. □ **shawl collar** a rolled collar extended down the front of a garment without lapel notches. □□ **shawled** *adj.* [Urdu, etc. f. Pers. *šāl*, prob. f. *Shāliāt* in India]
■ see WRAP *n.* 1.

shawm /shawm/ *n. Mus.* a medieval double-reed wind instrument with a sharp penetrating tone. [ME f. OF *chalemie*, *chalemel*, *chalemeaus* (pl.), ult. f. L *calamus* f. Gk *kalamos* reed]

Shawnee /shawnee, shaa-/ *n.* **1 a** a N. American people native to the central Ohio valley. **b** a member of this people. **2** the language of this people.

she /shee/ *pron. & n.* ● *pron.* (*obj.* **her;** *poss.* **her;** *pl.* **they**) **1** the woman or girl or female animal previously named or in question. **2** a thing regarded as female, e.g., a vehicle or ship. **3** esp. *Austral. & NZ colloq.* it; the state of affairs (*she'll be right*). ● *n.* **1** a female; a woman. **2** (in *comb.*) female (*she-goat*). □ **she-devil** a malicious or spiteful woman. [ME *scæ*, *sche*, etc., f. OE fem. demonstr. pron. & adj. *sīo*, *sēo*, acc. *sīe*]
■ □ **she-devil** see FURY 5.

s/he *pron.* a written representation of "he or she" used to indicate both sexes.

shea /shee, shay/ *n.* a W. African tree, *Vitellaria paradoxa*, bearing nuts containing a large amount of fat. □ **shea butter** a butter made from this fat. [Mandingo *si*, *se*, *sye*]

sheaf /sheef/ *n. & v.* ● *n.* (*pl.* **sheaves** /sheevz/) a group of things laid lengthways together and usu. tied, esp. a bundle of grain stalks tied after reaping, or a collection of papers. ● *v.tr.* make into sheaves. [OE *scēaf* f. Gmc (as SHOVE)]
■ *n.* see BUNDLE *n.* 1.

shealing var. of SHIELING.

shear /sheer/ *v. & n.* ● *v.* (*past* **sheared**, *archaic* **shore** /shor/; *past part.* **shorn** /shorn/ or **sheared**) **1** *tr.* cut with scissors or shears, etc. **2** *tr.* remove or take off by cutting. **3** *tr.* clip the wool off (a sheep, etc.). **4** *tr.* (foll. by *of*) **a** strip bare. **b** deprive. **5** *tr. & intr.* (often foll. by *off*) distort or be distorted, or break, from a structural strain. ● *n.* **1** *Mech. & Geol.* a strain produced by pressure in the structure of a substance, when its layers are laterally shifted in relation to each other. **2** (in *pl.*) (also **pair of shears** *sing.*) a large clipping or cutting instrument shaped like scissors for use in gardens, etc. □□ **shearer** *n.* [OE *sceran* f. Gmc]
■ *v.* **1–3** see CUT *v.* 3a. **4 a** see STRIP¹ *v.* 1. ● *n.* **2** (**shears**) see SNIP *n.* 4.

shearling /sheerling/ *n.* **1** a sheep that has been shorn once. **2** wool from a shearling.

shearwater /sheerwawtər, -wotər/ *n.* **1** any long-winged seabird of the genus *Puffinus*, usu. flying near the surface of the water. **2** = SKIMMER 4.

sheatfish /sheetfish/ *n.* (*pl.* same or **sheatfishes**) a large freshwater catfish, *Silurus glanis*, native to European waters. [earlier *sheath-fish*, prob. after G *Scheid*]

sheath /sheeth/ *n.* (*pl.* **sheaths** /sheethz, sheeths/) **1** a close-fitting cover, esp. for the blade of a knife or sword. **2** a condom. **3** *Bot., Anat., & Zool.* an enclosing case or tissue. **4** the protective covering around an electric cable. **5** a woman's close-fitting dress. □ **sheath knife** a daggerlike knife carried in a sheath. □□ **sheathless** *adj.* [OE *scæth*, *scēath*]

sheathe /sheeth/ *v.tr.* **1** put into a sheath. **2** encase; protect with a sheath. [ME f. SHEATH]
■ see COVER *v.* 3a.

sheathing /sheething/ *n.* a protective casing or covering.

sheave¹ /sheev/ *v.tr.* make into sheaves.

/.../ **pronunciation**	● **part of speech**

□ **phrases, idioms, and compounds**

□□ **derivatives**   ■ **synonym section**

cross-references appear in SMALL CAPITALS or *italics*

sheave[2] /sheev/ *n.* a grooved wheel in a pulley block, etc., for a rope to run on. [ME f. OE *scife* (unrecorded) f. Gmc]
■ see TACKLE *n.* 2.

sheaves *pl.* of SHEAF.

shebang /shibáng/ *n. sl.* **1** a matter or affair (esp. *the whole shebang*). **2** a shed or hut. [19th c.: orig. unkn.]

shebeen /shibeén/ *n.* esp. *Ir.* an unlicensed house selling alcoholic liquor. [Anglo-Ir. *síbín* f. *séibe* mugful]

shed[1] /shed/ *n.* **1** a one-story structure usu. of wood for storage or shelter for animals, etc., or as a workshop. **2** a large roofed structure with one side open, for storing or maintaining machinery, etc. [app. var. of SHADE]
■ **1** hut, shack, stall, booth, cote, hutch.

shed[2] /shed/ *v.tr.* (**shedding**; *past* and *past part.* **shed**) **1** let or cause to fall off (*trees shed their leaves*). **2** take off (clothes). **3** reduce (an electrical power load) by disconnection, etc. **4** cause to fall or flow (*shed blood*; *shed tears*). **5** disperse; diffuse; radiate (*shed light*). □ **shed light on** see LIGHT[1]. [OE *sc(e)adan* f. Gmc]
■ **1** let fall, drop, spill, scatter; molt, cast. **2** take off, remove, strip, cast, discard, divest oneself of, *literary* doff. **4** spill, drop, pour out *or* forth, discharge, emit, emanate. **5** disperse, diffuse, dissipate, radiate, spread; emanate, emit, send forth *or* out.

she'd /sheed/ *contr.* **1** she had. **2** she would.

shedder /shédər/ *n.* **1** a person or thing that sheds. **2** a female salmon after spawning.

sheen /sheen/ *n.* **1** a gloss or luster on a surface. **2** radiance; brightness. □□ **sheeny** *adj.* [obs. *sheen* beautiful, resplendent f. OE *scēne*: sense assim. to SHINE]
■ shine, gleam, polish, luster, shininess, burnish, brightness, gloss, glow, glimmer, shimmer, radiance, glint, dazzle.

sheep /sheep/ *n.* (*pl.* same) **1** any ruminant mammal of the genus *Ovis* with a thick woolly coat, esp. kept in flocks for its wool or meat, and noted for its timidity. **2** a bashful, timid, or silly person. **3** (usu. in *pl.*) **a** a member of a minister's congregation. **b** a parishioner. □ **separate the sheep from the goats** divide into superior and inferior groups (cf. Matt. 25:33). **sheep-dip 1** a preparation for cleansing sheep of vermin or preserving their wool. **2** the place where sheep are dipped in this. □□ **sheeplike** *adj.* [OE *scēp*, *scæp*, *scēap*]
■ **1** *Austral. colloq.* jumbuck, *joc.* mutton.

sheepdog /sheépdawg, -dog/ *n.* **1** a dog trained to guard and herd sheep. **2 a** a dog of various breeds suitable for this. **b** any of these breeds.

sheepfold /sheépfōld/ *n.* an enclosure for penning sheep.

sheepish /sheépish/ *adj.* **1** bashful; shy; reticent. **2** embarrassed through shame. □□ **sheepishly** *adv.* **sheepishness** *n.*
■ **1** bashful, shy, reticent, timid, withdrawn, passive, docile, obedient, compliant, sheeplike, manipulable, tractable, pliable, meek, amenable. **2** see SHAMEFACED 1.

sheepshank /sheépshangk/ *n.* a knot used to shorten a rope temporarily.

sheepskin /sheépskin/ *n.* **1** a garment or rug of sheep's skin with the wool on. **2** leather from a sheep's skin used in bookbinding.

sheepwalk /sheépwawk/ *n. Brit.* a tract of land on which sheep are pastured.

sheer[1] /sheer/ *adj.* & *adv.* ● *adj.* **1** no more or less than; mere; unqualified; absolute (*sheer luck*; *sheer determination*). **2** (of a cliff or ascent, etc.) perpendicular; very steep. **3** (of a textile) very thin; diaphanous. ● *adv.* **1** directly; outright. **2** perpendicularly. □□ **sheerly** *adv.* **sheerness** *n.* [ME *schere* prob. f. dial. *shire* pure, clear f. OE *scīr* f. Gmc]
■ *adj.* **1** absolute, unmitigated, unqualified, downright, out-and-out, unalloyed, unadulterated, pure, unmixed, plain, simple, mere, rank, total, complete, arrant, thorough, thoroughgoing, utter. **2** steep, precipitous, abrupt, perpendicular, bluff, vertical. **3** transparent, see-through, thin, diaphanous, filmy, gauzy, gossamer, translucent, peekaboo.

sheer[2] /sheer/ *v.* & *n.* ● *v.intr.* **1** esp. *Naut.* swerve or change course. **2** (foll. by *away*, *off*) go away, esp. from a person or topic one dislikes or fears. ● *n. Naut.* a deviation from a course. [perh. f. MLG *scheren* = SHEAR *v.*]

sheer[3] /sheer/ *n.* the upward slope of a ship's lines toward the bow and stern. [prob. f. SHEAR *n.*]

sheerlegs /sheérlegz/ *n.pl.* (treated as *sing.*) a hoisting apparatus made from poles joined at or near the top and separated at the bottom for masting ships, installing engines, etc. [*sheer*, var. of SHEAR *n.* + LEG]

sheet[1] /sheet/ *n.* & *v.* ● *n.* **1** a large rectangular piece of cotton or other fabric, used esp. in pairs as inner bedclothes. **2 a** a broad usu. thin flat piece of material (e.g., paper or metal). **b** (*attrib.*) made in sheets (*sheet iron*). **3** a wide continuous surface or expanse of water, ice, flame, falling rain, etc. **4** a set of unseparated postage stamps. **5** *derog.* a newspaper, esp. a disreputable one. **6** a complete piece of paper of the size in which it was made, for printing and folding as part of a book. ● *v.* **1** *tr.* provide or cover with sheets. **2** *tr.* form into sheets. **3** *intr.* (of rain, etc.) fall in sheets. □ **sheet lightning** a lightning flash with its brightness diffused by reflection. **sheet metal** metal formed into thin sheets by rolling, hammering, etc. **sheet music** music published in cut or folded sheets, not bound. [OE *scēte*, *scīete* f. Gmc]
■ *n.* **2a, 3** pane, panel, plate, slab; lamina, lamination, layer, stratum, veneer, membrane; area, expanse, stretch, film, coat, coating, covering, blanket, cover, surface, skin. **5** newspaper, journal, paper, tabloid, gazette, daily, weekly, monthly, *derog.* rag. **6** leaf, folio, page.

sheet[2] /sheet/ *n.* **1** a rope or chain attached to the lower corner of a sail for securing or controlling it. **2** (in *pl.*) the space at the bow or stern of an open boat. □ **flowing sheets** sheets eased for free movement in the wind. **sheet anchor 1** a second anchor for use in emergencies. **2** a person or thing depended on in the last resort. **sheet bend** a method of temporarily fastening one rope through the loop of another. [ME f. OE *scēata*, ON *skaut* (as SHEET[1])]

sheeting /sheéting/ *n.* fabric for making bed linen.

sheikh /sheek, shayk/ *n.* (also **sheik**, **shaikh**) **1** a chief or head of an Arab tribe, family, or village. **2** a Muslim leader. □□ **sheikhdom** *n.* [ult. f. Arab. *šayk* old man, sheikh, f. *šāka* be or grow old]

sheila /sheélə/ *n. Austral.* & *NZ sl.* a girl or young woman. [orig. *shaler* (of unkn. orig.): assim. to the name *Sheila*]

shekel /shékəl/ *n.* **1** the chief monetary unit of modern Israel. **2** *hist.* a silver coin and unit of weight used in ancient Israel and the Middle East. **3** (in *pl.*) *colloq.* money; riches. [Heb. *šekel* f. *šākal* weigh]
■ **3** (*shekels*) see MONEY 1, 3.

shelduck /shélduk/ *n.* (*pl.* same or **shelducks**; *masc.* **sheldrake**, *pl.* same or **sheldrakes**) any bright-plumaged coastal wild duck of the genus *Tadorna*, esp. *T. tadorna*. [ME prob. f. dial. *sheld* pied, rel. to MDu. *schillede* variegated, + DUCK[1], DRAKE]

shelf[1] /shelf/ *n.* (*pl.* **shelves** /shelvz/) **1 a** a thin flat piece of wood or metal, etc., projecting from a wall, or as part of a unit, used to support books, etc. **b** a flat-topped recess in a wall, etc., used for supporting objects. **2 a** a projecting horizontal ledge in a cliff face, etc. **b** a reef or sandbank under water. **c** = *continental shelf*. □ **on the shelf 1** (of a woman) past the age when she might expect to be married. **2** (esp. of a retired person) no longer active or of use. **3** postponed, as a plan or project. **shelf life** the amount of time for which a stored item of medicine, food, etc., remains usable. **shelf mark** a notation on a book showing its place in a library. □□ **shelved** /shelvd/ *adj.* **shelfful** *n.* (*pl.* **-fuls**). **shelflike** *adj.* [ME f. (M)LG *schelf*, rel. to OE *scylfe* partition, *scylf* crag]
■ **1** see LEDGE. **2 a** see OVERHANG *n.* **b** see SHALLOW *n.*

shelf[2] /shelf/ *n.* & *v. Austral. sl.* ● *n.* an informer. ● *v.tr.* inform upon. [20th c.: orig. uncert.]

shell /shel/ *n.* & *v.* ● *n.* **1 a** the hard outer case of many marine mollusks (*mussel shell*). **b** the esp. hard but fragile outer covering of a bird's, reptile's, etc., egg. **c** the usu. hard outer case of a nut kernel, seed, etc. **d** the carapace of a

tortoise, turtle, etc. **e** the elytron or cocoon, etc., of many insects, etc. **2 a** an explosive projectile or bomb for use in a big gun or mortar. **b** a hollow metal or paper case used as a container for fireworks, explosives, cartridges, etc. **c** a cartridge. **3** a mere semblance or outer form without substance. **4** any of several things resembling a shell in being an outer case, esp.: **a** a light racing boat. **b** a hollow pastry case. **c** the metal framework of a vehicle body, etc. **d** the walls of an unfinished or gutted building, ship, etc. **e** an inner or roughly made coffin. **f** a building shaped like a conch. **g** the handguard of a sword. **5** a group of electrons with almost equal energy in an atom. ● *v.* **1** *tr.* remove the shell or pod from. **2** *tr.* bombard (a town, troops, etc.) with shells. **3** *tr.* provide or cover with a shell or shells. **4** *intr.* (usu. foll. by *off*) (of metal, etc.) come off in scales. **5** *intr.* (of a seed, etc.) be released from a shell. □ **come out of one's shell** cease to be shy; become communicative. **shell jacket** an army officer's tight-fitting jacket reaching to the waist. **shell money** shells used as a medium of exchange, e.g., wampum. **shell out** (also *absol.*) *colloq.* **1** pay (money). **2** hand over (a required sum). **shell pink** a delicate pale pink. **shell shock** a nervous breakdown resulting from exposure to battle. **shell-shocked** suffering from shell shock. □□ **shelled** *adj.* **shell-less** *adj.* **shell-like** *adj.* **shellproof** *adj.* (in sense 2a of *n.*). **shelly** *adj.* [OE *sc(i)ell* f. Gmc: cf. SCALE¹]
■ *n.* **1** case, cover, covering, shield; armor, carapace, integument, pellicle, wing case, pupa case, cocoon; shuck, husk, rind, crust, pod. **2** cartridge, projectile, shot, bomb; case, casing. **3** see FRONT *n.* 5b. **4 c, d** exterior, outside, façade, framework, frame, chassis, external(s), skeleton, hull. ● *v.* **1** husk, peel, hull, decorticate, shuck. **2** fire on or upon, bombard, cannonade. □ **shell out** pay out, give out, disburse, spend, expend, lay out, ante up, *sl.* fork out *or* up; hand over, hand out, *sl.* dish out.

she'll /sheel, shil/ *contr.* she will; she shall.

shellac /shəlák/ *n.* & *v.* ● *n.* lac resin melted into thin flakes and used for making varnish (cf. LAC¹). ● *v.tr.* (**shellacked**, **shellacking**) **1** varnish with shellac. **2** *sl.* defeat or thrash soundly. [SHELL + LAC, transl. F *laque en écailles* lac in thin plates]
■ *n.* see GLAZE *n.* ● *v.* **1** see GLAZE *v.* 6. **2** see BEAT *v.* 3a.

shellback /shélbak/ *n.* *sl.* an old sailor.
■ see SAILOR.

shellfish /shélfish/ *n.* **1** an aquatic shelled mollusk, e.g., an oyster, mussel, etc. **2** a crustacean, e.g., a crab, shrimp, etc.

shellwork /shélwərk/ *n.* ornamentation consisting of shells cemented onto wood, etc.

shelter /shéltər/ *n.* & *v.* ● *n.* **1** anything serving as a shield or protection from danger, bad weather, etc. **2 a** a place of refuge provided esp. for the homeless, etc. **b** an animal sanctuary. **3** a shielded condition; protection (*took shelter under a tree*). ● *v.* **1** *tr.* act or serve as shelter to; protect; conceal; defend (*sheltered them from the storm; had a sheltered upbringing*). **2** *intr.* & *refl.* find refuge; take cover (*sheltered under a tree; sheltered themselves behind the wall*). □ **shelter belt** *Brit.* = WINDBREAK. a line of trees, etc., planted to protect crops, etc., from the wind. □□ **shelterer** *n.* **shelterless** *adj.* [16th c.: perh. f. obs. *sheltron* phalanx f. OE *scieldtruma* (as SHIELD, *truma* troop)]
■ *n.* **1, 3** protection, cover, shield, refuge, asylum, sanctuary, haven, safety, security; covering, concealment, screen, umbrella. **2 a** habitation, home, housing, accommodation, hostel, *formal* dwelling (plac●). ● *v.* **1** protect, screen, shield, defend, safeguard, guard, keep, secure, harbor, conceal. **2** seek *or* take *or* find refuge *or* shelter *or* cover, lie low, *colloq.* hole up.

sheltie /shéltee/ *n.* (also **shelty**) (*pl.* **-ies**) a Shetland pony or sheepdog. [prob. repr. ON *Hjalti* Shetlander, as pronounced in Orkney]

shelve¹ /shelv/ *v.tr.* **1** put (books, etc.) on a shelf. **2 a** abandon or defer (a plan, etc.). **b** remove (a person) from active work, etc. **3** fit (a cupboard, etc.) with shelves. □□ **shelver** *n.* **shelving** *n.* [*shelves* pl. of SHELF]

■ **2 a** postpone, defer, put off *or* aside, pigeonhole, table, lay aside, hold in abeyance, *colloq.* put on ice; abandon.

shelve² /shelv/ *v.intr.* (of ground, etc.) slope in a specified direction (*land shelved away to the horizon*). [perh. f. *shelvy* (adj.) having underwater reefs f. *shelve* (n.) ledge, f. SHELVE¹]

shelves *pl.* of SHELF.

shemozzle /shimózəl/ *n.* (also **schemozzle**) *sl.* **1** a brawl or commotion. **2** a muddle. [Yiddish after LHeb. *šel-lō'-mazzāl* of no luck]

shenanigan /shinánigən/ *n.* (esp. in *pl.*) *colloq.* **1** high-spirited behavior; nonsense. **2** trickery; dubious maneuvers. [19th c.: orig. unkn.]
■ **1** (*shenanigans*) see HANKY-PANKY 1.

Sheol /shee-ōl/ *n.* the Hebrew underworld abode of the dead. [Heb. *š°ôl*]
■ see HELL 1.

shepherd /shépərd/ *n.* & *v.* ● *n.* **1** (*fem.* **shepherdess** /shépərdis/) a person employed to tend sheep, esp. at pasture. **2** a member of the clergy, etc., who cares for and guides a congregation. ● *v.tr.* **1 a** tend (sheep, etc.) as a shepherd. **b** guide (followers, etc.). **2** marshal or drive (a crowd, etc.) like sheep. □ **the Good Shepherd** Christ. **shepherd dog** a sheepdog. **shepherd's check** (or **plaid**) **1** a small black and white check pattern. **2** woolen cloth with this pattern. **shepherd's crook** a staff with a hook at one end used by shepherds. **shepherd's needle** a white-flowered common plant, *Scandix pecten-veneris*, with spiny fruit. **shepherd's pie** a dish of ground or diced meat under a layer of mashed potato. **shepherd's purse** a white-flowered, hairy weed, *Capsella bursa-pastoris*, with triangular or cordate pods. [OE *scēaphierde* (as SHEEP, HERD)]
■ *v.* **1** see TEND² 1. **1b, 2** lead, convoy, escort, conduct, guide, usher, marshal, drive, take, pursue.

sherardize /shérərdiz/ *v.tr.* coat (iron or steel) with zinc by heating in contact with zinc dust. [*Sherard* Cowper-Coles, Engl. inventor d. 1936]

Sheraton /shérət'n/ *n.* (often *attrib.*) a style of furniture introduced in England *c.*1790, with delicate and graceful forms. [T. *Sheraton*, Engl. furniture maker d. 1806]

sherbet /shárbət/ *n.* **1 a** a fruit-flavored ice confection. **b** *Brit.* a flavored sweet effervescent powder or drink. **2** a cooling drink of sweet, diluted fruit juices, used esp. in the Middle East. **3** *Austral. joc.* beer. [Turk. *şerbet*, Pers. *šerbet* f. Arab. *šarba* drink f. *šariba* to drink: cf. SHRUB², SYRUP]

sherd /shərd/ *n.* = POTSHERD. [var. of SHARD]

shereef (also **sherif**) var. of SHARIF.

sheriff /shérif/ *n.* **1** an elected officer in a county, responsible for keeping the peace. **2** *Brit.* **a** (also **High Sheriff**) the chief executive officer of the Crown in a county, administering justice, etc. **b** an honorary officer elected annually in some towns. □□ **sheriffalty** *n.* (*pl.* **-ies**). **sheriffdom** *n.* **sheriffhood** *n.* **sheriffship** *n.* [OE *scīr-gerēfa* (as SHIRE, REEVE¹)]

Sherpa /shárpə/ *n.* (*pl.* same or **Sherpas**) **1** a Himalayan people living on the borders of Nepal and Tibet, and skilled in mountaineering. **2** a member of this people. [native name]

sherry /shéree/ *n.* (*pl.* **-ies**) **1** a fortified wine orig. from S. Spain. **2** a glass of this. □ **sherry cobbler** see COBBLER 2. **sherry glass** a small wineglass used for sherry. [earlier *sherris* f. Sp. (*vino de*) *Xeres* (now Jerez de la Frontera) in Andalusia]

she's /sheez/ *contr.* **1** she is. **2** she has.

Shetlander /shétləndər/ *n.* a native of the Shetland Islands, NNE of the mainland of Scotland.

Shetland pony *n.* **1** a pony of a small, hardy, rough-coated breed. **2** this breed.

Shetland sheepdog *n.* **1** a small dog of a collielike breed. **2** this breed.

/.../ **pronunciation**   ● **part of speech**

□ **phrases, idioms, and compounds**

□□ **derivatives**   ■ **synonym section**

cross-references appear in SMALL CAPITALS or *italics*

Shetland wool *n.* a fine, loosely twisted wool from Shetland sheep.

sheva var. of SCHWA.

shew *archaic* var. of SHOW.

shewbread /shṓbred/ *n.* twelve loaves that were displayed in a Jewish temple and renewed each sabbath.

Shia /shéeə/ *n.* one of the two main branches of Islam, esp. in Iran, that rejects the first three Sunni caliphs and regards Ali as Muhammad's first successor. [Arab. *šī'a* party (of Ali, Muhammad's cousin and son-in-law)]

shiatsu /shiátsoō/ *n.* a kind of therapy of Japanese origin, in which pressure is applied with the fingers to certain points of the body. [Jap., = finger pressure]

shibboleth /shíbəleth/ *n.* a long-standing formula, doctrine, or phrase, etc., held to be true by a party or sect (*must abandon outdated shibboleths*). [ME f. Heb. *šibbōleṯ* ear of corn, used as a test of nationality for its difficult pronunciation (Judg. 12:6)]

■ byword, watchword, password, catchword, catchphrase, buzzword; *colloq.* sacred cow; see also FORMULA 3b, DOCTRINE 2.

shicer /shísər/ *n. Austral.* **1** *Mining* an unproductive claim or mine. **2** *sl.* **a** a swindler, welsher, or cheat. **b** a worthless thing; a failure. [G *Scheisser* contemptible person]

shicker /shíkər/ *adj.* (also **shickered** /shíkərd/) *Austral.* & *NZ sl.* drunk. [Yiddish *shiker* f. Heb. *šikkôr* f. *šākar* be drunk]

shield /sheeld/ *n.* & *v.* ● *n.* **1 a** esp. *hist.* a piece of armor of esp. metal, carried on the arm or in the hand to deflect blows from the head or body. **b** a thing serving to protect (*insurance is a shield against disaster*). **2 a** a thing resembling a shield, esp.: **a** a trophy in the form of a shield. **b** a protective plate or screen in machinery, etc. **c** a shieldlike part of an animal, esp. a shell. **d** a similar part of a plant. **e** *Geol.* a large rigid area of the earth's crust, usu. of Precambrian rock, which has been unaffected by later orogenic episodes. **f** a police officer's shield-shaped badge. **3** *Heraldry* a stylized representation of a shield used for displaying a coat of arms, etc. ● *v.tr.* protect or screen, esp. from blame or lawful punishment. □□ **shieldless** *adj.* [OE *sc(i)eld* f. Gmc: prob. orig. = board, rel. to SCALE[1]]

■ *n.* **1 b** protection, guard, safeguard, defense, screen, bulwark, shelter. **2 c, d** see SHELL *n.* 1. ● *v.* protect, guard, safeguard, keep, defend, screen, shelter.

shieling /shéeling/ *n.* (also **shealing**) *Sc.* **1** a roughly constructed hut orig. esp. for pastoral use. **2** pasture for cattle. [Sc. *shiel* hut: ME, of unkn. orig.]

shier *compar.* of SHY[1].

shiest *superl.* of SHY[1].

shift /shift/ *v.* & *n.* ● *v.* **1** *intr.* & *tr.* change or move or cause to change or move from one position to another. **2** *tr. Brit.* remove, esp. with effort (*washing won't shift the stains*). **3** *Brit. sl.* **a** *intr.* hurry (*we'll have to shift!*). **b** *tr.* consume (food or drink) hastily or in bulk. **c** *tr.* sell (esp. dubious goods). **4** *intr.* contrive or manage as best one can. **5 a** *tr.* change (gear) in a vehicle. **b** *intr.* change gear. **6** *intr.* (of cargo) get shaken out of place. **7** *intr. archaic* be evasive or indirect. ● *n.* **1 a** the act or an instance of shifting. **b** the substitution of one thing for another; a rotation. **2 a** a relay of workers (*the night shift*). **b** the time for which they work (*an eight-hour shift*). **3 a** a device, stratagem, or expedient. **b** a dodge, trick, or evasion. **4 a** a woman's straight unwaisted dress. **b** *archaic* a loose-fitting undergarment. **5** a displacement of spectral lines, e.g., to the red end of the spectrum (*red shift*). **6** (also **sound shift**) a systematic change in pronunciation as a language evolves. **7** (in full **shift key**) a key on a keyboard used to switch between lowercase and uppercase, etc. **8** *Bridge* a change of suit in bidding. **b** a change of suit in play. **9** the positioning of successive rows of bricks so that their ends do not coincide. **10 a** a gear lever in a motor vehicle. **b** a mechanism for this. □ **make shift** *Brit.* manage or contrive; get along somehow (*made shift without it*). **shift for oneself** rely on one's own efforts. **shift one's ground** take up a new position in an argument, etc. **shift off** esp.

Brit. get rid of (responsibility, etc.) to another. □□ **shiftable** *adj.* **shifter** *n.* [OE *sciftan* arrange, divide, etc., f. Gmc]

■ *v.* **1** move, change position, switch; edge, budge; relocate, rearrange, transpose. **2** budge, get rid of; see also REMOVE *v.* 2b. **3 a** see HURRY *v.* 1. **b** see BOLT[1] *v.* 5, SWALLOW *v.* 1. **c** sell, market. **4** manage, make do, scrape by *or* through, *colloq.* get by. **7** see EQUIVOCATE. ● *n.* **1 a** change, movement, switch, transfer, deflection, swerve, veer. **b** see SUBSTITUTE *n.* 1a. **2 a** workforce, relay, crew, staff, squad, team, corps, group, gang; workers. **b** see STRATAGEM 1. **b** see TRICK *n.* 1, EVASION 2. **4 a** smock, muu-muu, caftan, *hist.* chemise. **b** *hist.* chemise. □ **make shift** see SHIFT *v.* 4 above. **shift for oneself** fend for oneself, look after oneself, make do (on one's own), take care of oneself, *colloq.* get by (on one's own). **shift one's ground** try another tack, change one's tack, wriggle.

shiftless /shíftlis/ *adj.* lacking resourcefulness; lazy; inefficient. □□ **shiftlessly** *adv.* **shiftlessness** *n.*

■ unambitious, lazy, indolent, idle, lackadaisical, aimless, slothful, unenterprising, inefficient, ineffective, ne'er-do-well, good-for-nothing, fainéant, inactive, uninspired, unmotivated, *archaic* otiose.

shifty /shíftee/ *adj. colloq.* (**shiftier**, **shiftiest**) not straightforward; evasive; deceitful. □□ **shiftily** *adv.* **shiftiness** *n.*

■ tricky, artful, shrewd, canny, cunning, foxy, wily, sharp, devious, slick, evasive, slippery, scheming, designing, conniving, calculating, underhand(ed), conspiratorial, treacherous, traitorous, deceitful, deceiving, duplicitous, two-faced, dishonest, untrustworthy, *colloq.* crooked, *sl.* bent.

shigella /shigélə/ *n.* (*pl.* **shigellae** /-lee/ or **shigellas**) any airborne bacterium of the genus *Shigella*, some of which cause dysentery. [mod.L f. K. *Shiga*, Jap. bacteriologist d. 1957 + dimin. suffix]

shih tzu /shée dzoō, shéetsoō/ *n.* **1** (*pl.* **shih tzus** or same) a dog of a breed with long silky hair and short legs. **2** this breed. [Chin. *shizi* lion]

Shiite /shée-it/ *n.* & *adj.* ● *n.* an adherent of the Shia branch of Islam. ● *adj.* of or relating to Shia. □□ **Shiism** /shée-izəm/ *n.*

shikar /shikaár/ *n. Ind.* hunting. [Urdu f. Pers. *šikār*]

shiksa /shíksə/ *n.* often *offens.* (used by Jews) a gentile girl or woman. [Yiddish *shikse* f. Heb. *šiqṣā* f. *sheqeṣ* detested thing + *-â* fem. suffix]

shill /shil/ *n.* a person employed to decoy or entice others into buying, gambling, etc. [prob. f. earlier *shillaber*, of unkn. orig.]

shillelagh /shiláylee, -lə/ *n.* a thick stick of blackthorn or oak used in Ireland esp. as a weapon. [*Shillelagh* in County Wicklow, Ireland]

■ see STAFF[1] *n.* 1a, b.

shilling /shíling/ *n.* **1** *hist.* a former British coin and monetary unit worth one-twentieth of a pound or twelve pence. **2** a monetary unit in Kenya, Tanzania, and Uganda. □ **shilling mark** *hist.* = SOLIDUS. **take the King's** (or **Queen's**) **shilling** *Brit. hist.* enlist as a soldier (formerly a soldier was paid a shilling on enlisting). [OE *scilling*, f. Gmc]

shilly-shally /shíleeshálee/ *v., adj.,* & *n.* ● *v.intr.* (**-ies, -ied**) hesitate to act or choose; be undecided; vacillate. ● *adj.* vacillating. ● *n.* indecision; vacillation. □□ **shilly-shallyer** *n.* (also **-shallier**). [orig. *shill I, shall I*, redupl. of *shall I*?]

■ *v.* hem and haw, seesaw, yo-yo, vacillate, waver, alternate, fluctuate, dither, falter, tergiversate, *Brit.* hum and haw, hum and ha, haver, *colloq.* dillydally; delay, hesitate, dawdle. ● *n.* see INDECISION.

shily var. of SHYLY (see SHY[1]).

shim /shim/ *n.* & *v.* ● *n.* a thin strip of material used in machinery, etc., to make parts fit. ● *v.tr.* (**shimmed**, **shimming**) fit or fill up with a shim. [18th c.: orig. unkn.]

shimmer /shímər/ *v.* & *n.* ● *v.intr.* shine with a tremulous or faint diffused light. ● *n.* such a light. □□ **shimmeringly** *adv.* **shimmery** *adj.* [OE *scymrian* f. Gmc: cf. SHINE]

■ *v.* shine, gleam, glow, glimmer, glint, glisten, ripple,

flicker. ● *n.* shimmering, shine, gleam, glow, glimmer, glint, gloss, flicker, light.

shimmy /shímee/ *n. & v.* ● *n.* (*pl.* **-ies**) **1** *hist.* a kind of ragtime dance in which the whole body is shaken. **2** *archaic colloq.* = CHEMISE. **3** an abnormal vibration of esp. the front wheels of a motor vehicle. ● *v.intr.* (**-ies, -ied**) **1 a** *hist.* dance a shimmy. **b** move in a similar manner. **2** shake or vibrate abnormally. [20th c.: orig. uncert.]

■ *v.* **2** see SHAKE *v.* 1, 2, 5.

shin /shin/ *n. & v.* ● *n.* **1** the front of the leg below the knee. **2** a cut of beef from the lower foreleg. ● *v.tr. & (usu.* foll. by *up, down*) *intr.* (**shinned, shinning**) climb quickly by clinging with the arms and legs. □ **shin guard** a protective pad for the shins, worn when playing football, etc. [OE *sinu*]

■ *v.* climb, clamber, scramble, *colloq.* shinny; (*shin up*) scale.

shinbone /shínbōn/ = TIBIA.

shindig /shíndig/ *n. colloq.* **1** a festive, esp. noisy, party. **2** = SHINDY 1. [prob. f. SHINDY]

■ **1** see PARTY[1] *n.* 1.

shindy /shíndee/ *n.* (*pl.* **-ies**) *colloq.* **1** a brawl, disturbance, or noise (*kicked up a shindy*). **2** = SHINDIG 1. [perh. alt. of SHINTY]

shine /shīn/ *v. & n.* ● *v.* (*past* and *past part.* **shone** /shon/ or **shined**) **1** *intr.* emit or reflect light; be bright; glow (*the lamp was shining; his face shone with gratitude*). **2** *intr.* (of the sun, a star, etc.) not be obscured by clouds, etc.; be visible. **3** *tr.* cause (a lamp, etc.) to shine. **4** *tr.* (*past* and *past part.* **shined**) make bright; polish (*shined his shoes*). **5** *intr.* be brilliant in some respect; excel (*does not shine in conversation; is a shining example*). ● *n.* **1** light; brightness, esp. reflected. **2** a high polish; luster. **3** the act or an instance of shining esp. shoes. □ **shine up to** seek to ingratiate oneself with. **take the shine out of 1** spoil the brilliance or newness of. **2** throw into the shade by surpassing. **take a shine to** *colloq.* take a fancy to; like. □□ **shiningly** *adv.* [OE *scīnan* f. Gmc]

■ *v.* **1** gleam, glow, shimmer, radiate, beam, glare, flare, glisten, glitter, coruscate, twinkle, sparkle, scintillate, glint, flash, flicker. **4** polish, burnish, rub, buff, brush, brighten. **5** excel, stand out, be brilliant *or* outstanding *or* preeminent *or* excellent. ● *n.* **1, 2** gleam, glow, shimmer, sparkle, brightness, radiance, light, gloss, luster, sheen, glaze. □ **shine up to** see INGRATIATE. **take the shine out of 1** see MAR 1. **2** see ECLIPSE *v.* 3. **take a shine to** see LIKE[2] *v.* 1.

shiner /shínər/ *n.* **1** a thing that shines. **2** *colloq.* a black eye. **3** any of various small silvery freshwater fish, esp. of the genus *Notropis*. **4** (usu. in *pl.*) *sl.* **a** *archaic* money. **b** a jewel.

shingle[1] /shínggəl/ *n.* (in *sing.* or *pl.*) small rounded pebbles, esp. on a seashore. □□ **shingly** *adj.* [16th c.: orig. uncert.]

■ □□ **shingly** see STONY 1.

shingle[2] /shínggəl/ *n. & v.* ● *n.* **1** a rectangular wooden tile used on roofs, spires, or esp. walls. **2** *archaic* a shingled hair. **b** the act of shingling hair. **3** a small signboard, esp. of a doctor, lawyer, etc. ● *v.tr.* **1** roof or clad with shingles. **2** *archaic* **a** cut (a woman's hair) very short. **b** cut the hair of (a person or head) in this way. [ME app. f. L *scindula*, earlier *scandula*]

■ *n.* **3** see SIGN *n.* 4.

shingles /shínggəlz/ *n.pl.* (usu. treated as *sing.*) an acute painful viral inflammation of the nerve ganglia, with a skin eruption often forming a girdle around the middle of the body. [ME f. med.L *cingulus* f. L *cingulum* girdle f. *cingere* gird]

shinny /shínee/ *v.intr.* (**-ies, -ied**) (usu. foll. by *up, down*) *colloq.* shin (up or down a tree, etc.).

■ see SHIN *v.*

Shinto /shíntō/ *n.* the official religion of Japan incorporating the worship of ancestors and nature spirits. □□ **Shintoism** *n.* **Shintoist** *n.* [Jap. f. Chin. *shen dao* way of the gods]

shinty /shíntee/ *n.* (*pl.* **-ies**) *Brit.* **1** a game like hockey played with a ball and curved sticks, and taller goalposts. **2** a stick or ball used in shinty. [earlier *shinny*, app. f. the cry used in the game *shin ye, shin you, shin t' ye*, of unkn. orig.]

shiny /shínee/ *adj.* (**shinier, shiniest**) **1** having a shine; glis-

tening; polished; bright. **2** (of clothing, esp. the seat of pants, etc.) having the nap worn off. □□ **shinily** *adv.* **shininess** *n.* [SHINE]

■ **1** gleaming, glowing, shimmering, glossy, shimmery, lustrous, radiant, bright, beaming, glistening, polished, burnished, glittering, dazzling, coruscating, twinkling, sparkling, scintillating, glinting, flashing, flickering, lambent, *poet. or rhet.* fulgent.

ship /ship/ *n. & v.* ● *n.* **1 a** any large seagoing vessel (cf. BOAT). **b** a sailing vessel with a bowsprit and three, four, or five square-rigged masts. **2** an aircraft. **3** a spaceship. **4** *colloq.* a boat, esp. a racing boat. ● *v.* (**shipped, shipping**) **1** *tr.* put, take, or send away (goods, passengers, sailors, etc.) on board ship. **2** *tr.* **a** take in (water) over the side of a ship, boat, etc. **b** take (oars) from the rowlocks and lay them inside a boat. **c** fix (a rudder, etc.) in its place on a ship, etc. **d** step (a mast). **3** *intr.* **a** take ship; embark. **b** (of a sailor) take service on a ship (*shipped for Africa*). **4** *tr.* deliver (goods) to a forwarding agent for conveyance. □ **ship biscuit** (or **bread**) *hist.* a hard, coarse kind of biscuit kept and eaten on board ship. **ship burial** *Archaeol.* burial in a wooden ship under a mound. **ship-canal** a canal large enough for ships to pass inland. **ship of the desert** the camel. **ship off 1** send or transport by ship. **2** *colloq.* send (a person) away. **ship of the line** *hist.* a large battleship fighting in the front line of battle. **ship-rigged** square-rigged. **ship's boat** a small boat carried on board a ship. **ship's company** a ship's crew. **ship's papers** documents establishing the ownership, nationality, nature of the cargo, etc., of a ship. **take ship** embark. **when a person's ship comes in** when a person's fortune is made. □□ **shipless** *adj.* **shippable** *adj.* [OE *scip, scipian* f. Gmc]

■ *n.* **1 a** vessel. ● *v.* **1, 4** send, deliver, dispatch, freight, haul; ferry, transport, carry. **3 a** take ship, embark, set sail, leave, depart. □ **ship off 2** see *send off*. **take ship** see SHIP *v.* 3a.

-ship /ship/ *suffix* forming nouns denoting: **1** a quality or condition (*friendship; hardship*). **2** status, office, or honor (*authorship; lordship*). **3** a tenure of office (*chairmanship*). **4** a skill in a certain capacity (*workmanship*). **5** the collective individuals of a group (*membership*). [OE *-scipe*, etc., f. Gmc]

shipboard /shípbawrd/ *n.* (usu. *attrib.*) used or occurring on board a ship (*a shipboard romance*). □ **on shipboard** on board ship.

shipbuilder /shípbildər/ *n.* a person, company, etc., that constructs ships. □□ **shipbuilding** *n.*

shiplap /shíplap/ *v. & n.* ● *v.tr.* fit (boards) together for cladding, etc., so that each overlaps the one below. ● *n.* such cladding.

shipload /shíplōd/ *n.* a quantity of goods forming a cargo.

■ see CARGO.

shipmaster /shípmastər/ *n.* a ship's captain.

shipmate /shípmayt/ *n.* a fellow member of a ship's crew.

shipment /shípmənt/ *n.* **1** an amount of goods shipped; a consignment. **2** the act or an instance of shipping goods, etc.

■ **1** see LOAD *n.* 1. **2** see TRANSPORT *n.* 1a.

shipowner /shípōnər/ *n.* a person owning a ship or ships or shares in ships.

shipper /shípər/ *n.* a person or company that sends or receives goods by ship, or by land or air. [OE *scipere* (as SHIP)]

■ see CARRIER 1, 2.

shipping /shíping/ *n.* **1** the act or an instance of shipping goods, etc. **2** ships, esp. the ships of a country, port, etc. □ **shipping agent** a person acting for a ship or ships at a port, etc.

■ **1** see TRANSPORT *n.* 1a.

shipshape /shípshayp/ *adv. & predic.adj.* in good order; trim and neat.

/.../ **pronunciation**	● **part of speech**
□ **phrases, idioms, and compounds**	
□□ **derivatives**	■ **synonym section**
cross-references appear in SMALL CAPITALS or *italics*	

■ neat, trim, spotless, orderly, spick-and-span, tidy, *orig*.

shipway /shípway/ *n.* a slope on which a ship is built and down which it slides to be launched.

shipworm /shípwərm/ *n.* = TEREDO.

shipwreck /shíprek/ *n.* & *v.* ● *n.* **1 a** the destruction of a ship by a storm, foundering, etc. **b** a ship so destroyed. **2** (often foll. by *of*) the destruction of hopes, dreams, etc. ● *v.* **1** *tr.* inflict shipwreck on (a ship, a person's hopes, etc.). **2** *intr.* suffer shipwreck.
   ■ *n.* **1 b** wreck, hulk, ruins. ● *v.* see WRECK *v.*

shipwright /shíprīt/ *n.* **1** a shipbuilder. **2** a ship's carpenter.

shipyard /shípyaard/ *n.* a place where ships are built, repaired, etc.

shiralee /shírəlee/ *n. Austral.* a tramp's swag or bundle. [20th c.: orig. unkn.]

shire /shīr/ *n. Brit.* **1** a county. **2** (**the Shires**) **a** a group of English counties with names ending or formerly ending in *-shire*, extending NE from Hampshire and Devon. **b** the midland counties of England. **c** the fox-hunting district of mainly Leicestershire and Northants. **3** *Austral.* a rural area with its own elected council. [OE *scīr*, OHG *scīra* care, official charge: orig. unkn.]

-shire /shər, sheer/ *suffix* forming the names of counties (*Derbyshire; Hampshire*).

shirk /shərk/ *v.* & *n.* ● *v.tr.* (also *absol.*) shrink from; avoid; get out of (duty, work, responsibility, fighting, etc.). ● *n.* a person who shirks. □□ **shirker** *n.* [obs. *shirk* (n.) sponger, perh. f. G *Schurke* scoundrel]
   ■ *v.* avoid, evade, shun, dodge, get out of, shrink from, *colloq*. duck (out of). ● *n.* see TRUANT *n.* □□ **shirker** see TRUANT *n.*

shirr /shər/ *n.* & *v.* ● *n.* **1** two or more rows of esp. elastic gathered threads in a garment, etc., forming smocking. **2** elastic webbing. ● *v.tr.* **1** gather (material) with parallel threads. **2** bake (eggs) without shells. □□ **shirring** *n.* [19th c.: orig. unkn.]
   ■ *v.* **1** gather, ruffle, pucker.

shirt /shərt/ *n.* **1** an upper-body garment of cotton, etc., having a collar, sleeves, and esp. buttons down the front, and often worn under a jacket or sweater; a blouse. **2 a** an undershirt. **b** a T-shirt. **3** = NIGHTSHIRT. □ **keep one's shirt on** *colloq*. keep one's temper. **lose one's shirt** lose all that one has, as through gambling, etc. **the shirt off one's back** *colloq*. one's last remaining possessions. □□ **shirted** *adj*. **shirting** *n.* **shirtless** *adj*. [OE *scyrte*, corresp. to ON *skyrta* (cf. SKIRT) f. Gmc: cf. SHORT]

shirtdress /shártdress/ *n.* = SHIRTWAIST sense 2. [SHIRT, DRESS]

shirtfront /shártfrunt/ the breast of a shirt, esp. of a stiffened evening shirt.

shirtsleeve /shártsleev/ *n.* (usu. in *pl.*) the sleeve of a shirt. □ **in shirtsleeves** wearing a shirt with no jacket, etc., over it.

shirttail /shárttayl/ the lower curved part of a shirt below the waist.

shirtwaist /shártwayst/ *n.* **1** a woman's dress with a bodice like a shirt. **2** a woman's blouse resembling a shirt. [SHIRT, WAIST]

shirty /shártee/ *adj.* (**shirtier, shirtiest**) *Brit. colloq.* angry; annoyed. □□ **shirtily** *adv.* **shirtiness** *n.*

shish kebab /shísh kibób/ *n.* a dish of pieces of marinated meat and vegetables cooked and served on skewers. [Turk. *şiş kebabı* f. *şiş* skewer, KEBAB roast meat]

shit /shit/ *v., n.,* & *int. coarse sl.* ¶ Usually considered a taboo word. ● *v.* (**shitting**; *past* and *past part.* **shit** or **shat**) *intr.* & *tr.* expel feces from the body or cause (feces, etc.) to be expelled. ● *n.* **1** feces. **2** an act of defecating. **3** a contemptible or worthless person or thing. **4** nonsense. **5** an intoxicating drug, esp. cannabis. ● *int.* an exclamation of disgust, anger, etc. [OE *scītan* (unrecorded) f. Gmc]
   ■ *v.* see DEFECATE. ● *n.* **1** feces, excrement, excreta, motion(s), stool(s), *sl.* pooh, *coarse sl.* crap.
   2 bowel movement, movement, motion, defecation, evacuation, *sl.* pooh, *coarse sl.* crap. **3** see STINKER *n.* 2, JUNK¹ *n.* 1, 2.

shitty /shítee/ *adj.* (**shittier, shittiest**) *coarse sl.* **1** disgusting; contemptible. **2** covered with excrement.

Shiva var. of SIVA.

shivaree var. of CHARIVARI.

shiver¹ /shívər/ *v.* & *n.* ● *v.intr.* **1** tremble with cold, fear, etc. **2** suffer a quick trembling movement of the body; shudder. ● *n.* **1** a momentary shivering movement. **2** (in *pl.*) an attack of shivering, esp. from fear or horror (*got the shivers in the dark*). □□ **shiverer** *n.* **shiveringly** *adv.* **shivery** *adj.* [ME *chivere*, perh. f. *chavele* chatter (as JOWL¹)]
   ■ *v.* shake, quake, tremble, shudder, quiver, quaver, tremor, oscillate, vibrate. ● *n.* **1** shake, tremble, shudder, quiver, trembling, shivering, tremor, flutter.
   2 (*shivers*) trembling, shivering; (*the shivers*) the shakes.

shiver² /shívər/ *n.* & *v.* ● *n.* (esp. in *pl.*) each of the small pieces into which esp. glass is shattered when broken; a splinter. ● *v.tr.* & *intr.* break into shivers. □ **shiver my** (or **me**) **timbers** a reputed piratical curse. [ME *scifre*, rel. to OHG *scivaro* splinter f. Gmc]
   ■ *n.* splinter, fragment, piece, shard, chip, sliver.
   ● *v.* shatter, fragment, splinter, disintegrate, explode, implode, smash (to smithereens).

shivoo /shivōō/ *n. Austral. colloq.* a party or celebration.

shoal¹ /shōl/ *n.* & *v.* ● *n.* **1** a great number of fish swimming together (cf. SCHOOL²). **2** a multitude; a crowd (*shoals of letters*). ● *v.intr.* (of fish) form shoals. [prob. readoption of MDu. *schōle* SCHOOL²]
   ■ *n.* see SWARM¹ *n.* 1–3.

shoal² /shōl/ *n., v.,* & *adj.* ● *n.* **1 a** an area of shallow water. **b** a submerged sandbank visible at low water. **2** (esp. in *pl.*) hidden danger or difficulty. ● *v.* **1** *intr.* (of water) get shallower. **2** *tr.* (of a ship, etc.) move into a shallower part of (water). ● *adj. archaic* (of water) shallow. □□ **shoaly** *adj.* [OE *sceald* f. Gmc, rel. to SHALLOW]
   ■ *n.* **1** see SHALLOW *n.*

shoat /shōt/ *n.* a young pig, esp. newly weaned. [ME: cf. W.Flem. *schote*]

shock¹ /shok/ *n.* & *v.* ● *n.* **1** a violent collision, impact, tremor, etc. **2** a sudden and disturbing effect on the emotions, physical reactions, etc. (*the news was a great shock*). **3** an acute state of prostration following a wound, pain, etc., esp. when much blood is lost (*died of shock*). **4** = *electric shock*. **5** a disturbance in stability causing fluctuations in an organization, monetary system, etc. ● *v.* **1** *tr.* **a** affect with shock; horrify; outrage; disgust; sadden. **b** (*absol.*) cause shock. **2** *tr.* (esp. in *passive*) affect with an electric or pathological shock. **3** *intr.* experience shock (*I don't shock easily*). **4** *intr. archaic* collide violently. □ **shock absorber** a device on a vehicle, etc., for absorbing shocks, vibrations, etc. **shock tactics 1** sudden and violent action. **2** *Mil.* a massed cavalry charge. **shock therapy** (or **treatment**) *Psychol.* a method of treating depressive patients by electric shock or drugs inducing coma and convulsions. **shock troops** troops specially trained for assault. **shock wave** a sharp change of pressure in a narrow region traveling through air, etc., caused by explosion or by a body moving faster than sound. □□ **shockable** *adj.* **shockability** *n.* [F *choc, choquer,* of unkn. orig.]
   ■ *n.* **1** jolt, tremor, collision; see also IMPACT *n.* 1. **2** surprise, thunderbolt, bolt from the blue, bombshell, revelation, jolt, *colloq.* shocker, eye-opener; trauma.
   ● *v.* **1** horrify, frighten, scare, petrify, traumatize, appall; outrage, disgust, nauseate, repel, revolt, sicken, upset, sadden, disquiet, disturb, perturb, discompose, unsettle, startle, surprise, stagger, jar, jolt, shake (up), astonish, astound; stun, numb, paralyze, daze, stupefy, dumbfound, *colloq.* bowl over, throw, flabbergast, give a person a turn. **3** scare, frighten.

shock² /shok/ *n.* & *v.* ● *n.* a group of usu. twelve sheaves of grain stood up with their heads together in a field. ● *v.tr.* arrange (grain) in shocks. [ME, perh. repr. OE *sc(e)oc* (unrecorded)]

shock³ /shok/ *n.* an unkempt or shaggy mass of hair. [cf. obs. *shock(-dog)*, earlier *shough*, shaggy-haired poodle]

shocker /shókər/ *n. colloq.* **1** a shocking, horrifying, unacceptable, etc., person or thing. **2** *hist.* a sordid or sensational novel, etc. **3** *Brit.* a shock absorber.

■ **1** see TERROR 2, FRIGHT *n.* 2.

shocking /shóking/ *adj. & adv.* ● *adj.* **1** causing indignation or disgust. **2** *Brit. colloq.* very bad (*shocking weather*). ● *adv. colloq.* shockingly (*shocking bad manners*). □ **shocking pink** a vibrant shade of pink. □□ **shockingly** *adv.* **shockingness** *n.*

■ *adj.* **1** disgusting, revolting, nauseating, nauseous, sickening, repulsive, abominable, hideous, horrible, horrifying, horrific, horrid, foul, loathsome, abhorrent, ghastly, hideous, unspeakable, dreadful, distressing, outrageous, appalling, monstrous, scandalous.

shockproof /shókproŏf/ *adj.* resistant to the effects of (esp. physical) shock.

shod *past* and *past part.* of SHOE.

shoddy /shódee/ *adj. & n.* ● *adj.* (**shoddier, shoddiest**) **1** trashy; shabby; poorly made. **2** counterfeit. ● *n.* (*pl.* **-ies**) **1 a** an inferior cloth made partly from the shredded fiber of old woolen cloth. **b** such fiber. **2** any thing of shoddy quality. □□ **shoddily** *adv.* **shoddiness** *n.* [19th c.: orig. dial.]

■ *adj.* **1** shabby, inferior, poor, cheapjack, rubbishy, cheap, pinchbeck, meretricious, tawdry, gaudy, brummagem, plastic, plasticky, tinsel, tinselly, second-rate, trashy, *colloq.* tatty, tacky. **2** see COUNTERFEIT *adj.* 1.

shoe /shoŏ/ *n. & v.* ● *n.* **1** either of a pair of protective foot coverings of leather, plastic, etc., having a sturdy sole and not reaching above the ankle. **2** a metal rim nailed to the hoof of a horse, etc.; a horseshoe. **3** anything resembling a shoe in shape or use, esp.: **a** a drag for a wheel. **b** = *brake shoe* (SEE BRAKE[1]). **c** a socket. **d** a ferrule, esp. on a sled runner. **e** a mast step. **f** a box from which cards are dealt in casinos at baccarat, etc. ● *v.tr.* (**shoes, shoeing;** *past* and *past part.* **shod** /shod/) **1** fit (esp. a horse, etc.) with a shoe or shoes. **2** protect (the end of a pole, etc.) with a metal shoe. **3** (as **shod** *adj.*) (in *comb.*) having shoes, etc., of a specified kind (*dry-shod; roughshod*). □ **be in a person's shoes** be in his or her situation, difficulty, etc. **dead men's shoes** property or a position, etc., coveted by a prospective successor. **if the shoe fits** (said of a generalized comment) it seems to be true (of a particular person). **shoe buckle** a buckle worn as ornament or as a fastening on a shoe. **shoe leather** leather for shoes, esp. when worn through by walking. **shoe tree** a shaped block for keeping a shoe in shape when not worn. **where the shoe pinches** where one's difficulty or trouble is. □□ **shoeless** *adj.* [OE *scōh, scōg(e)an* f. Gmc]

shoebill /shoŏbil/ *n.* an African storklike bird, *Balaeniceps rex,* with a large flattened bill for catching aquatic prey.

shoeblack /shoŏblak/ *n.* esp. *Brit.* = BOOTBLACK.

shoebox /shoŏboks/ *n.* **1** a box for packing shoes. **2** a very small space or dwelling.

shoehorn /shoŏhawrn/ *n.* a curved piece of horn, metal, etc., for easing the heel into a shoe.

shoelace /shoŏlays/ *n.* a cord for lacing up shoes.

■ see LACE *n.* 2.

shoemaker /shoŏmaykər/ *n.* a maker of boots and shoes. □□ **shoemaking** *n.*

shoeshine /shoŏshīn/ *n.* a polish given to shoes.

shoestring /shoŏstring/ *n.* **1** a shoelace. **2** *colloq.* a small esp. inadequate amount of money (*living on a shoestring*). **3** (*attrib.*) barely adequate; precarious (*a shoestring majority*).

■ **1** see LACE *n.* 2.

shofar /shṓfər, shawfaár/ *n.* (*pl.* **shofroth** /shōfrōt/) a ram's-horn trumpet used by Jews in religious ceremonies and as an ancient battle signal. [Heb. *šōpār,* pl. *šōpārôt*]

shogun /shṓgən, -gun/ *n. hist.* any of a succession of Japanese hereditary commanders in chief and virtual rulers before 1868. □□ **shogunate** /-nət, -nayt/ *n.* [Jap., = general, f. Chin. *jiang jun*]

shone *past* and *past part.* of SHINE.

shoo /shoŏ/ *int. & v.* ● *int.* an exclamation used to frighten away birds, children, etc. ● *v.* (**shoos, shooed**) **1** *intr.* utter the word "shoo!" **2** *tr.* (usu. foll. by *away*) drive (birds, etc.) away by shooing. □ **shoo-in** something easy or certain to succeed (*she's a shoo-in to win the election*). [imit.]

■ *int.* go away, go, away *or* be off (with you), *colloq.* scat, scram, *poet.* begone, *sl.* beat it, get lost. ● *v.* **2** (*shoo away*) scare off, frighten away, drive away, force to leave. □ **shoo-in** see BREEZE[1] *n.* 4.

shook[1] /shoŏk/ *past* of SHAKE. ● *predic.adj. colloq.* **1** (foll. by *up*) emotionally or physically disturbed; upset. **2** (foll. by *on*) *Austral. & NZ* keen on; enthusiastic about (*not too shook on the English climate*).

shook[2] /shoŏk/ *n.* a set of staves and headings for a cask, ready for fitting together. [18th c.: orig. unkn.]

shoot /shoŏt/ *v., n., & int.* ● *v.* (*past* and *past part.* **shot** /shot/) **1** *tr.* **a** cause (a gun, bow, etc.) to fire. **b** discharge (a bullet, arrow, etc.) from a gun, bow, etc. **c** kill or wound (a person, animal, etc.) with a bullet, arrow, etc. from a gun, bow, etc. **2** *intr.* discharge a gun, etc., esp. in a specified way (*shoots well*). **3** *tr.* send out, discharge, propel, etc., esp. violently or swiftly (*shot out the contents; shot a glance at his neighbor*). **4** *intr.* (often foll. by *out, along, forth,* etc.) come or go swiftly or vigorously. **5** *intr.* **a** (of a plant, etc.) put forth buds, etc. **b** (of a bud, etc.) appear. **6** *intr.* **a** hunt game, etc., with a gun. **b** (usu. foll. by *over*) shoot game over an estate, etc. **7** *tr.* shoot game in or on (coverts, an estate, etc.). **8** *tr.* film or photograph (a scene, film, etc.). **9** *tr.* (also *absol.*) Basketball, etc. **a** score (a goal). **b** take a shot at (the goal). **10** *tr.* (of a boat) sweep swiftly down or under (a bridge, rapids, falls, etc.). **11** *tr.* move (a door bolt) to fasten or unfasten a door, etc. **12** *tr.* let (trash, a load, etc.) fall or slide from a container, truck, etc. **13** *intr.* **a** (usu. foll. by *through, up,* etc.) (of a pain) pass with a stabbing sensation. **b** (of part of the body) be intermittently painful. **14** *intr.* (often foll. by *out*) project abruptly (*the mountain shoots out against the sky*). **15** *tr.* (often foll. by *up*) *sl.* inject esp. oneself with (a drug). **16** *tr. colloq.* **a** play a game of (craps, pool, etc.). **b** throw (a die or dice). **17** *tr.* Golf *colloq.* make (a specified score) for a round or hole. **18** *tr. colloq.* pass (traffic lights at red). **19** *tr.* plane (the edge of a board) accurately. ● *n.* **1** the act or an instance of shooting. **2 a** a young branch or sucker. **b** the new growth of a plant. **3** *Brit.* **a** a hunting party, expedition, etc. **b** land shot over for game. **4** = CHUTE[1]. **5** a rapid in a stream. ● *int. colloq.* **1** a demand for a reply, information, etc. **2** *euphem.* an exclamation of disgust, anger, etc. (see SHIT). □ **shoot ahead** come quickly to the front of competitors, etc. **shoot one's bolt** see BOLT[1]. **shoot down 1** kill (a person) by shooting. **2** cause (an aircraft, its pilot, etc.) to crash by shooting. **3** argue effectively against (a person, argument, etc.). **shoot from the hip** speak or act in haste. **shoot it out** *sl.* engage in a decisive gun battle. **shoot one's mouth off** *sl.* talk too much or indiscreetly. **shoot-out** *colloq.* a decisive gun battle; showdown. **shoot up 1** grow rapidly, esp. (of a person) grow taller. **2** rise suddenly. **3** terrorize (a district) by indiscriminate shooting. **4** *sl.* = sense 15 of *v.* □□ **shootable** *adj.* [OE *scēotan* f. Gmc: cf. SHEET[1], SHOT[1], SHUT]

■ *v.* **1 b** discharge, fire, let fly, launch, propel, project. **c** wound, hurt, harm, injure; kill, *literary or joc.* slay; gun (down), pot, *colloq.* blast, *sl.* plug. **3** see EJECT 1a, 5. **4** dart, whisk, speed, bolt, run, race, rush, flash, fly, dash, hurtle, streak, scuttle, bound, leap, spring, *colloq.* scoot, zip, whiz. **5** sprout, germinate; grow, spring up; mushroom, develop. **14** stand out, jut out; see also *stick out* (STICK[1]). ● *n.* **2** sprout, stem, bud, branch, offshoot, slip, scion, sucker. **2** *int. colloq.* spill the beans, spit it out, out with it. **2** damn, blast, esp. *Brit.* bother, *colloq.* hell, *euphem.* sugar. □ **shoot down 3** pull apart, take to pieces; see also ATTACK *v.* 3. **shoot one's mouth off** see PRATTLE *v.*

/. . . . /	**pronunciation**	● **part of speech**
□ **phrases, idioms, and compounds**		
□□ **derivatives**		■ **synonym section**
cross-references appear in SMALL CAPITALS or *italics*		

shooter /shŏŏtər/ n. **1** a person or thing that shoots. **2 a** (in comb.) a gun or other device for shooting (peashooter; six-shooter). **b** sl. a pistol, etc. **3** a player who shoots or is able to shoot a goal in basketball, etc. **4** a person who throws a die or dice.

shooting /shŏŏting/ n. & adj. ● n. **1** the act or an instance of shooting. **2 a** the right of shooting over an area of land. **b** an estate, etc., rented to shoot over. ● adj. moving, growing, etc., quickly (a shooting pain in the arm). □ **shooting box** (or **lodge**) Brit. a lodge used by hunters in the shooting season. **shooting brake** Brit. = station wagon. **shooting gallery** a place used for shooting at targets with rifles, etc. **shooting iron** colloq. a firearm. **shooting range** a ground with butts for rifle practice. **shooting star** a small meteor moving rapidly and burning up on entering the earth's atmosphere. **shooting stick** a walking stick with a foldable seat. **shooting war** a war in which there is shooting (opp. cold war, war of nerves, etc.). **the whole shooting match** colloq. everything.
■ n. **1** see DISCHARGE n. 4. ● adj. see ACUTE adj. 1b.
□ **shooting iron** see PISTOL n.

shop /shop/ n. & v. ● n. **1** a building, room, etc., for the retail sale of goods or services (dress shop; beauty shop); a store. **2** a place in which manufacture or repairing is done; a workshop (metal shop). **3** a profession, trade, business, etc., esp. as a subject of conversation (talk shop). **4** colloq. an institution, establishment, place of business, etc. ● v. (**shopped**, **shopping**) **1** intr. **a** go to a shop or shops to buy goods. **b** = window-shop. **2** tr. esp. Brit. sl. inform against (a criminal, etc.). □ **all over the shop** Brit. colloq. **1** in disorder (scattered all over the shop). **2** in every place (looked for it all over the shop). **3** wildly (hitting out all over the shop). **set up shop** establish oneself in business, etc. **shop around** look for the best bargain. **shop assistant** Brit. a person who serves customers in a shop. **shop boy** (or **girl**) an assistant in a shop. **shop steward** a person elected by workers in a factory, etc., to represent them in dealings with management. □□ **shopless** adj. **shoppy** adj. [ME f. AF & OF eschoppe booth f. MLG schoppe, OHG scopf porch]
■ n. **1** boutique, store. **2** workshop, machine shop; see also FACTORY. **4** see ESTABLISHMENT 2a. ● v. **2** betray, inform on or against, give away, colloq. peach on, rat on, blow the whistle on, sl. snitch on; see also INFORM 2.

shopkeeper /shópkeepər/ n. the owner and manager of a store. □□ **shopkeeping** n.
■ see TRADESMAN.

shoplifter /shópliftər/ n. a person who steals goods while appearing to shop. □□ **shoplift** v.tr. & intr. **shoplifting** n.
■ see THIEF. □□ **shoplifting** see THEFT.

shopper /shópər/ n. **1** a person who makes purchases in a store. **2** Brit. a shopping bag or carriage. **3** Brit. sl. an informer.
■ **1** client, customer; patron.

shopping /shóping/ n. **1** (often attrib.) the purchase of goods, etc. (shopping expedition). **2** goods purchased (put the shopping on the table). □ **shopping center** an area or complex of stores, with associated facilities.

shopwalker /shópwawkər/ n. Brit. = FLOORWALKER.

shopworn /shópwawrn/ adj. **1** (of an article) soiled or faded by display in a shop. **2** (of a person, idea, etc.) grubby; tarnished; no longer fresh or new.

shoran /sháwran/ n. a system of aircraft navigation using the return of two radar signals by two ground stations. [short range navigation]

shore[1] /shawr/ n. **1** the land that adjoins the sea or a large body of water. **2** (usu. in pl.) a country; a seacoast (often visits these shores; on a distant shore). **3** Law land between ordinary high and low water marks. □ **shore-based** operating from a base on shore. **shore leave** Naut. **1** permission to go ashore. **2** a period of time ashore. □□ **shoreless** adj. **shoreward** adj. & adv. **shorewards** adv. [ME f. MDu., MLG schōre, perh. f. the root of SHEAR]
■ **1** see COAST n.

shore[2] /shawr/ v. & n. ● v.tr. (often foll. by up) support with

or as if with a shore or shores; hold up. ● n. a prop or beam set obliquely against a ship, wall, tree, etc., as a support. □□ **shoring** n. [ME f. MDu., MLG schōre prop, of unkn. orig.]
■ v. see SUPPORT v. 1, 2; 4, 6. ● n. see PROP[1] n. 1.

shore[3] see SHEAR.

shoreline /sháwrlin/ n. the line along which a stretch of water, esp. a sea or lake, meets the shore.

shoreweed /sháwrweed/ n. a stoloniferous plant, Littorella uniflora, growing in shallow water.

shorn past part. of SHEAR.

short /shawrt/ adj., adv., n., & v. ● adj. **1 a** measuring little; not long from end to end (a short distance). **b** not long in duration; brief (a short time ago; had a short life). **c** seeming less than the stated amount (a few short years of happiness). **2** of small height; not tall (a short square tower; was shorter than average). **3 a** (usu. foll. by of, on) having a partial or total lack; deficient; scanty (short of spoons; is rather short on sense). **b** colloq. having little money. **c** not far-reaching; acting or being near at hand (within short range). **4 a** concise; brief (kept his speech short). **b** curt; uncivil (was short with her). **5** (of the memory) unable to remember distant events. **6** Phonet. & Prosody of a vowel or syllable: **a** having the lesser of the two recognized durations. **b** unstressed. **c** (of an English vowel) having a sound other than that called long (cf. LONG[1] adj. 8). **7 a** (of pastry) crumbling; not holding together. **b** (of clay) having poor plasticity. **8** esp. Stock Exch. **a** (of stocks, a stockbroker, crops, etc.) sold or selling when the amount is not in hand, with reliance on getting the deficit in time for delivery. **b** (of a bill of exchange) maturing at an early date. **9** Brit. (of a drink of liquor) undiluted. ● adv. **1** before the natural or expected time or place; abruptly (pulled up short; cut short the celebrations). **2** rudely; uncivilly (spoke to him short). ● n. **1** a short circuit. **2** a short movie. **3** Brit. colloq. a short drink, esp. liquor. **4** Stock Exch. **a** a person who sells short. **b** (in pl.) short-dated stocks. **5** Phonet. **a** a short syllable or vowel. **b** a mark indicating that a vowel is short. **6** (in pl.) a mixture of bran and coarse flour. ● v.tr. & intr. short-circuit. □ **be caught** (or Brit. **taken**) **short 1** be put at a disadvantage. **2** be unprepared. **3** Brit. colloq. urgently need to urinate or defecate. **bring up** (or **pull up**) **short** check or pause abruptly. **come short** be inadequate or disappointing. **come short of** fail to reach or amount to. **for short** as a short name (Tom for short). **get** (or **have**) **by the short hairs** colloq. be in complete control of (a person). **go short** (often foll. by of) not have enough. **in short** to use few words; briefly. **in short order** immediately. **in the short run** over a short period of time. **in short supply** scarce. **in the short term** = in the short run. **make short work of** accomplish, dispose of, destroy, consume, etc., quickly. **short and sweet** esp. iron. brief and pleasant. **short-arm** (of a blow, etc.) delivered with the arm not fully extended. **short circuit** an electric circuit through small resistance, esp. instead of the resistance of a normal circuit. **short-circuit** v. **1** cause a short circuit or a short circuit in. **2** shorten or avoid (a journey, work, etc.) by taking a more direct route, etc. **short commons** Brit. insufficient food. **short cut 1** a route shortening the distance traveled. **2** a quick way of accomplishing something. **short-day** (of a plant) needing the period of light each day to fall below some limit to cause flowering. **short division** Math. division in which the quotient is written directly without being worked out in writing. **short drink** a strong alcoholic drink served in small measures. **short-eared owl** an owl, Asio flammeus, frequenting open country and hunting at dawn or dusk. **short end of the stick** the less or least favorable of the lot (his younger brother always got the short end of the stick). **short for** an abbreviation for ("Bob" is short for "Robert"). **short fuse** colloq. a quick temper. **short game** Golf approaching and putting. **short haul 1** the transport of goods over a short distance. **2** a short-term effort. **short hundredweight** see HUNDREDWEIGHT. **short-list** v.tr. put on a shortlist. **short-lived** ephemeral; not long-lasting. **short mark** = BREVE 2. **short measure** less than the professed amount. **short meter** Prosody a hymn stanza of four lines with 6, 6, 8, and 6 syllables. **short notice** an insufficient length of warning time. **short odds** nearly equal stakes or chances in betting. **short of 1** see sense 3a of *adj.* **2** less than (*nothing short of a miracle*). **3** distant from (*two miles short of home*). **4** without going so far as; except (*did everything short of destroying it*). **short of breath** panting, short-winded. **short on** *colloq.* see sense 3a of *adj.* **short-order a** prepared or provided quickly, esp. simple restaurant fare. **b** pertaining to one who provides this (*a short-order cook*). **short-range 1** having a short range. **2** relating to a fairly immediate future time (*short-range possibilities*). **short score** *Mus.* a score not giving all parts. **short shrift** curt or dismissive treatment. **short sight** the inability to focus except on comparatively near objects. **short-sleeved** with sleeves not reaching below the elbow. **short-staffed** having insufficient staff. **short story** a story with a fully developed theme but shorter than a novel. **short temper** self-control soon or easily lost. **short-tempered** quick to lose one's temper; irascible. **short-term** occurring in or relating to a short period of time. **short title** an abbreviated form of a title of a book, etc. **short ton** see TON. **short view** a consideration of the present only, not the future. **short waist 1** a high or shallow waist of a dress. **2** a short upper body. **short weight** weight less than it is alleged to be. **short-winded 1** quickly exhausted of breath. **2** incapable of sustained effort. ▫▫ **shortish** *adj.* **shortness** *n.* [OE *sceort* f. Gmc: cf. SHIRT, SKIRT]

■ *adj.* **1 b** quick, limited; short-lived; see also BRIEF *adj.* 1. **2** small, little, diminutive, elfin; midget, dwarfish, squat, runty, undersized, stubby, stunted, *colloq.* pint-size, sawed-off. **3 a** (*short of* or *on*) deficient in, lacking in, needful of, wanting in, low on, *colloq.* shy. **b** impecunious, straitened, pinched, underfunded, deficient; see also BROKE. **c** close, near. **4 a** concise, compact, pocket, abbreviated, abridged, cut; laconic, terse, succinct, pithy, sententious, epigrammatic; direct, straight, straightforward, short and sweet; see also BRIEF *adj.* 2. **b** curt, terse, sharp, blunt, bluff, brusque, offhand, gruff, discourteous, uncivil, impolite; see also ABRUPT 2. ● *adv.* **1** abruptly, suddenly, peremptorily, without warning, instantly, unexpectedly, hurriedly, hastily. **2** bluntly, shortly, curtly, rudely, brusquely, sharply, abruptly, uncivilly, direct, straight ● *n.* **3** nip, short drink; see also SHOT¹ 11a. ▫ **be caught** (or *Brit.* **taken**) **short 1** be handicapped or constrained or trammeled or impeded, be out on a limb, be caught napping, *archaic* be on the hip. **bring up short** see CHECK¹ *v.* 2a. **come short of** fail, disappoint, be or prove inadequate or insufficient to. **get** (or **have**) **by the short hairs** have at one's beck and call, have under control; see also *twist around one's finger* (FINGER). **in short** briefly, in a word, to cut a long story short, in a nutshell. **in short order** see IMMEDIATELY *adv.* 1. **in the short run** in the short term. **in short supply** rare, scarce, unplentiful, thin on the ground, hard to come by, at a premium, limited, few and far between. **short-lived** ephemeral, evanescent, temporary, fleeting, transitory, transient, passing, *literary* fugacious. **short of 4** excepting, except for, leaving out, apart from, setting aside, excluding, exclusive of, barring. **short-staffed** undermanned, shorthanded, understaffed. **short-tempered** testy, irascible, curt, abrupt, gruff, bluff, terse, brusque, crabbed, crabby, touchy, petulant, peevish, bearish, snappish, waspish, shrewish, curmudgeonly, crusty, surly, *colloq.* grouchy; see also IRRITABLE 1. **short-winded 1** short of or out of breath, winded, breathless, panting, huffing (and puffing), gasping (for air or for breath), *Med.* dyspneal.

shortage /sháwrtij/ *n.* (often foll. by *of*) a deficiency; an amount lacking (*a shortage of 100 tons*).

■ deficit, deficiency, shortfall, dearth, scarcity, lack, want, paucity.

shortbread /sháwrtbred/ *n.* a crisp, rich, crumbly type of cookie made with butter, flour, and sugar.

shortcake /sháwrtkayk/ *n.* **1** = SHORTBREAD. **2** a cake made of short pastry and filled with fruit and cream.

shortchange /sháwrtcháynj/ *v.tr.* rob or cheat by giving insufficient money as change.

shortcoming /sháwrtkuming/ *n.* failure to come up to a standard; a defect.

■ defect, deficiency, weakness, frailty, drawback, liability, imperfection, weak point, flaw, *formal* defalcation.

shorten /sháwrt'n/ *v.* **1** *intr.* & *tr.* become or make shorter or short; curtail. **2** *tr. Naut.* reduce the amount of (sail spread). **3** *intr.* & *tr.* (with reference to gambling odds, prices, etc.) become or make shorter; decrease.

■ **1** cut, curtail, cut off or down or short, reduce, diminish, condense, abridge, abbreviate, digest, compress; trim.

shortening /sháwrt'ning, sháwrtning/ *n.* fat used for making pastry, bread, etc.

shortfall /sháwrtfawl/ *n.* a deficit below what was expected.

■ see DEFICIT.

shorthand /sháwrt-hand/ *n.* **1** (often *attrib.*) a method of rapid writing in abbreviations and symbols esp. for taking dictation. **2** an abbreviated or symbolic mode of expression.

■ **1** stenography, tachygraphy, phonography.

shorthanded /shawrt-hánded/ *adj.* undermanned or under-staffed.

shorthorn /sháwrt-horn/ *n.* **1** an animal of a breed of cattle with short horns. **2** this breed.

shortie var. of SHORTY.

shortlist /sháwrtlist/ *n.* a selective list of candidates from which a final choice is made.

shortly /sháwrtlee/ *adv.* **1** (often foll. by *before, after*) before long; soon (*will arrive shortly*; *arrived shortly after him*). **2** in a few words; briefly. **3** curtly. [OE *scortlice* (as SHORT, -LY²)]

■ **1** soon, presently, before long, in a (little) while, by and by, *archaic or literary* anon, *poet.* or *archaic* ere long. **3** abruptly, peremptorily, curtly, brusquely, bluntly, sharply, tersely, gruffly, rudely.

shorts /shawrts/ *n.pl.* **1** pants reaching only to the knees or higher. **2** underpants.

■ **1** Bermudas, lederhosen, trunks, knee breeches,. **2** see BRIEF *n.* 1.

shortsighted /sháwrtsítid/ *adj.* **1** esp. *Brit.* = NEARSIGHTED. **2** lacking imagination or foresight. ▫▫ **shortsightedly** *adv.* **shortsightedness** *n.*

■ **2** unimaginative, unprogressive, improvident, imprudent, injudicious, rash, impolitic, limited, thoughtless, unmindful.

shortstop /sháwrtstop/ *n.* a baseball fielder positioned between second and third base.

shortwave /sháwrtwáyv/ *n.* a radio wave of frequency greater than 3 MHz.

shorty /sháwrtee/ *n.* (also **shortie**) (*pl.* **-ies**) *colloq.* **1** a person shorter than average. **2** a short garment, esp. a nightgown or raincoat.

Shoshone /shəshṓn, -shṓnee/ *n.* (also **Shoshoni**) **1 a** a N. American people native to the western US. **b** a member of this people. **2** the language of this people. ▫▫ **Shoshonean** *adj.*

shot¹ /shot/ *n.* **1** the act or an instance of firing a gun, cannon, etc. (*several shots were heard*). **2** an attempt to hit by shooting or throwing, etc. (*took a shot at him*). **3 a** a single nonexplosive missile for a cannon, gun, etc. **b** (*pl.* same or **shots**) a small lead pellet used in quantity in a single charge or cartridge in a shotgun. **c** (as *pl.*) these collectively. **4 a** a photograph. **b** a film sequence photographed continuously by one camera. **5 a** a stroke or a kick in a ball game. **b** *colloq.* an attempt to guess or do something (*let her have a shot at it*). **6** *colloq.* a person having a specified skill with a gun, etc. (*is not a good shot*). **7** a heavy ball thrown by a shot-putter.

/.../ **pronunciation**	● **part of speech**
▫ **phrases, idioms, and compounds**	
▫▫ **derivatives**	■ **synonym section**
cross-references appear in SMALL CAPITALS or *italics*	

8 the launch of a space rocket (*a moonshot*). **9** the range, reach, or distance to or at which a thing will carry or act (*out of earshot*). **10** a remark aimed at a person. **11** *colloq.* **a** a drink of esp. liquor. **b** an injection of a drug, vaccine, etc. (*has had his shots*). □ **like a shot** *colloq.* without hesitation; willingly; quickly. **shot in the arm** *colloq.* **1** stimulus or encouragement. **2** *Brit.* an alcoholic drink. **shot in the dark** a mere guess. **shot put** an athletic contest in which a shot is thrown a great distance. **shot-putter** an athlete who puts the shot. **shot tower** *hist.* a tower in which shot was made from molten lead poured through sieves at the top and falling into water at the bottom. □□ **shotproof** *adj.* [OE *sc(e)ot*, *gesc(e)ot* f. Gmc: cf. SHOOT]

■ **1** blast. **3** bullet, ball, slug, cannonball, pellet, projectile, missile; buckshot. **4 a** photograph, print, snapshot, picture, snap, photo, *colloq.* pic. **5 a** see KICK *n.* 1. **b** attempt, try, opportunity, chance, endeavor, *colloq.* stab, crack, go, whirl, *sl.* bash. **6** marksman, shooter. **8** (space) launch *or* launching. **9** see RANGE *n.* 1a–c. **11 a** drink, jigger, dram, nip, slug, esp. *Brit.* tot, *colloq.* swig, finger, spot, snort. **b** injection, inoculation, vaccination, *colloq.* jab. □ **like a shot** quickly, swiftly, rapidly, speedily, hurriedly, hastily, at once, like a flash, immediately, instantly, instantaneously, in two shakes of a lamb's tail, before you can say Jack Robinson, *colloq.* like greased lightning; without hesitation, without a murmur, uncomplainingly; see also *willingly* (WILLING). **shot in the arm 1** stimulus, encouragement, incentive, inducement, provocation, motivation, *colloq.* boost. **shot in the dark** see GUESS *n.*

shot² /shot/ *past* and *past part.* of SHOOT. ● *adj.* **1** (of colored material) woven so as to show different colors at different angles. **2** *colloq.* **a** exhausted; finished. **b** drunk. **3** (of a board edge) accurately planed. □ **be** (or **get**) **shot of** *Brit. sl.* be (or get) rid of. **shot through** permeated or suffused. [past part. of SHOOT]

shot³ /shot/ *n. Brit. colloq.* a reckoning, a bill, esp. at an inn, etc. (*paid his shot*). [ME, = SHOT¹: cf. OE *scēotan* shoot, pay, contribute, and SCOT]

shotgun /shótgun/ *n.* a smoothbore gun for firing small shot at short range. □ **shotgun marriage** (or **wedding**) *colloq.* an enforced or hurried wedding, esp. because of the bride's pregnancy.

should /shòod/ *v.aux.* (*3rd sing.* **should**) *past* of SHALL, used esp.: **1** in reported speech, esp. with the reported element in the 1st person (*I said I should be home by evening*). ¶ Cf. WILL¹, WOULD, now more common in this sense, esp. to avoid implications of sense 2. **2 a** to express a duty, obligation, or likelihood; = OUGHT¹ (*I should tell you; you should have been more careful; they should have arrived by now*). **b** (in the 1st person) to express a tentative suggestion (*I should like to say something*). **3 a** expressing the conditional mood in the 1st person (cf. WOULD) (*I should have been killed if I had gone*). **b** forming a conditional protasis or indefinite clause (*if you should see him; should they arrive, tell them where to go*). **4** expressing purpose = MAY, MIGHT¹ (*in order that we should not worry*).

■ **2 a** see MUST¹ *v.*

shoulder /shòldər/ *n. & v.* ● *n.* **1 a** the part of the body at which the arm, foreleg, or wing is attached. **b** (in full **shoulder joint**) the end of the upper arm joining with the clavicle and scapula. **c** either of the two projections below the neck from which the arms hang. **2** the upper foreleg and shoulder blade of a pig, lamb, etc., when butchered. **3** (often in *pl.*) **a** the upper part of the back and arms. **b** this part of the body regarded as capable of bearing a burden or blame, providing comfort, etc. (*needs a shoulder to cry on*). **4** a strip of land next to a paved road (*pulled over onto the shoulder*). **5** a part of a garment covering the shoulder. **6** a part of anything resembling a shoulder in form or function, as in a bottle, mountain, tool, etc. ● *v.* **1 a** *tr.* push with the shoulder; jostle. **b** *intr.* make one's way by jostling (*shouldered through the crowd*). **2** *tr.* take (a burden, etc.) on one's shoulders (*shouldered the family's problems*). □ **put** (or **set**) **one's shoulder to the wheel** make an effort. **shoulder arms**

hold a rifle with the barrel against the shoulder and the butt in the hand. **shoulder bag** a handbag that can be hung from the shoulder. **shoulder belt** a seat belt that passes over one shoulder and under the opposite arm. **shoulder blade** *Anat.* either of the large flat bones of the upper back; the scapula. **shoulder board** (or **mark**) the stiffened shoulder strap of a naval officer bearing insignia of rank. **shoulder-high** up to or as high as the shoulders. **shoulder holster** a gun holster worn in the armpit. **shoulder knot** a knot of ribbon, metal, lace, etc., worn as part of a ceremonial dress. **shoulder loop** the shoulder strap of an army, air force, or marines officer. **shoulder note** *Printing* a marginal note at the top of a page. **shoulder-of-mutton sail** = *leg-of-mutton sail*. **shoulder strap 1** a strip of fabric, leather, etc., suspending a bag or garment from the shoulder. **2** a strip of cloth from shoulder to collar on a military uniform bearing a symbol of rank, etc. **3** a similar strip on a raincoat. **shoulder to shoulder 1** side by side. **2** with closed ranks or united effort. □□ **shouldered** *adj.* (also in *comb.*). [OE *sculdor* f. WG]

■ *n.* **4** side, edge, *Brit.* verge, hard shoulder. ● *v.* **1 a** push, shove, jostle, hustle, thrust, elbow, force. **2** support, carry, bear, take upon oneself, take on, accept, assume. □ **put** (or **set**) **one's shoulder to the wheel** make every effort, make an effort, strive, work hard, pitch in, apply oneself, roll up one's sleeves, set *or* get to work, knuckle down, buckle down, keep one's nose to the grindstone. **shoulder to shoulder** side by side, united, as one, cooperatively, jointly, together, arm in arm, hand in hand, in partnership.

shouldn't /shòod'nt/ *contr.* should not.

shout /showt/ *v. & n.* ● *v.* **1** *intr.* make a loud cry or vocal sound; speak loudly (*shouted for attention*). **2** *tr.* say or express loudly; call out (*shouted that the coast was clear*). **3** *tr.* (*also absol.*) *Austral. & NZ colloq.* treat (another person) to drinks, etc. ● *n.* **1** a loud cry expressing joy, etc., or calling attention. **2** *Brit., Austral., & NZ colloq.* one's turn to order and pay for a round of drinks, etc. (*your shout, I think*). □ **all over but the shouting** *colloq.* the contest is virtually decided. **shout at** speak loudly to, etc. **shout down** reduce to silence by shouting. **shout for** call for by shouting. **shout-up** *Brit. colloq.* a noisy argument. □□ **shouter** *n.* [ME, perh. rel. to SHOOT: cf. ON *skúta* SCOUT]

■ *v.* **1, 2** bellow, bawl, roar (out), cry (out), call (out), yell, scream, *colloq.* holler. ● *n.* **1** yell, scream, bellow, howl, yelp, roar, cry, call, whoop, *colloq.* holler. **2** round. □ **all over bar** (or **but**) **the shouting** almost over *or* finished, nearly over; fait accompli.

shove /shuv/ *v. & n.* ● *v.* **1** *tr.* (*also absol.*) push vigorously; move by hard or rough pushing (*shoved him out of the way*). **2** *intr.* (*usu. foll. by* *along, past, through*, etc.) make one's way by pushing (*shoved through the crowd*). **3** *tr. colloq.* put somewhere (*shoved it in the drawer*). ● *n.* an act of shoving or of prompting a person into action. □ **shove-halfpenny** (in the UK) a form of shuffleboard played with coins, etc., on a table, esp. in a bar or pub. **shove off 1** start from the shore in a boat. **2** *sl.* depart; go away (*told him to shove off*). [OE *scūfan* f. Gmc]

■ *v.* **1** see PUSH *v.* 1. **2** thrust *or* elbow *or* force *or* jostle one's way; see also PUSH *v.* 6. **3** see STUFF *v.* 2. ● *n.* push, thrust, nudge. □ **shove off 1** push off.
2 see *push off*.

shovel /shúvəl/ *n. & v.* ● *n.* **1 a** a spadelike tool for shifting quantities of coal, earth, etc., esp. having the sides curved upward. **b** the amount contained in a shovel; a shovelful. **2** a machine or part of a machine having a similar form or function. ● *v.tr.* **1** shift or clear (coal, etc.) with or as if with a shovel. **2** *colloq.* move (esp. food) in large quantities or roughly (*shoveled peas into his mouth*). □ **shovel hat** a broad-brimmed hat esp. worn by some English clergymen. □□ **shovelful** *n.* (*pl.* **-fuls**). [OE *scofl* f. Gmc (see SHOVE)]

shovelboard /shúvəlbawrd/ *n. Brit.* var. of SHUFFLEBOARD.

shovelhead /shúvəlhed/ *n.* a shark, *Sphyrna tiburo*, like the hammerhead but smaller. Also called BONNETHEAD.

shoveler /shúvələr, shúvlər/ *n.* (also esp. **Brit. shoveller**) **1**

a person or thing that shovels. **2** a duck, *Anas clypeata*, with a broad shovellike beak. [SHOVEL: sense 2 earlier *shovelard* f. -ARD, perh. after *mallard*]

show /shō/ *v. & n.* ● *v.* (*past part.* **shown** /shōn/ or **showed**) **1** *intr. & tr.* be, or allow or cause to be, visible; manifest; appear (*the buds are beginning to show*; *white shows the dirt*). **2** *tr.* (often foll. by *to*) offer, exhibit, or produce (a thing) for scrutiny, etc. (*show your tickets please*; *showed him my poems*). **3** *tr.* **a** indicate (one's feelings) by one's behavior, etc. (*showed mercy to him*). **b** indicate (one's feelings to a person, etc.) **c** (of feelings, etc.) be manifest (*his dislike shows*). **5** *tr.* **a** demonstrate; point out; prove (*has shown it to be false*; *showed that he knew the answer*). **b** (usu. foll. by *how to* + infin.) cause (a person) to understand or be capable of doing (*showed them how to knit*). **6** *tr.* (*refl.*) exhibit oneself as being (*showed herself to be fair*). **7** *tr. & intr.* (with ref. to a movie) be presented or cause to be presented. **8** *tr.* exhibit (a picture, animal, flower, etc.) in a show. **9** *tr.* (often foll. by *in, out, up*, etc.) conduct or lead (*showed them to their rooms*). **10** *intr.* = show up 3 (*waited but he didn't show*). **11** *intr.* finish third or among the first three in a race. ● *n.* **1** the act or an instance of showing; the state of being shown. **2 a** a spectacle, display, exhibition, etc. (*a fine show of blossom*). **b** a collection of things, etc., shown for public entertainment or in competition (*dog show*; *flower show*). **3 a** a play, etc., esp. a musical. **b** an entertainment program on television, etc. **c** any public entertainment or performance. **4 a** an outward appearance, semblance, or display (*made a show of agreeing*; *a show of strength*). **b** empty appearance; mere display (*did it for show*; *that's all show*). **5** *colloq.* an undertaking, business, etc. (*sold the whole show*). **6** esp. *Brit. colloq.* an opportunity of acting, defending oneself, etc. (*gave him a fair show*; *made a good show of it*). **7** *Med.* a discharge of blood, etc., from the vagina at the onset of childbirth. □ **get the show on the road** *colloq.* get started, begin an undertaking. **give the show** (or **whole show**) **away** demonstrate the inadequacies or reveal the truth. **good** (or **bad** or **poor**) **show!** esp. *Brit. colloq.* **1** that was well (or badly) done. **2** that was lucky (or unlucky). **nothing to show for** no visible result of (effort, etc.). **on show** being exhibited. **show business** *colloq.* the theatrical profession. **show one's cards** = *show one's hand.* **show cause** *Law* allege with justification. **show a clean pair of heels** *colloq.* retreat speedily; run away. **show one's colors** make one's opinion clear. **show a person the door** dismiss or eject a person. **show one's face** make an appearance; let oneself be seen. **show fight** be persistent or belligerent. **show the flag** see FLAG¹. **show forth** *archaic* exhibit; expound. **show one's hand 1** disclose one's plans. **2** reveal one's cards. **show in** see sense 9 of *v.* **show a leg** *Brit. colloq.* get out of bed. **show jumping** the sport of riding horses over a course of fences and other obstacles, with penalty points for errors. **show off 1** display to advantage. **2** *colloq.* act pretentiously; display one's wealth, knowledge, etc. **show-off** *n. colloq.* a person who shows off. **show of force** proof that one is prepared to use force. **show of hands** raised hands indicating a vote for or against, usu. without being counted. **show oneself 1** be seen in public. **2** see sense 6 of *v.* **show out** see sense 9 of *v.* **show around** take (a person) to places of interest; act as guide for (a person) in a building, etc. **show one's teeth** esp. *Brit.* reveal one's strength; be aggressive. **show through 1** be visible although supposedly concealed. **2** (of real feelings, etc.) be revealed inadvertently. **show trial** esp. *hist.* a judicial trial designed by the government to terrorize or impress the public. **show up 1** make or be conspicuous or clearly visible. **2** expose (a fraud, impostor, inferiority, etc.). **3** *colloq.* appear; be present; arrive. **4** *colloq.* embarrass or humiliate (*don't show me up by wearing jeans*). **show the way 1** indicate what has to be done, etc., by attempting it first. **2** show others which way to go, etc. **show the white feather** *Brit.* appear cowardly (see also *white feather*). **show willing** esp. *Brit.* display a willingness to help, etc. **show window** a window for exhibiting goods, etc. [ME f. OE *scēawian* f. WG: cf. SHEEN]

■ *v.* **1** appear, become or be visible, peek through, be seen; represent, symbolize, depict, portray, picture, illustrate; see also DISPLAY *v.* **1. 2** display, present, exhibit. **3** demonstrate, indicate, register; (lay) bare, disclose, reveal, expose, betray, make known, divulge, express, make clear or plain or manifest; grant, accord, bestow. **4** be apparent or manifest, show through. **5 a** prove, demonstrate, point out, illustrate, confirm, corroborate, verify, substantiate, bear out, certify, authenticate; exhibit, reveal, indicate, display, register. **b** teach, instruct, tell, inform, give an idea of, give a lesson in. **7** present, put on, screen; play, be presented or played or screened. **9** escort, accompany, conduct, usher, lead, guide, direct. ● *n.* **2 a** see DISPLAY *n.* 2. **b** display, exhibition, exposition, fair, expo. **3** production, presentation, play, musical, entertainment. **4 a** see SEMBLANCE 1. **b** display, appearance, pretense; see also OSTENTATION. **5** see UNDERTAKING 1. □ **give the show** (or **whole show**) **away** see let on 1 (LET¹). **good show!** **1** bravo, well done, good for you, congratulations. **on show** in the public eye, in the limelight, under the spotlight, high-profile. **show a clean pair of heels** see RUN *v.* 2. **show a person the door** see DISMISS *v.* 2. **show one's face** make or put in an appearance, show oneself, be seen, turn up; see also APPEAR 1. **show forth** see set forth 2 (SET¹). **show one's hand** see put one's cards on the table (CARD¹). **show a leg** get up, rise, greet the dawn, get out of bed, *colloq.* surface. **show off** make an exhibition or a spectacle of, flaunt, advertise, display, parade; pose, swagger, posture, boast, brag. **show-off** braggart, exhibitionist, swaggerer, egotist, boaster, *archaic* scaramouche, *colloq.* blowhard, *Austral. sl.* lair. **show up 1** stand out, be conspicuous, be noticeable, contrast; make visible, reveal, show. **2** expose, reveal; see also give away 3. **3** make or put in an appearance, appear, show, show one's face, arrive, come, turn up. **4** embarrass, (put to) shame, mortify, humiliate.

showbiz /shōbiz/ *n. colloq.* = *show business.*

showboat /shōbōt/ *n.* a river steamer on which theatrical performances are given.

showcase /shōkays/ *n. & v.* ● *n.* **1** a glass case used for exhibiting goods, etc. **2** a place or medium for presenting (esp. attractively) to general attention. ● *v.tr.* display in or as if in a showcase.

showdown /shōdown/ *n.* **1** a final test or confrontation; a decisive situation. **2** the laying down face up of the players' cards in poker.

■ **1** confrontation, climax, moment of truth, final settlement, moment of decision, *colloq.* crunch.

shower /showr/ *n. & v.* ● *n.* **1** a brief fall of esp. rain, hail, sleet, or snow. **2 a** a brisk flurry of arrows, bullets, dust, stones, sparks, etc. **b** a similar flurry of gifts, letters, honors, praise, etc. **3** (in full **shower bath**) **a** a cubicle, bath, etc. in which one stands under a spray of water. **b** the apparatus, etc., used for this. **c** the act of bathing in a shower. **4** a group of particles initiated by a cosmic-ray particle in the earth's atmosphere. **5** a party for giving presents to a prospective bride, expectant mother, etc. **6** *Brit. sl.* a contemptible or unpleasant person or group of people. ● *v.* **1** *tr.* **a** discharge (water, missiles, etc.) in a shower. **b** make wet (or as if with) a shower. **2** *intr.* use a shower bath. **3** *tr.* (usu. foll. by *on, upon*) lavishly bestow (gifts, etc.). **4** *intr.* descend or come in a shower (*it showered on and off all day*). □□ **showery** *adj.* [OE *scūr* f. Gmc]

■ *n.* **1** sprinkle, sprinkling, fall, drizzle, precipitation. **2** flurry, deluge, torrent, flood, influx, stream, barrage, overflow, abundance, profusion. **3 b, c** *Brit.* douche. ● *v.* **1** sprinkle, rain, pour, spray, splash, hail. **2** *Brit.* douche. **3** lavish, bestow, heap. **4** fall, descend, hail,

---

/.../ **pronunciation**	● **part of speech**
□ **phrases, idioms, and compounds**	
□□ **derivatives**	■ **synonym section**
cross-references appear in SMALL CAPITALS or *italics*	

pelt; rain, sprinkle, pour, drizzle, mizzle. ▫▫ **showery** see WET *adj.* 2.

showerproof /shówrpro͞of/ *adj. & v.* • *adj.* resistant to light rain. • *v.tr.* render showerproof.

showgirl /shógərl/ *n.* an actress who sings and dances in musicals, variety shows, etc.

showing /shóing/ *n.* **1** the act or an instance of showing. **2** a usu. specified quality of performance (*made a poor showing*). **3** the presentation of a case; evidence (*on present showing it must be true*). [OE *scēawung* (as SHOW)]
  ■ **1** exhibition; see also DEMONSTRATION 3.

showman /shómən/ *n.* (*pl.* **-men**) **1** the proprietor or manager of a circus, etc. **2** a person skilled in self-advertisement or publicity. ▫▫ **showmanship** *n.*
  ■ **1** producer, impresario, director, manager, regisseur.
  ▫▫ **showmanship** éclat, pyrotechnics, show, staginess, *sl.* razzle-dazzle; see also VERVE.

shown *past part.* of SHOW.

showpiece /shóopees/ *n.* **1** an item of work presented for exhibition or display. **2** an outstanding example or specimen.
  ■ **showpiece 2** masterpiece; see also MODEL *n.* 5a.

showplace /shóoplays/ *n.* a house, etc., that tourists go to see.

showroom /shóro͞om, -ro͝om/ *n.* a room in a factory, office building, etc., used to display goods for sale.

showstopper /shóstopər/ *n. colloq.* an act or performance receiving prolonged applause.

showy /shóee/ *adj.* (**showier, showiest**) **1** brilliant; gaudy, esp. vulgarly so. **2** striking. ▫▫ **showily** *adv.* **showiness** *n.*
  ■ flashy, garish, flamboyant, brilliant, conspicuous, striking, imposing, ostentatious, pretentious, grandiose, bravura, gaudy, lurid, loud, *colloq.* flash; elaborate, fancy, florid, flowery, ornate, fussy, intricate, baroque, rococo, Byzantine, arabesque.

s.h.p. *abbr.* shaft horsepower.

shrank *past* of SHRINK.

shrapnel /shrápnəl/ *n.* **1** fragments of a bomb, etc., thrown out by an explosion. **2** a shell containing bullets or pieces of metal timed to burst short of impact. [Gen. H. *Shrapnel*, Brit. soldier d. 1842, inventor of the shell]

shred /shred/ *n. & v.* • *n.* **1** a scrap, fragment, or strip of esp. cloth, paper, etc. **2** the least amount; remnant (*not a shred of evidence*). • *v.tr.* (**shredded, shredding**) tear or cut into shreds. □ **tear to shreds** completely refute (an argument, etc.). [OE *scrēad* (unrecorded) piece cut off, *scrēadian* f. WG: see SHROUD]
  ■ *n.* **1** scrap, fragment, bit, remnant, snippet, piece, tatter, strip, rag, sliver, chip. **2** atom, trace, whit, grain, jot (or tittle), tittle, scintilla, hint, suggestion, iota, speck, *Austral. colloq.* skerrick; see also FRAGMENT *n.*
  • *v.* tear (up), rip (up), fragment, *archaic or rhet.* rend; destroy, demolish.

shredder /shrédər/ *n.* **1** a machine used to reduce documents to shreds. **2** any device used for shredding.

shrew /shro͞o/ *n.* **1** any small, usu. insect-eating, mouselike mammal of the family Soricidae, with a long pointed snout. **2** a bad-tempered or scolding woman. ▫▫ **shrewish** *adj.* (in sense 2). **shrewishly** *adv.* **shrewishness** *n.* [OE *scrēawa, scrēawa* shrew-mouse: cf. OHG *scrawaz* dwarf, MHG *schrawaz,* etc. devil]
  ■ **2** harridan, virago, termagant, vixen, fishwife, nag, fury, spitfire, maenad, harpy, witch, hag, crone, hellcat, dragon, Xanthippe, *Ir. & Sc.* banshee, *archaic* scold, beldam, *colloq.* battleaxe, *sl. offens.* bitch. ▫▫ **shrewish** see *short-tempered.*

shrewd /shro͞od/ *adj.* **1 a** showing astute powers of judgment; clever and judicious (*a shrewd observer; made a shrewd guess*). **b** (of a face, etc.) shrewd-looking. **2** *archaic* **a** (of pain, cold, etc.) sharp; biting. **b** (of a blow, thrust, etc.) severe; hard. **c** mischievous; malicious. ▫▫ **shrewdly** *adv.* **shrewdness** *n.* [ME, = malignant, f. SHREW in sense 'evil person or thing,' or past part. of obs. *shrew* to curse, f. SHREW]
  ■ **1 a** clever, smart, astute, cunning, canny, acute, sharp, keen-minded, keen, quick-witted, crafty, artful,

manipulative, calculating, calculated, judicious, foxy, sly, wily, knowing, perceptive, percipient, perspicacious, discerning, wise, sage, sagacious, prudent, longheaded, farsighted, farseeing, intelligent, adroit, *colloq.* wide awake, *Brit. sl.* fly. ▫▫ **shrewdness** see JUDGMENT 1, 2.

shriek /shreek/ *v. & n.* • *v.* **1** *intr.* **a** utter a shrill screeching sound or words esp. in pain or terror. **b** (foll. by *of*) provide a clear or blatant indication of. **2** *tr.* **a** utter (sounds or words) by shrieking (*shrieked his name*). **b** indicate clearly or blatantly. • *n.* a high-pitched piercing cry or sound; a scream. □ **shriek out** say in shrill tones. **shriek with laughter** laugh uncontrollably. ▫▫ **shrieker** *n.* [imit.: cf. dial. *screak,* ON *skrækja,* and SCREECH]
  ■ *v. & n.* scream, cry, screech, squeal, squawk, squall.

shrieval /shreévəl/ *adj.* of or relating to a sheriff. [*shrieve* obs. var. of SHERIFF]

shrievalty /shreévəltee/ *n.* (*pl.* **-ies**) **1** a sheriff's office or jurisdiction. **2** the tenure of this. [as SHRIEVAL + *-alty* as in mayoralty, etc.]

shrift /shrift/ *n. archaic* **1** confession to a priest. **2** confession and absolution. □ **short shrift 1** curt treatment. **2** *archaic* little time between condemnation and execution or punishment. [OE *scrift* (verbal noun) f. SHRIVE]
  ■ **2** see FORGIVENESS 1.

shrike /shrik/ *n.* any bird of the family Laniidae, with a strong hooked and toothed bill, that impales its prey of small birds and insects on thorns. Also called *butcher-bird.* [perh. rel. to OE *scric* thrush, MLG *schrik* corncrake (imit.): cf. SHRIEK]

shrill /shril/ *adj. & v.* • *adj.* **1** piercing and high-pitched in sound. **2** *derog.* (esp. of a protester) sharp; unrestrained; unreasoning. • *v.* **1** *intr.* (of a cry, etc.) sound shrilly. **2** *tr.* (of a person, etc.) utter or send out (a song, complaint, etc.) shrilly. ▫▫ **shrilly** *adv.* **shrillness** *n.* [ME, rel. to LG *schrell* sharp in tone or taste f. Gmc]
  ■ *adj.* **1** high-pitched, high, earsplitting, piercing, ear-piercing, sharp, piping, screeching, screechy, penetrating.

shrimp /shrimp/ *n. & v.* • *n.* **1** (*pl.* same or **shrimps**) any of various small (esp. marine) edible crustaceans, with ten legs, gray-green when alive and pink when cooked. **2** *colloq.* a very small slight person. • *v.intr.* go catching shrimps. □ **shrimp plant** an evergreen shrub, *Justicia brandegeana,* bearing small white flowers in clusters of pinkish-brown bracts. ▫▫ **shrimper** *n.* [ME, prob. rel. to MLG *schrempen* wrinkle, MHG *schrimpfen* contract, and SCRIMP]

shrine /shrin/ *n. & v.* • *n.* **1** esp. *RC Ch.* **a** a chapel, church, altar, etc., sacred to a saint, holy person, relic, etc. **b** the tomb of a saint, etc. **c** a casket, esp. containing sacred relics; a reliquary. **d** a niche containing a holy statue, etc. **2** a place associated with or containing memorabilia of a particular person, event, etc. **3** a Shinto place of worship. • *v.tr. poet.* enshrine. [OE *scrin* f. Gmc f. L *scrinium* case for books, etc.]
  ■ *n.* **1 a** see SANCTUARY 1.

shrink /shringk/ *v. & n.* • *v.* (*past* **shrank** /shrangk/; *past part.* **shrunk** /shrungk/ or (esp. as *adj.*) **shrunken** /shrúngkən/) **1** *tr. & intr.* make or become smaller; contract, esp. by the action of moisture, heat, or cold. **2** *intr.* (usu. foll. by *from*) **a** retire; recoil; flinch; cower (*shrank from her touch*). **b** be averse from doing (*shrinks from meeting them*). **3** (as **shrunken** *adj.*) (esp. of a face, person, etc.) having grown smaller esp. because of age, illness, etc. **b** the act or an instance of shrinking; shrinkage. **2** *sl.* a psychiatrist (from "headshrinker"). □ **shrinking violet** an exaggeratedly shy person. **shrink into oneself** become withdrawn. **shrink-resistant** (of textiles, etc.) resistant to shrinkage when wet, etc. **shrink-wrap** *v. & n.* • *v.tr.* (**-wrapped, -wrapping**) enclose (an article) in (esp. transparent) film that shrinks tightly on to it. • *n.* plastic film used to shrink-wrap. ▫▫ **shrinkable** *adj.* **shrinker** *n.* **shrinkingly** *adv.* **shrinkproof** *adj.* [OE *scrincan:* cf. Sw. *skrynka* to shrink]
  ■ *v.* **1** wither, shrivel (up), contract, compress; diminish, dwindle, decrease; reduce. **2 a** withdraw, draw back, retire, recoil, back away or off, retreat, shy away; cower, cringe, flinch, wince. **b** (*shrink from*) see SCRUPLE *v.* 1.

3 (**shrunken**) see *emaciated* (EMACIATE). • *n.* **2** see *therapist* (THERAPY).

shrinkage /shríngkij/ *n.* **1 a** the process or fact of shrinking. **b** the degree or amount of shrinking. **2** an allowance made for the reduction in takings due to wastage, theft, etc.
■ **1** erosion, depletion, waste, wastage; see also DECREASE *n.*

shrive /shrīv/ *v.tr.* (*past* **shrove** /shrōv/; *past part.* **shriven** /shrívən/) *Eccl. archaic* **1** (of a priest) hear the confession of, assign penance to, and absolve. **2** (*refl.*) (of a penitent) submit oneself to a priest for confession, etc. [OE *scrīfan* impose as penance, WG f. L *scribere* write]

shrivel /shrívəl/ *v.tr. & intr.* contract or wither into a wrinkled, folded, rolled-up, contorted, or dried-up state. [perh. f. ON: cf. Sw. dial. *skryvla* to wrinkle]
■ shrivel up, shrink, wrinkle, pucker (up), curl (up), wizen, contract; wither, wilt, dry up, desiccate, dehydrate.

shriven *past part.* of SHRIVE.

shroud /shrowd/ *n. & v.* • *n.* **1 a** sheetlike garment for wrapping a corpse for burial. **2** anything that conceals like a shroud (*wrapped in a shroud of mystery*). **3** (in *pl.*) *Naut.* a set of ropes forming part of the standing rigging and supporting the mast or topmast. • *v.tr.* **1** clothe (a body) for burial. **2** cover, conceal, or disguise (*hills shrouded in mist*). □ **shroud-laid** (of a rope) having four strands laid right-handed on a core. □□ **shroudless** *adj.* [OE *scrūd* f. Gmc: see SHRED]
■ *n.* **1** winding-sheet, graveclothes, *hist.* cerecloth, *literary* cerement. **2** veil, cover, shield, cloak, blanket, mask, mantle, pall, screen, covering, cloud. • *v.* **2** swathe, wrap, cover, clothe, protect; screen, veil, mask, disguise, camouflage, shield, cloak, blanket, mantle, shade, obscure, hide, conceal; see also ENVELOP.

shrove *past* of SHRIVE.

Shrovetide /shrōvtíd/ *n.* Shrove Tuesday and the two days preceding it when it was formerly customary to be shriven. [ME *shrove* abnormally f. SHROVE]

Shrove Tuesday /shrōv/ *n.* the day before Ash Wednesday.

shrub[1] /shrub/ *n.* a woody plant smaller than a tree and having a very short stem with branches near the ground. □□ **shrubby** *adj.* [ME f. OE *scrubb, scrybb* shrubbery: cf. NFris. *skrobb* brushwood, WFlem. *schrobbe* vetch, Norw. *skrubba* dwarf cornel, and SCRUB[2]]

shrub[2] /shrub/ *n.* a cordial made of sweetened fruit juice and spirits, esp. rum. [Arab. *šurb, šarāb* f. *šariba* to drink: cf. SHERBET, SYRUP]

shrubbery /shrúbəree/ *n.* (*pl.* **-ies**) an area planted with shrubs.
■ shrubs, planting(s), hedge(s), hedging, hedgerow, thicket, brake, bracken, coppice, copse, undergrowth, underbrush.

shrug /shrug/ *v. & n.* • *v.* (**shrugged, shrugging**) **1** *intr.* slightly and momentarily raise the shoulders to express indifference, helplessness, contempt, etc. **2** *tr.* **a** raise (the shoulders) in this way. **b** shrug the shoulders to express (indifference, etc.) (*shrugged his consent*). • *n.* the act or an instance of shrugging. □ **shrug off** dismiss as unimportant, etc., by or as if by shrugging. [ME: orig. unkn.]
■ □ **shrug off** see DISMISS 4.

shrunk (also **shrunken**) *past part.* of SHRINK.

shtick /shtik/ *n. sl.* a theatrical routine, gimmick, etc. [Yiddish f. G *Stück* piece]
■ see ACT *n.* 3a.

shuck /shuk/ *n. & v.* • *n.* **1** a husk or pod. **2** the shell of an oyster or clam. **3** (in *pl.*) *colloq.* an expression of contempt or regret or self-deprecation in response to praise. • *v.tr.* **1** remove the shucks of; shell. **2** peel off or remove (*shucked his coat*). □□ **shucker** *n.* [17th c.: orig. unkn.]
■ *n.* **1, 2** see SHELL *n.* 1. • *v.* see SHELL *v.* 1.

shudder /shúdər/ *v. & n.* • *v.intr.* **1** shiver esp. convulsively from fear, cold, repugnance, etc. **2** feel strong repugnance, etc. (*shudder to think what might happen*). **3** (of a machine, etc.) vibrate or quiver. • *n.* **1** the act or an instance of shuddering. **2** (in *pl.*; prec. by *the*) *colloq.* a state of shuddering.

□□ **shudderingly** *adv.* **shuddery** *adj.* [ME *shod(d)er* f. MDu. *schūderen,* MLG *schōderen* f. Gmc]
■ *v.* **1** quiver, shake, tremble, shiver, jerk, convulse, quaver, quake. **2** see DREAD *v.* **3** vibrate, rattle, quiver, shake, quake, quaver, esp. *Brit.* judder. • *n.* **1** quiver, shake, tremble, tremor, twitch, shiver, convulsion, paroxysm, spasm, quaver; vibration, rattle, esp. *Brit.* judder. **2** (*the shudders*) see SHAKE *n.* 3.

shuffle /shúfəl/ *v. & n.* • *v.* **1** *tr. & intr.* move with a scraping, sliding, or dragging motion (*shuffles along; shuffling his feet*). **2** *tr.* **a** (also *absol.*) rearrange (a pack of cards) by sliding them over each other quickly. **b** rearrange; intermingle; confuse (*shuffled the documents*). **3** *tr.* (usu. foll. by *on, off, into*) assume or remove (clothes, a burden, etc.) esp. clumsily or evasively (*shuffled on his clothes; shuffled off responsibility*). **4** *intr.* **a** equivocate; prevaricate. **b** continually shift one's position; fidget. **5** *intr.* (foll. by *out of*) escape evasively (*shuffled out of the blame*). • *n.* **1** a shuffling movement. **2** the act or an instance of shuffling cards. **3** a general change of relative positions. **4** a piece of equivocation; sharp practice. **5** a quick alternation of the position of the feet in dancing. □ **shuffle the cards** change policy, etc. □□ **shuffler** *n.* [perh. f. LG *schuffeln* walk clumsily f. Gmc: cf. SHOVE]
■ *v.* **1** scuff *or* drag (one's feet), scrape along, shamble; see also HOBBLE *v.* 1. **2 b** mix (up), intermix, intermingle, disarrange, rearrange, interfile, intersperse, jumble, confuse, scramble; shift (about), mess up, turn topsy-turvy, scatter, disorganize. **4 a** equivocate, bumble, cavil, fence, be evasive, dodge, niggle, split hairs, quibble, prevaricate, hem and haw, *archaic* shift, *colloq.* be shifty, esp. *Brit. colloq.* waffle. **b** see FIDGET *v.* 1. **5** (*shuffle out of*) see EVADE 1, 2. • *n.* **1** shamble, shambling, scuffing, scraping. **3** rearrangement, reorganization, reshuffle, shake-up. **4** sidestep, evasion, subterfuge, trick, dodge, shift, prevarication, quibble.

shuffleboard /shúfəlbawrd/ *n.* a game played by pushing disks with the hand or esp. with a long-handled cue over a marked surface. [earlier *shoveboard* f. SHOVE + BOARD]

shun /shun/ *v.tr.* (**shunned, shunning**) avoid; keep clear of (*shuns human company*). [OE *scunian,* of unkn. orig.]
■ avoid, keep *or* shy away from, keep *or* steer clear of, shrink from, fight shy of, run *or* turn (away) from, flee *or* escape from, *literary* eschew; forgo, give up; disdain, spurn, rebuff, reject, cold-shoulder, give the cold shoulder to.

shunt /shunt/ *v. & n.* • *v.* **1** *intr. & tr.* diverge or cause (a train) to be diverted esp. onto a siding. **2** *tr. Electr.* provide (a current) with a shunt. **3** *tr.* **a** postpone or evade. **b** divert (a decision, etc.) on to another person, etc. • *n.* **1** the act or an instance of shunting on to a siding. **2** *Electr.* a conductor joining two points of a circuit, through which more or less of a current may be diverted. **3** *Surgery* an alternative path for the circulation of the blood. **4** *Brit. sl.* a motor vehicle accident, esp. a collision of vehicles traveling one close behind another. □□ **shunter** *n.* [ME, perh. f. SHUN]
■ *v.* **1** sidetrack, divert. **3 a** see DEFER[1].

shush /shŏŏsh, shush/ *int. & v.* • *int.* = HUSH *int.* • *v.* **1** *intr.* **a** call for silence by saying *shush.* **b** be silent (*they shushed at once*). **2** *tr.* make or attempt to make silent. [imit.]
■ *v.* see SILENCE *v.*

shut /shut/ *v.* (**shutting;** *past and past part.* **shut**) **1** *tr.* **a** move (a door, window, lid, lips, etc.) into position so as to block an aperture (*shut the lid*). **b** close or seal (a room, window, box, eye, mouth, etc.) by moving a door, etc. (*shut the box*). **2** *intr.* become or be capable of being closed or sealed (*the door shut with a bang; the lid shuts automatically*). **3** *intr. & tr.* esp. *Brit.* become or make (a store, business, etc.) closed for trade (*the shops shut at five; shuts his shop at five*). **4** *tr.* bring (a book, hand, telescope, etc.) into a folded-up or

---

/. . ./ **pronunciation**   • **part of speech**
□ **phrases, idioms, and compounds**
□□ **derivatives**   ■ **synonym section**
cross-references appear in SMALL CAPITALS or *italics*

contracted state. **5** *tr.* (usu. foll. by *in*, *out*) keep (a person, sound, etc.) in or out of a room, etc., by shutting a door, etc. (*shut out the noise*; *shut them in*). **6** *tr.* (usu. foll. by *in*) catch (a finger, dress, etc.) by shutting something on it (*shut her finger in the door*). **7** *tr.* bar access to (a place, etc.) (*this entrance is shut*). □ **be** (or **get**) **shut of** *sl.* be (or get) rid of (*were glad to get shut of him*). **shut the door on** refuse to consider; make impossible. **shut down 1** stop (a factory, nuclear reactor, etc.) from operating. **2** (of a factory, etc.) stop operating. **3** push or pull (a window sash, etc.) down into a closed position. **shut-eye** *colloq.* sleep. **shut one's eyes** (or **ears** or **heart** or **mind**) **to** pretend not, or refuse, to see (or hear or feel sympathy for or think about). **shut in** (of hills, houses, etc.) encircle, prevent access, etc., to or escape from (*were shut in by the sea on three sides*) (see also sense 5). **shut-in** a person confined to home, bed, etc., due to infirmity, etc. **shut off 1** stop the flow of (water, gas, etc.) by shutting a valve. **2** separate from society, etc. **shut out 1** exclude (a person, light, etc.) from a place, situation, etc. **2** screen (landscape, etc.) from view. **3** prevent (a possibility, etc.). **4** block (a painful memory, etc.) from the mind. **5** prevent (an opponent) from scoring (see also sense 5). **shut up 1** close all doors and windows of (a house, etc.); bolt and bar. **2** imprison (a person). **3** close (a box, etc.) securely. **4** *colloq.* reduce to silence by rebuke, etc. **5** put (a thing) away in a box, etc. **6** (esp. in *imper.*) *colloq.* stop talking. **shut your face** (or **head** or **mouth** or **trap**)! *sl.* an impolite request to stop talking. [OE *scyttan* f. WG: cf. SHOOT]

■ **1, 2** close (up), fasten, shut up, secure, bolt, lock (up), seal (up); latch. **3, 4, 7** close. **5** (*shut in*) confine, seclude, keep in, secure; see also *shut up* 2 below; (*shut out*) see *shut out* 1 below. **6** catch, trap, jam, squash, crush. □ **shut down 1, 2** switch *or* turn *or* shut off, stop; close down, discontinue, cease, suspend, halt, leave off, shut up. **shut-eye** see NAP[1] *n.* **shut one's eyes to** see OVERLOOK 1. **shut in** see ENCLOSE 1, 6, SHUT *v.* 5 above. **shut off 1** switch *or* turn off; shut (down), kill, douse, close (off), cut (off), disconnect. **2** separate, isolate, seclude, segregate, sequester, bar, shut out, cut off, send to Coventry. **shut out 1** exclude, eliminate, bar, debar, lock out, ban, keep out *or* away; screen, block out, cut out. **2** screen, mask, hide, conceal, veil, cover. **3** see PRECLUDE. **4** block out, keep out, exclude, repress. **shut up 1, 3** see SHUT 1 above. **2** confine, shut in, coop (up), cage (in); imprison, jail, incarcerate, intern, immure. **4** silence, keep quiet, stifle, mute, gag, hush, *Brit.* quieten. **6** (*imper.*) see *wrap up* 3. **shut up shop** see *close down* (CLOSE[2]). **shut your face** (or **head** or **mouth** or **trap**)! see *wrap up* 3.

shutdown /shútdown/ *n.* the closure of a factory, etc.

shutoff /shútawf/ *n.* **1** something used for stopping an operation. **2** a cessation of flow, supply, or activity.

shutout /shútowt/ *n.* **1** a competition or game in which the losing side fails to score. **2** a preemptive bid in bridge.

shutter /shútər/ *n. & v.* ● *n.* **1** a person or thing that shuts. **2 a** each of a pair or set of panels fixed inside or outside a window for security or privacy or to keep the light in or out. **b** a structure of slats on rollers used for the same purpose. **3** a device that exposes the film in a photographic camera. **4** *Mus.* the blind of a swell box in an organ used for controlling the sound level. ● *v.tr.* **1** put up the shutters of. **2** provide with shutters. □ **put up the shutters 1** cease business for the day. **2** cease business, etc., permanently. □□ **shutterless** *adj.*

■ □ **put up the shutters 2** see *close down*.

shutterbug /shútərbəg/ *n. colloq.* an amateur photographer who takes a great many pictures.

shuttering /shútəring/ *n.* esp. *Brit.* **1** = FORMWORK. **2** material for making shutters.

shuttle /shút'l/ *n. & v.* ● *n.* **1 a** a bobbin with two pointed ends used for carrying the weft thread across between the warp threads in weaving. **b** a bobbin carrying the lower thread in a sewing machine. **2** a train, bus, etc., going to

and fro over a short route continuously. **3** = SHUTTLECOCK. **4** = *space shuttle*. ● *v.* **1** *intr. & tr.* move or cause to move back and forth like a shuttle. **2** *intr.* travel in a shuttle. □ **shuttle armature** *Electr.* an armature with a single coil wound on an elongated iron bobbin. **shuttle diplomacy** negotiations conducted by a mediator who travels successively to several countries. **shuttle service** a train or bus, etc., service operating back and forth over a short route. [OE *scytel* dart f. Gmc: cf. SHOOT]

■ *v.* **2** commute; alternate.

shuttlecock /shút'lkok/ *n.* **1** a cork with a ring of feathers, or a similar device of plastic, used instead of a ball in badminton and in battledore. **2** a thing passed repeatedly back and forth. [SHUTTLE + COCK[1], prob. f. the flying motion]

shy[1] /shī/ *adj., v., & n.* ● *adj.* (**shyer, shyest** or **shier, shiest**) **1 a** diffident or uneasy in company; timid. **b** (of an animal, bird, etc.) easily startled; timid. **2** (foll. by *of*) avoiding; wary of (*shy of his aunt*; *shy of going to meetings*). **3** (in *comb.*) showing fear of or distaste for (*gun-shy*; *work-shy*). **4** (often foll. by *of, on*) *colloq.* having lost; short of (*I'm shy three dollars*; *shy of the price of admission*). ● *v.intr.* (**shies, shied**) **1** (usu. foll. by *at*) (esp. of a horse) start suddenly aside (at an object, noise, etc.) in fright. **2** (usu. foll. by *away from, at*) avoid accepting or becoming involved in (a proposal, etc.) in alarm. ● *n.* a sudden startled movement. □□ **shyer** *n.* **shyly** *adv.* (also **shyly**). **shyness** *n.* [OE *sceoh* f. Gmc]

■ *adj.* **1** diffident, coy, bashful, retiring, withdrawn, withdrawing, reserved, reticent, timid, quiet, meek, modest, sheepish, mousy, unconfident, self-conscious, introverted, nervous, apprehensive, timorous, uneasy. **2** cautious, wary, chary, guarded, afraid, fearful, frightened, anxious, worried, suspicious, distrustful, *sl.* leery. **4** missing, lacking, deficient in, short of. ● *v.* **1** see START *v.* 11. **2** (*shy (away) from*) see SHUN.

shy[2] /shī/ *v. & n.* ● *v.tr.* (**shies, shied**) (also *absol.*) fling or throw (a stone, etc.). ● *n.* (*pl.* **shies**) the act or an instance of shying. □ **have a shy at** *colloq.* **1** try to hit with a stone, etc. **2** make an attempt at. **3** jeer at. □□ **shyer** *n.* [18th c.: orig. unkn.]

Shylock /shílok/ *n.* a hard-hearted moneylender; a miser. [character in Shakesp. *Merchant of Venice*]

shyster /shístər/ *n. colloq.* a person, esp. a lawyer, who uses unscrupulous methods. [19th c.: orig. uncert.]

■ cheat, confidence man, mountebank, deceiver, fraud, *colloq.* crook, *sl.* con man.

SI *abbr.* **1** the international system of units of measurement (F *Système International*). **2** (Order of the) Star of India.

Si *symb. Chem.* the element silicon.

si /see/ *n. Mus.* = TE. [F f. It., perh. f. the initials of *Sancte Iohannes*: see GAMUT]

sialogogue /siáləgawg, -gog/ *n. & adj.* ● *n.* a medicine inducing the flow of saliva. ● *adj.* inducing such a flow. [F f. Gk *sialon* saliva + *agōgos* leading]

siamang /seéəmang/ *n.* a large black gibbon, *Hylobates syndactylus*, native to Sumatra and the Malay peninsula. [Malay]

Siamese /síəmeéz/ *n. & adj.* ● *n.* (*pl.* same) **1 a** a native of Siam (now Thailand) in SE Asia. **b** the language of Siam. **2** (in full **Siamese cat**) **a** a cat of a cream-colored short-haired breed with a brown face and ears and blue eyes. **b** this breed. ● *adj.* of or concerning Siam, its people, or language. □ **Siamese twins 1** twins joined at any part of the body and sometimes sharing organs, etc. **2** any closely associated pair.

sib /sib/ *n. & adj.* ● *n.* **1** a brother or sister (cf. SIBLING). **2 a** blood relative. **3** a group of people recognized by an individual as his or her kindred. ● *adj.* (usu. foll. by *to*) esp. *Sc.* related; akin. [OE *sib(b)*]

Siberian /sibeéreeən/ *n. & adj.* ● *n.* **1** a native of Siberia in the northeastern part of the Russian Federation. **2** a person of Siberian descent. ● *adj.* **1** of or relating to Siberia. **2** *colloq.* (esp. of weather) extremely cold.

sibilant /síbilənt/ *adj. & n.* ● *adj.* **1** (of a letter or set of letters, as *s*, *sh*) sounded with a hiss. **2** hissing (*a sibilant whisper*).

● *n.* a sibilant letter or letters. ▢▢ **sibilance** *n.* **sibilancy** *n.* [L *sibilare sibilant-* hiss]

■ ▢▢ **sibilance** hiss, hissing; see also RUSTLE *n.*

sibilate /síbilayt/ *v.tr. & intr.* pronounce with or utter a hissing sound. ▢▢ **sibilation** /-láyshən/ *n.*

sibling /síbling/ *n.* each of two or more children having one or both parents in common. [SIB + -LING[1]]

■ brother, sister, sib.

sibship /síbship/ *n.* **1** the state of belonging to a sib or the same sib. **2** a group of children having the same two parents.

sibyl /síbil/ *n.* **1** any of certain women in ancient times supposed to utter the oracles and prophecies of a god. **2** a prophetess, fortune-teller, or witch. [ME f. OF *Sibile* or med.L *Sibilla* f. L *Sibylla* f. Gk *Sibulla*]

■ see PROPHET 2a.

sibylline /síbilin, -leen/ *adj.* **1** of or from a sibyl. **2** oracular; prophetic. ▢ **the Sibylline books** a collection of oracles belonging to the ancient Roman State and used for guidance by magistrates, etc. [L *Sibyllinus* (as SIBYL)]

■ **2** see PROPHETIC.

sic[1] /sik/ *v.tr.* (**sicced, siccing;** also **sicked** /sikt/, **sicking**) (usu. in *imper.*) (esp. to a dog) set upon (a rat, etc.). [19th c., dial. var. of SEEK]

sic[2] /sik, seek/ *adv.* (usu. in brackets) used, spelled, etc., as written (confirming, or calling attention to, the form of quoted or copied words). [L, = so, thus]

■ see *to the letter* (LETTER).

siccative /síkətiv/ *n. & adj.* ● *n.* a substance causing drying, esp. mixed with oil paint, etc., for quick drying. ● *adj.* having such properties. [LL *siccativus* f. *siccare* to dry]

sice[1] /sīs/ *n. Brit.* the six on dice. [ME f. OF *sis* f. L *sex* six]

sice[2] var. of SYCE.

Sicilian /sisílyən/ *n. & adj.* ● *n.* **1** a native of Sicily, an island off the S. coast of Italy. **2** a person of Sicilian descent. **3** the Italian dialect of Sicily. ● *adj.* of or relating to Sicily. [L *Sicilia* Sicily]

sick[1] /sik/ *adj., n., & v.* ● *adj.* **1** (often in *comb.*) vomiting or tending to vomit (*I think I'm going to be sick; seasick*). **2** ill; affected by illness (*has been sick for a week; a sick man; sick with measles*). **3 a** (often foll. by *at*) esp. mentally perturbed; disordered (*the product of a sick mind; sick at heart*). **b** (often foll. by *for*, or in *comb.*) pining; longing (*sick for a sight of home; lovesick*). **4** (often foll. by *of*) *colloq.* **a** disgusted; surfeited (*sick of chocolates*). **b** angry, esp. because of surfeit (*am sick of being teased*). **5** *colloq.* (of humor, etc.) jeering at misfortune, illness, death, etc.; morbid (*sick joke*). **6** (of a ship) needing repair (esp. of a specified kind) (*paint-sick*). ● *n. Brit. colloq.* vomit. ● *v.tr.* (usu. foll. by *up*) *Brit. colloq.* vomit (*sicked up his dinner*). ▢ **look sick** *colloq.* be unimpressive or embarrassed. **sick at** (or **to**) **one's stomach** vomiting or tending to vomit. **sick building syndrome** a high incidence of illness in office workers, attributed to the immediate working surroundings. **sick call 1** a visit by a doctor to a sick person, etc. **2** *Mil.* a summons for sick individuals to attend. **sick flag** a yellow flag indicating disease at a quarantine station or on ship. **sick headache** a migraine headache with vomiting. **sick leave** leave of absence granted because of illness. **sick list** a list of the sick, esp. in a regiment, ship, etc. **sick pay** pay given to an employee, etc., on sick leave. **take sick** *colloq.* be taken ill. ▢▢ **sickish** *adj.* [OE *sēoc* f. Gmc]

■ *adj.* **1** nauseated, queasy, squeamish, qualmish, bilious; green *or* white around the gills, seasick, carsick, airsick, sick to one's stomach. **2** ill, unwell, unhealthy, sickly, poorly, indisposed, laid up, infirm, ailing, diseased, afflicted, on the sick list, *colloq.* under the weather, not (feeling) up to snuff, *Austral. & NZ colloq.* crook, *Brit. colloq.* (a bit) off. **3 a** affected, troubled, perturbed, heartsick, wretched, miserable, burdened, weighed down, *archaic* stricken; mad, insane, deranged, disturbed, neurotic, unbalanced, psychoneurotic, psychotic, *colloq.* mental, crazy, *sl.* off one's trolley, off one's rocker. **4** sickened, put out, upset, appalled, disgusted, revolted, repulsed, offended, repelled, nauseated; annoyed, chagrined, irritated; surfeited,

jaded; *colloq.* turned off; (*sick of*) (sick and) tired of, bored with, weary of, fed up with, glutted with, sated with. **5** peculiar, unconventional, far-out, strange, weird, odd, bizarre, grotesque, macabre, shocking, ghoulish, morbid, gruesome, stomach-turning, sadistic, masochistic, sadomasochistic, warped, perverted, *colloq.* kinky, colloq. off, *sl.* bent; black. ● *n.* vomit, *sl.* barf, *Austral. sl.* chunder. ● *v.* see VOMIT *v.* 1. **take sick** see SICKEN 2a.

sick[2] var. of SIC[1].

sickbay /síkbay/ *n.* **1** part of a ship used as a hospital. **2** any room, etc., for sick people.

sickbed /síkbed/ *n.* **1** an invalid's bed. **2** the state of being an invalid.

sicken /síkən/ *v.* **1** *tr.* affect with loathing or disgust. **2** *intr.* **a** *Brit.* (often foll. by *for*) show symptoms of illness (*is sickening for measles*). **b** (often foll. by *at*, or *to* + infin.) feel nausea or disgust (*he sickened at the sight*). **3** (as **sickening** *adj.*) **a** loathsome; disgusting. **b** *colloq.* very annoying. ▢▢ **sickeningly** *adv.*

■ **1** make ill *or* sick, afflict, affect, disgust, nauseate, turn one's stomach, upset, appall, shock, repel, revolt, repulse, offend, make one's gorge rise; put off, *colloq.* turn off. **2 a** fall *or* take ill, take sick, fail, weaken; (*sicken for*) contract, catch, come down with, *archaic* be stricken by *or* with. **3** (**sickening**) **a** see DISGUSTING.

sickle /síkəl/ *n.* **1** a short-handled farming tool with a semicircular blade, used for cutting grain, lopping, or trimming. **2** anything sickle-shaped, esp. the crescent moon. ▢ **sickle cell** a sickle-shaped blood cell, esp. as found in a type of severe hereditary anemia. **sickle feather** each of the long middle feathers of a rooster's tail. [OE *sicol, sicel* f. L *secula* f. *secare* cut]

sickly /síklee/ *adj.* (**sicklier, sickliest**) **1 a** of weak health; apt to be ill. **b** (of a person's complexion, look, etc.) languid, faint, or pale, suggesting sickness (*a sickly smile*). **c** (of light or color) faint; pale; feeble. **2** causing ill health (*a sickly climate*). **3** (of a book, etc.) sentimental or mawkish. **4** inducing or connected with nausea (*a sickly taste*). **5** (of a color, etc.) of an unpleasant shade inducing nausea (*a sickly green*). ▢▢ **sickliness** *n.* [ME, prob. after ON *sjuklígr* (as SICK[1])]

■ **1 a** see SICK[1] *adj.* 2. **b** languid, ailing, feeble, delicate, wan, weak, faint, pallid, drawn, pasty, peaked, peaky, peakish; see also PALE *adj.* 1. **c** faint, feeble, weak, colorless, wishy-washy; see also PALE *adj.* 2. **2** see UNHEALTHY 2. **3** sentimental, mushy, mawkish, maudlin, cloying, syrupy, saccharine, treacly, insipid, weak, watery, sloppy, *colloq.* soppy. **4** nauseating, cloying; see also DISGUSTING. **5** *colloq.* icky, *sl.* yucky; see also REVOLTING. **sickliness** see *infirmity* (INFIRM).

sickness /síknis/ *n.* **1** the state of being ill; disease. **2** a specified disease (*sleeping sickness*). **3** vomiting or a tendency to vomit. [OE *sēocnesse* (as SICK[1], -NESS)]

■ **1, 2** see DISEASE.

sicko /síkō/ *n.* (also **sickie** /síkee/) *sl.* a person who is mentally deranged or morally debased.

sickroom /síkroom, -room/ *n.* **1** a room occupied by a sick person. **2** a room adapted for sick people.

sidalcea /sidálseeə/ *n.* any mallowlike plant of the genus *Sidalcea*, bearing racemes of white, pink, or purple flowers. [mod.L f. *Sida* + *Alcea*, names of related genera]

side /sīd/ *n. & v.* ● *n.* **1 a** each of the more or less flat surfaces bounding an object (*a cube has six sides; this side up*). **b** a more or less vertical inner or outer plane or surface (*the side of a house; a mountainside*). **c** such a vertical lateral surface or plane as distinct from the top or bottom, front or back, or ends (*at the side of the house*). **2 a** the half of a person or animal that is on the right or the left, esp. of the torso (*has a pain in his right side*). **b** the left or right half of a specified

/.../ pronunciation	● part of speech
▢ phrases, idioms, and compounds	
▢▢ derivatives	■ synonym section
cross-references appear in SMALL CAPITALS or *italics*	

part of a thing, area, building, etc. (*put the box on that side*). **c** (often in *comb.*) a position next to a person or thing (*graveside*; *seaside*; *stood at my side*). **d** a specified direction relating to a person or thing (*on the north side of*; *came from all sides*). **e** half of a butchered carcass (*a side of bacon*). **3 a** either surface of a thing regarded as having two surfaces. **b** the amount of writing needed to fill one side of a sheet of paper (*write three sides*). **4** any of several aspects of a question, character, etc. (*many sides to his character*; *look on the bright side*). **5 a** each of two sets of opponents in war, politics, games, etc. (*the side that bats first*; *much to be said on both sides*). **b** a cause or philosophical position, etc., regarded as being in conflict with another (*on the side of right*). **6 a** a part or region near the edge and remote from the center (*at the side of the room*). **b** (*attrib.*) a subordinate, peripheral, or detached part (*a side road*; *a side table*). **7 a** each of the bounding lines of a plane rectilinear figure (*a hexagon has six sides*). **b** each of two quantities stated to be equal in an equation. **8** a position nearer or farther than, or right or left of, a dividing line (*on this side of the Alps*; *on the other side of the road*). **9** a line of hereditary descent through the father or the mother. **10** (in full **side spin**) *Brit.* = ᵉnglish *n.* 3. **11** *Brit. sl.* boastfulness; swagger (*has no side about him*). **12** *Brit. colloq.* a television channel (*shall we try another side?*). ● *v.intr.* (usu. foll. by *with*) take part or be on the same side as a disputant, etc. (*sided with his father*). □ **by the side of 1** close to. **2** compared with. **from side to side 1** right across. **2** alternately each way from a central line. **let the side down** *Brit.* fail one's colleagues, esp. by frustrating their efforts or embarrassing them. **on one side 1** not in the main or central position. **2** aside (*took him on one side to explain*). **on the . . . side** fairly; somewhat (qualifying an adjective: *on the high side*). **on the side 1** as a sideline; in addition to one's regular work, etc. **2** secretly or illicitly. **3** as a side dish. **on this side of the grave** in life. **side arms** swords, bayonets, or pistols. **side bet** a bet between opponents, esp. in card games, over and above the ordinary stakes. **side by side** standing close together, esp. for mutual support. **side chapel** a chapel off the side aisle or at the side of a church. **side dish** an extra dish subsidiary to the main course. **side door 1** a door in or at the side of a building. **2** an indirect means of access. **side drum** = *snare drum*. **side effect** a secondary, usu. undesirable, effect. **side-glance** a sideways or brief glance. **side issue** a point that distracts attention from what is important. **side note** a marginal note. **side-on** *adv.* from the side. ● *adj.* **1** from or toward one side. **2** (of a collision) involving the side of a vehicle. **side road** a minor or subsidiary road, esp. joining or diverging from a main road. **side salad** a salad served as a side dish. **side seat** a seat in a vehicle, etc., in which the occupant has his back to the side of the vehicle. **side street** a minor or subsidiary street. **side table** a table placed at the side of a room or apart from the main table. **side trip** a minor excursion during a voyage or trip; a detour. **side view 1** a view obtained sideways. **2** a profile. **side-wheeler** a steamboat with paddle wheels. **side-whiskers** whiskers growing on the cheeks. **side wind 1** wind from the side. **2** an indirect agency or influence. **take sides** support one or other cause, etc. □□ **sideless** *adj.* [OE *side* f. Gmc]

■ *n.* **1** a surface, face, plane; facet. **b** flank, edge, face, elevation. **4** see ASPECT 1a. **5 a** army; faction, interest, party, part, sect, camp; team, string, squad. **b** (point of) view, viewpoint, aspect, opinion, standpoint, stand, cause, angle, position, attitude, school, philosophy. **6 a** edge, margin, verge, bank, rim, brim, brink, border, boundary, limit; perimeter, periphery. **b** (*attrib.*) secondary, incidental, subordinate, tangential, subsidiary, auxiliary, indirect, ancillary, lesser, minor, unimportant, inconsequential, inconsiderable, insignificant, marginal, peripheral. **11** affectation, pretension, haughtiness, arrogance, insolence, boastfulness, pretentiousness, airs, swagger, *colloq.* swank. ● *v.* (*side with*) take sides with, show preference for, be partial to, show favoritism to *or* for, sympathize with, support, back, stand up for, stand by,

favor, prefer, go in *or* along with, join ((up) with), ally with, be *or* become allied with, team up with, throw in one's lot with. □ **on the side 2** see *on the sly* (SLY). **side by side** together, jointly, cheek by jowl, shoulder to shoulder. **side note** see NOTE *n.* 2, 5. **side road** exit, turnoff. **side trip** see EXCURSION 1. **side view** profile, outline, contour, silhouette. **take sides** show preference, be partial, show favoritism; see also SIDE *v.* above. **side-whiskers** muttonchops, muttonchop whiskers; sideburns, *Brit. colloq.* sideboards.

sideband /sídband/ *n.* a range of frequencies near the carrier frequency of a radio wave, concerned in modulation.

sidebar /sídbaar/ *n.* **1** a short news article, printed alongside a major news story, that contains related incidental information. **2** *Law* discussion or consultation between a trial judge and counsel that the jury is not permitted to hear.

sideboard /sídbawrd/ *n.* a table or esp. a flat-topped cupboard at the side of a dining room for supporting and containing dishes, table linen, decanters, etc.

sideboards /sídbawrdz/ *n.pl. Brit. colloq.* = SIDEBURNS.

sideburns /sídbərnz/ *n.pl. colloq.* hair grown by a man down the sides of his face; side-whiskers. [*burnsides* pl. of *burnside* f. General *Burnside* d. 1881 who affected this style]

sidecar /sídkaar/ *n.* **1** a small car for a passenger or passengers attached to the side of a motorcycle. **2** a cocktail of orange liqueur, lemon juice, and brandy.

sided /sídid/ *adj.* **1** having sides. **2** (in *comb.*) having a specified side or sides (*one-sided*). □□ **-sidedly** *adv.* **sidedness** *n.* (also in *comb.*).

sidehill /sídhil/ *n.* a hillside.

sidekick /sídkik/ *n. colloq.* a close associate.

■ see ACCOMPLICE.

sidelight /sídlīt/ *n.* **1** a light from the side. **2** incidental information, etc. **3** esp. *Brit.* a light at the side of the front of a motor vehicle to warn of its presence. **4** *Naut.* the red port or green starboard light on a ship under way.

sideline /sídlin/ *n. & v.* ● *n.* **1** work, etc., done in addition to one's main activity. **2** (usu. in *pl.*) **a** a line bounding the side of a football field, tennis court, etc. **b** the space next to these where spectators, etc., sit. ● *v.tr.* remove (a player) from a team through injury, suspension, etc. □ **on** (or **from**) **the sidelines** in (or from) a position removed from the main action.

■ *n.* **1** see HOBBY¹ 1. □ **on the sidelines** in the wings, standing by, aside, alongside; see also *in reserve* (RESERVE).

sidelong /sídlawng, -long/ *adj. & adv.* ● *adj.* inclining to one side; oblique (*a sidelong glance*). ● *adv.* obliquely (*moved sidelong*). [*sideling* (as SIDE, -LING²): see -LONG]

■ *adj.* oblique, indirect, sideways, lateral, covert, surreptitious, sly. ● *adv.* see SIDEWAYS *adv.*

sidereal /sīdeéreeəl/ *adj.* of or concerning the constellations or fixed stars. □ **sidereal clock** a clock showing sidereal time. **sidereal day** the time between successive meridional transits of a star or esp. of the first point of Aries, about four minutes shorter than the solar day. **sidereal time** time measured by the apparent diurnal motion of the stars. **sidereal year** a year longer than the solar year by 20 minutes 23 seconds because of precession. [L *sidereus* f. *sidus sideris* star]

■ stellar, astral, star.

siderite /sídərīt/ *n.* **1** a mineral form of ferrous carbonate. **2** a meteorite consisting mainly of nickel and iron. [Gk *sidēros* iron]

siderostat /sídərəstat/ *n.* an instrument used for keeping the image of a celestial body in a fixed position. [L *sidus sideris* star, after *heliostat*]

sidesaddle /sídsadˈl/ *n. & adv.* ● *n.* a saddle for a woman rider having supports for both feet on the same side of the horse. ● *adv.* sitting in this position on a horse.

sideshow /sídshō/ *n.* **1** a minor show or attraction in an exhibition or entertainment. **2** a minor incident or issue.

sideslip /sídslip/ *n. & v.* ● *n.* **1** a skid. **2** *Aeron.* a sideways movement instead of forward. ● *v.intr.* **1** skid. **2** *Aeron.* move sideways instead of forward.

sidesplitting /sídspliting/ *adj.* causing violent laughter.

sidestep /sídstep/ *n. & v.* ● *n.* a step taken sideways. ● *v.tr.* (**-stepped, -stepping**) **1** esp. *Football* avoid (esp. a tackle) by stepping sideways. **2** evade. □□ **sidestepper** *n.*
■ *v.* avoid, dodge, circumvent, skirt, bypass, evade, shun, steer clear of, shirk, get out of, *colloq.* duck.

sidestroke /sídstrōk/ *n.* **1** a stroke toward or from a side. **2** an incidental action. **3** a swimming stroke in which the swimmer lies on his or her side.

sideswipe /sídswīp/ *n. & v.* ● *n.* **1** a glancing blow along the side. **2** incidental criticism, etc. ● *v.tr.* hit with or as if with a sideswipe.

sidetrack /sídtrak/ *n. & v.* ● *n.* a railroad siding. ● *v.tr.* **1** turn into a siding; shunt. **2 a** postpone, evade, or divert treatment or consideration of. **b** divert (a person) from considering, etc.
■ *n.* (railroad) siding. ● *v.* **1** shunt, divert. **2** divert, deflect, draw off *or* away, distract, turn aside.

sidewalk /sídwawk/ *n.* a usu. paved pedestrian path at the side of a road.
■ walk, footpath, footway.

sidewall /sídwawl/ *n.* **1** the part of a tire between the tread and the wheel rim. **2** a wall that forms the side of a structure.

sideward /sídwərd/ *adj. & adv.* ● *adj.* = SIDEWAYS. ● *adv.* (also **sidewards** /-wərdz/) = SIDEWAYS.

sideways /sídwayz/ *adv. & adj.* ● *adv.* **1** to or from a side (*moved sideways*). **2** with one side facing forward (*sat sideways on the bus*). ● *adj.* to or from a side (*a sideways movement*). □□ **sidewise** *adv. & adj.*
■ *adv.* obliquely, laterally, edgeways, edgewise, edge on, sidelong, crabwise; indirectly. ● *adj.* see SIDELONG *adj.*

sidewinder /sídwīndər/ *n.* **1** a desert rattlesnake, *Crotalus cerastes*, native to N. America, moving with a lateral motion. **2** a sideways blow.

siding /sídiṅg/ *n.* **1** a short track at the side of and opening on to a railroad line, used for switching trains. **2** material for the outside of a building, e.g., clapboards, shingles, etc.

sidle /sídʼl/ *v. & n.* ● *v.intr.* (usu. foll. by *along, up*) walk in a timid, furtive, stealthy, or cringing manner. ● *n.* the act or an instance of sidling. [back-form. f. *sideling*, SIDELONG]
■ *v.* edge, slink, steal; see also CREEP *v.* 2.

SIDS /sīds/ *abbr.* sudden infant death syndrome; crib death.

siege /seej/ *n.* **1 a** a military operation in which an attacking force seeks to compel the surrender of a fortified place by surrounding it and cutting off supplies, etc. **b** a similar operation by police, etc., to force the surrender of an armed person. **c** the period during which a siege lasts. **2** a persistent attack or campaign of persuasion. □ **lay siege to** esp. *Mil.* conduct the siege of. **raise the siege of** abandon or cause the abandonment of an attempt to take (a place) by siege. [ME f. OF *sege* seat f. *assegier* BESIEGE]
■ **1** blockade, encirclement. □ **lay siege to** besiege, blockade, beleaguer, cordon off, encircle, box *or* pen *or* shut in, bottle up.

siemens /seémənz/ *n. Electr.* the SI unit of conductance, equal to one reciprocal ohm. ¶ Abbr.: **S**. [W. von *Siemens*, Ger. electrical engineer, d. 1892]

sienna /seénə/ *n.* **1** a kind of ferruginous earth used as a pigment in paint. **2** its color of yellowish-brown (**raw sienna**) or reddish-brown (**burnt sienna**). [It. (*terra di*) *Siena* (earth of) Siena in Tuscany]

sierra /seérə/ *n.* a long jagged mountain chain, esp. in Spain or Spanish America. [Sp. f. L *serra* saw]

siesta /seéstə/ *n.* an afternoon sleep or rest esp. in hot countries. [Sp. f. L *sexta (hora)* sixth hour]
■ see REST¹ *n.* 1.

sieve /siv/ *n. & v.* ● *n.* a utensil having a perforated or meshed bottom for separating solids or coarse material from liquids or fine particles, or for reducing a soft solid to a fine pulp. ● *v.tr.* **1** put through or sift with a sieve. **2** examine (evidence, etc.) to select or separate. □ **head like a sieve** *colloq.* a memory that retains little. □□ **sievelike** *adj.* [OE *sife* f. WG]
■ *n.* see MESH *n.* 1–3a. ● *v.* **1** see SIFT 1–3. **2** see SIFT 4.

sift /sift/ *v.* **1** *tr.* sieve (material) into finer and coarser parts. **2** *tr.* (usu. foll. by *from, out*) separate (finer or coarser parts)

from material. **3** *tr.* sprinkle (esp. sugar) from a perforated container. **4** *tr.* examine (evidence, facts, etc.) in order to assess authenticity, etc. **5** *intr.* (of snow, light, etc.) fall as if from a sieve. □ **sift through** examine by sifting. □□ **sifter** *n.* (also in *comb.*). [OE *siftan* f. WG]
■ **1** strain, sieve, riddle, filter, screen, bolt, winnow. **2** (*sift out*) winnow, separate, weed out, filter out, sort out; select, choose, pick. **3** sprinkle, dredge, sieve. **4** sift through, examine, analyze, study, probe, screen, scrutinize, investigate. □□ **sifter** riddle, sieve, colander.

Sig. *abbr.* Signor.

sigh /sī/ *v. & n.* ● *v.* **1** *intr.* emit a long, deep, audible breath expressive of sadness, weariness, longing, relief, etc. **2** *intr.* (foll. by *for*) yearn for (a lost person or thing). **3** *tr.* utter or express with sighs (*"Never!" he sighed*). **4** *intr.* (of the wind, etc.) make a sound like sighing. ● *n.* **1** the act or an instance of sighing. **2** a sound made in sighing (*a sigh of relief*). [ME *sihen*, etc., prob. back-form. f. *sihte* past of *sihen* f. OE *sican*]
■ *v.* **1** breathe, sough; groan, moan. **2** (*sigh for*) yearn *or* long *or* pine for; bemoan, lament *or* mourn *or* grieve *or* weep for, bewail. **3** sough, moan. ● *n.* **1** exhalation. **2** murmur, sound.

sight /sīt/ *n. & v.* ● *n.* **1 a** the faculty of seeing with the eyes (*lost his sight*). **b** the act or an instance of seeing; the state of being seen. **2** a thing seen; a display, show, or spectacle (*not a pretty sight; a beautiful sight*). **3** a way of looking at or considering a thing (*in my sight he can do no wrong*). **4** a range of space within which a person, etc., can see or an object be seen (*he's out of sight; they are just coming into sight*). **5** (usu. in *pl.*) noteworthy features of a town, area, etc. (*went to see the sights*). **6 a** a device on a gun or optical instrument used for assisting the precise aim or observation. **b** the aim or observation so gained (*got a sight of him*). **7** *colloq.* a person or thing having a ridiculous, repulsive, or disheveled appearance (*looked a perfect sight*). **8** *colloq.* a great quantity (*will cost a sight of money; is a sight better than he was*). ● *v.tr.* **1** get sight of, esp. by approaching (*they sighted land*). **2** observe the presence of (esp. aircraft, animals, etc.) (*sighted buffalo*). **3** take observations of (a star, etc.) with an instrument. **4 a** provide (a gun, quadrant, etc.) with sights. **b** adjust the sight of (a gun, etc.). **c** aim (a gun, etc.) with sights. □ **at first sight** on first glimpse or impression. **at** (or **on**) **sight** as soon as a person or a thing has been seen (*plays music at sight; liked him on sight*). **catch** (or **lose**) **sight of** begin (or cease) to see or be aware of. **get a sight of** manage to see; glimpse. **have lost sight of** no longer know the whereabouts of. **in sight 1** visible. **2** near at hand (*salvation is in sight*). **in** (or **within**) **sight of** so as to see or be seen from. **lower one's sights** become less ambitious. **out of my sight!** go at once! **out of sight 1** not visible. **2** *colloq.* excellent; delightful. **out of sight out of mind** we forget the absent. **put out of sight** hide; ignore. **set one's sights on** aim at (*set her sights on a directorship*). **sight for sore eyes** a welcome person or thing, esp. a visitor. **sighting shot** an experimental shot to guide riflemen in adjusting their sights. **sight line** a hypothetical line from a person's eye to what is seen. **sight-read** (*past* and *past part.* **-read** /-red/) read and perform (music) at sight. **sight reader** a person who sight-reads. **sight unseen** without previous inspection. □□ **sighter** *n.* [OE *(ge)sihth*]
■ *n.* **1 a** eyesight, vision, eyes, visual acuity. **b** glimpse, peep, peek, glance, look; see also VIEW *n.* 3. **2** spectacle, scene, display, show; rarity, marvel, wonder, phenomenon; pageant. **3** view, opinion, judgment. **4** field of view *or* vision, range of vision, ken, perception, view, eyeshot, gaze. **7** mess, disaster, eyesore, monstrosity, fright, *colloq.* atrocity. **8** see LOT *n.* 1. ● *v.* **1–3** spot, see, catch sight of, mark, observe, view, distinguish, discern, identify, note, notice, remark,

---

/.../ **pronunciation**	● **part of speech**
□ **phrases, idioms, and compounds**	
□□ **derivatives**	■ **synonym section**
cross-references appear in SMALL CAPITALS or *italics*	

glimpse, spy, *literary* behold, descry, espy. □ **catch** (or **lose**) **sight of** (*catch sight of*) spot, notice, spy, glance at, glimpse, catch a glimpse of, (get a) look *or* peep *or* peek at, *colloq.* get a look-see at, *sl.* take a gander at, get a load of; see also SIGHT *v.* 1–3 above; (*lose sight of*) see *lose track of* (TRACK¹). **in sight 1** see OUT *adv.* 2a, b, 3a, 12. **2** see *at hand* (HAND). **out of sight 1** remote, distant, far away, unseeable, imperceptible, invisible. **2** unusual, rare, extraordinary, outrageous, imaginative, awe inspiring, incredible, shocking, moving, jolting, excellent, splendid, superb, delightful, far-out, *colloq.* out of this world, brilliant, *colloq.* brill, *sl.* cool, neat; *US & Austral. sl.* unreal. **set one's sights on** see AIM *v.* 1, 4. **sight for sore eyes** vision, welcome sight, dream, picture.

sighted /sítid/ *adj.* **1** capable of seeing; not blind. **2** (in *comb.*) having a specified kind of sight (*farsighted*).

sightless /sítlis/ *adj.* **1** blind. **2** *poet.* invisible. □□ **sightlessly** *adv.* **sightlessness** *n.*
■ **1** see BLIND *adj.* 1.

sightly /sítlee/ *adj.* attractive to the sight; not unsightly. □□ **sightliness** *n.*

sightseer /sítseeər/ *n.* a person who visits places of interest; a tourist. □□ **sightsee** *v.intr. & tr.* **sightseeing** *n.*
■ tourist, traveler, globetrotter, visitor, esp. *Brit.* holidaymaker, tripper, day-tripper, *colloq.* rubberneck.
□□ **sightsee** see TRIP *v.* 4.

sightworthy /sítwurthee/ *adj.* worth seeing.

sigillate /síjilət/ *adj.* **1** (of pottery) having impressed patterns. **2** *Bot.* having seallike marks. [L *sigillatus* f. *sigillum* seal dimin. of *signum* sign]

sigma /sígmə/ *n.* the eighteenth letter of the Greek alphabet (Σ, σ, or, when final, ς). [L f. Gk]

sigmate /sígmət, -mayt/ *adj.* **1** sigma-shaped. **2** S-shaped.

sigmoid /sígmoyd/ *adj. & n.* ● *adj.* **1** curved like the uncial sigma (Ϲ); crescent-shaped. **2** S-shaped. ● *n.* (in full **sigmoid flexure**) *Anat.* the curved part of the intestine between the colon and the rectum. [Gk *sigmoeidēs* (as SIGMA)]

sign /sin/ *n. & v.* ● *n.* **1 a** a thing indicating or suggesting a quality or state, etc.; a thing perceived as indicating a future state or occurrence (*violence is a sign of weakness*; *shows all the signs of decay*). **b** a miracle evidencing supernatural power; a portent (*did signs and wonders*). **2 a** a mark, symbol, or device used to represent something or to distinguish the thing on which it is put (*marked the jar with a sign*). **b** a technical symbol used in algebra, music, etc. (*a minus sign*; *a repeat sign*). **3** a gesture or action used to convey information, an order, request, etc. (*gave him a sign to leave*; *conversed by signs*). **4** a publicly displayed board, etc., giving information; a signboard or signpost. **5** any objective evidence of a disease, usu. specified (*Babinski's sign*). **6** a password (*advanced and gave the sign*). **7** any of the twelve divisions of the zodiac, named from the constellations formerly situated in them (*the sign of Cancer*). **8** the trail of a wild animal. **9** *Math.*, etc., the positiveness or negativeness of a quantity. **10** = *sign language.* ● *v.* **1** *tr.* **a** (also *absol.*) write (one's name, initials, etc.) on a document, etc., indicating that one has authorized it. **b** write one's name, etc., on (a document) as authorization. **2** *intr. & tr.* communicate by gesture, esp. using sign language (*signed to me to come*; *signed her speech to the hearing impaired in the audience*). **3** *tr. & intr.* engage or be engaged by signing a contract, etc. (see also *sign on*, *sign up*). **4** *tr.* mark with a sign (esp. with the sign of the cross in baptism). □ **make no sign** seem unconscious; not protest. **sign and countersign** secret words, etc., used as passwords. **sign away** convey (one's right, property, etc.) by signing a deed, etc. **sign for** acknowledge receipt of by signing. **sign language** a system of communication by hand gestures, used esp. by the hearing impaired. **sign of the cross** a Christian sign made in blessing or prayer, by tracing a cross from the forehead to the chest and to each shoulder, or in the air. **sign off 1** end work, broadcasting, a letter, etc., esp. by writing or speaking one's name. **2** acknowledge by signature. **sign of the times** a portent, etc., showing a likely trend. **sign on 1** agree to a

contract, employment, etc. **2** begin work, broadcasting, etc., esp. by writing or announcing one's name. **3** employ (a person). **sign painter** (or **writer**) a person who paints signboards, etc. **sign up 1** engage or employ (a person). **2** enlist in the armed forces. **3 a** commit (another person or oneself) by signing, etc. (*signed you up for dinner*). **b** enroll (*signed up for evening classes*). □□ **signable** *adj.* **signer** *n.* [ME f. OF *signe*, *signer* f. L *signum*, *signare*]
■ *n.* **1** token, symbol, indication, mark, signal, indicator; notice; trace, evidence, manifestation, proof, reminder, pointer, clue, hint, suggestion, vestige; omen, augury, warning, forewarning, portent, writing on the wall, prophecy, prognostication, foreshadowing. **2** device, mark, symbol, representation, emblem, trademark, badge, insignia, brand, stamp, seal, ideogram, ideograph, phonogram, hieroglyph, rebus, logo(type), colophon, ensign, standard, banner, flag; monogram, initials, cipher, *Archaeol.* cartouche, *Linguistics* grapheme. **3** movement, gesture, motion, signal, cue, gesticulation; nod, wave. **4** signboard, advertisement, billboard, placard, poster, notice, announcement; shingle; signpost. **5** see SYMPTOM. **6** password, watchword, countersign. **8** see TRAIL *n.* 1. ● *v.* **1** inscribe, mark, subscribe; sign on the dotted line; autograph, put one's signature on *or* to, countersign, endorse, witness, put *or* set one's hand to. **2** see SIGNAL¹ *v.* 1, 2a. □ **sign away** forgo, relinquish, give up, abandon (claim to), quit claim to, waive, release, surrender, dispose of, sacrifice, get rid of; sign over, assign, consign, transfer, make over, deliver, give, donate, present, dispose of, turn over. **sign off 1** close down, end (off), terminate *or* discontinue. **sign on 1** sign up, enroll, enlist, register, volunteer, join (up), contract. **3** sign up, enroll, enlist, hire, employ, put under contract, retain, engage, take on. **sign up 1** see *sign on* 3 above. **2, 3b** see *sign on* 1 above.

signal¹ /sígnəl/ *n. & v.* ● *n.* **1 a** a usu. prearranged sign conveying information, guidance, etc., esp. at a distance (*waved as a signal to begin*). **b** a message made up of such signs (*signals made with flags*). **2** an immediate occasion for or cause of movement, action, etc. (*the uprising was a signal for repression*). **3** *Electr.* **a** an electrical impulse or impulses or radio waves transmitted as a signal. **b** a sequence of these. **4** a light, semaphore, etc., on a railroad giving instructions or warnings to train engineers, etc. **5** *Bridge* a prearranged mode of bidding or play to convey information to one's partner. ● *v.* **1** *intr.* make signals. **2** *tr.* **a** (often foll. by *to* + infin.) make signals to; direct. **b** transmit (an order, information, etc.) by signal; announce (*signaled her agreement*; *signaled that the town had been taken*). □ **signal book** a list of signals arranged for sending esp. naval and military messages. **signal box** *Brit.* = *signal tower*. **signal of distress** esp. *Naut.* an appeal for help, esp. from a ship, by firing flares. **signal tower** a building beside a railroad track from which signals are controlled. □□ **signaler** or **signaller** *n.* [ME f. OF f. Rmc & med.L *signale* neut. of LL *signalis* f. L *signum* SIGN]
■ *n.* **1** see SIGN *n.* 1, 3. **2** incitement, stimulus, spur, impetus, goad, *archaic* prick. ● *v.* **1, 2a** motion, indicate, gesture, gesticulate, whistle, wink, blink, nod, beckon, flag, semaphore, wave, sign; direct. **2 b** announce; see also COMMUNICATE 1a.

signal² /sígnəl/ *adj.* remarkably good or bad; noteworthy (*a signal victory*). □□ **signally** *adv.* [F *signalé* f. It. past part. *segnalato* distinguished f. *segnale* SIGNAL¹]
■ remarkable, conspicuous, striking, extraordinary, unusual, unique, singular, special, noteworthy, notable, exceptional, significant, important, outstanding, momentous, consequential, weighty. □□ **signally** see *notably* (NOTABLE).

signalize /sígnəliz/ *v.tr.* **1** make noteworthy or remarkable. **2** lend distinction or luster to. **3** indicate.

signalman /sígnəlmən/ *n.* (*pl.* **-men**) **1** a railroad employee responsible for operating signals and switches. **2** a person who displays or receives naval, etc., signals.

signary /sígnəree/ n. (pl. **-ies**) a list of signs constituting the syllabic or alphabetic symbols of a language. [L signum SIGN + -ARY[1], after syllabary]

signatory /sígnətawree/ n. & adj. • n. (pl. **-ies**) a party or esp. a nation that has signed an agreement or esp. a treaty. • adj. having signed such an agreement, etc. [L signatorius of sealing f. signare signat- mark]
■ n. see PARTY[1] n. 4.

signature /sígnəchər/ n. **1 a** a person's name, initials, or mark used in signing a letter, document, etc. **b** the act of signing a document, etc. **2** archaic a distinctive action, characteristic, etc. **3** Mus. **a** = key signature. **b** = time signature. **4** Printing **a** a letter or figure placed at the foot of one or more pages of each sheet of a book as a guide for binding. **b** such a sheet after folding. **5** written directions given to a patient as part of a medical prescription. □ **signature tune** esp. Brit. a distinctive tune used to introduce a particular program or performer on television or radio; theme song. [med.L signatura (LL = marking of sheep), as SIGNATORY]
■ **1 a** see STAMP n. 2, 4. **2** see TOUCH n. 5.

signboard /sínbawrd/ n. a board with a name or symbol, etc., displayed outside a store or hotel, etc.
■ see SIGN n. 4.

signet /sígnit/ n. **1** a seal used instead of or with a signature as authentication. **2** (prec. by the) the royal seal formerly used for special purposes in England and Scotland, and in Scotland later as the seal of the Court of Session. □ **signet ring** a ring with a seal set in it. [ME f. OF signet or med.L signetum (as SIGN)]
■ **1** see SANCTION n. 2.

significance /signífikəns/ n. **1** importance; noteworthiness (his opinion is of no significance). **2** a concealed or real meaning (what is the significance of her statement?). **3** the state of being significant. **4** Statistics the extent to which a result deviates from a hypothesis such that the difference is due to more than errors in sampling. [OF significance or L significantia (as SIGNIFY)]
■ **1** importance, weight, weightiness, consequence, moment, relevance, noteworthiness, value, import. **2** meaning, sense, signification, denotation, message, idea, point, import, purport, implication, portent, content, pith, essence; gist, drift, vein, impression, connotation.

significant /signífikənt/ adj. **1** having a meaning; indicative. **2** having an unstated or secret meaning; suggestive (refused it with a significant gesture). **3** noteworthy; important; consequential (a significant figure in history). **4** Statistics of or relating to the significance in the difference between an observed and calculated result. □ **significant digit** (or **figure**) Math. a digit in a numerical expression that is given to show the precision of the expression, and not a zero used simply to fill vacant space at the beginning or end. **significant other** a person who is very important in one's life, esp. a spouse or lover. □□ **significantly** adv. [L significare: see SIGNIFY]
■ **1, 2** meaningful, informative, indicative; eloquent, pithy, expressive, telling, pregnant, suggestive, telltale. **3** important, weighty, momentous, consequential, critical, considerable, goodly, substantial, major, great, noteworthy, notable, valuable, valued, meritorious, outstanding, impressive, historic, relevant, signal, archaic substantive. □□ **significantly** see MATERIALLY.

signification /sígnifikáyshən/ n. **1** the act of signifying. **2** (usu. foll. by of) exact meaning or sense, esp. of a word or phrase. [ME f. OF f. L significatio -onis (as SIGNIFY)]
■ **2** see MEANING n. 1, 2.

significative /signífikaytiv/ adj. **1** (esp. of a symbol, etc.) signifying. **2** having a meaning. **3** (usu. foll. by of) serving as a sign or evidence. [ME f. OF significatif -ive, or LL significativus (as SIGNIFY)]

signify /sígnifī/ v. (**-ies, -ied**) **1** tr. be a sign or indication of (a yawn signifies boredom). **2** tr. mean; have as its meaning ("Dr" signifies "doctor"). **3** tr. communicate; make known (signified their agreement). **4** intr. be of importance; matter

(it signifies little). □□ **signifier** n. [ME f. OF signifier f. L significare (as SIGN)]
■ **1, 2** indicate, be a sign of, symbolize, betoken, represent, express, denote, say, mean, stand for, specify, spell; imply, connote, intimate, suggest, reveal, disclose. **3** sign, signal, communicate, make known, convey, announce, tell, show, declare, express, intimate, indicate. **4** matter, count, be significant, be important, be consequential, be of significance, be of importance, be of consequence, carry weight, stand out, deserve or merit consideration.

signor /seenyáwr/ n. (pl. **signori** /-nyóree/) **1** a title or form of address used of or to an Italian-speaking man, corresponding to Mr or sir. **2** an Italian man. [It. f. L senior: see SENIOR]

signora /seenyáwrə/ n. **1** a title or form of address used of or to an Italian-speaking married woman, corresponding to Mrs. or madam. **2** a married Italian woman. [It., fem. of SIGNOR]

signorina /seenyəreenə/ n. **1** a title or form of address used of or to an Italian-speaking unmarried woman. **2** an Italian unmarried woman. [It., dimin. of SIGNORA]

signory /seenyəree/ n. (pl. **-ies**) **1** = SEIGNIORY. **2** hist. the governing body of a medieval Italian republic. [ME f. OF s(e)ignorie (as SEIGNEUR)]

signpost /sínpōst/ n. & v. • n. **1** a post erected at a crossroads with arms indicating the direction to and sometimes also the distance from various places. **2** a means of guidance; an indication. • v.tr. **1** provide with a signpost or signposts. **2** esp. Brit. indicate (a course of action, direction, etc.).
■ n. **1** see MARK[1] n. 6. **2** see CLUE n. 1, 2.

sika /seekə/ n. a small forest-dwelling deer, Cervus nippon, native to Japan. [Jap. shika]

Sikh /seek/ n. a member of an E. Indian monotheistic faith founded in the 16th c. [Hindi, = disciple, f. Skr. sishya]

Sikhism /seekizəm/ n. the religious tenets of the Sikhs.

silage /sílij/ n. & v. • n. **1** storage in a silo. **2** green fodder that has been stored in a silo. • v.tr. put into a silo. [alt. of ENSILAGE after silo]
■ n. **2** see FEED n. 1.

sild /silt/ n. a small immature herring, esp. one caught in N. European seas. [Da. & Norw.]

silence /síləns/ n. & v. • n. **1** absence of sound. **2** abstinence from speech or noise. **3** the avoidance of mentioning a thing, betraying a secret, etc. **4** oblivion; the state of not being mentioned. • v.tr. make silent, esp. by coercion or superior argument. □ **in silence** without speech or other sound. **reduce** (or **put**) **to silence** refute in argument. [ME f. OF f. L silentium (as SILENT)]
■ n. **1** quiet, quietness, stillness, soundlessness, noiselessness, calm, calmness, hush, quietude, tranquility, peace, peacefulness, serenity. **2, 3** speechlessness, muteness, dumbness; reticence, taciturnity, reserve, uncommunicativeness, secretiveness. • v. quiet, mute, hush, still, shush, calm, tranquilize, soothe, Brit. quieten; mollify, take the sting out of, propitiate, pacify, blunt, suppress, repress, restrain, subdue, inhibit, put down, damp (down), squelch, quash, emasculate, muzzle, muffle, shut off, gag, stifle, smother, deaden (the effect of), colloq. shut up. □□ **in silence** see quietly (QUIET).

silencer /sílənsər/ n. any of various devices for reducing the noise emitted by a gun, etc.

silent /sílənt/ adj. **1** not speaking; not uttering or making or accompanied by any sound. **2** (of a letter) written but not pronounced, e.g., b in doubt. **3** (of a movie) without a synchronized soundtrack. **4** (of a person) taciturn; speaking little. **5** (of an agreement) unspoken; unrecorded. **6** saying or recording nothing on some subject (the records are silent on

/.../ **pronunciation**	● **part of speech**
□ **phrases, idioms, and compounds**	
□□ **derivatives**	■ **synonym section**
cross-references appear in SMALL CAPITALS or italics	

the incident). **7** *Brit.* (of liquor) unflavored. □ **silent majority** those of moderate opinions who rarely assert them. **silent partner** a partner not sharing in the actual work of a firm. □□ **silently** *adv.* [L *silēre silent-* be silent]

■ **1** unspeaking, mute, dumb, speechless; quiet, still, soundless, noiseless, tranquil, hushed, shushed; calm, serene, placid, peaceful, pacific, unagitated, unruffled, untroubled, undisturbed, *poet.* stilly. **2** unpronounced, unuttered, unsounded. **4** uncommunicative, mute, closemouthed, taciturn, reticent, reserved, tight-lipped, secretive, *colloq.* mum. **5** unspoken, unexpressed, unrecorded, tacit, understood, implicit, implied, unstated. □ **silent majority** see PEOPLE *n.* 2. **silent partner** inactive partner, nonparticipating partner, passive partner, quiescent partner, *Brit.* sleeping partner. □□ **silently** quietly, soundlessly, noiselessly, with catlike tread, as quiet(ly) as a mouse, stealthily; wordlessly, speechlessly, mutely.

silenus /sīlêenəs/ *n.* (*pl.* **sileni** /-nī/) (in Greek mythology) a bearded old man like a satyr, sometimes with the tail and legs of a horse. [L f. Gk *seilēnos*]

silex /sīleks/ *n.* a kind of glass made of fused quartz. [L (as SILICA)]

silhouette /sīlōō-ét/ *n.* & *v.* ● *n.* **1** a representation of a person or thing showing the outline only, usu. done in solid black on white or cut from paper. **2** the dark shadow or outline of a person or thing against a lighter background. ● *v.tr.* represent or (usu. in *passive*) show in silhouette. □ **in silhouette** seen or placed in outline. [Étienne de *Silhouette*, Fr. author and politician d. 1767]

■ *n.* outline, profile, contour, form, figure, shape, shadow, configuration, periphery, perimeter.

silica /sīlikə/ *n.* silicon dioxide, occurring as quartz, etc., and as a principal constituent of sandstone and other rocks. □ **silica gel** hydrated silica in a hard granular form used as a desiccant. □□ **siliceous** /-líshəs/ *adj.* (also **silicious**). **silicic** /-lísik/ *adj.* **silicify** /-lísifī/ *v.tr.* & *intr.* (**-ies, -ied**). **silicification** /-fikáyshən/ *n.* [L *silex -icis* flint, after *alumina*, etc.]

silicate /sīlikayt, -kət/ *n.* any of the many insoluble compounds of a metal combined with silicon and oxygen, occurring widely in the rocks of the earth's crust.

silicon /sīlikən, -kon/ *n. Chem.* a nonmetallic element occurring widely in silica and silicates, and used in the manufacture of glass. ¶ Symb.: **Si**. □ **silicon chip** a silicon microchip. **silicon carbide** = CARBORUNDUM. **Silicon Valley** an area southeast of San Francisco, CA, with a high concentration of electronics industries. [L *silex -icis* flint (after *carbon*, *boron*), alt. of earlier *silicium*]

silicone /sīlikōn/ *n.* any of the many polymeric organic compounds of silicon and oxygen with high resistance to cold, heat, water, and the passage of electricity.

silicosis /sīlikósis/ *n.* lung fibrosis caused by the inhalation of dust containing silica. □□ **silicotic** /-kótik/ *adj.*

silique /sīlêek/ the long, narrow seedpod of a cruciferous plant. □□ **siliquose** /sīlikwōs/ *adj.* **siliquous** /-kwəs/ *adj.* [L, = pod]

silk /silk/ *n.* **1** a fine, strong, soft lustrous fiber produced by silkworms in making cocoons. **2** a similar fiber spun by some spiders, etc. **3 a** a thread or cloth made from silk fiber. **b** a thread or fabric resembling silk. **4** (in *pl.*) kinds of silk cloth or garments made from it, esp. as worn by a jockey in a horse-owner's colors. **5** *Brit. colloq.* Queen's (or King's) Counsel, as having the right to wear a silk gown. **6** (*attrib.*) made of silk (*silk blouse*). **7** the silky styles of the female corn flower. □ **silk cotton** kapok or a similar substance. **silk gland** a gland secreting the substance produced as silk. **silk hat** a tall cylindrical hat covered with silk plush. **silk moth** any of various large moths of the family Saturniidae, esp. *Hyalophora cecropia*. **silk-screen printing** = *screen printing*. □□ **silklike** *adj.* [OE *sioloc, seolec* (cf. ON *silki*) f. LL *sericum* neut. of L *sericus* f. *seres* f. Gk *Sēres* an oriental people]

■ □□ **silklike** see SILKY 1.

silken /sílkən/ *adj.* **1** made of silk. **2** wearing silk. **3** soft or

lustrous as silk. **4** (of a person's manner, etc.) suave or insinuating. [OE *seolcen* (as SILK)]

■ **1, 3** see SILKY 1. **4** see SMOOTH *adj.* 9.

silkworm /sílkwərm/ *n.* the caterpillar of the moth *Bombyx mori*, which spins its cocoon of silk.

silky /sílkee/ *adj.* (**silkier, silkiest**) **1** like silk in smoothness, softness, fineness, or luster. **2** (of a person's manner, etc.) suave; insinuating. □□ **silkily** *adv.* **silkiness** *n.*

■ **1** silken, silklike, delicate, fine, sleek, soft, smooth, satiny, shiny, glossy, lustrous, *Bot.* & *Zool.* sericeous. **2** see SMOOTH *adj.* 9.

sill /sil/ *n.* (also *Brit.* **cill**) **1** a shelf or slab of stone, wood, or metal at the foot of a window or doorway. **2** a horizontal timber at the bottom of a dock or lock entrance, against which the gates close. **3** *Geol.* a tabular sheet of igneous rock intruded between other rocks and parallel with their planar structure. [OE *syll, sylle*]

■ **1** see LEDGE.

sillabub var. of SYLLABUB.

sillimanite /sílimənīt/ *n.* an aluminum silicate occurring in orthorhombic crystals or fibrous masses. [B. *Silliman*, Amer. chemist d. 1864]

silly /sílee/ *adj.* & *n.* ● *adj.* (**sillier, silliest**) **1** lacking sense; foolish; imprudent; unwise. **2** weak-minded. **3** *Cricket* (of a fielder or position) very close to the batsman (*silly mid off*). **4** *archaic* innocent; simple; helpless. **5** *colloq.* stunned (as) by a blow (*I was knocked silly*). ● *n.* (*pl.* **-ies**) *colloq.* a foolish person. □ **the silly season** the time of year, usu. midsummer, when newspapers, etc., often publish trivial material for lack of important news. □□ **sillily** *adv.* **silliness** *n.* [later form of ME *sely* (dial. *seely*) happy, repr. OE *sǣlig* (recorded in *unsǣlig* unhappy) f. Gmc]

■ *adj.* **1** senseless, nonsensical, absurd, ridiculous, ludicrous, laughable, risible, farcical, asinine, apish, anserine, inane, preposterous, idiotic, childish, puerile, foolish, foolhardy, irresponsible, unreasonable, illogical, irrational, pointless, fatuous, stupid, unwise, imprudent, harebrained, mad, insane, *colloq.* imbecilic, crazy, esp. *Brit. colloq.* daft. **2** see *halfwitted* (HALFWIT). **5** stunned, stupefied, dazed, giddy, dizzy, muzzy, benumbed. ● *n.* fool, nincompoop, dunce, clown, ninny, simpleton, numskull, booby, dolt, jackass, dodo, blockhead, ignoramus, *colloq.* idiot, dimwit, nitwit, halfwit, dummy, thickhead, knucklehead, fathead, chump, goose, drip, silly billy, *Brit. colloq.* clot, *sl.*, nerd, bonehead, clod, twerp, goof, dope, jerk, *Austral. sl.* nong, galah, *Austral.* & *NZ sl.* drongo, *Brit. sl.* muggins, twit, mug.

silo /sílō/ *n.* & *v.* ● *n.* (*pl.* **-os**) **1** a pit or airtight structure in which green crops are pressed and kept for fodder, undergoing fermentation. **2** a pit or tower for the storage of grain, cement, etc. **3** an underground chamber in which a guided missile is kept ready for firing. ● *v.tr.* (**-oes, -oed**) make silage of. [Sp. f. L *sirus* f. Gk *siros* corn pit]

silt /silt/ *n.* & *v.* ● *n.* sediment deposited by water in a channel, harbor, etc. ● *v.tr.* & *intr.* (often foll. by *up*) choke or be choked with silt. □□ **siltation** /-táyshən/ *n.* **silty** *adj.* [ME, perh. rel. to Da., Norw. *sylt*, OLG *sulta*, OHG *sulza* salt marsh, formed as SALT]

■ *n.* deposit, sediment, alluvium, ooze, sludge, slime, mud. ● *v.* silt up *or* over; clog, choke, block, obstruct, dam, congest; become clogged *or* choked *or* blocked *or* obstructed *or* dammed *or* congested.

siltstone /síltstōn/ *n.* rock of consolidated silt.

Silurian /silōreeən, sī-/ *adj.* & *n. Geol.* ● *adj.* of or relating to the third period of the Paleozoic era with evidence of the first fish and land plants, and the formation of mountains and new land areas. ¶ Cf. Appendix VII. ● *n.* this period or system. [L *Silures*, a people of ancient SE Wales]

silva /sílvə/ *n.* (also **sylva**) (pl. **sylvae** /-vee/ or **sylvas**) **1** the trees of a region, epoch, or environment. **2** a treatise on or a list of such trees. [L *silva* a wood]

silvan var. of SYLVAN.

silver /sílvər/ *n.*, *adj.*, & *v.* ● *n. Chem.* **1** a grayish-white, lustrous, malleable, ductile, precious metallic element, oc-

curring naturally as the element and in mineral form, and used chiefly with an admixture of harder metals for coin, plate, and ornaments, as a subordinate monetary medium, and in compounds for photography, etc. ¶ Symb.: **Ag. 2** the color of silver. **3** silver or cupronickel coins. **4** esp. *Sc.* money. **5** silver vessels or implements, esp. cutlery. **6** household cutlery of any material. **7** = *silver medal.* ● *adj.* **1** made wholly or chiefly of silver. **2** colored like silver. ● *v.* **1** *tr.* coat or plate with silver. **2** *tr.* provide (a mirror glass) with a backing of tin amalgam, etc. **3** *tr.* (of the moon or a white light) give a silvery appearance to. **4 a** *tr.* turn (the hair) gray or white. **b** *intr.* (of the hair) turn gray or white. □ **silver age** a period regarded as inferior to a golden age, e.g., that of postclassical Latin literature in the early Imperial period. **silver band** *Brit.* a band playing silver-plated instruments. **silver birch** a common birch, *Betula alba*, with silver-colored bark. **silver fir** any fir of the genus *Abies*, with the undersides of its leaves colored silver. **silver fox 1** an American red fox at a time when its fur is black with white tips. **2** its fur. **silver gilt 1** gilded silver. **2** an imitation gilding of yellow lacquer over silver leaf. **silver-gray** a lustrous gray. **silver jubilee** a 25th anniversary. **silver Latin** literary Latin of the early Imperial period. **silver leaf** silver beaten into a very thin sheet. **silver lining** a consolation or hopeful feature in misfortune. **silver medal** a medal of silver, usu. awarded as second prize. **silver nitrate** a colorless solid that is soluble in water and formerly used in photography. **silver paper** *Brit.* **1** a fine, white tissue paper for wrapping silver. **2** aluminum or tin foil. **silver plate** vessels, spoons, etc., of copper, etc., plated with silver. **silver salmon** a coho. **silver screen** (usu. prec. by *the*) motion pictures collectively. **silver solder** solder containing silver. **silver spoon** a sign of future prosperity. **silver standard** a system by which the value of a currency is defined in terms of silver, for which the currency may be exchanged. **Silver Star** *US Mil.* a decoration awarded for gallantry in action. **silver tongue** eloquence. **silver wedding** the 25th anniversary of a wedding. [OE *seolfor* f. Gmc]
■ *n.* **2** grayish, whitish, whitish-gray, grayish-white, silver-gray, gray. **4** see MONEY 1. **5, 6** silverware, sterling, (silver) plate; hollowware; cutlery, flatware. ● *adj.* **2** silvery, shiny, shining, polished, burnished, lustrous, pearly, nacreous, bright, gleaming; silver-gray, whitish-gray, gray, grayish, grayish-white, white; *Heraldry* argent.

silverfish /sílvərfish/ *n.* (*pl.* same or **-fishes**) **1** any small silvery wingless insect of the order Thysanura, esp. *Lepisma saccharina* in houses and other buildings. **2** a silver-colored fish, esp. a colorless variety of goldfish.

silvern /sílvərn/ *adj. archaic* or *poet.* = SILVER *adj.* [OE *seolfren, silfren* (as SILVER)]

silverside /sílvərsid/ *n. Brit.* the upper side of a round of beef from the outside of the leg.

silversmith /sílvərsmith/ *n.* a worker in silver; a manufacturer of silver articles. □□ **silversmithing** *n.*

silverware /sílvərwair/ *n.* **1** articles made of or coated with silver. **2** tableware of any metal.
■ see SILVER *n.* 5, 6.

silverweed /sílvərweed/ *n.* a plant with silvery leaves, esp. a potentilla, *Potentilla anserina*, with silver-colored leaves.

silvery /sílvəree/ *adj.* **1** like silver in color or appearance. **2** having a clear, gentle, ringing sound. **3** (of the hair) white and lustrous. □□ **silveriness** *n.*
■ **1** see SILVER *adj.* **2** silver-toned, silver-tongued; see also MELODIOUS 2.

silviculture /sílvikulchər/ *n.* (also **sylviculture**) the growing and tending of trees as a branch of forestry. □□ **silvicultural** /-kúlchərəl/ *adj.* **silviculturist** /-kúlchərist/ [F f. L *silva* a wood + F *culture* CULTURE]

simian /símeeən/ *adj. & n.* ● *adj.* **1** of or concerning the anthropoid apes. **2** like an ape or monkey (*a simian walk*). ● *n.* an ape or monkey. [L *simia* ape, perh. f. L *simus* f. Gk *simos* flat-nosed]
■ *n.* monkey, ape, primate.

similar /símilər/ *adj.* **1** like; alike. **2** (often foll. by *to*) having

a resemblance. **3** of the same kind, nature, or amount. **4** *Geom.* shaped alike. □□ **similarity** /-láritee/ *n.* (*pl.* **-ies**). **similarly** *adv.* [F *similaire* or med.L *similaris* f. L *similis* like]
■ **1, 3** like, almost identical, comparable, equivalent, nearly the same; alike, akin, kindred, related, of a piece, of the same sort *or* kind *or* type. **2** (*similar to*) resembling, like, corresponding to, comparable with, reminiscent of, redolent of, along the same lines as. □□ **similarity** see LIKENESS 1, UNIFORMITY. **similarly** see ALIKE *adv.*

simile /símilee/ *n.* **1** a figure of speech involving the comparison of one thing with another of a different kind, as an illustration or ornament (e.g., *as brave as a lion*). **2** the use of such comparison. [ME f. L, neut. of *similis* like]
■ see METAPHOR.

similitude /símílitood, -tyood/ *n.* **1** the likeness, guise, or outward appearance of a thing or person. **2** a comparison or the expression of a comparison. **3** *archaic* a counterpart or facsimile. [ME f. OF *similitude* or L *similitudo* (as SIMILE)]
■ **1** see LIKENESS 1, 2.

simmer /símər/ *v. & n.* ● *v.* **1** *intr. & tr.* be or keep bubbling or boiling gently. **2** *intr.* be in a state of suppressed anger or excitement. ● *n.* a simmering condition. □ **simmer down** become calm or less agitated. [alt. of ME (now dial.) *simper*, perh. imit.]
■ *v.* **1** stew, cook, boil, bubble, *archaic* seethe. **2** chafe, seethe, stew, steam, smolder, fume, rage, burn.
□ **simmer down** calm *or* cool down, cool off, calm oneself, become quiet, control oneself, get control of *or* over oneself, quiet down, *Brit.* quieten down, *sl.* cool it.

simnel cake /símnəl/ *n. Brit.* a rich fruit cake, usu. with a marzipan layer and decoration, eaten esp. at Easter or during Lent. [ME f. OF *simenel*, ult. f. L *simila* or Gk *semidalis* fine flour]

simon-pure /símənpyoor/ *adj.* real; genuine. [(*the real*) *Simon Pure*, a character in Centlivre's *Bold Stroke for a Wife* (1717)]

simony /símənee, sím-/ *n.* the buying or selling of ecclesiastical privileges, e.g., pardons or benefices. □□ **simoniac** /-móneeak/ *adj. & n.* **simoniacal** /-níəkəl/ *adj.* [ME f. OF *simonie* f. LL *simonia* f. *Simon Magus* (Acts 8:18)]
■ □□ **simoniacal** see VENAL.

simoom /simoóm/ *n.* (also **simoon** /-moón/) a hot, dry, dust-laden wind blowing at intervals esp. in the Arabian desert. [Arab. *samūm* f. *samma* to poison]
■ see STORM *n.* 1.

simp /simp/ *n. colloq.* a simpleton. [abbr.]

simpatico /simpátikō/ *adj.* congenial; likable. [It. & Sp. (as SYMPATHY)]
■ see LIKABLE.

simper /símpər/ *v. & n.* ● *v.* **1** *intr.* smile in a silly or affected way. **2** *tr.* express by or with simpering. ● *n.* such a smile. □□ **simperingly** *adv.* [16th c.: cf. Du. and Scand. *semper, simper*, G *zimp(f)er* elegant, delicate]
■ *v.* **1** see SMILE *v.* 1. **2** twitter, warble, trill, tweet, prattle, giggle, titter, snicker, snigger. ● *n.* grin, smile, smirk.

simple /símpəl/ *adj. & n.* ● *adj.* **1** easily understood or done; presenting no difficulty (*a simple explanation; a simple task*). **2** not complicated or elaborate; without luxury or sophistication. **3** not compound; consisting of or involving only one element or operation, etc. **4** absolute; unqualified; straightforward (*the simple truth; a simple majority*). **5** foolish or ignorant; gullible, feeble-minded (*am not so simple as to agree to that*). **6** plain in appearance or manner; unsophisticated; ingenuous; artless. **7** of low rank; humble; insignificant (*simple people*). **8** *Bot.* **a** consisting of one part. **b** (of fruit) formed from one pistil. ● *n. archaic* **1** an herb used medicinally. **2** a medicine made from it. □ **simple eye** an eye of an insect, having only one lens. **simple fracture** a fracture of the bone only, without a skin wound. **simple harmonic motion** see HARMONIC. **simple interest** interest payable on a capital sum only (cf. *compound interest* (see COMPOUND)). **simple interval** *Mus.* an interval of one octave or less. **simple machine** any of the basic mechanical devices for applying a force (e.g., an inclined plane, wedge, or lever). **simple sentence** a sentence with a single subject and predicate. **Simple Simon** a foolish person (from the nursery-rhyme character). **simple time** *Mus.* a time with two, three, or four beats in a bar. □□ **simpleness** *n.* [ME f. OF f. L *simplus*]

■ *adj.* **1** uncomplicated, plain, uninvolved, unsophisticated, understandable, intelligible, (easily) understood, comprehensible, clear, lucid, obvious, straightforward, easy, painless, effortless, elementary, basic, esp. *Computing* user-friendly. **2** uncomplicated; plain, unadorned, undecorated, unembellished, unadulterated, unsophisticated, basic, fundamental, elementary, elemental, mere, unostentatious, unassuming, unpretentious, modest, classic, uncluttered, stark, clean, severe, austere, Spartan, homely; unvarnished, naked, honest. **4** see PURE 8. **5** foolish, ignorant, naive, green, gullible, credulous, slow, slow-witted, stupid, thick, simpleminded, feebleminded, oafish, bovine, dense, obtuse, dull, dull-witted, witless, halfwitted, brainless, backward, *colloq.* imbecilic, imbecile, thickheaded, moronic, cretinous, dumb. **6** sincere, frank, candid, open, unaffected, uncomplicated, unpretentious, straightforward, aboveboard, simple-hearted, uncontrived, direct, upright, square, forthright, foursquare, righteous, honest, naive, guileless, artless, undesigning, childlike, ingenuous, unsophisticated, innocent. **7** lowly, humble, inferior, mean, base, subservient, common, subordinate, insignificant.

simpleminded /símpəlmíndid/ *adj.* **1** natural; unsophisticated. **2** feeble-minded. □□ **simplemindedly** *adv.* **simplemindedness** *n.*

■ **1** see NAÏVE. **2** see FOOLISH. □□ **simplemindedness** see *stupidity* (STUPID).

simpleton /símpəltən/ *n.* a foolish, gullible, or half-witted person. [SIMPLE after surnames f. place-names in -*ton*]

■ see FOOL[1] *n.* 1.

simplex /símpleks/ *adj.* & *n.* ● *adj.* **1** simple; not compounded. **2** *Computing* (of a circuit) allowing transmission of signals in one direction only. ● *n.* a simple or uncompounded thing, esp. a word. [L, = single, var. of *simplus* simple]

simplicity /simplísitee/ *n.* the fact or condition of being simple. [OF *simplicité* or L *simplicitas* (as SIMPLEX)]

■ understandability, comprehensibility, lucidity, straightforwardness, clarity, intelligibility, decipherability; uncomplicatedness; plainness, cleanness, severity, starkness, austerity, asceticism; restraint, bareness, purity; stupidity, foolishness, slow-wittedness, simplemindedness, feeblemindedness, oafishness, cloddishness, obtuseness, dullness, dull-wittedness, witlessness, imbecility, brainlessness, *colloq.* thickheadedness, halfwittedness; sincerity, openness, artlessness, candor, guilelessness, frankness, unsophisticatedness, ingenuousness, forthrightness, unaffectedness, unpretentiousness, modesty, naïveté; directness, inelegance, rusticity, pastoralism.

simplify /símplifī/ *v.tr.* (-**ies**, -**ied**) make simple; make easy or easier to do or understand. □□ **simplification** /-fikáyshən/ *n.* [F *simplifier* f. med.L *simplificare* (as SIMPLE)]

■ clarify, clear up, make easy, paraphrase, explain, explicate, disentangle, untangle, unravel, streamline. □□ **simplification** see *interpretation* (INTERPRET).

simplism /símplizəm/ *n.* **1** affected simplicity. **2** the unjustifiable simplification of a problem, etc.

simplistic /simplístik/ *adj.* **1** excessively or affectedly simple. **2** oversimplified so as to conceal or distort difficulties. □□ **simplistically** *adv.*

■ see LITERAL *adj.* 1, 2.

simply /símplee/ *adv.* **1** in a simple manner. **2** absolutely;

without doubt (*simply astonishing*). **3** merely (*was simply trying to please*).

■ **1** distinctly, unambiguously, obviously, unmistakably; naively, artlessly, guilelessly, openly, innocently, ingenuously, unaffectedly, unpretentiously, plainly, naturally; modestly, starkly, severely, sparely, sparsely, austerely, ascetically. **2** totally, completely, absolutely, altogether, entirely, fully, wholly, just, plainly, obviously, really, unreservedly, unqualifiedly. **3** merely, purely, only, solely, just.

simulacrum /símyəláykrəm, -lák-/ *n.* (*pl.* **simulacra** /-krə/) **1** an image of something. **2 a** a shadowy likeness; a deceptive substitute. **b** mere pretense. [L (as SIMULATE)]

■ **1** see IMAGE *n.* 3. **2** a see IMAGE *n.* 5.

simulate /símyəlayt/ *v.tr.* **1 a** pretend to have or feel (an attribute or feeling). **b** pretend to be. **2** imitate or counterfeit. **3 a** imitate the conditions of (a situation, etc.), e.g., for training. **b** produce a computer model of (a process). **4** (as **simulated** *adj.*) made to resemble the real thing but not genuinely such (*simulated fur*). **5** (of a word) take or have an altered form suggested by (a word wrongly taken to be its source, e.g., *amuck*). □□ **simulation** /-láyshən/ *n.* **simulative** /-lətiv/ *adj.* [L *simulare* f. *similis* like]

■ **1** see FAKE[1] *v.* 2. **2**, **3a** see IMITATE 3. **4** (**simulated**) see FALSE 2a. □□ **simulation** see IMITATION *n.*

simulator /símyəlaytər/ *n.* **1** a person or thing that simulates. **2** a device designed to simulate the operations of a complex system, used esp. in training.

simulcast /síməlkast, sím-/ *n.* simultaneous transmission of the same program, as on radio and television. [SIMULTANEOUS + BROADCAST]

simultaneous /síməltáyneeəs, sím-/ *adj.* (often foll. by *with*) occurring or operating at the same time. □ **simultaneous equations** equations involving two or more unknowns that are to have the same values in each equation. □□ **simultaneity** /-tənáyitee/ *n.* **simultaneously** *adv.* **simultaneousness** *n.* [med.L *simultaneus* f. L *simul* at the same time, prob. after *instantaneus*, etc.]

■ coincident, coinciding, concurrent, contemporaneous, synchronous; contemporary. □□ **simultaneity** see COINCIDENCE 1. **simultaneously** see *at once* 2 (ONCE).

sin[1] /sin/ *n.* & *v.* ● *n.* **1 a** the breaking of divine or moral law, esp. by a conscious act. **b** such an act. **2** an offense against good taste or propriety, etc. ● *v.* (**sinned**, **sinning**) **1** *intr.* commit a sin. **2** *intr.* (foll. by *against*) offend. **3** *tr.* *archaic* commit (a sin). □ **as sin** *colloq.* extremely (*ugly as sin*). **for one's sins** *joc.* as a judgment on one for something done. **like sin** *colloq.* vehemently or forcefully. **live in sin** *colloq.* live together without being married. □□ **sinless** *adj.* **sinlessly** *adv.* **sinlessness** *n.* [OE *syn(n)*]

■ *n.* **1** wickedness, sinfulness, vice, corruption, ungodliness, unrighteousness, badness, evil, wrongfulness, iniquity, iniquitousness, immorality, depravity, impiety, irreverence, impiousness, sacrilege; transgression, offense, wrong, misdeed, profanation, desecration, devilry, crime, infraction, dereliction, infringement, violation, misdemeanor, fault, foible, peccadillo, *archaic* trespass. **2** see SCANDAL 1b. ● *v.* **1** transgress, offend, fall (from grace), lapse, go wrong, stray, go astray, err, *literary or archaic* trespass. **2** (*sin against*) offend (against), err against, *literary or archaic* trespass against. □ **live in sin** live together, cohabit. □□ **sinless** see HOLY 1, 2. **sinlessness** see PURITY 2.

sin[2] /sin/ *abbr.* sine.

Sinaitic /sínayítik/ *adj.* of or relating to Mount Sinai or of the Sinai peninsula. [var. of *Sinaic* f. *Sinai* f. Heb. *sīnay*, with *t* added for euphony]

sinanthropus /sinánthrəpəs, si-/ /sínanthrōpəs, sín-/ *n.* an apelike human of the extinct genus *Sinanthropus*. [mod.L, as SINO- Chinese (remains having been found near Peking) + Gk *anthrōpos* man]

since /sins/ *prep., conj.,* & *adv.* ● *prep.* throughout, or at a point in, the period between (a specified time, event, etc.) and the time present or being considered (*must have happened since yesterday; has been going on since June; the greatest* *composer since Beethoven*). ● *conj.* **1** during or in the time after (*what have you been doing since we met?*; *has not spoken since the dog died*). **2** for the reason that, because; inasmuch as (*since you are drunk I will drive you home*). **3** (*ellipt.*) as being (*a more useful, since better designed, tool*). ● *adv.* **1** from that time or event until now or the time being considered (*have not seen them since*); *had been healthy ever since*; *has since been cut down*). **2** ago (*happened many years since*). [ME, reduced form of obs. *sithence* or f. dial. *sin* (f. *sithen*) f. OE *siththon*]

sincere /sinseér/ *adj.* (**sincerer, sincerest**) **1** free from pretense or deceit; the same in reality as in appearance. **2** genuine; honest; frank. □□ **sincereness** *n.* **sincerity** /-séritee/ *n.* [L *sincerus* clean, pure]

■ honest, truthful, true, genuine, bona fide, heartfelt, earnest, truehearted, wholehearted, undissembling, unfeigned, open, (open and) aboveboard, straightforward, direct, frank, candid, guileless, artless, *colloq.* upfront, on the level, on the up and up, *Austral.* & *NZ colloq.* dinkum, *formal* veracious. □□ **sincerity** honesty, truthfulness, straightforwardness, openness, forthrightness, frankness, candor, candidness, seriousness, genuineness, uprightness.

sincerely /sinseérlee/ *adv.* in a sincere manner. □ **yours sincerely** a formula for ending an informal letter.

■ truly, honestly, really, wholeheartedly, candidly, frankly, unequivocally, seriously, earnestly, genuinely, deeply, fervently.

sinciput /sínsipoot/ *n. Anat.* the front of the skull from the forehead to the crown. □□ **sincipital** /-sípitəl/ *adj.* [L f. *semi-* half + *caput* head]

sine /sin/ *n. Math.* **1** the trigonometric function that is equal to the ratio of the side opposite a given angle (in a right triangle) to the hypotenuse. **2** a function of the line drawn from one end of an arc perpendicularly to the radius through the other. □ **sine curve** (or **wave**) a curve representing periodic oscillations of constant amplitude as given by a sine function: also called SINUSOID. [L *sinus* curve, fold of a toga, used in med.L as transl. of Arab. *jayb* bosom, sine]

sinecure /sínikyoor, sín-/ *n.* a position that requires little or no work but usu. yields profit or honor. □□ **sinecurism** *n.* **sinecurist** *n.* [L *sine cura* without care]

sine die /sínee dí-ee, sínay deé-ay/ *adv.* (of business adjourned indefinitely) with no appointed date. [L, = without day]

sine qua non /sínay kwaa nón/ *n.* an indispensable condition or qualification. [L, = without which not]

■ see PRECONDITION *n.*

sinew /sínyoo/ *n. & v.* ● *n.* **1** tough fibrous tissue uniting muscle to bone; a tendon. **2** (in *pl.*) muscles; bodily strength; wiriness. **3** (in *pl.*) that which forms the strength or framework of a plan, city, organization, etc. ● *v.tr. poet.* serve as the sinews of; sustain; hold together. □ **the sinews of war** money. □□ **sinewless** *adj.* **sinewy** *adj.* [OE *sin(e)we* f. Gmc]

■ *n.* **1** ligament, tendon. **2** (*sinews*) muscles, strength, force, power, energy, brawn, vigor, might, stamina, vitality; wiriness. □□ **sinewy** strong, powerful, muscular, mighty, stout, wiry, robust, tough, stringy; strapping, brawny, burly.

sinfonia /sínfəneéə/ *n. Mus.* **1** a symphony. **2** (in Baroque music) an orchestral piece used as an introduction to an opera, cantata, or suite. **3** (**Sinfonia**; usu. in names) a symphony orchestra. [It., = SYMPHONY]

sinfonietta /sínfənyétə/ *n. Mus.* **1** a short or simple symphony. **2** (**Sinfonietta**; usu. in names) a small symphony orchestra. [It., dimin. of *sinfonia*: see SINFONIA]

sinful /sínfool/ *adj.* **1** (of a person) committing sin, esp. habitually. **2** (of an act) involving or characterized by sin. □□ **sinfully** *adv.* **sinfulness** *n.* [OE *synfull* (as SIN, -FUL)]

■ corrupt, evil, wicked, bad, iniquitous, vile, base, profane, immoral, profligate, depraved, dissolute, criminal, sacrilegious, ungodly, unholy, unrighteous, godless, demonic, diabolic(al), irreligious, impious, irreverent, wrong, wrongful. □□ **sinfulness** see SIN *n.* 1.

sing /sing/ *v. & n.* ● *v.* (*past* **sang** /sang/; *past part.* **sung** /sung/) **1** *intr.* utter musical sounds with the voice, esp. words with a set tune. **2** *tr.* utter or produce by singing (*sing another song*). **3** *intr.* (of the wind, a kettle, etc.) make inarticulate melodious or humming, buzzing, or whistling sounds. **4** *intr.* (of the ears) be affected as with a buzzing sound. **5** *intr. sl.* turn informer; confess. **6** *intr. archaic* compose poetry. **7** *tr.* & (foll. by *of*) *intr. celebrate* in verse. **8** *tr.* (foll. by *in, out*) usher (esp. the new or old year) in or out with singing. **9** *tr.* bring to a specified state by singing (*sang the child to sleep*). ● *n.* **1** an act or spell of singing. **2** a meeting for amateur singing. □ **sing-along 1** a tune, etc., to which one can sing in accompaniment. **2** a gathering at which such tunes, etc., are sung. **sing out** call out loudly; shout. **sing the praises of** see PRAISE. **sing up** sing more loudly. □□ **singable** *adj.* **singer** *n.* **singingly** *adv.* [OE *singan* f. Gmc]

■ *v.* **1, 2** chant, intone, carol, serenade, vocalize, trill, croon, pipe, chirp, warble; chorus; yodel. **3** whistle, peep, tootle; drone, hum, whir, purr, murmur; buzz. **5** tell, tattle, name names; confess; *colloq.* rat, blow the whistle, spill the beans, peach, *sl.* snitch, squeal. □□ **singer** vocalist, soloist, songster, crooner, chanteuse, nightingale, minstrel, troubadour, balladeer, caroler, chorister, choirboy, choir girl, choir member, chorus boy, chorus girl, chorus member.

sing. *abbr.* singular.

singe /sinj/ *v. & n.* ● *v.* (**singeing**) **1** *tr.* & *intr.* burn superficially or lightly. **2** *tr.* burn the bristles or down off (the carcass of a pig or fowl) to prepare it for cooking. **3** *tr.* burn off the tips of (the hair) in hairdressing. ● *n.* a superficial burn. □ **singe one's wings** suffer some harm esp. in a risky attempt. [OE *sencgan* f. WG]

■ *v.* char, blacken, sear, scorch, burn.

Singh /sing/ *n.* **1** a title adopted by the warrior castes of N. India. **2** a surname adopted by male Sikhs. [Hind. *singh* f. Skr. *sinhá* lion]

Singhalese var. of SINHALESE.

single /sínggəl/ *adj., n., & v.* ● *adj.* **1** one only; not double or multiple. **2** united or undivided. **3 a** designed or suitable for one person (*single room*). **b** used or done by one person, etc., or one set or pair. **4** one by itself; not one of several (*a single tree*). **5** regarded separately (*every single thing*). **6** not married. **7** *Brit.* (of a ticket) valid for a one-way trip only, not for the return. **8** (with *neg.* or *interrog.*) even one; not to speak of more (*did not see a single person*). **9** (of a flower) having only one circle of petals. **10** lonely; unaided. **11** *archaic* free from duplicity, sincere, consistent, guileless, ingenuous. ● *n.* **1** a single thing, or item in a series. **2** esp. *Brit.* a one-way ticket. **3 a** a recording with one piece of music, etc., on each side. **b** the piece of music, etc., on one side of a single. **4** *Baseball* a hit that allows the batter to reach first base safely. **5** *Cricket* a hit for one run. **6** (usu. *in pl.*) a game, esp. tennis, with one player on each side. **7** an unmarried person (*young singles*). **8** *sl.* a one-dollar note. ● *v.* **1** *tr.* (foll. by *out*) choose as an example or as distinguishable or to serve some purpose. **2** *intr. Baseball* hit a single. □ **single acrostic** see ACROSTIC. **single-acting** (of an engine, etc.) having pressure applied only to one side of the piston. **single-breasted** (of a coat, etc.) having only one set of buttons and buttonholes, not overlapping. **single combat** a duel. **single cream** *Brit.* thin cream with a relatively low fat content. **single-cut** (of a file) with grooves cut in one direction only, not crossing. **single-decker** esp. *Brit.* a bus having only one deck. **single entry** a system of bookkeeping in which each transaction is entered in one account only. **single file** a line of people or things arranged one behind another. **single-handed** *adv.* **1** without help from another.

2 with one hand. ● *adj.* **1** done, etc., single-handed. **2** for one hand. **single-handedly** in a single-handed way. **single-lens reflex** denoting a reflex camera in which a single lens serves the film and the viewfinder. **single-minded** having or intent on only one purpose. **single parent** a person bringing up a child or children without a partner. **singles bar** a bar for single people seeking company. **single-seater** a vehicle with one seat. □□ **singleness** *n.* **singly** *adv.* [ME f. OF f. L *singulus*, rel. to *simplus* SIMPLE]

▪ *adj.* **1, 4** one, only, sole, lone, unique, isolated, solitary; singular, individual, distinct. **5** separate, distinct, individual, solitary. **6** unmarried, unwed, unattached, free. **7** one-way. **10** alone, unaccompanied, unaided, unsupported; see also LONELY 1. ● *v.* **1** (*single out*) select, choose, pick (out), separate, target, take aside *or* apart, put aside *or* apart, set aside *or* apart, earmark, distinguish, cull, segregate, fix *or* fasten on. □ **single-handed** (*adv.*) **1** single-handedly, by oneself, alone, solo, on one's own, independently. (*adj.*) **1** solo, lone, solitary, independent, unaided, unassisted. **single-handedly** see *single-handed* (*adv.*) above. **single-minded** dedicated, devoted, resolute, steadfast, persevering, firm, determined, dogged, unswerving, unwavering, tireless, purposeful. □□ **singleness** bachelorhood, spinsterhood, celibacy; see also UNITY 1. **singly** one at a time, separately, individually, one by one, successively, one after the other, seriatim.

singlestick /sínggəlstik/ *n.* **1** a basket-hilted stick of about a sword's length. **2** one-handed fencing with this.

singlet /síngglit/ *n.* **1 a** a sleeveless athletic shirt. **b** *Brit.* a garment worn under or instead of a shirt; an undershirt. **2** a single unresolvable line in a spectrum. [SINGLE + -ET¹, after *doublet*, the garment being unlined]

singleton /sínggəltən/ *n.* **1** *Cards* one card only of a suit, esp. as dealt to a player. **2 a** a single person or thing. **b** an only child. **3** a single child or animal born, not a twin, etc. [SINGLE, after *simpleton*]

singletree /sínggəltree/ *n.* = WHIFFLETREE.

singsong /síngsawng, -song/ *adj., n.,* & *v.* ● *adj.* uttered with a monotonous rhythm or cadence. ● *n.* **1** a singsong manner. **2** *Brit.* an informal gathering for singing; a songfest. ● *v.intr.* & *tr.* (*past* and *past part.* **singsonged**) speak or recite in a singsong manner.

▪ *v.* see CHANT *v.* 1.

singular /síngyələr/ *adj.* & *n.* ● *adj.* **1** unique; much beyond the average; extraordinary. **2** eccentric or strange. **3** *Gram.* (of a word or form) denoting or referring to a single person or thing. **4** *Math.* possessing unique properties. **5** single; individual. ● *n. Gram.* **1** a singular word or form. **2** the singular number. □□ **singularly** *adv.* [ME f. OF *singuler* f. L *singularis* (as SINGLE)]

▪ *adj.* **1** unique, outstanding, prominent, eminent, preeminent, noteworthy, significant, important, conspicuous, particular, notable, signal, exceptional, superior, unparalleled, matchless, extraordinary, remarkable, special. **2** unusual, different, atypical, abnormal, eccentric, uncommon, strange, odd, peculiar, bizarre, outlandish, curious, queer, outré, offbeat, far-out. **5** lone, isolated, single, separate, uncommon, rare, unique, individual, distinct, one of a kind. □□ **singularly** see ESPECIALLY.

singularity /síngyəláritee/ *n.* (*pl.* **-ies**) **1** the state or condition of being singular. **2** an odd trait or peculiarity. **3** *Physics* & *Math.* a point at which a function takes an infinite value, esp. in space-time when matter is infinitely dense. [ME f. OF *singularité* f. LL *singularitas* (as SINGULAR)]

▪ **1** individuality, distinctiveness, uniqueness, strangeness, oddness, queerness, eccentricity, peculiarity, outlandishness, uncommonness. **2** idiosyncrasy, eccentricity, quirk, trait, foible, oddity, peculiarity, curiosity, kink.

singularize /síngyələriz/ *v.tr.* **1** distinguish; individualize. **2** make singular. □□ **singularization** *n.*

sinh /sinch, sináych/ *abbr. Math.* hyperbolic sine. [*sine* + *hyperbolic*]

Sinhalese /sínhəléez, sínə-/ *n.* & *adj.* (also **Singhalese** /síngə-/) ● *n.* (*pl.* same) **1** a member of a people originally from N. India and now forming the majority of the population of Sri Lanka. **2** an Indic language spoken by this people. ● *adj.* of or relating to this people or language. [Skr. *sinhalam* Sri Lanka (Ceylon) + -ESE]

sinister /sínistər/ *adj.* **1** suggestive of evil; looking malignant or villainous. **2** wicked or criminal (*a sinister motive*). **3** of evil omen. **4** *Heraldry* of or on the left-hand side of a shield, etc. (i.e., to the observer's right). **5** *archaic* left-hand. □□ **sinisterly** *adv.* **sinisterness** *n.* [ME f. OF *sinistre* or L *sinister* left]

▪ **1, 3** dark, gloomy, black; alarming, disquieting, frightening; fateful, inauspicious, unfavorable, forbidding, threatening, menacing, minatory, portentous, ominous, unpropitious, disastrous. **2** evil, bad, corrupt, base, malevolent, malignant, malign, harmful, pernicious, treacherous, nefarious, wicked, criminal, devilish, diabolic(al), satanic, infernal, baleful, villainous, insidious, sneaky, furtive, underhand(ed).

sinistral /sínistrəl/ *adj.* & *n.* ● *adj.* **1** left-handed. **2** of or on the left. **3** (of a flatfish) with the left side uppermost. **4** (of a spiral shell) with whorls rising to the left and not (as usually) to the right. ● *n.* a left-handed person. □□ **sinistrality** /-trálitee/ *n.* **sinistrally** *adv.*

▪ *adj.* **1** left-handed, *colloq.* southpaw. **2** see LEFT¹ *adj.*

sinistrorse /sínistrawrs/ *adj.* rising toward the left, esp. of the spiral stem of a plant. [L *sinistrorsus* f. *sinister* left + *versus* past part. of *vertere* turn]

sink /singk/ *v.* & *n.* ● *v.* (*past* **sank** /sangk/ or **sunk** /sungk/; *past part.* **sunk** or **sunken**) **1** *intr.* fall or come slowly downward. **2** *intr.* disappear below the horizon (*the sun is sinking*). **3** *intr.* **a** go or penetrate below the surface esp. of a liquid. **b** (of a ship) go to the bottom of the sea, etc. **4** *intr.* settle down comfortably (*sank into a chair*). **5** *intr.* **a** gradually lose strength or value or quality, etc.; decline (*my heart sank*). **b** (of the voice) descend in pitch or volume. **c** (of a sick person) approach death. **6** *tr.* send (a ship) to the bottom of the sea, etc. **7** *tr.* cause or allow to sink or penetrate (*sank its teeth into my leg*). **8** *tr.* cause the failure of (a plan, etc.) or the discomfiture of (a person). **9** *tr.* dig (a well) or bore (a shaft). **10** *tr.* engrave (a die) or inlay (a design). **11** *tr.* **a** invest (money) (*sunk a large sum into the business*). **b** lose (money) by investment. **12** *tr.* **a** cause (a ball) to enter a pocket in billiards, a hole at golf, etc. **b** achieve this by (a stroke). **13** *tr.* overlook or forget; keep in the background (*sank their differences*). **14** *intr.* (of a price, etc.) become lower. **15** *intr.* (of a storm or river) subside. **16** *intr.* (of ground) slope down, or reach a lower level by subsidence. **17** *intr.* (foll. by *on, upon*) (of darkness) descend (on a place). **18** *tr.* lower the level of. **19** *tr.* (usu. in *passive*; foll. by *in*) absorb; hold the attention of (*be sunk in thought*). ● *n.* **1** a fixed basin with a water supply and outflow pipe. **2** a place where foul liquid collects. **3** a place of vice or corruption. **4** a pool or marsh in which a river's water disappears by evaporation or percolation. **5** *Physics* a body or process used to absorb or dissipate heat. **6** = SINKHOLE. □ **sink in 1** penetrate or make its way in. **2** become gradually comprehended (*paused to let the words sink in*). **sinking feeling** a bodily sensation caused by hunger or apprehension. **sinking fund** money set aside for the gradual repayment of a debt. **sink or swim** even at the risk of complete failure (*determined to try, sink or swim*). □□ **sinkable** *adj.* **sinkage** *n.* [OE *sincan* f. Gmc]

▪ *v.* **1** descend, go down *or* downward(s), drop, fall, move down *or* downward(s), come down *or* downward(s); sag, droop, slump; settle, precipitate. **2** set, go down, go lower, descend, decline, drop; disappear, vanish, fade away, *poet.* droop. **3** become submerged, go down, go under, plunge, descend, be engulfed, dive; see also FOUNDER² *v.* 1a. **5 a, c** decline, weaken, worsen, degenerate, subside, deteriorate, dwindle, flag, ebb, wane, fail, diminish, slip, fade (away), waste (away), die, expire; languish; *colloq.* go downhill. **6** scupper, scuttle. **7** submerge, immerse, plunge, dig. **8** see WRECK *v.* 2, FOIL¹ *v.* 1. **9** bore, put down, drill, dig, excavate, drive. **11 a** invest, venture, risk, put. **12 a** pocket; hole. **15** see SUBSIDE 1, 4. **16** subside, cave in, collapse, settle, drop, fall in, go down, slip away. **19** see IMMERSE 2. ● *n.* **1** basin, washbasin, washbowl, lavabo; *Ch.* font, stoup, piscina. **3** cesspool, cesspit, pit, hellhole, den of iniquity, *colloq.* dive. □ **sink in 1** (*sink into*) seep in, soak in, permeate; see also PENETRATE 1b. **2** be absorbed, be understood, penetrate, register, make an impression, get through.

sinker /síngkər/ *n.* **1 a** weight used to sink a fishing line or sounding line. **2** *Baseball* (in full **sinkerball**) pitch thrown so that it curves sharply downward. **3** *colloq.* a doughnut.
■ **1** see PLUMB¹ *n.*

sinkhole /síngkhōl/ *n. Geol.* a cavity in limestone, etc., into which a stream, etc., disappears.
■ sink, *Brit.* sink-hole.

sinner /sínər/ *n.* a person who sins, esp. habitually.
■ transgressor, wrongdoer, miscreant, offender, evildoer, malefactor, reprobate, *literary or archaic* trespasser.

sinnet var. of SENNIT.

Sinn Fein /shin fáyn/ *n.* a political movement and party seeking a united republican Ireland, often linked to the IRA.
□□ **Sinn Feiner** *n.* [Ir. *sinn féin* we ourselves]

Sino- /síno/ *comb. form* Chinese; Chinese and (*Sino-American*). [Gk *Sinai* the Chinese]

sinologue /sínəlawg, -log, sín-/ *n.* an expert in sinology; sinologist. [F, formed as SINO- + Gk -*logos* speaking]

sinology /sīnóləjee, sin-/ *n.* the study of Chinese language, history, customs, etc. □□ **sinological** /-nəlójikəl/ *adj.* **sinologist** *n.*

sinter /síntər/ *n. & v.* ● *n.* **1 a** siliceous or calcareous rock formed by deposition from springs. **2** a substance formed by sintering. ● *v.intr. & tr.* coalesce or cause to coalesce from powder into solid by heating. [G, = E *sinder* CINDER]

sinuate /sínyooət, -ayt/ *adj. esp. Bot.* wavy-edged; with distinct inward and outward bends along the edge. [L *sinuatus* past part. of *sinuare* bend]

sinuosity /sínyoo-ósitee/ *n.* (*pl.* -**ies**) **1** the state of being sinuous. **2** a bend, esp. in a stream or road. [F *sinuosité* or med.L *sinuositas* (as SINUOUS)]
■ **2** see TURN *n.* 4.

sinuous /sínyooəs/ *adj.* with many curves; tortuous; undulating. □□ **sinuously** *adv.* **sinuousness** *n.* [F *sinueux* or L *sinuosus* (as SINUS)]
■ see TORTUOUS 1.

sinus /sínəs/ *n.* **1** a cavity of bone or tissue, esp. in the skull connecting with the nostrils. **2** *Med.* a fistula esp. to a deep abscess. **3** *Bot.* the curve between the lobes of a leaf. [L, = bosom, recess]

sinusitis /sínəsítis/ *n.* inflammation of a nasal sinus.

sinusoid /sínəsoyd/ *n.* **1** a curve having the form of a sine wave. **2** a small irregular-shaped blood vessel, esp. found in the liver. □□ **sinusoidal** /-sóyd'l/ *adj.* [F *sinusoïde* f. L *sinus*: see SINUS]

Sion var. of ZION.

-sion /shən, zhən/ *suffix* forming nouns (see -ION) from Latin participial stems in -*s*- (*mansion; mission; persuasion*).

Sioux /soō/ *n. & adj.* ● *n.* (*pl.* same) **1** a member of a group of native N. American peoples, also called Dakota. **2** the language of this group. ● *adj.* of or relating to this people or language. □□ **Siouan** /soōən/ *adj. & n.* [F f. a native name]

sip /sip/ *v. & n.* ● *v.tr. & intr.* (**sipped**, **sipping**) drink in one or more small amounts or by spoonfuls. ● *n.* **1** a small mouthful of liquid (*a sip of brandy*). **2** the act of taking this. □□ **sipper** *n.* [ME: perh. a modification of SUP¹]
■ *v.* taste, sample, sup. ● *n.* taste, sample, soupçon, drop, bit, mouthful, spoonful, thimbleful, nip, dram; sup, swallow, draft, drink, *colloq.* swig.

siphon /sífən/ *n. & v.* (also **syphon**) ● *n.* **1** a pipe or tube shaped like an inverted V or U with unequal legs to convey a liquid from a container to a lower level by atmospheric pressure. **2** (in full **siphon bottle**) an aerated-water bottle

from which liquid is forced out through a tube by the pressure of gas. **3** *Zool.* **a** a canal or conduit esp. in cephalopods. **b** the sucking tube of some insects, etc. ● *v.tr. & intr.* (often foll. by *off*) **1** conduct or flow through a siphon. **2** divert or set aside (funds, etc.). □□ **siphonage** *n.* **siphonal** *adj.* **siphonic** /-fónik/ *adj.* [F *siphon* or L *sipho -onis* f. Gk *siphōn* pipe]
■ *v.* **1** see PUMP¹ *v.* 1, 3a, 5. **2** see DIVERT 1a.

siphonophore /sifónəfawr/ *n.* any usu. translucent marine hydrozoan of the order Siphonophora, e.g., the Portuguese man-of-war. [Gk *siphōno-* (as SIPHON, -PHORE)]

sippet /sípit/ *n.* **1** a small piece of bread, etc., soaked in liquid. **2** a piece of toast or fried bread as a garnish. **3** a fragment. [app. dimin. of SOP]

sir /sər/ *n.* **1** a polite or respectful form of address or mode of reference to a man. **2** (**Sir**) a titular prefix to the forename of a knight or baronet. [ME, reduced form of SIRE]

sirdar /sərdaar/ *n. Ind.*, etc. **1** a person of high political or military rank. **2** a Sikh. [Urdu *sardār* f. Pers. *sar* head + *dār* possessor]

sire /sīr/ *n. & v.* ● *n.* **1** the male parent of an animal, esp. a stallion kept for breeding. **2** *archaic* a respectful form of address, now esp. to a king. **3** *archaic poet.* a father or male ancestor. ● *v.tr.* (esp. of a stallion) beget. [ME f. OF ult. f. L *senior*: see SENIOR]
■ *n.* **1** father, progenitor. ● *v.* see FATHER *v.* 1.

siren /sírən/ *n.* **1 a** a device for making a loud prolonged signal or warning sound, esp. by revolving a perforated disk over a jet of compressed air or steam. **b** the sound made by this. **2** (in Greek mythology) each of a number of women or winged creatures whose singing lured unwary sailors onto rocks. **3** a sweet singer. **4 a** a dangerously fascinating woman; a temptress. **b** a tempting pursuit, etc. **5** (*attrib.*) irresistibly tempting. **6** an eel-shaped tailed amphibian of the family Sirenidae. [ME f. OF *sereine, sirene* f. LL *Sirena* fem. f. L f. Gk *Seirēn*]
■ **1** whistle, horn, foghorn; signal, alarm, warning, alert, tocsin. **4 a** temptress, seductress, enchantress, charmer, sorceress, femme fatale, Circe, *colloq.* vamp.

sirenian /sīreéneeən/ *adj. & n.* ● *adj.* of the order Sirenia of large aquatic plant-eating mammals, e.g., the manatee and dugong. ● *n.* any mammal of this order. [mod.L *Sirenia* (as SIREN)]

sirloin /sərloyn/ *n.* the upper and choicer part of a loin of beef. [OF (as SUR-¹, LOIN)]

sirocco /siróko/ *n.* (also **scirocco**) (*pl.* -**os**) **1** a Saharan simoom reaching the northern shores of the Mediterranean. **2** a warm sultry rainy wind in S. Europe. [F f. It. *scirocco*, ult. f. Arab. *S'arūk* east wind]
■ **1** see STORM *n.* 1.

sirrah /sírə/ *n. archaic* = SIR (as a form of address). [prob. f. ME *sīrĕ* SIR]

sirree /sireé/ *int. colloq.* as an emphatic, esp. after *yes* or *no*. [SIR + emphatic suffix]

sirup var. of SYRUP.

sis /sis/ *n. colloq.* a sister. [abbr.]

sisal /sísəl/ *n.* **1** a Mexican plant, *Agave sisalana*, with large fleshy leaves. **2** the fiber made from this plant, used for cordage, ropes, etc. [*Sisal*, the port of Yucatan, Mexico]

siskin /sískin/ *n.* a dark-streaked, yellowish-green songbird, *Carduelis spinus*, allied to the goldfinch. [MDu. *siseken* dimin., rel. to MLG *sīsek*, MHG *zīse, zīsec*, of Slav. origin]

sissy /sísee/ *n. & adj.* (also *Brit.* **cissy**) *colloq.* ● *n.* (*pl.* -**ies**) an effeminate or cowardly person. ● *adj.* (**sissier, sissiest**) effeminate; cowardly. □□ **sissified** *adj.* **sissiness** *n.* **sissyish** *adj.* [SIS + -Y²]
■ *n.* milksop, namby-pamby, weakling, coward, baby, crybaby, mollycoddle, *colloq.* softy, mama's boy, *Brit. colloq.* wet, mummy's boy, *Austral. & NZ sl.* derog.

/.../ **pronunciation**	● **part of speech**
□ **phrases, idioms, and compounds**	
□□ **derivatives**	■ **synonym section**
cross-references appear in SMALL CAPITALS or *italics*	

sook. ● *adj.* see EFFEMINATE, SOFT *adj.* 11b.
□□ **sissified** see SOFT *adj.* 11b.

sister /sístər/ *n.* **1** a woman or girl in relation to sons and other daughters of her parents. **2 a** (often as a form of address) a close female friend or associate. **b** a female fellow member of a trade union, class, sect, or the human race. **3** a member of a female religious order. **4** (*attrib.*) of the same type or design or origin, etc. (*sister ship*; *prose, the younger sister of verse*). **5** *Brit.* a senior female nurse. □ **sister german** see GERMAN. **sister-in-law** (*pl.* **sisters-in-law**) **1** the sister of one's wife or husband. **2** the wife of one's brother. **3** the wife of one's brother-in-law. **Sister of Mercy** a member of an educational or charitable order of women, esp. that founded in Dublin in 1827. **sister uterine** see UTERINE. □□ **sisterless** *adj.* **sisterly** *adj.* **sisterliness** *n.* [ME *sister* (f. ON), *suster*, etc. (repr. OE *sweoster* f. Gmc)]
■ **2** see INTIMATE¹ *n.* **5** see ASSOCIATE *adj.* 2.

sisterhood /sístərhŏŏd/ *n.* **1 a** the relationship between sisters. **b** sisterly friendliness; companionship; mutual support. **2 a** a society or association of women, esp. when bound by monastic vows or devoting themselves to religious or charitable work or to the feminist cause. **b** its members collectively.
■ **1** see LOVE *n.* 1. **2** see SOCIETY 8.

Sistine /sísteen, sisteén/ *adj.* of any of the Popes called Sixtus, esp. Sixtus IV. □ **Sistine Chapel** a chapel in the Vatican, with frescoes by Michelangelo and other painters. [It. *Sistino* f. *Sisto* Sixtus]

sistrum /sístrəm/ *n.* (*pl.* **sistra** /-trə/) a jingling metal instrument used by the ancient Egyptians esp. in the worship of Isis. [ME f. L f. Gk *seistron* f. *seiō* shake]
■ rattle, noisemaker.

Sisyphean /sísifeéən/ *adj.* (of toil) endless and fruitless like that of Sisyphus in Greek mythology (whose task in Hades was to push uphill a stone that at once rolled down again).
■ see BOOTLESS.

sit /sit/ *v. & n.* ● *v.* (**sitting**; *past* and *past part.* **sat** /sat/) **1** *intr.* adopt or be in a position in which the body is supported more or less upright by the buttocks resting on the ground or a raised seat, etc., with the thighs usu. horizontal. **2** *tr.* cause to sit; place in a sitting position. **3** *intr.* **a** (of a bird) perch. **b** (of an animal) rest with the hind legs bent and the body close to the ground. **4** *intr.* (of a bird) remain on its nest to hatch its eggs. **5** *intr.* **a** be engaged in an occupation in which the sitting position is usual. **b** (of a committee, legislative body, etc.) be engaged in business. **c** (of an individual) be entitled to hold some office or position (*sat as a magistrate*). **6** *intr.* (usu. foll. by *for*) pose in a sitting position (for a portrait). **7** *intr.* (foll. by *for*) *Brit.* be a member of Parliament for (a constituency). **8** *tr.* & (foll. by *for*) *intr. Brit.* be a candidate for (an examination). **9** *intr.* be in a more or less permanent position or condition (esp. of inactivity or being out of use or out of place). **10** *intr.* (of clothes, etc.) fit or hang in a certain way. **11** *tr.* keep or have one's seat on (a horse, etc.). **12** *intr.* act as a babysitter. **13** *intr.* (often foll. by *before*) (of an army) take a position outside a city, etc., to besiege it. **14** *tr.* = SEAT *v.* 2a. ● *n.* the way a dress, etc., sits on a person. □ **be sitting pretty** be comfortably or advantageously placed. **make a person sit up** *colloq.* surprise or interest a person. **sit at a person's feet** be a person's pupil. **sit at home** be inactive. **sit back** relax one's efforts. **sit by** look on without interfering. **sit down 1** sit after standing. **2** cause to sit. **3** *Brit.* (foll. by *under*) submit tamely to (an insult, etc.). **sit-down** *adj.* (of a meal) eaten sitting at a table. **sit-down strike** a strike in which workers refuse to leave their place of work. **sit in 1** occupy a place as a protest. **2** (foll. by *for*) take the place of. **3** (foll. by *on*) be present as a guest or observer at (a meeting, etc.). **sit-in** *n.* a protest involving sitting in. **sit in judgment** assume the right of judging others; be censorious. **sit loosely on** not be very binding. **sit on 1** be a member of (a committee, etc.). **2** hold a session or inquiry concerning. **3** *colloq.* delay action about (*the government has been sitting on the report*). **4** *colloq.* repress or rebuke or snub (*felt rather sat on*). **sit on the fence** see FENCE. **sit on one's hands 1** take no action. **2** refuse to applaud. **sit out 1** take no part in (a dance, etc.).

2 stay till the end of (esp. an ordeal). **3** esp. *Brit.* sit outdoors. **4** *Brit.* outstay (other visitors). **sit tight** *colloq.* **1** remain firmly in one's place. **2** not be shaken off or move away or yield to distractions. **sit up 1** rise from a lying to a sitting position. **2** sit firmly upright. **3** go to bed later than the usual time. **4** *colloq.* become interested or aroused, etc. **sit-up** *n.* a physical exercise in which a person sits up without raising the legs from the ground. **sit up and take notice** *colloq.* have one's interest aroused, esp. suddenly. **sit-upon** *Brit. colloq.* the buttocks. **sit well** esp. *Brit.* have a good seat in riding. **sit well on** esp. *Brit.* suit or fit. [OE *sittan* f. Gmc]
■ *v.* **1** be *or* get seated, settle, sit down, take a seat, rest, perch, *colloq.* take the weight off one's feet. **2** seat, sit down, install, ensconce, place, put. **3 a** perch, nest, roost, rest. **4** brood, incubate. **5 b** hold a session, be in session, assemble, meet, convene; gather, get together, congregate. **6** pose, model. **9** remain, stay, lie, rest; relax, mark time, *archaic* abide, *literary* dwell. **10** fit, hang; seem, appear, look. □ **sit back** see RELAX *v.* 1c, 4. **sit-down strike** see STRIKE *n.* 2. **sit in 2** (*sit in for*) substitute for, fill in for, stand in for, double for, take the place of, cover for, deputize for, *colloq.* sub for. **3** (*sit in on*) observe, watch, be present at, attend; join in, participate in, take part in. **sit-in** see DEMONSTRATION 2. **sit on 1** have *or* hold *or* occupy a seat on, participate in, be a member of. **sit out 2** wait out, last through, live through. **4** outwait, outstay, outlast, outlive. **sit tight** wait, hang back, hold back, be patient, bide one's time, play a waiting game, take no action, delay, temporize, *colloq.* hold one's horses. **sit up 4** awaken, pay attention, notice, take notice, become alert *or* interested *or* concerned, *colloq.* sit up and take notice. **sit well on** sit well *or* right (with), suit, fit, befit, look good *or* well on, become, agree with, be agreeable to.

sitar /sitaár, sítaar/ *n.* a long-necked E. Indian lute with movable frets. □□ **sitarist** /sitaárist/ *n.* [Hindi *sitār*]

sitcom /sítkom/ *n. colloq.* a situation comedy. [abbr.]

site /sit/ *n. & v.* ● *n.* **1** the ground chosen or used for a town or building. **2** a place where some activity is or has been conducted (*camping site*; *launching site*). ● *v.tr.* **1** locate or place. **2** provide with a site. [ME f. AF *site* or L *situs* local position]
■ *n.* location, place, plot, ground, spot, setting, locale, area, milieu, neighborhood, locality, purlieu, placement, position; situation, orientation, plat.
● *v.* locate, position, place, put, situate, install.

Sitka /sítkə/ *n.* (in full **Sitka spruce**) a fast-growing spruce, *Picea sitchensis*, native to N. America and yielding timber. [*Sitka* in Alaska]

sitrep /sítrep/ *n. Brit.* a report on the current military situation in an area. [situation *rep*ort]

sits vac /sits vák/ *abbr. Brit.* situations vacant, i.e., work available.

sitter /sítər/ *n.* **1** = baby-sitter (see BABY). **2** a person who sits, esp. for a portrait. **3** *Brit. colloq.* **a** an easy catch or shot. **b** an easy task. **4** a sitting hen. **5** *colloq.* the buttocks.
■ **2** model, subject, poser.

sitting /síting/ *n. & adj.* ● *n.* **1** a continuous period of being seated, esp. engaged in an activity (*finished the book in one sitting*). **2** a time during which an assembly is engaged in business. **3** a session in which a meal is served (*dinner will be served in two sittings*). **4** *Brit. Law* = TERM 5c. **5** a clutch of eggs. ● *adj.* **1** having sat down. **2** (of an animal or bird) not running or flying. **3** (of a hen) engaged in hatching. □ **sitting duck** (*or* **target**) *colloq.* a vulnerable person or thing. **sitting pretty** see PRETTY. **sitting room 1** esp. *Brit.* a room in a house for relaxed sitting in; living room. **2** space enough to accommodate seated persons.
■ *n.* **2** see SESSION 1, 2. ● *adj.* **1** sedentary, seated.
□ **sitting room 1** see PARLOR.

situate *v. & adj.* ● *v.tr.* /síchŏŏ-ayt/ (usu. in *passive*) **1** put in a certain position or circumstances (*is situated at the top of a hill*; *how are you situated at the moment?*). **2** establish or indicate the place of; put in a context. ● *adj.* /síchŏŏət/ *Law* or *archaic* situated. [med.L *situare situat-* f. L *situs* site]

■ *v.* **1** place in a position *or* situation *or* location, place, position, locate, set, site, spot, put, install.

situation /síchoo-áyshən/ *n.* **1** a place and its surroundings (*the house stands in a fine situation*). **2** a set of circumstances; a position in which one finds oneself; a state of affairs (*came out of a difficult situation with credit*). **3** an employee's position or job. **4** a critical point or complication in a drama. □ **situation comedy 1** a comedy in which the humor derives from the situations the characters are placed in. **2** a television series featuring such humor. **situations vacant** (or **wanted**) esp. *Brit.* lists of employment offered and sought. □□ **situational** *adj.* [ME f. F *situation* or med.L *situatio* (as SITUATE)]

■ **1** place, position, location, spot, site, locale, setting. **2** state (of affairs *or* things *or* play), condition, circumstances, case, status (quo), lie of the land, picture; plight, predicament, kettle of fish; *colloq.* ball game. **3** position, place, job, employment, post, *colloq.* berth, billet.

sitz bath /sítsbath, zíts-/ *n.* **1** a usu. portable bath in which a person sits. **2** the bath taken by such means. [partial transl. of G *Sitzbad* f. *sitzen* sit + *Bad* bath]

Siva /seévə, sheévə/ *n.* (also **Shiva** /sheévə/) a Hindu deity associated with the powers of reproduction and dissolution, regarded by some as the supreme being and by others as a member of the triad. □□ **Sivaism** *n.* **Sivaite** *n.* & *adj.* [Skr. *Śiva,* lit. the auspicious one]

six /siks/ *n.* & *adj.* ● *n.* **1** one more than five, or four less than ten; the product of two units and three units. **2** a symbol for this (6, vi, VI). **3** a size, etc., denoted by six. **4** a set or team of six individuals. **5** *Cricket* a hit scoring six runs by clearing the boundary without bouncing. **6** the time of six o'clock (*is it six yet?*). **7** a card, etc., with six pips. ● *adj.* that amount to six. □ **at sixes and sevens** in confusion or disagreement. **knock for six** *Brit. colloq.* utterly surprise or overcome (a person). **six-gun** = *six-shooter.* **six of one and half a dozen of the other** a situation of little real difference between the alternatives. **six-pack** six cans or bottles, as of beer, a soft drink, etc., packaged and sold as a unit. **six-shooter** a revolver with six chambers. [OE *siex,* etc. f. Gmc]

■ □ **at sixes and sevens** see *chaotic* (CHAOS).

sixain /síksayn/ *n.* a six-line stanza. [F f. *six* six]

sixfold /síksfōld/ *adj.* & *adv.* **1** six times as much or as many. **2** consisting of six parts.

sixpence /síkspəns/ *n. Brit.* **1** the sum of six pence, esp. before decimalization. **2** *hist.* a coin worth six old pence. □ **turn on a sixpence** *colloq.* make a sharp turn in a motor vehicle.

sixpenny /síkspənee, -penee/ *adj. Brit.* costing or worth six pence, esp. before decimalization.

sixte /síkst/ *n. Fencing* the sixth of the eight parrying positions. [F f. L *sextus* sixth]

sixteen /síksteén/ *n.* & *adj.* ● *n.* **1** one more than fifteen, or six more than ten. **2** a symbol for this (16, xvi, XVI). **3** a size, etc., denoted by sixteen. ● *adj.* that amount to sixteen. □ **sixteenth note** *Mus.* a note having the time value of one-sixteenth of a whole note and represented by a large dot with a two-hooked stem. □□ **sixteenth** *adj.* & *n.* [OE *siextiene* (as SIX, -TEEN)]

sixteenmo /síksteénmō/ *n.* (*pl.* **-os**) sextodecimo. [English reading of the symbol 16mo]

sixth /siksth/ *n.* & *adj.* ● *n.* **1** the position in a sequence corresponding to that of the number 6 in the sequence 1–6. **2** something occupying this position. **3** any of six equal parts of a thing. **4** *Mus.* **a** an interval or chord spanning six consecutive notes in the diatonic scale (e.g., C to A). **b** a note separated from another by this interval. ● *adj.* that is the sixth. □ **sixth sense 1** a supposed faculty giving intuitive or extrasensory knowledge. **2** such knowledge. □□ **sixthly** *adv.* [SIX]

■ □ **sixth sense** see INTUITION.

Sixtine /síksteen, -tīn/ *adj.* = SISTINE. [mod.L *Sixtinus* f. *Sixtus*]

sixty /síkstee/ *n.* & *adj.* ● *n.* (*pl.* **-ies**) **1** the product of six and ten. **2** a symbol for this (60, lx, LX). **3** (in *pl.*) the

numbers from 60 to 69, esp. the years of a century or of a person's life. **4** a set of sixty persons or things. ● *adj.* that amount to sixty. □ **sixty-first, -second,** etc., the ordinal numbers between sixtieth and seventieth. **sixty-fourmo** /síksteefáwrmō/ (*pl.* **-os**) **1** a size of book in which each leaf is one-sixty-fourth of a printing-sheet. **2** a book of this size (*after* DUODECIMO, etc.). **sixty-fourth note** *Mus.* a note having the time value of one-sixty-fourth of a whole note and represented by a large dot with a four-hooked stem. **sixty-four thousand** (or **sixty-four**) **dollar question** a difficult and crucial question (from the top prize in a broadcast quiz show). **sixty-nine** sexual activity between two people involving mutual oral stimulation of the genitals. **sixty-one, -two,** etc., the cardinal numbers between sixty and seventy. □□ **sixtieth** *adj.* & *n.* **sixtyfold** *adj.* & *adv.* [OE *siextig* (as SIX, -TY²)]

sizable /sízəbəl/ *adj.* (also **sizeable**) large or fairly large. □□ **sizably** *adv.*

■ see LARGE *adj.* 1, 2.

sizar /sízər/ *n.* a student at Cambridge or at Trinity College, Dublin, paying reduced fees and formerly having certain menial duties. □□ **sizarship** *n.* [SIZE¹ = ration]

size¹ /sīz/ *n.* & *v.* ● *n.* **1** the relative bigness or extent of a thing; dimensions; magnitude (*is of vast size; size matters less than quality*). **2** each of the classes, usu. numbered, into which things otherwise similar, esp. garments, are divided according to size (*is made in several sizes; takes size 7 in gloves; is three sizes too big*). ● *v.tr.* sort or group in sizes or according to size. □ **of a size** having the same size. **of some size** fairly large. **the size of** as big as. **the size of it** *colloq.* a true account of the matter (*that is the size of it*). **size up 1** estimate the size of. **2** *colloq.* form a judgment of. **what size?** how big? □□ **sized** *adj.* (also in *comb.*). **sizer** *n.* [ME f. OF *sise* f. *assise* ASSIZE, or f. ASSIZE]

■ *n.* **1** magnitude, largeness, bigness, bulk, extent, scope, range, dimensions, proportions, measurement(s), expanse, area, square footage, volume, capacity, mass, weight; breadth, width, length, height, depth; amount; hugeness, immensity, greatness, vastness, enormousness. ● *v.* see SORT *v.* □ **size up 1** see ESTIMATE *v.* 1–3. **2** assess, judge, evaluate, measure, take the measure of, appraise, assay, make an estimate of, estimate, value, gauge, rate.

size² /sīz/ *n.* & *v.* ● *n.* a gelatinous solution used in glazing paper, stiffening textiles, preparing plastered walls for decoration, etc. ● *v.tr.* glaze or stiffen or treat with size. [ME, perh. = SIZE¹]

sizeable var. of SIZABLE.

sizzle /sízəl/ *v.* & *n.* ● *v.intr.* **1** make a sputtering or hissing sound as of frying. **2** *colloq.* be in a state of great heat or excitement or marked effectiveness. ● *n.* **1** a sizzling sound. **2** *colloq.* a state of great heat or excitement. □□ **sizzler** *n.* **sizzling** *adj.* & *adv.* (*sizzling hot*). [imit.]

■ *v.* **1** see FIZZ *v.* 1. **2** see BOIL¹ *v.* 3b. □□ **sizzling** (*adj.*) see HOT *adj.* 1.

SJ *abbr.* Society of Jesus.

sjambok /shámbok/ *n.* & *v.* ● *n.* (in S. Africa) a rhinoceros-hide whip. ● *v.tr.* flog with a sjambok. [Afrik. f. Malay *samboq, chambok* f. Urdu *chābuk*]

skald /skawld/ *n.* (also **scald**) (in ancient Scandinavia) a composer and reciter of poems honoring heroes and their deeds. □□ **skaldic** *adj.* [ON *skáld,* of unkn. orig.]

■ see MINSTREL.

skat /skat/ *n.* a three-handed card game with bidding. [G f. It. *scarto* a discard f. *scartare* discard]

skate¹ /skayt/ *n.* & *v.* ● *n.* **1** each of a pair of steel blades (or of boots with blades attached) for gliding on ice. **2** (in full **roller skate**) each of a pair of metal frames with small wheels, fitted to shoes for riding on a hard surface. **3** a device

/.../	pronunciation	●	part of speech
□	phrases, idioms, and compounds		
□□	derivatives	■	synonym section
cross-references appear in SMALL CAPITALS or *italics*			

on which a heavy object moves. • v. **1 a** *intr.* move on skates. **b** *tr.* perform (a specified figure) on skates. **2** *intr.* (foll. by *over*) refer fleetingly to; disregard. □ **get one's skates on** *Brit. sl.* make haste. **skate on thin ice** *colloq.* behave rashly; risk danger, esp. by dealing with a subject needing tactful treatment. **skating rink** a piece of ice artificially made, or a floor used, for skating. □□ **skater** *n.* [orig. *scates* (pl.) f. Du. *schaats* (sing.) f. ONF *escace*, OF *eschasse* stilt]

■ v. **1 a** see SLIDE v. 1, 2. □ **skate on thin ice** see *sail close to the wind.*

skate[2] /skayt/ *n.* (*pl.* same or **skates**) any ray of the family Rajidae, esp. *Raja batis*, a large, flat, rhomboidal fish used as food. [ME f. ON *skata*]

skate[3] /skayt/ *n. sl.* a contemptible, mean, or dishonest person (esp. *cheap skate*). [19th c.: orig. uncert.]

skateboard /skáytbawrd/ *n. & v.* • *n.* a short narrow board on roller-skate wheels for riding on while standing. • *v.intr.* ride on a skateboard. □□ **skateboarder** *n.*

skean /skeen, skeé·ən/ *n. hist.* a Gaelic dagger formerly used in Ireland and Scotland. □ **skean-dhu** /-dōō/ *n.* a dagger worn in the stocking as part of Highland costume. [Gael. *sgian* knife, *dubh* black]

■ see DAGGER.

sked /sked/ *n. & v.* esp. *Brit. colloq.* • *n.* = SCHEDULE *n.* • *v.tr.* (**skedded, skedding**) = SCHEDULE *v.* [abbr.]

skedaddle /skidád'l/ *v. & n. colloq.* • *v.intr.* run away; depart quickly; flee. • *n.* a hurried departure or flight. [19th c.: orig. unkn.]

■ v. see FLEE 1.

skeet /skeet/ *n.* a shooting sport in which a clay target is thrown from a trap to simulate the flight of a bird. [ON *skjóta* SHOOT]

skeeter[1] /skeétər/ *n. US dial., Austral. sl.* a mosquito. [abbr.]

skeeter[2] var. of SKITTER.

skeg /skeg/ *n.* **1** a fin underneath the rear of a surfboard. **2** the after part of a vessel's keel or a projection from it. [ON *skeg* beard, perh. via Du. *scheg(ge)*]

skein /skayn/ *n.* **1** a loosely-coiled bundle of yarn or thread. **2** a flock of wild geese, etc., in flight. **3** a tangle or confusion. [ME f. OF *escaigne*, of unkn. orig.]

■ **2** see FLIGHT[1] *n.* 3a. **3** see TANGLE[1] *n.* 1.

skeleton /skélit'n/ *n.* **1 a** a hard internal or external framework of bones, cartilage, shell, woody fiber, etc., supporting or containing the body of an animal or plant. **b** the dried bones of a human being or other animal fastened together in the same relative positions as in life. **2** the supporting framework or structure or essential part of a thing. **3** a very thin or emaciated person or animal. **4** the remaining part of anything after its life or usefulness is gone. **5** an outline sketch; an epitome or abstract. **6** (*attrib.*) having only the essential or minimum number of persons, parts, etc. (*skeleton plan; skeleton staff*). □ **skeleton at the feast** something that spoils one's pleasure; an intrusive worry. **skeleton in the closet** (or esp. *Brit.* **cupboard**) a discreditable or embarrassing fact kept secret. **skeleton key** a key designed to fit many locks by having the interior of the bit hollowed. □□ **skeletal** *adj.* **skeletally** *adv.* **skeletonize** *v.tr.* [mod.L f. Gk, neut. of *skeletos* dried-up f. *skellō* dry up]

■ **1 a** see FRAME *n.* 4. **2** see FRAME *n.* 2. **5** see OUTLINE *n.* 1, 2. □ **skeleton in the closet** (or esp. *Brit.* **cupboard**) see SCANDAL 1a. **skeleton key** key, passkey, opener. □□ **skeletal** see *emaciated* (EMACIATE).

skep /skep/ *n.* **1 a** a wooden or wicker basket of any of various forms. **b** the quantity contained in this. **2** a straw or wicker beehive. [ME f. ON *skeppa*]

skepsis /sképsis/ *n.* (*Brit.* **scepsis**) **1** philosophic doubt. **2** skeptical philosophy. [Gk *skepsis* inquiry, doubt f. *skeptomai* consider]

■ Pyrrhonism; see also *skepticism* (SKEPTIC).

skeptic /sképtik/ *n. & adj.* (*Brit.* **sceptic**) • *n.* **1** a person inclined to doubt all accepted opinions; a cynic. **2** a person who doubts the truth of Christianity and other religions. **3** *hist.* a person who accepts the philosophy of Pyrrhonism.

• *adj.* = SKEPTICAL. □□ **skepticism** /-tisizəm/ *n.* [F *sceptique* or L *scepticus* f. Gk *skeptikos* (as SCEPSIS)]

■ *n.* **1** doubter, questioner, doubting Thomas, Pyrrhonist, scoffer, cynic. **2** disbeliever, nullifidian, agnostic, dissenter; see also INFIDEL *n.* □□ **skepticism** doubt, dubiousness, doubtfulness, skepsis, Pyrrhonism, disbelief, unbelief, incredulity, incredulousness, cynicism, mistrust, distrust, mistrustfulness, distrustfulness, *literary* dubiety; agnosticism.

skeptical /sképtikəl/ *adj.* (*Brit.* **sceptical**) **1** inclined to question the truth or soundness of accepted ideas, facts, etc.; critical; incredulous. **2** *Philos.* of or accepting the philosophy of Pyrrhonism, denying the possibility of knowledge. □□ **skeptically** *adv.*

■ **1** doubting, dubious, doubtful, questioning, critical, incredulous, scoffing, cynical, mistrustful, distrustful, disbelieving; agnostic.

skerrick /skérik/ *n.* (usu. with *neg.*) *Austral. colloq.* the smallest bit (*not a skerrick left*). [No. of Engl. dial.; orig. uncert.]

skerry /skéree/ *n.* (*pl.* **-ies**) *Sc.* a reef or rocky island. [Orkney dial. f. ON *sker*: cf. SCAR[2]]

sketch /skech/ *n. & v.* • *n.* **1** a rough, slight, merely outlined, or unfinished drawing or painting, often made to assist in making a more finished picture. **2** a brief account without many details conveying a general idea of something; a rough draft or general outline. **3** a very short play, usu. humorous and limited to one scene. **4** a short descriptive piece of writing. **5** a musical composition of a single movement. **6** *colloq.* a comical person or thing. • *v.* **1** *tr.* make or give a sketch of. **2** *intr.* draw sketches esp. of landscape (*went out sketching*). **3** *tr.* (often foll. by *in, out*) indicate briefly or in outline. □ **sketch map** a roughly-drawn map with few details. **sketch pad** = SKETCHBOOK. □□ **sketcher** *n.* [Du. *schets* or G *Skizze* f. It. *schizzo* f. *schizzare* make a sketch ult. f. Gk *skhēdios* extempore]

■ *n.* **1** see DRAWING. **2** see OUTLINE *n.* 1, 2. **3** see ACT *n.* 3a. **4, 5** see PIECE *n.* 3. • *v.* **1** see ROUGH *v.* **2** see DRAW *v.* 10. **3** see OUTLINE *v.*

sketchbook /skéchbŏŏk/ *n.* a book or pad of drawing paper for doing sketches on.

sketchy /skéchee/ *adj.* (**sketchier, sketchiest**) **1** giving only a slight or rough outline, like a sketch. **2** *colloq.* unsubstantial or imperfect esp. through haste. □□ **sketchily** *adv.* **sketchiness** *n.*

■ cursory, superficial, incomplete, patchy, unsubstantial, rough, perfunctory, skimpy, imperfect, crude, hasty, hurried, vague, ill-defined, fuzzy, indistinct, inexact, imprecise, unrefined, unpolished, rough-hewn, unfinished. □□ **sketchily** cursorily, superficially, incompletely, patchily, roughly, perfunctorily, skimpily, vaguely, imperfectly, crudely, hastily, hurriedly.

skeuomorph /skyŏŏəmawrf/ *n.* **1** an object or feature copying the design of a similar artifact in another material. **2** an ornamental design resulting from the nature of the material used or the method of working it. □□ **skeuomorphic** /-máwrfik/ *adj.* [Gk *skeuos* vessel, implement + *morphē* form]

skew /skyŏŏ/ *adj., n., & v.* • *adj.* **1** oblique; slanting; set askew. **2** *Math.* **a** lying in three dimensions (*skew curve*). **b** (of lines) not coplanar. **c** (of a statistical distribution) not symmetrical. • *n.* **1** a slant. **2** *Statistics* skewness. • *v.* **1** *tr.* make skew. **2** *tr.* distort. **3** *intr.* move obliquely. **4** *intr.* twist. □ **on the skew** askew. **skew arch** (or **bridge**) an arch (or bridge) with the line of the arch not at right angles to the abutment. **skew chisel** a chisel with an oblique edge. **skew-eyed** *Brit.* squinting. **skew gear** a gear consisting of two cogwheels having nonparallel, nonintersecting axes. **skew-whiff** /skyŏŏwíf/ *Brit. colloq.* askew. □□ **skewness** *n.* [ONF *eskiu(w)er* (v.) = OF *eschuer*: see ESCHEW]

■ *adj.* **1** see IRREGULAR *adj.* 1, 2. • *n.* **1** see TWIST *n.* 4, SLOPE *n.* 1–3. **2** bias, skewness, distortion. • *v.* **2** see BIAS *v.* **3** see SWERVE *v.*

skewback /skyŏŏbak/ *n.* the sloping face of the abutment on which an extremity of an arch rests.

skewbald /skyŏŏbawld/ *adj. & n.* • *adj.* (of an animal) with irregular patches of white and another color (properly not

black) (cf. PIEBALD). ● *n.* a skewbald animal, esp. a horse. [ME *skued* (orig. uncert.), after PIEBALD]
■ *adj.* see SPOTTY 1.

skewer /skyŏŏər/ *n. & v.* ● *n.* a long pin designed for holding meat compactly together while cooking. ● *v.tr.* **1** fasten together or pierce with or as with a skewer. **2** criticize sharply. [17th c., var. of dial. *skiver*: orig. unkn.]
■ *n.* see SPIKE¹ *n.* 1b. ● *v.* see PIERCE 1a, b.

ski /skee/ *n. & v.* ● *n.* (*pl.* **skis** or **ski**) **1** each of a pair of long narrow pieces of wood, etc., usu. pointed and turned up at the front, fastened under the feet for traveling over snow. **2** a similar device under a vehicle or aircraft. **3** = *water ski.* **4** (*attrib.*) for wear when skiing (*ski boots*). ● *v.* (**skis, skied** /skeed/; **skiing**) **1** *intr.* travel on skis. **2** *tr.* ski at (a place). □ **ski jump 1** a steep slope leveling off before a sharp drop to allow a skier to leap through the air. **2** a jump made from this. **ski jumper** a person who takes part in ski jumping. **ski jumping** the sport of leaping off a ski jump with marks awarded for style and distance attained. **ski lift** a device for carrying skiers up a slope, usu. on seats hung from an overhead cable. **ski run** a slope prepared for skiing. □□ **skiable** *adj.* [Norw. f. ON *skíth* billet, snow shoe]

skiagraphy /skīágrəfee/ *n.* (also *Brit.* **sciagraphy**) the art of shading in drawing, etc. □□ **skiagram** /skíəgram/ *n.* **skiagraph** /skíəgraf/ *n. & v.tr.* **skiagraphic** /-gráfik/ *adj.* [F *sciagraphie* f. L *sciagraphia* f. Gk *skiagraphia* f. *skia* shadow]

skibob /skéebob/ *n. & v.* ● *n.* a machine like a bicycle with skis instead of wheels. ● *v.intr.* (**-bobbed, -bobbing**) ride a skibob. □□ **skibobber** *n.*

skid /skid/ *v. & n.* ● *v.* (**skidded, skidding**) **1** *intr.* (of a vehicle, a wheel, or a driver) slide on slippery ground, esp. sideways or obliquely. **2** *tr.* cause (a vehicle, etc.) to skid. **3** *intr.* slip; slide. **4** *intr. colloq.* fail or decline or err. **5** *tr.* support or move or protect or check with a skid. ● *n.* **1** the act or an instance of skidding. **2 a** a supporting plank, low platform, pallet, etc., usu. made of wood. **b** a piece of wood, etc., serving as a support, ship's fender, inclined plane, etc. **3** a braking device, esp. a wooden or metal shoe preventing a wheel from revolving or used as a drag. **4** a runner beneath an aircraft for use when landing. □ **hit the skids** *colloq.* enter a rapid decline or deterioration. **on the skids** *colloq.* **1** about to be discarded or defeated. **2** esp. *Brit.* ready for launching. **put the skids under** *colloq.* **1** hasten the downfall or failure of. **2** cause to hasten. **skid road 1** a road for hauling logs along. **2** = *skid row.* **skid row** *colloq.* a part of a town frequented by vagrants, alcoholics, etc. [17th c.: orig. unkn.]
■ *v.* **1–3** see SLIDE *v.* 1, 2. □ **on the skids 1** see *on the decline* (DECLINE). **skid row** see SLUM *n.* 1.

skiddoo /skidŏŏ/ *v.intr.* (also **skidoo**) (**-oos, -ooed**) *sl.* go away; depart. [perh. f. SKEDADDLE]

skier /skéeər/ *n.* a person who skis.

skiff /skif/ *n.* a light rowboat or scull. [F *esquif* f. It. *schifo*, rel. to SHIP]
■ see BOAT *n.*

skiffle /skífəl/ *n.* a kind of folk music played by a small group, mainly with a rhythmic accompaniment to a singing guitarist, etc. [perh. imit.]

skijoring /skéejáwring/ *n.* a winter sport in which a skier is towed by a horse or vehicle. □□ **skijorer** *n.* [Norw. *skikjøring* (as SKI, *kjøre* drive)]

skill /skil/ *n.* (often foll. by *in*) expertness; practiced ability; facility in an action; dexterity or tact. □□ **skill-less** *adj.* (archaic **skilless**). [ME f. ON *skil* distinction]
■ talent, ability, aptitude, expertness, expertise, facility, prowess, skillfulness, art, artistry, cleverness, adeptness, adroitness, mastery, dexterity, handiness, ingenuity, experience, proficiency, finesse, knack, quickness, deftness, technique; accomplishment, forte, strength, gift, capability, know-how, faculty.

skilled /skild/ *adj.* **1** (often foll. by *in*) having or showing skill; skillful. **2** (of a worker) highly trained or experienced. **3** (of work) requiring skill or special training.
■ **1** see SKILLFUL. **2** see EXPERIENCED 2.

skillet /skílit/ *n.* **1** a frying pan. **2** *Brit.* a small metal kettle

or saucepan with a long handle and usu. legs. [ME, perh. f. OF *escuelete* dimin. of *escuele* platter f. LL *scutella*]
■ see PAN¹ *n.* 1.

skillful /skílfŏŏl/ *adj.* (*Brit.* **skilful**) (often foll. by *at, in*) having or showing skill; practiced, expert, adroit, ingenious. □□ **skillfully** *adv.* **skillfulness** *n.*
■ skilled, accomplished, adept, adroit, dexterous, expert, proficient, masterly, masterful, gifted, ingenious, brilliant, apt, able, clever, talented, capable, consummate, professional, trained, qualified, experienced, practiced. □□ **skillfulness** see SKILL.

skim /skim/ *v. & n.* ● *v.* (**skimmed, skimming**) **1** *tr.* **a** take scum or cream or a floating layer from the surface of (a liquid). **b** take (cream, etc.) from the surface of a liquid. **2** *tr.* **a** keep touching lightly or nearly touching (a surface) in passing over. **b** deal with or treat (a subject) superficially. **3** *intr.* **a** (often foll. by *over, along*) go lightly over a surface, glide along in the air. **b** (foll. by *over*) = sense 2b of *v.* **4 a** *tr.* read superficially; look over cursorily; gather the salient facts contained in. **b** *intr.* (usu. foll. by *through*) read or look over cursorily. **5** *tr. sl.* conceal or divert (income) to avoid paying tax. ● *n.* **1** the act or an instance of skimming. **2 a** thin covering on a liquid (*skim of ice*). □ **skim the cream off** take the best part of. **skim** (or **skimmed**) **milk** milk from which the cream has been skimmed. [ME, back-form. f. SKIMMER]
■ *v.* **1 a** cream (off). **b** skim off, separate, scoop or ladle off, take off, remove. **3 a** soar, glide, skate, slide, sail, scud, fly, plane, aquaplane, coast. **4** skim through or over, scan, flip or thumb or leaf through, skip through, glance at or through, dip into.

skimmer /skímər/ *n.* **1** a device for skimming liquids. **2** a person who skims. **3** a flat hat, esp. a broad-brimmed straw hat. **4** any long-winged marine bird of the genus *Rynchops* that feeds by skimming over water with its knifelike lower mandible immersed. **5** a hydroplane, hydrofoil, hovercraft, or other vessel that has little or no displacement at speed. **6** a sheathlike dress. [ME f. OF *escumoir* f. *escumer* f. *escume* SCUM]

skimmia /skímeeə/ *n.* any evergreen shrub of the genus *Skimmia,* native to E. Asia, with red berries. [mod.L f. Jap.]

skimobile /skéemōbeel/ *n.* = SNOWMOBILE.

skimp /skimp/ *v., adj., & n.* ● *v.* **1** *tr.* (often foll. by *in*) supply (a person, etc.) meagerly with food, money, etc. **2** *tr.* use a meager or insufficient amount of; stint (material, expenses, etc.). **3** *intr.* be parsimonious. ● *adj.* scanty. ● *n. colloq.* a small or scanty thing, esp. a skimpy garment. [18th c.: orig. unkn.: cf. SCRIMP]
■ *v.* see STINT *v.*

skimpy /skímpee/ *adj.* (**skimpier, skimpiest**) meager; not ample or sufficient. □□ **skimpily** *adv.* **skimpiness** *n.*
■ see MEAGER 1. □□ **skimpily** see POORLY.

skin /skin/ *n. & v.* ● *n.* **1** the flexible continuous covering of a human or other animal body. **2 a** the skin of a flayed animal with or without the hair, etc. **b** a material prepared from skins, esp. of smaller animals (opp. HIDE²). **3** a person's skin with reference to its color or complexion (*has a fair skin*). **4** an outer layer or covering, esp. the coating of a plant, fruit, or sausage. **5** a film like skin on the surface of a liquid, etc. **6** a container for liquid, made of an animal's skin. **7 a** the planking or plating of a ship or boat, inside or outside the ribs. **b** the outer covering of any craft or vehicle, esp. an aircraft or spacecraft. **8** *Brit. sl.* a skinhead. **9** *Cards* a game in which each player has one card which he bets will not be the first to be matched by a card dealt from the pack. **10** = *goldbeater's skin.* **11** *sl.* a condom. ● *v.* (**skinned, skinning**) **1** *tr.* remove the skin from. **2** (often foll. by *over*) **a** *tr.* cover (a sore, etc.) with or as with skin. **b** *intr.* (of a wound, etc.) become covered with new skin. **3** *tr. sl.* fleece or swindle. □ **be skin and bone** be very thin. **by** (or **with**) **the skin of one's teeth** by a very narrow margin. **change one's skin** undergo an impossible change of character, etc. **get under a person's skin** *colloq.* interest or annoy a person intensely. **have a thick** (or **thin**) **skin** be insensitive (or sensitive) to criticism, etc. **no skin off one's nose** *colloq.* a matter of indifference or even benefit to one. **skin-deep** (of a wound, or of an emotion, an impression, beauty, etc.) superficial; not deep or lasting. **skin diver** a person who swims underwater without a diving suit, usu. with a mask, snorkel, flippers, etc. **skin diving** such swimming. **skin effect** *Electr.* the tendency of a high-frequency alternating current to flow through the outer layer only of a conductor. **skin flick** *sl.* an explicitly pornographic film. **skin friction** friction at the surface of a solid and a fluid in relative motion. **skin game** *sl.* a swindling game; a swindle. **skin graft 1** the surgical transplanting of skin. **2** a piece of skin transferred in this way. **skin test** a test to determine whether an immune reaction is elicited when a substance is applied to or injected into the skin. **to the skin** through all one's clothing (*soaked to the skin*). **with a whole skin** unwounded. □□ **skinless** *adj.* **skinlike** *adj.* **skinned** *adj.* (also in *comb.*). [OE *scin(n)* f. ON *skinn*]

■ *n.* **1, 3** epidermis, dermis. **2 a** hide, pelt, fleece, fell. **4** coat, film, coating, covering, casing, integument, crust, incrustation, husk, peel, rind, outside, shell, pellicle, veneer, outer layer, lamina, overlay. **5** membrane, sheet, pellicle; see also FILM *n.* 1. ● *v.* **1** flay, strip, decorticate, excoriate; peel, hull, husk, shell; abrade, scrape, graze, bark. **3** see FLEECE *v.* 1. □ **by** (or **with**) **the skin of one's teeth** see *narrowly* (NARROW). **get under a person's skin** see INTRIGUE *v.* 2, IRRITATE 1. **skin-deep** superficial, shallow, surface, slight, external, unimportant, trivial, unprofound, insubstantial. **skin game** see SWINDLE *n.* 1, 3.

skinflint /skínflint/ *n.* a miserly person.
■ see MISER.

skinful /skínfŏŏl/ *n.* (*pl.* **-fuls**) *colloq.* enough liquor to make one drunk.

skinhead /skínhed/ *n.* **1** a youth with close-cropped hair, esp. one of an aggressive gang. **2** a U.S. Marine recruit.
■ **1** see BARBARIAN *n.* 1.

skink /skingk/ *n.* any small lizard of the family Scincidae. [F *scinc* or L *scincus* f. Gk *skigkos*]

skinner /skínər/ *n.* **1** a person who skins animals or prepares skins. **2** a dealer in skins; a furrier. **3** *Austral. Racing sl.* a result very profitable to bookmakers.

skinny /skíne/ *adj.* (**skinnier**, **skinniest**) **1** thin or emaciated. **2** (of clothing) tight-fitting. **3** made of or like skin. □ **skinny-dipping** *colloq.* swimming in the nude. □□ **skinniness** *n.*
■ **1** thin, underweight, gaunt, bony, scraggy, scrawny, rangy, lean, lank, lanky, gangly, gangling, rawboned, meager, spare, emaciated, half-starved, undernourished, pinched, hollow-cheeked, wasted, shrunken.

skint /skint/ *adj. Brit. sl.* having no money left. [= *skinned*, past part. of SKIN]
■ see BROKE.

skintight /skíntít/ *adj.* (of a garment) very close-fitting.

skip¹ /skip/ *v. & n.* ● *v.* (**skipped**, **skipping**) **1** *intr.* **a** move along lightly, esp. by taking two steps with each foot in turn. **b** jump lightly from the ground, esp. so as to clear a jump rope. **c** jump about; gambol; caper; frisk. **2** *intr.* (often foll. by *from, off, to*) move quickly from one point, subject, or occupation to another; be desultory. **3** *tr.* (also *absol.*) omit in dealing with a series or in reading (*skip every tenth row*; *always skips the small print*). **4** *tr. colloq.* not participate in. **5** *tr. colloq.* depart quickly from; leave hurriedly. **6** *intr.* (often foll. by *out, off*) *colloq.* make off; disappear. **7** *tr.* make (a stone) ricochet on the surface of water. ● *n.* **1** a skipping movement or action. **2** *Computing* the action of passing over part of a sequence of data or instructions. **3** *colloq.* a person who defaults or absconds. □ **skip it** *sl.* **1** abandon a topic, etc. **2** make off; disappear. **skip** (or *Brit.* **skipping**) **rope** =

jump rope. **skip zone** the annular region around a broadcasting station where neither direct nor reflected waves are received. [ME, prob. f. Scand.]

■ *v.* **1** leap, caper, gambol, frisk, prance, spring, jump, hop, romp, bound, dance, *sl.* cavort. **2** see FLIT *v.* 1. **3** omit, leave out, pass by, overlook, pass over, avoid, ignore, disregard, steer clear of, cut. **4** see AVOID 1. **5** see LEAVE¹ *v.* 1b, 3, 4. **6** see *make away*. ● *n.* **1** leap, caper, gambol, frisk, prance, jump, bound, dance, hop, romp. □ **skip it 2** see *make away*.

skip² /skip/ *n.* **1** a cage, bucket, etc., in which workers or materials are lowered and raised in mines and quarries. **2** *Brit.* a large container for builders' refuse, etc. **3** = SKEP. [var. of SKEP]

skip³ /skip/ *n. & v.* ● *n.* the captain or director of a side at bowling or curling. ● *v.tr.* (**skipped**, **skipping**) be the skip of. [abbr. of SKIPPER¹]

skipjack /skípjak/ *n.* **1** (in full **skipjack tuna**) a small striped Pacific tuna, *Katsuwonus pelamus*, used as food. **2** a click beetle. **3** a kind of sailboat used off the east coast of the US. [SKIP¹ + JACK¹]

skiplane /skéeplayn/ *n.* an airplane having its undercarriage fitted with skis for landing on snow or ice.

skipper¹ /skípər/ *n. & v.* ● *n.* **1** a sea captain, esp. the master of a small trading or fishing vessel. **2** the captain of an aircraft. **3** the captain of a side in games. ● *v.tr.* act as captain of. [ME f. MDu., MLG *schipper* f. *schip* SHIP]
■ *n.* captain, master, commander; leader, chief, director, *colloq.* boss. ● *v.* see LEAD *v.* 6, 7a.

skipper² /skípər/ *n.* **1** a person who skips. **2** any brown, thick-bodied butterfly of the family Hesperiidae.

skippet /skípit/ *n.* a small, round wooden box to enclose and protect a seal attached to a document. [ME: orig. unkn.]

skirl /skərl/ *n. & v.* ● *n.* the shrill sound characteristic of bagpipes. ● *v.intr.* make a skirl. [prob. Scand.: ult. imit.]
■ *v.* pipe, tootle, whistle.

skirmish /skɔ́rmish/ *n. & v.* ● *n.* **1** a piece of irregular or unpremeditated fighting, esp. between small or outlying parts of armies or fleets; a slight engagement. **2** a short argument or contest of wit, etc. ● *v.intr.* engage in a skirmish. □□ **skirmisher** *n.* [ME f. OF *eskirmir, escremir* f. Frank.]
■ *n.* **1** fight, encounter, fray, brush, clash, engagement, confrontation, showdown, combat, battle, conflict, struggle, contest, incident, scrimmage, fracas, tussle, melee, affray, *colloq.* scrap, dustup, set-to. **2** see ARGUMENT 1. ● *v.* fight, clash, struggle, battle, tussle.

skirr /skər/ *v.intr.* move rapidly, esp. with a whirring sound. [perh. rel. to SCOUR¹ or SCOUR²]

skirret /skírit/ *n.* a perennial umbelliferous plant, *Sium sisarum*, formerly cultivated in Europe for its edible root. [ME *skirwhit(e)*, perh. formed as SHEER¹, WHITE]

skirt /skərt/ *n. & v.* ● *n.* **1** a woman's outer garment hanging from the waist. **2** the part of a coat, etc., that hangs below the waist. **3** a hanging part around the base of a hovercraft. **4** (in *sing.* or *pl.*) an edge, border, or extreme part. **5** (also esp. *Brit.* **bit of skirt**) *sl. offens.* a woman regarded as an object of sexual desire. **6** (in full **skirt of beef**, etc.) **a** the diaphragm and other membranes as food. **b** *Brit.* a cut of meat from the lower flank. **7** a flap of a saddle. **8** a surface that conceals or protects the wheels or underside of a vehicle or aircraft. ● *v.* **1** *tr.* go along or around or past the edge of. **2** *tr.* be situated along. **3** *tr.* avoid dealing with (an issue, etc.). **4** *intr.* (foll. by *along*) go along the coast, a wall, etc. □ **skirt dance** a dance with graceful manipulation of a full skirt. □□ **skirted** *adj.* (also in *comb.*). **skirtless** *adj.* [ME f. ON *skyrta* shirt, corresp. to OE *scyrte*: see SHIRT]
■ *n.* **5** see *bit of fluff* (FLUFF). ● *v.* **1, 3** see BYPASS *v.*

skirting /skɔ́rting/ *n.* **1** fabric suitable for skirt making. **2** a border or edge. **3** *Brit.* = BASEBOARD.

skit /skit/ *n.* (often foll. by *on*) a light, usu. short, piece of satire or burlesque. [rel. to *skit* move lightly and rapidly, perh. f. ON (cf. *skjóta* SHOOT)]
■ see ACT *n.* 3a.

skite /skīt/ *v. & n.* ● *v.intr. Austral. & NZ colloq.* boast, brag. ● *n.* **1** *Austral. & NZ colloq.* **a** a boaster. **b** boasting; boastfulness. **2** *Sc.* a drinking bout; a spree (*on the skite*). [Sc. & No. of Engl. dial., = a person regarded with contempt: cf. BLATHERSKITE]

skitter /skítər/ *v.intr.* (also **skeeter** /skéetər/) **1 a** (usu. foll. by *along*, *across*) move lightly or hastily. **b** (usu. foll. by *about*, *off*) hurry about; dart off. **2** fish by drawing bait jerkily across the surface of the water. [app. frequent. of dial. *skite*, perh. formed as SKIT]
■ **1** see DASH *v.* 1. **2** see HURRY *v.* 1.

skittery /skítəree/ *adj.* skittish; restless.

skittish /skítish/ *adj.* **1** lively; playful. **2** (of a horse, etc.) nervous; inclined to shy; fidgety. □□ **skittishly** *adv.* **skittishness** *n.* [ME, perh. formed as SKIT]
■ **1** see LIVELY 1. **2** see NERVOUS 1–3, 5. □□ **skittishness** playfulness, impishness, mischievousness; see also JUMP *n.* 2b.

skittle /skít'l/ *n. & v.* ● *n.* **1 a** a pin used in the game of skittles. **2** (in *pl.*; usu. treated as *sing.*) (esp in the UK) **a** a game like ninepins played with usu. nine wooden pins set up at the end of an alley to be knocked down, usu. with wooden balls or a wooden disk. **b** (in full **table skittles**) a game played with similar pins set up on a board to be knocked down by swinging a suspended ball. **c** *Brit. colloq.* chess not played seriously. ● *v.tr.* (often foll. by *out*) *Cricket* get (batsmen) out in rapid succession. [17th c. (also *kittle-pins*: orig. unkn.]

skive /skīv/ *v. & n.* ● *v.* **1** *tr.* split or pare (hides, leather, etc.). **2** *intr. Brit. sl.* **a** evade a duty; shirk. **b** (often foll. by *off*) avoid work by absenting oneself; play truant. ● *n. sl.* **1** an instance of shirking. **2** an easy option. □□ **skiver** *n.* [ON *skifa*, rel. to ME *schive* slice]

skivvy /skívee/ *n.* (*pl.* **-ies**) **1 a** (in *pl.*) underwear of T-shirt and shorts. **b** a thin high-necked long-sleeved garment. **2** *Brit. colloq. derog.* a female domestic servant. [20th c.: orig. unkn.]
■ **1 a** (*skivvies*) see UNDERCLOTHES. **2** see SLAVE *n.* 1.

skoal /skōl/ *int.* used as a toast in drinking. [Da. *skaal*, Sw. *skål*, f. ON *skál* bowl]
■ see *bottoms up!* (BOTTOM).

skua /skyõõə/ *n.* **1** any of several predatory seabirds of the genus *Catharacta*, esp. the great skua *C. skua*. **2** *Brit.* = JAEGER 2. [mod.L f. Faroese *skúgvur*, ON *skúfr*]

skulduggery /skuldúgəree/ *n.* (also **sculduggery, skullduggery**) trickery; unscrupulous behavior. [earlier *sculduddery*, orig. Sc. = unchastity (18th c.: orig. unkn.)]
■ see TRICKERY.

skulk /skulk/ *v. & n.* ● *v.intr.* **1** move stealthily, lurk, or keep oneself concealed, esp. in a cowardly or sinister way. **2** stay or sneak away in time of danger. **3** *Brit.* shirk duty. ● *n.* **1** a person who skulks. **2** a group of foxes. □□ **skulker** *n.* [ME f. Scand.: cf. Norw. *skulka* lurk, Da. *skulke*, Sw. *skolka* shirk]
■ *v.* **1** see LURK *v.* 1, 2. **2** see SNEAK *v.* 1.

skull /skul/ *n.* **1** the bony case of the brain of a vertebrate. **2 a** the part of the skeleton corresponding to the head. **b** this with the skin and soft internal parts removed. **c** a representation of this. **3** the head as the seat of intelligence. □ **out of one's skull** *sl.* out of one's mind; crazy. **skull and crossbones** a representation of a skull with two thighbones crossed below it as an emblem of piracy or death. **skull session** *sl.* a discussion or conference. □□ **skulled** *adj.* (also in *comb.*). [ME *scolle*: orig. unkn.]
■ **3** see HEAD *n.* 1, 2.

skullcap /skúlkap/ *n.* **1** a small, close-fitting, peakless cap. **2** the top part of the skull. **3** any plant of the genus *Scutellaria*, with helmet-shaped bilabiate flowers.

skunk /skungk/ *n. & v.* ● *n.* **1 a** any of various cat-sized flesh-eating mammals of the family Mustelidae, esp. *Mephitis mephitis* having a distinctive black and white striped fur and able to emit a powerful stench from a liquid secreted by its anal glands as a defense. **b** its fur. **2** *colloq.* a thoroughly contemptible person. ● *v.tr.* **1** *sl.* defeat soundly. **2** fail to pay (a bill, etc.). □ **skunk bear** *colloq.* a wolverine. **skunk cabbage** one of two N. American herbaceous plants, esp. *Symplocarpus foetidus*, with an offensive-smelling spathe. [Algonquian *segankw*, *segongw*]

■ *n.* **2** see STINKER. ● *v.* **1** see BEAT *v.* 3a.

sky /ski/ *n. & v.* ● *n.* (*pl.* **skies**) (in *sing.* or *pl.*) **1** the region of the atmosphere and outer space seen from the earth. **2** the weather or climate evidenced by this. ● *v.tr.* (**skies**, **skied**) **1** *Baseball*, etc., hit (a ball) high into the air. **2** hang (a picture) high on a wall. □ **sky blue** a bright, clear blue. **sky-blue pink** an imaginary color. **sky-clad** *sl.* esp. *Brit.* naked (esp. in witchcraft). **sky cloth** *Theatr.* a backcloth painted or colored to represent the sky. **sky-high** *adv. & adj.* as if reaching the sky; very high. **the sky is the limit** there is practically no limit. **sky pilot** *sl.* a clergyman. **sky wave** a radio wave reflected from the ionosphere. **to the skies** very highly; without reserve (*praised to the skies*). **under the open sky** out of doors. □□ **skyey** *adj.* **skyless** *adj.* [ME *ski(es)* cloud(s) f. ON *ský*]
■ *n.* **1** heaven(s), skies, arch *or* vault of heaven, (wild) blue (yonder), ether, atmosphere, space, empyrean, *literary* firmament, *poet.* welkin, azure. □ **sky-high** see *towering* (TOWER *v.* 3a). **sky pilot** see MINISTER *n.* 2. **to the skies** excessively, extravagantly, unreservedly, fulsomely, profusely, inordinately, highly, overly.

skybox /skíboks/ *n.* an elevated enclosure in a sports stadium containing plush seating, food services, and other amenities.

skycap /skíkap/ *n.* a person who carries baggage for passengers at airports.

skydiving /skídiving/ *n.* the sport of performing acrobatic maneuvers under free fall with a parachute. □□ **skydive** *v.intr.* **skydiver** *n.*

Skye terrier /ski/ *n.* a small, long-bodied, short-legged, long-haired, slate- or fawn-colored variety of Scottish terrier. [*Skye*, an island of the Inner Hebrides]

skyjack /skíjak/ *n. & v.* ● *v.tr.* hijack (an aircraft). ● *n.* an act of skyjacking. □□ **skyjacker** *n.* [SKY + HIJACK]

skylark /skílaark/ *n. & v.* ● *n.* a lark, *Alauda arvensis*, of Eurasia and N. Africa, that sings while hovering in flight. ● *v.intr.* play tricks or practical jokes; indulge in horseplay; frolic. [SKY + LARK¹: (v.) with pun on LARK²]
■ *v.* see FROLIC *v.*

skylight /skílit/ *n.* a window set in the plane of a roof or ceiling.

skyline /skílin/ *n.* the outline of hills, buildings, etc., defined against the sky; the visible horizon.

skyrocket /skírokkit/ *n. & v.* ● *n.* a rocket exploding high in the air. ● *v.intr.* (esp. of prices, etc.) rise very steeply or rapidly.
■ *v.* see SOAR 2.

skysail /skísayl, -səl/ *n.* a light sail above the royal in a square-rigged ship.

skyscape /skískayp/ *n.* **1** a picture chiefly representing the sky. **2** a view of the sky.

skyscraper /skískraypər/ *n.* a very tall building of many stories.

skyward /skíwərd/ *adv. & adj.* ● *adv.* (also **skywards** /-wərdz/) toward the sky. ● *adj.* moving skyward.

skywatch /skíwoch/ *n.* the activity of watching the sky for aircraft, etc.

skyway /skíway/ *n.* **1** a route used by aircraft. **2** the sky as a medium of transport.

skywriting /skíriting/ *n.* legible smoke trails made by an airplane, esp. for advertising.

slab /slab/ *n. & v.* ● *n.* **1** a flat, broad, fairly thick, usu. square or rectangular piece of solid material, esp. stone. **2** a large flat piece of cake, chocolate, etc. **3** (of lumber) an outer piece sawn from a log. **4** esp. *Brit.* a mortuary table. ● *v.tr.* (**slabbed**, **slabbing**) remove slabs from (a log or tree) to prepare it for sawing into planks. [ME: orig. unkn.]
■ *n.* **1, 2** slice, wedge, piece, hunk, chunk, block, brick, cake, tablet, *Brit. colloq.* wodge.

slack¹ /slak/ *adj., n., v., & adv.* ● *adj.* **1** (of rope, etc.) not

---

/.../ **pronunciation**	● **part of speech**
□ **phrases, idioms, and compounds**	
□□ **derivatives**	■ **synonym section**
cross-references appear in SMALL CAPITALS or *italics*	

taut. **2** inactive or sluggish. **3** negligent or remiss. **4** (of tide, etc.) neither ebbing nor flowing. **5** (of trade or business or a market) with little happening. **6** loose. **7** *Phonet.* lax. **8** relaxed; languid. ● *n.* **1** the slack part of a rope (*haul in the slack*). **2** a slack time in trade, etc. **3** *colloq.* a spell of inactivity or laziness. **4** (in *pl.*) full-length loosely-cut trousers for informal wear. ● *v.* **1 a** *tr.* & *intr.* slacken. **b** *tr.* loosen (rope, etc.). **2** *intr. Brit. colloq.* take a rest; be lazy. **3** *tr.* slake (lime). ● *adv.* **1** slackly. **2** slowly or insufficiently (*dry slack*; *bake slack*). □ **slack hand** lack of full control in riding or governing. **slack lime** slaked lime. **slack off 1** loosen. **2** lose or cause to lose vigor. **slack rein** = *slack hand.* **slack suit** casual clothes of slacks and a matching jacket or shirt. **slack up** reduce the speed of a train, etc., before stopping. **slack water** a time near the turn of the tide, esp. at low tide. **take up the slack** use up a surplus or make up a deficiency; avoid an undesirable lull. □□ **slackly** *adv.* **slackness** *n.* [OE *slæc* f. Gmc]

■ *adj.* **1** loose, limp, lax. **2** indolent, lazy, idle, slothful, inactive, sluggish, lethargic, laggard, shiftless, fainéant, *archaic* otiose. **3** remiss, careless, negligent, lax, neglectful, delinquent, inattentive, dilatory, tardy, easygoing, do-nothing, *colloq.* asleep at the wheel *or* on the job. **5** inactive, slow, flat, quiet, sluggish. **6** loose, flabby, flaccid, soft, limp, baggy, droopy, saggy, floppy. ● *n.* **2** lull, pause, inactivity, cutback, lessening, reduction, abatement, drop-off, downturn, diminution, decline, falloff, decrease, dwindling. ● *v.* **1** slack off *or* up, slacken (off *or* up), relax, ease (out *or* off), let up (on); slow (down *or* up), delay, reduce speed, tire, decline, decrease, diminish, moderate, abate, weaken; loose, loosen, let go, let run, let loose, release. **2** shirk, skulk, *sl.* goof around *or* off, *Brit. sl.* skive (off); relax, rest. □ **slack off 1** see SLACK¹ *v.* 1 above. **slack up** see SLACK¹ *v.* 1 above. □□ **slackness** looseness, play, give, leeway; see also NEGLECT *n.* 1.

slack² /slak/ *n.* coal dust or small pieces of coal. [ME prob. f. LG or Du.]

slacken /slákən/ *v.tr.* & *intr.* make or become slack. □ **slacken off** = *slack off* (see SLACK¹).

■ see LOOSE *v.* 2–4.

slacker /slákər/ *n.* a shirker; an indolent person.

■ shirker, loafer, idler, skulker, gold brick, *Brit. sl.* skiver, *Brit. sl.,* esp. *Mil.* scrimshanker.

slag /slag/ *n.* & *v.* ● *n.* **1** vitreous refuse left after ore has been smelted; dross separated in a fused state in the reduction of ore; clinkers. **2** volcanic scoria. **3** *Brit. sl. derog.* **a** a prostitute or promiscuous woman. **b** a worthless or insignificant person. ● *v.* (**slagged, slagging**) **1** *intr.* **a** form slag. **b** cohere into a mass like slag. **2** *tr.* (often foll. by *off*) *Brit. sl.* criticize; insult. □ **slag heap** a hill of refuse from a mine, etc. **slag wool** = *mineral wool.* □□ **slaggy** *adj.* (**slaggier, slaggiest**). [MLG *slagge*, perh. f. *slagen* strike, with ref. to fragments formed by hammering]

slain *past part.* of SLAY¹.

slainte /sláánchə/ *int.* a Gaelic toast: good health! [Gael. *sláinte*, lit. 'health']

slake /slayk/ *v.tr.* **1** assuage or satisfy (thirst, revenge, etc.). **2** disintegrate (quicklime) by chemical combination with water. [OE *slacian* f. *slæc* SLACK¹]

■ **1** satisfy, quench, gratify, satiate, sate, allay, assuage, ease, relieve.

slalom /sláaləm/ *n.* **1** a ski race down a zigzag course defined by artificial obstacles. **2** an obstacle race in canoes or cars or on skateboards or water skis. [Norw., lit. 'sloping track']

slam¹ /slam/ *v.* & *n.* ● *v.* (**slammed, slamming**) **1** *tr.* & *intr.* shut forcefully and loudly. **2** *tr.* put down (an object) with a similar sound. **3** *intr.* move violently (*he slammed out of the room*). **4** *tr.* & *intr.* put or come into sudden action (*slam the brakes on*). **5** *tr. sl.* criticize severely. **6** *tr. sl.* hit. **7** *tr. sl.* gain an easy victory over. ● *n.* **1** a sound of or as of a slammed door. **2** the shutting of a door, etc., with a loud bang. **3** (usu. prec. by *the*) *sl.* prison. □ **slam-bang** *adv.* with the sound of a slam. ● *adj. colloq.* impressive, exciting, or energetic. [prob. f. Scand.: cf. ON *slam(b)ra*]

■ *v.* **1** shut, fling closed, bang; go bang. **4** jam, ram. **5** criticize, attack, vilify, pillory, run down, disparage, denigrate, denounce, put down, flay, pounce on *or* upon, shoot down, *colloq.* pan, *Brit. colloq.* slate. **6** hit, slap, bang, smack; smash, crash, ram. ● *n.* **1** see IMPACT *n.* 1. **3** see JAIL *n.* 1.

slam² /slam/ *n. Cards* the winning of every trick in a game. □ **grand slam 1** *Bridge* the winning of 13 tricks. **2** the winning of all of a group of championships or matches in a sport. **small** (or **little**) **slam** *Bridge* the winning of 12 tricks. [orig. name of a card game: perh. f. obs. *slampant* trickery]

slammer /slámər/ *n.* (usu. prec. by *the*) *sl.* prison.

■ see PRISON *n.* 1.

slander /slándər/ *n.* & *v.* ● *n.* **1** a malicious, false, and injurious statement spoken about a person. **2** the uttering of such statements; calumny. **3** *Law* false oral defamation (cf. LIBEL). ● *v.tr.* utter slander about; defame falsely. □□ **slanderer** *n.* **slanderous** *adj.* **slanderously** *adv.* [ME *sclaundre* f. AF *esclaundre*, OF *esclandre* alt. f. *escandle* f. LL *scandalum*: see SCANDAL]

■ *n.* defamation (of character), calumny, obloquy, misrepresentation, vilification, denigration, traducement; slur, smear. ● *v.* defame, calumniate, calumny, disparage, discredit, traduce, malign, smear, vilify, decry, slur. □□ **slanderous** defamatory, calumnious, calumniatory, disparaging, smear, injurious, scandalous, malicious, vituperative, deprecatory, depreciative, discrediting, decrying.

slang /slang/ *n.* & *v.* ● *n.* words, phrases, and uses that are regarded as very informal and are often restricted to special contexts or are peculiar to a specified profession, class, etc. (*racing slang*; *schoolboy slang*). ● *v.* **1** *tr.* use abusive language to. **2** *intr.* use such language. □ **slanging match** *Brit.* a prolonged exchange of insults. [18th-c. cant: orig. unkn.]

■ *n.* see DIALECT 2.

slangy /slángee/ *adj.* (**slangier, slangiest**) **1** of the character of slang. **2** fond of using slang. □□ **slangily** *adv.* **slanginess** *n.*

slant /slant/ *v., n.,* & *adj.* ● *v.* **1** *intr.* slope; diverge from a line; lie or go obliquely to a vertical or horizontal line. **2** *tr.* cause to do this. **3** *tr.* (often as **slanted** *adj.*) present (information) from a particular angle, esp. in a biased or unfair way. ● *n.* **1** a slope; an oblique position. **2** a way of regarding a thing; a point of view, esp. a biased one. ● *adj.* sloping; oblique. □ **on a** (or **the**) **slant** aslant. **slant-eyed** having slanting eyes. **slant height** the height of a cone from the vertex to the periphery of the base. [aphetic form of ASLANT: (v.) rel. to ME *slent* f. ON *sletta* dash, throw]

■ *v.* **1, 2** tilt, angle, incline, pitch, cant, slope, bend, lean, list, tip, bevel, shelve. **3** bend, distort, deviate, twist, warp, color, weight, bias. ● *n.* **1** slope, incline, tilt, ramp, gradient, pitch, lean, leaning, deflection, angle, rake, cant, camber. **2** angle, viewpoint, (point of) view, standpoint, approach, twist, idea, aspect, attitude, position; bias, prejudice, partiality, one-sidedness, turn, bent. ● *adj.* see OBLIQUE 1.

slantwise /slántwīz/ (also **slantways** /slántwayz/) *adv.* aslant.

slap /slap/ *v., n.,* & *adv.* ● *v.* (**slapped, slapping**) **1** *tr.* & *intr.* strike with the palm of the hand or a flat object, or so as to make a similar noise. **2** *tr.* lay forcefully (*slapped the money on the table*; *slapped a writ on the offender*). **3** *tr.* put hastily or carelessly (*slap some paint on the walls*). **4** *tr.* (often foll. by *down*) *colloq.* reprimand or snub. ● *n.* **1** a blow with the palm of the hand or a flat object. **2** a slapping sound. ● *adv.* **1** with the suddenness or effectiveness or true aim of a blow; suddenly; fully; directly (*ran slap into him*; *hit me slap in the eye*). **2** = *slap-bang.* □ **slap and tickle** *Brit. colloq.* lighthearted amorous amusement. **slap-bang** violently; noisily; headlong. **slap in the face** a rebuff or affront. **slap on the back** *n.* congratulations. ● *v.tr.* congratulate. **slap on the wrist** *n. colloq.* a mild reprimand or rebuke. ● *v.tr. colloq.* reprimand. **slap shot** *Ice Hockey* a powerful shot made with a full swing of the stick. **slap-up** esp. *Brit. colloq.* excellent;

lavish; done regardless of expense (*slap-up meal*). [LG *slapp* (imit.)]

■ *v.* **1** smack, cuff, rap, *colloq.* whack; spank; clout, *sl.* wallop; flap, whip, beat, bat; see also HIT *v.* 1a. **3** fling, toss, splash, hurl, throw, sling. ● *n.* **1** smack, blow, cuff, whack, rap, clout, *sl.* wallop. ● *adv.* **1** exactly, directly, precisely, straight, point-blank, right, squarely, plumb, fully, smack, *colloq.* bang, spang. □ **slap-bang** violently, noisily; headlong; see also PELL-MELL *adv.* 1. **slap in the face** reprimand, reproof, rebuff, criticism, censure, rebuke, attack, insult, offense, *colloq.* put-down, smack in the eye. **slap on the back** (*v.*) congratulate, felicitate, compliment. **slap-up** see LUXURIOUS 1, PLUSH.

slapdash /sláp-dash/ *adj. & adv.* ● *adj.* hasty and careless. ● *adv.* in a slapdash manner.

■ *adj.* see CARELESS 1. ● *adv.* see PELL-MELL *adv.*

slaphappy /sláp-hápee/ *adj. colloq.* **1** cheerfully casual or flippant. **2** punch-drunk.

slapjack /sláp-jak/ *n.* **1** a card game in which face-up jacks are slapped by the players' open hands. **2** a kind of pancake cooked on a griddle. [SLAP + JACK[1]]

slapstick /sláp-stik/ *n.* **1** boisterous knockabout comedy. **2** a flexible divided lath used by a clown. [SLAP + STICK[1]]

slash /slash/ *v. & n.* ● *v.* **1** *intr.* make a sweeping or random cut or cuts with a knife, sword, whip, etc. **2** *tr.* make such a cut or cuts at. **3** *tr.* make a long narrow gash or gashes in. **4** *tr.* reduce (prices, etc.) drastically. **5** *tr.* censure vigorously. **6** *tr.* make (one's way) by slashing. **7** *tr.* **a** lash (a person, etc.) with a whip. **b** crack (a whip). ● *n.* **1 a** a slashing cut or stroke. **b** a wound or slit made by this. **2** an oblique stroke; a solidus. **3** *Brit. sl.* an act of urinating. **4** debris resulting from the felling or destruction of trees. □ **slash-and-burn** (of cultivation) in which vegetation is cut down, allowed to dry, and then burned off before seeds are planted. □□ **slasher** *n.* [ME perh. f. OF *esclachier* break in pieces]

■ *v.* **2, 3** cut, gash, hack, score, slit, slice, knife, lacerate; wound; scar. **4** cut, reduce, decrease, drop, mark down, trim, lower. **6** cut, hack. **7 a** lash, whip, scourge, flog, beat, horsewhip, flail, flagellate, flay, lambaste, thrash. ● *n.* **1** cut, gash, incision, slit, slice, gouge, rent, rip, score, laceration; wound. **2** solidus, stroke.

slashed /slasht/ *adj.* (of a sleeve, etc.) having slits to show a lining or puffing of other material.

slashing /sláshing/ *adj.* vigorously incisive or effective.

slat /slat/ *n.* a thin narrow piece of wood or plastic or metal, esp. used in an overlapping series as in a fence or Venetian blind. [ME *s(c)lat* f. OF *esclat* splinter, etc. f. *esclater* split f. Rmc]

■ see STRIP[2] *n.*

slate /slayt/ *n., v., & adj.* ● *n.* **1** a fine-grained, gray, green, or bluish-purple metamorphic rock easily split into flat smooth plates. **2** a piece of such a plate used as roofing material. **3** a piece of such a plate used for writing on, usu. framed in wood. **4** the color of slate. **5** a list of nominees for office, etc. ● *v.tr.* **1** cover with slates esp. as roofing. **2** *Brit. colloq.* criticize severely; scold. **3** make arrangements for (an event, etc.). **4** propose or nominate for office, etc. ● *adj.* made of slate. □ **on the slate** *Brit.* recorded as a debt to be paid. **slate blue** (or **black**) a shade of blue (or black) occurring in slate. **slate-colored** a dark bluish or greenish gray. **slate gray** a shade of gray occurring in slate. **slate pencil** a small rod of soft slate used for writing on slate. **wipe the slate clean** forgive or cancel the record of past offenses. □□ **slating** *n.* **slaty** *adj.* [ME *s(c)late* f. OF *esclate,* fem. form of *esclat* SLAT]

■ *n.* **5** see LIST[1] *n.* **3** see SCHEDULE *v.*

slater /sláytər/ *n.* **1** a person who slates roofs, etc. **2** a woodlouse or similar crustacean.

slather /sláthər/ *n. & v.* ● *n.* **1** (usu. in *pl.*) *colloq.* a large amount. **2** (often **open slather**) *Austral. & NZ sl.* unrestricted scope for action. ● *v.tr. colloq.* **1** spread thickly. **2** squander. [19th c.: orig. unkn.]

slatted /slátid/ *adj.* having slats.

slattern /slátərn/ *n.* a slovenly woman. □□ **slatternly** *adj.* **slatternliness** *n.* [17th c.: rel. to *slattering* slovenly, f. dial. *slatter* to spill, slop, waste, frequent. of *slat* strike]

■ see SLUT. □□ **slatternly** see UNTIDY.

slaughter /sláwtər/ *n. & v.* ● *n.* **1** the killing of an animal or animals for food. **2** the killing of many persons or animals at once or continuously; carnage; massacre. ● *v.tr.* **1** kill (people) in a ruthless manner or on a great scale. **2** kill for food; butcher. **3** *colloq.* defeat utterly. □□ **slaughterer** *n.* **slaughterous** *adj.* [ME *slahter* ult. f. ON *slátr* butcher's meat, rel. to SLAY[1]]

■ *n.* **1** butchery, butchering. **2** massacre, killing, bloodshed, bloodbath, murder, homicide, manslaughter, carnage, extermination, execution, liquidation, slaying, butchery, pogrom, genocide, mass murder *or* execution *or* extermination, holocaust, sacrifice, hecatomb, bloodletting. ● *v.* **1** butcher, kill, murder, execute, exterminate, massacre, put to the sword, put to death, liquidate, destroy, *literary or joc.* slay. **2** butcher, kill. **3** defeat, beat, win (out) over, overcome, overwhelm, smash, crush, thrash, destroy, rout, upset, trounce, whitewash, *literary* vanquish, *sl.* clobber. □□ **slaughterer** see BUTCHER *n.* **slaughterous** see SANGUINARY.

slaughterhouse /sláwtərhows/ *n.* **1** a place for the slaughter of animals as food. **2** a place of carnage.

■ **1** abattoir.

Slav /slaav/ *n. & adj.* ● *n.* a member of a group of peoples in Central and Eastern Europe speaking Slavic languages. ● *adj.* **1** of or relating to the Slavs. **2** Slavic. □□ **Slavism** *n.* [ME *Sclave* f. med.L *Sclavus,* late Gk *Sklabos,* & f. med.L *Slavus*]

slave /slayv/ *n. & v.* ● *n.* **1** a person who is the legal property of another or others and is bound to absolute obedience, a human chattel. **2** a drudge; a person working very hard. **3** (foll. by *of, to*) a helpless victim of some dominating influence (*slave of fashion; slave to duty*). **4** a machine, or part of one, directly controlled by another. ● *v.* **1** *intr.* (often foll. by *at, over*) work very hard. **2** *tr.* (foll. by *to*) subject (a device) to control by another. □ **slave bracelet** a bangle or chain of gold, etc., worn around the ankle. **slave-drive** (*past* **-drove;** *past part.* **-driven**) work (a person) hard, esp. excessively. **slave driver 1** an overseer of slaves at work. **2** a person who works others hard. **slave labor** forced labor. **slave ship** *hist.* a ship transporting slaves, esp. from Africa. **Slave State** *hist.* any of the southern states of the US in which slavery was legal before the Civil War. **slave trade** *hist.* the procuring, transporting, and selling of human beings, esp. African blacks, as slaves. **slave trader** *hist.* a person engaged in the slave trade. [ME f. OF *esclave* = med.L *sclavus, sclava* Slav (captive): see SLAV]

■ *n.* **1** lackey, bondsman, *archaic* scullion, *colloq.* slavey, *Brit. colloq. derog.* skivvy, *hist.* serf, helot, odalisque, vassal, blackbird, *literary* thrall. **2** drudge, workhorse, hack, grind, toiler, laborer, serf, *Brit.* fag, *colloq.* dogsbody, slavey, *sl.* gofer. ● *v.* **1** labor, toil, grind, grub, drudge, sweat, burn the midnight oil, work one's fingers to the bone, work like a Trojan, *archaic* moil, *literary* lucubrate. □ **slave driver 1** see MASTER *n.* 1. **2** see *oppressor* (OPPRESS). **slave ship** see SLAVER[1]. **slave trade** slavery, white slavery, *hist.* blackbirding. **slave trader** see SLAVER[1].

slaver[1] /sláyvər/ *n. hist.* a ship or person engaged in the slave trade.

■ slave ship; slave trader, white slaver.

slaver[2] /slávər/ *n. & v.* ● *n.* **1** saliva running from the mouth. **2 a** fulsome or servile flattery. **b** drivel; nonsense. ● *v.intr.* **1** let saliva run from the mouth; dribble. **2** (foll. by *over*) show excessive sentimentality over, or desire for. [ME prob. f. LG or Du.: cf. SLOBBER]

■ *n.* **1** drool, saliva, drivel, dribble, spit, spittle. **2 a** see FLATTERY. **b** nonsense, drivel, rubbish, twaddle, *colloq.* piffle; see also FLANNEL *n.* 3. ● *v.* dribble, drivel, spit; drool, salivate, slobber.

slavery /sláyvəree, sláyvree/ *n.* **1** the condition of a slave. **2** exhausting labor; drudgery. **3** the custom of having slaves.

■ **1** enslavement, bondage, enthrallment, servitude, serfdom, vassalage, yoke, *literary* thralldom, thrall; subjugation, captivity. **2** toil, drudgery, grind, strain, (hard) labor, *archaic* moil, *literary* travail, *Austral. sl.* (hard) yakka.

slavey /sláyvee/ *n.* (*pl.* **-eys**) *Brit. colloq.* a maidservant, esp. a hard-worked one.

■ see SLAVE *n.* 2.

Slavic /slaávik/ *adj.* & *n.* ● *adj.* **1** of or relating to the group of Indo-European languages including Russian, Polish, and Czech. **2** of or relating to the Slavs. ● *n.* the Slavic language group.

slavish /sláyvish/ *adj.* **1** of, like, or as of slaves. **2** showing no attempt at originality or development. **3** abject; servile; base. □□ **slavishly** *adv.* **slavishness** *n.*

■ **3** see SERVILE. □□ **slavishness** see *servility* (SERVILE).

Slavonic /sləvónik/ *adj.* & *n.* = SLAVIC.

slaw /slaw/ *n.* coleslaw. [Du. *sla*, shortened f. *salade* SALAD]

slay[1] /slay/ *v.tr.* (*past* **slew** /slōo/; *past part.* **slain** /slayn/) **1** *literary* or *joc.* kill. **2** *sl.* overwhelm with delight; convulse with laughter. □□ **slayer** *n.* [OE *slēan* f. Gmc]

■ **1** see KILL *v.* 1a. □□ **slayer** see KILLER 1.

slay[2] var. of SLEY.

SLBM *abbr.* **1** submarine-launched ballistic missile. **2** sea-launched ballistic missile.

sleaze /sleez/ *n.* & *v. colloq.* ● *n.* **1** sleaziness. **2** a person of low moral standards. ● *v.intr.* move in a sleazy fashion. [back-form. f. SLEAZY]

sleazy /sleézee/ *adj.* (**sleazier**, **sleaziest**) **1** squalid; tawdry. **2** slatternly. **3** (of textiles, etc.) flimsy. □□ **sleazily** *adv.* **sleaziness** *n.* [17th c.: orig. unkn.]

■ **1** disreputable, lower-class, low-grade, squalid, dirty, filthy, shabby, mangy, seedy, sordid, base, contemptible, run-down, slummy, dilapidated, ramshackle, rickety, gimcrack, jerry-built, slipshod, mean, cheap, poor, tawdry, trashy, worthless, chintzy, *colloq.* crummy, tatty, tacky, *sl.* cheesy. **2** slovenly, slatternly, shabby, dirty, untidy, sloppy. **3** unsubstantial, insubstantial, flimsy, thin, slight.

sled /sled/ *n.* & *v.* ● *n.* **1** a vehicle on runners for conveying loads or passengers esp. over snow, drawn by horses, dogs, or reindeer or pushed or pulled by one or more persons. **2** a toboggan. ● *v.intr.* (**sledded**, **sledding**) ride on a sled. [MLG *sledde*, rel. to SLIDE]

■ toboggan, *Brit.* sledge.

sledge[1] /slej/ *n.* & *v.* ● *n.* a heavy sled, esp. one drawn by draft animals. ● *v.intr.* & *tr.* travel or convey by sledge. [MDu. *sleedse*, rel. to SLED]

sledge[2] /slej/ *n.* = SLEDGEHAMMER.

sledgehammer /sléjhamər/ *n.* **1** a large heavy hammer used to break stone, etc. **2** (*attrib.*) heavy or powerful (*a sledgehammer blow*). [OE *slecg*, rel. to SLAY[1]]

sleek /sleek/ *adj.* & *v.* ● *adj.* **1** (of hair, fur, or skin, or an animal or person with such hair, etc.) smooth and glossy. **2** looking well-fed and comfortable. **3** ingratiating. **4** (of a thing) smooth and polished. ● *v.tr.* make sleek, esp. by stroking or pressing down. □□ **sleekly** *adv.* **sleekness** *n.* **sleeky** *adj.* [later var. of SLICK]

■ *adj.* **1** smooth, velvety, lustrous, shiny, shining, glossy, silky, silken, *colloq.* slick. **2** well-fed, contented, complacent, comfortable, thriving. **3** suave, unctuous, slimy, fawning, oily, specious, hypocritical, smooth, *colloq.* slick, smarmy. **4** polished, glossy, lustrous, shining, shiny, smooth; graceful, trim, streamlined.

sleep /sleep/ *n.* & *v.* ● *n.* **1** a condition of body and mind such as that which normally recurs for several hours every night, in which the nervous system is inactive, the eyes

closed, the postural muscles relaxed, and consciousness practically suspended. **2** a period of sleep (*shall try to get a sleep*). **3** a state like sleep, such as rest, quiet, negligence, or death. **4** the prolonged inert condition of hibernating animals. **5** a substance found in the corners of the eyes after sleep. ● *v.* (*past* and *past part.* **slept** /slept/) **1** *intr.* **a** be in a state of sleep. **b** fall asleep. **2** *intr.* (foll. by *at, in,* etc.) spend the night. **3** *tr.* provide sleeping accommodation for (*the house sleeps six*). **4** *intr.* (foll. by *with, together*) have sexual intercourse, esp. in bed. **5** *intr.* (foll. by *on, over*) not decide (a question) until the next day. **6** *intr.* (foll. by *through*) fail to be woken by. **7** *intr.* be inactive or dormant. **8** *intr.* be dead; lie in the grave. **9** *tr.* **a** (foll. by *off*) remedy by sleeping (*slept off his hangover*). **b** (foll. by *away*) spend in sleeping (*sleep the hours away*). **10** *intr.* (of a top) spin so steadily as to seem motionless. □ **get to sleep** manage to fall asleep. **go to sleep 1** enter a state of sleep. **2** (of a limb) become numbed by pressure. **in one's sleep** while asleep. **last sleep** death. **let sleeping dogs lie** avoid stirring up trouble. **put to sleep 1** anesthetize. **2** kill (an animal) painlessly. **sleep around** *colloq.* be sexually promiscuous. **sleep in 1** remain asleep later than usual in the morning. **2** sleep by night at one's place of work, as a domestic. **sleeping bag** a lined or padded bag to sleep in esp. when camping, etc. **Sleeping Beauty** a fairy-tale heroine who slept for 100 years. **sleeping car** a railroad car provided with beds or berths; a Pullman. **sleeping partner** *Brit.* = *silent partner* (see SILENT). **sleeping pill** a pill to induce sleep. **sleeping policeman** *Brit.* a ramp, etc., in the road intended to cause traffic to reduce speed. **sleeping sickness 1** any of several tropical diseases with extreme lethargy caused by a trypanosome transmitted by a tsetse fly bite. **2** *encephalitis lethargica*, a viral infection of the brain, with drowsiness and sometimes a coma. **sleep like a log** (or *top*) sleep soundly. **the sleep of the just** sound sleep. **sleep out** sleep by night out of doors, or not at one's place of work. [OE *slēp, slæp* (n.), *slēpan, slǣpan* (v.) f. Gmc]

■ *n.* **2** nap, doze, rest, siesta, beauty sleep, catnap, *colloq.* forty winks, snooze, shut-eye, *Brit.* zizz, *poet. rhet.* slumber, *Brit. sl.* kip. **4** hibernation, dormancy. ● *v.* **1** doze, (take a) nap, (have a) catnap, rest, repose, drowse, be in the land of Nod, snore, *colloq.* snooze, drop *or* nod off, crash, catch forty winks, *poet. rhet.* slumber, *sl.* catch some Z's, count sheep, conk off, *Brit. sl.* kip. □ **put to sleep 2** see *put down* 7 (PUT[1]). **sleeping pill** see SEDATIVE *n.*

sleeper /sleépər/ *n.* **1** a person or animal that sleeps. **2** a wooden or concrete beam laid horizontally as a support, esp. for railroad track. **3 a** a sleeping car. **b** a berth in this. **4 a** a ring worn on an earlobe to pierce it gradually. **b** a ring worn in a pierced ear to keep the hole from closing. **5** a thing that is suddenly successful after being undistinguished. **6** a child's one-piece night garment. **7** a spy or saboteur, etc., who remains inactive while establishing a secure position.

■ **2** (railroad) tie.

sleepless /sleéplis/ *adj.* **1** characterized by lack of sleep (*a sleepless night*). **2** unable to sleep. **3** continually active or moving. □□ **sleeplessly** *adv.* **sleeplessness** *n.*

■ **1, 2** restless, wakeful; disturbed; insomniac, alert, watchful, vigilant, unsleeping, awake.

sleepwalk /sleépwawk/ *v.intr.* walk or perform other actions while asleep. □□ **sleepwalker** *n.* **sleepwalking** *n.*

■ □□ **sleepwalker** somnambulist, noctambulist. **sleepwalking** somnambulism, noctambulism.

sleepy /sleépee/ *adj.* (**sleepier**, **sleepiest**) **1** drowsy; ready for sleep; about to fall asleep. **2** lacking activity or bustle (*a sleepy little town*). **3** habitually indolent; unobservant; etc. □ **sleepy sickness** *Brit.* = *sleeping sickness*, 2 (SLEEP). □□ **sleepily** *adv.* **sleepiness** *n.*

■ **1** drowsy, somnolent, tired, nodding, dozy, lethargic, torpid, comatose, sluggish, *poet.* & *rhet.* slumberous; weary, fatigued, exhausted, *colloq.* dead on one's feet, knocked out, fagged (out), dopey, pooped, *sl.* beat.

2 boring, inactive, dull, quiet, soporific, slow, sluggish, dormant; gentle, relaxed, *colloq.* laid-back.

sleepyhead /sleepeehed/ *n.* (esp. as a form of address) a sleepy or inattentive person.

sleet /sleet/ *n. & v.* ● *n.* **1** a mixture of snow and rain falling together. **2** hail or snow melting as it falls. **3** a thin coating of ice. ● *v.intr.* (prec. by *it* as subject) sleet falls (*it is sleeting*; *if it sleets*). □□ **sleety** *adj.* [ME prob. f. OE: rel. to MLG *slōten* (pl.) hail, MHG *slōz(e)* f. Gmc]

■ *n.* **1, 2** see PRECIPITATION *n.* 3a. ● *v.* see STORM *v.* 4.

sleeve /sleev/ *n.* **1** the part of a garment that wholly or partly covers an arm. **2** the cover of a phonograph record. **3** a tube enclosing a rod or smaller tube. **4 a** a wind sock. **b** a drogue towed by an aircraft. □ **roll up one's sleeves** prepare to fight or work. **sleeve coupling** a tube for connecting shafts or pipes. **sleeve note** a descriptive note on a record sleeve; liner note. **sleeve nut** a long nut with right-hand and left-hand screw threads for drawing together pipes or shafts conversely threaded. **sleeve valve** a valve in the form of a cylinder with a sliding movement. **up one's sleeve** concealed but ready for use, in reserve. □□ **sleeved** *adj.* (also in *comb.*). **sleeveless** *adj.* [OE *slēfe*, *slīefe*, *slȳf*]

sleeving /sleeving/ *n.* tubular covering for electric cable, etc.

sleigh /slay/ *n. & v.* ● *n.* a sled, esp. one for riding on. ● *v.intr.* travel on a sleigh. □ **sleigh bell** any of a number of tinkling bells attached to the harness of a sleigh-horse, etc. [orig. US, f. Du. *slee*, rel. to SLED]

sleight /slit/ *n.* *archaic* **1** a deceptive trick or device or movement. **2** dexterity. **3** cunning. □ **sleight of hand 1** dexterity, esp. in conjuring or fencing. **2** a display of dexterity, esp. a conjuring trick. [ME *sleghth* f. ON *slœgth* f. *slœgr* SLY]

■ □ **sleight of hand 1** see DEXTERITY 1. **2** see TRICK *n.* 4.

slender /sléndər/ *adj.* (**slenderer, slenderest**) **1 a** of small girth or breadth (*a slender pillar*). **b** gracefully thin (*a slender waist*). **2** relatively small or scanty; slight; meager; inadequate (*slender hopes; slender resources*). □ **slender loris** see LORIS. □□ **slenderly** *adv.* **slenderness** *n.* [ME: orig. unkn.]

■ **1** slim, lean, willowy, sylphlike, svelte, lissom, lithe, graceful, thin, spare, slight, lanky, fine; attenuated, tenuous. **2** slim, slight, small, little, scanty; narrow, unlikely, remote; meager, poor, weak, feeble; limited, inadequate, insufficient, insignificant, trifling.

slenderize /sléndəriz/ *v.* **1** *tr.* **a** make (a thing) slender. **b** make (one's figure) appear slender. **2** *intr.* make oneself slender; slim.

■ see SLIM *v.*

slept *past* and *past part.* of SLEEP.

sleuth /slooth/ *n. & v. colloq.* ● *n.* a detective. ● *v.* **1** *intr.* act as a detective. **2** *tr.* investigate. [orig. in *sleuthhound*: ME f. *sleuth* f. ON *slóth* track, trail: cf. SLOT²]

■ *n.* (private) detective, (private) investigator, *colloq.* private eye, sleuthhound, snoop, *sl.* dick, tec, shamus, gumshoe.

sleuthhound /sloothhownd/ *n.* **1** a bloodhound. **2** *colloq.* a detective; an investigator.

slew¹ /sloo/ *v. & n.* (also **slue**) ● *v.tr. & intr.* (often foll. by *around*) turn or swing forcibly or with effort out of the forward or ordinary position. ● *n.* such a change of position. [18th-c. Naut.: orig. unkn.]

■ *v.* see WIND² *v.* 1.

slew² *past* of SLAY¹.

slew³ /sloo/ *n. colloq.* a large number or quantity. [Ir. *sluagh*]

■ see HEAP *n.* 2.

sley /slay/ *n.* (also **slay**) a weaver's reed. [OE *slege*, rel. to SLAY¹]

slice /slis/ *n. & v.* ● *n.* **1** a thin, broad piece or wedge cut off or out esp. from meat or bread or a cake, pie, or large fruit. **2** a share; a part taken or allotted or gained (*a slice of territory; a slice of the profits*). **3** an implement with a broad flat blade for serving fish, etc., or for scraping or chipping; spatula. **4** *Golf & Tennis* a slicing stroke. ● *v.* **1** *tr.* (often foll. by *up*) cut into slices. **2** *tr.* (foll. by *off*) cut (a piece) off. **3** *intr.* (foll. by *into, through*) cut with or like a knife. **4** *tr.* (also *absol.*) **a** *Golf* strike (the ball) so that it deviates away from the striker. **b** (in other sports) propel (the ball) forward

at an angle. **5** *tr.* go through (air, etc.) with a cutting motion. □ **slice of life** a realistic representation of everyday experience. □□ **sliceable** *adj.* **slicer** *n.* (also in *comb.*). [ME f. OF *esclice, esclicier* splinter f. Frank. *slītjan*, rel. to SLIT]

■ *n.* **1** piece, portion, segment, slab, wedge, sliver, helping; rasher, collop, escalope, shaving, layer. **2** share, helping, cut, portion, piece, part. **3** spatula; slicer, fish slice. ● *v.* **1-3** divide, cut, *Biol.* section; shear; carve.

slick /slik/ *adj., n., & v.* ● *adj. colloq.* **1 a** (of a person or action) skillful or efficient; dexterous (*gave a slick performance*). **b** superficially or pretentiously smooth and dexterous. **c** glib. **2 a** sleek; smooth. **b** slippery. ● *n.* **1** a smooth patch of oil, etc., esp. on the sea. **2** *Motor Racing* a smooth tire. **3** *colloq.* a glossy magazine. **4** *sl.* a slick person. ● *v.tr. colloq.* **1** make sleek or smart. **2** (usu. foll. by *down*) flatten (one's hair, etc.). □□ **slickly** *adv.* **slickness** *n.* [ME *slike(n)*, prob. f. OE: cf. SLEEK]

■ *adj.* **1 a** smooth, clever, skillful, adroit, dexterous, efficient, professional, ingenious, imaginative, inventive, creative, neat. **b** superficial, shallow, meretricious, specious, glib. **c** smooth, urbane, suave, smooth-spoken, glib, smug, plausible; disingenuous, artful, wily, cunning, *colloq.* shifty; sycophantic, unctuous, oily, *colloq.* smarmy. **2 a** smooth, sleek, glossy, silky, silken, shiny, shining. **b** slippery, glassy, greasy, oily, *colloq.* slippy. ● *v.* **2** slick down, smooth, flatten, plaster down, grease, oil.

slicker /slíkər/ *n.* **1** *colloq.* **a** a plausible rogue. **b** a smart and sophisticated city dweller (cf. *city slicker*). **2** a raincoat of smooth material.

■ **1 a** confidence man, cheat, swindler, mountebank, *sl.* con man. **b** city dweller, *usu. derog.* city slicker, *derog.* townie. **2** raincoat, oilskin, mackintosh.

slide /slid/ *v. & n.* ● *v.* (*past* and *past part.* **slid** /slid/) **1 a** *intr.* move along a smooth surface with continuous contact on the same part of the thing moving (cf. ROLL). **b** *tr.* cause to do this (*slide the drawer into place*). **2** *intr.* move quietly; glide; go smoothly along. **3** *intr.* pass gradually or imperceptibly. **4** *intr.* glide over ice on one or both feet without skates (under gravity or with momentum got by running). **5** *intr.* (foll. by *over*) barely touch upon (a delicate subject, etc.). **6** *intr. & tr.* (often foll. by *into*) move or cause to move quietly or unobtrusively (*slid his hand into mine*). **7** *intr.* take its own course (*let it slide*). **8** *intr.* decline (*shares slid to a new low*). ● *n.* **1 a** the act or an instance of sliding. **b** a rapid decline. **2** an inclined plane down which children, goods, etc., slide; a chute. **3 a** a track made by or for sliding, esp. on ice. **b** a slope prepared with snow or ice for tobogganing. **4** a part of a machine or instrument that slides, esp. a slide valve. **5 a** a thing slid into place, esp. a piece of glass holding an object for a microscope. **b** a mounted transparency usu. placed in a projector for viewing on a screen. **6** = *sliding seat.* **7** a part or parts of a machine on or between which a sliding part works. □ **let things slide** be negligent; allow deterioration. **slide fastener** *Brit.* = ZIPPER. **slide rule** a ruler with a sliding central strip, graduated logarithmically for making rapid calculations, esp. multiplication and division. **slide valve** a sliding piece that opens and closes an aperture by sliding across it. **sliding door** a door drawn across an aperture on a slide, not turning on hinges. **sliding keel** *Naut. Brit.* a centerboard. **sliding roof** esp. *Brit.* = SUNROOF. **sliding scale** a scale of fees, taxes, wages, etc., that varies as a whole in accordance with variation of some standard. **sliding seat** a seat able to slide to and fro on runners, etc., esp. in a racing scull to adjust the length of a stroke. □□ **slidable** *adj.* **slidably** *adv.* **slider** *n.* [OE *slīdan*]

■ *v.* **1, 2** glide, slip; coast, skim, glissade, skate, plane, skid, toboggan, slither. **6** creep, steal, slip, slink, move.

7 (*let slide*) forget, ignore, neglect, gloss *or* pass over, pay no heed *or* mind to. **8** decline, decrease, drop, fall. ● *n.* **1 b** see DECLINE *n.* 1, 4. **2** see CHUTE 1, 2.

slideway /slídway/ *n.* = SLIDE *n.* 7.

slight /slīt/ *adj., v.,* & *n.* ● *adj.* **1 a** inconsiderable; of little significance (*has a slight cold*; *the damage is very slight*). **b** barely perceptible (*a slight smell of gas*). **c** not much or great or thorough; inadequate; scanty (*a conclusion based on very slight observation*; *paid him slight attention*). **2** slender; frail-looking (*saw a slight figure approaching*; *supported by a slight framework*). **3** (in *superl.,* with *neg.* or *interrog.*) any whatever (*paid not the slightest attention*). ● *v.tr.* **1** treat or speak of (a person, etc.) as not worth attention, fail in courtesy or respect toward; markedly neglect. **2** *hist.* make militarily useless; raze (a fortification, etc.). ● *n.* a marked piece of neglect; a failure to show due respect. □ **not in the slightest** not at all. **put a slight upon** = sense 1 of *v.* □□ **slightingly** *adv.* **slightish** *adj.* **slightly** *adv.* **slightness** *n.* [ME *slyght, sleght* f. ON *sléttr* level, smooth f. Gmc]

■ *adj.* **1 a** small, little, minor, negligible, insignificant, inconsequential, inconsiderable. **b** trifling, tiny, slender, minute, infinitesimal. **c** see SCANTY, SLENDER 2. **2** slender, slim, thin, small, short, petite, diminutive, tiny, miniature, bantam, wee, *colloq.* pint-sized; insubstantial, unsubstantial, weak, feeble, delicate, dainty, frail, unstable, fragile, flimsy, lightly made *or* built, precarious, inadequate, rickety, insecure. ● *v.* **1** disregard, ignore, disdain, scorn, snub, rebuff, cut, cold-shoulder; insult, offend, affront, mortify, diminish, minimize, depreciate, disparage, put a slight upon. ● *n.* snub, insult, affront, slur, indignity, outrage, offense, disrespect. □□ **slightly** a little, somewhat, to a certain extent *or* degree *or* measure, to a slight extent *or* degree *or* measure, to a minor extent *or* degree *or* measure, marginally; moderately, rather.

slily var. of SLYLY (see SLY).

slim /slim/ *adj., v.,* & *n.* ● *adj.* (**slimmer, slimmest**) **1 a** of small girth or thickness; of long, narrow shape. **b** gracefully thin; slenderly built. **c** not fat nor overweight. **2** small, insufficient (*a slim chance of success*). **3** clever; artful; crafty; unscrupulous. ● *v.* (**slimmed, slimming**) **1** *intr.* esp. *Brit.* make oneself slimmer by dieting, exercise, etc. **2** *tr.* make slim or slimmer. ● *n.* esp. *Brit.* a course of slimming. □□ **slimly** *adv.* **slimmer** *n.* **slimming** *n.* & *adj.* **slimmish** *adj.* **slimness** *n.* [LG or Du. f. Gmc]

■ *adj.* **1** see SLENDER 1. **2** see SLENDER 2. ● *v.* **1** reduce, lose *or* shed weight, diet, slenderize.

slime /slīm/ *n.* & *v.* ● *n.* thick slippery mud or a substance of similar consistency, e.g., liquid bitumen or a mucus exuded by fish, etc. ● *v.tr.* cover with slime. □ **slime mold** a spore-bearing microorganism secreting slime. [OE *slīm* f. Gmc, rel. to L *limus* mud, Gk *limnē* marsh]

■ *n.* see MUD 1.

slimline /slímlin/ *adj.* of slender design.

slimy /slímee/ *adj.* (**slimier, slimiest**) **1** of the consistency of slime. **2** covered, smeared with, or full of slime. **3** disgustingly dishonest, meek, or flattering. **4** slippery; hard to hold. □□ **slimily** *adv.* **sliminess** *n.*

■ **1, 2** oozy, slippery, mucky, squashy, squishy, viscous, sticky, gluey, mucilaginous, glutinous, mucous, clammy, mushy, *Bot.* uliginose, *sl.* gooey, gunky. **3** slippery, unctuous, oily, slick, obsequious, sycophantic, toadying, servile, creeping, crawling, fawning, groveling, abject, *colloq.* smarmy. **4** see SLIPPERY 1, 2.

sling¹ /sling/ *n.* & *v.* ● *n.* **1** a strap, belt, etc., used to support or raise a hanging weight, e.g., a rifle, a ship's boat, or goods being transferred. **2** a bandage looped around the neck to support an injured arm. **3** a strap or string used with the hand to give impetus to a small missile, esp. a stone. **4** *Austral. sl.* a tip or bribe. ● *v.tr.* (*past* and *past part.* **slung** /slung/) **1** (also *absol.*) hurl (a stone, etc.) from a sling. **2** *colloq.* throw. **3** suspend with a sling; allow to swing suspended; arrange so as to be supported from above; hoist or transfer with a sling. □ **sling-back** an open-backed shoe

held in place by a strap above the heel. **sling off at** *Austral.* & *NZ sl.* disparage; mock; make fun of. [ME, prob. f. ON *slyngva* (v.)]

■ *n.* **1, 2** support, strap, band; belt. **3** catapult, slingshot, *hist.* trebuchet. ● *v.* **1, 2** catapult, propel, hurl, shy, fling, fire, shoot, let fly, launch; toss, throw, cast, pitch, heave, lob; *colloq.* chuck. **3** suspend, hang, dangle, swing, drape, string.

sling² /sling/ *n.* a sweetened drink of liquor (esp. gin) and water. [18th c.: orig. unkn.]

slinger /slíngər/ *n.* a person who slings, esp. the user of a sling.

slingshot /slíngshot/ *n.* a forked stick, etc., with elastic for shooting stones, etc.

■ see SLING¹ *n.* 3.

slink¹ /slingk/ *v.intr.* (*past* and *past part.* **slunk** /slungk/) (often foll. by *off, away, by*) move in a stealthy or guilty or sneaking manner. [OE *slincan* crawl]

■ sneak, creep, steal, prowl, skulk, slip.

slink² /slingk/ *v.* & *n.* ● *v.tr.* (also *absol.*) (of an animal) produce (young) prematurely. ● *n.* **1** an animal, esp. a calf, so born. **2** its flesh. [app. f. SLINK¹]

slinky /slíngkee/ *adj.* (**slinkier, slinkiest**) **1** stealthy. **2** (of a garment) close-fitting and flowing; sinuous. **3** gracefully slender. □□ **slinkily** *adv.* **slinkiness** *n.*

slip¹ /slip/ *v.* & *n.* ● *v.* (**slipped, slipping**) **1** *intr.* slide unintentionally esp. for a short distance; lose one's footing or balance or place by unintended sliding. **2** *intr.* go or move with a sliding motion (*as the door closes the catch slips into place*; *slipped into her nightgown*). **3** *intr.* escape restraint or capture by being slippery or hard to hold or by not being grasped (*the eel slipped through his fingers*). **4** *intr.* **a** make one's or its way unobserved or quietly or quickly (*just slip across to the baker's*; *errors will slip in*). **b** (foll. by *by*) (of time) go by rapidly or unnoticed. **5** *intr.* **a** make a careless or casual mistake. **b** fall below the normal standard; deteriorate; lapse. **6** *tr.* insert or transfer stealthily or casually or with a sliding motion (*slipped a coin into his hand*; *slipped the papers into his pocket*). **7** *tr.* **a** release from restraint (*slipped the greyhounds from the leash*). **b** detach (an anchor) from a ship. **c** *Brit.* detach (a railroad car) from a moving train. **d** release (the clutch of a motor vehicle) for a moment. **e** (of an animal) produce (young) prematurely. **8** *tr.* move (a stitch) to the other needle without knitting it. **9** *tr.* (foll. by *on, off*) pull (a garment) hastily on or off. **10** *tr.* escape from; give the slip to (*the dog slipped its collar*; *point slipped my mind*). ● *n.* **1** the act or an instance of slipping. **2** an accidental or slight error. **3** a loose covering or garment, esp. a petticoat or pillowcase. **4 a** a reduction in the movement of a pulley, etc., due to slipping of the belt. **b** a reduction in the distance traveled by a ship or aircraft arising from the nature of the medium in which its propeller revolves. **5** (in *sing.* or *pl.*) **a** an artificial slope of stone, etc., on which boats are landed. **b** an inclined structure on which ships are built or repaired. **6** *Cricket* **a** a fielder stationed for balls glancing off the bat to the off side. **b** (in *sing.* or *pl.*) the position of such a fielder (*caught in the slips*; *caught at slip*). **7** *Brit.* a leash to slip dogs. □ **give a person the slip** escape from or evade him or her. **let slip 1** release accidentally or deliberately, esp. from a leash. **2** miss (an opportunity). **3** utter inadvertently. **let slip the dogs of war** *poet.* open hostilities. **let slip through one's fingers 1** lose hold of. **2** miss the opportunity of having. **slip away** depart without leave-taking, etc. **slip carriage** *Brit.* a railroad car on an express for detaching at a station where the rest of the train does not stop. **slip coach** *Brit.* = *slip carriage.* **slip form** a mold in which a structure of uniform cross section is cast by filling it with concrete and continually moving and refilling it. **slip hook** a hook with a contrivance for releasing it readily when necessary; pelican hook. **slip off** depart without leave-taking, etc. **slip of the pen** (or **tongue**) a small mistake in which something is written (or said) unintentionally. **slip-on** *adj.* (of shoes or clothes) that can be easily slipped on and off. ● *n.* a slip-on shoe or garment. **slipped disk** a disk between vertebrae that has become displaced and causes lumbar pain. **slip**

ring a ring for sliding contact in a dynamo or electric motor.
slip rope *Naut.* a rope with both ends on board so that casting loose either end frees the ship from its moorings.
slip sheet *Printing* a sheet of paper placed between newly printed sheets to prevent offset or smudging. **slip something over on** *colloq.* outwit. **slip stitch 1** a loose stitch joining layers of fabric and not visible externally. **2** a stitch moved to the other needle without being knitted. **slip-stitch** *v.tr.* sew with slip stitch. **slip up** *colloq.* make a mistake. **there's many a slip 'twixt cup and lip** nothing is certain till it has happened. [ME prob. f. MLG *slippen*: cf. SLIPPERY]

■ *v.* **1** slide, skid, glide, aquaplane, slither; stumble, lose one's footing *or* balance, miss one's footing, trip; fall, tumble. **4 a** sneak, slink, steal, creep, edge, skulk; (*slip in*) enter, get in, sneak in. **b** (*slip by*) pass, elapse, vanish, go by. **5 a** see *slip up* below. **b** SEE DETERIORATE.
● *n.* **2** blunder, error, mistake, fault, oversight, slip of the tongue *or* pen, Freudian slip, *lapsus linguae*, gaffe, inadvertence, indiscretion, impropriety, transgression, peccadillo, faux pas, *colloq.* slipup, blooper, *sl.* bloomer, booboo, fluff, *Brit. sl.* boob. □ **give a person the slip** see ELUDE 1. **let slip** 2 see MISS¹ *v.* 8. **3** reveal, divulge, blurt out, leak, let out, disclose, expose, come out with, blab. **slip away, slip off** slip out, escape, disappear, leave, vanish, steal away, go away *or* off *or* out, run away *or* off *or* out, break away, get away, sneak away *or* off *or* out. **slip of the pen** (or **tongue**) see SLIP¹ *n.* above. **slip something over on** see OUTSMART. **slip up** slip, err, blunder, make a mistake, miscalculate, botch (up), *sl.* screw up, goof.

slip² /slip/ *n.* **1 a** a small piece of paper esp. for writing on. **b** a long, narrow strip of thin wood, paper, etc. **c** esp. *Brit.* a printer's proof on such paper; a galley proof. **2** a cutting taken from a plant for grafting or planting; a scion. □ **slip of a** small and slim (*a slip of a girl*). [ME, prob. f. MDu., MLG *slippe* cut, strip, etc.]

■ **1** paper, note, chit; permit, permission, pass, document; piece, scrap, strip, sliver. **2** shoot, scion, cutting, set, sprig, twig, sprout, runner, offshoot.

slip³ /slip/ *n.* clay in a creamy mixture with water, used mainly for decorating earthenware. □ **slip casting** the manufacture of ceramic ware by allowing slip to solidify in a mold. **slip-ware** pottery decorated with slip. [OE *slipa, slyppe* slime: cf. COWSLIP]

slipcase /slípcays/ *n.* a close-fitting case for a book.
slipcover /slípkəvər/ *n. & v.* ● *n.* **1** a removable covering for usu. upholstered furniture. **2** a jacket or slipcase for a book. ● *v.tr* cover with a slipcover.
slipknot /slípnot/ *n.* **1** a knot that can be undone by a pull. **2** a running knot.
slipover /slípōvər/ *adj. & n.* ● *adj.* (of a garment) to be slipped on over the head. ● *n.* a garment thus put on.
slippage /slípij/ *n.* **1** the act or an instance of slipping. **2 a** a decline, esp. in popularity or value. **b** failure to meet a deadline or fulfill a promise; delay.
slipper /slípər/ *n. & v.* ● *n.* **1** a light, loose, comfortable indoor shoe. **2** a light slip-on shoe for dancing, etc. ● *v.tr.* *Brit.* beat or strike with a slipper. □□ **slippered** *adj.*
slipperwort /slípərwərt, -wawrt/ *n.* calceolaria.
slippery /slípəree/ *adj.* **1** difficult to hold firmly because of smoothness, wetness, sliminess, or elusive motion. **2** (of a surface) difficult to stand on, causing slips by its smoothness or muddiness. **3** unreliable; unscrupulous; shifty. **4** (of a subject) requiring tactful handling. □ **slippery elm 1** the N. American red elm, *Ulmus rubra.* **2** the medicinal inner bark of this. **slippery slope** a course leading to disaster. □□ **slipperily** *adv.* **slipperiness** *n.* [prob. coined by Coverdale (1535) after Luther's *schlipfferig*, MHG *slipferig* f. *slipfern, slipfen* f. Gmc: partly f. *slipper* slippery (now dial.) f. OE *slipor* f. Gmc]

■ **1, 2** slick, sleek, slimy, icy, glassy, smooth, slithery, greasy, oily, lubricated, *colloq.* slippy. **3** evasive, devious, unreliable, undependable, questionable, untrustworthy, dishonest, treacherous, disloyal,

perfidious, slick, crafty, sly, foxy, cunning, tricky, sneaky, false, reptilian, faithless, shady, *colloq.* shifty.
slippy /slípee/ *adj.* (**slippier, slippiest**) *colloq.* slippery. □ **look** (or **be**) **slippy** *Brit.* look sharp; make haste. □□ **slippiness** *n.*
slipshod /slípshod/ *adj.* **1** (of speech or writing, a speaker or writer, a method of work, etc.) careless; unsystematic; loose in arrangement. **2** slovenly. **3** having shoes down at the heel.
■ **1, 2** careless, slapdash, haphazard, messy, untidy, disorganized, lax, unorganized, unmethodical, unsystematic, slovenly, sloppy, shoddy.
slipstream /slípstreem/ *n. & v.* ● *n.* **1** a current of air or water driven back by a revolving propeller or a moving vehicle. **2** an assisting force regarded as drawing something along with or behind something else. ● *v.tr.* **1** follow closely behind (another vehicle). **2** pass after traveling in another's slipstream.
slipup /slípəp/ *n.* a mistake; a blunder.
slipway /slípway/ *n.* a slip for building ships or landing boats.
slit /slit/ *n. & v.* ● *n.* **1** a long, straight, narrow incision. **2** a long, narrow opening comparable to a cut. ● *v.tr.* (**slitting**; *past* and *past part.* **slit**) **1** make a slit in; cut or tear lengthwise. **2** cut into strips. □ **slit-eyed** having long, narrow eyes. **slit-pocket** a pocket with a vertical opening giving access to the pocket or to a garment beneath. **slit trench** a narrow trench for a soldier or a weapon. □□ **slitter** *n.* [ME *slitte*, rel. to OE *slītan*, f. Gmc]
■ *n.* split, cut, gash, incision, fissure, groove, slash, rift, crack, cleft, vent, aperture, opening. ● *v.* **1** split, cut, slash, gash, slice, tear, rip, *literary* cleave.
slither /slíthər/ *v. & n.* ● *v.intr.* slide unsteadily; go with an irregular slipping motion. ● *n.* an instance of slithering. □□ **slithery** *adj.* [ME var. of *slidder* (now dial.) f. OE *slid(e)rian* frequent. f. *slid-*, weak grade of *slīdan* SLIDE]
■ *v.* slide, worm, snake, slip, slink, glide, skitter, creep, crawl.
slitty /slítee/ *adj.* (**slittier, slittiest**) (of the eyes) long and narrow.
sliver /slívər/ *n. & v.* ● *n.* **1** a long, thin piece cut or split off. **2** a piece of wood torn from a tree or from lumber. **3** a splinter, esp. from an exploded shell. **4** a strip of loose textile fibers after carding. ● *v.tr. & intr.* **1** break off as a sliver. **2** break up into slivers. **3** form into slivers. [ME, rel. to *slive* cleave (now dial.) f. OE]
■ *n.* **1–3** fragment, piece, shard, shred, splinter, slip, shaving, paring, flake, chip, bit, scrap, strip, slice, snippet, snip.
slivovitz /slívəvits/ *n.* a plum brandy made esp. in Romania and the former Yugoslavia. [Serbo-Croat *šljivovica* f. *šljiva* plum]
slob /slob/ *n.* **1** *colloq.* a stupid, careless, coarse, or fat person. **2** *Ir.* muddy land. □□ **slobbish** *adj.* [Ir. *slab* mud f. E *slab* ooze, sludge, prob. f. Scand.]
■ **1** oaf, boor, lout, churl, yahoo, barbarian, *colloq.* pig, galoot, *Brit. sl.* yob, yobbo.
slobber /slóbər/ *v. & n.* ● *v.intr.* **1** slaver. **2** (foll. by *over*) show excessive sentiment. ● *n.* saliva running from the mouth; slaver. □□ **slobbery** *adj.* [ME, = Du. *slobbern*, of imit. orig.]
■ *v.* **1** see SLAVER² *v.*
sloe /slō/ *n.* **1** = BLACKTHORN. **2** its small bluish-black fruit with a sharp sour taste. □ **sloe-eyed 1** having eyes of this color. **2** slant-eyed. **sloe gin** a liqueur of sloes steeped in gin. [OE *slā(h)* f. Gmc]
■ □ **sloe-eyed** 2 slit-eyed, slant-eyed.
slog /slog/ *v. & n.* ● *v.* (**slogged, slogging**) **1** *intr.* & *tr.* hit hard and usu. wildly, esp. in boxing or at cricket. **2** *intr.* (often foll. by *away, on*) walk or work doggedly. ● *n.* **1** a

/. . ./ **pronunciation**	● **part of speech**
□ **phrases, idioms, and compounds**	
□□ **derivatives**	■ **synonym section**
cross-references appear in SMALL CAPITALS or *italics*	

hard random hit. **2 a** hard steady work or walking. **b** a spell of this. □□ **slogger** *n.* [19th c.: orig. unkn.: cf. SLUG²]

■ *v.* **1** see STRIKE *v.* 1. **2** see WALK *v.* 1, 2. ● *n.* **2** see *drudgery* (DRUDGE), WALK *n.* 2.

slogan /slṓgən/ *n.* **1** a short catchy phrase used in advertising, etc. **2** a party cry; a watchword or motto. **3** *hist.* a Scottish Highland war cry. [Gael. *sluagh-ghairm* f. *sluagh* army + *gairm* shout]

■ catchword, watchword, byword, catchphrase; motto, jingle, saying; war cry, battle cry, rallying cry.

sloop /slṓop/ *n.* **1** a small, one-masted, fore-and-aft-rigged vessel with mainsail and jib. **2** (in full **sloop of war**) *hist.* a small warship with guns on the upper deck only. □ **sloop-rigged** rigged like a sloop. [Du. *sloep(e)*, of unkn. orig.]

slop¹ /slop/ *v.* & *n.* ● *v.* (**slopped, slopping**) **1** (often foll. by *over*) **a** *intr.* spill or flow over the edge of a vessel. **b** *tr.* allow to do this. **2** *tr.* make (the floor, clothes, etc.) wet or messy by slopping; spill or splash liquid on. **3** *intr.* (usu. foll. by *over*) gush; be effusive or maudlin. ● *n.* **1** a quantity of liquid spilled or splashed. **2** weakly sentimental language. **3** (in *pl.*) waste liquid, esp. dirty water or the waste contents of kitchen, bedroom, or prison vessels. **4** (in *sing.* or *pl.*) unappetizing weak liquid food. **5** *Naut.* a choppy sea. □ **slop about** *Brit.* move about in a slovenly manner. **slop basin** (or **bowl**) *Brit.* a basin for the dregs of cups at the table. **slop jar** a jar or pail for removing household slops. **slop out** *Brit.* carry slops out (in prison, etc.). **slop pail** *n.* **1** a pail for carrying slops to feed livestock, esp. pigs. **2** a slop jar. [earlier sense 'slush,' prob. rel. to *slyppe*: cf. COWSLIP]

■ *v.* **1** see SPILL¹ *v.* 1. ● *n.* **3** (*slops*) see GARBAGE 1a.

slop² /slop/ *n.* **1** a worker's loose outer garment. **2** (in *pl.*) esp. *Brit.* ready-made or cheap clothing. **3** (in *pl.*) clothes and bedding supplied to sailors in the navy. **4** (in *pl.*) *archaic* wide baggy trousers esp. as worn by sailors. [ME: cf. OE *oferslop* surplice f. Gmc]

slope /slṓp/ *n.* & *v.* ● *n.* **1** an inclined position or direction; a state in which one end or side is at a higher level than another; a position in a line neither parallel nor perpendicular to level ground nor to a line serving as a standard. **2** a piece of rising or falling ground. **3 a** a difference in level between the two ends or sides of a thing (*a slope of 5 yards*). **b** the rate at which this increases with distance, etc. **4** a place for skiing on the side of a hill or mountain. **5** (prec. by *the*) the position of a rifle when sloped. ● *v.* **1** *intr.* have or take a slope; slant esp. up or down; lie or tend obliquely, esp. to ground level. **2** *tr.* place or arrange or make in or at a slope. □ **slope arms** place one's rifle in a sloping position against one's shoulder. **slope off** esp. *Brit. sl.* go away, esp. to evade work, etc. [shortening of ASLOPE]

■ *n.* **1–3** incline, decline, ascent, descent, acclivity, declivity, rise, fall, ramp, dip, sink, drop, angle, slant, pitch, tilt, rake, tip, camber, cant, bevel, hill, bank, scarp, gradient, grade, upgrade, downgrade. **4** trail, track, piste. ● *v.* **1** incline, decline, ascend, descend, rise, fall, dip, sink, drop (off), angle, slant, cant, pitch, tilt, tip, lean, list. **2** slant, angle, bevel, cant, grade, incline, tilt, lean, tip. □ **slope off** see *beat it*.

sloppy /slópee/ *adj.* (**sloppier, sloppiest**) **1 a** (of the ground) wet with rain; full of puddles. **b** (of food, etc.) watery and disagreeable. **c** (of a floor, table, etc.) wet with slops, having water, etc., spilled on it. **2** unsystematic; careless; not thorough. **3** (of a garment) ill-fitting or untidy; (of a person) wearing such garments. **4** (of sentiment or talk) weakly emotional; maudlin. **5** *colloq.* (of the sea) choppy. □□ **sloppily** *adv.* **sloppiness** *n.*

■ **1 a, c** wet, slushy, soggy, soppy, sopping, sodden, sloshy, muddy, rainy. **b** watery, thin, runny, liquid, messy, slushy, *sl.* gooey. **2** slovenly, careless, slipshod, shoddy, slapdash, lax, unsystematic, untidy, messy, disordered, disorderly. **3** ill-fitting, shabby, dirty, untidy, messy, dowdy, frumpy, frumpish; draggle-tailed, bedraggled, disheveled, unkempt, *colloq.* scruffy. **4** sentimental, gushy, gushing, mawkish, maudlin, mushy, overemotional, romantic, sloshy, *colloq.* slushy, *Brit. colloq.* wet, soppy.

slosh /slosh/ *v.* & *n.* ● *v.* **1** *intr.* (often foll. by *about*) splash or flounder about; move with a splashing sound. **2** *tr. Brit. sl.* hit esp. heavily. **3** *tr. colloq.* **a** pour (liquid) clumsily. **b** pour liquid on. ● *n.* **1** slush. **2 a** an instance of splashing. **b** the sound of this. **3** *Brit. sl.* a heavy blow. **4** a quantity of liquid. [var. of SLUSH]

■ *v.* **1** see SPLASH *v.* 3. **2** see HIT *v.* 1a. ● *n.* **2** see SPLASH *n.* 2. **3** see BLOW² 1.

sloshed /slosht/ *adj. sl.* drunk.

■ see DRUNK *adj.* 1.

sloshy /slóshee/ *adj.* (**sloshier, sloshiest**) **1** slushy. **2** sloppy; sentimental.

■ **1** see SLOPPY 1a, c. **2** see SLOPPY 4.

slot¹ /slot/ *n.* & *v.* ● *n.* **1** a slit or other aperture in a machine, etc., for something (esp. a coin) to be inserted. **2** a slit, groove, channel, or long aperture into which something fits or in which something works. **3** an allotted place in an arrangement or scheme, esp. in a broadcasting schedule. ● *v.* (**slotted, slotting**) **1** *tr.* & *intr.* place or be placed into or as if into a slot. **2** *tr.* provide with a slot or slots. □ **slot machine** a machine worked by the insertion of a coin in a slot, esp. a gambling machine operated by a pulled handle. [ME, = hollow of the breast, f. OF *esclot*, of unkn. orig.]

■ *n.* **1, 2** groove, fissure, notch, slit, opening, hollow, depression, channel, track, *Anat.* sulcus. **3** opening, position, vacancy, job, place, assignment, niche, space, spot, pigeonhole, time. ● *v.* **1** assign, schedule, place, position, pigeonhole, fit. **2** groove, fissure, notch, slit, hollow out.

slot² /slot/ *n.* **1** the track of a deer, etc., esp. as shown by footprints. **2** a deer's foot. [OF *esclot* hoofprint of a horse, prob. f. ON *slóth* trail: cf. SLEUTH]

sloth /slawth, slṓth/ *n.* **1** laziness or indolence; reluctance to make an effort. **2** any slow-moving nocturnal mammal of the family Bradypodidae or Megalonychidae of S. America, having long limbs and hooked claws for hanging upside down from branches of trees. □ **sloth bear** a large-lipped black shaggy bear, *Melursus ursinus*, of India. [ME f. SLOW + -TH²]

■ **1** idleness, laziness, indolence, slothfulness, inertia, apathy, indifference, accidie, torpor, torpidity, sluggishness, languor, languidness, lethargy, phlegm, *literary* hebetude.

slothful /slawthfool, slṓth-/ *adj.* lazy; characterized by sloth. □□ **slothfully** *adv.* **slothfulness** *n.*

■ idle, lazy, indolent, apathetic, indifferent, torpid, inert, slack, lax, shiftless, fainéant, inactive, supine, do-nothing, sluggish, sluggardly, slow, laggard, languorous, languid, lethargic, lackadaisical, phlegmatic.

slouch /slowch/ *v.* & *n.* ● *v.* **1** *intr.* stand or move or sit in a drooping, ungainly fashion. **2** *tr.* bend one side of the brim of (a hat) downward (opp. COCK¹). **3** *intr.* droop; hang down loosely. ● *n.* **1** a slouching posture or movement, a stoop. **2** a downward bend of a hat brim (opp. COCK¹). **3** *sl.* an incompetent or slovenly worker or operator or performance (*he's no slouch*). □ **slouch hat** a hat with a wide flexible brim. □□ **slouchy** *adj.* (**slouchier, slouchiest**). [16th c.: orig. unkn.]

■ *v.* **1** droop, sag, stoop, loll, slump; hunch. ● *n.* **1** stoop, sag, droop, slump; hunch. **3** sloven, loafer, sluggard, laggard, idler, malingerer, *colloq.* lazybones.

slough¹ /slow, slṓo (for 2)/ *n.* **1** a swamp; a miry place; a quagmire. **2** a marshy pond, backwater, etc. □ **Slough of Despond** a state of hopeless depression (with ref. to Bunyan's *Pilgrim's Progress*). □□ **sloughy** *adj.* [OE *slōh, slō(g)*]

■ see SWAMP *n.*

slough² /sluf/ *n.* & *v.* ● *n.* **1** a part that an animal casts or molts, esp. a snake's cast skin. **2** dead tissue that drops off from living flesh, etc. **3** a habit, etc., that has been abandoned. ● *v.* **1** *tr.* cast off as a slough. **2** *intr.* (often foll. by *off*) drop off as a slough. **3** *intr.* cast off a slough. **4** *intr.* (often foll. by *away, down*) (of soil, rock, etc.) collapse or slide into a hole or depression. □□ **sloughy** *adj.* [ME, perh. rel. to LG *slu(we)* husk]

Slovak /slṓvaak, -vak/ *n. & adj.* ● *n.* **1** a member of a Slavic people inhabiting Slovakia in central Europe, formerly part of Czechoslovakia and now an independent republic. **2** the West Slavic language of this people. ● *adj.* of or relating to this people or language. [Slovak, etc., *Slovák*, rel. to SLO-VENE]

sloven /slúvən/ *n.* a person who is habitually untidy or careless. [ME perh. f. Flem. *sloef* dirty or Du. *slof* careless]
■ see SLOUCH *n.* 3.

Slovene /slṓveen, sləveén/ (also **Slovenian** /-veéneeən/) *n. & adj.* ● *n.* **1** a member of a Slavic people in Slovenia in the former Yugoslavia. **2** the language of this people. ● *adj.* of or relating to Slovenia or its people or language. [G *Slovene* f. Styrian, etc., *Slovenec* f. OSlav. *Slov-*, perh. rel. to *slovo* word]

slovenly /slúvənlee/ *adj. & adv.* ● *adj.* careless and untidy; unmethodical. ● *adv.* in a slovenly manner. □□ **slovenliness** *n.*
■ *adj.* see UNTIDY.

slow /slṓ/ *adj., adv., & v.* ● *adj.* **1 a** taking a relatively long time to do a thing or cover a distance (also foll. by *of*: *slow of speech*). **b** not quick; acting or moving or done without speed. **2** gradual; obtained over a length of time (*slow growth*). **3** not producing, allowing, or conducive to speed (*in the slow lane*). **4** (of a clock, etc.) showing a time earlier than is the case. **5** (of a person) not understanding readily; not learning easily. **6** dull; uninteresting; tedious. **7** slack or sluggish (*business is slow*). **8** (of a fire or oven) giving little heat. **9** *Photog.* **a** (of a film) needing long exposure. **b** (of a lens) having a small aperture. **10 a** reluctant; tardy (*not slow to defend himself*). **b** not hasty or easily moved (*slow to take offense*). **11** (of a tennis court, putting green, etc.) on which the ball bounces or runs slowly. ● *adv.* **1** at a slow pace; slowly. **2** (in *comb.*) (*slow-moving traffic*). ● *v.* (usu. foll. by *down, up*) **1** intr. & tr. reduce one's speed or the speed of (a vehicle, etc.). **2** intr. reduce one's pace of life; live or work less intensely. □ **slow and sure** of the attitude that haste is risky. **slow but sure** achieving the required result eventually. **slow handclap** *Brit.* slow clapping by an audience as a sign of displeasure or boredom. **slow loris** see LORIS. **slow march** the marching time adopted by troops in a funeral procession, etc. **slow match** a slow-burning match for lighting explosives, etc. **slow motion 1** the operation or speed of a film using slower projection or more rapid exposure so that actions, etc., appear much slower than usual. **2** the simulation of this in real action. **slow neutron** a neutron with low kinetic energy esp. after moderation (cf. *fast neutron* (see FAST[1])). **slow poison** a poison eventually causing death by repeated doses. **slow reactor** *Physics* a nuclear reactor using mainly slow neutrons (cf. *fast reactor* (see FAST[1])). **slow virus** a progressive disease caused by a virus or viruslike organism that multiplies slowly in the host organism and has a long incubation period, such as scrapie. **slow-witted** stupid. □□ **slowish** *adj.* **slowly** *adv.* **slowness** *n.* [OE *slāw* f. Gmc]
■ *adj.* **1** lagging, laggard, dawdling, sluggish, sluggardly, slow-moving, leaden, ponderous, unhurried, plodding, snaillike, tortoiselike, torpid, leaden-footed, creeping, crawling, dilatory, deliberate, slow-paced, leisurely, gradual, easy, relaxed, lax, lackadaisical, lazy, *sl.* lallygagging; see also LATE *adj.* 1. **2** gradual, progressive, moderate, perceptible, almost imperceptible, measurable. **4** behindhand, unpunctual, behind time. **5** dense, dull, slow-witted, dull-witted, obtuse, backward, retarded, bovine, dim, dimwitted, stupid, unresponsive, blockish, cloddish, unintelligent, doltish, simple, stolid, unimaginative, *colloq.* slow on the uptake, not with it, thick, dumb. **6** boring, dull, tiresome, tedious, sleepy, somnolent, torpid, soporific; wearisome, dryasdust, uninteresting, monotonous, tame, uneventful, humdrum, dead, *Brit.* dead-and-alive. **7** slack, inactive, quiet, sluggish; unproductive. **10** reluctant, unwilling, hesitant, disinclined, averse, loath, indisposed; not quick, not hasty, tardy, dilatory. ● *adv.* **1** slowly, unhurriedly, cautiously, carefully,

circumspectly; easy, leisurely, easily; tardily, unpunctually, late, behindhand. ● *v.* (*slow down* or *up*) **1** slack *or* slacken off, reduce speed, decelerate, go slower, hold back, put on the brakes, take it easy; see also RETARD *v.* **2** relax, take it easy, ease up, let up. □□ **slowly** see *gradually* (GRADUAL), SLOW *adv.* above.

slowcoach /slṓkōch/ *n. Brit.* = SLOWPOKE.

slowdown /slṓdown/ *n.* the action of slowing down, as in productivity.

slowpoke /slṓpōk/ *n.* **1** a slow or lazy person. **2** a dull-witted person. **3** a person behind the times in opinions, etc.
■ **1** see LAGGARD *n.*

slowworm /slṓwərm/ *n.* a small European legless lizard, *Anguis fragilis*, giving birth to live young. Also called BLIND-WORM. [OE *slā-wyrm*: first element of uncert. orig., assim. to SLOW]

SLR *abbr.* **1** *Photog.* single-lens reflex. **2** self-loading rifle.

slub[1] /slub/ *n. & adj.* ● *n.* **1** a lump or thick place in yarn or thread. **2** fabric woven from thread, etc., with slubs. ● *adj.* (of material, etc.) with an irregular appearance caused by uneven thickness of the warp. [19th c.: orig. unkn.]

slub[2] /slub/ *n. & v.* ● *n.* wool slightly twisted in preparation for spinning. ● *v.tr.* (**slubbed, slubbing**) twist (wool) in this way. [18th c.: orig. unkn.]

sludge /sluj/ *n.* **1** thick, greasy mud. **2** muddy or slushy sediment. **3** sewage. **4** *Mech.* an accumulation of dirty oil, esp. in the sump of an internal-combustion engine. **5** *Geol.* sea ice newly formed in small pieces. **6** (usu. *attrib.*) a muddy color (*sludge green*). □□ **sludgy** *adj.* [cf. SLUSH]
■ **1, 2** mire, ooze, mud, slime, dregs, silt, residue, precipitate, slush, goo, *colloq.* muck, *sl.* gunk.

slue var. of SLEW[1].

slug[1] /slug/ *n.* **1** a small shell-less mollusk of the class Gastropoda, usu. destructive to plants. **2 a** a bullet esp. of irregular shape. **b** a missile for an airgun. **3** *Printing* **a** a metal bar used in spacing. **b** a line of type in Linotype printing. **4** a shot of liquor. **5** a unit of mass, given an acceleration of 1 foot per second per second by a force of 1 lb. **6** a roundish lump of metal. **7** a disk-shaped metal piece, often used fraudulently as a coin or token. [ME *slugg(e)* sluggard, prob. f. Scand.]
■ **2** see SHOT[1] 3. **4** see DRINK *n.* 1b.

slug[2] /slug/ *v. & n.* ● *v.tr.* (**slugged, slugging**) strike with a hard blow. ● *n.* a hard blow. □ **slug it out 1** fight it out. **2** endure; stick it out. □□ **slugging** [19th c.: orig. unkn.]
■ *v.* see PUNCH[1] *v.* 1. ● *n.* see PUNCH[1] *n.* 1. □□ **slugger** see PUGILIST.

slugabed /slúgəbed/ *n. archaic* a lazy person who lies late in bed. [*slug* (v.) (see SLUGGARD) + ABED]
■ see IDLER.

sluggard /slúgərd/ *n.* a lazy, sluggish person. □□ **sluggardly** *adj.* **sluggardliness** *n.* [ME f. *slug* (v.) be slothful (prob. f. Scand.: cf. SLUG[1]) + -ARD]
■ see IDLER.

sluggish /slúgish/ *adj.* inert; inactive; slow-moving; torpid; indolent (*a sluggish circulation; a sluggish stream*). □□ **sluggishly** *adv.* **sluggishness** *n.* [ME f. SLUG[1] or *slug* (v.): see SLUGGARD]
■ see TORPID 1. □□ **sluggishness** sloth, laziness, slothfulness, indolence, idleness, languor, lassitude, lethargy, languidness, laggardness, torpor, phlegm, lifelessness, stagnation, inactivity, inertia, shiftlessness, fainéance, accidie, *literary* hebetude.

sluice /slōōs/ *n. & v.* ● *n.* **1** (also **sluice gate**, **sluice valve**) a sliding gate or other contrivance for controlling the volume or flow of water. **2** a sluiceway, esp. one for washing ore. **3** a place for rinsing. **4** the act or an instance of rinsing. **5** the water above or below or issuing through a floodgate. ● *v.* **1** *tr.* provide or wash with a sluice or sluices. **2** *tr.* rinse, pour

---

/.../ **pronunciation**	● **part of speech**
□ **phrases, idioms, and compounds**	
□□ **derivatives**	■ **synonym section**
cross-references appear in SMALL CAPITALS or *italics*	

or throw water freely upon. **3** *tr.* (foll. by *out*, *away*) wash out or away with a flow of water. **4** *tr.* flood with water from a sluice. **5** *intr.* (of water) rush out from a sluice, or as if from a sluice. [ME f. OF *escluse* ult. f. L *excludere* EXCLUDE]
■ *n.* **1** lock. **2** see CHANNEL¹ *n.* 5a, 6.

sluiceway /slōōsway/ *n.* an artificial channel in which the flow of water is controlled by a sluice.

slum /slum/ *n. & v.* ● *n.* **1** an overcrowded and squalid back street, district, etc., usu. in a city and inhabited by very poor people. **2** a house or building unfit for human habitation. ● *v.intr.* (**slummed**, **slumming**) **1** live in slumlike conditions. **2** go about the slums through curiosity, to examine the condition of the inhabitants, or for charitable purposes. □ **slum clearance** the demolition of slums and rehousing of their inhabitants. **slum it** *colloq.* put up with conditions less comfortable than usual. □□ **slummy** *adj.* (**slummier**, **slummiest**). **slumminess** *n.* [19th c.: orig. cant]
■ *n.* **1** slums, ghetto, warren, shanty town, *colloq.* skid row *or* road. **2** see HOLE *n.* 4a. □□ **slummy** see SHABBY 1, 2.

slumber /slúmbər/ *v. & n. poet. rhet.* ● *v.intr.* **1** sleep, esp. in a specified manner. **2** be idle, drowsy, or inactive. ● *n.* a sleep, esp. of a specified kind (*fell into a fitful slumber*). □ **slumber away** spend (time) in slumber. □□ **slumberer** *n.* **slumberous** *adj.* **slumbrous** *adj.* [ME *slūmere*, etc. f. *slūmen* (v.) or *slūme* (n.) f. OE *slūma*: -*b*- as in *number*]
■ *v.* **1** see SLEEP *v.* ● *n.* see SLEEP *n.* 2. □□ **slumberous** see SLEEPY 1.

slumlord /slúmlawrd/ *n.* the landlord of substandard housing, esp. one who fails to maintain the property while charging high rents.

slump /slump/ *n. & v.* ● *n.* **1** a sudden severe or prolonged fall in prices or values of commodities or securities. **2** a sharp or sudden decline in trade or business usu. bringing widespread unemployment. **3** a lessening of interest or commitment in a subject or undertaking. ● *v.intr.* **1** undergo a slump; fail; fall in price. **2** sit or fall heavily or limply (*slumped into a chair*). **3** lean or subside. [17th c., orig. 'sink in a bog': imit.]
■ *n.* **1, 2** dip, trough, depreciation, decline, downturn, recession, depression, falling off, falloff, fall, drop, plunge, descent, crash, collapse, failure; nosedive, tailspin. ● *v.* **1** decline, slip, recede, fall (off), drop, plunge, descend, sink, crash, collapse, fail, tumble, dive, plummet, take a nosedive *or* tailspin, go into a nosedive *or* tailspin. **2** fall, sink, flop, drop, collapse, tumble, crash. **3** lean, subside, sink; see also SLOUCH *v.*

slung *past* and *past part.* of SLING¹.

slunk *past* and *past part.* of SLINK¹.

slur /slər/ *v. & n.* ● *v.* (**slurred**, **slurring**) **1** *tr. & intr.* pronounce or write indistinctly so that the sounds or letters run into one another. **2** *tr. Mus.* **a** perform (a group of two or more notes) legato. **b** mark (notes) with a slur. **3** *tr.* put a slur on (a person or a person's character); make insinuations against. **4** *tr.* (usu. foll. by *over*) pass over (a fact, fault, etc.) lightly; conceal or minimize. ● *n.* **1** an imputation of wrongdoing; blame; stigma (*a slur on my reputation*). **2** the act or an instance of slurring in pronunciation, singing, or writing. **3** *Mus.* a curved line to show that two or more notes are to be sung to one syllable or played or sung legato. [17th c.: orig. unkn.]
■ *v.* **1** mumble, garble, stutter, lisp. **3** see SLANDER *v.* **4** (*slur over*) gloss over, pass over, disregard, overlook, give short shrift to, ignore, conceal, minimize. ● *n.* **1** smear, insult, calumny, aspersion, affront, stigma, stain, blot, spot, (black) mark, discredit, insinuation, innuendo, imputation, slander, libel, slight, *colloq.* put-down.

slurp /slərp/ *v. & n.* ● *v.tr.* eat or drink noisily. ● *n.* the sound of this; a slurping gulp. [Du. *slurpen*, *slorpen*]

slurry /slúree/ *n.* (*pl.* **-ies**) **1** a semiliquid mixture of fine particles and water; thin mud. **2** thin liquid cement. **3** a fluid form of manure. **4** a residue of water and particles of coal left at coal-mine washing plants. [ME, rel. to dial. *slur* thin mud]

slush /slush/ *n.* **1** watery mud or thawing snow. **2** silly sentiment. □ **slush fund** reserve funding, esp. as used for political bribery. [17th c., also *sludge* and *slutch*: orig. unkn.]
■ **1** see SLUDGE.

slushy /slúshee/ *adj.* (**slushier**, **slushiest**) **1** like slush; watery. **2** *colloq.* weakly sentimental; insipid. □□ **slushiness** *n.*
■ **1** see SLOPPY 1b. **2** see SENTIMENTAL.

slut /slut/ *n. derog.* a slovenly woman; a slattern; a hussy. □□ **sluttish** *adj.* **sluttishness** *n.* [ME: orig. unkn.]
■ sloven, slattern, trollop; whore, prostitute, streetwalker, lady of the evening, woman of ill repute, loose *or* fallen woman, call girl, *archaic* harlot, trull, *derog.* jade, hussy, *literary* wanton, *sl.* tart, hooker, hustler, *sl. derog.* tramp.

sly /slī/ *adj.* (**slier**, **sliest** *or* **slyer**, **slyest**) **1** cunning; crafty; wily. **2 a** (of a person) practicing secrecy or stealth. **b** (of an action, etc.) done, etc., in secret. **3** hypocritical; ironic. **4** knowing; arch; bantering; insinuating. **5** *Austral. & NZ sl.* (esp. of liquor) illicit. □ **on the sly** privately; covertly; without publicity (*smuggled some through on the sly*). **sly dog** *colloq.* a person who is discreet about mistakes or pleasures. □□ **slyly** *adv.* (also **slily**). **slyness** *n.* [ME *sleh*, etc., f. ON *slœgr* cunning, orig. 'able to strike' f. *slóg-* past stem of *slá* strike: cf. SLEIGHT]
■ **1** cunning, artful, crafty, clever, wily, guileful, underhand(ed), deceitful, treacherous, foxy, scheming, plotting, designing, conniving, furtive, shrewd, sneaky, insidious, devious, disingenuous, tricky, sharp, canny, shady, *colloq.* shifty. **2** see STEALTHY. **3** see INSINCERE. **4** knowing, impish, elfish, roguish, mischievous, puckish, devilish, scampish, naughty, arch, waggish. **5** see ILLEGAL 2. □ **on the sly** slyly, quietly, surreptitiously, privately, covertly, stealthily, furtively, sneakily, underhandedly, clandestinely, secretly, by stealth, on the side, on the quiet, *colloq.* on the q.t. □□ **slyly** see *on the sly* (SLY) above. **slyness** see STEALTH.

slyboots /slībōōts/ *n. colloq.* a sly person.
■ see DEVIL *n.* 3b.

slype /slīp/ *n.* a covered way or passage between a cathedral, etc., transept and the chapter house or deanery. [perh. = *slipe* a long narrow piece of ground, = SLIP² 1]

SM *abbr.* **1** sadomasochism. **2** sergeant major.

Sm *symb. Chem.* the element samarium.

smack¹ /smak/ *n., v., & adv.* ● *n.* **1** a sharp slap or blow esp. with the palm of the hand or a flat object. **2** a hard hit in baseball, etc. **3** a loud kiss (*gave her a hearty smack*). **4** a loud, sharp sound (*heard the smack as it hit the floor*). ● *v.* **1** *tr.* strike with the open hand, etc. **2** *tr.* part (one's lips) noisily in eager anticipation or enjoyment of food or another delight. **3** *tr.* crack (a whip). **4** *tr. & intr.* move, hit, etc., with a smack. ● *adv. colloq.* **1** with a smack. **2** suddenly; directly; violently (*landed smack on my desk*). **3** exactly (*hit it smack in the center*). □ **have a smack at** *colloq.* make an attempt, attack, etc., at. **a smack in the eye** (*or* **face**) *colloq.* a rebuff; a setback. [MDu. *smack(en)* of imit. orig.]
■ *n.* **1** see SLAP *n.* **2** see HIT *n.* 1a. **3** see KISS *n.* ● *v.* **1** see SLAP *v.* 1. **4** see HIT *v.* 1a. ● *adv.* **2, 3** see SLAP *adv.* □ **smack in the eye** (*or* **face**) see *slap in the face*.

smack² /smak/ *v. & n.* (foll. by *of*) ● *v.intr.* **1** have a flavor of; taste of (*smacked of garlic*). **2** suggest the presence or effects of (*it smacks of nepotism*). ● *n.* **1** a flavor; a taste that suggests the presence of something. **2** (in a person's character, etc.) a barely discernible quality (*just a smack of superciliousness*). **3** (in food, etc.) a very small amount (*add a smack of ginger*). [OE *smæc*]
■ *v.* **1** taste, savor, have a *or* the flavor. **2** see SUGGEST 2. ● *n.* **1** see TASTE *n.* 1a. **2, 3** see TOUCH *n.* 3.

smack³ /smak/ *n.* a single-masted sailboat for coasting or fishing. [Du. *smak* f. earlier *smacke*; orig. unkn.]

smack⁴ /smak/ *n. sl.* a hard drug, esp. heroin, sold or used illegally. [prob. alt. of Yiddish *schmeck* sniff]

smacker /smákər/ *n. sl.* **1** a loud kiss. **2** a resounding blow. **3** (usu. in *pl.*) *sl.* a dollar.
■ **1** see KISS *n.*

small /smawl/ *adj., n., & adv.* ● *adj.* **1** not large or big. **2** slender; thin. **3** not great in importance, amount, number, strength, or power. **4** not much; trifling (*a small token; paid small attention*). **5** insignificant; unimportant (*a small matter; from small beginnings*). **6** consisting of small particles (*small gravel; small shot*). **7** doing something on a small scale (*a small farmer*). **8** socially undistinguished; poor or humble. **9** petty; mean; ungenerous; paltry (*a small spiteful nature*). **10** lacking in imagination (*they have such small minds*). **11** young; not fully grown nor developed (*a small child*). ● *n.* **1** the slenderest part of something (esp. *small of the back*). **2** (in *pl.*) *Brit. colloq.* small items of laundry, esp. underwear. ● *adv.* into small pieces (*chop it small*). □ **feel** (or **look**) **small** be humiliated; appear mean or humiliated. **in a small way** unambitiously; on a small scale. **no small** considerable; a good deal of (*no small excitement about it*). **small arms** portable firearms, esp. rifles, pistols, light machine guns, submachine guns, etc. **small beer 1** esp. *Brit.* a trifling matter; something unimportant. **2** weak beer. **small-bore** (of a firearm) with a narrow bore, in international and Olympic shooting usu. .22-inch caliber (5.6-millimeter bore). **small capital** a capital letter which is of the same dimensions as the lowercase letters in the same typeface minus ascenders and descenders, as THIS. **small change 1** money in the form of coins as opposed to paper money. **2** trivial remarks. **small circle** see CIRCLE. **small-claims court** a local court in which claims for small amounts can be heard and decided quickly and cheaply without legal representation. **small craft** a general term for small boats and fishing vessels. **small fry 1** young children or the young of various species. **2** small or insignificant things or people. **small hours** the early hours of the morning after midnight. **small intestine** see INTESTINE. **small potatoes** an insignificant person or thing. **small print 1** printed matter in small type. **2** inconspicuous and usu. unfavorable limitations, etc., in a contract. **small profits and quick returns** the policy of an inexpensive store, etc., relying on large trade. **small-scale** made or occurring in small amounts or to a lesser degree. **small screen** television. **small slam** see SLAM². **small talk** light social conversation. **small-time** *colloq.* unimportant or petty. **small-town** relating to or characteristic of a small town; unsophisticated; provincial. **small wonder** not very surprising. □□ **smallish** *adj.* **smallness** *n.* [OE *smæl* f. Gmc]

■ *adj.* **1** little, tiny, short, diminutive, petite, elfin, lilliputian, midget, miniature, minute, minuscule, baby, pygmy, dwarf, pocket(-size), mini-, undersized, stunted; poky, compact; wee, *colloq.* teeny, teeny-weeny, weeny, pint-size. **2** see THIN *adj.* 4. **3–5** slight, secondary, insignificant, trivial, inconsequential, lesser, puny, negligible, minor, trifling, nugatory, unimportant, paltry, tiny, little; diminished, limited, reduced. **7, 8** small-scale, small-time, minor; humble, modest, poor, unpretentious, insignificant, undistinguished. **9** skimpy, niggardly, stingy, uncharitable, ungenerous, scanty, meager, cheap, petty, parsimonious, grudging, stinting, selfish, mean, miserly, tight, tightfisted, closefisted, close; paltry, poor, insignificant, inadequate, insufficient, unsatisfactory, negligible, trifling, *colloq.* piddling, measly. **10** unimaginitive, shallow, unoriginal, mundane, everyday, limited, unprofound, uninspired, commonplace, matter-of-fact, flat, two-dimensional. **11** young, immature, under age, baby, undeveloped. □ **feel** (or **look**) **small** feel embarrassed *or* ashamed *or* shamed *or* humiliated *or* foolish, feel discomfited *or* disconcerted *or* uncomfortable, feel mortified *or* chagrined, *colloq.* feel put down. **small change 1** coins, coppers, silver, cash, specie. **small craft** see BOAT *n.* **small fry 1** see YOUNG *n.* **small potatoes** peanuts, chicken feed, nothing; see also *triviality* (TRIVIAL). **small print 2** see CONDITION *n.* 1, CATCH *n.* 3b. **small-scale** see LITTLE *adj.* 1, 2, 6, 7. **small talk** see CHAT¹ *n.* 1. **small-time** small, small-scale, unimportant, petty, piddling, minor, insignificant, trifling, trivial. **small-town** see PROVINCIAL *adj.* 2.

smallholder /smáwlhōldər/ *n. Brit.* a person who farms a smallholding.
smallholding /smáwlhōlding/ *n. Brit.* an agricultural holding smaller than a farm.
small-minded /smáwlmíndid/ *adj.* petty; of rigid opinions or narrow outlook. □□ **small-mindedly** *adv.* **small-mindedness** *n.*

■ small, petty, selfish, stingy, grudging, niggardly, ungenerous, mean, narrow-minded, close-minded, narrow, uncharitable, hidebound, rigid, intolerant, bigoted, illiberal, prejudiced, unimaginative, shortsighted, myopic, nearsighted.

smallpox /smáwlpoks/ *n. hist.* an acute contagious viral disease, with fever and pustules, usu. leaving permanent scars.
smallsword /smáwlsáwrd/ *n.* a light, tapering thrusting sword, esp. *hist.* for dueling.
smalt /smawlt/ *n.* **1** glass colored blue with cobalt. **2** a pigment made by pulverizing this. [F f. It. *smalto* f. Gmc, rel. to SMELT¹]
smarm /smaarm/ *v.tr. Brit. colloq.* **1** (often foll. by *down*) smooth or plaster down (hair, etc.) usu. with cream or oil. **2** flatter fulsomely. [orig. dial. (also *smalm*), of uncert. orig.]
smarmy /smáarmee/ *adj.* (**smarmier, smarmiest**) ingratiating; flattering; obsequious. □□ **smarmily** *adv.* **smarminess** *n.*

■ see OBSEQUIOUS. □□ **smarminess** see *servility* (SERVILE).

smart /smaart/ *adj., v., n., & adv.* ● *adj.* **1 a** clever; ingenious; quickwitted (*a smart talker; gave a smart answer*). **b** keen in bargaining; quick to take advantage. **c** (of transactions, etc.) unscrupulous to the point of dishonesty. **2** well-groomed; neat; bright and fresh in appearance (*a smart suit*). **3** in good repair; showing bright colors, new paint, etc. (*a smart red bicycle*). **4** stylish; fashionable; prominent in society (*in all the smart restaurants; the smart set*). **5** quick; brisk (*set a smart pace*). **6** painfully severe; sharp; vigorous (*a smart blow*). ● *v.intr.* **1** (of a person or a part of the body) feel or give acute pain or distress (*my eye smarts; smarting from the insult*). **2** (of an insult, grievance, etc.) rankle. **3** (foll. by *for*) suffer the consequences of (*you will smart for this*). ● *n.* a bodily or mental sharp pain; a stinging sensation. ● *adv.* smartly; in a smart manner. □ **look smart** esp. *Brit.* make haste. **smart-ass** *sl.* = SMART ALECK. **smart bomb** a bomb that can be guided directly to its target by use of radio waves, television, or lasers. **smart money 1** money paid or exacted as a penalty or compensation. **2** money invested by persons with expert knowledge. □□ **smartingly** *adv.* **smartish** *Brit. adj. & adv.* **smartly** *adv.* **smartness** *n.* [OE *smeart, smeortan*]

■ *adj.* **1 a** intelligent, clever, bright, brilliant, quick-witted, sharp, acute, astute, capable, able, adept, apt, quick, ingenious; pert, pointed, saucy, witty, nimble-witted, poignant, trenchant, effective; canny, perspicacious, perceptive, percipient, discerning, knowledgeable, *au fait*, well-educated, well-read, erudite, learned, well-versed, aware, shrewd, streetwise, *sl.* hip, tuned in, *sl.* savvy. **2** well-groomed, trim, neat, dapper, spruce, soigné(e), elegant, chic, stylish, *colloq.* snappy, natty, swagger. **3** spick and span, bright, gleaming, shipshape, spotless, shiny. **4** see STYLISH 1, PROMINENT 3. **5** brisk, vigorous, animated, active, energetic, spirited, lively; quick, swift, alert, jaunty, perky, breezy, fast, speedy, spanking, rattling, *colloq.* snappy, *sl.* cracking. **6** severe, stiff, smarting, stinging, sharp, vigorous. ● *v.* **1** sting, hurt, pinch, pain, ache, tingle, prickle, burn, throb, stab, pierce. ● *n.* injury, harm, pain, pang, twinge, affliction, suffering. □ **look smart** see HURRY *v.* 1. □□ **smartness** see INGENUITY, PANACHE.

smart aleck /álik/ *n.* (also **alec**) *colloq.* a person displaying

/.../ **pronunciation**	● **part of speech**
□ **phrases, idioms, and compounds**	
□□ **derivatives**	■ **synonym section**
cross-references appear in SMALL CAPITALS or *italics*	

ostentatious or smug cleverness. □□ **smart-alecky** *adj.*
[SMART + *Alec*, dimin. of the name *Alexander*]
■ see *wise guy* (WISE¹).
smarten /smáart'n/ *v.tr.* & *intr.* (usu. foll. by *up*) make or
become smart or smarter.
■ see SPRUCE¹ *v.*
smarty /smáartee/ *n.* (*pl.* **-ies**) *colloq.* **1** a know-it-all; a smart
aleck. **2** *esp. Brit.* a smartly-dressed person; a member of a
smart set. □ **smarty-pants** = SMARTY 1. [SMART]
■ **1** see *wise guy.*
smash /smash/ *v., n.,* & *adv.* ● *v.* **1** *tr.* & *intr.* (often foll. by
up) **a** break into pieces; shatter. **b** bring or come to sudden
or complete destruction, defeat, or disaster. **2** *tr.* (foll. by
into, through) (of a vehicle, etc.) move with great force and
impact. **3** *tr.* & *intr.* (foll. by *in*) break in with a crushing
blow (*smashed in the window*). **4** *tr.* (in tennis, squash, etc.)
hit (a ball, etc.) with great force, esp. downward (*smashed it
back over the net*). **5** *intr.* esp. *Brit.* (of a business, etc.) go
bankrupt; come to grief. **6** *tr.* (as **smashed** *adj.*) *sl.* intoxicated. ● *n.* **1** the act or an instance of smashing; a violent
fall, collision, or disaster. **2** the sound of this. **3** (in full
smash hit) a very successful play, song, performer, etc. **4**
a stroke in tennis, squash, etc., in which the ball is hit, esp.
downward with great force. **5** a violent blow with a fist, etc.
6 esp. *Brit.* bankruptcy; a series of commercial failures. **7** a
mixture of liquor (usu. brandy) with flavored water and ice.
● *adv.* with a smash (*fell smash on the floor*). □ **go to smash**
Brit. be ruined, etc. [18th c., prob. imit. after *smack, smite*
and *bash, mash,* etc.]
■ *v.* **1a, 3** see SHATTER 1. **1 b** see DESTROY 1, 2. **2** see
BUMP *v.* 1, 2. **5** go bankrupt, go under, go to the wall,
crash, flounder, collapse, fail, *colloq.* go belly up. **6**
(**smashed**) see DRUNK *adj.* 1. ● *n.* **1** see COLLISION 1.
2 see CRASH¹ *n.* 1a. **3** see HIT *n.* 3. **5** see BLOW² 1.
smasher /smáshər/ *n.* **1** a person or thing that smashes. **2**
Brit. colloq. a very beautiful or pleasing person or thing.
smashing /smáshing/ *adj. colloq.* superlative; excellent; wonderful; beautiful. □□ **smashingly** *adv.*
■ see EXCELLENT. □□ **smashingly** see *beautifully*
(BEAUTIFUL).
smashup /smáshəp/ *n. colloq.* a violent collision, esp. of motor
vehicles; a complete smash.
smatter /smátər/ *n.* (also **smattering**) **1** a slight superficial
knowledge of a language or subject. **2** *colloq.* a small quantity. □□ **smatterer** *n.* [ME *smatter* talk ignorantly, prate:
orig. unkn.]
■ **2** see TOUCH *n.* 3.
smear /smeer/ *v.* & *n.* ● *v.tr.* **1** daub or mark with a greasy
or sticky substance or with something that stains. **2** blot;
smudge; obscure the outline of (writing, artwork, etc.). **3**
defame the character of; slander; attempt to or succeed in
discrediting (a person or his or her name) publicly. ● *n.* **1**
the act or an instance of smearing. **2** *Med.* **a** material
smeared on a microscopic slide, etc., for examination. **b** a
specimen of this. □ **smear test** = *cervical smear.* □□ **smearer**
n. **smeary** *adj.* [OE *smierwan* f. Gmc]
■ *v.* **1** daub, rub, anoint, spread, cover, coat, wipe,
plaster, bedaub, dab; besmirch, dirty, smudge, stain,
soil, begrime. **2** blot, smudge, blur. **3** blacken,
besmirch, smirch, soil, sully, calumniate, slander,
discredit, defame, denigrate, tarnish, defile, vilify,
scandalize, stigmatize. ● *n.* **1** smudge, daub, stain,
blot, taint, spot, blotch, streak, *colloq.* splotch; slander,
scandal, libel, vilification, defamation, calumny,
aspersion, reflection.
smegma /smégmə/ *n.* a sebaceous secretion in the folds of
the skin, esp. of the foreskin. □□ **smegmatic** /-mátik/ *adj.*
[L f. Gk *smēgma -atos* detergent f. *smēkhō* cleanse]
smell /smel/ *n.* & *v.* ● *n.* **1** the faculty of perceiving odors or
scents (*has a fine sense of smell*). **2** the quality in substances
that is perceived by this (*the smell of thyme; this rose has no
smell*). **3** an unpleasant odor. **4** the act of inhaling to ascertain smell. ● *v.* (*past* and *past part.* **smelled** or **smelt**
/smelt/) **1** *tr.* perceive the smell of; examine by smell
(*thought I could smell gas*). **2** *intr.* emit odor. **3** *intr.* seem by

smell to be (*this milk smells sour*). **4** *intr.* (foll. by *of*) **a** be
redolent of (*smells of fish*). **b** be suggestive of (*smells of dishonesty*). **5** *intr.* stink; be rank. **6** *tr.* perceive as if by smell;
detect; discern; suspect (*smell a bargain; smell blood*). **7** *intr.*
have or use a sense of smell. **8** *intr.* (foll. by *about*) sniff or
search about. **9** *intr.* (foll. by *at*) inhale the smell of. □ **smelling salts** ammonium carbonate mixed with scent to be
sniffed as a restorative in faintness, etc. **smell out 1** detect
by smell; find out by investigation. **2** (of a dog, etc.) hunt
out by smell. **smell a rat** begin to suspect trickery, etc.
□□ **smellable** *adj.* **smeller** *n.* **smell-less** *adj.* [ME *smel(le)*,
prob. f. OE]
■ *n.* **2** odor, scent, aroma, perfume, fragrance, bouquet,
breath, whiff, redolence. **3** stink, stench, fetor,
fetidness, mephitis, effluvium, *Brit. colloq.* pong, hum.
● *v.* **1** scent, sniff, nose (out), get a whiff of, get wind
of. **4** (*smell of*) **a** savor of, be redolent of. **b** smack of,
savor of, suggest, imply. **5** stink, reek, *Brit. colloq.* pong,
hum. **6** see DETECT. □ **smell out** see *track down.* **smell
a rat** mistrust, doubt, be suspicious, suspect, have
misgivings, have *or* harbor suspicions.
smelly /smélee/ *adj.* (**smellier, smelliest**) having a strong or
unpleasant smell. □□ **smelliness** *n.*
■ malodorous, evil-smelling, foul-smelling, foul,
mephitic, fetid, putrid, reeky, stinking, rank, offensive,
odoriferous, rancid, strong, high, gamy, *archaic*
miasmic, miasmatic, miasmal, *colloq.* whiffy, *Brit. colloq.*
pongy, *literary* noisome, *Austral. sl.* on the nose.
smelt¹ /smelt/ *v.tr.* **1** separate metal from (ore) by melting.
2 extract or refine (metal) in this way. □□ **smelter** *n.* **smelt-
ery** *n.* (*pl.* **-ies**). [MDu., MLG *smelten,* rel. to MELT]
smelt² *past* and *past part.* of SMELL.
smelt³ /smelt/ *n.* (*pl.* same or **smelts**) any small green and
silver fish of the genus *Osmerus,* etc., allied to salmon and
used as food. [OE, of uncert. orig.: cf. SMOLT]
smew /smyōō/ *n.* a small merganser, *Mergus albellus.* [17th c.,
rel. to *smeath, smee* = smew, widgeon, etc.]
smidgen /smíjən/ *n.* (also **smidgin**) *colloq.* a small bit or
amount. [perh. f. *smitch* in the same sense: cf. dial. *smitch*
wood smoke]
■ see BIT¹ 1.
smilax /smílaks/ *n.* **1** any climbing shrub of the genus *Smilax,*
the roots of some species of which yield sarsaparilla. **2** a
climbing kind of asparagus, *Asparagus medeoloides,* used decoratively by florists. [L f. Gk, = bindweed]
smile /smīl/ *v.* & *n.* ● *v.* **1** *intr.* relax the features into a
pleased or kind or gently skeptical expression or a forced
imitation of these, usu. with the lips parted and the corners
of the mouth turned up. **2** *tr.* express by smiling (*smiled their
consent*). **3** *tr.* give (a smile) of a specified kind (*smiled a
sardonic smile*). **4** *intr.* (foll. by *on, upon*) adopt a favorable
attitude toward; encourage (*fortune smiled on me*). **5** *intr.*
have a bright or favorable aspect (*the smiling countryside*). **6**
tr. (foll. by *away*) drive (a person's anger, etc.) away (*smiled
their tears away*). **7** *intr.* (foll. by *at*) **a** ridicule or show indifference to (*smiled at my feeble attempts*). **b** favor; smile on.
8 *tr.* (foll. by *into, out of*) bring (a person) into or out of a
specified mood, etc., by smiling (*smiled them into agreement*).
● *n.* **1** the act or an instance of smiling. **2** a smiling expression or aspect. □ **come up smiling** *colloq.* recover from adversity and cheerfully face what is to come. □□ **smileless** *adj.*
smiler *n.* **smiley** *adj.* **smilingly** *adv.* [ME perh. f. Scand.,
rel. to SMIRK: cf. OHG *smīlenter*]
■ *v.* **1** grin, beam; smirk, simper, sneer. **4** (*smile on or
upon*) see FAVOR *v.* 3b. ● *n.* grin; smirk, simper, sneer.
smirch /smərch/ *v.* & *n.* ● *v.tr.* mark, soil, or smear (a thing,
a person's reputation, etc.). ● *n.* **1** a spot or stain. **2** a blot
(on one's character, etc.). [ME: orig. unkn.]
■ *v.* see MUDDY *v.,* STAIN *v.* 2. ● *n.* **1** see STAIN *n.* 1.
2 see STAIN *n.* 2.
smirk /smərk/ *n.* & *v.* ● *n.* an affected, conceited, or silly
smile. ● *v.intr.* put on or wear a smirk. □□ **smirker** *n.*
smirkingly *adv.* **smirky** *adj.* **smirkily** *adv.* [OE
sme(a)rcian]

■ *n.* leer, sneer, grin, grimace, simper, simpering smile.
● *v.* sneer, grin, grimace, leer, simper.

smit /smit/ *archaic past part.* of SMITE.

smite /smīt/ *v. & n.* ● *v.* (*past* **smote** /smōt/; *past part.* **smitten** /smit'n/) *archaic* or *literary* **1** *tr.* strike or hit. **2** *tr.* chastise; defeat. **3** *tr.* (in *passive*) **a** have a sudden strong effect on (*was smitten by his conscience*). **b** infatuate; fascinate (*was smitten by her beauty*). **4** *intr.* (foll. by *on, upon*) come forcibly or abruptly upon. ● *n.* a blow or stroke. □□ **smiter** *n.* [OE *smītan* smear f. Gmc]

■ *v.* **1** see HIT *v.* 1a. **3** (*smitten*) **a** affected, afflicted, beset, troubled, distressed, burdened, crushed, plagued, haunted, worried, bothered, vexed, *archaic* stricken. **b** captivated, fascinated, enthralled, struck, bewitched, enchanted, beguiled, charmed, enraptured, infatuated, enamored, swept off one's feet, besotted, *colloq.* bowled over, *sl.* gaga.

smith /smith/ *n. & v.* ● *n.* **1** (esp. in *comb.*) a worker in metal (*goldsmith*; *tinsmith*). **2** a person who forges iron; a blacksmith. **3** a craftsman (*wordsmith*). ● *v.tr.* make or treat by forging. [OE f. Gmc]

smithereens /smíthəreénz/ *n.pl.* (also **smithers** /smíthərz/) small fragments (*smash into smithereens*). [19th c.: orig. unkn.]

■ see FRAGMENT *n.*

smithery /smíthəree/ *n.* (*pl.* **-ies**) **1** a smith's work. **2** (esp. in naval dockyards) a smithy.

smithy /smíthee/ *n.* (*pl.* **-ies**) a blacksmith's workshop; a forge. [ME f. ON *smithja*]

smitten *past part.* of SMITE.

smock /smok/ *n. & v.* ● *n.* **1** a loose shirtlike garment with the upper part closely gathered in smocking. **2** a loose overall. ● *v.tr.* adorn with smocking. [OE *smoc*, prob. rel. to OE *smūgan* creep, ON *smjúga* put on a garment]

■ *n.* see SHIFT *n.* 4a.

smocking /smóking/ *n.* an ornamental effect on cloth made by gathering the material tightly into pleats, often with embroidered stitches in a decorative pattern.

smog /smog, smawg/ *n.* fog intensified by smoke. □□ **smoggy** *adj.* (**smoggier, smoggiest**). [portmanteau word]

■ see FOG *n.* 1. □□ **smoggy** see THICK *adj.* 6.

smoke /smōk/ *n. & v.* ● *n.* **1** a visible suspension of carbon, etc., in air, emitted from a burning substance. **2** an act or period of smoking tobacco (*had a quiet smoke*). **3** *colloq.* a cigarette or cigar (*got a smoke?*). **4** (**the Smoke**) *Brit.* & *Austral. colloq.* a big city, esp. London. ● *v.* **1** *intr.* **a** emit smoke or visible vapor (*smoking ruins*). **b** (of a lamp, etc.) burn badly with the emission of smoke. **c** (of a chimney or fire) discharge smoke into the room. **2 a** *intr.* inhale and exhale the smoke of a cigarette or cigar or pipe. **b** *intr.* do this habitually. **c** *tr.* use (a cigarette, etc.) in this way. **3** *tr.* darken or preserve by the action of smoke (*smoked salmon*). **4** *tr.* spoil the taste of in cooking. **5** *tr.* **a** rid of insects, etc., by the action of smoke. **b** subdue (insects, esp. bees) in this way. **6** *tr. archaic* make fun of. **7** *tr.* bring (oneself) into a specified state by smoking. □ **go up in smoke** *colloq.* **1** be destroyed by fire. **2** (of a plan, etc.) come to nothing. **smoke bomb** a bomb that emits dense smoke on exploding. **smoke bush** = *smoke tree*. **smoked glass** glass darkened with smoke. **smoke-dried** cured in smoke. **smoke out 1** drive out by means of smoke. **2** drive out of hiding or secrecy, etc. **smoke ring** smoke from a cigarette, etc., exhaled in the shape of a ring. **smoke room** *Brit.* = *smoking room*. **smoke screen 1** a cloud of smoke diffused to conceal (esp. military) operations. **2** a device or ruse for disguising one's activities. **smoke tree** any ornamental shrub of the genus *Cotinus*, with feathery smokelike fruit stalks. □□ **smokable** *adj.* (also **smokeable**). [OE *smoca* f. weak grade of the stem of *smēocan* emit smoke]

■ *n.* **1** see FUME *n.* 1. **3** see CIGARETTE 1. **4** see TOWN 1. ● *v.* **1** see FUME *v.* 1. **2** see PUFF *v.* 2. **3** see PRESERVE *v.* 4a. **6** see JEER *v.* 2. □ **smoke out 2** see LOCATE 1, 3. **smoke screen 2** see COVER *n.* 4.

smokeless /smōklis/ *adj.* having or producing little or no smoke.

smoker /smōkər/ *n.* **1** a person or thing that smokes, esp. a person who habitually smokes tobacco. **2** a compartment on a train, in which smoking is allowed. **3** an informal social gathering of men. □ **smoker's cough** an ailment caused by excessive smoking.

smokestack /smōkstak/ *n.* **1** a chimney or funnel for discharging the smoke of a locomotive or steamer. **2** a tall chimney.

■ stack, chimney, chimney stack, funnel.

smoking /smōking/ *n. & adj.* ● *n.* the act of inhaling and exhaling from a cigarette, cigar, etc. ● *adj.* giving off smoke. □ **smoking gun** something that serves as indisputable proof, esp. of a crime. **smoking jacket** an ornamental jacket formerly worn by men while smoking. **smoking room** a room in a hotel, club, house, etc., kept for smoking in. [pres. part. of SMOKE]

smoky /smōkee/ *adj.* (also **smokey**) (**smokier, smokiest**) **1** emitting, veiled or filled with, or obscured by, smoke (*smoky fire*; *smoky room*). **2** stained with or colored like smoke (*smoky glass*). **3** having the taste or flavor of smoked food (*smoky bacon*). □ **smoky quartz** (or **topaz**) cairngorm. □□ **smokily** *adv.* **smokiness** *n.*

■ **1** see THICK *adj.* 6. **2** see GRAY *adj.* 1.

smolder /smōldər/ *v. & n.* (*Brit.* **smoulder**) ● *v.intr.* **1** burn slowly with smoke but without a flame; slowly burn internally or invisibly. **2** (of emotions, etc.) exist in a suppressed or concealed state. **3** (of a person) show silent or suppressed anger, hatred, etc. ● *n.* a smoldering or slow-burning fire. [ME, rel. to LG *smöln*, MDu. *smölen*]

■ *v.* **1** burn, smoke. **2, 3** burn, seethe, simmer, chafe, rage, fume, foam, boil, stew, fester; get hot under the collar, see red, *colloq.* get (all) steamed up, *sl.* get (all) burned up.

smolt /smōlt/ *n.* a young salmon migrating to the sea for the first time. [ME (orig. Sc. & N.Engl.): orig. unkn.]

smooch /smooch/ *n. & v. colloq.* ● *n.* **1** a spell of kissing and caressing. **2** *Brit.* a period of slow dancing close together. ● *v.intr.* engage in a smooch. □□ **smoocher** *n.* **smoochy** *adj.* (**smoochier, smoochiest**). [dial. *smouch* imit.]

■ *n.* **2** see KISS *n.* **v.** see KISS *v.* 3.

smoodge /smooj/ *v.intr.* (also **smooge**) *Austral.* & *NZ* **1** behave in a fawning or ingratiating manner. **2** behave amorously. [prob. var. of dial. *smudge* kiss, sidle up to, beg in a sneaking way]

smooth /smooth/ *adj., v., n., & adv.* ● *adj.* **1** having a relatively even and regular surface; free from perceptible projections, lumps, indentations, and roughness. **2** not wrinkled, pitted, scored, or hairy (*smooth skin*). **3** that can be traversed without check. **4** (of liquids) of even consistency; without lumps (*mix to a smooth paste*). **5** (of the sea, etc.) without waves or undulations. **6** (of a journey, passage, progress, etc.) untroubled by difficulties or adverse conditions. **7** having an easy flow or correct rhythm (*smooth breathing*; *a smooth meter*). **8 a** not harsh in sound or taste. **b** (of wine, etc.) not astringent. **9** (of a person, his or her manner, etc.) suave, conciliatory, flattering, unruffled, or polite (*a smooth talker*; *he's very smooth*). **10** (of movement, etc.) not suddenly varying; not jerky. ● *v.* **1** *tr. & intr.* (often foll. by *out, down*) make or become smooth. **2** (often foll. by *out, down, over, away*) **a** *tr.* reduce or get rid of (differences, faults, difficulties, etc.) in fact or appearance. **b** *intr.* (of difficulties, etc.) diminish; become less obtrusive (*it will all smooth over*). **3** *tr.* modify (a graph, curve, etc.) so as to lessen irregularities. **4** *tr.* free from impediments or discomfort (*smooth the way*; *smooth the declining years*). ● *n.* **1** a smoothing touch or stroke (*gave his hair a smooth*). **2** the easy part of life (*take the rough with the smooth*). ● *adv.* smoothly (*the course of true love never did run smooth*). □ **smooth-faced 1** beardless. **2** hypocritically friendly. **smoothing iron** *hist.* a

---

/.../ pronunciation	● part of speech
□ phrases, idioms, and compounds	
□□ derivatives	■ synonym section
cross-references appear in SMALL CAPITALS or *italics*	

flatiron. **smooth muscle** a muscle without striations, usu. occurring in hollow organs and performing involuntary functions. **smooth talk** *colloq.* bland specious language. **smooth-talk** *v. tr.* address or persuade with this. **smooth-tongued** insincerely flattering. □□ **smoothable** *adj.* **smoother** *n.* **smoothish** *adj.* **smoothly** *adv.* **smoothness** *n.* [OE *smōth*]

■ *adj.* **1** regular, even, flush, flat, level, plane; unbroken. **2** unwrinkled, uniform, slick, sleek, shiny, glossy, glassy, mirrorlike, polished, burnished; silky, silken, velvety, satiny; hairless, bald, bare, naked, clean-shaven, smooth-shaven, smooth-skinned, depilated, glabrous. **4** creamy, flowing. **5** calm, serene, tranquil, peaceful, glassy, flat, still, unruffled, unbroken, undisturbed. **6** unobstructed, easy, effortless, free, uncluttered, even, steady, orderly, well-ordered, uneventful, flowing, unconstrained, uninterrupted. **8 a** sweet, dulcet, mellow, well-modulated, silver-tongued. **b** mellow, pleasant, mild, suave. **9** suave, slippery, unctuous, silken, silky, glib, urbane, soigné(e), agreeable, winning, facile, nonchalant, unruffled, courtly, eloquent, smooth-spoken, smooth-tongued, persuasive, flattering, oily, slimy, syrupy, conciliatory; scheming, conniving, crafty, shrewd, cunning, tricky, sly, foxy, machiavellian, sophistic(al), plausible, credible, believable, *colloq.* slick, shifty, smarmy. **10** see GRACEFUL. ● *v.* **1** flatten, even, level, iron, press, calender, esp. *Brit. hist.* mangle; sand, plane, polish, buff, burnish. **2 a** assuage, allay, calm, gloss over, minimize, mitigate, lessen, soothe, reduce, temper, mollify, soften, palliate, appease, *formal* ameliorate. **4** prepare, lay, pave, ease, ready, clear, open, prime, lubricate, facilitate. □ **smooth-tongued** see SMOOTH *adj.* 9 above. □□ **smoothly** see EASILY 1. **smoothness** see FLUENCY, SAVOIR FAIRE.

smoothbore /smōōthbawr/ *adj. & n.* ● *adj.* (of a gun) having an unrifled barrel. ● *n.* a gun with an unrifled barrel.

smoothie /smōōthee/ *n. colloq.* a person who is smooth (*see* SMOOTH *adj.* 9). [SMOOTH]

■ see *charmer* (CHARM).

smorgasbord /smáwrgəsbawrd/ *n.* a buffet offering a variety of hot and cold meats, salads, hors d'oeuvres, etc. [Sw. f. *smör* butter + *gås* goose, lump of butter + *bord* table]

■ see HORS D´OEUVRE.

smorzando /smawrtsaándō/ *adj., adv., & n. Mus.* ● *adj. & adv.* dying away. ● *n.* (*pl.* **-os** or **smorzandi** /-dee/) a smorzando passage. [It., gerund of *smorzare* extinguish]

smote *past of* SMITE.

smother /smúthər/ *v. & n.* ● *v.* **1** *tr.* suffocate; stifle; kill by stopping the breath of or excluding air from. **2** *tr.* (foll. by *with*) overwhelm with (kisses, gifts, kindness, etc.) (*smothered with affection*). **3** *tr.* (foll. by *in, with*) cover entirely in or with (*chicken smothered in mayonnaise*). **4** *tr.* extinguish or deaden (a fire or flame) by covering it or heaping it with ashes, etc. **5** *intr.* **a** die of suffocation. **b** have difficulty breathing. **6** *tr.* (often foll. by *up*) suppress or conceal; keep from notice or publicity. **7** *tr.* defeat rapidly or utterly. ● *n.* **1** a cloud of dust or smoke. **2** obscurity caused by this. □ **smothered mate** *Chess* checkmate in which the king, having no vacant square to move to, is checkmated by a knight. [ME *smorther* f. the stem of OE *smorian* suffocate]

■ *v.* **1** suffocate, stifle, choke, asphyxiate. **2, 3** overwhelm, overcome, blanket, inundate, shower, drench; cover, envelop, wrap, surround, *literary* enshroud. **4** extinguish, put out, snuff out, quench, deaden. **5 a** suffocate, be suffocated *or* stifled *or* asphyxiated, be choked. **6** repress, subdue, suppress, conceal, hide, keep *or* hold back, cover up, mask, choke back *or* down, check; stifle, muffle, blanket, blank out; silence.

smothery /smúthəree/ *adj.* tending to smother; stifling.

smoulder *Brit.* var. of SMOLDER.

Smriti /smrítee/ *n.* Hindu traditional teachings on religion, etc. [Skr. *smṛti* remembrance]

smudge[1] /smuj/ *n. & v.* ● *n.* **1** a blurred or smeared line or mark; a blot; a smear of dirt. **2** a stain or blot on a person's character, etc. ● *v.* **1** *tr.* make a smudge on. **2** *intr.* become smeared or blurred (*smudges easily*). **3** *tr.* smear or blur the lines of (writing, drawing, etc.) (*smudge the outline*). **4** *tr.* defile, sully, stain, or disgrace (a person's name, character, etc.). □□ **smudgeless** *adj.* [ME: orig. unkn.]

■ *n.* **1** see BLOT *n.* 1. **2** see STAIN *n.* 2. ● *v.* **1–3** see SMEAR *v.* 1, 2.

smudge[2] /smuj/ *n.* an outdoor fire with dense smoke made to keep off insects, protect plants against frost, etc. □ **smudge pot** a container holding burning material that produces a smudge. [*smudge* (v.) cure (herring) by smoking (16th c.: orig. unkn.)]

smudgy /smújee/ *adj.* (**smudgier, smudgiest**) **1** smudged. **2** likely to produce smudges. □□ **smudgily** *adv.* **smudginess** *n.*

smug /smug/ *adj.* (**smugger, smuggest**) self-satisfied; complacent. □□ **smugly** *adv.* **smugness** *n.* [16th c., orig. 'neat' f. LG *smuk* pretty]

■ self-satisfied, complacent, holier-than-thou, self-important, self-righteous, overconfident, conceited, *colloq.* slick. □□ **smugness** see PRIDE *n.* 2.

smuggle /smúgəl/ *v. tr.* **1** (also *absol.*) import or export (goods) illegally, esp. without payment of customs duties. **2** (foll. by *in, out*) convey secretly. **3** (foll. by *away*) put into concealment. □□ **smuggler** *n.* **smuggling** *n.* [17th c. (also *smuckle*) f. LG *smukkeln smuggelen*]

■ **1, 2** see RUN *v.* 24.

smut /smut/ *n. & v.* ● *n.* **1** a small flake of soot, etc. **2** a spot or smudge made by this. **3** obscene or lascivious talk, pictures, or stories. **4 a** a fungal disease of cereals in which the affected parts change to black powder. **b** any fungus of the order Ustilaginales causing this. ● *v.* (**smutted, smutting**) **1** *tr.* mark with smuts. **2** *tr.* infect (a plant) with smut. **3** *intr.* (of a plant) contract smut. □□ **smutty** *adj.* (**smuttier, smuttiest**) (esp. in sense 3 of *n.*). **smuttily** *adv.* **smuttiness** *n.* [rel. to LG *smutt*, MHG *smutz(en)*, etc.: cf. OE *smitt(ian)* smear, and SMUDGE[1]]

■ *n.* **3** see DIRT 3. **4** see MOLD[2]. □□ **smutty** see OBSCENE 1. **smuttiness** see RIBALDRY.

Sn *symb. Chem.* the element tin.

snack /snak/ *n. & v.* ● *n.* **1** a light, casual, or hurried meal. **2** a small amount of food eaten between meals. **3** *Austral. sl.* something easy to accomplish. ● *v. intr.* eat a snack. □ **snack bar** a place where snacks are sold. [ME, orig. a snap or bite, f. MDu. *snac(k)* f. *snacken* (v.), var. of *snappen*]

■ *n.* **1, 2** bite, nibble, morsel, tidbit, refreshment(s), *Brit. colloq.* elevenses, tuck, *sl.* nosh. **3** see PUSHOVER 1. ● *v.* nibble, pick, *sl.* nosh.

snaffle /snáfəl/ *n. & v.* ● *n.* (in full **snaffle bit**) a simple bridle bit without a curb and usu. with a single rein. ● *v. tr.* **1** put a snaffle on. **2** *Brit. colloq.* steal; seize; appropriate. [prob. f. LG or Du.: cf. MLG, MDu. *snavel* beak, mouth]

snafu /snafōō/ *adj. & n. sl.* ● *adj.* in utter confusion or chaos. ● *n.* this state. [acronym for "situation *normal: all* fouled (or fucked) *up*"]

■ *adj.* see *confused* (CONFUSE 5). ● *n.* see CHAOS *n.* 1a.

snag[1] /snag/ *n. & v.* ● *n.* **1** an unexpected or hidden obstacle or drawback. **2** a jagged or projecting point or broken stump. **3** a tear in material, etc. **4** a short tine of an antler. ● *v. tr.* (**snagged, snagging**) **1** catch or tear on a snag. **2** clear (land, a waterway, a tree trunk, etc.) of snags. **3** catch or obtain by quick action. □□ **snagged** *adj.* **snaggy** *adj.* [prob. f. Scand.: cf. Norw. dial. *snag(e)* sharp point]

■ *n.* **1** hitch, catch, problem, (stumbling) block, stricture, bottleneck, complication, obstacle, impediment, obstruction, hindrance, difficulty, drawback, *sl.* hang-up. ● *v.* **1** catch, tear, rip.

snag[2] /snag/ *n.* (usu. in *pl.*) *Austral. sl.* a sausage. [20th c.: orig. unkn.]

snaggletooth /snágəl/ *n.* (*pl.* **snaggleteeth**) an irregular or projecting tooth. □□ **snaggletoothed** *adj.* [SNAG[1] + -LE[2]]

snail /snayl/ *n.* **1** any slow-moving gastropod mollusk with a spiral shell able to enclose the whole body. **2** a slow or lazy person; a dawdler. □ **snail's pace** a very slow movement. □□ **snaillike** *adj.* [OE *snæg(e)l* f. Gmc]

■ **2** see LAGGARD *n.* □□ **snaillike** see SLOW *adj.* 1.

snake /snayk/ *n. & v.* ● *n.* **1 a** any long, limbless reptile of the suborder Ophidia, including boas, pythons, and poisonous forms such as cobras and vipers. **b** a limbless lizard or amphibian. **2** (also **snake in the grass**) a treacherous person or secret enemy. **3 a** a plumber's snakelike device for clearing obstructed pipes. **b** an electrician's wirepuller. ● *v.intr.* move or twist like a snake. □ **snake charmer** a person appearing to make snakes move by music, etc. **snake oil 1** any of various concoctions sold as medicine but without medicinal value. **2** speech, writing, or actions intended to deceive; bunkum. **snake pit 1** a pit containing snakes. **2** a scene of vicious behavior. **3** a mental hospital in which inhumane treatment is known or suspect. **snake's-head** a bulbous plant, *Fritillaria meleagris*, with bell-shaped pendent flowers. □□ **snakelike** *adj.* [OE *snaca*]

■ *n.* **1a** reptile, ophidian, viper, cobra, boa, python, *usu. literary* serpent. **2** viper, serpent, traitor, turncoat, Judas, quisling, betrayer, double-crosser, informer, rat, ratfink, fink. ● *v.* slither, glide, creep, crawl, worm, wriggle; twist, wind, curve, bend, turn, zigzag, wander, loop, coil, crook, meander. □□ **snakelike** see SERPENTINE *adj.* 2.

snakebird /snáykbərd/ *n.* a fish-eating bird, *Anhinga anhinga*, with a long slender neck.

snakeroot /snáykrŏŏt, -rŏŏt/ *n.* any of various N. American plants, esp. *Cimicifuga racemosa*, with roots reputed to contain an antidote to snake's poison.

snaky /snáykee/ *adj.* **1** of or like a snake. **2** winding; sinuous. **3** showing coldness, ingratitude, venom, or guile. **4 a** infested with snakes. **b** (esp. of the hair of the Furies) composed of snakes. **5** *Austral. sl.* angry; irritable. □□ **snakily** *adv.* **snakiness** *n.*

snap /snap/ *v., n., adv., & adj.* ● *v.* (**snapped, snapping**) **1** *intr. & tr.* break suddenly or with a snap. **2** *intr. & tr.* emit or cause to emit a sudden sharp sound or crack. **3** *intr. & tr.* open or close with a snapping sound (*the bag snapped shut*). **4 a** *intr.* (often foll. by *at*) speak irritably or spitefully (to a person) (*did not mean to snap at you*). **b** *tr.* say irritably or spitefully. **5** *intr.* (often foll. by *at*) (esp. of a dog, etc.) make a sudden audible bite. **6** *tr. & intr.* move quickly (*snap into action*). **7** *tr.* take a snapshot of. **8** *tr. Football* put (the ball) into play on the ground by a quick backward movement. ● *n.* **1** an act or sound of snapping. **2** (often in *comb.*) a crisp cookie (*gingersnap*). **3** a snapshot. **4** (in full **cold snap**) a sudden brief spell of cold weather. **5** esp. *Brit.* **a** a card game in which players call "snap" when two similar cards are exposed. **b** (as *int.*) on noticing the (often unexpected) similarity of two things. **6** crispness of style; fresh vigor or liveliness in action; zest; dash; spring. **7** *sl.* an easy task (*it was a snap*). **8** = *snap fastener*. **9** *Football* the beginning of a play, when the ball is passed quickly back. ● *adv.* with the sound of a snap (*heard it go snap*). ● *adj.* done or taken on the spur of the moment, unexpectedly, or without notice (*snap decision*). □ **snap at 1** accept (bait, a chance, etc.) eagerly **2** see senses 4a and 5 of *v.* **snap bean** a bean grown for its pods, which are broken into pieces and eaten as a vegetable. **snap bolt** (or **lock**) a bolt, etc., which locks automatically when a door or window closes. **snap-brim** (of a hat) with a brim that can be turned up and down at opposite sides. **snap fastener** a two-piece device that snaps together, used esp. on garments, etc. (e.g., instead of buttons). **snap one's fingers 1** make an audible fillip, esp. in rhythm to music, etc. **2** (often foll. by *at*) defy; show contempt for. **snap hook** a hook with a spring allowing the entrance but barring the escape of a cord, link, etc. **snap off** break off or bite off. **snap out** say irritably. **snap out of** *sl.* get rid of (a mood, habit, etc.) by a sudden effort. **snapping turtle** any large American freshwater turtle of the family Chelydridae which seizes prey with a snap of its jaws. **snap up 1** accept (an offer, a bargain) quickly or eagerly. **2** pick up or catch hastily or smartly. **3** interrupt (another person) before he or she has finished speaking. □□ **snappable**

adj. **snappingly** *adv.* [prob. f. MDu. or MLG *snappen*, partly imit.]

■ *v.* **1** break (off), separate, crack; split, fracture, give way, part, *literary* cleave. **2, 3** click; pop; crack. **4** (*snap at*) **a** attack, lunge at, lash out at, snarl at, growl at, bark at, be brusque *or* short *or* curt with, snap off a person's head, *colloq.* jump down a person's throat, fly off the handle at. **5** (*snap at*) bite at, nip, gnash at, snatch at. **6** jump, leap; see also SPRING *v.* 1. **7** shoot, photograph, catch. ● *n.* **1** crack, crackle, pop, click. **3** snapshot, photograph, photo, picture. **4** spell, period, interval, wave. **6** energy, vigor, animation, liveliness, vitality, bounce, spring, alertness, sprightliness, élan, dash, sparkle, verve, zip, zest, *colloq.* zing, get-up-and-go, pep, *sl.* pizzazz. **7** easy job, *colloq.* cinch, pushover, picnic, breeze, *Austral. sl.* snack. ● *adj.* abrupt, sudden, precipitate, hurried, hasty, incautious, rash, unpremeditated, unplanned, not well-thought-out, quick, instantaneous, instant. □ **snap at 1** see *snap up* below. **snap fastener** fastener, fastening, clasp; *Brit.* press-stud. **snap one's fingers 2** (*snap one's fingers at*) disdain, scorn, flout, dismiss, disregard, ignore, defy, mock, deride, thumb one's nose at, *literary* contemn, *sl.* cock a snook at. **snap out of** get rid of, shake off; (*snap out of it*) recover, come around, revive, awaken, wake up, perk up, liven up, cheer up, rally; get a grip on *or* of oneself, get (a) hold on *or* of oneself, pull oneself together, (re)gain control of oneself. **snap up 1, 2** accept, snap at, grab (up), snatch (up), seize, pluck, pounce on *or* upon, make off with, take (away), capture, catch, get, secure.

snapdragon /snápdragən/ *n.* a plant, *Antirrhinum majus*, with a bag-shaped flower like a dragon's mouth.

snapper /snápər/ *n.* **1** a person or thing that snaps. **2** any of several fish of the family Lutjanidae, used as food. **3** a snapping turtle. **4** a party cracker (as a toy).

snappish /snápish/ *adj.* **1** (of a person's manner or a remark) curt; ill-tempered; sharp. **2** (of a dog, etc.) inclined to snap. □□ **snappishly** *adv.* **snappishness** *n.*

■ **1** curt, short, abrupt, brusque, curmudgeonly, cantankerous, sharp, cross, grouchy, gruff, crusty, crabby, crabbed, acid, tart, acerbic, churlish, dyspeptic, choleric, splenetic, ill-humored, ill-tempered, temperamental, moody, short-tempered, testy, petulant, peevish, irritable, prickly, touchy, irascible, quick to anger, quick-tempered, hot-tempered, waspish, cranky, *colloq.* snappy.

snappy /snápee/ *adj.* (**snappier, snappiest**) *colloq.* **1** brisk; full of zest. **2** neat and elegant (*a snappy dresser*). **3** snappish. □ **make it snappy** be quick about it. □□ **snappily** *adv.* **snappiness** *n.*

■ **1** quick, sharp, brisk, smart, crisp, rapid, speedy, lively, energetic, vigorous. **2** fashionable, chic, sharp, smart, stylish, dapper, modish, *colloq.* natty, *colloq. often derog.* trendy. **3** see SNAPPISH.

snapshot /snápshot/ *n.* a casual photograph taken quickly with a hand-held camera.

■ see PHOTOGRAPH *n.*

snare /snair/ *n. & v.* ● *n.* **1** a trap for catching birds or animals, esp. with a noose of wire or cord. **2** a thing that acts as a temptation. **3** a device for tempting an enemy, etc., to expose himself or herself to danger, failure, loss, capture, defeat, etc. **4** (in *sing.* or *pl.*) *Mus.* twisted strings of gut, hide, or wire stretched across the lower head of a snare drum to produce a rattling sound. **5** (in full **snare drum**) a small, double-headed drum fitted with snares, usu. played in a jazz or military band. **6** *Surgery* a wire loop for extracting polyps, etc. ● *v.tr.* **1** catch (a bird, etc.) in a snare. **2** ensnare; lure or trap (a person) with a snare. □□ **snarer** *n.* (also in *comb.*).

[OE *sneare* f. ON *snara*: senses 4 & 5 prob. f. MLG or MDu.]

■ *n.* **1** trap, net, springe, noose, gin, booby trap, pitfall, deadfall. **2** see TEMPTATION 2. ● *v.* trap, catch, entrap, seize, capture, ensnare; net, bag, hook; lure, decoy.

snark /snaark/ *n.* a fabulous animal, orig. the subject of a nonsense poem. [*The Hunting of the Snark* (1876) by Lewis Carroll]

snarl[1] /snaarl/ *v. & n.* ● *v.* **1** *intr.* (of a dog) make an angry growl with bared teeth. **2** *intr.* (of a person) speak cynically; make bad-tempered complaints or criticisms. **3** *tr.* (often foll. by *out*) **a** utter in a snarling tone. **b** express (discontent, etc.) by snarling. ● *n.* the act or sound of snarling. □□ **snarler** *n.* **snarlingly** *adv.* **snarly** *adj.* (**snarlier, snarliest**). [earlier *snar* f. (M)LG, MHG *snarren*]

■ *v.* **1, 3** growl; snap. **2** see COMPLAIN 1, 2b, CARP[2].
● *n.* growl.

snarl[2] /snaarl/ *v. & n.* ● *v.* **1** *tr.* (often foll. by *up*) twist; entangle; confuse and hamper the movement of (traffic, etc.). **2** *intr.* (often foll. by *up*) become entangled, congested, or confused. **3** *tr.* adorn the exterior of (a narrow metal vessel) with raised work. ● *n.* a knot or tangle. □ **snarl-up** *colloq.* a traffic jam; a muddle; a mistake. [ME f. *snare* (n. & v.): sense 3 perh. f. noun in dial. sense 'knot in wood']

■ *v.* **1** tangle, entangle, complicate, confuse; impede, hinder, hamper, obstruct; scramble, muddle, twist, mix *or* mess up, *sl.* screw up. **2** tangle, entangle, twist, ravel, jam, kink. ● *n.* knot, tangle, entanglement, snag, jungle, maze, labyrinth. □ **snarl-up** jam, holdup, hitch, blockage; complexity, snag, problem, difficulty, complication, muddle, mess, predicament, fix, quandary, tight spot, *disp.* dilemma; mix-up, mistake, bungle; *colloq.* pickle.

snatch /snach/ *v. & n.* ● *v.tr.* **1** seize quickly, eagerly, or unexpectedly, esp. with outstretched hands. **2** steal (a wallet, handbag, etc.); kidnap. **3** secure with difficulty (*snatched an hour's rest*). **4** (foll. by *away, from*) take away or from, esp. suddenly (*snatched away my hand*). **5** (foll. by *from*) rescue narrowly (*snatched from the jaws of death*). **6** (foll. by *at*) **a** try to seize by stretching or grasping suddenly. **b** take (an offer, etc.) eagerly. ● *n.* **1** an act of snatching (*made a snatch at it*). **2** a fragment of a song or talk, etc. (*caught a snatch of their conversation*). **3** *sl.* a kidnapping. **4** (in weight lifting) the rapid raising of a weight from the floor to above the head. **5** a short spell of activity, etc. □ **in** (or **by**) **snatches** in fits and starts. □□ **snatcher** *n.* (esp. in sense 3 of *n.*). **snatchy** *adj.* [ME *snecchen, sna(c)che*, perh. rel. to SNACK]

■ *v.* **1, 3** grab, grasp, seize, clasp, clutch, pluck, take (hold of), catch, lay hold of, wrest, latch on to, capture, snap up, win, get, lay *or* get one's hands on. **2** see PILFER, KIDNAP. **5** save, rescue, deliver; remove. **6 b** see *jump at.* ● *n.* **1** grab, clutch, grasp. **2** scrap, bit, fragment, snippet, segment, morsel; specimen, sample.

snazzy /snázee/ *adj.* (**snazzier, snazziest**) *sl.* smart or attractive, esp. in an ostentatious way. □□ **snazzily** *adv.* **snazziness** *n.* [20th c.: orig. unkn.]

■ see STYLISH 1.

sneak /sneek/ *v., n., & adj.* ● *v.* **1** *intr. & tr.* (foll. by *in, out, past, away*, etc.) go or convey furtively; slink. **2** *tr. sl.* steal unobserved; make off with. **3** *intr. Brit. school sl.* tell tales; turn informer. **4** *intr.* (as **sneaking** *adj.*) **a** furtive; undisclosed (*have a sneaking affection for him*). **b** persistent in one's mind; nagging (*a sneaking feeling that it is not right*). ● *n.* **1** a mean-spirited, cowardly, underhanded person. **2** *Brit. school sl.* a tattletale. ● *adj.* acting or done without warning; secret (*a sneak attack*). □ **sneak thief** a thief who steals without breaking in; a pickpocket. □□ **sneakingly** *adv.* [16th c., prob. dial.: perh. rel. to ME *snike*, OE *snīcan* creep]

■ *v.* **1** lurk, slink, steal, creep, skulk, cower, pad, prowl, sidle, slip, pussyfoot, tiptoe; smuggle. **2** see STEAL *v.* 1. **3** see INFORM 2. **4** (**sneaking**) **a** innate, intuitive, inherent, private, secret, furtive, suppressed, hidden, unexpressed, undeclared, unvoiced, unavowed, unconfessed, unrevealed, unadmitted, undivulged,

undisclosed, covert. **b** persistent, lingering, lurking, nagging, worrying, worrisome, niggling, intuitive, deep-rooted, deep-seated, gut. ● *n.* **2** informer, telltale, talebearer, stool pigeon, tattletale, *sl.* snitch, ratfink, fink, stoolie, *Brit. sl.* nark.

sneaker /snéekər/ *n.* each of a pair of rubber-soled canvas, etc., shoes.

■ sports shoe, tennis shoe, gym shoe, *Brit.* plimsoll.

sneaky /snéekee/ *adj.* (**sneakier, sneakiest**) given to or characterized by sneaking; furtive; mean. □□ **sneakily** *adv.* **sneakiness** *n.*

■ underhand(ed), devious, furtive, sly, slippery, stealthy, disingenuous, deceitful, dishonest, unscrupulous, treacherous, crafty, mean, low-down, *colloq.* shifty. □□ **sneakily** see *in private* (PRIVATE). **sneakiness** see STEALTH.

sneck /snek/ *n. & v. Sc. & No. of Engl.* ● *n.* a latch. ● *v.tr.* latch (a door, etc.); close or fasten with a sneck. [ME, rel. to SNATCH]

sneer /sneer/ *n. & v.* ● *n.* a derisive smile or remark. ● *v.* **1** *intr.* (often foll. by *at*) smile derisively. **2** *tr.* say sneeringly. **3** *intr.* (often foll. by *at*) speak derisively, esp. covertly or ironically (*sneered at his attempts*). □□ **sneerer** *n.* **sneeringly** *adv.* [16th c.: orig. unkn.]

■ *n.* jeer, scoff, boo, hiss, hoot, gibe, taunt. ● *v.* **1** smirk, curl one's lip. **3** (*sneer at*) scorn, disdain, despise, sniff at, scoff at, jeer at, laugh at, deride, mock, ridicule; underrate, pooh-pooh, *literary* contemn; *colloq.* turn up one's nose at, *sl.* knock.

sneeze /sneez/ *n. & v.* ● *n.* **1** a sudden involuntary expulsion of air from the nose and mouth caused by irritation of the nostrils. **2** the sound of this. ● *v.intr.* make a sneeze. □ **not to be sneezed at** *colloq.* not contemptible; considerable; notable. □□ **sneezer** *n.* **sneezy** *adj.* [ME *snese*, app. alt. of obs. *fnese* f. OE *-fnēsan*, ON *fnýsa* & replacing earlier and less expressive *nese*]

sneezewort /snéezwərt, -wawrt/ *n.* a kind of yarrow, *Achillea ptarmica*, whose dried leaves are used to induce sneezing.

Snell's law /snelz/ *n. Physics* the law that the ratio of the sines of the angles of incidence and refraction of a wave are constant when it passes between two given media. [W. *Snell*, Du. mathematician d. 1626]

snib /snib/ *v. & n. Sc. & Ir.* ● *v.tr.* (**snibbed, snibbing**) bolt, fasten, or lock (a door, etc.). ● *n.* a lock, catch, or fastening for a door or window. [19th c.: orig. uncert.]

snick /snik/ *v. & n.* ● *v.tr.* **1** cut a small notch in. **2** make a small incision in. **3** *Cricket* deflect (the ball) slightly with the bat. ● *n.* **1** a small notch or cut. **2** *Cricket* a slight deflection of the ball by the bat. [18th c.: prob. f. *snick-a-snee* fight with knives]

snicker /sníkər/ *v. & n.* ● *v.intr.* **1** = SNIGGER *v.* **2** whinny; neigh. ● *n.* **1** = SNIGGER *n.* **2** a whinny, a neigh. □□ **snickeringly** *adv.* [imit.]

■ *v.* **2** whinny, neigh, bray. ● *n.* **2** whinny, neigh.

snicket /sníkit/ *n. Brit. dial.* a narrow passage between houses; an alleyway. [orig. unkn.]

snide /snid/ *adj. & n.* ● *adj.* **1** sneering; slyly derogatory; insinuating. **2** counterfeit; bogus. **3** mean; underhanded. ● *n.* a snide person or remark. □□ **snidely** *adv.* **snideness** *n.* [19th-c. colloq.: orig. unkn.]

■ *adj.* **1** see SCORNFUL. **3** see SLY 1.

sniff /snif/ *v. & n.* ● *v.* **1** *intr.* draw up air audibly through the nose to stop it running or to detect a smell or as an expression of contempt. **2** *tr.* (often foll. by *up*) draw in (a scent, drug, liquid, or air) through the nose. **3** *tr.* draw in the scent of (food, drink, flowers, etc.) through the nose. ● *n.* **1** an act or sound of sniffing. **2** the amount of air, etc., sniffed up. □ **sniff at 1** try the smell of; show interest in. **2** show contempt for or discontent with. **sniff out** detect; discover by investigation. □□ **sniffingly** *adv.* [ME, imit.]

■ *v.* **1** snivel, sniffle, snuffle. **2** snuff, draw in, breathe in, inhale, *sl.* snort. **3** smell, scent, nose (out). ● *n.* **1** sniffle, snuffle. **2** whiff, breath, odor, scent. □ **sniff at 2** see SNEER *v.* 3. **sniff out** see DETECT *v.*

sniffer /snífər/ *n.* **1** a person who sniffs, esp. one who sniffs a drug or toxic substances (often in *comb.*: *glue-sniffer*). **2** *sl.* the nose. **3** *colloq.* any device for detecting gas, radiation, etc. □ **sniffer dog** *colloq.* a dog trained to sniff out drugs or explosives.

sniffle /snífəl/ *v. & n.* ● *v.intr.* sniff slightly or repeatedly. ● *n.* **1** the act of sniffling. **2** (in *sing.* or *pl.*) a cold in the head causing a running nose and sniffling. □□ **sniffler** *n.* **sniffly** *adj.* [imit.: cf. SNIVEL]
■ *v.* sniff, snivel, snuffle. ● *n.* **1** sniff, snuffle.

sniffy /snífee/ *adj. colloq.* (**sniffier, sniffiest**) **1** inclined to sniff. **2** disdainful; contemptuous. □□ **sniffily** *adv.* **sniffiness** *n.*

snifter /snífter/ *n.* **1** *sl.* a small drink of alcohol. **2** a balloon glass for brandy. □ **snifter valve** a valve in a steam engine to allow air in or out. [dial. *snift* sniff, perh. f. Scand.: imit.]
■ **1** see DRINK *n.* 2b.

snigger /snígər/ *n. & v.* ● *n.* a half-suppressed secretive laugh. ● *v.intr.* utter such a laugh. □□ **sniggerer** *n.* **sniggeringly** *adv.* [var. of SNICKER]
■ *n.* snicker, chuckle, giggle, titter, *Brit.* tee-hee; laugh. ● *v.* snicker, chuckle, giggle, titter, laugh up one's sleeve, tee-hee.

sniggle /snígəl/ *v.intr.* fish (for eels) by pushing bait into a hole. [ME *snig* small eel, of unkn. orig.]

snip /snip/ *v. & n.* ● *v.tr.* (**snipped, snipping**) (also *absol.*) cut (cloth, a hole, etc.) with scissors or shears, esp. in small, quick strokes. ● *n.* **1** an act of snipping. **2** a piece of material, etc., snipped off. **3** *sl.* **a** something easily achieved. **b** *Brit.* a bargain; something cheaply acquired. **4** (in *pl.*) hand shears for metal cutting (*tin snips*). □ **snip at 1** make snipping strokes at. **2** be curt and nasty toward. □□ **snipping** *n.* [LG & Du. *snippen* imit.]
■ *v.* nip, clip, crop, cut, lop, prune, dock, trim. ● *n.* **1** cut, slit, gash, slash, incision, nick. **2** bit, scrap, shred, snippet, fragment, sliver, patch, cutting, clipping, sample, remnant, morsel. **3 a** see BREEZE[1] *n.* 5. **4** (*snips*) scissors, shears, hand shears, tinsnips, clippers.

snipe /snip/ *n. & v.* ● *n.* (*pl.* same or **snipes**) any of various wading birds frequenting marshes, esp. of the genus *Gallinago*, with a long, straight bill. ● *v.* **1** *intr.* fire shots from hiding, usu. at long range. **2** *tr.* kill by sniping. **3** *intr.* (foll. by *at*) make a sly critical attack. **4** *intr.* go snipe shooting. □ **snipe eel** any eel of the family Nemichthyidae, having a long, slender snout. **snipe fish** any marine fish of the family Macrorhamphosidae, with a long, slender snout. □□ **sniper** *n.* [ME, prob. f. Scand.: cf. Icel. *mýrisnípa*, & MDu., MLG *snippe*, OHG *snepfa*]
■ *v.* **1** shoot, fire. **3** (*snipe at*) attack, criticize, deride, find fault with, carp at, pick apart. □□ **sniper** see SHOT[1] 6.

snippet /snípit/ *n.* **1** a small piece cut off. **2** (usu. in *pl.*; often foll. by *of*) **a** a scrap or fragment of information, knowledge, etc. **b** a short extract from a book, newspaper, etc. □□ **snippety** *adj.*
■ **1, 2a** see FRAGMENT *n.* **2 b** see CLIP[2] *n.* 3.

snippy /snípee/ *adj.* (**snippier, snippiest**) *colloq.* faultfinding, snappish, sharp. □□ **snippily** *adv.* **snippiness** *n.*

snit /snit/ *n.* a rage; a sulk (esp. *in a snit*). [20th c.: orig. unkn.]

snitch /snich/ *v. & n.* ● *v.* **1** *tr.* steal. **2** *intr.* (often foll. by *on*) inform on a person. ● *n.* an informer. [17th c.: orig. unkn.]
■ *v.* **1** see STEAL *v.* 1. **2** see INFORM 2. ● *n.* see INFORMER 1.

snivel /snívəl/ *v. & n.* ● *v.intr.* **1** weep with sniffling. **2** run at the nose; make a repeated sniffing sound. **3** show weak or tearful sentiment. ● *n.* **1** running mucus. **2** hypocritical talk; cant. □□ **sniveler** *n.* **sniveling** *adj.* **snivelingly** *adv.* [ME f. OE *snyflan* (unrecorded) f. *snofl* mucus: cf. SNUFFLE]
■ *v.* **1, 2** sniffle, snuffle, sniff; blubber, whimper, whine, mewl; cry, weep, *Austral. colloq.* whinge, *literary* pule. □□ **sniveling** see TEARFUL 1, *groveling* (GROVEL).

snob /snob/ *n.* **1 a** a person with an exaggerated respect for social position or wealth and who despises socially inferior connections. **b** (*attrib.*) related to or characteristic of this attitude. **2** a person who behaves with servility to social superiors. **3** a person who despises others whose (usu. speci-

fied) tastes or attainments are considered inferior (*an intellectual snob; a wine snob*). □□ **snobbery** *n.* (*pl.* **-ies**). **snobbish** *adj.* **snobbishly** *adv.* **snobbishness** *n.* **snobby** *adj.* (**snobbier, snobbiest**). [18th c. (now dial.) 'cobbler': orig. unkn.]
■ □□ **snobbery, snobbishness** pretentiousness, pretension, hauteur, haughtiness, superciliousness, condescension, loftiness, contemptuousness, presumptuousness, lordliness, disdainfulness, disdain, pompousness, pomposity, affectation, inflatedness, self-importance, conceit, arrogance; vainness, vanity, narcissism, self-admiration, self-centeredness, egotism; smugness, *colloq.* snootiness, esp. *Brit. colloq.* uppishness, *sl.* snottiness. **snobbish** condescending, superior, patronizing, arrogant, haughty, lordly, lofty, putting on airs, disdainful, supercilious, contemptuous, pretentious, smug, scornful, self-important, affected, conceited, egotistic(al), vain, self-satisfied, complacent, pompous, hoity-toity, *colloq.* snooty, highfalutin, on one's high horse, uppity, high and mighty, high-hat, stuck-up, esp. *Brit. colloq.* uppish, *sl.* snotty, *Brit. sl.* toffee-nosed.

snood /snoʊd/ *n.* **1** an ornamental hairnet usu. worn at the back of the head. **2** a ring of woolen, etc., material worn as a hood. **3** a short line attaching a hook to a main line in sea fishing. **4** *hist.* a ribbon or band worn by unmarried women in Scotland to confine their hair. [OE *snōd*]

snook[1] /snoʊk, snoʊk/ *n. sl.* a contemptuous gesture with the thumb to the nose and the fingers spread out. □ **cock a snook** = *thumb one's nose.* [19th c.: orig. unkn.]

snook[2] /snoʊk, snoʊk/ *n.* a marine fish, *Centropomus undecimalis*, used as food. [Du. *snoek* = PIKE[1], f. MLG *snōk*, prob. rel. to SNACK]

snooker /snoʊkər, snoʊk-/ *n. & v.* ● *n.* **1** a game similar to pool in which the players use a cue ball (white) to pocket the other balls (15 red and 6 colored) in a set order. **2** a position in this game in which a direct shot at a permitted ball is impossible. ● *v.tr.* **1** (also *refl.*) subject (oneself or another player) to a snooker. **2** (esp. as **snookered** *adj.*) *sl.* defeat; thwart. [19th c.: orig. unkn.]
■ *v.* **2** see BEAT *v.* 3a.

snoop /snoʊp/ *v. & n. colloq.* ● *v.intr.* **1** pry into matters one need not be concerned with. **2** (often foll. by *about, around*) investigate in order to find out transgressions of the law, etc. ● *n.* **1** an act of snooping. **2** a person who snoops, a detective. □□ **snooper** *n.* **snoopy** *adj.* [Du. *snoepen* eat on the sly]
■ *v.* **1** pry, spy, interfere, meddle, intrude, nose around *or* about, butt in, *colloq.* be nosy, stick *or* poke one's nose in, *Austral. & NZ sl.* stickybeak. ● *n.* **2** busybody, meddler, spy, intruder, snooper; private detective *or* investigator, *colloq.* private eye, sleuth, esp. *Brit. colloq.* Nosy Parker, *sl.* peeper, shamus, *Austral. & NZ sl.* stickybeak. □□ **snoopy** see NOSY.

snooperscope /snoʊpərskoʊp/ *n.* a device which converts infrared radiation into a visible image, esp. used for seeing in the dark.

snoot /snoʊt/ *n. sl.* the nose. [var. of SNOUT]

snooty /snoʊtee/ *adj.* (**snootier, snootiest**) *colloq.* supercilious; conceited. □□ **snootily** *adv.* **snootiness** *n.* [20th c.: orig. unkn.]
■ see SUPERCILIOUS. □□ **snootiness** see *snobbery* (SNOB).

snooze /snoʊz/ *n. & v. colloq.* ● *n.* a short sleep, esp. in the daytime. ● *v.intr.* take a snooze. □□ **snoozer** *n.* **snoozy** *adj.* (**snoozier, snooziest**). [18th-c. *sl.*: orig. unkn.]
■ *n.* see SLEEP *n.* 2. ● *v.* see SLEEP *v.*

snore /snawr/ *n. & v.* ● *n.* a snorting or grunting sound in breathing during sleep. ● *v.intr.* make this sound. □ **snore away** pass (time) sleeping or snoring. □□ **snorer** *n.* **snoringly** *adv.* [ME, prob. imit.: cf. SNORT]

/.../ **pronunciation**	● **part of speech**
□ **phrases, idioms, and compounds**	
□□ **derivatives**	■ **synonym section**
cross-references appear in SMALL CAPITALS or *italics*	

snorkel /snáwrkəl/ *n. & v.* ● *n.* **1** a breathing tube for an underwater swimmer. **2** a device for supplying air to a submerged submarine. ● *v.intr.* use a snorkel. □□ **snorkeler** *n.* [G *Schnorchel*]

snort /snawrt/ *n. & v.* ● *n.* **1** an explosive sound made by the sudden forcing of breath through the nose, esp. expressing indignation or incredulity. **2** a similar sound made by an engine, etc. **3** *colloq.* a small drink of liquor. **4** *sl.* an inhaled dose of a (usu. illegal) powdered drug. ● *v.* **1** *intr.* make a snort. **2** *intr.* (of an engine, etc.) make a sound resembling this. **3** *tr.* (also *absol.*) *sl.* inhale (a usu. illegal narcotic drug, esp. cocaine or heroin). **4** *tr.* express (defiance, etc.) by snorting. □ **snort out** express (words, emotions, etc.) by snorting. [ME, prob. imit.: cf. SNORE]
■ *n.* **1** see GASP *n.* **3** see DRINK *n.* 2b. ● *v.* **3** see SNIFF *v.* 2.

snorter /snáwrtər/ *n.* esp. *Brit. colloq.* **1** something very impressive or difficult. **2** something vigorous or violent.

snot /snot/ *n. sl.* **1** nasal mucus. **2** a term of contempt for a person. □ **snot-rag** *coarse* a handkerchief. [prob. f. MDu., MLG *snotte*, MHG *snuz*, rel. to SNOUT]
■ **2** see STINKER.

snotty /snótee/ *adj.* (**snottier, snottiest**) *sl.* **1** running or foul with nasal mucus. **2** *colloq.* contemptible. **3** *colloq.* supercilious; conceited. □□ **snottily** *adv.* **snottiness** *n.*
■ **3** see CONCEITED. □□ **snottiness** see *snobbery* (SNOB).

snout /snowt/ *n.* **1** the projecting nose and mouth of an animal. **2** *derog.* a person's nose. **3** the pointed front of a thing; a nozzle. **4** *Brit. sl.* tobacco or a cigarette. □ **snout beetle** a weevil. □□ **snouted** *adj.* (also in *comb.*). **snoutlike** *adj.* **snouty** *adj.* [ME f. MDu., MLG *snūt*]
■ **1** muzzle, trunk, proboscis; see also MOUTH *n.* 1.
2 nose, *sl.* snoot, beak, *Brit. sl.* conk, hooter.

snow /snō/ *n. & v.* ● *n.* **1** atmospheric vapor frozen into ice crystals and falling to earth in light white flakes. **2** a fall of this, or a layer of it on the ground. **3** a thing resembling snow in whiteness or texture, etc. **4** a mass of flickering white spots on a television or radar screen, caused by interference or a poor signal. **5** *sl.* cocaine. **6** a dessert or other dish resembling snow. **7** frozen carbon dioxide. ● *v.* **1** *intr.* (prec. by *it* as subject) snow falls (*it is snowing; if it snows*). **2** *tr.* (foll. by *in, over, up*, etc.) confine or block with large quantities of snow. **3** *tr. & intr.* sprinkle or scatter or fall as or like snow. **4** *intr.* come in large numbers or quantities. **5** *tr. sl.* deceive or charm with plausible words. □ **be snowed under** be overwhelmed, esp. with work. **snow-blind** temporarily blinded by the glare of light reflected by large expanses of snow. **snow blindness** this blindness. **snow boot** *Brit.* an overboot of rubber and cloth. **snow-broth** melted or melting snow. **snow goose** a white Arctic goose, *Anser caerulescens*, with black-tipped wings. **snow job** *sl.* an attempt at flattery or deception. **snow-job** *v.tr. sl.* do a snow job on (a person). **snow leopard** = OUNCE². **snow line** the level above which snow never melts entirely. **snow owl** = *snowy owl*. **snow partridge** a mainly white partridge, *Lerwa lerwa*. **snow-white** pure white. □□ **snowless** *adj.* **snowlike** *adj.* [OE *snāw* f. Gmc]
■ *n.* **1, 2** see PRECIPITATION 3a. **4** see INTERFERENCE 2.
● *v.* **1** see STORM *v.* 4. **5** see FOOL¹ *v.* 1, 3. □ **snow-white** see WHITE *adj.* 1.

snowball /snóbawl/ *n. & v.* ● *n.* **1** snow pressed together into a ball, esp. for throwing in play. **2** anything that grows or increases rapidly like a snowball rolled on snow. ● *v.* **1** *intr. & tr.* throw or pelt with snowballs. **2** *intr.* increase rapidly. □ **snowball bush 1** any of several shrubs of the genus *Viburnum*. **2** a guelder rose.
■ *v.* **2** see INCREASE *v.* 1.

snowberry /snóberee/ *n.* (*pl.* **-ies**) any shrub of the genus *Symphoricarpos*, with white berries.

snowbird /snóbərd/ *n.* **1** a bird, such as the junco, commonly seen in snowy regions. **2** *colloq.* a person who moves from a cold climate to a warmer climate during the winter.

snowblink /snóblingk/ *n.* the reflection in the sky of snow or ice fields.

snowblower /snóblōər/ *n.* a machine that clears snow by blowing it to the side of the road, etc.

snowboard /snóbawrd/ *n.* a board similar to a wide ski, ridden over snow in an upright or surfing position. □□ **snowboarder** *n.*

snowbound /snóbownd/ *adj.* prevented by snow from going out or traveling.

snowcap /snókap/ *n.* **1** the tip of a mountain when covered with snow. **2** a white-crowned hummingbird, *Microchera albocoronata*, native to Central America. □□ **snowcapped** *adj.*

snowdrift /snódrift/ *n.* a bank of snow heaped up by the action of the wind.

snowdrop /snódrop/ *n.* a bulbous plant, *Galanthus nivalis*, with white drooping flowers in the early spring.

snowfall /snófawl/ *n.* **1** a fall of snow. **2** *Meteorol.* the amount of snow that falls on one occasion or on a given area within a given time.
■ see PRECIPITATION 3a.

snowfield /snófeeld/ *n.* a permanent wide expanse of snow in mountainous or polar regions.

snowflake /snóflayk/ *n.* **1** each of the small collections of crystals in which snow falls. **2 a** any bulbous plant of the genus *Leucojum*, with snowdroplike flowers. **b** the white flower of this plant.
■ **1** flake.

snowman /snóman/ *n.* (*pl.* **-men**) a figure resembling a man, made of compressed snow.

snowmobile /snóməbeel, -mō-/ *n.* a motor vehicle, esp. with runners or revolving treads, for traveling over snow.

snowplow /snóplow/ *n.* a device, or a vehicle equipped with one, for clearing roads of thick snow.

snowshoe /snóshōō/ *n. & v.* ● *n.* a flat device like a racket attached to a boot for walking on snow without sinking in. ● *v.intr.* travel on snowshoes. □□ **snowshoer** *n.*

snowslide /snóslid/ *n.* an avalanche of snow.

snowslip /snóslip/ *n. Brit.* = SNOWSLIDE.

snowstorm /snóstawrm/ *n.* a heavy fall of snow, esp. with a high wind.
■ see STORM *n.* 1.

snowy /snóee/ *adj.* (**snowier, snowiest**) **1** of or like snow. **2** (of the weather, etc.) with much snow. □ **snowy owl** a large white owl, *Nyctea scandiaca*, native to the Arctic. □□ **snowily** *adv.* **snowiness** *n.*
■ **1** see WHITE *adj.* 1. **2** see WINTRY 1.

Snr. *abbr.* esp. *Brit.* senior.

snub /snub/ *v., n., & adj.* ● *v.tr.* (**snubbed, snubbing**) **1** rebuff or humiliate with sharp words or a marked lack of cordiality. **2** check the movement of (a boat, horse, etc.) esp. by a rope wound around a post, etc. ● *n.* an act of snubbing; a rebuff. ● *adj.* short and blunt in shape. □ **snub nose** a short turned-up nose. **snub-nosed 1** having a snub nose. **2** (of a gun) having a very short barrel. □□ **snubber** *n.* **snubbingly** *adv.* [ME f. ON *snubba* chide, check the growth of]
■ *v.* **1** see REBUFF *v.* ● *n.* see REBUFF *n.*

snuff¹ /snuf/ *n. & v.* ● *n.* the charred part of a candlewick. ● *v.tr.* trim the snuff from (a candle). □ **snuff it** *Brit. sl.* die. **snuff out 1** extinguish by snuffing. **2** kill; put an end to. [ME *snoffe, snuffe*: orig. unkn.]
■ □ **snuff it** see DIE¹ 1. **snuff out 1** see QUENCH 2. **2** see KILL¹ *v.* 1.

snuff² /snuf/ *n. & v.* ● *n.* powdered tobacco or medicine taken by sniffing it up the nostrils. ● *v.intr.* take snuff. □ **snuff-colored** dark yellowish-brown. **up to snuff** *colloq.* **1** up to standard. **2** *Brit.* knowing; not easily deceived. [Du. *snuf* (*tabak* tobacco) f. MDu. *snuffen* snuffle]
■ *v.* see SNIFF *v.* 2. □ **up to snuff 1** see *up to scratch* (SCRATCH).

snuffbox /snúfboks/ *n.* a small usu. ornamental box for holding snuff.

snuffer /snúfər/ *n.* **1** a small hollow cone with a handle used to extinguish a candle. **2** (in *pl.*) an implement like scissors used to extinguish a candle or trim its wick.

snuffle /snúfəl/ *v. & n.* ● *v.* **1** *intr.* make sniffing sounds. **2 a** *intr.* speak nasally, whiningly, or like one with a cold. **b** *tr.* (often foll. by *out*) say in this way. **3** *intr.* breathe noisily as through a partially blocked nose. **4** *intr.* sniff. ● *n.* **1** a snuffling sound or tone. **2** (in *pl.*) a partial blockage of the nose causing snuffling. **3** a sniff. □□ **snuffler** *n.* **snuffly** *adj.* [prob. f. LG & Du. *snuffelen* (as SNUFF²): cf. SNIVEL]

■ *v.* **1, 4** sniff, snivel, sniffle. ● *n.* **1, 3** sniffle, snuffle.

snuffy¹ /snúfee/ *adj.* (**snuffier, snuffiest**) **1** annoyed. **2** irritable. **3** supercilious or contemptuous. [SNUFF¹ + -Y¹]

snuffy² /snúfee/ *adj.* like snuff in color or substance. [SNUFF² + -Y²]

snug /snug/ *adj.* & *n.* ● *adj.* (**snugger, snuggest**) **1 a** cozy, comfortable; sheltered; well enclosed or placed or arranged. **b** cozily protected from the weather or cold. **c** close-fitting. **2** (of an income, etc.) allowing comfort and comparative ease. ● *n. Brit.* a small room in a pub or inn. □□ **snugly** *adv.* **snugness** *n.* [16th c. (orig. Naut.): prob. of LG or Du. orig.]

■ *adj.* **1a, b** cozy, comfortable, intimate, relaxing, restful, warm, sheltered, secure, friendly, easy, homely, casual, *colloq.* comfy. **c** see TIGHT *adj.* 1, 2a.

snuggery /snúgəree/ *n. Brit.* (*pl.* **-ies**) **1** a snug place, esp. a person's private room or den. **2** = SNUG *n.*

■ **1** see NEST *n.* 2, 3.

snuggle /snúgəl/ *v.intr.* & *tr.* (usu. foll. by *down, up, together*) settle or draw into a warm comfortable position. [SNUG + -LE⁴]

■ cuddle, nestle, nuzzle.

So. *abbr.* South.

so¹ /sō/ *adv.* & *conj.* ● *adv.* **1** (often foll. by *that* + clause) to such an extent, or to the extent implied (*why are you so angry?*; *stop complaining so*; *they were so pleased that they gave us a bonus*). **2** (with *neg.*; often foll. by *as* + clause) to the extent to which . . . is or does, etc., or to the extent implied (*was not so late as I expected*; *am not so eager as you*). ¶ In positive constructions *as . . . as . . .* is used: see AS¹. **3** (foll. by *that* or *as* + clause) to the degree or in the manner implied (*so expensive that few can afford it*; *so small as to be invisible*; *am not so foolish as to agree to that*). **4** (adding emphasis) to that extent; in that or a similar manner (*I want to leave and so does she*; *you said it was good, and so it is*). **5** to a great or notable degree (*I am so glad*). **6** (with verbs of state) in the way described (*am not very fond of it but may become so*). **7** (with verb of saying or thinking, etc.) as previously mentioned or described (*I think so*; *so he said*; *so I should hope*). ● *conj.* (often foll. by *that* + clause) **1** with the result that (*there was none left, so we had to go without*). **2** in order that (*came home early so that I could see you*). **3** and then; as the next step (*so then the car broke down*; *and so to bed*). **4 a** (introducing a question) then; after that (*so what did you tell them?*). **b** (*absol.*) = *so what?* □ **and so on** (or **forth**) **1** and others of the same kind. **2** and in other similar ways. **so as** (foll. by *to* + infin.) in order to (*did it so as to get it finished*). **so be it** an expression of acceptance or resignation. **so-called** commonly designated or known as, often incorrectly. **so far** see FAR. **so far as** see FAR. **so far so good** see FAR. **so long!** *colloq.* good-bye until we meet again. **so long as** see LONG¹. **so much 1** a certain amount (of). **2** a great deal of (*is so much nonsense*). **3** (with *neg.*) **a** less than; to a lesser extent (*not so much forgotten as ignored*). **b** not even (*didn't give me so much as a penny*). **so much for** that is all that need be done or said about. **so-so** *adj.* (usu. *predic.*) indifferent; not very good. ● *adv.* indifferently; only moderately well. **so to say** (or **speak**) an expression of reserve or apology for an exaggeration or neologism, etc. **so what?** *colloq.* why should that be considered significant? [OE *swā*, etc.]

■ *conj.* **1** see CONSEQUENTLY. **2** see *in order that* (ORDER). □ **so-called** self-styled, *soi-disant*, professed, alleged, pretended, supposed, ostensible; misnamed, misdesignated; suspect. **so long!** see GOOD-BYE *int.* **so-so** (*adj.*) mediocre, all right, average, undistinguished, passable, not (too) bad *or* good, adequate, fair (to middling), middling, indifferent, ordinary, tolerable, *comme ci, comme ça*, modest, *colloq.* OK. **so to say** (or **speak**) as it were, in a manner of speaking, figuratively *or* metaphorically (speaking); see also *in effect* (EFFECT). **so what?** *colloq.* big deal, so?, I couldn't care less.

so² var. of SOL.

-so /sō/ *comb. form* = -SOEVER.

soak /sōk/ *v.* & *n.* ● *v.* **1** *tr.* & *intr.* make or become thoroughly wet through saturation with or in liquid. **2** *tr.* (of rain, etc.) drench. **3** *tr.* (foll. by *in, up*) **a** absorb (liquid). **b** acquire (knowledge, etc.) copiously. **4** *refl.* (often foll. by *in*) steep (oneself) in a subject of study, etc. **5** *intr.* (foll. by *in, into, through*) (of liquid) make its way or penetrate by saturation. **6** *tr. colloq.* extract money from by an extortionate charge, taxation, etc. (*soak the rich*). **7** *intr. colloq.* drink persistently; booze. **8** *tr.* (as **soaked** *adj.*) very drunk. ● *n.* **1** the act of soaking or the state of being soaked. **2** a drinking bout. **3** *colloq.* a hard drinker. □□ **soakage** *n.* **soaker** *n.*

soaking *n.* & *adj.* [OE *socian* rel. to *soc* sucking at the breast, *sūcan* SUCK]

■ *v.* **1** drench, saturate, wet; immerse, submerge, souse, douse, sop, bathe, steep, inundate, flood, ret; macerate; marinate. **2** drench, saturate, wet. **3** (*soak up*) **a** absorb, take in *or* up, sponge up, sop up. **b** acquire, absorb, take in, assimilate, learn. **4** see *steep in* (STEEP²). **5** see IMPREGNATE *v.* 1, 2. **6** see STING *v.* 4. **8** (**soaked**) see DRUNK *adj.* 1. ● *n.* **2** see BENDER. **3** alcoholic, drunkard, drunk, dipsomaniac, drinker, tippler, sot, *archaic or literary* toper, *colloq.* sponge, souse, boozer, *sl.* lush, juicer. □□ **soaking** (*n.*) drenching, wetting, dousing, immersing, saturating. (*adj.*) wet, sopping, drenched, dripping, saturated, soaked, wringing wet, streaming, sodden, waterlogged.

so-and-so /sōandsō/ *n.* (*pl.* **so-and-sos**) **1** a particular person or thing not needing to be specified (*told me to do so-and-so*). **2** *colloq.* a person disliked or regarded with disfavor (*the so-and-so left me behind*).

■ **1** such and such, something or other. **2** see STINKER.

soap /sōp/ *n.* & *v.* ● *n.* **1** a cleansing agent that is a compound of fatty acid with soda or potash (or (**insoluble soap**) with another metallic oxide, of which the soluble kinds when rubbed in water yield a lather used in washing. **2** *colloq.* = *soap opera*. ● *v.tr.* **1** apply soap to. **2** scrub or rub with soap. □ **soap opera** a broadcast drama, usu. serialized in many episodes, dealing with sentimental or melodramatic domestic themes (so called because orig. sponsored in the US by soap manufacturers). □□ **soapless** *adj.* **soaplike** *adj.* [OE *sāpe* f. WG]

■ *n.* **1** see DETERGENT *n.* ● *v.* see WASH *v.* 1, 3. □ **soap powder** see DETERGENT *n.*

soapbark /sōpbaark/ *n.* an American tree, *Quillaja saponaria*, with bark yielding saponin.

soapberry /sōpberee/ *n.* (*pl.* **-ies**) any of various tropical American shrubs, esp. of the genus *Sapindus*, with fruits yielding saponin.

soapbox /sōpboks/ *n.* **1** a box for holding soap. **2** a makeshift stand for a public speaker.

soapstone /sōpstōn/ *n.* steatite.

soapsuds /sōpsudz/ *n.pl.* = SUDS 1.

soapwort /sōpwərt, -wawrt/ *n.* a European plant, *Saponaria officinalis*, with pink or white flowers and leaves yielding a soapy substance.

soapy /sōpee/ *adj.* (**soapier, soapiest**) **1** of or like soap. **2** containing or smeared with soap. **3** (of a person or manner) unctuous or flattering. □□ **soapily** *adv.* **soapiness** *n.*

■ **1, 2** see OILY 1, 2. **3** see OILY 3.

soar /sawr/ *v.intr.* **1** fly or rise high. **2** reach a high level or standard (*prices soared*). **3** maintain height in the air without flapping the wings or using power. □□ **soarer** *n.* **soaringly** *adv.* [ME f. OF *essorer* ult. f. L (as EX-¹, *aura* breeze)]

■ **1** rise, ascend, fly. **2** rise, increase, escalate, climb, mount, spiral upward, shoot up *or* upward, rocket, skyrocket. **3** fly, hover, float, hang, glide.

S.O.B. *abbr. sl.* (also **SOB**) = *son of a bitch*.

/.../ **pronunciation**	● **part of speech**
□ **phrases, idioms, and compounds**	
□□ **derivatives**	■ **synonym section**
cross-references appear in SMALL CAPITALS or *italics*	

sob /sob/ v. & n. ● v. (**sobbed, sobbing**) **1** intr. draw breath in convulsive gasps usu. with weeping under mental distress or physical exhaustion. **2** tr. (usu. foll. by *out*) utter with sobs. **3** tr. bring (oneself) to a specified state by sobbing (*sobbed themselves to sleep*). ● n. a convulsive drawing of breath, esp. in weeping. □ **sob sister** a journalist who writes or edits sentimental stories. **sob story** a story or explanation appealing mainly to the emotions. □□ **sobber** n. **sobbingly** adv. [ME *sobbe* (prob. imit.)]

▪ v. cry, shed tears, weep, blubber, snivel, whimper, sniff, snuffle, wail, moan, mewl, bawl, howl, yowl, *literary* pule. ● n. cry, snivel, whimper, sniff, snuffle, wail, moan, howl, yowl.

sober /sṓbər/ adj. & v. ● adj. (**soberer, soberest**) **1** not affected by alcohol. **2** not given to excessive drinking of alcohol. **3** moderate; well-balanced; tranquil; sedate. **4** not fanciful or exaggerated (*the sober truth*). **5** (of a color, etc.) quiet and inconspicuous. ● v.tr. & intr. (often foll. by *down, up*) make or become sober or less wild, reckless, enthusiastic, visionary, etc. (*a sobering thought*). □ **as sober as a judge** completely sober. □□ **soberingly** adv. **soberly** adv. [ME f. OF *sobre* f. L *sobrius*]

▪ adj. **1** clear-headed, lucid, rational, sensible, in control, steady, composed, collected, calm. **2** temperate, abstemious; teetotal, sl. on the (water) wagon. **3** serious, solemn, earnest, dispassionate, unruffled, unflustered, unexcited, unperturbed, steady, sedate, staid, composed, dignified, cool, calm, serene, tranquil, collected, cool-headed, level-headed, sane, balanced, moderate, practical, realistic, rational, clear-headed, *colloq.* together. **4** see MATTER-OF-FACT 1. **5** sedate, somber, plain, simple, subdued, quiet, inconspicuous, dreary, dark, drab, colorless, neutral. ● v. detoxify, recover, dry out.

sobriety /səbrí-itee/ n. the state of being sober. [ME f. OF *sobrieté* or L *sobrietas* (as SOBER)]

▪ abstemiousness, temperance, teetotalism, abstention, abstinence, nonindulgence; seriousness, solemnity, staidness, gravity, temperateness, sedateness, formality, dignity.

sobriquet /sṓbrikay, -ket/ n. (also **soubriquet** /sṓo-/) **1** a nickname. **2** an assumed name. [F, orig. = 'tap under the chin']

▪ see NICKNAME n.

Soc. abbr. **1** Socialist. **2** Society.

socage /sókij/ n. (also **soccage**) a feudal tenure of land involving payment of rent or other non-military service. [ME f. AF *socage* f. *soc* f. OE *sócn* SOKE]

soccer /sókər/ n. a game played by two teams of eleven players with a round ball that cannot be touched with the hands during play except by the goalkeepers. [shortening of Association football + -ER³]

sociable /sṓshəbəl/ adj. & n. ● adj. **1** fitted for or liking the society of other people; ready and willing to talk and act with others. **2** (of a person's manner or behavior, etc.) friendly. **3** (of a meeting, etc.) marked by friendliness; not stiff or formal. ● n. **1** an open carriage with facing side seats. **2** esp. Brit. an S-shaped couch for two occupants partly facing each other. **3** a social. □□ **sociability** /-bílitee/ n. **sociableness** n. **sociably** adv. [F *sociable* or L *sociabilis* f. *sociare* to unite f. *socius* companion]

▪ adj. **1, 2** social, gregarious, outgoing, extrovert(ed), companionable, accessible, approachable, friendly, affable, amiable, genial, congenial, convivial, warm, cozy, cordial, neighborly, hospitable, welcoming, hail-fellow-well-met, *colloq.* chummy. □□ **sociability, sociableness** see FRIENDSHIP 2.

social /sṓshəl/ adj. & n. ● adj. **1** of or relating to society or its organization. **2** concerned with the mutual relations of human beings or of classes of human beings. **3** living in organized communities; unfitted for a solitary life (*a human is a social animal*). **4 a** needing companionship; gregarious; interdependent. **b** cooperative; practicing the division of labor. **5** existing only as a member of a compound organism. **6 a** (of insects) living together in organized communities. **b**

(of birds) nesting near each other in communities. **7** (of plants) growing thickly together and monopolizing the ground they grow on. ● n. a social gathering, esp. one organized by a club, congregation, etc. □ **social anthropology** the comparative study of peoples through their culture and kinship systems. **social climber** derog. a person anxious to gain a higher social status. **social contract** (or **compact**) an agreement to cooperate for social benefits, e.g., by sacrificing some individual freedom for government protection. **social democracy** a socialist system achieved by democratic means. **social democrat** a person who advocates social democracy. **social disease** a venereal disease. **social order** the network of human relationships in society. **social realism** the expression of social or political views in art. **social science a** the scientific study of human society and social relationships. **b** a branch of this (e.g., politics or economics). **social scientist** a student of or expert in the social sciences. **social secretary** a person who makes arrangements for the social activities of a person or organization. **social security** (usu. **Social Security**) a US government program of assistance to the elderly, disabled, etc., funded by mandatory contributions from employers and employees. **social service** philanthropic activity. **social services** services provided by the government for the community, esp. education, health, and housing. **social war** hist. a war fought between allies. **social work** work of benefit to those in need of help or welfare, esp. done by specially trained personnel. **social worker** a person trained to do social work. □□ **sociality** /sṓsheeálitee/ n. **socially** adv. [F *social* or L *socialis* allied f. *socius* friend]

▪ adj. **1, 2** communal, community, common, collective, group, public, popular, societal. **4 a** see SOCIABLE. **b** cooperative, collective, collaborative. ● n. **1** see DANCE n., RECEPTION 3. □ **social climber** see PARVENU n.

socialism /sṓshəlizəm/ n. **1** a political and economic theory of social organization which advocates that the community as a whole should own and control the means of production, distribution, and exchange. **2** policy or practice based on this theory. □□ **socialist** n. & adj. **socialistic** adj. **socialistically** adv. [F *socialisme* (as SOCIAL)]

▪ □□ **socialist** (n.) see left-winger (LEFT¹). (adj.) see PINK¹ adj. 2.

socialite /sṓshəlīt/ n. a person prominent in fashionable society.

socialize /sṓshəlīz/ v. **1** intr. act in a sociable manner. **2** tr. make social. **3** tr. organize on socialistic principles. □ **socialized medicine** the provision of medical services for all from public funds. □□ **socialization** n.

▪ **1** mix, get together, fraternize, keep company, go out, get out; associate, hobnob, rub elbows or esp. Brit. shoulders.

society /səsíətee/ n. (pl. **-ies**) **1** the sum of human conditions and activity regarded as a whole functioning interdependently. **2** a social community (*all societies must have firm laws*). **3 a** a social mode of life. **b** the customs and organization of an ordered community. **4** Ecol. a plant community. **5 a** the socially advantaged or prominent members of a community (*society would not approve*). **b** this, or a part of it, qualified in some way (*is not done in polite society*). **6** participation in hospitality; other people's homes or company (*avoids society*). **7** companionship; company (*avoids the society of such people*). **8** an association of persons united by a common aim or interest or principle (*formed a music society*). □ **Society of Friends** see QUAKER. **Society of Jesus** see JESUIT. □□ **societal** adj. (esp. in sense 1). **societally** adv. [F *société* f. L *societas -tatis* f. *socius* companion]

▪ **2, 3** culture, civilization, community, way of life, world; organization, system. **5 a** high society, haut monde, beau monde, upper classes, polite society, elite, gentry, *colloq.* upper crust. **b** circles, company, spheres, set. **6** company, people. **7** companionship, company, camaraderie, friendship, fellowship, association, intercourse. **8** organization, club, association, circle, league, institute, academy, alliance, guild, group, fraternity, sorority, confraternity, brotherhood, sisterhood, fellowship, union, sodality. □□ **societal** see PUBLIC *adj.* 1.

socio- /sṓseeō, sṓsheeō/ *comb. form* **1** of society (and). **2** of or relating to sociology (and). [L *socius* companion]

sociobiology /sṓseeōbīólǝjee, sṓsheeō-/ *n.* the scientific study of the biological aspects of social behavior. □□ **sociobiological** /-bīǝlójikǝl/ *adj.* **sociobiologically** *adv.* **sociobiologist** *n.*

sociocultural /sṓseeōkúlchǝrǝl, sṓsheeō-/ *adj.* combining social and cultural factors. □□ **socioculturally** *adv.*

socioeconomic /sṓseeōékǝnómik, -eékǝ-,sṓsheeō-/ *adj.* relating to or concerned with the interaction of social and economic factors. □□ **socioeconomically** *adv.*

sociolinguistic /sṓseeōlinggwístik, sṓsheeō-/ *adj.* relating to or concerned with language in its social aspects. □□ **sociolinguist** *n.* **sociolinguistically** *adv.*

sociolinguistics /sṓseeōlinggwístiks, sṓsheeō-/ *n.* the study of language in relation to social factors.

sociology /sṓseeólǝjee, sṓshee-/ *n.* **1** the study of the development, structure, and functioning of human society. **2** the study of social problems. □□ **sociological** /-ǝlójikǝl/ *adj.* **sociologically** *adv.* **sociologist** *n.* [F *sociologie* (as SOCIO-, -LOGY)]

sociometry /sṓseeómitree, sṓshee-/ *n.* the study of relationships within a group of people. □□ **sociometric** /-ǝmétrik/ *adj.* **sociometrically** *adv.* **sociometrist** *n.*

sociopath /sṓseeōpáth, sṓshee-/ *n. Psychol.* a person who is asocial or anti-social and who lacks a social conscience, as a psychopath. □□ **sociopathic** *adj.*

sock[1] /sok/ *n.* (*pl.* **socks** or *colloq.* **sox** /soks/) **1** a short knitted covering for the foot, usu. not reaching the knee. **2** a removable inner sole put into a shoe for warmth, etc. **3** an ancient Greek or Roman comic actor's light shoe. **4** comic drama. □ **pull one's socks up** *Brit. colloq.* make an effort to improve. **put a sock in it** *sl.* be quiet. **sock away** put away money as savings. [OE *socc* f. L *soccus* comic actor's shoe, light low-heeled slipper, f. Gk *sukkhos*]

sock[2] /sok/ *v. & n. colloq.* ● *v.tr.* hit (esp. a person) forcefully. ● *n.* **1** a hard blow. **2** the power to deliver a blow. □ **sock it to** attack or address (a person) vigorously. [*c.*1700 (cant): orig. unkn.]

■ *v.* see HIT *v.* 1a. ● *n.* **1** see HIT *n.* 1a.

socket /sókit/ *n. & v.* ● *n.* **1** a natural or artificial hollow for something to fit into or stand firm or revolve in. **2** *Electr.* a device receiving a plug, lightbulb, etc., to make a connection. **3** *Golf* the part of an iron club into which the shaft is fitted. ● *v.tr.* (**socketed, socketing**) **1** place in or fit with a socket. **2** *Golf* hit (a ball) with the socket of a club. [ME f. AF, dimin. of OF *soc* plowshare, prob. f. Celt. orig.]

sockeye /sókī/ *n.* a blue-backed salmon of Alaska, etc., *Oncorhynchus nerka*. [Salish *sukai* fish of fishes]

socking /sóking/ *adv. & adj. Brit.* ● *adv. colloq.* exceedingly; very (*a socking great diamond ring*). ● *adj. sl.* confounded.

socle /sókǝl/ *n. Archit.* a plain low block or plinth serving as a support for a column, urn, statue, etc., or as the foundation of a wall. [F f. It. *zoccolo* orig. 'wooden shoe' f. L *socculus* f. *soccus* SOCK[1]]

■ see PEDESTAL *n.*

Socratic /sǝkrátik, sō-/ *adj. & n.* ● *adj.* of or relating to the Greek philosopher Socrates (d. 399 BC) or his philosophy, esp. the method associated with him of seeking the truth by a series of questions and answers. ● *n.* a follower of Socrates. □ **Socratic irony** a pose of ignorance assumed in order to entice others into making statements that can then be challenged. □□ **Socratically** *adv.* [L *Socraticus* f. Gk *Sōkratikos* f. *Sōkratēs*]

sod[1] /sod/ *n. & v.* ● *n.* **1** turf or a piece of turf. **2** the surface of the ground. ● *v.tr.* (**sodded, sodding**) cover (the ground) with sods. □ **under the sod** in the grave. [ME f. MDu., MLG *sode*, of unkn. orig.]

■ *n.* **1** see TURF *n.* 1. **2** see EARTH *n.* 2b.

sod[2] /sod/ *n. & v.* esp. *Brit. coarse sl.* ¶ Often considered a taboo word. ● *n.* **1** an unpleasant or awkward person or thing. **2** a person of a specified kind; a fellow (*the lucky sod*). ● *v.tr.* (**sodded, sodding**) **1** (often *absol.* or as *int.*) an ex-

clamation of annoyance (*sod them, I don't care!*). **2** (as **sodding** *adj.*) a general term of contempt. □ **sod off** go away. **Sod's Law** = MURPHY's LAW. [abbr. of SODOMITE]

soda /sṓdǝ/ *n.* **1** any of various compounds of sodium in common use, e.g., washing soda, baking soda. **2** (in full **soda water**) water made effervescent by impregnation with carbon dioxide under pressure and used alone or with alcohol as a drink (orig. made with sodium bicarbonate). **3** (also **soda pop**) esp. *US Regional* a sweet effervescent soft drink. □ **soda biscuit 1** a biscuit made with baking soda and either sour milk or buttermilk. **2** (also **soda cracker**) a cracker made with baking soda. **soda bread** bread leavened with baking soda. **soda fountain 1** a device supplying soda water. **2** a store or counter equipped with this. **3** a store or counter for preparing and serving sodas, sundaes, and ice cream. **soda lime** a mixture of calcium oxide and sodium hydroxide. [med.L, perh. f. *sodanum* glasswort (used as a remedy for headaches) f. *soda* headache f. Arab. *ṣudā'* f. *ṣadaʿa* split]

■ **2** see WATER *n.* **3** pop, soft drink.

sodality /sōdálitee/ *n.* (*pl.* **-ies**) a confraternity or association, esp. a Roman Catholic devotional or charitable group. [F *sodalité* or L *sodalitas* f. *sodalis* comrade]

■ fraternity, brotherhood.

sodden /sódǝn/ *adj. & v.* ● *adj.* **1** saturated with liquid; soaked through. **2** rendered stupid or dull, etc., with drunkenness. **3** (of bread, etc.) doughy; heavy and moist. ● *v.intr. & tr.* become or make sodden. □□ **soddenly** *adv.* **soddenness** *n.* [archaic past part. of SEETHE]

■ *adj.* **1** see *soaking* (SOAK).

sodium /sṓdeeǝm/ *n. Chem.* a soft silver white reactive metallic element, occurring naturally in soda, salt, etc., that is important in industry and is an essential element in living organisms. ¶ Symb.: **Na**. □ **sodium bicarbonate** a white soluble powder used in the manufacture of fire extinguishers and effervescent drinks. **sodium carbonate** a white powder with many commercial applications including the manufacture of soap and glass. **sodium chloride** a colorless crystalline compound occurring naturally in sea water and halite; common salt. **sodium hydroxide** a deliquescent compound which is strongly alkaline and used in the manufacture of soap and paper: also called *caustic soda*. **sodium nitrate** a white powdery compound used mainly in the manufacture of fertilizers. **sodium-vapor lamp** (or **sodium lamp**) a lamp using an electrical discharge in sodium vapor and giving a yellow light. □□ **sodic** *adj.* [SODA + -IUM]

■ □ **sodium chloride** salt, sea salt, rock salt.

Sodom /sódǝm/ *n.* a wicked or depraved place. [*Sodom* in ancient Palestine, destroyed for its wickedness (Gen. 18–19)]

sodomite /sódǝmīt/ *n.* a person who practices sodomy. [ME f. OF f. LL *Sodomita* f. Gk *Sodomitēs* inhabitant of Sodom f. *Sodoma* Sodom]

sodomy /sódǝmee/ *n.* sexual intercourse involving anal or oral copulation. □□ **sodomize** *v.tr.* [ME f. med.L *sodomia* f. LL *peccatum Sodomiticum* sin of Sodom: see SODOM]

soever /sō-évǝr/ *adv. literary* of any kind; to any extent (*how great soever it may be*).

-soever /sō-évǝr/ *comb. form* (added to relative pronouns, adverbs, and adjectives) of any kind; to any extent (*whatsoever; howsoever*).

sofa /sṓfǝ/ *n.* a long upholstered seat with a back and arms, for two or more people. □ **sofa bed** a sofa that can be converted into a temporary bed. [F, ult. f. Arab. *ṣuffa*]

■ see COUCH[1] *n.*

soffit /sófit/ *n.* the underside of an architrave, arch, balcony, etc. [F *soffite* or It. *soffitta, -itto* ult. f. L *suffixus* (as SUFFIX)]

S. of S. *abbr.* Song of Songs (Old Testament).

soft /sawft, soft/ *adj., adv., & n.* ● *adj.* **1** (of a substance,

---

> /.../ **pronunciation**   ● **part of speech**
> □ **phrases, idioms, and compounds**
> □□ **derivatives**   ■ **synonym section**
> **cross-references** appear in SMALL CAPITALS or *italics*

material, etc.) lacking hardness or firmness; yielding to pressure; easily cut. **2** (of cloth, etc.) having a smooth surface or texture; not rough or coarse. **3** (of air, etc.) mellow; mild; balmy; not noticeably cold or hot. **4** (of water) free from mineral salts and therefore good for lathering. **5** (of a light or color, etc.) not brilliant or glaring. **6** (of a voice or sounds) gentle and pleasing. **7** *Phonet.* **a** (of a consonant) sibilant or palatal (as *c* in *ice*, *g* in *age*). **b** voiced or unaspirated. **8** (of an outline, etc.) not sharply defined. **9** (of an action or manner, etc.) gentle; conciliatory; complimentary; amorous. **10** (of the heart or feelings, etc.) compassionate; sympathetic. **11** (of a person) **a** feeble; lenient; silly; sentimental. **b** weak; not robust. **12** *colloq.* (of a job, etc.) easy. **13** (of drugs) mild; not likely to cause addiction. **14** (of radiation) having little penetrating power. **15** (also **soft-core**) (of pornography) suggestive or erotic but not explicit. **16** *Stock Exch.* (of currency, prices, etc.) likely to fall in value. **17** *Polit.* moderate; willing to compromise (*the soft left*). **18** peaceful (*soft slumbers*). **19** *Brit.* (of the weather, etc.) rainy or moist or thawing. ● *adv.* softly (*play soft*). ● *n.* a silly weak person. □ **be soft on** *colloq.* **1** be lenient toward. **2** be infatuated with. **have a soft spot for** be fond of or affectionate toward (a person). **soft-boiled** (of an egg) lightly boiled with the yolk soft or liquid. **soft-centered** (of a person) softhearted; sentimental. **soft coal** bituminous coal. **soft drink** a nonalcoholic usu. effervescent drink. **soft focus** *Photog.* the slight deliberate blurring of a picture. **soft fruit** *Brit.* small stoneless fruit (strawberry, currant, etc.). **soft furnishings** *Brit.* curtains, rugs, etc. **soft goods** textiles. **soft-headed** feebleminded. **soft-headedness** feeblemindedness. **soft in the head** feebleminded. **soft landing** a landing by a spacecraft without its suffering major damage. **soft option** the easier alternative. **soft palate** the rear part of the palate. **soft paste** denoting an 'artificial' porcelain containing glassy materials and fired at a comparatively low temperature. **soft pedal** a pedal on a piano that makes the tone softer. **soft-pedal** *v.tr.* & (often foll. by *on*) *intr.* (**pedaled** or **-pedalled**, **pedaling** or **-pedalling**) **1** refrain from emphasizing; be restrained (about). **2** play with the soft pedal down. **soft roe** see ROE[1]. **soft sell** restrained or subtly persuasive salesmanship. **soft-sell** *v.tr.* (*past* and *past part.* **-sold**) sell by this method. **soft soap 1** a semifluid soap made with potash. **2** *colloq.* persuasive flattery. **soft-soap** *v.tr. colloq.* persuade (a person) with flattery. **soft-spoken** speaking with a gentle voice. **soft tissues** tissues of the body that are not bony or cartilaginous. **soft touch** *colloq.* a gullible person, esp. over money. □□ **softish** *adj.* **softness** *n.* [OE *sōfte* agreeable, earlier *sēfte* f. WG]

■ *adj.* **1** yielding, cushiony, plushy, spongy, flabby, squeezable, compressible, squashy, squashable, flexible, plastic, pliable, pliant, malleable, supple, springy, unstarched, *archaic* flexile. **2** downy, silky, silken, satiny, furry, fluffy, feathery, fleecy, fuzzy, velvety, smooth (as a baby's bottom). **3** gentle, mild, balmy, mellow, pleasant, moderate, warm, halcyon, springlike, summery, restful, tranquil, relaxing, lazy. **5** pastel, pale, faint, delicate, fine, subdued, light, matte, quiet, muted, toned down, diffuse(d), soothing, gentle. **6** subdued, toned *or* turned down, muted, low, quiet, melodious, mellifluous, mellifluent, mellow, gentle, faint, softened, soothing, smooth. **8** fuzzy, woolly, blurred, blurry, foggy, hazy, indistinct, diffuse(d). **9** gentle, good-tempered, mild, conciliatory, soothing, complimentary, pacific; amorous. **10** compassionate, tender-hearted, sympathetic, understanding, caring, humane, benign, merciful, kind-hearted, kind. **11 a** easygoing, tolerant, gentle, merciful, lenient, indulgent, permissive, liberal, lax, easy, docile, tame, submissive, deferential; soft in the head, feeble-minded, foolish, silly, simple, sentimental, esp. *Brit. colloq.* daft. **b** weak, feeble, frail, effete, delicate, nonphysical, nonmuscular, puny, flabby, out of training *or* condition *or* shape, pampered; namby-pamby, effeminate, unmanly, unmanful, *colloq.* sissified, sissy. **12** easy, comfortable, undemanding, *colloq.* cushy. **13** harmless, mild,

nonaddictive. □ **have a soft spot for** favor, be partial *or* predisposed to, be fond of, have a weakness *or* liking for, feel an attraction to *or* toward, *disp.* feel an affinity to *or* for. **soft drink** pop, soda. **soft-headed, soft in the head** see *weak-minded* 1. **soft-pedal 1** see SOFTEN 1. **2** see MUTE *v.* **soft sell** see *promotion* (PROMOTE), PERSUASION 1. **soft soap 2** nonsense, rubbish, *colloq.* hogwash, sweet talk, *sl.* eyewash, bull. **soft-soap** see FLATTER 1. **soft touch** see PUSHOVER 2.

softball /sáwftbawl, sóft-/ *n.* **1** a ball like a baseball but larger and pitched underhand. **2** a modified form of baseball using this.

softcover /sáwftcəvər/ *adj.* & *n.* ● *adj.* (of a book) bound in flexible covers. ● *n.* a softcover book.

soften /sáwfən, sófən/ *v.* **1** *tr.* & *intr.* make or become soft or softer. **2** *tr.* (often foll. by *up*) **a** reduce the strength of (defenses) by bombing or some other preliminary attack. **b** reduce the resistance of (a person). □ **softening of the brain** a morbid degeneration of the brain, esp. in old age. □□ **softener** *n.*

■ **1** muffle, deaden, damp, soft-pedal, lower, still, quiet, tone down, subdue, lessen, diminish, lighten, turn down, quell, mitigate, assuage, moderate, reduce, cushion, buffer, weaken, allay, alleviate, ease, abate, temper, relieve, *Brit.* quieten. **2 b** soften up, melt, affect, mollify, mellow, palliate, soothe, relax, appease.

softhearted /sáwft-haártid, sóft-/ *adj.* tender; compassionate; easily moved. □□ **softheartedness** *n.*

■ tenderhearted, compassionate, tender, warmhearted, sentimental, charitable, generous, giving, sympathetic, indulgent, merciful, forgiving, soft, kind, kindhearted, responsive. □□ **softheartedness** see MERCY 1, 2.

softie var. of SOFTY.

softly /sáwftlee, sóft-/ *adv.* in a soft, gentle, or quiet manner. □ **softly softly** (of an approach or strategy) cautious; discreet and cunning.

■ see *quietly* (QUIET).

software /sáwftwair, sóft-/ *n.* the programs and other operating information used by a computer (opp. HARDWARE 3).

softwood /sáwftwŏŏd, sóft-/ *n.* the wood of pine, spruce, or other conifers; easily sawn.

softy /sáwftee, sóftee/ *n.* (also **softie**) *colloq.* a weak or silly or softhearted person.

■ see WEAKLING.

soggy /sógee/ *adj.* (**soggier, soggiest**) sodden; saturated; dank. □□ **soggily** *adv.* **sogginess** *n.* [dial. *sog* a swamp]

■ see WET *adj.* 1.

soi-disant /swáadeezón/ *adj.* self-styled or pretended. [F f. *soi* oneself + *disant* saying]

■ see SELF-STYLED.

soigné /swaanyáy/ *adj.* (*fem.* **soignée** *pronunc.* same) carefully finished or arranged; well-groomed. [past part. of F *soigner* take care of f. *soin* care]

■ see ELEGANT 1, 2.

soil[1] /soyl/ *n.* **1** the upper layer of earth in which plants grow, consisting of disintegrated rock usu. with an admixture of organic remains (*alluvial soil*; *rich soil*). **2** ground belonging to a nation; territory (*on British soil*). □ **soil mechanics** the study of the properties of soil as affecting its use in civil engineering. **soil science** pedology. □□ **soilless** *adj.* **soily** *adj.* [ME f. AF, perh. f. L *solium* seat, taken in sense of L *solum* ground]

■ **1** earth, loam, dirt, ground, turf, humus; clay, marl. **2** ground, territory, land.

soil[2] /soyl/ *v.* & *n.* ● *v.tr.* **1** make dirty; smear or stain with dirt (*soiled linen*). **2** tarnish; defile; bring discredit to (*would not soil my hands with it*). ● *n.* **1** a dirty mark; a stain, smear, or defilement. **2** filth; refuse matter. □ **soil pipe** the discharge pipe of a toilet. [ME f. OF *suiller*, *soiller*, etc., ult. f. L *sucula* dimin. of *sus* pig]

■ *v.* **1** dirty, stain, begrime, muddy, smear, spot. **2** pollute, contaminate, sully, defile, foul, tarnish, besmirch, disgrace, muddy, smear, blacken, *poet.* befoul; blot. ● *n.* **2** dirt, filth, muck, mire, mud, sludge, dregs, refuse; excrement, waste (matter), sewage.

soil³ /soyl/ *v.tr.* feed (cattle) on fresh green fodder (orig. for purging). [perh. f. SOIL²]

soirée /swaaráy/ *n.* an evening party, usu. in a private house, for conversation or music. [F f. *soir* evening]
■ see PARTY¹ *n.* 1.

sojourn /sójərn/ *n. & v.* ● *n.* a temporary stay. ● *v.intr.* stay temporarily. □□ **sojourner** *n.* [ME f. OF *sojorn*, etc. f. LL SUB- + *diurnum* day]
■ *n.* stay, stop, stopover, visit, rest, holiday, vacation.
● *v.* stay, stop (over), visit, rest, holiday, vacation, *archaic or literary* tarry.

soke /sōk/ *n. Brit. hist.* 1 a right of local jurisdiction. 2 a district under a particular jurisdiction and administration. [ME f. AL *sōca* f. OE *sōcn* prosecution f. Gmc]

Sol /sol/ *n.* (in Roman mythology) the sun, esp. as a personification. [ME f. L]

sol¹ /sōl/ *n.* (also **so** /sō/) *Mus.* 1 (in tonic sol-fa) the fifth note of a major scale. 2 the note G in the fixed do system. [*sol* f. ME *sol* f. L *solve*: see GAMUT]

sol² /sol/ *n. Chem.* a liquid suspension of a colloid. [abbr. of SOLUTION]

sola¹ /sṓlə/ *n.* a pithy E. Indian swamp plant, *Aeschynomene indica.* □ **sola topi** an Indian sun helmet made from its pith. [Urdu & Bengali *solā*, Hindi *sholā*]

sola² *fem.* of SOLUS.

solace /sóləs/ *n. & v.* ● *n.* comfort in distress, disappointment, or tedium. ● *v.tr.* give solace to. □ **solace oneself with** find compensation or relief in. [ME f. OF *solas* f. L *solatium* f. *solari* CONSOLE¹]
■ *n.* comfort, consolation, condolence, relief, balm, support, help, succor; reassurance, cheer.
● *v.* comfort, console, condole, support, help, succor, soothe, allay, alleviate, assuage, relieve, *formal* ameliorate; cheer (up), reassure, hearten.

solan /sṓlən/ *n.* (in full **solan goose**) a gannet, *Sula bassana.* [prob. f. ON *súla* gannet + *önd*, *and-* duck]

solanaceous /sólənáyshəs/ *adj.* of or relating to the plant family Solanaceae, including potatoes, nightshades, and tobacco. [mod.L *solanaceae* f. L *sōlānum* nightshade]

solar /sṓlər/ *adj. & n.* ● *adj.* of, relating to, or reckoned by the sun (*solar eclipse*; *solar time*). ● *n. Brit.* 1 a solarium. 2 an upper chamber in a medieval house. □ **solar battery** (or **cell**) a device converting solar radiation into electricity. **solar constant** the quantity of heat reaching the earth from the sun. **solar day** the interval between successive meridian transits of the sun at a place. **solar month** one twelfth of the solar year. **solar panel** a panel designed to absorb the sun's rays as a source of energy for operating electricity or heating. **solar plexus** a complex of radiating nerves at the pit of the stomach. **solar system** the sun and the celestial bodies whose motion it governs. **solar wind** the continuous flow of charged particles from the sun. **solar year** the time taken for the earth to travel once around the sun, equal to 365 days, 5 hours, 48 minutes, and 46 seconds. [ME f. L *solaris* f. *sol* sun]

solarium /səláireeəm/ *n.* (*pl.* **solaria** /-reeə/) a room equipped with sunlamps or fitted with extensive areas of glass for exposure to the sun. [L, = sundial, sunning place (as SOLAR)]

solarize /sṓlərīz/ *v.intr. & tr. Photog.* undergo or cause to undergo change in the relative darkness of parts of an image by long exposure. □□ **solarization** *n.*

solatium /səláysheeəm/ *n.* (*pl.* **solatia** /-sheeə/) a thing given as a compensation or consolation. [L, = SOLACE]

sold *past* and *past part.* of SELL.

solder /sódər/ *n. & v.* ● *n.* 1 a fusible alloy used to join less fusible metals or wires, etc. 2 a cementing or joining agency. ● *v.tr.* join with solder. □ **soldering iron** a tool used for applying solder. □□ **solderable** *n.* **solderer** *n.* [ME f. OF *soudure* f. *souder* f. L *solidare* fasten f. *solidus* SOLID]
■ *n.* see CEMENT *n.* 2. ● *v.* see JOIN *v.* 1, 2.

soldier /sṓljər/ *n. & v.* ● *n.* 1 a person serving in or having

served in an army. 2 (in full **common soldier**) an enlisted person in an army. 3 a military commander of specified ability (*a great soldier*). 4 (in full **soldier ant**) a wingless ant or termite with a large head and jaws for fighting in defense of its colony. 5 (in full **soldier beetle**) a reddish colored beetle, *Rhagonycha fulva*, with flesh-eating larvae. ● *v.intr.* serve as a soldier (*was off soldiering*). □ **soldier of Christ** an active or proselytizing Christian. **soldier of fortune** an adventurous person ready to take service under any government or person; a mercenary. **soldier on** *colloq.* persevere doggedly. □□ **soldierly** *adj.* **soldiership** *n.* [ME *souder*, etc. f. OF *soudier*, *soldier* f. *soulde* (soldier's) pay f. L *solidus*: see SOLIDUS]
■ *n.* 1, 2 serviceman, servicewoman, regular (soldier), GI, recruit, draftee, conscript, fighter, infantryman, foot soldier, trooper, warrior, military man, enlisted man, *archaic* man-at-arms, *colloq.* doughboy, *Brit.* Tommy (Atkins); mercenary; private, NCO, noncommissioned officer. ● *v.* serve (in the army).
□ **soldier of fortune** mercenary, *usu. derog.* hireling; see also ADVENTURER 1. **soldier on** continue, persist, persevere, battle on, struggle on, endure, keep going, keep on, grind away. □□ **soldierly** see MARTIAL.

soldiery /sṓljəree/ *n.* (*pl.* **-ies**) 1 soldiers, esp. of a specified character. 2 a group of soldiers.
■ 1 see MILITARY *n.*

sole¹ /sōl/ *n. & v.* ● *n.* 1 the undersurface of the foot. 2 the part of a shoe, sock, etc., corresponding to this (esp. excluding the heel). 3 the lower surface or base of an implement, e.g., a plow, golf club head, etc. 4 the floor of a ship's cabin. ● *v.tr.* provide (a shoe, etc.) with a sole. □□ **-soled** *adj.* (in *comb.*). [OF ult. f. L *solea* sandal, sill: cf. OE unrecorded *solu* or *sola* f. *solum* bottom, pavement, sole]

sole² /sōl/ *n.* any flatfish of the family Soleidae, esp. *Solea solea*, used as food. [ME f. OF f. Prov. *sola* ult. f. L *solea* (as SOLE¹, named from its shape)]

sole³ /sōl/ *adj.* 1 (*attrib.*) one and only; single; exclusive (*the sole reason*; *has the sole right*). 2 *archaic* or *Law* (esp. of a woman) unmarried. 3 *archaic* alone; unaccompanied. □□ **solely** *adv.* [ME f. OF *soule* f. L *sola* fem. of *solus* alone]
■ 1 lone, (one and) only, single, singular, unique, solitary; particular, exclusive, individual, personal.

solecism /sólisizəm/ *n.* 1 a mistake of grammar or idiom; a blunder in speaking or writing. 2 a piece of bad manners or incorrect behavior. □□ **solecist** *n.* **solecistic** *adj.* [F *solécisme* or L *soloecismus* f. Gk *soloikismos* f. *soloikos* speaking incorrectly]
■ catachresis; error, slip, impropriety, fault, breach, violation, lapse, mistake, misusage, incongruity, inconsistency, barbarism, blunder, gaffe, bungle, fumble, gaucherie, faux pas, botch, *colloq.* blooper, flub, *sl.* booboo, boner, bloomer, *Brit. sl.* boob.

solemn /sóləm/ *adj.* 1 serious and dignified (*a solemn occasion*). 2 formal; accompanied by ceremony (*a solemn oath*). 3 mysteriously impressive. 4 (of a person) serious or cheerless in manner (*looks rather solemn*). 5 full of importance; weighty (*a solemn warning*). 6 grave; sober; deliberate; slow in movement or action (*a solemn promise*; *solemn music*). □ **solemn mass** = *high mass* (see MASS²). □□ **solemnly** *adv.* **solemnness** *n.* [ME f. OF *solemne* f. L *sol(l)emnis* customary, celebrated at a fixed date f. *sollus* entire]
■ 1 serious, dignified, ceremonial, ceremonious, ritual, formal, stately, grand, august, imposing, impressive, awe-inspiring, awesome, important, momentous. 2 formal, ceremonial, sacramental, ritual, ritualistic, liturgical, religious, official. 3 imposing, impressive, awe-inspiring, awesome. 4 serious, sober, reflective, grave, earnest, sedate, staid, taciturn; morose, mirthless, cheerless, sad, unsmiling, gloomy,

---

/ . . ./ **pronunciation**   ● **part** [...]
□ **phrases, idioms, and compo**[...]
□□ **derivatives**   ■ **synon**[...]
cross-references appear in [...]

somber, grim; glum, long-faced, saturnine. **5** important, weighty, grave, serious. **6** grave, sober, deliberate, earnest, measured. □□ **solemness** see SOLEMNITY 1.

solemnity /səlémnitee/ n. (pl. **-ies**) **1** the state of being solemn; a solemn character or feeling; solemn behavior. **2** a rite or celebration; a piece of ceremony. [ME f. OF solem(p)nité f. L sollemnitas -tatis (as SOLEMN)]
■ **1** solemnity, gravity, seriousness, soberness, reserve, sedateness, taciturnity, staidness, earnestness, impressiveness, grandeur, importance, momentousness, consequence. **2** see RITE.

solemnize /sóləmnīz/ v.tr. **1** duly perform (a ceremony, esp. of marriage). **2** celebrate (a festival, etc.). **3** make solemn. □□ **solemnization** n. [ME f. OF solem(p)niser f. med.L solemnizare (as SOLEMN)]
■ **1, 2** see CELEBRATE v. 1, 2. □□ **solemnization** see celebration (CELEBRATE).

solenoid /sólənoyd, sól-/ n. a cylindrical coil of wire acting as a magnet when carrying electric current. □□ **solenoidal** /-nóyd'l/ adj. [F solénoïde (as SOLEN)]

sol-fa /sólfaa/ n. & v. ● n. = SOLMIZATION; (cf. tonic sol-fa). ● v.tr. (**-fas, -faed**) sing (a tune) with sol-fa syllables. [SOL[1] + FA]

solfatara /sólfətaárə/ n. a volcanic vent emitting only sulfurous and other vapors. [name of a volcano near Naples, f. It. solfo sulfur]

solfeggio /solféjeeō/ n. (pl. **solfeggi** /-jee/) (also **solfège**) Mus. **1** an exercise in singing using sol-fa syllables. **2** solmization. [It. (as SOL-FA)]

soli pl. of SOLO.

solicit /səlísit/ v. (**solicited, soliciting**) **1** tr. & (foll. by for) intr. ask repeatedly or earnestly for or seek or invite (business, etc.). **2** tr. (often foll. by for) make a request or petition to (a person). **3** tr. accost (a person) and offer one's services as a prostitute. □□ **solicitation** n. [ME f. OF solliciter f. L sollicitare agitate f. sollicitus anxious f. sollus entire + citus past part., = set in motion]
■ **1, 2** entreat, beseech, ask (for), implore, petition (for), importune, appeal for or to, call on or upon, beg, supplicate, pray (for), request; crave, seek. **3** accost, approach, entice, lure, accost. proposition, sl. hustle.

solicitor /səlísitər/ n. **1** a person who solicits. **2** a canvasser. **3** the chief law officer of a city, county, etc. **4** Brit. a member of the legal profession qualified to deal with conveyancing, draw up wills, etc., and to advise clients and instruct barristers. □ **Solicitor General 1** (in the US) the law officer below the Attorney General. **2** (in the UK) the Crown law officer below the Attorney General or (in Scotland) below the Lord Advocate. [ME f. OF solliciteur (as SOLICIT)]
■ **4** lawyer, legal practitioner, attorney, conveyancer.

solicitous /səlísitəs/ adj. **1** (often foll. by of, about, etc.) showing interest or concern. **2** (foll. by to + infin.) eager; anxious. □□ **solicitously** adv. **solicitousness** n. [L sollicitus (as SOLICIT)]
■ **1** concerned, caring, considerate, thoughtful, tender, attentive, uneasy, troubled, anxious, apprehensive, worried. **2** eager, earnest, keen, anxious, desirous, ardent, avid. □□ **solicitousness** see SOLICITUDE, SYMPATHY 2.

solicitude /səlísitŏod, -tyŏod/ n. **1** the state of being solicitous; solicitous behavior. **2** anxiety or concern. [ME f. OF sollicitude f. L sollicitudo (as SOLICITOUS)]
■ concern, consideration, regard, solicitousness, disquiet, disquietude, uneasiness, anxiety, apprehension, worry, nervousness, fear, fearfulness, alarm.

solid /sólid/ adj. & n. ● adj. (**solider, solidest**) **1** firm and in shape; not liquid or fluid (solid food; water becomes ... 32°F). **2** of one material throughout, not hollow or ... ing cavities (a solid sphere). **3** of the same substance ... ut (solid silver). **4** of strong material or construction ... not flimsy or slender, etc. **5 a** having three dimen... ... ncerned with solids (solid geometry). **6 a** sound ...; genuine (solid arguments). **b** staunch and de... ... olid Republican). **7** sound but without any spe-

cial flair, etc. (a solid piece of work). **8** financially sound. **9** (of time) uninterrupted; continuous (spend four solid hours on it). **10 a** unanimous; undivided (support has been pretty solid so far). **b** (foll. by for) united in favor of. **11** (of printing) without spaces between the lines, etc. **12** (of a tire) without a central air space. **13** (foll. by with) colloq. on good terms. **14** Austral. & NZ colloq. severe; unreasonable. ● n. **1** a solid substance or body. **2** (in pl.) solid food. **3** Geom. a body or magnitude having three dimensions. □ **solid angle** an angle formed by planes, etc., meeting at a point. **solid color** color covering the whole of an object, without a pattern, etc. **solid-drawn** (of a tube, etc.) pressed or drawn out from a solid bar of metal. **solid solution** solid material containing one substance uniformly distributed in another. **solid state** the state of matter that retains its boundaries without support. **solid-state** adj. using the electronic properties of solids (e.g., a semiconductor) to replace those of vacuum tubes, etc. □□ **solidly** adv. **solidness** n. [ME f. OF solide f. L solidus, rel. to salvus safe, sollus entire]
■ adj. **1** firm, hard, compact, stable, rigid. **2** see DENSE 1. **3** consistent, homogeneous, uniform, unalloyed, unmixed, pure, continuous, unbroken, real, authentic, true, genuine, 24-karat, unadulterated, colloq. honest-to-God. **4** stable, sturdy, strong, substantial, sound, firm, well-built, well-constructed, well-made, tough, durable, robust, rugged, stout. **5** three-dimensional, cubic. **6 a** cogent, sound, concrete, weighty, proved, proven, provable, valid, reasonable, sensible, rational, sober, well-founded, authoritative, indisputable, incontrovertible, irrefutable, incontestable, reliable, genuine, good, strong, powerful, potent, forceful, telling, convincing, persuasive. **b** staunch, dependable, reliable, steady, steadfast, unshakable, stalwart, sober, straight, estimable, sure, trustworthy, true-blue, loyal, worthy, law-abiding, upstanding, upright, decent, stout, archaic or joc. trusty. **8** see SOLVENT adj. **9** continuous, uninterrupted, undivided, unbroken, unrelieved. **10** see UNITED 3. □□ **solidly** see firmly (FIRM[1]), SURELY 3.

solidarity /sólidáritee/ n. **1** unity or agreement of feeling or action, esp. among individuals with a common interest. **2** mutual dependence. [F solidarité f. solidaire f. solide SOLID]
■ **1** unity, unanimity, accord, concord, concordance, harmony, concurrence, like-mindedness, agreement, single-mindedness, singleness (of purpose), community of interest, esprit de corps, camaraderie, comradeship.

solidi pl. of SOLIDUS.

solidify /səlídifī/ v.tr. & intr. (**-ies, -ied**) make or become solid. □□ **solidification** /-fikáyshən/ n. **solidifier** n.
■ harden, freeze, set, firm up, thicken, cake, clot, congeal, coagulate, sinter, consolidate, crystallize, Chem. sublimate, sublime; compact, compress, literary inspissate; gel, jell.

solidity /səlíditee/ n. the state of being solid; firmness.
■ see STABILITY.

solidus /sólidəs/ n. (pl. **solidi** /-dī/) **1** an oblique stroke (/) used in writing fractions (¾), to separate other figures and letters, or to denote alternatives (and/or) and ratios (miles/day). **2** (in full **solidus curve**) a curve in a graph of the temperature and composition of a mixture, below which the substance is entirely solid. **3** hist. a gold coin of the later Roman Empire. [ME (in sense 3) f. L: see SOLID]
■ **1** see LINE[1] n. 1.

solifluction /sóliflúkshən, sól-/ n. the gradual movement of wet soil, etc., down a slope. [L solum soil + L fluctio flowing f. fluere fluct- flow]

soliloquy /səlíləkwee/ n. (pl. **-ies**) **1** the act of talking when alone or regardless of any hearers, esp. in drama. **2** part of a play involving this. □□ **soliloquist** n. **soliloquize** v.intr. [LL soliloquium f. L solus alone + loqui speak]

soliped /sóliped/ adj. & n. ● adj. (of an animal) solid hoofed. ● n. a solid hoofed animal. [F solipède or mod.L solipes -pedis f. L solidipes f. solidus solid + pes foot]

solipsism /sólipsizəm/ n. Philos. the view that the self is all that exists or can be known. □□ **solipsist** *n.* **solipsistic** *adj.* **solipsistically** *adv.* [L *solus* alone + *ipse* self]

solitaire /sólitáir/ *n.* **1** a diamond or other gem set by itself. **2** a ring having a single gem. **3** any of several card games for one player. **4** any of various extinct dodolike flightless birds of the family Raphidae. **5** any American thrush of the genus *Myadestes*. [F f. L *solitarius* (as SOLITARY)]

solitary /sóliteree/ *adj. & n.* ● *adj.* **1** living alone; not gregarious; without companions; lonely (*a solitary existence*). **2** (of a place) secluded or unfrequented. **3** single or sole (*a solitary instance*). **4** (of an insect) not living in communities. **5** *Bot.* growing singly; not in a cluster. ● *n.* (*pl.* **-ies**) **1** a recluse or anchorite. **2** *colloq.* = *solitary confinement*. □ **solitary confinement** isolation of a prisoner in a separate cell as a punishment. □□ **solitarily** *adv.* **solitariness** *n.* [ME f. L *solitarius* f. *solus* alone]

■ *adj.* **1** alone, single; unattended, solo, companionless, friendless, lonesome, lonely, unsocial, cloistered, secluded, reclusive, separate, eremitic(al), hermitic(al), remote, withdrawn, distant, *literary* unfriended. **2** secluded, remote, distant, out-of-the-way, unfrequented, lonely, desolate. **3** single, lone, sole, individual, isolated; unique. ● *n.* **1** see HERMIT. □ **solitary confinement** isolation, separation, *colloq.* solitary; see also SEGREGATION. □□ **solitarily** see SOLO *adv.* **solitariness** see SOLITUDE 1.

solitude /sólitōōd, -tyōōd/ *n.* **1** the state of being solitary. **2** a lonely place. [ME f. OF *solitude* or L *solitudo* f. *solus* alone]

■ **1** solitariness, aloneness, isolation, seclusion, privacy; loneliness, remoteness. **2** emptiness, wilderness; desert island.

solmization /sólmizáyshən/ *n. Mus.* a system of associating each note of a scale with a particular syllable, now usu. *do re mi fa sol la ti*, with do as C in the fixed-do system and as the keynote in the movable-do or tonic sol-fa system. □□ **solmizate** /sólmizayt/ *v.intr. & tr.* [F *solmisation* (as SOL¹, MI)]

solo /sṓlō/ *n., v., & adv.* ● *n.* (*pl.* **-os**) **1** (*pl.* **-os** or **soli** /-lee/) **a** a vocal or instrumental piece or passage, or a dance, performed by one person with or without accompaniment. **b** (*attrib.*) performed or performing as a solo (*solo passage; solo violin*). **2 a** an unaccompanied flight by a pilot in an aircraft. **b** anything done by one person unaccompanied. **c** (*attrib.*) unaccompanied; alone. **3** (in full **solo whist**) **a** a card game like whist in which one player may oppose the others. **b** a declaration or the act of playing to win five tricks at this. ● *v.* (**-oes, -oed**) **1** *intr.* perform a solo, esp. a solo flight. **2** *tr.* perform or achieve as a solo. ● *adv.* unaccompanied; alone (*flew solo for the first time*). [It. f. L *solus* alone]

■ *n.* **1b, 2c** (*attrib.*) unaccompanied, individual, solitary; single-handed, unaided. ● *adv.* alone, unaccompanied, solus, on one's own, single-handed(ly).

soloist /sṓlōist/ *n.* a performer of a solo, esp. in music.

Solomon /sóləmən/ *n.* a very wise person. □ **Solomon's seal 1** a figure like the Star of David. **2** any liliaceous plant of the genus *Polygonatum*, with arching stems and drooping green and white flowers. □□ **Solomonic** /sóləmónik/ *adj.* [*Solomon*, king of Israel in the 10th c. BC, famed for his wisdom]

■ see SAGE² *n.* 1.

solstice /sólstis, sól-, sáwl-/ *n.* **1** either of the times when the sun is farthest from the equator. **2** the point in its ecliptic reached by the sun at a solstice. □ **summer solstice** the time at which the sun is farthest north from the equator, about June 21 in the northern hemisphere. **winter solstice** the time at which the sun is farthest south from the equator, about Dec. 22 in the northern hemisphere. □□ **solstitial** /-stíshəl/ *adj.* [ME f. OF f. L *solstitium* f. *sol* sun + *sistere stit-* make stand]

solubilize /sólyəbiliz/ *v.tr.* make soluble or more soluble. □□ **solubilization** /-lizáyshən/ *n.*

soluble /sólyəbəl/ *adj.* **1** that can be dissolved, esp. in water. **2** that can be solved. □ **soluble glass** = *water glass*. □□ **solubility** /-bílitee/ *n.* [ME f. OF f. LL *solubilis* (as SOLVE)]

solus /sṓləs/ *predic.adj.* (*fem.* **sola** /-lə/) (esp. in a stage direction) alone; unaccompanied. [L]

solute /sólyōōt, sṓlōōt/ *n.* a dissolved substance. [L *solutum*, neut. of *solutus*: see SOLVE]

solution /səlōōshən/ *n.* **1 a** the act or a means of solving a problem or difficulty. **b** an explanation, answer, or decision. **2 a** the conversion of a solid or gas into a liquid by mixture with a liquid solvent. **b** a liquid mixture produced by this. **c** the state resulting from this (*held in solution*). **3** the act of dissolving or the state of being dissolved. **4** the act of separating or breaking. □ **solution set** *Math.* the set of all the solutions of an equation or condition. [ME f. OF f. L *solutio -onis* (as SOLVE)]

■ **1** solving, working *or* figuring out, unraveling, explication, decipherment, elucidation, clarification, explanation; answer, decision, key; settlement, resolution, result. **2a, 3** dissolving, mixing, blending. **2b** mixture, blend, compound, infusion; liquid, fluid; emulsion, suspension, *Chem.* colloid, colloidal solution, colloidal suspension.

Solutrean /səlōōtreeən/ *adj. & n.* (also **Solutrian**) ● *adj.* of the Paleolithic period in Europe following the Aurignacian and preceding the Magdalenian. ● *n.* the culture of this period. [*Solutré* in E. France, where remains of it were found]

solvate /sólvayt/ *v.intr. & tr.* enter or cause to enter combination with a solvent. □□ **solvation** /-váyshən/ *n.*

solve /solv/ *v.tr.* find an answer to, or an action or course that removes or effectively deals with (a problem or difficulty). □□ **solvable** *adj.* **solver** *n.* [ME, = loosen, f. L *solvere solut-* unfasten, release]

■ work *or* figure out, unravel, disentangle, untangle, sort out, clarify, clear up, make plain *or* clear, interpret, explicate, decipher, explain, elucidate, reveal, answer, resolve, *colloq.* crack, *Brit. sl.* suss out.

solvent /sólvənt/ *adj. & n.* ● *adj.* **1** able to dissolve or form a solution with something. **2** having enough money to meet one's liabilities. ● *n.* **1** a solvent liquid, etc. **2** a dissolving or weakening agent. □□ **solvency** *n.* (in sense 2).

■ *adj.* **2** creditworthy, (financially) sound, solid, reliable, debt-free; profitable.

soma¹ /sṓmə/ *n.* **1** the body as distinct from the soul. **2** the body of an organism as distinct from its reproductive cells. [Gk *sōma -atos* body]

soma² /sṓmə/ *n.* **1** an intoxicating drink used in Vedic ritual. **2** a plant yielding this. [Skr. *sōma*]

Somali /sōmáalee, sə-/ *n. & adj.* ● *n.* **1** (*pl.* same or **Somalis**) a member of a Hamitic Muslim people of Somalia in NE Africa. **2** the Cushitic language of this people. ● *adj.* of or relating to this people or language. □□ **Somalian** *adj.* [native name]

somatic /sōmátik, sə-/ *adj.* of or relating to the body, esp. as distinct from the mind. □ **somatic cell** any cell of a living organism except the reproductive cells. □□ **somatically** *adv.* [Gk *sōmatikos* (as SOMA¹)]

■ see PHYSICAL *adj.* 2.

somato- /sṓmátō-, sṓmətō-/ *comb. form* the human body. [Gk *sōma -atos* body]

somatogenic /sōmátōjénik, sṓmə-/ *adj.* originating in the body.

somatology /sṓmətóləjee/ *n.* the study of the physical characteristics of living bodies.

somatotonic /sōmátōtónik, sṓmə-/ *adj.* like a mesomorph in temperament, with predominantly physical interests.

somatotrophin /sōmátətrṓfin, sṓmə-/ (also **somatotropin**) *n.* a growth hormone secreted by the pituitary gland. [as SOMATO-, TROPHIC]

somatotype /sōmátətīp, sṓmətə-/ *n.* physique expressed in relation to various extreme types.

/.../ **pronunciation**	● **part of speech**
□ **phrases, idioms, and compounds**	
□□ **derivatives**	■ **synonym section**
cross-references appear in SMALL CAPITALS or *italics*	

somber /sómbər/ *adj.* (also **sombre**) **1** dark; gloomy (*a somber sky*). **2** oppressively solemn or sober. **3** dismal, foreboding (*a somber prospect*). □□ **somberly** *adv.* **somberness** *n.* [F *sombre* f. OF *sombre* (n.) ult. f. L SUB- + *umbra* shade]

■ **1** dark, shadowy, murky, leaden, gray, black, overcast, louring, dusky, dim, dingy, dull, *formal* subfusc, *poet.* darkling; gloomy, foreboding, bleak, depressing, dismal, dreary, cheerless. **2** gloomy, morose, lugubrious, funereal, morbid, lowering, melancholy, sad, dismal, unhappy, cheerless, joyless, serious, sober, staid, sedate, solemn, doleful, mournful, depressed, depressing, grave, grim, grim-faced, melancholic, *literary* grim-visaged, *literary or joc.* dolorous, *poet.* darksome. **3** gloomy, foreboding, bleak, depressing, dismal, dreary, cheerless. □□ **somberly** see *sadly* (SAD). **somberness** see GRAVITY 3b.

sombrero /sombráirō/ *n.* (*pl.* **-os**) a broad-brimmed felt or straw hat worn esp. in Mexico and the southwest US. [Sp. f. *sombra* shade (as SOMBER)]

some /sum/ *adj., pron.,* & *adv.* ● *adj.* **1** an unspecified amount or number of (*some water; some apples; some of them*). **2** that is unknown or unnamed (*will return some day; some fool has locked the door; to some extent*). **3** denoting an approximate number (*waited some twenty minutes*). **4** a considerable amount or number of (*went to some trouble*). **5** (usu. stressed) **a** at least a small amount of (*do have some consideration*). **b** such to a certain extent (*that is some help*). **c** *colloq.* notably such (*I call that some story*). ● *pron.* some people or things; some number or amount (*I have some already; would you like some more?*). ● *adv. colloq.* to some extent (*we talked some; do it some more*). □ **and then some** *sl.* and plenty more than that. **some few** see FEW. [OE *sum* f. Gmc]

■ *adj.* **1** see SEVERAL *adj.*

-some[1] /səm/ *suffix* forming adjectives meaning: **1** adapted to; productive of (*cuddlesome; fearsome*). **2** characterized by being (*fulsome; lithesome*). **3** apt to (*tiresome; meddlesome*). [OE *-sum*]

-some[2] /səm/ *suffix* forming nouns from numerals, meaning 'a group of (so many)' (*foursome*). [OE *sum* SOME, used after numerals in genit. pl.]

-some[3] /sōm/ *comb. form* denoting a portion of a body, esp. of a cell (*chromosome; ribosome*). [Gk *sōma* body]

somebody /súmbodee, -budee, -bədee/ *pron.* & *n.* ● *pron.* some person. ● *n.* (*pl.* **-ies**) a person of importance (*is really somebody now*).

■ *pron.* one, someone, some person. ● *n.* personage, celebrity, dignitary, VIP, luminary, notable, star, superstar, megastar, *colloq.* bigwig, big shot, big noise, hot stuff, heavyweight, *colloq.* hotshot, *sl.* big gun, bigtimer, big daddy, (big) cheese, big wheel, Mr. Big.

someday /súmday/ *adv.* at some time in the future.

■ see SOMETIME *adv.* 1.

somehow /súmhow/ *adv.* **1** for some reason or other (*somehow I never liked them*). **2** in some unspecified or unknown way (*he somehow dropped behind*). **3** no matter how (*must get it finished somehow*).

■ **2, 3** (in) one way or another, in some way, somehow or other, no matter how, by hook or by crook, by fair means or foul, come hell or high water.

someone /súmwun/ *n.* & *pron.* = SOMEBODY.

someplace /súmplays/ *adv. colloq.* = SOMEWHERE.

somersault /súmərsawlt/ *n.* & *v.* (also **summersault**) ● *n.* an acrobatic movement in which a person turns head over heels in the air or on the ground and lands on the feet. ● *v.intr.* perform a somersault. [OF *sombresault* alt. f. *sobresault* ult. f. L *supra* above + *saltus* leap f. *salire* to leap]

■ *n.* tumble, roll.

something /súmthing/ *n., pron.,* & *adv.* ● *n.* & *pron.* **1 a** some unspecified or unknown thing (*have something to tell you; something has happened*). **b** (in full **something or other**) as a substitute for an unknown or forgotten description (*a student of something or other*). **2** a known or understood but unexpressed quantity, quality, or extent (*there is something about it I do not like; is something of a fool*). **3** *colloq.* an important or notable person or thing (*the party was quite something*). ● *adv. archaic* in some degree. □ **or something** or some unspecified alternative possibility (*must have run away or something*). **see something of** encounter (a person) briefly or occasionally. **something else 1** something different. **2** *colloq.* something exceptional. **something like 1** an amount in the region of (*left something like a million dollars*). **2** somewhat like (*shaped something like a cigar*). **3** *colloq.* impressive; a fine specimen of. **something of** to some extent; in some sense (*is something of an expert*). [OE *sum thing* (as SOME, THING)]

sometime /súmtīm/ *adv.* & *adj.* ● *adv.* **1** at some unspecified time. **2** formerly. ● *attrib.adj.* **1** former (*the sometime mayor*). **2** occasional.

■ *adv.* **1** at some time or other, someday, one day, any time, on a future occasion, when *or* if the opportunity arises, soon, by and by, one of these days, sooner or later, in (due) time, in the fullness of time, in due course, in the long run, one fine day, eventually, when all is said and done, before long, before you know it. **2** see FORMERLY. ● *adj.* **1** former, erstwhile, past, recent, one-time, quondam, late, ex-.

sometimes /súmtīmz/ *adv.* at some times; occasionally.

■ occasionally, on occasion, (every) now and then, now and again, off and on, on and off, at (some) times, from time to time, every so often, (every) once in a while.

somewhat /súmhwut, -hwot, -hwət, -wut, -wot, -wət/ *adv., n.,* & *pron.* ● *adv.* to some extent (*behavior that was somewhat strange; answered somewhat hastily*). ● *n.* & *pron. archaic* something (*loses somewhat of its force*). □ **more than somewhat** *colloq.* very (*was more than somewhat perplexed*).

■ *adv.* rather, quite, relatively, more or less, moderately, pretty, fairly, to some extent *or* degree *or* measure, to a certain extent *or* degree *or* measure, slightly, a bit, a little, *colloq.* sort of, kind of.

somewhen /súmhwen, -wen/ *adv. colloq.* at some time.

somewhere /súmhwair, -wair/ *adv.* & *pron.* ● *adv.* in or to some place. ● *pron.* some unspecified place. □ **get somewhere** *colloq.* achieve success. **somewhere about** approximately.

somite /sómīt/ *n.* each body division of a metamerically segmented animal. □□ **somitic** /sōmítik/ *adj.* [Gk *sōma* body + -ITE[1]]

sommelier /suməlyáy, saw-/ *n.* a wine steward. [F, = butler, f. *somme* pack (as SUMPTER)]

somnambulism /somnámbyəlizəm/ *n.* **1** sleepwalking. **2** a condition of the brain inducing this. □□ **somnambulant** *adj.* **somnambulantly** *adv.* **somnambulist** *n.* **somnambulistic** *adj.* **somnambulistically** *adv.* [L *somnus* sleep + *ambulare* walk]

■ **1** sleepwalking, noctambulism.

somniferous /somnífərəs/ *adj.* inducing sleep; soporific. [L *somnifer* f. *somnium* dream]

somnolent /sómnələnt/ *adj.* **1** sleepy; drowsy. **2** inducing drowsiness. **3** *Med.* in a state between sleeping and waking. □□ **somnolence** *n.* **somnolency** *n.* **somnolently** *adv.* [ME f. OF *sompnolent* or L *somnolentus* f. *somnus* sleep]

■ **1** see SLEEPY 1. **2** see NARCOTIC *adj.* □□ **somnolence** see TORPOR.

son /sun/ *n.* **1** a boy or man in relation to either or both of his parents. **2 a** a male descendant. **b** (foll. by *of*) a male member of a family, nation, etc. **3** a person regarded as inheriting an occupation, quality, etc., or associated with a particular attribute (*sons of freedom; sons of the soil*). **4** (in full **my son**) a form of address, esp. to a boy. **5** (**the Son**) (in Christian belief) the second person of the Trinity. □ **son-in-law** (*pl.* **sons-in-law**) the husband of one's daughter. **son of a bitch** *coarse sl.* a general term of contempt. **son of a gun** *colloq.* a jocular or affectionate form of address or reference. □□ **sonless** *adj.* **sonship** *n.* [OE *sunu* f. Gmc]

■ □ **son of a bitch** see STINKER, WRETCH 2.

sonant /sónənt/ *adj.* & *n. Phonet.* ● *adj.* (of a sound) voiced and syllabic. ● *n.* a voiced sound, esp. other than a vowel and capable of forming a syllable, e.g., *l, m, n, ng, r*. □□ **sonancy** *n*. [L *sonare sonant-* sound]

sonar /sṓnaar/ *n*. **1** a system for the underwater detection of objects by reflected or emitted sound. **2** an apparatus for this. [*sound navigation and ranging*, after *radar*]

sonata /sənáatə/ *n*. a composition for one instrument or two (one usu. being a piano accompaniment), usu. in several movements with one (esp. the first) or more in sonata form. □ **sonata form** a type of composition in three sections (exposition, development, and recapitulation) in which two themes (or subjects) are explored according to set key relationships. [It., = sounded (orig. as distinct from sung): fem. past part. of *sonare* sound]

sonatina /sónəteénə/ *n*. a simple or short sonata. [It., dimin. of SONATA]

sonde /sond/ *n*. a device sent up to obtain information about atmospheric conditions, esp. = RADIOSONDE. [F, = sounding(-line)]

sone /sōn/ *n*. a unit of subjective loudness, equal to 40 phons. [L *sonus* sound]

son et lumière /sáwn ay lōōmyair/ *n*. an entertainment by night at a historic monument, building, etc., using lighting effects and recorded sound to give a dramatic narrative of its history. [F, = sound and light]

song /sawng, song/ *n*. **1** a short poem or other set of words set to music or meant to be sung. **2** singing or vocal music (*burst into song*). **3** a musical composition suggestive of a song. **4** the musical cry of some birds. **5** a short poem in rhymed stanzas. **6** *archaic* poetry or verse. □ **for a song** *colloq.* very cheaply. **on song** *Brit. colloq.* performing exceptionally well. **song and dance** *colloq.* **1** a fuss or commotion. **2** an elaborate or complicated story, esp. one intended to distract or confuse. **song cycle** a set of musically linked songs with a unifying theme. **Song of Songs** (or **of Solomon**) a poetic Old Testament book traditionally attributed to Solomon. **song sparrow** a N. American sparrow, *Melospiza melodia*, with a characteristic musical song. **song thrush** a thrush, *Turdus philomelos*, of Europe and W. Asia, with a song partly mimicked from other birds. □□ **songless** *adj.* [OE *sang* f. Gmc (as SING)]

  ■ **1** tune, air, melody, strain, ditty, number; chant, lay, ballad, madrigal, serenade, shanty, jingle; hymn, carol, anthem. □ **for a song** cheaply, inexpensively, at a bargain price, on the cheap. **song and dance 1** fuss, to-do, commotion, bother, ado, *Brit.* palaver, *colloq.* flap, performance.

songbird /sáwngbərd, sóng-/ *n*. a bird with a musical call.

songbook /sáwngbŏok, sóng-/ *n*. a collection of songs with music.

songsmith /sáwngsmith, sóng-/ *n*. a writer of songs.

songster /sáwngstər, sóng-/ *n*. (*fem.* **songstress** /-stris/) **1** a singer, esp. a fluent and skillful one. **2** a songbird. **3** a poet. **4** a songbook. [OE *sangestre* (as SONG, -STER)]

  ■ **1** see *singer* (SING).

songwriter /sáwng-rītər, sóng-/ *n*. a writer of songs or the music for them.

sonic /sónik/ *adj.* of or relating to or using sound or sound waves. □ **sonic barrier** = *sound barrier* (see SOUND¹). **sonic boom** a loud explosive noise caused by the shock wave from an aircraft when it passes the speed of sound. **sonic mine** a mine exploded by the sound of a passing ship. □□ **sonically** *adv.* [L *sonus* sound]

sonnet /sónit/ *n. & v.* ● *n.* a poem of 14 lines (usu. pentameters) using any of a number of formal rhyme schemes, in English usu. having ten syllables per line. ● *v.* (**sonneted, sonneting**) **1** *intr.* write sonnets. **2** *tr.* address sonnets to. [F *sonnet* or It. *sonetto* dimin. of *suono* SOUND¹]

sonneteer /sónitéer/ *n.* a writer of sonnets.

  ■ see POET.

sonny /súnee/ *n. colloq.* a familiar form of address to a young boy.

sonobuoy /sónəbōō-ee, -boy/ *n.* a buoy for detecting underwater sounds and transmitting them by radio. [L *sonus* sound + BUOY]

sonogram /sónəgram/ *n. Med.* an image of internal organs

or structures produced by ultrasound waves, used for diagnostic purposes.

sonometer /sənómitər/ *n.* **1** an instrument for measuring the vibration frequency of a string, etc. **2** an audiometer. [L *sonus* sound + -METER]

sonorous /sónərəs, sənáwrəs/ *adj.* **1** having a loud, full, or deep sound; resonant. **2** (of a speech, style, etc.) imposing; grand. □□ **sonority** /sənáwritee/ *n.* **sonorously** *adv.* **sonorousness** *n.* [L *sonorus* f. *sonor* sound]

  ■ **1** see DEEP *adj.* 5. **2** see ROTUND 2. □□ **sonority**, **sonorousness** see TONE *n.* 1.

sonsy /sónsee/ *adj.* (also **sonsie**) (**sonsier, sonsiest**) *Sc.* **1** plump; buxom. **2** of a cheerful disposition. **3** bringing good fortune. [ult. f. Ir. & Gael. *sonas* good fortune f. *sona* fortunate]

sook /sŏok/ *n. Austral. & NZ sl.* **1** *derog.* a timid bashful person; a coward or sissy. **2** a hand-reared calf. [E dial. *suck*, call word for a calf]

soon /sōon/ *adv.* **1** after no long interval of time (*shall soon know the result*). **2** relatively early (*must you go so soon?*). **3** (prec. by *how*) early (with relative rather than distinctive sense) (*how soon will it be ready?*). **4** readily or willingly (in expressing choice or preference: *which would you sooner do?*; *would as soon stay behind*). □ **as** (or **so**) **soon as** (implying a causal or temporal connection) at the moment that; not later than; as early as (*came as soon as I heard about it*; *disappears as soon as it's time to pay*). **no sooner ... than** at the very moment that (*we no sooner arrived than the rain stopped*). **sooner or later** at some future time; eventually. □□ **soonish** *adv.* [OE *sōna* f. WG]

  ■ **1** before long, presently, in the near future, any minute (now), before you know it, in good time, in a little while, in a minute, in a moment, shortly, quickly, speedily, swiftly, at once, promptly, immediately, directly, without delay, straight away, right away, forthwith, at the double, in a second, in two shakes (of a lamb's tail), in a wink, tout de suite, in short order, momentarily, *archaic or literary* anon, *colloq.* in a jiffy, pronto, lickety-split, *poet. or archaic* ere long. **2, 3** early, fast; quickly, swiftly, speedily. **4** willingly, gladly, happily, readily, *archaic* lief. □ **as soon as** as quickly as, as speedily as, as swiftly as, as promptly as, as early as; see also IMMEDIATELY *conj.* **sooner or later** at some time or other, some time, one day, in time, in due course, eventually, ultimately, in the end, at the end of the day, in the long run, when all is said and done, in the last *or* final analysis.

soot /sŏot/ *n. & v.* ● *n.* a black carbonaceous substance rising in fine flakes in the smoke of wood, coal, oil, etc., and deposited on the sides of a chimney, etc. ● *v.tr.* cover with soot. [OE *sōt* f. Gmc]

  ■ *n.* see DIRT 1.

sooth /sōoth/ *n. archaic* truth; fact. □ **in sooth** really; truly. [OE *sōth* (orig. adj., = true) f. Gmc]

soothe /sōoth/ *v.tr.* **1** calm (a person or feelings). **2** soften or mitigate (pain). **3** *archaic* flatter or humor. □□ **soother** *n.* **soothing** *adj.* **soothingly** *adv.* [OE *sōthian* verify f. *sōth* true: see SOOTH]

  ■ **1** see CALM *v.* **2** see MITIGATE. **3** see FLATTER 1, HUMOR *v.* □□ **soothing** relaxing, restful, serene, peaceful, pacifying, sedative, calm, calming, quiet, soft, quieting; mollifying, comforting, palliative, balsamic, emollient, lenitive, demulcent.

soothsayer /sōothsayər/ *n.* a diviner or seer. [ME, = one who says the truth: see SOOTH]

  ■ see SEER¹.

sooty /sŏotee/ *adj.* (**sootier, sootiest**) **1** covered with or full of soot. **2** (esp. of an animal or bird) black or brownish black. □□ **sootily** *adv.* **sootiness** *n.*

/ . . . / **pronunciation**   ● **part of speech**
□ **phrases, idioms, and compounds**
□□ **derivatives**   ■ **synonym section**
cross-references appear in SMALL CAPITALS or *italics*

■ **1** see DIRTY *adj.* 1. **2** see BLACK *adj.* 1.

SOP *abbr.* (also **S.O.P.**) standard operating procedure.

sop /sop/ *n. & v.* ● *n.* **1 a** a piece of bread, etc., dipped in gravy, etc. **2** a thing given or done to pacify or bribe. ● *v.* (**sopped, sopping**) **1** *intr.* be drenched (*came home sopping*). **2** *tr.* (foll. by *up*) absorb (liquid) in a towel, etc. **3** *tr.* wet thoroughly; soak. [OE *sopp*, corresp. to MLG *soppe*, OHG *sopfa* bread and milk, prob. f. a weak grade of the base of OE *sūpan*: see SUP¹]

soph. /sof/ *abbr.* sophomore.

sophism /sófizm/ *n.* a false argument, esp. one intended to deceive. [ME f. OF *sophime* f. L f. Gk *sophisma* clever device f. *sophizomai* become wise f. *sophos* wise]

■ see QUIBBLE *n.* 3.

sophist /sófist/ *n.* **1** one who reasons with clever but fallacious arguments. **2** *Gk Antiq.* a paid teacher of philosophy and rhetoric, esp. one associated with moral skepticism and specious reasoning. □□ **sophistic** /-fístik/ *adj.* **sophistical** *adj.* **sophistically** *adv.* [L *sophistes* f. Gk *sophistēs* f. *sophizomai*: see SOPHISM]

■ □□ **sophistic, sophistical** specious, fallacious, deceptive, deceitful, misleading, meretricious, hypocritical, false, unsound, baseless, groundless, casuistic(al), captious, bogus, sham, untenable, *often offens.* jesuitic(al).

sophisticate *v., adj., & n.* ● *v.* /səfístikayt/ **1** *tr.* make (a person, etc.) educated, cultured, or refined. **2** *tr.* make (equipment or techniques, etc.) highly developed or complex. **3** *tr.* **a** involve (a subject) in sophistry. **b** mislead (a person) by sophistry. **4** *tr.* deprive (a person or thing) of its natural simplicity, make artificial by worldly experience, etc. **5** *tr.* tamper with (a text, etc.) for purposes of argument, etc. **6** *tr.* adulterate (wine, etc.). **7** *intr.* use sophistry. ● *adj.* /səfístikət/ sophisticated. ● *n.* /səfístikət/ a sophisticated person. □□ **sophistication** /-káyshən/ *n.* [med.L *sophisticare* tamper with f. *sophisticus* (as SOPHISM)]

■ □□ **sophistication** worldliness, urbanity, culture, refinement, knowledge, knowledgeability, cosmopolitanism, polish, elegance, poise, suavity, savoir faire, savoir vivre, finesse, discrimination, discernment, awareness, taste, tastefulness, style; complexity, intricacy, subtlety, refinement.

sophisticated /səfístikaytid/ *adj.* **1** (of a person) educated and refined; discriminating in taste and judgment. **2** (of a thing, idea, etc.) highly developed and complex. □□ **sophisticatedly** *adv.*

■ **1** cultivated, cultured, refined, educated, experienced, worldly, cosmopolitan, discriminating, polished, elegant, urbane, worldly-wise, knowledgeable, knowing, suave, soigné(e), blasé, chichi, *colloq.* slick, with it, *sl.* hip, hep, cool. **2** advanced, complex, complicated, intricate, elaborate, subtle, refined, multifaceted.

sophistry /sófistree/ *n.* (*pl.* **-ies**) **1** the use of sophisms. **2** a sophism.

■ **1** see EVASION 2.

sophomore /sófəmawr, sófmawr/ *n.* a second year college or high school student. [earlier *sophumer* f. *sophum*, obs. var. of SOPHISM]

sophomoric /sofəmáwrik, -mór-/ *adj.* **1** of or relating to a sophomore. **2** overconfident and intellectually pretentious but immature and lacking judgment.

Sophy /sófee/ *n.* (*pl.* **-ies**) *hist.* a ruler of Persia in the 16th–17th c. [Pers. *ṣafī* surname of the dynasty, f. Arab. *ṣafī-ud-dīn* pure of religion, title of the founder's ancestor]

soporific /sópərífik/ *adj. & n.* ● *adj.* tending to produce sleep. ● *n.* a soporific drug or influence. □□ **soporiferous** *adj.* **soporifically** *adv.* [L *sopor* sleep + -FIC]

■ *adj.* see TIRESOME 1. ● *n.* see SEDATIVE *n.*

sopping /sóping/ *adj.* (also **sopping wet**) soaked with liquid; wet through. [pres. part. of SOP *v.*]

■ see WET *adj.* 1.

soppy /sópee/ *adj.* (**soppier, soppiest**) **1** *colloq.* **a** silly or foolish in a feeble or self-indulgent way. **b** mawkishly sentimen-

tal. **2** *Brit. colloq.* (foll. by *on*) foolishly infatuated with. **3** soaked with water. □□ **soppily** *adv.* **soppiness** *n.* [SOP + -Y¹]

■ **1 b** see SENTIMENTAL. **3** see WET *adj.* 1. □□ **soppiness** see *sentimentality* (SENTIMENTAL).

sopranino /sóprəneenō/ *n.* (*pl.* **-os**) *Mus.* an instrument higher than soprano, esp. a recorder or saxophone. [It., dimin. of SOPRANO]

soprano /səpránō, -praá-/ *n.* (*pl.* **-os** or **soprani** /-nee/) **1 a** the highest singing voice. **b** a female or boy singer with this voice. **c** a part written for it. **2 a** an instrument of a high or the highest pitch in its family. **b** its player. □ **soprano clef** an obsolete clef placing middle C on the lowest line of the staff. [It. f. *sopra* above f. L *supra*]

sora /sáwrə/ *n.* (in full **sora rail**) a bird, *Porzana carolina*, frequenting N. American marshes. [prob. a native name]

sorb /sawrb/ *n.* **1** = *service tree* (see SERVICE²). **2** (in full **sorb apple**) its fruit. [F *sorbe* or L *sorbus* service tree, *sorbum* service berry]

sorbefacient /sáwrbifáyshənt/ *adj. & n. Med.* ● *adj.* causing absorption. ● *n.* a sorbefacient drug, etc. [L *sorbēre* suck in + -FACIENT]

sorbet /sáwrbay, sáwrbit/ *n.* **1** a frozen confection of water, sugar, and usu. fruit flavoring. **2** = SHERBET. [F f. It. *sorbetto* f. Turk. *şerbet* f. Arab. *šarba* to drink: cf. SHERBET]

Sorbian /sáwrbeeən/ *n. & adj.* (pertaining to) a west Slavic people or their language; also called Lusatian or Wendish.

sorcerer /sáwrsərər/ *n.* (*fem.* **sorceress** /-ris/) a person who claims to use magic powers; a magician or wizard. □□ **sorcerous** *adj.* **sorcery** *n.* (*pl.* **-ies**). [obs. *sorcer* f. OF *sorcier* ult. f. L *sors sortis* lot]

■ magus, necromancer, wizard, enchanter, magician, thaumaturgist, thaumaturge, shaman, witch doctor, medicine man, *archaic* warlock; (*sorceress*) witch, enchantress, *Sc.* spaewife. □□ **sorcery** witchcraft, enchantment, sortilege, necromancy, wizardry, (black *or* white) magic, shamanism, black art, diabolism, the occult.

sordid /sáwrdid/ *adj.* **1** dirty or squalid. **2** ignoble, mean, or mercenary. **3** avaricious or niggardly. **4** dull colored. □□ **sordidly** *adv.* **sordidness** *n.* [F *sordide* or L *sordidus* f. *sordēre* be dirty]

■ **1** dirty, foul, filthy, squalid, unclean, untidy, mean, slummy, seamy, seedy, unsanitary, insanitary, offensive, defiled, polluted, fetid, feculent, mucky, maggoty, putrid, flyblown, slimy; wretched, miserable, poor, poverty-stricken, down-and-out, impoverished, ramshackle, hovel-like, tumbledown, dingy, deteriorated, sleazy. **2** base, vile, corrupt, low, ignoble, debased, degraded, abased, mean, mercenary, ignominious, dishonorable, despicable, disreputable, shabby, shameful, scurvy, rotten, execrable. **3** avaricious, greedy, grasping, mercenary, mean, piggish, hoggish, selfish, rapacious, penny-pinching, stingy, parsimonious, niggardly, *colloq.* moneygrubbing.

□□ **sordidness** see MISERY 1.

sordino /sawrdeenō/ *n.* (*pl.* **sordini** /-nee/) *Mus.* a mute for a bowed or wind instrument. [It. f. *sordo* mute f. L *surdus*]

sore /sawr/ *adj., n., & adv.* ● *adj.* **1** (of a part of the body) painful from injury or disease (*has a sore arm*). **2** (of a person) suffering pain. **3** (often foll. by *about, at*) angry or vexed. **4** *archaic* grievous or severe (*in sore need*). ● *n.* **1** a sore place on the body. **2** a source of distress or annoyance (*reopen old sores*). ● *adv. archaic* grievously; severely. □ **sore point** a subject causing distress or annoyance. **sore throat** an inflammation of the membrane lining the back of the mouth, etc. □□ **soreness** *n.* [OE *sār* (n. & adj.), *sāre* (adv.), f. Gmc]

■ *adj.* **1** painful, sensitive, tender, raw, angry, burning, stinging, smarting, aching, hurting; irritated, inflamed, chafed. **3** angry, angered, aggrieved, annoyed, irritated, vexed, irked, upset, *colloq.* peeved. **4** dire, serious, grievous, severe, acute, extreme, critical, urgent, pressing, desperate; painful, troublesome, distressing, distressful, harrowing, agonizing, bitter, fierce, burdensome, onerous, heavy, oppressive. ● *n.* **1** swelling, rawness, infection, inflammation, bruise, abrasion, cut, laceration, scrape, burn, canker, ulcer.

sorehead /sáwrhed/ *n.* a touchy or disgruntled person.

sorel /sáwrəl/ *n. Brit.* a male fallow deer in its third year. [var. of SORREL²]

sorely /sáwrlee/ *adv.* **1** extremely; badly (*am sorely tempted; sorely in need of repair*). **2** severely (*am sorely vexed*). [OE *sārlīce* (as SORE, -LY²)]

sorghum /sáwrgəm/ *n.* any tropical cereal grass of the genus *Sorghum,* e.g., durra. [mod.L f. It. *sorgo,* perh. f. unrecorded Rmc *syricum* (*gramen*) Syrian (grass)]

sori *pl.* of SORUS.

Soroptimist /səróptimist/ *n.* a member of an international association of clubs for professional and business women. [L *soror* sister + *optimist* (as OPTIMISM)]

sorority /səráwritee, -rór-/ *n.* (*pl.* **-ies**) a female students' society in a university or college, usu. for social purposes. [med.L *sororitas* or L *soror* sister, after *fraternity*]

sorosis /sərōsis/ *n.* (*pl.* **soroses** /-seez/) *Bot.* a fleshy compound fruit, e.g., a pineapple or mulberry. [mod.L f. Gk *sōros* heap]

sorption /sáwrpshən/ *n.* absorption or adsorption happening jointly or separately. [back-form. f. *absorption, adsorption*]

sorrel¹ /sáwrəl, sór-/ *n.* any acid leaved herb of the genus *Rumex,* used in salads and for flavoring. [ME f. OF *surele, sorele* f. Gmc]

sorrel² /sáwrəl, sór-/ *adj. & n.* ● *adj.* of a light reddish-brown color. ● *n.* **1** this color. **2** a sorrel animal, esp. a horse. **3** *Brit.* a sorel. [ME f. OF *sorel* f. *sor* yellowish f. Frank.]

sorrow /sáwrō, sór-/ *n. & v.* ● *n.* **1** mental distress caused by loss or disappointment, etc. **2** a cause of sorrow. **3** lamentation. ● *v.intr.* **1** feel sorrow. **2** mourn. □□ **sorrower** *n.* **sorrowing** *adj.* [OE *sorh, sorg*]

■ *n.* **1** sadness, heartbreak, grief, unhappiness, melancholy, misery, anguish, distress, suffering, torment, agony, wretchedness, heartache, desolation, desolateness, *archaic or literary* woe, *literary* dolor. **2** affliction, trouble, trial, tribulation, misfortune, hardship, adversity, bad *or* hard luck, cares, pressure, strain, *literary* travail. ● *v.* grieve, lament, mourn, weep, keen, agonize, moan, wail; (*sorrow for* or *over*) regret, bemoan, bewail.

sorrowful /sáwrōfōol, sór-/ *adj.* **1** feeling or showing sorrow. **2** distressing; lamentable. □□ **sorrowfully** *adv.* **sorrowfulness** *n.* [OE *sorhful* (as SORROW, -FUL)]

■ **1** sad, unhappy, regretful, sorry, depressed, dejected, crestfallen, chapfallen, gloomy, downcast, blue, dispirited, melancholy, in the doldrums, wretched, woebegone, miserable, heartsick, disheartened, piteous, heavyhearted, brokenhearted, heartbroken, rueful, woeful, tearful, disconsolate, inconsolable, grief-stricken, *colloq.* down in the mouth, in the dumps. **2** distressing, lamentable, doleful, unfortunate, bitter, distressful, grievous, unlucky, hapless, afflictive, *archaic or literary* troublous. □□ **sorrowfulness** see *penitence* (PENITENT), *sadness* (SAD).

sorry /sáwree, sór-/ *adj.* (**sorrier, sorriest**) **1** (*predic.*) pained or regretful or penitent (*were sorry for what they had done; am sorry that you have to go*). **2** (*predic.;* foll. by *for*) feeling pity or sympathy for (a person). **3** as an expression of apology. **4** wretched; in a poor state (*a sorry sight*). □ **sorry for oneself** dejected. □□ **sorrily** *adv.* **sorriness** *n.* [OE *sārig* f. WG (as SORE, -Y²)]

■ **1** regretful, penitent, remorseful, contrite, conscience-stricken, guilt-ridden, repentant, apologetic, penitential; see also SORROWFUL 1. **2** (*feel sorry for*) see PITY *v.* **4** abject, miserable, depressing, wretched, woeful, pitiful, pitiable, lamentable, pathetic, deplorable, stark, grim, sordid, dismal, base; ill-starred, *archaic* star-crossed.

sort /sawrt/ *n. & v.* ● *n.* **1** a group of things, etc., with common attributes; a class or kind. **2** (foll. by *of*) roughly of the kind specified (*is some sort of doctor*). **3** *colloq.* a person of a specified character or kind (*a good sort*). **4** *Printing* a letter or piece in a font of type. **5** *Computing* the arrangement of

data in a prescribed sequence. **6** *archaic* a manner or way. ● *v.tr.* (often foll. by *out, over*) arrange systematically or according to type, class, etc. □ **after a sort** after a fashion. **in some sort** to a certain extent. **of a sort** (or **of sorts**) *colloq.* not fully deserving the name (*a holiday of sorts*). **out of sorts 1** slightly unwell. **2** in low spirits; irritable. **sort of** *colloq.* as it were; to some extent (*I sort of expected it*). **sort out 1** separate into sorts. **2** select (things of one or more sorts) from a miscellaneous group. **3** disentangle or put into order. **4** resolve (a problem or difficulty). **5** *colloq.* deal with or reprimand (a person). □□ **sortable** *adj.* **sorter** *n.* **sorting** *n.* [ME f. OF *sorte* ult. f. L *sors sortis* lot, condition]

■ *n.* **1** kind, variety, type, class, classification, group, category, brand, make, mark, stamp, description, mold, stripe, kidney, character, nature, *colloq. disp.* ilk; manner; species, genus, family, phylum, subgenus, subspecies, race, breed, strain, stock. **2** kind, type, *archaic* manner. **3** person, individual, type. ● *v.* assort, classify, file, order, rank, grade, class, size, categorize, separate, divide, combine, merge, arrange, organize, systemize, systematize, catalog, group, esp. *Biol.* & *Med.* type; describe, characterize. □ **out of sorts 1** not oneself, unwell, ailing, indisposed, (slightly) ill, low, poorly, *colloq.* under the weather, *Brit. colloq.* not up to snuff. **2** see MOODY *adj.* **sort of** see SOMEWHAT *adv.* **sort out 1** see SORT *v.* above. **2** choose, select, pick out; separate. **3** disentangle, untangle, unravel, set *or* put straight, straighten out, tidy (up), clear up. **4** resolve, solve, straighten out, clarify, clear up, rectify, put right *or* straight, fix, settle.

sortie /sáwrtee, sawrtée/ *n. & v.* ● *n.* **1** a sally, esp. from a besieged garrison. **2** an operational flight by a single military aircraft. ● *v.intr.* (**sorties, sortied, sortieing**) make a sortie; sally. [F, fem. past part. of *sortir* go out]

■ *n.* **1** see CHARGE *n.* 4a.

sortilege /sáwrt'lij/ *n.* divination by lots. [ME f. OF f. med.L *sortilegium* sorcery f. L *sortilegus* sorcerer (as SORT, *legere* choose)]

■ see *sorcery* (SORCERER).

sorus /sáwrəs/ *n.* (*pl.* **sori** /-rī/) *Bot.* a heap or cluster, esp. of spore cases on the underside of a fern leaf, or in a fungus or lichen. [mod.L f. Gk *sōros* heap]

SOS /éss-ó-éss/ *n.* (*pl.* **SOSs**) **1** an international code signal of extreme distress, used esp. by ships at sea. **2** an urgent appeal for help. **3** *Brit.* a message broadcast to an untraceable person in an emergency. [chosen as being easily transmitted and recognized in Morse code]

sostenuto /sóstənōōtō/ *adv., adj., & n. Mus.* ● *adv. & adj.* in a sustained or prolonged manner. ● *n.* (*pl.* **-os**) a passage to be played in this way. [It., past part. of *sostenere* SUSTAIN]

sot /sot/ *n. & v.* ● *n.* a habitual drunkard. ● *v.intr.* (**sotted, sotting**) *Brit.* drink alcohol habitually. □□ **sottish** *adj.* [OE *sott* & OF *sot* foolish, f. med.L *sottus,* of unkn. orig.]

■ *n.* see DRUNK *n.* 1. ● *v.* see DRINK *v.* 2.

soteriology /sətéereeóləjee/ *n. Theol.* the doctrine of salvation. [Gk *sōtēria* salvation + -LOGY]

Sothic /sōthik, sóth-/ *adj.* of or relating to the Dog Star, esp. with ref. to the ancient Egyptian year fixed by its heliacal rising. [Gk *Sōthis* f. the Egypt. name of the Dog Star]

sotto voce /sótō vōchee, sáwt-tō vávche/ *adv.* in an undertone or aside. [It. *sotto* under + *voce* voice]

sou /sōo/ *n.* **1** *hist.* a former French coin of low value. **2** (usu. with *neg.*) *colloq.* a very small amount of money (*hasn't a sou*). [F, orig. pl. *sous* f. OF *sout* f. L SOLIDUS]

soubrette /sōobrét/ *n.* **1** a coquettish maidservant or similar female character in a comedy. **2** an actress taking this part. [F f. Prov. *soubreto* fem. of *soubret* coy f. *sobrar* f. L *superare* be above]

soubriquet var. of SOBRIQUET.

/.../ pronunciation   ● part of speech

□ phrases, idioms, and compounds

□□ derivatives   ■ synonym section

cross-references appear in SMALL CAPITALS or *italics*

---

souchong /so˘ochóng, -shóng/ *n.* a fine variety of black tea. [Chin. *xiao* small + *zhong* sort]

souffle /soˉofəl/ *n.* *Med.* a low murmur heard in the auscultation of various organs, etc. [F f. *souffler* blow f. L *sufflare*]

soufflé /soˉofláy/ *n.* & *adj.* ● *n.* **1** a light dish usu. made with flavored egg yolks added to stiffly beaten egg whites and baked (*cheese soufflé*). **2** any of various light dishes made with beaten egg whites. ● *adj.* **1** light and frothy (*omelette soufflé*). **2** (of ceramics) decorated with small spots. [F past part. (as SOUFFLE)]

sough /sow, suf/ *v.* & *n.* ● *v.intr.* make a moaning, whistling, or rushing sound as of the wind in trees, etc. ● *n.* this sound. [OE *swōgan* resound]
■ *v.* sigh, groan, moan.

sought *past* and *past part.* of SEEK.

souk /soˉok/ *n.* (also **suk, sukh, suq**) a marketplace in Arab countries. [Arab. *sūk*]
■ bazaar.

soul /sōl/ *n.* **1** the spiritual or immaterial part of a human being, often regarded as immortal. **2** the moral or emotional or intellectual nature of a person or animal. **3** the personification or pattern of something (*the very soul of discretion*). **4** an individual (*not a soul in sight*). **5 a** a person regarded with familiarity or pity, etc. (*the poor soul was utterly confused*). **b** a person regarded as embodying moral or intellectual qualities (*left that to meaner souls*). **6** a person regarded as the animating or essential part of something (*the life and soul of the party*). **7** emotional or intellectual energy or intensity, esp. as revealed in a work of art (*pictures that lack soul*). **8** African-American culture, music, ethnic pride, etc. □ **soul-destroying** (of an activity, etc.) deadeningly monotonous. **soul food** traditional southern African-American foods. **soul mate** a person ideally suited to another. **soul music** a kind of music incorporating elements of rhythm and blues and gospel music, popularized by African Americans. **the soul of honor** a person incapable of dishonorable conduct. **soul-searching** *n.* the examination of one's emotions and motives. ● *adj.* characterized by this. **upon my soul** an exclamation of surprise. □□ **-souled** *adj.* (in *comb.*). [OE *sāwol, sāwel, sāwl,* f. Gmc]
■ **1, 2** (vital) spirit *or* force, being, (inner *or* true) self, essence, psyche, heart, mind, intellect, reason, *Psychol.* anima. **3** incarnation, embodiment, epitome, personification, typification, essence, quintessence, example, model, pattern. **4** person, individual, man, woman, mortal, (human) being. **7** emotion, feeling, sentiment, sincerity, fervor, ardor, warmth, dynamism, vivacity, energy, spirit, vitality, force. □ **soul-destroying** see TEDIOUS. **upon my soul** see GRACIOUS *int.*

soulful /sōlfoˉol/ *adj.* **1** having or expressing or evoking deep feeling. **2** *collog.* overly emotional. □□ **soulfully** *adv.* **soulfulness** *n.*
■ **1** sincere, deep, profound, heartfelt, moving, emotional, warm, ardent, intense, fervent, expressive, eloquent.

soulless /sōl-lis/ *adj.* **1** lacking sensitivity or noble qualities. **2** having no soul. **3** undistinguished or uninteresting. □□ **soullessly** *adv.* **soullessness** *n.*

sound[1] /sownd/ *n.* & *v.* ● *n.* **1** a sensation caused in the ear by the vibration of the surrounding air or other medium. **2 a** vibrations causing this sensation. **b** similar vibrations whether audible or not. **3** what is or may be heard. **4** an idea or impression conveyed by words (*don't like the sound of that*). **5** mere words (*sound and fury*). **6** (in full **musical sound**) sound produced by continuous and regular vibrations (opp. NOISE *n.* 3). **7** any of a series of articulate utterances (*vowel and consonant sounds*). **8** music, speech, etc., accompanying a movie or other visual presentation. **9** (often *attrib.*) broadcasting by radio as distinct from television. **10** a distinctive musical style or set of characteristics (*pop music with a classical sound*). ● *v.* **1** *intr.* & *tr.* emit or cause to emit sound. **2** *tr.* utter or pronounce (*sound a note of alarm*). **3** *intr.* convey an impression when heard (*you sound worried*). **4** *tr.* give an audible signal for (an alarm, etc.). **5** *tr.*

test (the lungs, etc.) by noting the sound produced. **6** *tr.* cause to resound; make known (*sound their praises*). □ **sound barrier** the high resistance of air to objects moving at speeds near that of sound. **sound bite** a short extract from a recorded interview, chosen for its pungency or appropriateness. **sound box** the hollow chamber providing resonance and forming the body of a stringed musical instrument. **sound effect** a sound other than speech or music made artificially for use in a play, movie, etc. **sound engineer** an engineer dealing with acoustics, etc. **sound hole** an aperture in the belly of some stringed instruments. **sound off** talk loudly or express one's opinions forcefully. **sound post** a small prop between the belly and back of some stringed instruments. **sound shift** see SHIFT *n.* 6. **sound spectrograph** an instrument for analyzing sound into its frequency components. **sound wave** a wave of compression and rarefaction, by which sound is propagated in an elastic medium, e.g., air. □□ **soundless** *adj.* **soundlessly** *adv.* **soundlessness** *n.* [ME f. AF *soun*, OF *son* (n.), AF *suner*, OF *soner* (v.) f. L *sonus*]
■ *n.* **1** tone, noise, din, cacophony, report. **4** ring, tone, idea, quality, effect, aspect, look, feel. **8** soundtrack, voice-over, narration. ● *v.* **1** resound, reverberate, echo, resonate; see also BLARE *v.*, RING[2] *v.* 1. **2** articulate, pronounce, enunciate, utter; voice, vocalize. **3** seem, appear; strike a person as, give a person the impression *or* feeling *or* sense that. **4** ring, activate, set *or* touch off, signal. **6** shout (out), cry out, yell (out); make known, proclaim. □ **sound off** vituperate, complain, bluster, grumble, *collog.* bitch; go on. □□ **soundless** see NOISELESS. **soundlessly** see *silently* (SILENT). **soundlessness** see SILENCE *n.* 1.

sound[2] /sownd/ *adj.* & *adv.* ● *adj.* **1** healthy; not diseased or injured. **2** undamaged; in good condition. **3** (of an opinion or policy, etc.) correct; orthodox; well-founded; judicious; legally valid. **4** financially secure (*a sound investment*). **5** undisturbed (*a sound sleep*). **6** severe; hard (*a sound blow*). ● *adv.* soundly (*sound asleep*). □□ **soundly** *adv.* **soundness** *n.* [ME *sund, isund* f. OE *gesund* f. WG]
■ *adj.* **1** healthy, hale (and hearty), fit (as a fiddle), in good condition *or* shape, robust, vigorous, blooming, rosy, ruddy; undiseased, uninjured. **2** undamaged, whole, unmarred, intact, unimpaired, unscathed; in good condition, firm, solid, substantial, strong, sturdy, dependable. **3** correct, orthodox, well-founded, valid, good, judicious, reliable, useful; sane, balanced, normal, rational, wholesome, reasoning, reasonable, clearheaded, lucid, right-minded, responsible, practical, prudent, politic, wise, sensible, logical, commonsense, commonsensical, astute, farsighted, perceptive, perspicacious, percipient. **4** safe, secure, good, conservative, nonspeculative, solid, riskless; profitable. **5** unbroken, uninterrupted, continuous, undisturbed, untroubled, peaceful, deep, heavy. □□ **soundly** see FAST[1] *adv.* 2. **soundness** see STRENGTH 1.

sound[3] /sownd/ *v.* & *n.* ● *v.tr.* & *intr.* **1** *tr.* test the depth or quality of the bottom of (the sea or a river, etc.). **2** *tr.* (often foll. by *out*) inquire (esp. cautiously or discreetly) into the opinions or feelings of (a person). **3** *tr.* find the depth of water in (a ship's hold). **4** *tr.* get records of temperature, humidity, pressure, etc., from (the upper atmosphere). **5** *tr.* examine (a person's bladder, etc.) with a probe. **6** *intr.* (of a whale or fish) dive to the bottom. ● *n.* a surgeon's probe. □□ **sounder** *n.* [ME f. OF *sonder* ult. f. L SUB- + *unda* wave]
■ *v.* **1** plumb, probe, fathom, test. **2** plumb, probe, test, check (into), inquire of, question, poll, canvass, investigate, examine, survey, check out. **6** see DIVE *v.* 1, 2.

sound[4] /sownd/ *n.* **1 a** a narrow passage of water connecting two seas or a sea with a lake, etc. **b** an arm of the sea. **2** a fish's air bladder. [OE *sund*, = ON *sund* swimming, strait, f. Gmc (as SWIM)]
■ **1** strait(s), inlet, fiord, firth, arm of the sea, cove.

soundboard /sówndbawrd/ *n.* a thin sheet of wood over

which the strings of a piano, etc., pass to increase the sound produced.

sounding[1] /sównding/ *n.* **1 a** the action or process of measuring the depth of water, now usu. by means of echo. **b** an instance of this (*took a sounding*). **2** (in *pl.*) **a** a region close to the shore of the right depth for sounding. **b** *Naut.* measurements taken by sounding. **c** cautious investigation (*made soundings as to his suitability*). **3 a** the determination of any physical property at a depth in the sea or at a height in the atmosphere. **b** an instance of this. □ **sounding balloon** a balloon used to obtain information about the upper atmosphere. **sounding board 1** a canopy over a pulpit, etc., to direct sound toward the congregation. **2** = SOUNDBOARD. **3 a** a means of causing opinions, etc., to be more widely known (*used his students as a sounding board*). **b** a person, etc., used as a trial audience. **sounding line** a line used in sounding the depth of water. **sounding rod** a rod used in finding the depth of water in a ship's hold (see SOUND[3]).

sounding[2] /sównding/ *adj.* **1** giving forth (esp. loud or resonant) sound (*sounding brass*). **2** emptily boastful, resonant, or imposing (*sounding promises*).

soundproof /sówndproof/ *adj. & v.* ● *adj.* impervious to sound. ● *v.tr.* make soundproof.

soundtrack /sówndtrak/ *n.* **1** the recorded sound element of a movie, television broadcast, etc. **2** this recorded on the edge of a film, videotype, etc., in optical or magnetic form.

soup /soop/ *n. & v.* ● *n.* **1** a liquid dish made by boiling meat, fish, or vegetables, etc., in stock or water. **2** *sl.* nitroglycerine or gelignite, esp. for safe-cracking. **3** *sl.* the chemicals in which film is developed. **4** *colloq.* fog; thick cloud. ● *v.tr.* (usu. foll. by *up*) *colloq.* **1** increase the power and efficiency of (an engine). **2** increase the power or impact of (writing, music, etc.). □ **in the soup** *colloq.* in difficulties. **soup and fish** *colloq.* evening dress. **soup kitchen** a place dispensing soup, etc., to the poor. **soup plate** a deep wide-rimmed plate for serving soup. [F *soupe* sop, broth, f. LL *suppa* f. Gmc: cf. SOP, SUP[1]]
■ *n.* **1** see BROTH.

soupçon /soopsáwn, soopsón/ *n.* a very small quantity; a dash. [F f. OF *sou(s)peçon* f. med.L *suspectio -onis*: see SUSPICION]
■ see DASH *n.* 7.

soupspoon /soopspoon/ *n.* a spoon, usu. with a large rounded bowl, for eating soup.

soupy /soopee/ *adj.* (**soupier**, **soupiest**) **1** of or resembling soup. **2** *colloq.* sentimental; mawkish. □□ **soupily** *adv.* **soupiness** *n.*
■ **1** see THICK *adj.* 6. **2** see MAUDLIN *adj.*

sour /sowr/ *adj., n., & v.* ● *adj.* **1** having an acid taste like lemon or vinegar, esp. because of unripeness (*sour apples*). **2 a** (of food, esp. milk or bread) bad because of fermentation. **b** smelling or tasting rancid or unpleasant. **3** (of a person, temper, etc.) harsh; morose; bitter. **4** (of a thing) unpleasant; distasteful. **5** (of the soil) deficient in lime and usually dank. ● *n.* **1** a drink with lemon or lime juice (*whiskey sour*). **2** an acid solution used in bleaching, etc. ● *v.tr. & intr.* make or become sour (*soured the cream; soured by misfortune*). □ **go** (or **turn**) **sour 1** (of food, etc.) become sour. **2** turn out badly (*the job went sour on him*). **3** lose one's enthusiasm. **sour cream** cream deliberately fermented by adding bacteria. **sour grapes** resentful disparagement of something one cannot personally acquire. **sour mash** a brewing or distilling mash made acid to promote fermentation. □□ **sourish** *adj.* **sourly** *adv.* **sourness** *n.* [OE *sūr* f. Gmc]
■ *adj.* **1** acid, acidic, tart, vinegary, lemony, sharp, acidulous, acidulated, acerbic. **2** turned, bad, fermented, curdled, rancid, spoiled, esp. *Brit.* (gone) off. **3** acrimonious, bitter, embittered, harsh, unpleasant, churlish, ill-natured, ill-tempered, bad-tempered, crusty, curmudgeonly, crabbed, crabby, cross, testy, petulant, impatient, abrupt, nasty, curt, caustic, brusque, peevish, snappish, edgy, sullen, morose, gloomy, glum, discontented, cranky, *colloq.* grouchy. **4** disagreeable, unpleasant, distasteful, bad,

nasty, bitter. ● *v.* turn, spoil, curdle, go bad, ferment; embitter, disenchant, exasperate, vex, *colloq.* peeve.

source /sawrs/ *n. & v.* ● *n.* **1** a spring or fountainhead from which a stream issues (*the sources of the Nile*). **2** a place, person, or thing from which something originates (*the source of all our troubles*). **3** a person or document, etc., providing evidence (*reliable sources of information; historical source material*). **4 a** a body emitting radiation, etc. **b** *Physics* a place from which a fluid or current flows. **c** *Electronics* a part of a transistor from which carriers flow into the interelectrode channel. ● *v.tr.* obtain (esp. components) from a specified source. □ **at source** at the point of origin or issue. **source criticism** the evaluation of different, esp. successive, literary or historical sources. [ME f. OF *sors, sourse*, past part. of *sourdre* rise f. L *surgere*]
■ *n.* **1** (fountain)head, wellhead, (well)spring, origin; provenance, inception, start, beginning, root(s), rise, provenience, *formal* commencement. **2** originator, initiator, author, creator, begetter, cause, origin, root. **3** authority, documentation; informant, horse's mouth.

sourcebook /sáwrsbook/ *n.* a collection of documentary sources for the study of a subject.

sourdough /sówrdō/ *n.* **1** fermenting dough, esp. that left over from a previous baking, used as leaven. **2** an old-timer in Alaska, etc. [dial., = leaven, in allusion to piece of sour dough for raising bread baked in winter]

sourpuss /sówrpoos/ *n. colloq.* an ill-tempered person. [SOUR + PUSS = face]
■ see MISERY 3.

soursop /sówrsop/ *n.* **1** a W. Indian evergreen tree, *Annona muricata.* **2** the large succulent fruit of this tree.

sous- /soo/ *prefix* (in words adopted from French) subordinate; under (*sous-chef*). [F]

sousaphone /soozəfōn/ *n.* a large brass bass wind instrument encircling the player's body. □□ **sousaphonist** *n.* [J. P. Sousa, Amer. bandmaster d. 1932, after *saxophone*]

souse /sows/ *v. & n.* ● *v.* **1** *tr.* put (pickles, fish, etc.) in brine. **2** *tr. & intr.* plunge into liquid. **3** *tr.* (as **soused** *adj.*) *colloq.* drunk. **4** *tr.* (usu. foll. by *in*) soak (a thing) in liquid. **5** *tr.* (usu. foll. by *over*) throw (liquid) over a thing. ● *n.* **1** a pickling brine made with salt. **b** food, esp. a pig's head, etc., in pickle. **2** a dip, plunge, or drenching in water. **3** *colloq.* **a** a drinking bout. **b** a drunkard. [ME f. OF *sous, souz* pickle f. OS *sultia*, OHG *sulza* brine f. Gmc: cf. SALT]
■ *v.* **1** see SALT *v.* 1. **2, 4** see SOAK *v.* 1. **3** (**soused**) see DRUNK *adj.* 1. ● *n.* **3 a** see JAG[2] 1. **b** see DRUNK *n.* 1.

soutache /sootásh/ *n.* a narrow flat ornamental braid used to trim garments. [F f. Magyar *sujtás*]
■ see BRAID *n.* 1.

soutane /sootáan/ *n. RC Ch., Anglican Ch.* a cassock worn by a priest. [F f. It. *sottana* f. *sotto* under f. L *subtus*]

souter /sootər/ *n. Sc. & No. of Engl.* a shoemaker; a cobbler. [OE *sūtere* f. L *sutor* f. *suere* sut- sew]

souterrain /sootərayn/ *n.* esp. *Archaeol.* an underground chamber or passage. [F f. *sous* under + *terre* earth]

south /sowth/ *n., adj., adv., & v.* ● *n.* **1** the point of the horizon 90° clockwise from east. **2** the compass point corresponding to this. **3** the direction in which this lies. **4** (usu. **the South**) **a** the part of the world or a country or a town lying to the south. **b** the southern states of the US. **5** *Bridge* a player occupying the position designated 'south'. ● *adj.* **1** toward, at, near, or facing the south (*a south wall; south country*). **2** coming from the south (*south wind*). ● *adv.* **1** toward, at, or near the south (*they traveled south*). **2** (foll. by *of*) further south than. ● *v.intr.* **1** move toward the south. **2** (of a celestial body) cross the meridian. □ **South African** *adj.* of or relating to the republic of South Africa. ● *n.* **1** a native or inhabitant of South Africa. **2** a person of South African descent. **South American** *adj.* of or relating to

South America. ● *n.* a native or inhabitant of South America. **south by east** (or **west**) between south and south-southeast (or south-southwest). **southeast** *n.* **1** the point of the horizon midway between south and east. **2** the compass point corresponding to this. **3** the direction in which this lies. ● *adj.* of, toward, or coming from the southeast. ● *adv.* toward, at, or near the southeast. **Southeast** the part of a country or town lying to the southeast. **southeasterly** *adj.* & *adv.* = *southeast.* **southeastern** lying on the southeast side. **south pole** see POLE². **South Sea** the southern Pacific Ocean. **south-southeast** the point or direction midway between south and southeast. **south-southwest** the point or direction midway between south and southwest. **southwest** *n.* **1** the point of the horizon midway between south and west. **2** the compass point corresponding to this. **3** the direction in which this lies. ● *adj.* of, toward, or coming from the southwest. ● *adv.* toward, at, or near the southwest. **Southwest** the part of a country or town lying to the southwest. **southwesterly** *adj.* & *adv.* = *southwest.* **southwestern** lying on the southwest side. **south wind** a wind blowing from the south. **to the south** (often foll. by *of*) in a southerly direction. [OE *sūth*]

southbound /sówthbownd/ *adj.* traveling or leading southward.

Southdown /sówthdown/ *n.* **1** a sheep of a breed raised esp. for mutton, orig. in England. **2** this breed.

southeaster /sówtheéstər, sou-eéstər/ *n.* a southeast wind.

souther /sówthər/ *n.* a south wind.

southerly /súthərlee/ *adj.*, *adv.*, & *n.* ● *adj.* & *adv.* **1** in a southern position or direction. **2** (of a wind) blowing from the south. ● *n.* (*pl.* **-ies**) a southerly wind.

southern /súthərn/ *adj.* esp. *Geog.* **1** of or in the south; inhabiting the south. **2** lying or directed toward the south (*at the southern end*). □ **Southern Cross** a southern constellation in the shape of a cross. **southern hemisphere** the half of the earth below the equator. **southern lights** the aurora australis. **southern states** the states in the south, esp. the southeast, of the US, esp. those identified with the Confederacy. □□ **southernmost** *adj.* [OE *sútherne* (as SOUTH, -ERN)]

southerner /súthərnər/ *n.* a native or inhabitant of the south.

southernwood /súthərnwŏod/ *n.* a bushy kind of wormwood, *Artemisia abrotanum.*

southing /sówthing/ *n.* **1** a southern movement. **2** *Naut.* the distance traveled or measured southward. **3** *Astron.* the angular distance of a star, etc., south of the celestial equator.

southpaw /sówthpaw/ *n.* & *adj. colloq.* ● *n.* a left-handed person, esp. a left-handed pitcher in baseball. ● *adj.* left-handed.

southward /sówthwərd/ *adj.*, *adv.*, & *n.* ● *adj.* & *adv.* (also **southwards**) toward the south. ● *n.* a southward direction or region.

southwester /sówthwéstər, sow-wéstər/ *n.* a southwest wind.

souvenir /sŏovəneér/ *n.* & *v.* ● *n.* (often foll. by *of*) a memento of an occasion, place, etc. ● *v.tr. Brit. sl.* take as a "souvenir"; pilfer; steal. [F f. *souvenir* remember f. L *subvenire* occur to the mind (as SUB-, *venire* come)]

■ *n.* see MEMENTO.

souvlaki /sŏovláakee/ *n.* (*pl.* **souvlakia** /-keeə/) a Greek dish of pieces of meat (usu. lamb) grilled on a skewer. [mod. Gk]

sou'wester /sow-wéstər/ *n.* **1** = SOUTHWESTER. **2** a waterproof hat with a broad flap covering the neck.

sov. /sov/ *abbr. Brit.* sovereign.

sovereign /sóvrin/ *n.* & *adj.* ● *n.* **1** a supreme ruler, esp. a monarch. **2** *Brit. hist.* a gold coin nominally worth £1. ● *adj.* **1 a** supreme (*sovereign power*). **b** unmitigated (*sovereign contempt*). **2** excellent; effective (*a sovereign remedy*). **3** possessing independent national power (*a sovereign state*). **4** royal (*our sovereign lord*). □□ **sovereignly** *adv.* **sovereignty** *n.* (*pl.* **-ies**) [ME f. OF *so(u)verain* f. L: *-g-* by assoc. with *reign*]

■ *n.* **1** monarch, ruler, emperor, empress, czar, king, queen, prince, princess, elector, grand duke *or* duchess, potentate, supremo, chief, master, mistress, emir,

sheikh, sultan, *hist.* shah. ● *adj.* **1** supreme, paramount, highest, principal, foremost, greatest, predominant, dominant, ranking, leading, chief, superior, preeminent, ruling, regnant, reigning, governing, all-powerful, absolute, unlimited, unmitigated, unqualified. **3** see INDEPENDENT *adj.* 1b. **4** royal, regal, majestic, noble, lordly, aristocratic, kingly, queenly. □□ **sovereignty** suzerainty, hegemony, dominion, rule, reign, preeminence, power, jurisdiction, authority, leadership, command, sway, supremacy, ascendancy, primacy; kingship, queenship.

soviet /sóveeət, sóv-/ *n.* & *adj. hist.* ● *n.* **1** an elected local, district, or national council in the former USSR. **2** (**Soviet**) a citizen of the former USSR. **3** a revolutionary council of workers, peasants, etc., before 1917. ● *adj.* (usu. **Soviet**) of or concerning the former Soviet Union. □□ **Sovietize** *v.tr.* **Sovietization** *n.* [Russ. *sovet* council]

sovietologist /sóveeətóləjist, sóv-/ *n.* a person who studies the former Soviet Union.

sow¹ /sō/ *v.tr.* (*past* **sowed** /sōd/; *past part.* **sown** /sōn/ or **sowed**) **1** (also *absol.*) **a** scatter or put (seed) on or in the earth. **b** (often foll. by *with*) plant (a field, etc.) with seed. **2** initiate; arouse (*sowed doubt in her mind*). **3** (foll. by *with*) cover thickly with. □ **sow the seed** (or **seeds**) **of** first give rise to; implant (an idea, etc.). □□ **sower** *n.* **sowing** *n.* [OE *sāwan* f. Gmc]

■ **1** plant, strew, scatter, spread; broadcast; seed. **2** see PLANT *v.* 6.

sow² /sow/ *n.* **1 a** a female adult pig, esp. after farrowing. **b** a female guinea pig. **c** the female of some other species. **2 a** the main trough through which molten iron runs into side channels to form pigs. **b** a large block of iron so formed. **3** (in full **sow bug**) a woodlouse. [OE *sugu*]

sowbread /sówbred/ *n.* a tuberous plant, *Cyclamen hederifolium,* with solitary nodding flowers.

sown *past part.* of SOW¹.

sow thistle /sów thisəl/ *n.* any plant of the genus *Sonchus* with thistle-like leaves and milky juice.

sox *colloq. pl.* of SOCK¹.

soy /soy/ *n.* (also **soya** /sóyə/) **1** (also **soy sauce**) a sauce made esp. in Asia from pickled soya beans. **2** (in full **soy bean**) = *soya bean.* [Jap. *shō-yu* f. Chin. *shi-you* f. *shi* salted beans + *you* oil]

soya /sóyə/ *n.* (in full **soya bean**) **1 a** a leguminous plant, *Glycine soja,* orig. of SE Asia, cultivated for the edible oil and flour it yields, and used as a replacement for animal protein in certain foods. **b** the seed of this. **2** (also **soya sauce**) = SOY 1. [Du. *soja* f. Malay *soi* (as SOY)]

sozzled /sózəld/ *adj. colloq.* very drunk. [past part. of dial. *sozzle* mix sloppily (prob. imit.)]

■ see DRUNK *adj.* 1.

SP *abbr.* starting price.

spa /spaa/ *n.* **1** a curative mineral spring. **2** a place or resort with this. **3** a fashionable resort or hotel. **4** a hot tub, esp. one with a whirlpool device. **5** *health spa.* [*Spa* in Belgium]

■ **1** see SPRING *n.* 6.

space /spays/ *n.* & *v.* ● *n.* **1 a** a continuous unlimited area or expanse which may or may not contain objects, etc. **b** an interval between one, two, or three dimensional points or objects (*a space of 10 feet*). **c** an empty area; room (*clear a space in the corner*; *occupies too much space*). **2 a** large unoccupied region (*the wide open spaces*). **3** = *outer space.* **4** a place, seat, berth, etc., made available (*no space on the bus*). **5** an interval of time (*in the space of an hour*). **6** the amount of paper used in writing, etc. (*hadn't the space to discuss it*). **7 a** a blank between printed, typed, or written words, etc. **b** a piece of metal providing this. **8** *Mus.* each of the blanks between the lines of a staff. ● *v.tr.* **1** set or arrange at intervals. **2** put spaces between (esp. words, letters, lines, etc,. in printing, typing, or writing). **3** (as **spaced** *adj.*) (often foll. by *out*) *sl.* in a state of euphoria, esp. from taking drugs. □ **space age** the era when space travel has become possible. **space bar** a long key on a keyboard for making a space between words, etc. **space cadet** *sl.* a person who appears absentminded or removed from reality. **space flight 1** a journey through space. **2** = *space travel*. **space heater** a heater, usu. electric, that warms a limited space, as a room. **space probe** = PROBE *n.* 4. **space-saving** occupying little space. **space shuttle** a rocket for repeated use carrying people and cargo between the earth and space. **space station** an artificial satellite used as a base for operations in space. **space-time** (or **space-time continuum**) the fusion of the concepts of space and time, esp. as a four-dimensional continuum. **space travel** travel through outer space. **space traveler** a traveler in outer space; an astronaut. **space walk** any physical activity by an astronaut in space outside a spacecraft. □□ **spacer** *n.* **spacing** *n.* (esp. in sense 2 of *v.*). [ME f. OF *espace* f. L *spatium*]

■ *n.* **1 a** expanse, area, extent, compass, tract. **b** interval, interspace, interstice, gap, opening, lacuna, hiatus, window, daylight, clearance. **c** place, area, capacity, room, elbowroom, leeway, margin, latitude, clearance, play. **5** interval, lapse, period, time, hiatus, lacuna, span, while, duration, extent, spell, stretch, pause, wait, intermission, gap, break, interruption. **7** blank, gap. ● *v.* **1** arrange, organize, array, set out, align, range, order, rank, lay out, measure (out). **3** (*spaced out*) see HIGH *adj.* 8b.

spacecraft /spáyskraft/ *n.* a vehicle used for traveling in space.

■ see CRAFT *n.* 3.

spaceman /spáysman/ *n.* (*pl.* **-men**; *fem.* **spacewoman**, *pl.* **-women**) = *space traveler*.

spaceship /spáys-ship/ *n.* a spacecraft, esp. one controlled by its crew.

■ see CRAFT *n.* 3.

spacesuit /spáys-soōt, -syoōt/ *n.* a garment designed to allow an astronaut to survive in space.

spacey /spáysee/ *adj.* (also **spacy**) *sl.* **1** seemingly out of touch with reality; disoriented. **2** being in a confused or dazed state because of the influence of mind-altering drugs.

spacial var. of SPATIAL.

spacious /spáyshǝs/ *adj.* having ample space; covering a large area; roomy. □□ **spaciously** *adv.* **spaciousness** *n.* [ME f. OF *spacios* or L *spatiosus* (as SPACE)]

■ vast, large, extensive, enormous, wide, broad, commodious, ample, expansive, roomy, huge, sizable, capacious, great, immense, outsized, voluminous, oversize(d).

Spackle /spákǝl/ *n. propr.* a pastelike compound used for filling holes and cracks in plasterboard.

spade[1] /spayd/ *n. & v.* ● *n.* **1** a tool used for digging or cutting the ground, etc., with a sharp-edged metal blade and a long handle. **2** a tool of a similar shape for various purposes, e.g., for removing the blubber from a whale. **3** anything resembling a spade. ● *v.tr.* dig over (ground) with a spade. □ **call a spade a spade** speak plainly or bluntly. **spade beard** an oblong-shaped beard. **spade foot** a square spadelike enlargement at the end of a chair leg. □□ **spadeful** *n.* (*pl.* **-fuls**). [OE *spadu, spada*]

■ □ **call a spade a spade** talk straight, not mince (one's) words.

spade[2] /spayd/ *n.* **1 a** a playing card of a suit denoted by black inverted heart-shaped figures with small stalks. **b** (in *pl.*) this suit. **2** *sl. offens.* an African-American. □ **in spades** *sl.* to a high degree; with great force. [It. *spade* pl. of *spada* sword f. L *spatha* f. Gk *spathē*, rel. to SPADE¹: assoc. with the shape of a pointed spade]

spadework /spáydwǝrk/ *n.* hard or routine preparatory work.

■ see PREPARATION 1.

spadille /spǝdíl/ *n.* **1** the ace of spades in ombre and quadrille. **2** the highest trump, esp. the ace of spades. [F f. Sp. *espadilla* dimin. of *espada* sword (as SPADE²)]

spadix /spáydiks/ *n.* (*pl.* **spadices** /-seez/) *Bot.* a spike of flowers closely arranged round a fleshy axis and usu. enclosed in a spathe. □□ **spadiceous** /-díshǝs/ *adj.* [L f. Gk, = palm branch]

spae /spay/ *v.intr. & tr. Sc.* foretell; prophesy. [ME f. ON *spá*]

spaghetti /spǝgétee/ *n.* pasta made in solid strings, between macaroni and vermicelli in thickness. □ **spaghetti squash**

a type of squash whose flesh forms spaghettilike strands when cooked. **spaghetti western** a movie about the American West made cheaply in Italy. [It., pl. of dimin. of *spago* string: *Bolognese* It., = of Bologna]

spahi /spaáhee/ *n. hist.* **1** a member of the Turkish irregular cavalry. **2** a member of the Algerian cavalry in French service. [Turk. *sipāhī* formed as SEPOY]

spake /spayk/ *archaic past* of SPEAK.

spall /spawl/ *n. & v.* ● *n.* a splinter or chip, esp. of rock ● *v.intr. & tr.* break up or cause (ore) to break up in preparation for sorting. [ME (also *spale*): orig. unkn.]

spallation /spawláyshǝn/ *n. Physics* the breakup of a bombarded nucleus into several parts.

spalpeen /spalpeén/ *n. Ir.* **1** a rascal; a villain. **2** a youngster. [Ir. *spailpín*, of unkn. orig.]

Spam /spam/ *n. propr.* a canned meat product made mainly from ham. [*spiced ham*]

span[1] /span/ *n. & v.* ● *n.* **1** the full extent from end to end in space or time (*the span of a bridge; the whole span of history*). **2** each arch or part of a bridge between piers or supports. **3** the maximum lateral extent of an airplane, its wing, a bird's wing, etc. **4 a** the maximum distance between the tips of the thumb and little finger. **b** this as a measurement, equal to 9 inches. **5** a short distance or time (*our life is but a span*). ● *v.* (**spanned, spanning**) **1** *tr.* **a** (of a bridge, arch, etc.) stretch from side to side of; extend across (*the bridge spanned the river*). **b** (of a builder, etc.) bridge (a river, etc.). **2** *tr.* extend across (space or a period of time, etc.). **3** *tr.* measure or cover the extent of (a thing) with one's hand with the fingers stretched (*spanned a tenth on the piano*). □ **span roof** a roof with two inclined sides (opp. PENTHOUSE 2, *lean-to* (see LEAN¹)). [OE *span(n)* or OF *espan*]

■ *n.* **1** extent, reach, spread, sweep, breadth, width; course, interval, stretch, duration, period, time. **5** see SPELL³ *n.* 1. ● *v.* **1, 2** cross, stretch over or across, reach over or across, extend over or across, go over or across, bridge, straddle.

span[2] /span/ *n.* **1** *Naut.* a rope with both ends fastened to take purchase in a loop. **2** a matched pair of horses, mules, etc. **3** *S.Afr.* a team of two or more pairs of oxen. [LG & Du. *span* f. *spannen* unite]

span[3] see SPICK-AND-SPAN.

span[4] /span/ *archaic past* of SPIN.

spandrel /spándril/ *n. Archit.* **1** the almost triangular space between one side of the outer curve of an arch, a wall, and the ceiling or framework. **2** the space between the shoulders of adjoining arches and the ceiling or molding above. □ **spandrel wall** a wall built on the curve of an arch, filling in the spandrel. [perh. f. AF *spaund(e)re*, or f. *espaundre* EXPAND]

spang /spang/ *adv. colloq.* exactly; completely (*spang in the middle*). [20th c.: orig. unkn.]

■ see SLAP *adv.*

spangle /spánggǝl/ *n. & v.* ● *n.* **1** a small thin piece of glittering material esp. used in quantity to ornament a dress, etc.; a sequin. **2** a small sparkling object. **3** (in full **spangle gall**) a spongy excrescence on oak-leaves. ● *v.tr.* (esp. as **spangled** *adj.*) cover with or as with spangles (*spangled costume*). □□ **spangly** /spángglee/ *adj.* [ME f. *spang* f. MDu. *spange*, OHG *spanga*, ON *spöng* brooch f. Gmc]

Spaniard /spányǝrd/ *n.* **1 a** a native or inhabitant of Spain in southern Europe. **b** a person of Spanish descent. **2** *NZ* a spear grass. [ME f. OF *Espaignart* f. *Espaigne* Spain]

spaniel /spányǝl/ *n.* **1 a** a dog of any of various breeds with a long silky coat and drooping ears. **b** any of these breeds. **2** an obsequious or fawning person. [ME f. OF *espaigneul* Spanish (dog) f. Rmc *Hispaniolus* (unrecorded) f. *Hispania* Spain]

■ **2** see YES-MAN.

/.../ **pronunciation**   ● **part of speech**
□ **phrases, idioms, and compounds**
□□ **derivatives**   ■ **synonym section**
cross-references appear in SMALL CAPITALS or *italics*

Spanish /spánish/ *adj. & n.* ● *adj.* of or relating to Spain or its people or language. ● *n.* **1** the language of Spain and Spanish America. **2** (prec. by *the*; treated as *pl.*) the people of Spain. □ **Spanish America** those parts of America orig. settled by Spaniards, including Central and South America and part of the West Indies. **Spanish Armada** *hist.* the Spanish war fleet sent against England in 1588. **Spanish bayonet** a yucca, *Yucca aloifolia*, with stiff sharp-pointed leaves. **Spanish chestnut** = CHESTNUT *n.* 1b. **Spanish fly** a bright green beetle, *Lytta vesicatoria*, formerly dried and used for raising blisters, as a supposed aphrodisiac, etc. **Spanish guitar** the standard six-stringed acoustic guitar, used esp. for classical and folk music. **Spanish mackerel** any of various large mackerels, esp. *Scomberomorus colias* or *S. maculatus*. **Spanish Main** *hist.* the NE coast of South America between the Orinoco River and Panama, and adjoining parts of the Caribbean Sea. **Spanish moss** an epiphytic plant, *Tillandsia usneoides*, common in the southern US, with grayish-green fronds that hang from the branches of trees. **Spanish omelet** an omelet served with a sauce of tomatoes, onions, and green peppers. **Spanish onion** a large mild-flavored onion. **Spanish rice** rice cooked with chopped onions, peppers, tomatoes, spices, etc. [ME f. *Spain*, with shortening of the first element]

spank /spangk/ *v. & n.* ● *v.* **1** *tr.* slap, esp. on the buttocks, with the open hand. **2** *intr.* (of a horse, etc.) move briskly, esp. between a trot and a gallop. ● *n.* a slap, esp. with the open hand on the buttocks. [perh. imit.]
  ■ *v.* **1** slap, smack, put *or* take over one's knee, thrash, hit, paddle, *colloq.* whack, give a person a (good) licking *or* hiding, *sl.* wallop, tan (a person's hide). ● *n.* see SLAP *n.*

spanker /spángkər/ *n.* **1** a person or thing that spanks. **2** *Naut.* a fore-and-aft sail set on the after side of the mizzenmast. **3** a fast horse. **4** *colloq.* a person or thing of notable size or quality.

spanking /spángking/ *adj., adv., & n.* ● *adj.* **1** (esp. of a horse) moving quickly; lively; brisk (*at a spanking trot*). **2** *colloq.* striking; excellent. ● *adv. colloq.* very; exceedingly (*spanking clean*). ● *n.* the act or an instance of slapping, esp. on the buttocks as a punishment for children.
  ■ *adj.* **1** quick, rapid, swift, lively, fast, smart, energetic, vigorous, brisk, *colloq.* snappy; crisp, bracing, fresh, freshening, rattling, strong, stiff. **2** see EXCELLENT. ● *adv.* see EXCEEDINGLY 1. ● *n.* see WHIPPING 1.

spanner /spánər/ *n.* **1** the crossbrace of a bridge, etc. **2** *Brit.* an instrument for turning or gripping a nut on a screw, etc. (cf. WRENCH). □ **a spanner in the works** *Brit. colloq.* a drawback or impediment. [G *spannen* draw tight: see SPAN²]

spar¹ /spaar/ *n.* **1** a stout pole esp. used for the mast, yard, etc., of a ship. **2** the main longitudinal beam of an airplane wing. □ **spar buoy** a buoy made of a spar with one end moored so that the other stands up. **spar deck** the light upper deck of a vessel. [ME *sparre*, *sperre* f. OF *esparre* or ON *sperra* or direct f. Gmc: cf. MDu., MLG *sparre*, OS, OHG *sparro*]
  ■ **1** mast, yard, yardarm, boom, gaff, jigger(mast), mizzen, pole, *Naut. sl.* stick.

spar² /spaar/ *v. & n.* ● *v.intr.* (**sparred**, **sparring**) **1** (often foll. by *at*) make the motions of boxing without landing heavy blows. **2** engage in argument (*they are always sparring*). **3** (of a gamecock) fight with the feet or spurs. ● *n.* **1 a** a sparring motion. **b** a boxing match. **2** a cockfight. **3** an argument or dispute. □ **sparring partner 1** a boxer employed to engage in sparring with another as training. **2** a person with whom one enjoys arguing. [ME f. OE *sperran*, *spyrran*, of unkn. orig.: cf. ON *sperrask* kick out]
  ■ *v.* **1** fight, box, exchange blows; shadowbox. **2** dispute, argue, quarrel, bicker, squabble, wrangle, bandy words, have words; fight, *colloq.* scrap. ● *n.* **3** see ARGUMENT 1.

spar³ /spaar/ *n.* any crystalline, easily cleavable, and non-lustrous mineral, e.g., calcite or fluorspar. □□ **sparry** *adj.* [MLG, rel. to OE *spæren* of plaster, *spærstān* gypsum]

spare /spair/ *adj., n., & v.* ● *adj.* **1 a** not required for ordinary use; extra (*have no spare cash*; *spare time*). **b** reserved for emergency or occasional use (*slept in the spare room*). **2** lean; thin. **3** scanty; frugal; not copious (*a spare diet*; *a spare prose style*). **4** *colloq.* not wanted or used by others (*a spare seat in the front row*). ● *n.* **1** a spare part; a duplicate. **2** *Bowling* the knocking down of all the pins with the first two balls. ● *v.* **1** *tr.* afford to give or do without; dispense with (*cannot spare him just now*; *can spare you a couple*). **2** *tr.* **a** abstain from killing, hurting, wounding, etc. (*spared his feelings*; *spared her life*). **b** abstain from inflicting or causing; relieve from (*spare me this talk*; *spare my blushes*). **3** *tr.* be frugal or grudging of (*no expense spared*). **4** *intr. archaic* be frugal. □ **go spare** *Brit. colloq.* **1** become extremely angry or distraught. **2** be unwanted by others. **not spare oneself** exert one's utmost efforts. **spare part** a duplicate part to replace a lost or damaged part of a machine, etc. **spare tire 1** an extra tire carried in a motor vehicle for emergencies. **2** *colloq.* a roll of fat round the waist. **to spare** left over; additional (*an hour to spare*). □□ **sparely** *adv.* **spareness** *n.* **sparer** *n.* [OE *spær*, *sparian* f. Gmc]
  ■ *adj.* **1** extra, surplus, excess, supernumerary, auxiliary, supplementary, additional; odd, left over; unoccupied, leisure, free; in reserve, in addition. **2** thin, lean, skinny, scrawny, cadaverous, gaunt, rawboned, meager, gangling, lank(y), wiry, slim, slender; all skin and bones. **3** meager, small, skimpy, modest, scanty; frugal, economical, mean, sparing; plain, sparse, stark, austere, clean. **4** unoccupied, free, unused, unwanted, unneeded, not spoken for. ● *v.* **1** allow, relinquish, let go (of), give, award, bestow, afford, let a person have, donate, part with, yield, dispense with, manage *or* do without, forgo, forsake, surrender, give up, sacrifice. **2 a** pardon, let go, release, have mercy on, let off, free, liberate. **b** save from, rescue from, deliver from, redeem from; relieve from, exempt from. □ **spare tire 2** see STOMACH *n.* 2b. □□ **sparely** see SIMPLY 1.
  spareness plainness, cleanness, severity, starkness, austerity.

spareribs /spáir-ribs/ *n.* closely trimmed ribs of esp. pork. [prob. f. MLG *ribbesper*, by transposition and assoc. with SPARE]

sparge /spaarj/ *v.tr.* moisten by sprinkling, esp. in brewing. □□ **sparger** *n.* [app. f. L *spargere* sprinkle]

sparing /spáiring/ *adj.* **1** inclined to save; economical. **2** restrained; limited. □□ **sparingly** *adv.* **sparingness** *n.*
  ■ **1** thrifty, saving, frugal, spare, careful, prudent, parsimonious, economical; penurious, mean, penny-pinching, stingy, niggardly, miserly, close, closefisted, cheap, *colloq.* tight, tightfisted, mingy. **2** sparse, meager, scant, little, limited, restrained, inappreciable, not much, insignificant. □□ **sparingness** see THRIFT.

spark¹ /spaark/ *n. & v.* ● *n.* **1** a fiery particle thrown off from a fire, or remaining lit in ashes, or produced by a flint, match, etc. **2** (often foll. by *of*) a particle of a quality, etc. (*not a spark of life*; *a spark of interest*). **3** *Electr.* **a** a light produced by a sudden disruptive discharge through the air, etc. **b** such a discharge serving to ignite the explosive mixture in an internal combustion engine. **4 a** a flash of wit, etc. **b** anything causing interest, excitement, etc. **c** a witty or lively person. **5** a small bright object or point, e.g., in a gem. **6** (**Sparks**) a nickname for a radio operator or an electrician. ● *v.* **1** *intr.* emit sparks of fire or electricity. **2** *tr.* (often foll. by *off*) stir into activity; initiate (a process) suddenly. **3** *intr. Electr.* produce sparks at the point where a circuit is interrupted. □ **spark chamber** an apparatus designed to show ionizing particles. **spark gap** the space between electric terminals where sparks occur. **sparking plug** *Brit.* = spark plug. **spark plug** a device for firing the explosive mixture in an internal combustion engine. □□ **sparkless** *adj.* **sparky** *adj.* [ME f. OE *spærca*, *spearca*]
  ■ *n.* **2** scintilla, flicker, glimmer, glint, sparkle, speck, hint, suggestion, vestige, atom, particle, whit, jot (or tittle), iota. **3** see FLASH *n.* 1. ● *v.* **1** see FLASH *v.* 2. **2** set *or* touch off, ignite, kindle, electrify, animate, trigger, energize, galvanize, activate, excite, inspire,

inspirit, stimulate, *literary* enkindle; set in motion, bring about, start (up), begin, initiate, provoke, precipitate.

spark² /spaark/ *n.* & *v.* ● *n.* **1** a lively young fellow. **2** a gallant; a beau. ● *v.intr.* play the gallant. □□ **sparkish** *adj.* [prob. a fig. use of SPARK¹]

sparkle /spaárkəl/ *v.* & *n.* ● *v.intr.* **1 a** emit or seem to emit sparks; glitter; glisten (*her eyes sparkled*). **b** be witty; scintillate (*sparkling repartee*). **2** (of wine, etc.) effervesce (cf. STILL¹ *adj.* 4). ● *n.* **1** a gleam or spark. **2** vivacity; liveliness. □□ **sparkly** *adj.* [ME f. SPARK¹ + -LE⁴]
■ *v.* **1 a** glitter, glisten, scintillate, glint, gleam, flicker, shine, twinkle, wink, blink, glimmer, flash, coruscate, blaze, burn, flame. **b** scintillate, dazzle. **2** effervesce, fizz, bubble. ● *n.* **1** glitter, scintillation, twinkle, coruscation, dazzle, spark, gleam, brightness, brilliance, radiance. **2** vivacity, liveliness, fire, brightness, wittiness, effervescence, ebullience, excitement, animation, vigor, energy, spirit, cheer, joy, lightheartedness, élan, zeal, zip, gusto, dash, life, gaiety, cheer, cheerfulness, *colloq.* vim, zing, *sl.* pizzazz, oomph.

sparkler /spaárklər/ *n.* **1** a person or thing that sparkles. **2** a handheld sparkling firework. **3** *colloq.* a diamond or other gem.
■ **3** see JEWEL *n.* 1a.

sparling /spaárling/ *n.* a European smelt, *Osmerus eperlanus.* [ME f. OF *esperlinge,* of Gmc orig.]

sparoid /spároyd/ *n.* & *adj.* ● *n.* any marine fish of the family Sparidae, e.g., a porgy. ● *adj.* of or concerning the Sparidae. [mod.L *Sparoides* f. L *sparus* f. Gk *sparos* sea bream]

sparrow /spárō/ *n.* **1** any small brownish gray bird of the genus *Passer,* esp. the house sparrow and tree sparrow. **2** any of various birds of similar appearance such as the hedge sparrow. [OE *spearwa* f. Gmc]

sparrowgrass /spárōgras/ *n. dial.* or *colloq.* asparagus.

sparrowhawk /spárōhawk/ *n.* a small hawk, *Accipiter nisus,* that preys on small birds.

sparse /spaars/ *adj.* thinly dispersed or scattered; not dense (*sparse population; sparse graying hair*). □□ **sparsely** *adv.* **sparseness** *n.* **sparsity** *n.* [L *sparsus* past part. of *spargere* scatter]
■ thin (on the ground), few (and far between), meager, scanty, (thinly *or* widely) dispersed, (thinly *or* widely) scattered, spread out, in short supply, scarce. □□ **sparseness, sparsity** see DEARTH.

Spartan /spaárt'n/ *adj.* & *n.* ● *adj.* **1** of or relating to Sparta in ancient Greece. **2 a** possessing the qualities of courage, endurance, stern frugality, etc., associated with Sparta. **b** (of a regime, conditions, etc.) lacking comfort; austere. ● *n.* a citizen of Sparta. [ME f. L *Spartanus* f. *Sparta* f. Gk *Sparta,* -*tē*]
■ *adj.* **2** austere, strict, severe, harsh, hard, stern, rigorous, rigid, simple, plain, frugal, ascetic, stringent, controlled, disciplined, self-denying, abstinent, abstemious.

spartina /spaarteénə/ *n.* any grass of the genus *Spartina,* with rhizomatous roots and growing in wet or marshy ground. [Gk *spartinē* rope]

spasm /spázəm/ *n.* **1** a sudden involuntary muscular contraction. **2** a sudden convulsive movement or emotion, etc. (*a spasm of coughing*). **3** (usu. foll. by *of*) *colloq.* a brief spell of an activity. [ME f. OF *spasme* or L *spasmus* f. Gk *spasmos, spasma* f. *spaō* pull]
■ **1** convulsion, throe, fit, twitch, tic, paroxysm, shudder. **2** fit, seizure, convulsion, paroxysm, outburst, attack. **3** spell, burst, eruption, spurt.

spasmodic /spazmódik/ *adj.* **1** of, caused by, or subject to, a spasm or spasms (*a spasmodic jerk; spasmodic asthma*). **2** occurring or done by fits and starts (*spasmodic efforts*). □□ **spasmodically** *adv.* [mod.L *spasmodicus* f. Gk *spasmōdēs* (as SPASM)]
■ **1** paroxysmal, convulsive, jerky, jerking, sudden, *Med.* spastic. **2** fitful, irregular, intermittent, random, interrupted, sporadic, erratic, occasional, periodic,

unsustained, discontinuous, pulsating, cyclic(al), broken. □□ **spasmodically** see *by fits and starts* (FIT²).

spastic /spástik/ *adj.* & *n.* ● *adj.* **1** *Med.* suffering from a spasm or spasms of the muscles. **2** *sl. offens.* weak; feeble; incompetent. **3** spasmodic. ● *n. Med. offens.* a person suffering from cerebral palsy. □□ **spastically** *adv.* **spasticity** /-tísitee/ *n.* [L *spasticus* f. Gk *spastikos* pulling f. *spaō* pull]
■ *adj.* **3** see SPASMODIC 1.

spat¹ *past* and *past part.* of SPIT¹.

spat² /spat/ *n.* **1** (usu. in *pl.*) *hist.* a short cloth gaiter protecting the shoe from mud, etc. **2** a cover for an aircraft wheel. [abbr. of SPATTERDASH]

spat³ /spat/ *n.* & *v. colloq.* ● *n.* **1** a petty quarrel. **2** a slight amount. ● *v.intr.* (**spatted, spatting**) quarrel pettily. [prob. imit.]
■ *n.* **1** see QUARREL¹ *n.* 1. ● *v.* see ARGUE 1.

spat⁴ /spat/ *n.* & *v.* ● *n.* the spawn of shellfish, esp. the oyster. ● *v.* (**spatted, spatting**) **1** *intr.* (of an oyster) spawn. **2** *tr.* shed (spawn). [AF, of unkn. orig.]

spatchcock /spáchkok/ *n.* & *v.* ● *n.* a chicken or esp. game bird split open and grilled. ● *v.tr.* **1** treat (poultry) in this way. **2** esp. *Brit. colloq.* insert or interpolate (a phrase, sentence, story, etc.) esp. incongruously. [orig. in Ir. use, expl. by Grose (1785) as f. *dispatch-cock,* but cf. SPITCHCOCK]

spate /spayt/ *n.* **1** a river flood (*the river is in spate*). **2** a large or excessive amount (*a spate of inquiries*). [ME, Sc. & North Engl.: orig. unkn.]
■ **1** flood, inundation, deluge, torrent. **2** flood, inundation, onrush, rush, deluge, torrent.

spathe /spayth/ *n. Bot.* a large bract or pair of bracts enveloping a spadix or flower cluster. □□ **spathaceous** /spəthǽyshəs/ *adj.* [L f. Gk *spathē* broad blade, etc.]

spathic /spáthik/ *adj.* (of a mineral) like spar (see SPAR³), esp. in cleavage. □ **spathic iron ore** = SIDERITE. □□ **spathose** *adj.* [*spath* spar f. G *Spath*]

spatial /spáyshəl/ *adj.* (also **spacial**) of or concerning space (*spatial extent*). □□ **spatiality** /-sheeálitee/ *n.* **spatialize** *v.tr.* **spatially** *adv.* [L *spatium* space]

spatiotemporal /spáysheeōtémpərəl/ *adj. Physics* & *Philos.* belonging to both space and time or to space-time. □□ **spatiotemporally** *adv.* [formed as SPATIAL + TEMPORAL]

spatter /spátər/ *v.* & *n.* ● *v.* **1** *tr.* **a** (often foll. by *with*) splash (a person, etc.) (*spattered him with mud*). **b** scatter or splash (liquid, mud, etc.) here and there. **2** *intr.* (of rain, etc.) fall here and there (*glass spattered down*). **3** *tr.* slander (a person's honor, etc.). ● *n.* **1** (usu. foll. by *of*) a splash (*a spatter of mud*). **2** a quick pattering sound. [frequent. f. base as in Du., LG *spatten* burst, spout]
■ *v.* **1 a** splash, speckle, pepper, bespatter, spray, shower, scatter, dabble, daub, bedaub, sprinkle, besprinkle, splatter, *colloq.* splotch, *Brit. colloq.* splodge. **b** splash, bespatter, spray, shower, scatter, daub, sprinkle, splatter. **2** see FALL *v.* 1. ● *n.* **1** see SPLASH *n.* 2, 3. **2** see PATTER¹ *n.*

spatterdash /spátərdash/ *n.* **1** (usu. in *pl.*) *hist.* a cloth or other legging to protect the stockings, etc., from mud, etc. **2** = ROUGHCAST.

spatula /spáchələ/ *n.* **1** a broad-bladed flat implement used for spreading, lifting, stirring, mixing (food), etc. **2** *Brit.* = *tongue depressor.* [L, var. of *spathula,* dimin. of *spatha* SPATHE]

spatulate /spáchələt/ *adj.* **1** spatula shaped. **2** (esp. of a leaf) having a broad rounded end. [SPATULA]

spavin /spávin/ *n. Vet.* a disease of a horse's hock with a hard bony tumor or excrescence. □ **blood** (or **bog**) **spavin** a distension of the joint by effusion of lymph or fluid. **bone spavin** a deposit of bony substance uniting the bones. □□ **spavined** *adj.* [ME f. OF *espavin,* var. of *esparvain* f. Gmc]

/.../ **pronunciation**	● **part of speech**
□ **phrases, idioms, and compounds**	
□□ **derivatives**	■ **synonym section**
cross-references appear in SMALL CAPITALS or *italics*	

spawn /spawn/ *v.* & *n.* ● *v.* **1** *tr.* (also *absol.*) (of a fish, frog, mollusk, or crustacean) produce (eggs). **b** *intr.* be produced as eggs or young. **2** *tr. derog.* or *colloq.* (of people) produce (offspring). **3** *tr.* produce or generate, esp. in large numbers. ● *n.* **1** the eggs of fish, frogs, etc. **2** *derog.* human or other offspring. **3** a white fibrous matter from which fungi are produced; mycelium. □□ **spawner** *n.* [ME f. AF *espaundre* shed roe, OF *espandre* EXPAND]

■ *v.* **1a** produce, yield, bear. **2** give birth to, bring forth, breed, create, father, sire, *literary* beget. **3** generate, give rise to, bring about, produce, cause, give birth to, bring forth, breed, beget, create, father, sire, *archaic* engender, *literary* beget. ● *n.* **2** see ISSUE *n.* 5.

spay /spay/ *v.tr.* sterilize (a female animal) by removing the ovaries. [ME f. AF *espeier*, OF *espeer* cut with a sword f. *espee* sword f. L *spatha*: see SPATHE]

■ see STERILIZE 2.

SPCA *abbr.* Society for the Prevention of Cruelty to Animals.

speak /speek/ *v.* (*past* **spoke** /spōk/; *past part.* **spoken** /spṓkən/) **1** *intr.* make articulate verbal utterances in an ordinary (not singing) voice. **2** *tr.* **a** utter (words). **b** make known or communicate (one's opinion, the truth, etc.) in this way (*never speaks sense*). **3** *intr.* **a** (foll. by *to, with*) hold a conversation (*spoke to him for an hour; spoke with them about their work*). **b** (foll. by *of*) mention in writing, etc. (*speaks of it in her novel*). **c** (foll. by *for*) articulate the feelings of (another person, etc.) in speech or writing (*speaks for our generation*). **4** *intr.* (foll. by *to*) **a** address; converse with (a person, etc.). **b** speak in confirmation of or with reference to (*spoke to the resolution; can speak to his innocence*). **c** *colloq.* reprove (*spoke to them about their lateness*). **5** *intr.* make a speech before an audience, etc. (*spoke for an hour on the topic; has a good speaking voice*). **6** *tr.* use or be able to use (a specified language) (*cannot speak French*). **7** *intr.* (of a gun, a musical instrument, etc.) make a sound. **8** *intr.* (usu. foll. by *to*) *poet.* communicate feeling, etc.; affect; touch (*the sunset spoke to her*). **9** *intr.* (of a hound) bark. **10** *tr.* hail and hold communication with (a ship). **11** *tr. archaic* **a** (of conduct, etc.) show (a person) to be (*his conduct speaks him generous*). **b** be evidence of (*the loud laugh speaks the vacant mind*). □ **not** (or **nothing**) **to speak of** not (or nothing) worth mentioning; practically not (or nothing). **speak for itself** need no supporting evidence. **speak for oneself 1** give one's own opinions. **2** not presume to speak for others. **speak one's mind** speak bluntly or frankly. **speak out** speak loudly or freely; give one's opinion. **speak up** = *speak out.* **speak volumes** (of a fact, etc.) be very significant. **speak volumes** (or **well**, etc.) **for 1** be abundant evidence of. **2** place in a favorable light. □□ **speakable** *adj.* [OE *sprecan*, later *specan*]

■ **1** talk, converse, discourse, vocalize. **2** express, utter, talk, say, state, tell, pronounce, enunciate, voice, vocalize, mouth; articulate, make known, communicate, reveal, indicate, verbalize. **3 a** (*speak to* or *with*) talk to or with, converse or discourse with, communicate with, address, say something to, chat to or with. **b** (*speak of*) mention, allude to, refer to, make reference to, comment on, speak or talk about, *literary* advert to. **c** (*speak for*) act in or for. **4** (*speak to*) **a** accost, address, talk to; apostrophize. **b** see SPEAK 5 below, VOUCH. **c** reprove, scold, talk to, reprimand, rebuke, admonish, warn, lecture. **5** (*speak on* or *about*) discuss, address, discourse upon or on, lecture on, talk about, treat (of), deal with, examine, touch upon or on. **6** talk, communicate in, discourse in, converse in, utter in, articulate in, use. **8** (*speak to*) be meaningful to, appeal to, influence, affect, touch. **11 b** bespeak, show to be; symbolize, betoken, signify, communicate, convey, indicate. □ **speak for itself** be self-evident, be obvious, be significant. **speak one's mind** talk freely or unreservedly, express one's opinion, speak out or up, declare, pipe up, come out with it, state one's position, voice one's thoughts, take a stand. **speak out, speak**

up talk (more) loudly or clearly, make oneself heard, raise one's voice; see also *speak one's mind* above.

speakeasy /speékeezee/ *n.* (*pl.* **-ies**) an illicit liquor store or drinking club during Prohibition in the US.

speaker /speékər/ *n.* **1** a person who speaks, esp. in public. **2** a person who speaks a specified language (esp. in *comb.*: *a French speaker*). **3** (**Speaker**) the presiding officer in a legislative assembly, esp. the House of Representatives (in the US) or the House of Commons (in the UK). **4** = LOUD-SPEAKER. □□ **speakership** *n.*

■ **1** orator, lecturer, speechmaker, talker, preacher; spokesperson, spokesman, spokeswoman; rabble-rouser, demagogue, *colloq.* tub-thumper, *sl.* spieler.

speakerphone /speékərfōn/ *n.* a telephone equipped with a microphone and loudspeaker, allowing it to be used without picking up the handset.

speaking /speéking/ *n.* & *adj.* ● *n.* the act or an instance of uttering words, etc. ● *adj.* **1** that speaks; capable of articulate speech. **2** (of a portrait) lifelike; true to its subject (*a speaking likeness*). **3** (in *comb.*) speaking or capable of speaking a specified foreign language (*French-speaking*). **4** with a reference or from a point of view specified (*roughly speaking; professionally speaking*). □ **on speaking terms** (foll. by *with*) **1** slightly acquainted. **2** on friendly terms. **speaking acquaintance 1** a person one knows slightly. **2** this degree of familiarity. **speaking tube** a tube for conveying the voice from one room, building, etc., to another.

■ *n.* see SPEECH 1. □ **on speaking terms 1** (*be on speaking terms with*) see *be acquainted with* (ACQUAINT).

spear /speer/ *n.* & *v.* ● *n.* **1** a thrusting or throwing weapon with a pointed usu. steel tip and a long shaft. **2** a similar barbed instrument used for catching fish, etc. **3** *archaic* a spearman. **4** a pointed stem of asparagus, etc. ● *v.tr.* **1** pierce or strike with or as if with a spear (*speared an olive*). **2** catch (a baseball, etc.) with a thrusting motion. □ **spear gun** a gun used to propel a spear in underwater fishing. **spear side** the male side of a family. [OE *spere*]

■ *n.* **1, 2** see LANCE *n.* ● *v.* **1** see PIERCE 1a, b.

spearhead /speérhed/ *n.* & *v.* ● *n.* **1** the point of a spear. **2** an individual or group chosen to lead a thrust or attack. ● *v.tr.* act as the spearhead of (an attack, etc.).

■ *n.* **2** vanguard, advance guard, van, forefront, front line, cutting edge, leader(s), pioneer(s), trailblazer(s). ● *v.* **1** launch, initiate, lead (the way in), take the initiative in, pioneer, blaze the trail for, take the lead in, be in the van or vanguard or forefront of.

spearman /speérmən/ *n.* (*pl.* **-men**) *archaic* a person, esp. a soldier, who uses a spear.

spearmint /speérmint/ *n.* a common garden mint, *Mentha spicata*, used in cooking and to flavor chewing gum.

spearwort /speérwərt,-wawrt/ *n.* an aquatic plant, *Ranunculus lingua*, with thick hollow stems, long narrow spear-shaped leaves, and yellow flowers.

spec¹ /spek/ *n. colloq.* a commercial speculation or venture. □ **on spec** in the hope of success; as a gamble; on the off chance. [abbr. of SPECULATION]

spec² /spek/ *n. colloq.* a detailed working description; a specification. [abbr. of SPECIFICATION]

special /spéshəl/ *adj.* & *n.* ● *adj.* **1 a** particularly good; exceptional; out of the ordinary (*bought them a special present; today is a special day; took special trouble*). **b** peculiar; specific; not general (*lacks the special qualities required; the word has a special sense*). **2** for a particular purpose (*sent on a special assignment*). **3** in which a person specializes (*statistics is his special field*). **4** denoting education for children with particular needs, e.g., the handicapped. ● *n.* a special person or thing, e.g., a special train, examination, edition of a newspaper, dish on a menu, etc. □ **Special Branch** (in the UK) a police department dealing with political security. **special case 1** a written statement of fact presented by litigants to a court. **2** an exceptional or unusual case. **special correspondent** a journalist writing for a newspaper on special events or a special area of interest. **special delivery** a delivery of mail in advance of the regular delivery. **special drawing rights** the right to purchase extra foreign currency from the International Monetary Fund. **special edition** an extra edition of a newspaper including later news than the ordinary edition. **special effects** movie or television illusions created by props, or camera work, or generated by computer. **Special Forces** U.S. Army personnel specially trained in guerrilla warfare. **special intention** see INTENTION. **special interest (group)** an organization, corporation, etc., that seeks advantage, usu. by lobbying for favorable legislation. **special jury** = *blue-ribbon jury*. **Special Olympics** a program modeled on the Olympics that features sports competitions for physically and mentally handicapped persons. **special pleading 1** *Law* pleading with reference to new facts in a case. **2** (in general use) a specious or unfair argument favoring the speaker's point of view. **special verdict** *Law* a verdict stating the facts as proved but leaving the court to draw conclusions from them. □□ **specially** *adv.* **specialness** *n.* [ME f. OF *especial* ESPECIAL or L *specialis* (as SPECIES)]

■ *adj.* **1 a** exceptional, uncommon, especial, rare, unusual, out of the ordinary, extraordinary, remarkable, inimitable; distinguished, notable, noteworthy, particularly good; significant, important, momentous, earthshaking, memorable, red-letter; gala, festive, celebratory; particular, extra, pointed, concerted, deliberate, determined. **b** specific, particular, different, unorthodox, unconventional, unique, precise, individual, singular, distinctive, specialized, certain, idiosyncratic, curious, peculiar, odd, strange, bizarre, weird, one of a kind. **2** exclusive, express, individual, tailor-made, specialized, specific. ● *n.* extra, *Brit. colloq.* one-off; see also SPECIALTY 1. □□ **specially** especially, particularly, custom-, expressly, exclusively, specifically.

specialist /spéshəlist/ *n.* (usu. foll. by *in*) **1** a person who is trained in a particular branch of a profession, esp. medicine (*a specialist in dermatology*). **2** a person who especially or exclusively studies a subject or a particular branch of a subject. □□ **specialism** *n.* **specialistic** /-lístik/ *adj.*

■ **1** consultant, expert. **2** expert, authority, professional, master, connoisseur, maestro, artiste, artist, adept.

speciality /spésheeálitee/ *n.* (*pl.* **-ies**) *Brit.* = SPECIALTY 1. [ME f. OF *especialité* or LL *specialitas* (as SPECIAL)]

specialize /spéshəliz/ *v.* **1** *intr.* (often foll. by *in*) **a** be or become a specialist (*specializes in optics*). **b** devote oneself to an area of interest, skill, etc. (*specializes in insulting people*). **2** *Biol.* **a** *tr.* (esp. in *passive*) adapt or set apart (an organ, etc.) for a particular purpose. **b** *intr.* (of an organ, etc.) become adapted, etc., in this way. **3** *tr.* make specific or individual. **4** *tr.* modify or limit (an idea, statement, etc.). □□ **specialization** *n.* [F *spécialiser* (as SPECIAL)]

■ **2, 4** see DIFFERENTIATE 3. □□ **specialization** see FIELD *n.* 8.

specialty /spéshəltee/ *n.* (*pl.* **-ies**) **1** a special pursuit, product, operation, etc., to which a company or a person gives special attention. **2** *Law* an instrument under seal; a sealed contract. [ME f. OF *(e)specialté* (as SPECIAL)]

■ **1** expertise, talent, genius, gift, skill, aptitude, trade, craft, accomplishment, ability, strength, forte, strong point, art, pièce de résistance, special, *Brit.* speciality; sphere, field, area, line, subject, concentration, specialization, métier, baby, *colloq.* thing, cup of tea, claim to fame, *sl.* bag.

speciation /spéesheeáyshən, spées-/ *n.* *Biol.* the formation of a new species in the course of evolution.

specie /spéeshee, -see/ *n.* coin money as opposed to paper money. [L, ablat. of SPECIES in phrase *in specie*]

■ see COIN *n.*

species /spéesheez, -seez/ *n.* (*pl.* same) **1** a class of things having some characteristics in common. **2** *Biol.* a category in the system of classification of living organisms consisting of similar individuals capable of exchanging genes or interbreeding. **3** a kind or sort. **4** *Logic* a group subordinate to a genus and containing individuals agreeing in some common attribute(s) and called by a common name. **5** *Law* a form or shape given to materials. **6** *Eccl.* the visible form of each

of the elements of consecrated bread and wine in the Eucharist. [L, = appearance, kind, beauty, f. *specere* look]

■ **2** breed, stock, strain. **3** see SORT *n.* 1.

specific /spisífik/ *adj.* & *n.* ● *adj.* **1** clearly defined; definite (*has no specific name*; *told me so in specific terms*). **2** relating to a particular subject; peculiar (*a style specific to that*). **3 a** of or concerning a species (*the specific name for a plant*). **b** possessing, or concerned with, the properties that characterize a species (*the specific forms of animals*). **4** (of a duty or a tax) assessed by quantity or amount, not by the value of goods. ● *n.* **1** *archaic* a specific medicine or remedy. **2** a specific aspect or factor (*shall we discuss specifics?*). □ **specific cause** the cause of a particular form of a disease. **specific difference** a factor that differentiates a species. **specific disease** a disease caused by one identifiable agent. **specific gravity** the ratio of the density of a substance to the density of a standard, as water for a liquid and air for a gas. **specific heat capacity** the heat required to raise the temperature of the unit mass of a given substance by a given amount (usu. one degree). **specific performance** *Law* the performance of a contractual duty, as ordered in cases where damages would not be adequate remedy. □□ **specifically** *adv.* **specificity** /spésifísitee/ *n.* **specificness** *n.* [LL *specificus* (as SPECIES)]

■ *adj.* **1** definite, precise, exact, particular, explicit, express, unambiguous, definitive, clear-cut, unequivocal, categorical, (well-)defined, determined, specified, certain, limited, indicated, predetermined, established, spelled out, delineated, set, distinct, fixed, circumscribed, restricted. **2** unique (to), typical (of), characteristic (of), peculiar (to), personal (to), discrete, distinctive (to), special (to), individual, *sui generis*, proper to, relating to, identified with, associated with. ● *n.* **1** see REMEDY *n.* 1. **2** see DETAIL *n.* 1.

specification /spésifikáyshən/ *n.* **1** the act or an instance of specifying; the state of being specified. **2** (esp. in *pl.*) a detailed description of the construction, workmanship, materials, etc., of work done or to be done, prepared by an architect, engineer, etc. **3** a description by an applicant for a patent of the construction and use of his invention. **4** *Law* the conversion of materials into a new product not held to be the property of the owner of the materials. [med.L *specificatio* (as SPECIFY)]

■ **1** identification, description, particularization, naming; requirement, qualification, stipulation, condition, restriction, consideration. **2** (*specifications*) itemization, list, listing, checklist, inventory, list of particulars, detail(s), enumeration, description.

specify /spésifí/ *v.tr.* (**-ies, -ied**) **1** (also *absol.*) name or mention expressly (*specified the type he needed*). **2** (usu. foll. by *that* + clause) name as a condition (*specified that he must be paid at once*). **3** include in specifications (*a French window was not specified*). □□ **specifiable** /-fíəbəl/ *adj.* **specifier** *n.* [ME f. OF *specifier* or LL *specificare* (as SPECIFIC)]

■ particularize, enumerate, itemize, name, denominate, be specific about, list, indicate, mention, identify, cite, define, detail, stipulate, spell out, set out *or* forth, individualize, disambiguate, delineate, determine, establish.

specimen /spésimən/ *n.* **1** an individual or part taken as an example of a class or whole, esp. when used for investigation or scientific examination (*specimens of copper ore*; *a specimen of your handwriting*). **2** *Med.* a sample of urine for testing. **3** *colloq.* a person of a specified sort. [L f. *specere* look]

■ **1** sample, example, instance, exemplar, representative, representation; illustration, case (in point), type, model, pattern.

speciology /spéeseeóləjee/ *n.* the scientific study of species or of their origin, etc. □□ **speciological** /-seeəlójikəl/ *adj.*

/.../ pronunciation   ● part of speech

□ phrases, idioms, and compounds

□□ derivatives   ■ synonym section

cross-references appear in SMALL CAPITALS or *italics*

....

specious /spéeshəs/ *adj.* **1** superficially plausible but actually wrong (*a specious argument*). **2** misleadingly attractive in appearance. □□ **speciosity** /-sheeósitee/ *n.* **speciously** *adv.* **speciousness** *n.* [ME, = beautiful, f. L *speciosus* (as SPE-CIES)]

■ **1** deceptive, superficial, casuistic, ostensible, misleading, fallacious, sophistic(al), plausible, likely. □□ **speciously** see *seemingly* (SEEMING[1]).

speck /spek/ *n.* & *v.* ● *n.* **1** a small spot, dot, or stain. **2** (foll. by *of*) a particle (*speck of dirt*). **3** a rotten spot in fruit. ● *v.tr.* (esp. as **specked** *adj.*) marked with specks. □□ **speckless** *adj.* [OE *specca*: cf. SPECKLE]

■ *n.* **1** see SPOT *n.* 1a, b. **2** spot, dot, fleck, mote, speckle, mark, bit, particle; crumb, iota, jot (or tittle), whit, atom, molecule, touch, hint, suggestion, suspicion, tinge, trace, modicum, amount, grain, *colloq.* smidgen. ● *v.* (**specked**) see *speckled* (SPECKLE *v.*).

speckle /spékəl/ *n.* & *v.* ● *n.* a small spot, mark, or stain, esp. in quantity on the skin, a bird's egg, etc. ● *v.tr.* (esp. as **speckled** *adj.*) mark with speckles or patches. [ME f. MDu. *spekkel*]

■ *n.* see SPOT *n.* 1a, b. ● *v.* (**speckled**) spotted, mottled, dotted, sprinkled, flecked, specked, stippled, dappled, freckled, brindled; discolored, spattered, bespattered, spotty.

specs /speks/ *n.pl. colloq.* a pair of eyeglasses. [abbr.]

spectacle /spéktəkəl/ *n.* **1** a public show, ceremony, etc. **2** anything attracting public attention (*a charming spectacle*; *a disgusting spectacle*). □ **make a spectacle of oneself** make oneself an object of ridicule. [ME f. OF f. L *spectaculum* f. *spectare* frequent. of *specere* look]

■ **1** show, display, performance, event, presentation, exhibition, exposition, demonstration, extravaganza, spectacular, ceremony. **2** sight, exhibit, exhibition, marvel, wonder, sensation, curiosity. □ **make a spectacle of oneself** make a fool *or* a laughingstock *or* an exhibition of oneself.

spectacled /spéktəkəld/ *adj.* **1** wearing spectacles. **2** (of an animal) having facial markings resembling spectacles. □ **spectacled bear** a S. American bear, *Tremarctos ornatus*. **spectacled cobra** the Indian cobra.

spectacles /spéktəkəlz/ *n.pl. Old-fashioned or jocular* eyeglasses.

spectacular /spektákyələr/ *adj.* & *n.* ● *adj.* **1** of or like a public show; striking; amazing; lavish. **2** strikingly large or obvious (*a spectacular increase in output*). ● *n.* an event intended to be spectacular, esp. a musical movie or play. □□ **spectacularly** *adv.* [SPECTACLE, after *oracular*, etc.]

■ *adj.* **1** see SENSATIONAL. ● *n.* see EXTRAVAGANZA 2. □□ **spectacularly** see FAMOUSLY 1.

spectate /spéktayt/ *v.intr.* be a spectator, esp. at a sporting event. [back-form. f. SPECTATOR]

spectator /spéktáytər/ *n.* a person who looks on at a show, game, incident, etc. □ **spectator sport** a sport attracting spectators rather than participants. □□ **spectatorial** /-tətáwreeəl/ *adj.* [F *spectateur* or L *spectator* f. *spectare*: see SPEC-TACLE]

■ witness, eyewitness, observer, viewer, onlooker, looker-on, watcher, beholder, bystander.

specter /spéktər/ *n.* (*Brit.* **spectre**) **1** a ghost. **2** a haunting presentiment or preoccupation (*the specter of war*). **3** (in *comb.*) used in the names of some animals because of their thinness, transparency, etc. (*specter bat*; *specter crab*). □ **Specter of the Brocken** a huge shadowy image of the observer projected on mists about a mountaintop (observed on the Brocken in Germany). [F *specter* or L *spectrum*: see SPECTRUM]

■ **1** ghost, phantom, wraith, apparition, vision, spirit, revenant, doppelgänger, chimera, bogeyman, poltergeist, *colloq.* spook, *literary* shade. **2** shadow, image, vision, (mental) picture; presentiment.

spectra *pl.* of SPECTRUM.

spectral /spéktrəl/ *adj.* **1 a** of or relating to specters or ghosts. **b** ghostlike. **2** of or concerning spectra or the spectrum (*spectral colors*; *spectral analysis*). □□ **spectrally** *adv.*

■ **1** ghostly, ghostlike, phantom, eerie, wraithlike, incorporeal, disembodied, unearthly, supernatural, weird, *colloq.* spooky.

spectro- /spéktrō/ *comb. form* a spectrum.

spectrochemistry /spéktrōkémistree/ *n.* chemistry based on the study of the spectra of substances.

spectrogram /spéktrəgram/ *n.* a record obtained with a spectrograph.

spectrograph /spéktrəgraf/ *n.* an apparatus for photographing or otherwise recording spectra. □□ **spectrographic** *adj.* **spectrographically** *adv.* **spectrography** /spektrógrəfee/ *n.*

spectroheliograph /spéktrōhéeleeəgraf/ *n.* an instrument for taking photographs of the sun in the light of one wavelength only.

spectrohelioscope /spéktrōhéeleeəskōp/ *n.* a device similar to a spectroheliograph, for visual observation.

spectrometer /spektrómitər/ *n.* an instrument used for the measurement of observed spectra. □□ **spectrometric** /spéktrəmétrik/ *adj.* **spectrometry** *n.* [G *Spektrometer* or F *spectromètre* (as SPECTRO-, -METER)]

spectrophotometer /spéktrōfōtómitər/ *n.* an instrument for measuring and recording the intensity of light in various parts of the spectrum. □□ **spectrophotometric** /-təmétrik/ *adj.* **spectrophotometry** *n.*

spectroscope /spéktrəskōp/ *n.* an instrument for producing and recording spectra for examination. □□ **spectroscopic** /-skópik/ *adj.* **spectroscopical** *adj.* **spectroscopist** /-tróskəpist/ *n.* **spectroscopy** /-tróskəpee/ *n.* [G *Spektroskop* or F *spectroscope* (as SPECTRO-, -SCOPE)]

spectrum /spéktrəm/ *n.* (*pl.* **spectra** /-trə/) **1** the band of colors, as seen in a rainbow, etc., arranged in a progressive series according to their refrangibility or wavelength. **2** the entire range of wavelengths of electromagnetic radiation. **3 a** an image or distribution of parts of electromagnetic radiation arranged in a progressive series according to wavelength. **b** this as characteristic of a body or substance when emitting or absorbing radiation. **4** a similar image or distribution of energy, mass, etc., arranged according to frequency, charge, etc. **5** the entire range or a wide range of anything arranged by degree or quality, etc. **6** (in full **ocular spectrum**) an afterimage. □ **spectrum** (or **spectral**) **analysis** chemical analysis by means of a spectroscope. [L, = image, apparition f. *specere* look]

■ **5** see GAMUT.

specula *pl.* of SPECULUM.

specular /spékyələr/ *adj.* **1** of or having the nature of a speculum. **2** reflecting. □ **specular iron ore** lustrous hematite. [L *specularis* (as SPECULUM)]

speculate /spékyəlayt/ *v.* **1** *intr.* (usu. foll. by *on, upon, about*) form a theory or conjecture, esp. without a firm factual basis; meditate (*speculated on their prospects*). **2** *tr.* (foll. by *that, how*, etc., + clause) conjecture; consider (*speculated how he might achieve it*). **3** *intr.* **a** invest in stocks, etc., in the hope of gain but with the possibility of loss. **b** gamble recklessly. □□ **speculator** *n.* [L *speculari* spy out, observe f. *specula* watchtower f. *specere* look]

■ **1, 2** reflect, meditate, cogitate, think, mull (over), chew on *or* over, ruminate, wonder, deliberate, surmise, theorize, conjecture, postulate, hypothesize, *literary* muse; ponder, contemplate; consider, weigh, judge. **3** gamble, wager, play the market, take a chance *or* risk, *colloq.* plunge, *Brit. sl.* have a flutter. □□ **speculator** see PUNTER 1.

speculation /spékyəláyshən/ *n.* **1** the act or an instance of speculating; a theory or conjecture (*made no speculation as to her age; is given to speculation*). **2 a** a speculative investment or enterprise (*bought it as a speculation*). **b** the practice of business speculating. [ME f. OF *speculation* or LL *speculatio* (as SPECULATE)]

■ **1** thinking, rumination, cogitation, reflection, meditation, contemplation, consideration, cerebration, pondering, wondering, deliberation, evaluation; conjecture, guess, hypothesis, theory, guesswork, postulation, surmise, supposition, opinion. **2** gamble, wager, esp. *Brit.* flutter; gambling, wagering, taking a chance *or* risk, chance-taking, risk-taking.

speculative /spékyələtiv, -lay-/ *adj.* **1** of, based on, engaged in, or inclined to speculation. **2** (of a business investment) involving the risk of loss (*a speculative builder*). □□ **speculatively** *adv.* **speculativeness** *n.* [ME f. OF *speculatif -ive* or LL *speculativus* (as SPECULATE)]

■ **1** intellectual, ideational, abstract, cogitative, notional, theoretical, hypothetical, conjectural, suppositional, supposititious, suppositious, suppositive, rational, ratiocinative, ideal, idealized, idealistic, unrealistic, unpractical, impractical, analytical; groundless, unfounded. **2** risky, hazardous, uncertain, unreliable, untrustworthy, doubtful, dubious, untested, unproven, unproved, chancy, *colloq.* iffy, esp. *Brit. colloq.* dodgy, *sl.* dicey.

speculum /spékyələm/ *n.* (*pl.* **specula** /-lə/) **1** *Surgery* an instrument for dilating the cavities of the human body for inspection. **2** a mirror, usu. of polished metal, esp. in a reflecting telescope. **3** *Ornithol.* a lustrous colored area on the wing of some birds, esp. ducks. □ **speculum metal** an alloy of copper and tin used as a mirror, esp. in a telescope. [L, = mirror, f. *specere* look]

■ **2** see MIRROR *n.* 1.

sped *past* and *past part.* of SPEED.

speech /speech/ *n.* **1** the faculty or act of speaking. **2** a usu. formal address or discourse delivered to an audience or assembly. **3** a manner of speaking (*a man of blunt speech*). **4** a remark (*after this speech he was silent*). **5** the language of a nation, region, group, etc. **6** *Mus.* the act of sounding in an organ pipe, etc. □ **the Queen's** (or **King's**) **Speech (in the UK)** a statement including the Government's proposed measures read by the sovereign at the opening of Parliament. **speech day** *Brit.* an annual prize-giving day in many schools, usu. marked by speeches, etc. **speech therapist** a person who practices speech therapy. **speech therapy** treatment to improve defective speech. □□ **speechful** *adj.* [OE *sprēc*, later *spēc* f. WG, rel. to SPEAK]

■ **1** communication, speaking, talking, language, articulation. **2** oration, address, lecture, talk, disquisition, sermon, homily, *literary* discourse; monologue, soliloquy, tirade, harangue, philippic; *colloq.* blast, song and dance, line, (sales) pitch; *sl.* spiel. **3** articulation, diction, expression, enunciation, elocution, speech pattern, speaking, talking. **5** dialect, idiolect, jargon, parlance, idiom, language, tongue, *colloq.* lingo.

speechify /speechifī/ *v.intr.* (**-ies**, **-ied**) *joc.* or *derog.* make esp. boring or long speeches. □□ **speechification** /-fikáyshən/ *n.* **speechifier** *n.*

■ see *hold forth* 2 (HOLD¹).

speechless /speechlis/ *adj.* **1** temporarily unable to speak because of emotion, etc. (*speechless with rage*). **2** mute. □□ **speechlessly** *adv.* **speechlessness** *n.* [OE *spǣclēas* (as SPEECH, -LESS)]

■ **1** dumbfounded, dumbstruck, wordless, silent, struck dumb, tongue-tied, thunderstruck, shocked, dazed, inarticulate, paralyzed, nonplussed. **2** mute, dumb, voiceless. □□ **speechlessly** see *silently* (SILENT). **speechlessness** see SILENCE *n.* 2, 3.

speed /speed/ *n.* & *v.* ● *n.* **1** rapidity of movement (*with all speed*; *at full speed*). **2** a rate of progress or motion over a distance in time (*attains a high speed*). **3** an arrangement of gears yielding a specific ratio in a bicycle or automobile transmission. **4** *Photog.* **a** the sensitivity of film to light. **b** the light-gathering power of a lens. **c** the duration of an exposure. **5** *sl.* an amphetamine drug, esp. methamphetamine. **6** *archaic* success; prosperity (*send me good speed*). ● *v.* (*past* and *past part.* **sped** /sped/) **1** *intr.* go fast (*sped down the street*). **2** (*past* and *past part.* **speeded**) **a** *intr.* (of a motorist, etc.) travel at an illegal or dangerous speed. **b** *tr.* regulate the speed of (an engine, etc.). **c** *tr.* cause (an engine, etc.) to go at a fixed speed. **3** *tr.* send fast or on its way (*speed an arrow from the bow*). **4** *intr.* & *tr. archaic* be or make prosperous or successful (*God speed you!*). □ **at speed** esp. *Brit.*

moving quickly. **speed bump** (or *Brit.* **hump**) a transverse ridge in the road to control the speed of vehicles. **speed limit** the maximum speed at which a road vehicle may legally be driven in a particular area, etc. **speed merchant** *colloq.* a motorist who enjoys driving fast. **speed up** move or work at greater speed. □□ **speeder** *n.* [OE *spēd*, *spēdan* f. Gmc]

■ *n.* **1** rapidity, quickness, speediness, swiftness, velocity, dispatch, hurry, hurriedness, haste, hastiness, alacrity, expeditiousness, expedition, briskness, promptness, timeliness, *archaic or literary* celerity, *poet. or literary* fleetness; suddenness, precipitousness, abruptness. **2** see PACE *n.* 2. ● *v.* **1** hasten, make haste, hurry, rush, charge, dart, bolt, shoot, run, race, sprint, fly, streak, scurry, tear, hustle, scramble, scamper, career, bowl along, rattle along, zip, zoom, go *or* fly like the wind, *colloq.* go hell(bent) for leather, go like a bat out of hell, step on it, step on the gas, put one's foot down, skedaddle, go like a shot, go like greased lightning, make tracks, hightail it, *sl.* belt along. **speed up** accelerate, hurry up, quicken, pick up speed, *colloq.* get a move on.

speedball /speedbawl/ *n. sl.* a mixture of cocaine with heroin or morphine.

speedboat /speedbōt/ *n.* a motor boat designed for high speed.

■ motorboat, powerboat.

speedo /speedō/ *n.* (*pl.* **-os**) *Brit. colloq.* = SPEEDOMETER. [abbr.]

speedometer /spidómitər/ *n.* an instrument on a motor vehicle, etc., indicating its speed to the driver. [SPEED + METER¹]

speedway /speedway/ *n.* **1 a** a road or track used for automobile racing. **b** a highway for high-speed travel. **2 a** motorcycle racing. **b** a stadium or track used for this.

speedwell /speedwel/ *n.* any small herb of the genus *Veronica*, with a creeping or ascending stem and tiny blue or pink flowers. [app. f. SPEED + WELL¹]

speedy /speedee/ *adj.* (**speedier**, **speediest**) **1** moving quickly; rapid. **2** done without delay; prompt (*a speedy answer*). □□ **speedily** *adv.* **speediness** *n.*

■ **1** nimble, wing-footed, winged, fast, quick, rapid, swift, brisk, *poet. or literary* fleet. **2** prompt, immediate, expeditious, quick, swift, rapid, hasty, precipitate, precipitous, hurried, summary, *colloq.* snappy. □□ **speedily** see *promptly* (PROMPT), *quickly* (QUICK). **speediness** see SPEED *n.* 1.

speiss /spīs/ *n.* a compound of arsenic, iron, etc., formed in smelting certain lead ores. [G *Speise* food, amalgam]

speleology /speeleeóləjee/ *n.* **1** the scientific study of caves. **2** the exploration of caves. □□ **speleological** /-leeəlójikəl/ *adj.* **speleologist** *n.* [F *spéléologie* f. L *spelaeum* f. Gk *spēlaion* cave]

■ **2** see CAVING.

spell¹ /spel/ *v.tr.* (*past* and *past part.* **spelled** or esp. *Brit.* **spelt**) **1** (also *absol.*) write or name the letters that form (a word, etc.) in correct sequence (*spell 'exaggerate'*; *cannot spell properly*). **2 a** (of letters) make up or form (a word, etc.). **b** (of circumstances, a scheme, etc.) result in; involve (*spell ruin*). □ **spell out 1** make out (words, writing, etc.) letter by letter. **2** explain in detail (*spelled out what the change would mean*). □□ **spellable** *adj.* [ME f. OF *espel(l)er*, f. Frank. (as SPELL²)]

■ **2 b** augur, portend, presage, promise, hold promise of, signify, point to, indicate, omen, bode, look like, amount to, mean, involve, result in. □ **spell out 2** specify, delineate, make clear *or* plain *or* explicit, clarify, elucidate, explain.

spell² /spel/ *n.* **1** a form of words used as a magical charm or incantation. **2** an attraction or fascination exercised by a person, activity, quality, etc. □ **under a spell** mastered by or as if by a spell. [OE *spel*(*l*) f. Gmc]

■ **1** incantation, formula, charm, conjuration. **2** attraction, lure, allure, appeal, draw, pull, magnetism, influence, mesmerism, hypnotic effect, enchantment, fascination, captivation, enthrallment, charm, magic, witchcraft, witchery.

spell³ /spel/ *n. & v.* ● *n.* **1** a short or fairly short period (*a cold spell in April*). **2** a turn of work (*did a spell of woodwork*). **3** *Austral.* a period of rest from work. ● *v.* **1** *tr.* **a** relieve or take the place of (a person) in work, etc. **b** allow to rest briefly. **2** *intr. Austral.* take a brief rest. [earlier as verb: later form of dial. *spele* take place of f. OE *spelian*, of unkn. orig.]

■ *n.* **1** period, interval, time, term, season; snap. **2** stint, turn, run, course, shift, tour (of duty), watch, round, stretch. ● *v.* **1** relieve, replace, substitute for, take over for or from.

spellbind /spélbind/ *v.tr.* (*past* and *past part.* **spellbound**) **1** bind with or as if with a spell; entrance. **2** (as **spellbound** *adj.*) entranced or fascinated, esp. by a speaker, activity, quality, etc. □□ **spellbinder** *n.* **spellbindingly** *adv.*

■ **1** bewitch, cast a spell on or over, charm, entrance, mesmerize, hypnotize; captivate, fascinate, enthrall, enchant, enrapture, overpower. **2** (**spellbound**) see RAPT 1. □□ **spellbinder** see *talker* (TALK).

speller /spélər/ *n.* **1** a person who spells, esp. in a specified way (*is a poor speller*). **2** a book on spelling.

spellican var. of SPILLIKIN.

spelling /spéling/ *n.* **1** the process or activity of writing or naming the letters of a word, etc. **2** the way a word is spelled. **3** the ability to spell (*his spelling is weak*). □ **spelling bee** a spelling competition.

spelt¹ esp. *Brit. past* and *past part.* of SPELL¹.

spelt² /spelt/ *n.* a species of wheat, *Triticum aestivum*. [OE f. OS *spelta* (OHG *spelza*), ME f. MLG, MDu. *spelte*]

spelter /spéltər/ *n.* impure zinc, esp. for commercial purposes. [corresp. to OF *espeautre*, MDu. *speauter*, G *Spialter*, rel. to PEWTER]

spelunker /spilúngkər, speélung-/ *n.* a person who explores caves, esp. as a hobby. □□ **spelunking** *n.* [obs. *spelunk* cave f. L *spelunca*]

spence /spens/ *n.* esp. *Brit. archaic* a pantry or larder. [ME f. OF *despense* f. L *dispensa* fem. past part. of *dispendere*: see DISPENSE]

spencer¹ /spénsər/ *n.* **1** a short close-fitting jacket. **2** esp. *Brit.* a woman's thin usu. woolen undershirt worn for extra warmth in winter. [prob. f. the 2nd Earl *Spencer*, Engl. politician d. 1834]

spencer² /spénsər/ *n. Naut.* a trysail. [perh. f. K. *Spencer* (early 19th c.)]

spend /spend/ *v.tr.* (*past* and *past part.* **spent** /spent/) **1** (usu. foll. by *on*) **a** (also *absol.*) pay out (money) in making a purchase, etc. (*spent $5 on a new pen*). **b** pay out (money) for a particular person's benefit or for the improvement of a thing (*had to spend $200 on the car*). **2 a** use or consume (time or energy) (*shall spend no more effort; how do you spend your Sundays?*). **b** (also *refl.*) use up; exhaust; wear out (*their ammunition was all spent; his anger was soon spent; spent herself campaigning for justice*). **3** *tr.* (as **spent** *adj.*) having lost its original force or strength; exhausted (*the storm is spent; spent bullets*). □ **spending money** pocket money. **spend a penny** *Brit. colloq.* urinate or defecate (from the coin-operated locks of public toilets). □□ **spendable** *adj.* **spender** *n.* [OE *spendan* f. L *expendere* (see EXPEND): in ME perh. also f. obs. *dispend* f. OF *despendre* expend f. L *dispendere*: see DISPENSE]

■ **1** pay out, disburse, expend, lay out, squander, throw away, fritter away, waste, lavish, dissipate, *colloq.* go through, shell out, splurge, *sl.* fork out, dish out, cough up, blow. **2 a** use, consume, devote, allot, assign, invest, put in, pass, occupy, fill, while away, fritter away. **b** use up, consume, expend, drain, deplete; exhaust, tire, fatigue, weary, prostrate, fag out, wear out, burn out, *colloq.* do in. **3** (**spent**) exhausted, used (up), emptied, gone, expended, finished, played out,

consumed, depleted; drained, prostrate, tired (out), fatigued, weary, wearied, worn out, dog-tired, burned-out, *colloq.* done in or up or for, all in, fagged (out), pooped, *sl.* (dead) beat. □□ **spender** see SPENDTHRIFT *n.*

spendthrift /spéndthrift/ *n. & adj.* ● *n.* an extravagant person; a prodigal. ● *adj.* extravagant; prodigal.

■ *n.* profligate, wastrel, waster, (big) spender, squanderer, prodigal. ● *adj.* wasteful, free-spending, prodigal, profligate, squandering, extravagant, improvident.

Spenserian /spenseéreeən/ *adj.* of, relating to, or in the style of Edmund Spenser, Engl. poet d. 1599. □ **Spenserian stanza** the stanza used by Spenser in the *Faerie Queene*, with eight iambic pentameters and an alexandrine, rhyming ababbcbcc. [E. *Spenser*]

spent *past* and *past part.* of SPEND.

sperm /spərm/ *n.* (*pl.* same or **sperms**) **1** = SPERMATOZOON. **2** the male reproductive fluid containing spermatozoa; semen. **3** = *sperm whale*. **4** = SPERMACETI. **5** = *sperm oil*. □ **sperm bank** a supply of semen stored for use in artificial insemination. **sperm count** the number of spermatozoa in one ejaculation or a measured amount of semen. **sperm oil** an oil obtained from the head of a sperm whale, and used as a lubricant. **sperm whale** a large whale, *Physeter macrocephalus*, hunted for the spermaceti and sperm oil contained in its bulbous head, and for the ambergris found in its intestines: also called CACHALOT. [ME f. LL *sperma* f. Gk *sperma* -*atos* seed f. *speirō* sow: in *sperm whale* an abbr. of SPERMACETI]

spermaceti /spə́rməsétee/ *n.* a white waxy substance produced by the sperm whale to aid buoyancy, and used in the manufacture of candles, ointments, etc. □□ **spermacetic** *adj.* [ME f. med.L f. LL *sperma* sperm + *ceti* genit. of *cetus* f. Gk *kētos* whale, from the belief that it was whale spawn]

spermary /spérməree/ *n.* (*pl.* **-ies**) an organ in which human or animal sperm are generated. [mod.L *spermarium* (as SPERM)]

spermatic /spərmátik/ *adj.* of or relating to a sperm or spermary. □ **spermatic cord** a bundle of nerves, ducts, and blood vessels passing to the testicles. [LL *spermaticus* f. Gk *spermatikos* (as SPERM)]

spermatid /spérmətid/ *n. Biol.* an immature male sex cell formed from a spermatocyte, which may develop into a spermatozoon. □□ **spermatidal** /-tíd'l/ *adj.*

spermato- /spərmátō, spə́rmətō/ *comb. form Biol.* a sperm or seed.

spermatocyte /spərmátəsit, spə́rmətō-/ *n.* a cell produced from a spermatogonium and which may divide by meiosis into spermatids.

spermatogenesis /spərmátəjénisis, spə́rmətə-/ *n.* the production or development of mature spermatozoa. □□ **spermatogenetic** /-jinétik/ *adj.*

spermatogonium /spərmátəgŏneeəm, spə́rmə-/ *n.* (*pl.* **spermatogonia** /-neeə/) a cell produced at an early stage in the formation of spermatozoa, from which spermatocytes develop. [SPERM + mod.L *gonium* f. Gk *gonos* offspring, seed]

spermatophore /spərmátəfawr, spə́rmə-/ *n.* an albuminous capsule containing spermatozoa found in various invertebrates. □□ **spermatophoric** /-fáwrik, -fór-/ *adj.*

spermatophyte /spərmátəfit, spə́rmə-/ *n.* any seed-bearing plant.

spermatozoid /spərmátəzŏid, spə́rmə-/ *n.* the mature motile male sex cell of some plants.

spermatozoon /spərmátəzŏ-on, -ən, spə́rmə-/ *n.* (*pl.* **spermatozoa** /-zŏə/) the mature motile sex cell in animals. □□ **spermatozoal** *adj.* **spermatozoan** *adj.* **spermatozoic** *adj.* [SPERM + Gk *zōion* animal]

spermicide /spérmisid/ *n.* a substance able to kill spermatozoa. □□ **spermicidal** /-síd'l/ *adj.*

spermo- /spérmō/ *comb. form* = SPERMATO-.

spew /spyoō/ *v.* (also **spue**) **1** *tr. & intr.* vomit. **2** (often foll. by *out*) **a** *tr.* expel (contents) rapidly and forcibly. **b** *intr.* (of contents) be expelled in this way. □□ **spewer** *n.* [OE *spīwan*, *spēowan* f. Gmc]

■ **1** see VOMIT *v.* 1. **2** spew forth *or* out *or* up, belch (up *or* out *or* forth), spout, discharge, gush, pour forth, spurt; vomit (up *or* forth), throw up *or* out, spit up *or* out, expectorate, expel, emit, eject, disgorge, send forth.

SPF *abbr.* sun protection factor.

sp. gr. *abbr.* specific gravity.

sphagnum /sfágnəm/ *n.* (*pl.* **sphagna** /-nə/) (in full **sphagnum moss**) any moss of the genus *Sphagnum*, growing in bogs and peat, and used as packing for plants, as fertilizer, etc. [mod.L f. Gk *sphagnos* a moss]

sphalerite /sfálərīt/ *n.* a common zinc ore principally composed of zinc sulfide. [Gk *sphaleros* deceptive: cf. BLENDE]

spheno- /sfe̅énō/ *comb. form Anat.* the sphenoid bone. [Gk f. *sphēn* wedge]

sphenoid /sfe̅énoyd/ *adj. & n.* ● *adj.* **1** wedge shaped. **2** of or relating to the sphenoid bone. ● *n.* (in full **sphenoid bone**) a large compound bone forming the base of the cranium behind the eyes. □□ **sphenoidal** /-nóyd'l/ *adj.* [mod.L *sphenoides* f. Gk *sphēnoeidēs* f. *sphēn* wedge]

sphere /sfeer/ *n. & v.* ● *n.* **1** a solid figure, or its surface, with every point on its surface equidistant from its center. **2** an object having this shape; a ball or globe. **3 a** any celestial body. **b** a globe representing the earth. **c** *poet.* the heavens; the sky. **d** the sky perceived as a vault upon or in which celestial bodies are represented as lying. **e** *hist.* each of a series of revolving concentrically arranged spherical shells in which celestial bodies were formerly thought to be set in a fixed relationship. **4 a** a field of action, influence, or existence (*have done much within their own sphere*). **b** a (usu. specified) stratum of society or social class (*moves in quite another sphere*). ● *v. tr. archaic or poet.* **1** enclose in or as in a sphere. **2** form into a sphere. □ **music** (or **harmony**) **of the spheres** the natural harmonic tones supposedly produced by the movement of the celestial spheres (see sense 3e of *n.*) or the bodies fixed in them. **oblique** (or **parallel** or **right**) **sphere** the sphere of the apparent heavens at a place where there is an oblique, zero, or right angle between the equator and the horizon. **sphere of influence** the claimed or recognized area of a nation's interests, an individual's control, etc. □□ **spheral** *adj.* [ME *sper(e)* f. OF *espere* f. LL *sphera*, L f. Gk *sphaira* ball]

■ *n.* **1, 2** globe, orb, ball, globule, spherule; bubble; spheroid. **4 a** area, field, province, territory, subject, discipline, range, specialty, forte, *colloq.* department, thing, *joc.* bailiwick, *sl.* bag. **b** society, class, level, caste, rank, domain, milieu, world, circle, walk of life, station, stratum, position.

-sphere /sfeer/ *comb. form* **1** having the form of a sphere (*bathysphere*). **2** a region around the earth (*atmosphere*).

spheric /sfe̅érik, sfér-/ *adj.* = SPHERICAL. □□ **sphericity** /-rísitee/ *n.*

spherical /sfe̅érikəl, sfér-/ *adj.* **1** shaped like a sphere; globular. **2 a** of or relating to the properties of spheres (*spherical geometry*). **b** formed inside or on the surface of a sphere (*spherical triangle*). □ **spherical aberration** a loss of definition in the image produced by a spherically curved mirror or lens. **spherical angle** an angle formed by the intersection of two great circles of a sphere. □□ **spherically** *adv.* [LL *sphaericus* f. Gk *sphairikos* (as SPHERE)]

■ **1** spheric, spheral, globular, round, ball-shaped, balllike, globelike, globe-shaped, globose, globulous, globoid, spherelike, spheroidal.

spheroid /sfe̅éroyd/ *n.* **1** a spherelike but not perfectly spherical body. **2** a solid generated by a half-revolution of an ellipse about its major axis (**prolate spheroid**) or minor axis (**oblate spheroid**). □□ **spheroidal** /-óyd'l/ *adj.* **spheroidicity** /-dísitee/ *n.*

■ □□ **spheroidal** see SPHERICAL.

spherometer /sfeerómitər/ *n.* an instrument for finding the radius of a sphere and for the exact measurement of the thickness of small bodies. [F *sphéromètre* (as SPHERE, -METER)]

spherule /sfe̅éro̅o̅l, -yo̅o̅l, sfér-/ *n.* a small sphere. □□ **spherular** *adj.* [LL *sphaerula* dimin. of L *sphaera* (as SPHERE)]

■ see SPHERE *n.* 1, 2.

spherulite /sfe̅éryəlīt, sfeérə-, sfér-/ *n.* a vitreous globule as a constituent of volcanic rocks. □□ **spherulitic** /-lítik/ *adj.*

sphincter /sfíngktər/ *n. Anat.* a ring of muscle surrounding and serving to guard or close an opening or tube, esp. the anus. □□ **sphincteral** *adj.* **sphinctered** *adj.* **sphincterial** /-te̅éreeəl/ *adj.* **sphincteric** /-térik/ *adj.* [L f. Gk *sphigktēr* f. *sphiggō* bind tight]

sphingid /sfínggid/ *n.* any hawk moth of the family Sphingidae. [as SPHINX + -ID³]

sphinx /sfingks/ *n.* **1** (**Sphinx**) (in Greek mythology) the winged monster of Thebes, having a woman's head and a lion's body, whose riddle Oedipus guessed and who consequently killed herself. **2** *Antiq.* **a** any of several ancient Egyptian stone figures having a lion's body and a human or animal head. **b** (**the Sphinx**) the huge stone figure of a sphinx near the Pyramids at Giza. **3** an enigmatic or inscrutable person. **4 a** a hawk moth. **b** a species of baboon, *Papio sphinx*. [L f. Gk *Sphigx*, app. f. *sphiggō* draw tight]

sphragistics /sfrəjístiks/ *n.pl.* (also treated as *sing.*) the study of engraved seals. [F *sphragistique* (n. & adj.) f. Gk *sphragistikos* f. *sphragis* seal]

sphygmo- /sfígmō/ *comb. form Physiol.* a pulse or pulsation. [Gk *sphugmo-* f. *sphugmos* pulse f. *sphuzō* to throb]

sphygmogram /sfígməgram/ *n.* a record produced by a sphygmograph.

sphygmograph /sfígməgraf/ *n.* an instrument for showing the character of a pulse in a series of curves. □□ **sphygmographic** *adj.* **sphygmographically** *adv.* **sphygmography** /-mógrəfee/ *n.*

sphygmology /sfigmóləjee/ *n.* the scientific study of the pulse. □□ **sphygmological** /-məlójikəl/ *adj.*

sphygmomanometer /sfígmōmənómitər/ *n.* an instrument for measuring blood pressure. □□ **sphygmomanometric** /-nəmétrik/ *adj.*

spica /spíkə/ *n.* **1** *Bot.* a spike or spikelike form. **2** *Surgery* a spiral bandage with reversed turns, suggesting an ear of corn. □□ **spicate** /-kayt/ *adj.* **spicated** /-káytid/ *adj.* [L, = spike, ear of corn, rel. to *spina* SPINE: in sense 2 after Gk *stakhus*]

spiccato /spikaáto̅/ *n., adj., & adv. Mus.* ● *n.* (*pl.* **-os**) **1** a style of staccato playing on stringed instruments involving bouncing the bow on the strings. **2** a passage in this style. ● *adj.* performed or to be performed in this style. ● *adv.* in this style. [It., = detailed, distinct]

spice /spīs/ *n. & v.* ● *n.* **1** an aromatic or pungent vegetable substance used to flavor food, e.g., cloves, pepper, or mace. **2** spices collectively (*a dealer in spice*). **3 a** an interesting or piquant quality. **b** (foll. by *of*) a slight flavor or suggestion (*a spice of malice*). ● *v.tr.* **1** flavor with spice. **2** add an interesting or piquant quality to (*a book spiced with humor*). [ME f. OF *espice(r)* f. L *species* specific kind: in LL pl. = merchandise]

■ *n.* **1** condiment, relish, seasoning, flavor(ing); herb. **3 a** zest, spiciness, piquancy, tang, pungency, bite, sharpness, poignancy, salt, seasoning, ginger, gusto, excitement, dash, élan, color, life, vigor, zip, interest, stimulation, stimulant, spirit, *colloq.* vim, pep, kick, punch, *sl.* pizzazz. **b** see TOUCH *n.* 3. ● *v.* **1** season, flavor. **2** spice up, enliven, inspirit, stimulate, invigorate.

spicebush /spísbo̅o̅sh/ *n.* any aromatic shrub of the genus *Lindera* or *Calycanthus*, native to America.

spick-and-span /spík ənd spán/ (also **spic-and-span**) *adj.* **1** fresh and new. **2** neat and clean. [16th-c. *spick and span new*, emphatic extension of ME *span new* f. ON *spán-nýr* f. *spánn* chip + *nýr* new]

■ **1** see SMART *adj.* 3. **2** see NEAT¹ 1.

spicule /spíkyo̅o̅l/ *n.* **1** any small sharply pointed body. **2**

/.../ pronunciation	● part of speech
□ phrases, idioms, and compounds	
□□ derivatives	■ synonym section
cross-references appear in SMALL CAPITALS or *italics*	

Zool. a small hard calcareous or siliceous body, esp. in the framework of a sponge. **3** *Bot.* a small or secondary spike. **4** *Astron.* a spikelike prominence, esp. one appearing as a jet of gas in the sun's corona. □□ **spicular** *adj.* **spiculate** /-lət/ *adj.* [mod.L *spicula, spiculum,* dimins. of SPICA]
■ **1–3** see SPINE 2. ● ■ **spiculate** see PRICKLY 1.

spicy /spísee/ *adj.* (**spicier, spiciest**) **1** of, flavored with, or fragrant with spice. **2** piquant; pungent; sensational or improper (*a spicy story*). □□ **spicily** *adv.* **spiciness** *n.*
■ **1** zesty, zestful, piquant, tangy, (well-)spiced, (well-)seasoned, hot, peppery, sharp, pungent, biting, full-bodied, aromatic, savory, flavorsome, flavorful. **2** piquant, pungent; indelicate, suggestive, risqué, improper, indecent, indecorous, ribald, racy, bawdy, unseemly, offensive, titillating, sexy, off-color; scandalous, sensational, outrageous, notorious, revealing, revelatory, intimate, *colloq.* juicy. □□ **spiciness** see SPICE *n.* 3a.

spider /spídər/ *n.* & *v.* ● *n.* **1 a** any eight-legged arthropod of the order Araneae with a round unsegmented body, many of which spin webs for the capture of insects as food. **b** any of various similar or related arachnids, e.g., a red spider. **2** any object comparable to a spider, esp. as having numerous or prominent legs or radiating spokes. **3** a frying pan, esp. one with legs or feet. **4** *Brit.* a radiating series of elastic ties used to hold a load in place on a vehicle, etc. ● *v.intr.* **1** move in a scuttling manner suggestive of a spider (*fingers spidered across the map*). **2** cause to move or appear in this way. **3** (as **spidering** *adj.*) spiderlike in form, manner, or movement (*spidering streets*). □ **spider crab** any of various crabs of the family Majidæ with a pear-shaped body and long thin legs. **spider mite** any of various mites of the family Tetranychidae infesting hothouse plants, esp. vines. **spider monkey** any S. American monkey of the genus *Ateles,* with long limbs and a prehensile tail. **spider plant** any of various house plants with long narrow striped leaves. □□ **spiderish** *adj.* [OE *spīthra* (as SPIN)]

spiderman /spídərman/ *n.* (*pl.* **-men**) *Brit. colloq.* a person who works at great heights in building construction.

spiderwort /spídərwərt, -wawrt/ *n.* any plant of the genus *Tradescantia,* esp. *T. virginiana,* having flowers with long hairy stamens.

spidery /spídəree/ *adj.* elongated and thin (*spidery handwriting*).

spiegeleisen /spee´gəlizən/ *n.* an alloy of iron and manganese, used in steel making. [G f. *Spiegel* mirror + *Eisen* iron]

spiel /speel, shpeel/ *n.* & *v. sl.* ● *n.* a glib speech or story, esp. a salesman's patter. ● *v.* **1** *intr.* speak glibly; hold forth. **2** *tr.* reel off (patter, etc.). □□ **spieler** *n.* □□ [G, = play, game]
■ *n.* see SPEECH 2. ● *v.* **1** see LECTURE *v.* 1.

spiff /spif/ *v. tr. colloq.* (usu. foll. by *up*) remodel; refurbish; make neat or clean.

spiffing /spifing/ *adj. Brit. archaic sl.* **1** excellent. **2** smart; handsome. [19th c.: orig. unkn.]

spiffy /spífee/ *adj.* (**spiffier, spiffiest**) *sl.* stylish; smart. □□ **spiffily** *adv.*

spiflicate /spíflikayt/ *v.tr.* (also **spifflicate**) esp. *Brit. joc.* **1** destroy. **2** beat (in a fight, etc.). [18th c.: fanciful]

spigot /spígət/ *n.* **1** a small peg or plug, esp. for insertion into the vent hole of a cask. **2 a** a faucet. **b** a device for controlling the flow of liquid in a faucet. **3** the plain end of a pipe section fitting into the socket of the next one. [ME, perh. f. Prov. *espigou(n)* f. L *spiculum* dimin. of *spicum* = SPICA]
■ **1** see STOPPER *n.* 2 see TAP¹ *n.* 1.

spike¹ /spīk/ *n.* & *v.* ● *n.* **1 a** a sharp point. **b** a pointed piece of metal, esp. the top of an iron railing, etc. **2 a** any of several metal points set into the sole of a running shoe to prevent slipping. **b** (in *pl.*) a pair of running shoes with spikes. **3** = SPINDLE *n.* 7. **4** a large stout nail esp. as used for railways. **5** *sl.* a hypodermic needle. **6** *Brit. sl.* a doss house. **7** *Electronics* a pulse of very short duration in which a rapid increase in voltage is followed by a rapid decrease. **8** the act of propelling a volleyball, football, etc., rapidly downward. ● *v.tr.* **1 a** fasten or provide with spikes. **b** fix on or pierce with spikes.

2 (of a newspaper editor, etc.) reject (a story), esp. by filing it on a spike. **3** *colloq.* **a** lace (a drink) with alcohol, a drug, etc. **b** contaminate (a substance) with something added. **4** make useless; put an end to; thwart (an idea, etc.). **5** propel (a volleyball, football, etc.) rapidly downward. **6** *hist.* plug up the vent of (a gun) with a spike. □ **spike heel** a high tapering heel of a woman's shoe. [ME perh. f. MLG, MDu. *spiker,* rel. to SPOKE¹]
■ *n.* **1 a** see POINT *n.* 1. **b** skewer, spit, stake, prong, tine, treenail, nail, peg, picket, pin, spine, barb, *hist.* pike. ● *v.* **1** impale, transfix, stab, stick, skewer, spear, pierce, spit, lance, pin, rivet. **3 a** lace, strengthen, *sl.* slip a Mickey Finn into; drug, poison, *colloq.* doctor. **4** disable, thwart, stymie, nullify, disarm, block, frustrate, foil, void, balk, check, cancel, annul, put an end to.

spike² /spīk/ *n. Bot.* **1** a flower cluster formed of many flower heads attached closely on a long stem. **2** a separate sprig of any plant in which flowers form a spikelike cluster. □□ **spikelet** *n.* [ME, = ear of corn, f. L SPICA]

spikenard /spíknaard/ *n.* **1** *Bot.* an E. Indian plant, *Nardostachys grandiflora.* **2** *hist.* a costly perfumed ointment made from this. [ME ult. f. med.L *spica nardi* (as SPIKE², NARD) after Gk *nardostakhus*]

spiky¹ /spíkee/ *adj.* (**spikier, spikiest**) **1** like a spike; having many spikes. **2** *colloq.* easily offended; prickly. □□ **spikily** *adv.* **spikiness** *n.*
■ **1** see PRICKLY 1. **2** see PRICKLY 2a.

spiky² /spíkee/ *adj. Bot.* having spikes or ears.

spile /spīl/ *n.* & *v.* ● *n.* **1** a wooden peg or spigot. **2** a large timber or pile for driving into the ground. **3** a small spout for tapping the sap from a sugar maple, etc. ● *v.tr.* tap (a cask, etc.) with a spile in order to draw off liquid. [MDu., MLG, = wooden peg, etc.: in sense 'pile' app. alt. of PILE²]
■ *n.* **1** see STOPPER *n.* 1.

spill¹ /spil/ *v.* & *n.* ● *v.* (*past* and *past part.* **spilled** or **spilt**) **1** *intr.* & *tr.* fall or run or cause (a liquid, powder, etc.) to fall or run out of a vessel, esp. unintentionally. **2 a** *tr.* & *intr.* throw (a person, etc.) from a vehicle, saddle, etc. **b** *intr.* (esp. of a crowd) tumble out quickly from a place, etc. (*the fans spilled into the street*). **3** *tr. sl.* disclose (information, etc.). **4** *tr. Naut.* **a** empty (a sail) of wind. **b** lose (wind) from a sail. ● *n.* **1 a** the act or an instance of spilling or being spilled. **b** a quantity spilled. **2** a tumble or fall, esp. from a horse, etc. (*had a nasty spill*). **3** *Austral.* the vacating of all or several posts of a parliamentary party to allow reorganization. □ **spill the beans** *colloq.* divulge information, etc., esp. unintentionally or indiscreetly. **spill blood** be guilty of bloodshed. **spill the blood of** kill or injure (a person). **spill over 1** overflow. **2** (of a surplus population) be forced to move (cf. OVERSPILL). □□ **spillage** /spílij/ *n.* **spiller** *n.* [OE *spillan* kill, rel. to OE *spildan* destroy: orig. unkn.]
■ *v.* **1** pour (out *or* over), overflow, slop *or* run *or* brim over; leak, escape; see also UPSET *v.* 1a. **2 a** dislodge, throw, unseat, unhorse; shed, discharge, tip. **b** see STREAM *v.* 1. **3** see DISCLOSE 1. ● *n.* **1** spillage, spilth, outpouring, flood, leak, leakage. **2** fall, tumble, accident, mishap, *sl.* cropper. **3** reshuffle, shuffle, rearrangement. □ **spill the beans** reveal all *or* everything, tell all *or* everything, disclose all *or* everything, divulge all *or* everything, blab, tattle, let the cat out of the bag, give the show away, confess, be a stool pigeon, *sl.* squeal, sing (like a canary), be a stoolie. □□ **spillage** see SPILL *n.*¹ 1 above.

spill² /spil/ *n.* a thin strip of wood, folded or twisted paper, etc., used for lighting a fire, candles, a pipe, etc. [ME, rel. to SPILE]

spillikin /spílikin/ *n.* (also **spellican** /spélikən/) **1** a jackstraw. **2** (in *pl.*) a game of jackstraws. [SPILL² + -KIN]

spillover /spílōvər/ *n.* **1 a** the process or an instance of spilling over. **b** a thing that spills over. **2** a consequence, repercussion, or by-product.

spillway /spílway/ *n.* a passage for surplus water from a dam.

spilt *past* and *past part.* of SPILL¹.

spilth /spilth/ *n.* **1** material that is spilled. **2** the act or an instance of spilling. **3** an excess or surplus.

spin /spin/ *v. & n.* ● *v.* (**spinning**; *past* and *past part.* **spun** /spun/) **1** *intr. & tr.* turn or cause (a person or thing) to turn or whirl around quickly. **2** *tr.* (also *absol.*) **a** draw out and twist (wool, cotton, etc.) into threads. **b** make (yarn) in this way. **c** make a similar type of thread from (a synthetic substance, etc.). **3** *tr.* (of a spider, silkworm, etc.) make (a web, gossamer, a cocoon, etc.) by extruding a fine viscous thread. **4** *tr.* tell or write (a story, essay, article, etc.) (*spins a good tale*). **5** *tr.* impart spin to (a ball). **6** *intr.* (of a person's head, etc.) be dizzy through excitement, astonishment, etc. **7** *tr.* attempt to interpret or slant (a media report) a certain way. **8** *tr.* shape (metal) on a mold in a lathe, etc. **9** *intr.* (of a ball) move through the air with spin. **10** *tr.* (as **spun** *adj.*) converted into threads (*spun glass*; *spun gold*; *spun sugar*). **11** *tr.* fish in (a stream, pool, etc.) with a spinner. **12** *tr.* toss (a coin). **13** *tr.* = *spin-dry*. **14** *intr.* (of an airplane) to descend in a spin. ● *n.* **1** a spinning motion; a whirl. **2** an aircraft's diving descent combined with rotation. **3 a** a revolving motion through the air, esp. in a rifle bullet or in a billiard, tennis, or table tennis ball struck aslant. **b** *Baseball* a twisting motion given to the ball in pitching. **4** *colloq.* a brief drive in a motor vehicle, airplane, etc., esp. for pleasure. **5** *Physics* the intrinsic angular momentum of an elementary particle. **6** emphasis; interpretation. **7** *Austral. & NZ sl.* a piece of good or bad luck. □ **spin doctor** a political pundit who is employed to promote a favorable interpretation of political developments to the media. **spin-drier** (or **-dryer**) a machine for drying wet clothes, etc., centrifugally in a revolving drum. **spin-dry** (**-dries, -dried**) dry (clothes, etc.) in this way. **spin off 1** throw off by centrifugal force in spinning. **2** create or establish as a by-product or derivative endeavor. **spin-off** *n.* an incidental result or results, esp. as a side benefit from industrial technology. **spin out 1** prolong (a discussion, etc.). **2** make (a story, money, etc.) last as long as possible. **3** spend or consume (time, one's life, etc., by discussion or in an occupation, etc.). **spin a yarn** *orig. Naut.* tell a story. **spun silk** a cheap material made of short-fibered and waste silk. **spun yarn** *Naut.* a line formed of rope yarns twisted together. [OE *spinnan*]
■ *v.* **1** revolve, turn, rotate, wheel, gyrate, twirl, swirl, twist, reel, pirouette, pivot, swivel. **4** invent, concoct, make up, devise, produce, fabricate; weave, relate, retail, recount, narrate, tell, write, unfold. **6** be dizzy, suffer vertigo, swim, whirl, reel, be giddy. ● *n.* **1, 3** whirl, twirl, turn, gyration, reel, pirouette, revolution, rotation. **4** drive, whirl, ride, tour, excursion, outing, jaunt, *colloq.* joyride. □ **spin off 1** throw off, separate. **spin-off** see OFFSHOOT 2. **spin out 1, 2** prolong, protract, drag *or* draw out, stretch *or* string out, perpetuate, continue, extend, keep alive, keep going; pad out, lengthen.

spina bifida /spínə bífidə/ *n.* a congenital defect of the spine, in which part of the spinal cord and its meninges are exposed through a gap in the backbone. [mod.L (as SPINE, BIFID)]

spinach /spínich, -nij/ *n.* **1** a green garden vegetable, *Spinacia oleracea*, with succulent leaves. **2** the leaves of this plant used as food. □ **spinach beet** a variety of beet cultivated for its edible leaves. □□ **spinaceous** /-náyshəs/ *adj.* **spinachy** *adj.* [prob. MDu. *spinaetse, spinag(i)e*, f. OF *espinage, espinache* f. med.L *spinac(h)ia*, etc. f. Arab. *'isfānāk* f. Pers. *ispānāk*: perh. assim. to L *spina* SPINE, with ref. to its prickly seeds]

spinal /spín'l/ *adj.* of or relating to the spine (*spinal curvature*; *spinal disease*). □ **spinal canal** a cavity through the vertebrae containing the spinal cord. **spinal column** the spine. **spinal cord** a cylindrical structure of the central nervous system enclosed in the spine, connecting all parts of the body with the brain. □□ **spinally** *adv.* [LL *spinalis* (as SPINE)]
■ □ **spinal column** backbone, spine, vertebrae.

spindle /spínd'l/ *n. & v.* ● *n.* **1 a** a pin in a spinning wheel used for twisting and winding the thread. **b** a small bar with tapered ends used for the same purpose in hand spinning. **c** a pin bearing the bobbin of a spinning machine. **2** a pin or axis that revolves or on which something revolves. **3** a turned piece of wood used as a banister, chair leg, etc. **4**

Biol. a spindle-shaped mass of microtubules formed when a cell divides. **5** a varying measure of length for yarn. **6** a slender person or thing. **7 a** a pointed metal rod standing on a base and used for filing news items, etc., esp. when rejected for publication. **b** a similar spike used for bills, etc. ● *v.intr.* have, or grow into, a long slender form. □ **spindle berry** the fruit of the spindle tree. **spindle-shanked** having long thin legs. **spindle-shanks** a person with such legs. **spindle-shaped** having a circular cross section and tapering toward each end. **spindle side** = *distaff side*. **spindle tree** any shrub or small tree of the genus *Euonymus*, esp. *E. europaeus* with greenish white flowers, pink or red berries, and hard wood used for spindles. [OE *spinel* (as SPIN)]
■ *n.* **2** see PIVOT *n.* 1. **3** leg, cabriole.

spindly /spíndlee/ *adj.* (**spindlier, spindliest**) long or tall and thin; thin and weak.
■ see THIN *adj.* 4.

spindrift /spíndrift/ *n.* spray blown along the surface of the sea. [Sc. var. of *spoondrift* f. *spoon* run before wind or sea + DRIFT]
■ see SPRAY¹ *n.* 1.

spine /spin/ *n.* **1** a series of vertebrae extending from the skull to the small of the back, enclosing the spinal cord and providing support for the thorax and abdomen; the backbone. **2** *Zool. & Bot.* any hard pointed process or structure. **3** a sharp ridge or projection, esp. of a mountain range or slope. **4** a central feature, main support, or source of strength. **5** the part of a book's jacket or cover that encloses the fastened edges of the pages and usu. faces outwards on a shelf. □ **spine chiller** a frightening story, movie, etc. **spine-chilling** (esp. of a story, etc.) frightening. **spine-tingling** thrilling; pleasurably exciting. □□ **spined** *adj.* [ME f. OF *espine* or L *spina* thorn, backbone]
■ **1** backbone, spinal column, vertebrae. **2** thorn, needle, barb, spike, spur, prong, quill, ray, barbel, bristle, prickle, barbule, spicule. **3** see CREST *n.* 2, RIDGE. **4** see BACKBONE 2, 3. □ **spine-chilling** see SCARY. **spine-tingling** see *thrilling* (THRILL).

spinel /spinél/ *n.* **1** any of a group of hard crystalline minerals of various colors, consisting chiefly of oxides of magnesium and aluminum. **2** any substance of similar composition or properties. □ **spinel ruby** a deep red variety of spinel used as a gem. [F *spinelle* f. It. *spinella*, dimin. of *spina*: see SPINE]

spineless /spínlis/ *adj.* **1 a** having no spine; invertebrate. **b** (of a fish) having no spines on the fins. **2** (of a person) lacking energy or resolution; weak and purposeless. □□ **spinelessly** *adv.* **spinelessness** *n.*
■ **1 a** invertebrate. **2** weak, feeble, flabby, irresolute, weak-willed, weak-kneed, indecisive, ineffectual, ineffective, impotent, powerless, purposeless, invertebrate; cowardly, dastardly, pusillanimous, timorous, lily-livered, craven, fearful, timid, spiritless, squeamish, chicken hearted, *colloq.* yellow, chicken, yellow-bellied, wimpish, gutless.

spinet /spínit, spinét/ *n. Mus.* **1** *hist.* a small harpsichord with oblique strings. **2** a small upright piano. [obs. F *espinette* f. It. *spinetta* virginal, spinet, dimin. of *spina* thorn, etc. (as SPINE), with ref. to the plucked strings]

spinifex /spínifeks/ *n.* any Australian grass of the genus *Spinifex*, with coarse, spiny leaves. [mod.L f. L *spina* SPINE + *-fex* maker f. *facere* make]

spinnaker /spínəkər/ *n.* a large triangular sail carried opposite the mainsail of a racing yacht running before the wind. [fanciful f. *Sphinx*, name of yacht first using it, perh. after *spanker*]

spinner /spínər/ *n.* **1** a person or thing that spins. **2** *Cricket* **a** a spin bowler. **b** a spun ball. **3** a spin-drier. **4 a** a real or artificial fly for esp. trout fishing. **b** revolving bait. **5** a manufacturer or merchant engaged in (esp. cotton) spinning. **6**

/.../ **pronunciation**	● **part of speech**
□ **phrases, idioms, and compounds**	
□□ **derivatives**	■ **synonym section**
cross-references appear in SMALL CAPITALS or *italics*	

a fairing attached to and moving with an airplane propellor. **7** = SPINNERET. **8** *archaic* a spider.

spinneret /spínəret/ *n.* **1** the spinning organ in a spider, silkworm, etc. **2** a device for forming filaments of synthetic fiber.

spinney /spínee/ *n.* (*pl.* **-eys**) *Brit.* a small wood; a thicket. [OF *espinei* f. L *spinetum* thicket f. *spina* thorn]

spinning /spíning/ *n.* the act or an instance of spinning. □ **spinning jenny** *hist.* a machine for spinning with more than one spindle at a time. **spinning machine** a machine that spins fibers continuously. **spinning top** = TOP². **spinning wheel** a household machine for spinning yarn or thread with a spindle driven by a wheel attached to a crank or treadle.
■ see TWIRL *n.* 1.

spinose /spínōs/ *adj.* (also **spinous** /-nəs/) *Bot.* (of a plant) having many spines.
■ see THORNY 1.

Spinozism /spinṓzizəm/ *n. Philos.* the doctrine of Spinoza that there is one infinite substance of which extension and thought are attributes and human beings are changing forms. □□ **Spinozist** *n.* **Spinozistic** *adj.* [B. de *Spinoza*, Du. philosopher d. 1677]

spinster /spínstər/ *n.* **1** an unmarried woman. **2** a woman, esp. elderly, thought unlikely to marry. □□ **spinsterhood** *n.* **spinsterish** *adj.* **spinsterishness** *n.* [ME, orig. = woman who spins]
■ celibate, *derog.* old maid.

spinthariscope /spintháriskōp/ *n.* an instrument with a fluorescent screen showing the incidence of alpha particles by flashes. [irreg. f. Gk *spintharis* spark + -SCOPE]

spinule /spínyōōl/ *n. Bot. & Zool.* a small spine. □□ **spinulose** *adj.* **spinulous** *adj.* [L *spinula* dimin. of *spina* SPINE]
■ □□ **spinulose, spinulous** see THORNY 1.

spiny /spínee/ *adj.* (**spinier**, **spiniest**) **1** full of spines; prickly. **2** perplexing; troublesome; thorny. □ **spiny anteater** = ECHIDNA. **spiny lobster** any of various large edible crustaceans of the family Palinuridae, esp. *Palinuris vulgaris*, with a spiny shell and no large anterior claws. □□ **spininess** *n.*
■ **1** see THORNY 1. **2** see THORNY 2.

spiracle /spírəkəl/ *n.* (also **spiraculum** /spírákyələm/) (*pl.* **spiracles** or **spiracula** /-rákyələ/) an external respiratory opening in insects, whales, and some fish. □□ **spiracular** /-rákyələr/ *adj.* [L *spiraculum* f. *spirare* breathe]
■ see VENT¹ *n.* 1.

spiraea var. of SPIREA.

spiral /spírəl/ *adj., n., & v.* ● *adj.* **1** winding about a center in an enlarging or decreasing continuous circular motion, either on a flat plane or rising in a cone; coiled. **2** winding continuously along or as if along a cylinder, like the thread of a screw. ● *n.* **1** a plane or three-dimensional spiral curve. **2** a spiral spring. **3** a spiral formation in a shell, etc. **4** a spiral galaxy. **5** a progressive rise or fall of prices, wages, etc., each responding to an upward or downward stimulus provided by the other (*a spiral of rising prices and wages*). **6** *Football.* a kick or pass in which the ball rotates on its long axis while in the air. ● *v.* (**spiraled** or **spiralled**, **spiraling** or **spiralling**) **1** *intr.* move in a spiral course, esp. upwards or downwards. **2** *tr.* make spiral. **3** *intr.* esp. *Econ.* (of prices, wages, etc.) rise or fall, esp. rapidly (cf. sense 5 of *n.*). □ **spiral balance** a device for measuring weight by the torsion of a spiral spring. **spiral galaxy** a galaxy in which the matter is concentrated mainly in one or more spiral arms. **spiral staircase** a staircase rising in a spiral round a central axis. □□ **spirality** /-rálitee/ *n.* **spirally** *adv.* [F *spiral* or med.L *spiralis* (as SPIRE²)]
■ *adj.* helical, coiled, screw, corkscrew, cochlear; scrolled, volute(d), whorled. ● *n.* **1** helix, coil, corkscrew, screw, scroll; whorl, volute, turn, curl. ● *v.* **1** see TWIRL *v.* 3 (*spiral downwards*) see DROP *v.* 8a; (*spiral upwards*) see SOAR 2.

spirant /spírənt/ *adj. & n. Phonet.* ● *adj.* (of a consonant) uttered with a continuous expulsion of breath, esp. fricative. ● *n.* such a consonant. [L *spirare spirant-* breathe]

spire¹ /spīr/ *n. & v.* ● *n.* **1** a tapering cone- or pyramid-shaped structure built esp. on a church tower (cf. STEEPLE). **2** the continuation of a tree trunk above the point where branching begins. **3** any tapering thing, e.g., the spike of a flower. ● *v.tr.* **1** extend upward like a spire. **2** provide with a spire. □□ **spiry** /spíree/ *adj.* [OE *spīr*]
■ *n.* **1** pinnacle, flèche; column, belfry; steeple. **3** top, pinnacle, apex, peak, summit, acme, tip, crest, crown, vertex.

spire² /spīr/ *n.* **1 a** a spiral; a coil. **b** a single twist of this. **2** the upper part of a spiral shell. [F f. L *spira* f. Gk *speira* coil]

spirea /spíreeə/ *n.* (also **spiraea**) any rosaceous shrub of the genus *Spiraea*, with clusters of small white or pink flowers. [L f. Gk *speiraia* f. *speira* coil]

spirillum /spīríləm/ *n.* (*pl.* **spirilla** /-lə/) **1** any bacterium of the genus *Spirillum*, characterized by a rigid spiral structure. **2** any bacterium with a similar shape. [mod.L, irreg. dimin. of L *spira* SPIRE²]

spirit /spírit/ *n. & v.* ● *n.* **1 a** the vital animating essence of a person or animal (*was sadly broken in spirit*). **b** the intelligent nonphysical part of a person; the soul. **2 a** a rational or intelligent being without a material body. **b** a supernatural being such as a ghost, fairy, etc. (*haunted by spirits*). **3** a prevailing mental or moral condition or attitude; a mood; a tendency (*public spirit*; *took it in the wrong spirit*). **4 a** (in *pl.*) strong distilled liquor, e.g., brandy, whiskey, gin, rum. **b** a distilled volatile liquid (*wood spirits*). **c** purified alcohol (*methylated spirits*). **d** a solution of a volatile principle in alcohol; a tincture (*spirits of ammonia*). **5 a** a person's mental or moral nature or qualities, usu. specified (*has an unbending spirit*). **b** a person viewed as possessing these (*is an ardent spirit*). **c** (in full **high spirit**) courage; energy; vivacity; dash (*played with spirit*; *infused him with spirit*). **6** the real meaning as opposed to lip service or verbal expression (*the spirit of the law*). **7** *archaic* an immaterial principle thought to govern vital phenomena (*animal spirits*). ● *v.tr.* (**spirited**, **spiriting**) **1** (usu. foll. by *away*, *off*, etc.) convey rapidly and secretly by or as if by spirits. **2** animate or cheer up a person. □ **in** (or **in the**) **spirit** inwardly (*shall be with you in spirit*). **spirit gum** a quick-drying solution of gum used esp. for attaching false hair. **spirit lamp** a lamp burning methylated alcohol or other liquid fuel instead of oil. **spirit level** a bent glass tube nearly filled with alcohol used to test horizontality by the position of an air bubble. **the spirit moves a person** he or she feels inclined (to do something) (orig. in Quaker use). **spirit** (or **spirits**) **of wine** *archaic* purified alcohol. **spirits of salt** *archaic* hydrochloric acid. [ME f. AF (*e*)*spirit*, OF *esp*(*e*)*rit*, f. L *spiritus* breath, spirit f. *spirare* breathe]
■ *n.* **1** breath, life, vitality, vital spirit, soul, consciousness, psyche, self, heart, essence, *Psychol.* anima. **2 b** see SPECTER 1. **3** attitude, principle, thought, idea, inspiration, notion, feeling, inclination, tendency, impulse; atmosphere, mood; temper, sentiment, cheer, humor, frame of mind; morale, esprit de corps, team spirit. **4 a** (*spirits*) alcohol, liquor, strong drink, *colloq.* booze, firewater, *colloq.* hooch. **5 a** character, temperament, temper, nature, persona, disposition, heart, mind, will, willpower, attitude, bent, inclination. **b** character, soul. **c** bravery, courage, grit, backbone, valor, pluck, daring, mettle, stoutheartedness, manfulness, manliness, gameness, resoluteness, resolution, resolve, will, willpower; energy, ardor, desire, impetus, drive, urge, eagerness, enthusiasm, motivation, intention, enterprise; zest, zeal, zealousness, fire, passion, pungency, piquancy, warmth, animation, life, liveliness, vivacity, vivaciousness, panache, élan, dash, spice, *colloq.* sauce; vim, spunk, get-up-and-go, (right) stuff, guts, sand. **6** meaning, sense, tenor, signification, purport, intent, intention, purpose, aim, implication, message, essence, quintessence, core, heart, meat, pith, substance, marrow. ● *v.* **1** (*spirit away* or *off*) abduct, make off *or* away with, carry off, transport, take away, kidnap, steal (off *or* away with), whisk away, abscond with; make disappear.

spirited /spíritid/ *adj.* **1** full of spirit; animated, lively, brisk, or courageous (*a spirited attack*; *a spirited translation*). **2** having a spirit or spirits of a specified kind (*high spirited*; *mean spirited*). □□ **spiritedly** *adv.* **spiritedness** *n.*
■ **1** lively, sprightly, energetic, vigorous, racy, animated, brisk, sparkling, dynamic, buoyant, effervescent, vivacious; frisky, playful, sportive; ardent, fervent, impassioned; plucky, mettlesome, venturesome, courageous; *colloq.* spunky. □□ **spiritedly** see *vigorously* (VIGOROUS). **spiritedness** see ANIMATION.

spiritless /spíritlis/ *adj.* lacking courage, vigor, or vivacity. □□ **spiritlessly** *adv.* **spiritlessness** *n.*
■ see LIFELESS 3.

spiritual /spírichōōəl/ *adj.* & *n.* ● *adj.* **1** of or concerning the spirit as opposed to matter. **2** concerned with sacred or religious things; holy; divine; inspired (*the spiritual life*; *spiritual songs*). **3** (of the mind, etc.) refined; sensitive; not concerned with the material. **4** (of a relationship, etc.) concerned with the soul or spirit, etc., not with external reality (*his spiritual home*). ● *n.* a religious song derived from the musical traditions of African-American people in the southern US. □□ **spirituality** /-chōō-álitee/ *n.* **spiritually** *adv.* **spiritualness** *n.* [ME f. OF *spirituel* f. L *spiritualis* (as SPIRIT)]
■ *adj.* **1, 4** nonmaterial, incorporeal, psychic(al), mental, psychological, inner. **2** sacred, ecclesiastic(al), churchly, clerical, priestly, devotional, holy, divine, sacerdotal, religious, nonsecular; inspired. □□ **spirituality** see DEVOTION 2c.

spiritualism /spírichōōəlizəm/ *n.* **1 a** the belief that the spirits of the dead can communicate with the living, esp. through mediums. **b** the practice of this. **2** *Philos.* the doctrine that the spirit exists as distinct from matter, or that spirit is the only reality (cf. MATERIALISM). □□ **spiritualist** *n.* **spiritualistic** *adj.*
■ □□ **spiritualist** see PSYCHIC *n.* **spiritualistic** see PSYCHIC *adj.* 1b.

spiritualize /spírichōōəlīz/ *v.tr.* **1** make (a person or a person's character, thoughts, etc.) spiritual; elevate. **2** attach a spiritual as opposed to a literal meaning to. □□ **spiritualization** *n.*

spirituel /spírichōō-él/ *adj.* (also **spirituelle**) (of the mind) refined and yet spirited; witty. [F *spirituel*, fem. *-elle* (as SPIRITUAL)]

spirituous /spírichōōəs/ *adj.* **1** containing much alcohol. **2** distilled, as whiskey, rum, etc. (*spirituous liquor*). □□ **spirituousness** *n.* [L *spiritus* spirit, or F *spiritueux*]
■ **1** hard, potent; see also STRONG *adj.* 14.

spiro-¹ /spírō/ *comb. form* a coil. [L *spira*, Gk *speira* coil]

spiro-² /spírō/ *comb. form* breath. [irreg. f. L *spirare* breathe]

spirochete /spírōkeet/ *n.* (also **spirochaete**) any of various flexible spiral-shaped bacteria. [SPIRO-¹ + Gk *khaitē* long hair]

spirograph /spírəgraf/ *n.* an instrument for recording breathing movements. □□ **spirographic** *adj.* **spirographically** *adv.*

spirogyra /spírōjírə/ *n.* any freshwater alga of the genus *Spirogyra*, with cells containing spiral bands of chlorophyll. [mod.L f. SPIRO-¹ + Gk *guros gura* round]

spirometer /spírómitər/ *n.* an instrument for measuring the air capacity of the lungs.

spirt var. of SPURT.

spit¹ /spit/ *v.* & *n.* ● *v.* (**spitting**; *past* and *past part.* **spat** /spat/ or **spit**) **1** *intr.* **a** eject saliva from the mouth. **b** do this as a sign of hatred or contempt (*spat at him*). **2** *tr.* (usu. foll. by *out*) **a** eject (saliva, blood, food, etc.) from the mouth (*spat the meat out*). **b** utter (oaths, threats, etc.) vehemently (*"Damn you!" he spat*). **3** *intr.* (of a fire, pen, pan, etc.) send out sparks, ink, hot fat, etc. **4** *intr.* (of rain) fall lightly (*it's only spitting*). **5** *intr.* (esp. of a cat) make a spitting or hissing noise in anger or hostility. ● *n.* **1** spittle. **2** the act or an instance of spitting. **3** the foamy liquid secretion of some insects used to protect their young. □ **the spit of** *colloq.* the exact double of (cf. *spitting image*). **spit and polish 1** the cleaning and polishing duties of a soldier, etc. **2** exaggerated

neatness and smartness. **spit chips** *Austral. sl.* **1** feel extreme thirst. **2** be angry or frustrated. **spit curl** a tight curl usu. pressed against the forehead, cheek, or temple. **spit it out** *colloq.* say what is on one's mind. **spitting cobra** the African black-necked cobra, *Naja nigricollis*, that ejects venom by spitting, not striking. **spitting distance** a very short distance. **spitting image** (foll. by *of*) *colloq.* the exact double of (another person or thing). **spit up** regurgitate; vomit. □□ **spitter** *n.* [OE *spittan*, of imit. orig.: cf. SPEW]
■ *v.* **1 a** expectorate; dribble, salivate, drool, slaver. **2** expectorate, discharge, spew (forth), eject. **2b, 3** hiss, sputter, splutter; fizz. ● *n.* **1** spittle, saliva, drool, sputum, slaver. □ **spitting image** twin, duplicate, double, clone, image, counterpart, likeness, look-alike, copy, *colloq.* (very) spit, *sl.* (dead) ringer.

spit² /spit/ *n.* & *v.* ● *n.* **1** a slender rod on which meat is skewered before being roasted on a fire, etc.; a skewer. **2 a** a small point of land projecting into the sea. **b** a long narrow underwater bank. ● *v.tr.* (**spitted**, **spitting**) **1** thrust a spit through (meat, etc.). **2** pierce or transfix with a sword, etc. □ **spit roast** cook on a spit. □□ **spitty** *adj.* [OE *spitu* f. WG]

spit³ /spit/ *n.* esp. *Brit.* (*pl.* same or **spits**) a spade-depth of earth (*dig it two spit deep*). [MDu. & MLG, = OE *spittan* dig with spade, prob. rel. to SPIT²]

spitball /spítbawl/ *n.* & *v.* ● *n.* **1** a ball of chewed paper, etc., used as a missile. **2** a baseball moistened by the pitcher to affect its flight. ● *v.intr.* throw out suggestions for discussion. □□ **spitballer** *n.*

spitchcock /spíchkok/ *n.* & *v.* ● *n.* an eel split and grilled or fried. ● *v.tr.* prepare (an eel, fish, bird, etc.) in this way. [16th c.: orig. unkn.: cf. SPATCHCOCK]

spite /spīt/ *n.* & *v.* ● *n.* **1** ill will; malice toward a person (*did it from spite*). **2** a grudge. ● *v.tr.* thwart; mortify; annoy (*does it to spite me*). □ **in spite of** notwithstanding. **in spite of oneself**, etc., though one would rather have done otherwise. [ME f. OF *despit* DESPITE]
■ *n.* **1** spitefulness, maliciousness, malice, malevolence, malignity, ill will, venom, spleen, rancor, animosity, gall (and wormwood), resentment, bitterness, hostility, antagonism, hatred, hate, *sl.* bitchiness. **2** grudge, grievance, resentment. ● *v.* annoy, irritate, vex, upset, disconcert, offend, provoke, discomfit, pique, put out, hurt, injure, wound, mortify, thwart, *colloq.* peeve, get under a person's skin, needle. □ **in spite of** despite, notwithstanding, regardless of, ignoring, in defiance of.

spiteful /spítfool/ *adj.* motivated by spite; malevolent. □□ **spitefully** *adv.* **spitefulness** *n.*
■ malevolent, malicious, malignant, venomous, vindictive, hateful, invidious, hostile, antagonistic, unfriendly, unforgiving, retaliative, retaliatory, punitive, retributive, retributory, *sl.* bitchy. □□ **spitefulness** see SPITE *n.* 1.

spitfire /spítfir/ *n.* a person with a fiery temper.
■ see SHREW.

spittle /spít'l/ *n.* saliva, esp. as ejected from the mouth. □□ **spittly** *adj.* [alt. of ME (now dial.) *spattle* = OE *spātl* f. *spǣtan* to spit, after SPIT¹]
■ see SPIT¹ *n.*

spittoon /spitōōn/ *n.* a metal or earthenware pot with esp. a funnel shaped top, used for spitting into.

spitz /spits/ *n.* **1** any of a stocky type of dog with a pointed muzzle and a tail curved over the back, as a Pomeranian, Samoyed, etc. **2** this breed. [G *Spitz(hund)* f. *spitz* pointed + *Hund* dog]

spiv /spiv/ *n. Brit. colloq.* a man, often characterized by flashy dress, who makes a living by illicit or unscrupulous dealings. □□ **spivvish** *adj.* **spivvy** *adj.* [20th c.: orig. unkn.]

splanchnic /splángknik/ *adj.* of or relating to the viscera; in-

/.../ pronunciation	● part of speech
□ phrases, idioms, and compounds	
□□ derivatives	■ synonym section
cross-references appear in SMALL CAPITALS or *italics*	

testinal. [mod.L *splanchnicus* f. Gk *splagkhnikos* f. *splagkhna* entrails]

splash /splash/ *v. & n.* ● *v.* **1** *intr. & tr.* spatter or cause (liquid) to spatter in small drops. **2** *tr.* cause (a person) to be spattered with liquid, etc. (*splashed them with mud*). **3** *intr.* **a** (of a person) cause liquid to spatter (*was splashing about in the bath*). **b** (usu. foll. by *across, along*, etc.) move while spattering liquid, etc. (*splashed across the carpet in his boots*). **c** step, fall, or plunge, etc., into a liquid, etc., so as to cause a splash (*splashed into the sea*). **d** (foll. by *down*) (of a spacecraft) land in the sea after flight. **4** *tr.* display (news) prominently. **5** *tr.* decorate with scattered color. **6** *tr. Brit.* spend (money) ostentatiously. ● *n.* **1** the act or an instance of splashing. **2 a** a quantity of liquid splashed. **b** the resulting noise (*heard a splash*). **3** a spot or patch of dirt, etc., splashed on to a thing. **4** a prominent news feature, etc. **5** a daub or patch of color, esp. on an animal's coat. **6** *colloq.* a small quantity of liquid, esp. of soda water, etc., to dilute liquor. □ **make a splash** attract much attention, esp. by extravagance. **splash out** *Brit. colloq.* spend money freely. □□ **splashy** *adj.* (**splashier, splashiest**). [alt. of PLASH¹]

■ *v.* **1** spatter, bespatter, spray, shower, scatter, daub, sprinkle, splatter, *colloq.* slosh. **2** spatter, speckle, bespatter, spray, shower, scatter, dabble, daub, bedaub, sprinkle, besprinkle, splatter, *colloq.* slosh, splotch. **3** splatter, slosh, plash, wade, dabble, paddle, *colloq.* splosh. **4** blazon, display, spread, plaster. ● *n.* **2** splatter, spatter, slosh, *colloq.* splosh. **3** spatter, spray, sprinkle, spot, stain, smear, smudge, blotch, *colloq.* splotch. **5** patch, daub, blotch, *colloq.* splotch. **6** see DASH *n.* 7. □ **make a splash** make an impression or impact, cause a sensation *or* brouhaha *or* to-do *or* commotion, cause an uproar.

splashboard /spláshbawrd/ (*Brit.* **splashback**) *n.* a panel behind a sink, etc., to protect the wall from splashes.

splashdown /spláshdown/ *n.* the landing of a spacecraft in the sea.

splat¹ /splat/ *n.* a flat piece of thin wood in the center of a chair back. [*splat* (v.) split up, rel. to SPLIT]

splat² /splat/ *n., adv., & v. colloq.* ● *n.* a sharp cracking or slapping sound (*hit the wall with a splat*). ● *adv.* with a splat (*fell splat into the puddle*). ● *v.intr. & tr.* (**splatted, splatting**) fall or hit with a splat. [abbr. of SPLATTER]

splatter /splátər/ *v. & n.* ● *v.* **1** *tr. & intr.* splash esp. with a continuous noisy action. **2** *tr.* (often foll. by *with*) make wet or dirty by splashing. ● *n.* a noisy splashing sound. [imit.]

■ *v.* see SPLASH *v.* 1–3. ● *n.* see SPLASH *n.* 2.

splay /splay/ *v., n., & adj.* ● *v.* **1** *tr.* (usu. foll. by *out*) spread (the elbows, feet, etc.) out. **2** *intr.* (of an aperture or its sides) diverge in shape or position. **3** *tr.* construct (a window, doorway, aperture, etc.) so that it diverges or is wider at one side of the wall than the other. ● *n.* a surface making an oblique angle with another, e.g., the splayed side of a window or embrasure. ● *adj.* **1** wide and flat. **2** turned outward. [ME f. DISPLAY]

splayfoot /spláyfŏŏt/ *n.* a broad flat foot turned outward. □□ **splayfooted** *adj.*

spleen /spleen/ *n.* **1** an abdominal organ involved in maintaining the proper condition of blood in most vertebrates. **2** lowness of spirits; moroseness, ill temper, spite (from the earlier belief that the spleen was the seat of such feelings) (*a fit of spleen; vented their spleen*). □□ **spleenful** *adj.* **spleeny** *adj.* [ME f. OF *esplen* f. L *splen* f. Gk *splēn*]

■ **2** see SPITE *n.* 1.

spleenwort /spleenwərt, -wawrt/ *n.* any fern of the genus *Asplenium*, formerly used as a remedy for disorders of the spleen.

splen- /spleen/ *comb. form Anat.* the spleen. [Gk (as SPLEEN)]

splendent /spléndənt/ *adj. formal* **1** shining; lustrous. **2** illustrious. [ME f. L *splendēre* to shine]

splendid /spléndid/ *adj.* **1** magnificent; gorgeous; brilliant; sumptuous (*a splendid palace; a splendid achievement*). **2** dignified; impressive (*splendid isolation*). **3** excellent; fine (*a splendid chance*). □□ **splendidly** *adv.* **splendidness** *n.* [F *splendide* or L *splendidus* (as SPLENDENT)]

■ **1** magnificent, resplendent, dazzling, gorgeous, showy, dashing, marvelous, spectacular, grand, glorious, lavish, ornate, sumptuous, majestic, brilliant, extraordinary, exceptional, superb, supreme, imposing, impressive, awe-inspiring, awesome, lush, plush, rich, luxurious, swanky, *colloq.* posh, ritzy, swank, *colloq. or joc.* splendiferous; eminent, prominent, superior, noteworthy, notable, celebrated, illustrious, famous, distinguished, dignified, exemplary, remarkable, admirable, conspicuous, outstanding, sublime, striking, successful, meritorious, creditable, *formal* splendent. **3** excellent, superior, preeminent, fine, marvelous, extraordinary, exceptional, unbelievable, incredible, far-out, first-class, unequaled, unsurpassed, stupendous, peerless, matchless, nonpareil, superlative, praiseworthy, admirable, laudable, *colloq.* great, colossal, fabulous, fab, fantastic, terrific, super, smashing, A1, tiptop, capital, way-out, out of sight, keen, brilliant, dandy, *sl.* cool, neat. □□ **splendidness** see SPLENDOR 2.

splendiferous /splendífərəs/ *adj. colloq. or joc.* splendid. □□ **splendiferously** *adv.* **splendiferousness** *n.* [irreg. f. SPLENDOR]

■ see SPLENDID 1.

splendor /spléndər/ *n.* (*Brit.* **splendour**) **1** great or dazzling brightness. **2** magnificence; grandeur. [ME f. AF *splendour* or L *splendor* (as SPLENDENT)]

■ **1** brilliance, shine, luster, light, brightness, glitter, dazzle, luminosity, luminousness, gloss, *literary* effulgence, refulgence. **2** magnificence, grandeur, brilliance, display, radiance, resplendence, sumptuousness, stateliness, majesty, panoply, spectacle, show, glory, pomp, gorgeousness, dazzle, beauty, splendidness, exquisiteness, luxuriousness, richness, lavishness, luxury, swankiness, *colloq.* poshness, swank, ritziness, *colloq. or joc.* splendiferousness, *literary* refulgence.

splenectomy /splinéktəmee/ *n.* (*pl.* **-ies**) the surgical excision of the spleen.

splenetic /splinétik/ *adj. & n.* ● *adj.* **1** ill-tempered; peevish. **2** of or concerning the spleen. ● *n.* a splenetic person. □□ **splenetically** *adv.* [LL *spleneticus* (as SPLEEN)]

■ *adj.* **1** see PEEVISH.

splenic /splénik/ *adj.* of or in the spleen. □ **splenic fever** anthrax. □□ **splenoid** /spléenoyd/ *adj.* [F *splénique* or L *splenicus* f. Gk *splēnikos* (as SPLEEN)]

splenitis /spleenítis/ *n.* inflammation of the spleen.

splenius /spléeneeəs/ *n.* (*pl.* **splenii** /-nee-ī/) *Anat.* either section of muscle on each side of the neck and back serving to draw back the head. □□ **splenial** *adj.* [mod.L f. Gk *splēnion* bandage]

splenology /spleenóləjee/ *n.* the scientific study of the spleen.

splenomegaly /spléenəmégəlee/ *n.* a pathological enlargement of the spleen. [SPLEN- + *megaly* (as MEGALO-)]

splenotomy /spleenótəmee/ *n.* (*pl.* **-ies**) a surgical incision into or dissection of the spleen.

splice /splīs/ *v. & n.* ● *v.tr.* **1** join the ends of (ropes) by interweaving strands. **2** join (pieces of timber, magnetic tape, film, etc.) in an overlapping position. **3** artificially combine genetic materials. **4** (esp. as **spliced** *adj.*) *colloq.* join in marriage. ● *n.* a joint consisting of two ropes, pieces of wood, film, etc., made by splicing. □ **splice the main brace** *Naut. hist.* issue an extra tot of rum. □□ **splicer** *n.* [prob. f. MDu. *splissen*, of uncert. orig.]

■ *v.* **1** entwine, intertwine, braid, plait, twist, interlace, interweave, knit. **2** dovetail, mesh, fit (together), knit, interlock, engage. **4** join, unite, marry, bind, conjoin. ● *n.* union, joint, connection, tie, bond, binding, fastening, linkage.

spliff /splif/ *n.* (also **splif**) *sl.* a marijuana cigarette. [20th c.: orig. unkn.]

spline /splīn/ *n. & v.* ● *n.* **1** a rectangular key fitting into grooves in the hub and shaft of a wheel and allowing longitudinal play. **2** a slat. **3** a flexible wood or rubber strip used esp. in drawing large curves. ● *v.tr.* fit with a spline (sense 1). [orig. E. Anglian dial., perh. rel. to SPLINTER]

splint /splint/ *n. & v.* ● *n.* **1 a** a strip of rigid material used for holding a broken bone, etc., when set. **b** a rigid or flexible strip of esp. wood used in basketwork, etc. **2** a tumor or bony excrescence on the inside of a horse's leg. **3** a thin strip of wood, etc., used to light a fire, pipe, etc. **4** = *splint bone.* ● *v.tr.* secure (a broken limb, etc.) with a splint or splints. □ **splint bone 1** either of two small bones in a horse's foreleg lying behind and close to the cannon bone. **2** the human fibula. **splint coal** hard bituminous laminated coal burning with great heat. [ME *splent(e)* f. MDu. *splinte* or MLG *splinte, splente* metal plate or pin, rel. to SPLINTER]

splinter /splíntər/ *v. & n.* ● *v.tr. & intr.* break into fragments. ● *n.* a small thin sharp-edged piece broken off from wood, stone, etc. □ **splinter group** (or **party**) a group or party that has broken away from a larger one. □□ **splintery** *adj.* [ME f. MDu. (= LG) *splinter, splenter,* rel. to SPLINT]

■ *v.* shatter, break, fragment, split, disintegrate, shiver, smash to smithereens. ● *n.* sliver, shiver, fragment, piece; scrap, shard, shred, chip.

split /split/ *v. & n.* ● *v.* (**splitting**; *past* and *past part.* **split**) **1** *intr. & tr.* **a** break or cause to break forcibly into parts, esp. with the grain or into halves. **b** (often foll. by *up*) divide into parts (*split into groups*; *split up the money equally*). **c** *intr. Stock Exch.* divide into two or more shares for each share owned. **2** *tr. & intr.* (often foll. by *off, away*) remove or be removed by breaking, separating, or dividing (*split away from the main group*). **3** *intr. & tr.* **a** (usu. foll. by *up, on, over,* etc.) separate esp. through discord (*split up after ten years*; *they were split on the question of picketing*). **b** (foll. by *with*) quarrel or cease association with (another person, etc.). **4** *tr.* cause the fission of (an atom). **5** *intr. & tr. sl.* leave, esp. suddenly. **6** *intr.* (usu. foll. by *on*) *Brit. colloq.* betray secrets; inform (*split on them to the police*). **7** *intr.* **a** (as **splitting** *adj.*) (esp. of a headache) very painful; acute. **b** (of the head) suffer great pain from a headache, noise, etc. **8** *intr.* (of a ship) be wrecked. **9** *tr. colloq.* dilute (whiskey, etc.) with water. ● *n.* **1** the act or an instance of splitting; the state of being split. **2** a fissure, vent, crack, cleft, etc. **3** a separation into parties; a schism. **4** (in *pl.*) the athletic feat of leaping in the air or sitting down with the legs at right angles to the body in front and behind, or at the sides with the trunk facing forward. **5** a split willow shoot, etc., used for parts of basketwork. **6** each strip of steel, cane, etc., of the reed in a loom. **7** a single thickness of split hide. **8** the turning up of two cards of equal value in faro, so that the stakes are divided. **9 a** half a bottle of mineral water. **b** half a glass of liquor. **10** *colloq.* a division of money, esp. the proceeds of crime. **11** = *banana split.* □ **split the difference** take the average of two proposed amounts. **split gear** (or **pulley** or **wheel**) a gear, etc., made in halves for removal from a shaft. **split hairs** make small and insignificant distinctions. **split infinitive** a phrase consisting of an infinitive with an adverb, etc., inserted between *to* and the verb, e.g., *seems to really like it.* **split-level** (of a building) having a room or rooms a fraction of a story higher than other parts. **split pea** a dried pea split in half for cooking. **split personality** the alteration or dissociation of personality occurring in some mental illnesses, esp. schizophrenia and hysteria. **split ring** a small steel ring with two spiral turns, such as a key ring. **split screen** a screen on which two or more separate images are displayed. **split second** a very brief moment of time. **split shift** a shift comprising two or more separate periods of duty. **split one's sides** be convulsed with laughter. **split the ticket** (or **one's vote**) vote for candidates of more than one party in one election. **split the vote** (of a candidate or minority party) attract votes from another so that both are defeated by a third. □□ **splitter** *n.* [orig. Naut. f. MDu. *splitten,* rel. to *spletten, splīten,* MHG *splīzen*]

■ *v.* **1 a** split up *or* apart, divide, separate, cut *or* chop apart, cut *or* chop in two, pull *or* tear apart, break *or* snap apart, break *or* snap in two, break up, fracture, come apart, fall apart, rupture, partition, detach, become detached, *archaic or rhet.* rend, *literary* cleave;

bisect, dichotomize, halve; burst, *colloq.* bust. **b** divide (up), apportion, deal out, dole out, distribute, allot, allocate, share *or* parcel out, carve up; branch, fork, bifurcate, diverge, separate. **3 a** (*split up*) divorce, separate, go separate ways, break up, part company, *colloq.* bust up. **5** see LEAVE[1] *v.* 1b, 3, 4. **7 a** (**splitting**) severe, bad, acute, *colloq.* awful, thumping. **9** see DILUTE *v.* ● *n.* **1** see SEPARATION. **2** crack, cleft, fissure, chink, cranny, slit, slot, crevice, cleavage, groove, furrow, channel; gap, hiatus, lacuna, opening, separation, division, chasm; rift, break, rupture, fracture; slash, gash, tear, rip, rent, vent; *Anat.* sulcus. **3** division, dichotomy, schism, breach, rupture, partition, disunion, dissociation, discord; break, separation, divorce. □ **split hairs** see QUIBBLE *v.* **split second** see SECOND[2]. **split one's sides** see LAUGH *v.* 1.

splodge /sploj/ *n. & v.tr. Brit.* = SPLOTCH.

splosh /splosh/ *v. & n. colloq.* ● *v.tr. & intr.* move with a splashing sound. ● *n.* **1** a splashing sound. **2** a splash of water, etc. **3** *Brit. sl.* money. [imit.]

splotch /sploch/ *n. & v.tr. colloq.* ● *n.* a daub, blot, or smear. ● *v.tr.* make a large, esp. irregular, spot or patch on. □□ **splodgy** /splójee/ *adj.* [imit., or alt. of SPLOTCH] □□ **splotchy** *adj.* [perh. f. SPOT + obs. *plotch* BLOTCH]

■ *n.* see BLOT *n.* 1. ● *v.* see SPLASH *v.* 2.

splurge /splərj/ *n. & v. colloq.* ● *n.* **1** an ostentatious display or effort. **2** an instance of sudden great extravagance. ● *v.intr.* (usu. foll. by *on*) spend effort or esp. large sums of money (*splurged on new furniture*). [19th-c. US: prob. imit.]

■ *n.* **1** display, show, ostentatiousness, ostentation, splash, burst, outburst, access. **2** extravagance, indulgence, fling, *colloq.* spree. ● *v.* squander *or* dissipate *or* waste money, burn (up) money, throw away money, show off one's money, flaunt one's money, esp. *Brit.* lash out, *sl.* blow one's money.

splutter /splútər/ *v. & n.* ● *v.* **1** *intr.* **a** speak in a hurried, vehement, or choking manner. **b** emit particles from the mouth, sparks, hot oil, etc., with spitting sounds. **2** *tr.* **a** speak or utter (words, threats, a language, etc.) rapidly or incoherently. **b** emit (food, sparks, hot oil, etc.) with a spitting sound. ● *n.* spluttering speech. □□ **splutterer** *n.* **splutteringly** *adv.* [SPUTTER by assoc. with *splash*]

■ *v.* **1b, 2b** see SPIT[1] *v.* 2b, 3.

Spode /spōd/ *n.* a type of fine pottery or porcelain. [J. *Spode,* Engl. maker of china d. 1827]

spoil /spoyl/ *v. & n.* ● *v.* (*past* and *past part.* **spoiled** or esp. *Brit.* **spoilt**) **1** *tr.* **a** damage; diminish the value of (*was spoiled by the rain*; *will spoil all the fun*). **b** reduce a person's enjoyment, etc., of (*the news spoiled his dinner*). **2** *tr.* injure the character of (esp. a child, pet, etc.) by excessive indulgence. **3** *intr.* **a** (of food) go bad; decay; become unfit for eating. **b** (usu. in *neg.*) (of a joke, secret, etc.) become stale through long keeping. **4** *tr.* render (a ballot) invalid by improper marking. **5** *tr.* (foll. by *of*) *archaic* or *literary* plunder or deprive (a person of a thing) by force or stealth (*spoiled him of all his possessions*). ● *n.* **1** (usu. in *pl.*) **a** plunder taken from an enemy in war, or seized by force. **b** esp. *joc.* profit or advantages gained by succeeding to public office, high position, etc. **2** earth, etc., thrown up in excavating, dredging, etc. □ **be spoiling for** aggressively seek (a fight, etc.). **spoils system** the practice of giving public office to the adherents of a successful party. **spoilt for choice** esp. *Brit.* having so many choices that it is difficult to choose. [ME f. OF *espoillier, espoille* f. L *spoliare* f. *spolium* spoil, plunder, or f. DESPOIL]

■ *v.* **1** ruin, destroy, wreck, blight, queer, mess up, bungle, botch, upset, demolish, sabotage, undermine, harm, damage, vitiate, mar, injure, debase, deface, disfigure, mutilate, scar, blemish, kill, *colloq.* make a

---

/. . ./ **pronunciation**	● **part of speech**
□ **phrases, idioms, and compounds**	
□□ **derivatives**	■ **synonym section**
cross-references appear in SMALL CAPITALS or *italics*	

hash of, fluff, *sl.* blow. **2** baby, mollycoddle, coddle, cosset, indulge, overindulge, pamper, dote on, spoonfeed. **3 a** turn, go off, go bad, deteriorate, curdle, molder, decay, decompose, perish, become addle(d), rot, putrefy, mildew. ● *n.* **1** (*spoils*) **a** loot, booty, plunder, pillage, prizes, pickings, takings, take, *sl.* swag, boodle. **b** benefits, advantages, perquisites, *colloq.* perks. □ **be spoiling for** itch for *or* after, yearn for, be eager for, be keen for, look for, be bent on, be desirous of, crave, be after. **spoilt for choice** (*be spoiled for choice*) have an *embarras de choix* or *richesse(s)*.

spoilage /spóylij/ *n.* **1** paper spoiled in printing. **2** the spoiling of food, etc., by decay.

spoiler /spóylǝr/ *n.* **1** a person or thing that spoils. **2 a** a device on an aircraft to retard its speed or reduce lift by interrupting the air flow. **b** a similar device on a vehicle to improve its road-holding at speed.

spoilsman /spóylzmǝn/ *n.* (*pl.* **-men**) esp. *Polit.* **1** an advocate of the spoils system. **2** a person who seeks to profit by it.

spoilsport /spóylspawrt/ *n.* a person who spoils others' pleasure or enjoyment.
■ killjoy, damper, dog in the manger, *colloq.* wet blanket, *sl.* party pooper, *Austral. sl.* wowser.

spoilt esp. *Brit.* past and past part. of SPOIL.

spoke[1] /spōk/ *n. & v.* ● *n.* **1** each of the bars running from the hub to the rim of a wheel. **2** a rung of a ladder. **3** each radial handle of the wheel of a ship, etc. ● *v.tr.* **1** provide with spokes. **2** obstruct (a wheel, etc.) by thrusting a spoke in. □ **put a spoke in a person's wheel** *Brit.* thwart or hinder a person. □□ **spokewise** *adv.* [OE *spāca* f. WG]

spoke[2] past of SPEAK.

spoken /spōkǝn/ past part. of SPEAK. ● *adj.* (in *comb.*) speaking in a specified way (*smooth-spoken; well-spoken*). □ **spoken for** claimed; requisitioned (*this seat is spoken for*).
■ *adj.* speaking. □ **spoken for** reserved, bespoke, set aside, accounted for, chosen, selected, claimed, requisitioned, engaged, betrothed, attached.

spokeshave /spōkshayv/ *n.* a blade set between two handles, used for shaping spokes and other esp. curved work where an ordinary plane is not suitable.

spokesman /spōksmǝn/ *n.* (*pl.* **-men**; *fem.* **spokeswoman**, *pl.* **-women**) **1** a person who speaks on behalf of others, esp. in the course of public relations. **2** a person deputed to express the views of a group, etc. [irreg. f. SPOKE[2] after *craftsman*, etc.]

spokesperson /spōkspǝrsǝn/ *n.* (*pl.* **-persons** or **-people**) a spokesman or spokeswoman.

spoliation /spōleeáyshǝn/ *n.* **1 a** plunder or pillage, esp. of neutral vessels in war. **b** extortion. **2** *Eccl.* the taking of the fruits of a benefice under a pretended title, etc. **3** *Law* the destruction, mutilation, or alteration of a document to prevent its being used as evidence. □□ **spoliator** /-leeáytǝr/ *n.* **spoliatory** /-leeǝtáwree/ *adj.* [ME f. L *spoliatio* (as SPOIL)]

spondaic /spondáyik/ *adj.* **1** of or concerning spondees. **2** (of a hexameter) having a spondee as a fifth foot. [F *spondaïque* or LL *spondaicus* = LL *spondiacus* f. Gk *spondeiakos* (as SPONDEE)]

spondee /spóndee/ *n.* *Prosody* a foot consisting of two long (or stressed) syllables. [ME f. OF *spondee* or L *spondeus* f. Gk *spondeios* (*pous* foot) f. *spondē* libation, as being characteristic of music accompanying libations)]

spondylitis /spóndǝlítis/ *n.* inflammation of the vertebrae. [L *spondylus* vertebra f. Gk *spondulos* + -ITIS]

sponge /spunj/ *n. & v.* ● *n.* **1** any aquatic animal of the phylum Porifera, with pores in its body wall and a rigid internal skeleton. **2 a** the skeleton of a sponge, esp. the soft light elastic absorbent kind used in bathing, cleaning surfaces, etc. **b** a piece of porous rubber or plastic, etc., used similarly. **3** a thing of spongelike absorbency or consistency, e.g., a sponge cake, porous metal, etc. (*lemon sponge*). **4** = SPONGER. **5** *colloq.* a person who drinks heavily. **6** cleaning with or as with a sponge (*gave the stove a quick sponge*). ● *v.* **1** *tr.* wipe or clean with a sponge. **2** *tr.* (also *absol.*; often foll. by *down, over*) sluice water over (the body, a car, etc.). **3** *tr.*

(often foll. by *out, away,* etc.) wipe off or efface (writing, a memory, etc.) with or as with a sponge. **4** *tr.* (often foll. by *up*) absorb with or as with a sponge. **5** *intr.* (often foll. by *on, off*) live as a parasite; be dependent upon (another person). **6** *tr.* obtain (drink, etc.) by sponging. **7** *intr.* gather sponges. **8** *tr.* apply paint with a sponge to (walls, furniture, etc.). □ **sponge cake** a very light cake with a spongelike consistency. **sponge cloth 1** soft, lightly woven cloth with a slightly wrinkled surface. **2** a thin spongy material used for cleaning. **sponge pudding** *Brit.* a steamed or baked dessert dish of shortening, flour, and eggs with a usu. specified flavor. **sponge rubber** liquid rubber latex processed into a spongelike substance. **sponge tree** a spiny tropical acacia, *Acacia farnesiana*, with globose heads of fragrant yellow flowers yielding a perfume: also called *opopanax*. □□ **spongeable** *adj.* **spongelike** *adj.* **spongiform** *adj.* (esp. in senses 1, 2). [OE f. L *spongia* f. Gk *spoggia, spoggos*]
■ *n.* **5** see DRUNK *n.* 1. ● *v.* **1, 2** see CLEAN *v.* 1. **3** see ERASE. **4** (*sponge up*) see SOAK *v.* 3a. **5** (*sponge off*) *sl.* bum off. **6** see BUM[2] *v.* 2. □□ **spongelike** see POROUS 1, 2.

sponger /spúnjǝr/ *n.* a person who contrives to live at another's expense.
■ see PARASITE.

spongy /spúnjee/ *adj.* (**spongier, spongiest**) **1** like a sponge, esp. in being porous, compressible, elastic, or absorbent. **2** (of metal) finely divided and loosely coherent. □□ **spongily** *adv.* **sponginess** *n.*
■ **1** see POROUS 1, 2, SOFT *adj.* 1.

sponsion /spónshǝn/ *n.* **1** being a surety for another. **2** a pledge or promise made on behalf of the government by an agent not authorized to do so. [L *sponsio* f. *spondēre spons-* promise solemnly]

sponson /spónsǝn/ *n.* **1** a projection from the side of a warship or tank to enable a gun to be trained forward and aft. **2** a short subsidiary wing to stabilize a seaplane. **3** a triangular platform supporting the wheel on a paddle-steamer. **4** a flotation chamber along the gunwale of a canoe. [19th c.: orig. unkn.]

sponsor /spónsǝr/ *n. & v.* ● *n.* **1** a person who supports an activity done for charity by pledging money in advance. **2 a** a person or organization that promotes or supports an artistic or sporting activity, etc. **b** a business organization that promotes a broadcast program in return for advertising time. **3** an organization lending support to an election candidate. **4** a person who introduces a proposal for legislation. **5** *Eccles.* a godparent at baptism or esp. a person who presents a candidate for confirmation. **6** a person who makes himself or herself responsible for another. ● *v.tr.* be a sponsor for. □□ **sponsorial** /sponsáwreeǝl/ *adj.* **sponsorship** *n.* [L (as SPONSION)]
■ *n.* **1, 2a, 3** backer, supporter, promoter, patron, Maecenas, benefactor, subsidizer, *sl.* angel. **2 b** (radio *or* television) advertiser. ● *v.* back, support, promote, fund, patronize, subsidize, finance, underwrite. □□ **sponsorship** see BACKING 1a, b.

spontaneous /spontáyneeǝs/ *adj.* **1** acting or done or occurring without external cause. **2** voluntary; without external incitement (*made a spontaneous offer of his services*). **3** *Biol.* (of structural changes in plants and muscular activity esp. in young animals) instinctive; automatic; prompted by no motive. **4** (of bodily movement, literary style, etc.) gracefully natural and unconstrained. **5** (of sudden movement, etc.) involuntary; not due to conscious volition. **6** growing naturally without cultivation. □ **spontaneous combustion** the ignition of a mineral or vegetable substance (e.g., a heap of rags soaked with oil, a mass of wet coal) from heat engendered within itself, usu. by rapid oxidation. **spontaneous generation** the supposed production of living from nonliving matter as inferred from the appearance of life (due in fact to bacteria, etc.) in some infusions; abiogenesis. □□ **spontaneity** /spóntǝnéeitee, -náyitee/ *n.* **spontaneously** *adv.* **spontaneousness** *n.* [LL *spontaneus* f. *sponte* of one's own accord]
■ **2** see VOLUNTARY *adj.* 1. **4** unconstrained, unforced,

natural, unstudied, unaffected. **5** involuntary, instinctive, instinctual, unconscious, reflex, automatic, mechanical, immediate, offhand, unguarded, unthinking, unwitting, impetuous, impulsive, knee-jerk. □□ **spontaneously** see *automatically* (AUTOMATIC), *voluntarily* (VOLUNTARY).

spoof /spoof/ *n. & v. colloq.* ● *n.* **1** a parody. **2** a hoax or swindle. ● *v.tr.* **1** parody. **2** hoax; swindle. □□ **spoofer** *n.* **spoofery** *n.* [invented by A. Roberts, English comedian d. 1933]
■ *n.* **1** see PARODY *n.* 1. ● *v.* **1** see PARODY *v.*

spook /spook/ *n. & v.* ● *n.* **1** *colloq.* a ghost. **2** *sl.* a spy. ● *v. sl.* **1** *tr.* frighten; unnerve; alarm. **2** *intr.* take fright; become alarmed. [Du., = MLG *spōk*, of unkn. orig.]
■ *n.* **1** see GHOST *n.* 1. **2** see AGENT 1b. ● *v.* **1** see SCARE *v.* 1. **2** scare, frighten, *sl.* spook.

spooky /spookee/ *adj.* (**spookier**, **spookiest**) **1** *colloq.* ghostly; eerie. **2** *sl.* nervous; easily frightened. **3** *sl.* of spies or espionage. □□ **spookily** *adv.* **spookiness** *n.*
■ **1** see GHOSTLY. **2** see JUMPY 1.

spool /spool/ *n. & v.* ● *n.* **1 a** a reel for winding magnetic tape, photographic film, etc., on. **b** a reel for winding yarn, thread, or wire on. **c** a quantity of tape, yarn, etc., wound on a spool. **2** the revolving cylinder of an angler's reel. ● *v.tr.* wind on a spool. [ME f. OF *espole* or f. MLG *spōle*, MDu. *spoele*, OHG *spuolo*, of unkn. orig.]
■ *n.* **1 c** see ROLL *n.* 5a, TAPE *n.* 4b. ● *v.* reel, wind.

spoon /spoon/ *n. & v.* ● *n.* **1 a** a utensil consisting of an oval or round bowl and a handle for conveying food (esp. liquid) to the mouth, for stirring, etc. **b** a spoonful, esp. of sugar. **c** (in *pl.*) *Mus.* a pair of spoons held in the hand and beaten together rhythmically. **2** a spoon shaped thing, esp.: **a** (in full **spoon-bait**) a bright revolving piece of metal used as a lure in fishing. **b** an oar with a broad curved blade. **c** a wooden-headed golf club. **3** *colloq.* **a** a silly or demonstratively fond lover. **b** a simpleton. ● *v.* **1** *tr.* (often foll. by *up*, *out*) take (liquid, etc.) with a spoon. **2** *colloq.* **a** *intr.* behave in an amorous way, esp. foolishly. **b** *tr. archaic* woo in a silly or sentimental way. □ **born with a silver spoon in one's mouth** born into affluence. **spoon bread** soft corn bread. □□ **spooner** *n.* **spoonful** *n.* (*pl.* **-fuls**). [OE *spōn* chip of wood f. Gmc]
■ *n.* **1 a** see SCOOP *n.* 1b. ● *v.* **1** (*spoon out*) see SCOOP *v.* 1. **2 a** see KISS *v.* 3. □□ **spoonful** see MOUTHFUL 1.

spoonbill /spoonbil/ *n.* **1** any large wading bird of the subfamily Plataleidae, having a bill with a very broad flat tip. **2** a shoveler duck.

spoonerism /spoonərizəm/ *n.* a transposition, usu. accidental, of the initial letters, etc., of two or more words, e.g., *you have hissed the mystery lectures*. [Rev. W. A. *Spooner*, English scholar d. 1930, reputed to make such errors in speaking]

spoonfeed /spoonfeed/ *v.tr.* (*past* and *past part.* **-fed**) **1** feed (a baby, etc.) with a spoon. **2** provide help, information, etc., to (a person) without requiring any effort on the recipient's part. **3** artificially encourage (an industry) by subsidies or import duties.
■ **2** see SPOIL *v.* 2.

spoony /spoonee/ *adj. & n. colloq. archaic* ● *adj.* (**spoonier**, **spooniest**) **1** (often foll. by *on*) sentimental; amorous. **2** foolish; silly. ● *n.* (*pl.* **-ies**) a simpleton. □□ **spoonily** *adv.* **spooniness** *n.*

spoor /spoor/ *n. & v.* ● *n.* the track, droppings, or scent of an animal. ● *v.tr. & intr.* follow by the spoor. □□ **spoorer** *n.* [Afrik. f. MDu. *spo(o)r* f. Gmc]
■ *n.* see TRACK[1] *n.* 1. ● *v.* see TRACK *v.* 1.

sporadic /spərádik, spaw-/ *adj.* occurring only here and there or occasionally; separate; scattered. □□ **sporadically** *adv.* [med.L *sporadicus* f. Gk *sporadikos* f. *sporas -ados* scattered: cf. *speirō* to sow]
■ occasional, intermittent, random, casual, odd, irregular, patchy, spotty, scattered, uneven, erratic, chance, unexpected; spasmodic(al), fitful, periodic(al); separate. □□ **sporadically** see *occasionally* (OCCASIONAL).

sporangium /spəránjeeəm/ *n.* (*pl.* **sporangia** /-jeeə/) *Bot.*

a receptacle in which spores are found. □□ **sporangial** *adj.* [mod.L f. Gk *spora* SPORE + *aggeion* vessel]

spore /spawr/ *n.* **1** a specialized reproductive cell of many plants and microorganisms. **2** these collectively. [mod.L *spora* f. Gk *spora* sowing, seed f. *speirō* sow]
■ **1** see SEED *n.* 1a.

sporo- /spáwrō/ *comb. form Biol.* a spore. [Gk *spora* (as SPORE)]

sporogenesis /spáwrəjénisis/ *n.* the process of spore formation.

sporogenous /spərójinəs/ *adj.* producing spores.

sporophyte /spáwrəfīt/ *n.* a spore-producing form of plant with alternating sexual and asexual generations. □□ **sporophytic** /-fítik/ *adj.* **sporophytically** *adv.*

sporran /spáwrən, spór-/ *n.* a pouch, usu. of leather or sealskin covered with fur, etc., worn by a Highland Scot in front of the kilt. [Gael. *sporan* f. med.L *bursa* PURSE]

sport /spawrt/ *n. & v.* ● *n.* **1 a** a game or competitive activity, esp. an outdoor one involving physical exertion, e.g., baseball, football, racing, hunting. **b** (usu. in *pl.*) such activities collectively (*the world of sports*). **2** (in *pl.*) *Brit.* **a** a meeting for competing in sports, esp. track and field (*school sports*). **b** athletics. **3** amusement; diversion; fun. **4** *colloq.* **a** a fair or generous person. **b** a person behaving in a specified way, esp. regarding games, rules, etc. (*a bad sport at tennis*). **c** a form of address, esp. between males. **5** *Biol.* an animal or plant deviating suddenly or strikingly from the normal type. **6** a plaything or laughingstock (*was the sport of Fortune*). ● *v.* **1** *intr.* **a** divert oneself; take part in a pastime. **b** frolic; gambol. **2** *tr.* wear, exhibit, or produce, esp. ostentatiously (*sported a gold tiepin*). **3** *intr. Biol.* become or produce a sport. □ **in sport** jestingly. **make sport of** make fun of; ridicule. **the sport of kings** horseracing (less often war, hunting, or surfing). **sports car** a usu. open, low-built fast car. **sports coat** (or **jacket**) a man's jacket for informal wear. **sports writer** a person who writes (esp. as a journalist) on sports. □□ **sporter** *n.* [ME f. DISPORT]
■ *n.* **1 a** game, activity, pastime, recreation. **b** games, recreation, play. **3** recreation, diversion, amusement, entertainment, play, distraction, relaxation, divertissement, pleasure, enjoyment, fun, dalliance. **4 a, b** sportsman, sportswoman. ● *v.* **1** amuse oneself, divert oneself; frolic, gambol, romp, caper, play, frisk, rollick, skip about, *colloq.* lark, *literary* wanton, *sl.* cavort. **2** show off, exhibit, flaunt, display, wear, parade, flourish. □ **in sport** in jest, jestingly, jokingly, in fun, teasingly, playfully. **make sport of** make fun of, tease, deride, make a laughingstock of, (hold up to) ridicule, make a fool of.

sporting /spáwrting/ *adj.* **1** interested in sports (*a sporting man*). **2** sportsmanlike; generous (*a sporting offer*). **3** concerned about or involved in sports (*a sporting dog*; *sporting news*). □ **a sporting chance** some possibility of success. □□ **sportingly** *adv.*
■ **2** see LAVISH *adj.* 2.

sportive /spáwrtiv/ *adj.* playful. □□ **sportively** *adv.* **sportiveness** *n.*
■ frisky, gamboling, frolicking, romping, capering, rollicking, sprightly, coltish, skittish, spirited, frolicsome, buoyant, gamesome, gay, kittenish, merry, playful, gleeful, lighthearted, mischievous, puckish, impish, prankish, waggish, *poet.* blithe, *sl.* cavorting.

sportscast /spáwrtskast/ *n.* a broadcast of a sports event or information about sports. □□ **sportscaster** *n.*

sportsman /spáwrtsmən/ *n.* (*pl.* **-men**; *fem.* **sportswoman**, *pl.* **-women**) **1** a person who takes part in sports, esp. professionally. **2** a person who behaves fairly and generously. □□ **sportsmanlike** *adj.* **sportsmanly** *adj.* **sportsmanship** *n.*
■ **1** see PLAYER 1a. **2** *colloq.* sport. □□ **sportsmanship** fair

/.../ **pronunciation**	● **part of speech**
□ **phrases, idioms, and compounds**	
□□ **derivatives**	■ **synonym section**
cross-references appear in SMALL CAPITALS or *italics*	

play, fairness, honorableness, honesty, honor, probity, scrupulousness, integrity, uprightness, justice, justness.

sportswear /spáwrtswair/ *n.* clothes worn for sports or for casual use.

sporty /spáwrtee/ *adj.* (**sportier, sportiest**) *colloq.* **1** fond of sports. **2** rakish; showy. □□ **sportily** *adv.* **sportiness** *n.*
■ **2** informal, casual; stylish, chic, smart, fashionable, modish, à la mode, up to date, showy, rakish, swanky, loud, flashy, *colloq.* classy, sharp, swell, swank, *colloq. often derog.* trendy, *sl.* snazzy, spiffy.

sporule /spáwryŏŏl/ *n.* a small spore or a single spore. □□ **sporular** *adj.* [F *sporule* or mod.L *sporula* (as SPORE)]

spot /spot/ *n. & v.* ● *n.* **1 a** a small part of the surface of a thing distinguished by color, texture, etc., usu. round or less elongated than a streak or stripe (*a blue tie with pink spots*). **b** a small mark or stain. **c** a pimple. **d** a small circle or other shape used in various numbers to distinguish faces of dice, playing cards in a suit, etc. **e** a moral blemish or stain (*without a spot on his reputation*). **2 a** a particular place; a definite locality (*dropped it on this precise spot; the spot where Columbus landed*). **b** a place used for a particular activity (often in *comb.*: *nightspot*). **c** (*prec. by the*) *Soccer* the place from which a penalty kick is taken. **3** a particular part of one's body or aspect of one's character. **4 a** *colloq.* one's esp. regular position in an organization, program of events, etc. **b** a place or position in a performance or show (*did the spot before intermission*). **5** *Brit. a colloq.* a small quantity of anything (*a spot of lunch; a spot of trouble*). **b** a drop (*a spot of rain*). **c** *colloq.* a drink. **6** = SPOTLIGHT. **7** *colloq.* an awkward or difficult situation (esp. in *in a* (*tight*, etc.) *spot*). **8** (usu. *attrib.*) money paid or goods delivered immediately after a sale (*spot cash; spot silver*). **9** *Billiards*, etc. **a** a small round black patch to mark the position where a ball is placed at certain times. **b** (in full **spot ball**) the white ball distinguished from the other by two black spots. ● *v.* (**spotted, spotting**) **1** *tr.* **a** *colloq.* single out beforehand (the winner of a race, etc.). **b** *colloq.* recognize the identity, nationality, etc., of (*spotted him at once as the murderer*). **c** watch for and take note of (trains, talent, etc.). **d** *colloq.* catch sight of. **e** *Mil.* locate (an enemy's position), esp. from the air. **2 a** *tr. & intr.* mark or become marked with spots. **b** *tr.* stain; soil (a person's character, etc.). **3** *intr.* rain slightly (*it was spotting with rain*). **4** *tr.* *Billiards* place (a ball) on a spot. □ **on the spot 1** at the scene of an action or event. **2** *colloq.* in a position such that response or action is required. **3** without delay or change of place; then and there. **4** (of a person) wide awake, equal to the situation, in good form at a game, etc. **put on the spot** *sl.* make to feel uncomfortable, awkward, etc. **spot check** a test made on the spot or on a randomly selected subject. **spot height 1** the altitude of a point. **2** a figure on a map showing this. **spot on** *Brit. colloq. adj.* precise; on target. ● *adv.* precisely. **spot weld** a weld made in spot welding. **spot-weld** *v.tr.* join by spot welding. **spot welding** welding two surfaces together in a series of discrete points. [ME, perh. f. MDu. *spotte*, LG *spot*, ON *spotti* small piece]
■ *n.* **1 a, b** mark, patch, dot, speck, blot, blotch, blemish, speckle, fleck, particle, mote, macula, smudge, stain, stigma, discoloration, splotch. **c** eruption, pimple, pustule, blackhead, whitehead; boil, blain, wen; pockmark; *Med.* comedo *sl.* zit; (*spots*) acne. **d** pip. **e** stain, blemish, blot (on the escutcheon); see also STIGMA 1. **2 a, b** site, place, locale, location, position, locality, scene, setting, section, area, neighborhood, quarter. **4** see SLOT¹ *n.* 3. **5 a** bit, bite, morsel, *colloq.* smidgen; see also MODICUM. **b** drop, blob, bead. **7** predicament, tricky *or* difficult situation, quandary, mess, trouble, straits, *colloq.* pickle, jam, fix. ● *v.* **1** identify, pick out, distinguish, single out, detect, locate, recognize, discern, see, catch sight of, sight, glimpse, make out, *literary* descry. **2** mark, stain, fleck, speckle, spray, splash, spatter, bespatter, soil, dirty, taint, besmirch, smudge, *poet.* sully. □ **on the spot 3** see *on the nail* (NAIL). **spot on** (*adj.*) see ACCURATE. (*adv.*) precisely, exactly; *Brit. colloq.* bang on, *sl.* on the nose.

spotless /spótlis/ *adj.* immaculate; absolutely clean or pure. □□ **spotlessly** *adv.* **spotlessness** *n.*
■ immaculate, clean, gleaming, shiny, polished, unspotted, spick and span; pure, unsullied, flawless, faultless, impeccable, untarnished, unassailable, blameless, irreproachable.

spotlight /spótlīt/ *n. & v.* ● *n.* **1** a beam of light directed on a small area, esp. on a particular part of a theater stage or of the road in front of a vehicle. **2** a lamp projecting this. **3** full attention or publicity. ● *v.tr.* (*past* and *past part.* **-lighted** or **-lit**) **1** direct a spotlight on. **2** make conspicuous; draw attention to.
■ *n.* **1, 2** arc light, searchlight, spot. **3** focus (of attention), limelight, public eye. ● *v.* light (up), illuminate, focus light upon *or* on, shine light upon *or* on, shed light upon *or* on, throw light upon *or* on, cast light upon *or* on; emphasize, highlight, make conspicuous, draw attention to, focus upon *or* on, feature, give prominence to, stress, accentuate, accent, point up, underscore, underline.

spotted /spótid/ *adj.* marked or decorated with spots. □ **spotted dick** (or **dog**) *Brit.* **1** a suet pudding containing currants. **2** a Dalmatian dog. **spotted fever 1** cerebrospinal meningitis. **2** typhus. □□ **spottedness** *n.*
■ see SPOTTY 1.

spotter /spótar/ *n.* **1** a person who watches over a gymnast, weightlifter, etc., during practice to avoid or prevent injuries. **2** (often in *comb.*) a person who spots people or things (*train spotter*). **3** an aviator or aircraft employed in locating enemy positions, etc.

spotty /spótee/ *adj.* (**spottier, spottiest**) **1** marked with spots. **2** patchy; irregular. □□ **spottily** *adv.* **spottiness** *n.*
■ **1** spotted, dotted, speckled, freckled, flecked, blotched, blotchy, stained, marked, pied, piebald, brindle(d), skewbald, mottled, motley, dapple(d), macular, foxed; soiled, dirty; *colloq.* splotchy, splotched; pimply, pimpled, acned, pockmarked, pocky, bad. **2** patchy, uneven, erratic, sporadic, capricious, fitful; see also IRREGULAR 4.

spouse /spows, spowz/ *n.* a husband or wife. [ME *spūs(e)* f. OF *sp(o)us* (masc.), *sp(o)use* (fem.), vars. of *espous(e)* f. L *sponsus sponsa* past part. of *spondēre* betroth]
■ see MATE¹ *n.* 3b.

spout /spowt/ *n. & v.* ● *n.* **1 a** a projecting tube or lip through which a liquid, etc., is poured from a teapot, kettle, pitcher, etc., or issues from a fountain, pump, etc. **b** a sloping trough down which a thing may be shot into a receptacle. **c** *hist.* a lift serving a pawnbroker's storeroom. **2** a jet or column of liquid, grain, etc. **3** (in full **spout hole**) a whale's blowhole. ● *v.tr. & intr.* **1** discharge or issue forcibly in a jet. **2** utter (verses, etc.) or speak in a declamatory manner; speechify. □ **up the spout** *Brit. sl.* **1** useless; ruined; hopeless. **2** pawned. **3** pregnant. □□ **spouter** *n.* **spoutless** *adj.* [ME f. MDu. *spouten*, orig. imit.]
■ *n.* **1 a** lip, gargoyle, duct, waterspout, drain, outlet, conduit, downspout, *Brit.* downpipe. **2** see GUSH *n.* 1. ● *v.* **1** discharge, squirt, spurt, spit, shoot, gush, pour (out *or* forth), spew (up *or* out *or* forth), disgorge; emit, eject, vomit (up *or* forth); flow, issue, stream, jet, erupt. **2** ramble on, rant, rave, carry on, pontificate, declaim, hold forth, maunder (on), expatiate, talk, *colloq.* go on. *joc. or derog.* speechify, esp. *joc. or derog.* orate. □ **up the spout 1** gone, lost, destroyed, ruined, hopeless, useless, beyond hope *or* recovery, to be written off *or* abandoned, *colloq.* down the drain. **2** *colloq.* hocked, in hock.

SPQR *abbr. hist.* the Senate and people of Rome. [L *Senatus Populusque Romanus*]

sprag /sprag/ *n.* **1** a thick piece of wood or similar device used as a brake. **2** a support prop in a coal mine. [19th c.: orig. unkn.]

sprain /sprayn/ *v. & n.* ● *v.tr.* wrench (an ankle, wrist, etc.) violently so as to cause pain and swelling but not dislocation. ● *n.* **1** such a wrench. **2** the resulting inflammation and swelling. [17th c.: orig. unkn.]

■ *v.* see WRENCH *v.* 1b. ● *n.* **1** see STRAIN[1] *n.* 2.

sprang *past* of SPRING.

sprat /sprat/ *n. & v.* ● *n.* **1** a small European herring-like fish, *Sprattus sprattus*, much used as food. **2** a similar fish, e.g., a sand eel or a young herring. ● *v.intr.* (**spratted, spratting**) fish for sprats. □ **a sprat to catch a mackerel** a small risk to gain much. □□ **spratter** *n.* **spratting** *n.* [OE *sprot*]

sprauncy /spráwnsee/ *adj.* (**sprauncier, sprauncest**) *Brit. sl.* smart or showy. [20th c.: perh. rel. to dial. *sprouncey* cheerful]

sprawl /sprawl/ *v. & n.* ● *v.* **1 a** *intr.* sit or lie or fall with limbs flung out or in an ungainly way. **b** *tr.* spread (one's limbs) in this way. **2** *intr.* (of handwriting, a plant, a town, etc.) be of irregular or straggling form. ● *n.* **1** a sprawling movement or attitude. **2** a straggling group or mass. **3** the straggling expansion of an urban or industrial area. □□ **sprawlingly** *adv.* [OE *spreawlian*]

■ *v.* **1 a** spread out, stretch out, loll, lounge, slouch, slump, recline, lie about *or* around. **2** spread (out), stretch (out), ramble, meander, wander, straggle, branch out. ● *n.* **3** spread, stretch, expansion, extension.

spray[1] /spray/ *n. & v.* ● *n.* **1** water or other liquid flying in small drops from the force of the wind, the dashing of waves, or the action of an atomizer, etc. **2** a liquid preparation to be applied in this form with an atomizer, etc., esp. for medical purposes. **3** an instrument or apparatus for such application. ● *v.tr.* (also *absol.*) **1** throw (liquid) in the form of spray. **2** sprinkle (an object) with small drops or particles, esp. (a plant) with an insecticide. **3** (*absol.*) (of a tomcat) mark its environment with the smell of its urine, as an attraction to females. □ **spray gun** a gunlike device for spraying paint, etc. **spray paint** paint (a surface) by means of a spray. □□ **sprayable** *adj.* **sprayer** *n.* [earlier *spry*, perh. rel. to MDu. *spra(e)yen*, MHG *spræjen* sprinkle]

■ *n.* **1** shower, sprinkling, drizzle, mist, sprinkle, spindrift. **3** atomizer, sprayer, sprinkler, vaporizer, aerosol, spray gun. ● *v.* **1** sprinkle, shower, spatter, scatter, disperse, diffuse, spread. **2** sprinkle, shower, spatter, besprinkle; see also WATER *v.* 1. □□ **sprayer** see SPRAY[1] *n.* 3 above.

spray[2] /spray/ *n.* **1** a sprig of flowers or leaves, or a branch of a tree with branchlets or flowers, esp. a slender or graceful one. **2** an ornament in a similar form (*a spray of diamonds*). □□ **sprayey** *adj.* [ME f. OE *spræg* (unrecorded)]

■ **1** flower *or* floral arrangement, nosegay, posy, bouquet, sprig; branch, bough.

spread /spred/ *v. & n.* ● *v.* (*past* and *past part.* **spread**) **1** *tr.* (often foll. by *out*) **a** open or extend the surface of. **b** cause to cover a larger surface (*spread butter on bread*). **c** display to the eye or the mind (*the view was spread out before us*). **2** *intr.* (often foll. by *out*) have a wide or specified or increasing extent (*on every side spread a vast desert; spreading trees*). **3** *intr. & tr.* become or make widely known, felt, etc. (*rumors are spreading; spread a little happiness*). **4** *tr.* **a** cover the surface of (*spread the wall with paint; a meadow spread with daisies*). **b** lay (a table). ● *n.* **1** the act or an instance of spreading. **2** capability of expanding (*has a large spread*). **3** diffusion (*spread of learning*). **4** breadth; compass (*arches of equal spread*). **5** an aircraft's wingspan. **6** increased bodily girth (*middle-aged spread*). **7** the difference between two rates, prices, scores, etc. **8** *colloq.* an elaborate meal. **9** a food paste for spreading on bread, etc. **10** a bedspread. **11** printed matter spread across two facing pages or across more than one column. **12** a ranch with extensive land. □ **spread eagle 1** a representation of an eagle with legs and wings extended as an emblem. **2** *hist.* a person secured with arms and legs spread out, esp. to be flogged. **spread-eagle** *v.tr.* (usu. as **spread-eagled** *adj.*) **1** place (a person) in this position. **2** defeat utterly. **3** spread out. ● *adj.* bombastic, esp. noisily patriotic. **spread oneself** be lavish or discursive. **spread one's wings** see WING. □□ **spreadable** *adj.* **spreader** *n.* [OE *-sprædan* f. WG]

■ *v.* **1 a** unfold, draw out, display, stretch out, open out,

extend, lay out, fan out, unroll, unfurl. **b** smear, apply, smooth, put, rub, cover, layer, plaster, paint; diffuse, distribute, disperse, disseminate, broadcast, sow, scatter, strew. **c** lay out, unfurl, unfold. **2** grow, develop, increase, broaden, expand, extend, widen, enlarge, mushroom, proliferate, sprawl, branch out, *Physiol.* metastasize. **3** spread about *or* around, broadcast, publicize, make known, bruit about, air, televise, circulate, publish, distribute, disseminate, trumpet, announce, pronounce, promulgate, advertise, make public, tell the world, repeat, recite. **4 a** cover, smear, rub, plaster, plate, layer, coat, suffuse, wash, glaze, paint, varnish, overlay, overspread; strew; cloak, mantle, swaddle, swathe, wrap, blanket. **b** set, lay, arrange. ● *n.* **1** extension, expansion, enlargement, development, increase, proliferation, broadening, growth, widening, mushrooming, dispersion, dispersal, dissemination, distribution, dispensation. **3** see CIRCULATION 2a. **4** extent, expanse, area, span, sweep, vastness, stretch, reach, breadth, depth, size, dimensions, compass, scope, limits, bounds, boundary, boundaries. **7** range, extent, scope, span, difference. **8** feast, banquet, meal, dinner, barbecue, *formal* repast; table; *colloq.* feed. **9** butter, margarine, oleomargarine, jam, jelly, preserve, conserve, paste, pâté. **10** bedspread, counterpane, coverlet, bedcover, cover, quilt, eiderdown, duvet, afghan, comforter, throw. **12** ranch, landholding, holding, property, place, plantation, farm, homestead, *Austral. & NZ* station. □ **spread-eagled 1, 3** see FLAT[1] 1.

spreadsheet /sprédsheet/ *n.* a computer program allowing manipulation and flexible retrieval of esp. tabulated numerical data.

spree /spree/ *n. & v. colloq.* ● *n.* **1** a lively extravagant outing (*shopping spree*). **2** a bout of fun or drinking, etc. ● *v.intr.* (**sprees, spreed**) have a spree. □ **on a spree** engaged in a spree. [19th c.: orig. unkn.]

■ *n.* **1** outing, trip, jaunt, fling, *colloq.* splurge. **2** frolic, romp, escapade, revel, wild party, fling, debauch, orgy, bacchanal, bacchanalia, saturnalia, *colloq.* lark; drinking bout, carousal, carouse, blowout, *sl.* bender, binge, jag, tear. ● *v.* see REVEL *v.* 1.

sprig[1] /sprig/ *n. & v.* ● *n.* **1** a small branch or shoot. **2** an ornament resembling this, esp. on fabric. **3** usu. *derog.* a youth or young man (*a sprig of the nobility*). ● *v.tr.* (**sprigged, sprigging**) **1** ornament with sprigs (*a dress of sprigged muslin*). **2** (usu. as **sprigging** *n.*) decorate (ceramic ware) with ornaments in applied relief. □□ **spriggy** *adj.* [ME f. or rel. to LG *sprick*]

■ *n.* **1** see TWIG[1].

sprig[2] /sprig/ *n.* a small tapering headless tack; a brad. [ME: orig. unkn.]

sprightly /sprítlee/ *adj.* (**sprightlier, sprightliest**) vivacious, lively; brisk. □□ **sprightliness** *n.* [*spright* var. of SPRITE + -LY[1]]

■ lively, spry, vivacious, cheerful, gay, brisk, animated, sportive, active, alert, nimble, agile, energetic, vigorous, jaunty, perky, playful, spirited, *colloq.* chipper. □□ **sprightliness** see LIFE 8.

spring /spring/ *v. & n.* ● *v.* (*past* **sprang** /sprang/ also **sprung** /sprung/; *past part.* **sprung**) **1** *intr.* jump; move rapidly or suddenly (*sprang from his seat; sprang through the gap; sprang to their assistance*). **2** *intr.* move rapidly as from a constrained position or by the action of a spring (*the branch sprang back; the door sprang to*). **3** *intr.* (usu. foll. by *from*) originate or arise (*springs from an old family; their actions spring from a false conviction*). **4** *intr.* (usu. foll. by *up*) come into being; appear, esp. suddenly (*a breeze sprang up; the belief has sprung up*). **5** *tr.* cause to act suddenly, esp. by

/.../ **pronunciation**	● **part of speech**
□ **phrases, idioms, and compounds**	
□□ **derivatives**	■ **synonym section**
cross-references appear in SMALL CAPITALS or *italics*	

means of a spring (*spring a trap*). **6** *tr.* (often foll. by *on*) produce or develop or make known suddenly or unexpectedly (*has sprung a new theory*; *loves to spring surprises*). **7** *tr. sl.* contrive the escape or release of. **8** *tr.* rouse (game) from earth or covert. **9 a** *intr.* become warped or split. **b** *tr.* split; crack (wood or a wooden implement). **10** *tr.* (usu. as **sprung** *adj.*) provide (a motor vehicle, etc.) with springs. **11 a** *tr. colloq.* spend (money). **b** *intr.* (usu. foll. by *for*) *sl.* pay for a meal, drink, etc. **12** *tr.* cause (a mine) to explode. ● *n.* **1** a jump (*took a spring*; *rose with a spring*). **2** a backward movement from a constrained position; a recoil, e.g., of a bow. **3** elasticity; ability to spring back strongly (*a mattress with plenty of spring*). **4** a resilient device usu. of bent or coiled metal used esp. to drive clockwork or for cushioning in furniture or vehicles. **5 a** the season in which vegetation begins to appear, the first season of the year, in the N. hemisphere from March to May and in the S. hemisphere from September to November. **b** *Astron.* the period from the vernal equinox to the summer solstice. **c** (often foll. by *of*) the early stage of life, etc. **d** = *spring tide*. **6** a place where water, oil, etc., wells up from the earth; the basin or flow so formed (*hot springs*; *mineral springs*). **7** the motive for or origin of an action, custom, etc. (*the springs of human action*). **8** *sl.* an escape or release from prison. **9** the upward curve of a beam, etc., from a horizontal line. **10** the splitting or yielding of a plank, etc., under strain. □ **spring balance** a balance that measures weight by the tension of a spring. **spring bed** a bed with a spring mattress. **spring chicken 1** a young fowl for eating (orig. available only in spring). **2** (esp. with *neg.*) a young person (*she's no spring chicken*). **spring-clean** *n.* esp. *Brit.* a thorough cleaning of a house or room, esp. in spring. ● *v.tr.* clean (a house or room) in this way. **spring fever** a restless or lethargic feeling sometimes associated with spring. **spring a leak** develop a leak (orig. *Naut.*, from timbers springing out of position). **spring-loaded** containing a compressed or stretched spring pressing one part against another. **spring mattress** a mattress containing or consisting of springs. **spring onion** esp. *Brit.* an onion taken from the ground before the bulb has formed, and eaten raw in salad. **spring roll** an Asian snack consisting of a pancake filled with vegetables, etc., and fried. **spring tide** a tide just after new and full moon when there is the greatest difference between high and low water. **spring water** water from a spring, as opposed to river or rain water. □□ **springless** *adj.* **springlet** *n.* **springlike** *adj.* [OE *springan* f. Gmc]
■ *v.* **1** leap, bound, jump, hop, vault, fly, bounce, start. **3** originate, begin, start, arise, evolve; proceed, stem, issue, descend, derive, come, develop. **4** arise, appear, grow, develop, come up, rise, come into being *or* existence, be born, emerge, sprout, shoot up, burst forth, start up. **6** produce suddenly *or* unexpectedly, develop suddenly *or* unexpectedly, broach, pop, introduce suddenly *or* unexpectedly, divulge suddenly *or* unexpectedly, reveal suddenly *or* unexpectedly, disclose suddenly *or* unexpectedly. **11 b** (*spring for*) pay for, foot the bill for, treat a person to, *Austral. & NZ colloq.* shout a person to. ● *n.* **1** leap, bound, jump, hop, vault, bounce, skip. **3** bounciness, bounce, resiliency, resilience, springiness, buoyancy, elasticity, give, sprightliness, airiness, flexibility. **5 a–c** springtime, Eastertide, Maytime, *poet.* springtide; (*attrib.*) vernal. **6** source, fountain, fountainhead, wellspring, well, spa, geyser, origin, beginning, root, *poet.* fount. □□ **springlike** see SOFT *adj.* 3.
springboard /spríngbawrd/ *n.* **1** a springy board giving impetus in leaping, diving, etc. **2** a source of impetus in any activity. **3** a platform inserted in the side of a tree, on which a lumberjack stands to chop at some height from the ground.
springbok /spríngbok/ *n.* **1** a southern African gazelle, *Antidorcas marsupialis*, with the ability to run with high springing jumps. **2** (**Springbok**) a South African, esp. one who has played for South Africa in international sporting competitions. [Afrik. f. Du. *springen* SPRING + *bok* antelope]

springe /sprinj/ *n.* a noose or snare for catching small game. [ME, rel. to obs. *sprenge*, and SPRING]
■ see SNARE *n.* 1.
springer /spríngər/ *n.* **1** a person or thing that springs. **2 a** a small spaniel of a breed used to spring game. **b** this breed. **3** *Archit.* **a** the part of an arch where the curve begins. **b** the lowest stone of this. **c** the bottom stone of the coping of a gable. **d** a rib of a groined roof or vault. **4** a springbok.
springtail /spríngtayl/ *n.* any wingless insect of the order Collembola, leaping by means of a springlike caudal part.
springtide /spríngtīd/ *n. poet.* = SPRINGTIME.
springtime /spríngtīm/ *n.* **1** the season of spring. **2** a time compared to this.
■ **1** see SPRING *n.* 5a–c. **2** see PRIME[1] *n.* 1.
springy /spríngee/ *adj.* (**springier, springiest**) **1** springing back quickly when squeezed or stretched; elastic. **2** (of movements) as of a springy substance. □□ **springily** *adv.* **springiness** *n.*
■ see ELASTIC *adj.* 1, 2. □□ **springiness** see *elasticity* (ELASTIC).
sprinkle /spríngkəl/ *v. & n.* ● *v.tr.* **1** scatter (liquid, ashes, crumbs, etc.) in small drops or particles. **2** (often foll. by *with*) subject (the ground or an object) to sprinkling with liquid, etc. **3** (of liquid, etc.) fall on in this way. **4** distribute in small amounts. ● *n.* (usu. foll. by *of*) **1** a light shower. **2** = SPRINKLING. **3** (in *pl.*) candy particles used as a dessert topping, as on ice cream. [ME, perh. f. MDu. *sprenkelen*]
■ *v.* **1, 4** see SCATTER *v.* 1a. ● *n.* **1** see SHOWER *n.* 1.
sprinkler /spríngklər/ *n.* a person or thing that sprinkles, esp. a device for sprinkling water on a lawn or to extinguish fires.
■ see SPRAY[1] *n.* 3.
sprinkling /spríngkling/ *n.* (usu. foll. by *of*) a small thinly distributed number or amount.
■ see HANDFUL 2.
sprint /sprint/ *v. & n.* ● *v.* **1** *intr.* run a short distance at full speed. **2** *tr.* run (a specified distance) in this way. ● *n.* **1** such a run. **2** a similar short spell of maximum effort in cycling, swimming, auto racing, etc. □□ **sprinter** *n.* [ON *sprinta* (unrecorded), of unkn. orig.]
■ *v.* **1** see RUN *v.* 1, 3. **2** see RUN *v.* 15. ● *n.* **1** see RUN *n.* 1. □□ **sprinter** see RUNNER 1.
sprit /sprit/ *n.* a small spar reaching diagonally from the mast to the upper outer corner of the sail. [OE *sprēot* pole, rel. to SPROUT]
sprite /sprit/ *n.* an elf, fairy, or goblin. [ME f. *sprit* var. of SPIRIT]
■ see IMP *n.* 2.
spritsail /sprítsəl, -sayl/ *n.* **1** a sail extended by a sprit. **2** *hist.* a sail extended by a yard set under the bowsprit.
spritz /sprits/ *v. & n.* ● *v.tr.* sprinkle, squirt, or spray. ● *n.* the act or an instance of spritzing. [G *spritzen* to squirt]
spritzer /sprítsər/ *n.* a mixture of wine and soda water. [G *Spritzer* a splash]
sprocket /sprókit/ *n.* **1** each of several teeth on a wheel engaging with links of a chain, e.g., on a bicycle, or with holes in film or tape or paper. **2** (also **sprocket wheel**) a wheel with sprockets. [16th c.: orig. unkn.]
■ **1** cog, tooth, gear tooth.
sprog /sprog/ *n. Brit. sl.* a child; a baby. [orig. services' sl., = new recruit: perh. f. obs. *sprag* lively young man]
sprout /sprowt/ *v. & n.* ● *v.* **1** *tr.* put forth; produce (shoots, hair, etc.) (*has sprouted a mustache*). **2** *intr.* begin to grow; put forth shoots. **3** *intr.* spring up, grow to a height. ● *n.* **1** a shoot of a plant. **2** = BRUSSELS SPROUT. [OE *sprūtan* (unrecorded) f. WG]
■ *v.* **1** grow, put forth. **2** bud, germinate, come up, arise, begin, *literary* burgeon. **3** spring up, shoot up, grow, develop. ● *n.* **1** see SHOOT *n.*
spruce[1] /sprōōs/ *adj. & v.* ● *adj.* neat in dress and appearance; trim; neat and fashionable. ● *v.tr. & intr.* (also *refl.*; usu. foll. by *up*) make or become neat and fashionable. □□ **sprucely** *adv.* **spruceness** *n.* [perh. f. SPRUCE[2] in obs. sense 'Prussian,' in the collocation *spruce* (*leather*) *jerkin*]
■ *adj.* neat, dapper, smart, tidy, well turned out, well-groomed, elegant, *colloq.* natty. ● *v.* tidy (up),

neaten (up), primp, preen, clean (up), straighten out or up, smarten (up), *colloq.* titivate.

spruce² /sprōōs/ *n.* **1** any coniferous tree of the genus *Picea*, with dense foliage growing in a distinctive conical shape. **2** the wood of this tree used as timber. □ **spruce beer** a fermented beverage using spruce twigs and needles as flavoring. [alt. of obs. *Pruce* Prussia: cf. PRUSSIAN]

spruce³ /sprōōs/ *v. Brit. sl.* **1** *tr.* deceive. **2** *intr.* lie; practice deception. **3** *intr.* evade a duty; malinger. □□ **sprucer** *n.* [20th c.: orig. unkn.]

sprue¹ /sprōō/ *n.* **1** a channel through which metal or plastic is poured into a mold. **2** a piece of metal or plastic which has filled a sprue and solidified there. [19th c.: orig. unkn.]

sprue² /sprōō/ *n.* **1** = *celiac disease.* **2** a tropical disease with ulceration of the mucous membrane of the mouth and chronic enteritis. [Du. *spruw* THRUSH²; cf. Flem. *spruwen* sprinkle]

sprung see SPRING.

sprung rhythm /sprung rĭthəm/ *n.* a poetic meter approximating to speech, each foot having one stressed syllable followed by a varying number of unstressed.

spry /sprī/ *adj.* (**spryer, spryest**) lively; active; lively. □□ **spryly** *adv.* **spryness** *n.* [18th c., dial. & US: orig. unkn.]
■ see LIVELY 1.

spud /spud/ *n.* & *v.* ● *n.* **1** *sl.* a potato. **2** a small narrow spade for cutting the roots of weeds, etc. ● *v. tr.* (**spudded, spudding**) **1** (foll. by *up, out*) remove (weeds) with a spud. **2** (also *absol.*; often foll. by *in*) make the initial drilling for (an oil well). □ **spud-bashing** *Brit. sl.* a lengthy spell of peeling potatoes. [ME: orig. unkn.]

spue var. of SPEW.

spumante /spōōmaˈantee, -tay/ *n.* a sparkling wine, esp. a sweet white Italian sparkling wine (cf. ASTI). [It., = 'sparkling']

spume /spyōōm/ *n.* & *v.intr.* froth; foam. □□ **spumous** *adj.* **spumy** *adj.* (**spumier, spumiest**). [ME f. OF (*e*)*spume* or L *spuma*]
■ *n.* see FROTH *n.* 1a. ● *v.* see FROTH *v.* 1.

spumoni /spōōmōˈnee/ *n.* an ice-cream dessert of different colors and flavors, usu. layered, with nuts and candied fruits. [It. *spumone* f. *spuma* SPUME]

spun *past* and *past part.* of SPIN.

spunk /spungk/ *n.* **1** touchwood. **2** *colloq.* courage; mettle; spirit. **3** *Brit. coarse sl.* semen. ¶ Usually considered a taboo use. [16th c.: orig. unkn.: cf. PUNK]
■ **2** nerve, courage, pluck, spirit, gameness, resolve, resolution, mettle, heart, grit, backbone, marrow, *colloq.* guts, gumption, sand.

spunky /spúngkee/ *adj.* (**spunkier, spunkiest**) *colloq.* brave; spirited. □□ **spunkily** *adv.*
■ see SPIRITED.

spur /spər/ *n.* & *v.* ● *n.* **1** a device with a small spike or a spiked wheel worn on a rider's heel for urging a horse forward. **2** a stimulus or incentive. **3** a spur-shaped thing, esp.: **a** a projection from a mountain or mountain range. **b** a branch road or railway. **c** a hard projection on a cock's leg. **d** a steel point fastened to the leg of a gamecock. **e** a climbing iron. **f** a small support for ceramic ware in a kiln. **4** *Bot.* **a** a slender hollow projection from part of a flower. **b** a short fruit-bearing shoot. ● *v.* (**spurred, spurring**) **1** *tr.* prick (a horse) with spurs. **2** *tr.* **a** (often foll. by *on*) incite (a person) (*spurred him on to greater efforts; spurred her to try again*). **b** stimulate (interest, etc.). **3** *intr.* (often foll. by *on, forward*) ride a horse hard. **4** *tr.* (esp. as **spurred** *adj.*) provide (a person, boots, a gamecock) with spurs. □ **on the spur of the moment** on a momentary impulse; impromptu. **put** (or **set**) **spurs to 1** spur (a horse). **2** stimulate (resolution, etc.). **spur gear** = *spur wheel.* **spur-of-the-moment** *adj.* unpremeditated; impromptu. **spur wheel** a cog wheel with radial teeth. □□ **spurless** *adj.* [OE *spora, spura* f. Gmc. rel. to SPURN]
■ *n.* **2** goad, prod, impulse, impetus, incitement, instigation, pressure, stimulus, stimulation, incentive, provocation, inducement, enticement, encouragement, motive, motivation. **3** projection, prong, spike, spine,

gaff, barb, quill, tine, barbel, barbule, *Anat., Zool.,* & *Bot.* process. ● *v.* **2** goad, prod, urge, egg on, impel, incite, prompt, press, push, pressure, pressurize, drive, motivate; stimulate, provoke, induce, encourage, excite, animate, inspire. □ **on the spur of the moment** impetuously, impulsively, unthinkingly, unpremeditatedly, impromptu, offhand, on the spot; rashly, thoughtlessly, recklessly, hastily, brashly, incautiously, unexpectedly, suddenly.

spurge /spərj/ *n.* any plant of the genus *Euphorbia*, exuding an acrid milky juice once used medicinally as a purgative. □ **spurge laurel** any shrub of the genus *Daphne*, esp. *D. laureola*, with small yellow flowers. [ME f. OF *espurge* f. *espurgier* f. L *expurgare* (as EX-¹, PURGE)]

spurious /spyōōreeəs/ *adj.* **1** not genuine; not being what it purports to be; not proceeding from the pretended source (*a spurious excuse*). **2** having an outward similarity of form or function only. **3** (of offspring) illegitimate. □□ **spuriously** *adv.* **spuriousness** *n.* [L *spurius* false]
■ **1** false, counterfeit, sham, fake, fraudulent, bogus, mock, imitation, simulated, unauthentic, ungenuine, forged, feigned, pretended, deceitful, meretricious, contrived, factitious, artificial, ersatz, synthetic, pseudo, *colloq.* phony. □□ **spuriousness** see *falsity* (FALSE) .

spurn /spərn/ *v.* & *n.* ● *v.* **1** reject with disdain; treat with contempt. **2** repel or thrust back with one's foot. ● *n.* an act of spurning. □□ **spurner** *n.* [OE *spurnan, spornan,* rel. to SPUR]
■ *v.* **1** reject, disdain, scorn, despise, rebuff, repudiate, refuse, sneer at, snub, cold-shoulder, brush off, turn down, turn one's back on *or* upon, look down on *or* upon, *colloq.* turn up one's nose at, *literary* contemn.

spurry /spáree, spúree/ *n.* (also **spurrey**) (*pl.* **-ies** or **-eys**) a slender plant of the genus *Spergula*, esp. the corn spurry, a white-flowered weed in fields, etc. [Du. *spurrie,* prob. rel. to med.L *spergula*]

spurt /spərt/ *v.* & *n.* ● *v.* **1** (also **spirt**) **a** *intr.* gush out in a jet or stream. **b** *tr.* cause (liquid, etc.) to do this. **2** *intr.* make a sudden effort. ● *n.* **1** (also **spirt**) a sudden gushing out; a jet. **2** a short sudden effort or increase of pace, esp. in racing. [16th c.: orig. unkn.]
■ *v.* **1 a** gush, spew, squirt, shoot, spout, stream, spray, jet, erupt, burst, surge. **b** spew, squirt, shoot, spout, stream, spray. ● *n.* **1** see GUSH *n.* 1. **2** burst, access, effort, outbreak; increase, advance, acceleration, rise, improvement; see also DASH *n.* 1.

sputnik /spŏŏtnik, spút-/ *n.* each of a series of Russian artificial satellites launched from 1957. [Russ., = fellow traveler]
■ satellite, spaceship, spacecraft, rocket.

sputter /spútər/ *v.* & *n.* ● *v.* **1** *intr.* emit spitting sounds, esp. when being heated. **2** *intr.* (often foll. by *at*) speak in a hurried or vehement fashion. **3** *tr.* emit a spitting sound. **4** *tr.* speak or utter (words, threats, a language, etc.) rapidly or incoherently. **5** *tr. Physics* deposit (metal) by using fast ions, etc., to eject particles of it from a target. ● *n.* a sputtering sound, esp. sputtering speech. □□ **sputterer** *n.* [Du. *sputteren* (imit.)]
■ *v.* **1, 3** see SPIT¹ *v.* 2b, 3.

sputum /spyōōtəm/ *n.* (*pl.* **sputa** /-tə/) **1** saliva; spittle. **2** a mixture of saliva and mucus expectorated from the respiratory tract, usu. a sign of disease. [L, neut. past part. of *spuere* spit]
■ **1** see SPIT¹ *n.*

spy /spī/ *n.* & *v.* ● *n.* (*pl.* **spies**) **1** a person who secretly collects and reports information on the activities, movements, etc., of an enemy, competitor, etc. **2** a person who keeps watch on others, esp. furtively. ● *v.* (**spies, spied**) **1** *tr.* discern or make out, esp. by careful observation (*spied a*

/.../ pronunciation	● part of speech
□ **phrases, idioms, and compounds**	
□□ **derivatives**	■ **synonym section**
cross-references appear in SMALL CAPITALS or *italics*	

house in the distance). **2** *intr.* (often foll. by *on*) act as a spy; keep a close and secret watch. **3** *intr.* (often foll. by *into*) pry. □ **I spy** a children's game of guessing a visible object from the initial letter of its name. **spy out** explore or discover, esp. secretly. □□ **spying** *n.* [ME f. OF *espie* espying, *espier* espy f. Gmc]

■ *n.* double agent, foreign agent, secret(-service) agent, intelligence agent, undercover agent, fifth columnist, CIA man *or* woman *or* agent, MI5 man *or* woman *or* agent, MI6 man *or* woman *or* agent; informer, informant, stool pigeon, *colloq.* mole, snoop, snooper, fink, *sl.* ratfink, stoolie. ● *v.* **1** glimpse, spot, catch sight of, sight, catch a glimpse of, make out, note, notice, see, discern, *literary* espy, descry. **2** (*spy on*) follow, shadow, trail, watch, observe, reconnoiter, keep under surveillance, check out, *colloq.* tail, *sl.* case. **3** see SNOOP *v.* □□ **spying** espionage, undercover work, intelligence, surveillance.

spyglass /spíglas/ *n.* a small telescope.
■ see TELESCOPE *n.*

spyhole /spíhōl/ *n.* a peephole.

sq. *abbr.* square.

squab /skwob/ *n. & adj.* ● *n.* **1** a short fat person. **2** a young, esp. unfledged, pigeon or other bird. **3 a** a stuffed cushion. **b** *Brit.* the padded back or side of a car seat. **4** a sofa or couch. ● *adj.* short and fat; squat. □ **squab chick** an unfledged bird. [17th c.: orig. unkn.: cf. obs. *quab* shapeless thing, Sw. dial. *sqvabba* fat woman]

squabble /skwóbəl/ *n. & v.* ● *n.* a petty or noisy quarrel. ● *v.intr.* engage in a squabble. □□ **squabbler** *n.* [prob. imit.: cf. Sw. dial. *sqvabbel* a dispute]
■ *n.* see QUARREL *n.* 1. ● *v.* see QUARREL *v.* 2.

squabby /skwóbee/ *adj.* (**squabbier, squabbiest**) short and fat; squat.

squad /skwod/ *n.* **1** a small group of people sharing a task, etc. **2** *Mil.* a small number of soldiers assembled for drill, etc. **3** *Sports* a group of players forming a team. **4** (often in *comb.*) a specialized unit within a police force (*drug squad*). **5** a group or class of people of a specified kind (*the awkward squad*). □ **squad car** a police car having a radio link with headquarters. [F *escouade* var. of *escadre* f. It. *squadra* SQUARE]
■ unit, team, band, company, crew, force, troop, cohort, corps, detail, detachment, cadre, squadron, platoon, party, gang, section, group.

squadron /skwódrən/ *n.* **1** an organized body of persons. **2** a principal division of a cavalry regiment or armored formation, consisting of two troops. **3** a detachment of warships employed on a particular duty. **4 a** (in the US) a unit of the US Air Force with two or more flights. **b** (in the UK) a unit of the Royal Air Force with 10 to 18 aircraft. [It. *squadrone* (as SQUAD)]
■ see SQUAD.

squalid /skwólid/ *adj.* **1** filthy; repulsively dirty. **2** degraded or poor in appearance. **3** wretched; sordid. □□ **squalidity** *n.* /-líditee/ **squalidly** *adv.* **squalidness** *n.* [L *squalidus* f. *squalēre* be rough or dirty]
■ **1** see FILTHY *adj.* 1. **2, 3** see MEAN² 3, 4, SORDID 1.

squall /skwawl/ *n. & v.* ● *n.* **1** a sudden or violent gust or storm of wind, esp. with rain or snow or sleet. **2** a discordant cry; a scream (esp. of a baby). **3** (esp. in *pl.*) trouble; difficulty. ● *v.* **1** *intr.* utter a squall; scream; cry out violently as in fear or pain. **2** *tr.* utter in a screaming or discordant voice. □□ **squally** *adj.* [prob. f. SQUEAL after BAWL]
■ *n.* **1** see TEMPEST 1. **2** see SHRIEK *n.* ● *v.* see SHRIEK *v.*
□□ **squally** see INCLEMENT.

squalor /skwólər/ *n.* the state of being filthy or squalid. [L, as SQUALID]
■ see MISERY 1, IMPURITY 1.

squama /skwáymə/ *n.* (*pl.* **squamae** /-mee/) **1** a scale on an animal or plant. **2** a thin scalelike plate of bone. **3** a scalelike feather. □□ **squamate** /-mayt/ *adj.* **squamose** *adj.* **squamous** *adj.* **squamule** *n.* [L *squama*]
■ **1, 3** scale, flake, feather, tuft, flock. □□ **squamose**, **squamous** see SCALY.

squander /skwóndər/ *v.tr.* **1** spend (money, time, etc.) wastefully. **2** dissipate (a fortune, etc.) wastefully. □□ **squanderer** *n.* [16th c.: orig. unkn.]
■ see WASTE *v.* 1. □□ **squanderer** see PROFLIGATE *n.*

square /skwair/ *n., adj., adv., & v.* ● *n.* **1** an equilateral rectangle. **2 a** an object of this shape or approximately this shape. **b** a small square area on a game board. **c** a square scarf. **d** *Brit.* an academic cap with a stiff square top; a mortarboard. **3 a** an open (usu. four-sided) area surrounded by buildings, esp. one planted with trees, etc., and surrounded by houses. **b** an open area at the meeting of streets. **c** an area within barracks, etc., for drill. **d** a block of buildings bounded by four streets. **4** the product of a number multiplied by itself (*81 is the square of 9*). **5** an L-shaped or T-shaped instrument for obtaining or testing right angles. **6** *sl.* a conventional or old-fashioned person, one ignorant of or opposed to current trends. **7** a square arrangement of letters, figures, etc. **8** a body of infantry drawn up in rectangular form. **9** a unit of 100 sq. ft. as a measure of flooring, etc. **10** a square meal (*three squares a day*). ● *adj.* **1** having the shape of a square. **2** having or in the form of a right angle (*table with square corners*). **3** angular and not round; of square section (*has a square jaw*). **4** designating a unit of measure equal to the area of a square whose side is one of the unit specified (*square meter*). **5** (often foll. by *with*) **a** level; parallel. **b** on a proper footing; even; quits. **6 a** (usu. foll. by *to*) at right angles. **b** *Cricket* on a line through the stumps at right angles to the wicket. **7** having the breadth more nearly equal to the length or height than is usual (*a man of square frame*). **8** properly arranged; in good order; settled (*get things square*). **9** (also **all square**) **a** not in debt; with no money owed. **b** having equal scores, esp. *Golf* having won the same number of holes as one's opponent. **c** (of scores) equal. **10** fair and honest (*his dealings are not always quite square*). **11** uncompromising; direct; thorough (*was met with a square refusal*). **12** *sl.* conventional or old-fashioned; unsophisticated; conservative (cf. sense 6 of *n.*). **13** *Mus.* (of rhythm) simple; straightforward. ● *adv.* **1** squarely (*sat square on her seat*). **2** fairly; honestly (*play square*). ● *v.* **1** *tr.* make square or rectangular; give a rectangular cross-section to (timber, etc.). **2** *tr.* multiply (a number) by itself (*3 squared is 9*). **3** *tr. & intr.* (usu. foll. by *to, with*) adjust; make or be suitable or consistent; reconcile (*the results do not square with your conclusions*). **4** *tr.* mark out in squares. **5** *tr.* settle or pay (a bill, etc.). **6** *tr.* place (one's shoulders, etc.) squarely facing forward. **7** *tr. colloq.* **a** pay or bribe. **b** secure the acquiescence, etc., of (a person) in this way. **8** *tr.* (also *absol.*) make the scores of (a match, etc.) all square. **9** *tr.* assume the attitude of a boxer. **10** *tr. Naut.* **a** lay (yards) at right angles with the keel making them at the same time horizontal. **b** get (deadeyes) horizontal. **c** get (ratlines) horizontal and parallel to one another. □ **back to square one** *colloq.* back to the starting point with no progress made. **get square with** pay or compound with (a creditor). **on the square** *adj. colloq.* honest; fair. ● *adv. colloq.* honestly; fairly (*can be trusted to act on the square*). **out of square** not at right angles. **perfect square** = *square number.* **square accounts with** see ACCOUNT. **square away** neaten up. **square brackets** brackets of the form [ ]. **square-built** of comparatively broad shape. **square the circle 1** construct a square equal in area to a given circle (a problem incapable of a purely geometrical solution). **2** do what is impossible. **square dance** a dance with usu. four couples facing inwards from four sides. **square deal** a fair bargain; fair treatment. **squared paper** esp. *Brit.* paper marked out in squares, esp. for plotting graphs. **square-eyed** *joc. Brit.* affected by or given to excessive viewing of television. **square meal** a substantial and satisfying meal. **square measure** measure expressed in square units. **square number** the square of an integer e.g., 1, 4, 9, 16. **square off 1** assume the attitude of a boxer. **2** *Austral.* placate or conciliate. **3** mark out in squares. **square peg in a round hole** see PEG. **square piano** an early type of piano, small and oblong in shape. **square-rigged** with the principal sails at right angles to the length of the ship and extended by horizontal yards slung to the mast by the middle (opp. *fore-and-aft rigged*). **square root** the number that multiplied by itself gives a specified number (*3 is the square root of 9*). **square sail** a four-cornered sail extended on a yard slung to the mast by the middle. **square shooter** a person who is honest, fair, and straightforward. **square-shouldered** with broad and not sloping shoulders (cf. *round-shouldered*). **square-toed 1** (of shoes or boots) having square toes. **2** wearing such shoes or boots. **3** formal; prim. **square up** settle an account, etc. **square up to 1** move toward (a person) in a fighting attitude. **2** face and tackle (a difficulty, etc.) resolutely. **square wave** *Physics* a wave with periodic sudden alternations between only two values of quantity. □□ **squarely** *adv.* **squareness** *n.* **squarer** *n.* **squarish** *adj.* [ME f. OF *esquare*, *esquarré*, *esquarrer*, ult. f. EX-¹ + L *quadra* square]

■ *n.* **3 a** plaza, piazza, place, park, (village) green, marketplace, market (square), quadrangle.
c paradeground, parade, ground. **6** conservative, conformist, traditionalist, bourgeois, (old) fogy, diehard; *colloq.* straight, stuffed shirt, stick-in-the-mud, *sl.* fuddy-duddy, nerd, dweeb. ● *adj.* **1** equilateral, quadrangular, rectangular, quadrilateral, four-sided, boxy. **2** right-angled. **5** equal, on a par, even, level, parallel; on equal *or* even terms, quits, settled, balanced. **8** straight, straightened out, settled, in order, organized, arranged. **9 b, c** equal, even, level, drawn, tied, neck and neck. **10** honorable, upright, honest, straightforward, fair (and square), decent, ethical, open, (open and) aboveboard, right, (right and) proper, clean, just, equitable, *colloq.* on the level, on the up and up. **12** conservative, conventional, unsophisticated, provincial, old-fashioned, behind the times, conformist, straitlaced, bourgeois, unimaginative, predictable, stuffy, *colloq.* antediluvian, not with it, not in the know, straight, uptight, *sl.* not hip *or* hep, unhip. ● *adv.* **1** see FULL¹ *adv.* 3. **2** see HONESTLY 1. ● *v.* **3** adapt, adjust, change, modify, harmonize, accommodate, arrange, fit; (*square with*) meet, match (with), conform to *or* with, comply with, obey, correspond to *or* with, tally with, line up with, make *or* be consistent with, accord with, agree with, reconcile with *or* to. **5** see SETTLE¹ 9. **6** stiffen, throw back, straighten (up), tense. **7** see BRIBE *v.* □□ **squarely** see FULL¹ *adv.* 3.

squarrose /skwáirōs, skwór-/ *adj. Bot. & Zool.* rough with scalelike projections. [L *squarrosus* scurfy, scabby]

squash¹ /skwosh/ *v. & n.* ● *v.* **1** *tr.* crush or squeeze flat or into pulp. **2** *intr.* (often foll. by *into*) make one's way by squeezing. **3** *tr.* pack tight; crowd. **4** *tr.* **a** silence (a person) with a crushing retort, etc. **b** dismiss (a proposal, etc.). **c** quash (a rebellion). ● *n.* **1** a crowd; a crowded assembly. **2** a sound of or as of something being squashed, or of a soft body falling. **3** *Brit.* a concentrated drink made of crushed fruit, etc., diluted with water. **4** a game played with rackets and a small ball against the walls of a closed court. **5** a squashed thing or mass. □ **squash tennis** a game similar to squash, played with a tennis ball. □□ **squashy** *adj.* (**squashier, squashiest**). **squashily** *adv.* **squashiness** *n.* [alt. of QUASH]

■ *v.* **1** see SQUEEZE *v.* 1. **3** see SQUEEZE *v.* 3a, b. **4 c** see WHIP *v.* 5b. ● *n.* **1** see SQUEEZE *n.* 3. □□ **squashy** see *mushy* (MUSH¹).

squash² /skwosh/ *n.* (*pl.* same or **squashes**) **1** any of various gourdlike trailing plants of the genus *Cucurbita*, esp. *C. maxima*, *C. moschata*, and *C. melopepo*, whose fruits may be used as a vegetable. **2** the fruit of these cooked and eaten. [obs. (*i*)*squoutersquash* f. Narragansett *asquutasquash* f. *asq* uncooked + *squash* green]

squat /skwot/ *v., adj., & n.* ● *v.* (**squatted, squatting**) **1** *intr.* **a** crouch with the buttocks resting on the backs of the heels. **b** sit on the ground, etc., with the knees drawn up and the heels close to or touching the hams. **2** *tr.* put (a person) into a squatting position. **3** *intr. colloq.* sit down. **4 a** *intr.* act as a squatter. **b** *tr.* occupy (a building) as a squatter. **5** *intr.* (of an animal) crouch close to the ground. ● *adj.*

(**squatter, squattest**) **1** (of a person, etc.) short and thick; dumpy. **2** in a squatting posture. ● *n.* **1** a squatting posture. **2 a** a place occupied by a squatter or squatters. **b** being a squatter. □□ **squatly** *adv.* **squatness** *n.* [ME f. OF *esquatir* flatten f. *es-* EX-¹ + *quatir* press down, crouch ult. f. L *coactus* past part. of *cogere* compel: see COGENT]

■ *v.* **1, 5** see CROUCH *v.* ● *adj.* **1** see DUMPY. ● *n.* **1** crouch, stoop, hunch.

squatter /skwótər/ *n.* **1** a person who takes unauthorized possession of unoccupied premises. **2** *Austral.* **a** a sheepfarmer, esp. on a large scale. **b** *hist.* a person who gets the right of pasturage from the government on easy terms. **3** a person who settles on new, esp. public, land without title. **4** a person who squats.

■ **1, 3** see INTRUDER.

squaw /skwaw/ *n. often offens.* a Native American woman or wife. □ **squaw man** a white married to a squaw. **squaw winter** (in N. America) a brief wintry spell before an Indian summer. [Narragansett *squaws*, Massachusetts *squaw* woman]

squawk /skwawk/ *n. & v.* ● *n.* **1** a loud harsh cry, esp. of a bird. **2** a complaint. ● *v.tr. & intr.* utter with or make a squawk. □ **squawk box** *colloq.* a loudspeaker or intercom. □□ **squawker** *n.* [imit.]

■ *n.* **1** screech, shriek, yell, yowl, whoop, hoot, scream, call, cry, wail, squall, cackle. **2** complaint, grumble, whine, protest, objection, *colloq.* gripe, grouse, grouch, *sl.* beef. ● *v.* screech, shriek, yell, yowl, whoop, hoot, scream, call, cry, wail, squall, cackle; complain, grumble, whine, protest, object, kick, (make a) fuss, kick up (a fuss), *colloq.* bitch, gripe, grouse, grouch, yap, *Brit.* whinge, *sl.* bellyache, beef.

squeak /skweek/ *n. & v.* ● *n.* **1 a** a short shrill cry as of a mouse. **b** a slight high-pitched sound as of an unoiled hinge. **2** (also **squeaker** or **narrow squeak**) a narrow escape; a success barely attained; a game or election won by a narrow margin. ● *v.* **1** *intr.* make a squeak. **2** *tr.* utter (words) shrilly. **3** *intr.* (foll. by *by, through*) *colloq.* pass narrowly. **4** *intr. sl.* turn informer. [ME, imit.: cf. SQUEAL, SHRIEK, and Sw. *skväka* croak]

■ *n.* **1 a** see PEEP² *n.* 1. **2** see *near miss*. ● *v.* **1, 2** see PEEP² *v.*, SING *v.* 1, 2. **3** (*squeak by, through*) see SCRAPE *v.* 8b. **4** see INFORM 2.

squeaker /skweekər/ *n.* **1** a person or thing that squeaks. **2** a young bird, esp. a pigeon. **3** *colloq.* a close contest.

■ **1** see INFORMER *n.* 1.

squeaky /skweekee/ *adj.* (**squeakier, squeakiest**) making a squeaking sound. □ **squeaky clean 1** completely clean. **2** above criticism; beyond reproach. □□ **squeakily** *adv.* **squeakiness** *n.*

■ see HIGH *adj.* 9.

squeal /skweel/ *n. & v.* ● *n.* a prolonged shrill sound, esp. a cry of a child or a pig. ● *v.* **1** *intr.* make a squeal. **2** *tr.* utter (words) with a squeal. **3** *intr. sl.* turn informer. **4** *intr. sl.* protest loudly or excitedly. □□ **squealer** *n.* [ME, imit.]

■ *n.* see SHRIEK *n.* ● *v.* **1, 2** see SHRIEK *v.* **3** see INFORM 2. □□ **squealer** see INFORMER 1.

squeamish /skweemish/ *adj.* **1** easily nauseated or disgusted. **2** fastidious or overscrupulous in questions of propriety, honesty, etc. □□ **squeamishly** *adv.* **squeamishness** *n.* [ME var. of *squeamous* (now dial.), f. AF *escoymos*, of unkn. orig.]

■ **1** qualmish, queasy, easily disgusted *or* revolted *or* nauseated. **2** dainty, delicate, prudish, qualmish, punctilious, demanding, critical, exacting, difficult, fussy, overscrupulous, scrupulous, fastidious, meticulous, painstaking, finicky, finical, *colloq.* persnickety, *sl.* fuddy-duddy. □□ **squeamishness** see *prudery* (PRUDE).

/.../ **pronunciation**	● **part of speech**
□ **phrases, idioms, and compounds**	
□□ **derivatives**	■ **synonym section**
cross-references appear in SMALL CAPITALS or *italics*	

squeegee /skweéjee/ *n. & v.* ● *n.* **1** a rubber-edged implement often set on a long handle and used for cleaning windows, etc. **2** a small similar instrument or roller used in photography. ● *v.tr.* (**squeegees, squeegeed**) treat with a squeegee. [*squeeze*, strengthened form of SQUEEZE]

squeeze /skweez/ *v. & n.* ● *v.* **1** *tr.* **a** exert pressure on from opposite or all sides, esp. in order to extract moisture or reduce size. **b** compress with one's hand or between two bodies. **c** reduce the size of or alter the shape of by squeezing. **2** *tr.* (often foll. by *out*) extract (moisture) by squeezing. **3 a** *tr.* force (a person or thing) into or through a small or narrow space. **b** *intr.* make one's way by squeezing. **c** *tr.* make (one's way) by squeezing. **4** *tr.* **a** harass by exactions; extort money, etc., from. **b** constrain; bring pressure to bear on. **c** (usu. foll. by *out of*) obtain (money, etc.) by extortion, entreaty, etc. **d** *Bridge* subject (a player) to a squeeze. **5** *tr.* press or hold closely as a sign of sympathy, affection, etc. **6** *tr.* (often foll. by *out*) produce with effort (*squeezed out a tear*). ● *n.* **1** an instance of squeezing; the state of being squeezed. **2 a** a close embrace. **b** *sl.* a close friend of the opposite sex, esp. a girlfriend or boyfriend. **3** a crowd or crowded state; a crush. **4** a small quantity produced by squeezing (*a squeeze of lemon*). **5** a sum of money extorted or exacted, esp. an illicit commission. **6** *Econ.* a restriction on borrowing, investment, etc., in a financial crisis. **7** an impression of a coin, etc., taken by pressing damp paper, wax, etc., against it. **8** (in full **squeeze play**) **a** *Bridge* leading winning cards until an opponent is forced to discard an important card. **b** *Baseball* bunting a ball to the infield to enable a runner on third base to start for home as soon as the ball is pitched. **9** *colloq.* a difficult situation; an emergency. □ **put the squeeze on** *colloq.* coerce or pressure (a person). **squeeze bottle** a flexible container whose contents are extracted by squeezing it. □□ **squeezable** *adj.* **squeezer** *n.* [earlier *squise*, intensive of obs. *queise*, of unkn. orig.]

■ *v.* **1** press, compress, compact, constrict, crush, squash, wring, pinch, nip, grip, tweak. **2** see EXPRESS¹ 4. **3 a, b** ram, jam, pack, squash, stuff, cram, crowd, force, press, wedge. **c** inch, force, push, drive, thrust, propel; (*squeeze one's way*) see THREAD *v.* 4. **4 a** milk, bleed, screw, *colloq.* lean on, put the screws on, put the squeeze on, twist a person's arm, *sl.* shake down, *Austral. sl.* put the acid on. **c** extract, wrest, exact, extort, screw, wrench, tear, pry. **5** clasp, clench, hold, clutch, grip, clip; embrace, hug, enfold, *poet.* fold. ● *n.* **1** pinch, nip, tweak, grip. **2 a** clasp, embrace, hug, clutch, grasp, grip, *colloq.* clinch. **b** sweetheart, lover, girlfriend, boyfriend. **3** crush, jam, crowd, squash, press. **6** pressure, restrictions. **9** see DILEMMA 3, EMERGENCY 1. □ **put the squeeze on** press, bring pressure to bear on, put the screws on, twist a person's arm, coerce, urge, influence, pressurize, pressure.

squelch /skwelch/ *v. & n.* ● *v.* **1** *intr.* **a** make a sucking sound as of treading in thick mud. **b** move with a squelching sound. **2** *tr.* **a** disconcert; silence. **b** stamp on; crush flat; put an end to. ● *n.* **1** an instance of squelching. **2** *Electronics.* a circuit in a radio receiver that eliminates output noise when the receiver is tuned to a frequency at which there is no signal or a very low signal. □□ **squelcher** *n.* **squelchy** *adj.* [imit.]

■ *v.* **2 a** suppress, subdue, silence, put down, quell, quash, defeat, overcome, humiliate, disconcert, shoot down, take a person down a peg or two, take the wind out of a person's sails, *colloq.* slap down, settle a person's hash. **b** stamp on, suppress, squash, crush, quash, quell, put an end to.

squib /skwib/ *n. & v.* ● *n.* **1** a small firework burning with a hissing sound and usu. with a final explosion. **2** a short satirical composition; a lampoon. ● *v.* (**squibbed, squibbing**) **1** *tr. Football* kick (the ball) a comparatively short distance on a kickoff; execute (a kick) in this way. **2** *archaic* **a** *intr.* write lampoons. **b** *tr.* lampoon. [16th c.: orig. unkn.: perh. imit.]

■ *n.* **2** see LAMPOON *n.* ● *v.* **2b** see LAMPOON *v.*

squid /skwid/ *n. & v.* ● *n.* **1** any of various ten-armed ceph-

alopods, esp. of the genus *Loligo*, used as bait or food. **2** artificial bait for fish imitating a squid in form. ● *v.intr.* (**squidded, squidding**) fish with squid as bait. [17th c.: orig. unkn.]

squiffed /skwift/ *adj. sl.* = SQUIFFY.

squiffy /skwífee/ *adj.* (**squiffier, squiffiest**) esp. *Brit. sl.* slightly drunk. [19th c.: orig. unkn.]

■ see DRUNK *adj.* 1.

squiggle /skwígəl/ *n. & v.* ● *n.* a short curly line, esp. in handwriting or doodling. ● *v.* **1** *tr.* write in a squiggly manner; scrawl. **2** *intr.* wriggle; squirm. □□ **squiggly** *adj.* [imit.]

■ *n.* zigzag, curly *or* wavy *or* squiggly line, doodle, scrawl, scribble. ● *v.* **1** doodle, scrawl, scribble. **2** see WRIGGLE *v.*

squill /skwil/ *n.* **1** any bulbous plant of the genus *Scilla*, esp. *S. autumnalis*. **2** a seashore plant, *Urginea maritima*, having bulbs used in diuretic and purgative preparations. Also called *sea onion*. **3** any crustacean of the genus *Squilla*. [ME f. L *squilla, scilla* f. Gk *skilla*]

squinch /skwinch/ *n.* a straight or arched structure across an interior angle of a square tower to carry a superstructure, e.g., a dome. [var. of obs. *scunch*, abbr. of SCUNCHEON]

squint /skwint/ *v., n., & adj.* ● *v.* **1** *intr.* have the eyes turned in different directions; have a squint. **2** *intr.* (often foll. by *at*) look obliquely or with half closed eyes. **3** *tr.* close (one's eyes) quickly, hold (one's eyes) half shut. ● *n.* **1** = STRABISMUS. **2** a stealthy or sidelong glance. **3** *colloq.* a glance or look (*had a squint at it*). **4** an oblique opening through the wall of a church affording a view of the altar. **5** a leaning or inclination toward a particular object or aim. ● *adj.* **1** squinting. **2** looking different ways. □ **squint-eyed 1** squinting. **2** malignant; ill-willed. □□ **squinter** *n.* **squinty** *adj.* [ASQUINT: (adj.) perh. f. *squint-eyed* f. obs. *squint* (adv.) f. ASQUINT]

■ *v.* **2** see PEEP¹ *v.* ● *n.* **2, 3** see PEEP¹ *n.*

squire /skwir/ *n. & v.* ● *n.* **1** a country gentleman, esp. the chief landowner in a country district. **2** *hist.* a knight's attendant. **3** *Brit. colloq.* a jocular form of address to a man. **4** a local magistrate or judge in some rural districts. **5** *Austral.* a young snapper fish. ● *v.tr.* (of a man) attend upon or escort (a woman). □□ **squiredom** *n.* **squirehood** *n.* **squirelet** *n.* **squireling** *n.* **squirely** *adj.* **squireship** *n.* [ME f. OF *esquier* ESQUIRE]

■ *n.* **1** gentleman, landowner, landholder, landed proprietor, *archaic* esquire. ● *v.* attend upon, escort, accompany, conduct, go with.

squirearchy /skwíraarkee/ *n.* (also **squirarchy**) (*pl.* **-ies**) landowners collectively, esp. as a class having political or social influence; a class or body of squires. [SQUIRE, after HIERARCHY, etc.]

■ see GENTRY 1.

squirl /skwərl/ *n. colloq.* a flourish or twirl, esp. in handwriting. [perh. f. SQUIGGLE + TWIRL *or* WHIRL]

squirm /skwərm/ *v. & n.* ● *v.intr.* **1** wriggle; writhe. **2** show or feel embarrassment or discomfiture. ● *n.* a squirming movement. □□ **squirmer** *n.* **squirmy** *adj.* (**squirmier, squirmiest**). [imit., prob. assoc. with WORM]

■ *v.* **1** wriggle, writhe, twist, flounder, shift, fidget. **2** be (very) embarrassed *or* uncomfortable, agonize, sweat. ● *n.* see WRIGGLE *n.*

squirrel /skwórəl, skwúr-/ *n. & v.* ● *n.* **1** any rodent of the family Sciuridae, e.g., the red squirrel, gray squirrel, etc., often of arboreal habits, with a bushy tail arching over its back, and pointed ears. **2** the fur of this animal. **3** a person who hoards objects, food, etc. ● *v.* (**squirreled** or **squirrelled, squirreling** or **squirrelling**) **1** *tr.* (often foll. by *away*) hoard (objects, food, time, etc.) (*squirreled it away in the cupboard*). **2** *intr.* (often foll. by *around*) bustle around. □ **squirrel cage 1** a small cage containing a revolving cylinder like a treadmill, on which a captive squirrel may exercise. **2** a form of rotor used in small electric motors, resembling the cylinder of a squirrel cage. **3** a monotonous or repetitive way of life. **squirrel** (or **squirrel tail**) **grass** a grass, *Hordeum jubatum*, with bushy spikelets. **squirrelmonkey** a small yellow-haired monkey, *Saimiri sciureus*, native to S. America. [ME f. AF *esquirel*, OF *esquireul*, ult. f. L *sciurus* f. Gk *skiouros* f. *skia* shade + *oura* tail]

■ *v.* **1** (*squirrel away*) see HOARD *v.* 1.

squirrelly /skwə́rəlee, skwúr-/ *adj.* **1** like a squirrel. **2 a** inclined to bustle around. **b** (of a person) unpredictable; nervous; demented.

squirt /skwərt/ *v. & n.* ● *v.* **1** *tr.* eject (liquid or powder) in a jet as from a syringe. **2** *intr.* (of liquid or powder) be discharged in this way. **3** *tr.* splash with liquid or powder ejected by squirting. ● *n.* **1 a** a jet of water, etc. **b** a small quantity produced by squirting. **2 a** a syringe. **b** (in full **squirt gun**) a kind of toy gun using water as ammunition. **3** *colloq.* an insignificant but presumptuous person. □□ **squirter** *n.* [ME, imit.]

■ *v.* **1** see SPURT *v.* 1b. **2** see SPURT *v.* 1a.

squish /skwish/ *n. & v.* ● *n.* a slight squelching sound. ● *v.* **1** *intr.* move with a squish. **2** *tr. colloq.* squash; squeeze. □□ **squishy** *adj.* (**squishier, squishiest**). [imit.]

■ *v.* **2** see TRAMPLE *v.* 2. □□ **squishy** see *mushy* (MUSH[1]).

squitch /skwich/ *n.* couch grass. [alt. f. QUITCH]

squiz /skwiz/ *n. Austral. & NZ sl.* a look or glance. [prob. f. QUIZ[2]]

Sr *symb. Chem.* the element strontium.

Sr. *abbr.* **1** Senior. **2** Señor. **3** Signor. **4** *Eccl.* Sister.

sr *abbr.* steradian(s).

Sri Lankan /shree lángkən, sree/ *n. & adj.* ● *n.* **1** a native or inhabitant of Sri Lanka (formerly Ceylon), an island in the Indian Ocean. **2** a person of Sri Lankan descent. ● *adj.* of or relating to Sri Lanka or its people.

SRO *abbr.* standing room only.

SS *abbr.* **1** steamship. **2** Saints. **3** *hist.* Nazi special police force. [sense 3 f. G *Schutz-Staffel*]

SSA *abbr.* Social Security Administration.

SSE *abbr.* south-southeast.

SSS *abbr.* Selective Service System.

SST *abbr.* supersonic transport.

SSW *abbr.* south-southwest.

St. *abbr.* **1** Street. **2** Saint.

st. *abbr.* stone (in weight).

-st var. of -EST[2].

sta. *abbr.* station.

stab /stab/ *v. & n.* ● *v.* (**stabbed, stabbing**) **1** *tr.* pierce or wound with a (usu. short) pointed tool or weapon, e.g., a knife or dagger. **2** *intr.* (often foll. by *at*) aim a blow with such a weapon. **3** *intr.* cause a sensation like being stabbed (*stabbing pain*). **4** *tr.* hurt or distress (a person, feelings, conscience, etc.). **5** *intr.* (foll. by *at*) aim a blow at a person's reputation, etc. ● *n.* **1 a** an instance of stabbing. **b** a blow or thrust with a knife, etc. **2** a wound made in this way. **3** a sharply painful (physical or mental) sensation; a blow inflicted on a person's feelings. **4** *colloq.* an attempt; a try. □ **stab in the back** *n.* a treacherous or slanderous attack. ● *v.tr.* slander or betray. □□ **stabber** *n.* [ME: cf. dial. *stob* in sense 1 of *v.*]

■ *v.* **1** stick, puncture, prick, lance, jab, pierce, run through, impale, gore, transfix, knife, bayonet, skewer, spike, spit, spear, pin. **2** lunge, poke, thrust. **3** see SMART *v.* ● *n.* **1, 2** thrust, stab; prick, puncture, (stab) wound. **3** pang, twinge, sting, pain, ache, hurt, stitch. **4** attempt, try, *formal* essay; guess, conjecture; *colloq.* crack, go, shot. □ **stab in the back** (*n.*) treachery, betrayal, double cross, kiss of death, duplicity. (*v.*) harm, sell out, double-cross, play false with; see also DISPARAGE 2, BETRAY 2.

stabile /stáybeel, -bil/ *n.* a rigid, freestanding abstract sculpture or structure of wire, sheet metal, etc. [L *stabilis* STABLE[1], after MOBILE]

stability /stəbílitee/ *n.* the quality or state of being stable. [ME f. OF *stableté* f. L *stabilitas* f. *stabilis* STABLE[1]]

■ steadiness, solidity, firmness, soundness, sturdiness, strength; steadfastness, constancy, dependability, reliability, tenacity, resolve, resoluteness, perseverance, determination, persistence, durability, lasting quality, permanence.

stabilize /stáybilīz/ *v.tr. & intr.* make or become stable. □□ **stabilization** *n.*

■ see STEADY *v.* □□ **stabilization** see SETTLEMENT 1.

stabilizer /stáybilīzər/ *n.* a device or substance used to keep something stable, esp.: **1** a gyroscope device to prevent rolling of a ship. **2** the horizontal airfoil in the tail assembly of an aircraft. **3** (in *pl.*) *Brit.* a pair of small wheels fitted to the rear wheel of a child's bicycle.

■ see ANCHOR *n.* 2.

stable[1] /stáybəl/ *adj.* (**stabler, stablest**) **1** firmly fixed or established; not easily adjusted, destroyed, or altered (*a stable structure; a stable government*). **2 a** firm; resolute; not wavering or fickle (*a stable and steadfast friend*). **b** (of a person) well-adjusted; sane; sensible. **3** *Chem.* (of a compound) not readily decomposing. **4** *Physics* (of an isotope) not subject to radioactive decay. □ **stable equilibrium** a state in which a body when disturbed tends to return to equilibrium. □□ **stableness** *n.* **stably** *adv.* [ME f. AF *stable*, OF *estable* f. L *stabilis* f. *stare* stand]

■ **1** steady, solid, firm, sound, sturdy, strong, durable, well-founded, fast, fixed, sure, established, deep-rooted, stout. **2 a** lasting, enduring, long-lasting, long-standing, secure, steadfast, steady, strong, unchanging, unchanged, changeless, unchangeable, unalterable, fixed, invariable, firm, resolute, unwavering, immutable, permanent, constant. **b** sane, (well-) balanced, responsible, reasonable, sensible, well-adjusted; competent, accountable.

stable[2] /stáybəl/ *n. & v.* ● *n.* **1** a building set apart and adapted for keeping horses. **2** an establishment where racehorses are kept and trained. **3** the racehorses of a particular stable. **4** persons, products, etc., having a common origin or affiliation. **5** such an origin or affiliation. ● *v.tr.* put or keep (a horse) in a stable. □□ **stableful** *n.* (*pl.* **-fuls**). [ME f. OF *estable* f. L *stabulum* f. *stare* stand]

stableman /stáybəlmən/ *n.* (*pl.* **-men**; *fem.* **stablewoman**, *pl.* **-women**) a person employed in a stable.

■ see GROOM *n.*

stabling /stáybling/ *n.* accommodation for horses.

stablish /stáblish/ *v.tr. archaic* fix firmly; establish; set up. [var. of ESTABLISH]

staccato /stəkáatō/ *adv., adj., & n. esp. Mus.* ● *adv. & adj.* with each successive note or note sharply detached or separated from the others (cf. LEGATO, TENUTO). ● *n.* (*pl.* **-os**) **1** a staccato passage in music, etc. **2** staccato delivery or presentation. □ **staccato mark** a dot or stroke above or below a note, indicating that it is to be played staccato. [It., past part. of *staccare* = *distaccare* DETACH]

stack /stak/ *n. & v.* ● *n.* **1** a pile or heap, esp. in orderly arrangement. **2** a circular or rectangular pile of hay, straw, etc., or of grain in sheaf, often with a sloping thatched top; a rick. **3** *colloq.* a large quantity (*a stack of work; has stacks of money*). **4 a** a number of chimneys in a group. **b** = SMOKESTACK. **c** a tall factory chimney. **5** a stacked group of aircraft. **6** (also **stacks** or *Brit.* **stack-room**) a part of a library where books are compactly stored, esp. one to which the public does not have direct access. **7** *Brit.* a high detached rock, esp. off the coast of Scotland and the Orkneys. **8** a pyramidal group of rifles, a pile. **9** *Computing* a set of storage locations which store data in such a way that the most recently stored item is the first to be retrieved. **10** *Brit.* a measure for a pile of wood of 108 cu. ft. (30.1 cubic meters). ● *v.tr.* **1** pile in a stack or stacks. **2 a** arrange (cards) secretly for cheating. **b** manipulate (circumstances, etc.) to one's advantage. **3** cause (aircraft) to fly round the same point at different levels while waiting to land at an airport. □ **stack up** *colloq.* present oneself; measure up. □□ **stackable** *adj.* **stacker** *n.* [ME f. ON *stakkr* haystack f. Gmc]

■ *n.* **1** pile, heap, mound, mass, accumulation, hill,

mountain, store, stock, bank, deposit, supply, stockpile, hoard, load, bundle, bale, *colloq.* stash. **2** haystack, mow, cock, haycock, rick, hayrick. **3** collection, aggregation, accumulation, mass, load, lot, pile, pack, abundance, plenty, profusion, sea, throng, multitude, swarm, host. **4** smokestack, chimney, chimney stack, funnel. ● *v.* **1** stack up, pile (up), heap, accumulate, amass, store, stock, stockpile, hoard, collect, gather, aggregate, agglomerate, squirrel away, *colloq.* stash (away). □ **stack up** present oneself, measure up; (*stack up to* or *with*) compare with, hold a candle to, be on a par with, be as good as.

stacte /stáktee/ *n.* a sweet spice used by the ancient Jews in making incense. [ME f. L f. Gk *staktē* f. *stazō* drip]

staddle /stádǝl/ *n.* a platform or framework supporting a rick, etc. □ **staddle-stone** a stone supporting a staddle or rick, etc. [OE *stathol* base f. Gmc, rel. to STAND]

stadium /stáydeeǝm/ *n.* (*pl.* **stadiums**) **1** an athletic or sports *arena* with tiers of seats for spectators. **2** (*pl.* **stadiums** or **stadia** /-deeǝ/) *Antiq.* **a** a course for a footrace or chariot race. **b** a measure of length, about 607 feet or 185 meters. **3** a stage or period of development, etc. [ME f. L f. Gk *stadion*]

■ **1** arena, (sports *or* athletic) field, amphitheater, hippodrome, colosseum, *Rom. Antiq.* circus.

stadtholder /stáadhōldǝr, staát-/ *n.* (also **stadholder**) *hist.* **1** the chief magistrate of the United Provinces of the Netherlands. **2** the viceroy or governor of a province or town in the Netherlands. □□ **stadtholdership** *n.* [Du. *stadhouder* deputy f. *stad* STEAD + *houder* HOLDER, after med.L LOCUM TENENS]

staff[1] /staf/ *n.* & *v.* ● *n.* **1 a** a stick or pole for use in walking or climbing or as a weapon. **b** a stick or pole as a sign of office or authority. **c** a person or thing that supports or sustains. **d** a flagstaff. **e** *Surveying* a rod for measuring distances, heights, etc. **f** *Brit.* a token given to a driver on a single-track railroad as authority to proceed over a given section of line. **g** *Brit.* a spindle in a watch. **2 a** a body of persons employed in a business, etc. (*editorial staff of a newspaper*). **b** those in authority within an organization, esp. the teachers in a school. **c** *Mil.*, etc., a body of officers assisting an officer in high command and concerned with an army, regiment, fleet, or air force as a whole (*general staff*). **3** (*pl.* **staffs** or **staves** /stayvz/) *Mus.* a set of usu. five parallel lines on any one or between any adjacent two of which a note is placed to indicate its pitch. ● *v.tr.* provide (an institution, etc.) with staff. □ **staff notation** *Mus.* notation by means of a staff, esp. as distinct from tonic sol-fa. **staff nurse** *Brit.* a nurse ranking just below a sister. **staff sergeant** a noncommissioned officer ranking just above sergeant. □□ **staffed** *adj.* (also in *comb.*). [OE *stæf* f. Gmc]

■ *n.* **1 a, b** stick, pole, standard, baton, rod, pikestaff, pike, stake, cane, stave, shaft, alpenstock, shillelagh, club, truncheon, mace, crook, crozier, scepter, wand, verge, caduceus. **d** flagstaff, flagpole, pole. **2** personnel, employees, help, workforce, crew, team, organization. ● *v.* man, people, crew.

staff[2] /staf/ *n.* a mixture with a base of plaster of Paris used as a temporary building material. [19th c.: orig. unkn.]

staffage /stǝfáazh/ *n.* accessory items in a painting, esp. figures or animals in a landscape picture. [G f. *staffieren* decorate, perh. f. OF *estoffer*: see STUFF]

staffer /stáfǝr/ *n.* a member of a staff, esp. of a newspaper.
■ see JOURNALIST.

Staffs. *abbr.* Staffordshire.

stag /stag/ *n.*, *adj.*, & *v.* ● *n.* **1** an adult male deer, esp. one with a set of antlers. **2** a man who attends a social gathering unaccompanied by a woman. **3** *Brit. Stock Exch.* a person who applies for shares of a new issue with a view to selling at once for a profit. ● *adj.* **1** for men only, as a party. **2** intended for men only, esp. pornographic material (*stag films*). **3** unaccompanied by a date. ● *v.tr.* (**stagged, stagging**) **1** to attend a gathering unaccompanied. **2** *Brit. Stock Exch.* deal in (shares) as a stag. □ **stag beetle** any beetle of the family Lucanidae, the male of which has large branched

mandibles resembling a stag's antlers. **stag night** (or **party**) an all-male celebration, esp. in honor of a man about to marry. [ME f. OE *stacga, stagga* (unrecorded): cf. *docga* dog, *frogga* frog, etc., and ON *steggr, steggi* male bird]

stage /stayj/ *n.* & *v.* ● *n.* **1** a point or period in a process or development (*reached a critical stage; is in the larval stage*). **2 a** a raised floor or platform, esp. one on which plays, etc., are performed before an audience. **b** (prec. by *the*) the acting or theatrical profession, dramatic art or literature. **c** the scene of action (*the stage of politics*). **d** = *landing stage*. **3 a** a regular stopping place on a route. **b** the distance between two stopping places. **4** *Astronaut.* a section of a rocket with a separate engine, jettisoned when its propellant is exhausted. **5** *Geol.* a range of strata forming a subdivision of a series. **6** *Electronics* a single amplifying transistor or valve with the associated equipment. **7** the surface on which an object is placed for inspection through a microscope. ● *v.tr.* **1** present (a play, etc.) on stage. **2** arrange the occurrence of (*staged a demonstration; staged a comeback*). □ **go on the stage** become an actor. **hold the stage** dominate a conversation, etc. **set the stage for** prepare the way for; provide the basis for. **stage direction** an instruction in the text of a play as to the movement, position, tone, etc., of an actor, or sound effects, etc. **stage door** an actors' and workers' entrance from the street to a theater behind the stage. **stage effect 1** an effect produced in acting or on the stage. **2** an artificial or theatrical effect produced in real life. **stage fright** nervousness on facing an audience, esp. for the first time. **stage left** (or **right**) on the left (or right) side of the stage, facing the audience. **stage manager** the person responsible for lighting, scenery, and other mechanical arrangements for a play, etc. **stage name** a name assumed for professional purposes by an actor. **stage play** a play performed on stage rather than broadcast, etc. **stage rights** exclusive rights to perform a particular play. **stage-struck** filled with an inordinate desire to go on the stage. **stage whisper 1** an aside. **2** a loud whisper meant to be heard by others than the person addressed. □□ **stageable** *adj.* **stageability** /stáyjǝbílitee/ *n.* **stager** *n.* [ME f. OF *estage* dwelling ult. f. L *stare* stand]

■ *n.* **1** position, situation, grade, level, step, station, place, point, spot, juncture, period, division, phase, lap; status, condition. **2 a** platform, dais, podium; rostrum. **b** (*the stage*) show business, the theater, the boards, the footlights; acting, thespianism; *colloq.* showbiz. **3 b** see SECTION *n.* 2. ● *v.* **1** put on, produce, present, mount, exhibit. **2** put on, contrive, organize, arrange, originate, devise, make up, concoct, fake, trump up, stage-manage, manipulate. □ **stage-manage 2** see STAGE *v.* 2 above. **stage name** see PSEUDONYM. **stage play** see DRAMA 1.

stagecoach /stáyjkōch/ *n. hist.* a large enclosed horse-drawn coach running regularly by stages between two places.

stagecraft /stáyjkraft/ *n.* skill or experience in writing or staging plays.
■ see THEATER 2a.

stagehand /stáyjhand/ *n.* a person handling scenery, etc., during a performance on stage.

stagey var. of STAGY.

stagflation /stagfláyshǝn/ *n. Econ.* a state of inflation without a corresponding increase of demand and employment. [*stagnation* (as STAGNATE) + INFLATION]

stagger /stágǝr/ *v.* & *n.* ● *v.* **1 a** *intr.* walk unsteadily; totter. **b** *tr.* cause to totter (*was staggered by the blow*). **2 a** *tr.* shock; confuse; cause to hesitate or waver (*the question staggered them; they were staggered at the suggestion*). **b** *intr.* hesitate; waver in purpose. **3** *tr.* arrange (events, hours of work, etc.) so that they do not coincide. **4** *tr.* arrange (objects) so that they are not in line, esp.: **a** arrange (a road intersection) so that the side roads are not in line. **b** set (the spokes of a wheel) to incline alternately to right and left. ● *n.* **1** a tottering movement. **2** (in *pl.*) **a** a disease of the brain and spinal cord, esp. in horses and cattle, causing staggering. **b** giddiness. **3** an overhanging or slantwise or zigzag arrangement of like parts in a structure, etc. □□ **staggerer** *n.* [alt.

of ME *stacker* (now dial.) f. ON *stakra* frequent. of *staka* push, stagger]

■ *v.* **1** totter, dodder, reel, lurch, teeter, sway, walk unsteadily *or* shakily, stumble, falter, waver, pitch, rock, wobble. **2 a** surprise, amaze, astound, astonish, overwhelm, overcome, dumbfound, shock, stupefy, stun, nonplus, confound, confuse, bewilder, startle, jolt, shake (up), take a person's breath away, make a person's head swim, take aback, throw off balance, tax, burden, *colloq.* flabbergast, flummox, bowl over, floor, *sl.* blow a person's mind. **3, 4** alternate, space (out), vary, rearrange.

staggering /stágəring/ *adj.* **1** astonishing; bewildering. **2** that staggers. □□ **staggeringly** *adv.*

■ **1** see *amazing* (AMAZE).

staghound /stághownd/ *n.* **1** any large dog of a breed used for hunting deer by sight or scent. **2** this breed.

staging /stáyjing/ *n.* **1** the presentation of a play, etc. **2 a** a platform or support or scaffolding, esp. temporary. **b** *Brit.* shelves for plants in a greenhouse. □ **staging area** an intermediate assembly point for troops, etc., in transit. **staging post** a regular stopping place, esp. on an air route.

■ **1** see PRODUCTION 1. **2 a** see SUPPORT *n.* 2.

stagnant /stágnənt/ *adj.* **1** (of liquid) motionless, having no current; stale or foul due to this. **2** (of life, action, the mind, business, a person) showing no activity, dull, sluggish. □□ **stagnancy** *n.* **stagnantly** *adv.* [L *stagnare stagnant-* f. *stagnum* pool]

■ **1** motionless, standing, still, quiet, sluggish, unmoving, immobile, flat; stale, foul, putrid, putrescent, putrefied, polluted, dirty, contaminated, filthy. **2** see INACTIVE 1, 2.

stagnate /stágnayt/ *v.intr.* be or become stagnant. □□ **stagnation** /-náyshən/ *n.*

■ languish, idle, vegetate, deteriorate, degenerate, decline, decay, rust, molder, decompose, spoil, rot, *colloq.* go to seed *or* pot.

stagy /stáyjee/ *adj.* (also **stagey**) (**stagier**, **stagiest**) theatrical; artificial; exaggerated. □□ **stagily** *adv.* **staginess** *n.*

■ see THEATRICAL *adj.* □□ **staginess** see THEATER 2c, PRETENSE 4.

staid /stayd/ *adj.* of quiet and steady character; sedate. □□ **staidly** *adv.* **staidness** *n.* [= *stayed*, past part. of STAY¹]

■ sedate, rigid, stiff, prim, dignified, sober, calm, composed, quiet, restrained, steady, solemn, serious, serious-minded, grave. □□ **staidness** see SOBRIETY.

stain /stayn/ *v. & n.* ● *v.* **1** *tr. & intr.* discolor or be discolored by the action of liquid sinking in. **2** *tr.* sully; blemish; spoil; damage (a reputation, character, etc.). **3** *tr.* color (wood, glass, etc.) by a process other than painting or covering the surface. **4** *tr.* impregnate (a specimen) for microscopic examination with coloring matter that makes the structure visible by being deposited in some parts more than in others. **5** *tr.* print colors on (wallpaper). ● *n.* **1** a discoloration, a spot or mark caused esp. by contact with foreign matter and not easily removed (*a cloth covered with tea stains*). **2 a** a blot or blemish. **b** damage to a reputation, etc. (*a stain on one's character*). **3** a substance used in staining. □ **stained glass** dyed or colored glass, esp. in a lead framework in a window (also (with hyphen) *attrib.*: *stained-glass window*). □□ **stainable** *adj.* **stainer** *n.* [ME f. *distain* f. OF *desteindre desteign-* (as DIS-, TINGE)]

■ *v.* **1** blot, mark, spot, discolor, blotch, speckle, dye, spatter, splatter, tinge, smudge, splash. **2** spoil, defile, ruin, smirch, besmirch, taint, tarnish, stigmatize, shame, disgrace, sully, contaminate, soil, corrupt, blemish, damage. ● *n.* **1** blot, mark, spot, discoloration, blotch, smirch, speck, *colloq.* splotch. **2** mark, blot (on the escutcheon), stigma, blemish, damage, smirch, smudge, blot on one's copybook. **3** dye, color, coloring, colorant, tint, tinge, pigment.

stainless /stáynlis/ *adj.* **1** (esp. of a reputation) without stains. **2** not liable to stain. □ **stainless steel** chrome steel not liable to rust or tarnish under ordinary conditions.

■ **1** see IMMACULATE 1, 3.

stair /stair/ *n.* **1** each of a set of fixed indoor steps (*on the top stair but one*). **2** (usu. in *pl.*) a set of esp. indoor steps (*passed him on the stairs*; *down a winding stair*). **3** (in *pl.*) a landing stage. □ **stair rod** a rod for securing a carpet against the base of the riser. [OE *stæger* f. Gmc]

■ **1, 2** see STEP *n.* 4a.

staircase /stáirkays/ *n.* **1** a flight of stairs and the supporting structure. **2** a part of a building containing a staircase.

stairhead /stáirhed/ *n.* a level space at the top of stairs.

stairway /stáirway/ *n.* **1** a flight of stairs; a staircase. **2** the way up this.

stairwell /stáirwel/ *n.* the shaft in which a staircase is built.

stake¹ /stayk/ *n. & v.* ● *n.* **1** a stout stick or post sharpened at one end and driven into the ground as a support, boundary mark, etc. **2** *hist.* **a** the post to which a person was tied to be burned alive. **b** (prec. by *the*) death by burning as a punishment (*was condemned to the stake*). **3** a long vertical rod in basket-making. **4** a metalworker's small anvil fixed on a bench by a pointed prop. ● *v.tr.* **1** fasten, secure, or support with a stake or stakes. **2** (foll. by *off*, *out*) mark off (an area) with stakes. **3** state or establish (a claim). □ **pull** (or **pull up**) **stakes** depart; go to live elsewhere. **stake boat** a boat anchored to mark the course for a boat race, etc. **stake body** (*pl.* **-ies**) a body for a truck, etc., having a flat open platform with removable posts along the sides. **stake net** a fishing net hung on stakes. **stake out** *colloq.* **1** place under surveillance. **2** place (a person) to maintain surveillance. [OE *staca* f. WG, rel. to STICK²]

■ *n.* **1** stick, post, spike, picket, paling, pale, pole, pike, stave; palisade, upright, pillar, column. ● *v.* **1** tether, tie (up), secure, fasten, picket, lash, leash, hitch, chain; support. **2** (*stake off* or *out*) mark off *or* out, define, delimit, outline, demarcate, delineate, circumscribe; fence (in *or off*), enclose, close in *or* off, wall in. □ **pull** (or **pull up**) **stakes** move (house), resettle, move on, migrate, emigrate, leave, depart, *colloq.* clear off *or* out.

stake² /stayk/ *n. & v.* ● *n.* **1** a sum of money, etc., wagered on an event, esp. deposited with a stakeholder. **2** (often foll. by *in*) an interest or concern, esp. financial. **3** (in *pl.*) a money offered as a prize, esp. in a horse race. **b** such a race (*maiden stakes*; *trial stakes*). ● *v.tr.* **1 a** wager (*staked $5 on the next race*). **b** risk (*staked everything on convincing him*). **2** *colloq.* give financial or other support to. □ **at stake 1** risked; to be won or lost (*life itself is at stake*). **2** at issue; in question. □□ **staker** *n.* [16th c.: perh. f. STAKE¹]

■ *n.* **1** bet, wager, ante, risk, hazard, *Brit.* punt. **2** investment, interest, share, involvement, concern. **3 a** (*stakes*) see PRIZE¹ *n.* 2. ● *v.* **1** wager, bet, gamble, put, risk, venture, chance, hazard, *Brit. colloq.* punt. □ **at stake 1** at hazard, hazarded, at risk, risked, on the table, in jeopardy, jeopardized. **2** at issue, in question, concerned, involved, to be decided *or* resolved.

stakeholder /stáyk-hōldər/ *n.* an independent party with whom each of those who make a wager deposits the money, etc., wagered.

stakeout /stáykowt/ *n. colloq.* a period of surveillance.

Stakhanovite /stəkáanəvīt/ *n.* a worker (esp. in the former USSR) who increases his or her output to an exceptional extent, and so gains special awards. □□ **Stakhanovism** *n.* **Stakhanovist** *n. & adj.* [A. G. *Stakhanov*, Russian coal miner d. 1977]

stalactite /stəláktīt, stálək-/ *n.* a deposit of calcium carbonate having the shape of a large icicle, formed by the trickling of water from the roof of a cave, cliff overhang, etc. □□ **stalactic** /-láktik/ *adj.* **stalactiform** /-láktifawrm/ *adj.* **stalactitic** /-títik/ *adj.* [mod.L *stalactites* f. Gk *stalaktos* dripping f. *stalassō* drip]

stalag /stáalaag, stálag/ *n. hist.* a German prison camp, esp.

/.../	**pronunciation**	●	**part of speech**
	□ **phrases, idioms, and compounds**		
	□□ **derivatives**	■	**synonym section**
	cross-references appear in SMALL CAPITALS or *italics*		

for noncommissioned officers and privates. [G f. *Stamm* base, main stock, *Lager* camp]

stalagmite /stəlágmit, stálǝg-/ *n.* a deposit of calcium carbonate formed by the dripping of water into the shape of a large inverted icicle rising from the floor of a cave, etc., often uniting with a stalactite. □□ **stalagmitic** /-mítik/ *adj.* [mod.L *stalagmites* f. Gk *stalagma* a drop f. *stalassō* (as STALACTITE)]

stale[1] /stayl/ *adj. & v.* ● *adj.* (**staler, stalest**) **1 a** not fresh; not quite new (*stale bread is best for toast*). **b** musty, insipid, or otherwise the worse for age or use. **2** trite or unoriginal (*a stale joke; stale news*). **3** (of an athlete or other performer) having ability impaired by excessive exertion or practice. **4** *Law* (esp. of a claim) having been left dormant for an unreasonably long time. ● *v.tr. & intr.* make or become stale. □□ **stalely** *adv.* **staleness** *n.* [ME, prob. f. AF & OF f. *estaler* halt: cf. STALL[1]]

■ *adj.* **1** old, past its prime, dry, dried-out, hardened, limp, wilted, withered, flat, sour, rank, rancid, turned, (gone) off, moldy, musty, spoiled, rotten. **2** old, banal, overused, antiquated, old-fashioned, threadbare, trite, clichéd, unoriginal, hackneyed, stereotyped, ready-made, tired, weary, boring, tiresome, shopworn, familiar, stock, well-known, hand-me-down, warmed-over, *Brit.* reach-me-down.

stale[2] /stayl/ *n. & v.* ● *n.* the urine of horses and cattle. ● *v.intr.* (esp. of horses and cattle) urinate. [ME, perh. f. OF *estaler* adopt a position (cf. STALE[1])]

stalemate /stáylmayt/ *n. & v.* ● *n.* **1** *Chess* a position counting as a draw, in which a player is not in check but cannot move except into check. **2** a deadlock or drawn contest. ● *v.tr.* **1** *Chess* bring (a player) to a stalemate. **2** bring to a standstill. [obs. *stale* (f. AF *estale* f. *estaler* be placed: cf. STALE[1]) + MATE[2]]

■ *n.* **2** impasse, deadlock, standstill, (dead *or* full) stop, tie, draw, checkmate, stand-off.

Stalinism /staálinizəm/ *n.* **1** the policies followed by Stalin in the government of the former USSR, esp. centralization, totalitarianism, and the pursuit of socialism. **2** any rigid centralized authoritarian form of socialism. □□ **Stalinist** *n.* [J. V. *Stalin* (Dzhugashvili), Soviet statesman d. 1953]

■ **2** totalitarianism.

stalk[1] /stawk/ *n.* **1** the main stem of a herbaceous plant. **2** the slender attachment or support of a leaf, flower, fruit, etc. **3** a similar support for an organ, etc., in an animal. **4** a slender support or linking shaft in a machine, object, etc., e.g., the stem of a wineglass. **5** the tall chimney of a factory, etc. □ **stalk-eyed** (of crabs, snails, etc.) having the eyes mounted on stalks. □□ **stalked** *adj.* (also in *comb.*). **stalkless** *adj.* **stalklet** *n.* **stalklike** *adj.* **stalky** *adj.* [ME *stalke*, prob. dimin. of (now dial.) *stale* rung of a ladder, long handle, f. OE *stalu*]

■ **1** stem, trunk, cane, main axis, shaft. **2** leafstalk, stem, shaft, spike, shoot, bine, *Bot.* petiole, pedicel, peduncle. **3** *Zool.* peduncle, pedicel.

stalk[2] /stawk/ *v. & n.* ● *v.* **1 a** *tr.* pursue or approach (game or an enemy) stealthily. **b** *intr.* steal up to game under cover. **2** *intr.* stride, walk in a stately or haughty manner. ● *n.* **1** the stalking of game. **2** an imposing gait. □ **stalking-horse 1** a horse behind which a hunter is concealed. **2** a pretext concealing one's real intentions or actions. □□ **stalker** *n.* (also in *comb.*). [OE f. Gmc, rel. to STEAL]

■ *v.* **1 a** follow, dog, haunt, shadow, trail, track (down), hunt (down), prey on, pursue, hound, chase, *colloq.* tail. **2** see WALK *v.* 1, 2. □□ **stalker** see HUNTER 1a.

stall[1] /stawl/ *n. & v.* ● *n.* **1 a** a trader's stand or booth in a market, etc., or outdoors. **b** a compartment in a building for the sale of goods. **c** a table in this on which goods are exposed. **2 a** a stable or cowhouse. **b** a compartment for one animal in this. **3 a** a fixed seat in the choir or chancel of a church, more or less enclosed at the back and sides and often canopied, esp. one appropriated to a clergyman (*canon's stall; dean's stall*). **b** the office or dignity of a canon, etc. **4** (usu. in *pl.*) *Brit.* each of a set of seats in a theater, usu. on the ground floor. **5 a** a compartment for one person in

a shower, toilet, etc. **b** a compartment for one horse at the start of a race. **6 a** the stalling of an engine or aircraft. **b** the condition resulting from this. **7** a receptacle for one object. ● *v.* **1 a** *intr.* (of a motor vehicle or its engine) stop because of an overload on the engine or an inadequate supply of fuel to it. **b** *intr.* (of an aircraft or its pilot) reach a condition where the speed is too low to allow effective operation of the controls. **c** *tr.* cause (an engine or vehicle or aircraft) to stall. **2** *tr.* **a** put or keep (cattle, etc.) in a stall or stalls esp. for fattening (*a stalled ox*). **b** furnish (a stable, etc.) with stalls. **3** *intr.* **a** (of a horse or cart) stick fast as in mud or snow. **b** (of a car) be stuck in mud or snow. □ **stall-feed** fatten (cattle) in a stall. [OE *steall* f. Gmc, rel. to STAND: partly f. OF *estal* f. Frank.]

■ *n.* **1** stand, booth, cubicle, kiosk; compartment, alcove, section, space, area, slot, enclosure, quarters; counter, table. **2** shed, pen, cote, fold, coop, sty, enclosure, cowshed, barn, stable, corral, *Brit.* byre. ● *v.* **1 a** stop, halt, die, shut down, fail, cease operating, come to a standstill, quit, *colloq.* conk out.

stall[2] /stawl/ *v. & n.* ● *v.* **1** *intr.* play for time when being questioned, etc. **2** *tr.* delay; obstruct; block. ● *n.* the act or an instance of stalling. □ **stall off** evade or deceive. [*stall* pickpocket's confederate, orig. 'decoy' f. AF *estal(e)*, prob. rel. to STALL[1]]

■ *v.* **1** delay, dawdle, dally, temporize, equivocate, hesitate, prevaricate, play for time, waste time, stonewall, be obstructive, put a person *or* thing off; vacillate, dither, hedge, procrastinate; beat about the bush, drag one's feet, give a person the runaround, *Brit.* haver, *colloq.* dillydally. **2** see OBSTRUCT 2. ● *n.* delay, hedge, pretext, subterfuge, wile, trick, ruse, artifice, stratagem, maneuver, move, runaround, stalling, stonewalling, obstructionism, playing for time, procrastination, beating about the bush.

stallage /stáwlij/ *n. Brit.* **1** space for a stall or stalls in a market, etc. **2** the rent for such a stall. **3** the right to erect such a stall. [ME f. OF *estalage* f. *estal* STALL[1]]

stallholder /stáwlhōldər/ *n. Brit.* a person in charge of a stall at a market, etc.

stallion /stályən/ *n.* an uncastrated adult male horse, esp. one kept for breeding. [ME f. OF *estalon* ult. f. a Gmc root rel. to STALL[1]]

stalwart /stáwlwərt/ *adj. & n.* ● *adj.* **1** strongly built; sturdy. **2** courageous; resolute; determined (*stalwart supporters*). ● *n.* a stalwart person, esp. a loyal uncompromising partisan. □□ **stalwartly** *adv.* **stalwartness** *n.* [Sc. var. of obs. *stalworth* f. OE *stælwierthe* f. *stæl* place, WORTH]

■ *adj.* **1** robust, stout, strong, mighty, powerful, rugged, staunch, hardy, sturdy, vigorous, lusty, indomitable, solid, able-bodied, brawny, husky, hefty, beefy, sinewy, muscular, fit, healthy, hale, (hale and) hearty. **2** brave, courageous, daring, intrepid, valiant, heroic, manly, manful, fearless, indomitable, stouthearted, bold, audacious, game, red-blooded, plucky, mettlesome, lionhearted, spirited; redoubtable, undaunted, resolute, firm, determined, unbending, steadfast, staunch, tenacious, unswerving, unwavering, unfaltering, unflinching, uncompromising, unyielding, persevering, persistent, unflagging, relentless, tireless, untiring, indefatigable. ● *n.* supporter, upholder, sustainer, partisan, loyalist, (party) faithful, trouper; hero, heroine. □□ **stalwartly** see *vigorously* (VIGOROUS). **stalwartness** see BRAVERY, STAMINA.

stamen /stáymən/ *n.* the male fertilizing organ of a flowering plant, including the anther containing pollen. □□ **staminiferous** /stáminífərəs/ *adj.* [L *stamen staminis* warp in an upright loom, thread]

stamina /stáminə/ *n.* the ability to endure prolonged physical or mental strain; staying power; power of endurance. [L, pl. of STAMEN in sense 'warp, threads spun by the Fates']

■ ruggedness, vigor, vigorousness, fortitude, robustness, indefatigability, staying power, endurance, energy, power, might, mettle, (inner) strength, staunchness, stalwartness, courage, indomitability, *colloq.* grit, guts, sand.

staminate /stáminət, -nayt/ *adj.* (of a plant) having stamens, esp. stamens but not pistils.

stammer /stámər/ *v. & n.* ● *v.* **1** *intr.* speak (habitually, or on occasion from embarrassment, etc.) with halting articulation, esp. with pauses or rapid repetitions of the same syllable. **2** *tr.* (often foll. by *out*) utter (words) in this way (*stammered out an excuse*). ● *n.* **1** a tendency to stammer. **2** an instance of stammering. □□ **stammerer** *n.* **stammeringly** *adv.* [OE *stamerian* f. WG]

■ *v.* **1** stutter, hesitate, hem and haw, stumble, falter, pause, *Brit.* hum and haw. ● *n.* stutter.

stamp /stamp/ *v. & n.* ● *v.* **1 a** *tr.* bring down (one's foot) heavily on the ground, etc. **b** *tr.* crush, flatten, or bring into a specified state in this way (*stamped down the earth around the plant*). **c** *intr.* bring down one's foot heavily; walk with heavy steps. **2** *tr.* impress (a pattern, mark, etc.) on metal, paper, butter, etc., with a die or similar instrument of metal, wood, rubber, etc. **b** impress (a surface) with a pattern, etc., in this way. **3** *tr.* affix a postage or other stamp to (an envelope or document). **4** *tr.* assign a specific character to; characterize; mark out (*stamps the story an invention*). **5** *tr.* crush or pulverize (ore, etc.). ● *n.* **1** an instrument for stamping a pattern or mark. **2 a** a mark or pattern made by this. **b** the impression of an official mark required to be made for revenue purposes on deeds, bills of exchange, etc., as evidence of payment of tax. **3** a small adhesive piece of paper indicating that a price, fee, or tax has been paid, esp. a postage stamp. **4** a mark impressed on or label, etc., affixed to a commodity as evidence of quality, etc. **5 a** a heavy downward blow with the foot. **b** the sound of this. **6 a** a characteristic mark or impression (*bears the stamp of genius*). **b** character; kind (*avoid people of that stamp*). **7** the block that crushes ore in a stamp mill. □ **Stamp Act** an act concerned with stamp duty, esp. that imposing the duty on the American colonies in 1765 and repealed in 1766. **stamp collecting** the collecting of postage stamps as objects of interest or value. **stamp collector** a person engaged in stamp collecting. **stamp duty** (or **tax**) a duty imposed on certain kinds of legal document. **stamp hinge** see HINGE. **stamping ground** a favorite haunt or place of action. **stamp mill** a mill for crushing ore, etc. **stamp on 1** impress (an idea, etc.) on (the memory, etc.). **2** suppress. **stamp out 1** produce by cutting out with a die, etc. **2** put an end to; crush; destroy. □□ **stamper** *n.* [prob. f. OE *stampian* (v.) (unrecorded) f. Gmc: infl. by OF *estamper* (v.) and F *estampe* (n.) also f. Gmc]

■ *v.* **1 b** trample, tramp, crush, flatten, squash, press, tread on, *colloq.* squish. **c** tramp, stomp, thump; tread *or* step heavily. **2** impress, mark, imprint, print, brand; engrave, emboss, inscribe. **4** brand, label, mark, tag, term, name, style, identify, categorize, classify, characterize, designate, denominate, show to be. ● *n.* **1** die, block, punch, seal, matrix, plate, die stamp, stereotype; rubber stamp, signet (ring). **2, 4** seal, (trade) mark, brand, logotype, symbol, representation, colophon, imprint, emblem, insignia, label, monogram, sign, crest, coat of arms, escutcheon, signature, initials, *Archit.* & *Archaeol.* cartouche, *colloq.* logo. **6 a** mark, sign, impress, hallmark, earmark, trait(s), feature(s), characteristic(s). **b** character, kind, sort, make, fashion, type, cast, mold, grade, style, cut, genre, class, level, kidney, classification, species, genus, variety, description, stripe. □ **stamp collecting** philately. **stamp collector** philatelist. **stamping ground** see HAUNT *n.* **stamp on 1** impress on, imprint on, etch on, engrave on, inscribe on, print on, record in, document in, register in, log in. **2** see SQUELCH *v.* 2b. **stamp out 2** eliminate, eradicate, abolish, get rid of, annihilate, exterminate, kill, snuff out, terminate, end, put an end to, destroy, put down, put out, extinguish, extirpate; crush, quell, subdue, suppress, squelch, repress.

stampede /stampéed/ *n. & v.* ● *n.* **1** a sudden flight and scattering of a number of horses, cattle, etc. **2** a sudden flight or hurried movement of people due to interest or panic. **3** the spontaneous response of many persons to a common impulse. **4** *W. US* and *Canada* a festival combining a rodeo and other events and competitions. ● *v.* **1** *intr.* take part in a stampede. **2** *tr.* cause to do this. **3** *tr.* cause to act hurriedly or unreasoningly. □□ **stampeder** *n.* [Sp. *estampida* crash, uproar, ult. f. Gmc, rel. to STAMP]

■ *n.* **1, 2** rout, flight, scattering, panic, rush, dash. ● *v.* **1** rush, run, race, charge, take to one's heels, dash, flee, take flight. **2** panic, frighten, rush, scatter, rout, put to flight. **3** see RAILROAD *v.*

stance /stans/ *n.* **1** an attitude or position of the body, esp. when hitting a ball, etc. **2** a standpoint; an attitude of mind. **3** *Sc.* a site for a market, taxi stand, etc. [F f. It. *stanza*: see STANZA]

■ **1** position, posture, attitude, stand, carriage, bearing, deportment. **2** standpoint, viewpoint, point of view, attitude, stand; see also POSITION *n.* 5.

stanch[1] /stawnch, stanch, staanch/ *v.tr.* (also **staunch**) **1** restrain the flow of (esp. blood). **2** restrain the flow from (esp. a wound). [ME f. OF *estanchier* f. Rmc]

■ **1** stem, halt, check, arrest, end, cease, prevent, *archaic or literary* stay; see also STOP *v.* 1b.

stanch[2] var. of STAUNCH[1].

stanchion /stánshən, -chən/ *n. & v.* ● *n.* **1** a post or pillar; an upright support; a vertical strut. **2** an upright bar, pair of bars, or frame for confining cattle in a stall. ● *v.tr.* **1** supply with a stanchion. **2** fasten (cattle) to a stanchion. [ME f. AF *stanchon*, OF *estanchon* f. *estance* prob. ult. f. L *stare* stand]

■ *n.* **1** see POST[1] *n.*

stand /stand/ *v. & n.* ● *v.* (*past* and *past part.* **stood** /stŏŏd/) **1** *intr.* have or take or maintain an upright position, esp. on the feet or a base. **2** *intr.* be situated or located (*here once stood a village*). **3** *intr.* be of a specified height (*stands six foot three*). **4** *intr.* be in a specified condition (*stands accused*; *the thermometer stood at 90°*; *the matter stands as follows*; *stood in awe of them*). **5** *tr.* place or set in an upright or specified position (*stood it against the wall*). **6** *intr.* a move to and remain in a specified position (*stand aside*). **b** take a specified attitude (*stand aloof*). **7** *intr.* maintain a position; avoid falling or moving or being moved (*the house will stand for another century*; *stood for hours arguing*). **8** *intr.* assume a stationary position; cease to move (*now stand still*). **9** *intr.* remain valid or unaltered; hold good (*the former conditions must stand*). **10** *intr.* *Naut.* hold a specified course (*stand in for the shore*). **11** *tr.* endure without yielding or complaining; tolerate (*cannot stand the pain*; *how can you stand him?*). **12** *tr.* provide for another or others at one's own expense (*stood him a drink*). **13** *intr.* (often foll. by *for*) esp. *Brit.* be a candidate (for an office, legislature, or constituency) (*stood for Parliament*). **14** *intr.* act in a specified capacity (*stood proxy*). **15** *tr.* undergo (trial). **16** *intr.* *Cricket* act as umpire. **17** *intr.* (of a dog) point; set. **18** *intr.* (in full **stand at stud**) (of a stallion) be available for breeding. ● *n.* **1** a cessation from motion or progress; a stoppage. **2 a** a halt made, or a stationary condition assumed, for the purpose of resistance. **b** resistance to attack or compulsion (esp. *make a stand*). **3 a** a position taken up (*took his stand near the door*). **b** an attitude adopted. **4** a rack, set of shelves, table, etc., on or in which things may be placed (*music stand*; *hatstand*). **5 a** a small open-fronted structure for a trader outdoors or in a market, etc. **b** esp. *Brit.* a structure occupied by a participating organization at an exhibition. **6** a standing place for vehicles (*cab stand*). **7 a** (usu. in *pl.*) a raised structure for persons to sit or stand on. **b** a witness box (*take the stand*). **8 a** *Theatr.*, etc., each halt made on a tour to give one or more performances. **b** *Sports* each place in which a traveling team plays one or more games (*5-game stand in Boston*). **9** a group of growing plants (*stand of trees*; *stand of clover*). □ **as it**

/. . ./ **pronunciation**	● **part of speech**
□ **phrases, idioms, and compounds**	
□□ **derivatives**	■ **synonym section**
cross-references appear in SMALL CAPITALS or *italics*	

stands 1 in its present condition; unaltered. **2** in the present circumstances. **it stands to reason** see REASON. **stand alone** be unequaled. **stand-alone** (of a computer) operating independently of a network or other system. **stand and deliver!** *hist.* a highwayman's order to hand over valuables, etc. **stand at bay** see BAY⁵. **stand back 1** withdraw; take up a position further from the front. **2** withdraw psychologically in order to take an objective view. **stand by 1** stand nearby; look on without interfering (*will not stand by and see him ill-treated*). **2** uphold; support; side with (a person). **3** adhere to; abide by (terms or promises). **4** *Naut.* stand ready to take hold of or operate (an anchor, etc.). **5** (often foll. by *for*) wait; stand ready for. **stand a chance** see CHANCE. **stand corrected** accept correction. **stand down 1** withdraw (a person) or retire from a team, witness box, or similar position. **2** *Brit.* cease to be a candidate, etc. **3** *Brit. Mil.* go off duty. **stand easy!** see EASY. **stand for 1** represent; signify; imply (*"US" stands for "United States"*; *democracy stands for a great deal more than that*). **2** (often with *neg.*) *colloq.* endure tolerate; acquiesce in. **3** espouse the cause of. **stand one's ground** maintain one's position, not yield. **stand high** be high in status, price, etc. **stand in** (usu. foll. by *for*) deputize; act in place of another. **stand-in** *n.* a deputy or substitute, esp. for an actor when the latter's acting ability is not needed. **stand in the breach** see BREACH. **stand in good stead** see STEAD. **stand in with** be in league with. **stand of arms** *Brit. Mil.* a complete set of weapons for one individual. **stand of colors** *Brit. Mil.* a regiment's flags. **stand off 1** move or keep away; keep one's distance. **2** *Brit.* temporarily dispense with the services of (an employee). **stand-off** *n.* a deadlock. **stand on 1** insist on; observe scrupulously (*stand on ceremony*; *stand on one's dignity*). **2** *Naut.* continue on the same course. **stand on me** esp. *Brit. sl.* rely on me; believe me. **stand on one's own (two) feet** (or **legs**) be self-reliant or independent. **stand out 1** be prominent or conspicuous or outstanding. **2** (usu. foll. by *against, for*) hold out; persist in opposition or support or endurance. **stand over 1** stand close to (a person) to watch, control, threaten, etc. **2** be postponed, be left for later settlement, etc. **stand pat** see PAT². **stand to 1** *Mil.* stand ready for an attack (esp. before dawn or after dark). **2** abide by; adhere to (terms or promises). **3** be likely or certain to (*stands to lose everything*). **4** uphold, support, or side with (a person). **stand treat** esp. *Brit.* bear the expense of entertainment, etc. **stand up 1 a** rise to one's feet from a sitting or other position. **b** come to or remain in or place in a standing position. **2** (of an argument, etc.) be valid. **3** *colloq.* fail to keep an appointment with. **stand-up** *attrib.adj.* **1** (of a meal) eaten standing. **2** (of a fight) violent, thorough, or fair and square. **3** (of a collar) upright, not turned down. **4** (of a comedian) performing by standing before an audience and telling jokes. **stand up for 1** support; side with; maintain (a person or cause). **2** serve as best man, maid of honor, or other attendant in a wedding. **stand upon** = *stand on.* **stand up to 1** meet or face (an opponent) courageously. **2** be resistant to the harmful effects of (wear, use, etc.). **stand well** (usu. foll. by *with*) be on good terms or in good repute. **take one's stand on** base one's argument, etc., on; rely on. □□ **stander** *n.* [OE *standan* f. Gmc]

■ *v.* **1** stand up, rise, get up, be upstanding, be upright, esp. *archaic & poet.* arise; stay, remain (standing). **2** be, be located *or* situated *or* positioned, exist, lie. **5** stand up, set, place (upright), position, put, move; upend. **8** stop, remain, halt, *archaic or literary* stay. **9** continue, remain, persist, be *or* remain in effect, be *or* remain in force, prevail, obtain, apply, hold good, exist. **11** endure, survive, tolerate, countenance, face, confront, last through, abide, allow, accept, take, suffer, bear, withstand, undergo, experience, cope with, brave, stand *or* bear up under, stand for, stomach, weather, handle, put up with, *literary* brook. **12** treat to, buy, *Austral. & NZ colloq.* shout. **13** campaign, run, be a candidate, present oneself as a candidate, seek election. **15** see UNDERGO. ● *n.* **1** see STANDSTILL. **2 b** defense, resistance, effort. **3** position, place. **b** position,

attitude, stance, posture, policy, philosophy, point of view, viewpoint, standpoint, belief, opinion, sentiment, feeling, line. **4** rack, frame, bracket; hatstand, coatrack; easel; tripod. **5** counter, booth, stall, kiosk; table; wagon, barrow, cart. **6** lot, *Brit.* rank. **7 a** platform, dais, stage, staging, rostrum, bandstand. **b** witness box, witness stand. **8** stop, stopover, halt, stay; performance, show. **9** copse, grove, wood, thicket, brake, coppice, *Brit.* spinney. □ **stand by 1** wait (in the wings), stand *or* wait *or* stay *or* remain on the sidelines, stand back, stand aside *or* alongside, be *or* stand ready, be *or* stand available, be *or* stand accessible, be *or* stand in readiness. **2** support, defend, back, stand up for, stick up for, stand behind, stand alongside, be *or* remain loyal to, be *or* remain faithful to, uphold, take the side of, side with, stand to, sympathize with. **3** stick to, adhere to, support, maintain, persist in, affirm, reaffirm, confirm, abide by, stand to. **stand down 1, 2** lay off, suspend, *Brit.* stand off; resign, quit, step aside, step down, withdraw, pull out, retire. **stand for 1** symbolize, betoken, represent, signify, mean, be emblematic of, be short for, exemplify, epitomize, illustrate, typify, refer to, allude to, imply. **2** see STAND *v.* 11 above. **3** support, advocate, favor, sponsor, promote, espouse (the cause of), subscribe to, back, champion, lend support to, lend one's name to, second. **stand in** (*stand in for*) substitute for, understudy for, replace, relieve, double for, cover for, deputize for, take the place of. **stand-in** double, substitute, stunt man; surrogate, replacement, standby, backup, understudy, second, deputy, alternate, pinch hitter. **stand off 2** stand down, lay off, suspend. **stand-off** see STALEMATE *n.* **stand out 1** be prominent, be conspicuous, be noticeable, be notable, be noteworthy, be outstanding; protrude, project, stick out, jut out, bulge, obtrude, beetle, overhang, extend. **stand to 2** see *stand by* 3 above. **4** see *stand by* 2 above. **stand up 1 a** stand, rise, get to one's feet, get up, be upstanding, esp. *archaic & poet.* arise. **b** see STAND *v.* 1 above. **2** see *hold good* (HOLD¹). **3** jilt, break an appointment with, fail to keep an appointment with. **stand up for 1** support, defend, take the side of, side with, champion, uphold, maintain, stick up for, stand by. **stand up to 1** confront, face (up to), brave, stick up to, challenge, dispute, question, tackle, oppose, resist, defy, withstand. **2** resist, defy, withstand, endure, outlast, last through, survive, suffer.

standard /stándərd/ *n. & adj.* ● *n.* **1** an object or quality or measure serving as a basis or example or principle to which others conform or should conform or by which the accuracy or quality of others is judged (*by present-day standards*). **2 a** the degree of excellence, etc., required for a particular purpose (*not up to standard*). **b** average quality (*of a low standard*). **3** the ordinary procedure, or quality or design of a product, without added or novel features. **4** a distinctive flag, esp. the flag of a cavalry regiment as distinct from the *colors* of an infantry regiment. **5 a** an upright support. **b** an upright water or gas pipe. **6 a** a tree or shrub that grows on an erect stem of full height and stands alone without support. **b** a shrub grafted on an upright stem and trained in tree form (*standard rose*). **7** a thing recognized as a model for imitation, etc. **8** a tune or song of established popularity. **9 a** a system by which the value of a currency is defined in terms of gold or silver or both. **b** the prescribed proportion of the weight of fine metal in gold or silver coins. **10** a measure for lumber, equivalent to 165 cu. ft. (4.7 cubic meters). ● *adj.* **1** serving or used as a standard (*a standard size*). **2** of a normal or prescribed but not exceptional quality or size, etc. **3** having recognized and permanent value; authoritative (*the standard book on the subject*). **4** (of language) conforming to established educated usage (*Standard English*). □ **standard-bearer 1** a soldier who carries a standard. **2** a prominent leader in a cause. **standard deviation** see DEVIATION. **standard lamp** *Brit.* = *floor lamp.* **standard of living** the degree of material comfort available to a person or class or community. **standard time** a uniform time for places in approximately the same longitude, established in a country or region by law or custom. [ME f. AF *estaundart*, OF *estendart* f. *estendre*, as EXTEND: in senses 5 and 6 of *n*. affected by association with STAND]

■ *n*. **1, 8** model, pattern, archetype, paradigm, paragon, exemplar, example, sample, type, ideal, beau ideal; criterion, measure, benchmark, touchstone, yardstick, gauge, guide, guideline, rule, canon, law, requirement, precept, principle. **2** quality, grade, level, rating. **3** mean, average, norm, par, usual. **4** flag, banner, ensign, jack, emblem, pennant, burgee, insignia, guidon, gonfalon, labarum. **5 a** upright, pole, post, stanchion, lamppost, column, pillar, support, pedestal, pier, footing, (upright) bar *or* rod *or* timber. ● *adj*. **2–4** recognized, prevailing, prevalent, usual, customary, habitual, orthodox, set, established, prescribed, defined, required, regular, familiar, ordinary, traditional, accepted, approved, recognized, classic, textbook, definitive, authoritative, official, regulative, regulatory. □ **standard-bearer 2** see PROTAGONIST 3.

Standardbred /stándərdbred/ *n*. **1** a horse of an American breed able to attain a specified speed, developed esp. for harness racing. **2** this breed.

standardize /stándərdīz/ *v.tr.* **1** cause to conform to a standard. **2** determine the properties of by comparison with a standard. □□ **standardizable** *adj*. **standardization** *n*. **standardizer** *n*.

■ **1** regiment, systematize, codify, normalize, regularize, homogenize, equalize.

standby /stándbī/ *n*. (*pl.* **standbys**) **1** a person or thing ready if needed in an emergency, etc. **2** readiness for duty (*on standby*). ● *adj*. **1** ready for immediate use. **2** (of air travel) not booked in advance but allocated on the basis of earliest availability.

standee /standeé/ *n. colloq.* a person who stands, esp. when all seats are occupied.

standing /stánding/ *n. & adj.* ● *n*. **1** esteem or repute, esp. high; status; position (*people of high standing; is of no standing*). **2** duration (*a dispute of long standing*). **3** length of service, membership, etc. ● *adj*. **1** that stands; upright. **2 a** established; permanent (*a standing rule*). **b** not made, raised, etc., for the occasion (*a standing army*). **3** (of a jump, start, race, etc.) performed from rest or from a standing position. **4** (of water) stagnant. **5** (of grain) unreaped. **6** (of a stallion) that stands at stud. **7** *Printing* (formerly, of type) not yet distributed after use. □ **all standing 1** *Naut.* without time to lower the sails. **2** taken by surprise. **in good standing** fully paid-up as a member, etc. **leave a person standing** make far more rapid progress than he or she. **standing committee** see COMMITTEE. **standing joke** an object of permanent ridicule. **standing order** an instruction to follow a prescribed procedure in certain circumstances, as to a publisher, etc., for a regular supply of a periodical, etc. **standing orders** the rules governing the manner in which all business shall be conducted in a parliament, council, society, etc. **standing ovation** see OVATION. **standing rigging** rigging which is fixed in position. **standing room** space to stand in. **standing wave** *Physics* the vibration of a system in which some particular points remain fixed while others between them vibrate with the maximum amplitude (cf. *traveling wave*).

■ *n*. **1** eminence, prominence, esteem, repute, reputation; status, rank, station, footing, position, place, grade, order, level, stratum. **2** duration; endurance, longevity. **3** experience, seniority. ● *adj*. **1** erect, upright, on one's feet, vertical, unseated. **2 a** established, set, standard, conventional, customary, usual, normal, regular, fixed, permanent, continued, continuing, continuous, ongoing, perpetual, unbroken. **b** permanent, regular, established. **4** stagnant, motionless, unmoving, stationary, still, static.

standoffish /stándáwfish, -óf-/ *adj*. cold or distant in manner. □□ **standoffishly** *adv*. **standoffishness** *n*.

■ aloof, haughty, unsocial, reserved, cool, cold, frosty,

frigid, withdrawn, remote, removed, distant, detached, unapproachable, inaccessible, uncongenial, unfriendly, unsociable; Olympian, lordly, pompous, *colloq.* highfalutin, snooty. □□ **standoffishness** see RESERVE *n*. 3.

standout /stándowt/ *n*. a remarkable person or thing.

standpipe /stándpīp/ *n*. a vertical pipe extending from a water supply, esp. one connecting a temporary faucet to the main water supply.

standpoint /stándpoynt/ *n*. **1** the position from which a thing is viewed. **2** a mental attitude.

■ viewpoint, point of view, vantage point, position, stance, perspective, angle, aspect, slant; view, outlook, attitude, opinion.

standstill /stándstil/ *n*. a stoppage; an inability to proceed.

■ (dead *or* full) stop, halt, stand, stoppage, deadlock, stalemate, impasse.

stanhope /stánhōp/ *n*. a light open carriage for one with two or four wheels. [Fitzroy *Stanhope*, Engl. clergyman d. 1864, for whom the first one was made]

stank past of STINK.

stannary /stánəree/ *n*. (*pl.* **-ies**) *Brit.* **1** a tin mine. **2** (usu. in *pl.*) a tin-mining district in Cornwall and Devon. □ **stannary court** a legal body for the regulation of tin miners in the stannaries. [med.L *stannaria* (pl.) f. LL *stannum* tin]

stannic /stánik/ *adj. Chem.* of or relating to tetravalent tin (*stannic acid; stannic chloride*). [LL *stannum* tin]

stannous /stánəs/ *adj. Chem.* of or relating to bivalent tin (*stannous salts; stannous chloride*).

stanza /stánzə/ *n*. **1** the basic metrical unit in a poem or verse consisting of a recurring group of lines (often four lines and usu. not more than twelve) which may or may not rhyme. **2** a group of four lines in some Greek and Latin meters. □□ **stanza'd** *adj*. (also **stanzaed**) (also in *comb.*). **stanzaic** /-záyik/ *adj*. [It., = standing place, chamber, stanza, ult. f. L *stare* stand]

■ see PASSAGE¹ 6.

stapelia /stəpeéleeə/ *n*. any S. African plant of the genus *Stapelia*, with flowers having an unpleasant smell. [mod.L f. J. B. von *Stapel*, Du. botanist d. 1636]

stapes /stáypeez/ *n*. (*pl.* same) a small stirrup-shaped bone in the ear of a mammal. [mod.L f. med.L *stapes* stirrup]

staphylococcus /stáfiləkókəs/ *n*. (*pl.* **staphylococci** /-kóksī, kóki/) any bacterium of the genus *Staphylococcus*, occurring in grapelike clusters, and sometimes causing pus formation usu. in the skin and mucous membranes of animals. □□ **staphylococcal** *adj*. [mod.L f. Gk *staphulē* bunch of grapes + *kokkos* berry]

staple¹ /stáypəl/ *n. & v.* ● *n*. a U-shaped metal bar or piece of wire with pointed ends for driving into, securing, or fastening together various materials or for driving through and clinching papers, netting, electric wire, etc. ● *v.tr.* provide or fasten with a staple. □ **staple gun** a handheld device for driving in staples. □□ **stapler** *n*. [OE *stapol* f. Gmc]

staple² /stáypəl/ *n., adj., & v.* ● *n*. **1** the principal or an important article of commerce (*the staples of local industry*). **2** the chief element or a main component, e.g., of a diet. **3** a raw material. **4** the fiber of cotton or wool, etc., as determining its quality (*cotton of fine staple*). ● *adj*. **1** main or principal (*staple commodities*). **2** important as a product or an export. ● *v.tr.* sort or classify (wool, etc.) according to fiber. [ME f. OF *estaple* market f. MLG, MDu. *stapel* market (as STAPLE¹)]

■ *n*. **1, 2** necessity, essential, basic, fundamental. ● *adj*. **1** basic, elementary, essential, necessary, requisite, required, vital, indispensable, critical, fundamental, primary, principal, main, chief; standard, usual, habitual, ordinary, customary, prevailing, normal, conventional, universal.

/ . . . / **pronunciation**   ● **part of speech**
□ **phrases, idioms, and compounds**
□□ **derivatives**   ■ **synonym section**
cross-references appear in SMALL CAPITALS or *italics*

star /staar/ *n. & v.* ● *n.* **1** a celestial body appearing as a luminous point in the night sky. **2** (in full **fixed star**) such a body so far from the earth as to appear motionless (cf. PLANET, COMET). **3** a large naturally luminous gaseous body such as the sun. **4** a celestial body regarded as influencing a person's fortunes, etc. (*born under a lucky star*). **5** a thing resembling a star in shape or appearance. **6** a star-shaped mark, esp. a white mark on a horse's forehead. **7** a figure or object with radiating points esp. as the insignia of an order, as a decoration or mark of rank, or showing a category of excellence (*a five-star hotel; was awarded a gold star*). **8 a** a famous or brilliant person; the principal or most prominent performer in a play, movie, etc. (*the star of the show*). **b** (*attrib.*) outstanding; particularly brilliant (*star pupil*). **9** (in full **star connection**) esp. *Brit. Electr.* a Y-shaped arrangement of three-phase windings. ● *v.* (**starred, starring**) **1 a** *tr.* (of a movie, etc.) feature as a principal performer. **b** *intr.* (of a performer) be featured in a movie, etc. **2** (esp. as **starred** *adj.*) **a** a mark, set, or adorn with a star or stars. **b** put an asterisk or star beside (a name, an item in a list, etc.). □ **my stars!** *Old-fashioned colloq.* an expression of surprise. **star apple** an edible, purple, applelike fruit (with a starlike cross section) of a tropical evergreen tree, *Chrysophyllum cainito*. **Star Chamber** *Brit. Law* **1** *hist.* a court of civil and criminal jurisdiction noted for its arbitrary procedure, and abolished in 1640. **2** any arbitrary or oppressive tribunal. **star-crossed** *archaic* ill-fated. **star fruit** = CARAMBOLA. **star of Bethlehem** any of various plants with starlike flowers esp. *Ornithogalum umbellatum* with white star-shaped flowers striped with green on the outside (see Matt. 2:9). **Star of David** a figure consisting of two interlaced equilateral triangles used as a Jewish and Israeli symbol. **star route** a rural mail delivery route served by private contractors. **Stars and Bars** the flag of the Confederate States of the US. **Stars and Stripes** the national flag of the US. **star sapphire** a cabochon sapphire reflecting a starlike image due to its regular internal structure. **star shell** an explosive projectile designed to burst in the air and light up the enemy's position. **star-spangled** (esp. of the US national flag) covered or glittering with stars. **star stream** a systematic drift of stars. **star-studded** containing or covered with many stars, esp. featuring many famous performers. **star turn** *Brit.* the principal item in an entertainment or performance. **Star Wars** *colloq.* the strategic defense initiative. □□ **stardom** *n.* **starless** *adj.* **starlike** *adj.* [OE *steorra* f. Gmc]

▪ *n.* **1** celestial body, heavenly body; fixed star, evening star, morning star, falling star, shooting star, comet, lodestar, pole star; nova, supernova. **5** asterisk, pentagram. **8 a** celebrity, personage, dignitary, VIP, name, somebody, luminary, leading light, leading man, leading woman *or* lady, lead, principal, diva, prima donna, hero, heroine, idol, superstar, megastar, big name, (big) draw, pinup, headliner, *colloq.* bigwig, big noise *or* shot *or* wheel, celeb, *sl.* big-timer. **b** principal, major, leading, important, celebrated, famous, famed, prominent, eminent, preeminent, outstanding, distinguished, brilliant, illustrious, unequaled, peerless, matchless, incomparable, unrivaled, inimitable, unmatched, unparalleled, top, foremost. ● *v.* **1 a** feature. **b** be featured; play *or* perform *or* act *or* take the lead *or* leading part *or* leading role. □ **Star Chamber 2** interrogation, third degree, grilling, *usu derog.* inquisition; esp. *hist.* show trial. **star-crossed** see *doomed* (DOOM *v.* 2). □□ **stardom** see FAME 1, 2. **starless** see BLACK *adj.* 2.

starboard /staarbərd/ *n. & v. Naut. & Aeron.* ● *n.* the right-hand side (looking forward) of a ship, boat, or aircraft (cf. PORT³). ● *v.tr.* (also *absol.*) turn (the helm) to starboard. □ **starboard tack** see TACK¹ 4. **starboard watch** see WATCH *n.* 3b. [OE *stēorbord* = rudder side (see STEER, BOARD), early Teutonic ships being steered with a paddle over the right side]

▪ *n.* right (side *or* hand).

starch /staarch/ *n. & v.* ● *n.* **1** an odorless tasteless polysac-

charide occurring widely in plants and obtained chiefly from cereals and potatoes, forming an important constituent of the human diet. **2** a preparation of this for stiffening fabric before ironing. **3** stiffness of manner; formality. ● *v.tr.* stiffen (clothing) with starch. □□ **starcher** *n.* [earlier as verb: ME *sterche* f. OE *stercan* (unrecorded) stiffen f. Gmc: cf. STARK]

starchy /staarchee/ *adj.* (**starchier, starchiest**) **1 a** of or like starch. **b** containing much starch. **2** (of a person) precise; overly formal. □□ **starchily** *adv.* **starchiness** *n.*
▪ **2** see STIFF *adj.* 5.

stardust /staardust/ *n.* **1** a twinkling mass. **2** a romantic mystical look or sensation. **3** a multitude of stars looking like dust.

stare /stair/ *v. & n.* ● *v.* **1** *intr.* (usu. foll. by *at*) look fixedly with eyes open, esp. as the result of curiosity, surprise, bewilderment, admiration, horror, etc. (*sat staring at the door; stared in amazement*). **2** *intr.* (of eyes) be wide open and fixed. **3** *intr.* be unpleasantly prominent or striking. **4** *tr.* (foll. by *into*) reduce (a person) to a specified condition by staring (*stared me into silence*). ● *n.* a staring gaze. □ **stare down** (or **out**) outstare. **stare a person in the face** be evident or imminent. □□ **starer** *n.* [OE *starian* f. Gmc]

▪ *v.* **1** gaze, gape, goggle, watch, peer, glare; ogle; *archaic* quiz, *colloq.* gawk, rubberneck, *Brit. colloq.* gawp. ● *n.* (fixed *or* blank) look; goggle, gaze, glare.

starfish /staarfish/ *n.* an echinoderm of the class Asteroidea with five or more radiating arms.

stargaze /staargayz/ *v.intr.* **1** gaze at or study the stars. **2** gaze intently.

stargazer /staargayzər/ *n.* **1** *colloq.* usu. *derog.* or *joc.* an astronomer or astrologer. **2** *Austral. sl.* a horse that turns its head when galloping.

stark /staark/ *adj. & adv.* ● *adj.* **1** desolate; bare (*a stark landscape*). **2** sharply evident; brutally simple. (*in stark contrast; the stark reality*). **3** downright; sheer (*stark madness*). **4** completely naked. **5** *archaic* strong; stiff; rigid. ● *adv.* completely; wholly (*stark mad; stark naked*). □□ **starkly** *adv.* **starkness** *n.* [OE *stearc* f. Gmc: stark naked f. earlier *start-naked* f. obs. *start* tail: cf. REDSTART]

▪ *adj.* **1** harsh, severe, bleak, barren, desolate, dreary, gray, cold, cheerless, depressing, grim, ravaged, empty, vacant, austere, bare, plain, simple, Spartan, unembellished, unadorned, *poet.* drear. **2** clear, plain, evident, obvious, patent, manifest, overt, conspicuous, flagrant, blatant, gross, rank; bare, blunt, unadorned, unembellished, harsh, hard, grim. **3** sheer, complete, utter, absolute, perfect, pure, thorough, thoroughgoing, arrant, unmitigated, out-and-out, downright, outright, total, unconditional, unqualified. **4** see NAKED 1. ● *adv.* completely, utterly, unqualifiedly, wholly, absolutely, entirely, quite, totally, fully, altogether, plainly, obviously, clearly. □□ **starkly** see *clearly* (CLEAR), *severely* (SEVERE). **starkness** see *severity* (SEVERE).

Stark effect /staark/ *n. Physics* the splitting of a spectrum line into several components by the application of an electric field. [J. *Stark*, Ger. physicist d. 1957]

starkers /staarkərz/ *adj. Brit. sl.* stark naked.

starlet /staarlit/ *n.* **1** a promising young performer, esp. a woman. **2** a little star.

starlight /staarlit/ *n.* **1** the light of the stars (*walked home by starlight*). **2** (*attrib.*) = STARLIT (*a starlight night*).

starling¹ /staarling/ *n.* **1** a small gregarious partly migratory bird, *Sturnus vulgaris*, with blackish-brown speckled iridescent plumage, chiefly inhabiting cultivated areas. **2** any similar bird of the family Sturnidae. [OE *stærlinc* f. *stær* starling f. Gmc: cf. -LING¹]

starling² /staarling/ *n.* piles built around or upstream of a bridge or pier to protect it from floating debris, etc. [perh. corrupt. of (now dial.) *staddling* STADDLE]

starlit /staarlit/ *adj.* **1** lighted by stars. **2** with stars visible.

starry /staaree/ *adj.* (**starrier, starriest**) **1** covered with stars. **2** resembling a star. □ **starry-eyed** *colloq.* **1** visionary;

enthusiastic but impractical. **2** euphoric. □□ **starrily** *adv.* **starriness** *n.*

■ □ **starry-eyed** see *idealistic* (IDEALISM).

START /staart/ *abbr.* Strategic Arms Reduction Treaty (or Talks).

start /staart/ *v. & n.* ● *v.* **1** *tr. & intr.* begin; commence (*started work*; *started crying*; *started to shout*; *the play starts at eight*). **2** *tr.* set (proceedings, an event, etc.) in motion (*start the meeting*; *started a fire*). **3** *intr.* (often foll. by *on*) make a beginning (*started on a new project*). **4** *intr.* (often foll. by *after*, *for*) set oneself in motion or action ('*wait!*' he shouted, *and started after her*). **5** *intr.* set out; begin a journey, etc. (*we start at 6 a.m.*). **6** (often foll. by *up*) **a** *intr.* (of a machine) begin operating (*the car wouldn't start*). **b** *tr.* cause (a machine, etc.) to begin operating (*tried to start the engine*). **7** *tr.* **a** cause or enable (a person) to make a beginning (with something) (*started me in business with $10,000*). **b** (foll. by pres. part.) cause (a person) to begin (doing something) (*the smoke started me coughing*). **c** *colloq.* complain or be critical (*don't you start*). **8** *tr.* (often foll. by *up*) found or establish; originate. **9** *intr.* (foll. by *at*, *with*) have as the first of a series of items, e.g., in a meal (*we started with soup*). **10** *tr.* give a signal to (competitors) to start in a race. **11** *intr.* (often foll. by *up*, *from*, etc.) make a sudden movement from surprise, pain, etc. (*started at the sound of my voice*). **12** *intr.* (foll. by *out*, *up*, *from*, etc.) spring out, up, etc. (*started up from the chair*). **13** *tr.* conceive (a baby). **14** *tr.* rouse (game, etc.) from its lair. **15 a** *intr.* (of boards, etc.) spring from their proper position; give way. **b** *tr.* cause or experience (boards, etc.) to do this. **16** *intr.* (foll. by *out*, *to*, etc.) (of a thing) move or appear suddenly (*tears started to his eyes*). **17** *intr.* (foll. by *from*) (of eyes, usu. with exaggeration) burst forward (from their sockets, etc.). **18** *tr.* pour out (alcoholic beverages) from a cask. ● *n.* **1** a beginning of an event, action, journey, etc. (*missed the start*; *an early start tomorrow*; *made a fresh start*). **2** the place from which a race, etc., begins. **3** an advantage given at the beginning of a race, etc. (*a 15-second start*). **4** an advantageous initial position in life, business, etc. (*a good start in life*). **5** a sudden movement of surprise, pain, etc. (*you gave me a start*). **6** an intermittent or spasmodic effort or movement (esp. *in* or *by fits and starts*). **7** *colloq.* a surprising occurrence (*an odd start*). □ **for a start** *colloq.* as a beginning; in the first place. **get the start of** gain an advantage over. **start a hare** see HARE. **start in** *colloq.* **1** begin. **2** (foll. by *on*) make a beginning on. **start off 1** begin; commence (*started off on a lengthy monologue*). **2** begin to move (*it's time we started off*). **start out 1** begin a journey. **2** *colloq.* (foll. by *to* + infin.) proceed as intending (to do something). **start over** begin again. **start something** *colloq.* cause trouble. **start up** arise; occur. **to start with 1** in the first place; before anything else is considered (*should never have been there to start with*). **2** at the beginning (*had six members to start with*). [OE (orig. in sense 11) f. Gmc]

■ *v.* **1, 2** start off *or* up, begin, get going, get under way, open, set in motion, activate, trigger (off), get *or* start the ball rolling, *colloq.* get off the ground, kick off, start in, *formal* commence. **3** (start on) embark on, enter upon, begin on, take up, strike out on, *colloq.* start in on. **4, 5** start off *or* up *or* out, go, leave, depart, get going, move (off *or* out *or* on), make a move, get under way, be on one's way, set off *or* out *or* forth, *colloq.* start in, get the show on the road, *sl.* hit the road, hit the trail. **6 b** start up, turn on, switch on, crank up, activate, set in motion. **8** establish, found, begin, set up, launch, introduce, inaugurate, initiate, instigate, institute, originate, create, pioneer, father, give birth to, *archaic* engender, *literary* beget. **9** begin, open, *formal* commence. **11** jump, flinch, blench, quail, shy, recoil, wince, shrink, draw back. **12** see SPRING *v.* 1. **14** rouse, cause to spring *or* leap *or* dart *or* jump *or* bound. **16** see WELL² *v.* **17** bulge, protrude, stick out. ● *n.* **1** beginning(s), opening, outset, onset, inception, initiation, rise, genesis, creation, emergence, origin, inauguration, launch, founding, foundation,

introduction, institution, establishment, *formal* commencement, *rhet.* birth; dawn, threshold, brink, verge, start-up; *colloq.* kickoff. **2** starting line, starting gate, starting post; starting point. **3** head start, advantage, lead, edge, *colloq.* jump, drop. **4** advantage, head start, opportunity, chance, beginning, opening, *colloq.* break. **5** see JUMP *n.* 2a, TURN *n.* 13. □ **start in 1** see START *v.* 1, 2 above. **2** (*start in on*) see START *v.* 3 above. **start off 1** see START *v.* 1, 2 above; (*start off on*) see START *v.* 3 above. **2** see START *v.* 4, 5 above. **start out 1** see START *v.* 4, 5 above. **start up** start (off *or* in), arise, occur, come up, come to be, come into being, emerge, crop up, develop, begin, get under way, originate, *formal* commence. **to start with** see FIRST *adv.* 1.

starter /staartər/ *n.* **1** a person or thing that starts. **2** an esp. automatic device for starting the engine of a motor vehicle, etc. **3** a person giving the signal for the start of a race. **4** a horse or competitor starting in a race, game, etc. (*a list of probable starters*). **5** *Baseball* **a** the pitcher who pitches first in a game. **b** a pitcher who normally starts games. **6** *Brit.* the first course of a meal. **7** the initial action, etc. □ **for starters** *sl.* to start with. **under starter's orders** (of racehorses, etc.) in a position to start a race and awaiting the starting signal.

■ **1** see APPRENTICE *n.* **6** see HORS D'OEUVRE.

starting /staarting/ *n.* in senses of START *v.* □ **starting block** a shaped rigid block for bracing the feet of a runner at the start of a race. **starting gate** a movable barrier for securing a fair start in horse races. **starting pistol** a pistol used to give the signal for the start of a race. **starting point** the point from which a journey, process, argument, etc., begins. **starting post** the post from which competitors start in a race. **starting price** the odds ruling at the start of a horse race. **starting stall** a compartment for one horse at the start of a race.

■ □ **starting point** see BASE¹ *n.* 2, 3.

startle /staart'l/ *v.tr.* give a shock or surprise to; cause (a person, etc.) to start with surprise or sudden alarm. □□ **startler** *n.* [OE *steartlian* (as START, -LE⁴)]

■ frighten, alarm, surprise, scare, disturb, unsettle, upset, discompose, catch unawares, make a person jump, jolt, jar, dismay, perturb, stun, take aback, take by surprise, shock, astound, astonish, shake up, give a person a start, *colloq.* give a person a turn, *joc.* discombobulate.

startling /staartling/ *adj.* **1** surprising. **2** alarming (*startling news*). □□ **startlingly** *adv.*

■ surprising, amazing, astounding, astonishing, awesome, staggering, shocking, unexpected, unforeseen, jarring, disturbing, unsettling, upsetting, alarming, terrifying, frightening.

starve /staarv/ *v.* **1** *intr.* die of hunger; suffer from malnourishment. **2** *tr.* cause to die of hunger or suffer from lack of food. **3** *intr.* suffer from extreme poverty. **4** *intr. colloq.* (esp. as **starved** or **starving** *adjs.*) feel very hungry (*I'm starving*). **5** *intr.* **a** suffer from mental or spiritual want. **b** (foll. by *for*) feel a strong craving for (sympathy, amusement, knowledge, etc.). **6** *tr.* **a** (foll. by *for*, *of*) deprive of; keep scantily supplied with (*starved for affection*). **b** cause to suffer from mental or spiritual want. **7** *tr.* **a** (foll. by *into*) compel by starving (*starved into submission*). **b** (foll. by *out*) compel to surrender, etc., by starving (*starved them out*). **8** *intr.* archaic or dial. perish with or suffer from cold. □□ **starvation** /-váyshən/ *n.* [OE *steorfan* die]

■ **4** (starved or starving) (extremely) hungry, famished, ravenous. **5 b** (starve for) yearn for, hanker for, hunger for, pine for, long for, crave (for), thirst for *or* after, desire, ache for; (be starving for) be dying for, be hungry for, be burning for, be desirous of. **6** (starve for,

/.../ **pronunciation**	● **part of speech**
□ **phrases, idioms, and compounds**	
□□ **derivatives**	■ **synonym section**
cross-references appear in SMALL CAPITALS or *italics*	

of) deprive of; (*be starved for, of*) be in need *or* want of, be lacking, be bereft of. □□ **starvation** hunger, deprivation, undernourishment, malnutrition, malnourishment, *archaic* famine.

starveling /staárvling/ *n.* & *adj. archaic* ● *n.* a starving or ill-fed person or animal. ● *adj.* **1** starving. **2** meager.

starwort /staárwərt, -wawrt/ *n.* a plant of the genus *Stellaria* with starlike flowers.

stash /stash/ *v.* & *n. colloq.* ● *v.tr.* (often foll. by *away*) **1** conceal; put in a safe or hidden place. **2** hoard; stow; store. ● *n.* **1** a hiding place or hideout. **2** a thing hidden; a cache. [18th c.: orig. unkn.]
■ *v.* see CACHE *v.* ● *n.* **1** see CACHE *n.* 1. **2** see CACHE *n.* 2.

stasis /stáysis, stásis/ *n.* (*pl.* **stases** /-seez/) **1** inactivity; stagnation; a state of equilibrium. **2** a stoppage of circulation of any of the body fluids. [mod.L f. Gk f. *sta-* STAND]

-stasis /stásis, stáysis/ *comb. form* (*pl.* **-stases** /-seez/) *Physiol.* forming nouns denoting a slowing or stopping (*hemostasis*). □□ **-static** *comb. form* forming adjectives.

-stat /stat/ *comb. form* forming nouns with ref. to keeping fixed or stationary (*rheostat*). [Gk *statos* stationary]

stat. *abbr.* **1** at once. [L *statim*] **2** statistics. **3** statute.

state /stayt/ *n.* & *v.* ● *n.* **1** the existing condition or position of a person or thing (*in a bad state of repair*; *in a precarious state of health*). **2** *colloq.* **a** an excited, anxious, or agitated mental condition (esp. *in a state*). **b** an untidy condition. **3 a** an organized political community under one government; a commonwealth; a nation. **b** such a community forming part of a federal republic, esp. the United States of America. **c** (**the States**) the US. **4** (*attrib.*) **a** of, for, or concerned with the state (*state documents*). **b** reserved for or done on occasions of ceremony (*state apartments*; *state visit*). **5** (also **State**) civil government (*church and state*; *Secretary of State*). **6 a** pomp; rank; dignity (*as befits their state*). **b** imposing display; ceremony; splendor (*arrive in state*). **7** (**the States**) the legislative body in the UK islands of Jersey, Guernsey, and Alderney. **8** *Bibliog.* one of two or more variant forms of a single edition of a book. **9 a** an etched or engraved plate at a particular stage of its progress. **b** an impression taken from this. ● *v.tr.* **1** express, esp. fully or clearly, in speech or writing (*have stated my opinion*; *must state full particulars*). **2** fix; specify (*at stated intervals*). **3** *Law* specify the facts of (a case) for consideration. **4** *Mus.* play (a theme, etc.) so as to make it known to the listener. □ **in state** with all due ceremony. **of state** concerning politics or government. **state capitalism** a system of state control and use of capital. **State Department** the federal government department concerned with foreign affairs. **state house** the building where the legislature of a state meets. **state of the art 1** the current stage of development of a practical or technological subject. **2** (usu. **state-of-the-art**) (*attrib.*) using the latest techniques or equipment (*state-of-the-art weaponry*). **state of grace** the condition of being free from grave sin. **state of life** rank and occupation. **state of things** (or **affairs** or esp. *Brit.* **play**) the circumstances; the current situation. **state of war** the situation when war has been declared or is in progress. **state's evidence** see EVIDENCE. **States General** *hist.* the legislative body in the Netherlands, and in France before 1789. **state socialism** a system of state control of industries and services. **states' rights** the rights and powers not assumed by the federal government of the United States but reserved to its individual states. **state trial** prosecution by the government. **state university** a university managed by the public authorities of a state. □□ **statable** *adj.* **statedly** *adv.* **statehood** *n.* [ME: partly f. ESTATE, partly f. L STATUS]
■ *n.* **1** condition(s), circumstance(s), situation, state of affairs, status, position; shape, structure, form, constitution, phase, stage; trim, order, repair, fettle; see also *frame of mind* (FRAME *n.* 7). **2 a** see STEW¹ *n.* 2. **b** see SHAMBLES. **3 a** nation, country, land, commonwealth, body politic, domain, *formal* esp. *Law* realm. **4** (*attrib.*) **a** governmental, government, national, federal. **b, c** ceremonial, formal, dignified,

stately, solemn, official; presidential, royal, regal, imperial, majestic. **5** government, administration. **6 b** grandeur, pomp, style, ceremony, splendor, magnificence, glory, brilliance. ● *v.* **1** assert, asseverate, declare, affirm, express, report, articulate, formulate, enunciate, voice, communicate, announce, proclaim, specify, delineate, claim, maintain, allege, submit, confirm, *formal* aver; say, testify, hold, have it that. **2** fix, specify, define, delineate, designate, determine, set. □ **state of things** (or **affairs** or **play**) see SITUATION 2. **state school** public school, government school.

statecraft /stáytkraft/ *n.* the art of conducting affairs of state.
■ see POLITICS 1.

statehood /stáythŏŏd/ *n.* the condition or status of being a state, esp. a state of the United States.

stateless /stáytlis/ *adj.* **1** (of a person) having no nationality or citizenship. **2** without a state. □□ **statelessness** *n.*

stately /stáytlee/ *adj.* (**statelier, stateliest**) dignified; imposing; grand. □ **stately home** *Brit.* a large magnificent house, esp. one open to the public. □□ **stateliness** *n.*
■ dignified, august, solemn, distinguished, impressive, striking, imposing, awesome, grand, lofty, elevated, noble, majestic, regal, royal, imperial. □□ **stateliness** see DIGNITY 1.

statement /stáytmənt/ *n.* **1** the act or an instance of stating or being stated; expression in words. **2** a thing stated; a declaration (*that statement is unfounded*). **3** a formal account of facts, esp. to the police or in a court of law (*make a statement*). **4** a record of transactions in a bank account, etc. **5** a formal notification of an amount due.
■ **1–3** assertion, allegation, declaration, affirmation, asseveration, averment, announcement, annunciation, proclamation, profession, utterance, expression, disclosure, communication; communiqué, proposition, report, account, testimony, *Law* deposition, affidavit. **5** account, bill, invoice.

stater /stáytər/ *n.* an ancient Greek gold or silver coin. [ME f. LL f. Gk *statēr*]

stateroom /stáytrŏŏm, -rŏŏm/ *n.* **1** a private compartment in a passenger ship or train. **2** a state apartment in a palace, hotel, etc.

stateside /stáytsīd/ *adj. colloq.* of, in, or toward the United States.

statesman /stáytsmən/ *n.* (*pl.* **-men**; *fem.* **stateswoman**, *pl.* **-women**) **1** a person skilled in affairs of state, esp. one taking an active part in politics. **2** a distinguished and capable politician. □□ **statesmanlike** *adj.* **statesmanly** *adj.* **statesmanship** *n.* [= *state's man* after F *homme d'état*]
■ see POLITICIAN. □□ **statesmanship** see POLITICS 1.

statewide /stáytwīd/ *adj.* so as to include or cover a whole state.

static /státik/ *adj.* & *n.* ● *adj.* **1** stationary; not acting or changing; passive. **2** *Physics* **a** concerned with bodies at rest or forces in equilibrium (opp. DYNAMIC). **b** acting as weight but not moving (*static pressure*). **c** of statics. ● *n.* **1** static electricity. **2** electrical disturbances in the atmosphere or the interference with telecommunications caused by this. **3** *sl.* aggravation; fuss; criticism. □ **static electricity** electricity not flowing as a current as that produced by friction. **static line** a length of cord attached to an aircraft, etc., which releases a parachute without the use of a ripcord. [mod.L *staticus* f. Gk *statikos* f. *sta-* stand]
■ *adj.* **1** immovable, immobile, unmoving, motionless, stationary, fixed, stagnant, inert, still, passive, unchanging, unchanged, changeless, unvarying, invariable, constant, steady. ● *n.* **2** interference, noise, atmospherics. **3** difficulty, trouble, problem(s), aggravation, fuss, confusion, interference, *colloq.* hassle; flak, criticism.

statical /státikəl/ *adj.* = STATIC. □□ **statically** *adv.*

statice /státisee, státis/ *n.* **1** sea lavender. **2** sea pink. [L f. Gk, fem. of *statikos* STATIC (with ref. to stanching of blood)]

statics /státiks/ *n.pl.* (usu. treated as *sing.*) **1** the science of bodies at rest or of forces in equilibrium (opp. DYNAMICS). **2** = STATIC. [STATIC *n.* in the same senses + -ICS]

station /stáyshən/ *n. & v.* ● *n.* **1 a** a regular stopping place on a public transportation route, esp. one on a railroad line with a platform and often one or more buildings. **b** these buildings (see also *bus station*). **2** a place or building, etc., where a person or thing stands or is placed, esp. habitually or for a definite purpose. **3 a** a designated point or establishment where a particular service or activity is based or organized (*police station; polling station; research station*). **b** a branch post office. **4** an establishment involved in radio or television broadcasting. **5 a** a military or naval base esp. *hist.* in India. **b** the inhabitants of this. **6** position in life; rank or status (*ideas above your station*). **7** *Austral. & NZ* a large sheep or cattle farm. **8** *Bot.* a particular place where an unusual species, etc., grows. ● *v.tr.* **1** assign a station to. **2** put in position. □ **station-bill** *Naut.* a list showing the prescribed stations of a ship's crew for various drills or in an emergency. **station break** a pause between or within broadcast programs for an announcement of the identity of the station transmitting them. **station hand** *Austral.* a worker on a large sheep or cattle farm. **station house** a police or fire station. **station of the cross** *RC Ch., Anglican Ch.* **a** each of a series of usu. 14 images or pictures, representing the events in Christ's passion, before which devotions are performed. **b** each of these devotions. **station wagon** a car with passenger seating and storage or extra seating area in the rear, accessible by a rear door. [ME, = standing, f. OF f. L *statio -onis* f. *stare* stand]
  ■ *n.* **1** railroad station, train station; stopping place, stop, stage; terminus, terminal; bus station, coach station, depot. **2** place, position, spot, point, post, site, location, situation. **3 a** base, headquarters, center, depot, office. **4** broadcaster, transmitter; channel. **5 a** see BASE[1] *n.* 3. **6** position, place, status, rank, caste, standing, class, level. ● *v.* **1** assign, appoint, post, install, garrison, billet, quarter. **2** position, place, spot, post, site, situate, locate, install, put, set, stand.

stationary /stáyshəneree/ *adj.* **1** remaining in one place; not moving (*hit a stationary car*). **2** not meant to be moved; not portable (*stationary troops; stationary engine*). **3** not changing in magnitude, number, quality, efficiency, etc. (*stationary temperature*). **4** (of a planet) having no apparent motion in longitude. □ **stationary bicycle** a fixed exercise apparatus resembling a bicycle. **stationary point** *Math.* a point on a curve where the gradient is zero. **stationary wave** = *standing wave.* □□ **stationariness** *n.* [ME f. L *stationarius* (as STATION)]
  ■ **1, 3** see STATIC *adj.* **2** see IMMOVABLE *adj.* 1.

stationer /stáyshənər/ *n.* a person who sells writing materials, etc. □ **Stationers' Hall** *Brit.* the hall of the Stationers' Company in London, at which a book was formerly registered for purposes of copyright. [ME, = bookseller (as STATIONARY in med.L sense 'shopkeeper,' esp. bookseller, as opposed to peddler)]

stationery /stáyshəneree/ *n.* **1** writing materials such as pens, paper, etc. **2** writing paper, esp. with matching envelopes.
  ■ writing paper, letterhead(s), paper and envelopes, writing materials *or* implements *or* supplies; office supplies *or* equipment.

stationmaster /stáyshənmastər/ *n.* the official in charge of a railroad station.

statism /stáytizəm/ *n.* centralized government administration and control of social and economic affairs.

statist /státist, stáytist/ *n.* **1** a statistician. **2** a supporter of statism. [orig. 'politician' f. It. *statista* (as STATE)]

statistic /stətístik/ *n. & adj.* ● *n.* a statistical fact or item. ● *adj.* = STATISTICAL. [G *statistisch, Statistik* f. *Statist* (as STATIST)]

statistical /stətístikəl/ *adj.* of or relating to statistics. □ **statistical physics** physics as it is concerned with large numbers of particles to which statistics can be applied. **statistical significance** = SIGNIFICANCE 4. □□ **statistically** *adv.*

statistics /stətístiks/ *n.pl.* **1** (usu. treated as *sing.*) the science of collecting and analyzing numerical data, esp. in or for

large quantities, and usu. inferring proportions in a whole from proportions in a representative sample. **2** any systematic collection or presentation of such facts. □□ **statistician** /státistíshən/ *n.*
  ■ **2** see DATA.

stator /stáytər/ *n. Electr.* the stationary part of a machine, esp. of an electric motor or generator. [STATIONARY, after ROTOR]

statoscope /státəskōp/ *n.* an aneroid barometer used to show minute variations of pressure, esp. to indicate the altitude of an aircraft. [Gk *statos* fixed f. *sta-* stand + -SCOPE]

statuary /státchōoeree/ *adj. & n.* ● *adj.* of or for statues (*statuary art*). ● *n.* (*pl.* **-ies**) **1** statues collectively. **2** the art of making statues. **3** a sculptor. □ **statuary marble** fine-grained white marble. [L *statuarius* (as STATUE)]

statue /státchōo/ *n.* a sculptured, cast, carved, or molded figure of a person or animal, esp. life-size or larger (cf. STATUETTE). □□ **statued** *adj.* [ME f. OF f. L *statua* f. *stare* stand]
  ■ sculpture, figure, figurine, statuette, carving, casting, model, bronze, image, icon, effigy, representation, likeness; bust, colossus, figurehead, *Archit.* caryatid, *Bibl.* graven image.

statuesque /státchōo-ésk/ *adj.* like, or having the dignity or beauty of, a statue. □□ **statuesquely** *adv.* **statuesqueness** *n.* [STATUE + -ESQUE, after *picturesque*]
  ■ imposing, impressive, majestic, regal, stately, magnificent, noble, dignified, august, grand, well-proportioned, comely, handsome, queenly.

statuette /státchōo-ét/ *n.* a small statue; a statue less than life-size. [F, dimin. of *statue*]
  ■ see STATUE.

stature /státchər/ *n.* **1** the height of a (esp. human) body. **2** a degree of eminence, social standing, or advancement (*recruit someone of his stature*). □□ **statured** *adj.* (also in *comb.*). [ME f. OF f. L *statura* f. *stare stat-* stand]
  ■ **2** see STATUS 2.

status /stáytəs, stát-/ *n.* **1** rank; social position; relation to others; relative importance (*not sure of their status in the hierarchy*). **2** a superior social, etc., position (*considering your status in the business*). **3** *Law* a person's legal standing which determines his or her rights and duties, e.g., citizen, alien, civilian, etc. **4** the state of affairs (*let me know if the status changes*). □ **status symbol** a possession, etc., taken to indicate a person's high status. [L, = standing f. *stare* stand]
  ■ **1** see STANDING *n.* 1. **2** eminence, prominence, preeminence, standing, stature, importance, significance, repute, reputation, prestige, rank, station. **4** see SITUATION 2.

status quo /stáytəs kwó, státəs/ *n.* the existing state of affairs. [L, = the state in which]
  ■ see SCORE *n.* 7.

statutable /státchōotəbəl/ *adj.* = STATUTORY, esp. in amount or value. □□ **statutably** *adv.*

statute /státchōot/ *n.* **1** a written law passed by a legislative body. **2** a rule of a corporation, founder, etc., intended to be permanent (*against the university statutes*). **3** divine law (*kept thy statutes*). □ **statute book 1** a book or books containing the statute law. **2** the body of a country's statutes. **statute law 1** (*collect.*) the body of principles and rules of law laid down in statutes as distinct from rules formulated in practical application (cf. *common law, case law* (see CASE[1])). **2** a statute. **statute mile** see MILE 1. **statute of limitations** a statute that sets a time limit during which legal action can be taken. **statute roll 1** (in the UK) the rolls in the Public Records Office containing the statutes of the Parliament of England. **2** = *statute book.* **statutes at large** the statutes as originally enacted, regardless of later modifications. [ME f. OF *statut* f. LL *statutum* neut. past part. of L *statuere* set up f. *status*: see STATUS]
  ■ **1** see LAW 1b. **2** see RULE *n.* 1.

statutory /stáchətawree/ *adj.* **1** required, permitted, or enacted by statute (*statutory minimum; statutory provisions*). **2** (of a criminal offense) carrying a penalty prescribed by statute. □ **statutory rape** the offense of sexual intercourse with a minor. □□ **statutorily** *adv.*
■ **1** legal, constitutional, statutable.

staunch[1] /stawnch, staanch/ *adj.* (also **stanch**) **1** trustworthy; loyal (*my staunch friend and supporter*). **2** (of a ship, joint, etc.) strong, watertight, airtight, etc. □□ **staunchly** *adv.* **staunchness** *n.* [ME f. OF *estanche* fem. of *estanc* f. Rmc: see STANCH[1]]
■ **1** steadfast, loyal, firm, unflinching, steady, unshrinking, unswerving, dependable, reliable, stalwart, (tried and) true, devoted, constant, true-blue, trustworthy, trusted, faithful, unfaltering, undeviating, unwavering, *archaic or joc.* trusty. **2** strong, solid, sturdy, sound, well-built, stout, substantial, well-constructed, well-made, tough, rugged, long-lasting; watertight, seaworthy; airtight. □□ **staunchly** see *firmly* (FIRM[1]). **staunchness** see *tenacity* (TENACIOUS).

staunch[2] var. of STANCH[1].

stave /stayv/ *n. & v.* ● *n.* **1** each of the curved pieces of wood forming the sides of a cask, barrel, etc. **2** = STAFF[1] *n.* 3. **3** a stanza or verse. **4** the rung of a ladder. ● *v.tr.* (*past* and *past part.* **stove** /stōv/ or **staved**) **1** break a hole in. **2** crush or knock out of shape. **3** fit or furnish (a cask, etc.) with staves. □ **stave in** crush by forcing inwards. **stave off** avert or defer (danger or misfortune). **stave rhyme** alliteration, esp. in old Germanic poetry. [ME, back-form. f. *staves*, pl. of STAFF[1]]
■ □ **stave off** see PREVENT 1.

staves pl. of STAFF[1] *n.* 3.

stavesacre /stáyvzaykər/ *n.* a larkspur, *Delphinium staphisagria*, yielding seeds used as poison for vermin. [ME f. L *staphisagria* f. Gk *staphis agria* wild raisin]

stay[1] /stay/ *v. & n.* ● *v.* **1** *intr.* continue to be in the same place or condition; not depart or change (*stay here until I come back*). **2** *intr.* **a** (often foll. by *at, in, with*) have temporary residence as a visitor, etc. (*stayed with them for Christmas*). **b** *Sc. & S.Afr.* dwell permanently. **3** *archaic or literary* **a** *tr.* stop or check (progress, the inroads of a disease, etc.). **b** *intr.* (esp. in *imper.*) pause in movement, action, speech, etc. (*Stay! You forget one thing*). **4** *tr.* postpone (judgment, decision, execution, etc.). **5** *tr.* assuage (hunger, etc.) esp. for a short time. **6 a** *intr.* show endurance. **b** *tr.* show endurance to the end of (a race, etc.). **7** *tr.* (often foll. by *up*) *literary* support; prop up (as or with a buttress, etc.). **8** *intr.* (foll. by *for, to*) wait long enough to share or join in an activity, etc. (*stay to supper; stay for the video*). **9** call a poker bet without a raise. ● *n.* **1 a** the act or an instance of staying or dwelling in one place. **b** the duration of this (*just a ten minute stay; a long stay in London*). **2** a suspension or postponement of a sentence, judgment, etc. (*was granted a stay of execution*). **3** *archaic or literary* a check or restraint (*will endure no stay; a stay upon his activity*). **4** endurance; staying power. **5** a prop or support. **6** (in *pl.*) *hist.* a corset esp. with whalebone, etc., stiffening, and laced. □ **has come** (or **is here**) **to stay** *colloq.* must be regarded as permanent. **stay-at-home** *adj.* remaining habitually at home. ● *n.* a person who does this. **stay the course** pursue a course of action or endure a struggle, etc., to the end. **stay one's hand** see HAND. **stay in** remain indoors or at home, esp. in school after hours as a punishment. **staying power** endurance; stamina. **stay the night** remain until the next day. **stay put** *colloq.* remain where it is placed or where one is. **stay up** not go to bed (until late at night). □□ **stayer** *n.* [AF *estai*-stem of OF *ester* f. L *stare* stand: sense 5 f. OF *estaye(r)* prop, formed as STAY[2]]
■ *v.* **1** remain, stop, wait, linger, loiter, hang about *or* around, *archaic or literary* tarry; stand, freeze; continue (to be), keep; *archaic or dial.* bide. **2** remain, stop, sojourn, visit; lodge, reside, live, *archaic* abide, *literary* dwell. **3 a** stop, arrest, thwart, prevent, put an end to, halt, interrupt, discontinue, block, check; stanch, stem, curb, retard, slow, delay, impede, foil, obstruct,

hamper, hinder, discourage, deter. **4** delay, put off, defer, prorogue; see also POSTPONE. **6 a** see LAST[2]. **7** see PROP[1] *v.* **8** remain, linger, wait, hang about *or* around, *archaic or literary* tarry. ● *n.* **1** stopover, sojourn, visit, stop, stopoff, layover. **2** suspension, delay, postponement, deferment, deferral, reprieve; moratorium. **3** see CHECK[1] *n.* 2c. **4** see ENDURANCE 2. **5** see SUPPORT *n.* 2. □ **staying power** see ENDURANCE 2. **stay put** see REMAIN 2.

stay[2] /stay/ *n. & v.* ● *n.* **1** *Naut.* a rope or guy supporting a mast, spar, flagstaff, etc. **2** a tie-piece in an aircraft, etc. ● *v.tr.* **1** support (a mast, etc.) by stays. **2** put (a ship) on another tack. □ **be in stays** (of a sailing ship) be head to the wind with sails shaking while tacking. **miss stays** fail to be in stays. [OE *stæg* be firm, f. Gmc]
■ *n.* **1** guy, line, rope, cable, chain, support, brace, reinforcement; *Naut.* (running) backstay, forestay, mainstay, mizzen-stay. ● *v.* **1** support, strengthen, secure, reinforce, brace, buttress, shore (up), *literary* gird.

staysail /stáysayl, stáysəl/ *n.* a triangular fore-and-aft sail extended on a stay.

STD *abbr.* **1** Doctor of Sacred Theology. **2** sexually transmitted disease. [sense 1 f. L *Sanctae Theologiae Doctor*]

std. *abbr.* standard.

stead /sted/ *n.* □ **in a person's** (or **thing's**) **stead** as a substitute; instead of him or her or it. **stand a person in good stead** be advantageous or serviceable to him or her. [OE *stede* f. Gmc]
■ □ **in a person's** (or **thing's**) **stead** see INSTEAD 1.

steadfast /stédfast/ *adj.* constant; firm; unwavering. □□ **steadfastly** *adv.* **steadfastness** *n.* [OE *stedefæst* (as STEAD, FAST[1])]
■ resolute, determined, persevering, resolved, single-minded, steady, unflinching, unfaltering, unwavering, unswerving, indefatigable, dependable, immovable, immutable, stable, firm, fixed, constant, persistent, unflagging, tireless, enduring, dedicated, deep-rooted, faithful, true, loyal, staunch. □□ **steadfastness** see PERSEVERANCE.

steading /stéding/ *n.* esp. *Brit.* a farmstead.
■ see FARM *n.* 1.

steady /stédee/ *adj., v., adv., int., & n.* ● *adj.* (**steadier, steadiest**) **1** firmly fixed or supported or standing or balanced; not tottering, rocking, or wavering. **2** done or operating or happening in a uniform and regular manner (*a steady pace; a steady increase*). **3 a** constant in mind or conduct; not changeable. **b** persistent. **4** (of a person) serious and dependable in behavior; of industrious and temperate habits; safe; cautious. **5** regular; established (*a steady girlfriend*). **6** accurately directed; not faltering; controlled (*a steady hand; a steady eye; steady nerves*). **7** (of a ship) on course and upright. ● *v.tr. & intr.* (**-ies, -ied**) make or become steady (*steady the boat*). ● *adv.* steadily (*hold it steady*). ● *int.* as a command or warning to take care. ● *n.* (*pl.* **-ies**) *colloq.* a regular boyfriend or girlfriend. □ **go steady** (often foll. by *with*) *colloq.* have as a regular boyfriend or girlfriend. **steady down** become steady. **steady-going** staid; sober. **steady on!** *Brit.* a call to take care. **steady state** an unvarying condition, esp. in a physical process, e.g., of the universe having no beginning and no end. □□ **steadier** *n.* **steadily** *adv.* **steadiness** *n.* [STEAD = place, + -Y[1]]
■ *adj.* **1** stable, balanced, poised, settled, firm, fast, secure, solid. **2** even, regular, uniform, invariable, unvarying, unfluctuating, unwavering, undeviating, changeless, unchanging, continuous, constant; perpetual, nonstop, around-the-clock, persistent, uninterrupted, unbroken, unrelieved, unceasing, ceaseless, incessant, relentless, unremitting, sustained, never-ending, unending, endless. **3** see STEADFAST. **4** staid, sedate, sober, temperate, moderate, dignified, poised, sensible, down-to-earth, settled, serious, levelheaded, reliable, dependable, industrious, diligent, conscientious, safe, cautious, careful, *colloq.* unflappable. **5** regular, established, devoted,

firm, staunch, faithful, loyal, constant, long-standing, inveterate, consistent, confirmed, serious, persistent. **6** unflinching, unblinking, fixed, constant, continuous, unfaltering, accurate, direct; controlled, calm, cool, balanced, equable. ● *v.* stabilize, balance, hold fast; brace, secure, support. ● *adv.* firmly, fast, immovably, solidly, securely; steadily. ● *n.* (regular) boyfriend *or* girlfriend, sweetheart, woman, *colloq.* (regular) fellow *or* girl, man, guy, *sl. gal.* □ **go steady** keep company, consort, *colloq.* date regularly. □□ **steadily** see SURELY 3.

steadiness see *regularity* (REGULAR), STABILITY.

steak /stayk/ *n.* **1** a thick slice of meat (esp. beef) or fish, often cut for grilling, frying, etc. **2** beef cut for stewing or braising. □ **steak house** a restaurant specializing in serving beefsteaks. **steak knife** a table knife with a serrated steel blade for cutting steak. [ME f. ON *steik* rel. to *steikja* roast on spit, *stikna* be roasted]

steal /steel/ *v. & n.* ● *v.* (*past* **stole** /stōl/; *past part.* **stolen** /stōlən/) **1** *tr.* (also *absol.*) **a** take (another person's property) illegally. **b** take (property, etc.) without right or permission, esp. in secret with the intention of not returning it. **2** *tr.* obtain surreptitiously or by surprise (*stole a kiss*). **3** *tr.* **a** gain insidiously or artfully. **b** (often foll. by *away*) win or get possession of (a person's affections, etc.), esp. insidiously (*stole her heart away*). **4** *intr.* (foll. by *in, out, away, up,* etc.) **a** move, esp. silently or stealthily (*stole out of the room*). **b** (of a sound, etc.) become gradually perceptible. **5** *tr.* **a** (in various sports) gain (a run, the ball, etc.) surreptitiously or by luck. **b** *Baseball* run to (a base) while the pitcher is in the act of delivery. ● *n.* **1** *colloq.* the act or an instance of stealing or theft. **2** *colloq.* an unexpectedly easy task or good bargain. □ **steal a march on** get an advantage over by surreptitious means; anticipate. **steal the show** outshine other performers, esp. unexpectedly. **steal a person's thunder** use another person's words, ideas, etc., without permission and without giving credit. □□ **stealer** *n.* (also in *comb.*). **stealing** *n.* [OE *stelan* f. Gmc]

■ *v.* **1** take (away), appropriate, filch, thieve, shoplift, pilfer, plunder, make off with, walk off *or* away with, get away with; embezzle, misappropriate, peculate; hijack, usurp; plagiarize, pirate, borrow, poach, copy, imitate; *colloq.* lift, swipe, *formal or joc.* purloin, *sl.* pinch, snitch, sneak, knock off, hook, heist, liberate, *Austral. sl.* duff, *Brit. sl.* nick. **4 a** sneak, creep, slip, slink, tiptoe, prowl, lurk, skulk, pussyfoot. ● *n.* **2** bargain, (good) buy, *colloq.* giveaway. □ **steal a march on** see OUTSMART. □□ **stealer** see THIEF. **stealing** see THEFT.

stealth /stelth/ *n. & adj.* ● *n.* secrecy; a secret procedure. ● *adj. Mil. Aeron.* of an aircraft design intended to avoid detection by radar. □ **by stealth** surreptitiously. [ME f. OE (as STEAL, -TH²)]

■ stealthiness, furtiveness, secrecy, clandestinity, clandestineness, surreptitiousness, sneakiness, slyness, underhandedness. □ **by stealth** see *on the sly* (SLY).

stealthy /stélthee/ *adj.* (**stealthier, stealthiest**) **1** (of an action) done with stealth; proceeding imperceptibly. **2** (of a person or thing) acting or moving with stealth. □□ **stealthily** *adv.* **stealthiness** *n.*

■ furtive, secret, sly, clandestine, hugger-mugger, surreptitious, stealthful, insidious, sneaky, sneaking, undercover, underground, underhand(ed), covert, closet, backstairs; secretive, skulking. □□ **stealthily** see *on the sly* (SLY). **stealthiness** see STEALTH.

steam /steem/ *n. & v.* ● *n.* **1 a** the gas into which water is changed by boiling, used as a source of power by virtue of its expansion of volume. **b** a mist of liquid particles of water produced by the condensation of this gas. **2** any similar vapor. **3 a** energy or power provided by a steam engine or other machine. **b** *colloq.* power or energy generally. **4** repressed or pent up feelings, etc. ● *v.* **1** *tr.* **a** cook (food) in steam. **b** soften or make pliable (lumber, etc.) or otherwise treat with steam. **2** *intr.* give off steam or other vapor, esp. visibly. **3** *intr.* **a** move under steam power (*the ship steamed down the river*). **b** (foll. by *ahead, away,* etc.) *colloq.* proceed

or travel fast or with vigor. **4** *tr. & intr.* (usu. foll. by *up*) **a** cover or become covered with condensed steam. **b** (as **steamed up** *adj.*) *colloq.* angry or excited. **5** *tr.* (foll. by *open,* etc.) apply steam to the adhesive of (a sealed envelope) to get it open. □ **get up steam 1** generate enough power to work a steam engine. **2** work oneself into an energetic or angry state. **let** (or **blow**) **off steam** relieve one's pent up feelings or energy. **run out of steam** lose one's impetus or energy. **steam age** the era when trains were drawn by steam locomotives. **steam bath** a room, etc., filled with steam for bathing in. **steam boiler** a vessel (in a steam engine, etc.) in which water is boiled to generate steam. **steam engine 1** an engine which uses the expansion or rapid condensation of steam to generate power. **2** a locomotive powered by this. **steam gauge** a pressure gauge attached to a steam boiler. **steam heat** the warmth given out by steam-heated radiators, etc. **steam iron** an electric iron that emits steam from holes in its flat surface, to improve its ironing ability. **steam organ** a pipe organ driven by a steam engine and played by means of a keyboard or a system of punched cards. **steam power** the force of steam applied to machinery, etc. **steam shovel** an excavator powered by steam. **steam train** a train driven by a steam engine. **steam turbine** a turbine in which a high-velocity jet of steam rotates a bladed disk or drum. **under one's own steam** without assistance; unaided. [OE *stēam* f. Gmc]

■ *n.* **1** vapor, mist, fog, cloud, haze. ● *v.* **2** see REEK *v.* 3. **4 a** (*steam up*) see MIST *v.* **b** (*steamed up*) see ANGRY 1. □ **steam organ** calliope.

steamboat /steémbōt/ *n.* a boat propelled by a steam engine.

steamer /steémər/ *n.* **1** a person or thing that steams. **2** a vessel propelled by steam, esp. a ship. **3** a vessel in which things are steamed, esp. cooked by steam. □ **steamer rug** a small blanket used as a covering by passengers seated in deck chairs on a ship, etc.

steamroller /steémrōlər/ *n. & v.* ● *n.* **1** a heavy slow-moving vehicle with a roller, used to flatten new-made roads. **2** a crushing power or force. ● *v.tr.* **1** crush forcibly or indiscriminately. **2** (foll. by *through*) force (a measure, etc.) through a legislature by overriding opposition.

steamship /steémship/ *n.* a ship propelled by a steam engine.

steamy /steémee/ *adj.* (**steamier, steamiest**) **1** like or full of steam. **2** *colloq.* erotic; salacious. □□ **steamily** *adv.* **steaminess** *n.*

■ **1** humid, steaming, damp, moist, muggy, sticky, dank, sweaty, sweltering, sodden, sultry, boiling, wet; steamed (up), fogged (up), befogged, misty, misted, hazy, clouded, cloudy, beclouded, dim, blurred. **2** erotic, passionate, (sexually) exciting, salacious, arousing, hot, torrid, sexy, *colloq.* raunchy.

stearic /steérik, steeárik/ *adj.* derived from stearin. □ **stearic acid** a solid saturated fatty acid obtained from animal or vegetable fats. □□ **stearate** /-rayt/ *n.* [F *stéarique* f. Gk *stear steatos* tallow]

stearin /steérin/ *n.* **1** a glyceryl ester of stearic acid, esp. in the form of a white crystalline constituent of tallow, etc. **2** a mixture of fatty acids used in candle making. [F *stéarine* f. Gk *stear steatos* tallow]

steatite /steéətīt/ *n.* a soapstone or other impure form of talc. □□ **steatitic** /-títik/ *adj.* [L *steatitis* f. Gk *steatītēs* f. *stear steatos* tallow]

steatopygia /steeátəpíjeeə, steéətə-/ *n.* an excess of fat on the buttocks. □□ **steatopygous** /-pígəs, -tópigəs/ *adj.* [mod.L (as STEATITE + Gk *pugē* rump)]

steed /steed/ *n. archaic* or *poet.* a horse, esp. a fast powerful one. [OE *stēda* stallion, rel. to STUD²]

■ see MOUNT¹ *n.* 3a.

steel /steel/ *n., adj., & v.* ● *n.* **1** any of various alloys of iron and carbon with other elements increasing strength and malleability, much used for making tools, weapons, etc., and capable of being tempered to many different degrees of hardness. **2** hardness of character; strength; firmness (*nerves of steel*). **3 a** a rod of steel, usu. roughened and tapering, on which knives are sharpened. **b** a strip of steel for expanding a skirt or stiffening a corset. **c** a piece of steel used with flint for starting fires. **4** (not in *pl.*) *literary* a sword, lance, etc. (*foemen worthy of their steel*). • *adj.* **1** made of steel. **2** like or having the characteristics of steel. • *v.tr. & refl.* harden or make resolute (*steeled myself for a shock*). □ **cold steel** cutting or thrusting weapons. **pressed steel** steel molded under pressure. **steel band** a group of usu. W. Indian musicians with percussion instruments made from oil drums. **steel-clad** wearing armor. **steel engraving** the process of engraving on or an impression taken from a steel-coated copper plate. **steel wool** an abrasive substance consisting of a mass of fine steel shavings. [OE *stýle*, *stēli* f. Gmc, rel. to STAY²]

■ *n.* **4** sword, dagger, knife, dirk, stiletto, lance, *poet.* blade. • *adj.* **2** see STEELY. • *v.* inure, insulate, protect; brace, nerve, stiffen, strengthen, fortify, prepare; (*steel oneself*) grit one's teeth, bear up, screw up one's courage; *sl.* bite the bullet.

steelhead /stḗelhed/ *n.* a large N. American rainbow trout.

steelwork /stḗelwərk/ *n.* articles of steel.

steelworks /stḗelwərks/ *n.pl.* (usu. treated as *sing.*) a place where steel is manufactured. □□ **steelworker** *n.*

steely /stḗelee/ *adj.* (**steelier, steeliest**) **1** of, or hard as, steel. **2** inflexibly severe; cold; ruthless (*steely composure; steely-eyed glance*). □□ **steeliness** *n.*

■ **1** steel; grayish, gray; hard, iron, tough, strong, unyielding, inflexible. **2** iron, tough, severe, obdurate, adamant, adamantine, hard, strong, rugged, unyielding, unimpressionable, flinty, sturdy; ruthless; see also STONY 2.

steelyard /stḗelyaard/ *n.* a kind of balance with a short arm to take the item to be weighed and a long graduated arm along which a weight is moved until it balances.

steenbok /stḗenbok, stáyn-/ *n.* an African dwarf antelope, *Raphicerus campestris*. [Du. f. *steen* STONE + *bok* BUCK¹]

steep¹ /steep/ *adj. & n.* • *adj.* **1** sloping sharply; almost perpendicular (*a steep hill; steep stairs*). **2** (of a rise or fall) rapid (*a steep drop in stock prices*). **3** (*predic.*) *colloq.* **a** (of a demand, price, etc.) exorbitant; unreasonable (esp. *a bit steep*). **b** (of a story, etc.) exaggerated; incredible. • *n.* a steep slope; a precipice. □□ **steepen** *v.intr. & tr.* **steepish** *adj.* **steeply** *adv.* **steepness** *n.* [OE *stēap* f. WG, rel. to STOOP¹]

■ *adj.* **1** sheer, abrupt, precipitous, scarped, bluff, sharp, nearly vertical *or* perpendicular *or* upright, high-pitched. **2** sharp, rapid, abrupt, sudden. **3 a** dear, high, exorbitant, excessive, extravagant, extortionate, gouging, *Brit.* over the odds, *colloq.* stiff; unreasonable, outrageous, *colloq.* over-the-top. **b** see TALL 4.

steep² /steep/ *v. & n.* • *v.tr.* soak or bathe in liquid. • *n.* **1** the act or process of steeping. **2** the liquid for steeping. □ **steep in 1** pervade or imbue with (*steeped in misery*). **2** make deeply acquainted with (a subject, etc.) (*steeped in the classics*). [ME f. OE f. Gmc (as STOUP)]

■ *v.* soak, submerge, souse, drench, immerse, bathe, saturate, douse, wet, ret; pickle, marinate. □ **steep in** imbue with, fill with, impregnate with, pervade with, saturate with, immerse in, inundate with, soak in; bury in.

steeple /stḗepəl/ *n.* a tall tower, esp. one surmounted by a spire, above the roof of a church. □ **steeple-crowned** (of a hat) with a tall pointed crown. □□ **steepled** *adj.* [OE *stēpel* *stýpel* f. Gmc (as STEEP¹)]

■ see SPIRE¹ *n.* 1.

steeplechase /stḗepəlchays/ *n.* **1** a horse race (orig. with a steeple as the goal) across the countryside or on a racetrack with ditches, hedges, etc., to jump. **2** a cross-country foot race. □□ **steeplechaser** *n.* **steeplechasing** *n.*

steeplejack /stḗepəljak/ *n.* a person who climbs tall chimneys, steeples, etc., to do repairs, etc.

steer¹ /steer/ *v. & n.* • *v.* **1** *tr.* **a** guide (a vehicle, aircraft, etc.) by a wheel, etc. **b** guide (a vessel) by a rudder or helm. **2** *intr.* guide a vessel or vehicle in a specified direction (*tried to steer left*). **3** *tr.* direct (one's course). **4** *intr.* direct one's course in a specified direction (*steered for the railroad station*). **5** *tr.* guide the movement or trend of (*steered them into the garden; steered the conversation away from that subject*). • *n.* steering; guidance. □ **steer clear of** take care to avoid. **steering column** the shaft or column which connects the steering wheel, handlebars, etc., of a vehicle to the rest of the steering mechanism. **steering committee** a committee deciding the order of dealing with business, or priorities and the general course of operations. **steering wheel** a wheel by which a vehicle, etc., is steered. □□ **steerable** *adj.* **steerer** *n.* **steering** *n.* (esp. in senses 1, 2 of *v.*). [OE *stieran* f. Gmc]

■ *v.* **1** guide, pilot, direct, navigate; manage, control. **4** see HEAD *v.* 4a. **5** see GUIDE *v.* 1, 3. • *n.* steering; guidance, advice, tip, suggestion, hint, information. □ **steer clear of** avoid, dodge, keep away from, shun, circumvent, give a wide berth to, fight shy of. □□ **steerable** see NAVIGABLE 2, 3. **steering** see NAVIGATION.

steer² /steer/ *n.* a young male bovine animal castrated before sexual maturity, esp. one raised for beef. [OE *stēor* f. Gmc]

steerage /stḗerij/ *n.* **1** the act of steering. **2** the effect of the helm on a ship. **3** the part of a ship allotted to passengers traveling at the cheapest rate. **4** *hist.* (in a warship) quarters assigned to midshipmen, etc., just forward of the wardroom.

steersman /stḗerzmən/ *n.* (*pl.* **-men**) a helmsman.

■ see NAVIGATOR.

steeve¹ /steev/ *n. & v. Naut.* • *n.* the angle of the bowsprit in relation to the horizontal. • *v.* **1** *intr.* (of a bowsprit) make an angle with the horizontal. **2** *tr.* cause (the bowsprit) to do this. [17th c.: orig. unkn.]

steeve² /steev/ *n. & v. Naut.* • *n.* a long spar used in stowing cargo. • *v.tr.* stow with a steeve. [ME f. OF *estiver* or Sp. *estivar* f. L *stipare* pack tight]

stegosaurus /stégəsáwrəs/ *n.* any of a group of plant-eating dinosaurs with a double row of large bony plates along the spine. [mod. L f. Gk *stegē* covering + *sauros* lizard]

stein /stin/ *n.* a large earthenware, pewter, etc., mug, esp. for beer. [G, lit. 'stone']

■ see MUG¹ *n.* 1.

steinbock /stinbok/ *n.* **1** an ibex native to the Alps. **2** = STEENBOK. [G f. *Stein* STONE + *Bock* BUCK¹]

stela /stḗelə/ *n.* (*pl.* **stelae** /-lee/) *Archaeol.* an upright slab or pillar usu. with an inscription and sculpture, esp. as a gravestone. [L f. Gk (as STELE)]

stele /steel, stḗelee/ *n.* **1** *Bot.* the axial cylinder of vascular tissue in the stem and roots of most plants. **2** *Archaeol.* = STELA. □□ **stelar** *adj.* [Gk *stēlē* standing block]

stellar /stélər/ *adj.* **1** of or relating to a star or stars. **2** having the quality of a star entertainer or performer; leading; outstanding. □□ **stelliform** *adj.* [LL *stellaris* f. L *stella* star]

■ **1** astral, sidereal, star. **2** chief, starring, principal, leading, main, headlining.

stellate /stélayt/ *adj.* (also **stellated** /stélaytid/) **1** arranged like a star; radiating. **2** *Bot.* (of leaves) surrounding the stem in a whorl. [L *stellatus* f. *stella* star]

stellular /stélyələr/ *adj.* shaped like, or set with, small stars. [LL *stellula* dimin. of L *stella* star]

stem¹ /stem/ *n. & v.* • *n.* **1** the main body or stalk of a plant or shrub, usu. rising into light, but occasionally subterranean. **2** the stalk supporting a fruit, flower, or leaf, and attaching it to a larger branch, twig, or stalk. **3** a stem-shaped part of an object: **a** the slender part of a wineglass between the body and the foot. **b** the tube of a tobacco pipe. **c** a vertical stroke in a letter or musical note. **d** the winding shaft of a watch. **4** *Gram.* the root or main part of a noun, verb, etc., to which inflections are added; the part that appears unchanged throughout the cases and derivatives of a noun, persons of a tense, etc. **5** *Naut.* the main upright timber or metal piece at the bow of a ship to which the ship's sides are joined at the fore end (*from stem to stern*). **6** a line of ancestry, branch of a family, etc. (*descended from an ancient stem*). **7** (in full **drill stem**) a rotating rod, cylinder, etc., used in drilling. ● *v.* (**stemmed, stemming**) **1** *intr.* (foll. by *from*) spring or originate from (*stems from a desire to win*). **2** *tr.* remove the stem or stems from (fruit, tobacco, etc.). **3** *tr.* (of a vessel, etc.) hold its own or make headway against (the tide, etc.). □ **stem cell** *Biol.* an undifferentiated cell from which specialized cells develop. **stem stitch** an embroidery stitch used for narrow stems, etc. **stem-winder 1** a watch wound by turning a head on the end of a stem rather than by a key. **2** a rousing political speech. □□ **stemless** *adj.* **stemlet** *n.* **stemlike** *adj.* **stemmed** *adj.* (also in *comb.*). [OE *stemn, stefn* f. Gmc, rel. to STAND]

■ *n.* **1** trunk, stalk, cane, stock; *Bot.* peduncle. **2** stalk, shoot, bine, twig, *Bot.* peduncle, pedicel, petiole. **3** shaft, shank, stalk, support, upright. **4** see BASE¹ *n.* 12. **5** *Naut.* bow(s), prow, stem post. ● *v.* **1** come, arise, develop, derive, issue, flow, generate, originate, spring, emanate, sprout, grow, descend, result, proceed. **3** resist, withstand, make headway *or* progress against, go *or* advance against, hold its own against, prevail over *or* against.

stem² /stem/ *v. & n.* ● *v.* (**stemmed, stemming**) **1** *tr.* check or stop. **2** *tr.* dam up (a stream, etc.). **3** *intr.* slide the tail of one ski or both skis outwards usu. in order to turn or slow down. ● *n.* an act of stemming on skis. □ **stem turn** a turn on skis made by stemming with one ski. [ON *stemma* f. Gmc: cf. STAMMER]

■ *v.* **1** check, stop, halt, stanch, staunch, arrest, curb, control, quell, suppress, *archaic or literary* stay; retard, slow, lessen, diminish, reduce, cut, cut back (on). **2** dam up, block, obstruct, hold back, restrain, stop.

stemma /stémə/ *n.* (*pl.* **stemmata** /stémətə/) **1** a family tree; a pedigree. **2** the line of descent, e.g., of variant texts of a work. **3** *Zool.* a simple eye; a facet of a compound eye. [L f. Gk *stemma* wreath f. *stephō* wreathe]

stemware /stémwair/ *n.* glasses with stems.

stench /stench/ *n.* an offensive or foul smell. □ **stench trap** a trap in a sewer, etc., to prevent the upward passage of gas. [OE *stenc* smell f. Gmc, rel. to STINK]

■ stink, reek, mephitis, fetor, foul odor, effluvium, *Brit. colloq.* pong, *literary* noisomeness.

stencil /sténsil/ *n. & v.* ● *n.* **1** a thin sheet of plastic, metal, card, etc., in which a pattern or lettering is cut, used to produce a corresponding pattern on the surface beneath it by applying ink, paint, etc. **2** the pattern, lettering, etc., produced by a stencil. **3** a waxed sheet, etc., from which a stencil is made by means of a typewriter. ● *v.tr.* (**stenciled** or **stencilled, stenciling** or **stencilling**) **1** (often foll. by *on*) produce (a pattern) with a stencil. **2** decorate or mark (a surface) in this way. [ME f. OF *estanceler* sparkle, cover with stars, f. *estencele* spark ult. f. L *scintilla*]

■ *n.* **1** see PATTERN *n.* 3.

Sten gun /sten/ *n.* a type of lightweight submachine gun. [*S* and *T* (the initials of the inventors' surnames, Shepherd and Turpin) + -*en* after BREN]

steno /sténō/ *n.* (*pl.* -**os**) *colloq.* a stenographer. [abbr.]

stenography /stənógrəfee/ *n.* shorthand or the art of writing this. □□ **stenographer** *n.* **stenographic** /sténəgráfik/ *adj.* [Gk *stenos* narrow + -GRAPHY]

■ shorthand, tachygraphy, phonography, speedwriting. □□ **stenographer** secretary, amanuensis, stenotypist, tachygrapher, phonographer, *colloq.* steno.

stenosis /stinṓsis/ *n. Med.* the abnormal narrowing of a passage in the body. □□ **stenotic** /-nótik/ *adj.* [mod.L f. Gk *stenōsis* narrowing f. *stenoō* make narrow f. *stenos* narrow]

stenotype /sténətip/ *n.* **1** a machine like a typewriter for recording speech in syllables or phonemes. **2** a symbol or the symbols used in this process. □□ **stenotypist** *n.* [STENOGRAPHY + TYPE]

Stentor /sténtər/ *n.* (also **stentor**) a person with a powerful voice. □□ **stentorian** /-táwreeən/ *adj.* [Gk *Stentōr*, herald in the Trojan War (Homer, *Iliad* v. 785)]

■ □□ **stentorian** see LOUD *adj.* 1.

step /step/ *n. & v.* ● *n.* **1 a** the complete movement of one leg in walking or running (*took a step forward*). **b** the distance covered by this. **c** (in *pl.*) the course followed by a person

in walking, etc. **2** a unit of movement in dancing. **3** a measure taken, esp. one of several in a course of action (*took steps to prevent it; considered it a wise step*). **4 a** a surface on which a foot is placed on ascending or descending a stair or tread. **b** a block of stone or other platform before a door, altar, etc. **c** the rung of a ladder. **d** a notch cut for a foot in climbing ice. **e** a platform, etc., in a vehicle provided for ease in stepping up or down. **5** a short distance (*only a step from my door*). **6** the sound or mark made by a foot in walking, etc. (*heard a step on the stairs*). **7** the manner of walking, etc., as seen or heard (*know her by her step*). **8 a** a degree in the scale of promotion, advancement, or precedence. **b** one of a series of fixed points on a payscale, etc. **9 a** stepping (or not stepping) in time with others or music (esp. *in* or *out of step*). **b** the state of conforming to what others are doing (*refuses to keep step with the team*). **10** (in *pl.*) (also **pair of steps** *sing.*) *Brit.* = STEPLADDER. **11** *Mus.* a melodic interval of one degree of the scale, i.e. a tone or semitone. **12** *Naut.* a block, socket, or platform supporting a mast. ● *v.* (**stepped, stepping**) **1** *intr.* lift and set down one's foot or alternate feet in walking. **2** *intr.* come or go in a specified direction by stepping. **3** *intr.* make progress in a specified way (*stepped into a new job*). **4** *tr.* (foll. by *off, out*) measure (distance) by stepping. **5** *tr.* perform (a dance). **6** *tr. Naut.* set up (a mast) in a step. □ **in a person's (foot)steps** following a person's example. **step aerobics** an exercise regimen using a step-climbing motion. **step-by-step** gradually; cautiously; by stages or degrees. **step cut** (of a gem) cut in straight facets around the center. **step down 1** resign from a position, etc. **2** *Electr.* decrease (voltage) by using a transformer. **step in 1** enter a room, house, etc. **2 a** intervene to help or hinder. **b** act as a substitute. **step-in** *attrib.adj.* (of a garment or shoe) put on by being stepped into without unfastening. ● *n.* such a garment or shoe. **step on it** (or **on the gas**) *colloq.* **1** accelerate a motor vehicle. **2** hurry up. **step out 1** leave a room, house, etc. **2 b** be active socially. **3** take large steps. **stepping-stone 1** a raised stone, usu. one of a set in a stream, muddy place, etc., to help in crossing. **2** a means or stage of progress to an end. **step stool** a stool with usu. folding steps used to reach high kitchen shelves, etc. **step this way** a deferential formula meaning 'follow me.' **step up 1** increase; intensify (*must step up production*). **2** *Electr.* increase (voltage) using a transformer. **take a step** (or **steps**) implement a course of action leading to a specific result; proceed. **turn one's steps** go in a specified direction. **watch one's step** be careful. □□ **steplike** *adj.* **stepped** *adj.* **stepwise** *adv. & adj.* [OE *stæpe, stepe* (n.), *stæppan, steppan* (v.), f. Gmc]

■ *n.* **1a, b, 5** pace, footstep, stride. **1 c** (*steps*) course, way, route, direction, path, movement, passage; journey, journeying, travels, traveling. **2** movement, move. **3** action, initiative, measure, activity, procedure, move, motion; *démarche.* **4** a stair, tread, *Brit.* treadboard; (*steps*) stairs, stair, stairway, staircase, stoop. **b** doorstep, ledge, sill. **6** footfall, footstep, tread; footprint, trace, spoor, track, mark, impression; imprint. **7** see WALK *n.* 1. **8** see NOTCH *n.* 3. **9** (*in step*) in time, in line, in keeping, in harmony, in agreement, in accord, in conformity, in tune; harmonious, agreeable, according, concordant, attuned, consonant, consistent, conforming, appropriate, fitting; conventional, traditional, routine; (*out of step*) not in time, out of *or* not in keeping, out of *or* not in line, out of *or* not in harmony, out of *or* not in agreement, out of *or* not in tune, not harmonious, not agreeable, not according, discordant, not concordant, not attuned, not consonant, inconsistent, nonconforming, inappropriate, not fitting; offbeat, unconventional, eccentric, kinky. ● *v.* **1, 2** tread, move; pace, stride;

/.../ **pronunciation**	● **part of speech**
□ **phrases, idioms, and compounds**	
□□ **derivatives**	■ **synonym section**
cross-references appear in SMALL CAPITALS or *italics*	

see also WALK *v.* 1, 2. **4** pace, measure. □ **step-by-step** gradually, a step at a time, by stages, by degrees, slowly, steadily, stealthily, cautiously. **step down 1** resign, abdicate, quit, bow out, retire. **2** decrease, diminish, reduce. **step in 1** enter, go in, come in. **2 a** intervene, interfere, intercede, become involved. **b** (*step in for*) see SUBSTITUTE *v.* 1. **step on it** (or **on the gas**) **1** accelerate, speed up, *colloq.* put one's foot down. **2** hurry (up), make haste, hasten, speed up, get a move on. **step out 1** go outside, go out of doors, leave. **2** go out, socialize. **3** pace, stride. **step up** increase, raise, intensify, strengthen, escalate, up, augment, *colloq.* boost. **take a step** (or **steps**) proceed, move, begin *or* start to act *or* to take action, do something, *formal* commence to act. **turn one's steps** see HEAD *v.* 4a. **watch one's step** tread carefully *or* cautiously, be cautious, be careful, exercise care *or* caution, be wary, be discreet, be on the qui vive, be *or* remain alert, be on one's guard, keep one's wits about one, watch it, watch oneself, take care *or* heed, pussyfoot (about *or* around).

step- /step/ *comb. form* denoting a relationship like the one specified but resulting from a parent's remarriage. [OE *stēop-* orphan-]

stepbrother /stépbrudhər/ *n.* a son of a stepparent by a marriage other than with one's father or mother.

stepchild /stépchīld/ *n.* a child of one's husband or wife by a previous marriage. [OE *stēopcīld* (as STEP-, CHILD)]

stepdaughter /stépdawtər/ *n.* a female stepchild. [OE *stēopdohtor* (as STEP-, DAUGHTER)]

stepfather /stépfaathər/ *n.* a male stepparent. [OE *stēopfæder* (as STEP-, FATHER)]

■ see PARENT *n.* 2.

stephanotis /stéfənōtis/ *n.* any climbing tropical plant of the genus *Stephanotis*, cultivated for its fragrant waxy usu. white flowers. [mod.L f. Gk, = fit for a wreath f. *stephanos* wreath]

stepladder /stépladər/ *n.* a short ladder with flat steps and a folding support, used without being leaned against a surface.

stepmother /stépmudhər/ *n.* a female stepparent. [OE *stēopmōdor* (as STEP-, MOTHER)]

■ see PARENT *n.* 2.

stepparent /stép-pairənt/ *n.* a mother's or father's later husband or wife.

steppe /step/ *n.* a level grassy unforested plain, esp. in SE Europe and Siberia. [Russ *step'*]

■ see PLAIN¹ *n.*

stepsister /stépsistər/ *n.* a daughter of a stepparent by a marriage other than with one's father or mother.

stepson /stépsun/ *n.* a male stepchild. [OE *stēopsunu* (as STEP-, SON)]

-ster /stər/ *suffix* denoting a person engaged in or associated with a particular activity or thing (*gangster*; *youngster*). [OE *-estre*, etc. f. Gmc]

steradian /stəráydeeən/ *n.* a solid angle equal to the angle at the center of a sphere subtended by a part of the surface equal in area to the square of the radius. ¶ Abbr.: **sr**. [Gk *stereos* solid + RADIAN]

stercoraceous /stérkəráyshəs/ *adj.* **1** consisting of or resembling dung or feces. **2** living in dung. [L *stercus -oris* dung]

stere /steer/ *n.* a unit of volume equal to one cubic meter. [F *stère* f. Gk *stereos* solid]

stereo /stéreeō, steéreeō/ *n. & adj.* ● *n.* (*pl.* **-os**) **1 a** a stereophonic record player, tape recorder, etc. **b** = *stereophony* (see STEREOPHONIC). **2** = STEREOSCOPE. ● *adj.* **1** = STEREOPHONIC. **2** = *stereoscopic* (see STEREOSCOPE). [abbr.]

stereo- /stéreeō, steéreeō/ *comb. form* solid; having three dimensions. [Gk *stereos* solid]

stereobate /stéreeəbayt, steéreeə-/ *n. Archit.* a solid mass of masonry as a foundation for a building. [F *stéréobate* f. L *stereobata* f. Gk *stereobatēs* (as STEREO-, *bainō* walk)]

stereochemistry /stéreeōkémistree, steéreeō-/ *n.* the branch of chemistry dealing with the three-dimensional arrangement of atoms in molecules.

stereography /stéreeógrəfee, steéree-/ *n.* the art of depicting solid bodies in a plane.

stereoisomer /stéreeō-ísəmər, steéreeō-/ *n. Chem.* any of two or more compounds differing only in their spatial arrangement of atoms.

stereometry /stéreeómitree, steéree-/ *n.* the measurement of solid bodies.

stereophonic /stéreeōfónik, steéreeō-/ *adj.* (of sound reproduction) using two or more channels so that the sound has the effect of being distributed and of coming from more than one source. □□ **stereophonically** *adv.* **stereophony** /-reeófənee/ *n.*

stereoscope /stéreeəskōp, steéreeə-/ *n.* a device by which two photographs of the same object taken at slightly different angles are viewed together, giving an impression of depth and solidity as in ordinary human vision. □□ **stereoscopic** /-skópik/ *adj.* **stereoscopically** *adv.* **stereoscopy** /-reeóskəpee/ *n.*

stereotype /stéreeətīp, steéree-/ *n. & v.* ● *n.* **1 a** a person or thing that conforms to an unjustifiably fixed, usu. standardized, mental picture. **b** such an impression or attitude. **2** a printing plate cast from a mold of composed type. ● *v.tr.* **1** (esp. as **stereotyped** *adj.*) standardize; cause to conform to a type. **2 a** print from a stereotype. **b** make a stereotype of. □□ **stereotypic** /-típik/ *adj.* **stereotypical** *adj.* **stereotypically** *adv.* **stereotypy** *n.* [F *stéréotype* (adj.) (as STEREO-, TYPE)]

■ *n.* **1** see CLICHÉ. **2** see STAMP *n.* 1. ● *v.* **1** (**stereotyped**) see STOCK *adj.* 2. □□ **stereotypical** see BANAL.

steric /stérik, steér-/ *adj. Chem.* relating to the spatial arrangement of atoms in a molecule. □ **steric hindrance** the inhibiting of a chemical reaction by the obstruction of reacting atoms. [irreg. f. Gk *stereos* solid]

sterile /stérəl, -īl/ *adj.* **1** not able to produce seeds or fruit or (of an animal) young; barren. **2** unfruitful; unproductive (*sterile discussions*). **3** free from living microorganisms, etc. **4** lacking originality or emotive force; mentally barren. □□ **sterilely** *adv.* **sterility** /stərílitee/ *n.* [F *stérile* or L *sterilis*]

■ **1** barren, fruitless, unfruitful, childless, unproductive, lifeless, arid, infertile. **2** barren, unfruitful, unproductive, fruitless, unprofitable, ineffectual, useless, abortive, *archaic* bootless. **3** pure, aseptic, uninfected, unpolluted, uncontaminated, disinfected, sanitary, sterilized, germfree, hygienic, antiseptic, clean. **4** barren, unproductive, stale, unoriginal, unimaginative, dull, uninspired, uninspiring, effete.

sterilize /stériliz/ *v.tr.* **1** make sterile. **2** deprive of the power of reproduction. □□ **sterilizable** *adj.* **sterilization** *n.* **sterilizer** *n.*

■ **1** purify, disinfect, clean, fumigate, depurate, pasteurize, decontaminate, *usu. formal* cleanse. **2** castrate, emasculate, hysterectomize, vasectomize; geld, spay, desex, neuter, caponize, fix, cut, alter. □□ **sterilizer** see DISINFECTANT *n.*

sterlet /stárlit/ *n.* a small sturgeon, *Acipenser ruthenus*, found in the Caspian Sea area and yielding fine caviar. [Russ. *sterlyad'*]

sterling /stárling/ *adj. & n.* ● *adj.* **1** of or in British money (*pound sterling*). **2** (of a coin or precious metal) genuine; of standard value or purity. **3** (of a person or qualities, etc.) of solid worth; genuine; reliable (*sterling work*). ● *n.* **1** = *sterling silver*. **2** British money (*paid in sterling*). □ **sterling area** a group of countries with currencies tied to British sterling and holding reserves mainly in sterling. **sterling silver** silver of 92¹⁄₂% purity. □□ **sterlingness** *n.* [prob. f. late OE *steorling* (unrecorded) f. *steorra* star + -LING¹ (because some early Norman pennies bore a small star): recorded earlier in OF *esterlin*]

■ *adj.* **2** genuine, authentic, real, true, pure. **3** excellent, superior, superb, superlative, first-class, exceptional, matchless, peerless, unequaled, nonpareil, incomparable, fine, very good, worthy, worthwhile, estimable, admirable; solid, reliable, genuine.

stern[1] /stərn/ adj. severe; grim; strict; enforcing discipline or submission (a stern expression; stern treatment). □□ **sternly** adv. **sternness** n. [OE styrne, prob. f. a Gmc root = be rigid]
■ severe, serious, frowning, grim, forbidding, grave, gloomy, dour, somber, saturnine, lugubrious, gruff, taciturn, crabby, crabbed, crusty, churlish, sour; austere, Spartan, strict, stringent, demanding, critical, rigid, rigorous, flinty, steely, authoritarian, uncompromising, hard, tough, inflexible, firm, immovable, unmoved, unrelenting, unremitting, steadfast, resolute, determined, unyielding, adamant, adamantine, obdurate, hard-hearted, stony, stonyhearted, unsparing, unforgiving, unsympathetic, harsh. □□ **sternly** see ROUGHLY 1, severely (SEVERE). **sternness** see severity (SEVERE).

stern[2] /stərn/ n. **1** the rear part of a ship or boat. **2** any rear part. □ **stern foremost** moving backward. **stern on** with the stern presented. □□ **sterned** adj. (also in comb.). **sternmost** adj. **sternward** adj. & adv. **sternwards** adv. [ME prob. f. ON stjórn steering f. stýra STEER[1]]

sternal /stərnəl/ adj. of or relating to the sternum. □ **sternal rib** = true rib.

sternum /stərnəm/ n. (pl. **sternums** or **sterna** /-nə/) the breastbone. [mod.L f. Gk sternon chest]

sternutation /stərnyətáyshən/ n. Med. or joc. a sneeze or attack of sneezing. [L sternutatio f. sternutare frequent. of sternuere sneeze]

sternutator /stərnyətaytər/ n. a substance, esp. poison gas, that causes nasal irritation, violent coughing, etc. □□ **sternutatory** /-nyŏŏtətawree/ adj. & n. (pl. **-ies**)

sternway /stərnway/ n. Naut. a backward motion or impetus of a ship.

steroid /steéroyd, stér-/ n. Biochem. any of a group of organic compounds with a characteristic structure of four rings of carbon atoms, including many hormones, alkaloids, and vitamins. □□ **steroidal** /-róyd'l/ adj. [STEROL + -OID]

sterol /steérawl, -ol, stér-/ n. Chem. any of a group of naturally occurring steroid alcohols. [CHOLESTEROL, ERGOSTEROL, etc.]

stertorous /stərtərəs/ adj. (of breathing, etc.) labored and noisy; sounding like snoring. □□ **stertorously** adv. **stertorousness** n. [stertor, mod.L f. L stertere snore]

stet /stet/ v. (**stetted, stetting**) **1** intr. (usu. as an instruction written on a proof, etc.) ignore or cancel the correction or alteration; let the original form stand. **2** tr. write 'stet' against; cancel the correction of. [L, = let it stand, f. stare stand]

stethoscope /stéthəskōp/ n. an instrument used in listening to the action of the heart, lungs, etc., usu. consisting of a circular piece placed against the chest, with tubes leading to earpieces. □□ **stethoscopic** /-skópik/ adj. **stethoscopically** adv. **stethoscopist** /stethóskəpist/ n. **stethoscopy** /stethóskəpee/ n. [F stéthoscope f. Gk stēthos breast: see -SCOPE]

Stetson /stétsən/ n.propr. a felt hat with a very wide brim and a high crown. [J. B. Stetson, Amer. hat maker d. 1906]

stevedore /steévədawr/ n. a person employed in loading and unloading ships. [Sp. estivador f. estivar stow a cargo f. L stipare: see STEEVE[2]]
■ see DOCKER.

Stevengraph /steévəngraf/ n. a colorful woven silk picture. [T. Stevens, Engl. weaver d. 1888, whose firm made them]

stew[1] /stōō, styōō/ v. & n. ● v. **1** tr. & intr. cook by long simmering in a closed pot with liquid. **2** intr. colloq. be oppressed by heat or humidity, esp. in a confined space. **3** intr. colloq. **a** suffer prolonged embarrassment, anxiety, etc. **b** (foll. by over) fret or be anxious. **4** tr. Brit. make (tea) bitter or strong with prolonged brewing. **5** tr. (as **stewed** adj.) colloq. drunk. **6** intr. (often foll. by over) colloq. study hard. ● n. **1** a dish of stewed meat, etc. **2** colloq. an agitated or angry state (be in a stew). **3** archaic **a** a hot bath. **b** (in pl.) a brothel. □ **stew in one's own juice** be left to suffer the consequences of one's actions. [ME f. OF estuve, estuver prob. ult. f. EX-[1] + Gk tuphos smoke, steam]

■ v. **1** casserole, braise, boil, simmer, jug. **2** roast, swelter, colloq. boil. **3** agonize, fret, dither, chafe, burn, smolder, simmer, seethe, be anxious, sweat, colloq. get steamed up, work oneself (up) into a sweat or lather or state. **5** (**stewed**) see DRUNK adj. 1. **6** study, cram, burn the midnight oil, Brit. colloq. swot. ● n. **1** casserole, fricassee, cassoulet, ragout, hotpot, hodgepodge, goulash, olla podrida, olio. **2** state of excitement or alarm or anxiety, bother, lather, colloq. sweat, tizzy, dither, state, literary pother. **3 b** (stews) see BROTHEL.

stew[2] /stōō, styōō/ n. Brit. **1** an artificial oyster bed. **2** a pond or large tank for keeping fish for eating. [ME f. F estui f. estoier confine ult. f. L studium: see STUDY]

steward /stōōərd, styōō-/ n. & v. ● n. **1** a passengers' attendant on a ship or aircraft or train. **2** an official appointed to keep order or supervise arrangements at a meeting or show or demonstration, etc. **3** = shop steward. **4** a person responsible for supplies of food, etc., for a college or club, etc. **5** a person employed to manage another's property. **6** Brit. the title of several officers of the government or the royal household (Lord High Steward). ● v.tr. act as a steward of (will steward the meeting). □□ **stewardship** n. [OE stīweard f. stig prob. = house, hall + weard WARD]
■ n. **1** see ATTENDANT n. □□ **stewardship** see MANAGEMENT 1.

stewardess /stōōərdis, styōō-/ n. a female steward, esp. on a ship or aircraft.
■ see ATTENDANT n.

stg. abbr. sterling.

stick[1] /stik/ n. **1 a** a short slender branch or length of wood broken or cut from a tree. **b** this trimmed for use as a support or weapon. **2** a thin rod or spike of wood, etc., for a particular purpose. **3 a** an implement used to propel the ball in hockey or polo, etc. **b** (in pl.) the raising of the stick above the shoulder in field hockey. **4** a gear lever, esp. in a motor vehicle. **5** the lever controlling the ailerons and elevators in an airplane. **6** a conductor's baton. **7 a** a slender piece of a thing, e.g., celery, dynamite, deodorant, etc. **b** a number of bombs or paratroops released rapidly from aircraft. **8** (often prec. by the) punishment, esp. by beating. **9** esp. Brit. colloq. adverse criticism; censure; reproof (took a lot of stick). **10** colloq. a piece of wood as part of a house or furniture (a few sticks of furniture). **11** colloq. a person, esp. one who is dull or unsociable (a funny old stick). **12** (in pl.; prec. by the) colloq. remote rural areas. **13** (in pl.) Austral. sl. goalposts. **14** Naut. sl. a mast or spar. □ **stick insect** any usu. wingless female insect of the family Phasmidae with a twiglike body. **up sticks** Brit. colloq. go to live elsewhere. □□ **stickless** adj. **sticklike** adj. [OE sticca f. WG]
■ **1 a** branch, twig, stalk, switch. **b** stake, pole, pike, rod, mace, wand, staff, cane, walking stick, crook; club, cudgel, truncheon, bludgeon, Austral. & NZ waddy. **8** see PUNISHMENT 1, 2. **11** person, man, woman, colloq. fellow, chap, guy, bird, codger, sl. geezer, Brit. sl. bloke. **12** (the sticks) the country, the provinces, the countryside, the backwoods, the middle of nowhere, the back of beyond, the hinterland, esp. Austral. the outback, esp. Austral. & Afr. the bush, sl. the boondocks, the boonies.

stick[2] /stik/ v. (past and past part. **stuck** /stuk/) **1** tr. (foll. by in, into, through) insert or thrust (a thing or its point) (stuck a finger in my eye; stick a pin through it). **2** tr. insert a pointed thing into; stab. **3** tr. & intr. (foll. by in, into, on, etc.) **a** fix or be fixed on a pointed thing. **b** fix or be fixed by or as by a pointed end. **4** tr. & intr. fix or become or remain fixed by or as by adhesive, etc. (stick a label on it; the label won't stick). **5** intr. endure; make a continued impression (the scene stuck in my mind; the name stuck). **6** intr. lose or be deprived of the power of motion or action through adhesion or jamming

/. . . ./	pronunciation	● part of speech
□	phrases, idioms, and compounds	
□□	derivatives	■ synonym section
cross-references	appear in SMALL CAPITALS or italics	

or other impediment. **7** *colloq.* **a** *tr.* put in a specified position or place, esp. quickly or haphazardly (*stick them down anywhere*). **b** *intr.* remain in a place (*stuck indoors*). **8** *colloq.* **a** *intr.* (of an accusation, etc.) be convincing or regarded as valid (*could not make the charges stick*). **b** *tr.* (foll. by *on*) place the blame for (a thing) on (a person). **9** *tr. Brit. colloq.* endure; tolerate (*could not stick it any longer*). **10** *tr.* (foll. by *at*) *colloq.* persevere with. □ **be stuck for** be at a loss for or in need of. **be stuck on** *colloq.* be infatuated with. **be stuck with** *colloq.* be unable to get rid of or escape from; be permanently involved with. **get stuck in** (or **into**) *sl.* begin in earnest. **stick around** *colloq.* linger; remain at the same place. **stick at it** *colloq.* persevere. **stick at nothing** allow nothing, esp. no scruples, to deter one. **stick by** (or **with**) stay loyal or close to. **stick 'em up!** *colloq.* hands up! **stick fast** adhere or become firmly fixed or trapped in a position or place. **stick in one's gizzard** see GIZZARD. **sticking plaster** *Brit.* an adhesive bandage for wounds, etc. **sticking point** the limit of progress, agreement, etc. **stick-in-the-mud** *colloq.* an unprogressive or old-fashioned person. **stick in one's throat** be against one's principles. **stick it on** *Brit. sl.* **1** make high charges. **2** tell an exaggerated story. **stick it out** *colloq.* put up with or persevere with a burden, etc., to the end. **stick one's neck** (or **chin**) **out** expose oneself to censure, etc., by acting or speaking boldly. **stick out** protrude or cause to protrude or project (*stuck his tongue out*; *stick out your chest*). **stick out for** persist in demanding. **stick out a mile** (or **like a sore thumb**) *colloq.* be very obvious or incongruous. **stick pigs** engage in pigsticking. **stick to 1** remain close to or fixed on or to. **2** remain faithful to. **3** keep to (a subject, etc.) (*stick to the point*). **stick to a person's fingers** *colloq.* (of money) be embezzled by a person. **stick together** *colloq.* become or remain united or mutually loyal. **stick to one's guns** see GUN. **stick to it** persevere. **stick to one's last** see LAST³. **stick up 1** be or make erect or protruding upwards. **2** fasten to an upright surface. **3** *colloq.* rob or threaten with a gun. **stick-up** *n. colloq.* an armed robbery. **stick up for** support or defend or champion (a person or cause). **stick up to** be assertive in the face of; offer resistance to. **stick with** *colloq.* remain in touch with or faithful to; persevere with. **stuck-up** *colloq.* affectedly superior and aloof; snobbish. □□ **stickability** /stíkəbílitee/ *n.* [OE *stician* f. Gmc]

■ **1** put, poke, push, thrust, prod, dig, jab; insert. **2** pierce, stab, transfix, pin, spike, impale, spear, skewer, spit, run through, poke, gore, jab, prick, puncture, punch, penetrate, drill, bore, riddle, perforate. **3** attach, affix, fix, nail, pin, tack. **4** fix, affix, attach, fasten, glue, cement, paste, gum, weld, solder, bind, tie, tape, wire; bond, melt, fuse, unite, join; cohere, adhere, stay *or* remain *or* cling together, *literary* cleave together. **5** endure, linger, remain (fixed), continue, stay, *literary* dwell. **6** become lodged *or* embedded, be jammed, be wedged, be trapped, become fixed *or* fast, become entangled, become bogged down; catch, wedge, jam, lodge, remain (fixed), stay. **7 a** put, drop, place, deposit, plop, plunk, *colloq.* shove, *Brit. sl.* bung. **b** remain, stay, linger. **8 a** hold, go through, be upheld, be *or* remain effective. **9** stand, abide, tolerate, endure, bear, put up with, suffer, *colloq.* lump. **10** (*stick at*) see PERSEVERE. □ **be stuck for** be at a loss for, be stumped for; be in need *or* want of, need. **be stuck on** be infatuated with, be in love with, be taken with, be enamored of, be fond of, be keen on, be mad about, *colloq.* be sweet on, have a thing about, be wild *or* nuts *or* crazy about, *sl.* be bats about. **be stuck with** be burdened *or* encumbered *or* saddled *or* charged with, be weighed down with. **get stuck in** (or **into**) see *get a move on* 2 (MOVE). **stick around** wait, linger, stay, stand by, remain, hang around or about, *archaic or literary* tarry, *colloq.* hang on. **stick at it** see PERSEVERE. **stick at nothing** stop *or* hesitate *or* pause *or* balk at nothing. **stick by** (or **with**) stick to, support, be loyal *or* faithful to, stand by, stick up for. **stick-in-the-mud** (old) fogy, conservative, anachronism, dodo,

colloq. fossil, *derog.* museum piece, troglodyte, *sl.* fuddy-duddy, square, back number. **stick in one's throat** see SCANDALIZE. **stick it out** persevere, persist, stand fast, bear it, be resolute, hold one's ground, grin and bear it, see it through, weather it, *colloq.* stick it, tough it out, soldier on. **stick one's neck** (or **chin**) **out** see *sail close to the wind* 2. **stick out** protrude, jut (out), extend, project, poke (out); bulge, obtrude, stand out, overhang, beetle. **stick shift** a manual automotive transmission with a shift lever on the vehicle's floor or steering column. **stick to 2** see *stick by* above. **3** see KEEP *v.* 7a. **stick together** be *or* remain united, be *or* remain loyal, be as one, hang together, work together, cooperate; unite, unify, join (forces), consolidate, merge, confederate, amalgamate. **stick to it** see PERSEVERE. **stick up 1** stand up *or* out, poke out *or* up, protrude, jut, extend, project, obtrude. **2** put up, post, affix, display. **3** rob, mug, hold up, *Austral. & NZ* bail up, *sl.* heist. **stick-up** see *hold-up* 2 (HOLD¹). **stick up for** rally to the support of, support, stand by, stand up for, defend, champion, speak for, speak on *or* in behalf of, take up the cudgels for. **stick up to** see *stand up to* 1. **stick with** stick by *or* to, stand by, support, be loyal *or* faithful to, stay *or* remain *or* continue with; persevere with, persist in, stay *or* remain *or* continue with, not change one's mind about. **stuck-up** see *snobbish* (SNOB).

stickball /stíkbawl/ *n.* a form of baseball played with a stick or broom handle and a rubber ball.

sticker /stíkər/ *n.* **1** an adhesive label or notice, etc. **2** a person or thing that sticks. **3** a persistent person. □ **sticker price** the full price of a new item, esp. the price listed on a sticker attached to a new automobile. **sticker shock** *colloq.* surprise at a higher-than-expected retail price.

■ **1** see LABEL *n.* 1.

stickleback /stíkəlbak/ *n.* any small fish of the family Gasterosteidae with sharp spines along the back. [ME f. OE *sticel* thorn, sting + *bæc* BACK]

stickler /stíklər/ *n.* (foll. by *for*) a person who insists on something (*a stickler for accuracy*). [obs. *stickle* be umpire, ME *stightle* control, frequent. of *stight* f. OE *stiht(i)an* set in order]

■ see *perfectionist* (PERFECTIONISM).

stickpin /stíkpin/ *n.* an ornamental tiepin.

■ see PIN *n.* 1c, d.

stickweed /stíkweed/ *n.* = RAGWEED 2.

sticky /stíkee/ *adj. & n.* ● *adj.* (**stickier, stickiest**) **1** tending or intended to stick or adhere. **2** glutinous; viscous. **3** (of the weather) humid. **4** *colloq.* awkward or uncooperative; intransigent (*was very sticky about giving me leave*). **5** *colloq.* difficult; awkward (*a sticky problem*). **6** *Brit. colloq.* very unpleasant or painful (*came to a sticky end*). ● *n. colloq.* glue. □ **sticky wicket 1** *Cricket* a playing field that has been drying after rain and is difficult for the batsman. **2** *colloq.* difficult or awkward circumstances. □□ **stickily** *adv.* **stickiness** *n.*

■ *adj.* **1** adhesive, gummed, glued; clinging. **2** gluey, gummy, viscous, tacky, glutinous, viscid, mucilaginous, *sl.* gooey. **3** humid, clammy, dank, damp, muggy, close, sultry, oppressive, sweltering, steamy. **5** awkward, ticklish, tricky, difficult, sensitive, delicate, uncomfortable, discomfiting, discomforting, embarrassing, *sl.* hairy. ● *n.* see GLUE *n.* □□ **stickiness** see *tenacity* (TENACIOUS).

stickybeak /stíkeebeek/ *n. & v. Austral. & NZ sl.* ● *n.* an inquisitive person. ● *v.intr.* pry.

stiff /stif/ *adj. & n.* ● *adj.* **1** rigid; not flexible. **2** hard to bend or move or turn, etc.; not working freely. **3** hard to cope with; needing strength or effort (*a stiff test; a stiff climb*). **4** severe or strong (*a stiff breeze; a stiff penalty; stiff opposition*). **5** (of a person or manner) formal; constrained; lacking spontaneity. **6** (of a muscle or limb, etc., or a person affected by these) aching when used, owing to previous exertion, injury, etc. **7** (of an alcoholic or medicinal drink) strong. **8** (*predic.*) *colloq.* to an extreme degree (*bored stiff; scared stiff*). **9** (foll. by *with*) *colloq.* abounding in (*a place stiff with tourists*). **10**

colloq. (of a price, demand, etc.) unusually high; excessive. ● *n. sl.* **1** a corpse. **2 a** a foolish or useless person (*you big stiff*). **b** any person (*lucky stiff*). □ **stiff neck** a rheumatic condition in which the head cannot be turned without pain. **stiff-necked** obstinate or haughty. **stiff upper lip** determination; fortitude. □□ **stiffish** *adj.* **stiffly** *adv.* **stiffness** *n.* [OE *stīf* f. Gmc]

■ *adj.* **1, 2** firm, rigid, inelastic, unbending, inflexible, hard, unbendable, tough, solid, solidified, stiffened, unyielding, brittle; semisolid, semifluid, viscous, heavy, thick, dense, compact. **3** difficult, hard, steep, uphill, laborious, arduous, onerous, tiring, fatiguing, exhausting, harrowing, toilsome, rigorous, challenging, demanding, exacting, rough, tough. **4** strong, steady, powerful, fresh, brisk, gusty, forceful, howling; severe, harsh, punitive, hurtful, punishing, abusive, torturous, distressing, afflictive, painful, overwhelming, unbearable, tormenting, merciless, strict, stringent, tough, excruciating, cruel, drastic; vigorous, energetic, staunch, dogged, tenacious, resolute, resolved, determined, stubborn, obstinate, unyielding, indomitable, relentless. **5** cool, haughty, rigid, wooden, stuffy, aloof, tense, intense, unrelaxed, starchy, forced, pompous, pedantic, turgid, stilted, constrained, artificial, labored, mannered, ceremonious, austere, formal, prim, chilly, cold, frigid, unfriendly, standoffish, reserved, snobbish, *colloq.* snooty, uptight. **7** strong, potent, powerful, overpowering, alcoholic. **10** excessive, exorbitant, high, *colloq.* steep; unreasonable, extortionate. ● *n.* **1** corpse, body, esp. *Med.* cadaver. □ **stiff-necked** see SELF-WILLED. □□ **stiffish** see THICK *adj.* 5a.

stiffen /stífən/ *v.tr.* & *intr.* make or become stiff. □□ **stiffener** *n.* **stiffening** *n.*

■ thicken, coagulate, clot, harden, set, solidify, congeal, crystallize, *colloq.* jell; brace, reinforce, tauten, tighten, rigidify, toughen, strengthen. □□ **stiffener** thickener, hardener; see also BRACE *n.* 1b.

stifle[1] /stífəl/ *v.* **1** *tr.* smother; suppress (*stifled a yawn*). **2** *intr.* & *tr.* experience or cause to experience constraint of breathing (*stifling heat*). **3** *tr.* kill by suffocating. □□ **stifler** /stíflər/ *n.* **stiflingly** *adv.* [perh. alt. of ME *stuffe, stuffle* f. OF *estouffer*]

■ **1** smother, choke back, keep *or* hold back, withhold, repress, suppress, hold in, restrain, prevent, curb, check, cover up, control, silence, muffle, stop, destroy, crush, demolish, extinguish, dampen, stamp out, kill, quash. **2, 3** suffocate, smother, choke, strangle, throttle, asphyxiate.

stifle[2] /stífəl/ *n.* (in full **stifle joint**) a joint in the legs of horses, dogs, etc., equivalent to the knee in humans. □ **stifle bone** the bone in front of this joint. [ME: orig. unkn.]

stigma /stígmə/ *n.* (*pl.* **stigmas** or esp. in sense 4 **stigmata** /-mətə, -maátə/) **1** a mark or sign of disgrace or discredit. **2** (foll. by *of*) a distinguishing mark or characteristic. **3** the part of a pistil that receives the pollen in pollination. **4** (in *pl.*) *Eccl.* (in Christian belief) marks corresponding to those left on Christ's body by the Crucifixion, said to have appeared on the bodies of St. Francis of Assisi and others. **5** a mark or spot on the skin or on a butterfly wing. **6** *Med.* a visible sign or characteristic of a disease. **7** an insect's spiracle. [L f. Gk *stigma -atos* a mark made by a pointed instrument, a brand, a dot: rel. to STICK[1]]

■ **1** brand, (bad) mark, blot, smirch, stain, spot, taint, blemish, demerit, blot on the escutcheon, *Brit.* blot in one's copybook. **2** see MARK[1] *n.* 2a, 3, 4a.

stigmatic /stigmátik/ *adj.* & *n.* ● *adj.* **1** of or relating to a stigma or stigmas. **2** = ANASTIGMATIC. ● *n. Eccl.* a person bearing stigmata. □□ **stigmatically** *adv.*

stigmatist /stígmətist/ *n. Eccl.* = STIGMATIC *n.*

stigmatize /stígmətīz/ *v.tr.* **1** (often foll. by *as*) describe as unworthy or disgraceful. **2** *Eccl.* produce stigmata on. □□ **stigmatization** *n.* [F *stigmatiser* or med.L *stigmatizo* f. Gk *stigmatizō* (as STIGMA)]

■ **1** brand, disparage, depreciate, discredit, denounce, condemn, calumniate, defame, pillory, slander, vilify.

stilb /stilb/ *n.* a unit of luminance equal to one candela per square centimeter. [F f. Gk *stilbō* glitter]

stilbene /stílbeen/ *n. Chem.* an aromatic hydrocarbon forming phosphorescent crystals. [as STILB + -ENE]

stilbestrol /stilbéstrawl, -rol/ *n.* (*Brit.* **stilboestrol**) a powerful synthetic estrogen derived from stilbene. [STILBENE + ESTRUS]

stile[1] /stīl/ *n.* an arrangement of steps allowing people but not animals to climb over a fence or wall. [OE *stigel* f. a Gmc root *stig-* (unrecorded) climb]

stile[2] /stīl/ *n.* a vertical piece in the frame of a paneled door, wainscot, etc. (cf. RAIL[1] *n.* 5). [prob. f. Du. *stijl* pillar, doorpost]

stiletto /stilétō/ *n.* (*pl.* **-os**) **1** a short dagger with a thick blade. **2** a pointed instrument for making eyelets, etc. **3** (in full **stiletto heel**) **a** a long tapering heel of a woman's shoe. **b** a shoe with such a heel. [It., dimin. of *stilo* dagger (as STYLUS)]

■ **1** see DAGGER.

still[1] /stil/ *adj., n., adv.,* & *v.* ● *adj.* **1** not or hardly moving. **2** with little or no sound; calm and tranquil (*a still evening*). **3** (of sounds) hushed; stilled. **4** (of a drink) not effervescent. **5** designed for or concerned with static photographs (*a still camera*). ● *n.* **1** deep silence (*in the still of the night*). **2** an ordinary static photograph (as opposed to a motion picture), esp. a single shot from a movie or videotape. ● *adv.* **1** without moving (*stand still*). **2** even now or at a particular time (*they still did not understand*; *why are you still here?*). **3** nevertheless; all the same. **4** (with *compar.*, etc.) even; yet; increasingly (*still greater efforts*; *still another explanation*). ● *v.tr.* & *intr.* make or become still. □ **still and all** *colloq.* nevertheless. **still life** (*pl.* **still lifes**) **1** a painting or drawing of inanimate objects such as fruit or flowers. **2** this genre of painting. **still waters run deep** a quiet manner conceals depths of feeling or knowledge or cunning. □□ **stillness** *n.* [OE *stille* (adj. & adv.), *stillan* (v.), f. WG]

■ *adj.* **1** quiet, serene, placid, calm, tranquil, motionless, unmoving, immobile, peaceful, pacific, at rest, quiescent, inert, inactive, even, flat, smooth, undisturbed, unruffled, stationary, static, standing, stagnant. **2** silent, quiet, noiseless, soundless; calm, tranquil, hushed, restful, *poet.* stilly. **3** hushed, stilled, quiet. **4** see FLAT[1] *adj.* 4. ● *n.* **1** stillness, hush, quiet, silence, tranquility, quietness, quietude, noiselessness, soundlessness, peace, peacefulness, serenity, calm. ● *adv.* **1** motionlessly, quietly, silently, stock-still. **2** even now *or* then, at this *or* that time, till this *or* that time, until this *or* that time, (up) till *or* until now *or* then, to this day, yet. **3** notwithstanding, yet, all the same, even then *or* so, *colloq.* still and all; see also NEVERTHELESS. ● *v.* calm, allay, assuage, alleviate, relieve, pacify, tranquilize, soothe, mollify, appease, subdue, suppress; silence, lull, quiet, hush, *Brit.* quieten. □ **still and all** see YET *adv.* 6. □□ **stillness** see STILL[1] *n.* above.

still[2] /stil/ *n.* an apparatus for distilling alcohol, etc. [obs. *still* (v.), ME f. DISTILL]

stillage /stílij/ *n.* a bench, frame, etc., for keeping articles off the floor while draining, drying, waiting to be packed, etc. [app. f. Du. *stellagie* scaffold f. *stellen* to place + F *-age*]

stillbirth /stílbərth/ *n.* the birth of a dead child.

stillborn /stílbawrn/ *adj.* **1** (of a child) born dead. **2** (of an idea, plan, etc.) abortive; not able to succeed.

Stillson /stílsən/ *n.* (in full **Stillson wrench**) a large wrench with jaws that tighten as pressure is increased. [D. C. *Stillson*, its inventor d. 1899]

/.../ pronunciation	● part of speech
□ phrases, idioms, and compounds	
□□ derivatives	■ synonym section
cross-references appear in SMALL CAPITALS or *italics*	

stilly | stint

stilly /stílee/ adv. & adj. • adv. in a still manner. • adj. poet. still; quiet. [(adv.) OE stillīce: (adj.) f. STILL¹]

stilt /stilt/ n. **1** either of a pair of poles with supports for the feet enabling the user to walk at a distance above the ground. **2** each of a set of piles or posts supporting a building, etc. **3 a** any wading bird of the genus Himantopus with long legs. **b** (in comb.) denoting a long-legged kind of bird (stilt-petrel). **4** a three-legged support for ceramic ware in a kiln. □ **on stilts 1** supported by stilts. **2** bombastic; stilted. □□ **stiltless** adj. [ME & LG stilte f. Gmc]

stilted /stíltid/ adj. **1** (of a literary style, etc.) stiff and unnatural; bombastic. **2** standing on stilts. **3** Archit. (of an arch) with pieces of upright masonry between the imposts and the springers. □□ **stiltedly** adv. **stiltedness** n.
■ **1** awkward, ungraceful, graceless, clumsy, wooden, stiff, turgid, affected, artificial, unnatural, mannered, forced, labored; pretentious, formal, pompous, lofty, bombastic, grandiloquent, high-flown, inflated.

Stilton /stílt'n/ n. propr. a kind of strong rich cheese, often with blue veins, orig. sold in Stilton in East Anglia.

stimulant /stímyələnt/ adj. & n. • adj. that stimulates, esp. bodily or mental activity. • n. **1** a stimulant substance, esp. a drug or alcoholic drink. **2** a stimulating influence. [L stimulare stimulant- urge, goad]
■ adj. see TONIC adj. • n. **1** energizer, antidepressant, tonic, restorative, analeptic, pick-me-up, colloq. bracer, shot in the arm, pep pill, sl. upper, speed. **2** stimulus, incentive, provocation, spur, prompt, goad, urge, prod, fillip, impetus, incitement, drive, impulse, push, pull, draw, colloq. boost.

stimulate /stímyəlayt/ v.tr. **1** apply or act as a stimulus to. **2** animate; excite; arouse. **3** be a stimulant to. □□ **stimulating** adj. **stimulatingly** adv. **stimulation** /-láyshən/ n. **stimulative** adj. **stimulator** n.
■ rouse, arouse, waken, awaken, wake up, excite, incite, inspire, encourage, spur, sting, quicken, animate, inflame, foment, fire, kindle, fuel, nourish, whet, activate, whip or stir up, goad, galvanize, energize, jog, jolt, fillip, inspirit, impassion, work up, literary enkindle; increase, encourage, prompt, provoke, quicken; see also VITALIZE. □□ **stimulating** exciting, inspirational, inspiring, arousing, rousing, stirring, animating, invigorating, tonic, exhilarating, thrilling, provocative, thought-provoking, challenging. **stimulation** see SPUR n. 2, THRILL n. 1.

stimulus /stímyələs/ n. (pl. **stimuli** /-lī/) **1** a thing that rouses to activity or energy. **2** a stimulating or rousing effect. **3** a thing that evokes a specific functional reaction in an organ or tissue. [L, = goad, spur, incentive]
■ **1** see incitement (INCITE). **2** see INSPIRATION 1a.

stimy var. of STYMIE.

sting /sting/ n. & v. • n. **1** a sharp often poisonous wounding organ of an insect, snake, nettle, etc. **2 a** the act of inflicting a wound with this. **b** the wound itself or the pain caused by it. **3** a wounding or painful quality or effect (the sting of hunger; stings of remorse). **4** pungency; sharpness; vigor (a sting in the voice). **5** sl. a swindle or robbery. • v. (past and past part. **stung** /stung/) **1 a** tr. wound or pierce with a sting. **b** intr. be able to sting; have a sting. **2** intr. & tr. feel or cause to feel a tingling physical or sharp mental pain. **3** tr. (foll. by into) incite by a strong or painful mental effect (was stung into replying). **4** tr. sl. swindle or charge exorbitantly. □ **stinging nettle** a nettle, Urtica dioica, having stinging hairs. **sting in the tail** unexpected pain or difficulty at the end. □□ **stingingly** adv. **stingless** adj. **stinglike** adj. [OE sting (n.), stingan (v.), f. Gmc]
■ n. **2 b** pain, tingle; see also PRICK n. 3. • v. **1 a** prick, stab, pierce, stick, wound; bite, nip. **2** hurt, ache, smart; wound, pain, injure, distress, nettle, pique, prick, cut to the quick. **3** see STIMULATE. **4** cheat, overcharge, swindle, fleece, rook, defraud, colloq. rip off, take for a ride, diddle, colloq. rob, soak, sl. chisel, gyp.

stingaree /stíngəreé/ n. US & Austral. = STINGRAY.

stinger /stíngər/ n. **1 a** = STING n. 1. **b** a stinging insect, snake, nettle, etc. **2** a sharp painful blow.

stingray /stíng-ray/ n. any of various broad flatfish, esp. of the family Dasyatidae, having a long poisonous serrated spine at the base of its tail.

stingy /stínjee/ adj. (**stingier**, **stingiest**) ungenerous; mean. □□ **stingily** adv. **stinginess** n. [perh. f. dial. stinge STING]
■ see MEAN² 1. □□ **stinginess** see THRIFT.

stink /stingk/ v. & n. • v. (past **stank** /stangk/ or **stunk** /stungk/; past part. **stunk**) **1** intr. emit a strong offensive smell. **2** tr. (often foll. by out) fill (a place) with a stink. **3** tr. (foll. by out, etc.) drive (a person) out, etc., by a stink. **4** intr. colloq. be or seem very unpleasant, contemptible, or scandalous. **5** intr. (foll. by of) colloq. have plenty of (esp. money). • n. **1** a strong or offensive smell; a stench. **2** colloq. an outcry or fuss (the affair caused quite a stink). □ **like stink** Brit. colloq. intensely; extremely hard or fast, etc. (working like stink). **stink bomb** a device emitting a stink when exploded. [OE stincan ult. f. WG: cf. STENCH]
■ v. **1** see SMELL v. 5. • n. **1** see SMELL n. 3. **2** see FUSS n. 1, 2a. □ **like stink** intensely; like a bat out of hell, like a demon, colloq. like a bomb, like greased lightning, like nobody's business, like blazes; see also quickly (QUICK).

stinker /stíngkər/ n. **1** a person or thing that stinks. **2** sl. an objectionable person or thing. **3** sl. **a** a difficult task. **b** Brit. a letter, etc., conveying strong disapproval.
■ **2** wretch, villain, scoundrel, cad, beast, cur, viper, snake in the grass, blackguard, rogue, knave, archaic dastard, whoreson, archaic or joc. varlet, colloq. rat, skunk, swine, nasty piece of work, so-and-so, heel, colloq. or joc. bounder, Brit. colloq. blighter, poet. or archaic (base) caitiff, sl. louse, creep, stinkpot, ratbag, (rotten) bastard, son of a bitch, sl. S.O.B., bum, esp. Brit. sl. rotter.

stinkhorn /stíngk-hawrn/ n. any foul-smelling fungus of the order Phallales.

stinking /stíngking/ adj. & adv. • adj. **1** that stinks. **2** sl. very objectionable. • adv. sl. extremely and usu. objectionably (stinking rich). □ **stinking badger** a teledu. □□ **stinkingly** adv.
■ adj. **1** foul-smelling, evil-smelling, smelly, fetid, mephitic, rank, malodorous, reeky, reeking, putrid, rancid, gamy, high, off, archaic miasmal, miasmatic, miasmatical, miasmic, colloq. whiffy, Brit. colloq. pongy, literary noisome **2** wretched, villainous, beastly, vile, contemptible, objectionable, low, despicable, mean, nasty, disgusting, dastardly, colloq. terrible, awful, lousy, sl. rotten. • adv. colloq. horribly, disgustingly; see also extremely (EXTREME).

stinko /stíngkō/ adj. sl. drunk.
■ see DRUNK adj. 1.

stinkpot /stíngkpot/ n. sl. **1** a term of contempt for a person. **2** a vehicle or boat that emits foul exhaust fumes.
■ **1** see STINKER.

stinkweed /stíngkweed/ n. any of several foul-smelling plants.

stinkwood /stíngkwŏŏd/ n. an African tree, Ocotea bullata, with foul-smelling timber.

stint /stint/ v. & n. • v. **1 a** tr. supply (food or aid, etc.) in an ungenerous amount or grudgingly. **b** intr. (foll. by on) be grudging or mean about. **2** (often refl.) supply (a person, etc.) in this way. • n. **1** a limitation of supply or effort (without stint). **2** a fixed or allotted time or amount of work (do one's stint). **3** a small sandpiper, esp. a dunlin. □□ **stinter** n. **stintless** adj. [OE styntan to blunt, dull, f. Gmc, rel. to STUNT¹]
■ v. **1** skimp, scrimp, hold back (on), withhold; be stingy, be mean, be cheap, be niggardly, be penurious, be parsimonious, be sparing, be frugal, economize, pinch (pennies), cut corners, Brit. colloq. be mingy. **2** control, curb, limit, restrict. • n. **1** control, curb, limit, limitation, restriction, check, restraint, constraint, condition, qualification, reservation. **2** share, quota,

1498

allotment, assignment, stretch, shift, term, time, spell, bout, turn, tour, *colloq.* bit, *sl.* whack.

stipe /stīp/ *n. Bot. & Zool.* a stalk or stem, esp. the support of a carpel, the stalk of a frond, the stem of a fungus, or an eyestalk. □□ **stipiform** *adj.* **stipitate** /stípitayt/ *adj.* **stipitiform** /stípitiform/ *adj.* [F f. L *stipes:* see STIPES]

stipel /stípəl/ *n. Bot.* a secondary stipule at the base of the leaflets of a compound leaf. □□ **stipellate** /stípélayt/ *adj.* [F *stipelle* f. mod.L *stipella* dimin. (as STIPULE)]

stipend /stípend/ *n.* a fixed regular allowance or salary. [ME f. OF *stipend(i)e* or L *stipendium* f. *stips* wages + *pendere* to pay]

■ pay, salary, wage, payment, remuneration, remittance, recompense, compensation, reward, emolument, fee, earnings, income; grant, subvention, scholarship, subsidy, allowance, allotment, (financial) support.

stipendiary /stipéndee-eree/ *adj. & n.* ● *adj.* **1** receiving a stipend. **2** working for pay, not voluntarily. ● *n.* (*pl.* **-ies**) a person receiving a stipend. [L *stipendiarius* (as STIPEND)]

stipes /stípeez/ *n.* (*pl.* **stipites** /stípiteez/) = STIPE. [L, = log, tree trunk]

stipple /stípəl/ *v. & n.* ● *v.* **1** *tr. & intr.* draw or paint or engrave, etc., with dots instead of lines. **2** *tr.* roughen the surface of (paint, cement, etc.). ● *n.* **1** the process or technique of stippling. **2** the effect of stippling. □□ **stippler** *n.* **stippling** *n.* [Du. *stippelen* frequent. of *stippen* to prick f. *stip* point]

stipulate[1] /stípyəlayt/ *v.tr.* **1** demand or specify as part of a bargain or agreement. **2** (foll. by *for*) mention or insist upon as an essential condition. **3** (as **stipulated** *adj.*) laid down in the terms of an agreement. □□ **stipulation** /-láyshən/ *n.* **stipulator** *n.* [L *stipulari*]

■ **1** specify, demand, require, covenant, set forth, prescribe, lay down, agree (to), provide (for), guarantee, warrant, promise, insist upon *or* on; call for. □□ **stipulation** condition, demand, essential, given, requirement, requisite, prerequisite, precondition, qualification, specification, undertaking, obligation, covenant, clause, proviso, term, agreement, provision, guarantee, warranty, promise.

stipulate[2] /stípyələt, -layt/ *adj. Bot.* having stipules. [L *stipula* (as STIPULE)]

stipule /stípyoōl/ *n.* a small leaflike appendage to a leaf, usu. at the base of a leaf stem. □□ **stipular** *adj.* [F *stipule* or L *stipula* straw]

stir[1] /stər/ *v. & n.* ● *v.* (**stirred, stirring**) **1** *tr.* move a spoon or other implement around and around in (a liquid, etc.) to mix the ingredients or constituents. **2 a** *tr.* cause to move or be disturbed, esp. slightly (*a breeze stirred the lake*). **b** *intr.* be or begin to be in motion (*not a creature was stirring*). **c** *refl.* rouse (oneself), esp. from a lethargic state. **3** *intr.* rise from sleep (*is still not stirring*). **4** *intr.* (foll. by *out of*) leave; go out of (esp. one's house). **5** *tr.* arouse or inspire or excite (the emotions, etc., or a person as regards these) (*was stirred to anger; it stirred the imagination*). **6** *esp. Austral. colloq.* **a** *tr.* annoy; tease. **b** *intr.* cause trouble. ● *n.* **1** an act of stirring (*give it a good stir*). **2** commotion or excitement; public attention (*caused quite a stir*). **3** the slightest movement (*not a stir*). □ **not stir a finger** make no effort to help. **stir the blood** inspire enthusiasm, etc. **stir in** mix (an added ingredient) with a substance by stirring. **stir one's stumps** *Brit. colloq.* **1** begin to move. **2** become active. **stir up 1** mix thoroughly by stirring. **2** incite (trouble, etc.) (*loved stirring things up*). **3** stimulate; excite; arouse (*stirred up their curiosity*). □□ **stirless** *adj.* [OE *styrian* f. Gmc]

■ *v.* **1** stir up, agitate, mix (up), scramble, amalgamate, mingle, intermingle, merge, blend, fold (in), churn (up), beat, whip (up), whisk, *literary* commingle. **2 a** disturb, ruffle, shake (up). **b** see MOVE *v.* 1, 4. **c** (*stir oneself*) rouse oneself, bestir oneself, get up, get moving, *colloq.* get a move on, shake a leg, look *or* step lively, look alive, stir one's stumps, *sl.* get a wiggle on. **3** rise, get up, wake up, waken, awaken, esp. *archaic & poet.* arise; start *or* begin the day, be up and about, *colloq.* turn out. **5** arouse, rouse, inspire, excite, affect,

stimulate, energize, galvanize, electrify, animate, provoke, activate. **6 a** see ANNOY 1, TEASE *v.* 1. **b** see *make difficulties* (DIFFICULTY). ● *n.* **1** beat, whisk, whip, mix, blend, shake. **2** bustle, activity, movement, stirring, action, commotion, flurry, confusion, tumult, ado, to-do, fuss, disturbance, excitement, hubbub. **3** movement, stirring, move, flicker. □ **stir one's stumps** see STIR[1] *v.* 2c above. **stir up 1** see STIR[1] *v.* 1 above. **2** incite, whip up, provoke, inspire, foment, instigate; motivate, move, encourage, spur, prod, induce; (*stir up trouble*) make *or* cause trouble. **3** stimulate, energize, galvanize, electrify, animate, quicken, excite, inspire, provoke, rouse, arouse, awaken; revive, resuscitate.

stir[2] /stər/ *n. sl.* a prison (esp. *in stir*). □ **stir-crazy** deranged from long imprisonment or confinement. [19th c.: orig. unkn.]

■ see PRISON *n.* 1. □ **stir-crazy** see *deranged* (DERANGE 2).

stir-fry /stərfrī/ *v. & n.* ● *v.tr.* (**-ies, -ied**) fry rapidly while stirring and tossing. ● *n.* a dish consisting of stir-fried meat, vegetables, etc.

stirk /stərk/ *n. Brit. dial.* a yearling bullock or heifer. [OE *stirc*, perh. dimin. of *stēor* STEER[2]: see -OCK]

stirps /stərps/ *n.* (*pl.* **stirpes** /-peez/) **1** *Biol.* a classificatory group. **2** *Law* **a** a branch of a family. **b** its progenitor. [L, = stock]

stirrer /stərər/ *n.* **1** a thing or a person that stirs. **2** *Brit. colloq.* a troublemaker; an agitator.

stirring /stəring/ *adj.* **1** stimulating; exciting; arousing. **2** actively occupied (*lead a stirring life*). □□ **stirringly** *adv.* [OE *styrende* (as STIR[1])]

■ **1** moving, telling, emotional, emotive, emotion-charged, impassioned, rousing, stimulating, inspiring, affecting, gripping, evocative, exciting, thrilling, melodramatic, dramatic, heady, intoxicating, spirited, inspiriting, exhilarating, awe-inspiring. **2** see BUSY *adj.* 2.

stirrup /stərəp, stír-/ *n.* **1** each of a pair of devices attached to each side of a horse's saddle, in the form of a loop with a flat base to support the rider's foot. **2** (*attrib.*) having the shape of a stirrup. **3** (in full **stirrup bone**) = STAPES. □ **stirrup cup** a cup of wine, etc., offered to a person about to depart, orig. on horseback. **stirrup iron** the metal loop of a stirrup. **stirrup leather** (or **strap**) the strap attaching a stirrup to a saddle. **stirrup pump** a hand-operated water pump with a foot rest, used to extinguish small fires. [OE *stigrāp* f. *stigan* climb (as STILE[1]) + ROPE]

■ □ **stirrup cup** see DRINK *n.* 2b.

stitch /stich/ *n. & v.* ● *n.* **1 a** (in sewing or knitting or crocheting, etc.) a single pass of a needle or the thread or loop, etc., resulting from this. **b** a particular method of sewing or knitting, etc. (*am learning a new stitch*). **2** (usu. in *pl.*) *Surgery* each of the loops of material used in sewing up a wound. **3** the least bit of clothing (*hadn't a stitch on*). **4** an acute pain in the side of the body induced by running, etc. ● *v.tr.* **1** sew; make stitches (in). **2** join or close with stitches. □ **in stitches** *colloq.* laughing uncontrollably. **a stitch in time** a timely remedy. **stitch up 1** join or mend by sewing or stitching. **2** *Brit. sl.* betray or cheat. □□ **stitcher** *n.* **stitchery** *n.* **stitchless** *adj.* [OE *stice* f. Gmc, rel. to STICK[2]]

■ *n.* **1 a** tack, basting (stitch). **4** see TWINGE *n.* ● *v.* see SEW.

stitchwort /stíchwərt, -wawrt/ *n.* any plant of the genus *Stellaria*, esp. *S. media* with an erect stem and white starry flowers, once thought to cure a stitch in the side.

stiver /stívər/ *n.* the smallest quantity or amount (*don't care a stiver*). [Du. *stuiver* a small coin, prob. rel. to STUB]

stoa /stōə/ *n.* (*pl.* **stoas**) **1** a portico or roofed colonnade in ancient Greek architecture. **2** (**the Stoa**) the Stoic school of philosophy. [Gk: cf. STOIC]

/. . ./ **pronunciation**	● **part of speech**
□ **phrases, idioms, and compounds**	
□□ **derivatives**	■ **synonym section**
cross-references appear in SMALL CAPITALS or *italics*	

stoat /stōt/ *n.* a carnivorous mammal, *Mustela erminea*, of the weasel family, having brown fur in the summer turning mainly white in the winter. Also called ERMINE. [ME: orig. unkn.]

stochastic /stōkástik/ *adj.* **1** determined by a random distribution of probabilities. **2** (of a process) characterized by a sequence of random variables. **3** governed by the laws of probability. □□ **stochastically** *adv.* [Gk *stokhastikos* f. *stokhazomai* aim at, guess f. *stokhos* aim]

stock /stok/ *n., adj., & v.* ● *n.* **1** a store of goods, etc., ready for sale or distribution, etc. **2** a supply or quantity of anything for use (*lay in winter stocks of fuel*; *a great stock of information*). **3** equipment or raw material for manufacture or trade, etc. (*rolling stock*; *paper stock*). **4 a** farm animals or equipment. **b** = FATSTOCK. **5 a** the capital of a business company. **b** shares in this. **6 a** one's reputation or popularity (*his stock is rising*). **b** an estimate or assessment. **c** confidence, esp. in reliability. **7 a** money lent to a government at fixed interest. **b** the right to receive such interest. **8** a line of ancestry; family origins (*comes from German stock*). **9** liquid made by stewing bones, vegetables, fish, etc., as a basis for soup, gravy, sauce, etc. **10** any of various fragrant-flowered cruciferous plants of the genus *Matthiola* or *Malcolmia* (orig. *stock-gillyflower*, so-called because it had a stronger stem than the clove gillyflower). **11** a plant into which a graft is inserted. **12** the main trunk of a tree, stem of a plant, etc. **13** (in *pl.*) *hist.* a wooden frame with holes for the feet and occas. the hands and head, in which offenders were locked as a public punishment. **14 a** = *stock company*. **b** the repertory of this. **15 a** a base or support or handle for an implement or machine. **b** the crossbar of an anchor. **16** the butt of a rifle, etc. **17 a** = HEADSTOCK. **b** = TAILSTOCK. **18** (in *pl.*) the supports for a ship during building. **19** a band of material worn round the neck esp. in horseback riding or below a clerical collar. **20** hard solid brick pressed in a mold. ● *adj.* **1** kept in stock and so regularly available (*stock sizes*). **2** perpetually repeated; hackneyed; conventional (*a stock answer*). ● *v.tr.* **1** have or keep (goods) in stock. **2 a** provide (a store or a farm, etc.) with goods, equipment, or livestock. **b** fill with items needed (*shelves well-stocked with books*). **3** fit (a gun, etc.) with a stock. □ **in stock** available immediately for sale, etc. **on the stocks** in construction or preparation. **out of stock** not immediately available for sale. **stock book** a book or ledger showing amounts of goods, stocks or stores, etc., acquired and disposed of. **stock car 1** a specially modified production car for use in racing. **2** a railroad boxcar for transporting livestock. **stock company** a repertory company performing mainly at a particular theater. **stock dove** a European wild pigeon, *Columba oenas*, with a shorter tail and squarer head than a wood pigeon and breeding in tree trunks. **stock exchange 1** a place where stocks and shares are bought and sold. **2** the dealers working there. **stock-in-trade 1** goods kept on sale by a retailer, dealer, etc. **2** all the requisites of a trade or profession. **3** a ready supply of characteristic phrases, attitudes, etc. **stock market 1** = *stock exchange*. **2** transactions on this. **stock-still** without moving. **stock up 1** provide with or get stocks or supplies. **2** (foll. by *with*, *on*) get in or gather a stock of (food, fuel, etc.). **take stock 1** make an inventory of one's stock. **2** (often foll. by *of*) make a review or estimate of (a situation, etc.). **3** (foll. by *of*) concern oneself with. □□ **stocker** *n.* **stockless** *adj.* [OE *stoc, stocc* f. Gmc]

■ *n.* **1, 2** supply, store, inventory, stockpile, reserve, reservoir, cache, hoard, accumulation, quantity; wares, merchandise, goods, commodities, resources. **4** livestock, (domestic *or* farm) animals, cattle, beasts; horses, cows, oxen, sheep, goats. **5** capital, funds; property, assets. **6 a** see REPUTATION 2. **8** pedigree, bloodline, blood, house, dynasty, (line of) descent, extraction, roots, origins, lineage, family, ancestry, parentage, breeding, heritage. **9** see BROTH. **12** see TRUNK 1. **16** butt, handle. ● *adj.* **1** standard, ordinary, regular, routine, staple. **2** routine, stereotyped, banal, clichéd, unoriginal, commonplace, usual, hackneyed, ordinary, stale, staple, ready-made, run-of-the-mill,

tired, old, everyday, customary, set, standard, predictable, traditional, conventional, trite, worn out, *colloq.* corny. ● *v.* **1** carry, have, have *or* make available, handle, deal in, market, sell, supply, furnish, provide, offer, trade in, keep. **2 a** see OUTFIT *v.* **b** fill, supply, provide, furnish. □ **in stock** available, on the shelf, for sale. **out of stock** unavailable, sold out. **stock exchange 1** see EXCHANGE *n.* 4. **stock-in-trade 1** see WARE¹. **stock market 1** see EXCHANGE *n.* 4. **stock-still** see STILL¹ *adv.* 1. **stock up 2** (*stock up with* or *on*) accumulate, amass, pile up, stockpile, gather, garner, hoard, store (up), cache, lay in, get in, buy in. **take stock 2** (*take stock of*) weigh (up), estimate, review, appraise, look at, *colloq.* size up.

stockade /stokáyd/ *n. & v.* ● *n.* **1** a line or enclosure of upright stakes. **2** a military prison. ● *v.tr.* fortify with a stockade. [obs. F *estocade*, alt. of *estacade* f. Sp. *estacada*: rel. to STAKE¹]

■ *n.* **1** see WALL *n.* 1.

stockbreeder /stókbreedər/ *n.* a farmer who raises livestock. □□ **stockbreeding** *n.*

stockbroker /stókbrōkər/ *n.* = BROKER 2. □ **stockbroker belt** *Brit.* an affluent residential area, esp. near a business center such as London. □□ **stockbrokerage** *n.* **stockbroking** *n.*

stockfish /stókfish/ *n.* cod or a similar fish split and dried in the open air without salt.

stockholder /stók-hōldər/ *n.* an owner of stocks or shares. □□ **stockholding** *n.*

stockinette /stókinét/ *n.* (also **stockinet**) an elastic, knitted, usu. cotton material. [prob. f. *stocking net*]

stocking /stóking/ *n.* **1 a** either of a pair of long separate coverings for the legs and feet, usu. closely woven in wool or nylon and worn esp. by women and girls. **b** = SOCK¹. **2** any close-fitting garment resembling a stocking (*bodystocking*). **3** a differently colored, usu. white, lower part of the leg of a horse, etc. □ **in one's stocking** (or **stockinged**) **feet** without shoes (esp. while being measured). **stocking cap** a knitted usu. conical cap. **stocking stuffer** a small present suitable for a Christmas stocking. □□ **stockinged** *adj.* (also in *comb.*). **stockingless** *adj.* [STOCK in (now dial.) sense 'stocking' + -ING¹]

stockjobber /stókjobər/ *n.* **1** *US* = JOBBER 1b. **2** *Brit.* = JOBBER 2. □□ **stockjobbing** *n.*

stocklist /stóklist/ *n. Brit.* a regular publication stating a dealer's stock of goods with current prices, etc.

stockman /stókmən/ *n.* (*pl.* **-men**) **1 a** an owner of livestock. **b** *Austral.* a man in charge of livestock. **2** a person in charge of a stock of goods in a warehouse, etc.

stockpile /stókpil/ *n. & v.* ● *n.* an accumulated stock of goods, materials, weapons, etc., held in reserve. ● *v.tr.* accumulate a stockpile of. □□ **stockpiler** *n.*

■ *n.* see ACCUMULATION 2. ● *v.* see ACCUMULATE 1.

stockpot /stókpot/ *n.* a pot for cooking stock for soup, etc.

stockroom /stókrōōm, -rōōm/ *n.* a room for storing goods in stock.

■ see WAREHOUSE.

stocktaking /stóktayking/ *n.* **1** the process of making an inventory of stock in a store, warehouse, etc. **2** a review of one's position and resources.

stocky /stókee/ *adj.* (**stockier, stockiest**) (of a person, plant, or animal) short and strongly built; thickset. □□ **stockily** *adv.* **stockiness** *n.*

■ thickset, sturdy, chunky, dumpy, solid, stumpy, burly, beefy, heavyset, squat, mesomorphic, *Anthropol.* pyknic.

stockyard /stókyaard/ *n.* an enclosure with pens, etc., for the sorting or temporary keeping of cattle.

stodge /stoj/ *n. & v. esp. Brit. colloq.* ● *n.* **1** food, esp. of a thick heavy kind. **2** an unimaginative person or idea. ● *v.tr.* stuff with food, etc. [earlier as verb: imit., after *stuff* and *podge*]

stodgy /stójee/ *adj.* (**stodgier, stodgiest**) **1** dull and uninteresting. **2** (of a literary style, etc.) turgid and dull. **3** esp.

Brit. (of food) heavy and indigestible. □□ **stodgily** *adv.* **stodginess** *n.*

■ **1** heavy, indigestible, solid, filling. **2, 3** stuffy, dull, heavy, ponderous, boring, tedious, humdrum, tiresome, turgid, uninteresting, unimaginative, dreary, bland, *colloq.* deadly.

stoep /stoop/ *n. S.Afr.* a terraced veranda in front of a house. [Du., rel. to STEP]

stogy /stṓgee/ *n.* (also **stogie**) (*pl.* **-ies**) **1** a long narrow roughly-made cigar. **2** a rough heavy boot. [orig. *stoga*, short for *Conestoga* in Pennsylvania]

Stoic /stṓik/ *n. & adj.* ● *n.* **1** a member of the ancient Greek school of philosophy founded at Athens by Zeno *c.*308 BC, which sought virtue as the greatest good and taught control of one's feelings and passions. **2** (**stoic**) a stoical person. ● *adj.* **1** of or like the Stoics. **2** (**stoic**) = STOICAL. [ME f. L *stoicus* f. Gk *stōikos* f. STOA (with ref. to Zeno's teaching in the *Stoa Poikilē* or Painted Porch at Athens)]

stoical /stṓikəl/ *adj.* having or showing great self-control in adversity. □□ **stoically** *adv.*

■ stoic, impassive, resigned, cool, unemotional, emotionless, imperturbable, calm, philosophical, dispassionate, indifferent, phlegmatic, long-suffering, patient, stolid, disciplined, self-possessed, (self-) controlled, *colloq.* unflappable.

stoichiometry /stóykeeómitree/ *n. Chem.* **1** the fixed, usu. rational numerical relationship between the relative quantities of substances in a reaction or compound. **2** the determination or measurement of these quantities. □□ **stoichiometric** /-keeəmétrik/ *adj.* [Gk *stoikheion* element + -METRY]

Stoicism /stṓisizəm/ *n.* **1** the philosophy of the Stoics. **2** (**stoicism**) a stoical attitude.

■ **2** (**stoicism**) self-possession, austerity, self-control, fortitude, calmness, calm, coolness, imperturbability, forbearance, patience, fatalism, resignation, philosophy, *colloq.* unflappability.

stoke /stōk/ *v.* (often foll. by *up*) **1 a** *tr.* feed and tend (a fire or furnace, etc.). **b** *intr.* act as a stoker. **2** *intr. colloq.* consume food, esp. steadily and in large quantities. [back-form. f. STOKER]

stokehold /stṓk-hōld/ *n.* a compartment in a steamship, containing its boilers and furnace.

stokehole /stṓk-hōl/ *n.* a space for stokers in front of a furnace.

stoker /stṓkər/ *n.* a person who tends to the furnace on a steamship. [Du. f. *stoken* stoke f. MDu. *stoken* push, rel. to STICK¹]

stokes /stōks/ *n.* (*pl.* same) the cgs unit of kinematic viscosity, corresponding to a dynamic viscosity of 1 poise and a density of 1 gram per cubic centimeter, equivalent to 10^{-4} square meters per second. [Sir G. G. *Stokes*, Brit. physicist d. 1903]

STOL *abbr. Aeron.* short take-off and landing.

stole¹ /stōl/ *n.* **1** a woman's long garment like a scarf, worn around the shoulders. **2** a strip of silk, etc., worn over the shoulders as a vestment by a priest. [OE *stol, stole* (orig. a long robe) f. L *stola* f. Gk *stolē* equipment, clothing]

■ **1** tippet, scarf, boa, shawl, wrap, cape.

stole² *past* of STEAL.

stolen *past part.* of STEAL.

stolid /stólid/ *adj.* **1** lacking or concealing emotion or animation. **2** not easily excited or moved. □□ **stolidity** /-líditee/ *n.* **stolidly** *adv.* **stolidness** *n.* [obs. F *stolide* or L *stolidus*]

■ impassive, exanimate, phlegmatic, unemotional, stoical; vegetating, lethargic, apathetic, indifferent, uninterested; wooden, slow, lumpish. □□ **stolidity** see INDIFFERENCE 1.

stolon /stólon/ *n.* **1** *Bot.* a horizontal stem or branch that takes root at points along its length, forming new plants. **2** *Zool.* a branched stemlike structure in some invertebrates such as corals. □□ **stolonate** /-nayt/ *adj.* **stoloniferous** /-nífərəs/ *adj.* [L *stolo -onis*]

stoma /stṓmə/ *n.* (*pl.* **stomas** or **stomata** /-mətə/) **1** *Bot.* a minute pore in the epidermis of a leaf. **2 a** *Zool.* a small mouthlike opening in some lower animals. **b** *Surgery* a sim-

ilar artificial orifice made in the stomach. □□ **stomal** *adj.* [mod.L f. Gk *stoma -atos* mouth]

■ **1** see PORE¹.

stomach /stúmək/ *n. & v.* ● *n.* **1 a** the internal organ in which the first part of digestion occurs, being in humans a pear-shaped enlargement of the alimentary canal linking the esophagus to the small intestine. **b** any of several such organs in animals, esp. ruminants, in which there are four (cf. RUMEN, RETICULUM, OMASUM, ABOMASUM). **2 a** the belly, abdomen, or lower front of the body (*pit of the stomach*). **b** a protuberant belly (*what a stomach he has got!*). **3** (usu. foll. by *for*) **a** an appetite (for food). **b** liking, readiness, or inclination (for controversy, conflict, danger, or an undertaking) (*had no stomach for the fight*). ● *v.tr.* **1** find sufficiently palatable to swallow or keep down. **2** submit to or endure (an affront, etc.) (usu. with *neg.: cannot stomach it*). □ **on an empty stomach** not having eaten recently. **on a full stomach** soon after a large meal. **stomach ache** a pain in the abdomen or bowels. **stomach pump** a syringe for forcing liquid, etc., into or esp. out of the stomach. **stomach tube** a tube introduced into the stomach via the gullet for emptying it. □□ **stomachful** *n.* (*pl.* **-fuls**). **stomachless** *adj.* [ME *stomak* f. OF *stomaque, estomac* f. L *stomachus* f. Gk *stomakhos* gullet f. *stoma* mouth]

■ *n.* **2 a** abdomen, belly, gut, paunch, *colloq.* tummy, insides, guts, *Austral. colloq.* bingy, *sl.* bread basket. **b** potbelly, pot, paunch, beer belly, *colloq.* spare tire, *joc.* corporation. **3 b** tolerance; taste, appetite, desire, hunger, thirst, craving, need; inclination, relish; see also LIKING 2. ● *v.* **1** swallow, keep down, digest, eat. **2** abide, tolerate, endure, stand, bear, suffer, take, accept, swallow, resign *or* reconcile oneself to, put up with, submit to, countenance, *colloq.* stick, *literary* brook. □ **stomach ache** see INDIGESTION.

stomacher /stúmәkәr/ *n. hist.* **1** a front piece of a woman's dress covering the breast and pit of the stomach, often jeweled or embroidered. **2** an ornament worn on the front of a bodice. [ME, prob. f. OF *estomachier* (as STOMACH)]

stomachic /stəmákik/ *adj. & n.* ● *adj.* **1** of or relating to the stomach. **2** promoting the appetite or assisting digestion. ● *n.* a medicine or stimulant for the stomach. [F *stomachique* or L *stomachicus* f. Gk *stomakhikos* (as STOMACH)]

stomata *pl.* of STOMA.

stomatitis /stṓmətītis/ *n. Med.* inflammation of the mucous membrane of the mouth.

stomatology /stṓmətóləjee/ *n.* the scientific study of the mouth or its diseases. □□ **stomatological** /-təlójikəl/ *adj.* **stomatologist** *n.*

stomp /stomp/ *v. & n.* ● *v.intr.* tread or stamp heavily. ● *n.* a lively jazz dance with heavy stamping. □□ **stomper** *n.* [US dial. var. of STAMP]

■ *v.* see STAMP *v.* 1c.

stone /stōn/ *n. & v.* ● *n.* **1 a** a solid nonmetallic mineral matter, of which rock is made. **b** a piece of this, esp. a small piece. **2** *Building* **a** = LIMESTONE (*Portland stone*). **b** = SANDSTONE (*Bath stone*). **3** *Mineral.* = precious stone. **4** a stony meteorite; an aerolite. **5** (often in *comb.*) a piece of stone of a definite shape or for a particular purpose (*tombstone; stepping-stone*). **6 a** a thing resembling stone in hardness or form, e.g., the hard case of the kernel in some fruits. **b** *Med.* (often in *pl.*) a hard morbid concretion in the body esp. in the kidney or gallbladder (*gallstones*). **7** (*pl.* same) *Brit.* a unit of weight equal to 14 lb. (6.35 kg). **8** (*attrib.*) **a** made of stone. **b** of the color of stone. ● *v.tr.* **1** pelt with stones. **2** remove the stones from (fruit). **3** face or pave, etc., with stone. **4** sharpen, polish, etc., by rubbing with or against a stone. □ **cast** (or **throw**) **stones** (or **the first stone**) make aspersions on a person's character, etc. **leave no stone unturned** try all possible means. **Stone Age** a prehistoric pe-

─────────────────────────

/.../ **pronunciation**	● **part of speech**
□ **phrases, idioms, and compounds**	
□□ **derivatives**	■ **synonym section**
cross-references appear in SMALL CAPITALS or *italics*	

riod when weapons and tools were made of stone. **stone coal** anthracite. **stone cold** completely cold. **stone sober** completely sober. **stone the crows** *Brit. sl.* an exclamation of surprise or disgust. **stone-dead** completely dead. **stone-deaf** completely deaf. **stone fruit** a fruit with flesh or pulp enclosing a stone. **stone parsley** an umbelliferous hedge plant, *Sison amomum*, with aromatic seeds. **stone pine** a S. European pine tree, *Pinus pinea*, with branches at the top spreading like an umbrella. **stone pit** a quarry. **a stone's throw** a short distance. □□ **stoned** *adj.* (also in *comb.*). **stoneless** *adj.* **stoner** *n.* [OE *stān* f. Gmc]

■ *n.* **1 b** see ROCK¹ 4. **5** see TABLET 3. **6 a** pip, seed, pit. □ **stone cold** see COLD *adj.* 1. **stone the crows** *sl.* well blow me down, well knock me down with a feather; see also *well I'll be damned* (DAMN). **stone-deaf** deaf, hard of hearing.

stonechat /stŏnchat/ *n.* any small brown bird of the thrush family with black and white markings, esp. *Saxicola torquata* with a call like stones being knocked together.

stonecrop /stŏnkrop/ *n.* any succulent plant of the genus *Sedum*, usu. having yellow or white flowers and growing among rocks or in walls.

stonecutter /stŏnkutər/ *n.* a person or machine that cuts or carves stone.

stoned /stŏnd/ *adj. sl.* under the influence of alcohol or drugs.
■ see DRUNK *adj.* 1, HIGH *adj.* 8b.

stonefish /stŏnfish/ *n.* (*pl.* same) a venomous tropical fish, *Synanceia verrucosa*, with poison glands underlying its erect dorsal spines. Also called DEVILFISH.

stonefly /stŏnflī/ *n.* (*pl.* **-flies**) any insect of the order Plecoptera, with aquatic larvae found under stones.

stone-ground /stŏn-grownd/ *adj.* (of grain) ground with millstones.

stonehatch /stŏnhach/ *n.* a ringed plover.

stonemason /stŏnmaysən/ *n.* a person who cuts, prepares, and builds with stone. □□ **stonemasonry** *n.*

stonewall /stŏnwawl/ *v. tr. & intr.* obstruct (discussion or investigation) or be obstructive with evasive answers or denials, etc. □□ **stonewaller** *n.* **stonewalling** *n.*
■ see STALL² *v.* 1.

stoneware /stŏnwair/ *n.* ceramic ware that is impermeable and partly vitrified but opaque.
■ see POTTERY.

stonewashed /stŏnwawsht, -wosht/ *adj.* (of a garment or fabric, esp. denim) washed with abrasives to produce a worn or faded appearance.

stonework /stŏnwərk/ *n.* **1** masonry. **2** the parts of a building made of stone. □□ **stoneworker** *n.*

stonewort /stŏnwərt, -wawrt/ *n.* **1** = *stone parsley*. **2** any plant of the genus *Chara*, with a calcareous deposit on the stem.

stony /stŏnee/ *adj.* (**stonier**, **stoniest**) **1** full of or covered with stones (*stony soil*; *a stony road*). **2 a** hard; rigid. **b** cold; unfeeling; uncompromising (*a stony stare*; *a stony silence*). □ **stony-broke** *Brit. sl.* entirely without money. **stony-hearted** unfeeling; obdurate. □□ **stonily** *adv.* **stoniness** *n.* [OE *stānig* (as STONE)]

■ **1** rocky, pebbly, shingly, shingled, gravelly; rough, rugged. **2** hard, obdurate, adamant, adamantine, heartless, stony-hearted, hard-hearted, indifferent, unsympathetic, implacable, intractable, insensitive, insensible, unfeeling, unresponsive, unsentimental, merciless, pitiless, cold, coldhearted, chilly, frigid, icy, tough, hard-boiled, callous, steely, rigid, inflexible, uncompromising. □ **stony-broke** bankrupt, penniless, indigent, penurious, poverty-stricken, poor, *colloq.* broke, *Brit. sl.* skint. **stony-hearted** see STONY 2 above.

stood past and past part. of STAND.

stooge /stŏoj/ *n. & v. colloq.* ● *n.* **1** a butt or foil, esp. for a comedian; straight man. **2** an assistant or subordinate, esp. for routine or unpleasant work. **3** a compliant person; a puppet. ● *v.intr.* **1** (foll. by *for*) act as a stooge for. **2** *Brit.* (foll. by *about*, *around*, etc.) move about aimlessly. [20th c.: orig. unkn.]

■ *n.* **1** see FOOL *n.* 3. **2** see INFERIOR *n.* 1. **3** see PUPPET.

stook /stŏok, stŏok/ *n. & v. Brit.* ● *n.* a group of sheaves of grain stood on end in a field. ● *v.tr.* arrange in stooks. [ME *stouk*, from or rel. to MLG *stūke*]

stool /stŏol/ *n. & v.* ● *n.* **1** a seat without a back or arms, usu. for one person and consisting of a wooden slab on three or four short legs. **2 a** = FOOTSTOOL. **b** a low bench for kneeling on. **3** (usu. in *pl.*) = FECES. **4** the root or stump of a tree or plant from which the shoots spring. **5** a decoy bird in hunting. ● *v.intr.* (of a plant) throw up shoots from the root. □ **fall between two stools** fail from vacillation between two courses, etc. **stool pigeon 1** a person acting as a decoy (orig. a decoy of a pigeon fixed to a stool). **2** a police informer. [OE *stōl* f. Gmc, rel. to STAND]

■ *n.* **1** see SEAT *n.* 1. □ **stool pigeon 1** see DECOY *n.* **2** see INFORMER 1.

stoolie /stŏolee/ *n. sl.* a person acting as a stool pigeon.
■ see INFORMER 1.

stoop¹ /stŏop/ *v. & n.* ● *v.* **1** *tr.* bend (one's head or body) forward and downward. **2** *intr.* carry one's head and shoulders bowed forward. **3** *intr.* (often foll. by *down*) lower the body by bending forward, sometimes also bending at the knee. **4** *intr.* (foll. by *to* + infin.) deign or condescend. **5** *intr.* (foll. by *to*) descend or lower oneself to (some conduct) (*has stooped to crime*). **6** *intr.* (of a hawk, etc.) swoop on its prey. ● *n.* **1** a stooping posture. **2** the downward swoop of a hawk, etc. [OE *stūpian* f. Gmc, rel. to STEEP¹]

■ *v.* **1** bend, bow, duck, lean, hunch, double up. **3** stoop down, bend, bow (down), bow, duck (down), lean (down), crouch (down), squat, scrunch down, hunch (down). **4, 5** condescend, deign, lower *or* abase *or* degrade oneself, sink, descend, humble oneself. **6** see SWOOP *v.* 1. ● *n.* **1** hunch, slouch, crouch, *Med.* kyphosis, curvature of the spine. **2** see SWOOP *n.*

stoop² /stŏop/ *n.* a porch or small veranda or set of steps in front of a house. [Du. *stoep*: see STOEP]

stoop³ var. of STOUP.

stop /stop/ *v. & n.* ● *v.* (**stopped**, **stopping**) **1** *tr.* **a** put an end to (motion, etc.); completely check the progress or motion or operation of. **b** effectively hinder or prevent (*stopped them playing so loudly*). **c** discontinue (an action or sequence of actions) (*stopped playing*; *stopped my visits*). **2** *intr.* come to an end; cease (*supplies suddenly stopped*). **3** *intr.* cease from motion or speaking or action; make a halt or pause (*the car stopped at the lights*; *he stopped in the middle of a sentence*; *my watch has stopped*). **4** *tr.* cause to cease action; defeat. **5** *sl.* receive (a blow, etc.). **6** *intr.* esp. *Brit.* remain; stay for a short time. **7** *tr.* (often foll. by *up*) block or close up (a hole or leak, etc.). **8** *tr.* not permit or supply as usual; discontinue or withhold (*shall stop their wages*). **9** *tr.* (in full **stop payment of** or **on**) instruct a bank to withhold payment on (a check). **10** *tr. Brit.* put a filling in (a tooth). **11** *tr.* obtain the required pitch from (the string of a violin, etc.) by pressing at the appropriate point with the finger. **12** *tr.* plug the upper end of (an organ pipe), giving a note an octave lower. **13** *tr. Bridge* be able to prevent opponents from taking all the tricks in (a suit). **14** *tr.* make (a sound) inaudible. **15** *tr. Boxing* **a** parry (a blow). **b** knock out (an opponent). **16** *tr. Hort.* pinch back (a plant). **17** *tr.* make (a clock, factory, etc.) cease working. **18** *tr. Naut.* make fast; stopper (a cable, etc.). ● *n.* **1** the act or an instance of stopping; the state of being stopped (*put a stop to; the vehicle was brought to a stop*). **2** a place designated for a bus or train, etc., to stop. **3** *Brit.* a punctuation mark, esp. a sentence-ending period. **4** a device for stopping motion at a particular point. **5** a change of pitch effected by stopping a string. **6 a** (in an organ) a row of pipes of one character. **b** a knob, etc., operating these. **7** a manner of speech adopted to produce a particular effect. **8** *Optics & Photog.* = DIAPHRAGM 3. **9 a** the effective diameter of a lens. **b** a device for reducing this. **c** a unit of change of relative aperture or exposure (with a reduction of one stop equivalent to halving it). **10** (of sound) = PLOSIVE. **11** (in telegrams, etc.) a period. **12** *Bridge* a card or cards stopping a suit. **13** *Naut.* a small line used as a lashing. □ **put a stop to** cause to end, esp. abruptly. **stop-and-go** alternate stopping and restarting, esp. in traffic. **stop at nothing** be ruthless. **stop by** (also *absol.*) call at (a place). **stop dead** (or **short**) cease abruptly. **stop down** *Photog.* reduce the aperture of (a lens) with a diaphragm. **stop drill** a drill with a shoulder limiting the depth of penetration. **stop one's ears 1** put one's fingers in one's ears to avoid hearing. **2** refuse to listen. **stop-go 1** = *stop-and-go.* **2** *Brit.* the alternate restriction and stimulation of economic demand. **stop in** pay a brief visit. **stop knob** a knob controlling an organ stop. **stop light 1** a red traffic light. **2** a light on the rear of a vehicle showing when the brakes are applied. **stop off** (or **over**) break one's journey. **stop out 1** stay out. **2** cover (part of an area) to prevent printing, etching, etc. **stop press** *Brit.* **1** (often *attrib.*) late news inserted in a newspaper after printing has begun. **2** a column in a newspaper reserved for this. **stop valve** a valve closing a pipe against the passage of liquid. **stop volley** (esp. in tennis) a checked volley close to the net, dropping the ball dead on the other side. **with all the stops out** exerting extreme effort. □□ **stopless** *adj.* **stoppable** *adj.* [ME f. OE -*stoppian* f. LL *stuppare* STUFF: see ESTOP]

■ *v.* **1 a** put an end to, put a stop to, bring to a stop *or* halt *or* close *or* standstill, immobilize, paralyze, freeze, deactivate, bring to an end, shut down, check, arrest, nip in the bud; see also ABOLISH. **b** curb, restrain, thwart, frustrate, put a stopper on; block, bar, obstruct, intercept, dam, keep *or* hold back, prevent, preclude, hinder, hamper, delay; slow, impede, stem, stanch. **c** discontinue, halt, terminate, cease, break off, cut off, interrupt, suspend, give up, quit, leave off, finish, end, conclude, refrain from, abstain from, abandon, drop, *colloq.* cut (out), lay off, knock off, pack in *or* up, *literary* desist (from). **2** draw to a close, be over, come to a stop *or* halt *or* close, come to an end, expire, cease, end, finish, halt, cut out, peter out, run out. **3** halt, pause, pull up, draw up, come to a stop *or* halt *or* standstill, come to rest, cut out, end up, turn up, arrive; pull in *or* over. **4** see DEFEAT *v.* 2. **6** pause, break, take a break, *archaic or literary* tarry; sojourn, rest, remain, stay, put up, lodge, visit, stop off *or* over. **7** obstruct, block (up), jam (up), plug (up), bung (up), clog (up), choke (up), stuff (up), fill (up), caulk, occlude, seal, close (up *or* off). **8** discontinue, terminate, suspend, withhold, keep *or* hold back. **10** fill. ● *n.* **1** stop off, stopover, halt, end, finish, cessation, termination, ban, prohibition; close, standstill, conclusion; stoppage; see also *interruption* (INTERRUPT). **2** stopping place, station, terminal, stage, terminus, depot. **3** period, point, *Brit.* full stop. □ **put a stop to** see STOP *v.* 1a above. **stop-and-go** see INTERMITTENT. **stop at nothing** see PERSEVERE. **stop by** see VISIT *v.* 1. **stop dead** see FREEZE *v.* 6a. **stop in** see VISIT *v.* 1. **stop off** (or **over**) see STOP *v.* 6 above.

stopbank /stópbangk/ *n. Austral. & NZ* an embankment built to prevent river flooding.

stopcock /stópkok/ *n.* an externally operated valve regulating the flow of a liquid or gas through a pipe, etc.

■ see TAP¹ *n.* 1.

stope /stōp/ *n.* a steplike part of a mine where ore, etc., is being extracted. [app. rel. to STEP *n.*]

stopgap /stópgap/ *n.* (often *attrib.*) a temporary substitute.

■ improvisation; (*often attrib.*) makeshift, substitute, stand-in, standby, temporary, emergency; (*attrib.*) improvised, impromptu, provisional, *Naut.* jury-rigged.

stopoff /stópawf, -of/ *n.* = STOPOVER.

stopover /stópōvər/ *n.* a break in one's journey.

stoppage /stópij/ *n.* **1** the condition of being blocked or stopped. **2** a stopping (of pay). **3** a stopping or interruption of work in a factory, etc.

■ **1** blockage, blocking, obstruction, block. **3** see *interruption* (INTERRUPT).

stopper /stópər/ *n. & v.* ● *n.* **1** a plug for closing a bottle, etc. **2** a person or thing that stops something. **3** *Naut.* a rope or clamp, etc., for checking and holding a rope cable or chain cable. ● *v.tr.* close or secure with a stopper. □ **put a**

stopper on 1 put an end to (a thing). **2** keep (a person) quiet.

■ *n.* **1** stopple, cork, plug, bung, peg, spigot, spile. ● *v.* see PLUG *v.* 1. □ **put a stopper on 1** see END *v.* 1, 2. **2** see GAG *v.* 2.

stopping /stóping/ *n. Brit.* a filling for a tooth.

stopple /stópəl/ *n. & v.* ● *n.* a stopper or plug. ● *v.tr.* close with a stopple. [ME: partly f. STOP + -LE¹, partly f. ESTOPPEL]

■ *n.* see STOPPER *n.* ● *v.* see PLUG *v.* 1.

stopwatch /stópwoch/ *n.* a watch with a mechanism for recording elapsed time, used to time races, etc.

storage /stáwrij/ *n.* **1 a** the storing of goods, etc. **b** a particular method of storing or the space available for it. **2** the cost of storing. **3** the electronic retention of data in a computer, etc. □ **storage battery** (or **cell**) a battery (or cell) for storing electricity.

storax /stáwraks/ *n.* **1 a** a fragrant resin, obtained from the tree *Styrax officinalis* and formerly used in perfume. **b** this tree. **2** (in full **Levant** or **liquid storax**) a balsam obtained from the tree *Liquidambar orientalis.* [L f. Gk, var. of STYRAX]

store /stawr/ *n. & v.* ● *n.* **1** a quantity of something kept available for use (*a store of wine*; *a store of wit*). **2** (in *pl.*) **a** articles for a particular purpose accumulated for use (*naval stores*). **b** a supply of these or the place where they are kept. **3 a** = *department store.* **b** a retail outlet or shop. **c** a shop selling basic necessities (*general store*). **4** *Brit.* a warehouse for the temporary keeping of furniture, etc. **5** *Brit.* a device in a computer for storing retrievable data; a memory. ● *v.tr.* **1** put (furniture, etc.) in storage. **2** (often foll. by *up, away*) accumulate (provisions, energy, electricity, etc.) for future use. **3** stock or provide with something useful (*a mind stored with facts*). **4** (of a receptacle) have storage capacity for. **5** enter or retain (data) for retrieval. □ **in store 1** kept in readiness. **2** coming in the future. **3** (foll. by *for*) destined or intended. **set** (or **lay** or **put**) **store by** (or **on**) consider important or valuable. □□ **storable** *adj.* **storer** *n.* [ME f. obs. *astore* (n. & v.) f. OF *estore, estorer* f. L *instaurare* renew: cf. RESTORE]

■ *n.* **1** supply, inventory, collection, accumulation, stock, stockpile, reservoir, reserve, hoard, cache, fund, quantity, wealth, mine. **2** (*stores*) **a** see PROVISION *n.* 2. **b** see STOREHOUSE. **3 a** department store, emporium. **b** shop, market, retailer, outlet, cooperative (store), supermarket, esp. *Brit.* warehouse, *Brit.* hypermarket. ● *v.* **1** keep, hold, stow (away), preserve, warehouse, house. **2** stock, collect, accumulate, put by, lay away, set aside, pile (up), stockpile, aggregate, amass, cumulate; hoard. **3** stock, supply, provide, fill. □ **in store 1** see *in reserve* (RESERVE). **2** see *impending* (IMPEND). **set** (or **lay** or **put**) **store by** (or **on**) give credence to, believe (in), have faith *or* trust in, trust (in), bank *or* rely on, depend (up)on, count on, value.

storefront /stáwrfrunt/ *n.* **1** the side of a store facing the street. **2** a room at the front of a store.

storehouse /stáwrhows/ *n.* a place where things are stored.

■ warehouse, depository, repository, storeroom, bank, store(s), depot, godown; treasury; arsenal, magazine, armory.

storekeeper /stáwrkeepər/ *n.* the owner or manager of a store.

■ **2** see DEALER.

storeman /stáwrmən/ *n.* (*pl.* **-men**) *Brit.* a person responsible for stored goods.

storeroom /stáwr-rōōm, -rŏŏm/ *n.* a room in which items are stored.

■ see WAREHOUSE *n.*

storey *Brit.* var. of STORY².

storiated /stáwreeaytid/ *adj.* decorated with historical, legendary, or emblematic designs. □□ **storiation** /-áyshən/ *n.* [shortening of HISTORIATED]

storied /stáwreed/ *adj. literary* celebrated in or associated with stories or legends.

stork /stawrk/ *n.* **1** any long-legged large wading bird of the family Ciconiidae, esp. *Ciconia ciconia* with white plumage, black wingtips, a long reddish beak, and red feet, nesting esp. on tall buildings. **2** this bird as the pretended bringer of babies. □ **stork's-bill** a plant of the genus *Pelargonium* or *Erodium*. [OE *storc*, prob. rel. to STARK (from its rigid posture)]

storm /stawrm/ *n.* & *v.* ● *n.* **1** a violent disturbance of the atmosphere with strong winds and usu. with thunder and rain or snow, etc. **2** *Meteorol.* a wind intermediate between gale and hurricane, esp. (on the Beaufort scale) of 55–72 m.p.h. **3** a violent disturbance of the established order in human affairs. **4** (foll. by *of*) **a** a violent shower of missiles or blows. **b** an outbreak of applause, indignation, hisses, etc. (*they were greeted by a storm of abuse*). **5 a** a direct assault by troops on a fortified place. **b** the capture of a place by such an assault. ● *v.* **1** *intr.* (often foll. by *at*, *away*) talk violently; rage; bluster. **2** *intr.* (usu. foll. by *in*, *out of*, etc.) move violently or angrily (*stormed out of the meeting*). **3** *tr.* attack or capture by storm. **4** *intr.* (of wind, rain, etc.) rage; be violent. □ **storm bird** = **storm petrel**. **storm cellar** an underground shelter for refuge from severe storms. **storm center 1** the point to which the wind blows spirally inward in a cyclonic storm. **2** a subject, etc., upon which agitation or disturbance is concentrated. **storm cloud 1** a heavy rain cloud. **2** a threatening state of affairs. **storm collar** a high coat collar that can be turned up and fastened. **storm door** an additional outer door for protection in bad weather or winter. **storm glass** a sealed tube containing a solution of which the clarity is thought to change when storms approach. **storming party** a detachment of troops ordered to begin an assault. **storm in a teacup** *Brit.* great excitement over a trivial matter. **storm petrel 1** a small petrel, *Hydrobates pelagicus*, of the North Atlantic, with black and white plumage. **2** a person causing unrest. **storm sail** a sail of smaller size and stouter canvas than the corresponding one used in ordinary weather. **storm signal** a device warning of an approaching storm. **storm trooper 1** *hist.* a member of the Nazi political militia. **2** a member of the shock troops. **storm troops 1** = *shock troops* (see SHOCK[1]). **2** *hist.* the Nazi political militia. **storm window** an additional outer window used like a storm door. **take by storm 1** capture by direct assault. **2** rapidly captivate (a person, audience, etc.). □□ **stormless** *adj.* **stormproof** *adj.* [OE f. Gmc]
■ *n.* **1** tempest, disturbance, turbulence; mistral, gale, whirlwind, hurricane, tornado, typhoon, cyclone; shower, cloudburst, downpour, rainstorm, deluge, monsoon, thundershower, thunderstorm, electrical storm; dust storm, sandstorm, harmattan, khamsin, sirocco; snowstorm, blizzard; hailstorm; *Austral.* willy-willy. **3** disturbance, stir, commotion, agitation, uproar, furor, to-do, tumult, *colloq.* rumpus; turbulence, strife, turmoil, disorder. **4** shower, torrent, flood, deluge, hail, volley, barrage, bombardment; outburst, outbreak, outcry, explosion, eruption, outpouring. ● *v.* **1** rage, rant, rave, bluster, fume, explode, thunder, roar, *colloq.* raise the roof, raise hell, raise Cain, raise the devil, fly off the handle, blow one's top, blow one's stack. **2** charge, stamp, stomp, ramp, march, fling, stride. **3** attack, assault, assail, raid, rush, charge, take *or* capture by storm, take over, *colloq.* blitz. **4** blow, rage, bluster, howl. □ **take by storm 1** see STORM *v.* 3 above.

stormbound /stáwrmbownd/ *adj.* prevented by storms from leaving port or continuing a voyage.

stormy /stáwrmee/ *adj.* (**stormier**, **stormiest**) **1** of or affected by storms. **2** (of a wind, etc.) violent; raging; vehement. **3** full of angry feeling or outbursts; lively; boisterous (*a stormy meeting*). □ **stormy petrel** = *storm petrel*. □□ **stormily** *adv.* **storminess** *n.*
■ **1** foul, nasty, bad, inclement, wild, rough, squally,

blustery, choppy, gusty, windy, thundery, boisterous. **2** violent, tempestuous, blustery, turbulent, wild, vehement, howling, raging, roaring. **3** violent, tempestuous, turbulent, fierce, fiery, frantic, frenetic, nerve-racking, frenzied, feverish, raving, wild, boisterous, noisy, impassioned, *joc.* lively. □□ **storminess** see *severity* (SEVERE).

story[1] /stáwree/ *n.* (*pl.* **-ies**) **1** an account of imaginary or past events; a narrative, tale, or anecdote. **2** the past course of the life of a person or institution, etc. (*my story is a strange one*). **3** (in full **story line**) the narrative or plot of a novel or play, etc. **4** facts or experiences that deserve narration. **5** *colloq.* a fib or lie. **6** a narrative or descriptive item of news. □ **the old** (or **same old**) **story** the familiar or predictable course of events. **the story goes** it is said. **to cut** (or **make**) **a long story short** a formula excusing the omission of details. [ME *storie* f. AF *estorie* (OF *estoire*) f. L *historia* (as HISTORY)]
■ **1** narrative, tale, recounting, anecdote, yarn; account, recital, chronicle, record, history; legend, myth, fairy tale *or* story, novel, novelette, romance, fable, fabliau; epic, saga, *Edda*; allegory, parable; article, piece, composition; joke, gag; mystery, detective story, thriller, horror story, *colloq.* whodunit; testimony, version, statement, representation, description, contention, assertion, allegation. **2, 4** biography, curriculum vitae, life (story); tale, yarn, saga. **3** story line, plot, scenario, (plot) outline, thread, summary, narrative. **5** fib, lie, excuse, untruth, falsehood, fabrication, *disp.* alibi; tall tale, *Austral. sl.* furphy. **6** article, piece, item, report, dispatch, news, release, information, copy, feature, *literary* tidings; scoop, exclusive.

story[2] /stáwree/ *n.* (also *Brit.* **storey**) (*pl.* **-ies**) **1** any of the parts into which a building is divided horizontally; the whole of the rooms, etc., having a continuous floor (*a third-story window*; *a house of five stories*). **2** a thing forming a horizontal division. □□ **-storied** (in *comb.*). [ME f. AL *historia* HISTORY (perh. orig. meaning a tier of painted windows or sculpture)]
■ **1** floor, level, tier.

storyboard /stáwreebawrd/ *n.* a displayed sequence of pictures, etc., outlining the plan of a movie, television advertisement, etc.

storybook /stáwreebŏŏk/ *n.* **1** a book of stories for children. **2** (*attrib.*) unreal, romantic (*a storybook ending*).

storyteller /stáwreetelər/ *n.* **1** a person who tells stories. **2** *colloq.* a liar. □□ **storytelling** *n.* & *adj.*
■ **1** see RACONTEUR. **2** see LIAR. □□ **storytelling** (*adj.*) see NARRATIVE *adj.*

stoup /stŏŏp/ *n.* (also **stoop**) **1** a basin for holy water. **2** *archaic* a flagon, beaker, or drinking vessel. [ME f. ON *staup* (= OE *stēap*) f. Gmc, rel. to STEEP[2]]
■ **1** see SINK *n.* 1. **2** see MUG[1] *n.* 1.

stout /stowt/ *adj.* & *n.* ● *adj.* **1** somewhat fat; corpulent; bulky. **2** of considerable thickness or strength (*a stout stick*). **3** brave; resolute; vigorous (*a stout fellow*; *put up stout resistance*). ● *n.* a strong dark beer brewed with roasted malt or barley. □ **a stout heart** courage; resolve. □□ **stoutish** *adj.* **stoutly** *adv.* **stoutness** *n.* [ME f. AF & dial. OF *stout* f. WG, perh. rel. to STILT]
■ *adj.* **1** fat, obese, tubby, overweight, thickset, heavyset, stocky, big, bulky, burly, corpulent, fleshy, heavy, plump, portly, rotund, *colloq.* hulking; brawny, beefy, husky, sturdy. **2** thick, fat, solid, sturdy, strong, robust, substantial. **3** valiant, brave, undaunted, dauntless, hardy, courageous, gallant, plucky, valorous, staunch, resolute, determined, steadfast, stalwart, vigorous, bold, *archaic or joc.* doughty. □□ **stoutness** see *fatness* (FAT), STRENGTH 1.

stouthearted /stówt-hártəd/ *adj.* courageous. □□ **stoutheartedly** *adj.* **stoutheartedness** *n.*
■ see BRAVE *adj.* 1. **stoutheartedness** see PLUCK *n.*

stove[1] /stōv/ *n.* & *v.* ● *n.* **1** a closed apparatus burning fuel or electricity for heating or cooking. **2** *Brit. Hort.* a hothouse with artificial heat. ● *v.tr. Brit.* force or raise (plants) in a stove. □ **stove-enamel** a heatproof enamel produced by the treatment of enameled objects in a stove. [ME = sweating room, f. MDu., MLG *stove*, OHG *stuba* f. Gmc, perh. rel. to STEW¹]

■ *n.* 1 see RANGE *n.* 6b.

stove² *past* and *past part.* of STAVE *v.*

stovepipe /stṓvpīp/ *n.* a pipe conducting smoke and gases from a stove to a chimney. □ **stovepipe hat** *colloq.* a tall silk hat.

stow /stō/ *v.tr.* 1 pack (goods, etc.) tidily and compactly. 2 *Naut.* place (a cargo or provisions) in its proper place and order. 3 fill (a receptacle) with articles compactly arranged. 4 (usu. in *imper.*) *sl.* abstain or cease from (*stow the noise!*). □ **stow away** 1 place (a thing) where it will not cause an obstruction. 2 be a stowaway on a ship, etc. 3 eat; consume (*he stowed away three servings of pie*). [ME, f. BESTOW: in Naut. use perh. infl. by Du. *stouwen*]

■ 1, 2 pack, store, load, deposit, put (away), place, tuck away, *colloq.* stash (away). 3 fill, pack, load, jam, cram. 4 see REFRAIN¹.

stowage /stṓij/ *n.* 1 the act or an instance of stowing. 2 a place for this.

stowaway /stṓəway/ *n.* a person who hides on board a ship or aircraft, etc., to get free passage.

STP *abbr.* 1 standard temperature and pressure. 2 a hallucinogen related to amphetamine.

str. *abbr.* 1 strait. 2 stroke (of an oar).

strabismus /strəbízməs/ *n. Med.* the abnormal condition of one or both eyes not correctly aligned in direction; a squint. □□ **strabismal adj. strabismic** *adj.* [mod.L f. Gk *strabismos* f. *strabizō* squint f. *strabos* squinting]

Strad /strad/ *n. colloq.* a Stradivarius. [abbr.]

straddle /strádʼl/ *v. & n.* ● *v.* 1 *tr.* **a** sit or stand across (a thing) with the legs wide apart. **b** be situated across or on both sides of (*the town straddles the border*). 2 *intr.* **a** sit or stand in this way. **b** (of the legs) be wide apart. 3 *tr.* part (one's legs) widely. 4 *tr.* drop shots or bombs short of and beyond (a target). 5 *tr.* vacillate between two policies, etc., regarding (an issue). ● *n.* 1 the act or an instance of straddling. 2 *Stock Exch.* an option giving the holder the right of either calling for or delivering stock at a fixed price. □□ **straddler** *n.* [alt. of *striddle*, back-form. f. *striddlings* astride f. *strid-* = STRIDE]

■ *v.* 1 **b** see SPAN *v.* 1, 2.

Stradivarius /strádiváireəs/ *n.* a violin or other stringed instrument made by Antonio Stradivari of Cremona (d. 1737) or his followers. [Latinized f. *Stradivari*]

strafe /strayf/ *v. & n.* ● *v.tr.* 1 bombard; harass with gunfire. 2 reprimand. 3 abuse. 4 beat soundly. ● *n.* an act of strafing. [joc. adaptation of G catchword (1914) *Gott strafe England* may God punish England]

■ *v.* 1 see PELT¹ *v.* 1. 2 see CASTIGATE. 3 see ABUSE *v.* 3. 4 see BEAT *v.* 1.

straggle /strágəl/ *v. & n.* ● *v.intr.* 1 lack or lose compactness or tidiness. 2 be or become dispersed or sporadic. 3 trail behind others in a march or race, etc. 4 (of a plant, beard, etc.) grow long and loose. ● *n.* a body or group of straggling or scattered persons or things. □□ **straggler** *n.* **straggly** *adj.* (**stragglier, straggliest**). [ME, perh. rel. to dial. *strake* go, rel. to STRETCH]

■ *v.* 1 see SPRAWL *v.* 2. 2 (be) spread (out), disperse, scatter, thin out. 3 stray, ramble, rove, prowl, range, drift, wander, meander, *sl.* mosey; see also TRAIL *v.* 4. □□ **straggler** stray; see also LAGGARD *n.* **straggly** unkempt, untidy, loose, lank, *colloq.* ratty; see also RAMBLING 3.

straight /strayt/ *adj., n., & adv.* ● *adj.* 1 **a** extending uniformly in the same direction; without a curve or bend, etc. **b** *Geom.* (of a line) lying on the shortest path between any two of its points. 2 successive; uninterrupted (*three straight wins*). 3 in proper order or place or condition; duly arranged; level; symmetrical (*is the picture straight?*; *put things straight*). 4 honest; candid; not evasive (*a straight answer*). 5 (of thinking, etc.) logical; unemotional. 6 (of drama, etc.)

serious as opposed to popular or comic; employing the conventional techniques of its art form. 7 **a** unmodified. **b** (of a drink) undiluted. 8 *Brit. colloq.* (of music) classical. 9 *colloq.* **a** (of a person, etc.) conventional or respectable. **b** heterosexual. 10 (of an arch) flat-topped. 11 (of a person's back) not bowed. 12 (of the hair) not curly or wavy. 13 (of a knee) not bent. 14 (of the legs) not bowed or knock-kneed. 15 (of a garment) not flared. 16 coming direct from its source. 17 (of an aim, look, blow, or course) going direct to the mark. ● *n.* 1 the straight part of something, esp. the concluding stretch of a racetrack. 2 a straight condition. 3 a sequence of five cards in poker. 4 *colloq.* **a** a conventional person. **b** a heterosexual. ● *adv.* 1 in a straight line; direct; without deviation or circumlocution (*came straight from Paris*; *I told them straight*). 2 in the right direction; with a good aim (*shoot straight*). 3 correctly (*can't see straight*). 4 *archaic* at once or immediately. □ **go straight** live an honest life after being a criminal. **the straight and narrow** morally correct behavior. **straight angle** an angle of 180°. **straight away** at once; immediately. **straight cut** (of tobacco) cut lengthwise into long silky fibers. **straight eight** 1 an internal combustion engine with eight cylinders in line. 2 a vehicle having this. **straight eye** the ability to detect deviation from the straight. **straight face** an intentionally expressionless face, esp. avoiding a show of amusement. **straight-faced** having a straight face. **straight fight** *Brit. Polit.* a direct contest between two candidates. **straight flush** see FLUSH³. **straight from the shoulder** 1 (of a blow) well delivered. 2 (of a verbal attack) delivered in a frank or direct manner. **straight man** a comedian's stooge. **straight off** *colloq.* without hesitation, deliberation, etc. (*cannot tell you straight off*). **straight-out** 1 uncompromising. 2 straightforward; genuine. **straight razor** a razor with a straight blade that is hinged to a handle into which it can be folded. **straight up** *colloq.* 1 truthfully; honestly. 2 **a** (of food, drink, etc.) without admixture or dilution. **b** (of liquor) without ice. □□ **straightish** *adj.* **straightly** *adv.* **straightness** *n.* [ME, past part. of STRETCH]

■ *adj.* 1 direct, unbending, undeviating, unswerving, uncurved, regular, linear. 2 see SUCCESSIVE. 3 shipshape, orderly, neat, tidy, in order, arranged, organized, sorted out, straightened out; even, square, true, right, flat, smooth, horizontal, level; vertical, upright, perpendicular, plumb; symmetrical. 4 honest, frank, candid, straightforward, direct, downright, forthright, legitimate, (fair and) square, fair, equitable, just, aboveboard, upright, upstanding, respectable, decent, trustworthy, honorable, dependable, reliable; unequivocal, unambiguous, plain, simple, explicit, blunt, unembellished, unelaborated, unqualified, outright, accurate, point-blank, straight-from-the-shoulder, no-nonsense, *colloq.* upfront. 5 see LOGICAL 2, 3. 7 undiluted, neat, unmixed, pure, unadulterated, uncut, unmodified, unaltered, unalloyed, *colloq.* straight up. 9 **a** see CONSERVATIVE *adj.* 1, RESPECTABLE 3a, b. **b** heterosexual, *colloq.* hetero. 11 erect, vertical, upright, perpendicular, plumb. 16 see DIRECT *adj.* 3. 17 direct, unswerving, undeviating. ● *n.* 1 home stretch, *Brit.* home straight. 4 **a** see SQUARE *n.* 6. **b** heterosexual, *colloq.* hetero. ● *adv.* 1 directly, right, undeviatingly, unswervingly; as the crow flies, in a beeline; (straight) ahead; unequivocally, unambiguously, forthrightly, straightforwardly, point-blank, candidly, frankly, plainly, simply, in plain *or* simple English, straight from the shoulder, explicitly, outright, honestly, straight-out, *colloq.* straight up. 2 accurately, precisely. 3 properly, correctly. 4 see *straight away* below. □ **go straight** reform, mend one's ways, turn over a new leaf. **straight away** immediately, at once, without delay,

---

instantly, posthaste, summarily, directly, right (away *or* off*), promptly, right off the bat, *archaic* straight, straightway, *colloq.* p.d.q. **straight-faced** sober, staid, sedate, serious, unsmiling, unemotional, impassive, emotionless, taciturn, composed. **straight from the shoulder 2** directly, straightforwardly, candidly, frankly, honestly, openly, unabashedly, unashamedly, unambiguously, unequivocally, plainly, bluntly, man to man, (with) no holds barred, outright, without beating about the bush, without pulling (any) punches, *colloq.* straight up. **straight off** see *straight away* above. **straight up 1** see STRAIGHT *adv.* 1, *straight from the shoulder* above. **2** neat, without ice, undiluted, pure, straight.

straightaway /stráytəway/ *adj. & n.* ● *adj.* **1** (of a course, etc.) straight. **2** straightforward. *n.* a straight course, track, road, etc.

straightedge /stráytej/ *n.* a bar with one edge accurately straight, used for testing.

straighten /stráyt'n/ *v.tr. & intr.* **1** (often foll. by *out*) make or become straight. **2** (foll. by *up*) stand erect after bending. □□ **straightener** *n.*
■ **1** uncurl, untangle, disentangle, unsnarl, unravel, unkink, unbend, untwist; straighten up, tidy (up), arrange, rearrange, neaten, spruce up, put in order, clean (up); (*straighten out*) clear (up), settle, resolve, patch up, sort out, set *or* put straight, set *or* put right, set *or* put to rights, correct, adjust, rectify; reform, rehabilitate, organize, reorganize.

straightforward /stráytfáwrwərd/ *adj.* **1** honest or frank. **2** (of a task, etc.) uncomplicated. □□ **straightforwardly** *adv.* **straightforwardness** *n.*
■ **1** see HONEST *adj.* 2. **2** see EASY *adj.* 1.
□□ **straightforwardly** see HONESTLY 1. **straightforwardness** see HONESTY 2.

straightway /stráytway/ *adv. archaic* = *straight away*.

strain[1] /strayn/ *v. & n.* ● *v.* **1** *tr. & intr.* stretch tightly; make or become taut or tense. **2** *tr.* exercise (oneself, one's senses, a thing, etc.) intensely or excessively; press to extremes. **3 a** *intr.* make an intensive effort. **b** *intr.* (foll. by *after*) strive intensely for (*straining after perfection*). **4** *intr.* (foll. by *at*) tug; pull (*the dog strained at the leash*). **5** *intr.* hold out with difficulty under pressure (*straining under the load*). **6** *tr.* **a** distort from the true intention or meaning. **b** apply (authority, laws, etc.) beyond their province or in violation of their true intention. **7** *tr.* overtask or injure by overuse or excessive demands (*strain a muscle; strained their loyalty*). **8 a** *tr.* clear (a liquid) of solid matter by passing it through a sieve, etc. **b** *tr.* (foll. by *out*) filter (solids) out from a liquid. **c** *intr.* (of a liquid) percolate. **9** *tr.* hug or squeeze tightly. **10** *tr.* use (one's ears, eyes, voice, etc.) to the best of one's power. ● *n.* **1 a** the act or an instance of straining. **b** the force exerted in this. **2** an injury caused by straining a muscle, etc. **3 a** a severe demand on physical strength or resources. **b** the exertion needed to meet this (*is suffering from strain*). **4** (*in sing. or pl.*) a snatch or spell of music or poetry. **5** a tone or tendency in speech or writing (*more in the same strain*). **6** *Physics* **a** the condition of a body subjected to stress; molecular displacement. **b** a quantity measuring this, equal to the amount of deformation usu. divided by the original dimension. □ **strain every nerve** make every possible effort. **strain oneself 1** injure oneself by effort. **2** make undue efforts. □□ **strainable** *adj.* [ME f. OF *estreindre estreign*- f. L *stringere strict*- draw tight]
■ *v.* **1** stretch, crane, tense, tauten, tension; see also TIGHTEN. **2** see TAX *v.* 3. **3** try (hard), struggle, strive, labor, toil, push, make an effort, exert oneself. **4** push, pull, tug, heave, stretch, twist, wrench, struggle. **6** see STRETCH *v.* 6. **7** injure, hurt, harm, impair, damage, pull, tear, twist, sprain, wrick, wrench; stretch, force, tax, overtax, burden, overburden, overwork, overtask, overextend, push. **8 a, b** filter, sift, drain, screen, sieve, riddle; leach, winnow, separate. **c** percolate, seep, filter, drain. ● *n.* **1 a** see *exertion* (EXERT). **2** sprain, wrick, injury, damage, harm, wrench, pull. **3 a** tax,

demand, burden, stress, pressure, obligation. **b** stress, tension, pressure, overexertion, overwork; anxiety, worry. **4** air, melody, tune, song, sound, music, phrase, cadence. **5** tenor, tone, drift, inclination, tendency, quality, spirit, mood, humor, character, complexion, cast, impression, thread, vein, theme. □ **strain every nerve** move mountains, strain oneself, go all out, give it one's all, give it all one has, *colloq.* bust a gut.

strain[2] /strayn/ *n.* **1** a breed or stock of animals, plants, etc. **2** a moral tendency as part of a person's character (*a strain of aggression*). [ME, = progeny, f. OE *strēon* (recorded in *ġestrēonan* beget), rel. to L *struere* build]
■ **1** family, stock, ancestry, roots, extraction, derivation, background, heritage, descent, parentage, lineage, pedigree, bloodline, race, line, breed, variety. **2** trace, hint, suggestion, suspicion, soupçon, streak, trait, tendency, mark, indication, vestige, evidence, sign.

strained /straynd/ *adj.* **1** constrained; forced; artificial. **2** (of a relationship) mutually distrustful or tense. **3** (of an interpretation) involving an unreasonable assumption; farfetched; labored.
■ **1** labored, forced, artificial, false, constrained, stiff, self-conscious, unnatural, insincere, put-on. **2** tense, awkward, uneasy, uncomfortable, difficult, fraught, tension-ridden. **3** see *far-fetched*.

strainer /stráynər/ *n.* a device for straining liquids, vegetables, etc.

strait /strayt/ *n. & adj.* ● *n.* **1** (*in sing. or pl.*) a narrow passage of water connecting two seas or large bodies of water. **2** (usu. in *pl.*) difficulty, trouble, or distress (usu. *in dire or desperate straits*). ● *adj. archaic* **1** narrow; limited; confined or confining. **2** strict or rigorous. □□ **straitly** *adv.* **straitness** *n.* [ME *streit* f. OF *estreit* tight, narrow f. L *strictus* STRICT]
■ *n.* **1** narrows, channel, sound, neck. **2** (*dire or desperate* or *sore straits*) bad *or* poor state, bad *or* poor condition, trouble, difficulty, distress, need, predicament, plight, mess, tight spot, *colloq.* hot water, bind, pickle, jam, fix, scrape, pretty *or* fine kettle of fish, *disp.* dilemma. ● *adj.* **1** narrow, tight, constricted, constricting, confining, confined, restricting, restricted, limited, limiting, rigorous, demanding, exacting; difficult, straitened. **2** see STRICT 1.

straiten /stráyt'n/ *v.* **1** *tr.* restrict in range or scope. **2** *tr.* (as **straitened** *adj.*) (esp. of circumstances) characterized by poverty. **3** *tr. & intr. archaic* make or become narrow.
■ **1** restrict, confine, limit. **2** (**straitened**) reduced; poverty-stricken, impoverished.

straitjacket /stráytjakit/ *n. & v.* (also **straightjacket**) ● *n.* **1** a strong garment with long arms for confining the arms of a violent prisoner, mental patient, etc. **2** restrictive measures. ● *v.tr.* (**-jacketed**, **-jacketing**) **1** restrain with a straitjacket. **2** severely restrict.

straitlaced /stráytláyst/ *adj.* (also **straightlaced**) severely virtuous; morally scrupulous; puritanical.
■ priggish, prim, conservative, old-fashioned, Victorian, old-maidish, proper, prudish, puritanical, moralistic, stuffy, strict, narrow-minded, (over)scrupulous, fussy, *colloq.* goody-goody, persnickety, *sl.* square.

strake /strayk/ *n.* **1** a continuous line of planking or plates from the stem to the stern of a ship. **2** a section of the iron rim of a wheel. [ME: prob. rel. to OE *streccan* STRETCH]

stramonium /strəmṓneəm/ *n.* **1** datura. **2** the dried leaves of this plant used in the treatment of asthma. [mod.L, perh. f. Tartar *turman* horse medicine]

strand[1] /strand/ *v. & n.* ● *v.* **1** *tr. & intr.* run aground. **2** *tr.* (as **stranded** *adj.*) in difficulties, esp. without money or means of transport. **3** *tr. Baseball* leave a runner on base at the end of an inning. ● *n. rhet. or poet.* the margin of a sea, lake, or river, esp. the foreshore. [OE]
■ *v.* **1** see BEACH *v.* 2. **2** (**stranded**) see *deserted* (DESERT[1] 5). ● *n.* see BEACH *n.* 1.

strand[2] /strand/ *n. & v.* ● *n.* **1** each of the threads or wires twisted around each other to make a rope or cable. **2 a** a single thread or strip of fiber. **b** a constituent filament. **3** something resembling a strand or rope (*strand of pearls*). **4**

a lock of hair. **5** an element or strain in any composite whole. ● *v.tr.* **1** break a strand in (a rope). **2** arrange in strands. [ME: orig. unkn.]

■ *n.* **1, 2** see THREAD *n.* 1. **4** see LOCK² 1a. **5** thread, element, strain; aspect.

strange /straynj/ *adj.* **1** unusual; peculiar; surprising; eccentric; novel. **2 a** (often foll. by *to*) unfamiliar; alien; foreign (*lost in a strange land*). **b** not one's own (*strange gods*). **3** (foll. by *to*) unaccustomed. **4** not at ease; out of one's element (*felt strange in such company*). □ **feel strange** be unwell. **strange particle** *Physics* an elementary particle classified as having a nonzero value for strangeness. **strange to say** it is surprising or unusual (that). □□ **strangely** *adv.* [ME f. OF *estrange* f. L *estraneus* EXTRANEOUS]

■ **1** odd, peculiar, bizarre, weird, curious, uncommon, unusual, unwonted, rare, singular, exceptional, eccentric, funny, quaint, fantastic, out of the ordinary, extraordinary, out-of-the-way, far-out, offbeat, unconventional, queer, outlandish, unheard-of, grotesque, abnormal, atypical, remarkable, surprising, inexplicable, unaccountable, uncanny, novel, new, different, *colloq.* way-out, kinky, esp. *Brit. colloq.* rum, *sl.* kooky. **2** unknown, alien, foreign, exotic, new; see also UNFAMILIAR. **3** see UNACCUSTOMED 1. **4** ill at ease, uneasy, uncomfortable, awkward, out of one's element, out of place, like a fish out of water, lost, not at home. □ **feel strange** feel sick *or* ill *or* unwell *or* queasy *or* poorly, *colloq.* feel under the weather. □□ **strangely** see *notably* (NOTABLE).

strangeness /stráynjnis/ *n.* **1** the state or fact of being strange or unfamiliar, etc. **2** *Physics* a property of certain elementary particles that is conserved in strong interactions.

■ **1** see ODDITY 3.

stranger /stráynjər/ *n.* **1** a person who does not know or is not known in a particular place or company. **2** (often foll. by *to*) a person one does not know (*was a complete stranger to me*). **3** (foll. by *to*) a person entirely unaccustomed to (a feeling, experience, etc.) (*no stranger to controversy*). **4** a floating tea leaf, etc., held to foretell the arrival of a visitor. **5** *Parl.* (in the UK) a person who is not a member or official of the House of Commons. [ME f. OF *estrangier* ult. f. L (as STRANGE)]

■ **1** foreigner, outlander, outsider, alien, newcomer, visitor.

strangle /stránggəl/ *v.tr.* **1** squeeze the windpipe or neck of, esp. so as to kill. **2** hamper or suppress (a movement, impulse, cry, etc.). □□ **strangler** *n.* [ME f. OF *estrangler* f. L *strangulare* f. Gk *straggalaō* f. *straggalē* halter: cf. *straggos* twisted]

■ **1** throttle, choke, garrotte. **2** see SUPPRESS.

stranglehold /stránggəlhōld/ *n.* **1** an illegal wrestling hold that throttles an opponent. **2** a deadly grip. **3** complete and exclusive control.

strangles /stránggəlz/ *n.pl.* (usu. treated as *sing.*) an infectious streptococcal fever, esp. affecting the respiratory tract, in a horse, donkey, etc. [pl. of *strangle* (n.) f. STRANGLE]

strangulate /strángyəlayt/ *v.tr. Surgery* **1** prevent circulation through (a vein, intestine, etc.) by compression. **2** remove (a tumor, etc.) by binding with a cord. □ **strangulated hernia** *Med.* a hernia in which the protruding part is constricted, preventing circulation. [L *strangulare strangulat-* (as STRANGLE)]

strangulation /strángyəláyshən/ *n.* **1** the act of strangling or the state of being strangled. **2** the act of strangulating. [L *strangulatio* (as STRANGULATE)]

strangury /stránggyəree/ *n.* a condition in which urine is passed painfully and in drops. □□ **strangurious** /-gyŏōreeəs/ *adj.* [ME f. L *stranguria* f. Gk *straggouria* f. *stragx -ggos* drop squeezed out + *ouron* urine]

strap /strap/ *n. & v.* ● *n.* **1** a strip of leather or other flexible material, often with a buckle or other fastening for holding things together, etc. **2** a thing like this for keeping a garment in place. **3** a loop for grasping to steady oneself in a moving vehicle. **4 a** a strip of metal used to secure or connect. **b** a leaf of a hinge. **5** *Bot.* a tongue-shaped part in a floret. **6**

(prec. by *the*) punishment by beating with a strap. ● *v.tr.* (**strapped, strapping**) **1** (often foll. by *down*, *up*, etc.) secure or bind with a strap. **2** beat with a strap. **3** (esp. as **strapped** *adj.*) *colloq.* subject to a shortage. **4** *Brit.* (often foll. by *up*) close (a wound) or bind (a part) with an adhesive bandage. □ **strap-work** ornamentation imitating braided straps. □□ **strapper** *n.* **strappy** *adj.* [dial. form of STROP]

■ *n.* **1, 2** see TAPE *n.* 1. **3** see TAB¹ *n.* 1. ● *v.* **1** see CONNECT 1a, b. **2** see FLOG 1a. **3** (**strapped**) see *straitened* (STRAITEN 2).

straphanger /stráp-hangər/ *n. sl.* a standing passenger in a bus or subway, esp. a regular commuter. □□ **straphang** *v.intr.*

strapless /stráplis/ *adj.* (of a garment) without straps, esp. shoulder straps.

strappado /strəpáydō, -páa-/ *n.* (*pl.* **-os**) *hist.* **1** a form of torture in which the victim is raised from the ground by a rope and made to fall from a height almost to the ground then stopped with a jerk. **2** an application of this. **3** the instrument used. [F (*e*)*strapade* f. It. *strappata* f. *strappare* snatch]

strapping /stráping/ *adj.* (esp. of a person) large and sturdy.

■ see STURDY *adj.* 1.

strata *pl.* of STRATUM.

stratagem /strátəjəm/ *n.* **1** a cunning plan or scheme, esp. for deceiving an enemy. **2** trickery. [ME f. F *stratagème* f. L *stratagema* f. Gk *stratēgēma* f. *stratēgeō* be a general (*stratēgos*) f. *stratos* army + *agō* lead]

■ **1** trick, artifice, device, dodge, subterfuge, lure, wile, ruse, deceit, deception, plan, scheme, plot, intrigue, maneuver, tactic, *colloq.* ploy. **2** see TRICKERY.

stratal see STRATUM.

strategic /strəteéjik/ *adj.* **1** of or serving the ends of strategy; useful or important with regard to strategy (*strategic considerations*; *strategic move*). **2** (of materials) essential in fighting a war. **3** (of bombing or weapons) done or for use against an enemy's home territory as a longer-term military objective (opp. TACTICAL). □ **strategic defense initiative** a proposed US system of defense against nuclear weapons using satellites. □□ **strategical** *adj.* **strategically** *adv.* **strategics** *n.pl.* (usu. treated as *sing.*). [F *stratégique* f. Gk *stratēgikos* (as STRATAGEM)]

■ **1** calculated, planned, deliberate, politic, tactical, well-thought-out, well-considered, prudent, judicious, wise, clever.

strategy /strátijee/ *n.* (*pl.* **-ies**) **1** the art of war. **2 a** the management of an army or armies in a campaign. **b** the art of moving troops, ships, aircraft, etc., into favorable positions (cf. TACTICS). **c** an instance of this or a plan formed according to it. **3** a plan of action or policy in business or politics, etc. (*economic strategy*). □□ **strategist** *n.* [F *stratégie* f. Gk *stratēgia* generalship f. *stratēgos*: see STRATAGEM]

■ **1** generalship, military science. **2c, 3** plan, tactic(s), design, policy, procedure, approach, maneuver, scheme, blueprint, scenario, master plan, game plan. □□ **strategist** see *tactician* (TACTICS).

strath /strath/ *n. Sc.* a broad mountain valley. [Gael. *srath*]

strathspey /strathspáy/ *n.* **1** a slow Scottish dance. **2** the music for this. [*Strathspey*, valley of the river Spey]

strati *pl.* of STRATUS.

straticulate /strətikyələt/ *adj. Geol.* (of rock formations) arranged in thin strata. [STRATUM, after *vermiculate*, etc.]

stratify /strátifī/ *v.tr.* (**-ies, -ied**) **1** (esp. as **stratified** *adj.*) arrange in strata. **2** construct in layers, social grades, etc. □□ **stratification** /-fikáyshən/ *n.* [F *stratifier* (as STRATUM)]

■ □□ **stratification** see STRATUM 1–3.

stratigraphy /strətigrəfee/ *n. Geol. & Archaeol.* **1** the order and relative position of strata. **2** the study of this as a means

---

/.../ **pronunciation**	● **part of speech**
□ **phrases, idioms, and compounds**	
□□ **derivatives**	■ **synonym section**
cross-references appear in SMALL CAPITALS or *italics*	

of historical interpretation. □□ **stratigraphic** /strátigráfik/ *adj.* **stratigraphical** *adj.* [STRATUM + -GRAPHY]

strato- /strátō/ *comb. form* stratus.

stratocirrus /strátōsírəs/ *n.* clouds combining stratus and cirrus features.

stratocracy /strətókrəsee/ *n.* (*pl.* **-ies**) **1** a military government. **2** domination by soldiers. [Gk *stratos* army + -CRACY]

stratocumulus /strátōkyŏŏmyələs/ *n.* clouds combining cumulus and stratus features.

stratopause /strátōpawz/ *n.* the interface between the stratosphere and the ionosphere.

stratosphere /strátəsfeer/ *n.* **1** a layer of atmospheric air above the troposphere extending to about 50 km above the earth's surface, in which the lower part changes little in temperature and the upper part increases in temperature with height (cf. IONOSPHERE). **2** a very high or the highest place, degree, etc. □□ **stratospheric** /-feérik, -férik/ *adj.* [STRATUM + SPHERE after *atmosphere*]

stratum /stráytəm, strát-/ *n.* (*pl.* **strata** /-tə/) **1** esp. *Geol.* or *Archaeol.* a layer or set of successive layers of any deposited substance. **2** an atmospheric layer. **3** a layer of tissue, etc. **4 a** a social grade, class, etc. (*the various strata of society*). **b** *Statistics* each of the groups into which a population is divided in stratified sampling. □□ **stratal** *adj.* [L, = something spread or laid down, neut. past part. of *sternere* strew]

■ **1–3** layer, level, stratification; lamina, sheet, thickness, vein, seam; table, plane. **4 a** level, caste, class, rank, echelon, station, status, standing, bracket, group, *archaic or literary* estate.

stratus /stráytəs, strát-/ *n.* (*pl.* **strati** /-tī/) a continuous horizontal sheet of cloud. [L, past part. of *sternere*: see STRATUM]

straw /straw/ *n.* **1** dry cut stalks of grain for use as fodder or as material for thatching, packing, making hats, etc. **2** a single stalk or piece of straw. **3** a thin hollow paper or plastic tube for sucking a drink from a glass, etc. **4** an insignificant thing (*not worth a straw*). **5** the pale yellow color of straw. **6** a straw hat. □ **catch** (or **grasp**) **at straws** resort to an utterly inadequate expedient in desperation, like a person drowning. **straw boss** an assistant foreman. **straw-color** pale yellow. **straw-colored** of pale yellow. **straw in the wind** a slight hint of future developments. **straw man 1** an insubstantial person; an imaginary person set up as an opponent. **2** a stuffed effigy. **3** a person undertaking a financial commitment without adequate means. **straw vote** (or **poll**) an unofficial ballot as a test of opinion. **straw-worm** a caddisworm. □□ **strawy** *adj.* [OE *strēaw* f. Gmc, rel. to STREW]

■ **4** see PIN *n.* 3. □ **straw boss** see FOREMAN.

strawberry /stráwberee/ *n.* (*pl.* **-ies**) **1 a** any plant of the genus *Fragaria*, esp. any of various cultivated varieties, with white flowers, trifoliate leaves, and runners. **b** the pulpy red edible fruit of this, having a seed-studded surface. **2** a deep pinkish-red color. □ **strawberry blond 1** reddish blond hair. **2** a person with such hair. **strawberry mark** a soft reddish birthmark. **strawberry pear 1** a W. Indian cactaceous plant, *Hylocereus undatus*. **2** the fruit of this. **strawberry roan** see ROAN[1]. **strawberry tree** an evergreen tree, *Arbutus unedo*, bearing strawberrylike fruit. [OE *strēa(w)berige*, *strēowberige* (as STRAW, BERRY): reason for the name unkn.]

stray /stray/ *v., n., & adj.* ● *v.intr.* **1 a** wander from the right place; become separated from one's companions, etc.; go astray. **b** (often foll. by *from*, *off*) digress. **2** deviate morally. **3** (as **strayed** *adj.*) that has gone astray. ● *n.* **1** a person or thing that has strayed, esp. a domestic animal. **2** (esp. in *pl.*) electrical phenomena interfering with radio reception; static. ● *adj.* **1** strayed or lost. **2** isolated; found or occurring occasionally (*a stray customer or two; hit by a stray bullet*). **3** *Physics* wasted or unwanted (*eliminate stray magnetic fields*). □□ **strayer** *n.* [ME f. AF & OF *estrayer* (v.), AF *strey* (n. & adj.) f. OF *estraié* (as ASTRAY)]

■ *v.* **1** wander, roam, rove, range, straggle, drift, meander, go astray; deviate, diverge, digress, ramble, get *or* go off the track, get *or* go off the subject, go off on *or* at a tangent, get sidetracked, *literary* divagate. **2** see SIN[1] *v.* 1. **3** (**strayed**) see STRAY *adj.* 1 below. ● *n.*

1 straggler, vagrant, dogie. ● *adj.* **1** strayed, vagrant, lost, roving, roaming, wandering, homeless. **2** isolated, separate(d), lone, odd, single; random, casual, chance, accidental, haphazard, singular, freak, unexpected.

streak /streek/ *n. & v.* ● *n.* **1** a long thin usu. irregular line or band, esp. distinguished by color (*black with red streaks*; *a streak of light above the horizon*). **2** a strain or element in a person's character (*has a streak of mischief*). **3** a spell or series (*a winning streak*). **4** a line of bacteria, etc., placed on a culture medium. ● *v.* **1** *tr.* **a** mark with streaks. **b** lighten (strands of hair) chemically for a streaked effect. **2** *intr.* move very rapidly. **3** *intr. colloq.* run naked in a public place as a stunt. □ **streak of lightning** a sudden prominent flash of lightning. □□ **streaker** *n.* **streaking** *n.* [OE *strica* pen stroke f. Gmc: rel. to STRIKE]

■ *n.* **1** stripe, strip, stroke, bar, band, line, mark, smear, slash, dash, touch, daub, fleck, trace; vein, layer, seam, stratum, *Anat.*, *Bot.*, & *Zool.* striation. **2** see VEIN 6. **3** spell, period, stretch, run, spate, series. ● *v.* **1** stripe, line, bar, mark, smear, daub, slash, *Anat.*, *Bot.*, & *Zool.* striate. **2** race, run, rush, dash, sprint, dart, hurtle, fly, flit, speed, hasten, hurry, whistle, zip, zoom, *colloq.* whiz, tear, scoot.

streaky /streékee/ *adj.* (**streakier**, **streakiest**) **1** full of streaks. **2** *Brit.* (of bacon) with alternate streaks of fat and lean. □□ **streakily** *adv.* **streakiness** *n.*

■ **1** see *mottled* (MOTTLE *v.*).

stream /streem/ *n. & v.* ● *n.* **1** a flowing body of water, esp. a small river. **2 a** the flow of a fluid or of a mass of people (*a stream of lava*). **b** (in *sing.* or *pl.*) a large quantity of something that flows or moves along. **3** a current or direction in which things are moving or tending (*against the stream*). **4** *Brit.* a group of schoolchildren taught together as being of similar ability for a given age. ● *v.* **1** *intr.* flow or move as a stream. **2** *intr.* run with liquid (*my eyes were streaming*). **3** *intr.* (of a banner or hair, etc.) float or wave in the wind. **4** *tr.* emit a stream of (blood, etc.). **5** *tr. Brit.* arrange (schoolchildren) in streams. □ **go with the stream** *Brit.* do as others do. **on stream** (of a factory, etc.) in operation. **stream anchor** an anchor intermediate in size between a bower and a kedge, esp. for use in warping. **stream of consciousness 1** *Psychol.* a person's thoughts and conscious reactions to events perceived as a continuous flow. **2** a literary style depicting events in such a flow in the mind of a character. □□ **streamless** *adj.* **streamlet** *n.* [OE *strēam* f. Gmc]

■ *n.* **1** brook, brooklet, streamlet, rivulet, river, tributary, branch, freshet, run, watercourse, waterway, channel, runlet, rill, creek, runnel, anabranch, *dial.* kill, *No. of Engl.* beck, *Sc.* burn. **2** flow, current, outpouring, effluence, efflux, effusion, rush, spurt, surge, fountain, geyser, gush, torrent, flood, deluge, shower, cataract, cascade; swarm, tide, spate, succession, series, row, line, string, chain, barrage, esp. *Brit.* queue. **3** current, course, direction, tide, mainstream; see also TREND *n.* ● *v.* **1** run, flow, course, glide, rush, slide, slip, surge; pour, issue, emanate, gush, flood, spout, well up *or* out *or* forth, squirt, spurt, shoot, jet, cascade, spill; teem, swarm; file, proceed, march, walk, move. **3** float, flutter, flap, waft, blow; see also WAVE *v.* 2.

streamer /streémər/ *n.* **1** a long narrow flag. **2** a long narrow strip of ribbon or paper, esp. in a coil that unrolls when thrown. **3** a banner headline. **4** (in *pl.*) the aurora borealis or australis.

■ **1** pennant, banner, pennon, flag, banderole, gonfalon, jack, ensign, burgee.

streamline /streémlin/ *v. & n.* ● *v.tr.* **1** give (a vehicle, etc.) the form which presents the least resistance to motion. **2** make (an organization, process, etc.) simple or more efficient or better organized. **3** (as **streamlined** *adj.*) **a** having a smooth, slender, or elongated form; aerodynamic. **b** having a simplified and more efficient structure or organization. ● *n.* **1** the natural course of water or air currents. **2** (often *attrib.*) the shape of an aircraft, car, etc., calculated to cause the least air resistance.

■ *v.* **3** (**streamlined**) **a** aerodynamic, curved,

curvilinear; smooth, flowing, sleek. **b** modernized, up-to-date, modernistic, time-saving, labor-saving, (well-)organized, efficient, automated, well-run, smooth, efficient, automated, simplified.

street /street/ *n.* **1 a** a public road in a city, town, or village. **b** this with the houses or other buildings on each side. **2** the persons who live or work on a particular street. □ **in the street 1** in the area outside the houses. **2** (of Stock Exchange business) done after closing time. **on the streets 1** living by prostitution. **2** homeless. **street Arab** *often offens.* **1** a homeless child. **2** an urchin. **streets ahead** (often foll. by *of*) *Brit. colloq.* much superior (to). **street smarts** social savvy gained from hard experience. **street value** the value of drugs sold illicitly. **take to the streets** gather outdoors in order to protest, etc. **up** (or **right up**) **a person's street** esp. *Brit.* see ALLEY. □□ **streeted** *adj.* (also in *comb.*). **streetward** *adj. & adv.* [OE *strēt* f. LL *strāta* (*via*) paved (way), fem. past part. of *sternere* lay down]

■ **1** thoroughfare, way, road, main road, roadway, avenue, concourse, boulevard, lane, drive, terrace, crescent, cul-de-sac, row, passage, alley, byway, side street, esp. *Brit.* high road. □ **on the streets 2** see HOMELESS *adj.*

streetcar /stree̅tkaar/ *n.* a commuter vehicle that operates on rails in city streets.

■ see TRAM[1].

streetwalker /stree̅twawkər/ *n.* a prostitute seeking customers in the street. □□ **streetwalking** *n. & adj.*

■ see PROSTITUTE *n.* 1a.

streetwise /stree̅twiz/ *n.* familiar with the ways of modern urban life.

■ see SMART *adj.* 1a.

strength /strengkth, strength, strenth/ *n.* **1** the state of being strong; the degree or respect in which a person or thing is strong. **2 a** a person or thing affording strength or support. **b** an attribute making for strength of character (*patience is your great strength*). **3** the number of persons present or available. **4** a full complement (*below strength*). □ **from strength** from a strong position. **from strength to strength** with ever-increasing success. **in strength** in large numbers. **on the strength of** relying on; on the basis of. **the strength of** the essence or main features of. □□ **strengthless** *adj.* [OE *strengthu* f. Gmc (as STRONG)]

■ **1** power, might, force, mightiness, robustness, toughness, stoutness, sturdiness, brawn, brawniness, muscle, sinew, vigor, energy; durability, reliability, resistance, solidity, stamina, ruggedness, endurance; fortitude, backbone, tenacity, tenaciousness, willpower, perseverance, persistence, resoluteness, resolution, pertinacity, nerve, pluck, determination, gameness, intrepidity, firmness, stability; concentration, intensity, potency, efficacy, persuasiveness, cogency, weight, convincingness, incisiveness, soundness; *colloq.* guts, grit, gutsiness, spunk. **2 a** see PILLAR 2. **b** talent, ability, aptitude, endowment, gift, strong point *or* suit, forte, asset, long suit. □ **on the strength of** on the basis of, according to, by *or* in virtue of. **the strength of** see ESSENCE 1.

strengthen /strengkthən, stren-/ *v.tr. & intr.* make or become stronger. □ **strengthen a person's hand** (or **hands**) encourage a person to vigorous action. □□ **strengthener** *n.*

■ reinforce, renew, bolster, fortify, toughen, stiffen, support, brace (up), buttress; confirm, consolidate, back up, corroborate, substantiate; step up, increase, intensify, heighten, enhance; encourage, hearten, invigorate, rejuvenate, nourish, energize, vitalize, steel, *colloq.* boost.

strenuous /strenyoōōs/ *adj.* **1** requiring or using great effort. **2** energetic or unrelaxing. □□ **strenuously** *adv.* **strenuousness** *n.* [L *strenuus* brisk]

■ **1** demanding, taxing, tough, arduous, laborious, toilsome, burdensome, tiring, exhausting, grueling, punishing, difficult, hard, uphill. **2** energetic, active, vigorous, enthusiastic, zealous, earnest, dynamic, intense, indefatigable, tireless, unremitting, persistent,

dogged, determined, tenacious, pertinacious, resolute, sincere, eager. □□ **strenuously** see HARD *adv.* 1.

strep /strep/ *n. colloq.* = STREPTOCOCCUS. **strep throat** an acute sore throat caused by hemolytic streptococci and characterized by fever and inflammation. [abbr.]

streptococcus /streptəkókəs/ *n.* (*pl.* **streptococci** /-kóksī, -kókī/) any bacterium of the genus *Streptococcus*, usu. occurring in chains, some of which cause infectious diseases. □□ **streptococcal** *adj.* [Gk *streptos* twisted f. *strephō* turn + COCCUS]

streptomycin /streptəmísin/ *n.* an antibiotic produced by the bacterium *Streptomyces griseus*, effective against many disease-producing bacteria. [Gk *streptos* (as STREPTOCOCCUS) + *mukēs* fungus]

stress /stres/ *n. & v.* ● *n.* **1 a** pressure or tension exerted on a material object. **b** a quantity measuring this. **2 a** demand on physical or mental energy. **b** distress caused by this (*suffering from stress*). **3 a** emphasis (*the stress was on the need for success*). **b** accentuation; emphasis laid on a syllable or word. **c** an accent, esp. the principal one in a word (*the stress is on the first syllable*). **4** *Mech.* force per unit area exerted between contiguous bodies or parts of a body. ● *v.tr.* **1** lay stress on; emphasize. **2** subject to mechanical or physical or mental stress. □ **lay stress on** indicate as important. □□ **stressless** *adj.* [ME f. DISTRESS, or partly f. OF *estresse* narrowness, oppression, ult. f. L *strictus* STRICT]

■ *n.* **1** see PRESSURE *n.* 1a, b, TENSION *n.* 1. **2** (stress and) strain, burden, anxiety, worry, distress, pain, grief, suffering, anguish, pressure, tenseness, tension. **3 a** emphasis, importance, weight, force, insistence. **b, c** emphasis, force, forcefulness, accentuation, accent, prominence, *Prosody* ictus. ● *v.* **1** emphasize, accent, accentuate, lay stress *or* emphasis on, underscore, underline, mark, note, make a point of, bring home, dwell on, insist on, focus on, bring into prominence, spotlight, feature, highlight. **2** strain, put under strain *or* stress, upset, disturb, burden, worry, distress, pressurize, pressure.

stressful /stresfoōl/ *adj.* causing stress; mentally tiring (*had a stressful day*). □□ **stressfully** *adv.* **stressfulness** *n.*

■ see TRYING.

stretch /strech/ *v. & n.* ● *v.* **1** *tr. & intr.* draw or be drawn or admit of being drawn out into greater length or size. **2** *tr. & intr.* make or become taut. **3** *tr. & intr.* place or lie at full length or spread out (*with a canopy stretched over them*). **4** *tr.* (also *absol.*) **a** extend (an arm, leg, etc.). **b** (often *refl.*) thrust out one's limbs and tighten one's muscles after being relaxed. **5** *intr.* have a specified length or extension; extend (*farmland stretches for many miles*). **6** *tr.* strain or exert extremely or excessively; exaggerate (*stretch the truth*). **7** *intr.* (as **stretched** *adj.*) elongated or extended. ● *n.* **1** a continuous extent or expanse or period (*a stretch of open road*). **2** the act or an instance of stretching; the state of being stretched. **3** (*attrib.*) able to stretch; elastic (*stretch fabric*). **4 a** *colloq.* a period of imprisonment. **b** a period of service. **5** the straight side of a racetrack. **6** *Naut.* the distance covered on one tack. □ **at full stretch** working to capacity. **at a stretch 1** in one continuous period (*slept for two hours at a stretch*). **2** with much effort. **stretch one's legs** exercise oneself by walking. **stretch marks** marks on the skin resulting from a gain of weight, or on the abdomen after pregnancy. **stretch out 1** *tr.* extend (a hand or foot, etc.). **2** *intr. & tr.* last for a longer period; prolong. **3** *tr.* make (money, etc.) last for a sufficient time. **stretch a point** agree to something not normally allowed. **stretch one's wings** see WING. □□ **stretchable** *adj.* **stretchability** /strechəbílitee/ *n.* **stretchy** *adj.* **stretchiness** *n.* [OE *streccan* f. WG: cf. STRAIGHT]

■ *v.* **1** distend, lengthen, elongate, widen, broaden, swell,

---

/.../ **pronunciation**	● **part of speech**
□ **phrases, idioms, and compounds**	
□□ **derivatives**	■ **synonym section**
cross-references appear in SMALL CAPITALS or *italics*	

draw *or* pull out, balloon, inflate, enlarge, expand, extend, increase, dilate, blow up. **2** see TENSE *v.* **3** see SPREAD *v.* 1a. **5** extend, reach, continue; span, spread. **6** overtax, overextend, overburden, tax; warp, strain, distort, bend, break; exaggerate, overstate. ● *n.* **1** extent, reach, span, distance, length, spread, expanse, sweep, range, area, tract, section; see also PERIOD *n.* 1. **3** (*attrib.*) see ELASTIC *adj.* 1, 2. **4** stint, period, spell, term; *colloq.* time; tour (of duty), *sl.* hitch. **5** straight. □ **stretch one's legs** (take *or* go for a) walk, (take *or* get some) exercise. **stretch out 1** see REACH *v.* 1, 2. **2** see PROLONG 1. □□ **stretchable, stretchy** see ELASTIC 1, 2. **stretchability, stretchiness** see *elasticity* (ELASTIC).

stretcher /stréchǝr/ *n. & v.* ● *n.* **1** a framework of two poles with canvas, etc., between, for carrying sick, injured, or dead persons in a lying position. **2** a brick or stone laid with its long side along the face of a wall (cf. HEADER). **3** a board in a boat against which a rower presses the feet. **4** a rod or bar as a tie between chair legs, etc. **5** a wooden frame over which a canvas is stretched ready for painting. **6** *archaic sl.* an exaggeration or lie. ● *v.tr.* (often foll. by *off*) convey (a sick or injured person) on a stretcher.
■ *n.* **1** see LITTER *n.* 4, 5.

stretto /strétō/ *adv. Mus.* in quicker time. [It., = narrow]

strew /strōō/ *v.tr.* (*past part.* **strewn** or **strewed**) **1** scatter or spread about over a surface. **2** (usu. foll. by *with*) spread (a surface) with scattered things. □□ **strewer** *n.* [OE *stre(o)wian*]
■ scatter, bestrew, sprinkle, spread, litter; disperse, toss, distribute.

stria /stríǝ/ *n.* (*pl.* **-ae** /stríee/) **1** *Anat., Zool., Bot.,* & *Geol.* **a** a linear mark on a surface. **b** a slight ridge, furrow, or score. **2** *Archit.* a fillet between the flutes of a column. [L]
■ see GROOVE *n.* 1a.

striate *adj. & v. Anat., Zool., Bot.,* & *Geol.* ● *adj.* /stríǝt/ (also **striated** /stríaytid/) marked with striae. ● *v.tr.* /stríayt/ mark with striae. □□ **striation** /stríáyshǝn/ *n.*
■ *adj.* (**striated**) see STRIPED. ● *v.* see STREAK *v.* 1.
□□ **striation** see STRIPE 1.

stricken /stríkǝn/ *adj.* **1** affected or overcome with illness or misfortune, etc. (*stricken with measles; grief-stricken*). **2** leveled with a strickle. **3** (often foll. by *from,* etc.) *Law* deleted. □ **stricken in years** *archaic* enfeebled by age. [archaic past part. of STRIKE]
■ **1** broken, crushed, demoralized, broken-hearted, grief-stricken; (*stricken by* or *with*) struck (down) by, hit by, laid low by *or* with, affected by *or* with, afflicted with, racked by *or* with, overwhelmed by *or* with, overcome by *or* with, plagued by *or* with, tormented by, troubled by, *archaic or literary* smitten by. □ **stricken in years** enfeebled, infirm, doddering, doddery, faltering, shaky, frail; see also AGED 2.

strickle /stríkǝl/ *n.* **1** a rod used in strike measure. **2** a whetting tool. [OE *stricel,* rel. to STRIKE]

strict /strikt/ *adj.* **1** precisely limited or defined; without exception or deviation (*lives in strict seclusion*). **2 a** (of a person) severe; rigorous in upholding standards of conscience or morality. **b** requiring complete compliance or exact performance; enforced rigidly (*gave strict orders*). □□ **strictness** *n.* [L *strictus* past part. of *stringere* tighten]
■ **1** rigorous, narrow, close, undeviating, confining, constricting, constrictive, rigid, defined, precise, accurate, exact, exacting, stringent, meticulous, compulsive, punctilious, finicky, finical, scrupulous, attentive, conscientious, faithful, literal, thorough, complete, *archaic* strait. **2 a** severe, austere, authoritarian, autocratic, stern, firm, hard, tough, uncompromising, inflexible, cold-blooded, tyrannical, harsh, ruthless, pitiless, unsympathetic **b** rigid, set, unalterable, invariable, hard-and-fast, tight, binding, stringent. □□ **strictness** see PRECISION 1, *severity* (SEVERE).

strictly /stríktlee/ *adv.* **1** in a strict manner. **2** (also **strictly speaking**) applying words in their strict sense (*he is, strictly, an absconder*). **3** *colloq.* definitely.

stricture /stríkchǝr/ *n.* **1** (usu. in *pl.*; often foll. by *on, upon*) a critical or censorious remark. **2** *Med.* a morbid narrowing of a canal or duct in the body. □□ **strictured** *adj.* [ME f. L *strictura* (as STRICT)]
■ **1** criticism, censure, condemnation. **2** constriction, narrowing.

stride /strīd/ *v. & n.* ● *v.* (*past* **strode** /strōd/; *past part.* **stridden** /stríd'n/) **1** *intr. & tr.* walk with long firm steps. **2** *tr.* cross with one step. **3** *tr.* bestride; straddle. ● *n.* **1 a** a single long step. **b** the length of this. **2** a person's gait as determined by the length of stride. **3** (usu. in *pl.*) progress (*has made great strides*). **4** a settled rate of progress (*get into one's stride; be thrown out of one's stride*). **5** (in *pl.*) *sl. Brit.* trousers. **6** the distance between the feet parted either laterally or as in walking. □ **take in one's stride 1** clear (an obstacle) without changing one's gait to jump. **2** manage without difficulty. □□ **strider** *n.* [OE *strīdan*]
■ *v.* **1** see WALK *v.* 1, 2. ● *n.* **1** see STEP *n.* 1a, b, 5. **2** see WALK *n.* 1. **3** (**strides**) progress, advances, steps.

strident /strīd'nt/ *adj.* loud and harsh. □□ **stridency** *n.* **stridently** *adv.* [L *stridere strident-* creak]
■ shrill, raucous, harsh, loud, clamorous, noisy, grating, stridulant, scraping, scratching, scratchy, screeching, grinding, hoarse, rough, guttural, gravelly, rasping, jarring, discordant, inconsonant, unharmonious, unmelodious, unmusical, cacophonous, croaking, creaking.

stridulate /stríjǝlayt/ *v.intr.* (of insects, esp. the cicada and grasshopper) make a shrill sound by rubbing esp. the legs or wing cases together. □□ **stridulant** *adj.* **stridulation** /-láyshǝn/ *n.* [F *striduler* f. L *stridulus* creaking (as STRIDENT)]

strife /strīf/ *n.* **1** conflict; struggle between opposed persons or things. **2** *Austral. colloq.* trouble of any kind. [ME f. OF *estrif:* cf. OF *estriver* STRIVE]
■ **1** discord, disharmony, disagreement, difference, conflict, rivalry, competition, contention, dispute, dissension, struggle, squabbling, bickering, arguing, quarreling; animosity, friction, hard feelings, bad feeling(s), bad blood, antagonism, ill will, hatred, enmity, hostility, unfriendliness.

strigil /stríjil/ *n.* **1** *Gk & Rom. Antiq.* a skin scraper used by bathers after exercise. **2** a structure on the leg of an insect used to clean its antennae, etc. [L *strigilis* f. *stringere* graze]

strigose /strígōs/ *adj.* **1** (of leaves, etc.) having short stiff hairs or scales. **2** (of an insect, etc.) streaked, striped, or ridged. [L *striga* swath, furrow]
■ **1** see HAIRY 1.

strike /strīk/ *v. & n.* ● *v.* (*past* **struck** /struk/; *past part.* **struck** or *archaic* **stricken** /stríkǝn/) **1 a** *tr.* subject to an impact. **b** *tr.* deliver (a blow) or inflict a blow on. **2** *tr.* come or bring sharply into contact with (*the ship struck a rock*). **3** *tr.* propel or divert with a blow (*struck the ball into the pond*). **4** *intr.* (foll. by *at*) try to hit. **5** *tr.* cause to penetrate (*struck terror into him*). **6** *tr.* ignite (a match) or produce (sparks, etc.) by rubbing. **7** *tr.* make (a coin) by stamping. **8** *tr.* produce (a musical note) by striking. **9 a** *tr.* (also *absol.*) (of a clock) indicate (the time) by the sounding of a chime, etc. **b** *intr.* (of time) be indicated in this way. **10** *tr.* **a** attack or affect suddenly (*was struck with sudden terror*). **b** (of a disease) afflict. **11** *tr.* cause to become suddenly (*was struck dumb*). **12** *tr.* reach or achieve (*strike a balance*). **13** *tr.* agree on (a bargain). **14** *tr.* assume (an attitude) suddenly and dramatically. **15** *tr.* **a** discover or come across. **b** find (oil, etc.) by drilling. **c** encounter (an unusual thing, etc.). **16** come to the attention of or appear to (*it strikes me as silly; an idea suddenly struck me*). **17 a** *intr.* (of employees) engage in a strike; cease work as a protest. **b** *tr.* act in this way against (an employer). **18 a** *tr.* lower or take down (a flag, tent, stage set, etc.). **b** *intr.* signify surrender by striking a flag; surrender. **19** *intr.* take a specified direction (*struck east*). **20** *tr.* **a** (also *absol.*) secure a hook in the mouth of (a fish) by jerking the tackle. **b** (of a fish) snatch at (bait, the hook, etc.). **21** *tr.* (of a snake) wound with its fangs. **22** *intr.* (of oysters) attach themselves to a bed. **23 a** *tr.* insert (the cutting of a plant) in soil to take root. **b** *tr.* (also *absol.*) (of a plant or cutting, etc.) put forth (roots). **24** *tr.* level (grain, etc., or the measure) in strike measure. **25** *tr.* **a** ascertain (a balance) by deducting credit or debit from the other. **b** arrive at (an average, state of balance) by equalizing all items. **26** compose (a jury) esp. by allowing both sides to reject the same number. **27** cancel; cross out. ● *n.* **1** the act or an instance of striking. **2 a** the organized refusal by employees to work until some grievance is remedied. **b** a similar refusal to participate in some other expected activity. **3** a sudden find or success (*a lucky strike*). **4** an attack, esp. from the air. **5** *Baseball* a pitched ball counted against a batter, either for failure to hit it into fair territory or because it passes through the strike zone. **6** the act of knocking down all the pins with the first ball in bowling. **7** horizontal direction in a geological structure. **8** a strickle. □ **on strike** taking part in an industrial, etc., strike. **strike at the root** (or **roots**) **of** see ROOT¹. **strike back 1** strike or attack in return. **2** (of a gas burner) burn from an internal point before the gas has become mixed with air. **strike down 1** knock down. **2** bring low; afflict (*struck down by a virus*). **strike home 1** deal an effective blow. **2** have an intended effect (*my words struck home*). **strike in 1** intervene in a conversation, etc. **2** (of a disease) attack the interior of the body from the surface. **strike it rich** *colloq.* find a source of abundance or success. **strike a light 1** produce a light by striking a match. **2** *Brit. sl.* an expression of surprise, disgust, etc. **strike lucky** esp. *Brit.* have a lucky success. **strike measure** measurement by passing a rod across the top of a heaped measure to ensure that it is exactly full. **strike off 1** remove with a stroke. **2** delete (a name, etc.) from a list. **3** produce (copies of a document). **strike oil 1** find oil by sinking a shaft. **2** attain prosperity or success. **strike out 1** hit out. **2** act vigorously. **3** delete (an item or name, etc.). **4** set off or begin (*struck out eastwards*). **5** use the arms and legs in swimming. **6** forge or devise (a plan, etc.). **7** *Baseball* **a** dismiss (a batter) by means of three strikes. **b** be dismissed in this way. **c** *sl.* fail. **strike pay** an allowance paid to strikers by their trade union. **strike through** delete (a word, etc.) with a stroke of one's pen. **strike up 1** start (an acquaintance, conversation, etc.) esp. casually. **2** (also *absol.*) begin playing (a tune, etc.). **strike upon 1** have (an idea, etc.) luckily occur to one. **2** (of light) illuminate. **strike while the iron is hot** act promptly at a good opportunity. **strike zone** *Baseball* an area between a batter's knees and armpits and over home plate through which a pitch must pass in order to be called a strike. **struck on** *Brit. colloq.* infatuated with. □□ **strikable** *adj.* [OE *strīcan* go, stroke f. WG]

■ *v.* **1** hit, deal a blow to, knock, smack, thump, trounce, crown, cuff, punch, slog, slap, spank, bash, clout; beat, hammer, belabor, batter, pummel, pommel, pelt, buffet, thrash; cudgel, bludgeon, club, whip, horsewhip, scourge, lash, cane, flog, birch, slug, *archaic or literary* smite, *colloq.* whack, thwack, sock, lambaste, bop, swipe, *sl.* belt, clobber, wallop, conk, *Austral. & NZ sl.* stoush; deliver, deal, administer, inflict, aim, direct. **2** hit, collide with, land on *or* in *or* against, smash *or* bump *or* bang *or* knock *or* ram *or* crash *or* dash into, go *or* run into. **3** see HIT *v.* 9a. **4** see SWIPE *v.* 1. **5** instill, implant, induce. **6** light, ignite. **7** impress, print, stamp, punch, mint, make. **9 a** see CHIME¹ *v.* 1. **10 a** seize, beset, overcome, attack, afflict, infect, assail; penetrate, affect, get to *or* at, hit; see also CONSUME 3. **b** afflict, affect, attack, hit, *archaic or literary* smite; see also *strike down* 2 below. **12** reach, arrive at, attain, achieve; see also REALIZE 4. **13** make, reach, attain, conclude; agree *or* settle (on), ratify, confirm. **14** assume, adopt, put on, display, affect, take on, feign. **15** encounter, come *or* happen *or* hit upon, come across, chance upon, discover, stumble on, find. **16** occur *or* come to, dawn on *or* upon, hit, register with. **17 a** walk out (of the job), go on strike, stop *or* quit working, *Brit.* come out, take industrial action. **18 a** remove, take away, take apart, dismantle, knock down; take *or* pull *or* haul down, lower. ● *n.* **1** see HIT *n.* 1a. **2** walkout, sit-down (strike), sit-in, stoppage,

Brit. industrial action. **3** see WINDFALL. **4** see ASSAULT *n.* 1, 5. □ **strike back 1** see RETALIATE 1. **strike down 1** see *knock down* 1. **2** afflict, attack, bring low, indispose, incapacitate, disable, cripple, invalid. **strike home 2** hit home. **strike in 1** see INTERVENE. **strike it rich** see *go places* (PLACE). **strike off 1, 2** cross off *or* out, cancel, scratch, obliterate, expunge, erase, eradicate, remove, blot out, delete, eliminate, rub out, wipe out. **strike out 3** see *strike off* above. **4** see START *v.* 4, 5. **strike up 1** begin, start, *formal* commence. **strike upon 1** dream up, devise, conjure up, improvise, work out, invent, contrive, come up with, hit on *or* upon, arrive at. **strike while the iron is hot** take the opportunity, seize the day, make hay while the sun shines. **struck on** infatuated with, enamored of, besotted by, impressed with, *archaic or literary* smitten by, *colloq.* bowled over by, stuck on.

strikebound /stríkbownd/ *adj.* immobilized or closed by a strike.

strikebreaker /stríkbraykər/ *n.* a person working or employed in place of others who are on strike. □□ **strikebreak** *v.intr.*
■ see *scab n.* 2.

strikeout /stríkowt/ *n. Baseball* an out charged against a batter who has three strikes and credited to the pitcher.

striker /stríkər/ *n.* **1** a person or thing that strikes. **2** an employee on strike. **3** *Sports* the player who is to strike, or who is to be the next to strike, the ball. **4** *Soccer* an attacking dplayer positioned well forward in order to score goals. **5** *Brit.* a device striking the primer in a gun.
■ **2** see PICKET *n.* 1. **4** forward.

striking /stríking/ *adj. & n.* ● *adj.* **1** impressive; attracting attention. **2** (of a clock) making a chime to indicate the hours, etc. ● *n.* the act or an instance of striking. □ **striking (strike) force** a military body ready to attack at short notice. **within striking distance** near enough to hit or achieve. □□ **strikingly** *adv.* **strikingness** *n.*
■ *adj.* **1** remarkable, astounding, astonishing, amazing, awe-inspiring, awesome, impressive, imposing, great, grand, out of the ordinary, unusual, rare, exceptional, marvelous, extraordinary, magnificent, superb, splendid, stupendous; conspicuous, noticeable, prominent, salient, pronounced, marked, arresting, telling; *colloq.* smashing, fabulous, stunning, ripsnorting, *Brit. colloq.* top-hole, *poet.* wondrous, *sl.* bang-up, *Brit. archaic sl.* ripping, topping. ● *n.* see TOLL² *n.* □□ **strikingly** see ESPECIALLY.

Strine /strin/ *n.* **1** a comic transliteration of Australian speech, e.g., *Emma Chissitt* = 'How much is it?'. **2** (esp. uneducated) Australian English. [= *Australian* in Strine]

string /string/ *n. & v.* ● *n.* **1** twine or narrow cord. **2 a** piece of this or of similar material used for tying or holding together, pulling, etc. **3** a length of catgut or wire, etc., on a musical instrument, producing a note by vibration. **4 a** (in *pl.*) the stringed instruments in an orchestra, etc. **b** (*attrib.*) relating to or consisting of stringed instruments (*string quartet*). **5** (in *pl.*) an awkward condition or complication (*the offer has no strings*). **6** a set of things strung together; a series or line of persons or things (*a string of beads; a string of oaths*). **7** a group of racehorses trained at one stable. **8** a tough piece connecting the two halves of a peapod, etc. **9** a piece of catgut, etc., interwoven with others to form the head of a tennis, etc., racket. **10** = STRINGBOARD. **11** *Sports* a group of players that normally play together as a team. ● *v.* (*past* and *past part.* **strung** /strung/) **1** *tr.* supply with a string or strings. **2** *tr.* tie with string. **3** *tr.* thread (beads, etc.) on a string. **4** *tr.* arrange in or as a string. **5** *tr.* remove the strings from (a bean, etc.). **6** *tr.* place a string ready for use on (a bow). **7** *tr. colloq.* hoax. **8** *intr.* (of glue, etc.) become stringy.

/.../ **pronunciation**	● **part of speech**
□ **phrases, idioms, and compounds**	
□□ **derivatives**	■ **synonym section**
cross-references appear in SMALL CAPITALS or *italics*	

9 *intr. Billiards* make the preliminary strokes that decide which player begins. □ **on a string** under one's control or influence. **string along** *colloq.* **1** deceive, esp. by appearing to comply with (a person). **2** (often foll. by *with*) keep company (with). **string bass** *Mus.* a double bass. **string bean 1** any of various beans eaten in their fibrous pods, esp. runner beans or snap beans. **2** *colloq.* a tall thin person. **string out** extend; prolong (esp. unduly). **string theory** *Physics* a proposed structure for the mathematical representation of elementary particles. **string tie** a very narrow necktie. **string up 1** hang up on strings, etc. **2** kill by hanging. **3** *Brit.* make tense. **string vest** a loosely-woven mesh vest. □□ **stringless** *adj.* **stringlike** *adj.* [OE *streng* f. Gmc: cf. STRONG]

■ *n.* **1** line, cord, thread, twine, fiber, rope, cable, strand, filament. **2** tie, lace, cord, line; leash, lead, leader. **5** (*strings*) conditions, stipulations, provisos, qualifications, requirements, prerequisites, terms, obligations, limitations, provisions, catches, complications, *colloq.* musts. **6** line, row, series, sequence, succession, chain, concatenation, procession, stream, run, train, file, column, esp. *Brit.* queue. ● *v.* **2** tie, join, lace. **4** line up, align, array, connect, link, join, chain together, concatenate, loop. **7** see CHEAT *v.* 1a. □ **string along 1** fool, deceive, bluff, dupe, cheat, trick, hoax; keep dangling, keep on tenterhooks, play fast and loose with. **2** (*string along with*) accompany, go *or* tag along with, keep company with, associate with, hang around with, go *or* be with. **string out** stretch, extend; prolong, drag out, protract, spin out. **string up 1** festoon, loop, drape, suspend, sling, hang, array. **2** hang, lynch. □□ **stringlike** see THIN *adj.* 2.

stringboard /stríngbawrd/ *n.* a supporting timber or skirting in which the ends of a staircase steps are set.

stringed /stringd/ *adj.* (of musical instruments) having strings (also in *comb.*: *twelve-stringed guitar*).

stringendo /strinjéndō/ *adj.* & *adv. Mus.* with increasing speed. [It. f. *stringere* press: see STRINGENT]

stringent /strínjənt/ *adj.* **1** (of rules, etc.) strict; precise; requiring exact performance; leaving no loophole or discretion. **2** (of a money market, etc.) tight; hampered by scarcity; unaccommodating; hard to operate in. □□ **stringency** *n.* **stringently** *adv.* [L *stringere* draw tight]

■ **1** see STRICT 1. □□ **stringency** see *severity* (SEVERE). **stringently** see *severely* (SEVERE).

stringer /stríngər/ *n.* **1** a longitudinal structural member in a framework, esp. of a ship or aircraft. **2** *colloq.* a newspaper correspondent not on the regular staff. **3** = STRINGBOARD.

■ **2** see CORRESPONDENT *n.*

stringhalt /strínghawlt/ *n.* spasmodic movement of a horse's hind leg.

stringy /stríngee/ *adj.* (**stringier, stringiest**) **1** (of food, etc.) fibrous; tough. **2** of or like string. **3** (of a person) tall, wiry, and thin. **4** (of a liquid) viscous; forming strings. □□ **stringily** *adv.* **stringiness** *n.*

■ **1** fibrous, chewy, sinewy, gristly, leathery, tough. **2** stringlike, ropy, threadlike, fibrous, filamentous. **3** gangling, rangy, leggy, long-legged, wiry; see also LANKY.

strip[1] /strip/ *v.* & *n.* ● *v.* (**stripped, stripping**) **1** *tr.* (often foll. by *of*) remove the clothes or covering from (a person or thing). **2** *intr.* (often foll. by *off*) undress oneself. **3** *tr.* (often foll. by *of*) deprive (a person) of property or titles. **4** *tr.* leave bare of accessories or fittings. **5** *tr.* remove bark and branches from (a tree). **6** *tr.* (often foll. by *down*) remove the accessory fittings of or take apart (a machine, etc.) to inspect or adjust it. **7** *tr.* milk (a cow) to the last drop. **8** *tr.* remove the old hair from (a dog). **9** *tr.* remove the stems from (tobacco). **10** *tr.* tear the thread from (a screw). **11** *tr.* tear the teeth from (a gearwheel). **12** *tr.* remove (paint) or remove paint from (a surface) with solvent. **13** *tr.* (often foll. by *from*) pull or tear (a covering or property, etc.) off (*stripped the masks from their faces*). **14** *intr.* (of a screw) lose its thread. **15** *intr.* (of a bullet) issue from a rifled gun without spin owing to a loss of surface. ● *n.* **1** an act of stripping,

esp. of undressing in striptease. **2** *Brit. colloq.* the identifying outfit worn by the members of a sports team while playing. □ **strip club** a club at which striptease performances are given. **strip mine** a mine worked by removing the material that overlies the ore, etc. **strip search** *n.* a search of a person involving the removal of all clothes. ● *v.tr.* search in this way. [ME f. OE *bestrīepan* plunder f. Gmc]

■ *v.* **1** disrobe, undress, strip to the skin, divest a person of clothes, *joc.* strip a person to his *or* her birthday suit; peel, skin, bare, uncover, expose, denude, lay bare, flay, excoriate; fleece, shear, pluck; defoliate. **2** get undressed, undress, undress (oneself), unclothe (oneself), shed *or* remove one's clothes, take off one's clothes, get naked, strip down to nothing, peel off one's clothes, divest oneself of one's clothes, *colloq.* strip to the buff, *joc.* strip to one's birthday suit, *literary* doff one's clothes; (do a) striptease. **3** see DEPRIVE 1. **4** clear; gut, clean out, clear out, empty. **5** decorticate, debark, denude; lop. **6** dismantle, take apart. **13** take off, peel off, remove. ● *n.* **1** striptease.

strip[2] /strip/ *n.* **1** a long narrow piece (*a strip of land*). **2** a narrow flat bar of iron or steel. **3** (in full **strip cartoon**) = *comic strip*. □ **strip light** a tubular fluorescent lamp. **strip mill** a mill in which steel slabs are rolled into strips. [ME, from or rel. to MLG *strippe* strap, thong, prob. rel. to STRIPE]

■ **1** band, ribbon, fillet, belt, swathe, stripe, slat, lath, sliver, shred.

stripe /strīp/ *n.* **1** a long narrow band or strip differing in color or texture from the surface on either side of it (*black with a red stripe*). **2** *Mil.* a chevron, etc., denoting military rank. **3** a category of character, opinion, etc. (*a man of that stripe*). **4** (usu. in *pl.*) *archaic* a blow with a scourge or lash. **5** (in *pl.*, treated as *sing.*) *colloq.* a tiger. [perh. back-form. f. *striped*: cf. MDu., MLG *strīpe*, MHG *strīfe*]

■ **1** band, bar, striation, strip, streak, vein, thread, line, stroke, slash, length, *Anat.* & *Zool.* striation. **3** style, kind, sort, class, category, type, complexion, character, nature, description, persuasion, kidney. **4** see LASH *n.* 1a.

striped /strīpt/ *adj.* marked with stripes (also in *comb.*: *red-striped*). □ **striped bass** a fish, *Morone saxatilis*, with dark stripes along its sides, used for food and game along the N. American coasts.

■ stripy, streaked, lined, banded, *Anat.* & *Zool.* striated.

stripling /strípling/ *n.* a youth not yet fully grown. [ME, prob. f. STRIP[2] + -LING[1], in the sense of having a figure not yet filled out]

■ lad, boy, adolescent, juvenile, minor, schoolboy, youngster, teenager, youth, young fellow *or* man, fledgling, *Ir.* gossoon, *colloq.* hobbledehoy, young 'un.

stripper /strípər/ *n.* **1** a person or thing that strips something. **2** a device or solvent for removing paint, etc. **3** a striptease performer.

striptease /strípteéz/ *n.* & *v.* ● *n.* an entertainment in which the performer gradually undresses before the audience. ● *v.intr.* perform a striptease. □□ **stripteaser** *n.*

stripy /strípee/ *adj.* (**stripier, stripiest**) striped; having many stripes.

strive /strīv/ *v.intr.* (*past* **strove** /strōv/; *past part.* **striven** /strívən/) **1** (often foll. by *for*, or *to* + infin.) try hard; make efforts (*strive to succeed*). **2** (often foll. by *with, against*) struggle or contend. □□ **striver** *n.* [ME f. OF *estriver*, rel. to *estrif* STRIFE]

■ **1** endeavor, strain, struggle, make an *or* every effort, take pains, attempt, work, try (hard), aim, do one's best *or* utmost; exert oneself, work at, give (it) one's all, go all out. **2** compete, contend, fight, struggle, battle.

strobe /strōb/ *n. colloq.* **1** a stroboscope. **2** a stroboscopic lamp. [abbr.]

strobila /strōbílə/ *n.* (*pl.* **strobilae** /-lee/) **1** a chain of proglottids in a tapeworm. **2** a sessile polyplike form which divides horizontally to produce jellyfish larvae. [mod.L f. Gk *strobilē* twisted lint plug f. *strephō* twist]

strobile /strṓbil, -bəl/ *n.* **1** the cone of a pine, etc. **2** the layered flower of the hop. [F *strobile* or LL *strobilus* f. Gk *strobilos* f. *strephō* twist]

strobilus /strŏbiləs/ *n.* (*pl.* **strobili** /-lī/) *Bot.* = STROBILE 1. [LL (as STROBILE)]

stroboscope /strŏbəskōp/ *n.* **1** *Physics* an instrument for determining speeds of rotation, etc., by shining a bright light at intervals so that a rotating object appears stationary. **2** a lamp made to flash intermittently, esp. for this purpose. □□ **stroboscopic** /-skópik/ *adj.* **stroboscopical** *adj.* **stroboscopically** *adv.* [Gk *strobos* whirling + -SCOPE]

strode *past* OF STRIDE.

stroganoff /strάwgənawf, strŏ-/ *adj.* (of meat) cut into strips and cooked in a sour cream sauce (*beef stroganoff*). [P. *stroganoff*, 19th-c. Russ. diplomat]

stroke /strōk/ *n.* & *v.* ● *n.* **1** the act or an instance of striking; a blow or hit (*with a single stroke*; *a stroke of lightning*). **2** a sudden disabling attack or loss of consciousness caused by an interruption in the flow of blood to the brain, esp. through thrombosis; apoplexy. **3 a** an action or movement esp. as one of a series. **b** the time or way in which such movements are done. **c** the slightest such action (*has not done a stroke of work*). **4** the whole of the motion (of a wing, oar, etc.) until the starting position is regained. **5** (in rowing) the mode or action of moving the oar (*row a fast stroke*). **6** the whole motion (of a piston) in either direction. **7** *Golf* the action of hitting (or hitting at) a ball with a club, as a unit of scoring. **8** a mode of moving the arms and legs in swimming. **9** a method of striking with the bat, etc., in games, etc. (*hits with an unorthodox stroke*). **10** a specially successful or skillful effort (*a stroke of diplomacy*). **11 a** a mark made by the movement in one direction of a pen or pencil or paintbrush. **b** a similar mark printed. **12** a detail contributing to the general effect in a description. **13** the sound made by a striking clock. **14** (in full **stroke oar**) the oar or oarsman nearest the stern, setting the time of the stroke. **15** the act or a spell of stroking. ● *v.tr.* **1** pass one's hand gently along the surface of (hair or fur, etc.); caress lightly. **2** act as the stroke of (a boat or crew). **3** hit (a ball), esp. smoothly or well. **4** *colloq.* flatter; seek to influence by flattery. □ **at a stroke** by a single action. **finishing stroke** a coup de grâce; a final and fatal stroke. **off one's stroke** not performing as well as usual. **on the stroke** punctually. **stroke of genius** an original or strikingly successful idea. **stroke of luck** (or **good luck**) an unforeseen opportune occurrence. **stroke play** *Golf* play in which the score is reckoned by counting the number of strokes taken for the round (cf. *match play* (see MATCH[1])). **stroke a person the wrong way** irritate a person. [OE *strācian* f. Gmc, rel. to STRIKE]

■ *n.* **1** blow, rap, tap, thump, knock, hit, lash, smack, slam, strike, drive, *colloq.* whack, swipe, *sl.* wallop. **2** attack, seizure, fit, apoplexy, apoplectic fit, spasm, paralytic attack *or* fit; *Med.* embolism, thrombosis, cerebrovascular accident, aneurysm, ictus. **3 a** action, motion, go, move, movement, feat, achievement. **c** bit, jot (or tittle), scrap, iota, touch, stitch. **10** achievement, accomplishment; feat, act, action, work; example; touch. **11** flourish, movement, gesture; mark, dash, sweep. **15** pat, touch, caress, rub, massage. ● *v.* **1** caress, pet, pat, fondle; massage, rub, soothe. □ **at a stroke** see *at once* 1 (ONCE). **finishing stroke** see CLINCHER. **off one's stroke** not up to par. **stroke of luck** (or **good luck**) see FLUKE[1] *n.*

stroll /strōl/ *v.* & *n.* ● *v.intr.* saunter or walk in a leisurely way. ● *n.* a short leisurely walk (*go for a stroll*). □ **strolling players** actors, musicians, etc., going from place to place to give performances. [orig. of a vagrant, prob. f. G *strollen*, *strolchen* f. *Strolch* vagabond, of unkn. orig.]

■ *v.* amble, saunter, ramble, walk, wander, promenade, meander, *sl.* mosey. ● *n.* amble, ramble, saunter, walk, wander, promenade, meander, constitutional.

stroller /strŏlər/ *n.* **1** a person who strolls. **2** a folding chair on wheels, for pushing a child in.

■ **1** see PEDESTRIAN *n.*

stroma /strŏmə/ *n.* (*pl.* **stromata** /-mətə/) *Biol.* **1** the framework of an organ or cell. **2** a fungous tissue containing

spore-producing bodies. □□ **stromatic** /-mátik/ *adj.* [mod.L f. LL f. Gk *strōma* coverlet]

strong /strawng, strong/ *adj.* & *adv.* ● *adj.* (**stronger** /strάwnggər, stróng-/; **strongest** /strάwnggist, stróng-/) **1** having the power of resistance; able to withstand great force or opposition; not easily damaged or overcome (*strong material*; *strong faith*; *a strong character*). **2** (of a person's constitution) able to overcome, or not liable to, disease. **3** (of a person's nerves) proof against fright, irritation, etc. **4** (of a patient) restored to health. **5** (of an economy) stable and prosperous; (of a market) having steadily high or rising prices. **6** capable of exerting great force or of doing much; muscular; powerful. **7** forceful or powerful in effect (*a strong wind*; *a strong protest*). **8** decided or firmly held (*a strong suspicion*; *strong views*). **9** (of an argument, etc.) convincing or striking. **10** powerfully affecting the senses or emotions (*a strong light*; *strong acting*). **11** powerful in terms of size or numbers or quality (*a strong army*). **12** capable of doing much when united (*a strong combination*). **13 a** formidable; likely to succeed (*a strong candidate*). **b** tending to assert or dominate (*a strong personality*). **14** (of a solution or drink, etc.) containing a large proportion of a substance in water or another solvent (*strong tea*). **15** *Chem.* (of an acid or base) fully ionized into cations and anions in aqueous solution. **16** (of a group) having a specified number (*200 strong*). **17** (of a voice) loud or penetrating. **18** (of food or its flavor) pungent. **19** (esp. of a person's breath) bad smelling. **20** (of a literary style) vivid and terse. **21** (of a measure) drastic. **22** *Gram.* in Germanic languages: **a** (of a verb) forming inflections by change of vowel within the stem rather than by the addition of a suffix (e.g., *swim*, *swam*). **b** (of a noun or adjective) belonging to a declension in which the stem originally ended otherwise than in -*n* (opp. WEAK 9). **23** having validity or credence (*a stong possibility*; *a strong chance*). **24** unmistakable; noticeable (*a strong resemblance*; *a strong accent*). ● *adv.* strongly (*the tide is running strong*). □ **come it strong** *Brit. colloq.* go to great lengths; use exaggeration. **come on strong** act aggressively, flamboyantly, etc. **going strong** *colloq.* continuing action vigorously; in good health. **strong-arm** using force (*strong-arm tactics*). **strong drink** see DRINK. **strong interaction** (or **force**) *Physics* interaction between certain elementary particles that is very strong but is effective only at short distances. **strong language** forceful language; swearing. **strong-minded** having determination. **strong-mindedness** determination. **strong point 1** a thing at which one excels. **2** a specially fortified defensive position. **strong stomach** a stomach not easily affected by nausea. **strong suit 1** a suit at cards in which one can take tricks. **2** a thing at which one excels. □□ **strongish** *adj.* **strongly** *adv.* [OE f. Gmc: cf. STRING]

■ *adj.* **1** solid, sturdy, substantial, stout, tough, sound, well-built, reinforced, heavy-duty, durable, indestructible, unbreakable, hardwearing. **4** see HEALTHY 1. **5** steady, stable, firm, balanced, sound, solvent, resilient, buoyant; prosperous, flourishing, thriving. **6** powerful, muscular, mighty, brawny, strapping, robust, sturdy, stalwart, burly, stout, sinewy, wiry, beefy, hefty, husky. **7** vigorous, forceful, powerful, heavy; urgent, strongly worded, emphatic, assertive; effective, efficacious, effectual, formidable. **8** firm, decided, definite, unshakable, unwavering; deep-felt, deep-seated, deep-rooted, basic, intense, fervent, fierce, passionate, deep, earnest, keen. **9** well-supported, irrefutable, well-substantiated, cogent, forceful, powerful, potent, substantial, weighty, solid, convincing, persuasive, influential, compelling, telling, striking, conclusive. **10** dazzling, glaring, bright, garish, brilliant, vivid, bold, blinding; affecting, impressive, powerful, compelling. **11** large, considerable, great,

/.../	**pronunciation**	● **part of speech**
□	**phrases, idioms, and compounds**	
□□	**derivatives**	■ **synonym section**
cross-references appear in SMALL CAPITALS or *italics*		

sizable, numerous; redoubtable, substantial, powerful, mighty, formidable; invincible, unconquerable; well-established, well-founded. **13 a** formidable, likely; competent, talented, able, experienced, efficient, capable. **b** forthright, positive, willful, forceful, impressive, dominating, assertive; self-willed, opinionated, doctrinaire, stubborn, obstinate, dogmatic. **14** concentrated, undiluted, potent, intensified; fortified, stiff, alcoholic. **16** numerically, in number, in strength. **17** see *penetrating* (PENETRATE 5b). **18** powerful, concentrated, intense, pungent, potent, sharp, piquant, acrid, heady, aromatic, fragrant, hot, spicy. **19** smelly, odoriferous, malodorous, stinking, foul, bad smelling, evil-smelling, rank, mephitic, putrid, putrescent, rotten, *archaic* miasmic, *literary* noisome. **20** pithy, forceful, racy, vigorous, sharp, trenchant, incisive, terse, vivid. **21** drastic, extreme, draconian, high-handed, severe, forceful, rigorous, harsh, stringent, aggressive, strenuous, stiff, tough, *colloq.* hard-nosed. **23** likely, substantial, good, reasonable, better than average. **24** definite, clear-cut, clear, pronounced, distinct, striking, marked, decided, unmistakable, noticeable, obvious. □ **going strong** on good form, up to par. **strong-arm** threatening, menacing, bullying, high-pressure, thuggish, violent, brutal, brutish, aggressive, terrorist, intimidating. **strong language** cursing, swearing, bad language, profanity. **strong-minded** strong-willed, obstinate, firm, determined, tenacious, uncompromising, resolute, resolved, independent. **strong-mindedness** see *tenacity* (TENACIOUS). **strong point 1** see FORTE¹. **strong suit 2** see FORTE¹. □□ **strongly** see *deeply* (DEEP), *vigorously* (VIGOROUS).

strongbox /stráwngboks, stróng-/ *n.* a strongly made small chest for valuables.
■ see SAFE *n.*

stronghold /stráwnghōld, stróng-/ *n.* **1** a fortified place. **2** a secure refuge. **3** a center of support for a cause, etc.
■ **1** fortress, bulwark, bastion, fastness, fortification, fort, citadel, garrison, castle. **2** see REFUGE 1, 2. **3** bastion, fortress, bulwark.

strongroom /stráwngrŏŏm, -rŏŏm, stróng-/ *n.* a room designed to protect valuables against fire and theft.

strontia /strónshə/ *n. Chem.* strontium oxide. [*strontian* native strontium carbonate f. Strontian in the Highland region of Scotland, where it was discovered]

strontium /stróntee∂m/ *n. Chem.* a soft silver white metallic element occurring naturally in various minerals. ¶ Symb.: **Sr.** □ **strontium 90** a radioactive isotope of strontium concentrated selectively in bones and teeth when taken into the body. **strontium oxide** a white compound used in the manufacture of fireworks. [STRONTIA + -IUM]

strop /strop/ *n. & v.* ● *n.* **1** a device, esp. a strip of leather, for sharpening razors. **2** *Naut.* a collar of leather or spliced rope or iron used for handling cargo. ● *v.tr.* (**stropped**, **stropping**) sharpen on or with a strop. [ME f. MDu., MLG *strop*, OHG *strupf*, WG f. L *stroppus*]
■ *v.* see SHARPEN.

strophanthin /strəfánthin/ *n.* a white crystalline poisonous glucoside extracted from various tropical plants of the genus *Strophanthus* and used as a heart medication. [mod.L *strophanthus* f. Gk *strophos* twisted cord + *anthos* flower]

strophe /strṓfee/ *n.* **1 a** a turn in dancing made by an ancient Greek chorus. **b** lines recited during this. **c** the first section of an ancient Greek choral ode or of one division of it. **2** a group of lines forming a section of a lyric poem. □□ **strophic** *adj.* [Gk *strophē*, lit. turning, f. *strephō* turn]

stroppy /strópee/ *adj.* (**stroppier**, **stroppiest**) *Brit. colloq.* bad-tempered; awkward to deal with. □□ **stroppily** *adv.* **stroppiness** *n.* [20th c.: perh. abbr. of OBSTREPEROUS]
■ awkward, difficult; see also PERVERSE 3.

strove *past* of STRIVE.

strow /strō/ *v.tr.* (*past part.* **strown** /strōn/ or **strowed**) *archaic* = STREW. [var. of STREW]

struck *past* and *past part.* of STRIKE.

structural /strúkchərəl/ *adj.* of, concerning, or having a structure. □ **structural engineering** the branch of civil engineering concerned with the structures of esp. large buildings, etc. **structural formula** *Chem.* a formula showing the arrangement of atoms in the molecule of a compound. **structural linguistics** the study of language as a system of interrelated elements. **structural psychology** the study of the arrangement and composition of mental states and conscious experiences. **structural steel** strong mild steel in shapes suited to construction work. □□ **structurally** *adv.*
■ see ORGANIC 5.

structuralism /strúkchərəlizəm/ *n.* **1** the doctrine that structure rather than function is important. **2** structural linguistics. **3** structural psychology. □□ **structuralist** *n. & adj.*

structure /strúkchər/ *n. & v.* ● *n.* **1 a** a whole constructed unit, esp. a building. **b** the way in which a building, etc., is constructed (*has a flimsy structure*). **2** a set of interconnecting parts of any complex thing; a framework (*the structure of a sentence*; *a new wages structure*). ● *v.tr.* give structure to; organize; frame. □□ **structured** *adj.* (also in *comb.*). **structureless** *adj.* [ME f. OF *structure* or L *structura* f. *struere struct-* build]
■ *n.* **1 a** building, edifice, house, construction. **b** construction, fabric, framework, design. **2** form, shape, configuration, construction, organization, arrangement, makeup, fabric, composition, constitution, framework, layout, order, design, formation; system, setup, mechanism, nature, character. ● *v.* construct, build, frame, organize, design, form, shape, arrange, systematize. □□ **structured** see ORGANIC 6.

strudel /strŏŏd'l/ *n.* a confection of thin pastry rolled up around a filling and baked (*apple strudel*). [G]

struggle /strúgəl/ *v. & n.* ● *v.intr.* **1** make forceful or violent efforts to get free of restraint or constriction. **2** (often foll. by *for*, or *to* + infin.) make violent or determined efforts under difficulties; strive hard (*struggled for supremacy*; *struggled to get the words out*). **3** (foll. by *with*, *against*) contend; fight strenuously (*struggled with the disease*; *struggled against superior numbers*). **4** (foll. by *along*, *up*, etc.) make one's way with difficulty (*struggled to my feet*). **5** (esp. as **struggling** *adj.*) have difficulty in gaining recognition or a living (*a struggling artist*). ● *n.* **1** the act or a spell of struggling. **2** a hard or confused contest. **3 a** determined effort under difficulties. □ **the struggle for existence** (or **life**) the competition between organisms esp. as an element in natural selection, or between persons seeking a livelihood. □□ **struggler** *n.* [ME *strugle* frequent. of uncert. orig. (perh. imit.)]
■ *v.* **1, 2** strive, strain, expend energy, exert oneself, schlep, labor, toil, wrestle, endeavor, try, attempt; wriggle, squirm, writhe, twist, worm, *colloq.* wiggle. **3** contend, fight, wrestle, battle, war, grapple; tussle, scuffle. **4** see FLOUNDER¹ *v.*, SCRAMBLE *v.* 1. ● *n.* **1, 3** effort, exertion, strain, endeavor; toil, work, labor, drudgery, schlep, *literary* travail; trial, *colloq.* grind. **2** contention, competition, contest, battle, fight, combat, tussle, scrimmage, scuffle, match, conflict, clash, encounter.

strum /strum/ *v. & n.* ● *v.tr.* (**strummed, strumming**) **1** play on (a stringed or keyboard instrument), esp. carelessly or unskillfully. **2** play (a tune, etc.) in this way. ● *n.* the sound made by strumming. □□ **strummer** *n.* [imit.: cf. THRUM¹]

struma /strŏŏmə/ *n.* (*pl.* **strumae** /-mee/) **1** *Med.* **a** = SCROFULA. **b** = GOITER. **2** *Bot.* a cushion-like swelling of an organ. □□ **strumose** *adj.* **strumous** *adj.* [L, = scrofulous tumor]

strumpet /strúmpit/ *n. archaic* or *rhet.* a prostitute. [ME: orig. unkn.]
■ see PROSTITUTE *n.* 1a.

strung *past* and *past part.* of STRING. □ **strung out** *sl.* **1 a** debilitated from long drug use. **b** addicted to a drug. **c** stupefied or agitated or incoherent from using drugs. **2** exhausted physically or emotionally.

strut /strut/ *n. & v.* ● *n.* **1** a bar forming part of a framework and designed to resist compression. **2** a strutting gait. ● *v.*

(**strutted**, **strutting**) 1 *intr.* walk with a pompous or affected stiff erect gait. 2 *tr.* brace with a strut or struts. □□ **strutter** *n.* **struttingly** *adv.* [ME 'bulge, swell, strive,' earlier *stroute* f. OE *strūtian* be rigid (?)]
■ *n.* 1 see BRACE *n.* 1b. 2 prance, swagger. ● *v.* 1 swagger, parade, promenade, prance. 2 see BRACE *v.* 2.

struthious /stroōtheeəs/ *adj.* of or like an ostrich. [L *struthio* ostrich]

strychnine /stríknīn, -nin, -neen/ *n.* a vegetable alkaloid obtained from plants of the genus *Strychnos* (esp. nux vomica), bitter and highly poisonous, formerly used as a stimulant and (in small amounts) a medication. □□ **strychnic** *adj.* [F f. L *strychnos* f. Gk *strukhnos* a kind of nightshade]

Sts. *abbr.* Saints.

Stuart /stoōərt, styoō-/ *adj.* & *n.* ● *adj.* of or relating to the royal family ruling Scotland 1371–1714 and England 1603–1649 and 1660–1714. ● *n.* a member of this family.

stub /stub/ *n.* & *v.* ● *n.* 1 the remnant of a pencil, cigarette, etc., after use. 2 part of a check, receipt, etc., retained as a record. 3 a stunted tail, etc. 4 the stump of a tree, tooth, etc. 5 (*attrib.*) going only part of the way through (*stub mortise*; *stub tenon*). ● *v.tr.* (**stubbed**, **stubbing**) 1 strike (one's toe) against something. 2 (usu. foll. by *out*) extinguish (a lighted cigarette) by pressing the lighted end against something. 3 (foll. by *up*) grub up by the roots. 4 clear (land) of stubs. □ **stub-axle** an axle supporting only one wheel of a pair. [OE *stub*, *stubb* f. Gmc]
■ *n.* 1, 4 butt (end), end, stump, tail (end), remnant, fag end. 2 esp. *Brit.* counterfoil; tally, receipt, check, ticket. ● *v.* 1 bump, knock, hit, strike. 2 (*stub out*) extinguish, put out.

stubble /stúbəl/ *n.* 1 the cut stalks of cereal plants left sticking up after the harvest. 2 **a** cropped hair or a cropped beard. **b** a short growth of unshaven hair. □□ **stubbled** *adj.* **stubbly** *adj.* [ME f. AF *stuble*, OF *estuble* f. L *stupla*, *stupula* var. of *stipula* straw]

stubborn /stúbərn/ *adj.* 1 unreasonably obstinate. 2 unyielding; obdurate; inflexible. 3 refractory; intractable. □□ **stubbornly** *adj.* **stubbornness** *n.* [ME *stiborn*, *stoburn*, etc., of unkn. orig.]
■ obstinate, unyielding, inflexible, obdurate, intransigent, intractable, uncompromising, mulish, pigheaded, adamant, bullheaded, headstrong, persistent, tenacious, pertinacious, unrelenting, dogged, determined, refractory, wayward, perverse, defiant, recalcitrant, disobedient. □□ **stubbornness** see *obstinacy* (OBSTINATE).

stubby /stúbee/ *adj.* & *n.* ● *adj.* (**stubbier**, **stubbiest**) short and thick. ● *n.* (*pl.* **-ies**) *Austral. colloq.* a small squat bottle of beer. □□ **stubbily** *adv.* **stubbiness** *n.*
■ *adj.* see SHORT *adj.* 2.

stucco /stúkō/ *n.* & *v.* ● *n.* (*pl.* **-oes**) plaster or cement used for coating wall surfaces or molding into architectural decorations. ● *v.tr.* (**-oes**, **-oed**) coat with stucco. [It., of Gmc orig.]

stuck *past* and *past part.* of STICK².

stuck-up see STICK².

stud¹ /stud/ *n.* & *v.* ● *n.* 1 a large-headed nail, boss, or knob, projecting from a surface esp. for ornament. 2 a double button esp. for use with two buttonholes in a shirt front. 3 a small object projecting slightly from a road surface as a marker, etc. 4 a rivet or crosspiece in each link of a chain cable. 5 **a** a post to which laths, plasterboard, etc., are nailed. **b** the height of a room as indicated by the length of this. 6 a metal or rubber projection on an automobile tire providing greater traction. ● *v.tr.* (**studded**, **studding**) 1 set with or as with studs. 2 (as **studded** *adj.*) (foll. by *with*) thickly set or strewn (*studded with diamonds*). 3 be scattered over or about (a surface). [OE *studu*, *stuthu* post, prop, rel. to G *stützen* to prop]
■ 1 see KNOB *n.* 1a. 5 a see BEAM *n.* 1.

stud² /stud/ *n.* 1 **a** a number of horses kept for breeding, etc. **b** a place where these are kept. 2 (in full **stud horse**) a stallion. 3 *colloq.* a young man (esp. one noted for sexual prowess). 4 (in full **stud poker**) a form of poker with bet-

ting after the dealing of successive rounds of cards face up. □ **at stud** (of a male horse) publicly available for breeding on payment of a fee. **stud farm** a place where horses are bred. [OE *stōd* f. Gmc: rel. to STAND]
■ 3 see *philanderer* (PHILANDER).

studbook /stúdbŏŏk/ *n.* a book containing the pedigrees of horses.

studding /stúding/ *n.* the woodwork of a lath-and-plaster or plasterboard wall.

studding sail /stúdingsayl, stúnsəl/ *n.* a sail set on a small extra yard and boom beyond the leech of a square sail in light winds. [16th c.: orig. uncert.: perh. f. MLG, MDu. *stōtinge* a thrusting]

student /stoōd'nt, styoōd-/ *n.* 1 a person who is studying, esp. at university or another place of higher education. 2 (*attrib.*) studying in order to become (*a student nurse*). 3 a person of studious habits. 4 *Brit.* a graduate recipient of a stipend from the foundation of a college, esp. a fellow of Christ Church, Oxford. □ **student driver** a person who is learning to drive a motor vehicle and has not yet passed a driving test. [ME f. L *studēre* f. *studium* STUDY]
■ 1 pupil, learner, undergraduate, postgraduate, schoolboy, schoolgirl, schoolchild, trainee, apprentice, disciple, protégé, *archaic* scholar. 3 *colloq.* grind, *Brit. colloq.* swot.

studio /stoōdeeō, styoō-/ *n.* (*pl.* **-os**) 1 the workroom of a painter or photographer, etc. 2 a place where movies or recordings are made or where television or radio programs are made or produced. □ **studio couch** a couch that can be converted into a bed. **studio** (**apartment**) an apartment having only one main room, a kitchenette, and bath. [It. f. L (as STUDY)]
■ 1 see STUDY *n.* 3.

studious /stoōdeeəs, styoō-/ *adj.* 1 devoted to or assiduous in study or reading. 2 studied; deliberate; painstaking (*with studious care*). 3 (foll. by *to* + infin. or *in* + verbal noun) showing care or attention. 4 (foll. by *of* + verbal noun) anxiously desirous. □□ **studiously** *adv.* **studiousness** *n.* [ME f. L *studiosus* (as STUDY)]
■ 1 scholarly, bookish, academic. 2, 3 assiduous, sedulous, diligent, industrious, attentive, careful, painstaking, thorough, deliberate, tireless; see also *studied* (STUDY *v.* 6). □□ **studiously** see *intently* (INTENT).

study /stúdee/ *n.* & *v.* ● *n.* (*pl.* **-ies**) 1 the devotion of time and attention to acquiring information or knowledge, esp. from books. 2 (in *pl.*) the pursuit of academic knowledge (*continued their studies abroad*). 3 a room used for reading, writing, etc. 4 a piece of work, esp. a drawing, done for practice or as an experiment (*a study of a head*). 5 the portrayal in literature or another art form of an aspect of behavior or character, etc. 6 a musical composition designed to develop a player's skill. 7 a thing worth observing closely (*your face was a study*). 8 a thing that has been or deserves to be investigated. 9 *Theatr.* **a** the act of memorizing a role. **b** a person who memorizes a role. 10 *archaic* a thing to be secured by pains or attention. ● *v.* (**-ies**, **-ied**) 1 *tr.* make a study of; investigate or examine (a subject) (*study law*). 2 *intr.* (often foll. by *for*) apply oneself to study. 3 *tr.* scrutinize or earnestly contemplate (*studied their faces*; *studying the problem*). 4 *tr.* try to learn (the words of one's role, etc.). 5 *tr.* take pains to achieve (a result) or pay regard to (a subject or principle, etc.). 6 *tr.* (as **studied** *adj.*) deliberate; intentional; affected (*with studied politeness*). 7 *tr.* read (a book) attentively. 8 *tr.* (foll. by *to* + infin.) *archaic* a be on the watch. **b** try constantly to manage. □ **in a brown study** in a reverie; absorbed in one's thoughts. **make a study of** investigate carefully. **study group** a group of people meeting from time to time to study a particular subject or topic.

□□ **studiedly** *adv.* **studiedness** *n.* [ME f. OF *estudie* f. L *studium* zeal, study]

■ *n.* **1, 2** learning, lessons, schooling, education, training, instruction, bookwork, work, reading, contemplation, investigation, research, cramming, *colloq.* boning up, *Brit. colloq.* swotting. **3** library, reading room, study hall, haunt, studio, retreat, den, workroom, office, *colloq.* sanctum. **4, 5** see PORTRAIT 1, 2. **8** project, program; analysis, review, examination, survey, inquiry, investigation, research, exploration. ● *v.* **1, 3** make a study of, look into *or* over *or* at, go into *or* over, scan, examine, analyze, inspect, investigate, scrutinize, survey, monitor, observe, contemplate; learn (about), read; consider, reflect on, think over *or* about, ruminate on, chew over, turn over, weigh, ponder, deliberate over *or* on *or* about, mull over, meditate on *or* about *or* over, *literary* muse about *or* on. **2** burn the midnight oil, cram, *colloq.* bone up, *Brit. colloq.* swot, *literary* lucubrate. **4** memorize, practice, rehearse, go over, run through, learn (by heart), *archaic* con; *colloq.* bone up on, *Brit. colloq.* swot (up). **5** pay *or* give regard *or* attention to, give thought to, consider. **6** (**studied**) premeditated, deliberate, calculated, measured, planned, intentional, willful, well-thought-out, conscious, contrived, feigned, affected, forced, labored. **7** see EXAMINE 1, 2. □ **in a brown study** see PENSIVE 1. **make a study of** see STUDY *v.* 1, 3 above.

stuff /stuf/ *n. & v.* ● *n.* **1** the material that a thing is made of; material that may be used for some purpose. **2** a substance or things or belongings of an indeterminate kind or a quality not needing to be specified (*there's a lot of stuff about it in the newspapers*). **3** a particular knowledge or activity (*know one's stuff*). **4** *Brit.* woolen fabric (esp. as distinct from silk, cotton, and linen). **5** valueless matter; trash; refuse; nonsense (*take that stuff away*). **6** (prec. by *the*) *a colloq.* an available supply of something, esp. alcohol or drugs. **b** *sl.* money. ● *v.* **1** *tr.* pack (a receptacle) tightly (*stuff a cushion with feathers; a head stuffed with weird notions*). **2** *tr.* (foll. by *in, into*) force or cram (a thing) (*stuffed the socks in the drawer*). **3** *tr.* fill out the skin of (an animal or bird, etc.) with material to restore the original shape (*a stuffed owl*). **4** *tr.* fill (poultry, vegetables, etc.) with a mixture, as of rice or seasoned bread crumbs, esp. before cooking. **5 a** *tr. & refl.* fill (a person or oneself) with food. **b** *tr. & intr.* eat greedily. **6** *tr.* push, esp. hastily or clumsily (*stuffed the note behind the cushion*). **7** *tr.* (usu. in *passive*; foll. by *up*) block up (a person's nose, etc.). **8** *tr. sl.* (esp. as an expression of contemptuous dismissal) dispose of as unwanted (*you can stuff the job*). **9** *tr.* place bogus votes in (a ballot box). **10** *tr. Brit. coarse sl. offens.* have sexual intercourse with (a woman). □ **bit of stuff** *Brit. sl. offens.* a woman regarded as an object of sexual desire. **do one's stuff** *colloq.* do what one has to. **get stuffed** *Brit. sl.* an exclamation of dismissal, contempt, etc. **stuff and nonsense** *Brit.* an exclamation of incredulity or ridicule. **stuffed shirt** *colloq.* a pompous person. **stuff it** *sl.* an expression of rejection or disdain. **that's the stuff** *colloq.* that is what is wanted. □□ **stuffer** *n.* (also in *comb.*). [ME *stoffe* f. OF *estoffe* (n.), *estoffer* (v.) equip, furnish f. Gk *stuphō* draw together]

■ *n.* **1** substance, material, matter, fabric, ingredients, constituents, essence, essentials, fundamentals, building blocks, makings. **2** matter, substance, material; things, articles, objects, creations, accomplishments, works; bits and pieces, goods, gear, equipment, materials, trappings, kit, tackle, accessories, paraphernalia, accoutrements, effects, belongings, possessions, impedimenta, baggage, property, chattels, lumber, junk, esp. *Brit.* rubbish, *colloq.* traps. **5** refuse, junk, esp. *Brit.* rubbish; garbage; trash; nonsense, stuff and nonsense, twaddle, humbug, bunkum, balderdash, claptrap, drivel, *colloq.* tripe, malarkey, hogwash, piffle, flapdoodle, *sl.* poppycock, bunk, baloney, bosh, bull, rot, tommyrot, *Brit. sl.* codswallop. **6 b** see MONEY 1. ● *v.* **1, 3, 4** line, fill, pack, pad. **2** jam, ram, cram, crowd, compress, pack, press, squeeze, squash, shove,

thrust, force. **5 a** fill, overfeed, satiate, glut, surfeit, pall; (*stuff oneself*) overeat, gorge, overindulge, gormandize, gluttonize, make a pig *or* hog of oneself. **b** see DEVOUR 1. **6** push, shove, thrust, *colloq.* stick, stash, *Brit. colloq.* bung. **7** (*stuff up*) clog (up), congest, block (up), bung up; choke, plug (up), obstruct, stop up. □ **get stuffed** *colloq.* shut up, *sl.* go take a running jump *or* a flying leap. **stuffed shirt** see PRIG.

stuffing /stúfing/ *n.* **1** padding used to stuff cushions, etc. **2** a mixture used to stuff poultry, vegetables, etc., esp. before cooking. □ **knock** (or **take**) **the stuffing out of** *colloq.* beat soundly; defeat. **stuffing box** a box packed with material, to allow the working of an axle while remaining airtight.

■ **1** see PAD¹ *n.* 1.

stuffy /stúfee/ *adj.* (**stuffier, stuffiest**) **1** (of a room or the atmosphere in it) lacking fresh air or ventilation; close. **2** dull or uninteresting. **3** (of a person's nose, etc.) stuffed up. **4** (of a person) dull and conventional. □□ **stuffily** *adv.* **stuffiness** *n.*

■ **1** close, airless, unventilated, oppressive, stifling, suffocating, stale, musty, fusty, moldy, mildewy, muggy, fetid, frowzy, *Brit.* frowsty. **2** dull, dreary, uninteresting; see also BORING. **3** stuffed up, blocked up, congested, clogged up. **4** pompous, pedantic, narrow-minded, self-important, self-centered, stodgy, dull, old-fogyish, old-fashioned, strait-laced, staid, conventional, prim (and proper), priggish, niminy-piminy, stilted, stiff, rigid, formal, *colloq.* uptight, *sl.* fuddy-duddy, square.

stultify /stúltifī/ *v.tr.* (**-ies, -ied**) **1** make ineffective, useless, or futile, esp. as a result of tedious routine (*stultifying boredom*). **2** cause to appear foolish or absurd. **3** negate or neutralize. □□ **stultification** /-fikáyshən/ *n.* **stultifier** *n.* [LL *stultificare* f. L *stultus* foolish]

stum /stum/ *n. & v.* ● *n.* unfermented grape juice; must. ● *v.tr.* (**stummed, stumming**) **1** prevent from fermenting, or secure (wine) against further fermentation in a cask, by the use of sulfur, etc. **2** renew the fermentation of (wine) by adding stum. [Du. *stommen* (v.), *stom* (n.) f. *stom* (adj.) dumb]

stumble /stúmbəl/ *v. & n.* ● *v.* **1** *intr.* lurch forward or have a partial fall from catching or striking or misplacing one's foot. **2** *intr.* (often foll. by *along*) walk with repeated stumbles. **3** *intr.* make a mistake or repeated mistakes in speaking, etc. **4** *intr.* (foll. by *on, upon, across*) find or encounter by chance (*stumbled on a disused well*). ● *n.* an act of stumbling. □ **stumbling block** an obstacle or circumstance causing difficulty or hesitation. □□ **stumbler** *n.* **stumblingly** *adv.* [ME *stumble* (with euphonic *b*) corresp. to Norw. *stumla*: rel. to STAMMER]

■ *v.* **1** miss one's footing, slip, trip, stagger, lurch, flounder, totter, tumble, fall, falter. **2** see HOBBLE *v.* 1. **3** pause, hesitate, stammer, stutter, blunder. **4** (*stumble on or upon or across*) chance *or* come *or* happen (up)on, hit *or* light (up)on, come *or* run across, find, discover, encounter, *colloq.* bump into. ● *n.* see TRIP *n.* 2. □ **stumbling block** impediment, obstacle, bar, block, obstruction, hurdle, hindrance, balk, barrier, difficulty, snag.

stumblebum /stúmbəlbum/ *n. colloq.* a clumsy or inept person.

stump /stump/ *n. & v.* ● *n.* **1** the projecting remnant of a cut or fallen tree. **2** the similar remnant of anything else (e.g., a branch or limb) cut off or worn down. **3** *Cricket* each of the three uprights of a wicket. **4** (in *pl.*) *joc.* the legs. **5** the stump of a tree, or other place, used by an orator to address a meeting. **6** a cylinder of rolled paper or other material with conical ends for shading, blending, softening pencil marks and other uses in drawing. ● *v.* **1** *tr.* (of a question, etc.) be too hard for; puzzle. **2** *tr.* (as **stumped** *adj.*) at a loss; baffled. **3** *tr. Cricket* (esp. of a wicket-keeper) put (a batsman) out by touching the stumps with the ball while the batsman is out of the crease. **4** *intr.* walk stiffly or noisily as on a wooden leg. **5** *tr.* (also *absol.*) traverse (a district) making political speeches. **6** *tr.* use a stump on (a drawing, line, etc.). □ **on the stump** *colloq.* engaged in political speech-making or agitation. **stump up** *Brit. colloq.* pay or produce (the money required). **up a stump** in difficulties. [ME *stompe* f. MDu. *stomp*, OHG *stumpf*]

■ *n.* **1, 2** stub, butt, end, remnant. **4** (*stumps*) see LEG *n.* 1, 3. ● *v.* **1** be beyond, mystify, confuse, perplex, bewilder, foil, puzzle, baffle, confound, dumbfound, stop, stymie, nonplus, bring up short, esp. *Brit.* catch out, *colloq.* flummox, throw. **2** (**stumped**) see *confused* (CONFUSE 4b). **5** campaign, electioneer, canvass, barnstorm. □ **stump up** pay up *or* out, contribute, donate, *colloq.* chip in, shell out, *sl.* cough up, fork out *or* up. **up a stump** see *in trouble* 1 (TROUBLE).

stumper /stúmpər/ *n. colloq.* **1** a puzzling question. **2** *Cricket* a wicket-keeper.

stumpy /stúmpee/ *adj.* (**stumpier, stumpiest**) short and thick. □□ **stumpily** *adv.* **stumpiness** *n.*

■ see STOCKY.

stun /stun/ *v.tr.* (**stunned, stunning**) **1** knock senseless; stupefy. **2** bewilder or shock. **3** (of a sound) deafen temporarily. [ME f. OF *estoner* ASTONISH]

■ **1** daze, numb, benumb, knock out; stupefy, paralyze. **2** astonish, daze, paralyze, stagger, stupefy, transfix, overcome, overwhelm, astound, jar, shock, jolt, strike dumb, dumbfound, amaze, confound, bewilder, disconcert, take a person's breath away, shake up, *colloq.* bowl over, flabbergast, *joc.* discombobulate.

stung *past* and *past part.* of STING.

stunk *past* and *past part.* of STINK.

stunner /stúnər/ *n. colloq.* a stunning person or thing.

■ see KNOCKOUT 4.

stunning /stúning/ *adj. colloq.* extremely impressive or attractive. □□ **stunningly** *adv.*

■ beautiful, dazzling, brilliant, spectacular, ravishing, sensational, extraordinary, impressive, prodigious, remarkable, marvelous, stupendous, wonderful, superb, grand, sublime, lovely, exquisite, glorious, astonishing, astounding, amazing, striking, splendid, phenomenal, staggering, overpowering, earth-shattering, earthshaking, magnificent, *colloq.* fabulous, fantastic, mind-boggling, gorgeous, divine, heavenly, super. □□ **stunningly** see *notably* (NOTABLE).

stunt[1] /stunt/ *v.tr.* **1** retard the growth or development of. **2** dwarf; cramp. □□ **stuntedness** *n.* [*stunt* foolish (now dial.), MHG *stunz*, ON *stuttr* short f. Gmc, perh. rel. to STUMP]

■ **1** impede, hamper, hinder, inhibit, slow (down), retard. **2** dwarf, cramp, limit, delimit, restrict, check, curb, stop, arrest, put an end to, end.

stunt[2] /stunt/ *n. & v.* ● *n.* **1** something unusual done to attract attention. **2** a trick or daring maneuver. **3** a display of concentrated energy. ● *v.intr.* perform stunts. □ **stunt man** (or **woman**) a man (or woman) employed to take an actor's place in performing dangerous stunts. [orig. unkn.: first used in 19th-c. US college sports]

■ *n.* **1, 2** feat, act, deed, tour de force, exploit, trick.

stupa /stóopə/ *n.* a round usu. domed building erected as a Buddhist shrine. [Skr. *stúpa*]

stupe[1] /stóop, styóop/ *n. & v.* ● *n.* a soft cloth, etc., soaked in hot water, wrung out, and applied as a poultice. ● *v.tr.* treat with this. [ME f. L f. Gk *stupē* tow]

stupe[2] /stóop, styóop/ *n. sl.* a foolish or stupid person.

stupefy /stóopifī, styóo-/ *v.tr.* (**-ies, -ied**) **1** make stupid or insensible (*stupefied with drink*). **2** stun with astonishment (*the news was stupefying*). □□ **stupefacient** /-fáyshənt/ *adj. & n.* **stupefaction** /-fákshən/ *n.* **stupefactive** *adj.* **stupefier** *n.* **stupefying** *adj.* **stupefyingly** *adv.* [F *stupéfier* f. L *stupefacere* f. *stupēre* be amazed]

■ **1** see DRUG *v.* 2b. **2** see STUN 2. □□ **stupefacient** (*adj.*) see NARCOTIC *adj.* (*n.*) see NARCOTIC *n.* **stupefaction** see *astonishment* (ASTONISH). **stupefactive** see NARCOTIC *adj.* **stupefying** see NARCOTIC *adj.*, OVERWHELMING.

stupendous /stóopéndəs, styóo-/ *adj.* amazing or prodigious, esp. in terms of size or degree (*a stupendous achievement*). □□ **stupendously** *adv.* **stupendousness** *n.* [L *stupendus* gerundive of *stupēre* be amazed at]

■ see *amazing* (AMAZE).

stupid /stóopid, styóo-/ *adj. & n.* (**stupider, stupidest**) ● *adj.* **1** unintelligent; slow-witted; foolish (*a stupid fellow*). **2** typical of stupid persons (*put it in a stupid place*). **3** uninteresting or boring. **4** in a state of stupor or lethargy. **5** obtuse; lacking in sensibility. ● *n. colloq.* a stupid person. □□ **stupidity** /-píditee/ *n.* (*pl.* **-ies**). **stupidly** *adv.* [F *stupide* or L *stupidus* (as STUPENDOUS)]

■ *adj.* **1, 5** unintelligent, fatuous, foolish, obtuse, bovine, dull, lumpish, doltish, cloddish, simple, simpleminded, *colloq.* moronic, imbecilic, cretinous; subnormal, feebleminded, weak-minded, stolid, dull-witted, thick-witted, thick-skulled, slow-witted, witless, brainless, mindless, empty-headed, featherbrained, featherheaded, oxlike, addlebrained, addled, imbecile, *colloq.* dopey, dim, dim-witted, halfwitted, thick, thickheaded, dense, pinheaded, birdbrained, *colloq.* dumb, esp. *Brit. colloq.* gormless, *sl.* boneheaded. **2** foolish, silly, frivolous, asinine, harebrained, insane, mad, scatterbrained, absurd, inane, idiotic, lunatic, ridiculous, risible, laughable, ludicrous, nonsensical, senseless, irresponsible, irrational, ill-advised, imprudent, unwise, foolhardy, half-baked, *colloq.* crazy, crackbrained, cockeyed, esp. *Brit. colloq.* daft, *sl.* cuckoo, balmy, *Brit. sl.* barmy. **3** insipid, dull, tedious, boring, tiresome, humdrum, prosaic, monotonous, unimaginative, uninspired, uninteresting, vapid, vacuous, *colloq.* ho-hum. **4** stupefied, stunned, dazed, senseless, insensible, unconscious, semiconscious, sluggish, lethargic. □□ **stupidity** fatuity, fatuousness, obtuseness, dullness, denseness, lumpishness, doltishness, simplicity, simplemindedness, feeblemindedness, weak-mindedness, stolidity, dull-wittedness, thick-wittedness, slow-wittedness, witlessness, brainlessness, mindlessness, empty-headedness, featherheadedness, *archaic* bootlessness, *colloq.* dimness, dim-wittedness, halfwittedness, thickheadedness, dopiness, imbecility, cretinism, *sl.* boneheadedness; foolishness, folly, asininity, insanity, madness, absurdity, absurdness, inanity, idiocy, silliness, ridiculousness, risibility, ludicrousness, nonsense, senselessness, irresponsibility, irrationality, foolhardiness, *colloq.* craziness. **stupidly** see MADLY 1.

stupor /stóopər, styóo-/ *n.* a dazed, torpid, or helplessly amazed state. □□ **stuporous** *adj.* [ME f. L (as STUPENDOUS)]

■ insensibility, stupefaction, torpor, torpidity, lethargy, listlessness, languor, laziness, lassitude, lifelessness, supineness, inertia; inertness, coma, trance, daze, unconsciousness, numbness. □□ **stuporous** see *lethargic* (LETHARGY).

sturdy /stɔ́rdee/ *adj. & n.* ● *adj.* (**sturdier, sturdiest**) **1** robust; strongly built. **2** vigorous and determined (*sturdy resistance*). ● *n.* vertigo in sheep caused by a tapeworm larva encysted in the brain. □□ **sturdied** *adj.* (in sense of *n.*). **sturdily** *adv.* **sturdiness** *n.* [ME 'reckless, violent,' f. OF *esturdi, estourdi* past part. of *estourdir* stun, daze ult. f. L *ex* EX-[1] + *turdus* thrush (taken as a type of drunkenness)]

■ *adj.* **1** strong, solid, stout, rugged, tough, well-built, substantial, well-made; sound, durable; strapping, muscular, powerful, brawny, burly, robust, well-muscled, athletic, hardy, husky, hefty, stocky. **2** stalwart, staunch, steadfast, resolute, firm, vigorous, determined, uncompromising, unyielding, unwavering, unswerving, unfaltering, enduring, indomitable. ● *n.* SEE VERTIGO. □□ **sturdiness** see BACKBONE 3, STRENGTH 1.

sturgeon /stɔ́rjən/ *n.* any large sharklike fish of the family Acipenseridae, etc., swimming up river to spawn, used as

---

/.../ **pronunciation**	● **part of speech**
□ **phrases, idioms, and compounds**	
□□ **derivatives**	■ **synonym section**
cross-references appear in SMALL CAPITALS or *italics*	

food and a source of caviar and isinglass. [ME f. AF *sturgeon*, OF *esturgeon* ult. f. Gmc]

Sturm und Drang /shtŏŏrm ŏŏnt dráng/ *n.* a literary and artistic movement in Germany in the late 18th c., characterized by the expression of emotional unrest and strong feeling. [G, = storm and stress]

stutter /stútər/ *v. & n.* ● *v.* **1** *intr.* stammer, esp. by involuntarily repeating the first consonants of words. **2** *tr.* (often foll. by *out*) utter (words) in this way. ● *n.* **1** the act or habit of stuttering. **2** an instance of stuttering. □□ **stutterer** *n.* **stutteringly** *adv.* [frequent. of ME (now dial.) *stut* f. Gmc]
■ *v.* see STAMMER *v.* ● *n.* see STAMMER *n.*

sty[1] /stī/ *n. & v.* ● *n.* (*pl.* **sties**) **1** a pen or enclosure for pigs. **2** a filthy room or dwelling. **3** a place of debauchery. ● *v.tr. & intr.* (**sties, stied**) lodge in a sty. [OE *stī*, prob. = *stig* hall (cf. STEWARD), f. Gmc]
■ *n.* **1** see ENCLOSURE 2. **2** slum, *colloq.* dump, hole, hellhole.

sty[2] /stī/ *n.* (also **stye**) (*pl.* **sties** or **styes**) an inflamed swelling on the edge of an eyelid. [*styany* (now dial.) = *styan eye* f. OE *stīgend* sty, lit. 'riser' f. *stīgan* rise + EYE, shortened as if = *sty on eye*]

Stygian /stíjeeən/ *adj.* **1** (in Greek mythology) of or relating to the Styx, a river in Hades. **2** *literary* dark; gloomy; indistinct. [L *stugius* f. Gk *stugios* f. *Stux -ugos* Styx f. *stugnos* hateful, gloomy]
■ **2** see GLOOMY 1.

style /stīl/ *n. & v.* ● *n.* **1** a kind or sort, esp. in regard to appearance and form (*an elegant style of house*). **2** a manner of writing or speaking or performing (*written in a florid style*; *started off in fine style*). **3** the distinctive manner of a person or school or period, esp. in relation to painting, architecture, furniture, dress, etc. **4** the correct way of designating a person or thing. **5 a** a superior quality or manner (*do it in style*). **b** = FORM *n.* 9 (*bad style*). **c** state of popularity; fashion. **6** a particular make, shape, or pattern (*in all sizes and styles*). **7** a method of reckoning dates (*old style*; *new style*). **8** = STYLUS 2. **9** the gnomon of a sundial. **10** *Bot.* the narrow extension of the ovary supporting the stigma. **11** (in *comb.*) = -WISE. ● *v.tr.* **1** design or make, etc., in a particular (esp. fashionable) style. **2** designate in a specified way. □□ **styleless** *adj.* **stylelessness** *n.* **styler** *n.* [ME f. OF *stile, style* f. L *stilus*: spelling *style* due to assoc. with Gk *stulos* column]
■ *n.* **1, 6** type, kind, variety, category, genre, sort, manner, mode, make, design, fashion, look, pattern, configuration, line, cut, shape, form, version. **2, 3** quality, character, approach, treatment, vein, coloring, spirit, mood, form, technique, way, manner, method; tenor, tone, wording, phraseology, phrasing, mode of expression, language, vocabulary, word choice, diction, sentence structure; presentation; fashion, trend, vogue, mode, look, rage, craze, fad, *colloq.* (latest) thing. **4** see NAME *n.* 1, 2. **5 a** chic, stylishness, taste, smartness, flair, dash, élan, panache, cachet, tastefulness, fashionableness, elegance, refinement, finesse, polish, sophistication, sophisticatedness, cosmopolitanism; luxury, high style, comfort, opulence, splendor; *colloq.* class, ritziness, *sl.* pizzazz. **8, 9** stylus. ● *v.* **1** fashion, design, arrange, set, do, cut, tailor, shape, form. **2** characterize, designate, denominate, call, name, term, label, tag, brand, title, *archaic* entitle.

stylet /stílit/ *n.* **1** a slender pointed instrument; a stiletto. **2** *Med.* the stiffening wire of a catheter; a probe. [F *stilet* f. It. STILETTO]

styli *pl.* of STYLUS.

stylish /stílish/ *adj.* **1** fashionable; elegant. **2** having a superior quality, manner, etc. □□ **stylishly** *adv.* **stylishness** *n.*
■ **1** chic, fashionable, smart, à la mode, modish, in style *or* fashion *or* vogue, elegant, neat, dapper; chichi, *colloq.* with it, classy, swanky, swell, natty, *Brit.* swagger, *colloq. often derog.* trendy, *sl.* snazzy, spiffy.
2 see POSH *adj.* 1. □□ **stylishness** see STYLE *n.* 5a.

stylist /stílist/ *n.* **1 a** a designer of fashionable styles, etc. **b** a hairdresser. **2 a** a writer noted for or aspiring to good literary

style. **b** (in sports or music) a person who performs with style.

stylistic /stilístik/ *adj.* of or concerning esp. literary style. □□ **stylistically** *adv.* [STYLIST + -IC, after G *stilistisch*]
■ see RHETORICAL 2, 3.

stylistics /stilístiks/ *n.* the study of literary style.

stylite /stílīt/ *n. Eccl. hist.* an ancient or medieval ascetic living on top of a pillar. [eccl.Gk *stulitēs* f. *stulos* pillar]

stylize /stílīz/ *v.tr.* (esp. as **stylized** *adj.*) paint, draw, etc., (a subject) in a conventional nonrealistic style. □□ **stylization** *n.* [STYLE + -IZE, after G *stilisieren*]

stylo /stílō/ *n.* (*pl.* **-os**) *colloq.* = STYLOGRAPH. [abbr.]

stylobate /stíləbayt/ *n. Archit.* a continuous base supporting a row of columns. [L *stylobata* f. Gk *stulobatēs* f. *stulos* pillar, *bainō* walk]

stylograph /stíləgraf/ *n.* a kind of fountain pen having a point instead of a split nib. □□ **stylographic** *adj.* [STYLUS + -GRAPH]

styloid /stíloyd/ *adj. & n.* ● *adj.* resembling a stylus or pen. ● *n.* (in full **styloid process**) a spine of bone, esp. that projecting from the base of the temporal bone. [mod.L *styloides* f. Gk *stuloeidēs* f. *stulos* pillar]

stylus /stíləs/ *n.* (*pl.* **-li** /-lī/ or **-luses**) **1 a** a hard, esp. diamond or sapphire, point following a groove in a phonoraph record and transmitting the recorded sound for reproduction. **b** a similar point producing such a groove when recording sound. **2 a** an ancient writing implement, a small rod with a pointed end for scratching letters on wax-covered tablets and a blunt end for obliterating them. **b** a thing of a similar shape esp. for engraving, tracing, etc. **3** *Computing* a pointing device used esp. with a graphics tablet. [erron. spelling of L *stilus*: cf. STYLE]

stymie /stímee/ *n. & v.* (also **stimy**) ● *n.* (*pl.* **-ies**) **1** *Golf* a situation where an opponent's ball lies between the player and the hole, forming a possible obstruction to play (*lay a stymie*). **2** a difficult situation. ● *v.tr.* (**stymies, stymied, stymying** or **stymieing**) **1** obstruct; thwart. **2** *Golf* block (an opponent, a ball, or oneself) with a stymie. [19th c.: orig. unkn.]
■ *n.* **2** see DILEMMA 3. ● *v.* **1** thwart, obstruct, block, frustrate, defeat, spike, ruin, foil, confound, stump, nonplus, hinder, impede, *colloq.* flummox, *sl.* snooker.

styptic /stíptik/ *adj. & n.* ● *adj.* (of a drug, etc.) that checks bleeding. ● *n.* a styptic drug or substance. **styptic pencil** a pencil-shaped wand containing a styptic substance used to check bleeding from minor cuts, as from shaving. [ME f. L *stypticus* f. Gk *stuptikos* f. *stuphō* contract]

styrax /stíraks/ *n.* **1** storax resin. **2** any tree or shrub of the genus *Styrax*, e.g., the storax tree. [L f. Gk *sturax*: cf. STORAX]

styrene /stíreen/ *n. Chem.* a liquid hydrocarbon easily polymerized and used in making plastics, etc. [STYRAX + -ENE]

Styrofoam /stírəfōm/ *n. propr.* a brand of expanded rigid lightweight polystyrene plastic.

suable /sóōəbəl/ *adj.* capable of being sued. □□ **suability** /-bílitee/ *n.*

suasion /swáyzhən/ *n. formal* persuasion as opposed to force (*moral suasion*). □□ **suasive** /swáysiv/ *adj.* [ME f. OF *suasion* or L *suasio* f. *suadēre suas-* urge]

suave /swaav/ *adj.* **1** (of a person) smooth; polite; sophisticated. **2** (of a wine, etc.) bland; smooth. □□ **suavely** *adv.* **suaveness** *n.* **suavity** /-vitee/ *n.* (*pl.* **-ies**). [F *suave* or L *suavis* agreeable: cf. SWEET]
■ **1** debonair, sophisticated, urbane, cosmopolitan, worldly, smooth, gracious, nonchalant, civilized, cultivated, well-bred, courteous, diplomatic, polite, charming, agreeable, affable, bland. **2** see SMOOTH *adj.* 8b. □□ **suaveness, suavity** see REFINEMENT 3.

sub /sub/ *n. & v. colloq.* ● *n.* **1** a submarine. **2** a subscription. **3** a substitute. **4** *Brit.* a subeditor. **5** *Brit. Mil.* a subaltern. **6** *Brit.* an advance or loan against expected income. ● *v.* (**subbed, subbing**) **1** *intr.* (usu. foll. by *for*) act as a substitute for a person. **2** *tr. Brit. colloq.* lend or advance (a sum) to (a person) against expected income. **3** *tr. Brit.* subedit. [abbr.]

■ *n.* **2** see SUBSCRIPTION 2. **3** see SUBSTITUTE *n.* 1a. ● *v.* **1** see SUBSTITUTE *v.*

sub- /sub, səb/ *prefix* (also **suc-** before *c*, **suf-** before *f*, **sug-** before *g*, **sup-** before *p*, **sur-** before *r*, **sus-** before *c, p, t*) **1** at or to or from a lower position (*subordinate*; *submerge*; *subtract*; *subsoil*). **2** secondary or inferior in rank or position (*subclass*; *subcommittee*; *sub-lieutenant*; *subtotal*). **3** somewhat; nearly; more or less (*subacid*; *subarctic*; *subaquatic*). **4** (forming verbs) denoting secondary action (*subdivide*; *sublet*). **5** denoting support (*subvention*). **6** *Chem.* (of a salt) basic (*subacetate*). [from or after L *sub-* f. *sub* under, close to, toward]

subabdominal /súbabdómínəl/ *adj.* below the abdomen.

subacid /súbásid/ *adj.* moderately acid or tart (*subacid fruit*; *a subacid remark*). □□ **subacidity** /súbəsíditee/ *n.* [L *subacidus* (as SUB-, ACID)]

subacute /súbəkyŏot/ *adj.* *Med.* (of a condition) between acute and chronic.

subagency /súbáyjənsee/ *n.* (*pl.* **-ies**) a secondary or subordinate agency. □□ **subagent** *n.*

subalpine /súbálpïn/ *adj.* of or situated in the higher slopes of mountains just below the timberline.

subaltern /subáwltərn/ *n.* & *adj.* ● *n. Brit. Mil.* an officer below the rank of captain, esp. a second lieutenant. ● *adj.* **1** of inferior rank. **2** /súbəltərn/ *Logic* (of a proposition) particular; not universal. [LL *subalternus* f. *alternus* ALTERNATE *adj.*]

subantarctic /súbantaárktik, -aártik/ *adj.* of or like regions immediately north of the Antarctic Circle.

subaquatic /súbəkwátik, -əkwótik/ *adj.* **1** of more or less aquatic habits or kind. **2** underwater.

subaqueous /súbáykweeəs, -ák-/ *adj.* **1** existing, formed, or taking place under water. **2** lacking in substance or strength; wishy-washy.

subarctic /súbaárktik, -aártik/ *adj.* of or like regions immediately south of the Arctic Circle.

subastral /súbástrəl/ *adj.* terrestrial.

■ see TERRESTRIAL *adj.* 1, 4.

subatomic /súbətómik/ *adj.* occurring in or smaller than an atom.

subaudition /súbawdíshən/ *n.* **1** the act of mentally supplying an omitted word or words in speech. **2** the act or process of understanding the unexpressed; reading between the lines. [LL *subauditio* f. *subaudire* understand (as SUB-, AUDITION)]

subaxillary /súbáksileree/ *adj.* **1** *Bot.* in or growing beneath the axil. **2** beneath the armpit.

subbasement /súbbaysmənt/ *n.* a story below a basement.

subbranch /súbbranch/ *n.* a secondary or subordinate branch.

subbreed /súbbreed/ *n.* a secondary or inferior breed.

subcategory /súbkátigawree/ *n.* (*pl.* **-ies**) a secondary or subordinate category. □□ **subcategorize** *v.tr.* **subcategorization** *n.*

subcaudal /súbkáwdəl/ *adj.* of or concerning the region under the tail or the back part of the body.

subclass /súbklas/ *n.* **1** a secondary or subordinate class. **2** *Biol.* a taxonomic category below a class.

subclause /súbklawz/ *n.* **1** esp. *Law* a subsidiary section of a clause. **2** *Gram.* a subordinate clause.

subclavian /súbkláyveeən/ *adj.* & *n.* ● *adj.* (of an artery, etc.) lying or extending under the collar bone. ● *n.* such an artery. [mod.L *subclavius* (as SUB-, *clavis* key): cf. CLAVICLE]

subclinical /súbklínikəl/ *adj.* *Med.* (of a disease) not yet presenting definite symptoms.

subcommissioner /súbkəmishənər/ *n.* a deputy commissioner.

subcommittee /súbkəmitee/ *n.* a secondary committee.

subcompact /səbkómpakt/ *n.* & *adj.* a car that is smaller than a compact.

subconical /súbkónikəl/ *adj.* approximately conical.

subconscious /súbkónshəs/ *adj.* & *n.* ● *adj.* of or concerning the part of the mind which is not fully conscious but influences actions, etc. ● *n.* this part of the mind. □□ **subconsciously** *adv.* **subconsciousness** *n.*

● *adj.* subliminal, unconscious, suppressed, preconscious, hidden, latent, repressed, inner, innermost, underlying, deep-rooted; intuitive, instinctive; *Psychol.* Freudian. ● *n.* unconscious, inner self, psyche, id; heart.
□□ **subconsciously** see *vaguely* (VAGUE).

subcontinent /súbkóntinənt/ *n.* **1** a large land mass, smaller than a continent. **2** a large geographically or politically independent part of a continent. □□ **subcontinental** /-nént'l/ *adj.*

subcontract *v.* & *n.* ● *v.* /súbkəntrákt/ **1** *tr.* employ a firm, etc., to do (work) as part of a larger project. **2** *intr.* make or carry out a subcontract. ● *n.* /súbkóntrakt/ a secondary contract, esp. to supply materials, labor, etc. □□ **subcontractor** /-kóntraktər/ *n.*

■ *v.* **1** see LET[1] *v.* 5.

subcontrary /súbkóntreree/ *adj.* & *n. Logic* ● *adj.* (of a proposition) incapable of being false at the same time as another. ● *n.* (*pl.* **-ies**) such a proposition. [LL *subcontrarius* (as SUB-, CONTRARY), transl. Gk *hupenantios*]

subcordate /súbkáwrdayt/ *adj.* approximately heart-shaped.

subcortical /súbkáwrtikəl/ *adj.* *Anat.* below the cortex.

subcostal /súbkóstəl/ *adj.* *Anat.* below the ribs.

subcranial /súbkráyneeəl/ *adj.* *Anat.* below the cranium.

subcritical /súbkrítikəl/ *adj.* *Physics* of less than critical mass, etc.

subculture /súbkulchər/ *n.* a cultural group within a larger culture, often having beliefs or interests at variance with those of the larger culture. □□ **subcultural** /-kúlchərəl/ *adj.*

subcutaneous /súbkyŏotáyneeəs/ *adj.* under the skin. □□ **subcutaneously** *adv.*

subdeacon /súbdeékən/ *n.* *Eccl.* a minister of the order immediately below a deacon. □□ **subdiaconate** /-dīákənayt, -nət/ *n.* **subdeaconate** /-deékənit/ *n.*

subdean /súbdeén/ *n.* an official ranking immediately below, or acting as a deputy for, a dean. □□ **subdeanery** *n.* (*pl.* **-ies**). **subdecanal** /-dikáyn'l/ *adj.*

subdelirious /súbdileereeəs/ *adj.* capable of becoming delirious; mildly delirious. □□ **subdelirium** *n.*

subdivide /súbdivíd/ *v.tr.* & *intr.* divide again after a first division. [ME f. L *subdividere* (as SUB-, DIVIDE)]

■ see DIVIDE *v.* 1, 3a.

subdivision /súbdivízhən/ *n.* **1** the act or an instance of subdividing. **2** a secondary or subordinate division. **3 a** an area of land divided into plots for sale. **b** a housing development in such an area.

■ **2** see SECTION *n.* 3, 4.

subdominant /súbdóminənt/ *n.* *Mus.* the fourth note of the diatonic scale of any key.

subdue /səbdŏo, -dyŏo/ *v.tr.* (**subdues, subdued, subduing**) **1** conquer, subjugate, or tame (an enemy, nature, one's emotions, etc.). **2** (as **subdued** *adj.*) softened; lacking in intensity; toned down (*subdued light*; *in a subdued mood*). □□ **subduable** *adj.* **subdual** *n.* [ME *sodewe* f. OF *so(u)duire* f. L *subducere* (as SUB-, *ducere* lead, bring) used with the sense of *subdere* conquer (as SUB-, *-dere* put)]

■ **1** put down, beat down, quell, repress, suppress, quash, crush, control, master, overpower, conquer, defeat, overcome, gain mastery *or* control over, gain the upper hand over, get the better of, dominate, subjugate, subject, triumph over, hold *or* keep in check, restrain, check, curb, bridle, tame, chasten, *literary* vanquish. **2** (**subdued**) quiet, mellow(ed), toned down, moderate(d), tempered, hushed, muted, softened, soft; low-key, unenthusiastic, repressed, restrained, peaceful, tranquil, placid, calm(ed), temperate, reserved; chastened, sober, sobered, solemn, saddened, dejected, sad, crestfallen, downcast, grave, serious, *colloq.* down in the mouth.

subeditor /súbéditər/ *n.* *Brit.* **1** an assistant editor. **2** a per-

---

/.../ **pronunciation**   ● **part of speech**
□ **phrases, idioms, and compounds**
□□ **derivatives**   ■ **synonym section**
cross-references appear in SMALL CAPITALS or *italics*

son who edits material for printing in a book, newspaper, etc. □□ **subedit** *v.tr.* (**-edited, -editing**). **subeditorial** /-táwreeəl/ *adj.*
■ **2** copy editor, copyreader.

suberect /súbirékt/ *adj.* (of an animal, plant, etc.) almost erect.

subereous /soōbeéreeəs/ *adj.* (also **suberic** /soōbérik/, **suberose** /soōbərōs/) **1** of or concerning cork. **2** corky. [L *suber* cork, cork oak]

subfamily /súbfamilee/ *n.* (*pl.* **-ies**) **1** *Biol.* a taxonomic category below a family. **2** any subdivision of a group.

subfloor /súbflawr/ (also **subflooring**) *n.* a foundation for a floor in a building.

subform /súbfawrm/ *n.* a subordinate or secondary form.

subfusc /súbfusk/ *adj.* & *n.* ● *adj. formal* dull; dusky; gloomy. ● *n. Brit.* formal clothing at some universities. [L *subfuscus* f. *fuscus* dark brown]
■ *adj.* see DARK *adj.* 1.

subgenus /súbjeenəs/ *n.* (*pl.* **subgenera** /-jénərə/) *Biol.* a taxonomic category below a genus. □□ **subgeneric** /-jinérik/ *adj.*

subglacial /súbgláyshəl/ *adj.* next to or at the bottom of a glacier.

subgroup /súbgroōp/ *n. Math.,* etc., a subset of a group.

subhead /súbhed/ *n.* (also **subheading**) **1** a subordinate heading or title in a chapter, article, etc. **2** a subordinate division in a classification.
■ **1** see TITLE *n.* 2.

subhuman /súbhyoŌmən/ *adj.* **1** (of an animal) closely related to humans. **2** (of behavior, intelligence, etc.) less than human.
■ **2** see ANIMAL *adj* 3.

subj. *abbr.* **1** subject. **2** subjective. **3** subjunctive.

subjacent /súbjáysənt/ *adj.* underlying; situated below. [L *subjacēre* (as SUB-, *jacēre* lie)]

subject *n., adj., adv.,* & *v.* ● *n.* /súbjikt/ **1 a** a matter, theme, etc., to be discussed, described, represented, dealt with, etc. **b** (foll. by *for*) a person, circumstance, etc., giving rise to specified feeling, action, etc. (*a subject for congratulation*). **2** a department or field of study (*his best subject is geography*). **3** *Gram.* a noun or its equivalent about which a sentence is predicated and with which the verb agrees. **4 a** any person except a monarch living under a monarchy or any other form of government (*the ruler and his subjects*). **b** any person owing obedience to another. **5** *Philos.* **a** a thinking or feeling entity; the conscious mind; the ego, esp. as opposed to anything external to the mind. **b** the central substance or core of a thing as opposed to its attributes. **6** *Mus.* a theme of a fugue or sonata; a leading phrase or motif. **7** a person of specified mental or physical tendencies (*a hysterical subject*). **8** *Logic* the part of a proposition about which a statement is made. **9 a** a person or animal undergoing treatment, examination, or experimentation. **b** a dead body for dissection. ● *adj.* /súbjikt/ **1** (often foll. by *to*) owing obedience to a government, colonizing power, force, etc.; in subjection. **2** (foll. by *to*) liable, exposed, or prone to (*is subject to infection*). **3** (foll. by *to*) conditional upon; on the assumption of (*the arrangement is subject to your approval*). ● *adv.* /súbjikt/ (foll. by *to*) conditionally upon (*subject to your consent, I propose to try again*). ● *v.tr.* /səbjékt/ **1** (foll. by *to*) make liable; expose; treat (*subjected us to hours of waiting*). **2** (usu. foll. by *to*) subdue (a nation, person, etc.) to one's control, etc. □ **subject and object** *Psychol.* the ego or self and the non-ego; consciousness and that of which it is or may be conscious. **subject catalog** a catalog, esp. in a library, arranged according to the subjects treated. **subject heading** a heading in an index collecting references to a subject. **subject matter** the matter treated of in a book, lawsuit, etc. □□ **subjection** /səbjékshən/ *n.* **subjectless** /súbjiktlis/ *adj.* [ME *soget,* etc. f. OF *suget,* etc. f. L *subjectus* past part. of *subjicere* (as SUB-, *jacere* throw)]
■ *n.* **1 a** (subject) matter, topic; issue, theme, thesis, gist, substance, business, affair, concern, point. **b** cause, ground(s), motive, reason, basis, source, rationale; excuse. **2** course (of study), field, area, discipline,

department, branch of knowledge. **4** citizen, national; taxpayer, voter; subordinate, servant, *hist.* liegeman, vassal. **6** see MOTIF. **9 a** participant, case, patient, guinea pig, testee. ● *adj.* **1** dependent, subjugated, enslaved, captive; under someone's thumb; (*subject to*) answerable to, accountable to, amenable to, responsible to, bound by, obedient to, subservient to, submissive to, controlled by, under the control of. **2** (*subject to*) exposed to, open to, vulnerable to, susceptible to, prone to, disposed to, at the mercy of, liable to (suffer or undergo). **3** (*subject to*) dependent (up)on, conditional (up)on, contingent (up)on. ● *v.* **1** (*subject to*) expose to, lay open to, submit to, treat to, put through, impose on, cause to undergo, make liable to. **2** conquer, subjugate, dominate, subdue, enslave, enthrall, crush, humble. □ **subject matter** see CONTENT² 3. □□ **subjection** subordination, domination, conquest, subjugation, enslavement, servitude, bondage, enthrallment, humbling, humiliation, *hist.* vassalage.

subjective /səbjéktiv/ *adj.* & *n.* ● *adj.* **1** (of art, literature, written history, a person's views, etc.) proceeding from personal idiosyncrasy or individuality; not impartial or literal. **2** esp. *Philos.* proceeding from or belonging to the individual consciousness or perception; imaginary, partial, or distorted. **3** *Gram.* of or concerning the subject. ● *n. Gram.* the subjective case. □ **subjective case** *Gram.* the nominative. □□ **subjectively** *adv.* **subjectiveness** *n.* **subjectivity** /subjektívitee/ *n.* [ME f. L *subjectivus* (as SUBJECT)]
■ *adj.* **1, 2** personal, individual, idiosyncratic; prejudiced, biased, partial, distorted; self-centered, egoistic, egocentric, selfish, self-serving. ● *n.* subjective case, nominative.

subjectivism /səbjéktivizəm/ *n. Philos.* the doctrine that knowledge is merely subjective and that there is no external or objective truth. □□ **subjectivist** *n.*

subjoin /súbjóyn/ *v.tr.* add or append (an illustration, anecdote, etc.) at the end. [obs. F *subjoindre* f. L *subjungere* (as SUB-, *jungere junct-* join)]
■ see SUFFIX *v.*

subjoint /súbjoynt/ *n.* a secondary joint (in an insect's leg, etc.).

sub judice /sub joŌdisee, soŌb yoŌdikay/ *adj. Law* under judicial consideration and therefore prohibited from public discussion elsewhere. [L, = under a judge]

subjugate /súbjəgayt/ *v.tr.* bring into subjection; subdue; vanquish. □□ **subjugable** /-gəbəl/ *adj.* **subjugation** /-gáyshən/ *n.* **subjugator** *n.* [ME f. LL *subjugare* bring under the yoke (as SUB-, *jugum* yoke)]
■ dominate, subordinate, enslave, enthrall, crush, humble, subject, oppress, suppress, put down, tyrannize, subdue, reduce, quell, overcome, overpower, conquer, make subservient or subordinate or submissive, humiliate, *literary* vanquish. □□ **subjugation** see *subjection* (SUBJECT).

subjunctive /səbjúngktiv/ *adj.* & *n. Gram.* ● *adj.* (of a mood) denoting what is imagined or wished or possible (e.g., *if I were you, God help you; be that as it may*). ● *n.* **1** the subjunctive mood. **2** a verb in this mood. □□ **subjunctively** *adv.* [F *subjonctif -ive* or LL *subjunctivus* f. L (as SUBJOIN), transl. Gk *hupotaktikos,* as being used in subjoined clauses]

subkingdom /súbkingdəm/ *n. Biol.* a taxonomic category below a kingdom.

sublease *n.* & *v.* ● *n.* /súblees/ a lease of a property by a tenant to a subtenant. ● *v.tr.* /súbleés/ lease (a property) to a subtenant.

sublessee /súbleseé/ *n.* a person who holds a sublease.

sublessor /súblesáwr/ *n.* a person who grants a sublease.

sublet *n.* & *v.* ● *n.* /súblet/ = SUBLEASE *n.* ● *v.tr.* /súblét/ (**-letting;** *past* and *past part.* **-let**) = SUBLEASE *v.*

sublieutenant /súbloōténənt/ *n. Brit.* a naval officer ranking immediately below lieutenant.

sublimate *v., adj.,* & *n.* ● *v.* /súblimayt/ **1** *tr.* & *intr.* divert (the energy of a primitive impulse, esp. sexual) into a culturally more acceptable activity. **2** *tr.* & *intr. Chem.* convert (a substance) from the solid state directly to its vapor by heat, and usu. allow it to solidify again. **3** *tr.* refine; purify; idealize. ● *adj.* /súblimət, -mayt/ **1** *Chem.* (of a substance) sublimated. **2** purified; refined. ● *n.* /súblimət/ *Chem.* **1** a sublimated substance. **2** = *corrosive sublimate.* □□ **sublimation** /-máyshən/ *n.* [L *sublimare sublimat-* SUBLIME *v.*]

■ *v.* **1** transmute, alter, transform; channel, divert, redirect. **3** sublime, refine, purify, rarefy; idealize, elevate.

sublime /səblím/ *adj. & v.* ● *adj.* (**sublimer, sublimest**) **1** of the most exalted, grand, or noble kind; awe inspiring (*sublime genius*). **2** (of indifference, impudence, etc.) arrogantly unruffled; extreme (*sublime ignorance*). ● *v.* **1** *tr. & intr. Chem.* = SUBLIMATE *v.* 2. **2** *tr.* purify or elevate by or as if by sublimation; make sublime. **3** *intr.* become pure by or as if by sublimation. □ **Sublime Porte** see PORTE. □□ **sublimely** *adv.* **sublimity** /-límitee/ *n.* [L *sublimis* (as SUB-, second element perh. rel. to *limen* threshold, *limus* oblique)]

■ *adj.* **1** lofty, high, supreme, exalted, elevated, empyrean, empyreal, heavenly, noble, glorious, grand, high-minded; honorable, ennobled, eminent, glorified, canonized, sanctified, *RC Ch.* beatified; great, magnificent, majestic, splendid, transcendent; awesome, overwhelming, inspiring, overpowering, humbling, awe-inspiring, *colloq.* mind-boggling. **2** extreme, lofty, supreme, utmost. ● *v.* **2** see SUBLIMATE *v.* 3. □□ **sublimely** see PERFECTLY 3. **sublimity** see NOBILITY 1.

subliminal /səblímínəl/ *adj. Psychol.* (of a stimulus, etc.) below the threshold of sensation or consciousness. □ **subliminal advertising** the use of subliminal images in advertising on television, etc., to influence the viewer at an unconscious level. **subliminal self** the part of one's personality outside conscious awareness. □□ **subliminally** *adv.* [SUB- + L *limen -inis* threshold]

■ subconscious, unconscious, vague, indefinable. □□ **subliminally** see *vaguely* (VAGUE).

sublingual /súblínggwəl/ *adj.* under the tongue. [SUB- + L *lingua* tongue]

sublittoral /súblítərəl/ *adj.* **1** (of plants, animals, deposits, etc.) living or found on the seashore just below the low tide line. **2** of or concerning the seashore.

sublunary /súbloonéree, sublooonəree/ *adj.* **1** beneath the moon. **2** *Astron.* **a** within the moon's orbit. **b** subject to the moon's influence. **3** of this world; earthly. [LL *sublunaris* (as SUB-, LUNAR)]

■ **3** see TERRESTRIAL *adj* 1, 4.

submachine gun /súbməsheén/ *n.* a hand-held lightweight machine gun.

submarginal /súbmaárjinəl/ *adj.* **1** esp. *Econ.* not reaching minimum requirements. **2** (of land) that cannot be farmed profitably.

submarine /súbməreén/ *n. & adj.* ● *n.* **1** a vessel, esp. a warship, capable of operating under water and usu. equipped with torpedoes, missiles, and a periscope. **2** = *submarine sandwich.* ● *adj.* existing, occurring, done, or used under the surface of the sea (*submarine cable*). □ **submarine sandwich** a large sandwich usu. consisting of a halved roll, meat, cheese, lettuce, tomato, etc. □□ **submariner** /-mareénər, səbmárinər/ *n.*

■ **submarine sandwich** hero, hoagy *or* hoagie, sub, grinder, torpedo, wedge, poor boy.

submaxillary /submáksileree/ *adj.* beneath the lower jaw.

submediant /súbmeédeeənt/ *n. Mus.* the sixth note of the diatonic scale of any key.

submental /súbmént'l/ *adj.* under the chin.

submerge /səbmérj/ *v.* **1** *tr.* **a** place under water; flood; inundate. **b** flood or inundate with work, problems, etc. **2** *intr.* (of a submarine, its crew, a diver, etc.) dive below the surface of water. □□ **submergence** *n.* **submergible** *adj.* **submersion** /-mérzhən, -shən/ *n.* [L *submergere* (as SUB-, *mergere mers-* dip)]

■ **1** flood, immerse, inundate, swamp, engulf, ingurgitate, overwhelm, deluge, drown, bury; plunge, submerse, dip, wash, soak, drench, saturate, wet, douse, souse,

dunk, steep. **2** dive, plunge, go down, descend, sink, sound, plummet. □□ **submersion** see PLUNGE *n.*

submersible /səbmérsibəl/ *n. & adj.* ● *n.* a submarine operating under water for short periods, esp. one used for deep-sea diving. ● *adj.* capable of being submerged. [*submerse* (v.) = SUBMERGE]

submicroscopic /súbmíkrəskópik/ *adj.* too small to be seen by an ordinary microscope.

subminiature /súbmíneeəchər, -choor/ *adj.* **1** of greatly reduced size. **2** (of a camera) very small and using 16-mm film.

submission /səbmíshən/ *n.* **1 a** the act or an instance of submitting; the state of being submitted. **b** anything that is submitted. **2** humility; meekness; obedience; submissiveness (*showed great submission of spirit*). **3** *Law* a theory, etc., submitted by a lawyer to a judge or jury. **4** (in wrestling) the surrender of a participant yielding to the pain of a hold. [ME f. OF *submission* or L *submissio* (as SUBMIT)]

■ **1 a** concession, acquiescence, capitulation, surrender, yielding, giving in. **b** offering, tender, proposal, proposition, suggestion, contribution, entry. **2** obedience, compliance, deference, resignation, submissiveness, tractability; humility, meekness, docility, passivity, timidity, unassertiveness. **3** theory, proposition, proposal, contention, claim, suggestion. **4** surrender, capitulation, giving in.

submissive /səbmísiv/ *adj.* **1** humble; obedient. **2** yielding to power or authority; willing to submit. □□ **submissively** *adv.* **submissiveness** *n.* [SUBMISSION after *remissive*, etc.]

■ humble, obedient, deferential, biddable, compliant, yielding, acquiescent, tractable, amenable, agreeable, accommodating, passive, unresisting, pliant, flexible, manageable, unassertive, docile, meek, timid, resigned, uncomplaining; obsequious, abject, subservient, servile, slavish, ingratiating, truckling, sycophantic, toadying, *colloq.* bootlicking. □□ **submissively** see *cap in hand.* **submissiveness** see HUMILITY 1.

submit /səbmít/ *v.* (**submitted, submitting**) **1** (usu. foll. by *to*) **a** *intr.* cease resistance; give way; yield (*had to submit to defeat; will never submit*). **b** *refl.* surrender (oneself) to the control of another, etc. **2** *tr.* present for consideration or decision. **3** *tr.* (usu. foll. by *to*) subject (a person or thing) to an operation, process, treatment, etc. (*submitted it to the flames*). **4** *tr.* esp. *Law* urge or represent esp. deferentially (*that, I submit, is a misrepresentation*). □□ **submitter** *n.* [ME f. L *submittere* (as SUB-, *mittere miss-* send)]

■ **1 a** surrender, yield, capitulate, give in *or* up *or* way, throw in the towel, throw in the sponge; bow *or* bend, succumb, truckle, knuckle under; agree, concede, consent, accede, defer; (*submit to*) respect, accept, comply with, resign oneself to, be *or* become resigned to, put up with. **2** offer, proffer, tender, put in, advance, put forward, enter, propose, propound, present, deliver; hand *or* give in. **3** (*submit to*) see SUBJECT *v.* 1. **4** suggest, urge, represent, exhort, plead, supplicate.

submultiple /súbmúltipəl/ *n. & adj.* ● *n.* a number that can be divided exactly into a specified number. ● *adj.* being such a number.

subnormal /súbnáwrməl/ *adj.* **1** (esp. as regards intelligence) below normal. **2** less than normal. □□ **subnormality** /-málitee/ *n.*

■ **1** see DEFECTIVE *adj.* 2.

subnuclear /súbnóokleeər, -nyóo-/ *adj. Physics* occurring in or smaller than an atomic nucleus.

subocular /súbókyələr/ *adj.* situated below or under the eyes.

suborbital /súbáwrbit'l/ *adj.* **1** situated below the orbit of the eye. **2** (of a spaceship, etc.) not completing a full orbit of the earth.

/.../ pronunciation	● part of speech
□ phrases, idioms, and compounds	
□□ derivatives	■ synonym section
cross-references appear in SMALL CAPITALS or *italics*	

suborder /súbawrdər/ *n.* a taxonomic category between an order and a family. □□ **subordinal** /-órdin'l/ *adj.*

subordinary /súbáwrd'neree/ *n.* (*pl.* **-ies**) *Heraldry* a device or bearing that is common but less so than ordinaries.

subordinate *adj., n.,* & *v.* ● *adj.* /səbáwrd'nət/ (usu. foll. by *to*) of inferior importance or rank; secondary; subservient. ● *n.* /səbáwrd'nət/ a person working under another's control or orders. ● *v.tr.* /səbáwrd'nayt/ (usu. foll. by *to*) **1** make subordinate; treat or regard as of minor importance. **2** make subservient. □ **subordinate clause** a clause serving as an adjective, adverb, or noun in a main sentence because of its position or a preceding conjunction. □□ **subordinately** *adv.* **subordination** /-náyshən/ *n.* **subordinative** /səbáwrd'nətiv/ *adj.* [med.L *subordinare, subordinat-* (as SUB-, L *ordinare* ordain)]

■ *adj.* minor; inferior, lower, lesser, secondary, second, junior, subsidiary, subservient; (*subordinate to*) next to, below, beneath, under. ● *n.* assistant, aide, junior, staff member; staffer; inferior, servant, slave; *Brit. Mil.* subaltern, *hist. or rhet.* vassal; *usu. derog.* flunky, lackey, menial, hireling, underling. ● *v.* **1** see REDUCE 6. **2** see SUBJUGATE. □□ **subordination** see *subjection* (SUBJECT).

suborn /səbáwrn/ *v.tr.* induce by bribery, etc., to commit perjury or any other unlawful act. □□ **subornation** *n.* **suborner** *n.* [L *subornare* incite secretly (as SUB-, *ornare* equip)]

■ see BRIBE *v.*

suboxide /súbóksid/ *n. Chem.* an oxide containing the smallest proportion of oxygen.

subphylum /súbfíləm/ *n.* (*pl.* **subphyla** /-lə/) *Biol.* a taxonomic category below a phylum.

subplot /súbplot/ *n.* a subordinate plot in a play, etc.

subpoena /səpeénə/ *n.* & *v.* ● *n.* a writ ordering a person to appear in court. ● *v.tr.* (*past* and *past part.* **subpoenaed** or **subpoena'd**) serve a subpoena on. [ME f. L *sub poena* under penalty (the first words of the writ)]

■ *n.* see WARRANT *n.* 2. ● *v.* see INDICT.

subregion /súbreejən/ *n.* a division of a region, esp. with regard to natural life. □□ **subregional** /-reejənəl/ *adj.*

subreption /səbrépshən/ *n. formal* the obtaining of a thing by surprise or misrepresentation. [L *subreptio* purloining f. *subripere* (as SUB-, *rapere* snatch)]

■ see DECEIT 2.

subrogation /súbrəgáyshən/ *n. Law* the substitution of one party for another as creditor, with the transfer of rights and duties. □□ **subrogate** /súbrəgayt/ *v.tr.* [LL *subrogatio* f. *subrogare* choose as substitute (as SUB-, *rogare* ask)]

sub rosa /sub rózə/ *adj.* & *adv.* (of communication, consultation, etc.) in secrecy or confidence. [L, lit. 'under the rose,' as emblem of secrecy]

■ see *secretly* (SECRET).

subroutine /súbrooteen/ *n. Computing* a routine designed to perform a frequently used operation within a program.

subscribe /səbskríb/ *v.* **1** (usu. foll. by *to, for*) **a** *tr.* & *intr.* contribute (a specified sum) or make or promise a contribution to a fund, project, charity, etc., esp. regularly. **b** *intr.* enter one's name in a list of contributors to a charity, etc. **c** *tr.* raise or guarantee raising (a sum) by so subscribing. **2** *intr.* (usu. foll. by *to*) express one's agreement with an opinion, resolution, etc. (*cannot subscribe to that*). **3** *tr.* **a** write (esp. one's name) at the foot of a document, etc. (*subscribed a motto*). **b** write one's name at the foot of, sign (a document, picture, etc.). **4** *tr.* & *intr.* arrange to receive a periodical; cable television service, etc., regularly. [ME f. L *subscribere* (as SUB-, *scribere script-* write)]

■ **1** (*subscribe to*) contribute to, support, give to, donate to, pledge to, promise to, sign (up) for, *colloq.* chip in to or for. **2** (*subscribe to*) endorse, support, underwrite, advocate, back (up), approve of, agree with *or* to, accept, consent to, assent to, sanction, countenance, tolerate, condone, go along with, hold with, allow, permit, *literary* brook. **3 a** append, tack on. **b** see SIGN *v.* 1.

subscriber /səbskríbər/ *n.* **1** a person who subscribes. **2** a person paying for the renting of a telephone line, television cable connection, etc.

■ **1** see PROPONENT *n.*

subscript /súbskript/ *adj.* & *n.* ● *adj.* written or printed below the line, esp. *Math.* (of a symbol) written below and to the right of another symbol. ● *n.* a subscript number or symbol. [L *subscriptus* (as SUBSCRIBE)]

subscription /səbskrípshən/ *n.* **1 a** the act or an instance of subscribing. **b** money subscribed. **2 a** an agreement to take and pay for usu. a specified number of issues of a newspaper, magazine, etc. **b** the money paid by this. **3** a signature on a document, etc. **4** *Brit.* a fee for the membership of a society, etc., esp. paid regularly. □ **subscription concert**, etc., each of a series of concerts, etc., for which tickets are sold in advance. [ME f. L *subscriptio* (as SUBSCRIBE)]

■ **1 a** obligation, pledge, promise, commitment, underwriting. **b** payment, remittance, investment; contribution. **2** dues, fee, contribution, *Brit. colloq.* sub. **3 b** fee, payment, remittance, price, cost.

subsection /súbsekshən/ *n.* a division of a section.

■ see BRANCH *n.* 2, 3.

subsellium /səbséleeəm/ *n.* (*pl.* **subsellia** /-leeə/) = MISERICORD 1. [L f. *sella* seat]

subsequence[1] /súbsikwəns/ *n.* a subsequent incident; a consequence.

subsequence[2] /súbseékwəns/ *n.* a sequence forming part of a larger one.

subsequent /súbsikwənt/ *adj.* (usu. foll. by *to*) following a specified event, etc., in time, esp. as a consequence. □□ **subsequently** *adv.* [ME f. OF *subsequent* or L *subsequi* (as SUB-, *sequi* follow)]

■ succeeding, following, ensuing, next, future, later, posterior, successive; resultant, resulting, consequent; (*subsequent to*) after, following, succeeding, in the wake or aftermath of. □□ **subsequently** later (on), afterwards, afterward.

subserve /səbsárv/ *v.tr.* serve as a means of furthering (a purpose, action, etc.). [L *subservire* (as SUB-, SERVE)]

subservient /səbsárveeənt/ *adj.* **1** cringing; obsequious. **2** (usu. foll. by *to*) serving as a means; instrumental. **3** (usu. foll. by *to*) subordinate. □□ **subservience** *n.* **subserviency** *n.* **subserviently** *adv.* [L *subserviens subservient-* (as SUBSERVE)]

■ **1** see OBSEQUIOUS. **2** see INSTRUMENTAL *adj.* **3** see SUBORDINATE *adj.* □□ **subservience** see *servility* (SERVILE). **subserviently** see *cap in hand.*

subset /súbset/ *n.* **1** a secondary part of a set. **2** *Math.* a set all the elements of which are contained in another set.

subshrub /súbshrub/ *n.* a low-growing or small shrub.

subside /səbsíd/ *v.intr.* **1** cease from agitation; become tranquil; abate (*excitement subsided*). **2** (of water, suspended matter, etc.) sink. **3** (of the ground) cave in; sink. **4** (of a building, ship, etc.) sink lower in the ground or water. **5** (of a swelling, etc.) become less. **6** usu. *joc.* (of a person) sink into a sitting, kneeling, or lying posture. □□ **subsidence** /-síd'ns, súbsíd'ns/ *n.* [L *subsidere* (as SUB-, *sidere* settle rel. to *sedēre* sit)]

■ **1** abate, quiet *or Brit.* quieten (down), calm (down), moderate, let up, decrease, diminish, lessen, slacken, die (down *or* off *or* out), ebb, pass (away), wear off, wane. **2** sink (down), drop (down), go down, recede, descend, decline; settle, *Chem. or Physics* precipitate. **3** cave in, collapse, fall in, sink, drop, settle. **4** sink (down), drop (down), go down, settle. **5** go down, lessen, decrease, reduce, abate. **6** sink, collapse, flop, drop, slump, settle. □□ **subsidence** see SAG *n.* 2, WANE *n.*

subsidiarity /səbsídeeáritee/ *n.* (*pl.* **-ies**) **1** the quality of being subsidiary. **2** the principle that a central authority should perform only tasks which cannot be performed effectively at a local level.

subsidiary /səbsídee-airee/ *adj.* & *n.* ● *adj.* **1** serving to assist or supplement; auxiliary. **2** (of a company) controlled by another. **3** (of troops): **a** paid for by subsidy. **b** hired by another nation. ● *n.* (*pl.* **-ies**) **1** a subsidiary thing or person; an accessory. **2** a subsidiary company. □□ **subsidiarily** *adv.* [L *subsidiarius* (as SUBSIDY)]

■ *adj.* **1** ancillary, auxiliary, additional, supplementary, supplemental, complementary, accessory, adjuvant, secondary, lesser, minor, subordinate. ● *n.* **1** accessory, auxiliary, extra, assistant, adjuvant, subordinate; adjunct, supplement.

subsidize /súbsidīz/ *v.tr.* **1** pay a subsidy to. **2** reduce the cost of by subsidy (*subsidized lunches*). □□ **subsidization** *n.* **subsidizer** *n.*

■ **1** fund, finance, support, aid, sponsor, maintain, underwrite; capitalize, *colloq.* bankroll.

subsidy /súbsidee/ *n.* (*pl.* **-ies**) **1** money granted by the government or a public body, etc., to keep down the price of commodities, etc. (*housing subsidy*). **b** money granted to a charity or other undertaking held to be in the public interest. **c** any grant or contribution of money. **2** money paid by one nation to another in return for military, naval, or other aid. **3** *hist.* **a** a parliamentary grant to the sovereign for government needs. **b** a tax levied on a particular occasion. [ME f. AF *subsidie*, OF *subside* f. L *subsidium* assistance]

■ **1** funding, sponsorship, assistance, aid, contribution, support, grant, bounty, endowment, subvention, maintenance, backing, capitalization.

subsist /səbsíst/ *v.* **1** *intr.* (often foll. by *on*) keep oneself alive; be kept alive (*subsists on vegetables*). **2** *intr.* remain in being; exist. **3** *intr.* (foll. by *in*) be attributable to (*its excellence subsists in its freshness*). **4** *tr.* *archaic* provide sustenance for. □□ **subsistent** *adj.* [L *subsistere* stand firm (as SUB-, *sistere* set, stand)]

■ **1, 2** see EXIST 5.

subsistence /səbsístəns/ *n.* **1** the state or an instance of subsisting. **2 a** the means of supporting life; a livelihood. **b** a minimal level of existence or the income providing this (*a bare subsistence*). □ **subsistence allowance** (or **money**) an allowance or advance on pay granted esp. as traveling expenses. **subsistence farming** farming which directly supports the farmer's household without producing a significant surplus for trade.

■ **1** existence, living, survival, subsisting, being. **2** see MAINTENANCE 2a.

subsoil /súbsoyl/ *n.* soil lying immediately under the surface soil (opp. TOPSOIL).

subsonic /súbsónik/ *adj.* relating to speeds less than that of sound. □□ **subsonically** *adv.*

subspecies /súbspeesheez, -seez/ *n.* (*pl.* same) *Biol.* a taxonomic category below a species, usu. a fairly permanent geographically isolated variety. □□ **subspecific** /-spəsifik/ *adj.*

subst. *abbr.* **1** substantive. **2** substitute.

substance /súbstəns/ *n.* **1 a** the essential material, esp. solid, forming a thing (*the substance was transparent*). **b** a particular kind of material having uniform properties (*this substance is salt*). **2 a** reality; solidity (*ghosts have no substance*). **b** seriousness or steadiness of character (*there is no substance in him*). **3** additive drugs or alcohol, etc. (*problems of substance abuse*). **4** the theme or subject of esp. a work of art, argument, etc. (*prefer the substance to the style*). **5** the real meaning or essence of a thing. **6** wealth and possessions (*a woman of substance*). **7** *Philos.* the essential nature underlying phenomena, which is subject to changes and accidents. □ **in substance** generally; apart from details. [ME f. OF f. L *substantia* (as SUB-, *stare* stand)]

■ **1** material, matter, stuff; fabric; composition, makeup. **2 a** reality, corporeality, solidity, actuality, concreteness. **3** theme, subject, gist, thrust, burden, point, content. **4** meaning, import, significance, purport, signification, point; essence, quintessence, pith, heart, core, meat, kernel, nub, crux, gravamen; sum total; *Philos.* quiddity, haecceity. **5** means, wealth, property, possessions, riches, resources, affluence, assets. □ **in substance** see *substantially* (SUBSTANTIAL).

substandard /súbstándərd/ *adj.* **1** of less than the required or normal quality or size; inferior. **2** (of language) not conforming to standard usage.

■ **1** see INFERIOR *adj.* 2.

substantial /səbstánshəl/ *adj.* **1 a** of real importance, value, or validity (*made a substantial contribution*). **b** of large size or amount (*awarded substantial damages*). **2** of solid material or structure; stout (*a man of substantial build*; *a substantial house*). **3** commercially successful; wealthy. **4** essential; true in large part (*substantial truth*). **5** having substance; real. □□ **substantiality** /-sheeálitee/ *n.* **substantially** *adv.* [ME f. OF *substantiel* or LL *substantialis* (as SUBSTANCE)]

■ **1 a** material, considerable, significant, great, worthwhile, consequential, important, valuable; well-founded, sound, weighty, solid, well-established, telling, good, valid, actual. **b** ample, goodly, respectable, abundant, generous, big, large, sizable, major, *colloq.* tidy, healthy. **2** strong, solid, well-built, durable, sound, stout, sturdy, hefty; big, large, massive, huge, sizable, impressive, vast. **3** wealthy, well-to-do, rich, affluent, prosperous, profitable, successful; landed, propertied. **4** basic, fundamental; virtual; see also ESSENTIAL *adj.* 2. **5** see MATERIAL *adj.* 1. □□ **substantially** essentially, at bottom, fundamentally, basically, in essence, intrinsically, in reality, at heart, truly, actually, veritably, indeed, in fact, as a matter of fact, *literary* in truth; in substance; largely, to a large extent, in large measure, materially, practically, in the main, for the most part, mostly, virtually, to all intents and purposes; *archaic* verily.

substantialism /səbstánshəlizəm/ *n.* *Philos.* the doctrine that behind phenomena there are substantial realities. □□ **substantialist** *n.*

substantialize /səbstánshəliz/ *v.tr.* & *intr.* invest with or acquire substance or actual existence.

substantiate /səbstánsheeayt/ *v.tr.* prove the truth of (a charge, statement, claim, etc.); give good grounds for. □□ **substantiation** /-áyshən/ *n.* [med.L *substantiare* give substance to (as SUBSTANCE)]

■ confirm, affirm, attest, corroborate, support, sustain, back up, bear out, authenticate, show (clearly), prove, document, verify, certify, validate, give substance to. □□ **substantiation** see PROOF *n.* 1.

substantive /súbstəntiv/ *adj.* & *n.* ● *adj.* /also səbstántiv/ **1** having separate and independent existence. **2** *Law* relating to rights and duties. **3** (of an enactment, motion, resolution, etc.) made in due form as such; not amended. **4** *Gram.* expressing existence. **5** (of a dye) not needing a mordant. **6** *Mil.* (of a rank, etc.) permanent, not acting or temporary. **7** *archaic* denoting a substance. ● *n.* *Gram.* = NOUN. □ **the substantive verb** the verb 'to be'. □□ **substantival** /-tívəl/ *adj.* **substantively** *adv.* esp. *Gram.* [ME f. OF *substantif* -*ive*, or LL *substantivus* (as SUBSTANCE)]

■ *adj.* **1** see INDEPENDENT *adj.* 1a, 5.

substation /súbstayshən/ *n.* a subordinate station, esp. one reducing the high voltage of electric power transmission to that suitable for supply to consumers.

substituent /səbstíchŏŏənt/ *adj.* & *n.* *Chem.* ● *adj.* (of a group of atoms) replacing another atom or group in a compound. ● *n.* such a group. [L *substituere substituent*- (as SUBSTITUTE)]

substitute /súbstitŏŏt, -tyŏŏt/ *n.* & *v.* ● *n.* **1 a** (also *attrib.*) a person or thing acting or serving in place of another. **b** an artificial alternative to a natural substance (*butter substitute*). **2** *Sc. Law* a deputy. ● *v.* **1** *intr.* & *tr.* (often foll. by *for*) act or cause to act as a substitute; put or serve in exchange (*substituted for her mother*; *substituted it for the broken one*). **2** *tr.* (usu. foll. by *by*, *with*) *colloq.* replace (a person or thing) with another. **3** *tr.* *Chem.* replace (an atom or group in a molecule) with another. □□ **substitutable** *adj.* **substitutability** *n.* **substitution** /-tŏŏshən, -tyŏŏ-/ *n.* **substitutional** *adj.* **substitutionary** /-tŏŏshənəree, -tyŏŏ-/ *adj.* **substitu-**

tive adj. [ME f. L substitutus past part. of substituere (as SUB-, statuere set up)]
- n. **1 a** substitution, replacement, alternative, relief, supply, representative, proxy, deputy, delegate, stand-in, standby, stopgap, reserve, surrogate, succedaneum, locum tenens, alternate, pinch-hitter, esp. Theatr. understudy, colloq. locum, sub. **b** alternative, replacement, ersatz, imitation. ● v. **1** (substitute for) take the place of, stand in for, step in for, fill in for, double for, deputize for, cover for, relieve, colloq. sub for; replace; supersede, displace, supplant. **2, 3** replace. □□ **substitution** see SUBSTITUTE n. 1a above, CHANGE n. 4.

substrate /súbstrayt/ n. **1** = SUBSTRATUM. **2** a surface to be painted, printed, etc., on. **3** Biol. **a** the substance upon which an enzyme acts. **b** the surface or material on which any particular organism grows. [Anglicized f. SUBSTRATUM]

substratum /súbstraytəm, -strát-/ n. (pl. **substrata** /-tə/) **1** an underlying layer or substance. **2** a layer of rock or soil beneath the surface. **3** a foundation or basis (there is a substratum of truth in it). [mod.L, past part. of L substernere (as SUB-, sternere strew): cf. STRATUM]
- substrate, foundation, basis, base, substructure, groundwork.

substructure /súbstrukchər/ n. an underlying or supporting structure. □□ **substructural** adj.
- see SUPPORT n. 2.

subsume /səbsốom, -syốom/ v.tr. (usu. foll. by under) include (an instance, idea, category, etc.) in a rule, class, category, etc. □□ **subsumable** adj. **subsumption** /-súmpshən/ n. [med.L subsumere (as SUB-, sumere sumpt- take)]
- see INCLUDE 1.

subtenant /súbténənt/ n. a person who leases a property from a tenant. □□ **subtenancy** n.

subtend /səbténd/ v.tr. **1 a** (usu. foll. by at) (of a line, arc, figure, etc.) form (an angle) at a particular point when its extremities are joined at that point. **b** (of an angle or chord) have bounding lines or points that meet or coincide with those of (a line or arc). **2** Bot. (of a bract, etc.) extend under so as to embrace or enfold. [L subtendere (as SUB-, tendere stretch)]

subterfuge /súbtərfyōoj/ n. **1 a** an attempt to avoid blame or defeat, esp. by lying or deceit. **b** a statement, etc., resorted to for such a purpose. **2** this as a practice or policy. [F subterfuge or LL subterfugium f. L subterfugere escape secretly f. subter beneath + fugere flee]
- **1** artifice, trick, device, stratagem, maneuver, scheme, evasion, deception, dodge, feint, shift, excuse, expedient, ruse, wile, contrivance, intrigue, colloq. ploy, Austral. sl. lurk. **2** see DECEIT 1.

subterminal /súbtərminəl/ adj. nearly at the end.

subterranean /súbtəráyneeən/ adj. **1** existing, occurring, or done under the earth's surface. **2** secret; underground; concealed. □□ **subterraneously** adv. [L subterraneus (as SUB-, terra earth)]
- **1** see UNDERGROUND adj. 1.

subtext /súbtekst/ n. an underlying often distinct theme in a piece of writing or conversation.

subtilize /sút'liz/ v. **1** tr. **a** make subtle. **b** elevate; refine. **2** intr. (usu. foll. by upon) argue or reason subtly. □□ **subtilization** n. [F subtiliser or med.L subtilizare (as SUBTLE)]
- **1 b** see REFINE 4.

subtitle /súbtit'l/ n. & v. ● n. **1** a secondary or additional title of a book, etc. **2** a printed caption at the bottom of a movie, etc., esp. translating dialogue. ● v.tr. provide with a subtitle or subtitles.
- n. **1** see TITLE n. 2.

subtle /sút'l/ adj. (**subtler, subtlest**) **1** evasive or mysterious; hard to grasp (subtle charm; a subtle distinction). **2** (of scent, color, etc.) faint; delicate; elusive (subtle perfume). **3 a** capable of making fine distinctions; perceptive; acute (subtle intellect; subtle senses). **b** ingenious; elaborate; clever (a subtle device). **4** archaic crafty; cunning. □□ **subtleness** n. **subtly** adv. [ME f. OF sotil f. L subtilis]
- **1** abstruse, arcane, recondite, remote, deep, profound,

concealed, hidden, shadowy, nebulous, vague, obscure, veiled, thin, airy, insubstantial, elusive, evasive, mysterious, faint; sophistic(al); refined, fine, nice. **2** delicate, fine, refined, exquisite, nice; faint, elusive. **3 a** see ACUTE adj. 2. **b** see SOPHISTICATED 2. **4** tricky, shrewd, cunning, wily, sly, devious, crafty, smart, clever, foxy, artful, scheming, designing, underhand(ed), deceptive, machiavellian, ingenious, skillful, strategic, insidious, casuistic, slimy, colloq. shifty, slick, smarmy, often offens. jesuitical. □□ **subtleness** see SUBTLETY 1.

subtlety /sút'ltee/ n. (pl. **-ies**) **1** something subtle; the quality of being subtle. **2 a** fine distinction; an instance of hairsplitting. [ME f. OF s(o)utilté f. L subtilitas -tatis (as SUBTLE)]
- **1** treachery, guile, insidiousness, casuistry, cunning, artfulness, craftiness, deviousness, slyness, deceptiveness, subtleness; refinement, nicety, delicacy, exquisiteness, intricacy, fineness, acuteness, elegance, sophistication. **2** see REFINEMENT 6.

subtonic /súbtónik/ n. Mus. the note below the tonic, the seventh note of the diatonic scale of any key.

subtotal /súbtōt'l/ n. the total of one part of a group of figures to be added.

subtract /səbtrákt/ v.tr. (often foll. by from) deduct (a part, quantity, or number) from another. □□ **subtracter** n. (cf. SUBTRACTOR). **subtraction** /-trákshən/ n. **subtractive** adj. [L subtrahere subtract- (as SUB-, trahere draw)]
- deduct, take away or off; (subtract from) take from. □□ **subtraction** see DEDUCTION 1a.

subtractor /səbtráktər/ n. Electronics a circuit or device that produces an output dependent on the difference of two inputs.

subtrahend /súbtrəhend/ n. Math. a quantity or number to be subtracted. [L subtrahendus gerundive of subtrahere: see SUBTRACT]

subtropics /súbtrópiks/ n.pl. the regions adjacent to or bordering on the tropics. □□ **subtropical** adj.

subulate /súbyələt/ adj. Bot. & Zool. slender and tapering. [L subula awl]

suburb /súbərb/ n. an outlying district of a city, esp. residential. [ME f. OF suburbe or L suburbium (as SUB-, urbs urbis city)]
- see MUNICIPALITY.

suburban /səbárbən/ adj. **1** of or characteristic of suburbs. **2** derog. provincial, uncultured, or naïve. □□ **suburbanite** n. **suburbanize** v.tr. **suburbanization** n. [L suburbanus (as SUBURB)]

suburbia /səbárbeeə/ n. often derog. the suburbs, their inhabitants, and their way of life.

subvention /səbvénshən/ n. a grant of money from a government, etc.; a subsidy. [ME f. OF f. LL subventio -onis f. L subvenire subvent- assist (as SUB-, venire come)]
- see GRANT n.

subversive /səbvársiv/ adj. & n. ● adj. (of a person, group, organization, activity, etc.) seeking to subvert (esp. a government). ● n. a subversive person; a revolutionary. □□ **subversion** /-várzhən, -shən/ n. **subversively** adv. **subversiveness** n. [med.L subversivus (as SUBVERT)]
- adj. seditious, treasonous, treacherous, traitorous, mutinous, revolutionary, insurrectionary; undermining, destabilizing. ● n. traitor, insurgent, subverter, saboteur, fifth columnist, collaborator, collaborationist, quisling, radical, revolutionary, insurrectionist; dissident, defector. □□ **subversion** overthrow, ruin, destruction, undermining, destabilization, upheaval, displacement; see also MUTINY n.

subvert /səbvárt/ v.tr. esp. Polit. overturn, overthrow, or upset (religion, government, morality, etc.). □□ **subverter** n. [ME f. OF subvertir or L subvertere (as SUB-, vertere vers-turn)]
- overthrow, overturn, ruin, destroy, undermine, destabilize, topple, upset, disrupt, demolish, wreck, sabotage, corrupt, pervert.

subway /súbway/ n. **1** an underground, usu. electrically powered, railroad. **2 a** a tunnel beneath a road, etc., for pedestrians. **b** an underground passage for pipes, cables, etc. ■ **1** underground (railroad), metro, esp. *Brit. colloq.* (the) tube. **2 a** tunnel, underpass.

subzero /súbzeʹerō/ *adj.* (esp. of temperature) lower than zero.

suc- /suk, sək/ *prefix* assim. form of SUB- before *c*.

succedaneum /súksidáyneeəm/ *n.* (*pl.* **succedanea** /-neeə/) a substitute, esp. for a medicine or drug. □□ **succedaneous** *adj.* [mod.L, neut. of L *succedaneus* (as SUCCEED)]
■ see SUBSTITUTE *n.* 1a.

succeed /səkseéd/ *v.* **1** *intr.* **a** (often foll. by *in*) accomplish one's purpose; have success; prosper (*succeeded in his ambition*). **b** (of a plan, etc.) be successful. **2 a** *tr.* follow in order; come immediately after (*night succeeded day*). **b** *intr.* (foll. by *to*) come next; be subsequent. **3** *intr.* (often foll. by *to*) come by an inheritance, office, title, or property (*succeeded to the throne*). **4** *tr.* take over an office, property, inheritance, etc., from (*succeeded his father*; *succeeded the manager*). □ **nothing succeeds like success** one success leads to others. □□ **succeeder** *n.* [ME f. OF *succeder* or L *succedere* (as SUB-, *cedere cess-* go)]
■ **1 a** make good, thrive, prosper, flourish, be a success, be successful, progress, advance, get ahead *or* on, go *or* come up in the world, attain *or* gain *or* achieve success, win, triumph, be victorious, prevail, *colloq.* make it, arrive, go places, come *or* get to the top, get there. **b** be successful *or* effective, work, bear fruit. **2** follow, come (next) after, be subsequent to. **3** (*succeed to*) see INHERIT 1. **4** be successor to, follow, be heir to, replace, take the place of, inherit from, take over from.

succentor /səkséntər/ *n. Eccl.* a precentor's deputy in some cathedrals. □□ **succentorship** *n.* [LL f. L *succinere* (as SUB-, *canere* sing)]

succès de scandale /sōōksáy də skoNdaáal/ *n.* a book, play, etc., having great success because of its scandalous nature or associations. [F]

success /səksés/ *n.* **1** the accomplishment of an aim; a favorable outcome (*their efforts met with success*). **2** the attainment of wealth, fame, or position (*spoiled by success*). **3** a thing or person that turns out well. **4** *archaic* a usu. specified outcome of an undertaking (*ill success*). [L *successus* (as SUCCEED)]
■ **1** good *or* happy result, good *or* happy outcome, good fortune, achievement, triumph, victory, attainment, ascendancy, prosperity. **3** star, superstar, megastar, success story, celebrity, (big) name, headliner; sensation, *colloq.* winner, hit.

successful /səksésfŏŏl/ *adj.* having success; prosperous. □□ **successfully** *adv.* **successfulness** *n.*
■ victorious, triumphant, first, winning; famous, well-known, famed, celebrated, renowned, eminent; prominent, preeminent, popular, leading, top, best-selling; effective; lucrative, booming, profitable, fruitful, moneymaking, remunerative; wealthy, rich, prosperous, fortunate, lucky, flourishing, thriving, well-to-do, affluent, *colloq.* well-heeled, flush, in the money, *sl.* loaded. □ **successfully** see SWIMMINGLY.

succession /səkséshən/ *n.* **1 a** the process of following in order; succeeding. **b** a series of things or people in succession. **2 a** the right of succeeding to a throne, an office, inheritance, etc. **b** the act or process of so succeeding. **c** those having such a right. **3** *Biol.* the order of development of a species or community; = SERE³. □ **in quick succession** following one another at short intervals. **in succession** one after another, without intervention. **in succession to** as the successor of. **law of succession** the law regulating inheritance. **settle the succession** determine who shall succeed. **succession state** a nation resulting from the partition of a previously existing country. □□ **successional** *adj.* [ME f. OF *succession* or L *successio* (as SUCCEED)]
■ **1** sequence, progression, order, series, course, flow, run, chain, train, string, line, procession, round, cycle, esp. *Brit.* queue. **2 a** birthright, privilege. **b** accession,

assumption, attainment, elevation, promotion; inheritance; passing (on), handing down *or* on, descent, transmittal, transmission, transfer, transferral, shift, conveyance. **c** lineage, descent, dynasty, ancestry, descendants, bloodline. □ **in succession** one after *or* behind the other, at intervals, successively, consecutively, in a row, running, without interruption, uninterruptedly, in order, in line, in turn.

successive /səksésiv/ *adj.* following one after another; running; consecutive. □□ **successively** *adv.* **successiveness** *n.* [ME f. med.L *successivus* (as SUCCEED)]
■ uninterrupted, continuous, unbroken, consecutive, straight, succeeding, following, running. □□ **successively** see *in succession* (SUCCESSION).

successor /səksésər/ *n.* (often foll. by *to*) a person or thing that succeeds another. [ME f. OF *successour* f. L *successor* (as SUCCEED)]
■ see HEIR.

succinct /səksíngkt/ *adj.* briefly expressed; terse; concise. □□ **succinctly** *adv.* **succinctness** *n.* [ME f. L *succinctus* past part. of *succingere* tuck up (as SUB-, *cingere* gird)]
■ compact, brief, concise, pithy, terse, short, compressed, condensed, epigrammatic. □□ **succinctly** see *in brief* (BRIEF). **succinctness** see BREVITY.

succinic acid /suksínik/ *n. Chem.* a crystalline dibasic acid derived from amber, etc. □□ **succinate** /súksinayt/ *n.* [F *succinique* f. L *succinum* amber]

succor /súkər/ *n.* & *v.* ● *n.* **1** aid; assistance, esp. in time of need. **2** (in *pl.*) *archaic* reinforcements of troops. ● *v.tr.* assist or aid (esp. a person in danger or distress). □□ **succorless** *adj.* [ME f. OF *socours* f. med.L *succursus* f. L *succurrere* (as SUB-, *currere curs-* run)]
■ *n.* **1** see AID *n.* 1. ● *v.* see AID *v.* 1.

succory /súkəree/ *n.* = CHICORY 1. [alt. f. *cicoree*, etc., early forms of CHICORY]

succotash /súkətash/ *n.* a dish of green corn and beans boiled together. [Narragansett *msiquatash*]

Succoth /sŏŏkəs, sŏŏkŏt/ *n.* (also **Sukkoth**) the Jewish autumn thanksgiving festival commemorating the sheltering in the wilderness. [Heb. *sukkôt* pl. of *sukkāh* thicket, hut]

succour *Brit.* var. of SUCCOR.

succubus /súkyəbəs/ *n.* (*pl.* **succubi** /-bī/) a female demon believed to have sexual intercourse with sleeping men. [LL *succuba* prostitute, med.L *succubus* f. *succubare* (as SUB-, *cubare* lie)]

succulent /súkyələnt/ *adj.* & *n.* ● *adj.* **1** juicy; palatable. **2** *colloq.* desirable. **3** *Bot.* (of a plant, its leaves, or stems) thick and fleshy. ● *n. Bot.* a succulent plant, esp. a cactus. □□ **succulence** *n.* **succulently** *adv.* [L *succulentus* f. *succus* juice]
■ *adj.* **1** juicy, rich, luscious, mouthwatering, toothsome, palatable, tasty. **2** desirable, tempting, tantalizing, attractive, enticing, inviting. **3** fleshy; lush.

succumb /səkúm/ *v.intr.* (usu. foll. by *to*) **1** be forced to give way; be overcome (*succumbed to temptation*). **2** be overcome by death (*succumbed to his injuries*). [ME f. OF *succomber* or L *succumbere* (as SUB-, *cumbere* lie)]
■ **1** yield, give in, give up, give way, surrender, accede, submit, capitulate, fall, bow, cave in.

such /such/ *adj.* & *pron.* ● *adj.* **1** (often foll. by *as*) of the kind or degree in question or under consideration (*such a person*; *such people*; *people such as these*). **2** (usu. foll. by *as to* + infin. or *that* + clause) so great; in such high degree (*not such a fool as to believe them*; *had such a fright that he fainted*). **3** of a more than normal kind or degree (*we had such an enjoyable evening*; *such crude language*). **4** of the kind or degree already indicated, or implied by the context (*there are no such things*; *such is life*). **5** *Law* or *formal* the aforesaid; of the aforesaid kind. ● *pron.* **1** the thing or action in question or referred to (*such were his words*; *such was not my intention*). **2 a** *Commerce* or *colloq.* the aforesaid thing or things; it, they, or them (*those without tickets should purchase such*). **b** similar things; suchlike (*brought sandwiches and such*). □ **as such** as being what has been indicated or named (*a stranger is welcomed as such*; *there is no theater as such*). **such and such** ● *adj.* of a particular kind but not needing to be specified. ● *n.* a person or thing of this kind. **such and such a person** someone; so-and-so. **such as 1** of a kind that; like (*a person such as we all admire*). **2** for example (*insects, such as moths and bees*). **3** those who (*such as don't need help*). **such as it is** despite its shortcomings (*you are welcome to it, such as it is*). **such a one 1** (usu. foll. by *as*) such a person or such a thing. **2** *archaic* some person or thing unspecified. [OE *swilc*, *swylc* f. Gmc: cf. LIKE[1]]

■ □ **such as 1, 2** see LIKE[1] *adj.* 1b.

suchlike /súchlik/ *adj.* & *n.* *colloq.* ● *adj.* of such a kind. ● *n.* things, people, etc., of such a kind.

suck /suk/ *v.* & *n.* ● *v.* **1** *tr.* draw (a fluid) into the mouth by making a partial vacuum. **2** *tr.* (also *absol.*) **a** draw milk or other fluid from or through (the breast, etc., or a container). **b** extract juice from (a fruit) by sucking. **3** *tr.* **a** draw sustenance, knowledge, or advantage from (a book, etc.). **b** imbibe or gain (knowledge, advantage, etc.) as if by sucking. **4** *tr.* roll the tongue around (a candy, teeth, one's thumb, etc.). **5** *intr.* make a sucking action or sound (*sucking at his pipe*). **6** *intr.* (of a pump, etc.) make a gurgling or drawing sound. **7** *tr.* (usu. foll. by *down, in*) engulf, smother, or drown in a sucking movement. **8** *intr. sl.* be or seem very unpleasant, contemptible, or unfair. ● *n.* **1** the act or an instance of sucking, esp. at the breast. **2** the drawing action or sound of a whirlpool, etc. **3** (often foll. by *of*) a small drink of alcohol. **4** (in *pl.*; esp. as *int.*) *Brit. colloq.* **a** an expression of disappointment. **b** an expression of derision or amusement at another's discomfiture. □ **give suck** *archaic* (of a mother, dam, etc.) suckle. **suck dry 1** exhaust the contents of (a bottle, the breast, etc.) by sucking. **2** exhaust (a person's sympathy, resources, etc.) as if by sucking. **suck in 1** absorb. **2** = sense 7 of *v.* **3** involve (a person) in an activity, etc., esp. against his or her will. **suck up 1** (often foll. by *to*) *colloq.* behave obsequiously, esp. for one's own advantage. **2** absorb. [OE *sūcan*, = L *sugere*]

■ □ **suck in 3** see *lead on* 1 (LEAD[1]). **suck up 1** (*suck up to*) see FLATTER 1.

sucker /súkər/ *n.* & *v.* ● *n.* **1 a** a person or thing that sucks. **b** a sucking pig, newborn whale, etc. **2** *sl.* **a** a gullible or easily deceived person. **b** (foll. by *for*) a person especially susceptible to. **3 a** a rubber cup, etc., that adheres to a surface by suction. **b** an organ enabling an organism to cling to a surface by suction. **4** *Bot.* a shoot springing from the rooted part of a stem, from the root at a distance from the main stem, from an axil, or occasionally from a branch. **5** any of various fish that has a mouth capable of or seeming to be capable of adhering by suction. **6 a** the piston of a suction pump. **b** a pipe through which liquid is drawn by suction. **7** *colloq.* a lollipop. ● *v. Bot.* **1** *tr.* remove suckers from. **2** *intr.* produce suckers. **3** *tr. sl.* cheat; fool.

■ *n.* **2** dupe, pigeon, victim, butt, cat's-paw, fool, greenhorn, easy or fair game, *colloq.* goat, chump, pushover, soft touch, *sl.* (easy) mark, sap, fall guy, patsy, *Brit. sl.* mug. **4** see OFFSHOOT 1a.

sucking /súking/ *adj.* **1** (of a child, animal, etc.) not yet weaned. **2** *Zool.* unfledged (*sucking dove*). □ **sucking fish** = REMORA.

suckle /súkəl/ *v.* **1** *tr.* **a** feed (young) from the breast or udder. **b** nourish (*suckled his talent*). **2** *intr.* feed by sucking the breast, etc. □□ **suckler** *n.* [ME, prob. back-form. f. SUCKLING]

■ **1 a** see NURSE *v.* 2.

suckling /súkling/ *n.* an unweaned child or animal.

sucrose /sóŏkrōs/ *n. Chem.* sugar; a disaccharide obtained from sugar cane, sugar beet, etc. [F *sucre* SUGAR]

suction /súkshən/ *n.* **1** the act or an instance of sucking. **2 a** the production of a partial vacuum by the removal of air, etc., in order to force in liquid, etc., or procure adhesion. **b**

the force produced by this process (*suction keeps the lid on*). □ **suction pump** a pump for drawing liquid through a pipe into a chamber emptied by a piston. [LL *suctio* f. L *sugere* *suct-* SUCK]

suctorial /suktáwreeəl/ *adj. Zool.* **1** adapted for or capable of sucking. **2** having a sucker for feeding or adhering. □□ **suctorian** *n.* [mod.L *suctorius* (as SUCTION)]

Sudanese /sóŏdəneéz/ *adj.* & *n.* ● *adj.* of or relating to Sudan, a republic in NE Africa, or the Sudan region south of the Sahara. ● *n.* (*pl.* same) **1** a native, national, or inhabitant of Sudan. **2** a person of Sudanese descent.

sudatorium /sóŏdətáwreeəm/ *n.* (*pl.* **sudatoria** /-reeə/) esp. *Rom. Antiq.* **1** a hot air or steam bath. **2** a room where such a bath is taken. [L, neut. of *sudatorius*: see SUDATORY]

sudatory /sóŏdətawree/ *adj.* & *n.* ● *adj.* promoting perspiration. ● *n.* (*pl.* **-ies**) **1** a sudatory drug. **2** = SUDATORIUM. [L *sudatorius* f. *sudare* sweat]

sudd /sud/ *n.* floating vegetation impeding the navigation of the White Nile. [Arab., = obstruction]

sudden /súd'n/ *adj.* & *n.* ● *adj.* occurring or done unexpectedly or without warning; abrupt; hurried; hasty (*a sudden storm*; *a sudden departure*). ● *n. archaic* a hasty or abrupt occurrence. □ **all of a sudden** unexpectedly; hurriedly; suddenly. **sudden death** *colloq.* a decision in a tied game, etc., dependent on one move, card, toss of a coin, etc. **sudden infant death syndrome** *Med.* the death of a seemingly healthy infant from an unknown cause; crib death. □□ **suddenly** *adv.* **suddenness** *n.* [ME f. AF *sodein*, *sudein*, OF *soudain* f. LL *subitanus* f. L *subitaneus* f. *subitus* sudden]

■ *adj.* unexpected, unannounced, unanticipated, unforeseen; surprising, startling; precipitate, abrupt, quick, immediate, rapid, swift, brisk, hurried, whirlwind; impetuous, hasty, rash, impulsive, snap. □ **all of a sudden** see *suddenly* (SUDDEN) below. □□ **suddenly** in a flash, in a moment, in a split second, all at once, instantly, instantaneously, fleetingly, in the twinkling of an eye, in a trice, momentarily; quickly, abruptly, swiftly, speedily, rapidly; all of a sudden, out of the blue, unexpectedly, without warning, on the spur of the moment, hastily, hurriedly, feverishly, *archaic* on a sudden. **suddenness** see SPEED *n.* 1.

sudoriferous /sóŏdərífərəs/ *adj.* (of a gland, etc.) secreting sweat. [LL *sudorifer* f. L *sudor* sweat]

sudorific /sóŏdərífik/ *adj.* & *n.* ● *adj.* (of a drug) causing sweating. ● *n.* a sudorific drug. [mod.L *sudorificus* f. L *sudor* sweat]

Sudra /sóŏdrə/ *n.* a member of the lowest of the four great Hindu castes. [Skr. *śūdra*]

suds /sudz/ *n.* & *v.* ● *n.pl.* **1** froth of soap and water. **2** *colloq.* beer. ● *v.* **1** *intr.* form suds. **2** *tr.* lather, cover, or wash in soapy water. □□ **sudsy** *adj.* [orig. = fen waters, etc., of uncert. orig.: cf. MDu., MLG *sudde*, MDu. *sudse* marsh, bog, prob. rel. to SEETHE]

■ *n.* **1** see FROTH *n.* 1a. ● *v.* **1** see FOAM *v.*

sue /sóŏ/ *v.* (**sues**, **sued**, **suing**) **1** *tr.* (also *absol.*) *Law* institute legal proceedings against (a person). **2** *tr.* (also *absol.*) entreat (a person). **3** *intr.* (often foll. by *to, for*) *Law* make application to a court of law for redress. **4** *intr.* (often foll. by *to, for*) make entreaty to a person for a favor. **5** *tr.* (often foll. by *out*) make a petition in a court of law for and obtain (a writ, pardon, etc.). □□ **suer** *n.* [ME f. AF *suer*, *siwer*, etc., f. OF *siu-*, etc., stem of *sivre* f. L *sequi* follow]

■ **1** proceed or move or act (against), take (legal) action (against), bring suit (against), prefer charges (against), prosecute; summon(s), charge, accuse. **2, 4** petition, beg, plead (with), entreat, pray, request, solicit, beseech, implore, supplicate; apply (to), appeal (to). □□ **suer** see LITIGANT *n.*

suede /swayd/ *n.* (often *attrib.*) **1** leather, esp. kidskin, with the flesh side rubbed to make a velvety nap. **2** (also **suede cloth**) a woven fabric resembling suede. [F (*gants de*) *Suède* (gloves of) Sweden]

suet /sóŏ-it/ *n.* the hard white fat on the kidneys or loins of oxen, sheep, etc., used in cooking, etc. □ **suet pudding** a pudding of chopped suet, flour, spices, etc., usu. boiled or steamed. □□ **suety** *adj.* [ME f. AF f. OF *seu* f. L *sebum* tallow]

suf- /suf, səf/ *prefix* assim. form of SUB- before *f*.

suffer /súfər/ *v.* **1** *intr.* **a** undergo pain, grief, etc. (*suffers acutely*; *suffers from neglect*). **b** be damaged; decline (*your reputation will suffer*). **2** *tr.* undergo, experience, or be subjected to (pain, loss, grief, defeat, change, etc.) (*suffered banishment*). **3** *tr.* put up with; tolerate (*does not suffer fools gladly*). **4** *intr.* undergo martyrdom. **5** *tr.* (foll. by *to* + infin.) *archaic* allow. □□ **sufferable** *adj.* **sufferer** *n.* **suffering** *n.* [ME f. AF *suffrir, soeffrir*, OF *sof(f)rir* f. L *sufferre* (as SUB-, *ferre* bear)]

■ **1 a** agonize, smart, hurt, writhe, sweat, ache. **b** decline, deteriorate, diminish, go down, fall off, be reduced *or* diminished; pay (dearly). **2** endure, undergo, experience, feel, bear, live *or* go through, withstand, sustain, take, submit to. **3** tolerate, take, abide, put up with, bear, stand, indulge. **5** allow, permit, let. □□ **sufferable** see *supportable* (SUPPORT). **sufferer** see INVALID[1] *n.* 1, VICTIM 1, 2. **suffering** pain, agony, anguish, distress, misery, grief, sorrow, affliction, hardship, hurt, torment, torture, tribulation, trials, *archaic or literary* woe.

sufferance /súfərəns, súfrəns/ *n.* **1** tacit consent; abstinence from objection. **2** *archaic* submissiveness. □ **on sufferance** with toleration implied by lack of consent or objection. [ME f. AF, OF *suffraunce* f. LL *sufferentia* (as SUFFER)]

■ **1** see TOLERANCE 1.

suffice /səfís/ *v.* **1** *intr.* (often foll. by *for*, or *to* + infin.) be enough or adequate (*that will suffice for our purpose*; *suffices to prove it*). **2** *tr.* meet the needs of; satisfy (*six sufficed him*). □ **suffice it to say** I shall content myself with saying. [ME f. OF *suffire* (*suffis-*) f. L *sufficere* (as SUB-, *facere* make)]

■ **1** serve, do, be sufficient *or* enough *or* adequate, answer, *colloq.* do the trick. **2** satisfy, sate, satiate, do, serve, meet the needs of.

sufficiency /səfíshənsee/ *n.* (*pl.* **-ies**) **1** (often foll. by *of*) an adequate amount or adequate resources. **2** *archaic* being sufficient; ability; efficiency. [LL *sufficientia* (as SUFFICIENT)]

■ **1** see ENOUGH *n.*

sufficient /səfíshənt/ *adj.* **1** sufficing; adequate; enough (*is sufficient for a family*; *didn't have sufficient funds*). **2** = SELF-SUFFICIENT. **3** *archaic* competent; of adequate ability, resources, etc. □□ **sufficiently** *adv.* [ME f. OF *sufficient* or L *sufficiens* (as SUFFICE)]

■ **1** adequate, enough; ample. **3** see *up to scratch* (SCRATCH). □□ **sufficiently** see ENOUGH *adv.* 1, 2.

suffix /súfiks/ *n. & v.* ● *n.* **1** a verbal element added at the end of a word to form a derivative (e.g., *-ation, -fy, -ing, -itis*). **2** *Math.* = SUBSCRIPT. ● *v.tr.* /also səfíks/ append, esp. as a suffix. □□ **suffixation** *n.* [*suffixum, suffixus* past part. of L *suffigere* (as SUB-, *figere fix-* fasten)]

■ *n.* **1** ending, termination, addition; *Gram.* affix.
● *v.* add (on), join, fasten to, subjoin, append, tack on.

suffocate /súfəkayt/ *v.* **1** *tr.* choke or kill by stopping breathing, esp. by pressure, fumes, etc. **2** *tr.* (often foll. by *by, with*) produce a choking or breathless sensation in, esp. by excitement, terror, etc. **3** *intr.* be or feel suffocated or breathless. □□ **suffocating** *adj.* **suffocatingly** *adv.* **suffocation** /-káyshən/ *n.* [L *suffocare* (as SUB-, *fauces* throat)]

■ **1** see CHOKE[1] *v.* 1. □□ **suffocating** see STUFFY 1.

Suffolk /súfək/ *n.* **1** a sheep of a black-faced breed raised for food. **2** this breed. [*Suffolk* in S. England]

suffragan /súfrəgən/ *n.* (in full **suffragan bishop** or **bishop suffragan**) **1** a bishop appointed to help a diocesan bishop in the administration of a diocese. **2** a bishop in relation to his archbishop or metropolitan. □ **suffragan see** the see of a suffragan bishop. □□ **suffraganship** *n.* [ME f. AF & OF, repr. med.L *suffraganeus* assistant (bishop) f. L *suffragium* (see SUFFRAGE): orig. of a bishop summoned to vote in synod]

suffrage /súfrij/ *n.* **1 a** the right to vote in political elections (*full adult suffrage*). **b** a view expressed by voting; a vote (*gave their suffrages for and against*). **c** opinion in support of

a proposal, etc. **2** (esp. in *pl.*) *Eccl.* **a** a prayer made by a priest in the liturgy. **b** a short prayer made by a congregation, esp. in response to a priest. **c** *archaic* an intercessory prayer. [ME f. L *suffragium*, partly through F *suffrage*]

■ **1** (right to) vote, voting right(s), franchise, voice, say, ballot, option, choice.

suffragette /súfrəjét/ *n. hist.* a woman seeking the right to vote through organized protest. [SUFFRAGE + -ETTE]

suffragist /súfrəjist/ *n.* esp. *hist.* a person who advocates the extension of suffrage, esp. to women. □□ **suffragism** *n.*

suffuse /səfyōōz/ *v.tr.* **1** (of color, moisture, etc.) spread from within to color or moisten (*a blush suffused her cheeks*). **2** cover with color, etc. □□ **suffusion** /-fyōōzhən/ *n.* [L *suffundere suffus-* (as SUB-, *fundere* pour)]

■ overspread, imbue, spread through *or* over, permeate, pervade, flood, flush, charge, penetrate, saturate, mantle, infuse, transfuse, cover, bathe, pour over, *literary* imbrue.

Sufi /sōōfee/ *n.* (*pl.* **Sufis**) a Muslim ascetic and mystic. □□ **Sufic** *adj.* **Sufism** *n.* [Arab. *ṣūfī*, perh. f. *ṣūf* wool (from the woolen garment worn)]

sug- /sug, səg/ *prefix* assim. form of SUB- before *g*.

sugar /shōōgər/ *n., v., & int.* ● *n.* **1** a sweet crystalline substance obtained from various plants, esp. the sugar cane and sugar beet, used in cooking, confectionery, brewing, etc.; sucrose. **2** *Chem.* any of a group of soluble usu. sweet-tasting crystalline carbohydrates found esp. in plants, e.g., glucose. **3** *colloq.* darling; dear (used as a term of address). **4** sweet words; flattery. **5** anything comparable to sugar encasing a pill in reconciling a person to what is unpalatable. **6** *sl.* a narcotic drug, esp. heroin or LSD (taken on a lump of sugar). ● *v.tr.* **1** sweeten with sugar. **2** make (one's words, meaning, etc.) more pleasant or welcome. **3** coat with sugar (*sugared almond*). **4** spread a sugar mixture on (a tree) to catch moths. **5** make maple syrup or maple sugar by sugaring off. ● *int. euphem.* = SHIT *int.* □ **sugar beet** a beet, *Beta vulgaris*, from which sugar is extracted. **sugar candy** see CANDY 1. **sugar cane** *Bot.* any perennial tropical grass of the genus *Saccharum*, esp. *S. officinarum*, with tall stout jointed stems from which sugar is made. **sugar-coated 1** (of food) enclosed in sugar. **2** made superficially attractive. **sugar daddy** (*pl.* **-ies**) *sl.* an older man who lavishes gifts on a younger partner. **sugar-gum** *Bot.* an Australian eucalyptus, *Eucalyptus cladocalyx*, with sweet foliage eaten by cattle. **sugar loaf** a conical molded mass of sugar. **sugar maple** any of various trees, esp. *Acer saccharum*, from the sap of which sugar is made. **sugar of lead** *Chem.* = lead acetate (see LEAD[2]). **sugar off** boil down maple sap into maple syrup and sugar. **sugar pea** a variety of pea eaten whole including the pod. **sugar the pill** see PILL. **sugar soap** *Brit.* an alkaline compound for cleaning or removing paint. □□ **sugarless** *adj.* [ME f. OF *çukre, sukere* f. It. *zucchero* prob. f. med.L *succarum* f. Arab. *sukkar*]

■ *n.* **4** cajolery, sweet words, flattery, *colloq.* sweet talk, soft soap, *sl.* snow job, *Brit. sl.* flannel. **6** see JUNK[1] *n.* 3.
● *v.* **1** sweeten, sugarcoat.

sugarplum /shōōgərplum/ *n. archaic* a small round candy of flavored boiled sugar.

sugary /shōōgəree/ *adj.* **1** containing or resembling sugar. **2** excessively sweet or esp. sentimental. **3** falsely sweet or pleasant (*sugary compliments*). □□ **sugariness** *n.*

■ **1** see SWEET *adj.* 1. **2** see ROMANTIC *adj.* 1. **3** see *flattering* (FLATTER).

suggest /səgjést, səjést/ *v.tr.* **1** (often foll. by *that* + clause) propose (a theory, plan, or hypothesis) (*suggested to them that they should wait*; *suggested a different plan*). **2 a** cause (an idea, memory, association, etc.) to present itself; evoke (*this poem suggests peace*). **b** hint at (*his behavior suggests guilt*). □ **suggest**

itself (of an idea, etc.) come into the mind. □□ **suggester** *n.* [L *suggerere suggest-* (as SUB-, *gerere* bring)]

▪ **1** propose, advance, propound, recommend, endorse, commend, urge, advise, advocate, offer, proffer, put *or* set forward, present, mention, introduce. **2** call to mind, evoke, bring up, hint (at), imply, insinuate, intimate, make a person think of, lead a person to believe, indicate, communicate.

suggestible /səgjéstəbəl, səjés-/ *adj.* **1** capable of being suggested. **2** open to suggestion; easily swayed. □□ **suggestibility** *n.*

▪ **2** impressionable, susceptible, receptive, impressible, susceptive, open (to suggestion), moldable. □□ **suggestibility** susceptibility, impressionability, receptiveness, vulnerability, frailty.

suggestion /səgjéschən, səjés-/ *n.* **1** the act or an instance of suggesting; the state of being suggested. **2** a theory, plan, etc., suggested (*made a helpful suggestion*). **3** a slight trace; a hint (*a suggestion of garlic*). **4** *Psychol.* **a** the insinuation of a belief, etc., into the mind. **b** such a belief, etc. [ME f. OF f. L *suggestio -onis* (as SUGGEST)]

▪ **1** counseling, prompting, urging, inducement. **2** proposal, proposition, recommendation, plan, advice, counsel, exhortation, tip, idea, notion, opinion, theory. **3** indication, trace, whisper, hint, soupçon, touch, tinge, suspicion, breath; iota, jot (or tittle).

suggestive /səgjéstiv, səjés-/ *adj.* **1** (usu. foll. by *of*) conveying a suggestion; evocative. **2** (esp. of a remark, joke, etc.) indecent; improper; racy. □□ **suggestively** *adv.* **suggestiveness** *n.*

▪ **1** reminiscent, redolent, evocative, indicative, symptomatic, expressive; pregnant, significant, meaningful, eloquent. **2** provocative, risqué, ribald, racy, bawdy, earthy, lusty, rude, indelicate, unseemly, immodest, improper, indecent, obscene, prurient, blue, offensive, vulgar, smutty, dirty, pornographic, lewd, salacious, sexy, spicy, off color, *colloq.* raunchy, *colloq. joc.* naughty. □□ **suggestiveness** see IMPROPRIETY 1.

suicidal /sŏŏisíd'l/ *adj.* **1** inclined to commit suicide. **2** of or concerning suicide. **3** self-destructive; fatally or disastrously rash. □□ **suicidally** *adv.*

suicide /sŏŏisīd/ *n. & v.* ● *n.* **1 a** the intentional killing of oneself. **b** a person who commits suicide. **2** a self-destructive action or course (*political suicide*). **3** (*attrib.*) *Mil.* designating a highly dangerous or deliberately suicidal operation, etc. (*a suicide mission*). ● *v.intr.* commit suicide. □ **suicide pact** an agreement between two or more people to commit suicide together. [mod.L *suicida*, *suicidium* f. L *sui* of oneself]

sui generis /sŏŏ-ī jénəris, sŏŏ-ee, sŏŏ-ee gén-/ *adj.* of its own kind; unique. [L]

▪ see UNIQUE *adj.* 1.

sui juris /sŏŏ-ī jŏŏris, sŏŏ-ee, sŏŏ-ee yŏŏris/ *adj. Law* of age; independent. [L]

suint /swint/ *n.* the natural grease in sheep's wool. [F f. *suer* sweat]

suit /sŏŏt/ *n. & v.* ● *n.* **1 a** a set of outer clothes of matching material for men, consisting usu. of a jacket, trousers, and sometimes a vest. **b** a similar set of clothes for women usu. having a skirt instead of trousers. **c** (esp. in *comb.*) a set of clothes for a special occasion, occupation, etc. (*playsuit; swimsuit*). **2 a** any of the four sets (spades, hearts, diamonds, clubs) into which a pack of cards is divided. **b** a player's holding in a suit (*his strong suit was clubs*). **c** *Bridge* one of the suits as proposed trumps in bidding, frequently as opposed to no trumps. **3** (in full **suit at law**) a lawsuit (*criminal suit*). **4 a** a petition, esp. to a person in authority. **b** the process of courting a woman (*paid suit to her*). **5** (usu. foll. by *of*) a set of sails, armor, etc. ● *v.* **1** *tr.* go well with (a person's figure, features, character, etc.); become. **2** *tr.* (also *absol.*) meet the demands or requirements of; satisfy; agree with (*does not suit all tastes; that date will suit*). **3** *tr.* make fitting or appropriate; accommodate, adjust (*suited his style to his audience*). **4** *tr.* (as **suited** *adj.*) appropriate; well-fitted (*not suited to be an engineer*). **5** *intr.* (usu. foll. by *with*) go

well with the appearance, etc., of a person (*red hair suits with her complexion*). □ **suit the action to the word** carry out a promise or threat at once. **suit oneself 1** do as one chooses. **2** find something that satisfies one. [ME f. AF *siute*, OF *si(e)ute* f. fem. past part. of Rmc *sequere* (unrecorded) follow: see SUE]

▪ *n.* **1** costume, outfit, two-piece, ensemble; uniform, habit; garb, clothing, clothes, livery. **3** lawsuit, action, case, proceeding, process, cause, trial; litigation. **4 a** petition, plea, request, entreaty, prayer, solicitation, application, appeal, supplication. **b** courtship, wooing; court, attentions, addresses. ● *v.* **1** go well with; become, befit, look good on, be appropriate *or* suitable for. **2** please, satisfy, fill *or* meet *or* answer a person's needs, gratify, be acceptable (to *or* for), be suitable (to *or* for), be convenient (to *or* for), befit; conform (to), agree with, fit in (with). **3** adapt, accommodate, fit, adjust, tailor, gear, make appropriate *or* suitable. **4** (**suited**) see APPROPRIATE *adj.*, tailor-made 2.

suitable /sŏŏtəbəl/ *adj.* (usu. foll. by *to, for*) well fitted for the purpose; appropriate. □□ **suitability** / *n.* **suitableness** *n.* **suitably** *adv.* [SUIT + -ABLE, after *agreeable*]

▪ appropriate, apt, apposite, fit, fitting, befitting, becoming, right, proper, correct, acceptable, satisfactory, applicable, qualified, eligible, seemly; pertinent, relevant, apropos; timely, opportune, convenient, *archaic* meet. □□ **suitability, suitableness** see *fitness* (FIT¹). **suitably** see *appropriately* (APPROPRIATE).

suitcase /sŏŏtkays/ *n.* a usu. oblong case for carrying clothes, etc., having a handle and often a flat hinged lid. □□ **suitcaseful** *n.* (*pl.* **-fuls**).

▪ bag, case, trunk, overnight bag, traveling bag, valise, esp. *Brit.* portmanteau.

suite /sweet/ *n.* **1** a set of things belonging together, esp.: **a** a set of rooms in a hotel, etc. **b** furniture intended for the same room and of the same design. **2** *Mus.* **a** a set of instrumental compositions, orig. in dance style, to be played in succession. **b** a set of selected pieces from an opera, musical, etc., arranged to be played as one instrumental work. **3** a set of people in attendance; a retinue. [F (as SUIT)]

▪ **1** set, series, collection, number; arrangement. **3** following, retinue, entourage, train, cortège, convoy, escort; followers, attendants, *hist.* retainers.

suiting /sŏŏting/ *n.* cloth used for making suits.

suitor /sŏŏtər/ *n.* **1** a man seeking to marry a specified woman; a wooer. **2** a plaintiff or petitioner in a lawsuit. [ME f. AF *seutor, suitour*, etc., f. L *secutor -oris* f. *sequi secut-* follow]

▪ **1** admirer, wooer, beau; boyfriend, lover, inamorato, escort, *archaic or derog.* paramour, *poet.* swain. **2** see LITIGANT *n.*

suk (also **sukh**) var. of SOUK.

sukiyaki /sŏŏkeeyaákee, skeeyaá-/ *n.* a Japanese dish of sliced meat simmered with vegetables and sauce. [Jap.]

Sukkoth var. of SUCCOTH.

sulcate /súlkayt/ *adj.* grooved; fluted; channeled. [L *sulcatus*, past part. of *sulcare* furrow (as SULCUS)]

sulcus /súlkəs/ *n.* (*pl.* **sulci** /-sī/) *Anat.* a groove or furrow, esp. on the surface of the brain. [L]

▪ see FURROW *n.*

sulfa /súlfə/ *n.* any drug derived from sulfanilamide (often *attrib.*: *sulfa drug*). [abbr.]

sulfamic acid /sulfámik/ *n.* a strong acid used in weedkiller, an amide of sulfuric acid. □□ **sulfamate** /súlfəmayt/ *n.* [SULFUR + AMIDE]

sulfanilamide /súlfəníləmīd/ *n.* a colorless sulfonamide drug with anti-bacterial properties. [*sulfanilic* (SULFUR, ANILINE) + AMIDE]

sulfate /súlfayt/ *n.* a salt or ester of sulfuric acid. [F *sulfate* f. L *sulfur*]

sulfide /súlfīd/ *n. Chem.* a binary compound of sulfur.

sulfite /súlfīt/ *n. Chem.* a salt or ester of sulfurous acid. [F *sulfite* alt. of *sulfate* SULFATE]

sulfonamide /sulfónəmīd/ *n.* a substance derived from an amide of a sulfonic acid, able to prevent the multiplication of some pathogenic bacteria. [SULFONE + AMIDE]

sulfonate /súlfənayt/ n. & v. Chem. ● n. a salt or ester of sulfonic acid. ● v.tr. convert into a sulfonate by reaction with sulfuric acid.

sulfone /súlfōn/ n. an organic compound containing the SO_2 group united directly to two carbon atoms. □□ **sulfonic** /-fónik/ adj. [G Sulfon (as SULFUR)]

sulfur /súlfər/ n. & v. ● n. **1 a** a pale yellow nonmetallic element having crystalline and amorphous forms, burning with a blue flame and a suffocating smell, and used in making gunpowder, matches, and sulfuric acid, in the vulcanizing of rubber, and in the treatment of skin diseases. ¶ Symb.: S. **b** (attrib.) like or containing sulfur. **2** the material of which hellfire and lightning were believed to consist. **3** any yellow butterfly of the family Pieridae. **4** a pale greenish yellow color. ● v.tr. **1** treat with sulfur. **2** fumigate with sulfur. □ **sulfur candle** a candle burned to produce sulfur dioxide for fumigating. **sulfur dioxide** a colorless pungent gas formed by burning sulfur in air and used as a food preservative. **sulfur spring** a spring impregnated with sulfur or its compounds. □□ **sulfury** adj. [ME f. AF sulf(e)re, OF soufre f. L sulfur, sulp(h)ur]
■ n. **1, 2** archaic brimstone.

sulfurate /súlfyərayt, -fə-/ v.tr. impregnate, fumigate, or treat with sulfur, esp. in bleaching. □□ **sulfuration** /-ráyshən/ n. **sulfurator** n.

sulfureous /sulfyŏoréeəs/ adj. **1** of, like, or suggesting sulfur. **2** sulfur-colored; yellow. [L sulphureus f. SULFUR]

sulfureted /súlfyŏorétid/ adj. archaic containing sulfur in combination. □ **sulfureted hydrogen** hydrogen sulfide. [sulphuret sulfide f. mod.L sulphuretum]

sulfuric /sulfyŏorik/ adj. Chem. containing sexivalent sulfur. □ **sulfuric acid** a dense, oily, colorless, highly acid and corrosive fluid much used in the chemical industry. ¶ Chem. formula: H_2SO_4. [F sulfurique (as SULFUR)]

sulfurize /súlfyəriz, -fə-/ v.tr. = SULFURATE. □□ **sulfurization** n. [F sulfuriser (as SULFUR)]

sulfurous /súlfərəs, -fyŏōr-/ adj. **1** relating to or suggestive of sulfur, esp. in color. **2** Chem. containing quadrivalent sulfur. □ **sulfurous acid** an unstable weak acid used as a reducing and bleaching acid. [L sulphurosus f. SULFUR]

sulk /sulk/ v. & n. ● v.intr. indulge in a sulk; be sulky. ● n. (also in pl., prec. by the) a period of sullen, esp. resentful, silence (having a sulk; got the sulks). □□ **sulker** n. [perh. back-form. f. SULKY]
■ v. mope, brood, pout, lower, be sullen or moody or ill-humored.

sulky /súlkee/ adj. & n. ● adj. (**sulkier, sulkiest**) **1** sullen, morose, or silent, esp. from resentment or ill temper. **2** sluggish. ● n. (pl. **-ies**) a light two-wheeled horse-drawn vehicle for one, esp. used in harness racing. □□ **sulkily** adv. **sulkiness** n. [perh. f. obs. sulke hard to dispose of]
■ adj. **1** see SULLEN adj. 1.

sullage /súlij/ n. filth; refuse; sewage. [perh. f. AF suillage f. souiller SOIL²]
■ see FILTH 1.

sullen /súlən/ adj. & n. ● adj. **1** morose; resentful; sulky; unforgiving; unsociable. **2 a** (of a thing) slow moving. **b** dismal; melancholy (a sullen sky). ● n. (in pl., usu. prec. by the) archaic a sullen frame of mind; depression. □□ **sullenly** adv. **sullenness** n. [16th-c. alt. of ME solein f. AF f. sol SOLE³]
■ adj. **1** sulky, sulking, morose, brooding, broody, pouting, gloomy, moody, temperamental, dour, lugubrious, funereal, dismal, dreary, grim, depressed, churlish, ill-humored, glum, grumpy, somber, out of humor, antisocial, unsociable, resentful, cross, petulant, perverse, crusty, crotchety, choleric, crabby, ill-natured, ill-tempered, bad-tempered, splenetic, peevish, dyspeptic, out of sorts, cranky. **2 b** see LEADEN 4.

sully /súlee/ v.tr. (**-ies, -ied**) **1** disgrace or tarnish (a person's reputation or character, a victory, etc.). **2** poet. dirty; soil. [perh. f. F souiller (as SOIL²)]

■ besmirch, stain, smirch, blemish, mar, defile, soil, disgrace, dirty, tarnish, pollute, contaminate, spoil.

sulph- Brit. var. of words in SULF-.

sultan /súlt'n/ n. **1 a** a Muslim sovereign. **b** (**the Sultan**) hist. the sultan of Turkey. **2** a variety of white domestic fowl from Turkey. □□ **sultanate** /-nayt/ n. [F sultan or med.L sultanus f. Arab. sulṭān power, ruler f. saluṭa rule]
■ **1** see SOVEREIGN n.

sultana /sultánə, -táänə/ n. **1 a** a seedless raisin used in cakes, etc. **b** the small, pale yellow grape producing this. **2** the mother, wife, concubine, or daughter of a sultan. [It., fem. of sultano = SULTAN]

sultry /súltree/ adj. (**sultrier, sultriest**) **1** (of the atmosphere or the weather) hot or oppressive; close. **2** (of a person, character, etc.) passionate; sensual. □□ **sultrily** adv. **sultriness** n. [obs. sulter SWELTER]
■ **1** hot, humid, sticky, stuffy, oppressive, close, muggy, steamy, steaming, moist, damp, sweltering, suffocating. **2** lusty, lustful, passionate, erotic, seductive, voluptuous, provocative, sensual, sexy, hot.

sum /sum/ n. & v. ● n. **1** the total amount resulting from the addition of two or more items, facts, ideas, feelings, etc. (the sum of two and three is five; the sum of their objections is this). **2** a particular amount of money (paid a large sum for it). **3 a** an arithmetical problem (could not work out the sum). **b** (esp. pl.) esp. Brit. colloq. arithmetic work, esp. at an elementary level (was good at sums). ● v.tr. (**summed, summing**) find the sum of. □ **in sum** in brief. **summing-up 1** a review of evidence and a direction given by a judge to a jury. **2** a recapitulation of the main points of an argument, case, etc. **sum total** = sense 1 of n. **sum up 1** (esp. of a judge) recapitulate or review the evidence in a case, etc. **2** form or express an idea of the character of (a person, situation, etc.). **3** collect into or express as a total or whole. [ME f. OF summe, somme f. L summa main part, fem. of summus highest]
■ n. **1** total, aggregate, grand total, sum total, whole, totality; result, tally, score. **2** amount, figure, quantity. **3 a** problem, question. **b** (sums) arithmetic, figures, numbers, calculation, computation; mathematics, colloq. math, Brit. colloq. maths. ● v. see ADD 2.
□ **in sum** see in brief (BRIEF). **summing-up** review, recapitulation, summarization, summary, summation, synopsis, rundown. **sum up 1** recapitulate, summarize, encapsulate, synopsize, digest, abridge, condense, consolidate, epitomize, review. **2** estimate, evaluate, assess, size up, measure (up), take the measure of. **3** reckon, add up, calculate, total, tot up, sum.

sumac /sóomak, shóo-/ n. (also **sumach**) **1** any shrub or tree of the genus Rhus, having reddish cone-shaped fruits used as a spice in cooking. **2** the dried and ground leaves of this used in tanning and dyeing. [ME f. OF sumac or med.L sumac(h) f. Arab. summāk]

Sumerian /sōoméereeən, -mér-/ adj. & n. ● adj. of or relating to the early and non-Semitic element in the civilization of ancient Babylonia. ● n. **1** a member of the early non-Semitic people of ancient Babylonia. **2** the Sumerian language. [F sumérien f. Sumer in Babylonia]

summa /sóomə, súmə/ n. (pl. **summae** /-mee/) a summary of what is known of a subject. [ME f. L: see SUM]

summa cum laude /sóomə kŏōm lówday, -də, -dee/ adv. & adj. (of a degree, diploma, etc.) of the highest standard; with the highest distinction. [L, = with highest praise]

summarize /súməriz/ v.tr. make or be a summary of; sum up. □□ **summarist** n. **summarizable** adj. **summarization** n. **summarizer** n.
■ see sum up 1. □□ **summarization** see SUMMARY n.

summary /súmaree/ n. & adj. ● n. (pl. **-ies**) a brief account; an abridgment. ● adj. **1** dispensing with needless details or formalities; brief (*a summary account*). **2** *Law* (of a trial, etc.) without the customary legal formalities (*summary justice*). □ **summary conviction** a conviction made by a judge or magistrates without a jury. **summary jurisdiction** the authority of a court to use summary proceedings and arrive at a judgment. **summary offense** an offense within the scope of a summary court. □□ **summarily** /səmáirilee/ *adv*. **summariness** *n*. [ME f. L *summarium* f. L *summa* SUM]

■ *n*. summarization, recapitulation, encapsulation, compendium, synopsis, abstract, digest, abridgment, condensation, shortening, consolidation, epitome, epitomization, review, distillate, conspectus, outline, précis, résumé, *Law* brief. ● *adj*. **1** abrupt, sudden, short, quick, brief, laconic, perfunctory, curt, terse, concise, succinct. **2** peremptory; see also SPEEDY 2. □□ **summarily** immediately, at once, straightaway, directly, quickly, without delay, unhesitatingly, without hesitation, forthwith, promptly, swiftly, speedily, expeditiously, instantly; suddenly, without warning, abruptly, peremptorily, precipitately; *colloq*. p.d.q. (= "pretty damn quick").

summation /səmáyshən/ *n*. **1** the finding of a total or sum; an addition. **2** a summing-up. □□ **summational** *adj*.

summer[1] /súmər/ *n*. & *v*. ● *n*. **1** the warmest season of the year, in the N. hemisphere from June to August and in the S. hemisphere from December to February. **2** *Astron.* the period from the summer solstice to the autumnal equinox. **3** the hot weather typical of summer. **4** (often foll. by *of*) the mature stage of life; the height of achievement, powers, etc. **5** (esp. in *pl.*) *poet.* a year (esp. of a person's age) (*a child of ten summers*). **6** (*attrib.*) characteristic of or suitable for summer (*summer clothes*). ● *v*. **1** *intr.* (usu. foll. by *at, in*) pass the summer. **2** *tr.* (often foll. by *at, in*) pasture (cattle). □ **summer lightning** sheet lightning without thunder, resulting from a distant storm. **summer school** **1** a course of lectures, etc., held during the summer vacation, esp. at a university. **2** a course or series of courses held during the summer vacation allowing students to make up work missed or failed, or to accelerate toward their degrees. **summer solstice** see SOLSTICE. **summer squash** any of various cultivated squashes whose fruit is used as a vegetable. **summer time** *Brit.* the period between March and October during which the clocks are advanced an hour (cf. SUMMERTIME). **summer-weight** (of clothes) suitable for use in summer, esp. because of their light weight. □□ **summerless** *adj*. **summerly** *adv*. **summery** *adj*. [OE *sumor*]

■ □□ **summery** see SOFT *adj*. 3.

summer[2] /súmər/ *n*. (in full **summertree**) a horizontal bearing beam, esp. one supporting joists or rafters. [ME f. AF *sumer, somer* packhorse, beam, OF *somier* f. LL *sagmarius* f. *sagma* f. Gk *sagma* packsaddle]

summersault var. of SOMERSAULT.

summertime /súmərtīm/ *n*. the season or period of summer (cf. *summer time*).

summit /súmit/ *n*. **1** the highest point, esp. of a mountain; the apex. **2** the highest degree of power, ambition, etc. **3** (in full **summit meeting, talks,** etc.) a discussion, esp. on disarmament, etc., between heads of government. □□ **summitless** *adj*. [ME f. OF *somet, som(m)ete* f. *som* top f. L *summum* neut. of *summus*]

■ **1, 2** peak, top, apex, acme, pinnacle, zenith, crown, height; culmination, apogee, climax.

summon /súmən/ *v.tr.* **1** call upon to appear, esp. as a defendant or witness in a court of law. **2** (usu. foll. by *to* + infin.) call upon (*summoned her to assist*). **3** call together for a meeting or some other purpose (*summoned the members to attend*). □ **summon up** (often foll. by *to, for*) gather (courage, spirits, resources, etc.) (*summoned up her strength for the task*). □□ **summonable** *adj*. **summoner** *n*. [ME f. OF *somondre* f. L *summonēre* (as SUB-, *monēre* warn)]

■ **1, 2** subpoena, summons; call upon, send for, command, order. **3** call, assemble, convene, send for, invite, muster, get *or* gather together, rally, arouse, rouse, *formal* convoke. □ **summon up** call *or* draw

(up)on, draw up, mobilize, muster (up), work up, whip up, gather, invoke.

summons /súmənz/ *n*. & *v*. ● *n*. (*pl.* **summonses**) **1** an authoritative or urgent call to attend on some occasion or do something. **2 a** a call to appear before a judge or magistrate. **b** the writ containing such a summons. ● *v.tr.* esp. *Law* serve with a summons. [ME f. OF *somonce, sumunse* f. L *summonita* fem. past part. of *summonēre*: see SUMMON]

■ *n*. **1, 2a** see CALL *n*. 5. **2 b** see WARRANT *n*. 2. ● *v*. see INDICT.

summum bonum /soomam bónam/ *n*. the highest good, esp. as the end or determining principle in an ethical system. [L]

sumo /soomō/ *n*. (*pl.* **-os**) **1** a style of Japanese wrestling in which a participant is defeated by touching the ground with any part of the body except the soles of the feet or by moving outside the marked area. **2** a sumo wrestler. [Jap.]

sump /sump/ *n*. **1** a pit, well, hole, etc., in which superfluous liquid collects in mines, machines, etc. **2** a cesspool. [ME, = marsh f. MDu., MLG *sump*, or (mining) G *Sumpf*, rel. to SWAMP]

sumpter /súmptər/ *n*. *archaic* **1** a packhorse. **2** any pack animal (*sumpter-mule*). [ME f. OF *som(m)etier* f. LL f. Gk *sagma -atos* packsaddle: cf. SUMMER[2]]

sumptuary /súmpchōoeree/ *adj*. **1** regulating expenditure. **2** (of a law or edict, etc.) limiting private expenditure in the interests of the government. [L *sumptuarius* f. *sumptus* cost f. *sumere sumpt-* take]

sumptuous /súmpchōoəs/ *adj*. rich; lavish; costly (*a sumptuous setting*). □□ **sumptuosity** /-ósitee/ *n*. **sumptuously** *adv*. **sumptuousness** *n*. [ME f. OF *sompteux* f. L *sumptuosus* (as SUMPTUARY)]

■ expensive, costly, extravagant, exorbitant, dear, rich; lavish, luxurious, deluxe, opulent, palatial, royal, majestic, regal, magnificent, dazzling, splendid, gorgeous, grand, showy, plush, *colloq.* posh, plushy, ritzy. □□ **sumptuously** see RICHLY 1. **sumptuousness** see LUXURY 1.

Sun. *abbr.* Sunday.

sun /sun/ *n*. & *v*. ● *n*. **1 a** the star around which the earth orbits and from which it receives light and warmth. **b** any similar star in the universe with or without planets. **2** the light or warmth received from the sun (*pull down the blinds and keep out the sun*). **3** *poet.* a day or a year. **4** *poet.* a person or thing regarded as a source of glory, radiance, etc. ● *v*. (**sunned, sunning**) **1** *refl.* bask in the sun. **2** *tr.* expose to the sun. **3** *intr.* sun oneself. □ **against the sun** counterclockwise. **beneath** (or **under**) **the sun** anywhere in the world. **in the sun** exposed to the sun's rays. **sun and planet** a system of gearing cog wheels. **sun bear** a small black bear, *Helarctos malayanus*, of SE Asia, with a light-colored mark on its chest. **sun-blind** *Brit.* a window awning. **sun dance** a dance of some Native American tribes in honor of the sun. **sun deck** the upper deck of a cruise ship, etc. **sun disk** a winged disk, emblematic of the sun god. **sun dog** = PARHELION. **sun-dried** dried by the sun, not by artificial heat. **sun god** the sun worshiped as a deity. **sun hat** a hat designed to protect the head from the sun. **sun helmet** a helmet of cork, etc., formerly worn in the tropics. **sun in splendor** *Heraldry* the sun with rays and a human face. **one's sun is set** the time of one's prosperity is over. **sun-kissed** warmed or affected by the sun. **sun lamp 1** a lamp giving ultraviolet rays for an artificial suntan, therapy, etc. **2** *Cinematog.* a large lamp with a parabolic reflector used in film-making. **sun lounge** *Brit.* = *sun parlor*. **sun parlor** a room with large windows, designed to receive sunlight. **sun rays 1** sunbeams. **2** ultraviolet rays used therapeutically. **sun stone** a cat's eye gem, esp. feldspar with embedded flecks of hematite, etc. **sun visor** a fixed or movable shield at the top of a vehicle windshield to shield the eyes from the sun. **take** (or **shoot**) **the sun** *Naut.* ascertain the altitude of the sun with a sextant in order to fix the latitude. **with the sun** clockwise. □□ **sunless** *adj*. **sunlessness** *n*. **sunlike** *adj*. **sunproof** *adj*. **sunward** *adj*. & *adv*. **sunwards** *adv*. [OE *sunne, sunna*]

■ *n*. **2** sunshine, sunlight. ● *v*. **1, 3** bask, bake, sun oneself; tan, suntan, sunbathe, brown, bronze. **2** tan, bake, brown, bronze. □ **beneath** (or **under**) **the sun** see BELOW *adv.* 5. □□ **sunless** dark, dull, grim, cheerless, unhappy, joyless, funereal, depressing, dreary, somber, gloomy, overcast, gray, black, pitchy, inky, shadowy, unlit, unlighted, dusky, *formal* subfusc, *literary* tenebrous, stygian, *poet.* darkling, drear.

sunbath /súnbath/ *n.* a period of exposing the body to the sun.

sunbathe /súnbayth/ *v.intr.* bask in the sun, esp. to tan the body. □□ **sunbather** *n.*
■ see SUN *v.* 1, 3.

sunbeam /súnbeem/ *n.* a ray of sunlight.

sunbed /súnbed/ *n.* **1** *Brit.* a lightweight, usu. folding, chair with a seat long enough to support the legs, used for sunbathing. **2** a bed for lying on under a sun lamp.

sunbelt /súnbelt/ *n.* a strip of territory receiving a high amount of sunshine, esp. the region in the southern US stretching from California to Florida.

sunbird /súnbərd/ *n.* any small brightly plumaged Old World bird of the family Nectariniidae, resembling a hummingbird.

sunblock /súnblok/ *n.* a cream or lotion for protecting the skin from the sun.

sunburn /súnbərn/ *n. & v.* ● *n.* reddening and inflammation of the skin caused by overexposure to the sun. ● *v.intr.* **1** suffer from sunburn. **2** (as **sunburned** or **sunburnt** *adj.*) suffering from sunburn; brown or tanned.

sunburst /súnbərst/ *n.* **1** something resembling the sun and its rays, esp.: **a** an ornament, brooch, etc. **b** a firework. **2** the sun shining suddenly from behind clouds.

sundae /súnday, -dee/ *n.* a dish of ice cream with fruit, nuts, syrup, etc. [perh. f. SUNDAY]

Sunday /súnday, -dee/ *n. & adv.* ● *n.* **1** the first day of the week, a Christian holiday and day of worship. **2** a newspaper published on a Sunday. ● *adv. colloq.* **1** on Sunday. **2** (**Sundays**) on Sundays; each Sunday. □ **Sunday best** a person's best clothes, kept for Sunday use. **Sunday letter** = *dominical letter.* **Sunday painter** an amateur painter, esp. one with little training. **Sunday school** a school for the religious instruction of children on Sundays. [OE *sunnandæg,* transl. of L *dies solis,* Gk *hēmera hēliou* day of the sun]
■ □ **Sunday best** see FINERY[1].

sunder /súndər/ *v.tr. & intr. archaic* or *literary* separate; sever. □ **in sunder** apart. [OE *sundrian,* f. *āsundrian,* etc.: *in sunder* f. ME f. *o(n)sunder* ASUNDER]
■ see DIVIDE *v.* 1, 3a.

sundew /súndōō, -dyōō/ *n.* any small insect-consuming bog plant of the family Droseraceae, esp. of the genus *Drosera* with hairs secreting drops of moisture.

sundial /súndiəl/ *n.* an instrument showing the time by the shadow of a pointer cast by the sun onto a graduated disk.

sundown /súndown/ *n.* sunset.
■ see EVENING *n.* 1.

sundowner /súndownər/ *n.* **1** *Austral.* a tramp who arrives at a sheep station, etc., in the evening for food and shelter too late to do any work. **2** *Brit. colloq.* an alcoholic drink taken at sunset.

sundress /súndres/ *n.* a dress without sleeves and with a low neck and back, designed for warm weather.

sundry /súndree/ *adj. & n.* ● *adj.* various; several (*sundry items*). ● *n.* (*pl.* **-ies**) **1** (in *pl.*) items or oddments not mentioned individually. **2** *Austral. Cricket* = EXTRA *n.* 5. [OE *syndrig* separate, rel. to SUNDER]
■ *adj.* various, varied, miscellaneous, assorted, different, mixed, diversified, diverse, several, *archaic* or *literary* divers. ● *n.* **1** (*sundries*) miscellanea, oddments, et ceteras.

sunfast /súnfast/ *adj.* (of dye) not subject to fading by sunlight.

sunfish /súnfish/ *n.* any of various almost spherical fish, esp. a large ocean fish, *Mola mola.*

sunflower /súnflowr/ *n.* any very tall plant of the genus *Helianthus,* esp. *H. annus* with very large, showy, golden-rayed flowers, grown also for its seeds which yield an edible oil.

sung *past part.* of SING.

sunglasses /súnglasiz/ *n.* glasses tinted to protect the eyes from sunlight or glare.
■ *colloq.* shades.

sunk *past* and *past part.* of SINK.

sunken /súngkən/ *adj.* **1** that has been sunk. **2** beneath the surface; submerged. **3** (of the eyes, cheeks, etc.) hollow; depressed. □ **sunken garden** a garden placed below the general level of its surroundings. [past part. of SINK]
■ **1** buried, underground, in-ground, belowground, settled, lowered. **2** submerged, undersea, underwater. **3** hollow, depressed; haggard, drawn.

sunlight /súnlit/ *n.* light from the sun.
■ see LIGHT[1] *n.* 2.

sunlit /súnlit/ *adj.* illuminated by sunlight.
■ see SUNNY 1.

sunn /sun/ *n.* (in full **sunn hemp**) an E. Indian hemplike fiber. [Urdu & Hindi *san* f. Skr. *śaṇá* hempen]

Sunna /sóōnə/ *n.* a traditional portion of Muslim law based on Muhammad's words or acts, accepted by Muslims as authoritative. [Arab., = form, way, course, rule]

Sunni /sóōnee/ *n. & adj.* ● *n.* (*pl.* same or **Sunnis**) **1** one of the two main branches of Islam, regarding the Sunna as equal in authority to the Koran (cf. SHIA). **2** an adherent of this branch of Islam. ● *adj.* (also **Sunnite**) of or relating to Sunni.

sunny /súnee/ *adj.* (**sunnier, sunniest**) **1 a** bright with sunlight. **b** exposed to or warmed by the sun. **2** cheery and bright in temperament. □ **the sunny side 1** the side of a house, street, etc., that gets most sun. **2** the more cheerful aspect of circumstances, etc. (*always looks on the sunny side*). □□ **sunnily** *adv.* **sunniness** *n.*
■ **1** sunlit, sunshiny, brilliant, bright, radiant, fair, fine, cloudless, clear, unclouded. **2** cheerful, cheery, bright, happy, joyous, joyful, lighthearted, smiling, beaming, buoyant, gay, mirthful, jolly, bubbly, ebullient, genial, warm, friendly, outgoing, *poet.* blithe.

sunnyside up /súneesid/ *adj.* (of an egg) fried on one side and served.

sunrise /súnriz/ *n.* **1** the sun's rising at dawn. **2** the colored sky associated with this. **3** the time at which sunrise occurs. □ **sunrise industry** any newly established industry, esp. in electronics and telecommunications, regarded as signaling prosperity.
■ **1, 3** see DAWN *n.* 1.

sunroof /súnrōōf/ *n.* a section of an automobile roof that can be slid open.

sunset /súnset/ *n. & adj.* ● *n.* **1** the sun's setting in the evening. **2** the colored sky associated with this. **3** the time at which sunset occurs. **4** the declining period of life. ● *adj.* pertaining to a law or government program subject to review for its continuation.
■ **1, 3** see DUSK *n.* 1.

sunshade /súnshayd/ *n.* **1** a parasol. **2** an awning.

sunshine /súnshin/ *n.* **1 a** the light of the sun. **b** an area lit by the sun. **2** good weather. **3** cheerfulness; joy (*brought sunshine into her life*). **4** *Brit. colloq.* a form of address. □ **sunshine roof** *Brit.* = SUNROOF. □□ **sunshiny** *adj.*
■ **1 a** see DAYLIGHT 1. **3** see JOY *n.* 1.

sunspot /súnspot/ *n.* one of the dark patches, changing in shape and size and lasting for varying periods, observed on the sun's surface.

sunstar /súnstaar/ *n.* any starfish of the genus *Solaster,* with many rays.

sunstroke /súnstrōk/ *n.* acute prostration or collapse from the excessive heat of the sun.

suntan /súntan/ *n. & v.* ● *n.* the brownish coloring of skin caused by exposure to the sun. ● *v.intr.* (**-tanned, -tanning**) color the skin with a suntan.

/. . ./ **pronunciation**	● **part of speech**
□ **phrases, idioms, and compounds**	
□□ **derivatives**	■ **synonym section**
cross-references appear in SMALL CAPITALS or *italics*	

■ *v.* see SUN *v.* 1, 3.

suntrap /súntrap/ *n. Brit.* a place sheltered from the wind and suitable for catching the sunshine.

sunup /súnup/ *n.* sunrise.

■ see DAWN *n.* 1.

sup[1] /sup/ *v. & n.* ● *v.tr.* (**supped, supping**) **1** take (soup, tea, etc.) by sips or spoonfuls. **2** esp. *No. of Engl. colloq.* drink (alcohol). ● *n.* a sip of liquid. [OE *sūpan*]

■ *v.* **1** see SIP *v.* **2** see DRINK *v.* 2. ● *n.* see SIP *n.*

sup[2] /sup/ *v.intr.* (**supped, supping**) (usu. foll. by *off, on*) *archaic* take supper. [OF *super, soper*]

■ see DINE.

sup- /sup, səp/ *prefix* assim. form of SUB- before *p.*

super /sŏŏpər/ *adj. & n.* ● *adj.* **1** (also **super-duper** /-dŏŏpər/) *colloq.* (also as *int.*) exceptional; splendid. **2** esp. *Brit. Commerce* superfine. **3** esp. *Brit. Commerce* (of a measure) superficial, in square (not lineal or solid) measure (*120 super ft.; 120 ft. super*). ● *n. colloq.* **1** *Theatr.* a supernumerary actor. **2** a superintendent. **3** superphosphate. **4** an extra, unwanted, or unimportant person; a supernumerary. **5** *Commerce* superfine cloth or manufacture. [abbr.]

■ *adj.* **1** see SUPERB. ● *n.* **1** see EXTRA *n.* 3. **2** see SUPERINTENDENT *n.* 1.

super- /sŏŏpər/ *comb. form* forming nouns, adjectives, and verbs, meaning: **1** above, beyond, or over in place or time or conceptually (*superstructure; supernormal; superimpose*). **2** to a great or extreme degree (*superabundant; superhuman*). **3** extra good or large of its kind (*supertanker*). **4** of a higher kind, esp. in names of classificatory divisions (*superclass*). [from or after L *super-* f. *super* above, beyond]

superable /sŏŏpərəbəl/ *adj.* able to be overcome. [L *superabilis* f. *superare* overcome]

superabound /sŏŏpərəbównd/ *v.intr.* be very or too abundant. [LL *superabundare* (as SUPER-, ABOUND)]

superabundant /sŏŏpərəbúndənt/ *adj.* abounding beyond what is normal or right. □□ **superabundance** *n.* **superabundantly** *adv.* [ME f. LL *superabundare*: see SUPERABOUND]

■ see ABUNDANT 1. □□ **superabundance** see ABUNDANCE 1.

superadd /sŏŏpərád/ *v.tr.* add over and above. □□ **superaddition** /-ədíshən/ *n.* [ME f. L *superaddere* (as SUPER-, ADD)]

superaltar /sŏŏpərawltər/ *n. Eccl.* a portable slab of stone consecrated for use on an unconsecrated altar, etc. [ME f. med.L *superaltare* (as SUPER-, ALTAR)]

superannuate /sŏŏpərányŏŏayt/ *v.tr.* **1** retire (a person) with a pension. **2** dismiss or discard as too old for use, work, etc. **3** (as **superannuated** *adj.*) too old for work or use; obsolete. □□ **superannuable** *adj.* [back-form. f. *superannuated* f. med.L *superannuatus* f. L SUPER- + *annus* year]

■ **1** see *pension off* (PENSION[1]). **3** (**superannuated**) see OBSOLETE.

superannuation /sŏŏpərányŏŏ-áyshən/ *n.* **1** a pension paid to a retired person. **2** *Brit.* a regular payment made toward this by an employed person. **3** the process or an instance of superannuating.

■ **1** see PENSION[1] *n.* 1.

superaqueous /sŏŏpəráykweeəs, -ák-/ *adj.* above water.

superb /sŏŏpérb/ *adj.* **1** of the most impressive, splendid, grand, or majestic kind (*superb courage; a superb specimen*). **2** *colloq.* excellent; fine. □□ **superbly** *adv.* **superbness** *n.* [F *superbe* or L *superbus* proud]

■ wonderful, marvelous, excellent, superior, gorgeous, glorious, grand, majestic, magnificent, outstanding, exquisite, fine, splendid, unequaled, sensational, noteworthy, great, impressive, admirable, peerless, matchless, unrivaled, first-rate, superlative, perfect, classic, exceptional, extraordinary, striking, brilliant, dazzling, miraculous, incredible, unbelievable, stupendous, staggering, breathtaking, *colloq.* far-out, smashing, magic, terrific, fantastic, fabulous, out-of-sight, out of this world, divine, mind-boggling, super, super-duper, top-notch, crack, *sl.* unreal, cool, bad, *Austral. sl.* grouse. □□ **superbly** see *beautifully* (BEAUTIFUL).

supercalender /sŏŏpərkálindər/ *v.tr.* give a highly glazed finish to (paper) by extra calendering.

supercargo /sŏŏpərkaargō/ *n.* (*pl.* **-oes**) an officer in a merchant ship managing sales, etc., of cargo. [earlier *supracargo* f. Sp. *sobrecargo* f. *sobre* over + *cargo* CARGO]

supercelestial /sŏŏpərsiléschəl/ *adj.* **1** above the heavens. **2** more than heavenly. [LL *supercaelestis* (as SUPER-, CELESTIAL)]

supercharge /sŏŏpərchaarj/ *v.tr.* **1** (usu. foll. by *with*) charge (the atmosphere, etc.) with energy, emotion, etc. **2** use a supercharger on (an internal combustion engine).

supercharger /sŏŏpərchaarjər/ *n.* a device supplying air or fuel to an internal combustion engine at above normal pressure to increase efficiency.

superciliary /sŏŏpərsílee-eree/ *adj. Anat.* of or concerning the eyebrow; over the eye. [L *supercilium* eyebrow (as SUPER-, *cilium* eyelid)]

supercilious /sŏŏpərsíleeəs/ *adj.* assuming an air of contemptuous indifference or superiority. □□ **superciliously** *adv.* **superciliousness** *n.* [L *superciliosus* (as SUPERCILIARY)]

■ haughty, contemptuous, superior, snobbish, disdainful, arrogant, condescending, patronizing, overbearing, scornful, lordly, high and mighty, pompous, lofty, pretentious, hoity-toity, *colloq.* highfalutin, uppity, snooty, stuck-up, la-di-da, esp. *Brit. colloq.* uppish, esp. *Brit. sl.* toffee-nosed. □□ **superciliousness** see *snobbery* (SNOB).

superclass /sŏŏpərklas/ *n.* a taxonomic category between class and phylum.

supercolumnar /sŏŏpərkəlúmnər/ *adj. Archit.* having one order or set of columns above another. □□ **supercolumniation** /-neeáyshən/ *n.*

supercomputer /sŏŏpərkəmpyŏŏtər/ *n.* a powerful computer capable of dealing with complex problems. □□ **supercomputing** *n.*

superconductivity /sŏŏpərkónduktívitee/ *n. Physics* the property of zero electrical resistance in some substances at very low absolute temperatures. □□ **superconducting** /-kəndúkting/ *adj.* **superconductive** /-kəndúktiv/ *adj.*

superconductor /sŏŏpərkəndúktər/ *n. Physics* a substance having superconductivity.

superconscious /sŏŏpərkónshəs/ *adj.* transcending human consciousness. □□ **superconsciously** *adv.* **superconsciousness** *n.*

supercool /sŏŏpərkŏŏl/ *v. & adj.* ● *v. Chem.* **1** *tr.* cool (a liquid) below its freezing point without solidification or crystallization. **2** *intr.* (of a liquid) be cooled in this way. ● *adj. sl.* very cool, relaxed, etc.

supercritical /sŏŏpərkrítikəl/ *adj. Physics* of more than critical mass, etc.

super-duper var. of SUPER *adj.* 1.

superego /sŏŏpəreegō, -égō/ *n.* (*pl.* **-os**) *Psychol.* the part of the mind that acts as a conscience and responds to social rules.

superelevation /sŏŏpəréliváyshən/ *n.* the amount by which the outer edge of a curve on a road or railroad is above the inner edge.

supereminent /sŏŏpəréminənt/ *adj.* supremely eminent, exalted, or remarkable. □□ **supereminence** *n.* **supereminently** *adv.* [L *supereminēre* rise above (as SUPER-, EMINENT)]

supererogation /sŏŏpərérəgáyshən/ *n.* the performance of more than duty requires. □ **works of supererogation** *RC Ch.* actions believed to form a reserve fund of merit that can be drawn on by prayer in favor of sinners. □□ **supererogatory** /-irógətawree/ *adj.* [LL *supererogatio* f. *supererogare* pay in addition (as SUPER-, *erogare* pay out)]

■ see EXCESS *n.* 1. □□ **supererogatory** see SUPERFLUOUS.

superexcellent /sŏŏpəréksələnt/ *adj.* very or supremely excellent. □□ **superexcellence** *n.* **superexcellently** *adv.* [LL *superexcellens* (as SUPER-, EXCELLENT)]

superfamily /sŏŏpərfamilee/ *n.* (*pl.* **-ies**) a taxonomic category between family and order.

superfatted /sŏŏpərfátid/ *adj.* (of soap) containing extra fat.

superfecundation /sŏŏpərfeekəndáyshən, -fékən-/ *n.* = SUPERFETATION 1.

superfetation /sōōpərfeetáyshən/ *n.* **1** *Med.* & *Zool.* a second conception during pregnancy giving rise to embryos of different ages in the uterus. **2** *Bot.* the fertilization of the same ovule by different kinds of pollen. **3** the accretion of one thing on another. [F *superfétation* or f. mod.L *superfetatio* f. L *superfetare* (as SUPER-, *fetus* FETUS)]

superficial /sōōpərfíshəl/ *adj.* **1** of or on the surface; lacking depth (*a superficial knowledge*; *superficial wounds*). **2** swift or cursory (*a superficial examination*). **3** apparent but not real (*a superficial resemblance*). **4** (esp. of a person) having no depth of character or knowlege; trivial; shallow. **5** esp. *Brit.* *Commerce* (of a measure) square (cf. SUPER *adj.* 3). □□ **superficiality** /-sheeálitee/ *n.* (*pl.* **-ies**). **superficially** *adv.* **superficialness** *n.* [LL *superficialis* f. L (as SUPERFICIES)]

■ **1** surface, external, exterior, shallow, skin-deep, slight, outside. **2** cursory, slapdash, quick, swift, hurried, hasty, perfunctory, passing. **3** surface, slight, external, apparent, skin-deep, outward, insignificant, passing, unimportant, empty, insubstantial, nominal, token, meaningless; paying lip service, for appearances' sake, cosmetic. **4** trivial, frivolous, shallow, empty-headed, hollow, mindless. □□ **superficially** see *outwardly* (OUTWARD).

superficies /sōōpərfísheez, -fishee-eez/ *n.* (*pl.* same) *Geom.* a surface. [L (as SUPER-, *facies* face)]

■ (outer) surface, facade, face, externals, outside.

superfine /sōōpərfín/ *adj.* **1** *Commerce* of high quality. **2** pretending great refinement. [med.L *superfinus* (as SUPER-, FINE[1])]

superfluity /sōōpərflōōitee/ *n.* (*pl.* **-ies**) **1** the state of being superfluous. **2** a superfluous amount or thing. [ME f. OF *superfluité* f. LL *superfluitas -tatis* f. L *superfluus*: see SUPERFLUOUS]

■ **1** excess, superabundance, overabundance, surplus, surfeit, glut, superfluousness, profusion, plethora, oversupply, supersaturation. **2** excess, surplus, leftovers, overflow.

superfluous /sōōpərflōōəs/ *adj.* more than enough; redundant; needless. □□ **superfluously** *adv.* **superfluousness** *n.* [ME f. L *superfluus* (as SUPER-, *fluere* to flow)]

■ excessive, excess, superabundant, overabundant, supererogatory, surplus, unneeded, uncalled-for, unnecessary, redundant, extra, nonessential; needless, dispensable, gratuitous. □□ **superfluousness** see SUPERFLUITY 1.

supergiant /sōōpərjìənt/ *n.* a star of very great luminosity and size.

superglue /sōōpərglōō/ *n.* any of various adhesives with an exceptional bonding capability.

supergrass /sōōpərgras/ *n. Brit. colloq.* a police informer who implicates a large number of people.

superheat /sōōpərhéet/ *v.tr. Physics* **1** heat (a liquid) above its boiling point without vaporization. **2** heat (a vapor) above its boiling point (*superheated steam*). □□ **superheater** *n.*

superhet /sōōpərhét/ *n. colloq.* = SUPERHETERODYNE.

superheterodyne /sōōpərhétərōdīn/ *adj.* & *n.* ● *adj.* denoting or characteristic of a system of radio reception in which a local variable oscillator is tuned to beat at a constant ultrasonic frequency with carrier wave frequencies, making it unnecessary to vary the amplifier tuning and securing greater selectivity. ● *n.* a superheterodyne receiver. [SUPERSONIC + HETERODYNE]

superhighway /sōōpərhíway/ *n.* a multilane main road for fast traffic.

■ see ROAD[1] 1.

superhuman /sōōpərhyōōmən/ *adj.* **1** beyond normal human capability. **2** higher than man. □□ **superhumanly** *adv.* [LL *superhumanus* (as SUPER-, HUMAN)]

■ **1** heroic, Herculean, godlike, legendary, valiant, courageous, brave, daring, dangerous, death-defying, extraordinary, miraculous, phenomenal, incredible, fabulous, fantastic, unbelievable, amazing, prodigious. **2** see DIVINE *adj.* 2a.

superhumeral /sōōpərhyōōmərəl/ *n. Eccl.* a vestment worn over the shoulders, e.g., an amice, ephod, or pallium. [LL *superhumerale* (as SUPER-, HUMERAL)]

superimpose /sōōpərimpōz/ *v.tr.* (usu. foll. by *on*) lay (a thing) on something else. □□ **superimposition** /-pəzishən/ *n.*

■ see LAY[1] *v.* 1.

superincumbent /sōōpərinkúmbənt/ *adj.* lying on something else.

superinduce /sōōpərindōōs, -dyōōs/ *v.tr.* introduce or induce in addition. [L *superinducere* cover over, bring from outside (as SUPER-, INDUCE)]

superintend /sōōpərinténd/ *v.tr.* & *intr.* be responsible for the management or arrangement of (an activity, etc.); supervise and inspect. □□ **superintendence** *n.* **superintendency** *n.* [eccl.L *superintendere* (as SUPER-, INTEND), transl. Gk *episkopō*]

■ see SUPERVISE. □□ **superintendence** see MANAGEMENT 1.

superintendent /sōōpərinténdənt/ *n.* & *adj.* ● *n.* **1 a** a person who superintends. **b** a director of an institution, etc. **2 a** *US* a high-ranking official, often the chief of a police department. **b** *Brit.* a police officer above the rank of inspector. **3** the caretaker of a building. ● *adj.* superintending. [eccl.L *superintendent-* part. stem of *superintendere*: see SUPERINTEND]

■ *n.* **1** supervisor, foreman, overseer, manager, administrator, chief, head; governor, controller, director, conductor; *colloq.* boss, super, *Brit. colloq.* gaffer. **3** see PORTER[2].

superior /sōōpéeree·ər/ *adj.* & *n.* ● *adj.* **1** in a higher position; of higher rank (*a superior officer*; *a superior court*). **2 a** above the average in quality, etc. (*made of superior leather*). **b** having or showing a high opinion of oneself; supercilious (*had a superior air*). **3** (often foll. by *to*) **a** better or greater in some respect (*superior to its rivals in speed*). **b** above yielding, making concessions, paying attention, etc. (*is superior to bribery*; *superior to temptation*). **4** further above or out; higher, esp.: **a** *Astron.* (of a planet) having an orbit further from the sun than the earth's. **b** *Zool.* (of an insect's wings) folding over others. **c** *Printing* (of figures or letters) placed above the line. **d** *Bot.* (of the calyx) above the ovary. **e** *Bot.* (of the ovary) above the calyx. ● *n.* **1** a person superior to another in rank, character, etc. (*is deferential to his superiors*; *is her superior in courage*). **2** (*fem.* **superioress** /-ris/) *Eccl.* the head of a monastery or other religious institution (*Mother Superior*; *Father Superior*). **3** *Printing* a superior letter or figure. □□ **superiorly** *adv.* [ME f. OF *superiour* f. L *superior -oris*, compar. of *superus* that is above f. *super* above]

■ *adj.* **1** higher, upper, loftier, higher-ranking, higher-level, higher-class, higher-caliber, upper-level, upper-class, nobler, senior; of a higher order *or* status *or* standing, greater. **2 a** high-class, elevated, first-rate, distinguished, exceptional, excellent, better, preferred, choice, select, élitist, outstanding, superlative, matchless, unequaled, peerless, nonpareil, sterling, supreme, fine, noteworthy, notable, worthy, estimable, *colloq.* classier, tonier. **b** see SUPERCILIOUS. **3 b** (*superior to*) see ABOVE *prep.* 4b. ● *n.* **1** better, senior, elder; see also *supervisor* (SUPERVISE).

superiority /sōōpéeree-áwritee, -ór-/ *n.* the state of being superior. □ **superiority complex** *Psychol.* an undue conviction of one's own superiority to others.

■ ascendancy, preeminence, supremacy, leadership, lead, dominance, predominance, primacy, precedence, advantage, hegemony; excellence, greatness, peerlessness, matchlessness, inimitability, superlativeness, prominence, eminence, importance, distinction, prestige, renown.

/.../ **pronunciation**	● **part of speech**
□ **phrases, idioms, and compounds**	
□□ **derivatives**	■ **synonym section**
cross-references appear in SMALL CAPITALS or *italics*	

superjacent /sŏŏpərjáysənt/ *adj.* overlying; superincumbent. [L *superjacēre* (as SUPER-, *jacēre* lie)]

superlative /sŏŏpə́rlətiv/ *adj. & n.* ● *adj.* **1** of the highest quality or degree (*superlative wisdom*). **2** *Gram.* (of an adjective or adverb) expressing the highest or a very high degree of a quality (e.g., *bravest, most fiercely*) (cf. POSITIVE, COMPARATIVE). **3** exaggerated; excessive. ● *n.* **1** *Gram.* **a** the superlative expression or form of an adjective or adverb. **b** a word in the superlative. **2** something embodying excellence; the highest form of a thing. **3** an exaggerated or excessive statement, comment, expression, etc. □□ **superlatively** *adv.* **superlativeness** *n.* [ME f. OF *superlatif -ive* f. LL *superlativus* f. L *superlatus* (as SUPER-, *latus* past part. of *ferre* take)]

▪ *adj.* **1** unsurpassed, paramount, supreme, consummate, superior, best, choicest, finest, matchless, peerless, unequaled, unrivaled, unbeatable, singular, unique, incomparable, excellent, superb, dazzling, first-rate, first-class, exceptional, extraordinary, marvelous, spectacular, *colloq.* tiptop, capital, super, smashing, great, terrific, fantastic, crack, *sl.* ace. □□ **superlatively** see PERFECTLY 3. **superlativeness** see SUPERIORITY.

superlunary /sŏŏpərlŏ́ōnəree/ *adj.* **1** situated beyond the moon. **2** belonging to a higher world; celestial. [med.L *superlunaris* (as SUPER-, LUNAR)]

superman /sŏŏpərman/ *n.* (*pl.* **-men**) **1** esp. *Philos.* the ideal superior man of the future. **2** *colloq.* a man of exceptional strength or ability. [SUPER- + MAN, formed by G. B. Shaw after Nietzsche's G *Übermensch*]

▪ **2** hero, Hercules, Titan.

supermarket /sŏŏpərmaarkit/ *n.* a large self-service store selling foods, household goods, etc.

▪ see STORE *n.* 3b.

supermundane /sŏŏpərmundáyn/ *adj.* superior to earthly things.

▪ see PSYCHIC *adj.* 1b.

supernal /sŏŏpə́rnəl/ *adj.* esp. *poet.* **1** heavenly; divine. **2** of or concerning the sky. **3** lofty. □□ **supernally** *adv.* [ME f. OF *supernal* or med.L *supernalis* f. L *supernus* f. *super* above]

▪ **1** see HEAVENLY 1.

supernatant /sŏŏpərnáyt'nt/ *adj. & n.* esp. *Chem.* ● *adj.* floating on the surface of a liquid. ● *n.* a supernatant substance. [SUPER- + *natant* swimming (as NATATION)]

supernatural /sŏŏpərnáchərəl/ *adj. & n.* ● *adj.* attributed to or thought to reveal some force above the laws of nature; magical; mystical. ● *n.* (prec. by *the*) supernatural, occult, or magical forces, effects, etc. □□ **supernaturalism** *n.* **supernaturalist** *n.* **supernaturalize** *v.tr.* **supernaturally** *adv.* **supernaturalness** *n.*

▪ *adj.* preternatural, unusual, extraordinary, exceptional, unnatural, miraculous, remarkable, fabulous, preterhuman, ghostly, spectral, abnormal, supernormal, inexplicable, unexplainable; metaphysical, hyperphysical, superphysical, otherworldly, unearthly, ultramundane, supramundane, extramundane, divine, occult, mystic(al), paranormal, psychic, uncanny, weird, mysterious, arcane, unreal, magical, dark. ● *n.* see *the occult* (OCCULT). □□ **supernaturalism** see MYSTIQUE 1.

supernormal /sŏŏpərnáwrməl/ *adj.* beyond what is normal or natural. □□ **supernormality** /-málitee/ *n.*

supernova /sŏŏpərnṓvə/ *n.* (*pl.* **-novae** /-vee/ or **-novas**) *Astron.* a star that suddenly increases very greatly in brightness because of an explosion ejecting most of its mass.

▪ see STAR *n.* 1.

supernumerary /sŏŏpərnŏ́ōməreree, -nyŏ́ō-/ *adj. & n.* ● *adj.* **1** in excess of the normal number; extra. **2** (of a person) engaged for extra work. **3** (of an actor) appearing on stage but not speaking. ● *n.* (*pl.* **-ies**) **1** an extra or unwanted person or thing. **2** a supernumerary actor; extra. **3** a person engaged for extra work. [LL *supernumerarius* (soldier) added to a legion already complete, f. L *super numerum* beyond the number]

▪ *adj.* **1** see SPARE *adj.* 1. ● *n.* **1** see UNNECESSARY *n.* **2** see THESPIAN *n.*

superorder /sŏŏpərawrdər/ *n. Biol.* a taxonomic category between order and class. □□ **superordinal** /-órdin'l/ *adj.*

superordinate /sŏŏpəráwrd'nət/ *adj.* (usu. foll. by *to*) of superior importance or rank. [SUPER-, after *subordinate*]

superphosphate /sŏŏpərfósfayt/ *n.* a fertilizer made by treating phosphate rock with sulfuric or phosphoric acid.

superphysical /sŏŏpərfízikəl/ *adj.* **1** unexplainable by physical causes; supernatural. **2** beyond what is physical.

superpose /sŏŏpərpṓz/ *v.tr.* (usu. foll. by *on*) esp. *Geom.* place (a thing or a geometric figure) on or above something else, esp. so as to coincide. □□ **superposition** /-pəzíshən/ *n.* [F *superposer* (as SUPER-, POSE¹)]

▪ superimpose, place; see also LAY¹ *v.* 1.

superpower /sŏŏpərpowr/ *n.* a nation of supreme power and influence, esp. the US and the former USSR.

supersaturate /sŏŏpəsáchərayt/ *v.tr.* add to (esp. a solution) beyond saturation point. □□ **supersaturation** /-ráyshən/ *n.*

▪ □□ **supersaturation** see SUPERFLUITY 1.

superscribe /sŏŏpərskríb/ *v.tr.* **1** write (an inscription) at the top of or on the outside of a document, etc. **2** write an inscription over or on (a thing). □□ **superscription** /-skrípshən/ *n.* [L *superscribere* (as SUPER-, *scribere* script-write)]

superscript /sŏŏpərskript/ *adj. & n.* ● *adj.* written or printed above the line, esp. *Math.* (of a symbol) written above and to the right of another. ● *n.* a superscript number or symbol. [L *superscriptus* past part. of *superscribere*: see SUPERSCRIBE]

supersede /sŏŏpərseéd/ *v.tr.* **1 a** adopt or appoint another person or thing in place of. **b** set aside; cease to employ. **2** (of a person or thing) take the place of. □□ **supersedence** *n.* **supersedure** /-seéjər/ *n.* **supersession** /-séshən/ *n.* [OF *superseder* f. L *supersedēre* be superior to (as SUPER-, *sedēre* sess-sit)]

▪ **1** replace, put in place of, change. **2** replace, succeed, displace, supplant, oust, take the place of, take over from, substitute for.

supersonic /sŏŏpərsónik/ *adj.* designating or having a speed greater than that of sound. □□ **supersonically** *adv.*

supersonics /sŏŏpərsóniks/ *n.pl.* (treated as *sing.*) = ULTRASONICS.

superstar /sŏŏpərstaar/ *n.* an extremely famous or renowned actor, movie star, athlete, etc. □□ **superstardom** *n.*

▪ see CELEBRITY 1.

superstition /sŏŏpərstíshən/ *n.* **1** credulity regarding the supernatural. **2** an irrational fear of the unknown or mysterious. **3** misdirected reverence. **4** a practice, opinion, or religion based on these tendencies. **5** a widely held but unjustified idea of the effects or nature of a thing. □□ **superstitious** *adj.* **superstitiously** *adv.* **superstitiousness** *n.* [ME f. OF *superstition* or L *superstitio* (as SUPER-, *stare* stat-stand)]

superstore /sŏŏpərstawr/ *n.* a very large store selling a wide range of goods.

▪ see STORE *n.* 3b.

superstratum /sŏŏpərstraytəm, -strat-/ *n.* (*pl.* **-strata** /-tə/) an overlying stratum.

superstructure /sŏŏpərstrukchər/ *n.* **1** the part of a building above its foundations. **2** a structure built on top of something else. **3** a concept or idea based on others. □□ **superstructural** *adj.*

supersubtle /sŏŏpərsút'l/ *adj.* extremely or excessively subtle. □□ **supersubtlety** *n.*

supertanker /sŏŏpərtangkər/ *n.* a very large tanker ship.

supertax /sŏŏpərtaks/ *n.* esp. *Brit.* a tax on incomes above a certain level, esp. a surtax.

superterrestrial /sŏŏpərtəréstreeəl/ *adj.* **1** in or belonging to a region above the earth. **2** celestial.

supertitle var. of SURTITLE.

supertonic /sŏŏpərtónik/ *n. Mus.* the note above the tonic, the second note of the diatonic scale of any key.

supervene /sŏŏpərveén/ *v.intr.* occur as an interruption in or a change from some state. □□ **supervenient** *adj.* **supervention** /-vénshən/ *n.* [L *supervenire supervent-* (as SUPER-, *venire* come)]

■ see SUCCEED 2. □□ **supervenient** see SUPPLEMENTARY.

supervise /sо̄о̄pərviz/ *v.tr.* **1** superintend; oversee the execution of (a task, etc.). **2** oversee the actions or work of (a person). □□ **supervision** /-vízhən/ *n.* **supervisor** *n.* **supervisory** *adj.* [med.L *supervidēre supervis-* (as SUPER-, *vidēre* see)]

■ oversee, overlook, watch (over), manage, run, control, superintend, govern, direct, head, be in *or* have charge of, handle, keep an eye on, administer. □□ **supervision** see *leadership* (LEADER). **supervisor** overseer, foreman, manager, controller, superintendent, superior, director, chief, head, administrator; invigilator; *colloq.* boss, super, *Brit. colloq.* gaffer, *sl.* honcho, *Brit. sl.* governor. **supervisory** managerial, administrative, executive.

superwoman /sо̄о̄pərwŏŏmən/ *n.* (*pl.* **-women**) *colloq.* a woman of exceptional strength or ability.

supinate /sо̄о̄pinayt/ *v.tr.* put (a hand or foreleg, etc.) into a supine position (cf. PRONATE). □□ **supination** /-náyshən/ *n.* [back-form. f. *supination* f. L *supinatio* f. *supinare* f. *supinus*: see SUPINE]

supinator /sо̄о̄pinaytər/ *n. Anat.* a muscle in the forearm effecting supination.

supine *adj. & n.* ● *adj.* sо̄о̄pín/ **1** lying face upwards (cf. PRONE). **2** having the front or ventral part upwards; (of the hand) with the palm upwards. **3** inert; indolent; morally or mentally inactive. ● *n.* /sо̄о̄pín/ a Latin verbal noun used only in the accusative and ablative cases, esp. to denote purpose (e.g., *mirabile dictu* wonderful to relate). □□ **supinely** /-pínlee/ *adv.* **supineness** *n.* [L *supinus*, rel. to *super*: (n.) f. LL *supinum* neut. (reason unkn.)]

■ *adj.* **1** face upwards, flat (on one's back); lying (down), recumbent, *Bot. & Zool.* decumbent. **3** indolent, lazy, lethargic, idle, listless, indifferent, apathetic, unconcerned, uninterested, torpid, languid, languorous, sluggish, slothful, phlegmatic, lymphatic, lackadaisical, inert, inactive, passive, motionless, inanimate, spiritless, abject. □□ **supineness** see STUPOR.

supper /súpər/ *n.* a light evening meal. □ **sing for one's supper** do something in return for a benefit. □□ **supperless** *adj.* [ME f. OF *soper, super*]

■ see MEAL¹.

supplant /səplánt/ *v.tr.* dispossess and take the place of, esp. by underhand means. □□ **supplanter** *n.* [ME f. OF *supplanter* or L *supplantare* trip up (as SUB-, *planta* sole)]

■ replace, displace, oust, turn out, eject, remove, expel, dismiss, unseat, supersede, take the place of, substitute for.

supple /súpəl/ *adj. & v.* ● *adj.* (**suppler, supplest**) **1** flexible; pliant; easily bent. **2** compliant; avoiding overt resistance; artfully or servilely submissive. ● *v.tr. & intr.* make or become supple. □□ **suppleness** *n.* [ME f. OF *souple* ult. f. L *supplex supplicis* submissive]

■ *adj.* **1** flexible, pliant, bendable, elastic, resilient, pliable; willowy, lithe, limber, nimble, lissome, graceful, athletic, *archaic* flexile. **2** tractable, compliant, yielding, accommodating, obliging, complaisant, acquiescent, submissive, unresistant, unresisting, servile, obsequious, ingratiating, fawning, toadying. □□ **suppleness** see *flexibility* (FLEXIBLE).

supplejack /súpəljak/ *n.* any of various strong twining tropical shrubs, esp. *Berchemia scandens.* [SUPPLE + JACK¹]

supplely var. of SUPPLY².

supplement *n. & v.* ● *n.* /súplimənt/ **1** a thing or part added to remedy deficiencies (*dietary supplement*). **2** a part added to a book, etc., to provide further information. **3** a separate section, esp. a color magazine, added to a newspaper or periodical. **4** *Geom.* the amount by which an angle is less than 180° (cf. COMPLEMENT). ● *v.tr.* /súplimént/ provide a supplement for. □□ **supplemental** /-mént'l/ *adj.* **supplementally** *adv.* **supplementation** /-mentáyshən/ *n.* [ME f. L *supplementum* (as SUB-, *plēre* fill)]

■ *n.* **1** addition, extension, appendage, adjunct, appurtenance, accessory, prosthetic; surcharge, extra; supplementation, suppletion. **2** addendum, addition, appendix, epilogue, end piece, postscript, codicil, rider,

insert, extension, continuation, annex. **3** insert, appendix, extra; (color) magazine, *Brit.* color supplement. ● *v.* add to, extend, augment, *colloq.* boost; complement, esp. *Brit.* top up. □□ **supplemental** see SUPPLEMENTARY.

supplementary /súpliméntəree/ *adj.* forming or serving as a supplement; additional. □□ **supplementarily** *adv.*

■ additional, added, annexed, adjunct, new; supplemental, supportive, contributory, ancillary, secondary, subordinate, attached, appended, subsidiary, auxiliary, accessory; extraneous, adventitious, supervenient, extra, excess, further; *Linguistics* suppletive.

suppletion /səpleéshən/ *n.* the act or an instance of supplementing, esp. *Linguistics* the occurrence of unrelated forms to supply gaps in conjugation (e.g., *went* as the past of *go*). □□ **suppletive** *adj.* [ME f. OF f. med.L *suppletio -onis* (as SUPPLY¹)]

■ see SUPPLEMENT *n.* 1. □□ **suppletive** see SUPPLEMENTARY.

suppliant /súpleeənt/ *adj. & n.* ● *adj.* **1** supplicating. **2** expressing supplication. ● *n.* a supplicating person. □□ **suppliantly** *adv.* [ME f. F *supplier* beseech f. L (as SUPPLICATE)]

■ *adj.* see *supplicant adj.* (SUPPLICATE). ● *n.* see *supplicant n.* (SUPPLICATE).

supplicate /súplikayt/ *v.* **1** *tr.* petition humbly to (a person) or for (a thing). **2** *intr.* (foll. by *to, for*) make a petition. □□ **supplicant** *adj. & n.* **supplication** /-áyshən/ *n.* **supplicatory** *adj.* [ME f. L *supplicare* (as SUB-, *plicare* bend)]

■ **1** see PETITION *v.* 2. □□ **supplicant** (*adj.*) supplicatory, suppliant, imploring, solicitous, importunate, mendicant. (*n.*) applicant, suppliant, petitioner, beseecher, suitor, aspirant, beggar, mendicant; *Law* pleader, appellant, plaintiff. **supplication** entreaty, petition, prayer, appeal, pleading, plea, request, suit, solicitation, obsecration.

supply¹ /səplí/ *v. & n.* ● *v.tr.* (**-ies, -ied**) **1** provide or furnish (a thing needed). **2** (often foll. by *with*) provide (a person, etc., with a thing needed). **3** meet or make up for (a deficiency or need, etc.). **4** fill (a vacancy, place, etc.) as a substitute. ● *n.* (*pl.* **-ies**) **1** the act or an instance of providing what is needed. **2** a stock, store, amount, etc., of something provided or obtainable (*a large supply of water; the gas supply*). **3** (in *pl.*) **a** the collected provisions and equipment for an army, expedition, etc. **b** *Brit.* a grant of money by Parliament for the costs of government. **c** *Brit.* a money allowance to a person. **4** (often *attrib.*) a person, esp. a schoolteacher or clergyman, acting as a temporary substitute for another. **5** (*attrib.*) providing supplies or a supply (*supply officer*). □ **in short supply** available in limited quantity. **supply and demand** *Econ.* quantities available and required as factors regulating the price of commodities. **supply-side** *Econ.* denoting a policy of low taxation and other incentives to produce goods and invest. □□ **supplier** *n.* [ME f. OF *so(u)pleer*, etc., f. L *supplēre* (as SUB-, *plēre* fill)]

■ *v.* **1, 2** furnish, provide, give, endow, donate, present, purvey, deliver, come up with, yield, contribute, distribute, sell; stock, accommodate, afford, equip, outfit, gear (up), rig (out), fit (out), provision, fullfill, minister (with), esp. *Brit.* kit out *or* up; victual. **3** satisfy, meet, replenish, fill. ● *n.* **1** provision, purveyance, distribution, delivery. **2** stock, stockpile, store, inventory, quantity, reservoir, reserve, cache, hoard, accumulation, fund. **3** (*supplies*) **a** see KIT¹ *n.* 1, PROVISION *n.* 2. **4** see SUBSTITUTE *n.* 1a. □ **in short supply** see LIMITED 1. □□ **supplier** see DEALER, DONOR.

supply² /súplee/ *adv.* (also **supplely** /súpəlee/) in a supple manner.

support /səpáwrt/ *v. & n.* ● *v.tr.* **1** carry all or part of the weight of. **2** keep from falling or sinking or failing. **3** provide with a home and the necessities of life (*has a family to support*). **4** enable to last out; give strength to; encourage. **5** bear out; tend to substantiate or corroborate (a statement, charge, theory, etc.). **6** give help or countenance to; back up; second; further. **7** speak in favor of (a resolution, etc.). **8** be actively interested in (a particular team or sport). **9** take a part that is secondary to (a principal actor, etc.). **10** assist (a lecturer, etc.) by one's presence. **11** endure; tolerate (*can no longer support the noise*). **12** maintain or represent (a part or character) adequately. **13** back (an institution, etc.) financially. ● *n.* **1** the act or an instance of supporting; the process of being supported. **2** a person or thing that supports. □ **in support of** in order to support. **support price** a minimum price guaranteed to a farmer for agricultural produce and maintained by subsidy, etc. □□ **supportable** *adj.* **supportability** *n.* **supportably** *adv.* **supportingly** *adv.* **supportless** *adj.* [ME f. OF *supporter* f. L *supportare* (as SUB-, *portare* carry)]

■ *v.* **1, 2** carry, bear, take, hold up, sustain; brace, prop (up); strengthen, shore up, reinforce, fortify, buttress, bolster, underpin. **3** maintain, keep, provide for; pay for, fund, finance. **4, 6** back (up), stand by, stick by, help, assist, aid, bolster, uphold, brace, strengthen, fortify, buttress, prop (up), shore up, reinforce, encourage, sustain, *colloq.* boost; champion, take up the cudgels for, back (up), promote, forward, further, second, advance, advocate, stand up for, be supportive (of *or* in), stick up for. **5** verify, corroborate, authenticate, vouch for, endorse, confirm, affirm, bear out, attest to, certify, substantiate, validate, ratify. **7** speak *or* plead *or* argue for, speak *or* plead *or* argue in favor of, recommend, advocate, favor. **11** tolerate, bear, stand (for), suffer, submit to, undergo, stomach, endure, abide, countenance, face, weather, put up with, esp. *Brit. colloq.* stick, *literary* brook. **13** give to, contribute to, donate to, finance, fund, subsidize, underwrite, patronize, sponsor, *colloq.* bankroll. ● *n.* **1** help, backing, backup, reinforcement, encouragement, assistance, aid, succor, sustenance; contribution, allegiance, patronage, sponsorship. **2** brace, prop, stay, frame, foundation, underpinning, substructure, shoring, staging, truss, beam, joist, column, pillar, stilt, post, stanchion, strut, guy, guy wire, mainstay, crutch, bracket, buttress, bolster, reinforcement; sustenance, (living) expenses, keep, maintenance, subsistence, upkeep; finances, funding; see also SUPPORTER. □ **in support of** see *in favor* (FAVOR). □□ **supportable** tolerable, bearable, endurable, acceptable, sufferable; defensible, confirmable, verifiable, demonstrable, tenable, believable.

supporter /səpáwrtər/ *n.* **1** a person or thing that supports, esp. a person supporting a team, sport, political candidate, etc. **2** *Heraldry* the representation of an animal, etc., usu. one of a pair, holding up or standing beside an escutcheon. **3** = JOCKSTRAP 1.

■ **1** enthusiast, champion, promoter, fan, aficionado, devotee, admirer, backer, follower, support, advocate, defender, seconder, exponent, adherent, aid, assistant, ally, helper, benefactor, patron.

supportive /səpáwrtiv/ *adj.* providing support or encouragement. □□ **supportively** *adv.* **supportiveness** *n.*

■ helpful, sustaining, supporting, encouraging, sympathetic, understanding, reassuring.

suppose /səpṓz/ *v.tr.* (often foll. by *that* + clause) **1** assume, esp. in default of knowledge; be inclined to think (*I suppose they will return*; *what do you suppose he meant?*). **2** take as a possibility or hypothesis (*let us suppose you are right*). **3** (in *imper.*) as a formula of proposal (*suppose we go to the party*). **4** (of a theory or result, etc.) require as a condition (*design in creation supposes a creator*). **5** (in *imper.* or *pres. part.* forming a question) in the circumstances that; if (*suppose he won't let you*; *supposing we stay*). **6** (as **supposed** *adj.*) generally accepted as being so; believed (*his supposed brother*; *generally supposed to be wealthy*). **7** (in *passive*; foll. by *to* + infin.) **a**

be expected or required (*was supposed to write to you*). **b** (with *neg.*) not have to; not be allowed to (*you are not supposed to go in there*). □ **I suppose so** an expression of hesitant agreement. □□ **supposable** *adj.* [ME f. OF *supposer* (as SUB-, POSE¹)]

■ **1** assume, presume, presuppose, surmise, take, take as given, take for granted; believe, think, fancy, imagine; take it. **2** hypothesize, theorize, postulate, posit, assume. **4** require, presuppose, assume; see also INVOLVE 2. **5** (*supposing*) if, even if, *disp.* in the event that. **6** (**supposed**) alleged, assumed, putative, reputed, presumed; hypothetical, theoretical, theorized, suppositious, supposititious; believed, purported, thought, imagined. **7 a** (*be supposed*) be obliged, be expected, be required; be meant, be intended.

supposedly /səpṓzidlee/ *adv.* as is generally supposed.

■ allegedly, reputedly, theoretically, hypothetically, presumably; (as) rumor has it.

supposition /súpəzíshən/ *n.* **1** a fact or idea, etc., supposed. **2** the act or an instance of supposing. □□ **suppositional** *adj.*

■ **1, 2** assumption, presumption, surmise, inference, conjecture, speculation; belief, thought, fancy, idea, guess, theory, hypothesis, postulate, proposal, proposition; postulation, guesswork, inference, conjecture, surmise, speculation. □□ **suppositional** see HYPOTHETICAL.

suppositious /súpəzíshəs/ *adj.* hypothetical; assumed. □□ **suppositiously** *adv.* **suppositiousness** *n.* [partly f. SUPPOSITITIOUS, partly f. SUPPOSITION + -OUS]

■ see HYPOTHETICAL.

supposititious /səpózitíshəs/ *adj.* spurious; substituted for the real. □□ **supposititiously** *adv.* **supposititiousness** *n.* [L *supposititius*, *-icius* f. *supponere supposit-* substitute (as SUB-*ponere* place)]

suppository /səpózitawree/ *n.* (*pl.* **-ies**) a medical preparation in the form of a cone, cylinder, etc., to be inserted into the rectum or vagina to melt. [ME f. med.L *suppositorium*, neut. of LL *suppositorius* placed underneath (as SUPPOSITITIOUS)]

suppress /səprés/ *v.tr.* **1** end the activity or existence of, esp. forcibly. **2** prevent (information, feelings, a reaction, etc.) from being seen, heard, or known (*tried to suppress the report*; *suppressed a yawn*). **3 a** partly or wholly eliminate (electrical interference, etc.). **b** equip (a device) to reduce such interference due to it. **4** *Psychol.* keep out of one's consciousness. □□ **suppressible** *adj.* **suppression** *n.* **suppressive** *adj.* **suppressor** *n.* [ME f. L *supprimere suppress-* (as SUB-, *premere* press)]

■ **1** end, discontinue, cut off, cease, stop, terminate, put an end to, halt, prohibit, preclude, prevent, repress, forbid, interdict, block, obstruct, stifle, inhibit, hinder, arrest; put down, quell, crush, squelch, quash, overcome, overpower, subdue, check, stamp out, snuff out, smother, extinguish, quench, *colloq.* crack down on. **2** keep down, control, keep under control, keep *or* hold in check, restrain, hold in *or* back, bottle up, swallow, stifle, repress, cover up, censor, conceal, hide, keep quiet *or* secret, mute, muffle, quiet, silence, *Brit.* quieten. □□ **suppression** end, discontinuation, cutoff, cessation, stop, termination, halt, prohibition, preclusion, prevention, repression, censorship, forbiddance, interdiction, obstruction, *literary* surcease; check, extinction, elimination, *colloq.* crackdown; control, restraint, concealment. **suppressive** see PROHIBITIVE 1, *repressive* (REPRESS).

suppressant /səprésənt/ *n.* a suppressing or restraining agent, esp. a drug that suppresses the appetite.

suppurate /súpyərayt/ *v.intr.* **1** form pus. **2** fester. □□ **suppuration** /-ráyshən/ *n.* **suppurative** /-rətiv/ *adj.* [L *suppurare* (as SUB-, *purare* as PUS)]

■ **2** see FESTER 1. □□ **suppuration** see DISCHARGE *n.* 5. **suppurative** see *ulcerous* (ULCER).

supra /sóōprə/ *adv.* above or earlier on (in a book, etc.). [L, = above]

supra- /sóōprə/ *prefix* **1** above. **2** beyond; transcending (*su-*

pranational). [from or after L *supra*- f. *supra* above, beyond, before in time]

supramaxillary /sŏŏprəmáksileree/ *adj.* of or relating to the upper jaw.

supramundane /sŏŏprəmundáyn/ *adj.* above or superior to the world.

■ see SUPERNATURAL *adj.*

supranational /sŏŏprənáshənəl/ *adj.* transcending national limits. □□ **supranationalism** *n.* **supranationality** /-nálitee/ / *n.*

■ see INTERNATIONAL *adj.*

supraorbital /sŏŏprəáwrbit'l/ *adj.* situated above the orbit of the eye.

suprarenal /sŏŏprəreénəl/ *adj.* situated above the kidneys.

supremacist /sŏŏpréməsist/ *n. & adj.* ● *n.* an advocate of the supremacy of a particular group, esp. determined by race or sex. ● *adj.* relating to or advocating such supremacy. □□ **supremacism** *n.*

■ *n.* bigot, racist, racialist, dogmatist, zealot, fanatic, chauvinist.

supremacy /sŏŏprémǝsee/ *n.* (*pl.* **-ies**) **1** the state of being supreme. **2** supreme authority. □ **Act of Supremacy** (in the UK) an act securing ecclesiastical supremacy to the Crown and excluding the authority of the Pope.

■ **1** transcendency, preeminence, supremeness, superiority, ascendancy, predominance, excellence, primacy, peerlessness, matchlessness, incomparability, inimitability. **2** sovereignty, dominion, sway, mastery, control, dominance, (supreme *or* absolute) rule, (supreme *or* absolute) authority, autarchy, omnipotence, hegemony.

supreme /sŏŏpreém/ *adj. & n.* ● *adj.* **1** highest in authority or rank. **2** greatest; most important. **3** (of a penalty or sacrifice, etc.) involving death. ● *n.* **1** a rich cream sauce. **2** a dish served in this. □ **the Supreme Being** a name for God. **Supreme Court** the highest judicial court in a nation, etc. **supreme pontiff** see PONTIFF. □□ **supremely** *adv.* **supremeness** *n.* [L *supremus*, superl. of *superus* that is above f. *super* above]

■ *adj.* **1** highest, loftiest, topmost, greatest, first, foremost, principal, unsurpassed, top, uppermost, chief, paramount, sovereign. **2** best, greatest, first, outstanding, preeminent, first-rate, prime, primary, unexcelled, leading, crowning, consummate; superlative, matchless, peerless, incomparable, unparalleled, surpassing, transcendent, inimitable, sublime. **3** greatest, maximum, extreme, uttermost, utmost, ultimate. □□ **supremely** very, extremely, exceedingly, completely, perfectly, superlatively, sublimely, transcendently; see also *preeminently* (PREEMINENT). **supremeness** see SUPREMACY 1.

suprême /sŏŏprém/ *n.* = SUPREME *n.* [F]

supremo /sŏŏpreémō/ *n. Brit.* (*pl.* **-os**) **1** a supreme leader or ruler. **2** a person in overall charge. [Sp., = SUPREME]

■ see CHIEF *n.*

suprv. *abbr.* supervisor.

Supt. *abbr.* Superintendent.

sur-[1] /sər/ *prefix* = SUPER- (*surcharge*; *surrealism*). [OF]

sur-[2] /sər/ *prefix* assim. form of SUB- before *r*.

sura /sŏŏrə/ *n.* (also **surah**) a chapter or section of the Koran. [Arab. *sūra*]

surah /sŏŏrə/ *n.* a soft twilled silk for scarves, etc. [F pronunc. of *Surat* in India, where it was orig. made]

sural /sŏŏrəl/ *adj.* of or relating to the calf of the leg (*sural artery*). [mod.L *suralis* f. L *sura* calf]

surcease /sərsees, sərseés/ *n. & v. literary* ● *n.* a cessation. ● *v.intr. & tr.* cease. [ME f. OF *sursis*, -*ise* (cf. AF *sursise* omission), past part. of OF *surseoir* refrain, delay f. L (as SUPERSEDE), with assim. to CEASE]

■ *n.* see *interruption* (INTERRUPT).

surcharge *n. & v.* ● *n.* /sɜrchaarj/ **1** an additional charge or payment. **2** a charge made by assessors as a penalty for false returns of taxable property. **3** a mark printed on a postage stamp changing its value. **4** an additional or excessive load. **5** *Brit.* an amount in an official account not passed by the

auditor and having to be refunded by the person responsible. **6** the showing of an omission in an account for which credit should have been given. ● *v.tr.* /sɜrchaarj, -chaárj/ **1** exact a surcharge from. **2** exact (a sum) as a surcharge. **3** mark (a postage stamp) with a surcharge. **4** overload. **5** fill or saturate to excess. [ME f. OF *surcharger* (as SUR-[1], CHARGE)]

■ *n.* **1** see EXTRA *n.* 2. **2** see TRIBUTE 2. **4** see OVERLOAD *n.*

surcingle /sɜrsinggəl/ *n.* a band round a horse's body usu. to keep a pack, etc., in place. [ME f. OF *surcengle* (as SUR-[1], *cengle* girth f. L *cingula* f. *cingere* gird)]

surcoat /sɜrkōt/ *n.* **1** *hist.* a loose robe worn over armor. **2** a similar sleeveless garment worn as part of the insignia of an order of knighthood. **3** *hist.* an outer coat of rich material. [ME f. OF *surcot* (as SUR-[1], *cot* coat)]

surculose /sɜrkyəlōs/ *adj. Bot.* producing suckers. [L *surculosus* f. *surculus* twig]

surd /sərd/ *adj. & n.* ● *adj.* **1** *Math.* (of a number) irrational. **2** *Phonet.* (of a sound) uttered with the breath and not the voice (e.g., *f*, *k*, *p*, *s*, *t*). ● *n.* **1** *Math.* a surd number, esp. the root of an integer. **2** *Phonet.* a surd sound. [L *surdus* deaf, mute: sense 1 by mistransl. into L of Gk *alogos* irrational, speechless, through Arab. *jaḏr aṣamm* deaf root]

sure /shŏŏr/ *adj. & adv.* ● *adj.* **1** having or seeming to have adequate reason for a belief or assertion. **2** (often foll. by *of*, or *that* + clause) convinced. **3** (foll. by *of*) having a certain prospect or confident anticipation or satisfactory knowledge of. **4** reliable or unfailing (*there is one sure way to find out*). **5** (foll. by *to* + infin.) certain. **6** undoubtedly true or truthful. ● *adv. colloq.* certainly. □ **be sure** (in *imper.* or *infin.*; foll. by *that* + clause or *to* + infin.) take care to; not fail to (*be sure to turn the lights out*). **for sure** *colloq.* without doubt. **make sure 1** make or become certain; ensure. **2** (foll. by *of*) establish the truth or ensure the existence or happening of. **sure enough** *colloq.* **1** in fact; certainly. **2** with near certainty (*they will come sure enough*). **sure-fire** *colloq.* certain to succeed. **sure-footed** never stumbling or making a mistake. **sure-footedly** in a sure-footed way. **sure-footedness** being sure-footed. **sure thing** *n.* a certainty. ● *int. colloq.* certainly. **to be sure 1** it is undeniable or admitted. **2** it must be admitted. □□ **sureness** *n.* [ME f. OF *sur sure* (earlier *seur*) f. L *securus* SECURE]

■ *adj.* **1, 2** certain, assured, convinced, persuaded, positive, definite; unwavering, unswerving, unflinching, steadfast, steady, unshakable, undeviating, unfaltering. **3** confident, satisfied, certain. **4** accurate, reliable, dependable, tried-and-true, unfailing, unerring, infallible, foolproof, effective; established, firm, solid, stable, steadfast, steady, faithful, secure, safe, trustworthy; certain, inevitable, indubitable, unavoidable, ineluctable, inescapable, guaranteed, *colloq.* sure-fire. **5** see CERTAIN *adj.* 2. **6** see CERTAIN *adj.* 1b. ● *adv.* see SURELY 1. □ **for sure** see SURELY 1. **make sure 1** see ENSURE 1. **2** see ASSURE 2. **sure-fire** see SURE *adj.* 4 above. **sure thing** (*n.*) certainty, *colloq.* cinch. (*int.*) see ABSOLUTELY 6. **to be sure** see DEFINITELY *adv.* 2. □□ **sureness** see CONVICTION 2a.

surely /shŏŏrlee/ *adv.* **1** with certainty (*the time approaches slowly but surely*). **2** as an appeal to likelihood or reason (*surely that can't be right*). **3** with safety; securely (*the goat plants its feet surely*).

■ **1** certainly, to be sure, positively, absolutely, definitely, undoubtedly, indubitably, unquestionably, beyond the shadow of a doubt, beyond question, doubtless, doubtlessly, assuredly, *colloq.* sure, for sure. **3** firmly, solidly, confidently, unfalteringly, steadily, unswervingly, unhesitatingly, determinedly, doggedly, securely.

surety /shŏŏritee/ *n.* (*pl.* **-ies**) **1** a person who takes respon-

sibility for another's performance of an undertaking, e.g., to appear in court, or payment of a debt. **2** *archaic* a certainty. □ **of** (or **for**) **a surety** *archaic* certainly. **stand surety** become a surety; stand bail. □□ **suretyship** *n.* [ME f. OF *surté*, *seurté* f. L *securitas -tatis* SECURITY]
■ **1** see PLEDGE *n.* 2. **2** see CERTAINTY 1a.

surf /sərf/ *n.* & *v.* ● *n.* **1** the swell of the sea breaking on the shore or reefs. **2** the foam produced by this. ● *v.intr.* ride the surf, with or as with a surfboard. □ **surf casting** fishing by casting a line into the sea from the shore. □□ **surfer** *n.* **surfy** *adj.* [app. f. obs. *suff*, perh. assim. to *surge*: orig. applied to the Indian coast]

surface /sórfis/ *n.* & *v.* ● *n.* **1 a** the outside of a material body. **b** the area of this. **2** any of the limits terminating a solid. **3** the upper boundary of a liquid or of the ground, etc. **4** the outward aspect of anything; what is apparent on a casual view or consideration (*presents a large surface to view; all is quiet on the surface*). **5** *Geom.* a set of points that has length and breadth but no thickness. **6** (*attrib.*) **a** of or on the surface (*surface area*). **b** superficial (*surface politeness*). ● *v.* **1** *tr.* give the required surface to (a road, paper, etc.). **2** *intr.* & *tr.* rise or bring to the surface. **3** *intr.* become visible or known. **4** *intr. colloq.* become conscious; wake up. □ **come to the surface** become perceptible after being hidden. **surface-active** (of a substance, e.g., a detergent) able to affect the wetting properties of a liquid. **surface mail** mail carried over land and by sea, and not by air. **surface noise** extraneous noise in playing a phonograph record, caused by imperfections in the grooves. **surface tension** the tension of the surface film of a liquid, tending to minimize its surface area. □□ **surfaced** *adj.* (usu. in *comb.*). **surfacer** *n.* [F (as SUR-¹, FACE)]
■ *n.* **1** exterior, covering, outside, top, skin, integument, façade, face, boundary. **2** side, face; boundary, limit, *Geom.* superficies, esp. *Physics* interface. **3** top; surface film; *Physics* meniscus. **4** exterior, outside, top, skin, façade, face; (*on the surface*) superficially, to all appearances, at first glance, outwardly, to the casual observer, extrinsically, ostensibly. **5** plane, *Geom.* superficies. **6** (*attrib.*) **a** see SUPERFICIAL 1. **b** see SUPERFICIAL 3. ● *v.* **1** coat, finish, top; pavement, concrete, tar, tarmac. **2, 3** appear, show up, rise, come up, pop up, crop up, emerge, arise, *colloq.* materialize. **4** see AWAKE *v.* 1a.

surfactant /surfáktənt/ *n.* a substance which reduces surface tension. [*surface-active*]
■ see DETERGENT *n.*

surfboard /súrfbawrd/ *n.* a long narrow board used in surfing.

surfeit /súrfit/ *n.* & *v.* ● *n.* **1** an excess, esp. in eating or drinking. **2** a feeling of satiety or disgust resulting from this. ● *v.* (**surfeited, surfeiting**) **1** *tr.* overfeed. **2** *intr.* overeat. **3** *intr.* & *tr.* (foll. by *with*) be or cause to be wearied through excess. [ME f. OF *sorfe(i)t*, *surfe(i)t* (as SUPER-, L *facere* factdo)]
■ *n.* **1** over-abundance, superabundance, plethora, glut, excess, surplus, oversupply, overdose, satiety, overindulgence, overflow, flood, deluge, superfluity. **2** satiety, nausea, sickness, disgust. ● *v.* **1** overfeed, gorge, satiate, sate, stuff. **2** see OVEREAT. **3** sate, satiate, cloy, glut, pall.

surficial /surfíshəl/ *adj. Geol.* of or relating to the earth's surface. □□ **surficially** *adv.* [SURFACE after *superficial*]

surg. *abbr.* **1** surgeon. **2** surgery. **3** surgical.

surge /surj/ *n.* & *v.* ● *n.* **1** a sudden or impetuous onset (*a surge of anger*). **2** the swell of the waves at sea. **3** a heavy forward or upward motion. **4** a rapid increase in price, activity, etc. over a short period. **5** a sudden marked increase in voltage of an electric current. ● *v.intr.* **1** (of waves, the sea, etc.) rise and fall or move heavily forward. **2** (of a crowd, etc.) move suddenly and powerfully forward in large numbers. **3** (of an electric current, etc.) increase suddenly. **4** *Naut.* (of a rope, chain, or windlass) slip back with a jerk. [OF *sourdre sourge-*, or *sorgir* f. Cat., f. L *surgere* rise]

■ *n.* **1** see OUTBURST. **2** swell, surf, upsurge, eddy, rush, gush, flood, stream, flow; see also WAVE *n.* 6a. **4** see SWELL *n.* 1. ● *v.* **1** swell, billow, bulge, heave, roll, undulate, well forth *or* up, rise and fall, ebb and flow, pulsate, rush, gush, pour, flood, stream, flow. **2** rush, pour, flood, stream, flow.

surgeon /súrjən/ *n.* **1** a medical practitioner qualified to practice surgery. **2** a medical officer in a navy or army or military hospital. □ **surgeon fish** any tropical marine fish of the genus *Acanthurus* with movable lancet-shaped spines on each side of the tail. **surgeon general** (*pl.* **surgeons general**) the head of a public health service or of an army, etc., medical service. **surgeon's knot** a reef-knot with a double twist. [ME f. AF *surgien* f. OF *serurgien* (as SURGERY)]
■ see PHYSICIAN.

surgery /súrjəree/ *n.* (*pl.* **-ies**) **1** the branch of medicine concerned with treatment of injuries or disorders of the body by incision, manipulation or alteration of organs, etc., with the hands or with instruments. **2** *Brit.* **a** a place where a doctor, dentist, etc., treats patients. **b** the occasion of this (*the doctor will see you after surgery*). **3** *Brit.* **a** a place where a member of Parliament, lawyer, or other professional person gives advice. **b** the occasion of this. [ME f. OF *surgerie* f. L *chirurgia* f. Gk *kheirourgia* handiwork, surgery f. *kheir* hand + *erg-* work]

surgical /súrjikəl/ *adj.* **1** of or relating to or done by surgeons or surgery. **2** resulting from surgery (*surgical fever*). **3 a** used in surgery. **b** (of a special garment, etc.) worn to correct a deformity, etc. **4** extremely precise. □ **surgical spirit** methylated alcohol used in surgery for cleansing, disinfecting, etc. □□ **surgically** *adv.* [earlier *chirurgical* f. *chirurgy* f. OF *sirurgie*: see SURGEON]

suricate /sŏorikayt/ *n.* a South African burrowing mongoose, *Suricata suricatta*, with gray and black stripes. [F f. S.Afr. native name]

Surinam toad /sŏorinám, -naám/ *n.* = PIPA. [*Surinam* in S. America]

surly /sórlee/ *adj.* (**surlier, surliest**) bad-tempered and unfriendly; churlish. □□ **surlily** *adv.* **surliness** *n.* [alt. spelling of obs. *sirly* haughty f. SIR + -LY¹]
■ unpleasant, unfriendly, rude, crusty, cantankerous, curmudgeonly, churlish, crabby, crabbed, choleric, splenetic, dyspeptic, bilious, temperamental, cross, crotchety, irritable, grumpy, bearish, gruff, sullen, testy, touchy, tetchy, short-tempered, ill-tempered, bad-tempered, ill-natured, bad-natured, ill-humored, peevish, quarrelsome, argumentative, obnoxious, uncivil, rough, obstreperous, *colloq.* grouchy. □□ **surliness** see TEMPER *n.* 3.

surmise /sərmíz/ *n.* & *v.* ● *n.* a conjecture or suspicion about the existence or truth of something. ● *v.* **1** *tr.* (often foll. by *that* + clause) infer doubtfully; make a surmise about. **2** *tr.* suspect the existence of. **3** *intr.* make a guess. [ME f. AF & OF fem. past part. of *surmettre* accuse f. LL *supermittere supermiss-* (as SUPER-, *mittere* send)]
■ *n.* guess, conjecture, speculation, notion, hypothesis, theory, supposition, assumption, presumption, conclusion, understanding, fancy, suspicion, feeling, sense. ● *v.* **1** imagine, guess, conjecture, speculate, suppose, hypothesize, theorize, assume, presume, conclude, gather, infer, deduce, understand, fancy, suspect, feel, sense. **3** guess, conjecture, speculate.

surmount /sərmównt/ *v.tr.* **1** overcome or get over (a difficulty or obstacle). **2** (usu. in *passive*) cap or crown (*peaks surmounted with snow*). □□ **surmountable** *adj.* [ME f. OF *surmonter* (as SUR-¹, MOUNT¹)]
■ **1** see *get over* 2. **2** see CROWN *v.* 4.

surmullet /sərmúlit, sərmul-/ *n.* the red mullet. [F *surmulet* f. OF *sor* red + *mulet* MULLET]

surname /sárnaym/ *n.* & *v.* ● *n.* **1** a hereditary name common to members of a family, as distinct from a Christian or first name. **2** *archaic* an additional descriptive or allusive name attached to a person, sometimes becoming hereditary. ● *v.tr.* **1** give a surname to. **2** give (a person a surname). **3**

(as **surnamed** *adj.*) having as a family name. [ME, alt. of *surnoun* f. AF (as SUR-[1], NOUN name)]

▪ *n.* **1** family name, last name.

surpass /sərpás/ *v.tr.* **1** outdo; be greater or better than. **2** (as **surpassing** *adj.*) preeminent; matchless (*of surpassing intelligence*). □□ **surpassingly** *adv.* [F *surpasser* (as SUR-[1], PASS[1])]

▪ **1** exceed, excel, go *or* pass beyond, outdo, beat, worst, better, outstrip, outdistance, outperform, outclass, outshine, eclipse, overshadow, top, cap, transcend, prevail over, leave behind, *colloq.* best. **2** (**surpassing**) excessive, extraordinary, great, enormous, preeminent, incomparable, unrivaled, unparalleled, matchless, peerless, unmatched, unequaled, unsurpassed. □□ **surpassingly** exceedingly, extraordinarily, incomparably.

surplice /sɔ́rplis/ *n.* a loose white linen vestment reaching the knees, worn over a cassock by clergy and choristers at services. □□ **surpliced** *adj.* [ME f. AF *surplis*, OF *sourpelis*, f. med.L *superpellicium* (as SUPER-, *pellicia* PELISSE)]

surplus /sɔ́rpləs, -plus/ *n. & adj.* ▪ *n.* **1** an amount left over when requirements have been met. **2 a** an excess of revenue over expenditure in a given period, esp. a financial year (opp. DEFICIT). **b** the excess value of a company's assets over the face value of its stock. ▪ *adj.* exceeding what is needed or used. □ **surplus value** *Econ.* the difference between the value of work done and wages paid. [ME f. AF *surplus*, OF *s(o)urplus* f. med.L *superplus* (as SUPER-, + *plus* more)]

▪ *n.* **1** overage, excess, superfluity, surfeit, overabundance, oversupply, overdose, glut; leftovers, remainder, residue, balance. ▪ *adj.* excess, leftover, extra, spare, overabundant, superfluous, unused, redundant.

surprise /sərpríz/ *n. & v.* ▪ *n.* **1** an unexpected or astonishing event or circumstance. **2** the emotion caused by this. **3** the act of catching a person, etc., unawares, or the process of being caught unawares. **4** (*attrib.*) unexpected; made or done, etc., without warning (*a surprise visit*). ▪ *v.tr.* **1** affect with surprise; turn out contrary to the expectations of (*your answer surprised me; I surprised her by arriving early*). **2** (usu. in *passive*; foll. by *at*) shock; scandalize (*I am surprised at you*). **3** capture or attack by surprise. **4** come upon (a person) unawares (*surprised him taking a cookie*). **5** (foll. by *into*) startle (a person) by surprise into an action, etc. (*surprised them into consenting*). □ **take by surprise** affect with surprise, esp. by an unexpected encounter or statement. □□ **surprisedly** /-prízidlee/ *adv.* **surprising** *adj.* **surprisingly** *adv.* **surprisingness** *n.* [OF, fem. past part. of *surprendre* (as SUR-[1], *prendre* f. L *praehendere* seize)]

▪ *n.* **1** blow, jolt, bolt from *or* out of the blue, bombshell, *colloq.* shocker, eye-opener. **2** shock, astonishment, amazement, stupefaction, wonder, incredulity. **4** (*attrib.*) see UNFORESEEN. ▪ *v.* **1** shock, astound, astonish, amaze, take by surprise, disconcert, nonplus, dumbfound, confound, stagger, startle, stupefy, stun, take aback, strike, *colloq.* floor, bowl over, flabbergast, knock (*or* throw) one for a loop. **2** shock, scandalize, appall, dismay, horrify, outrage. **3, 4** ambush, ambuscade, pounce on, swoop on, startle; take *or* catch unawares, take by surprise, catch red-handed, catch in the act, catch in flagrante delicto, catch napping, catch off guard, discover, detect, come upon, catch out, *colloq.* catch someone with his *or* her pants down. □□ **surprising** see *amazing* (AMAZE). **surprisingly** see PARTICULARLY 1.

surra /sŏ́rə/ *n.* a febrile disease transmitted by bites of flies and affecting horses and cattle in the tropics. [Marathi]

surreal /sərée∍l/ *adj.* **1** having the qualities of surrealism. **2** strange; bizarre. □□ **surreality** /-ree-álitee/ *n.* **surreally** *adv.* [back-form. f. SURREALISM, etc.]

▪ **2** see *dreamlike* (DREAM).

surrealism /sərée∍lizəm/ *n.* a 20th-c. movement in art and literature aiming at expressing the subconscious mind, e.g., by the irrational juxtaposition of images. □□ **surrealist** *n. &*

adj. **surrealistic** *adj.* **surrealistically** *adv.* [F *surréalisme* (as SUR-[1], REALISM)]

surrebutter /sɔ́ribútər/ *n. Law* the plaintiff's reply to the defendant's rebutter. [SUR-[1] + REBUTTER, after SURREJOINDER]

▪ see ANSWER *n.* 1.

surrejoinder /sɔ́rijóyndər/ *n. Law* the plaintiff's reply to the defendant's rejoinder. [SUR-[1] + REJOINDER]

▪ see ANSWER *n.* 1.

surrender /səréndər/ *v. & n.* ▪ *v.* **1** *tr.* hand over; relinquish possession of, esp. on compulsion or demand; give into another's power or control. **2** *intr.* **a** accept an enemy's demand for submission. **b** give oneself up; cease from resistance; submit. **3** *intr. & refl.* (foll. by *to*) give oneself over to a habit, emotion, influence, etc. **4** *tr.* give up rights under (a life-insurance policy) in return for a smaller sum received immediately. **5** *tr.* give up (a lease) before its expiration. **6** *tr.* abandon (hope, etc.). ▪ *n.* the act or an instance of surrendering. □ **surrender by bail** duly appear in a court of law after release on bail. **surrender value** the amount payable to one who surrenders a life-insurance policy. [ME f. AF f. OF *surrendre* (as SUR-[1], RENDER)]

▪ *v.* **1** give up, yield, let go (of), relinquish, deliver (up), hand over, forgo, forsake, turn over, turn in, part with, cede, concede. **2** give (oneself) up, yield, quit, cry quits, capitulate, throw in the sponge, throw in the towel, raise the white flag, throw up one's hands, succumb, submit, give way, acquiesce, comply, give in, concede, crumble, cave in. **6** abandon, give up. ▪ *n.* submission, capitulation, yielding, renunciation, relinquishment, forfeiture; transferral, transfer, transference, handover, conveyancing, ceding, cession, concession.

surreptitious /sɔ́rəptíshəs/ *adj.* **1** covert; kept secret. **2** done by stealth; clandestine. □□ **surreptitiously** *adv.* **surreptitiousness** *n.* [ME f. L *surrepticius -itius* f. *surripere surrept-* (as SUR-[1], *rapere* seize)]

▪ furtive, secret, clandestine, stealthy, underhand(ed), devious, covert, sly, secretive, private, concealed, hidden, veiled, sneaky. □□ **surreptitiously** see *secretly* (SECRET). **surreptitiousness** see SECRECY.

surrey /sɔ́ree, súree/ *n.* (*pl.* **surreys**) a light four-wheeled carriage with two seats facing forward. [orig. of an adaptation of the *Surrey cart*, orig. made in *Surrey* in England]

surrogate /sɔ́rəgət, -gayt, súr-/ *n.* **1** a substitute, esp. for a person in a specific role or office. **2** *Brit.* a deputy, esp. of a bishop in granting marriage licenses. **3** a judge in charge of probate, inheritance, and guardianship. □ **surrogate mother 1** a person acting the role of mother. **2** a woman who bears a child on behalf of another woman, usu. from her own egg fertilized by the other woman's partner. □□ **surrogacy** *n.* **surrogateship** *n.* [L *surrogatus* past part. of *surrogare* elect as a substitute (as SUR-[1], *rogare* ask)]

▪ **1** see SUBSTITUTE *n.* 1a. **3** see JUDGE *n.* 1.

surround /sərównd/ *v. & n.* ▪ *v.tr.* **1** come or be all around; encircle; enclose. **2** (in *passive*; foll. by *by, with*) have on all sides (*the house is surrounded by trees*). ▪ *n.* **1** an area or substance surrounding something. **2** *Brit.* **a** a border or edging, esp. an area between the walls and carpet of a room. **b** a floor-covering for this. □□ **surrounding** *adj.* [ME = overflow, f. AF *sur(o)under*, OF *s(o)uronder* f. LL *superundare* (as SUPER-, *undare* flow f. *unda* wave)]

▪ *v.* encompass, encircle, envelop, enclose, hem in, hedge in, fence in, box in, ring, circle, skirt; cover, coat, encase, beset, besiege. ▪ *n.* **1** environs, environment, surroundings, atmosphere, ambience, setting. □□ **surrounding** nearby, neighboring, local, adjoining, neighborhood, adjacent, bordering, abutting, circumambient, circumjacent.

/.../ **pronunciation**	● **part of speech**
□ **phrases, idioms, and compounds**	
□□ **derivatives**	▪ **synonym section**
cross-references appear in SMALL CAPITALS or *italics*	

surroundings /sərówndingz/ *n.pl.* the things in the neighborhood of, or the conditions affecting, a person or thing. ■ see ENVIRONMENT 1, 2.

surtax /sə́rtaks/ *n. & v.* ● *n.* an additional tax, esp. levied on incomes above a certain level. ● *v.tr.* impose a surtax on. [F *surtaxe* (as SUR-¹, TAX)]

surtitle /sə́rtit'l/ *n.* (also **supertitle** /sŏŏpərtit'l/) (esp. in opera) each of a sequence of captions projected above the stage, translating the text being sung.

surtout /sərtŏŏ, -tŏŏt/ *n. hist.* a man's heavy overcoat or frock coat. [F f. *sur* over + *tout* everything]

surveillance /sərváyləns/ *n.* close observation, esp. of a suspected person. [F f. *surveiller* (as SUR-¹, *veiller* f. L *vigilare* keep watch)]
■ watch, scrutiny, reconnaissance; see also OBSERVATION 1, 2, 4.

survey *v. & n.* ● *v.tr.* /sərváy/ **1** take or present a general view of. **2** examine the condition of (a building, etc.). **3** determine the boundaries, extent, ownership, etc., of (a district, etc.). **4** poll the opinions of a group of people, esp. by a statistical sample. ● *n.* /sə́rvay/ **1** a general view or consideration of something. **2 a** the act of surveying opinions, etc. **b** the result or findings of this, esp. in a written report. **3** an inspection or investigation. **4** a map or plan made by surveying an area. **5** a department carrying out the surveying of land. [ME f. AF *survei(e)r*, OF *so(u)rveeir* (pres. stem *survey-*) f. med.L *supervidēre* (as SUPER-, *vidēre* see)]
■ *v.* **1, 2** view, look at, get a bird's-eye view of, contemplate, scan, observe; consider, review; examine, appraise, evaluate, inspect, study, scrutinize, assess, investigate, look into *or* over. **3** measure, size up, take the measure of; plot, map (out), triangulate; explore, reconnoiter. ● *n.* **1, 3** view, observation, sight, contemplation, consideration; examination, appraisal, evaluation, assessment, review, measure, study, scan, scrutiny, inquiry, measurement, investigation, probe, inspection; canvass, poll, census.

surveyor /sərváyər/ *n.* **1** a person who surveys land and buildings, esp. professionally. **2** *Brit.* an official inspector, esp. for measurement and valuation. **3** a person who carries out surveys. □□ **surveyorship** *n.* (esp. in sense 2). [ME f. AF & OF *surve(i)our* (as SURVEY)]

survival /sərvívəl/ *n.* **1** the process or an instance of surviving. **2** a person, thing, or practice that has remained from a former time. □ **survival kit** emergency rations, etc., esp. carried by military personnel, hikers, etc. **survival of the fittest** the process or result of natural selection.
■ **1** see ENDURANCE 3, SUBSISTENCE 1. **2** hangover.

survivalism /sərvívəlizəm/ *n.* the practicing of outdoor survival skills as a sport or hobby, esp. in the belief that these skills will be necessary at the collapse of civilization. □□ **survivalist** *adj. & n.*

survive /sərvív/ *v.* **1** *intr.* continue to live or exist; be still alive or existent. **2** *tr.* live or exist longer than. **3** *tr.* remain alive after going through, or continue to exist in spite of (a danger, accident, etc.). [ME f. AF *survivre*, OF *sourvivre* f. L *supervivere* (as SUPER, *vivere* live)]
■ **1** continue, last, live (on), carry on, persist, subsist, exist, pull through, endure, keep going, remain. **2** outlast, outlive. **3** see WEATHER *v.*

survivor /sərvívər/ *n.* **1** a person who survives or has survived. **2** *Law* a joint tenant who has the right to the whole estate on the other's death.

sus- /sus, səs/ *prefix* assim. form of SUB- before *c, p, t.*

susceptibility /səséptibílitee/ *n.* (*pl.* **-ies**) **1** the state of being susceptible. **2** (in *pl.*) a person's sensitive feelings. **3** *Physics* the ratio of magnetization to a magnetizing force.
■ **1** see SENSITIVITY. **2** (*susceptibilities*) see SENSIBILITY 3.

susceptible /səséptibəl/ *adj.* **1** impressionable; sensitive; easily moved by emotion. **2** (*predic.*) **a** (foll. by *to*) likely to be affected by; liable or vulnerable to (*susceptible to pain*). **b** (foll. by *of*) allowing; admitting of (*facts not susceptible of proof*). □□ **susceptibly** *adv.* [LL *susceptibilis* f. L *suscipere suscept-* (as SUB-, *capere* take)]
■ **1** impressionable, influenceable, vulnerable, reachable,

accessible, credulous, suggestible, gullible, naive; sensitive, susceptive; emotional. **2 a** (*susceptible to*) open to, liable to, prone to, subject to, disposed to, predisposed to, receptive to, affected by, vulnerable to, responsive to. **b** (*susceptible of*) allowing, permitting; admitting of, capable of.

susceptive /səséptiv/ *adj.* **1** concerned with the receiving of emotional impressions or ideas. **2** receptive. **3** = SUSCEPTIBLE. [LL *susceptivus* (as SUSCEPTIBLE)]
■ **1** see SENSITIVE *adj.* 2. **2** see RECEPTIVE.

sushi /sŏŏshee/ *n.* a Japanese dish of balls of cold rice flavored and garnished, esp. with raw fish or shellfish. [Jap.]

suslik /súslik/ *n.* an E. European and Asian ground squirrel, *Citellus citellus.* [Russ.]

suspect *v., n.,* & *adj.* ● *v.tr.* /səspékt/ **1** have an impression of the existence or presence of (*suspects poisoning*). **2** (foll. by *to be*) believe tentatively, without clear ground. **3** (foll. by *that* + clause) be inclined to think. **4** (often foll. by *of*) be inclined to mentally accuse; doubt the innocence of (*suspect him of complicity*). **5** doubt the genuineness or truth of. ● *n.* /súspekt/ a suspected person. ● *adj.* /súspekt/ subject to or deserving suspicion or distrust; not sound or trustworthy. [ME f. L *suspicere suspect-* (as SUB-, *specere* look)]
■ *v.* **3** feel, think, believe, sense, have a feeling, fancy, imagine, theorize, guess, surmise, suppose, have a sneaking suspicion, think it likely *or* probable, *colloq.* expect. **4, 5** disbelieve, doubt, mistrust, distrust, harbor suspicions about *or* of, have suspicions about *or* of, have misgivings about, be suspicious of, *Brit. sl.* suss. ● *adj.* suspicious, questionable, open to question *or* suspicion, doubtful, dubious, unreliable, untrustworthy, shady; suspected; *sl.* fishy.

suspend /səspénd/ *v.tr.* **1** hang up. **2** keep inoperative or undecided for a time; defer. **3** bar temporarily from a school, function, office, privilege, etc. **4** (as **suspended** *adj.*) (of solid particles or a body in a fluid medium) sustained somewhere between top and bottom. □ **suspended animation** a temporary cessation of the vital functions without death. **suspended sentence** a judicial sentence left unenforced subject to good behavior during a specified period. **suspend payment** (of a company) fail to meet its financial obligations; admit insolvency. □□ **suspensible** /səspénsibəl/ *adj.* [ME f. OF *suspendre* or L *suspendere suspens-* (as SUB-, *pendere* hang)]
■ **1** hang (up), attach, fasten, dangle, swing, sling. **2** hold up *or* off (on), withhold, put off, put in *or* into abeyance, hold *or* keep in abeyance, shelve, postpone, delay, defer, interrupt, intermit, stop *or* check *or* cease *or* discontinue temporarily, table. **3** bar, exclude, eliminate, reject, expel, eject, evict; blackball; see also lay off 1 (LAY¹).

suspender /səspéndər/ *n.* **1** (in *pl.*) straps worn across the shoulders and supporting trousers, a skirt, etc. **2** *Brit.* an attachment to hold up a stocking or sock by its top.

suspense /səspéns/ *n.* **1** a state of anxious uncertainty or expectation. **2** *Law* a suspension; the temporary cessation of a right, etc. □ **keep in suspense** delay informing (a person) of urgent information. **suspense account** an account in which items are entered temporarily before allocation to the right account. □□ **suspenseful** *adj.* [ME f. AF & OF *suspens* f. past part. of L *suspendere* SUSPEND]
■ **1** anxiety, tension, apprehension, nervousness, agitation, anxiousness, anticipation, expectation, excitement; uncertainty, indefiniteness, insecurity, incertitude, doubt, irresolution, expectancy, indecision, not knowing. **2** see SUSPENSION.

suspension /səspénshən/ *n.* **1** the act of suspending or the condition of being suspended. **2** the means by which a vehicle is supported on its axles. **3** a substance consisting of particles suspended in a medium. **4** *Mus.* the prolongation of a note of a chord to form a discord with the following chord. □ **suspension bridge** a bridge with a roadway suspended from cables supported by structures at each end. [F *suspension* or L *suspensio* (as SUSPEND)]
■ **1** intermission, moratorium, deferral, deferment,

holdup, delay, interruption, break, postponement, discontinuation, stay; debarment, exclusion, elimination, rejection, expulsion, ejection, eviction; disbarment; *Law* suspense.

suspensive /səspénsiv/ *adj.* **1** having the power or tendency to suspend or postpone. **2** causing suspense. □□ **suspensively** *adv.* **suspensiveness** *n.* [F *suspensif -ive* or med.L *suspensivus* (as SUSPEND)]

suspensory /səspénsəree/ *adj.* (of a ligament, muscle, bandage, etc.) holding an organ, etc., suspended. [F *suspensoire* (as SUSPENSION)]

suspicion /səspíshən/ *n.* **1** the feeling or thought of a person who suspects. **2** the act or an instance of suspecting; the state of being suspected. **3** (foll. by *of*) a slight trace of. □ **above suspicion** too obviously good, etc., to be suspected. **under suspicion** suspected. [ME f. AF *suspeciun* (OF *sospeçon*) f. med.L *suspectio -onis* f. L *suspicere* (as SUSPECT): assim. to F *suspicion* & L *suspicio*]

■ **1** (funny) feeling, hunch, guess, presentiment, premonition, intuition, idea, notion, impression; qualm, doubt, misgiving; dubiousness, mistrust, distrust, skepticism, wariness, apprehension, apprehensiveness, cautiousness, hesitation, second thoughts, uncertainty, *literary* dubiety, leeriness; *colloq.* bad vibes. **3** inkling, suggestion, hint, trace, vestige, flavor, soupçon, taste, dash, glimmer, tinge, touch, shadow, shade, whisper, scintilla, speck, *colloq.* tad. □ **above suspicion** see IRREPROACHABLE. **under suspicion** see SUSPICIOUS 3.

suspicious /səspíshəs/ *adj.* **1** prone to or feeling suspicion. **2** indicating suspicion (*a suspicious glance*). **3** inviting or justifying suspicion (*a suspicious lack of surprise*). □□ **suspiciously** *adv.* **suspiciousness** *n.* [ME f. AF & OF f. L *suspiciosus* (as SUSPICION)]

■ **1, 2** mistrustful, distrustful, doubtful, in doubt, skeptical, suspecting, disbelieving, unbelieving, incredulous, doubting, questioning, apprehensive, wary, chary, uncertain, uneasy, *sl.* leery. **3** doubtful, in doubt, dubious, questionable, debatable, suspect, suspected, under suspicion, untrustworthy, open to doubt *or* question *or* misconstruction, shady, *sl.* fishy. □□ **suspiciously** see *jealously* (JEALOUS).

suss /sus/ *v.* & *n.* (also **sus**) esp. *Brit. sl.* ● *v.tr.* (**sussed**, **sussing**) **1** suspect of a crime. **2** (usu. foll. by *out*) **a** investigate; inspect (*go and suss out the restaurants*). **b** work out; grasp; understand; realize (*he had the market sussed*). ● *n.* **1** a suspect. **2** a suspicion; suspicious behavior. □ **on suss** on suspicion (of having committed a crime). [abbr. of SUSPECT, SUSPICION]

■ *v.* **2 a** see INSPECT. **b** see *find out* 4. ● *n.* **2** see SUSPICION 1.

Sussex /súsiks/ *n.* **1** a speckled or red domestic chicken of an English breed. **2** this breed. [*Sussex* in S. England]

sustain /səstáyn/ *v.tr.* **1** support, bear the weight of, esp. for a long period. **2** give strength to; encourage; support. **3** (of food) give nourishment to. **4** endure; stand; bear up against. **5** undergo or suffer (defeat or injury, etc.). **6** (of a court, etc.) uphold or decide in favor of (an objection, etc.). **7** substantiate or corroborate (a statement or charge). **8 a** maintain or keep (a sound, effort, etc.) going continuously. **b** (as **sustained** *adj.*) maintained continuously over a long period. **9** continue to represent (a part, character, etc.) adequately. □□ **sustainable** *adj.* **sustainedly** /-stáynidlee/ *adv.* **sustainer** *n.* **sustainment** *n.* [ME f. AF *sustein-*, OF *so(u)stein-* stressed stem of *so(u)stenir* f. L *sustinēre sustent-* (as SUB-, *tenēre* hold)]

■ **1** bear, carry, support, take, hold. **2** support, carry, bear, bolster, buoy (up), reinforce, keep a person going, encourage, strengthen, shore up, underpin, prop up, buttress. **3** nourish, feed, support, keep (alive); maintain. **4, 5** endure, stand, withstand, bear up under *or* against, put up with, suffer, undergo, experience, tolerate, weather, brave. **6** uphold, recognize, allow, admit, approve, ratify, sanction, authorize, endorse, validate. **7** see SUBSTANTIATE. **8a, 9** uphold, support,

keep up, maintain, continue, keep going, keep alive, preserve; prolong, persist in. **8 b** (**sustained**) continued, continuous, continual, prolonged, *Mus.* sostenuto; steady, even, level. □□ **sustainable** see VIABLE. **sustainer** see STALWART *n.*

sustenance /sústinəns/ *n.* **1 a** nourishment; food. **b** the process of nourishing. **2** a means of support; a livelihood. [ME f. AF *sustenaunce*, OF *so(u)stenance* (as SUSTAIN)]

■ **1 a** nutriment, nourishment, food (and drink), daily bread, rations, victuals, provisions, groceries, edibles, eatables, foodstuff(s), *archaic* meat, *colloq.* grub, eats, scoff, *formal* aliment, viands, *joc.* provender, *sl.* chow, nosh. **2** livelihood, (means of) support, maintenance, upkeep, keep, (means of) subsistence, daily bread, living.

sustentation /sústəntáyshən/ *n. formal* **1** the support of life. **2** maintenance. [ME f. OF *sustentation* or L *sustentatio* f. *sustentare* frequent. of *sustinēre* SUSTAIN]

■ see MAINTENANCE 1.

susurration /soˉosəráyshən/ *n.* (also **susurrus** /sooˉsə́rəs/) *literary* a sound of whispering or rustling. [ME f. LL *susurratio* f. L *susurrare*]

■ see RUSTLE *n.*

sutler /sútlər/ *n. hist.* a person following an army and selling provisions, etc., to the soldiers. [obs. Du. *soeteler* f. *soetelen* befoul, perform mean duties, f. Gmc]

Sutra /sooˉtrə/ *n.* **1** an aphorism or set of aphorisms in Hindu literature. **2** a narrative part of Buddhist literature. **3** Jainist scripture. [Skr. *sūtra* thread, rule, f. *siv* SEW]

suttee /sutee, sútee/ *n.* (also **sati**) (*pl.* **suttees** or **satis**) esp. *hist.* **1** the Hindu practice of a widow immolating herself on her husband's funeral pyre. **2** a widow who undergoes or has undergone this. [Hindi & Urdu f. Skr. *satī* faithful wife f. *sat* good]

suture /sooˉchər/ *n.* & *v.* ● *n.* **1** *Surgery* **a** the joining of the edges of a wound or incision by stitching. **b** the thread or wire used for this. **2** the seamlike junction of two bones, esp. in the skull. **3** *Bot.* & *Zool.* a similar junction of parts. ● *v.tr. Surgery* stitch up (a wound or incision) with a suture. □□ **sutural** *adj.* **sutured** *adj.* [F *suture* or L *sutura* f. *suere sut-* sew]

■ **2, 3** see JUNCTION 1.

suzerain /sooˉzərən, -rayn/ *n.* **1** a feudal overlord. **2** a sovereign state having some control over another state that is internally autonomous. □□ **suzerainty** *n.* [F, app. f. *sus* above f. L *su(r)sum* upward, after *souverain* SOVEREIGN]

■ □□ **suzerainty** see *sovereignty* (SOVEREIGN).

s.v. *abbr.* (in a reference) under the word or heading given. [f. L *sub voce* (or *verbo*)]

svelte /svelt/ *adj.* slender; graceful. [F f. It. *svelto*]

■ see SLENDER 1.

sw *abbr.* (also **SW**) **1** southwest. **2** southwestern. **3** switch. **4** short wave.

swab /swob/ *n.* & *v.* (also **swob**) ● *n.* **1** a mop or other absorbent device for cleaning or mopping up. **2 a** an absorbent pad used in surgery, esp. one with a long stick handle. **b** a specimen of a possibly morbid secretion taken with a swab for examination. **3** *sl.* a sailor. **4** *sl.* a term of contempt for a person. ● *v.tr.* (**swabbed**, **swabbing**) **1** clean with a swab. **2** (foll. by *up*) absorb (moisture) with a swab. [backform. f. *swabber* f. early mod.Du. *zwabber* f. a Gmc base = 'splash, sway']

■ *v.* see WIPE *v.* 1.

swaddle /swód'l/ *v.tr.* swathe (esp. an infant) in garments or bandages, etc. □ **swaddling clothes** narrow bandages formerly wrapped round a newborn child to restrain its movements and quieten it. [ME f. SWATHE + -LE⁴]

■ see SWATHE *v.*

swag /swag/ *n.* & *v.* ● *n.* **1** *sl.* **a** the booty carried off by burglars, etc. **b** illicit gains. **2 a** an ornamental festoon of

/.../ **pronunciation**	● **part of speech**
□ **phrases, idioms, and compounds**	
□□ **derivatives**	■ **synonym section**
cross-references appear in SMALL CAPITALS or *italics*	

flowers, etc. **b** a carved, etc., representation of this. **c** drapery of similar appearance. **3** *Austral.* & *NZ* a traveler's or miner's bundle of personal belongings. ● *v.* (**swagged, swagging**) **1** *tr.* arrange (a curtain, etc.) in swags. **2** *intr.* **a** hang heavily. **b** sway from side to side. **3** *tr.* cause to sway or sag. [16th c.: prob. f. Scand.]

■ *n.* **1 a** see BOOTY 1. ● *v.* **2 a** see SAG *v.* 1, 2.

swage /swayj/ *n. & v.* ● *n.* **1** a die or stamp for shaping wrought iron, etc., by hammering or pressure. **2** a tool for bending metal, etc. ● *v.tr.* shape with a swage. □ **swage block** a block with various perforations, grooves, etc., for shaping metal. [F *s(o)uage* decorative groove, of unkn. orig.]

swagger /swágǝr/ *v., n.,* & *adj.* ● *v.intr.* **1** walk arrogantly or self-importantly. **2** behave arrogantly; be domineering. ● *n.* **1** a swaggering gait or manner. **2** swaggering behavior. **3** a dashing or confident air or way of doing something. **4** *Brit.* stylishness. ● *adj.* **1** *Brit. colloq.* stylish or fashionable. **2** (of a coat) cut with a loose flare from the shoulders. □ **swagger stick** a short cane carried by a military officer. □□ **swaggerer** *n.* **swaggeringly** *adv.* [app. f. SWAG *v.* + -ER⁴]

■ *v.* **1** strut, prance, parade, *archaic* swash, *colloq.* sashay. **2** boast, brag, crow, *colloq.* show off, swank, *literary* vaunt; see also *lord it over.* ● *n.* **1** strut, prance, caper. **2** show, display, ostentation, braggadocio, arrogance, bravado, bluster, boastfulness, *colloq.* showing off. **3, 4** see PANACHE. □□ **swaggerer** see BRAGGART *n.*

swagman /swágman/ *n.* (*pl.* **-men**) *Austral.* & *NZ* a tramp carrying a swag (see SWAG *n.* 3).

■ see TRAMP *n.* 1.

Swahili /swaaheelee/ *n.* (*pl.* same) **1** a member of a Bantu people of Zanzibar and adjacent coasts. **2** their language, used widely as a lingua franca in E. Africa. [Arab. *sawāhil* pl. of *sāhil* coast]

swain /swayn/ *n.* **1** *archaic* a country youth. **2** *poet.* a young male lover or suitor. [ME *swein* f. ON *sveinn* lad = OE *swān* swineherd, f. Gmc]

■ **1** see PEASANT. **2** see SUITOR 1.

swallow¹ /swólō/ *v. & n.* ● *v.* **1** *tr.* cause or allow (food, etc.) to pass down the throat. **2** *intr.* perform the muscular movement of the esophagus required to do this. **3** *tr.* **a** accept meekly; put up with (an affront, etc.). **b** accept credulously (an unlikely assertion, etc.). **4** *tr.* repress; resist the expression of (a feeling, etc.) (*swallow one's pride*). **5** *tr.* articulate (words, etc.) indistinctly. **6** *tr.* (often foll. by *up*) engulf or absorb; exhaust; cause to disappear. ● *n.* **1** the act of swallowing. **2** an amount swallowed in one action. □□ **swallowable** *adj.* **swallower** *n.* [OE *swelg* (n.), *swelgan* (v.) f. Gmc]

■ *v.* **1** eat, consume, devour, ingest, dispatch; guzzle, gobble, bolt, wolf; drink, imbibe, gulp, swill, lap up, put away, *colloq.* down, swig, *literary* quaff. **3 a** see TOLERATE. **b** accept, allow, credit, believe, take, *colloq.* fall for, *sl.* buy. **4** keep back *or* down, choke back *or* down, repress, suppress, hold in, control, stifle, smother, overcome, conquer. **5** see MUMBLE *v.* **6** absorb, make disappear, swamp, engulf, envelop, enfold, consume, assimilate. ● *n.* drink, gulp, guzzle, sip, sup, *colloq.* swig; bite, nibble, morsel, mouthful, nip, draft, dram, tot. □ **swallow-hole** *Geol.* sink(hole).

swallow² /swólō/ *n.* any of various migratory swift-flying insect-eating birds of the family Hirundinidae, esp. *Hirundo rustica*, with a forked tail and long pointed wings. □ **one swallow does not make a summer** a warning against a hasty inference from one instance. **swallow dive** *Brit.* = **swan dive**. **swallow-tailed** having a swallowtail. [OE *swealwe* f. Gmc]

swallowtail /swólōtayl/ *n.* **1** a deeply forked tail. **2** anything resembling this shape. **3** any butterfly of this family Papilionidae with wings extended at the back to this shape.

swam *past* of SWIM.

swami /swaamee/ *n.* (*pl.* **swamis**) a Hindu male religious teacher. [Hindi *swāmī* master, prince, f. Skr. *svāmin*]

■ see MASTER *n.* 2.

swamp /swaamp/ *n. & v.* ● *n.* a piece of waterlogged ground; a bog or marsh. ● *v.* **1 a** *tr.* overwhelm, flood, or soak with water. **b** *intr.* become swamped. **2** *tr.* overwhelm or make

invisible, etc., with an excess or large amount of something. □□ **swampy** *adj.* (**swampier, swampiest**). [17th c., = dial. *swamp* sunk (14th c.), prob. of Gmc orig.]

■ *n.* **1** bog, fen, marsh, quagmire, mire, slough; marshland, wetlands; moor, *Sc.* & *No. of Engl.* moss, *literary* morass. ● *v.* overwhelm, flood, inundate, submerge, immerse, deluge; soak, drench, engulf, swallow up; overcome, overload, overtax, overburden, snow under. □□ **swampy** see MUDDY *adj.* 2.

swan /swon/ *n. & v.* ● *n.* **1** a large water bird of the genus *Cygnus*, etc., having a long flexible neck, webbed feet, and in most species snow-white plumage. **2** *literary* a poet. ● *v.intr.* (**swanned, swanning**) (usu. foll. by *about, off,* etc.) *Brit. colloq.* move or go aimlessly or casually or with a superior air. □ **swan dive** a dive with the arms outspread until close to the water. **swan-neck** a curved structure shaped like a swan's neck. **Swan of Avon** *Brit. literary* Shakespeare. **swan song 1** a person's last work or act before death or retirement, etc. **2** a song like that fabled to be sung by a dying swan. □□ **swanlike** *adj.* & *adv.* [OE f. Gmc]

swank /swangk/ *n., v.,* & *adj. colloq.* ● *n.* ostentation; swagger; bluff. ● *v.intr.* behave with swank; show off. ● *adj.* = SWANKY. [19th c.: orig. uncert.]

■ *n.* see SPLENDOR 2. ● *v.* see SWAGGER *v.* 2.

swankpot /swángkpot/ *n. Brit. colloq.* a person behaving with swank.

swanky /swángkee/ *adj.* (**swankier, swankiest**) **1** marked by swank; ostentatiously smart or showy. **2** (of a person) inclined to swank; boastful. □□ **swankily** *adv.* **swankiness** *n.*

■ **1** smart, stylish, fashionable, chic, chichi, fancy, showy, luxurious, grand, elegant, plush, *colloq.* nifty, plushy, posh, ritzy, swell, swank, *Brit. colloq.*, swish, swagger, *sl.* snazzy, neat. **2** see BOASTFUL. □□ **swankiness** see SPLENDOR 2.

swannery /swónǝree/ *n.* (*pl.* **-ies**) a place where swans are bred.

swansdown /swónzdown/ *n.* **1** the fine down of a swan, used in trimming clothing, etc. **2** a kind of thick cotton cloth with a soft nap on one side.

swap /swop/ *v. & n.* (also **swop**) ● *v.tr.* & *intr.* (**swapped, swapping**) exchange or barter (one thing for another). ● *n.* **1** an act of swapping. **2** a thing suitable for swapping. **3** a thing swapped. □□ **swapper** *n.* [ME, orig. = 'hit': prob. imit.]

■ *v.* see EXCHANGE *v.* ● *n.* **1** see EXCHANGE *n.* 1.

swaraj /swǝraaj/ *n. hist.* self-government or independence for India. □□ **swarajist** *n.* [Skr., = self-ruling: cf. RAJ]

sward /swawrd/ *n. literary* **1** an expanse of short grass. **2** turf. □□ **swarded** *adj.* [OE *sweard* skin]

■ see TURF *n.* 1.

sware /swair/ *archaic past* of SWEAR.

swarf /swawrf/ *n.* **1** fine chips or filings of stone, metal, etc. **2** wax, etc., removed in cutting a phonograph record. [ON *svarf* file dust]

swarm¹ /swawrm/ *n. & v.* ● *n.* **1** a cluster of bees leaving the hive with the queen to establish a new colony. **2** a large number of insects or birds moving in a cluster. **3** a large group of people, esp. moving over or filling a large area. **4** (in *pl.*; foll. by *of*) great numbers. **5** a group of zoospores. ● *v.intr.* **1** move in or form a swarm. **2** gather or move in large numbers. **3** (foll. by *with*) (of a place) be overrun, crowded, or infested (*was swarming with tourists*). [OE *swearm* f. Gmc]

■ *n.* **1–3** throng, horde, army, host, multitude, hive, herd, mob, mass, drove, flood, stream, cloud, flock, pack, shoal, bunch. **4** (*swarms*) see SCORE *n.* 3. ● *v.* **1, 2** throng, mass, crowd, congregate, cluster, flock, herd, gather, mob, flood, stream, flow, pour, surge. **3** (*swarm with*) crawl with, abound in *or* with, throng with, teem with, burst with, bristle with, be alive with, be crowded with, be overrun with, be infested with.

swarm² /swawrm/ *v.intr.* (foll. by *up*) & *tr.* climb (a rope or tree, etc.), esp. in a rush, by clasping or clinging with the hands and knees, etc. [16th c.: orig. unkn.]

swart /swawrt/ *adj. archaic* swarthy; dark-hued. [OE *sweart* f. Gmc]
- see SWARTHY.

swarthy /swáwrthee/ *adj.* (**swarthier, swarthiest**) dark; dark-complexioned. □□ **swarthily** *adv.* **swarthiness** *n.* [var. of obs. *swarty* (as SWART)]
- dark, dusky, brown, tanned, weather-beaten, *archaic* swart.

swash[1] /swosh/ *v. & n.* ● *v.* **1** *intr.* (of water, etc.) wash about; make the sound of washing or rising and falling. **2** *tr. archaic* strike violently. **3** *intr. archaic* swagger. ● *n.* the motion or sound of swashing water. [imit.]
- *v.* **3** see SWAGGER *v.* 1.

swash[2] /swosh/ *adj.* **1** inclined obliquely. **2** (of a letter) having a flourished stroke or strokes. □ **swash plate** an inclined disk revolving on an axle and giving reciprocating motion to a part in contact with it. [17th c.: orig. unkn.]

swashbuckler /swóshbuklər/ *n.* **1** a swaggering bully or ruffian. **2** a dashing or daring adventurer, esp. in a novel, movie, etc. □□ **swashbuckling** *adj. & n.* [SWASH[1] + BUCKLER]
- see ADVENTURER 1, BULLY[1] *n.* □□ **swashbuckling** (*adj.*) adventurous, daring, daredevil, swaggering, roisterous, bold, dashing, flamboyant, macho.

swastika /swóstikə/ *n.* **1** an ancient symbol formed by an equal-armed cross with each arm continued at a right angle. **2** this with clockwise continuations as the symbol of Nazi Germany. [Skr. *svastika* f. *svasti* well-being f. *sú* good + *asti* being]
- hakenkreuz.

swat /swot/ *v. & n.* ● *v.tr.* (**swatted, swatting**) **1** crush (a fly, etc.) with a sharp blow. **2** hit hard and abruptly. ● *n.* **1** a swatting blow. **2** a homerun in baseball. [17th c. in the sense 'sit down': No. of Engl. dial. & US var. of SQUAT]
- *v.* see HIT *v.* 1a. ● *n.* **1** see HIT *n.* 1a.

swatch /swoch/ *n.* **1** a sample, esp. of cloth or fabric. **2** a collection of samples. [17th c.: orig. unkn.]

swath /swoth, swawth/ *n.* (also **swathe** /swoth, swayth/) (*pl.* **swaths** /swoths, swawths/ or **swathes** swothz, swaythz/) **1** a ridge of grass or grain, etc., lying after being cut. **2** a space left clear after the passage of a mower, etc. **3** a broad strip. □ **cut a wide swath** be effective in destruction. [OE *swæth, swathu*]
- ridge, path, belt, strip, ribbon.

swathe /swoth, swayth/ *v. & n.* ● *v.tr.* bind or enclose in bandages or garments, etc. ● *n.* a bandage or wrapping. [OE *swathian*]
- *v.* tie, bind, bandage, wrap, swaddle, bundle (up), envelop, shroud, muffle (up), *literary* enwrap. ● *n.* bandage, wrapping, covering, wrapper, cover.

swatter /swótər/ *n.* an implement for swatting flies.

sway /sway/ *v. & n.* ● *v.* **1** *intr. & tr.* lean or cause to lean unsteadily in different directions alternately. **2** *intr.* oscillate irregularly; waver. **3** *tr.* **a** control the motion or direction of. **b** have influence or rule over. ● *n.* **1** rule, influence, or government (*hold sway*). **2** a swaying motion or position. [ME: cf. LG *swajen* be blown to and fro, Du. *zwaaien* swing, wave]
- *v.* **1** bend, lean, roll, rock, swing (to and fro *or* back and forth *or* from side to side *or* backward and forward), move to and fro *or* back and forth *or* from side to side *or* backward and forward, wave, fluctuate, undulate, reel, totter, lurch. **2** see OSCILLATE. **3 a** move, incline, divert, veer, tilt, lean, slant, bias, swing. **b** influence, persuade, impress, win over, bring around, convince, talk into; move, incline, affect, bias, swing. ● *n.* **1** influence, control, power, command, authority, jurisdiction, dominion, rule, government, sovereignty, leadership, mastery, domination; grip, clutches, grasp; *colloq.* clout. **2** sweep, wave, swing, (period of) oscillation, libration.

swear /swair/ *v. & n.* ● *v.* (*past* **swore** /swor/; *past part.* **sworn** /sworn/) **1** *tr.* **a** (often foll. by *to* + infin. or *that* + clause) state or promise solemnly or on oath. **b** take (an oath). **2** *tr. colloq.* say emphatically; insist (*swore he had not seen it*). **3** *tr.* cause to take an oath (*swore them to secrecy*). **4** *intr.* (often foll. by *at*) use profane or indecent language, esp. as an expletive or from anger. **5** *tr.* (often foll. by *against*) make a sworn affirmation of (an offense) (*swear treason against*). **6** *intr.* (foll. by *by*) **a** appeal to as a witness in taking an oath (*swear by Almighty God*). **b** *colloq.* have or express great confidence in (*swears by yoga*). **7** *intr.* (foll. by *to*; usu. in *neg.*) admit the certainty of (*could not swear to it*). **8** *intr.* (foll. by *at*) *Brit. colloq.* (of colors, etc.) fail to harmonize with. ● *n.* a spell of swearing. □ **swear blind** *Brit. colloq.* affirm emphatically. **swear in** induct into office, etc., by administering an oath. **swear off** *colloq.* promise to abstain from (drink, etc.). **swear out** obtain an arrest warrant by making an accusation under oath. □□ **swearer** *n.* [OE *swerian* f. Gmc, rel. to ANSWER]
- *v.* **1a, 2** asseverate, declare, insist, assert, solemnly affirm *or* state, testify, promise, take an oath, state under *or* on oath, undertake, vow, avow, warrant, pledge, give one's word, agree, *Law* depose, *formal* aver. **4** curse, blaspheme, imprecate, use profanity, utter profanities, *colloq.* cuss. **6 b** (*swear by*) trust (in), believe in, rely on, have confidence in, count on. **7** (*swear to*) see PROVE 1. **8** (*swear off*) see CLASH *v.* 3b. □ **swear in** see INDUCT 1. **swear off** forswear, renounce, abjure, go off, forgo, shun, avoid, give up, forsake, throw over, *literary* eschew.

sweat /swet/ *n. & v.* ● *n.* **1** moisture exuded through the pores of the skin, esp. from heat or nervousness. **2** a state or period of sweating. **3** *colloq.* a state of anxiety (*was in a sweat about it*). **4** *colloq.* **a** drudgery; effort. **b** a laborious task or undertaking. **5** condensed moisture on a surface. ● *v.* (*past* and *past part.* **sweat** or **sweated**) **1** *intr.* exude sweat; perspire. **2** *intr.* be terrified, suffering, etc. **3** *intr.* (of a wall, etc.) exhibit surface moisture. **4** *intr.* drudge; toil. **5** *tr.* heat (meat or vegetables) slowly in fat or water to extract the juices. **6** *tr.* emit (blood, gum, etc.) like sweat. **7** *tr.* make (a horse, athlete, etc.) sweat by exercise. **8** *tr.* **a** cause to drudge or toil. **b** (as **sweat** *adj.*) (of goods, workers, or labor) produced by or subjected to long hours under poor conditions. **9** *tr.* subject (hides or tobacco) to fermentation in manufacturing. **10** join (metal pipes, tubing, etc.) by heating and usu. soldering. □ **by the sweat of one's brow** by one's own hard work. **no sweat** *colloq.* there is no need to worry. **sweat blood** *colloq.* **1** work strenuously. **2** be extremely anxious. **sweat bullets 1** = *sweat blood*. **2** sweat excessively or profusely. **sweat gland** *Anat.* a spiral tubular gland below the skin secreting sweat. **sweating sickness** an epidemic fever with sweating prevalent in England in the 15th–16th c. **sweat it out** *colloq.* endure a difficult experience to the end. [ME *swet(e)*, alt. (after *swete* v. f. OE *swǣtan* OHG *sweizzen* roast) of *swote* f. OE *swāt* f. Gmc]
- *n.* **1, 2** perspiration, lather, *Med.* diaphoresis. **3** state of confusion *or* upset *or* excitement *or* distraction *or* agitation *or* anxiety *or* distress *or* worry; *colloq.* dither, tizzy, stew, flap, *literary* pother; (*in a sweat*) see NERVOUS 1–3, 5. **4 a** (hard) work, labor, effort, exertion, laboriousness, toil, drudgery, *archaic* moil, *colloq.* grind, *Brit. colloq.* swot, *Austral. sl.* (hard) yakka. **b** slog, labor, chore, *colloq.* grind. ● *v.* **1** perspire, glow. **2** worry, be anxious, agonize, anguish, bite one's nails, be on pins and needles, fret, fuss, torture *or* torment oneself, lose sleep, *colloq.* sweat blood, stew, be in a tizzy *or* stew. **4** slave (away), labor, drudge, grind, toil, slog, work like a Trojan, *archaic* toil and moil, *Brit. colloq.* swot. **6** ooze, exude, squeeze out, transude, emit. □ **no sweat** don't worry, everything is taken care of, all is well, that presents no difficulty, *colloq.* no problem(s), no worries, not to worry. **sweat it out** see ENDURE 1.

/. . ./ **pronunciation**	● **part of speech**
□ **phrases, idioms, and compounds**	
□□ **derivatives**	■ **synonym section**
cross-references appear in SMALL CAPITALS or *italics*	

sweatband /swétband/ *n.* a band of absorbent material inside a hat or around a wrist, etc., to soak up sweat.

sweater /swétər/ *n.* **1** a knitted jersey, pullover, or cardigan. **2** an employer who works employees hard in poor conditions for low pay.

sweatpants /swétpants/ *n.pl.* loose pants of absorbent cotton material worn for exercise, etc.

sweatshirt /swétshərt/ *n.* a sleeved cotton pullover of absorbent material, as worn by athletes before and after exercise.

sweatshop /swétshop/ *n.* a workshop where sweat labor is used.

sweatsuit /swétsōōt/ *n.* a suit of a jacket or sweatshirt and pants intended for exercise, etc.

sweaty /swétee/ *adj.* (**sweatier, sweatiest**) **1** sweating; covered with sweat. **2** causing sweat. □□ **sweatily** *adv.* **sweatiness** *n.*

■ **2** see STEAMY 1.

Swede /sweed/ *n.* **1 a** a native or national of Sweden. **b** a person of Swedish descent. **2** (**swede**) (in full **swede turnip**) *Brit.* = RUTABAGA. [MLG & MDu. *Swēde*, prob. f. ON *Svíthjóth* f. *Svíar* Swedes + *thjóth* people]

Swedish /sweedish/ *adj. & n.* ● *adj.* of or relating to Sweden or its people or language. ● *n.* the language of Sweden.

sweep /sweep/ *v. & n.* ● *v.* (*past* and *past part.* **swept** /swept/) **1** *tr.* clean or clear (a room or area, etc.) with or as with a broom. **2** *intr.* (often foll. by *up*) clean a room, etc., in this way. **3** *tr.* (often foll. by *up*) collect or remove (dirt or litter, etc.) by sweeping. **4** *tr.* (foll. by *aside, away,* etc.) **a** a push with or as with a broom. **b** dismiss or reject abruptly (*their objections were swept aside*). **5** *tr.* (foll. by *along, down,* etc.) carry or drive along with force. **6** *tr.* (foll. by *off, away,* etc.) remove or clear forcefully. **7** *tr.* traverse swiftly or lightly (*the wind swept the hillside*). **8** *tr.* impart a sweeping motion to (*swept his hand across*). **9** *tr.* swiftly cover or affect (*a new fashion swept the country*). **10** *intr.* **a** glide swiftly; speed along with unchecked motion. **b** go majestically. **11** *intr.* (of geographical features, etc.) have continuous extent. **12** *tr.* drag (a river bottom, etc.) to search for something. **13** *tr.* (of artillery, etc.) include in the line of fire; cover the whole of. **14** *tr.* propel (a barge, etc.) with sweeps. **15** *tr.* win every game, etc., in (a series) (*the team swept their latest home stand*). ● *n.* **1** the act or motion or an instance of sweeping. **2** a curve in the road, a sweeping line of a hill, etc. **3** range or scope (*beyond the sweep of the human mind*). **4** = *chimney sweep*. **5** a sortie by aircraft. **6** *colloq.* = SWEEPSTAKE. **7** a long oar worked from a barge, etc. **8** the sail of a windmill. **9** a long pole mounted as a lever for raising buckets from a well. **10** *Electronics* the movement of a beam across the screen of a cathode-ray tube. **11** (in *pl.*) a period during which television ratings are monitored and advertising rates are set. □ **make a clean sweep of 1** completely abolish or expel. **2** win all the prizes, etc., in (a competition, etc.). **sweep away 1** abolish swiftly. **2** (usu. in *passive*) powerfully affect, esp. emotionally. **sweep-secondhand** a second hand on a clock or watch, moving on the same dial as the other hands. **sweep under the carpet** see CARPET. **swept-back** (of an aircraft wing) fixed at an acute angle to the fuselage, inclining outwards toward the rear. **swept-up** (of hair) = UPSWEPT. **swept-wing** (of an aircraft) having swept-back wings. [ME *swepe* (earlier *swōpe*) f. OE *swāpan*]

■ *v.* **1** brush, clean, dust, clear, tidy up. **4 b** (*sweep aside*) see REJECT *v.* 1, 3. **6** remove, clear, wash away; expel, eliminate, get rid of, dispose of. **10 a** glide, sail; swoop, skim, dash, charge, fly, speed, rush, zoom, *colloq.* tear. **b** sail, glide, flounce, march, parade. **11** curve, arc, arch, bend, bow, circle, turn. ● *n.* **1** see WHISK *n.* 1. **2** curve, arc, arch, bow, bend, turn, curvature, flexure. **3** range, extent, compass, reach, stretch, scope, swing, span. **7** see PADDLE[1] *n.* □ **make a clean sweep of 1** see ABOLISH. **sweep away 1** see ABOLISH. **2** see INSPIRE 1, 2.

sweepback /sweepbak/ *n.* the angle at which an aircraft's wing is set back from a position at right angles to the body.

sweeper /sweepər/ *n.* **1** a person who cleans by sweeping. **2** a device for sweeping carpets, etc. **3** *Soccer* a defensive player positioned close to the goalkeeper.

sweeping /sweeping/ *adj. & n.* ● *adj.* **1** wide in range or effect (*sweeping changes*). **2** taking no account of particular cases or exceptions (*a sweeping statement*). ● *n.* (in *pl.*) dirt, etc., collected by sweeping. □□ **sweepingly** *adv.* **sweepingness** *n.*

■ *adj.* **1** comprehensive, (all-)inclusive, general, extensive, universal, all-embracing, broad, widespread, wide(-ranging), far-ranging, blanket, umbrella, catholic, exhaustive, radical, thorough(going), out-and-out, across-the-board, wholesale, complete, total, overwhelming, *colloq.* wall-to-wall. **2** broad, generalized, unspecific, nonspecific, imprecise, inexact, unqualified, oversimplified, general. ● *n.* (*sweepings*) see DIRT 6.

sweepstake /sweepstayk/ *n.* **1** a form of gambling on horse races or other contests in which all competitors' stakes are paid to the winners. **2** a race with betting of this kind. **3** a prize or prizes won in a sweepstake.

■ see LOTTERY.

sweet /sweet/ *adj. & n.* ● *adj.* **1** having the pleasant taste characteristic of sugar. **2** smelling pleasant like roses or perfume, etc.; fragrant. **3** (of sound, etc.) melodious or harmonious. **4 a** not salt, sour, or bitter. **b** fresh, with flavor unimpaired by rottenness. **c** (of water) fresh and readily drinkable. **5** (of wine) having a sweet taste (opp. DRY). **6** highly gratifying or attractive. **7** amiable; pleasant (*has a sweet nature*). **8** *colloq.* (of a person or thing) pretty; charming; endearing. **9** (foll. by *on*) *colloq.* fond of; in love with. ● *n.* **1** a sweet part of something; sweetness. **2** *Brit.* candy. **3** *Brit.* a dessert. **4** (in *pl.*) delights; gratification. **5** (esp. as a form of address) sweetheart, etc. □ **she's sweet** *Austral. sl.* all is well. **sweet-and-sour** cooked in a sauce containing sugar and vinegar or lemon, etc. **sweet basil** see BASIL. **sweet bay** = BAY[2]. **sweet chestnut** see CHESTNUT. **sweet cicely** a white-flowered aromatic plant, *Myrrhis odorata.* **sweet corn 1** a kind of corn with kernels having a high sugar content. **2** these kernels, eaten as a vegetable when young. **sweet flag** a marsh herb, *Acorus calamus,* of the arum family with an aromatic rootstock. **sweet gale** see GALE[2]. **sweet pea** any dwarf or climbing plant of the genus *Lathyrus,* esp. *L. odoratus* with fragrant flowers in many colors. **sweet pepper** see PEPPER. **sweet potato 1** a tropical climbing plant, *Ipomoea batatas,* with sweet tuberous roots used for food. **2** the root of this. **sweet rocket** see ROCKET[2]. **sweet rush** (or **sedge**) a kind of sedge with a thick creeping aromatic rootstock used in medicine and confectionery. **sweet sultan** a sweet-scented plant, *Centaurea moschata* or *C. suaveoleus.* **sweet talk** *colloq.* flattery; blandishment. **sweet-talk** *v.tr. colloq.* flatter in order to persuade. **sweet-tempered** amiable. **sweet tooth** a liking for sweet-tasting foods. **sweet violet** a sweet-scented violet, *Viola odorata.* **sweet william** a plant, *Dianthus barbatus,* with clusters of vivid fragrant flowers. **sweet william catchfly** a pink-flowered European pink, *Silene armeria.* □□ **sweetish** *adj.* **sweetly** *adv.* [OE *swēte* f. Gmc]

■ *adj.* **1** sugary, honeylike, honeyed, sweetened; luscious, saccharine, cloying, sickly, treacly, syrupy. **2** fragrant, perfumed, scented, aromatic, ambrosial, sweet-smelling, sweet-scented, balmy, redolent. **3** harmonious, melodious, sweet-sounding, euphonious, dulcet, musical, tuneful, euphonic, mellifluous, mellow, lyric, silvery, bell-like, golden. **4 c** drinkable, potable, fresh, clean. **6** gratifying, satisfying, pleasant, nice, attractive; dear, beloved, precious, prized, treasured, wonderful, marvelous, splendid, *colloq.* great. **7** gentle, amiable, agreeable, genial, warm, friendly, nice, pleasant, unassuming, easygoing; considerate, attentive, solicitous, thoughtful, sympathetic, compassionate, kind, kindhearted, generous, gracious, accommodating. **8** attractive, appealing, charming, endearing, winning, pleasant, pleasing, lovely; pretty, *colloq.* cute; dear, nice. **9** (*sweet on*) fond of, taken with, keen on, devoted to, enamored of, infatuated with, (head over heels) in love with, mad about, *colloq.* wild *or* crazy about, nuts about *or* on *or* over, stuck on, esp. *Brit. colloq.* daft about, *sl.* gone on, batty about. ● *n.* **2** bonbon, chocolate, confection, sweetmeat, fondant, toffee, candy, *archaic* comfit, *Austral. colloq.* lolly. **3** dessert, *Brit.* pudding, *Brit. colloq.* afters, pud; (*sweets*) confectionery, candy. **5** see DEAR *n.* □ **sweet talk** see *cajolery* (CAJOLE).

■ **sweet-talk** flatter, *colloq.* soft-soap; see also CAJOLE.

sweetbread /sweétbred/ *n.* the pancreas or thymus of an animal, esp. as food.

sweetbrier /sweétbrɪər/ *n.* a wild rose, *Rosa eglanteria* of Europe and central Asia; with hooked thorns and small fragrant pink flowers.

sweeten /sweét'n/ *v.tr. & intr.* **1** make or become sweet or sweeter. **2** make agreeable or less painful. □ **sweeten the pill** see PILL. □□ **sweetening** *n.*

■ **1** sugar, sugarcoat. **2** dress up, make more attractive *or* agreeable, sugarcoat, embellish, embroider; make less painful, mitigate, alleviate, assuage, lighten, soften, palliate, mollify, ease, allay, moderate, mellow, temper.

sweetener /sweét'nər/ *n.* **1** a substance used to sweeten food or drink. **2** *colloq.* a bribe or inducement.

sweetheart /sweét-haart/ *n.* **1** a lover or darling. **2** a term of endearment (esp. as a form of address). □ **sweetheart agreement** (or **contract** or **deal**) *colloq.* an industrial agreement reached privately by employers and labor union representatives that is beneficial to them but not to the workers.

■ **1** girlfriend, boyfriend, friend, admirer, darling, dear, love, beloved, lover, inamorato, inamorata, ladylove, betrothed, fiancé(e), beau, *archaic* sweeting, *archaic or derog.* paramour, *archaic or poet.* mistress, *colloq.* intended, heartthrob, flame, steady, *poet.* swain. **2** see DEAR *n.*

sweetie /sweétee/ *n. colloq.* **1** a sweetheart. **2** *Brit.* a candy. **3** (also **sweetie-pie**) a term of endearment (esp. as a form of address).

■ **2** see DEAR *n.*

sweeting /sweéting/ *n.* **1** a sweet-flavored variety of apple. **2** *archaic* darling.

sweetmeal /sweétmeel/ *n. Brit.* **1** sweetened wholemeal. **2** a sweetmeal biscuit.

sweetmeat /sweétmeet/ *n.* **1** a candy. **2** a small fancy cake.

■ **1** see SWEET *n.* 1. **2** see DELICACY 4.

sweetness /sweétnis/ *n.* the quality of being sweet; fragrance, melodiousness, etc. □ **sweetness and light** a display of (esp. uncharacteristic) mildness and reason.

■ see MELODY 4, *sentimentality* (SENTIMENTAL).

sweetshop /sweétshop/ *n. Brit.* a store selling candy as its main item.

sweetsop /sweétsop/ *n.* **1** a tropical American evergreen shrub, *Annona squamosa.* **2** the fruit of this, having a green rind and a sweet pulp.

swell /swel/ *v., n.,* & *adj.* ● *v.* (*past part.* **swollen** /swólən/ or **swelled**) **1** *intr. & tr.* grow or cause to grow bigger or louder or more intense; expand; increase in force or intensity. **2** *intr.* (often foll. by *up*) & *tr.* rise or raise up from the surrounding surface. **3** *intr.* (foll. by *out*) bulge. **4** *intr.* (of the heart as the seat of emotion) feel full of joy, pride, relief, etc. **5** *intr.* (foll. by *with*) be hardly able to restrain (pride, etc.). **6** (as **swollen** *adj.*) distended or bulging. ● *n.* **1** an act or the state of swelling. **2** the heaving of the sea with waves that do not break, e.g., after a storm. **3 a** a crescendo. **b** a mechanism in an organ, etc., for obtaining a crescendo or diminuendo. **4** *colloq.* a person of distinction or of dashing or fashionable appearance. **5** a protuberant part. ● *adj.* **1** *colloq.* fine; splendid; excellent. **2** *colloq.* smart, fashionable. □ **swell box** *Mus.* a box in which organ pipes are enclosed, with a shutter for controlling the sound level. **swelled** (or **swollen**) **head** *colloq.* conceit. **swell organ** *Mus.* a section of an organ with pipes in a swell-box. □□ **swellish** *adj.* [OE *swellan* f. Gmc]

■ *v.* **1** grow, increase, enlarge, expand, blow up *or* out, dilate, wax, extend; mushroom, snowball, multiply, accumulate, mount, rise, escalate; raise, augment, step

up, build up, intensify, heighten, *colloq.* boost. **3** bloat, bulge, billow, belly, balloon, fatten, puff up *or* out, blow up *or* out, distend, inflate, tumefy. **5** (*swell with*) be filled with, be full of, be bursting with, brim with, overflow with. **6** (**swollen**) distended, enlarged, bulging, bulbous, tumid, tumescent. ● *n.* **1** enlargement, broadening, increase, extension, spread, swelling, inflation, expansion, growth, rise, surge, upsurge. **2** surge, waves, rollers, billows. **4** fop, dandy, coxcomb, *colloq.* clotheshorse, lounge lizard, *colloq. usu. archaic* gay blade, *hist.* macaroni, *sl.* dude, *Austral. sl.* lair, *Brit. sl.* nob, toff. ● *adj.* **1** marvelous, thrilling, splendid, spectacular, first-rate, excellent, fine, *colloq.* great, super, terrific. **2** smart, chic, stylish, fashionable, modish, dapper; grand, luxurious, deluxe, elegant, first-rate, first-class, top-grade, swanky, *colloq.* posh, ritzy, swank.

swelling /sweéling/ *n.* an abnormal protuberance on or in the body.

■ enlargement, distension, tumescence, protuberance, bump, prominence, bulge, lump, excrescence, protrusion, tumor, node, nodule; boil, blister, bunion.

swelter /sweéltər/ *v. & n.* ● *v.intr.* (usu. as **sweltering** *adj.*) be uncomfortably hot. ● *n.* a sweltering atmosphere or condition. □□ **swelteringly** *adv.* [base of (now dial.) *swelt* f. OE *sweltan* perish f. Gmc]

■ *v.* (**sweltering**) hot, torrid, steamy, sultry, stifling, sticky, suffocating, roasting, blistering, burning, tropical, close, *colloq.* baking, boiling, scorching.

swept *past* and *past part.* of SWEEP.

swerve /swərv/ *v. & n.* ● *v.intr. & tr.* change or cause to change direction, esp. abruptly. ● *n.* **1** a swerving movement. **2** divergence from a course. □□ **swerveless** *adj.* **swerver** *n.* [ME, repr. OE *sweorfan* SCOUR[1]]

■ *v.* veer, career, swing, diverge, deviate, dodge, sheer off, skew, stray, turn (aside), careen.

SWG *abbr.* standard wire gauge.

swift /swift/ *adj., adv.,* & *n.* ● *adj.* **1** quick; rapid; soon coming or passing. **2** speedy; prompt (*a swift response; was swift to act*). ● *adv.* (*archaic* except in *comb.*) swiftly (*swift-moving*). ● *n.* **1** any swift-flying insect-eating bird of the family Apodidae, with long wings and a superficial resemblance to a swallow. **2** a revolving frame for winding yarn, etc., from. □□ **swiftly** *adv.* **swiftness** *n.* [OE, rel. to *swīfan* move in a course]

■ *adj.* fast, rapid, speedy, hasty, quick, *poet. or literary* fleet; lively, nimble, *poet. or literary* fleet-footed; brisk, sudden, abrupt; meteoric, whirlwind, express; prompt, expeditious. □□ **swiftly** fast, quick(ly), speedily, rapidly, expeditiously, *literary* apace; briskly, hurriedly, hastily, posthaste, suddenly, abruptly, in a flash, in a trice, in the wink of an eye, in an instant, in no time, like the wind, precipitately, unexpectedly, *colloq.* like a bat out of hell, before you can say Jack Robinson, like a shot, like greased lightning, lickety-split, in a jiff(y), pronto, p.d.q., *joc.* in less than no time. **swiftness** see SPEED *n.* 1.

swiftie /swíftee/ *n. Austral. sl.* **1** a deceptive trick. **2** a person who acts or thinks quickly.

swiftlet /swíftlit/ *n.* a small swift of the genus *Collocalia.*

swig /swig/ *v. & n. colloq.* ● *v.tr. & intr.* (**swigged, swigging**) drink in large swallows. ● *n.* a swallow of drink, esp. a large amount. □□ **swigger** *n.* [16th c., orig. as noun in obs. sense 'liquor': orig. unkn.]

■ *v.* see DRINK *v.* 1. ● *n.* see DRINK *n.* 1b.

swill /swil/ *v. & n.* ● *v.* **1** *tr. & intr.* drink greedily. **2** *tr.* (often foll. by *out*) *Brit.* rinse or flush; pour water over or through. ● *n.* **1** mainly liquid refuse as pig food. **2** inferior liquor. **3**

worthless matter, trash. **4** *Brit.* an act of rinsing. □□ **swiller**
n. [OE *swillan, swilian*, of unkn. orig.]

■ *v.* **1** drink, guzzle, swallow, toss off, polish off, *colloq.*
swig, *literary* quaff, *sl.* knock back. ● *n.* **1, 3** hogwash,
pigswill, refuse, pigwash, slop(s), garbage, waste,
rubbish. **4** rinse, clean, wash.

swim /swim/ *v. & n.* ● *v.* (**swimming**; *past* **swam** /swam/;
past part. **swum** /swum/) **1** *intr.* propel the body through
water by working the arms and legs, or (of a fish) the fins
and tail. **2** *tr.* **a** traverse (a stretch of water or its distance)
by swimming. **b** compete in (a race) by swimming. **c** use (a
particular stroke) in swimming. **3** *intr.* float on or at the
surface of a liquid (*bubbles swimming on the surface*). **4** *intr.*
appear to undulate or reel or whirl. **5** *intr.* have a dizzy effect
or sensation (*my head swam*). **6** *intr.* (foll. by *in, with*) be
flooded. ● *n.* **1** a spell or the act of swimming. **2** a deep
pool frequented by fish in a river. □ **in the swim** involved
in or acquainted with what is going on. **swim bladder** a
gas-filled sac in fishes used to maintain buoyancy. **swimming pool** an indoor or outdoor pool for swimming. **swim-
ming-costume** *Brit.* = SWIMSUIT. □□ **swimmable** *adj.*
swimmer *n.* [OE *swimman* f. Gmc]

■ *v.* **3** see FLOAT *v.* 2. **5** see SPIN *v.* 6. ● *n.* **1** see DIP *n.* 3.
□ **in the swim** see SWINGING.

swimmeret /swiməret/ *n.* a swimming foot in crustaceans.

swimmingly /swiminglee/ *adv.* with easy and unobstructed
progress.

■ smoothly, easily, effortlessly, well, successfully, without
a hitch *or* problem, like clockwork, like a house on fire,
without difficulty, readily, *colloq.* like a dream.

swimsuit /swimsoot/ *n.* garment worn for swimming.
□□ **swimsuited** *adj.*

swimwear /swimwair/ *n.* clothing worn for swimming.

swindle /swind'l/ *v. & n.* ● *v.tr.* (often foll. by *out of*) **1** cheat
(a person) of money, possessions, etc. (*was swindled out of
all his savings*). **2** cheat a person of (money, etc.) (*swindled
all his savings out of him*). ● *n.* **1** an act of swindling. **2** a
person or thing represented as what it is not. **3** a fraudulent
scheme. □□ **swindler** *n.* [back-form. f. *swindler* f. G *Schwin-
dler* extravagant maker of schemes, swindler, f. *schwindeln*
be dizzy]

■ *v.* **1** cheat, defraud, deceive, double-cross, hoodwink,
take in, flimflam, fleece, rook, dupe, fool, mulct, gull,
make a fool (out) of, victimize, exploit, trick, hoax,
euchre, screw, *colloq.* bamboozle, diddle, pull a fast one
on, take for a ride, rip off, *literary* cozen, *sl.* con, fiddle,
chisel, *sl.* take to the cleaners, bilk, sting, pluck, gyp,
buffalo, bunco. ● *n.* **1, 3** fraud, confidence trick,
deception, racket, trick, chicane; confidence game,
colloq. fiddle, rip-off, *sl.* con, gyp, scam, skin game,
bunco; double-dealing, trickery, sharp practice,
thimblerigging, chicanery, knavery. **2** see DECEIT 2.
□□ **swindler** cheat, confidence man, hoaxer,
mountebank, charlatan, knave, scoundrel, sharper,
racketeer, fraud, trickster, thimblerigger, villain,
flimflam man, four-flusher, *colloq.* sharp, shark, *formal*
defalcator, *sl.* con man, *Austral. sl.* shicer, bunco artist.

swine /swin/ *n.* (*pl.* same) **1** a pig. **2** *colloq.* (*pl.* **swine** or
swines) **a** a term of contempt or disgust for a person. **b** a
very unpleasant or difficult thing. □ **swine fever** an intestinal viral disease of pigs. □□ **swinish** *adj.* (esp. in sense 2).
swinishly *adv.* **swinishness** *n.* [OE *swin* f. Gmc]

■ **2** see WRETCH 2.

swineherd /swinhərd/ *n.* a person who tends pigs.

swing /swing/ *v. & n.* ● *v.* (*past* and *past part.* **swung**
/swung/) **1** *intr. & tr.* move or cause to move with a to-and-
fro or curving motion, as of an object attached at one end
and hanging free at the other. **2** *intr. & tr.* **a** sway. **b** hang
so as to be free to sway. **c** oscillate or cause to oscillate. **3**
intr. & tr. revolve or cause to revolve. **4** *intr.* move by gripping something and leaping, etc. (*swung from tree to tree*). **5**
intr. go with a swinging gait (*swung out of the room*). **6** *intr.*
(foll. by *around*) move around to the opposite direction. **7**
intr. change from one opinion or mood to another. **8** *intr.*
(foll. by *at*) attempt to hit or punch. **9 a** *intr.* (also **swing**

it) play music with a swing rhythm. **b** *tr.* play (a tune) with
swing. **10** *intr. colloq.* **a** be lively or up to date; enjoy oneself.
b be promiscuous. **11** *intr. colloq.* (of a party, etc.) be lively,
successful, etc. **12** *tr.* have a decisive influence on (esp. voting, etc.). **13** *tr. colloq.* deal with or achieve; manage. **14** *intr.
colloq.* be executed by hanging. ● *n.* **1** the act or an instance
of swinging. **2** the motion of swinging. **3** the extent of swinging. **4** a swinging or smooth gait or rhythm or action. **5 a** a
seat slung by ropes or chains, etc., for swinging on or in. **b**
a spell of swinging on this. **6** an easy but vigorous continued
action. **7 a** jazz or dance music with an easy flowing rhythm.
b the rhythmic feeling or drive of this music. **8** a discernible
change in opinion, esp. the amount by which votes or points
scored, etc., change from one side to another. **9** *colloq.* the
regular procedure or course of events (*get into the swing of
things*). □ **swing bridge** a bridge that can be swung to one
side to allow the passage of ships. **swing the lead** *Brit. colloq.* malinger; shirk one's duty. **swings and roundabouts**
Brit. a situation affording no eventual gain or loss (from the
phr. *lose on the swings what you make on the roundabouts*).
swing shift a work shift from afternoon to late evening.
swung dash a dash (~) with alternate curves used in printing to represent a word or part of a word previously spelled
out. □□ **swinger** *n.* (esp. in sense 10 of *v.*). [OE *swingan* to
beat f. Gmc]

■ *v.* **1, 2a, c** sway, move *or* go to and fro, move *or* go
back and forth, move *or* go backward and forward,
come and go, rock, wave, flourish, flap, fluctuate,
oscillate, vibrate, waver, zigzag, wobble, *colloq.* waggle,
wigwag. **2 b** hang, dangle, sling, suspend; be
suspended. **6** see WHEEL *v.* 2. **7** see OSCILLATE. **8** swipe,
lash out. **12** see SWAY *v.* 3. **13** see ACCOMPLISH, WANGLE
v. 1. **14** hang, be hanged, be strung up. ● *n.* **1, 2**
sway, toing and froing, fluctuation, flap, oscillation,
vibration, libration, waver, wobble, zigzag, flourish,
colloq. waggle, wigwag; stroke, *colloq.* swipe. **3** sweep,
scope, range, extent, compass, limit(s). **8** change,
switch, shift, movement, trend, fluctuation, variation,
oscillation. **9** pace, pattern, routine, groove.

swinge /swinj/ *v.tr.* (**swingeing**) *archaic* strike hard; beat.
[alt. f. ME *swenge* f. OE *swengan* shake, shatter, f. Gmc]

swingeing /swinjing/ *adj.* esp. *Brit.* **1** (of a blow) forcible. **2**
huge or far-reaching, esp. in severity (*swingeing economies*).
□□ **swingeingly** *adv.*

swinging /swinging/ *adj.* **1** (of gait, melody, etc.) vigorously
rhythmical. **2** *colloq.* **a** lively; up to date; excellent. **b** promiscuous. □ **swinging door** a door able to open in either
direction and close itself when released. □□ **swingingly** *adv.*

■ **2** a fashionable, chic, up to date, modern, lively, in the
swim, *colloq.* with-it, *colloq. often derog.* trendy, *sl.* hip,
groovy, in the groove.

swingle /swinggəl/ *n. & v.* ● *n.* **1** a wooden instrument for
beating flax and removing the woody parts from it. **2** the
swinging part of a flail. ● *v.tr.* clean (flax) with a swingle.
[ME f. MDu. *swinghel* (as SWING, -LE¹)]

swingletree /swinggəltree/ esp. *Brit.* = WHIFFLETREE.

swingy /swingee/ *adj.* (**swingier, swingiest**) **1** (of music)
characterized by swing (see SWING *n.* 7). **2** (of a skirt or
dress) designed to swing with body movement.

swipe /swip/ *v. & n. colloq.* ● *v.* **1** *tr. &* (often foll. by *at*) *intr.*
hit hard and recklessly. **2** *tr.* steal. **3** run (a credit card, etc.)
through an electronic card reader. ● *n.* a reckless hard hit
or attempted hit. □□ **swiper** *n.* [perh. var. of SWEEP]

■ *v.* **1** strike, hit, *sl.* belt, wallop; (*swipe at*) lash out at,
swing at. **2** steal, filch, pilfer, snatch, *colloq.* lift, snaffle,
formal or joc. purloin, *sl.* pinch, snitch, *Brit. sl.* nick.
● *n.* swing, strike, hit, stroke, clip.

swipple /swipəl/ *n.* the swingle of a flail. [ME, prob. formed
as SWEEP + -LE¹]

swirl /swərl/ *v. & n.* ● *v.intr. & tr.* move or flow or carry
along with a whirling motion. ● *n.* **1** a swirling motion of
or in water, air, etc. **2** the act of swirling. **3** a twist or curl,
esp. as part of a pattern or design. □□ **swirly** *adj.* [ME (orig.
as noun): orig. Sc., perh. of LG or Du. orig.]

■ *v.* whirl, spin, eddy, churn, circulate, gyrate, surge,

boil, seethe; twist, curl, roll, furl, curve, spiral, twirl, wind (around). ● *n.* twist, whirl, curl, roll, twirl, spiral; see also EDDY *n.*

swish /swish/ *v., n.,* & *adj.* ● *v.* **1** *tr.* swing (a scythe or stick, etc.) audibly through the air, grass, etc. **2** *intr.* move with or make a swishing sound. **3** *tr.* (foll. by *off*) cut (a flower, etc.) in this way. ● *n.* a swishing action or sound. ● *adj. colloq.* smart, fashionable. □□ **swishy** *adj.* [imit.]
  ■ *v.* **2** hiss, whisk, rustle, whoosh, swoosh, whisper. ● *n.* hiss, hissing sound, whoosh, swoosh, rustle, whistle. ● *adj.* elegant, fashionable, stylish, de rigueur, smart, plush, swanky, *colloq.* posh, plushy, ritzy, swell, swank, *sl.* snazzy.

Swiss /swis/ *adj.* & *n.* ● *adj.* of or relating to Switzerland in Western Europe or its people. ● *n.* (*pl.* same) **1** a native or inhabitant of Switzerland. **2** a person of Swiss descent. □ **Swiss chard** = CHARD. **Swiss cheese** a type of hard cheese with large holes that form during ripening. **Swiss steak** a slice of beef that is flattened, floured, and braised with vegetables, etc. [F *Suisse* f. MHG *Swīz*]

switch /swich/ *n.* & *v.* ● *n.* **1** a device for making and breaking the connection in an electric circuit. **2 a** a transfer, change-over, or deviation. **b** an exchange. **3** a slender flexible shoot cut from a tree. **4** a light tapering rod. **5** a device at the junction of railroad tracks for transferring a train from one track to another. **6** a tress of false or detached hair tied at one end used in hairdressing. ● *v.* **1** *tr.* (foll. by *on, off*) turn (an electrical device) on or off. **2** *intr.* change or transfer position, subject, etc. **3** *tr.* change or transfer. **4** *tr.* reverse the positions of; exchange (*switched chairs*). **5** *tr. esp. Brit.* swing or snatch (a thing) suddenly (*switched it out of my hand*). **6** *tr.* beat or flick with a switch. □ **switched-on** *colloq.* **1** up to date; aware of what is going on. **2** excited; turned on. **switch off** *colloq.* cease to pay attention. **switch over** change or exchange. □□ **switcher** *n.* [earlier *swits, switz,* prob. f. LG]
  ■ *n.* **1** circuit breaker. **2 a** change, alteration, shift, changeover, transfer, reversal, deflection, deviation. **b** trade, swap; see also EXCHANGE *n.* 1. **3, 4** twitch, lash, whip, rod, birch (rod), scourge. ● *v.* **1** (*switch on*) see *turn on* 1; (*switch off*) see *turn off* 1. **2** change, deviate, shift, seesaw. **3** change, shift, transfer, turn, rechannel, redirect, direct. **4** change, shift, swap, reverse, replace, substitute, exchange, switch over. **5** swing, swish; whisk, whip, snatch. **6** lash, whip, birch, beat, strike, thrash, scourge, flog; flick.

switchback /swíchbak/ *n.* **1** (often *attrib.*) a railroad or road with alternate sharp ascents and descents. **2** *Brit.* = *roller coaster.*

switchblade /swíchblayd/ *n.* a pocket knife with the blade released by a spring.

switchboard /swíchbawrd/ *n.* an apparatus for varying connections between electric circuits, esp. for completing telephone calls.

swither /swíthər/ *v.* & *n. Sc.* ● *v.intr.* hesitate; be uncertain. ● *n.* doubt or uncertainty. [16th c.: orig. unkn.]

swivel /swívəl/ *n.* & *v.* ● *n.* a coupling between two parts enabling one to revolve without turning the other. ● *v.tr.* & *intr.* (**swiveled, swiveling** or **swivelled, swivelling**) turn on or as on a swivel. □ **swivel chair** a chair with a seat able to be turned horizontally. [ME f. weak grade *swif-* of OE *swīfan* sweep + -LE¹: cf. SWIFT]
  ■ *n.* pivot, elbow joint, gimbals, ball-and-socket joint. ● *v.* pivot, turn, rotate, spin, revolve, wheel, twirl, pirouette, gyrate, move freely.

swizz /swiz/ *n.* (also **swiz**) (*pl.* **swizzes**) *Brit. colloq.* **1** something unfair or disappointing. **2** a swindle. [abbr. of SWIZZLE²]

swizzle¹ /swízəl/ *n.* & *v. colloq.* ● *n.* a mixed alcoholic drink, esp. of rum, made frothy by stirring. ● *v.tr.* stir with a swizzle stick. □ **swizzle stick** a stick used for stirring drinks. [19th c.: orig. unkn.]

swizzle² /swízəl/ *n. Brit. colloq.* = SWIZZ. [20th c.: prob. alt. of SWINDLE]

swob var. of SWAB.

swollen *past part.* OF SWELL.

swoon /swoon/ *v.* & *n. literary* ● *v.intr.* faint; fall into a fainting fit. ● *n.* an occurrence of fainting. [ME *swoune* perh. back-form. f. *swogning* (n.) f. *iswogen* f. OE *geswogen* overcome]
  ■ *v.* see FAINT *v.* 1. ● *n.* see FAINT *n.*

swoop /swoop/ *v.* & *n.* ● *v.* **1** *intr.* (often foll. by *down*) descend rapidly like a bird of prey. **2** *intr.* (often foll. by *on*) make a sudden attack from a distance. **3** *tr.* (often foll. by *up*) *colloq.* snatch the whole of at one swoop. ● *n.* a swooping or snatching movement or action. □ **at** (or **in**) **one fell swoop** see FELL⁴. [perh. dial. var. of obs. *swōpe* f. OE *swāpan*: see SWEEP]
  ■ *v.* **1** descend, dive, sweep down, pounce, stoop, plunge, plummet, nosedive. **2** see RAID *v.* 1. **3** (*swoop on*) scoop up, sweep up; see also SNATCH *v.* 1, 3. ● *n.* descent, dive, sweep, pounce, stoop, stroke, blow, rush.

swoosh /swoosh/ *n.* & *v.* ● *n.* the noise of a sudden rush of liquid, air, etc. ● *v.intr.* move with this noise. [imit.]
  ■ *n.* see SWISH *n.* ● *v.* see SWISH *v.*

swop var. of SWAP.

sword /sawrd/ *n.* **1** a weapon usu. of metal with a long blade and hilt with a handguard, used esp. for thrusting or striking, and often worn as part of ceremonial dress. **2** (prec. by *the*) **a** war. **b** military power. □ **put to the sword** kill, esp. in war. **sword-bearer** *Brit.* an official carrying the sovereign's, etc., sword on a formal occasion. **sword dance** a dance in which the performers brandish swords or step about swords laid on the ground. **sword grass** a grass, *Scirpus americanus,* with swordlike leaves. **sword knot** a ribbon or tassel attached to a sword hilt orig. for securing it to the wrist. **sword lily** = GLADIOLUS. **sword of Damocles** /dáməkleez/ an imminent danger (from *Damokles,* flatterer of Dionysius of Syracuse (4th c. BC) made to feast while a sword hung by a hair over him). **the sword of justice** judicial authority. **Sword of State** *Brit.* a sword borne before the sovereign on state occasions. **sword swallower** a person ostensibly or actually swallowing sword blades as entertainment. □□ **swordlike** *adj.* [OE *sw(e)ord* f. Gmc]
  ■ **1** see BLADE 6.

swordbill /sáwrdbil/ *n.* a long-billed humming bird, *Ensifera ensifera.*

swordfish /sáwrdfish/ *n.* a large marine fish, *Xiphias gladius,* with an extended swordlike upper jaw.

swordplay /sáwrdplay/ *n.* **1** fencing. **2** repartee; cut-and-thrust argument.

swordsman /sáwrdzmən/ *n.* (*pl.* **-men**) a person of (usu. specified) skill with a sword. □□ **swordsmanship** *n.*

swordstick /sáwrdstik/ *n.* a hollow walking stick containing a blade that can be used as a sword.

swordtail /sáwrdtayl/ *n.* **1** a tropical fish, *Xiphophorus helleri,* with a long tail. **2** = *horseshoe crab.*

swore *past* of SWEAR.

sworn /swawrn/ **1** *past part.* of SWEAR. **2** *adj.* bound by or as by an oath (*sworn enemies*).
  ■ **2** see PROFESSED 1.

swot /swot/ *v.* & *n. Brit. colloq.* ● *v.* (**swotted, swotting**) **1** *intr.* study assiduously. **2** *tr.* (often foll. by *up*) study (a subject) hard or hurriedly. ● *n.* **1** a person who swots. **2 a** hard study. **b** a thing that requires this. [dial. var. of SWEAT]

swum *past part.* of SWIM.

swung *past* and *past part.* of SWING.

sybarite /síbərīt/ *n.* & *adj.* ● *n.* a person who is self-indulgent or devoted to sensuous luxury. ● *adj.* fond of luxury or sensuousness. □□ **sybaritic** /-rítik/ *adj.* **sybaritical** *adj.* **sybaritically** *adv.* **sybaritism** *n.* [orig. an inhabitant of Sybaris in S. Italy, noted for luxury, f. L *sybarita* f. Gk *subaritēs*]

/. . ./ **pronunciation**	● **part of speech**
□ **phrases, idioms, and compounds**	
□□ **derivatives**	■ **synonym section**
cross-references appear in SMALL CAPITALS or *italics*	

■ *n.* epicure, epicurean, hedonist, voluptuary, sensualist, aesthete, gastronome, gourmet, bon vivant, pleasure seeker, playboy, *colloq.* jet-setter. ● *adj.* see *epicurean* (EPICUREAN *adj.* 2). ▫▫ **sybaritic, sybaritical** see *epicurean* (EPICUREAN *adj.* 2). **sybaritism** see LUXURY 1.

sycamine /síkəmin, -min/ *n. Bibl.* the black mulberry tree, *Morus nigra* (see Luke 17:6; in modern versions translated as 'mulberry tree'). [L *sycaminus* f. Gk *sukaminos* mulberry tree f. Heb. *šiḳmāh* sycamore, assim. to Gk *sukon* fig]

sycamore /síkəmawr/ *n.* **1** any pf several plane trees, esp. *Platanus occidentalis* of N. America, or its wood. **2** (in full **sycamore maple**) **a** a large maple, *Acer pseudoplatanus*, with winged seeds, grown for its shade and timber. **b** its wood. **3** *Bibl.* a fig tree, *Ficus sycomorus*, growing in Egypt, Syria, etc. [var. of SYCOMORE]

syce /sīs/ *n.* (also **sice**) *Anglo-Ind.* a groom. [Hind. f. Arab. *sā'is, sāyis*]

sycomore /síkəmawr/ *n. Bot.* = SYCAMORE 3. [ME f. OF *sic(h)amor* f. L *sycomorus* f. Gk *sukomoros* f. *sukon* fig + *moron* mulberry]

syconium /sīkṓneeəm/ *n.* (*pl.* **syconia**) *Bot.* a fleshy hollow receptacle developing into a multiple fruit as in the fig. [mod.L f. Gk *sukon* fig]

sycophant /síkəfant, síkə-/ *n.* a servile flatterer; a toady. ▫▫ **sycophancy** *n.* **sycophantic** /-fántik/ *adj.* **sycophantically** *adv.* [F *sycophante* or L *sycophanta* f. Gk *sukophantēs* informer f. *sukon* fig + *phainō* show: the reason for the name is uncert., and association with informing against the illegal exportation of figs from ancient Athens (recorded by Plutarch) cannot be substantiated]

■ see *flatterer* (FLATTER). ▫▫ **sycophancy** see *servility* (SERVILE). **sycophantic** see OBSEQUIOUS.

sycosis /sīkṓsis/ *n.* a skin disease of the bearded part of the face with inflammation of the hair follicles. [mod.L f. Gk *sukōsis* f. *sukon* fig: orig. of a figlike ulcer]

syenite /sī́ənīt/ *n.* a gray crystalline rock of feldspar and hornblende with or without quartz. ▫▫ **syenitic** /-nítik/ *adj.* [F *syénite* f. L *Syenites* (*lapis*) (stone) of *Syene* in Egypt]

syl- /sil/ *prefix* assim. form of SYN- before *l*.

syllabary /síləberee/ *n.* (*pl.* **-ies**) a list of characters representing syllables and (in some languages or stages of writing) serving the purpose of an alphabet. [mod.L *syllabarium* (as SYLLABLE)]

syllabi *pl.* of SYLLABUS.

syllabic /silábik/ *adj.* **1** of, relating to, or based on syllables. **2** *Prosody* based on the number of syllables. **3** (of a symbol) representing a whole syllable. **4** articulated in syllables. ▫▫ **syllabically** *adv.* **syllabicity** /-ləbísitee/ *n.* [F *syllabique* or LL *syllabicus* f. Gk *sullabikos* (as SYLLABLE)]

syllabication /sílabikáyshən/ *n.* (also **syllabification**) (/-bifikáyshən/) division into or articulation by syllables. ▫▫ **syllabify** *v.tr.* (**-ies, -ied**). [med.L *syllabicatio* f. *syllabicare* f. L *syllaba*: see SYLLABLE]

syllabize /síləbīz/ *v.tr.* divide into or articulate by syllables. [med.L *syllabizare* f. Gk *sullabizō* (as SYLLABLE)]

syllable /síləbəl/ *n.* & *v.* ● *n.* **1** a unit of pronunciation uttered without interruption, forming the whole or a part of a word and usu. having one vowel sound often with a consonant or consonants before or after: there are two syllables in *water* and three in *inferno*. **2** a character or characters representing a syllable. **3** (usu. with *neg.*) the least amount of speech or writing (*did not utter a syllable*). ● *v.tr.* pronounce by syllables; articulate distinctly. ▫▫ **syllabled** *adj.* (also in *comb.*). [ME f. AF *sillable* f. OF *sillabe* f. L *syllaba* f. Gk *sullabē* (as SYN-, *lambanō* take)]

syllabub /síləbub/ *n.* (also **sillabub**) **1** a drink of milk or cream mixed with wine or cider. **2** a dessert made of cream or milk flavored with wine or liquor, sweetened, and whipped to thicken it. [16th c.: orig. unkn.]

syllabus /síləbəs/ *n.* (*pl.* **syllabuses** or **syllabi** /-bī/) **1 a** the program or outline of a course of study, teaching, etc. **b** a statement of the requirements for a particular examination. **2** *RC Ch.* a summary of points decided by papal decree regarding heretical doctrines or practices. [mod.L, orig. a misreading of L *sittybas* accus. pl. of *sittyba* f. Gk *sittuba* title or label]

■ **1** see PROGRAM *n.* 4. **2** see EPITOME 3.

syllepsis /silépsis/ *n.* (*pl.* **syllepses** /-seez/) a figure of speech in which a word is applied to two others in different senses (e.g., *caught the train and a bad cold*) or to two others of which it grammatically suits one only (e.g., *neither they nor it is working*) (cf. ZEUGMA). ▫▫ **sylleptic** *adj.* **sylleptically** *adv.* [LL f. Gk *sullēpsis* taking together f. *sullambanō*: see SYLLABLE]

syllogism /síləjizəm/ *n.* **1** a form of reasoning in which a conclusion is drawn from two given or assumed propositions (premises): a common or middle term is present in the two premises but not in the conclusion, which may be invalid (e.g., *all trains are long; some buses are long; therefore some buses are trains*: the common term is *long*). **2** deductive reasoning as distinct from induction. ▫▫ **syllogistic** *adj.* **syllogistically** *adv.* [ME f. OF *silogisme* or L *syllogismus* f. Gk *sullogismos* f. *sullogizomai* (as SYN-, *logizomai* to reason f. *logos* reason)]

■ ▫▫ **syllogistic** see LOGICAL 1.

syllogize /síləjīz/ *v.* **1** *intr.* use syllogisms. **2** *tr.* put (facts or an argument) in the form of syllogism. [ME f. OF *sillogiser* or LL *syllogizare* f. Gk *sullogizomai* (as SYLLOGISM)]

sylph /silf/ *n.* **1** an elemental spirit of the air. **2** a slender graceful woman or girl. **3** any hummingbird of the genus *Aglaiocercus* with a long forked tail. ▫▫ **sylphlike** *adj.* [mod.L *sylphes*, G *Sylphen* (pl.), perh. based on L *sylvestris* of the woods + *nympha* nymph]

■ ▫▫ **sylphlike** see SLENDER 1.

sylva var. of SILVA.

sylvan /sílvən/ *adj.* (also **silvan**) **1 a** of the woods. **b** having woods; wooded. **2** rural. [F *sylvain* (obs. *silvain*) or L *Silvanus* woodland deity f. *silva* a wood]

■ **1 b** see WOODED. **2** see RURAL 1.

sylviculture var. of SILVICULTURE.

sym. *abbr.* **1** symbol. **2** symphony.

sym- /sim/ *prefix* assim. form of SYN- before *b, m, p*.

symbiont /símbeeont, -ənt/ *n.* an organism living in symbiosis. [Gk *sumbiōn -ountos* part. of *sumbioō* live together (as SYMBIOSIS)]

symbiosis /símbee-ṓsis, -bī-/ *n.* (*pl.* **symbioses** /-seez/) **1 a** an interaction between two different organisms living in close physical association, usu. to the advantage of both (cf. ANTIBIOSIS). **b** an instance of this. **2 a** a mutually advantageous association or relationship between persons. **b** an instance of this. ▫▫ **symbiotic** /-bīótik/ *adj.* **symbiotically** /-bīótikəlee/ *adv.* [mod.L f. Gk *sumbiōsis* a living together f. *sumbioō* live together, *sumbios* companion (as SYN-, *bios* life)]

symbol /símbəl/ *n.* & *v.* ● *n.* **1** a thing conventionally regarded as typifying, representing, or recalling something, esp. an idea or quality (*white is a symbol of purity*). **2** a mark or character taken as the conventional sign of some object, idea, function, or process, e.g., the letters standing for the chemical elements or the characters in musical notation. ● *v.tr.* (**symboled, symboling** or **symbolled, symbolling**) symbolize. ▫▫ **symbology** /-bóləjee/ *n.* [ME f. L *symbolum* f. Gk *sumbolon* mark, token (as SYN-, *ballō* throw)]

■ *n.* representation, figure, metaphor, allegory, token, sign, image, emblem; insignia, badge, logotype, mark, hallmark, stamp, trademark, colophon, brand, code, abbreviation, character, phonogram, logogram, pictogram, pictograph, ideogram, ideograph, initialism, cryptogram, acronym, monogram, password, shibboleth, watchword, code word; arms, bearing, armorial bearing, crest, escutcheon, coat of arms, banner, flag, pennant, standard, *colloq.* logo. ● *v.* see SYMBOLIZE.

symbolic /simbólik/ *adj.* (also **symbolical** /-bólikəl/) **1** of or serving as a symbol. **2** involving the use of symbols or symbolism. ▫ **symbolic logic** the use of symbols to denote propositions, etc., in order to assist reasoning. ▫▫ **symbolically** *adv.* [F *symbolique* or LL *symbolicus* f. Gk *sumbolikos*]

■ symbolical, figurative, allegoric(al), metaphoric(al); emblematic, typical, representative, token,

symptomatic, characteristic, allusive, denotative, connotative, suggestive, mnemonic.

symbolism /símbəlizəm/ *n.* **1 a** the use of symbols to represent ideas. **b** symbols collectively. **2** an artistic and poetic movement or style using symbols and indirect suggestion to express ideas, emotions, etc. □□ **symbolist** *n.* **symbolistic** *adj.*
■ **1 a** see IMAGERY 1.

symbolize /símbəlīz/ *v.tr.* **1** be a symbol of. **2** represent by means of symbols. □□ **symbolization** *n.* [F *symboliser* f. *symbole* SYMBOL]
■ **1** represent, stand for, denote, connote, suggest, express, imply, signify, mean, indicate, typify, exemplify, betoken, illustrate, embody, epitomize, symbol.

symmetry /símitree/ *n.* (*pl.* **-ies**) **1 a** correct proportion of the parts of a thing; balance; harmony. **b** beauty resulting from this. **2 a** a structure that allows an object to be divided into parts of an equal shape and size and similar position to the point or line or plane of division. **b** the possession of such a structure. **c** approximation to such a structure. **3** the repetition of exactly similar parts facing each other or a center. **4** *Bot.* the possession by a flower of sepals and petals and stamens and pistils in the same number or multiples of the same number. □□ **symmetric** /símétrik/ *adj.* **symmetrical** *adj.* **symmetrically** *adv.* **symmetrize** *v.tr.* [obs. F *symmétrie* or L *summetria* f. Gk (as SYN-, *metron* measure)]
■ **1, 3** balance, proportion, evenness, order, orderliness, regularity, uniformity, congruity, congruousness, correspondence, agreement, harmony, consistency, equality. □□ **symmetric, symmetrical** (well-)balanced, proportionate, proportional, well-proportioned, orderly, (well-)ordered, in proportion, even, regular, congruous, congruent, uniform, harmonious; equal, mirror image, mirror like.

sympathectomy /símpəthéktəmee/ *n.* (*pl.* **-ies**) the surgical removal of a sympathetic ganglion, etc.

sympathetic /símpəthétik/ *adj. & n.* ● *adj.* **1** of, showing, or expressing sympathy. **2** due to sympathy. **3** likable or capable of evoking sympathy. **4** (of a person) friendly and cooperative. **5** (foll. by *to*) inclined to favor (a proposal, etc.) (*was most sympathetic to the idea*). **6** (of a landscape, etc.) that touches the feelings by association, etc. **7** (of a pain, etc.) caused by a pain or injury to someone else or in another part of the body. **8** (of a sound, resonance, or string) sounding by a vibration communicated from another vibrating object. **9 a** designating the part of the nervous system consisting of nerves leaving the thoracic and lumbar regions of the spinal cord and connecting with the nerve cells in or near the viscera (see PARASYMPATHETIC). **b** (of a nerve or ganglion) belonging to this system. ● *n.* **1** a sympathetic nerve. **2** the sympathetic system. □ **sympathetic magic** a type of magic that seeks to achieve an effect by performing an associated action or using an associated thing. □□ **sympathetically** *adv.* [SYMPATHY, after *pathetic*]
■ *adj.* **1** compassionate, commiserative, understanding, supportive, caring, concerned, interested, solicitous, warmhearted, kindhearted, kindly, softhearted, tenderhearted, merciful, responsive, well-meaning, well-intentioned, good-natured, considerate, empathetic, empathic; like-minded; comforting, consoling. **3** likable, appealing, congenial, agreeable, attractive, pleasant, simpatico. **4** friendly, cooperative, responsive, congenial; see also CONSIDERATE. **5** (*sympathetic to*) well-disposed to, favorably disposed to, supportive of, approving of, agreeable to. □□ **sympathetically** compassionately, kindly, benignantly, considerately, supportively, empathetically; see also *favorably* (FAVORABLE).

sympathize /símpəthīz/ *v.intr.* (often foll. by *with*) **1** feel or express sympathy; share a feeling or opinion. **2** agree with a sentiment or opinion. □□ **sympathizer** *n.* [F *sympathiser* (as SYMPATHY)]
■ **1** (*sympathize with*) suffer *or* grieve *or* mourn with, feel (sorry) for, have pity for, condole with, commiserate

with, offer condolences to; empathize with, harmonize with, get along with, relate to, identify with, see eye to eye with, side with, understand, be in sympathy with, have (a) rapport with, *colloq.* be on the same wavelength with *or* as. **2** (*sympathize with*) agree with, go along with, favor, support, understand, appreciate, relate to, identify with, *sl.* dig. □□ **sympathizer** condoner, approver, conspirator, co-conspirator, collaborator, accomplice, accessory, supporter, ally, fellow traveler, *Polit.* comrade; see also PATRON 1.

sympathy /símpəthee/ *n.* (*pl.* **-ies**) **1 a** the state of being simultaneously affected with the same feeling as another. **b** the capacity for this. **2** (often foll. by *with*) **a** the act of sharing or tendency to share (with a person, etc.) in an emotion or sensation or condition of another person or thing. **b** (in *sing.* or *pl.*) compassion or commiseration; condolences. **3** (often foll. by *for*) a favorable attitude; approval. **4** (in *sing.* or *pl.*; often foll. by *with*) agreement (with a person, etc.) in opinion or desire. **5** (*attrib.*) in support of another cause (*sympathy strike*). □ **in sympathy** (often foll. by *with*) **1** having or showing or resulting from sympathy (with another). **2** by way of sympathetic action (*working to rule in sympathy*). [L *sympathia* f. Gk *sumpatheia* (as SYN-, *pathēs* f. *pathos* feeling)]
■ **2** compassion, commiseration, pity, concern, feeling, fellow feeling, tenderness, empathy, understanding, solicitousness, warmth, tenderheartedness, warmheartedness; condolences. **3** see PATRONAGE 1, AGREEMENT 1, 2. **4** agreement, harmony, compatibility, rapport, concord, accord, affinity, closeness, unity, unanimity; fellow feeling, congeniality, communion, fellowship, camaraderie. □ **in sympathy 1** in agreement, in accord, agreed, united, unanimous.

sympetalous /simpét'ləs/ *adj. Bot.* having the petals united.

symphonic /simfónik/ *adj.* (of music) relating to or having the form or character of a symphony. □ **symphonic poem** an extended orchestral piece, usu. in one movement, on a descriptive or rhapsodic theme. □□ **symphonically** *adv.*
■ □ **symphonic poem** tone poem.

symphonist /símfənist/ *n.* a composer of symphonies.

symphony /símfənee/ *n.* (*pl.* **-ies**) **1** an elaborate composition usu. for full orchestra, and in several movements with one or more in sonata form. **2** an interlude for orchestra alone in a large-scale vocal work. **3** = *symphony orchestra*. □ **symphony orchestra** a large orchestra suitable for playing symphonies, etc. [ME, = harmony of sound, f. OF *symphonie* f. L *symphonia* f. Gk *sumphōnia* (as SYN-, *-phōnos* f. *phōnē* sound)]

symphyllous /simfíləs/ *adj. Bot.* having the leaves united. [SYN- + Gk *phullon* leaf]

symphysis /símfisis/ *n.* (*pl.* **symphyses** /-seez/) **1** the process of growing together. **2 a** a union between two bones, esp. in the median plane of the body. **b** the place or line of this. □□ **symphyseal** /-físeeəl, -fízeeəl/ *adj.* **symphysial** /-fízeeəl/ *adj.* [mod.L f. Gk *sumphusis* (as SYN-, *phusis* growth)]

sympodium /simpódeeəm/ *n.* (*pl.* **sympodia** /-deeə/) *Bot.* the apparent main axis or stem of a vine, etc., made up of successive secondary axes. □□ **sympodial** *adj.* [mod.L (as SYN-, Gk *pous podos* foot)]

symposium /simpózeeəm/ *n.* (*pl.* **symposia** /-zeeə/) **1 a** a conference or meeting to discuss a particular subject. **b** a collection of essays or papers for this purpose. **2** a philosophical or other friendly discussion. **3** a drinking party, esp. of the ancient Greeks with conversation, etc., after a banquet. [L f. Gk *symposion* in sense 3 (as SYN-, *-potēs* drinker)]
■ **1 a** see CONFERENCE 2.

symptom /símptəm/ *n.* **1** *Med.* a change in the physical or mental condition of a person, regarded as evidence of a dis-

/.../ **pronunciation**	● **part of speech**
□ **phrases, idioms, and compounds**	
□□ **derivatives**	■ **synonym section**
cross-references appear in SMALL CAPITALS or *italics*	

order (cf. SIGN 5). **2** a sign of the existence of something. [ME *synthoma* f. med.L *sinthoma*, & f. LL *symptoma* f. Gk *sumptōma -atos* chance, symptom, f. *sumpiptō* happen (as SYN-, *piptō* fall)]

■ manifestation, evidence, mark, token, indication, indicator, cue, clue, (warning) sign, characteristic, trait, feature, earmark, marker, *colloq.* pointer.

symptomatic /símptəmátik/ *adj.* serving as a symptom. □□ **symptomatically** *adv.*

■ indicative, representative, suggestive, characteristic, emblematic, symbolic, typical.

symptomatology /símptəmətóləjee/ *n.* the branch of medicine concerned with the study and interpretation of symptoms.

syn. *abbr.* **1** synonym. **2** synonymous. **3** synonymy.

syn- /sin/ *prefix* with, together, alike. [from or after Gk *sun-* f. *sun* with]

synaeresis *Brit.* var. of SYNERESIS.

synaesthesia *Brit.* var. of SYNESTHESIA.

synagogue /sínəgog/ *n.* **1** the house of worship where a Jewish assembly or congregation meets for religious observance and instruction. **2** the assembly itself. □□ **synagogal** /-gógəl/ *adj.* **synagogical** /-gójikəl/ *adj.* [ME f. OF *sinagoge* f. LL *synagoga* f. Gk *sunagōgē* meeting (as SYN-, *agō* bring)]

■ **1** see TEMPLE¹.

synapse /sínaps, sináps/ *n. Anat.* a junction of two nerve cells. [Gk *synapsis* (as SYN-, *hapsis* f. *haptō* join)]

synapsis /sinápsis/ *n.* (*pl.* **synapses** /-seez/) **1** *Anat.* = SYNAPSE. **2** *Biol.* the fusion of chromosome pairs at the start of meiosis. □□ **synaptic** /-náptik/ *adj.* **synaptically** *adv.*

synarthrosis /sínaarthrṓsis/ *n.* (*pl.* **synarthroses** /-seez/) *Anat.* an immovably fixed bone joint, e.g., the sutures of the skull. [SYN- + Gk *arthrōsis* jointing f. *arthron* joint]

sync /singk/ *n. & v.* (also **synch**) *colloq.* ● *n.* synchronization. ● *v.tr. & intr.* synchronize. □ **in** (or **out of**) **sync** (often foll. by *with*) harmonizing or agreeing well (or badly). [abbr.]

■ □ **out of sync** see WRONG *adj.* 4.

syncarp /sínkaarp/ *n.* a compound fruit from a flower with several carpels, e.g., a blackberry. [SYN- + Gk *karpos* fruit]

syncarpous /sinkaárpəs/ *adj.* (of a flower or fruit) having the carpels united (opp. APOCARPOUS). [SYN- + Gk *karpos* fruit]

synch var. of SYNC.

synchondrosis /síngkondrṓsis/ *n.* (*pl.* **synchondroses** /-seez/) *Anat.* an almost immovable bone joint bound by a layer of cartilage, as in the spinal vertebrae. [SYN- + Gk *khondros* cartilage]

synchro- /síngkrō/ *comb. form* synchronized; synchronous.

synchrocyclotron /síngkrōsíklətron/ *n.* a cyclotron able to achieve higher energies by decreasing the frequency of the accelerating electric field as the particles increase in energy and mass.

synchromesh /síngkrōmesh/ *n. & adj.* ● *n.* a system of changing gears, esp. in motor vehicles, in which the driving and driven gearwheels are made to revolve at the same speed during engagement by means of a set of friction clutches, thereby easing the change. ● *adj.* relating to or using this system. [abbr. of *synchronized mesh*]

synchronic /singkrónik/ *adj.* describing a subject (esp. a language) as it exists at one point in time (opp. DIACHRONIC). □□ **synchronically** *adv.* [LL *synchronus*: see SYNCHRONOUS]

■ see CONTEMPORARY *adj.* 1.

synchronism /síngkrənizəm/ *n.* **1** = SYNCHRONY. **2** the process of synchronizing sound and picture in cinematography, television, etc. □□ **synchronistic** *adj.* **synchronistically** *adv.* [Gk *sugkhronismos* (as SYNCHRONOUS)]

synchronize /síngkrəniz/ *v.* **1** *intr.* (often foll. by *with*) occur at the same time; be simultaneous. **2** *tr.* cause to occur at the same time. **3** *tr.* carry out the synchronism of (a movie, etc.). **4** *tr.* ascertain or set forth the correspondence in the date of (events). **5 a** *tr.* cause (clocks, etc.) to show a standard or uniform time. **b** *intr.* (of clocks, etc.) be synchronized. □ **synchronized swimming** a form of swimming in which participants make coordinated leg and arm movements in time to music. □□ **synchronization** *n.* **synchronizer** *n.*

■ **1** see COINCIDE 1, 2. **2, 5a** see COORDINATE *v.* 1.

synchronous /síngkrənəs/ *adj.* (often foll. by *with*) existing or occurring at the same time. □ **synchronous motor** *Electr.* a motor having a speed exactly proportional to the current frequency. □□ **synchronously** *adv.* [LL *synchronus* f. Gk *sugkhronos* (as SYN-, *khronos* time)]

■ see SIMULTANEOUS.

synchrony /síngkrənee/ *n.* **1** the state of being synchronic or synchronous. **2** the treatment of events, etc., as being synchronous. [Gk *sugkhronos*: see SYNCHRONOUS]

■ **1** see COINCIDENCE 1.

synchrotron /síngkrətron/ *n. Physics* a cyclotron in which the magnetic field strength increases with the energy of the particles to keep their orbital radius constant.

syncline /síngklin/ *n.* a rock bed forming a trough. □□ **synclinal** *adj.* [*synclinal* (as SYN-, Gk *klinō* lean)]

syncopate /síngkəpayt/ *v.tr.* **1** *Mus.* displace the beats or accents in (a passage) so that strong beats become weak and vice versa. **2** shorten (a word) by dropping interior sounds or letters, as *symbology* for *symbolology*, *Gloster* for *Gloucester*. □□ **syncopation** /-páyshən/ *n.* **syncopator** *n.* [LL *syncopare* swoon (as SYNCOPE)]

syncope /síngkəpee/ *n.* **1** *Gram.* the omission of interior sounds or letters in a word (see SYNCOPATE 2). **2** *Med.* a temporary loss of consciousness caused by a fall in blood pressure. □□ **syncopal** *adj.* [ME f. LL *syncopē* f. Gk *sugkopē* (as SYN-, *koptō* strike, cut off)]

■ **2** see FAINT *n.*

syncretism /síngkrətizəm/ *n.* **1** *Philos. & Theol.* the process or an instance of syncretizing (see SYNCRETIZE). **2** *Philol.* the merging of different inflectional varieties in the development of a language. □□ **syncretic** /-krétik/ *adj.* **syncretist** *n.* **syncretistic** /-krətístik/ *adj.* [mod.L *syncretismus* f. Gk *sugkrētismos* f. *sugkrētizō* (of two parties) combine against a third f. *krēs* Cretan (orig. of ancient Cretan communities)]

syncretize /síngkrətiz/ *v.tr. Philos. & Theol.* attempt, esp. inconsistently, to unify or reconcile differing schools of thought.

syncytium /sinsísheeəm/ *n.* (*pl.* **syncytia** /-sheeə/) *Biol.* a mass of cytoplasm with several nuclei, not divided into separate cells. □□ **syncytial** /-síshəl/ *adj.* [formed as SYN- + -CYTE + -IUM]

synd. *abbr.* **1** syndicate. **2** syndicated.

syndactyl /sindáktil/ *adj.* (of an animal) having digits united as in webbed feet, etc. □□ **syndactylism** *n.* **syndactylous** *adj.*

syndesis /síndisis/ *n.* (*pl.* **syndeses** /-seez/) *Biol.* = SYNAPSIS 2. [mod.L f. Gk *syndesis* binding together f. *sundeō* bind together]

syndesmosis /síndezmṓsis/ *n.* the union and articulation of bones by means of ligaments. [mod.L f. Gk *sundesmos* binding, fastening + -OSIS]

syndetic /sindétik/ *adj. Gram.* of or using conjunctions. [Gk *sundetikos* (as SYNDESIS)]

syndic /síndik/ *n.* **1** a government official in various countries. **2** *Brit.* a business agent of certain universities and corporations. □□ **syndical** *adj.* [F f. LL *syndicus* f. Gk *sundikos* (as SYN-, *-dikos* f. *dikē* justice)]

syndicalism /síndikəlizəm/ *n. hist.* a movement for transferring the ownership and control of the means of production and distribution to workers' unions. □□ **syndicalist** *n.* [F *syndicalisme* f. *syndical* (as SYNDIC)]

syndicate *n. & v.* ● *n.* /síndikət/ **1** a combination of individuals or commercial firms to promote some common interest. **2** an association or agency supplying material simultaneously to a number of newspapers or periodicals. **3** a group of people who combine to buy or rent property, gamble, organize crime, etc. **4** a committee of syndics. ● *v.tr.* /síndikayt/ **1** form into a syndicate. **2** publish (material) through a syndicate. □□ **syndication** /-káyshən/ *n.* [F *syndicat* f. med.L *syndicatus* f. LL *syndicus*: see SYNDIC]

■ *n.* **1, 3** trust, monopoly, pool, bloc, cartel, syndication, group, association, alliance, combine, consortium, cooperative, collective, federation, confederation, coalition, league, union; Cosa Nostra, mafia.

● *v.* **1** ally, associate, amalgamate, consolidate, league, confederate, synthesize, combine.

syndrome /síndrōm/ *n.* **1** a group of concurrent symptoms of a disease. **2** a characteristic combination of opinions, emotions, behavior, etc. □□ **syndromic** /-drómik/ *adj.* [mod.L f. Gk *sundromē* (as SYN-, *dromē* f. *dramein* to run)]

syne /sin/ *adv., conj.,* & *prep. Sc.* since. [contr. f. ME *sithen* SINCE]

synecdoche /sinékdəkee/ *n.* a figure of speech in which a part is made to represent the whole or vice versa (e.g., *new faces at the meeting*). □□ **synecdochic** /-dókik/ *adj.* [ME f. L f. Gk *sunekdokhē* (as SYN-, *ekdokhē* f. *ekdekhomai* take up)]

synecology /sínikólǝjee/ *n.* the ecological study of plant or animal communities. □□ **synecological** /-kǝlójikǝl/ *adj.* **synecologist** *n.*

syneresis /sináirisis/ *n.* (*pl.* **synereses** /-seez/) the contraction of two vowels into a diphthong or single vowel. [LL f. Gk *sunairesis* (as SYN-, *hairesis* f. *haireō* take)]

synergism /sínǝrjizǝm/ *n.* (also **synergy** /sínǝrjee/) the combined effect of drugs, organs, etc., that exceeds the sum of their individual effects. □□ **synergetic** /-jétik/ *adj.* **synergic** /-nárjik/ *adj.* **synergistic** *adj.* **synergistically** *adv.* [Gk *sunergos* working together (as SYN-, *ergon* work)]

■ □□ **synergetic, synergistic** see UNITED 2a.

synergist /sínǝrjist/ *n.* a medicine or a bodily organ (e.g., a muscle) that cooperates with another or others.

synesthesia /sínis-theézhǝ, -zeeǝ/ *n.* **1** *Psychol.* the production of a mental sense impression relating to one sense by the stimulation of another sense. **2** a sensation produced in a part of the body by stimulation of another part. □□ **synesthetic** /-thétik/ *adj.* [mod.L f. SYN- after *anesthesia*]

syngamy /sínggǝmee/ *n. Biol.* the fusion of gametes or nuclei in reproduction. □□ **syngamous** *adj.* [SYN- + Gk *gamos* marriage]

syngenesis /sinjénisis/ *n.* sexual reproduction from combined male and female elements.

synod /sínǝd/ *n.* **1** an Episcopal council attended by delegated clergy and sometimes laity (see also *General Synod*). **2** a Presbyterian ecclesiastical court above the presbyteries and subject to the General Assembly. **3** any meeting for debate. [ME f. LL *synodus* f. Gk *sunodos* meeting (as SYN-, *hodos* way)]

■ **1, 3** see ASSEMBLY 1, 2a.

synodic /sinódik/ *adj. Astron.* relating to or involving the conjunction of stars, planets, etc. □ **synodic period** the time between the successive conjunctions of a planet with the sun. [LL *synodicus* f. Gk *sunodikos* (as SYNOD)]

synodical /sinódikǝl/ *adj.* **1** (also **synodal** /sínǝd'l/) of, relating to, or constituted as a synod. **2** = SYNODIC.

synonym /sínǝnim/ *n.* **1** a word or phrase that means exactly or nearly the same as another in the same language (e.g., *shut* and *close*). **2** a word denoting the same thing as another but suitable to a different context (e.g., *serpent* for *snake*). **3** a word equivalent to another in some but not all senses (e.g., *ship* and *vessel*). □□ **synonymic** /-nímik/ *adj.* **synonymity** /-nímitee/ *n.* [ME f. L *synonymum* f. Gk *sunōnumon* neut. of *sunōnumos* (as SYN-, *onoma* name): cf. ANONYMOUS]

synonymous /sinónimǝs/ *adj.* (often foll. by *with*) **1** having the same meaning; being a synonym (of). **2** (of a name, idea, etc.) suggestive of or associated with another (*excessive drinking regarded as synonymous with violence*). □□ **synonymously** *adv.* **synonymousness** *n.*

■ **1** (*synonymous with*) equal to, equivalent to; tantamount to; transposable with, exchangeable with, identical to or with, interchangeable with, the same as. **2** (*synonymous with*) identified with, associated with, suggestive of, corresponding to or with.

synonymy /sinónimee/ *n.* (*pl.* **-ies**) **1** the state of being synonymous. **2** the collocation of synonyms for emphasis (e.g., *in any shape or form*). **3 a** a system or collection of synonyms. **b** a treatise on synonyms. [LL *synonymia* f. Gk *sunōnumia* (as SYNONYM)]

■ **3 a** see THESAURUS 1b.

synopsis /sinópsis/ *n.* (*pl.* **synopses** /-seez/) **1** a summary

or outline. **2** a brief general survey. □□ **synopsize** *v.tr.* [LL f. Gk (as SYN-, *opsis* seeing)]

■ **1** summary, condensation, abridgment, epitomization, outline, abstract, digest, précis, epitome, compendium, conspectus, *aperçu,* résumé, roundup. **2** survey, runthrough, review, conspectus, *aperçu.* □□ **synopsize** see *sum up* 1.

synoptic /sinóptik/ *adj.* & *n.* ● *adj.* **1** of, forming, or giving a synopsis. **2** taking or affording a comprehensive mental view. **3** of the Synoptic Gospels. **4** giving a general view of weather conditions. ● *n.* **1** a Synoptic Gospel. **2** the writer of a Synoptic Gospel. □ **Synoptic Gospels** the Gospels of Matthew, Mark, and Luke, describing events from a similar point of view. □□ **synoptical** *adj.* **synoptically** *adv.* [Gk *sunoptikos* (as SYNOPSIS)]

synoptist /sinóptist/ *n.* the writer of a Synoptic Gospel.

synostosis /sínostōsis/ *n.* the joining of bones by ankylosis, etc. [SYN- + Gk *osteon* bone + -OSIS]

synovia /sinōveeǝ, si-/ *n. Physiol.* a viscous fluid lubricating joints and tendon sheaths. □ **synovial membrane** a dense membrane of connective tissue secreting synovia. □□ **synovial** *adj.* [mod.L, formed prob. arbitrarily by Paracelsus]

synovitis /sinōvítis, si-/ *n.* inflammation of the synovial membrane.

syntactic /sintáktik/ *adj.* of or according to syntax. □□ **syntactical** *adj.* **syntactically** *adv.* [Gk *suntaktikos* (as SYNTAX)]

syntagma /sintágmǝ/ *n.* (*pl.* **syntagmas** or **syntagmata** /-mǝtǝ/) **1** a word or phrase forming a syntactic unit. **2** a systematic collection of statements. □□ **syntagmatic** /-mátik/ *adj.* **syntagmic** /-mik/ *adj.* [LL f. Gk *suntagma* (as SYNTAX)]

syntax /síntaks/ *n.* **1** the grammatical arrangement of words, showing their connection and relation. **2** a set of rules for or an analysis of this. [F *syntaxe* or LL *syntaxis* f. Gk *suntaxis* (as SYN-, *taxis* f. *tassō* arrange)]

synth /sinth/ *n. colloq.* = SYNTHESIZER.

synthesis /sínthisis/ *n.* (*pl.* **syntheses** /-seez/) **1** the process or result of building up separate elements, esp. ideas, into a connected whole, esp. into a theory or system. **2** a combination or composition. **3** *Chem.* the artificial production of compounds from their constituents as distinct from extraction from plants, etc. **4** *Gram.* **a** the process of making compound and derivative words. **b** the tendency in a language to use inflected forms rather than groups of words, prepositions, etc. **5** the joining of divided parts in surgery. □□ **synthesist** *n.* [L f. Gk *sunthesis* (as SYN-, THESIS)]

■ **1, 2** combination, composition, union, amalgamation, coalescence, integration, fusion, unification, mix; compounding, combining, blending, merging, integrating, mixing, fusing, unifying, synthesizing; blend, compound, amalgam, merger, composite, mixture, concoction. **3** manufacture, production, making.

synthesize /sínthisiz/ *v.tr.* (also **synthetize** /-tiz/) **1** make a synthesis of. **2** combine into a coherent whole.

■ see COMBINE *v.* 3.

synthesizer /sínthisizǝr/ *n.* an electronic musical instrument, esp. operated by a keyboard, producing a wide variety of sounds by generating and combining signals of different frequencies.

synthetic /sinthétik/ *adj.* & *n.* ● *adj.* **1** made by chemical synthesis, esp. to imitate a natural product (*synthetic rubber*). **2** (of emotions, etc.) affected; insincere. **3** *Logic* (of a proposition) having truth or falsity determinable by recourse to experience (cf. ANALYTIC 3). **4** *Philol.* using combinations of simple words or elements in compounded or complex words (cf. ANALYTICAL). ● *n. Chem.* a synthetic substance. □ **synthetic resin** *Chem.* see RESIN *n.* 2. □□ **synthetical** *adj.* **syn-**

/. . ./ **pronunciation**	● **part of speech**
□ **phrases, idioms, and compounds**	
□□ **derivatives**	■ **synonym section**
cross-references appear in SMALL CAPITALS or *italics*	

thetically *adv.* [F *synthétique* or mod.L *syntheticus* f. Gk *sun-thetikos* f. *sunthetos* f. *suntithēmi* (as SYN-, *tithēmi* put)]
■ *adj.* **1** artificial, man-made, manufactured, ersatz; fake, false, counterfeit, sham, bogus, spurious, mock, imitation, pseudo, plastic, *colloq.* phony. **2** see ARTIFICIAL 3.

syphilis /sífilis/ *n.* a contagious venereal disease progressing from infection of the genitals via the skin and mucous membranes to the bones, muscles, and brain. □□ **syphilitic** /-lítik/ *adj.* **syphilize** /-līz/ *v.tr.* **syphiloid** /-loyd/ *adj.* [mod.L f. title (*Syphilis, sive Morbus Gallicus*) of a Latin poem (1530), f. *Syphilus*, a character in it, the supposed first sufferer from the disease]
■ □□ **syphilitic** see VENEREAL 2.

syphon var. of SIPHON.

Syriac /sírreeak/ *n. & adj.* ● *n.* the language of ancient Syria; western Aramaic. ● *adj.* in or relating to this language. [L *Syriacus* f. Gk *Suriakos* f. *Suria* Syria]

Syrian /sírreeən/ *n. & adj.* ● *n.* **1** a native or inhabitant of the modern nation of Syria in the Middle East; a person of Syrian descent. **2** a native or inhabitant of the region of Syria in antiquity or later. ● *adj.* of or relating to the region or state of Syria.

syringa /sírínggə/ *n. Bot.* **1** = *mock orange.* **2** any plant of the genus *Syringa*, esp. the lilac. [mod.L, formed as SYRINX (with ref. to the use of its stems as pipe stems)]

syringe /sírínj/ *n. & v.* ● *n.* **1** *Med.* **a** a tube with a nozzle and piston or bulb for sucking in and ejecting liquid in a fine stream, used in surgery. **b** (in full **hypodermic syringe**) a similar device with a hollow needle for insertion under the skin. **2** any similar device used in gardening, cooking, etc. ● *v.tr.* sluice or spray (the ear, a plant, etc.) with a syringe. [ME f. med.L *syringa* (as SYRINX)]

syrinx /síringks/ *n.* (*pl.* **syrinxes** or **syringes** /sírínjeez/) **1** a set of panpipes. **2** *Archaeol.* a narrow gallery cut in rock in an ancient Egyptian tomb. **3** the lower larynx or song organ of birds. □□ **syringeal** /sírínjeeəl/ *adj.* [L *syrinx -ngis* f. Gk *surigx suriggos* pipe, channel]

Syro- /síró/ *comb. form* Syrian; Syrian and (*Syro-Phoenician*). [Gk *Suro-* f. *Suros* a Syrian]

syrup /sírəp, sər-/ *n.* (also **sirup**) **1 a** a sweet sauce made by dissolving sugar in boiling water, often used for preserving fruit, etc. **b** a similar sauce of a specified flavor as a drink, medicine, etc. (*rose hip syrup*). **2** the condensed juice of various plants, such as sugarcane or the sugar maple; part of this remaining uncrystallized at various stages of refining; molasses. **3** excessive sweetness of style or manner. □□ **syrupy** *adj.* [ME f. OF *sirop* or med.L *siropus* f. Arab. *šarāb* beverage: cf. SHERBET, SHRUB²]
■ □□ **syrupy** see SWEET *adj.* 1.

syssarcosis /sísaarkósis/ *n.* (*pl.* **syssarcoses** /-seez/) *Anat.* a connection between bones formed by intervening muscle. [mod.L f. Gk *sussarkōsis* (as SYN-, *sarx, sarkos* flesh)]

systaltic /sistáltik, sistáwl-/ *adj.* (esp. of the heart) contracting and dilating rhythmically; pulsatory (cf. SYSTOLE, DIASTOLE). [LL *systalticus* f. Gk *sustaltikos* (as SYN-, *staltos* f. *stellō* put)]

system /sístəm/ *n.* **1 a** a complex whole; a set of connected things or parts; an organized body of material or immaterial things. **b** the composition of such a body; arrangement; setup. **2** a set of devices (e.g., pulleys) functioning together. **3** *Physiol.* **a** a set of organs in the body with a common structure or function (*the digestive system*). **b** the human or animal body as a whole. **4 a** method; considered principles of procedure or classification. **b** classification. **5** orderliness. **6 a** a body of theory or practice relating to or prescribing a particular form of government, religion, etc. **b** (prec. by *the*) the prevailing political or social order, esp. regarded as oppressive and intransigent. **7** a method of choosing one's procedure in gambling, etc. **8** *Computing* a group of related hardware units or programs or both, esp. when dedicated to a single application. **9** one of seven general types of crystal structure. **10** a major group of geological strata (*the Devonian system*). **11** *Physics* a group of associated bodies moving under mutual gravitation, etc. **12** *Mus.* the braced staves of a score. □ **get a thing out of one's system** *colloq.* be rid of a preoccupation or anxiety. **systems analysis** the analysis of a complex process or operation in order to improve its efficiency, esp. by applying a computer system. □□ **systemless** *adj.* [F *système* or LL *systema* f. Gk *sustēma -atos* (as SYN-, *histēmi* set up)]
■ **1** organized whole, organization, set, group, combination, network; structure, arrangement, setup; see also FRAME *n.* 6. **4 a** scheme, method, approach, modus operandi, way, procedure, methodology, technique, plan, process, practice, routine; logic, principles, rules. **b** classification, organization, categorization, codification, arrangement, grouping, division, ordering, taxonomy. **5** see ORDER *n.* 1. **6 a** see CODE *n.* 5. **b** regime, government, bureaucracy, (prevailing) order, status quo, Establishment, powers that be, *archaic* regimen.

systematic /sístəmátik/ *adj.* **1** methodical; done or conceived according to a plan or system. **2** regular; deliberate (*a systematic liar*). □ **systematic theology** a form of theology in which the aim is to arrange religious truths in a self-consistent whole. □□ **systematically** *adv.* **systematism** /sístəmətizəm/ *n.* **systematist** /sístəmátist/ *n.* [F *systématique* f. LL *systematicus* f. late Gk *sustēmatikos* (as SYSTEM)]
■ **1** organized, systematized, planned, methodical, businesslike, orderly, well-organized, well-ordered, regular, routine, standardized, standard. **2** deliberate, regular, habitual, inveterate, persistent, *colloq. disp.* chronic.

systematics /sístəmátiks/ *n.pl.* (usu. treated as *sing.*) the study or a system of classification; taxonomy.

systematize /sístəmətīz/ *v.tr.* **1** make systematic. **2** devise a system for. □□ **systematization** *n.* **systematizer** *n.*
■ see ORGANIZE 1. □□ **systematization** see ORGANIZATION 1.

systemic /sistémik/ *adj.* **1** *Physiol.* **a** of or concerning the whole body; not confined to a particular part (*systemic infection*). **b** (of blood circulation) other than pulmonary. **2** *Hort.* (of an insecticide, fungicide, etc.) entering the plant via the roots or shoots and passing through the tissues. □□ **systemically** *adv.* [irreg. f. SYSTEM]

systemize /sístəmīz/ *v.tr.* = SYSTEMATIZE. □□ **systemization** *n.* **systemizer** *n.*

systole /sístəlee/ *n. Physiol.* the contraction of the heart, when blood is pumped into the arteries (cf. DIASTOLE). □□ **systolic** /sistólik/ *adj.* [LL f. Gk *sustolē* f. *sustellō* contract (as SYSTALTIC)]

syzygy /sízijee/ *n.* (*pl.* **-ies**) **1** *Astron.* conjunction or opposition, esp. of the moon with the sun. **2** a pair of connected or correlated things. [LL *syzygia* f. Gk *suzugia* f. *suzugos* yoked, paired (as SYN-, *zugon* yoke)]

Tt

T¹ /tee/ *n.* (also **t**) (*pl.* **Ts** or **T's**) **1** the twentieth letter of the alphabet. **2** a T-shaped thing (esp. *attrib.*: *T-joint*). □ **to a T** exactly; to perfection.
■ □ **to a T** see EXACTLY 1.

T² *abbr.* **1** tera-. **2** tesla. **3** tablespoon. **4** temperature.

T³ *symb. Chem.* the isotope tritium.

t. *abbr.* **1** ton(s). **2** teaspoon. **3** temperature.

't *pron. contr.* of IT¹ (*'tis*).

-t¹ /t/ *suffix* = -ED¹ (*crept*; *sent*).

-t² /t/ *suffix* = -EST² (*shalt*).

Ta *symb. Chem.* the element tantalum.

ta /taa/ *int. Brit. colloq.* thank you. [infantile form]

Taal /taal/ *n.* (prec. by *the*) *hist.* an early form of Afrikaans. [Du., = language, rel. to TALE]

tab¹ /tab/ *n. & v.* ● *n.* **1 a** a small flap or strip of material attached for grasping, fastening, or hanging up, or for identification. **b** a similar object as part of a garment, etc. **2** *colloq.* a bill or check (*picked up the tab*). **3** *Brit. Mil.* a marking on the collar distinguishing a staff officer. **4** a small or drawn-aside stage curtain. ● *v.tr.* (**tabbed, tabbing**) provide with a tab or tabs. □ **keep tabs** (or **a tab**) **on** *colloq.* **1** keep account of. **2** have under observation. [prob. f. dial.: cf. TAG¹]
■ *n.* **1** flap, tag, loop, ticket, sticker, label, flag, lappet, strap, handle. **2** charge, bill, account, reckoning, check.
● *v.* see TAG¹ *v.* 1.

tab² /tab/ *n.* **1 a** a device on a typewriter for advancing to a sequence of set positions in tabular work. **b** a programmable key on a computer keyboard that moves the cursor forward a designated number of spaces. **2** = TABULATOR 3. [abbr.]

tabard /tábərd/ *n.* **1** a herald's official coat emblazoned with the arms of his master. **2** a woman's or girl's sleeveless jerkin. **3** *hist.* a knight's short emblazoned garment worn over armor. [ME f. OF *tabart*, of unkn. orig.]

tabaret /tábərit/ *n.* an upholstery fabric of alternate satin and plain stripes. [prob. f. TABBY]

Tabasco /təbáskō/ *n. propr.* a pungent pepper sauce made from the fruit of *Capsicum frutescens*. [*Tabasco* in Mexico]

tabbouleh /təbŏŏlə, -lee/ *n.* an Arabic vegetable salad made with cracked wheat. [Arab. *tabbûla*]

tabby /tábee/ *n.* (*pl.* **-ies**) **1** (in full **tabby cat**) **a** a gray orange, or brownish cat mottled or streaked with dark stripes. **b** any domestic cat, esp. female. **2** a kind of watered silk. **3** a plain weave. [F *tabis* (in sense 2) f. Arab. *al-´attabiya* the quarter of Baghdad where tabby was manufactured: connection of other senses uncert.]

tabernacle /tábərnakəl/ *n.* **1** *hist.* a tent used as a sanctuary for the Ark of the Covenant by the Israelites during the Exodus. **2** *Eccl.* a canopied niche or receptacle esp. for the Eucharistic elements. **3** a place of worship, esp. in some Christian denominations. **4** *Bibl.* a fixed or movable habitation usu. of light construction. **5** *Naut.* a socket or double post for a hinged mast that can be lowered to pass under low bridges. □ **feast of Tabernacles** = SUCCOTH. □□ **tabernacled** *adj.* [ME f. OF *tabernacle* or L *tabernaculum* tent, dimin. of *taberna* hut]

tabes /táybeez/ *n. Med.* **1** emaciation. **2** (in full **tabes dorsalis**) locomotor ataxia, a form of neurosyphilis. □□ **tabetic** /təbétik/ *adj.* [L, = wasting away]

tabla /taáblə, túb-/ *n. Ind. Mus.* a pair of small drums played with the hands. [Hind. f. Arab. *tabla* drum]

tablature /tábləchər/ *n. Mus.* an early form of notation indicating fingering (esp. in playing the lute), rhythm, and features other than notes. [F f. It. *tavolatura* f. *tavolare* set to music]

table /táybəl/ *n. & v.* ● *n.* **1** a piece of furniture with a flat top and one or more legs, providing a level surface for eating, writing, or working at, playing games on, etc. **2** a flat surface serving a specified purpose (*altar table*; *bird table*). **3 a** food provided in a household (*keeps a good table*). **b** a group seated at a table for dinner, etc. **4 a** a set of facts or figures systematically displayed, esp. in columns (*a table of contents*). **b** matter contained in this. **c** = *multiplication table*. **5** a flat surface for working on or for machinery to operate on. **6 a** a slab of wood or stone, etc., for bearing an inscription. **b** matter inscribed on this. **7** = TABLELAND. **8** *Archit.* **a** a flat usu. rectangular vertical surface. **b** a horizontal molding, esp. a cornice. **9 a** a flat surface of a gem. **b** a cut gem with two flat faces. **10** each half or quarter of a folding board for backgammon. **11** (prec. by *the*) *Bridge* the dummy hand. ● *v.tr.* **1** postpone consideration of (a matter). **2** *Brit.* bring forward for discussion or consideration at a meeting. **3** *Naut.* strengthen (a sail) with a wide hem. □ **at table** esp. *Brit.* taking a meal at a table. **lay on the table 1** submit for discussion. **2** postpone indefinitely. **on the table** offered for discussion. **table knife** a knife for use at meals, esp. in eating a main course. **table linen** tablecloths, napkins, etc. **table manners** decorum or correct behavior while eating. **table salt** salt for use at meals. **table talk** miscellaneous informal talk at table. **table tennis** an indoor game based on tennis, played with paddles and a ball bounced on a table divided by a net. **table wine** ordinary wine for drinking with a meal. **turn the tables** (often foll. by *on*) reverse one's relations (with), esp. by turning an inferior into a superior position (orig. in backgammon). **under the table** *colloq.* **1** drunk. **2** (esp. of a payment) covertly; secretly. □□ **tableful** *n.* (*pl.* **-fuls**). **tabling** *n.* [ME f. OF f. L *tabula* plank, tablet, list]
■ *n.* **3 a** food, victuals, edibles, eatables, fare, provisions, *archaic* board, *formal or joc.* comestibles, *joc.* provender. **4 a** list, listing, register, record, tabulation, chart, catalog, index, inventory, itemization, précis; table of contents. **5** counter, bench. **6 a** see TABLET 3. **7** tableland, plateau. ● *v.* **1** submit, present, offer, proffer, bring forward, lay on the table, bring up, propose. **2** shelve, postpone, defer, suspend, put off, stay, pigeonhole, mothball, *colloq.* put on ice.
□ **table linen** tablecloths, napkins, *Sc. or archaic* napery. **table tennis** Ping-Pong. **under the table 1** see DRUNK *adj.* 1.

tableau /tablŏ, táblō/ *n.* (*pl.* **tableaux** /-lōz/) **1** a picturesque presentation. **2** = TABLEAU VIVANT. **3** a dramatic or effective situation suddenly brought about. □ **tableau curtains** *Theatr.* a pair of curtains drawn open by a diagonal cord. [F, = picture, dimin. of *table*: see TABLE]

▪ **1** scene, sight, spectacle, picture, image, presentation, representation, view. **2** composition, arrangement, grouping, *Theatr. tableau vivant.*

tableau vivant /veeva·áN/ *n.* (*pl.* **tableaux vivants** *pronunc.* same) *Theatr.* a silent and motionless group of people arranged to represent a scene. [F, lit. 'living picture']

tablecloth /táybəlklawth, -kloth/ *n.* a cloth spread over the top of a table, esp. for meals.

table d'hôte /táabəl dṓt, táablə/ *n.* a meal consisting of a set menu at a fixed price, esp. in a hotel (cf. À LA CARTE). [F, = host's table]

tableland /táybəl-land/ *n.* an extensive elevated region with a level surface; a plateau.

tablespoon /táybəlspōon/ *n.* **1** a large spoon for serving food. **2** an amount held by this. **3** a unit of measure equal to 15 ml. or ½ fl. oz. □□ **tablespoonful** *n.* (*pl.* **-fuls**).

tablet /táblit/ *n.* **1** a small measured and compressed amount of a substance, esp. of a medicine or drug. **2** a small flat piece of soap, etc. **3** a flat slab of stone or wood, esp. for display or an inscription. **4** *Archit.* = TABLE 8. **5** a writing pad. [ME f. OF *tablete* f. Rmc, dimin. of L *tabula* TABLE]
▪ **1** pill, capsule, troche, pellet, pastille, drop, lozenge, bolus. **2** block, bar, cake, slab, chunk, piece. **3** slab, plaque, plate, panel, table, plaquette; stone, gravestone, headstone, tombstone, memorial. **5** (scribbling *or* writing *or* memo) pad, notepad, (spiral (-bound)) notebook, jotter, scratch pad.

tabletop /táybəltop/ *n.* **1** the top or surface of a table. **2** (*attrib.*) that can be placed or used on a tabletop.

tableware /táybəlwair/ *n.* dishes, plates, utensils, etc., for use at meals.

tabloid /tábloyd/ *n. & adj.* ● *n.* **1** a newspaper, usu. popular in style with bold headlines and large photographs, having pages of half size. **2** anything in a compressed or concentrated form. ● *adj.* printed on newsprint and folded once lengthwise so as to be read like a magazine. [orig. the propr. name of a medicine sold in tablets]

taboo /təbōo, ta-/ *n., adj., & v.* (also **tabu**) ● *n.* (*pl.* **taboos** or **tabus**) **1** a system or the act of setting a person or thing apart as sacred or accursed. **2** a prohibition or restriction imposed by social custom. ● *adj.* **1** avoided or prohibited, esp. by social custom (*taboo words*). **2** designated as sacred and prohibited. ● *v.tr.* (**taboos, tabooed** or **tabus, tabued**) **1** put (a thing, practice, etc.) under taboo. **2** exclude or prohibit by authority or social influence. [Tongan *tabu*]
▪ *n.* **1** anathema, excommunication, curse; consecration, sanctification. **2** interdict, interdiction, proscription, ban, prohibition, restriction; see also BOYCOTT *n.*
● *adj.* anathema, forbidden, interdicted, off limits, out of bounds, verboten, proscribed, banned, prohibited, restricted, unmentionable, unspeakable; censored, censorable, unacceptable, rude, impolite, indecorous, dirty, explicit; outlawed, illegal, illicit, unlawful.
● *v.* forbid, interdict, proscribe, ban, prohibit, exclude.

tabor /táybər/ *n. hist.* a small drum, esp. one used to accompany a pipe. [ME f. OF *tabor, tabur*: cf. TABLA, Pers. *tabīra* drum]

taboret /tábərit, tabərét, -ráy/ *n.* (*Brit.* **tabouret**) a low seat usu. without arms or a back. [F, = stool, dimin. as TABOR]

tabu var. of TABOO.

tabular /tábyələr/ *adj.* **1** of or arranged in tables or lists. **2** broad and flat like a table. **3** (of a crystal) having two broad flat faces. **4** formed in thin plates. □□ **tabularly** *adv.* [L *tabularis* (as TABLE)]

tabula rasa /tábyələ ráasə, -zə/ *n.* **1** an erased tablet. **2** the human mind (esp. at birth) viewed as having no innate ideas. [L, = scraped tablet]

tabulate /tábyəlayt/ *v.tr.* arrange (figures or facts) in tabular form. □□ **tabulation** /-láyshən/ *n.* [LL *tabulare tabulat-* f. *tabula* table]
▪ systematize, organize, order, group, list, arrange, classify, categorize, rate, grade, catalog, codify, pigeonhole, sort, assort, index, itemize; record, note. □□ **tabulation** see TABLE *n.* 4a.

tabulator /tábyəlaytər/ *n.* **1** a person or thing that tabulates. **2** = TAB ². **3** *Computing* a machine that produces lists or tables from a data storage medium such as punched cards.

tacamahac /tákəməhak/ *n.* **1** a resinous gum obtained from certain tropical trees esp. of the genus *Calophyllum.* **2 a** the balsam poplar. **b** the resin of this. [obs. Sp. *tacamahaca* f. Aztec *tecomahiyac*]

tacet /tásit, táy-, táaket/ *v.intr. Mus.* an instruction for a particular voice or instrument to be silent. [L, = is silent]

tachism /táshizəm/ *n.* (also **tachisme**) a form of action painting with dabs of color arranged randomly to evoke a subconscious feeling. [F *tachisme* f. *tache* stain]

tachistoscope /təkístəskōp/ *n.* an instrument for very brief measured exposure of objects to the eye. □□ **tachistoscopic** /-skópik/ *adj.* [Gk *takhistos* swiftest + -SCOPE]

tacho /tákō/ *n.* (*pl.* **-os**) *Brit. colloq.* = TACHOMETER. [abbr.]

tacho- /tákō/ *comb. form* speed. [Gk *takhos* speed]

tachograph /tákəgraf/ *n.* a device used esp. in heavy trucks and buses, etc., for automatically recording speed and travel time.

tachometer /təkómitər, ta-/ *n.* **1** an instrument for measuring the rate of rotation of a shaft and hence the speed of an engine or the speed or velocity of a vehicle. **2** a device for indicating the number or rate of revolutions of an engine, etc.

tachy- /tákee/ *comb. form* swift. [Gk *takhus* swift]

tachycardia /tákikáardeeə/ *n. Med.* an abnormally rapid heart rate. [TACHY- + Gk *kardia* heart]

tachygraphy /təkígrəfee/ *n.* **1** stenography, esp. that of the ancient Greeks and Romans. **2** the abbreviated medieval writing of Greek and Latin. □□ **tachygrapher** *n.* **tachygraphic** /tákigráfik/ *adj.* **tachygraphical** *adj.*

tachymeter /təkímitər, ta-/ *n.* **1** *Surveying* an instrument used to locate points rapidly. **2** a speed indicator.

tacit /tásit/ *adj.* understood or implied without being stated (*tacit consent*). □□ **tacitly** *adv.* [L *tacitus* silent f. *tacēre* be silent]
▪ unspoken, undeclared, unsaid, unstated, unvoiced, unuttered, silent, mute, understood, unexpressed, implied, implicit.

taciturn /tásitərn/ *adj.* reserved in speech; saying little; uncommunicative. □□ **taciturnity** /-tə́rnitee/ *n.* **taciturnly** *adv.* [F *taciturne* or L *taciturnus* (as TACIT)]
▪ silent, uncommunicative, mute, reticent, reserved, unforthcoming, tight-lipped, closemouthed, untalkative, quiet, secretive. □□ **taciturnity** see SILENCE *n.* 2, 3.

tack[1] /tak/ *n. & v.* ● *n.* **1** a small sharp broad-headed nail. **2** a pin used to attach papers, etc., to a bulletin board or other surface. **3** a long stitch used in fastening fabrics, etc., lightly or temporarily together. **4 a** the direction in which a ship moves as determined by the position of its sails and regarded in terms of the direction of the wind (*starboard tack*). **b** a temporary change of direction in sailing to take advantage of a side wind, etc. **5** a course of action or policy (*try another tack*). **6** *Naut.* **a** a rope for securing the corner of some sails. **b** the corner to which this is fastened. **7** a sticky condition of varnish, etc. **8** *Brit.* an extraneous clause appended to a bill in Parliament. ● *v.* **1** *tr.* (often foll. by *down*, etc.) fasten with tacks. **2** *tr.* stitch (pieces of cloth, etc.) lightly together. **3** *tr.* (foll. by *to, on*) annex (a thing). **4** *intr.* **a** change a ship's course by turning its head to the wind (cf. WEAR²). **b** make a series of tacks. **5** *intr.* change one's conduct or policy, etc. **6** *tr. Brit.* append (a clause) to a bill. □□ **tacker** *n.* [ME *tak*, etc., of uncert. orig.: cf. Bibl. *tache* clasp, link f. OF *tache*]
▪ *n.* **1** nail. **2** thumbtack; pin, *Brit.* tintack, drawing pin. **3** fastening, stitch, baste. **4** direction, bearing, heading, course. **5** approach, way, path, direction, course, policy, procedure, method, technique, attack, line, angle. ● *v.* **1** pin, attach, fasten, secure, join, couple, unite, combine, stick, fix, affix, staple, nail, skewer, peg, screw, bolt, rivet. **2** baste, stitch, sew, bind. **3** (*tack on*) add (on), append, annex, attach, join on, tag

on. **4** change direction *or* heading *or* course; zigzag; veer off *or* away, *Naut.* go about, beat.

tack² / tak/ *n.* the saddle, bridle, etc., of a horse. [shortened f. TACKLE]

■ harness, saddlery, bridle, tackle, gear, equipment, equipage, fittings, fitments, kit, outfit, rig, rigging, accoutrements.

tack³ / tak/ *n. colloq.* cheap or shoddy material; kitsch. [back-form. f. TACKY²]

tackle / tákəl/ *n. & v.* ● *n.* **1** equipment for a task or sport (*fishing tackle*). **2** a mechanism, esp. of ropes, pulley blocks, hooks, etc., for lifting weights, managing sails, etc. (*block and tackle*). **3** a windlass with its ropes and hooks. **4** an act of tackling in football, etc. **5** *Football* **a** the position next to the end of the forward line. **b** the player in this position. ● *v.tr.* **1** try to deal with (a problem or difficulty). **2** grapple with or try to overcome (an opponent). **3** enter into discussion with. **4** obstruct, intercept, or seize and stop (a player running with the ball). **5** secure by means of tackle. □ **tackle block** a pulley over which a rope runs. **tackle fall** a rope for applying force to the blocks of a tackle. □□ **tackler** *n.* **tackling** *n.* [ME, prob. f. MLG *takel* f. *taken* lay hold of]

■ *n.* **1** gear, rig, fittings, equipment, things, equipage, rig(ging), paraphernalia, kit, outfit, tools, implements, apparatus, trappings, accoutrements. **2** block (and tackle), hoisting gear, pulley, hoist, sheave. **3** windlass. ● *v.* **1** come *or* get to grips with, grapple with, approach, take on, try to solve, (try to) deal *or* cope with, stand *or* face up to, face, confront, address (oneself to), attend to, set about, pursue, have a go at, *colloq.* have a crack at. **2, 4** grapple with, take on, attack, contend with, challenge; intercept, obstruct, block, stop, seize.

tacky¹ / tákee/ *adj.* (**tackier, tackiest**) (of glue or paint, etc.) still slightly sticky after application. □□ **tackiness** *n.* [TACK¹ + -Y¹]

■ sticky, gluey, gummy, adhesive, ropy, viscous, viscid, glutinous, *sl.* gooey.

tacky² / tákee/ *adj.* (**tackier, tackiest**) *colloq.* **1** showing poor taste or style. **2** shoddy or seedy. □□ **tackily** *adv.* **tackiness** *n.* [19th c.: orig. unkn.]

■ **1** tawdry, cheap, brummagem, gaudy, chintzy, tasteless, vulgar, flashy, kitsch(y), *colloq.* flash. **2** shabby, sleazy, shoddy, seedy, dowdy, *colloq.* tatty.

taco / taákō/ *n.* (*pl.* -**os**) a Mexican-style dish of usu. meat, cheese, lettuce, tomatoes, etc., in a folded or rolled fried tortilla. [Mex. Sp.]

tact / takt/ *n.* **1** adroitness in dealing with others or with difficulties arising from personal feeling. **2** intuitive perception of the right thing to do or say. [F f. L *tactus* touch, sense of touch f. *tangere tact-* touch]

■ tactfulness, discretion, diplomacy, sensitivity, savoir faire, judgment, politesse, delicacy, finesse, cleverness, prudence, care, carefulness, dexterity, dexterousness, discernment, judiciousness, adroitness, skill, acumen, acuteness, perception, understanding, consideration, thoughtfulness, politeness, courtesy.

tactful / táktfŏol/ *adj.* having or showing tact. □□ **tactfully** *adv.* **tactfulness** *n.*

■ discreet, diplomatic, sensitive, politic, judicious, delicate, clever, prudent, careful, dexterous, discerning, adroit, skillful, acute, perceptive, understanding, considerate, thoughtful, polite, courteous. □□ **tactfulness** see TACT.

tactic / táktik/ *n.* **1** a tactical maneuver. **2** = TACTICS. [mod.L *tactica* f. Gk *taktikē* (*tekhnē* art): see TACTICS]

■ **1** move, maneuver, caper, plan, strategy, stratagem, policy, line, tack, device, ruse, plot, scheme, design, *colloq.* ploy.

tactical / táktikəl/ *adj.* **1** of, relating to, or constituting tactics (*a tactical retreat*). **2** (of bombing or weapons) done or for use in immediate support of military or naval operations (opp. STRATEGIC). **3** adroitly planning or planned. **4** *Brit.* (of voting) aimed at preventing the strongest candidate from

winning by supporting the next strongest. □□ **tactically** *adv.* [Gk *taktikos* (as TACTICS)]

■ **1, 3** artful, clever, cunning, shrewd, adroit, strategic, planned, calculated, skillful, adept, politic, smart, tactful.

tactics / táktiks/ *n.pl.* **1** (also treated as *sing.*) the art of disposing armed forces esp. in contact with an enemy (cf. STRATEGY). **2 a** the plans and means adopted in carrying out a scheme or achieving some end. **b** a skillful device or devices. □□ **tactician** / taktíshən/ *n.* [mod.L *tactica* f. Gk *taktika* neut.pl. f. *taktos* ordered f. *tassō* arrange]

■ **1** military science, military operation(s), generalship, maneuvering. **2 a** maneuvers, strategy, plans, campaign, orchestration, engineering, masterminding, approach, game plan. **b** device(s), ruse(s), plot(s), scheme(s), stratagem(s), trick(s), dodge(s), *colloq.* ploy(s). □□ **tactician** strategist, campaigner, mastermind, intriguer, plotter, planner, schemer, manipulator, maneuverer, orchestrator, *colloq.* operator.

tactile / táktəl, -tīl/ *adj.* **1** of or connected with the sense of touch. **2** perceived by touch. **3** tangible. **4** *Art* (in painting) producing or concerning the effect of three-dimensional solidity. □□ **tactual** / tákchŏoəl/ *adj.* (in senses 1, 2). **tactility** /-tílitee/ *n.* [L *tactilis* f. *tangere tact-* touch]

tactless / táktlis/ *adj.* having or showing no tact. □□ **tactlessly** *adv.* **tactlessness** *n.*

■ coarse, boorish, uncivilized, unsophisticated, rough, rude, uncouth, discourteous, ungentlemanly, unladylike, crude, gruff, bluff, abrupt, blunt, brusque, impertinent, disrespectful, uncivil, impolite, insensitive, awkward, bungling, clumsy, maladroit, inept, undiplomatic, thoughtless, unthinking, gauche, unskillful, impolitic, imprudent, inconsiderate, injudicious, indiscreet, unwise. □□ **tactlessness** see INCIVILITY, *impudence* (IMPUDENT).

tad / tad/ *n. colloq.* a small amount (often used adverbially: *a tad salty*). [19th c.: orig. unkn.]

■ see DASH *n.* 7.

tadpole / tádpōl/ *n.* a larva of an amphibian, esp. a frog, toad, or newt in its aquatic stage and breathing through gills. [ME *taddepolle* (as TOAD, POLL from the size of its head)]

taedium vitae / teédeeəm veétī, vītee/ *n.* weariness of life (often as a pathological state, with a tendency to suicide). [L]

tae kwon do / tí kwón dố/ *n.* a Korean martial art similar to karate. [Korean *t'ae* trample + *kwŏn* fist + -*do* way]

taenia / teéneeə/ *n.* (also **tenia**) (*pl.* **taeniae** /-nee-ee/ *or* **taenias**) **1** *Archit.* a fillet between a Doric architrave and frieze. **2** *Anat.* any flat ribbonlike structure, esp. the muscles of the colon. **3** any large tapeworm of the genus *Taenia*, esp. *T. saginata* and *T. soleum*, parasitic on humans. **4** *Gk Antiq.* a fillet or headband. □□ **taenioid** *adj.* [L f. Gk *tainia* ribbon]

taffeta / táfitə/ *n.* a fine lustrous silk or silklike fabric. [ME f. OF *taffetas* or med.L *taffata*, ult. f. Pers. *tāfta* past part. of *tāftan* twist]

taffrail / táfrayl, -rəl/ *n. Naut.* a rail round a ship's stern. [earlier *tafferel* f. Du. *taffereel* panel, dimin. of *tafel* (as TABLE): assim. to RAIL¹]

Taffy / táfee/ *n.* (*pl.* -**ies**) *Brit. colloq.* often *offens.* a Welshman. [supposed Welsh pronunc. of *Davy* = *David* (Welsh *Dafydd*)]

taffy / táfee/ *n.* (*pl.* -**ies**) **1** a chewy boiled sugar or molasses candy. **2** insincere flattery. [19th c.: orig. unkn.]

tafia / táfeeə/ *n. W.Ind.* rum distilled from molasses, etc. [18th c.: orig. uncert.]

tag¹ / tag/ *n. & v.* ● *n.* **1 a** a label, esp. one for tying on an object to show its address, price, etc. **b** *colloq.* an epithet or popular name serving to identify a person or thing. **c** *sl.* the signature or identifying mark of a graffiti artist. **2** a metal or

/ . . . / **pronunciation**	● **part of speech**
□ **phrases, idioms, and compounds**	
□□ **derivatives**	■ **synonym section**
cross-references appear in SMALL CAPITALS *or italics*	

plastic point at the end of a lace, etc., to assist insertion. **3** a loop at the back of a boot used in pulling it on. **4** a license plate of a motor vehicle. **5** a loose or ragged end of anything. **6** a ragged lock of wool on a sheep. **7** *Theatr.* a closing speech addressed to the audience. **8** a trite quotation or stock phrase. **9 a** the refrain of a song. **b** a musical phrase added to the end of a piece. **10** an animal's tail, or its tip. ● *v.tr.* (**tagged, tagging**) **1** provide with a tag or tags. **2** (often foll. by *on, on to*) join or attach. **3** esp. *Brit. colloq.* follow closely or trail behind. **4** *Computing* identify (an item of data) by its type for later retrieval. **5** label radioactively (see LABEL *v.* 3). **6 a** find rhymes for (verses). **b** string (rhymes) together. **7** shear away tags from (sheep). **8** to give a ticket to, as for a traffic or parking violation. □ **tag along** (often foll. by *with*) go along or accompany passively. **tag end** esp. the last remnant of something. [ME: orig. unkn.]
■ *n.* **1 a** label, name *or* price tag, mark, marker, tab, tally, ticket, sticker, stub, docket. **b** name, epithet, label, designation, title, nickname, byname, *colloq.* handle, *formal* appellation, *sl.* moniker. **9 a** see REFRAIN². **10** see TAIL¹ *n.* 1. ● *v.* **1** label, mark, ticket, identify, earmark, tab; name, call, dub, nickname, style, christen, baptize, *archaic* entitle. **2** (*tag on*) see TACK¹ *v.* 3. **3** follow, trail behind *or* after, shadow, *colloq.* tail. □ **tag along** go along; (*tag along with*) accompany, attend, escort; trail (along) after. **tag end** see REAR¹ *n.* 1.

tag² /tag/ *n. & v.* ● *n.* **1** a children's game in which one chases the rest, and anyone who is caught then becomes the pursuer. **2** *Baseball* the act of tagging a runner. ● *v.tr.* (**tagged, tagging**) **1** touch in a game of tag. **2** (often foll. by *out*) put (a runner) out by touching with the ball or with the hand holding the ball. [18th c.: orig. unkn.]

Tagalog /təgaʹaʹləg, -lawg/ *n. & adj.* ● *n.* **1** a member of the principal people of the Philippine Islands. **2** the language of this people. ● *adj.* of or relating to this people or language. [Tagalog f. *taga* native + *ilog* river]

tagliatelle /taʹalyətelʹee/ *n.* a form of pasta in narrow ribbons. [It.]

Tahitian /təheʹeshən/ *n. & adj.* ● *n.* **1** a native or inhabitant of Tahiti in the S. Pacific. **2** the language of Tahiti. ● *adj.* of or relating to Tahiti or its people or language.

tahr /taar/ *n.* any goatlike mammal of the genus *Hemitragus*, esp. *H. jemlahicus* of the Himalayas. [native name in Nepal]

tahsil /taaseʹel/ *n.* an administrative area in parts of India. [Urdu *taḥsīl* f. Arab., = collection]

t'ai chi ch'uan /tíʹ chee chwaʹan/ *n.* (also **t'ai chi**) a Chinese martial art and system of calisthenics consisting of sequences of very slow controlled movements. [Chin., = great ultimate boxing]

Taig /tayg/ *n.* esp. *Brit.* and *Ir. sl. offens.* (in Northern Ireland) a Protestant name for a Catholic. [var. of *Teague*, Anglicized spelling of the Irish name *Tadhg*, a nickname for an Irishman]

taiga /tíʹgə/ *n.* coniferous forest lying between tundra and steppe, esp. in Siberia. [Russ.]

tail¹ /tayl/ *n. & v.* ● *n.* **1** the hindmost part of an animal, esp. when prolonged beyond the rest of the body. **2 a** a thing like a tail in form or position, esp. something extending downwards or outwards at an extremity. **b** the rear end of anything, e.g., of a procession. **c** a long train or line of people, vehicles, etc. **3 a** the rear part of an airplane, with the horizontal stabilizer and rudder, or of a rocket. **b** the rear part of a motor vehicle. **4** the luminous trail of particles following a comet. **5** the inferior or weaker part of anything, esp. in a sequence. **6 a** the part of a shirt below the waist. **b** the hanging part of the back of a coat. **7** (in *pl.*) *colloq.* **a** a tailcoat. **b** evening dress including this. **8** (in *pl.*) the reverse of a coin as a choice when tossing. **9** *colloq.* a person following or shadowing another. **10** an extra strip attached to the lower end of a kite. **11** the stem of a note in music. **12** the part of a letter (e.g., *y*) below the line. **13 a** the exposed end of a slate or tile in a roof. **b** the unexposed end of a brick or stone in a wall. **14** the slender backward prolongation of a butterfly's wing. **15** a comparative calm at the end of a gale. **16** a calm stretch following rough water in a

stream. **17 a** the buttocks. **b** *sl. offens.* a (usu. female) sexual partner. ● *v.* **1** *tr.* remove the stalks of (fruit). **2** *tr. & (*foll. by *after*) *intr. colloq.* shadow or follow closely. **3** *tr.* provide with a tail. **4** *tr.* dock the tail of (a lamb, etc.). **5** *tr.* (often foll. by *on to*) join (one thing to another). □ **on a person's tail** closely following a person. **tail back** *Brit.* (of traffic) form a tailback. **tail covert** any of the feathers covering the base of a bird's tail feathers. **tail end 1** the hindmost or lowest or last part. **2** (sense 5 of the *n.*). **tail in** fasten (timber) by one end into a wall, etc. **tail off** (or **away**) **1** become fewer, smaller, or fainter. **2** fall behind or away in a scattered line. **tail off** *n.* a decline or gradual reduction, esp. in demand. **tail skid** a support for the tail of an aircraft when on the ground. **tail wind** a wind blowing in the direction of travel of a vehicle or aircraft, etc. **with one's tail between one's legs** in a state of dejection or humiliation. **with one's tail up** in good spirits; cheerful. □□ **tailed** *adj.* (also in *comb.*). **tailless** *adj.* [OE *tægl, tægel* f. Gmc]
■ *n.* **1** appendage, brush (*of a fox*), scut (*of a hare, rabbit,* or *deer*), dock, caudal fin (*of a fish*), uropygium (*of a bird*), tailpiece, tag *facetious* parson's nose; tail end, buttocks, seat, croup, rump, posterior(s), *colloq.* backside, bottom, behind, rear (end), *Brit. sl.* bum. **2 b** see REAR¹ *n.* 1. **c** see QUEUE *n.* 1. **3** rear, back. **5** tail end, bottom, tag end, fag end. **8** (*tails*) reverse. ● *v.* **2** dog, follow, pursue, trail, stalk, shadow, track. □ **tail end 1** see REAR¹ *n.* 1. **tail off** (or **away**) **1** see DECLINE *v.* 1, 7. **tail off** see DECREASE *n.*

tail² /tayl/ *n. & adj. Law* ● *n.* limitation of ownership, esp. of an estate limited to a person and that person's heirs. ● *adj.* so limited (*estate tail; fee tail*). □ **in tail** under such a limitation. [ME f. OF *taille* notch, cut, tax, f. *taillier* cut ult. f. L *talea* twig]

tailback /táylbak/ *n.* **1** *Football* on offense, a player positioned behind the quarterback. **2** *Brit.* a long line of traffic extending back from an obstruction.

tailboard /táylbawrd/ *n. Brit.* = TAILGATE 1.

tailcoat /táylkōt/ *n.* a man's morning or evening coat with a long skirt divided at the back into tails and cut away in front, worn as part of formal dress.

tailgate /táylgayt/ *n. & v.* ● *n.* **1 a** a hinged or removable flap at the rear of a station wagon, truck, etc. **b** the tail door of a station wagon or hatchback. **2** the lower end of a canal lock. ● *v. colloq.* **1** *intr.* drive too closely behind another vehicle. **2** *tr.* follow (a vehicle) too closely. □□ **tailgater** *n.*

tailing /táyling/ *n.* **1** (in *pl.*) the refuse or inferior part of grain or ore, etc. **2** the part of a beam or projecting brick, etc., embedded in a wall.

taillight /táyllīt/ *n.* a usu. red light at the rear of a train, motor vehicle, or bicycle.

tailor /táylər/ *n. & v.* ● *n.* a maker of clothes, esp. one who makes men's outer garments to measure. ● *v.* **1** *tr.* make (clothes) as a tailor. **2** *tr.* make or adapt for a special purpose. **3** *intr.* work as or be a tailor. **4** *tr.* (esp. as **tailored** *adj.*) make clothes for. **5** *tr.* (as **tailored** *adj.*) = tailor-made. □ **tailor-made 1** (of clothing) made to order by a tailor. **2** made or suited for a particular purpose (*a job tailor-made for me*). ● *n.* a tailor-made garment. **tailor's chair** a chair without legs for sitting cross-legged like a tailor at work. **tailor's twist** a fine strong silk thread used by tailors. □□ **tailoring** *n.* [ME & AF *taillour*, OF *tailleur* cutter, formed as TAIL²]
■ *n.* couturier, couturière, clothier, garment maker, outfitter, costumier, costumer, seamstress, dressmaker, modiste. ● *v.* **2** fit, adapt, suit, adjust, alter, accommodate, gear, modify, change, convert, cut, fashion, mold, stretch. □ **tailor-made** *adj.* **1** fitted, tailored, custom-made, made to measure, made to order, bespoke. **2** ideal, perfect, customized, made to order, custom-made, suited, suitable, (just) right, *colloq.* (right) up one's street *or* alley.

tailored /táylərd/ *adj.* (of clothing) well or closely fitted.

tailpiece /táylpees/ *n.* **1** an appendage at the rear of anything. **2** the final part of a thing. **3** a decoration in a blank space at the end of a chapter, etc., in a book. **4** a piece of wood to which the strings of some musical instruments are attached at their lower ends.

tailpipe /táylpīp/ *n.* the rear section of the exhaust pipe of a motor vehicle.

tailplane /táylplayn/ *n. Brit.* = *horizontal stabilizer.*

tailspin /táylspin/ *n. & v.* ● *n.* **1** a spin (see SPIN *n.* 2) by an aircraft with the tail spiraling. **2** a state of chaos or panic. ● *v.intr.* (**-spinning;** *past* and *past part.* **-spun**) perform a tailspin.

tailstock /táylstok/ *n.* the adjustable part of a lathe holding the fixed spindle.

taint /taynt/ *n. & v.* ● *n.* **1** a spot or trace of decay, infection, or some bad quality. **2** a corrupt condition or infection. ● *v.* **1** *tr.* affect with a taint. **2** *tr.* (foll. by *with*) affect slightly. **3** *intr.* become tainted. □□ **taintless** *adj.* [ME, partly f. OF *teint(e)* f. L *tinctus* f. *tingere* dye, partly f. ATTAINT]

■ *n.* stain, blot, blemish, slur, tarnish, tinge, tincture, (black *or* bad) mark, stigma, imperfection, flaw, scar, defect; discredit, dishonor. ● *v.* **1** sully, tarnish, stain, stigmatize, smear, harm, hurt, damage, debase, vitiate, blacken, foul, contaminate, pollute, adulterate, dirty, muddy, smirch, besmirch, blemish, soil, corrupt, spoil, defile, ruin, destroy, infect, poison. **2** see TINT *v.*

taipan¹ /típán/ *n.* the head of a foreign business in China. [Chin.]

taipan² /típan/ *n.* a large venomous Australian snake, *Oxyuranus scutellatus.* [Aboriginal]

takahe /taákahee/ *n.* = NOTORNIS. [Maori]

take /tayk/ *v. & n.* ● *v.* (**took** /took/; **taken** /táykən/) **1** *tr.* lay hold of; get into one's hands. **2** *tr.* acquire; get possession of; capture, earn, or win. **3** *tr.* get the use of by purchase or formal agreement (*take an apartment*). **4** *tr.* (in a recipe) avail oneself of; use. **5** *tr.* use as a means of transport (*took a taxi*). **6** *tr.* regularly buy or subscribe to (a particular newspaper or periodical, etc.). **7** *tr.* obtain after fulfilling the required conditions (*take a degree*). **8** *tr.* occupy (*take a chair*). **9** *tr.* make use of (*take precautions*). **10** *tr.* consume as food or medicine (*took the pills*). **11** *intr.* **a** be successful or effective (*the inoculation did not take*). **b** (of a plant, seed, etc.) begin to grow. **12** *tr.* **a** require or use up (*will only take a minute; these things take time*). **b** accommodate; have room for (*the elevator takes three people*). **13** *tr.* cause to come or go with one; convey (*take the book home; the bus will take you all the way*). **14** *tr.* **a** remove; dispossess a person of (*someone has taken my pen*). **b** destroy; annihilate (*took her own life*). **c** (often foll. by *for*) *sl.* defraud; swindle. **15** *tr.* catch or be infected with (fire or fever, etc.). **16** *tr.* **a** experience or be affected by (*take fright; take pleasure*). **b** give play to (*take comfort*). **c** exert (*take courage; take no notice*). **d** exact; get (*take revenge*). **17** *tr.* find out and note (a name and address; a person's temperature, etc.) by inquiry or measurement. **18** *tr.* grasp mentally; understand (*I take your point; I took you to mean yes*). **19** *tr.* treat or regard in a specified way (*took the news calmly; took it badly*). **20** *tr.* (foll. by *for* or *to be*) regard as being (*do you take me for an idiot?*). **21** *tr.* **a** accept (*take the offer*). **b** submit to (*take a joke; take no nonsense; took a risk*). **22** *tr.* choose or assume (*took a different view; took a job; took the initiative; took responsibility*). **23** *tr.* derive (*takes its name from the inventor*). **24** *tr.* (foll. by *from*) subtract (*take 3 from 9*). **25** *tr.* execute, make, or undertake; perform or effect (*take notes; take an oath; take a decision; take a look*). **26** *tr.* occupy or engage oneself in; indulge in; enjoy (*take a rest; take exercise; take a vacation*). **27** *tr.* conduct (*took the early class*). **28** *tr.* deal with in a certain way (*took the corner too fast*). **29** *tr.* **a** teach or be taught (a subject). **b** be examined in (a subject). **30** *tr.* make (a photograph) with a camera; photograph (a person or thing). **31** *tr.* use as an instance (*let us take Napoleon*). **32** *tr. Gram.* have or require as part of the appropriate construction (*this verb takes an object*). **33** *tr.* have sexual intercourse with (a woman). **34** *tr.* (in *passive;* foll. by *by, with*) be attracted or charmed by. **35** *tr. Baseball* to refrain from swinging at (a pitch). ● *n.* **1** an amount taken or caught in one session or attempt, etc. **2** a scene or sequence of film or videotape photographed continuously at one time. **3** money received

by a business, esp. money received at a theater for seats. **4** *Printing* the amount of copy set up at one time. **5** a visible or emotional reaction, as to a surprise, etc. □ **be taken ill** become ill, esp. suddenly. **have what it takes** *colloq.* have the necessary qualities, etc., for success. **on the take** *sl.* accepting bribes. **take account of** see ACCOUNT. **take action** see ACTION. **take advantage of** see ADVANTAGE. **take advice** see ADVICE. **take after** resemble (esp. a parent or ancestor). **take against** *Brit.* begin to dislike, esp. impulsively. **take aim** see AIM. **take apart 1** dismantle. **2** *colloq.* beat or defeat. **take aside** see ASIDE. **take as read** esp. *Brit.* accept without reading or discussing. **take away 1** remove or carry elsewhere. **2** subtract. **3** *Brit.* buy (food, etc.) at a store or restaurant for eating elsewhere. **take-away** *Brit. attrib.adj.* = *take-out.* ● *n. Brit.* **1** an establishment selling take-out food. **2** the food itself. **take back 1** retract (a statement). **2** convey (a person or thing) to his or her or its original position. **3** carry (a person) in thought to a past time. **4** *Printing* transfer to the previous line. **take a bath** *sl.* lose money. **take a bow** see BOW². **take the cake** *colloq.* be the most remarkable. **take care of** see CARE. **take a chance,** etc., see CHANCE. **take down 1** write down (spoken words). **2** remove (a structure) by separating it into pieces. **3** humiliate. **take effect** see EFFECT. **take five** (or **ten**) take a break, esp. from work. **take for granted** see GRANT. **take fright** see FRIGHT. **take from** diminish; weaken; detract from. **take heart** be encouraged. **take the heat** endure criticism, punishment, etc. **take hold** see HOLD¹. **take home** earn. **take-home pay** the pay received by an employee after the deduction of taxes, etc. **take ill** (**sick**) *colloq.* be taken ill. **take in 1** accepts as a boarder, etc. **2** undertake (work) at home. **3** make (a garment, etc.) smaller. **4** understand (*did you take that in?*). **5** cheat (*managed to take them all in*). **6** include or comprise. **7** *colloq.* visit (a place) on the way to another (*shall we take in the White House*). **8** furl (a sail). **9** regularly buy (a newspaper, etc.). **10** attend; watch (*take in a show*). **11** arrest. **take-in** *n.* a deception. **take in hand 1** undertake; start doing or dealing with. **2** undertake the control or reform of (a person). **take into account** see ACCOUNT. **take it 1** (often foll. by *that* + clause) assume (*I take it that you have finished*). **2** see TAKE *v.* 19. **take it easy** see EASY. **take it from me** (or **take my word for it**) I can assure you. **take it ill** resent it. **take it into one's head** see HEAD. **take it on one** (or **oneself**) (foll. by *to* + infin.) venture or presume. **take it or leave it** (esp. in *imper.*) an expression of indifference or impatience about another's decision after making an offer. **take it out of 1** exhaust the strength of. **2** penalize. **take it out on** relieve one's frustration by attacking or treating harshly. **take one's leave of** see LEAVE². **take a lot of** (or **some**) **doing** be hard to do. **take a person's name in vain** see VAIN. **take off 1 a** remove (clothing) from one's or another's body. **b** remove or lead away. **2** deduct (part of an amount). **3** depart, esp. hastily (*took off in a fast car*). **4** *colloq.* mimic humorously. **5** jump from the ground. **6** become airborne. **7** (of a scheme, enterprise, etc.) become successful or popular. **8** have (a period) away from work. **take oneself off** go away. **take on 1** undertake (work, a responsibility, etc.). **2** engage (an employee). **3** be willing or ready to meet (an adversary in a sport, an argument, etc., esp. a stronger one). **4** acquire (a new meaning, etc.). **5** esp. *Brit. colloq.* show strong emotion. **take orders** see ORDER. **take out 1** remove from within a place; extract. **2** escort on an outing. **3** get (a license or summons, etc.) issued. **4** buy (food) at a store, restaurant, etc., for eating elsewhere. **5** *Bridge* remove (a partner or a partner's call) from a suit by bidding a different one or no trumps. **6** murder or destroy. **take-out** *adj.* (of food) bought at a shop or restaurant for eating elsewhere. ● *n.* food sold for consumption elsewhere. **take a person out of himself** or **herself** make a person forget his or her worries. **take over 1** succeed to the management or ownership of. **2** take control. **3** *Printing* transfer to the next line. **take part** see PART. **take place** see PLACE. **take a person's point** see POINT. **take shape** assume a distinct form; develop into something definite. **take sides** see SIDE. **take stock** see STOCK. **take the sun** see SUN. **take that!** an exclamation accompanying a blow, etc. **take one's time** not hurry. **take to 1** begin or fall into the habit of (*took to drink*). **2** have recourse to. **3** adapt oneself to. **4** form a liking for. **5** make for (*took to the hills*). **take to heart** see HEART. **take to one's heels** see HEEL[1]. **take to pieces** see PIECE. **take the trouble** see TROUBLE. **take up 1** become interested or engaged in (a pursuit, a cause, etc.). **2** adopt as a protégé. **3** occupy (time or space). **4** begin (residence, etc.). **5** resume after an interruption. **6** interrupt or question (a speaker). **7** accept (an offer, etc.). **8** shorten (a garment). **9** lift up. **10** absorb (*sponges take up water*). **11** take (a person) into a vehicle. **12** pursue (a matter, etc.) further. **take a person up on** accept (a person's offer, etc.). **take up with** begin to associate with. □□ **takable** *adj.* (also **takeable**). [OE *tacan* f. ON *taka*]

■ *v.* **1** grip, seize, grasp, clasp, get, get or take hold of, hold, grab, snatch, clutch, pluck, lay hold of, lay hands on, *sl.* nab. **2** obtain, procure, acquire, get, gain (possession of), take possession of, lay one's hands on, carry off, capture, catch, abduct; earn, secure, win. **3** reserve, book, engage, get the use of; hire, rent, lease, borrow. **5** catch, use, travel by; get on(to) or in(to), board. **6** buy, subscribe to, get, *Brit.* take in. **9** use, employ, make use of, establish, put in(to) place, adopt, put into effect, apply; resort to, have recourse to, turn to. **10** swallow, eat, consume, ingest, devour, gulp down, gobble up or down, wolf, bolt; drink, imbibe, *literary* quaff; inhale. **11 a** prove or be effective, prove or be efficacious, take effect, take hold, operate, function, work, *colloq.* do the trick. **b** strike, take root, germinate. **12 a** require, demand, need, necessitate, call for; use up, consume. **b** hold, contain, accommodate, have room for, accept, fit in. **13** conduct, escort, lead, convoy, guide, accompany; carry, convey, bear, transport, run, bring, deliver, ferry, haul, cart. **14 a** appropriate, carry off or away, steal, pilfer, filch, palm, pocket, remove, walk off or away with, run off or away with, make off or away with, help oneself to, dispossess a person of; embezzle, misappropriate, peculate; plagiarize, pirate; *colloq.* lift, swipe, rip off, bag, snaffle, *euphem.* abstract, *formal or joc.* purloin, *sl.* knock off, hook, pinch, liberate, snitch, nab, *Brit. sl.* nick. **b** end, terminate, annihilate, wipe out. **c** cheat, swindle, defraud, *sl.* bilk, con, fiddle. **16 a** experience, entertain, feel, be affected by; get, derive. **d** exact, extract, get. **18** understand, gather, interpret, perceive, apprehend, deduce, conclude, construe, infer, judge, assume, suppose, imagine, see, *formal* deem. **19** bear, accept, receive; treat, regard. **20** believe, think, judge, hold, feel, *formal* deem; (*take for*) assess as, consider (as), regard as, view as. **21 a** accept, take up, jump at. **b** accept, bear, withstand, stand, endure, weather, tolerate, abide, brave, go through, undergo, suffer, submit to, swallow, put up with, stomach, *colloq.* stick, *literary* brook. **22** pick, select, choose, opt for, settle or decide or fasten (up)on; assume, bear, undertake, adopt, arrogate (to oneself); acknowledge, accept. **23** acquire, get, adopt; derive, obtain, draw, receive, inherit. **24** subtract, deduct, remove, take away or off. **26** occupy or engage oneself in, partake of, have, experience, indulge in, enjoy. **27** conduct, lead, direct, preside over, chair. **28** clear, get over or past or around or through, go over or past or around or through; negotiate. **29 a** teach; take up, study, be involved in or with, be occupied in or with, apply oneself to, learn, have lessons in; read, tackle. **30** see PHOTOGRAPH *v.* **34** (*be taken*) be captivated, be entranced, be enchanted, be attracted, be charmed, be bewitched, be infatuated.

● *n.* **3** revenue, takings, yield, return, receipts,

proceeds, gain, profit(s); gate (money). □ **take after** resemble, look like, be the spitting image or spit and image of, favor, remind a person of. **take apart 1** see *knock down* 5. **take away 1** see CONFISCATE, REMOVE *v.* 2a. **2** see SUBTRACT. **take back 1** retract, withdraw, recant, disavow, repudiate, rescind. **2** see RETURN *v.* 2. **take down 1** note, make a note or memo or memorandum of, write down, record, put or set down, put in writing, document, transcribe, chronicle. **2** see *knock down* 5. **3** debase, deflate, lower, diminish, belittle, depreciate, deprecate, humble, humiliate, shame, disparage, degrade, disgrace. **take from** see DETRACT. **take home** see EARN 1. **take-home pay** see PAY[1] *n.* **take ill** see SICKEN 2a. **take in 1** accommodate, receive, let in, quarter, billet, board, lodge, house, put up. **4** see COMPREHEND 1. **5** deceive, fool, trick, impose upon, overcharge, cheat, mulct, defraud, dupe, gull, mislead, hoax, hoodwink, swindle, pull the wool over a person's eyes, *colloq.* bamboozle, *literary* cozen, *sl.* bilk, con, do. **6** include, subsume, embrace, comprise, cover, encompass, contain, incorporate. **7** see VISIT *v.* 1. **take it 1** see SUPPOSE 1. **take it out of 1** see EXHAUST *v.* 2. **take off 1 a** remove, strip or peel off, discard, shed, divest (oneself) of, *literary* doff. **2** see DEDUCT. **3** depart, leave, go (away), decamp, flee; *colloq.* skedaddle, make oneself scarce, scram, *sl.* beat it, split, hit the road or trail. **4** satirize, lampoon, caricature, mock, parody, travesty, burlesque, mimic, imitate, *colloq.* spoof, *Brit. colloq.* send up. **6** fly (off), become airborne, take to the air, take wing, lift off, blast off. **take on 1** assume, accept, undertake, tackle; shoulder, carry. **2** hire, engage, employ, enroll, enlist, sign up, retain, appoint, recruit. **3** challenge, face, contend with, oppose, match or pit oneself against, vie with, fight. **5** see SEETHE 2. **take out 1** see EXTRACT *v.* 1. **2** entertain, escort, invite out; court, woo. **6** see MURDER *v.* 1. **take over 1** seize, arrogate (to oneself), assume, assume control or possession or command of, take control or possession or command of, usurp control or possession or command of, take, usurp, gain control or possession or command of. **take shape** see JELL 1. **take one's time** dawdle, dilly-dally, delay, linger, loiter. **take to 2** see RESORT *v.* 1. **4** like, find pleasant or pleasing, feel affection or liking for, find suitable, *disp.* feel affinity for. **5** leave for, depart for, take off for, run for, head for, flee to, make for. **take up 1** become interested or involved or engaged in; embark on, start, begin, *formal* commence; espouse, embrace, support, sponsor, advocate. **3** occupy, cover, use (up), consume, fill (up), eat up. **5** resume, carry on, continue, go on with, follow on with, pick up. **7** accept, agree to, acquiesce to, accede to. **9** raise (up), lift (up), pick up. **12** pursue, deal with, treat, consider, discuss, bring up, raise. **take up with** see FRATERNIZE.

takeoff /táykawf/ *n.* **1** the act of becoming airborne. **2** *colloq.* an act of mimicking. **3** a place from which one jumps.

■ **1** launch, lift-off, blast-off, taking off, departure, leaving, going; flight, flying. **2** satire, lampoon, caricature, mockery, parody, travesty, burlesque, imitation, *colloq.* spoof, send-up.

takeover /táykōvər/ *n.* the assumption of control (esp. of a business); the buying out of one company by another.

taker /táykər/ *n.* **1** a person who takes a bet. **2** a person who accepts an offer.

takin /taákin/ *n.* a large Tibetan horned ruminant, *Budorcas taxicolor*. [Mishmi]

taking /táyking/ *adj. & n.* ● *adj.* **1** attractive or captivating. **2** *archaic* catching or infectious. ● *n.* (in *pl.*) esp. *Brit.* an amount of money taken in business. □□ **takingly** *adv.* **takingness** *n.*

■ *adj.* **1** attractive, alluring, engaging, captivating, winning, winsome, charming, entrancing, enchanting, bewitching, fetching, fascinating, delightful, irresistible, compelling, intriguing, prepossessing. **2** see INFECTIOUS 2, 3. ● *n.* (*takings*) see REVENUE.

tala /taálə/ *n.* any of the traditional rhythmic patterns of Indian music. [Skr.]

talaria /təláireeə/ *n.pl.* (in Roman mythology) winged sandals as an attribute of Mercury, Iris, and others. [L, neut. pl. of *talaris* f. *talus* ankle]

talc /talk/ *n. & v.* ● *n.* **1** talcum powder. **2** any crystalline form of magnesium silicate that occurs in soft flat plates, usu. white or pale green in color and used as a lubricant, etc. ● *v.tr.* (**talcked, talcking**) treat (a surface) with talc to lubricate or dry it. □□ **talcose** *adj.* **talcous** *adj.* **talcy** *adj.* (in sense 1). [F *talc* or med.L *talcum*, f. Arab. *ṭalk* f. Pers. *ṭalk*]

talcum /tálkəm/ *n.* **1** = TALC. **2** (in full **talcum powder**) powdered talc for toilet and cosmetic use, usu. perfumed. [med.L: see TALC]

tale /tayl/ *n.* **1** a narrative or story, esp. fictitious and imaginatively treated. **2** a report of an alleged fact, often malicious or in breach of confidence (*all sorts of tales will get about*). **3** a lie; a falsehood. **4** *archaic* or *literary* a number or total (*the tale is complete*). □ **tale of a tub** an idle fiction. [OE *talu* f. Gmc: cf. TELL¹]

■ **1** story, narrative, report, account, record, chronicle, history, saga, narration, recital, anecdote, myth, legend, romance, fable; fiction, fabrication, fairy story *or* tale, shaggy-dog story, cock-and-bull story, *colloq.* yarn, tall tale *or* story, *sl.* fishy story. **2** rumor, gossip, slander, allegation, tittle-tattle, libel, story, *colloq.* scuttlebutt; see also LIE² *n.*

talebearer /táylbairər/ *n.* a person who maliciously gossips or reveals secrets. □□ **talebearing** *n. & adj.*

■ gossip, rumormonger, gossipmonger, taleteller, scandalmonger, newsmonger, telltale, tattler, informer, stool pigeon, rat, blabbermouth, tattletale, *archaic* quidnunc, *colloq.* bigmouth, *sl.* squealer, ratfink, fink, stoolie, narc, sneak.

talent /tálənt/ *n.* **1** a special aptitude or faculty (*a talent for music; has real talent*). **2** high mental ability. **3** a person or persons of talent (*is a real talent; plenty of local talent*). **4** an ancient weight and unit of currency, esp. among the Greeks. □ **talent scout** (or *Brit.* **spotter**) a person looking for talented performers, esp. in sports and entertainment. □□ **talented** *adj.* **talentless** *adj.* [OE *talente* & OF *talent* f. L *talentum* inclination of mind f. Gk *talanton* balance, weight, sum of money]

■ **1** ability, power, gift, faculty, flair, genius, brilliance, facility, aptitude, capacity, knack, ingenuity, expertise, forte, strength; endowment; see also BENT¹ *n.* 2. **3 a** see VIRTUOSO 1a. □□ **talented** gifted, accomplished, brilliant, skilled, skillful, masterful, expert, adept, adroit, dexterous, deft, clever, good, polished, proficient, first-rate, excellent, *colloq.* crack, top-notch, top-drawer, *sl.* ace, crackerjack, *Brit. sl.* wizard.

tales /taylz, táyleez/ *n. Law* **1** a writ for summoning jurors when a panel is deficient. **2** a list of persons who may be summoned. [ME f. L *tales* (*de circumstantibus*) such (of the bystanders), the first words of the writ]

talesman /taylzmən, táyleez-/ *n.* (*pl.* **-men**) *Law* a person summoned by a tales.

taleteller /táyltelər/ *n.* **1** a person who tells stories. **2** a person who spreads malicious reports.

tali *pl.* of TALUS¹.

talion /táleeən/ *n.* = LEX TALIONIS. [ME f. OF f. L *talio -onis* f. *talis* such]

talipes /tálipeez/ *n. Med.* = CLUBFOOT. [mod.L f. L *talus* ankle + *pes* foot]

talipot /tálipot/ *n.* a tall S. Indian palm, *Corypha umbraculifera*, with very large fan-shaped leaves that are used as sunshades, etc. [Malayalam *tālipat*, Hindi *tālpāt* f. Skr. *tālapattra* f. *tāla* palm + *pattra* leaf]

talisman /tálizmən/ *n.* (*pl.* **talismans**) **1** an object, esp. an inscribed ring or stone, supposed to be endowed with magic powers esp. of averting evil from or bringing good luck to its holder. **2** a charm or amulet; a thing supposed to be capable of working wonders. □□ **talismanic** /-mánik/ *adj.*

[F & *Sp.*, = It. *talismano*, f. med.Gk *telesmon*, Gk *telesma* completion, religious rite f. *teleō* complete f. *telos* end]

■ amulet, charm, fetish, juju, periapt, mascot; wishbone, rabbit's foot, esp. *Brit.* merry thought.

talk /tawk/ *v. & n.* ● *v.* **1** *intr.* (often foll. by *to, with*) converse or communicate ideas by spoken words. **2** *intr.* have the power of speech. **3** *intr.* (foll. by *about*) **a** have as the subject of discussion. **b** (in *imper.*) *colloq.* as an emphatic statement (*talk about expense! It cost me $50*). **4** *tr.* express or utter in words; discuss (*you are talking nonsense; talked football all day*). **5** *tr.* use (a language) in speech (*is talking Spanish*). **6** *intr.* (foll. by *at*) address pompously. **7** *tr.* (usu. foll. by *into, out of*) bring into a specified condition, etc., by talking (*talked himself hoarse; how did you talk them into it?; talked them out of the difficulty*). **8** *intr.* reveal (esp. secret) information; betray secrets. **9** *intr. colloq.* gossip (*people are beginning to talk*). **10** *intr.* have influence (*money talks*). **11** *intr.* communicate by radio. ● *n.* **1** conversation or talking. **2** a particular mode of speech (*baby talk*). **3** an informal address or lecture. **4 a** rumor or gossip (*there is talk of a merger*). **b** its theme (*their success was the talk of the town*). **c** empty words; verbiage (*mere talk*). **5** (often in *pl.*) extended discussions or negotiations. □ **know what one is talking about** be expert or authoritative. **now you're talking** *colloq.* I like what you say, suggest, etc. **talk away 1** consume (time) in talking. **2** carry on talking (*talk away! I'm listening*). **talk back 1** reply defiantly. **2** respond on a two-way radio system. **talk big** *colloq.* talk boastfully. **talk down** denigrate; belittle. **talk down to** speak patronizingly or condescendingly to. **talk a person down 1** silence a person by greater loudness or persistence. **2** bring (a pilot or aircraft) to landing by radio instructions from the ground. **talk of 1** discuss or mention. **2** (often foll. by verbal noun) express some intention of (*talked of moving to Dallas*). **talk of the town** what is being talked about generally. **talk out** *Brit.* block the course of (a bill in Parliament) by prolonging discussion to the time of adjournment. **talk over** discuss at length. **talk a person over** (or **around**) gain agreement or compliance from a person by talking. **talk shop** talk, esp. tediously or inopportunely, about one's occupation, business, etc. **talk show** a television or radio program featuring discussionof topical issues. **talk tall** boast. **talk through one's hat** (or *Brit.* **neck**) *colloq.* **1** exaggerate. **2** bluff. **3** talk wildly or nonsensically. **talk to** reprove or scold (a person). **talk to oneself** soliloquize. **talk turkey** see TURKEY. **talk up** discuss (a subject) in order to arouse interest in it. **you can't** (or **can**) **talk** *colloq.* a reproof that the person addressed is just as culpable, etc., in the matter at issue. □□ **talker** *n.* [ME *talken* frequent. verb f. TALE or TELL¹]

■ *v.* **1, 3a** speak, give *or* deliver a speech, give *or* deliver a talk, give *or* deliver an address, lecture; converse, communicate, confer, consult, parley, negotiate, have a (little) talk, (have a) chat, confabulate; chatter, prate, prattle, jabber, blather, blether, gibber, gabble, cackle, babble, patter, rattle on, gossip, palaver, *Austral. & NZ colloq.* yabber; have a bull session, *colloq.* confab, gab, gas, jaw, natter, go on, *sl.* rap, chin-wag, chew the fat *or* rag. **2** speak, communicate, vocalize. **4** see DISCUSS 1, SPEAK 2. **5** talk in, speak in, use, communicate in, converse in, express oneself in, discourse in. **7** (*talk into*) convince that, bring around to, persuade to, argue into, prevail (up)on to; (*talk out of*) discourage from, dissuade from, deter from, put off from, divert from, argue out of. **8** confess, give the game away, tell, *colloq.* come clean, spill the beans, rat, *sl.* squeal, sing. **9** see GOSSIP *v.* ● *n.* **1** conversation, conference, discussion, meeting, consultation, dialogue, colloquy, parley, chat, tête-à-tête, powwow, confabulation, *literary* discourse; palaver, gossip, claptrap, patter, prattle, prattling,

─────────────────────────

/. . . / **pronunciation**	● **part of speech**
□ **phrases, idioms, and compounds**	
□□ **derivatives**	■ **synonym section**
cross-references appear in SMALL CAPITALS or *italics*	

chatter, verbiage, jabber, cackle; *colloq.* confab, chitchat, *Austral.* & *NZ colloq.* yabber, *sl.* chin-wag, rap session. **2** dialect, speech, way *or* manner of speaking, language, jargon, argot, cant, patois, accent, *colloq.* lingo. **3** oration, lecture, address, presentation, speech, report, disquisition, dissertation, *literary* discourse; sermon; harangue, tirade, *sl.* spiel. **4 a** gossip, rumor, hearsay, news, report. **b** subject *or* topic of conversation, subject *or* topic of gossip, subject *or* topic of rumor, information, news, *colloq.* info, *sl.* dope. **c** empty words, palaver, gossip, claptrap, prattle, prattling, chatter, verbiage, jabber, cackle, bunkum, nonsense, rubbish, balderdash, stuff and nonsense, twaddle, *colloq.* malarkey, tripe, hogwash, esp. *Brit. colloq.* tosh, *sl.* bunk, bilge(water), bull, guff, hot air, bosh, poppycock, hooey, hokum. **5** see *negotiation* (NEGOTIATE). □ **talk back 1** answer back. **talk big** boast, brag, crow, bluster, exaggerate, blow one's own trumpet, *colloq.* swank, show off, blow, *Austral.* & *NZ colloq.* skite, *literary* vaunt. **talk down** deprecate, deprecate, denigrate, disparage, belittle, minimize, diminish, criticize, *colloq.* knock, pan, put down. **talk down to** condescend to, patronize. **talk of 1** see DISCUSS 1, MENTION *v.* 1, 2. **talk over** see DISCUSS 1. **talk a person over** (or **around**) see *win over.* **talk to** see SPEAK 4c. **talk up** promote, support, sponsor, advertise, publicize, push, *colloq.* plug, *sl.* hype. □□ **talker** speaker, lecturer, orator, speechmaker, spellbinder, rabble-rouser, demagogue, haranguer, ranter; blusterer, blatherskite, swaggerer, show-off, *colloq.* tub-thumper, windbag, blowhard, *sl.* gasbag, lot of hot air, spieler.

talkathon /táwkəthon/ *n. colloq.* a prolonged session of talking or discussion. [TALK + MARATHON]

talkative /táwkətiv/ *adj.* fond of or given to talking. □□ **talkatively** *adv.* **talkativeness** *n.*

■ garrulous, loquacious, verbose, long-winded, voluble, prolix, wordy, chatty, gossipy, effusive, expansive, communicative, forthcoming, logorrheic, *colloq.* gabby, windy.

talkback /táwkbak/ *n.* (often *attrib.*) a system of two-way communication by loudspeaker.

talkie /táwkee/ *n.* esp. *hist.* a movie with a soundtrack, as distinct from a silent movie. [TALK + -IE, after *movie*]

talking /táwking/ *adj.* & *n.* ● *adj.* **1** that talks. **2** having the power of speech (*a talking parrot*). **3** expressive (*talking eyes*). ● *n.* in senses of TALK *v.* □ **talking book** a recorded reading of a book, esp. for the blind. **talking head** *colloq.* a commentator, etc., on television, speaking to the camera and viewed in close-up. **talking point** a topic for discussion or argument. **talking-to** *colloq.* a reproof or reprimand (*gave them a good talking-to*).

tall /tawl/ *adj.* & *adv.* ● *adj.* **1** of more than average height. **2** of a specified height (*looks about six feet tall*). **3** higher than the surrounding objects (*a tall building*). **4** *colloq.* extravagant or excessive (*a tall story; tall talk*). ● *adv.* as if tall; proudly; in a tall or extravagant way (*sit tall*). □ **tall drink** a drink served in a tall glass. **tall hat** = *top hat* (see TOP[1]). **tall order** an exorbitant or unreasonable demand. **tall ship** a sailing ship with more than one high mast. □□ **tallish** *adj.* **tallness** *n.* [ME, repr. OE *getæl* swift; prompt]

■ *adj.* **1** lanky, gangling, rangy, leggy, long-legged, *colloq.* long; big, giant, huge, gigantic, large. **3** high, towering, big, soaring, giant, gigantic, *literary* lofty; multistory. **4** exaggerated, overblown, far-fetched, improbable, unbelievable, incredible, preposterous, outrageous, extravagant, excessive, overdone, absurd, *colloq.* steep. □□ **tallness** height, size.

tallage /tálij/ *n. hist.* **1** a form of taxation on towns, etc., abolished in the 14th c. **2** a tax on feudal dependants, etc. [ME f. OF *taillage* f. *tailler* cut: see TAIL[2]]

tallboy /táwlboy/ *n.* a tall chest of drawers sometimes in lower and upper sections or mounted on legs.

■ see *chest of drawers.*

tallith /taális, taaleét/ *n.* a scarf worn by Jewish men esp. at prayer. [Rabbinical Heb. *ṭallīt* f. *ṭillel* to cover]

tallow /tálō/ *n.* & *v.* ● *n.* the harder kinds of (esp. animal) fat melted down for use in making candles, soap, etc. ● *v.tr.* grease with tallow. □ **tallow tree** any of various trees, esp. *Sapium sebiferum* of China, yielding vegetable tallow. **vegetable tallow** a vegetable fat used as tallow. □□ **tallowish** *adj.* **tallowy** *adj.* [ME *talg, talug,* f. MLG *talg, talch,* of unkn. orig.]

tally /tálee/ *n.* & *v.* ● *n.* (*pl.* **-ies**) **1** the reckoning of a debt or score. **2** a total score or amount. **3 a** a mark registering a fixed number of objects delivered or received. **b** such a number as a unit. **4** *hist.* **a** a piece of wood scored across with notches for the items of an account and then split into halves, each party keeping one. **b** an account kept in this way. **5** a ticket or label for identification. **6** a corresponding thing, counterpart, or duplicate. ● *v.* (**-ies, -ied**) (often foll. by *with*) **1** *intr.* agree or correspond. **2** *tr.* record or reckon by tally. □□ **tallier** *n.* [ME f. AF *tallie,* AL *tallia, talia* f. L *talea:* cf. TAIL[2]]

■ *n.* **1** reckoning, count, enumeration, record, account, register, addition, tabulation, itemization, listing, calculation, computation. **2** total, sum, score. **5** ticket, label, mark, marker, tag, tab. **6** esp. *Brit.* stub, counterpart, duplicate, mate, counterfoil. ● *v.* **1** agree, coincide, accord, correspond, fit, compare, match (up), square, conform, concur, harmonize, *colloq.* jibe. **2** tally up, count (up *or* out), enumerate, record, register, reckon, add (up), total (up), tot (up), tabulate, itemize, list, calculate, compute.

tallyho /táleehó/ *int., n.,* & *v.* ● *int.* a huntsman's cry to the hounds on sighting a fox. ● *n.* (*pl.* **-hos**) an utterance of this. ● *v.* (**-hoes, -hoed**) **1** *intr.* utter a cry of "tallyho." **2** *tr.* indicate (a fox) or urge (hounds) with this cry. [cf. F *taïaut*]

tallyman /táleemən/ *n.* (*pl.* **-men**) **1** a person who keeps a tally. **2** *Brit.* a person who sells goods on credit, esp. from door to door.

Talmud /taálmŏod, -məd, tál-/ *n.* the body of Jewish civil and ceremonial law and legend comprising the Mishnah and the Gemara. □□ **Talmudic** /-mŏodik, myŏo-/ *adj.* **Talmudical** *adj.* **Talmudist** *n.* [late Heb. *talmûd* instruction f. Heb. *lāmad* learn]

talon /tálən/ *n.* **1** a claw, esp. of a bird of prey. **2** the cards left after the deal in a card game. **3** the shoulder of a bolt against which the key presses in shooting it in a lock. **4** an ogee molding. □□ **taloned** *adj.* (also in *comb.*). [ME f. OF, = heel, ult. f. L *talus:* see TALUS[1]]

talus[1] /táyləs, tál-/ *n.* (*pl.* **tali** /-lī/) *Anat.* the ankle bone supporting the tibia. Also called ASTRAGALUS. [L, = ankle, heel]

talus[2] /táyləs/ *n.* (*pl.* **taluses**) **1** the slope of a wall that tapers to the top or rests against a bank. **2** *Geol.* a sloping mass of fragments at the foot of a cliff. [F: orig. unkn.]

tam /tam/ *n.* a tam-o'-shanter. [abbr.]

tamable /táyməbəl/ *adj.* capable of being tamed. □□ **tamability** /-bílitee/ *n.* **tamableness** *n.*

tamale /təmaálee/ *n.* a Mexican food of seasoned meat and corn flour steamed or baked in corn husks. [Mex. Sp. *tamal,* pl. *tamales*]

tamandua /təmándyŏoə/ *n.* any small Central and S. American arboreal anteater of the genus *Tamandua,* with a prehensile tail used in climbing. [Port. f. Tupi *tamanduà*]

tamarack /támərak/ *n.* **1** an American larch, *Larix laricina.* **2** the wood from this. [f. Native Amer. lang.]

tamarillo /támərílō, -reèyō/ *n.* (*pl.* **-os**) a South American shrub, *Cyphomandra betacea,* with egg-shaped red fruit. [arbitrary marketing name: cf. Sp. *tomatillo* dimin. of *tomate* TOMATO]

tamarin /támərin/ *n.* any S. American usu. insectivorous monkey of the genus *Saguinus,* having hairy crests and mustaches. [F f. Carib]

tamarind /támərind/ *n.* **1** a tropical evergreen tree, *Tamarindus indica.* **2** the fruit of this, containing an acid pulp used as food and in making drinks. [med.L *tamarindus* f. Arab. *tamr-hindī* Indian date]

tamarisk /támərisk/ *n.* any shrub of the genus *Tamarix*, usu. with long slender branches and small pink or white flowers, that thrives by the sea. [ME f. LL *tamariscus*, L *tamarix*]

tambour /támboor/ *n.* & *v.* ● *n.* **1** a drum. **2 a** a circular frame for holding fabric taut while it is being embroidered. **b** material embroidered in this way. **3** *Archit.* each of a sequence of cylindrical stones forming the shaft of a column. **4** *Archit.* the circular part of various structures. **5** *Archit.* a lobby with a ceiling and folding doors in a church porch, etc., to obviate drafts. **6** a sloping buttress or projection in some court games. **7** a rolling top or front for a desk, etc., made of strips of wood glued to a canvas backing. ● *v.tr.* (also *absol.*) decorate or embroider on a tambour. [F f. *tabor* TABOR]

tamboura /tamboorə/ *n.* *Mus.* an E. Indian stringed instrument used as a drone. [Arab. *ṭanbūra*]

tambourin /támbərin/ *n.* **1** a long narrow drum used in the Provence region of France. **2 a** a dance accompanied by a tambourin. **b** the music for this. [F, dimin. of TAMBOUR]

tambourine /támbəreén/ *n.* a percussion instrument consisting of a hoop with a parchment stretched over one side and jingling disks in slots around the hoop. □□ **tambourinist** *n.* [F, dimin. of TAMBOUR]

tame /taym/ *adj.* & *v.* ● *adj.* **1** (of an animal) domesticated; not wild or shy. **2** insipid; lacking spirit or interest; dull (*tame acquiescence*). **3** (of a person) amenable and available. **4 a** (of land) cultivated. **b** (of a plant) produced by cultivation. ● *v.tr.* **1** make tame; domesticate; break in. **2** subdue; curb; humble; break the spirit of. □□ **tamely** *adv.* **tameness** *n.* **tamer** *n.* (also in *comb.*). [OE *tam* f. Gmc]
■ *adj.* **1** tamed, docile, disciplined, obedient, domesticated, housebroken, trained, broken, *Brit.* house-trained; mild, gentle, fearless, unafraid. **2** boring, tedious, tiresome, dull, insipid, bland, lifeless, flat, vapid, prosaic, humdrum, bland, unexciting, uninspired, uninspiring, run-of-the-mill, ordinary, uninteresting, dead, wishy-washy. **3** tractable, amenable, pliant, compliant, meek, submissive, passive, mild, under a person's control *or* thumb, subdued, suppressed; unassertive, ineffectual. ● *v.* **1** break, domesticate, train, gentle, master, subdue, subjugate. **2** calm, subdue, control, mollify, humble, pacify, mute, temper, soften, curb, tone down, moderate, mitigate, tranquilize.

tameable var. of TAMABLE.

Tamil /támil, túm-, taá-/ *n.* & *adj.* ● *n.* **1** a member of a Dravidian people inhabiting South India and Sri Lanka. **2** the language of this people. ● *adj.* of this people or their language. □□ **Tamilian** /-míleeən/ *adj.* [native name *Tamiḷ*, rel. to DRAVIDIAN]

Tammany /támənee/ *n.* (also **Tammany Hall**) **1** a corrupt political organization or group. **2** corrupt political activities. □□ **Tammanyism** *n.* [orig. the name of a benevolent society in New York with headquarters at Tammany Hall, which later became the headquarters of the Democratic Party in New York]

tammy /támee/ *n.* (*pl.* **-ies**) = TAM-O´-SHANTER.

tam-o'-shanter /táməshántər/ *n.* a round woolen or cloth cap of Scottish origin fitting closely round the brows but large and full above. [the hero of Burns's *Tam o' Shanter*]

tamp /tamp/ *v.tr.* **1** ram down (concrete, pipe tobacco, etc.). **2** pack (a detonation hole) full of clay, etc., to get the full force of an explosion. □□ **tamper** *n.* **tamping** *n.* (in sense 1). [perh. back-form. f. F *tampin* (var. of TAMPION, taken as = *tamping*)]

tamper /támpər/ *v.intr.* (foll. by *with*) **1** meddle with or make unauthorized changes in. **2** exert a secret or corrupt influence upon; bribe. □□ **tamperer** *n.* **tamperproof** *adj.* [var. of TEMPER]
■ **1** interfere, meddle, tinker, mess (about *or* around), fiddle *or* fool (about *or* around), monkey (around); see also JUGGLE *v.* 3b.

tampion /támpeeən/ *n.* (also **tompion** /tóm-/) **1** a wooden

stopper for the muzzle of a gun. **2** a plug, e.g., for the top of an organ pipe. [ME f. F *tampon*, nasalized var. of *tapon*, rel. to TAP¹]

tampon /támpon/ *n.* & *v.* ● *n.* a plug of soft material used to absorb fluid, esp. one inserted into the vagina during menstruation. ● *v.tr.* (**tamponed, tamponing**) plug with a tampon. [F: see TAMPION]

tam-tam /támtam/ *n.* a large metal gong. [Hindi: see TOM-TOM]

tan¹ /tan/ *n., adj.,* & *v.* ● *n.* **1** a brown skin color resulting from exposure to ultraviolet light. **2** a yellowish-brown color. **3** = TANBARK. **4** (in full **spent tan**) tan from which the tannic acid has been extracted, used for covering roads, etc. ● *adj.* yellowish-brown. ● *v.* (**tanned, tanning**) **1** *tr.* & *intr.* make or become brown by exposure to ultraviolet light. **2** *tr.* convert (raw hide) into leather by soaking in a liquid containing tannic acid or by the use of mineral salts, etc. **3** *tr. sl.* beat; whip. □□ **tannable** *adj.* **tanning** *n.* **tannish** *adj.* [OE *tannian*, prob. f. med.L *tanare, tannare*, perh. f. Celtic]
■ *v.* **1** see SUN *v.* 2. **3** see BEAT *v.* 1. □□ **tanning** see *thrashing* (THRASH).

tan² /tan/ *abbr.* tangent.

tanager /tánəjər/ *n.* any small American bird of the subfamily Thraupidae, the male usu. having brightly-colored plumage. [mod.L *tanagra* f. Tupi *tangara*]

tanbark /tánbaark/ *n.* **1** the bark of oak and other trees, used to obtain tannin. **2** bark, esp. of oak, bruised and used to tan hides.

tandem /tándəm/ *n.* & *adv.* ● *n.* **1** a bicycle or tricycle with two or more seats one behind another. **2 a** a group of two persons or machines, etc., with one behind or following the other. **b** (in full **tandem trailer**) a truck hauling two or more trailers. **3** a carriage driven tandem. ● *adv.* with two or more horses harnessed one behind another (*drive tandem*). □ **in tandem** one behind another. [L, = at length (of time), used punningly]

tandoor /tándoor/ *n.* a clay oven. [Hind.]

tandoori /tandooree/ *n.* food cooked over charcoal in a tandoor (often *attrib.*: *tandoori chicken*). [Hind.]

Tang /tang/ *n.* **1** a dynasty ruling China 618–*c*.906. **2** (*attrib.*) designating art and artifacts of this period. [Chin. *táng*]

tang¹ /tang/ *n.* **1** a strong taste or flavor or smell. **2 a** a characteristic quality. **b** a trace; a slight hint of some quality, ingredient, etc. **3** the projection on the blade of a tool, esp. a knife, by which the blade is held firm in the handle. [ME f. ON *tange* point, tang of a knife]
■ **1** pungency, piquancy, bite, zest, zestiness, sharpness, poignancy, spiciness, nip, edge, spice, taste, flavor, savor, aroma, smell, odor, *colloq.* kick. **2 a** flavor, quality, character, feel, essence, smack, touch, taste. **b** tinge, hint, suggestion, suspicion, soupçon, trace, dab, smack, touch, smattering. **3** tab, projection, tongue, strip, shank, pin, spike.

tang² /tang/ *v.* & *n.* ● *v.tr.* & *intr.* ring, clang; sound loudly. ● *n.* a tanging sound. [imit.]

tangelo /tánjəlō/ *n.* (*pl.* **-os**) a hybrid of the tangerine and grapefruit. [TANGERINE + POMELO]

tangent /tánjənt/ *n.* & *adj.* ● *n.* **1** a straight line, curve, or surface that meets another curve or curved surface at a point, but if extended does not intersect it at that point. **2** the ratio of the sides opposite and adjacent to an angle in a right-angled triangle. ● *adj.* **1** (of a line or surface) that is a tangent. **2** touching. □ **on a tangent** diverging from a previous course of action or thought, etc. (*go off on a tangent*). **tangent galvanometer** a galvanometer with a coil through which the current to be measured is passed, its strength being proportional to the tangent of the angle of deflection. □□ **tangency** *n.* [L *tangere tangent-* touch]

/.../ pronunciation   ● part of speech
□ phrases, idioms, and compounds
□□ derivatives   ■ synonym section
cross-references appear in SMALL CAPITALS or *italics*

tangential /tanjénshəl/ *adj.* **1** of or along a tangent. **2** divergent. **3** peripheral. □□ **tangentially** *adv.*
■ **2** divergent. **3** digressive, off *or* beside the point, peripheral, irrelevant, extraneous, unrelated.

tangerine /tánjəreén/ *n.* **1** a small sweet orange-colored citrus fruit with a thin skin; a mandarin. **2** a deep orange-yellow color. [*Tangier* in Morocco]

tangible /tánjəbəl/ *adj.* **1** perceptible by touch. **2** definite; clearly intelligible; not elusive or visionary (*tangible proof*). □□ **tangibility** *n.* **tangibleness** *n.* **tangibly** *adv.* [F *tangible* or LL *tangibilis* f. *tangere* touch]
■ **1** touchable, tactile, palpable. **2** definite, material, real, physical, corporeal, solid, concrete, manifest, palpable, evident, actual, substantial, visible, seeable, discernible, intelligible, perceptible, objective, ostensive, *literary* ponderable.

tangle¹ /tánggəl/ *v. & n.* ● *v.* **1 a** *tr.* intertwine (threads or hairs, etc.) in a confused mass; entangle. **b** *intr.* become tangled. **2** *intr.* (foll. by *with*) *colloq.* become involved (esp. in conflict or argument) with (*don't tangle with me*). **3** *tr.* complicate (*a tangled affair*). ● *n.* **1** a confused mass of intertwined threads, etc. **2** a confused or complicated state (*be in a tangle; a love tangle*). [ME var. of obs. *tagle*, of uncert. orig.]
■ *v.* **1** confuse, knot, entangle, intertwist, interweave, entwine, jumble, mess up, scramble, shuffle, muddle; tangle up, mesh, snarl, twist, kink, ravel, jam, snag, intertwine, interlace. **2** (*tangle with*) wrangle with, contend with, fight with *or* against, (come into) conflict with, come *or* go up against, lock horns with, dispute with, cross swords with, disagree with, become involved with. **3** see COMPLICATE. ● *n.* **1** confusion, knot, mesh, snarl, twist, kink, entanglement, jam, snag, jumble, mess, skein, web, coil. **2** muddle, jumble, puzzle, scramble, mishmash, mix-up, hodgepodge, disorder, jungle, morass, maze, labyrinth.

tangle² /tánggəl/ *n.* any of various seaweeds, esp. of the genus *Laminaria* or *Fucus*. [prob. f. Norw. *taangel* f. ON *thöngull*]

tangly /tángglee/ *adj.* (**tanglier, tangliest**) tangled.

tango /tánggō/ *n. & v.* ● *n.* (*pl.* **-os**) **1** a slow S. American ballroom dance. **2** the music for this. ● *v.intr.* (**-oes, -oed**) dance the tango. [Amer. Sp.]

tangram /tánggram/ *n.* a Chinese puzzle square cut into seven pieces to be combined into various figures. [19th c.: orig. unkn.]

tangy /tángee/ *adj.* (**tangier, tangiest**) having a strong usu. spicy tang. □□ **tanginess** *n.*
■ see SPICY 1.

tanh /tansh, tanáych/ *abbr.* hyperbolic tangent.

tanist /tánist/ *n. hist.* the heir apparent to a Celtic chief, usu. his most vigorous adult relation, chosen by election. □□ **tanistry** *n.* [Ir. & Gael. *tánaiste* heir]

tank /tangk/ *n. & v.* ● *n.* **1** a large receptacle or storage chamber usu. for liquid or gas. **2** a heavy armored fighting vehicle carrying guns and moving on a tracked carriage. **3** a container for the fuel supply in a motor vehicle. **4** the part of a locomotive tender containing water for the boiler. **5** a reservoir. **6** *colloq.* a prison cell or holding cell. **7** = *tank top*. ● *v.* (usu. foll. by *up*) **1** *tr.* store or place in a tank. **2** *tr.* fill the tank of (a vehicle, etc.) with fuel. **3** *intr. & colloq. tr.* (in *passive*) drink heavily; become drunk. □ **tank engine** a train engine carrying fuel and water receptacles in its own frame, not in a tender. **tank farm** a tract of land with several large storage tanks. **tank farming** = HYDROPONICS. **tank top** a sleeveless, close-fitting, collarless upper garment. □□ **tankful** *n.* (*pl.* **-fuls**). **tankless** *adj.* [Gujurati *tānkh*, etc., perh. f. Skr. *tadāga* pond]

tanka /tángkə/ *n.* a Japanese poem in five lines and thirty-one syllables giving a complete picture of an event or mood. [Jap.]

tankage /tángkij/ *n.* **1 a** storage in tanks. **b** a charge made for this. **2** the cubic content of a tank. **3** a kind of fertilizer obtained from animal bones, offal, etc.

tankard /tángkərd/ *n.* **1** a tall mug with a handle and sometimes a hinged lid, esp. of silver or pewter for beer. **2** the

contents of or an amount held by a tankard (*drank a tankard of ale*). [ME: orig. unkn.: cf. MDu. *tanckaert*]

tanker /tángkər/ *n.* a ship, aircraft, or truck for carrying liquids or gases in bulk.

tanner¹ /tánər/ *n.* a person who tans hides.

tanner² /tánər/ *n. Brit. hist. sl.* a sixpence. [19th c.: orig. unkn.]

tannery /tánəree/ *n.* (*pl.* **-ies**) a place where hides are tanned.

tannic /tánik/ *adj.* **1** of or produced from tan. **2** (of wine) astringent; tasting of tannin. □ **tannic acid** a complex natural organic compound of a yellowish color used as a mordant and astringent. □□ **tannate** /-nayt/ *n.* [F *tannique* (as TANNIN)]

tannin /tánin/ *n.* any of a group of complex organic compounds found in certain tree barks and oak galls, used in leather production and ink manufacture. [F *tanin* (as TAN¹, -IN)]

tannish see TAN¹.

tanrec var. of TENREC.

tansy /tánzee/ *n.* (*pl.* **-ies**) any plant of the genus *Tanacetum*, esp. *T. vulgare* with yellow button-like flowers and aromatic leaves, formerly used in medicines and cooking. [ME f. OF *tanesie* f. med.L *athanasia* immortality f. Gk]

tantalite /tántəlīt/ *n.* a rare dense black mineral, the principal source of the element tantalum. [G & Sw. *tantalit* (as TANTALUM)]

tantalize /tántəlīz/ *v.tr.* **1** torment or tease by the sight or promise of what is unobtainable. **2** raise and then dash the hopes of; torment with disappointment. □□ **tantalization** *n.* **tantalizer** *n.* **tantalizingly** *adv.* [Gk *Tantalos* mythical king of Phrygia condemned to stand in water that receded when he tried to drink it and under branches that drew back when he tried to pick the fruit]
■ tease, taunt, provoke, torment, torture, bait, tempt, lead on, flirt with, plague, frustrate.

tantalum /tántələm/ *n. Chem.* a rare hard white metallic element occurring naturally in tantalite, resistant to heat and the action of acids, and used in surgery and for electronic components. ¶ Symb.: **Ta**. □□ **tantalic** /-tálik/ *adj.* [formed as TANTALUS with ref. to its nonabsorbent quality]

tantalus /tántələs/ *n.* **1** *Brit.* a stand in which liquor decanters may be locked up but visible. **2** a wood ibis, *Mycteria americana*. [see TANTALIZE]

tantamount /tántəmownt/ *predic.adj.* (foll. by *to*) equivalent to (*was tantamount to a denial*). [f. obs. verb f. It. *tanto montare* amount to so much]
■ (*tantamount to*) amounting to, as good as, virtually the same as, (pretty) much the same as, equal to, equivalent to, like, comparable to, commensurate with.

tantivy /tantívee/ *n. & adj. archaic* ● *n.* (*pl.* **-ies**) **1** a hunting cry. **2** a swift movement; a gallop or rush. ● *adj.* swift. [17th c.: perh. an imit. of hoofbeats]

tant mieux /taan myő/ *int.* so much the better. [F]

tant pis /taan pée/ *int.* so much the worse. [F]

tantra /tántrə, tún-/ *n.* any of a class of Hindu or Buddhist mystical and magical writings. □□ **tantric** *adj.* **tantrism** *n.* **tantrist** *n.* [Skr., = loom, groundwork, doctrine f. *tan* stretch]

tantrum /tántrəm/ *n.* an outburst of bad temper or petulance (*threw a tantrum*). [18th c.: orig. unkn.]
■ fit (of anger *or* passion *or* temper), outburst, eruption, explosion, flare-up, storm, rage, fury, *colloq.* blowup, esp. *Brit. sl.* wax.

Taoiseach /teeshəkh/ *n.* the Prime Minister of the Irish Republic. [Ir., = chief, leader]

Taoism /tówizəm, dów-/ *n.* a Chinese philosophy based on the writings of Lao-tzu (*c.*500 BC), advocating humility and religious piety. □□ **Taoist** /-ist/ *n.* **Taoistic** /-ístik/ *adj.* [Chin. *dao* (right) way]

Taos /tows/ *n.* **1 a** a N. American people native to New Mexico. **b** a member of this people. **2** the language of this people.

tap¹ /tap/ *n. & v.* ● *n.* **1** = FAUCET 1. **2** an act of tapping a telephone, etc.; also, the device used for this. **3** *Brit.* a taproom. **4** an instrument for cutting the thread of a female

screw. ● *v.tr.* (**tapped, tapping**) **1 a** provide (a cask) with a tap. **b** let out (a liquid) by means of, or as if by means of, a tap. **2** draw sap from (a tree) by cutting into it. **3 a** obtain information or supplies or resources from. **b** establish communication or trade with. **4** connect a listening device to (a telephone or telegraph line, etc.) to listen to a call or transmission. **5** cut a female screw thread in. □ **on tap 1** ready to be drawn off by tap. **2** *colloq.* ready for immediate use; freely available. **tap root** a tapering root growing vertically downwards. **tap water** water from a piped supply. □□ **tapless** *adj.* **tappable** *adj.* [OE *tæppian* (v.), *tæppa* (n.) f. Gmc]
■ *n.* **1** faucet, spigot, cock, stopcock, seacock, spout, valve, bung, stopper, cork, spile, plug, stopple, peg. **2** wiretapping, bugging, electronic eavesdropping; wiretap, bug, listening device, electronic eavesdropper. ● *v.* **1 b** drain, draw (off), siphon off *or* out, extract, withdraw, broach. **2** sap, milk. **3 a** sap, bleed, milk, mine, use, utilize, make use of, put to use, draw on *or* upon, exploit, turn to account. **4** eavesdrop on, listen in to *or* on, wiretap, *sl.* bug. □ **on tap 1** on draft, out of the barrel *or* keg. **2** ready, available, on *or* at hand, waiting, in reserve, on call. **tap root** see ROOT¹ *n.* 1a.
tap water see WATER *n.*

tap² / tap/ *v. & n.* ● *v.* (**tapped, tapping**) **1** *intr.* (foll. by *at, on*) strike a gentle but audible blow. **2** *tr.* strike lightly (*tapped me on the shoulder*). **3** *tr.* (foll. by *against*, etc.) cause (a thing) to strike lightly (*tapped a stick against the window*). **4** select as if by tapping (*tapped for membership*). **5** *intr.* = *tap-dance v.* (*can you tap?*). ● *n.* **1 a** a light blow; a rap. **b** the sound of this (*heard a tap at the door*). **2 a** = *tap dance n.* (*goes to tap classes*). **b** a piece of metal attached to the toe and heel of a tap dancer's shoe to make the tapping sound. **3** (in *pl.*, usu. treated as *sing.*) **a** a bugle call for lights to be put out in army quarters. **b** a similar call played at a military funeral. **tap dance** *n.* a form of display dance performed wearing shoes fitted with metal taps, with rhythmical tapping of the toes and heels. ● *v.intr.* (**tap-dance**) perform a tap dance. □ **tap-tap** a repeated tap; a series of taps. □□ **tap dancer** *n.* **tap dancing** *n.* **tapper** *n.* [ME *tappe* (imit.), perh. through F *taper*]
■ *v.* **1, 2** rap, knock, dab, pat, strike, hit, peck; drum, beat. **3** knock, beat, rap, drum. ● *n.* **1** rap, knock, dab, strike, peck, pat; tapping, rapping, knocking, pecking, beat, beating, patter, pattering.

tapa¹ / taápə/ *n.* **1** the bark of a paper mulberry tree. **2** cloth made from this, used in the Pacific islands. [Polynesian]

tapa² / taápə/ *n.* (usu. *pl.*) a Spanish-style appetizer typically served with wine or beer. [Sp., = cover, lid, perh. f. Gmc]

tape / tayp/ *n. & v.* ● *n.* **1** a narrow strip of woven material for tying up, fastening, etc. **2 a** a strip of material stretched across the finishing line of a race. **b** a similar strip for marking off an area or forming a notional barrier. **3** (in full **adhesive tape**) a strip of opaque or transparent paper or plastic, etc., esp. coated with adhesive for fastening, sticking, masking, insulating, etc. **4 a** = *magnetic tape.* **b** a tape recording or tape cassette. **5** = *tape measure.* ● *v.tr.* **1 a** tie up or join, etc., with tape. **b** apply tape to. **2** (foll. by *off*) seal or mark off an area or thing with tape. **3** record on magnetic tape. **4** measure with tape. □ **break the tape** win a race. **have** (or **get**) **a person** or **thing taped** *Brit. colloq.* understand a person or thing fully. **on tape** recorded on magnetic tape. **tape deck** an audio device for playing and usu. recording magnetic tape. **tape measure** a strip of tape or thin flexible metal marked for measuring lengths. **tape-record** record (sounds) on magnetic tape. **tape recorder** apparatus for recording sounds on magnetic tape and afterwards reproducing them. **tape recording** a recording on magnetic tape. □□ **tapeable** *adj.* (esp. in sense 3 of *v.*). **tapeless** *adj.* **tapelike** *adj.* [OE *tæppa, tæppe*, of unkn. orig.]
■ *n.* **1** strip, band, fillet, stripe, strap, binding, belt, ribbon, braid. **4 b** (tape) recording, reel, spool, cassette, video, videotape. ● *v.* **1** strap, band, bind; fasten, fix, join, seal, stick. **3** record, tape-record, video, videotape.

taper / taýpər/ *n. & v.* ● *n.* **1** a wick coated with wax, etc.,

for lighting fires, candles, etc. **2** a slender candle. ● *v.* (often foll. by *off*) **1** *intr. & tr.* diminish or reduce in thickness toward one end. **2** *tr. & intr.* make or become gradually less. [OE *tapur, -or, -er* wax candle, f. L PAPYRUS, whose pith was used for candle wicks]
■ *n.* **1** see LIGHT¹ *n.* 7. ● *v.* **1** narrow (down), thin, diminish, attenuate. **2** taper off, diminish, reduce, thin out, wind down, decrease, fade, lessen, peter out, tail off, wane, subside, let up, slacken, die away *or* down *or* off *or* out, decline, slow (down *or* up), weaken, abate, ebb, slump, drop (off), fall (off), plummet.

tapestry / tápistree/ *n.* (*pl.* **-ies**) **1 a** a thick textile fabric in which colored weft threads are woven to form pictures or designs. **b** embroidery imitating this, usu. in wools on canvas. **c** a piece of such embroidery. **2** events or circumstances, etc., compared with a tapestry in being intricate, interwoven, etc. (*life's rich tapestry*). □□ **tapestried** *adj.* [ME, alt. f. *tapissery* f. OF *tapisserie* f. *tapissier* tapestry worker or *tapisser* to carpet, f. *tapis*: see TAPIS]

tapetum / tápéètəm/ *n.* a membranous layer of the choroid membrane in the eyes of certain mammals, e.g., cats. [LL f. L *tapete* carpet]

tapeworm / táypwərm/ *n.* any flatworm of the class Cestoda, with a body like segmented tape, living as a parasite in the intestines.

tapioca / tápeeókə/ *n.* a starchy substance in hard white grains obtained from cassava and used for puddings, etc. [Tupi-Guarani *tipioca* f. *tipi* dregs + *og, ok* squeeze out]

tapir / táypər, təpeér/ *n.* any nocturnal hoofed mammal of the genus *Tapirus*, native to Central and S. America and Malaysia, having a short flexible protruding snout used for feeding on vegetation. □□ **tapiroid** *adj. & n.* [Tupi *tapira*]

tapis / tápee/ *n.* a covering or tapestry. □ **on the tapis** (of a subject) under consideration or discussion. [ME, a kind of cloth, f. OF *tapiz* f. LL *tapetium* f. Gk *tapétion* dimin. of *tapēs tapētos* tapestry]

tapotement / təpótmənt/ *n. Med.* rapid and repeated striking of the body as massage treatment. [F f. *tapoter* tap]

tapper see TAP².

tappet / tápit/ *n.* a lever or projecting part used in machinery to give intermittent motion, often in conjunction with a cam. [app. f. TAP² + -ET¹]

taproom / táprōōm, -rŏŏm/ *n.* a room in which alcoholic drinks are available on tap; a barroom.

tapster / tápstər/ *n.* a bartender. [OE *tæppestre* orig. fem. (as TAP¹, -STER)]

tapu / taápōō/ *n. & adj. NZ* = TABOO. [Maori]

tar¹ / taar/ *n. & v.* ● *n.* **1** a dark, thick, flammable liquid distilled from wood or coal, etc., and used as a preservative of wood and iron, in making roads, as an antiseptic, etc. **2** a similar substance formed in the combustion of tobacco, etc. ● *v.tr.* (**tarred, tarring**) cover with tar. □ **tar and feather** smear with tar and then cover with feathers as a punishment. **tarred with the same brush** having the same faults. [OE *te(o)ru* f. Gmc, rel. to TREE]

tar² / taar/ *n. colloq.* a sailor. [abbr. of TARPAULIN]

taradiddle / táradid'l/ *n.* (also **tarradiddle**) *colloq.* **1** a petty lie. **2** pretentious nonsense. [18th c.: cf. DIDDLE]
■ **2** see NONSENSE.

tarantella / táræntélə/ *n.* (also **tarantelle** /-tél/) **1** a rapid whirling S. Italian dance. **2** the music for this. [It., f. *Taranto* in Italy (because the dance was once thought to be a cure for a tarantula bite): cf. TARANTISM]

tarantism / táræntizəm/ *n. hist.* dancing mania, esp. that originating in S. Italy among those who had (actually or supposedly) been bitten by a tarantula. [mod.L *tarantismus*, It. *tarantismo* f. *Taranto* in S. Italy f. L *Tarentum*]

tarantula / təránchələ/ *n.* **1** any large, hairy, tropical spider of the family Theraphosidae. **2** a large black S. European spider, *Lycosa tarentula*, whose bite was formerly held to cause tarantism. [med.L f. It. *tarantola* (as TARANTISM)]

taraxacum /təráksəkəm/ *n.* **1** any composite plant of the genus *Taraxacum*, including the dandelion. **2** a tonic, etc., prepared from the dried roots of this. [med.L f. Arab. *ṭarakšakūk* f. Pers. *talk* bitter + *chakūk* purslane]

tarboosh /taarboŏsh/ *n.* a cap like a fez, sometimes worn as part of a turban. [Egypt. Arab. *ṭarbūš*, ult. f. Pers. *sar-būš* head cover]

Tardenoisian /taard'nóyzeeən/ *n.* & *adj. Archaeol.* ● *n.* a Mesolithic culture using small flint implements. ● *adj.* of or relating to this culture. [*Tardenois* in NE France, where remains of it were found]

tardigrade /taárdigrayd/ *n.* & *adj.* ● *n.* any minute fresh-water animal of the phylum Tardigrada, having a short plump body and four pairs of short legs. Also called *water bear.* ● *adj.* of or relating to this phylum. [F *tardigrade* f. L *tardigradus* f. *tardus* slow + *gradi* walk]

tardy /taárdee/ *adj.* (**tardier, tardiest**) **1** slow to act or come or happen. **2** delaying or delayed beyond the right or expected time. □□ **tardily** *adv.* **tardiness** *n.* [F *tardif, tardive* ult. f. L *tardus* slow]

■ **1** slow, dilatory, belated, slack, retarded, sluggish, reluctant, indolent, lackadaisical, listless, phlegmatic, slothful, lethargic, languid. **2** late, unpunctual, delayed, behind schedule, overdue, behindhand; belated.
□□ **tardily** see SLOW *adv.*

tare[1] /tair/ *n.* **1** vetch, esp. as a weed or fodder. **2** (in *pl.*) *Bibl.* an injurious grain weed (Matt. 13:24-30). [ME: orig. unkn.]

tare[2] /tair/ *n.* **1** an allowance made for the weight of the packing or wrapping around goods. **2** the weight of a motor vehicle without its fuel or load. □ **tare and tret** the arithmetical rule for computing a tare. [ME f. F, = deficiency, tare, f. med.L *tara* f. Arab. *ṭarḥa* what is rejected f. *ṭaraha* reject]

targe /taarj/ *n. archaic* = TARGET *n.* 5. [ME f. OF]

target /taárgit/ *n.* & *v.* ● *n.* **1** a mark or point fired or aimed at, esp. a round or rectangular object marked with concentric circles. **2** a person or thing aimed at, or exposed to gunfire, etc. (*they were an easy target*). **3** (also *attrib.*) an objective or result aimed at (*our export targets; target date*). **4** a person or thing against whom criticism, abuse, etc., is or may be directed. **5** *archaic* a shield or buckler, esp. a small round one. ● *v.tr.* (**targeted, targeting**) **1** identify or single out (a person or thing) as an object of attention or attack. **2** aim or direct (*missiles targeted on major cities; should target our efforts where needed*). □□ **targetable** *adj.* [ME, dimin. of ME and OF *targe* shield]

■ *n.* **1, 3** goal, mark, object, objective, aim, end. **4** butt, quarry, prey, victim, object. ● *v.* **1** see SINGLE *v.* **2** see DIRECT *v.* 4.

tariff /tárif/ *n.* & *v.* ● *n.* **1** a table of fixed charges. **2 a** a duty on a particular class of imports or exports. **b** a list of duties or customs to be paid. **3** esp. *Brit.* standard charges agreed between insurers, etc. ● *v.tr.* subject (goods) to a tariff. [F *tarif* f. It. *tariffa* f. Turk. *tarife* f. Arab. *ta'rīf*(a) f. *'arrafa* notify]

■ *n.* **1** schedule (of charges), price list. **2 a** tax, assessment, duty, excise, levy, impost, toll. ● *v.* tax, impose or levy a tax on.

tarlatan /taárlət'n/ *n.* a thin, stiff, open-weave muslin. [F *tarlatane*, prob. of Ind. orig.]

Tarmac /taármak/ *n.* & *v. propr.* **1** = TARMACADAM. **2** a surface made of this, e.g., a runway. ● *v.tr.* (**tarmac**) (**tarmacked, tarmacking**) apply tarmacadam to. [abbr.]

tarmacadam /taárməkádəm/ *n.* a material of stone or slag bound with tar, used in paving roads, etc. [TAR[1] + MACADAM]

tarn /taarn/ *n.* a small mountain lake. [ME *terne, tarne* f. ON]

tarnation /taarnáyshən/ *int.* esp. *dial. sl.* damn; blast. [alt. of DAMNATION, *darnation*]

■ see BOTHER *int.*

tarnish /taárnish/ *v.* & *n.* ● *v.* **1** *tr.* lessen or destroy the luster of (metal, etc.). **2** *tr.* impair (one's reputation, etc.). **3** *intr.* (of metal, etc.) lose luster. ● *n.* **1 a** a loss of luster. **b** a film of color formed on an exposed surface of a mineral

or metal. **2** a blemish; a stain. □□ **tarnishable** *adj.* [F *ternir* f. *terne* dark]

■ *v.* **1, 3** dull, blacken, stain, discolor. **2** sully, disgrace, taint, blacken, blemish, stain, blot, soil, spot, smirch, besmirch, dirty, contaminate, defame, injure, spoil, ruin, mar, damage, harm, hurt, stigmatize, debase, degrade, denigrate, dishonor. ● *n.* **2** see DISCREDIT *n.* 1.

taro /taáro͞, táro͞/ *n.* (*pl.* **-os**) a tropical plant of the arum family, *Colocasia esculenta*, with tuberous roots used as food. Also called EDDO. [Polynesian]

tarot /táro͞, tərő̄/ *n.* **1** (in *sing.* or *pl.*) **a** any of several games played with a pack of cards having five suits, the last of which is a set of permanent trumps. **b** a similar pack used in fortune-telling. **2 a** any of the trump cards. **b** any of the cards from a fortune-telling pack. [F *tarot*, It. *tarocchi*, of unkn. orig.]

tarp /taarp/ *n. colloq.* tarpaulin. [abbr.]

tarpan /taárpan/ *n.* an extinct N. European primitive wild horse. [Kirghiz Tartar]

tarpaulin /taarpáwlin, taárpə-/ *n.* **1** heavy-duty waterproof cloth, esp. of tarred canvas or heavy plastic. **2** a sheet or covering of this. **3 a** a sailor's tarred or oilskin hat. **b** *archaic* a sailor. [prob. f. TAR[1] + PALL[1] + -ING[1]]

tarpon /taárpon/ *n.* **1** a large silvery fish, *Tarpon atlanticus*, common in the tropical Atlantic. **2** a similar fish, *Megalops cyprinoides*, of the Pacific ocean. [Du. *tarpoen*, of unkn. orig.]

tarradiddle var. of TARADIDDLE.

tarragon /tárəgon/ *n.* a bushy herb, *Artemisia dracunculus*, with leaves used to flavor salads, stuffings, vinegar, etc. [= med.L *tarchon* f. med. Gk *tarkhōn*, perh. through Arab. f. Gk *drakōn* dragon]

tarry[1] /taáree/ *adj.* (**tarrier, tarriest**) of or like or smeared with tar. □□ **tarriness** *n.*

tarry[2] /táree/ *v.intr.* (**-ies, -ied**) *archaic* or *literary* **1** defer coming or going. **2** linger; stay; wait. **3** be tardy. □□ **tarrier** *n.* [ME: orig. uncert.]

■ **1** delay, pause, wait, linger, loiter, stall, procrastinate, dawdle, dally, temporize, hang back *or* about *or* (a)round, *colloq.* hang on, dilly-dally. **2** remain, sojourn, stay, stop, rest, linger, wait, bide one's time, settle, *archaic* or *dial.* bide.

tarsal /taársəl/ *adj.* & *n.* ● *adj.* of or relating to the bones in the ankle. ● *n.* a tarsal bone. [TARSUS + -AL]

tarsi *pl.* of TARSUS.

tarsi- /taársee/ *comb. form* (also **tarso-** /taárso͞/) tarsus.

tarsia /taárseeə/ *n.* = INTARSIA. [It.]

tarsier /taárseeər/ *n.* any small, large-eyed, arboreal, nocturnal primate of the genus *Tarsius*, native to Borneo, the Philippines, etc., with a long tail and long hind legs used for leaping from tree to tree. [F (as TARSUS), from the structure of its foot]

tarso- *comb. form* var. of TARSI-.

tarsus /taársəs/ *n.* (*pl.* **tarsi** /-sī, -see/) **1 a** the group of bones forming the ankle and upper foot. **b** the shank of a bird's leg. **c** the terminal segment of a limb in insects. **2** the fibrous connective tissue of the eyelid. [mod.L f. Gk *tarsos* flat of the foot, rim of the eyelid]

tart[1] /taart/ *n.* **1** a small pie containing jam, fruit, etc., having no upper crust. **2** a pie with a fruit or sweet filling. □□ **tartlet** *n.* [ME f. OF *tarte* = med.L *tarta*, of unkn. orig.]

■ **1** tartlet, pastry, flan, quiche. **2** pie, turnover, patty, pasty.

tart[2] /taart/ *n.* & *v.* ● *n. sl.* **1** a prostitute; a promiscuous woman. **2** *sl. offens.* a girl or woman. ● *v.* (foll. by *up*) *colloq.* **1** *tr.* (usu. *refl.*) dress (oneself or a thing) up, esp. flashily or gaudily. **2** *intr.* dress up gaudily. [prob. abbr. of SWEETHEART]

■ *n.* **1** streetwalker, prostitute, fallen woman, trollop, *fille de joie*, call girl, loose woman, drab, demimondaine, woman of ill repute, lady of the night, lady of easy virtue, *archaic* trull, demirep, harlot, *archaic or rhet.* strumpet, *colloq.* floozy, vamp, *derog.* hussy, whore, slut, jade, *literary* doxy, wanton, courtesan, *sl.* hooker, working girl, *sl. derog.* tramp. ● *v.* **1** see DECORATE 1; (*tart oneself up*) see PRIMP 2. **2** see PRIMP 2.

tart³ /taart/ *adj.* **1** sharp or acid in taste. **2** (of a remark, etc.) cutting; bitter. □□ **tartly** *adv.* **tartness** *n.* [OE *teart*, of unkn. orig.]

■ **1** sour, acidic, acidulous, acidulated, lemony, citrous, vinegary, acetic, acetous; sharp, tangy, astringent, acerb, acerbic, acrid, bitter, pungent, piquant, harsh. **2** biting, bitter, caustic, acid, corrosive, mordant, astringent, acrimonious, trenchant, harsh, scathing, stinging, acerbic, incisive, cutting, keen, sharp, barbed, nasty, curmudgeonly, testy, crusty, abusive, virulent, sarcastic, sardonic, satiric(al), vicious, cynical.

tartan¹ /taárt'n/ *n.* **1** a pattern of colored stripes crossing at right angles, esp. the distinctive plaid worn by the Scottish Highlanders to denote their clan. **2** woolen fabric woven in this pattern (often *attrib.*: *a tartan scarf*). [perh. f. OF *tertaine, tiretaine*]

tartan² /taárt'n/ *n.* a lateen-sailed single-masted ship used in the Mediterranean. [F *tartane* f. It. *tartana*, perh. f. Arab. *ṭarīda*]

Tartar /taártər/ *n. & adj.* (also **Tatar** /taátər/ except in sense 2 of *n.*) ● *n.* **1 a** a member of a group of Central Asian peoples including Mongols and Turks. **b** the Turkic language of these peoples. **2** (**tartar**) a violent-tempered or intractable person. ● *adj.* **1** of or relating to the Tartars. **2** of or relating to Central Asia E. of the Caspian Sea. □ **tartar sauce** a sauce of mayonnaise and chopped pickles, capers, etc. □□ **Tartarian** /-táireeən/ *adj.* [ME *tartre* f. OF *Tartare* or med.L *Tartarus*]

tartar /taártər/ *n.* **1** a hard deposit of saliva, calcium phosphate, etc., that forms on the teeth. **2** a deposit of acid potassium tartrate that forms a hard crust on the inside of a cask during the fermentation of wine. □ **tartar emetic** potassium antimony tartrate used as a mordant and in medicine (formerly as an emetic). □□ **tartarize** *v.tr.* [ME f. med.L f. med.Gk *tartaron*]

tartare /taartaár/ *adj.* (in full **sauce tartare**) = *tartar sauce* (see TARTAR). [F, = tartar]

tartaric /taartárik/ *adj. Chem.* of or produced from tartar. □ **tartaric acid** a natural carboxylic acid found esp. in unripe grapes, used in baking powders and as a food additive. [F *tartarique* f. med.L *tartarum*: see TARTAR]

Tartarus /taártərəs/ *n.* (in Greek mythology): **1** an abyss below Hades where the Titans were confined. **2** a place of punishment in Hades. □□ **Tartarean** /-táireeən/ *adj.* [L f. Gk *Tartaros*]

tartrate /taártrayt/ *n. Chem.* any salt or ester of tartaric acid. [F (as TARTAR, -ATE¹)]

tartrazine /taártrəzeen/ *n. Chem.* a brilliant yellow dye derived from tartaric acid and used to color food, drugs, and cosmetics. [as TARTAR + AZO- + -INE⁴]

tarty /taártee/ *adj. colloq.* (**tartier, tartiest**) (esp. of a woman) vulgar; gaudy; promiscuous. □□ **tartily** *adv.* **tartiness** *n.* [TART² + -Y¹]

Tarzan /taárzən, -zan/ *n.* a man of great agility and powerful physique. [name of the hero of stories by E. R. Burroughs, Amer. writer d. 1950]

Tas. *abbr.* Tasmania.

Tashi lama /taáshee laámə/ *n.* = PANCHEN LAMA.

task /task/ *n. & v.* ● *n.* a piece of work to be done or undertaken. ● *v.tr.* **1** make great demands on (a person's powers, etc.). **2** assign a task to. □ **take to task** rebuke; scold. **task force** (or **group**) **1** *Mil.* an armed force organized for a special operation. **2** a unit specially organized for a task. [ME f. ONF *tasque* = OF *tasche* f. med.L *tasca*, perh. f. *taxa* f. L *taxare* TAX]

■ *n.* duty, assignment, business, job, charge, function, role, office, stint, mission, (piece of) work, chore, commission, errand, undertaking; (major) effort, test (of strength), struggle, strain. ● *v.* **1** see TAX *v.* 3. □ **take to task** scold, reprimand, call to account, blame, censure, reproach, reprove, rebuke, castigate, criticize, lecture, upbraid, reprehend, *archaic or literary* chide, *colloq.* tell off. **task force 1** see FLEET¹.

taskmaster /táskmastər/ *n.* (*fem.* **taskmistress** /-mistris/) a person who imposes a task or burden, esp. regularly or severely.

■ see DISCIPLINARIAN.

Tasmanian /tazmáyneeən/ *n. & adj.* ● *n.* **1** a native of Tasmania, an island state of Australia. **2** a person of Tasmanian descent. ● *adj.* of or relating to Tasmania. □ **Tasmanian devil** a nocturnal carnivorous marsupial similar to a badger, *Sarcophilus harrisii*, now found only in Tasmania. [*Tasmania* f. A. J. *Tasman*, Du. navigator d. 1659, who discovered the island]

Tass /tas, taas/ *n. hist.* the official news agency of the former Soviet Union. [the initials of Russ. *Telegrafnoe agentstvo Sovetskogo Soyuza* Telegraphic Agency of the Soviet Union]

tass /tas/ *n. Sc.* **1** a cup or small goblet. **2** a small draft of brandy, etc. [ME f. OF *tasse* cup f. Arab. *ṭāsa* basin f. Pers. *tast*]

tassel¹ /tásəl/ *n. & v.* ● *n.* **1** a tuft of loosely hanging threads or cords, etc., attached for decoration to a cushion, scarf, cap, etc. **2** a tassellike head of some plants, esp. a flowerhead with prominent stamens at the top of a corn stalk. ● *v.* (**tasseled, tasseling** or **tasselled, tasselling**) **1** *tr.* provide with a tassel or tassels. **2** *intr.* (of corn, etc.) form tassels. **3** *tr.* remove the tassels from (corn, etc.). [ME f. OF *tas(s)el* clasp, of unkn. orig.]

tassel² /tásəl/ *n.* (also **torsel** /tór-/) a small piece of stone, wood, etc., supporting the end of a beam or joist. [OF ult. f. L *taxillus* small die, and *tessella*: see TESSELLATE]

tassie /tásee/ *n. Sc.* a small cup.

taste /tayst/ *n. & v.* ● *n.* **1 a** the sensation characteristic of a soluble substance caused in the mouth and throat by contact with that substance (*disliked the taste of garlic*). **b** the faculty of perceiving this sensation (*was bitter to the taste*). **2 a** a small portion of food or drink taken as a sample. **b** a hint or touch of some ingredient or quality. **3** a slight experience (*a taste of success*). **4** (often foll. by *for*) a liking or predilection (*has expensive tastes*; *is not to my taste*). **5 a** aesthetic discernment in art, literature, conduct, etc., esp. of a specified kind (*a person of taste*; *dresses in poor taste*). **b** a style or manner based on this (*a novel of Victorian taste*). ● *v.* **1** *tr.* sample or test the flavor of (food, etc.) by taking it into the mouth. **2** *tr.* (also *absol.*) perceive the flavor of (*could taste the lemon*; *cannot taste with a cold*). **3** *tr.* (esp. with *neg.*) eat or drink a small portion of (*had not tasted food for days*). **4** *tr.* have experience of (*had never tasted failure*). **5** *intr.* (often foll. by *of*) have a specified flavor (*tastes bitter*; *tastes of onions*). □ **a bad** (or **bitter**, etc.) **taste** *colloq.* a strong feeling of regret or unease. **taste blood** see BLOOD. **taste bud** any of the cells or nerve endings on the surface of the tongue by which things are tasted. **to taste** in the amount needed for a pleasing result (*add salt and pepper to taste*). □□ **tasteable** *adj.* [ME, = touch, taste, f. OF *tast, taster* touch, try, taste, ult. perh. f. L *tangere* touch + *gustare* taste]

■ *n.* **1 a** flavor, savor, relish, smack, tang. **2 a** sample, morsel, mouthful, bite, nibble, tidbit, esp. *Brit.* titbit; sip, sup, nip, swallow. **b** drop, soupçon, suspicion, dash, pinch, smack, touch, hint, suggestion, grain, trace, bit. **3** sample, experience. **4** palate, desire, inclination, leaning, partiality, disposition, penchant, liking, fancy, preference, predilection, fondness, appetite, relish, stomach, tolerance. **5 a** discernment, discrimination, perception, judgment, cultivation, refinement, stylishness, style, grace, polish, finesse, elegance; decorum, discretion, tactfulness, delicacy, politesse, politeness, correctness, propriety, tastefulness. **b** style, mode, fashion, manner, form, design. ● *v.* **1** savor, sample, examine, try, test. **3** sup, sip, nibble; see also TOUCH *v.* 6c. **4** experience, sample, know, have knowledge of, undergo, encounter, meet

---

/.../ **pronunciation**	● **part of speech**
□ **phrases, idioms, and compounds**	
□□ **derivatives**	■ **synonym section**
cross-references appear in SMALL CAPITALS or *italics*	

(with), come up against. **5** (*taste of*) smack of, savor of, have the flavor of.

tasteful /táystfŏŏl/ *adj.* having, or done in, good taste. ▫▫ **tastefully** *adv.* **tastefulness** *n.*

■ in good taste, decorous, refined, finished, tactful, polite, polished, restrained, correct, harmonious, fitting, fit, proper, discriminating, aesthetic, attractive, discriminative, fastidious, cultivated, *comme il faut*, elegant, stylish, graceful, charming. ▫▫ **tastefulness** see GRACE *n.* 2.

tasteless /táystlis/ *adj.* **1** lacking flavor. **2** having, or done in, bad taste. ▫▫ **tastelessly** *adv.* **tastelessness** *n.*

■ **1** insipid, bland, dull, flat, watery, weak, vapid, flavorless, wishy-washy. **2** in bad *or* poor taste, garish, gaudy, loud, kitsch(y), tawdry, meretricious, cheap, flashy, unrefined, inelegant, unaesthetic, *colloq.* tarty; improper, wrong, indecorous, indelicate, unseemly, uncultivated, uncouth, uncultured, gauche, boorish, maladroit, distasteful, unsavory, coarse, crude, gross, vulgar, base, low, tacky.

taster /táystər/ *n.* **1** a person employed to test food or drink by tasting it, esp. for quality or *hist.* to detect poisoning. **2** a small cup used by a wine taster. **3** an instrument for extracting a small sample from within a cheese. **4** a sample of food, etc. [ME f. AF *tastour*, OF *tasteur* f. *taster*: see TASTE]

tasting /táysting/ *n.* a gathering at which food or drink (esp. wine) is tasted and evaluated.

tasty /táystee/ *adj.* (**tastier, tastiest**) (of food) pleasing in flavor; appetizing. ▫▫ **tastily** *adv.* **tastiness** *n.*

■ delicious, luscious, flavorous, flavorsome, flavorful, piquant, savory, toothsome, palatable, appetizing, mouthwatering, ambrosial, *colloq.* yummy, scrumptious, *literary* delectable, sapid. ▫▫ **tastiness** see FLAVOR *n.* 1.

tat[1] /tat/ *n. Brit. colloq.* **1 a** a tatty or tasteless clothes; worthless goods. **b** rubbish; junk. **2** a shabby person. [back-form. f. TATTY]

tat[2] /tat/ *v.* (**tatted, tatting**) **1** *intr.* do tatting. **2** *tr.* make by tatting. [19th c.: orig. unkn.]

tat[3] see TIT[2].

ta-ta /taatáa/ *int. joc.* good-bye. [19th c.: orig. unkn.]

■ see GOOD-BYE *int.*

Tatar var. of TARTAR.

tater /táytər/ *n.* (also *Brit.* **tatie** /-tee/, **tato** /-tō/) *sl.* = POTATO. [abbr.]

tatler *archaic* var. of TATTLER.

tatter /tátər/ *n.* (usu. in *pl.*) a rag; an irregularly torn piece of cloth or paper, etc. ▫ **in tatters** *colloq.* (of a negotiation, argument, etc.) ruined; demolished. ▫▫ **tattery** *adj.* [ME f. ON *tötrar* rags: cf. Icel. *töturr*]

■ (*tatters*) scraps, rags, shreds, bits, pieces. ▫ **in tatters** in ruins, in shreds, in pieces, destroyed, ruined, shattered, in disarray, demolished.

tattered /tátərd/ *adj.* in tatters; ragged.

■ ragged, torn, shredded, rent, ripped, frayed, threadbare, worn out, holey, in holes, in tatters, shabby, *colloq.* tatty.

tattersall /tátərsawl/ *n.* (in full **tattersall check**) a fabric with a pattern of colored lines forming squares like a tartan. [R. *Tattersall*, Engl. horseman d. 1795: from the traditional design of horse blankets]

tatting /táting/ *n.* **1** a kind of knotted lace made by hand with a small shuttle and used as trim, etc. **2** the process of making this. [19th c.: orig. unkn.]

tattle /tát'l/ *v. & n.* ● *v.* **1** *intr.* prattle; chatter; gossip idly; speak indiscreetly. **2** *tr.* utter (words) idly; reveal (secrets). ● *n.* gossip; idle or trivial talk. [ME f. MFlem. *tatelen, tateren* (imit.)]

■ *v.* **1** gossip, prattle, prate, babble, chatter, jabber, blather, blether, *colloq.* natter, *sl. derog.* yack; blab, tittle-tattle, tell, reveal *or* divulge *or* give away secrets, *sl.* squeal. **2** see BLURT. ● *n.* talk, small talk; see also CHATTER *n.*

tattler /tátlər/ *n.* a prattler; a gossip.

tattletale /tát'ltayl/ *n.* one who tells tales or informs, esp. a child.

■ informer, tattler, telltale, talebearer, *sl.* fink, rat, squealer, stool pigeon, stoolie, *Brit. sl.* nark.

tattoo[1] /tatŏ̄/ *n.* (*pl.* **tattoos**) **1** an evening drum or bugle signal recalling soldiers to their quarters. **2** an elaboration of this with music and marching, presented as an entertainment. **3** a rhythmic tapping or drumming. [17th-c. *tap-too* f. Du. *taptoe*, lit. 'close the tap' (of the cask)]

■ see PATTER[1] *n.*

tattoo[2] /tatŏ̄/ *v. & n.* ● *v.tr.* (**tattoos, tattooed**) **1** mark (the skin) with an indelible design by puncturing it and inserting pigment. **2** make (a design) in this way. ● *n.* (*pl.* **tattoos**) a design made by tattooing. ▫▫ **tattooer** *n.* **tattooist** *n.* [Polynesian]

tatty /tátee/ *adj.* (**tattier, tattiest**) esp. *Brit. colloq.* **1** tattered; worn and shabby. **2** inferior. **3** tawdry. ▫▫ **tattily** *adv.* **tattiness** *n.* [orig. Sc., = shaggy, app. rel. to OE *tættec* rag, TATTER]

■ **1** see SHABBY 1, 2. **2** see INFERIOR *adj.* 2. **3** see TAWDRY *adj.*

tau /tow, taw/ *n.* the nineteenth letter of the Greek alphabet (Τ, τ). ▫ **tau cross** a T-shaped cross. **tau particle** *Physics* an unstable, heavy, charged elementary particle of the lepton class. [ME f. Gk]

taught *past* and *past part.* of TEACH.

taunt /tawnt/ *n. & v.* ● *n.* a thing said in order to anger or wound a person. ● *v.tr.* **1** assail with taunts. **2** reproach (a person) contemptuously. ▫▫ **taunter** *n.* **tauntingly** *adv.* [16th c., in phr. *taunt for taunt* f. F *tant pour tant* tit for tat, hence a clever rejoinder]

■ *n.* jeer, gibe, brickbat, insult, scoff, sneer, slap (in the face), *colloq.* dig. ● *v.* tease, jeer (at), twit, mock, torment, annoy, make fun *or* sport of, poke fun at, deride, heckle, sneer at, scoff at, insult, ridicule, burlesque, lampoon, guy, ride, *Austral. & NZ* chiack, *colloq.* kid, rib, needle, put down, hassle, *sl.* bug, rag.

taupe /tōp/ *n.* a gray with a tinge of another color, usu. brown. [F, = MOLE[1]]

taurine /táwreen, -rīn/ *adj.* of or like a bull; bullish. [L *taurinus* f. *taurus* bull]

Taurus /táwrəs/ *n.* **1** a constellation. **2 a** the second sign of the zodiac (the Bull). **b** a person born under this sign. ▫▫ **Taurean** *adj. & n.* [ME f. L, = bull]

taut /tawt/ *adj.* **1** (of a rope, muscles, etc.) tight; not slack. **2** (of nerves) tense. **3** (of a ship, etc.) in good order or condition. ▫▫ **tauten** *v.tr. & intr.* **tautly** *adv.* **tautness** *n.* [ME *touht, togt*, perh. = TOUGH, infl. by *tog-* past part. stem of obs. *tee* (OE *tēon*) pull]

■ **1** tight, tense, strained, stretched, rigid, stiff. **2** tense, strained. **3** neat, tidy, shipshape, spruce, (in) trim, smart, orderly, well-organized; well-disciplined, *orig. Naut.* Bristol fashion. ▫▫ **tauten** see TENSE[1] *v.* **tautness** see TENSION 1, 2.

tauto- /táwtō/ *comb. form* the same. [Gk, f. *tauto, to auto* the same]

tautog /tawtóg/ *n.* a fish, *Tautoga onitis*, found off the Atlantic coast of N. America, used as food. [Narragansett *tautauog* (pl.)]

tautology /tawtóləjee/ *n.* (*pl.* **-ies**) **1** the saying of the same thing twice over in different words, esp. as a fault of style (e.g., *arrived one after the other in succession*). **2** a statement that is necessarily true. ▫▫ **tautologic** /-t'lójik/ *adj.* **tautological** *adj.* **tautologically** *adv.* **tautologist** *n.* **tautologize** *v.intr.* **tautologous** /-ləgəs/ *adj.* [LL *tautologia* f. Gk (as TAUTO-, -LOGY)]

■ **1** repetition, redundancy, pleonasm, iteration, duplication; repetitiousness, repetitiveness, wordiness, prolixity, verbiage, verbosity, long-windedness. ▫▫ **tautological, tautologous** see REPETITIOUS.

tautomer /táwtəmər/ *n. Chem.* a substance that exists as two mutually convertible isomers in equilibrium. ▫▫ **tautomeric** /-mérik/ *adj.* **tautomerism** /-tómərizəm/ *n.* [TAUTO- + -MER]

tautophony /tawtófənee/ *n.* repetition of the same sound. [TAUTO- + Gk *phōnē* sound]

tavern /távərn/ *n.* an inn or bar. [ME f. OF *taverne* f. L *taberna* hut, tavern]

taverna /təvə́rnə/ *n.* a Greek eating house. [mod. Gk (as TAVERN)]

taw[1] /taw/ *v.tr.* make (hide) into leather without the use of tannin, esp. by soaking in a solution of alum and salt. □□ **tawer** *n.* [OE *tawian* f. Gmc]

taw[2] /taw/ *n.* **1** a large marble. **2** a game of marbles. **3** a line from which players throw marbles. [18th c.: orig. unkn.]

tawdry /táwdree/ *adj. & n.* ● *adj.* (**tawdrier, tawdriest**) **1** showy but worthless. **2** overly ornamented; gaudy; vulgar. ● *n.* cheap or gaudy finery. □□ **tawdrily** *adv.* **tawdriness** *n.* [earlier as noun: short for *tawdry lace*, orig. *St. Audrey's lace* f. *Audrey* = *Etheldrida*, patron saint of Ely]
■ *adj.* gaudy, cheap, worthless, flashy, brummagem, showy, meretricious, garish, loud, vulgar, tasteless, tinsel, tinselly, plastic, tinny, shabby, cheapjack, *colloq.* tatty, tacky. □□ **tawdriness** see GLARE[1] *n.* 3.

tawny /táwnee/ *adj.* (**tawnier, tawniest**) of an orangish or yellowish brown color. □ **tawny eagle** a brownish African or Asian eagle, *Aquila rapax.* **tawny owl** a reddish brown European owl, *Strix aluco.* □□ **tawniness** *n.* [ME f. AF *tauné*, OF *tané* f. *tan* TAN[1]]

taws /tawz/ *n.* (also **tawse**) *Sc. hist. & Ir. hist.* a leather strap with a slit end formerly used in schools for punishing children. [app. pl. of obs. *taw* tawed leather, f. TAW[1]]

tax /taks/ *n. & v.* ● *n.* **1** a contribution to government revenue compulsorily levied on individuals, property, or businesses (often foll. by *on*: *a tax on luxury goods*). **2** (usu. foll. by *on, upon*) a strain or heavy demand; an oppressive or burdensome obligation. ● *v.tr.* **1** impose a tax on (persons or goods, etc.). **2** deduct tax from (income, etc.). **3** make heavy demands on (a person's powers or resources, etc.) (*you really tax my patience*). **4** (foll. by *with*) confront (a person) with a wrongdoing, etc. **5** call to account. **6** *Law* examine and assess (costs, etc.). □ **tax-deductible** (of expenditure) that may be paid out of income before the deduction of income tax. **tax evasion** the illegal nonpayment or underpayment of income tax. **tax-exempt 1** exempt from taxes. **2** bearing tax-exempt interest. **tax-free** = *tax-exempt.* **tax haven** a country, etc., where income tax is low. **tax return** a declaration of income for taxation purposes. **tax shelter** a means of organizing business affairs, etc., to minimize payment of tax. **tax year** see *financial year.* □□ **taxable** *adj.* **taxer** *n.* **taxless** *adj.* [ME f. OF *taxer* f. L *taxare* censure, charge, compute, perh. f. Gk *tassō* fix]
■ *n.* **1** levy, impost, duty, tariff, assessment, tribute, toll, excise, customs, dues, charge, contribution, octroi, tithe, *hist.* scot, *Brit.* rate(s). **2** onus, burden, weight, load, encumbrance, imposition, drain, strain, pressure, demand, obligation. ● *v.* **1** assess, exact *or* demand a tax from, charge, impose *or* levy a tax on, mulct, tithe. **3** burden, strain, put a strain on, try, task; load, overload, overwork, stretch, exhaust, tire, drain; encumber, weigh down, saddle, pressurize, pressure.

taxa *pl.* of TAXON.

taxation /taksáyshən/ *n.* the imposition or payment of tax. [ME f. AF *taxacioun*, OF *taxation* f. L *taxatio -onis* f. *taxare*: see TAX]

taxi /táksee/ *n. & v.* ● *n.* (*pl.* **taxis**) **1** (in full **taxicab**) an automobile licensed to carry passengers for a fee and usu. fitted with a taximeter. **2** a boat, airplane, etc., similarly used. ● *v.* (**taxis, taxied, taxiing** or **taxying**) **1 a** *intr.* (of an aircraft or pilot) move along the ground under the machine's own power before takeoff or after landing. **b** *tr.* cause (an aircraft) to taxi. **2** *intr. & tr.* go or convey in a taxi. □ **taxi dancer** a dancing partner available for a fee. **taxi driver** a driver of a taxi. **taxi stand** (*Brit.* **rank**) a place where taxis wait to be hired. [abbr. of *taximeter cab*]
■ *n.* **1** taxicab, cab, hackney carriage, hack, *Brit.* minicab. ● *v.* **2** drive, chauffeur; take a taxi *or* cab.

taxidermy /táksidərmee/ *n.* the art of preparing, stuffing, and mounting the skins of animals with lifelike effect. □□ **taxidermal** /-də́rməl/ *adj.* **taxidermic** /-də́rmik/ *adj.* **taxidermist** *n.* [Gk *taxis* arrangement + *derma* skin]

taximeter /tákseemeetər/ *n.* an automatic device fitted to a taxi, recording the distance traveled and the fare payable. [F *taximètre* f. *taxe* tariff, TAX + -METER]

taxis /táksis/ *n.* **1** *Surgery* the restoration of displaced bones or organs by manual pressure. **2** *Biol.* the movement of a cell or organism in response to an external stimulus. **3** *Gram.* order or arrangement of words. [Gk f. *tassō* arrange]

taxman /táksman/ *n. colloq.* (*pl.* **-men**) an inspector or collector of taxes.

taxon /táksən/ *n.* (*pl.* **taxa** /táksə/) any taxonomic group. [back-form. f. TAXONOMY]

taxonomy /taksónəmee/ *n.* **1** the science of the classification of living and extinct organisms. **2** the practice of this. □□ **taxonomic** /-sənómik/ *adj.* **taxonomical** /-sənómikəl/ *adj.* **taxonomically** /-sənómiklee/ *adv.* **taxonomist** *n.* [F *taxonomie* (as TAXIS, Gk *-nomia* distribution)]

taxpayer /tákspayər/ *n.* a person who pays taxes.

tazza /taátsə/ *n.* a saucer-shaped cup, esp. one mounted on a pedestal. [It.]

TB *abbr.* **1** tubercle bacillus. **2** tuberculosis.

Tb *symb. Chem.* the element terbium.

T-bone /teébōn/ *n.* a T-shaped bone, esp. in steak from the thin end of a loin.

tbs. or **tbsp.** *abbr.* tablespoon.

Tc *symb. Chem.* the element technetium.

TD *abbr.* **1** touchdown. **2** Treasury Department.

Te *symb. Chem.* the element tellurium.

te var. of TI[2].

tea /tee/ *n. & v.* ● *n.* **1 a** (in full **tea plant**) an evergreen shrub or small tree, *Camellia sinensis*, of India, China, etc. **b** its dried leaves. **2** a drink made by infusing tea leaves in boiling water. **3** a similar drink made from the leaves of other plants or from another substance (*chamomile tea; beef tea*). **4 a** *Brit.* a light afternoon meal consisting of tea, bread, cakes, etc. **b** a cooked evening meal. **5** an afternoon party or reception at which tea is served. ● *v. Brit.* (**teaed** or **tea'd** /teed/) **1** *intr.* take tea. **2** *tr.* give tea to (a person). □ **tea and sympathy** *colloq.* hospitable behavior toward a troubled person. **tea bag** a small porous bag of tea leaves for infusion. **tea ball** a ball of perforated metal to hold tea leaves for infusion. **tea bread** light or sweet bread for eating at tea. **tea break** *Brit.* a pause in work, etc., to drink tea. **tea caddy** a container for tea. **tea ceremony** an elaborate Japanese ritual of serving and drinking tea, as an expression of Zen Buddhist philosophy. **tea chest** a light metal-lined wooden box in which tea is transported. **tea cozy** a cover to keep a teapot warm. **tea dance** an afternoon tea with dancing. **tea garden** a garden in which afternoon tea is served to the public. **tea leaf 1** a dried leaf of tea, used to make a drink of tea. **2** (esp. in *pl.*) these after infusion or as dregs. **tea rose** a hybrid shrub, *Rosa odorata*, with a scent resembling that of tea. **tea set** a set of china or silver, etc., for serving tea. **tea shop** esp. *Brit.* = TEAROOM. **tea towel** esp. *Brit.* a towel for drying washed dishes, etc. **tea tree** *Austral. & NZ* an aromatic evergreen flowering shrub, *Leptospermum scoparium*; the manuka. **tea wagon** (*Brit.* **trolley**) a small wheeled cart from which tea is served. [17th-c. *tay, tey*, prob. f. Du. *tee* f. Chin. (Amoy dial.) *te*, = Mandarin dial. *cha*]

teacake /teékayk/ *n.* a light, usu. sweet cake, cookie, etc., eaten at tea.

teach /teech/ *v.tr.* (*past* and *past part.* **taught** /tawt/) **1 a** give systematic information to (a person) or about (a subject or skill). **b** (*absol.*) practice this professionally. **c** enable (a person) to do something by instruction and training (*taught me to swim; taught me how to dance*). **2** advocate as a moral,

---

/. . ./ **pronunciation**	● **part of speech**
□ **phrases, idioms, and compounds**	
□□ **derivatives**	■ **synonym section**
cross-references appear in SMALL CAPITALS or *italics*	

etc., principle (*my parents taught me tolerance*). **3** (foll. by *to* + infin.) **a** induce (a person) by example or punishment to do or not to do a thing (*that will teach you to sit still*; *that will teach you not to laugh*). **b** *colloq.* make (a person) disinclined to do a thing (*I will teach you to interfere*). □ **teach-in 1** an informal lecture and discussion on a subject of public interest. **2** a series of these. **teach a person a lesson** see LESSON. **teach school** be a teacher in a school. [OE *tǣcan* f. a Gmc root = 'show']

■ **1** show, inform about, familiarize *or* acquaint with; instruct, drill, discipline, educate, school, give a person lessons, guide, train, tutor, coach, enlighten, edify, indoctrinate; communicate, demonstrate, inculcate, instill, give lessons in; teach school. **2** instill (in), din (into), inculcate (in), preach (to); imbue (with), indoctrinate (with).

teachable /teéchəbəl/ *adj.* **1** apt at learning. **2** (of a subject) that can be taught. □□ **teachability** /-bílitee/ *n.* **teachableness** *n.*

teacher /teéchər/ *n.* a person who teaches, esp. in a school. □□ **teacherly** *adj.*

■ schoolteacher, educator, instructor, professor, tutor, fellow, lecturer, reader, preceptor, master, mistress, schoolmaster, schoolmistress, coach, trainer, guide, mentor, guru, cicerone, counselor, governess, educationalist, educationist; rabbi; don, *Sc.* dominie, *archaic* doctor, *archaic or derog.* pedagogue, *old-fashioned* schoolma'm, *Brit. sl.* beak.

teaching /teéching/ *n.* **1** the profession of a teacher. **2** (often in *pl.*) what is taught; a doctrine. □ **teaching hospital** a hospital where medical students are taught. **teaching machine** any of various devices for giving instruction according to a program measuring pupils' responses.

■ **1** see EDUCATION 1a. **2** see DOCTRINE.

teacup /teékup/ *n.* **1** a cup from which tea or other hot beverages are drunk. **2** an amount held by this, about 4 fluid ounces. □□ **teacupful** *n.* (*pl.* **-fuls**).

teak /teek/ *n.* **1** a large deciduous tree, *Tectona grandis*, native to India and SE Asia. **2** its hard durable wood, used in shipbuilding and for furniture. [Port. *teca* f. Malayalam *tēkka*]

teal /teel/ *n.* (*pl.* same) **1** any of various small freshwater ducks of the genus *Anas*, esp. *A. crecca*. **2** a dark greenish blue color. [rel. to MDu. *tēling*, of unkn. orig.]

team /teem/ *n. & v.* ● *n.* **1** a set of players forming one side in a game, debate, etc. (*a hockey team*). **2** two or more persons working together. **3 a** a set of draft animals. **b** one animal or more in harness with a vehicle. ● *v.* **1** *intr. & tr.* (usu. foll. by *up*) join in a team or in common action (*decided to team up with them*). **2** *tr.* harness (horses, etc.) in a team. **3** *tr.* (foll. by *with*) match or coordinate (clothes). □ **team spirit** willingness to act as a member of a group rather than as an individual. **team teaching** teaching by a team of teachers working together. [OE *tēam* offspring f. a Gmc root = 'pull,' rel. to TOW¹]

■ *n.* **1** side, lineup, club, squad. **2** pair, group, partnership, band, gang, alliance, body, corps, crew, cadre, squad, party, troupe. **3** pair, yoke, span, duo, set, rig, tandem. ● *v.* **1** join (up *or* together), band *or* club *or* get *or* work together, join forces, unite, ally, combine, link (up), cooperate, collaborate; conspire. **3** match, pair, mate, put together, coordinate, complement. **team spirit** esprit de corps, unity, morale.

teammate /teémmayt/ *n.* a member of the same team or group.

■ see COLLEAGUE.

teamster /teémstər/ *n.* **1 a** a truck driver. **b** a member of the Teamsters Union. **2** a driver of a team of animals. □ **Teamsters Union** a shortened name referring to the International Brotherhood of Teamsters, Chauffeurs, Warehousemen, and Helpers of America.

teamwork /teémwərk/ *n.* the combined action of a team, group, etc., esp. when effective and efficient.

■ see COOPERATION.

teapot /teépot/ *n.* a pot with a handle, spout, and lid, in which tea is brewed and from which it is poured.

teapoy /teépoy/ *n.* a small three- or four-legged table esp. for tea. [Hindi *tīn*, *tir-* three + Pers. *pāī* foot: sense and spelling infl. by TEA]

tear¹ /tair/ *v. & n.* ● *v.* (*past* **tore** /tor/; *past part.* **torn** /torn/) **1** *tr.* (often foll. by *up*) pull apart or to pieces with some force (*tear it in half*; *tore up the letter*). **2** *tr.* **a** make a hole or rent in by tearing (*have torn my coat*). **b** make (a hole or rent). **3** *tr.* (foll. by *away*, *off*, etc.) pull violently or with some force (*tore the book away from me*; *tore off the cover*; *tore a page out*; *tore down the notice*). **4** *tr.* violently disrupt or divide (*the country was torn by civil war*; *torn by conflicting emotions*). **5** *intr. colloq.* go or travel hurriedly or impetuously (*tore across the road*). **6** *intr.* undergo tearing (*the curtain tore down the middle*). **7** *intr.* (foll. by *at*, etc.) pull violently or with some force. ● *n.* **1** a hole or other damage caused by tearing. **2** the torn part of a piece of cloth, etc. **3** *sl.* a spree; a drinking bout. □ **be torn between** have difficulty in choosing between. **tear apart 1** search (a place) exhaustively. **2** criticize forcefully. **tear into 1** attack verbally; reprimand. **2** make a vigorous start on (an activity). **tear oneself away** leave despite a strong desire to stay. **tear one's hair out** behave with extreme desperation or anger. **tear sheet** a page that can be removed from a newspaper or magazine, etc., for use separately. **tear to shreds** *colloq.* refute or criticize thoroughly. **that's torn it** *Brit. colloq.* that has spoiled things, caused a problem, etc. □□ **tearable** *adj.* **tearer** *n.* [OE *teran* f. Gmc]

■ *v.* **1** rip, rupture, pull apart, shred, mutilate, mangle, claw, split, divide, separate, sever, *archaic or poet.* rive, *archaic or rhet.* rend. **2 a** rip, gash, lacerate, pierce, split, slit, snag. **b** rip, pierce. **3** pull, rip, snatch, seize, wrench. **4** disrupt, divide, split, disunite, *archaic or poet.* rive, *archaic or rhet.* rend. **5** dash, fly, run, gallop, race, rush, shoot, sprint, speed, bolt, dart, flit, scurry, scuttle, career, zoom, hurry, hasten, hurtle, spurt, zip, *colloq.* whiz, scoot. ● *n.* **1** rip, rent, rupture, hole, split, slash, gore, cut, score, slit, gash, fissure, rift, laceration. **3** see BENDER. □ **tear apart 1** see SCOUR². **tear into 1** see *pitch into* (PITCH¹). **tear one's hair out** see FRET¹ 1a.

tear² /teer/ *n.* **1** a drop of clear salty liquid secreted by glands that serves to moisten and wash the eye and is shed from it in grief or other strong emotions. **2** a tearlike thing; a drop. □ **in tears** crying; shedding tears. **tear duct** a drain for carrying tears to the eye or from the eye to the nose. **tear gas** gas that disables by causing severe irritation to the eyes. **without tears** presented so as to be learned or done easily. □□ **tearlike** *adj.* [OE *tēar*]

tearaway /táirəway/ *n. Brit.* **1** an impetuous or reckless young person. **2** a hooligan.

tearful /teérfŏŏl/ *adj.* **1** crying or inclined to cry. **2** causing or accompanied with tears; sad (*a tearful event*). □□ **tearfully** *adv.* **tearfulness** *n.*

■ **1** weeping, crying, in tears, sobbing, whimpering, dewy-eyed, blubbering, sniveling, maudlin, *colloq.* weepy, *formal* lachrymose. **2** see SAD 2, SENTIMENTAL. □□ **tearfulness** see sentimentality (SENTIMENTAL).

tearing /táiring/ *adj.* extreme; overwhelming; violent (*in a tearing hurry*).

tearjerker /teérjərkər/ *n. colloq.* a story, film, etc., calculated to evoke sadness or sympathy.

tearless /teérlis/ *adj.* not shedding tears. □□ **tearlessly** *adv.* **tearlessness** *n.*

tearoom /teérŏŏm, -rŏŏm/ *n.* a small restaurant or café where tea is served.

tease /teez/ *v. & n.* ● *v.tr.* (also *absol.*) **1 a** make fun of (a person or animal) playfully or unkindly or annoyingly. **b** tempt or allure, esp. sexually, while refusing to satisfy the desire aroused. **2** pick (wool, hair, etc.) into separate fibers. **3** dress (cloth) esp. with teasels. ● *n.* **1** *colloq.* a person fond of teasing. **2** an instance of teasing (*it was only a tease*). **3** = TEASER 3. □ **tease out 1** separate (strands, etc.) by disentan-

gling. **2** search out; elicit (information, etc.). □□ **teasingly**
adv. [OE *tǣsan* f. WG]

■ *v.* **1** bait, taunt, torment, harass, bedevil, bother,
nettle, plague, chaff, pester, annoy, irritate, goad,
badger, provoke, vex, twit, tantalize, frustrate, pick on,
drive mad *or* crazy, guy, make fun of, deride, laugh at,
mock, gibe at, pull a person's leg, *colloq.* needle, rib,
have on, drive up the wall, *disp.* aggravate, *sl.* rag, razz,
bug, ride, get *or* take a rise out of, *Austral.* & *NZ sl.*
poke borak at; see also FLIRT *v.* 1. ● *n.* **1** see NUISANCE,
FLIRT *n.* □ **tease out 2** elicit, search out, coax *or* worry
or winkle *or* work out. □□ **teasingly** see *in fun* (FUN).

teasel /téezəl/ *n.* & *v.* (also **teazel, teazle**) ● *n.* **1** any plant
of the genus *Dipsacus*, with large prickly heads that are dried
and used to raise the nap on woven cloth. **2** a device used
as a substitute for teasels. ● *v.tr.* dress (cloth) with teasels.
□□ **teaseler** *n.* [OE *tǣs(e)l,* = OHG *zeisala* (as TEASE)]

teaser /téezər/ *n.* **1** *colloq.* a hard question or task. **2** a teasing
person. **3** (also **tease**) a short introductory advertisement,
etc.

teaspoon /téespoon/ *n.* **1** a small spoon for stirring tea. **2** an
amount held by this. **3** a unit of measure equal to ⅓ tablespoon, approx. 5 ml. or ⅙ fl. oz. □□ **teaspoonful** *n.* (*pl.*
-fuls).

teat /teet/ *n.* **1** a mammary nipple, esp. of an animal. **2** *Brit.*
a thing resembling this, esp. a device of rubber, etc., for
sucking milk from a bottle; a nipple. [ME f. OF *tete,* prob.
of Gmc orig., replacing TIT³]

teatime /téetim/ esp. *Brit. n.* the time in the afternoon when
tea is served.

teazel (also **teazle**) var. of TEASEL.

tec /tek/ *n. colloq.* a detective. [abbr.]

tech /tek/ *n. colloq.* **1** a technician. **2** a technical college.
[abbr.]

technetium /teknéeshəm, -sheeəm/ *n. Chem.* an artificially
produced radioactive metallic element occurring in the fission products of uranium. ¶ Symb.: **Tc**. [mod.L f. Gk *tekhn-
ētos* artificial f. *tekhnē* art]

technic /téknik/ *n.* **1** (usu. in *pl.*) **a** technology. **b** technical
terms, details, methods, etc. **2** technique. □□ **technicist**
/-nisist/ *n.* [L *technicus* f. Gk *tekhnikos* f. *tekhnē* art]

technical /téknikəl/ *adj.* **1** of or involving or concerned with
the mechanical arts and applied sciences (*technical college; a
technical education*). **2** of or relating to a particular subject or
craft, etc., or its techniques (*technical terms; technical merit*).
3 (of a book or discourse, etc.) using technical language;
requiring special knowledge to be understood. **4** due to mechanical failure (*a technical hitch*). **5** legally such; such in
strict interpretation (*technical assault; lost on a technical
point*). □ **technical hitch** a temporary breakdown or problem in machinery, etc. **technical knockout** *Boxing* a termination of a fight by the referee on the grounds of a contestant's inability to continue, the opponent being declared
the winner. □□ **technically** *adv.* **technicalness** *n.*

■ **1** mechanical, applied, industrial, polytechnic,
technological. **2, 3** complex, complicated, detailed,
intricate, esoteric, specialized. **4** mechanical.

technicality /téknikálitee/ *n.* (*pl.* **-ies**) **1** the state of being
technical. **2** a technical expression. **3** a technical point or
detail (*was acquitted on a technicality*).

■ **3** see DETAIL *n.* 1, *triviality* (TRIVIAL).

technician /teknishən/ *n.* **1** an expert in the practical application of a science. **2** a person skilled in the technique of an
art or craft. **3** a person employed to look after technical
equipment and do practical work in a laboratory, etc.

Technicolor /téknikulər/ *n.* (often *attrib.*) **1** *propr.* a process
of color cinematography using synchronized monochrome
films, each of a different color, to produce a color print. **2**
(usu. **technicolor**) *colloq.* **a** vivid color. **b** artificial brilliance. □□ **technicolored** *adj.* [TECHNICAL + COLOR]

technique /teknéek/ *n.* **1** mechanical skill in an art. **2** a
means of achieving one's purpose, esp. skillfully. **3** a manner
of artistic execution in music, painting, etc. [F (as TECHNIC)]

■ **1** technic, art, craftsmanship, artistry, craft, knack,
touch, skill, skillfulness, adroitness, adeptness,

dexterousness, facility, competence, faculty, ability,
aptitude, performance, proficiency, talent, gift, genius,
expertise. **2** technic, method, approach, manner, mode,
means, fashion, style, procedure, system, way, knack,
tack, line, modus operandi, m.o., standard operating
procedure.

technobabble /téknōbábəl/ *n. colloq.* incomprehensible
technical jargon.

technocracy /teknókrəsee/ *n.* (*pl.* **-ies**) **1** the government
or control of society or industry by technical experts. **2** an
instance or application of this. [Gk *tekhnē* art + -CRACY]

technocrat /téknəkrat/ *n.* an exponent or advocate of technocracy. □□ **technocratic** /-krátik/ *adj.* **technocratically**
adv.

technological /téknəlójikəl/ *adj.* of, using, or ascribable to
technology. □□ **technologically** *adv.*

technology /teknóləjee/ *n.* (*pl.* **-ies**) **1** the study or use of
the mechanical arts and applied sciences. **2** these subjects
collectively. □□ **technologist** *n.* [Gk *tekhnologia* systematic
treatment f. *tekhnē* art]

techy var. of TETCHY.

tectonic /tektónik/ *adj.* **1** *Geol.* relating to the deformation
of the earth's crust or to the structural changes caused by
this (see *plate tectonics*). **2** of or relating to building or construction. □□ **tectonically** *adv.* [LL *tectonicus* f. Gk *tektoni-
kos* f. *tektōn -onos* carpenter]

tectonics /tektóniks/ *n.pl.* (usu. treated as *sing.*) **1** *Geol.* the
study of large-scale structural features (cf. *plate tectonics*). **2**
Archit. the art and process of producing practical and aesthetically pleasing buildings.

tectorial /tektáwreeəl/ *adj. Anat.* **1** forming a covering. **2** (in
full **tectorial membrane**) the membrane covering the or-
gan of Corti (see CORTI) in the inner ear. [L *tectorium* a cover
(as TECTRIX)]

tectrix /téktriks/ *n.* (*pl.* **tectrices** /-triseez, -tríseez/) = CO-
VERT *n.* 2. [mod.L f. L *tegere tect-* cover]

ted /ted/ *v.tr.* (**tedded, tedding**) turn over and spread out
(grass, hay, or straw) to dry or for a bedding, etc. □□ **tedder**
n. [ME f. ON *tethja* spread manure f. *tad* dung, *toddi* small
piece]

teddy /tédee/ *n.* (also **Teddy**) (*pl.* **-ies**) (in full **teddy bear**)
a stuffed toy bear. [*Teddy,* nickname of *Theodore* Roosevelt,
US president d. 1919, famous as a bear hunter]

Teddy boy /tédee/ *n. Brit. colloq.* **1** a youth, esp. of the 1950s,
affecting an Edwardian style of dress and appearance. **2** a
young rowdy male. [*Teddy,* nickname for *Edward*]

Te Deum /tee déeəm, tay dáyəm/ **1 a** a hymn beginning *Te
Deum laudamus,* 'We praise Thee, O God'. **b** the music for
this. **2** an expression of thanksgiving or exultation. [L]

tedious /téedeeəs/ *adj.* tiresomely long; wearisome. □□ **tediously** *adv.* **tediousness** *n.* [ME f. OF *tedieus* or LL *tae-
diosus* (as TEDIUM)]

■ over long, long-drawn-out, prolonged, endless,
unending, monotonous, unchanging, changeless,
unvarying, laborious, long-winded, wearing, wearying,
wearisome, tiring, exhausting, fatiguing, tiresome,
boring, dreary, dull, dead, dryasdust, drab, colorless,
vapid, insipid, flat, uninteresting, banal, unexciting,
prosaic, prosy, soporific, humdrum, routine,
repetitious, repetitive, mechanical, soul-destroying,
automaton-like, automatic. □□ **tediousness** see TEDIUM.

tedium /téedeeəm/ *n.* the state of being tedious; boredom.
[L *taedium* f. *taedēre* to weary]

■ tediousness, monotony, changelessness, invariability,
long-windedness, wearisomeness, tiresomeness,
boredom, ennui, dreariness, dullness, drabness,
colorlessness, vapidity, insipidity, insipidness,
vapidness, banality, routine, repetitiousness.

tee¹ /tee/ *n.* = T¹. [phonet. spelling]

/.../ **pronunciation**	● **part of speech**
□ **phrases, idioms, and compounds**	
□□ **derivatives**	■ **synonym section**
cross-references appear in SMALL CAPITALS or *italics*	

tee² /tee/ *n. & v.* ● *n.* **1** *Golf* **a** a cleared space from which a golf ball is struck at the beginning of play for each hole. **b** a small support of wood or plastic from which a ball is struck at a tee. **2** a mark aimed at in bowls, quoits, curling, etc. ● *v.tr.* (**tees, teed**) (often foll. by *up*) *Golf* place (a ball) on a tee ready to strike it. □ **tee off 1** *Golf* play a ball from a tee. **2** *colloq.* start; begin. [earlier (17th-c.) *teaz*, of unkn. orig.: in sense 2 perh. = TEE¹]

tee-hee /teehee/ *n. & v.* (also **te-hee**) ● *n.* **1** a titter. **2** a restrained or contemptuous laugh. ● *v.intr.* (**tee-hees, tee-heed**) titter or laugh in this way. [imit.]

teem¹ /teem/ *v.intr.* **1** be abundant (*fish teem in these waters*). **2** (foll. by *with*) be full of or swarming with (*teeming with fish*; *teeming with ideas*). [OE *tēman*, etc., give birth to f. Gmc, rel. to TEAM]
■ **1** proliferate, be prolific, abound, be abundant. **2** (*teem with*) be prolific in, abound in *or* with, be abundant in, swarm with, be alive with, crawl with, bristle with, overflow with, be overrun with, be full of, brim with, *colloq.* be lousy with.

teem² /teem/ *v.intr.* (often foll. by *down*) (of water, etc.) flow copiously; pour (*it was teeming with rain*). [ME *tēmen* f. ON *tœma* f. *tómr* (adj.) empty]
■ pour, rain, stream (down), pelt (down), come down (in buckets), *colloq.* rain cats and dogs.

teen /teen/ *adj. & n.* ● *adj.* = TEENAGE. ● *n.* = TEENAGER. [abbr. of TEENAGE, TEENAGER]

-teen /teen/ *suffix* forming the names of numerals from 13 to 19. [OE inflected form of TEN]

teenage /teenayj/ *adj.* relating to or characteristic of teenagers. □□ **teenaged** *adj.*
■ see ADOLESCENT *adj.*

teenager /teenayjər/ *n.* a person from 13 to 19 years of age.
■ teen, adolescent, youth, boy, girl, young man, young lady *or* woman, stripling, juvenile, minor, *colloq.* kid.

teens /teenz/ *n.pl.* the years of one's age from 13 to 19 (*in one's teens*).

teensy /teensee/ *adj.* (**teensier, teensiest**) *colloq.* = TEENY. □ **teensy-weensy** = *teeny-weeny*.

teeny /teenee/ *adj.* (**teenier, teeniest**) *colloq.* tiny. □ **teeny-weeny** very tiny. [var. of TINY]
■ see TINY .

teenybopper /teeneebopər/ *n. colloq.* a young teenager, usu. a girl, who follows the latest fashions in clothes, pop music, etc.

teepee var. of TEPEE.

teeshirt var. of T-SHIRT.

teeter /teetər/ *v.intr.* **1** totter; stand or move unsteadily. **2** hesitate; be indecisive. □ **teeter on the brink** (or **edge**) be in imminent danger (of disaster, etc.). [var. of dial. *titter*]
■ **1** wobble, rock, sway, totter, waver, tremble, stagger. **2** see SEESAW *v.*

teeth *pl.* of TOOTH.

teethe /teeth/ *v.intr.* grow or cut teeth, esp. baby teeth. □ **teething ring** a small ring for an infant to bite on while teething. **teething troubles** initial difficulties in an enterprise, etc., regarded as temporary. □□ **teething** *n.*

teetotal /teetṓt'l/ *adj.* advocating or characterized by total abstinence from alcohol. □□ **teetotalism** *n.* [redupl. of TOTAL]
■ see SOBER *adj.* 2. □□ **teetotalism** see TEMPERANCE 2a.

teetotaler /teetṓt'lər/ *n.* (also **teetotaller**) a person advocating or practicing abstinence from alcoholic beverages.

teetotum /teetṓtəm/ *n.* **1** a top with four sides lettered to determine whether the spinner has won or lost. **2** any top spun with the fingers. [*T* (the letter on one side) + L *totum* the whole (stakes), for which *T* stood]

teff /tef/ *n.* an African cereal, *Eragrostis tef.* [Amharic *ṭēf*]

TEFL *abbr.* teaching of English as a foreign language.

Teflon /téflon/ *n. propr.* polytetrafluoroethylene, esp. used as a nonstick coating for kitchen utensils, etc. [*tetra-* + *fluor-* + *-on*]

tegular /tégyələr/ *adj.* **1** of or like tiles. **2** arranged like tiles. □□ **tegularly** *adv.* [L *tegula* tile f. *tegere* cover]

tegument /tégyəmənt/ *n.* the natural covering of an animal's body or part of its body. □□ **tegumental** /-mént'l/ *adj.* **tegumentary** /-méntəree/ *adj.* [L *tegumentum* f. *tegere* cover]

te-hee var. of TEE-HEE.

tektite /téktīt/ *n. Geol.* a small roundish glassy body of unknown origin occurring in various parts of the earth. [G *Tektit* f. Gk *tēktos* molten f. *tēkō* melt]

Tel. *abbr.* **1** Telephone. **2 a** Telegraph. **b** Telegraphic.

telaesthesia *Brit.* var. of TELESTHESIA.

telamon /téləmon/ *n.* (*pl.* **telamones** /-mṓneez/) *Archit.* a male figure used as a pillar to support an entablature. [L *telamones* f. Gk *telamōnes* pl. of *Telamōn*, name of a mythical hero]

tele- /télee/ *comb. form* **1** at or to a distance (*telekinesis*). **2** forming names of instruments for operating over long distances (*telescope*). **3** television (*telecast*). **4** done by means of the telephone (*teleconference*). [Gk *tēle-* f. *tēle* far off: sense 3 f. TELEVISION: sense 4 f. TELEPHONE]

telecamera /télikamrə, -mərə/ *n.* **1** a television camera. **2** a telephotographic camera.

telecast /télikast/ *n. & v.* ● *n.* a television broadcast. ● *v.tr.* transmit by television. □□ **telecaster** *n.* [TELE- + BROADCAST]
■ *n.* see BROADCAST *n.* ● *v.* see BROADCAST *v.* 1a.

telecine /télisinee/ *n.* **1** the broadcasting of a movie or film on television. **2** equipment for doing this. [TELE- + CINE]

telecommunication /télikəmyo͞onikáyshən/ *n.* **1** communication over a distance by cable, telegraph, telephone, or broadcasting. **2** (usu. in *pl.*) the branch of technology concerned with this. [F *télécommunication* (as TELE-, COMMUNICATION)]

telecommute /télikəmyo͞ot/ *v.intr.* (**telecommuted, telecommuting**) work, esp. at home, communicating electronically with one's employer, etc., by computer, fax, and telephone.

teleconference /télikónfərəns, -frəns/ *n.* a conference with participants in different locations linked by telecommunication devices. □□ **teleconferencing** *n.*

telefacsimile /télifaksímilee/ *n.* facsimile transmission (see FACSIMILE *n.* 2).

telefax /télifaks/ *n. propr.* = TELEFACSIMILE. [abbr.]

telefilm /télifilm/ *n.* = TELECINE.

telegenic /télijénik/ *adj.* having an appearance or manner that looks attractive on television. [TELEVISION + -*genic* in PHOTOGENIC]

telegony /tilégənee/ *n. Biol.* the formerly supposed influence of a previous sire on the offspring of a dam with other sires. □□ **telegonic** /téligónik/ *adj.* [TELE- + Gk -*gonia* begetting]

telegram /téligram/ *n.* a message sent by telegraph. [TELE- + -GRAM, after TELEGRAPH]
■ cable, cablegram, radiogram, radiotelegram, telex, *Brit.* telemessage, *colloq.* wire, *trade mark* Mailgram.

telegraph /téligraf/ *n. & v.* ● *n.* **1 a** a system of or device for transmitting messages or signals over a distance esp. by making and breaking an electrical connection. **b** (*attrib.*) used in this system (*telegraph pole*; *telegraph wire*). **2** (in full **telegraph board**) *Brit.* = SCOREBOARD. ● *v.* **1** *tr.* send a message to by telegraph. **2** *tr.* send by telegraph. **3** *tr.* give an advance indication of. **4** *intr.* make signals (*telegraphed to me to come up*). □ **telegraph key** a device for making and breaking the electric circuit of a telegraph system. **telegraph plant** an E. Indian plant, *Desmodium motorium*, whose leaves have a spontaneous jerking motion. □□ **telegrapher** /tilégrəfər, téligrafər/ *n.* [F *télégraphe* (as TELE-, -GRAPH)]
■ *v.* **1, 2** see TRANSMIT 1a. **4** see SIGNAL *v.* 1, 2a.

telegraphese /téligrəfeez/ *n. colloq.* or *joc.* an abbreviated style usual in telegrams.

telegraphic /téligráfik/ *adj.* **1** of or by telegraphs or telegrams. **2** economically worded. □ **telegraphic address** an abbreviated or other registered address for use in telegrams. □□ **telegraphically** *adv.*

telegraphist /tilégrəfist/ *n.* a person skilled or employed in telegraphy.

telegraphy /tiégrəfee/ *n.* the science or practice of using or constructing communication systems for the reproduction of information.

telekinesis /télikineéesis, -kī/ *n. Psychol.* movement of objects at a distance supposedly by paranormal means. □□ **telekinetic** /-nétik/ *adj.* [mod.L (as TELE-, Gk *kinēsis* motion f. *kineō* move)]
■ □□ **telekinetic** see PSYCHIC *adj.* 1b.

telemark /télimaark/ *n. & v. Skiing* ● *n.* a swing turn with one ski advanced and the knee bent, used to change direction or stop short. ● *v.intr.* perform this turn. [*Telemark* in Norway]

telemarketing /télimaárkiting/ *n.* the marketing of goods, etc., by means of usu. unsolicited telephone calls. □□ **telemarketer** *n.*

telemessage /télimesij/ *n. Brit.* a message sent by telephone or telex and delivered in written form.
■ see TELEGRAM.

telemeter /tilémitər, télimeetər/ *n. & v.* ● *n.* an apparatus for recording the readings of an instrument and transmitting them by radio. ● *v.* **1** *intr.* record readings in this way. **2** *tr.* transmit (readings, etc.) to a distant receiving set or station. □□ **telemetric** /teləmétrik/ *adj.* **telemetry** /tilémitree/ *n.*

teleology /téleeóləjee, teé-/ *n.* (*pl.* **-ies**) *Philos.* **1** the explanation of phenomena by the purpose they serve rather than by postulated causes. **2** *Theol.* the doctrine of design and purpose in the material world. □□ **teleologic** /-leeəlójik/ *adj.* **teleological** *adj.* **teleologically** *adv.* **teleologism** *n.* **teleologist** *n.* [mod.L *teleologia* f. Gk *telos teleos* end + -LOGY]

teleost /téleeost, teé-/ *n.* any fish of the subclass Teleostei of bony fish, including eels, plaice, salmon, etc. [Gk *teleo-* complete + *osteon* bone]

telepath /télipath/ *n.* a telepathic person. [back-form. f. TELEPATHY]

telepathy /təlépəthee/ *n.* the supposed communication of thoughts or ideas otherwise than by the known senses. □□ **telepathic** /télipáthik/ *adj.* **telepathically** *adv.* **telepathist** *n.* **telepathize** *v.tr. & intr.*
■ □□ **telepathic** clairvoyant, magical; see also PSYCHIC *adj.* 1b.

telephone /télifōn/ *n. & v.* ● *n.* **1** an apparatus for transmitting sound (esp. speech) over a distance by wire or cord or radio, esp. by converting acoustic vibrations to electrical signals. **2** a transmitting and receiving instrument used in this. **3** a system of communication using a network of telephones. ● *v.* **1** *tr.* speak to (a person) by telephone. **2** *tr.* send (a message) by telephone. **3** *intr.* make a telephone call. □ **on the telephone** by use of or using the telephone. **over the telephone** by use of or using the telephone. **telephone book** a book listing telephone subscribers and numbers in a particular area. **telephone booth** (or *Brit.* **box** or **kiosk**) a public booth or enclosure from which telephone calls can be made. **telephone call** = CALL *n.* 4. **telephone directory** = *telephone book.* **telephone exchange** = EXCHANGE *n.* 3. **telephone number** a number assigned to a particular telephone and used in making connections to it. **telephone operator** an operator in a telephone exchange or at a switchboard. □□ **telephoner** *n.* **telephonic** /-fónik/ *adj.* **telephonically** /-fóniklee/ *adv.*
■ *n.* **1, 2** handset, *colloq.* phone, horn, esp. *Brit. sl.* blower. ● *v.* **1, 3** call (up), esp. *Brit.* ring (up), dial, *colloq.* phone, get a person on the horn, give a person a ring *or* call, *Brit. colloq.* get a person on the blower, give a person a tinkle, *sl.* buzz, give a person a buzz. **2** see TRANSMIT 1a.

telephonist /tiléfənist/ *n. Brit.* an operator in a telephone exchange or at a switchboard.

telephony /təléfənee/ *n.* the use or a system of telephones.

telephoto /télifōtō/ *n.* (*pl.* **-os**) (in full **telephoto lens**) a lens used in telephotography.

telephotographic /télifōtəgráfik/ *adj.* of or for or using telephotography. □□ **telephotographically** *adv.*

telephotography /télifətógrəfee/ *n.* the photographing of distant objects with a system of lenses giving a large image.

teleport /télipawrt/ *v.tr. Psychol.* move by telekinesis. □□ **teleportation** *n.* [TELE- + PORT⁴ 3]

teleprinter /téliprintər/ *n.* esp. *Brit.* = TELETYPEWRITER.

TelePrompTer /télipromptər/ *n. propr.* a device used in tele-

vision and film-making to project a speaker's script out of sight of the audience (cf. AUTOCUE).

telesales /télisaylz/ *n.pl.* selling by means of the telephone.

telescope /téliskōp/ *n. & v.* ● *n.* **1** an optical instrument using lenses or mirrors or both to make distant objects appear nearer and larger. **2** = *radio telescope.* ● *v.* **1** *tr.* press or drive (sections of a tube, colliding vehicles, etc.) together so that one slides into another like the sections of a folding telescope. **2** *intr.* close or be driven or be capable of closing in this way. **3** *tr.* compress so as to occupy less space or time. [It. *telescopio* or mod.L *telescopium* (as TELE-, -SCOPE)]
■ *n.* **1** spyglass, glass; refracting telescope, reflecting telescope. ● *v.* **1** concertina, squash, crush. **3** shorten, compress, compact, abbreviate, contract, condense, summarize, précis, digest, tighten (up), boil down, abridge, abstract.

telescopic /téliskópik/ *adj.* **1 a** of, relating to, or made with a telescope (*telescopic observations*). **b** visible only through a telescope (*telescopic stars*). **2** (esp. of a lens) able to focus on and magnify distant objects. **3** consisting of sections that telescope. □ **telescopic sight** a telescope used for sighting on a rifle, etc. □□ **telescopically** *adv.*

telesoftware /télisawftwair, -sóft-/ *n.* software transmitted or broadcast to receiving terminals.

telesthesia /télis-theézhə/ *n.* (*Brit.* **telaesthesia**) *Psychol.* the supposed perception of distant occurrences or objects otherwise than by the recognized senses. □□ **telesthetic** /-thétik/ *adj.* [mod.L, formed as TELE- + Gk *aisthēsis* perception]

teletext /télitekst/ *n.* a news and information service, in the form of text and graphics, from a computer source transmitted to televisions with appropriate receivers.

telethon /télithon/ *n.* an exceptionally long television program, esp. to raise money for a charity. [TELE- + -*thon* in MARATHON]

Teletype /télitip/ *n. & v.* ● *n. propr.* a kind of teletypewriter. ● *v.* (**teletype**) **1** *intr.* operate a teletypewriter. **2** *tr.* send by means of a teletypewriter.

teletypewriter /télitípritər/ *n.* a device for transmitting telegraph messages as they are keyed, and for printing messages received.

televangelist /télivánjəlist/ *n.* an evangelical preacher who appears regularly on television to promote beliefs and appeal for funds.

televiewer /télivyōōər/ *v.tr.* a person who watches television. □□ **televiewing** *adj.*

televise /télivīz/ *v.tr.* transmit by television. □□ **televisable** *adj.* [back-form. f. TELEVISION]
■ see BROADCAST *v.* 1a.

television /télivízhən/ *n.* **1** a system for reproducing on a screen visual images transmitted (usu. with sound) by radio waves. **2** (in full **television set**) a device with a screen for receiving these signals. **3** the medium, art form, or occupation of broadcasting on television; the content of television programs.
■ **2, 3** TV, receiver, video (receiver), small screen, *colloq.* box, idiot box, tube, esp. *Brit. colloq.* telly, *Brit. colloq.* goggle-box, *sl.* boob tube.

televisual /télivízhooəl/ *adj.* esp. *Brit.* relating to or suitable for television. □□ **televisually** *adv.*

telex /téleks/ *n. & v.* (also **Telex**) ● *n.* an international system of telegraphy with printed messages transmitted and received by teletypewriters using the public telecommunications network. ● *v.tr.* send or communicate with by telex. [TELEPRINTER + EXCHANGE]
■ *v.* see TRANSMIT 1a.

tell¹ /tel/ *v.* (*past* and *past part.* **told** /tōld/) **1** *tr.* relate or narrate in speech or writing; give an account of (*tell me a story*). **2** *tr.* make known; express in words; divulge (*tell me*

/. . ./ pronunciation	● part of speech
□ phrases, idioms, and compounds	
□□ derivatives	■ synonym section
cross-references appear in SMALL CAPITALS or *italics*	

your name; *tell me what you want*). **3** *tr.* reveal or signify to (a person) (*your face tells me everything*). **4** *tr.* **a** utter (*don't tell lies*). **b** warn (*I told you so*). **5** *intr.* **a** (often foll. by *of, about*) divulge information or a description; reveal a secret (*I told of the plan; promise you won't tell*). **b** (foll. by *on*) *colloq.* inform against (a person). **6** *tr.* (foll. by *to* + infin.) give (a person) a direction or order (*tell them to wait; do as you are told*). **7** *tr.* assure (*it's true, I tell you*). **8** *tr.* explain in writing; instruct (*this book tells you how to cook*). **9** *tr.* decide; predict; determine; distinguish (*cannot tell what might happen; how do you tell one from the other?*). **10** *intr.* **a** (often foll. by *on*) produce a noticeable effect (*every disappointment tells; the strain was beginning to tell on me*). **b** reveal the truth (*time will tell*). **c** have an influence (*the evidence tells against you*). **11** *tr.* (often *absol.*) count (votes) at a meeting, election, etc. □ **tell apart** distinguish between (usu. with *neg.* or *interrog.*: *could not tell them apart*). **tell me another** *colloq.* an expression of incredulity. **tell off 1** *colloq.* reprimand; scold. **2** count off or detach for duty. **tell a tale** (or **its own tale**) be significant or revealing. **tell tales** report a discreditable fact about another. **tell (the) time** determine the time from the face of a clock or watch. **there is no telling** it is impossible to know (*there's no telling what may happen*). **you're telling me** *colloq.* I agree wholeheartedly. □□ **tellable** *adj.* [OE *tellan* f. Gmc, rel. to TALE]

■ **1** relate, narrate, recount, recite, report, chronicle. **2** say, mention, utter, state, declare, proclaim, announce, publish, broadcast, communicate, make known, report, impart, indicate, advertise, trumpet, herald, intimate, hint at, refer to, touch on, acknowledge, confess, apprise, advise, inform, let a person know, notify, acquaint a person with a thing; recount, describe, delineate, outline, portray, depict, express, put, word, explain; disclose, divulge, release, break, let a thing be known, bring to light, leak, admit, betray, blab, tattle, let out, let slip, *colloq.* get a thing off one's chest. **3** reveal, express, show, convey, communicate, signify, impart, indicate. **4 a** see SPEAK 2. **b** warn, advise, counsel, caution, forewarn, alert, inform, apprise. **5 a** unbosom oneself, unburden *or* disburden oneself, blab, tattle, talk, let the cat out of the bag, give the (whole) show away, *colloq.* spill the beans. **b** (*tell on*) denounce, tattle on, inform against, betray, report (on), sell, *archaic* delate, *colloq.* blow the whistle on, rat on, peach on *or* against, split on, *sl.* squeal on, squeak on, esp. *Brit. sl.* shop, *Brit. sl.* sneak on. **6** order, command, require, charge, direct, instruct, *archaic or literary* bid. **7** assure, swear to, promise. **8** recount, describe, delineate, detail, outline, depict; inform, instruct, explain, teach. **9** ascertain, determine, decide, perceive, understand, know; predict, prophesy, forecast, foretell, foresee; say, confirm, know for sure *or* certain, be sure *or* certain *or* positive; make out, discern, identify, recognize, distinguish, discriminate, differentiate. **10 a** be effective, have (an) effect, be noticeable, register. **b** show, reveal the truth. **c** carry weight, be influential. □ **tell apart** see DISTINGUISH 1. **tell off 1** scold, reprimand, berate, castigate, censure, take to task, upbraid, admonish, rebuke, lecture, reproach, reprove, give a person a tongue-lashing, haul over the coals, give a person a piece of one's mind, *archaic or literary* chide, *colloq.* tear into, bawl out, chew out, *Austral. & NZ colloq.* go crook on. **tell tales** tattle, tittle-tattle, gossip, blab, *colloq.* name names.

tell[2] /tel/ *n. Archaeol.* an artificial mound in the Middle East, etc., formed by the accumulated remains of ancient settlements. [Arab. *tall* hillock]

■ tumulus, mound, barrow, hillock.

teller /télər/ *n.* **1** a person employed to receive and pay out money in a bank, etc. **2** a person who counts (votes). **3** a person who tells esp. stories (*a teller of tales*). □□ **tellership** *n.*

telling /téling/ *adj.* **1** having a marked effect; striking. **2** significant. □ **telling off** esp. *Brit. colloq.* a reproof or reprimand. □□ **tellingly** *adv.*

■ effective, effectual, influential, weighty, important, powerful, forceful, potent, strong, compelling, significant, considerable, striking. □ **telling off** see REPRIMAND *n.*

telltale /téltayl/ *n.* **1** a person who reveals (esp. discreditable) information about another's private affairs or behavior. **2** (*attrib.*) that reveals or betrays (*a telltale smile*). **3** a device for automatic indicating, monitoring, or registering of a process, etc.

■ **2** (*attrib.*) see MEANINGFUL.

tellurian /teloóreeən/ *adj.* & *n.* ● *adj.* of or inhabiting the earth. ● *n.* an inhabitant of the earth. [L *tellus -uris* earth]

telluric /teloórik/ *adj.* **1** of the earth as a planet. **2** of the soil. **3** *Chem.* of tellurium, esp. with valence 6. □□ **tellurate** /télyoórət/ *n.* [L *tellus -uris* earth: sense 3 f. TELLURIUM]

tellurium /teloóreeəm/ *n. Chem.* a rare brittle lustrous silver-white element occurring naturally in ores of gold and silver, used in semiconductors. ¶ Symb.: **Te.** □□ **telluride** /télyərīd/ *n.* **tellurite** /télyərit/ *n.* **tellurous** *adj.* [L *tellus -uris* earth, prob. named in contrast to *uranium*]

telly /télee/ *n.* (*pl.* **-ies**) esp. *Brit. colloq.* **1** television. **2** a television set. [abbr.]

telpher /télfər/ *n.* a system for transporting goods, etc., by electrically driven trucks or cable cars. □□ **telpherage** *n.* [TELE- + -PHORE]

telson /télsən/ *n.* the last segment in the abdomen of crustaceans, etc. [Gk, = limit]

Telugu /téləgoō/ *n.* (also **Telegu**) (*pl.* same or **Telegus**) **1** a member of a Dravidian people in SE India. **2** the language of this people. [Telugu]

temerarious /téməráireeəs/ *adj.* reckless; rash. [L *temerarius* f. *temere* rashly]

■ see FOOLHARDY .

temerity /timéritee/ *n.* **1** rashness. **2** audacity; impudence. [L *temeritas* f. *temere* rashly]

■ **2** see EFFRONTERY.

temp /temp/ *n.* & *v. colloq.* ● *n.* a temporary employee. ● *v.intr.* work as a temp. [abbr.]

temp.[1] /temp/ *abbr.* temperature.

temp.[2] /temp/ *abbr.* in the time of (*temp. Henry I*). [L *tempore* ablat. of *tempus* time]

temper /témpər/ *n.* & *v.* ● *n.* **1** habitual or temporary disposition of mind esp. as regards composure (*a person of calm temper*). **2 a** irritation or anger (*in a fit of temper*). **b** an instance of this (*flew into a temper*). **3** a tendency to have fits of anger (*have a temper*). **4** composure or calmness (*keep one's temper; lose one's temper*). **5** the condition of metal as regards hardness and elasticity. ● *v.tr.* **1** bring (metal or clay) to a proper hardness or consistency. **2** (often foll. by *with*) moderate or mitigate (*temper justice with mercy*). **3** tune or modulate (a piano, etc.) so as to distance intervals correctly. □ **in a bad temper** angry; peevish. **in a good temper** in an amiable mood. **out of temper** angry; peevish. **show temper** be petulant. □□ **temperable** *adj.* **temperative** /-pərətiv/ *adj.* **tempered** *adj.* **temperedly** *adv.* **temperer** *n.* [OE *temprian* (v.) f. L *temperare* mingle: infl. by OF *temprer, tremper*]

■ *n.* **1** disposition, temperament, character, personality, nature, makeup, constitution; mood, humor, state *or* frame of mind. **2 a** anger, irritation, passion, rage. **b** (*temper*) tantrum, fury, fit (of pique), rage, *literary* ire, esp. *Brit. sl.* wax. **3** ill humor, ill temper, foul temper, irascibility, irritability, petulance, volatility, peevishness, huffiness, surliness, churlishness, hot temper, hotheadedness, hot-bloodedness. **4** composure, self-control, self-possession, calmness, equanimity, balance, sangfroid, coolness, *sl.* cool. ● *v.* **1** anneal, toughen, strengthen, harden. **2** modify, moderate, assuage, mollify, soften, cushion, tone down, allay, soothe, mitigate, palliate, reduce, relax, slacken, lighten, appease. **3** see MODULATE. □ **in a bad temper**, **out of temper** see ANGRY 1. □□ **tempered** see *subdued* (SUBDUE 2).

tempera /témpərə/ *n.* a method of painting using an emulsion, e.g., of pigment with egg, esp. on canvas. [It.: cf. DIS-TEMPER[1]]

temperament /témprəmənt/ n. **1** a person's distinct nature and character, esp. as determined by physical constitution and permanently affecting behavior (*a nervous temperament*; *the artistic temperament*). **2** a creative or spirited personality (*was full of temperament*). **3 a** an adjustment of intervals in tuning a piano, etc., so as to fit the scale for use in all keys. **b** (**equal temperament**) an adjustment in which the 12 semitones are at equal intervals. [ME f. L *temperamentum* (as TEMPER)]

■ **1** see DISPOSITION 1.

temperamental /témprəmént'l/ adj. **1** of or having temperament. **2 a** (of a person) liable to erratic or moody behavior. **b** (of a thing, e.g., a machine) working unpredictably; unreliable. □□ **temperamentally** adv.

■ **2 a** moody, erratic, sensitive, touchy, hypersensitive, volatile, mercurial, changeable, irascible, petulant, testy, short-tempered, hot-tempered, hotheaded, hot-blooded, excitable, explosive, capricious, impatient, ill-humored, *colloq.* on a short fuse; see also IRRITABLE 1. **b** erratic, unreliable, inconsistent, undependable, unpredictable, capricious.

temperance /témpərəns, témprəns/ n. **1** moderation or self-restraint esp. in eating and drinking. **2 a** total or partial abstinence from alcohol. **b** (*attrib.*) advocating or concerned with abstinence. [ME f. AF *temperaunce* f. L *temperantia* (as TEMPER)]

■ **1** (self-)restraint, moderation, abstemiousness, (self-)control, forbearance, (self-)discipline, continence. **2 a** teetotalism, abstinence, sobriety, nonindulgence; prohibition.

temperate /témpərət, témprət/ adj. **1** avoiding excess; self-restrained. **2** moderate. **3** (of a region or climate) characterized by mild temperatures. **4** abstemious. □ **temperate zone** the belt of the earth between the frigid and the torrid zones. □□ **temperately** adv. **temperateness** n. [ME f. L *temperatus* past part. of *temperare*: see TEMPER]

■ **1, 2** moderate, reasonable, (self-)restrained, disciplined, controlled, forbearing, reasonable, sensible, sane, rational, not excessive, composed, steady, stable, even-tempered, equable, sober, sober-minded, mild, dispassionate, unimpassioned, cool, coolheaded, unexcited, calm, unruffled, tranquil, imperturbable, unperturbed, self-possessed, quiet, serene. **3** see MILD 3. **4** abstemious, teetotal, abstinent, continent, moderate, sober, self-restrained; chaste, celibate, austere, ascetic, self-denying, puritanical. □□ **temperately** see EASY adv. **temperateness** see SOBRIETY.

temperature /témprichər/ n. **1** the degree or intensity of heat of a body, air mass, etc., in relation to others, esp. as shown by a thermometer or perceived by touch, etc. **2** *Med.* the degree of internal heat of the body. **3** *colloq.* a body temperature above the normal (*have a temperature*). **4** the degree of excitement in a discussion, etc. □ **take a person's temperature** ascertain a person's body temperature, esp. as a diagnostic aid. **temperature-humidity index** a quantity giving the measure of discomfort due to the combined effects of the temperature and humidity of the air. [F *température* or L *temperatura* (as TEMPER)]

-tempered /témpərd/ comb. form having a specified temper or disposition (*bad-tempered*; *hot-tempered*). □□ **-temperedly** adv. **-temperedness** n.

tempest /témpist/ n. **1** a violent windy storm. **2** violent agitation or tumult. [ME f. OF *tempest(e)* ult. f. L *tempestas* season, storm, f. *tempus* time]

■ **1** storm, hailstorm, rainstorm, hurricane, typhoon, tornado, cyclone, squall, thunderstorm, *Naut.* gale. **2** storm, commotion, disturbance, upheaval, disruption, furor, turbulence, ferment, tumult, agitation, perturbation, hurly-burly, disorder, outbreak, unrest, riot, chaos, uproar, brouhaha, *sl.* hoo-ha.

tempestuous /tempéschŏoͻs/ adj. **1** stormy. **2** (of a person,

emotion, etc.) turbulent; violent; passionate. □□ **tempestuously** adv. **tempestuousness** n. [LL *tempestuosus* (as TEMPEST)]

■ **1** see STORMY 1, 2. **2** stormy, wild, uncontrolled, uncontrollable, disrupting, disruptive, turbulent, tumultuous, riotous, chaotic, uproarious, boisterous, frantic, frenzied, frenetic, furious, vehement, violent, fiery, impassioned, passionate, fierce, *literary* wrathful. □□ **tempestuousness** see FURY 2.

tempi pl. of TEMPO.

Templar /témplər/ n. **1** a lawyer or law student in London. **2** (in full **Knight Templar**) *hist.* a member of a religious and military order for the protection of pilgrims to the Holy Land, suppressed in 1312. [ME f. AF *templer*, OF *templier*, med.L *templarius* (as TEMPLE[1])]

template /témplit, -playt/ n. (also **templet**) **1 a** a pattern or gauge, usu. a piece of thin board or metal plate, used as a guide in cutting or drilling metal, stone, wood, etc. **b** a flat card or plastic pattern esp. for cutting cloth for patchwork, etc. **2** a timber or plate used to distribute the weight in a wall or under a beam, etc. **3** *Biochem.* the molecular pattern governing the assembly of a protein, etc. [orig. *templet*: prob. f. TEMPLE[3] + -ET[1], alt. after *plate*]

■ **1** pattern, mold, guide, model, die.

temple[1] /témpəl/ n. **1** a building devoted to the worship, or regarded as the dwelling place, of a god or gods or other objects of religious reverence. **2** *hist.* any of three successive religious buildings of the Jews in Jerusalem. **3** a Reform or Conservative synagogue. **4** a place of Christian public worship, esp. a Protestant church in France. **5** any place in which God is regarded as residing, as the body of a Christian (I Cor. 6:19). □ **temple block** a percussion instrument consisting of a hollow block of wood that is struck with a stick. [OE *temp(e)l*, reinforced in ME by OF *temple*, f. L *templum* open or consecrated space]

■ **1** place *or* house of worship, holy place, house of God, church, synagogue, mosque, pagoda, stupa, tope, gurdwara, cathedral, sanctuary, chapel, tabernacle, shrine.

temple[2] /témpəl/ n. the flat part of either side of the head between the forehead and the ear. [ME f. OF ult. f. L *tempora* pl. of *tempus*]

temple[3] /témpəl/ n. a device in a loom for keeping the cloth stretched. [ME f. OF, orig. the same word as TEMPLE[2]]

templet var. of TEMPLATE.

tempo /témpō/ n. (pl. **-os** or **tempi** /-pee/) **1** *Mus.* the speed at which music is or should be played, esp. as characteristic (*waltz tempo*). **2** the rate of motion or activity (*the tempo of the war is quickening*). [It. f. L *tempus* time]

■ **1** cadence, rhythm, beat, time, pulse, meter, measure. **2** pace, speed, rate.

temporal /témpərəl, témprəl/ adj. **1** of worldly as opposed to spiritual affairs; of this life; secular. **2** of or relating to time. **3** *Gram.* relating to or denoting time or tense (*temporal conjunction*). **4** of the temples of the head (*temporal artery*; *temporal bone*). □ **temporal power** the power of an ecclesiastic, esp. the Pope, in temporal matters. □□ **temporally** adv. [ME f. OF *temporel* or f. L *temporalis* f. *tempus -oris* time]

■ **1** earthly, terrestrial, terrene, mundane, worldly, nonspiritual, nonclerical, lay, laic(al), secular, nonreligious, nonecclesiastic(al), material, civil, profane, fleshly, mortal.

temporality /témpərálitee/ n. (pl. **-ies**) **1** temporariness. **2** (usu. in pl.) a secular possession, esp. the properties and revenues of a religious corporation or an ecclesiastic. [ME f. LL *temporalitas* (as TEMPORAL)]

temporary /témpəréree/ adj. & n. ● adj. lasting or meant to last only for a limited time (*temporary buildings*; *temporary relief*). ● n. (pl. **-ies**) a person employed temporarily (cf.

/. . ./	**pronunciation**	● **part of speech**
□	**phrases, idioms, and compounds**	
□□	**derivatives**	■ **synonym section**
	cross-references appear in SMALL CAPITALS or *italics*	

TEMP). □□ **temporarily** /-pəráirilee/*adv.* **temporariness** *n.* [L *temporarius* f. *tempus -oris* time]
■ *adj.* impermanent, makeshift, stopgap, standby, provisional, acting, interim; *pro tempore*, ad interim, transitory, transient, fleeting, fugitive, passing, ephemeral, evanescent, brief, short-lived, momentary, *colloq.* pro tem. ● *n.* stopgap, stand-in, *colloq.* temp. □□ **temporarily** for the time being, in the interim, ad interim, *pro tempore*, (in *or* for the) meantime, (in *or* for the) meanwhile, for now; briefly, fleetingly, for a (short *or* little) while, for a (short *or* little) time, for the moment, *colloq.* pro tem.

temporize /témpəriz/ *v.intr.* **1** avoid committing oneself so as to gain time; employ delaying tactics. **2** comply temporarily with the requirements of the occasion; adopt a time-serving policy. □□ **temporization** *n.* **temporizer** *n.* [F *temporiser* bide one's time f. med. L *temporizare* delay f. *tempus -oris* time]
■ **1** see PROCRASTINATE .

tempt /tempt/ *v.tr.* **1** entice or incite (a person) to do a wrong or forbidden thing (*tempted him to steal it*). **2** allure; attract. **3** risk provoking (esp. an abstract force or power) (*would be tempting fate to try it*). **4** *archaic* make trial of; try the resolution of (*God did tempt Abraham*). □ **be tempted to** be strongly disposed to (*I am tempted to question this*). □□ **temptable** *adj.* **temptability** /témptəbílitee/ *n.* [ME f. OF *tenter, tempter* test f. L *temptare* handle, test, try]
■ **1** lead, induce, entice, incite, persuade, prompt, move, incline, dispose, coax, cajole, inveigle. **2** attract, entice, lure, allure, draw (in), invite, lead on, whet a person's appetite, seduce, captivate. **3** provoke, dare, (put to the) test. **4** try, test, *archaic* prove.

temptation /temptáyshən/ *n.* **1 a** the act or an instance of tempting; the state of being tempted; incitement esp. to wrongdoing. **b** (**the Temptation**) the tempting of Christ by the Devil (see Matt. 4). **2** an attractive thing or course of action. **3** *archaic* putting to the test. [ME f. OF *tentacion, temptacion* f. L *temptatio -onis* (as TEMPT)]
■ **1 a** enticement, leading on, seduction, captivation, persuasion, coaxing, cajoling, incitement. **2** enticement, allurement, invitation, attraction, draw, lure, inducement, incentive, snare, pull, bait, *sl.* come-on.

tempter /témptər/ *n.* (*fem.* **temptress** /-tris/) **1** a person who tempts. **2** (**the Tempter**) the Devil. [ME f. OF *tempteur* f. eccl.L *temptator -oris* (as TEMPT)]
■ **1** charmer, seducer, enchanter; (*temptress*) seductress, siren, femme fatale, coquette, flirt, enchantress, Circe, *colloq.* sexpot, vamp, *sl.* foxy lady, fox. **2** see DEVIL *n.* 1, 2.

tempting /témpting/ *adj.* **1** attractive; inviting. **2** enticing to evil. □□ **temptingly** *adv.*
■ **1** seductive, enticing, inviting, alluring, captivating, attractive, tantalizing, titillating, exciting, appealing, irresistible; (*of food*) appetizing, mouthwatering, delicious, savory, succulent, luscious, toothsome, *literary* delectable.

tempura /tempŏŏrə/ *n.* a Japanese dish of fish, shellfish, or vegetables, dipped in batter and deep-fried. [Jap.]

ten /ten/ *n. & adj.* ● *n.* **1** one more than nine. **2** a symbol for this (10, x, X). **3** a size, etc., denoted by ten. **4** the time of ten o'clock (*is it ten yet?*). **5** a playing card with ten pips. **6** a ten-dollar bill. **7** a set of ten. ● *adj.* **1** that amount to ten. **2** (as a round number) several (*ten times as easy*). □ **the Ten Commandments** see COMMANDMENT. **ten-gallon hat** a cowboy's large wide-brimmed hat. [OE *tīen, tēn* f. Gmc]

ten. *abbr.* **1** tenor. **2** tenuto.

tenable /ténəbəl/ *adj.* **1** that can be maintained or defended against attack or objection (*a tenable position; a tenable theory*). **2** (foll. by *for, by*) (of an office, etc.) that can be held for (a specified period) or by (a specified class of person). □□ **tenability** *n.* **tenableness** *n.* [F f. *tenir* hold f. L *tenēre*]
■ **1** defensible, supportable, justifiable, maintainable, sustainable, workable, viable, defendable, plausible, reasonable, rational, arguable, believable, credible, creditable, imaginable, conceivable, possible.

tenace /ténáys/ *n.* **1** two cards, one ranking immediately above, and the other immediately below, a card held by an opponent. **2** the holding of such cards. [F f. Sp. *tenaza*, lit. 'pincers']

tenacious /tináyshəs/ *adj.* **1** (often foll. by *of*) keeping a firm hold of property, principles, life, etc.; not readily relinquishing. **2** (of memory) retentive. **3** holding fast. **4** strongly cohesive. **5** persistent; resolute. **6** adhesive; sticky. □□ **tenaciously** *adv.* **tenaciousness** *n.* **tenacity** /tinásitee/ *n.* [L *tenax -acis* f. *tenēre* hold]
■ **1** (*tenacious of*) clinging to, grasping, maintaining, keeping (up), staying with, retentive of, persisting *or* persistent in, retaining. **2** retentive, good. **3** firm, strong, sturdy, rigid, fast, secure, tight. **4** cohesive, strong, tough. **5** persistent, dogged, unfaltering, pertinacious, unswerving, determined, diligent, resolute, staunch, stalwart, steadfast, strong, sturdy, unwavering, strong-willed, strong-minded, unshaken, unshakable, obstinate, intransigent, stubborn, adamant, obdurate, refractory, immovable, inflexible, rigid, firm, unyielding, uncompromising. **6** adhesive, sticky, clinging; gummy, gluey, mucilaginous, glutinous, viscous, viscid. □□ **tenaciousness, tenacity** persistence, doggedness, perseverance, pertinacity, determination, grit, diligence, resoluteness, resolution, purposefulness, resolve, staunchness, steadfastness, stamina, assiduity, sedulousness, strength, strong-mindedness, unshakability, obstinacy, intransigence, stubbornness, obduracy, inflexibility, rigidity, firmness, uncompromisingness, *colloq.* sand; cohesiveness, power, toughness, resilience; adhesiveness, stickiness, clinginess, gumminess, glueyness, mucilaginousness, glutinousness, viscousness, viscosity, viscidity.

tenaculum /tənákyələm/ *n.* (*pl.* **tenacula** /-lə/) a surgeon's sharp hook for picking up arteries, etc. [L, = holding instrument, f. *tenēre* hold]

tenancy /ténənsee/ *n.* (*pl.* **-ies**) **1** the status of a tenant; possession as a tenant. **2** the duration or period of this.
■ occupancy, occupation, possession, holding, tenure, residence, residency.

tenant /ténənt/ *n. & v.* ● *n.* **1** a person who rents land or property from a landlord. **2** (often foll. by *of*) the occupant of a place. **3** *Law* a person holding real property by private ownership. ● *v.tr.* occupy as a tenant. □ **tenant farmer** a person who farms rented land. □□ **tenantable** *adj.* **tenantless** *adj.* [ME f. OF, pres. part. of *tenir* hold f. L *tenēre*]
■ *n.* **1** lessee, renter, leaseholder. **2** occupant, resident, inhabitant, *Brit.* occupier, *poet.* denizen. ● *v.* see OCCUPY 1. □□ **tenantless** see UNINHABITED.

tenantry /ténəntree/ *n.* the tenants of an estate, etc.

tench /tench/ *n.* (*pl.* same) a European freshwater fish, *Tinca tinca*, of the carp family. [ME f. OF *tenche* f. LL *tinca*]

tend¹ /tend/ *v.intr.* **1** (usu. foll. by *to*) be apt or inclined (*tends to lose his temper*). **2** serve; conduce. **3** be moving; be directed; hold a course (*tends in our direction; tends downwards*); tends to the same conclusion). [ME f. OF *tendre* stretch f. L *tendere tens-* or *tent-*]
■ **1** be inclined *or* disposed *or* prone, be apt *or* likely, have *or* show *or* exhibit *or* demonstrate a tendency, *disp.* be liable. **3** incline, lean, verge, gravitate, trend, be biased; (*tend to*) favor.

tend² /tend/ *v.* **1** *tr.* take care of; look after (a person, esp. an invalid; animals, esp. sheep; a machine). **2** *intr.* (foll. by *on, upon*) wait on. **3** *intr.* (foll. by *to*) give attention to. □□ **tendance** *n. archaic.* [ME f. ATTEND]
■ **1** care for, take care of, look after, look out for, watch over, mind, attend to, see to, keep an eye on, cater for, minister to, nurse, nurture, cherish, protect. **2** (*tend on*) attend on, wait on, serve, minister to. **3** (*tend to*) attend to, see to, turn to, deal with, take care of, handle.

tendency /téndənsee/ *n.* (*pl.* **-ies**) **1** (often foll. by *to, toward*) a leaning or inclination; a way of tending. **2** a group within a larger political party or movement. [med.L *tendentia* (as TEND[1])]

■ **1** inclination, bent, leaning, disposition, propensity, instinct, predisposition, proclivity, predilection, penchant, susceptibility, proneness, readiness, partiality, affinity, bias, drift, direction, course, trend, movement.

tendentious /tendénshəs/ *adj. derog.* (of writing, etc.) calculated to promote a particular cause or viewpoint; having an underlying purpose. □□ **tendentiously** *adv.* **tendentiousness** *n.* [as TENDENCY + -OUS]

■ see PARTISAN *adj.* 2. □□ **tendentiousness** see BIAS *n.* 1.

tender[1] /téndər/ *adj.* (**tenderer**, **tenderest**) **1** easily cut or chewed; not tough (*tender steak*). **2** easily touched or wounded; susceptible to pain or grief (*a tender heart; a tender conscience*). **3** easily hurt; sensitive (*tender skin; a tender place*). **4 a** delicate; fragile (*a tender plant*). **b** gentle; soft (*a tender touch*). **5** loving; affectionate; fond (*tender parents; wrote tender verses*). **6** requiring tact or careful handling; ticklish (*a tender subject*). **7** (of age) early; immature (*of tender years*). **8** (usu. foll. by *of*) solicitous; concerned (*tender of his honor*). □ **tender-hearted** having a tender heart; easily moved by pity, etc. **tender-heartedness** being tender-hearted. **tender mercies** *iron.* attention or treatment which is not in the best interests of its recipient. **tender spot** a subject on which a person is touchy. □□ **tenderly** *adv.* **tenderness** *n.* [ME f. OF *tendre* f. L *tener*]

■ **1** chewable, edible, eatable, soft. **2** see SENSITIVE 2. **3** sore, raw, painful, sensitive, inflamed; smarting, burning, hurting, aching. **4 a** sensitive, delicate, fragile, frail, infirm, unstable, shaky, weak, feeble, unwell, sickly, ailing, unsound. **b** gentle, soft, delicate, light, sensitive, soothing. **5** loving, affectionate, fond, kind, kindhearted, gentle, mild, compassionate, considerate, humane, benevolent, sympathetic, feeling, thoughtful, softhearted, warm, caring, merciful, solicitous, tender-hearted, warmhearted, good-natured; touching, emotional, moving, stirring, soul-stirring, heartrending, heartfelt, passionate, impassioned, poignant, sentimental, mawkish, maudlin; amatory, amorous, adoring, romantic. **6** sensitive, touchy, ticklish, troublesome, provocative, difficult, tricky, controversial. **7** young, youthful, immature, juvenile, inexperienced, impressionable, vulnerable, green, new, raw, undeveloped, untrained, uninitiated, callow. **8** solicitous, concerned, thoughtful, mindful, heedful, caring. □ **tender-hearted** see SYMPATHETIC *adj.* 1. **tender-heartedness** see MERCY 1, 2. □□ **tenderly** see *warmly* (WARM). **tenderness** see FEELING *n.* 3.

tender[2] /téndər/ *v.* & *n.* ● *v.* **1** *tr.* **a** offer; present (one's services, apologies, resignation, etc.). **b** offer (money, etc.) as payment. **2** *intr.* (often foll. by *for*) make a tender for the supply of a thing or the execution of work. ● *n.* an offer, esp. an offer in writing to execute work or supply goods at a fixed price. □ **legal tender** see LEGAL. **plea of tender** *Law* a plea that the defendant has always been ready to satisfy the plaintiff's claim and now brings the sum into court. **put out to tender** seek tenders or bids for (work, etc.). □□ **tenderer** *n.* [OF *tendre*: see TEND[1]]

■ *v.* **1** offer, proffer, present, propose, put forward, extend, hold out, submit, advance, put up, set before, hand in, give. **2** bid, put in a bid, quote. ● *n.* offer, bid, presentation, proposal, proposition, submission, quotation, *colloq.* quote.

tender[3] /téndər/ *n.* **1** a person who looks after people or things. **2** a vessel attending a larger one to supply stores, convey passengers or orders, etc. **3** a special car closely coupled to a steam locomotive to carry fuel, water, etc. [ME f. TEND[2] or f. *attender* (as ATTEND)]

■ **2** dinghy, gig, skiff, launch, boat, jolly (boat), rowboat, *Brit.* rowing-boat.

tenderfoot /téndərfŏŏt/ *n.* a newcomer or novice, esp. to the outdoor life or to the Scouts.

tenderize /téndəriz/ *v.tr.* make tender, esp. make (meat) tender by beating, etc. □□ **tenderizer** *n.*

tenderloin /téndərloyn/ *n.* **1** a long tender cut of beef or pork from the loin, along the vertebrae. **2** *sl.* a district of a city where vice and corruption are prominent.

tendon /téndən/ *n.* **1** a cord or strand of strong tissue attaching a muscle to a bone, etc. **2** (in a quadruped) = HAMSTRING. □□ **tendinitis** /téndinítis/ *n.* **tendinous** /-dinəs/ *adj.* [F *tendon* or med.L *tendo -dinis* f. Gk *tenōn* sinew f. *teinō* stretch]

tendril /téndril/ *n.* **1** each of the slender leafless shoots by which some climbing plants cling for support. **2** a slender curl of hair, etc. [prob. f. obs. F *tendrillon* dimin. of obs. *tendron* young shoot ult. f. L *tener* TENDER[1]]

Tenebrae /ténəbray, -bree/ *n.pl.* **1** *RC Ch. hist.* church services for the last three days of Holy Week, at which candles are successively extinguished. **2** this office set to music. [L, = darkness]

tenebrous /ténibrəs/ *adj. literary* dark; gloomy. [ME f. OF *tenebrus* f. L *tenebrosus* (as TENEBRAE)]

■ see DARK *adj.* 1.

tenement /ténimənt/ *n.* **1** a room or a set of rooms forming a separate residence within a house or apartment building. **2** a house divided into and rented in tenements, esp. one that is overcrowded, in poor condition, etc. **3** a dwelling place. **4 a** a piece of land held by an owner. **b** *Law* any kind of permanent property, e.g., lands or rents, held from another. □ **tenement house** = sense 2. □□ **tenemental** /-mént'l/ *adj.* **tenementary** /-méntəree/ *adj.* [ME f. OF f. med.L *tenementum* f. *tenēre* hold]

tenesmus /tinézmʌs/ *n. Med.* a continual inclination to evacuate the bowels or bladder accompanied by painful straining. [med.L f. Gk *teinesmos* straining f. *teinō* stretch]

tenet /ténit/ *n.* a doctrine, dogma, or principle held by a group or person. [L, = he, etc., holds f. *tenēre* hold]

■ belief, credo, creed, article of faith, ideology, precept, conviction, principle, dogma, idea, opinion, position, view, viewpoint, maxim, axiom, canon, teaching, doctrine.

tenfold /ténfold/ *adj.* & *adv.* **1** ten times as much or as many. **2** consisting of ten parts.

tenia var. of TAENIA.

Tenn. *abbr.* Tennessee.

tenné /ténee/ *n.* & (usu. placed after noun) adj. (also **tenny**) *Heraldry* orange-brown. [obs. F, var. of *tanné* TAWNY]

tenner /ténər/ *n. colloq.* a ten-dollar bill or ten-pound note. [TEN]

tennis /ténis/ *n.* a game in which two or four players strike a ball with rackets over a net stretched across a court. □ **tennis ball** a ball used in playing tennis. **tennis court** a court used in playing tennis. **tennis elbow** chronic inflammation caused by or as by playing tennis. **tennis racket** a racket used in playing tennis. **tennis shoe** a light canvas or leather rubbersoled shoe suitable for tennis or general casual wear. [ME *tenetz, tenes,* etc., app. f. OF *tenez* 'take, receive,' called by the server to an opponent, imper. of *tenir* take]

tenny var. of TENNÉ.

Tennysonian /ténisōneeən/ *adj.* relating to or in the style of Alfred (Lord) Tennyson, Engl. poet d. 1892.

tenon /ténən/ *n.* & *v.* ● *n.* a projecting piece of wood made for insertion into a corresponding cavity (esp. a mortise) in another piece. ● *v.tr.* **1** cut as a tenon. **2** join by means of a tenon. □ **tenon saw** a small saw with a strong brass or steel back for fine work. □□ **tenoner** *n.* [ME f. F f. *tenir* hold f. L *tenēre*]

tenor /ténər/ *n.* **1 a** a singing voice between baritone and alto or countertenor, the highest of the ordinary adult male range. **b** a singer with this voice. **c** a part written for it. **2 a** an instrument, esp. a viola, recorder, or saxophone, of which the range is roughly that of a tenor voice. **b** (in full **tenor**

bell) the largest bell of a peal or set. **3** (usu. foll. by *of*) the general purport or drift of a document or speech. **4** (usu. foll. by *of*) a settled or prevailing course or direction, esp. the course of a person's life or habits. **5** *Law* **a** the actual wording of a document. **b** an exact copy. **6** the subject to which a metaphor refers (opp. VEHICLE 4). □ **tenor clef** *Mus.* a clef placing middle C on the second highest line of the staff. [ME f. AF *tenur*, OF *tenour* f. L *tenor -oris* f. *tenēre* hold]

■ **3** drift, tone, spirit, essence, character, gist, bias, import, substance, effect, significance, meaning, sense, connotation, theme, thread, implication, intent, purpose, tendency, purport, direction. **4** course, direction, tendency, inclination, trend.

tenosynovitis /ténōsínəvítis/ *n.* inflammation and swelling of a tendon, usu. in the wrist, often caused by repetitive movements such as typing. [Gk *tenōn* tendon + SYNOVITIS]

tenotomy /tənótəmee/ *n.* (*pl.* **-ies**) the surgical cutting of a tendon, esp. as a remedy for a clubfoot. [F *ténotomie*, irreg. f. Gk *tenōn -ontos* tendon]

tenpin /ténpin/ *n.* **1** a pin used in tenpin bowling. **2** (in *pl.*) = *tenpin bowling*. □ **tenpin bowling** a game developed from ninepins in which ten pins are set up at the end of an alley and bowled at to be knocked down.

tenrec /ténrek/ *n.* (also **tanrec** /tán-/) any hedgehoglike, tailless, insectivorous mammal of the family Tenrecidae, esp. *Tenrec ecaudatus* native to Madagascar. [F *tanrec*, f. Malagasy *tàndraka*]

tense[1] /tens/ *adj. & v.* ● *adj.* **1** stretched tight; strained (*tense cord*; *tense muscle*; *tense nerves*; *tense emotion*). **2** causing tenseness (*a tense moment*). **3** *Phonet.* pronounced with the vocal muscles tense. ● *v.tr. & intr.* make or become tense. □ **tense up** become tense. □□ **tensely** *adv.* **tenseness** *n.* **tensity** *n.* [L *tensus* past part. of *tendere* stretch]

■ *adj.* **1** taut, strained, stretched, tight, stiff, under tension, rigid; intense, nervous, anxious, under (a) strain, high-strung, on edge, wrought up, keyed up, worked up, on tenterhooks, apprehensive, distressed, upset, disturbed, worried, edgy, on pins and needles, jumpy, fidgety, uneasy, overwrought, strung up, *colloq.* wound up, jittery, having a case of the jitters, uptight, antsy. **2** nervous, anxious, worrying, worrisome, distressing, disturbing, stressful, nerve-racking, fraught, disquieting. ● *v.* tense up; tighten, stretch, strain, tauten, tension, stiffen; string up. □□ **tensely** see *tightly* (TIGHT). **tenseness** see TENSION *n.* 1, 2, STRESS *n.* 2.

tense[2] /tens/ *n. Gram.* a form taken by a verb to indicate the time (also the continuance or completeness) of the action, etc. (*present tense*; *imperfect tense*). **2** a set of such forms for the various persons and numbers. □□ **tenseless** *adj.* [ME f. OF *tens* f. L *tempus* time]

tensile /ténsəl, -síl/ *adj.* **1** of or relating to tension. **2** capable of being drawn out or stretched. □ **tensile strength** resistance to breaking under tension. □□ **tensility** /tensílitee/ *n.* [med.L *tensilis* (as TENSE[1])]

■ **2** see FLEXIBLE 1.

tensimeter /tensímitər/ *n.* **1** an instrument for measuring vapor pressure. **2** a manometer. [TENSION + -METER]

tension /ténshən/ *n. & v.* ● *n.* **1** the act or an instance of stretching; the state of being stretched; tenseness. **2** mental strain or excitement. **3** a strained (political, social, etc.) state or relationship. **4** *Mech.* the stress by which a bar, cord, etc., is pulled when it is part of a system in equilibrium or motion. **5** electromagnetic force (*high tension*; *low tension*). ● *v.tr.* subject to tension. □□ **tensional** *adj.* **tensionally** *adv.* **tensionless** *adj.* [F *tension* or L *tensio* (as TEND[1])]

■ *n.* **1** stress, tightness, tautness, strain, pull, traction, pressure, tenseness, force. **2** nervousness, anxiety, anxiousness, strain, edginess, apprehension, suspense, stress, tautness, distress, upset, worry, jumpiness, fidgetiness, *colloq.* jitteriness, (a case of) the jitters; see also *excitement* (EXCITE). **3** strain, stress, pressure. ● *v.* see TENSE[1] *v.*

tenson /ténsən, tensôn/ *n.* (also **tenzon** /teénzən, tenzôn/) **1** a contest in versifying between troubadours. **2** a piece of

verse composed for this. [F *tenson*, = Prov. *tenso* (as TENSION)]

tensor /ténsər/ *n.* **1** *Anat.* a muscle that tightens or stretches a part. **2** *Math.* a generalized form of vector involving an arbitrary number of indices. □□ **tensorial** /-sáwreeəl/ *adj.* [mod.L (as TEND[1])]

tent[1] /tent/ *n. & v.* ● *n.* **1** a portable shelter or dwelling of canvas, cloth, etc., supported by a pole or poles and stretched by cords attached to pegs driven into the ground. **2** *Med.* a tentlike enclosure for control of the air supply to a patient. ● *v.* **1** *tr.* cover with or as with a tent. **2** *intr.* **a** encamp in a tent. **b** dwell temporarily. □ **tent bed** a bed with a tentlike canopy, or for a patient in a tent. **tent caterpillar** any of several caterpillars of the genus *Malacosoma*, including *M. americanum* and *M. disstria* (forest tent caterpillar), that construct and live in large tentlike webs in trees. **tent coat** (or **dress**) a coat (or dress) cut very full with no waistline. **tent fly** (*pl.* **flies**) **1** a flap at the entrance to a tent. **2** a piece of canvas stretched over the ridgepole of a tent leaving an open space but keeping off sun and rain. **tent peg** any of the pegs to which the cords of a tent are attached. **tent pegging** a sport in which a rider tries at full gallop to carry off on the point of a lance a tent peg fixed in the ground. **tent stitch 1** a series of parallel diagonal embroidery stitches. **2** such a stitch. [ME f. OF *tente* ult. f. L *tendere* stretch: *tent stitch* may be f. another word]

tent[2] /tent/ *n.* a deep red sweet wine chiefly from Spain, used esp. as sacramental wine. [Sp. *tinto* deep-colored f. L *tinctus* past part.: see TINGE]

tent[3] /tent/ *n. Surgery* a piece (esp. a roll) of lint, linen, etc., inserted into a wound or natural opening to keep it open. [ME f. OF *tente* f. *tenter* probe (as TEMPT)]

tentacle /téntəkəl/ *n.* **1** a long slender flexible appendage of an (esp. invertebrate) animal, used for feeling, grasping, or moving. **2** a thing used like a tentacle as a feeler, etc. **3** *Bot.* a sensitive hair or filament. □□ **tentacled** *adj.* (also in *comb.*). **tentacular** /-tákyələr/ *adj.* **tentaculate** /-tákyələt, -layt/ *adj.* [mod.L *tentaculum* f. L *tentare = temptare* (see TEMPT) + -*culum* -CULE]

■ **1** feeler, antenna, palp. **2** see FEELER 3.

tentative /téntətiv/ *adj. & n.* ● *adj.* **1** done by way of trial; experimental. **2** hesitant; not definite (*tentative suggestion*; *tentative acceptance*). ● *n.* an experimental proposal or theory. □□ **tentatively** *adv.* **tentativeness** *n.* [med.L *tentativus* (as TENTACLE)]

■ *adj.* **1** experimental, speculative, exploratory, trial, provisional. **2** unsure, hesitant, uncertain, indecisive, noncommittal, indefinite, cautious, timid, shy, diffident, uneasy, apprehensive. □□ **tentatively** see GINGERLY *adv.*

tenter[1] /téntər/ *n.* **1** a machine for stretching cloth to dry in shape. **2** = TENTERHOOK. [ME ult. f. med.L *tentorium* (as TEND[1])]

tenter[2] /téntər/ *n. Brit.* **1** a person in charge of something, esp. of machinery in a factory. **2** a worker's unskilled assistant. [*tent* (now Sc.) pay attention, perh. f. *tent* attention f. INTENT or obs. *attent* (as ATTEND)]

tenterhook /téntərhoŏk/ *n.* any of the hooks to which cloth is fastened on a tenter. □ **on tenterhooks** in a state of suspense or mental agitation due to uncertainty.

■ □ **on tenterhooks** see TENSE[1] *adj.* 1.

tenth /tenth/ *n. & adj.* ● *n.* **1** the position in a sequence corresponding to the number 10 in the sequence 1-10. **2** something occupying this position. **3** one of ten equal parts of a thing. **4** *Mus.* **a** an interval or chord spanning an octave and a third in the diatonic scale. **b** a note separated from another by this interval. ● *adj.* that is the tenth. □ **tenth-rate** of extremely poor quality. □□ **tenthly** *adv.* [ME *tenthe*, alt. of OE *teogotha*]

tenuis /tényoŏis/ *n.* (*pl.* **tenues** /-yoo-eez/) *Phonet.* a voiceless stop, e.g., *k*, *p*, *t*. [L, = thin, transl. Gk *psilos* smooth]

tenuity /tinoŏitee, -nyoŏ-/ *n.* **1** slenderness. **2** (of a fluid, esp. air) rarity; thinness. [L *tenuitas* (as TENUIS)]

tenuous /tényoŏəs/ *adj.* **1** slight; of little substance (*tenuous connection*). **2** (of a distinction, etc.) oversubtle. **3** thin; slender; small. **4** rarefied. □□ **tenuously** *adv.* **tenuousness** *n.* [L *tenuis*]

■ **1** flimsy, slight, slender, insubstantial, unsubstantial, paltry, weak, feeble, frail, shaky, meager, vague, negligible, insignificant, trifling, sketchy, hazy, nebulous. **2** overfine, oversubtle, overnice, hairsplitting, quibbling, dubious, doubtful, *colloq.* nit-picking. **3** thin, slender, slight, small, fine, attenuated, delicate, gossamer, diaphanous, fragile. **4** see *rarefied* (RAREFY 1).

tenure /tényər/ *n.* **1** a condition, or form of right or title, under which (esp. real) property is held. **2** (often foll. by *of*) **a** the holding or possession of an office or property. **b** the period of this (*during his tenure of office*). **3** guaranteed permanent employment, esp. as a teacher or professor after a probationary period. [ME f. OF f. *tenir* hold f. L *tenēre*]

■ **1, 2** right, title, possession, holding, ownership, occupancy, incumbency. **3** (job) security, permanence, permanency.

tenured /tényərd/ *adj.* **1** (of an official position) carrying a guarantee of permanent employment. **2** (of a teacher, professor, etc.) having guaranteed tenure of office.

tenurial /tenyŏōreeəl/ *adj.* of the tenure of land. □□ **tenurially** *adv.* [med.L *tenūra* TENURE]

tenuto /tənŏōtō/ *adv., adj.,* & *n. Mus.* ● *adv.* & *adj.* (of a note, etc.) sustained; given its full time value (cf. LEGATO, STACCATO). ● *n.* (*pl.* **-os**) a note or chord played tenuto. [It., = held]

tenzon var. of TENSON.

teocalli /tee‑əkálee/ *n.* (*pl.* **teocallis**) a temple of the Aztecs or other Mexican peoples, usu. on a truncated pyramid. [Nahuatl f. *teotl* god + *calli* house]

tepee /téepee/ *n.* (also **teepee**) a conical tent, made of skins, cloth, or canvas on a frame of poles, orig. used by Native Americans. [Sioux or Dakota *tipī*]

tephra /téfrə/ *n.* fragmented rock, etc., ejected by a volcanic eruption. [Gk, = ash]

tepid /tépid/ *adj.* **1** slightly warm. **2** unenthusiastic. □□ **tepidity** /tipíditee/ *n.* **tepidly** *adv.* **tepidness** *n.* [L *tepidus* f. *tepēre* be lukewarm]

■ **1** lukewarm, warmish. **2** lukewarm, unenthusiastic, cool, indifferent, apathetic, uninterested, unconcerned, nonchalant, uncaring, neutral, halfhearted, blasé.

tequila /tekéelə/ *n.* a Mexican liquor made from an agave. [*Tequila* in Mexico]

ter- /ter/ *comb. form* three; threefold (*tercentenary*; *tervalent*). [L *ter* thrice]

tera- /térə/ *comb. form* denoting a factor of 10^{12}. [Gk *teras* monster]

terai /təri/ *n.* (in full **terai hat**) a wide-brimmed felt hat, often with a double crown, worn by travelers, etc., in subtropical regions. [*Terai*, belt of marshy jungle between Himalayan foothills and plains, f. Hindi *tarāī* moist (land)]

teraph /térəf/ *n.* (*pl.* **teraphim**, also used as *sing.*) a small image as a domestic deity or oracle of the ancient Hebrews. [ME f. LL *theraphim*, Gk *theraphin* f. Heb. *tᵉrāpĭm*]

terato- /térətō/ *comb. form* monster. [Gk *teras -atos* monster]

teratogen /tərátəjən/ *n. Med.* an agent or factor causing malformation of an embryo. □□ **teratogenic** /térətəjénik/ *adj.* **teratogeny** /térətójənee/ *n.*

teratology /térətóləjee/ *n.* **1** *Biol.* the scientific study of animal or vegetable monstrosities. **2** mythology relating to fantastic creatures, monsters, etc. □□ **teratological** /-təlójikəl/ *adj.* **teratologist** *n.*

teratoma /térətṓmə/ *n. Med.* a tumor of heterogeneous tissues.

terbium /tárbeeəm/ *n. Chem.* a silvery metallic element of the lanthanide series. ¶ Symb.: **Tb**. [mod.L f. *Ytterby* in Sweden]

terce /ters/ *n. Eccl.* **1** the office of the canonical hour of prayer appointed for the third daytime hour (i.e., 9 a.m.). **2** this hour. [var. of TIERCE]

tercel /tɔ́rsəl/ *n.* (also **tiercel** /téersəl/) *Falconry* the male of the hawk, esp. a peregrine or goshawk. [ME f. OF *tercel*, ult. a dimin. of L *tertius* third, perh. from a belief that the third

egg of a clutch produced a male bird, or that the male was one-third smaller than the female]

tercentenary /tɔ́rsenténəree, tərséntineree/ *n.* & *adj.* ● *n.* (*pl.* **-ies**) **1** a three-hundredth anniversary. **2** a celebration of this. ● *adj.* of this anniversary.

tercentennial /tɔ́rsenténeeəl/ *adj.* & *n.* ● *adj.* **1** occurring every three hundred years. **2** lasting three hundred years. ● *n.* a tercentenary.

tercet /térsit/ *n.* (also **tiercet** /téer-/) *Prosody* a set or group of three lines rhyming together or connected by rhyme with an adjacent triplet. [F f. It. *terzetto* dimin. of *terzo* third f. L *tertius*]

terebene /téribeen/ *n.* a mixture of terpenes prepared by treating oil of turpentine with sulfuric acid, used as an expectorant, etc. [TEREBINTH + -ENE]

terebinth /téribinth/ *n.* a small Southern European tree, *Pistacia terebinthus*, yielding turpentine. [ME f. OF *terebinte* or L *terebinthus* f. Gk *terebinthos*]

terebinthine /téribínthin, -thīn/ *adj.* **1** of the terebinth. **2** of turpentine. [L *terebinthinus* f. Gk *terebinthinos* (as TEREBINTH)]

teredo /təréedō/ *n.* (*pl.* **-os**) any bivalve mollusk of the genus *Teredo*, esp. *T. navalis*, that bores into submerged wood, damaging ships, etc. Also called SHIPWORM. [L f. Gk *terēdōn* f. *teirō* rub hard, wear away, bore]

terete /tərēet/ *adj. Biol.* smooth and rounded; cylindrical. [L *teres -etis*]

tergal /tɔ́rgəl/ *adj.* of or relating to the back; dorsal. [L *tergum* back]

tergiversate /tɔ́rjiversáyt/ *v.intr.* **1** be apostate; change one's party or principles. **2** equivocate; make conflicting or evasive statements. **3** turn one's back on something. □□ **tergiversation** /-sáyshən/ *n.* **tergiversator** *n.* [L *tergiversari* turn one's back f. *tergum* back + *vertere vers-* turn]

■ **1** recant, apostatize; see also DEFECT *v.* **2** see EQUIVOCATE. **3** see SECEDE. □□ **tergiversator** see TURNCOAT.

teriyaki /tereeyókee/ *n.* a dish consisting of meat, poultry, or fish that is marinated in seasoned soy sauce and grilled, sautéed, or broiled. [Jap. *teri* glaze + *yaki* broil]

term /tərm/ *n.* & *v.* ● *n.* **1** a word used to express a definite concept, esp. in a particular branch of study, etc. (*a technical term*). **2** (in *pl.*) language used; mode of expression (*answered in no uncertain terms*). **3** (in *pl.*) a relation or footing (*we are on familiar terms*). **4** (in *pl.*) **a** conditions or stipulations (*cannot accept your terms*; *do it on your own terms*). **b** charge or price (*his terms are $20 a lesson*). **5 a** a limited period of some state or activity (*for a term of five years*). **b** a period over which operations are conducted or results contemplated (*in the short term*). **c** a period of some weeks, alternating with holidays or vacation, during which instruction is given in a school, college, or university, or during which a court of law holds sessions. **d** a period of imprisonment. **e** a period of tenure. **6** *Logic* a word or words that may be the subject or predicate of a proposition. **7** *Math.* **a** each of the two quantities in a ratio. **b** each quantity in a series. **c** a part of an expression joined to the rest by + or − (e.g., *a*, *b*, *c* in *a + b − c*). **8** the completion of a normal length of pregnancy. **9** an appointed day, time, etc. **10** (in full US **term for years** or *Brit.* **term of years**) *Law* an interest in land for a fixed period. **11** = TERMINUS 6. **12** *archaic* a boundary or limit, esp. of time. ● *v.tr.* denominate; call; assign a term to (*the music termed classical*). □ **bring to terms** cause to accept conditions. **come to terms** yield; give way. **come to terms with 1** reconcile oneself to (a difficulty, etc.). **2** conclude an agreement with. **in set terms** in definite terms. **in terms** explicitly. **in terms of 1** in the language peculiar to; using as a basis of expression or thought. **2** by way of. **make terms** conclude

---

/.../ **pronunciation**	● **part of speech**
□ **phrases, idioms, and compounds**	
□□ **derivatives**	■ **synonym section**
cross-references appear in SMALL CAPITALS or *italics*	

an agreement. **on terms** on terms of friendship or equality. **term paper** an essay or dissertation representative of the work done during a term. **terms of reference** *Brit.* points referred to an individual or body of persons for decision or report; the scope of an inquiry, etc.; a definition of this. □□ **termless** *adj.* **termly** *adj.* & *adv.* [ME f. OF *terme* f. L TERMINUS]

■ *n.* **1** name, title, designation, denomination, label, *formal* appellation; word, expression, locution, phrase. **2** (*terms*) language, words, phrases. **3** (*terms*) standing, position, basis, relationship, relation, relations, footing. **4** (*terms*) **a** conditions, provisions, articles, clauses, provisos; stipulations, qualifications, assumptions, basis. **b** payment, schedule, charges, prices, rates. **5 a, b** time, period (of time), interval, length of time, span (of time), duration, spell, stint, course, while. **c** semester, trimester; sitting, session. **d** stretch. **e** incumbency, administration. ● *v.* call, name, label, designate, denominate, title, style, dub, *archaic* entitle; nickname. □ **come to terms** agree, yield, give way, assent, come to *or* reach an agreement, come to *or* reach an arrangement, come to *or* reach an understanding, be reconciled, settle, compromise. **come to terms with 1** accept, reconcile *or* resign oneself to, adjust to, cope with, face up to. **2** agree with, come to *or* reach an agreement with, come to *or* reach an arrangement with, come to *or* reach an understanding with, settle with. **in terms of 2** by way of, as, in the way of, as regards, concerning, regarding, with regard to, in the matter of. □□ **termly** terminal (ly).

termagant /tə́rməgənt/ *n.* & *adj.* ● *n.* **1** an overbearing or brawling woman; a virago or shrew. **2** (**Termagant**) *hist.* an imaginary deity of violent and turbulent character, often appearing in morality plays. ● *adj.* violent; turbulent; shrewish. [ME *Tervagant* f. OF *Tervagan* f. It. *Trivigante*]
■ *n.* **1** see SHREW.

terminable /tə́rminəbəl/ *adj.* **1** that may be terminated. **2** coming to an end after a certain time (*terminable annuity*). □□ **terminableness** *n.*

terminal /tə́rminəl/ *adj.* & *n.* ● *adj.* **1 a** (of a disease) ending in death; fatal. **b** (of a patient) in the last stage of a fatal disease. **c** (of a morbid condition) forming the last stage of a fatal disease. **d** *colloq.* ruinous; disastrous; very great (*terminal laziness*). **2** of or forming a limit or terminus (*terminal station*). **3** a *Zool.*, etc., ending a series (*terminal joints*). **b** *Bot.* growing at the end of a stem, etc. **4** of or done, etc., each term (*terminal accounts*; *terminal examinations*). ● *n.* **1** a terminating thing; an extremity. **2** a terminus for trains or long-distance buses. **3** a departure and arrival building for air passengers. **4** a point of connection for closing an electric circuit. **5** an apparatus for transmission of messages between a user and a computer, communications system, etc. **6** (in full **terminal figure**) = TERMINUS 6. **7** an installation where oil is stored at the end of a pipeline or at a port. □ **terminal velocity** a velocity of a falling body such that the resistance of the air, etc., prevents further increase of speed under gravity. □□ **terminally** *adv.* [L *terminalis* (as TERMINUS)]
■ *adj.* **1 a** deadly, mortal, fatal, lethal, incurable. **b** dying. **c** final, last. **2** closing, concluding, terminating, ending, final, ultimate, extreme. **4** termly. ● *n.* **1** see TIP[1] *n.* 1. **2** terminus, (terminal) station, end of the line, depot. **4** connection, wire, connector, coupler, coupling, conductor. **5** keyboard, monitor, position, (work) station, visual display unit, (personal) computer, esp. *Brit.* VDU, PC, module, CRT, screen, (control) panel. □□ **terminally** see *severely* (SEVERE).

terminate /tə́rminayt/ *v.* **1** *tr.* & *intr.* bring or come to an end. **2** *intr.* (foll. by *in*) (of a word) end in (a specified letter or syllable, etc.). **3** *tr.* end (a pregnancy) before term by artificial means. **4** *tr.* bound; limit. [L *terminare* (as TERMINUS)]
■ **1, 2** stop, end, finish, cease, conclude; put an end to, complete, discontinue, drop, bring to an end *or* close,

wind up *or* down, cut off; come to an end, expire, sign off. **3** abort.

termination /tə̀rmináyshən/ *n.* **1** the act or an instance of terminating; the state of being terminated. **2** *Med.* an induced abortion. **3** an ending or result of a specified kind (*a happy termination*). **4** a word's final syllable or letters or letter esp. as an element in inflection or derivation. □ **put a termination to** (or **bring to a termination**) make an end of. □□ **terminational** *adj.* [ME f. OF *termination* or L *terminatio* (as TERMINATE)]
■ **1, 3** end, ending, stop, stoppage, cessation, discontinuation, cancellation, expiration, windup, close, dissolution, finish, conclusion, completion. **2** abortion. **4** suffix, ending.

terminator /tə́rminaytər/ *n.* **1** a person or thing that terminates. **2** the dividing line between the light and dark part of a planetary body.

terminer see OYER AND TERMINER.

termini *pl.* of TERMINUS.

terminological /tə̀rminəlójikəl/ *adj.* of terminology. □ **terminological inexactitude** *joc.* a lie. □□ **terminologically** *adv.*

terminology /tə̀rminóləjee/ *n.* (*pl.* **-ies**) **1** the system of terms used in a particular subject. **2** the science of the proper use of terms. □□ **terminologist** *n.* [G *Terminologie* f. med.L TERMINUS term]
■ **1** nomenclature, vocabulary, language, words, locutions, wording, terms, phraseology, phrasing, jargon, argot, cant, *colloq.* lingo, *often derog.* -ese.

terminus /tə́rminəs/ *n.* (*pl.* **termini** /-nī/ or **terminuses**) **1** a station or destination at the end of a railroad or bus route. **2** a point at the end of a pipeline, etc. **3** a final point; a goal. **4** a starting point. **5** *Math.* the end point of a vector, etc. **6** *Archit.* a figure of a human bust or an animal ending in a square pillar from which it appears to spring, orig. as a boundary marker. □ **terminus ad quem** /ad kwém/ the finishing point of an argument, policy, period, etc. **terminus ante quem** /ántee kwém/ the finishing point of a period. **terminus a quo** /aa kwó/ the starting point of an argument, policy, period, etc. **terminus post quem** /pōst kwém/ the starting point of a period. [L, = end, limit, boundary]
■ **1** see TERMINAL *n.* 2. **3** see DESTINATION.

termitary /tə́rmiteree/ *n.* (*pl.* **-ies**) a nest of termites, usu. a large mound of earth.

termite /tə́rmīt/ *n.* a small antlike social insect of the order Isoptera, chiefly tropical and destructive to wood. [LL *termes -mitis*, alt. of L *tarmes* (*termes* where *terere* rub]

termor /tə́rmər/ *n.* *Law* a person who holds lands, etc., for a term of years, or for life. [ME f. AF *termer* (as TERM)]

tern[1] /tərn/ *n.* any marine bird of the subfamily Sterninae, like a gull but usu. smaller and with a long forked tail. [of Scand. orig.: cf. Da. *terne*, Sw. *tärna* f. ON *therna*]

tern[2] /tərn/ *n.* **1** a set of three, esp. three lottery numbers that when drawn together win a large prize. **2** such a prize. [F *terne* f. L *terni* three each]

ternary /tə́rnəree/ *adj.* **1** composed of three parts. **2** *Math.* using three as a base (*ternary scale*). □ **ternary form** *Mus.* the form of a movement in which the first subject is repeated after an interposed second subject in a related key. [ME f. L *ternarius* f. *terni* three each]

ternate /tə́rnayt/ *adj.* **1** arranged in threes. **2** *Bot.* (of a leaf): **a** having three leaflets. **b** whorled in threes. □□ **ternately** *adv.* [mod.L *ternatus* (as TERNARY)]

terne /tərn/ *n.* (in full **terneplate**) inferior tin plate alloyed with four parts lead. [prob. f. F *terne* dull: cf. TARNISH]

terotechnology /tèrōteknóləjee, teér-/ *n.* esp. *Brit.* the branch of technology and engineering concerned with the installation and maintenance of equipment. [Gk *tēreō* take care of + TECHNOLOGY]

terpene /tə́rpeen/ *n.* *Chem.* any of a large group of unsaturated cyclic hydrocarbons found in the essential oils of plants, esp. conifers and oranges. [*terpentin* obs. var. of TURPENTINE]

terpsichorean /tə̀rpsikəréeən, -káwreeən/ *adj.* of or relating to dancing. [*Terpsichore* Muse of dancing]

terr. *abbr.* **1** terrace. **2** territory.

terra alba /tə́rə álbə/ *n.* a white mineral, esp. pipe clay or pulverized gypsum. [L, = white earth]

terrace /térəs/ *n. & v.* ● *n.* **1** each of a series of flat areas formed on a slope and used for cultivation. **2** a level paved area next to a house. **3 a** a row of houses on a raised level or along the top or face of a slope. **b** *Brit.* a row of houses built in one block of uniform style; a set of row houses. **4** *Brit.* a flight of wide shallow steps as for spectators at a sports ground. **5** *Geol.* a raised beach, or a similar formation beside a river, etc. ● *v.tr.* form into or provide with a terrace or terraces. □ **terraced house** *Brit.* = *row house.* **terraced roof** a flat roof. **terrace house** *Brit.* = *row house.* [OF ult. f. L *terra* earth]

terra-cotta /térəkótə/ *n.* **1 a** unglazed usu. brownish red earthenware used chiefly as an ornamental building material and in modeling. **b** a statuette of this. **2** its color. [It. *terra cotta* baked earth]

terra firma /térə fə́rmə/ *n.* dry land; firm ground. [L, = firm land]

■ see LAND *n.* 1.

terrain /təráyn/ *n.* a tract of land as regarded by the physical geographer or the military tactician. [F, ult. f. L *terrenum* neut. of *terrenus* TERRENE]

■ topography, landscape, ground, land, country, territory, zone.

terra incognita /térə inkógneetə, ínkognéetə/ *n.* an unknown or unexplored region. [L, = unknown land]

terramara /térəmaárə/ *n.* (*pl.* **terramare** /-ray/) = TERRAMARE. [It. dial.: see TERRAMARE]

terramare /térəmaaree/ *n.* **1** an ammoniacal earthy deposit found in mounds in prehistoric lake dwellings or settlements esp. in Italy. **2** such a dwelling or settlement. [F f. It. dial. *terra mara* f. *marna* marl]

terrapin /térəpin/ *n.* any of various N. American edible freshwater turtles of the family Emydidae. [Algonquian]

terrarium /teráireeəm/ *n.* (*pl.* **terrariums** or **terraria** /-reeə/) **1** a vivarium for small land animals. **2** a sealed transparent globe, etc., containing growing plants. [mod.L f. L *terra* earth, after AQUARIUM]

terra sigillata /térə sigilaátə, sijiláytə/ *n.* **1** astringent clay from Lemnos or Samos. **2** Samian ware. [med.L, = sealed earth]

terrazzo /təraázō, -raátsō/ *n.* (*pl.* **-os**) a flooring material of stone chips set in concrete and given a smooth surface. [It., = terrace]

terrene /teréen/ *adj.* **1** of the earth; earthy; worldly. **2** of earth; earthly. **3** of dry land; terrestrial. [ME f. AF f. L *terrenus* f. *terra* earth]

■ **1** see EARTHLY 1. **3** terrestrial, earthbound, telluric.

terreplein /táirplayn, térə-/ *n.* a level space where a battery of guns is mounted. [orig. a sloping bank behind a rampart f. F *terre-plein* f. It. *terrapieno* f. *terrapienare* fill with earth f. *terra* earth + *pieno* f. L *plenus* full]

terrestrial /təréstreeəl/ *adj. & n.* ● *adj.* **1** of or on or relating to the earth; earthly. **2 a** of or on dry land. **b** *Zool.* living on or in the ground (opp. AQUATIC, ARBOREAL, AERIAL). **c** *Bot.* growing in the soil (opp. AQUATIC, *epiphytic*). **3** *Astron.* (of a planet) similar in size or composition to the earth. **4** of this world; worldly (*terrestrial sins; terrestrial interests*). ● *n.* an inhabitant of the earth. □ **a terrestrial globe** a globe representing the earth. **the terrestrial globe** the earth. **terrestrial magnetism** the magnetic properties of the earth as a whole. **terrestrial telescope** a telescope giving an erect image for observation of terrestrial objects. □□ **terrestrially** *adv.* [ME f. L *terrestris* f. *terra* earth]

■ *adj.* **1** earthly, earthbound, terrene, tellurian, telluric, global, sublunary, subastral. **2** earthbound, terrene, telluric, terricolous. **4** worldly, terrene, mundane, temporal, secular. ● *n.* earthman, earthwoman, earthperson, earthling, tellurian, mortal, human.

terret /térit/ *n.* (also **territ**) each of the loops or rings on a harness pad for the driving reins to pass through. [ME, var. of *toret* (now dial.) f. OF *to(u)ret* dimin. of TOUR]

terre verte /táir váirt/ *n.* a soft green earth used as a pigment. [F, = green earth]

terrible /téribəl/ *adj.* **1** *colloq.* very great or bad (*a terrible bore*). **2** *colloq.* very incompetent (*terrible at tennis*). **3** causing terror; fit to cause terror; awful; dreadful; formidable. **4** (*predic.*; usu. foll. by *about*) *colloq.* full of remorse; sorry (*I felt terrible about it*). □□ **terribleness** *n.* [ME f. F f. L *terribilis* f. *terrēre* frighten]

■ **1** bad, serious, grave, severe, acute, distressing, nasty, foul, unbearable, loathsome, hideous, intolerable, egregious, atrocious; unhappy, unpleasant, disagreeable, miserable, woeful, joyless, lamentable, wretched, unfortunate; *colloq.* awful, dreadful, vile, ghastly, lousy, beastly, abysmal, *sl.* rotten. **2** see INCOMPETENT *adj.* 2. **3** gruesome, grisly, macabre, gory, grotesque, brutal, savage, horrible, horrendous, terrifying, terrific, harrowing, horrid, horrifying, horrific, ghastly, frightening, frightful, fearsome, formidable, redoubtable, awesome, awe-inspiring, unspeakable, monstrous, wicked, grievous, dread, appalling, shocking, alarming, awful, dreadful, foul, disgusting, revolting, nauseating, nauseous, offensive, vomit-provoking, obnoxious, stomach-turning, abominable, noxious, loathsome, hideous, evil, vile, rotten, *literary* noisome. **4** remorseful, regretful, rueful, sorry, contrite, ashamed, conscience-stricken, guilty, distressed.

terribly /tériblee/ *adv.* **1** *colloq.* very; extremely (*he was terribly nice about it*). **2** in a terrible manner.

■ **1** very, extremely, exceedingly, thoroughly, decidedly, really, unbelievably, incredibly, monumentally, outrageously, awfully, fabulously, *colloq.* frightfully. **2** dreadfully, fearfully, awfully, frightfully; see also BADLY 1.

terricolous /teríkələs/ *adj.* living on or in the ground. [L *terricola* earth dweller f. *terra* earth + *colere* inhabit]

terrier[1] /téreeər/ *n.* **1 a** a small dog of various breeds originally used for driving out foxes, etc., from their holes. **b** any of these breeds. **2** an eager or tenacious person or animal. [ME f. OF (*chien*) *terrier* f. med.L *terrarius* f. L *terra* earth]

terrier[2] /téreeər/ *n. hist.* **1** a book recording the site, boundaries, etc., of the land of private persons or corporations. **2** a rent roll. **3** a collection of acknowledgments of vassals or tenants of a lordship. [ME f. OF *terrier* (adj.) = med.L *terrarius liber* (as TERRIER[1])]

terrific /tərífik/ *adj.* **1** *colloq.* **a** of great size or intensity. **b** excellent (*did a terrific job*). **c** excessive (*making a terrific noise*). **2** causing terror. □□ **terrifically** *adv.* [L *terrificus* f. *terrēre* frighten]

■ **1 a** see HUGE 1, INTENSE 1, 3. **b** wonderful, marvelous, splendid, breathtaking, extraordinary, outstanding, magnificent, exceptional, unbelievable, stupendous, sensational, superb, excellent, first-class, superior, *colloq.* great, fantastic, fabulous, mind-boggling, incredible, smashing, super, *sl.* ace, awesome. **c** see EXCESSIVE 1. **2** see TERRIBLE 3.

terrify /térifī/ *v.tr.* (**-ies, -ied**) fill with terror; frighten severely (*terrified them into submission; is terrified of dogs*). □□ **terrifier** *n.* **terrifying** *adj.* **terrifyingly** *adv.* [L *terrificare* (as TERRIFIC)]

■ alarm, frighten, scare, terrorize, shock, make one's flesh crawl *or* creep, horrify, make one's blood run cold, make a person's hair stand on end, stun, paralyze, petrify; see also SCARE *v.* 1. □□ **terrifying** alarming, frightening, shocking, horrifying, paralyzing, petrifying, *colloq.* scary.

terrigenous /teríjinəs/ *adj.* produced by the earth or the land (*terrigenous deposits*). [L *terrigenus* earthborn]

terrine /təréen/ *n.* **1** an earthenware vessel, esp. one in which

---

/.../ **pronunciation**	● **part of speech**
□ **phrases, idioms, and compounds**	
□□ **derivatives**	■ **synonym section**
cross-references appear in SMALL CAPITALS or *italics*	

pâté, etc., is cooked or sold. **2** pâté or similar food. [orig. form of TUREEN]

territ var. of TERRET.

territorial /tèritáwreeəl/ *adj.* **1** of territory (*territorial possessions*). **2** limited to a district (*the right was strictly territorial*). **3** (of a person or animal, etc.) tending to defend an area of territory. **4** of any of the territories of the US or Canada. □ **territorial waters** the waters under the jurisdiction of a nation, esp. the part of the sea within a stated distance of the shore (traditionally three miles from the low water mark). □□ **territoriality** /-reeálitee/ *n.* **territorialize** *v.tr.* **territorialization** *n.* **territorially** *adv.* [LL *territorialis* (as TERRITORY)]

territory /téritawree/ *n.* (*pl.* **-ies**) **1** the extent of the land under the jurisdiction of a ruler, nation, city, etc. **2** (**Territory**) an organized division of a country, esp. one not yet admitted to the full rights of a state. **3** a sphere of action or thought; a province. **4** the area over which a sales representative or distributor operates. **5** *Zool.* an area defended by an animal or animals against others of the same species. **6** an area defended by a team or player in a game. **7** a large tract of land. [ME f. L *territorium* f. *terra* land]
■ **1, 7** area, region, district, neighborhood, zone, sector, tract, land, terrain, country, precinct, quarter, domain, demesne, vicinage, vicinity, purlieu, enclave. **3** area, domain, sphere, province, preserve, haunt, stamping ground, *colloq.* patch, *joc.* bailiwick, *sl.* turf. **5** area, domain, stamping ground.

terror /térər/ *n.* **1** extreme fear. **2 a** a person or thing that causes terror. **b** (also **holy terror**) *colloq.* a formidable person; a troublesome person or thing (*the twins are little terrors*). **3** the use of organized intimidation; terrorism. □ **reign of terror** a period of remorseless repression or bloodshed, esp. a period of the French Revolution 1793–94. **terror-stricken** (or **-struck**) affected with terror. [ME f. OF *terrour* f. L *terror -oris* f. *terrēre* frighten]
■ **1** fright, dread, fear, horror, panic, shock, alarm, anxiety, dismay, consternation, trepidation, intimidation, awe. **2** scourge, demon, brute, monster, fiend, devil, horror, dread. □ **terror-stricken** (or **-struck**) see *panic-stricken* (PANIC¹).

terrorist /térərist/ *n.* (also *attrib.*) a person who uses or favors violent and intimidating methods of coercing a government or community. □□ **terrorism** *n.* **terroristic** *adj.* **terroristically** *adv.* [F *terroriste* (as TERROR)]
■ subversive, radical, insurgent, revolutionary, freedom fighter, anarchist, nihilist; bomber, arsonist, incendiary; hijacker; desperado, gunman, thug, felon, criminal. □□ **terroristic** see *strong-arm*.

terrorize /térərīz/ *v.tr.* **1** fill with terror. **2** use terrorism against. □□ **terrorization** *n.* **terrorizer** *n.*
■ **1** see INTIMIDATE.

terry /téree/ *n.* & *adj.* ● *n.* (*pl.* **-ies**) a pile fabric with the loops uncut, used esp. for towels. ● *adj.* of this fabric. [18th c.: orig. unkn.]

terse /ters/ *adj.* (**terser**, **tersest**) **1** (of language) brief; concise; to the point. **2** curt; abrupt. □□ **tersely** *adv.* **terseness** *n.* [L *tersus* past part. of *tergēre* wipe, polish]
■ **1** concise, brief, short, compact, pithy, succinct, summary, laconic, short and sweet, to the point, sententious, crisp, epigrammatic, aphoristic; distilled, condensed, compendious, abbreviated, abridged, shortened, concentrated. **2** abrupt, curt, short, brusque, blunt, gruff, bluff, ungracious, petulant, tart, rude. □□ **terseness** see ECONOMY 3.

tertian /tśrshən/ *adj.* (of a fever) recurring every third day by inclusive counting. [ME (*fever*) *tersiane* f. L (*febris*) *tertiana* (as TERTIARY)]

tertiary /tśrshee-eree, -shəri/ *adj.* & *n.* ● *adj.* **1** third in order or rank, etc. **2** (**Tertiary**) *Geol.* of or relating to the first period in the Cenozoic era with evidence of the development of mammals and flowering plants (cf. PALEOCENE, EOCENE, OLIGOCENE, MIOCENE, PLIOCENE). ¶ Cf. Appendix VII. ● *n.* **1** *Geol.* this period or system. **2** a member of the third order of a monastic body. [L *tertiarius* f. *tertius* third]

tertium quid /tśrsheeəm kwid, tértee-ōōm/ *n.* a third something, esp. intermediate between mind and matter or between opposite things. [L, app. transl. Gk *triton ti*]

tervalent /tśrváylənt/ *adj. Chem.* having a valence of three; trivalent. [TER- + *valent-* part. stem (as VALENCE¹)]

terza rima /táirtsə réemə/ *n. Prosody* an arrangement of (esp. iambic pentameter) triplets rhyming *aba bcb cdc*, etc., as in Dante's *Divina Commedia*. [It., = third rhyme]

terzetto /tairtséttō/ *n.* (*pl.* **-os** or **terzetti** /-tee/) *Mus.* a vocal or instrumental trio. [It.: see TERCET]

TESL *abbr.* teaching of English as a second language.

tesla /téslə/ *n.* a unit of magnetic flux density. □ **Tesla coil** a form of induction coil for producing high-frequency alternating currents. [N. *Tesla*, Croatian-born Amer. scientist d. 1943]

TESOL /tésawl, -ol/ *abbr.* teaching of English to speakers of other languages.

tessellate /tésəlayt/ *v.tr.* **1** make from tesserae. **2** *Math.* cover (a plane surface) by repeated use of a single shape. [L *tessellare* f. *tessella* dimin. of TESSERA]

tessellated /tésəlaytid/ *adj.* **1** of or resembling mosaic. **2** *Bot.* & *Zool.* regularly checkered. [L *tessellatus* or It. *tessellato* (as TESSELLATE)]

tessellation /tésəláyshən/ *n.* **1** the act or an instance of tessellating; the state of being tessellated. **2** an arrangement of polygons without gaps or overlapping, esp. in a repeated pattern.

tessera /tésərə/ *n.* (*pl.* **tesserae** /-ree/) **1** a small square block used in mosaic. **2** *Gk & Rom. Antiq.* a small square of bone, etc., used as a token, ticket, etc. □□ **tesseral** *adj.* [L f. Gk, neut. of *tesseres, tessares* four]

tessitura /tésitōōrə/ *n. Mus.* the range within which most tones of a voice part fall. [It., = TEXTURE]

test¹ /test/ *n.* & *v.* ● *n.* **1** a critical examination or trial of a person's or thing's qualities. **2** the means of so examining; a standard for comparison or trial; circumstances suitable for this (*success is not a fair test*). **3** a minor examination, esp. in school (*spelling test*). **4** *Brit. colloq.* a test match in cricket or rugby. **5** a ground for admission or rejection (*is excluded by our test*). **6** *Chem.* a reagent or a procedure employed to reveal the presence of another in a compound. **7** *Brit.* a movable hearth in a reverberating furnace with a cupel used in separating gold or silver from lead. **8** (*attrib.*) done or performed in order to test (*a test run*). ● *v.tr.* **1** put to the test; make trial of (a person or thing or quality). **2** try severely; tax a person's powers of endurance, etc. **3** *Chem.* examine by means of a reagent. **4** *Brit.* refine or assay (metal). □ **put to the test** cause to undergo a test. **Test Act** *Brit. hist.* **1** an act in force 1672–1828, requiring all persons before holding office in Britain to take oaths of supremacy and allegiance or an equivalent test. **2** an act of 1871 relaxing conditions for university degrees. **test bed** equipment for testing aircraft engines before acceptance for general use. **test card** *Brit.* = *test pattern.* **test case** *Law* a case setting a precedent for other cases involving the same question of law. **test drive** a drive taken to determine the qualities of a motor vehicle with a view to its regular use. **test-drive** *v.tr.* (*past* **-drove**; *past part.* **-driven**) drive (a vehicle) for this purpose. **test flight** a flight during which the performance of an aircraft is tested. **test-fly** *v.tr.* (**-flies**; *past* **-flew**; *past part.* **-flown**) fly (an aircraft) for this purpose. **test match** a cricket or rugby match between teams of certain countries, usu. each of a series in a tour. **test out** put (a theory, etc.) to a practical test. **test paper 1** a minor examination paper. **2** *Chem.* a paper impregnated with a substance changing color under known conditions. **test pattern** a still television picture transmitted outside normal program hours and designed for use in judging the quality and position of the image. **test pilot** a pilot who test-flies aircraft. **test tube** a thin glass tube closed at one end used for chemical tests, etc. **test-tube baby** *colloq.* a baby conceived by *in vitro* fertilization. □□ **testable** *adj.* **testability** *n.* **testee** /testée/ *n.* [ME f. OF f. L *testu(m)* earthen pot, collateral form of *testa* TEST²]

■ *n.* **1** trial, examination, exam, tryout, experiment, evaluation, check, checkup, investigation, inspection, appraisal, assessment, study, analysis. **2** see PROOF *n.* 4. **3** examination, exam, trial. **6** assay, analysis. ● *v.* **1** try (out), check (up) (on), examine, question, quiz, evaluate, appraise, assess, prove, put to the test, probe, sound out, vet, inspect, screen, audition, sample, experiment with, check out. **2** see TAX *v.* 3. **3, 4** assay, analyze. □ **put to the test** see TEST¹ *v.* 1 above.
□□ **testee** examinee, candidate.

test² /test/ *n.* the shell of some invertebrates, esp. foraminiferans and tunicates. [L *testa* tile, jug, shell, etc.: cf. TEST¹]

Test. *abbr.* Testament.

testa /téstə/ *n.* (*pl.* **testae** /-tee/) *Bot.* a seed coat. [L (as TEST²)]

testaceous /testáyshəs/ *adj.* **1** *Biol.* having a hard continuous outer covering. **2** *Bot.* & *Zool.* of a brick red color. [L *testaceus* (as TEST²)]

testament /téstəmənt/ *n.* **1** a will (esp. *last will and testament*). **2** (usu. foll. by *to*) evidence; proof (*is testament to his loyalty*). **3** *Bibl.* **a** a covenant or dispensation. **b** (**Testament**) a division of the Christian Bible (see *Old Testament*, *New Testament*). **c** (**Testament**) a copy of the New Testament. [ME f. L *testamentum* will (as TESTATE): in early Christian L rendering Gk *diathēkē* covenant]
■ **1** will, (last will and) testament, last wishes. **2** see MONUMENT 4, PROOF *n.* 1.

testamentary /téstəméntəree/ *adj.* of or by or in a will. [L *testamentarius* (as TESTAMENT)]

testate /téstayt/ *adj.* & *n.* ● *adj.* having left a valid will at death. ● *n.* a testate person. □□ **testacy** *n.* (*pl.* **-ies**). [L *testatus* past part. of *testari* testify, make a will, f. *testis* witness]

testator /téstaytər, testáytər/ *n.* (*fem.* **testatrix** /testáytriks/) a person who has made a will, esp. one who dies testate. [ME f. AF *testatour* f. L *testator* (as TESTATE)]

tester¹ /téstər/ *n.* **1** a person or thing that tests. **2** a sample of a cosmetic, etc., allowing customers to try it before purchase.

tester² /téstər/ *n.* a canopy, esp. over a four-poster bed. [ME f. med.L *testerium*, *testrum*, *testura*, ult. f. L *testa* tile]

testes *pl.* of TESTIS.

testicle /téstikəl/ *n.* a male organ that produces spermatozoa, etc., esp. one of a pair enclosed in the scrotum behind the penis of a man and most mammals. □□ **testicular** /-stíkyələr/ *adj.* [ME f. L *testiculus* dimin. of *testis* witness (of virility)]

testiculate /testíkyələt/ *adj.* **1** having or shaped like testicles. **2** *Bot.* (esp. of an orchid) having pairs of tubers so shaped. [LL *testiculatus* (as TESTICLE)]

testify /téstifī/ *v.* (**-ies, -ied**) **1** *intr.* (of a person or thing) bear witness (*testified to the facts*). **2** *intr. Law* give evidence. **3** *tr.* affirm or declare (*testified his regret; testified that she had been present*). **4** *tr.* (of a thing) be evidence of; evince. □□ **testifier** *n.* [ME f. L *testificari* f. *testis* witness]
■ **1** attest, (bear) witness. **2** give evidence *or* testimony. **3** state, assert, attest, swear, say, affirm, declare, avow, proclaim, announce, *formal* aver, vouchsafe. **4** see EVIDENCE *v.* □□ **testifier** see WITNESS *n.* 2.

testimonial /téstimóneeəl/ *n.* **1** a certificate of character, conduct, or qualifications. **2** a gift presented to a person (esp. in public) as a mark of esteem, in acknowledgment of services, etc. [ME f. OF *testimoignal* (adj.) f. *tesmoin* or LL *testimonialis* (as TESTIMONY)]
■ **1** endorsement, certification, commendation, (letter of) recommendation, reference, blurb. **2** see TRIBUTE 1.

testimony /téstimōnee/ *n.* (*pl.* **-ies**) **1** *Law* an oral or written statement under oath or affirmation. **2** declaration or statement of fact. **3** evidence; demonstration (*called him in testimony; produce testimony*). **4** *Bibl.* the Ten Commandments. **5** *archaic* a solemn protest or confession. [ME f. L *testimonium* f. *testis* witness]
■ **1, 2** evidence, attestation, affirmation, avowal, deposition, statement, affidavit, declaration, assertion,

claim, averment, asseveration; confirmation, verification, authentication, corroboration. **3** see DEMONSTRATION 4. **5** profession, admission, confession, protest, declaration, avowal, announcement.

testis /téstis/ *n.* (*pl.* **testes** /-teez/) *Anat.* & *Zool.* a testicle. [L, = witness: cf. TESTICLE]

testosterone /testóstərōn/ *n.* a steroid androgen formed in the testicles. [TESTIS + STEROL + -ONE]

testudinal /testoõd′nəl, -tyoõd-/ *adj.* of or shaped like a tortoise. [as TESTUDO]

testudo /testoõdō, testyoõ-/ *n.* (*pl.* **-os** or **testudines** /-dineez/) *Rom.Hist.* **1** a screen formed by a body of troops in close array with overlapping shields. **2** a movable screen to protect besieging troops. [L *testudo -dinis*, lit. 'tortoise' (as TEST²)]

testy /téstee/ *adj.* (**testier, testiest**) irritable; touchy. □□ **testily** *adv.* **testiness** *n.* [ME f. AF *testif* f. OF *teste* head (as TEST²)]
■ irritable, bad-tempered, irascible, short-tempered, petulant, touchy, tetchy, querulous, peevish, hot-tempered, crusty, cross, grumpy, bearish, crabby, crabbed, fretful, captious, waspish, snappish, prickly, quarrelsome, fractious, contentious, choleric, splenetic, ill-humored, disagreeable, ill-tempered, edgy, on edge, quick-tempered, crotchety, cantankerous, cranky, *colloq.* grouchy, shirty, ornery, *Brit. colloq.* stroppy, *Austral. sl.* snaky. □□ **testily** see SHORTLY 3.

tetanic /titánik/ *adj.* of or such as occurs in tetanus. □□ **tetanically** *adv.* [L *tetanicus* f. Gk *tetanikos* (as TETANUS)]

tetanus /tét′nəs/ *n.* **1** a bacterial disease affecting the nervous system and marked by tonic spasm of the voluntary muscles. **2** *Physiol.* the prolonged contraction of a muscle caused by rapidly repeated stimuli. □□ **tetanize** *v.tr.* **tetanoid** *adj.* [ME f. L f. Gk *tetanos* muscular spasm f. *teinō* stretch]

tetany /tét′nee/ *n.* a disease with intermittent muscular spasms caused by malfunction of the parathyroid glands and a consequent deficiency of calcium. [F *tétanie* (as TETANUS)]

tetchy /téchee/ *adj.* (also **techy**) (**-ier, -iest**) peevish; irritable. □□ **tetchily** *adv.* **tetchiness** *n.* [prob. f. *tecche, tache* blemish, fault f. OF *teche, tache*]
■ see PEEVISH.

tête-à-tête /táytaatáyt, tétaatét/ *n., adv.,* & *adj.* ● *n.* **1** a private conversation or interview usu. between two persons. **2** an S-shaped sofa for two people to sit face to face. ● *adv.* together in private (*dined tête-à-tête*). ● *adj.* **1** private; confidential. **2** concerning only two persons. [F, lit. 'head-to-head']
■ *n.* **1** (cozy *or* personal) chat, dialogue, causerie, heart-to-heart, private talk *or* word *or* conversation, parley, interview, *colloq.* confab, one-on-one. **2** see COUCH¹ *n.* ● *adv.* intimately, privately, in private, face to face, heart to heart, confidentially, secretly, à deux, in secret, *colloq.* one-on-one. ● *adj.* **1** intimate, private, heart-to-heart, cozy.

tête-bêche /taytbésh, tét-/ *adj.* (of a postage stamp) printed upside down or sideways relative to another. [F f. *tête* head + *béchevet* double bedhead]

tether /téthər/ *n.* & *v.* ● *n.* **1** a rope, etc., by which an animal is tied to confine it to the spot. **2** the extent of one's knowledge, authority, etc.; scope; limit. ● *v.tr.* tie (an animal) with a tether. □ **at the end of one's tether** having reached the limit of one's patience, resources, abilities, etc. [ME f. ON *tjóthr* f. Gmc]
■ *n.* **1** lead, leash, rope, cord, fetter, restraint, halter, tie, chain. ● *v.* tie (up *or* down), restrain, fetter, chain (up *or* down), leash, rope, manacle, secure, shackle, fasten, picket, stake. □ **at the end of one's tether** see DESPERATE 1.

/.../ **pronunciation**	● **part of speech**
□ **phrases, idioms, and compounds**	
□□ **derivatives**	■ **synonym section**
cross-references appear in SMALL CAPITALS or *italics*	

tetra- /tétrə/ *comb. form* (also **tetr-** before a vowel) **1** four (*tetrapod*). **2** *Chem.* (forming names of compounds) containing four atoms or groups of a specified kind (*tetroxide*). [Gk f. *tettares* four]

tetrachord /tétrəkawrd/ *n. Mus.* **1** a scale pattern of four notes, the interval between the first and last being a perfect fourth. **2** a musical instrument with four strings.

tetracyclic /tétrəsíklik, -sí-/ *adj.* **1** *Bot.* having four circles or whorls. **2** *Chem.* (of a compound) having a molecular structure of four fused hydrocarbon rings.

tetracycline /tétrəsíkleen, -klin/ *n.* an antibiotic with a molecule of four rings. [TETRACYCLIC + -INE⁴]

tetrad /tétrad/ *n.* **1** a group of four. **2** the number four. [Gk *tetras -ados* (as TETRA-)]

tetradactyl /tétrədáktil/ *n. Zool.* an animal with four toes on each foot. □□ **tetradactylous** *adj.*

tetraethyl lead /tétrəéthəl/ *n.* a liquid formerly added to gasoline as an antiknock agent.

tetragon /tétrəgon/ *n.* a plane figure with four angles and four sides. [Gk *tetragōnon* quadrangle (as TETRA-, -GON)]

tetragonal /tetrágənəl/ *adj.* **1** of or like a tetragon. **2** *Crystallog.* (of a crystal) having three axes at right angles, two of them equal. □□ **tetragonally** *adv.*

tetragram /tétrəgram/ *n.* a word of four letters.

Tetragrammaton /tétrəgrámətən/ *n.* the Hebrew name of God written in four letters, articulated as *Yahweh*, etc. [Gk (as TETRA-, *gramma*, *-atos* letter)]

tetragynous /titrájinəs/ *adj. Bot.* having four pistils.

tetrahedron /tétrəheédrən/ *n.* (*pl.* **tetrahedra** /-drə/ or **tetrahedrons**) a four-sided solid; a triangular pyramid. □□ **tetrahedral** /late Gk *tetraedron* neut. of *tetraedros* foursided (as TETRA-, -HEDRON)]

tetralogy /tetráləjee, -tról-/ *n.* (*pl.* **-ies**) **1** a group of four related literary or operatic works. **2** *Gk Antiq.* a trilogy of tragedies with a satyric drama.

tetramerous /tetrámərəs/ *adj.* having four parts.

tetrameter /tetrámitər/ *n. Prosody* a verse of four measures. [LL *tetrametrus* f. Gk *tetrametros* (as TETRA-, *metron* measure)]

tetrandrous /tetrándrəs/ *adj. Bot.* having four stamens.

tetraplegia /tétrəpleéjeeə, -jə/ *n. Med.* = QUADRIPLEGIA. □□ **tetraplegic** *adj. & n.* [mod.L (as TETRA-, Gk *plēgē* blow, strike)]

tetraploid /tétrəployd/ *adj. & n. Biol.* ● *adj.* (of an organism or cell) having four times the haploid set of chromosomes. ● *n.* a tetraploid organism or cell.

tetrapod /tétrəpod/ *n.* **1** *Zool.* an animal with four feet. **2** a structure supported by four feet radiating from a center. □□ **tetrapodous** /titrápədəs/ *adj.* [mod.L *tetrapodus* f. Gk *tetrapous* (as TETRA-, *pous podos* foot)]

tetrapterous /tetráptərəs/ *adj. Zool.* having four wings. [mod.L *tetrapterus* f. Gk *tetrapteros* (as TETRA-, *pteron* wing)]

tetrarch /tétraark/ *n.* **1** *Rom.Hist.* **a** the governor of a fourth part of a country or province. **b** a subordinate ruler. **2** one of four joint rulers. □□ **tetrarchate** /-kayt/ *n.* **tetrarchical** /-raárkikəl/ *adj.* **tetrarchy** *n.* (*pl.* **-ies**). [ME f. LL *tetrarcha* f. L *tetrarches* f. Gk *tetrarkhēs* (as TETRA-, *arkhō* rule)]

tetrastich /tétrəstik/ *n. Prosody* a group of four lines of verse. [L *tetrastichon* f. Gk (as TETRA-, *stikhon* line)]

tetrastyle /tétrəstil/ *n. & adj.* ● *n.* a building with four pillars, esp. forming a portico in front or supporting a ceiling. ● *adj.* (of a building) built in this way. [L *tetrastylos* f. Gk *tetrastulos* (as TETRA-, STYLE)]

tetrasyllable /tétrəsíləbəl/ *n.* a word of four syllables. □□ **tetrasyllabic** /-lábik-/ *adj.*

tetrathlon /tetráthlən/ *n.* a contest comprising four events, esp. riding, shooting, swimming, and running. [TETRA- + Gk *athlon* contest, after PENTATHLON]

tetratomic /tétrətómik/ *adj. Chem.* having four atoms (of a specified kind) in the molecule.

tetravalent /tétrəváylənt/ *adj. Chem.* having a valence of four; quadrivalent.

tetrode /tétrōd/ *n.* a thermionic valve having four electrodes. [TETRA- + Gk *hodos* way]

tetter /tétər/ *n. archaic* or *dial.* a pustular skin eruption, e.g.,

eczema. [OE *teter*: cf. OHG *zittaroh*, G dial. *Zitteroch*, Skr. *dadru*]

Teut. *abbr.* Teutonic.

Teuto- /tōōtō, tōō-/ *comb. form* = TEUTON.

Teuton /tōōt'n, tyōōtən/ *n.* **1** a member of a Teutonic nation, esp. a German. **2** *hist.* a member of a N. European tribe which attacked the Roman republic *c.* 110 BC. [L *Teutones*, *Teutoni*, f. an IE base meaning 'people' or 'country']

Teutonic /tōōtónik, tyōō-/ *adj. & n.* ● *adj.* **1** relating to or characteristic of the Germanic peoples or their languages. **2** German. ● *n.* the early language usu. called Germanic. □□ **Teutonicism** /-isizəm/ *n.* [F *teutonique* f. L *Teutonicus* (as TEUTON)]

Tex. *abbr.* Texas.

Texan /téksən/ *n. & adj.* ● *n.* a native or inhabitant of Texas. ● *adj.* of or relating to Texas.

Tex-Mex /téksméks/ *adj.* combining cultural elements from Texas and Mexico, as in cooking, music, etc.

text /tekst/ *n.* **1** the main body of a book as distinct from notes, appendices, pictures, etc. **2** the original words of an author or document, esp. as distinct from a paraphrase of or commentary on them. **3** a passage quoted from Scripture, esp. as the subject of a sermon. **4** a subject or theme. **5** (in *pl.*) books prescribed for study. **6** a textbook. **7** (in full **text hand**) a large kind of handwriting esp. for manuscripts. **8** lyrics, as to a song or poem. □ **text editor** *Computing* a system or program allowing the user to enter and edit text. **text processing** *Computing* the manipulation of text, esp. transforming it from one format to another. □□ **textless** *adj.* [ME f. ONF *tixte*, *texte* f. L *textus* tissue, literary style (in med.L = Gospel) f. L *texere text-* weave]

■ **1** wording, words, content, (subject) matter; printed matter, (main) body (text), contents. **2** wording, words, script, transcript. **3** extract, abstract, section, quotation, part, paragraph, passage, verse, line; lesson. **4** subject (matter), topic, theme, motif, issue, focus. **5** (*texts*) (set) books, works, writings, literary texts, literature. **6** textbook, schoolbook, reader, manual, handbook, primer, workbook, exercise book.

textbook /tékstbōōk/ *n. & adj.* ● *n.* a book for use in studying, esp. a standard account of a subject. ● *attrib.adj.* **1** exemplary; accurate (cf. COPYBOOK). **2** instructively typical. □□ **textbookish** *adj.*

textile /tékstil/ *n. & adj.* ● *n.* **1** any woven material. **2** any cloth. ● *adj.* **1** of weaving or cloth (*textile industry*). **2** woven (*textile fabrics*). **3** suitable for weaving (*textile materials*). [L *textilis* (as TEXT)]

■ *n. & adj.* cloth, fabric, material.

textual /tékschōōəl/ *adj.* of, in, or concerning a text (*textual errors*). □ **textual criticism** the process of attempting to ascertain the correct reading of a text. □□ **textually** *adv.* [ME f. med.L *textualis* (as TEXT)]

textualist /tékschōōəlist/ *n.* a person who adheres strictly to the letter of the text. □□ **textualism** *n.*

texture /tékschər/ *n. & v.* ● *n.* **1** the feel or appearance of a surface or substance. **2** the arrangement of threads, etc., in textile fabric. **3** the arrangement of small constituent parts. **4** *Art* the representation of the structure and detail of objects. **5** *Mus.* the quality of sound formed by combining parts. **6** the quality of a piece of writing, esp. with reference to imagery, alliteration, etc. **7** quality or style resulting from composition (*the texture of her life*). ● *v.tr.* (usu. as **textured** *adj.*) provide with a texture. □□ **textural** *adj.* **texturally** *adv.* **textureless** *adj.* [ME f. L *textura* weaving (as TEXT)]

■ *n.* **1, 2** feel, surface, finish, nap, character, grain, features, consistency, weave, appearance. **3** configuration, composition, constitution, structure. **4–7** nature, structure, fabric, constitution, substance, quality, style.

texturize /tékschəriz/ *v.tr.* (usu. as **texturized** *adj.*) impart a particular texture to (fabrics or food).

Th *symb. Chem.* the element thorium.

Th. *abbr.* Thursday.

-th¹ /th/ *suffix* (also **-eth** /ith/) forming ordinal and fractional numbers from *four* onwards (*fourth*; *thirtieth*). [OE *-tha, -the, -otha, -othe*]

-th[2] /th/ *suffix* forming nouns denoting an action or process: **1** from verbs (*birth*; *growth*). **2** from adjectives (*breadth*; *filth*; *length*). [OE *-thu, -tho, -th*]

-th[3] var. of -ETH[2].

Thai /tī/ *n. & adj.* ● *n.* (*pl.* same or **Thais**) **1 a** a native or inhabitant of Thailand in SE Asia; a member of the largest ethnic group in Thailand. **b** a person of Thai descent. **2** the language of Thailand. ● *adj.* of or relating to Thailand or its people or language. [Thai, = free]

thalamus /thálamas/ *n.* (*pl.* **thalami** /-mī/) **1** *Anat.* either of two masses of gray matter in the forebrain, serving as relay stations for sensory tracts. **2** *Bot.* the receptacle of a flower. **3** *Gk Antiq.* an inner room or women's apartment. □□ **thalamic** /thalámik, thálamik/ *adj.* (in senses 1 and 2). [L f. Gk *thalamos*]

thalassic /thalásik/ *adj.* of the sea or seas, esp. small or inland seas. [F *thalassique* f. Gk *thalassa* sea]
■ see MARINE *adj.* 1.

thaler /taálar/ *n. hist.* a German silver coin. [G *T(h)aler*: see DOLLAR]

thalidomide /thalídamīd/ *n.* a drug formerly used as a sedative but found in 1961 to cause fetal malformation when taken by a mother early in pregnancy. □ **thalidomide baby** (or **child**) a baby or child born deformed from the effects of thalidomide. [ph*thalidomide* *mide*]

thalli *pl.* of THALLUS.

thallium /tháleeəm/ *n. Chem.* a rare soft white metallic element, occurring naturally in zinc blende and some iron ores. □□ **thallic** *adj.* **thallous** *adj.* [formed as THALLUS, from the green line in its spectrum]

thallophyte /tháləfīt/ *n. Bot.* a plant having a thallus, e.g., algae, fungus, or lichen. [mod.L *Thallophyta* (as THALLUS) + -PHYTE]

thallus /tháləs/ *n.* (*pl.* **thalli** /-lī/) a plant body without vascular tissue and not differentiated into root, stem, and leaves. □□ **thalloid** *adj.* [L f. Gk *thallos* green shoot f. *thallō* bloom]

thalweg /taálveg/ *n.* **1** *Geog.* a line where opposite slopes meet at the bottom of a valley, river, or lake. **2** *Law* a boundary between states along the center of a river, etc. [G f. *Thal* valley + *Weg* way]

than /than, thən/ *conj.* **1** introducing the second element in a comparison (*you are older than he is*; *you are older than he*). ¶ It is also possible to say *you are older than him*, with *than* treated as a preposition, esp. in less formal contexts. **2** introducing the second element in a statement of difference (*anyone other than me*). [OE *thanne*, etc., orig. the same word as THEN]

thanage /tháynij/ *n. hist.* **1** the rank of thane. **2** the land granted to a thane. [ME f. AF *thanage* (as THANE)]

thanatology /thánətólajee/ *n.* the scientific study of death and its associated phenomena and practices. [Gk *thanatos* death + -LOGY]

thane /thayn/ *n. hist.* **1** a man who held land from an English king or other superior by military service, ranking between ordinary freemen and hereditary nobles. **2** a man who held land from a Scottish king and ranked with an earl's son; the chief of a clan. □□ **thanedom** *n.* [OE *theg(e)n* servant, soldier f. Gmc]

thank /thangk/ *v. & n.* ● *v.tr.* **1** express gratitude to (*thanked him for the present*). **2** hold responsible (*you can thank yourself for that*). ● *n.* (in *pl.*) **1** gratitude (*expressed his heartfelt thanks*). **2** an expression of gratitude (*give thanks to all who helped*). **3** (as a formula) thank you (*thanks for your help*; *thanks very much*). □ **give thanks** say grace at a meal. **I will thank you** esp. *Brit.* a polite formula, now usu. *iron.* implying reproach (*I will thank you to go away*). **no** (or **small**) **thanks to** despite. **thank goodness** (or **God** or **heavens**, etc.) **1** *colloq.* an expression of relief or pleasure. **2** an expression of pious gratitude. **thanks to** as the (good or bad) result of (*thanks to my foresight*; *thanks to your obstinacy*). **thank you** a polite formula acknowledging a gift or service or an offer accepted or refused. **thank-you** *n. colloq.* an in-

stance of expressing thanks. [OE *thancian, thanc* f. Gmc, rel. to THINK]
■ *v.* **1** express *or* show (one's) gratitude to, express *or* show (one's) thanks to, express *or* show (one's) appreciation to, say thank you *or* thanks to, give *or* offer *or* tender thanks to. **2** blame, hold responsible, credit, acknowledge. ● *n.* (*thanks*) **1** gratitude, appreciation, gratefulness, acknowledgment, recognition. **2** thanksgiving. □ **thanks to** owing to, because of, as a result of, in consequence of, as a consequence of, by reason of, through, by virtue of, by dint of, on account of, *disp.* due to.

thankful /thángkfŏŏl/ *adj.* **1** grateful; pleased. **2** (of words or acts) expressive of thanks. □□ **thankfulness** *n.* [OE *thancful* (as THANK, -FUL)]
■ **1** grateful, appreciative, indebted, pleased, glad, obliged, obligated, under (an) obligation, beholden. **2** grateful, appreciative. □□ **thankfulness** see GRATITUDE.

thankfully /thángkfŏŏlee/ *adv.* **1** in a thankful manner. **2** *disp.* let us be thankful; fortunately (*thankfully, nobody was hurt*). [OE *thancfullice* (as THANKFUL, -LY[2])]
■ **2** see *happily* (HAPPY).

thankless /thángklis/ *adj.* **1** not expressing or feeling gratitude. **2** (of a task, etc.) giving no pleasure or profit. **3** not deserving thanks. □□ **thanklessly** *adv.* **thanklessness** *n.*
■ **1** ungrateful, unappreciative, unthankful. **2** unappreciated, unacknowledged, unrecognized, unrewarded, useless, unrewarding, fruitless, unprofitable, profitless, vain, futile, *archaic* bootless. □□ **thanklessness** see INGRATITUDE.

thanksgiving /thángksgíving/ *n.* **1 a** the expression of gratitude, esp. as a prayer. **b** a form of words for this. **2** (**Thanksgiving** or **Thanksgiving Day**) a national holiday for giving thanks, the fourth Thursday in November in the US, usu. the second Monday in October in Canada. □ **General Thanksgiving** *Anglican Ch.* a form of thanksgiving in the Book of Common Prayer or the Alternative Service Book.
■ **1** see GRATITUDE.

thar var. of TAHR.

that /that/ *pron., adj., adv., & conj.* ● *demons.pron.* (*pl.* **those** /thōz/) **1** the person or thing indicated, named, or understood, esp. when observed by the speaker or when familiar to the person addressed (*I heard that*; *who is that in the yard?*; *I knew all that before*; *that is not fair*). **2** (contrasted with *this*) the further or less immediate or obvious, etc., of two (*this bag is much heavier than that*). **3** the action, behavior, or circumstances just observed or mentioned (*don't do that again*). **4** *Brit.* (on the telephone, etc.) the person spoken to (*who is that?*). **5** esp. *Brit. colloq.* referring to a strong feeling just mentioned ('*Are you glad?*' '*I am that*'). **6** (esp. in relative constructions) the one, the person, etc., described or specified in some way (*those who have cars can take the luggage*; *those unfit for use*; *a table like that described above*). **7** /that/ (*pl.* **that**) used instead of *which* or *whom* to introduce a defining clause, esp. one essential to identification (*the book that you sent me*; *there is nothing here that matters*). ¶ As a relative *that* usually specifies, whereas *who* or *which* need not: compare *the book that you sent me is lost* with *the book, which I gave you, is lost.* ● *demons.adj.* (*pl.* **those** /thōz/) **1** designating the person or thing indicated, named, understood, etc. (cf. sense 1 of *pron.*) (*look at that dog*; *what was that noise?*; *things were easier in those days*). **2** contrasted with *this* (cf. sense 2 of *pron.*) (*this bag is heavier than that one*). **3** expressing strong feeling (*shall not easily forget that day*). ● *adv.* **1** to such a degree; so (*have done that much*; *will go that far*). **2** *colloq.* very (*not that good*). **3** /thət/ at which, on which, etc. (*at the speed that he was going he could not stop*; *the day that I first met her*). ¶ Often omitted in this sense: *the*

/.../ **pronunciation**	● **part of speech**
□ **phrases, idioms, and compounds**	
□□ **derivatives**	■ **synonym section**
cross-references appear in SMALL CAPITALS or *italics*	

day I first met her. ● *conj.* /th**ǝ**t except when stressed/ introducing a subordinate clause indicating: **1** a statement or hypothesis (*they say that he is better; there is no doubt that he meant it; the result was that the handle fell off*). **2** a purpose (*we live that we may eat*). **3** a result (*am so sleepy that I cannot keep my eyes open*). **4** a reason or cause (*it is rather that he lacks the time*). **5** a wish (*Oh, that summer were here!*). ¶ Often omitted in senses 1, 3: *they say he is better.* □ **all that** very (*not all that good*). **and all that** (or **and that** *colloq.*) and all or various things associated with or similar to what has been mentioned; and so forth. **like that 1** of that kind (*is fond of books like that*). **2** in that manner; as you are doing; as he has been doing; etc. (*wish they would not talk like that*). **3** *colloq.* without effort (*did the job like that*). **4** of that character (*he would not accept any payment &em. he is like that*). **that is** (or **that is to say**) a formula introducing or following an explanation of a preceding word or words. **that's** *colloq.* you are (by virtue of present or future obedience, etc.) (*that's a good boy*). **that's more like it** an acknowledgment of improvement. **that's right** an expression of approval or *colloq.* assent. **that's that** a formula concluding a narrative or discussion or indicating completion of a task. **that there** *sl.* = sense 1 of *adj.* **that will do** no more is needed or desirable. [OE *thæt*, nom. & acc. sing. neut. of demons. pron. & adj. *se, sēo, thæt* f. Gmc; *those* f. OE *thās* pl. of *thes* THIS]

▪ □ **that is (to say)** see NAMELY, LIKE[1] *adj.* 1b.

thatch /thach/ *n. & v.* ● *n.* **1** a roofing material of straw, reeds, palm leaves, or similar material. **2** *colloq.* the hair of the head esp. when extremely thick. ● *v.tr.* (also *absol.*) cover (a roof or a building) with thatch. □□ **thatcher** *n.* [n. late collateral form of *thack* (now dial.) f. OE *thæc*, after v. f. OE *theccan* f. Gmc, assim. to *thack*]

thaumatrope /tháwmǝtrōp/ *n. hist.* **1** a disk or card with two different pictures on its two sides, which combine into one by the persistence of visual impressions when the disk is rapidly rotated. **2** a zoetrope. [irreg. f. Gk *thauma* marvel + *-tropos* -turning]

thaumaturge /tháwmǝtǝrj/ *n.* a worker of miracles; a wonder-worker. □□ **thaumaturgic** /-túrjik/ *adj.* **thaumaturgical** /-túrjikǝl/ *adj.* **thaumaturgist** *n.* **thaumaturgy** *n.* [med.L *thaumaturgus* f. Gk *thaumatourgos* (adj.) f. *thauma -matos* marvel + *-ergos* -working]

thaw /thaw/ *v. & n.* ● *v.* **1** *intr.* (often foll. by *out*) (of ice or snow or a frozen thing) pass into a liquid or unfrozen state. **2** *intr.* (usu. prec. by *it* as subject) (of the weather) become warm enough to melt ice, etc. (*it began to thaw*). **3** *intr.* become warm enough to lose numbness, etc. **4** *intr.* become less cold or stiff in manner; become genial. **5** *tr.* (often foll. by *out*) cause to thaw. **6** *tr.* make cordial or animated. ● *n.* **1** the act or an instance of thawing. **2** the warmth of weather that thaws (*a thaw has set in*). **3** *Polit.* a relaxation of control or restriction. □□ **thawless** *adj.* [OE *thawian* f. WG; orig. unkn.]

▪ *v.* **1, 5** melt, defrost, warm (up), heat (up), unfreeze, *Chem.* liquefy. **2, 3** warm (up), heat (up). **4, 6** soften, warm, melt, become (more) cordial *or* friendly, relax, yield, relent, unbend, let oneself go. ● *n.* **1** thawing, unfreezing, defrosting, melting, warming up, heating up.

the /before a vowel *thee*, before a consonant *thǝ*, when stressed *thee*/ *adj. & adv.* ● *adj.* (called the definite article) **1** denoting one or more persons or things already mentioned, under discussion, implied, or familiar (*gave the man a wave; shall let the matter drop; hurt myself in the arm; went to the theater*). **2** serving to describe as unique (*the President; the Mississippi*). **3 a** (foll. by defining adj.) which is, who are, etc. (*ignored the embarrassed Mr. Smith; Edward the Seventh*). **b** (foll. by adj. used *absol.*) denoting a class described (*from the sublime to the ridiculous*). **4** best known or best entitled to the name (with *the* stressed: *no relation to the Hemingway; this is the book on this subject*). **5** used to indicate a following defining clause or phrase (*the book that you borrowed; the best I can do for you; the bottom of a well*). **6 a** used to indicate that a singular noun represents a species, class, etc. (*the cat loves comfort; has the novel a future?; plays the harp well*). **b**

used with a noun which figuratively represents an occupation, pursuit, etc. (*went on the stage; too fond of the bottle*). **c** (foll. by the name of a unit) a; per (*$5 the square yard; allow 8 minutes to the mile*). **d** *colloq.* designating a disease, affliction, etc. (*the measles; the toothache; the blues*). **7** (foll. by a unit of time) the present; the current (*man of the moment; questions of the day; book of the month*). **8** *colloq.* my; our (*the dog; the car*). **9** used before the surname of the chief of a Scottish or Irish clan (*the Macnab*). ● *adv.* (preceding comparatives in expressions of proportional variation) in or by that (or such a) degree; on that account (*the more the merrier; the more he gets the more he wants*). □ **all the** in the full degree to be expected (*that makes it all the worse*). **so much the** (tautologically) in that degree (*so much the more; so much the worse for him*). [((adj.) OE, replacing *se, sēo, thæt* (= THAT), f. Gmc: (adv.) f. OE *thȳ, thē*, instrumental case]

theandric /theeándrik/ *adj.* of the union, or by the joint agency, of the divine and human natures in Christ. [eccl.Gk *theandrikos* f. *theos* god + *anēr andros* man]

theanthropic /theeanthrópik/ *adj.* **1** both divine and human. **2** tending to embody deity in human form. [eccl.Gk *theanthrōpos* god man f. *theos* god + *anthrōpos* human being]

thearchy /thee-aarkee/ *n.* (*pl.* **-ies**) **1** government by a god or gods. **2** a system or order of gods (*the Olympian thearchy*). [eccl.Gk *thearkhia* godhead f. *theos* god + *-arkhia* f. *arkhō* rule]

theat. *abbr.* **1** theater. **2** theatrical.

theater /thee-ǝtǝr/ *n.* (*Brit.* **theatre**) **1 a** a building or outdoor area for dramatic performances. **b** (in full **movie theater**) a building used for showing movies. **2 a** the writing and production of plays. **b** effective material for the stage (*makes good theater*). **c** action with a dramatic quality; dramatic character or effect. **3** a room or hall for lectures, etc., with seats in tiers. **4** (in full **operating theater**) **a** a room or lecture hall with rising tiers of seats to accommodate students' viewing of surgical procedures **b** *Brit.* = *operating room*. **5 a** a scene or field of action (*the theater of war*). **b** (*attrib.*) designating weapons intermediate between tactical and strategic (*theater nuclear missiles*). **6** a natural land formation in a gradually rising part-circle like ancient Greek and Roman theaters. □ **theater-goer** a frequenter of theaters. **theater-going** frequenting theaters. **theater-in-the-round** a dramatic performance on a stage surrounded by spectators. **theater sister** *Brit.* a nurse supervising the nursing team in an operating theater. [ME f. OF *t(h)eatre* or f. L *theatrum* f. Gk *theatron* f. *theaomai* behold]

▪ **1 a** playhouse, (opera) house, (music) hall, auditorium, amphitheater, theater-in-the-round, colosseum, hippodrome, arena. **b** *colloq.* movie house, *Brit.* cinema. **2 a** drama, stagecraft, dramaturgy, melodrama, theatrics, histrionics, acting, performing, performance; the stage, dramatic *or* thespian *or* histrionic art(s), the boards, show business, *colloq.* showbiz. **b** drama, entertainment. **c** drama, melodrama, staginess, theatricalism, theatrics, histrionics; (dramatic) effect. **5 a** area, arena, scene, sphere *or* place *or* field of action, setting, site.

theatric /theeátrik/ *adj. & n.* ● *adj.* = THEATRICAL. ● *n.* (in *pl.*) theatrical actions.

▪ *n.* (*theatrics*) see DRAMA 4.

theatrical /theeátrikǝl/ *adj. & n.* ● *adj.* **1** of or for the theater; of acting or actors. **2** (of a manner, speech, gesture, or person) calculated for effect; showy; artificial; affected. ● *n.* (in *pl.*) **1** dramatic performances (*amateur theatricals*). **2** theatrical actions. □□ **theatricalism** *n.* **theatricality** /-kálitee/ *n.* **theatricalize** *v.tr.* **theatricalization** *n.* **theatrically** *adv.* [LL *theatricus* f. Gk *theatrikos* f. *theatron* THEATER]

▪ *adj.* **1** theatric, dramatic, stage, histrionic, thespian; repertory. **2** stagy, overdone, melodramatic, histrionic, overwrought, exaggerated, forced, overacted, sensational, sensationalistic, mannered, affected, unnatural, artificial, fake, false, showy, ostentatious, spectacular, extravagant, *colloq.* phony, camp, campy, hammy, *sl.* ham. ● *n.* **2** (*theatricals*) see DRAMA 3.

□□ **theatricalism, theatricality** see DRAMA 4.

Theban /theéebən/ adj. & n. ● adj. of or relating to Thebes in ancient Egypt or ancient Greece. ● n. a native or inhabitant of Thebes. [ME f. L *Thebanus* f. *Thebae* Thebes f. Gk *Thēbai*]

theca /theékə/ n. (pl. **thecae** /theésee/) **1** Bot. a part of a plant serving as a receptacle. **2** Zool. a case or sheath enclosing an organ or organism. □□ **thecate** adj. [L f. Gk *thēkē* case]

thé dansant /táy donSÓN/ n. = tea dance. [F]

thee /thee/ pron. objective case of THOU¹. [OE]

theft /theft/ n. **1** the act or an instance of stealing. **2** Law dishonest appropriation of another's property with intent to deprive him or her of it permanently. [OE *thīefth*, *thēofth*, later *thēoft*, f. Gmc (as THIEF)]

■ **1** robbery, stealing, larceny, pilferage, pilfering, filching, shoplifting, thievery, thieving, embezzlement, peculation, fraud, pocketing, colloq. lifting, swiping, rip-off, ripping off, formal or joc. purloining, sl. pinching, snitching, knocking off, heist, Austral. sl. duffing, Brit. sl. nicking.

thegn /thayn/ n. hist. an English thane. [OE: see THANE]

theine /theéin, theé-een/ n. = CAFFEINE. [mod.L *thea* tea + -INE⁴]

their /thair/ poss.pron. (attrib.) **1** of or belonging to them or themselves (their house; their own business). **2** (**Their**) (in the UK) (in titles) that they are (Their Majesties). **3** disp. as a third person sing. indefinite meaning 'his or her' (has anyone lost their purse?). [ME f. ON their(r)a of them, genit. pl. of *sá* THE, THAT]

theirs /thairz/ poss.pron. the one or ones belonging to or associated with them (it is theirs; theirs are over here). □ **of theirs** of or belonging to them (a friend of theirs). [ME f. THEIR]

theism /theéizəm/ n. belief in the existence of gods or a god, esp. a God supernaturally revealed to man (cf. DEISM) and sustaining a personal relation to his creatures. □□ **theist** n. **theistic** adj. **theistical** adj. **theistically** adv. [Gk *theos* god + -ISM]

them /them, thəm/ pron. & adj. ● pron. **1** objective case of THEY (I saw them). **2** colloq. they (it's them again; is older than them). **3** archaic themselves (they fell and hurt them). ● adj. sl. or dial. those (them bones). [ME *theim* f. ON: see THEY]

thematic /theemátik/ adj. **1** of or relating to subjects or topics (thematic philately; the arrangement of the anthology is thematic). **2** Mus. of melodic subjects (thematic treatment). **3** Gram. **a** of or belonging to a theme (thematic vowel; thematic form). **b** (of a form of a verb) having a thematic vowel. □ **thematic catalog** Mus. a catalog giving the opening themes of works as well as their names and other details. □□ **thematically** adv. [Gk *thematikos* (as THEME)]

theme /theem/ n. **1** a subject or topic on which a person speaks, writes, or thinks. **2** Mus. a prominent or frequently recurring melody or group of notes in a composition. **3** a school exercise, esp. an essay, on a given subject. **4** Gram. the stem of a noun or verb; the part to which inflections are added, esp. composed of the root and an added vowel. **5** hist. any of the 29 provinces in the Byzantine empire. □ **theme park** an amusement park organized around a unifying idea. **theme song 1** a recurrent melody in a musical play or movie. **2** a signature tune. [ME *teme* ult. f. Gk *thema* -matos f. *tithēmi* set, place]

■ **1** subject (matter), topic, idea, notion, concept, thesis, text, thread, keynote, gist, core, substance, point, essence, argument, question, issue. **2** see MOTIF. **3** essay, paper, composition, review, article, story, piece, exposition, study, exercise, tract, thesis, dissertation, disquisition. **4** see BASE¹ n. 12.

themselves /themsélvz, -thəm-/ pron. **1 a** emphat. form of THEY or THEM. **b** refl. form of THEM; (cf. HERSELF). **2** in their normal state of body or mind (are quite themselves again). □ **be themselves** act in their normal, unconstrained manner.

■ **2** see NORMAL adj. 2.

then /then/ adv., adj., & n. ● adv. **1** at that time; at the time in question (was then too busy; then comes the trouble; the then existing laws). **2 a** next; afterwards; after that (then he told me to come in). **b** and also (then, there are the children to consider). **c** after all (it is a problem, but then that is what we are here for). **3 a** in that case; therefore; it follows that (then you should have said so). **b** if what you say is true (but then why did you take it?). **c** (implying grudging or impatient concession) if you must have it so (all right then, have it your own way). **d** used parenthetically to resume a narrative, etc. (the policeman, then, knocked on the door). ● adj. that or who was such at the time in question (the then Senator). ● n. that time (until then). □ **then and there** immediately and on the spot. [OE *thanne*, *thonne*, etc., f. Gmc, rel. to THAT, THE]

■ adv. **2 b** see FURTHER adv. **c** see YET adv. **6**. **3 a, b** see THUS **2**. □ **then and there** see IMMEDIATELY adv. **1**.

thenar /theénər/ n. Anat. the ball of muscle at the base of the thumb. [earlier = palm of the hand: mod.L f. Gk]

thence /thens/ adv. (also **from thence**) archaic or literary **1** from that place or source. **2** for that reason. [ME *thannes*, *thennes* f. *thanne*, *thenne* f. OE *thanon(e)*, etc. f. WG]

■ **2** see THEREFORE.

thenceforth /thénsfáwrth/ adv. (also **from thenceforth**) formal from that time onward.

thenceforward /thénsfáwrwərd/ adv. formal thenceforth.

theo- /theé-ō/ comb. form God or gods. [Gk f. *theos* god]

theobromine /theéəbrŏmin, -meen/ n. a bitter white alkaloid obtained from cacao seeds, related to caffeine. [*Theobroma* cacao genus: mod.L f. Gk *theos* god + *brōma* food, + -INE⁴]

theocentric /theéəséntrik/ adj. having God or a god as its center.

theocracy /theeókrəsee/ n. (pl. **-ies**) **1** a form of government by God or a god directly or through a priestly order, etc. **2** (**the Theocracy**) the Jewish commonwealth from Moses to the monarchy. □□ **theocrat** /theéəkrat/ n. **theocratic** /theéəkrátik/ adj. **theocratically** adv.

theocrasy /theeókrəsee/ n. **1** the mingling of deities into one personality. **2** the union of the soul with God through contemplation (among Neoplatonists, etc.). [THEO- + Gk *krasis* mingling]

theodicy /theeódisee/ n. (pl. **-ies**) **1** the vindication of divine providence in view of the existence of evil. **2** an instance of this. □□ **theodicean** /-seéən/ adj. [THEO- + Gk *dikē* justice]

theodolite /theeód'lit/ n. a surveying instrument for measuring horizontal and vertical angles with a rotating telescope. □□ **theodolitic** /-lítik/ adj. [16th c. *theodelitus*, of unkn. orig.]

theogony /theeógənee/ n. (pl. **-ies**) **1** the genealogy of the gods. **2** an account of this. [THEO- + Gk *-gonia* begetting]

theol. abbr. **1** theological. **2** theology.

theologian /theéəlōjən/ n. a person trained in theology. [ME f. OF *theologien* (as THEOLOGY)]

theological /theéəlójikəl/ adj. of theology. □ **theological virtues** faith, hope, and charity. □□ **theologically** adv. [med.L *theologicalis* f. L *theologicus* f. Gk *theologikos* (as THEOLOGY)]

theology /theeólajee/ n. (pl. **-ies**) **1 a** the study of theistic (esp. Christian) religion. **b** a system of theistic (esp. Christian) religion. **c** the rational analysis of a religious faith. **2** a system of theoretical principles, esp. an impractical or rigid ideology. □□ **theologist** n. **theologize** v.tr. & intr. [ME f. OF *theologie* f. L *theologia* f. Gk (as THEO-, -LOGY)]

theomachy /theeóməkee/ n. (pl. **-ies**) strife among or against the gods. [THEO- + Gk *makhē* fight]

theophany /theeófənee/ n. (pl. **-ies**) a visible manifestation of God or a god to man.

theophoric /theéəfórik/ adj. bearing the name of a god.

theophylline /theéəfíleen, -lin/ n. an alkaloid similar to

/. . ./ pronunciation	● part of speech
□ phrases, idioms, and compounds	
□□ derivatives	■ synonym section
cross-references appear in SMALL CAPITALS or *italics*	

theobromine, found in tea leaves. [irreg. f. mod.L *thea* tea + Gk *phullon* leaf + -INE⁴]

theorbo /thee-áwrbō/ *n.* (*pl.* -os) a two-necked musical instrument of the lute class much used in the seventeenth century. □□ **theorbist** *n.* [It. *tiorba*, of unkn. orig.]

theorem /theéərəm, theérəm/ *n.* esp. *Math.* 1 a general proposition not self-evident but proved by a chain of reasoning; a truth established by means of accepted truths (cf. PROBLEM). 2 a rule in algebra, etc., esp. one expressed by symbols or formulae (*binomial theorem*). □□ **theorematic** /-mátik/ *adj.* [F *théorème* or LL *theorema* f. Gk *theōrēma* speculation, proposition f. *theōreō* look at]
■ 1 hypothesis, proposition, assumption, conjecture, statement, deduction, thesis, postulate. 2 rule, formula, principle.

theoretic /theeərétik/ *adj.* & *n.* ● *adj.* = THEORETICAL. ● *n.* (in *sing.* or *pl.*) the theoretical part of a science, etc. [LL *theoreticus* f. Gk *theōrētikos* (as THEORY)]

theoretical /theeərétikəl/ *adj.* 1 concerned with knowledge but not with its practical application. 2 based on theory rather than experience or practice. □□ **theoretically** *adv.*
■ 1 impractical, unrealistic, pure, ideal, abstract, academic, theoretic. 2 hypothetical, conjectural, speculative, assumed, untested, unproved, unproven, moot, putative, debatable, tentative, unsubstantiated, suppositious, suppositional, theoretic.
□□ **theoretically** see *ideally* (IDEAL).

theoretician /theeəritishən, -theérit/ *n.* a person concerned with the theoretical aspects of a subject.

theorist /theéərist, theérist/ *n.* a holder or inventor of a theory or theories.
■ theoretician, speculator, hypothesizer, theorizer, philosopher, dreamer.

theorize /theéəriz, theériz/ *v.intr.* evolve or indulge in theories. □□ **theorizer** *n.*
■ hypothesize, conjecture, speculate, surmise, guess.
□□ **theorizer** see THEORIST.

theory /theéəree, theéree/ *n.* (*pl.* -ies) 1 a supposition or system of ideas explaining something, esp. one based on general principles independent of the particular things to be explained (cf. HYPOTHESIS) (*atomic theory*; *theory of evolution*). 2 a speculative (esp. fanciful) view (*one of my pet theories*). 3 the sphere of abstract knowledge or speculative thought (*this is all very well in theory, but how will it work in practice?*). 4 the exposition of the principles of a science, etc. (*the theory of music*). 5 *Math.* a collection of propositions to illustrate the principles of a subject (*probability theory*; *theory of equations*). [LL *theoria* f. Gk *theōria* f. *theōros* spectator f. *theōreō* look at]
■ 1 see DOCTRINE 2. 2 see VIEW *n.* 5, FEELING 4a. 4 see LAW 11.

theosophy /theeósəfee/ *n.* (*pl.* -ies) any of various philosophies professing to achieve a knowledge of God by spiritual ecstasy, direct intuition, or special individual relations, esp. a modern movement following Hindu and Buddhist teachings and seeking universal brotherhood. □□ **theosopher** *n.* **theosophic** /theeəsófik/ *adj.* **theosophical** *adj.* **theosophically** *adv.* **theosophist** *n.* [med.L *theosophia* f. late Gk *theosophia* f. *theosophos* wise concerning God (as THEO-, *sophos* wise)]

therapeutic /thérəpyōōtik/ *adj.* 1 of, for, or contributing to the cure of disease. 2 contributing to general, esp. mental, well-being (*finds walking therapeutic*). □□ **therapeutical** *adj.* **therapeutically** *adv.* **therapeutist** *n.* [attrib. use of *therapeutic*, orig. form of THERAPEUTICS]
■ 1 therapeutical, healing, curative, remedial, restorative, corrective, medical, medicinal. 2 therapeutical, health-giving, healthy, beneficial, salubrious, *archaic* salutary.
□□ **therapeutist** see *therapist* (THERAPY).

therapeutics /thérəpyōōtiks/ *n.pl.* (usu. treated as *sing.*) the branch of medicine concerned with the treatment of disease and the action of remedial agents. [F *thérapeutique* or LL *therapeutica* (pl.) f. Gk *therapeutika* neut. pl. of *therapeutikos* f. *therapeuō* wait on, cure]

therapy /thérəpee/ *n.* (*pl.* -ies) 1 the treatment of physical or mental disorders, other than by surgery. 2 a a particular type of such treatment. b psychotherapy. □□ **therapist** *n.* [mod.L *therapia* f. Gk *therapeia* healing]
■ 1 treatment, healing, cure. 2 a technique, treatment, remedy, remedial program. b psychotherapy, psychoanalysis, analysis, counseling, group therapy.
□□ **therapist** healer, practitioner, therapeutist; psychotherapist, psychologist, analyst, psychiatrist, psychoanalyst, counselor, adviser, *sl.* shrink.

Theravada /thérəvaádə/ *n.* a more conservative form of Buddhism, practiced in Burma (now Myanmar), Thailand, etc. [Pali *theravāda* f. *thera* elder, old + *vāda* speech, doctrine]

there /thair/ *adv., n., & int.* ● *adv.* 1 in, at, or to that place or position (*lived there for some years*; *goes there every day*). 2 at that point (in speech, performance, writing, etc.) (*there he stopped*). 3 in that respect (*I agree with you there*). 4 used for emphasis in calling attention (*you there!*; *there goes the bell*). 5 used to indicate the fact or existence of something (*there is a house on the corner*). ● *n.* that place (*lives somewhere near there*). ● *int.* 1 expressing confirmation, triumph, dismay, etc. (*there! what did I tell you?*). 2 used to soothe a child, etc. (*there, there, never mind*). □ **have been there before** *sl.* know all about it. **so there** *colloq.* that is my final decision (whether you like it or not). **there and then** immediately and on the spot. **there it is 1** that is the trouble. 2 nothing can be done about it. **there's** *Brit. colloq.* you are (by virtue of present or future obedience, etc.) (*there's a dear*). **there you are** (or **go**) *colloq.* 1 this is what you wanted, etc. 2 expressing confirmation, triumph, resignation, etc. [OE *thǽr*, *thēr* f. Gmc, rel. to THAT, THE]
■ □ **there and then** see IMMEDIATELY *adv.* 1.

thereabouts /tháirəbówts/ *adv.* (also **thereabout**) 1 near that place (*ought to be somewhere thereabouts*). 2 near that number, quantity, etc. (*two acres or thereabouts*).

thereafter /tháiráftər/ *adv.* after that.

thereanent /tháirənént/ *adv. Sc.* about that matter.

thereat /tháirát/ *adv. archaic* 1 at that place. 2 on that account. 3 after that.

thereby /tháirbí/ *adv.* by that means; as a result of that. □ **thereby hangs a tale** much could be said about that.

therefor /tháirfáwr/ *adv. archaic* for that object or purpose.

therefore /tháirfawr/ *adv.* for that reason; accordingly; consequently.
■ consequently, so, as a result *or* consequence, hence, ergo, for that reason, accordingly, then, that being so *or* the case, *archaic* wherefore, *archaic or literary* thence, *formal* thus.

therefrom /tháirfrúm, -fróm/ *adv. formal* from that or it.

therein /tháirín/ *adv. formal* 1 in that place, etc. 2 in that respect.

thereinafter /tháirinnáftər/ *adv. formal* later in the same document, etc.

thereinbefore /tháirinbifáwr/ *adv. formal* earlier in the same document, etc.

thereinto /tháiríntōō/ *adv. archaic* into that place.

thereof /tháirúv, -óv/ *adv. formal* of that or it.

thereon /tháirón, -áwn/ *adv. archaic* on that or it (of motion or position).

thereout /tháirówt/ *adv. archaic* out of that; from that source.

thereto /tháirtōō/ *adv. formal* 1 to that or it. 2 in addition; to boot.

theretofore /tháirtōōfáwr/ *adv. formal* before that time.
■ see *previously* (PREVIOUS).

thereunto /tháiruntōō/ *adv. archaic* to that or it.

thereupon /tháirəpón, -páwn/ *adv.* 1 in consequence of that. 2 soon or immediately after that. 3 *archaic* upon that (of motion or position).

therewith /tháirwíth, -wíth/ *adv. archaic* 1 with that. 2 soon or immediately after that.

therewithal /tháirwitháwl, -wíth-/ *adv. archaic* in addition; besides.

theriac /theéreeak/ *n. archaic* an antidote to the bites of poisonous animals, esp. snakes. [L *theriaca* f. Gk *thēriakē* antidote, fem. of *thēriakos* f. *thēr* wild beast]

therianthropic /theereeanthrópik/ *adj.* of or worshiping beings represented in combined human and animal forms. [Gk *thērion* dimin. of *thēr* wild beast + *anthrōpos* human being]

theriomorphic /theereeəmáwrfik/ *adj.* (esp. of a deity) having an animal form. [as THERIANTHROPIC + Gk *morphē* form]

therm /thərm/ *n.* a unit of heat, equivalent to 100,000 British thermal units or 1.055 x 10^8 joules. [Gk *thermē* heat]

thermae /thə́rmee/ *n.pl. Gk* & *Rom. Antiq.* public baths. [L f. Gk *thermai* (pl.) (as THERM)]

thermal /thə́rməl/ *adj.* & *n.* ● *adj.* **1** of, for, or producing heat. **2** promoting the retention of heat (*thermal underwear*). ● *n.* a rising current of heated air (used by gliders, balloons, and birds to gain height). □ **British thermal unit** the amount of heat needed to raise 1 lb. of water at maximum density through one degree Fahrenheit, equivalent to 1.055 x 10^3 joules. **thermal printer** *Comp.* a printer that makes a text image by application of heat to thermally sensitive paper. □□ **thermalize** *v.tr.* & *intr.* **thermalization** *n.* **thermally** *adv.* [F (as THERM)]

thermic /thə́rmik/ *adj.* of or relating to heat.

thermidor see LOBSTER.

thermion /thə́rmíon/ *n.* an ion or electron emitted by a substance at high temperature. [THERMO- + ION]

thermionic /thərmiónik/ *adj.* of or relating to electrons emitted from a substance at very high temperature. □ **thermionic emission** the emission of electrons from a heated source. **thermionic valve** *Brit.* = *vacuum tube* 1.

thermionics /thərmióniks/ *n.pl.* (treated as *sing.*) the branch of science and technology concerned with thermionic emission.

thermistor /thərmístər/ *n. Electr.* a resistor whose resistance is greatly reduced by heating, used for measurement and control. [*thermal resistor*]

thermite /thə́rmīt/ *n.* (also **thermit** /-mit/) a mixture of finely powdered aluminum and iron oxide that produces a very high temperature on combustion (used in welding and for incendiary bombs). [G *Thermit* (as THERMO-, -ITE^1)]

thermo- /thə́rmō/ *comb. form* denoting heat. [Gk f. *thermos* hot, *thermē* heat]

thermochemistry /thərmōkémistree/ *n.* the branch of chemistry dealing with the quantities of heat evolved or absorbed during chemical reactions. □□ **thermochemical** *adj.*

thermocouple /thə́rmōkupəl/ *n.* a pair of different metals in contact at a point, generating a thermoelectric voltage that can serve as a measure of temperature at this point relative to their other parts.

thermodynamics /thərmōdínámiks/ *n.pl.* (usu. treated as *sing.*) the science of the relations between heat and other (mechanical, electrical, etc.) forms of energy. □□ **thermodynamic** *adj.* **thermodynamical** *adj.* **thermodynamically** *adv.* **thermodynamicist** /-misist/ *n.*

thermoelectric /thərmōiléktrik/ *adj.* producing electricity by a difference of temperatures. □□ **thermoelectrically** *adv.* **thermoelectricity** /-ilektrísitee/ *n.*

thermogenesis /thərmōjénisis/ *n.* the production of heat, esp. in a human or animal body.

thermogram /thə́rməgram/ *n.* a record made by a thermograph.

thermograph /thə́rməgraf/ *n.* **1** an instrument that gives a continuous record of temperature. **2** an apparatus used to obtain an image produced by infrared radiation from a human or animal body. □□ **thermographic** /-gráfik/ *adj.*

thermography /thərmógrəfee/ *n. Med.* the taking or use of infrared thermograms, esp. to detect tumors.

thermolabile /thə́rmōláybīl, -bil/ *adj.* (of a substance) unstable when heated.

thermoluminescence /thə́rmōlōōminésəns/ *n.* the property of becoming luminescent when pretreated and subjected to high temperatures, used as a means of dating ancient artifacts. □□ **thermoluminescent** *adj.*

thermolysis /thərmólisis/ *n.* decomposition by the action of heat. □□ **thermolytic** /-məlítik/ *adj.*

thermometer /thərmómitər/ *n.* an instrument for measuring temperature, esp. a graduated glass tube with a small bore containing mercury or alcohol which expands when heated. □□ **thermometric** /thərməmétrik/ *adj.* **thermometrical** *adj.* **thermometry** *n.* [F *thermomètre* or mod.L *thermometrum* (as THERMO-, -METER)]

thermonuclear /thərmōnōōkleeər, -nyōō-/ *adj.* **1** relating to or using nuclear reactions that occur only at very high temperatures. **2** relating to or characterized by weapons using thermonuclear reactions.

thermophile /thə́rmōfīl/ *n.* & *adj.* (also **thermophil** /-fil/) ● *n.* a bacterium, etc., growing optimally at high temperatures. ● *adj.* of or being a thermophile. □□ **thermophilic** /-fílik/ *adj.*

thermopile /thə́rmōpīl/ *n.* a set of thermocouples, esp. arranged for measuring small quantities of radiant heat.

thermoplastic /thə́rmōplástik/ *adj.* & *n.* ● *adj.* (of a substance) that becomes plastic on heating and hardens on cooling, and is able to repeat these processes. ● *n.* a thermoplastic substance.

thermos /thə́rmos/ *n.* (in full **thermos bottle** or **flask**) *propr.* a bottle, etc., with a double wall enclosing a vacuum so that the liquid in the inner receptacle retains its temperature. [Gk (as THERMO-)]

thermosetting /thə́rmōséting/ *adj.* (of plastics) setting permanently when heated. □□ **thermoset** *adj.*

thermosphere /thə́rməsfeer/ *n.* the region of the atmosphere beyond the mesosphere.

thermostable /thə́rmōstáybəl/ *adj.* (of a substance) stable when heated.

thermostat /thə́rməstat/ *n.* a device that automatically regulates temperature, or that activates a device when the temperature reaches a certain point. □□ **thermostatic** *adj.* **thermostatically** *adv.* [THERMO- + Gk *statos* standing]

thermotaxis /thə́rmōtáksis/ *n.* **1** the regulation of heat or temperature, esp. in warm-blooded animals. **2** movement or stimulation in a living organism caused by heat. □□ **thermotactic** *adj.* **thermotaxic** *adj.*

thermotropism /thərmótrəpizəm/ *n.* the growing or bending of a plant toward or away from a source of heat. □□ **thermotropic** /thə́rmōtrópik/ *adj.*

thesaurus /thisáwrəs/ *n.* (*pl.* **thesauri** /-rī/ or **thesauruses**) **1 a** a collection of concepts or words arranged according to sense. **b** a book of synonyms and antonyms. **2** a dictionary or encyclopedia. [L f. Gk *thēsauros* treasure]

■ **1 b** synonym dictionary, synonymy. **2** dictionary, lexicon, encyclopedia, wordfinder.

these *pl.* of THIS.

thesis /theesis/ *n.* (*pl.* **theses** /-seez/) **1** a proposition to be maintained or proved. **2** a dissertation, esp. by a candidate for a degree. **3** (also *Brit.* /thésis/) an unstressed syllable or part of a metrical foot in Greek or Latin verse (opp. ARSIS). [ME f. LL f. Gk, = putting, placing, a proposition, etc., f. *the-* root of *tithēmi* place]

■ **1** argument, theory, proposition, point, contention, belief, idea, premise, assumption, view, assertion, precept, opinion, notion, theorem, axiom, postulate, hypothesis. **2** dissertation, disquisition, treatise, tract, monograph, paper, essay, *literary* discourse.

thespian /théspeeən/ *adj.* & *n.* ● *adj.* of or relating to tragedy or drama. ● *n.* an actor or actress. [Gk *Thespis* the traditional originator of Greek tragedy]

■ *adj.* dramatic, theatric(al), histrionic, acting, performing; *colloq.* hammy, *sl.* ham. ● *n.* actor, actress, performer, trouper, player; supernumerary, extra; matinée idol, star; *sl.* ham.

Thess. *abbr.* Thessalonians (New Testament).

theta /tháytə, theé-/ *n.* the eighth letter of the Greek alphabet (Θ, θ). [Gk]

theurgy /theé-ərjee/ *n.* **1 a** supernatural or divine agency,

---

/.../ **pronunciation**	● **part of speech**
□ **phrases, idioms, and compounds**	
□□ **derivatives**	■ **synonym section**
cross-references appear in SMALL CAPITALS or *italics*	

esp. in human affairs. **b** the art of securing this. **2** the magical science of the Neoplatonists. □□ **theurgic** /-ȯrjik/ *adj.* **theurgical** *adj.* **theurgist** *n.* [LL *theurgia* f. Gk *theourgia* f. *theos* god + *-ergos* working]

thew /thyoō/ *n.* (often in *pl.*) *literary* **1** muscular strength. **2** mental or moral vigor. [OE *thēaw* usage, conduct, of unkn. orig.]

they /thay/ *pron.* (*obj.* **them**; *poss.* **their, theirs**) **1** the people, animals, or things previously named or in question (*pl.* of HE, SHE, IT[1]). **2** people in general (*they say we are wrong*). **3** those in authority (*they have raised the fees*). **4** *disp.* as a third person sing. indefinite pronoun meaning 'he or she' (*anyone can come if they want to*). [ME *thei*, obj. *theim*, f. ON *their* nom. pl. masc., *theim* dat. pl. of *sá* THE that]

they'd /thayd/ *contr.* **1** they had. **2** they would.

they'll /thayl/ *contr.* **1** they will. **2** they shall.

they're /thair/ *contr.* they are.

they've /thayv/ *contr.* they have.

THI *abbr.* temperature-humidity index.

thiamine /thíəmin, -meen/ *n.* (also **thiamin**) a vitamin of the B complex, found in unrefined cereals, beans, and liver, a deficiency of which causes beriberi. Also called *vitamin B₁*, or ANEURIN. [THIO- + *amin* from VITAMIN]

thick /thik/ *adj.*, *n.*, & *adv.* ● *adj.* **1 a** of great or specified extent between opposite surfaces (*a thick wall*; *a wall two meters thick*). **b** of large diameter (*a thick rope*). **2 a** (of a line, etc.) broad; not fine. **b** (of script or type, etc.) consisting of thick lines. **3 a** arranged closely; crowded together; dense. **b** numerous (*fell thick as peas*). **c** bushy; luxuriant (*thick hair*; *thick growth*). **4** (usu. foll. by *with*) densely covered or filled (*air thick with snow*). **5 a** firm in consistency; containing much solid matter; viscous (*a thick paste*; *thick soup*). **b** made of thick material (*a thick coat*). **6** muddy; cloudy; impenetrable by sight (*thick darkness*). **7** *colloq.* (of a person) stupid; dull. **8 a** (of a voice) indistinct. **b** (of an accent) pronounced; exaggerated. **9** *colloq.* intimate or very friendly (esp. *thick as thieves*). ● *n.* a thick part of anything. ● *adv.* thickly (*snow was falling thick*; *blows rained down thick and fast*). □ **a bit thick** *colloq.* unreasonable or intolerable. **in the thick of 1** at the busiest part of. **2** heavily occupied with. **thick ear** *Brit. sl.* the external ear swollen as a result of a blow (esp. *give a person a thick ear*). **thick-skinned** not sensitive to reproach or criticism. **thick-skulled** (or **-witted**) stupid; dull; slow to learn. **through thick and thin** under all conditions; in spite of all difficulties. □□ **thickish** *adj.* **thickly** *adv.* [OE *thicce* (adj. & adv.) f. Gmc]

■ *adj.* **1 a** broad, wide, solid, thickset, burly, ample, bulky, fat, substantial, beamy, chunky, stout, broad-beamed. **2** broad, fat, wide. **3 a** compact, condensed, compressed, choking, packed, solid, impenetrable, impassable, dense, close, thickset, serried. **b** abundant, plentiful, numerous. **c** abundant, plentiful, bushy, luxuriant, lush. **4** dense, solid, packed, close-packed, crowded, choked, filled, full, deep, clotted, covered, chock-full, chockablock, teeming, swarming, alive, bristling, crawling, bursting, crammed, jammed, brimming, *colloq.* lousy. **5 a** dense, viscid, viscous, gelatinous, mucilaginous, gluey, glutinous, ropy, condensed, concentrated, coagulated, clotted, congealed, jelled, jellied, stiffish; stiff, firm, rigid, solid, *literary* inspissated. **b** heavy, bulky, chunky. **6** soupy, murky, misty, foggy, smoggy, smoky, opaque, impenetrable, obscure, obscuring, hazy, muddy, cloudy. **7** thickheaded, thick-witted, thick-skulled, dense, stupid, slow, slow-witted, dull, dull-witted, stolid, obtuse, fatheaded, addlebrained, halfwitted, blockheaded, doltish, imbecilic; insensitive, thick-skinned; *colloq.* moronic, cretinous, dim-witted, dopey, pinheaded, dumb, wooden-headed, esp. *Brit. colloq.* gormless, *sl.* boneheaded. **8 a** guttural, hoarse, throaty, raspy, rasping, rough, husky, grating, gravelly, indistinct, distorted, inarticulate; gruff, raucous. **b** marked, pronounced, exaggerated, strong, broad, decided, obvious, noticeable. **9** close, friendly, inseparable, devoted, hand in glove, on good terms,

on the best (of) terms, intimate, esp. *Brit.* matey, *colloq.* chummy, pally, like that, (as) thick as thieves, palsy-walsy. ● *n.* core, heart, center, middle, focus, midst. □ **in the thick of 1** see AMID. **thick-skinned** insensitive, insensate, dull, obtuse, stolid, callous, numb(ed), steeled, hardened, toughened, tough, unsusceptible, inured, unfeeling, case-hardened, impervious, pachydermatous, *colloq.* hard-boiled. **thick-skulled** (or **-witted**) see THICK *adj.* 7 above.

thicken /thíkən/ *v.* **1** *tr.* & *intr.* make or become thick or thicker. **2** *intr.* become more complicated (*the plot thickens*). □□ **thickener** *n.*

■ **1** coagulate, clot, congeal, gel, set, solidify, stiffen, harden, firm up, cake, *colloq.* jell, *literary* inspissate.

thickening /thíkəning/ *n.* **1** the process of becoming thick or thicker. **2** a substance used to thicken liquid. **3** a thickened part.

thicket /thíkit/ *n.* a tangle of shrubs or trees. [OE *thiccet* (as THICK, -ET[1])]

■ copse, brake, grove, coppice, thickset, covert, wood, brush, *Brit.* spinney.

thickhead /thík-hed/ *n.* **1** *colloq.* a stupid person; a blockhead. **2** *Austral.* any bird of the genus *Pachycephala*; a whistler. □□ **thickheaded** *adj.* **thickheadedness** *n.*

■ **1** see FOOL[1] *n.* 1. □□ **thickheaded** see STUPID *adj.* 1, 5. **thickheadedness** see *stupidity* (STUPID).

thickness /thíknis/ *n.* **1** the state of being thick. **2** the extent to which a thing is thick. **3** a layer of material of a certain thickness (*three thicknesses of cardboard*). **4** a part that is thick or lies between opposite surfaces (*steps cut in the thickness of the wall*). [OE *thicness* (as THICK, -NESS)]

■ **1** see BODY *n.* 8, *stupidity* (STUPID). **2** see BREADTH 1. **3** see PLY[1] 1.

thickset /thíkset/ *adj.* & *n.* ● *adj.* **1** heavily or solidly built. **2** set or growing close together. ● *n.* a thicket.

■ *adj.* **1** see STOCKY. **2** see THICK *adj.* 3a. ● *n.* see THICKET.

thief /theef/ *n.* (*pl.* **thieves** /theevz/) a person who steals, esp. secretly and without violence. [OE *thēof* f. Gmc]

■ robber, burglar, cat burglar, housebreaker, picklock, sneak thief, safecracker, pilferer, shoplifter, stealer, kleptomaniac, *formal or joc.* purloiner; embezzler, peculator; pickpocket, purse snatcher, mugger, highwayman, footpad, brigand, bandit, thug, dacoit, outlaw, plunderer, looter; poacher; pirate, (sea) rover, picaroon, corsair, freebooter, buccaneer, marauder; cheat, swindler, confidence man, mountebank, charlatan, sharper, trickster, thimblerigger, *archaic* cutpurse, *Austral. hist.* bushranger, *sl.* cracksman, con man, con artist, highbinder.

thieve /theev/ *v.* **1** *intr.* be a thief. **2** *tr.* steal (a thing). [OE *thēofian* (as THIEF)]

■ **2** see STEAL *v.* 1.

thievery /theévəree/ *n.* the act or practice of stealing.

■ see THEFT.

thieves *pl.* of THIEF.

thievish /theévish/ *adj.* given to stealing. □□ **thievishly** *adv.* **thievishness** *n.*

thigh /thī/ *n.* **1** the part of the human leg between the hip and the knee. **2** a corresponding part in other animals. □ **thigh-slapper** *colloq.* an exceptionally funny joke, etc. □□ **-thighed** *adj.* (in *comb.*). [OE *thēh*, *thēoh*, *thīoh*, OHG *dioh*, ON *thjó* f. Gmc]

thill /thil/ *n.* a shaft of a cart or carriage, esp. one of a pair. [ME: orig. unkn.]

thill-horse /thílhawrs/ *n.* (also **thiller** /thílər/) a horse put between thills.

thimble /thímbəl/ *n.* **1** a metal or plastic cap, usu. with a closed end, worn to protect the finger and push the needle in sewing. **2** *Mech.* a short metal tube or ferrule, etc. **3** *Naut.* a metal ring concave on the outside and fitting in a loop of spliced rope to prevent chafing. [OE *thȳmel* (as THUMB, -LE[1])]

thimbleful /thímbəlfool/ *n.* (*pl.* **-fuls**) a small quantity, esp. of liquid to drink.

■ see DROP n. 1b, SIP n.

thimblerig /thímbəlrig/ n. a game often involving sleight of hand, in which three inverted thimbles or cups are moved about, contestants having to spot which is the one with a pea or other object beneath. □□ **thimblerigger** n. [THIMBLE + RIG² in sense 'trick, dodge']

thin /thin/ adj., adv., & v. ● adj. (**thinner, thinnest**) **1** having the opposite surfaces close together; of small thickness or diameter. **2 a** (of a line) narrow or fine. **b** (of a script or type, etc.) consisting of thin lines. **3** made of thin material (a thin dress). **4** lean; not plump. **5 a** not dense or copious (thin hair; a thin haze). **b** not full or closely packed (a thin audience). **6** of slight consistency (a thin paste). **7** weak; lacking an important ingredient (thin blood; a thin voice). **8** (of an excuse, argument, disguise, etc.) flimsy or transparent. ● adv. thinly (cut the bread very thin). ● v. (**thinned, thinning**) **1** tr. & intr. make or become thin or thinner. **2** tr. & intr. (often foll. by out) reduce; make or become less dense or crowded or numerous. **3** tr. (often foll. by out) remove some of a crop of (seedlings, saplings, etc.) or some young fruit from (a vine or tree) to improve the growth of the rest. □ **on thin ice** see ICE. **thin air** a state of invisibility or non-existence (vanished into thin air). **thin end of the wedge** see WEDGE¹. **thin on the ground** see GROUND¹. **thin on top** balding. **thin-skinned** sensitive to reproach or criticism; easily upset. □□ **thinly** adv. **thinness** n. **thinnish** adj. [OE thynne f. Gmc]

■ adj. **1** slim, slender, spindly, skinny. **2** attenuated, threadlike, stringlike, pencil-thin, fine; narrow. **3** airy, filmy, diaphanous, gossamer, sheer, light, delicate, chiffon, silky, silken, gauzy, flimsy, fine, translucent, see-through, transparent. **4** slim, slender, lean, spare, slight, small, lanky, spindly, skinny, thin as a rail or reed or rake, wispy, willowy, twiggy, wiry, skeletal, gaunt, gangling, bony, emaciated, cadaverous, meager, scrawny, all skin and bones, rawboned, scraggy, thinnish, undernourished, underfed, underweight, undersized, puny, sparse, hollow-cheeked, (half-) starved, pinched, withered, shrunken, shriveled (up). **5** sparse, unsubstantial, poor, scant, scanty, insufficient, inadequate, slight, worthless, deficient, skimpy, unplentiful, meager, paltry. **6** watery, runny, watered down, dilute(d), weak, unsatisfying. **8** flimsy, weak, feeble, slight, unsubstantial, insubstantial, tenuous, threadbare, transparent, fragile, frail, poor, lame; unbelievable, unconvincing. ● v. **1** thin down, draw out, attenuate, reduce, trim, cut down, prune; sharpen, taper. **2** thin down or out, dilute, water (down), weaken, decrease, reduce, diminish. □ **thin-skinned** see SENSITIVE adj. 2.

thine /thīn/ poss.pron. archaic or dial. **1** (predic. or absol.) of or belonging to thee. **2** (attrib. before a vowel) = THY. [OE thīn f. Gmc]

thing /thing/ n. **1** a material or nonmaterial entity, idea, action, etc., that is or may be thought about or perceived. **2** an inanimate material object (take that thing away). **3** an unspecified object or item (have a few things to buy). **4** an act, idea, or utterance (a silly thing to do). **5** an event (an unfortunate thing to happen). **6** a quality (patience is a useful thing). **7** (with ref. to a person) expressing pity, contempt, or affection (poor thing!; a dear old thing). **8** a specimen or type of something (quarks are an important thing in physics). **9** colloq. **a** one's special interest or concern (not my thing at all). **b** an obsession, fear, or prejudice (spiders are a thing of mine). **10** esp. Brit. colloq. something remarkable (now there's a thing!). **11** (prec. by the) colloq. **a** what is conventionally proper or fashionable. **b** what is needed or required (your suggestion was just the thing). **c** what is to be considered (the thing is, shall we go or not?). **d** what is important (the thing about them is their reliability). **12** (in pl.) personal belongings or clothing (where have I left my things?). **13** (in pl.) equipment (painting things). **14** (in pl.) affairs in general (not in the nature of things). **15** (in pl.) circumstances or conditions (things look good). **16** (in pl. with a following adjective) all that is so describable (all things Greek). **17** (in pl.) Law prop-

erty. □ **do one's own thing** colloq. pursue one's own interests or inclinations. **do things to** colloq. affect remarkably. **have a thing about** colloq. be obsessed, fearful, or prejudiced about. **make a thing of** colloq. **1** regard as essential. **2** cause a fuss about. **one** (or **just one**) **of those things** colloq. something unavoidable or to be accepted. [OE f. Gmc]

■ **2, 3** device, item, gadget, (inanimate) object, entity, article, possession, commodity, mechanism, contrivance, apparatus, instrument, utensil; whatnot, doodad, colloq. whatchamacallit, what-do-you-call-it, what's-its-name, whatsit, thingummy, thingy, thingamajig, thingamabob, affair, sl. gizmo. **4** act, action, deed, activity, proceeding; chore, task, job, responsibility, matter; idea, statement; item, subject, matter, detail, feature, aspect, affair, constituent, element, factor, point, particular. **5** event, happening, circumstance, occurrence, incident, phenomenon. **6** quality, attribute, property. **7** soul, dear. **9 a** interest, concern, fancy, love, passion, mania, fetish; see also BAG n. 9. **b** obsession, fixation, fetish, idée fixe; fear, phobia, terror, loathing, horror, detestation, dislike, aversion, sl. hang-up; prejudice, bias. **11 a** fad, trend, fashion, mode, rage. **12** (things) belongings, luggage, baggage, impedimenta, possessions, paraphernalia, effects, clothes, clothing, goods, chattels, stuff, junk, bits and pieces, colloq. gear, traps. **13** (things) equipment, tools, utensils, implements, apparatus, stuff, paraphernalia, gear, outfit, tackle, kit. **14** (things) affairs, matters, business, concerns. **15** (things) circumstances, events, happenings, conditions, life. □ **have a thing about** have a feeling about or toward, have a reaction to, have an attitude to or toward, have an emotional attachment to; be preoccupied or obsessed with, be fixated on, like, be passionate about or partial to, colloq. fancy, love; fear, be afraid of, shudder at, recoil from, sl. be hung up on; hate, loathe, detest, abominate, execrate.

thingamabob /thíngəməbob/ (also **thingamajig** /thíngəmajig/, n. Brit. **thingummy** /thíngəmee/) colloq. a person or thing whose name one has forgotten or does not know or does not wish to mention. [THING + meaningless suffix]

■ see THING 2, 3.

thingy /thíngee/ n. (pl. **-ies**) = THINGAMABOB.

think /thingk/ v. & n. ● v. (past and past part. **thought** /thawt/) **1** tr. (foll. by that + clause) be of the opinion (we think that they will come). **2** tr. (foll. by that + clause or to + infin.) judge or consider (is thought to be a fraud). **3** intr. exercise the mind positively with one's ideas, etc. (let me think for a moment). **4** tr. (foll. by of or about) **a** consider; be or become mentally aware of (think of you constantly). **b** form or entertain the idea of; imagine to oneself (couldn't think of such a thing). **c** choose mentally; hit upon (think of a number). **d** form or have an opinion of (what do you think of them?). **5** tr. have a half-formed intention (I think I'll stay). **6** tr. form a conception of (cannot think how you do it). **7** tr. reduce to a specified condition by thinking (cannot think away a toothache). **8** tr. recognize the presence or existence of (the child thought no harm). **9** tr. (foll. by to + infin.) intend or expect (thinks to deceive us). **10** tr. (foll. by to + infin.) remember (did not think to lock the door). ● n. colloq. an act of thinking (must have a think about that). □ **think again** revise one's plans or opinions. **think out loud** (or **aloud**) utter one's thoughts as soon as they occur. **think back** to recall (a past event or time). **think better of** change one's mind about (an intention) after reconsideration. **think big** see BIG. **think fit** see FIT¹. **think for oneself** have an independent mind or attitude. **think little** (or **nothing**) **of** consider to be insignificant or unremarkable. **think much**

/.../ **pronunciation**	● **part of speech**
□ **phrases, idioms, and compounds**	
□□ **derivatives**	■ **synonym section**
cross-references appear in SMALL CAPITALS or italics	

(or **highly**) **of** have a high opinion of. **think on** (or **upon**) *archaic* think of or about. **think out 1** consider carefully. **2** produce (an idea, etc.) by thinking. **think over** reflect upon in order to reach a decision. **think tank** a body of experts providing advice and ideas on specific national or commercial problems. **think through** reflect fully upon (a problem, etc.). **think twice** use careful consideration, avoid hasty action, etc. **think up** *colloq.* devise; produce by thought. □□ **thinkable** *adj.* [OE *thencan thōhte gethōht* f. Gmc]

■ *v.* **1** see BELIEVE 2. **2** judge, reckon, consider, regard as, characterize as, view as, believe, assume, *formal* deem. **3** contemplate, cogitate, ruminate, reflect, meditate, ponder, deliberate, reason, concentrate, cudgel *or* rack one's brains, use one's head, *literary* muse. **4** (*think of* or *about*) **a** see CONSIDER 4. **b** consider, ponder, weigh, contemplate, imagine, mull over, entertain the idea *or* notion of, have in mind, propose, *literary* muse over. **c** see *hit on*. **d** see VIEW *v.* 3. **5** believe, imagine, expect, dream, fancy, fantasize, suppose. **6** see CONCEIVE 3. **9** intend, have in mind, mean, design, purpose, plan, propose, expect. □ **think back to** recall, remember, recollect, call *or* bring to mind. **think better of** reconsider, think twice about, change one's mind about. **think little** (or **nothing**) **of** see UNDERESTIMATE *v.* **think much** (or **highly**) **of** see RESPECT *v.* 1. **think over** contemplate, consider, cogitate on *or* over *or* about, ruminate over *or* about, ponder (over *or* on), reflect on, meditate on *or* over *or* about, deliberate on *or* over *or* about, mull over, chew over, think about *or* of, *literary* muse on *or* over *or* about. **think through** see PUZZLE *v.* 4. **think twice** see SCRUPLE *v.* 2; (*think twice about*) see SCRUPLE *v.* 1. **think up** think of, devise, concoct, contrive, come up with, invent, conceive (of), dream up, create, make up, improvise, mastermind. □□ **thinkable** conceivable, possible, imaginable, feasible, reasonable, tenable, not unlikely, plausible, believable, credible.

thinker /thíngkər/ *n.* **1** a person who thinks, esp. in a specified way (*an original thinker*). **2** a person with a skilled or powerful mind.

■ **2** sage, wise man, savant, savante, Solomon, pundit, mastermind, philosopher, scholar, intellectual, learned person, mentor, expert.

thinking /thíngking/ *adj. & n.* ● *adj.* using thought or rational judgment. ● *n.* **1** opinion or judgment. **2** thought; train of thought. □ **put on one's thinking cap** *colloq.* meditate on a problem.

■ *adj.* rational, sensible, intelligent, reasoning, reasonable; meditative, contemplative, reflective, philosophical, cogitative, pensive, thoughtful, intellectual, *literary* ratiocinative. ● *n.* **1** opinion, judgment, belief, thought, point of view, viewpoint, assessment, evaluation, theory, reasoning, conclusion, idea, philosophy, outlook.

thinner /thínər/ *n.* a volatile liquid used to dilute paint, etc.

thio- /thí-ō/ *comb. form* sulfur, esp. replacing oxygen in compounds (*thio acid*). [Gk *theion* sulfur]

thiol /thíawl, -ol/ *n. Chem.* any organic compound containing an alcohol-like group but with sulfur in place of oxygen. [THIO- + -OL¹]

thiosulfate /thí-ōsúlfayt/ *n.* a sulfate in which one oxygen atom is replaced by sulfur.

thiourea /thí-ōyŏŏreeə/ *n.* a crystalline compound used in photography and the manufacture of synthetic resins.

third /thərd/ *n. & adj.* ● *n.* **1** the position in a sequence corresponding to that of the number 3 in the sequence 1–3. **2** something occupying this position. **3** each of three equal parts of a thing. **4** = *third gear*. **5** *Mus.* **a** an interval or chord spanning three consecutive notes in the diatonic scale (e.g., C to E). **b** a note separated from another by this interval. **6** = *third base*. **7** *Brit.* **a** a place in the third class in an examination. **b** a person having this. ● *adj.* that is the third. □ **third base 1** the third base (counterclockwise from home plate) in baseball. **2** the area around this base as defended by a fielder. **third-best** *adj.* of third quality. ● *n.* a

thing in this category. **third class** the third-best group or category, esp. of hotel and train accommodation. **third-class** *adj.* **1** belonging to or traveling by the third class. **2** of lower quality; inferior. ● *adv.* by the third class (*travels third-class*). **third degree** long and severe questioning, esp. by police to obtain information or a confession. **third-degree** *Med.* denoting burns of the most severe kind, affecting lower layers of tissue. **third eye 1** *Hinduism & Buddhism* the 'eye of insight' in the forehead of an image of a deity, esp. the god Siva. **2** the faculty of intuitive insight. **third force** a political group or party acting as a check on conflict between two opposing parties. **third gear** the third in a sequence of gears. **third man** *Cricket* **1** a fielder positioned near the boundary behind the slips. **2** this position. **third part** each of three equal parts into which a thing is or might be divided. **third party 1** another party besides the two principals. **2** a bystander, etc. **third person 1** = *third party*. **2** *Gram.* see PERSON. **third rail** a metal rail that provides power to the trains of an electric railroad. **third-rate** inferior; very poor in quality. **third reading** a third presentation of a bill to a legislative assembly, in the US to consider it for the last time, in the UK to debate committee reports. **Third Reich** see REICH. **Third World** (usu. prec. by *the*) the developing countries of Asia, Africa, and Latin America. □□ **thirdly** *adv.* [OE *third(d)a, thridda* f. Gmc]

thirst /thərst/ *n. & v.* ● *n.* **1** a physical need to drink liquid, or the feeling of discomfort caused by this. **2** a strong desire or craving (*a thirst for power*). ● *v.intr.* (often foll. by *for* or *after*) **1** feel thirst. **2** have a strong desire. [OE *thurst, thyrstan* f. WG]

■ *n.* **1** thirstiness, dryness. **2** craving, desire, appetite, hunger, eagerness, avidity, ravenousness, voracity, voraciousness, lust, passion, enthusiasm, fancy, hankering, longing, yearning, itch, *colloq.* yen. ● *v.* **2** (*thirst for* or *after*) crave, desire, want, hunger for *or* after, lust for *or* after, fancy, hanker for *or* after, pant for, long for, yearn for, wish for.

thirsty /thársteе/ *adj.* (**thirstier, thirstiest**) **1** feeling thirst. **2** (of land, a season, etc.) dry or parched. **3** (often foll. by *for* or *after*) eager. **4** *colloq.* causing thirst (*thirsty work*). □□ **thirstily** *adv.* **thirstiness** *n.* [OE *thurstig, thyrstig* (as THIRST, -Y¹)]

■ **1** parched, dry, dehydrated. **2** parched, dry, arid. **3** desirous, hungry, avid, eager, ravenous, voracious, burning, greedy, hankering, yearning, longing, craving, itching.

thirteen /thártéen/ *n. & adj.* ● *n.* **1** one more than twelve, or three more than ten. **2** a symbol for this (13, xiii, XIII). **3** a size, etc., denoted by thirteen. ● *adj.* that amount to thirteen. □□ **thirteenth** *adj. & n.* [OE *thrēotīene* (as THREE, -TEEN)]

thirty /thártее/ *n. & adj.* ● *n.* (*pl.* **-ies**) **1** the product of three and ten. **2** a symbol for this (30, xxx, XXX). **3** (in *pl.*) the numbers from 30 to 39, esp. the years of a century or of a person's life. ● *adj.* that amount to thirty. □ **thirty-first, -second,** etc., the ordinal numbers between thirtieth and fortieth. **thirty-one, -two,** etc., the cardinal numbers between thirty and forty. **thirty-second note** *Mus.* a note having the time value of half a semiquaver and represented by a large dot with a three-hooked stem. Also called *demisemiquaver*. □□ **thirtieth** *adj. & n.* **thirtyfold** *adj. & adv.* [OE *thrītig* (as THREE, -TY²)]

this /this/ *pron., adj., & adv.* ● *demons.pron.* (*pl.* **these** /theez/) **1** the person or thing close at hand or indicated or already named or understood (*can you see this?; this is my cousin*). **2** (contrasted with *that*) the person or thing nearer to hand or more immediately in mind. **3** the action, behavior, or circumstances under consideration (*this won't do at all; what do you think of this?*). **4** (on the telephone): **a** the person spoken to. **b** the person speaking. ● *demons.adj.* (*pl.* **these** /theez/) **1** designating the person or thing close at hand, etc. (cf. senses 1, 2 of *pron.*). **2** (of time): **a** the present or current (*am busy all this week*). **b** relating to today (*this morning*). **c** just past or to come (*have been asking for it these three weeks*). **3** *colloq.* (in narrative) designating a person or thing previously unspecified (*then up came this policeman*). ● *adv.* to this degree or extent (*knew him when he was this high*; *did not reach this far*). □ **this and that** *colloq.* various unspecified examples of things (esp. trivial). **this here** *sl.* this particular (person or thing). **this much** the amount or extent about to be stated (*I know this much, that he was not there*). **this world** mortal life. [OE, neut. of *thes*]

thistle /thísəl/ *n.* **1** any of various prickly composite herbaceous plants of the genus *Cirsium, Carlina,* or *Carduus,* etc., usu. with globular heads of purple flowers. **2** this as the Scottish national emblem. [OE *thistel* f. Gmc]

thistledown /thísəldown/ *n.* a light fluffy stuff attached to thistle seeds and blown about in the wind.

thistly /thíslee/ *adj.* overgrown with thistles.

thither /thíthər, thi-/ *adv.* archaic or formal to or toward that place. [OE *thider,* alt. (after HITHER) of *thæder*]

thixotropy /thiksótrəpee/ *n.* the property of becoming temporarily liquid when shaken or stirred, etc., and returning to a gel on standing. □□ **thixotropic** /thíksətrópik/ *adj.* [Gk *thixis* touching + *tropē* turning]

tho' var. of THOUGH.

thole[1] /thōl/ *n.* **1** a pin in the gunwale of a boat as the fulcrum for an oar. **2** each of two such pins forming an oarlock. [OE *thol* fir tree, peg]

thole[2] /thōl/ *v.tr.* Sc. or archaic undergo or suffer (pain, grief, etc.). [OE *tholian* f. Gmc]

tholepin /thōlpin/ *n.* = THOLE[1].

tholos /thólos/ *n.* (*pl.* **tholoi** /-loy/) Gk Antiq. a dome-shaped tomb, esp. of the Mycenaean period. [Gk]

Thomism /tōmizəm/ *n.* the doctrine of Thomas Aquinas, Italian scholastic philosopher and theologian d. 1274, or of his followers. □□ **Thomist** *n.* **Thomistic** /-místik/ *adj.* **Thomistical** /-místikəl/ *adj.*

thong /thong/ *n. & v.* ● *n.* **1** a narrow strip of hide or leather used as the lash of a whip, as a halter or rein, etc. **2** = FLIP-FLOP 1. ● *v.tr.* **1** provide with a thong. **2** strike with a thong. [OE *thwang, thwong* f. Gmc]

thorax /tháwraks, thór-/ *n.* (*pl.* **thoraxes** or **thoraces** /tháwrəseez/) **1** Anat. & Zool. the part of the trunk between the neck and the abdomen. **2** Gk Antiq. a breastplate or cuirass. □□ **thoracal** /thórəkəl/ *adj.* **thoracic** /thawrásik/ *adj.* [L f. Gk *thōrax -akos*]

thoria /tháwreeə, thór-/ *n.* the oxide of thorium, used esp. in incandescent mantles.

thorium /tháwreeəm, thór-/ *n.* Chem. a radioactive metallic element occurring naturally in monazite and used in alloys and for nuclear power. ¶ Symb.: **Th**. [*Thor,* Scand. god of thunder]

thorn /thawrn/ *n.* **1** a stiff sharp-pointed projection on a plant. **2** a thorn-bearing shrub or tree. **3** the name of an Old English and Icelandic runic letter, = th. □ **thorn apple 1** a poisonous plant of the nightshade family, *Datura stramonium*; jimsonweed. **2** the prickly fruit of this. **a thorn in one's side** (or **flesh**) a constant annoyance. □□ **thornless** *adj.* **thornproof** *adj.* [OE f. Gmc]

■ **1** barb, spine, spike, prickle, bristle, brier, burr, point, bramble. □ **a thorn in one's side** (or **flesh**) bother, irritation, annoyance, nuisance, vexation, torment, torture, trial, scourge, plague, pest, affliction, irritant, bane, burr, colloq. headache, pain in the neck, sl. pain in the butt.

thornback /tháwrnbak/ *n.* a ray, *Raja clavata,* with spines on the back and tail.

thorny /tháwrnee/ *adj.* (**thornier, thorniest**) **1** having many thorns. **2** (of a subject) hard to handle without offense; problematic. □□ **thornily** *adv.* **thorniness** *n.*

■ **1** prickly, barbed, spiny, spiked, brambly, Bot. spinous, spicular, spinose, spiculate, Bot. & Zool. setaceous, setiferous, setigerous, setose, spinulose, spinulous. **2** difficult, hard, tough, prickly, nettlesome, painful, ticklish, delicate, intricate, critical, complex, complicated, problematic, vexatious, knotty, tangled, involved, tricky, troublesome, controversial, nasty, worrying, colloq. sticky, sl. hairy.

thorough /thúrō/ *adj.* **1** complete and unqualified; not su-

perficial (*needs a thorough change*). **2** acting or done with great care and completeness (*the report is most thorough*). **3** absolute (*a thorough nuisance*). □ **thorough-paced 1** (of a horse) trained in all paces. **2** complete or unqualified. □□ **thoroughly** *adv.* **thoroughness** *n.* [orig. as adv. and prep. in the senses of *through,* f. OE *thuruh* var. of *thurh* THROUGH]

■ **1** extensive, exhaustive, detailed, in-depth, comprehensive, full, complete, all-inclusive, unqualified, total, all-embracing, encyclopedic, universal, A-to-Z, all-out, thoroughgoing, profound. **2** exhaustive, extensive, searching, painstaking, meticulous, assiduous, careful, scrupulous, particular, conscientious, methodical, intensive. **3** thoroughgoing, complete, downright, perfect, total, real, unmitigated, undiluted, unmixed, unalloyed, out-and-out, unqualified, sheer, utter, arrant, absolute, ingrained, colloq. positive, proper, colloq. or archaic right. □□ **thoroughly** carefully, painstakingly, exhaustively, extensively, assiduously, sedulously, methodically, conscientiously, scrupulously, meticulously, intensively, comprehensively, throughout, from top to bottom, from stem to stern, backward and forward, in every nook and cranny; completely, downright, perfectly, totally, unqualifiedly, utterly, absolutely, entirely, extremely, profoundly, unreservedly, wholly, fully, positively, definitely, quite.

thoroughbass /thúrəbays/ *n.* = CONTINUO.

thoroughbred /thúrōbred, thór-/ *adj. & n.* ● *adj.* **1** of pure breeding. **2** high-spirited. ● *n.* **1** a thoroughbred animal, esp. a horse. **2** (**Thoroughbred**) **a** a breed of racehorses originating from English mares and Arab stallions. **b** a horse of this breed.

thoroughfare /thúrōfair, thór-, thúr-/ *n.* a road or path open at both ends, esp. for traffic.

■ see ROAD[1] 1, PATH 1, PASSAGEWAY.

thoroughgoing /thúrōgōing, thór-, thúr-/ *adj.* **1** uncompromising; not superficial. **2** (usu. attrib.) extreme; out-and-out.

■ **1** see EXHAUSTIVE . **2** see out-and-out 1.

thorp /thawrp/ *n.* (also **thorpe**) archaic a village or hamlet. ¶ Now usually only in place-names. [OE *thorp, throp,* f. Gmc]

Thos. abbr. Thomas.

those pl. of THAT.

thou[1] /thow/ *pron.* (obj. **thee** /thee/; poss. **thy** or **thine**; pl. **ye** or **you**) second person singular pronoun, now replaced by you except in some formal, liturgical, dialect, and poetic uses. [OE *thu* f. Gmc]

thou[2] /thow/ *n.* (pl. same or **thous**) colloq. **1** a thousand. **2** one thousandth. [abbr.]

though /thō/ *conj. & adv.* ● *conj.* **1** despite the fact that (*though it was early we went to bed; though annoyed, I agreed*). **2** (introducing a possibility) even if (*ask him though he may refuse; would not attend though the Queen herself were there*). **3** and yet; nevertheless (*she read on, though not to the very end*). **4** in spite of being (*ready though unwilling*). ● *adv.* colloq. however; all the same (*I wish you had told me, though*). [ME *thoh,* etc., f. ON *thó,* etc., corresp. to OE *thēah,* f. Gmc]

■ *conj.* **1** although, even though, whilst, in spite of or despite the fact that, notwithstanding that, granted, granting or conceding that, allowing or admitting that, esp. Brit. whilst, archaic whiles. **2** even if, supposing, although, even though. **4** although, in spite of or despite being, literary albeit. ● *adv.* however, nonetheless, nevertheless, yet, but, still, even so, be that as it may, all the same, notwithstanding, for all that, Austral., NZ, & Sc. but, colloq. still and all.

thought[1] /thawt/ *n.* **1** the process or power of thinking; the faculty of reason. **2** a way of thinking characteristic of or

---

/.../ **pronunciation**	● **part of speech**
□ **phrases, idioms, and compounds**	
□□ **derivatives**	■ **synonym section**
cross-references appear in SMALL CAPITALS or *italics*	

associated with a particular time, people, group, etc. (*medieval European thought*). **3 a** sober reflection or consideration (*gave it much thought*). **b** care; regard; concern (*had no thought for others*). **4** an idea or piece of reasoning produced by thinking (*many good thoughts came out of the discussion*). **5** (foll. by *of* + verbal noun or *to* + infin.) a partly formed intention or hope (*gave up all thoughts of winning*; *had no thought to go*). **6** (usu. in *pl.*) what one is thinking; one's opinion (*have you any thoughts on this?*). **7** the subject of one's thinking (*my one thought was to get away*). **8** (prec. by *a*) *Brit.* somewhat (*seems to me a thought arrogant*). □ **give thought to** consider; think about. **in thought** thinking; meditating. **take thought** consider matters. **thought-provoking** stimulating serious thought. **thought-reader** a person supposedly able to perceive another's thoughts; a mind-reader. **thought-reading** the supposed perception of what another is thinking; mind-reading. □□ **-thoughted** *adj.* (in *comb.*). [OE *thōht* (as THINK)]

■ **1** thinking, intellect, intelligence, reasoning, rationality, reason, *literary* ratiocination. **2** see THINKING *n.* **3 a** reflection, meditation, contemplation, cogitation, musing, pondering, rumination, brooding, mental activity, mentation, introspection; brainwork, cerebration, concentration, deliberation, consideration, *literary* lucubration. **3 b** thoughtfulness, consideration, care, kindliness, kindheartedness, concern, compassion, tenderness, kindness, sympathy, attention, attentiveness, regard, solicitude. **4** idea, notion, observation, conclusion, conjecture, concept, conception, brainstorm, *colloq.* brainwave. **5** consideration, contemplation, planning, plan, scheme, design, intention, objective, expectation, hope, prospect, anticipation, dream, vision. **6** see OPINION 1, 3. **7** notion, idea, concept, concern. **8** bit, trifle, touch, little, *colloq.* tad. □ **give thought to** see NOTE *v.* 1. **thought-provoking** see *stimulating* (STIMULATE).

thought² *past and past part.* of THINK.

thoughtful /tháwtfööl/ *adj.* **1** engaged in or given to meditation. **2** (of a book, writer, remark, etc.) giving signs of serious thought. **3** (often foll. by *of*) (of a person or conduct) considerate; not haphazard or unfeeling. □□ **thoughtfully** *adv.* **thoughtfulness** *n.*

■ **1** contemplative, pensive, reflective, musing, in a brown study, pondering, meditative, cogitative, engrossed, absorbed, introspective, rapt, wistful, brooding, broody, wool-gathering, daydreaming. **2** see THINKING *adj.* **3** considerate, kind, kindly, kindhearted, compassionate, caring, tender, sympathetic, attentive, solicitous, concerned, helpful, obliging, charitable; prudent, wary, cautious, mindful, heedful, thinking, circumspect, careful. □□ **thoughtfully** see KINDLY 1. **thoughtfulness** see CONSIDERATION 2.

thoughtless /tháwtlis/ *adj.* **1** careless of consequences or of others' feelings. **2** due to lack of thought. □□ **thoughtlessly** *adv.* **thoughtlessness** *n.*

■ **1** unthinking, inconsiderate, rude, impolite, insensitive, tactless, undiplomatic, untactful, indiscreet, uncaring, unfeeling; rash, imprudent, negligent, neglectful, reckless, heedless, careless; remiss, unreflective, absentminded, forgetful, inattentive. **2** rash, imprudent, negligent, neglectful, reckless, heedless, careless; foolish, stupid, silly, ill-considered, inadvertent. □□ **thoughtlessly** see *blindly* (BLIND). **thoughtlessness** see *imprudence* (IMPRUDENT).

thousand /thówzənd/ *n. & adj.* ● *n.* (*pl.* **thousands** or (in sense 1) **thousand**) (in *sing.* prec. by *a* or *one*) **1** the product of a hundred and ten. **2** a symbol for this (1,000, m, M). **3** a set of a thousand things. **4** (in *sing.* or *pl.*) *colloq.* a large number. ● *adj.* that amount to a thousand. □□ **thousandfold** *adj. & adv.* **thousandth** *adj. & n.* [OE *thūsend* f. Gmc]

■ *n.* **4** (*thousands*) see SCORE *n.* 3.

thrall /thrawl/ *n. literary* **1** (often foll. by *of*, *to*) a slave (of a person, power, or influence). **2** bondage; a state of slavery or servitude (*in thrall*). □□ **thralldom** *n.* (also **thraldom**). [OE *thrǣl* f. ON *thrǽll*, perh. f. a Gmc root = run]

thrash /thrash/ *v. & n.* ● *v.* **1** *tr.* beat severely, esp. with a stick or whip. **2** *tr.* defeat thoroughly in a contest. **3** *intr.* (of a paddle wheel, branch, etc.) act like a flail; deliver repeated blows. **4** *intr.* (foll. by *about*, *around*) move or fling the limbs about violently or in panic. **5** *intr.* (of a ship) keep striking the waves; make way against the wind or tide (*thrash to windward*). **6** *tr.* = THRESH 1. ● *n.* **1** an act of thrashing. **2** *Brit. colloq.* a party, esp. a lavish one. □ **thrash out** discuss to a conclusion. □□ **thrashing** *n.* [OE *therscan*, later *threscan*, f. Gmc]

■ *v.* **1** see BEAT *v.* 1. **2** see DEFEAT *v.* 1. **4** (*thrash about or around*) see FLAP *v.* 1. ● *n.* **1** see *thrashing* (THRASH) below. □ **thrash out** see DEBATE *v.*, RESOLVE *v.* 1. □□ **thrashing** beating, drubbing, whipping, flogging, caning, belting, mauling, lashing, trouncing, basting, battering, pounding, thrash, assault; punishment, chastisement, disciplining, discipline, castigation, *colloq.* hiding, lambasting, hammering, *sl.* tanning, pasting, walloping.

thrasher¹ /tráshər/ *n.* **1** a person or thing that thrashes. **2** = THRESHER.

thrasher² /tráshər/ *n.* any of various long-tailed N. American thrushlike birds of the family Mimidae. [perh. f. E dial. *thrusher* = THRUSH¹]

thrawn /thrawn/ *adj. Sc.* **1** perverse or ill-tempered. **2** misshapen; crooked. [Sc. form of *thrown* in obs. senses]

thread /thred/ *n. & v.* ● *n.* **1 a** a spun filament of cotton, silk, or glass, etc.; yarn. **b** a length of this. **2** a thin cord of twisted yarns used esp. in sewing and weaving. **3** anything regarded as threadlike with reference to its continuity or connectedness (*the thread of life*; *lost the thread of his argument*). **4** the spiral ridge of a screw. **5** (in *pl.*) *sl.* clothes. **6** a thin seam or vein of ore. ● *v.tr.* **1** pass a thread through the eye of (a needle). **2** put (beads) on a thread. **3** arrange (material in a strip form, e.g., film or magnetic tape) in the proper position on equipment. **4** make (one's way) carefully through a crowded place, over a difficult route, etc. **5** streak (hair, etc.) as with threads. **6** form a screw thread on. □ **hang by a thread** be in a precarious state, position, etc. **thread mark** a mark in the form of a thin line made in paper money with highly colored silk fibers to prevent photographic counterfeiting. □□ **threader** *n.* **threadlike** *adj.* [OE *thrēd* f. Gmc]

■ *n.* **1** fiber, filament, strand, (piece of) yarn; cotton, silk, wool. **2** string, line, cord, twine; cotton, silk, wool. **3** theme, plot, storyline, subject, motif, thesis, course, drift, direction, tenor, train (of thought), sequence *or* train *or* chain of events. **5** (*threads*) see CLOTHES. **6** see VEIN 5. ● *v.* **2** string, lace. **4** (*thread one's way*) file, weave, wind (one's way), pass, squeeze, pick *or* make one's way, inch *or* ease (one's way). □□ **threadlike** see FINE¹ *adj.* 7c.

threadbare /thrédbair/ *adj.* **1** (of cloth) so worn that the nap is lost and the thread visible. **2** (of a person) wearing such clothes. **3 a** hackneyed. **b** feeble or insubstantial (*a threadbare excuse*).

■ **1** frayed, worn (out), ragged, moth-eaten, tattered, tatty, shabby, torn, *colloq.* worn to a frazzle. **2** ragged, scruffy, shabby, seedy, wretched, sorry, slovenly. **3 a** trite, hackneyed, overused, overworked, reworked, stale, tired, timeworn, stereotyped, commonplace, clichéd, cliché-ridden, banal, prosaic, dull, monotonous, tedious, tiresome, boring, played out, *colloq.* old hat. **b** see THIN *adj.* 8.

threadfin /thrédfin/ *n.* any small tropical fish of the family Polynemidae, with long streamers from its pectoral fins.

threadworm /thrédwərm/ *n.* any of various, esp. parasitic, threadlike nematode worms, e.g., the pinworm.

thready /thrédee/ *adj.* (**threadier**, **threadiest**) **1** of or like a thread. **2** (of a person's pulse) scarcely perceptible.

threat /thret/ *n.* **1 a** a declaration of an intention to punish or hurt. **b** *Law* a menace of bodily hurt or injury, such as may restrain a person's freedom of action. **2** an indication of something undesirable coming (*the threat of war*). **3** a person or thing as a likely cause of harm, etc. [OE *thrēat* affliction, etc., f. Gmc]

■ **1 a** intimidation, menace, commination, sword of Damocles, warning, duress. **2** omen, presage, portent, foreboding, forewarning, warning, intimation. **3** menace, danger, hazard, peril.

threaten /thrét'n/ *v.tr.* **1 a** make a threat or threats against. **b** constitute a threat to; be likely to harm; put into danger. **2** be a sign or indication of (something undesirable). **3** (foll. by *to* + infin.) announce one's intention to do an undesirable or unexpected thing (*threatened to resign*). **4** (also *absol.*) give warning of the infliction of (harm, etc.) (*the clouds were threatening rain*). □□ **threatener** *n.* **threatening** *adj.* **threateningly** *adv.* [OE *thrēatnian* (as THREAT)]

■ **1 a** intimidate, menace, terrorize, daunt, cow, bully, browbeat, warn, caution. **b** imperil, put at risk, endanger, jeopardize, put in jeopardy. **4** augur, portend, presage, forebode, forewarn of, warn of; impend, loom, lower. □ **threatening** intimidating, menacing, minatory, comminatory; ominous, portentous, sinister, looming, inauspicious, foreboding, imminent, impending.

three /three/ *n. & adj.* ● *n.* **1 a** one more than two, or seven less than ten. **b** a symbol for this (3, iii, III). **2** a size, etc., denoted by three. **3** the time of three o'clock. **4** a set of three. **5** a card with three pips. ● *adj.* that amount to three. □ **three-card monte** (or **trick**) a game in which bets are made on which is the queen (or other identified card) among three cards lying face downwards. **three cheers** see CHEER. **three-color process** a process of reproducing natural colors by combining photographic images in the three primary colors. **three-cornered 1** triangular. **2** (of a contest, etc.) between three parties as individuals. **three-decker 1** a warship with three gun decks. **2** a novel in three volumes. **3** a sandwich with three slices of bread. **three-dimensional** having or appearing to have length, breadth, and depth. **three-handed 1** having or using three hands. **2** involving three players. **three-legged race** a running race between pairs, one member of each pair having the left leg tied to the right leg of the other. **three parts** three quarters. **three-phase** see PHASE. **three-piece** consisting of three items (esp. of a suit of clothes or a suite of furniture). **three-ply** *adj.* of three strands, webs, or thicknesses. ● *n.* **1** three-ply wool. **2** three-ply wood made by gluing together three layers with the grain in different directions. **three-point landing** *Aeron.* the landing of an aircraft on the two main wheels and the tail wheel or skid or front wheel simultaneously. **three-point turn** a method of turning a vehicle around in a narrow space by moving forward, backward, and forward again in a sequence of arcs. **three-quarter 1** consisting of three-fourths of something. **2** (of a portrait) going down to the hips or showing three-fourths of the face (between full face and profile). **three-quarters** three parts out of four. **three-ring circus 1** a circus with three rings for simultaneous performances. **2** an extravagant display. **the three Rs** reading, writing (*joc.* 'riting), and arithmetic (*joc.* 'rithmetic), regarded as the fundamentals of learning. **three-way** involving three ways or participants. **three-wheeler** a vehicle with three wheels. [OE *thrī* f. Gmc]

■ *n.* **4** see TRIO.

threefold /threefōld/ *adj. & adv.* **1** three times as much or as many. **2** consisting of three parts.

threepence /thrépəns, thrōōpəns/ *n. Brit.* the sum of three pence, esp. before decimalization.

threepenny /thrípənee, thrōōpənee/ *adj. Brit.* costing three pence, esp. before decimalization. □ **threepenny bit** *hist.* a former coin worth three old pence.

threescore /threeskáwr/ *n. archaic* sixty.

threesome /threesəm/ *n.* **1** a group of three persons. **2** a game, etc., for three.

■ **1** see TRIO.

thremmatology /thrémətóləjee/ *n.* the science of breeding animals and plants. [Gk *thremma -matos* nursling + -LOGY]

threnody /thrénədee/ *n.* (also **threnode** /thrénōd/) (*pl.* **-ies** or **threnodes**) **1** a lamentation, esp. on a person's death. **2**

a song of lamentation. □□ **threnodial** /-nṓdeeəl/ *adj.* **threnodic** /-nódik/ *adj.* **threnodist** /thrénədist/ *n.* [Gk *thrēnōidia* f. *thrēnos* wailing + *ōidē* ODE]

threonine /threeəneen, -nin/ *n. Biochem.* an amino acid, considered essential for growth. [*threose* (name of a tetrose sugar) ult. f. Gk *eruthros* red + -INE⁴]

thresh /thresh/ *v.* **1** *tr.* beat out or separate grain from (wheat, etc.). **2** *intr.* = THRASH *v.* 4. **3** *tr.* (foll. by *over*) analyze (a problem, etc.) in search of a solution. □ **threshing floor** a hard level floor for threshing, esp. with flails. **threshing machine** a power-driven machine for separating the grain from the straw or husk. **thresh out** = *thrash out.* [var. of THRASH]

■ **3** (*thresh over*) see CONSIDER 1.

thresher /thréshər/ *n.* **1** a person or machine that threshes. **2** a shark, *Alopias vulpinus*, with a long upper lobe to its tail, that it can lash about.

threshold /thréshōld, thrésh-hōld/ *n.* **1** a strip of wood or stone forming the bottom of a doorway and crossed in entering a house or room, etc. **2** a point of entry or beginning (*on the threshold of a new century*). **3** *Physiol. & Psychol.* a limit below which a stimulus causes no reaction (*pain threshold*). **4** *Physics* a limit below which no reaction occurs, esp. a minimum dose of radiation producing a specified effect. **5** esp. *Brit.* (often *attrib.*) a step in a scale of wages or taxation, usu. operative in specified conditions. [OE *therscold, threscold,* etc., rel. to THRASH in the sense 'tread']

■ **1** sill, doorsill, doorstep; doorway, entrance. **2** brink, verge, edge, beginning, inception, outset, start, dawn, *formal* commencement.

threw *past* of THROW.

thrice /thris/ *adv. archaic* or *literary* **1** three times. **2** (esp. in *comb.*) highly (*thrice-blessed*). [ME *thries* f. *thrie* (adv.) f. OE *thrīwa, thrīga* (as THREE, -s³)]

thrift /thrift/ *n.* **1** frugality; economical management. **2** a plant of the genus *Armeria*, esp. the sea pink. **3** a savings and loan association or savings bank. □ **thrift shop** (or **store**) a shop selling secondhand items usu. for charity. [ME f. ON (as THRIVE)]

■ **1** economy, husbandry, care, carefulness, prudence, providence, parsimony, frugality, thriftiness, sparingness, scrimping, skimping; penuriousness, closefistedness, tightfistedness, niggardliness, stinginess, miserliness.

thriftless /thriftlis/ *adj.* wasteful; improvident. □□ **thriftlessly** *adv.* **thriftlessness** *n.*

■ see IMPROVIDENT 2.

thrifty /thriftee/ *adj.* (**thriftier, thriftiest**) **1** economical; frugal. **2** thriving; prosperous. □□ **thriftily** *adv.* **thriftiness** *n.*

■ **1** economical, careful, prudent, parsimonious, frugal, sparing, scrimping, skimping; penurious, closefisted, tightfisted, niggardly, stingy, miserly, penny-pinching, cheap. **2** see SUCCESSFUL. □□ **thriftiness** see THRIFT.

thrill /thril/ *n. & v.* ● *n.* **1 a** a wave or nervous tremor of emotion or sensation (*a thrill of joy; a thrill of recognition*). **b** a thrilling experience (*seeking new thrills*). **2** a throb or pulsation. **3** *Med.* a vibratory movement or resonance heard in auscultation. ● *v.* **1** *intr.* & *tr.* feel or cause to feel a thrill (*thrilled to the sound; a voice that thrilled millions*). **2** *intr.* quiver or throb with or as with emotion. **3** *intr.* (foll. by *through, over, along*) (of an emotion, etc.) pass with a thrill through, etc. (*fear thrilled through my veins*). □ **thrills and spills** the excitement of potentially dangerous activities. □□ **thrilling** *adj.* **thrillingly** *adv.* [*thirl* (now dial.) f. OE *thyrlian* pierce f. *thyrel* hole f. *thurh* THROUGH]

■ *n.* **1 a** excitement, titillation, frisson, shiver, tingle, tingling (sensation), stimulation, tremor, quiver, shudder, tremble, flutter, *colloq.* kick, *sl.* buzz. **2** tremor, quiver, shudder, tremble, flutter, throb,

/. . ./ **pronunciation**	● **part of speech**
□ **phrases, idioms, and compounds**	
□□ **derivatives**	■ **synonym section**
cross-references appear in SMALL CAPITALS or *italics*	

pulsation, vibration. ● *v.* **1** (*tr.*) excite, stimulate, animate, electrify, galvanize, enliven, stir, titillate, touch, strike, move, impassion, arouse, rouse, *colloq.* give a person a kick, *sl.* send. □□ **thrilling** exciting, stimulating, animating, electrifying, galvanizing, enlivening, stirring, titillating, striking, moving, arousing, rousing, gripping, wild, sensational, riveting, spine-tingling, soul-stirring.

thriller /thrílər/ *n.* an exciting or sensational story or play, etc., esp. one involving crime or espionage.

thrips /thrips/ *n.* (*pl.* same) any insect of the order Thysanoptera, esp. a pest injurious to plants. [L f. Gk, = woodworm]

thrive /thrīv/ *v.intr.* (*past* **throve** /thrōv/ or **thrived**; *past part.* **thriven** /thrívən/ or **thrived**) **1** prosper or flourish. **2** grow rich. **3** (of a child, animal, or plant) grow vigorously. [ME f. ON *thrífask* refl. of *thrífa* grasp]

■ **1** succeed, prosper, boom, advance, flourish, do well. **3** grow, flourish, bloom, blossom, develop, wax, increase, fructify, ripen, *literary* burgeon.

throat /thrōt/ *n.* **1 a** the windpipe or gullet. **b** the front part of the neck containing this. **2** *literary* **a** a voice, esp. of a songbird. **b** a thing compared to a throat, esp. a narrow passage, entrance, or exit. **3** *Naut.* the forward upper corner of a fore-and-aft sail. □ **cut one's own throat** bring about one's own downfall. **ram** (or **thrust**) **down a person's throat** force (a thing) on a person's attention. □□ **-throated** *adj.* (in *comb.*). [OE *throte*, *throtu* f. Gmc]

throaty /thrōtee/ *adj.* (**throatier**, **throatiest**) **1** (of a voice) deficient in clarity; hoarsely resonant. **2** guttural; uttered in the throat. **3** having a prominent or capacious throat. □□ **throatily** *adv.* **throatiness** *n.*

■ **1, 2** see GRUFF 1a, THICK *adj.* 8a.

throb /throb/ *v. & n.* ● *v.intr.* (**throbbed**, **throbbing**) **1** palpitate or pulsate, esp. with more than the usual force or rapidity. **2** vibrate or quiver with a persistent rhythm or with emotion. ● *n.* **1** a throbbing. **2** a palpitation or (esp. violent) pulsation. [ME, app. imit.]

■ *v.* see PULSATE, ACHE *v.* 1, VIBRATE 1, 2, 4; 3. ● *n.* see PULSE¹ n. 5, 6, THRILL n. 2.

throe /thrō/ *n.* (usu. in *pl.*) **1** a violent pang, esp. of childbirth or death. **2** anguish. □ **in the throes of** struggling with the task of. [ME *throwe* perh. f. OE *thréa*, *thrawu* calamity, alt. perh. by assoc. with *woe*]

■ **1** pang, agony, pain, paroxysm, spasm; fit, seizure, convulsion, *Med.* ictus. **2** (*throes*) anguish, struggle, turmoil, tumult; see also AGONY 1.

thrombi *pl.* of THROMBUS.

thrombin /thrómbin/ *n.* an enzyme promoting the clotting of blood. [as THROMBUS + -IN]

thrombocyte /thrómbəsīt/ *n.* a blood platelet, a small plate of protoplasm concerned in the coagulation of blood. [as THROMBUS + -CYTE]

thrombose /thrombōz/ *v.tr. & intr.* affect with or undergo thrombosis. [back-form. f. THROMBOSIS]

thrombosis /thrombṓsis/ *n.* (*pl.* **thromboses** /-seez/) the coagulation of the blood in a blood vessel or organ. □□ **thrombotic** /-bótik/ *adj.* [mod.L f. Gk *thrombōsis* curdling (as THROMBUS)]

thrombus /thrómbəs/ *n.* (*pl.* **thrombi** /-bī/) a bloodclot formed in the vascular system and impeding blood flow. [mod.L f. Gk *thrombos* lump, bloodclot]

throne /thrōn/ *n. & v.* ● *n.* **1** a chair of state for a sovereign or bishop, etc. **2** sovereign power (*came to the throne*). **3** (in *pl.*) the third order of the ninefold celestial hierarchy. **4** *colloq.* a toilet seat and bowl. ● *v.tr.* place on a throne. □□ **throneless** *adj.* [ME f. OF *trone* f. L *thronus* f. Gk *thronos* high seat]

throng /thrawng, throng/ *n. & v.* ● *n.* **1** a crowd of people. **2** (often foll. by *of*) a multitude, esp. in a small space. ● *v.* **1** *intr.* come in great numbers (*crowds thronged to the stadium*). **2** *tr.* flock into or crowd around; fill with or as with a crowd (*crowds thronged the streets*). [ME *thrang*, *throng*, OE *gethrang*, f. verbal stem *thring- thrang-*]

■ *n.* horde, crowd, host, assemblage, assembly,

gathering, mass, crush, jam, multitude, congregation, rabble, army, press, swarm, herd, flock, mob, pack, bevy, drove. ● *v.* **1** crowd, swarm, flock; assemble, gather, mass, congregate. **2** crowd into *or* around, fill, pack (into), cram (into), crush into, jam into, pour into, press into *or* around, swarm into *or* around, herd into *or* around, flock into *or* to *or* around; assemble in *or* at *or* around, gather in *or* at *or* around, mass in *or* at *or* around, congregate in *or* at *or* around.

throstle /thrósəl/ *n.* **1** *Brit.* a song thrush. **2** (in full **throstle frame**) a machine for continuously spinning wool or cotton, etc. [OE f. Gmc: rel. to THRUSH¹]

throttle /thrót'l/ *n. & v.* ● *n.* **1 a** (in full **throttle valve**) a valve controlling the flow of fuel or steam, etc., in an engine. **b** (in full **throttle lever**) a lever or pedal operating this valve. **2** the throat, gullet, or windpipe. ● *v.tr.* **1** choke or strangle. **2** prevent the utterance, etc., of. **3** control (an engine or steam, etc.) with a throttle. □ **throttle back** (or **down**) reduce the speed of (an engine or vehicle) by throttling. □□ **throttler** *n.* [ME *throtel* (v.), perh. f. THROAT + -LE⁴: (n.) perh. a dimin. of THROAT]

■ *v.* **1** see CHOKE¹ *v.* 1. **2** see GAG *v.* 2.

through /throo/ *prep., adv., & adj.* (also **thru**) ● *prep.* **1 a** from end to end or from side to side of. **b** going in one side or end and out the other of. **2** between or among (*swam through the waves*). **3** from beginning to end of (*read through the letter*; *went through many difficulties*; *through the years*). **4** because of; by the agency, means, or fault of (*lost it through carelessness*). **5** up to and including (*Monday through Friday*). ● *adv.* **1** through a thing; from side to side, end to end, or beginning to end; completely; thoroughly (*went through to the garden*; *would not let us through*). **2** having completed (esp. successfully) (*are through their exams*). **3** so as to be connected by telephone (*will put you through*). ● *attrib.adj.* **1** (of a journey, route, etc.) done without a change of line or vehicle, etc., or with one ticket. **2** (of traffic) going through a place to its destination. □ **be through** *colloq.* **1** (often foll. by *with*) have finished. **2** (often foll. by *with*) cease to have dealings. **3** have no further prospects (*is through as a politician*). **through and through 1** thoroughly; completely. **2** through again and again. [OE *thurh* f. WG]

■ *prep.* **1** see OVER *prep.* 3, 4. **3** during, throughout, in *or* during the course of. **4** because of, on account of, owing to, as a consequence *or* result of, by virtue of, via, by means of, by way of, with the aid *or* help of, under the aegis *or* auspices of, *disp.* due to. ● *adv.* **1** by, past; entirely, through and through, completely, thoroughly, totally, wholly, utterly, fully, to the core, from head to foot *or* toe, from top to toe, from top to bottom, from stem to stern, from one end to the other, in every way, in all respects. ● *adj.* **1** direct, unbroken, nonstop. □ **be through 1** have done *or* finished. **2** (*be through with*) have finished with, be at the end of one's tether with, have washed *or* be washing one's hands of. **3** be finished, be played out, *sl.* be washed up.

through and through 1 see THROUGH *adv.* above.

throughout /throo-ówt/ *prep. & adv.* ● *prep.* right through; from end to end of (*throughout the town*; *throughout the 18th century*). ● *adv.* in every part or respect (*the timber was rotten throughout*).

■ *prep.* during, all (the way) through, from the beginning to the end of; everywhere in, all over, in every part of, in every nook and cranny of, from one end to the other of. ● *adv.* all (the way) through, through and through, everywhere, from one end to the other, from top to bottom, in every part, wholly, entirely, completely, fully.

throughput /throoput/ *n.* the amount of material put through a process, esp. in manufacturing or computing.

throughway /throo-way/ *n.* (also **thruway**) a thoroughfare, esp. a highway.

■ see ROAD¹ 1.

throve *past* of THRIVE.

throw /thrō/ *v. & n.* ● *v.tr.* (*past* **threw** /throo/; *past part.* **thrown** /thrōn/) **1** propel with some force through the air or in a particular direction. **2** force violently into a specified position or state (*the ship was thrown on the rocks*; *threw themselves down*). **3** compel suddenly to be in a specified condition (*was thrown out of work*). **4** turn or move (part of the body) quickly or suddenly (*threw an arm out*). **5** project or cast (light, a shadow, a spell, etc.). **6 a** bring to the ground in wrestling. **b** (of a horse) unseat (its rider). **7** *colloq.* disconcert (*the question threw me for a moment*). **8** (foll. by *on*, *off*, etc.) put (clothes, etc.) hastily on or off, etc. **9 a** cause (dice) to fall on a table. **b** obtain (a specified number) by throwing dice. **10** cause to pass or extend suddenly to another state or position (*threw in the army*; *threw a bridge across the river*). **11** move (a switch or lever) so as to operate it. **12 a** form (pottery) on a potter's wheel. **b** turn (wood, etc.) on a lathe. **13** have (a fit or tantrum, etc.). **14** give (a party). **15** *colloq.* lose (a contest or race, etc.) intentionally. **16** *Cricket* bowl (a ball) with an illegitimate sudden straightening of the elbow. **17** (of a snake) cast (its skin). **18** (of an animal) give birth to (young). **19** twist (silk, etc.) into thread or yarn. **20** (often foll. by *into*) put into another form or language, etc. ● *n.* **1** an act of throwing. **2** the distance a thing is or may be thrown (*a record throw with the hammer*). **3** the act of being thrown in wrestling. **4** *Geol. & Mining* **a** a fault in strata. **b** the amount of vertical displacement caused by this. **5** a machine or device giving rapid rotary motion. **6 a** the movement of a crank or cam, etc. **b** the extent of this. **7** the distance moved by the pointer of an instrument, etc. **8 a** a light cover for furniture. **b** (in full **throw rug**) a light rug. **c** a shawl or scarf. **9** (prec. by *a*) *sl.* each; per item (*sold at $10 a throw*). □ **throw around** (or **about**) **1** throw in various directions. **2** spend (one's money) ostentatiously. **throw away 1** discard as useless or unwanted. **2** waste or fail to make use of (an opportunity, etc.). **3** discard (a card). **4** *Theatr.* speak (lines) with deliberate underemphasis. **5** (in *passive*; often foll. by *on*) be wasted (*the advice was thrown away on him*). **throw back 1** revert to ancestral character. **2** (usu. in *passive*; foll. by *on*) compel to rely on (*was thrown back on his savings*). **throw cold water on** see COLD. **throw down** cause to fall. **throw down the gauntlet** (or **glove**) issue a challenge. **throw good money after bad** incur further loss in a hopeless attempt to recoup a previous loss. **throw one's hand in 1** abandon one's chances in a card game, esp. poker. **2** give up; withdraw from a contest. **throw in 1** interpose (a word or remark). **2** include at no extra cost. **3** throw (a soccer ball) from the edge of the field where it has gone out of play. **4** *Baseball & Cricket* return (the ball) from the outfield. **5** *Cards* give (a player) the lead, to the player's disadvantage. **throw-in** *n.* the throwing in of a soccer ball during play. **throw in one's lot with** see LOT. **throw in the towel** (or **the sponge**) admit defeat. **throw light on** see LIGHT¹. **throw off 1** discard; contrive to get rid of. **2** write or utter in an offhand manner. **3** confuse or distract (a person speaking, thinking, or acting) from the matter in hand. **4** (of hounds or a hunt) begin hunting; make a start. **throw-off** the start in a hunt or race. **throw oneself at** seek blatantly as a spouse or sexual partner. **throw oneself into** engage vigorously in. **throw oneself on** (or **upon**) **1** rely completely on. **2** attack. **throw open** (often foll. by *to*) **1** cause to be suddenly or widely open. **2** make accessible. **throw out 1** put out forcibly or suddenly. **2** discard as unwanted. **3** expel (a troublemaker, etc.). **4** *Brit.* build (a wing of a house, a pier, or a projecting or prominent thing). **5** put forward tentatively. **6** reject (a proposal, etc.) **7** *Brit.* = throw off 3. **8** dislocate; strain (*threw out her shoulder*). **9** *Baseball & Cricket* put out (an opponent) by throwing the ball to the base or wicket. **throw over** desert or abandon. **throw stones** cast aspersions. **throw together 1** assemble hastily. **2** bring into casual contact. **throw up 1** abandon. **2** resign from. **3** *colloq.* vomit. **4** erect hastily. **5** bring to notice. **6** lift (a window) quickly. **throw one's weight around** (or **about**) *colloq.* act with unpleasant self-assertiveness. □□ **throwable** *adj.* **thrower** *n.* (also in *comb.*). [OE *thrāwan* twist, turn f. WG]

■ *v.* **1, 2** toss, cast, hurl, fling, pitch, dash, propel, project, shy, bowl, send, precipitate, launch, lob, put, *colloq.* chuck, heave, sling, *Brit. sl.* bung. **3** hurl, fling, cast. **4** fling. **5** cast, shed, project, emit. **6 b** unseat, unhorse, dislodge, buck off. **7** dismay, confound, confuse, dumbfound, baffle, disconcert, unnerve, throw off *or* out, unsettle, put off, put a person off his *or* her stride *or* pace *or* stroke, *colloq.* rattle, faze, *US joc.* discombobulate. ● *n.* **1** toss, lob, pitch, heave, shy, fling, hurl, launch, put, delivery. **8 a** see SPREAD *n.* 10. □ **throw away 1** discard, cast off, dispose of, jettison, get rid of, scrap, junk, throw out, toss away *or* out, dispense with, dump, *colloq.* chuck out, trash, *sl.* ditch. **2** waste, squander, lose, forgo, fritter away, fail to exploit *or* take advantage of, *sl.* blow. **throw down** bring down, floor, fell, knock down *or* over, overthrow, upset, overturn, topple. **throw down the gauntlet** challenge a person, enter the lists. **throw in 1** interpose, put in, interpolate, cut in with. **throw in the towel** see SURRENDER *v.* 2. **throw off 1** shake off, rid *or* free oneself of, get rid of, discard, reject, renounce, repudiate. **3** see *throw out* 7 below. **throw oneself on** (or **upon**) **2** see ATTACK *v.* 1. **throw out 1** see *cast out*. **2** see *throw away* 1 above. **3** expel, eject, force out, evict, turn *or* toss *or* boot out, *Brit. colloq.* turf out, *sl.* bounce, kick out. **6** reject, say no to, veto, turn down; see also QUASH 1. **7** distract, divert, bewilder, confound, confuse, *colloq.* flummox, faze; see also THROW *v.* 7 above. **throw over** jilt, leave, abandon, desert, forsake, break *or* split up with, walk out on, *colloq.* chuck, drop, dump, *sl.* ditch. **throw together 1** see *throw up* 4 below. **2** see LUMP¹ *v.* **throw up 1, 2** abandon, quit, leave, throw over, give up, relinquish, resign (from), renounce, *colloq.* chuck. **3** vomit, spit up, spew (up), be sick; regurgitate, disgorge, *Brit. colloq.* sick up, *sl.* puke, barf, *Austral. sl.* chunder. **4** throw *or* slap *or* knock together. **5** reveal, bring out *or* up, bring to the surface *or* top, bring forward *or* forth, bring to light *or* notice.

throwaway /thrṓəway/ *adj.* **1** meant to be thrown away after (one) use. **2** (of lines, etc.) deliberately underemphasized. ● *n.* a thing to be thrown away after (one) use.

■ **1** see DISPOSABLE *adj.* 1.

throwback /thrṓbak/ *n.* **1** reversion to ancestral character. **2** an instance of this.

throwster /thrṓstər/ *n.* a person who throws silk.

thru var. of THROUGH.

thrum¹ /thrum/ *v. & n.* ● *v.* (**thrummed, thrumming**) **1** *tr.* play (a stringed instrument) monotonously or unskillfully. **2** *intr.* (often foll. by *on*) beat or drum idly or monotonously. ● *n.* **1** such playing. **2** the resulting sound. [imit.]

■ *v.* **1** strum, pluck, pick, *usu. derog.* twang. **2** see PULSATE. ● *n.* **1** strumming. **2** see PATTER¹ *n.*

thrum² /thrum/ *n. & v.* ● *n.* **1** the unwoven end of a warp thread, or the whole of such ends, left when the finished web is cut away. **2** any short loose thread. ● *v.tr.* (**thrummed, thrumming**) make of or cover with thrums. □□ **thrummer** *n.* **thrummy** *adj.* [OE f. Gmc]

thrush¹ /thrush/ *n.* any small or medium-sized songbird of the family Turdidae, esp. a song thrush or mistle thrush (see *song thrush*). [OE *thrysce* f. Gmc: cf. THROSTLE]

thrush² /thrush/ *n.* **1 a** a fungal disease, esp. of children, marked by whitish vesicles in the mouth and throat. **b** a similar disease of the vagina. **2** inflammation affecting the frog of a horse's foot. [17th c.: orig. unkn.]

thrust /thrust/ *v. & n.* ● *v.* (*past* and *past part.* **thrust**) **1** *tr.* push with a sudden impulse or with force (*thrust the letter into my pocket*). **2** *tr.* (foll. by *on*) impose (a thing) forcibly; enforce acceptance of (a thing) (*had it thrust on me*). **3** *intr.* (foll. by *at, through*) pierce or stab; make a sudden lunge. **4** *tr.* make (one's way) forcibly. **5** *intr.* (foll. by *through, past,* etc.) force oneself (*thrust past me abruptly*). ● *n.* **1** a sudden or forcible push or lunge. **2** The propulsive force developed by a jet or rocket engine. **3** a strong attempt to penetrate an enemy's line or territory. **4** a remark aimed at a person. **5** the stress between the parts of an arch, etc. **6** (often foll. by *of*) the chief theme or gist of remarks, etc. **7** an attack with the point of a weapon. **8** (in full **thrust fault**) *Geol.* a low-angle reverse fault, with older strata displaced horizontally over newer. □ **thrust oneself** (or **one's nose**) **in** obtrude; interfere. **thrust stage** a stage extending into the audience. [ME *thruste*, etc. f. ON *þrýsta*]

▪ *v.* **1** push, shove, drive, force, stuff, wedge, stick, jam, impel, ram, propel, urge, press. **2** press, impose, force, urge, foist, intrude. **3** stab, jab, poke, pierce, prod; lunge. **4** push, shove, drive, force, propel, urge, press, elbow, butt, jostle. **5** shoulder, jostle, elbow; push, shove, force oneself, press. ● *n.* **1, 7** shove, push, drive, lunge, poke, prod, stab, jab. **2** propulsion, force, power, energy, impetus, drive. **4** see GIBE *n.* **6** see IMPORT *n.* 3. □ **thrust oneself** (or **one's nose**) **in** see OBTRUDE, INTERFERE 2.

thruster /thrúster/ *n.* **1** a person or thing that thrusts. **2** a small rocket engine used to provide extra or correcting thrust on a spacecraft.

thruway var. of THROUGHWAY.

thud /thud/ *n. & v.* ● *n.* a low dull sound as of a blow on a nonresonant surface. ● *v.intr.* (**thudded, thudding**) make or fall with a thud. □□ **thuddingly** *adv.* [prob. f. OE *þyddan* thrust]

▪ *n.* clunk, thump, clonk, bump, *colloq.* wham.
● *v.* clunk, clonk, thump, bump, plump, clump, clomp.

thug /thug/ *n.* **1** a vicious or brutal gangster or ruffian. **2** (**Thug**) *hist.* a member of a religious organization of robbers and assassins in India. □□ **thuggery** *n.* **thuggish** *adj.* **thuggishly** *adv.* **thuggishness** *n.* [Hindi & Marathi *þag* swindler]

▪ **1** hooligan, gangster, desperado, gunman, hoodlum, ruffian, apache, tough, rough, mugger, *Austral.* larrikin, *colloq.* heavy, bruiser, *sl.* mobster, goon, hood, mug, *Brit. sl.* yob. □□ **thuggish** see strong-arm.

thuggee /thugée/ *n. hist.* murder practiced by the Thugs. □□ **thuggism** *n.* [Hindi *þagī* (as THUG)]

thuja /thóoya/ *n.* (also **thuya**) any evergreen coniferous tree of the genus *Thuja*, with small leaves closely pressed to the branches; arborvitae. [mod.L f. Gk *thuia*, an Afr. tree]

thulium /thóoleeam, thyóo-/ *n. Chem.* a soft metallic element of the lanthanide series, occurring naturally in apatite. ¶ Symb.: **Tm**. [mod.L f. L *Thule* name of a region in the remote north]

thumb /thum/ *n. & v.* ● *n.* **1 a** a short thick terminal projection on the human hand, set lower and apart from the other four and opposable to them. **b** a digit of other animals corresponding to this. **2** part of a glove, etc., for a thumb. ● *v.* **1** *tr.* wear or soil (pages, etc.) with a thumb (*a well-thumbed book*). **2** *intr.* turn over pages with or as with a thumb (*thumbed through the directory*). **3** *tr.* request or obtain (a lift in a passing vehicle) by signaling with a raised thumb. **4** *tr.* gesture at (a person) with the thumb. □ **be all thumbs** be clumsy with one's hands. **thumb index** *n.* a set of lettered grooves cut down the side of a diary, dictionary, etc., for easy reference. ● *v.tr.* provide (a book, etc.) with these. **thumb one's nose 1** put one's thumb up to one's nose with fingers extended up, a gesture of contempt. **2** display contempt or disdain. **thumbs-down** an indication of rejection or failure. **thumbs-up** an indication of satisfaction or approval. **under a person's thumb** completely dominated by a person. □□ **thumbed** *adj.* (also in *comb.*). **thumbless** *adj.* [OE *þūma* f. a WG root = swell]

▪ *n.* **1** pollex. ● *v.* **2** leaf, flick, flip, riffle, skim, browse. **3** *colloq.* hitch. □ **be all thumbs** be awkward, be clumsy, be maladroit, *colloq.* be a butterfingers, be ham-fisted. **thumb one's nose 2** scoff at, deride, jeer at, mock, dismiss, scorn, flout, be contemptuous of, show contempt for, exhibit defiance of (*or* for), be

defiant of, *literary* contemn. **thumbs-down** see VETO *n.* **thumbs-up** see APPROVAL. **under a person's thumb** under a person's control, wrapped around a person's little finger, in the palm of a person's hand, eating out of a person's hand, at a person's beck and call.

thumbnail /thúmnayl/ *n.* **1** the nail of a thumb. **2** (*attrib.*) denoting conciseness (*a thumbnail sketch*).

▪ **2** (*attrib.*) rough, undetailed, cursory, sketchy, superficial; brief, short, quick; compact, concise, pithy, succinct.

thumbprint /thúmprint/ *n.* an impression of a thumb, esp. as used for identification.

thumbscrew /thúmskroo/ *n.* **1** an instrument of torture for crushing the thumbs. **2** a screw with a flattened head for turning with the thumb and forefinger.

thumbtack /thúmtak/ *n.* a tack with a flat head pressing in with the thumb.

thump /thump/ *v. & n.* ● *v.* **1** *tr.* beat or strike heavily, esp. with the fist (*thumped the table for attention*). **2** *intr.* throb or pulsate strongly (*my heart was thumping*). **3** *intr.* (foll. by *at, on,* etc.) deliver blows, esp. to attract attention (*thumped on the door*). **4** *tr.* (often foll. by *out*) play (a tune on a piano, etc.) with a heavy touch. **5** *intr.* tread heavily. ● *n.* **1** a heavy blow. **2** the sound of this. □□ **thumper** *n.* [imit.]

▪ *v.* **1** see BEAT *v.* 1. **2** see PULSATE 3. **3** see KNOCK *v.* 1.
● *n.* see KNOCK *n.*

thumping /thúmping/ *adj. colloq.* big; prominent (*a thumping majority; a thumping lie*).

▪ great, huge, colossal, stupendous, gigantic, enormous, immense, monumental, massive, titanic, elephantine, gargantuan, mammoth, hefty, *colloq.* thundering, jumbo, *sl.* whopping, walloping; complete, utter, unmitigated, 24-karat, perfect.

thunder /thúnder/ *n. & v.* ● *n.* **1** a loud rumbling or crashing noise heard after a lightning flash and due to the expansion of rapidly heated air. **2** a resounding loud deep noise (*the thunder of an explosion*). **3** strong censure or denunciation. ● *v.* **1** *intr.* (prec. by *it* as subject) thunder sounds (*it is thundering; if it thunders*). **2** *intr.* make or proceed with a noise suggestive of thunder (*the applause thundered in my ears; the crowd thundered past*). **3** *tr.* utter or communicate (approval, disapproval, etc.) loudly or impressively. **4** *intr.* (foll. by *against*, etc.) **a** make violent threats, etc., against. **b** criticize violently. □ **steal a person's thunder** spoil the effect of another's idea, action, etc., by expressing or doing it first. **thunder-box** *Brit. colloq.* a primitive toilet. □□ **thunderer** *n.* **thunderless** *adj.* **thundery** *adj.* [OE *þunor* f. Gmc]

▪ *n.* **1, 2** rumble, rumbling, roll, reverberation, boom, booming, roar, roaring, peal; crash, crashing, crack, cracking, explosion, blast. ● *v.* **2** roll, reverberate, boom, roar, rumble, resound; explode, crash, crack, blast. **3** shout, yell, scream, bellow, bark, bawl, roar. **4** (*thunder against* or *at*) **a** threaten, intimidate, menace; denounce, fulminate against, swear at, rail against *or* at, curse at, execrate.

thunderbolt /thúnderbōlt/ *n.* **1 a** a flash of lightning with a simultaneous crash of thunder. **b** a stone, etc., imagined to be a destructive bolt. **2** a sudden or unexpected occurrence or item of news. **3** a supposed bolt or shaft as a destructive agent, esp. as an attribute of a god.

▪ **2** see SHOCK¹ *n.* 2.

thunderclap /thúnderklap/ *n.* **1** a crash of thunder. **2** something startling or unexpected.

thundercloud /thúnderklowd/ *n.* a cumulus cloud with a tall diffuse top, charged with electricity and producing thunder and lightning.

thunderhead /thúnderhed/ *n.* a rounded cumulus cloud projecting upwards and heralding a thunderstorm.

thundering /thúndering/ *adj. colloq.* very big or great (*a thundering nuisance*). □□ **thunderingly** *adv.*

▪ see THUMPING .

thunderous /thúnderas/ *adj.* **1** like thunder. **2** very loud. □□ **thunderously** *adv.* **thunderousness** *n.*

■ roaring, booming, thundering, tumultuous, noisy, loud, ear-splitting, deafening.

thundershower /thúndərshowər/ *n.* a brief rain shower accompanied by thunder and sometimes lightning.

thunderstorm /thúndərstawrm/ *n.* a storm with thunder and lightning and usu. heavy rain or hail.

thunderstruck /thúndərstruk/ *adj.* amazed; overwhelmingly surprised or startled.

■ dumbfounded, astonished, astounded, awestruck, awed, speechless, struck dumb, dumbstruck, amazed, taken aback, staggered, stunned, shocked, dazed, numb, paralyzed, aghast, openmouthed, nonplussed, *colloq.* flabbergasted, floored, bowled over, knocked for six.

Thur. *abbr.* Thursday.

thurible /thōoribəl, thyōo-/ *n.* a censer. [ME f. OF *thurible* or L *t(h)uribulum* f. *thus thur-* incense (as THURIFER)]

thurifer /thōorifər, thyōo-/ *n.* an acolyte carrying a censer. [LL f. *thus thuris* incense f. Gk *thuos* sacrifice + *-fer* -bearing]

Thurs. *abbr.* Thursday.

Thursday /thɔrzday, -dee/ *n. & adv.* ● *n.* the fifth day of the week, following Wednesday. ● *adv. colloq.* **1** on Thursday. **2 (Thursdays)** on Thursdays; each Thursday. [OE *thunresdæg, thur(e)sdæg*, day of thunder, representing LL *Jovis dies* day of Jupiter]

thus /thus/ *adv. formal* **1 a** in this way. **b** as indicated. **2 a** accordingly. **b** as a result or inference. **3** to this extent; so (*thus far*; *thus much*). □□ **thusly** *adv. colloq.* [OE (= OS *thus*), of unkn. orig.]

■ **1** so, in this manner *or* way *or* fashion, as follows, as indicated, *archaic* in this wise, *colloq.* like so, thusly. **2** therefore, ergo, consequently, as a consequence, as a result, accordingly, (and) so, then, for this *or* that reason, hence, in which case *or* event, that being the case, that being so.

thuya var. of THUJA.

thwack /thwak/ *v. & n. colloq.* ● *v.tr.* hit with a heavy blow; whack. ● *n.* a heavy blow. [imit.]

■ *v.* see HIT *v.* 1a. ● *n.* see HIT *n.* 1a.

thwaite /thwayt/ *n. Brit. dial.* a piece of wild land made arable. ¶ Now usually only in place-names. [ON *thveit(i)* paddock, rel. to OE *thwītan* to cut]

thwart /thwawrt/ *v., n., prep., & adv.* ● *v.tr.* frustrate or foil (a person or purpose, etc.). ● *n.* a rower's seat placed across a boat. ● *prep. & adv. archaic* across; athwart. [ME *thwert* (adv.) f. ON *thvert* neut. of *thverr* transverse = OE *thwe(o)rh* f. Gmc]

■ *v.* frustrate, impede, check, stymie, baffle, stop, foil, hinder, obstruct, balk, block, stand in the way of, oppose, negate, nullify, short-circuit, *Brit. sl.* scupper. ● *n.* brace; (rowing) seat, bench.

thy /thī/ *poss.pron.* (*attrib.*) (also **thine** /thīn/ before a vowel) of or belonging to thee: now replaced by *your* except in some formal, liturgical, dialect, and poetic uses. [ME *thī*, reduced f. *thīn* THINE]

thyme /tīm/ *n.* any herb or shrub of the genus *Thymus* with aromatic leaves, esp. *T. vulgaris* grown for culinary use. □□ **thymy** *adj.* [ME f. OF *thym* f. L *thymum* f. Gk *thumon* f. *thuō* burn a sacrifice]

thymi *pl.* of THYMUS.

thymine /thímeen/ *n. Biochem.* a pyrimidine derivative found in all living tissue as a component base of DNA. [*thymic* (as THYMUS) + -INE⁴]

thymol /thímawl, -ōl/ *n. Chem.* a white crystalline phenol obtained from oil of thyme and used as an antiseptic. [as THYME + -OL¹]

thymus /thíməs/ *n.* (*pl.* **-muses** or **-mi** /-mī/) (in full **thymus gland**) *Anat.* a lymphoid organ situated in the neck of vertebrates (in humans becoming much smaller at the approach of puberty) producing lymphocytes for the immune response. [mod.L f. Gk *thumos*]

thyristor /thírístər/ *n. Electronics* a semiconductor rectifier in which the current between two electrodes is controlled by a signal applied to a third electrode. [Gk *thura* gate + TRANSISTOR]

thyro- /thírō/ *comb. form* (also **thyreo-** /-reō/) thyroid.

thyroid /thíroyd/ *n. & adj.* ● *n.* (in full **thyroid gland**) **1** a large ductless gland in the neck of vertebrates secreting a hormone which regulates growth and development through the rate of metabolism. **2** an extract prepared from the thyroid gland of animals and used in treating goiter, etc. ● *adj. Anat. & Zool.* **1** connected with the thyroid cartilage (*thyroid artery*). **2** shield shaped. □ **thyroid cartilage** a large cartilage of the larynx, the projection of which in humans forms the Adam's apple. [obs.F *thyroide* or mod.L *thyroides*, irreg. f. Gk *thureoeidēs* f. *thureos* oblong shield]

thyroxine /thíróksin, -seen/ *n.* the main hormone produced by the thyroid gland, involved in controlling the rate of metabolic processes. [THYROID + OX- + -INE⁴]

thyrsus /thɔrsəs/ *n.* (*pl.* **thyrsi** /-sī/) **1** *Gk & Rom. Antiq.* a staff tipped with an ornament like a pinecone, an attribute of Bacchus. **2** *Bot.* (also **thyrse**) an inflorescence as in lilac, with the primary axis racemose and the secondary axis cymose. [L f. Gk *thursos*]

thyself /thīsélf/ *pron. archaic* emphat. & refl. form of THOU¹, THEE.

Ti *symb. Chem.* the element titanium.

ti¹ /tee/ *n.* any woody liliaceous plant of the genus *Cordyline*, esp. *C. terminalis* with edible roots. [Tahitian, Maori, etc.]

ti² /tee/ *n.* (also **te**) **1** (in tonic sol-fa) the seventh note of a major scale. **2** the note B in the fixed-do system. [earlier *si*: F f. It., perh. f. *Sancte Iohannes*: see GAMUT]

tiara /teeárə, -aárə, -áirə/ *n.* **1** a jeweled ornamental band worn on the front of a woman's hair. **2** a three-crowned diadem worn by a pope. **3** *hist.* a turban worn by ancient Persian kings. □□ **tiaraed** *adj.* (also **tiara'd**). [L f. Gk, of unkn. orig.]

Tibetan /tibét'n/ *n. & adj.* ● *n.* **1 a** a native of Tibet. **b** a person of Tibetan descent. **2** the language of Tibet. ● *adj.* of or relating to Tibet or its language.

tibia /tíbeeə/ *n.* (*pl.* **tibiae** /-bee-ee/) **1** *Anat.* the inner and usu. larger of two bones extending from the knee to the ankle. **2** the tibiotarsus of a bird. **3** the fourth segment of the leg in insects. □□ **tibial** *adj.* [L, = shinbone]

tibiotarsus /tíbeeōtaársəs/ *n.* (*pl.* **tibiotarsi** /-sī/) the bone in a bird corresponding to the tibia fused at the lower end with some bones of the tarsus. [TIBIA + TARSUS]

tic /tik/ *n.* **1** a habitual spasmodic contraction of the muscles, esp. of the face. **2** a personality or behavioral quirk. □ **tic douloureux** /dōōlərōō, -rɔ́/ trigeminal neuralgia. [F f. It. *ticchio*: *douloureux* F, = painful]

tice /tis/ *n. Brit.* **1** *Cricket* a ball bowled so that it pitches immediately under the bat (also called *yorker*). **2** *Croquet* a stroke tempting an opponent to aim at one's ball. [*tice* (now dial.), = ENTICE]

tick¹ /tik/ *n. & v.* ● *n.* **1** a slight recurring click, esp. that of a watch or clock. **2** esp. *Brit. colloq.* a moment; an instant. **3** *Brit.* a mark (√) to denote correctness, check items in a list, etc. ● *v.* **1** *intr.* **a** (of a clock, etc.) make ticks. **b** (foll. by *away*) (of time, etc.) pass. **2** *intr.* (of a mechanism) work; function (*take it apart to see how it ticks*). **3** *tr. Brit.* **a** mark (a written answer, etc.) with a tick. **b** (often foll. by *off*) mark (an item in a list, etc.) with a tick in checking. □ **in two ticks** *Brit. colloq.* in a very short time. **tick off 1** *sl.* annoy, anger; dispirit. **2** *Brit. colloq.* reprimand. **tick over** *Brit.* **1** (of an engine, etc.) idle. **2** (of a person, project, etc.) be working or functioning at a basic or minimum level. **tick-tack** (or **tic-tac**) *Brit.* a kind of manual semaphore signaling used by bookmakers to exchange information. **tick-tack-toe** (also **tic-tac-toe**) a game in which players alternate turns, seeking to complete a series of three Xs or Os marked in a nine-square grid. **what makes a person tick** *colloq.* a person's motivation. □□ **tickless** *adj.* [ME: cf. Du. *tik*, LG *tikk* touch, tick]

■ *n.* **2** see MOMENT 1, 2. **3** check. ● *v.* **1b** (*tick away*) see GO¹ *v.* 9. **2** see WORK *v.* 5. **3** check off, mark. □ **tick off 1** see ANNOY 1.

tick² /tik/ *n.* **1** any of various arachnids of the order Acarina, parasitic on the skin of warm-blooded vertebrates. **2** any of various insects of the family Hippoboscidae, parasitic on sheep and birds, etc. **3** *colloq.* an unpleasant or despicable person. □ **tick fever** a bacterial or rickettsial fever transmitted by the bite of a tick. [OE *ticca* (recorded as *ticia*); ME *teke, tyke:* cf. MDu., MLG *tēke*, OHG *zēcho*]

tick³ /tik/ *n.* *Brit. colloq.* credit (*buy goods on tick*). [app. an abbr. of TICKET in phr. *on the ticket*]

tick⁴ /tik/ *n.* **1** the cover of a mattress or pillow. **2** = TICKING. [ME *tikke, tēke* f. WG f. L *theca* f. Gk *thēkē* case]

ticker /tikər/ *n.* *colloq.* **1** the heart. **2** a watch. **3** a machine that receives and prints telegraphed messages onto paper tape. □ **ticker tape 1** a paper strip from a ticker. **2** this or similar material thrown from windows, etc., along the route of a parade honoring a hero, etc.

ticket /tikit/ *n.* & *v.* ● *n.* **1** a written or printed piece of paper or card entitling the holder to enter a place, participate in an event, travel by public transport, use a public amenity, etc. **2** an official notification of a traffic offense, etc. (*parking ticket*). **3** *Brit.* a certificate of discharge from the army. **4** a certificate of qualification as a ship's master, ship or airplane pilot, etc. **5** a label attached to a thing and giving its price or other details. **6** a list of candidates put forward by one group, esp. a political party. **7** (*prec. by the*) *colloq.* what is correct or needed. ● *v.tr.* (**ticketed, ticketing**) attach or serve a ticket to. □ **have tickets on oneself** *Austral. colloq.* be conceited. **ticket office** an office or kiosk where tickets are sold for transport, entertainment, etc. **ticket-of-leave man** *Brit. hist.* a prisoner or convict who had served part of his time and was granted certain concessions, esp. leave. □□ **ticketed** *adj.* **ticketless** *adj.* [obs.F *étiquet* f. OF *estiquet(te)* f. *estiquier, estechier* fix f. MDu. *steken*]

■ *n.* **5** see TAG¹ *n.* 1a. ● *v.* see TAG¹ *v.* 1.

tickety-boo /tikəteeboō/ *adj.* *Brit. colloq.* all right; in order. [20th c.: orig. uncert.]

ticking /tiking/ *n.* a stout usu. striped material used to cover mattresses, etc. [TICK⁴ + -ING¹]

tickle /tikəl/ *v.* & *n.* ● *v.* **1 a** *tr.* apply light touches or strokes to (a person or part of a person's body) so as to excite the nerves and usu. produce laughter and spasmodic movement. **b** *intr.* feel this sensation (*my foot tickles*). **2** *tr.* excite agreeably; amuse or divert (a person, a sense of humor, vanity, etc.) (*was tickled at the idea; this will tickle your fancy*). **3** *tr.* catch (a trout, etc.) by rubbing it so that it moves backward into the hand. ● *n.* **1** an act of tickling. **2** a tickling sensation. □ **tickled pink** (or **to death**) *colloq.* extremely amused or pleased. □□ **tickler** *n.* **tickly** *adj.* [ME, prob. frequent. of TICK¹]

■ *v.* **1 a** titillate. **2** titillate, delight, please, gratify, amuse, entertain, divert, captivate, thrill, excite, *colloq.* tickle pink *or* to death. ● *n.* **2** see ITCH *n.* 1. □ **tickled pink** (or **to death**) see GLAD¹ *adj.* 1.

ticklish /tiklish/ *adj.* **1** sensitive to tickling. **2** (of a matter or person to be dealt with) difficult; requiring careful handling. □□ **ticklishly** *adv.* **ticklishness** *n.*

■ **2** uncertain, unsteady, unsure, unstable, unsettled, fickle, touch and go; delicate, precarious, risky, hazardous, dangerous, critical, thorny, fragile, awkward, difficult, tricky; sensitive, oversensitive, hypersensitive, touchy, prickly. □□ **ticklishness** see DELICACY 3.

tic-tac var. of *tic-tack* (see TICK¹).

tidal /tid'l/ *adj.* relating to, like, or affected by tides (*tidal basin; tidal river*). □ **tidal bore** a large wave or bore caused by constriction of the spring tide as it enters a long narrow shallow inlet. **tidal wave 1** *Geog.* an exceptionally large ocean wave, esp. one caused by an underwater earthquake or volcanic eruption. **2** a widespread manifestation of feeling, etc. □□ **tidally** *adv.*

■ □ **tidal wave 2** see FLOOD *n.* 2b.

tidbit /tidbit/ *n.* (*Brit.* **titbit** /tit-/) **1** a small morsel. **2** a choice item of news, etc. [perh. f. dial. *tid* tender + BIT¹]

■ **1** delicacy, (dainty) morsel, treat, choice item, *bonne bouche*, goody, *Brit.* titbit.

tiddledy-winks var. of TIDDLY-WINKS.

tiddler /tidlər/ *n.* *Brit. colloq.* **1** a small fish, esp. a stickleback or minnow. **2** an unusually small thing or person. [perh. rel. to TIDDLY² and *tittlebat*, a childish form of *stickleback*]

tiddly¹ /tidlee/ *adj.* (**tiddlier, tiddliest**) esp. *Brit. colloq.* slightly drunk. [19th c., earlier = a drink: orig. unkn.]

tiddly² /tidlee/ *adj.* (**tiddlier, tiddliest**) *Brit. colloq.* little.

tiddly-winks /tidleewingks/ *n.* (also **tiddledy-** /tid'ldee-/) a game played by flicking counters into a cup, etc. [19th c.: perh. rel. to TIDDLY¹]

tide /tid/ *n.* & *v.* ● *n.* **1 a** the periodic rise and fall of the sea due to the attraction of the moon and sun (see EBB *n.* 1, FLOOD *n.* 3). **b** the water as affected by this. **2** a time or season (usu. in *comb.: Whitsuntide*). **3** a marked trend of opinion, fortune, or events. ● *v.intr.* drift with the tide, esp. move in or out of a harbor with the help of the tide. □ **tide mill** a mill with a waterwheel driven by the tide. **tide over** enable or help (a person) to deal with an awkward situation, difficult period, etc. (*the money will tide me over until Friday*). **work double tides** *Brit.* work twice the normal time, or extra hard. □□ **tideless** *adj.* [OE *tid* f. Gmc, rel. to TIME]

■ *n.* **3** see WAVE *n.* 6a, TREND *n.*

tideland /tidland/ *n.* **1** land that is submerged at high tide. **2** land below the low-water mark but within a nation's territorial waters.

tidemark /tidmaark/ *n.* **1** a mark made by the tide at esp. high water. **2** esp. *Brit.* **a** a mark left round a bathtub at the level of the water in it. **b** a line on a person's body, garment, etc., marking the extent to which it has been washed.

tidetable /tidtaybəl/ *n.* a table indicating the times of high and low tides at a place.

tidewaiter /tidwaytər/ *n.* *hist.* a customs officer who boarded ships on their arrival to enforce the customs regulations.

tidewater /tidwawtər, -wotər/ *n.* **1** water brought by or affected by tides. **2** (*attrib.*) affected by tides (*tidewater region*).

tidewave /tidwayv/ *n.* an undulation of water passing round the earth and causing high and low tides.

tideway /tidway/ *n.* **1** a channel in which a tide runs, esp. the tidal part of a river. **2** the ebb or flow in a tidal channel.

tidings /tidingz/ *n.* (as *sing.* or *pl.*) news; information. [OE *tidung*, prob. f. ON *títhindi* events f. *tithr* occurring]

■ see NEWS 1, 3.

tidy /tidee/ *adj., n.,* & *v.* ● *adj.* (**tidier, tidiest**) **1** neat; orderly; methodically arranged. **2** (of a person) methodically inclined. **3** *colloq.* considerable (*it cost a tidy sum*). ● *n.* (*pl.* **-ies**) **1** a receptacle for holding small objects. **2** esp. *Brit.* an act or spell of tidying. **3** a detachable ornamental cover for a chair back, arms, etc. ● *v.tr.* (**-ies, -ied**) (also *absol.*; often foll. by *up*) put in good order; make (oneself, a room, etc.) tidy. □□ **tidily** *adv.* **tidiness** *n.* [ME, = timely, etc., f. TIDE + -Y¹]

■ *adj.* **1** neat, orderly, trim, shipshape, spruce, spick-and-span, clean, smart, well-kept, well-groomed; well-organized, organized, well-ordered, methodical, systematic. **2** well-organized, organized, methodical, meticulous, systematic. **3** respectable, sizable, significant, considerable, substantial, appreciable, good, goodly, good-sized, handsome, large, big, fair, generous, not insignificant; *colloq.* not to be sneezed at. ● *v.* tidy up, neaten (up), straighten (out *or* up), clean (up), clear up, put in order, fix (up), spruce up, organize, reorganize, arrange, rearrange, square away; see also GROOM *v.* 1. □□ **tidiness** see ORDER *n.* 1.

tie /ti/ *v.* & *n.* ● *v.* (**tying**) **1** *tr.* **a** attach or fasten with string or cord, etc. (*tie the dog to the gate; tie his hands together; tied on a label*). **b** link conceptually. **2** *tr.* **a** form (a string, ribbon, shoelace, necktie, etc.) into a knot or bow. **b** form (a knot or bow) in this way. **3** *tr.* restrict or limit (a person) as to conditions, occupation, place, etc. (*is tied to his family*). **4**

intr. (often foll. by *with*) achieve the same score or place as another competitor (*they tied at ten games each*; *tied with her for first place*). **5** *tr.* hold (rafters, etc.) together by a cross-piece, etc. **6** *tr. Mus.* **a** unite (written notes) by a tie. **b** perform (two notes) as one unbroken note. ● *n.* **1** a cord, line, or chain, etc., used for fastening. **2** a strip of material worn round the collar and tied in a knot at the front with the ends hanging down. **3** a thing that unites or restricts persons; a bond or obligation (*family ties*; *ties of friendship*). **4** a draw, dead heat, or equality of score among competitors. **5** *Brit.* a match between any pair from a group of competing players or teams. **6** (also **tie beam**, etc.) a rod or beam holding parts of a structure together. **7** *Mus.* a curved line above or below two notes of the same pitch indicating that they are to be played for the combined duration of their time values. **8** a beam laid horizontally as a support for railroad rails. **9** a shoe tied with a lace. □ **fit to be tied** *colloq.* very angry. **tie down** = TIE *v.* 3 above. **tie-dye** (or **tie and dye**) a method of producing dyed patterns by tying string, etc., to protect parts of the fabric from the dye. **tie in** (foll. by *with*) bring into or have a close association or agreement. **tie-in** *n.* **1** a connection or association. **2** (often *attrib.*) a form of sale or advertising that offers or requires more than a single purchase. **3** the joint promotion of related commodities, etc. (e.g., a book and a movie). **tie the knot** *colloq.* get married. **tie-line** a transmission line connecting parts of a system, esp. a telephone line connecting two private branch exchanges. **tie up 1** bind or fasten securely with cord, etc. **2** invest or reserve (capital, etc.) so that it is not immediately available for use. **3** moor (a boat). **4** secure (an animal). **5** obstruct; prevent from acting freely. **6** secure or complete (an undertaking, etc.). **7** (often foll. by *with*) = *tie in*. **8** (usu. in *passive*) fully occupy (a person). □□ **tieless** *adj.* [OE *tīgan*, *tēgan* (v.), *tēah*, *tēg* (n.) f. Gmc]

■ *v.* **1 a** bind, fasten, make fast, tie up, lash, secure, truss (up), pinion, attach, hitch, tether, rope, chain, moor; connect, join, knot, link, couple, splice, unite. **b** connect, associate, unite, join, link, bind (up), affiliate, ally, league, team (up). **3** restrict, confine, restrain; limit, tie down, constrain, curtail, curb, cramp, hamper, hinder. **4** (*tie with*) equal, even, be equal *or* even with, match, be neck and neck with, draw with. ● *n.* **1** string, cord, lace, rope, thong, ribbon, band, ligature, shoelace, line, leash, lead, chain, *Naut.* stop. **2** cravat, bow tie, string tie, necktie. **3** link, fastening, bond, band, connection, tie-in, relationship, affiliation, liaison, involvement, entanglement. **4** equality, dead heat, deadlock, draw, stalemate. **7** ligature. **8** railroad tie, esp. *Brit.* sleeper. **9** lace-up. □ **fit to be tied** see ANGRY 1. **tie in** relate, connect, link, associate, coordinate; be consistent, make sense, correspond, coincide, fit (in), tie up, be logical, coordinate. **tie-in 1** relationship, association, connection, link, linkage. **tie up 1, 3** see TIE *v.* 1a above. **2** commit, invest, sink, obligate. **4** see TETHER *v.* **5** stop, halt, bring to a standstill; see also OBSTRUCT 2. **6** clinch, secure, confirm, complete, wrap up, nail down. **8** occupy, engage, (keep) busy, engross.

tied /tīd/ *adj. Brit.* **1** (of a house) occupied subject to the tenant's working for its owner. **2** (of a bar, etc.) bound to supply the products of a particular brewery only.

tiepin /tīpin/ *n.* an ornamental pin or clip for holding a tie in place.

tier /teer/ *n.* **1** a row or rank or unit of a structure, as one of several placed one above another (*tiers of seats*). **2** a layer or rank. **3** *Naut.* **a** a circle of coiled cable. **b** a place for a coiled cable. □□ **tiered** *adj.* (also in *comb.*). [earlier *tire* f. F f. *tirer* draw, elongate f. Rmc]

■ **1** row, line, level, order, range, course, series, stratum, layer, echelon, file, rank, story. □□ **tiered** see SERRIED.

tierce /teers/ *n.* **1** *Eccl.* = TERCE. **2** *Mus.* an interval of a major or minor third. **3** a sequence of three cards. **4** *Fencing* **a** the third of eight parrying positions. **b** the corresponding thrust. **5** *archaic* **a** a former wine measure of one-third of a pipe. **b** a cask containing a certain quantity (varying with the con-

tents), esp. of provisions. [ME f. OF *t(i)erce* f. L *tertia* fem. of *tertius* third]

tierced /teerst/ *adj. Heraldry* divided into three parts of different tinctures.

tiercel var. of TERCEL.

tiercet var. of TERCET.

tiff /tif/ *n.* & *v.* ● *n.* **1** a slight or petty quarrel. **2** a fit of peevishness. ● *v.intr.* have a petty quarrel; bicker. [18th c.: orig. unkn.]

■ *n.* **1** (petty) quarrel, disagreement, misunderstanding, dispute, argument, difference (of opinion), altercation, squabble, wrangle, *colloq.* row, spat, *Brit. colloq.* barney. ● *v.* see BICKER.

tiffany /tifənee/ *n.* (*pl.* **-ies**) thin gauze muslin. [orig. dress worn on Twelfth Night, f. OF *tifanie* f. eccl.L *theophania* f. Gk *theophaneia* Epiphany]

tiffin /tifin/ *n.* & *v. Brit.* & *Ind.* ● *n.* a light meal, esp. lunch. ● *v.intr.* (**tiffined, tiffining**) take lunch, etc. [app. f. *tiffing* sipping]

tiger /tīgər/ *n.* **1 a** a large Asian feline, *Panthera tigris*, having a yellowish brown coat with black stripes. **b** a similar feline, as the jaguar or ocelot. **2** a domestic cat with similar striping. **3** a fierce, energetic, or formidable person. □ **tiger beetle** any carnivorous beetle of the family Cicindelidae, with spotted or striped wing covers. **tiger cat 1** any moderate-sized feline resembling the tiger, e.g., the ocelot, serval, or margay. **2** *Austral.* any of various carnivorous marsupials of the genus *Dasyurus*, including the Tasmanian devil. **3** = sense 2. **tiger-eye** (or **tiger's-eye**) **1** a yellowish brown striped gem of brilliant luster. **2** a pottery glaze of similar appearance. **tiger lily** a tall garden lily, *Lilium tigrinum*, with flowers of dull orange spotted with black and purple. **tiger moth** any moth of the family Arctiidae, esp. *Arctia caja*, having richly spotted and streaked wings suggesting a tiger's skin. **tiger wood** a striped or streaked wood used for cabinet-making. □□ **tigerish** *adj.* **tigerishly** *adv.* [ME f. OF *tigre* f. L *tigris* f. Gk *tigris*]

tight /tīt/ *adj.*, *n.*, & *adv.* ● *adj.* **1** closely held, drawn, fastened, fitting, etc. (*a tight hold*; *a tight skirt*). **2 a** closely and firmly put together (*a tight joint*). **b** close; evenly matched (*a tight finish*). **3** (of clothes, etc.) too closely fitting (*my shoes are rather tight*). **4** impermeable, impervious, esp. (in *comb.*) to a specified thing (*watertight*). **5** tense; stretched so as to leave no slack (*a tight bowstring*). **6** *colloq.* drunk. **7** *colloq.* (of a person) mean; stingy. **8 a** (of money or materials) not easily obtainable. **b** (of a money market) in which money is tight. **9 a** (of precautions, a program, a schedule, etc.) stringent; demanding. **b** presenting difficulties (*a tight situation*). **c** (of an organization, group, or member) strict; disciplined. **10** produced by or requiring great exertion or pressure (*a tight squeeze*). **11** (of control, etc.) strictly imposed. **12** *colloq.* friendly; close (*the two girls quickly became tight*) ● *adv.* tightly (*hold tight!*). □ **tight corner** (or **place** or **spot**) a difficult situation. **tight-fisted** stingy. **tight-fitting** (of a garment) fitting (often too) close to the body. **tight-lipped** with or as with the lips compressed to restrain emotion or speech. □□ **tightly** *adv.* **tightness** *n.* [prob. alt. of *thight* f. ON *thēttr* watertight, of close texture]

■ *adj.* **1, 2a** secure, firm, fast, fixed, secured, close-fitting, tight-fitting, snug. **2 b** close, (almost) even, (highly) competitive, evenly matched, dingdong. **3** constricting, (too) small, ill-fitting, tight-fitting. **4** sealed, hermetically sealed, leakproof, hermetic, impervious, impenetrable, impermeable, airtight, watertight, waterproof. **5** taut, stretched, tense. **6** tipsy, drunk, intoxicated, *colloq.* high, woozy, under the influence, esp. *Brit. colloq.* tiddly; see also DRUNK *adj.* 1. **7** stingy, niggardly, mean, penurious, miserly, parsimonious, penny-pinching, tight-fisted, closefisted,

Brit. colloq. mingy. **8 a** scarce, scanty, hard to find *or* come by, rare; dear, expensive. **9 a** strict, binding, restrictive, stringent, severe, tough, uncompromising, unyielding, rigorous, stern, austere, autocratic, harsh, hard and fast, inflexible; demanding, exacting. **b** difficult, trying, dangerous, perilous, risky, hazardous, touchy, problematic, tricky, ticklish, precarious, touch-and-go, *colloq.* sticky, *sl.* hairy. **c** (well-)disciplined, orderly, well-organized, strict. **11** see sense 9a above. ● *adv.* tightly, securely, firmly, fast; compactly, densely, solidly, closely. □ **tight corner** (or **place** or **spot**) see BIND *n.* 1b. **tight-fisted** see TIGHT *adj.* 7 above. **tight-lipped** closemouthed, silent, quiet, mute, close-lipped, noncommittal, reticent, secretive, taciturn, unforthcoming, uncommunicative, reserved, *colloq.* mum. □□ **tightly** closely, tensely, vigorously, rigorously; compactly, densely, solidly; securely, firmly, fast, tight. **tightness** see TENSION *n.* 1.

tighten /títʼn/ *v.tr.* & *intr.* (also foll. by *up*) make or become tight or tighter. □ **tighten one's belt** see BELT.
■ make *or* become tighter *or* tenser *or* stronger, strengthen; tauten, stiffen, tense, close; anchor, fasten, fix, secure; make *or* become more rigorous *or* strict *or* stringent *or* severe *or* restrictive, close gaps in.

tightrope /títrōp/ *n.* a rope stretched tightly high above the ground, on which acrobats perform.

tights /tits/ *n.pl.* **1** a thin but not sheer close-fitting wool or nylon, etc., garment covering the legs and the lower part of the torso. **2** a similar garment worn by a dancer, acrobat, etc.
■ **1** panty hose, *Brit.* pantihose.

tightwad /títwod/ *n. colloq.* a person who is miserly or stingy.

tiglon /tíglən/ (also **tigon** /tígən/) *n.* the offspring of a tiger and a lioness (cf. LIGER). [portmanteau word f. TIGER + LION]

tigress /tígris/ *n.* **1** a female tiger. **2** a fierce or passionate woman.

tike var. of TYKE.

tiki /teékee/ *n.* (*pl.* **tikis**) esp. *NZ* a large wooden or small ornamental greenstone image representing a human figure. [Maori]

tilbury /tílberee, -bəree/ *n.* (*pl.* **-ies**) *hist.* a light open two-wheeled carriage. [after the inventor's name]

tilde /tíldə/ *n.* a mark (˜), put over a letter, e.g., over a Spanish *n* when pronounced *ny* (as in *señor*) or a Portuguese *a* or *o* when nasalized (as in *São Paulo*). [Sp., ult. f. L *titulus* TITLE]

tile /til/ *n.* & *v.* ● *n.* **1** a thin slab of concrete or baked clay, etc., used in series for covering a roof or pavement, etc. **2** a similar slab of glazed pottery, cork, linoleum, etc., for covering a floor, wall, etc. **3** a thin flat piece used in a game (esp. mah-jongg). ● *v.tr.* cover with tiles. □ **on the tiles** *Brit. colloq.* having a spree. [OE *tigule, -ele,* f. L *tegula*]

tiler /tílər/ *n.* **1** a person who makes or lays tiles. **2** the doorkeeper of a Freemasons' lodge.

tiling /tíling/ *n.* **1** the process of fixing tiles. **2** an area of tiles.

till¹ /til/ *prep.* & *conj.* ● *prep.* **1** up to or as late as (*wait till six o'clock; did not return till night*). **2** up to the time of (*faithful till death; waited till the end*). ● *conj.* **1** up to the time when (*wait till I return*). **2** so long that (*laughed till I cried*). ¶ *Until* is more usual when beginning a sentence. [OE & ON *til* to, rel. to TILL³]

till² /til/ *n.* **1** a drawer for money in a store or bank, etc., esp. with a device recording the amount of each purchase. **2** a supply of money. [ME: orig. unkn.]
■ **1** money drawer, cashdrawer, cashbox, cash register.

till³ /til/ *v.tr.* prepare and cultivate (land) for crops. □□ **tillable** *adj.* **tiller** *n.* [OE *tilian* strive for, cultivate, f. Gmc]
■ plow, cultivate, farm, work, dig, hoe, harrow, manure, *poet.* delve.

till⁴ /til/ *n.* stiff clay containing boulders, sand, etc., deposited by melting glaciers and ice sheets. [17th c. (Sc.): orig. unkn.]

tillage /tílij/ *n.* **1** the preparation of land for bearing crops. **2** tilled land.

tiller¹ /tílər/ *n.* a horizontal bar fitted to the head of a boat's rudder to turn it in steering. [ME f. AF *telier* weaver's beam f. med.L *telarium* f. L *tela* web]

tiller² /tílər/ *n.* & *v.* ● *n.* **1** a shoot of a plant springing from the bottom of the original stalk. **2** a sapling. **3** a sucker. ● *v.intr.* put forth tillers. [app. repr. OE *telgor* extended f. *telga* bough]

tilt /tilt/ *v.* & *n.* ● *v.* **1 a** *intr.* & *tr.* assume or cause to assume a sloping position; heel over. **b** incline or lean or cause to lean toward one side of an opinion, action, controversy, etc. **2** *intr.* (foll. by *at*) strike, thrust, or run at with a weapon, esp. in jousting. **3** *intr.* (foll. by *with*) engage in a contest. **4** *tr.* forge or work (steel, etc.) with a tilt hammer. ● *n.* **1** the act or an instance of tilting. **2** a sloping position. **3** an inclination or bias. **4** (of medieval knights, etc.) the act of charging with a lance against an opponent or at a mark, done for exercise or as a sport. **5** an encounter between opponents; an attack, esp. with argument or satire (*have a tilt at*). **6** = *tilt hammer.* □ **full** (or **at full**) **tilt 1** at full speed. **2** with full force. **tilt hammer** a heavy pivoted hammer used in forging. □□ **tilter** *n.* [ME *tilte* perh. f. an OE form rel. to *tealt* unsteady f. Gmc: weapon senses of unkn. orig.]
■ *v.* **1 a** lean, slant, incline, slope, angle, tip, heel over, pitch, list, cant, careen. **2** (*tilt at*) strike at, thrust at, run at, lunge at, attack, *hist.* joust with. **3** (*tilt with*) compete with, battle with *or* against, contend with, spar with, cross swords with, attack, *hist.* joust with. ● *n.* **2** lean, slant, incline, slope, angle, tip, heel, list, pitch, cant, inclination. **4, 5** tourney, tournament, meeting, tilting, engagement, encounter, match, contest, test, trial, fight, combat, *hist.* joust; dispute, argument, difference, quarrel, altercation, squabble, tiff, attack, *colloq.* set-to, spat. □ **full** (or **at full**) **tilt 1** see *posthaste.* **2** see *at full blast* (BLAST).

tilth /tilth/ *n.* **1** tillage; cultivation. **2** the condition of tilled soil (*in good tilth*). [OE *tilth(e)* (as TILL³)]

Tim. *abbr.* Timothy (New Testament).

timbal /tímbəl/ *n.* a kettledrum. [F *timbale,* earlier *tamballe* f. Sp. *atabal* f. Arab. *aṭ-ṭabl* the drum]

timbale /tímbəl, taNbaál/ *n.* a drum-shaped dish of ground meat or fish baked in a mold or pastry shell. [F: see TIMBAL]

timber /tímbər/ *n.* **1** large standing trees suitable for lumber; woods or forest. **2** (esp. as *int.*) a warning cry that a tree is about to fall. **3** a prepaid piece of wood or beam, esp. as the rib of a vessel. **4** *Brit.* wood prepared for building, carpentry, etc. □ **timber hitch** a knot used in attaching a rope to a log or spar. **timber wolf** a type of large N. American gray wolf. □□ **timbering** *n.* [OE, = building, f. Gmc]
■ **3** wood, beams, boards, planks, lumber. **1** see WOOD 2.

timbered /tímbərd/ *adj.* **1** (esp. of a building) made wholly or partly of lumber, esp. with partly exposed beams. **2** (of country) wooded.

timberland /tímbərland/ *n.* land covered with forest yielding timber.

timberline /tímbərlin/ *n.* (on a mountain) the line or level above which no trees grow.

timbre /támbər, taNbrə/ (also **timber**) *n.* the distinctive character of a musical sound or voice apart from its pitch and intensity. [F f. Rmc f. med.Gk *timbanon* f. Gk *tumpanon* drum]
■ tone (color *or* quality), tonality, color, resonance.

timbrel /tímbrəl/ *n. archaic* a tambourine or similar instrument. [dimin. of ME *timbre* f. OF (as TIMBRE, -LE²)]

Timbuktu /tímbuktóō/ *n.* any distant or remote place. [*Timbuktu* in W. Africa]

time /tim/ *n.* & *v.* ● *n.* **1** the indefinite continued progress of existence, events, etc., in past, present, and future regarded as a whole. **2 a** the progress of this as affecting persons or things (*stood the test of time*). **b** (**Time**) (in full **Father Time**) the personification of time, esp. as an old man with a scythe and hourglass. **3** a more or less definite portion of time belonging to particular events or circumstances (*the time of the Plague; prehistoric times; the scientists of the time*). **4** an allotted, available, or measurable portion of time; the period of time at one's disposal (*am wasting my time; had no* time to visit; *how much time do you need?*). **5** a point of time, esp. in hours and minutes (*the time is 7:30*; *what time is it?*). **6** (prec. by *a*) an indefinite period (*waited for a time*). **7** time or an amount of time as reckoned by a conventional standard (*the time allowed is one hour*; *ran the mile in record time*; *eight o'clock Eastern Standard time*). **8 a** an occasion (*last time I saw you*). **b** an event or occasion qualified in some way (*had a good time*). **9** a moment or definite portion of time destined or suitable for a purpose, etc. (*now is the time to act*; *shall we set a time?*). **10** (in *pl.*) expressing multiplication (*is four times as old*; *five times six is thirty*). **11** a lifetime (*will last my time*). **12** (in *sing.* or *pl.*) **a** the conditions of life or of a period (*hard times*; *times have changed*). **b** (prec. by *the*) the present age, or that being considered. **13** *colloq.* a prison sentence (*is doing time*). **14 a** an apprenticeship (*served his time*). **b** a period of military service. **15** a period of gestation. **16** the date or expected date of childbirth (*is near her time*) or of death (*my time is drawing near*). **17** measured time spent in work (*put them on short time*). **18 a** any of several rhythmic patterns of music (*in waltz time*). **b** the duration of a note as indicated by a quarter note, whole note, etc. **19** *Brit.* the moment at which a bar closes. **20** = *time out*. ● *v.tr.* **1** choose the time or occasion for (*time your remarks carefully*). **2** do at a chosen or correct time. **3** arrange the time of arrival of. **4** ascertain the time taken by (a process or activity, or a person doing it). **5** regulate the duration or interval of; set times for (*trains are timed to arrive every hour*). □ **against time** with utmost speed; so as to finish by a specified time (*working against time*). **ahead of time** earlier than expected. **ahead of one's time** having ideas too enlightened or advanced to be accepted by one's contemporaries. **all the time 1** during the whole of the time referred to (often despite some contrary expectation, etc.) (*we never noticed, but he was there all the time*). **2** constantly (*nags all the time*). **3** at all times (*leaves a light on all the time*). **at one time 1** in or during a known but unspecified past period. **2** simultaneously (*ran three businesses at one time*). **at the same time 1** simultaneously; at a time that is the same for all. **2** nevertheless (*at the same time, I do not want to offend you*). **at a time** separately in the specified groups or numbers (*came three at a time*). **at times** occasionally; intermittently. **before time** (usu. prec. by *not*) before the due or expected time. **before one's time** prematurely (*old before his time*). **for the time being** for the present; until some other arrangement is made. **half the time** *colloq.* as often as not. **have no time for 1** be unable or unwilling to spend time on. **2** dislike. **have the time 1** be able to spend the time needed. **2** know from a watch, etc., what time it is. **have a time of it** undergo trouble or difficulty. **in no** (or **less than no**) **time 1** very soon. **2** very quickly. **in one's own good time** at a time and a rate decided by oneself. **in time 1** not late; punctual (*was in time to catch the bus*). **2** eventually (*in time you may agree*). **3** in accordance with a given rhythm or tempo, esp. of music. **in one's time** at or during some previous period of one's life (*in his time he was a great hurdler*). **keep good** (or **bad**) **time 1** (of a clock, etc.) record time accurately (or inaccurately). **2** be habitually punctual (or not punctual). **keep time** move or sing, etc., in time. **know the time of day** be well informed. **lose no time** (often foll. by *in* + verbal noun) act immediately (*lost no time in cashing the check*). **not before time** not too soon; timely. **on** (also **in**) **one's own time** outside working hours. **on time** see ON. **no time** *colloq.* a very short interval (*it was no time before they came*). **out of time 1** unseasonable; unseasonably. **2** not in rhythm. **pass the time of day** *colloq.* exchange a greeting or casual remarks. **time after time 1** repeatedly; on many occasions. **2** in many instances. **time and** (or **time and time**) **again** on many occasions. **time and a half** a rate of payment for work at one and a half times the normal rate. **time and motion** (usu. *attrib.*) concerned with measuring the efficiency of industrial and other operations. **time bomb** a bomb designed to explode at a preset time. **time capsule** a box, etc., containing objects typical of the present time, buried for discovery in the future. **time clock 1** a clock with a device for recording workers' hours of work. **2**

a switch mechanism activated at preset times by a built-in clock. **time-consuming** using much or too much time. **time exposure** the exposure of photographic film for longer than the maximum normal shutter setting. **time factor** the passage of time as a limitation on what can be achieved. **time frame** period of time during which an action occurs or will occur. **time fuse** a fuse calculated to burn for or explode at a given time. **time-honored** esteemed by tradition or through custom. **time immemorial** (or **out of mind**) a longer time than anyone can remember or trace. **time lag** an interval of time between an event, a cause, etc., and its effect. **time-lapse** (of photography) using frames taken at long intervals to photograph a slow process, and shown continuously as if at normal speed. **time limit** the limit of time within which a task must be done. **the time of day** the hour by the clock. **time off** time for rest or recreation, etc. **the time of one's life** a period or occasion of exceptional enjoyment. **time out 1** a brief intermission in a game, etc. **2** = *time off*. **time-served** having completed a period of apprenticeship or training. **time-server** a person who changes his or her view to suit the prevailing circumstances, fashion, etc. **time-serving** self-seeking or obsequious. **time-share** a share in a property under a time-sharing arrangement. **time-sharing 1** the operation of a computer system by several users for different operations at one time. **2** the use of a vacation home at agreed different times by several joint owners. **time sheet** a sheet of paper for recording hours of work, etc. **time signal** an audible (esp. broadcast) signal or announcement of the exact time of day. **time signature** *Mus.* an indication of tempo following a clef, expressed as a fraction with the numerator giving the number of beats in each bar and the denominator giving the kind of note getting one beat. **time switch** a switch acting automatically at a preset time. **time warp** an imaginary distortion of space in relation to time, whereby persons or objects of one age can be moved to another. **time was** there was a time (*time was when I could do that*). **time zone** a range of longitudes where a common standard time is used. [OE *tima* f. Gmc]

■ *n.* **3** age, period, epoch, era, lifetime, heyday, day(s). **4, 6** period, interval, stretch, spell, patch, while, span, space, phase, season, term, session, duration. **5, 9** hour; point, moment, instant, juncture, date. **8 a** opportunity, chance, occasion. **b** experience. **11** see LIFE 3. **12 a** life, things, circumstances, conditions, everything, culture, mores, habits, values. **18 a** tempo, beat, rhythm, meter, measure. ● *v.* **2, 3** schedule, timetable, program, set, organize, adjust, fix, arrange. **4** *colloq.* clock. **5** schedule, timetable, set, regulate, control. □ **ahead of time** (bright and) early, prematurely, beforehand, in good time. **all the time 2** always, ever, constantly, continuously, continually, perpetually, everlastingly, unceasingly, *literary* without surcease. **3** at all times, continuously, constantly, always, permanently, perpetually. **at one time 1** once, once upon a time, on one occasion, previously, formerly, in the (good) old days, *formal* heretofore, *literary* in days of yore. **2** simultaneously, (all) at once, at the same time, together, all together, in unison. **at the same time 1** see *at one time* 2 (TIME) above. **2** all the same, nonetheless, yet, even so, but, however, be that as it may, nevertheless, notwithstanding, just the same. **at times** from time to time, occasionally, (every) now and then, once in a while, on occasion, every so often, at intervals, intermittently, sometimes. **for the time being** for now, for the present, for the moment, meanwhile, temporarily, for the nonce, *pro tempore*, *colloq.* pro tem. **in no** (or **less than no**) **time 1** at once, forthwith, straightaway, immediately, (very)

/. . ./ **pronunciation**	● **part of speech**
□ **phrases, idioms, and compounds**	
□□ **derivatives**	■ **synonym section**
cross-references appear in SMALL CAPITALS or *italics*	

soon, promptly, without delay, before you know it, right away. **2** quickly, speedily, swiftly, expeditiously, rapidly, in a flash *or* trice *or* moment, in an instant. **in one's own good time** at one's ease, at one's leisure, at one's (own) convenience. **in time 1** punctually, in timely fashion, early, in good time, in the nick of time. **2** soon, one of these days, sometime, someday, one day, eventually, sooner or later, *archaic or literary* anon. **time and** (or **time and time**) **again** again (and again), repeatedly, (over and) over again, time after time, frequently, often, many times, on many occasions. **time-consuming** see LONG¹ *adj.* 1–3, 5–7. **time-honored** established, traditional, traditionary, habitual, customary, rooted, conventional, age-old, set, fixed; venerable, venerated, respected, revered, honored. **time off** see BREAK¹ *n.* 2. **time-server** see *yes-man.* **time-serving** self-seeking, self-serving, selfish, self-indulgent, ambitious, mercenary, venal, greedy, opportunistic, hypocritical; obsequious, sycophantic, toadying, toadyish, subservient, cringing, groveling, *colloq.* bootlicking, crawling, smarmy, on the make. **time was** see FORMERLY.

timekeeper /tímkeepər/ *n.* **1** a person who records time, esp. of workers or in a game. **2 a** a watch or clock as regards accuracy (*a good timekeeper*). **b** a person as regards punctuality. □□ **timekeeping** *n.*

timeless /tímlis/ *adj.* not affected by the passage of time; eternal. □□ **timelessly** *adv.* **timelessness** *n.*
■ eternal, everlasting, immortal, undying, endless, unending, ceaseless, abiding, deathless, ageless, changeless, unchanged, immutable, unchanging, perpetual, permanent, indestructible, *rhet.* sempiternal. □□ **timelessness** see ETERNITY 1, 3.

timely /tímlee/ *adj.* (**timelier, timeliest**) opportune; coming at the right time. □□ **timeliness** *n.*
■ well-timed, propitious, opportune, seasonable, convenient, favorable, auspicious.

timepiece /tímpees/ *n.* an instrument, such as a clock or watch, for measuring time.

timer /tímər/ *n.* **1** a person or device that measures or records time taken. **2** an automatic mechanism for activating a device, etc., at a preset time.

timetable /tímtaybəl/ *n. & v.* ● *n.* a list of times at which events are scheduled to take place, esp. the arrival and departure of buses or trains, etc., or *Brit.* a lesson plan in a school or college. ● *v.tr.* include in or arrange to a timetable; schedule.
■ *n.* schedule, calendar, curriculum, program, agenda, plan, diary. ● *v.* see SCHEDULE *v.*

timework /tímwərk/ *n.* work paid for by the time it takes.

timeworn /tímwawrn/ *adj.* impaired by age.
■ aging, old, tired, worn, time-scarred, decrepit, dilapidated, tumbledown, ramshackle, run-down, dog-eared, ragged, moth-eaten, threadbare, seedy, shabby, archaic, antique, well-worn, worn out, *passé,* broken-down, old-fashioned, outdated, dated, antiquated, ancient, obsolescent, obsolete, stereotyped, stereotypic(al), hackneyed, clichéd, stale, trite, overused, *colloq.* old hat.

timid /tímid/ *adj.* (**timider, timidest**) easily frightened; apprehensive; shy. □□ **timidity** /-míditee/ *n.* **timidly** *adv.* **timidness** *n.* [F *timide* or L *timidus* f. *timēre* fear]
■ shy, retiring, modest, coy, bashful, diffident, timorous, fearful, apprehensive, fainthearted, mousy, scared, frightened, nervous, cowardly, pusillanimous, craven, chickenhearted, chicken-livered, lily-livered, *colloq.* yellow, yellow-bellied, chicken, gutless. □□ **timidity, timidness** see COWARDICE. **timidly** see *fearfully* (FEARFUL).

timing /tíming/ *n.* **1** the way an action or process is timed, esp. in relation to others. **2** the regulation of the opening and closing of valves in an internal combustion engine.

timocracy /timókrəsee/ *n.* (*pl.* **-ies**) **1** a form of government in which possession of property is required in order to hold office. **2** a form of government in which rulers are motivated by love of honor. □□ **timocratic** /tíməkrátik/ *adj.* [OF *timocracie* f. med.L *timocratia* f. Gk *timokratia* f. *timē* honor, worth + *kratia* -CRACY]

timorous /tímərəs/ *adj.* **1** timid; easily alarmed. **2** frightened. □□ **timorously** *adv.* **timorousness** *n.* [ME f. OF *temoreus* f. med.L *timorosus* f. L *timor* f. *timēre* fear]
■ **1** see TIMID. **2** see AFRAID. □□ **timorously** see *fearfully* (FEARFUL), GINGERLY *adv.* **timorousness** see COWARDICE, HUMILITY 1.

timothy /tíməthee/ *n.* (in full **timothy grass**) a fodder grass, *Phleum pratense.* [*Timothy* Hanson, who introduced it in Carolina *c.*1720]

timothy² /tíməthee/ *n. Austral. sl.* a brothel. [20th c.: orig. unkn.]

timpani /tímpənee/ *n.pl.* (also **tympani**) kettledrums. □□ **timpanist** *n.* [It., pl. of *timpano* = TYMPANUM]

tin /tin/ *n. & v.* ● *n.* **1** *Chem.* a silvery white malleable metallic element resisting corrosion, occurring naturally in cassiterite and other ores, and used esp. in alloys and for plating thin iron or steel sheets to form tin plate. ¶ Symb.: **Sn.** **2 a** a vessel or container made of tin or tin-plated iron. **b** esp. *Brit.* an airtight sealed container made of tin plate or aluminum for preserving food. **3** = *tin plate.* **4** *Brit. sl.* money. ● *v.tr.* (**tinned, tinning**) **1** esp. *Brit.* seal (food) in an airtight can for preservation. **2** cover or coat with tin. □ **tin can** a tin container (see sense 2 of *n.*), esp. an empty one. **tin foil** foil made of tin, aluminum, or tin alloy, used for wrapping food for cooking or storing. **tin god 1** an object of unjustified veneration. **2** a self-important person. **tin hat** *colloq.* a military steel helmet. **tin Lizzie** *colloq.* an old or decrepit car. **Tin Pan Alley** the world of composers and publishers of popular music. **tin plate** sheet iron or sheet steel coated with tin. **tin-plate** *v.tr.* coat with tin. **tin soldier** a toy soldier made of metal. **tin whistle** = *penny whistle.* [OE f. Gmc]

tinamou /tínəmoō/ *n.* any South American bird of the family Tinamidae, resembling a grouse but related to the rhea. [F f. Galibi *tinamu*]

tinctorial /tingktáwreeəl/ *adj.* **1** of or relating to color or dyeing. **2** producing color. [L *tinctorius* f. *tinctor* dyer: see TINGE]

tincture /tíngkchər/ *n. & v.* ● *n.* (often foll. by *of*) **1** a slight flavor or trace. **2** a tinge (of a color). **3** a medicinal solution (of a drug) in alcohol (*tincture of quinine*). **4** *Heraldry* an inclusive term for the metals, colors, and furs used in coats of arms. **5** *Brit. colloq.* an alcoholic drink. ● *v.tr.* **1** color slightly; tinge, flavor. **2** (often foll. by *with*) affect slightly (with a quality). [ME f. L *tinctura* dyeing (as TINGE)]
■ **1, 2** see TINT *n.* 1, 2.

tinder /tíndər/ *n.* a dry substance such as wood that readily catches fire from a spark. □□ **tindery** *adj.* [OE *tynder, tyndre* f. Gmc]

tinderbox /tíndərboks/ *n.* **1** *hist.* a box containing tinder, flint, and steel, formerly used for kindling fires. **2** a potentially explosive or violent person, place, situation, etc.

tine /tin/ *n.* a prong or tooth or point of a fork, comb, antler, etc. □□ **tined** *adj.* (also in *comb.*). [OE *tind*]

tinea /tíneeə/ *n. Med.* ringworm. [L, = moth, worm]

ting /ting/ *n. & v.* ● *n.* a tinkling sound as of a bell. ● *v.intr. & tr.* emit or cause to emit this sound. [imit.]

tinge /tinj/ *v. & n.* ● *v.tr.* (also **tingeing**) (often foll. by *with*; often in *passive*) **1** color slightly (*is tinged with red*). **2** affect slightly (*regret tinged with satisfaction*). ● *n.* **1** a tendency toward or trace of some color. **2** a slight admixture of a feeling or quality. [ME f. L *tingere tinct-* dye, stain]
■ *v.* **1** see COLOR *v.* 1. **2** see TINT *v.* ● *n.* **1** see TINT *n.* 1. **2** see SHADE *n.* 6.

tingle /tínggəl/ *v. & n.* ● *v.* **1** *intr.* **a** feel a slight prickling, stinging, or throbbing sensation. **b** cause this (*the reply tingled in my ears*). **2** *tr.* make (the ear, etc.) tingle. ● *n.* a tingling sensation. [ME, perh. var. of TINKLE]
■ *v.* **1** see PRICKLE *v.* ● *n.* see PRICKLE *n.* 3.

tingly /tínglee/ *adj.* (**tinglier, tingliest**) causing or characterized by tingling.

tinhorn /tínhawrn/ *n. & adj. sl.* ● *n.* a pretentious but unimpressive person. ● *adj.* cheap; pretentious.

tinker /tíngkər/ *n. & v.* ● *n.* **1** an itinerant mender of kettles and pans, etc. **2** *Sc. & Ir.* a gypsy. **3** *Brit. colloq.* a mischievous person or animal. **4** a spell of tinkering. **5** a rough-and-ready worker. ● *v.* **1** *intr.* (foll. by *at, with*) work in an amateurish or desultory way, esp. to adjust or mend machinery, etc. **2 a** *intr.* work as a tinker. **b** *tr.* repair (pots and pans). □□ **tinkerer** *n.* [ME: orig. unkn.]

■ *v.* **1** trifle, dabble, meddle, tamper, mess (around *or* about), toy, fool (around *or* about), play (around *or* about), fiddle (about *or* around), monkey about *or* around, putter (about *or* around), esp. *Brit.* potter (about *or* around), *Brit. colloq.* muck (about *or* around).

tinkle /tíngkəl/ *v. & n.* ● *v.* **1** *intr. & tr.* make or cause to make a succession of short light ringing sounds. **2** *intr. colloq.* urinate. ● *n.* **1** a tinkling sound. **2** *Brit. colloq.* a telephone call (*will give you a tinkle on Monday*). **3** *colloq.* an act of urinating. [ME f. obs. *tink* to chink (imit.)]

■ *v.* **1** see RING² *v.* 1. **2** see URINATE. ● *n.* **1** see RING² *n.* 1. **3** *babytalk* weewee, *colloq.* piddle, pee, *sl.* leak, esp. *Brit. sl.* wee, *Brit. sl.* slash.

tinner /tínər/ *n.* **1** a tin miner. **2** a tinsmith.

tinnitus /tínîtəs, tíni-/ *n. Med.* a ringing in the ears. [L f. *tinnire tinnit-* ring, tinkle, of imit. orig.]

tinny /tínee/ *adj. & n.* ● *adj.* (**tinnier, tinniest**) **1** of or like tin. **2** (of a metal object) flimsy; insubstantial; of poor quality. **3 a** sounding like struck tin. **b** (of reproduced sound) thin and metallic, lacking low frequencies. **4** *Austral. sl.* lucky. ● *n.* (also **tinnie**) (*pl.* **-ies**) *Austral. sl.* a can of beer. □□ **tinnily** *adv.* **tinniness** *n.*

■ *adj.* **2** shabby, flimsy, flimsily *or* poorly made, shoddy, inferior, cheap, tawdry, insubstantial, tinpot. **3 b** metallic, harsh, twangy, thin.

tinpot /tínpot/ *adj.* cheap; inferior.

■ see CHEAP *adj.* 3.

tinsel /tínsəl/ *n. & v.* ● *n.* **1** glittering metallic strips, threads, etc., used as decoration to give a sparkling effect. **2** a fabric adorned with tinsel. **3** superficial brilliance or splendor. **4** (*attrib.*) showy; gaudy; flashy. ● *v.tr.* (**tinseled, tinseling** or **tinselled, tinselling**) adorn with or as with tinsel. □□ **tinseled** *adj.* **tinselly** *adj.* [OF *estincele* spark f. L *scintilla*]

tinsmith /tínsmith/ *n.* a worker in tin and tin plate.

tinsnips /tínsnips/ *n.* a pair of clippers for cutting sheet metal.

tinstone /tínstōn/ *n. Geol.* = CASSITERITE.

tint /tint/ *n. & v.* ● *n.* **1** a variety of a color, esp. one made lighter by adding white. **2** a tendency toward or admixture of a different color (*red with a blue tint*). **3** a faint color spread over a surface, esp. as a background for printing on. **4** a set of parallel engraved lines to give uniform shading. **5** a dye for the hair. ● *v.tr.* apply a tint to; color. □□ **tinter** *n.* [alt. of earlier *tinct* f. L *tinctus* dyeing (as TINGE), perh. infl. by It. *tinto*]

■ *n.* **1** hue, color, cast, shade, tone. **2** tincture, tinge, touch, hint, trace, dash, coloring, suggestion, nuance. **3** dye, rinse, wash, stain, tincture, colorant, coloring.

● *v.* dye, stain, color, tinge; influence, affect, taint.

tintinnabulation /tíntinábyəláyshən/ *n.* a ringing or tinkling of bells. [as L *tintinnabulum* tinkling bell f. *tintinnare* redupl. form of *tinnire* ring]

tinware /tínwair/ *n.* articles made of tin or tin plate.

tiny /tínee/ *adj.* (**tinier, tiniest**) very small or slight. □□ **tinily** *adv.* **tininess** *n.* [obs. *tine, tyne* (adj. & n.) small, a little: ME, of unkn. orig.]

■ microscopic, infinitesimal, minute, minuscule, ultramicroscopic, diminutive, small, little, miniature, micro-, mini-, pocket, pocket-size, bantam, pygmy, midget, lilliputian, petite, delicate, dainty, elfin, slight, insignificant, imperceptible, negligible, trifling, paltry, inconsequential, puny, *colloq.* pint-size, wee, weeny, teeny, teeny-weeny, teensy-weensy, itty-bitty, itsy-bitsy.

-tion /shən/ *suffix* forming nouns of action, condition, etc. (see -ION, -ATION, -ITION, -UTION). [from or after F *-tion* or L *-tio -tionis*]

tip¹ /tip/ *n. & v.* ● *n.* **1** an extremity or end, esp. of a small or tapering thing (*tips of the fingers*). **2** a small piece or part

attached to the end of a thing, e.g., a ferrule on a stick. **3** a leaf bud of tea. ● *v.tr.* (**tipped, tipping**) **1** provide with a tip. **2** (foll. by *in*) attach (a loose sheet) to a page at the inside edge. □ **on the tip of one's tongue** about to be said, esp. after difficulty in recalling to mind. **the tip of the iceberg** a small evident part of something much larger or more significant. □□ **tipless** *adj.* **tippy** *adj.* (in sense 3). [ME f. ON *typpi* (n.), *typpa* (v.), *typptr* tipped f. Gmc (rel. to TOP¹): prob. reinforced by MDu. & MLG *tip*]

■ *n.* **1** end, extremity, peak, apex, summit, vertex, cap, top, pinnacle, crown, head, terminal, nib, point, *Archit.* finial, *Sc. & No. of Engl.* neb, *colloq.* tip-top. **2** cap, ferrule, nib. ● *v.* **1** top, cap, crown, surmount.

tip² /tip/ *v. & n.* ● *v.* (**tipped, tipping**) **1 a** *intr.* lean or slant. **b** *tr.* cause to do this. **2** *tr.* (foll. by *into*, etc.) **a** overturn or cause to overbalance (*was tipped into the pond*). **b** discharge the contents of (a container, etc.) in this way. ● *n.* **1 a** a slight push or tilt. **b** a glancing stroke, esp. in baseball. **2** *Brit.* a place where material (esp. trash) is dumped. □ **tip the balance** make the critical difference. **tip the scales** see SCALE². [17th c.: orig. uncert.]

■ *v.* **1** slant, lean, incline, list, heel over, tilt, cant, careen. **2 a** tip over, upset, overthrow, knock *or* cast *or* throw down, upend, knock over, overturn, topple (over), capsize. **b** empty, unload, dump, deposit, discharge, spill, pour out, *sl.* ditch. ● *n.* **1 a** see LIST² *n.* **2** (trash *or* garbage *or* rubbish) dump, rubbish *or* refuse *or* trash heap, trash pile, dumping ground.

tip³ /tip/ *v. & n.* ● *v.* (**tipped, tipping**) **1** *tr.* make a small present of money to, esp. for a service given (*have you tipped the waiter?*). **2** *tr.* name as the likely winner of a race or contest, etc. **3** *tr.* strike or touch lightly. **4** *tr. sl.* give; hand; pass (esp. in *tip the wink* below). ● *n.* **1** a small gift of money, esp. for a service given. **2** a piece of private or special information, esp. regarding betting or investment. **3** a small or casual piece of advice. □ **tip off 1** give (a person) a hint or piece of special information or warning, esp. discreetly or confidentially. **2** *Basketball* start play by throwing the ball up between two opponents. **tip-off 1** a hint or warning, etc., given discreetly or confidentially. **2** *Basketball* the act of starting play with a tip off. **tip a person the wink** *Brit.* give a person private information. □□ **tipper** *n.* [ME: orig. uncert.]

■ *v.* **1** reward, remunerate. ● *n.* **1** gratuity, baksheesh, *pourboire*, present, gift, *colloq.* little something, sweetener. **2** tip-off, bit of (inside) information, warning, piece of advice, suggestion, clue, hint, forecast, prediction, *colloq.* pointer, *Austral. sl.* drum. **3** suggestion, hint, clue, piece of information, piece of advice, warning, recommendation, *colloq.* pointer. □ **tip off 1** advise, warn, caution, alert, forewarn, notify, let a person know, let a person in on. **tip-off 1** see TIP³ *n.* 2 above.

tipcat /típkat/ *n.* **1** a game with a short piece of wood tapering at the ends and struck with a stick. **2** this piece of wood.

tipper /típər/ *n.* a person or thing that tips.

tippet /típit/ *n.* **1** a covering of fur, etc., for the shoulders formerly worn by women. **2** a similar garment worn as part of some official costumes, esp. by the clergy. **3** *hist.* a long narrow strip of cloth as part of or an attachment to a hood, etc. [ME, prob. f. TIP¹]

tipple /típəl/ *v. & n.* ● *v.* **1** *intr.* drink intoxicating liquor habitually. **2** *tr.* drink (liquor) repeatedly in small amounts. ● *n. colloq.* a drink, esp. a strong one. □□ **tippler** *n.* [ME, back-form. f. *tippler*, of unkn. orig.]

■ *v.* **1** see DRINK *v.* 2. ● *n.* see DRINK *n.* 2b.

tipstaff /típstaf/ *n.* **1** a sheriff's officer. **2** a metal-tipped staff carried as a symbol of office. [contr. of *tipped staff*, i.e., tipped with metal]

/.../ **pronunciation**	● **part of speech**
□ **phrases, idioms, and compounds**	
□□ **derivatives**	■ **synonym section**
cross-references appear in SMALL CAPITALS or *italics*	

tipster /típstər/ n. a person who gives tips, esp. about betting at horse races.
- ■ tout, *Brit.* barker, touter.

tipsy /típsee/ adj. (**tipsier, tipsiest**) **1** slightly intoxicated. **2** caused by or showing intoxication (*a tipsy leer*). □ **tipsy cake** *Brit.* a sponge cake soaked in wine or liquor and served with custard. □□ **tipsily** adv. **tipsiness** n. [prob. f. TIP² = inclined to lean, unsteady: for -*sy* cf. FLIMSY, TRICKSY]
- ■ see TIGHT adj. 6.

tiptoe /típtō/ n., v., & adv. ● n. the tips of the toes. ● v.intr. (**tiptoes, tiptoed, tiptoeing**) walk on tiptoe, or very stealthily. ● adv. (also **on tiptoe**) with the heels off the ground and the weight on the balls of the feet.
- ■ v. see STEAL v. 4a.

tip-top /típtóp/ adj., adv., & n. colloq. ● adj. & adv. highest in excellence; very best. ● n. the highest point of excellence.
- ■ adj. see EXCELLENT.

tirade /tírayd, tīráyd/ n. a long vehement denunciation or declamation. [F, = long speech, f. It. *tirata* volley f. *tirare* pull f. Rmc]
- ■ declamation, harangue, diatribe, philippic, outburst, onslaught, screed, jeremiad, denunciation, rant, stream of abuse, invective.

tirailleur /teéraayőr, tírəlőr/ n. **1** a sharpshooter. **2** a skirmisher. [F f. *tirailler* shoot independently f. *tirer* shoot, draw, f. Rmc]

tire¹ /tīr/ v. **1** tr. & intr. make or grow weary. **2** tr. exhaust the patience or interest of; bore. **3** tr. (in *passive*; foll. by *of*) have had enough of; be fed up with (*was tired of arguing*). [OE *tēorian*, of unkn. orig.]
- ■ **1** weary, tire out, fatigue, exhaust, wear out, drain, sap, enervate, debilitate, weaken, take it out of, fag (out). **2** bore, exasperate, weary, irk, irritate, annoy, bother. **3** (*be tired of*) be weary of, have had enough of, be bored with, be exasperated by, be irked *or* irritated *or* annoyed *or* bothered by, be fed up (to here) with, *colloq.* be sick (and tired) of.

tire² /tīr/ n. **1** a rubber covering, usu. inflatable, that fits around a wheel rim. **2** a band of metal placed around the rim of a wheel to strengthen it. [ME, perh. = archaic *tire* headdress]

tired /tīrd/ adj. **1** weary; exhausted; ready for sleep. **2** (of an idea, etc.) hackneyed. □□ **tiredly** adv. **tiredness** n.
- ■ **1** exhausted, tired out, worn out, weary, fatigued, enervated, lethargic, sleepy, drowsy, spent, drained, jaded, dogtired, ready to drop, dead tired, *colloq.* fagged (out), knocked out, all in, done in, *colloq.* bushed, pooped, (dead) beat, tuckered out, esp. *Brit. colloq.* whacked, *sl.* wiped out, *Brit. sl.* knackered. **2** overworked, overused, clichéd, stereotyped, stereotypic(al), hackneyed, unimaginative, trite, stale, worn out, unoriginal, commonplace. □□ **tiredness** see FATIGUE n. 1.

tireless /tīrlis/ adj. having inexhaustible energy. □□ **tirelessly** adv. **tirelessness** n.
- ■ energetic, vital, vigorous, dynamic, spirited, lively, indefatigable, hardworking, industrious, untiring, unflagging, unfaltering, unfailing, persistent, dogged, tenacious, pertinacious, persevering, staunch, sedulous, diligent, unwavering, unswerving, undeviating, steady, steadfast, resolute, determined. □□ **tirelessly** see NONSTOP adv. **tirelessness** see PERSEVERANCE.

tiresome /tírsəm/ adj. **1** wearisome; tedious. **2** *Brit. colloq.* annoying (*how tiresome of you!*). □□ **tiresomely** adv. **tiresomeness** n.
- ■ **1** boring, dull, fatiguing, humdrum, monotonous, flat, tedious, wearisome, tiring, uninteresting, insipid, bland, dryasdust, fatiguing, soporific, hypnotic, *colloq.* deadly. **2** irritating, irksome, vexing, vexatious, annoying, bothersome, exasperating, trying, disagreeable, troublesome, unpleasant, *colloq.* infernal. □□ **tiresomeness** see TEDIUM.

tiro *Brit.* var. of TYRO.

'tis /tiz/ archaic it is. [contr.]

tisane /tizán, -zaán/ n. an infusion of dried herbs, etc. [F: see PTISAN]

tissue /tíshōō/ n. **1** any of the coherent collections of specialized cells of which animals or plants are made (*muscular tissue; nervous tissue*). **2** = *tissue paper*. **3** a disposable piece of thin soft absorbent paper for wiping, drying, etc. **4** fine woven esp. gauzy fabric. **5** (foll. by *of*) a connected series; a web (*a tissue of lies*). □ **tissue paper** thin soft paper for wrapping or protecting fragile or delicate articles. [ME f. OF *tissu* rich material, past part. of *tistre* f. L *texere* weave]
- ■ **5** fabric, network, web, interweaving, combination, chain, series, accumulation, conglomeration, concatenation, pile, mass, pack.

Tit. abbr. Titus (New Testament).

tit¹ /tit/ n. any of various small birds, esp. of the family Paridae. [prob. f. Scand.]

tit² /tit/ n. □ **tit for tat** /tat/ blow for blow; retaliation. [= earlier *tip* (TIP²) *for tap*]

tit³ /tit/ n. **1** *colloq.* a nipple. **2** *coarse sl.* a woman's breast. ¶ Usually considered a taboo word in sense 2. □ **get on a person's tits** *Brit. coarse sl.* annoy; irritate. [OE: cf. MLG *titte*]
- ■ see BREAST n. 1a.

tit⁴ /tit/ n. *Brit. coarse sl.* a term of contempt for a person. [20th c.: perh. f. TIT³]

Titan /tít'n/ n. **1** (often **titan**) a person of very great strength, intellect, or importance. **2** (in Greek mythology) a member of a family of early gigantic gods, the offspring of Heaven and Earth. [ME f. L f. Gk]

titanic¹ /tītánik/ adj. **1** of or like the Titans. **2** gigantic; colossal. □□ **titanically** adv. [Gk *titanikos* (as TITAN)]
- ■ **2** see GIGANTIC.

titanic² /tītánik, tee-/ adj. *Chem.* of titanium, esp. in quadrivalent form. □□ **titanate** /tít'nayt, tit-/ n.

titanium /tītáyneeəm, tee-/ n. *Chem.* a gray metallic element occurring naturally in many clays, etc., and used to make strong light alloys that are resistant to corrosion. ¶ Symb.: **Ti**. □ **titanium dioxide** (or **oxide**) a white oxide occurring naturally and used as a white pigment. [Gk (as TITAN) + -IUM, after *uranium*]

titbit *Brit.* var. of TIDBIT.

titch /tich/ n. (also **tich**) *Brit. colloq.* a small person. [*Tich*, stage name of Harry Relph (d. 1928), Engl. music hall comedian]

titchy /tíchee/ adj. (**titchier, titchiest**) *Brit. colloq.* very small.
- ■ see TINY.

titer /títər/ n. *Chem.* the strength of a solution or the quantity of a constituent as determined by titration. [F, = TITLE]

titfer /títfər/ n. *Brit. sl.* a hat. [abbr. of *tit for tat*, rhyming sl.]

tithe /tīth/ n. & v. ● n. **1** one tenth of the annual product of land or labor, formerly taken as a tax for the support of the church and clergy. **2** a tenth part. ● v. **1** tr. subject to tithes. **2** intr. pay tithes. □ **tithe barn** a barn built to hold tithes paid in kind. □□ **tithable** adj. [OE *teogotha* tenth]

tithing /títhing/ n. **1** the practice of taking or paying a tithe. **2** *Brit. hist.* **a** ten householders living near each other and collectively responsible for each other's behavior. **b** the area occupied by them. [OE *tīgething* (as TITHE, -ING¹)]

titi /teétee/ n. (*pl.* **titis**) any South American monkey of the genus *Callicebus*. [Tupi]

Titian /tíshən/ adj. (in full **Titian red**) (of hair) reddish brown. [name of *Tiziano* Vecelli, It. painter d. 1576]

titillate /tít'layt/ v.tr. **1** excite pleasantly. **2** tickle. □□ **titillatingly** adv. **titillation** /-láyshən/ n. [L *titillare titillat-*]
- ■ **1** see EXCITE 1c. □□ **titillation** see THRILL n. 1.

titivate /títivayt/ v.tr. (also **tittivate**) colloq. **1** adorn; smarten; spruce up. **2** (often *refl.*) put the finishing touches to. □□ **titivation** /-váyshən/ n. [earlier *tidivate*, perh. f. TIDY after *cultivate*]
- ■ see BEAUTIFY, SPRUCE¹ v.

titlark /títlaark/ n. a pipit, esp. the meadow pipit.

title /tít'l/ n. & v. ● n. **1** the name of a book, work of art, piece of music, etc. **2** the heading of a chapter, poem, document, etc. **3 a** the contents of the title page of a book. **b** a book regarded in terms of its title (*published 20 new titles*).

4 a caption or credit in a movie, broadcast, etc. **5** a form of nomenclature indicating a person's status (e.g., *professor*, *queen*) or used as a form of address or reference (e.g., *Lord*, *Mr.*). **6** a sports championship. **7** *Law* **a** the right to ownership of property with or without possession. **b** the facts constituting this. **c** (foll. by *to*) a just or recognized claim. **8** *Eccl.* **a** a fixed sphere of work and source of income as a condition for ordination. **b** a parish church in Rome under a cardinal. ● *v.tr.* **1** give a title to. **2** call by a title; term. □ **title deed** a legal instrument as evidence of a right, esp. to property. **title page** a page at the beginning of a book giving the title and particulars of authorship, etc. **title role** the part in a play, etc., that gives it its name (e.g., *Othello*). [ME f. OF f. L *titulus* placard, title]

■ *n.* **1** name. **2** caption, inscription, headline, head, heading, subtitle, legend, subhead, subheading, rubric. **4** caption, credit. **5** designation, epithet, form of address; office, position, status, rank, *formal* appellation. **6** championship, crown. **7 a** right, interest, privilege, entitlement, ownership, possession, tenure. **b** (title) deed, documentation of ownership. **c** (*title to*) claim *or* right to. ● *v.* name, call, designate, style, label, term, christen, baptize, nickname, denominate, tag, dub, *archaic* entitle. □ **title deed** see DEED *n.* 4. **title role** see PROTAGONIST 1, 2.

titled /tít'ld/ *adj.* having a title of nobility or rank.

titling[1] /títling/ *n.* the impressing of a title in gold leaf, etc., on the cover of a book.

titling[2] /títling/ *n.* **1** a titlark. **2** a titmouse.

titmouse /títmows/ *n.* (*pl.* **titmice** /-mīs/) any of various small tits, esp. of the genus *Parus*. [ME *titmōse* f. TIT[1] + OE *māse* titmouse, assim. to MOUSE]

titrate /títrayt/ *v.tr. Chem.* ascertain the amount of a constituent in (a solution) by measuring the volume of a known concentration of reagent required to complete the reaction. □□ **titratable** *adj.* **titration** /-tráyshən/ *n.*

titre *Brit.* var. of TITER.

titter /títər/ *v. & n.* ● *v.intr.* laugh in a furtive or restrained way; giggle. ● *n.* a furtive or restrained laugh. □□ **titterer** *n.* **titteringly** *adv.* [imit.]

■ *v.* chuckle, snicker, chortle, giggle, snigger; laugh. ● *n.* chuckle, snicker, giggle, (suppressed) laugh *or* laughter, chortle, snigger.

tittivate var. of TITIVATE.

tittle /tít'l/ *n.* **1** a small written or printed stroke or dot. **2** a particle; a whit (esp. in *not one jot or tittle*). [ME f. L (as TITLE)]

tittlebat /tít'lbat/ *n. Brit.* a stickleback. [fanciful var.]

tittle-tattle /tít'ltat'l/ *n. & v.* ● *n.* petty gossip. ● *v.intr.* gossip; chatter. [redupl. of TATTLE]

■ *n.* talk, small talk; see also CHATTER *n.* ● *v.* see BABBLE *v.* 1a, b.

tittup /títəp/ *v. & n.* ● *v.intr.* (**tittupped**, **tittupping** or **tittuped**, **tittuping**) go about friskily or jerkily; bob up and down; canter. ● *n.* such a gait or movement. [perh. imit. of hoofbeats]

titty /títee/ *n.* (*pl.* **-ies**) *sl.* = TIT[3].

titubation /tíchōōbáyshən/ *n. Med.* unsteadiness, esp. as caused by nervous disorder. [L *titubatio* f. *titubare* totter]

titular /tíchələr/ *adj. & n.* ● *adj.* **1** of or relating to a title (*the book's titular hero*). **2** existing, or being what is specified, in name or title only (*titular ruler*; *titular sovereignty*). ● *n.* **1** the holder of an office, etc., esp. a benefice, without the corresponding functions or obligations. **2** a titular saint. □ **titular bishop** a bishop with a no longer existent see. **titular saint** the patron saint of a particular church. □□ **titularly** *adv.* [F *titulaire* or mod.L *titularis* f. *titulus* TITLE]

■ *adj.* **2** nominal, so-called, token, putative, theoretical.

tizzy /tízee/ *n.* (*pl.* **-ies**) (also **tizz**, **tiz**) *colloq.* a state of nervous agitation (*in a tizzy*). [20th c.: orig. unkn.]

■ see STEW[1] *n.* 2, FLAP *n.* 3.

TKO *abbr. Boxing* technical knockout.

Tl *symb. Chem.* the element thallium.

TLC *abbr. colloq.* tender loving care.

Tlingit /tlíngkət, -gət, klíng-/ *n. & adj.* ● *n.* **1 a** a N. American people native to southern Alaska. **b** a member of this people. **2** the language of this people. ● *adj.* of or relating to this people or their language.

TM *abbr.* Transcendental Meditation.

Tm *symb. Chem.* the element thulium.

tmesis /tméesis/ *n.* (*pl.* **tmeses** /-seez/) *Gram.* the separation of parts of a compound word by an intervening word or words (esp. in colloq. speech, e.g., *can't find it any-damnedwhere*). [Gk *tmēsis* cutting f. *temnō* cut]

TN *abbr.* Tennessee (in official postal use).

tn *abbr.* **1** ton(s). **2** town.

tnpk. *abbr.* turnpike.

TNT *abbr.* trinitrotoluene, a high explosive formed from toluene by substitution of three hydrogen atoms with nitro groups.

to /tōō; tə (when unstressed)/ *prep. & adv.* ● *prep.* **1** introducing a noun: **a** expressing what is reached, approached, or touched (*fell to the ground*; *went to Paris*; *put her face to the window*; *five minutes to six*). **b** expressing what is aimed at: often introducing the indirect object of a verb (*throw it to me*; *explained the problem to them*). **c** as far as; up to (*went on to the end*; *have to stay from Tuesday to Friday*). **d** to the extent of (*were all drunk to a man*; *was starved to death*). **e** expressing what is followed (*according to instructions*; *made to order*). **f** expressing what is considered or affected (*am used to that*; *that is nothing to me*). **g** expressing what is caused or produced (*turn to stone*; *tear to shreds*). **h** expressing what is compared (*nothing to what it once was*; *comparable to any other*; *equal to the occasion*; *won by three to two*). **i** expressing what is increased (*add it to mine*). **j** expressing what is involved or composed as specified (*there is nothing to it*; *more to him than meets the eye*). **k** *archaic* for; by way of (*took her to wife*). **2** introducing the infinitive: **a** as a verbal noun (*to get there is the priority*). **b** expressing purpose, consequence, or cause (*we eat to live*; *left him to starve*; *am sorry to hear that*). **c** as a substitute for *to* + infinitive (*wanted to come but was unable to*). ● *adv.* **1** in the normal or required position or condition (*come to*; *heave to*). **2** (of a door) in a nearly closed position. □ **to and fro** **1** backward and forward. **2** repeatedly between the same points. [OE *tō* (adv. & prep.) f. WG]

toad /tōd/ *n.* **1** any froglike amphibian of the family Bufonidae, esp. of the genus *Bufo*, breeding in water but living chiefly on land. **2** any of various similar amphibians including the Surinam toad. **3** a repulsive or detestable person. □ **toad-in-the-hole** *Brit.* sausages or other meat baked in batter. □□ **toadish** *adj.* [OE *tādige*, *tādde*, *tāda*, of unkn. orig.]

toadfish /tódfish/ *n.* any marine fish of the family Batrachoididae, with a large head and wide mouth, making grunting noises by vibrating the walls of its swim bladder.

toadflax /tódflaks/ *n.* **1** any plant of the genus *Linaria* or *Chaenorrhinum*, with flaxlike leaves and spurred yellow or purple flowers. **2** a related plant, *Cymbalaria muralis*, with lilac flowers and ivy-shaped leaves.

toadstone /tódstōn/ *n.* a stone, sometimes precious, supposed to resemble or to have been formed in the body of a toad, formerly used as an amulet, etc.

toadstool /tódstōōl/ *n.* the spore-bearing structure of various fungi, usu. poisonous, with a round top and slender stalk.

toady /tódee/ *n. & v.* ● *n.* (*pl.* **-ies**) a sycophant; an obsequious hanger-on. ● *v.tr.* & (foll. by *to*) intr. (**-ies**, **-ied**) behave servilely to; fawn upon. □□ **toadyish** *adj.* **toadyism** *n.* [contr. of *toadeater*, a charlatan's attendant who ate toads (regarded as poisonous)]

■ *n.* see FLUNKY 2. ● *v.* see TRUCKLE *v.* □□ **toadyish** see OBSEQUIOUS, SERVILE. **toadyism** see *servility* (SERVILE).

toast /tōst/ *n. & v.* ● *n.* **1** bread in slices browned on both sides by radiant heat. **2 a** a person (orig. esp. a woman) or

---

/.../ pronunciation	● part of speech
□ phrases, idioms, and compounds	
□□ derivatives	■ synonym section
cross-references appear in SMALL CAPITALS or *italics*	

thing in whose honor a company is requested to drink. **b** a call to drink or an instance of drinking in this way. ● *v.* **1** *tr.* cook or brown (bread, etc.) by radiant heat. **2** *intr.* (of bread, etc.) become brown in this way. **3** *tr.* warm (one's feet, oneself, etc.) at a fire, etc. **4** *tr.* drink to the health or in honor of (a person or thing). □ **have a person on toast** *Brit. colloq.* be in a position to deal with a person as one wishes. [ME (orig. as verb) f. OF *toster* roast, ult. f. L *torrēre tost-* parch: sense 2 of the noun reflects the notion that a woman's name flavors the drink as spiced toast would]
■ *n.* **2 a** heroine, hero, favorite, darling, idol. **b** health, pledge. ● *v.* **1** brown, grill. **4** pay tribute to, salute, drink (a toast) to, drink the health of, raise one's glass to, pledge.

toaster /tṓstər/ *n.* an electrical device for making toast.

toastmaster /tṓstmastər/ *n.* (*fem.* **toastmistress** /-mistris/) an official responsible for announcing toasts at a public occasion.

tobacco /təbákō/ *n.* (*pl.* **-os**) **1** any plant of the genus *Nicotiana*, of American origin, with narcotic leaves used for smoking, chewing, or snuff. **2** its leaves, esp. as prepared for smoking. □ **tobacco mosaic virus** a virus that causes mosaic disease in tobacco, much used in biochemical research. [Sp. *tabaco*, perh. f. an Amer. Indian lang.]

tobacconist /təbákənist/ *n.* a retail dealer in tobacco and cigarettes, etc.

toboggan /təbógən/ *n.* & *v.* ● *n.* a long light narrow sled curled up at the front for sliding downhill, esp. over compacted snow or ice. ● *v.intr.* ride on a toboggan. □□ **tobogganer** *n.* **tobogganing** *n.* **tobogganist** *n.* [Can. F *tabaganne* f. Algonquian]

toby jug /tṓbee/ *n.* (also **toby, Toby**) a pitcher or mug for ale, etc., usu. in the form of a stout old man wearing a three-cornered hat. [familiar form of the name *Tobias*]

toccata /təkaátə/ *n.* a musical composition for a keyboard instrument designed to exhibit the performer's touch and technique. [It., fem. past part. of *toccare* touch]

Tocharian /təkáireeən/ *n.* & *adj.* ● *n.* **1** an extinct Indo-European language of a central Asian people in the first millennium AD. **2** a member of the people speaking this language. ● *adj.* of or in this language. [F *tocharien* f. L *Tochari* f. Gk *Tokharoi* a Scythian tribe]

tocopherol /tōkófərawl, -rol/ *n.* any of several closely related vitamins, found in wheat germ oil, egg yolk, and leafy vegetables, and important in the stabilization of cell membranes, etc. Also called *vitamin E*. [Gk *tokos* offspring + *pherō* bear + -OL¹]

tocsin /tóksin/ *n.* an alarm bell or signal. [F f. OF *touquesain, toquassen* f. Prov. *tocasenh* f. *tocar* TOUCH + *senh* signal bell]
■ see ALARM *n.* 2a.

today /tədáy/ *adv.* & *n.* ● *adv.* **1** on or in the course of this present day (*shall we go today?*). **2** nowadays; in modern times. ● *n.* **1** this present day (*today is my birthday*). **2** modern times. □ **today week** (or **fortnight**, etc.) *Brit.* a week (or fortnight, etc.) from today. [OE *tō dæg* on (this) day (as TO, DAY)]
■ *adv.* **2** see NOW *adv.* 1, 4.

toddle /tód'l/ *v.* & *n.* ● *v.intr.* **1** walk with short unsteady steps like those of a small child. **2** *colloq.* **a** (often foll. by *around, to*, etc.) take a casual or leisurely walk. **b** (usu. foll. by *off*) depart. ● *n.* **1** a toddling walk. **2** *colloq.* a stroll or short walk. [16th-c. *todle* (Sc. & No. of Engl.), of unkn. orig.]
■ *v.* **1** see WADDLE *v.* **2 a** see STROLL *v.* **b** see DEPART 1.
● *n.* **2** see STROLL *n.*

toddler /tódlər/ *n.* a child who is just beginning to walk. □□ **toddlerhood** *n.*
■ see TOT¹ 1.

toddy /tódee/ *n.* (*pl.* **-ies**) **1** a drink of liquor with hot water and sugar or spices. **2** the sap of some kinds of palm, fermented to produce arrack. [Hind. *tāṛī* f. *tār* palm f. Skr. *tāla* palmyra]

to-do /tədṓo/ *n.* a commotion or fuss. [*to do* as in *what's to do* (= to be done)]
■ see FUSS *n.* 1, 2a.

tody /tṓdee/ *n.* (*pl.* **-ies**) any small insectivorous West Indian bird of the genus *Todus*, related to the kingfisher. [F *todier* f. L *todus*, a small bird]

toe /tō/ *n.* & *v.* ● *n.* **1** any of the five terminal projections of the foot. **2** the corresponding part of an animal. **3** the part of an item of footwear that covers the toes. **4** the lower end or tip of an implement, etc. **5** *Archit.* a projection from the foot of a buttress, etc., to give stability. **6** *Austral. & NZ sl.* speed; energy. ● *v.* (**toes, toed, toeing**) **1** *tr.* touch (a starting line, etc.) with the toes before starting a race. **2** *tr.* **a** mend the toe of (a sock, etc.). **b** provide with a toe. **3** *intr.* (foll. by *in, out*) **a** walk with the toes pointed in (or out). **b** (of a pair of wheels) converge (or diverge) slightly at the front. **4** *tr.* *Golf* strike (the ball) with a part of the club too near the toe. □ **on one's toes** alert; eager. **toe clip** a clip on a bicycle pedal to prevent the foot from slipping. **toe the line** conform to a general policy or principle, esp. unwillingly or under pressure. **turn up one's toes** *colloq.* die. □□ **toed** *adj.* (also in *comb.*). **toeless** *adj.* [OE *tā* f. Gmc]
■ *n.* □ **on one's toes** see ALERT *adj.* 1. **turn up one's toes** see DIE¹ 1.

toecap /tṓkap/ *n.* the (usu. strengthened) outer covering of the toe of a boot or shoe.

toenail /tṓnayl/ *n.* **1** the nail at the tip of each toe. **2** a nail driven obliquely through the end of a board, etc.

toerag /tṓrag/ *n.* *Brit. sl.* a term of contempt for a person. [earlier = tramp, vagrant, f. the rag wrapped round the foot in place of a sock]

toey /tṓee/ *adj.* *Austral. sl.* restless; nervous; touchy.

toff /tof/ *n.* & *v.* *Brit. sl.* ● *n.* a distinguished or well-dressed person; a dandy. ● *v.tr.* (foll. by *up*) dress up smartly. [perh. a perversion of *tuft* = titled undergraduate (from the gold tassel formerly worn on the cap)]

toffee /táwfee, tóf-/ *n.* (also **toffy**) (*pl.* **toffees** or **toffies**) **1** a kind of firm or hard candy softening when sucked or chewed, made by boiling sugar, butter, etc. **2** a small piece of this. □ **for toffee** *Brit. sl.* (prec. by *can't*, etc.) (denoting incompetence) at all (*they couldn't sing for toffee*). **toffee-nosed** esp. *Brit. sl.* snobbish; pretentious. [earlier TAFFY]
■ □ **toffee-nosed** see snobbish (SNOB).

toft /toft/ *n.* *Brit.* **1** a homestead. **2** land once occupied by this. [OE f. ON *topt*]

tofu /tṓfoo/ *n.* a curd made from mashed soy beans. [Jap. *tōfu* f. Chin., = curdled beans]

tog¹ /tog/ *n.* & *v.* *colloq.* ● *n.* (usu. in *pl.*) **1** an item of clothing. **2** *Austral. & NZ colloq.* a bathing suit. ● *v.tr.* & *intr.* (**togged, togging**) (foll. by *out, up*) dress, esp. elaborately. [app. abbr. of 16th-c. cant *togeman(s), togman*, f. F *toge* or L *toga*: see TOGA]
■ *n.* **1** (*togs*) see CLOTHES. ● *v.* see CLOTHE 1.

toga /tṓgə/ *n.* *hist.* an ancient Roman citizen's loose flowing outer garment. □□ **togaed** *adj.* [L, rel. to *tegere* cover]

together /təgéthər/ *adv.* & *adj.* ● *adv.* **1** in company or conjunction (*walking together; built it together; were at school together*). **2** simultaneously; at the same time (*both shouted together*). **3** one with another (*were talking together*). **4** into conjunction; so as to unite (*tied them together; put two and two together*). **5** into company or companionship (*came together in friendship*). **6** uninterruptedly (*could talk for hours together*). ● *adj. colloq.* well organized or controlled. □ **together with** as well as; and also. [OE *tōgædere* f. TO + *gædre* together: cf. GATHER]
■ *adv.* **2** see at once 2 (ONCE), at one time 2 (TIME).
● *adj.* see POISED 1. □ **together with** see PLUS *prep.*

togetherness /təgéthərnis/ *n.* **1** the condition of being together. **2** a feeling of comfort from being together.

toggery /tógəree/ *n. colloq.* clothes; togs.

toggle /tógəl/ *n.* & *v.* ● *n.* **1** a device for fastening (esp. a garment), consisting of a crosspiece which can pass through a hole or loop in one position but not in another. **2** a pin or other crosspiece put through the eye of a rope, a link of a chain, etc., to keep it in place. **3** a pivoted barb on a harpoon. **4** *Computing* a switch action that is operated the same way but with opposite effect on successive occasions. ● *v.tr.* provide or fasten with a toggle. □ **toggle switch** an electric switch with a projecting lever to be moved usu. up and down. [18th-c. Naut.: orig. unkn.]

Togolese /tŏgəlee'z/ *adj. & n.* ● *adj.* of or relating to Togo in W. Africa. ● *n.* (*pl.* same) **1** a native or inhabitant of Togo. **2** a person of Togolese descent.

toil /toyl/ *v. & n.* ● *v.intr.* **1** work laboriously or incessantly. **2** make slow painful progress (*toiled along the path*). ● *n.* prolonged or intensive labor; drudgery. □ □□ **toiler** *n.* [ME f. AF *toiler* (v.), *toil* (n.), dispute, OF *tooilier*, *tooil*, f. L *tudiculare* stir about f. *tudicula* machine for bruising olives, rel. to *tundere* beat]

■ **1** see LABOR *v.* 1, 2. **2** see LABOR *v.* 5. ● *n.* see LABOR *n.* 1.

toile /twaal/ *n.* **1** a type of sheer fabric. **2** a garment reproduced in muslin or other cheap material for fitting or for making copies. [F *toile* cloth f. L *tela* web]

toilet /tóylit/ *n.* **1 a** a fixture, as in a bathroom, etc., for defecating and urinating. **b** a bathroom or lavatory. **2** the process of washing oneself, dressing, etc. (*make one's toilet*). **3** the cleansing of part of the body after an operation or at the time of childbirth. □ **toilet paper** (or **tissue**) paper for cleaning oneself after excreting. **toilet roll** a roll of toilet paper. **toilet set** a set of hairbrushes, combs, etc. **toilet soap** mild soap for washing oneself. **toilet table** a dressing table usu. with a mirror. **toilet train** cause (a young child) to undergo toilet training. **toilet training** the training of a young child to use a toilet. **toilet water** a diluted form of perfume used esp. after washing. [F *toilette* cloth, wrapper, dimin. f. *toile*: see TOILE]

■ **1** lavatory, bathroom, rest room, washroom, outhouse, privy, water closet, WC, men's room, ladies' room, powder room, (public) convenience, facility *or* facilities, urinal, *pissoir*; *Mil.* latrine, *Naut.* head, *Brit.* the Ladies('), *euphem.* comfort station, *Brit. colloq.* loo, the Gents, *Brit. euphem.* cloakroom, *sl.* john, can, *Austral. sl.* toot, dunny, *Brit. sl.* bog. **2** grooming, dressing, making up, toilette. □ **toilet water** see PERFUME *n.* 2.

toiletry /tóylitree/ *n.* (*pl.* **-ies**) (usu. in *pl.*) any of various articles or cosmetics used in washing, dressing, etc.

toilette /twaalét/ *n.* = TOILET 2. [F: see TOILET]

toils /toylz/ *n.pl.* a net or snare. [pl. of *toil* f. OF *toile* cloth f. L *tela* web]

toilsome /tóylsəm/ *adj.* involving toil; laborious. □□ **toilsomely** *adv.* **toilsomeness** *n.*

■ arduous, laborious, tough, hard, difficult, strenuous, stiff, burdensome, onerous, backbreaking, exhausting, fatiguing, tiring, enervating, wearying, draining.

to-ing and fro-ing /tŏoing ənd frŏing/ *n.* constant movement to and fro; bustle; dispersed activity. [TO *adv.* + FRO + -ING[1]]

■ see ACTIVITY 1.

Tokay /tōkáy/ *n.* **1** a sweet aromatic wine made near Tokaj in Hungary. **2** a similar wine produced elsewhere.

token /tŏkən/ *n.* **1** a thing serving as a symbol, reminder, or distinctive mark of something (*as a token of affection*; *in token of my esteem*). **2** a thing serving as evidence of authenticity or as a guarantee. **3** a voucher exchangeable for goods (often of a specified kind), given as a gift. **4** anything used to represent something else, esp. a metal disk, etc., used instead of money in coin-operated machines, as subway fare, etc. **5** (*attrib.*) **a** nominal or perfunctory (*token effort*). **b** conducted briefly to demonstrate strength of feeling (*token resistance*; *token strike*). **c** serving to acknowledge a principle only (*token payment*). **d** chosen by way of tokenism to represent a particular group (*the token woman on the committee*). □ **by the same** (or **this**) **token 1** similarly. **2** moreover. **token money** coins having a higher face value than their worth as metal. **token vote** (in the UK) a parliamentary vote of money, the stipulated amount of which is not meant to be binding. [OE *tāc(e)n* f. Gmc, rel. to TEACH]

■ **1, 2** symbol, sign, mark, marker, badge, emblem, indication, proof, evidence; souvenir, memento, keepsake, reminder, remembrance. **3** voucher, coupon. **4** coin, disk, counter. **5** (*attrib.*) **a, b** superficial,

cosmetic, surface, perfunctory, minimal, slight, nominal. **d** symbolic, emblematic, representative.

tokenism /tŏkənizəm/ *n.* **1** esp. *Polit.* the principle or practice of granting minimum concessions, esp. to appease radical demands, etc. (cf. TOKEN 5d). **2** making only a token effort.

tolbooth var. of TOLLBOOTH 2, 3.

told *past* and *past part.* of TELL[1].

Toledo /təleedō/ *n.* (*pl.* **-os**) a fine sword or sword blade made in Toledo in Spain.

tolerable /tólərəbəl/ *adj.* **1** able to be endured. **2** fairly good; mediocre. □□ **tolerability** /-bílitee/ *n.* **tolerableness** *n.* **tolerably** *adv.* [ME f. OF f. L *tolerabilis* (as TOLERATE)]

■ **1** bearable, supportable, allowable, endurable, permissible, acceptable, sufferable. **2** acceptable, unexceptional, common, fair, fair to middling, middling, *comme ci, comme ça*, ordinary, average, so-so, mediocre, adequate, run-of-the-mill, passable, indifferent, fairly good, *colloq.* OK, okay, not (too) bad, pretty good *Brit. colloq.* common or garden. □□ **tolerably** see FAIRLY 2.

tolerance /tólərəns/ *n.* **1** a willingness or ability to tolerate; forbearance. **2** the capacity to tolerate. **3** an allowable variation in any measurable property. **4** the ability to tolerate the effects of a drug, etc., after continued use. [ME f. OF f. L *tolerantia* (as TOLERATE)]

■ **1** open-mindedness, toleration, forbearance, broadmindedness, permissiveness, magnanimity, lenience, indulgence, sufferance, acceptance, patience, freedom from bigotry *or* prejudice, understanding. **3** play, clearance, allowance, variation. **4** toleration, resistance, endurance, imperviousness; immunity, insensitivity.

tolerant /tólərənt/ *adj.* **1** disposed or accustomed to tolerate others or their acts or opinions. **2** (foll. by *of*) enduring or patient. **3** exhibiting tolerance of a drug, etc. □□ **tolerantly** *adv.* [F *tolérant* f. L *tolerare* (as TOLERATE)]

■ **1** open-minded, objective, forbearing, forgiving, unprejudiced, unbigoted, dispassionate, broad-minded, indulgent, lenient, magnanimous, patient, generous, charitable, catholic, latitudinarian, permissive, liberal, easygoing, bighearted, fair, evenhanded, understanding, considerate.

tolerate /tólərayt/ *v.tr.* **1** allow the existence or occurrence of without authoritative interference. **2** leave unmolested. **3** endure or permit, esp. with forbearance. **4** sustain or endure (suffering, etc.). **5** be capable of continued subjection to (a drug, radiation, etc.) without harm. **6** find or treat as endurable. □□ **tolerator** *n.* [L *tolerare tolerat-* endure]

■ **1, 3, 6** stand (for), allow, permit, bear, endure, suffer, countenance, accept, abide, admit, sanction, condone, swallow, stomach, turn a blind eye to, put up with, *colloq.* stick, lump, *literary* brook, *sl.* hack. **4, 5** bear, stand, submit to, sustain, endure, weather, take, accept, put up with, undergo.

toleration /tóləráyshən/ *n.* the process or practice of tolerating, esp. the allowing of differences in religious opinion without discrimination. [F *tolération* f. L *toleratio* (as TOLERATE)]

■ see TOLERANCE 1, 4.

toll[1] /tōl/ *n.* **1** a charge payable for permission to pass a barrier or use a bridge or road, etc. **2** the cost or damage caused by a disaster, battle, etc., or incurred in an achievement (*death toll*). **3** a charge for a long distance telephone call. **take its toll** be accompanied by loss or injury, etc. **toll bridge** a bridge at which a toll is charged. **toll road** a road maintained by the tolls collected on it. [OE f. med.L *toloneum* f. LL *teloneum* f. Gk *telōnion* tollhouse f. *telos* tax]

■ **1** charge, fee, dues, assessment, tariff; excise, duty,

/.../ **pronunciation**	● **part of speech**
□ **phrases, idioms, and compounds**	
□□ **derivatives**	■ **synonym section**
cross-references appear in SMALL CAPITALS or *italics*	

impost, levy, tribute, tax. **2** loss, penalty, cost, damage(s); exaction.

toll² /tōl/ *v. & n.* ● *v.* **1 a** *intr.* (of a bell) sound with a slow uniform succession of strokes. **b** *tr.* ring (a bell) in this way. **c** *tr.* (of a bell) announce or mark (a death, etc.) in this way. **2** *tr.* strike (the hour). ● *n.* **1** the act of tolling. **2** a stroke of a bell. [ME, special use of (now dial.) *toll* entice, pull, f. an OE root *-tyllan* (recorded in *fortyllan* seduce)]
■ *v.* ring, peal, chime, strike, sound, knell. ● *n.* ring, peal, chime, striking, sound, knell.

tollbooth /tōlbōōth/ *n.* **1** a booth on a toll road or toll bridge, etc., from which tolls are collected. **2** (also **tolbooth**) *Sc. archaic* a town hall. **3** (also **tolbooth**) *Sc. archaic* a town jail.

tollgate /tōlgayt/ *n.* a gate preventing passage until a toll is paid.

tollhouse /tōlhows/ *n.* a house at a tollgate or toll bridge, used by a toll collector.

Toltec /tōltek, tól-/ *n.* **1** a member of a Native American people that flourished in Mexico before the Aztecs. **2** the language of this people. □□ **Toltecan** *adj.*

tolu /təlōō, tōlōō/ *n.* a fragrant brown balsam obtained from either of two South American trees, *Myroxylon balsamum* or *M. toluifera*, and used in perfumery and medicine. [Santiago de *Tolu* in Colombia]

toluene /tólyōō-een/ *n.* a colorless aromatic liquid hydrocarbon derivative of benzene, orig. obtained from tolu, used in the manufacture of explosives, etc. Also called *methyl benzene*. □□ **toluic** *adj.* **toluol** *n.* [TOLU + -ENE]

tom /tom/ *n.* a male of various animals, esp. (in full **tomcat**) a male cat. [abbr. of the name *Thomas*]

tomahawk /tóməhawk/ *n. & v.* ● *n.* **1** a Native American war ax with a stone or iron head. **2** *Austral.* a hatchet. ● *v.tr.* strike, cut, or kill with a tomahawk. [Renape *tämähäk* f. *tämäham* he, etc., cuts]

tomato /təmáytō, -maá-/ *n.* (*pl.* **-oes**) **1** a glossy red or yellow pulpy edible fruit. **2** a solanaceous plant, *Lycopersicon esculentum*, bearing this. □□ **tomatoey** *adj.* [17th-c. *tomate*, = F or Sp. & Port., f. Mex. *tomatl*]

tomb /tōōm/ *n.* **1** a large, esp. underground, vault for the burial of the dead. **2** an enclosure cut in the earth or in rock to receive a dead body. **3** a sepulchral monument. **4** (prec. by *the*) the state of death. [ME *t(o)umbe* f. AF *tumbe*, OF *tombe* f. LL *tumba* f. Gk *tumbos*]
■ **1, 2** sepulcher, crypt, vault, grave, catacomb, burial chamber, charnel house, final *or* last resting place. **3** monument, mausoleum, pyramid, dolmen, cromlech.

tombac /tómbak/ *n.* an alloy of copper and zinc used esp. as material for cheap jewelry. [F f. Malay *tambāga* copper]

tombolo /tómbəlō/ *n.* (*pl.* **-os**) a spit joining an island to the mainland. [It., = sand dune]

tomboy /tómboy/ *n.* a girl who behaves in a boisterous boyish way. □□ **tomboyish** *adj.* **tomboyishness** *n.*

tombstone /tōōmstōn/ *n.* a stone standing or laid over a grave, usu. with an epitaph.
■ gravestone, headstone, tablet, marker, monument, cenotaph.

Tom Collins /tom kólinz/ *n.* a tall iced drink of gin with soda, lemon or lime juice, and sugar. [20th c.: orig. unkn.]

Tom, Dick, and Harry /tóm dik ənd háree/ *n.* (usu. prec. by *any, every*) ordinary people taken at random; anyone.

tome /tōm/ *n.* a large heavy book or volume. [F f. L *tomus* f. Gk *tomos* section, volume f. *temnō* cut]
■ see BOOK *n.* 1.

tome /tōm/ *comb. form* forming nouns meaning: **1** an instrument for cutting (*microtome*). **2** a section or segment. [Gk *tomē* a cutting, *-tomos* -cutting, f. *temnō* cut]

tomentum /tōméntəm/ *n.* (*pl.* **tomenta** /-tə/) **1** *Bot.* matted woolly down on stems and leaves. **2** *Anat.* the tufted inner surface of the pia mater in the brain. □□ **tomentose** /-tōs/ *adj.* **tomentous** *adj.* [L, = cushion stuffing]

tomfool /tómfōōl/ *n.* **1** a foolish person. **2** (*attrib.*) silly; foolish (*a tomfool idea*).

tomfoolery /tómfōōləree/ *n.* (*pl.* **-ies**) **1** foolish behavior; nonsense. **2** an instance of this.

■ see NONSENSE.

Tommy /tómee/ *n.* (*pl.* **-ies**) *colloq.* a British enlisted soldier. [*Tommy* (*Thomas*) *Atkins*, a name used in specimens of completed official forms]

tommy bar /tómee/ *n.* a short bar adding leverage when used with a wrench, etc.

tommy gun /tómee/ *n.* a type of submachine gun. [J. T. Thompson, US Army officer d. 1940, its co-inventor]

tommyrot /tómeerot/ *n. sl.* nonsense.

tomogram /tóməgram/ *n.* a record obtained by tomography.

tomography /təmógrəfee/ *n.* a method of radiography displaying details in a selected plane within the body. [Gk *tomē* a cutting + -GRAPHY]

tomorrow /təmáwrō, -mór-/ *adv. & n.* ● *adv.* **1** on the day after today. **2** at some future time. ● *n.* **1** the day after today. **2** the near future. □ **tomorrow morning** (or **afternoon**, etc.) in the morning (or afternoon, etc.) of tomorrow. **tomorrow week** *Brit.* a week from tomorrow. [TO + MORROW: cf. TODAY]
■ *n.* **2** future, days *or* time to come.

tompion var. of TAMPION.

Tom Thumb /tom thúm/ *n.* **1** a dwarf or midget. **2** a dwarf variety of various plants. [the name of a tiny person in fairy tales]

tomtit /tómtit/ *n.* any of various tit birds, esp. a blue tit.

tom-tom /tómtom/ *n.* **1** an early drum beaten with the hands. **2** a tall drum beaten with the hands and used in jazz bands, etc. [Hindi *tamtam*, imit.]

-tomy /təmee/ *comb. form* forming nouns denoting cutting, esp. in surgery (*laparotomy*). [Gk *-tomia* cutting f. *temnō* cut]

ton¹ /tun/ *n.* **1** (in full **short ton**) a unit of weight equal to 2,000 lb. (907.19 kg). **2** (in full **long ton**) a unit of weight equal to 2,240 lb. (1016.05 kg). **3** = *metric ton*. **4 a** (in full **displacement ton**) a unit of measurement of a ship's weight or volume in terms of its displacement of water with the loadline just immersed, equal to 2,240 lb. or 35 cu. ft. (0.99 cubic meters). **b** (in full **freight ton**) a unit of weight or volume of cargo, equal to a metric ton (1,000 kg) or 40 cu. ft. **5 a** (in full **gross ton**) a unit of gross internal capacity, equal to 100 cu. ft. (2.83 cubic meters). **b** (in full **net** or **register ton**) an equivalent unit of net internal capacity. **6** a unit of refrigerating power able to freeze 2,000 lb. of ice at 0°C in 24 hours. **7** a measure of capacity for various materials, esp. 40 cu. ft. of timber. **8** (usu. in *pl.*) *colloq.* a large number or amount (*tons of money*). **9** esp. *Brit. sl.* **a** a speed of 100 m.p.h. **b** a sum of £100. **c** a score of 100. □ **ton-mile** one ton of goods carried one mile, as a unit of traffic. **weigh a ton** *colloq.* be very heavy. [orig. the same word as TUN: differentiated in the 17th c.]
■ **8** see HEAP *n.* 2, MANY *n.* 1.

ton² /toN/ *n.* **1** a prevailing mode or fashion. **2** fashionable society. [F]

tonal /tōnəl/ *adj.* **1** of or relating to tone or tonality. **2** (of a fugue, etc.) having repetitions of the subject at different pitches in the same key. □□ **tonally** *adv.* [med.L *tonalis* (as TONE)]

tonality /tōnálitee/ *n.* (*pl.* **-ies**) **1** *Mus.* **a** the relationship between the tones of a musical scale. **b** the observance of a single tonic key as the basis of a composition. **2** the tone or color scheme of a picture. **3** *Linguistics* the differentiation of words, syllables, etc., by a change of vocal pitch.

tondo /tóndō/ *n.* (*pl.* **tondi** /-dee/) a circular painting or relief. [It., = round (plate), f. *rotondo* f. L *rotundus* round]

tone /tōn/ *n. & v.* ● *n.* **1** a musical or vocal sound, esp. with reference to its pitch, quality, and strength. **2** (often in *pl.*) modulation of the voice expressing a particular feeling or mood (*a cheerful tone; suspicious tones*). **3** a manner of expression in writing. **4** *Mus.* **a** a musical sound, esp. of a definite pitch and character. **b** an interval of a major second, e.g., C–D. **5 a** the general effect of color or of light and shade in a picture. **b** the tint or shade of a color. **6 a** the prevailing character of the morals and sentiments, etc., in a group. **b** an attitude or sentiment expressed, esp. in a letter, etc. **7** the proper firmness of bodily organs. **8** a state of good or specified health or quality. **9** *Phonet.* **a** an accent on one

syllable of a word. **b** the pitch of a word to distinguish it from others of a similar sound (*Mandarin has four tones*). ● *v.* **1** *tr.* give the desired tone to. **2** *tr.* modify the tone of. **3** *intr.* (often foll. by *to*) attune. **4** *intr.* (foll. by *with*) be in harmony (esp. of color) (*does not tone with the wallpaper*). **5** *tr. Photog.* give (a monochrome picture) an altered color in finishing by means of a chemical solution. **6** *intr.* undergo a change in color by toning. □ **tone arm** the movable arm supporting the pickup of a record player. **tone-deaf** unable to perceive differences of musical pitch accurately. **tone deafness** the condition of being tone-deaf. **tone down 1** make or become softer in tone of sound or color. **2** make (a statement, etc.) less harsh or emphatic. **tone poem** = *symphonic poem*. **tone row** *Mus.* a series of varying tones that recur in sequence throughout a composition. **tone up 1** make or become stronger in tone of sound or color. **2** make (a statement, etc.) more emphatic. **3** make (muscles) firm by exercise, etc.; make or become fitter. **whole tone scale** see WHOLE. □□ **toneless** *adj.* **tonelessly** *adv.* **toner** *n.* [ME f. OF *ton* or L *tonus* f. Gk *tonos* tension, tone f. *teino* stretch]
■ *n.* **1** sound, note. **2** stress, emphasis, force, accent, intonation, modulation, phrasing, inflection, pitch, tonality, timbre, sound (color), tone color *or* quality, color *or* coloring, resonance, sonorousness, sonority, fullness, richness, expression, note, tone of voice. **3** manner, style, approach, mode of expression. **5** tint, tinge, shade, hue, color, coloring, cast. **6 b** attitude, feeling, sentiment, air, atmosphere, mood, aspect, character, note, tenor, drift, temper, vein, spirit. ● *v.* **4** go with, be harmonious with, match. □ **tone down 1** temper, modify, reduce, moderate, modulate, soften, quiet, lower, dampen, dull, subdue, mute, soft-pedal, *Brit.* quieten. **2** see MITIGATE. **tone up 1, 2** see INTENSIFY. **3** (re)invigorate, tune (up), firm (up), brighten (up), (re)vitalize, freshen (up), limber up, get into condition or shape. □□ **toneless** muffled, dull, flat, low; see also NEUTRAL *adj.* 3, 5.

toneburst /tṓnbərst/ *n.* an audio signal used in testing the transient response of audio components.

toneme /tṓneem/ *n.* a phoneme distinguished from another only by its tone. □□ **tonemic** /-neémik/ *adj.* [TONE after *phoneme*]

tong /tawng, tong/ *n.* a Chinese guild, association, or secret society. [Chin. *tang* meeting place]

tonga /tóngga/ *n.* a light horse-drawn two-wheeled vehicle used in India. [Hindi *tāngā*]

tongs /tawngz, tongz/ *n.pl.* (also **pair of tongs** *sing.*) an instrument with two hinged or sprung arms for grasping and holding. [pl. of *tong* f. OE *tang(e)* f. Gmc]

tongue /tung/ *n. & v.* ● *n.* **1** the fleshy muscular organ in the mouth used in tasting, licking, and swallowing, and (in humans) for speech. **2** the tongue of an ox, etc., as food. **3** the faculty of or a tendency in speech (*a sharp tongue*). **4** a particular language (*the German tongue*). **5** a thing like a tongue in shape or position, esp.: **a** a long low promontory. **b** a strip of leather, etc., attached at one end only, under the laces in a shoe. **c** the clapper of a bell. **d** the pin of a buckle. **e** the projecting strip on a wooden, etc., board fitting into the groove of another. **f** a vibrating slip in the reed of some musical instruments. **g** a jet of flame. ● *v.* (**tongues**, **tongued**, **tonguing**) **1** *tr.* produce staccato, etc., effects with (a flute, etc.) by means of tonguing. **2** *intr.* use the tongue in this way. □ **find** (or **lose**) **one's tongue** be able (or unable) to express oneself after a shock, etc. **the gift of tongues** the power of speaking in unknown languages, regarded in some Christian denominations as one of the gifts of the Holy Spirit (Acts 2). **keep a civil tongue in one's head** avoid rudeness. **tongue-and-groove** applied to boards in which a tongue along one edge fits into a groove along the edge of the next, each board having a tongue on one edge and a groove on the other. **tongue depressor** a doctor's implement for holding the tongue in place while examining the throat or mouth. **tongue-in-cheek** *adj.* ironic; slyly humorous. ● *adv.* insincerely or ironically. **tongue-lashing** a severe scolding or reprimand. **tongue-**

tie a speech impediment due to a malformation of the tongue. **tongue-tied 1** too shy or embarrassed to speak. **2** having a tongue-tie. **tongue twister** a sequence of words difficult to pronounce quickly and correctly. **with one's tongue hanging out** eagerly or expectantly. □□ **tongued** *adj.* (also in *comb.*). **tongueless** *adj.* [OE *tunge* f. Gmc, rel. to L *lingua*]
■ *n.* **4** language, speech; dialect, patois, Creole, idiom, parlance, argot, talk, vernacular. □ **tongue-in-cheek** *adj.* see PLAYFUL 2. ● *adv.* facetiously, whimsically, ironically, jocularly, jokingly, teasingly, not seriously, in jest, jestingly, in fun, to be funny, insincerely, *colloq.* kiddingly. **tongue-lashing** scolding, berating, reproof, rebuke, reprimand, lecture; (verbal) abuse, castigation, chastisement, vituperation, revilement, *colloq.* dressing-down, bawling-out, telling-off, talking-to, *Brit. colloq.* ticking-off, wigging, slating. **tongue-tied 1** speechless, at a loss for words, struck dumb, dumbfounded, mute, inarticulate.

tonguing /túnging/ *n. Mus.* the technique of playing a wind instrument using the tongue to articulate certain notes.

tonic /tónik/ *n. & adj.* ● *n.* **1** an invigorating medicine. **2** anything serving to invigorate. **3** = *tonic water*. **4** *Mus.* the first degree of a scale, forming the keynote of a piece (see KEYNOTE 3). ● *adj.* **1** serving as a tonic; invigorating. **2** *Mus.* denoting the first degree of a scale. **3 a** producing tension, esp. of the muscles. **b** restoring normal tone to organs. □ **tonic accent** an accent marked by a change of pitch within a syllable. **tonic sol-fa** *Mus.* a system of notation used esp. in teaching singing, with do as the keynote of all major keys and la as the keynote of all minor keys. **tonic spasm** continuous muscular contraction (cf. CLONUS). **tonic water** a carbonated mineral water containing quinine. □□ **tonically** *adv.* [F *tonique* f. Gk *tonikos* (as TONE)]
■ *n.* **1, 2** stimulant, restorative, pick-me-up, refresher, *colloq.* boost, shot in the arm; ptisan, tisane, analeptic, *Med.* roborant, *colloq.* bracer, pickup, picker-upper. ● *adj.* **1** stimulant, stimulating, restorative, invigorating, fortifying, bracing, strengthening, reviving, enlivening, refreshing, analeptic, *Med.* roborant.

tonicity /tōnísitee/ *n.* **1** the state of being tonic. **2** a healthy elasticity of muscles, etc. **3** *Linguistics* phonetic emphasis at a certain place in an intonation pattern.

tonight /tənít/ *adv. & n.* ● *adv.* on the present or approaching evening or night. ● *n.* the evening or night of the present day. [TO + NIGHT: cf. TODAY]

tonka bean /tóngkə/ *n.* the black fragrant seed of a South American tree, *Dipteryx odorata*, used in perfumery, etc. [*tonka*, its name in Guyana, + BEAN]

tonnage /túnij/ *n.* **1** a ship's internal cubic capacity or freight-carrying capacity, measured in tons. **2** the total carrying capacity, esp. of a country's merchant marine. **3** a charge per ton on freight or cargo. [orig. in sense 'duty on a tun of wine': OF *tonnage* f. *tonne* TUN: later f. TON¹]

tonne /tun/ *n.* = *metric ton*. [F: see TUN]

tonneau /tonṓ, tónō/ *n.* the part of an automobile occupied by the back seats, esp. in an open car. □ **tonneau cover** a removable flexible cover for the passenger seats in an open car, boat, etc., when they are not in use. [F, lit. cask, tun]

tonometer /tōnómitər/ *n.* **1** a tuning fork or other instrument for measuring the pitch of tones. **2** an instrument for measuring the pressure of fluid. [formed as TONE + -METER]

tonsil /tónsəl/ *n.* either of two small masses of lymphoid tissue on each side of the root of the tongue. □□ **tonsillar** *adj.* [F *tonsilles* or L *tonsillae* (pl.)]

tonsillectomy /tónsiléktəmee/ *n.* (*pl.* **-ies**) the surgical removal of the tonsils.

tonsillitis /tónsilítis/ *n.* inflammation of the tonsils.

tonsorial /tonsáwreeəl/ *adj.* usu. *joc.* of or relating to a hair-

---

/. . . / **pronunciation**	● **part of speech**
□ **phrases, idioms, and compounds**	
□□ **derivatives**	■ **synonym section**
cross-references appear in SMALL CAPITALS or *italics*	

dresser or barber or hairdressing. [L *tonsorius* f. *tonsor* barber f. *tondēre tons-* shave]

tonsure /tónshər/ *n. & v.* ● *n.* **1** the shaving of the crown of the head or the entire head, esp. of a person entering a priesthood or monastic order. **2** a bare patch made in this way. ● *v.tr.* give a tonsure to. [ME f. OF *tonsure* or L *tonsura* (as TONSORIAL)]

tontine /tontéen/ *n.* an annuity shared by subscribers to a loan, the shares increasing as subscribers die until the last survivor gets all, or until a specified date when the remaining survivors share the proceeds. [F, f. the name of Lorenzo *Tonti* of Naples, originator of tontines in France *c.* 1653]

tony /tónee/ *adj.* (**tonier, toniest**) *colloq.* having 'tone'; stylish; fashionable.

too /too/ *adv.* **1** to a greater extent than is desirable, permissible, or possible for a specified or understood purpose (*too colorful for my taste; too large to fit*). **2** *colloq.* extremely (*you're too kind*). **3** in addition (*are they coming too?*). **4** moreover (*we must consider, too, the time of year*). □ **none too 1** somewhat less than (*feeling none too good*). **2** barely. **too bad** see BAD. **too much, too much for** see MUCH. **too right** see RIGHT. **too-too** *adj. & adv. colloq.* extreme; excessive(ly). [stressed form of TO, f. 16th-c. spelling *too*]

■ **1** see OVERLY. **2** see VERY *adv.* **3** see *in addition* (ADDITION). **4** see MOREOVER.

toodle-oo /toodlóo/ *int.* (also *Brit.* **toodle-pip**) *colloq.* goodbye. [20th c.: orig. unkn.: perh. alt. of F *à tout à l'heure* see you soon]

took past of TAKE.

tool /tool/ *n. & v.* ● *n.* **1** any device or implement used to carry out mechanical functions whether manually or by a machine. **2** a thing used in an occupation or pursuit (*the tools of one's trade; literary tools*). **3** a person used as a mere instrument by another. **4** *coarse sl.* the penis. ¶ Usually considered a taboo use. **5 a** a distinct figure in the tooling of a book. **b** a small stamp or roller used to make this. ● *v.tr.* **1** dress (stone) with a chisel. **2** impress a design on (a leather book cover). **3** (foll. by *along, around,* etc.) *sl.* drive or ride, esp. in a casual or leisurely manner. **4** (often foll. by *up*) equip with tools. □ **tool up 1** *sl.* arm oneself. **2** equip oneself. □□ **tooler** *n.* [OE *tōl* f. Gmc]

■ *n.* **1** utensil, implement, instrument, device, apparatus, appliance, contrivance, aid, machine, mechanism, gadget; *colloq.* gimmick, *often derog. or joc.* contraption, *sl.* gizmo; (*tools*) hardware, kit, gear. **2** instrument, gadget; (*tools*) kit, gear, tackle, paraphernalia; technique, method, methodology, agency, medium, vehicle. **3** puppet, cat's-paw, pawn, instrument, dupe, *colloq.* stooge, *sl.* sucker. ● *v.* **1** work, carve, cut, dress, shape. **2** embellish, decorate, ornament. **3** see DRIVE *v.* 3b.

tooling /tooling/ *n.* **1** the process of dressing stone with a chisel. **2** the ornamentation of a book cover with designs impressed by heated tools.

toolmaker /toolmaykər/ *n.* a person who makes precision tools, esp. tools used in a press. □□ **toolmaking** *n.*

toot[1] /toot/ *n. & v.* ● *n.* **1** a short sharp sound as made by a horn, trumpet, or whistle. **2** *sl.* cocaine or a snort (see SNORT *n.* 4) **of cocaine. 3** *sl.* a drinking session; a binge; a spree. ● *v.* **1** *tr.* sound (a horn, etc.) with a short sharp sound. **2** *intr.* give out such a sound. □□ **tooter** *n.* [prob. f. MLG *tūten*, or imit.]

■ *n.* **3** see CAROUSE *n.*

toot[2] /toot/ *n. Austral. sl.* a toilet. [20th c.: orig. unkn.]

tooth /tooth/ *n. & v.* ● *n.* (*pl.* **teeth** /teeth/) **1** each of a set of hard bony enamel-coated structures in the jaws of most vertebrates, used for biting and chewing. **2** a toothlike part or projection, e.g., the cog of a gearwheel, the point of a saw or comb, etc. **3** (often foll. by *for*) one's sense of taste; an appetite or liking. **4** (in *pl.*) force or effectiveness (*the penalties give the contract teeth*). ● *v.* **1** *tr.* provide with teeth. **2** *intr.* (of cogwheels) engage, interlock. □ **armed to the teeth** completely and elaborately armed or equipped. **fight tooth and nail** fight very fiercely. **get** (or **sink**) **one's teeth into** devote oneself seriously to. **in the teeth of 1** in spite

of (opposition or difficulty, etc.). **2** contrary to (instructions, etc.). **3** directly against (the wind, etc.). **set a person's teeth on edge** see EDGE. **tooth-billed** (of a bird) having toothlike projections on the cutting edges of the bill. **tooth comb** *Brit.* = *fine-tooth comb* (see FINE[1]). **tooth powder** powder for cleaning the teeth. **tooth shell** = *tusk shell*. □□ **toothed** *adj.* (also in *comb.*). **toothless** *adj.* **toothlike** *adj.* [OE *tōth* (pl. *tēth*) f. Gmc]

■ □ **in the teeth of 1** see DESPITE *prep.*

toothache /toothayk/ *n.* a (usu. prolonged) pain in a tooth or teeth.

toothbrush /toothbrush/ *n.* a brush for cleaning the teeth.

toothing /toothing/ *n.* projecting bricks or stones left at the end of a wall to allow its continuation.

toothpaste /toothpayst/ *n.* a paste for cleaning the teeth.

toothpick /toothpik/ *n.* a small sharp instrument for removing small pieces of food lodged between the teeth.

toothsome /toothsəm/ *adj.* **1** (of food) delicious; appetizing. **2** attractive, esp. sexually. □□ **toothsomely** *adv.* **toothsomeness** *n.*

■ see DELICIOUS.

toothwort /toothwərt, -wawrt/ *n.* a parasitic plant, *Lathraea squamaria*, with toothlike root scales.

toothy /toothee/ *adj.* (**toothier, toothiest**) having or showing large, numerous, or prominent teeth (*a toothy grin*). □□ **toothily** *adv.*

tootle /tootl/ *v.intr.* **1** toot gently or repeatedly. **2** (usu. foll. by *along, around,* etc.) *colloq.* move casually or aimlessly. □□ **tootler** *n.*

■ **1** pipe, skirl, whistle. **2** see STROLL *v.*

tootsy /tootsee/ *n.* (also **tootsie**) (*pl.* **-ies**) *sl.* usu. *joc.* a foot. [E joc. dimin.: cf. FOOTSIE]

top[1] /top/ *n., adj., & v.* ● *n.* **1** the highest point or part (*the top of the house*). **2 a** the highest rank or place (*at the top of the school*). **b** a person occupying this (*was top in spelling*). **c** esp. *Brit.* the upper end or head (*the top of the table*). **3** the upper surface of a thing, esp. of the ground, a table, etc. **4** the upper part of a thing, esp.: **a** a blouse, sweater, etc., for wearing with a skirt or pants. **b** the upper part of a shoe or boot. **c** the stopper of a bottle. **d** the lid of a jar, saucepan, etc. **e** the creamy part of unhomogenized milk. **f** the folding roof of a car, carriage, etc. **g** the upper edge or edges of a page or pages in a book (*gilt top*). **5** the utmost degree; height (*called at the top of his voice*). **6** (in *pl.*) *colloq.* a person or thing of the best quality (*he's tops at swimming*). **7** (esp. in *pl.*) the leaves, etc., of a plant grown esp. for its root (*turnip tops*). **8** (usu. in *pl.*) a bundle of long wool fibers prepared for spinning. **9** *Naut.* a platform around the head of the lower mast, serving to extend the topmost rigging or carry guns. **10** (in *pl.*) esp. *Bridge* the two or three highest cards of a suit. **11** *Baseball* the first half of an inning. **12** *Brit.* = *top gear* (*climbed the hill in top*). **13** = TOPSPIN. ● *adj.* **1** highest in position (*the top shelf*). **2** highest in degree or importance (*at top speed; the top job*). ● *v.tr.* (**topped, topping**) **1** provide with a top, cap, etc. (*cake topped with icing*). **2** remove the top of (a plant, fruit, etc.), esp. to improve growth, prepare for cooking, etc. **3** be higher or better than; surpass; be at the top of (*topped the list*). **4** *Brit. sl.* **a** execute, esp. by hanging; kill. **b** (*refl.*) commit suicide. **5** reach the top of (a hill, etc.). **6 a** hit (a ball) above the center. **b** make (a hit or stroke) in this way. □ **come to the top** *colloq.* win distinction. **from top to toe** from head to foot; completely. **off the top of one's head** see HEAD. **on top 1** in a superior position; above. **2** on the upper part of the head (*bald on top*). **on top of 1** fully in command of. **2** in close proximity to. **3** in addition to. **4** above; over. **on top of the world** *colloq.* exuberant. **over the top 1** over the parapet of a trench (and into battle). **2** into a final or decisive state. **3** to excess; beyond reasonable limits (*that joke was over the top*). **top banana 1** *Theatr. sl.* a comedian who tops the bill of a show. **2** *sl.* a leader; the head of an organization, etc. **top boot** esp. *hist.* a boot with a high top, esp. of a different material or color. **top brass** esp. *Mil. colloq.* the highest ranking officers, heads of industries, etc. **top copy** the uppermost typed copy (cf. *carbon copy*). **top dog** *colloq.* a victor or master. **top drawer 1** the uppermost drawer in a chest, etc. **2** *colloq.* high social position or origin. **top-drawer** *colloq.* of high social standing; of the highest level or quality. **top-dress** apply manure or fertilizer on the top of (soil) instead of plowing it in. **top dressing 1** this process. **2** manure so applied. **3** a superficial show. **top fruit** *Brit.* fruit grown on trees, not bushes. **top gear** esp. *Brit.* the highest gear in a motor vehicle or bicycle. **top-hamper** an encumbrance on top, esp. the upper sails and rigging of a ship. **top hat** a man's tall silk hat. **top-hole** *Brit. colloq.* first-rate. **top level** of the highest level of importance, prestige, etc. **top notch** *colloq.* first rate. **top off** (or **up**) **1** put an end or the finishing touch to (a thing). **2** fill up, esp. a container already partly full. **top out** put the highest stone on (a building). **top one's part** *Theatr.* act or discharge one's part to perfection. **top-sawyer 1** a sawyer in the upper position in a sawmill. **2** *Brit.* a person who holds a superior position; a distinguished person. **top secret** of the highest secrecy. **top ten** (or **twenty**, etc.) the first ten (or twenty, etc.) records, movies, etc., at a given time in terms of sales, popularity, etc. **top up 1 a** esp. *Brit.* complete (an amount or number). **b** fill up (a glass, fuel tank, or other partly full container). **2** top up something for (a person) (*may I top you up with coffee?*). **top-up** *n.* an addition; something that serves to top up (esp. a partly full glass). □□ **topmost** *adj.* [OE *topp*]

■ *n.* **1** summit, apex, peak, acme, crest, head, pinnacle, tip, vertex, zenith, meridian, crown, culmination, high point, height, apogee. **4 c, d** stopper, cork, bung; lid, cover, cap, covering. **6** (*tops*) see *high-class.* ● *adj.* **1** uppermost, topmost, highest. **2** greatest, highest, maximum, topmost; best, foremost, leading, preeminent, topping, eminent, first, first-rate, principal, prime, premier, finest, choicest; excellent, superior, superb, top-grade, top-level, supreme, peerless, unequaled, incomparable, topflight, *colloq.* crack, A1, top-drawer, top-notch, *Brit. colloq.* top-hole, *sl.* ace. ● *v.* **1** surmount, cover, cap, crown, tip; finish, complete, garnish. **2** trim, crop, lop *or* cut off, clip, prune, nip, pinch (back). **3** surpass, better, best, outstrip, exceed, outdo, excel, beat, cap, transcend. **5** scale, climb, ascend, surmount. □ **from top to toe** see THROUGH *adv.* **on top 1** above, overhead, on high, aloft; upstairs. **on top of 3** see *in addition to* (ADDITION). **4** see OVER *prep.* **1. on top of the world** ecstatic, delighted, elated, happy, exultant, exuberant, overjoyed, rapturous, *Brit.* over the moon, in seventh heaven; *colloq.* on cloud nine *or* seven. **top banana 2** see HEAD *n.* 6a. **top dog** see MASTER *n.* 1, VICTOR. **top-drawer** see *high-class.* **top-level** see IMPORTANT 2. **top-notch** see *first-rate adj.* **top off 1** (or **up**) see COMPLEMENT *v.* **1. top up 1 b** fill (up), refresh, refill, replenish, freshen (up). □□ **topmost** see TOP¹ *adj.* above, UPPERMOST *adj.* 1.

top² /top/ *n.* a wooden or metal toy, usu. conical, spherical, or pearshaped, spinning on a point when set in motion by hand, string, etc. [OE, of uncert. orig.]

topaz /tṓpaz/ *n.* **1** a transparent or translucent aluminum silicate mineral, usu. yellow, used as a gem. **2** any South American hummingbird of the genus *Topaza.* [ME f. OF *topace, topaze* f. L *topazus* f. Gk *topazos*]

topazolite /təpázəlīt/ *n.* a yellow or green kind of garnet. [TOPAZ + -LITE]

topcoat /tópkōt/ *n.* **1** an overcoat. **2** an outer coat of paint, etc.

tope¹ /tōp/ *v.intr.* drink alcohol to excess, esp. habitually. □□ **toper** *n.* [perh. f. obs. *top* quaff]

tope² /tōp/ *n. Ind.* a grove, esp. of mangoes. [Telugu *tōpu,* Tamil *tōppu*]

tope³ /tōp/ *n.* = STUPA. [Punjab *tōp* f. Prakrit & Pali *thūpo* f. Skr. STUPA]

tope⁴ /tōp/ *n.* a small shark, *Galeorhinus galeus.* [perh. f. Corn.]

topee /tṓpee/ *n.* (also **topi**) (pl. **topees** or **topis**) *Anglo-Ind.* a lightweight hat or helmet, often made of pith. [Hindi *topī*]

topgallant /topgálənt, təgálənt/ *n. Naut.* the mast, sail, yard, or rigging immediately above the topmast and topsail.

top-heavy /tóphévee/ *adj.* **1** disproportionately heavy at the top so as to be in danger of toppling. **2 a** (of an organization, business, etc.) having a disproportionately large number of people in senior administrative positions. **b** overcapitalized. **3** *colloq.* (of a woman) having a disproportionately large bust. □□ **top-heavily** *adv.* **top-heaviness** *n.*

Tophet /tófit, -fet/ *n. Bibl.* hell. [name of a place in the Valley of Hinnom near Jerusalem used for idolatrous worship and later for burning refuse: f. Heb. *tōpet*]

tophus /tófəs/ *n.* (pl. **tophi** /-fī/) **1** *Med.* a gouty deposit of crystalline uric acid and other substances at the surface of joints. **2** *Geol.* = TUFA. [L, name of loose porous stones]

topi var. of TOPEE.

topiary /tṓpee-eree/ *adj. & n.* ● *adj.* concerned with or formed by clipping shrubs, trees, etc., into ornamental shapes. ● *n.* (pl. **-ies**) **1** topiary art. **2** an example of this. □□ **topiarian** /-peeáireeən/ *adj.* **topiarist** *n.* [F *topiaire* f. L *topiarius* landscape gardener f. *topia opera* fancy gardening f. Gk *topia* pl. dimin. of *topos* place]

topic /tópik/ *n.* **1** a theme for a book, discourse, essay, sermon, etc. **2** the subject of a conversation or argument. [L *topica* f. Gk (*ta*) *topika* topics, as title of a treatise by Aristotle f. *topos* a place, a commonplace]

■ subject (matter), matter, issue, question, point, talking point, thesis, theme, text, keynote, field *or* area of study, field *or* area of inquiry.

topical /tópikəl/ *adj.* **1** dealing with the news, current affairs, etc. (*a topical song*). **2** dealing with a place; local. **3** *Med.* (of an ailment, medicine, etc.) affecting a part of the body. **4** of or concerning topics. □□ **topicality** /-kálitee/ *n.* **topically** *adv.*

■ **1** contemporary, current, up-to-date, timely. **3** local, localized.

topknot /tópnot/ *n.* a knot, tuft, crest, or bow worn or growing on the head.

topless /tóplis/ *adj.* **1** without or seeming to be without a top. **2 a** (of clothes) having no upper part. **b** (of a person) wearing such clothes; barebreasted. **c** (of a place, esp. a beach, bar, etc.) where women go topless. □□ **toplessness** *n.*

toplofty /tóplawftee, -lóf-/ *adj. colloq.* haughty.

topman /tópmən/ *n.* (pl. **-men**) *Naut.* a man doing duty in a top.

topmast /tópmast/ *n. Naut.* the mast next above the lower mast.

topography /təpógrəfee/ *n.* **1 a** a detailed description, representation on a map, etc., of the natural and artificial features of a town, district, etc. **b** such features. **2** *Anat.* the mapping of the surface of the body with reference to the parts beneath. □□ **topographer** *n.* **topographic** /tópəgráfik/ *adj.* **topographical** *adj.* **topographically** *adv.* [ME f. LL *topographia* f. Gk f. *topos* place]

topoi pl. of TOPOS.

topology /təpóləjee/ *n. Math.* the study of geometrical properties and spatial relations unaffected by the continuous change of shape or size of figures. □□ **topological** /tópəlójikəl/ *adj.* **topologically** *adv.* **topologist** *n.* [G *Topologie* f. Gk *topos* place]

toponym /tópənim/ *n.* **1** a place-name. **2** a descriptive place-name, usu. derived from a topographical feature of the place. [TOPONYMY]

toponymy /təpónimee/ *n.* the study of the place-names of a region. □□ **toponymic** /tópənímik/ *adj.* [Gk *topos* place + *onoma* name]

topos /tópōs, -pos/ *n.* (pl. **topoi** /-poy/) a stock theme in literature, etc. [Gk, = commonplace]

/.../ **pronunciation**	● **part of speech**
□ **phrases, idioms, and compounds**	
□□ **derivatives**	■ **synonym section**
cross-references appear in SMALL CAPITALS or *italics*	

topper /tópər/ *n.* **1** a thing that tops. **2** *colloq.* = *top hat* (see TOP¹). **3** *Brit. colloq.* a good fellow; a good sort.

topping /tóping/ *adj. & n.* ● *adj.* **1** preeminent in position, rank, etc. **2** *Brit. archaic sl.* excellent. ● *n.* anything that tops something else, esp. icing, etc., on a cake.

topple /tópəl/ *v.intr. & tr.* (usu. foll. by *over, down*) **1 a** fall or cause to fall as if top-heavy. **b** fall or cause to fall from power. **2** totter or cause to totter and fall. [TOP¹ + -LE⁴]
■ **1 a** fall (over *or* down), drop, collapse, founder, overbalance, keel over, tumble down; upset, upend, knock down *or* over, fell, capsize. **b** bring *or* throw down, overthrow, defeat, overcome, overturn, subvert, unseat, oust, *literary* vanquish. **2** see TOTTER *v.*

topsail /tópsayl, -səl/ *n.* a square sail next above the lowest fore-and-aft sail on a gaff.

topside /tópsid/ *n.* **1** the side of a ship above the waterline. **2** *Brit.* the outer side of a round of beef.

topsoil /tópsoyl/ *n.* the top layer of soil (opp. SUBSOIL).

topspin /tópspin/ *n.* a fast forward spinning motion imparted to a ball in tennis, etc., by hitting it forward and upward.

topsy-turvy /tópseetérvee/ *adv., adj., & n.* ● *adv. & adj.* **1** upside down. **2** in utter confusion. ● *n.* utter confusion. □□ **topsy-turvily** *adv.* **topsy-turviness** *n.* [app. f. TOP¹ + obs. *terve* overturn]
■ *adj.* **1** upside down, wrong side up, head over heels, inverted, reversed, backward, vice versa. **2** chaotic, muddled, jumbled, disorderly, disordered, disorganized, confused, mixed-up, messy, untidy, in a muddle, higgledy-piggledy, *colloq.* every which way.

toque /tōk/ *n.* **1** a woman's small brimless hat. **2** *hist.* a small cap or bonnet for a man or woman. [F, app. = It. *tocca*, Sp. *toca*, of unkn. orig.]

toquilla /təkée'yə/ *n.* **1** a palmlike tree, *Carludovica palmata*, native to S. America. **2** a fiber produced from the leaves of this. [Sp., = small gauze headdress, dimin. of *toca* toque]

tor /tor/ *n.* a hill or rocky peak. [OE *torr*: cf. Gael. *tòrr* bulging hill]

Torah /tőrə, táwrə, tōráə/ *n.* **1** (usu. prec. by *the*) **a** the Pentateuch. **b** a scroll containing this. **2** the will of God as revealed in Mosaic law. [Heb. *tōrāh* instruction]

torc var. of TORQUE 1.

torch /tawrch/ *n. & v.* ● *n.* **1 a** a piece of wood, cloth, etc., soaked in tallow and lighted for illumination. **b** any similar lamp, e.g., an oil lamp on a pole. **2** a source of heat, illumination, or enlightenment (*bore aloft the torch of freedom*). **3** = BLOWTORCH. **4** *sl.* an arsonist. **5** (also **electric torch**) *Brit.* = FLASHLIGHT 2. ● *v.tr. sl.* set alight with or as with a torch. □ **carry a torch for** suffer from unrequited love for. **put to the torch** destroy by burning. **torch-race** *Gk Antiq.* a festival performance of runners handing lighted torches to others in relays. **torch singer** a woman who sings torch songs. **torch song** a popular song of unrequited love. [ME f. OF *torche* f. L *torqua* f. *torquēre* twist]
■ *n.* **1** flambeau, lamp, light, *hist.* link, *poet.* brand. **5** flashlight.

torchère /tawrsháir/ *n.* **1** a tall stand with a small table for a candlestick, etc. **2** a tall floor lamp giving indirect light. [F (as TORCH)]

torchlight /táwrchlīt/ *n.* the light of a torch or torches.

torchon /táwrshon/ *n.* (in full **torchon lace**) coarse bobbin lace with geometrical designs. [F, = duster, dishcloth f. *torcher* wipe]

tore¹ *past* of TEAR¹.

tore² /tawr/ *n.* = TORUS 1, 4. [F f. L *torus*: see TORUS]

toreador /táwreeədor/ *n.* a bullfighter, esp. on horseback. □ **toreador pants** close-fitting calf-length women's slacks. [Sp. f. *torear* fight bulls f. *toro* bull f. L *taurus*]

torero /tawráirō/ *n.* (*pl.* **-os**) a bullfighter. [Sp. f. *toro*: see TOREADOR]

toreutic /tərőōtik/ *adj. & n.* ● *adj.* of or concerning the chasing, carving, and embossing of esp. metal. ● *n.* (in *pl.*) the art or practice of this. [Gk *toreutikos* f. *toreuō* work in relief]

tori *pl.* of TORUS.

toric /táwrik/ *adj. Geom.* having the form of a torus or part of a torus.

torii /táwree-ee/ *n.* (*pl.* same) the gateway of a Shinto shrine, with two uprights and two crosspieces. [Jap.]

torment *n. & v.* ● *n.* /táwrment/ **1** severe physical or mental suffering (*was in torment*). **2** a cause of this. **3** *archaic* **a** torture. **b** an instrument of torture. ● *v.tr.* /tawrmént/ **1** subject to torment (*tormented with worry*). **2** tease or worry excessively (*enjoyed tormenting the teacher*). □□ **tormentedly** *adv.* **tormentingly** *adv.* **tormentor** *n.* [ME f. OF *torment, tormenter* f. L *tormentum* missile engine f. *torquēre* to twist]
■ *n.* **1** agony, wretchedness, anguish, distress, misery, pain, painfulness, torture, suffering, hell, *archaic or literary* woe. **2** worry, vexation, annoyance, harassment, ordeal, persecution, nuisance, bane, irritation, bother, affliction, curse, plague, scourge, torture, *colloq.* needling. ● *v.* **1** torture, abuse, maltreat, mistreat, molest, distress, agonize, excruciate, crucify, harrow, rack, pain. **2** worry, trouble, plague, annoy, bedevil, vex, harry, badger, hector, harass, pester, nag, persecute, victimize, bully, nettle, irk, irritate, bother, torture, afflict, chivy; tease, taunt, bait, chaff, *colloq.* needle, *sl.* rag. □□ **tormentor** see *oppressor* (OPPRESS).

tormentil /táwrməntil/ *n.* a low-growing plant, *Potentilla erecta*, with bright yellow flowers and a highly astringent rootstock used in medicine. [ME f. OF *tormentille* f. med.L *tormentilla*, of unkn. orig.]

torn *past part.* of TEAR¹.

tornado /tawrnáydō/ *n.* (*pl.* **-oes**) **1** a violent storm of small extent with whirling winds, esp.: **a** over a narrow path often accompanied by a funnel-shaped cloud. **b** in West Africa at the beginning and end of the rainy season. **2** an outburst or volley of cheers, hisses, missiles, etc. □□ **tornadic** /-nádik/ *adj.* [app. assim. of Sp. *tronada* thunderstorm (f. *tronar* to thunder) to Sp. *tornar* to turn]

toroid /táwroyd/ *n.* a figure of toroidal shape.

toroidal /tawróyd'l/ *adj. Geom.* of or resembling a torus. □□ **toroidally** *adv.*

torose /táwrōs/ *adj.* **1** *Bot.* (of plants, esp. their stalks) cylindrical with bulges at intervals. **2** *Zool.* knobby; bulging. [L *torosus* f. *torus*: see TORUS]

torpedo /tawrpéedō/ *n. & v.* ● *n.* (*pl.* **-oes**) **1 a** a cigar-shaped self-propelled underwater missile that explodes on impact with a ship. **b** a similar device dropped from an aircraft. **2** *Zool.* an electric ray. **3** a type of explosive device or firework. ● *v.tr.* (**-oes, -oed**) **1** destroy or attack with a torpedo. **2** make (a policy, institution, plan, etc.) ineffective or inoperative; destroy. □ **torpedo boat** a small fast lightly armed warship for carrying or discharging torpedoes. **torpedo net** (or **netting**) netting of steel wire hung around a ship to intercept torpedoes. **torpedo tube** a tube from which torpedoes are fired. □□ **torpedolike** *adj.* [L, = numbness, electric ray f. *torpēre* be numb]

torpefy /táwrpifī/ *v.tr.* (**-ies, -ied**) make numb or torpid. [L *torpefacere* f. *torpēre* be numb]

torpid /táwrpid/ *adj.* **1** sluggish; inactive; dull; apathetic. **2** numb. **3** (of a hibernating animal) dormant. □□ **torpidity** /-píditee/ *n.* **torpidly** *adv.* **torpidness** *n.* [L *torpidus* (as TORPOR)]
■ **1** sluggish, slow, slow-moving, slow-paced, tortoise-like, lethargic, apathetic, indolent, passive, slothful, dull, stupefied, sleepy, somnolent, inactive, inert, languid, languorous, phlegmatic, spiritless, lifeless, listless, fainéant, lackadaisical, indifferent, uncaring, unconcerned, insouciant. **2** see INSENSIBLE 1. **3** see DORMANT 1. □□ **torpidity, torpidness** see TORPOR.

torpor /táwrpər/ *n.* torpidity. □□ **torporific** /-pərífik/ *adj.* [L f. *torpēre* be sluggish]
■ torpidity, torpidness, sluggishness, sloth, lethargy, apathy, indolence, passivity, slothfulness, dullness, stupefaction, drowsiness, sleepiness, somnolence, inactivity, inertia, inertness, languor, laziness, phlegm, lifelessness, listlessness, idleness, fainéance, accidie, indifference, unconcern.

torquate /táwrkwayt/ *adj. Zool.* (of an animal) with a ring of distinctive color or texture of hair or plumage round the neck. [L *torquatus* (as TORQUE)]

torque /tawrk/ n. **1** (also **torc**) hist. a necklace of twisted metal, esp. of the ancient Gauls and Britons. **2** Mech. the moment of a system of forces tending to cause rotation. □ **torque converter** a device to transmit the correct torque from the engine to the axle in a motor vehicle. [(sense 1 F f. L torques) f. L torquēre to twist]

torr /tawr/ n. (pl. same) a unit of pressure used in measuring partial vacuums, equal to 133.32 pascals. [E. Torricelli, It. physicist d. 1647]

torrefy /táwrifī, tór-/ v.tr. (-ies, -ied) **1** roast or dry (metallic ore, a drug, etc.). **2** parch or scorch with heat. □□ **torrefaction** /-fákshən/ n. [F torréfier f. L torrefacere f. torrēre scorch]

torrent /táwrənt, tór-/ n. **1** a rushing stream of water, lava, etc. **2** (usu. in pl.) a great downpour of rain (came down in torrents). **3** (usu. foll. by of) a violent or copious flow (uttered a torrent of abuse). □□ **torrential** /tərénshəl/ adj. **torrentially** /tərénshəlee/ adv. [F f. It. torrente f. L torrens -entis scorching, boiling, roaring f. torrēre scorch]

■ **1, 3** stream, rush, flood, deluge, effusion, gushing, outburst, outpouring, spate, inundation, flow, overflow, tide, cascade. **2** see DOWNPOUR. □□ **torrential** rushing, streaming, copious, profuse, teeming, relentless, violent; fierce, vehement, vociferous, ferocious.

Torricellian vacuum /táwrichéleeən/ n. a vacuum formed when mercury in a long tube closed at one end is inverted with the open end in a reservoir of mercury (the principle on which a barometer is made). [Torricelli: see TORR]

torrid /táwrid, tór-/ adj. **1 a** (of the weather) very hot and dry. **b** (of land, etc.) parched by such weather. **2** (of language or actions) emotionally charged; passionate; intense. □ **torrid zone** the central belt of the earth between the Tropics of Cancer and Capricorn. □□ **torridity** /-ríditee/ n. **torridly** adv. **torridness** n. [F torride or L torridus f. torrēre parch]

■ **1 a** hot, fiery, sultry, stifling, sweltering, sizzling, roasting, blazing, burning, baking, cooking, boiling, blistering, scorching, parching, broiling; tropical. **b** scorched, parched, arid, dry, hot. **2** fervent, fervid, passionate, intense, ardent, inflamed, impassioned, lustful, amorous, erotic, sexy, hot. □□ **torridity**, **torridness** see HEAT n. 1a, b.

torse /tawrs/ n. Heraldry a wreath. [obs. F torse, torce wreath ult. f. L torta fem. past part. (as TORT)]

torsel var. of TASSEL².

torsion /táwrshən/ n. **1** twisting, esp. of one end of a body while the other is held fixed. **2** Math. the extent to which a curve departs from being planar. **3** Bot. the state of being twisted into a spiral. **4** Med. the twisting of the cut end of an artery after surgery, etc., to impede bleeding. □ **torsion balance** an instrument for measuring very weak forces by their effect upon a system of fine twisted wire. **torsion bar** a bar forming part of a vehicle suspension, twisting in response to the motion of the wheels, and absorbing their vertical movement. **torsion pendulum** a pendulum working by rotation rather than by swinging. □□ **torsional** adj. **torsionally** adv. **torsionless** adj. [ME f. OF f. LL torsio -onis f. L tortio (as TORT)]

torsk /tawrsk/ n. a fish of the cod family, Brosmius brosme, abundant in northern waters and often dried for food. [Norw. to(r)sk f. ON tho(r)skr prob. rel. to thurr dry]

torso /táwrsō/ n. (pl. -os or -i) **1** the trunk of the human body. **2** a statue of a human consisting of the trunk alone, without head or limbs. **3** an unfinished or mutilated work (esp. of art, literature, etc.). [It., = stalk, stump, torso, f. L thyrsus]

tort /tawrt/ n. Law a breach of duty (other than under contract) leading to liability for damages. [ME f. OF f. med.L tortum wrong, neut. past part. of L torquēre tort- twist]

torte /táwrt/ n. (pl. **torten** /táwrt'n/ or **tortes**) an elaborate sweet cake. [G]

tortfeasor /táwrtfeezər/ n. Law a person guilty of tort. [OF tort-fesor, tort-faiseur, etc. f. tort wrong, -fesor, faiseur doer]

torticollis /tawrtikólis/ n. Med. a rheumatic, etc., disease of the muscles of the neck, causing twisting and stiffness. [mod.L f. L tortus crooked + collum neck]

tortilla /tawrtéeyə/ n. a thin flat orig. Mexican corn or wheat bread eaten hot or cold with or without a filling. [Sp. dimin. of torta cake f. LL]

tortious /táwrshəs/ adj. Law constituting a tort; wrongful. □□ **tortiously** adv. [AF torcious f. torcion extortion f. LL tortio torture: see TORSION]

tortoise /táwrtəs/ n. **1** any slow-moving, esp. land reptile of the family Testudinidae, encased in a scaly or leathery domed shell, and having a retractile head and elephantine legs. **2** Rom. Antiq. = TESTUDO. □□ **tortoiselike** adj. & adv. [ME tortuce, OF tortue, f. med.L tortuca, of uncert. orig.]

tortoiseshell /táwrtəs-shel/ n. & adj. ● n. **1** the yellowish brown mottled or clouded outer shell of some turtles, used for decorative combs, jewelry, etc. **2 a** = tortoiseshell cat. **b** = tortoiseshell butterfly. ● adj. having the coloring or appearance of tortoiseshell. □ **tortoiseshell butterfly** any of various butterflies, esp. of the genus Nymphalis, with wings mottled like tortoiseshell. **tortoiseshell cat** a domestic cat with markings resembling tortoiseshell.

tortrix /táwrtriks/ n. (also **tortricid**) any moth of the family Tortricidae, esp. Tortrix viridana, the larvae of which live inside rolled leaves. [mod.L, fem. of L tortor twister: see TORT]

tortuous /táwrchōōəs/ adj. **1** full of twists and turns (followed a tortuous route). **2** devious; circuitous; crooked (has a tortuous mind). □□ **tortuosity** /-ósitee/ n. (pl. -ies). **tortuously** adv. **tortuousness** n. [ME f. OF f. L tortuosus f. tortus a twist (as TORT)]

■ **1** twisted, twisting, winding, wandering, serpentine, meandering, turning, crooked, sinuous, bent, curled, curling, curving, curved, curvy, curviform, curvilinear, flexuous, anfractuous, convoluted, involuted, zigzag, mazelike, mazy, labyrinthine. **2** roundabout, indirect, devious, tricky, intricate, involved, involuted, unstraightforward, complicated, ambiguous, circuitous, convoluted, warped, crooked, tricky, misleading, deceptive. □□ **tortuosity** see MEANDER n.

torture /táwrchər/ n. & v. ● n. **1** the infliction of severe bodily pain, esp. as a punishment or a means of persuasion. **2** severe physical or mental suffering (the torture of defeat). ● v.tr. **1** subject to torture (tortured by guilt). **2** force out of a natural position or state; deform; pervert. □□ **torturable** adj. **torturer** n. **torturous** adj. **torturously** adv. [F f. LL tortura twisting (as TORT)]

■ n. **1** see PERSECUTION. **2** see TORMENT n. 1. ● v. **1** see PERSECUTE, TORMENT v. 2 see DISTORT.

torula /táwryələ, -ələ, tór-/ n. (pl. **torulae** /-lee/) **1** a yeast, Candida utilis, used medicinally as a food additive. **2** any yeast-like fungus of the genus Torula, growing on dead vegetation. [mod.L, dimin. of torus: see TORUS]

torus /táwrəs/ n. (pl. **tori** /-rī/) **1** Archit. a large convex molding, esp. as the lowest part of the base of a column. **2** Bot. the receptacle of a flower. **3** Anat. a smooth ridge of bone or muscle. **4** Geom. a surface or solid formed by rotating a closed curve, esp. a circle, about a line in its plane but not intersecting it. [L, = swelling, bulge, cushion, etc.]

Tory /táwree/ n. & adj. ● n. (pl. -ies) **1** esp. Brit. colloq. = CONSERVATIVE n. 2. **2** Brit. hist. a member of the party that opposed the exclusion of James II and later supported the established religious and political order and gave rise to the Conservative party (opp. WHIG). **3** a colonist loyal to the English during the American Revolution. ● adj. colloq. = CONSERVATIVE adj. 3. □□ **Toryism** n. [orig. = Irish outlaw, prob. f. Ir. f. tóir pursue]

tosh /tosh/ n. esp. Brit. colloq. rubbish; nonsense. [19th c.: orig. unkn.]

■ see RUBBISH n. 3.

/.../ **pronunciation**   ● **part of speech**
□ **phrases, idioms, and compounds**
□□ **derivatives**   ■ **synonym section**
cross-references appear in SMALL CAPITALS or italics

toss /taws, tos/ *v. & n.* ● *v.* **1** *tr.* throw up (a ball, etc.) esp. with the hand. **2** *tr. & intr.* roll about, throw, or be thrown, restlessly or from side to side (*the ship tossed on the ocean; was tossing and turning all night; tossed her head angrily*). **3** *tr.* (usu. foll. by *to, away, aside, out,* etc.) throw (a thing) lightly or carelessly (*tossed the letter away*). **4** *tr.* **a** (of a coin) into the air to decide a choice, etc., by the side on which it lands. **b** (also *absol.*; often foll. by *for*) settle a question or dispute with (a person) in this way (*tossed him for the armchair; tossed for it*). **5** *tr.* **a** (of a ball, etc.) throw (a person, etc.) up with the horns. **b** (of a horse, etc.) throw (a rider) off its back. **6** *tr.* coat (food) with dressing, etc., by mixing or shaking. **7** *tr.* bandy about in debate; discuss (*tossed the question back and forth*). ● *n.* **1** the act or an instance of tossing (a coin, the head, etc.). **2** a fall, esp. from a horse. □ **tossing the caber** the Scottish sport of throwing a tree trunk. **toss oars** *Brit.* raise oars to an upright position in salute. **toss off 1** drink off at one swallow. **2** dispatch (work) rapidly or without effort (*tossed off an omelette*). **3** *Brit. coarse sl.* masturbate. **toss up** toss a coin to decide a choice, etc. **toss-up** *n.* **1** a doubtful matter; a close thing (*it's a toss-up whether he wins*). **2** the tossing of a coin. □□ **tosser** *n.* [16th c.: orig. unkn.]
  ■ *v.* **1, 5** throw, cast, lob, pitch, fling, hurl, heave, shy, launch, send, let fly, propel, catapult, sling, bowl, *colloq.* chuck. **2** pitch, yaw, roll, welter, lurch, bob, undulate, plunge; shake (up), jerk, stir (up), agitate, fling, throw, jiggle, tumble, joggle; wave, lash; writhe, wriggle, squirm, toss and turn, thrash. **4 a** flip, spin, flick. ● *n.* **1** throw, lob, pitch, heave, shy, fling, hurl, launch. □ **toss off 1** see DRINK *v.* 1.

tostada /tōstaadə/ *n.* a crisp fried tortilla, often topped with meat, cheese, etc. [Mex. Sp.]

tot¹ /tot/ *n.* **1** a small child (*a tiny tot*). **2** esp. *Brit.* a dram of liquor. [18th c., of dial. orig.]
  ■ **1** child, toddler, infant, baby. **2** see NIP² 1.

tot² /tot/ *v. & n.* esp. *Brit.* ● *v.* (**totted, totting**) **1** *tr.* (usu. foll. by *up*) add (numbers, etc.). **2** *intr.* (foll. by *up*) (of items) mount up. ● *n. Brit. archaic* a set of figures to be added. □ **totting-up 1** the adding of separate items. **2** *Brit.* the adding of convictions for driving offenses to cause disqualification. **tot up to** amount to. [abbr. of TOTAL or of L *totum* the whole]

tot³ /tot/ *v. & n. Brit. sl.* ● *v.intr.* (**totted, totting**) collect salable items from refuse as an occupation. ● *n.* an article collected from refuse. [19th c.: orig. unkn.]

total /tốt'l/ *adj., n., & v.* ● *adj.* **1** complete; comprising the whole (*the total number of people*). **2** absolute; unqualified (*in total ignorance; total abstinence*). ● *n.* a total number or amount. ● *v.* (**totaled, totaling** or **totalled, totalling**) **1** *tr.* **a** amount in number to (*they totaled 131*). **b** find the total of (things, a set of numbers, etc.). **2** *intr.* (foll. by *to, up to*) amount to; mount up to. **3** *tr. sl.* wreck completely; demolish. □ **total abstinence** abstaining completely from alcohol. **total eclipse** an eclipse in which the whole disk (of the sun, moon, etc.) is obscured. **total internal reflection** reflection without refraction of a light ray meeting the interface between two media at more than a certain critical angle to the normal. **total recall** the ability to remember every detail of one's experience clearly. **total war** a war in which all available weapons and resources are employed. □□ **totally** *adv.* [ME f. OF f. med.L *totalis* f. *totus* entire]
  ■ *adj.* **1** whole, entire, complete, full, gross, overall, comprehensive. **2** complete, unalloyed, unmitigated, unqualified, unconditional, utter, out-and-out, thorough, thoroughgoing, perfect, outright, downright, all-out, absolute, *Brit. colloq.* blithering. ● *n.* sum (total), totality, aggregate, whole, amount, total number. ● *v.* **1 b** add (up), tot up, sum (up), reckon, compute. **2** (*total up to*) amount to, add up to, come to, mount up to, tot up to, make. **3** see TRASH *v.* 1. □□ **totally** completely, utterly, entirely, fully, unqualifiedly, unconditionally, perfectly, absolutely, thoroughly, wholly, consummately.

totalitarian /tōtálitáireeən/ *adj. & n.* ● *adj.* of or relating to a centralized dictatorial form of government requiring complete subservience to the state. ● *n.* a person advocating such a system. □□ **totalitarianism** *n.*
  ■ *adj.* absolute, absolutist, arbitrary, authoritarian, autocratic, dictatorial, fascist(ic), undemocratic, illiberal, monolithic, Nazi, oppressive, despotic, tyrannical. ● *n.* absolutist, authoritarian, fascist, Nazi. □□ **totalitarianism** see DESPOTISM.

totality /tōtálitee/ *n.* **1** the complete amount or sum. **2** *Astron.* the time during which an eclipse is total.
  ■ **1** total, aggregate, sum (total), whole, entirety, beginning and end, alpha and omega, be-all and end-all.

totalizator /tốt'lizaytər/ *n.* (also **totalisator**) = PARI-MUTUEL 2.

totalize /tốt'līz/ *v.tr.* collect into a total; find the total of. □□ **totalization** /-izáyshən/ *n.*

totalizer /tốt'lizər/ *n.* = TOTALIZATOR.

tote¹ /tōt/ *n. sl.* **1** a totalizator. **2** a lottery. [abbr.]

tote² /tōt/ *v.tr. colloq.* carry or convey, esp. a heavy load (*toting a gun*). □ **tote bag** a large open-topped bag for shopping, etc. **tote box** a small container for tools, etc. □□ **toter** *n.* (also in *comb.*). [17th-c. US, prob. of dial. orig.]
  ■ see CARRY *v.* 1, 2.

totem /tốtəm/ *n.* **1** a natural object, esp. an animal, adopted by Native American people as an emblem of a clan or an individual. **2** an image of this. □ **totem pole 1** a pole on which totems are carved or hung. **2** a hierarchy. □□ **totemic** /-témik/ *adj.* **totemism** *n.* **totemist** *n.* **totemistic** /-təmístik/ *adj.* [Algonquian]

tother /túthər/ *adj. & pron.* (also **t'other**) *dial.* or *joc.* the other. ● *tell tother from which Brit. joc.* tell one from the other. [ME *the tother*, for earlier *thet other* 'that other'; now understood as = *the other*]

totter /tótər/ *v. & n.* ● *v.intr.* **1** stand or walk unsteadily or feebly (*tottered out of the bar*). **2 a** (of a building, etc.) shake or rock as if about to collapse. **b** (of a system of government, etc.) be about to fall. ● *n.* an unsteady or shaky movement or gait. □□ **totterer** *n.* **tottery** *adj.* [ME f. MDu. *touteren* to swing]
  ■ *v.* dodder, falter, stagger, stumble, shiver; waver, topple, tremble, teeter, sway, rock, reel, wobble, quiver, shake, quake.

toucan /tōokan/ *n.* any tropical American fruit-eating bird of the family Ramphastidae, with an immense beak and brightly colored plumage. [Tupi *tucana*, Guarani *tucã*]

touch /tuch/ *v. & n.* ● *v.* **1** *tr.* come into or be in physical contact with (another thing) at one or more points. **2** *tr.* (often foll. by *with*) bring the hand, etc., into contact with (*touched her arm*). **3 a** *intr.* (of two things, etc.) be in or come into contact with one another (*the balls were touching*). **b** *tr.* bring (two things) into mutual contact (*they touched hands*). **4** *tr.* rouse tender or painful feelings in (*was touched by his appeal*). **5** *tr.* strike lightly (*just touched the wall with the back bumper*). **6** *tr.* (usu. with *neg.*) **a** disturb or harm (*don't touch my things*). **b** have any dealings with (*won't touch bricklaying*). **c** consume; use up; make use of (*dare not touch alcohol; has not touched her breakfast; need not touch your savings*). **d** cope with; affect; manage (*soap won't touch this dirt*). **7** *tr.* **a** deal with (a subject) lightly or in passing (*touched the matter of their expenses*). **b** concern (*it touches you closely*). **8** *tr.* **a** reach or rise as far as, esp. momentarily (*the thermometer touched 90°*). **b** (usu. with *neg.*) approach in excellence, etc. (*can't touch him for style*). **9** *tr.* affect slightly; modify (*pity touched with fear*). **10** *tr.* (as **touched** *adj.*) slightly mad. **11** *tr.* esp. *Art* mark lightly; put in (features, etc.) with a brush, pencil, etc. **12** *tr.* **a** strike (the keys, strings, etc., of a musical instrument). **b** strike the keys or strings of (a piano, etc.). **13** *tr.* (usu. foll. by *for*) *sl.* ask for and get money, etc., from (a person) as a loan or gift (*touched him for $5*). **14** *tr.* injure slightly (*blossom touched by frost*). **15** *tr. Geom.* be tangent to (a curve). ● *n.* **1** the act or an instance of touching, esp. with the body or hand (*felt a touch on my arm*). **2 a** the faculty of perception through physical contact, esp. with the fingers (*has no sense of touch in her right hand*). **b** the qualities of an object, etc., as perceived in this way (*the soft touch of silk*). **3** a small amount; a slight trace (*a touch of salt*; *a touch of irony*). **4 a** a musician's manner of playing keys or strings. **b** the manner in which the keys or strings respond to touch. **c** an artist's or writer's style of workmanship, writing, etc. (*has a delicate touch*). **5** a distinguishing quality or trait (*a professional touch*). **6** (esp. in *pl.*) **a** a light stroke with a pen, pencil, etc. **b** a slight alteration or improvement (*speech needs a few touches*). **7** = TAG². **8** (prec. by *a*) slightly (*is a touch too arrogant*). **9** *sl.* **a** the act of asking for and getting money, etc., from a person. **b** a person from whom money, etc., is so obtained. **10** *Soccer & Rugby* the part of the field outside the side limits. **11** *archaic* a test with or as if with a touchstone (*put it to the touch*). □ **at a touch** if touched, however lightly (*opened at a touch*). **easy touch** *sl.* a person who readily parts with money. **finishing touch** (or **touches**) the final details completing and enhancing a piece of work, etc. **get** (or **put**) **in** (or **into**) **touch with** come or cause to come into communication with; contact. **in touch** (often foll. by *with*) **1** in communication (*we're still in touch after all these years*). **2** up to date, esp. regarding news, etc. (*keeps in touch with events*). **3** aware; conscious; empathetic (*not in touch with her own feelings*). **keep in touch** (often foll. by *with*) **1** remain informed (*kept in touch with the latest developments*). **2** continue correspondence, a friendship, etc. **lose touch** (often foll. by *with*) **1** cease to be informed. **2** cease to correspond with or be in contact with another person. **lose one's touch** not show one's customary skill. **the Nelson touch** *Brit.* a masterly or sympathetic approach to a problem (from Horatio Nelson, Admiral at Trafalgar). **out of touch** (often foll. by *with*) **1** not in correspondence. **2** not up to date or modern. **3** lacking in awareness or sympathy (*out of touch with his son's beliefs*). **personal touch** a characteristic or individual approach to a situation. **soft touch** = *easy touch* (see TOUCH). **to the touch** when touched (*was cold to the touch*). **touch and go** uncertain regarding a result; risky (*it was touch and go whether we'd catch the train*). **touch-and-go** an airplane landing and immediate takeoff done esp. as practice. **touch at** (of a ship) call at (a port, etc.). **touch base** (**with**) make contact with; briefly communicate with. **touch bottom 1** reach the bottom of water with one's feet. **2** be at the lowest or worst point. **3** be in possession of the full facts. **touch down** (of an aircraft or spacecraft) make contact with the ground in landing. **touch football** football with touching in place of tackling. **touch-in-goal** *Soccer* each of the four corners enclosed by continuations of the touchlines and goal lines. **touch-me-not** any of various plants of the genus *Impatiens*, with ripe seed capsules bursting open when touched. **touch-needle** a needle of gold or silver alloy of known composition used as a standard in testing other alloys on a touchstone. **touch off 1** represent exactly (in a portrait, etc.). **2** explode by touching with a match, etc. **3** initiate (a process) suddenly (*touched off a run on the peso*). **touch of nature 1** a natural trait. **2** *colloq.* an exhibition of human feeling with which others sympathize (from a misinterpretation of Shakesp. *Troilus and Cressida* III. iii. 169). **touch of the sun 1** a slight attack of sunstroke. **2** a little sunlight. **touch on** (or **upon**) **1** treat (a subject) briefly, refer to or mention casually. **2** verge on (*that touches on impudence*). **touch paper** paper impregnated with niter, for firing gunpowder, fireworks, etc. **touch-tone 1** of or relating to a tone dialing telephone system. **2** (**Touch-Tone**) *propr.* a telephone that produces tones when buttons are pushed. **touch the spot** = *hit the spot*. **touch-type** type without looking at the keys. **touch typing** this skill. **touch-typist** a person who touch-types. **touch up 1** give finishing touches to or retouch (a picture, writing, etc.). **2** *Brit. sl.* **a** caress so as to excite sexually. **b** sexually molest. **3** strike (a horse) lightly with a whip. **touch wood** esp. *Brit.* touch something wooden with the hand to avert bad luck. **would not touch with a bargepole** see BARGEPOLE. □□ **touchable** *adj.* **toucher** *n.* [ME f. OF *tochier*, *tuchier* (v.), *touche* (n.): prob. imit., imitating a knock]

■ *v.* **1** be in contact with, border, adjoin, meet, come into contact with, come up against, be (up) against, butt against, push *or* press *or* lean (up) against, brush *or* rub (up) against, abut. **2** put one's hand on, feel, handle; lay a hand *or* finger on; see also FONDLE. **3 a** be in contact, come *or* be together, meet. **b** bring into contact, place *or* put *or* bring together. **4** affect, impress, influence, disturb, move, stir, arouse, excite, impassion, stimulate, strike, *colloq.* get (to). **5** brush, graze, tap, knock. **6 a** lay a hand *or* finger on; disturb, harm, meddle with, have to do with, interfere with, tamper with; come near, approach. **b** have to do with, have dealings with, handle. **c** drink, eat, consume, partake of, take, taste, have to do with; have access to, access, use, employ, make use of, put to use, avail oneself of, get, take advantage of. **7 a** see *touch on* 1 below. **b** see CONCERN *v.* 1a. **8 a** reach, attain, rise to. **b** rival, match, equal, compare with, come up to, be on a par with, be a match for, be in the same league as *or* with, be in the same class as *or* with, be on an equal footing with, reach, come *or* get near *or* close to, hold a candle to, measure up to *or* against, *colloq.* stack up to. **10** (**touched**) see MAD *adj.* 1. **13** (*touch for*) see BORROW 1. ● *n.* **1** pat, tap, dab, blow, hit, stroke, brush, caress. **2 a** feel, feeling. **b** feeling, feel, texture. **3** dash, hint, intimation, suggestion, soupçon, bit, pinch, jot, spot, trace, tinge, taste, suspicion, smattering, coloring, smack, speck, dab, drop, whiff, odor, scent, smell. **4 a, c** approach, style, manner, technique, execution, method; feel, feeling, sensitivity; see also INSTINCT *n.* 2. **b** response, feel, responsiveness, feeling, movement, operation, performance level. **5** trade mark, characteristic, quality, feature, trait, influence, *archaic* signature. □ **easy touch** see MUG¹ *n.* 3. **get** (or **put**) **in** (or **into**) **touch with** see CONTACT *v.* **in touch 2** see INFORMED 1. **3** (*in touch with*) see SENSIBLE 4. **touch and go** see PRECARIOUS. **touch down** land, alight, come to earth. **touch off 2** detonate, spark (off), set alight, set off, ignite, light, fire, put a match to. **3** instigate, initiate, begin, start, set in motion, ignite, set off, trigger, provoke, foment, cause, give rise to. **touch on** (or **upon**) **1** touch, refer to, have reference to, pertain to, relate to, have a bearing on, regard, mention, allude to, speak *or* write of, tell of, bring up *or* in, raise, broach, deal with, cover. **2** verge on *or* upon, border on, approach, resemble. **touch up 1** retouch, patch up; edit, polish; beautify, enhance, titivate, renovate, restore, spruce up. **touch wood** keep one's fingers crossed, cross one's fingers, knock (on) wood. □□ **touchable** tangible, tactile, palpable.

touchback /túchbak/ *n. Football* a play in which the ball is downed behind the goal line after it has been caught there; the ball is put back in play at the 20-yard line of the team making the catch, who then take over on offense.

touchdown /túchdown/ *n.* **1** the act or an instance of an aircraft or spacecraft making contact with the ground during landing. **2** *Football* the act or an instance of scoring by crossing the goal line.

■ **1** see LANDING 1a, b.

touché /tōōsháy/ *int.* **1** the acknowledgment of a hit by a fencing opponent. **2** the acknowledgment of a justified accusation, a witticism, or a point made in reply to one's own. [F, past part. of *toucher* TOUCH]

touching /túching/ *adj. & prep.* ● *adj.* moving; pathetic (*a touching incident*; *touching confidence*). ● *prep.* concerning; about. □□ **touchingly** *adv.* **touchingness** *n.* [ME f. TOUCH: (prep.) f. OF *touchant* pres. part. (as TOUCH)]

■ *adj.* moving, stirring, emotional, tender, heartwarming, poignant, pathetic, soul-stirring, heartrending, heartbreaking, sad, pitiful, distressing, distressful. ● *prep.* see ABOUT *prep.* 1a, b, d.

/.../ **pronunciation**	● **part of speech**
□ **phrases, idioms, and compounds**	
□□ **derivatives**	■ **synonym section**
cross-references appear in SMALL CAPITALS or *italics*	

touchline /túchlin/ *n.* (in various sports) either of the lines marking the side boundaries of the field.

touchmark /túchmaark/ *n.* the maker's mark on pewter.

touchstone /túchstōn/ *n.* **1** a fine-grained dark schist or jasper used for testing alloys of gold, etc., by marking it with them and observing the color of the mark. **2** a standard or criterion.

■ **2** standard, yardstick, criterion, reference, benchmark, test, norm, measure.

touchwood /túchwŏŏd/ *n.* readily flammable wood, esp. when made soft by fungi, used as tinder.

touchy /túchee/ *adj.* (**touchier, touchiest**) **1** apt to take offense; overly sensitive. **2** not to be touched without danger; ticklish; risky; awkward. □□ **touchily** *adv.* **touchiness** *n.* [perh. alt. of TETCHY after TOUCH]

■ **1** (over)sensitive, supersensitive, hypersensitive, highstrung, highly strung, tense, thin-skinned, crabby, crabbed, testy, irascible, irritable, tetchy, prickly, edgy, temperamental, peevish, querulous, petulant, pettish, splenetic, captious, bad-tempered, short-tempered, hot-tempered, quick-tempered, crusty, cross, curmudgeonly, cantankerous, choleric, dyspeptic, waspish, bearish, snarling, snappish, snappy, argumentative, disputatious, contentious, *colloq.* grouchy, cranky. **2** critical, touch and go, sensitive, ticklish, risky, precarious, hazardous, chancy, unsure, uncertain, close, hairbreadth, dangerous, hair-raising, frightening, terrifying, nerve-racking, *archaic or joc.* parlous, *sl.* hairy; see also AWKWARD 4. □□ **touchiness** see SENSITIVITY.

tough /tuf/ *adj. & n.* ● *adj.* **1** hard to break, cut, tear, or chew; durable; strong. **2** (of a person) able to endure hardship; hardy. **3** unyielding; stubborn; difficult (*it was a tough job; a tough customer*). **4** *colloq.* **a** acting sternly; hard (*get tough with*). **b** (of circumstances, luck, etc.) severe; unpleasant; hard; unjust. **5** *colloq.* criminal or violent (*tough guys*). ● *n.* a tough person, esp. a gangster or criminal. □ **tough guy** *colloq.* **1** a hard unyielding person. **2** a violent aggressive person. **tough it out** *colloq.* endure or withstand difficult conditions. **tough-minded** realistic; not sentimental. **tough-mindedness** being tough-minded. □□ **toughen** *v.tr. & intr.* **toughener** *n.* **toughish** *adj.* **toughly** *adv.* **toughness** *n.* [OE *tōh*]

■ *adj.* **1** hard, firm, durable, long-lasting, wear-resistant, hard-wearing, serviceable, heavy-duty, substantial, strong, stout, rugged, sturdy, sound, well-built, solid, indestructible, unbreakable, resilient; stiff, leathery, inflexible, chewy, fibrous, cartilaginous, cartilaginoid, gristly, sinewy, ropy, wiry, stringy. **2** strong, stalwart, brawny, burly, beefy, muscular, powerful, virile, manly, sturdy, intrepid, stout, rough, vigorous, robust, strapping, athletic, hardy, *archaic or joc.* doughty. **3** difficult, demanding, exacting, hard, troublesome; laborious, arduous, taxing, strenuous; baffling, thorny, puzzling, perplexing, mystifying, tricky, knotty, irksome; stubborn, obstinate, obdurate, inflexible, refractory, intractable, adamant, resolute, unyielding. **4 a** hardened, inured, hard, harsh, severe, stern, strict, inflexible, adamant, unyielding, ungiving, rigid, unbending, uncompromising, unsentimental, unfeeling, unsympathetic, merciless, ruthless, callous, hard-boiled, uncaring, cold, cool, icy, stony, *colloq.* hard-nosed. **b** see SEVERE 1, 5. ● *n.* hooligan, bully(boy), rowdy, thug, troublemaker, rough, *colloq.* roughneck, bruiser, tough guy, toughie, *sl.* hood. □ **tough guy 2** see TOUGH *n.* above. **tough it out** see *stick it out* (STICK²). **tough-minded** see REALISTIC 2. □□ **toughen** see STRENGTHEN. **toughness** see STRENGTH 1.

toughie (also **toughy**) /túfee/ *n. colloq.* a tough person or problem.

toupee /tōōpáy/ *n.* a wig or artificial hairpiece to cover a bald spot. [F *toupet* hair tuft dimin. of OF *toup* tuft (as TOP¹)]

tour /tŏŏr/ *n. & v.* ● *n.* **1 a** a journey from place to place as a vacation. **b** an excursion, ramble, or walk (*made a tour of the yard*). **2 a** a period of duty on military or diplomatic

service. **b** the time to be spent at a particular post. **3** a series of performances, games, etc., at different places on a route through a country, etc. ● *v.* **1** *intr.* (usu. foll. by *through*) make a tour (*toured through Italy*). **2** *tr.* make a tour of (a country, etc.). □ **on tour** (esp. of a team, theater company, etc.) touring. **touring car** a car with room for passengers and much luggage. **tour operator** a travel agent specializing in package tours. [ME f. OF *to(u)r* f. L *tornus* f. Gk *tornos* lathe]

■ *n.* **1 a** journey, trip, excursion, outing, expedition, voyage, trek, jaunt, junket, *archaic or joc.* peregrination. **b** stroll, perambulation, ramble, walk, drive, ride, excursion, *Austral.* walkabout; esp. *Brit.* round, circuit, ambit. **2** spell, shift, stint, assignment, turn, stretch, *Mil.* period of service *or* enlistment. ● *v.* **1** journey, travel, voyage, trip, trek, sightsee, cruise; *colloq.* globetrot. **2** visit, see, sightsee, explore, go around, *colloq.* take in, do.

touraco var. of TURACO.

tour de force /tŏŏr də fáwrs/ *n.* a feat of strength or skill. [F]

■ see FEAT.

tourer /tŏŏrər/ *n.* a vehicle, esp. a car, for touring. [TOUR]

tourism /tŏŏrizəm/ *n.* the organization and operation of tours, esp. as a commercial enterprise.

■ tourist *or* leisure industry, travel trade; see also TRAVEL *n.* 1a.

tourist /tŏŏrist/ *n.* a person making a visit or tour as a vacation; a traveler. (often *attrib.*: *tourist accommodations*). □ **tourist class** the lowest class of passenger accommodations in a ship, aircraft, etc. □□ **touristic** *adj.* **touristically** *adv.*

■ traveler, voyager, visitor, sightseer, day-tripper, vacationer, vacationist, esp. *Brit.* holidaymaker, *Brit.* tripper, *colloq.* rubberneck, out-of-towner.

touristy /tŏŏristee/ *adj.* usu. *derog.* appealing to or visited by many tourists.

tourmaline /tŏŏrməlin, -leen/ *n.* a boron aluminum silicate mineral of various colors, possessing unusual electrical properties, and used in electrical and optical instruments and as a gemstone. [F f. Sinh. *toramalli* porcelain]

tournament /tŏŏrnəmənt, tár-/ *n.* **1** any contest of skill between a number of competitors, esp. played in heats or a series of games (*chess tournament; tennis tournament*). **2** (in the UK) a display of military exercises, etc. (*Royal Tournament*). **3** *hist.* **a** a pageant in which jousting with blunted weapons took place. **b** a meeting for jousting between single knights for a prize, etc. [ME f. OF *torneiement* f. *torneier* TOURNEY]

■ **1** tourney, competition, contest, championship, match, meeting, event, meet. **3** tilt, *hist.* joust.

tournedos /tŏŏrnədō/ *n.* (*pl.* same /-dōz/) a small round thick cut from a tenderloin of beef. [F]

tourney /tŏŏrnee, tár-/ *n. & v.* ● *n.* (*pl.* **-eys**) a tournament. ● *v.intr.* (**-eys, -eyed**) take part in a tournament. [ME f. OF *tornei* (n.), *torneier* (v.), ult. f. L *tornus* a turn]

■ *n.* see TOURNAMENT 1.

tourniquet /tŏŏrnikit, tŏŏr-/ *n.* a device for stopping the flow of blood through an artery by twisting a dowel, etc., in a ligature or bandage. [F prob. f. OF *tournicle* coat of mail, TUNICLE, infl. by *tourner* TURN]

tousle /tówzəl/ *v.tr.* **1** make (esp. the hair) untidy; rumple. **2** handle roughly or rudely. [frequent. of (now dial.) *touse*, ME f. OE rel. to OHG -*zuson*]

■ **1** dishevel, disorder, ruffle, disarrange, tangle (up), mess (up), rumple, disarray, *colloq.* muss (up).

tous-les-mois /tŏŏlaymwaá/ *n.* **1** food starch obtained from tubers of a canna, *Canna indica.* **2** this plant. [F, lit. = every month, prob. corrupt. of W.Ind. *toloman*]

tout /towt/ *v. & n.* ● *v.* **1** *intr.* (usu. foll. by *for*) solicit patronage persistently; pester customer s (*touting for business*). **2** *tr.* solicit the patronage of (a person) or for (a thing). **3** *intr.* **a** *Brit.* spy out the movements and condition of racehorses in training. **b** offer racing tips for a share of the resulting profit. ● *n.* a person employed in touting. □□ **touter**

n. [ME *tūte* look out = ME (now dial.) *toot* (OE *tōtian*) f. Gmc]

■ *v.* **2** (*tout* (*a thing*)) hawk, peddle, sell, promote, talk up, push, *colloq.* plug. ● *n.* barker, tipster, touter.

tout de suite /tŏŏt sweét/ *adv.* at once, immediately. [F]

■ see IMMEDIATELY *adv.* 1.

tovarich /təvaárish/ *n.* (also **tovarish**) (in esp. communist Russia) comrade (esp. as a form of address). [Russ. *tovarishch*]

tow[1] /tō/ *v.* & *n.* ● *v.tr.* **1** (of a motor vehicle, horse, or person controlling it) pull (a boat, another motor vehicle, a trailer, etc.) along by a rope, tow bar, etc. **2** pull (a person or thing) along behind one. ● *n.* the act or an instance of towing; the state of being towed. □ **have in** (or **on**) **tow 1** be towing. **2** be accompanied by and often in charge of (a person). **tow bar** a bar for towing, esp. a trailer or camper. **tow** (or **towing**) **net** a net used for dragging through water to collect specimens. □□ **towable** *adj.* **towage** /tóij/ *n.* [OE *togian* f. Gmc, rel. to TUG]

■ *v.* pull, drag, draw, haul, lug, trail, tug, trawl. ● *n.* pull, drag, haul, lug, tug, trawl.

tow[2] /tō/ *n.* **1** the coarse and broken part of flax or hemp prepared for spinning. **2** a loose bunch of rayon, etc., strands. □ **tow-colored** (of hair) very light. □□ **towy** /tóee/ *adj.* [ME f. MLG *touw* f. OS *tou*, rel. to ON *tó* wool: cf. TOOL]

toward /tawrd, təwáwrd, twawrd/ *prep.* & *adj.* (also **towards** /tawrdz, təwáwrdz, twawrdz/) ● *prep.* **1** in the direction of (*set out toward town*). **2** as regards; in relation to (*his attitude toward death*). **3** as a contribution to; for (*put this toward your expenses*). **4** near (*toward the end of our journey*). ● *adj.* *archaic* **1** about to take place; in process. **2** docile; apt. **3** promising; auspicious. □□ **towardness** *n.* (in sense of *adj.*). [OE *tōweard* (adj.) future (as TO, -WARD)]

■ *prep.* **1** toward, in the direction of, to; for, so as to approach *or* near, on the way *or* road to. **2** toward, as regards, in *or* with regard to, in relation to, concerning, about, regarding, with respect to. **3** toward, to, for, as a help to, supporting, promoting, assisting. **4** toward, near, nearing, close to, approaching, shortly before.

towel /tówəl/ *n.* & *v.* ● *n.* **1 a** a piece of absorbent cloth used for drying oneself or a thing after washing. **b** absorbent paper used for this. **c** a cloth used for drying plates, dishes, etc.; a dish towel. **2** *Brit.* = sanitary napkin. ● *v.* (**toweled, toweling** or **towelled, towelling**) **1** *tr.* (often *refl.*) wipe or dry with a towel. **2** *intr.* wipe or dry oneself with a towel. **3** *tr. sl.* thrash. □ **towel rack** (or **horse or rail**) a frame for hanging towels on. □□ **toweling** or **towelling** *n.* [ME f. OF *toail(l)e* f. Gmc]

tower /tówər/ *n.* & *v.* ● *n.* **1 a** a tall esp. square or circular structure, often part of a church, castle, etc. **b** a fortress, etc., comprising or including a tower. **c** a tall structure housing machinery, apparatus, operators, etc. (*cooling tower*; *control tower*). **2** a place of defense; a protection. ● *v.intr.* **1** (usu. foll. by *above, high*) reach or be high or above; be superior. **2** (of a bird) soar or hover. **3** (as **towering** *adj.*) **a** high, lofty (*towering intellect*). **b** violent (*towering rage*). □ **tower block** *Brit.* a tall building containing offices or apartments. **tower of strength** a person who gives strong and reliable support. □□ **towered** /tówərd/ *adj.* **towery** *adj.* [OE *torr*, & ME *tūr*, AF & OF *tur*, etc., f. L *turris* f. Gk]

■ *n.* **1 a** bell tower, campanile, minaret, pagoda, obelisk; belfry, turret, steeple, flèche. **b** fortress, citadel, stronghold, castle, fastness; prison, *archaic* dungeon, *hist.* keep. **2** see PROTECTION 1b, c. ● *v.* **1** loom, soar, rise, ascend, rear; (*tower above*) see OVERSHADOW 1. **2** soar, rise, hover. **3** (**towering**) **a** tall, high, soaring, outstanding, elevated, skyscraping, sky-high, *literary* lofty; great, impressive, imposing, huge, gigantic, mighty, supreme, superior, paramount, extraordinary, unmatched, unequaled, unrivaled, unparalleled, unsurpassed. **b** violent, fiery, burning, passionate, excessive, vehement, intense, consuming, mighty, overwhelming, unrestrained, immoderate, inordinate, intemperate, extreme, colossal, enormous.

towhead /tóhed/ *n.* **1** tow-colored or blond hair. **2** a person with such hair. □□ **towheaded** *adj.*

town /town/ *n.* **1 a** an urban area with a name, defined boundaries, and local government, being larger than a village and usu. not incorporated as a city. **b** any densely populated area, esp. as opposed to the country or suburbs. **c** the people of a town (*the whole town knows of it*). **2 a** *Brit.* London or the chief city or town in an area (*went up to town*). **b** the central business or shopping area in a neighborhood (*just going into town*). **3** the permanent residents of a university town as distinct from the members of the university (cf. GOWN). □ **go to town** *colloq.* act or work with energy or enthusiasm. **on the town** *colloq.* enjoying the entertainments, esp. the nightlife, of a town; celebrating. **town clerk** the officer of a town in charge of records, etc. **town council** (esp. in the UK) the elective governing body in a municipality. **town councilor** (esp. in the UK) an elected member of this. **town crier** see CRIER. **town hall** a building for the administration of local government, having public meeting rooms, etc. **town house 1** a town residence, esp. of a person with a house in the country. **2** a row house. **3** a house in a development. **4** *Brit.* a town hall. **town meeting** a meeting of the voters of a town for the transaction of public business. **town planning** the planning of the construction and growth of towns. □□ **townish** *adj.* **townless** *adj.* **townlet** *n.* **townward** *adj.* & *adv.* **townwards** *adv.* [OE *tūn* enclosure f. Gmc]

■ **1** community, townlet; municipality, city, metropolis, borough, *Austral.* & *NZ* township, *hist.* burgh, *Brit. sl.* big smoke. **2 b** central business district, town *or* city center, downtown.

townie /tównee/ *n.* (also *Brit.* **townee**) *colloq.* a person living in a town, esp. as opposed to a student, etc.

townscape /tównskayp/ *n.* **1** the visual appearance of a town or towns. **2** a picture of a town.

townsfolk /tównzfōk/ *n.* the inhabitants of a particular town or towns.

township /tównship/ *n.* **1** *S.Afr.* **a** an urban area formerly set aside for black residents. **b** a white urban area (esp. if new or about to be developed). **2** *US* & *Can.* **a** a division of a county in some states with some corporate powers. **b** a district six miles square in some states. **3** *Brit. hist.* **a** a community inhabiting a manor, parish, etc. **b** a manor or parish as a territorial division. **c** a small town or village forming part of a large parish. **4** *Austral.* & *NZ* a small town; a town site. [OE *tūnscipe* (as TOWN, -SHIP)]

townsman /tównzmən/ *n.* (*pl.* **-men**; *fem.* **townswoman**, *pl.* **-women**) an inhabitant of a town; a fellow citizen.

■ see CITIZEN 2a.

townspeople /tównzpeepəl/ *n.pl.* the people of a town.

towy see TOW[2].

toxemia /tokseémeeə/ *n.* (*Brit.* **toxaemia**) **1** blood poisoning. **2** a condition in pregnancy characterized by increased blood pressure. □□ **toxemic** *adj.* [as TOXI- + -EMIA]

toxi- /tóksee/ *comb. form* (also **toxico-** /tóksikō/, **toxo-** /tóksō/) poison; poisonous; toxic.

toxic /tóksik/ *adj.* **1** of or relating to poison (*toxic symptoms*). **2** poisonous (*toxic gas*). **3** caused by poison (*toxic anemia*). □□ **toxically** *adv.* **toxicity** /-sísitee/ *n.* [med.L *toxicus* poisoned f. L *toxicum* f. Gk *toxikon* (*pharmakon*) (poison for) arrows f. *toxon* bow, *toxa* arrows]

■ **2** see *poisonous* (POISON). □□ **toxicity** see *virulence* (VIRULENT).

toxicology /tóksikóləjee/ *n.* the scientific study of poisons. □□ **toxicological** /-kəlójikəl/ *adj.* **toxicologist** *n.*

toxin /tóksin/ *n.* a poison produced by a living organism, esp. one formed in the body and stimulating the production of antibodies. [TOXIC + -IN]

■ see POISON *n.* 1.

---

toxocara /tóksōkáarə/ *n.* any nematode worm of the genus *Toxocara*, parasitic in the alimentary canal of dogs and cats. □□ **toxocariasis** /-kəríasis/ *n.* [*toxo-* (see TOXI-) + Gk *kara* head]

toxophilite /toksófilīt/ *n.* & *adj.* ● *n.* a student or lover of archery. ● *adj.* of or concerning archery. □□ **toxophily** *n.* [*Ascham's Toxophilus* (1545) f. Gk *toxon* bow + *-philos* -PHILE]

toy /toy/ *n.* & *v.* ● *n.* **1 a** a plaything, esp. for a child. **b** (often *attrib.*) a model or miniature replica of a thing, esp. as a plaything (*toy gun*). **2 a** a thing, esp. a gadget or instrument, regarded as providing amusement or pleasure. **b** a task or undertaking regarded in an unserious way. **3** (usu. *attrib.*) a diminutive breed or variety of dog, etc. ● *v.intr.* (usu. foll. by *with*) **1** trifle; amuse oneself, esp. with a person's affections; flirt (*toyed with the idea of going to Africa*). **2 a** move a material object idly (*toyed with her necklace*). **b** nibble at food, etc., unenthusiastically (*toyed with a peach*). □ **toy box** a usu. wooden box for keeping toys in. **toy boy** (also **boy toy**) *colloq.* a woman's much younger male lover. **toy soldier 1** a miniature figure of a soldier. **2** *sl.* a soldier in a peacetime army. [16th c.: earlier = dallying, fun, jest, whim, trifle: orig. unkn.]

■ *n.* **1 a** plaything. **b** (*attrib.*) imitation, fake, simulated, artificial, *colloq.* phony; see also LITTLE *adj.* 1, 2a. **2** trifle, trinket, bauble, gewgaw, gimcrack, knickknack, bagatelle, bit of frippery, kickshaw. **3** miniature, tiny, diminutive, small, dwarf. ● *v.* **1** (*toy with*) flirt with, dally with, play with, deal with carelessly, amuse oneself with, *colloq.* dillydally with. **2 a** (*toy with*) trifle with, dally with, play with, sport with, fool with, fiddle with, tinker with, finger, twiddle (with).

tp. *abbr.* **1** (also **t.p.**) title page. **2** township. **3** troop.

tpk. *abbr.* turnpike.

trabeation /tráybeeáyshən/ *n.* the use of beams instead of arches or vaulting in construction. □□ **trabeate** /tráybeeət, -ayt/ *adj.* [L *trabs trabis* beam]

trabecula /trəbékyələ/ *n.* (*pl.* **trabeculae** /-lee/) **1** *Anat.* a supporting band or bar of connective or bony tissue, esp. dividing an organ into chambers. **2** *Bot.* a beamlike projection or process within a hollow structure. □□ **trabecular** *adj.* **trabeculate** /-lət, -layt/ *adj.* [L, dimin. of *trabs* beam]

trace[1] /trays/ *v.* & *n.* ● *v.tr.* **1 a** observe, discover, or find vestiges or signs of by investigation. **b** (often foll. by *along*, *through*, *to*, etc.) follow or mark the track or position of (*traced their footprints in the mud*; *traced the outlines of a wall*). **c** (often foll. by *back*) follow to its origins (*can trace my family to the 12th century*; *the report has been traced back to you*). **2** (often foll. by *over*) copy (a drawing, etc.) by drawing over its lines on a superimposed piece of translucent paper, or by using carbon paper. **3** (often foll. by *out*) mark out, delineate, sketch, or write, often laboriously (*traced out a plan of the district*; *traced out his vision of the future*). **4** pursue one's way along (a path, etc.). ● *n.* **1 a** a sign or mark or other indication of something having existed; a vestige (*no trace remains of the castle*; *has the traces of a vanished beauty*). **b** a very small quantity. **c** an amount of rainfall, etc., too small to be measured. **2** a track or footprint left by a person or animal. **3** a track left by the moving pen of an instrument, etc. **4** a line on the screen of a cathode-ray tube showing the path of a moving spot. **5** a curve's projection on or intersection with a plane, etc. **6** a change in the brain caused by learning processes. □ **trace element 1** a chemical element occurring in minute amounts. **2** a chemical element required only in minute amounts by living organisms for normal growth. **trace fossil** a fossil that represents a burrow, footprint, etc., of an organism. □□ **traceable** *adj.* **traceability** /tráysəbílitee/ *n.* **traceless** *adj.* [ME f. OF *trace* (n.), *tracier* (v.) f. L *tractus* drawing: see TRACT[1]]

■ *v.* **1 a, c** investigate, discover, ascertain, detect, determine, find, seek, search for, hunt down or up, unearth, track, follow, observe. **b** dog, pursue, follow (in the footsteps of), stalk, track (down), locate, shadow, trail, *colloq.* tail. **2** copy, reproduce, go over, mark out, draw over. **3** delineate, outline, describe,

draw, map, chart, mark (out), record, sketch. ● *n.* **1 a** hint, intimation, sign, token, suggestion, vestige, relic, remains, remnant, indication, mark, record, evidence, clue. **b** bit, spot, speck, streak, grain, jot, drop, dash, touch, suspicion, remnant, fragment, shred, tinge, taste, soupçon, iota, whiff, flicker, gleam, ray, shadow, suggestion, trifle, *Austral. colloq.* skerrick. **2** track(s), trail, spoor, footprint(s), print(s), footmark(s).

trace[2] /trays/ *n.* each of the two straps, chains, or ropes by which a horse draws a vehicle. □ **kick over the traces** become insubordinate or reckless. **trace horse** a horse that draws in traces or by a single trace, esp. one hitched on to help draw uphill, etc. [ME f. OF *trais*, pl. of TRAIT]

tracer /tráysər/ *n.* **1** a person or thing that traces. **2** *Mil.* a bullet, etc., that is visible in flight because of flames, etc., emitted. **3** an artificially produced radioactive isotope capable of being followed through the body by the radiation it produces.

tracery /tráysəree/ *n.* (*pl.* **-ies**) **1** ornamental stone openwork, esp. in the upper part of a Gothic window. **2** a fine decorative pattern. **3** a natural object finely patterned. □□ **traceried** *adj.*

trachea /tráykeeə/ *n.* (*pl.* **tracheae** /-kee-ee/ or **tracheas**) **1** the passage, reinforced by rings of cartilage, through which air reaches the bronchial tubes from the larynx; the windpipe. **2** each of the air passages in the body of an insect, etc. **3** any duct or vessel in a plant. □□ **tracheal** /tráykeeəl/ *adj.* **tracheate** /tráykeeayt/ *adj.* [ME f. med.L, = LL *trachia* f. Gk *trakheia* (*artēria*) rough (artery), f. *trakhus* rough]

tracheo- /tráykeeō/ *comb. form.*

tracheotomy /traykeeótəmee/ *n.* (also **tracheostomy** /-óstəmee/) (*pl.* **-ies**) an incision made in the trachea to relieve an obstruction to breathing. □ **tracheotomy tube** a breathing tube inserted into this incision.

trachoma /trəkṓmə/ *n.* a contagious disease of the eye with inflamed granulation on the inner surface of the lids. □□ **trachomatous** /-kṓmətəs, -kómətəs/ *adj.* [mod.L f. Gk *trakhōma* f. *trakhus* rough]

trachyte /trákīt, tráyk-/ *n.* a light-colored volcanic rock rough to the touch. □□ **trachytic** /trəkítik/ *adj.* [F f. Gk *trakhutēs* roughness (as TRACHOMA)]

tracing /tráysing/ *n.* **1** a copy of a drawing, etc., made by tracing. **2** = TRACE[1] *n.* 3. **3** the act or an instance of tracing. □ **tracing paper** translucent paper used for making tracings.

track[1] /trak/ *n.* & *v.* ● *n.* **1 a** a mark or marks left by a person, animal, or thing in passing. **b** (in *pl.*) such marks, esp. footprints. **2** a rough path, esp. one beaten by use. **3** a continuous railway line (*laid three miles of track*). **4 a** a course for racing horses, dogs, etc. **b** a prepared course for runners, etc. **c** various sports performed on a track, as running or hurdles. **5 a** a groove on a phonograph record. **b** a section of a phonograph record, compact disk, etc., containing one song, etc. (*this side has six tracks*). **c** a lengthwise strip of magnetic tape containing one sequence of signals. **6 a** a line of travel, passage, or motion (*followed the track of the hurricane*; *Canada followed in the same track*). **b** the path traveled by a ship, aircraft, etc. (cf. COURSE *n.* 2c). **7** a continuous band around the wheels of a tank, tractor, etc. **8** the transverse distance between a vehicle's wheels. **9** = SOUNDTRACK. **10** a line of reasoning or thought (*this track proved fruitless*). **11** any of several levels of instruction to which students are assigned based on their abilities, interests, etc. **12** a course of action or planned future (*management track*). ● *v.* **1** *tr.* follow the track of (an animal, person, spacecraft, etc.). **2** *tr.* make out (a course, development, etc.); trace by vestiges. **3** *intr.* (often foll. by *back*, *in*, etc.) (of a movie or television camera) move in relation to the subject being filmed. **4** *intr.* (of wheels) run so that the back ones are exactly in the track of the front ones. **5** *intr.* (of a record stylus) follow a groove. **6** *tr.* make a track with (dirt, etc.) from the feet. **b** leave such a track on (a floor, etc.). □ **in one's tracks** *colloq.* where one stands; then and there (*stopped him in his tracks*). **keep** (or **lose**) **track of** follow (or fail to follow) the course or development of. **make tracks** *colloq.* go or run away.

make tracks for *colloq.* go in pursuit of or toward. **off the track** away from the subject. **on a person's track 1** in pursuit of him or her. **2** in possession of a clue to a person's conduct, plans, etc. **on the wrong side of** (or **across**) **the tracks** *colloq.* in an inferior or dubious part of town. **on the wrong** (or **right**) **track** following the wrong (or right) line of inquiry. **track down** reach or capture by tracking. **track events** running races as opposed to jumping, etc. (cf. *field events*). **tracking station** an establishment set up to track objects in the sky. **track-laying** (of a vehicle) having a caterpillar tread. **track record** a person's past performance or achievements. **track shoe** a spiked shoe worn by a runner. **track suit** a loose warm suit worn by an athlete, etc., for exercising or jogging. **track system** a system of grouping children of similar ability in education. **track with** *Austral. sl.* associate with; court. □□ **trackage** *n.* [ME f. OF *trac*, perh. f. LG or Du. *tre(c)k* draft, etc.]

■ *n.* **1** spoor, trail, footprint(s), print(s), trace(s), mark(s), footmark(s), scent, slot, wake. **2** path, trail, route, footpath, course, road, street, alley. **3** line, rail(s), way, railway, railroad. **4** racecourse, course, racetrack, *Brit.* circuit. **6** see COURSE *n.* 2. **10** see LINE[1] 19. ● *v.* **1** follow, dog, pursue, trace, stalk, shadow, trail, spoor, hunt down, chase, *colloq.* tail. **2** see *keep track of* (TRACK[1]) below. □ **keep track of** trace, track, keep an eye on, follow, pursue, monitor, supervise, oversee, keep up with *or* on, watch, keep a record of *or* on, record. **lose track of** lose, misplace, mislay, lose sight of, forget. **make tracks** see *make away*. **track down** find, discover, seek out, ferret out, hunt down, trace, catch, apprehend, capture, recover, smell *or* sniff out, run to earth *or* ground, run down. **track record** see RECORD *n.* 5.

track[2] /trak/ *Brit. v.* **1** *tr.* tow (a boat) by rope, etc., from a bank. **2** *intr.* travel by being towed. [app. f. Du. *trekken* to draw, etc., assim. to TRACK[1]]

tracker /trákər/ *n.* **1** a person or thing that tracks. **2** a police dog tracking by scent. **3** a wooden connecting rod in the mechanism of an organ.

tracking /tráking/ *n.* **1** assignment of students in a track system. **2** *Electr.* the formation of a conducting path over the surface of an insulating material.

tracklayer /tráklayər/ *n.* **1** a person employed in laying or repairing railroad tracks. **2** a tractor or other vehicle equipped with continuous tracks (see TRACK[1] *n.* 7).

trackless /tráklis/ *adj.* **1** without a track or tracks; untrodden. **2** leaving no track or trace. **3** not running on a track. □ **trackless trolley** an electric bus running on the road, powered by a trolley wire.

■ **1** empty, pathless, untrodden, unexplored, uncharted, virgin.

trackman /trákmən/ *n.* (*pl.* **-men**) a tracklayer.

trackway /trákway/ *n.* a beaten path; an ancient roadway.

tract[1] /trakt/ *n.* **1** a region or area of indefinite, esp. large, extent (*pathless desert tracts*). **2** *Anat.* an area of an organ or system (*respiratory tract*). **3** *Brit. archaic* a period of time, etc. [L *tractus* drawing f. *trahere tract-* draw, pull]

■ **1** region, area, stretch, territory, expanse, zone, portion, section, sector, quarter, district; patch, plot, parcel, lot.

tract[2] /trakt/ *n.* a short treatise in pamphlet form, esp. on a religious subject. [app. abbr. of L *tractatus* TRACTATE]

■ treatise, monograph, essay, article, paper, dissertation, disquisition, homily, sermon; pamphlet, booklet, brochure, leaflet.

tract[3] /trakt/ *n. RC Ch. & Mus.* an anthem replacing the alleluia in some Masses. [med.L *tractus (cantus)* drawn out (song), past part. of L *trahere* draw]

tractable /tráktəbəl/ *adj.* **1** (of a person) easily handled; manageable; docile. **2** (of material, etc.) pliant; malleable. □□ **tractability** /-bílitee/ *n.* **tractableness** *n.* **tractably** *adv.* [L *tractabilis* f. *tractare* handle, frequent. of *trahere tract-* draw]

■ **1** docile, amenable, tame, manageable, biddable, persuadable, persuasible, compliant, easygoing,

willing, submissive, obedient, governable, yielding. **2** manageable, handleable, workable, adaptable, malleable, pliable, pliant, flexible, plastic, ductile. □□ **tractability, tractableness** see *flexibility* (FLEXIBLE).

Tractarianism /traktáireeənizəm/ *n. hist.* = OXFORD MOVEMENT. □□ **Tractarian** *adj. & n.* [after *Tracts for the Times*, published in Oxford 1833–41 and outlining the movement's principles]

tractate /tráktayt/ *n.* a treatise. [L *tractatus* f. *tractare*: see TRACTABLE]

traction /trákshən/ *n.* **1** the act of drawing or pulling a thing over a surface, esp. a road or track (*steam traction*). **2 a** sustained pulling on a limb, muscle, etc., by means of pulleys, weights, etc. **b** contraction, e.g., of a muscle. **3** the grip of a tire on a road, a wheel on a rail, etc. □ **traction engine** a steam or diesel engine for drawing heavy loads on roads, fields, etc. **traction wheel** the driving wheel of a locomotive, etc. □□ **tractional** *adj.* **tractive** /tráktiv/ *adj.* [F *traction* or med.L *tractio* f. L *trahere tract-* draw]

■ **2 a** see TENSION *n.* 1. **3** grip, gripping power, drag, purchase, friction, adhesion.

tractor /tráktər/ *n.* **1** a motor vehicle used for hauling, esp. farm machinery, heavy loads, etc. **2** a traction engine. □ **tractor-trailer** a truck consisting of a tractor or cab unit attached to a trailer. [LL *tractor* (as TRACTION)]

trad /trad/ *n. & adj. esp. Brit. colloq.* ● *n.* traditional jazz. ● *adj.* traditional. [abbr.]

trade /trayd/ *n. & v.* ● *n.* **1 a** buying and selling. **b** buying and selling conducted between nations, etc. **c** business conducted for profit (esp. as distinct from a profession) (*a butcher by trade*). **d** business of a specified nature or time (*Christmas trade*; *tourist trade*). **2** a skilled craft, esp. requiring an apprenticeship (*learned a trade*; *his trade is plumbing*). **3** (usu. prec. by *the*) **a** the people engaged in a specific trade (*the trade will never agree to it*; *trade inquiries only*). **b** *Brit. colloq.* licensed victuallers. **4** a transaction, esp. a swap. **5** (usu. in *pl.*) a trade wind. ● *v.* **1** *intr.* (often foll. by *in*, *with*) engage in trade; buy and sell (*trades in plastic novelties*; *we trade with Japan*). **2** *tr.* **a** exchange in commerce; barter (goods). **b** exchange (insults, blows, etc.). **3** *intr.* (usu. foll. by *with*, *for*) have a transaction with a person for a thing. □ **be in trade** *Brit. esp. derog.* be in commerce, esp. keep a shop. **foreign trade** international trade. **Trade Board** *Brit. hist.* a statutory body for settling disputes, etc., in certain industries. **trade book** a book published by a commercial publisher and intended for general readership. **trade cycle** *Brit.* recurring periods of boom and recession. **trade deficit** (or **gap**) the extent by which a country's imports exceed its exports. **trade in** (often foll. by *for*) exchange (esp. a used car, etc.) in esp. part payment for another. **trade-in** *n.* a thing, esp. a car, exchanged in this way. **trade journal** a periodical containing news, etc., concerning a particular trade. **trade-last** a compliment from a third person that is reported to the person complimented in exchange for one to the reporter. **trade name 1** a name by which a thing is called in a trade. **2** a name given to a product. **3** a name under which a business trades. **trade off** exchange, esp. as a compromise. **trade-off** *n.* such an exchange. **trade on** take advantage of (a person's credulity, one's reputation, etc.). **trade paper** = *trade journal*. **trade price** a wholesale price charged to the dealer before goods are retailed. **trade secret 1** a secret device or technique used esp. in a trade. **2** *joc.* any secret. **Trades Union Congress** *Brit.* the official representative body of British trade unions, meeting annually. **trade** (or **trades**) **union** *Brit.* = *labor union* (LABOR). **trade wind** a wind blowing continually toward the equator and deflected westward, f. obs. *blow trade* = blow regularly.

/.../ **pronunciation**	● **part of speech**
□ **phrases, idioms, and compounds**	
□□ **derivatives**	■ **synonym section**
cross-references appear in SMALL CAPITALS or *italics*	

□□ **tradable**, **tradeable** *adj.* [ME f. MLG *trade* track f. OS *trada*, OHG *trata*: cf. TREAD]

■ *n.* **1 a, b** commerce, business, traffic, exchange, barter, dealing(s), buying and selling, merchandising, marketing, truck. **d** business; customers, clientele, custom, patrons, following, patronage, shoppers. **2** calling, occupation, pursuit, work, business, employment, line (of work), métier, job, vocation, craft, handicraft, career, profession. **4** swap, exchange, interchange, barter, transaction, *colloq.* deal.

● *v.* **1** transact *or* do business, buy, sell, deal, traffic, merchandise, have dealings. **2** exchange, swap, interchange, switch, barter; return. □ **trade in** see REDEEM 3. **trade name 2, 3** see BRAND *n.* 1 b. **trade on** see *play on.*

trademark /tráydmaark/ *n.* **1** a device, word, or words, secured by legal registration or established by use as representing a company, product, etc. **2** a distinctive characteristic, etc.

■ **trademark 1** see BRAND *n.* 1 b. **2** see HALLMARK *n.* 2.

trader /tráydər/ *n.* **1** a person engaged in trade. **2** a merchant ship.

■ **1** dealer, merchant, businessman, businesswoman, business person, broker, merchandiser, distributor, seller, salesman, saleswoman, salesperson, vendor, buyer, purchaser, shopkeeper, supplier, retailer, wholesaler, *Brit.* stockist; tradesman, tradeswoman; trafficker.

tradescantia /trádiskánteeə/ *n.* any usu. trailing plant of the genus *Tradescantia*, with large blue, white, or pink flowers. [mod.L f. J. *Tradescant*, Engl. naturalist d. 1638]

tradesman /tráydzmən/ *n.* (*pl.* **-men**; *fem.* **tradeswoman**, *pl.* **-women**) a person engaged in trading or a trade, as a skilled craftsman *or Brit.* a shopkeeper.

■ craftsman, journeyman, handicraftsman, *Brit.* roundsman.

tradespeople /tráydzpeepəl/ *n.pl.* people engaged in trade.

trading /tráyding/ *n.* the act of engaging in trade. □ **trading estate** esp. *Brit.* a specially designed industrial and commercial area. **trading post** a store, etc., established in a remote or unsettled region. **trading stamp** a stamp given to customers by some stores that is exchangeable in large numbers for various articles.

tradition /trədíshən/ *n.* **1 a** a custom, opinion, or belief handed down to posterity, esp. orally or by practice. **b** this process of handing down. **2** esp. *joc.* an established practice or custom (*it's a tradition to complain about the weather*). **3** artistic, literary, etc., principles based on experience and practice; any one of these (*stage tradition; traditions of the Dutch School*). **4** *Theol.* doctrine or a particular doctrine, etc., claimed to have divine authority without documentary evidence, esp.: **a** the oral teaching of Christ and the Apostles. **b** the laws held by the Pharisees to have been delivered by God to Moses. **c** the words and deeds of Muhammad not in the Koran. **5** *Law* the formal delivery of property, etc. □□ **traditionary** *adj.* **traditionist** *n.* **traditionless** *adj.* [ME f. OF *tradicion* or L *traditio* f. *tradere* hand on, betray (as TRANS-, *dare* give)]

■ **1, 2** custom, practice, habit, usage, convention, ritual, rite, unwritten law, institution, form, praxis, belief, lore, folklore.

traditional /trədíshənəl/ *adj.* **1** of, based on, or obtained by tradition. **2** (of jazz) in the style of the early 20th c. □□ **traditionally** *adv.*

■ **1** customary, usual, routine, habitual, standard, household, stock, time-honored, traditionary, classical, established, well-known, conventional, orthodox, ritual, unwritten, accustomed, historic, old, ancestral.

traditionalism /trədíshənalizəm/ *n.* **1** respect, esp. excessive, for tradition, esp. in religion. **2** a philosophical system referring all religious knowledge to divine revelation and tradition. □□ **traditionalist** *n.* **traditionalistic** *adj.*

■ □□ **traditionalistic** see REACTIONARY *adj.*, ORTHODOX.

traduce /trədóōs, -dyóōs/ *v.tr.* speak ill of; misrepresent.

□□ **traducement** *n.* **traducer** *n.* [L *traducere* disgrace (as TRANS-, *ducere duct-* lead)]

■ see DISPARAGE.

traffic /tráfik/ *n. & v.* ● *n.* **1** (often *attrib.*) **a** vehicles moving on a public highway, esp. of a specified kind, density, etc. (*heavy traffic on the interstate; traffic cop*). **b** such movement in the air or at sea. **2** (usu. foll. by *in*) trade, esp. illegal (*the traffic in drugs*). **3 a** the transportation of goods; the coming and going of people or goods by road, rail, air, sea, etc. **b** the persons or goods so transported. **4** dealings or communication between people, etc. (*had no traffic with them*). **5** the messages, signals, etc., transmitted through a communications system; the flow or volume of such business. ● *v.* (**trafficked**, **trafficking**) **1** *intr.* (usu. foll. by *in*) deal in something, esp. illegally (*trafficked in narcotics; traffics in innuendo*). **2** *tr.* deal in; barter. □ **traffic circle** a road junction at which traffic moves in one direction around a central island. **traffic island** a paved or grassy area in a road to divert traffic and provide a space for pedestrians. **traffic jam** traffic at a standstill because of construction, an accident, etc. **traffic light** (or **traffic signal**) a usu. automatic signal with colored lights to control road traffic, esp. at intersections. **traffic warden** *Brit.* a uniformed official employed to help control road traffic and esp. parking. □□ **trafficker** *n.* **trafficless** *adj.* [F *traf(f)ique,* Sp. *tráfico,* It. *traffico,* of unkn. orig.]

■ *n.* **2** see TRADE *n.* 1a, b. **3** movement, conveyance, shipping, transport, freight, transportation. **4** see DEALINGS. ● *v.* (*traffic in*) see DEAL[1] *v.* 2. □ **traffic circle** rotary, *Brit.* roundabout. **traffic jam** jam, gridlock, delay, congestion, stoppage, backup, esp. *Brit.* traffic queue, *colloq.* snarl-up.

tragacanth /trágəkanth, tráj-/ *n.* a white or reddish gum from a plant, *Astragalus gummifer,* used in pharmaceuticals, calico printing, etc., as a vehicle for drugs, dye, etc. [F *tragacante* f. L *tragacantha* f. Gk *tragakantha,* name of a shrub, f. *tragos* goat + *akantha* thorn]

tragedian /trəjeédeeən/ *n.* **1** a writer of tragedies. **2** an actor in tragedy. [ME f. OF *tragediane* (as TRAGEDY)]

tragedienne /trəjeédee-én/ *n.* an actress in tragedy. [F fem. (as TRAGEDIAN)]

tragedy /trájidee/ *n.* (*pl.* **-ies**) **1** a serious accident, crime, or natural catastrophe. **2** a sad event; a calamity (*the team's defeat is a tragedy*). **3 a** a play in verse or prose dealing with tragic events and with an unhappy ending, esp. concerning the downfall of the protagonist. **b** tragic plays as a genre (cf. COMEDY). [ME f. OF *tragedie* f. L *tragoedia* f. Gk *tragōidia* app. goat song f. *tragos* goat + *ōidē* song]

■ **1, 2** catastrophe, calamity, disaster, misfortune, adversity, blow.

tragic /trájik/ *adj.* **1** (also **tragical** /-kəl/) sad; calamitous; greatly distressing (*a tragic tale*). **2** of, or in the style of, tragedy (*tragic drama; a tragic actor*). □ **tragic irony** a device, orig. in Greek tragedy, by which words carry a tragic, esp. prophetic, meaning to the audience, unknown to the character speaking. □□ **tragically** *adv.* [F *tragique* f. L *tragicus* f. Gk *tragikos* f. *tragos* goat: see TRAGEDY]

■ **1** sad, depressing, lamentable, unhappy, funereal, forlorn, melancholy, cheerless, mournful, grievous, morose, lugubrious, dismal, piteous, pitiable, pitiful, pathetic(al), appalling, wretched, dreadful, awful, terrible, horrible, deplorable, miserable, distressing, heartrending, disturbing, upsetting, shocking, unlucky, unfortunate, hapless, ill-fated, inauspicious, ill-omened, ill-starred, calamitous, catastrophic, crushing, disastrous, *archaic* star-crossed, *formal* lachrymose, *literary or joc.* dolorous; tragical.

tragicomedy /trájikómidee/ *n.* (*pl.* **-ies**) **1 a** a play having a mixture of comedy and tragedy. **b** plays of this kind as a genre. **2** an event, etc., having tragic and comic elements. □□ **tragicomic** /-kómik/ *adj.* **tragicomically** *adv.* [F *tragicomédie* or It. *tragicomedia* f. LL *tragicomoedia* f. L *tragicomoedia* (as TRAGIC, COMEDY)]

tragopan /trágəpan/ *n.* any Asian pheasant of the genus

Tragopan, with erect fleshy horns on its head. [L f. Gk f. *tragos* goat + *Pan* the god Pan]

trail /trayl/ *n. & v.* ● *n.* **1 a** a track left by a thing, person, etc., moving over a surface (*left a trail of wreckage; a slug's slimy trail*). **b** a track or scent followed in hunting, seeking, etc. (*he's on the trail*). **2** a beaten path or track, esp. through a wild region. **3** a part dragging behind a thing or person; an appendage (*a trail of smoke; a condensation trail*). **4** the rear end of a gun carriage stock. ● *v.* **1** *tr. & intr.* draw or be drawn along behind, esp. on the ground. **2** *intr.* (often foll. by *behind*) walk wearily; lag; straggle. **3** *tr.* follow the trail of; pursue (*trailed him to his home*). **4** *intr.* be losing in a game or other contest (*trailing by three points*). **5** *intr.* (usu. foll. by *away, off*) peter out; tail off. **6** *intr.* **a** (of a plant, etc.) grow or hang over a wall, along the ground, etc. **b** (of a garment, etc.) hang loosely. **7** *tr.* (often *refl.*) drag (oneself, one's limbs, etc.) along wearily, etc. **8** *tr.* advertise (a movie, a radio or television program, etc.) in advance by showing extracts, etc. **9** *tr.* apply (slip) through a nozzle or spout to decorate pottery. □ **trail bike** a light motorcycle for use in rough terrain. **trail one's coat** deliberately provoke a quarrel, fight, etc. **trailing edge 1** the rear edge of an aircraft's wing, etc. **2** *Electronics* the part of a pulse in which the amplitude diminishes (opp. *leading edge* (see LEADING¹)). **trailing wheel** a wheel not given direct motive power. [ME (earlier as verb) f. OF *traillier* to tow, or f. MLG *treilen* haul f. L *tragula* dragnet]

■ *n.* **1** track, spoor, scent, smell, trace, footsteps, footprints, path, wake, sign. **2** (beaten) path, way, pathway, footpath, route, track, course. ● *v.* **1** tow, draw, drag (along), haul, pull, tag along, trawl, bring along (behind), carry along (behind); move, be drawn, stream, sweep, dangle. **2** lag (behind), dawdle, loiter, linger, follow, straggle, bring up the rear, hang back, fall *or* drop behind. **3** follow, pursue, dog, trace, shadow, stalk, track, chase, hunt, *colloq.* tail. **4** lag (behind), be losing, fall *or* drop behind, be down. **5** (*trail off* or *away*) diminish, decrease, fade away *or* out, disappear, dwindle, lessen, die out *or* away, peter out, subside, taper off, tail off, weaken, grow faint *or* dim.

trailblazer /tráylblayzər/ *n.* **1** a person who marks a new track through wild country. **2** a pioneer; an innovator.

trailblazing /tráylblayzing/ *n. & adj.* the act or process of blazing a trail. ● *attrib.adj.* that blazes a trail; pioneering.

trailer /tráylər/ *n.* **1** a person or thing that trails. **2** a series of brief extracts from a movie, etc., used to advertise it in advance. **3** a vehicle towed by another, esp.: **a** the rear section of a tractor-trailer. **b** an open cart. **c** a platform for transporting a boat, etc. **d** a camper. **4** a mobile home. **5** a trailing plant. □ **trailer park** a place where trailers are parked as dwellings, often with special amenities.

train /trayn/ *v. & n.* ● *v.* **1 a** *tr.* (often foll. by *to* + infin.) teach (a person, animal, oneself, etc.) a specified skill, esp. by practice (*trained the dog to beg; was trained in midwifery*). **b** *intr.* undergo this process (*trained as a teacher*). **2** *tr. & intr.* bring or come into a state of physical fitness by exercise, diet, etc.; undergo physical exercise, esp. for a specific purpose (*trained me for the high jump; the team trains every evening*). **3** *tr.* cause (a plant) to grow in a required shape (*trained the peach tree up the wall*). **4** (usu. as **trained** *adj.*) make (the mind, eye, etc.) sharp or discerning as a result of instruction, practice, etc. **5** *tr.* (often foll. by *on*) point or aim (a gun, camera, etc.) at an object, etc. **6** *colloq.* **a** *intr.* go by train. **b** *tr.* esp. *Brit.* (foll. by *it* as object) make a journey by train (*trained it to Aberdeen*). **7** *tr.* (usu. foll. by *away*) *archaic* entice; lure. ● *n.* **1** a series of railroad cars drawn by an engine. **2** something dragged along behind or forming the back part of a dress, robe, etc. (*wore a dress with a long train; the train of the peacock*). **3** a succession or series of people, things, events, etc. (*a long train of camels; interrupted my train of thought; a train of ideas*). **4** a body of followers; a retinue (*a train of admirers*). **5** a succession of military vehicles, etc., including artillery, supplies, etc. (*baggage train*). **6** a line of gunpowder, etc., to fire an explosive charge. **7** a series of connected wheels or parts in machinery.

□ **in train** properly arranged or directed. **in a person's train** following behind a person. **in the train of** as a sequel of. **train down** *Brit.* train with exercise or diet to lower one's weight. **train oil** oil obtained from the blubber of a whale (esp. of a right whale). □□ **trainable** *adj.* **trainability** /tráynəbílitee/ *n.* **trainee** /-neé/ *n.* **trainless** *adj.* [ME f. OF *traïner, trahiner*, ult. f. L *trahere* draw]

■ *v.* **1 a** discipline, exercise, tutor, teach, coach, drill, school, instruct, prepare, fit, educate, edify, guide, bring up, indoctrinate, condition, rear, raise. **2** work out, exercise, practice. **4** (**trained**) see EXPERIENCED 2, SHARP *adj.* 9. **5** see AIM *v.* 2. ● *n.* **1** *colloq.* (*esp. as a child's word*) choo-choo. **3, 5** line, procession, succession, string, set, series, sequence, chain, concatenation, progression, stream, caravan, cavalcade, parade, column, file, row, esp. *Brit.* queue. **4** retinue, entourage, cortège, suite, following, escort, guard, attendants, followers, *hist.* retainers; staff, court, household. □□ **trainable** see MANAGEABLE. **trainee** see NOVICE.

trainband /tráynband/ *n. hist.* any of several divisions of 16th or 17th c. citizen soldiers in England or America.

trainer /tráynər/ *n.* **1** a person who trains. **2** a person who trains or provides medical assistance, etc., to horses, athletes, etc., as a profession. **3** an aircraft or device simulating it used to train pilots. **4** *Brit.* a soft running shoe of leather, canvas, etc.

■ **2** see TEACHER.

training /tráyning/ *n.* the act or process of teaching or learning a skill, discipline, etc. (*physical training*). □ **go into training** begin physical training. **in training 1** undergoing physical training. **2** physically fit as a result of this. **out of training 1** no longer training. **2** physically unfit. **training college** *Brit.* a college or school for training esp. prospective teachers. **training ship** a ship on which young people are taught seamanship, etc.

■ warming up, exercise, working out; drilling, practice, preparation, rehearsal; see also EDUCATION 1a.

trainman /tráynmən/ *n.* (*pl.* **-men**) a railroad employee working on trains.

trainsick /tráynsik/ *adj.* affected with nausea by the motion of a train. □□ **trainsickness** *n.*

traipse /trayps/ *v. & n. colloq.* or *dial.* ● *v.intr.* **1** tramp or trudge wearily. **2** esp. *Brit.* (often foll. by *about*) go on errands. ● *n.* **1** a tedious journey on foot. **2** *archaic* a slattern. [16th-c. *trapes* (v.), of unkn. orig.]

■ *v.* **1** see TRAMP *v.* 1a.

trait /trayt/ *n.* a distinguishing feature or characteristic, esp. of a person. [F f. L *tractus* (as TRACT¹)]

■ feature, characteristic, attribute, quality, peculiarity, idiosyncrasy, quirk, lineament, mark, property, hallmark.

traitor /tráytər/ *n.* (*fem.* **traitress** /-tris/) (often foll. by *to*) a person who is treacherous or disloyal, esp. to his or her country. □□ **traitorous** *adj.* **traitorously** *adv.* [ME f. OF *traït(o)ur* f. L *traditor -oris* f. *tradere*: see TRADITION]

■ turncoat, Judas, quisling, betrayer, informer, renegade, fifth columnist, double-crosser, snake (in the grass), viper in one's bosom, double-dealer, collaborator, *colloq.* two-timer, *hist.* traditor. □□ **traitorous** treacherous, perfidious, seditious, subversive, insurrectionist, insurrectionary, renegade, insurgent, disloyal, deceitful, untrue, unfaithful, faithless; treasonable, double-crossing, double-dealing, *colloq.* two-timing. **traitorously** treacherously, perfidiously, seditiously, subversively, disloyally, deceitfully, insidiously, behind a person's back.

trajectory /trəjéktəree/ *n.* (*pl.* **-ies**) **1** the path described by a projectile flying or an object moving under the action of

/. . ./ **pronunciation**	● **part of speech**
□ **phrases, idioms, and compounds**	
□□ **derivatives**	■ **synonym section**
cross-references appear in SMALL CAPITALS or *italics*	

given forces. **2** *Geom.* a curve or surface cutting a system of curves or surfaces at a constant angle. [(orig. adj.) f. med.L *trajectorius* f. L *traicere traject-* (as TRANS-, *jacere* throw)]
■ **1** flight path, course, track.

tra-la /traalaá/ *int.* an expression of joy or gaiety, esp. as in a song. [imit. of song]

tram[1] /tram/ *n.* **1** *Brit.* = STREETCAR. **2** a four-wheeled vehicle used in coal mines. [MLG & MDu. *trame* balk, beam, barrow shaft]

tram[2] /tram/ *n.* (in full **tram silk**) double silk thread used for the weft of some velvets and silks. [F *trame* f. L *trama* weft]

tramcar /trámkaar/ *n. Brit.* = TRAM[1] 1.

tramlines /trámlinz/ *n.pl. Brit.* **1** rails for a streetcar. **2** *colloq.* **a** either pair of two sets of long parallel lines at the sides of a lawn tennis court. **b** similar lines at the side or back of a badminton court. **3** inflexible principles or courses of action, etc.

trammel /trámɘl/ *n. & v.* ● *n.* **1** (usu. in *pl.*) an impediment to free movement; a hindrance (*the trammels of domesticity*). **2** a triple dragnet for fish, which are trapped in a pocket formed when they attempt to swim through. **3** an instrument for drawing ellipses, etc., with a bar sliding in upright grooves. **4** a beam compass. **5** a hook in a fireplace for a kettle, etc. ● *v.tr.* (**trammeled, trammeling** or **trammelled, trammelling**) confine or hamper with or as if with trammels. [in sense 'net' ME f. OF *tramail* f. med.L *tramaculum, tremaculum,* perh. formed as TRI- + *macula* (MAIL[2]): later history uncert.]
■ *n.* **1** impediment(s), hindrance(s), shackle(s), handicap(s), check(s), restriction(s), restraint(s), curb(s), deterrent(s), constraint(s), hitch(es), snag(s), (stumbling) block(s), obstacle(s). ● *v.* impede, hinder, handicap, check, restrain, curb, deter, constrain, block, obstruct, fetter, confine.

tramontana /traámontaána, -tánɘ/ *n.* a cold north wind in the Adriatic. [It.: see TRAMONTANE]

tramontane /trɘmóntayn, trámɘn-/ *adj. & n.* ● *adj.* **1** situated or living on the other side of mountains, esp. the Alps as seen from Italy. **2** (from the Italian point of view) foreign; barbarous. ● *n.* **1** a tramontane person. **2** = TRAMONTANA. [ME f. It. *tramontano* f. L *transmontanus* beyond the mountains (as TRANS-, *mons montis* mountain)]
■ *adj.* **1** transalpine, transmontane.

tramp /tramp/ *v. & n.* ● *v.* **1** *intr.* **a** walk heavily and firmly (*tramping about upstairs*). **b** go on foot, esp. a distance. **2** *tr.* **a** cross on foot, esp. wearily or reluctantly. **b** cover (a distance) in this way (*tramped forty miles*). **3** *tr.* (often foll. by *down*) tread on; trample; stamp on. **4** *tr. Austral. colloq.* dismiss from employment; fire. **5** *intr.* live as a tramp. ● *n.* **1** an itinerant vagrant or beggar. **2** the sound of a person, or esp. people, walking, marching, etc., or of horses' hooves. **3** a journey on foot, esp. protracted. **4 a** an iron plate protecting the sole of a boot used for digging. **b** the part of a spade that it strikes. **5** *sl. derog.* a promiscuous woman. **6** (also **tramp steamer**) a merchant ship that takes on any cargo available. □□ **tramper** *n.* **trampish** *adj.* [ME *trampe* f. Gmc]
■ *v.* **1 a** plod, stamp, stomp, stump, clump, clomp, trudge, lumber, *colloq.* galumph, *colloq. or dial.* traipse. **b** march, hike, trudge, plod, slog, footslog, plow, tread, trek, walk, mush. **2** see TRAVERSE *v.* 1, WALK *v.* 1, 2. **3** see TRAMPLE *v.* 1. ● *n.* **1** derelict, vagabond, vagrant, drifter, hobo, bum, bagman, beachcomber, down-and-outer, *Austral.* sundowner, swagman, *colloq.* knight of the road. **2** step, tread, footfall, footstep. **3** march, trudge, plod, slog, footslog, trek, hike, walk, *colloq. or dial.* traipse. **5** see SLUT.

trample /trámpɘl/ *v. & n.* ● *v.tr.* **1** tread underfoot. **2** press down or crush in this way. ● *n.* the sound or act of trampling. □ **trample on** (or **underfoot**) **1** tread heavily on. **2** treat roughly or with contempt; disregard (a person's feelings, etc.). □□ **trampler** *n.* [ME f. TRAMP + -LE[4]]
■ *v.* **1** trample on, tramp (down *or* on *or* upon), stamp (on), stomp (on *or* upon), tread (down *or* on), step on.

2 crush, press, squash, flatten, *colloq.* squish; stamp out, extinguish, put out, destroy, rout, defeat. □ **trample on** (or **underfoot**) **2** trample upon, violate, damage, harm, hurt, infringe *or* encroach on, ride roughshod over, set at naught, scorn, disdain, defy, disregard, ignore, fly in the face of, fling *or* cast *or* throw to the winds, *literary* contemn.

trampoline /trámpɘleen/ *n. & v.* ● *n.* a strong fabric sheet connected by springs to a horizontal frame, used by gymnasts, etc., for somersaults, as a springboard, etc. ● *v.intr.* use a trampoline. □□ **trampolinist** *n.* [It. *trampolino* f. *trampoli* stilts]

tramway /trámway/ *n. Brit.* **1** rails for a streetcar. **2** a streetcar system.

trance /trans/ *n. & v.* ● *n.* **1 a** a sleeplike or half-conscious state without response to stimuli. **b** a hypnotic or cataleptic state. **2** such a state as entered into by a medium. **3** a state of extreme exaltation or rapture; ecstasy. ● *v.tr. poet.* = ENTRANCE[2]. □□ **trancelike** *adj.* [ME f. OF *transe* f. *transir* depart, fall into trance f. L *transire:* see TRANSIT]
■ *n.* **1, 2** daze, stupor, semiconscious *or* half-conscious *or* hypnotic *or* cataleptic *or* sleeplike *or* dream state, state of semiconsciousness *or* half-consciousness *or* catalepsy *or* suspended animation *or* stupefaction *or* abstraction *or* (complete) absorption; brown study, reverie. **3** exaltation, rapture; see also ECSTASY. □□ **trancelike** see GLASSY *adj.* 2.

tranche /traansh/ *n.* a portion, esp. of income, or of a block of bonds or stocks. [F, = slice (as TRENCH)]
■ see PORTION *n.* 1, SLAB *n.*

tranny /tránee/ *n.* (*pl.* -ies) **1** *sl.* a vehicle transmission. **2** esp. *Brit. colloq.* a transistor radio. [abbr.]

tranquil /trángkwil/ *adj.* calm; serene; unruffled. □□ **tranquillity** /-kwílitee/ *n.* **tranquilly** *adv.* [F *tranquille* or L *tranquillus*]
■ calm, serene, placid, quiet, peaceful, still, smooth, unagitated, halcyon, relaxed, restful; unruffled, sedate, steady, regular, even, dispassionate, self-possessed, cool, self-controlled, collected, composed, coolheaded, unexcited, undisturbed, untroubled, unperturbed. □□ **tranquillity** see CALM *n.* 1. **tranquilly** see EASY *adv.*

tranquilize /trángkwiliz/ *v.tr.* make tranquil, esp. by a drug, etc.
■ calm, soothe, pacify, still, quiet, relax, lull, compose, settle, sedate, *Brit.* quieten.

tranquilizer /trángkwilizɘr/ *n.* a drug used to diminish anxiety.
■ barbiturate, opiate, sedative, antipsychotic, antianxiety drug, *Med.* calmative, palliative, lenitive, *Pharm.* bromide, *sl.* downer.

trans- /trans, tranz/ *prefix* **1** across; beyond (*transcontinental; transgress*). **2** on or to the other side of (*transatlantic*) (opp. CIS-). **3** through (*transonic*). **4** into another state or place (*transform; transcribe*). **5** surpassing; transcending (*transfinite*). **6** *Chem.* **a** (of an isomer) having the same atom or group on opposite sides of a given plane in the molecule (cf. CIS- 4). **b** having a higher atomic number than (*transuranic*). [from or after L *trans* across]

trans. *abbr.* **1** transaction. **2** transfer. **3** transitive. **4** (also **transl.**) translated. **5** (also **transl.**) translation. **6** (also **transl.**) translator. **7** transmission. **8** transportation. **9** transpose. **10** transposition. **11** transverse.

transact /tranzákt, -sákt/ *v.tr.* perform or carry through (business). □□ **transactor** *n.* [L *transigere transact-* (as TRANS-, *agere* do)]
■ do, carry on *or* out, conduct, manage, handle, negotiate, administer, discharge, perform, enact, settle, conclude, complete, finish.

transaction /tranzákshɘn, -sák-/ *n.* **1 a** a piece of esp. commercial business done; a deal (*a profitable transaction*). **b** the management of business, etc. **2** (in *pl.*) published reports of discussions, papers read, etc., at the meetings of a learned society. □□ **transactional** *adj.* **transactionally** *adv.* [ME f. LL *transactio* (as TRANSACT)]
■ **1 a** deal, dealing, negotiation, matter, affair, business,

action, proceeding, agreement, arrangement, bargain. **2** (*transactions*) proceedings, record(s), acts, minutes, annals, report(s).

transalpine /tránzálpin, trans-/ *adj.* beyond the Alps, esp. from the Italian point of view. [L *transalpinus* (as TRANS-, *alpinus* ALPINE)]
■ see TRAMONTANE *adj.*

transatlantic /tránzətlántik, trans-/ *adj.* **1** beyond the Atlantic, esp.: **a** European. **b** *Brit.* American. **2** crossing the Atlantic (*a transatlantic flight*).

transaxle /tranzáksəl/ *n.* a unit in front-wheel drive vehicles that combines the functions of the transmission and differential.

transceiver /transeévər/ *n.* a combined radio transmitter and receiver.

transcend /transénd/ *v.tr.* **1** be beyond the range or grasp of (human experience, reason, belief, etc.). **2** excel; surpass. [ME f. OF *transcendre* or L *transcendere* (as TRANS-, *scandere* climb)]
■ **1** go beyond, lie outside, exceed. **2** surpass, outstrip, exceed, outdistance, outdo, excel, overshadow, top, rise above, outshine, eclipse, beat.

transcendent /transéndənt/ *adj. & n.* ● *adj.* **1** excelling; surpassing (*transcendent merit*). **2** transcending human experience. **3** *Philos.* **a** higher than or not included in any of Aristotle's ten categories in scholastic philosophy. **b** not realizable in experience in Kantian philosophy. **4** (esp. of the supreme being) existing apart from, not subject to the limitations of, the material universe (opp. IMMANENT). ● *n. Philos.* a transcendent thing. □□ **transcendence** *n.* **transcendency** *n.* **transcendently** *adv.*
■ *adj.* **1** peerless, incomparable, unequaled, matchless, unrivaled, unparalleled, unique, consummate, paramount, superior, surpassing, supreme, preeminent, sublime, excelling, superb, magnificent, marvelous, transcendental. □□ **transcendence, transcendency** see *predominance* (PREDOMINANT). **transcendently** see *supremely* (SUPREME).

transcendental /tránsendént'l/ *adj. & n.* ● *adj.* **1** = TRANSCENDENT. **2 a** (in Kantian philosophy) presupposed in and necessary to experience; a priori. **b** (in Schelling's philosophy) explaining matter and objective things as products of the subjective mind. **c** (esp. in Emerson's philosophy) regarding the divine as the guiding principle in man. **3 a** visionary; abstract. **b** vague; obscure. **4** *Math.* (of a function) not capable of being produced by the algebraical operations of addition, multiplication, and involution, or the inverse operations. ● *n.* a transcendental term, conception, etc. □ **transcendental meditation** a method of detaching oneself from problems, anxiety, etc., by silent meditation and repetition of a mantra. □□ **transcendentally** *adv.* [med.L *transcendentalis* (as TRANSCENDENT)]
■ *adj.* **3 a** see OCCULT *adj.* 1, 3. **b** see OCCULT *adj.* 2.

transcendentalism /tránsendént'lizəm/ *n.* **1** transcendental philosophy. **2** exalted or visionary language. □□ **transcendentalist** *n.* **transcendentalize** *v.tr.*

transcode /tranzkṓd, trans-/ *v.tr. & intr.* convert from one form of coded representation to another.

transcontinental /tránzkontinént'l, trans-/ *adj. & n.* ● *adj.* (of a railroad, etc.) extending across a continent. ● *n.* a transcontinental railroad or train. □□ **transcontinentally** *adv.*

transcribe /transkríb/ *v.tr.* **1** make a copy of, esp. in writing. **2** transliterate. **3** write out (shorthand, notes, etc.) in ordinary characters or continuous prose. **4 a** record for subsequent reproduction. **b** broadcast in this form. **5** arrange (music) for a different instrument, etc. □□ **transcriber** *n.* **transcription** /-skrípshən/ *n.* **transcriptional** *adj.* **transcriptive** /-skríptiv/ *adj.* [L *transcribere transcript-* (as TRANS-, *scribere* write)]
■ **1** copy, reproduce, replicate, duplicate, record. **2, 3** translate, transliterate, write out, render, represent, show, interpret. **4 a** see RECORD *v.* □□ **transcriber** see SCRIBE *n.* 1. **transcription** see TRANSCRIPT 1.

transcript /tránskript/ *n.* **1** a written or recorded copy. **2** any

copy. [ME f. OF *transcrit* f. L *transcriptum* neut. past part.: see TRANSCRIBE]
■ **1** transcription, record, copy, transliteration. **2** (carbon *or* machine *or* photostatic *or* xerographic) copy, carbon, duplicate, photocopy, facsimile, fax, reproduction, *propr.* Xerox, Photostat.

transducer /tranzdṓosər, -dyṓo-, trans-/ *n.* any device for converting a nonelectrical signal into an electrical one, e.g., pressure into voltage. [L *transducere* lead across (as TRANS-, *ducere* lead)]

transect /transékt/ *v.tr.* cut across or transversely. □□ **transection** *n.* [TRANS- + L *secare sect-* cut]

transept /tránsept/ *n.* **1** either arm of the part of a cross-shaped church at right angles to the nave (*north transept*; *south transept*). **2** this part as a whole. □□ **transeptal** *adj.* [mod.L *transeptum* (as TRANS-, SEPTUM)]

transfer *v. & n.* ● *v.* /transfɚr/ (**transferred, transferring**) **1** *tr.* (often foll. by *to*) **a** convey, remove, or hand over (a thing, etc.) (*transferred the bag from the car to the station*). **b** make over the possession of (property, a ticket, rights, etc.) to a person (*transferred his membership to his son*). **2** *tr. & intr.* change or move to another group, club, department, school, etc. **3** *intr.* change from one station, route, etc., to another on a journey. **4** *tr.* **a** convey (a drawing, etc.) from one surface to another, esp. to a lithographic stone by means of transfer paper. **b** remove (a picture) from one surface to another, esp. from wood or a wall to canvas. **5** *tr.* change (the sense of a word, etc.) by extension or metaphor. ● *n.* /tránsfɚr/ **1** the act or an instance of transferring or being transferred. **2 a** a design, etc., conveyed or to be conveyed from one surface to another. **b** a small usu. colored picture or design on paper, which is transferable to another surface; a decal. **3** a student, etc., who is or is to be transferred. **4 a** the conveyance of property, a right, etc. **b** a document effecting this. **5** a ticket allowing a journey to be continued on another route, etc. □ **transfer company** a company conveying passengers or luggage between stations. **transfer ink** ink used for making designs on a lithographic stone or transfer paper. **transfer paper** specially coated paper to receive the impression of transfer ink and transfer it to stone. **transfer RNA** RNA conveying an amino acid molecule from the cytoplasm to a ribosome for use in protein synthesis, etc. □□ **transferee** /-reé/ *n.* **transferor** /-fɚrər/ esp. *Law n.* **transferrer** /-fɚrər/ *n.* [ME f. F *transférer* or L *transferre* (as TRANS-, *ferre lat-* bear)]
■ *v.* **1 a** move, transport, translocate, convey, remove, carry, take, deliver, bring, transmit, cart, haul, shift, hand (on *or* over), turn over, give, pass (on *or* along *or* over). **b** see *make over* 1. **2** change, switch; see also TRANSPLANT *v.* 1, MOVE *v.* 7. **3** change, switch. ● *n.* **1** move, conveyance, transmittal, transmission, delivery, change, transferal, transference.

transferable /tránsfərəbəl/ *adj.* capable of being transferred. □□ **transferability** /-bílitee/ *n.*
■ see MOVABLE *adj.*

transference /transfɚrəns, tránsfər-/ *n.* **1** the act or an instance of transferring; the state of being transferred. **2** *Psychol.* the redirection of childhood emotions to a new object, esp. to a psychoanalyst.
■ **1** see DISPOSITION 4a, SURRENDER *n.*, TRANSMISSION 1, TRANSIT *n.* 1.

transferral /transfɚrəl/ *n.* = TRANSFER *n.* 1.

transferrin /transférin/ *n.* a protein transporting iron in the blood serum. [TRANS- + L *ferrum* iron]

transfiguration /transfigyəráyshən/ *n.* **1** a change of form or appearance. **2 a** Christ's appearance in radiant glory to three of his disciples (Matt. 17:2, Mark 9:2–3). **b** (**Transfiguration**) the festival of Christ's transfiguration, Aug. 6. [ME f. OF *transfiguration* or L *transfiguratio* (as TRANSFIGURE)]

/.../ **pronunciation**	● **part of speech**
□ **phrases, idioms, and compounds**	
□□ **derivatives**	■ **synonym section**
cross-references appear in SMALL CAPITALS or *italics*	

■ **1** see TRANSFORMATION.

transfigure /transfígyər/ *v.tr.* change in form or appearance, esp. so as to elevate or idealize. [ME f. OF *transfigurer* or L *transfigurare* (as TRANS-, FIGURE)]

■ see TRANSFORM *v.*

transfinite /tránsfínit/ *adj.* **1** beyond or surpassing the finite. **2** *Math.* (of a number) exceeding all finite numbers.

transfix /transfíks/ *v.tr.* **1** pierce with a sharp implement or weapon. **2** root (a person) to the spot with horror or astonishment; paralyze the faculties of. □□ **transfixion** /-fíkshən/ *n.* [L *transfigere transfix-* (as TRANS-, FIX)]

■ **1** pin, fix, impale, skewer, nail, pierce, transpierce, spear, spike, spit, stick, stab. **2** enrapture, hypnotize, mesmerize, rivet, fascinate, bewitch, enchant, engross, root to the spot, stun, paralyze, freeze, stop dead, *colloq.* stop a person in his or her tracks.

transform *v. & n.* ● *v.* /transfáwrm/ **1 a** *tr.* make a thorough or dramatic change in the form, outward appearance, character, etc., of. **b** *intr.* (often foll. by *into, to*) undergo such a change. **2** *tr. Electr.* change the voltage, etc., of (a current). **3** *tr. Math.* change (a mathematical entity) by transformation. ● *n.* /tránsfawrm/ *Math. & Linguistics* the product of a transformation. □□ **transformable** *adj.* **transformative** *adj.* [ME f. OF *transformer* or L *transformare* (as TRANS-, FORM)]

■ *v.* **1** change, modify, transfigure, alter, transmute, metamorphose, turn into, convert, mutate, permute, revolutionize, *joc.* transmogrify. □□ **transformable** see CHANGEABLE 2.

transformation /tránsfərmáyshən/ *n.* **1** the act or an instance of transforming; the state of being transformed. **2** *Zool.* a change of form at metamorphosis, esp. of insects, amphibians, etc. **3** the induced or spontaneous change of one element into another. **4** *Math.* a change from one geometrical figure, expression, or function to another of the same value, magnitude, etc. **5** *Biol.* the modification of a eukaryotic cell from its normal state to a malignant state. **6** *Linguistics* a process, with reference to particular rules, by which one grammatical pattern of sentence structure can be converted into another, or the underlying meaning of a sentence can be converted into a statement of syntax. [ME f. OF *transformation* or LL *transformatio* (as TRANSFORM)]

■ **1–3** change, modification, transfiguration, alteration, transmutation, metamorphosis, conversion, mutation, permutation, revolution, *joc.* transmogrification.

transformational /tránsfərmáyshənəl/ *adj.* relating to or involving transformation. □ **transformational grammar** *Linguistics* a grammar that describes a language by means of transformation (see TRANSFORMATION 6). □□ **transformationally** *adv.*

transformer /transfáwrmər/ *n.* **1** an apparatus for reducing or increasing the voltage of an alternating current. **2** a person or thing that transforms.

transfuse /transfyóoz/ *v.tr.* **1 a** permeate (*purple dye transfused the water*). **b** instill (an influence, quality, etc.) into (*transfused enthusiasm into everyone*). **2 a** transfer (blood) from one person or animal to another. **b** inject (liquid) into a blood vessel to replace lost fluid. **3** cause (fluid, etc.) to pass from one vessel, etc., to another. □□ **transfusion** /-fyóozhən/ *n.* [ME f. L *transfundere transfus-* (as TRANS-, *fundere* pour)]

■ **1 a** infuse, permeate, suffuse, imbue, percolate through. **b** instill, transmit, transfer, inject.

transgenic /tranzjénik/ *adj. Biol.* (of an animal or plant) having genetic material introduced from another species.

transgress /tranzgrés/ *v.tr.* (also *absol.*) **1** go beyond the bounds or limits set by (a commandment, law, etc.); violate; infringe. **2** *Geol.* (of the sea) to spread over (the land). □□ **transgression** /-gréshən/ *n.* **transgressive** *adj.* **transgressor** *n.* [F *transgresser* or L *transgredi transgress-* (as TRANS-, *gradi* go)]

■ **1** sin, offend, err, lapse, fall from grace, misbehave, go wrong or astray, do wrong, *literary or archaic* trespass; (*transgress the law*) break or violate or contravene or go beyond or exceed or overstep or infringe or breach or

defy or disobey the law. □□ **transgression** sin, offense, error, lapse, fall from grace, disobedience, misbehavior, wrong, violation, fault, misdeed, misdemeanor, crime, wrongdoing, infraction, peccadillo, *archaic* trespass.

transgressor sinner, offender, criminal, felon, culprit, lawbreaker, wrongdoer, evildoer, reprobate, villain, miscreant, malefactor, delinquent, *archaic* trespasser.

tranship var. of TRANSSHIP.

transhumance /tranz-hyóomǝns/ *n.* the seasonal moving of livestock to a different region. [F f. *transhumer* f. L TRANS- + *humus* ground]

transient /tránzhǝnt, -shǝnt, -zeeǝnt/ *adj. & n.* ● *adj.* **1** of short duration; momentary; passing; impermanent (*life is transient; of transient interest*). **2** *Mus.* serving only to connect; inessential (*a transient chord*). ● *n.* **1** a temporary visitor, worker, etc. **2** *Electr.* a brief current, etc. □□ **transience** *n.* **transiency** *n.* **transiently** *adv.* [L *transire* (as TRANS-, *ire* go)]

■ *adj.* **1** transitory, temporary, brief, fleeting, momentary, passing, ephemeral, fugitive, evanescent, short-lived, short-term, impermanent, fly-by-night, volatile, *literary* fugacious. ● *n.* **1** see MIGRANT *n.*

transilluminate /tránzilóominayt/ *v.tr.* pass a strong light through for inspection, esp. for medical diagnosis. □□ **transillumination** /-náyshǝn/ *n.*

transire /transír/ *n. Brit.* a customs permit for the passage of goods. [L *transire* go across (as TRANSIENT)]

transistor /tranzístǝr/ *n.* **1** a semiconductor device with three connections, capable of amplification in addition to rectification. **2** (in full **transistor radio**) a portable radio with transistors. [portmanteau word, f. TRANSFER + RESISTOR]

■ **2** see RADIO *n.*

transit /tránzit, -sit/ *n. & v.* ● *n.* **1** the act or process of going, conveying, or being conveyed, esp. over a distance (*transit by rail; made a transit of the lake*). **2** a passage or route (*the overland transit*). **3 a** the apparent passage of a celestial body across the meridian of a place. **b** such an apparent passage across the sun or a planet. **4** the local conveyance of passengers on public transportation. **5** a surveying instrument consisting of a theodolite with a telescope mounted so it can be turned in a vertical plane. ● *v.* (**transited, transiting**) **1** *tr.* make a transit across. **2** *intr.* make a transit. □ **in transit** while going or being conveyed. **transit camp** a camp for the temporary accommodation of soldiers, refugees, etc. **transit circle** (or **instrument**) an instrument for observing the transit of a celestial body across the meridian. **transit compass** (or **theodolite**) a surveyor's instrument for measuring a horizontal angle. **transit duty** duty paid on goods passing through a country. **transit lounge** a lounge at an airport for passengers waiting between flights. **transit visa** a visa allowing only passage through a country. [ME f. L *transitus* f. *transire* (as TRANSIENT)]

■ *n.* **1** moving, movement, travel, traveling, motion, passing, progress, progression, transition; passage, traverse, traversal, traversing; transport, transportation, carriage, haulage, cartage, conveyance, transfer, transference, transferral, transmittal. **2** passage, route. ● *v.* **1** cross, traverse, go across or over or through, move across or over or through, pass across or over or through, travel across or over or through. □ **in transit** see *on the move* 2 (MOVE).

transition /tranzíshǝn, -síshǝn/ *n.* **1** a passing or change from one place, state, condition, etc., to another (*an age of transition; a transition from plains to hills*). **2** *Mus.* a momentary modulation. **3** *Art* a change from one style to another, esp. *Archit.* from Norman to Early English. **4** *Physics* a change in an atomic nucleus or orbital electron with emission or absorption of radiation. □ **transition metal** (or **element**) *Chem.* any of a set of elements in the periodic table characterized by partly filled d or f orbitals and the ability to form colored complexes. **transition point** *Physics* the point at which different phases of the same substance can be in equilibrium. □□ **transitional** *adj.* **transitionally** *adv.* **transitionary** *adj.* [F *transition* or L *transitio* (as TRANSIT)]

■ **1** change, alteration, metamorphosis, changeover, transformation, transmutation, mutation, development, evolution, conversion, modification, *Physiol.* metastasis; movement, motion, passing, progress, progression, transit, passage. □□ **transitional, transitionary** see INTERMEDIATE *adj.*

transitive /tránzitiv, -si-/ *adj.* **1** *Gram.* (of a verb or sense of a verb) that takes a direct object (whether expressed or implied), e.g., *saw* in *saw the donkey, saw that she was ill* (opp. INTRANSITIVE). **2** *Logic* (of a relation) such as to be valid for any two members of a sequence if it is valid for every pair of successive members. □□ **transitively** *adv.* **transitiveness** *n.* **transitivity** /-tívitee/ *n.* [LL *transitivus* (as TRANSIT)]

transitory /tránzitawree/ *adj.* not permanent; brief; transient. □□ **transitorily** /-táwrilee/ *adv.* **transitoriness** /-táwreenis/ *n.* [ME f. AF *transitorie*, OF *transitoire* f. L *transitorius* (as TRANSIT)]

■ see BRIEF *adj.* 1, TRANSIENT *adj.*

transl. *abbr.* **1** translated. **2** translation. **3** translator.

translate /tránzláyt, tráns-/ *v.* **1** *tr.* (also *absol.*) **a** (often foll. by *into*) express the sense of (a word, sentence, speech, book, etc.) in another language. **b** do this as a profession, etc. (*translates for the UN*). **2** *intr.* (of a literary work, etc.) be translatable; bear translation (*does not translate well*). **3** *tr.* express (an idea, book, etc.) in another, esp. simpler, form. **4** *tr.* interpret the significance of; infer as (*translated his silence as dissent*). **5** *tr.* move or change, esp. from one person, place, or condition, to another (*was translated by joy*). **6** *intr.* (foll. by *into*) result in; be converted into; manifest itself as. **7** *tr. Eccl.* **a** remove (a bishop) to another see. **b** remove (a saint's relics, etc.) to another place. *Bibl.* convey to heaven without death; transform. **9** *tr. Mech.* **a** cause (a body) to move so that all its parts travel in the same direction. **b** impart motion without rotation to. □□ **translatable** *adj.* **translatability** /-laytəbílitee/ *n.* [ME f. L *translatus*, past part. of *transferre*: see TRANSFER]

■ **1** convert (into), paraphrase (in), change (into), rewrite (in), interpret (in), transcribe (into); render in, turn into; decode, decipher, metaphrase. **3** interpret, rewrite, explain, rephrase, reword, metaphrase, elucidate, spell out. **4** interpret, construe, take, understand, read; infer as. **5** transform, convert, change, mutate, turn, transmute, metamorphose, alter, *joc.* transmogrify; transfer, convey, carry, move, transport, send.

translation /tranzláyshən, trans-/ *n.* **1** the act or an instance of translating. **2** a written or spoken expression of the meaning of a word, speech, book, etc., in another language. □□ **translational** *adj.* **translationally** *adv.*

■ **1** interpretation, rewriting, rewrite, explanation, rewording, metaphrase, elucidation; metamorphosis, change, alteration, transmutation, transfiguration, transformation, conversion, *joc.* transmogrification; transfer, transference, transferral, conveyance, movement, transportation, transport, transmittal, transmission. **2** conversion, paraphrase, interpretation, transcription, transliteration, rendering, rendition, version, rewrite, rewriting, rewording, rephrasing, metaphrase, gloss, decipherment, decoding, explanation, elucidation.

translator /tránzláytər, trans-/ *n.* **1** a person who translates from one language into another. **2** a television relay transmitter. **3** a program that translates from one (esp. programming) language into another.

transliterate /tranzlítərayt, trans-/ *v.tr.* represent (a word, etc.) in the closest corresponding letters or characters of a different alphabet or language. □□ **transliteration** /-ráyshən/ *n.* **transliterator** *n.* [TRANS- + L *littera* letter]

■ see TRANSCRIBE 2, 3. □□ **transliteration** see TRANSCRIPT *n.* 1, TRANSLATION 2.

translocate /tranzlṓkayt, trans-/ *v.tr.* **1** move from one place to another. **2** (usu. in *passive*) *Bot.* move (substances in a plant) from one part to another. □□ **translocation** /-káyshən/ *n.*

translucent /tranzlṓsənt, tráns-/ *adj.* **1** allowing light to

pass through diffusely; semitransparent. **2** transparent. □□ **translucence** *n.* **translucency** *n.* **translucently** *adv.* [L *translucēre* (as TRANS-, *lucēre* shine)]

■ see CLEAR *adj.* 3a, *see-through* (SEE¹).

translunar /tránzlṓnər, tráns-/ *adj.* **1** lying beyond the moon. **2** of or relating to space travel or a trajectory toward the moon.

transmarine /tránzmərén, tráns-/ *adj.* situated or going beyond the sea. [L *transmarinus* f. *marinus* MARINE]

transmigrant /tranzmígrənt, trans-/ *adj. & n.* ● *adj.* passing through, esp. a country on the way to another. ● *n.* a migrant or alien passing through a country, etc. [L *transmigrant-*, part. stem of *transmigrare* (as TRANSMIGRATE)]

transmigrate /tránzmígráyt, trans-/ *v.intr.* **1** (of the soul) pass into a different body; undergo metempsychosis. **2** migrate. □□ **transmigration** /-gráyshən/ *n.* **transmigrator** *n.* **transmigratory** /-mígrətawree/ *adj.* [ME f. L *transmigrare* (as TRANS-, MIGRATE)]

transmission /tranzmíshən, trans-/ *n.* **1** the act or an instance of transmitting; the state of being transmitted. **2** a broadcast radio or television program. **3** the mechanism by which power is transmitted from an engine to the axle in a motor vehicle. □ **transmission line** a conductor or conductors carrying electricity over large distances with minimum losses. [L *transmissio* (as TRANS-, MISSION)]

■ **1** transfer, transference, transferral, conveyance, carriage, movement, transportation, transport, forwarding, shipping, shipment, transmittal, dispatch; broadcasting, dissemination, communication, telecasting. **2** broadcast, telecast, program, show.

transmit /tranzmít, trans-/ *v.tr.* (**transmitted, transmitting**) **1 a** pass or hand on; transfer (*transmitted the message*; *how diseases are transmitted*). **b** communicate (ideas, emotions, etc.). **2 a** allow (heat, light, sound, electricity, etc.) to pass through; be a medium for. **b** be a medium for (ideas, emotions, etc.) (*his message transmits hope*). **3** broadcast (a radio or television program). □□ **transmissible** /-mísəbəl/ *adj.* **transmissive** /-mísiv/ *adj.* **transmittable** *adj.* **transmittal** *n.* [ME f. L *transmittere* (as TRANS-, *mittere* miss- send)]

■ **1 a** send, transfer, convey, communicate, pass *or* hand on, relay, deliver, forward, dispatch; post, ship, cable, radio, telegraph, fax, telex, telephone, mail, *colloq.* phone, wire. **b** see COMMUNICATE 1a. **2** pass on, send, direct, conduct, channel. **3** see BROADCAST *v.* 1a. □□ **transmissible** see CATCHING 1a. **transmittal** see TRANSMISSION 1.

transmitter /tránzmítər, trans-/ *n.* **1** a person or thing that transmits. **2** a set of equipment used to generate and transmit electromagnetic waves carrying messages, signals, etc., esp. those of radio or television. **3** = NEUROTRANSMITTER.

transmogrify /tranzmógrifi, trans-/ *v.tr.* (**-ies, -ied**) *joc.* transform, esp. in a magical or surprising manner. □□ **transmogrification** /-fikáyshən/ *n.* [17th c.: orig. unkn.]

■ see TRANSFORM *v.* □□ **transmogrification** see TRANSFORMATION.

transmontane /transmóntayn, tranz-/ *adj.* = TRAMONTANE. [L *transmontanus*: see TRAMONTANE]

■ see TRAMONTANE *adj.*

transmutation /tránzmyōōtáyshən, tráns-/ *n.* **1** the act or an instance of transmuting or changing into another form, etc. **2** *Alchemy hist.* the supposed process of changing base metals into gold. **3** *Physics* the changing of one element into another by nuclear bombardment, etc. **4** *Geom.* the changing of a figure or body into another of the same area or volume. **5** *Biol.* Lamarck's theory of the change of one species into another. □□ **transmutational** *adj.* **transmutationist** *n.* [ME f. OF *transmutation* or LL *transmutatio* (as TRANSMUTE)]

/ . . . / **pronunciation** ● **part of speech**
□ **phrases, idioms, and compounds**
□□ **derivatives** ■ **synonym section**
cross-references appear in SMALL CAPITALS or *italics*

■ **1** see TRANSFORMATION.

transmute /tranzmyŏŏt, trans-/ *v.tr.* **1** change the form, nature, or substance of. **2** *Alchemy hist.* subject (base metals) to transmutation. □□ **transmutable** *adj.* **transmutability** /-təbílitee/ *n.* **transmutative** /-myŏŏtətiv/ *adj.* **transmuter** *n.* [ME f. L *transmutare* (as TRANS-, *mutare* change)]

■ see TRANSFORM *v.*

transnational /tránznáshənəl, tráns-/ *adj.* extending beyond national boundaries.

transoceanic /tránzŏshiánik, tráns-/ *adj.* **1** situated beyond the ocean. **2** concerned with crossing the ocean (*transoceanic flight*).

transom /tránsəm/ *n.* **1** a horizontal bar of wood or stone across a window or the top of a door (cf. MULLION). **2** each of several beams fixed across the sternpost of a ship. **3** a beam across a saw pit to support a log. **4** a strengthening crossbar. **5** = *transom window*. □ **transom window 1** a window divided by a transom. **2** a window placed above the transom of a door or larger window; a fanlight. □□ **transomed** *adj.* [ME *traversayn, transyn, -ing,* f. OF *traversin* f. *traverse* TRAVERSE]

transonic /transónik/ *adj.* (also **transsonic**) relating to speeds close to that of sound. [TRANS- + SONIC, after *supersonic*, etc.]

transpacific /tránzpəsífik, tráns-/ *adj.* **1** beyond the Pacific. **2** crossing the Pacific.

transparence /tranzpárəns, traanz-, -páirəns/ *n.* = TRANSPARENCY 1.

transparency /tranzpárənsee, -páirənsee, trans-/ *n.* (*pl.* **-ies**) **1** the condition of being transparent. **2** *Photog.* a positive transparent photograph on glass or in a frame to be viewed using a slide projector, etc. **3** a picture, inscription, etc., made visible by a light behind it. [med.L *transparentia* (as TRANSPARENT)]

■ **1** see CLARITY. **2** slide.

transparent /tranzpáirənt, -párənt, trans-/ *adj.* **1** allowing light to pass through so that bodies can be distinctly seen (cf. TRANSLUCENT). **2 a** (of a disguise, pretext, etc.) easily seen through. **b** (of a motive, quality, etc.) easily discerned; evident; obvious. **3** (of a person, etc.) easily understood; frank; open. **4** *Physics* transmitting heat or other electromagnetic rays without distortion. □□ **transparently** *adv.* **transparentness** *n.* [ME f. OF f. med.L *transparens* f. L *transparēre* shine through (as TRANS-, *parēre* appear)]

■ **1** (crystal) clear, pellucid, diaphanous, see-through, limpid, crystalline, sheer. **2** plain, apparent, obvious, evident, unambiguous, patent, manifest, unmistakable, (crystal) clear, as plain as day, as plain as the nose on one's face, undisguised, recognizable, understandable. **3** candid, open, frank, plainspoken, direct, unambiguous, unequivocal, straightforward, ingenuous, forthright, aboveboard, artless, guileless, simple, naive, undissembling, *colloq.* on the level, upfront.

transpierce /tranzpéers, trans-/ *v.tr.* pierce through.

transpire /transpír/ *v.* **1** *intr.* (of a secret or something unknown) leak out; come to be known. **2** *intr. disp.* **a** (prec. by *it* as subject) turn out; prove to be the case (*it transpired he knew nothing about it*). **b** occur; happen. **3** *tr. & intr.* emit (vapor, sweat, etc.), or be emitted, through the skin or lungs; perspire. **4** *intr.* (of a plant or leaf) release water vapor. □□ **transpirable** *adj.* **transpiration** /-spiráyshən/ *n.* **transpiratory** /-spírətawree/ *adj.* [F *transpirer* or med.L *transpirare* (as TRANS-, L *spirare* breathe)]

■ **1** become known, be rumored, be revealed, come to light, leak out, come out, get out, emerge. **2 a** turn out, emerge, be revealed. **b** happen, occur, take place, come about, come to pass, materialize, arise.

transplant *v. & n.* ● *v.tr.* /tranzplánt, trans-/ **1 a** plant in another place (*transplanted the daffodils*). **b** move to another place (*whole nations were transplanted*). **2** *Surgery* transfer (living tissue or an organ) and implant in another part of the body or in another body. ● *n.* /tránzplant, trans-/ **1** *Surgery* **a** the transplanting of an organ or tissue. **b** such an organ, etc. **2** a thing, esp. a plant, transplanted. □□ **trans-**

plantable *adj.* **transplantation** /-táyshən/ *n.* **transplanter** *n.* [ME f. LL *transplantare* (as TRANS-, PLANT)]

■ *v.* **1** displace, move, relocate, shift, uproot, resettle, transfer, *formal* remove. **2** graft. ● *n.* **1 a** transplantation, implantation. **b** implant, graft.

transponder /tranzpóndər, trans-/ *n.* a device for receiving a radio signal and automatically transmitting a different signal. [TRANSMIT + RESPOND]

transpontine /tránzpóntin, tráns-/ *adj.* on the other side of a bridge, esp. *Brit.* on the south side of the Thames. [TRANS- + L *pons pontis* bridge]

transport *v. & n.* ● *v.tr.* /tranzpáwrt, trans-/ **1** take or carry (a person, goods, troops, baggage, etc.) from one place to another. **2** *hist.* take (a criminal) to a penal colony; deport. **3** (as **transported** *adj.*) (usu. foll. by *with*) affected with strong emotion. ● *n.* /tránzpawrt, tráns-/ **1 a** a system of conveying people, goods, etc., from place to place. **b** esp. *Brit.* the means of this (*our transport has arrived*). **2** a ship, aircraft, etc., used to carry soldiers, stores, etc. **3** (esp. in *pl.*) vehement emotion (*transports of joy*). **4** *hist.* a transported convict. [ME f. OF *transporter* or L *transportare* (as TRANS-, *portare* carry)]

■ *v.* **1** carry, bear, convey, move, remove, transfer, ferry, deliver, fetch, bring, get, take, ship, haul, cart, transmit, send, forward, freight. **2** exile, banish, deport, send away. **3** (**transported**) carried away, enraptured, captivated, delighted, charmed, spellbound, bewitched, fascinated, enchanted, entranced, enthralled, hypnotized, mesmerized, electrified, ravished; rapt, overjoyed, ecstatic, elated. ● *n.* **1 a** transportation, conveyance, shipping, transfer, transferral, shipment, haulage, cartage, carriage, moving. **b** carrier, conveyance, transporter, transportation. **3** rapture, ecstasy.

transportable /tranzpáwrtəbəl, trans-/ *adj.* **1** capable of being transported. **2** *hist.* (of an offender or an offense) punishable by transportation. □□ **transportability** /-bílitee/ *n.*

■ **1** see PORTABLE *adj.*

transportation /tránzpərtáyshən, tráns-/ *n.* **1** the act of conveying or the process of being conveyed. **2 a** a system of conveying. **b** the means of this. **3** *hist.* removal to a penal colony.

■ **1, 2** see TRANSIT *n.* 1. **3** see EXILE *n.* 1.

transporter /tránzpáwrtər, tráns-/ *n.* **1** a person or device that transports. **2** a vehicle used to transport other vehicles or large pieces of machinery, etc., by road. □ **transporter bridge** a bridge carrying vehicles, etc., across water on a suspended moving platform.

■ **1** see CARRIER 1, 2.

transpose /tranzpóz, trans-/ *v.tr.* **1 a** cause (two or more things) to change places. **b** change the position of (a thing) in a series. **2** change the order or position of (words or a word) in a sentence. **3** *Mus.* write or play in a different key. **4** *Algebra* transfer (a term) with a changed sign to the other side of an equation. □□ **transposable** *adj.* **transposal** *n.* **transposer** *n.* [ME, = transform f. OF *transposer* (as TRANS-, L *ponere* put)]

■ **1, 2** exchange, interchange, rearrange, reverse, switch, swap, trade, commute, transfer.

transposition /tránzpəzíshən, tráns-/ *n.* the act or an instance of transposing; the state of being transposed. □□ **transpositional** *adj.* **transpositive** /-pózitiv/ *adj.* [F *transposition* or LL *transpositio* (as TRANS-, POSITION)]

transsexual /tránsékshŏŏəl/ *adj. & n.* ● *adj.* having the physical characteristics of one sex and the supposed psychological characteristics of the other. ● *n.* **1** a transsexual person. **2** a person whose sex has been changed by surgery. □□ **transsexualism** *n.*

transship /tranz-shíp, trans-/ *v.tr.* (also **tranship**) *intr.* (**-shipped, -shipping**) transfer from one ship or form of transport to another. □□ **transshipment** *n.*

transsonic var. of TRANSONIC.

transubstantiation /tránsəbstánsheeáyshən/ *n. Theol. & RC Ch.* the conversion of the Eucharistic elements wholly into the body and blood of Christ, only the appearance of bread and wine still remaining. [med.L (as TRANS-, SUBSTANCE)]

transude /transṓod/ *v.intr.* (of a fluid) pass through the pores or interstices of a membrane, etc. □□ **transudation** /-dáyshən/ *n.* **transudatory** /-dətawree/ *adj.* [F *transsuder* f. OF *tressuer* (as TRANS-, L *sudare* sweat)]
■ see PERCOLATE 1. □□ **transudation** see SECRETION 1a.

transuranic /tránzyŏŏránik, tráns-/ *adj. Chem.* (of an element) having a higher atomic number than uranium.

transversal /tranzvә́rsəl, trans-/ *adj. & n.* ● *adj.* (of a line) cutting a system of lines. ● *n.* a transversal line. □□ **transversality** /-sálitee/ *n.* **transversally** *adv.* [ME f. med.L *transversalis* (as TRANSVERSE)]

transverse /tránzvә́rs, tráns-/ *adj.* situated, arranged, or acting in a crosswise direction. □ **transverse magnet** a magnet with poles at the sides and not the ends. **transverse wave** *Physics* a wave in which the medium vibrates at right angles to the direction of its propagation. □□ **transversely** *adv.* [L *transvertere transvers-* turn across (as TRANS-, *vertere* turn)]

transvestism /tranzvéstizəm, trans-/ *n.* (also **transvestitism** /-véstitizəm/) the practice of wearing the clothes of the opposite sex, esp. as a sexual stimulus. □□ **transvestist** *n.* [G *Transvestismus* f. TRANS- + L *vestire* clothe]

transvestite /tranzvéstīt, trans-/ *n.* a person given to transvestism.

trap¹ /trap/ *n. & v.* ● *n.* **1 a** an enclosure or device, often baited, for catching animals, usu. by affording a way in but not a way out. **b** a device with bait for killing vermin, esp. = MOUSETRAP. **2** a trick betraying a person into speech or an act (*is this question a trap?*). **3** an arrangement to catch an unsuspecting person, e.g., a speeding motorist. **4** a device for hurling an object such as a clay pigeon into the air to be shot at. **5** a compartment from which a greyhound is released at the start of a race. **6** a shoe-shaped wooden device with a pivoted bar that sends a ball from its heel into the air on being struck at the other end with a bat. **7 a** a curve in a downpipe, etc., that fills with liquid and forms a seal against the upward passage of gases. **b** a device for preventing the passage of steam, etc. **8** *Golf* a bunker. **9** a device allowing pigeons to enter but not leave a loft. **10** a two-wheeled carriage (*a pony and trap*). **11** = TRAPDOOR. **12** *sl.* the mouth (esp. *shut one's trap*). **13** (esp. in *pl.*) *colloq.* a percussion instrument, esp. in a jazz band. ● *v.tr.* (**trapped, trapping**) **1** catch (an animal) in a trap. **2** catch (a person) by means of a trick, plan, etc. **3** stop and retain in or as in a trap. **4** provide (a place) with traps. □□ **traplike** *adj.* [OE *treppe, træppe,* rel. to MDu. *trappe,* med.L *trappa,* of uncert. orig.]
■ *n.* **1** snare, pitfall, gin, springe, deadfall. **2** trick, subterfuge, wile, ruse, stratagem, deception, artifice, *colloq.* ploy. **3** ambush, device, snare, pitfall, mantrap, booby trap, setup. **12** mouth, *sl.* yap, esp. *Brit. sl.* gob. ● *v.* **1** snare, ensnare, entrap, catch, capture, net, corner, ambush. **2** trick, deceive, fool, dupe, beguile, inveigle, catch, catch out. **3** imprison, confine, lock, hold, keep, pin down.

trap² /trap/ *v.tr.* (**trapped, trapping**) (often foll. by *out*) **1** provide with trappings. **2** adorn. [obs. *trap* (n.): ME f. OF *drap*: see DRAPE]

trap³ /trap/ *n.* (in full **traprock**) any dark-colored igneous rock, finegrained and columnar in structure, esp. basalt. [Sw. *trapp* f. *trappa* stair, f. the often stairlike appearance of its outcroppings]

trapdoor /trápdáwr/ *n.* a door or hatch in a floor, ceiling, or roof, usu. made flush with the surface. □ **trapdoor spider** any of various spiders, esp. of the family Ctenizidae, that make a hinged trapdoor at the top of their nest.

trapeze /trapéez/ *n.* a crossbar or set of crossbars suspended by ropes used as a swing for acrobatics, etc. [F *trapèze* f. LL *trapezium*: see TRAPEZIUM]

trapezium /trəpéezeeəm/ *n.* (*pl.* **trapezia** /-zeeə/ or **trapeziums**) **1** a quadrilateral with no two sides parallel. **2** *Brit.* = TRAPEZOID 1. [LL f. Gk *trapezion* f. *trapeza* table]

trapezoid /trápizoyd/ *n.* **1** a quadrilateral with only one pair

of sides parallel. **2** *Brit.* = TRAPEZIUM 1. □□ **trapezoidal** *adj.* [mod.L *trapezoides* f. Gk *trapezoeidēs* (as TRAPEZIUM)]

trapper /trápər/ *n.* a person who traps wild animals, esp. to obtain furs.

trappings /trápingz/ *n.pl.* **1** ornamental accessories, esp. as an indication of status (*the trappings of office*). **2** the harness of a horse, esp. when ornamental. [ME (as TRAP²)]
■ **1** accoutrements, panoply, caparison, equipage, apparatus, equipment, accompaniments, paraphernalia, appointments, furniture, gear, rig, decoration(s), embellishment(s), accessories, frippery, fripperies, adornment(s), ornaments, trimmings, fittings, finery, *archaic* raiment.

Trappist /trápist/ *n. & adj.* ● *n.* a member of a branch of the Cistercian order founded in 1664 at La Trappe in Normandy, France, and noted for an austere rule including a vow of silence. ● *adj.* of or relating to this order. [F *trappiste* f. *La Trappe*]

traps /traps/ *n.pl.* esp. *Brit. colloq.* personal belongings; baggage. [perh. contr. f. TRAPPINGS]

trash /trash/ *n. & v.* ● *n.* **1 a** worthless or poor quality stuff, esp. literature. **b** rubbish; refuse. **c** absurd talk or ideas; nonsense. **2** a worthless person or persons. **3** a thing of poor workmanship or material. **4** (in full **cane trash**) *W.Ind.* the refuse of crushed sugarcanes and dried stripped leaves and tops of sugarcane used as fuel. ● *v.tr.* **1** *colloq.* wreck. **2** strip (sugarcanes) of their outer leaves to speed up the ripening process. **3** *colloq.* expose the worthless nature of; disparage. **4** *colloq.* throw away; discard. [16th c.: orig. unkn.]
■ *n.* **1 a** junk, knickknacks, gewgaws, trifles, bric-a-brac, frippery, fripperies, bits and pieces, odds and ends, lumber, trinkets, tinsel, *Brit. colloq.* brummagem goods; rubbish, garbage. **b** rubbish, litter, garbage, waste, refuse, debris, rubble, scrap, dregs, dross, scoria, slag, dirt, sweepings. **c** rubbish, (stuff and) nonsense, balderdash, moonshine, gibberish, bunkum, garbage, twaddle, *colloq.* gobbledegook, flapdoodle, piffle, malarkey, hogwash, esp. *Brit. colloq.* tosh, gammon, *sl.* tommyrot, rot, bunk, hooey, poppycock, baloney, eyewash, bilgewater, bull, hokum, *Brit. sl.* codswallop. **2** see RABBLE¹ 2, 3. ● *v.* **1** destroy, ruin, wreck, vandalize, deface, *sl.* total. **3** see PAN¹ *v.* 1. **4** see DISCARD *v.*

trashy /tráshee/ *adj.* (**trashier, trashiest**) worthless; poorly made. □□ **trashily** *adv.* **trashiness** *n.*
■ see WORTHLESS.

trattoria /trátərée/ *n.* an Italian restaurant. [It.]

trauma /trówmə, tráw-/ *n.* (*pl.* **traumata** /-mətə/ or **traumas**) **1** any physical wound or injury. **2** physical shock following this, characterized by a drop in body temperature, mental confusion, etc. **3** *Psychol.* emotional shock following a stressful event, sometimes leading to long-term neurosis. □□ **traumatize** *v.tr.* **traumatization** *n.* [Gk *trauma traumatos* wound]
■ **1** see WOUND¹ *n.* 1. **2** shock. □□ **traumatize** see WOUND¹ *v.*, SHOCK¹ *v.* 1.

traumatic /trəmátik, trow-, traw-/ *adj.* **1** of or causing trauma. **2** *colloq.* (in general use) distressing; emotionally disturbing (*a traumatic experience*). **3** of or for wounds. □□ **traumatically** *adv.* [LL *traumaticus* f. Gk *traumatikos* (as TRAUMA)]
■ **1, 2** shocking, upsetting, disturbing, painful, agonizing, distressing, harmful, hurtful, injurious, damaging, wounding, harrowing, traumatizing.

traumatism /trówmətizəm, tráw-/ *n.* **1** the action of a trauma. **2** a condition produced by this.

trav. *abbr.* **1** travel. **2** traveler.

travail /trəváyl, trávayl/ *n. & v.* ● *n.* **1** painful or laborious effort. **2** the pangs of childbirth. ● *v.intr.* undergo a painful

---

/.../ **pronunciation**   ● **part of speech**
□ **phrases, idioms, and compounds**
□□ **derivatives**   ■ **synonym section**
cross-references appear in SMALL CAPITALS or *italics*

effort, esp. in childbirth. [ME f. OF *travail, travaillier* ult. f. med.L *trepalium* instrument of torture f. L *tres* three + *palus* stake]

■ *n.* **1** see LABOR *n.* 1. **2** see LABOR *n.* 3. ● *v.* see LABOR *v.* 1, 2.

travel /trávəl/ *v. & n.* ● *v.intr. & tr.* (**traveled, traveling** or **travelled, travelling**) **1** *intr.* go from one place to another; make a journey, esp. of some length or abroad. **2** *tr.* **a** journey along or through (a country). **b** cover (a distance) in traveling. **3** *intr. colloq.* withstand a long journey (*wines that do not travel*). **4** *intr.* go from place to place as a salesman. **5** *intr.* move or proceed in a specified manner or at a specified rate (*light travels faster than sound*). **6** *intr. colloq.* move quickly. **7** *intr.* pass esp. in a deliberate or systematic manner from point to point (*the photographer's eye traveled over the scene*). **8** *intr.* (of a machine or part) move or operate in a specified way. **9** *intr.* (of deer, etc.) move onward in feeding. ● *n.* **1 a** the act of traveling, esp. in foreign countries. **b** (often in *pl.*) a time or occurrence of this (*have returned from their travels*). **2** the range, rate, or mode of motion of a part in machinery. □ **travel agency** (or **bureau**) an agency that makes the necessary arrangements for travelers. **travel agent** a person or business acting as a travel agency. **traveling rug** *Brit.* = *lap robe* (see LAP¹). **traveling salesman** a person who travels to solicit orders as a representative of a company, etc. **traveling wave** *Physics* a wave in which the medium moves in the direction of propagation. □□ **traveling** *adj.* [ME, orig. = TRAVAIL]

■ *v.* **1** journey, go, move, proceed, roam, rove, tour, take *or* make a trip, take *or* make a tour, take *or* make an excursion, take *or* make a junket, take *or* make a journey, commute, trek, voyage, *archaic or joc.* peregrinate. **2** see TRAVERSE *v.* 1. **5** proceed, move, advance, progress, go. **7** pass, move, go, roam, rove, range, wander. ● *n.* **1 a** traveling, tourism, touring, globe-trotting. **b** trip(s), expedition(s), journey(s), excursion(s), tour(s), voyage(s), touring, trek(s), trekking, traveling, wandering(s), junket(s), pilgrimage(s), *archaic or joc.* peregrination(s). □□ **traveling** itinerant, wandering, peripatetic, roving, mobile, nomadic, touring, wayfaring, migratory, restless.

traveled /trávəld/ *adj.* experienced in traveling (also in *comb.*: *much traveled*).

traveler /trávələr, trávlər/ *n.* **1** a person who travels or is traveling. **2** *Brit.* a traveling salesman. **3** a Gypsy. **4** *Austral.* an itinerant worker; a swagman. **5** a moving mechanism, such as an overhead crane. □ **traveler's check** a check for a fixed amount that may be cashed on signature, usu. internationally.

■ **1** tourist, vacationer, voyager, sightseer, globe-trotter, wanderer, hiker, rover, wayfarer, bird of passage, day-tripper, commuter, passenger, esp. *Brit.* holiday maker, *Brit.* tripper, *colloq.* rubberneck, jet-setter.

travelogue /trávəlôg/ *n.* (also **travelog**) a movie or illustrated lecture about travel. [TRAVEL after *monologue*, etc.]

traverse /trávərs, trəvə́rs/ *v. & n.* ● *v.* **1** *tr.* travel or lie across (*traversed the country; a pit traversed by a beam*). **2** *tr.* consider or discuss the whole extent of (a subject). **3** *tr.* turn (a large gun) horizontally. **4** *tr. Law* deny (an allegation) in pleading. **5** *tr.* thwart, frustrate, or oppose (a plan or opinion). **6** *intr.* (of the needle of a compass, etc.) turn on or as on a pivot. **7** *intr.* (of a horse) walk obliquely. **8** *intr.* make a traverse in climbing. ● *n.* **1** a sideways movement. **2** an act of traversing. **3** a thing, esp. part of a structure, that crosses another. **4** a gallery extending from side to side of a church or other building. **5 a** a single line of survey, usu. plotted from compass bearings and with chained or paced distances between angular points. **b** a tract surveyed in this way. **6** *Naut.* a zigzag line taken by a ship because of contrary winds or currents. **7** a skier's similar movement on a slope. **8** the sideways movement of a part in a machine. **9 a** a sideways motion across a rock face from one practicable line of ascent or descent to another. **b** a place where this is necessary. **10** *Mil.* a pair of right-angle bends in a trench to

avoid enfilading fire. **11** *Law* a denial, esp. of an allegation of a matter of fact. **12** the act of turning a large gun horizontally to the required direction. □□ **traversable** *adj.* **traversal** *n.* **traverser** *n.* [OF *traverser* f. LL *traversare, transversare* (as TRANSVERSE)]

■ *v.* **1** cross, crisscross, pass over *or* through, move over *or* through, walk, cover, travel (over *or* through), roam, wander, range, tramp, tour; go across, lie across *or* athwart, extend across *or* athwart, bridge, span, intersect. **2** examine, look into, scrutinize, inspect, investigate, review, study, look at, consider, contemplate, scan, look over, check, survey, reconnoiter, observe. **5** oppose, cross, thwart, frustrate, go *or* act against, go *or* act in opposition to, go *or* act counter to, conflict (with), controvert, contravene, counter, obstruct, contradict, deny, *archaic or literary* gainsay. ● *n.* **2** see TRANSIT *n.* 1. □□ **traversable** see NAVIGABLE 1. **traversal** see PASSAGE¹ 1.

travertine /trávərteen/ *n.* a white or light-colored calcareous rock deposited from springs. [It. *travertino, tivertino* f. L *tiburtinus* of Tibur (Tivoli) near Rome]

travesty /trávistee/ *n. & v.* ● *n.* (*pl.* **-ies**) a grotesque misrepresentation or imitation (*a travesty of justice*). ● *v.tr.* (**-ies, -ied**) make or be a travesty of. [(orig. adj.) f. F *travesti* past part. of *travestir* disguise, change the clothes of, f. It. *travestire* (as TRANS-, *vestire* clothe)]

■ *n.* see PARODY *n.* 2, MOCKERY 1b, 2. ● *v.* see MOCK *v.* 2.

travois /trəvóy/ *n.* (*pl.* same /-vóyz/) a vehicle of two joined poles pulled by a horse, etc., for carrying a burden, orig. used by Native American people of the Plains. [earlier *travail* f. F, perh. the same word as TRAVAIL]

trawl /trawl/ *v. & n.* ● *v.* **1** *intr.* **a** fish with a trawl or seine. **b** seek a suitable candidate, etc., by sifting through a large number. **2** *tr.* **a** catch by trawling. **b** seek a suitable candidate, etc., from (a certain area or group, etc.) (*trawled the schools for new trainees*). ● *n.* **1** an act of trawling. **2** (in full **trawl net**) a large wide-mouthed fishing net dragged by a boat along the bottom. **3** (in full **trawl line**) a long sea fishing line buoyed and supporting short lines with baited hooks. [prob. f. MDu. *traghelen* to drag (cf. *traghel* dragnet), perh. f. L *tragula*]

trawler /tráwlər/ *n.* **1** a boat used for trawling. **2** a person who trawls.

tray /tray/ *n.* **1** a flat shallow vessel usu. with a raised rim for carrying dishes, etc., or containing small articles, papers, etc. **2** a shallow lidless box forming a compartment of a trunk. □□ **trayful** *n.* (*pl.* **-fuls**) [OE *trīg* f. Gmc, rel. to TREE]

treacherous /tréchərəs/ *adj.* **1** guilty of or involving treachery. **2** (of the weather, ice, the memory, etc.) not to be relied on; likely to fail or give way. □□ **treacherously** *adv.* **treacherousness** *n.* [ME f. OF *trecherous* f. *trecheor* a cheat f. *trechier, trichier*: see TRICK]

■ **1** see *perfidious* (PERFIDY), *traitorous* (TRAITOR). **2** see DANGEROUS. □□ **treacherously** see *behind a person's back.*

treachery /tréchəree/ *n.* (*pl.* **-ies**) **1** violation of faith or trust; betrayal. **2** an instance of this.

■ see *betrayal* (BETRAY).

treacle /treekəl/ *n.* **1** esp. *Brit.* **a** a syrup produced in refining sugar. **b** molasses. **2** cloying sentimentality or flattery. □□ **treacly** *adj.* [ME *triacle* f. OF f. L *theriaca* f. Gk *thēriakē* antidote against venom, fem. of *thēriakos* (adj.) f. *thērion* wild beast]

tread /tred/ *v. & n.* ● *v.* (**trod** /trod/; **trodden** /tród'n/ or **trod**) **1** *intr.* (often foll. by *on*) **a** set down one's foot; walk or step (*do not tread on the grass; trod on a snail*). **b** (of the foot) be set down. **2** *tr.* **a** walk on. **b** (often foll. by *down*) press or crush with the feet. **3** *tr.* perform (steps, etc.) by walking (*trod a few paces*). **4** *tr.* make (a hole, etc.) by treading. **5** *intr.* (foll. by *on*) suppress; subdue mercilessly. **6** *tr.* make a track with (dirt, etc.) from the feet. **7** *tr.* (often foll. by *in, into*) press down into the ground with the feet (*trod dirt into the carpet*). **8** *tr.* (also *absol.*) (of a male bird) copulate with (a hen). ● *n.* **1** a manner or sound of walking (*recog-*

nized the heavy tread). **2** the top surface of a step or stair. **3** the thick molded part of a vehicle tire for gripping the road. **4 a** the part of a wheel that touches the ground or rail. **b** the part of a rail that the wheels touch. **5** the part of the sole of a shoe that rests on the ground. **6** (of a male bird) copulation. □ **tread the boards** (or **stage**) be or become an actor; appear on the stage. **tread on air** see AIR. **tread on a person's toes** offend a person or encroach on a person's privileges, etc. **tread out** esp. *Brit.* **1** stamp out (a fire, etc.). **2** press out (wine or grain) with the feet. **tread water** maintain an upright position in the water by moving the feet with a walking movement and the hands with a downward circular motion. **tread wheel** a treadmill or similar machine. □□ **treader** *n.* [OE *tredan* f. WG]
■ *v.* **1, 3** see WALK *v.* 1, 2. **2** see TRAMPLE *v.* 1. ● *n.* **1** step, footstep, footfall. □ **tread on a person's toes** see OFFEND 1, 2.

treadle /trédəl/ *n. & v.* ● *n.* a lever worked by the foot and imparting motion to a machine. ● *v.intr.* work a treadle. [OE *tredel* stair (as TREAD)]

treadmill /trédmil/ *n.* **1** a device for producing motion by the weight of persons or animals stepping on movable steps on the inner surface of a revolving upright wheel. **2** monotonous routine work.
■ **2** see RUT 2, LABOR *n.* 1.

treason /tréezən/ *n.* **1** violation by a subject of allegiance to the sovereign or to the nation, esp. by attempting to kill or overthrow the sovereign or to overthrow the government. **2** *hist.* murder of one's master or husband, regarded as a form of treason. □□ **treasonous** *adj.* [ME f. AF *treisoun*, etc., OF *traïson*, f. L *traditio* handing over (as TRADITION)]
■ **1** see PERFIDY.

treasonable /tréezənəbəl/ *adj.* involving or guilty of treason. □□ **treasonably** *adv.*
■ see *perfidious* (PERFIDY), *traitorous* (TRAITOR).

treasure /trézhər/ *n. & v.* ● *n.* **1 a** precious metals or gems. **b** a hoard of these. **c** accumulated wealth. **2** a thing valued for its rarity, workmanship, associations, etc. (*art treasures*). **3** *colloq.* a much loved or highly valued person. ● *v.tr.* **1** (often foll. by *up*) store up as valuable. **2** value (esp. a long-kept possession) highly. □ **treasure hunt 1** a search for treasure. **2** a game in which players seek a hidden object from a series of clues. **treasure trove 1** *Law* treasure of unknown ownership found hidden. **2** a hidden store of valuables. [ME f. OF *tresor*, ult. f. Gk *thēsauros*: see THESAURUS]
■ *n.* **1** wealth, riches, money, fortune, valuables, cash, cache, hoard, trove, treasure trove. **3** pride (and joy), delight, joy, darling, ideal, apple of one's eye, jewel, gem, pearl, prize, find, catch. ● *v.* **2** hold dear, cherish, value, prize, esteem, rate *or* value highly, appreciate.

treasurer /trézhərər/ *n.* **1** a person appointed to administer the funds of a society or municipality, etc. **2** an officer authorized to receive and disburse public revenues. □□ **treasurership** *n.* [ME f. AF *tresorer*, OF *tresorier* f. *tresor* (see TREASURE) after LL *thesaurarius*]

treasury /trézhəree/ *n.* (*pl.* **-ies**) **1** a place or building where treasure is stored. **2** the funds or revenue of a nation, institution, or society. **3** (**Treasury**) **a** the department managing the public revenue of a country. **b** the offices and officers of this. **c** the place where the public revenues are kept. □ **treasury bill** a bill of exchange issued by the government to raise money for temporary needs. **treasury note** a note issued by the Treasury for use as currency or as a bond. [ME f. OF *tresorie* (as TREASURE)]
■ **1** store, storehouse, repository, mine, treasure trove, hoard, cache, bank, coffers. **2** exchequer, purse, resources, funds, finances, money(s), revenue, *Rom. Hist.* fisc. **3** exchequer.

treat /treet/ *v. & n.* ● *v.* **1** *tr.* act or behave toward or deal with (a person or thing) in a certain way (*treated me kindly*; *treat it as a joke*). **2** *tr.* deal with or apply a process to; act upon to obtain a particular result (*treat it with acid*). **3** *tr.* apply medical care or attention to. **4** *tr.* present or deal with (a subject) in literature or art. **5** *tr.* (often foll. by *to*) provide

with food or drink or entertainment, esp. at one's own expense (*treated us to dinner*). **6** *intr.* (often foll. by *with*) negotiate terms (with a person). **7** *intr.* (often foll. by *of*) give a spoken or written exposition. ● *n.* **1** an event or circumstance (esp. when unexpected or unusual) that gives great pleasure. **2** a meal, entertainment, etc., provided by one person for the enjoyment of another or others. **3** *Brit.* (prec. by *a*) extremely good or well (*they looked a treat*; *has come on a treat*). □□ **treatable** *adj.* **treater** *n.* **treating** *n.* [ME f. AF *treter*, OF *traitier* f. L *tractare* handle, frequent. of *trahere tract-* draw, pull]
■ *v.* **1** handle, manage, behave *or* act toward(s), deal with; use; consider, regard, look upon, view. **2** process, prepare, make, produce. **3** nurse, doctor, attend, care for, look after, tend, prescribe for, dose, medicate, vet. **4** handle, deal with, discuss, touch on *or* upon, present, consider, take up, study, examine, explore, investigate, scrutinize, analyze, go into, probe, survey, expound (on), criticize, review, critique. **5** take out, pay (the bill) for, buy for, regale, entertain, play host to; wine and dine; stand, *Austral. & NZ colloq.* shout, *sl.* spring for. **7** (*treat of*) see SPEAK 5. ● *n.* **1** see LUXURY 2, JOY *n.* 2. **2** favor, gift, present, boon, bonus, premium, *colloq.* freebie.

treatise /tréetis/ *n.* a written work dealing formally and systematically with a subject. [ME f. AF *tretis* f. OF *traitier* TREAT]
■ see PAPER *n.* 8.

treatment /tréetmənt/ *n.* **1** a process or manner of behaving toward or dealing with a person or thing (*received rough treatment*). **2** the application of medical care or attention to a patient. **3** a manner of treating a subject in literature or art. **4** (prec. by *the*) *colloq.* the customary way of dealing with a person, situation, etc. (*got the full treatment*).
■ **1** behavior, conduct, action, handling, care, management, dealing(s), manipulation, reception; usage, use. **2** therapy, care, curing, remedying, healing; remedy, cure, medication.

treaty /tréetee/ *n.* (*pl.* **-ies**) **1** a formally concluded and ratified agreement between nations. **2** an agreement between individuals or parties, esp. for the purchase of property. □ **treaty port** *hist.* a port that a country was bound by treaty to keep open to foreign trade. [ME f. AF *treté* f. L *tractatus* TRACTATE]
■ pact, agreement, alliance, concordat, entente, covenant, convention, contract, compact, accord, *colloq.* deal.

treble /trébəl/ *adj., n., & v.* ● *adj.* **1 a** threefold. **b** triple. **c** three times as much or many (*treble the amount*). **2** (of a voice) high-pitched. **3** *Mus.* = SOPRANO (esp. of an instrument or with ref. to a boy's voice). ● *n.* **1** a treble quantity or thing. **2** *Darts* a hit on the narrow ring enclosed by the two middle circles of a dartboard, scoring treble. **3 a** *Mus.* = SOPRANO (esp. a boy's voice or part, or an instrument). **b** a high-pitched voice. **4** the high-frequency output of a radio, record player, etc., corresponding to the treble in music. **5** *Brit.* a system of betting in which the winnings and stake from the first bet are transferred to a second and then (if successful) to a third. **6** *Brit. Sports* three victories or championships in the same game, sport, etc. ● *v.* **1** *tr. & intr.* make or become three times as much or many; increase threefold; multiply by three. **2** *tr.* amount to three times as much as. □ **treble clef** a clef placing G above middle C on the second lowest line of the staff. **treble rhyme** a rhyme including three syllables. □□ **trebly** *adv.* (in sense 1 of *adj.*). [ME f. OF f. L *triplus* TRIPLE]
■ *adj.* **2** see HIGH *adj.* 9.

trebuchet /trébyoōshét/ *n.* (also **trebucket** /trébəkít/, trebyoōkét/) *hist.* **1** a military machine used in siege warfare for throwing stones, etc. **2** a tilting balance for accurately weighing light articles. [ME f. OF f. *trebucher* overthrow, ult. f. Frank.]

trecento /traychéntō/ *n.* the style of Italian art and literature of the 14th c. □□ **trecentist** *n.* [It., = 300 used with reference to the years 1300-99]

tree /tree/ *n. & v.* ● *n.* **1 a** a perennial plant with a woody self-supporting main stem or trunk when mature and usu. unbranched for some distance above the ground (cf. SHRUB¹). **b** any similar plant having a tall erect usu. single stem, e.g., palm tree. **2** a piece or frame of wood, etc., for various purposes (*shoe tree*). **3** *archaic or poet.* **a** a gibbet. **b** a cross, esp. the one used for Christ's crucifixion. **4** (in full **tree diagram**) *Math.* a diagram with a structure of branching connecting lines. **5** = *family tree.* ● *v.tr.* **1** force to take refuge in a tree. **2** put into a difficult position. **3** stretch on a shoe tree. □ **tree agate** agate with treelike markings. **tree calf** a calf binding for books stained with a treelike design. **tree fern** a large fern, esp. of the family Cyatheaceae, with an upright trunklike stem. **tree frog** any arboreal tailless amphibian, esp. of the family Hylidae, climbing by means of adhesive pads on its digits. **tree hopper** any insect of the family Membracidae, living in trees. **tree house** a structure in a tree for children to play in. **tree line** = TIMBERLINE. **tree of heaven** an ornamental Asian tree, *Ailanthus altissima*, with foul-smelling flowers. **tree of life** = ARBOR VITAE. **tree ring** a ring in a cross section of a tree, from one year's growth. **tree shrew** any small insectivorous arboreal mammal of the family Tupaiidae having a pointed nose and bushy tail. **tree sparrow 1** a European sparrow, *Passer montanus*, inhabiting woodland areas. **2** a N. American finch, *Spizella arborea*, inhabiting grassland areas. **tree surgeon** a person who treats decayed trees in order to preserve them. **tree surgery** the art or practice of such treatment. **tree toad** = *tree frog.* **tree tomato** = TAMARILLO. **tree trunk** the trunk of a tree. **up a tree** cornered; nonplussed. □□ **treeless** *adj.* **treelessness** *n.* **treelike** *adj.* [OE *trēow* f. Gmc]

treecreeper /treékreepər/ *n.* any small creeping bird, esp. of the family Certhiidae, feeding on insects in the bark of trees.

treen /treen/ *n.* (treated as *pl.*) small domestic wooden objects, esp. antiques. [*treen* (adj.) wooden f. OE *trēowen* (as TREE)]

treenail /treénayl/ *n.* (also **trenail**) a hard wooden pin for securing timbers, etc.

treetop /treétop/ *n.* the topmost part of a tree.

tref /tráyf/ *adj.* (also **trefa** /tráyfə/ and other variants) not kosher. [Heb. *ṭrēpāh* the flesh of an animal torn f. *ṭarap* rend]

trefoil /treéfoyl, tréf-/ *n. & adj.* ● *n.* **1** any leguminous plant of the genus *Trifolium*, with leaves of three leaflets and flowers of various colors, esp. clover. **2** any plant with similar leaves. **3** a three-lobed ornamentation, esp. in tracery windows. **4** a thing arranged in or with three lobes. ● *adj.* of or concerning a three-lobed plant, window tracery, etc. □□ **trefoiled** *adj.* (also in *comb.*). [ME f. AF *trifoil* f. L *trifolium* (as TRI-, *folium* leaf)]

trek /trek/ *v. & n.* ● *v.intr.* (**trekked, trekking**) **1** travel or make one's way arduously (*trekking through the forest*). **2** esp. *S. Afr. hist.* migrate or journey with one's belongings by ox wagon. **3** (of an ox) draw a vehicle or pull a load. ● *n.* **1 a** a journey or walk made by trekking (*it was a trek to the nearest laundromat*). **b** each stage of such a journey. **2** an organized migration of a body of persons. □□ **trekker** *n.* [S.Afr. Du. *trek* (n.), *trekken* (v.) draw, travel]

■ *v.* **1** see TRAVEL *v.* 1, TRAMP *v.* 1b. ● *n.* **1** see TRAMP *n.* 3.

trellis /trélis/ *n. & v.* ● *n.* (in full **trelliswork**) a lattice or grating of light wooden or metal bars used esp. as a support for fruit trees or creepers and often fastened against a wall. ● *v.tr.* (**trellised, trellising**) **1** provide with a trellis. **2** support (a vine, etc.) with a trellis. [ME f. OF *trelis, trelice* ult. f. L *trilix* three-ply (as TRI-, *licium* warp-thread)]

trematode /trémətōd, treé-/ *n.* any parasitic flatworm of the class Trematoda, esp. a fluke, equipped with hooks or suck-

ers, e.g., a liver fluke. [mod.L Trematoda f. Gk *trēmatōdēs* perforated f. *trēma* hole]

tremble /trémbəl/ *v. & n.* ● *v.intr.* **1** shake involuntarily from fear, excitement, weakness, etc. **2** be in a state of extreme apprehension (*trembled at the very thought of it*). **3** move in a quivering manner (*leaves trembled in the breeze*). ● *n.* **1** a trembling state or movement; a quiver (*couldn't speak without a tremble*). **2** (in *pl.*) a disease (esp. of cattle) marked by trembling. □ **trembling poplar** an aspen. □□ **tremblingly** *adv.* [ME f. OF *trembler* f. med.L *tremulare* f. L *tremulus* TREMULOUS]

■ *v.* quiver, shake, quake, shiver, shudder, tremor, quaver; vibrate, rock, dodder. ● *n.* **1** quiver, shake, quake, shiver, shudder, quaver, tremor; vibration.

trembly /trémblee/ *adj.* (**tremblier, trembliest**) *colloq.* trembling; agitated.

■ see TREMULOUS 1.

tremendous /triméndəs/ *adj.* **1** awe inspiring; fearful; overpowering. **2** *colloq.* remarkable; considerable; excellent (*a tremendous explosion; gave a tremendous performance*). □□ **tremendously** *adv.* **tremendousness** *n.* [L *tremendus*, gerundive of *tremere* tremble]

■ **1** see OVERWHELMING. **2** see EXCELLENT, GREAT *adj.* 1a.

□□ **tremendously** see *extremely* (EXTREME).

tremolo /tréməlō/ *n. Mus.* **1** a tremulous effect in playing stringed and keyboard instruments or singing, esp. by rapid reiteration of a note; in other instruments, by rapid alternation between two notes (cf. VIBRATO). **2** a device in an organ producing a tremulous effect. [It. (as TREMULOUS)]

tremor /trémər/ *n. & v.* ● *n.* **1** a shaking or quivering. **2** a thrill (of fear or exultation, etc.). **3** a slight earthquake. ● *v.intr.* undergo a tremor or tremors. [ME f. OF *tremour* & L *tremor* f. *tremere* tremble]

■ *n.* **1** see QUIVER¹ *n.* **2** see THRILL *n.* 1. **3** earthquake, quake. ● *v.* see QUIVER¹ *v.*

tremulous /trémyələs/ *adj.* **1** trembling or quivering (*in a tremulous voice*). **2** (of a line, etc.) drawn by a tremulous hand. **3** timid or vacillating. □□ **tremulously** *adv.* **tremulousness** *n.* [L *tremulus* f. *tremere* tremble]

■ **1** trembling, atremble, quivering, shaking, quaking, shivering, shuddering, quavering, shaky, palpitating, *colloq.* trembly, all of a tremble. **3** timid, shy, bashful, anxious, worried, timorous, fearful, afraid, frightened, scared, nervous, jumpy; hesitant, vacillating, wavering, unsure, unsteady, faltering, doubtful; *colloq.* jittery.

trenail var. of TREENAIL.

trench /trench/ *n. & v.* ● *n.* **1** a long narrow usu. deep depression or ditch. **2** *Mil.* **a** this dug by troops to stand in and be sheltered from enemy fire. **b** (in *pl.*) a defensive system of these. **3** a long narrow deep depression in the ocean bed. ● *v.* **1** *tr.* dig a trench or trenches in (the ground). **2** *tr.* turn over the earth of (a field, garden, etc.) by digging a succession of adjoining ditches. **3** *intr.* (foll. by *on, upon*) *archaic* **a** encroach. **b** verge or border closely. □ **trench coat 1** a soldier's lined or padded waterproof coat. **2** a loose belted raincoat. **trench fever** a highly infectious disease, transmitted by lice, that infested soldiers in the trenches in World War I. **trench mortar** a light simple mortar throwing a bomb from one's own into the enemy trenches. **trench warfare** hostilities carried on from more or less permanent trenches. [ME f. OF *trenche* (n.) *trenchier* (v.), ult. f. L *truncare* TRUNCATE]

■ *n.* **1** see FURROW *n.*

trenchant /trénchənt/ *adj.* **1** (of a style or language, etc.) incisive; terse; vigorous. **2** *archaic or poet.* sharp; keen. □□ **trenchancy** *n.* **trenchantly** *adv.* [ME f. OF, part. of *trenchier*: see TRENCH]

■ **1** cutting, keen, acute, sharp, pointed, poignant, penetrating, incisive, biting, mordant, sarcastic, bitter, acerbic, acid, vitriolic, tart, acrid, acrimonious, acidulous, corrosive, caustic; terse, epigrammatic, vigorous.

trencher /trénchər/ *n.* **1** *hist.* a wooden or earthenware platter for serving food. **2** (in full **trencher cap**) a stiff square academic cap; a mortarboard. [ME f. AF *trenchour*, OF *trencheoir* f. *trenchier*: see TRENCH]

trencherman /trénchərmən/ *n.* (*pl.* **-men**) a person who eats well, or in a specified manner (*a good trencherman*).

trend /trend/ *n. & v.* ● *n.* a general direction and tendency (esp. of events, fashion, or opinion, etc.). ● *v.intr.* **1** bend or turn away in a specified direction. **2** be chiefly directed; have a general and continued tendency. [ME 'revolve,' etc., f. OE *trendan* f. Gmc: cf. TRUNDLE]
■ *n.* tendency, leaning, bias, bent, drift, course, inclination, direction; fashion, style, vogue, mode, look, rage, craze, fad, *colloq.* thing. ● *v.* **1** lean, bend, incline, veer, turn, swing, shift, drift, head. **2** tend, be directed, be biased, head.

trendsetter /tréndsetər/ *n.* a person who leads the way in fashion, etc. □□ **trendsetting** *adj.*
■ see PIONEER *n.* 1.

trendy /tréndee/ *adj. & n. colloq.* ● *adj.* (**trendier, trendiest**) often *derog.* fashionable; following fashionable trends. ● *n.* (*pl.* **-ies**) a fashionable person. □□ **trendily** *adv.* **trendiness** *n.*
■ *adj.* fashionable, stylish, à la mode, modern, latest, up-to-date, up-to-the-minute, in vogue, voguish, in, all the rage, *colloq.* with it, swinging, hot, *sl.* groovy, in the groove. ● *n.* coxcomb, dandy, exhibitionist, *colloq.* show-off, clotheshorse, pseud. □□ **trendiness** see *popularity* (POPULAR).

trepan /tripán/ *n. & v.* ● *n.* **1** a cylindrical saw formerly used by surgeons for removing part of the bone of the skull. **2** a borer for sinking shafts. ● *v.tr.* (**trepanned, trepanning**) perforate (the skull) with a trepan. □□ **trepanation** /trépənáyshən/ *n.* **trepanning** *n.* [ME f. med.L *trepanum* f. Gk *trupanon* f. *trupaō* bore f. *trupē* hole]

trepang /tripáng/ *n.* a kind of sea cucumber eaten in China, usu. in long dried strips. [Malay *trīpang*]

trephine /trifín, -feen/ *n. & v.* ● *n.* an improved form of trepan with a guiding center pin. ● *v.tr.* operate on with this. □□ **trephination** /tréfináyshən/ *n.* [orig. *trafine*, f. L *tres fines* three ends, app. formed after TREPAN]

trepidation /trépidáyshən/ *n.* **1** a feeling of fear or alarm; perturbation of the mind. **2** tremulous agitation. **3** the trembling of limbs, e.g., in paralysis. [L *trepidatio* f. *trepidare* be agitated, tremble, f. *trepidus* alarmed]
■ **1** see ALARM *n.* 3.

trespass /tréspəs, -pas/ *v. & n.* ● *v.intr.* **1** (usu. foll. by *on, upon*) make an unlawful or unwarrantable intrusion (esp. on land or property). **2** (foll. by *on*) make unwarrantable claims (*shall not trespass on your hospitality*). **3** (foll. by *against*) literary or archaic offend. ● *n.* **1** *Law* a voluntary wrongful act against the person or property of another, esp. unlawful entry to a person's land or property. **2** *archaic* a sin or offense. □□ **trespasser** *n.* [ME f. OF *trespasser* pass over, trespass, *trespas* (n.), f. med.L *transpassare* (as TRANS-, PASS¹)]
■ *v.* **1, 2** see ENCROACH 1. **3** see SIN¹ *v.* 2. ● *n.* **2** see SIN¹ *n.* 1. □□ **trespasser** see INTRUDER, SINNER.

tress /tres/ *n. & v.* ● *n.* **1** a long lock of human (esp. female) hair. **2** (in *pl.*) a woman's or girl's head of hair. ● *v.tr.* arrange (hair) in tresses. □□ **tressed** *adj.* (also in *comb.*). **tressy** *adj.* [ME f. OF *tresse*, perh. ult. f. Gk *trikha* threefold]
■ *n.* **1** see LOCK² 1a. **2** (*tresses*) hair, locks, *colloq.* mane.

trestle /trésəl/ *n.* **1** a supporting structure for a table, etc., consisting of two frames fixed at an angle or hinged or of a bar supported by two divergent pairs of legs. **2** (in full **trestle table**) a table consisting of a board or boards laid on trestles or other supports. **3** (also **trestlework**) an open braced framework to support a bridge, etc. **4** (also **trestletree**) *Naut.* each of a pair of horizontal pieces on a lower mast supporting the topmast, etc. [ME f. OF *trestel* ult. f. L *transtrum*]

tret /tret/ *n. hist.* an allowance of extra weight formerly made to purchasers of some goods for waste in transportation. [ME f. AF & OF, var. of *trait* draft: see TRAIT]

trevally /triválee/ *n.* (*pl.* **-ies**) any Australian fish of the genus *Caranx*, used as food. [prob. alt. f. *cavally*, a kind of fish, f. Sp. *caballo* horse f. L (as CAVALRY)]

trews /trooz/ *n.pl.* esp. *Brit.* trousers, esp. close-fitting tartan trousers worn by women. [Ir. *trius*, Gael. *triubhas* (sing.): cf. TROUSERS]

trey /tray/ *n.* (*pl.* **treys**) the three on dice or cards. [ME f. OF *trei, treis* three f. L *tres*]

tri- /trī/ *comb. form* forming nouns and adjectives meaning: **1** three or three times. **2** *Chem.* (forming the names of compounds) containing three atoms or groups of a specified kind (*triacetate*). [L & Gk f. L *tres*, Gk *treis* three]

triable /trīəbəl/ *adj.* **1** liable to a judicial trial. **2** that may be tried or attempted. [ME f. AF (as TRY)]

triacetate /trīásitayt/ *n.* a cellulose derivative containing three acetate groups, esp. as a base for manmade fibers.

triad /trīad/ *n.* **1** a group of three (esp. notes in a chord). **2** the number three. **3** a Chinese secret society, usu. criminal. **4** a Welsh form of literary composition with an arrangement in groups of three. □□ **triadic** *adj.* **triadically** *adv.* [F *triade* or LL *trias triad-* f. Gk *trias -ados* f. *treis* three]
■ **1** see TRIO.

triadelphous /trīədélfəs/ *adj. Bot.* having stamens united in three bundles. [TRI- + Gk *adelphos* brother]

triage /tree-aázh, treé-aazh/ *n.* **1** the act of sorting according to quality. **2** the assignment of degrees of urgency to decide the order of treatment of wounds, illnesses, etc. [F f. *trier*: cf. TRY]

trial /trīəl/ *n.* **1** a judicial examination and determination of issues between parties by a judge with or without a jury (*stood trial for murder*). **2 a** a process or mode of testing qualities. **b** experimental treatment. **c** a test (*will give you a trial*). **d** an attempt. **e** (*attrib.*) experimental. **3** a trying thing or experience or person, esp. hardship or trouble (*the trials of old age*). **4** a preliminary contest to test the ability of players eligible for selection to a team, etc. **5** *Brit.* a test of individual ability on a motorcycle over rough ground or on a road. **6** any of various contests involving performance by horses, dogs, or other animals. □ **on trial 1** being tried in a court of law. **2** being tested; to be chosen or retained only if suitable. **trial and error** repeated (usu. varied and unsystematic) attempts or experiments continued until successful. **trial balance** (of a ledger in double-entry bookkeeping), a comparison of the totals on either side, the inequality of which reveals errors in posting. **trial by ordeal** see ORDEAL 2. **trial jury** = *petit jury*. **trial run** a preliminary test of a vehicle, vessel, machine, etc. [AF *trial, triel* f. *trier* TRY]
■ **1** hearing, inquiry, examination, inquisition, litigation, judicial proceeding, lawsuit, contest. **2 a–c** test, testing, experiment, proof, tryout, trying out, trial run, dummy run, examination, check, checking, *colloq.* dry run. **d** try, attempt, endeavor, effort, venture, go, fling, *colloq.* shot, stab, whirl, crack, *formal* essay, *sl.* whack. **e** sample, experimental, exploratory, provisional, probationary, tentative, conditional, pilot. **3** trouble, affliction, tribulation, hardship, adversity, suffering, grief, misery, distress, bad *or* hard luck, misfortune, hard times, ordeal, *archaic or literary* woe; nuisance, irritation, bother, bane, annoyance, pest, irritant, thorn in one's flesh *or* side, *colloq.* plague, hassle, pain (in the neck), headache, pain in the butt. □ **trial run** see TRIAL 2a–c above.

triandrous /trīándrəs/ *adj. Bot.* having three stamens.

triangle /trīanggəl/ *n.* **1** a plane figure with three sides and angles. **2** any three things not in a straight line, with imaginary lines joining them. **3** an implement of this shape. **4** a musical instrument consisting of a steel rod bent into a triangle and sounded by striking it with a smaller steel rod. **5** a situation, esp. an emotional relationship, involving three people. **6** a right-angled triangle of wood, etc., as a drawing implement. **7** *Naut.* a device of three spars for raising weights. **8** *hist.* a frame of three halberds joined at the top

---

/. . ./ **pronunciation**	● **part of speech**
□ **phrases, idioms, and compounds**	
□□ **derivatives**	■ **synonym section**
cross-references appear in SMALL CAPITALS or *italics*	

to which a soldier was bound for flogging. □ **triangle of forces** a triangle whose sides represent in magnitude and direction three forces in equilibrium. [ME f. OF *triangle* or L *triangulum* neut. of *triangulus* three-cornered (as TRI-, ANGLE¹)]

triangular /trīánggyələr/ *adj.* **1** triangle-shaped; three-cornered. **2** (of a contest or treaty, etc.) between three persons or parties. **3** (of a pyramid) having a three-sided base. □□ **triangularity** /-láiritee/ *n.* **triangularly** *adv.* [LL *triangularis* (as TRIANGLE)]

triangulate *v.* & *adj.* ● *v.tr.* /trīánggyəlayt/ **1** divide (an area) into triangles for surveying purposes. **2 a** measure and map (an area) by the use of triangles with a known base length and base angles. **b** determine (a height, distance, etc.) in this way. ● *adj.* /trīánggyələt/ *Zool.* marked with triangles. □□ **triangulately** /-lətlee/ *adv.* **triangulation** /-láyshən/ *n.* [L *triangulatus* triangular (as TRIANGLE)]

Triassic /trīásik/ *adj.* & *n.* *Geol.* ● *adj.* of or relating to the earliest period of the Mesozoic era with evidence of an abundance of reptiles (including the earliest dinosaurs) and the emergence of mammals. ¶ Cf. Appendix VII. ● *n.* this period or system. [LL *trias* (as TRIAD), because the strata are divisible into three groups]

triathlon /trīáthlən, -lon/ *n.* an athletic contest consisting of three different events, esp. running, swimming, and bicycling. □□ **triathlete** /-leet/ *n.* [TRI- after DECATHLON]

triatomic /trīətómik/ *adj.* *Chem.* **1** having three atoms (of a specified kind) in the molecule. **2** having three replacement atoms or radicals.

triaxial /trīákseeəl/ *adj.* having three axes.

trib. *abbr.* **1** tribunal. **2** tribune. **3** tributary.

tribade /tríbəd/ *n.* a lesbian. □□ **tribadism** *n.* [F *tribade* or L *tribas* f. Gk f. *tribō* rub]

tribal /tríbəl/ *adj.* of, relating to, or characteristic of a tribe or tribes. □□ **tribally** *adv.*

tribalism /tríbəlizəm/ *n.* **1** tribal organization. **2** strong loyalty to one's tribe, group, etc. □□ **tribalist** *n.* **tribalistic** *adj.*

tribasic /tríbáysik/ *adj.* *Chem.* (of an acid) having three replaceable hydrogen atoms.

tribe /trīb/ *n.* **1** a group of (esp. primitive) families or communities, linked by social, economic, religious, or blood ties, and usu. having a common culture and dialect, and a recognized leader. **2** any similar natural or political division. **3** *Rom.Hist.* each of the political divisions of the Roman people. **4** each of the 12 divisions of the Israelites. **5** a set or number of persons, esp. of one profession, etc., or family (*the whole tribe of actors*). **6** *Biol.* a group of organisms usu. ranking between genus and the subfamily. **7** (in *pl.*) large numbers. [ME, orig. in pl. form *tribuz, tribus* f. OF or L *tribus* (sing. & pl.)]

■ **1, 2** race, stock, strain, nation, breed, people, (ethnic) group, clan, blood, pedigree, family, sept, dynasty, house, *archaic* seed; caste, class; *Anthropol.* gens.

tribesman /tríbzmən/ *n.* (*pl.* **-men**) a member of a tribe or of one's own tribe.

tribo- /tríbō, trí-/ *comb. form* rubbing; friction. [Gk *tribos* rubbing]

triboelectricity /tríbō-ílektrísitee, tríb-/ *n.* the generation of an electric charge by friction.

tribology /trībóləjee/ *n.* the study of friction, wear, lubrication, and the design of bearings; the science of interacting surfaces in relative motion. □□ **tribologist** *n.*

triboluminescence /tríbōlōōminésəns, tríb-/ *n.* the emission of light from a substance when rubbed, scratched, etc. □□ **triboluminescent** *adj.*

tribometer /trībómitər/ *n.* an instrument for measuring friction in sliding.

tribrach /tríbrak, tríb-/ *n. Prosody* a foot of three short or unstressed syllables. □□ **tribrachic** *adj.* [L *tribrachys* f. Gk *tribrakhus* (as TRI-, *brakhus* short)]

tribulation /tríbyəláyshən/ *n.* **1** great affliction or oppression. **2** a cause of this (*was a real tribulation to me*). [ME f. OF f. eccl.L *tribulatio -onis* f. L *tribulare* press, oppress, f. *tribulum* sledge for threshing, f. *terere trit-* rub]

■ **1** see AFFLICTION 1. **2** see AFFLICTION 2.

tribunal /trībyōōnəl, tri-/ *n.* **1** a board appointed to adjudicate in some matter, esp. one appointed by the government to investigate a matter of public concern. **2** a court of justice. **3** a seat or bench for a judge or judges. **4 a** a place of judgment. **b** judicial authority (*the tribunal of public opinion*). [F *tribunal* or L *tribunus* (as TRIBUNE²)]

■ **1** see BOARD *n.* 4. **2** court (of justice), bar, court of law, bench, judiciary *Brit.* lawcourt.

tribune¹ /tríbyōōn, tribyóōn/ *n.* **1** a popular leader or demagogue. **2** (in full **tribune of the people**) an official in ancient Rome chosen by the people to protect their interests. **3** (in full **military tribune**) a Roman legionary officer. □□ **tribunate** /-nət, -nayt/ *n.* **tribuneship** *n.* [ME f. L *tribunus*, prob. f. *tribus* tribe]

tribune² /tríbyōōn, tribyóōn/ *n.* **1** *Eccl.* **a** a bishop's throne in a basilica. **b** an apse containing this. **2** a dais or rostrum. **3** a raised area with seats. [F f. It. f. med.L *tribuna* TRIBUNAL]

tributary /tríbyəteree/ *n.* & *adj.* ● *n.* (*pl.* **-ies**) **1** a river or stream flowing into a larger river or lake. **2** *hist.* a person or nation paying or subject to tribute. ● *adj.* **1** (of a river, etc.) that is a tributary. **2** *hist.* **a** paying tribute. **b** serving as tribute. □□ **tributarily** /-táirilee/ *adv.* **tributariness** /-táireenis/ *n.* [ME f. L *tributarius* (as TRIBUTE)]

■ *n.* **1** branch, offshoot, streamlet, feeder, brook, brooklet, creek, rivulet, run, rill, runnel, runlet, *Sc.* burn, *No. of Engl.* beck.

tribute /tríbyōōt/ *n.* **1** a thing said or done or given as a mark of respect or affection, etc. (*paid tribute to their achievements*; *floral tributes*). **2** *hist.* **a** a payment made periodically by one nation or ruler to another, esp. as a sign of dependence. **b** an obligation to pay this (*was paid under tribute*). **3** (foll. by *to*) an indication of (some praiseworthy quality) (*their success is a tribute to their perseverance*). **4** a proportion of ore or its equivalent paid to a miner for his work, or to the owner of a mine. [ME f. L *tributum* neut. past part. of *tribuere tribut-* assign, orig. divide between tribes (*tribus*)]

■ **1** honor, homage, recognition, celebration, respect, esteem, testimonial, compliment, encomium, acknowledgment, acclaim, acclamation, commendation, praise, accolade, panegyric, eulogy, glorification, exaltation, *colloq.* kudos, *formal* laudation. **2** tax, exaction, impost, duty, excise, levy, dues, assessment, tariff, charge, surcharge, payment, contribution, offering, gift; ransom; tithe, *RC Ch.* Peter's pence.

trice /trīs/ *n.* □ **in a trice** in a moment; instantly. [ME *trice* (v.) pull, haul f. MDu. *trīsen*, MLG *trīssen*, rel. to MDu. *trīse* windlass, pulley]

■ □ **in a trice** see *at once* 1 (ONCE).

tricentenary /trísenténəree/ *n.* (*pl.* **-ies**) = TERCENTENARY.

triceps /tríseps/ *adj.* & *n.* ● *adj.* (of a muscle) having three heads or points of attachment. ● *n.* any triceps muscle, esp. the large muscle at the back of the upper arm. [L, = three-headed (as TRI-, *-ceps* f. *caput* head)]

triceratops /trísératops/ *n.* an herbivorous dinosaur with three sharp horns on the forehead and a wavy-edged collar around the neck. [mod.L f. Gk *trikeratos* three-horned + *ōps* face]

trichiasis /trikíəsis/ *n. Med.* ingrowth or introversion of the eyelashes. [LL f. Gk *trikhiasis* f. *trikhiaō* be hairy]

trichina /trikínə/ *n.* (*pl.* **trichinae** /-nee/) any hairlike parasitic nematode worm of the genus *Trichinella*, esp. *T. spiralis*, the adults of which live in the small intestine, and whose larvae become encysted in the muscle tissue of humans and carnivorous animals. □□ **trichinous** *adj.* [mod.L f. Gk *trikhinos* of hair: see TRICHO-]

trichinosis /trikinósis/ *n.* a disease caused by trichinae, usu. ingested in meat, and characterized by digestive disturbance, fever, and muscular rigidity.

tricho- /tríkō/ *comb. form* hair. [Gk *thrix trikhos* hair]

trichogenous /trikójənəs/ *adj.* causing or promoting the growth of hair.

trichology /trikóləjee/ *n.* the study of the structure, functions, and diseases of the hair. □□ **trichologist** *n.*

trichome /tríkōm/ *n. Bot.* a hair, scale, prickle, or other outgrowth from the epidermis of a plant. [Gk *trikhōma* f. *trikhoō* cover with hair (as TRICHO-)]

trichomonad /tríkəmónad, -mŏ-/ *n.* any flagellate protozoan of the genus *Trichomonas*, parasitic in humans, cattle, and fowls.

trichomoniasis /tríkəməníəsis/ *n.* any of various infections caused by trichomonads parasitic on the urinary tract, vagina, or digestive system.

trichopathy /trikópəthee/ *n.* the treatment of diseases of the hair. □□ **trichopathic** /tríkəpáthik/ *adj.*

trichotomy /trikótəmee/ *n.* (*pl.* **-ies**) a division (esp. sharply defined) into three categories, esp. of human nature into body, soul, and spirit. □□ **trichotomic** /-kətómik/ *adj.* [Gk *trikha* threefold f. *treis* three, after DICHOTOMY]

trichroic /tríkrŏik/ *adj.* (esp. of a crystal viewed in different directions) showing three colors. □□ **trichroism** /tríkrōizəm/ *n.* [Gk *trikhroos* (as TRI-, *khrōs* color)]

trichromatic /tríkrəmátik/ *adj.* **1** having or using three colors. **2** (of vision) having the normal three color sensations, i.e., red, green, and blue. □□ **trichromatism** /-krŏmətizəm/ *n.*

trick /trik/ *n., adj.,* & *v.* ● *n.* **1** an action or scheme undertaken to fool, outwit, or deceive. **2** an optical or other illusion (*a trick of the light*). **3** a special technique; a knack or special way of doing something. **4 a** a feat of skill or dexterity. **b** an unusual action (e.g., begging) learned by an animal. **5** a mischievous, foolish, or discreditable act; a practical joke (*a mean trick to play*). **6** a peculiar or characteristic habit or mannerism (*has a trick of repeating himself*). **7 a** the cards played in a single round of a card game, usu. one from each player. **b** such a round. **c** a point gained as a result of this. **8** (*attrib.*) done to deceive or mystify or to create an illusion (*trick photography*; *trick question*). **9** *Naut.* a sailor's turn at the helm, usu. two hours. **10 a** a prostitute's client. **b** a sexual act performed by a prostitute and a client. ● *adj.* unreliable or inclined to weaken suddenly (*trick knee*). ● *v.tr.* **1** deceive by a trick; outwit. **2** (often foll. by *out of*, or *into* + verbal noun) cheat; treat deceitfully so as to deprive (*were tricked into agreeing*; *were tricked out of their savings*). **3** (of a thing) foil or baffle; take by surprise; disappoint the calculations of. □ **do the trick** *colloq.* accomplish one's purpose; achieve the required result. **how's tricks?** *colloq.* how are you? **not miss a trick** see MISS¹. **trick of the trade** a special usu. ingenious technique or method of achieving a result in an industry or profession, etc. **trick or treat** a children's custom of calling at houses at Halloween with the threat of pranks if they are not given candy. **trick out** (or **up**) dress, decorate, or deck out, esp. showily. **turn tricks** engage in prostitution. **up to one's tricks** *colloq.* misbehaving. **up to a person's tricks** aware of what a person is likely to do by way of mischief. □□ **tricker** *n.* **trickish** *adj.* **trickless** *adj.* [ME f. OF dial. *trique*, OF *triche* f. *trichier* deceive, of unkn. orig.]

■ *n.* **1** ruse, artifice, device, stratagem, wile, deception, maneuver, deceit, fraud, hoax, imposture, intrigue, machination, conspiracy, subterfuge, dodge, confidence trick, sham, confidence game, *colloq.* put-on, *Austral. colloq.* lurk, sl. con. **2** illusion, deception. **3** art, knack, technique, skill, secret, gift, ability, *colloq.* hang. **4** feat, accomplishment, deed; legerdemain, magic, stunt, *archaic* sleight of hand. **5** prank, frolic, antic, (practical) joke, hoax, gag, tomfoolery, antic, caper, jape; sport, horseplay, mischief; *colloq.* leg-pull, shenanigans, dido. **6** trait, characteristic, peculiarity, idiosyncrasy, eccentricity, quirk, practice, habit, mannerism, crotchet, weakness, foible. ● *v.* **1, 2** fool, hoodwink, dupe, mislead, outwit, outmaneuver, deceive, misguide, misinform, gull, cheat, defraud, take in, swindle, humbug, rook, pull a person's leg, pull the wool over a person's eyes, put a thing over a person, *colloq.* bamboozle, take for a ride, outfox, *Brit. colloq.* gammon, *literary* cozen, *sl.* bilk, have. ■ **do the trick** work, answer, fulfill the need, suffice, be effective, solve *or* take care of the problem, fill *or* fit the bill, *colloq.* do

the needful *or* necessary. **trick out** (or **up**) see EMBELLISH 1.

trickery /tríkəree/ *n.* (*pl.* **-ies**) **1** the practice or an instance of deception. **2** the use of tricks.

■ chicanery, deception, deceit, guile, beguilement, shrewdness, craftiness, trickiness, slyness, shiftiness, evasiveness, artfulness, artifice, craft, imposture, swindling, knavery, duplicity, double-dealing, fraud, cheating, skulduggery, hocus-pocus, legerdemain, stratagem, *archaic* sleight of hand, *colloq.* monkey business, esp. *Brit. colloq.* jiggery-pokery, *sl.* funny business, hanky-panky.

trickle /tríkəl/ *v.* & *n.* ● *v.* **1** *intr.* & *tr.* flow or cause to flow in drops or a small stream (*water trickled through the crack*). **2** *intr.* come or go slowly or gradually (*information trickles out*). ● *n.* a trickling flow. □ **trickle charger** an electrical charger for batteries that works at a steady slow rate. [ME *trekel, trikle,* prob. imit.]

■ *v.* **1** drip, drop, dribble, drizzle, run, flow, spill; ooze, seep, leak, exude, percolate. ● *n.* drip, seepage, spill, dribble, runnel, runlet, rivulet.

trickster /tríkstər/ *n.* a deceiver or rogue.

■ see ROGUE *n.* 1.

tricksy /tríksee/ *adj.* (**tricksier, tricksiest**) full of tricks; playful. □□ **tricksily** *adv.* **tricksiness** *n.* [TRICK: for -*sy* cf. FLIMSY, TIPSY]

tricky /tríkee/ *adj.* (**trickier, trickiest**) **1** difficult or intricate; requiring care and adroitness (*a tricky job*). **2** crafty or deceitful. **3** resourceful or adroit. □□ **trickily** *adv.* **trickiness** *n.*

■ **1** ticklish, risky, hazardous, sensitive, delicate, touch-and-go, thorny, difficult, awkward, complex, complicated, intricate, knotty, uncertain, *colloq.* iffy, sticky, *sl.* dicey. **2** deceitful, shady, deceptive, dodgy, artful, guileful, crafty, duplicitous, shrewd, cunning, dishonest, devious, sly, wily, slippery, foxy, double-dealing, cheating, *colloq.* shifty; unsportsmanlike, unfair. **3** see SHREWD. □□ **trickiness** see ARTIFICE 2a.

triclinic /tríklínik/ *adj.* **1** (of a mineral) having three unequal oblique axes. **2** denoting the system classifying triclinic crystalline substances. [Gk TRI- + *klinō* incline]

triclinium /tríklíneeəm/ *n.* (*pl.* **triclinia** /-neeə/) *Rom. Antiq.* **1** a dining table with couches along three sides. **2** a room containing this. [L f. Gk *triklinion* (as TRI-, *klinē* couch)]

tricolor /tríkulər/ *n.* & *adj.* ● *n.* a flag of three colors, esp. the French national flag of blue, white, and red. ● *adj.* (also **tricolored**) having three colors. [F *tricolore* f. LL *tricolor* (as TRI-, COLOR)]

tricorn /tríkawrn/ *adj.* & *n.* (also **tricorne**) ● *adj.* **1** having three horns. **2** (of a hat) having a brim turned up on three sides. ● *n.* **1** an imaginary animal with three horns. **2** a tricorn hat. [F *tricorne* or L *tricornis* (as TRI-, *cornu* horn)]

tricot /treekō/ *n.* **1 a** a hand-knitted woolen fabric. **b** an imitation of this. **2** a ribbed woolen cloth. [F, = knitting f. *tricoter* knit, of unkn. orig.]

tricrotic /tríkrótik/ *adj.* (of the pulse) having a triple beat. [TRI- after DICROTIC]

tricuspid /tríkúspid/ *n.* & *adj.* ● *n.* **1** a tooth with three cusps or points. **2** a heart valve formed of three triangular segments. ● *adj.* (of a tooth) having three cusps or points.

tricycle /trísikəl/ *n.* & *v.* ● *n.* **1** a vehicle having three wheels, two on an axle at the back and one at the front, driven by pedals in the same way as a bicycle. **2** a three-wheeled motor vehicle for a disabled driver. ● *v.intr.* ride on a tricycle. □□ **tricyclist** *n.*

tridactyl /trídáktil/ *adj.* (also **tridactylous** /-dáktiləs/) having three fingers or toes.

trident /tríd'nt/ *n.* **1** a three-pronged spear, esp. as an attribute of Poseidon (Neptune) or Britannia. **2** (**Trident**) a type

---

/.../ **pronunciation**	● **part of speech**
□ **phrases, idioms, and compounds**	
□□ **derivatives**	■ **synonym section**
cross-references appear in SMALL CAPITALS *or italics*	

of submarine-launched ballistic missile. [L *tridens trident-* (as TRI-, *dens* tooth)]

tridentate /trīdéntayt/ *adj.* having three teeth or prongs. [TRI- + L *dentatus* toothed]

Tridentine /trīdéntin, -tīn, -teen/ *adj.* & *n.* ● *adj.* of or relating to the Council of Trent, held at Trento in Italy 1545–63, esp. as the basis of Roman Catholic doctrine. ● *n.* a Roman Catholic adhering to this traditional doctrine. □ **Tridentine mass** the eucharistic liturgy used by the Roman Catholic Church from 1570 to 1964. [med.L *Tridentinus* f. *Tridentum* Trent]

triduum /trījōŏəm, trīdyōŏəm/ *n. RC Ch.* esp. *hist.* three days' prayer in preparation for a saint's day or other religious occasion. [L (as TRI-, *dies* day)]

tridymite /trídimīt/ *n.* a crystallized form of silica, occurring in cavities of volcanic rocks. [G *Tridymit* f. Gk *tridumos* threefold (as TRI-, *didumos* twin), from its occurrence in groups of three crystals]

tried *past* and *past part.* of TRY.

triennial /trī-éneeəl/ *adj.* & *n.* ● *adj.* **1** lasting three years. **2** recurring every three years. ● *n.* a visitation of an Anglican diocese by its bishop every three years. □□ **triennially** *adv.* [LL *triennis* (as TRI-, L *annus* year)]

triennium /trī-éneeəm/ *n.* (*pl.* **trienniums** or **triennia** /-neeə/) a period of three years. [L (as TRIENNIAL)]

trier /trīər/ *n.* **1** a person who perseveres (*is a real trier*). **2** a tester, esp. of foodstuffs. **3** *Brit. Law* a person appointed to decide whether a challenge to a juror is well founded.

trifacial nerve /trīfáyshəl/ *n.* = TRIGEMINAL NERVE.

trifecta /trīféktə/ *n.* a form of betting in which the first three places in a race must be predicted in the correct order. [TRI- + PERFECTA]

trifid /trífid/ *adj.* esp. *Biol.* partly or wholly split into three divisions or lobes. [L *trifidus* (as TRI-, *findere fid-* split)]

trifle /trīfəl/ *n.* & *v.* ● *n.* **1** a thing of slight value or importance. **2 a** a small amount, esp. of money (*was sold for a trifle*). **b** (prec. by *a*) somewhat (*seems a trifle annoyed*). **3** *Brit.* a confection of sponge cake with custard, jelly, fruit, cream, etc. ● *v.* **1** *intr.* talk or act frivolously. **2** *intr.* (foll. by *with*) **a** treat or deal with frivolously or derisively; flirt heartlessly with. **b** refuse to take seriously. **3** *tr.* (foll. by *away*) waste (time, energies, money, etc.) frivolously. □□ **trifler** *n.* [ME f. OF *truf(f)le* by-form of *trufe* deceit, of unkn. orig.]

■ *n.* **1** knickknack, trinket, bauble, bagatelle, toy, gewgaw, nothing, plaything, bêtise, triviality, doodad, *Brit.* doodah. **2 b** little, bit, drop, iota, scintilla, suggestion, dash, dab, pinch, whiff, mite, whit, jot, tittle, *colloq.* smidgen, tad. ● *v.* **2** (*trifle with*) dally with, flirt with, mess about with, toy with, *literary* wanton with; play with, dabble in *or* at, fiddle with, dandle, tinker with, fidget with. **3** (*trifle away*) see FRITTER[1]. □□ **trifler** see DILETTANTE *n.*

trifling /trífling/ *adj.* **1** unimportant; petty. **2** frivolous. □□ **triflingly** *adv.*

■ **1** trivial, insignificant, unimportant, puny, minor, paltry, slight, petty, inconsequential, frivolous, superficial, incidental, negligible, commonplace, inconsiderable, shallow, valueless, worthless, picayune, *colloq.* piddling, piffling. **2** see IDLE *adj.* 5, 6.

trifocal /trīfōkəl/ *adj.* & *n.* ● *adj.* having three focuses, esp. of a lens with different focal lengths. ● *n.* (in *pl.*) trifocal eyeglasses.

trifoliate /trīfōleeət/ *adj.* **1** (of a compound leaf) having three leaflets. **2** (of a plant) having such leaves.

triforium /trīfáwreeəm/ *n.* (*pl.* **triforia** /-reeə/) a gallery or arcade above the arches of the nave, choir, and transepts of a church. [AL, of unkn. orig.]

triform /trífawrm/ *adj.* (also **triformed**) **1** formed of three parts. **2** having three forms or bodies.

trifurcate *v.* & *adj.* ● *v.tr.* & *intr.* /trífərkayt/ divide into three branches. ● *adj.* /trífərkət/ divided into three branches.

trig[1] /trig/ *n. colloq.* trigonometry. [abbr.]

trig[2] /trig/ *adj.* & *v. archaic* or *dial.* ● *adj.* trim or spruce.

● *v.tr.* (**trigged, trigging**) make trim; neaten. [ME, = trusty, f. ON *tryggr*, rel. to TRUE]

trigamous /trígəməs/ *adj.* **1 a** three times married. **b** having three wives or husbands at once. **2** *Bot.* having male, female, and hermaphroditic flowers in the same head. □□ **trigamist** *n.* **trigamy** *n.* [Gk *trigamos* (as TRI-, *gamos* marriage)]

trigeminal nerve /trījéminəl/ *n. Anat.* the largest cranial nerve, which divides into the ophthalmic, maxillary, and mandibular nerves. □ **trigeminal neuralgia** *Med.* neuralgia involving one or more of these branches, and often causing severe pain. [as TRIGEMINUS]

■ trifacial nerve, trigeminus.

trigeminus /trījéminəs/ *n.* (*pl.* **trigemini** /-nī/) the trigeminal nerve. [L, = born as a triplet (as TRI-, *geminus* born at the same birth)]

trigger /trígər/ *n.* & *v.* ● *n.* **1** a movable device for releasing a spring or catch and so setting off a mechanism (esp. that of a gun). **2** an event, occurrence, etc., that sets off a chain reaction. ● *v.tr.* **1** (often foll. by *off*) set (an action or process) in motion; initiate; precipitate. **2** fire (a gun) by the use of a trigger. □ **quick on the trigger** quick to respond. **trigger fish** any usu. tropical marine fish of the family Balistidae with a first dorsal fin spine that can be depressed by pressing on the second. **trigger-happy** apt to shoot without or with slight provocation. □□ **triggered** *adj.* [17th-c. *tricker* f. Du. *trekker* f. *trekken* pull: cf. TREK]

■ *v.* **1** see INITIATE *v.* 1.

triglyph /trīglif/ *n. Archit.* each of a series of tablets with three vertical grooves, alternating with metopes in a Doric frieze. □□ **triglyphic** /-glífik/ *adj.* **triglyphical** /-glífikəl/ *adj.* [L *triglyphus* f. Gk *trigluphos* (as TRI-, *gluphē* carving)]

trigon /trígon/ *n.* **1** a triangle. **2** an ancient triangular lyre or harp. **3** the cutting region of an upper molar tooth. [L *trigonum* f. Gk *trigōnon* neuter of *trigōnos* three-cornered (as TRI-, -GON)]

trigonal /trígənəl/ *adj.* **1** triangular; of or relating to a triangle. **2** *Biol.* triangular in cross section. **3** (of a crystal, etc.) having an axis with threefold symmetry. □□ **trigonally** *adv.* [med.L *trigonalis* (as TRIGON)]

trigonometry /trígənómitree/ *n.* the branch of mathematics dealing with the relations of the sides and angles of triangles and with the relevant functions of any angles. □□ **trigonometric** /-nəmétrik/ *adj.* **trigonometrical** *adj.* [mod.L *trigonometria* (as TRIGON, -METRY)]

trigraph /trígraf/ *n.* (also **trigram** /-gram/) **1** a group of three letters representing one sound. **2** a figure of three lines.

trigynous /tríjinəs/ *adj. Bot.* having three pistils.

trihedral /trīheedrəl/ *adj.* having three surfaces.

trihedron /trīheedrən/ *n.* a figure of three intersecting planes.

trihydric /trīhídrik/ *adj. Chem.* containing three hydroxyl groups.

trike /trīk/ *n.* & *v.intr. colloq.* tricycle. [abbr.]

trilabiate /trīláybeeət/ *adj. Bot.* & *Zool.* three-lipped.

trilateral /trīlátərəl/ *adj.* & *n.* ● *adj.* **1** of, on, or with three sides. **2** shared by or involving three parties, countries, etc. (*trilateral negotiations*). ● *n.* a figure having three sides.

trilby /trílbee/ *n.* (*pl.* **-ies**) *Brit.* a soft felt hat with a narrow brim and indented crown. □□ **trilbied** *adj.* [name of the heroine in G. du Maurier's novel *Trilby* (1894), in the stage version of which such a hat was worn]

trilinear /trīlíneeər/ *adj.* of or having three lines.

trilingual /trīlínggwəl/ *adj.* **1** able to speak three languages, esp. fluently. **2** spoken or written in three languages. □□ **trilingualism** *n.*

triliteral /trīlítərəl/ *adj.* **1** of three letters. **2** (of a Semitic language) having (most) roots with three consonants.

trilith /trílith/ *n.* (also **trilithon** /-lithən/) a monument consisting of three stones, esp. of two uprights and a lintel. □□ **trilithic** *adj.* [Gk *trilithon* (as TRI-, *lithos* stone)]

trill /tril/ *n.* & *v.* ● *n.* **1** a quavering or vibratory sound, esp. a rapid alternation of sung or played notes. **2** a bird's warbling sound. **3** the pronunciation of *r* with a vibration of the tongue. ● *v.* **1** *intr.* produce a trill. **2** warble (a song) or pronounce (*r*, etc.) with a trill. [It. *trillo* (n.), *trillare* (v.)]

■ *n.* **2** see CHIRP *n.* ● *v.* see CHIRP *v.*

trillion /trílyən/ n. (pl. same or (in sense 3) **trillions**) **1** a million million (1,000,000,000,000 or 10¹²). **2** esp. *Brit.* a million million million (1,000,000,000,000,000,000 or 10¹⁸). **3** (in *pl.*) *colloq.* a very large number (*trillions of times*). □□ **trillionth** adj. & n. [F *trillion* or It. *trilione* (as TRI-, MILLION), after *billion*]
■ **3** (*trillions*) see UMPTEEN adj.

trilobite /trílǝbīt/ n. any fossil marine arthropod of the class Trilobita of Palaeozoic times, characterized by a three-lobed body. [mod.L *Trilobites* (as TRI-, Gk *lobos* lobe)]

trilogy /trílǝjee/ n. (pl. **-ies**) **1** a group of three related literary or operatic works. **2** *Gk Antiq.* a set of three tragedies performed as a group. [Gk *trilogia* (as TRI-, -LOGY)]

trim /trim/ v., n., & adj. ● v. (**trimmed, trimming**) **1** tr. **a** set in good order. **b** make neat or of the required size or form, esp. by cutting away irregular or unwanted parts. **2** tr. (foll. by *off, away*) remove by cutting off (such parts). **3** tr. **a** (often foll. by *up*) make (a person) neat in dress and appearance. **b** ornament or decorate (esp. clothing, a hat, etc.), by adding ribbons, lace, etc.). **4** tr. adjust the balance of (a ship or aircraft) by the arrangement of its cargo, etc. **5** tr. arrange (sails) to suit the wind. **6** intr. **a** associate oneself with currently prevailing views, esp. to advance oneself. **b** hold a middle course in politics or opinion. **7** tr. *colloq.* **a** rebuke sharply. **b** thrash. **c** get the better of in a bargain, etc. ● n. **1** the state or degree of readiness or fitness (*found everything in perfect trim*). **2** ornament or decorative material. **3** dress or equipment. **4** the act of trimming a person's hair. **5** the inclination of an aircraft to the horizontal. ● adj. **1** neat, slim, or tidy. **2** in good condition or order; well arranged or equipped. □ **in trim 1** looking smart, healthy, etc. **2** *Naut.* in good order. □□ **trimly** adv. **trimness** n. [perh. f. OE *trymman, trymian* make firm, arrange: but there is no connecting evidence between OE and 1500]
■ v. **1 b** curtail, shorten, abbreviate, abridge, reduce, prune, pare, lop, crop, bob, clip, cut, whittle, shave, shear, mow, dock; barber; neaten, shape, tidy. **2** cut (off), snip (off), prune, pare, lop (off), crop, clip, shave, shear. **3 a** see NEATEN. **b** decorate, embellish, dress up, embroider, adorn, ornament, deck out, caparison, beautify. ● n. **1** condition, state, fettle, health, form, order, fitness, repair, shape. **2** trimming, edging, piping, purfling, rickrack, embroidery, border, hem, frill, fringe, ornament, ornamentation, decoration, embellishment, adornment. ● adj. **1** neat, tidy, orderly, well-ordered, well-groomed, well turned out, well-kept, smart, crisp, dapper, spick-and-span, spruce, shipshape (and Bristol fashion), *archaic or dial.* trig, *archaic sl.* spiffing, *colloq.* natty, *sl.* spiffy; slim, slender, clean-cut, shapely, streamlined, compact. **2** in good *or* fine fettle, fit (as a fiddle), in good shape *or* condition *or* order, athletic, *Brit. colloq.* as right as a trivet; neat, tidy, orderly, well-ordered, well-organized, organized, well-equipped, in apple-pie order, streamlined.

trimaran /trímǝran/ n. a vessel like a catamaran, with three hulls side by side. [TRI- + CATAMARAN]

trimer /trímǝr/ n. *Chem.* a polymer comprising three monomer units. □□ **trimeric** /-mérik/ adj. [TRI- + -MER]

trimerous /trímǝrǝs/ adj. having three parts.

trimester /tríméstǝr/ n. a period of three months, esp. of human gestation or as a college or university term. □□ **trimestral** adj. **trimestrial** adj. [F *trimestre* f. L *trimestris* (as TRI-, *-mestris* f. *mensis* month)]

trimeter /trímitǝr/ n. *Prosody* a verse of three measures. □□ **trimetric** /trimétrik/ adj. **trimetrical** adj. [L *trimetrus* f. Gk *trimetros* (as TRI-, *metron* measure)]

trimmer /trímǝr/ n. **1** a person who trims articles of dress. **2** a person who trims in politics, etc.; a person swayed by prevailing opinion. **3** an instrument for clipping, etc. **4** *Archit.* a short piece of lumber across an opening (e.g., for a hearth) to carry the ends of truncated joists. **5** a small capacitor, etc., used to tune a radio set. **6** *Austral. colloq.* a striking or outstanding person or thing.

trimming /tríming/ n. **1** ornamentation or decoration, esp.

for clothing. **2** (in *pl.*) *colloq.* the usual accompaniments, esp. of the main course of a meal. **3** (in *pl.*) pieces cut off in trimming.
■ **1** see ORNAMENT n. 1, 2. **2** (*trimmings*) see TRAPPINGS.

trimorphism /trīmáwrfizǝm/ n. *Bot., Zool.,* & *Crystallog.* existence in three distinct forms. □□ **trimorphic** adj. **trimorphous** adj.

trine /trīn/ adj. & n. ● adj. **1** threefold; triple; made up of three parts. **2** *Astrol.* denoting the aspect of two heavenly bodies 120° (one-third of the zodiac) apart. ● n. *Astrol.* a trine aspect. □□ **trinal** adj. [ME f. OF *trin trine* f. L *trinus* threefold f. *tres* three]

Trinitarian /trínitáireeǝn/ n. & adj. ● n. a person who believes in the doctrine of the Trinity. ● adj. of or relating to this belief. □□ **Trinitarianism** n.

trinitrotoluene /trīnítrōtólyo͞oeen/ n. (also **trinitrotoluol** /-tólyo͞o-awl, -ōl/) = TNT.

trinity /trínitee/ n. (pl. **-ies**) **1** the state of being three. **2** a group of three. **3** (**the Trinity** or **Holy Trinity**) *Theol.* the three persons of the Christian Godhead (Father, Son, and Holy Spirit). □ **Trinity Sunday** the next Sunday after Pentecost. **Trinity term** *Brit.* the university and law term beginning after Easter. [ME f. OF *trinité* f. L *trinitas -tatis* triad (as TRINE)]
■ **2** see TRIO.

trinket /tríngkit/ n. a trifling ornament, jewel, etc., esp. one worn on the person. □□ **trinketry** n. [16th c.: orig. unkn.]
■ see BAUBLE.

trinomial /trínṓmeeǝl/ adj. & n. ● adj. consisting of three terms. ● n. a scientific name or algebraic expression of three terms. [TRI- after BINOMIAL]

trio /tree-ṓ/ n. (pl. **-os**) **1** a set or group of three. **2** *Mus.* **a** a composition for three performers. **b** a group of three performers. **c** the central, usu. contrastive, section of a minuet, scherzo, or march. **3** (in piquet) three aces, kings, queens, or jacks in one hand. [F & It. f. L *tres* three, after *duo*]
■ **1** threesome, trilogy, triad, triple, troika, triptych, triumvirate, triplet, trinity, triunity, three.

triode /trí-ōd/ n. **1** a thermionic valve having three electrodes. **2** a semiconductor rectifier having three connections. [TRI- + ELECTRODE]

trioecious /tri-e͞eshǝs/ adj. *Bot.* having male, female, and hermaphroditic organs each on separate plants. [TRI- + Gk *oikos* house]

triolet /tree͞eláy, trí͞olit/ n. a poem of eight (usu. eight syllable) lines rhyming *abaaabab*, the first line recurring as the fourth and seventh and the second as the eighth. [F (as TRIO)]

trioxide /tríóksid/ n. *Chem.* an oxide containing three oxygen atoms.

trip /trip/ v. & n. ● v.intr. & tr. (**tripped, tripping**) **1** intr. **a** walk or dance with quick light steps. **b** (of a rhythm, etc.) run lightly. **2 a** intr. & tr. (often foll. by *up*) stumble or cause to stumble, esp. by catching or entangling the feet. **b** intr. & tr. (foll. by *up*) make or cause to make a slip or blunder. **3** tr. detect (a person) in a blunder. **4** intr. make an excursion to a place. **5** tr. release (part of a machine) suddenly by knocking aside a catch, etc. **6 a** release and raise (an anchor) from the bottom by means of a cable. **b** turn (a yard, etc.) from a horizontal to a vertical position for lowering. **7** intr. *colloq.* have a hallucinatory experience caused by a drug. ● n. **1** a journey or excursion, esp. for pleasure. **2 a** a stumble or blunder. **b** the act of tripping or the state of being tripped up. **3** a nimble step. **4** *colloq.* a hallucinatory experience caused by a drug. **5** a contrivance for a tripping mechanism, etc. □ **trip-hammer** a large tilt hammer operated by tripping. **trip the light fantastic** *joc.* dance. **trip wire** a wire stretched close to the ground, operating an alarm, etc., when disturbed. [ME f. OF *triper, tripper,* f. MDu. *trippen* skip, hop]

■ *v.* **1** dance, caper, skip, gambol, frolic, frisk, hop, spring, scamper, *sl.* cavort. **2 a** stumble, slip, blunder, misstep, fall (down), tumble, topple, dive, plunge, sprawl, lurch, flounder, stagger, falter. **b** (*trip up*) blunder, slip, err, *colloq.* slip up; trap, trick, unsettle, throw off, disconcert esp. *Brit.* catch out. **3** esp. *Brit.* catch out. **4** journey, travel, voyage, visit, tour, trek, sightsee, cruise; *colloq.* globe-trot. **5** detonate, set off, trigger, operate, activate, release, explode, spark off. **7** hallucinate, *colloq.* freak out, turn on. ● *n.* **1** tour, journey, excursion, outing, expedition, voyage, passage, trek, pilgrimage, jaunt, junket, drive, *archaic or joc.* peregrination. **2** stumble, slip, blunder, false step, misstep, fall; faux pas, error, mistake, indiscretion, lapse, slip of the tongue, *lapsus linguae*, erratum, oversight; Freudian slip; *colloq.* slipup, *Brit. sl.* boob.

tripartite /trìpáartìt/ *adj.* **1** consisting of three parts. **2** shared by or involving three parties. **3** *Bot.* (of a leaf) divided into three segments almost to the base. □□ **tripartitely** *adv.* **tripartition** /-tíshən/ *n.* [ME f. L *tripartitus* (as TRI-, *partitus* past part. of *partiri* divide)]

tripe /trìp/ *n.* **1** the first or second stomach of a ruminant, esp. an ox, as food. **2** *colloq.* nonsense; rubbish (*don't talk such tripe*). [ME f. OF, of unkn. orig.]

■ **2** see RUBBISH *n.* 3.

triphibious /trìfíbeeəs/ *adj.* (of military operations) on land, on sea, and in the air. [irreg. f. TRI- after *amphibious*]

triphthong /tríf-thawng, -thong, tríp-/ *n.* **1** a union of three vowels (letters or sounds) pronounced in one syllable (as in *fire*). **2** three vowel characters representing the sound of a single vowel (as in b*eau*). □□ **triphthongal** /-thónggəl/ *adj.* [F *triphtongue* (as TRI-, DIPHTHONG)]

triplane /tríplayn/ *n.* an early type of airplane having three sets of wings, one above the other.

triple /trípəl/ *adj., n., & v.* ● *adj.* **1** consisting of three usu. equal parts or things; threefold. **2** involving three parties. **3** three times as much or many (*triple the amount; triple thickness*). ● *n.* **1** a threefold number or amount. **2** a set of three. **3** a base hit allowing a batter to safely reach third base. **4** (in *pl.*) a peal of changes on seven bells. ● *v.intr. & tr.* **1** multiply or increase by three. **2** to hit a triple. □ **triple crown 1** *RC Ch.* the pope's tiara. **2** the act of winning all three of a group of important events in horse racing, etc. **triple jump** an athletic exercise or contest comprising a hop, a step, and a jump. **triple play** *Baseball* the act of making all three outs in a single play. **triple rhyme** a rhyme including three syllables. **triple time** *Mus.* that with three beats to the bar; waltz time. □□ **triply** *adv.* [OF *triple* or L *triplus* f. Gk *triplous*]

■ *n.* **2** see TRIO.

triplet /tríplit/ *n.* **1** each of three children or animals born at one birth. **2** a set of three things, esp. of equal notes played in the time of two or of verses rhyming together. [TRIPLE + -ET[1], after *doublet*]

■ **2** see TRIO.

triplex /trípleks, trí-/ *adj. & n.* ● *adj.* triple or threefold. ● *n.* (**Triplex**) *Brit. propr.* toughened or laminated safety glass for car windows, etc. [L *triplex -plicis* (as TRI-, *plic-* fold)]

triplicate *adj., n., & v.* ● *adj.* /tríplikət/ **1** existing in three examples or copies. **2** having three corresponding parts. **3** tripled. ● *n.* /tríplikət/ each of a set of three copies or corresponding parts. ● *v.tr.* /tríplikayt/ **1** make in three copies. **2** multiply by three. □ **in triplicate** consisting of three exact copies. □□ **triplication** /-káyshən/ *n.* [ME f. L *triplicatus* past part. of *triplicare* (as TRIPLEX)]

triplicity /tríplísitee/ *n.* (*pl.* **-ies**) **1** the state of being triple. **2** a group of three things. **3** *Astrol.* a set of three zodiacal signs. [ME f. LL *triplicitas* f. L TRIPLEX]

triploid /tríployd/ *n. & adj. Biol.* ● *n.* an organism or cell having three times the haploid set of chromosomes. ● *adj.* of or being a triploid. [mod.L *triploides* f. Gk (as TRIPLE)]

triploidy /tríploydee/ *n.* the condition of being triploid.

tripmeter /trípmeetər/ *n.* a vehicle instrument that can be set to record the distance of individual journeys.

tripod /trípod/ *n.* **1** a three-legged stand for supporting a

camera, etc. **2** a stool, table, or utensil resting on three feet or legs. **3** *Gk Antiq.* a bronze altar at Delphi on which a priestess sat to utter oracles. □□ **tripodal** /trípəd'l/ *adj.* [L *tripus tripodis* f. Gk *tripous* (as TRI-, *pous podos* foot)]

tripoli /trípəlee/ *n.* = ROTTENSTONE. [F f. *Tripoli* in N. Africa or in Syria]

tripos /trípos/ *n. Brit.* (at Cambridge University) the honors examination for the BA degree. [as TRIPOD, with ref. to the stool on which graduates sat to deliver a satirical speech at the degree ceremony]

tripper /trípər/ *n.* **1** *Brit.* a person who goes on a pleasure trip or excursion. **2** *colloq.* a person experiencing hallucinatory effects of a drug.

triptych /tríptik/ *n.* **1 a** a picture or relief carving on three panels, usu. hinged vertically together and often used as an altarpiece. **b** a set of three associated pictures placed in this way. **2** a set of three writing tablets hinged or tied together. **3** a set of three artistic works. [TRI-, after DIPTYCH]

triquetra /trikétrə/ *n.* (*pl.* **triquetrae** /-tree/) a symmetrical ornament of three interlaced arcs. [L, fem. of *triquetrus* three-cornered]

trireme /tríreem/ *n.* an ancient Greek warship, with three banks of oarsmen on each side. [F *trirème* or L *triremis* (as TRI-, *remus* oar)]

trisaccharide /trìsákərìd/ *n. Chem.* a sugar consisting of three linked monosaccharides.

trisect /trìsékt/ *v.tr.* cut or divide into three (usu. equal) parts. □□ **trisection** /-sékshən/ *n.* **trisector** *n.* [TRI- + L *se-care sect-* cut]

trishaw /tríshaw/ *n.* a light three-wheeled pedaled vehicle used in Asia. [TRI- + RICKSHA]

triskelion /triskéleeən, tri-/ *n.* a symbolic figure of three legs or lines from a common center. [Gk TRI- + *skelos* leg]

trismus /trízməs/ *n. Med.* a variety of tetanus with tonic spasm of the jaw muscles causing the mouth to remain tightly closed. [mod.L f. Gk *trismos* = *trigmos* a scream, grinding]

triste /treest/ *adj.* sad; melancholy; dreary. [F f. L *tristis*]

trisyllable /trísíləbəl, tri-/ *n.* a word or metrical foot of three syllables. □□ **trisyllabic** /-sìlábik/ *adj.*

tritagonist /tritágənist/ *n.* the third actor in a Greek play (cf. DEUTERAGONIST). [Gk *tritagōnistēs* (as TRITO-, *agōnistēs* actor)]

trite /trìt/ *adj.* (of a phrase, opinion, etc.) hackneyed; worn out by constant repetition. □□ **tritely** *adv.* **triteness** *n.* [L *tritus* past part. of *terere* rub]

■ see BANAL.

tritiate /tríteeayt/ *v.tr.* replace the ordinary hydrogen in (a substance) by tritium. □□ **tritiation** /-áyshən/ *n.*

tritium /tríteeəm/ *n. Chem.* a radioactive isotope of hydrogen with a mass about three times that of ordinary hydrogen. ¶ Symb.: **T**. [mod.L f. Gk *tritos* third]

trito- /trítō, trító/ *comb. form* third. [Gk *tritos* third]

Triton /trít'n/ *n.* **1** (in Greek mythology) a minor sea god usu. represented as a man with a fish's tail and carrying a trident and shell trumpet. **2** (**triton**) any marine gastropod mollusk of the family Cymatiidae, with a long conical shell. **3** (**triton**) a newt. [L f. Gk *Tritōn*]

triton /trít'n/ *n.* a nucleus of a tritium atom, consisting of a proton and two neutrons.

tritone /trítōn/ *n. Mus.* an interval of an augmented fourth, comprising three tones.

triturate /tríchərayt/ *v.tr.* **1** grind to a fine powder. **2** masticate thoroughly. □□ **triturable** *adj.* **trituration** /-ráyshən/ *n.* **triturator** *n.* [L *triturare* thresh wheat f. *tritura* rubbing (as TRITE)]

triumph /tríəmf, -umf/ *n. & v.* ● *n.* **1 a** the state of being victorious or successful (*returned home in triumph*). **b** a great success or achievement. **2** a supreme example (*a triumph of engineering*). **3** joy at success; exultation (*could see triumph in her face*). **4** the processional entry of a victorious general into ancient Rome. ● *v.intr.* **1** (often foll. by *over*) gain a victory; be successful; prevail. **2** ride in triumph. **3** (often foll. by *over*) exult. [ME f. OF *triumphe* (n.), *triumpher* (v.), f. L *triump(h)us* prob. f. Gk *thriambos* hymn to Bacchus]

■ *n.* **1 a** victory, success, ascendancy. **b** success, victory, conquest, win, achievement, accomplishment, attainment, coup, smash (hit), winner, *colloq.* knockout, hit. **3** exultation, rejoicing, exulting, elation, delight, rapture, exhilaration, jubilation, happiness, joy, celebration, glory. ● *v.* **1** win, succeed, carry the day, be victorious *or* successful, gain a victory, take the honors, thrive, dominate, prevail; (*triumph over*) defeat, beat, rout, best, conquer, overcome, overwhelm, subdue, *literary* vanquish. **3** see EXULT.

triumphal /trɪúmfəl/ *adj.* of or used in or celebrating a triumph. [ME f. OF *triumphal* or L *triumphalis* (as TRIUMPH)]
■ celebratory, rapturous, jubilant, joyful, glorious, exultant; commemorative.

triumphant /trɪúmfənt/ *adj.* **1** victorious or successful. **2** exultant. □□ **triumphantly** *adv.* [ME f. OF *triumphant* or L *triumphare* (as TRIUMPH)]
■ **1** victorious, successful, conquering, winning; undefeated. **2** see *exultant* (EXULT).

triumvir /trɪómveer, -úmvər/ *n.* (*pl.* **triumvirs** or **triumviri** /-rī/) **1** each of three men holding a joint office. **2** a member of a triumvirate. □□ **triumviral** *adj.* [L, orig. in pl. *triumviri*, back-form. f. *trium virorum* genit. of *tres viri* three men]

triumvirate /trɪúmvirət/ *n.* **1** a board or ruling group of three men, esp. in ancient Rome. **2** the office of triumvir.

triune /trɪyoon/ *adj.* three in one, esp. with ref. to the Trinity. □□ **triunity** /-yoonitee/ *n.* (*pl.* **-ies**). [TRI- + L *unus* one]

trivalent /trɪváylənt/ *adj. Chem.* having a valence of three. □□ **trivalence** *n.* **trivalency** *n.*

trivet /trívit/ *n.* **1** an iron tripod or bracket for a hot pot, kettle, or dish to stand on. **2** an iron bracket designed to hook on to bars of a grate for a similar purpose. □ **as right as a trivet** *colloq.* in a perfectly good state, esp. healthy. **trivet table** a table with three feet. [ME *trevet*, app. f. L *tripes* (as TRI-, *pes pedis* foot)]

trivia /tríveeə/ *n.pl.* **1** insignificant factual details. **2** trifles or trivialities. [mod.L, pl. of TRIVIUM, infl. by TRIVIAL]

trivial /tríveeəl/ *adj.* **1** of small value or importance; trifling (*raised trivial objections*). **2** (of a person) concerned only with trivial things. **3** *archaic* commonplace or humdrum (*the trivial round of daily life*). **4** *Biol. & Chem.* of a name: **a** popular; not scientific. **b** specific, as opposed to generic. **5** *Math.* giving rise to no difficulty or interest. □□ **triviality** /-veeálitee/ *n.* (*pl.* **-ies**). **trivially** *adv.* **trivialness** *n.* [L *trivialis* commonplace f. *trivium*: see TRIVIUM]
■ **1** see TRIFLING 1. **3** see BANAL. □□ **triviality**, **trivialness** smallness, unimportance, insignificance, meaninglessness, inconsequentiality, inconsequentialness, inconsequence, pettiness, paltriness; trifle, technicality, nonessential, small matter, unimportant *or* insignificant *or* inconsequential *or* petty detail, bêtise.

trivialize /tríveeəlīz/ *v.tr.* make trivial or apparently trivial; minimize. □□ **trivialization** *n.*
■ belittle, denigrate, lessen, minimize, undervalue, depreciate, underestimate, underrate, make light of, laugh off, underplay, dismiss, disparage, deprecate, slight, scoff at, scorn, run down, decry, play down, pooh-pooh, *colloq.* put down, *literary* misprize.

trivium /tríveeəm/ *n. hist.* the medieval university studies of grammar, rhetoric, and logic. [L, = place where three roads meet (as TRI-, *via* road)]

triweekly /trɪweéklee/ *adj.* produced or occurring three times a week or every three weeks.

-trix /triks/ *suffix* (*pl.* **-trices** /trisiz, tríseez/ or **-trixes**) forming feminine agent nouns corresponding to masculine nouns in *-tor*, esp. in Law (*executrix*). [L *-trix -tricis*]

tRNA *abbr.* transfer RNA.

trocar /trṓkaar/ *n.* an instrument used for withdrawing fluid from a body cavity, esp. in edema, etc. [F *trois-quarts, trocart* f. *trois* three + *carre* side, face of an instrument, after its triangular form]

trochaic /trōkáyik/ *adj. & n. Prosody* ● *adj.* of or using trochees. ● *n.* (usu. in *pl.*) trochaic verse. [L *trochaicus* f. Gk *trokhaikos* (as TROCHEE)]

trochal /trṓkəl/ *adj. Zool.* wheel-shaped. □ **trochal disk** *Zool.*

the retractable disk on the head of a rotifer bearing a crown of cilia, used for drawing in food or for propulsion. [Gk *trokhos* wheel]

trochanter /trōkántər/ *n.* **1** *Anat.* any of several bony protuberances by which muscles are attached to the upper part of the femur. **2** *Zool.* the second segment of the leg in insects. [F f. Gk *trokhantēr* f. *trekhō* run]

troche /trṓkee/ *n.* a small usu. circular medicated tablet or lozenge. [obs. *trochisk* f. OF *trochisque* f. LL *trochiscus* f. Gk *trokhiskos* dimin. of *trokhos* wheel]

trochee /trṓkee/ *n. Prosody* a foot consisting of one long or stressed syllable followed by one short or unstressed syllable. [L *trochaeus* f. Gk *trokhaios* (*pous*) running (foot) f. *trekhō* run]

trochlea /trṓkleeə/ *n.* (*pl.* **trochleae** /-lee-ee/) *Anat.* a pulley-like structure or arrangement of parts, e.g., the groove at the lower end of the humerus. □□ **trochlear** *adj.* [L, = pulley f. Gk *trokhilia*]

trochoid /trṓkoyd/ *adj. & n.* ● *adj.* **1** *Anat.* rotating on its own axis. **2** *Geom.* (of a curve) traced by a point on a radius of a circle rotating along a straight line or another circle. ● *n.* a trochoid joint or curve. □□ **trochoidal** *adj.* [Gk *trokhoeidēs* wheel-like f. *trokhos* wheel]

trod *past* and *past part.* of TREAD.

trodden *past part.* of TREAD.

trog /trog/ *n.* esp. *Brit. sl.* a term of contempt for a person; a boor or hooligan. [abbr. of TROGLODYTE]

troglodyte /tróglədīt/ *n.* **1** a cave dweller, esp. of prehistoric times. **2** a hermit. **3** *derog.* a willfully obscurantist or old-fashioned person. □□ **troglodytic** /-dítik/ *adj.* **troglodytical** /-dítikəl/ *adj.* **troglodytism** *n.* [L *troglodyta* f. Gk *trōglodutēs* f. the name of an Ethiopian people, after *trōglē* hole]

trogon /trṓgon/ *n.* any tropical bird of the family Trogonidae, with a long tail and brilliantly colored plumage. [mod.L f. Gk *trōgōn* f. *trōgō* gnaw]

troika /tróykə/ *n.* **1 a** a Russian vehicle with a team of three horses abreast. **b** this team. **2** a group of three people, esp. as an administrative council. [Russ. f. *troe* three]
■ **2** see TRIO.

troilism /tróylizəm/ *n.* sexual activity involving three participants. [perh. f. F *trois* three]

Trojan /trṓjən/ *adj. & n.* ● *adj.* of or relating to ancient Troy in Asia Minor. ● *n.* **1** a native or inhabitant of Troy. **2** a person who works, fights, etc., courageously (*works like a Trojan*). □ **Trojan Horse** a hollow wooden horse said to have been used by the Greeks to enter Troy. **2** a person or device secreted, intended to bring about ruin at a later time. **3** *Computing* a set of instructions hidden in a program that cause damage or mischief. [ME f. L *Troianus* f. *Troia* Troy]

troll[1] /trōl/ *n.* (in Scandinavian folklore) a fabled being, esp. a giant or dwarf dwelling in a cave. [ON & Sw. *troll*, Da. *trold*]

troll[2] /trōl/ *v. & n.* ● *v.* **1** *intr.* sing out in a carefree jovial manner. **2** *tr. & intr.* fish by drawing bait along in the water. **3** *intr.* esp. *Brit.* walk; stroll. ● *n.* **1** the act of trolling for fish. **2** a line or bait used in this. □□ **troller** *n.* [ME 'stroll, roll': cf. OF *troller* quest, MHG *trollen* stroll]

trolley /trṓlee/ *n.* (*pl.* **-eys**) **1** esp. *Brit.* a table, stand, or basket on wheels or castors for serving food, transporting luggage or shopping, gathering purchases in a supermarket, etc. **2** esp. *Brit.* a low truck running on rails. **3** (in full **trolley wheel**) a wheel attached to a pole, etc., used to carry current from an overhead electric wire to drive a vehicle. **4 a** = *trolley car*. **b** = *trolley bus*. □ **off one's trolley** *sl.* crazy. **trolley bus** a trackless trolley. **trolley car** an electric streetcar using a trolley wheel. [of dial. orig., perh. f. TROLL[2]]
■ □ **off one's trolley** see CRAZY 1.

trollop /tróləp/ *n.* **1** a disreputable girl or woman. **2** a pro

/.../ **pronunciation**	● **part of speech**
□ **phrases, idioms, and compounds**	
□□ **derivatives**	■ **synonym section**
cross-references appear in SMALL CAPITALS or *ita*	

titute. □□ **trollopish** *adj.* **trollopy** *adj.* [17th c.: perh. rel. to TRULL]

■ see TART² *n.*

trombone /trombṓn/ *n.* **1 a** a large brass wind instrument with a sliding tube. **b** its player. **2** an organ stop with the quality of a trombone. □□ **trombonist** *n.* [F or It. f. It. *tromba* TRUMPET]

trommel /trómǝl/ *n. Mining* a revolving cylindrical sieve for cleaning ore. [G, = drum]

tromometer /trǝmómitǝr/ *n.* an instrument for measuring very slight earthquake shocks. [Gk *tromos* trembling + -METER]

tromp /tromp, trawmp/ *v.* **1** *tr. & intr.* walk heavily; trample. **2** *tr.* defeat decisively; trounce. [prob. a var. of TRAMPLE]

trompe /tromp/ *n.* an apparatus for producing a blast in a furnace by using falling water to displace air. [F, = trumpet: see TRUMP¹]

trompe-l'œil /troNplṓyǝ, trámpláy, -loi/ *n.* a still life painting, etc., designed to give an illusion of reality. [F, lit. 'deceives the eye']

-tron /tron/ *suffix Physics* forming nouns denoting: **1** an elementary particle (*positron*). **2** a particle accelerator. **3** a thermionic valve. [after ELECTRON]

troop /troop/ *n. & v.* ● *n.* **1** an assembled company; an assemblage of people or animals. **2** (in *pl.*) soldiers or armed forces. **3** a cavalry unit commanded by a captain. **4** a unit of artillery and armored formation. **5** a unit of Girl Scouts, Boy Scouts, etc. ● *v.* **1** *intr.* (foll. by *in, out, off,* etc.) come together or move in large numbers. **2** *tr.* form (a regiment) into troops. □ **troop the color** esp. *Brit.* transfer a flag ceremonially at a public mounting or changing of garrison guards. [F *troupe,* back-form. f. *troupeau* dimin. of med.L *troppus* flock, prob. of Gmc orig.]

■ *n.* **1** see FLOCK¹ *n.* 2. **2** (*troops*) see SERVICE *n.* 8. ● *v.* **1** see FILE² *v.*

trooper /troopǝr/ *n.* **1** a soldier in a cavalry or armored unit. **2 a** a mounted police officer. **b** a state police officer. **3** a cavalry horse. **4** esp. *Brit.* a troopship. □ **swear like a trooper** swear extensively or forcefully.

trop. *abbr.* **1** tropic. **2** tropical.

trope /trōp/ *n.* a figurative (e.g., metaphorical or ironical) use of a word. [L *tropus* f. Gk *tropos* turn, way, trope f. *trepō* turn]

trophic /trófik, trṓ-/ *adj.* of or concerned with nutrition (*trophic nerves*). [Gk *trophikos* f. *trophē* nourishment f. *trephō* nourish]

-trophic /trófik, trṓ-/ *comb. form* relating to nutrition.

tropho- /trófō, trṓ-/ *comb. form* nourishment. [Gk *trophē*: see TROPHIC]

trophoblast /trófōblast, trṓ-/ *n.* a layer of tissue on the outside of a mammalian blastula, providing nourishment to an embryo.

trophy /trṓfee/ *n.* (*pl.* **-ies**) **1** a cup or other decorative object awarded as a prize or memento of victory or success in a contest, etc. **2** a memento or souvenir, e.g., a deer's antlers, taken in hunting. **3** *Gk & Rom. Antiq.* the weapons, etc., of a defeated army set up as a memorial of victory. **4** an ornamental group of symbolic or typical objects arranged for display. □□ **trophied** *adj.* (also in *comb.*). [F *trophée* f. L *trophaeum* f. Gk *tropaion* f. *tropē* rout f. *trepō* turn]

■ **1** prize, laurel (s), wreath, cup, award, reward, honor(s), medal, citation, palm, bays; gold (medal), silver (medal), bronze (medal). **2** memento, souvenir, token, record, reminder, remembrance, keepsake; booty, spoils.

ⁱⁱⁱⁱⁱⁱc /trópik/ *n. & adj.* ● *n.* **1** the parallel of latitude 23°27′ (**tropic of Cancer**) or south (**tropic of Capricorn**) Equator. **2** each of two corresponding circles on the ◌ sphere where the sun appears to turn after reaching ◌◌lination. **3** (**the Tropics**) the region between ◌ncer and Capricorn. ● *adj.* **1** = TROPICAL ◌ **tropic bird** any sea bird of the family ◌ very long central tail feathers. [ME f. ◌◌s f. *tropē* turning f. *trepō* turn]

-tropic /trópik/ *comb. form* **1** = -TROPHIC. **2** turning toward (*heliotropic*).

tropical /trópikǝl/ *adj.* **1** of, peculiar to, or suggesting the Tropics (*tropical fish; tropical diseases*). **2** very hot; passionate; luxuriant. **3** of or by way of a trope. □ **tropical year** see YEAR 1. □□ **tropically** *adv.*

■ **2** see *sweltering* (SWELTER *v.*)

tropism /trṓpizǝm/ *n. Biol.* the turning of all or part of an organism in a particular direction in response to an external stimulus. [Gk *tropos* turning f. *trepō* turn]

tropology /trǝpólǝjee/ *n.* **1** the figurative use of words. **2** figurative interpretation, esp. of the Scriptures. □□ **tropological** /trópǝlójikǝl, trṓ-/ *adj.* [LL *tropologia* f. Gk *tropologia* (as TROPE)]

tropopause /trópǝpawz, trṓ-/ *n.* the interface between the troposphere and the stratosphere. [TROPOSPHERE + PAUSE]

troposphere /trópǝsfeer, trṓ-/ *n.* a layer of atmospheric air extending upward from the earth's surface, in which the temperature falls with increasing height (cf. STRATOSPHERE, IONOSPHERE). □□ **tropospheric** /-sférik, -sfeer-/ *adj.* [Gk *tropos* turning + SPHERE]

troppo¹ /trópō, tráwpō/ *adv. Mus.* too much (qualifying a tempo indication). □ **ma non troppo** but not too much so. [It.]

troppo² /trópō/ *adj. Austral. sl.* mentally ill from exposure to a tropical climate.

trot /trot/ *v. & n.* ● *v.* (**trotted, trotting**) **1** *intr.* (of a person) run at a moderate pace, esp. with short strides. **2** *intr.* (of a horse) proceed at a steady pace faster than a walk lifting each diagonal pair of legs alternately. **3** *intr. colloq.* walk or go. **4** *tr.* cause (a horse or person) to trot. **5** *tr.* traverse (a distance) at a trot. ● *n.* **1** the action or exercise of trotting (*proceed at a trot; went for a trot*). **2** (**the trots**) *sl.* an attack of diarrhea. **3** a brisk steady movement or occupation. **4** (in *pl.*) *Austral. colloq.* **a** trotting races. **b** a meeting for these. **5** *sl.* a literal translation of a text used by students; a crib. □ **on the trot** *Brit. colloq.* **1** continually busy (*kept them on the trot*). **2** in succession (*five weeks on the trot*). **trot out 1** cause (a horse) to trot to show his paces. **2** produce or introduce (as if) for inspection and approval, esp. tediously or repeatedly. [ME f. OF *troter* f. Rmc & med.L *trottare,* of Gmc orig.]

■ *v.* **1** jog, run; bustle, hustle, hurry, hasten, scamper, *colloq.* scoot, skedaddle. ● *n.* **1** jog, jogtrot, lope; run. **5** translation, gloss, *colloq.* crib. □ **trot out 2** bring out, show, display, exhibit, flaunt, come out with, produce; dredge up, drag out; recite, repeat.

troth /trawth, trōth/ *n. archaic* **1** faith; loyalty. **2** truth. □ **pledge** (or **plight**) **one's troth** pledge one's word esp. in marriage or betrothal. [ME *trowthe,* for OE *trēowth* TRUTH]

Trotskyism /trótskeeizǝm/ *n.* the political or economic principles of L. Trotsky, Russian politician d. 1940, esp. as urging worldwide socialist revolution. □□ **Trotskyist** *n.* **Trotskyite** *n. derog.*

trotter /trótǝr/ *n.* **1** a horse bred or trained for trotting. **2** (usu. in *pl.*) **a** an animal's foot as food (*pig's trotters*). **b** *joc.* a human foot.

trotting /tróting/ *n.* racing for trotting horses pulling a two-wheeled vehicle and driver.

troubadour /troobǝdawr/ *n.* **1** any of a number of French medieval lyric poets composing and singing in Provençal in the 11th–13th c. on the theme of courtly love. **2** a singer or poet. [F f. Prov. *trobador* f. *trobar* find, invent, compose in verse]

■ see MINSTREL.

trouble /trúbǝl/ *n. & v.* ● *n.* **1** difficulty or distress; vexation; affliction (*am having trouble with my car*). **2 a** inconvenience; unpleasant exertion; bother (*went to a lot of trouble*). **b** a cause of this (*the child was no trouble*). **3** a cause of annoyance or concern (*the trouble with you is that you can't say no*). **4** a faulty condition or operation (*kidney trouble; engine trouble*). **5 a** fighting; disturbance (*crowd trouble; don't want any trouble*). **b** (in *pl.*) political or social unrest; public disturbances. **6** disagreement; strife (*is having trouble at home*). ● *v.* **1** *tr.* cause distress or anxiety to; disturb (*were much troubled by their debts*). **2** *intr.* be disturbed or worried (*don't trouble about* it). **3** *tr.* afflict; cause pain, etc., to (*am troubled with arthritis*). **4** *tr.* & *intr.* (often *refl.*) subject or be subjected to inconvenience or unpleasant exertion (*sorry to trouble you*; *don't trouble yourself*). □ **ask** (or **look**) **for trouble** *colloq.* invite trouble or difficulty by one's actions, behavior, etc.; behave rashly or indiscreetly. **be no trouble** cause no inconvenience, etc. **go to the trouble** (or **some trouble**, etc.) exert oneself to do something. **in trouble 1** involved in a matter likely to bring censure or punishment. **2** *colloq.* pregnant while unmarried. **take trouble** (or **the trouble**) exert oneself to do something. **trouble and strife** *rhyming sl.* wife. **trouble spot** a place where difficulties regularly occur. □□ **troubler** *n.* [ME f. OF *truble* (n.), *trubler*, *turbler* (v.) ult. f. L *turbidus* TURBID]

■ *n.* **1** distress, worry, concern, difficulty, discomfort, unpleasantness, inconvenience, vexation, grief, affliction, disquiet, suffering, tribulation, adversity, misfortune, hardship, anxiety, torment, anguish, *archaic or literary* woe, *colloq.* hassle. **2 a** inconvenience, bother, effort, pains, exertion, care. **b** annoyance, bother, torment, irritation, nuisance, burden, problem, pest. **3** see HEADACHE. **4** affliction, defect, fault, malfunction, disability, disease, ailment, illness, sickness, disorder, complaint, problem. **5, 6** disorder, agitation, disturbance, turbulence, tumult, upset, dissatisfaction, unrest, discord, dispute, disagreement, unpleasantness, turmoil, rebellion, revolt, uprising, outbreak, fighting, fight, skirmishing, skirmish, fracas, fuss, *colloq.* row. ● *v.* **1, 3** bother, upset, anguish, alarm, worry, afflict, agitate, disquiet, discomfit, make uncomfortable, grieve, distress, disturb, perturb, discommode, inconvenience, discompose, discountenance, put out, burden, encumber, weigh down, oppress; annoy, irritate, irk, vex, plague, pester, torment, harass, hector, harry, provoke, nettle, exasperate, ruffle, get *or* grate on a person's nerves, *archaic* ail, *colloq.* hassle, get under a person's skin, *sl.* bug. **4** discommode, incommode, impose on, inconvenience, put out; care, be concerned, take the trouble *or* time, go to *or* take the trouble, bother, exert oneself, concern oneself, take pains. □ **in trouble 1** in deep trouble, in a mess, in a predicament, in dire straits, in strife, in a bad way, in a corner, *colloq.* in a pickle, in hot water, in the soup, in a jam, on the spot, in a scrape, in a (tight) spot, *sl.* up the creek.

troubled /trúbəld/ *adj.* showing, experiencing, or reflecting trouble, anxiety, etc. (*a troubled mind*; *a troubled childhood*).
■ see ANXIOUS 1, DIFFICULT 3.

troublemaker /trúbəlmaykər/ *n.* a person who habitually causes trouble. □□ **troublemaking** *n.*
■ mischief-maker, rabble-rouser, gadfly, firebrand, agent provocateur, stormy petrel, incendiary, gossipmonger, scandalmonger, malcontent, instigator, ringleader, meddler, agitator, busybody, troubler; see also DELINQUENT *n.* □□ **troublemaking** see *rowdyism* (ROWDY).

troubleshooter /trúbəlshootər/ *n.* **1** a mediator in industrial or diplomatic, etc., disputes. **2** a person who traces and corrects faults in machinery, etc. □□ **troubleshooting** *n.*

troublesome /trúbəlsəm/ *adj.* **1** causing trouble. **2** vexing; annoying. □□ **troublesomely** *adv.* **troublesomeness** *n.*
■ **1** difficult, awkward, inconvenient, burdensome, onerous, problematical, niggling, trying, tough; uncooperative, unruly, unmanageable, refractory. **2** worrisome, worrying, annoying, irksome, irritating, vexatious, vexing, bothersome, wearisome, distressing, pestiferous, pestilential, *Brit.* tiresome, *colloq.* pesky. □□ **troublesomeness** see INCONVENIENCE *n.* 1.

troublous /trúbləs/ *adj. archaic or literary* full of troubles; agitated; disturbed (*troublous times*). [ME f. OF *troubleus* (as TROUBLE)]

trough /trawf, trof/ *n.* **1** a long narrow open receptacle for water, animal feed, etc. **2** a channel for conveying a liquid. **3** an elongated region of low barometric pressure. **4** a hollow between two wave crests. **5** the time of lowest economic

performance, etc. **6** a region around the minimum on a curve of variation of a quantity. **7** a low point or depression. [OE *trog* f. Gmc]
■ **2** see CHANNEL[1] 5a, 6. **5** see SLUMP *n.*

trounce /trowns/ *v.tr.* **1** defeat heavily. **2** beat; thrash. **3** punish severely. □□ **trouncer** *n.* **trouncing** *n.* [16th c., = afflict: orig. unkn.]
■ **1** see DEFEAT *v.* 1. **2** see BEAT *v.* 1. **3** see PUNISH 1.
□□ **trouncing** see DEFEAT *n.*, *thrashing* (THRASH), PUNISHMENT 1, 2.

troupe /troop/ *n.* a company of actors or acrobats, etc. [F, = TROOP]
■ see COMPANY *n.* 4.

trouper /troopər/ *n.* **1** a member of a theatrical troupe. **2** a staunch reliable person, esp. during difficult times.
■ **2** see STALWART *n.*

trousers /trówzərz/ *n.pl.* **1** = PANTS. **2** (**trouser**) (*attrib.*) designating parts of this (*trouser leg*). □□ **trouserless** *adj.* [archaic *trouse* (sing.) f. Ir. & Gael. *triubhas* TREWS: pl. form after *drawers*]

trousseau /troosō, troosō̄/ *n.* (*pl.* **trousseaus** or **trousseaux** /-sōz/) the clothes and other possessions collected by a bride for her marriage. [F, lit. bundle, dimin. of *trousse* TRUSS]

trout /trowt/ *n.* (*pl.* same or **trouts**) **1** any of various freshwater fish of the genus *Salmo* of the northern hemisphere, valued as food. **2** a similar fish of the family Salmonidae (see also *salmon trout*). **3** *Brit. sl. derog.* a woman, esp. an old or ill-tempered one (usu. *old trout*). □□ **troutlet** *n.* **troutling** *n.* **trouty** *adj.* [OE *truht* f. LL *tructa*]

trouvère /troováir/ *n.* a medieval epic poet in northern France in the 11th–14th c. [OF *trovere* f. *trover* find: cf. TROUBADOUR]
■ see MINSTREL.

trove /trōv/ *n.* = *treasure trove*. [AF *trové* f. *trover* find]

trover /trṓvər/ *n. Law* **1** finding and keeping personal property. **2** common law action to recover the value of personal property wrongfully taken, etc. [OF *trover* find]

trow /trow, trō/ *v.tr. archaic* think; believe. [OE *trūwian*, *trēowian*, rel. to TRUCE]

trowel /trówəl/ *n.* & *v.* ● *n.* **1** a small hand tool with a flat pointed blade, used to apply and spread mortar, etc. **2** a similar tool with a curved scoop for lifting plants or earth. ● *v.tr.* (**troweled**, **troweling** or **trowelled**, **trowelling**) **1** apply (plaster, etc.). **2** plaster (a wall, etc.) with a trowel. [ME f. OF *truele* f. med.L *truella* f. L *trulla* scoop, dimin. of *trua* ladle, etc.]

troy /troy/ *n.* (in full **troy weight**) a system of weights used for precious metals and gems, with a pound of 12 ounces or 5,760 grains. [ME, prob. f. *Troyes* in France]

truant /trōənt/ *n.*, *adj.*, & *v.* ● *n.* **1** a child who stays away from school without leave or explanation. **2** a person missing from work, etc. ● *adj.* (of a person, conduct, thoughts, etc.) shirking; idle; wandering. ● *v.intr.* (also **play truant**) stay away as a truant. □□ **truancy** *n.* [ME f. OF, prob. ult. f. Celt.: cf. Welsh *truan*, Gael. *truaghan* wretched]
■ *n.* malingerer, runaway, absentee, dodger, shirker, idler, loafer, layabout, *colloq.* goldbrick, *Brit. sl.* esp. *Mil.* scrimshanker. ● *adj.* malingering, runaway, absent, absentee, delinquent, shirking, loafing.
● *v.* play truant, absent oneself, be absent, stay away, desert, malinger, *sl.* play hookey. □□ **truancy** absenteeism, nonattendance, malingering, absence, *Brit. sl.* skiving (off).

truce /troos/ *n.* **1** a temporary agreement to cease hostilities. **2** a suspension of private feuding or bickering. □□ **truceless** *adj.* [ME *trew(e)s* (pl.) f. OE *trēow*, rel. to TRUE]
■ armistice, cease-fire, suspension of hostilities, lull, moratorium, respite, letup.

/.../ **pronunciation**	● **part of speech**
□ **phrases, idioms, and compounds**	
□□ **derivatives**	■ **synonym section**
cross-references appear in SMALL CAPITALS or *italics*	

T
V

truck[1] /truk/ *n. & v.* ● *n.* **1** a vehicle for carrying heavy or bulky cargo, etc. **2** *Brit.* a railroad freight car. **3** a vehicle for transporting troops, supplies, etc. **4** a swiveling wheel frame of a railroad car. **5** a wheeled stand for transporting goods; a handcart. **6 a** *Naut.* a wooden disk at the top of a mast with holes for halyards. **b** a small solid wheel. ● *v.* **1** *tr.* convey on or in a truck. **2** *intr.* drive a truck. **3** *intr. sl.* proceed; go. □ **truck stop** a facility, esp. for truck drivers, usu. by a major highway and including a gas station, restaurant, etc. □□ **truckage** *n.* [perh. short for TRUCKLE in sense 'wheel, pulley']

truck[2] /truk/ *n. & v.* ● *n.* **1** dealings; exchange; barter. **2** small wares. **3** small farm or garden produce (*truck farm*). **4** *colloq.* odds and ends. **5** *hist.* the payment of workers in kind. ● *v.tr. & intr. archaic* barter; exchange. □ **have no truck with** avoid dealing with. [ME f. OF *troquer* (unrecorded) = *trocare*, of unkn. orig.]

■ *n.* **1** dealing(s), traffic, business, transaction, trade, commerce, barter, exchange, communication, contact, connection, (business *or* social) relations. **2, 4** merchandise, commodities, goods, stock, wares, stuff, bits and pieces, odds and ends, sundries.

trucker /trúkər/ *n.* **1** a long-distance truck driver. **2** a firm dealing in long-distance transportation of goods.

truckie /trúkee/ *n. Austral. colloq.* a truck driver; a trucker.

trucking /trúking/ *n.* transportation of goods by truck.

truckle /trúkəl/ *n. & v.* ● *n.* **1** (in full **truckle bed**) = *trundle bed* (TRUNDLE). **2** *orig. dial.* a small barrel-shaped cheese. ● *v.intr.* (foll. by *to*) submit obsequiously. □□ **truckler** *n.* [orig. = wheel, pulley, f. AF *trocle* f. L *trochlea* pulley]

■ *v.* kowtow, be obsequious, toady, fawn, bow, scrape, genuflect, salaam, drop to the ground, drop to one's knees, drop down on one's knees, submit, yield, cower, cringe, grovel, crawl, quail, lick a person's boots, *Austral. & NZ* smoodge, *colloq.* suck up, bootlick; (*truckle to*) fawn on *or* upon, defer to, butter up.

□□ **truckler** see *flatterer* (FLATTER).

truculent /trúkyələnt/ *adj.* **1** aggressively defiant. **2** aggressive; pugnacious. **3** fierce; savage. □□ **truculence** *n.* **truculency** *n.* **truculently** *adv.* [L *truculentus* f. *trux trucis* fierce]

■ surly, sullen, bad-tempered, ill-tempered, unpleasant, nasty, obstreperous, defiant, rude, ferocious, fierce, savage, barbarous, harsh, scathing, virulent, combative, belligerent, antagonistic, aggressive, bellicose, hostile, contentious, warlike, violent, pugnacious, *Brit. colloq.* stroppy, *sl.* feisty.

trudge /truj/ *v. & n.* ● *v.* **1** *intr.* go on foot, esp. laboriously. **2** *tr.* traverse (a distance) in this way. ● *n.* a trudging walk. □□ **trudger** *n.* [16th c.: orig. unkn.]

■ *v.* see TRAMP *v.* 1.

trudgen /trújən/ *n.* a swimming stroke like the crawl with a scissors movement of the legs. [J. *Trudgen*, 19th-c. English swimmer]

true /troo/ *adj., adv., & v.* ● *adj.* **1** in accordance with fact or reality (*a true story*). **2** genuine; rightly or strictly so called; not spurious or counterfeit (*a true friend*; *the true heir to the throne*). **3** (often foll. by *to*) loyal or faithful (*true to one's word*). **4** (foll. by *to*) accurately conforming (to a standard or expectation, etc.) (*true to form*). **5** correctly positioned or balanced; upright; level. **6** exact; accurate (*a true aim*; *a true copy*). **7** (*absol.*) (also **it is true**) certainly; admittedly (*true, it would cost more*). **8** (of a note) exactly in tune. **9** *archaic* honest; upright (*twelve good men and true*). ● *adv.* **1** truly (*tell me true*). **2** accurately (*aim true*). **3** without variation (*breed true*). ● *v.tr.* (**trues, trued, trueing** or **truing**) bring (a tool, wheel, frame, etc.) into the exact position or form required. □ **come true** actually happen or be the case. **out of true** (or **the true**) not in the correct or exact position. **true bill** a bill of indictment endorsed by a grand jury as being sustained by evidence. **true-blue** *adj.* extremely loyal or orthodox. **true blue** *n.* a person who is true-blue. **true-hearted** faithful; loyal. **true lover's knot** a kind of knot with interlacing bows on each side, symbolizing true love. **true north**, etc., north, etc., according to the earth's axis,

not magnetic north. **true rib** a rib joined directly to the breastbone. **true to form** (or **type**) being or behaving, etc., as expected. **true to life** accurately representing life. □□ **trueish** *adj.* **trueness** *n.* [OE *trēowe, trȳwe*, f. the Gmc noun repr. by TRUCE]

■ *adj.* **1** accurate, correct, truthful, faithful, literal, authentic, actual, factual, realistic, genuine, right, valid, unelaborated, unvarnished, unadulterated, verified, verifiable, *formal* veracious. **2** genuine, authentic, bona fide, authorized, legitimate, rightful, legal, proper, real, veritable, *Austral. & NZ colloq.* dinkum. **3** staunch, faithful, devoted, dedicated, loyal, fast, firm, unswerving, steady, steadfast, trustworthy, dutiful, upright, honorable, constant, unwavering, stable, dependable, sincere, genuine, reliable, true-blue, true-hearted, *archaic* trusty. **5** square, parallel; see also LEVEL *adj.* 1. **6** proper, exact, accurate, unerring, correct, precise, right, *Brit. colloq.* spot on. **9** see HONEST *adj.* 1. ● *adv.* **1** truly, truthfully, honestly, accurately, candidly, frankly, sincerely, straightforwardly. **2** exactly, correctly, precisely, accurately, unerringly. □ **come true** come to pass, occur, take place, happen, be realized, become a reality, be fulfilled. **true-blue** (*adj.*) see STAUNCH[1] 1, CONSERVATIVE *adj.* 1a. **true-hearted** see TRUE *adj.* 3 above. **true to life** see LIFELIKE.

truffle /trúfəl/ *n.* **1** any strong-smelling underground fungus of the order Tuberales, used as a culinary delicacy and found esp. in France by trained dogs or pigs. **2** a usu. round candy made of chocolate mixture covered with cocoa, etc. [prob. f. Du. *truffel* f. obs. F *truffle* ult. f. L *tubera* pl. of TUBER]

trug /trug/ *n. Brit.* **1** a shallow oblong garden basket usu. of wood strips. **2** *archaic* a wooden milk pan. [perh. a dial. var. of TROUGH]

truism /trόoizəm/ *n.* **1** an obviously true or hackneyed statement. **2** a proposition that states nothing beyond what is implied in any of its terms. □□ **truistic** /-ístik/ *adj.*

■ **1** commonplace, platitude, bromide, axiom, cliché, maxim, saw.

trull /trul/ *n. archaic* a prostitute. [16th c.: cf. G *Trulle*, TROLLOP]

truly /trόolee/ *adv.* **1** sincerely; genuinely (*am truly grateful*). **2** really; indeed (*truly, I do not know*). **3** faithfully; loyally (*served them truly*). **4** accurately; truthfully (*is not truly depicted*; *has been truly stated*). **5** rightly; properly (*well and truly*). [OE *trēowlice* (as TRUE, -LY[2])]

■ **1** truthfully, actually, really, honestly, in fact, in actuality, in reality, in all honesty, sincerely, genuinely, *literary* in truth. **2** definitely, really, actually, undoubtedly, indubitably, beyond (the shadow of) a doubt, beyond question, without a doubt, indeed, unquestionably, absolutely, positively, decidedly, certainly, surely, *archaic* (yea,) verily, *archaic or joc.* forsooth, *literary* in truth. **3** faithfully, loyally, devotedly, steadfastly, unswervingly, staunchly. **4** accurately, truthfully, correctly, faithfully, literally, factually, *formal* veraciously. **5** properly, rightly, rightfully, justly, legitimately, justifiably, duly, well and truly.

trumeau /trōomṓ/ *n.* (*pl.* **trumeaux** /-mṓz/) a section of wall or a pillar between two openings, e.g., a pillar dividing a large doorway. [F]

trump[1] /trump/ *n. & v.* ● *n.* **1** a playing card of a suit ranking above the others. **2** an advantage, esp. involving surprise. **3** *colloq.* **a** a helpful or admired person. **b** *Austral. & NZ* a person in authority. ● *v.* **1 a** *tr.* defeat (a card or its player) with a trump. **b** *intr.* play a trump card when another suit has been led. **2** *tr. colloq.* gain a surprising advantage over (a person, proposal, etc.). □ **trump card 1** a card belonging to, or turned up to determine, a trump suit. **2** *colloq.* **a** a valuable resource. **b** a surprise move to gain an advantage. **trump up** fabricate or invent (an accusation, excuse, etc.) (*on a trumped-up charge*). **turn up trumps** *Brit. colloq.* **1** turn out better than expected. **2** be greatly successful or helpful. [corrupt. of TRIUMPH in the same (now obs.) sense]

■ *n.* **3 a** see BRICK *n.* 4. ● *v.* **2** see DISCOMFIT 1b, OUTDO.
□ **trump up** see FABRICATE 2.

trump² /trump/ *n. archaic* a trumpet blast. □ **the last trump** the trumpet blast to wake the dead on Judgment Day in Christian theology. [ME f. OF *trompe* f. Frank.: prob. imit.]

trumpery /trúmpəree/ *n. & adj.* ● *n.* (*pl.* **-ies**) **1 a** a worthless finery. **b** a worthless article. **2** junk. ● *adj.* **1** showy but worthless (*trumpery jewels*). **2** delusive; shallow (*trumpery arguments*). [ME f. OF *tromperie* f. *tromper* deceive]

trumpet /trúmpit/ *n. & v.* ● *n.* **1 a** a tubular or conical brass instrument with a flared bell and a bright penetrating tone. **b** its player. **c** an organ stop with a quality resembling a trumpet. **2 a** the tubular corona of a daffodil, etc. **b** a trumpet-shaped thing (*ear trumpet*). **3** a sound of or like a trumpet. ● *v.* (**trumpeted, trumpeting**) **1** *intr.* **a** blow a trumpet. **b** (of an enraged elephant, etc.) make a loud sound as of a trumpet. **2** *tr.* proclaim loudly (a person's or thing's merit). □ **trumpet call** an urgent summons to action. **trumpet major** the chief trumpeter of a cavalry regiment. □□ **trumpetless** *adj.* [ME f. OF *trompette* dimin. (as TRUMP²)]

■ *v.* **2** see PROCLAIM 1.

trumpeter /trúmpitər/ *n.* **1** a person who plays or sounds a trumpet, esp. a cavalry soldier giving signals. **2** a bird making a trumpet-like sound, esp.: **a** a variety of domestic pigeon. **b** a large black S. American cranelike bird of the genus *Psophia.* □ **trumpeter swan** a large N. American wild swan, *Cygnus buccinator.*

truncal /trúngkəl/ *adj.* of or relating to the trunk of a body or a tree.

truncate /trúngkayt/ *v. & adj.* ● *v.tr.* **1** cut the top or the end from (a tree, a body, a piece of writing, etc.). **2** *Crystallog.* replace (an edge or an angle) by a plane. ● *adj. Bot.* & *Zool.* (of a leaf or feather, etc.) ending abruptly as if cut off at the base or tip. □□ **truncately** *adv.* **truncation** /-káyshən/ *n.* [L *truncare truncat-* maim]

■ *v.* **1** see CUT *v.* 3a, c.

truncheon /trúnchən/ *n.* **1** a short club or cudgel, esp. carried by a policeman; a billy club. **2** a staff or baton as a symbol of authority, esp. (in the UK) that of the Earl Marshal. [ME f. OF *tronchon* stump ult. f. L *truncus* trunk]

trundle /trúnd'l/ *v.tr. & intr.* roll or move heavily or noisily, esp. on or as on wheels. □ **trundle bed** a low bed on wheels that can be stored under a larger bed. [var. of obs. or dial. *trendle, trindle,* f. OE *trendel* circle (as TREND)]

■ see ROLL *v.* 1, 3a.

trunk /trungk/ *n.* **1** the main stem of a tree as distinct from its branches and roots. **2** a person's or animal's body apart from the limbs and head. **3** the main part of any structure. **4** a large box with a hinged lid for transporting luggage, clothes, etc. **5** the luggage compartment of an automobile. **6** an elephant's elongated prehensile nose. **7** (in *pl.*) men's often close-fitting shorts worn for swimming, boxing, etc. **8** the main body of an artery, nerve, communications network, etc. **9** an enclosed shaft or conduit for cables, ventilation, etc. □ **trunk call** esp. *Brit.* a long-distance telephone call. **trunk line** a main line of a railway, telephone system, etc. **trunk road** esp. *Brit.* an important main road. □□ **trunkful** *n.* (*pl.* **-fuls**). **trunkless** *adj.* [ME f. OF *tronc* f. L *truncus*]

■ **1** main stem, stalk, stock, bole. **2** torso, body. **4** chest, locker, box, case, bin, coffer. **5** luggage compartment, *Brit.* boot. **6** snout, proboscis. **7** (*trunks*) see PANTS 2. □ **trunk call** long-distance call, toll call.

trunking /trúngking/ *n.* **1** a system of shafts or conduits for cables, ventilation, etc. **2** the use or arrangement of trunk lines.

trunnion /trúnyən/ *n.* **1** a supporting cylindrical projection on each side of a cannon or mortar. **2** a hollow gudgeon supporting a cylinder in a steam engine and giving passage to the steam. [F *trognon* core, tree trunk, of unkn. orig.]

truss /trus/ *n. & v.* ● *n.* **1** a framework, e.g., of rafters and struts, supporting a roof or bridge, etc. **2** a surgical appli-

ance worn to support a hernia. **3** *Brit.* a bundle of old hay (56 lb.) or new hay (60 lb.) or straw (36 lb.). **4** a compact terminal cluster of flowers or fruit. **5** a large corbel supporting a monument, etc. **6** *Naut.* a heavy iron ring securing the lower yards to a mast. ● *v.tr.* **1** tie up (a fowl) compactly for cooking. **2** (often foll. by *up*) tie (a person) up with the arms to the sides. **3** support (a roof or bridge, etc.) with a truss or trusses. □□ **trusser** *n.* [ME f. OF *trusser* (v.), *trusse* (n.), of unkn. orig.]

■ *v.* **2** see TIE *v.* 1a.

trust /trust/ *n. & v.* ● *n.* **1 a** a firm belief in the reliability or truth or strength, etc., of a person or thing. **b** the state of being relied on. **2** a confident expectation. **3 a** a thing or person committed to one's care. **b** the resulting obligation or responsibility (*am in a position of trust; have fulfilled my trust*). **4** a person or thing confided in (*is our sole trust*). **5** reliance on the truth of a statement, etc., without examination. **6** commercial credit (*obtained merchandise on trust*). **7** *Law* **a** confidence placed in a person by making that person the nominal owner of property to be used for another's benefit. **b** the right of the latter to benefit by such property. **c** the property so held. **d** the legal relation between the holder and the property so held. **8 a** a body of trustees. **b** an organization managed by trustees. **c** an organized association of several companies for the purpose of reducing or defeating competition, etc., esp. one in which all or most of the stock is transferred to a central committee and shareholders lose their voting power although remaining entitled to profits. ● *v.* **1** *tr.* place trust in; believe in; rely on the character or behavior of. **2** *tr.* (foll. by *with*) allow (a person) to have or use (a thing) from confidence in its proper use (*was reluctant to trust them with my books*). **3** *tr.* (often foll. by *that* + clause) have faith or confidence or hope that a thing will take place (*I trust you will not be late; I trust that she is recovering*). **4** *tr.* (foll. by *to*) consign (a thing) to (a person) with trust. **5** *tr.* (foll. by *for*) allow credit to (a customer) for (merchandise). **6** *intr.* (foll. by *in*) place reliance in (*we trust in you*). **7** *intr.* (foll. by *to*) place (esp. undue) reliance on (*shall have to trust to luck*). □ **in trust** *Law* held on the basis of trust (see sense 7 of *n.*). **on trust 1** on credit. **2** on the basis of trust or confidence. **take on trust** accept (an assertion, claim, etc.) without evidence or investigation. **trust company** a company formed to act as a trustee or to deal with trusts. **trust fund** a fund of money, etc., held in trust. **trust territory** a territory under the trusteeship of the United Nations or of a nation designated by them. □□ **trustable** *adj.* **truster** *n.* [ME *troste, truste* (n.) f. ON *traust* f. *traustr* strong: (v.) f. ON *treysta,* assim. to the noun]

■ *n.* **1, 5** confidence, reliance, faith, conviction, certitude, certainty, sureness, positiveness, assurance, belief, dependence, credence. **2** belief, conviction, expectation. **3 a** see RESPONSIBILITY 2. **b** see OBLIGATION 2. **6** credit, reliability, dependability, credibility, trustworthiness, esp. *Brit. colloq.* tick. **7 d** custody, care, keeping, charge, guardianship, protection, safe keeping, trusteeship. **8 c** monopoly, cartel; group, corporation, conglomerate, syndicate. ● *v.* **1** rely on *or* upon, believe in, have faith *or* confidence in, confide in, depend *or* bank *or* count on *or* upon, pin one's faith *or* hopes on *or* upon. **2** (*trust with*) entrust *or* charge with, empower to. **3** see HOPE *v.* 1, 2. **4** entrust, commit, commend, give, delegate, make *or* turn *or* sign *or* hand over, depute, assign, consign. **6** (*trust in*) see TRUST *v.* 1 above. **7** (*trust to*) see TRUST *v.* 1 above. □ **on trust 1** on credit, esp. *Brit. colloq.* on tick.

trustee /trustée/ *n.* **1** *Law* a person or member of a board given control or powers of administration of property in trust with a legal obligation to administer it solely for the

/.../ **pronunciation**	● **part of speech**
□ **phrases, idioms, and compounds**	
□□ **derivatives**	■ **synonym section**
cross-references appear in SMALL CAPITALS or *italics*	

purposes specified. **2** a nation made responsible for the government of an area. □□ **trusteeship** *n.*

trustful /trústfŏŏl/ *adj.* **1** full of trust or confidence. **2** not feeling or showing suspicion. □□ **trustfully** *adv.* **trustfulness** *n.*
■ see TRUSTING.

trusting /trústing/ *adj.* having trust (esp. characteristically); trustful. □□ **trustingly** *adv.* **trustingness** *n.*
■ trustful, unsuspicious, confiding, confident, unsuspecting, unquestioning; naive, innocent, gullible, incautious, credulous.

trustworthy /trústwurthee/ *adj.* deserving of trust; reliable. □□ **trustworthily** *adv.* **trustworthiness** *n.*
■ reliable, dependable, accurate; responsible, steady, steadfast, loyal, faithful, (tried and) true, honorable, honest, ethical, principled, moral, incorruptible, *archaic or joc.* trusty. □□ **trustworthiness** see LOYALTY, INTEGRITY 1.

trusty /trústee/ *adj. & n.* ● *adj.* (**trustier, trustiest**) **1** *archaic or joc.* trustworthy (*a trusty steed*). **2** *archaic* loyal (to a sovereign) (*my trusty subjects*). ● *n.* (*pl.* **-ies**) a prisoner who is given special privileges for good behavior. □□ **trustily** *adv.* **trustiness** *n.*
■ *adj.* **1** see TRUSTWORTHY. **2** see LOYAL.

truth /trŏŏth/ *n.* (*pl.* **truths** /trŏŏthz, trŏŏths/) **1** the quality or a state of being true or truthful (*doubted the truth of the statement; there may be some truth in it*). **2 a** what is true (*tell us the whole truth; the truth is that I forgot*). **b** what is accepted as true (*one of the fundamental truths*). □ **in truth** truly; really. **to tell the truth** (*or* **truth to tell**) to be frank. **truth drug** (*or* **serum**) any of various drugs supposedly able to induce a person to tell the truth. **truth table** a list indicating the truth or falsity of various propositions in logic, etc. □□ **truthless** *adj.* [OE *trīewth, trēowth* (as TRUE)]
■ **1** veracity, truthfulness, verity, genuineness, correctness, accuracy, authenticity, factuality, fact. **2 a** fact(s), reality, actuality. **b** axiom, maxim, truism, rule, law, principle, given, gospel. □ **in truth** in fact, truly, actually, really, in reality, *archaic* verily, *archaic or joc.* forsooth.

truthful /trŏŏthfŏŏl/ *adj.* **1** habitually speaking the truth. **2** (of a story, etc.) true. **3** (of a likeness, etc.) corresponding to reality. □□ **truthfully** *adv.* **truthfulness** *n.*
■ **1** honest, reliable, faithful, trustworthy, straightforward, candid, frank, sincere, earnest, forthright, *formal* veracious. **2** true, accurate, factual, correct, true to life, honest, reliable, faithful, trustworthy, unvarnished, unembellished, unadulterated, unelaborated, *formal* veracious. **3** true, accurate, true to life, realistic, faithful. □□ **truthfully** see TRULY 1. **truthfulness** see HONESTY 2.

try /trī/ *v. & n.* ● *v.* (**-ies, -ied**) **1** *intr.* make an effort with a view to success (often foll. by *to* + infin.; *colloq.* foll. by *and* + infin.: *tried to be on time; try and be early; I shall try hard*). ¶ Use with *and* is uncommon in the past tense and in negative contexts (except in *imper.*). **2** *tr.* make an effort to achieve (*tried my best; had better try something easier*). **3** *tr.* **a** test (the quality of a thing) by use or experiment. **b** test the qualities of (a person or thing) (*try it before you buy*). **4** *tr.* make severe demands on (a person, quality, etc.) (*my patience has been sorely tried*). **5** *tr.* examine the effectiveness or usefulness of for a purpose (*try cold water; have you tried kicking it?*). **6** *tr.* ascertain the state of fastening of (a door, window, etc.). **7** *tr.* **a** investigate and decide (a case or issue) judicially. **b** subject (a person) to trial (*will be tried for murder*). **8** *tr.* make an experiment in order to find out (*let us try which takes longest*). **9** *intr.* (foll. by *for*) **a** apply or compete for. **b** seek to reach or attain (*am going to try for a gold medal*). **10** *tr.* (often foll. by *out*) **a** extract (oil) from fat by heating. **b** treat (fat) in this way. **11** *tr.* (often foll. by *up*) smooth (roughly planed wood) with a plane to give an accurately flat surface. ● *n.* (*pl.* **-ies**) **1** an effort to accomplish something; an attempt (*give it a try*). **2** *Rugby* the act of touching the ball down behind the opposing goal line, scoring points and entitling the scoring side to a kick at the goal. **3** *Football*

an attempt to score one or two extra points after a touchdown. □ **tried and true** (*or* **tested**) proved reliable by experience; dependable. **try conclusions with** see CONCLUSION. **try a fall with** contend with. **try on for size** try out or test for suitability. **try one's hand** see how skillful one is, esp. at the first attempt. **trying-plane** a plane used in trying (see sense 11 of *v.*). **try it on** *Brit. colloq.* **1** test another's patience. **2** attempt to outwit or deceive another person. **try on** put on (clothes, etc.) to see if they fit or suit the wearer. **try-on** *n. Brit. colloq.* **1** an act of trying it on. **2** an attempt to fool or deceive. **try out 1** put to the test. **2** test thoroughly. **try square** a carpenter's square, usu. with one wooden and one metal limb. [ME, = separate, distinguish, etc., f. OF *trier* sift, of unkn. orig.]
■ *v.* **1, 2** attempt, endeavor, aim, undertake, venture, strive, struggle, make an effort, tackle, try one's hand (at), have a go (at), *archaic* seek, *colloq.* have a stab (at), take a shot *or* crack (at), *formal* essay, *sl.* have a whack (at). **3** test, try out, prove, evaluate, examine, inspect, investigate, sample, appraise, assay, look over, analyze, scrutinize, assess, judge, check out. **4** test, strain, tax, *archaic* prove. **7** hear, sit on, adjudicate, judge, adjudge. ● *n.* **1** attempt, endeavor, undertaking, venture, struggle, effort, turn, go, fling, *colloq.* stab, shot, crack, whirl, *formal* essay, *sl.* whack. □ **tried and true** (or **tested**) see SAFE *adj.* 3. **try out** see TRY *v.* 3 above.

trying /trí-ing/ *adj.* annoying; vexatious; hard to endure. □□ **tryingly** *adv.*
■ irritating, exasperating, frustrating, annoying, irksome, infuriating, maddening, bothersome, tiresome, vexing, vexatious, troublesome, worrying, worrisome, distressing, disquieting, upsetting, dispiriting, taxing, demanding, tough, stressful, difficult, tiring, fatiguing, *Austral. sl.* on the nose.

trypanosome /trípǝnǝsōm, tripánǝ-/ *n. Med.* any protozoan parasite of the genus *Trypanosoma* having a long trailing flagellum and infesting the blood, etc. [Gk *trupanon* borer + -SOME³]

trypanosomiasis /trípǝnǝsōmíǝsis, tripánǝ-/ *n.* any of several diseases caused by a trypanosome including sleeping sickness and Chagas' disease.

trypsin /trípsin/ *n.* a digestive enzyme acting on proteins and present in the pancreatic juice. □□ **tryptic** /tríptik/ *adj.* [Gk *tripsis* friction f. *tribō* rub (because it was first obtained by rubbing down the pancreas with glycerine)]

trypsinogen /tripsínǝjǝn/ *n.* a substance in the pancreas from which trypsin is formed.

tryptophan /tríptǝfan/ *n. Biochem.* an amino acid essential in the diet of vertebrates. [as TRYPSIN + -*phan* f. Gk *phainō* appear]

tryst /trist/ *n. & v. archaic* ● *n.* **1** a time and place for a meeting, esp. of lovers. **2** such a meeting (*keep a tryst; break one's tryst*). ● *v.intr.* (foll. by *with*) make a tryst. □□ **tryster** *n.* [ME, = obs. *trist* (= TRUST) f. OF *triste* an appointed station in hunting]
■ *n.* see MEETING 1.

tsar var. of CZAR.

tsarevich var. of CZAREVICH.

tsarina var. of CZARINA.

tsetse /tsétsee, tét-, tséetsee, teé-/ *n.* any fly of the genus *Glossina* native to Africa that feeds on human and animal blood with a needlelike proboscis and transmits trypanosomiasis. [Setswana]

TSH *abbr.* thyroid-stimulating hormone.

T-shirt /téeshǝrt/ *n.* (also **teeshirt**) a short-sleeved collarless casual top, usu. of knitted cotton and having the form of a T when spread out.

tsp. *abbr.* (*pl.* **tsps.**) teaspoon; teaspoonful.

T square /tée skwair/ *n.* a T-shaped instrument for drawing or testing right angles.

tsunami /tsŏŏnáamee/ *n.* (*pl.* **tsunamis**) a long high sea wave caused by underwater earthquakes or other disturbances; tidal wave. [Jap. f. *tsu* harbor + *nami* wave]

Tswana /tswáanǝ, swáa-/ *n.* (also **Setswana** /setswáanǝ/) **1**

a southern African people living in Botswana and neighboring areas. **2** a member of this people. **3** the Bantu language of this people. ¶ *Setswana* is now the preferred form for the language. [native name]

Tu. *abbr.* Tuesday.

tuatara /tŏŏətaˈärə/ *n.* a large lizardlike reptile, *Sphenodon punctatus*, unique to certain small islands of New Zealand, having a crest of soft spines extending along its back and a third eye on top of its head. [Maori f. *tua* on the back + *tara* spine]

tub /tub/ *n. & v.* ● *n.* **1** an open flat-bottomed usu. round container for various purposes. **2** a tub-shaped (usu. plastic) carton. **3** the amount a tub will hold. **4** *Brit. colloq.* a bath. **5 a** *colloq.* a clumsy slow boat. **b** a stout roomy boat for rowing practice. **6** (in mining) a container for conveying ore, coal, etc. ● *v.* (**tubbed, tubbing**) **1** *tr. & intr. esp. Brit.* plant, bathe, or wash in a tub. **2** *tr.* enclose in a tub. **3** *tr.* line (a mine shaft) with a wooden or iron casing. □ **tub chair** a chair with solid arms continuous with a usu. semicircular back. **tub-thumper** *colloq.* a ranting preacher or orator. **tub-thumping** *colloq.* ranting oratory. □□ **tubbable** *adj.* **tubbish** *adj.* **tubful** *n.* (*pl.* **-fuls**). [ME, prob. of LG or Du. orig.: cf. MLG, MDu. *tubbe*]

tuba /tŏŏbə, tyŏ́ŏ-/ *n.* (*pl.* **tubas**) **1 a** a low-pitched brass wind instrument. **b** its player. **2** an organ stop with the quality of a tuba. [It. f. L, = trumpet]

tubal /tŏŏbəl, tyŏ́ŏ-/ *adj. Anat.* of or relating to a tube, esp. the bronchial or Fallopian tubes.

tubby /túbee/ *adj.* (**tubbier, tubbiest**) **1** (of a person) short and fat; tub-shaped. **2** (of a violin) dull-sounding, lacking resonance. □□ **tubbiness** *n.*

■ **1** see FAT *adj.* 1. □□ **tubbiness** see FAT *n.*

tube /tŏŏb, tyŏŏb/ *n. & v.* ● *n.* **1** a long hollow rigid or flexible cylinder, esp. for holding or carrying air, liquids, etc. **2** a soft metal or plastic cylinder sealed at one end and having a screw cap at the other, for holding a semiliquid substance ready for use (*a tube of toothpaste*). **3** *Anat. & Zool.* a hollow cylindrical organ in the body (*bronchial tubes; Fallopian tubes*). **4** (often prec. by *the*) *colloq.* the London subway system. **5 a** a cathode-ray tube, esp. in a television set. **b** (prec. by *the*) *colloq.* television. **6** = *vacuum tube.* **7** = *inner tube.* **8** the cylindrical body of a wind instrument. **9** (in full **tube top**) an elasticized upper garment shaped like a tube. **10** *Austral. sl.* a can of beer. ● *v.tr.* **1** equip with tubes. **2** enclose in a tube. □□ **tubeless** *adj.* (esp. in sense 7 of *n.*). **tubelike** *adj.* [F *tube* or L *tubus*]

■ *n.* **1** see PIPE *n.* 1. **5 b** (*the tube*) see TELEVISION 2, 3.

tubectomy /tŏŏbéktəmee, tyŏŏ-/ *n.* (*pl.* **-ies**) *Surgery* removal of a Fallopian tube.

tuber /tŏŏbər, tyŏŏ-/ *n.* **1 a** the short thick rounded part of a stem or rhizome, usu. found underground and covered with modified buds, e.g., a potato. **b** the similar root of a dahlia, etc. **2** *Anat.* a lump or swelling. [L, = hump, swelling]

tubercle /tŏŏbərkəl, tyŏŏ-/ *n.* **1** a small rounded protuberance, esp. on a bone. **2** a small rounded swelling on the body or in an organ, esp. a nodular lesion characteristic of tuberculosis in the lungs, etc. **3** a small tuber; a wartlike growth. □ **tubercle bacillus** a bacterium causing tuberculosis. □□ **tuberculate** /-bərkyələt, -layt/ *adj.* **tuberculous** /-bərkyələs/ *adj.* [L *tuberculum*, dimin. of *tuber*: see TUBER]

tubercular /tŏŏbərkyələr, tyŏŏ-/ *adj. & n.* ● *adj.* of or having tubercles or tuberculosis. ● *n.* a person with tuberculosis. [f. L *tuberculum* (as TUBERCLE)]

tuberculation /tŏŏbərkyəláyshən, tyŏŏ-/ *n.* **1** the formation of tubercles. **2** a growth of tubercles. [f. L *tuberculum* (as TUBERCLE)]

tuberculin /tŏŏbərkyəlin, tyŏŏ-/ *n.* a sterile liquid from cultures of tubercle bacillus, used in the diagnosis and treatment of tuberculosis. □ **tuberculin test** a hypodermic injection of tuberculin to detect a tubercular infection. **tuberculin-tested** (of milk) from cows giving a negative response to a tuberculin test. [f. L *tuberculum* (as TUBERCLE)]

tuberculosis /tŏŏbərkyəlṓsis, tyŏŏ-/ *n.* an infectious disease caused by the bacillus *Mycobacterium tuberculosis*, characterized by tubercles, esp. in the lungs.

tuberose[1] /tŏŏbərōs, tyŏ́ŏ-/ *adj.* **1** covered with tubers; knobby. **2** of or resembling a tuber. **3** bearing tubers. □□ **tuberosity** /-rósitee/ *n.* [L *tuberosus* f. TUBER]

tuberose[2] /tŏŏbərōz, tyŏ́ŏ-/ *n.* a plant, *Polianthes tuberosa*, native to Mexico, having heavily scented white funnel-like flowers and strap-shaped leaves. [L *tuberosa* fem. (as TUBEROSE[1])]

tuberous /tŏŏbərəs, tyŏ́ŏ-/ *adj.* = TUBEROSE[1]. □ **tuberous root** a thick and fleshy root like a tuber but without buds. [F *tubéreux* or L *tuberosus* f. TUBER]

tubifex /tŏŏbifeks, tyŏ́ŏ-/ *n.* any red annelid worm of the genus *Tubifex*, found in mud at the bottom of rivers and lakes and used as food for aquarium fish. [mod.L f. L *tubus* tube + *-fex* f. *facere* make]

tubiform /tŏŏbifawrm, tyŏ́ŏ-/ *adj.* tube-shaped.

tubing /tŏŏbing, tyŏ́ŏ-/ *n.* **1** a length of tube. **2** a quantity of tubes.

tubular /tŏŏbyələr, tyŏ́ŏ-/ *adj.* **1** tube-shaped. **2** having or consisting of tubes. **3** (of furniture, etc.) made of tubular pieces. □ **tubular bells** an orchestral instrument consisting of a row of vertically suspended brass tubes that are struck with a hammer.

tubule /tŏŏbyŏŏl, tyŏ́ŏ-/ *n.* a small tube in a plant or an animal body. [L *tubulus*, dimin. of *tubus* tube]

tubulous /tŏŏbyələs, tyŏ́ŏ-/ *adj.* = TUBULAR.

tuck /tuk/ *v. & n.* ● *v.* **1** *tr.* (often foll. by *in, up*) **a** draw, fold, or turn the outer or end parts of (cloth or clothes, etc.) close together so as to be held; thrust in the edge of (a thing) so as to confine it (*tucked his shirt into his trousers; tucked the sheet under the mattress*). **b** thrust in the edges of bedclothes around (a person) (*came to tuck me in*). **2** *tr.* draw together into a small space (*tucked her legs under her; the bird tucked its head under its wing*). **3** *tr.* stow (a thing) away in a specified place or way (*tucked it in a corner; tucked it out of sight*). **4** *tr.* **a** make a stitched fold in (material, a garment, etc.). **b** shorten, tighten, or ornament with stitched folds. ● *n.* **1** a flattened usu. stitched fold in material, a garment, etc., often one of several parallel folds for shortening, tightening, or ornament. **2** *Brit. colloq.* food, esp. cake and candy eaten by children (also *attrib.*: *tuck box*). **3** *Naut.* the part of a ship's hull where the planks meet under the stern. **4** (in full **tuck position**) (in diving, gymnastics, etc.) a position with the knees bent upward into the chest and the hands clasped around the shins. □ **tuck away** (or **into**) *colloq.* eat (food) heartily (*tucked into their dinner; could really tuck it away*). **tuck in** *Brit. colloq.* eat food heartily. **tuck-in** *n. Brit. colloq.* a large meal. **tuck shop** *Brit.* a small shop, esp. near or in a school, selling food to children. [ME *tukke, tokke*, f. MDu., MLG *tucken*, = OHG *zucchen* pull, rel. to TUG]

tucker /túkər/ *n. & v.* ● *n.* **1** a person or thing that tucks. **2** *hist.* a piece of lace or linen, etc., in or on a woman's bodice. **3** *Austral. colloq.* food. ● *v.tr.* (esp. in *passive*; often foll. by *out*) *colloq.* tire; exhaust. □ **best bib and tucker** see BIB[1]. **tucker-bag** (or **-box**) *Austral. colloq.* a container for food.

tucket /túkit/ *n. archaic* a flourish on a trumpet. [ONF *toquer* beat (a drum)]

tucking /túking/ *n.* a series of usu. stitched tucks in material or a garment.

-tude /tŏŏd, tyŏŏd/ *suffix* forming abstract nouns (*altitude; attitude; solitude*). [from or after F *-tude* f. L *-tudo -tudinis*]

Tudor /tŏŏdər, tyŏ́ŏ-/ *adj. & n. hist.* ● *adj.* **1** of, characteristic of, or associated with the royal family of England ruling 1485–1603 or this period. **2** of or relating to the architectural style of this period, esp. with half-timbering and elaborately decorated houses. ● *n.* a member of the Tudor royal family. □ **Tudor rose** (in late Perpendicular decoration) a conventional five-lobed figure of a rose, esp. a red rose encircling a white one. [Owen *Tudor* of Wales, grandfather of Henry VII]

Tues. *abbr.* (also **Tue.**) Tuesday.

Tuesday /tōōzday, -dee, tyōōz-/ *n. & adv.* ● *n.* the third day of the week, following Monday. ● *adv.* **1** *colloq.* on Tuesday. **2** (**Tuesdays**) on Tuesdays; each Tuesday. [OE *Tiwesdæg* f. *Tiw* the Gmc god identified with Roman Mars]

tufa /tōōfə, tyōō-/ *n.* **1** a porous rock composed of calcium carbonate and formed around mineral springs. **2** = TUFF. □□ **tufaceous** /-fáyshəs/ *adj.* [It., var. of *tufo*: see TUFF]

tuff /tuf/ *n.* rock formed by the consolidation of volcanic ash. □□ **tuffaceous** /tufáyshəs/ *adj.* [F *tuf, tuffe* f. It. *tufo* f. LL *tofus*, L TOPHUS]

tuffet /túfit/ *n.* **1** = TUFT *n.* 1. **2** a low seat. [var. of TUFT]

tuft /tuft/ *n. & v.* ● *n.* **1** a bunch or collection of threads, grass, feathers, hair, etc., held or growing together at the base. **2** *Anat.* a bunch of small blood vessels. ● *v.* **1** *tr.* provide with a tuft or tufts. **2** *tr.* make depressions at regular intervals in (a mattress, etc.) by passing a thread through. **3** *intr.* grow in tufts. □□ **tufty** *adj.* [ME, prob. f. OF *tofe, toffe*, of unkn. orig.: for *-t* cf. GRAFT¹]

■ *n.* **1** see WISP.

tufted /túftid/ *adj.* **1** having or growing in a tuft or tufts. **2** (of a bird) having a tuft of feathers on the head.

tug /tug/ *v. & n.* ● *v.* (**tugged, tugging**) **1** *tr.* & (foll. by *at*) *intr.* pull hard or violently; jerk (*tugged it from my grasp; tugged at my sleeve*). **2** *tr.* tow (a ship, etc.) by means of a tugboat. ● *n.* **1** a hard, violent, or jerky pull (*gave a tug on the rope*). **2** a sudden strong emotional feeling (*felt a tug as I watched them go*). **3** a small powerful boat for towing larger boats and ships. **4** an aircraft towing a glider. **5** (of a horse's harness) a loop from a saddle supporting a shaft or trace. □ **tug-of-war 1** a trial of strength between two sides pulling against each other on a rope. **2** a decisive or severe contest. □□ **tugger** *n.* [ME *togge, tugge*, intensive f. Gmc: see TOW¹]

■ *v.* **1** pull, jerk, draw, drag, haul, lug, wrench, pluck, twitch, *colloq.* yank. **2** tow, pull, haul. ● *n.* **1** pull, tow, jerk, drag, haul, wrench, lug, *colloq.* yank. **2** wrench, pang.

tugboat /túgbōt/ *n.* = TUG *n.* 3.

tui /tōō-ee/ *n. NZ* a large honeyeater, *Prosthemadera novaeseelandiae*, native to New Zealand and having a long protrusible bill and glossy bluish black plumage with two white tufts at the throat. [Maori]

tuition /tōō-íshən, tyōō-/ *n.* **1** teaching or instruction, esp. if paid for (*driving tuition; music tuition*). **2** a fee for this. □□ **tuitional** *adj.* [ME f. OF f. L *tuitio -onis* f. *tueri tuit-* watch, guard]

■ **1** education, teaching, tutelage, training, schooling, instruction, guidance, preparation.

tularemia /tōōlərée'meeə/ *n.* a severe infectious disease of animals transmissible to humans; caused by the bacterium *Pasteurella tularense* and characterized by ulcers at the site of infection, fever, and loss of weight. □□ **tularemic** *adj.* [mod.L f. *Tulare* County in California, where it was first observed]

tulip /tōōlip, tyōō-/ *n.* **1** any bulbous spring-flowering plant of the genus *Tulipa*, esp. one of the many cultivated forms with showy cup-shaped flowers of various colors and markings. **2** a flower of this plant. □ **tulip tree** any of various trees, esp. of the genus *Liriodendron*, producing tulip-like flowers. [orig. *tulipa(n)* f. mod.L *tulipa* f. Turk. *tul(i)band* f. Pers. *dulband* TURBAN (from the shape of the expanded flower)]

tulle /tōōl/ *n.* a soft fine silk, etc., net for veils and dresses. [*Tulle* in SW France, where it was first made]

tum /tum/ *n. Brit. colloq.* stomach. [abbr. of TUMMY]

tumble /túmbəl/ *v. & n.* ● *v.* **1** *intr.* & *tr.* fall or cause to fall suddenly, clumsily, or headlong. **2** *intr.* fall rapidly in amount, etc. (*prices tumbled*). **3** *intr.* (often foll. by *about, around*) roll or toss erratically or helplessly to and fro. **4** *intr.* move or rush in a headlong or blundering manner (*the children tumbled out of the car*). **5** *intr.* (often foll. by *to*) *colloq.* grasp the meaning or hidden implication of an idea, circumstance, etc. (*they quickly tumbled to our intentions*). **6** *tr.* overturn; fling or push roughly or carelessly. **7** *intr.* perform acrobatic feats, esp. somersaults. **8** *tr.* rumple or disarrange;

disorder. **9** *tr.* dry (laundry) in a tumble dryer. **10** *tr.* clean (castings, gemstones, etc.) in a tumbling barrel. **11** *intr.* (of a pigeon) turn over backward in flight. ● *n.* **1** a sudden or headlong fall. **2** a somersault or other acrobatic feat. **3** an untidy or confused state. □ **tumble dryer** *n.* a machine for drying laundry in a heated rotating drum. **tumble dry** *v.tr. & intr.* (**dries, dried**) dry in a tumble dryer. **tumbling barrel** (or **box**, etc.) a revolving device containing an abrasive substance, in which castings, gemstones, etc., are cleaned by friction. **tumbling-bay 1** the outfall of a river, reservoir, etc. **2** a pool into which this flows. [ME *tumbel* f. MLG *tummelen*, OHG *tumalōn* frequent. of *tūmōn*: cf. OE *tumbian* dance]

■ *v.* **1** fall (down), pitch, fall *or* turn end over end, go *or* turn head over heels, roll, drop, flop, collapse, topple, stumble, *sl.* come a cropper. **2** fall, drop, topple, nosedive, plummet, take a dive. **3** see ROLL *v.* 1. **5** see the light, *colloq.* get the message, catch on, get wise, wise up, *Brit. colloq.* twig; (*tumble to*) understand, apprehend, perceive, comprehend, realize, *colloq.* catch on to, get wise to, *Brit. colloq.* twig (to), *sl.* dig. **6** fling, throw, toss, drop, dump, push, shove; see also OVERTURN *v.* 1, 3. **8** rumple, disarrange, disorder, tousle, ruffle, mess up, jumble. ● *n.* **1** fall, slip, stumble, spill, *colloq.* header. **2** somersault, roll.

tumbledown /túmbəldown/ *adj.* falling or fallen into ruin; dilapidated.

■ ramshackle, dilapidated, ruined, in ruins, decrepit, rickety, shaky, falling apart *or* to pieces, disintegrating, tottering, broken-down, crumbling, derelict, gone to rack and ruin.

tumbler /túmblər/ *n.* **1** a drinking glass with no handle or foot (formerly with a rounded bottom so as not to stand upright). **2** an acrobat, esp. one performing somersaults. **3** (in full **tumbler dryer**) = *tumble dryer*. **4 a** a pivoted piece in a lock that holds the bolt until lifted by a key. **b** a notched pivoted plate in a gunlock. **5** a kind of pigeon that turns over backward in flight. **6** an electrical switch worked by pushing a small sprung lever. **7** a toy figure that rocks when touched. **8** = *tumbling barrel* (see TUMBLE). □□ **tumblerful** *n.* (*pl.* **-fuls**).

■ **1** see GLASS *n.* 2a.

tumbleweed /túmbəlweed/ *n.* a plant, *Amaranthus albus*, that forms a globular bush that breaks off in late summer and is tumbled about by the wind.

tumbrel /túmbrəl/ *n.* (also **tumbril** /-ril/) *hist.* **1** an open cart in which condemned persons were conveyed to their execution, esp. to the guillotine during the French Revolution. **2** a two-wheeled covered cart for carrying tools, ammunition, etc. **3** a cart that tips to empty its load, esp. one carrying dung. [ME f. OF *tumberel, tomberel* f. *tomber* fall]

tumefy /tōōmifī, tyōō-/ *v.* (**-ies, -ied**) **1** *intr.* swell; inflate; be inflated. **2** *tr.* cause to do this. □□ **tumefacient** /-fáyshənt/ *adj.* **tumefaction** /-fákshən/ *n.* [F *tuméfier* f. L *tumefacere* f. *tumēre* swell]

tumescent /tōōmésənt, tyōō-/ *adj.* **1** becoming tumid; swelling. **2** swelling as a response to sexual stimulation. □□ **tumescence** *n.* **tumescently** *adv.* [L *tumescere* (as TUMEFY)]

tumid /tōōmid, tyōō-/ *adj.* **1** (of parts of the body, etc.) swollen; inflated. **2** (of a style, etc.) inflated; bombastic. □□ **tumidity** /-míditee/ *n.* **tumidly** *adv.* **tumidness** *n.* [L *tumidus* f. *tumēre* swell]

tummy /túmee/ *n.* (*pl.* **-ies**) *colloq.* the stomach. □ **tummy ache** an abdominal pain; indigestion. [childish pronunc. of STOMACH]

■ see STOMACH *n.* 2a.

tumor /tōōmər, tyōō-/ *n.* a swelling, esp. from an abnormal growth of tissue. □□ **tumorous** *adj.* [L *tumor* f. *tumēre* swell]

■ neoplasm, cancer, melanoma, sarcoma, malignancy, carcinoma, growth, lump, swelling, protuberance, excrescence.

tump /tump/ *n.* esp. *dial.* a hillock; a mound; a tumulus. [16th c.; orig. unkn.]

■ see HILL *n.* 1.

tumult /tōōmult, tyōō-/ *n.* **1** an uproar or din, esp. of a disorderly crowd. **2** an angry demonstration by a mob; a riot; a public disturbance. **3** a conflict of emotions in the mind. [ME f. OF *tumulte* or L *tumultus*]

■ **1, 2** commotion, disturbance, upset, uproar, din, riot, disorder, disquiet, insurrection, unrest, agitation, bedlam, chaos, brouhaha, fracas, hubbub, stir, pandemonium, hullabaloo, furor, brawl, donnybrook, affray, mêlée, turbulence, ferment, ado, turmoil, confusion, rampage, frenzy, rage, excitement, ruckus, *colloq.* rumpus, row. **3** turmoil, confusion, upset, disquiet, agitation.

tumultuous /tōōmúlchōōəs, tyōō-/ *adj.* **1** noisily vehement; uproarious; making a tumult (*a tumultuous welcome*). **2** disorderly. **3** agitated. □□ **tumultuously** *adv.* **tumultuousness** *n.* [OF *tumultuous* or L *tumultuosus* (as TUMULT)]

■ clamorous, noisy, boisterous, disorderly, turbulent, violent, vehement, uproarious, chaotic, frenzied, furious, excited, agitated, hectic, riotous, rowdy, unruly, unrestrained, fierce, savage, wild, hysterical, frantic, obstreperous, tempestuous, stormy, thunderous.

tumulus /tōōmyələs, tyōō-/ *n.* (*pl.* **tumuli** /-lī/) an ancient burial mound or barrow. □□ **tumular** *adj.* [L f. *tumēre* swell]

tun /tun/ *n. & v.* ● *n.* **1** a large beer or wine cask. **2** a brewer's fermenting vat. **3** a measure of capacity, equal to 252 gallons. ● *v.tr.* (**tunned, tunning**) store (wine, etc.) in a tun. [OE *tunne* f. med.L *tunna*, prob. of Gaulish orig.]

tuna[1] /tōōnə, tyōō-/ *n.* (*pl.* same or **tunas**) **1** any marine fish of the family Scombridae native to tropical and warm waters, having a round body and pointed snout, and used for food. Also called esp. *Brit.* TUNNY. **2** (in full **tuna fish**) the flesh of the tuna, usu. preserved in oil or brine. [Amer. Sp., perh. f. Sp. *atún* tunny]

tuna[2] /tōōnə, tyōō-/ *n.* **1** a prickly pear, esp. *Opuntia tuna*. **2** the fruit of this. [Sp. f. Haitian]

tundish /túndish/ *n.* **1** a wooden funnel, esp. in brewing. **2** an intermediate reservoir in metal-founding.

tundra /túndrə/ *n.* a vast level treeless Arctic region usu. with a marshy surface and underlying permafrost. [Lappish]

tune /tōōn, tyōōn/ *n. & v.* ● *n.* a melody with or without harmony. ● *v.* **1** *tr.* put (a musical instrument) in tune. **2 a** *tr.* adjust (a radio receiver, etc.) to the particular frequency of the required signals. **b** *intr.* (foll. by *in*) adjust a radio receiver to the required signal (*tuned in to the news*). **3** *tr.* adjust (an engine, etc.) to run smoothly and efficiently. **4** *tr.* (foll. by *to*) adjust or adapt to a required or different purpose, situation, etc. **5** *intr.* (foll. by *with*) be in harmony with. □ **in tune 1** having the correct pitch or intonation (*sings in tune*). **2** (usu. foll. by *with*) harmonizing with one's associates, surroundings, etc. **out of tune 1** not having the correct pitch or intonation (*always plays out of tune*). **2** (usu. foll. by *with*) clashing with one's associates, etc. **to the tune of** *colloq.* to the considerable sum or amount of. **tuned in 1** (of a radio, etc.) adjusted to a particular frequency, station, etc. **2** (foll. by *on, to*) *sl.* in rapport or harmony with. **3** *colloq.* up to date; aware of what is going on. **tune up 1** (of an orchestra) bring the instruments to the proper or uniform pitch. **2** begin to play or sing. **3** bring to the most efficient condition. □□ **tunable** *adj.* (also **tuneable**). [ME: unexpl. var. of TONE]

■ *n.* melody, air, song, strain, motif, theme. ● *v.* **1** tune up, attune, adjust, modulate, temper. **3, 4** calibrate, adjust, regulate, coordinate, adapt, attune, align, set, fine-tune. □ **in tune, out of tune** see STEP *n.* 9a.

tuneful /tōōnfŏŏl, tyōōn-/ *adj.* melodious; musical. □□ **tunefully** *adv.* **tunefulness** *n.*

■ melodic, musical, sweet-sounding, melodious, euphonious, dulcet, mellifluent, mellifluous, harmonic, catchy, mellow, smooth, rich, rhythmic, *colloq.* easy on the ear(s). □□ **tunefulness** see MELODY 4.

tuneless /tōōnlis, tyōōn-/ *adj.* **1** unmelodious; unmusical. **2** out of tune. □□ **tunelessly** *adv.* **tunelessness** *n.*

tuner /tōōnər, tyōō-/ *n.* **1** a person who tunes musical instruments, esp. pianos. **2** a device for tuning a radio receiver.

tung /tung/ *n.* (in full **tung tree**) a tree, *Aleurites fordii*, native

to China, bearing poisonous fruits containing seeds that yield oil. □ **tung oil** this oil used in paints and varnishes. [Chin. *tong*]

tungsten /túngstən/ *n. Chem.* a steel-gray dense metallic element with a very high melting point, occurring naturally in scheelite and used for the filaments of electric lamps and for alloying steel, etc. ¶ Symb.: **W**. □ **tungsten carbide** a very hard black substance used in making dies and cutting tools. □□ **tungstate** /-stayt/ *n.* **tungstic** /-stik/ *adj.* **tungstous** /-stəs/ *adj.* [Sw. f. *tung* heavy + *sten* stone]

tunic /tōōnik, tyōō-/ *n.* **1 a** a close-fitting short coat as part of a police or military, etc., uniform. **b** a loose, often sleeveless garment usu. reaching to about the knees, as worn in ancient Greece and Rome. **c** any of various loose, pleated dresses gathered at the waist with a belt or cord. **d** a tunicle. **2** *Zool.* the rubbery outer coat of an ascidian, etc. **3** *Bot.* **a** any of the concentric layers of a bulb. **b** the tough covering of a part of this. **4** *Anat.* a membrane enclosing or lining an organ. [F *tunique* or L *tunica*]

tunica /tōōnikə, tyōō-/ *n.* (*pl.* **tunicae** /-kee/) *Bot. & Anat.* = TUNIC 3, 4. [L]

tunicate /tōōnikət, -kayt, tyōō-/ *n. & adj.* ● *n.* any marine animal of the subphylum Urochordata having a rubbery or hard outer coat, including sea squirts. ● *adj.* **1** *Zool.* of or relating to this subphylum. **2 a** *Zool.* enclosed in a tunic. **b** *Bot.* having concentric layers. [L *tunicatus* past part. of *tunicare* clothe with a tunic (as TUNICA)]

tunicle /tōōnikəl, tyōō-/ *n.* a short vestment worn by a bishop or subdeacon at Mass, etc. [ME f. OF *tunicle* or L *tunicula* dimin. of TUNICA]

tuning /tōōning, tyōō-/ *n.* the process or a system of putting a musical instrument in tune. □ **tuning fork** a two-pronged steel fork that gives a particular note when struck, used in tuning. **tuning peg** (or **pin**, etc.) a peg or pin, etc., attached to the strings of a stringed instrument and turned to alter their tension in tuning.

tunnel /túnəl/ *n. & v.* ● *n.* **1** an artificial underground passage through a hill or under a road or river, etc., esp. for a railroad or road to pass through, or in a mine. **2** an underground passage dug by a burrowing animal. **3** a prolonged period of difficulty or suffering (esp. in metaphors, e.g., *the end of the tunnel*). **4** a tube containing a propeller shaft, etc. ● *v.* (**tunneled, tunneling** or **tunnelled, tunnelling**) **1** *intr.* (foll. by *through, into*, etc.) make a tunnel through (a hill, etc.). **2** *tr.* make (one's way) by tunneling. **3** *intr. Physics* pass through a potential barrier. □ **tunnel diode** *Electronics* a two-terminal semiconductor diode using tunneling electrons to perform high-speed switching operations. **tunnel net** a fishing net wide at the mouth and narrow at the other end. **tunnel vision 1** vision that is defective in not adequately including objects away from the center of the field of view. **2** *colloq.* inability to grasp the wider implications of a situation. □□ **tunneler** *n.* [ME f. OF *tonel* dimin. of *tonne* TUN]

■ *n.* **1** shaft, subway, (underground) passage(way), underpass. **2** burrow, hole, passage. ● *v.* **1** burrow, dig, hole, excavate, penetrate, mine, bore, drill.

tunny /túnee/ *n.* (*pl.* same or **-ies**) esp. *Brit.* = TUNA[1]. [F *thon* f. Prov. *ton*, f. L *thunnus* f. Gk *thunnos*]

tup /tup/ *n. & v.* ● *n.* **1** esp. *Brit.* a male sheep; a ram. **2** the striking head of a pile driver, etc. ● *v.tr.* (**tupped, tupping**) esp. *Brit.* (of a ram) copulate with (a ewe). [ME *toje*, *tupe*, of unkn. orig.]

tupelo /tōōpilō, tyōō-/ *n.* (*pl.* **-os**) **1** any of various Asian and N. American deciduous trees of the genus *Nyssa*, with colorful foliage and growing in swampy conditions. **2** the wood of this tree. [Creek f. *ito* tree + *opilwa* swamp]

Tupi /tōōpee/ *n. & adj.* ● *n.* (*pl.* same or **Tupis**) **1** a member of a Native American people native to the Amazon valley.

/ . . . / pronunciation		● **part of speech**
□ **phrases, idioms, and compounds**		
□□ **derivatives**		■ **synonym section**
cross-references appear in SMALL CAPITALS or *italics*		

2 the language of this people. ● *adj.* of or relating to this people or language. [native name]

tuppence /túpəns/ *n. Brit.* = TWOPENCE. [phonet. spelling]

tuppenny /túpənee/ *adj. Brit.* = TWOPENNY. [phonet. spelling]

Tupperware /túpərwair/ *n. propr.* a brand of plastic containers for storing food. [*Tupper*, name of the manufacturer, + WARE¹]

tuque /tŏŏk/ *n.* a Canadian stocking cap. [Can. F form of TOQUE]

turaco /tŏŏrəkō/ *n.* (also **touraco**) (*pl.* **-os**) any African bird of the family Musophagidae, with crimson and green plumage and a prominent crest. [F f. native W.Afr. name]

Turanian /tŏŏráyneeən, tyŏŏ-/ *n. & adj.* ● *n.* the group of Asian languages that are neither Semitic nor Indo-European, esp. the Ural-Altaic family. ● *adj.* of or relating to this group. [Pers. *Tūrān* region beyond the Oxus]

turban /tə́rbən/ *n.* **1** a man's headdress of cotton or silk wound around a cap or the head, worn esp. by Muslims and Sikhs. **2** a woman's headdress or hat resembling this. □□ **turbaned** *adj.* [16th c. (also *tulbant*, etc.), ult. f. Turk. *tülbent* f. Pers. *dulband*: cf. TULIP]

turbary /tə́rbəree/ *n.* (*pl.* **-ies**) *Brit.* **1** the right of digging turf on common ground or on another's ground. **2** a place where turf or peat is dug. [ME f. AF *turberie*, OF *tourberie* f. *tourbe* TURF]

turbellarian /tə́rbiláireeən/ *n. & adj.* ● *n.* any usu. free-living flatworm of the class Turbellaria, having a ciliated surface. ● *adj.* of or relating to this class. [mod.L *Turbellaria* f. L *turbella* dimin. of *turba* crowd: see TURBID]

turbid /tə́rbid/ *adj.* **1** (of a liquid or color) muddy; thick; not clear. **2** (of a style, etc.) confused; disordered. □□ **turbidity** /-bíditee/ *n.* **turbidly** *adv.* **turbidness** *n.* [L *turbidus* f. *turba* a crowd, a disturbance]

■ **1** see OPAQUE *adj.* 1, 2. **2** see INCOHERENT 2, DISORDERLY 1.

turbinate /tə́rbinət/ *adj.* **1** shaped like a top or inverted cone. **2** (of a shell) with whorls decreasing rapidly in size. **3** *Anat.* (esp. of some nasal bones) shaped like a scroll. □□ **turbinal** *adj.* **turbination** /-náyshən/ *n.* [L *turbinatus* (as TURBINE)]

turbine /tə́rbin, -bīn/ *n.* a rotary motor or engine driven by a flow of water, steam, gas, wind, etc., esp. to produce electrical power. [F f. L *turbo -binis* top, whirlwind]

turbit /tə́rbit/ *n.* a breed of domestic pigeon of stout build with a neck frill and short beak. [app. f. L *turbo* top, from its figure]

turbo /tə́rbō/ *n.* (*pl.* **-os**) = TURBOCHARGER.

turbo- /tə́rbō/ *comb. form* turbine.

turbocharger /tə́rbōchaarjər/ *n.* a supercharger driven by a turbine powered by the engine's exhaust gases.

turbofan /tə́rbōfan/ *n.* **1** a jet engine in which a turbine-driven fan provides additional thrust. **2** an aircraft powered by this.

turbojet /tə́rbōjet/ *n. Aeron.* **1** a jet engine in which the jet also operates a turbine-driven compressor for the air drawn into the engine. **2** an aircraft powered by this.

turboprop /tə́rbōprop/ *n. Aeron.* **1** a jet engine in which a turbine is used as in a turbojet and also to drive a propeller. **2** an aircraft powered by this.

turboshaft /tə́rbōshaft/ *n.* a gas turbine that powers a shaft for driving heavy vehicles, generators, pumps, etc.

turbosupercharger /tə́rbōsŏŏpərchaarjər/ *n.* = TURBO-CHARGER.

turbot /tə́rbət/ *n.* **1** a flatfish, *Psetta maxima*, having large bony tubercles on the body and head and prized as food. **2** any of various similar fishes including halibut. [ME f. OF f. OSw. *törnbut* f. *törn* thorn + *but* BUTT³]

turbulence /tə́rbyələns/ *n.* **1** an irregularly fluctuating flow of air or fluid. **2** *Meteorol.* stormy conditions as a result of atmospheric disturbance. **3** a disturbance, commotion, or tumult.

■ **3** see DISTURBANCE 1, 4; 2.

turbulent /tə́rbyələnt/ *adj.* **1** disturbed; in commotion. **2** (of a flow of air, etc.) varying irregularly; causing disturbance.

3 tumultuous. **4** insubordinate; riotous. □□ **turbulently** *adv.* [L *turbulentus* f. *turba* crowd]

■ **1, 3, 4** see DISORDERLY 2, TUMULTUOUS.

Turco- /tə́rkō/ *comb. form* (also **Turko-**) Turkish; Turkish and. [med.L (as TURK)]

Turcoman var. of TURKOMAN.

turd /tə́rd/ *n. coarse sl.* **1** a lump of excrement. **2** a term of contempt for a person. ¶ Often considered a taboo word, esp. in sense 2. [OE *tord* f. Gmc]

turdoid /tə́rdoyd/ *adj.* thrushlike. [L *turdus* THRUSH¹]

tureen /tŏŏréen, tyŏŏ-/ *n.* a deep covered dish for serving soup, etc. [earlier *terrine, -ene* f. F *terrine* large circular earthenware dish, fem. of OF *terrin* earthen ult. f. L *terra* earth]

turf /tərf/ *n. & v.* ● *n.* (*pl.* **turfs** or **turves**) **1 a** a layer of grass, etc., with earth and matted roots as the surface of grassland. **b** a piece of this cut from the ground. **c** an artificial ground covering, as on a playing field, etc. **2** a slab of peat for fuel. **3** (prec. by *the*) **a** a horse racing generally. **b** a general term for racetracks. **4** *sl.* a person's territory or sphere of influence. ● *v.tr.* **1** cover (ground) with turf. **2** (foll. by *out*) esp. *Brit. colloq.* expel or eject (a person or thing). □ **turf accountant** *Brit.* a bookmaker. [OE f. Gmc]

■ *n.* **1** sod, grass, lawn, green, *archaic or literary* greensward, *literary* sward. **3** (*the turf*) horse racing, racing, the racing world, racecourse, racetrack. **4** territory, area, neighborhood, backyard, stamping ground, home ground, haunt, province, preserve, *colloq.* patch, *joc.* bailiwick; field, domain, sphere (of influence). ● *v.* **1** grass (over). **2** (*turf out*) eject, dismiss, expel, throw *or* toss *or* turn out, oust, banish, exile, boot *or* kick out, *colloq.* sack, give a person the boot *or* sack, chuck out, *sl.* bounce, fire.

turfman /tə́rfmən/ *n.* (*pl.* **-men**) a devotee of horse racing.

turfy /tə́rfee/ *adj.* (**turfier, turfiest**) like turf; grassy.

turgescent /tərjésənt/ *adj.* becoming turgid; swelling. □□ **turgescence** *n.*

turgid /tə́rjid/ *adj.* **1** swollen; inflated; enlarged. **2** (of language) pompous; bombastic. □□ **turgidity** /-jíditee/ *n.* **turgidly** *adv.* **turgidness** *n.* [L *turgidus* f. *turgēre* swell]

■ **1** see *swollen* (SWELL *v.* 6). **2** see POMPOUS 2. □□ **turgidity** see RANT *n.*

turgor /tə́rgər/ *n. Bot.* the rigidity of cells due to the absorption of water. [LL (as TURGID)]

turion /tŏŏreeən, tyŏŏ-/ *n. Bot.* **1** a young shoot or sucker arising from an underground bud. **2** a bud formed by certain aquatic plants. [F f. L *turio -onis* shoot]

Turk /tərk/ *n.* **1 a** a native or inhabitant of Turkey in SE Europe and Asia Minor. **b** a person of Turkish descent. **2 a** member of a central Asian people from whom the Ottomans derived, speaking Turkic languages. **3** *offens.* a ferocious, wild, or unmanageable person. □ **Turk's cap** (or **Turks'-cap lily**) a martagon lily or other plant with turban-like flowers. **Turk's head** a turban-like ornamental knot. [ME, = F *Turc*, It., etc. *Turco*, med.L *Turcus*, Pers. & Arab. *Turk*, of unkn. orig.]

turkey /tə́rkee/ *n.* (*pl.* **-eys**) **1** a large mainly domesticated game bird, *Meleagris gallopavo*, orig. of N. America, having dark plumage with a green or bronze sheen, prized as food, esp. on festive occasions including Christmas and Thanksgiving. **2** the flesh of the turkey as food. **3** *sl.* **a** a theatrical failure; a flop. **b** a stupid or inept person. □ **talk turkey** *colloq.* talk frankly and straightforwardly; get down to business. **turkey cock 1** a male turkey. **2** a pompous or self-important person. **turkey vulture** (or **buzzard**) an American vulture, *Cathartes aura*. [16th c.: short for *turkeycock* or *turkeyhen*, orig. applied to the guinea-fowl, which was imported through Turkey, and then erron. to the Amer. bird]

Turkey red *n.* **1** a scarlet pigment obtained from the madder or alizarin. **2** a cotton cloth dyed with this.

Turki /tə́rkee/ *adj. & n.* ● *adj.* of or relating to a group of Ural-Altaic languages (including Turkish) and the peoples speaking them. ● *n.* the Turki group of languages. □□ **Turkic** /-kik/ *adj.* [Pers. *turkī* (as TURK)]

Turkish /tə́rkish/ *adj. & n.* ● *adj.* of or relating to Turkey in SE Europe and Asia Minor, or to the Turks or their language. ● *n*. this language. □ **Turkish bath 1** a hot air or steam bath followed by washing, massage, etc. **2** (in *sing.* or *pl.*) a building for this. **Turkish carpet** a wool carpet with a thick pile and traditional bold design. **Turkish coffee** a strong black coffee. **Turkish delight** a confection of lumps of flavored gelatin coated in powdered sugar. **Turkish towel** a towel made of cotton terry cloth.

Turko- var. of TURCO-.

Turkoman /tə́rkōmən/ *n.* (also **Turcoman**) (*pl.* **-mans**) **1** a member of any of various Turkic peoples in Turkmenistan in central Asia. **2** the language of these peoples. □ **Turkoman carpet** a traditional rich-colored carpet with a soft long nap. [Pers. *Turkumān* (as TURK, *mānistan* resemble)]

turmeric /tə́rmərik/ *n.* **1** an E. Indian plant, *Curcuma longa*, of the ginger family, yielding aromatic rhizomes used as a spice and for yellow dye. **2** this powdered rhizome used as a spice, esp. in curry powder. [16th-c. forms *tarmaret*, etc., perh. f. F *terre mérite* and mod.L *terra merita*, of unkn. orig.]

turmoil /tə́rmoyl/ *n.* **1** violent confusion; agitation. **2** din and bustle. [16th c.: orig. unkn.]

■ **1** see CONFUSION 2a. **2** see *excitement* (EXCITE).

turn /tərn/ *v.* & *n.* ● *v.* **1** *tr.* & *intr.* move around a point or axis so that the point or axis remains in a central position; give a rotary motion to or receive a rotary motion (*turned the wheel*; *the wheel turns*; *the key turns in the lock*). **2** *tr.* & *intr.* change in position so that a different side, end, or part becomes outermost or uppermost, etc.; invert or reverse or cause to be inverted or reversed (*turned inside out*; *turned it upside down*). **3 a** *tr.* give a new direction to (*turn your face this way*). **b** *intr.* take a new direction (*turn left here*; *my thoughts have often turned to you*). **4** *tr.* aim in a certain way (*turned the hose on them*). **5** *intr.* & *tr.* (foll. by *into*) change in nature, form, or condition to (*turned into a dragon*; *then turned him into a frog*; *turned the book into a play*). **6** *intr.* (foll. by *to*) **a** apply oneself to; set about (*turned to doing the ironing*). **b** have recourse to; begin to indulge in habitually (*turned to drink*; *turned to me for help*). **c** go on to consider next (*let us now turn to your report*). **7** *intr.* & *tr.* become or cause to become (*turned hostile*; *has turned informer*). **8 a** *tr.* & *intr.* (foll. by *against*) make or become hostile to (*has turned them against us*). **b** *intr.* (foll. by *on*, *upon*) become hostile to; attack (*suddenly turned on them*). **9** *intr.* (of hair or leaves) change color. **10** *intr.* (of milk) become sour. **11** *intr.* (of the stomach) be nauseated. **12** *intr.* (of the head) become giddy. **13** *tr.* cause (milk) to become sour, (the stomach) to be nauseated, or (the head) to become giddy. **14** *tr.* translate (*turn it into French*). **15** *tr.* move to the other side of; go around (*turned the corner*). **16** *tr.* pass the age or time of (*he has turned 40*; *it has now turned 4 o'clock*). **17** *intr.* (foll. by *on*) depend on; be determined by; concern (*it all turns on the weather tomorrow*; *the conversation turned on my motives*). **18** *tr.* send or put into a specified place or condition; cause to go (*was turned loose*; *turned the water out into a basin*). **19** *tr.* **a** perform (a somersault, etc.) with rotary motion. **b** twist (an ankle) out of position; sprain. **20** *tr.* remake (a garment or a sheet) putting the worn outer side on the inside. **21** *tr.* make (a profit). **22** *tr.* (also foll. by *aside*) deflect (something material or immaterial). **23** *tr.* blunt (the edge of a knife, slot of a screw, etc.). **24** *tr.* shape (an object) on a lathe. **25** *tr.* give an (esp. elegant) form to (*turn a compliment*). **26** *intr.* *Golf* begin the second half of a round. **27** *tr.* (esp. as **turned** *adj.*) *Printing* invert (type) to make it appear upside down (*a turned comma*). **28** *tr.* pass around (the flank, etc., of an army) so as to attack it from the side or rear. **29** *intr.* (of the tide) change from flood to ebb or vice versa. ● *n.* **1** the act or process or an instance of turning; rotary motion (*a single turn of the handle*). **2 a** a changed or a change of direction or tendency (*took a sudden turn to the left*). **b** a deflection or deflected part (*full of twists and turns*). **3** a point at which a turning or change occurs. **4** a turning of a road. **5** a change of the tide from ebb to flow or from flow to ebb. **6** a change in the course of events. **7** a tendency or disposition (*is of a mechanical turn of mind*). **8** an opportunity or obligation, etc., that comes successively to each of several persons, etc. (*your turn will come*; *my turn to read*). **9** a short

walk or ride (*shall take a turn around the block*). **10** a short performance on stage or in a circus, etc. **11** service of a specified kind (*did me a good turn*). **12** purpose (*served my turn*). **13** *colloq.* a momentary nervous shock or ill feeling (*gave me quite a turn*). **14** *Mus.* an ornament consisting of the principal note with those above and below it. **15** one round in a coil of rope, etc. **16** *Printing* **a** inverted type as a temporary substitute for a missing letter. **b** a letter turned wrong side up. **17 a** *Brit.* the difference between the buying and selling price of stocks, etc. **b** a profit made from this. □ **at every turn** continually; at each new stage, etc. **by turns** in rotation of individuals or groups; alternately. **in turn** in succession; one by one. **in one's turn** when one's turn or opportunity comes. **not know which way** (or **where**) **to turn** be completely at a loss, unsure how to act, etc. **not turn a hair** see HAIR. **on the turn 1** changing. **2** (of milk) becoming sour. **3** at the turning point. **out of turn 1** at a time when it is not one's turn. **2** inappropriately; inadvisedly or tactlessly (*did I speak out of turn?*). **take turns** (or **take it in turns**) act or work alternately or in succession. **to a turn** (esp. cooked) to exactly the right degree, etc. **turn about** move so as to face in a new direction. **turn and turn about** esp. *Brit.* alternately. **turn around** (or *Brit.* **round**) **1** turn so as to face in a new direction. **2 a** *Commerce* unload and reload (a ship, vehicle, etc.). **b** receive, process, and send out again; cause to progress through a system. **3** adopt new opinions or policy. **turn-around** (or *Brit.* **-round**) **1 a** the process of loading and unloading. **b** the process of receiving, processing, and sending out again; progress through a system. **2** the reversal of an opinion or tendency. **turn aside** see TURN *v.* 22 above. **turn away 1** turn to face in another direction. **2** refuse to accept; reject. **3** send away. **turn back 1** begin or cause to retrace one's steps. **2** fold back. **turn one's back on** see BACK. **turn the corner 1** pass around it into another street. **2** pass the critical point in an illness, difficulty, etc. **turn a deaf ear** see DEAF. **turn down 1** reject (a proposal, application, etc.). **2** reduce the volume or strength of (sound, heat, etc.) by turning a knob, etc. **3** fold down. **4** place downward. **turn one's hand to** see HAND. **turn a person's head** see HEAD. **turn an honest penny** see HONEST. **turn in 1** hand in or over; deliver. **2** achieve or register (a performance, score, etc.). **3** *colloq.* go to bed in the evening. **4** fold inward. **5** incline inward (*his toes turn in*). **6** *colloq.* abandon (a plan, etc.). **turn in one's grave** see GRAVE[1]. **turn inside out** see INSIDE. **turn off 1 a** stop the flow or operation of (water, electricity, etc.) by means of a faucet, switch, etc. **b** operate (a faucet, switch, etc.) to achieve this. **2 a** enter a side road. **b** (of a side road) lead off from another road. **3** *colloq.* repel; cause to lose interest (*turned me right off with their complaining*). **4** *Brit.* dismiss from employment. **turn of speed** the ability to go fast when necessary. **turn on 1 a** start the flow or operation of (water, electricity, etc.) by means of a faucet, switch, etc. **b** operate (a faucet, switch, etc.) to achieve this. **2** *colloq.* excite; stimulate the interest of, esp. sexually. **3** *tr.* & *intr.* *colloq.* intoxicate or become intoxicated with drugs. **turn-on** *n.* *colloq.* a person or thing that causes (esp. sexual) arousal. **turn one's stomach** make one nauseous or disgusted. **turn on one's heel** see HEEL[1]. **turn out 1** expel. **2** extinguish (an electric light, etc.). **3** dress or equip (*well turned out*). **4** produce (manufactured goods, etc.). **5** esp. *Brit.* empty or clean out (a room, etc.). **6** empty (a pocket) to see the contents. **7** *colloq.* **a** get out of bed. **b** go out of doors. **8** *colloq.* assemble; attend a meeting, etc. **9** (often foll. by *to* + infin. or *that* + clause) prove to be the case; result (*turned out to be true*; *we shall see how things turn out*). **10** *Mil.* call (a guard) from the guardroom. **turn over 1** reverse or cause to reverse vertical position; bring the underside or reverse into view (*turn over the page*). **2** upset; fall or cause to

---

/. . ./ **pronunciation**	● **part of speech**
□ **phrases, idioms, and compounds**	
□□ **derivatives**	■ **synonym section**
cross-references appear in SMALL CAPITALS or *italics*	

fall over. **3 a** cause (an engine) to run. **b** (of an engine) start running. **4** consider thoroughly. **5** (foll. by *to*) transfer the care or conduct of (a person or thing) to (a person) (*shall turn it all over to my deputy*; *turned him over to the authorities*). **6** do business to the amount of (*turns over $5,000 a week*). **turn over a new leaf** improve one's conduct or performance. **turn the scales** see SCALE². **turn the other cheek** respond meekly to insult or abuse. **turn signal** any of the flashing lights on the front or back of an automobile that are activated by a driver to indicate that the vehicle is about to turn or change lanes. **turn the tables** see TABLE. **turn tail** turn one's back; run away. **turn the tide** reverse the trend of events. **turn to** set about one's work (*came home and immediately turned to*). **turn to account** see ACCOUNT. **turn turtle** see TURTLE. **turn up 1** increase the volume or strength of (sound, heat, etc.) by turning a knob, etc. **2** place upward. **3** discover or reveal. **4** be found, esp. by chance (*it turned up on a trash heap*). **5** happen or present itself; (of a person) put in an appearance (*a few people turned up late*). **6** *Brit. colloq.* cause to vomit (*the sight turned me up*). **7** shorten (a garment) by increasing the size of the hem. **turn-up** *n. Brit.* **1** the lower turned up end of a trouser leg. **2** *colloq.* an unexpected (esp. welcome) happening; a surprise. **turn up one's nose** (or **turn one's nose up**) react with disdain. [OE *tyrnan, turnian* f. L *tornare* f. *tornus* lathe f. Gk *tornos* lathe, circular movement: prob. reinforced in ME f. OF *turner, torner*]

■ *v.* **1** rotate, revolve, spin, roll, reel, circle, gyrate, pirouette, whirl, wheel, go around *or* about, pivot, orbit, swivel, spiral, twirl. **2** reverse, invert, turn upside down, turn inside out, turn *or* flip *or* roll over. **3 b** go *or* pass *or* move around, veer, wheel, swing, swerve, corner, deviate, divert, shift, switch, move, face, head; twist, wind, snake, curve, bend, arc, coil, loop, meander, zigzag. **4** direct, aim, point. **5** alter, adapt, reorganize, remodel, modify, remake, refashion, reshape, reform, transform, make over, bring over; (*turn into*) become, change into *or* to, convert into *or* to, metamorphose into *or* to. **6** (*turn to*) **a** see *set about* 1 (SET¹). **b** appeal to, apply to, resort to, have recourse to. **c** proceed to, go on to, refer to, pick *or* take up, *literary* advert to. **7** become, grow; make. **8 a** (*turn against*) defy, mutiny *or* rebel *or* revolt *or* rise (up) against. **b** (*turn on*) be hostile to, attack, assail, set upon, tear into. **10** go bad, spoil, curdle, sour, go off. **14** see TRANSLATE 1. **15** round, go *or* pass *or* move *or* veer around. **17** (*turn on*) depend on *or* upon, be contingent on, hinge on *or* upon, hang on, be subject to; concern, revolve about *or* around, relate to. **19 b** twist, sprain, wrench. **22** turn aside *or* away, divert, block, avert, thwart, prevent, balk, parry, deflect, fend off, check. **25** form, make up, fashion, formulate, construct, cast, create, coin, concoct, express. ● *n.* **1** revolution, rotation, cycle, spin, whirl, circuit, round, roll, twirl; pirouette. **2** trend, direction, drift; deviation, turning, detour, shift, wind, deflection, change of direction *or* course *or* tendency. **3** turning point, turning, crossroads, junction, watershed. **4** curve, bend, turning, corner, angle, sinuosity, dogleg, hairpin bend *or* curve, irregularity, meander, twist, loop, zigzag. **6** change, alteration, shift, switch. **7** disposition, inclination, bent, bias, leaning, tendency. **8** opportunity, chance, say, round, spell, time, watch, shift, stint, tour (of duty), innings, move, trick, *colloq.* crack, shot, go, *sl.* whack. **9** airing, constitutional, ramble, saunter, stroll, walk, promenade, amble; drive, ride, *colloq.* spin. **10** see ACT *n.* 3a. **11** service, deed, act; (*bad turn*) disservice, harm, injury, wrong; (*good turn*) favor, good deed, (act of) kindness, courtesy, boon, mercy. **13** shock, fright, surprise, start, scare. **15** loop, coil, spiral, twist, round. □ **at every turn** everywhere, constantly, always, all the time, continually. **by turns** alternately, reciprocally, in rotation, successively, in succession. **in turn** sequentially, one after the other, in succession,

successively, in (proper) order. **out of turn 1** out of sequence, out of order. **2** imprudently, indiscreetly, improperly, disobediently, inappropriately, inadvisedly, tactlessly. **take turns** (or **take it in turns**) alternate, vary, rotate, exchange. **turn away 2** see DISQUALIFY. **3** see *send off.* **turn back 1** go back, retrace one's steps, return; reverse, repulse, repel, rebuff, drive back, beat back. **turn down 1** refuse, reject, rebuff, spurn, decline, forgo, pass up, deny. **2** decrease *or* diminish *or* lessen *or* lower *or* soften the sound of, mute; decrease *or* lower *or* lessen the heat of. **turn in 1** hand in *or* over, turn over, deliver, give in, submit, offer, proffer, tender, give back, return, surrender, yield; deliver up, inform on, betray, *colloq.* rat on, tell on, *sl.* squeal on, *sl.* finger. **3** go to bed *or* sleep, retire, withdraw, call it a day, *colloq.* hit the sack *or* hay. **turn off 1** stop, switch off, shut off, deactivate; extinguish; disconnect. **2** deviate, diverge, branch off. **3** disillusion, depress, cool (off), disenchant, disaffect, alienate, repel, repulse, bore, offend, put off, displease, sicken, nauseate, disgust. **4** see DISMISS 2. **turn on 1** start (up), switch on, energize, activate, set in motion, cause to function *or* operate. **2** excite, thrill, arouse, stimulate, titillate, work up, impassion. **3** see TRIP *v.* 7. **turn out 1** eject, evict, throw out, kick out, expel, oust, remove, dismiss, cashier, axe, *colloq.* sack, esp. *Brit. colloq.* turf out, *sl.* fire. **2** see EXTINGUISH 1. **3** dress, fit out, equip, rig out, accoutre. **4** make, form, shape, construct, build, fabricate, put together, assemble, manufacture, produce, put out, bring out. **8** come, arrive, appear, attend, assemble, meet, *colloq.* show (up), surface. **9** develop, evolve, happen, result, occur, arise, emerge, *formal* eventuate; prove, end up. **turn over 1** reverse, invert, turn upside down. **2** overturn, upset, knock *or* flip over; capsize, keel *or* fall *or* roll over, turn turtle. **3 b** rotate, revolve, spin, kick over. **4** consider, ruminate over *or* about, revolve, ponder (over), contemplate, reflect on, *literary* muse over *or* about. **6** sell. **turn over a new leaf** see REFORM *v.* 1. **turn tail** turn one's back; run away, flee, bolt, take to one's heels, beat a hasty retreat, take off, *colloq.* scoot, scram, skedaddle, show a clean pair of heels, *sl.* cut and run, beat it, *Brit. sl.* do a bunk. **turn to** get to work, pitch in, buckle *or* knuckle down, get going *or* started, set to, *colloq.* get cracking. **turn up 1** increase *or* raise *or* amplify *or* intensify the sound of; raise *or* increase *or* intensify the heat of. **3** uncover, discover, find, unearth, come across, hit upon, dig up, expose, disclose, reveal, bring to light. **4** see *come to light* (LIGHT¹). **5** come up, arise, happen, present itself, crop up, pop up; surface, appear, arrive, put in an appearance, show one's face, *colloq.* show (up).

turnabout /tɔ́rnəbowt/ *n.* **1** an act of turning about. **2** an abrupt change of policy, etc.
■ about-turn, volte-face, reversal, U-turn, about-face.

turnaround /tɔ́rnərownd/ *n.* **1** time taken in a car's, plane's, etc., round trip. **2** a change in one's opinion. **3** space needed for a vehicle to turn around.

turnbuckle /tɔ́rnbukəl/ *n.* a device for tightly connecting parts of a metal rod or wire.

turncoat /tɔ́rnkōt/ *n.* a person who changes sides in a conflict, dispute, etc.
■ renegade, traitor, betrayer, deserter, fifth columnist, double agent, apostate, tergiversator, defector, backslider, snake in the grass.

turndown /tɔ́rndown/ *n. & adj.* ● *n.* a rejection, a refusal.
● *adj.* (of a collar) turned down.
■ *n.* see *rejection* (REJECT).

turner /tɔ́rnər/ *n.* **1** a person or thing that turns. **2** a person who works with a lathe. [ME f. OF *tornere -eor* f. LL *tornator* (as TURN)]

turnery /tɔ́rnəree/ *n.* **1** objects made on a lathe. **2** work with a lathe.

turning /tɔ́rning/ *n.* **1 a** a road that branches off another; a turn. **b** a place where this occurs. **2 a** use of the lathe. **b** (in *pl.*) chips or shavings from a lathe. □ **turning circle** (or **radius**) the smallest circle in which a vehicle can turn without reversing. **turning point** a point at which a decisive change occurs.

turnip /tɔ́rnip/ *n.* **1** a cruciferous plant, *Brassica rapa*, with a large white globular root and sprouting leaves. **2** this root used as a vegetable. **3** a large thick old-fashioned watch. □□ **turnipy** *adj.* [earlier *turnep(e)* f. *neep* f. L *napus*: first element of uncert. orig.]

turnkey /tɔ́rnkee/ *n. & adj.* • *n.* (*pl.* **-eys**) *archaic* a jailer. • *adj.* (of a contract, etc.) providing for a supply of equipment in a state ready for operation. ■ see JAILER.

turnoff /tɔ́rnof/ *n.* **1** a turning off a main road. **2** *colloq.* something that repels or causes a loss of interest.

turnout /tɔ́rnowt/ *n.* **1** the number of people attending a meeting, voting in an election, etc. (*rain reduced the turnout*). **2** the quantity of goods produced in a given time. **3** a set or display of equipment, clothes, etc. **4 a** a railroad siding. **b** a place where a highway widens so cars may park, pass, etc. ■ **1** assemblage, attendance, audience, crowd, gate, throng, gathering. **2** output, production, outturn, volume; gross national product, GNP, gross domestic product, GDP. **3** gear, outfit, clothing, apparatus, equipment, trappings, fittings, equipage, *colloq.* rig, *formal* apparel.

turnover /tɔ́rnōvər/ *n.* **1** the act or an instance of turning over. **2** the amount of money taken in a business. **3** the number of people entering and leaving employment, etc. **4** a small pastry made by folding a piece of pastry crust over a filling. **5** a change in a business' goods as items are sold, new merchandise arrives, etc. **6** *Sports* a change in possession of the ball from one team to the other usu. from fumbling, committing a foul, etc. ■ **2** (gross) revenue, (total) business, volume. **4** see TART[1] 2.

turnpike /tɔ́rnpik/ *n.* **1** a highway, esp. one on which a toll is charged. **2** *hist.* **a** a tollgate. **b** a road on which a toll was collected at a tollgate. **3** *hist.* a defensive frame of spikes.

turnsole /tɔ́rnsōl/ *n.* any of various plants supposed to turn with the sun. [OF *tournesole* f. Prov. *tournasol* f. L *tornare* TURN + *sol* sun]

turnspit /tɔ́rnspit/ *n.* **1** *hist.* a person or small dog used to turn a spit. **2** a rotating spit.

turnstile /tɔ́rnstil/ *n.* a gate for admission or exit, with revolving arms allowing people through singly.

turnstone /tɔ́rnstōn/ *n.* any wading bird of the genus *Arenaria*, related to the plover, that looks under stones for small animals to eat.

turntable /tɔ́rntaybəl/ *n.* **1** a circular revolving plate supporting a phonograph record that is being played. **2** a circular revolving platform for turning a railroad locomotive or other vehicle.

turpentine /tɔ́rpəntin/ *n. & v.* • *n.* an oleoresin secreted by several trees, esp. of the genus *Pinus*, *Pistacia*, *Syncarpia*, or *Copaifera*, and used in various commercial preparations. • *v.tr.* apply turpentine to. □ **Chian turpentine** the type of turpentine secreted by the terebinth. **oil of turpentine** a volatile pungent oil distilled from turpentine, used in mixing paints and varnishes, and in medicine. [ME f. OF *ter(e)bentine* f. L *ter(e)binthina* (*resina* resin) (as TEREBINTH)]

turpeth /tɔ́rpith/ *n.* (in full **turpeth root**) the root of an E. Indian plant, *Ipomoea turpethum*, used as a cathartic. [ME f. med.L *turbit(h)um* f. Arab. & Pers. *turbid*]

turpitude /tɔ́rpitōod, -tyōod/ *n. formal* baseness; depravity; wickedness. [F *turpitude* or L *turpitudo* f. *turpis* disgraceful, base] ■ see EVIL *n.* 2.

turps /tɔrps/ *n. colloq.* oil of turpentine. [abbr.]

turquoise /tɔ́rkwoyz, -koyz/ *n. & adj.* • *n.* **1** a semiprecious stone, usu. opaque and greenish blue or blue, consisting of hydrated copper aluminum phosphate. **2** a greenish blue color. • *adj.* of this color. [ME *turkeis*, etc. f. OF *turqueise* (later *-oise*) Turkish (stone)]

turret /tɔ́rit, túr-/ *n.* **1** a small tower, usu. projecting from the

wall of a building as a decorative addition. **2** a low flat usu. revolving armored tower for a gun and gunners in a ship, aircraft, fort, or tank. **3** a rotating holder for tools in a lathe, lenses in a microscope, etc. □□ **turreted** *adj.* [ME f. OF *to(u)rete* dimin. of *to(u)r* TOWER]

turtle /tɔ́rt'l/ *n.* **1** any of various terrestrial, marine, or freshwater reptiles of the order Chelonia, encased in a shell of bony plates, and having flippers or webbed toes used in swimming. **2** the flesh of the turtle, esp. used for soup. **3** *Computing* a directional cursor in a computer graphics system for children that can be instructed to move around a screen. □ **turn turtle** capsize. [app. alt. of *tortue*: see TORTOISE] ■ □ **turn turtle** capsize, overturn, keel *or* turn over, upset, upend, go bottom up.

turtledove /tɔ́rt'lduv/ *n.* any wild dove of the genus *Streptopelia*, esp. *S. turtur*, noted for its soft cooing and its affection for its mate and young. [archaic *turtle* (in the same sense) f. OE *turtla*, *turtle* f. L *turtur*, of imit. orig.]

turtleneck /tɔ́rt'lnek/ *n.* **1** a high close-fitting turned over collar on a garment. **2** an upper garment with such a collar.

Tuscan /túskən/ *n. & adj.* • *n.* **1** an inhabitant of Tuscany in central Italy. **2** the classical Italian language of Tuscany. • *adj.* **1** of or relating to Tuscany or the Tuscans. **2** *Archit.* denoting the least ornamented of the classical orders. □ **Tuscan straw** fine yellow wheat straw used for hats, etc. [ME f. F f. L *Tuscanus* f. *Tuscus* Etruscan]

Tuscarora /təskərɔ́rə, -ráwr-/ *n.* **1 a** a N. American people native to N. Carolina and later to New York. **b** a member of this people. **2** the language of this people.

tush[1] /tush/ *int. archaic* expressing strong disapproval or scorn. [ME: imit.]

tush[2] /tush/ *n.* **1** a long pointed tooth, esp. a canine tooth of a horse. **2** an elephant's short tusk. [OE *tusc* TUSK]

tush[3] /tŏŏsh/ *n. sl.* the buttocks. [20th c.: abbr. or dimin. of *tokus* f. Yiddish *tokhes*] ■ see *buttocks* (BUTTOCK).

tusk /tusk/ *n. & v.* • *n.* **1** a long pointed tooth, esp. protruding from a closed mouth, as in the elephant, walrus, etc. **2** a tusklike tooth or other object. • *v.tr.* gore, thrust at, or tear up with a tusk or tusks. □ **tusk shell 1** any of various mollusks of the class Scaphopoda. **2** its long tubular tuskshaped shell. □□ **tusked** *adj.* (also in *comb.*). **tusky** *adj.* [ME alt. of OE *tux* var. of *tusc*: cf. TUSH[2]]

tusker /túskər/ *n.* an elephant or wild boar with well-developed tusks.

tussah /túsə/ *n.* (also **tussore** /túsawr/, **tusser** /túsər/) **1** an E. Indian or Chinese silkworm, *Antheraea mylitta*, yielding strong but coarse brown silk. **2** (in full **tussah silk**) silk from this and some other silkworms. [Urdu f. Hindi *tasar* f. Skr. *tasara* shuttle]

tussive /túsiv/ *adj.* of or relating to a cough. [L *tussis* cough]

tussle /túsəl/ *n. & v.* • *n.* a struggle or scuffle. • *v.intr.* engage in a tussle. [orig. Sc. & N.Engl., perh. dimin. of *touse*: see TOUSLE] ■ *n.* see STRUGGLE *n.* 2.

tussock /túsək/ *n.* **1** a clump of grass, etc. **2** (in full **tussock moth**) any moth of the genus *Orgyia*, etc., with tufted larvae. □ **tussock grass** grass growing in tussocks, esp. *Poa flabellata* from Patagonia, etc. □□ **tussocky** *adj.* [16th c.: perh. alt. f. dial. *tusk* tuft]

tut var. of TUT-TUT.

tutelage /tŏŏt'lij, tyŏŏ-/ *n.* **1** guardianship. **2** the state or duration of being under this. **3** instruction. [L *tutela* f. *tueri tuit-* or *tut-* watch] ■ **3** see TUITION.

tutelary /tŏŏt'lairee, tyŏŏ-/ *adj.* (also **tutelar** /-t'lər/) **1 a** serving as guardian. **b** relating to a guardian (*tutelary au-*

thority). **2** giving protection (*tutelary saint*). [LL *tutelaris*, L -*arius* f. *tutela*: see TUTELAGE]

tutenag /tŏŏt′nag/ *n.* **1** zinc imported from China and the E. Indies. **2** a white alloy like German silver. [Marathi *tuttināg* perh. f. Skr. *tuttha* copper sulfate + *nāga* tin, lead]

tutor /tŏŏtər, tyŏŏ-/ *n. & v.* ● *n.* **1** a private teacher, esp. in general charge of a person's education. **2** esp. *Brit.* a university teacher supervising the studies or welfare of assigned undergraduates. **3** *Brit.* a book of instruction in a subject. ● *v.* **1** *tr.* act as a tutor to. **2** *intr.* work as a tutor. **3** *tr.* receive instruction; discipline. **4** *intr.* receive instruction. □□ **tutorage** /-rij/ *n.* **tutorship** *n.* [ME f. AF, OF *tutour* or L *tutor* f. *tuēri* *tut*-watch]

■ *n.* **1, 2** teacher, instructor, instructress, educator, coach, mentor, guru. ● *v.* **1** teach, instruct, coach, educate, school, train, drill, enlighten, advise, direct, guide, prepare, ground, prime. **2** teach. **3** see DISCIPLINE *v.* 2.

tutorial /tŏŏtáwreeəl, tyŏŏ-/ *adj. & n.* ● *adj.* of or relating to a tutor or tuition. ● *n.* **1** a period of individual instruction given by a tutor. **2** *Computing* a routine that allows one to instruct oneself in using a software program. □□ **tutorially** *adv.* [L *tutorius* (as TUTOR)]

tutsan /tútsən/ *n.* a species of St. John's wort, *Hypericum androsaemum*, formerly used to heal wounds, etc. [ME f. AF *tutsaine* all healthy]

tutti /tŏŏtee/ *adv. & n. Mus.* ● *adv.* with all voices or instruments together. ● *n.* (*pl.* **tuttis**) a passage to be performed in this way. [It., pl. of *tutto* all]

tutti-frutti /tŏŏteefrŏŏtee/ *n.* (*pl.* **-fruttis**) a confection, esp. ice cream, of or flavored with mixed fruits. [It., = all fruits]

tut-tut /tut-tút/ *int., n., & v.* (also **tut** /tut/) ● *int.* expressing rebuke, impatience, or contempt. ● *n.* such an exclamation. ● *v.intr.* (**-tutted, -tutting**) exclaim this. [imit. of a click of the tongue against the teeth]

■ *v.* see OBJECT *v.*

tutty /tútee/ *n.* impure zinc oxide or carbonate used as a polishing powder. [ME f. OF *tutie* f. med.L *tutia* f. Arab. *tūtiyā*]

tutu[1] /tŏŏtŏŏ/ *n.* a ballet dancer's short skirt of stiffened projecting frills. [F]

tutu[2] /tŏŏtŏŏ/ *n. Bot.* a shrub, *Coriaria arborea*, native to New Zealand, bearing poisonous purplish black berries. [Maori]

tu-whit, tu-whoo /tŏŏwít tŏŏwŏŏ/ *n.* a representation of the cry of an owl. [imit.]

tux /tuks/ *n. colloq.* = TUXEDO.

tuxedo /tukseédō/ *n.* (*pl.* **-os** or **-oes**) **1** a man's short black formal jacket. **2** a suit of clothes including this. [after a country club at *Tuxedo* Park, New York]

tuyère /tweeyáir, tŏŏ-/ *n.* (also **tuyere, twyer**) a nozzle through which air is forced into a furnace, etc. [F f. *tuyau* pipe]

TV *abbr.* television. □ **TV dinner** a prepackaged frozen meal, usu. consisting of meat, potatoes, vegetable, and dessert.

TVA *abbr.* Tennessee Valley Authority.

TWP *abbr. propr.* textured vegetable protein (in foods made from vegetable but given a meatlike texture).

twaddle /twód'l/ *n. & v.* ● *n.* useless, senseless, or dull writing or talk. ● *v.intr.* indulge in this. □□ **twaddler** *n.* [alt. of earlier *twattle*, alt. of TATTLE]

■ *n.* see RUBBISH *n.* 3.

twain /twayn/ *adj. & n. archaic* two (usu. *in twain*). [OE *twegen*, masc. form of *twā* TWO]

twang /twang/ *n. & v.* ● *n.* **1** a strong ringing sound made by the plucked string of a musical instrument or bow. **2** the nasal quality of a voice compared to this. ● *v.* **1** *intr. & tr.* emit or cause to emit this sound. **2** *tr.* usu. *derog.* play (a tune or instrument) in this way. **3** *tr.* utter with a nasal twang. □□ **twangy** *adj.* [imit.]

'twas /twuz, twoz/ *archaic* it was. [contr.]

twat /twot/ *n. coarse sl.* ¶ Usually considered a taboo word. **1** the female genitals. **2** esp. *Brit.* a term of contempt for a person. [17th c.: orig. unkn.]

twayblade /twáyblayd/ *n.* any orchid of the genus *Listera*, etc., with green or purple flowers and a single pair of leaves. [*tway* var. of TWAIN + BLADE]

tweak /tweek/ *v. & n.* ● *v.tr.* **1** pinch and twist sharply; pull with a sharp jerk; twitch. **2** make small adjustments to (a mechanism). ● *n.* an instance of tweaking. [prob. alt. of dial. *twick* & TWITCH]

■ *v.* **1** pinch, nip, twitch, squeeze, jerk, grip, pull.

■ *n.* pinch, nip, twitch, squeeze, jerk, grip, pull.

twee /twee/ *adj.* (**tweer** /tweéər/; **tweest** /weé-ist/) *Brit.* usu. *derog.* affectedly dainty or quaint. □□ **tweely** *adv.* **tweeness** *n.* [childish pronunc. of SWEET]

■ precious, sweet, sentimental, quaint, dainty, bijou, *colloq.* cute.

tweed /tweed/ *n.* **1** a rough-surfaced woolen cloth, usu. of mixed colors, orig. produced in Scotland. **2** (in *pl.*) clothes made of tweed. [orig. a misreading of *tweel*, Sc. form of TWILL, infl. by assoc. with the river *Tweed*]

Tweedledum and Tweedledee /tweéd'ldúm, tweéd'ldeé/ *n.* a pair of persons or things that are virtually indistinguishable. [after the stock names of rival musicians]

tweedy /tweédee/ *adj.* (**tweedier, tweediest**) **1** of or relating to tweed cloth. **2** characteristic of the country gentry; heartily informal. □□ **tweedily** *adv.* **tweediness** *n.*

'tween /tween/ *prep. archaic* = BETWEEN. □ **'tween-decks** *Naut.* the space between decks. [contr.]

tweet /tweet/ *n. & v.* ● *n.* the chirp of a small bird. ● *v.intr.* make a chirping noise. [imit.]

■ *n.* see CHIRP *n.* ● *v.* see CHIRP *v.*

tweeter /tweétər/ *n.* a loudspeaker designed to reproduce high frequencies.

tweeze /tweez/ *v.tr.* pluck out with tweezers (*tweeze eyebrow hair*).

tweezers /tweézərz/ *n.pl.* a small pair of pincers for picking up small objects, plucking out hairs, etc. [extended form of *tweezes* (cf. *pincers*, etc.) pl. of obs. *tweeze* case for small instruments, f. *etweese* = *étuis*, pl. of ETUI]

twelfth /twelfth/ *n. & adj.* ● *n.* **1** the position in a sequence corresponding to the number 12 in the sequence 1–12. **2** something occupying this position. **3** each of twelve equal parts of a thing. **4** *Mus.* **a** an interval or chord spanning an octave and a fifth in the diatonic scale. **b** a note separated from another by this interval. ● *adj.* that is the twelfth. □ **Twelfth Day** Jan. 6, the twelfth day after Christmas, the festival of the Epiphany. **Twelfth Night** the evening of Jan. 5, the eve of the Epiphany. **twelfth part** = sense 3 of *n.* □□ **twelfthly** *adv.* [OE *twelfta* (as TWELVE)]

twelve /twelv/ *n. & adj.* ● *n.* **1** one more than eleven; the product of two units and six units. **2** a symbol for this (12, xii, XII). **3** a size, etc., denoted by twelve. **4** the time denoted by twelve o'clock (*is it twelve yet?*). **5** (**the Twelve**) the twelve apostles. ● *adj.* that amount to twelve. □ **twelve-tone** *Mus.* using the twelve chromatic notes of the octave on an equal basis without dependence on a key system. [OE *twelf(e)* f. Gmc, prob. rel. to TWO]

twelvefold /twélvfōld/ *adj. & adv.* **1** twelve times as much or as many. **2** consisting of twelve parts.

twelvemo /twélvmō/ *n.* = DUODECIMO.

twelvemonth /twélvmunth/ *n. archaic* a year; a period of twelve months.

twenty /twéntee/ *n. & adj.* ● *n.* (*pl.* **-ies**) **1** the product of two and ten. **2** a symbol for this (20, xx, XX). **3** (in *pl.*) the numbers from 20 to 29, esp. the years of a century or of a person's life. **4** *colloq.* a large indefinite number (*have told you twenty times*). ● *adj.* that amount to twenty. □ **twenty-first, -second**, etc., the ordinal numbers between twentieth and thirtieth. **twenty-one, -two**, etc., the cardinal numbers between twenty and thirty. **twenty-one** a card game in which players try to acquire cards with a face value totaling 21 points and no more. **twenty-twenty** (or **20/20**) **1** denoting vision of normal acuity. **2** *colloq.* denoting clear perception or hindsight. □□ **twentieth** *adj. & n.* **twentyfold** *adj. & adv.* [OE *twentig* (perh. as TWO, -TY[2])]

■ *n.* **1** score. **4** see SCORE *n.* 3.

'twere /twər/ *archaic* it were. [contr.]

twerp /twərp/ *n.* (also **twirp**) *sl.* a stupid or objectionable person. [20th c.: orig. unkn.]

■ see FOOL[1] *n.* 1.

twibill /twíbil/ *n.* a double-bladed battleax. [OE f. *twi-* double + BILL³]

twice /twis/ *adv.* **1** two times (esp. of multiplication); on two occasions. **2** in double degree or quantity (*twice as good*). [ME *twiges* f. OE *twige* (as TWO, -s³)]

twiddle /twíd'l/ *v. & n.* ● *v.* **1** *tr.* & (foll. by *with*, etc.) *intr.* twirl, adjust, or play randomly or idly. **2** *intr.* move twirlingly. ● *n.* **1** an act of twiddling. **2** a twirled mark or sign. □ **twiddle one's thumbs 1** make them rotate around each other. **2** have nothing to do. □□ **twiddler** *n.* **twiddly** *adj.* [app. imit., after *twirl*, *twist*, and *fiddle*, *piddle*]

■ *v.* **1** play with, twirl, fiddle (with), juggle, adjust, toy with, tinker with, fidget with, fool with, mess (about *or* around) with, monkey with, *colloq.* wiggle. ● *n.* **1** twirl, fiddle, jiggle, tinker, *colloq.* wiggle. □ **twiddle one's thumbs 2** do nothing, be idle, idle *or* while away (the) time, waste time.

twig¹ /twig/ *n.* **1** a small branch or shoot of a tree or shrub. **2** *Anat.* a small branch of an artery, etc. □□ **twigged** *adj.* (also in *comb.*). **twiggy** *adj.* [OE *twigge* f. a Gmc root *twi-* (unrecorded) as in TWICE, TWO]

■ **1** sprig, stem, shoot, offshoot, branchlet, stick, sucker, sprout, withe, tendril. □□ **twiggy** see THIN *adj.* 4.

twig² /twig/ *v.tr.* (**twigged**, **twigging**) *Brit. colloq.* **1** (also *absol.*) understand; grasp the meaning or nature of. **2** perceive; observe. [18th c.: orig. unkn.]

■ **1** understand, grasp, fathom, get, comprehend, see, know, sense, divine, perceive, apprehend, *colloq.* catch on (to), be *or* get *or* become wise to, tumble to, *sl.* dig.

twilight /twílit/ *n.* **1** the soft glowing light from the sky when the sun is below the horizon, esp. in the evening. **2** the period of this. **3** a faint light. **4** a state of imperfect knowledge or understanding. **5** a period of decline or destruction. **6** *attrib.* of, resembling, or occurring at twilight. □ **twilight sleep** *Med.* a state of partial narcosis, esp. to ease the pain of childbirth. **twilight zone 1** any physical or conceptual area that is undefined or intermediate, esp. one that is eerie or unreal. **2** *Brit.* an urban area that is becoming dilapidated. [ME f. OE *twi-* two (in uncert. sense) + LIGHT¹]

■ **1, 2** dusk, sunset, sundown, half-light, *poet.* gloaming. **2** evening, nightfall, *archaic or poet.* eventide. **5** decline, wane, waning, ebb, downturn, downswing, slump, decay, weakening, declination, diminution. **6** evening, crepuscular, dimming, twilit, darkening, darkish, shadowy, shady, dim, dark, obscure, somber, gloomy, *poet.* darksome, darkling. □ **twilight zone 2** limbo.

twilit /twílit/ *adj.* (also **twilighted** /-litid/) dimly illuminated by or as by twilight. [past part. of *twilight* (v.) f. TWILIGHT]

twill /twil/ *n. & v.* ● *n.* a fabric so woven as to have a surface of diagonal parallel ridges. ● *v.tr.* (esp. as **twilled** *adj.*) weave (fabric) in this way. □□ **twilled** *adj.* [No. of Engl. var. of obs. *twilly*, OE *twili*, f. *twi-* double, after L *bilix* (as BI-, *licium* thread)]

'twill /twil/ *archaic* it will. [contr.]

twin /twin/ *n., adj., & v.* ● *n.* **1** each of a closely related or associated pair, esp. of children or animals born at one birth. **2** the exact counterpart of a person or thing. **3** a compound crystal one part of which is in a reversed position with reference to the other. **4** (**the Twins**) the zodiacal sign or constellation Gemini. ● *adj.* **1** forming, or being one of, such a pair (*twin brothers*). **2** *Bot.* growing in pairs. **3** consisting of two closely connected and similar parts. ● *v.* (**twinned**, **twinning**) **1** *tr. & intr.* **a** join intimately together. **b** (foll. by *with*) pair. **2** *intr.* bear twins. **3** *intr.* grow as a twin crystal. □ **twin bed** each of a pair of single beds. **twin-engine** having two engines. **twin-screw** (of a ship) having two propellers on separate shafts with opposite twists. □□ **twinning** *n.* [OE *twinn* double, f. *twi-* two: cf. ON *tvinnr*]

■ *n.* **2** double, clone, duplicate, look-alike, counterpart, doppelgänger, image, *colloq.* spitting image, *sl.* (dead) ringer. ● *adj.* **1, 3** identical, matching, matched, duplicate, corresponding, look-alike. ● *v.* **1** pair, match, yoke, join, link, couple, combine, connect, associate.

twine /twin/ *n. & v.* ● *n.* **1** a strong thread or string of two or more strands of hemp or cotton, etc., twisted together. **2** a coil or twist. **3** a tangle; an interlacing. ● *v.* **1** *tr.* form (a string or thread, etc.) by twisting strands together. **2** *tr.* form (a garland, etc.) of interwoven material. **3** *tr.* (often foll. by *with*) garland (a brow, etc.). **4** *intr.* (often foll. by *around*, *about*) coil or wind. **5** *intr.* & *refl.* (of a plant) grow in this way. □□ **twiner** *n.* [OE *twin*, *twigin* linen, ult. f. the stem of *twi-* two]

■ *n.* **1** cord, string, thread; rope, cable, yarn. ● *v.* entwine, braid, twist, intertwine, curl, wreathe, spiral, wind, coil, weave, interweave, interlace, encircle, wrap.

twinge /twinj/ *n. & v.* ● *n.* a sharp momentary local pain or pang (*a twinge of toothache*; *a twinge of conscience*). ● *v.intr. & tr.* experience or cause to experience a twinge. [*twinge* (v.) pinch, wring f. OE *twengan* f. Gmc]

■ *n.* stab, pang, cramp, spasm, pinch, stitch, (sharp) pain, prick, smart, bite, gripe. ● *v.* see HURT *v.* 3.

twinkle /twíngkəl/ *v. & n.* ● *v.* **1** *intr.* (of a star or light, etc.) shine with rapidly intermittent gleams. **2** *intr.* (of the eyes) sparkle. **3** *intr.* (of the feet in dancing) move lightly and rapidly. **4** *tr.* emit (a light or signal) in quick gleams. **5** *tr.* blink or wink (one's eyes). ● *n.* **1 a** a sparkle or gleam of the eyes. **b** a blink or wink. **2** a slight flash of light; a glimmer. **3** a short rapid movement. □ **in a twinkle** (or **a twinkling** or **the twinkling of an eye**) in an instant. □□ **twinkler** *n.* **twinkly** *adj.* [OE *twinclian*]

■ *v.* **1, 2, 4** scintillate, sparkle, coruscate, glitter, shimmer, wink, flicker, glisten, glint, flash, spark, dance, blink, shine, gleam. ● *n.* **1a, 2** twinkling, scintillation, scintillating, sparkle, sparkling, coruscation, coruscating, glitter, glittering, glimmer, glimmering, shimmer, shimmering, winking, flicker, flickering, glistening, glint, flash, flashing, spark, sparking, dancing, blinking, shine, shining, gleam, gleaming, dazzle, dazzling. □ **in a twinkle** (or **a twinkling** or **the twinkling of an eye**) in a (split) second, in a flash, in the wink of an eye, in a wink, in an instant, in a moment, in a trice, in two shakes (of a lamb's tail), *colloq.* in a jiffy, esp. *Brit. colloq.* in a tick, in two ticks.

twirl /twərl/ *v. & n.* ● *v.tr. & intr.* spin or swing or twist quickly and lightly around. ● *n.* **1** a twirling motion. **2** a form made by twirling, esp. a flourish made with a pen. □□ **twirler** *n.* **twirly** *adj.* [16th c.: prob. alt. (after *whirl*) of obs. *tirl* TRILL]

■ *v.* spin, whirl, rotate, revolve, wheel, turn, gyrate, twist, pirouette, pivot, wind (about *or* around). ● *n.* **1** twirling, spin, spinning, whirl, whirling, turn, turning, revolution, pirouette. **2** whorl, winding, convolution, spiral, helix, coil, *Archit.* volute; flourish.

twirp var. of TWERP.

twist /twist/ *v. & n.* ● *v.* **1 a** *tr.* change the form of by rotating one end and not the other or the two ends in opposite directions. **b** *intr.* undergo such a change; take a twisted position (*twisted around in his seat*). **c** *tr.* wrench or pull out of shape with a twisting action (*twisted my ankle*). **2** *tr.* **a** wind (strands, etc.) around each other. **b** form (a rope, etc.) by winding the strands. **c** (foll. by *with*, *in with*) interweave. **d** form by interweaving or twining. **3 a** *tr.* give a spiral form to (a rod, column, cord, etc.) as by rotating the ends in opposite directions. **b** *intr.* take a spiral form. **4** *tr.* (foll. by *off*) break off or separate by twisting. **5** *tr.* distort or misrepresent the meaning of (words). **6 a** *intr.* take a winding course. **b** *tr.* make (one's way) in a winding manner. **7** *tr. Brit. colloq.* cheat (*twisted me out of my allowance*). **8** *tr.* cause (the ball, esp. in billiards) to rotate while following a curved path. **9** *tr.* (as **twisted** *adj.*) (of a person or mind) emotionally unbalanced. **10** *intr.* dance the twist. ● *n.* **1** the act or an instance of twisting. **2 a** a twisted state. **b** the manner or degree in which a thing is twisted. **3** a thing formed by or as by twisting, esp. a thread or rope, etc., made by winding strands together. **4** the point at which a thing twists or bends. **5** usu. *derog.* a peculiar tendency of mind or character, etc. **6 a** an unexpected development of events, esp. in a story, etc. **b** an unusual interpretation or variation. **c** a distortion or bias. **7** a fine strong silk thread used by tailors, etc. **8** a roll of bread, tobacco, etc., in the form of a twist. **9** *Brit.* a paper package with the ends twisted shut. **10** a curled piece of lemon, etc., peel to flavor a drink. **11** a spinning motion given to a ball in throwing, etc., to make it curve. **12 a** a twisting strain. **b** the amount of twisting of a rod, etc., or the angle showing this. **c** forward motion combined with rotation about an axis. **13** *Brit.* a drink made of two ingredients mixed together. **14** *Brit. colloq.* a swindle. **15** (prec. by *the*) a dance with a twisting movement of the body, popular in the 1960s. □ **round the twist** *Brit. sl.* crazy. **twist a person's arm** *colloq.* apply coercion, esp. by moral pressure. **twist around one's finger** see FINGER. □□ **twistable** *adj.* **twisty** *adj.* (**twistier, twistiest**). [ME, rel. to TWIN, TWINE]

■ *v.* **1 a, b** contort, screw up, distort, buckle, warp; crumple. **c** wrench, turn, sprain. **2** wind, plait, braid, weave, entwine, intertwine, twine, interweave, pleach, splice, wreathe, interlace, tangle, entangle. **3** see WIND² *v.* 4. **4** see WRENCH *v.* 1a. **5** distort, warp, contort, pervert, wrest, alter, change, slant, bias, color, falsify, misquote, misstate, garble, misrepresent, violate; misinterpret, mistranslate, misunderstand, misconstrue. **6 a** wind, snake, meander, turn, zigzag, worm, bend, curve, kink, loop. **b** wriggle, worm, squirm, writhe, *colloq.* wiggle. **9** (**twisted**) see UNSTABLE 2, 3. ● *n.* **1** rotation, turn, roll, twirl, spin, wind. **2** see TANGLE *n.* 1. **4** coil, spiral, corkscrew, helix, convolution, skew, zigzag, dogleg, turn, curve, angle, bend, wind, bow, kink, loop, curl, meander. **5** quirk, kink, idiosyncrasy, crotchet, peculiarity, oddity, trick, eccentricity, incongruity, inconsistency, irregularity; weakness, flaw, fault, foible, failing. **6 b** interpretation, analysis, understanding, slant, angle, construction, construal; treatment, approach, version, variation. **c** distortion, misinterpretation, contortion, perversion, warping, alteration, change, departure, bias, coloring, falsification, misquotation, misstatement, garbling, misrepresentation; mistranslation, misunderstanding, misconstrual, misconstruction. **8, 9** roll, coil, *Brit.* screw. **12 a** wrench, turn, sprain. **14** see SWINDLE *n.* 1, 3. □ **twist a person's arm** coerce *or* constrain *or* bully *or* pressurize *or* pressure a person, *colloq.* put the squeeze on, put the screws on.

twister /twístər/ *n.* **1** *colloq.* a tornado, waterspout, etc. **2** *Brit. colloq.* = *swindler* (SWINDLE). **3** a twisting ball in cricket or billiards, etc.

■ **1** tornado, cyclone, typhoon, hurricane, whirlwind; waterspout.

twit¹ /twit/ *n. sl.* a silly or foolish person. [orig. dial.: perh. f. TWIT²]

■ nincompoop, ass, ninny, fool, imbecile, blockhead, idiot, simpleton, *colloq.* nitwit, halfwit, chump, moron, silly billy, silly, lamebrain, *sl.* dope, jerk, twerp, nerd, *Austral. sl.* galah, nong.

twit² /twit/ *v.tr.* (**twitted, twitting**) reproach or taunt, usu. good-humoredly. [16th-c. *twite* f. *atwite* f. OE *ætwītan* reproach with f. *æt* at + *wītan* blame]

■ tease, cajole, taunt, jeer (at), make fun of, banter, rag, gibe, chaff, ridicule, mock; blame, berate, deride, scorn, censure, revile, reproach, upbraid, *literary* contemn; pull a person's leg, *colloq.* kid.

twitch /twich/ *v. & n.* ● *v.* **1** *intr.* (of the features, muscles, limbs, etc.) move or contract spasmodically. **2** *tr.* give a short sharp pull at. ● *n.* **1** a sudden involuntary contraction or movement. **2** a sudden pull or jerk. **3** *colloq.* a state of

nervousness. **4** a noose and stick for controlling a horse during a veterinary operation. □□ **twitchy** *adj.* (**twitchier, twitchiest**) (in sense 3 of *n.*). [ME f. Gmc: cf. OE *twiccian*, dial. *twick*]

■ *v.* **1** see JERK¹ *v.* 1. **2** see JERK¹ *v.* 2. ● *n.* **1, 2** see JERK¹ *n.* 1, 2.

twitcher /twíchər/ *n.* **1** *Brit. colloq.* a birdwatcher who tries to get sightings of rare birds. **2** a person or thing that twitches.

twitch grass /twich/ *n.* = COUCH². [var. of QUITCH]

twite /twīt/ *n.* a moorland finch, *Carduelis flavirostris*, resembling the linnet. [imit. of its cry]

twitter /twítər/ *v. & n.* ● *v.* **1** *intr.* (of or like a bird) emit a succession of light tremulous sounds. **2** *tr.* utter or express in this way. ● *n.* **1** the act or an instance of twittering. **2** *colloq.* a tremulously excited state. □□ **twitterer** *n.* **twittery** *adj.* [ME, imit.: cf. -ER⁴]

■ *v.* **1** peep, cheep, tweet, chirp, warble, trill, chirrup; chatter, prattle, gossip, giggle, prate, titter, snicker, snigger, simper. **2** chirp, warble, trill. ● *n.* **1** peep, peeping, cheep, cheeping, twittering, tweet, tweeting, chirrup, chirruping, chirp, chirping, warble, warbling, trill, trilling. **2** flutter, whirl, agitation, *colloq.* dither, stew, tizzy.

'twixt /twikst/ *prep. archaic* = BETWIXT. [contr.]

two /tōō/ *n. & adj.* ● *n.* **1** one more than one; the sum of one unit and another unit. **2** a symbol for this (2, ii, II). **3** a size, etc., denoted by two. **4** the time of two o'clock (*is it two yet?*). **5** a set of two. **6** a card with two pips. **7** a two-dollar bill. ● *adj.* that amount to two. □ **in two** in or into two pieces. **in two shakes** (or **ticks**) see SHAKE, TICK¹. **or two** denoting several (*a thing or two* = several things). **put two and two together** make (esp. an obvious) inference from what is known or evident. **that makes two of us** *colloq.* that is true of me also. **two-bit** *colloq.* cheap; petty. **two-by-four** a length of lumber with a rectangular cross section nominally 2 in. by 4 in. **by two** (or **two and two**) in pairs. **two can play at that game** *colloq.* another person's behavior can be copied to that person's disadvantage. **two-dimensional 1** having or appearing to have length and breadth but no depth. **2** lacking depth or substance; superficial. **two-edged** double-edged. **two-faced 1** having two faces. **2** insincere; deceitful. **two-handed 1** having, using, or requiring the use of two hands. **2** (of a card game) for two players. **two-piece** *adj.* (of a suit, etc.) consisting of two matching items. ● *n.* a two-piece suit, etc. **two-ply** *adj.* of two strands, webs, or thicknesses. ● *n.* **1** two-ply wool. **2** two-ply wood made by gluing together two layers with the grain in different directions. **two-sided 1** having two sides. **2** having two aspects; controversial. **two-step** a dance with a sliding step in march or polka time. **two-stroke** (or **-cycle**) (of an internal combustion engine) having its power cycle completed in one up-and-down movement of the piston. **two-time** *colloq.* **1** deceive or be unfaithful to (esp. a partner or lover). **2** swindle; double-cross. **two-timer** *colloq.* a person who is deceitful or unfaithful. **two-tone** having two colors or sounds. **two-way 1** involving two ways or participants. **2** (of a switch) permitting a current to be switched on or off from either of two points. **3** (of a radio) capable of transmitting and receiving signals. **4** (of a faucet, etc.) permitting fluid, etc., to flow in either of two channels or directions. **5** (of traffic, etc.) moving in two esp. opposite directions. **two-way mirror** a panel of glass that can be seen through from one side and is a mirror on the other. **two-wheeler** a vehicle with two wheels. [OE *twā* (fem. & neut.), *tū* (neut.), with Gmc cognates and rel. to Skr. *dwau*, *dwe*, Gk & L *duo*]

■ *n.* **5** set of two, couple, pair, brace, duo, duet, twosome. ● *adj.* a couple *or* pair *or* brace of. □ **put two and two together** see REASON *v.* 1. **two-bit** see CHEAP *adj.* 3. **two-dimensional 2** see SUPERFICIAL 1, 4. **two-faced 2** double-dealing, hypocritical, duplicitous, dissembling, deceitful, treacherous, dishonest, untrustworthy, insincere, disingenuous, scheming, designing, crafty, machiavellian, sly, perfidious, lying, mendacious. **two-time** see DECEIVE 1. **two-timer** see TRAITOR.

twofold /tŏŏfōld/ adj. & adv. **1** twice as much or as many. **2** consisting of two parts.

■ adj. **1** double. **2** dual.

twopence /túpəns/ n. Brit. **1** the sum of two pence, esp. before decimalization. **2** colloq. (esp. with neg.) a thing of little value (don't care twopence).

■ **2** see DAMN n. 2.

twopenny /túpənee/ adj. Brit. **1** costing two pence, esp. before decimalization. **2** colloq. cheap; worthless. □ **twopenny-halfpenny** /túpneeháypnee/ cheap; insignificant.

■ **2** see CHEAP adj. 3.

twosome /tŏŏsəm/ n. **1** two persons together. **2** a game, dance, etc., for two persons.

■ **1** couple, pair, duo.

'twould /twŏŏd/ archaic it would. [contr.]

twp. abbr. township.

TX abbr. Texas (in official postal use).

-ty[1] /tee/ suffix forming nouns denoting quality or condition (cruelty; plenty). [ME -tie, -tee, -te f. OF -té, -tet f. L -tas -tatis: cf. -ITY]

-ty[2] /tee/ suffix denoting tens (twenty; thirty; ninety). [OE -tig]

tychism /tíkizəm/ n. Philos. the theory that chance controls the universe. [Gk tukhē chance]

tycoon /tīkŏŏn/ n. **1** a business magnate. **2** hist. a title applied by foreigners to the shogun of Japan 1854–68. [Jap. taikun great lord]

■ **1** magnate, baron, financier, (multi)millionaire, billionaire, merchant prince, potentate, colloq. wheeler-dealer, mogul, big shot, (big-time) operator, bigwig, sl. big-timer, big cheese, honcho, big wheel.

tying pres. part. of TIE.

tyke /tīk/ n. (also **tike**) **1** a small child. **2** a mongrel. **3** esp. Brit. an unpleasant or coarse man. **4** Brit. sl. a Yorkshireman. **5** Austral. & NZ sl. offens. a Roman Catholic. [ME f. ON tik bitch: sense 5 assim. from TAIG]

tylopod /tíləpod/ n. & adj. Zool. ● n. any animal that bears its weight on the sole of the feet rather than on the hoofs, esp. the camel. ● adj. (of an animal) bearing its weight in this way. □□ **tylopodous** /-lópədəs/ adj. [Gk tulos knob or tulē callus, cushion + pous podos foot]

tympan /tímpən/ n. **1** Printing an appliance in a printing press used to equalize pressure between the platen, etc., and a printing sheet. **2** Archit. = TYMPANUM. [F tympan or L tympanum: see TYMPANUM]

tympana pl. of TYMPANUM.

tympani var. of TIMPANI.

tympanic /timpánik/ adj. **1** Anat. of, relating to, or having a tympanum. **2** resembling or acting like a drumhead. □ **tympanic bone** Anat. the bone supporting the tympanic membrane. **tympanic membrane** Anat. the membrane separating the outer ear and middle ear and transmitting vibrations resulting from sound waves to the inner ear.

tympanites /tímpəníteez/ n. a swelling of the abdomen caused by gas in the intestine, etc. □□ **tympanitic** /-nítik/ adj. [LL f. Gk tumpanitēs of a drum (as TYMPANUM)]

tympanum /tímpənəm/ n. (pl. **tympanums** or **tympana** /-nə/) **1** Anat. **a** the middle ear. **b** the tympanic membrane. **2** Zool. the membrane covering the hearing organ on the leg of an insect. **3** Archit. **a** a vertical triangular space forming the center of a pediment. **b** a similar space over a door between the lintel and the arch; a carving on this space. **4** a wheel, etc., for raising water from a stream. **5** the diaphragm in a telephone handset. [L f. Gk tumpanon drum f. tuptō strike]

Tynwald /tínwawld, -wəld/ n. the parliament of the UK's Isle of Man. [ON thing-völlr place of assembly f. thing assembly + völlr field]

type /tīp/ n. & v. ● n. **1 a** a class of things or persons having common characteristics. **b** a kind or sort (would like a different type of car). **2** a person, thing, or event serving as an illustration, symbol, or characteristic specimen of another,

or of a class. **3** (in comb.) made of, resembling, or functioning as (ceramic-type material; Cheddar-type cheese). **4** colloq. a person, esp. of a specified character (is rather a quiet type; is not really my type). **5** an object, conception, or work of art serving as a model for subsequent artists. **6** Printing **a** a piece of metal, etc., with a raised letter or character on its upper surface for use in printing. **b** a kind or size of such pieces (printed in large type). **c** a set or supply of these (ran short of type). **7** a device on either side of a medal or coin. **8** Theol. a foreshadowing in the Old Testament of a person or event of the New Testament. **9** Biol. an organism having or chosen as having the essential characteristics of its group and giving its name to the next highest group. ● v. **1** tr. be a type or example of. **2** tr. & intr. write with a typewriter or keyboard. **3** tr. esp. Biol. & Med. assign to a type; classify. **4** tr. = TYPECAST. □ **in type** Printing composed and ready for printing. **type founder** a designer and maker of metal types. **type foundry** a foundry where type is made. **type site** Archaeol. a site where objects regarded as defining the characteristics of a period, etc., are found. **type specimen** Biol. the specimen used for naming and describing a new species. □□ **typal** adj. [ME f. F type or L typus f. Gk tupos impression, figure, type, f. tuptō strike]

■ n. **1** class, category, classification, kind, sort, genre, run, order, variety, breed, race, species, strain, group, genus, kidney, nature, colloq. disp. ilk; brand, make, marque, line, model, cast, form, version. **2** prototype, paradigm, archetype, epitome, embodiment, avatar, exemplar, model, specimen, illustration, example, symbol, pattern, personification, standard, quintessence, typification, typifier. **4** person, character, individual, colloq. sort. **6** Printing typeface, font, print, printing, lettering, characters, Brit. fount. ● v. **2** formal typewrite; key (in), keyboard; transcribe. **3** see CLASS v.

typecast /típkast/ v.tr. (past and past part. **-cast**) assign (an actor or actress) repeatedly to the same type of role.

typeface /típfays/ n. Printing **1** a set of type or characters in a particular design. **2** the inked part of type, or the impression made by this.

■ see TYPE n. 6.

typescript /típskript/ n. a typewritten document.

typesetter /típsetər/ n. Printing **1** a person who composes type. **2** a composing machine. □□ **typesetting** n.

typewrite /típrīt/ v.tr. & intr. (past **-wrote**; past part. **-written**) = TYPE v. 2.

typewriter /típrītər/ n. a machine with keys for producing printlike characters one at a time on paper inserted around a roller.

typewritten /típrit'n/ adj. produced with a typewriter.

typhlitis /tiflítis/ n. inflammation of the cecum. □□ **typhlitic** /-lítik/ adj. [mod.L f. Gk tuphlon cecum or blind gut f. tuphlos blind + -ITIS]

typhoid /tífoyd/ n. & adj. ● n. **1** (in full **typhoid fever**) an infectious bacterial fever with an eruption of red spots on the chest and abdomen and severe intestinal irritation. **2** a similar disease of animals. ● adj. like typhus. □ **typhoid condition** (or **state**) a state of depressed vitality occurring in many acute diseases. □□ **typhoidal** adj. [TYPHUS + -OID]

typhoon /tīfŏŏn/ n. a violent hurricane in E. Asia. □□ **typhonic** /-fónik/ adj. [partly f. Port. tufão f. Arab. ṭūfān perh. f. Gk tuphōn whirlwind; partly f. Chin. dial. tai fung big wind]

■ see HURRICANE 1, 2.

typhus /tífəs/ n. an infectious fever caused by rickettsiae, characterized by a purple rash, headaches, fever, and usu. delirium. □□ **typhous** adj. [mod.L f. Gk tuphos smoke, stupor f. tuphō to smoke]

typical /típikəl/ adj. **1** serving as a characteristic example;

/.../	**pronunciation**	●	**part of speech**
□	**phrases, idioms, and compounds**		
□□	**derivatives**	■	**synonym section**
cross-references appear in SMALL CAPITALS or italics			

representative. **2** characteristic of or serving to distinguish a type. **3** (often foll. by *of*) conforming to expected behavior, attitudes, etc. (*is typical of them to forget*). **4** symbolic. □□ **typicality** /-kálitee/ *n.* **typically** *adv.* [med.L *typicalis* f. L *typicus* f. Gk *tupikos* (as TYPE)]

■ **1, 2** representative, characteristic, conventional, normal, standard, ordinary, average, regular, run-of-the-mill, orthodox, classic. **3** conventional, in character, in keeping, usual, commonplace, natural, customary, common, to be expected, proverbial, normal, ordinary. **4** see SYMBOLIC. □□ **typically** see *ordinarily* (ORDINARY).

typify /típifī/ *v.tr.* (**-ies, -ied**) **1** be a representative example of; embody the characteristics of. **2** represent by a type or symbol; serve as a type, figure, or emblem of; symbolize. □□ **typification** /-fikáyshən/ *n.* **typifier** *n.* [L *typus* TYPE + -FY]

■ **1** exemplify, instantiate, epitomize, personify, represent, characterize, embody, evince, symbolize. **2** represent, symbolize, characterize, stand for, suggest, emblematize, be emblematic of. □□ **typification** see SOUL 3, TYPE *n.* 2.

typist /típist/ *n.* a person who types at a typewriter or keyboard.

typo /típō/ *n.* (*pl.* **-os**) *colloq.* **1** a typographical error. **2** a typographer. [abbr.]

■ **1** see MISPRINT *n.*

typographer /típógrəfər/ *n.* a person skilled in typography.

typography /típógrəfee/ *n.* **1** printing as an art. **2** the style and appearance of printed matter. □□ **typographic** /-pəgráfik/ *adj.* **typographical** *adj.* **typographically** *adv.* [F *typographie* or mod.L *typographia* (as TYPE, -GRAPHY)]

typology /típóləjee/ *n.* the study and interpretation of (esp. biblical) types. □□ **typological** /típəlójikəl/ *adj.* **typologist** *n.* [Gk *tupos* TYPE + -LOGY]

tyrannical /tiránikəl/ *adj.* **1** acting like a tyrant; imperious; arbitrary. **2** given to or characteristic of tyranny. □□ **tyrannically** *adv.* [OF *tyrannique* f. L *tyrannicus* f. Gk *turannikos* (as TYRANT)]

■ tyrannous, oppressive, dictatorial, fascistic, despotic, autocratic, absolute, authoritarian, arbitrary, imperious, peremptory, overbearing, exacting, unjust, high-handed, severe, harsh, heavy-handed. □□ **tyrannically** see *severely* (SEVERE), *arbitrarily* (ARBITRARY).

tyrannicide /tiránisīd/ *n.* **1** the act or an instance of killing

a tyrant. **2** the killer of a tyrant. □□ **tyrannicidal** /-nisíd'l/ *adj.* [F f. L *tyrannicida, -cidium* (as TYRANT, -CIDE)]

tyrannize /tírəniz/ *v.tr.* & (foll. by *over*) *intr.* behave like a tyrant toward; rule or treat despotically or cruelly. [F *tyranniser* (as TYRANT)]

■ domineer over, bully, subjugate, enthrall, enslave, dominate, intimidate, dictate to, order about or around, ride roughshod over, browbeat, keep under one's thumb, oppress, persecute, subdue, suppress, keep down, grind down.

tyrannosaurus /tiránəsáwrəs/ *n.* (also **tyrannosaur**) any bipedal carnivorous dinosaur of the genus *Tyrannosaurus*, esp. *T. rex* having powerful hind legs, small clawlike front legs, and a long well-developed tail. [Gk *turannos* TYRANT, after *dinosaur*]

tyranny /tírənee/ *n.* (*pl.* **-ies**) **1** the cruel and arbitrary use of authority. **2** a tyrannical act; tyrannical behavior. **3 a** rule by a tyrant. **b** a period of this. **c** a nation ruled by a tyrant. □□ **tyrannous** /-rənəs/ *adj.* **tyrannously** *adv.* [ME f. OF *tyrannie* f. med.L *tyrannia* f. Gk *turannia* (as TYRANT)]

■ **1–3b** autocracy, authoritarianism, absolutism, despotism, dictatorship; arbitrariness, oppression, suppression, subjugation, enslavement, enthrallment, domination; fascism; Nazism; Stalinism. □□ **tyrannous** see TYRANNICAL.

tyrant /tírənt/ *n.* **1** an oppressive or cruel ruler. **2** a person exercising power arbitrarily or cruelly. **3** *Gk Hist.* an absolute ruler who seized power without the legal right. [ME *tyran, -ant,* f. OF *tiran, tyrant* f. L *tyrannus* f. Gk *turannos*]

■ **1, 2** dictator, despot, autocrat, martinet, Hitler, bully, oppressor, authoritarian, hard taskmaster, slave driver, overlord.

tyre *Brit.* var. of TIRE[2].

Tyrian /tíreeən/ *adj.* & *n.* ● *adj.* of or relating to ancient Tyre in Phoenicia. ● *n.* a native or citizen of Tyre. □ **Tyrian purple** see PURPLE *n.* 2. [L *Tyrius* f. *Tyrus* Tyre]

tyro /tírō/ *n.* (*Brit.* also **tiro**) (*pl.* **-os**) a beginner or novice. [L *tiro,* med.L *tyro,* recruit]

Tyrolean /tírōleeən, ti-/ *adj.* of or characteristic of the Tyrol, an Alpine province of Austria. □□ **Tyrolese** *adj.* & *n.*

Tyrrhene /tíreen/ *adj.* & *n.* (also **Tyrrhenian** /tireéneeən/) *archaic* or *poet.* = ETRUSCAN. [L *Tyrrhenus*]

tzigane /tsigaán/ *n.* **1** a Hungarian gypsy. **2** (*attrib.*) characteristic of the tziganes or (esp.) their music. [F f. Magyar *c(z)igány*]

Uu

U[1] /yōō/ n. (also **u**) (pl. **Us** or **U's**) **1** the twenty-first letter of the alphabet. **2** a U-shaped object or curve (esp. in comb.: U-bolt).

U[2] /yōō/ adj. esp. Brit. colloq. **1** upper class. **2** supposedly characteristic of the upper class. [abbr.]

U[3] /ōō/ adj. a Burmese title of respect before a man's name. [Burmese]

U[4] abbr. (also **U.**) university.

U[5] symb. Chem. the element uranium.

u prefix = MU 2 (μ).

UAE abbr. United Arab Emirates.

ubiety /yōōbíətee/ n. the fact or condition of being in a definite place; local relation. [med.L ubietas f. L ubi where]

-ubility /yōōbílitee/ suffix forming nouns from, or corresponding to, adjectives in -uble (solubility; volubility). [L -ubilitas: cf. -ITY]

ubiquitarian /yōōbíkwitáireeən/ adj. & n. Theol. ● adj. relating to or believing in the doctrine of the omnipresence of Christ's body. ● n. a believer in this. □□ **ubiquitarianism** n. [mod.L ubiquitarius (as UBIQUITOUS)]

ubiquitous /yōōbíkwitəs/ adj. **1** present everywhere or in several places simultaneously. **2** often encountered. □□ **ubiquitously** adv. **ubiquitousness** n. **ubiquity** n. [mod.L ubiquitas f. L ubique everywhere f. ubi where]

■ see PERVASIVE. □□ **ubiquitously** see EVERYWHERE.
ubiquitousness, ubiquity see prevalence (PREVALENT).

-uble /yəbəl/ suffix forming adjectives meaning 'that may or must be' (see -ABLE) (soluble; voluble). [F f. L -ubilis]

-ubly /yəblee/ suffix forming adverbs corresponding to adjectives in -uble.

U-boat /yōōbōt/ n. hist. a German submarine. [G U-boot = Unterseeboot undersea boat]

u.c. abbr. uppercase.

udder /údər/ n. the mammary gland of cattle, sheep, etc., hanging as a baglike organ with several teats. □□ **uddered** adj. (also in comb.). [OE ūder f. WG]

udometer /yōōdómitər/ n. formal a rain gauge. [F udomètre f. L udus damp]

UFO /yōō-ef-ō, yōōfō/ n. (also **ufo**) (pl. **UFOs** or **ufos**) unidentified flying object. [abbr.]

ufology /yōōfóləjee/ n. the study of UFOs. □□ **ufologist** n.

ugh /əkh, ug, ukh/ int. **1** expressing disgust or horror. **2** the sound of a cough or grunt. [imit.]

Ugli /úglee/ n. (pl. **Uglis** or **Uglies**) propr. a mottled green and yellow citrus fruit, a hybrid of a grapefruit and tangerine. [UGLY]

uglify /úglifī/ v.tr. (-ies, -ied) make ugly. □□ **uglification** /-fikáyshən/ n.

ugly /úglee/ adj. (**uglier, ugliest**) **1** unpleasing or repulsive to see or hear (an ugly scar; spoke with an ugly snarl). **2** unpleasantly suggestive; discreditable (ugly rumors are about). **3** threatening; dangerous (the sky has an ugly look; an ugly mood). **4** morally repulsive; vile (ugly vices). □ **ugly duckling** a person who turns out to be beautiful or talented, etc., against all expectations (with ref. to a cygnet in a brood of ducks in a tale by Andersen). □□ **uglily** adv. **ugliness** n. [ME f. ON ugglígr to be dreaded f. ugga to dread]

■ **1** unattractive, unlovely, unbeautiful, unhandsome, unshapely, unprepossessing, unpleasing, unsightly, hideous, grotesque, gruesome, ghastly, offensive, horrible, horrid, repulsive, plain, plain-featured, bad-featured, ill-favored, dreadful-looking, awful-looking, frightful-looking, homely. **2** see poisonous (POISON). **3** unpleasant, disagreeable, surly, hostile, nasty, spiteful, bad-tempered, ill-tempered, currish, irascible, curmudgeonly, cantankerous, crabby, crabbed, crotchety, cross, mean, cranky; disquieting, uncomfortable, discomforting, forbidding, sinister, troublesome, awkward, disadvantageous, ominous, threatening, menacing, dangerous, perilous, hazardous. **4** objectionable, disagreeable, unpleasant, offensive, nasty, loathsome, repellent, repugnant, repulsive, nauseating, nauseous, revolting, sickening, disgusting, obnoxious, rotten, corrupt, filthy, vile, heinous, bad, sordid, evil, foul, perverted, immoral, depraved, degenerate, base, debased, detestable, hateful, abominable, execrable, despicable, odious, literary noisome.

Ugrian /ōōgreeən/ adj. & n. (also **Ugric** /ōōgrik/) ● adj. of or relating to the eastern branch of Finnic peoples, esp. the Finns and Magyars. ● n. **1** a member of this people. **2** the language of this people. [Russ. Ugry name of a race dwelling E. of the Urals]

UHF abbr. ultrahigh frequency.

uh-huh /uhú/ int. colloq. expressing assent. [imit.]

uhlan /ōōlaan, yōōlən/ n. hist. a cavalryman armed with a lance in some European armies, esp. the former German army. [F & G f. Pol. (h)ulan f. Turk. oğlan youth, servant]

UHT abbr. **1** ultrahigh temperature. **2** ultra-heat-treated (esp. of milk, for long keeping).

Uitlander /íttlandər, áy-, óyt-/ n. S.Afr. a foreigner or alien, esp. before the Boer War. [Afrik. f. Du. uit out + land land]

UK abbr. United Kingdom.

ukase /yōōkáys, -káyz/ n. **1** an arbitrary command. **2** hist. an edict of the czarist Russian government. [Russ. ukaz ordinance, edict f. ukazat' show, decree]

Ukrainian /yōōkráyneeən/ n. & adj. ● n. **1** a native of Ukraine. **2** the language of Ukraine. ● adj. of or relating to Ukraine or its people or language. [Ukraine f. Russ. ukraina frontier region f. u at + krai edge]

ukulele /yōōkəláylee/ n. a small, four-stringed Hawaiian (orig. Portuguese) guitar. [Hawaiian, = jumping flea]

-ular /yələr/ suffix forming adjectives, sometimes corresp. to nouns in -ule (pustular) but often without diminutive force (angular; granular). □□ **-ularity** /-láritee/ suffix forming nouns. [from or after L -ularis (as -ULE, -AR¹)]

ulcer /úlsər/ n. **1** an open sore on an external or internal surface of the body, often forming pus. **2 a** a moral blemish. **b** a corroding or corrupting influence, etc. □□ **ulcered** adj. **ulcerous** adj. [ME f. L ulcus -eris, rel. to Gk helkos]

■ **1** sore, lesion, abscess, ulceration, canker, chancre, boil, gumboil, eruption, carbuncle, inflammation, Med. furuncle. **2** cancer, canker, festering spot, blight, scourge, poison, disease, pestilence, curse, bane,

---

/. . ./ **pronunciation** ● **part of speech**
□ **phrases, idioms, and compounds**
□□ **derivatives** ■ **synonym section**
cross-references appear in SMALL CAPITALS or italics

plague. □□ **ulcerous** ulcerative, cancerous, cankerous, festering, ulcerated, suppurating, suppurative, gangrenous, septic, *Med.* furuncular, furunculous, necrotic, necrosed.

ulcerate /úlsərayt/ *v.tr.* & *intr.* form into or affect with an ulcer. □□ **ulcerable** *adj.* **ulceration** /-ráyshən/ *n.* **ulcerative** *adj.* [ME f. L *ulcerare ulcerat-* (as ULCER)]

-ule /əl, yōōl/ *suffix* forming diminutive nouns (*capsule*; *globule*). [from or after L *-ulus, -ula, -ulum*]

ulema /ōōlimaa/ *n.* **1** a body of Muslim doctors of sacred law and theology. **2** a member of this. [Arab. '*ulamā* pl. of '*ālim* learned f. '*alama* know]

-ulent /yələnt/ *suffix* forming adjectives meaning 'abounding in; full of' (*fraudulent*; *turbulent*). □□ **-ulence** *suffix* forming nouns. [L *-ulentus*]

uliginose /yōōlíjinōs/ *adj.* (also **uliginous** /-nəs/) *Bot.* growing in wet or swampy places. [L *uliginosus* f. *uligo -ginis* moisture]

ullage /úlij/ *n.* **1** the amount by which a cask, etc., falls short of being full. **2** loss by evaporation or leakage. [ME f. AF *ulliage*, OF *ouillage* f. *ouiller* fill up, ult. f. L *oculus* eye, with ref. to the bunghole]

ulna /úlnə/ *n.* (*pl.* **ulnae** /-nee/) **1** the thinner and longer bone in the forearm, on the side opposite to the thumb (cf. RADIUS 3). **2** *Zool.* a corresponding bone in an animal's foreleg or a bird's wing. □□ **ulnar** *adj.* [L, rel. to Gk *ōlenē* and ELL]

ulotrichan /yōōlótrikən/ *adj.* & *n.* ● *adj.* (also **ulotrichous** /-kəs/) having tightly curled hair, esp. denoting a human type. ● *n.* a person having such hair. [mod.L *Ulotrichi* f. Gk *oulos* woolly, crisp + *thrix trikhos* hair]

-ulous /yələs/ *suffix* forming adjectives (*fabulous*; *populous*). [L *-ulosus, -ulus*]

ulster /úlstər/ *n.* a man's long, loose overcoat of rough cloth. [*Ulster* in Ireland, where it was orig. sold]

Ulsterman /úlstərmən/ *n.* (*pl.* **-men**; *fem.* **Ulsterwoman**; *pl.* **-women**) a native of Ulster, the northern part of Ireland.

ult. *abbr.* **1** ultimo. **2** ultimate.

ulterior /ultéereeər/ *adj.* **1** existing in the background, or beyond what is evident or admitted; hidden; secret (esp. *ulterior motive*). **2** situated beyond. **3** more remote; not immediate; in the future. □□ **ulteriorly** *adv.* [L, = further, more distant]

■ **1** hidden, concealed, covert, secret, unrevealed, undisclosed, unexpressed, private, personal, underlying, surreptitious, underhand(ed). **2** outside, beyond, further, farther, remote, more distant. **3** future, further, remote.

ultima /últimə/ *n.* the last syllable of a word. [L *ultima* (*syllaba*), fem. of *ultimus* last]

ultimata *pl.* of ULTIMATUM.

ultimate /últimət/ *adj.* & *n.* ● *adj.* **1** last; final. **2** beyond which no other exists or is possible (*the ultimate analysis*). **3** fundamental; primary; unanalyzable (*ultimate truths*). **4** maximum (*ultimate tensile strength*). ● *n.* **1** (prec. by *the*) the best achievable or imaginable. **2** a final or fundamental fact or principle. □□ **ultimately** *adj.* **ultimateness** *n.* [LL *ultimatus* past part. of *ultimare* come to an end]

■ *adj.* **1, 2** final, last, terminating, terminal, end, eventual, net, closing, conclusive, concluding, decisive, deciding, definitive; remotest, furthest, farthest, extreme, uttermost. **3** elemental, basic, fundamental, underlying, primary, root, essential, unanalyzable, final. **4** final, maximum, highest, greatest, supreme, utmost, paramount. □□ **ultimately** finally, at long last, in the final *or* last analysis, eventually, in the end, at the end of the day, when all is said and done, at (the) last, in the long run; fundamentally, essentially, basically, at bottom.

ultima Thule /últimə thōōlee, ōóltimaa tōōlee/ *n.* a faraway, unknown region. [L, = furthest Thule, a remote northern region]

ultimatum /últimáytəm/ *n.* (*pl.* **ultimatums** or **ultimata** /-tə/) a final demand or statement of terms by one party, the rejection of which by another could cause a breakdown

in relations, war, or an end of cooperation, etc. [L neut. past part.: see ULTIMATE]

■ (final) demand(s), term(s), condition(s), stipulation(s), requirement(s).

ultimo /últimō/ *adj. Commerce* of last month (*the 28th ultimo*). [L *ultimo mense* in the last month]

ultimogeniture /últimōjénichər/ *n.* a system in which the youngest son has the right of inheritance (cf. PRIMOGENITURE 2). [L *ultimus* last, after PRIMOGENITURE]

ultra /últrə/ *adj.* & *n.* ● *adj.* favoring extreme views or measures, esp. in religion or politics. ● *n.* an extremist. [orig. as abbr. of F *ultra-royaliste*: see ULTRA-]

■ *adj.* die-hard, rabid, unregenerate, unrepentant, unreformed, fundamentalist, extremist, prejudiced, opinionated, bigoted, *colloq.* hard-nosed. ● *n.* see EXTREMIST.

ultra- /últrə/ *comb. form* **1** beyond; on the other side of (opp. CIS-). **2** extreme(ly), excessive(ly) (*ultraconservative*; *ultramodern*). [L *ultra* beyond]

■ **1** beyond. **2** extreme(ly), immoderate(ly), excessive(ly), drastic(ally), radical (ly), fanatic, fanatical (ly), unmitigated(ly), outrageous(ly), unqualified(ly), uncompromising(ly), sheer, blatant(ly), out-and-out, complete(ly), thorough(ly), thoroughgoing, dyed-in-the-wool; arch-.

ultracentrifuge /últrəséntrifyōōj/ *n.* a high-speed centrifuge used to separate small particles and large molecules by their rate of sedimentation from sols.

ultrahigh /últrəhí/ *adj.* **1** (of a frequency) in the range 300 to 3,000 megahertz. **2** extremely high (*ultrahigh prices; ultrahigh suspension bridge*).

ultraist /últrəist/ *n.* the holder of extreme positions in politics, religion, etc. □□ **ultraism** *n.*
■ see EXTREMIST.

ultramarine /últrəməreén/ *n.* & *adj.* ● *n.* **1 a** a brilliant blue pigment orig. obtained from lapis lazuli. **b** an imitation of this from powdered fired clay, sodium carbonate, sulfur, and resin. **2** the color of this. ● *adj.* **1** of this color. **2** *archaic* situated beyond the sea. [obs. It. *oltramarino* & med.L *ultramarinus* beyond the sea (as ULTRA-, MARINE), because lapis lazuli was brought from beyond the sea]

ultramicroscope /últrəmíkrəskōp/ *n.* an optical microscope used to reveal very small particles by means of light scattered by them.

ultramicroscopic /últrəmíkrəskópik/ *adj.* **1** too small to be seen by an ordinary optical microscope. **2** of or relating to an ultramicroscope.

ultramontane /últrəmontáyn/ *adj.* & *n.* ● *adj.* **1** situated on the other side of the mountains (esp. the Alps) from the point of view of the speaker. **2** advocating supreme papal authority in matters of faith and discipline. ● *n.* **1** a person living on the other side of the mountains (esp. the Alps). **2** a person advocating supreme papal authority. [med.L *ultramontanus* (as ULTRA-, L *mons montis* mountain)]

ultramundane /últrəmúndayn/ *adj.* lying beyond the world or the solar system. [L *ultramundanus* (as ULTRA-, *mundanus* f. *mundus* world)]

ultrasonic /últrəsónik/ *adj.* of or involving sound waves with a frequency above the upper limit of human hearing. □□ **ultrasonically** *adv.*

ultrasonics /últrəsóniks/ *n.pl.* (usu. treated as *sing.*) the science and application of ultrasonic waves.

ultrasound /últrəsownd/ *n.* **1** sound having an ultrasonic frequency. **2** ultrasonic waves. □ **ultrasound cardiography** = ECHOCARDIOGRAPHY.

ultrastructure /últrəstrukchər/ *n. Biol.* fine structure not visible with an optical microscope.

ultraviolet /últrəvíələt/ *adj. Physics* **1** having a wavelength (just) beyond the violet end of the visible spectrum. **2** of or using such radiation.

ultra vires /últrə víreez, ōóltraa veérayz/ *adv.* & *predic.adj.* beyond one's legal power or authority. [L]

ululate /úlyəlayt, yōōl-/ *v.intr.* howl; wail; make a hooting cry. □□ **ululant** *adj.* **ululation** /-láyshən/ *n.* [L *ululare ululat-* (imit.)]

■ see HOWL v. 1. □□ **ululation** see HOWL n. 1.

um /um, əm/ int. expressing hesitation or a pause in speech. [imit.]

-um var. of -IUM 1.

umbel /úmbəl/ n. Bot. a flower cluster in which stalks nearly equal in length spring from a common center and form a flat or curved surface, as in parsley. □□ **umbellar** adj. **umbellate** /-bəlit, -layt, umbélit/ adj. **umbellule** /úmbəlyōōl, -bélyōōl/ adj. [obs. F umbelle or L umbella sunshade, dimin. of UMBRA]

umbellifer /umbélifər/ n. any plant of the family Umbelliferae bearing umbels, including parsley and parsnip. □□ **umbelliferous** /-bəlifərəs/ adj. [obs. F umbellifère f. L (as UMBEL, -fer bearing)]

umber /úmbər/ n. & adj. ● n. 1 a natural pigment like ocher but darker and browner. 2 the color of this. ● adj. 1 of this color. 2 dark; dusky. [F (terre d')ombre or It. (terra di) ombra = shadow (earth), f. L UMBRA or Umbra fem. of Umber Umbrian]

umbilical /umbílikəl/ adj. 1 of, situated near, or affecting the navel. 2 centrally placed. □ **umbilical cord** 1 a flexible, cordlike structure attaching a fetus to the placenta. 2 Astronaut. a supply cable linking a missile to its launcher, or an astronaut in space to a spacecraft. [obs. F umbilical or f. UMBILICUS]

umbilicate /umbílikət/ adj. 1 shaped like a navel. 2 having an umbilicus.

umbilicus /umbílikəs/ n. (pl. **umbilici** /-bílisī/ or **umbilicuses**) 1 Anat. the navel. 2 Bot. & Zool. a navellike formation. 3 Geom. a point in a surface through which all cross sections have the same curvature. [L, rel. to Gk omphalos and to NAVEL]

umbles /úmbəlz/ n.pl. the edible offal of deer, etc. (cf. eat humble pie). [ME var. of NUMBLES]

umbo /úmbō/ n. (pl. **-os** or **umbones** /-bṓneez/) 1 the boss of a shield, esp. in the center. 2 Bot. & Zool. a rounded knob or protuberance. □□ **umbonal** adj. **umbonate** /-bṓnət/ adj. [L umbo -onis]

umbra /úmbrə/ n. (pl. **umbras** or **umbrae** /-bree/) Astron. 1 a total shadow usu. cast on the earth by the moon during a solar eclipse. 2 the dark central part of a sunspot (cf. PENUMBRA). □□ **umbral** adj. [L, = shade]

umbrage /úmbrij/ n. 1 offense; a sense of slight or injury (esp. give or take umbrage at). b what gives shade. [ME f. OF ult. f. L umbraticus f. umbra: see UMBRA]

■ 1 (take umbrage) feel or be offended, take offense, be affronted, bridle, feel displeasure or annoyance or exasperation or indignation or vexation or bitterness or resentment, be piqued or displeased or annoyed or exasperated or indignant or vexed or resentful, take exception, harbor a grudge.

umbrella /umbrélə/ n. 1 a light, portable device for protection against rain, strong sun, etc., consisting of a usu. circular canopy of cloth mounted by means of a collapsible metal frame on a central stick. 2 protection or patronage. 3 (often attrib.) a coordinating or unifying agency (umbrella organization). 4 a screen of fighter aircraft or a curtain of fire put up as a protection against enemy aircraft. 5 Zool. the gelatinous disk of a jellyfish, etc., which it contracts and expands to move through the water. □ **umbrella bird** any S. American bird of the genus Cephalopterus, with a black radiating crest and long wattles. **umbrella pine 1** = stone pine. 2 a tall Japanese evergreen conifer, Sciadopitys verticillata, with leaves in umbrellalike whorls. **umbrella stand** a stand for holding closed, upright umbrellas. **umbrella tree** a small magnolia, Magnolia tripetala, with leaves in a whorl like an umbrella. □□ **umbrellaed** /-ləd/ adj. **umbrellalike** adj. [It. ombrella, dimin. of ombra shade f. L umbra: see UMBRA]

■ 1 parasol, sunshade; Brit. colloq. brolly. 2 protection, cover, coverage, aegis, shield, screen, patronage. 3 (attrib.) catchall, overall, blanket. 4 screen, shelter, shield, protection, cover, curtain.

Umbrian /úmbreeən/ adj. & n. ● adj. of or relating to Umbria in central Italy. ● n. 1 the language of ancient Umbria,

related to Latin. 2 an inhabitant of ancient Umbria. □ **Umbrian school** a Renaissance school of Italian painting, to which Raphael and Perugino belonged.

umbriferous /umbrífərəs/ adj. formal providing shade. [L umbrifer f. umbra shade: see -FEROUS]

umiak /ōōmeeak/ n. an Inuit skin-and-wood open boat propelled with paddles. [Eskimo umiaq women's boat]

umlaut /ōōmlowt/ n. & v. ● n. 1 a mark (¨) used over a vowel, esp. in Germanic languages, to indicate a vowel change. 2 such a vowel change, e.g., German Mann, Männer, English man, men, due to i, j, etc. (now usu. lost or altered) in the following syllable. ● v.tr. modify (a form or a sound) by an umlaut. [G f. um about + Laut sound]

ump /ump/ n. colloq. an umpire. [abbr.]

umpire /úmpir/ n. & v. ● n. 1 a person chosen to enforce the rules and settle disputes in various sports. 2 a person chosen to arbitrate between disputants, or to see fair play. ● v. 1 intr. (usu. foll. by for, in, etc.) act as umpire. 2 tr. act as umpire in (a game, etc.). □□ **umpirage** /-pìrij, -pərij/ n. **umpireship** n. [ME, later form of noumpere f. OF nonper not equal (as NON-, PEER²): for loss of n- cf. ADDER]

■ n. referee, arbiter, judge, moderator, go-between, adjudicator, arbitrator; official; colloq. ref.
● v. officiate; referee, arbitrate, judge, moderate, adjudicate.

umpteen /úmpteén/ adj. & pron. sl. ● adj. indefinitely many; a lot of. ● pron. indefinitely many. □□ **umpteenth** adj. [joc. form. on -TEEN]

■ adj. a lot of, many, innumerable, unnumbered, countless, a huge number of, very many, numerous, colloq. hundreds of, thousands of, millions of, billions of, trillions of, zillions of, masses of.

UN abbr. United Nations.

un-¹ /un/ prefix 1 added to adjectives and participles and their derivative nouns and adverbs, meaning: a not: denoting the absence of a quality or state (unusable; uncalled-for; uneducated; unfailing; unofficially; unhappiness). b the reverse of, usu. with an implication of approval or disapproval, or with some other special connotation (unselfish; unsociable; unscientific). ¶ Words formed in this way often have neutral counterparts in non- (see NON- 6) and counterparts in in- (see IN-¹), e.g., unadvisable. 2 (less often) added to nouns, meaning 'a lack of' (unrest; untruth). ¶ The number of words that can be formed with this prefix (and similarly with un-²) is potentially as large as the number of adjectives in use; consequently only a selection, being considered the most current or semantically noteworthy, can be given here. [OE f. Gmc, rel. to L in-]

un-² /un/ prefix added to verbs and (less often) nouns, forming verbs denoting: 1 the reversal or cancellation of an action or state (undress; unlock; unsettle). 2 deprivation or separation (unmask). 3 release from (unburden; uncage). 4 causing to be no longer (unman). ¶ See the note at un-¹. Both un-¹ and un-² can be understood in some forms in -able, -ed (especially), and -ing: for example, undressed can mean either 'not dressed' or 'no longer dressed'. [OE un-, on- f. Gmc]

'un /ən/ pron. colloq. one (that's a good 'un). [dial. var.]

unabashed /únəbásht/ adj. not abashed. □□ **unabashedly** /-shidlee/ adv.

■ unashamed, unblushing, unembarrassed, brazen, barefaced, blatant, bold, undaunted, not abashed, undeterred, unawed, undismayed, unconcerned. □□ **unabashedly** see OPENLY.

unabated /únəbáytid/ adj. not abated; undiminished. □□ **unabatedly** adv.

■ see RELENTLESS 2, UNMITIGATED 1.

unable /únáybəl/ adj. (usu. foll. by to + infin.) not able; lacking ability.

┌───┐
│ /.../ **pronunciation**   ● **part of speech** │
│ □ **phrases, idioms, and compounds**   │
│ □□ **derivatives**   ■ **synonym section** │
│ **cross-references** appear in SMALL CAPITALS or italics │
└───┘

■ not able, powerless, unfit, unqualified, impotent, incompetent.

unabridged /únəbríjd/ *adj.* (of a text, etc.) complete; not abridged.

■ uncut, whole, full-length, entire, complete, intact, not abridged, uncondensed, unshortened; not bowdlerized, unexpurgated; extensive, thorough, comprehensive, full, exhaustive, all-encompassing, (all-)inclusive.

unabsorbed /únəbzáwrbd, -sáwrbd/ *adj.* not absorbed.

unacademic /únakədémik/ *adj.* **1** not academic (esp. not scholarly or theoretical). **2** (of a person) not suited to academic study.

unaccented /únáksentid, -akséntid/ *adj.* not accented; not emphasized.

■ unstressed, unemphasized, unaccentuated, weak.

unacceptable /únəkséptəbəl/ *adj.* not acceptable. □□ **unacceptableness** *n.* **unacceptably** *adv.*

■ unsatisfactory, objectionable, exceptionable, wrong, bad, improper, unallowable, insupportable, intolerable, inadmissible, ineligible, undesirable, distasteful, disagreeable, unsuitable, inappropriate, alien, unpleasant, tasteless, beyond the pale, *colloq.* not on. □□ **unacceptably** see BADLY 1.

unacclaimed /únəkláymd/ *adj.* not acclaimed.

unaccommodating /únəkómədayting/ *adj.* not accommodating; disobliging.

■ see DIFFICULT 2, INFLEXIBLE 2, 3.

unaccompanied /únəkúmpəneed/ *adj.* **1** not accompanied. **2** *Mus.* without accompaniment.

■ **1** alone, solo, lone, on one's own, by oneself, unescorted, unchaperoned, unattended, *archaic* sole. **2** solo, *Mus.* a cappella.

unaccomplished /únəkómplisht/ *adj.* **1** not accomplished; uncompleted. **2** lacking accomplishments.

■ **1** see INCOMPLETE, UNDONE 1. **2** see UNREFINED, UNEDUCATED.

unaccountable /únəkówntəbəl/ *adj.* **1** unable to be explained. **2** unpredictable or strange in behavior. **3** not responsible. □□ **unaccountability** /-bílitee/ *n.* **unaccountableness** *n.* **unaccountably** *adv.*

■ **1, 2** unexplained, inexplicable, unexplainable, unaccounted for, mysterious, inscrutable, incomprehensible, unintelligible, enigmatic, strange, puzzling, baffling, mystifying, peculiar, odd, bizarre, unfathomable, unpredictable, weird, unheard-of, extraordinary, unusual, unorthodox, uncanny. **3** not answerable, not responsible.

unaccounted /únəkówntid/ *adj.* of which no account is given. □ **unaccounted for** unexplained; not included in an account.

■ □ **unaccounted for** see UNACCOUNTABLE 1, 2.

unaccustomed /únəkústəmd/ *adj.* **1** (usu. foll. by *to*) not accustomed. **2** not customary; unusual (*his unaccustomed silence*). □□ **unaccustomedly** *adv.*

■ **1** (*unaccustomed to*) unused to, inexperienced in *or* at, amateurish at, unpracticed in *or* at, unfamiliar with, uninitiated in. **2** unfamiliar, unusual, rare, unwonted, unexpected, uncommon, unprecedented, unanticipated, curious, peculiar, atypical, untypical.

unachievable /únəchéevəbəl/ *adj.* not achievable.

unacknowledged /únəknólijd/ *adj.* not acknowledged.

■ see THANKLESS 2, UNTHANKED.

unacquainted /únəkwáyntid/ *adj.* (usu. foll. by *with*) not acquainted.

■ (*unacquainted with*) see UNFAMILIAR.

unadaptable /únədáptəbəl/ *adj.* not adaptable.

■ see INFLEXIBLE 2, 3.

unadapted /únədáptid/ *adj.* not adapted.

unaddressed /únədrést/ *adj.* (esp. of a letter, etc.) without an address.

unadjacent /únəjáysənt/ *adj.* not adjacent.

unadopted /únədóptid/ *adj.* not adopted.

unadorned /únədáwrnd/ *adj.* not adorned; plain.

■ plain, simple, unembellished, undecorated, unornamented, stark, bare, austere.

unadulterated /únədúltəraytid/ *adj.* **1** not adulterated; pure; concentrated. **2** sheer; complete; utter (*unadulterated nonsense*).

■ **1** see PURE 1, 2. **2** see SHEER¹ *adj.* 1.

unadventurous /únədvénchərəs/ *adj.* not adventurous. □□ **unadventurously** *adv.*

unadvertised /únádvərtizd/ *adj.* not advertised.

■ see UNHERALDED.

unadvisable /únədvízəbəl/ *adj.* **1** not open to advice. **2** (of a thing) inadvisable.

■ **2** see *ill-advised* 2.

unadvised /únədvízd/ *adj.* **1** indiscreet; rash. **2** not having had advice. □□ **unadvisedly** /-zidlee/ *adv.* **unadvisedness** *n.*

■ **1** see *ill-advised* 2.

unaffected /únəféktid/ *adj.* **1** (usu. foll. by *by*) not affected. **2** free from affectation; genuine; sincere. □□ **unaffectedly** *adv.* **unaffectedness** *n.*

■ **1** (*unaffected by*) impervious to, immune to, untouched by, unmoved by, unresponsive to, above, aloof from, uninfluenced by, unimpressed by, remote from, cool *or* cold to, unconcerned by, unstirred by, insensible to. **2** genuine, real, sincere, natural, simple, plain, unpretentious, unassuming, ingenuous, unsophisticated, unstudied, honest, guileless, artless, unartificial, unspoiled, straightforward, unfeigned. □□ **unaffectedly** see NATURALLY 1. **unaffectedness** see *sincerity* (SINCERE).

unaffiliated /únəfíleeaytid/ *adj.* not affiliated.

■ see NONALIGNED.

unafraid /únəfráyd/ *adj.* not afraid.

■ see BRAVE *adj.* 1.

unaided /únáydid/ *adj.* not aided; without help.

■ see *single-handed adj.*

unalienable /únáyleeənəbəl/ *adj.* *Law* = INALIENABLE.

unaligned /únəlínd/ *adj.* **1** = NONALIGNED. **2** not physically aligned.

unalike /únəlík/ *adj.* not alike; different.

■ see DIFFERENT 1, 2.

unalive /únəlív/ *adj.* **1** lacking in vitality. **2** (foll. by *to*) not fully susceptible or awake to.

unalleviated /únəléeveeaytid/ *adj.* not alleviated; relentless.

■ see RELENTLESS 2, UNMITIGATED 1.

unallied /únəlíd/ *adj.* not allied; having no allies.

■ see NEUTRAL *adj.* 1, 2.

unallowable /únəlówəbəl/ *adj.* not allowable.

■ see INADMISSIBLE.

unalloyed /únəlóyd, únál-/ *adj.* **1** not alloyed; pure. **2** complete; utter (*unalloyed joy*).

■ **1** see PURE 1, 2. **2** see PURE 8.

unalterable /únáwltərəbl/ *adj.* not alterable. □□ **unalterableness** *n.* **unalterably** *adv.*

■ see INVARIABLE 1, CONSTANT *adj.* 3.

unaltered /únáwltərd/ *adj.* not altered; remaining the same.

■ see SAME *adj.* 2.

unamazed /únəmáyzd/ *adj.* not amazed.

unambiguous /únambígyōōəs/ *adj.* not ambiguous; clear or definite in meaning. □□ **unambiguity** /-gyōō-itee/ *n.* **unambiguously** *adv.*

■ see CLEAR *adj.* 6b. □□ **unambiguously** see *expressly* (EXPRESS²).

unambitious /únambíshəs/ *adj.* not ambitious; without ambition. □□ **unambitiously** *adv.* **unambitiousness** *n.*

■ see MEEK, SHIFTLESS.

unambivalent /únambívələnt/ *adj.* (of feelings, etc.) not ambivalent; straightforward. □□ **unambivalently** *adv.*

un-American /únəmérikən/ *adj.* **1** not in accordance with American characteristics, etc. **2** contrary to the interests of the US; (in the US) treasonable. □□ **un-Americanism** *n.*

unamiable /únáymeeəbəl/ *adj.* not amiable.

■ see UNSOCIAL.

unamplified /únámplifīd/ *adj.* not amplified.

unamused /únəmyōōzd/ *adj.* not amused.

unanalyzable /únánəlìzəbəl/ *adj.* not able to be analyzed.

unanalyzed /únánəlizd/ *adj.* not analyzed.

unaneled /únəneéld/ *adj.* *archaic* not having received extreme unction.

unanimous /yōōnániməs/ *adj.* **1** all in agreement (*the committee was unanimous*). **2** (of an opinion, vote, etc.) held or given by general consent (*the unanimous choice*). □□ **unanimity** /-nənímitee/ *n.* **unanimously** *adv.* **unanimousness** *n.* [LL *unanimis*, L *unanimus* f. *unus* one + *animus* mind]
  ■ **1** see UNITED 3. □□ **unanimity** see ACCORD *n.* 1.

unannounced /únənównst/ *adj.* not announced; without warning (of arrival, etc.).
  ■ see UNHERALDED.

unanswerable /únánsərəbəl/ *adj.* **1** unable to be refuted (*has an unanswerable case*). **2** unable to be answered (*an unanswerable question*). □□ **unanswerableness** *n.* **unanswerably** *adv.*
  ■ **1** see INCONTROVERTIBLE.

unanswered /únánsərd/ *adj.* not answered.
  ■ see UNRESOLVED 2.

unanticipated /únantísipaytid/ *adj.* not anticipated.
  ■ see UNFORESEEN.

unapparent /únəpárənt/ *adj.* not apparent.

unappealable /únəpeéləbəl/ *adj.* esp. *Law* not able to be appealed against.

unappealing /únəpeéling/ *adj.* not appealing; unattractive. □□ **unappealingly** *adv.*
  ■ see UNINVITING.

unappeasable /únəpeézəbəl/ *adj.* not appeasable.
  ■ see IMPLACABLE.

unappeased /únəpeézd/ *adj.* not appeased.

unappetizing /únápitīzing/ *adj.* not appetizing. □□ **unappetizingly** *adv.*
  ■ see UNPALATABLE 1, UNINVITING.

unapplied /únəplíd/ *adj.* not applied.
  ■ see ABSTRACT *adj.* 1a.

unappreciated /únəpreésheeaytid/ *adj.* not appreciated.
  ■ see THANKLESS 2, UNTHANKED.

unappreciative /únəpreéshətiv/ *adj.* not appreciative.
  ■ see UNGRATEFUL.

unapproachable /únəprōchəbəl/ *adj.* **1** not approachable; remote; inaccessible. **2** (of a person) unfriendly. □□ **unapproachability** *n.* **unapproachableness** *n.* **unapproachably** *adv.*
  ■ **1** inaccessible, remote, unreachable, out-of-the-way, out of reach, beyond reach. **2** distant, remote, aloof, reserved, standoffish, austere, withdrawn, unfriendly, unsociable, antisocial, forbidding, chilly, cool, cold, frigid.

unappropriated /únəprópreeaytid/ *adj.* **1** not allocated or assigned. **2** not taken into possession by anyone.

unapproved /únəprōōvd/ *adj.* not approved or sanctioned.
  ■ see UNAUTHORIZED.

unapt /únápt/ *adj.* **1** (usu. foll. by *for*) not suitable. **2** (usu. foll. by *to* + infin.) not apt. □□ **unaptly** *adv.* **unaptness** *n.*
  ■ **1** see INAPPROPRIATE. **2** see EXTRANEOUS 2b.

unarguable /únáargyōōəbəl/ *adj.* not arguable; certain.
  ■ see CERTAIN *adj.* 1b.

unarm /únáarm/ *v.tr.* deprive or free of arms or armor.
  ■ disarm, demilitarize.

unarmed /únáarmd/ *adj.* not armed; without weapons.
  ■ unprotected, defenseless, weaponless.

unarresting /únərésting/ *adj.* uninteresting; dull. □□ **unarrestingly** *adv.*

unarticulated /únaartíkyəlaytid/ *adj.* not articulated or distinct.

unartistic /únaartístik/ *adj.* not artistic, esp. not concerned with art. □□ **unartistically** *adv.*
  ■ see MATTER-OF-FACT 1.

unascertainable /únasərtáynəbəl/ *adj.* not ascertainable.
  ■ see UNCERTAIN 1.

unascertained /únasərtáynd/ *adj.* not ascertained; unknown.
  ■ see UNCERTAIN 1.

unashamed /únəsháymd/ *adj.* **1** feeling no guilt, shameless.

2 blatant; bold. □□ **unashamedly** /-midlee/ *adv.* **unashamedness** /-midnis/ *n.*
  ■ **1** see SHAMELESS. **2** see BLATANT 1. □□ **unashamedly** see OPENLY 2.

unasked /únáskt/ *adj.* (often foll. by *for*) not asked, requested, or invited.
  ■ uninvited, unrequested, undemanded, unsolicited, unsought, unwanted, unprompted, gratuitous, volunteered, voluntary, unbidden, spontaneous, unwelcome, uncalled(-for).

unassailable /únəsáyləbəl/ *adj.* unable to be attacked or questioned; impregnable. □□ **unassailability** /-bílitee/ *n.* **unassailableness** *n.* **unassailably** *adv.*
  ■ see INVINCIBLE, WATERTIGHT 2.

unassertive /únəsərtiv/ *adj.* (of a person) not assertive or forthcoming; reticent. □□ **unassertively** *adv.* **unassertiveness** *n.*
  ■ see PASSIVE 2. □□ **unassertiveness** see SUBMISSION 2.

unassignable /únəsínəbəl/ *adj.* not assignable.

unassigned /únəsínd/ *adj.* not assigned.

unassimilated /únəsímiláytid/ *adj.* not assimilated. □□ **unassimilable** *adj.*

unassisted /únəsístid/ *adj.* not assisted.
  ■ see *single-handed adj.*

unassuaged /únəswáyjd/ *adj.* not assuaged. □□ **unassuageable** *adj.*

unassuming /únəsōōming/ *adj.* not pretentious or arrogant; modest. □□ **unassumingly** *adv.* **unassumingness** *n.*
  ■ see MODEST 1, 2.

unatoned /únətōnd/ *adj.* not atoned for.

unattached /únətácht/ *adj.* **1** (often foll. by *to*) not attached, esp. to a particular body, organization, etc. **2** not engaged or married.
  ■ **1** separate, unconnected, detached, independent, unaffiliated, self-governing, self-regulating, autonomous, self-reliant, self-sustaining, self-sustained; see also *detached* (DETACH 3). **2** single, unmarried, uncommitted, unengaged, on one's own, not spoken for.

unattackable /únətákəbəl/ *adj.* unable to be attacked or damaged.

unattainable /únətáynəbəl/ *adj.* not attainable. □□ **unattainableness** *n.* **unattainably** *adv.*
  ■ see IMPOSSIBLE 1, UNAPPROACHABLE 1.

unattempted /únətémptid/ *adj.* not attempted.

unattended /únəténdid/ *adj.* **1** (usu. foll. by *to*) not attended. **2** (of a person, vehicle, etc.) not accompanied; alone; uncared for.
  ■ **2** see UNACCOMPANIED 1.

unattractive /únətráktiv/ *adj.* not attractive. □□ **unattractively** *adv.* **unattractiveness** *n.*
  ■ see UGLY 1, UNINVITING.

unattributable /únətríbyətəbəl/ *adj.* (esp. of information) that cannot or may not be attributed to a source, etc. □□ **unattributably** *adv.*

unauthentic /únawthéntik/ *adj.* not authentic. □□ **unauthentically** *adv.*
  ■ see FACTITIOUS.

unauthenticated /únawthéntikaytid/ *adj.* not authenticated.

unauthorized /únáwthərīzd/ *adj.* not authorized.
  ■ unsanctioned, unapproved, unofficial, unwarranted, unlawful, illegal, illicit, illegitimate.

unavailable /únəváyləbəl/ *adj.* not available. □□ **unavailability** *n.* **unavailableness** *n.*
  ■ unobtainable, inaccessible; spoken for.

unavailing /únəváyling/ *adj.* not availing; achieving nothing; ineffectual. □□ **unavailingly** *adv.*
  ■ see INEFFECTIVE 1, 3.

/.../ pronunciation	● part of speech
□ phrases, idioms, and compounds	
□□ derivatives	■ synonym section
cross-references appear in SMALL CAPITALS or *italics*	

unavoidable /únəvóydəbəl/ *adj.* not avoidable; inevitable. □□ **unavoidability** *n.* **unavoidableness** *n.* **unavoidably** *adv.*

▪ inescapable, ineluctable, inevitable, irresistible, inexorable, necessary, compulsory, automatic, sure, certain, fated, destined, predestined, determined, predetermined, unchangeable, unalterable, settled, fixed, definite. □□ **unavoidability** inevitability, inevitableness, unavoidableness, necessity, ineluctability, inescapability, indispensability, indispensableness, inexorability. **unavoidably** see NECESSARILY.

unavowed /únəvówd/ *adj.* not avowed.
▪ see SECRET *adj.* 1.

unaware /únəwáir/ *adj.* & *adv.* ● *adj.* **1** (usu. foll. by *of*, or *that* + clause) not aware; ignorant (*unaware of her presence*). **2** (of a person) insensitive; unperceptive. ● *adv.* = UNAWARES. □□ **unawareness** *n.*

▪ *adj.* **1** ignorant, oblivious, unknowing, unsuspecting, unwitting, unconscious, uninformed, unenlightened, incognizant, inobservant, insensible, heedless, unwary, unmindful. **2** see THOUGHTLESS 1. □□ **unawareness** see IGNORANCE.

unawares /únəwáirz/ *adv.* **1** unexpectedly (*met them unawares*). **2** inadvertently (*dropped it unawares*). [earlier *unware(s)* f. OE *unwær(es)*: see WARE²]

▪ **1** unexpectedly, abruptly, by surprise, suddenly, off (one's) guard. **2** inadvertently, unconsciously, unintentionally, unknowingly, unwittingly, unaware, by mistake, mistakenly, by accident, accidentally, in an unguarded moment.

unbacked /únbákt/ *adj.* **1** not supported. **2** (of a horse, etc.) having no backers. **3** (of a chair, picture, etc.) having no back or backing.

unbalance /únbáləns/ *v.* & *n.* ● *v.tr.* **1** upset the physical or mental balance of (*unbalanced by the blow*; *the shock unbalanced him*). **2** (as **unbalanced** *adj.*) **a** not balanced. **b** (of a mind or a person) unstable or deranged. ● *n.* lack of balance; instability, esp. mental.

▪ *v.* **2** (**unbalanced**) **a** uneven, asymmetric(al), unsymmetric(al), lopsided, off-center, unequal, overbalanced, unstable, wobbly, shaky, unsteady; one-sided, biased. **b** mad, demented, certifiable, crazy, insane, eccentric, *non compos* (*mentis*), touched (in the head), unstable, unhinged, deranged, disturbed, of unsound mind, dizzy, esp. *Brit. colloq.* daft, *sl.* daffy, nuts, nutty, bananas, batty, bonkers, off one's head *or* rocker, loco, out of one's head.

unban /únbán/ *v.tr.* (**unbanned, unbanning**) cease to ban; remove a ban from.

unbar /únbáar/ *v.tr.* (**unbarred, unbarring**) **1** remove a bar or bars from (a gate, etc.). **2** unlock; open.

unbearable /únbáirəbəl/ *adj.* not bearable. □□ **unbearableness** *n.* **unbearably** *adv.*

▪ intolerable, unsupportable, insupportable, unendurable, insufferable, unacceptable, oppressive, overwhelming, overpowering, *colloq.* too much.

unbeatable /únbéetəbəl/ *adj.* not beatable; excelling.
▪ unsurpassable, undefeatable, unconquerable, invincible, excellent, unexcelled, incomparable, matchless, unrivaled, peerless, unparalleled, superlative, supreme, transcendent.

unbeaten /únbéet'n/ *adj.* **1** not beaten. **2** (of a record, etc.) not surpassed.

unbeautiful /únbyóotifōol/ *adj.* not beautiful; ugly. □□ **unbeautifully** *adv.*
▪ see UGLY 1.

unbecoming /únbikúming/ *adj.* **1** (esp. of clothing) not flattering or suiting a person. **2** (usu. foll. by *to, for*) not fitting; indecorous or unsuitable. □□ **unbecomingly** *adv.* **unbecomingness** *n.*

▪ **1** unflattering, unsuitable. **2** unbefitting, unfitting, unfit; indecorous, unseemly, indelicate, improper, ungentlemanly, unladylike, offensive, tasteless;

unsuitable, inappropriate, unsuited, ill-suited, inapt, unapt, out of place.

unbefitting /únbifíting/ *adj.* not befitting; unsuitable. □□ **unbefittingly** *adv.* **unbefittingness** *n.*
▪ see INAPPROPRIATE.

unbefriended /únbifréndid/ *adj.* not befriended.

unbegotten /únbigót'n/ *adj.* not begotten.

unbeholden /únbihṓld'n/ *predic.adj.* (usu. foll. by *to*) under no obligation.

unbeknown /únbinṓn/ *adj.* (also **unbeknownst** /-nṓnst/) (foll. by *to*) without the knowledge of (*was there all the time unbeknown to us*). [UN-¹ + *beknown* (archaic) = KNOWN]
▪ (*unbeknown to*) see *unknown* to.

unbelief /únbiléef/ *n.* lack of belief, esp. in religious matters. □□ **unbeliever** *n.* **unbelieving** *adj.* **unbelievingly** *adv.* **unbelievingness** *n.*

▪ see *skepticism* (SKEPTIC) □□ **unbeliever** see NONBELIEVER. **unbelieving** incredulous, disbelieving, nonbelieving, doubting, mistrusting, distrusting, mistrustful, distrustful, suspicious, skeptical, unpersuaded, unconvinced; nonreligious, faithless, unreligious.

unbelievable /únbiléevəbəl/ *adj.* not believable; incredible. □□ **unbelievability** *n.* **unbelievableness** *n.* **unbelievably** *adv.*

▪ incredible, preposterous, inconceivable, unimaginable, implausible, improbable, unthinkable, beyond belief; amazing, extraordinary, fantastic, astounding, staggering, fabulous, *colloq.* mind-boggling, *sl.* mind-blowing. □□ **unbelievably** see TERRIBLY 1.

unbeloved /únbilúvd/ *adj.* not beloved.

unbelt /únbélt/ *v.tr.* remove or undo the belt of (a garment, etc.).

unbend /únbénd/ *v.* (*past* and *past part.* **unbent**) **1** *tr.* & *intr.* change from a bent position; straighten. **2** *intr.* relax from strain or severity; become affable. **3** *tr. Naut.* **a** unfasten (sails) from yards and stays. **b** cast (a cable) loose. **c** untie (a rope).

▪ **2** see THAW *v.* 4, 6.

unbending /únbénding/ *adj.* **1** not bending; inflexible. **2** firm; austere (*unbending rectitude*). **3** relaxing from strain, activity, or formality. □□ **unbendingly** *adv.* **unbendingness** *n.*

▪ **1** see INFLEXIBLE 1. **2** see INFLEXIBLE 2.

unbiased /únbíəst/ *adj.* (also esp. *Brit.* **unbiassed**) not biased; impartial.
▪ see IMPARTIAL.

unbiblical /únbíblikəl/ *adj.* **1** not in or authorized by the Bible. **2** contrary to the Bible.

unbiddable /únbídəbəl/ *adj. Brit.* disobedient; not docile.

unbidden /únbíd'n/ *adj.* not commanded or invited (*arrived unbidden*).
▪ see UNASKED.

unbind /únbínd/ *v.tr.* (*past* and *past part.* **unbound**) release from bonds or binding.

unbirthday /únbśrthday/ *n.* (often *attrib.*) *joc.* any day but one's birthday (*an unbirthday party*).

unbleached /únbléecht/ *adj.* not bleached.

unblemished /únblémisht/ *adj.* not blemished.
▪ see *flawless* (FLAW¹).

unblessed /únblést/ *adj.* (also **unblest**) not blessed.
▪ see UNFORTUNATE *adj.* 1.

unblinking /únblíngking/ *adj.* **1** not blinking. **2** steadfast; not hesitating. **3** stolid; cool. □□ **unblinkingly** *adv.*
▪ **1, 3** see STEADY *adj.* 6. **2** see STEADFAST.

unblock /únblók/ *v.tr.* **1** remove an obstruction from (esp. a pipe, drain, etc.). **2** (also *absol.*) *Cards* allow the later unobstructed play of (a suit) by playing a high card.
▪ **1** see CLEAR *v.* 2b.

unblown /únblṓn/ *adj.* **1** not blown. **2** *archaic* (of a flower) not yet in bloom.

unblushing /únblúshing/ *adj.* **1** not blushing. **2** unashamed; frank. □□ **unblushingly** *adv.*
▪ **2** see UNABASHED.

unbolt /únbṓlt/ *v.tr.* release (a door, etc.) by drawing back the bolt.

unbolted /únbṓltid/ *adj.* **1** not bolted. **2** (of flour, etc.) not sifted.

unbonnet /únbónit/ *v.* (**unbonneted, unbonneting**) **1** *tr.* remove the bonnet from. **2** *intr. archaic* remove one's hat or bonnet esp. in respect.

unbookish /únbŏŏkish/ *adj.* **1** not academic; not often inclined to read. **2** free from bookishness.

unboot /únbŏŏt/ *v.intr.* & *tr.* remove one's boots or the boots of (a person).

unborn /únbáwrn/ *adj.* **1** not yet born (*an unborn child*). **2** never to be brought into being (*unborn hopes*).

unbosom /únbŏŏzəm/ *v.tr.* **1** disclose (thoughts, secrets, etc.). **2** (*refl.*) unburden (oneself) of one's thoughts, secrets, etc.
- **1** see OPEN *v.* 9a.

unbothered /únbóthərd/ *adj.* not bothered; unconcerned.

unbound[1] /únbównd/ *adj.* **1** not bound or tied up. **2** unconstrained. **3 a** (of a book) not having a binding. **b** having paper covers. **4** (of a substance or particle) in a loose or free state.
- **1** see LOOSE *adj.* 1.

unbound[2] *past* and *past part.* of UNBIND.

unbounded /únbówndid/ *adj.* not bounded; infinite (*unbounded optimism*). □□ **unboundedly** *adv.* **unboundedness** *n.*
- see LIMITLESS.

unbrace /únbráys/ *v.tr.* **1** (also *absol.*) free from tension; relax (the nerves, etc.). **2** remove a brace or braces from.

unbreachable /únbreechəbəl/ *adj.* not able to be breached.

unbreakable /únbráykəbəl/ *adj.* not breakable.
- see INDESTRUCTIBLE.

unbreathable /únbreethəbəl/ *adj.* not able to be breathed.

unbribable /únbríbəbəl/ *adj.* not bribable.

unbridgeable /únbríjəbəl/ *adj.* unable to be bridged.

unbridle /únbríd'l/ *v.tr.* **1** remove a bridle from (a horse). **2** remove constraints from (one's tongue, a person, etc.). **3** (as **unbridled** *adj.*) unconstrained (*unbridled insolence*).
- **3** (**unbridled**) see UNINHIBITED.

unbroken /únbrŏkən/ *adj.* **1** not broken. **2** not tamed (*an unbroken horse*). **3** not interrupted (*unbroken sleep*). **4** not surpassed (*an unbroken record*). □□ **unbrokenly** *adv.* **unbrokenness** /-ən-nis/ *n.*
- **1** see INTACT 1. **2** see UNTAMED. **3** see CONTINUOUS.

unbruised /únbrŏŏzd/ *adj.* not bruised.

unbuckle /únbúkəl/ *v.tr.* release the buckle of (a strap, shoe, etc.).
- see UNDO 1.

unbuild /únbíld/ *v.tr.* (*past* and *past part.* **unbuilt**) **1** demolish or destroy (a building, theory, system, etc.). **2** (as **unbuilt** *adj.*) not yet built or (of land, etc.) not yet built on.

unburden /únbúrd'n/ *v.tr.* **1** relieve of a burden. **2** (esp. *refl.*; often foll. by *to*) relieve (oneself, one's conscience, etc.) by confession, etc. □□ **unburdened** *adj.*
- **1** (*unburden of*) see RELIEVE 6.

unburied /únbéreed/ *adj.* not buried.

unbury /únbéree/ *v.tr.* (**-ies, -ied**) **1** remove from the ground, etc., after burial. **2** unearth (a secret, etc.).

unbusinesslike /únbíznislik/ *adj.* not businesslike.

unbutton /únbút'n/ *v.tr.* **1 a** unfasten (a coat, etc.) by taking the buttons out of the buttonholes. **b** unbutton the clothes of (a person). **2** (*absol.*) *colloq.* relax from tension or formality, become communicative. **3** (as **unbuttoned** *adj.*) **a** not buttoned. **b** *colloq.* communicative; informal.
- **3 b** (**unbuttoned**) see INFORMAL.

uncage /únkáyj/ *v.tr.* **1** release from a cage. **2** release from constraint; liberate.

uncalled /únkáwld/ *adj.* not summoned or invited. □ **uncalled-for** (of an opinion, action, etc.) impertinent or unnecessary (*an uncalled-for remark*).
- □ **uncalled-for** see UNWARRANTED 2.

uncandid /únkándid/ *adj.* not candid; disingenuous.

uncanny /únkánee/ *adj.* (**uncannier, uncanniest**) seemingly supernatural; mysterious. □□ **uncannily** *adv.* **uncanniness** *n.* [(orig. Sc. & No. of Engl.) f. UN-[1] + CANNY]
- see EERIE.

uncanonical /únkənónikəl/ *adj.* not canonical. □□ **uncanonically** *adv.*

uncap /únkáp/ *v.tr.* (**uncapped, uncapping**) **1** remove the cap from (a jar, bottle, etc.). **2** remove a cap from (the head or another person).

uncared-for /únkáirdfawr/ *adj.* disregarded; neglected.

uncaring /únkáiring/ *adj.* lacking compassion or concern for others.

uncase /únkáys/ *v.tr.* remove from a cover or case.

uncashed /únkásht/ *adj.* not cashed.

uncaught /únkáwt/ *adj.* not caught.

unceasing /únseésing/ *adj.* not ceasing; continuous (*unceasing effort*). □□ **unceasingly** *adv.*
- see CONTINUOUS. □□ **unceasingly** see NONSTOP *adv.*

uncensored /únsénsərd/ *adj.* not censored.
- see ENTIRE *adj.* 1.

uncensured /únsénshərd/ *adj.* not censured.

unceremonious /únserimōneeəs/ *adj.* **1** lacking ceremony or formality. **2** abrupt; discourteous. □□ **unceremoniously** *adv.* **unceremoniousness** *n.*
- **1** see INFORMAL. **2** see CURT.

uncertain /únsə́rt'n/ *adj.* **1** not certainly knowing or known (*uncertain what it means; the result is uncertain*). **2** unreliable (*his aim is uncertain*). **3** changeable; erratic (*uncertain weather*). □ **in no uncertain terms** clearly and forcefully. □□ **uncertainly** *adv.*
- **1** unsure, of two minds, vacillating, wavering, undecided, unclear, ambivalent, irresolute, indecisive, hesitant, hesitating, undetermined, shilly-shallying; indeterminate, (up) in the air, indefinite, unpredictable, undeterminable, indeterminable, unforeseeable, unascertainable, unascertained, unresolved, unsettled, in the balance, conjectural, unconjecturable, speculative, debatable, arguable, touch and go, unreliable, doubtful, dubious, questionable, vague, hazy, obscure, ambiguous, equivocal. **2** unreliable, unsure, unpredictable, haphazard, chance, arbitrary, random, aleatory, hit-or-miss, casual. **3** variable, changeable, inconstant, unfixed, unsettled, irregular, fickle, erratic, fitful, unsteady, wavering, unreliable, sporadic, occasional; unmethodical, unsystematic.

uncertainty /únsə́rt'ntee/ *n.* (*pl.* **-ies**) **1** the fact or condition of being uncertain. **2** an uncertain matter or circumstance. □ **uncertainty principle** (in full **Heisenberg uncertainty principle** after W. Heisenberg, Ger. physicist d. 1976) *Physics* the principle that the momentum and position of a particle cannot both be precisely determined at the same time.
- **1** see DOUBT *n.* 1, AMBIGUITY 1a. **2** see QUESTION *n.* 4.

uncertified /únsə́rtifid/ *adj.* **1** not attested as certain. **2** not guaranteed by a certificate of competence, etc. **3** not certified as insane.

unchain /úncháyn/ *v.tr.* **1** remove the chains from. **2** release; liberate.
- **2** see RELEASE *v.* 1.

unchallengeable /únchálinjəbəl/ *adj.* not challengeable; unassailable. □□ **unchallengeably** *adv.*
- see INALIENABLE.

unchallenged /únchálinjd/ *adj.* not challenged.
- see UNDISPUTED.

unchangeable /úncháynjəbəl/ *adj.* not changeable; immutable; invariable. □□ **unchangeability** *n.* **unchangeableness** *n.* **unchangeably** *adv.*
- see INVARIABLE 1.

unchanged /úncháynjd/ *adj.* not changed; unaltered.
- see SAME *adj.* 2.

unchanging /úncháynjing/ *adj.* not changing; remaining the same. □□ **unchangingly** *adv.* **unchangingness** *n.*
- see ABIDING.

/.../	pronunciation	● part of speech
□	phrases, idioms, and compounds	
□□	derivatives	■ synonym section
cross-references	appear in SMALL CAPITALS or *italics*	

unchaperoned /únshápərŏnd/ *adj.* without a chaperon.
■ see UNACCOMPANIED 1.

uncharacteristic /únkariktərístik/ *adj.* not characteristic.
□□ **uncharacteristically** *adv.*
■ see UNNATURAL 1; (*uncharacteristic of*) see UNLIKE *adj.* 2.

uncharged /únchaárjd/ *adj.* not charged (esp. in senses 3, 7, 8 of CHARGE *v.*).

uncharitable /únchárritəbəl/ *adj.* censorious; severe in judgment. □□ **uncharitableness** *n.* **uncharitably** *adv.*
■ see UNKIND.

uncharted /únchaártid/ *adj.* not charted, mapped, or surveyed.
■ unmapped, unknown, unexplored, undiscovered, unfamiliar, strange, virgin, trackless.

unchartered /únchaártərd/ *adj.* **1** not furnished with a charter; not formally privileged or constituted. **2** unauthorized; illegal.

unchaste /úncháyst/ *adj.* not chaste. □□ **unchastely** *adv.* **unchasteness** *n.* **unchastity** /-chástitee/ *n.*
■ impure, wanton, immoral, unvirtuous, promiscuous, loose, dissolute, immodest, indecent, unclean, obscene, licentious, libertine, debased, lecherous, lewd, lascivious. □□ **unchastity** see IMPURITY 1.

unchecked /únchékt/ *adj.* **1** not checked. **2** freely allowed; unrestrained (*unchecked violence*).
■ see UNCONTROLLED, UNINHIBITED, UNIMPEDED.

unchivalrous /únshívəlrəs/ *adj.* not chivalrous; rude. □□ **unchivalrously** *adv.*

unchosen /únchṓzən/ *adj.* not chosen.

unchristian /únkríschən/ *adj.* **1 a** contrary to Christian principles, esp. uncaring or selfish. **b** not Christian. **2** *colloq.* outrageous. □□ **unchristianly** *adv.*
■ **1 a** see UNKIND.

unchurch /únchórch/ *v.tr.* **1** excommunicate. **2** deprive (a building) of its status as a church.

uncial /únsheeəl, únshəl/ *adj.* & *n.* ● *adj.* **1** of or written in majuscule writing with rounded, unjoined letters found in manuscripts of the 4th–8th c., from which modern capitals are derived. **2** of or relating to an inch or an ounce. ● *n.* **1** an uncial letter. **2** an uncial style or manuscript. [L *uncialis* f. *uncia* inch: sense 1 in LL sense of *unciales litterae*, the orig. application of which is unclear]

unciform /únsifawrm/ *n.* = UNCINATE.

uncinate /únsinət, -nayt/ *adj.* esp. *Anat.* hooked; crooked. [L *uncinatus* f. *uncinus* hook]

uncircumcised /únsórkəmsīzd/ *adj.* **1** not circumcised. **2** spiritually impure; heathen. □□ **uncircumcision** /-sízhən/ *n.*

uncivil /únsívil/ *adj.* **1** ill-mannered; impolite. **2** not public-spirited. □□ **uncivilly** *adv.*
■ **1** see IMPOLITE.

uncivilized /únsívilīzd/ *adj.* **1** not civilized. **2** rough; uncultured.
■ **1** barbarous, savage, wild, uncultivated, barbarian, barbaric, crude, primitive, brutish. **2** unrefined, uncultured, uncouth, loutish, coarse, uneducated, untutored, unpolished, churlish, boorish, philistine, provincial, rough, rude, unlearned, ill-mannered, unmannerly, unsophisticated, inelegant, gross, gauche.

unclad /únklád/ *adj.* not clad; naked.
■ see NAKED 1.

unclaimed /únkláymd/ *adj.* not claimed.

unclasp /únklásp/ *v.tr.* **1** loosen the clasp or clasps of. **2** release the grip of (a hand, etc.).

unclassifiable /únklásifíəbəl/ *adj.* not classifiable.

unclassified /únklásifīd/ *adj.* **1** not classified. **2** (of government information) not secret.

uncle /úngkəl/ *n.* **1 a** the brother of one's father or mother. **b** an aunt's husband. **2** *colloq.* a name given by children to a male family friend. **3** *sl.* esp. *hist.* a pawnbroker. □ **Uncle Sam** *colloq.* the federal government or citizens of the US (*will fight for Uncle Sam*). **Uncle Tom** *derog.* a black man considered to be servile, cringing, etc. (from the hero of H. B. Stowe's *Uncle Tom's Cabin*, 1852). [ME f. AF *uncle*, OF *oncle* f. LL *auunculus* f. L *avunculus* maternal uncle: see AVUNCULAR]

-uncle /ungkəl/ *suffix* forming nouns, usu. diminutives (*carbuncle*). [OF *-uncle*, *-oncle* or L *-unculus*, *-la*, a special form of *-ulus* -ULE]

unclean /únkleén/ *adj.* **1** not clean. **2** unchaste. **3** unfit to be eaten; ceremonially impure. **4** *Bibl.* (of a spirit) wicked. □□ **uncleanly** *adv.* **uncleanly** /-klénlee/ *adj.* **uncleanliness** /-klénleenis/ *n.* **uncleanness** *n.* [OE *unclǽne* (as UN-¹, CLEAN)]
■ **1** see DIRTY *adj.* 1. **2** see UNCHASTE. **3** profane, impure, adulterated, not kosher. □□ **uncleanness** see IMPURITY 1.

unclear /únkleér/ *adj.* **1** not clear or easy to understand; obscure; uncertain. **2** (of a person) doubtful; uncertain (*I'm unclear as to what you mean*). □□ **unclearly** *adv.* **unclearness** *n.*
■ **1** see OBSCURE *adj.* 1, 2, 4. **2** see UNCERTAIN 1.

unclench /únklénch/ *v.* **1** *tr.* release (clenched hands, features, teeth, etc.). **2** *intr.* (of clenched hands, etc.) become relaxed or open.

unclinch /únklínch/ *v.tr.* & *intr.* release or become released from a clinch.

uncloak /únklṓk/ *v.tr.* **1** expose; reveal. **2** remove a cloak from.

unclog /únklóg/ *v.tr.* (**unclogged**, **unclogging**) unblock (a drain, pipe, etc.).

unclose /únklṓz/ *v.* **1** *tr.* & *intr.* open. **2** *tr.* reveal; disclose.

unclothe /únklṓth/ *v.tr.* **1** remove the clothes from. **2** strip of leaves or vegetation (*trees unclothed by the wind*). **3** expose; reveal. □□ **unclothed** *adj.*
■ **1** see STRIP¹ *v.* 1. □□ **unclothed** see NAKED 1.

unclouded /únklówdid/ *adj.* **1** not clouded; clear; bright. **2** untroubled (*unclouded serenity*).
■ **1** see CLEAR *adj.* 2, 3, 6c. **2** see SERENE *adj.*

uncluttered /únklútərd/ *adj.* not cluttered; austere; simple.
■ see SIMPLE *adj.* 2, NEAT¹ 1.

unco /úngkō/ *adj.*, *adv.*, & *n.* *Sc.* ● *adj.* strange; unusual; notable. ● *adv.* remarkably; very. ● *n.* (*pl.* **-os**) **1** a stranger. **2** (in *pl.*) news. [ME, var. of UNCOUTH]

uncoil /únkóyl/ *v.tr.* & *intr.* unwind.
■ see *roll out*.

uncolored /únkúlərd/ *adj.* **1** having no color. **2** not influenced; impartial. **3** not exaggerated.
■ **2** see OBJECTIVE *adj.* 2.

uncombed /únkṓmd/ *adj.* (of hair or a person) not combed.
■ see UNKEMPT 2.

uncomely /únkúmlee/ *adj.* **1** improper; unseemly. **2** ugly.

uncomfortable /únkúmftəbəl, -kúmfərtə-/ *adj.* **1** not comfortable. **2** uneasy; causing or feeling disquiet (*an uncomfortable silence*). □□ **uncomfortableness** *n.* **uncomfortably** *adv.*
■ **1** see *cramped* (CRAMP 4b), ROCKY *adj.* 1, 2, OPPRESSIVE 3. **2** see AWKWARD 3, 4.

uncommercial /únkəmórshəl/ *adj.* **1** not commercial. **2** contrary to commercial principles.

uncommitted /únkəmítid/ *adj.* **1** not committed. **2** unattached to any specific political cause or group.
■ see NEUTRAL *adj.* 1, 2, NONALIGNED.

uncommon /únkómən/ *adj.* & *adv.* ● *adj.* **1** not common; unusual; remarkable. **2** remarkably great, etc. (*an uncommon fear of spiders*). ● *adv.* *archaic* uncommonly (*he was uncommon fat*). □□ **uncommonly** *adv.* **uncommonness** /-mən-nis/ *n.*
■ *adj.* **1** see UNUSUAL. **2** see EXTREME *adj.* 1.
□□ **uncommonly** see ESPECIALLY. **uncommonness** see RARITY 1, SINGULARITY 1.

uncommunicative /únkəmyóonikətiv/ *adj.* not wanting to communicate; taciturn. □□ **uncommunicatively** *adv.* **uncommunicativeness** *n.*
■ see TACITURN. □□ **uncommunicativeness** see SILENCE *n.* 2, 3.

uncompanionable /únkəmpányənəbəl/ *adj.* unsociable.

uncompensated /únkómpənsaytid/ *adj.* not compensated.

uncompetitive /únkəmpétitiv/ *adj.* not competitive.

uncomplaining /únkəmpláyning/ *adj.* not complaining; resigned. □□ **uncomplainingly** *adv.*
■ see SUBMISSIVE.

uncompleted /únkəmpleétid/ *adj.* not completed; incomplete.
■ see INCOMPLETE.

uncomplicated /únkómplikaytid/ *adj.* not complicated; simple; straightforward.
■ see SIMPLE *adj.* 1, 2.

uncomplimentary /únkomplimentəree/ *adj.* not complimentary; insulting.
■ see DEROGATORY.

uncompounded /únkəmpówndid/ *adj.* not compounded; unmixed.

uncomprehending /únkomprihénding/ *adj.* not comprehending. □□ **uncomprehendingly** *adv.* **uncomprehension** /-hénshən/ *n.*
■ see VACANT 2, *confused* (CONFUSE 4).

uncompromising /únkómprəmizing/ *adj.* unwilling to compromise; stubborn; unyielding. □□ **uncompromisingly** *adv.* **uncompromisingness** *n.*
■ see RESOLUTE. □□ **uncompromisingly** see DOWNRIGHT *adv.*

unconcealed /únkənseéld/ *adj.* not concealed; obvious.
■ see OBVIOUS.

unconcern /únkənsə́rn/ *n.* lack of concern; indifference; apathy. □□ **unconcerned** *adj.* **unconcernedly** /-nidlee/ *adv.*
■ see INDIFFERENCE 1, 2. □□ **unconcerned** see INDIFFERENT 4.

unconcluded /únkənklo͞odid/ *adj.* not concluded.

unconditional /únkəndíshənəl/ *adj.* not subject to conditions; complete (*unconditional surrender*). □□ **unconditionality** /-nálitee/ *n.* **unconditionally** *adv.*
■ see UNQUALIFIED 3, FULL¹ *adj.* 6.

unconditioned /únkəndíshənd/ *adj.* **1** not subject to conditions or to an antecedent condition. **2** (of behavior, etc.) not determined by conditioning; natural. □ **unconditioned reflex** an instinctive response to a stimulus.

unconfined /únkənfínd/ *adj.* not confined; boundless.
■ see FREE *adj.* 3, LIMITLESS.

unconfirmed /únkənfə́rmd/ *adj.* not confirmed.
■ see UNOFFICIAL 1.

unconformable /únkənfáwrməbəl/ *adj.* **1** not conformable or conforming. **2** (of rock strata) not having the same direction of stratification. **3** *hist.* not conforming to the provisions of the Act of Uniformity. □□ **unconformableness** *n.* **unconformably** *adv.* **unconformity** *n.*

uncongenial /únkənjeényəl/ *adj.* not congenial.
■ see UNSOCIAL.

unconjecturable /únkənjékchərəbəl/ *adj.* not conjecturable.
■ see UNCERTAIN 1.

unconnected /únkənéktid/ *adj.* **1** not physically joined. **2** not connected or associated. **3** (of speech, etc.) disconnected; not joined in order or sequence (*unconnected ideas*). **4** not related by family ties. □□ **unconnectedly** *adv.* **unconnectedness** *n.*
■ **1** see LOOSE *adj.* 2. **2** see UNRELATED, EXTRANEOUS 2b. **3** see DISCONNECTED 2.

unconquerable /únkóngkərəbəl/ *adj.* not conquerable. □□ **unconquerableness** *n.* **unconquerably** *adv.*
■ see IMPREGNABLE.

unconquered /únkóngkərd/ *adj.* not conquered or defeated.

unconscionable /únkónshənəbəl/ *adj.* **1 a** having no conscience. **b** contrary to conscience. **2 a** unreasonably excessive (*an unconscionable length of time*). **b** not right or reasonable. □□ **unconscionableness** *n.* **unconscionably** *adv.* [UN-¹ + obs. *conscionable* f. *conscions* obs. var. of CONSCIENCE]
■ **1** conscienceless, unscrupulous, amoral, unprincipled, immoral, unethical, evil, criminal, unjust, wicked, arrant. **2** excessive, extortionate, egregious, extreme, unwarranted, unreasonable, outrageous, inordinate, immoderate, exorbitant, indefensible, unpardonable, inexcusable, unforgivable.

unconscious /únkónshəs/ *adj.* & *n.* ● *adj.* not conscious (*unconscious of any change; fell unconscious on the floor; an*

unconscious prejudice). ● *n.* that part of the mind which is inaccessible to the conscious mind but which affects behavior, emotions, etc. (cf. *collective unconscious*). □□ **unconsciously** *adv.* **unconsciousness** *n.*
■ *adj.* insensible, knocked out, senseless, numb, stunned, comatose, blacked out, *colloq.* out (cold), dead to the world; heedless, unheeding, unheedful, insensitive, mindless, unmindful, reflex, automatic, involuntary, mechanical, unintentional, instinctive, subliminal, unthinking, unpremeditated, subconscious, unwitting; blind, unaware, oblivious, deaf. ● *n.* see SUBCONSCIOUS *n.* □□ **unconsciously** see UNAWARES 2. **unconsciousness** see FAINT *n.*, STUPOR.

unconsecrated /únkónsikraytid/ *adj.* not consecrated.

unconsenting /únkənsénting/ *adj.* not consenting.

unconsidered /únkənsídərd/ *adj.* **1** not considered; disregarded. **2** (of a response, etc.) immediate; not premeditated.
■ **1** ignored, overlooked, disregarded. **2** see IMPULSIVE, UNTHINKING 1.

unconsolable /únkənsóləbəl/ *adj.* unable to be consoled; inconsolable. □□ **unconsolably** *adv.*
■ see INCONSOLABLE.

unconstitutional /únkonstito͞oshənəl, -tyo͞o-/ *adj.* not in accordance with the political constitution or with procedural rules. □□ **unconstitutionality** /-nálitee/ *n.* **unconstitutionally** *adv.*

unconstrained /únkənstráynd/ *adj.* not constrained or compelled. □□ **unconstrainedly** /-nidlee/ *adv.*
■ see FREE *adj.* 3, 6, NATURAL *adj.* 4. □□ **unconstrainedly** see *freely* (FREE).

unconstraint /únkənstráynt/ *n.* freedom from constraint.
■ see FREEDOM 5.

unconstricted /únkənstríktid/ *adj.* not constricted.

unconsumed /únkənso͞omd/ *adj.* not consumed.
■ leftover, left, remaining, uneaten.

unconsummated /únkónsəmaytid/ *adj.* not consummated.

uncontainable /únkəntáynəbəl/ *adj.* not containable.
■ see IRREPRESSIBLE.

uncontaminated /únkəntáminaytid/ *adj.* not contaminated.
■ see CLEAN *adj.* 1.

uncontested /únkəntéstid/ *adj.* not contested. □□ **uncontestedly** *adv.*
■ see UNDISPUTED.

uncontradicted /únkontradíktid/ *adj.* not contradicted.

uncontrollable /únkəntróləbəl/ *adj.* not controllable. □□ **uncontrollableness** *n.* **uncontrollably** *adv.*
■ see INVOLUNTARY, IRREPRESSIBLE, UNRULY.

uncontrolled /únkəntróld/ *adj.* not controlled; unrestrained; unchecked.
■ unrestrained; ungoverned, unchecked, untrammeled, undisciplined, wild, unruly, boisterous, riotous, out of hand *or* control, rampant, frenzied, frantic; (going) berserk, running amok.

uncontroversial /únkontrəvə́rshəl/ *adj.* not controversial. □□ **uncontroversially** *adv.*

uncontroverted /únkóntrəvə́rtid/ *adj.* not controverted. □□ **uncontrovertible** *adj.*

unconventional /únkənvénshənəl/ *adj.* not bound by convention or custom; unusual; unorthodox. □□ **unconventionalism** *n.* **unconventionality** /-nálitee/ *n.* **unconventionally** *adv.*
■ see UNORTHODOX.

unconverted /únkənvə́rtid/ *adj.* not converted.

unconvinced /únkənvínst/ *adj.* not convinced.
■ see DOUBTFUL 1.

unconvincing /únkənvínsing/ *adj.* not convincing. □□ **unconvincingly** *adv.*
■ see *far-fetched* , WEAK 4.

uncooked /únko͞okt/ *adj.* not cooked; raw.

/.../ **pronunciation**	● **part of speech**
□ **phrases, idioms, and compounds**	
□□ **derivatives**	■ **synonym section**
cross-references appear in SMALL CAPITALS or *italics*	

■ fresh, raw.

uncool /únkōōl/ *adj. sl.* **1** unrelaxed; unpleasant. **2** (of jazz) not cool.

uncooperative /únkō-ópərətiv, -óprətiv/ *adj.* not cooperative. □□ **uncooperatively** *adv.*
■ see *resistant* (RESIST).

uncoordinated /únkō-áwrd'naytid/ *adj.* **1** not coordinated. **2** (of a person's movements, etc.) clumsy.
■ **1** see INDISCRIMINATE 2. **2** see CLUMSY 1.

uncopiable /únkópeeəbəl/ *adj.* not able to be copied.

uncord /únkáwrd/ *v.tr.* remove the cord from.

uncordial /únkáwrjəl/ *adj.* not congenial; unfriendly.

uncork /únkáwrk/ *v.tr.* **1** draw the cork from (a bottle). **2** allow (feelings, etc.) to be vented.

uncorroborated /únkəróbəraytid/ *adj.* (esp. of evidence, etc.) not corroborated.
■ see *ill-founded.*

uncorrupted /únkərúptid/ *adj.* not corrupted.
■ see HONORABLE 1a–c, INNOCENT *adj.* 1.

uncountable /únkówntəbəl/ *adj.* **1** inestimable; immense (*uncountable wealth*). **2** *Gram.* (of a noun) that cannot form a plural or be used with the indefinite article (e.g., *happiness*). □□ **uncountability** /-bílitee/ *n.* **uncountably** *adv.*
■ **1** see IMMEASURABLE.

uncounted /únkówntid/ *adj.* **1** not counted. **2** very many; innumerable.
■ **2** see NUMBERLESS.

uncouple /únkúpəl/ *v.tr.* **1** release (wagons) from couplings. **2** release (dogs, etc.) from couples. □□ **uncoupled** *adj.*

uncourtly /únkáwrtlee/ *adj.* not courteous; ill-mannered.

uncouth /únkōōth/ *adj.* **1** (of a person, manners, appearance, etc.) lacking in ease and polish; uncultured; rough (*uncouth voices; behavior was uncouth*). **2** *archaic* not known; desolate; wild; uncivilized (*an uncouth place*). □□ **uncouthly** *adv.* **uncouthness** *n.* [OE *uncūth* unknown (as UN-¹ + *cūth* past part. of *cunnan* know, CAN¹)]
■ **1** see ROUGH *adj.* 4a.

uncovenanted /únkúvənəntid/ *adj.* **1** not bound by a covenant. **2** not promised by or based on a covenant, esp. God's covenant.

uncover /únkúvər/ *v.* **1** *tr.* **a** remove a cover or covering from. **b** make known; disclose (*uncovered the truth at last*). **2** *intr. archaic* remove one's hat, cap, etc. **3** *tr.* (as **uncovered** *adj.*) **a** not covered by a roof, clothing, etc. **b** not wearing a hat.
■ **1 a** see BARE *v.* 1. **b** see BARE *v.* 2, DISCOVER 1a, b.
3 a (*uncovered*) see BARE *adj.* 1, VULNERABLE 1.

uncreate /únkree-áyt/ *v.tr. literary* annihilate.

uncreated /únkree-áytid/ *adj.* existing without having been created; not created. [UN-¹ + obs. *create* f. L *creatus* past part. of *creare*: see CREATE]

uncreative /únkree-áytiv/ *adj.* not creative.

uncritical /únkrítikəl/ *adj.* **1** not critical; complacently accepting. **2** not in accordance with the principles of criticism. □□ **uncritically** *adv.*
■ **1** see INDISCRIMINATE 1, PASSIVE 2.

uncropped /únkrópt/ *adj.* not cropped.

uncross /únkráws, -krós/ *v.tr.* **1** remove (the limbs, knives, etc.) from a crossed position. **2** (as **uncrossed** *adj.*) **a** (of a letter or symbol, etc.) not crossed (*I recognize his writing by the uncrossed t's*). **b** not thwarted or challenged. **c** not wearing a cross.

uncrown /únkrówn/ *v.tr.* **1** deprive (a monarch, etc.) of a crown. **2** deprive (a person) of a position. **3** (as **uncrowned** *adj.*) **a** not crowned. **b** having the status but not the name of (*the uncrowned king of boxing*).

uncrushable /únkrúshəbəl/ *adj.* not crushable.

uncrushed /únkrúsht/ *adj.* not crushed.

unction /úngkshən/ *n.* **1 a** the act of anointing with oil, etc., as a religious rite. **b** the oil, etc., so used. **2 a** soothing words or thought. **b** excessive or insincere flattery. **3 a** the act of anointing for medical purposes. **b** an ointment so used. **4 a** a fervent or sympathetic quality in words or tone caused by or causing deep emotion. **b** a pretense of this. [ME f. L *unctio* f. *ung(u)ere unct-* anoint]

unctuous /úngkchōōəs/ *adj.* **1** (of behavior, speech, etc.) unpleasantly flattering; oily. **2** (esp. of minerals) having a greasy or soapy feel; oily. □□ **unctuously** *adv.* **unctuousness** *n.* [ME f. med.L *unctuosus* f. L *unctus* anointing (as UNCTION)]
■ **1** see OILY 3. **2** see OILY 1, 2. □□ **unctuousness** see *servility* (SERVILE).

unculled /únkúld/ *adj.* not culled.

uncultivated /únkúltivaytid/ *adj.* (esp. of land) not cultivated.
■ see WILD *adj.* 3.

uncultured /únkúlchərd/ *adj.* **1** not cultured; unrefined. **2** (of soil or plants) not cultivated.
■ **1** see UNREFINED.

uncurb /únkárb/ *v.tr.* remove a curb or curbs from. □□ **uncurbed** *adj.*
■ □□ **uncurbed** see UNINHIBITED, LAVISH 3.

uncured /únkyōōrd/ *adj.* **1** not cured. **2** (of pork, etc.) not salted or smoked.

uncurl /únkárl/ *v.intr.* & *tr.* relax from a curled position; untwist.
■ see *roll out.*

uncurtailed /únkərtayld/ *adj.* not curtailed.

uncurtained /únkárt'nd/ *adj.* not curtained.

uncut /únkút/ *adj.* **1** not cut. **2** (of a book) with the pages not cut open or with untrimmed margins. **3** (of a book, film, etc.) complete; uncensored. **4** (of a stone, esp. a diamond) not shaped by cutting. **5** (of fabric) having its pile loops intact (*uncut moquette*).
■ **1** see INTACT 1. **3** see ENTIRE *adj.* 1.

undamaged /úndámijd/ *adj.* not damaged; intact.
■ see INTACT 2.

undated /úndáytid/ *adj.* not provided or marked with a date.

undaunted /úndáwntid/ *adj.* not daunted. □□ **undauntedly** *adv.* **undauntedness** *n.*
■ see INDOMITABLE 2.

undecagon /úndékəgon/ *n.* = HENDECAGON. [L *undecim* eleven, after *decagon*]

undeceive /úndiseév/ *v.tr.* (often foll. by *of*) free (a person) from a misconception, deception, or error.

undecided /úndisídid/ *adj.* **1** not settled or certain (*the question is undecided*). **2** hesitating; irresolute (*undecided about their relative merits*). □□ **undecidedly** *adv.*
■ **1** see UNRESOLVED 2. **2** see IRRESOLUTE 1.

undecipherable /úndisífərəbəl/ *adj.* not decipherable.
■ see ILLEGIBLE, INCOMPREHENSIBLE.

undeclared /úndiklaird/ *adj.* not declared.
■ see TACIT, *sneaking* (SNEAK *v.* 4a).

undefeated /úndifeétid/ *adj.* not defeated.
■ see TRIUMPHANT 1, INVINCIBLE.

undefended /úndiféndid/ *adj.* (esp. of a lawsuit) not defended.

undefiled /úndifíld/ *adj.* not defiled; pure.
■ see PURE 3, 4.

undefined /úndifínd/ *adj.* **1** not defined. **2** not clearly marked; vague; indefinite. □□ **undefinable** *adj.* **undefinably** *adv.*
■ see INDEFINITE 1.

undelivered /úndilívərd/ *adj.* **1** not delivered or handed over. **2** not set free or released. **3 a** (of a pregnant woman) not yet having given birth. **b** (of a child) not yet born.

undemanding /úndimánding/ *adj.* not demanding; easily satisfied. □□ **undemandingness** *n.*
■ see EASY *adj.* 1, 3.

undemocratic /úndeməkrátik/ *adj.* not democratic. □□ **undemocratically** *adv.*
■ see TOTALITARIAN *adj.*

undemonstrated /úndémənstráytid/ *adj.* not demonstrated.

undemonstrative /úndimónstrətiv/ *adj.* not expressing feelings, etc., outwardly; reserved. □□ **undemonstratively** *adv.* **undemonstrativeness** *n.*
■ see RESERVED.

undeniable /úndiníəbəl/ *adj.* **1** unable to be denied or disputed; certain. **2** excellent (*was of undeniable character*). □□ **undeniableness** *n.* **undeniably** *adv.*

■ **1** see CERTAIN *adj.* 1b. □□ **undeniably** see *undoubtedly* (UNDOUBTED).

undenied /úndiníd/ *adj.* not denied.

undependable /úndipéndəbəl/ *adj.* not to be depended upon; unreliable.

■ see UNRELIABLE.

under /úndər/ *prep., adv., & adj.* ● *prep.* **1 a** in or to a position lower than; below; beneath (*fell under the table; under the left eye*). **b** within; on the inside of (a surface, etc.) (*wore a vest under his jacket*). **2 a** inferior to; less than (*a captain is under a major; is under 18*). **b** at or for a lower cost than (*was under $20*). **3 a** subject or liable to; controlled or bound by (*lives under oppression; under pain of death; born under Saturn; the country prospered under him*). **b** undergoing (*is under repair*). **c** classified or subsumed in (*that book goes under biology; goes under many names*). **4** at the foot of or sheltered by (*hid under the wall; under the cliff*). **5** planted with (a crop). **6** powered by (sail, steam, etc.). **7** following (another player in a card game). **8** *archaic* attested by (esp. *under one's hand and seal* = signature). ● *adv.* **1** in or to a lower position or condition (*kept him under*). **2** *colloq.* in or into a state of unconsciousness (*put her under for the operation*). ● *adj.* lower (*the under jaw*). □ **under one's arm** see ARM[1]. **under arms** see ARM[2]. **under one's belt** see BELT. **under one's breath** see BREATH. **under canvas** see CANVAS. **under a cloud** see CLOUD. **under control** see CONTROL. **under the counter** see COUNTER[1]. **under cover** see COVER *n.* 4. **under fire** see FIRE. **under hatches** see HATCH[1]. **under a person's nose** see NOSE. **under the rose** see ROSE[1]. **under separate cover** in another envelope. **under the sun** anywhere in the world. **under way** in motion; in progress. **under the weather** see WEATHER. □□ **undermost** *adj.* [OE f. Gmc]

■ *prep.* **1 a** beneath, below, underneath. **b** inside, within, covered by, beneath, underneath. **2 a** inferior to, second to, secondary to, subservient to, below, beneath, underneath, junior to, subordinate to, answerable to; less than. **b** less than, lower than. **3 a** subject to, liable to, at the beck and call of, at the mercy of, under the control of, directed *or* supervised *or* controlled *or* bound by; under the aegis *or* protection *or* eye *or* guardianship *or* care of. **c** included in *or* under, comprised in *or* under, subsumed under. **4** at the foot of, under the lee of, sheltered by. ● *adv.* **1** below, underneath, beneath, down, out of sight; underwater. ● *adj.* lower, inferior, *archaic* nether. □ **under way** proceeding, progressing, on the move, in motion, moving, advancing, going, begun, started, in progress, in the pipeline, operating, functioning, at work, in work, *colloq.* in the works.

under- /úndər/ *prefix* in senses of UNDER: **1** below; beneath (*undercarriage; underground*). **2** lower in status; subordinate (*undersecretary*). **3** insufficiently; incompletely (*undercook; underdeveloped*). [OE (as UNDER)]

underachieve /úndərəcheév/ *v.intr.* do less well than might be expected (esp. scholastically). □□ **underachievement** *n.* **underachiever** *n.*

underact /úndərákt/ *v.* **1** *tr.* act (a part, etc.) with insufficient force. **2** *intr.* act a part in this way.

underage /úndəráyj/ *adj.* **1** not old enough, esp. not yet of adult status. **2** involving underage persons (*underage smoking and drinking*).

underarm /úndəraarm/ *adj., adv., & n.* ● *adj. & adv.* **1** *Sports* with the arm below shoulder level. **2** under the arm. **3** in the armpit. ● *n.* the armpit.

underbelly /úndərbélee/ *n.* (*pl.* **-ies**) the underside of an animal, vehicle, etc., esp. as an area vulnerable to attack.

underbid *v. & n.* ● *v.tr.* /úndərbíd/ (**-bidding**; *past* and *past part.* **-bid**) **1** make a lower bid than (a person). **2** (also *absol.*) *Bridge*, etc., bid less on (one's hand) than its strength warrants. ● *n.* /úndərbid/ **1** such a bid. **2** the act or an instance of underbidding.

underbidder /úndərbídər/ *n.* **1** the person who makes the bid next below the highest. **2** *Bridge*, etc., a player who underbids.

underbody /úndərbódee/ *n.* (*pl.* **-ies**) the underside of the body of an animal, vehicle, etc.

underbred /úndərbréd/ *adj.* **1** ill-bred; vulgar. **2** not of pure breeding.

underbrush /úndərbrúsh/ *n.* undergrowth in a forest.

undercarriage /úndərkárij/ *n.* **1** a wheeled structure beneath an aircraft, usu. retracted when not in use, to receive the impact on landing and support the aircraft on the ground, etc. **2** the supporting frame of a vehicle.

undercharge /úndərcháarj/ *v.tr.* **1** charge too little for (a thing) or to (a person). **2** give less than the proper charge to (a gun, an electric battery, etc.).

■ **1** see UNDERCUT *v.* 1.

underclass /úndərklas/ *n.* a subordinate social class.

underclay /úndərklay/ *n.* a clay bed under a coal seam.

undercliff /úndərklif/ *n.* a terrace or lower cliff formed by a landslide.

underclothes /úndərklōz, -klōthz/ *n.pl.* clothes worn under others, esp. next to the skin.

■ underclothing, underwear, undergarments, lingerie, skivvies, esp. *Brit.* underlinen, *colloq.* underthings, undies, *Brit. colloq.* smalls, *joc.* unmentionables.

underclothing /úndərklōthing/ *n.* underclothes collectively.

undercoat /úndərkōt/ *n. & v.* ● *n.* **1 a** a preliminary layer of paint under the finishing coat. **b** the paint used for this. **2** an animal's under layer of hair or down. **3** a coat worn under another. ● *v.tr.* seal the underpart of (esp. a motor vehicle against rust, etc.) with an undercoat. □□ **undercoating** *n.*

undercover /úndərkúvər/ *adj.* (usu. *attrib.*) **1** surreptitious. **2** engaged in spying, esp. by working with or among those to be observed (*undercover agent*).

■ secret, private, clandestine, surreptitious, covert, confidential, spying, underground, stealthy.

undercroft /úndərkrawft, -kroft/ *n.* a crypt. [ME f. UNDER- + *croft* crypt f. MDu. *crofte* cave f. med.L *crupta* for L *crypta*: see CRYPT]

undercurrent /úndərkɔ́rənt, -kur-/ *n.* **1** a current below the surface. **2** an underlying, often contrary, feeling, activity, or influence (*an undercurrent of protest*).

■ **1** undertow, crosscurrent, riptide, rip (current), *Naut.* underset, esp. *Brit.* underflow. **2** undertone, subcurrent, trend, tendency, overtone, tenor, suggestion, trace, hint, murmur, buzz, implication, connotation, sense, feeling, aura, tinge, flavor, atmosphere, ambience; vibrations, *colloq.* vibes.

undercut *v. & n.* ● *v.tr.* /úndərkút/ (**-cutting**; *past* and *past part.* **-cut**) **1** sell or work at a lower price or lower wages than. **2** *Golf* strike (a ball) so as to make it rise high. **3 a** cut away the part below or under (a thing). **b** cut away material to show (a carved design, etc.) in relief. **4** render unstable or less firm; undermine. ● *n.* /úndərkut/ **1** a notch cut in a tree trunk to guide its fall when felled. **2** any space formed by the removal or absence of material from the lower part of something. **3** *Brit.* the underside of a sirloin.

■ *v.* **1** underprice, undercharge, sell cheaply *or* at a loss, undersell. **3** undermine, excavate, hollow out, cut out *or* away, gouge out. **4** undermine, destabilize, weaken, debilitate, sabotage, subvert, impair, disable, damage.

underdeveloped /úndərdivéləpt/ *adj.* **1** not fully developed; immature. **2** (of a country, etc.) below its potential economic level. **3** *Photog.* not developed sufficiently to give a normal image. □□ **underdevelopment** *n.*

■ **1** see IMMATURE 1, 3.

underdog /úndərdawg, -dog/ *n.* **1** a dog, or usu. a person, losing a fight. **2** a person whose loss in a contest, etc., is expected. **3** a person who is in a state of inferiority or subjection.

■ loser, scapegoat, victim; little fellow *or* guy, *sl.* fall guy.

/. . ./ **pronunciation**	● **part of speech**
□ **phrases, idioms, and compounds**	
□□ **derivatives**	■ **synonym section**
cross-references appear in SMALL CAPITALS or *italics*	

underdone /úndərdún/ adj. **1** not thoroughly done. **2** (of food) lightly or insufficiently cooked.

underdress /úndərdrés/ v.tr. & intr. dress with too little formality or too lightly.

underemphasis /úndərémfəsis/ n. (pl. **-emphases** /-seez/) an insufficient degree of emphasis. □□ **underemphasize** /-síz/ v.tr.

underemployed /úndərimplóyd/ adj. **1** not fully employed. **2** having employment inadequate to one's abilities, education, etc. □□ **underemployment** n.

underestimate v. & n. • v.tr. /úndəréstimayt/ form too low an estimate of. • n. /úndəréstimət/ an estimate that is too low. □□ **underestimation** /-máyshən/ n.

■ v. undervalue, underrate, discount, misjudge, miscalculate, minimize, depreciate, belittle, trivialize, not do justice to, fail to appreciate, set (too) little store by, think (too) little of, *literary* misprize.

underexpose /úndərikspóz/ v.tr. Photog. expose (film) for too short a time or with insufficient light. □□ **underexposure** /-pózhər/ n.

underfed /úndərféd/ adj. insufficiently fed.

■ see THIN adj. 4.

underfloor /úndərflawr/ attrib.adj. Brit. situated or operating beneath the floor (underfloor heating).

underflow /úndərflō/ n. esp. Brit. an undercurrent.

■ see UNDERCURRENT 1.

underfoot /úndərfŏŏt/ adv. **1** under one's feet. **2** on the ground. **3** in a state of subjection. **4** so as to obstruct or inconvenience.

undergarment /úndərgaarmənt/ n. a piece of underclothing.

undergird /úndərgérd/ v.tr. **1** make secure underneath. **2** strengthen; support.

underglaze /úndərglayz/ adj. & n. • adj. **1** (of painting on porcelain, etc.) done before the glaze is applied. **2** (of colors) used in such painting. • n. underglaze painting.

undergo /úndərgṓ/ v.tr. (3rd sing. present **-goes**; past **-went**; past part. **-gone**) be subjected to; suffer; endure. [OE *undergān* (as UNDER-, GO¹)]

■ suffer, bear, endure, experience, live or go through, be subjected to, subject oneself to, sustain, submit to, weather, put up with, stand, withstand.

undergrad /úndərgrád/ n. colloq. = UNDERGRADUATE. [abbr.]

undergraduate /úndərgrájŏŏət/ n. a student at a college or university who has not yet taken a degree.

underground adv., adj., n., & v. • adv. /úndərgrównd/ **1** beneath the surface of the ground. **2** in or into secrecy or hiding. • adj. /úndərgrownd/ **1** situated underground. **2** secret, hidden, esp. working secretly to subvert a ruling power. **3** unconventional; experimental (underground press). • n. /úndərgrownd/ **1** a secret group or activity, esp. aiming to subvert the established order. **2** Brit. subway system. • v.tr. /úndərgrownd/ lay (cables) below ground level. □ **Underground Railroad** US hist. a covert system of escape through which abolitionists helped fugitive slaves reach safe destinations, before 1863.

■ adv. **1** see BENEATH adv. • adj. **1** subterranean, buried, belowground, sunken, covered. **2** secret, clandestine, concealed, hidden, covert, undercover, surreptitious, stealthy, private. **3** alternative, radical, experimental, avant-garde, nonconformist, unconventional, revolutionary. • n. **1** resistance, partisans, freedom fighters, Maquis, insurgents, insurrectionists, guerrillas, irregulars, extremists, revolutionaries; fifth columnists, fifth column, saboteurs, subversives. **2** subway, metro, underground railroad, colloq. tube.

undergrowth /úndərgrṓth/ n. a dense growth of shrubs, etc., esp. under large trees.

underhand adj. & adv. • adj. /úndərhand/ **1** secret; clandestine; not aboveboard. **2** deceptive; crafty. **3** Sports underarm. • adv. /úndərhánd/ in an underhand manner. [OE (as UNDER-, HAND)]

■ **1, 2** see FURTIVE 1, 2, DISHONEST.

underhanded /úndərhándid/ adj. & adv. = UNDERHAND.

underhung /úndərhúng/ adj. **1** (of the lower jaw) projecting beyond the upper jaw. **2** having an underhung jaw.

underlay¹ v. & n. • v.tr. /úndərláy/ (past and past part. **-laid**) lay something under (a thing) to support or raise it. • n. /úndərlay/ a thing laid under another, esp. material laid under a carpet or mattress as protection or support. [OE *underlecgan* (as UNDER-, LAY¹)]

underlay² past of UNDERLIE.

underlayment /úndərláymənt/ n. an underlay.

underlease n. /úndərlees/ v.tr. /úndərleés/ = SUBLEASE.

underlet /úndərlét/ v.tr. (**-letting**; past and past part. **-let**) **1** sublet. **2** let at less than the true value.

underlie /úndərlí/ v.tr. (**-lying**; past **-lay**; past part. **-lain**) **1** (also absol.) lie or be situated under (a stratum, etc.). **2** (also absol.) (esp. as **underlying** adj.) (of a principle, reason, etc.) be the basis of (a doctrine, law, conduct, etc.). **3** exist beneath the superficial aspect of. [OE *underlicgan* (as UNDER-, LIE¹)]

■ **2** (**underlying**) see BASIC adj. 2.

underline v. & n. • v.tr. /úndərlín/ **1** draw a line under (a word, etc.) to give emphasis or draw attention or indicate italic or other special type. **2** emphasize; stress. • n. /úndərlin/ **1** a line drawn under a word, etc. **2** a caption below an illustration.

■ **1** underscore. **2** see EMPHASIZE.

underlinen /úndərlinin/ n. esp. Brit. underclothes, esp. of linen.

■ see UNDERCLOTHES.

underling /úndərling/ n. usu. derog. a subordinate.

■ see SUBORDINATE n.

underlying pres. part. of UNDERLIE.

undermanned /úndərmánd/ adj. having too few people as crew or staff.

■ short-staffed, shorthanded, understaffed.

undermentioned /úndərménshənd/ adj. Brit. mentioned at a later place in a book, etc.

undermine /úndərmín/ v.tr. **1** injure (a person, reputation, influence, etc.) by secret or insidious means. **2** weaken, injure, or wear out (health, etc.) imperceptibly or insidiously. **3** wear away the base or foundation of (rivers undermine their banks). **4** make a mine or excavation under. □□ **underminer** n. **underminingly** adv. [ME f. UNDER- + MINE²]

■ **1, 2** sap, drain, disable, weaken, debilitate, emasculate, enfeeble, undercut, wear away, erode, threaten, sabotage, subvert, damage, injure, hurt, harm, impair, ruin, dash, destroy, wreck, spoil, sl. queer. **3** wear away, wash away, erode. **4** undercut, excavate, mine or dig or tunnel or burrow under, cut out or away, hollow or gouge out.

underneath /úndərnéeth/ prep., adv., n., & adj. • prep. **1** at or to a lower place than, below. **2** on the inside of, within. • adv. **1** at or to a lower place. **2** inside. • n. the lower surface or part. • adj. lower. [OE *underneothan* (as UNDER + neothan: cf. BENEATH)]

■ prep. **1** see BELOW prep. 1, 2. • adv. **1** see BELOW adv. 2a.

undernourished /úndərnórisht, -núr-/ adj. insufficiently nourished. □□ **undernourishment** n.

■ see THIN adj. 4.

underpaid past and past part. of UNDERPAY.

underpants /úndərpants/ n.pl. an undergarment, esp. men's, covering the lower part of the body and part of the legs.

■ see PANTS 1.

underpart /úndərpaart/ n. **1** a lower part, esp. of an animal. **2** a subordinate part in a play, etc.

underpass /úndərpas/ n. **1** a road, etc., passing under another. **2** a crossing of this form.

■ tunnel, esp. Brit. subway.

underpay /úndərpáy/ v.tr. (past and past part. **-paid**) pay too little to (a person) or for (a thing). □□ **underpayment** n.

underpin /úndərpín/ v.tr. (**-pinned**, **-pinning**) **1** support from below with masonry, etc. **2** support; strengthen.

■ **2** see SUSTAIN 2.

underpinning /úndərpíning/ n. **1** a physical or metaphorical foundation. **2** the action or process of supporting from below.

underplant /úndərplánt/ v.tr. (usu. foll. by with) plant or cultivate the ground about (a tall plant) with smaller ones.

underplay /úndərpláy/ v. **1** tr. play down the importance of. **2** intr. & tr. Theatr. **a** perform with deliberate restraint. **b** underact.
■ **1** see TRIVIALIZE.

underplot /úndərplot/ n. a subordinate plot in a play, etc.

underpopulated /úndərpópyəláytid/ adj. having an insufficient or very small population.

underprice /úndərprís/ v.tr. price lower than what is usual or appropriate.
■ see UNDERCUT v. 1.

underprivileged /úndərprívilijd, -prívlijd/ adj. **1** less privileged than others. **2** not enjoying the normal standard of living or rights in a society.
■ see deprived (DEPRIVE 2).

underproduction /úndərprədúkshən/ n. production of less than is usual or required.

underproof /úndərprōof/ adj. containing less alcohol than proof spirit does.

underprop /úndərpróp/ v.tr. (**-propped, -propping**) **1** support with a prop. **2** support; sustain.

underquote /úndərkwōt/ v.tr. **1** quote a lower price than (a person). **2** quote a lower price than others for (goods, etc.).

underrate /úndəráyt/ v.tr. have too low an opinion of.
■ see UNDERESTIMATE v.

underscore v. & n. ● v.tr. /úndərskáwr/ = UNDERLINE v.
● n. /úndərskawr/ = UNDERLINE n. 1.

undersea /úndərsee/ adj. below the sea or the surface of the sea; submarine.
■ see UNDERWATER adj.

undersecretary /úndərsékrəteree/ n. (pl. **-ies**) a subordinate official, esp. a junior minister or senior civil servant.

undersell /úndərsél/ v.tr. (past and past part. **-sold**) **1** sell at a lower price than (another seller). **2** sell at less than the true value.
■ see UNDERCUT v. 1.

underset v. & n. ● v.tr. /úndərsét/ (**-setting**; past and past part. **-set**) place something under (a thing). ● n. /úndərset/ Naut. an undercurrent.
■ n. see UNDERCURRENT 1.

undersexed /úndərsékst/ adj. having unusually weak sexual desires.

undersheriff /úndərsherif/ n. a deputy sheriff.

undershirt /úndərshərt/ n. an undergarment worn under a shirt.

undershoot v. & n. ● v.tr. /úndərshōot/ (past and past part. **-shot**) **1** (of an aircraft) land short of (a runway, etc.). **2** shoot short of or below. ● n. /úndərshōot/ the act or an instance of undershooting.

undershorts /úndərsháwrts/ n. short underpants; trunks.
■ see PANTS 2.

undershot /úndərshót/ adj. **1** (of a waterwheel) turned by water flowing under it. **2** = UNDERHUNG.

undershrub /úndərshrub/ n. = SUBSHRUB.

underside /úndərsíd/ n. the lower or under side or surface.
■ see REVERSE n. 5.

undersigned /úndərsínd/ adj. whose signature is appended (we, the undersigned, wish to state . . .).

undersized /úndərsízd/ adj. of less than the usual size.
■ undersize, little, short, small, petite, tiny, diminutive, puny, elfin, bantam, slight; stunted, underdeveloped, runty, dwarf, dwarfish, dwarfed, pygmy, squat; underweight, undeveloped; midget, baby.

underskirt /úndərskərt/ n. a skirt worn under another; a petticoat.

underslung /úndərslúng/ adj. **1** supported from above. **2** (of a vehicle chassis) hanging lower than the axles.

undersold past and past part. of UNDERSELL.

undersow /úndərsó/ v.tr. (past part. **-sown**) **1** sow (a later-growing crop) on land already seeded with another crop. **2** (foll. by with) sow land already seeded with (a crop) with a later-growing crop.

underspend /úndərspénd/ v. (past and past part. **-spent**) **1** tr. spend less than (a specified amount). **2** intr. & refl. spend too little.

understaffed /úndərstáft/ adj. having too few staff.
■ short-staffed, undermanned, shorthanded.

understand /úndərstánd/ v. (past and past part. **-stood** /-stŏod/) **1** tr. perceive the meaning of (words, a person, a language, etc.) (does not understand what you say; understood you perfectly; cannot understand French). **2** tr. perceive the significance or explanation or cause of (do not understand why he came; could not understand what the noise was about; do not understand the point of his remark). **3** tr. be sympathetically aware of the character or nature of, know how to deal with (quite understand your difficulty; cannot understand him at all; could never understand algebra). **4** tr. **a** (often foll. by that + clause) infer esp. from information received; take as implied; take for granted (I understand that it begins at noon; I understand him to be a distant relation; am I to understand that you refuse?). **b** (absol.) believe or assume from knowledge or inference (he is coming tomorrow, I understand). **5** tr. supply (a word) mentally (the verb may be either expressed or understood). **6** tr. accept (terms, conditions, etc.) as part of an agreement. **7** intr. have understanding (in general or in particular). □ **understand each other 1** know each other's views or feelings. **2** be in agreement or collusion. □□ **understandable** adj. **understandably** adv. **understander** n. [OE understandan (as UNDER-, STAND)]
■ **1, 2** grasp, comprehend, see, perceive, discern, make out, make sense of, get the drift or hang or gist of, follow, appreciate, interpret, take cognizance of, recognize, be aware or conscious of, be conversant with, know, realize, conceive of, apprehend, penetrate, fathom, colloq. get, catch on to, get there, tumble to, cotton on to, get a handle on, Brit. twig, sl. dig. **3** sympathize or empathize with, be in sympathy with, show compassion for, commiserate with; accept, tolerate, allow, forgive, condone. **4** hear, gather, get wind, take it, be told or informed or advised, have found out or learned, hear tell, be led to believe, infer, deduce, interpret, read, construe, surmise, assume, presume, suppose, believe, guess, conclude. **6** accept, agree (to), assent to; covenant. **7** be aware, colloq. get it, catch on, cotton on, twig. □□ **understandable** see INTELLIGIBLE.

understanding /úndərstánding/ n. & adj. ● n. **1 a** the ability to understand or think; intelligence. **b** the power of apprehension; the power of abstract thought. **2** an individual's perception or judgment of a situation, etc. **3** an agreement; a thing agreed upon, esp. informally (had an understanding with the rival company; consented only on this understanding). **4** harmony in opinion or feeling (disturbed the good understanding between them). **5** sympathetic awareness or tolerance. ● adj. **1** having understanding or insight or good judgment. **2** sympathetic to others' feelings. □□ **understandingly** adv. [OE (as UNDERSTAND)]
■ n. **1** intellect, intelligence, mind, brain, brainpower, sense, reason, reasoning power, wisdom, brains, acumen, penetration, insight, discernment, perception, perceptiveness, percipience, good sense, intuition, enlightenment, sagacity, sageness, literary sapience, sl. savvy; comprehension, apprehension, awareness, appreciation, cognizance, idea(s), knowledge; conception, grasp, command, mastery. **2** reading, interpretation, opinion, judgment, estimation, notion, view, perception, apperception, apprehension. **3** agreement, contract, arrangement, bargain, covenant, concession, pact, compact, accord, treaty, concordat, entente, alliance, truce, armistice, reconciliation, settlement. **4** harmony, agreement, sympathy, compatibility, rapport, entente, concord, accord,

/. . ./ **pronunciation**	● **part of speech**
□ **phrases, idioms, and compounds**	
□□ **derivatives**	■ **synonym section**
cross-references appear in SMALL CAPITALS or italics	

consensus, congeniality, closeness, affinity, unity.
5 sympathy, empathy, rapport, feeling, fellow feeling,
compassion, tolerance, sensitivity, sensitiveness.
● *adj.* **1** see JUDICIOUS. **2** see SYMPATHETIC *adj.* 1.

understate /úndərstáyt/ *v.tr.* (often as **understated** *adj.*) **1**
express in greatly or unduly restrained terms. **2** represent as
being less than it actually is. □□ **understatement** /ún-
dərstáytmənt/ *n.* **understater** *n.*
■ (**understated**) **1** subtle, restrained, low-key, simple,
basic, unembellished, unadorned.

understeer *n. & v.* ● *n.* /úndərsteer/ a tendency of a motor
vehicle to turn less sharply than was intended. ● *v.intr.*
/úndərsteér/ have such a tendency.

understood *past* and *past part.* of UNDERSTAND.

understory /úndərstáwree/ *n.* (*pl.* -**ies**) **1** a layer of vegetation beneath the main canopy of a forest. **2** the plants forming this.

understudy /úndərstúdee/ *n. & v.* esp. *Theatr.* ● *n.* (*pl.* -**ies**)
a person who studies another's role or duties in order to act
at short notice in the absence of the other. ● *v.tr.* (-**ies,**
-**ied**) **1** study (a role, etc.) as an understudy. **2** act as an
understudy to (a person).
■ *n.* second, substitute, stand-in, standby, backup,
double, reserve, alternate, pinch hitter, *colloq.* sub.
● *v.* **2** substitute for, stand in for, back up, double
for, second, replace.

undersubscribed /úndərsəbskríbd/ *adj.* without sufficient
subscribers, participants, etc.

undersurface /úndərsúrfis/ *n.* esp. *Brit.* = UNDERSIDE.

undertake /úndərtáyk/ *v.tr.* (*past* -**took**; *past part.* -**taken**)
1 bind oneself to perform; make oneself responsible for; engage in; enter upon (work, an enterprise, a responsibility).
2 (usu. foll. by to + infin.) accept an obligation; promise. **3**
guarantee; affirm (*I will undertake that he has not heard a
word*).
■ **1** assume, take on, take upon oneself, accept, take *or*
assume *or* bear the responsibility for, enter upon,
begin, start, set about, embark on, engage in, tackle,
try, attempt. **2** promise, covenant, agree, consent,
contract, pledge, vow, swear, warrant, guarantee,
bargain, commit oneself. **3** see SWEAR *v.* 1a, 2.

undertaker /úndərtaykər/ *n.* **1** a person whose business is to
make arrangements for funerals. **2** (also /-táykər/) a person
who undertakes to do something. **3** *hist.* an influential person in 17th-century England who undertook to procure particular legislation, esp. to obtain supplies from the House of
Commons if the king would grant some concession.
■ **1** funeral director, mortician.

undertaking /úndərtáyking/ *n.* **1** work, etc., undertaken, an
enterprise (*a serious undertaking*). **2** a pledge or promise. **3**
/úndərtayking/ the management of funerals as a profession.
■ **1** enterprise, affair, business, project, task, operation,
effort, endeavor, venture, mission, work, job, feat.
2 promise, pledge, commitment, assurance,
contract, agreement, vow, guarantee, warranty.

undertenant /úndərtenənt/ *n.* a subtenant. □□ **underten-
ancy** *n.* (*pl.* -**ies**).

underthings /úndərthingz/ *n.pl. colloq.* underclothes.
■ see UNDERCLOTHES.

undertint /úndərtint/ *n.* a subdued tint.

undertone /úndərtōn/ *n.* **1** a subdued tone of sound or color.
2 an underlying quality. **3** an undercurrent of feeling.
■ **1** see MURMUR *n.* 1, TINT *n.* 2. **2, 3** see UNDERCURRENT
2.

undertook *past* of UNDERTAKE.

undertow /úndərtō/ *n.* a current below the surface of the sea
moving in the opposite direction to the surface current.
■ see UNDERCURRENT 1.

undertrick /úndərtrik/ *n. Bridge* a trick by which the declarer
falls short of his or her contract.

undervalue /úndərvályōō/ *v.tr.* (-**values**, -**valued**, -**valuing**) **1** value insufficiently. **2** underestimate. □□ **underval-
uation** *n.*
■ **2** see UNDERESTIMATE *v.*

undervest /úndərvest/ *n. Brit.* an undershirt.

underwater /úndərwáwtər, -wótər/ *adj. & adv.* ● *adj.* situated or done under water. ● *adv.* in and covered by water.
■ *adj.* submarine; see also SUNKEN 2. ● *adv.* undersea,
submerged, inundated, flooded, immersed, sunken.

underway /úndərwáy/ *adj.* occurring while in progress or in
motion (*the ship's underway food service was excellent*).

underwear /úndərwair/ *n.* underclothes.
■ see UNDERCLOTHES.

underweight *adj. & n.* ● *adj.* /úndərwáyt/ weighing less than
is normal or desirable. ● *n.* /úndərwayt/ insufficient weight.
■ *adj.* see LIGHT² *adj.* 2b, UNDERSIZED.

underwent *past* of UNDERGO.

underwhelm /úndərhwelm, -wélm/ *v.tr. joc.* fail to impress.
[after OVERWHELM]

underwing /úndərwing/ *n.* a wing placed under or partly covered by another.

underwood /úndərwood/ *n.* undergrowth.

underwork /úndərwórk/ *v.* **1** *tr.* impose too little work on. **2**
intr. do too little work.

underworld /úndərwərld/ *n.* **1** the part of society comprising
those who live by organized crime and immorality. **2** the
mythical abode of the dead under the earth. **3** the antipodes.
■ **1** organized crime, syndicate, Mafia, Cosa Nostra,
criminals, criminal element, *colloq.* mob, gangland.
2 nether regions *or* world, lower regions *or* world,
abode of the dead, infernal regions, Hades, hell.

underwrite /úndər-rít/ *v.* (*past* -**wrote**; *past part.* -**written**)
1 a *tr.* sign, and accept liability under (an insurance policy,
esp. on shipping, etc.). **b** *tr.* accept (liability) in this way. **c**
intr. practice (marine) insurance. **2** *tr.* undertake to finance
or support. **3** *tr.* engage to buy all the stock in (a company,
etc.) not bought by the public. **4** *tr.* write below (*the under-
written names*). □□ **underwriter** /ún-/ *n.*
■ **1 a, b** subscribe to, endorse, sign, countersign, consent
to, agree to, confirm, accede to, sanction, ratify,
approve, validate, *colloq.* OK, okay. **2** back (up),
finance, support, invest in, subsidize, sponsor, uphold,
approve, insure, guarantee.

undescended /úndiséndid/ *adj. Med.* (of a testicle) remaining in the abdomen instead of descending normally into the
scrotum.

undeserved /úndizárvd/ *adj.* not deserved (as reward or
punishment). □□ **undeservedly** /-vidlee/ *adv.*
■ see UNWARRANTED 2.

undeserving /úndizárving/ *adj.* not deserving. □□ **undeserv-
ingly** *adv.*
■ see UNWORTHY 1.

undesigned /úndizínd/ *adj.* unintentional. □□ **undesignedly**
/-nidlee/ *adv.*

undesirable /úndizírəbəl/ *adj. & n.* ● *adj.* not desirable; objectionable; unpleasant. ● *n.* an undesirable person. □□ **un-
desirability** /-bílitee/ *n.* **undesirableness** *n.* **undesirably**
adv.
■ *adj.* unwanted, objectionable, offensive, unacceptable,
obnoxious, unsavory, unwelcome, disliked, distasteful,
repugnant, unfit, unbecoming, unsuitable, unpleasant.
● *n.* persona non grata, pariah, outcast, exile, reject,
leper.

undesired /úndizírd/ *adj.* not desired.
■ see UNWELCOME.

undesirous /úndizírəs/ *adj.* not desirous.

undetectable /úndiléktəbəl/ *adj.* not detectable. □□ **unde-
tectability** /-bílitee/ *n.* **undetectably** *adv.*
■ see IMPERCEPTIBLE 1.

undetected /úndiléktid/ *adj.* not detected.

undetermined /únditárminid/ *adj.* = UNDECIDED.

undeterred /únditérd/ *adj.* not deterred.
■ see INDOMITABLE 2, UNABASHED.

undeveloped /úndivélapt/ *adj.* not developed.
■ embryonic, premature, immature, rudimentary,
seminal, primitive, crude, incipient, inchoate,
potential, latent.

undeviating /úndeeveeayting/ *adj.* not deviating; steady;
constant. □□ **undeviatingly** *adv.*

■ see STEADY *adj.* 2, DIRECT *adj.* 1. □□ **undeviatingly** see DIRECTLY *adv.* 3.

undiagnosed /úndíəgnōst, -nōzd/ *adj.* not diagnosed.

undid *past* of UNDO.

undies /úndeez/ *n.pl. colloq.* (esp. women's) underclothes. [abbr.]

■ see UNDERCLOTHES.

undifferentiated /úndifərénsheeaytid/ *adj.* not differentiated; amorphous.

■ see INDISTINGUISHABLE.

undigested /úndijéstid, úndī-/ *adj.* **1** not digested. **2** (esp. of information, facts, etc.) not properly arranged or considered.

undignified /úndígnifīd/ *adj.* lacking dignity.

■ see UNSEEMLY 2.

undiluted /úndilốōtid/ *adj.* not diluted.

■ pure, neat, straight, unmixed, uncut, unblended, unadulterated, unwatered, concentrated, unalloyed; see also UNMITIGATED.

undiminished /úndimínisht/ *adj.* not diminished or lessened.

■ see UNMITIGATED 1.

undine /undeén, ún-/ *n.* a female water spirit. [mod.L *undina* (word invented by Paracelsus) f. L *unda* wave]

undiplomatic /úndipləmátik/ *adj.* tactless. □□ **undiplomatically** *adv.*

■ see TACTLESS.

undischarged /úndischaárjd/ *adj.* (esp. of a bankrupt or a debt) not discharged.

undiscipline /úndísiplin/ *n.* lack of discipline.

undisciplined /úndísiplind/ *adj.* lacking discipline; not disciplined.

■ untrained, unschooled, unprepared, untutored, uneducated, untaught, unpracticed, uncontrolled, disobedient, naughty, bad, willful, wayward, unrestrained, erratic, unpredictable, disorderly, unruly, wild.

undisclosed /úndisklốzd/ *adj.* not revealed or made known.

■ see PRIVATE *adj.* 3, 5.

undiscoverable /úndiskúvərəbəl/ *adj.* that cannot be discovered.

undiscovered /úndiskúvərd/ *adj.* not discovered.

■ see UNCHARTED, UNKNOWN *adj.*

undiscriminating /úndiskríminayting/ *adj.* not showing good judgment.

■ see INDISCRIMINATE 1, BLIND *adj.* 3.

undisguised /úndisgízd/ *adj.* not disguised. □□ **undisguisedly** /-zidlee/ *adv.*

■ open, out-and-out, unmistakable, overt, unconcealed, barefaced, bald, unreserved, unrestrained, unfeigned, unpretended, obvious, evident, patent, manifest, clear, explicit, transparent, sincere, heartfelt, unalloyed, unmitigated.

undismayed /úndismáyd/ *adj.* not dismayed.

■ see UNABASHED.

undisputed /úndispyốōtid/ *adj.* not disputed or called in question.

■ unquestioned, unquestionable, beyond question, accepted, acknowledged, admitted, indisputable, indubitable, undoubted, certain, sure, unmistakable, definite, explicit, clear, (self-)evident, obvious, uncontested, unchallenged, incontestable, irrefutable, incontrovertible, undeniable, conclusive.

undissolved /úndizólvd/ *adj.* not dissolved.

undistinguishable /úndistínggwishəbəl/ *adj.* (often foll. by *from*) indistinguishable.

undistinguished /úndistínggwisht/ *adj.* not distinguished; mediocre.

■ ordinary, commonplace, common, everyday, run-of-the-mill, pedestrian, unexceptional, plain, homespun, simple, prosaic, unremarkable, nothing special *or* unusual *or* extraordinary; mediocre, middling, indifferent, so-so, unexciting, unimpressive, unpretentious, homely, *colloq.* no great shakes, no big

deal, nothing to write home about, esp. *Brit.* common or garden.

undistributed /úndistríbyətid/ *adj.* not distributed. □ **undistributed middle** *Logic* a fallacy resulting from the failure of the middle term of a syllogism to refer to all the members of a class.

undisturbed /úndistárbd/ *adj.* not disturbed or interfered with.

■ untouched; see also CALM *adj.* 1, 2.

undivided /úndivídid/ *adj.* not divided or shared; whole, entire (*gave him my undivided attention*).

■ whole, entire, unbroken, uncut, intact, unseparated, unsplit; undiverted, devoted, wholehearted, concentrated, full, complete, exclusive, undistracted.

undo /úndốō/ *v.tr.* (*3rd sing. present* **-does**; *past* **-did**; *past part.* **-done**) **1 a** unfasten or untie (a coat, button, package, etc.). **b** unfasten the clothing of (a person). **2** annul; cancel (*cannot undo the past*). **3** ruin the prospects, reputation, or morals of. [OE *undōn* (as UN-², DO¹)]

■ **1** loosen, loose, open, unfasten, unhook, unlace, unzip, unbutton, unbuckle, unclasp, unclip, untie, unknot, ungird, unpin; unlock, unbolt, unhasp, unhinge, unlash, unlatch, unlink, unpeg; unwrap, uncover, unbind, unstrap; unpick, unravel; uncouple, detach, disconnect, disengage, release, free, unhitch, untether, unscrew, unplug, unrivet. **2** cancel, annul, rescind, nullify, void, declare null and void, reverse, invalidate. **3** see RUIN *v.* 1.

undock /úndók/ *v.tr.* **1** (also *absol.*) separate (a spacecraft) from another in space. **2** take (a ship) out of a dock.

undocumented /úndókyəmentid/ *adj.* **1** not having the appropriate document. **2** not proved by or recorded in documents.

■ **2** unrecorded; see also UNOFFICIAL 1.

undoing /úndốōing/ *n.* **1** ruin or a cause of ruin. **2** the process of reversing what has been done. **3** the action of opening or unfastening.

■ **1** ruin, ruination, destruction, devastation, defeat, downfall, overthrow, fall, collapse, descent, debasement, degradation, abasement, mortification, humiliation, shame, disgrace; curse, misfortune, affliction, trouble, blight, *poet.* bane.

undomesticated /úndəméstikaytid/ *adj.* not domesticated.

■ see UNTAMED.

undone /úndún/ *adj.* **1** not done; incomplete (*left the job undone*). **2** not fastened (*left the buttons undone*). **3** *archaic* ruined.

■ **1** unaccomplished, uncompleted, incomplete, unfinished, omitted, neglected, left (out), skipped, missed, passed over, forgotten, unattended to. **2** open, loose, loosened, untied, unfastened, detached, unhooked, unlaced, unzipped, unsnapped, unbuttoned, unbuckled, unclipped, unclasped, unpinned, unstuck. **3** ruined, lost, wrecked, crushed, destroyed, devastated, shattered, brought to ruin, defeated, prostrated, overcome.

undoubtable /úndówtəbəl/ *adj.* that cannot be doubted; indubitable.

undoubted /úndówtid/ *adj.* certain; not questioned; not regarded as doubtful. □□ **undoubtedly** *adv.*

■ see UNDISPUTED, CERTAIN *adj.* 1b. □□ **undoubtedly** indubitably, without (a) doubt, indisputably, unquestionably, beyond (a *or* the shadow of a) doubt, doubtless(ly), certainly, definitely, surely, assuredly, unmistakably, explicitly, clearly, obviously, of course, incontestably, irrefutably, incontrovertibly, undeniably.

undrained /úndráynd/ *adj.* not drained.

/ . . . / **pronunciation**   ● **part of speech**

□ **phrases, idioms, and compounds**

□□ **derivatives**   ■ **synonym section**

cross-references appear in SMALL CAPITALS or *italics*

undraped /úndráypt/ *adj.* **1** not covered with drapery. **2** naked.

undreamed /úndre͞emd, úndrémt/ *adj.* (also **undreamt** /úndrémt/) (often foll. by *of*) not dreamed or thought of or imagined.

■ (*undreamed of*) see UNFORESEEN, INCONCEIVABLE 1.

undress /úndrés/ *v. & n.* ● *v.* **1** *intr.* take off one's clothes. **2** *tr.* take the clothes off (a person). ● *n.* **1** ordinary dress as opposed to full dress or uniform. **2** casual or informal dress.

■ *v.* see STRIP¹ *v.* 1, 2.

undressed /úndrést/ *adj.* **1** not or no longer dressed; partly or wholly naked. **2** (of leather, etc.) not treated. **3** (of food) **a** not having a dressing (*undressed salad*). **b** prepared simply, with no sauce, stuffing, etc. (*undressed turkey*).

■ **1** see NAKED 1.

undrinkable /úndríngkəbəl/ *adj.* unfit for drinking.

undue /úndo͞o, -dyo͞o/ *adj.* **1** excessive; disproportionate. **2** not suitable. **3** not owed. □ **undue influence** *Law* influence by which a person is induced to act otherwise than by his or her own free will, or without adequate attention to the consequences. □□ **unduly** *adv.*

■ **1** see EXCESSIVE. **2** see UNWARRANTED 2. □□ **unduly** disproportionately, excessively, unnecessarily, inordinately, unreasonably, irrationally, unjustifiably, improperly, inappropriately, overly; immoderately, lavishly, profusely, extravagantly.

undulant /únjələnt, -dyə-, -də-/ *adj.* moving like waves; fluctuating. □ **undulant fever** brucellosis in humans. [L *undulare* (as UNDULATE)]

undulate *v. & adj.* ● *v.* /únjəlayt, -dyə-, -də-/ *intr. & tr.* have or cause to have a wavy motion or look. ● *adj.* /únjələt, -dyə-, -də-/ wavy; going alternately up and down or in and out (*leaves with undulate margins*). □□ **undulately** *adv.* [LL *undulatus* f. L *unda* wave]

■ *v.* see WAVE *v.* 2.

undulation /únjəláyshən, -dyə-, -də-/ *n.* **1** a wavy motion or form; a gentle rise and fall. **2** each wave of this. **3** a set of wavy lines.

undulatory /únjələtawree, -dyə-, -də-/ *adj.* **1** undulating; wavy. **2** of or due to undulation.

undutiful /úndo͞otifo͞ol, -dyo͞o-/ *adj.* not dutiful. □□ **undutifully** *adv.* **undutifulness** *n.*

■ see DISOBEDIENT, REMISS.

undyed /úndíd/ *adj.* not dyed.

undying /úndí-ing/ *adj.* **1** immortal. **2** never-ending (*undying love*). □□ **undyingly** *adv.*

■ see IMMORTAL *adj.* 1a. □□ **undyingly** see ALWAYS 4.

unearned /únárnd/ *adj.* not earned. □ **unearned income** income from interest payments, etc., as opposed to salary, wages, or fees.

unearth /únárth/ *v.tr.* **1 a** discover by searching or in the course of digging or rummaging. **b** dig out of the earth. **2** drive (a fox, etc.) from its earth.

■ **1** dig up, disinter, exhume; excavate, dredge up, mine, quarry, find, pull *or* root out, come across, discover, turn up, expose, uncover.

unearthly /únárthlee/ *adj.* **1** supernatural; mysterious. **2** *colloq.* absurdly early or inconvenient (*an unearthly hour*). **3** not earthly. □□ **unearthliness** *n.*

■ **1** supernatural, unnatural, preternatural, psychic(al), extrasensory, supersensory, out-of-body, incorporeal, metaphysical; weird, bizarre, macabre, nightmarish, uncanny, eerie, strange, mysterious, mystical, ghostly, spectral, unreal, eldritch, *colloq.* spooky, creepy. **2** strange, odd, peculiar, unusual, abnormal, absurd, out of the ordinary, extraordinary, outrageous; unheard-of, ridiculous, unreasonable, *colloq.* ungodly, *sl.* god-awful. **3** unworldly, otherworldly, extramundane, ultramundane, supramundane, extraterrestrial, sublime, celestial, heavenly, astral, divine, esp. *poet.* supernal.

unease /únée'z/ *n.* lack of ease; discomfort; distress.

■ see MISGIVING.

uneasy /únée'zee/ *adj.* (**uneasier, uneasiest**) **1** disturbed or uncomfortable in mind or body (*passed an uneasy night*). **2** disturbing (*had an uneasy suspicion*). □□ **uneasily** *adv.* **uneasiness** *n.*

■ **1** see ANXIOUS 1, RESTLESS 1, 2. **2** see *disturbing* (DISTURB).

uneatable /únée'təbəl/ *adj.* not able to be eaten, esp. because of its condition (cf. INEDIBLE).

■ see UNPALATABLE.

uneaten /únée't'n/ *adj.* not eaten; left undevoured.

■ see LEFTOVER *adj.*

uneconomic /únekənómik, -eekə-/ *adj.* not economic; incapable of being profitably operated, etc. □□ **uneconomically** *adv.*

■ see UNPROFITABLE, INEFFICIENT 1.

uneconomical /únekənómikəl, -eekə-/ *adj.* not economical; wasteful.

unedifying /únédifī-ing/ *adj.* not edifying, esp. uninstructive or degrading. □□ **unedifyingly** *adv.*

unedited /únéditid/ *adj.* not edited.

uneducated /únéjəkaytid/ *adj.* not educated. □□ **uneducable** /-kəbəl/ *adj.*

■ unschooled, untaught, unlearned, uncultivated, unread, uncultured, unaccomplished, illiterate, unlettered, ignorant, unenlightened.

unelectable /úníléktəbəl/ *adj.* (of a candidate, party, etc.) associated with or holding views likely to bring defeat at an election.

unembellished /únimbélisht/ *adj.* not embellished or decorated.

■ see PLAIN¹ *adj.* 3.

unemotional /únimṓshənəl/ *adj.* not emotional; lacking emotion. □□ **unemotionally** *adv.*

■ see COLD *adj.* 4, COOL *adj.* 3b.

unemphatic /únimfátik/ *adj.* not emphatic. □□ **unemphatically** *adv.*

unemployable /únimplóyəbəl/ *adj. & n.* ● *adj.* unfitted for paid employment. ● *n.* an unemployable person. □□ **unemployability** /-bíilitee/ *n.*

unemployed /únimplóyd/ *adj.* **1** not having paid employment; out of work. **2** not in use.

■ **1** out of work, jobless, unwaged, idle, laid off, out of a job, workless, unoccupied, inactive, *Brit.* redundant, between engagements *or* assignments, at leisure, on *or* collecting unemployment, *Brit. euphem.* resting, esp. *Brit. colloq.* on the dole. **2** unused, not in use, idle, inactive, unoccupied.

unemployment /únimplóymənt/ *n.* **1** the state of being unemployed. **2** the condition or extent of this in a country or region, etc. (*the Northeast has higher unemployment*). □ **unemployment benefit** a payment made by the government or a labor union to an unemployed person.

unenclosed /úninklṓzd/ *adj.* not enclosed.

■ see OPEN *adj.* 1–4, 13, 20.

unencumbered /úninkúmbərd/ *adj.* **1** (of an estate) not having any liabilities (e.g., a mortgage) on it. **2** having no encumbrance; free.

■ **2** see FREE *adj.* 3a.

unending /únénding/ *adj.* having or apparently having no end. □□ **unendingly** *adv.* **unendingness** *n.*

■ see ENDLESS 1. □□ **unendingly** see NONSTOP *adv.*, ALWAYS 4.

unendowed /únindówd/ *adj.* not endowed.

unendurable /únindo͞orəbəl, -dyo͞or-/ *adj.* that cannot be endured. □□ **unendurably** *adv.*

■ see UNBEARABLE.

unengaged /úningáyjd/ *adj.* not engaged; uncommitted.

un-English /úníngglish/ *adj.* **1** not characteristic of the English. **2** not English.

unenjoyable /úninjóyəbəl/ *adj.* not enjoyable.

unenlightened /úninlít'nd/ *adj.* not enlightened.

■ see IGNORANT 1a.

unenterprising /únéntərprizing/ *adj.* not enterprising.

■ see SHIFTLESS.

unenthusiastic /únintho͞ozeeástik/ *adj.* not enthusiastic. □□ **unenthusiastically** *adv.*

■ lukewarm, halfhearted, cool, cold, uninterested, indifferent, blasé, unresponsive, apathetic, lackadaisical, listless, phlegmatic, nonchalant, tepid, unexcited, unimpressed.

unenviable /únénveeəbəl/ *adj.* not enviable. □□ **unenviably** *adv.*

■ uncoveted, undesirable, unwished for, unattractive.

unenvied /únénveed/ *adj.* not envied.

unequal /úneékwəl/ *adj.* **1** (often foll. by *to*) not equal. **2** of varying quality. **3** lacking equal advantage to both sides (*an unequal bargain*). □□ **unequally** *adv.*

■ **1** see UNLIKE *adj.* 3, LOPSIDED; (*unequal to*) see UNLIKE *adj.* 1, INCAPABLE 1a. **3** see UNREASONABLE 1.

unequaled /úneékwəld/ *adj.* (also esp. *Brit.* **unequalled**) superior to all others.

■ see *peerless* (PEER²).

unequalize /úneékwəlīz/ *v.tr.* make unequal.

unequipped /únikwípt/ *adj.* not equipped.

■ see UNQUALIFIED 1, 2.

unequivocal /únikwívəkəl/ *adj.* not ambiguous; plain; unmistakable. □□ **unequivocally** *adv.* **unequivocalness** *n.*

■ see PLAIN¹ *adj.* 1, 2, CATEGORICAL. □□ **unequivocally** see *expressly* (EXPRESS).

unerring /únéring/ *adj.* not erring, failing, or missing the mark; true; certain. □□ **unerringly** *adv.* **unerringness** *n.*

■ see CERTAIN *adj.* 3, TRUE *adj.* 6. □□ **unerringly** see EXACTLY 1.

unescapable /úniskáypəbəl/ *adj.* inescapable.

UNESCO /yōōnéskō/ *abbr.* United Nations Educational, Scientific, and Cultural Organization.

unescorted /úniskáwrtid/ *adj.* not escorted.

■ see UNACCOMPANIED 1.

unessential /únisénshəl/ *adj. & n.* ● *adj.* **1** not essential (cf. INESSENTIAL). **2** not of the first importance. ● *n.* an unessential part or thing.

■ *adj.* see NONESSENTIAL.

unestablished /únistáblisht/ *adj.* not established.

unethical /únéthikəl/ *adj.* not ethical, esp. unscrupulous in business or professional conduct. □□ **unethically** *adv.*

■ see UNSCRUPULOUS, UNPROFESSIONAL 1.

unevangelical /úneevanjélikəl/ *adj.* not evangelical.

uneven /úneévən/ *adj.* **1** not level or smooth. **2** not uniform or equable. **3** (of a contest) unequal. □□ **unevenly** *adv.* **unevenness** *n.* [OE *unefen* (as UN-¹, EVEN¹)]

■ **1, 2** see IRREGULAR *adj.* 1, 2. **3** see DISPROPORTIONATE. □□ **unevenness** see *irregularity* (IRREGULAR), DISPROPORTION.

uneventful /únivéntfŏŏl/ *adj.* not eventful. □□ **uneventfully** *adv.* **uneventfulness** *n.*

■ see HUMDRUM *adj.*, SMOOTH *adj.* 6.

unexamined /únigzámind/ *adj.* not examined.

unexampled /únigzámpəld/ *adj.* having no precedent or parallel.

unexceptionable /úniksépshənəbəl/ *adj.* with which no fault can be found; entirely satisfactory. □□ **unexceptionableness** *n.* **unexceptionably** *adv.*

■ see FAULTLESS.

unexceptional /úniksépshənəl/ *adj.* not out of the ordinary; usual; normal. □□ **unexceptionally** *adv.*

unexcitable /úniksítəbəl/ *adj.* not easily excited. □□ **unexcitability** *n.*

■ see SERENE.

unexciting /úniksíting/ *adj.* not exciting; dull.

■ see TAME *adj.* 2.

unexecuted /únéksikyŏŏtid/ *adj.* not carried out or put into effect.

unexhausted /únigzáwstid/ *adj.* **1** not used up, expended, or brought to an end. **2** not emptied.

unexpected /únikspéktid/ *adj.* not expected; surprising. □□ **unexpectedly** *adv.* **unexpectedness** *n.*

■ see UNFORESEEN. □□ **unexpectedly** see *suddenly* (SUDDEN).

unexpired /únikspírd/ *adj.* that has not yet expired.

unexplainable /únikspláynəbəl/ *adj.* inexplicable. □□ **unexplainably** *adv.*

■ see INEXPLICABLE.

unexplained /únikspláynd/ *adj.* not explained.

■ see UNACCOUNTABLE 1, 2.

unexploited /úniksplóytid/ *adj.* (of resources, etc.) not exploited.

unexplored /únikspláwrd/ *adj.* not explored.

■ see UNCHARTED, UNKNOWN *adj.*

unexposed /únikspŏzd/ *adj.* not exposed.

■ see SECURE *adj.* 1, 2.

unexpressed /úniksprést/ *adj.* not expressed or made known (*unexpressed fears*).

■ see TACIT.

unexpurgated /únékspərgaytid/ *adj.* (esp. of a text, etc.) not expurgated; complete.

■ see UNABRIDGED.

unfaceable /únfáysəbəl/ *adj.* that cannot be faced or confronted.

unfading /únfáyding/ *adj.* that never fades. □□ **unfadingly** *adv.*

■ see IMMORTAL *adj.* 2.

unfailing /únfáyling/ *adj.* **1** not failing. **2** not running short. **3** constant. **4** reliable. □□ **unfailingly** *adv.* **unfailingness** *n.*

■ **1** see CERTAIN *adj.* 3. **2** see INEXHAUSTIBLE 1. **3** see CONSTANT *adj.* 3. **4** see RELIABLE. □□ **unfailingly** see *consistently* (CONSISTENT).

unfair /únfáir/ *adj.* **1** not equitable or honest (*obtained by unfair means*). **2** not impartial or according to the rules (*unfair play*). □□ **unfairly** *adv.* **unfairness** *n.* [OE *unfæger* (as UN-¹, FAIR¹)]

■ **1** see DISHONEST. **2** see IRREGULAR *adj.* 3, *prejudiced* (PREJUDICE). □□ **unfairly** see ILL *adv.* 1. **unfairness** see INJUSTICE 1.

unfaithful /únfáythfŏŏl/ *adj.* **1** not faithful, esp. adulterous. **2** not loyal. **3** treacherous. □□ **unfaithfully** *adv.* **unfaithfulness** *n.*

■ see UNTRUE 2. □□ **unfaithfulness** see INFIDELITY 1, PERFIDY.

unfaltering /únfáwltəring/ *adj.* not faltering; steady; resolute. □□ **unfalteringly** *adv.*

■ see STEADY *adj.* 6, RESOLUTE. □□ **unfalteringly** see SURELY 3.

unfamiliar /únfəmílyər/ *adj.* not familiar. □□ **unfamiliarity** /-leeáritee/ *n.*

■ new, novel, unknown, unheard-of, unconventional, unusual, different, uncommon, alien, foreign, strange, odd, peculiar, bizarre, exotic; (*unfamiliar with*) unacquainted with, unaccustomed to, inexperienced in *or* with, unused to, unconversant with, uninformed about, ignorant of, unpracticed in, unskilled in *or* at, uninitiated in, unversed in. □□ **unfamiliarity** see IGNORANCE.

unfashionable /únfáshənəbəl/ *adj.* not fashionable. □□ **unfashionableness** *n.* **unfashionably** *adv.*

■ see *old-fashioned*.

unfashioned /únfáshənd/ *adj.* not made into its proper shape.

unfasten /únfásən/ *v.* **1** *tr. & intr.* make or become loose. **2** *tr.* open the fastening(s) of. **3** *tr.* detach.

■ see LOOSEN, UNDO 1.

unfastened /únfásənd/ *adj.* **1** that has not been fastened. **2** that has been loosened, opened, or detached.

■ see UNDONE 2.

unfathered /únfáathərd/ *adj.* **1** having no known or acknowledged father; illegitimate. **2** of unknown origin (*unfathered rumors*).

unfatherly /únfáathərlee/ *adj.* not befitting a father. □□ **unfatherliness** *n.*

unfathomable /únfáthəməbəl/ *adj.* incapable of being fathomed. □□ **unfathomableness** *n.* **unfathomably** *adv.*

/.../ **pronunciation**   ● **part of speech**
□ **phrases, idioms, and compounds**
□□ **derivatives**   ■ **synonym section**
cross-references appear in SMALL CAPITALS or *italics*

■ see INCOMPREHENSIBLE, IMMEASURABLE.

unfathomed /únfáthəmd/ *adj.* **1** of unascertained depth. **2** not fully explored or known.

■ **1** see BOTTOMLESS 1.

unfavorable /únfáyvərəbəl/ *adj.* not favorable; adverse; hostile. □□ **unfavorableness** *n.* **unfavorably** *adv.*

■ see BAD *adj.* 2. □□ **unfavorably** see ILL *adv.* 3.

unfavorite /únfáyvərit, -fáyvrit/ *adj. colloq.* least favorite; most disliked.

unfazed /únfáyzd/ *adj. colloq.* untroubled; not disconcerted.

unfeasible /únféezibəl/ *adj.* not feasible; impractical. □□ **unfeasibility** /-bílitee/ *n.* **unfeasibly** *adv.*

■ see IMPOSSIBLE 1.

unfed /únféd/ *adj.* not fed.

unfeeling /únféeling/ *adj.* **1** unsympathetic; harsh; not caring about others' feelings. **2** lacking sensation or sensitivity. □□ **unfeelingly** *adv.* **unfeelingness** *n.* [OE *unfelende* (as UN-[1], FEELING)]

■ **1** see UNSYMPATHETIC. **2** see DEAD *adj.* 3.

unfeigned /únfáynd/ *adj.* genuine; sincere. □□ **unfeignedly** /-fáynidlee/ *adv.*

■ see SINCERE.

unfelt /únfélt/ *adj.* not felt.

unfeminine /únféminin/ *adj.* not in accordance with, or appropriate to, female character. □□ **unfemininity** /-nínitee/ *n.*

unfenced /únfénst/ *adj.* **1** not provided with fences. **2** unprotected.

unfermented /únfərméntid/ *adj.* not fermented.

unfertilized /únfért'lizd/ *adj.* not fertilized.

unfetter /únfétər/ *v.tr.* release from fetters.

unfettered /únfétərd/ *adj.* unrestrained; unrestricted.

■ see FREE *adj.* 3.

unfilial /únfíleeəl/ *adj.* not befitting a son or daughter. □□ **unfilially** *adv.*

unfilled /únfíld/ *adj.* not filled.

■ see EMPTY *adj.* 1, VACANT 1, OPEN *adj.* 12b.

unfiltered /únfíltərd/ *adj.* **1** not filtered. **2** (of a cigarette) not provided with a filter.

unfinished /únfínisht/ *adj.* not finished; incomplete.

■ see INCOMPLETE.

unfit /únfít/ *adj.* & *v.* ● *adj.* (often foll. by *for*, or *to* + infin.) not fit. ● *v.tr.* (**unfitted**, **unfitting**) (usu. foll. by *for*) make unsuitable. □□ **unfitly** *adv.* **unfitness** *n.*

■ *adj.* out of condition *or* shape; see also INELIGIBLE, UNBECOMING 2; (*unfit for*) see UNWORTHY 1.

unfitted /únfítid/ *adj.* **1** not fit. **2** not fitted or suited. **3** not provided with fittings.

unfitting /únfíting/ *adj.* not fitting or suitable; unbecoming. □□ **unfittingly** *adv.*

■ see UNBECOMING 2.

unfix /únfíks/ *v.tr.* **1** release or loosen from a fixed state. **2** detach.

unfixed /únfíkst/ *adj.* not fixed.

■ see FLUID *adj.* 2.

unflagging /únfláging/ *adj.* tireless; persistent. □□ **unflaggingly** *adv.*

■ see TIRELESS.

unflappable /únflápəbəl/ *adj. colloq.* imperturbable; remaining calm in a crisis. □□ **unflappability** /-bílitee/ *n.* **unflappably** *adv.*

■ see COOL *adj.* 3a. □□ **unflappability** see SERENITY.

unflattering /únflátəring/ *adj.* not flattering. □□ **unflatteringly** *adv.*

■ uncomplimentary, insulting, unfavorable, depreciatory, disparaging, derogatory, slighting, pejorative; harsh, unsympathetic; realistic, stark, candid, *colloq.* warts and all.

unflavored /únfláyvərd/ *adj.* not flavored.

unfledged /únfléjd/ *adj.* **1** (of a person) inexperienced. **2** (of a bird) not yet fledged.

■ **1** inexperienced, immature, green, callow, raw, new, young, uninitiated. **2** undeveloped, immature, young.

unfleshed /únflésht/ *adj.* **1** not covered with flesh. **2** stripped of flesh.

unflinching /únflínching/ *adj.* not flinching. □□ **unflinchingly** *adv.*

■ see STAUNCH[1] 1. □□ **unflinchingly** see *intently* (INTENT).

unfocused /únfṓkəst/ *adj.* (also esp. *Brit.* **unfocussed**) not focused.

unfold /únfṓld/ *v.* **1** *tr.* open the fold or folds of; spread out. **2** *tr.* reveal (thoughts, etc.). **3** *intr.* become opened out. **4** *intr.* develop. □□ **unfoldment** *n.* [OE *unfealdan* (as UN-[2], FOLD[1])]

■ **1, 3** open (out *or* up), spread (out), unfurl, stretch out, expand, extend, uncoil, unwind, straighten out. **2** see BARE *v.* 2. **4** develop, evolve, happen, take place, occur, be divulged, be disclosed *or* revealed.

unforced /únfáwrst/ *adj.* **1** not produced by effort; easy; natural. **2** not compelled or constrained. □□ **unforcedly** /-fáwrsidlee/ *adv.*

■ **1** see SPONTANEOUS 4. **2** see OPTIONAL.

unfordable /únfáwrdəbəl/ *adj.* that cannot be forded.

unforeseeable /únfawrseéəbəl/ *adj.* not foreseeable.

■ see CHANCE *adj.*, UNCERTAIN 1.

unforeseen /únfawrseén/ *adj.* not foreseen.

■ unexpected, surprising, unanticipated, unpredicted, unlooked-for, unsought, unhoped for, undreamed of, unthought of, startling, surprise, chance, accidental, fortuitous.

unforetold /únfawrtṓld/ *adj.* not foretold; unpredicted.

unforgettable /únfərgétəbəl/ *adj.* that cannot be forgotten; memorable; wonderful (*an unforgettable experience*). □□ **unforgettably** *adv.*

■ see MEMORABLE.

unforgivable /únfərgívəbəl/ *adj.* that cannot be forgiven. □□ **unforgivably** *adv.*

■ see INEXCUSABLE, UNCONSCIONABLE 2.

unforgiven /únfərgívən/ *adj.* not forgiven.

unforgiving /únfərgíving/ *adj.* not forgiving. □□ **unforgivingly** *adv.* **unforgivingness** *n.*

■ see IMPLACABLE.

unforgotten /únfərgót'n/ *adj.* not forgotten.

unformed /únfáwrmd/ *adj.* **1** not formed. **2** shapeless. **3** not developed.

■ **1** see FLUID *adj.* 2. **2** see SHAPELESS. **3** see IMMATURE 1.

unformulated /únfáwrmyəlaytid/ *adj.* not formulated.

unforthcoming /únfawrthkúming/ *adj.* not forthcoming.

■ see *tight-lipped*.

unfortified /únfáwrtifid/ *adj.* not fortified.

unfortunate /únfáwrchənət/ *adj.* & *n.* ● *adj.* **1** having bad fortune; unlucky. **2** unhappy. **3** regrettable. **4** disastrous. ● *n.* an unfortunate person.

■ *adj.* **1** unlucky, luckless, hapless; cursed, out of luck, unblessed, poor, doomed, ill-starred, ill-fated, *archaic* star-crossed, *colloq.* jinxed, down on one's luck. **2** miserable, wretched, woebegone, pathetic, dismal, unhappy, forlorn, pitiable, despondent, disconsolate, depressed, dejected. **3** deplorable, lamentable, regrettable, distressing, upsetting, disturbing. **4** catastrophic, disastrous, calamitous, tragic, grievous, ruinous, terrible, awful, dreadful, horrible, dire; inauspicious, untoward, unhappy. ● *n.* see WRETCH 1.

unfortunately /únfáwrchənətlee/ *adv.* **1** (qualifying a whole sentence) it is unfortunate that. **2** in an unfortunate manner.

■ **1** see *sadly* (SAD).

unfounded /únfówndid/ *adj.* having no foundation (*unfounded hopes*; *unfounded rumor*). □□ **unfoundedly** *adv.* **unfoundedness** *n.*

■ baseless, groundless, unwarranted, unjustified, unsupported, unsupportable, unsound, unjustifiable, unattested, unproven, unproved.

unframed /únfráymd/ *adj.* (esp. of a picture) not framed.

unfreeze /únfréez/ *v.* (*past* **unfroze**; *past part.* **unfrozen**) **1** *tr.* cause to thaw. **2** *intr.* thaw. **3** *tr.* remove restrictions from; make (assets, credits, etc.) realizable.

unfrequented /únfreékwentid, -frikwén-/ *adj.* not frequented.

■ see ISOLATED 1.

unfriended /únfréndid/ *adj. literary* without friends.

■ see SOLITARY *adj.* 1.

unfriendly /únfréndlee/ *adj.* (**unfriendlier, unfriendliest**) not friendly. □□ **unfriendliness** *n.*

■ see UNSOCIAL. □□ **unfriendliness** see CHILL *n.* 4, HOSTILITY 1.

unfrock /únfrók/ *v.tr.* = DEFROCK.

unfroze *past* of UNFREEZE.

unfrozen *past part.* of UNFREEZE.

unfruitful /únfróotfŏol/ *adj.* **1** not producing good results; unprofitable. **2** not producing fruit or crops. □□ **unfruitfully** *adv.* **unfruitfulness** *n.*

■ **1** see UNPROFITABLE.

unfulfilled /únfŏolfíld/ *adj.* not fulfilled. □□ **unfulfillable** *adj.*

■ see *dissatisfied* (DISSATISFY).

unfunded /únfúndid/ *adj.* (of a debt) not funded.

unfunny /únfúnee/ *adj.* (**unfunnier, unfunniest**) not amusing (though meant to be). □□ **unfunnily** *adv.* **unfunniness** *n.*

unfurl /únfərl/ *v.* **1** *tr.* spread out (a sail, umbrella, etc.). **2** *intr.* become spread out.

■ **1** see SPREAD *v.* 1a. **2** see *roll out.*

unfurnished /únfərnisht/ *adj.* **1** (usu. foll. by *with*) not supplied. **2** without furniture.

ungainly /úngáynlee/ *adj.* (of a person, animal, or movement) awkward; clumsy. □□ **ungainliness** *n.* [UN-¹ + obs. *gainly* graceful ult. f. ON *gegn* straight]

■ see AWKWARD 2.

ungallant /úngálənt/ *adj.* not gallant. □□ **ungallantly** *adv.*

ungenerous /únjénərəs/ *adj.* not generous; mean. □□ **ungenerously** *adv.* **ungenerousness** *n.*

■ see MEAN² 1.

ungenial /únjéenyəl, -jéeneeəl/ *adj.* not genial.

ungentle /únjént'l/ *adj.* not gentle. □□ **ungentleness** *n.* **ungently** *adv.*

ungentlemanly /únjéntəlmənlee/ *adj.* not gentlemanly. □□ **ungentlemanliness** *n.*

■ see RUDE 1.

ungifted /úngíftid/ *adj.* not gifted or talented.

ungird /úngərd/ *v.tr.* **1** release the girdle, belt, or girth of. **2** release or take off by undoing a belt or girth.

■ see UNDO 1.

unglazed /únglláyzd/ *adj.* not glazed.

ungloved /únglúvd/ *adj.* not wearing a glove or gloves.

ungodly /úngódlee/ *adj.* **1** impious; wicked. **2** *colloq.* outrageous (*an ungodly hour to arrive*). □□ **ungodliness** *n.*

■ **1** wicked, sinful, impious, blasphemous, heretical, irreligious, iconoclastic, atheist(ic), antireligious, sacrilegious, irreverent, demonic, demoniac(al), diabolic(al), satanic, fiendish, hellish, infernal; depraved, godless, corrupt, immoral, evil, iniquitous, bad, villainous, heinous, flagitious, profane, vile. **2** awful, outrageous, indecent, monstrous, unseemly, objectionable, nasty, dreadful, terrible, appalling, frightful, shocking, *colloq.* unearthly, beastly, *sl.* godawful. □□ **ungodliness** see SIN¹ *n.* 1.

ungovernable /úngúvərnəbəl/ *adj.* uncontrollable; violent. □□ **ungovernability** /-bílitee/ *n.* **ungovernably** *adv.*

■ unruly, intractable, unmanageable, uncontrollable, rebellious, wild, disobedient, defiant, unrestrainable, obstreperous, refractory, recalcitrant, incorrigible, self-willed, violent.

ungraceful /úngráysfŏol/ *adj.* not graceful. □□ **ungracefully** *adv.* **ungracefulness** *n.*

■ awkward, clumsy, ungainly, gauche, gawky, lubberly, uncoordinated, all thumbs, *colloq.* butterfingered, *sl.* klutzy; inelegant, graceless, coarse, crude, inartistic, vulgar, tasteless, unaesthetic, unrefined, barbarous, unlovely, ugly, unharmonious, inconsonant, unattractive, ill-proportioned, unsymmetrical, asymmetric(al).

ungracious /úngráyshəs/ *adj.* **1** not kindly or courteous; unkind. **2** unattractive. □□ **ungraciously** *adv.* **ungraciousness** *n.*

■ **1** discourteous, overbearing, churlish, gauche, rude, uncivil, impolite, ill-bred, ill-mannered, bad-mannered,

unmannerly, ungentlemanly, unladylike, unrefined, gruff, bluff, brusque, abrupt, surly, curmudgeonly; unkind, inconsiderate, insensitive.

ungrammatical /úngrəmátikəl/ *adj.* contrary to the rules of grammar. □□ **ungrammaticality** /-kálitee/ *n.* **ungrammatically** *adv.* **ungrammaticalness** *n.*

ungraspable /úngráspəbəl/ *adj.* that cannot be grasped or comprehended.

ungrateful /úngráytfŏol/ *adj.* **1** not feeling or showing gratitude. **2** not pleasant or acceptable. □□ **ungratefully** *adv.* **ungratefulness** *n.*

■ **1** unthankful, unappreciative, rude; selfish, heedless. □□ **ungratefulness** see INGRATITUDE.

ungrounded /úngrówndid/ *adj.* **1** having no basis or justification; unfounded. **2** *Electr.* not earthed. **3** (foll. by *in* a subject) not properly instructed. **4** (of an aircraft, ship, etc.) no longer grounded.

■ **1** see GRATUITOUS 2, UNFOUNDED.

ungrudging /úngrújing/ *adj.* not grudging. □□ **ungrudgingly** *adv.*

■ see UNSELFISH. □□ **ungrudgingly** see *willingly* (WILLING).

ungual /únggwəl/ *adj.* of, like, or bearing a nail, hoof, or claw. [L UNGUIS]

unguard /úngaard/ *v.tr. Cards* discard a low card that was protecting (a high card) from capture.

unguarded /úngaardid/ *adj.* **1** incautious; thoughtless (*an unguarded remark*). **2** not guarded; without a guard. □ **in an unguarded moment** unawares. □□ **unguardedly** *adv.* **unguardedness** *n.*

■ **1** indiscreet, careless, imprudent, unwise, hasty, unthinking, thoughtless; guileless, incautious; inattentive, heedless, inobservant, inadvertent, unwary, unwatchful, unvigilant. **2** defenseless, unprotected, undefended, unfortified, unshielded, open, uncovered, exposed, vulnerable. □ **in an unguarded moment** see UNAWARES 2.

unguent /únggwənt/ *n.* a soft substance used as ointment or for lubrication. [L *unguentum* f. *unguere* anoint]

■ see OINTMENT.

unguessable /úngésəbəl/ *adj.* that cannot be guessed or imagined.

unguiculate /unggwíkyələt, -layt/ *adj.* **1** *Zool.* having one or more nails or claws. **2** *Bot.* (of petals) having an unguis. [mod.L *unguiculatus* f. *unguiculus* dimin. of UNGUIS]

unguided /úngídid/ *adj.* not guided in a particular path or direction; left to take its own course.

unguis /únggwis/ *n.* (*pl.* **ungues** /-weez/) **1** *Bot.* the narrow base of a petal. **2** *Zool.* a nail or claw. [L]

ungula /úngyələ/ *n.* (*pl.* **ungulae** /-lee/) a hoof or claw. [L, dimin. of UNGUIS]

ungulate /úngyələt, -layt/ *adj.* & *n.* ● *adj.* hoofed. ● *n.* a hoofed mammal. [LL *ungulatus* f. UNGULA]

unhallowed /únhálōd/ *adj.* **1** not consecrated. **2** not sacred; unholy; wicked.

■ **1** see PROFANE *adj.* 1.

unhampered /únhámpərd/ *adj.* not hampered.

■ see UNIMPEDED.

unhand /únhánd/ *v.tr. rhet.* or *joc.* **1** take one's hands off (a person). **2** release from one's grasp.

unhandsome /únhánsəm/ *adj.* not handsome.

■ see UGLY 1.

unhandy /únhándee/ *adj.* **1** not easy to handle or manage; awkward. **2** not skillful in using the hands. □□ **unhandily** *adv.* **unhandiness** *n.*

unhang /únháng/ *v.tr.* (*past* and *past part.* **unhung**) take down from a hanging position.

unhappy /únhápee/ *adj.* (**unhappier, unhappiest**) **1** not happy; miserable. **2** unsuccessful; unfortunate. **3** causing

---

/. . ./ **pronunciation**	● **part of speech**
□ **phrases, idioms, and compounds**	
□□ **derivatives**	■ **synonym section**
cross-references appear in SMALL CAPITALS or *italics*	

misfortune. **4** disastrous. **5** inauspicious. □□ **unhappily** *adv.*
unhappiness *n.*

■ **1** sad, depressed, blue, dejected, melancholy, despondent, downcast, gloomy, dismal, downhearted, dispirited, disenchanted, heavyhearted, long-faced, disconsolate, sorrowful, miserable, woebegone, woeful, crestfallen, cheerless, joyless, forlorn, wretched, low-spirited, glum, distressed, disgruntled, tearful, *colloq.* down, down in the mouth, *formal* lachrymose. **2** unlucky, unfortunate, unsuccessful, luckless, hapless, cursed, wretched, doomed, frustrated, disappointed, let down, *colloq.* jinxed. **4** see UNFORTUNATE *adj.* 4. **5** unpropitious, inauspicious, unlucky, unfortunate, unfavorable; ill-omened, ill-fated, ill-starred, *archaic* star-crossed; infelicitous, unfitting, inappropriate, unsuitable, unsuited, wrong, inexpedient, ill-advised, poor, bad, unsatisfactory. □□ **unhappily** see *sadly* (SAD). **unhappiness** see MISERY 1.

unharmed /únha͞armd/ *adj.* not harmed.

■ see INTACT 2.

unharmful /únha͞armfŏŏl/ *adj.* not harmful.

unharmonious /únha͞armő́neeəs/ *adj.* not harmonious.

unharness /únha͞arnis/ *v.tr.* remove a harness from.

unhasp /únhásp/ *v.tr.* free from a hasp or catch; unfasten.

■ see UNDO 1.

unhatched /únhácht/ *adj.* (of an egg, etc.) not hatched.

unhealthful /únhélthfŏŏl/ *adj.* harmful to health; unwholesome. □□ **unhealthfulness** *n.*

unhealthy /únhélthee/ *adj.* (**unhealthier, unhealthiest**) **1** not in good health. **2 a** (of a place, etc.) harmful to health. **b** unwholesome. **c** *sl.* dangerous to life. □□ **unhealthily** *adv.* **unhealthiness** *n.*

■ **1** ailing, unwell, ill, sickly, infirm, feeble, frail, debilitated, unsound, sick, peaky, in poor health *or* condition, in delicate health *or* condition, indisposed, invalid, valetudinarian, valetudinary. **2 a, b** unwholesome, harmful, sickly, noxious, detrimental, insalubrious, unhealthful, damaging, injurious, destructive, deleterious, malign. **c** risky, dangerous, perilous, life-threatening, touch and go.

unheard /únhə́rd/ *adj.* **1** not heard. **2** (usu. **unheard-of**) unprecedented; unknown.

■ **1** see UNNOTICED. **2** (**unheard-of**) unknown, unfamiliar, obscure, unidentified, nameless, unsung, unimaginable, undreamed of, unprecedented, unimagined, unbelievable, inconceivable, unusual; shocking, offensive, outrageous, disgraceful, extreme, unthinkable, outlandish.

unheated /únhéėtid/ *adj.* not heated.

unheeded /únhéėdid/ *adj.* not heeded; disregarded.

unheedful /únhéėdfŏŏl/ *adj.* heedless; taking no notice.

unheeding /únhéėding/ *adj.* not giving heed; heedless. □□ **unheedingly** *adv.*

■ see UNCONSCIOUS *adj.*

unhelpful /únhélpfŏŏl/ *adj.* not helpful. □□ **unhelpfully** *adv.* **unhelpfulness** *n.*

■ see DIFFICULT 2, USELESS 1.

unheralded /únhérəldid/ *adj.* not heralded; unannounced.

■ unannounced, unpublicized, unadvertised; unexpected, surprise, unanticipated, unforeseen, unpredicted.

unheroic /únhirṓik/ *adj.* not heroic. □□ **unheroically** *adv.*

unhesitating /únhézitayting/ *adj.* without hesitation. □□ **unhesitatingly** *adv.* **unhesitatingness** *n.*

■ swift, rapid, quick, immediate, instantaneous, prompt, ready, unhesitant; unfaltering, unwavering, wholehearted, unqualified, unswerving, undeviating, staunch, steadfast, implicit, resolute, decided. □□ **unhesitatingly** see IMMEDIATELY *adv.* 1.

unhindered /únhíndərd/ *adj.* not hindered.

■ see UNIMPEDED.

unhinge /únhínj/ *v.tr.* **1** take (a door, etc.) off its hinges. **2** (esp. as **unhinged** *adj.*) unsettle or disorder (a person's mind, etc.), make (a person) crazy.

■ **1** see UNDO 1. **2** (**unhinged**) see CRAZY 1.

unhip /únhíp/ *adj. sl.* unaware of current fashions.

unhistoric /únhistáwrik, -histórik/ *adj.* not historic or historical.

unhistorical /únhistáwrikl, -histór-/ *adj.* not historical. □□ **unhistorically** *adv.*

unhitch /únhích/ *v.tr.* **1** release from a hitched state. **2** unhook; unfasten.

■ see DISCONNECT 1, UNDO 1.

unholy /únhṓlee/ *adj.* (**unholier, unholiest**) **1** impious; profane; wicked. **2** *colloq.* dreadful; outrageous (*made an unholy ordeal out of nothing*). **3** not holy. □□ **unholiness** *n.* [OE *unhālig* (as UN-[1], HOLY)]

■ **1** see IMPIOUS. **2** see DREADFUL *adj.* 1.

unhonored /únónərd/ *adj.* not honored.

unhook /únhŏŏk/ *v.tr.* **1** remove from a hook or hooks. **2** unfasten by releasing a hook or hooks.

■ see DISCONNECT 1, UNDO 1.

unhoped /únhṓpt/ *adj.* (foll. by *for*) not hoped for or expected.

■ (**unhoped for**) see UNFORESEEN.

unhorse /únháwrs/ *v.tr.* **1** throw or drag from a horse. **2** (of a horse) throw (a rider). **3** dislodge; overthrow.

unhouse /únhówz/ *v.tr.* deprive of shelter; turn out of a house.

unhuman /únhyŏŏmən/ *adj.* **1** not human. **2** superhuman. **3** inhuman; brutal.

unhung[1] /únhúng/ *adj.* **1** not (yet) executed by hanging. **2** not hung up (for exhibition).

unhung[2] *past* and *past part.* of UNHANG.

unhurried /únhə́rid, -húr-/ *adj.* not hurried. □□ **unhurriedly** *adv.*

■ leisurely, unrushed, easy, easygoing, relaxed, casual, gradual, deliberate, slow, steady, sedate, calm. □□ **unhurriedly** at one's leisure *or* convenience, in one's own time, slowly, sedately, steadily, calmly, deliberately.

unhurt /únhə́rt/ *adj.* not hurt.

■ see UNSCATHED.

unhusk /únhúsk/ *v.tr.* remove a husk or shell from.

unhygienic /únhijénik, -jee-én-/ *adj.* not hygienic. □□ **unhygienically** *adv.*

■ see UNWHOLESOME 1.

unhyphenated /únhífənaytid/ *adj.* not hyphenated.

uni /yŏŏnee/ *n.* (*pl.* **unis**) esp. *Brit., Austral., & NZ colloq.* a university. [abbr.]

uni- /yŏŏnee/ *comb. form* one; having or consisting of one. [L f. *unus* one]

Uniate /yŏŏneeit, -ayt/ *adj. & n.* (also **Uniat** /-at/) ● *adj.* of or relating to any community of Christians in E. Europe or the Near East that acknowledges papal supremacy but retains its own liturgy, etc. ● *n.* a member of such a community. [Russ. *uniyat* f. *uniya* f. L *unio* UNION]

uniaxial /yŏŏneeákseeəl/ *adj.* having a single axis. □□ **uniaxially** *adv.*

unicameral /yŏŏnikámərəl/ *adj.* with a single legislative chamber.

UNICEF /yŏŏnisef/ *abbr.* United Nations Children's (orig. International Children's Emergency) Fund.

unicellular /yŏŏnisélyələr/ *adj.* (of an organism, organ, tissue, etc.) consisting of a single cell.

unicolor /yŏŏnikulər/ *adj.* (also **unicolored**) of one color.

unicorn /yŏŏnikawrn/ *n.* **1 a** a mythical animal with a horse's body and a single straight horn. **b** a heraldic representation of this, with a twisted horn, a deer's feet, a goat's beard, and a lion's tail. **c** used in old translations of the Old Testament for the Hebrew *r'em*, a two-horned animal, probably a wild ox. **2 a** a pair of horses and a third horse in front. **b** an equipage with these. [ME f. OF *unicorne* f. L *unicornis* f. UNI- + *cornu* horn, transl. Gk *monocerōs*]

unicuspid /yŏŏnikúspid/ *adj. & n.* ● *adj.* with one cusp. ● *n.* a unicuspid tooth.

unicycle /yŏŏnisīkəl/ *n.* a single-wheeled cycle, esp. as used by acrobats. □□ **unicyclist** *n.*

unideal /únidéėəl/ *adj.* not ideal.

unidentifiable /únidéntifiəbəl/ *adj.* unable to be identified.

■ see NAMELESS 1, 3, 5.

unidentified /únidéntifid/ adj. not identified.

■ nameless, anonymous, unknown, incognito, unmarked, unnamed, unfamiliar, unrecognized, mysterious, unspecified.

unidimensional /yŏonidiménshənəl, -dī-/ adj. having (only) one dimension.

unidirectional /yŏonidirékshənəl, -dī-/ adj. having only one direction of motion, operation, etc. □□ **unidirectionality** /-nálitee/ n. **unidirectionally** adv.

unification /yŏonifikáyshən/ n. the act or an instance of unifying; the state of being unified. □ **Unification Church** a religious organization founded in 1954 in Korea by Sun Myung Moon (cf. MOONIE). □□ **unificatory** adj.

■ see UNION 1.

uniflow /yŏoniflō/ adj. involving flow (esp. of steam or waste gases) in one direction only.

uniform /yŏonifawrm/ adj., n., & v. ● adj. **1** not changing in form or character; the same; unvarying (*present a uniform appearance*; *all of uniform size and shape*). **2** conforming to the same standard, rules, or pattern. **3** constant in the course of time (*uniform acceleration*). **4** (of a tax, law, etc.) not varying with time or place. ● n. uniform distinctive clothing worn by members of the same body, e.g., by soldiers, police, and schoolchildren. ● v.tr. **1** clothe in uniform (*a uniformed officer*). **2** make uniform. □□ **uniformly** adv. [F *uniforme* or L *uniformis* (as UNI-, FORM)]

■ adj. **1, 2** homogeneous, consistent, unvaried, unchanged, unaltered, constant; unvarying, unchanging; invariable, unchangeable, unalterable, regimented, standard; ordered, orderly, equal, like, identical, (the) same; alike; even, unbroken, smooth, regular, flat. **3** see EVEN¹ adj. 2a. ● n. livery, habit, regalia, costume, outfit; regimentals. □□ **uniformly** see ALIKE adv.

uniformitarian /yŏonifáwrmitáireeən/ adj. & n. ● adj. of the theory that geological processes are always due to continuously and uniformly operating forces. ● n. a holder of this theory. □□ **uniformitarianism** n.

uniformity /yŏonifáwrmitee/ n. (pl. **-ies**) **1** being uniform; sameness; consistency. **2** an instance of this. [ME f. OF *uniformité* or LL *uniformitas* (as UNIFORM)]

■ regularity, similarity, sameness, homogeneity, consistency, symmetry, evenness, invariability, unchangeability, unchangeableness, similitude, conformity, agreement, concord, accord, harmoniousness; harmony, concordance, accordance, conformance, correspondence; dullness, monotony, drabness, tedium, featurelessness, flatness, lack of variety, changelessness.

unify /yŏonifī/ v.tr. (also absol.) (**-ies, -ied**) reduce to unity or uniformity. □ **unified field theory** Physics a theory that seeks to explain all the field phenomena (e.g., gravitation and electromagnetism: see FIELD n. 9) formerly treated by separate theories. □□ **unifier** n. [F *unifier* or LL *unificare* (as UNI-, -FY)]

■ consolidate, unite, combine, amalgamate, coalesce, bring together, fuse, join, weld, merge, confederate, incorporate, integrate.

unilateral /yŏonilátərəl/ adj. **1** performed by or affecting only one person or party (*unilateral disarmament*; *unilateral declaration of independence*). **2** one-sided. **3** (of the parking of vehicles) restricted to one side of the street. **4** (of leaves) all on the same side of the stem. **5** (of a line of descent) through ancestors of one sex only. □□ **unilaterally** adv.

■ **1, 2** see one-sided 2.

unilateralism /yŏonilátərəlizəm/ n. **1** unilateral disarmament. **2** the pursuit of a foreign policy without allies. □□ **unilateralist** n. & adj.

unilingual /yŏonilínggwəl/ adj. of or in only one language. □□ **unilingually** adv.

uniliteral /yŏonilítərəl/ adj. consisting of one letter.

unilluminated /únilóominaytid/ adj. not illuminated.

■ see DARK adj. 1.

unillustrated /únílləstraytid/ adj. (esp. of a book) without illustrations.

unilocular /yŏonilókyələr/ adj. Bot. & Zool. single-chambered.

unimaginable /únimájinəbəl/ adj. impossible to imagine. □□ **unimaginably** adv.

■ see INCONCEIVABLE 1, UNTOLD 2.

unimaginative /únimájinətiv/ adj. lacking imagination; stolid; dull. □□ **unimaginatively** adv. **unimaginativeness** n.

■ see PROSAIC.

unimpaired /únimpáird/ adj. not impaired.

■ see flawless (FLAW¹).

unimpassioned /únimpáshənd/ adj. not impassioned.

unimpeachable /únimpéechəbəl/ adj. giving no opportunity for censure; beyond reproach or question. □□ **unimpeachably** adv.

■ see IRREPROACHABLE.

unimpeded /únimpéedid/ adj. not impeded. □□ **unimpededly** adv.

■ unblocked, unchecked, free, unconstrained, unrestrained, unhindered, unhampered, unencumbered, open, clear, untrammeled, unrestricted, unobstructed.

unimportance /únimpáwrt'ns/ n. lack of importance.

■ see triviality (TRIVIAL).

unimportant /únimpáwrt'nt/ adj. not important.

■ see INSIGNIFICANT 1.

unimposing /únimpōzing/ adj. unimpressive. □□ **unimposingly** adv.

■ unimpressive, nugatory, trivial, trifling, minor, unimportant, insignificant, puny, inconsiderable, negligible, ordinary, unexceptional, humble, modest.

unimpressed /únimprést/ adj. not impressed.

■ see UNENTHUSIASTIC.

unimpressionable /únimpréshənəbəl/ adj. not impressionable.

unimpressive /únimprésiv/ adj. not impressive. □□ **unimpressively** adv. **unimpressiveness** n.

■ see UNDISTINGUISHED.

unimproved /únimprŏovd/ adj. **1** not made better. **2** not made use of. **3** (of land) not used for agriculture or building; not developed.

unincorporated /úninkáwrpəraytid/ adj. **1** not incorporated or united. **2** not formed into a corporation.

uninfected /úninféktid/ adj. not infected.

uninflamed /úninfláymd/ adj. not inflamed.

uninflammable /úninfláməbəl/ adj. not flammable.

uninflected /úninfléktid/ adj. **1** Gram. (of a language) not having inflections. **2** not changing or varying. **3** not bent or deflected.

uninfluenced /únínflŏoinst/ adj. (often foll. by by) not influenced.

■ (uninfluenced by) see UNAFFECTED 1.

uninfluential /úninflŏo-énshəl/ adj. having little or no influence.

uninformative /úninfáwrmətiv/ adj. not informative; giving little information.

uninformed /úninfáwrmd/ adj. **1** not informed or instructed. **2** ignorant, uneducated.

■ ignorant, unknowledgeable, unenlightened, uneducated, unschooled, untutored, untaught, uninstructed, unaware, incognizant, benighted, literary nescient.

uninhabitable /úninhábitəbəl/ adj. that cannot be inhabited. □□ **uninhabitableness** n.

■ see INHOSPITABLE 2, DERELICT adj. 1, 2.

uninhabited /úninhábitid/ adj. not inhabited.

■ desolate, empty, abandoned, deserted, unoccupied,

/.../ **pronunciation**	● **part of speech**
□ **phrases, idioms, and compounds**	
□□ **derivatives**	■ **synonym section**
cross-references appear in SMALL CAPITALS or italics	

vacant, vacated, tenantless, untenanted; desert, unpopulated, unpeopled, unlived-in, trackless, depopulated, waste, barren.

uninhibited /úninhíbitid/ *adj.* not inhibited. □□ **uninhibitedly** *adv.* **uninhibitedness** *n.*
- wild, unchecked, unbridled, uncurbed, rampant, intemperate, boisterous, unrepressed, unconstrained, unrestrained, abandoned, uncontrolled, unselfconscious, unreserved, relaxed, casual, easygoing, free (and easy), natural, spontaneous, open, frank, candid, outspoken, *colloq.* upfront.

uninitiated /úninísheeaytid/ *adj.* not initiated; not admitted or instructed.
- see *inexperienced* (INEXPERIENCE).

uninjured /únínjərd/ *adj.* not injured.
- see UNSCATHED.

uninspired /úninspírd/ *adj.* **1** not inspired. **2** (of oratory, etc.) commonplace.
- **2** see PROSAIC.

uninspiring /úninspíring/ *adj.* not inspiring. □□ **uninspiringly** *adv.*
- see PROSAIC.

uninstructed /úninstrúktid/ *adj.* not instructed or informed.
- see UNINFORMED.

uninsurable /úninshŏŏrəbəl/ *adj.* that cannot be insured.

uninsured /úninshŏŏrd/ *adj.* not insured.

unintelligent /úníntélijənt/ *adj.* not intelligent. □□ **unintelligently** *adv.*
- see STUPID *adj.* 1, 5.

unintelligible /úníntélijibəl/ *adj.* not intelligible. □□ **unintelligibility** *n.* **unintelligibleness** *n.* **unintelligibly** *adv.*
- see INCOMPREHENSIBLE.

unintended /únínténdid/ *adj.* not intended.
- see INADVERTENT 1, INVOLUNTARY.

unintentional /únínténshənəl/ *adj.* not intentional. □□ **unintentionally** *adv.*
- see INADVERTENT 1, INVOLUNTARY. □□ **unintentionally** see UNAWARES 2.

uninterested /úníntrəstid, -təristid, -tərəs-/ *adj.* **1** not interested. **2** unconcerned; indifferent. □□ **uninterestedly** *adv.* **uninterestedness** *n.*
- see UNENTHUSIASTIC, see INDIFFERENT 4.

uninteresting /úníntrəsting, -tərəsting, -tərəs-/ *adj.* not interesting. □□ **uninterestingly** *adv.* **uninterestingness** *n.*
- see PROSAIC.

uninterpretable /úníntərpritəbəl/ *adj.* that cannot be interpreted.

uninterruptable /úníntərúptəbəl/ *adj.* that cannot be interrupted.

uninterrupted /úníntərúptid/ *adj.* not interrupted. □□ **uninterruptedly** *adv.* **uninterruptedness** *n.*
- see NONSTOP *adj.*

uninucleate /yŏŏninŏŏkleeət, -ayt, -nyŏŏ-/ *adj.* *Biol.* having a single nucleus.

uninventive /úninvéntiv/ *adj.* not inventive. □□ **uninventively** *adv.* **uninventiveness** *n.*

uninvestigated /úninvéstigaytid/ *adj.* not investigated.

uninvited /úninvítid/ *adj.* not invited. □□ **uninvitedly** *adv.*
- see UNASKED.

uninviting /úninvíting/ *adj.* not inviting; unattractive; repellent. □□ **uninvitingly** *adv.*
- repulsive, repellent, offensive, unappealing, unattractive, unpleasant, inhospitable, disagreeable, distasteful, unappetizing, unsavory, sickening, revolting, nauseating, obnoxious, nasty, disgusting, *Brit.* off-putting.

uninvoked /úninvŏkt/ *adj.* not invoked.

uninvolved /úninvólvd/ *adj.* not involved.
- see *detached* (DETACH 3a), SIMPLE *adj.* 1.

union /yŏŏnyən/ *n.* **1** the act or an instance of uniting; the state of being united. **2 a** a whole resulting from the combination of parts or members. **b** a political unit formed in this way, esp. (**Union**) the US (esp. as distinct from the Confederacy during the Civil War), the UK, or South Africa. **3** = *labor union.* **4** marriage; matrimony. **5** concord;

agreement (*lived together in perfect union*). **6** (**Union**) (in the UK) **a** a general social club and debating society at some universities and colleges. **b** the buildings or accommodation of such a society. **7** *Math.* the totality of the members of two or more sets. **8** a part of a flag with a device emblematic of union, normally occupying the upper corner next to the staff. **9** a joint or coupling for pipes, etc. **10** a fabric of mixed materials, e.g., cotton with linen or silk. □ **union bashing** *Brit. colloq.* active opposition to labor unions and their rights. **union catalog** a catalog of the combined holdings of several libraries. **union down** (of a flag) hoisted with the union below as a signal of distress. **Union Jack** (or **flag**) the national ensign of the United Kingdom formed by the union of the crosses of St. George, St. Andrew, and St. Patrick. **union jack** a jack consisting of the union from a national flag. **union shop** a shop, factory, trade, etc., in which employees must belong to a labor union or join one within an agreed time. **union suit** a single undergarment for the body and legs; combinations. [ME f. OF *union* or eccl.L *unio* unity f. L *unus* one]
- **1** unification, combination, junction, conjunction, alliance, association, coalition, amalgamation, fusion, bonding, bond, marriage, confederation, confederacy, synthesis, blending, blend, mixing, mixture, merger, federation, coherence, cohesion, togetherness. **2** alliance, association, organization, society, circle, fraternity, club, fellowship, team, ring, gang, syndicate, coalition, party, confederation, confederacy, federation, league, consortium, bloc, cartel, trust. **4** marriage, matrimony, wedlock, partnership. **5** agreement, accord, harmony, harmoniousness, concord, congruity, coherence, compatibility, unanimity, unity. **9** joint, seam, splice, junction, conjunction, weld; coupling; graft.

unionist /yŏŏnyənist/ *n.* **1 a** a member of a labor union. **b** an advocate of labor unions. **2** (usu. **Unionist**) an advocate of union, esp.: **a** a person opposed to the rupture of the parliamentary union between Great Britain and Northern Ireland (formerly between Great Britain and Ireland). **b** *hist.* a person who opposed secession during the US Civil War. □□ **unionism** *n.* **unionistic** /-nístik/ *adj.*

unionize /yŏŏnyənīz/ *v.tr.* & *intr.* bring or come under labor-union organization or rules. □□ **unionization** *n.*

un-ionized /únī́ənīzd/ *adj.* not ionized.

uniparous /yŏŏnípərəs/ *adj.* **1** producing one offspring at a birth. **2** *Bot.* having one axis or branch.

uniped /yŏŏniped/ *n.* & *adj.* ● *n.* a person having only one foot or leg. ● *adj.* one-footed; one-legged. [UNI- + *pes pedis* foot]

unipersonal /yŏŏnípə́rsənəl/ *adj.* (of the Deity) existing only as one person.

uniplanar /yŏŏnipláynər/ *adj.* lying in one plane.

unipod /yŏŏnipod/ *n.* a one-legged support for a camera, etc. [UNI-, after TRIPOD]

unipolar /yŏŏnipṓlər/ *adj.* **1** (esp. of an electric or magnetic apparatus) showing only one kind of polarity. **2** *Biol.* (of a nerve cell, etc.) having only one pole. □□ **unipolarity** /-lárite/ *n.*

unique /yŏŏnéek/ *adj.* & *n.* ● *adj.* **1** of which there is only one; unequaled; having no like, equal, or parallel (*his position was unique; this vase is considered unique*). **2** *disp.* unusual; remarkable (*the most unique man I ever met*). ● *n.* a unique thing or person. □□ **uniquely** *adv.* **uniqueness** *n.* [F f. L *unicus* f. *unus* one]
- *adj.* **1** single, lone, (one and) only, solitary, one of a kind, sui generis, individual, distinctive, singular; unequaled, unparalleled, unrivaled, nonpareil, incomparable, inimitable, peerless, unmatched, unsurpassed, unexcelled, second to none, *Brit. colloq.* one-off. **2** see EXCEPTIONAL. □□ **uniqueness** see SINGULARITY 1.

unironed /únírnd/ *adj.* (esp. of clothing, linen, etc.) not ironed.

uniserial /yŏŏniseéreeəl/ *adj.* *Bot.* & *Zool.* arranged in one row.

unisex /yōōniseks/ *adj.* (of clothing, hairstyles, etc.) designed to be suitable for both sexes.

unisexual /yōōnisékshōōəl/ *adj.* **1 a** of one sex. **b** *Bot.* having stamens or pistils but not both. **2** unisex. □□ **unisexuality** /-shōōálitee/ *n.* **unisexually** *adv.*

unison /yōōnisən/ *n. & adj.* ● *n.* **1** *Mus.* **a** coincidence in pitch of sounds or notes. **b** this regarded as an interval. **2** *Mus.* a combination of voices or instruments at the same pitch or at pitches differing by one or more octaves (*sang in unison*). **3** agreement; concord (*acted in perfect unison*). ● *adj. Mus.* coinciding in pitch. □ **unison string** a string tuned in unison with another string and meant to be sounded with it. □□ **unisonant** /yōōnísənənt/ *adj.* **unisonous** /yōōnísənəs/ *adj.* [OF *unison* or LL *unisonus* (as UNI-, *sonus* SOUND¹)]

■ *n.* **3** see UNITY 2; (*in unison*) in harmony, together, as one, harmonious; (*in unison with*) corresponding exactly to *or* with, in (perfect) accord with, in consonance with, consonant with.

unissued /únishōōd/ *adj.* not issued.

unit /yōōnit/ *n.* **1 a** an individual thing, person, or group regarded as single and complete, esp. for purposes of calculation. **b** each of the (smallest) separate individuals or groups into which a complex whole may be analyzed (*the family as the unit of society*). **2 a** a quantity chosen as a standard in terms of which other quantities may be expressed (*unit of heat*; *SI unit*; *mass per unit volume*). **3** the smallest share in a unit trust. **4** a device with a specified function forming part of a complex mechanism. **5** a piece of furniture for fitting with others like it or made of complementary parts. **6** a group with a special function in an organization. **7** a group of buildings, wards, etc., in a hospital. **8** the number 'one'. □ **unit cell** *Crystallog.* the smallest repeating group of atoms, ions, or molecules in a crystal. **unit cost** the cost of producing one item of manufacture. **unit price** the price charged for each unit of goods supplied. **unit trust** *Brit.* = *mutual fund*. [L *unus*, prob. after DIGIT]

■ **1, 4, 5** element, component, entity, part, item, constituent, piece, portion, segment, member, section, module. **6** see SQUAD, DIVISION 6.

unitard /yōōnətaard/ *n.* a one-piece leotard that covers the legs as well as the torso.

Unitarian /yōōnitáireeən/ *n. & adj.* ● *n.* **1** a person who believes that God is not a Trinity but one being. **2** a member of a religious body maintaining this and advocating freedom from formal dogma or doctrine. ● *adj.* of or relating to the Unitarians. □□ **Unitarianism** *n.* [mod.L *unitarius* f. L *unitas* UNITY]

unitary /yōōniteree/ *adj.* **1** of a unit or units. **2** marked by unity or uniformity. □□ **unitarily** *adv.* **unitarity** /-téritee/ *n.*

unite /yōōnít/ *v.* **1** *tr. & intr.* join together; make or become one; combine. **2** *tr. & intr.* join together for a common purpose or action (*united in their struggle against injustice*). **3** *tr. & intr.* join in marriage. **4** *tr.* possess (qualities, features, etc.) in combination (*united anger with mercy*). **5** *intr. & tr.* form or cause to form a physical or chemical whole (*oil will not unite with water*). □□ **unitive** /yōōnitiv/ *adj.* **unitively** *adv.* [ME f. L *unire unit-* f. *unus* one]

■ **1, 5** bond, join *or* fuse *or* weld *or* solder *or* glue *or* stick *or* knit *or* splice *or* tie *or* bind *or* fasten *or* fix *or* fit (together); combine, integrate, incorporate, coalesce, compound, synthesize, blend, mix, intermix, amalgamate, consolidate, mingle, *literary* commingle. **2** combine, unify, merge, coalesce, amalgamate, consolidate, collaborate, ally, join forces, join (together); team up, band together, *colloq.* gang up. **3** join, unify, marry, link, connect, *colloq.* get spliced *or* hitched, *usu. formal or literary* wed. **4** combine, blend, compound, marry, mix, mingle.

united /yōōnítid/ *adj.* **1** that has united or been united. **2 a** of or produced by two or more persons or things in union; joint. **b** resulting from the union of two or more parts (esp. in the names of churches, societies, and athletic clubs). **3** in agreement; of like mind. □ **United Brethren** *Eccl.* the Moravians. **United Kingdom** Great Britain and Northern Ireland (until 1922, Great Britain and Ireland). **United Nations** (orig., in 1942) those united against the Axis powers in the war of 1939–45, (later) a supranational peaceseeking organization of these and many other nations. **United States** (in full **United States of America**) a federal republic of 50 states, mostly in N. America and including Alaska and Hawaii. □□ **unitedly** *adv.*

■ **1** merged, coalesced, unified, amalgamated, consolidated, combined, incorporated, connected, linked. **2 a** joint, common, communal, mutual, combined, allied, pooled, shared, collective; collaborative, cooperative, synergetic, synergistic, concerted, coordinated. **b** amalgamated, allied, unified, merged, combined, consolidated, incorporated. **3** agreed, unanimous, in agreement, of one mind, of like mind *or* opinion, like-minded, in accord, in harmony, harmonious.

unity /yōōnitee/ *n.* (*pl.* **-ies**) **1** oneness; being one, single, or individual; being formed of parts that constitute a whole; due interconnection and coherence of parts (*disturbs the unity of the idea*; *the pictures lack unity*; *national unity*). **2** harmony or concord between persons, etc. (*lived together in unity*). **3** a thing forming a complex whole (*a person regarded as a unity*). **4** *Math.* the number 'one,' the factor that leaves unchanged the quantity on which it operates. **5** *Theatr.* each of the three dramatic principles requiring limitation of the supposed time of a drama to that occupied in acting it or to a single day (**unity of time**), use of one scene throughout (**unity of place**), and concentration on the development of a single plot (**unity of action**). [ME f. OF *unité* f. L *unitas* -*tatis* f. *unus* one]

■ **1** oneness, singularity, integrity, singleness, congruity, uniformity, congruence, homogeneity, identity, sameness, resemblance, likeness, similarity, similitude; coherence, cohesion, unification, union. **2** consistency, unanimity, constancy, uniformity, sameness, consensus, agreement, union, harmony, harmoniousness, concord, unison, concordance, consonance, accord, solidarity, compatibility, concurrence, continuity, rapport, sympathy, like-mindedness.

Univ. *abbr.* University.

univalent *adj. & n.* ● *adj.* **1** /yōōniváylənt/ *Chem.* having a valence of one. **2** /yōōnívələnt/ *Biol.* (of a chromosome) remaining unpaired during meiosis. ● *n.* /yōōnívələnt/ *Biol.* a univalent chromosome. [UNI- + *valent-* pres. part. stem (as VALENCE¹)]

univalve /yōōnivalv/ *adj. & n.* *Zool.* ● *adj.* having one valve. ● *n.* a univalve mollusk.

universal /yōōnivársəl/ *adj. & n.* ● *adj.* **1** of, belonging to, or done, etc., by all persons or things in the world or in the class concerned; applicable to all cases (*the feeling was universal*; *met with universal approval*). **2** *Logic* (of a proposition) in which something is asserted of all of a class (opp. PARTICULAR 5). ● *n.* **1** *Logic* a universal proposition. **2** *Philos.* **a** a term or concept of general application. **b** a nature or essence signified by a general term. □ **universal agent** an agent empowered to do all that can be delegated. **universal compass** a compass with legs that may be extended for large circles. **universal joint** (or **coupling**) a joint or coupling which can transmit rotary power by a shaft at any selected angle. **universal language** an artificial language intended for use by all nations. **Universal Product Code** a bar code on products that can be read by an electronic scanner, usu. providing price and product identification. **universal suffrage** a suffrage extending to all adults with minor exceptions. **universal time** = GREENWICH MEAN TIME. □□ **universality** /-sálitee/ *n.* **universalize** *v.tr.* **universal-**

/. . ./ pronunciation	● part of speech
□ **phrases, idioms, and compounds**	
□□ **derivatives**	■ **synonym section**
cross-references appear in SMALL CAPITALS or *italics*	

ization /-lizáyshən/ *n.* **universally** *adv.* [ME f. OF *univer-sal* or L *universalis* (as UNIVERSE)]

■ *adj.* **1** prevalent, prevailing, general, global, worldwide, widespread, ubiquitous, omnipresent, common, pandemic, epidemic; cosmic, infinite, boundless, limitless, unlimited; measureless, endless, uncircumscribed, all-inclusive, all-embracing, all-encompassing, wide-ranging, comprehensive.
□□ **universality** see *prevalence* (PREVALENT).
universally in every case *or* instance, in all cases *or* instances, unexceptionally, without exception, uniformly, always, invariably, globally, extensively, widely, generally, everywhere.

universalist /yŏŏnivársəlist/ *n. Theol.* **1** a person who holds that all mankind will eventually be saved. **2** a member of an organized body of Christians who hold this. □□ **universalism** *n.* **universalistic** /-lístik/ *adj.*

universe /yŏŏnivərs/ *n.* **1 a** all existing things; the whole creation; the cosmos. **b** a sphere of existence, influence, activity, etc. **2** all mankind. **3** *Statistics & Logic* all the objects under consideration. □ **universe of discourse** *Logic* = sense 3. [F *univers* f. L *universum* neut. of *universus* combined into one, whole f. UNI- + *versus* past part. of *vertere* turn]

■ **1 a** cosmos, creation, macrocosm; world. **b** world, sphere, province, preserve, domain, circle, milieu, territory, corner, quarter, microcosm. **2** mankind, humanity, people, society, humankind, world, microcosm.

university /yŏŏnivársitee/ *n.* (*pl.* **-ies**) **1** an educational institution designed for instruction, examination, or both, of students in many branches of advanced learning, conferring degrees in various faculties, and often embodying colleges and similar institutions. **2** the members of this collectively. **3** *Brit.* a team, crew, etc., representing a university. □ **at university** esp. *Brit.* studying at a university. [ME f. OF *université* f. L *universitas -tatis* the whole (world), in LL college, guild (as UNIVERSE)]

univocal /yŏŏnívəkəl, yŏŏnivŏkəl/ *adj. & n.* ● *adj.* (of a word, etc.) having only one proper meaning. ● *n.* a univocal word. □□ **univocality** /yŏŏnivŏkálitee/ *n.* **univocally** *adv.*

unjoin /únjóyn/ *v.tr.* detach from being joined; separate.
unjoined /únjóynd/ *adj.* not joined.
unjoint /únjóynt/ *v.tr.* **1** separate the joints of. **2** disunite.
unjust /únjúst/ *adj.* not just; contrary to justice or fairness. □□ **unjustly** *adv.* **unjustness** *n.*
■ see UNREASONABLE 1, *one-sided* 1. □□ **unjustly** see ILL *adv.* 1.
unjustifiable /únjústifíəbəl/ *adj.* not justifiable. □□ **unjusti-fiably** *adv.*
■ see UNTENABLE, UNREASONABLE 1. □□ **unjustifiably** see *unduly* (UNDUE).
unjustified /únjústifīd/ *adj.* not justified.
■ see UNWARRANTED 2.
unkempt /únkémpt/ *adj.* **1** untidy; of neglected appearance. **2** uncombed; disheveled. □□ **unkemptly** *adv.* **unkempt-ness** *n.* [UN-¹ + archaic *kempt* past part. of *kemb* comb f. OE *cemban*]
■ **1** ungroomed, untidy, messy, messed up, bedraggled, shaggy, rumpled, slovenly, sloppy, frowzy, blowzy, draggle-tailed, *colloq.* scruffy, mussy, mussed (up). **2** disheveled, uncombed, tousled, disarranged, windblown, disordered, untidy, ungroomed, messy, messed-up, bedraggled, shaggy, blowzy, *colloq.* scruffy, mussy, mussed(-up).
unkept /únképt/ *adj.* **1** (of a promise, law, etc.) not observed; disregarded. **2** not tended; neglected.
unkillable /únkíləbəl/ *adj.* that cannot be killed.
unkind /únkínd/ *adj.* **1** not kind. **2** harsh; cruel. **3** unpleasant. □□ **unkindly** *adv.* **unkindness** *n.*
■ inconsiderate, unthoughtful, thoughtless, unfeeling, unconcerned, insensitive, unfriendly, unsympathetic, uncharitable, unchristian, uncaring, hard-hearted, heartless, flinty, coldhearted, hard, rigid, callous,

tough, inflexible, unyielding, unbending, severe, harsh, stern, cruel, malicious, mean, hurtful, inhuman, unpleasant, brutal, *colloq.* beastly. □□ **unkindly** see ROUGHLY 1. **unkindness** see DISSERVICE.
unking /únkíng/ *v.tr.* **1** deprive of the position of king; dethrone. **2** deprive (a country) of a king.
unkink /únkíngk/ *v.* **1** *tr.* remove the kinks from; straighten. **2** *intr.* lose kinks; become straight.
unknit /ún-nít/ *v.tr.* (**unknitted**, **unknitting**) separate (things joined, knotted, or interlocked).
unknot /ún-nót/ *v.tr.* (**unknotted**, **unknotting**) release the knot or knots of; untie.
■ see UNDO 1.
unknowable /ún-nŏ́əbəl/ *adj. & n.* ● *adj.* that cannot be known. ● *n.* **1** an unknowable thing. **2** (**the Unknowable**) the postulated absolute or ultimate reality.
unknowing /ún-nŏ́ing/ *adj. & n.* ● *adj.* (often foll. by *of*) not knowing; ignorant; unconscious. ● *n.* ignorance (*cloud of unknowing*). □□ **unknowingly** *adv.* **unknowingness** *n.*
■ *adj.* see UNAWARE *adj.* 1. □□ **unknowingly** see UNAWARES 2.
unknown /ún-nŏ́n/ *adj. & n.* ● *adj.* (often foll. by *to*) not known; unfamiliar (*his purpose was unknown to me*). ● *n.* **1** an unknown thing or person. **2** an unknown quantity (*equation in two unknowns*). □ **unknown country** see COUNTRY. **unknown quantity** a person or thing whose nature, significance, etc., cannot be determined. **Unknown Soldier** an unidentified representative member of a country's armed forces killed in war, given burial with special honors in a national memorial. **unknown to** without the knowledge of (*did it unknown to me*). **Unknown Warrior** = *Unknown Soldier*. □□ **unknownness** *n.*
■ *adj.* unrecognized, unfamiliar, strange, unnamed, anonymous, nameless, incognito, unidentified, unspecified; obscure, unheard-of, little-known, humble, undistinguished, unsung; unexplored, uninvestigated, unresearched, undiscovered, unrevealed, mysterious, uncharted, unmapped, untold, dark. ● *n.* **1** see NOBODY *n.* □ **unknown to** unbeknown(st) to.
unlabeled /únláybəld/ *adj.* not labeled; without a label.
unlabored /únláybərd/ *adj.* not labored.
unlace /únláys/ *v.tr.* **1** undo the lace or laces of. **2** unfasten or loosen in this way.
■ see UNDO 1.
unlade /únláyd/ *v.tr.* **1** take the cargo out of (a ship). **2** discharge (a cargo, etc.) from a ship.
unladen /únláyd'n/ *adj.* not laden. □ **unladen weight** the weight of a vehicle, etc., when not loaded with goods, etc.
unladylike /únláydeelīk/ *adj.* not ladylike.
■ see UNSEEMLY 2.
unlaid¹ /únláyd/ *adj.* not laid.
unlaid² past and *past part.* of UNLAY.
unlamented /únləméntid/ *adj.* not lamented.
■ unmissed, unmourned, unbemoaned, unbewailed, unloved.
unlash /únlásh/ *v.tr.* unfasten (a thing lashed down, etc.).
■ see UNDO 1.
unlatch /únlách/ *v.* **1** *tr.* release the latch of. **2** *tr. & intr.* open or be opened in this way.
■ see UNDO 1.
unlawful /únláwfŏŏl/ *adj.* not lawful; illegal; not permissible. □□ **unlawfully** *adv.* **unlawfulness** *n.*
■ illegal, illicit, against the law, illegitimate, criminal, felonious, wrong; outlawed, banned, prohibited, forbidden, interdicted, disallowed, proscribed, verboten; unauthorized, unlicensed, unsanctioned, *colloq.* crooked.
unlay /únláy/ *v.tr.* (*past* and *past part.* **unlaid**) *Naut.* untwist (a rope). [UN-² + LAY¹]
unleaded /únlédid/ *adj.* **1** (of gasoline, etc.) without added lead. **2** not covered, weighted, or framed with lead. **3** *Printing* not spaced with leads.
unlearn /únlárn/ *v.tr.* (*past* and *past part.* **unlearned** or **un-**

learnt) **1** discard from one's memory. **2** rid oneself of (a habit, false information, etc.).

unlearned[1] /únlə́rnid/ *adj.* not well educated; untaught; ignorant. □□ **unlearnedly** *adv.*

unlearned[2] /únlə́rnd/ *adj.* (also **unlearnt** /-lérnt/) that has not been learned.

unleash /únleésh/ *v.tr.* **1** release from a leash or restraint. **2** set free to engage in pursuit or attack.

■ **2** see RELEASE *v.* 1, LOOSE *v.* 5.

unleavened /únlévənd/ *adj.* not leavened; made without yeast or other raising agent.

unless /únlés, ən-/ *conj.* if not; except when (*shall go unless I hear from you*; *always walked unless I had a bicycle*). [ON or IN + LESS, assim. to UN-[1]]

unlettered /únlétərd/ *adj.* **1** illiterate. **2** not well educated.

unliberated /únlíbəraytid/ *adj.* not liberated.

unlicensed /únlísənst/ *adj.* not licensed, esp. (in the UK) without a license to sell alcoholic drink.

unlighted /únlítid/ *adj.* **1** not provided with light. **2** not set burning.

unlikable /únlíkəbəl/ *adj.* (also **unlikeable**) not easy to like; unpleasant.

■ see DISAGREEABLE 1.

unlike /únlík/ *adj.* & *prep.* ● *adj.* **1** not like; different from (*is unlike both his parents*). **2** uncharacteristic of (*such behavior is unlike him*). **3** dissimilar; different. ● *prep.* differently from (*acts quite unlike anyone else*). □ **unlike signs** *Math.* plus and minus. □□ **unlikeness** *n.* [perh. f. ON *úlíkr*, OE *ungelic*: see LIKE[1]]

■ *adj.* **1** different from, dissimilar to, distinct from, opposite from *or* to, contrasting with *or* to, contrastive with *or* to, separate from, divergent from, incompatible with, distinguishable from, far apart from, far from, distant from, ill-matched with, unequal to, unequivalent to. **2** atypical of, uncharacteristic of, untypical of. **3** unalike, different, dissimilar, distinct, disparate, opposite, contrasting, contrastive, divergent, diverse, varied, heterogeneous, distinguishable, separate, far apart, incompatible, ill-matched, unequal, unequivalent. ● *prep.* differently from, in contradistinction to, in contrast with *or* to, as opposed to. □□ **unlikeness** see DIFFERENCE *n.* 1.

unlikely /únlíklee/ *adj.* (**unlikelier**, **unlikeliest**) **1** improbable (*unlikely tale*). **2** (foll. by *to* + infin.) not to be expected to do something (*he's unlikely to be available*). **3** unpromising (*an unlikely candidate*). □□ **unlikelihood** *n.* **unlikeliness** *n.*

■ **1** improbable, doubtful, dubious, remote, unthinkable, unimaginable, inconceivable, implausible, unbelievable, incredible, unconvincing, far-fetched. **3** unpropitious, unpromising, inauspicious.

unlimited /únlímitid/ *adj.* without limit; unrestricted; very great in number or quantity (*has unlimited possibilities*; *an unlimited expanse of sea*). □□ **unlimitedly** *adv.* **unlimitedness** *n.*

■ unrestricted, unrestrained, limitless, unconstrained, unqualified, indefinite, full, absolute, unconditional, far-reaching, unchecked, uncontrolled; boundless, endless, vast, unbounded, immense, immeasurable, measureless, numberless, innumerable, inexhaustible, interminable, never-ending, infinite, extensive, *literary* myriad.

unlined[1] /únlínd/ *adj.* **1** (of paper, etc.) without lines. **2** (of a face, etc.) without wrinkles.

unlined[2] /únlínd/ *adj.* (of a garment, etc.) without lining.

unlink /únlíngk/ *v.tr.* **1** undo the links of (a chain, etc.). **2** detach or set free by undoing or unfastening a link or chain.

■ see UNDO 1.

unliquidated /únlíkwidaytid/ *adj.* not liquidated.

unlisted /únlístid/ *adj.* not included in a published list, esp. of stock exchange prices or of telephone numbers.

unlit /únlít/ *adj.* not lit.

■ see DARK *adj.* 1.

unlivable /únlívəbəl/ *adj.* that cannot be lived or lived in.

unlived-in /únlívdin/ *adj.* **1** appearing to be uninhabited. **2** unused by the inhabitants.

■ **1** see UNINHABITED.

unload /únlṓd/ *v.tr.* **1** (also *absol.*) remove a load from (a vehicle, etc.). **2** remove (a load) from a vehicle, etc. **3** remove the charge from (a firearm, etc.). **4** *colloq.* get rid of. **5** (often foll. by *on*) *colloq.* **a** divulge (information). **b** (also *absol.*) give vent to (feelings). □□ **unloader** *n.*

■ **1, 2** empty, dump, unpack, offload, discharge; disburden, unburden. **4** see DUMP *v.* 2. **5 a** see DISCLOSE 1. **b** see FREE *v.* 2, VENT *v.* 2.

unlock /únlók/ *v.tr.* **1 a** release the lock of (a door, box, etc.). **b** release or disclose by unlocking. **2** release thoughts, feelings, etc., from (one's mind, etc.).

■ **1 a** see OPEN *v.* 1–3, UNDO 1. **1b, 2** see RELEASE *v.* 1.

unlocked /únlókt/ *adj.* not locked.

■ see OPEN *adj.* 1–4, 13, 20.

unlooked-for /únlŏŏktfawr/ *adj.* unexpected; unforeseen.

■ see UNFORESEEN.

unloose /únlŏŏs/ *v.tr.* (also **unloosen**) loose; set free.

unlovable /únlúvəbəl/ *adj.* not lovable.

unloved /únlúvd/ *adj.* not loved.

■ see UNPOPULAR.

unlovely /únlúvlee/ *adj.* not attractive; unpleasant; ugly. □□ **unloveliness** *n.*

■ see UGLY 1.

unloving /únlúving/ *adj.* not loving. □□ **unlovingly** *adv.* **unlovingness** *n.*

unlucky /únlúkee/ *adj.* (**unluckier**, **unluckiest**) **1** not fortunate or successful. **2** wretched. **3** bringing bad luck. **4** ill-judged. □□ **unluckily** *adv.* **unluckiness** *n.*

■ **1** see UNFORTUNATE *adj.* 1, UNSUCCESSFUL. **2** see TRAGIC. **3** see INAUSPICIOUS 1. **4** see *ill-advised* 2. □□ **unluckily** see *sadly* (SAD).

unmade /únmáyd/ *adj.* **1** not made. **2** destroyed; annulled.

unmake /únmáyk/ *v.tr.* (*past* and *past part.* **unmade**) undo the making of; destroy; depose; annul.

unmalleable /únmáleeəbəl/ *adj.* not malleable.

unman /únmán/ *v.tr.* (**unmanned**, **unmanning**) **1** deprive of supposed manly qualities (e.g., self-control, courage); cause to weep, etc.; discourage. **2** deprive (a ship, etc.) of men.

unmanageable /únmánijəbəl/ *adj.* not (easily) managed, manipulated, or controlled. □□ **unmanageableness** *n.* **unmanageably** *adv.*

■ see DIFFICULT 2, UNWIELDY, WILD *adj.* 4.

unmanly /únmánlee/ *adj.* not manly. □□ **unmanliness** *n.*

■ see EFFEMINATE.

unmanned /únmánd/ *adj.* **1** not manned. **2** esp. *Brit.* overcome by emotion, etc.

unmannerly /únmánərlee/ *adj.* **1** without good manners. **2** (of actions, speech, etc.) showing a lack of good manners. □□ **unmannerliness** *n.*

■ see RUDE 1.

unmarked /únmaárkt/ *adj.* **1** not marked. **2** not noticed.

■ **1** see UNIDENTIFIED, UNSCATHED. **2** see UNNOTICED.

unmarketable /únmaárkitəbəl/ *adj.* not marketable.

unmarried /únmáreed/ *adj.* not married; single.

■ single, unwed(ded), celibate, bachelor, spinster, old-maid, maiden, free.

unmask /únmásk/ *v.* **1** *tr.* **a** remove the mask from. **b** expose the true character of. **2** *intr.* remove one's mask. □□ **unmasker** *n.*

■ **1 b** see EXPOSE 5.

unmatchable /únmáchəbəl/ *adj.* that cannot be matched. □□ **unmatchably** *adv.*

unmatched /únmácht/ *adj.* not matched or equaled.

■ see UNPARALLELED.

unmatured /únmətyŏŏrd, -tŏŏrd, -chŏŏrd/ *adj.* not yet matured.

unmeaning /únmeéning/ *adj.* having no meaning or signifi-

/.../ **pronunciation**	● **part of speech**
□ **phrases, idioms, and compounds**	
□□ **derivatives**	■ **synonym section**
cross-references appear in SMALL CAPITALS or *italics*	

cance; meaningless. □□ **unmeaningly** *adv.* **unmeaningness** *n.*

unmeant /únmént/ *adj.* not meant or intended.

unmeasurable /únmézhərəbəl/ *adj.* that cannot be measured. □□ **unmeasurably** *adv.*
- see IMMEASURABLE.

unmeasured /únmézhərd/ *adj.* **1** not measured. **2** limitless.

unmelodious /únmilṓdeeəs/ *adj.* not melodious; discordant. □□ **unmelodiously** *adv.*

unmelted /únméltid/ *adj.* not melted.

unmemorable /únmémərəbəl/ *adj.* not memorable. □□ **unmemorably** *adv.*

unmentionable /únménshənəbəl/ *adj. & n.* ● *adj.* that cannot (properly) be mentioned. ● *n.* **1** (in *pl.*) *joc.* **a** undergarments. **b** *archaic* trousers. **2** a person or thing not to be mentioned. □□ **unmentionability** /-bílitee/ *n.* **unmentionableness** *n.* **unmentionably** *adv.*
- *adj.* unspeakable, unutterable, unprintable, ineffable, indescribable, nameless, taboo, scandalous, forbidden, interdicted, proscribed, prohibited; disgraceful, indecent, rude, immodest, shameful, shocking, appalling, dishonorable, obscene, filthy. ● *n.* **1 a** (*unmentionables*) underclothes, underclothing, underwear, undergarments, lingerie, *colloq.* underthings, undies, skivvies, *Brit. colloq.* smalls.

unmentioned /únménshənd/ *adj.* not mentioned.

unmerchantable /únmə́rchəntəbəl/ *adj.* not merchantable.

unmerciful /únmə́rsifŏŏl/ *adj.* merciless. □□ **unmercifully** *adv.* **unmercifulness** *n.*
- merciless, pitiless, unsparing, unkind, relentless, unrelenting, inexorable, ruthless, unpitying, heartless, stonyhearted, hard-hearted, flinty, unfeeling, unsympathetic, unforgiving, inhuman, inhumane, harsh, mean, cruel, savage, brutal, brutish, vicious, barbarous. □□ **unmercifully** see ROUGHLY 1, *endlessly* (ENDLESS).

unmerited /únméritid/ *adj.* not merited.
- see UNWARRANTED 2.

unmet /únmét/ *adj.* (of a quota, demand, goal, etc.) not achieved or fulfilled.

unmetaled /únmét'ld/ *adj. Brit.* (of a road, etc.) not made with road metal.

unmethodical /únmithódikəl/ *adj.* not methodical. □□ **unmethodically** *adv.*
- see *chaotic* (CHAOS), INDISCRIMINATE 2.

unmetrical /únmétrikəl/ *adj.* not metrical.

unmilitary /únmíliteree/ *adj.* not military.

unmindful /únmíndfŏŏl/ *adj.* (often foll. by *of*) not mindful. □□ **unmindfully** *adv.* **unmindfulness** *n.*
- see UNAWARE *adj.* 1.

unmissable /únmísəbəl/ *adj.* that cannot or should not be missed.

unmistakable /únmistáykəbəl/ *adj.* that cannot be mistaken or doubted; clear. □□ **unmistakability** /-bílitee/ *n.* **unmistakableness** *n.* **unmistakably** *adv.*
- see CLEAR *adj.* 6, OBVIOUS. □□ **unmistakably** see *obviously* (OBVIOUS), *expressly* (EXPRESS²), *undoubtedly* (UNDOUBTED).

unmistaken /únmistáykən/ *adj.* not mistaken; right; correct.

unmitigated /únmítigaytid/ *adj.* **1** not mitigated or modified. **2** absolute; unqualified (*an unmitigated disaster*). □□ **unmitigatedly** *adv.*
- **1** undiluted, unalloyed, unmixed, untempered, unmoderated, unmodified, unabated, unlessened, undiminished, unreduced, unrelieved, oppressive, immoderate, unalleviated, unmollified, unsoftened, relentless. **2** unqualified, out-and-out, thorough, thoroughgoing, outright, downright, categorical, absolute, sheer, complete, consummate, total, perfect, true, positive, pure, arrant, utter, plain. □□ **unmitigatedly** see DOWNRIGHT *adv.*

unmixed /únmíkst/ *adj.* not mixed. □ **unmixed blessing** a thing having advantages and no disadvantages.
- see NEAT¹ 5, SEPARATE *adj.*

unmodified /únmódifīd/ *adj.* not modified.

- see SAME *adj.* 2, UNMITIGATED 1.

unmodulated /únmójəlaytid/ *adj.* not modulated.

unmolested /únmələstid/ *adj.* not molested.

unmoor /únmŏ́ŏr/ *v.tr.* **1** (also *absol.*) release the moorings of (a vessel). **2** weigh all but one anchor of (a vessel).

unmoral /únmáwrəl, -mór-/ *adj.* not concerned with morality (cf. IMMORAL). □□ **unmorality** /-rálitee/ *n.* **unmorally** *adv.*

unmotherly /únmúthərlee/ *adj.* not motherly.

unmotivated /únmṓtivaytid/ *adj.* without motivation; without a motive.
- see SHIFTLESS, WANTON 2.

unmounted /únmówntid/ *adj.* not mounted.

unmourned /únmáwrnd/ *adj.* not mourned.
- see UNLAMENTED.

unmoved /únmŏ́ŏvd/ *adj.* **1** not moved. **2** not changed in one's purpose. **3** not affected by emotion. □□ **unmovable** *adj.* (also **unmoveable**).
- **2** see RELENTLESS 1. **3** cool, aloof, calm, collected, unaffected, untouched, unsympathetic, unstirred, undisturbed, apathetic, stoic(al), impassive, dispassionate, unemotional, unfeeling, unconcerned, indifferent, unreactive, unresponsive, stolid, stony, adamant, stonyhearted, hard-hearted. □□ **unmovable** see IMMOVABLE *adj.*

unmown /únmṓn/ *adj.* not mown.

unmuffle /únmúfəl/ *v.tr.* **1** remove a muffler from (a face, bell, etc.). **2** free of something that muffles or conceals.

unmurmuring /únmə́rməring/ *adj.* not complaining. □□ **unmurmuringly** *adv.*

unmusical /únmyŏŏzikəl/ *adj.* **1** not pleasing to the ear. **2** unskilled in or indifferent to music. □□ **unmusicality** /-kálitee/ *n.* **unmusically** *adv.* **unmusicalness** *n.*
- **1** see DISCORDANT 2.

unmutilated /únmyŏ́ŏt'laytid/ *adj.* not mutilated.

unmuzzle /únmúzəl/ *v.tr.* **1** remove a muzzle from. **2** relieve of an obligation to remain silent.

unnail /ún-náyl/ *v.tr.* unfasten by the removal of nails.

unnameable /ún-náyməbəl/ *adj.* that cannot be named, esp. too bad to be named.

unnamed /ún-náymd/ *adj.* not named.
- see NAMELESS 1, 3, 5.

unnatural /ún-náchərəl/ *adj.* **1** contrary to nature or the usual course of nature; not normal. **2 a** lacking natural feelings. **b** extremely cruel or wicked. **3** artificial. **4** affected. □□ **unnaturally** *adv.* **unnaturalness** *n.*
- **1** outlandish, weird, uncanny, peculiar, strange, odd, unaccountable, supernatural, preternatural, queer, grotesque, bizarre, extraordinary, eccentric, freakish; abnormal, unexpected, unusual, uncharacteristic, out of character. **2** abnormal, perverse, perverted, monstrous, aberrant, improper, unseemly; deviant, depraved, degenerate, bestial; unfeeling, callous, inhuman, inhumane, cruel, wicked, sadistic, warped, twisted, corrupted, *colloq.* kinky, *sl.* bent. **3** see ARTIFICIAL 1, 2. **4** labored, forced, stilted, stiff, strained, restrained, artificial, false, insincere, sham, feigned, pretended, contrived, affected, mannered, self-conscious, theatrical, stagy, *colloq.* phony. □□ **unnaturalness** see ODDITY 3.

unnavigable /ún-návigəbəl/ *adj.* not navigable. □□ **unnavigability** /-bílitee/ *n.*

unnecessary /ún-nésəseree/ *adj. & n.* ● *adj.* **1** not necessary. **2** more than is necessary (*with unnecessary care*). ● *n.* (*pl.* **-ies**) (usu. in *pl.*) an unnecessary thing. □□ **unnecessarily** *adv.* **unnecessariness** *n.*
- *adj.* **1** unneeded, needless, unrequired, dispensable, disposable, expendable, unwanted, uncalled-for, inessential, unessential, nonessential. **2** surplus, superfluous, supererogatory, redundant, extra, de trop, undue, excessive. ● *n.* inessential, nonessential, supernumerary, extra. □□ **unnecessarily** see *unduly* (UNDUE).

unneeded /ún-neédid/ *adj.* not needed.
- see NEEDLESS.

unneighborly /ún-náybərlee/ *adj.* not neighborly. □□ **unneighborliness** *n.*

unnerve /ún-nə́rv/ *v.tr.* deprive of strength or resolution. □□ **unnervingly** *adv.*
■ upset, agitate, perturb, ruffle, fluster, discomfit, discompose, unsettle, disconcert, dismay, intimidate, stun, stupefy, rock, shatter, *colloq.* shake (up), rattle, faze, throw.

unnoticeable /ún-nṓtisəbəl/ *adj.* not easily seen or noticed. □□ **unnoticeably** *adv.*
■ see INCONSPICUOUS, IMPERCEPTIBLE.

unnoticed /ún-nṓtist/ *adj.* not noticed.
■ unnoted, overlooked, unobserved, undiscovered, unremarked, unmarked, unperceived; unseen, unheard.

unnumbered /ún-númbərd/ *adj.* **1** not marked with a number. **2** not counted. **3** countless.
■ **3** see UMPTEEN *adj.*

unobjectionable /únəbjékshənəbəl/ *adj.* not objectionable; acceptable. □□ **unobjectionableness** *n.* **unobjectionably** *adv.*
■ see INOFFENSIVE.

unobliging /únəblíjing/ *adj.* not obliging; unhelpful; uncooperative.

unobscured /únəbskyŏ́ord/ *adj.* not obscured.
■ see FULL¹ *adj.* 7b, DISTINCT 2.

unobservable /únəbzə́rvəbəl/ *adj.* not observable; imperceptible.

unobservant /únəbzə́rvənt/ *adj.* not observant. □□ **unobservantly** *adv.*
■ see *heedless* (HEED).

unobserved /únəbzə́rvd/ *adj.* not observed. □□ **unobservedly** /-vidlee/ *adv.*
■ see UNNOTICED.

unobstructed /únəbstrúktid/ *adj.* not obstructed.
■ see CLEAR *adj.* 10.

unobtainable /únəbtáynəbəl/ *adj.* that cannot be obtained.
■ unavailable, inaccessible, unreachable; out of stock, sold out.

unobtrusive /únəbtrŏ́osiv/ *adj.* not making oneself or itself noticed. □□ **unobtrusively** *adv.* **unobtrusiveness** *n.*
■ inconspicuous, unostentatious, low-key, retiring, modest, self-effacing, unpresuming, unpretentious, unassuming, quiet, humble, unassertive, nonassertive, subdued, reserved, reticent, suppressed, discreet, unnoticeable. □□ **unobtrusively** see *quietly* (QUIET).

unoccupied /únókyəpid/ *adj.* not occupied.
■ see IDLE *adj.* 2, VACANT 1.

unoffending /únəfénding/ *adj.* not offending; harmless; innocent. □□ **unoffended** *adj.*
■ see INOFFENSIVE.

unofficial /únəfíshəl/ *adj.* **1** not officially authorized or confirmed. **2** not characteristic of officials. □□ **unofficially** *adv.*
■ **1** informal, unauthorized, undocumented, unconfirmed, off the record, private, secret, unpublicized, unannounced. **2** see INFORMAL. □□ **unofficially** see *off the record* (RECORD).

unoiled /únóyld/ *adj.* not oiled.

unopened /únṓpənd/ *adj.* not opened.
■ closed, shut.

unopposed /únəpṓzd/ *adj.* not opposed, esp. in an election.

unordained /únawrdáynd/ *adj.* not ordained.

unordinary /únáwrd'neree/ *adj.* not ordinary.

unorganized /únáwrgənizd/ *adj.* not organized (cf. DISORGANIZE).
■ see *chaotic* (CHAOS).

unoriginal /únəríjinəl/ *adj.* lacking originality; derivative. □□ **unoriginality** /-nálitee/ *n.* **unoriginally** *adv.*
■ see TIRED 2, DERIVATIVE *adj.*

unornamental /únawrnəmént'l/ *adj.* not ornamental; plain.

unornamented /únáwrnəmentid/ *adj.* not ornamented.
■ see UNADORNED.

unorthodox /únáwrthədoks/ *adj.* not orthodox. □□ **unorthodoxly** *adv.* **unorthodoxy** *n.*
■ irregular, unconventional, nonconformist, unconforming, nonconforming, nonstandard, aberrant, aberrational, deviant, heretical, unsound, heteroclite, unusual, abnormal, uncustomary, uncommon, offbeat, *colloq.* way-out. □□ **unorthodoxy** see ORIGINALITY 1, 2.

unostentatious /únostentáyshəs/ *adj.* not ostentatious. □□ **unostentatiously** *adv.* **unostentatiousness** *n.*
■ see MODEST 5.

unowned /únṓnd/ *adj.* **1** unacknowledged. **2** having no owner.

unpack /únpák/ *v.tr.* **1** (also *absol.*) open and remove the contents of (a package, luggage, etc.). **2** take (a thing) out from a package, etc. □□ **unpacker** *n.*
■ **1** see UNLOAD 1, 2.

unpaged /únpáyjd/ *adj.* with pages not numbered.

unpaid /únpáyd/ *adj.* (of a debt or a person) not paid.
■ payable, outstanding, owed, owing, due, unsettled; unsalaried, voluntary, volunteer, honorary.

unpainted /únpáyntid/ *adj.* not painted.

unpaired /únpáird/ *adj.* **1** not arranged in pairs. **2** not forming one of a pair.

unpalatable /únpálətəbəl/ *adj.* **1** not pleasant to taste. **2** (of an idea, suggestion, etc.) disagreeable; distasteful. □□ **unpalatability** *n.* **unpalatableness** *n.*
■ rancid, sour, off, turned, bitter, inedible, uneatable; distasteful, disagreeable, unpleasant, unsavory, unappetizing, unattractive, repugnant, nasty, offensive, objectionable.

unparalleled /únpárəleld/ *adj.* having no parallel or equal.
■ unequaled, incomparable, matchless, peerless, unrivaled, unmatched, nonpareil, inimitable, unexcelled, superior, supreme, superlative, unsurpassed, hors concours, surpassing, transcendent, unusual, special, singular, rare, unique, exceptional, consummate.

unpardonable /únpaárd'nəbəl/ *adj.* that cannot be pardoned. □□ **unpardonableness** *n.* **unpardonably** *adv.*
■ see INEXCUSABLE.

unparliamentary /únpaarləméntəree/ *adj.* contrary to proper parliamentary usage. □ **unparliamentary language** oaths or abuse.

unpasteurized /únpáschərizd, -pástə-/ *adj.* not pasteurized.

unpatented /únpát'ntid/ *adj.* not patented.

unpatriotic /únpaytreeótik/ *adj.* not patriotic. □□ **unpatriotically** *adv.*

unpaved /únpáyvd/ *adj.* not paved.

unpeeled /únpéeld/ *adj.* not peeled.

unpeg /únpég/ *v.tr.* (**unpegged**, **unpegging**) **1** unfasten by the removal of pegs. **2** cease to maintain or stabilize (prices, etc.).
■ **1** see UNDO 1.

unpeople *v. & n.* ● *v.tr.* /únpéepəl/ depopulate. ● *n.pl.* /únpeepəl/ unpersons.

unperceived /únpərséevd/ *adj.* not perceived; unobserved.
■ see UNNOTICED.

unperceptive /únpərséptiv/ *adj.* not perceptive. □□ **unperceptively** *adv.* **unperceptiveness** *n.*
■ see BLIND *adj.* 2a.

unperfected /únpərféktid/ *adj.* not perfected.

unperforated /únpə́rfəraytid/ *adj.* not perforated.

unperformed /únpərfáwrmd/ *adj.* not performed.

unperfumed /únpə́rfyŏŏmd/ *adj.* not perfumed.
■ unscented, scentless, nonperfumed, plain, natural.

unperson /únpə́rsən/ *n.* a person whose name or existence is denied or ignored.

unpersuadable /únpərswáydəbəl/ *adj.* not able to be persuaded; obstinate.

unpersuaded /únpərswáydid/ *adj.* not persuaded.
■ see DOUBTFUL 1.

/.../ **pronunciation**	● **part of speech**
□ **phrases, idioms, and compounds**	
□□ **derivatives**	■ **synonym section**
cross-references appear in SMALL CAPITALS or *italics*	

unpersuasive /únpərswáysiv, -ziv/ *adj.* not persuasive. □□ **unpersuasively** *adv.*
■ see WEAK 4.

unperturbed /únpərtárbd/ *adj.* not perturbed. □□ **unperturbedly** /-bidlee/ *adv.*
■ see CALM *adj.* 2.

unphilosophical /únfiləsófikəl/ *adj.* (also **unphilosophic**) **1** not according to philosophical principles. **2** lacking philosophy. □□ **unphilosophically** *adv.*

unphysiological /únfizeeəlójikəl/ *adj.* (also **unphysiologic**) not in accordance with normal physiological functioning. □□ **unphysiologically** *adv.*

unpick /únpík/ *v.tr.* undo the sewing of (stitches, a garment, etc.).
■ see UNDO 1.

unpicked /únpíkt/ *adj.* **1** not selected. **2** (of a flower) not plucked.

unpicturesque /únpikchərésk/ *adj.* not picturesque.

unpin /únpín/ *v.tr.* (**unpinned**, **unpinning**) **1** unfasten or detach by removing a pin or pins. **2** *Chess* release (a piece that has been pinned).
■ **1** see UNDO 1.

unpitied /únpíteed/ *adj.* not pitied.

unpitying /únpíteeing/ *adj.* not pitying. □□ **unpityingly** *adv.*
■ see UNSYMPATHETIC.

unplaceable /únpláysəbəl/ *adj.* that cannot be placed or classified (*his accent was unplaceable*).

unplaced /únpláyst/ *adj.* not placed, esp. not placed as one of the first three finishing in a race, etc.

unplanned /únplánd/ *adj.* not planned.
■ see ACCIDENTAL *adj.* 1, IMPULSIVE, RAMBLING 2, 3.

unplanted /únplántid/ *adj.* not planted.

unplausible /únpláwzibəl/ *adj.* not plausible.
■ see IMPLAUSIBLE.

unplayable /únpláyəbəl/ *adj.* **1** *Sports* (of a ball) that cannot be struck or returned. **2** that cannot be played. □□ **unplayably** *adv.*

unpleasant /únplézənt/ *adj.* not pleasant; displeasing; disagreeable. □□ **unpleasantly** *adv.* **unpleasantness** *n.*
■ see NASTY 1, 5a, b;3. □□ **unpleasantly** see AWFULLY 1, *painfully* (PAINFUL). **unpleasantness** see TROUBLE *n.* 1.

unpleasing /únpleézing/ *adj.* not pleasing. □□ **unpleasingly** *adv.*
■ see DISAGREEABLE 1, UNWELCOME, UGLY 1.

unplowed /únplówd/ *adj.* not plowed.

unplucked /únplúkt/ *adj.* not plucked.

unplug /únplúg/ *v.tr.* (**unplugged**, **unplugging**) **1** disconnect (an electrical device) by removing its plug from the socket. **2** unstop.
■ **1** see UNDO 1.

unplumbed /únplúmd/ *adj.* **1** not plumbed. **2** not fully explored or understood. □□ **unplumbable** *adj.*

unpoetic /únpō-étik/ *adj.* (also **unpoetical**) not poetic.

unpointed /únpóyntid/ *adj.* **1** having no point or points. **2 a** not punctuated. **b** (of written Hebrew, etc.) without vowel points. **3** (of masonry or brickwork) not pointed.

unpolished /únpólisht/ *adj.* **1** not polished; rough. **2** without refinement; crude.
■ **2** see CRUDE *adj.* 1b.

unpolitic /únpólitik/ *adj.* impolitic; unwise.

unpolitical /únpəlítikəl/ *adj.* not concerned with politics. □□ **unpolitically** *adv.*

unpolled /únpṓld/ *adj.* **1** not having voted at an election. **2** not included in an opinion poll.

unpolluted /únpəlṓotid/ *adj.* not polluted.
■ see CLEAN *adj.* 1.

unpopular /únpópyələr/ *adj.* not popular; not liked by the public or by people in general. □□ **unpopularity** /-láritee/ *n.* **unpopularly** *adv.*
■ out of favor, in bad odor, unliked, disliked, shunned, avoided, snubbed, ignored, unsought-after, unaccepted, unwanted, rejected, outcast, despised, unwelcome, undesirable; unloved, friendless.

unpopulated /únpópyəlaytid/ *adj.* not populated.
■ see UNINHABITED.

unpossessed /únpəzést/ *adj.* **1** (foll. by *of*) not in possession of. **2** not possessed.

unpractical /únpráktikəl/ *adj.* **1** not practical. **2** (of a person) not having practical skill. □□ **unpracticality** /-kálitee/ *n.* **unpractically** *adv.*
■ see IMPRACTICAL 1.

unpracticed /únpráktist/ *adj.* **1** not experienced or skilled. **2** not put into practice.
■ **1** see *inexperienced* (INEXPERIENCE).

unprecedented /únprésidentid/ *adj.* **1** having no precedent; unparalleled. **2** novel. □□ **unprecedentedly** *adv.*
■ **1** see EXTRAORDINARY 1, 2. **2** see ORIGINAL *adj.* 2.

unpredictable /únpridíktəbəl/ *adj.* that cannot be predicted. □□ **unpredictability** *n.* **unpredictableness** *n.* **unpredictably** *adv.*
■ see ARBITRARY 1, VARIABLE *adj.* 2. □□ **unpredictability** see VICISSITUDE, *inconstancy* (INCONSTANT).

unpredicted /únpridíktid/ *adj.* not predicted or foretold.
■ see UNFORESEEN.

unprejudiced /únpréjədist/ *adj.* not prejudiced.
■ unbigoted, unbiased, impartial, not jaundiced, just, fair, objective, disinterested, neutral, fair-minded, nonpartisan, liberal, open-minded, undogmatic.

unpremeditated /únpriméditaytid/ *adj.* not previously thought over; not deliberately planned; unintentional. □□ **unpremeditatedly** *adv.*
■ unprepared, unplanned, unarranged, uncontrived, unstudied, unrehearsed, spontaneous, spur-of-the-moment, last-minute, impromptu, extemporaneous, extempory, extempore, ad lib, improvised, offhand, casual, impulsive, natural, involuntary, automatic, unconscious, unintended, unintentional, *colloq.* off-the-cuff. □□ **unpremeditatedly** see *on the spur of the moment* (SPUR).

unprepared /únpripáird/ *adj.* not prepared (in advance); not ready. □□ **unpreparedly** *adv.* **unpreparedness** *n.*
■ (*of a person*) unready, ill-equipped, surprised, taken aback, unwarned, not forewarned, (caught) napping *or* off guard, dumbfounded, at sixes and sevens, *colloq.* caught short, (caught) with one's pants down; (*of a thing*) unmade, not set up, unfinished, incomplete; (*of an action*) improvised, thrown together, *colloq.* done by the seat of one's pants; see also UNPREMEDITATED.

unprepossessing /únpreepəzésing/ *adj.* not prepossessing; unattractive.
■ see ORDINARY *adj.*

unprescribed /únpriskríbd/ *adj.* (esp. of drugs) not prescribed.

unpresentable /únprizéntəbəl/ *adj.* not presentable.

unpressed /únprést/ *adj.* not pressed, esp. (of clothing) unironed.

unpresuming /únprizṓoming/ *adj.* not presuming; modest.

unpresumptuous /únprizúmpchōoəs/ *adj.* not presumptuous.

unpretending /únpriténding/ *adj.* unpretentious. □□ **unpretendingly** *adv.* **unpretendingness** *n.*

unpretentious /únpriténshəs/ *adj.* not making a great display; simple; modest. □□ **unpretentiously** *adv.* **unpretentiousness** *n.*
■ see MODEST 1, 2, 5.

unpriced /únpríst/ *adj.* not having a price or prices fixed, marked, or stated.

unprimed /únprímd/ *adj.* not primed.

unprincipled /únprínsipəld/ *adj.* lacking or not based on good moral principles. □□ **unprincipledness** *n.*
■ see UNSCRUPULOUS.

unprintable /únpríntəbəl/ *adj.* that cannot be printed, esp. because too indecent or libelous or blasphemous. □□ **unprintably** *adv.*

unprinted /únpríntid/ *adj.* not printed.

unprivileged /únprívilijd, -prívlijd/ *adj.* not privileged.

unproblematic /únprobləmátik/ *adj.* causing no difficulty. □□ **unproblematically** *adv.*

unproclaimed /únprōkláymd, -prə-/ *adj.* not proclaimed.

unprocurable /únprōkyŏŏrəbəl, -prə-/ *adj.* that cannot be procured.

unproductive /únprədúktiv/ *adj.* not productive. □□ **unproductively** *adv.* **unproductiveness** *n.*
■ see FRUITLESS 1, 2.

unprofessional /únprəféshənəl/ *adj.* **1** contrary to professional standards of behavior, etc. **2** not belonging to a profession; amateur. □□ **unprofessionally** *adv.*
■ **1** unbecoming, improper, unethical, unprincipled, unseemly, undignified, unfitting, unbefitting, unworthy, unscholarly, negligent, lax; amateurish, inexpert, incompetent, unskillful, inferior, second-rate, inefficient, poor, shoddy, low-quality, sloppy. **2** amateur, nonprofessional, lay, unspecialized, nonspecialist, inexpert, inexperienced, untrained, untutored, unschooled, unskilled. □□ **unprofessionally** see POORLY *adv.*

unprofitable /únprófitəbəl/ *adj.* not profitable. □□ **unprofitableness** *n.* **unprofitably** *adv.*
■ profitless, ungainful, unremunerative, unfruitful, uneconomic, uncommercial; breaking even; losing, esp. *Brit.* loss-making; pointless, purposeless, unavailing, futile, fruitless, useless, unproductive, unrewarding, thankless, worthless, ineffective, inefficient, *archaic* bootless.

unprogressive /únprəgrésiv/ *adj.* not progressive.

unpromising /únprómising/ *adj.* not likely to turn out well. □□ **unpromisingly** *adv.*
■ inauspicious, unpropitious, unfavorable, gloomy, ominous, adverse, portentous, baleful, hopeless.

unprompted /únprómptid/ *adj.* spontaneous.
■ see VOLUNTARY *adj.* 1.

unpronounceable /únprənównsəbəl/ *adj.* that cannot be pronounced. □□ **unpronounceably** *adv.*

unpropitious /únprəpíshəs/ *adj.* not propitious. □□ **unpropitiously** *adv.*
■ see INAUSPICIOUS 1. □□ **unpropitiously** inauspiciously, unluckily, regrettably.

unprosperous /únpróspərəs/ *adj.* not prosperous. □□ **unprosperously** *adv.*

unprotected /únprətéktid/ *adj.* not protected. □□ **unprotectedness** *n.*
■ see *defenseless* (DEFENSE), OPEN *adj.* 1–4, 13, 20.

unprotesting /únprətésting/ *adj.* not protesting. □□ **unprotestingly** *adv.*

unprovable /únprŏŏvəbəl/ *adj.* that cannot be proved. □□ **unprovability** *n.* **unprovableness** *n.*

unproved /únprŏŏvd/ *adj.* (also **unproven** /-vən/) not proved.
■ see THEORETICAL 2.

unprovided /únprəvídid/ *adj.* (usu. foll. by *with*) not furnished, supplied, or equipped.

unprovoked /únprəvŏkt/ *adj.* (of a person or act) without provocation.
■ see UNWARRANTED 2, CALM *adj.* 2.

unpublished /únpúblisht/ *adj.* not published. □□ **unpublishable** *adj.*

unpunctual /únpúngkchŏŏəl/ *adj.* not punctual. □□ **unpunctuality** /-chŏŏálitee/ *n.*

unpunctuated /únpúngkchŏŏaytid/ *adj.* not punctuated.

unpunishable /únpúnishəbəl/ *adj.* that cannot be punished.

unpunished /únpúnisht/ *adj.* not punished.

unpurified /únpyŏŏrifīd/ *adj.* not purified.

unputdownable /únpŏŏtdównəbəl/ *adj. colloq.* (of a book) so engrossing that one has to go on reading it.

unqualified /únkwólifīd/ *adj.* **1** not competent (*unqualified to give an answer*). **2** not legally or officially qualified (*an unqualified practitioner*). **3** not modified or restricted; complete (*unqualified assent; unqualified success*).
■ **1** ineligible, unfit, incompetent, unable, ill-equipped, unsuited. **2** untrained, unequipped, unprepared, amateur. **3** unrestricted, unreserved, unconditional, categorical, outright, unmitigated, downright, out-and-out, wholehearted, pure (and simple), true, perfect, complete, utter, sheer, absolute, consummate.

unquenchable /únkwénchəbəl/ *adj.* that cannot be quenched. □□ **unquenchably** *adv.*
■ insatiable, unslakable, unsatisfiable; inextinguishable, unsuppressible, irrepressible, indestructible.

unquenched /únkwéncht/ *adj.* not quenched.

unquestionable /únkwéschənəbəl/ *adj.* that cannot be disputed or doubted. □□ **unquestionability** *n.* **unquestionableness** *n.* **unquestionably** *adv.*
■ unexceptionable, indubitable, undoubted, indisputable, incontestable, unimpeachable, undeniable, certain, sure, positive, irrefutable, manifest, obvious, patent, clear, definite, incontrovertible, unequivocal, unmistakable, conclusive. □□ **unquestionably** see *undoubtedly* (UNDOUBTED).

unquestioned /únkwéschənd/ *adj.* **1** not disputed or doubted; definite; certain. **2** not interrogated.
■ see UNDISPUTED.

unquestioning /únkwéschəning/ *adj.* **1** asking no questions. **2** done, etc., without asking questions. □□ **unquestioningly** *adv.*
■ **2** see IMPLICIT 3. □□ **unquestioningly** see *willingly* (WILLING), *implicitly* (IMPLICIT).

unquiet /únkwíət/ *adj.* **1** restless; agitated; stirring. **2** perturbed, anxious. □□ **unquietly** *adv.* **unquietness** *n.*

unquotable /únkwŏtəbəl/ *adj.* that cannot be quoted.

unquote /únkwŏt/ *v.tr.* (as *int.*) (in dictation, reading aloud, etc.) indicate the presence of closing quotation marks (cf. QUOTE *v.* 5 b).

unquoted /únkwŏtid/ *adj.* not quoted, esp. on a stock exchange.

unravel /únrávəl/ *v.* **1** *tr.* cause to be no longer raveled, tangled, or intertwined. **2** *tr.* probe and solve (a mystery, etc.). **3** *tr.* undo (a fabric, esp. a knitted one). **4** *intr.* become disentangled or unknitted.
■ **1** untangle, disentangle, unsnarl, sort out. **2** see SOLVE. **3** see UNDO 1.

unreachable /únréechəbəl/ *adj.* that cannot be reached. □□ **unreachableness** *n.* **unreachably** *adv.*
■ see INACCESSIBLE 1, 2.

unread /únréd/ *adj.* **1** (of a book, etc.) not read. **2** (of a person) not well-read.
■ **2** see UNEDUCATED.

unreadable /únréedəbəl/ *adj.* **1** too dull or too difficult to be worth reading. **2** illegible. □□ **unreadability** /-bílitee/ *n.* **unreadably** *adv.*
■ **2** see ILLEGIBLE.

unready[1] /únrédee/ *adj.* **1** not ready. **2** not prompt in action. □□ **unreadily** *adv.* **unreadiness** *n.*
■ see UNPREPARED.

unready[2] /únrédee/ *adj. archaic* lacking good advice; rash (*Ethelred the Unready*). [UN-[1] + REDE, assim. to UNREADY[1]]

unreal /únréeəl/ *adj.* **1** not real. **2** imaginary; illusory. **3** *sl.* incredible, amazing. □□ **unreality** /-reeálitee/ *n.* **unreally** *adv.*
■ **1** artificial, synthetic, synthesized, mock, false, fake(d), counterfeit, fraudulent, dummy, spurious, falsified, pretend(ed), sham, pseudo, make-believe. **2** imaginary, imagined, theoretical, hypothetical, mythical, made-up, invented, fictitious, fictional, fabulous, fantastic, chimeric(al), fanciful, fancied, illusory, make-believe, dreamlike, insubstantial, phantasmagoric(al), phantasmal, spectral, unrealistic, nonexistent. **3** see INCREDIBLE. □□ **unreality** see FANCY *n.* 6.

unrealistic /únreeəlístik/ *adj.* not realistic. □□ **unrealistically** *adv.*
■ unreal, unlifelike, unnatural, unauthentic, nonrepresentational, unrepresentative, inaccurate; impractical, illogical, unreasonable, unworkable, unrealizable, quixotic, idealistic, romantic, fanciful,

---

/. . ./ **pronunciation**	● **part of speech**
□ **phrases, idioms, and compounds**	
□□ **derivatives**	■ **synonym section**
cross-references appear in SMALL CAPITALS or *italics*	

1683

far-fetched, visionary, delusional, delusive, delusory, *colloq.* starry-eyed.

unrealizable /únree͡əlízəbəl/ *adj.* that cannot be realized.
■ see IMPOSSIBLE 1.

unrealized /únree͡əlizd/ *adj.* not realized.
■ see POTENTIAL *adj.*

unreason /únree͡əzən/ *n.* lack of reasonable thought or action. [ME, = injustice, f. UN-¹ + REASON]

unreasonable /únree͡əzənəbəl/ *adj.* **1** going beyond the limits of what is reasonable or equitable (*unreasonable demands*). **2** not guided by or listening to reason. □□ **unreasonableness** *n.* **unreasonably** *adv.*
■ **1** excessive, outrageous, exorbitant, extravagant, immoderate, extortionate, inordinate, unconscionable, unjust, unwarranted, inequitable, unfair, unequal, improper, unjustified, unjustifiable, uncalled-for; inappropriate, unapt, inapt, unsuitable, unbefitting, impractical, unrealistic. **2** irrational, illogical, unthinking, absurd, foolish, senseless, nonsensical, mindless, brainless, thoughtless, silly, mad, crazy, insane, idiotic, moronic, imbecilic, stupid, fatuous, ridiculous, ludicrous, laughable, preposterous, far-fetched; unperceptive, undiscerning, short-sighted, myopic, blind. □□ **unreasonableness** see ABSURDITY 1, 2, FOLLY 1. **unreasonably** see *unduly* (UNDUE).

unreasoned /únree͡əzənd/ *adj.* not reasoned.
■ see GROUNDLESS, ARBITRARY 1.

unreasoning /únree͡əzəning/ *adj.* not reasoning. □□ **unreasoningly** *adv.*
■ see BLIND *adj.* 3.

unreceptive /únriséptiv/ *adj.* not receptive.
■ see CHILLY 3.

unreciprocated /únrisíprəkaytid/ *adj.* not reciprocated.

unreckoned /únrékənd/ *adj.* not calculated or taken into account.

unreclaimed /únrikláymd/ *adj.* not reclaimed.

unrecognizable /únrékəgnízəbəl/ *adj.* that cannot be recognized. □□ **unrecognizableness** *n.* **unrecognizably** *adv.*
■ see INDEFINITE 1, INCOGNITO *adj.* & *adv.*

unrecognized /únrékəgnízd/ *adj.* not recognized.
■ see UNIDENTIFIED, THANKLESS 2.

unrecompensed /únrékəmpenst/ *adj.* not recompensed.

unreconciled /únrékənsild/ *adj.* not reconciled.

unreconstructed /únreekənstrúktid/ *adj.* **1** not reconciled or converted to the current political orthodoxy. **2** not rebuilt.

unrecorded /únrikáwrdid/ *adj.* not recorded. □□ **unrecordable** *adj.*

unrectified /únréktifid/ *adj.* not rectified.

unredeemable /únridee͡əməbəl/ *adj.* that cannot be redeemed. □□ **unredeemably** *adv.*

unredeemed /únridee͡əmd/ *adj.* not redeemed.

unredressed /únridrést/ *adj.* not redressed.

unreel /únree͡əl/ *v.tr.* & *intr.* unwind from a reel.

unreeve /únree͡əv/ *v.tr.* (*past* **unrove**) withdraw (a rope, etc.) from being reeved.

unrefined /únrifínd/ *adj.* not refined.
■ (*of a substance*) impure, unpurified, unclarified, raw, crude, coarse, untreated, unfinished, natural, unprocessed; (*of a person, behavior, etc.*) coarse, rude, rough, unsophisticated, uncultured, uncivilized, uncultivated, unaccomplished, unpolished, inelegant, ill-bred, impolite, discourteous, unmannerly, ill-mannered, bad-mannered, ignoble, plebeian, undignified, unladylike, ungentlemanlike, ungentlemanly, uncourtly, ungracious, boorish, loutish, gross, vulgar, uncouth, cloddish, awkward, gauche.

unreflecting /únriflékting/ *adj.* not thoughtful. □□ **unreflectingly** *adv.* **unreflectingness** *n.*

unreformed /únrifáwrmd/ *adj.* not reformed.

unregarded /únrigaárdid/ *adj.* not regarded.

unregenerate /únrijénərət/ *adj.* not regenerate; obstinately wrong or bad. □□ **unregeneracy** *n.* **unregenerately** *adv.*

unregistered /únréjistərd/ *adj.* not registered.

unregulated /únrégyələytid/ *adj.* not regulated.

■ see INDEPENDENT *adj.* 1a.

unrehearsed /únrihə́rst/ *adj.* not rehearsed.
■ see EXTEMPORANEOUS.

unrelated /únriláytid/ *adj.* not related. □□ **unrelatedness** *n.*
■ independent, separate, distinct, different, dissimilar, incompatible, inappropriate, irrelevant, extraneous, foreign, alien, unassociated, unaffiliated, unconnected, uncoupled, unlinked, unallied, uncoordinated.

unrelaxed /únrilákst/ *adj.* not relaxed.
■ see TENSE¹ *adj.*

unrelenting /únrilénting/ *adj.* **1** not relenting or yielding. **2** unmerciful. **3** not abating or relaxing. □□ **unrelentingly** *adv.* **unrelentingness** *n.*
■ **1, 2** see RELENTLESS 1. **3** see RELENTLESS 2.

unreliable /únrilíəbəl/ *adj.* not reliable; erratic. □□ **unreliability** *n.* **unreliableness** *n.* **unreliably** *adv.*
■ untrustworthy, undependable, irresponsible, uncertain, unpredictable, erratic, fickle, inconsistent, temperamental, unstable, unsound, treacherous, flimsy, weak, suspect, risky, chancy, *Brit. colloq.* dodgy, *sl.* dicey, iffy. □□ **unreliability** see *inconstancy* (INCONSTANT). **unreliably** see *by fits and starts* (FIT²).

unrelieved /únrilee͡əvd/ *adj.* **1** lacking the relief given by contrast or variation. **2** not aided or assisted. □□ **unrelievedly** /-vidlee/ *adv.*
■ **1** see UNMITIGATED 1.

unreligious /únrilíjəs/ *adj.* **1** not concerned with religion. **2** irreligious.
■ see *unbelieving* (UNBELIEF).

unremarkable /únrimaárkəbəl/ *adj.* not remarkable; uninteresting. □□ **unremarkably** *adv.*
■ see ORDINARY *adj.*

unremembered /únrimémbərd/ *adj.* not remembered; forgotten.

unremitting /únrimíting/ *adj.* never relaxing or slackening; incessant. □□ **unremittingly** *adv.* **unremittingness** *n.*
■ see RELENTLESS 2.

unremorseful /únrimáwrsfŏŏl/ *adj.* lacking remorse. □□ **unremorsefully** *adv.*
■ see UNREPENTANT.

unremovable /únrimŏŏvəbəl/ *adj.* that cannot be removed.

unremunerative /únrimyŏŏnərətiv, -raytiv/ *adj.* bringing no, or not enough, profit or income. □□ **unremuneratively** *adv.* **unremunerativeness** *n.*

unrenewable /únrinŏŏəbəl, -nyŏŏ-/ *adj.* that cannot be renewed. □□ **unrenewed** *adj.*

unrepealed /únripee͡əld/ *adj.* not repealed.

unrepeatable /únripee͡ətəbəl/ *adj.* **1** that cannot be done, made, or said again. **2** too indecent to be said again. □□ **unrepeatability** *n.*

unrepentant /únripéntənt/ *adj.* not repentant; impenitent. □□ **unrepentantly** *adv.*
■ unrepenting, unremorseful, impenitent, unapologetic, unregretful, unashamed, unembarrassed, unselfconscious, remorseless, unreformed, unrehabilitated, unregenerate, unreformable, incorrigible, incurable, hardened, recidivist(ic).

unreported /únripáwrtid/ *adj.* not reported.

unrepresentative /únreprizéntətiv/ *adj.* not representative. □□ **unrepresentativeness** *n.*
■ see UNUSUAL 2.

unrepresented /únreprizéntid/ *adj.* not represented.

unreproved /únriprŏŏvd/ *adj.* not reproved.

unrequested /únrikwéstid/ *adj.* not requested or asked for.
■ see UNASKED.

unrequited /únrikwítid/ *adj.* (of love, etc.) not returned. □□ **unrequitedly** *adv.* **unrequitedness** *n.*
■ see THANKLESS 2.

unreserve /únrizə́rv/ *n.* lack of reserve; frankness.

unreserved /únrizə́rvd/ *adj.* **1** not reserved (*unreserved seats*). **2** without reservations; absolute (*unreserved confidence*). **3** free from reserve (*an unreserved nature*). □□ **unreservedly** /-vidlee/ *adv.* **unreservedness** *n.*
■ **1** see FREE *adj.* 8b. **2** see WHOLEHEARTED. **3** see OPEN *adj.* 8a. □□ **unreservedly** see ABSOLUTELY 1.

unresisted /únrizístid/ *adj.* not resisted. □□ **unresistedly** *adv.*

unresisting /únrizísting/ *adj.* not resisting. □□ **unresistingly** *adv.* **unresistingness** *n.*
■ see PASSIVE 2.

unresolvable /únrizólvəbəl/ *adj.* (of a problem, conflict, etc.) that cannot be resolved.

unresolved /únrizólvd/ *adj.* **1 a** uncertain how to act; irresolute. **b** uncertain in opinion; undecided. **2** (of questions, etc.) undetermined; undecided; unsolved. **3** not broken up or dissolved. □□ **unresolvedly** /-vidlee/ *adv.* **unresolvedness** *n.*
■ **1** undecided, uncertain, unsure, ambivalent, of two minds, wavering, vacillating, shilly-shallying, dithering, hesitant, irresolute. **2** unsettled, undetermined, undecided, open, up in the air, moot, pending, debatable, arguable, problematic(al), indefinite, vague, open to question, questionable, unanswered, unsolved.

unresponsive /únrispónsiv/ *adj.* not responsive. □□ **unresponsively** *adv.* **unresponsiveness** *n.*
■ see UNMOVED 3, SLOW *adj.* 5, INERT 1, 2.

unrest /únrést/ *n.* **1** lack of rest. **2** restlessness; disturbance; agitation.
■ **2** disquiet, uneasiness, restlessness, distress, anxiety, anxiousness, nervousness, anguish, unease, worry, concern, agony, agitation, ferment, turmoil, disturbance, turbulence, tumult, rioting, trouble, strife, ruction.

unrested /únréstid/ *adj.* not refreshed by rest.

unrestful /únréstfŏŏl/ *adj.* not restful. □□ **unrestfully** *adv.*

unresting /únrésting/ *adj.* not resting. □□ **unrestingly** *adv.*

unrestored /únristáwrd/ *adj.* not restored.

unrestrainable /únristráynəbəl/ *adj.* that cannot be restrained; irrepressible; ungovernable.

unrestrained /únristráynd/ *adj.* not restrained. □□ **unrestrainedly** /-nidlee/ *adv.* **unrestrainedness** *n.*
■ see FREE *adj.* 3, UNCONTROLLED, LIMITLESS.
□□ **unrestrainedly** see *freely* (FREE).

unrestraint /únristráynt/ *n.* lack of restraint.

unrestricted /únristríktid/ *adj.* not restricted. □□ **unrestrictedly** *adv.* **unrestrictedness** *n.*
■ see ABSOLUTE *adj.* 2, FREE *adj.* 3a, LIMITLESS.

unreturned /únritórnd/ *adj.* **1** not reciprocated or responded to. **2** not having returned or been returned.

unrevealed /únriveéld/ *adj.* not revealed; secret.
■ see DORMANT 2b, UNTOLD 1.

unreversed /únrivórst/ *adj.* (esp. of a decision, etc.) not reversed.

unrevised /únrivízd/ *adj.* not revised; in an original form.

unrevoked /únrivŏkt/ *adj.* not revoked or annulled; still in force.

unrewarded /únriwáwrdid/ *adj.* not rewarded.

unrewarding /únriwáwrding/ *adj.* not rewarding or satisfying.
■ see FRUITLESS 2, THANKLESS 2.

unrhymed /únrímd/ *adj.* not rhymed.

unrhythmical /únríthmikəl/ *adj.* not rhythmical. □□ **unrhythmically** *adv.*

unridable /únrídəbəl/ *adj.* that cannot be ridden.

unridden /únríd'n/ *adj.* not ridden.

unriddle /únríd'l/ *v.tr.* solve or explain (a mystery, etc.). □□ **unriddler** *n.*

unrig /únríg/ *v.tr.* (**unrigged, unrigging**) **1** remove the rigging from (a ship). **2** *dial.* undress.

unrighteous /únríchəs/ *adj.* not righteous; unjust; wicked; dishonest. □□ **unrighteously** *adv.* **unrighteousness** *n.* [OE *unrihtwīs* (as UN-¹, RIGHTEOUS)]

unrip /únríp/ *v.tr.* (**unripped, unripping**) open by ripping.

unripe /únríp/ *adj.* not ripe. □□ **unripeness** *n.*
■ see GREEN *adj.* 3.

unrisen /únrízən/ *adj.* that has not risen.

unrivaled /únrívəld/ *adj.* having no equal; peerless.
■ see *peerless* (PEER²).

unrivet /únrívit/ *v.tr.* **1** undo, unfasten, or detach by the removal of rivets. **2** loosen; relax; undo; detach.

■ see UNDO 1.

unrobe /únrŏb/ *v.tr. & intr.* **1** disrobe. **2** undress.

unroll /únrŏl/ *v.tr. & intr.* **1** open out from a rolled-up state. **2** display or be displayed in this form.
■ see SPREAD *v.* 1a.

unromantic /únrəmántik/ *adj.* not romantic. □□ **unromantically** *adv.*
■ see PROSAIC.

unroof /únrŏŏf, -rŏŏf/ *v.tr.* remove the roof of.

unroofed /únrŏŏft, -rŏŏft/ *adj.* not provided with a roof.

unroot /únrŏŏt, -rŏŏt/ *v.tr.* **1** uproot. **2** eradicate.

unrope /únrŏp/ *v.* **1** *tr.* detach by undoing a rope. **2** *intr. Mountaineering* detach oneself from a rope.

unrounded /únrówndid/ *adj.* not rounded.

unrove *past* of UNREEVE.

unruffled /únrúfəld/ *adj.* **1** not agitated or disturbed; calm. **2** not physically ruffled.
■ **1** see CALM *adj.* 2. **2** see SMOOTH *adj.* 5.

unruled /únrŏŏld/ *adj.* **1** not ruled or governed. **2** not having ruled lines.

unruly /únrŏŏlee/ *adj.* (**unrulier, unruliest**) not easily controlled or disciplined; disorderly. □□ **unruliness** *n.* [ME f. UN-¹ + *ruly* f. RULE]
■ unmanageable, ungovernable, uncontrollable, uncontrolled, undisciplined, unregulated, lawless, disobedient, insubordinate, rebellious, mutinous, fractious, refractory, contumacious, obstreperous, willful, headstrong, stubborn, recalcitrant, intractable, defiant, uncooperative, wayward, disorderly, turbulent, riotous, rowdy, tumultuous, wild, violent, stormy, tempestuous, *colloq.* rambunctious.

UNRWA *abbr.* United Nations Relief and Works Agency.

unsaddle /únsád'l/ *v.tr.* **1** remove the saddle from (a horse, etc.). **2** dislodge from a saddle.

unsafe /únsáyf/ *adj.* not safe. □□ **unsafely** *adv.* **unsafeness** *n.*
■ see DANGEROUS, INSECURE 2a, b. □□ **unsafely** see *dangerously* (DANGEROUS).

unsaid¹ /únséd/ *adj.* not said or uttered.
■ see TACIT.

unsaid² *past* and *past part.* of UNSAY.

unsalable /únsáyləbəl/ *adj.* (also **unsaleable**) not salable. □□ **unsalability** *n.*

unsalaried /únsáləreed/ *adj.* not salaried.
■ see UNPAID.

unsalted /únsáwltid/ *adj.* not salted.

unsanctified /únsángktifīd/ *adj.* not sanctified.

unsanctioned /únsángkshənd/ *adj.* not sanctioned.
■ see UNAUTHORIZED.

unsanitary /únsániteree/ *adj.* not sanitary.
■ see SORDID 1.

unsatisfactory /únsatisfáktəree/ *adj.* not satisfactory; poor; unacceptable. □□ **unsatisfactorily** *adv.* **unsatisfactoriness** *n.*
■ insufficient, inadequate, inferior, substandard, poor, unacceptable, displeasing, disappointing, dissatisfying, unsatisfying, unworthy, inappropriate, deficient, weak, wanting, lacking, unsuitable, imperfect, flawed, defective, faulty, not up to par *or* scratch.
□□ **unsatisfactorily** see POORLY *adv.*

unsatisfied /únsátisfīd/ *adj.* not satisfied. □□ **unsatisfiedness** *n.*
■ see *dissatisfied* (DISSATISFY).

unsatisfying /únsátisfī-ing/ *adj.* not satisfying. □□ **unsatisfyingly** *adv.*
■ see *disappointing* (DISAPPOINT), THIN *adj.* 6.

unsaturated /únsáchəraytid/ *adj.* **1** *Chem.* (of a compound, esp. a fat or oil) having double or triple bonds in its molecule

/. . ./ **pronunciation**	● **part of speech**
□ **phrases, idioms, and compounds**	
□□ **derivatives**	■ **synonym section**
cross-references appear in SMALL CAPITALS or *italics*	

unsaved | unsettled

and therefore capable of further reaction. **2** not saturated. □□ **unsaturation** /-ráyshən/ n.

unsaved /únsáyvd/ adj. not saved.

unsavory /únsáyvəree/ adj. **1** disagreeable to the taste, smell, or feelings; disgusting. **2** disagreeable; unpleasant (an unsavory character). **3** morally offensive. □□ **unsavorily** adv. **unsavoriness** n.

■ unappetizing, unpalatable, inedible, uneatable; distasteful, objectionable, unpleasant, disagreeable, offensive, repugnant, obnoxious, repellent, nasty, repulsive, revolting, disgusting, nauseating, sickening, seamy, noxious, literary noisome.

unsay /únsáy/ v.tr. (past and past part. **unsaid**) retract (a statement).

unsayable /únsáyəbəl/ adj. that cannot be said.

unscalable /únskáyləbəl/ adj. that cannot be scaled.

unscarred /únskáard/ adj. not scarred or damaged.

■ unblemished, clear; see also UNSCATHED.

unscathed /únskáythd/ adj. without suffering any injury.

■ unharmed, unhurt, uninjured, unmarked, untouched, undamaged, unscarred, unscratched, safe and sound, sound, in one piece, intact, whole, as new, archaic scatheless, colloq. like new.

unscented /únséntid/ adj. not scented.

■ see UNPERFUMED.

unscheduled /únskéjōold/ adj. not scheduled.

■ see ACCIDENTAL adj. 1, OPEN adj. 17.

unscholarly /únskólərlee/ adj. not scholarly. □□ **unscholarliness** n.

unschooled /únskōold/ adj. **1** uneducated; untaught. **2** not sent to school. **3** untrained; undisciplined. **4** not made artificial by education.

■ **1** see UNEDUCATED. **3** see inexperienced (INEXPERIENCE), UNDISCIPLINED.

unscientific /únsīəntífik/ adj. **1** not in accordance with scientific principles. **2** not familiar with science. □□ **unscientifically** adv.

unscramble /únskrámbəl/ v.tr. restore from a scrambled state, esp. interpret (a scrambled transmission, etc.). □□ **unscrambler** n.

■ see DECIPHER 2.

unscreened /únskréend/ adj. **1 a** (esp. of coal) not passed through a screen or sieve. **b** not investigated or checked, esp. for security or medical problems. **2** not provided with a screen. **3** not shown on a screen.

unscrew /únskrōō/ v. **1** tr. & intr. unfasten or be unfastened by turning or removing a screw or screws or by twisting like a screw. **2** tr. loosen (a screw).

■ see UNDO 1.

unscripted /únskríptid/ adj. (of a speech, etc.) delivered without a prepared script.

■ see EXTEMPORANEOUS.

unscriptural /únskrípchərəl/ adj. against or not in accordance with Scripture. □□ **unscripturally** adv.

unscrupulous /únskrōōpyələs/ adj. having no scruples; unprincipled. □□ **unscrupulously** adv. **unscrupulousness** n.

■ unconscionable, conscienceless, unprincipled, amoral, unethical, immoral, dishonorable, corrupt, dishonest, deceitful, sly, cunning, artful, insidious, shady, sharp, sneaky, dirty, slippery, roguish, knavish, disingenuous, treacherous, perfidious, faithless, false, untrustworthy, wicked, evil, colloq. shifty, crooked.

unseal /únséel/ v.tr. break the seal of; open (a letter, receptacle, etc.).

unsealed /únséeld/ adj. not sealed.

■ see OPEN adj. 1–4, 13, 20.

unsearchable /únsérchəbəl/ adj. inscrutable. □□ **unsearchableness** n. **unsearchably** adv.

unsearched /únsércht/ adj. not searched.

unseasonable /únséezənəbəl/ adj. **1** not appropriate to the season. **2** untimely; inopportune. □□ **unseasonableness** n. **unseasonably** adv.

■ **2** unsuitable, inopportune, inappropriate, malapropos, untimely, ill-timed, inexpedient.

unseasoned /únséezənd/ adj. **1** not flavored with salt, herbs, etc. **2** (esp. of timber) not matured. **3** not habituated.

■ **2** see GREEN adj. 3. **3** see inexperienced (INEXPERIENCE).

unseat /únséet/ v.tr. **1** remove from a seat, esp. in an election. **2** dislodge from a seat, esp. on horseback.

■ **1** see TOPPLE 1b.

unseaworthy /únséewúrthee/ adj. not seaworthy.

unsecured /únsikyōórd/ adj. not secured.

■ see LOOSE adj. 2.

unseeable /únséeəbəl/ adj. that cannot be seen.

■ see INVISIBLE 1, 2.

unseeded /únséedid/ adj. Sports (of a player) not seeded.

unseeing /únséeing/ adj. **1** unobservant. **2** blind. □□ **unseeingly** adv.

unseemly /únséemlee/ adj. (**unseemlier**, **unseemliest**) **1** indecent. **2** unbecoming. □□ **unseemliness** n.

■ **1** improper, indecorous, indelicate, in poor or bad taste, risqué, naughty, indecent, shameful, offensive, lewd, lascivious, obscene, rude, coarse, off-color. **2** unbecoming, unrefined, unladylike, ungentlemanly, undignified, unworthy, disreputable, discreditable, impolitic, unwise, imprudent, inapt, inappropriate, uncalled-for, unsuitable, improper, inadvisable, ill-advised, unbefitting, unfitting, out of place or keeping, awkward, inauspicious, inexpedient, unfortunate, ill-timed, untimely. □□ **unseemliness** see IMPROPRIETY 1.

unseen /únséen/ adj. & n. ● adj. **1** not seen. **2** invisible. **3** esp. Brit. (of a translation) to be done without preparation. ● n. Brit. an unseen translation.

■ adj. **1** see UNNOTICED, BACKGROUND 2. **2** see INVISIBLE 1, 2.

unsegregated /únségrigaytid/ adj. not segregated.

unselect /únsilékt/ adj. not select.

unselective /únsiléktiv/ adj. not selective.

unself-conscious /únselfkónshəs/ adj. not self-conscious. □□ **unself-consciously** adv. **unself-consciousness** n.

■ see UNINHIBITED.

unselfish /únsélfish/ adj. mindful of others' interests. □□ **unselfishly** adv. **unselfishness** n.

■ generous, charitable, openhanded, ungrudging, unstinting, unsparing, free, liberal, giving, bighearted, magnanimous, considerate, thoughtful, philanthropic, humanitarian, altruistic, public-spirited, selfless, self-sacrificing. □□ **unselfishness** see ALTRUISM.

unsensational /únsensáyshənəl/ adj. not sensational. □□ **unsensationally** adv.

unsentimental /únsentimént'l/ adj. not sentimental. □□ **unsentimentality** /-tálitee/ n. **unsentimentally** adv.

■ see HARD adj. 4, 7b, REALISTIC 2.

unseparated /únsépəraytid/ adj. not separated.

■ see UNDIVIDED.

unserviceable /únsérvisəbəl/ adj. not serviceable; unfit for use. □□ **unserviceability** n.

■ see out of order 1 (ORDER), USELESS.

unsettle /únsét'l/ v. **1** tr. disturb the settled state or arrangement of; discompose. **2** tr. derange. **3** intr. become unsettled. □□ **unsettlement** n. **unsettling** adj.

■ **1** upset, agitate, perturb, ruffle, fluster, discomfit, discompose, unnerve, disconcert, dismay, pull the rug from under, colloq. shake (up), rattle, faze, throw; see also DISORDER v. **2** see UPSET v. **3**. □□ **unsettling** unnerving, upsetting, disturbing, perturbing, discomfiting, disconcerting, dismaying.

unsettled /únsét'ld/ adj. **1** not (yet) settled. **2** liable or open to change or further discussion. **3** (of a bill, etc.) unpaid. □□ **unsettledness** n.

■ **1** unfixed, unstable, changing, varying, variable, changeable, inconstant, ever-changing, protean, unpredictable, uncertain; disoriented, confused, mixed-up, unorganized, disorganized, disorderly, disordered, tumultuous; disturbed, turbulent, agitated, disquieted, disconcerted, upset, perturbed, ruffled, flustered, restive, restless, unnerved, colloq. rattled, riled, roiled. **2** see UNRESOLVED 2. **3** see UNPAID.

unsewn /únsṓn/ adj. not sewn. □ **unsewn binding** Brit. = perfect binding.

unsex /únséks/ v.tr. deprive (a person, esp. a woman) of the qualities of her or his sex.

unsexed /únsékst/ adj. having no sexual characteristics.

unshackle /únshákəl/ v.tr. **1** release from shackles. **2** set free.
■ see RELEASE v. 1.

unshaded /únsháydid/ adj. not shaded.

unshakable /únsháykəbəl/ adj. (also **unshakeable**) that cannot be shaken; firm; obstinate. □□ **unshakability** n. **unshakably** adv.
■ see FIRM¹ adj. 2a, b.

unshaken /únsháykən/ adj. not shaken. □□ **unshakenly** adv.

unshapely /únsháyplee/ adj. not shapely. □□ **unshapeliness** n.
■ see UGLY 1.

unsharp /únsháʹarp/ adj. Photog. not sharp. □□ **unsharpness** n.

unshaved /únsháyvd/ adj. not shaved.

unshaven /únsháyvən/ adj. not shaved.

unsheathe /únsheéth/ v.tr. remove (a knife, etc.) from a sheath.
■ see DRAW v. 7a.

unshed /únshéd/ adj. not shed.

unshell /únshél/ v.tr. (usu. as **unshelled** adj.) extract from its shell.

unsheltered /únshéltərd/ adj. not sheltered.
■ see OPEN adj.1–4, 13, 20.

unshielded /únsheéldid/ adj. not shielded or protected.
■ see VULNERABLE 1.

unship /únshíp/ v.tr. (**unshipped, unshipping**) **1** remove or discharge (a cargo or passenger) from a ship. **2** esp. Naut. remove (an object, esp. a mast or oar) from a fixed position.

unshockable /únshókəbəl/ adj. that cannot be shocked. □□ **unshockability** /-bílitee/ n. **unshockably** adv.

unshod /únshód/ adj. not wearing shoes.

unshorn /únsháwrn/ adj. not shorn.
■ see SHAGGY.

unshrinkable /únshríngkəbəl/ adj. (of fabric, etc.) not liable to shrink. □□ **unshrinkability** /-bílitee/ n.

unshrinking /únshríngking/ adj. unhesitating; fearless. □□ **unshrinkingly** adv.
■ see OUTSPOKEN, STAUNCH¹ 1.

unsighted /únsítid/ adj. **1** not sighted or seen. **2** prevented from seeing, esp. by an obstruction.

unsightly /únsítlee/ adj. unpleasant to look at; ugly. □□ **unsightliness** n.
■ ugly, hideous, awful-looking, horrible, horrible-looking, frightful-looking, dreadful-looking, terrible-looking, grotesque, ghastly, offensive, unattractive, unprepossessing, unlovely, unpretty, plain, homely.

unsigned /únsínd/ adj. not signed.

unsinkable /únsíngkəbəl/ adj. unable to be sunk. □□ **unsinkability** n.

unsized¹ /únsízd/ adj. **1** not made to a size. **2** not sorted by size.

unsized² /únsízd/ adj. not treated with size.

unskillful /únskílfōōl/ adj. not skillful. □□ **unskillfully** adv. **unskillfulness** n.
■ see CLUMSY 1, AMATEUR adj. □□ **unskillfully** see ROUGHLY 1.

unskilled /únskíld/ adj. lacking or not needing special skill or training.
■ see MENIAL adj., AMATEUR adj., inexperienced (INEXPERIENCE).

unskimmed /únskímd/ adj. (of milk) not skimmed.

unslakable /únsláykəbəl/ adj. (also **unslakeable**) that cannot be slaked or quenched.
■ see UNQUENCHABLE.

unsleeping /únsleéping/ adj. not or never sleeping. □□ **unsleepingly** adv.

unsliced /únslíst/ adj. (esp. of a loaf of bread when it is bought) not having been cut into slices.

unsling /únslíng/ v.tr. (past and past part. **unslung**) free from being slung or suspended.

unsmiling /únsmíling/ adj. not smiling. □□ **unsmilingly** adv. **unsmilingness** n.
■ see SOLEMN 4.

unsmoked /únsmṓkt/ adj. **1** not cured by smoking (unsmoked bacon). **2** not consumed by smoking (an unsmoked cigar).

unsnarl /únsnaárl/ v.tr. disentangle. [UN-² + SNARL²]

unsociable /únsṓshəbəl/ adj. not sociable; disliking the company of others. □□ **unsociability** /-bílitee/ n. **unsociableness** n. **unsociably** adv.
■ see UNSOCIAL.

unsocial /únsṓshəl/ adj. **1** not social; not suitable for, seeking, or conforming to society. **2** Brit. outside the normal working day (unsocial hours). **3** antisocial. □□ **unsocially** adv.
■ **1, 3** unsociable, unfriendly, cool, cold, chilly, aloof, uncongenial, unamiable, unforthcoming, standoffish, inhospitable, withdrawn, reserved, solitary, retiring, private, distant, detached, reclusive, hermitic, eremitic(al), anchoritic, anchoretic; antisocial, misanthropic(al), hostile.

unsoiled /únsóyld/ adj. not soiled or dirtied.
■ see CLEAN adj. 1.

unsold /únsṓld/ adj. not sold.

unsolder /únsódər/ v.tr. undo the soldering of.

unsoldierly /únsṓljərlee/ adj. not soldierly.

unsolicited /únsəlísitid/ adj. not asked for; given or done voluntarily. □□ **unsolicitedly** adv.
■ unlooked-for, unsought, not sought(-after), unrequested, unasked (for), uncalled-for, gratuitous, free, voluntary, uninvited, unbidden.

unsolvable /únsólvəbəl/ adj. that cannot be solved; insoluble. □□ **unsolvability** /-bílitee/ n. **unsolvableness** n.
■ see IMPOSSIBLE 1, MYSTERIOUS.

unsolved /únsólvd/ adj. not solved.
■ see UNRESOLVED 2, MYSTERIOUS.

unsophisticated /únsəfístikaytid/ adj. **1** artless; simple; natural; ingenuous. **2** not adulterated or artificial. □□ **unsophisticatedly** adv. **unsophisticatedness** n. **unsophistication** /-káyshən/ n.
■ **1** naive, inexperienced, callow, simple, childlike, unworldly, innocent, ingenuous, unaffected, artless, guileless, natural. **2** simple, plain, crude, undeveloped, primitive, rudimentary, uncomplicated, undetailed, uninvolved, unrefined, unadulterated, unembellished. □□ **unsophisticatedness** see NAÏVETÉ, SIMPLICITY. **unsophistication** see INEXPERIENCE.

unsorted /únsáwrtid/ adj. not sorted.

unsought /únsáwt/ adj. **1** not searched out or sought for. **2** unasked; without being requested.
■ **1** see UNFORESEEN, GRATUITOUS 2. **2** see UNASKED.

unsound /únsównd/ adj. **1** unhealthy; diseased. **2** rotten; weak. **3 a** ill-founded; fallacious. **b** unorthodox; heretical. **4** unreliable. **5** wicked. □ **of unsound mind** insane. □□ **unsoundly** adv. **unsoundness** n.
■ **1** unhealthy, diseased, ill, afflicted, in poor health, ailing, sickly, sick, unwell, delicate, injured, wounded. **2** weak, feeble, frail, flimsy, rickety, shaky, rocky, ramshackle, infirm, unstable, wobbly, tottering, teetering, unsteady, broken-down, crumbling, disintegrating, dilapidated, decrepit, defective, imperfect, faulty, decayed, rotten. **3 a** illogical, faulty, flawed, fallacious, untenable, invalid, groundless, unfounded, ill-founded, shaky, erroneous, defective, specious. **b** see UNORTHODOX. **4** see UNRELIABLE. □ **of unsound mind** mad, psychotic, unbalanced, unstable, unhinged, demented, deranged, lunatic, colloq. crazy, certifiable, mental, around the bend, not all there, sl. nuts, bats, bananas, bonkers; see also INSANE 1.

/. . ./ **pronunciation**   ● **part of speech**
□ **phrases, idioms, and compounds**
□□ **derivatives**   ■ **synonym section**
cross-references appear in SMALL CAPITALS or italics

unsounded[1] /únsówndid/ *adj.* **1** not uttered or pronounced. **2** not made to sound.

unsounded[2] /únsówndid/ *adj.* unfathomed.

unsoured /únsówrd/ *adj.* not soured.

unsown /únsṓn/ *adj.* not sown.

unsparing /únspáiring/ *adj.* **1** lavish; profuse. **2** merciless. □□ **unsparingly** *adv.* **unsparingness** *n.*

■ **1** see LAVISH *adj.* 1, 2. **2** see MERCILESS.

unspeakable /únspeéekəbəl/ *adj.* **1** that cannot be expressed in words. **2** indescribably bad or objectionable. □□ **unspeakableness** *n.* **unspeakably** *adv.*

■ see INEXPRESSIBLE, OUTRAGEOUS 3. □□ **unspeakably** see BADLY 1.

unspecialized /únspéshəlīzd/ *adj.* not specialized.

■ see GENERAL *adj.* 6, UNPROFESSIONAL 2.

unspecified /únspésifīd/ *adj.* not specified.

■ see VAGUE 1.

unspectacular /únspektákyələr/ *adj.* not spectacular; dull. □□ **unspectacularly** *adv.*

unspent /únspént/ *adj.* **1** not expended or used. **2** not exhausted or used up.

unspilled /únspíld/ *adj.* not spilled.

unspilt /únspílt/ *adj.* not spilled.

unspiritual /únspírichōōəl/ *adj.* not spiritual; earthly; worldly. □□ **unspirituality** /-chōō-álitee/ *n.* **unspiritually** *adv.* **unspiritualness** *n.*

unspoiled /únspóyld/ *adj.* **1** not spoiled. **2** not plundered.

■ **1** unsullied, pristine, perfect, virgin, whole, intact, unimpaired, undamaged, untainted, unstained, unblemished, immaculate, impeccable, uncorrupted, unpolluted, spotless, stainless, flawless, clean, esp. *Brit.* unspoilt.

unspoilt /únspóylt/ *adj.* not spoiled.

■ see UNSPOILED.

unspoken /únspṓkən/ *adj.* **1** not expressed in speech. **2** not uttered as speech.

■ see TACIT.

unsporting /únspáwrting/ *adj.* not sportsmanlike; not fair or generous. □□ **unsportingly** *adv.* **unsportingness** *n.*

■ see DIRTY *adj.* 5.

unsportsmanlike /únspáwrtsmənlik/ *adj.* unsporting.

■ see DIRTY *adj.* 5.

unspotted /únspótid/ *adj.* **1 a** not marked with a spot or spots. **b** morally pure. **2** unnoticed.

unsprung /únsprúng/ *adj.* not provided with a spring or springs; not resilient.

unstable /únstáybəl/ *adj.* (**unstabler**, **unstablest**) **1** not stable. **2** changeable. **3** showing a tendency to sudden mental or emotional changes. □ **unstable equilibrium** a state in which a body when disturbed tends to move farther from equilibrium. □□ **unstableness** *n.* **unstably** *adv.*

■ **1** see SHAKY. **2, 3** changeable, variable, unsteady, inconstant, inconsistent, insecure, capricious, fickle, irregular, unpredictable, unreliable, erratic, volatile, fluid, shifting, fluctuating, flighty, mercurial, moody, vacillating, tergiversating, indecisive, undecided, irresolute, unsteadfast, indefinite, unsettled, unbalanced, twisted.

unstained /únstáynd/ *adj.* not stained.

■ see CLEAN *adj.* 1, CHASTE 1.

unstamped /únstámpt/ *adj.* **1** not marked by stamping. **2** not having a stamp affixed.

unstarched /únstaárcht/ *adj.* not starched.

unstated /únstáytid/ *adj.* not stated or declared.

■ see TACIT.

unstatesmanlike /únstáytsmənlik/ *adj.* not statesmanlike.

unstatutable /únstáchōōtəbəl/ *adj.* contrary to a statute or statutes. □□ **unstatutably** *adv.*

unsteadfast /únstédfast/ *adj.* not steadfast.

■ see UNSTABLE 2, 3.

unsteady /únstédee/ *adj.* (**unsteadier**, **unsteadiest**) **1** not steady or firm. **2** changeable; fluctuating. **3** not uniform or regular. □□ **unsteadily** *adv.* **unsteadiness** *n.*

■ **1** see SHAKY, *doddering* (DODDER[1]), FAINT *adj.* 2. **2** see

VARIABLE *adj.* 2. □□ **unsteadiness** see *fluctuation* (FLUCTUATE), *inconstancy* (INCONSTANT).

unstick *v.* & *n.* ● *v.* /únstík/ (*past* and *past part.* **unstuck** /-stúk/) **1** *tr.* separate (a thing stuck to another). **2** *Aeron. colloq.* **a** *intr.* take off. **b** *tr.* cause (an aircraft) to take off. ● *n.* /únstik/ *Aeron. colloq.* the moment of takeoff. □ **come unstuck** *colloq.* come to grief; fail.

unstinted /únstíntid/ *adj.* not stinted. □□ **unstintedly** *adv.*

unstinting /únstínting/ *adj.* ungrudging; lavish. □□ **unstintingly** *adv.*

■ see GENEROUS 1, WHOLEHEARTED.

unstirred /únstírd/ *adj.* not stirred.

unstitch /únstích/ *v.tr.* undo the stitches of.

unstop /únstóp/ *v.tr.* (**unstopped**, **unstopping**) **1** free from obstruction. **2** remove the stopper from.

unstoppable /únstópəbəl/ *adj.* that cannot be stopped or prevented. □□ **unstoppability** /-bílitee/ *n.* **unstoppably** *adv.*

■ see INDOMITABLE 1, RELENTLESS.

unstopper /únstópər/ *v.tr.* remove the stopper from.

unstrained /únstráynd/ *adj.* **1** not subjected to straining or stretching. **2** not injured by overuse or excessive demands. **3** not forced or produced by effort. **4** not passed through a strainer.

■ **3** see EASY *adj.* 1, 3.

unstrap /únstráp/ *v.tr.* (**unstrapped**, **unstrapping**) undo the strap or straps of.

■ see UNDO 1.

unstressed /únstrést/ *adj.* **1** (of a word, syllable, etc.) not pronounced with stress. **2** not subjected to stress.

■ **1** see UNACCENTED.

unstring /únstríng/ *v.tr.* (*past* and *past part.* **unstrung**) **1** remove or relax the string or strings of (a bow, harp, etc.). **2** remove from a string. **3** (esp. as **unstrung** *adj.*) unnerve.

unstructured /únstrúkchərd/ *adj.* **1** not structured. **2** informal.

■ **1** see INCOHERENT 2, LOOSE *adj.* 6, 8, 9. **2** see INFORMAL.

unstuck *past* and *past part.* of UNSTICK.

unstudied /únstúdeed/ *adj.* easy; natural; spontaneous. □□ **unstudiedly** *adv.*

■ see NATURAL *adj.* 4.

unstuffed /únstúft/ *adj.* not stuffed.

unstuffy /únstúfee/ *adj.* **1** informal; casual. **2** not stuffy.

unsubdued /únsəbdōōd, -dyōōd/ *adj.* not subdued.

unsubjugated /únsúbjəgaytid/ *adj.* not subjugated.

unsubstantial /únsəbstánshəl/ *adj.* having little or no solidity, reality, or factual basis. □□ **unsubstantiality** /-sheeáli- tee/ *n.* **unsubstantially** *adv.*

■ see INSUBSTANTIAL.

unsubstantiated /únsəbstánsheeaytid/ *adj.* not substantiated.

■ see *ill-founded*, SHAKY.

unsuccess /únsəksés/ *n.* **1** lack of success; failure. **2** an instance of this.

unsuccessful /únsəksésfōōl/ *adj.* not successful. □□ **unsuccessfully** *adv.* **unsuccessfulness** *n.*

■ unfortunate, unavailing, vain, abortive, failed, useless, fruitless, unfruitful, unproductive, ineffective, ineffectual, inefficacious, worthless, unprofitable, sterile; unlucky, hapless, luckless, defeated, beaten, losing, cursed, foiled, frustrated, balked, *archaic* bootless, *colloq.* jinxed. □□ **unsuccessfully** see BADLY 1, *in vain* (VAIN).

unsugared /únshōōgərd/ *adj.* not sugared.

unsuggestive /únsəgjéstiv, -səjés-/ *adj.* not suggestive.

unsuitable /únsōōtəbəl/ *adj.* not suitable. □□ **unsuitability** *n.* **unsuitableness** *n.* **unsuitably** *adv.*

■ see INAPPROPRIATE, UNACCEPTABLE, UNSATISFACTORY. □□ **unsuitability** see IMPROPRIETY 4.

unsuited /únsōṓtid/ *adj.* **1** (usu. foll. by *for*) not fit for a purpose. **2** (usu. foll. by *to*) not adapted.

■ see INAPPROPRIATE, UNQUALIFIED 1, INCOMPATIBLE 1, 3.

unsullied /únsúleed/ *adj.* not sullied.

■ see CLEAN *adj.* 1, INNOCENT *adj.* 1.

unsummoned /únsúmənd/ *adj.* not summoned.

unsung /únsúng/ *adj.* **1** not celebrated in song; unknown. **2** not sung.

■ **1** uncelebrated, unrecognized, unglorified, unexalted, unpraised, unhonored, unnoticed, disregarded, unknown, unheard-of, anonymous, unidentified, nameless, obscure, insignificant, inconspicuous.

unsupervised /únsoॊoॊpərvizd/ *adj.* not supervised.

unsupportable /únsəpáwrtəbəl/ *adj.* **1** that cannot be endured. **2** indefensible. □□ **unsupportably** *adv.*

■ **1** see UNBEARABLE. **2** see UNTENABLE.

unsupported /únsəpáwrtid/ *adj.* not supported. □□ **unsupportedly** *adv.*

■ see GROUNDLESS, SHAKY.

unsure /únshoॊoॊr/ *adj.* not sure. □□ **unsurely** *adv.* **unsureness** *n.*

■ see UNCERTAIN 1, 2.

unsurpassable /únsərpásəbəl/ *adj.* that cannot be surpassed. □□ **unsurpassably** *adv.*

■ see UNBEATABLE.

unsurpassed /únsərpást/ *adj.* not surpassed.

■ see UNPARALLELED .

unsurprising /únsərprízing/ *adj.* not surprising. □□ **unsurprisingly** *adv.*

unsusceptible /únsəséptibəl/ *adj.* not susceptible. □□ **unsusceptibility** *n.*

■ (*unsusceptible to*) see IMMUNE 2.

unsuspected /únsəspéktid/ *adj.* not suspected. □□ **unsuspectedly** *adv.*

unsuspecting /únsəspékting/ *adj.* not suspecting. □□ **unsuspectingly** *adv.* **unsuspectingness** *n.*

■ unsuspicious, unwary, unknowing, ignorant, unconscious, gullible, green, credulous, naive, ingenuous, innocent, trusting; unaware, off guard.

unsuspicious /únsəspíshəs/ *adj.* not suspicious. □□ **unsuspiciously** *adv.* **unsuspiciousness** *n.*

unsustained /únsəstáynd/ *adj.* not sustained.

■ see SPASMODIC 2.

unswathe /unswoॊth, -swáyth/ *v.tr.* free from being swathed.

unswayed /únswáyd/ *adj.* uninfluenced; unaffected.

unsweetened /únsweॊeॊt'nd/ *adj.* not sweetened.

unswept /únswépt/ *adj.* not swept.

unswerving /únswórving/ *adj.* **1** steady; constant. **2** not turning aside. □□ **unswervingly** *adv.*

■ **1** see CONSTANT *adj.* 3. □□ **unswervingly** see *consistently* (CONSISTENT).

unsworn /únswáwrn/ *adj.* **1** (of a person) not subjected to or bound by an oath. **2** not confirmed by an oath.

unsymmetrical /únsimétrikəl/ *adj.* not symmetrical. □□ **unsymmetrically** *adv.*

■ see LOPSIDED.

unsympathetic /únsimpəthétik/ *adj.* not sympathetic. □□ **unsympathetically** *adv.*

■ uncaring, unconcerned, callous, unfeeling, unaffected, untouched, unmoved, indifferent, unemotional, dispassionate, unreactive, unresponsive, impassive, stolid, cold, cool, aloof, unstirred, apathetic, insensitive, stoic(al), stony, adamant, hostile, stonyhearted, hard-hearted, heartless, uncharitable, unkind, unpitying, pitiless, unmerciful, merciless, ruthless. □□ **unsympathetically** see ROUGHLY 1.

unsystematic /únsistəmátik/ *adj.* not systematic. □□ **unsystematically** *adv.*

■ see *chaotic* (CHAOS), RANDOM. □□ **unsystematically** see *at random* (RANDOM), HELTER-SKELTER *adv.*

untack /únták/ *v.tr.* detach, esp. by removing tacks.

untainted /úntáyntid/ *adj.* not tainted.

■ see PURE 1–4.

untalented /úntáləntid/ *adj.* not talented.

untamable /úntáyməbəl/ *adj.* (also **untameable**) that cannot be tamed.

untamed /úntáymd/ *adj.* not tamed; wild.

■ undomesticated, wild, unbroken, unsubdued, uncontrollable, savage, fierce, feral, ferocious.

untangle /úntánggəl/ *v.tr.* **1** free from a tangled state. **2** free from entanglement.

■ **1, 2** see STRAIGHTEN, EXTRICATE.

untanned /úntánd/ *adj.* not tanned.

untapped /úntápt/ *adj.* not (yet) tapped or wired (*untapped resources*).

untarnished /úntaॊarnisht/ *adj.* not tarnished.

■ unsoiled, unsullied, immaculate, spotless, unspotted, unstained, unblemished, untainted, faultless, flawless, impeccable, uncorrupted, unfouled, chaste, clean, pure, lily-white, undefiled, virginal.

untasted /úntáystid/ *adj.* not tasted.

untaught /úntáwt/ *adj.* **1** not instructed by teaching; ignorant. **2** not acquired by teaching; natural; spontaneous.

■ **1** see UNEDUCATED. **2** see INBORN, NATURAL *adj.* 4.

untaxed /úntákst/ *adj.* not required to pay or not attracting taxes.

unteach /únteॊech/ *v.tr.* (*past* and *past part.* **untaught**) **1** cause (a person) to forget or discard previous knowledge. **2** remove from the mind (something known or taught) by different teaching.

unteachable /únteॊechəbəl/ *adj.* **1** incapable of being instructed. **2** that cannot be imparted by teaching.

untearable /úntáirəbəl/ *adj.* that cannot be torn.

untechnical /úntéknikəl/ *adj.* not technical. □□ **untechnically** *adv.*

untempered /úntémpərd/ *adj.* (of metal, etc.) not brought to the proper hardness or consistency.

untenable /únténəbəl/ *adj.* not tenable; that cannot be defended. □□ **untenability** *n.* **untenableness** *n.* **untenably** *adv.*

■ insupportable, unsupportable, indefensible, unsustainable, unmaintainable, unjustified, unjustifiable, baseless, groundless, unfounded, flawed, faulty, weak, illogical, specious, implausible, unreasonable, unsound, invalid.

untended /únténdid/ *adj.* not tended; neglected.

untested /úntéstid/ *adj.* not tested or proved.

■ see GREEN *adj.* 5, THEORETICAL 2, NOVEL².

untether /úntéthər/ *v.tr.* release (an animal) from a tether.

untethered /úntéthərd/ *adj.* not tethered.

unthanked /únthángkt/ *adj.* not thanked.

■ unacknowledged, unrecognized, unappreciated.

unthankful /únthángkfoॊoॊl/ *adj.* not thankful. □□ **unthankfully** *adv.* **unthankfulness** *n.*

■ see UNGRATEFUL.

unthinkable /únthíngkəbəl/ *adj.* **1** that cannot be imagined or grasped by the mind. **2** *colloq.* highly unlikely or undesirable. □□ **unthinkability** /-bílitee/ *n.* **unthinkableness** *n.* **unthinkably** *adv.*

■ **1** inconceivable, unbelievable, unimaginable, incredible, incomprehensible, extraordinary, *colloq.* mind-boggling, *sl.* mind-blowing. **2** unacceptable, unattractive, absurd, illogical, impossible, improbable, unlikely, out of the question, beyond belief, preposterous, ridiculous, laughable, ludicrous.

unthinking /únthíngking/ *adj.* **1** thoughtless. **2** unintentional; inadvertent. □□ **unthinkingly** *adv.* **unthinkingness** *n.*

■ **1** thoughtless, inconsiderate, impolite, tactless, rude, undiplomatic, discourteous, uncivil, imprudent, unwise, indiscreet, neglectful, negligent, careless, mindless, heedless, undiscriminating, unconsidered, unreflecting, unthoughtful, irrational, unreasonable, illogical, unperceptive, unperceiving, undiscerning, witless, brainless, foolish, senseless, nonsensical, rash, impetuous, stupid, silly, mad, insane, idiotic, imbecilic, hasty, shortsighted, *colloq.* crazy, moronic. **2** see INADVERTENT 1. □□ **unthinkingly** see *blindly* (BLIND).

unthought /úntháwt/ *adj.* (often foll. by *of*) not thought of.

■ (*unthought of*) see INCONCEIVABLE 1, UNFORESEEN.

/. . ./ **pronunciation**	● **part of speech**
□ **phrases, idioms, and compounds**	
□□ **derivatives**	■ **synonym section**
cross-references appear in SMALL CAPITALS or *italics*	

unthoughtful /úntháwtfŏŏl/ *adj.* unthinking; unmindful; thoughtless. □□ **unthoughtfully** *adv.* **unthoughtfulness** *n.*
■ see UNTHINKING 1.

unthread /únthréd/ *v.tr.* **1** take the thread out of (a needle, etc.). **2** find one's way out of (a maze).

unthrifty /únthríftee/ *adj.* **1** wasteful; extravagant; prodigal. **2** not thriving or flourishing. □□ **unthriftily** *adv.* **unthriftiness** *n.*
■ **1** see WASTEFUL.

unthrone /únthrŏn/ *v.tr.* dethrone.

untidy /úntídee/ *adj.* (**untidier, untidiest**) not neat or orderly. □□ **untidily** *adv.* **untidiness** *n.*
■ disorderly, messy, disheveled, unkempt, ungroomed, slovenly, slatternly, bedraggled, rumpled, tousled, frowzy, sloppy, shabby, draggle-tailed, *colloq.* scruffy, tatty; littered, cluttered, chaotic, helter-skelter, jumbled, muddled, disorganized, disordered, disarranged, higgledy-piggledy, topsy-turvy, messed-up, mussy, mussed-up. □□ **untidiness** see DISORDER *n.* 1.

untie /úntí/ *v.tr.* (*pres. part.* **untying**) **1** undo (a knot, etc.). **2** unfasten the cords, etc., of (a package, etc.). **3** release from bonds or attachment. [OE *untígan* (as UN-², TIE)]
■ **1, 2** see UNDO 1. **3** see RELEASE *v.* 1.

untied /úntíd/ *adj.* not tied.
■ see LOOSE *adj.* 1, 2, UNDONE 2.

until /əntíl, un-/ *prep. & conj.* = TILL¹. ¶ Used esp. when beginning a sentence and in formal style, e.g., *until you told me, I had no idea*; *he resided there until his decease.* [orig. northern ME *untill* f. ON *und* as far as + TILL¹]

untilled /úntíld/ *adj.* not tilled.

untimely /úntímlee/ *adj. & adv.* ● *adj.* **1** inopportune. **2** (of death) premature. ● *adv. archaic* **1** inopportunely. **2** prematurely. □□ **untimeliness** *n.*
■ *adj.* **1** see INOPPORTUNE. **2** see PREMATURE 1.

untinged /úntínjd/ *adj.* not tinged.

untiring /úntíring/ *adj.* tireless. □□ **untiringly** *adv.*
■ unflagging, determined, indefatigable, dogged, persevering, persistent, assiduous, tireless, unwearying, unwearied, dedicated, unfailing, unfaltering, unwavering, steady. □□ **untiringly** see HARD *adv.* 1.

untitled /úntít'ld/ *adj.* having no title.

unto /úntŏŏ, úntə/ *prep. archaic* = TO *prep.* (in all uses except as the sign of the infinitive); (*do unto others*; *faithful unto death*; *take unto oneself*). [ME f. UNTIL, with TO replacing northern TILL¹]

untold /úntŏld/ *adj.* **1** not told. **2** not (able to be) counted or measured (*untold misery*). [OE *untēald* (as UN-¹, TOLD)]
■ **1** unrecounted, unnarrated, undescribed, unpublished, unrevealed, undisclosed, undivulged, unreported, private, hidden, secret. **2** countless, uncounted, uncountable, unnumbered, numberless, innumerable, incalculable, inestimable, *literary* myriad; immeasurable, measureless, unlimited; inexpressible, unutterable, indescribable, unimaginable, inconceivable, unthinkable, unspeakable.

untouchable /úntúchəbəl/ *adj. & n.* ● *adj.* that may not or cannot be touched. ● *n.* a member of a hereditary Hindu group held to defile members of higher castes on contact. ¶ Use of the term, and social restrictions accompanying it, were declared illegal under the Indian constitution in 1949. □□ **untouchability** *n.* **untouchableness** *n.*

untouched /úntúcht/ *adj.* **1** not touched. **2** not affected physically; not harmed, modified, used, or tasted. **3** not affected by emotion. **4** not discussed.
■ **2** see UNUSED 1b, UNSCATHED. **3** see UNMOVED 3.

untoward /úntáwrd, -təwáwrd/ *adj.* **1** inconvenient; unlucky. **2** awkward. **3** perverse, refractory. **4** unseemly. □□ **untowardly** *adv.* **untowardness** *n.*
■ **1** adverse, unfavorable, unlucky, unpropitious, discouraging, inopportune, inconvenient, unpromising, inauspicious, bad, unfortunate. **4** unbecoming, unfitting, inappropriate, unapt, unsuitable, improper, impolite, rude, boorish, ungentlemanly, unladylike, indecorous, indelicate, unwarranted, uncalled-for,

unrefined, unseemly, unwise, imprudent, undiplomatic, tactless, untactful; ill-conceived, silly, foolish, stupid, ill-timed.

untraceable /úntráysəbəl/ *adj.* that cannot be traced. □□ **untraceably** *adv.*

untraced /úntráyst/ *adj.* not traced.

untrained /úntráynd/ *adj.* not trained.
■ see AMATEUR *adj.*, *inexperienced* (INEXPERIENCE).

untrammeled /úntráməld/ *adj.* not trammeled, unhampered.
■ see UNIMPEDED.

untransferable /úntransfɚrəbəl, -tránsfər-/ *adj.* not transferable.
■ nontransferable, nonnegotiable; see also *fixed* (FIX *v.* 20c).

untranslatable /úntranzláytəbəl, -trans-, -tránzlayt-, -tráns-/ *adj.* that cannot be translated satisfactorily. □□ **untranslatability** *n.* **untranslatably** *adv.*

untransportable /úntranzpáwrtəbəl, -trans-/ *adj.* that cannot be transported.

untraveled /úntrávəld/ *adj.* **1** that has not traveled. **2** that has not been traveled over or through.

untreatable /úntreétəbəl/ *adj.* (of a disease, etc.) that cannot be treated.

untreated /úntreétid/ *adj.* not treated.

untried /úntríd/ *adj.* **1** not tried or tested. **2** inexperienced. **3** not yet tried by a judge.
■ **1** untested, unproved, unproven, new. **2** see RAW *adj.* 5.

untrodden /úntród'n/ *adj.* not trodden, stepped on, or traversed.
■ see NEW *adj.* 6, TRACKLESS.

untroubled /úntrúbəld/ *adj.* not troubled; calm; tranquil.
■ see TRANQUIL.

untrue /úntrŏŏ/ *adj.* **1** not true; contrary to what is the fact. **2** (often foll. by *to*) not faithful or loyal. **3** deviating from an accepted standard. □□ **untruly** *adv.* [OE *untrēowe*, etc. (as UN-¹, TRUE)]
■ **1** wrong, false, inaccurate, incorrect, erroneous, misleading, mistaken, distorted, invented, fictitious, made-up, fabricated, apocryphal. **2** unfaithful, faithless, disloyal, fickle, capricious, undependable, unreliable, dishonorable, untrustworthy, false, hypocritical, dishonest, insincere, two-faced, duplicitous, devious, deceitful, treacherous, traitorous, perfidious. **3** inexact, nonstandard, substandard, imprecise, imperfect.

untruss /úntrús/ *v.tr.* unfasten (a trussed fowl).

untrustworthy /úntrústwúrthee/ *adj.* not trustworthy. □□ **untrustworthiness** *n.*
■ see DISHONEST, IRRESPONSIBLE 1.

untruth /úntrŏŏth/ *n.* (*pl.* **untruths** /-trŏŏthz, -trŏŏths/) **1** the state of being untrue; falsehood. **2** a false statement (*told me an untruth*). [OE *untrēowth*, etc. (as UN-¹, TRUTH)]
■ **2** see LIE² *n.*

untruthful /úntrŏŏthfŏŏl/ *adj.* not truthful. □□ **untruthfully** *adv.* **untruthfulness** *n.*
■ see FALSE *adj.* 1, 2b, DECEITFUL. □□ **untruthfulness** see *falsity* (FALSE).

untuck /úntúk/ *v.tr.* free (bedclothes, etc.) from being tucked in or up.

untunable /úntŏŏnəbəl, -tyŏŏ-/ *adj.* (of a piano, etc.) that cannot be tuned.

untuned /úntŏŏnd, -tyŏŏnd/ *adj.* **1** not in tune; not made tuneful. **2** (of a radio receiver, etc.) not tuned to any one frequency. **3** not in harmony or concord; disordered.

untuneful /úntŏŏnfŏŏl, -tyŏŏn-/ *adj.* not tuneful. □□ **untunefully** *adv.* **untunefulness** *n.*

unturned /úntɚrnd/ *adj.* **1** not turned over, around, away, etc. **2** not shaped by turning.

untutored /úntŏŏtərd, -tyŏŏ-/ *adj.* uneducated; untaught.
■ see UNINFORMED.

untwine /úntwín/ *v.tr. & intr.* untwist; unwind.

untwist /úntwíst/ *v.tr. & intr.* open from a twisted or spiraled state.

untying *pres. part.* of UNTIE.

untypical /úntípikəl/ *adj.* not typical; unusual.

■ see UNUSUAL 2.

unusable /únyŏŏzəbəl/ adj. (also **unuseable**) not usable.

■ see USELESS 1, DUD adj. 1.

unused adj. **1** /únyŏŏzd/ **a** not in use. **b** never having been used. **2** /únyŏŏst/ (foll. by to) not accustomed.

■ **1 a** disused, abandoned, derelict, neglected, given up, idle, vacant, empty, free. **b** (brand-)new, untouched, pristine, original, intact, virgin, fresh, firsthand; unconsumed, leftover, remaining, surplus, left. **2** (unused to) unaccustomed to, unfamiliar with, inexperienced in or at, amateurish at, unpracticed in or at, unversed in, uninitiated in.

unusual /únyŏŏzhŏŏəl/ adj. **1** not usual. **2** exceptional; remarkable. □□ **unusually** adv. **unusualness** n.

■ **1** uncommon, rare, unexpected, surprising, unfamiliar, unaccustomed, unwonted, unprecedented, unconventional, unorthodox. **2** exceptional, atypical, untypical, different, singular, abnormal, irregular, out of the ordinary, extraordinary, odd, peculiar, curious, bizarre, strange, queer, remarkable, freakish, eccentric, weird, offbeat, colloq. way-out, disp. unique, sl. off-the-wall. □□ **unusually** see ESPECIALLY. **unusualness** see eccentricity (ECCENTRIC).

unutterable /únútərəbəl/ adj. inexpressible; beyond description (unutterable torment; an unutterable fool). □□ **unutterableness** n. **unutterably** adv.

■ see INEXPRESSIBLE.

unuttered /únútərd/ adj. not uttered or expressed.

■ see TACIT.

unvaccinated /únváksinaytid/ adj. not vaccinated.

unvalued /únvályŏŏd/ adj. **1** not regarded as valuable. **2** not having been valued.

unvanquished /únvángkwisht/ adj. not vanquished.

unvaried /únváirid/ adj. not varied.

■ see UNIFORM adj. 1, 2, HUMDRUM.

unvarnished /únvaárnisht/ adj. **1** not varnished. **2** (of a statement or person) plain and straightforward (the unvarnished truth).

■ **1** see FLAT¹ adj. 8a. **2** plain, simple, pure, unembellished, straightforward, straight, direct, honest, unelaborated, naked, stark, sincere, frank, candid, outspoken.

unvarying /únváireeing/ adj. not varying. □□ **unvaryingly** adv. **unvaryingness** n.

■ see UNIFORM adj. 1, 2, HUMDRUM.

unveil /únváyl/ v. **1** tr. remove a veil from. **2** tr. remove a covering from (a statue, plaque, etc.) as part of the ceremony of the first public display. **3** tr. disclose; reveal; make publicly known. **4** intr. remove one's veil.

■ **1–3** reveal, expose, uncover, disclose, lay bare or open, bare; divulge, make known, bring to light.

unventilated /únvént'laytid/ adj. **1** not provided with a means of ventilation. **2** not discussed.

unverifiable /únvérəfiəbəl/ adj. that cannot be verified.

unverified /únvérifid/ adj. not verified.

unversed /únvŏrst/ adj. (usu. foll. by in) not experienced or skilled.

■ (unversed in) see UNFAMILIAR.

unviable /únvíəbəl/ adj. not viable. □□ **unviability** /-bílitee/ n.

unviolated /únvíəlaytid/ adj. not violated.

unvisited /únvízitid/ adj. not visited.

unvitiated /únvísheeaytid/ adj. not vitiated.

unvoiced /únvóyst/ adj. **1** not spoken. **2** Phonet. not voiced.

■ **1** see TACIT, sneaking (SNEAK v. 4a).

unwaged /únwáyjd/ adj. not receiving a wage; out of work.

■ see UNEMPLOYED 1.

unwanted /únwóntid/ adj. not wanted.

■ see REDUNDANT 1, UNWELCOME.

unwarlike /únwáwrlik/ adj. not warlike.

unwarmed /únwáwrmd/ adj. not warmed.

unwarned /únwáwrnd/ adj. not warned or forewarned.

■ see UNPREPARED.

unwarrantable /únwáwrəntəbəl, -wór-/ adj. indefensible;

unjustifiable. □□ **unwarrantableness** n. **unwarrantably** adv.

unwarranted /únwáwrəntid, -wór-/ adj. **1** unauthorized. **2** unjustified.

■ **1** see UNAUTHORIZED. **2** uncalled-for, unasked (for), unjustified, indefensible, unjust, unfair, unconscionable, unworthy, improper, inexcusable, gratuitous, unmerited, undeserved, unprovoked, outrageous, excessive, inordinate, unreasonable, unrestrained, intemperate, untempered, immoderate, undue, unnecessary.

unwary /únwáiree/ adj. **1** not cautious. **2** (often foll. by of) not aware of possible danger, etc. □□ **unwarily** adv. **unwariness** n.

■ **1** heedless, careless, hasty, incautious, unguarded, unsuspecting, imprudent, rash, foolhardy, foolish, reckless, improvident, thoughtless, indiscreet, unthinking, mindless, unwise. **2** see UNAWARE adj. 1.

unwashed /únwósht, -wáwsht/ adj. **1** not washed. **2** not usually washed or clean. □ **the great unwashed** colloq. the rabble.

■ dirty, uncleaned, unclean, uncleansed; filthy, grimy, begrimed, soiled. □ **the great unwashed** the rabble, the masses, the hoi polloi, people (at large or in general), the population, the man in the street, the working class(es), most people, the (silent) majority, Middle America, esp. Brit. Mr. (& Mrs.) Average, colloq. usu. derog. the plebs, usu. derog. the mob, the populace.

unwatched /únwócht/ adj. not watched.

unwatchful /únwóchfŏŏl/ adj. not watchful.

unwatered /únwáwtərd, -wótərd/ adj. not watered.

unwavering /únwáyvəring/ adj. not wavering. □□ **unwaveringly** adv.

■ see CONSTANT adj. 1, 3.

unweaned /únweénd/ adj. not weaned.

unwearable /únwáirəbəl/ adj. that cannot be worn.

unwearied /únweéreed/ adj. **1** not wearied or tired. **2** never becoming weary; indefatigable. **3** unremitting. □□ **unweariedly** adv. **unweariedness** n.

unweary /únweéree/ adj. not weary.

unwearying /únweéreeing/ adj. **1** persistent. **2** not causing or producing weariness. □□ **unwearyingly** adv.

unwed /únwéd/ adj. unmarried.

■ see UNMARRIED.

unwedded /únwédid/ adj. unmarried. □□ **unweddedness** n.

unweeded /únweédid/ adj. not cleared of weeds.

unweighed /únwáyd/ adj. **1** not considered; hasty. **2** (of goods) not weighed.

unwelcome /únwélkəm/ adj. not welcome or acceptable. □□ **unwelcomely** adv. **unwelcomeness** n.

■ uninvited, unsought, unwished-for, undesired, undesirable, displeasing, unpleasing, distasteful, unpleasant, unpopular, disagreeable, unacceptable; unwanted, de trop, rejected, unaccepted, excluded.

unwell /únwél/ adj. **1** not in good health; (somewhat) ill. **2** indisposed.

■ see ILL adj. 1.

unwept /únwépt/ adj. **1** not wept for. **2** (of tears) not wept.

unwetted /únwétid/ adj. not wetted.

unwhipped /únhwípt, -wípt/ adj. **1** not punished by or as by whipping. **2** Brit. not subject to a party whip.

unwholesome /únhŏlsəm/ adj. **1** not promoting, or detrimental to, physical or moral health. **2** unhealthy; insalubrious. **3** unhealthy-looking. □□ **unwholesomely** adv. **unwholesomeness** n.

■ **1** unhealthy, unhealthful, detrimental, deleterious, pernicious, insalubrious, unhygienic, insanitary, harmful, noxious, toxic, injurious, destructive,

---

/.../ **pronunciation**   ● **part of speech**

□ **phrases, idioms, and compounds**

□□ **derivatives**   ■ **synonym section**

cross-references appear in SMALL CAPITALS or italics

damaging; corrupt, immoral, bad, wicked, evil, sinful, perverted; demoralizing, depraved, degrading, corrupting, perverting. **2** unhealthy, insalubrious. **3** ill, unhealthy, ailing, sickly, sick, pale, wan, anemic, pallid, pasty, peaky.

unwieldy /únweéldee/ *adj.* (**unwieldier, unwieldiest**) cumbersome, clumsy, or hard to manage, owing to size, shape, or weight. □□ **unwieldily** *adv.* **unwieldiness** *n.* [ME f. UN-¹ + *wieldy* active (now dial.) f. WIELD]
■ awkward, clumsy, bulky, oversized, cumbersome, burdensome, ungainly, unmanageable, unhandy, inconvenient, unmaneuverable. □□ **unwieldiness** see INCONVENIENCE *n.* 1.

unwilling /únwíling/ *adj.* not willing or inclined; reluctant. □□ **unwillingly** *adv.* **unwillingness** *n.* [OE *unwillende* (as UN-¹, WILLING)]
■ see RELUCTANT. □□ **unwillingly** see *under protest* (PROTEST).

unwind /únwínd/ *v.* (*past* and *past part.* **unwound** /-wównd/) **1 a** *tr.* draw out (a thing that has been wound). **b** *intr.* become drawn out after having been wound. **2** *intr.* & *tr. colloq.* relax.
■ **2** see RELAX 4.

unwinking /únwíngking/ *adj.* **1** not winking. **2** watchful; vigilant. □□ **unwinkingly** *adv.*

unwinnable /únwínəbəl/ *adj.* that cannot be won.

unwisdom /únwízdəm/ *n.* lack of wisdom; folly; imprudence. [OE *unwīsdōm* (as UN-¹, WISDOM)]

unwise /únwíz/ *adj.* **1** foolish; imprudent. **2** injudicious. □□ **unwisely** *adv.* [OE *unwīs* (as UN-¹, WISE¹)]
■ see IMPRUDENT.

unwished /únwísht/ *adj.* (usu. foll. by *for*) not wished for.
■ (*unwished-for*) see UNWELCOME.

unwithered /únwíthərd/ *adj.* not withered; still vigorous or fresh.

unwitnessed /únwítnist/ *adj.* not witnessed.

unwitting /únwíting/ *adj.* **1** unaware of the state of the case (*an unwitting offender*). **2** unintentional. □□ **unwittingly** *adv.* **unwittingness** *n.* [OE *unwitende* (as UN-¹, WIT²)]
■ **1** see UNAWARE *adj.* 1. **2** see INADVERTENT 1. □□ **unwittingly** see UNAWARES 2.

unwomanly /únwoomənlee/ *adj.* not womanly; not befitting a woman. □□ **unwomanliness** *n.*

unwonted /únwáwntid, -wón-, -wún-/ *adj.* not customary or usual. □□ **unwontedly** *adv.* **unwontedness** *n.*
■ infrequent, unusual, uncustomary, uncommon, unfamiliar, unprecedented, rare, singular, atypical, abnormal, peculiar, odd, strange, irregular, unconventional, unorthodox.

unwooded /únwoodid/ *adj.* not wooded; treeless.

unworkable /únwórkəbəl/ *adj.* not workable; impracticable. □□ **unworkability** *n.* **unworkableness** *n.* **unworkably** *adv.*
■ see IMPOSSIBLE 1.

unworked /únwórkt/ *adj.* **1** not wrought into shape. **2** not exploited or turned to account.

unworkmanlike /únwórkmənlīk/ *adj.* badly done or made.

unworldly /únwórldlee/ *adj.* **1** spiritually minded. **2** spiritual. □□ **unworldliness** *n.*
■ see UNEARTHLY 3, SPIRITUAL *adj.*

unworn /únwáwrn/ *adj.* not worn or impaired by wear.

unworried /únwáreed, -wúr-/ *adj.* not worried; calm.

unworthy /únwúrthee/ *adj.* (**unworthier, unworthiest**) **1** (often foll. by *of*) not worthy or befitting the character of a person, etc. **2** discreditable; unseemly. **3** contemptible; base. □□ **unworthily** *adv.* **unworthiness** *n.*
■ **1** unequal, meritless, unmerited, substandard, inferior, second-rate, menial, puny, petty, paltry, unprofessional, mediocre, unqualified, ineligible, undeserving, unbefitting; (*unworthy of*) unbecoming to, inappropriate to, unsuitable for, unfit for, out of character for, inconsistent with *or* for, out of place with *or* for, incongruous with *or* for, beneath, below. **2** dishonorable, ignoble, disreputable, discreditable,

improper, unseemly, unbecoming, undignified, shameful, disgraceful. **3** see CONTEMPTIBLE.

unwound¹ /únwównd/ *adj.* not wound or wound up.

unwound² *past* and *past part.* of UNWIND.

unwounded /únwoondid/ *adj.* not wounded; unhurt.

unwoven /únwóvən/ *adj.* not woven.

unwrap /únráp/ *v.* (**unwrapped, unwrapping**) **1** *tr.* remove the wrapping from. **2** *tr.* open or unfold. **3** *intr.* become unwrapped.
■ undo, open.

unwrinkled /únríngkəld/ *adj.* free from wrinkles; smooth.

unwritable /únrítəbəl/ *adj.* that cannot be written.

unwritten /únrít'n/ *adj.* **1** not written. **2** (of a law, etc.) resting originally on custom or judicial decision, not on statute.
■ **1** see VERBAL *adj.* 2.

unwrought /únráwt/ *adj.* (of metals) not hammered into shape or worked into a finished condition.

unyielding /únyeélding/ *adj.* **1** not yielding to pressure, etc. **2** firm; obstinate. □□ **unyieldingly** *adv.* **unyieldingness** *n.*
■ **1** see FIRM¹ *adj.* 1. **2** see FIRM¹ *adj.* 2a, b, OBSTINATE.

unyoke /únyók/ *v.* **1** *tr.* release from a yoke. **2** *intr.* cease work.

unzip /únzíp/ *v.tr.* (**unzipped, unzipping**) unfasten the zipper of.
■ see UNDO 1.

up /up/ *adv., prep., adj., n.,* & *v.* ● *adv.* **1** at, in, or toward a higher place or position (*jumped up in the air; what are they doing up there?*). **2** to or in a place regarded as higher, esp.: **a** northward (*up in New England*). **b** *Brit.* toward a major city or a university (*went up to London*). **3** *colloq.* ahead, etc., as indicated (*went up front*). **4 a** to or in an erect position or condition (*stood it up*). **b** to or in a prepared or required position (*wound up the watch*). **c** in or into a condition of efficiency, activity, or progress (*stirred up trouble; the house is up for sale; the hunt is up*). **5** in a stronger or winning position or condition (*our team was three goals up; am $10 up on the transaction*). **6** (of a computer) running and available for use. **7** to the place or time in question or where the speaker, etc., is (*a child came up to me; went straight up to the door; has been fine up till now*). **8** at or to a higher price or value (*our costs are up; shares are up*). **9 a** completely or effectually (*burn up; eat up; tear up; use up*). **b** more loudly or clearly (*speak up*). **10** in a state of completion; denoting the end of availability, supply, etc. (*time is up*). **11** into a compact, accumulated, or secure state (*pack up; save up; tie up*). **12 a** awake. **b** out of bed (*are you up yet?*). **13** (of the sun, etc.) having risen. **14** happening, esp. unusually or unexpectedly (*something is up*). **15** esp. *Brit.* (usu. foll. by *on* or *in*) taught or informed (*is well up in French*). **16** (usu. foll. by *before*) appearing for trial, etc. (*was up before the judge*). **17** *Brit.* (of a road, etc.) being repaired. **18** (of a jockey) in the saddle. **19** toward the source of a river. **20** inland. **21** (of the points, etc., in a game): **a** registered on the scoreboard. **b** forming the total score for the time being. **22** upstairs, esp. to bed (*are you going up yet?*). **23** (of a theater curtain) raised, etc., to reveal the stage. **24** (as *int.*) get up. **25** (of a ship's helm) with rudder to leeward. **26** in rebellion. **27** *Baseball* at bat (*he struck out his last time up*). ● *prep.* **1** upward along, through, or into (*climbed up the ladder*). **2** from the bottom to the top of. **3** along (*walked up the road*). **4 a** at or in a higher part of (*is situated up the street*). **b** toward the source of (a river). ● *adj.* **1** (often in *comb.*) directed upward (*upstroke*). **2** *Brit.* of travel toward a capital or center (*the up train; the up platform*). **3** *Brit.* (of beer, etc.) effervescent; frothy. ● *n.* a spell of good fortune. ● *v.* (**upped, upping**) **1** *intr. colloq.* start up; begin abruptly to say or do something (*upped and hit him*). **2** *intr.* (foll. by *with*) raise; pick up (*upped with his stick*). **3** *tr.* increase or raise, esp. abruptly (*upped all their prices*). □ **be all up with** be disastrous or hopeless for (a person). **on the up and up** *colloq.* **1** honest(ly); on the level. **2** *Brit.* steadily improving. **something is up** *colloq.* something unusual or undesirable is afoot or happening. **up against 1** close to. **2** in or into contact with. **3** *colloq.* confronted with (*up against a problem*). **up against it** *colloq.* in great difficulties. **up-anchor** *Naut.* weigh anchor. **up and about** (or doing) having risen from bed; active. **up-and-coming** *colloq.* (of a person) making good progress and likely to succeed. **up and down 1** to and fro (along). **2** in every direction. **3** *colloq.* in varying health or spirits. **up for** available for or being considered for (office, etc.). **up-front** *adv.* (usu. **up front**) **1** at the front; in front. **2** (of payments) in advance. ● *adj.* **1** honest, open, frank. **2** (of payments) made in advance. **3** at the front or most prominent. **up hill and down dale** up and down hills on an arduous journey. **up in arms** see ARM². **up the pole** see POLE¹. **ups and downs 1** rises and falls. **2** alternate good and bad fortune. **up to 1** until (*up to the present*). **2** not more than (*you can have up to five*). **3** less than or equal to (*adds up to $10*). **4** incumbent on (*it is up to you to say*). **5** capable of or fit for (*am not up to a long walk*). **6** occupied or busy with (*what have you been up to?*). **up-to-date** see DATE¹. **up to the mark** see MARK¹. **up-to-the-minute** see MINUTE¹. **up to snuff** see SNUFF². **up to one's tricks** see TRICK. **up to a person's tricks** see TRICK. **up with** *int.* expressing support for a stated person or thing. **what's up?** *colloq.* **1** what is going on? **2** what is the matter? [OE *up(p)*, *uppe*, rel. to OHG *ūf*]

■ *adv.* **1** see ALOFT 1, 2. **15** see INFORMED 1. □ **on the up and up 1** see SINCERE, ABOVEBOARD. **2** improving, getting better. **up against it** see *in trouble* 1 (TROUBLE). **up and down 1, 2** see ABOUT *adv.* 3. **up-front** *adj.* **1** open, straightforward, honest, direct, forthright, frank, candid. **3** see *in front* (FRONT). **ups and downs 2** vicissitudes. **up to 5** (*be up to*) see *be equal to* (EQUAL).

up- /up/ *prefix* in senses of UP, added: **1** as an adverb to verbs and verbal derivations, = 'upward' (*upcurved; update*). **2** as a preposition to nouns forming adverbs and adjectives (*upcountry; uphill*). **3** as an adjective to nouns (*upland; upstroke*). [OE *up(p)-*, = UP]

Upanishad /ōōpánishad, ōōpáanishaad/ *n.* each of a series of philosophical compositions concluding the exposition of the Vedas. [Skr. f. *upa* near + *ni-ṣad* sit down]

upas /yōōpəs/ *n.* **1** (in full **upas tree**) **a** a Javanese tree, *Antiaris toxicaria*, yielding a milky sap used as arrow poison. **b** *Mythol.* a Javanese tree thought to be fatal to whatever came near it. **c** a pernicious influence, practice, etc. **2** the poisonous sap of upas and other trees. [Malay *ūpas* poison]

upbeat /úpbeet/ *n.* & *adj.* ● *n.* an unaccented beat in music. ● *adj. colloq.* optimistic or cheerful.

■ *adj.* positive, optimistic, sanguine, favorable, cheerful, encouraging, heartening, buoyant, lighthearted.

upbraid /upbráyd/ *v.tr.* (often foll. by *with*, *for*) chide or reproach (a person). □□ **upbraiding** *n.* [OE *upbrēdan* (as UP-, *brēdan* = *bregdan* BRAID in obs. sense 'brandish')]

■ scold, rebuke, reprimand, reproach, berate, castigate, admonish, chastise, reprove, censure, take to task, give a person a piece of one's mind, call *or* haul a person over the coals, have a go at, *archaic or literary* chide, *colloq.* tell off, dress down, give a person a dressing-down, tell a person a thing or two, jump on, bawl out, chew out, esp. *Brit.* tick off. □□ **upbraiding** see REPRIMAND *n.*

upbringing /úpbringing/ *n.* the bringing up of a child; education. [obs. *upbring* to rear (as UP-, BRING)]

■ rearing, raising, bringing up, parenting, nurture, training, education, instruction, cultivation, breeding.

UPC *abbr.* = *Universal Product Code.*

upcast *n.* & *v.* ● *n.* /úpkast/ **1** the act of casting up; an upward throw. **2** *Mining* a shaft through which air leaves a mine. **3** *Geol.* = UPTHROW. ● *v.tr.* /úpkást/ (*past* and *past part.* **upcast**) cast up.

upchuck /úpchuk/ *v.tr.* & *intr. sl.* vomit.

upcoming /úpkúming/ *adj.* forthcoming; about to happen.

■ see FORTHCOMING 1.

up-country /úpkúntree/ *adv.* & *adj.* inland; toward the interior of a country.

update *v.* & *n.* ● *v.tr.* /úpdáyt/ bring up to date. ● *n.* /úpdayt/ **1** the act or an instance of updating. **2** an updated version; a set of updated information. □□ **updater** *n.*

■ *v.* see MODERNIZE, REVISE *v.* 1. ● *n.* see REVISION.

updraft /úpdraft/ *n.* an upward draft of gas, esp. smoke in a chimney.

upend /úpénd/ *v.tr.* & *intr.* set or rise up on end.

■ see TIP² *v.* 2a, *turn over* 1.

upfield /úpfeeld/ *adv.* in or to a position nearer to the opponents' end of a football, etc., field.

upfold /úpfōld/ *n. Geol.* an anticline.

upgrade *v.* & *n.* ● *v.tr.* /úpgráyd/ **1** raise in rank, etc. **2** improve (equipment, machinery, etc.) esp. by replacing components. ● *n.* /úpgrayd/ **1** the act or an instance of upgrading. **2** an upgraded piece of equipment, etc. **3** an upward slope. □ **on the upgrade 1** improving in health, etc. **2** advancing; progressing. □□ **upgrader** *n.*

■ *v.* **1** see PROMOTE 1. **2** see IMPROVE 1a. ● *n.* **1** see *promotion* (PROMOTE).

upgrowth /úpgrōth/ *n.* the process or result of growing upward.

upheaval /uphéevəl/ *n.* **1** a violent or sudden change or disruption. **2** *Geol.* an upward displacement of part of the earth's crust. **3** the act or an instance of heaving up.

■ **1** upset, unrest, commotion, change, revolution, cataclysm, turbulence, disruption, disturbance, disorder, confusion, chaos, havoc, uproar, furor. **2** uplift.

upheave /uphéev/ *v.* **1** *tr.* heave or lift up, esp. forcibly. **2** *intr.* rise up.

uphill *adv.*, *adj.*, & *n.* ● *adv.* /úphíl/ in an ascending direction up a hill, slope, etc. ● *adj.* /úphíl/ **1** sloping up; ascending. **2** arduous; difficult (*an uphill task*). ● *n.* /úphil/ an upward slope.

■ *adj.* **2** see LABORIOUS 1.

uphold /úphōld/ *v.tr.* (*past* and *past part.* **upheld** /-héld/) **1** confirm or maintain (a decision, etc., esp. of another). **2** give support or countenance to (a person, practice, etc.). □□ **upholder** *n.*

■ **1** see CONFIRM 1, 2. **2** support, maintain, sustain, preserve, hold up, defend, protect, advocate, promote, espouse, embrace, endorse, back, champion, stand by *or* behind, stick up for. □□ **upholder** see PROPONENT *n.*

upholster /uphōlstər, əpṓl-/ *v.tr.* **1** provide (furniture) with upholstery. **2** furnish (a room, etc.) with furniture, carpets, etc. □ **well-upholstered** *joc.* (of a person) fat. [back-form. f. UPHOLSTERER]

upholsterer /uphōlstərər, əpṓl-/ *n.* a person who upholsters furniture, esp. professionally. [obs. *upholster* (n.) f. UPHOLD (in obs. sense 'keep in repair') + -STER]

upholstery /uphōlstəree, əpṓl-/ *n.* **1** textile covering, padding, springs, etc., for furniture. **2** an upholsterer's work.

upkeep /úpkeep/ *n.* **1** maintenance in good condition. **2** the cost or means of this.

■ **1** maintenance, repair, support, preservation, conservation, running, operation. **2** (operating) costs, (running) expenses, outlay, expenditure, overhead, *Brit.* oncosts.

upland /úplənd/ *n.* & *adj.* ● *n.* the higher or inland parts of a country. ● *adj.* of or relating to these parts.

■ *n.* see HILL *n.* 1, INTERIOR *n.* 2.

uplift *v.* & *n.* ● *v.tr.* /úplíft/ **1** esp. *Brit.* raise; lift up. **2** elevate or stimulate morally or spiritually. ● *n.* /úplift/ **1** the act or an instance of being raised. **2** *Geol.* the raising of part of the earth's surface. **3** *colloq.* a morally or spiritually elevating influence. **4** support for the bust, etc., from a garment. □□ **uplifter** *n.* **uplifting** *adj.* (esp. in sense 2 of *v.*).

■ *v.* **1** see RAISE *v.* 1. **2** see INSPIRE 1, 2. □□ **uplifting** see *exhilarating* (EXHILARATE).

upmarket /úpmáarkit/ *adj.* & *adv.* = UPSCALE.

upmost var. of UPPERMOST.

upon /əpón, əpáwn/ *prep.* = ON. ¶ *Upon* is sometimes more formal, and is preferred in *once upon a time* and *upon my* *word*, and in uses such as *row upon row of seats* and *Christmas is almost upon us*. [ME f. UP + ON *prep.*, after ON *upp á*]

upper[1] /úpər/ *adj. & n.* ● *adj.* **1 a** higher in place; situated above another part (*the upper atmosphere*; *the upper lip*). **b** *Geol.* designating a younger (and usually shallower) part of a stratigraphic division, or the period of its formation (*the Upper Jurassic*). **2** higher in rank or dignity, etc. (*the upper class*). **3** situated on higher ground, further to the north, or further inland (*Upper Egypt*). ● *n.* the part of a boot or shoe above the sole. □ **on one's uppers** *colloq.* extremely short of money. **upper class** the highest class of society, esp. (in the UK) the aristocracy. **upper-class** *adj.* of the upper class. **the upper crust** *colloq.* (in the UK) the aristocracy. **upper-crust** *adj. colloq.* of the aristocracy. **the upper hand** dominance or control. **upper house** the higher house in a legislature, e.g., the U.S. Senate. **the upper regions 1** the sky. **2** heaven. **upper works** the part of a ship that is above the water when fully laden. [ME f. UP + -ER[2]]

■ *adj.* **1 a** higher (up), loftier, topmost, more elevated, uppermost, superior. **b** later, more recent. **2** see SUPERIOR *adj.* 1. **3** higher, upland, more elevated; (more) northerly, northern; inland. □ **on one's uppers** poor, indigent, destitute, poverty-stricken, impoverished, penniless, penurious, insolvent, needy, down and out, *colloq.* strapped (for cash), flat broke, up against it, *sl* stone-broke, *Brit. sl.* skint; see also BROKE. **upper class** see *the upper crust* below. **upper-class** élite, aristocratic, blue-blooded, well-born, noble, high-born, patrician; high-class, elegant, genteel, fancy, luxurious, first-rate, deluxe, royal, regal, sumptuous, *colloq.* ritzy, posh, swanky, swank. **the upper crust** upper class, élite, aristocracy, aristocrats, gentility, nobility, nobles, the blue-blooded, four hundred, *Brit. sl.* nobs. **the upper hand** the whip hand, advantage, control, authority, power, sway, superiority, supremacy, command, dominance, ascendancy, the edge.

upper[2] /úpər/ *n. sl.* a stimulant drug, esp. an amphetamine. [UP *v.* + -ER[2]]

uppercase /úpərkáys/ *adj., n., & v.* ● *adj.* (of letters) capital. ● *n.* capital letters. ● *v.tr.* set or print in uppercase.

uppercut /úpərkut/ *n. & v./* ● *n.* an upward blow delivered with the arm bent. ● *v.tr.* hit with an uppercut.

■ see PUNCH[1] *n.* 1.

uppermost /úpərmōst/ *adj. & adv.* ● *adj.* (also **upmost** /úpmōst/) **1** highest in place or rank. **2** predominant. ● *adv.* at or to the highest or most prominent position.

■ *adj.* **1** highest, topmost, loftiest, highest, top, supreme. **2** upmost, foremost, first, most important *or* prominent *or* influential *or* telling, principal, paramount, preeminent, predominant.

uppish /úpish/ *adj. esp. Brit. colloq.* self-assertive or arrogant; uppity. □□ **uppishly** *adv.* **uppishness** *n.*

■ affected, putting on airs, snobbish, conceited, overweening, self-important, self-assertive, arrogant, superior, supercilious, lofty, haughty, hoity-toity, *colloq.* uppity, snooty, high and mighty, highfalutin, stuck-up, on one's high horse, *sl.* snotty, esp. *Brit. sl.* toffee-nosed. □□ **uppishness** see *snobbery* (SNOB).

uppity /úpitee/ *adj. colloq.* arrogant; snobbish. [fanciful f. UP]

■ see *snobbish* (SNOB).

upraise /úpráyz/ *v.tr.* raise to a higher level.

■ see RAISE *v.* 1, DIGNIFY.

upright /úprīt/ *adj., adv., & n.* ● *adj.* **1** erect; vertical (*an upright posture*; *stood upright*). **2** (of a piano) with vertical strings. **3** (of a person or behavior) righteous; strictly honorable or honest. **4** (of a picture, book, etc.) greater in height than breadth. ● *adv.* in a vertical direction; vertically upward; into an upright position. ● *n.* **1** a post or rod fixed upright, esp. as a structural support. **2** an upright piano. □□ **uprightly** *adv.* **uprightness** *n.* [OE *upriht* (as UP, RIGHT)]

■ *adj.* **1** erect, perpendicular, vertical, on end, straight up and down, plumb, stand-up, standing (up), upstanding. **3** moral, principled, high-minded, ethical,

virtuous, upstanding, righteous, straightforward, honorable, honest, just, trustworthy, unimpeachable, uncorrupted, incorruptible, scrupulous, decent, good, *colloq.* straight. ● *adv.* perpendicularly, vertically, upward(s), straight up (and down); right side up. ● *n.* **1** post, pole, column, pillar, stanchion, standard, vertical, perpendicular. □□ **uprightly** see UPRIGHT *adv.* above, HONESTLY 1. **uprightness** see RECTITUDE.

uprise /úpríz/ *v.intr.* (**uprose, uprisen**) rise (to a standing position, etc.).

uprising /úprīzing/ *n.* a rebellion or revolt.

■ rebellion, revolt, mutiny, revolution, insurrection, rising, putsch, coup, coup d'état.

uproar /úprawr/ *n.* a tumult; a violent disturbance. [Du. *oproer* f. *op* up + *roer* confusion, assoc. with ROAR]

■ clamor, hubbub, disturbance, disorder, commotion, hullabaloo, brouhaha, din, racket, pandemonium, tumult, turmoil, turbulence, outcry, outburst, bedlam, chaos, confusion, agitation, frenzy, broil, fuss, to-do; affray, fracas, brawl; *colloq.* row, rumpus, *literary* pother, *sl.* hoo-ha, hoopla.

uproarious /upráwreeəs/ *adj.* **1** very noisy; tumultuous. **2** provoking loud laughter. □□ **uproariously** *adv.* **uproariousness** *n.*

■ **1** clamorous, noisy, deafening, tumultuous, turbulent, tempestuous, excited, frenzied, rowdy, riotous, disorderly, wild. **2** hilarious, (screamingly) funny, sidesplitting, too funny for words, *colloq.* hysterical, killing.

uproot /úprŏŏt, rŏŏt/ *v.tr.* **1** pull (a plant, etc.) up from the ground. **2** displace (a person) from an accustomed location. **3** eradicate; destroy. □□ **uprooter** *n.*

■ **1** pull up, root out, dig out *or* up, pluck out, tear out, grub up, weed out, *literary* deracinate. **2** transfer, transplant, move, displace; exile, banish. **3** extirpate, root out, dig out, pluck out, tear out, weed out; destroy, demolish, ruin, eradicate, eliminate, exterminate, annihilate, kill, devastate, ravage, *literary* deracinate.

uprose *past* of UPRISE.

uprush /úprush/ *n.* an upward rush, esp. *Psychol.* from the subconscious.

upsa-daisy var. of UPSY-DAISY.

upscale /úpskáyl/ *adj., v., & n.* ● *adj.* toward or relating to the more affluent or upper sector of society or the market. ● *v.tr.* improve the quality or value of. ● *n.* (as *pl.*) upscale persons collectively (*apartments built for the upscale*).

upset *v., n., & adj.* ● *v.* /úpsét/ (**upsetting**; *past* and *past part.* **upset**) **1 a** *tr. & intr.* overturn or be overturned. **b** *tr.* overcome; defeat. **2** *tr.* disturb the composure or digestion of (*was very upset by the news*; *ate something that upset me*). **3** *tr.* disrupt. **4** *tr.* shorten and thicken (metal, esp. a tire) by hammering or pressure. ● *n.* /úpset/ **1** a condition of upsetting or being upset (*a stomach upset*). **2** a surprising result in a game, etc. ● *adj.* /úpsét/ disturbed (*an upset stomach*). □ **upset price** the lowest acceptable selling price of a property in an auction, etc.; a reserve price. □□ **upsetter** *n.* **upsettingly** *adv.*

■ *v.* **1 a** overturn, capsize, topple, upend, upturn, tip over, knock over *or* down, invert, turn topsy-turvy *or* upside down, spill. **b** overthrow, topple, defeat, beat, worst, thrash, rout, conquer, overcome, win out over, get the better of, get *or* gain the advantage over, triumph over, be victorious over, *literary* vanquish. **2** disturb, agitate, distress, grieve, unsettle, put off, put out, offend, perturb, disquiet, fluster, ruffle, frighten, scare, disconcert, dismay, trouble, worry, bother, annoy, irritate, discompose, discomfit, make nervous, unnerve, *colloq.* rattle, *joc.* discombobulate. **3** disturb, derange, disrupt, disarrange, disorder, unsettle, mess up, disorganize, snarl up, jumble, muddle, confuse; defeat, ruin, wreck, spoil, thwart, interfere with, destroy, demolish, *colloq.* gum up, *sl.* screw up, put the kibosh on. ● *n.* **1** disorder, ailment, malady; see also DISTURBANCE 1, 4; 2. **2** surprise, unexpected event *or* occurrence; defeat, conquest, overthrow, rout, thrashing; triumph, victory. ● *adj.* (*of digestion*) sick, queasy; (*of a person*) perturbed, disturbed, disquieted, disconcerted, agitated, distressed, worried, troubled, unnerved, distracted, apprehensive, nervous, frightened, scared, afraid; angry, irate, furious, beside oneself, mad, *colloq.* fit to be tied, freaked out.

upshot /úpshot/ *n.* the final or eventual outcome or conclusion.
■ result, end (result), outcome, ending, (end) product, conclusion, termination, effect, aftereffect, fallout, wake, backwash, repercussion, feedback, resolution, culmination, denouement, issue, *sl.* payoff.

upside down /úpsid dówn/ *adv.* & *adj.* ● *adv.* **1** with the upper part where the lower part should be; in an inverted position. **2** in or into total disorder (*everything was turned upside down*). ● *adj.* (also **upside-down** *attrib.*) that is positioned upside down; inverted. □ **upside-down cake** a cake baked with fruit in a syrup at the bottom, and inverted for serving. [ME, orig. *up so down*, perh. = 'up as if down']
■ see TOPSY-TURVY.

upsides /úpsidz/ *adv. Brit. colloq.* (foll. by *with*) equal with (a person) by revenge, retaliation, etc. [*upside* = top part]

upsilon /úpsilon, yŏŏp-/ *n.* the twentieth letter of the Greek alphabet (Υ, υ). [Gk, = slender U f. *psilos* slender, with ref. to its later coincidence in sound with Gk *oi*]

upstage /úpstáyj/ *adj., adv., v.,* & *n.* ● *adj.* & *adv.* **1** nearer the back of a theater stage. **2** snobbish(ly). ● *v.tr.* **1** (of an actor) move upstage to make (another actor) face away from the audience. **2** divert attention from (a person) to oneself; outshine. ● *n.* the part of the stage farthest from the audience.
■ *v.* **2** see TRANSCEND 2.

upstairs /úpstáirz/ *adv., adj.,* & *n.* ● *adv.* to or on an upper floor. ● *adj.* (also **upstair**) situated upstairs. ● *n.* an upper floor.

upstanding /úpstánding/ *adj.* **1** standing up. **2** strong and healthy. **3** honest or straightforward.
■ **1** see UPRIGHT *adj.* 1. **3** see UPRIGHT *adj.* 3.

upstart /úpstaart/ *n.* & *adj.* ● *n.* a person who has risen suddenly to prominence, esp. one who behaves arrogantly. ● *adj.* **1** that is an upstart. **2** of or characteristic of an upstart.
■ *n.* parvenu(e), arriviste, nouveau riche, (social) climber, status seeker, pretender, nobody, whippersnapper. ● *adj.* parvenu(e), nouveau riche, social-climbing, status-seeking.

upstate /úpstáyt/ *n., adj.,* & *adv.* ● *n.* part of a state remote from its large cities, esp. the northern part (upstate New York). ● *adj.* of or relating to this part. ● *adv.* in or to this part. □□ **upstater** *n.*

upstream /úpstreém/ *adv.* & *adj.* ● *adv.* against the flow of a stream, etc. ● *adj.* moving upstream.

upstroke /úpstrōk/ *n.* a stroke made or written upward.

upsurge /úpsərj/ *n.* an upward surge; a rise (esp. in feelings, etc.).
■ see REVIVAL 5, RISE *n.* 3.

upswept /úpswept/ *adj.* **1** (of the hair) combed to the top of the head. **2** curved or sloped upward.

upswing /úpswing/ *n.* an upward movement or trend.
■ see REVIVAL 5, IMPROVEMENT 1, 2.

upsy-daisy /úpseedáyzee/ *int.* (also **upsa-daisy**) expressing encouragement to a child who is being lifted or has fallen. [earlier *up-a-daisy*: cf. LACKADAISICAL]

uptake /úptayk/ *n.* **1** *colloq.* understanding; comprehension (esp. *quick* or *slow on the uptake*). **2** the act or an instance of taking up.
■ **1** comprehension, understanding, apprehension, grasp, perception, insight, perspicaciousness, perspicacity, perceptiveness, sensitivity.

upthrow /úpthrō/ *n.* **1** the act or an instance of throwing upward. **2** *Geol.* an upward dislocation of strata.

upthrust /úpthrust/ *n.* **1** upward thrust, e.g., of a fluid on an immersed body. **2** *Geol.* = UPHEAVAL.

uptight /úptít/ *adj. colloq.* **1** nervously tense or angry. **2** rigidly conventional.

uptown /úptówn/ *adj., adv.,* & *n.* ● *adj.* **1** of or in the residential part of a town or city. **2** characteristic of or suitable to affluent or sophisticated people. ● *adv.* in or into this part. ● *n.* this part. □□ **uptowner** *n.*

upturn *n.* & *v.* ● *n.* /úptərn/ **1** an upward trend; an improvement. **2** an upheaval. ● *v.tr.* /úptúrn/ turn up or upside down.
■ *n.* **1** see REVIVAL 5, IMPROVEMENT 1, 2.

UPU *abbr.* Universal Postal Union.

upward /úpwərd/ *adv.* & *adj.* ● *adv.* (also **upwards**) toward what is higher, superior, larger in amount, more important, or earlier. ● *adj.* moving, extending, pointing, or leading upward. □ **upwards of** more than (*found upwards of forty specimens*). [OE *upweard(es)* (as UP, -WARD)]
■ □ **upwards of** see OVER *prep.* 10.

upwardly /úpwərdlee/ *adv.* in an upward direction. □ **upwardly mobile** able or aspiring to advance socially or professionally.

upwarp /úpwawrp/ *n. Geol.* a broad surface elevation; an anticline.

upwind /úpwínd/ *adj.* & *adv.* against the direction of the wind.

ur- /ŏŏr/ *comb. form* primitive; original; earliest. [G]

uracil /yŏŏrəsil/ *n. Biochem.* a pyrimidine derivative found in living tissue as a component base of RNA. [UREA + ACETIC]

uraemia *Brit.* var. of UREMIA.

uraeus /yŏŏreéəs/ *n.* the sacred serpent as an emblem of power represented on the headdress of Egyptian divinities and sovereigns. [mod.L f. Gk *ouraios*, repr. the Egypt. word for 'cobra']

Ural-Altaic /yŏŏrəlaltáyik/ *n.* & *adj.* ● *n. Philol.* a family of Finno-Ugric, Turkic, Mongolian, and other agglutinative languages of N. Europe and Asia. ● *adj.* **1** of or relating to this family of languages. **2** of or relating to the Ural and Altai mountain ranges in west and central Asia.

uranium /yŏŏráyneeəm/ *n. Chem.* a radioactive, gray, dense metallic element occurring naturally in pitchblende, and capable of nuclear fission and therefore used as a source of nuclear energy. ¶ Symb.: U. □□ **uranic** /-ránik/ *adj.* [mod.L, f. URANUS: cf. *tellurium*]

urano-¹ /yŏŏrəno, yŏŏráynō/ *comb. form* the heavens. [Gk *ouranos* heaven(s)]

urano-² /yŏŏrənō/ *comb. form* uranium.

uranography /yŏŏrənógrəfee/ *n.* the branch of astronomy concerned with describing and mapping the stars, planets, etc. □□ **uranographer** *n.* **uranographic** /-nəgráfik/ *adj.*

Uranus /yŏŏrənəs, yŏŏráynəs/ *n.* a planet discovered by Herschel in 1781, the outermost of the solar system except Neptune and Pluto. [L f. Gk *Ouranos* heaven, Uranus, in Gk Mythol. the son of Gaea (Earth) and father of Kronos (Saturn), the Titans, etc.]

urban /árbən/ *adj.* of, living in, or situated in a town or city (*an urban population*) (opp. RURAL). □ **urban renewal** slum clearance and redevelopment in a city or town. **urban sprawl** the uncontrolled expansion of urban areas. [L *urbanus* f. *urbs urbis* city]

urbane /árbáyn/ *adj.* courteous; suave; elegant and refined in manner. □□ **urbanely** *adv.* **urbaneness** *n.* [F *urbain* or L *urbanus*: see URBAN]
■ see COURTEOUS, ELEGANT 1, 2.

urbanism /árbənizəm/ *n.* **1** urban character or way of life. **2** a study of urban life. □□ **urbanist** *n.*

urbanite /árbənit/ *n.* a dweller in a city or town.

urbanity /ərbánitee/ *n.* **1** an urbane quality; refinement of manner. **2** urban life. [F *urbanité* or L *urbanitas* (as URBAN)]
■ **1** see REFINEMENT 3.

urbanize /árbəniz/ *v.tr.* **1** make urban. **2** destroy the rural quality of (a district). □□ **urbanization** /-záyshən/ *n.* [F *urbaniser* (as URBAN)]

/.../ **pronunciation**   ● **part of speech**
□ **phrases, idioms, and compounds**
□□ **derivatives**   ■ **synonym section**
cross-references appear in SMALL CAPITALS or *italics*

urceolate /ɔ́rseeələt, ɔrse'eəlayt/ *adj. Bot.* having the shape of a pitcher, with a large body and small mouth. [L *urceolus* dimin. of *urceus* pitcher]

urchin /ɔ́rchin/ *n.* **1** a mischievous child, esp. young and raggedly dressed. **2** = *sea urchin*. **3** *archaic* **a** a hedgehog. **b** a goblin. [ME *hirchon, urcheon* f. ONF *herichon,* OF *heriçon* ult. f. L (*h*)*ericius* hedgehog]
  ■ **1** see RAGAMUFFIN.

Urdu /ŏŏrdōō, ɔ́r-/ *n.* a language related to Hindi but with many Persian words, an official language of Pakistan and also used in India. [Hind. (*zabān i*) *urdū* (language of the) camp, f. Pers. *urdū* f. Turki *ordū*: see HORDE]

-ure /ər/ *suffix* forming: **1** nouns of action or process (*censure; closure; seizure*). **2** nouns of result (*creature; scripture*). **3** collective nouns (*legislature; nature*). **4** nouns of function (*judicature; ligature*). [from or after OF *-ure* f. L *-ura*]

urea /yŏŏree'ə/ *n. Biochem.* a soluble, colorless, crystalline, nitrogenous compound contained esp. in the urine of mammals. □□ **ureal** *adj.* [mod.L f. F *urée* f. Gk *ouron* urine]

uremia /yŏŏree'meeə/ *n.* (*Brit.* **uraemia**) *Med.* a morbid condition due to the presence in the blood of urinary matter normally eliminated by the kidneys. □□ **uremic** /-mik/ *adj.* [Gk *ouron* urine + *haima* blood]

ureter /yŏŏree'tər/ *n.* the duct by which urine passes from the kidney to the bladder or cloaca. □□ **ureteral** *adj.* **ureteric** /yóoritérik/ *adj.* **ureteritis** /-rítis/ *n.* [F *uretère* or mod.L *ureter* f. Gk *ourētēr* f. *oureō* urinate]

urethane /yŏŏríthayn/ *n. Chem.* a crystalline amide, ethyl carbamate, used in plastics and paints. [F *uréthane* (as UREA, ETHANE)]

urethra /yŏŏree'thrə/ *n.* (*pl.* **urethras** or **urethrae** /-ree/) the duct by which urine is discharged from the bladder. □□ **urethral** *adj.* **urethritis** /-rithrítis/ *n.* [LL f. Gk *ourēthra* (as URETER)]

urge /ərj/ *v. & n.* ● *v.tr.* **1** (often foll. by *on*) drive forcibly; impel; hasten (*urged them on; urged the horses forward*). **2** (often foll. by *to* + infin. or *that* + clause) encourage or entreat earnestly or persistently (*urged them to go; urged them to action; urged that they should go*). **3** (often foll. by *on, upon*) advocate (an action or argument, etc.) pressingly or emphatically (to a person). **4** adduce forcefully as a reason or justification (*urged the seriousness of the problem*). **5** ply (a person, etc.) hard with argument or entreaty. ● *n.* **1** an urging impulse or tendency. **2** a strong desire. [L *urgēre* press, drive]
  ■ *v.* **1** press, push, drive, force, impel, speed, accelerate, hurry, rush, hustle, hasten, move, goad, prod, egg on, spur. **2** press, goad, prod, egg on, spur, prompt, induce, incite, constrain, exhort, encourage, demand, request, ask, plead (with), beseech, beg, entreat, implore, importune, coax, persuade, prevail (up)on, campaign (with), sway, influence, talk into, advise, suggest, counsel. **3** advocate, adduce, advise, argue. **4** argue, set forth, affirm, state, allege, assert, hold. ● *n.* **1** pressure, impetus, compulsion, impulse, drive. **2** desire, longing, yearning, hankering, fancy, itch, hunger, thirst, craving, wish, *colloq.* yen.

urgent /ɔ́rjənt/ *adj.* **1** requiring immediate action or attention (*an urgent need for help*). **2** importunate; earnest and persistent in demand. □□ **urgency** *n.* **urgently** *adv.* [ME f. F (as URGE)]
  ■ **1** immediate, instant, imperative, pressing, compelling, vital, life-and-death, life-or-death, important, serious, grave, desperate, necessary, exigent, rush, emergency, high-priority. **2** supplicant, begging, solicitous, earnest, importunate, insistent, persistent, loud, clamorous, active, energetic, pertinacious, tenacious, forceful, firm. □□ **urgency** imperativeness, pressure, stress, extremity, importance, seriousness, importunity, necessity, need, insistence, exigency, emergency. **urgently** see HARD *adv.* 1.

urger /ɔ́rjər/ *n.* **1** a person who urges or incites. **2** *Austral. sl.* a person who obtains money dishonestly, esp. as a racing tipster.

-uria /yŏŏree'ə/ *comb. form* forming nouns denoting that a substance is (esp. excessively) present in the urine. [mod.L f. Gk *-ouria* (as URINE)]

uric /yŏŏrik/ *adj.* of or relating to urine. □ **uric acid** a crystalline acid forming a constituent of urine. [F *urique* (as URINE)]

urinal /yŏŏrinəl/ *n.* **1** a sanitary fitting, usu. against a wall, for men to urinate into. **2** a place or receptacle for urination. [ME f. OF f. LL *urinal* neut. of *urinalis* (as URINE)]

urinalysis /yŏŏrinálisis/ *n.* (*pl.* **urinalyses** /-seez/) the chemical analysis of urine, esp. for diagnostic purposes.

urinary /yŏŏrinəree/ *adj.* **1** of or relating to urine. **2** affecting or occurring in the urinary system (*urinary diseases*).

urinate /yŏŏrinayt/ *v.intr.* discharge urine. □□ **urination** /-náyshən/ *n.* [med.L *urinare* (as URINE)]
  ■ pass *or* make water, void, excrete, relieve oneself; *colloq.* (have a) pee, tinkle, piddle, esp. *Brit. sl.* (make *or* have a) wee, *babytalk* (go) weewee, *colloq.* take a pee, *Brit. colloq.* spend a penny, go to the loo, *euphem.* go to the men's *or* ladies' (room), go to the lavatory, excuse (oneself), wash (one's) hands, go to the bathroom, go to the powder room, go to the little boys' *or* girls' room, *sl.* (take *or* have a) piss. □□ **urination** passing water, voiding, excretion, *formal or Med.* micturition.

urine /yŏŏrin/ *n.* a pale-yellow fluid secreted as waste from the blood by the kidneys, stored in the bladder, and discharged through the urethra. □□ **urinous** *adj.* [ME f. OF f. L *urina*]

urn /ərn/ *n. & v.* ● *n.* **1** a vase with a foot and usu. a rounded body, esp. for storing the ashes of the cremated dead or as a vessel or measure. **2** a large vessel with a tap, in which tea or coffee, etc., is made or kept hot. **3** *poet.* anything in which a dead body or its remains are preserved, e.g., a grave. ● *v.tr.* enclose in an urn. □□ **urnful** *n.* (*pl.* **-fuls**). [ME f. L *urna*, rel. to *urceus* pitcher]

uro-[1] /yŏŏrō/ *comb. form* urine. [Gk *ouron* urine]

uro-[2] /yŏŏrō/ *comb. form* tail. [Gk *oura* tail]

urochord /yŏŏrōkawrd/ *n.* the notochord of a tunicate.

urodele /yŏŏrōdeel/ *n.* any amphibian of the order Urodela, having a tail when in the adult form, including newts and salamanders. [URO-[2] + Gk *dēlos* evident]

urogenital /yŏŏrəjénit'l/ *adj.* of or relating to urinary and genital products or organs.

urology /yŏŏróləjee/ *n.* the scientific study of the urinary system. □□ **urologic** /-rəlójik/ *adj.* **urologist** *n.*

uropygium /yŏŏrōpíjeeəm/ *n.* the rump of a bird. [med.L f. Gk *ouropugion*]

uroscopy /yŏŏróskəpee/ *n. Med. hist.* the examination of urine, esp. in diagnosis.

Ursa Major /ɔ́rsə máyjər/ *n.* = *Big Dipper.* [L, = greater bear]

Ursa Minor /ɔ́rsə mínər/ *n.* = *Little Dipper.* [L, = lesser bear]

ursine /ɔ́rsin/ *adj.* of or like a bear. [L *ursinus* f. *ursus* bear]

Ursuline /ɔ́rsəlin, -līn, -leen, ɔ́rsyə-/ *n. & adj.* ● *n.* a nun of an order founded by St. Angela in 1535 for nursing the sick and teaching girls. ● *adj.* of or relating to this order. [St. *Ursula*, the founder's patron saint]

urticaria /ɔ́rtikáireeə/ *n. Med.* skin rash, usu. from an allergic reaction; hives. [mod.L f. L *urtica* nettle f. *urere* burn]

urticate /ɔ́rtikayt/ *v.tr.* sting like a nettle. □□ **urtication** /-káyshən/ *n.* [med.L *urticare* f. L *urtica*: see URTICARIA]

urus /yŏŏrəs/ *n.* = AUROCHS. [L f. Gmc]

US *abbr.* **1** United States (of America). **2** *Brit.* undersecretary.

us /us, əs/ *pron.* **1** objective case of WE (*they saw us*). **2** *colloq.* = WE (*it's us again*). **3** *colloq.* = ME[1] (*give us a kiss*). [OE *ūs* f. Gmc]

USA *abbr.* **1** United States of America. **2** United States Army.

usable /yŏŏzəbəl/ *adj.* (also **useable**) that can be used. □□ **usability** /-bílitee/ *n.* **usableness** *n.*
  ■ see SERVICEABLE 1, 2, USEFUL.

USAF *abbr.* United States Air Force.

usage /yŏŏsij/ *n.* **1** a manner of using or treating; treatment (*damaged by rough usage*). **2** habitual or customary practice, esp. as creating a right, obligation, or standard. [ME f. OF f. *us* USE *n.*]

■ **1** treatment, use, management, handling, operation, manipulation, wear (and tear). **2** use (and wont), custom, habit, practice, routine, convention, form, tradition.

usance /yōōzəns/ *n.* the time allowed by commercial usage for the payment of foreign bills of exchange. [ME f. OF (as USE)]

U.S.C. *abbr. Law* United States Code.

USCG *abbr.* United States Coast Guard.

use *v. & n.* ● *v.tr.* /yōōz/ **1 a** cause to act or serve for a purpose; bring into service; avail oneself of (*rarely uses the car; use your discretion*). **b** consume by eating or drinking; take (alcohol, a drug, etc.), esp. habitually. **2** treat (a person) in a specified manner (*they used him shamefully*). **3** exploit for one's own ends (*they are just using you; used his position*). **4** (in *past* /yōōst/; foll. by *to* + infin.) did or had in the past (but no longer) as a customary practice or state (*I used to be an archaeologist; it used not (or did not use) to rain so often*). **5** (as **used** *adj.*) secondhand. **6** (as **used** /yōōst/ *predic. adj.*) (foll. by *to*) familiar by habit; accustomed (*not used to hard work*). **7** apply (a name or title, etc.) to oneself. ● *n.* /yōōs/ **1** the act of using or the state of being used; application to a purpose (*put it to good use; is in daily use; worn and polished with use*). **2** the right or power of using (*lost the use of my right arm*). **3 a** the ability to be used (*a flashlight would be of use*). **b** the purpose for which a thing can be used (*it's no use talking*). **4** custom or usage (*long use has reconciled me to it*). **5** the characteristic ritual and liturgy of a church or diocese, etc. **6** *Law hist.* the benefit or profit of lands, esp. in the possession of another who holds them solely for the beneficiary. □ **could use** *colloq.* would be glad to have; would be improved by having. **have no use for 1** be unable to find a use for. **2** dislike or be impatient with. **make use of 1** employ; apply. **2** benefit from. **use a person's name** quote a person as an authority or reference, etc. **use up 1** consume completely; use the whole of. **2** find a use for (something remaining). **3** exhaust or wear out, e.g., with overwork. [ME f. OF *us*, *user*, ult. f. L *uti us-* use]

■ *v.* **1 a** employ, make use of, put into practice *or* operation, practice, operate, utilize, exercise, exert, apply, administer, wield, ply, work, bring into play, have recourse to, resort to, put *or* press into service, put to use, avail oneself of. **b** consume, eat, drink, smoke, take, partake of, ingest, inject, *sl.* do, shoot (up). **2** treat, handle, deal with, act *or* behave toward. **3** exploit, make use of, take advantage of, manipulate, maneuver, abuse, misuse; utilize, capitalize on, turn to account, profit by *or* from, play, work. **5** (**used**) secondhand, cast-off, old, worn, hand-me-down, *Brit.* reach-me-down. **6** (*used to*) accustomed to, habituated to, acclimatized *or* acclimated to, adapted to, hardened to *or* against, toughened to *or* against, inured to *or* against, tempered to, tolerant of; familiar *or* acquainted with. **7** adopt, assume, take up. ● *n.* **1** usage, application, employment, utilization; using, handling; consumption. **2** usability, usefulness, utility, utilization, usage, function, functioning, service(s), serviceability, power. **3 a** utility, service. **b** advantage, benefit, good, service, interest, profit, avail; purpose, point, object, reason, basis, ground; demand, need, necessity, urgency, exigency. **4** see USAGE. □ **have no use for 2** execrate, detest, abhor, hate, despise, scorn, spurn, reject, dislike, *literary* contemn. **make use of 1** see USE *v.* 1a above. **2** see PROFIT *v.* 2, USE *v.* 3 above. **use up 1** consume, exhaust, expend, spend, run through, run out of, deplete; waste, squander, fritter away, pour down the drain, throw away, *sl.* blow. **3** see EXHAUST *v.* 2.

useful /yōōsfŏŏl/ *adj.* **1 a** of use; serviceable. **b** producing or able to produce good results (*gave me some useful hints*). **2** *colloq.* highly creditable or efficient (*a useful performance*). □ **make oneself useful** perform useful services. □□ **usefully** *adv.* **usefulness** *n.*

■ **1** utilitarian, functional, serviceable, practical, usable, of use, beneficial, salutary, advantageous, expedient,

profitable, valuable, gainful, helpful, constructive, fruitful, productive, effective, worthwhile. □□ **usefulness** utility, applicability, practicability, purpose, purposefulness, use, point, practicality, good, benefit, advantage, expediency, profit, profitability, value, gain, help, fruitfulness, effectiveness, worth.

useless /yōōslis/ *adj.* **1** serving no purpose; unavailing (*the contents were made useless by moisture; protest is useless*). **2** *colloq.* feeble or ineffectual (*am useless at swimming; a useless gadget*). □□ **uselessly** *adv.* **uselessness** *n.*

■ **1** ineffective, ineffectual, unserviceable, impractical, impracticable, unpractical, unavailing, vain, pointless, purposeless, idle, futile, unproductive, unprofitable, unsuccessful, impotent, sterile, barren, fruitless, abortive, unusable, worthless, *archaic* bootless. **2** inefficient, incompetent, unproductive, ineffectual, ineffective, no-good, hopeless, inept, feeble, *sl.* out to lunch; see also USELESS **1**. □□ **uselessness** see incompetence (INCOMPETENT), VANITY 2a.

user /yōōzər/ *n.* **1** a person who uses (esp. a particular commodity or service, or a computer). **2** *colloq.* a drug addict. **3** *Law* the continued use or enjoyment of a right, etc. □ **right of user** *Law* **1** a right to use. **2** a presumptive right arising from the user. **user-friendly** esp. *Computing* (of a machine or system) designed to be easy to use.

■ **1** consumer, owner; operator. **2** alcohol *or* drug, *etc.*, addict, alcohol *or* drug *or* substance, *etc.*, abuser. □ **user-friendly** simple, practicable, usable, explicit, accommodating, understandable, intelligible, comprehensible, accessible.

usher /úshər/ *n. & v.* ● *n.* **1** a person who shows people to their seats in an auditorium or theater, etc. **2** a doorkeeper at a court, etc. **3** *Brit.* an officer walking before a person of rank. **4** *archaic or joc.* an assistant teacher. ● *v.tr.* **1** act as usher to. **2** (usu. foll. by *in*) announce or show in, etc. (*ushered us into the room; ushered in a new era*). □□ **ushership** *n.* [ME f. AF *usser*, OF *uissier*, var. of *huissier* f. med.L *ustiarius* for L *ostiarius* f. *ostium* door]

■ *v.* see LEAD¹ *v.* 1.

usherette /úshərét/ *n.* a female usher, esp. in a movie theater.

USIA *abbr.* (also **U.S.I.A.**) United States Information Agency.

USM *abbr.* **1** United States Marines. **2** United States Mint.

USMC *abbr.* United States Marine Corps.

USN *abbr.* United States Navy.

USO *abbr.* (also **U.S.O.**) United Service Organizations.

USPS *abbr.* (also **U.S.P.S.**) United States Postal Service.

usquebaugh /úskwibaw/ *n.* esp. *Ir. & Sc.* whiskey. [Ir. & Sc. Gael. *uisge beatha* water of life: cf. WHISKEY]

USS *abbr.* United States Ship.

USSR *abbr. hist.* Union of Soviet Socialist Republics.

usu. *abbr.* **1** usual. **2** usually.

usual /yōōzhōōəl/ *adj.* **1** such as commonly occurs, or is observed or done; customary; habitual (*the usual formalities; it is usual to tip them; forgot my keys as usual*). **2** (prec. by *the, my*, etc.) *colloq.* a person's usual drink, etc. □□ **usualness** *n.* [ME f. OF *usual*, *usuel* or LL *usualis* (as USE)]

■ **1** same, customary, habitual, accustomed, familiar, well-known, common, everyday, established, traditional, set, time-honored, old, conventional, standard, workaday, stock, wonted, regular, ordinary, normal, expected, routine, typical, run-of-the-mill, stereotypic(al), hackneyed, trite, prosaic, worn out, shopworn, predictable, unexceptional, unoriginal, unremarkable, unimaginative. □□ **usually** customarily, as a rule, generally (speaking), in general, most of the time, for the most part, most often, mostly, almost always, inveterately, on the whole, normally,

/.../ **pronunciation**	● **part of speech**
□ **phrases, idioms, and compounds**	
□□ **derivatives**	■ **synonym section**
cross-references appear in SMALL CAPITALS or *italics*	

commonly, regularly, predominantly, chiefly, in the main, mainly, by and large, as usual, *colloq.* as per usual.

usucaption /yŏŏzəkápshən/ *n.* (also **usucapion** /-káy-peeən/) (in Roman and Scots law) the acquisition of a title or right to property by uninterrupted and undisputed possession for a prescribed term. [OF *usucap(t)ion* or L *usu-cap(t)io* f. *usucapere* acquire by prescription f. *usu* by use + *capere capt-* take]

usufruct /yŏŏzəfrukt, -sə-/ *n.* & *v.* ● *n.* (in Roman and Scots law) the right of enjoying the use and advantages of another's property short of the destruction or waste of its substance. ● *v.tr.* hold in usufruct. □□ **usufructuary** /-frúk-chŏoeree/ *adj.* & *n.* [med.L *usufructus* f. L *usus* (*et*) *fructus* f. *usus* USE + *fructus* FRUIT]

usurer /yŏŏzhərər/ *n.* a person who practices usury. [ME f. AF *usurer*, OF *usureor* f. *usure* f. L *usura*: see USURY]

usurious /yoozhŏŏreeəs/ *adj.* of, involving, or practicing usury. □□ **usuriously** *adv.*

usurp /yŏŏzə́rp, -sə́rp/ *v.* **1** *tr.* seize or assume (a throne or power, etc.) wrongfully. **2** *intr.* (foll. by *on, upon*) encroach. □□ **usurpation** /yŏŏzərpáyshən, -sər-/ *n.* **usurper** *n.* [ME f. OF *usurper* f. L *usurpare* seize for use]

■ **1** see APPROPRIATE *v.* 1.

usury /yŏŏzhəree/ *n.* **1** the act or practice of lending money at interest, esp. *Law* at an exorbitant rate. **2** interest at this rate. □ **with usury** *rhet.* or *poet.* with increased force, etc. [ME f. med.L *usuria* f. L *usura* (as USE)]

UT *abbr.* **1** Utah (in official postal use). **2** universal time.

Ute /yŏŏt/ *n.* (*pl.* **Ute** or **Utes**) **1** a member of a N. American people native to the area that is now Colorado, New Mexico, Utah, and Arizona. **2** the language of these people.

utensil /yŏŏténsəl/ *n.* an implement or vessel, esp. for domestic use (*cooking utensils*). [ME f. OF *utensile* f. med.L, neut. of L *utensilis* usable (as USE)]

uterine /yŏŏtərin, -rin/ *adj.* **1** of or relating to the uterus. **2** born of the same mother but not the same father (*sister uterine*). [ME f. LL *uterinus* (as UTERUS)]

uterus /yŏŏtərəs/ *n.* (*pl.* **uteri** /-rī/) the womb. □□ **uteritis** /-rítis/ *n.* [L]

utile /yŏŏtil, -tīl/ *adj.* useful; having utility. [ME f. OF f. L *utilis* f. *uti* use]

utilitarian /yŏŏtílitáireeən/ *adj.* & *n.* ● *adj.* **1** designed to be useful for a purpose rather than attractive; severely practical. **2** of utilitarianism. ● *n.* an adherent of utilitarianism.

■ *adj.* **1** see PRACTICAL *adj.* 2.

utilitarianism /yŏŏtílitáireeənizəm/ *n.* **1** the doctrine that actions are right if they are useful or for the benefit of a majority. **2** the doctrine that the greatest happiness of the greatest number should be the guiding principle of conduct.

utility /yŏŏtílitee/ *n.* (*pl.* **-ies**) **1** the condition of being useful or profitable. **2** a useful thing. **3** = *public utility*. **4** (*attrib.*) **a** severely practical and standardized (*utility furniture*). **b** made or serving for utility. □ **utility room** a room equipped with appliances for washing, ironing, and other domestic work. **utility vehicle** (or **truck**, etc.) a vehicle capable of serving various functions. [ME f. OF *utilité* f. L *utilitas -tatis* (as UTILE)]

■ **1** see *usefulness* (USEFUL).

utilize /yŏŏt'líz/ *v.tr.* make practical use of; turn to account; use effectively. □□ **utilizable** *adj.* **utilization** *n.* **utilizer** *n.* [F *utiliser* f. It. *utilizzare* (as UTILE)]

■ see USE *v.* 1a. □□ **utilization** see USE *n.* 1, 2.

-ution /ŏŏshən/ *suffix* forming nouns, = -ATION (*solution*). [F f. L *-utio*]

utmost /útmōst/ *adj.* & *n.* ● *adj.* furthest, extreme, or great-

est (*the utmost limits*; *showed the utmost reluctance*). ● *n.* (prec. by *the*) the utmost point or degree, etc. □ **do one's utmost** do all that one can. [OE *ūt(e)mest* (as OUT, -MOST)]

■ *adj.* see MAXIMUM *adj.* ● *n.* see MAXIMUM *n.*

Utopia /yŏŏtŏpeeə/ *n.* an imagined perfect place or state of things. [title of a book (1516) by Thomas More: mod.L f. Gk *ou* not + *topos* place]

■ paradise, heaven, seventh heaven, (Garden of) Eden, bliss, cloud-cuckoo-land, cloudland, never-never land, Shangri-la, heaven on earth, perfection.

Utopian /yŏŏtŏpeeən/ *adj.* & *n.* (also **utopian**) ● *adj.* characteristic of Utopia; idealistic. ● *n.* an idealistic reformer. □□ **Utopianism** *n.*

utricle /yŏŏtrikəl/ *n.* a small cell or sac in an animal or plant, esp. one in the inner ear. □□ **utricular** /-tríkyələr/ *adj.* [F *utricule* or L *utriculus* dimin. of *uter* leather bag]

utter[1] /útər/ *attrib.adj.* complete; total; absolute (*utter misery*; *saw the utter absurdity of it*). □□ **utterly** *adv.* **utterness** *n.* [OE *ūtera*, *ūttra*, compar. adj. f. *ūt* OUT: cf. OUTER]

■ see COMPLETE *adj.* 3, TOTAL *adj.* 2. □□ **utterly** completely, perfectly, absolutely, thoroughly, fully, entirely, wholly, unreservedly, totally, unqualifiedly, out-and-out, altogether, downright, overwhelmingly, unequivocally, categorically, positively, definitely, (with) no holds barred, body and soul, head over heels; extremely, *colloq.* properly, *Brit. dial.* or *colloq.* proper.

utter[2] /útər/ *v.tr.* **1** emit audibly (*uttered a startled cry*). **2** express in spoken or written words. **3** *Law* put (esp. forged money) into circulation. □□ **utterable** *adj.* **utterer** *n.* [ME f. MDu. *ūteren* make known, assim. to UTTER[1]]

■ **1, 2** see VOICE *v.*

utterance /útərəns/ *n.* **1** the act or an instance of uttering. **2** a thing spoken. **3 a** the power of speaking. **b** a manner of speaking. **4** *Linguistics* an uninterrupted chain of spoken or written words not necessarily corresponding to a single or complete grammatical unit.

■ **1** see EXPRESSION 1. **2** see STATEMENT 1–3, OBSERVATION 3.

uttermost /útərmōst/ *adj.* furthest; extreme.

■ see MAXIMUM *adj.*

U-turn /yŏŏtərn/ *n.* **1** the turning of a vehicle in a U-shaped course so as to face in the opposite direction. **2** a reversal of policy.

■ **2** see *reversal* (REVERSE).

UV *abbr.* ultraviolet.

uvea /yŏŏveeə/ *n.* the pigmented layer of the eye, lying beneath the outer layer. [med.L f. L *uva* grape]

uvula /yŏŏvyələ/ *n.* (*pl.* **uvulas** or **uvulae** /-lee/) **1** a fleshy extension of the soft palate hanging above the throat. **2** a similar process in the bladder or cerebellum. [ME f. LL, dimin. of L *uva* grape]

uvular /yŏŏvyələr/ *adj.* & *n.* ● *adj.* **1** of or relating to the uvula. **2** articulated with the back of the tongue and the uvula, as in *r* in French. ● *n.* a uvular consonant.

uxorial /uksáwreeəl, ugzáwr-/ *adj.* of or relating to a wife.

uxoricide /uksáwrisīd, ugzáwr-/ *n.* **1** the killing of one's wife. **2** a person who does this. □□ **uxoricidal** *adj.* [L *uxor* wife + -CIDE]

uxorious /uksáwreeəs, ugzáwr-/ *adj.* **1** greatly or excessively fond of one's wife. **2** (of behavior, etc.) showing such fondness. □□ **uxoriously** *adv.* **uxoriousness** *n.* [L *uxoriosus* f. *uxor* wife]

Uzbek /ŏŏzbek-, úz-/ *n.* (also **Uzbeg** /-beg/) **1** a member of a Turkic people living mainly in Uzbekistan, a country of south central Asia. **2** the language of this people. [Uzbek]

V¹ /vee/ *n.* (also **v**) (*pl.* **Vs** or **V's**) **1** the twenty-second letter of the alphabet. **2** a V-shaped thing. **3** (as a Roman numeral) five.

V² *abbr.* (also **V.**) volt(s).

V³ *symb. Chem.* the element vanadium.

v. *abbr.* **1** verse. **2** verso. **3** versus. **4** very. **5** *vide.*

VA *abbr.* **1** Veterans Administration. **2** Virginia (in official postal use). **3** vice admiral. **4** vicar apostolic. **5** (in the UK) Order of Victoria and Albert.

Va. *abbr.* Virginia.

vac /vak/ *n. colloq.* **1** vacuum cleaner. **2** *Brit.* vacation (esp. of universities). [abbr.]

vacancy /váykənsee/ *n.* (*pl.* **-ies**) **1 a** the state of being vacant or empty. **b** an instance of this; empty space. **2** an unoccupied position or job (*there are three vacancies for computer specialists*). **3** an available room in a hotel, etc. **4** emptiness of mind; idleness; listlessness.

▪ **1** emptiness, voidness, blankness, hollowness; void, gap, lacuna, hiatus, blank, deficiency, opening, breach, space, vacuum. **2** (job) opening, slot, position, post, situation, place; (*vacancies*) help wanted. **4** blankness, emptiness, vacuity, absentmindedness, inanity, vacuousness, incomprehension, fatuity, unawareness; idleness, listlessness.

vacant /váykənt/ *adj.* **1** not filled nor occupied; empty. **2** not mentally active; showing no interest (*had a vacant stare*). □ **vacant possession** *Brit.* ownership of a house, etc., with any previous occupant having moved out. □□ **vacantly** *adv.* [ME f. OF *vacant* or L *vacare* (as VACATE)]

▪ **1** free, unfilled, unused, unutilized, spare, extra, idle, unengaged, unspoken for; empty, void, hollow, unoccupied, untenanted, uninhabited, abandoned, deserted. **2** blank, expressionless, deadpan, empty, vacuous, dull, absentminded, inane, uncomprehending, fatuous, unaware. □□ **vacantly** vaguely, blankly, vacuously, absently, absentmindedly, idly, fatuously.

vacate /váykayt, vaykáyt/ *v.tr.* **1** leave vacant or cease to occupy (a house, room, etc.). **2** give up tenure of (a post, etc.). **3** *Law* annul (a judgment or contract, etc.). □□ **vacatable** *adj.* [L *vacare vacat-* be empty]

▪ **1** leave, depart (from), withdraw from, quit, evacuate, get *or* go out of; desert, abandon. **2** give up, relinquish, sacrifice, renounce, let go, resign, abdicate, cede, give up right *or* claim to, abandon. **3** annul, declare null and void, nullify, void, repudiate, override, overrule, rescind, revoke, recall, quash, set aside, invalidate.

vacation /vaykáyshən, və-/ *n. & v.* ● *n.* **1** a time of rest, recreation, etc., esp. spent away from home or in traveling, during which regular activities (esp. work or schooling) are suspended. **2** a fixed period of cessation from work, esp. in legislatures and courts of law. **3** the act of vacating (a house or post, etc.). ● *v.intr.* take a vacation, esp. away from home for pleasure and recreation. □□ **vacationer** *n.* **vacationist** *n.* [ME f. OF *vacation* or L *vacatio* (as VACATE)]

▪ *n.* **1** break, time off, respite, leave (of absence), recess, furlough.

vacationland /vaykáyshənland, və-/ *n.* an area providing attractions for vacationers.

vaccinate /váksinayt/ *v.tr.* inoculate with a vaccine to pro-

cure immunity from a disease; immunize. □□ **vaccination** /-náyshən/ *n.* **vaccinator** *n.*
▪ □□ **vaccination** see JAB *n.* 2.

vaccine /vákseen/ *n. & adj.* ● *n.* **1** an antigenic preparation used to stimulate the production of antibodies and procure immunity from one or several diseases. **2** *hist.* the cowpox virus used in vaccination against smallpox. ● *adj.* of or relating to cowpox or vaccination. □□ **vaccinal** /-sinəl/ *adj.* [L *vaccinus* f. *vacca* cow]

vaccinia /vaksíneeə/ *n. Med.* a virus used as a vaccine against smallpox. [mod.L (as VACCINE)]

vacillate /vásilayt/ *v.intr.* **1** fluctuate in opinion or resolution. **2** move from side to side; oscillate; waver. □□ **vacillation** /-láyshən/ *n.* **vacillator** *n.* [L *vacillare vacillat-* sway]
▪ see OSCILLATE. □□ **vacillation** see *fluctuation* (FLUCTUATE).

vacua *pl.* of VACUUM.

vacuity /vakyóoətee, və-/ *n.* **1** the condition, state, or quality of being vacuous. **2** complete lack of intelligence or thought; inanity. **3** something, such as a comment, that is senseless or inane. **4** an empty space.

vacuole /vákyoo-ōl/ *n. Biol.* a tiny space within the cytoplasm of a cell containing air, fluid, food particles, etc. □□ **vacuolar** /vakyōō-ōlər, vákyooələr/ *adj.* **vacuolation** /-láyshən/ *n.* [F, dimin. of L *vacuus* empty]

vacuous /vákyōōəs/ *adj.* **1** lacking expression (*a vacuous stare*). **2** unintelligent (*a vacuous remark*). **3** empty. □□ **vacuity** /vəkyōō-itee/ *n.* **vacuously** *adv.* **vacuousness** *n.* [L *vacuus* empty (as VACATE)]
▪ **1** see BLANK *adj.* 3a. **2** see INANE 1. □□ **vacuousness** see VACANCY 4.

vacuum /vákyōōəm, -yōōm, -yəm/ *n. & v.* ● *n.* (*pl.* **vacuums** or **vacua** /-yōōə/) **1** a space entirely devoid of matter. **2** a space or vessel from which the air has been completely or partly removed by a pump, etc. **3 a** the absence of the normal or previous content of a place, environment, etc. **b** the absence of former circumstances, activities, etc. **4** (*pl.* **vacuums**) *colloq.* a vacuum cleaner. **5** a decrease of pressure below the normal atmospheric value. ● *v. colloq.* **1** *tr.* clean with a vacuum cleaner. **2** *intr.* use a vacuum cleaner. □ **vacuum brake** a brake in which pressure is caused by the exhaustion of air. **vacuum cleaner** an apparatus for removing dust, etc., by suction. **vacuum flask** *Brit.* = THERMOS. **vacuum gauge** a gauge for testing the pressure after the production of a vacuum. **vacuum-packed** sealed after the partial removal of air. **vacuum pump** a pump for producing a vacuum. **vacuum tube** *Electronics* an evacuated glass tube that regulates the flow of thermionic electrons in one direction, used esp. in the rectification of a current and in radio reception. [mod.L, neut. of L *vacuus* empty]
▪ *n.* **3** see VOID *n.* 1.

vade mecum /vaadee máykəm, váydee meékəm/ *n.* a handbook, etc., carried constantly for use. [F f. mod.L, = go with me]

▪ handbook, manual, companion, ready reference, book, guide.

vagabond /vágəbond/ *n., adj., & v.* ● *n.* **1** a wanderer or vagrant, esp. an idle one. **2** *colloq.* a scamp or rascal. ● *adj.* having no fixed habitation; wandering. ● *v.intr.* wander about as a vagabond. □□ **vagabondage** *n.* [ME f. OF *vagabond* or L *vagabundus* f. *vagari* wander]

▪ *n.* **1** gypsy, tramp, vagrant, wayfarer, rover, drifter, hobo, wanderer, itinerant, migrant, nomad, bird of passage, rolling stone, beachcomber, derelict, *Austral.* & *NZ* swagman, *colloq.* panhandler, *sl.* bum. **2** see RASCAL. ● *adj.* vagrant, wayfaring, roving, wandering, itinerant, migrant, derelict, nomadic, gypsy, rambling, roaming, drifting, peripatetic, transient, homeless, *archaic or joc.* peregrinating.

vagal see VAGUS.

vagary /váygəree/ *n.* (*pl.* **-ies**) a caprice; an eccentric idea or act (*the vagaries of Fortune*). □□ **vagarious** /vəgáireeəs/ *adj.* [L *vagari* wander]

▪ see QUIRK 1.

vagi *pl.* of VAGUS.

vagina /vəjínə/ *n.* (*pl.* **vaginas** or **vaginae** /-nee/) **1** the canal between the uterus and vulva of a woman or other female mammal. **2** a sheath formed around a stem by the base of a leaf. □□ **vaginal** /vájin'l/ *adj.* **vaginitis** /vájinítis/ *n.* [L, = sheath, scabbard]

vaginismus /vájinízməs/ *n.* a painful spasmodic contraction of the vagina, usu. in response to pressure. [mod.L (as VAGINA)]

vagrant /váygrənt/ *n. & adj.* ● *n.* **1** a person without a settled home or regular work. **2** a wanderer or vagabond. ● *adj.* **1** wandering or roving (*a vagrant musician*). **2** being a vagrant. □□ **vagrancy** /-grənsee/ *n.* **vagrantly** *adv.* [ME f. AF *vag(a)raunt*, perh. alt. f. AF *wakerant*, etc., by assoc. with L *vagari* wander]

▪ *n.* see TRAMP *n.* 1.

vague /vayg/ *adj.* **1** of uncertain or ill-defined meaning or character (*gave a vague answer; has some vague idea of emigrating*). **2** (of a person or mind) imprecise; inexact in thought, expression, or understanding. □□ **vaguely** *adv.* **vagueness** *n.* **vaguish** *adj.* [F *vague* or L *vagus* wandering, uncertain]

▪ **1** indefinite, indistinct, imprecise, inexact, unclear, confused, woolly, loose, unspecified, nonspecified, undetermined, indeterminate, unfixed, general, generalized, unspecific, nonspecific, inexplicit, unexplicit, ambiguous, doubtful, in doubt, uncertain, equivocal; subliminal, subconscious, indefinable, unexplained; ill-defined, hazy, fuzzy, obscure, amorphous, shapeless, nebulous, blurred, blurry, filmy, dim, faint, shadowy, veiled, concealed, hidden, shrouded, bleary, foggy, misty, cloudy, clouded, hardly *or* barely distinguishable, hardly *or* barely discernible. **2** wishy-washy, imprecise, inexact, undecided, indecisive, irresolute, vacillating, wavering, inconstant, unsettled, uncertain; vacant, empty, blank, vacuous; see also ABSENTMINDED. □□ **vaguely** ambiguously, imprecisely, inexactly, unclearly, confusedly, confusingly, hazily, fuzzily, nebulously, obscurely; distantly, remotely, indefinitely, dimly, subliminally, subconsciously, inexplicably; idly, vacantly, detachedly, absentmindedly, dreamily, absently, distractedly. **vagueness** see *imprecision* (IMPRECISE).

vagus /váygəs/ *n.* (*pl.* **vagi** /-gī, -jī/) *Anat.* either of the tenth pair of cranial nerves with branches to the heart, lungs, and viscera. □□ **vagal** *adj.* [L: see VAGUE]

vail /vayl/ *v. archaic* **1** *tr.* lower or doff (one's plumes, pride, crown, etc.), esp. in token of submission. **2** *intr.* yield; give place; remove one's hat as a sign of respect, etc. [ME f. obs. *avale* f. OF *avaler* to lower f. *a* val down f. *val* VALE¹]

vain /vayn/ *adj.* **1** excessively proud or conceited, esp. about one's own attributes. **2** empty; trivial; unsubstantial (*vain boasts; vain triumphs*). **3** useless; followed by no good result (*in the vain hope of dissuading them*). □ **in vain** without result or success (*it was in vain that we protested*). **take a person's**

name in vain use it lightly or profanely. □□ **vainly** *adv.* **vainness** *n.* [ME f. OF f. L *vanus* empty, without substance]

▪ **1** proud, conceited, haughty, arrogant, boastful, puffed up, egotistical, cocky, self-important, *Psychol.* narcissistic, *colloq.* bigheaded, stuck-up, swellheaded, swelled-headed, *literary* vainglorious. **2** see EMPTY *adj.* 4a. **3** worthless, profitless, pointless, unsuccessful, futile, useless, unavailing, unproductive, fruitless, ineffective, *archaic* bootless; abortive. □ **in vain** vainly, futilely, unsuccessfully, fruitlessly, *archaic* bootlessly. **take a person's name in vain** use a person's name irreverently *or* blasphemously *or* disrespectfully *or* improperly *or* lightly *or* profanely. □□ **vainness** see VANITY.

vainglory /vayngláwree/ *n. literary* boastfulness; extreme vanity. □□ **vainglorious** *adj.* **vaingloriously** *adv.* **vaingloriousness** *n.* [ME, after OF *vaine gloire*, L *vana gloria*]

▪ see VANITY 1. □□ **vainglorious** see BOASTFUL, VAIN 1.

vair /vair/ *n.* **1** *archaic* or *hist.* a squirrel fur widely used for medieval linings and trimmings. **2** *Heraldry* fur represented by small shield-shaped or bell-shaped figures usu. alternately azure and argent. [ME f. OF f. L (as VARIOUS)]

Vaishnava /víshnəvə/ *n. Hinduism* a devotee of Vishnu. [Skr. *vaiṣṇavá*]

Vaisya /vísyə/ *n.* **1** the third of the four great Hindu castes, comprising the merchants and agriculturalists. **2** a member of this caste. [Skr. *vaíśya* peasant, laborer]

valance /váləns, váyl-/ *n.* (also **valence**) a short curtain around the frame or canopy of a bed, above a window, or under a shelf. □□ **valanced** *adj.* [ME ult. f. OF *avaler* descend: see VAIL]

▪ see FLOUNCE² *n.*

vale¹ /vayl/ *n. archaic* or *poet.* (except in place-names) a valley (*Vale of the White Horse*). □ **vale of tears** *literary* the world as a scene of life, trouble, etc. [ME f. OF *val* f. L *vallis*, *valles*]

▪ see VALLEY.

vale² /vaaleé, waaláy/ *int. & n. esp. Brit.* ● *int.* farewell. ● *n.* a farewell. [L, imper. of *valere* be well or strong]

valediction /válidíkshən/ *n.* **1** the act or an instance of bidding farewell. **2** the words used in this. [L *valedicere valedict-* (as VALE², *dicere* say), after *benediction*]

▪ **1** see FAREWELL *n.*

valedictorian /válidiktáwreeən/ *n.* a person who gives a valedictory, esp. the highest-ranking member of a graduating class.

valedictory /válidíktəree/ *adj. & n.* ● *adj.* serving as a farewell. ● *n.* (*pl.* **-ies**) a farewell address.

▪ *n.* see PARTING 1.

valence¹ /váyləns/ *n. Chem.* the combining power of an atom measured by the number of hydrogen atoms it can displace or combine with. □ **valence electron** an electron in the outermost shell of an atom involved in forming a chemical bond. [LL *valentia* power, competence f. *valere* be well or strong]

valence² var. of VALANCE.

Valenciennes /vəlénsee-énz, valoNsyén/ *n.* a rich kind of lace. [*Valenciennes* in NE France, where it was made in the 17th and 18th c.]

valency /váylənsee/ *n.* (*pl.* **-ies**) *Chem. Brit.* = VALENCE¹.

valentine /váləntin/ *n.* **1** a card or gift sent, often anonymously, as a mark of love or affection on St. Valentine's Day (Feb. 14). **2** a sweetheart chosen on this day. [ME f. OF *Valentin* f. L *Valentinus*, name of two saints]

valerian /vəleéreeən/ *n.* **1** any of various flowering plants of the family Valerianaceae. **2** the root of any of these used as a medicinal sedative. □ **common valerian 1** a valerian, *Valeriana officinalis*, with pink or white flowers and a strong smell liked by cats: also called *setwall*. **2** the root of this used as a medicinal sedative. [ME f. OF *valeriane* f. med.L *valeriana (herba)*, app. fem. of *Valerianus* of Valerius]

valeric acid /vəlérik, -leérik/ *n. Chem.* a colorless liquid carboxylic acid used in making perfumes, esp. that derived from valerian root. [VALERIAN + -IC]

valet /valáy, válit, -lay/ *n.* & *v.* ● *n.* **1** a gentleman's personal attendant who looks after his clothes, etc. **2** a hotel, etc., employee with similar duties. **3** a standing rack for holding one's suit, coat, etc. ● *v.* (**valeted, valeting**) **1** *intr.* work as a valet. **2** *tr.* act as a valet to. **3** *tr.* clean or clean out (a car). [F, = OF *valet, vaslet*, VARLET: rel. to VASSAL]
■ *n.* **1** see MAN *n.* 4b.

valetudinarian /válitōōd'náireeən, -tyōōd-/ *n.* & *adj.* ● *n.* a person of poor health or unduly anxious about health. ● *adj.* **1** of or being a valetudinarian. **2** of poor health. **3** seeking to recover one's health. □□ **valetudinarianism** *n.* [L *valetudinarius* in ill health f. *valetudo -dinis* health f. *valēre* be well]

valetudinary /válitōōd'neree/ *adj.* & *n.* (*pl.* **-ies**) = VALETUDINARIAN.

valgus /válgəs/ *n.* a deformity involving the outward displacement of the foot or hand from the midline. [L, = knock-kneed]

Valhalla /valhálə, vaalhaálə/ *n.* **1** (in Norse mythology) a palace in which the souls of slain heroes feasted for eternity. **2** a building used for honoring the illustrious. [mod.L f. ON *Valhöll* f. *valr* the slain + *höll* HALL]

valiant /vályənt/ *adj.* (of a person or conduct) brave; courageous. □□ **valiantly** *adv.* [ME f. AF *valiaunt*, OF *vaillant* ult. f. L *valēre* be strong]
■ see BRAVE *adj.* 1.

valid /válid/ *adj.* **1** (of a reason, objection, etc.) sound or defensible; well-grounded. **2 a** executed with the proper formalities (*a valid contract*). **b** legally acceptable (*a valid passport*). **c** not having reached its expiration date. □□ **validity** /-líditee/ *n.* **validly** *adv.* [F *valide* or L *validus* strong (as VALIANT)]
■ **1** see LEGITIMATE *adj.* 3. **2 a, b** see LEGITIMATE *adj.* 1, 2. **2 c** see *in force* (FORCE¹). □□ **validity** legitimacy, soundness, truth, correctness, genuineness, authenticity; see also FORCE¹ *n.* 4.

validate /válidayt/ *v.tr.* make valid; ratify; confirm. □□ **validation** /-dáyshən/ *n.* [med.L *validare* f. L (as VALID)]
■ see RATIFY. □□ **validation** see SANCTION *n.* 2.

valine /váyleen/ *n. Biochem.* an amino acid that is an essential nutrient for vertebrates and a general constituent of proteins. [VALERIC (ACID) + -INE⁴]

valise /vəlées/ *n.* **1** a small suitcase; traveling bag. **2** a knapsack. [F f. It. *valigia* corresp. to med.L *valisia*, of unkn. orig.]

Valium /váleeəm/ *n. propr.* the drug diazepam used as a tranquilizer and relaxant. [20th c.: orig. uncert.]

Valkyrie /valkeéree, válkiree/ *n.* (in Norse mythology) each of Odin's twelve handmaidens who selected heroes destined to be slain in battle. [ON *Valkyrja*, lit. 'chooser of the slain' f. *valr* the slain + (unrecorded) *kur-, kuz-* rel. to CHOOSE]

vallecula /vəlékyələ/ *n.* (*pl.* **valleculae** /-lee/) *Anat.* & *Bot.* a groove or furrow. □□ **vallecular** *adj.* **valleculate** /-layt/ *adj.* [LL, dimin. of L *vallis* valley]

valley /válee/ *n.* (*pl.* **-eys**) **1** a low area more or less enclosed by hills and usu. with a stream flowing through it. **2** any depression compared to this. **3** *Archit.* an internal angle formed by the intersecting planes of a roof. [ME f. AF *valey*, OF *valee* ult. f. L *vallis, valles*: cf. VALE¹]
■ **1, 2** glen, dale, dell, dingle, hollow, basin, gorge, ravine, gulch, canyon, gully, *Geol.* cirque, graben, esp. *Brit.* cwm, *Brit.* combe, *archaic or poet.* vale.

vallum /váləm/ *n. Rom. Antiq.* a rampart and stockade as a defense. [L, collect. f. *vallus* stake]

valonia /vəlṓneeə/ *n.* acorn cups of an evergreen oak, *Quercus macrolepis*, used in tanning, dyeing, and making ink. [It. *vallonia* ult. f. Gk *balanos* acorn]

valor /válər/ *n.* (*Brit.* **valour**) personal courage, esp. in battle. □□ **valorous** *adj.* [ME f. OF f. LL *valor -oris* f. *valēre* be strong]
■ see COURAGE.

valorize /váləriz/ *v.tr.* raise or fix the price of (a commodity, etc.) by artificial means, esp. by government action. □□ **valorization** *n.* [back-form. f. *valorization* f. F *valorisation* (as VALOR)]

valour *Brit.* var. of VALOR.

valse /vaals/ *n.* a waltz. [F f. G (as WALTZ)]

valuable /vályōōəbəl, vályə-/ *adj.* & *n.* ● *adj.* of great value, price, or worth (*a valuable property; valuable information*). ● *n.* (usu. in *pl.*) a valuable thing, esp. a small article of personal property. □□ **valuably** *adv.*
■ *adj.* see *advantageous* (ADVANTAGE), PRECIOUS *adj.* 1.

valuation /vályōō-áyshən/ *n.* **1 a** an estimation (esp. by a professional valuer) of a thing's worth. **b** the worth estimated. **2** the price set on a thing. □□ **valuate** *v.tr.*

valuator /vályoo-aytər/ *n.* a person who makes valuations; a valuer.

value /vályōō/ *n.* & *v.* ● *n.* **1** the worth, desirability, or utility of a thing, or the qualities on which these depend (*the value of regular exercise*). **2** worth as estimated; valuation (*set a high value on my time*). **3** the amount of money or goods for which a thing can be exchanged in the open market; purchasing power. **4** the equivalent of a thing; what represents or is represented by or may be substituted for a thing (*paid them the value of their lost property*). **5** (in full **value for money**) something well worth the money spent. **6** the ability of a thing to serve a purpose or cause an effect (*news value; nuisance value*). **7** (in *pl.*) one's principles or standards; one's judgment of what is valuable or important in life. **8** *Mus.* the duration of the sound signified by a note. **9** *Math.* the amount denoted by an algebraic term or expression. **10** (foll. by *of*) **a** the meaning (of a word, etc.). **b** the quality (of a spoken sound). **11** the relative rank or importance of a playing card, chess piece, etc., according to the rules of the game. **12** the relation of one part of a picture to others in respect of light and shade; the part being characterized by a particular tone. **13** *Physics* & *Chem.* the numerical measure of a quantity or a number denoting magnitude on some conventional scale (*the value of gravity at the equator*). ● *v.tr.* (**values, valued, valuing**) **1** estimate the value of; appraise (esp. professionally) (*valued the property at $200,000*). **2** have a high or specified opinion of; attach importance to (*a valued friend*). □ **value-added tax** a tax on the amount by which the value of an article has been increased at each stage of its production. **value judgment** a subjective estimate of quality, etc. **value received** money or its equivalent given for a bill of exchange. [ME f. OF, fem. past part. of *valoir* be worth f. L *valēre*]
■ *n.* **1** see *usefulness* (USEFUL). **3, 4** see PRICE *n.* 1. **7** (*values*) see PHILOSOPHY 2. ● *v.* **1** see ESTIMATE *v.* 2, 3. **2** see APPRECIATE 1a, b.

valueless /vályōōlis/ *adj.* having no value. □□ **valuelessness** *n.*
■ see WORTHLESS.

valuer /vályōōər/ *n. Brit.* a person who estimates or assesses values, esp. professionally.

valuta /vəlōōtə/ *n.* **1** the value of one currency with respect to another. **2** a currency considered in this way. [It., = VALUE]

valve /valv/ *n.* **1** a device for controlling the passage of fluid through a pipe, etc., esp. an automatic device allowing movement in one direction only. **2** *Anat.* & *Zool.* a membranous part of an organ, etc., allowing a flow of blood, etc., in one direction only. **3** *Brit.* = vacuum tube. **4** a device to vary the effective length of the tube in a brass musical instrument. **5** each of the two shells of an oyster, mussel, etc. **6** *Bot.* each of the segments into which a capsule or dry fruit dehisces. **7** *archaic* a leaf of a folding door. □□ **valvate** /-vayt/ *adj.* **valved** *adj.* (also in *comb.*). **valveless** *adj.* **valvule** *n.* [ME f. L *valva* leaf of a folding door]

valvular /vályələr/ *adj.* **1** having a valve or valves. **2** having the form or function of a valve. [mod.L *valvula*, dimin. of L *valva*]

/.../ pronunciation	● part of speech
□ phrases, idioms, and compounds	
□□ derivatives	■ synonym section
cross-references appear in SMALL CAPITALS or *italics*	

valvulitis /válvyəlítis/ *n.* inflammation of the valves of the heart.

vambrace /vámbrays/ *n. hist.* defensive armor for the forearm. [ME f. AF *vaunt-bras*, OF *avant-bras* f. *avant* before (see AVAUNT) + *bras* arm]

vamoose /vamoōs, və–/ *v.intr.* (esp. as *int.*) *sl.* depart hurriedly. [Sp. *vamos* let us go]
■ see LEAVE¹ *v.* 1b, 3, 4.

vamp¹ /vamp/ *n. & v.* ● *n.* **1** the upper front part of a boot or shoe. **2** a patched-up article. **3** an improvised musical accompaniment. ● *v.* **1** *tr.* (often foll. by *up*) repair or furbish. **2** *tr.* (foll. by *up*) make by patching or from odds and ends. **3 a** *tr. & intr.* improvise a musical accompaniment (to). **b** *tr.* improvise (a musical accompaniment). **4** *tr.* put a new vamp to (a boot or shoe). [ME f. OF *avantpié* f. *avant* before (see AVAUNT) + *pied* foot]

vamp² /vamp/ *n. & v. colloq.* ● *n.* **1** an unscrupulous flirt. **2** a woman who uses sexual attraction to exploit men. ● *v.* **1** *tr.* allure or exploit (a man). **2** *intr.* act as a vamp. [abbr. of VAMPIRE]

vampire /vámpīr/ *n.* **1** a ghost or reanimated corpse supposed to leave its grave at night to suck the blood of persons sleeping. **2** a person who preys ruthlessly on others. **3** (in full **vampire bat**) any tropical (esp. South American) bat of the family Desmodontidae, with incisors for piercing flesh and feeding on blood. **4** *Theatr.* a small spring trapdoor used for sudden disappearances. □□ **vampiric** /-pírik/ *adj.* [F *vampire* or G *Vampir* f. Magyar *vampir* perh. f. Turk. *uber* witch]

vampirism /vámpīrizəm/ *n.* **1** belief in the existence of vampires. **2** the practices of a vampire.

vamplate /vámplayt/ *n. hist.* an iron plate on a lance protecting the hand when the lance was couched. [ME f. AF *vauntplate* (as VAMBRACE, PLATE)]

van¹ /van/ *n.* **1** a covered vehicle for conveying goods, etc., esp. a large truck or trailer (*moving van*). **2** a smaller such vehicle, similar to a panel truck and used esp. for carrying passengers, traveling gear, etc. **3** *Brit.* a railroad car for luggage or for the use of the guard. **4** *Brit.* a gypsy trailer. [abbr. of CARAVAN]

van² /van/ *n.* **1** a vanguard. **2** the forefront (*in the van of progress*). [abbr. of VANGUARD]
■ **1** see SPEARHEAD *n.* **2** see FRONT *n.* 6; (*be in the van of*) see SPEARHEAD *v.*

van³ /van/ *n.* **1** the testing of ore quality by washing on a shovel or by machine. **2** *archaic* a winnowing fan. **3** *archaic* or *poet.* a wing. [ME, southern & western var. of FAN¹, perh. partly f. OF *van* or L *vannus*]

van⁴ /van/ *n. Brit. Tennis colloq.* = ADVANTAGE. [abbr.]

vanadium /vənáydeeəm/ *n. Chem.* a hard, gray, metallic transition element occurring naturally in several ores and used in small quantities for strengthening some steels. ¶ Symb.: **V.** □□ **vanadate** /vánədayt/ *n.* **vanadic** /-nádik/ *adj.* **vanadous** /vánədəs/ *adj.* [mod.L f. ON *Vanadís* name of the Scand. goddess Freyja + -IUM]

Van Allen belt /van álən/ *n.* (also **Van Allen layer**) each of two regions of intense radiation partly surrounding the earth at heights of several thousand miles. [J. A. *Van Allen*, US physicist b. 1914]

vandal /vánd'l/ *n. & adj.* ● *n.* **1** a person who willfully or maliciously destroys or damages property. **2** (**Vandal**) a member of a Germanic people that ravaged Gaul, Spain, N. Africa, and Rome in the 4th–5th c., destroying many books and works of art. ● *adj.* of or relating to the Vandals. □□ **Vandalic** /-dálik/ *adj.* (in sense 2 of *n.*). [L *Vandalus* f. Gmc]
■ **1** hooligan, ruffian, tough, hoodlum, *Austral.* larrikin, *sl.* punk, lug, hood, *Brit. sl.* yob, yobbo.

vandalism /vánd'lizəm/ *n.* willful or malicious destruction or damage to works of art or other property. □□ **vandalistic** *adj.* **vandalistically** *adv.*

vandalize /vánd'līz/ *v.tr.* destroy or damage willfully or maliciously.
■ see DAMAGE *v.* 1, MUTILATE 2.

Van de Graaff generator /ván də gráf/ *n. Electr.* a machine

devised to generate electrostatic charge by means of a vertical endless belt collecting charge from a voltage source and transferring it to a large insulated metal dome, where a high voltage is produced. [R. J. *Van de Graaff*, US physicist d. 1967]

van der Waals forces /ván dər wáwlz, waálz/ *n.pl. Chem.* short-range attractive forces between uncharged molecules arising from the interaction of dipole moments. [J. *van der Waals*, Dutch physicist d. 1923]

Vandyke /vandík/ *n. & adj.* ● *n.* **1** each of a series of large points forming a border to lace or cloth, etc. **2** a cape or collar, etc., with these. ● *adj.* in the style of dress, esp. with pointed borders, common in portraits by Van Dyck. □ **Vandyke beard** a neat, pointed beard. **Vandyke brown** a deep rich brown. [Sir A. *Van Dyck*, Anglicized *Vandyke*, Flem. painter d. 1641]

vane /vayn/ *n.* **1** (in full **weather vane**) a revolving pointer mounted on a church spire or other high place to show the direction of the wind (cf. WEATHERCOCK). **2** a blade of a screw propeller or a windmill, etc. **3** the sight of surveying instruments, a quadrant, etc. **4** the flat part of a bird's feather formed by the barbs. □□ **vaned** *adj.* **vaneless** *adj.* [ME, southern & western var. of obs. *fane* f. OE *fana* banner f. Gmc]

vanessa /vənésə/ *n.* any butterfly of the genus *Vanessa*, including the red admiral and the painted lady. [mod.L]

vang /vang/ *n. Naut.* each of two guy ropes running from the end of a gaff to the deck. [earlier *fang* = gripping device: OE f. ON *fang* grasp f. Gmc]

vanguard /vángaard/ *n.* **1** the foremost part of an army or fleet advancing or ready to advance. **2** the leaders of a movement or of opinion, etc. [earlier *vandgard*, (*a*)*vantgard*, f. OF *avan*(*t*)*garde* f. *avant* before (see AVAUNT) + *garde* GUARD]
■ see SPEARHEAD *n.*

vanilla /vənílə/ *n.* **1 a** any tropical climbing orchid of the genus *Vanilla*, esp. *V. planifolia*, with fragrant flowers. **b** (in full **vanilla bean**) the fruit of these. **2** a substance obtained from the vanilla bean or synthesized and used to flavor ice cream, chocolate, etc. [Sp. *vainilla* pod, dimin. of *vaina* sheath, pod, f. L VAGINA]

vanillin /vənílin/ *n.* **1** the fragrant principle of vanilla. **2** a synthetic preparation used as a vanillalike fragrance or flavoring.

vanish /vánish/ *v.* **1** *intr.* **a** disappear suddenly. **b** disappear gradually; fade away. **2** *intr.* cease to exist. **3** *intr.* Math. become zero. **4** *tr.* cause to disappear. □ **vanishing cream** an ointment that leaves no visible trace when rubbed into the skin. **vanishing point 1** the point at which receding parallel lines viewed in perspective appear to meet. **2** the state of complete disappearance of something. [ME f. OF *e*(*s*)*vaniss-* stem of *e*(*s*)*vanir* ult. f. L *evanescere* (as EX-¹, *vanus* empty)]
■ **1** see DISAPPEAR 1. **2** see DISAPPEAR 2.

vanity /vánitee/ *n.* (*pl.* **-ies**) **1** conceit and desire for admiration of one's personal attainments or attractions. **2 a** a futility or unsubstantiality (*the vanity of human achievement*). **b** an unreal thing. **3** ostentatious display. **4** a dressing table. **5** a unit consisting of a washbowl set into a flat top with cupboards beneath. □ **vanity bag** (or **case**) a bag or case for carrying a small mirror, makeup, etc. **vanity fair** (also **Vanity Fair**) the world (allegorized in Bunyan's *Pilgrim's Progress*) as a scene of vanity. [ME f. OF *vanité* f. L *vanitas* -*tatis* (as VAIN)]
■ **1** vainness, conceit, conceitedness, egotism, arrogance, cockiness, self-importance, haughtiness, pride, self-admiration, self-worship, *Psychol.* narcissism, *colloq.* bigheadedness, *literary* vainglory. **2 a** vainness, emptiness, hollowness, worthlessness, futility, unreality, insubstantiality, unsubstantiality, pointlessness, idleness, uselessness, folly, vapidity, silliness, vacuousness, vacuity, foolishness, fatuity, frivolousness, *archaic* bootlessness. **3** see OSTENTATION.

vanquish /vángkwish/ *v.tr. literary* conquer or overcome. □□ **vanquishable** *adj.* **vanquisher** *n.* [ME *venkus*, *-quis*, etc., f. OF *vencus* past part. and *venquis* past tenses of *veintre* f. L *vincere*: assim. to -ISH²]

■ see OVERCOME 1.

vantage /vántij/ *n.* **1** (also **vantage point** or **ground**) a place affording a good view or prospect. **2** *Tennis* = ADVANTAGE. **3** *archaic* an advantage or gain. [ME f. AF f. OF *avantage* ADVANTAGE]

■ **1** see PERCH¹ *n.*

vapid /vápid/ *adj.* insipid; lacking interest; flat; dull (*vapid moralizing*). □□ **vapidity** /-píditee/ *n.* **vapidly** *adv.* **vapidness** *n.* [L *vapidus*]

■ insipid, flavorless, tasteless, bland, watery, watered down, wishy-washy, jejune, colorless, unpalatable, flat, dull, dreary, tame, lifeless, boring, tedious, tiresome, uninteresting, trite, wearisome, wearying, humdrum, *colloq.* blah. □□ **vapidity** see TEDIUM.

vapor /váypər/ *n. & v.* (*Brit.* **vapour**) ● *n.* **1** moisture or another substance diffused or suspended in air, e.g., mist or smoke. **2** *Physics* a gaseous form of a normally liquid or solid substance (cf. GAS). **3** a medicinal agent for inhaling. **4** (in *pl.*) *archaic* a state of depression or melancholy thought to be caused by exhalations of vapor from the stomach. ● *v.intr.* **1** rise as vapor. **2** make idle boasts or empty talk. □ **vapor density** the density of a gas or vapor relative to hydrogen, etc. **vapor pressure** the pressure of a vapor in contact with its liquid or solid form. **vapor trail** a trail of condensed water from an aircraft or rocket at high altitude, seen as a white streak against the sky. □□ **vaporous** *adj.* **vaporously** *adv.* **vaporousness** *n.* **vaporer** *n.* **vaporing** *n.* **vaporish** *adj.* **vapory** *adj.* [ME f. OF *vapor* or L *vapor* steam, heat]

■ *n.* **1** mist, fog, haze, steam, cloud, smoke, smog, fumes, exhalation, *archaic* miasma. **3** inhalant, inhalation. **4** (*vapors*) morbidity, morbidness, melancholy, hypochondria, hysteria, nervousness, depression.

vaporific /váypərífik/ *adj.* concerned with or causing vapor or vaporization.

vaporimeter /váypərímitər/ *n.* an instrument for measuring the amount of vapor.

vaporize /váypəriz/ *v.tr. & intr.* convert or be converted into vapor. □□ **vaporizable** *adj.* (also **vaporable**). **vaporization** *n.*

■ see EVAPORATE 1, 2. □□ **vaporization** see *evaporation* (EVAPORATE).

vaporizer /váypərizər/ *n.* a device that vaporizes substances, esp. for medicinal inhalation.

■ see SPRAY¹ *n.* 3.

vapour *Brit.* var. of VAPOR.

var. *abbr.* **1** variant. **2** variety.

varactor /vəráktər/ *n.* a semiconductor diode with a capacitance dependent on the applied voltage. [*varying* re*actor*]

varec /várek/ *n.* **1** seaweed. **2** = KELP. [F *varec(h)* f. ON: rel. to WRECK]

variable /váireeəbəl/ *adj. & n.* ● *adj.* **1 a** that can be varied or adapted (*a rod of variable length; the pressure is variable*). **b** (of a gear) designed to give varying speeds. **2** apt to vary; not constant; unsteady (*a variable mood; variable fortunes*). **3** *Math.* (of a quantity) indeterminate; able to assume different numerical values. **4** (of wind or currents) tending to change direction. **5** *Astron.* (of a star) periodically varying in brightness. **6** *Bot. & Zool.* (of a species) including individuals or groups that depart from the type. **7** *Biol.* (of an organism or part of it) tending to change in structure or function. ● *n.* **1** a variable thing or quantity. **2** *Math.* a variable quantity. **3** *Naut.* **a** a shifting wind. **b** (in *pl.*) the region between the NE and SE trade winds. □□ **variability** /-bílitee/ *n.* **variableness** *n.* **variably** *adv.* [ME f. OF f. L *variabilis* (as VARY)]

■ *adj.* **1** adaptable, adjustable, alterable. **2** changeable, protean, changing, inconstant, fluid, varying, wavering, mercurial, fickle, capricious, erratic, fitful, unsteady, unfixed, unstable, uncertain, unreliable, undependable, unpredictable, inconsistent, fluctuating, vacillating, chameleonic, chameleonlike, *literary* mutable. □□ **variability** see *inconstancy* (INCONSTANT).

variance /váireeəns/ *n.* **1** difference of opinion; dispute; disagreement; lack of harmony (*at variance among ourselves; a theory at variance with all known facts*). **2** *Law* a discrepancy between statements or documents. **3** *Statistics* a quantity equal to the square of the standard deviation. [ME f. OF f. L *variantia* difference (as VARY)]

■ **1** disagreement, misunderstanding, discord, difference (of opinion), dissension, contention, dispute, dissent, controversy, quarrel, conflict, argument, debate, lack of harmony, falling out, schism, rift; (*at variance*) in dispute, in disagreement, quarreling, conflicting, clashing, disagreeing, in contention, in conflict, in opposition, at odds, at loggerheads, not in keeping, out of line. **2** variation, difference, disparity, discrepancy, disagreement, deviation, inconsistency, divergence, incongruity.

variant /váireeənt/ *adj. & n.* ● *adj.* **1** differing in form or details from the main one (*a variant spelling*). **2** having different forms (*forty variant types of pigeon*). **3** variable or changing. ● *n.* a variant form, spelling, type, reading, etc. [ME f. OF (as VARY)]

■ *adj.* **1** alternative, different, varying, deviant. **2** separate, distinct, different. **3** varying, variable, changing, altering, unstable, inconstant, fluctuating, deviant, deviating, different, differing. ● *n.* alternative, modification, variation, version.

variate /váireeət/ *n.* *Statistics* **1** a quantity having a numerical value for each member of a group. **2** a variable quantity, esp. one whose values occur according to a frequency distribution. [past part. of L *variare* (as VARY)]

variation /váireeáyshən/ *n.* **1** the act or an instance of varying. **2** departure from a former or normal condition, action, or amount, or from a standard or type (*prices are subject to variation*). **3** the extent of this. **4** a thing that varies from a type. **5** *Mus.* a repetition (usu. one of several) of a theme in a changed or elaborated form. **6** *Astron.* a deviation of a heavenly body from its mean orbit or motion. **7** *Math.* a change in a function, etc., due to small changes in the values of constants, etc. **8** *Ballet* a solo dance. □□ **variational** *adj.* [ME f. OF *variation* or L *variatio* (as VARY)]

■ **1** change, alteration, variety, modification, transformation, difference, diversification, diversity, modulation, fluctuation, conversion, permutation, mutation. **2, 3** variety, choice, novelty; diversity, inconsistency, departure (from the norm *or* usual), change of pace, divergence, deviation (from the norm). **4** see VARIANT *n.*

varicella /váriséla/ *n.* *Med.* = *chicken pox.* [mod.L, irreg. dimin. of VARIOLA]

varices *pl.* of VARIX.

varicocele /várikōseel/ *n.* a mass of varicose veins in the spermatic cord. [formed as VARIX + -CELE]

varicolored /váirikúlərd, vári-/ *adj.* (*Brit.* **varicoloured**) **1** variegated in color. **2** of various or different colors. [L *varius* VARIOUS + COLORED]

■ see VARIEGATE 1.

varicose /várikōs/ *adj.* (esp. of the veins of the legs) affected by a condition causing them to become dilated and swollen. □□ **varicosity** /-kósitee/ *n.* [L *varicosus* f. VARIX]

varied /váireed/ *adj.* showing variety; diverse. □□ **variedly** *adv.*

■ diverse, diversified, mixed, miscellaneous, assorted, heterogeneous; see also VARIOUS 1.

variegate /váirigayt, váireeə-, vár-/ *v.tr.* **1** (often as **variegated** *adj.*) mark with irregular patches of different colors. **2** diversify in appearance, esp. in color. **3** (as **variegated** *adj.*) *Bot.* (of plants) having leaves containing two or more colors. □□ **variegation** /-gáyshən/ *n.* [L *variegare variegat-* f. *varius* various]

/.../ **pronunciation**	● **part of speech**
□ **phrases, idioms, and compounds**	
□□ **derivatives**	■ **synonym section**
cross-references appear in SMALL CAPITALS or *italics*	

■ **1, 3** (**variegated**) multicolor(ed), particolor(ed), varicolored, many-colored, versicolored, motley, harlequin, pied, piebald, two-tone, brindle(d), mottled, marbled, polychrome, polychromatic; opalescent, opaline.

varietal /vəríət'l/ adj. **1** esp. Bot. & Zool. of, forming, or designating a variety. **2** (of wine) made from a single designated variety of grape. □□ **varietally** adv.

varietist /vəríətist/ n. a person whose habits, etc., differ from what is normal.

variety /vəríətee/ n. (pl. -ies) **1** diversity; absence of uniformity; many-sidedness; the condition of being various (not enough variety in our lives). **2** a quantity or collection of different things (for a variety of reasons). **3 a** a class of things different in some common qualities from the rest of a larger class to which they belong. **b** a specimen or member of such a class. **4** (foll. by of) a different form of a thing, quality, etc. **5** Biol. **a** a subspecies. **b** a cultivar. **c** an individual or group usually fertile within the species to which it belongs but differing from the species type in some qualities capable of perpetuation. **6** a mixed sequence of dances, songs, comedy acts, etc. (usu. attrib.: a variety show). □ **variety store** a retail store selling many kinds of small items. [F variété or L varietas (as VARIOUS)]

■ **1** difference, heterogeneity, discrepancy, diversity, disparity, variation, contrast, many-sidedness, multifariousness. **2** diversity, multiplicity, number, range, array, assortment, medley, mixture, mix, blend, miscellany, selection, collection, combination. **3** sort, brand, make, mark, kind, class, category, breed, type, order, genre, species, genus, strain. **4** see VERSION 3. **6** vaudeville, Brit. music hall.

varifocal /váirifōkəl/ adj. & n. ● adj. having a focal length that can be varied, esp. of a lens that allows an infinite number of focusing distances for near, intermediate, and far vision. ● n. (in pl.) varifocal spectacles.

variform /váirifawrm/ adj. having various forms. [L varius + -FORM]

variola /vəríələ/ n. Med. smallpox. □□ **variolar** adj. **varioloid** /váireeəloyd/ adj. **variolous** /med.L, = pustule, pock (as VARIOUS)]

variole /váireeōl/ n. **1** a shallow pit like a smallpox mark. **2** a small spherical mass in variolite. [med.L variola: see VARIOLA]

variolite /váireeəlit/ n. a rock with embedded small spherical masses causing on its surface an appearance like smallpox pustules. □□ **variolitic** /-lítik/ adj. [as VARIOLE + -ITE¹]

variometer /váireeómitər/ n. **1** a device for varying the inductance in an electric circuit. **2** a device for indicating an aircraft's rate of change of altitude. [as VARIOUS + -METER]

variorum /váiree-áwrəm/ adj. & n. ● adj. **1** (of an edition of a text) having notes by various editors or commentators. **2** (of an edition of an author's works) including variant readings. ● n. a variorum edition. [L f. editio cum notis variorum edition with notes by various (commentators): genit. pl. of varius VARIOUS]

various /váireeəs/ adj. **1** different; diverse (too various to form a group). **2** more than one; several (for various reasons). □□ **variously** adv. **variousness** n. [L varius changing, diverse]

■ **1** different, distinct, individual, diverse, varied, heterogeneous. **2** different, a number of, a variety of, diversified, diverse, several, many, numerous, sundry, multifarious, miscellaneous, assorted, archaic or literary divers, literary manifold.

varistor /vərístər/ n. a semiconductor diode with resistance dependent on the applied voltage. [varying resistor]

varix /váireeks/ n. (pl. varices /váirəseez/) **1** Med. **a** a permanent abnormal dilation of a vein or artery. **b** a vein, etc., dilated in this way. **2** each of the ridges across the whorls of a univalve shell. [ME f. L varix -icis]

varlet /váarlit/ n. **1** archaic or joc. a menial or rascal. **2** hist. a knight's attendant. □□ **varletry** n. [ME f. OF, var. of vaslet: see VALET]

■ **1** see WRETCH 2.

varmint /vaarmint/ n. dial. a mischievous or discreditable person or animal. [var. of varmin, VERMIN]

varna /vaárnə/ n. each of the four Hindu castes. [Skr., = color, class]

varnish /vaárnish/ n. & v. ● n. **1** a resinous solution used to give a hard shiny transparent coating to wood, metal, paintings, etc. **2** any other preparation for a similar purpose (nail varnish). **3** external appearance or display without an underlying reality. **4** artificial or natural glossiness. **5** a superficial polish of manner. ● v.tr. **1** apply varnish to. **2** gloss over (a fact). □□ **varnisher** n. [ME f. OF vernis f. med.L veronix fragrant resin, sandarac or med.Gk berenikē prob. f. Berenice in Cyrenaica]

varsity /vaársitee/ n. (pl. -ies) **1** a high school, college, etc., first team in a sport. **2** Brit. colloq. (esp. with ref. to sports) university. [abbr.]

varus /váirəs/ n. a deformity involving the inward displacement of the foot or hand from the midline. [L, = bent, crooked]

varve /vaarv/ n. annually deposited layers of clay and silt in a lake used to determine the chronology of glacial sediments. □□ **varved** adj. [Sw. varv layer]

vary /váiree/ v. (-ies, -ied) **1** tr. make different; modify; diversify (seldom varies the routine; the style is not sufficiently varied). **2** intr. **a** undergo change; become or be different (the temperature varies from 30° to 70°). **b** be of different kinds (his mood varies). **3** intr. (foll. by as) be in proportion to. □□ **varyingly** adv. [ME f. OF varier or L variare (as VARIOUS)]

■ **1** change, alter, diversify, transform, reshape, remodel, restyle, modify, adjust, reorganize. **2 a** change; depart, deviate, differ, diverge, shift, veer. **b** change, switch, alternate, fluctuate, vacillate, oscillate, see-saw, swing.

vas /vas/ n. (pl. vasa /váysə/) Anat. a vessel or duct. □ **vas deferens** /défərenz/ (pl. vasa deferentia /défərénsheeə/) Anat. the spermatic duct from the testicle to the urethra. □□ **vasal** /váysəl/ adj. [L, = vessel]

vascular /váskyələr/ adj. of, made up of, or containing vessels for conveying blood or sap, etc. (vascular functions; vascular tissue). □ **vascular plant** a plant with conducting tissue. □□ **vascularity** /-láritee/ n. **vascularize** v.tr. **vascularly** adv. [mod.L vascularis f. L VASCULUM]

vasculum /váskyələm/ n. (pl. vascula /-lə/) a botanist's (usu. metal) collecting case with a lengthwise opening. [L, dimin. of VAS]

vase /vays, vayz, vaaz/ n. a vessel, usu. tall and circular, used as an ornament or container, esp. for flowers. □□ **vaseful** n. (pl. -fuls). [F f. L VAS]

vasectomy /vəséktəmee/ n. (pl. -ies) the surgical removal of part of each vas deferens, esp. as a means of sterilization. □□ **vasectomize** v.tr.

Vaseline /vásileén/ n. propr. a type of petroleum jelly used as an ointment, lubricant, etc. [irreg. f. G Wasser + Gk elaion oil]

vasiform /váyzifawrm, váse-/ adj. **1** duct-shaped. **2** vase-shaped. [L vasi- f. vas + -FORM]

vaso- /váyzō/ comb. form a vessel, esp. a blood vessel (vasoconstrictive). [L vas: see VAS]

vasoactive /váyzō-áktiv/ adj. = VASOMOTOR.

vasoconstrictive /váyzōkənstríktiv/ adj. causing constriction of blood vessels.

vasodilating /váyzōdíláyting, -dílay-/ adj. causing dilatation of blood vessels. □□ **vasodilation** /-láyshən/ n.

vasomotor /váyzōmōtər/ adj. causing constriction or dilatation of blood vessels.

vasopressin /váyzōprésin/ n. a pituitary hormone acting to reduce diuresis and increase blood pressure. Also called ANTIDIURETIC HORMONE.

vassal /vásəl/ n. **1** hist. a holder of land by feudal tenure on conditions of homage and allegiance. **2** rhet. a humble dependant. □□ **vassalage** n. [ME f. OF f. med.L vassallus retainer, of Celt. orig.: the root vassus corresp. to Bret. gwaz, Welsh gwas, Ir. foss: cf. VAVASOR]

■ **2** see SLAVE n. 1.

vast /vast/ adj. & n. ● adj. **1** immense; huge; very great (a *vast expanse of water*; *a vast crowd*). **2** *colloq.* great; considerable (*makes a vast difference*). ● *n. poet.* or *rhet.* a vast space (*the vast of heaven*). □□ **vastly** *adv.* **vastness** *n.* [L *vastus* void, immense]

■ *adj.* **1** infinite, unlimited, boundless, limitless, unbounded, interminable, endless, never-ending, inexhaustible, indeterminate, immeasurable, incalculable, measureless, extensive; immense, enormous, huge, tremendous, great, prodigious, stupendous, gigantic, massive, voluminous, capacious, colossal, monumental, mammoth, elephantine, behemoth, cyclopean, titanic, *colloq.* jumbo, *sl.* humongous. **2** big, large, considerable, sizable, substantial, significant, great, goodly. □□ **vastly** immensely, greatly, hugely, enormously, considerably, substantially, (almost) entirely, infinitely, exceedingly, extremely, profoundly, very (much). **vastness** see SIZE[1] *n.*

VAT /vée-aytée, vat/ *abbr.* value-added tax.

vat /vat/ *n. & v.* ● *n.* **1** a large tank or other vessel, esp. for holding liquids or something in liquid in the process of brewing, tanning, dyeing, etc. **2** a dyeing liquor in which a textile is soaked to take up a colorless, soluble dye afterward colored by oxidation in air. ● *v.tr.* (**vatted, vatting**) place or treat in a vat. □□ **vatful** *n.* (*pl.* **-fuls**). [ME, southern & western var. of *fat*, OE *fæt* f. Gmc]

vatic /vátik/ *adj. formal* prophetic or inspired. [L *vates* prophet]

Vatican /vátikǝn/ *n.* **1** the palace and official residence of the Pope in Rome. **2** papal government. □ **Vatican City** an independent Papal State in Rome, instituted in 1929. **Vatican Council** an ecumenical council of the Roman Catholic Church, esp. that held in 1869–70 or that held in 1962–65. □□ **Vaticanism** *n.* **Vaticanist** *n.* [F *Vatican* or L *Vaticanus* name of a hill in Rome]

vaticinate /vatísinayt/ *v.tr. & intr. formal* prophesy. □□ **vaticinal** *adj.* **vaticination** /-náyshǝn/ *n.* **vaticinator** *n.* [L *vaticinari* f. *vates* prophet]

vaudeville /váwdvil, váwdǝ-/ *n.* **1** variety entertainment. **2** a stage play on a trivial theme with interspersed songs. **3** a satirical or topical song with a refrain. □□ **vaudevillian** /-vílyǝn/ *adj. & n.* [F, orig. of convivial song esp. any of those composed by O. Basselin, 15th-c. poet born at *Vau de Vire* in Normandy]

Vaudois[1] /vṓdwaá/ *n. & adj.* ● *n.* (*pl.* same) **1** a native of Vaud in W. Switzerland. **2** the French dialect spoken in Vaud. ● *adj.* of or relating to Vaud or its dialect. [F]

Vaudois[2] /vṓdwaá/ *n. & adj.* ● *n.* (*pl.* same) a member of the Waldenses. ● *adj.* of or relating to the Waldenses. [F, repr. med.L *Valdensis*: see WALDENSES]

vault /vawlt/ *n. & v.* ● *n.* **1 a** an arched roof. **b** a continuous arch. **c** a set or series of arches whose joints radiate from a central point or line. **2** a vaultlike covering (*the vault of heaven*). **3** an esp. underground chamber: **a** as a place of storage (*bank vaults*). **b** as a place of interment beneath a church or in a cemetery, etc. (*family vault*). **4** an act of vaulting. **5** *Anat.* the arched roof of a cavity. ● *v.* **1** *intr.* leap or spring, esp. while resting on one or both hands or with the help of a pole. **2** *tr.* spring over (a gate, etc.) in this way. **3** *tr.* (esp. as **vaulted**) **a** make in the form of a vault. **b** provide with a vault or vaults. □□ **vaulter** *n.* [OF *voute, vaute*, ult. f. L *volvere* roll]

■ *v.* **1, 2** see LEAP *v.* 1, 2.

vaulting /váwlting/ *n.* **1** arched work in a vaulted roof or ceiling. **2** a gymnastic or athletic exercise in which participants vault over obstacles. □ **vaulting horse** a wooden block to be vaulted over by gymnasts.

vaunt /vawnt/ *v. & n. literary* ● *v.* **1** *intr.* boast; brag. **2** *tr.* boast of; extol boastfully. ● *n.* a boast. □□ **vaunter** *n.* **vauntingly** *adv.* [ME f. AF *vaunter*, OF *vanter* f. LL *vantare* f. L *vanus* VAIN: partly obs. *avaunt* (v.) f. *avanter* f. *a-* intensive + *vanter*]

■ *v.* **1** see BOAST *v.* 1. **2** see DISPLAY *v.* 2.

vavasor /vávǝsawr, -sṓor/ *n. hist.* (also **vavasour**) a vassal owing allegiance to a great lord and having other vassals

under him. [ME f. OF *vavas(s)our* f. med.L *vavassor*, perh. f. *vassus vassorum* VASSAL of vassals]

vavasory /vávǝsawree/ *n.* (*pl.* **-ies**) *hist.* the estate of a vavasor. [OF *vavasorie* or med.L *vavasoria* (as VAVASOR)]

VC *abbr.* **1** vice-chairman. **2** vice-chancellor. **3** vice-consul. **4** Victoria Cross. **5** Vietcong.

VCR *abbr.* videocassette recorder.

VD *abbr.* venereal disease.

VDT *abbr.* video display terminal.

V-E *abbr.* Victory in Europe (in 1945). □ **V-E Day** May 8, the day marking this.

've *abbr.* (chiefly after pronouns) = HAVE (*I've*; *they've*).

veal /veel/ *n.* calf's flesh as food. □□ **vealy** *adj.* [ME f. AF *ve(e)l*, OF *veiaus veel* f. L *vitellus* dimin. of *vitulus* calf]

vector /véktǝr/ *n. & v.* ● *n.* **1** *Math. & Physics* a quantity having direction as well as magnitude, esp. as determining the position of one point in space relative to another (*radius vector*). **2** a carrier of disease. **3** a course to be taken by an aircraft. ● *v.tr.* direct (an aircraft in flight) to a desired point. □ **vector sum** *Math.* a force, etc., equivalent to two or more acting in different directions at the same point. □□ **vectorial** /-táwreeǝl/ *adj.* **vectorize** *v.tr.* (in sense 1 of *n.*). **vectorization** /-tǝrizáyshǝn/ *n.* [L, = carrier, f. *vehere vect-* convey]

Veda /váydǝ, vée-/ *n.* (in *sing.* or *pl.*) the most ancient Hindu scriptures, esp. four collections called Rig-Veda, Sāma-Veda, Yajur-Veda, and Atharva-Veda. [Skr. *veda*, lit. (sacred) knowledge]

Vedanta /vidaántǝ, vedán-/ *n.* **1** the Upanishads. **2** the Hindu philosophy based on these, esp. in its monistic form. □□ **Vedantic** *adj.* **Vedantist** *n.* [Skr. *vedānta* (as VEDA, *anta* end)]

Vedda /védǝ/ *n.* (also **Veddah**) a Sri Lankan aboriginal. [Sinh. *veddā* hunter]

vedette /vidét/ *n.* a mounted sentry positioned beyond an army's outposts to observe the movements of the enemy. [F, = scout, f. It. *vedetta, veletta* f. Sp. *vela(r)* watch f. L *vigilare*]

Vedic /váydik, vée-/ *adj. & n.* ● *adj.* of or relating to the Veda or Vedas. ● *n.* the language of the Vedas, an older form of Sanskrit. [F *Védique* or G *Vedisch* (as VEDA)]

vee /vee/ *n.* **1** the letter V. **2** a thing shaped like a V. [name of the letter]

veejay /véejay/ *n.* video jockey.

veer[1] /veer/ *v. & n.* ● *v.intr.* **1** change direction, esp. (of the wind) clockwise (cf. BACK *v.* 5). **2** change in course, opinion, conduct, emotions, etc. **3** *Naut.* = WEAR[2]. ● *n.* a change of course or direction. [F *virer* f. Rmc, perh. alt. f. L *gyrare* GYRATE]

■ *v.* **1** see DEVIATE *v.*

veer[2] /veer/ *v.tr. Naut.* slacken or let out (a rope, cable, etc.). [ME f. MDu. *vieren*]

veg /vej/ *n. & v.* ● *n. Brit. colloq.* a vegetable or vegetables. ● *v.* = VEGETATE[1]. [abbr.]

Vega /véegǝ, váy-/ *n. Astron.* a brilliant blue star in the constellation of the Lyra. [Sp. or med.L *Vega* f. Arab., = the falling vulture]

vegan /véjǝn, véegǝn/ *n. & adj.* ● *n.* a person who does not eat or use animal products. ● *adj.* using or containing no animal products. [VEG(ETABLE) + -AN]

vegetable /véjtǝbǝl, véjitǝbǝl/ *n. & adj.* ● *n.* **1** *Bot.* any of various plants, esp. a herbaceous plant used wholly or partly for food, e.g., a cabbage, potato, turnip, or bean. **2** *colloq.* **a** a person who is incapable of normal intellectual activity, esp. through brain injury, etc. **b** a person lacking in animation or living a monotonous life. ● *adj.* **1** of, derived from, relating to, or comprising plants or plant life, esp. as distinct from animal life or mineral substances. **2** of or relating to vegetables as food. **3 a** unresponsive to stimulus

---

/.../ pronunciation	● part of speech
□ phrases, idioms, and compounds	
□□ derivatives	■ synonym section
cross-references appear in SMALL CAPITALS or *italics*	

(*vegetable behavior*). **b** uneventful; monotonous (*a vegetable existence*). □ **vegetable ivory** see IVORY. **vegetable marrow** see MARROW 1. **vegetable oyster** = SALSIFY. **vegetable parchment** see PARCHMENT 2. **vegetable sponge** = LOOFAH. **vegetable tallow** see TALLOW. **vegetable wax** an exudation of certain plants such as sumac. [ME f. OF *vegetable* or LL *vegetabilis* animating (as VEGETATE)]

vegetal /véjit'l/ *adj.* **1** of or having the nature of plants (*vegetal growth*). **2** vegetative. [med.L *vegetalis* f. L *vegetare* animate]

vegetarian /véjitáireeən/ *n. & adj.* ● *n.* a person who abstains from animal food, esp. that from slaughtered animals, though often not eggs and dairy products. ● *adj.* excluding animal food, esp. meat (*a vegetarian diet*). □□ **vegetarianism** *n.* [irreg. f. VEGETABLE + -ARIAN]

vegetate /véjitayt/ *v.intr.* **1 a** live an uneventful or monotonous life. **b** spend time lazily or passively, exerting oneself neither mentally nor physically. **2** grow as plants do; fulfill vegetal functions. [L *vegetare* animate f. *vegetus* f. *vegēre* be active]

■ **1** see STAGNATE.

vegetation /véjitáyshən/ *n.* **1** plants collectively; plant life (*luxuriant vegetation*; *no sign of vegetation*). **2** the process of vegetating. □□ **vegetational** *adj.* [med.L *vegetatio* growth (as VEGETATE)]

vegetative /véjitaytiv/ *adj.* **1** concerned with growth and development as distinct from sexual reproduction. **2** of or relating to vegetation or plant life. □□ **vegetatively** *adv.* **vegetativeness** *n.* [ME f. OF *vegetatif -ive* or med.L *vegetativus* (as VEGETATE)]

veggie /véjee/ *n.* (also **vegie**) *colloq.* **1** a vegetable. **2** a vegetarian. [abbr.]

vehement /vée′əmənt/ *adj.* showing or caused by strong feeling; forceful; ardent (*a vehement protest*; *vehement desire*). □□ **vehemence** /-məns/ *n.* **vehemently** *adv.* [ME f. F *véhément* or L *vehemens -entis*, perh. f. *vemens* (unrecorded) deprived of mind, assoc. with *vehere* carry]

■ see IMPASSIONED. □□ **vehemence** see FERVOR 1. **vehemently** see *warmly* (WARM).

vehicle /vée′ikəl/ *n.* **1** any conveyance for transporting people, goods, etc., esp. on land. **2** a medium for thought, feeling, or action (*the stage is the best vehicle for their talents*). **3** a liquid, etc., as a medium for suspending pigments, drugs, etc. **4** the literal meaning of a word or words used metaphorically (opp. TENOR 6). □ **vehicle identification number** a combination of letters and numbers used to identify vehicles for insurance, registration, etc. □□ **vehicular** /vee-híkyələr/ *adj.* [F *véhicule* or L *vehiculum* f. *vehere* carry]

■ **1** conveyance. **2** medium, means, channel, mechanism, carrier, conduit, agency, instrument, agent, tool.

veil /vayl/ *n. & v.* ● *n.* **1** a piece of usu. more or less transparent fabric attached to a woman's hat, etc., esp. to conceal the face or protect against the sun, dust, etc. **2** a piece of linen, etc., as part of a nun's headdress, resting on the head and shoulders. **3** a curtain, esp. that separating the sanctuary in the Jewish temple. **4** a disguise; a pretext; a thing that conceals (*under the veil of friendship*; *a veil of mist*). **5** *Photog.* slight fogging. **6** huskiness of the voice. **7** = VELUM. ● *v.tr.* **1** cover with a veil. **2** (esp. as **veiled** *adj.*) partly conceal (*veiled threats*). □ **beyond the veil** in the unknown state of life after death. **draw a veil over** avoid discussing or calling attention to. **take the veil** become a nun. □□ **veilless** *adj.* [ME f. AF *veil(e)*, OF *voil(e)* f. L *vela* pl. of VELUM]

■ *n.* **1** covering, yashmak. **4** covering, cover, screen, camouflage, cloak, mantle, curtain, cloud, mask, shroud; disguise, pretext. ● *v.* cover, conceal, hide, camouflage, cloak, mask, disguise, shroud, shield, obscure, *literary* enshroud; (**veiled**) concealed, hidden, masked, obscure, unrevealed, covert, disguised, secret, sub rosa, subtle.

veiling /váyling/ *n.* light fabric used for veils, etc.

vein /vayn/ *n. & v.* ● *n.* **1 a** any of the tubes by which blood is conveyed to the heart (cf. ARTERY). **b** (in general use) any blood vessel (*has royal blood in his veins*). **2** a nervure of an

insect's wing. **3** a slender bundle of tissue forming a rib in the framework of a leaf. **4** a streak or stripe of a different color in wood, marble, cheese, etc. **5** a fissure in rock filled with ore or other deposited material. **6** a source of a particular characteristic (*a rich vein of humor*). **7** a distinctive character or tendency; a cast of mind or disposition; a mood (*spoke in a sarcastic vein*). ● *v.tr.* fill or cover with or as with veins. □□ **veinless** *n.* **veinlet** *n.* **veinlike** *adj.* **veiny** *adj.* (**veinier, veiniest**). [ME f. OF *veine* f. L *vena*]

■ *n.* **1** blood vessel; *Anat.* venule. **2, 3** nervure, rib. **4** streak, seam, stripe, thread, strand, line, *Biol. & Geol.* striation, stria. **5** seam, lode, stratum, course, deposit, bed, pocket. **6** thread, hint, suggestion, touch, trace, streak, line, strain. **7** tendency, inclination, proclivity; mood, spirit, tone, note, tenor, feeling, attitude, disposition, cast of mind, humor, temper; way, manner, course, fashion, style, mode, pattern.

veining /váyning/ *n.* a pattern of streaks or veins.

vela *pl.* of VELUM.

velamen /veláymən/ *n.* (*pl.* **velamina** /-minə/) an enveloping membrane, esp. of an aerial root of an orchid. [L f. *velare* cover]

velar /vée′lər/ *adj.* **1** of a veil or velum. **2** *Phonet.* (of a sound) pronounced with the back of the tongue near the soft palate. [L *velaris* f. *velum*: see VELUM]

Velcro /vélkrō/ *n. propr.* a fastener for clothes, etc., consisting of two strips of nylon fabric, one looped and one burred, which adhere when pressed together. □□ **Velcroed** *adj.* [F *velours croché* hooked velvet]

veld /velt, felt/ *n.* (also **veldt**) *S.Afr.* open country; grassland. [Afrik. f. Du., = FIELD]

velitation /vélitáyshən/ *n. archaic* a slight skirmish or controversy. [L *velitatio* f. *velitari* skirmish f. *veles velitis* light-armed skirmisher]

velleity /veléeitee/ *n. literary* **1** a low degree of volition not conducive to action. **2** a slight wish or inclination. [med.L *velleitas* f. L *velle* to wish]

vellum /véləm/ *n.* **1 a** fine parchment orig. from the skin of a calf. **b** a manuscript written on this. **2** smooth writing paper imitating vellum. [ME f. OF *velin* (as VEAL)]

velocimeter /vée′lōsímitər, vélō-/ *n.* an instrument for measuring velocity.

velocipede /vilósipeed/ *n.* **1** *hist.* an early form of bicycle propelled by pressure from the rider's feet on the ground. **2** a child's tricycle. □□ **velocipedist** *n.* [F *vélocipède* f. L *velox -ocis* swift + *pes pedis* foot]

velocity /vilósitee/ *n.* (*pl.* **-ies**) **1** the measure of the rate of movement of a usu. inanimate object in a given direction. **2** speed in a given direction. **3** (in general use) speed. □ **velocity of escape** = *escape velocity*. [F *vélocité* or L *velocitas* f. *velox -ocis* swift]

■ **3** speed, swiftness, rapidity, quickness, briskness, alacrity, pace, rate of speed, miles per hour, m.p.h., kilometers per hour, km/hr, *archaic or literary* celerity, *poet. or literary* fleetness.

velodrome /véladrōm/ *n.* a special place or building with a track for cycling. [F *vélodrome* f. *vélo* bicycle (as VELOCITY, -DROME)]

velour /vəloŏr/ *n.* (also **velours**) **1** a plushlike woven fabric or felt. **2** *archaic* a hat of this felt. [F *velours* velvet f. OF *velour, velous* f. L *villosus* hairy f. *villus*: see VELVET]

velouté /vəlootáy/ *n.* a sauce made from a roux of butter and flour with chicken, veal, or fish stock. [F, = velvety]

velum /vée′ləm/ *n.* (*pl.* **vela** /-lə/) a membrane, membranous covering, or flap. [L, = sail, curtain, covering, veil]

velutinous /viloot′nəs/ *adj.* covered with soft fine hairs. [perh. f. It. *vellutino* f. *velluto* VELVET]

velvet /vélvit/ *n. & adj.* ● *n.* **1** a closely woven fabric of silk, cotton, etc., with a thick short pile on one side. **2** the furry skin on a deer's growing antler. **3** anything smooth and soft like velvet. ● *adj.* of, like, or soft as velvet. □ **on** (or **in**) **velvet** in an advantageous or prosperous position. **velvet glove** outward gentleness, esp. cloaking firmness or strength (cf. *iron hand*). □□ **velveted** *adj.* **velvety** *adj.* [ME

f. OF *veluotte* f. *velu* velvety f. med.L *villutus* f. L *villus* tuft, down]
■ □□ **velvety** see SOFT *adj.* 2.

velveteen /vélviteén/ *n.* **1** a cotton fabric with a pile like velvet. **2** (in *pl.*) garments made of this.

Ven. *abbr.* Venerable (as the title of an archdeacon).

vena cava /veéna káyva/ *n.* (*pl.* **venae cavae** /-nee -vee/) each of usu. two veins carrying blood into the heart. [L, = hollow vein]

venal /veénal/ *adj.* **1** (of a person) able to be bribed or corrupted. **2** (of conduct, etc.) characteristic of a venal person. □□ **venality** /-nálitee/ *n.* **venally** *adv.* [L *venalis* f. *venum* thing for sale]
■ corruptible, bribable, buyable, purchasable, rapacious, avaricious, greedy, simoniacal, esp. Brit. dishonorable, *sl.* bent; corrupt, mercenary, unprincipled, *colloq.* crooked. □□ **venality** see VICE[1] 1, 2.

venation /vináyshan/ *n.* the arrangement of veins in a leaf or an insect's wing, etc., or the system of venous blood vessels in an organism. □□ **venational** *adj.* [L *vena* vein]

vend /vend/ *v.tr.* **1** offer (small wares) for sale. **2** *Law* sell. □ **vending machine** a machine that dispenses small articles for sale when a coin or token is inserted. □□ **vender** *n.* (usu. in *comb.*). **vendible** *adj.* [F *vendre* or L *vendere* sell (as VENAL, *dare* give)]

vendace /véndays/ *n.* a small delicate fish, *Coregonus albula*, found in some British lakes. [OF *vendese, -oise* f. Gaulish]

vendee /vendeé/ *n. Law* the buying party in a sale, esp. of property.

vendetta /vendéta/ *n.* **1 a** a blood feud in which the family of a murdered person seeks vengeance on the murderer or the murderer's family. **b** this practice as prevalent in Corsica and Sicily. **2** a prolonged bitter quarrel. [It. f. L *vindicta*: see VINDICTIVE]
■ **1** (blood) feud. **2** quarrel, dispute, feud, conflict, rivalry; enmity, hostility, bitterness, hatred, ill will, bad blood.

vendeuse /voNdóz/ *n.* a saleswoman, esp. in a fashionable dress shop. [F]

vendor /véndar/ *n.* **1** *Law* the seller in a sale, esp. of property. **2** = *vending machine* (see VEND). [AF *vendour* (as VEND)]
■ **1** see SELLER.

vendue /véndoo, -dyoo, vendoó, -dyoó/ *n.* a public auction. [Du. *vendu(e)* f. F *vendue* sale f. *vendre* VEND]

veneer /vineér/ *n. & v.* ● *n.* **1 a** a thin covering of fine wood or other surface material applied to a coarser wood. **b** a layer in plywood. **2** (often foll. by *of*) a deceptive outward appearance of a good quality, etc. ● *v.tr.* **1** apply a veneer to (wood, furniture, etc.). **2** disguise (an unattractive character, etc.) with a more attractive manner, etc. [earlier *fineer* f. G *furni(e)ren* f. OF *fournir* FURNISH]
■ *n.* **1** covering, coating, overlay, surface, exterior, finish, skin. **2** gloss, façade, exterior, pretense, cover, (false) front, (outward) show *or* display, appearance, semblance, mask, guise, face, aspect, surface. ● *v.* **1** see FACE *v.* 5a.

veneering /vineéring/ *n.* material used as veneer.

venepuncture var. of VENIPUNCTURE.

venerable /vénarabal/ *adj.* **1** entitled to veneration on account of character, age, associations, etc. (*a venerable priest; venerable relics*). **2** as the title of an archdeacon in the Church of England. **3** *RC Ch.* as the title of a deceased person who has attained a certain degree of sanctity but has not been fully beatified or canonized. □□ **venerability** *n.* **venerableness** *n.* **venerably** *adv.* [ME f. OF *venerable* or L *venerabilis* (as VENERATE)]
■ **1** respectable, honorable, estimable, respected, honored, esteemed, august, dignified, impressive, revered, reverenced, venerated, worshipped; old, ancient, aged.

venerate /vénarayt/ *v.tr.* **1** regard with deep respect. **2** revere on account of sanctity, etc. □□ **veneration** /-ráyshan/ *n.* **venerator** *n.* [L *venerari* adore, revere]
■ respect, honor, esteem, revere, reverence, worship, hallow, adore, admire, idolize, glorify, look up to, pay

homage to. □□ **veneration** respect, honor, esteem, reverence, deference, homage, devotion, worship, admiration, adoration, idolization, awe.

venereal /vineéreeal/ *adj.* **1** of or relating to sexual desire or intercourse. **2** relating to venereal disease. □ **venereal disease** any of various diseases contracted chiefly by sexual intercourse with a person already infected. □□ **venereally** *adv.* [ME f. L *venereus* f. *venus veneris* sexual love]
■ **1** see SEXUAL, EROTIC. **2** sexual; genital; sexually transmitted, gonorrheal, syphilitic.

venereology /vineéreeólajee/ *n.* the scientific study of venereal diseases. □□ **venereological** /-reeálójikal/ *adj.* **venereologist** *n.*

venery[1] /vénaree/ *n. archaic* sexual indulgence. [med.L *veneria* (as VENEREAL)]

venery[2] /vénaree/ *n. archaic* hunting. [ME f. OF *venerie* f. *vener* to hunt ult. f. L *venari*]

venesection /vénisekshan, veéna-/ *n.* (also **venisection**) phlebotomy. [med.L *venae sectio* cutting of a vein (as VEIN, SECTION)]

Venetian /vineéshan/ *n. & adj.* ● *n.* **1** a native or citizen of Venice in NE Italy. **2** the Italian dialect of Venice. **3** (**venetian**) = *venetian blind.* ● *adj.* of Venice. □ **venetian blind** a window blind of adjustable horizontal slats to control the light. **venetian** (or **Venetian**) **glass** delicate glassware made at Murano near Venice. **Venetian red** a reddish pigment of ferric oxides. **Venetian window** a window with three separate openings, the central one being arched and highest. □□ **venetianed** *adj.* (in sense 3 of *n.*). [ME f. OF *Venicien*, assim. to med.L *Venetianus* f. *Venetia* Venice]

vengeance /vénjans/ *n.* punishment inflicted or retribution exacted for wrong to oneself or to a person, etc., whose cause one supports. □ **with a vengeance** in a higher degree than was expected or desired; in the fullest sense (*punctuality with a vengeance*). [ME f. OF f. *venger* avenge f. L (as VINDICATE)]
■ revenge, retaliation, retribution, requital, reprisal, settling *or* squaring of accounts. □ **with a vengeance** violently, fiercely, ferociously, wildly, vehemently, furiously, forcefully, energetically; to the fullest extent, to the utmost *or* fullest *or* limit, (with) no holds barred, enthusiastically, wholeheartedly.

vengeful /vénjfool/ *adj.* vindictive; seeking vengeance. □□ **vengefully** *adv.* **vengefulness** *n.* [obs. *venge* avenge (as VENGEANCE)]
■ see VINDICTIVE 1. □□ **vengefulness** see RANCOR.

venial /veéneeal/ *adj.* (of a sin or fault) pardonable; excusable; not mortal. □□ **veniality** /-neeálitee/ *n.* **venially** *adv.* **venialness** *n.* [ME f. OF f. LL *venialis* f. *venia* forgiveness]
■ forgivable, excusable, pardonable, tolerable, tolerated, minor, petty, insignificant, unimportant, remittable, remissible.

venipuncture /vénipungkchar, veéna-/ *n.* (also **venepuncture**) *Med.* the puncture of a vein, esp. with a hypodermic needle, to withdraw blood or for an intravenous injection. [L *vena* vein + PUNCTURE]

venisection var. of VENESECTION.

venison /vénisan, -zan/ *n.* a deer's flesh as food. [ME f. OF *veneso(u)n* f. L *venatio -onis* hunting f. *venari* to hunt]

Venite /vinítee, veneétay/ *n.* **1** a canticle consisting of Psalm 95. **2** a musical setting of this. [ME f. L, = 'come ye,' its first word]

Venn diagram /ven/ *n.* a diagram of usu. circular areas representing mathematical sets, the areas intersecting where they have elements in common. [J. *Venn*, Engl. logician d. 1923]

venom /vénam/ *n.* **1** a poisonous fluid secreted by snakes, scorpions, etc., usu. transmitted by a bite or sting. **2** malignity; virulence of feeling, language, or conduct. □□ **ven-**

/.../ **pronunciation**	● **part of speech**
□ **phrases, idioms, and compounds**	
□□ **derivatives**	■ **synonym section**
cross-references appear in SMALL CAPITALS or *italics*	

omed *adj.* [ME f. OF *venim*, var. of *venin* ult. f. L *venenum* poison]

■ **1** poison, toxin. **2** malice, maliciousness, malevolence, ill will, malignity, animosity, hate, hatred, hostility, antagonism, spite, spitefulness, spleen, rancor, bitterness, embitterment, poison, poisonousness, virulence, *sl.* gall.

venomous /vénəməs/ *adj.* **1 a** containing, secreting, or injecting venom. **b** (of a snake, etc.) inflicting poisonous wounds by this means. **2** (of a person, etc.) virulent; spiteful; malignant. □□ **venomously** *adv.* **venomousness** *n.* [ME f. OF *venimeux* f. *venim*: see VENOM]

■ **1** poisonous, deadly, toxic, dangerous, life-threatening, lethal. **2** poisonous, virulent, malicious, malevolent, malign, malignant, savage, baleful, envenomed, hostile, antagonistic, spiteful, splenetic, acerbic, rancorous, bitter, embittered, mean, vicious. □□ **venomousness** see *virulence* (VIRULENT).

venose /veénōs/ *adj.* having many or very marked veins. [L *venosus* f. *vena* vein]

venous /veénəs/ *adj.* of, full of, or contained in veins. □□ **venosity** /vinósitee/ *n.* **venously** *adv.* [L *venosus* VENOSE or L *vena* vein + -OUS]

vent[1] /vent/ *n. & v.* ● *n.* **1** a hole or opening allowing motion of air, etc., out of or into a confined space. **2** an outlet; free passage or play (*gave vent to their indignation*). **3** the anus esp. of a lower animal, serving for both excretion and reproduction. **4** the venting of an otter, beaver, etc. **5** an aperture or outlet through which volcanic products are discharged at the earth's surface. **6** a touchhole of a gun. **7** a finger hole in a musical instrument. **8** a flue of a chimney. ● *v.* **1** *tr.* **a** make a vent in (a cask, etc.). **b** provide (a machine) with a vent. **2** *tr.* give vent or free expression to (*vented my anger on the cat*). **3** *intr.* (of an otter or beaver) come to the surface for breath. **4** *tr. & intr.* discharge. □ **vent one's spleen on** scold or ill-treat without cause. □□ **ventless** *adj.* [partly F *vent* f. L *ventus* wind, partly F *évent* f. *éventer* expose to air f. OF *esventer* ult. f. L *ventus* wind]

■ *n.* **1** opening, slit, slot, hole, aperture, airhole, ventilator, blowhole, vent hole, orifice, outlet, inlet, funnel, duct, passage, pipe. **2** outlet, expression, free play *or* passage. **5** blowhole, vent hole, fumarole, mofette, fissure. **8** chimney, flue, smoke duct, outlet, ventilator, vent hole, funnel. ● *v.* **2** give vent to, express, verbalize, air, articulate, enunciate, declare, voice, announce, communicate, pronounce, proclaim, reveal, release, let go, let loose, allow to become known, make known, disclose, blurt out, make public, broadcast. **4** discharge, release, emit, eject, issue, empty, dump, expel, send out *or* forth, pour out *or* forth, throw out, *colloq.* unload.

vent[2] /vent/ *n.* a slit in a garment, esp. in the lower edge of the back of a coat. [ME, var. of *fent* f. OF *fente* slip ult. f. L *findere* cleave]

ventiduct /véntidukt/ *n. Archit.* an air passage, esp. for ventilation. [L *ventus* wind + *ductus* DUCT]

ventifact /véntifakt/ *n.* a stone shaped by windblown sand. [L *ventus* wind + *factum* neut. past part. of *facere* make]

ventil /véntil/ *n. Mus.* **1** a valve in a wind instrument. **2** a shutter for regulating the airflow in an organ. [G f. It. *ventile* f. med.L *ventile* sluice f. L *ventus* wind]

ventilate /vént'layt/ *v.tr.* **1** cause air to circulate freely in (a room, etc.). **2** submit (a question, grievance, etc.) to public consideration and discussion. **3** *Med.* **a** oxygenate (the blood). **b** admit or force air into (the lungs). □□ **ventilation** /-láyshən/ *n.* **ventilative** /-láytiv/ *adj.* [L *ventilare ventilat-* blow, winnow, f. *ventus* wind]

■ **1** see AIR *v.* **2**. **2** see AIR *v.* **3**.

ventilator /véntilaytər/ *n.* **1** an appliance or aperture for ventilating a room, etc. **2** *Med.* = RESPIRATOR 2.

ventral /véntrəl/ *adj.* **1** *Anat. & Zool.* of or on the abdomen (cf. DORSAL). **2** *Bot.* of the front or lower surface. □ **ventral fin** either of the ventrally placed fins on a fish. □□ **ventrally** *adv.* [obs. *venter* abdomen f. L *venter ventr-*]

ventricle /véntrikəl/ *n. Anat.* **1** a cavity in the body. **2** a hollow part of an organ, esp. in the brain or heart. □□ **ventricular** /-tríkyələr/ *adj.* [ME f. L *ventriculus* dimin. of *venter* belly]

ventricose /véntrikōs/ *adj.* **1** having a protruding belly. **2** *Bot.* distended; inflated. [irreg. f. VENTRICLE + -OSE[1]]

ventriloquism /ventríləkwizəm/ *n.* the skill of speaking or uttering sounds so that they seem to come from the speaker's dummy or a source other than the speaker. □□ **ventriloquial** /véntrilőkweeəl/ *adj.* **ventriloquist** *n.* **ventriloquize** *v.intr.* [ult. f. L *ventriloquus* ventriloquist f. *venter* belly + *loqui* speak]

ventriloquy /ventríləkwee/ *n.* = VENTRILOQUISM.

venture /vénchər/ *n. & v.* ● *n.* **1 a** an undertaking of a risk. **b** a risky undertaking. **2** a commercial speculation. ● *v.* **1** *intr.* dare; not be afraid (*did not venture to stop them*). **2** *intr.* (usu. foll. by *out*, etc.) dare to go (out), esp. outdoors. **3** *tr.* dare to put forward (an opinion, suggestion, etc.). **4 a** *tr.* expose to risk; stake (a bet, etc.). **b** *intr.* take risks. **5** *intr.* (foll. by *on*, *upon*) dare to engage in, etc. (*ventured on a longer journey*). □ **at a venture** at random; without previous consideration. **venture capital** money put up for speculative business investment. [*aventure* = ADVENTURE]

■ *n.* risk, chance, hazardous undertaking, enterprise, experiment, speculation, gamble, plunge, fling. ● *v.* **1** dare, make bold, be *or* make so bold as, presume, take the liberty, attempt, try, endeavor. **3** dare, risk, hazard, volunteer, tender, offer, broach, advance, proffer, put forward. **4 a** jeopardize, risk, endanger, hazard, imperil; gamble, bet, wager, stake, chance, plunge, put down.

venturer /vénchərər/ *n. hist.* a person who undertakes or shares in a trading venture.

venturesome /vénchərsəm/ *adj.* **1** disposed to take risks. **2** risky. □□ **venturesomely** *adv.* **venturesomeness** *n.*

■ **1** daring, bold, intrepid, adventurous, courageous, plucky, adventuresome, audacious, daredevil, fearless, game, brave, spirited, sporting, *archaic or joc.* doughty. **2** risky, rash, reckless, daredevil, dangerous, perilous, hazardous.

venturi /ventŏŏree/ *n.* (*pl.* **venturis**) a short piece of narrow tube between wider sections for measuring flow rate or exerting suction. [G. B. *Venturi*, It. physicist d. 1822]

venue /vényŏŏ/ *n.* **1 a** an appointed meeting place, esp. for a sports event, meeting, concert, etc. **b** a rendezvous. **2** *Law hist.* the county or other place within which a jury must be gathered and a cause tried (orig. the neighborhood of the crime, etc.). [F, = a coming, fem. past part. of *venir* come f. L *venire*]

■ **1 a** see LOCALE.

venule /vényŏŏl/ *n. Anat.* a small vein adjoining the capillaries. [L *venula* dimin. of *vena* vein]

Venus /veénəs/ *n.* (*pl.* **Venuses**) **1** the planet second from the sun in the solar system. **2** *poet.* **a** a beautiful woman. **b** sexual love; amorous influences or desires. □ **Venus's** (or **Venus**) **flytrap** a carnivorous plant, *Dionaea muscipula*, with leaves that close on insects, etc. □□ **Venusian** /vinŏŏshən, -sheeən, -zeeən, -nyŏŏ-/ *adj. & n.* [OE f. L *Venus Veneris*, the goddess of love]

veracious /vəráyshəs/ *adj. formal* **1** speaking or disposed to speak the truth. **2** (of a statement, etc.) true or meant to be true. □□ **veraciously** *adv.* **veraciousness** *n.* [L *verax veracis* f. *verus* true]

■ **1** see TRUTHFUL 1. **2** see TRUTHFUL 2.

veracity /vərásitee/ *n.* **1** truthfulness; honesty. **2** accuracy (of a statement, etc.). [F *veracité* or med.L *veracitas* (as VERACIOUS)]

■ **1** see HONESTY 2. **2** see TRUTH 1.

veranda /vərándə/ *n.* (also **verandah**) **1** = PORCH[2]. **2** *Austral. & NZ* a roof over a pavement in front of a store. [Hindi *varandā* f. Port. *varanda*]

veratrine /vérətreen, -trin/ *n.* a poisonous compound obtained from sabadilla, etc., and used esp. as a local irritant in the treatment of neuralgia and rheumatism. [F *vératrine* f. L *veratrum* hellebore]

verb /vərb/ *n. Gram.* a word used to indicate an action, state, or occurrence, and forming the main part of the predicate of a sentence (e.g., *hear, become, happen*). [ME f. OF *verbe* or L *verbum* word, verb]

verbal /vərbəl/ *adj., n., & v.* ● *adj.* **1** of or concerned with words (*made a verbal distinction; verbal reasoning*). **2** oral; not written (*gave a verbal statement*). **3** *Gram.* of or in the nature of a verb (*verbal inflections*). **4** literal (*a verbal translation*). **5** talkative; articulate. ● *n.* **1** *Gram.* **a** a verbal noun. **b** a word or words functioning as a verb. **2** *Brit. sl.* a verbal statement, esp. one made to the police. **3** *Brit. sl.* an insult; abuse (*gave them the verbal*). ● *v.tr. Brit. sl.* attribute a damaging statement to (a suspect). □ **verbal noun** *Gram.* a noun formed as an inflection of a verb and partly sharing its constructions (e.g., *smoking* in *smoking is forbidden*: see -ING¹). □□ **verbally** *adv.* [ME f. F *verbal* or LL *verbalis* (as VERB)]

■ *adj.* **1** lexical; *attrib.* word, vocabulary. **2** spoken, oral, vocal, said, uttered, expressed, enunciated, articulated, colloquial, conversational, viva voce, word-of-mouth, unwritten. **4** word for word, verbatim, literal. ● *n.* **2** see STATEMENT 1–3.

verbalism /vərbəlizəm/ *n.* **1** minute attention to words; verbal criticism. **2** merely verbal expression. □□ **verbalist** *n.* **verbalistic** /-lístik/ *adj.*

verbalize /vərbəliz/ *v.* **1** *tr.* express in words. **2** *intr.* be verbose. **3** *tr.* make (a noun, etc.) into a verb. □□ **verbalizable** *adj.* **verbalization** *n.* **verbalizer** *n.*

■ **1** see EXPRESS¹ 1, 2. □□ **verbalization** see EXPRESSION 1.

verbatim /vərbáytim/ *adv. & adj.* in exactly the same words; word for word (*copied it verbatim; a verbatim report*). [ME f. med.L (adv.), f. L *verbum* word: cf. LITERATIM]

■ *adv.* word for word, verbatim et literatim, literally, exactly, precisely, accurately, faithfully, to the letter, strictly. ● *adj.* word-for-word, verbatim et literatim, literal, exact, precise, accurate, faithful, strict.

verbena /vərbeénə/ *n.* any plant of the genus *Verbena*, bearing clusters of fragrant flowers. [L, = sacred bough of olive, etc., in med.L vervain]

verbiage /vərbeeij/ *n.* needless accumulation of words; verbosity. [F f. obs. *verbeier* chatter f. *verbe* word: see VERB]

■ see *hot air.*

verbose /vərbṓs/ *adj.* using or expressed in more words than are needed. □□ **verbosely** *adv.* **verboseness** *n.* **verbosity** /-bósitee/ *n.* [L *verbosus* f. *verbum* word]

■ see WORDY. □□ **verbosity** see RHETORIC 2.

verboten /ferbṓt'n/ *adj.* forbidden, esp. by an authority. [G]

■ see TABOO *adj.*

verb sap /vərb/ *int.* expressing the absence of the need for a further explicit statement. [abbr. of L *verbum sapienti sat est* a word is enough for the wise person]

verdant /vərd'nt/ *adj.* **1** (of grass, etc.) green, fresh-colored. **2** (of a field, etc.) covered with green grass, etc. **3** (of a person) unsophisticated; raw; green. □□ **verdancy** /-d'nsee/ *n.* **verdantly** *adv.* [perh. f. OF *verdeant* part. of *verdoier* be green ult. f. L *viridis* green]

■ **1, 2** see LUSH¹ 1.

verd antique /vərd/ *n.* (also **verde antique**) **1** ornamental usu. green serpentine. **2** a green incrustation on ancient bronze. **3** green porphyry. [obs. F, = antique green]

verderer /vərdərər/ *n. Brit.* a judicial officer of royal forests. [AF (earlier *verder*), OF *verdier* ult. f. L *viridis* green]

verdict /vərdikt/ *n.* **1** a decision on an issue of fact in a civil or criminal cause or an inquest. **2** a decision; a judgment. [ME f. AF *verdit*, OF *voirdit* f. *voir*, *veir* true f. L *verus* + *dit* f. L DICTUM saying]

■ see DECISION 2, 3.

verdigris /vərdigrees, -gris, -gree/ *n.* **1 a** a green crystallized substance formed on copper by the action of acetic acid. **b** this used as a medicine or pigment. **2** green rust on copper or brass. [ME f. OF *verte-gres*, *vert de Grece* green of Greece]

verdure /vərjər/ *n.* **1** green vegetation. **2** the greenness of this. **3** *poet.* freshness. □□ **verdured** *adj.* **verdurous** *adj.* [ME f. OF f. *verd* green f. L *viridis*]

verge¹ /vərj/ *n.* **1** an edge or border. **2** an extreme limit beyond which something happens (*on the verge of tears*). **3** *Brit.* a grass edging of a road, flower bed, etc. **4** *Archit.* an edge of tiles projecting over a gable. **5** a wand or rod carried before a bishop, dean, etc., as an emblem of office. [ME f. OF f. L *virga* rod]

■ **1** edge, border, boundary, margin, brink, brim, bank, side, perimeter. **2** (*on the verge of*) about to, ready to, close to, near (to), on the brink of, on the (very) point of, on the threshold of; preparing to, soon to. **3** edging, border, edge. **5** see STAFF¹ *n.* 1a, b.

verge² /vərj/ *v.intr.* **1** incline downward or in a specified direction (*the now verging sun; verge to a close*). **2** (foll. by *on*) border on; approach closely (*verging on the ridiculous*). [L *vergere* bend, incline]

■ **1** incline, lean, tend, extend, stretch, turn; draw, move. **2** (*verge on*) border on, approach, come close to or near (to), be asymptotic to.

verger /vərjər/ *n.* **1** esp. *Brit.* an official in a church who acts as caretaker and attendant. **2** *Brit.* an officer who bears the staff before a bishop, etc. □□ **vergership** *n.* [ME f. AF (as VERGE¹)]

verglas /váirglaà/ *n.* a thin coating of ice or frozen rain. [F]

veridical /virídikəl/ *adj.* **1** *formal* truthful. **2** *Psychol.* (of visions, etc.) coinciding with reality. □□ **veridicality** /-kálitee/ *n.* **veridically** *adv.* [L *veridicus* f. *verus* true + *dicere* say]

veriest /véreeist/ *adj.* (*superl.* of VERY). *archaic* real; extreme (*the veriest fool knows that*).

verification /vérifikáyshən/ *n.* **1** the process or an instance of establishing the truth or validity of something. **2** *Philos.* the establishment of the validity of a proposition empirically. **3** the process of verifying procedures laid down in weapons agreements.

■ **1** see PROOF *n.* 3.

verify /vérifi/ *v.tr.* (**-ies, -ied**) **1** establish the truth or correctness of by examination or demonstration (*must verify the statement; verified my figures*). **2** (of an event, etc.) bear out or fulfill (a prediction or promise). **3** *Law* append an affidavit to (pleadings); support (a statement) by testimony or proofs. □□ **verifiable** *adj.* **verifiably** *adv.* **verifier** *n.* [ME f. OF *verifier* f. med.L *verificare* f. *verus* true]

■ affirm, confirm, check over or out, testify to, attest (to), bear witness to, vouch for, corroborate, support, substantiate, uphold, prove, demonstrate, show, bear out, authenticate, validate, certify, guarantee, back up, warrant. □□ **verifiable** see DEMONSTRABLE.

verily /vérilee/ *adv. archaic* really; truly. [ME f. VERY + -LY², after OF & AF]

■ see TRULY 2.

verisimilitude /vérisimílitōōd, -tyōōd/ *n.* **1** the appearance or semblance of being true or real. **2** a statement, etc., that seems true. □□ **verisimilar** /-símilər/ *adj.* [L *verisimilitudo* f. *verisimilis* probable f. *veri* genit. of *verus* true + *similis* like]

verism /veerizəm/ *n.* realism in literature or art. □□ **verist** *n.* **veristic** /-rístik/ *adj.* [L *verus* or It. *vero* true + -ISM]

verismo /verízmó/ *n.* (esp. of opera) realism. [It. (as VERISM)]

veritable /véritəbəl/ *adj.* real; rightly so called (*a veritable feast*). □□ **veritably** *adv.* [OF (as VERITY)]

■ real, true, genuine, proper, actual, legitimate, authentic. □□ **veritably** see FAIRLY 5.

verity /véritee/ *n.* (*pl.* **-ies**) **1** a true statement, esp. one of fundamental import. **2** truth. **3** a really existent thing. [ME f. OF *verité, verté* f. L *veritas -tatis* f. *verus* true]

verjuice /vərjōōs/ *n.* **1** an acid liquor obtained from crab apples, sour grapes, etc., and formerly used in cooking and medicine. **2** bitter feelings, thoughts, etc. [ME f. OF *vertjus* f. VERT green + *jus* JUICE]

vermeil /vərmil, vərmáyl/ *n.* **1** (/vərmáy/) silver gilt. **2** an orange-red garnet. **3** *poet.* vermilion. [ME f. OF: see VERMILION]

---

vermi- /vɚmee/ *comb. form* worm. [L *vermis* worm]

vermian /vɚmeeən/ *adj.* of worms; wormlike. [L *vermis* worm]

vermicelli /vɚmichélee/ *n.* **1** pasta made in long slender threads. **2** *Brit.* shreds of chocolate used as cake decoration, etc. [It., pl. of *vermicello* dimin. of *verme* f. L *vermis* worm]

vermicide /vɚmisīd/ *n.* a substance that kills worms.

vermicular /vɚmíkyələr/ *adj.* **1** like a worm in form or movement; vermiform. **2** *Med.* of or caused by intestinal worms. **3** marked with close wavy lines. [med.L *vermicularis* f. L *vermiculus* dimin. of *vermis* worm]

vermiculate /vɚmíkyələt/ *adj.* **1** = VERMICULAR. **2** worm-eaten. [L *vermiculatus* past part. of *vermiculari* be full of worms (as VERMICULAR)]

vermiculation /vɚmíkyəláyshən/ *n.* **1** the state or process of being eaten or infested by or converted into worms. **2** a vermicular marking. **3** a worm-eaten state. [L *vermiculatio* (as VERMICULATE)]

vermiculite /vɚmíkyəlīt/ *n.* a hydrous silicate mineral usu. resulting from alteration of mica, and expandable into sponge by heating, used as an insulation material. [as VERMICULATE + -ITE¹]

vermiform /vɚmifawrm/ *adj.* worm-shaped. □ **vermiform appendix** see APPENDIX 1.

vermifuge /vɚmifyōōj/ *adj.* & *n.* ● *adj.* that expels intestinal worms. ● *n.* a drug that does this.

vermilion /vɚmílyən/ *n.* & *adj.* ● *n.* **1** cinnabar. **2 a** a brilliant red pigment made by grinding this or artificially. **b** the color of this. ● *adj.* of this color. [ME f. OF *vermeillon* f. *vermeil* f. L *vermiculus* dimin. of *vermis* worm]

vermin /vɚmin/ *n.* (usu. treated as *pl.*) **1** mammals and birds injurious to game, crops, etc., e.g., foxes, rodents, and noxious insects. **2** parasitic worms or insects. **3** vile persons. □□ **verminous** *adj.* [ME f. OF *vermin*, *-ine* ult. f. L *vermis* worm]

■ **3** see RABBLE¹ 2.

verminate /vɚminayt/ *v.intr.* **1** breed vermin. **2** become infested with parasites. □□ **vermination** /-náyshən/ *n.* [L *verminare verminat-* f. *vermis* worm]

vermivorous /vɚmívərəs/ *adj.* feeding on worms.

vermouth /vɚmōōth/ *n.* a wine flavored with aromatic herbs. [F *vermout* f. G *Wermut* WORMWOOD]

vernacular /vɚnákyələr/ *n.* & *adj.* ● *n.* **1** the language or dialect of a particular country (*Latin gave place to the vernacular*). **2** the language of a particular clan or group. **3** homely speech. ● *adj.* **1** (of language) of one's native country; not of foreign origin or of learned formation. **2** (of architecture) concerned with ordinary rather than monumental buildings. □□ **vernacularism** *n.* **vernacularity** /-láritee/ *n.* **vernacularize** *v.tr.* **vernacularly** *adv.* [L *vernaculus* domestic, native f. *verna* home-born slave]

■ *n.* **1** language, dialect, tongue. **2** jargon, patois, argot, vulgate, cant, idiom, phraseology, parlance, language, talk, speech, *colloq.* lingo. ● *adj.* **1** native, local, regional, indigenous, autochthonous; popular, informal, colloquial, conversational, ordinary, familiar, everyday, spoken, vulgar; plain, simple, straightforward, easy.

vernal /vɚnəl/ *adj.* of, in, or appropriate to spring (*vernal equinox*; *vernal breezes*). □ **vernal grass** a sweet-scented European grass, *Anthoxanthum odoratum*, grown for hay. □□ **vernally** *adv.* [L *vernalis* f. *vernus* f. *ver* spring]

vernalization /vɚnəlizáyshən/ *n.* the cooling of seed before planting, in order to accelerate flowering. □□ **vernalize** /vɚnəlīz/ *v.tr.* [(transl. of Russ. *yarovizatsiya*) f. VERNAL]

vernation /vɚnáyshən/ *n.* *Bot.* the arrangement of leaves in a leaf bud (cf. ESTIVATION). [mod.L *vernatio* f. L *vernare* bloom (as VERNAL)]

vernicle /vɚnikəl/ *n.* = VERONICA 2. [ME f. OF (earlier *ver(o)nique*), f. med.L VERONICA]

vernier /vɚneeər/ *n.* a small, movable graduated scale for obtaining fractional parts of subdivisions on a fixed main scale of a barometer, sextant, etc. □ **vernier engine** an auxiliary engine for slight changes in the motion of a space rocket, etc. [P. *Vernier*, Fr. mathematician d. 1637]

Veronal /vérənəl/ *n. propr.* a sedative drug, a derivative of barbituric acid. [G, f. *Verona* in Italy]

veronica /vərónikə/ *n.* **1** any plant of the genus *Veronica* or *Hebe*, esp. speedwell. **2 a** a cloth supposedly impressed with an image of Christ's face. **b** any similar picture of Christ's face. **3** *Bullfighting* the movement of a matador's cape away from a charging bull. [med.L f. the name *Veronica*: in sense 2 from the association with St. Veronica]

verruca /vərōōkə/ *n.* (*pl.* **verrucae** /-rōōsee/ or **verrucas**) a wart or similar growth. □□ **verrucose** /vérookōz/ *adj.* **verrucous** /vérookəs/ *adj.* [L]

versant /vɚsənt/ *n.* **1** the extent of land sloping in one direction. **2** the general slope of land. [F f. *verser* f. L *versare* frequent. of *vertere vers-* turn]

versatile /vɚsət'l, -tīl/ *adj.* **1** turning easily or readily from one subject or occupation to another; capable of dealing with many subjects (*a versatile mind*). **2** (of a device, etc.) having many uses. **3** *Bot.* & *Zool.* moving freely about or up and down on a support (*versatile antenna*). **4** *archaic* changeable; inconstant. □□ **versatilely** *adv.* **versatility** /-tílitee/ *n.* [F *versatile* or L *versatilis* (as VERSANT)]

■ **1** adaptable, resourceful, all-around, multiskilled, many-sided, multifaceted, flexible, protean, dexterous, handy. **2** multipurpose, all-purpose, handy, adjustable, flexible. **4** variable, changeable, protean, changing, flexible, fluctuating, inconstant. □□ **versatility** adaptability, flexibility, adjustability.

verse /vɚs/ *n.* & *v.* ● *n.* **1 a** metrical composition in general (*wrote pages of verse*). **b** a particular type of this (*English verse*). **2 a** a metrical line in accordance with the rules of prosody. **b** a group of a definite number of such lines. **c** a stanza of a poem or song with or without refrain. **3** each of the short numbered divisions of a chapter in the Bible or other scripture. **4 a** a versicle. **b** a passage (of an anthem, etc.) for solo voice. ● *v.tr.* **1** express in verse. **2** (usu. *refl.*; foll. by *in*) instruct; make knowledgeable. □□ **verselet** *n.* [OE *fers* f. L *versus* a turn of the plow, a furrow, a line of writing f. *vertere vers-* turn: in ME reinforced by OF *vers* f. L *versus*]

■ *n.* **1** poetry, versification, *archaic* poesy; see also POEM.

versed¹ /vɚst/ *predic.adj.* (foll. by *in*) experienced or skilled in; knowledgeable about. [F *versé* or L *versatus* past part. of *versari* be engaged in (as VERSANT)]

■ (*versed in*) well-versed in, well-read in, (well-)informed in *or* about, (well-)trained in, (well-)grounded in, (well-)schooled in, (well-)educated in, (well-)tutored in, learned in, cultured in, lettered in, cultivated in, literate in, competent in, accomplished in, skilled in, (well-)posted on, knowledgeable in *or* about, proficient in *or* at, experienced in *or* at, practiced in *or* at, expert in *or* at, good in *or* at, conversant with, familiar with, (well-)acquainted with, esp. *Brit. colloq.* a dab hand at.

versed² /vɚst/ *adj.* *Math.* reversed. □ **versed sine** one minus cosine. [mod.L (*sinus*) *versus* turned (sine), formed as VERSE]

verset /vɚsit/ *n.* *Mus.* a short prelude or interlude for organ. [F: dimin. of *vers* VERSE]

versicle /vɚsikəl/ *n.* each of the short sentences in a liturgy said or sung by a priest, etc., and alternating with responses. □□ **versicular** /-síkyōōlər/ *adj.* [ME f. OF *versicule* or L *versiculus* dimin. of *versus* (as VERSE)]

versicolored /vɚsikúlərd/ *adj.* (*Brit.* **versicoloured**) **1** changing from one color to another in different lights. **2** variegated. [L *versicolor* f. *versus* past part. of *vertere* turn + *color* color]

■ **2** see variegated (VARIEGATE).

versify /vɚsifī/ *v.* (**-ies, -ied**) **1** *tr.* turn into or express in verse. **2** *intr.* compose verses. □□ **versification** /-fikáyshən/ *n.* **versifier** *n.* [ME f. OF *versifier* f. L *versificare* (as VERSE)]

versine /vɚsin/ *n.* (also **versin**) *Math.* = *versed sine* (see VERSED²).

version /vɚrzhən, -shən/ *n.* **1** an account of a matter from a particular person's point of view (*told them my version of the incident*). **2** a book or work, etc., in a particular edition or translation (*Authorized Version*). **3** a form or variant of a thing as performed, adapted, etc. **4** a piece of translation, esp. as a school exercise. **5** *Med.* the manual turning of a fetus in the womb to improve presentation. ▫▫ **versional** *adj.* [F *version* or med.L *versio* f. L *vertere* vers- turn]

■ **1** story, account, report, description, rendering, rendition, translation, interpretation, reading, understanding, view, side. **2** edition, adaptation, translation, interpretation, rendering. **3** form, variant, variation, type, model, style, design, kind, variety, manifestation, portrayal, adaptation, rendition, interpretation, construct, construction, conception, idea.

vers libre /vair le'ebrə/ = *free verse.* [F, = free verse]

verso /vársō/ *n.* (*pl.* **-os**) **1 a** the left-hand page of an open book. **b** the back of a printed leaf of paper or manuscript (opp. RECTO). **2** the reverse of a coin. [L *verso* (*folio*) on the turned (leaf)]

verst /vərst/ *n.* a Russian measure of length, about 0.66 mile (1.1 km). [Russ. *versta*]

versus /vársəs, -səz/ *prep.* against (esp. in legal and sports use). ¶ Abbr.: **v., vs.** [L, = toward, in med.L against]

vert /vərt/ *n.* & (usu. placed after noun) adj. *Heraldry* green. [ME f. OF f. L *viridis* green]

vertebra /vártibrə/ *n.* (*pl.* **vertebrae** /-bray, -bree/) **1** each segment of the backbone. **2** (in *pl.*) the backbone. ▫▫ **vertebral** *adj.* [L f. *vertere* turn]

■ **2** spine, backbone, spinal column.

vertebrate /vártibrət, -brayt/ *n.* & *adj.* ● *n.* any animal of the subphylum Vertebrata, having a spinal column, including mammals, birds, reptiles, amphibians, and fishes. ● *adj.* of or relating to the vertebrates. [L *vertebratus* jointed (as VERTEBRA)]

vertebration /vártibráyshən/ *n.* division into vertebrae or similar segments.

vertex /várteks/ *n.* (*pl.* **vertices** /-tiseez/ or **vertexes**) **1** the highest point; the top or apex. **2** *Geom.* **a** each angular point of a polygon, polyhedron, etc. **b** a meeting point of two lines that form an angle. **c** the point at which an axis meets a curve or surface. **d** the point opposite the base of a figure. **3** *Anat.* the crown of the head. [L *vertex -ticis* whirlpool, crown of a head, vertex, f. *vertere* turn]

■ **1** top, tip, extremity, zenith, meridian, apogee, peak, apex, acme, summit, pinnacle, crest, crown, cap, height(s).

vertical /vártikəl/ *adj.* & *n.* ● *adj.* **1** at right angles to a horizontal plane; perpendicular. **2** in a direction from top to bottom of a picture, etc. **3** of or at the vertex or highest point. **4** at, or passing through, the zenith. **5** *Anat.* of or relating to the crown of the head. **6** involving all the levels in an organizational hierarchy or stages in the production of a class of goods (*vertical integration*). ● *n.* a vertical line or plane. □ **out of the vertical** not vertical. **vertical angles** *Math.* each pair of opposite angles made by two intersecting lines. **vertical fin** *Zool.* a dorsal, anal, or caudal fin. **vertical plane** a plane at right angles to the horizontal. **vertical takeoff** the takeoff of an aircraft directly upward. ▫▫ **verticality** /-kálitee/ *n.* **verticalize** *v.tr.* **vertically** *adv.* [F *vertical* or LL *verticalis* (as VERTEX)]

■ *adj.* **1, 2** see PERPENDICULAR *adj.* 2. ▫▫ **vertically** see UPRIGHT *adv.*

verticil /vártisil/ *n. Bot.* & *Zool.* a whorl; a set of parts arranged in a circle around an axis. ▫▫ **verticillate** /-tísilət, -layt/ *adj.* [L *verticillus* whorl of a spindle, dimin. of VERTEX]

vertiginous /vərtíjinəs/ *adj.* of or causing vertigo. ▫▫ **vertiginously** *adv.* [L *vertiginosus* (as VERTIGO)]

■ see DIZZY *adj.* 1a, SHEER[1] 2, HIGH *adj.* 1a.

vertigo /vártigō/ *n.* a condition with a sensation of whirling and a tendency to lose balance; dizziness; giddiness. [L *vertigo -ginis* whirling f. *vertere* turn]

■ dizziness, light-headedness, giddiness, muzziness, instability, unsteadiness, esp. *Brit.* staggers; *colloq.* wooziness.

vertu var. of VIRTU.

vervain /várvayn/ *n. Bot.* any of various herbaceous plants of the genus *Verbena*, esp. *V. officinalis* with small blue, white, or purple flowers. [ME f. OF *verveine* f. L VERBENA]

verve /vərv/ *n.* enthusiasm; vigor; spirit, esp. in artistic or literary work. [F, earlier = a form of expression, f. L *verba* words]

■ spirit, vivacity, vivaciousness, vitality, life, liveliness, animation, sparkle, energy, vigor, exuberance, briskness, brio, esprit, élan, dash, flair, panache, flourish, enthusiasm, zeal, zest, gusto, zip, *colloq.* vim, get-up-and-go, pep, zing, *sl.* pizzazz, oomph.

vervet /várvit/ *n.* a small, gray African monkey, *Cercopithecus aethiops.* [F]

very /véree/ *adv.* & *adj.* ● *adv.* **1** in a high degree (*did it very easily; had a very bad cough; am very much better*). **2** in the fullest sense (foll. by *own* or superl. adj.: *at the very latest; do your very best; my very own room*). ● *adj.* **1** (usu. prec. by *the, this, his*, etc.) **a** real; true; actual; truly such (emphasizing identity, significance, or extreme degree: *the very thing we need; those were his very words*). **b** mere; sheer (*the very idea of it was horrible*). **2** *archaic* real; genuine (*very God*). □ **not very 1** in a low degree. **2** far from being. **very high frequency** (of radio frequency) in the range 30–300 megahertz. **Very Reverend** the title of a religious officer below the rank of bishop or abbot. **the very same** see SAME. [ME f. OF *verai* ult. f. L *verus* true]

■ *adv.* **1** extremely, truly, really, to a great extent, exceedingly, greatly, highly, (very) much, most, profoundly, deeply, acutely, perfectly, thoroughly, unusually, extraordinarily, uncommonly, exceptionally, especially, particularly, remarkably, absolutely, completely, entirely, utterly, altogether, totally, quite, rather, hugely, enormously, vastly, *archaic* right, *colloq.* damn(ed), terribly, awfully, darned, *Brit. colloq.* jolly, *sl.* plumb. ● *adj.* **1 a** exact, precise, perfect; same, selfsame, identical, particular; actual, real, true. **b** least, mere, merest, bare, barest, sheer, sheerest; utter, pure, simple. **2** real, true, genuine.

Very light /véree, vééree/ *n.* a flare projected from a pistol for signaling or temporarily illuminating the surroundings. [E. W. *Very*, Amer. inventor d. 1910]

Very pistol *n.* a gun for firing a Very light.

vesica /vesíkə, vésikə/ *n.* **1** *Anat.* & *Zool.* a bladder, esp. the urinary bladder. **2** (in full **vesica piscis** /písis/ or **piscium** /píseeəm/) *Art* a pointed oval used as an aureole in medieval sculpture and painting. ▫▫ **vesical** *adj.* [L]

vesicate /vésikayt/ *v.tr.* raise blisters on. ▫▫ **vesicant** /-kənt/ *adj.* & *n.* **vesication** /-káyshən/ *n.* **vesicatory** /-kətawree/ *adj.* & *n.* [LL *vesicare* vesicat- (as VESICA)]

vesicle /vésikəl/ *n.* **1** *Anat., Zool.,* & *Bot.* a small bladder, bubble, or hollow structure. **2** *Geol.* a small cavity in volcanic rock produced by gas bubbles. **3** *Med.* a blister. ▫▫ **vesicular** /-síkyələr/ *adj.* **vesiculate** /-síkyəlayt/ *adj.* **vesiculation** /-láyshən/ *n.* [F *vésicule* or L *vesicula* dimin. of VESICA]

vesper /véspər/ *n.* **1** Venus as the evening star. **2** *poet.* evening. **3** (in *pl.*) **a** the sixth of the canonical hours of prayer. **b** evensong. [L *vesper* evening (star): sense 3 partly f. OF *vespres* f. eccl.L *vesperas* f. L *vespera* evening]

vespertine /véspərtin, -tin/ *adj.* **1** *Bot.* (of a flower) opening in the evening. **2** *Zool.* active in the evening. **3** *Astron.* setting near the time of sunset. **4** of or occurring in the evening. [L *vespertinus* f. *vesper* evening]

vespiary /véspee-eree/ *n.* (*pl.* **-ies**) a nest of wasps. [irreg. f. L *vespa* wasp, after *apiary*]

vespine /véspīn/ *adj.* of or relating to wasps. [L *vespa* wasp]

vessel /vésəl/ *n.* **1** a hollow receptacle esp. for liquid, e.g., a cask, cup, pot, bottle, or dish. **2** a ship or boat, esp. a large one. **3 a** *Anat.* a duct or canal, etc., holding or conveying blood or other fluid, esp. = *blood vessel.* **b** *Bot.* a woody duct carrying or containing sap, etc. **4** *Bibl.* or *joc.* a person regarded as the recipient or exponent of a quality (*a weak*

/.../ pronunciation	● part of speech
□ phrases, idioms, and compounds	
▫▫ derivatives	■ synonym section
cross-references appear in SMALL CAPITALS or *italics*	

vessel). [ME f. AF *vessel(e)*, OF *vaissel(le)* f. LL *vascellum* dimin. of *vas* vessel]
- **1** container, receptacle, utensil, holder, repository. **2** craft, boat, ship, ark, *poet.* barque, bark, argosy. **3** duct, canal, tube; blood vessel, vein, *Anat.* venule.

vest /vest/ *n. & v.* ● *n.* **1** a waist-length close-fitting, sleeveless garment, often worn under a suit jacket, etc. **2** *Brit.* an undershirt. **3** a usu. V-shaped piece of material to fill the opening at the neck of a woman's dress. ● *v.* **1** *tr.* (esp. in *passive*; foll. by *with*) bestow or confer (powers, authority, etc.) on (a person). **2** *tr.* (foll. by *in*) confer (property or power) on (a person) with an immediate fixed right of immediate or future possession. **3** *intr.* (foll. by *in*) (of property, a right, etc.) come into the possession of (a person). **4** a *tr. poet.* clothe. **b** *intr. Eccl.* put on vestments. □ **vested interest 1** *Law* an interest (usu. in land or money held in trust) recognized as belonging to a person. **2** a personal interest in a state of affairs, usu. with an expectation of gain. **vest-pocket 1** small enough to fit into the pocket of a vest. **2** very small. [(n.) F *veste* f. It. *veste* f. L *vestis* garment: (v.) ME, orig. past part. f. OF *vestu* f. *vestir* f. L *vestire* *vestit-* clothe]

vesta /véstə/ *n. hist.* a short wooden or wax match. [*Vesta*, Roman goddess of the hearth and household]

vestal /vést'l/ *adj. & n.* ● *adj.* **1** chaste; pure. **2** of or relating to the Roman goddess Vesta. ● *n.* **1** a chaste woman, esp. a nun. **2** *Rom. Antiq.* a vestal virgin. □ **vestal virgin** *Rom. Antiq.* a virgin consecrated to Vesta and vowed to chastity, who shared the charge of maintaining the sacred fire burning on the goddess's altar. [ME f. L *vestalis* (adj. & n.) (as VESTA)]
- *adj.* **1** see PURE 3, 4.

vestee /vestee/ *n.* = VEST *n.* 3.

vestiary /véstee-eree, -chee-/ *n. & adj.* ● *n.* (*pl.* **-ies**) **1** a vestry. **2** cloakroom. ● *adj.* of or relating to clothes or dress. [ME f. OF *vestiarie*, *vestiaire*: see VESTRY]

vestibule /véstibyool/ *n.* **1** a an antechamber, hall, or lobby next to the outer door of a building. **b** a porch of a church, etc. **2** an enclosed entrance to a railroad car. **3** *Anat.* **a** a chamber or channel communicating with others. **b** part of the mouth outside the teeth. **c** the central cavity of the labyrinth of the inner ear. □□ **vestibular** /-stíbyoolər/ *adj.* [F *vestibule* or L *vestibulum* entrance court]
- **1 a** see HALL 1.

vestige /véstij/ *n.* **1** a trace or piece of evidence; a sign (*vestiges of an earlier civilization*; *found no vestige of their presence*). **2** a slight amount; a particle (*without a vestige of clothing*; *showed not a vestige of decency*). **3** *Biol.* a part or organ of an organism that is reduced or functionless but was well developed in its ancestors. [F f. L *vestigium* footprint]
- **1** trace, suggestion, hint, inkling, sign, evidence, mark, token, scent; remnant, scrap, fragment, memorial, residue, relic, remains. **2** particle, trace, suggestion, soupçon, hint, glimmer, suspicion, whiff, tinge, taste, touch; iota, jot, speck, scrap, shred, bit, fragment.

vestigial /vestíjeeəl, -jəl/ *adj.* **1** being a vestige or trace. **2** *Biol.* (of an organ) atrophied or functionless from the process of evolution (*a vestigial wing*). □□ **vestigially** *adv.*
- **2** imperfect, undeveloped, underdeveloped, rudimentary, incomplete.

vestiture /véstichər/ *n.* **1** *Zool.* hair, scales, etc., covering a surface. **2** *archaic* **a** clothing. **b** investiture. [ME f. med.L *vestitura* f. L *vestire*: see VEST]

vestment /véstmənt/ *n.* **1** any of the official robes of clergy, choristers, etc., worn during divine service, esp. a chasuble. **2** a garment, esp. an official or state robe. [ME f. OF *vestiment*, *vestement* f. L *vestimentum* (as VEST)]
- **2** (*vestments*) see ROBE *n.* 4.

vestry /véstree/ *n.* (*pl.* **-ies**) **1** a room or building attached to a church for keeping vestments in. **2** *hist.* **a** a meeting of parishioners usu. in a vestry for parochial business. **b** a body of parishioners meeting in this way. □□ **vestral** *adj.* [ME f. OF *vestiaire*, *vestiarie*, f. L *vestiarium* (as VEST)]

vestryman /véstreemən/ *n.* (*pl.* **-men**) a member of a vestry.

vesture /véschər/ *n. & v.* ● *n. poet.* **1** garments; dress. **2** a covering. ● *v.tr.* clothe. [ME f. OF f. med.L *vestitura* (as VEST)]

vet[1] /vet/ *n. & v.* ● *n. colloq.* a veterinary surgeon. ● *v.tr.* (**vetted, vetting**) **1** make a careful and critical examination of (a scheme, work, candidate, etc.). **2** examine or treat (an animal). [abbr.]
- *n.* veterinary, veterinarian, esp. *Brit.* veterinary surgeon.
- *v.* **1** examine, review, investigate, scrutinize, inspect, check, look over, scan, screen; validate, authenticate; check out, *colloq.* give a thing *or* person the once-over, size up. **2** see TREAT *v.* 3.

vet[2] /vet/ *n. colloq.* a veteran. [abbr.]

vetch /vech/ *n.* any plant of the genus *Vicia*, esp. *V. sativa*, largely used for silage or fodder. □□ **vetchy** *adj.* [ME f. AF & ONF *veche* f. L *vicia*]

vetchling /véchling/ *n.* any of various plants of the genus *Lathyrus*, related to vetch.

veteran /vétərən, vétrən/ *n.* **1** a person who has grown old in or had long experience of esp. military service or an occupation (*a war veteran*; *a veteran of the theater*; *a veteran marksman*). **2** an ex-serviceman or servicewoman. **3** (*attrib.*) of or for veterans. □ **veteran car** *Brit.* a car made before 1916, or (strictly) before 1905. **Veteran's Day** November 11, a legal holiday in the US, commemorating the end of World War I and of World War II, and honoring all veterans. [F *vétéran* or L *veteranus* (adj. & n.) f. *vetus -eris* old]
- **1** old hand, past master, trouper, *colloq.* warhorse, oldtimer. **2** ex-serviceman, ex-servicewoman, returned serviceman, returned servicewoman, returned soldier, *colloq. vet.* **3** (*attrib.*) experienced, practiced, seasoned, mature, long-serving, battle-scarred; old.

veterinarian /vétərináreeən, vétrə-/ *n.* a doctor who practices veterinary medicine or surgery. [L *veterinarius* (as VETERINARY)]

veterinary /vétərineree, vétrə-/ *adj. & n.* ● *adj.* of or for diseases and injuries of farm and domestic animals, or their treatment. ● *n.* (*pl.* **-ies**) a veterinary surgeon. □ **veterinary surgeon** *Brit.* a person qualified to treat diseased or injured animals. [L *veterinarius* f. *veterinae* cattle]

vetiver /vétivər/ *n.* = CUSCUS[1]. [F *vétiver* f. Tamil *veṭṭivēru* f. *vēr* root]

veto /véetō/ *n. & v.* ● *n.* (*pl.* **-oes**) **1 a** a constitutional right to reject a legislative enactment. **b** the right of a permanent member of the UN Security Council to reject a resolution. **c** such a rejection. **d** an official message conveying this. **2** a prohibition (*put one's veto on a proposal*). ● *v.tr.* (**-oes, -oed**) **1** exercise a veto against (a measure, etc.). **2** forbid authoritatively. □□ **vetoer** *n.* [L, = I forbid, with ref. to its use by Roman tribunes of the people in opposing measures of the Senate]
- *n.* denial, ban, stoppage, block, embargo, turndown, thumbs down, rejection, disallowance, quashing, prevention, prohibition, interdiction, taboo, proscription, preclusion. ● *v.* stop, block, deny, ban, turn down, say no to, reject, disallow, rule out, quash, prevent, prohibit, forbid, interdict, taboo, outlaw, proscribe, preclude, *colloq.* kill, *sl.* put the kibosh on, nix.

vex /veks/ *v.tr.* **1** anger by a slight or a petty annoyance; irritate. **2** *archaic* grieve; afflict. □□ **vexer** *n.* **vexing** *adj.* **vexingly** *adv.* [ME f. OF *vexer* f. L *vexare* shake, disturb]
- **1** see ANGER *v.* □□ **vexing** see IRKSOME.

vexation /veksáyshən/ *n.* **1** the act or an instance of vexing; the state of being vexed. **2** an annoying or distressing thing. [ME f. OF *vexation* or L *vexatio -onis* (as VEX)]
- **1** see ANGER *n.* **2** see PEST 1, WORRY *n.* 1.

vexatious /veksáyshəs/ *adj.* **1** such as to cause vexation. **2** *Law* not having sufficient grounds for action and seeking only to annoy the defendant. □□ **vexatiously** *adv.* **vexatiousness** *n.*
- **1** see IRKSOME.

vexed /vekst/ *adj.* **1** irritated; angered. **2** (of a problem, issue, etc.) difficult and much discussed; problematic. □□ **vexedly** /véksidlee/ *adv.*

■ **1** see ANGRY 1. **2** see DIFFICULT 1b.

vexillology /véksilólǝjee/ n. the study of flags. □□ **vexillological** adj. **vexillologist** n. [VEXILLUM + -LOGY]

vexillum /veksíləm/ n. (pl. **vexilla** /-lǝ/) **1** Rom. Antiq. **a** a military standard, esp. of a maniple. **b** a body of troops under this. **2** Bot. the large upper petal of a papilionaceous flower. **3** Zool. the vane of a feather. **4** Eccl. **a** a flag attached to a bishop's staff. **b** a processional banner or cross. [L = flag f. vehere vect- carry]

VF abbr. (also **V.F.**) **1** video frequency. **2** visual field.

VG abbr. **1** very good. **2** vicar-general.

VHF abbr. very high frequency.

VI abbr. Virgin Islands.

via /véeǝ, víǝ/ prep. by way of; through (New York to Washington via Philadelphia; send it via your secretary). [L, ablat. of via way, road]

■ by way of, by means of; see also THROUGH prep. 4.

viable /víǝbǝl/ adj. **1** (of a plan, etc.) feasible; practicable esp. from an economic standpoint. **2 a** (of a plant, animal, etc.) capable of living or existing in a particular climate, etc. **b** (of a fetus or newborn child) capable of maintaining life. **3** (of a seed or spore) able to germinate. □□ **viability** /-bílitee/ n. **viably** adv. [F f. vie life f. L vita]

■ **1** sustainable, supportable, sensible, reasonable, practical, practicable, applicable, workable, feasible, possible, achievable. □□ **viability** SEE FEASIBILITY.

viaduct /víǝdukt/ n. **1** a long, bridgelike structure, esp. a series of arches, carrying a road or railroad across a valley or dip in the ground. **2** such a road or railroad. [L via way, after AQUEDUCT]

vial /víǝl/ n. a small (usu. cylindrical glass) vessel esp. for holding liquid medicines. □□ **vialful** n. (pl. **-fuls**). [ME, var. of fiole, etc.: see VIAL]

via media /víǝ meédeeǝ, véeǝ médeeǝ/ n. literary a middle way or compromise between extremes. [L]

viand /víǝnd/ n. formal **1** an article of food. **2** (in pl.) provisions; victuals. [ME f. OF viande food, ult. f. L vivenda, neut. pl. gerundive of vivere to live]

viaticum /viátikǝm/ n. (pl. **viaticums** or **viatica** /-kǝ/) **1** the Eucharist as given to a person near or in danger of death. **2** provisions or an official allowance of money for a journey. [L, neut. of viaticus f. via road]

vibes /víbz/ n.pl. colloq. **1** vibrations, esp. in the sense of feelings or atmosphere communicated (the house had bad vibes). **2** = VIBRAPHONE. [abbr.]

■ **1** vibrations, feelings, sensations, resonance(s), rapport, empathy, sympathy.

vibraculum /víbrákyǝlǝm/ n. (pl. **vibracula** /-lǝ/) Zool. a whiplike structure of bryozoans used to bring food within reach by lashing movements. □□ **vibracular** adj. [mod.L (as VIBRATE)]

vibrant /víbrǝnt/ adj. **1** vibrating. **2** (often foll. by with) (of a person or thing) thrilling; quivering (vibrant with emotion). **3** (of sound) resonant. **4** (of color) bright and vivid. □□ **vibrancy** /-rǝnsee/ n. **vibrantly** adv. [L vibrare: see VIBRATE]

■ **2** see ANIMATED 1. **4** see RICH 8.

vibraphone /víbrǝfōn/ n. a percussion instrument of tuned metal bars with motor-driven resonators and metal tubes giving a vibrato effect. □□ **vibraphonist** n. [VIBRATO + -PHONE]

vibrate /víbráyt/ v. **1** intr. & tr. move or cause to move continuously and rapidly to and fro; oscillate. **2** intr. Physics move unceasingly to and fro, esp. rapidly. **3** intr. (of a sound) throb; continue to be heard. **4** intr. (foll. by with) quiver; thrill (vibrating with passion). **5** intr. (of a pendulum) swing to and fro. □□ **vibrative** /-rǝtiv/ adj. [L vibrare vibrat- shake, swing]

■ **1, 2, 4** quiver, shiver, shudder, fluctuate, quake, shake, tremble, throb, pulsate, palpitate, oscillate, pulse. **3** throb, pulse, pulsate, quaver, quiver, shake, tremble, reverberate, resonate, esp. Brit. judder. **5** swing, oscillate.

vibratile /víbrǝtil, -til/ adj. **1** capable of vibrating. **2** Biol. (of cilia, etc.) used in vibratory motion. [VIBRATORY, after pulsatile, etc.]

vibration /víbráyshǝn/ n. **1** the act or an instance of vibrating; oscillation. **2** Physics (esp. rapid) motion to and fro, esp. of the parts of a fluid or an elastic solid whose equilibrium has been disturbed or of an electromagnetic wave. **3** (in pl.) **a** a mental (esp. occult) influence. **b** a characteristic atmosphere or feeling in a place, regarded as communicable to people present in it. □□ **vibrational** adj. [L vibratio (as VIBRATE)]

vibrato /víbraátō/ n. Mus. a rapid slight variation in pitch in singing or playing a stringed or wind instrument, producing a tremulous effect (cf. TREMOLO). [It., past part. of vibrare VIBRATE]

vibrator /víbráytǝr/ n. **1** a device that vibrates or causes vibration, esp. an electric or other instrument used in massage or for sexual stimulation. **2** Mus. a reed in a reed organ.

vibratory /víbrǝtawree/ adj. causing vibration.

vibrissae /víbríssee/ n.pl. **1** stiff coarse hairs near the mouth of most mammals (e.g., a cat's whiskers) and in the human nostrils. **2** bristlelike feathers near the mouth of insect-eating birds. [L (as VIBRATE)]

viburnum /víbȯrnǝm, vee-/ n. Bot. any shrub of the genus Viburnum, usu. with white flowers, e.g., the guelder rose and snowball bush. [L, = wayfaring tree]

Vic. abbr. Victoria.

vicar /víkǝr/ n. **1 a** (in the Church of England) an incumbent of a parish where tithes formerly passed to a chapter or religious house or layman (cf. RECTOR). **b** (in an Episcopal Church) a member of the clergy deputizing for another. **2** RC Ch. a representative or deputy of a bishop. □ **vicar apostolic** RC Ch. a Roman Catholic missionary or titular bishop. **vicar-general** (pl. **vicars-general**) **1** an Anglican official assisting or representing a bishop, esp. in administrative matters. **2** RC Ch. a bishop's assistant in matters of jurisdiction, etc. **Vicar of Christ** the pope. □□ **vicariate** /-káireeǝt/ n. **vicarship** n. [ME f. AF viker(e), OF vicaire f. L vicarius substitute f. vicis: see VICE³]

vicarage /víkǝrij/ n. the residence or benefice of a vicar.

vicarial /vikáireeǝl/ adj. of or serving as a vicar.

vicarious /vikáireeǝs/ adj. **1** experienced in the imagination through another person (vicarious pleasure). **2** acting or done for another (vicarious suffering). **3** deputed; delegated (vicarious authority). □□ **vicariously** adv. **vicariousness** n. [L vicarius: see VICAR]

■ **1** indirect, secondhand. **2** substitute(d), surrogate. **3** delegated, deputed, commissioned, assigned.

vice¹ /vís/ n. **1 a** evil or grossly immoral conduct. **b** a particular form of this, esp. involving prostitution, drugs, etc. **2 a** depravity; evil. **b** an evil habit; a particular form of depravity (has the vice of gluttony). **3** a defect of character or behavior (drunkenness was not among his vices). **4** a fault or bad habit in a horse, etc. □ **vice ring** a group of criminals involved in organizing illegal prostitution. **vice squad** a police department enforcing laws against prostitution, drug abuse, etc. □□ **viceless** adj. [ME f. OF f. L vitium]

■ **1, 2** immorality, corruption, evil, badness, depravity, degradation, degeneracy, iniquity, villainy, venality, evildoing, wrongdoing, wickedness, profligacy, sin, sinning, sinfulness, transgression. **3** flaw, defect, fault, imperfection, blemish, shortcoming, failing, weakness, frailty, foible, infirmity, deficiency.

vice² esp. Brit. var. of VISE.

vice³ /vísee, -sǝ/ prep. in the place of; in succession to. [L, ablat. of vix (recorded in oblique forms in vic-) change]

vice⁴ /vís/ n. colloq. = VICE PRESIDENT, VICE ADMIRAL, etc. [abbr.]

vice- /vís/ comb. form forming nouns meaning: **1** acting as a substitute or deputy for (vice chancellor). **2** next in rank to (vice admiral). [as VICE⁴]

/.../ **pronunciation**	● **part of speech**
□ **phrases, idioms, and compounds**	
□□ **derivatives**	■ **synonym section**
cross-references appear in SMALL CAPITALS or italics	

vice admiral /vís/ *n.* a naval officer ranking below admiral and above rear admiral. □□ **vice admiralty** *n.* (*pl.* **-ies**).

vice-chancellor /vís-chánsələr/ *n.* a deputy chancellor, esp. of a university, discharging most of the administrative duties.

vicegerent /vísjérənt/ *adj.* & *n.* ● *adj.* exercising delegated power. ● *n.* a vicegerent person; a deputy. □□ **vicegerency** /-rənsee/ *n.* (*pl.* **-ies**). [med.L *vicegerens* (as VICE³, L *gerere* carry on)]

vicennial /viséneeəl/ *adj.* lasting for or occurring every twenty years. [LL *vicennium* period of 20 years f. *vicies* 20 times f. *viginti* 20 + *annus* year]

vice president /vís-prézidənt, -dent/ *n.* an official ranking below and deputizing for a president. □□ **vice presidency** *n.* (*pl.* **-ies**). **vice presidential** /-dénshəl/ *adj.*

viceregal /vísree̊gəl/ *adj.* of or relating to a viceroy. □□ **viceregally** *adv.*

vicereine /vísrayn/ *n.* **1** the wife of a viceroy. **2** a woman viceroy. [F (as VICE-, *reine* queen)]

viceroy /vísroy/ *n.* a ruler exercising authority on behalf of a sovereign in a colony, province, etc. □□ **viceroyal** *adj.* **viceroyalty** *n.* **viceroyship** *n.* [F (as VICE-, *roy* king)]

vice versa /vísə vársə, vís-/ *adv.* with the order of the terms or conditions changed; the other way around; conversely (*could go from left to right or vice versa*). [L, = the position being reversed (as VICE³, *versa* ablat. fem. past part. of *vertere* turn)]

▪ conversely, contrariwise, to *or* on the contrary, the reverse, the other way about *or* around.

vichyssoise /vísheeswaáz, veé-/ *n.* a creamy soup of pureed leeks and potatoes, usu. served chilled. [F *vichyssois -oise* of Vichy (in France)]

Vichy water /víshee, -veé/ *n.* an effervescent mineral water from Vichy in France.

vicinage /vísinij/ *n.* **1** a neighborhood; a surrounding district. **2** relation in terms of nearness, etc., to neighbors. [ME f. OF *vis(e)nage* ult. f. L *vicinus* neighbor]

vicinal /vísinəl/ *adj.* **1** neighboring; adjacent. **2** of a neighborhood; local. [F *vicinal* or L *vicinalis* f. *vicinus* neighbor]

vicinity /visínitee/ *n.* (*pl.* **-ies**) **1** a surrounding district. **2** (foll. by *to*) nearness or closeness of place or relationship. □ **in the vicinity** (often foll. by *of*) near (to). [L *vicinitas* (as VICINAL)]

▪ **1** area, neighborhood, locale, vicinage, environs, locality, precincts, purlieus, territory, district, region. **2** nearness, closeness, proximity, propinquity, contiguity. □ **in the vicinity** see NEARBY *adv.*

vicious /víshəs/ *adj.* **1** bad-tempered; spiteful (*a vicious dog*; *vicious remarks*). **2** violent; severe (*a vicious attack*). **3** of the nature of or addicted to vice. **4** (of language or reasoning, etc.) faulty or unsound. □ **vicious circle** see CIRCLE *n.* 11. **vicious spiral** continual harmful interaction of causes and effects, esp. as causing repeated rises in both prices and wages. □□ **viciously** *adv.* **viciousness** *n.* [ME f. OF *vicious* or L *vitiosus* f. *vitium* VICE¹]

▪ **1** savage, wild, untamed, ferocious, fearful, bad-tempered, brutal, fierce, fiendish, bestial, feral, brutish, ravening, *poet. or rhet.* fell; malicious, spiteful, mean, nasty, hateful, malevolent, malignant, bitter, acrimonious, rancorous, venomous, vindictive, defamatory, slanderous, scandalous, *sl.* rotten, bitchy. **2** see SAVAGE *adj.* 1. **3** immoral, unprincipled, amoral, barbarous, corrupt, evil, bad, base, depraved, vile, atrocious, execrable, degraded, degrading, degenerate, venal, iniquitous, heinous, odious, perverted, nefarious, wicked, flagitious, devilish, diabolic(al), fiendish, monstrous, profligate, shameful, shameless, abominable, sinful. □□ **viciousness** see BARBARITY 1.

vicissitude /visísitŏŏd, -tyŏŏd/ *n.* **1** a change of circumstances, esp. variation of fortune. **2** *archaic or poet.* regular change; alternation. □□ **vicissitudinous** *adj.* [F *vicissitude* or L *vicissitudo -dinis* f. *vicissim* by turns (as VICE³)]

▪ change, mutation, alteration, changeability, mutability, variation, variability, variety, alternation, shift, contrast,

flux, fluctuation, unpredictability, inconstancy, uncertainty, flukiness; (*vicissitudes*) ups and downs.

victim /víktim/ *n.* **1** a person injured or killed as a result of an event or circumstance (*a road victim*; *the victims of war*). **2** a person or thing injured or destroyed in pursuit of an object or in gratification of a passion, etc. (*the victim of their ruthless ambition*). **3** a prey; a dupe (*fell victim to a confidence scam*). **4** a living creature sacrificed to a deity or in a religious rite. [L *victima*]

▪ **1, 2** sufferer, casualty, fatality, injured party, martyr. **3** prey, quarry, target; dupe, gull, fool, butt, fair game, *colloq.* chump, schlemiel, *sl.* sucker, sap, fall guy, *sl.* patsy, schnook, *Austral. sl.* bunny, *Brit. sl.* mug. **4** sacrifice, sacrificial lamb, scapegoat, offering.

victimize /víktimīz/ *v.tr.* **1** single out (a person) for punishment or unfair treatment, esp. dismissal from employment. **2** make (a person, etc.) a victim. □□ **victimization** /-izáyshən/ *n.* **victimizer** *n.*

▪ prey on, pursue, go after, pick on, bully, take advantage of, persecute, oppress, torment, exploit, use; cheat, swindle, defraud, dupe, hoodwink, deceive, gull, fool, trick, outwit, take (in), flimflam, screw, rook, *colloq.* outsmart, outfox, shaft, suck in, *sl.* bilk. □□ **victimization** see PERSECUTION.

victor /víktər/ *n.* a winner in battle or in a contest. [ME f. AF *victo(u)r* or L *victor* f. *vincere vict-* conquer]

▪ winner, champion, conqueror, prizewinner, *literary* vanquisher, *colloq.* top dog.

victoria /viktáwreeə/ *n.* **1** a low, light, four-wheeled carriage with a collapsible top, seats for two passengers, and a raised driver's seat. **2** a gigantic S. American water lily, *Victoria amazonica*. **3 a** a species of crowned pigeon. **b** a variety of domestic pigeon. **4** (also **victoria plum**) *Brit.* a large, red, luscious variety of plum. [Queen *Victoria*, d. 1901]

Victoria Cross /viktáwreeə/ *n.* a UK decoration awarded for conspicuous bravery in the armed services, instituted by Queen Victoria in 1856.

Victorian /viktáwreeən/ *adj.* & *n.* ● *adj.* **1** of or characteristic of the time of Queen Victoria. **2** associated with attitudes attributed to this time, esp. of prudery and moral strictness. ● *n.* a person, esp. a writer, of this time. □□ **Victorianism** *n.*

Victoriana /viktáwreeánə, -aánə/ *n.pl.* **1** articles, esp. collectors' items, of the Victorian period. **2** attitudes characteristic of this period.

victorious /viktáwreeəs/ *adj.* **1** having won a victory; conquering; triumphant. **2** marked by victory (*victorious day*). □□ **victoriously** *adv.* **victoriousness** *n.* [ME f. AF *victorious*, OF *victorieux*, f. L *victoriosus* (as VICTORY)]

▪ **1** triumphant, successful, champion, conquering, prevailing, winning.

victory /víktəree/ *n.* (*pl.* **-ies**) **1** the process of defeating an enemy in battle or war or an opponent in a contest. **2** an instance of this; a triumph. [ME f. AF *victorie*, OF *victoire*, f. L *victoria* (as VICTOR)]

▪ **1** triumph, supremacy, superiority, success, overcoming, mastery, winning, quelling, crushing. **2** triumph, conquest, success, win, walkover.

victual /vít'l/ *n.* & *v.* ● *n.* (usu. in *pl.*) food, provisions, esp. as prepared for use. ● *v.* **1** *tr.* supply with victuals. **2** *intr.* obtain stores. **3** *intr.* eat victuals. □□ **victualless** *adj.* [ME f. OF *vitaille* f. LL *victualia*, neut. pl. of L *victualis* f. *victus* food, rel. to *vivere* live]

▪ *n.* (*victuals*) see FOOD 1.

victualler /vítlər/ *n.* (also **victualer**) **1 a** a person, etc., who supplies victuals. **b** (in full **licensed victualler**) *Brit.* a pub owner, etc., licensed to sell liquor. **2** a ship carrying stores for other ships. [ME f. OF *vitaill(i)er*, *vitaillour* (as VICTUAL)]

vicuña /víkōōnə, -nyə, -kyōō-, vi-/ *n.* (also **vicuna**) **1** a S. American mammal, *Vicugna vicugna*, related to the llama, with fine silky wool. **2 a** a cloth made from its wool. **b** an imitation of this. [Sp. f. Quechua]

vide /vídee, veéday/ *v.tr.* (as an instruction in a reference to a passage in a book, etc.) see; consult. [L, imper. of *vidēre* see]

videlicet /vidéliset, vī-/ adv. = VIZ. [ME f. L f. vidēre see + licet it is permissible]

video /vídeeō/ adj., n., & v. ● adj. **1** relating to the recording, reproducing, or broadcasting of visual images on magnetic tape. **2** relating to the broadcasting of television pictures. ● n. (pl. -os) **1** the process of recording, reproducing, or broadcasting visual images on magnetic tape. **2** the visual element of television broadcasts. **3** colloq. = videocassette recorder. **4** a movie, etc., recorded on a videotape. ● v.tr. (-oes, -oed) make a video recording of. □ **video display terminal** Computing a device displaying data as characters on a screen and usu. incorporating a keyboard. **video frequency** a frequency in the range used for video signals in television. **video game** a game played by electronically manipulating images produced by a computer program on a television screen. **video jockey** a person who introduces music videos, as on television. **video recorder** = videocassette recorder. **video signal** a signal containing information for producing a television image. [L vidēre see, after AUDIO] ▪ n. **4** see TAPE n. 4, FILM n. 3a. ● v. see TAPE v. 3, FILM v. 1.

videocassette /vīdeeōkasét, -kəsét/ n. a cassette of videotape. □ **videocassette recorder** an apparatus for recording and playing videotapes.

videodisc /vídeeōdisk/ n. (also **videodisk**) a metal-coated disk on which visual material is recorded for reproduction on a television screen.

videophone /vídeeōfōn/ n. a telephone device transmitting a visual image as well as sound.

videotape /vídeeōtayp/ n. & v. ● n. magnetic tape for recording television pictures and sound. ● v.tr. make a recording of (broadcast material, etc.) with this. □ **videotape recorder** = videocassette recorder. ▪ n. see TAPE n. 4. ● v. see TAPE v. 3, FILM v. 1.

videotex /vídeeōteks/ n. (also **videotext** /-tekst/) any electronic information system, esp. teletext or viewdata.

vie /vī/ v.intr. (**vying**) (often foll. by with) compete; strive for superiority (vied with each other for recognition). [prob. f. ME (as ENVY)] ▪ compete, contend, struggle, strive.

Viennese /veéəneéz/ adj. & n. ● adj. of, relating to, or associated with Vienna in Austria. ● n. (pl. same) a native or citizen of Vienna.

Vietnamese /vee-étnəmeéz/ adj. & n. ● adj. of or relating to Vietnam in SE Asia. ● n. (pl. same) **1** a native or national of Vietnam. **2** the language of Vietnam.

vieux jeu /vyö zhö́/ adj. old-fashioned; hackneyed. [F, lit. old game]

view /vyōo/ n. & v. ● n. **1** range of vision; extent of visibility (came into view; in full view of the crowd). **2 a** what is seen from a particular point; a scene or prospect (a fine view of the mountains; a room with a view). **b** a picture, etc., representing this. **3** an inspection by the eye or mind; a visual or mental survey. **4** an opportunity for visual inspection; a viewing (a private view of the exhibition). **5 a** an opinion (holds strong views on morality). **b** a mental attitude (took a favorable view of the matter). **c** a manner of considering a thing (took a long-term view of it). ● v. **1** tr. look at; survey visually; inspect (we are going to view the house). **2** tr. examine; survey mentally (different ways of viewing a subject). **3** tr. form a mental impression or opinion of; consider (does not view the matter in the same light). **4** intr. watch television. **5** tr. see (a fox) break cover. □ **have in view 1** have as one's object. **2** bear (a circumstance) in mind in forming a judgment, etc. **in view of** having regard to; considering. **on view** being shown (for observation or inspection); being exhibited. **view halloo** Hunting a shout on seeing a fox break cover. **with a view to 1** with the hope or intention of. **2** with the aim of attaining (with a view to marriage). □ **viewable** adj. [ME f. AF v(i)ewe, OF vēue fem. past part. f. vēoir see f. L vidēre] ▪ n. **1** sight, vision. **2 a** outlook, aspect, prospect, scene, perspective, vista, panorama, spectacle; landscape, seascape, cityscape. **b** representation, projection, perspective, panorama, picture, tableau; landscape, seascape, cityscape. **3** inspection, survey, observation,

scrutiny, examination, contemplation, study. **4** viewing, inspection. **5** opinion, point of view, angle, approach, position, judgment, belief, conviction, attitude, way of thinking, conception, understanding, impression, feeling, sentiment, notion. ● v. **1** look at or upon or over, see, take in, watch, observe, scrutinize, contemplate, gaze at, examine, inspect, survey, regard, witness, literary behold. **2** see SURVEY v. 1, 2. **3** regard, consider, think of, look on or upon, judge, believe, hold, estimate, rate, gauge, assess, formal deem. □ **in view of** in (the) light of, considering, in consideration of, having regard to, because of, on account of. **with a view to** with the aim or direction or intent or intention or purpose or objective or object or expectation or prospect or vision or hope or dream of. □□ **viewable** see PUBLIC adj. 3, OPEN adj. 9–11.

viewdata /vyṓodaytə, -data/ n. a news and information service from a computer source to which a television screen is connected by telephone link.

viewer /vyṓoər/ n. **1** a person who views. **2** a person watching television. **3** a device for looking at film transparencies, etc.

viewership /vyṓoərship/ n. a viewing audience, especially of a television program.

viewfinder /vyṓofindər/ n. a device on a camera showing the area covered by the lens in taking a photograph.

viewing /vyṓoing/ n. **1** an opportunity or occasion to view; an exhibition. **2** the act or practice of watching television.

viewless /vyṓolis/ adj. **1** not having or affording a view. **2** lacking opinions.

viewpoint /vyṓopoynt/ n. a point of view; a standpoint. ▪ standpoint, (point of) view, attitude, angle, slant, position, stance, vantage point, perspective, frame of reference, way of thinking, context.

vigesimal /vijésiməl/ adj. **1** of twentieths or twenty. **2** reckoning or reckoned by twenties. □□ **vigesimally** adv. [L vigesimus f. viginti twenty]

vigil /víjil/ n. **1 a** keeping awake during the time usually given to sleep, esp. to keep watch or pray (keep vigil). **b** a period of this. **2** Eccl. the eve of a festival or holy day. **3** (in pl.) nocturnal devotions. [ME f. OF vigile f. L vigilia f. vigil awake] ▪ **1** see WATCH n. 2, WAKE¹ n.

vigilance /víjiləns/ n. watchfulness; caution; circumspection. □ **vigilance committee** a self-appointed body for the maintenance of order, etc. [F vigilance or L vigilantia f. vigilare keep awake (as VIGIL)] ▪ watchfulness, alertness, observance, guardedness, circumspection, attentiveness, caution, care.

vigilant /víjilənt/ adj. watchful against danger, difficulty, etc. □□ **vigilantly** adv. [L vigilans -antis (as VIGILANCE)] ▪ watchful, alert, sharp, observant, guarded, circumspect, attentive, wakeful, awake, cautious, careful, wary, chary, on one's guard, on the alert, on the lookout, eagle-eyed, hawkeyed, Argus-eyed, on the qui vive, on one's toes, with one's eyes open or skinned or peeled. □□ **vigilantly** see attentively (ATTENTIVE).

vigilante /víjilántee/ n. a member of a vigilance committee or similar body. [Sp., = vigilant]

vigneron /veényəráwn/ n. a winegrower. [F f. vigne VINE]

vignette /vinyét/ n. & v. ● n. **1** a short descriptive essay or character sketch. **2** an illustration or decorative design, esp. on the title page of a book, not enclosed in a definite border. **3** a photograph or portrait showing only the head and shoulders with the background gradually shaded off. **4** a brief scene in a movie, etc. ● v.tr. **1** make a portrait of (a person) in vignette style. **2** shade off (a photograph or portrait). □□ **vignettist** n. [F, dimin. of vigne VINE] ▪ n. **1** see PROFILE n. 2a.

vigor /vígər/ n. (Brit. **vigour**) **1** active physical strength or energy. **2** a flourishing physical condition. **3** healthy growth; vitality; vital force. **4 a** mental strength or activity shown in thought or speech or in literary style. **b** forcefulness; trenchancy; animation. □□ **vigorless** *adj.* [ME f. OF *vigor* f. L *vigor -oris* f. *vigēre* be lively]

■ **1** vitality, resilience, strength, power, potency, energy, forcefulness, force, stamina, endurance, mettle, mettlesomeness, pith, dynamism, spirit, liveliness, animation, *joie de vivre*, verve, vivacity, exuberance, brio, dash, briskness, zest, zeal, zealousness, enthusiasm, gusto, drive, eagerness, *colloq.* spunk, pep, vim, zing, get-up-and-go, *sl.* pizzazz, oomph, zap. **3** see HEALTH 1.

vigorish /vígərish/ *n. sl.* **1** the percentage deducted by the organizers of a game from a gambler's winnings. **2** an excessive rate of interest on a loan. [prob. f. Yiddish f. Russ. *vyigrysh* gain, winnings]

vigoro /vígərō/ *n. Austral.* a team ball game combining elements of cricket and baseball. [app. f. VIGOROUS]

vigorous /vígərəs/ *adj.* **1** strong and active; robust. **2** (of a plant) growing strongly. **3** forceful; acting or done with physical or mental vigor; energetic. **4** full of vigor; showing or requiring physical strength or activity. □□ **vigorously** *adv.* **vigorousness** *n.* [ME f. OF f. med.L *vigorosus* f. L *vigor* (as VIGOR)]

■ **1, 3, 4** energetic, active, vivacious, dynamic, brisk, lively, spirited, forceful, zestful, robust, strong, strenuous, hardy, hale, hearty, vital, fit, lusty, stalwart, in good *or* fine fettle, spry, sprightly, resilient, *colloq.* peppy, full of pep, full of get-up-and-go, full of beans, zippy, snappy. **2** strong, robust, hardy, sturdy, flourishing, tough. □□ **vigorously** energetically, actively, vivaciously, animatedly, dynamically, briskly, spiritedly, robustly, strongly, forcefully, hardily, heartily, lustily, stalwartly, eagerly, with might and main, with a vengeance, strenuously, *colloq.* like mad, like crazy, hammer and tongs. **vigorousness** see STAMINA.

vigour *Brit.* var. of VIGOR.

vihara /vihaára/ *n.* a Buddhist temple or monastery. [Skr.]

Viking /víking/ *n. & adj.* • *n.* any of the Scandinavian seafaring pirates and traders who raided and settled in parts of NW Europe in the 8th–11th c. • *adj.* of or relating to the Vikings or their time. [ON *víkingr*, perh. f. OE *wícing* f. *wíc* camp]

vile /vil/ *adj.* **1** disgusting. **2** morally base; depraved; shameful. **3** *colloq.* abominably bad (*vile weather*). **4** *archaic* worthless. □□ **vilely** *adv.* **vileness** *n.* [ME f. OF *vil vile* f. L *vilis* cheap, base]

■ **1** disgusting, nasty, sickening, nauseous, nauseating, foul, loathsome, offensive, noxious, obnoxious, objectionable, revolting, repulsive, repellent, repugnant. **2** base, abject, contemptible, debased, degenerate, depraved, bad, iniquitous, execrable, atrocious, sordid, immoral, amoral, wicked, evil, sinful, hellish, fiendish, ignoble, revolting, repulsive, despicable, odious, heinous, monstrous, horrid, horrible, dreadful, terrible, corrupt, mean, wretched, miserable, degrading, ignominious, disgraceful, shameful, shameless. **3** atrocious, foul, unpleasant, bad, wretched, woeful, miserable, *colloq.* abominable, abysmal, villainous, lousy, dreadful, horrible, horrid, terrible, awful, *sl.* rotten, stinking. □□ **vileness** see EVIL *n.* 2.

vilify /vílifī/ *v.tr.* (**-ies**, **-ied**) defame; speak evil of. □□ **vilification** /-fikáyshən/ *n.* **vilifier** *n.* [ME in sense 'lower in value,' f. LL *vilificare* (as VILE)]

■ depreciate, devalue, deprecate, debase, disparage, denigrate, diminish, discredit, traduce, defame, speak ill of, revile, slander, libel, abuse, defile, sully, smear, blacken, tarnish, malign, calumniate, asperse, run down, decry, bad-mouth, *sl.* knock. □□ **vilification** see SLANDER *n.*

vill /vil/ *n. hist.* a feudal township. [AF f. OF *vile, ville* farm f. L (as VILLA)]

villa /vílə/ *n.* **1** *Rom. Antiq.* a large country house with an estate. **2** a country residence. **3** *Brit.* a detached or semidetached house in a residential district. **4** a rented holiday home, esp. abroad. [It. & L]

village /vílij/ *n.* **1 a** a group of houses and associated buildings, larger than a hamlet and smaller than a town, esp. in a rural area. **b** the inhabitants of a village regarded as a community. **2** *Brit.* a self-contained district or community within a town or city, regarded as having features characteristic of village life. **3** a small municipality with limited corporate powers. □□ **villager** *n.* **villagey** *adj.* [ME f. OF f. L *villa*]

villain /vílən/ *n.* **1** a person guilty or capable of great wickedness. **2** *colloq. usu. joc.* a rascal or rogue. **3** (also **villain of the piece**) (in a play, etc.) a character whose evil actions or motives are important in the plot. **4** *Brit. colloq.* a professional criminal. **5** *archaic* a rustic; a boor. [ME f. OF *vilein, vilain* ult. f. L *villa*: see VILLA]

■ **1, 3** wretch, evildoer, criminal, felon, lawbreaker, miscreant, blackguard, malefactor, wrongdoer, scoundrel, cur, viper, reptile, snake in the grass, *colloq.* crook, baddie. **2** rogue, cad, knave, scalawag, scoundrel, *archaic or joc.* rapscallion, *colloq.* rat, scamp, *colloq. or joc.* bounder, *Brit. colloq.* blighter, *often joc.* rascal, *poet. or archaic* caitiff, *sl.* bastard, son of a bitch, S.O.B. esp. *Brit. sl.* rotter.

villainous /vílənəs/ *adj.* **1** characteristic of a villain; wicked. **2** *colloq.* abominably bad; vile (*villainous weather*). □□ **villainously** *adv.* **villainousness** *n.*

■ **1** treacherous, perfidious, dishonest, unscrupulous, traitorous, corrupt, faithless, criminal, felonious, murderous; base, abject, contemptible, debased, degenerate, depraved, bad, iniquitous, execrable, atrocious, sordid, immoral, amoral, wicked, evil, sinful, hellish, fiendish, ignoble, revolting, despicable, rotten, horrid, horrible, dreadful, terrible, mean, wretched, miserable, degrading, ignominious, disgraceful, shameful, shameless, *colloq.* crooked. **2** see VILE 3. □□ **villainously** see BADLY 1.

villainy /vílənee/ *n.* (*pl.* **-ies**) **1** villainous behavior. **2** a wicked act. [OF *vilenie* (as VILLAIN)]

■ **1** see DEVILRY. **2** see ATROCITY 1.

villanelle /vílənél/ *n.* a *usu.* pastoral or lyrical poem of 19 lines, with only two rhymes throughout, and some lines repeated. [F f. It. *villanella* fem. of *villanello* rural, dimin. of *villano* (as VILLAIN)]

-ville /vil/ *comb. form colloq.* forming the names of fictitious places with ref. to a particular quality, etc. (*dragsville*; *squaresville*). [F *ville* town, as in many town names]

villein /vílin, -ayn, viláyn/ *n. hist.* a feudal tenant entirely subject to a lord or attached to a manor. [ME, var. of VILLAIN]

villeinage /vílinij/ *n. hist.* the tenure or status of a villein.

villus /víləs/ *n.* (*pl.* **villi** /-lī/) **1** *Anat.* each of the short, fingerlike processes on some membranes, esp. on the mucous membrane of the small intestine. **2** *Bot.* (in *pl.*) long, soft hairs covering fruit, flowers, etc. □□ **villiform** /víləfawrm/ *adj.* **villose** /vílōs/ *adj.* **villosity** /-lósitee/ *n.* **villous** /-əs/ *adj.* [L, = shaggy hair]

vim /vim/ *n. colloq.* vigor. [perh. f. L, accus. of *vis* energy]

■ see VIGOR 1.

vimineous /vimíneeəs/ *adj. Bot.* of or producing twigs or shoots. [L *vimineus* f. *vimen viminis* osier]

VIN *abbr.* = *vehicle identification number.*

vina /véenə/ *n.* an Indian four-stringed musical instrument with a fretted fingerboard and a gourd at each end. [Skr. & Hindi *viṇā*]

vinaceous /vináyshəs, vī-/ *adj.* wine-red. [L *vinaceus* f. *vinum* wine]

vinaigrette /vínigrét/ *n.* **1** (in full **vinaigrette sauce**) a salad dressing of oil, vinegar, and seasoning. **2** a small ornamental bottle for holding smelling salts. [F, dimin. of *vinaigre* VINEGAR]

vincible /vínsibəl/ *adj. literary* that can be overcome or conquered. □□ **vincibility** *n.* [L *vincibilis* f. *vincere* overcome]

vinculum /víngkyələm/ *n.* (*pl.* **vincula** /-lə/) **1** *Algebra* a horizontal line drawn over a group of terms to show they have a common relation to what follows or precedes (e.g., $a + b \times c = ac + bc$, but $a + \overline{b \times c} = a + bc$). **2** *Anat.* a ligament; a frenum. [L, = bond, f. *vincire* bind]

vindicate /víndikayt/ *v.tr.* **1** clear of blame or suspicion. **2** establish the existence, merits, or justice of (one's courage, conduct, assertion, etc.). **3** justify (a person, oneself, etc.) by evidence or argument. □□ **vindicable** /-kəbəl/ *adj.* **vindication** /-káyshən/ *n.* **vindicative** /vindíkətiv, víndikaytiv/ *adj.* **vindicator** *n.* [L *vindicare* claim, avenge f. *vindex -dicis* claimant, avenger]
  ■ **1** clear, exonerate, absolve, acquit, excuse, *formal* exculpate. **2** justify, support, uphold, prove, defend. **3** justify, defend, bear out, back up. □□ **vindication** see DEFENSE 4a.

vindicatory /víndikətawree/ *adj.* **1** tending to vindicate. **2** (of laws) punitive.

vindictive /vindíktiv/ *adj.* **1** tending to seek revenge. **2** spiteful. □ **vindictive damages** *Brit. Law* = *punitive damages.* □□ **vindictively** *adv.* **vindictiveness** *n.* [L *vindicta* vengeance (as VINDICATE)]
  ■ **1** avenging, vengeful, vindicatory, revengeful, retaliatory, retaliative, retributory, retributive, punitive. **2** spiteful, unforgiving, splenetic, malevolent, malicious, resentful, rancorous, implacable. □□ **vindictiveness** see REVENGE *n.* 3, RANCOR.

vine /vīn/ *n.* **1** any climbing or trailing woody-stemmed plant, esp. of the genus *Vitis*, bearing grapes. **2** a slender trailing or climbing stem. □□ **viny** *adj.* [ME f. OF *vi(g)ne* f. L *vinea* vineyard f. *vinum* wine]

vinedresser /víndréssər/ *n.* a person who prunes, trains, and cultivates vines, esp. grapevines.

vinegar /vínigər/ *n.* **1** a sour liquid obtained from wine, cider, etc., by fermentation and used as a condiment or for pickling. **2** sour behavior or character. □□ **vinegarish** *adj.* **vinegary** *adj.* [ME f. OF *vyn egre* ult. f. L *vinum* wine + *acer, acre* sour]
  ■ □□ **vinegary** see SOUR *adj.* 1.

vinery /vínəree/ *n.* (*pl.* **-ies**) **1** a greenhouse for grapevines. **2** a vineyard.

vineyard /vínyərd/ *n.* **1** a plantation of grapevines, esp. for wine-making. **2** *Bibl.* a sphere of action or labor (see Matt. 20:1). [ME f. VINE + YARD²]

vingt-et-un /vántayóN/ *n.* = BLACKJACK¹. [F, = twenty-one]

vini- /vínee/ *comb. form* wine. [L *vinum*]

viniculture /vínikulchər/ *n.* the cultivation of grapevines. □□ **vinicultural** *adj.* **viniculturist** *n.*

vinification /vínifikáyshən/ *n.* the conversion of grape juice, etc., into wine.

vining /víning/ *n.* the separation of leguminous crops from their vines and pods.

vino /veénō/ *n. sl.* wine, esp. a red Italian wine. [Sp. & It., = wine]

vin ordinaire /ván awrdináir/ *n.* inexpensive (usu. red) table wine. [F, = ordinary wine]

vinous /vínəs/ *adj.* **1** of, like, or associated with wine. **2** addicted to wine. □□ **vinosity** /-nósitee/ *n.* [L *vinum* wine]

vin rosé /ván rōzáy/ *n.* = ROSÉ. [F]

vint¹ /vint/ *v.tr.* make (wine). [back-form. f. VINTAGE]

vint² /vint/ *n.* a Russian card game like auction bridge. [Russ., = screw]

vintage /víntij/ *n. & adj.* ● *n.* **1 a** a season's produce of grapes. **b** the wine made from this. **2 a** the gathering of grapes for wine making. **b** the season of this. **3** a wine of high quality from a single identified year and district. **4 a** the year, etc., when a thing was made, etc. **b** a thing made, etc., in a particular year, etc. **5** *poet.* or *rhet.* wine. ● *adj.* **1** of high quality, esp. from the past or characteristic of the best period of a person's work. **2** of a past season. □ **vintage car** an automobile made in the early part of the twentieth century. [alt. (after VINTNER) of ME *vendage, vindage* f. OF *vendange* f. L *vindemia* f. *vinum* wine + *demere* remove]
  ■ *n.* **1** year, crop, harvest. **2** harvest. **4** year, date, period, generation, origin. ● *adj.* **1** quality, choice, superior,

better, good, high-quality, select, best, classic; aged, seasoned, mature(d), mellow(ed). **2** antiquated, old-fashioned, old-fogyish, antique, bygone, old-time, collector('s), *colloq.* over the hill.

vintager /víntijər/ *n.* a grape gatherer.

vintner /víntnər/ *n.* a wine merchant. [ME f. AL *vintenarius, vinetarius* f. AF *vineter*, OF *vinetier* f. med.L *vinetarius* f. L *vinetum* vineyard f. *vinum* wine]

viny see VINE.

vinyl /vínəl/ *n.* any plastic made by polymerizing a compound containing the vinyl group, esp. polyvinyl chloride. □ **vinyl group** the organic radical or group CH_2CH. [L *vinum* wine + -YL]

viol /víəl/ *n.* a medieval stringed musical instrument, played with a bow and held vertically on the knees or between the legs. [ME *viel*, etc., f. OF *viel(l)e*, alt. of *viole* f. Prov. *viola, viula*, prob. ult. f. L *vitulari* be joyful: cf. FIDDLE]

viola¹ /vee-ólə/ *n.* **1 a** an instrument of the violin family, larger than the violin and of lower pitch. **b** a viola player. **2** a viol. □ **viola da braccio** /də bráachō/ a viol corresponding to the modern viola. **viola da gamba** /də gámbə/ a viol held between the player's legs, esp. one corresponding to the modern cello. **viola d'amore** /damóray/ a sweet-toned tenor viol. [It. & Sp., prob. f. Prov.: see VIOL]

viola² /vi-ólə, vee-, víələ/ *n.* **1** any plant of the genus *Viola*, including the pansy and violet. **2** a cultivated hybrid of this genus. [L, = violet]

violaceous /víəláyshəs/ *adj.* **1** of a violet color. **2** *Bot.* of the violet family Violaceae. [L *violaceus* (as VIOLA²)]

violate /víəlayt/ *v.tr.* **1** disregard; fail to comply with (an oath, treaty, law, etc.). **2** treat (a sanctuary, etc.) profanely or with disrespect. **3** break in upon; disturb (a person's privacy, etc.). **4** assault sexually; rape. □□ **violable** *adj.* **violation** /-láyshən/ *n.* **violator** *n.* [ME f. L *violare* treat violently]
  ■ **1** break, breach, disobey, disregard, contravene, infringe, ignore. **2** dishonor, desecrate, profane, defile, degrade, debase, treat irreverently. **3** invade, disturb, abuse, intrude on, trespass on. **4** rape, debauch, deflower, ravish, ravage, molest, attack, assault (sexually), outrage. □□ **violation** infringement, breach, disregard, disobedience, contravention, abuse; profanation, sacrilege, desecration, defilement, degradation, dishonor, debasement; rape, ravishment, molestation, attack, outrage, assault.

violence /víələns/ *n.* **1** the quality of being violent. **2** violent conduct or treatment; outrage; injury. **3** *Law* **a** the unlawful exercise of physical force. **b** intimidation by the exhibition of this. □ **do violence to 1** act contrary to; outrage. **2** distort. [ME f. OF f. L *violentia* (as VIOLENT)]
  ■ **1** (brute *or* physical) force, might, power, strength, severity, intensity, energy, vehemence, ferocity, ferociousness, fierceness, fury, vigor; destructiveness, virulence; bestiality, brutality, barbarity, savagery, cruelty, bloodthirstiness, wildness, frenzy, passion, vehemence, murderousness. **2** see OUTRAGE *n.* 1.
  □ **do violence to 1** harm, damage, injure, outrage, offend, abuse, violate. **2** warp, twist, distort.

violent /víələnt/ *adj.* **1** involving or using great physical force (*a violent person; a violent storm; came into violent collision*). **2 a** intense; vehement; passionate; furious (*a violent contrast; violent dislike*). **b** vivid (*violent colors*). **3** (of death) resulting from external force or from poison (cf. NATURAL *adj.* 2). **4** involving an unlawful exercise of force (*laid violent hands on him*). □□ **violently** *adv.* [ME f. OF f. L *violentus*]
  ■ **1** wild, physical, brutal, brutish, beastly, nasty, cruel, mean, barbarous, inhuman, savage, fierce, ferocious, furious, frenzied, vicious, uncontrollable, untamed, ungovernable, raging, raving, irrational, insane, crazed, hotheaded, *colloq.* fit to be tied; harmful, injurious,

---

/.../ **pronunciation**	● **part of speech**
□ **phrases, idioms, and compounds**	
□□ **derivatives**	■ **synonym section**
cross-references appear in SMALL CAPITALS or *italics*	

damaging, detrimental, destructive, deleterious, catastrophic, cataclysmic, ruinous, devastating. **2 a** acute, serious, severe, extreme, harsh, trenchant, virulent, intense, energetic, forceful, vehement, passionate, impassioned, impetuous, tempestuous, stormy, furious. **b** see VIVID 1. □□ **violently** see MADLY 2a, *fiercely* (FIERCE).

violet /ví∂l∂t/ n. & adj. ● n. **1 a** any plant of the genus *Viola*, esp. the sweet violet, with usu. purple, blue, or white flowers. **b** any of various plants resembling the sweet violet. **2** the bluish-purple color seen at the end of the spectrum opposite red. **3 a** pigment of this color. **b** clothes or material of this color. ● adj. of this color. [ME f. OF *violet(te)* dimin. of *viole* f. L VIOLA²]

violin /víalín/ n. **1** a musical instrument with four strings of treble pitch played with a bow. **2** a violin player. □□ **violinist** n. [It. *violino* dimin. of VIOLA¹]
■ fiddle.

violist¹ /víalist/ n. a viol player.

violist² /vee-ólist/ n. a viola player.

violoncello /veéal∂nchélō, ví-/ n. (pl. **-os**) formal = CELLO. □□ **violoncellist** n. [It., dimin. of VIOLONE]

violone /veéalónay/ n. a double-bass viol. [It., augment. of VIOLA¹]

VIP abbr. very important person.
■ see DIGNITARY.

viper /vípar/ n. **1** any venomous snake of the family Viperidae, esp. the common viper (see ADDER). **2** a malignant or treacherous person. □ **viper's bugloss** a stiff, bristly blue-flowered plant, *Echium vulgare*. **viper's grass** scorzonera. □□ **viperine** /-in, -rin/ adj. **viperish** adj. **viperlike** adj. **viperous** adj. [F *vipère* or L *vipera* f. *vivus* alive + *parere* bring forth]
■ **2** see SNAKE n. 2.

virago /viraágō, -ráygō/ n. (pl. **-os**) **1** a fierce or abusive woman. **2** archaic a woman of masculine strength or spirit. [OE f. L, = female warrior, f. *vir* man]
■ see FURY 5.

viral /vír∂l/ adj. of or caused by a virus. □□ **virally** adv.

virelay /vírilay/ n. a short (esp. old French) lyric poem with two rhymes to a stanza variously arranged. [ME f. OF *virelai*]

vireo /víreeō/ n. (pl. **-os**) any small American songbird of the family Vireonidae. [L, perh. = greenfinch]

virescence /virésans/ n. **1** greenness. **2** Bot. abnormal greenness in petals, etc., normally of some bright color. □□ **virescent** adj. [L *virescere*, incept. of *virēre* be green]

virgate¹ /várgayt/ adj. Bot. & Zool. slim, straight, and erect. [L *virgatus* f. *virga* rod]

virgate² /várgat/ n. Brit. hist. a varying measure of land, esp. 30 acres. [med.L *virgata* (rendering OE *gierd-land* yardland) f. L *virga* rod]

virger var. of VERGER.

Virgilian /vərjileéan/ adj. of, or in the style of, the Roman poet Virgil (d. 19 BC). [L *Vergilianus* f. P. *Vergilius* Maro, Virgil]

virgin /várjin/ n. & adj. ● n. **1** a person (esp. a woman) who has never had sexual intercourse. **2 a** (**the Virgin**) Christ's mother the Blessed Virgin Mary. **b** a picture or statue of the Virgin. **3** (**the Virgin**) the zodiacal sign or constellation Virgo. **4** colloq. a naïve, innocent, or inexperienced person (*a political virgin*). **5** a member of any order of women under a vow to remain virgins. **6** a female insect producing eggs without impregnation. ● adj. **1** that is a virgin. **2** of or befitting a virgin (*virgin modesty*). **3** not yet used, penetrated, or tried (*virgin soil*). **4** undefiled; spotless. **5** (of clay) not fired. **6** (of metal) made from ore by smelting. **7** (of wool) not yet, or only once, spun or woven. **8** (of an insect) producing eggs without impregnation. □ **virgin birth 1** the doctrine of Christ's birth without a human father. **2** parthenogenesis. **virgin forest** a forest in its untouched natural state. **virgin honey** honey taken from a virgin comb, or drained from the comb without heat or pressure. **virgin queen** an unfertilized queen bee. **the Virgin Queen** Queen Elizabeth I of England. **virgin's bower** a clematis, *Clematis*

viticella. □□ **virginhood** n. [ME f. AF & OF *virgine* f. L *virgo* -*ginis*]
■ adj. **1, 2** see PURE 3, 4. **3** see UNUSED 1b, UNCHARTED. **4** see UNSPOILED.

virginal /várjin∂l/ adj. & n. ● adj. that is or befits or belongs to a virgin. ● n. (usu. in pl.) (in full **pair of virginals**) an early form of spinet in a box, used in the sixteenth and seventeenth centuries. □□ **virginalist** n. **virginally** adv. [ME f. OF *virginal* or L *virginalis* (as VIRGIN): name of the instrument perh. from its use by young women]
■ adj. see PURE 3, 4.

Virginia /vərjínyə/ n. **1** tobacco from Virginia. **2** a cigarette made of this. □ **Virginia creeper** a N. American vine, *Parthenocissus quinquefolia*, cultivated for ornament. **Virginia reel** a country dance. **Virginia** (or **Virginian**) **stock** a cruciferous plant, *Malcolmia maritima*, with white or pink flowers. □□ **Virginian** n. & adj. [*Virginia* in US, orig. the first English settlement (1607), f. *Virgin Queen*]

virginity /vərjínitee/ n. the state of being a virgin. [OF *virginité* f. L *virginitas* (as VIRGIN)]
■ see VIRTUE 3.

Virgo /várgō/ n. (pl. **-os**) **1** a constellation, traditionally regarded as contained in the figure of a woman. **2 a** the sixth sign of the zodiac (the Virgin). **b** a person born when the sun is in this sign. □□ **Virgoan** n. & adj. [OE f. L, = virgin]

virgule /várgyōōl/ n. **1** a slanting line used to mark division of words or lines. **2** = SOLIDUS 1. [F, = comma, f. L *virgula* dimin. of *virga* rod]

viridescent /víridésant/ adj. greenish, tending to become green. □□ **viridescence** /-sans/ n. [LL *viridescere* f. L *viridis*: see VIRIDIAN]

viridian /virideéan/ n. & adj. ● n. **1** a bluish-green chromium oxide pigment. **2** the color of this. ● adj. bluish-green. [L *viridis* green f. *virēre* be green]

viridity /viríditee/ n. literary greenness; verdancy. [ME f. OF *viridité* or L *viriditas* f. *viridis*: see VIRIDIAN]

virile /vír∂l, -il/ adj. **1** of or characteristic of a man; having masculine (esp. sexual) vigor or strength. **2** of or having procreative power. **3** of a man as distinct from a woman or child. □□ **virility** /virílitee/ n. [ME f. F *viril* or L *virilis* f. *vir* man]
■ **1** see MANLY 1. □□ **virility** see MACHISMO.

virilism /vírilizam/ n. Med. the development of secondary male characteristics in a female or precociously in a male.

viroid /víroyd/ n. an infectious entity affecting plants, similar to a virus but smaller and consisting only of nucleic acid without a protein coat.

virology /vírólajee/ n. the scientific study of viruses. □□ **virological** /-ralójikal/ adj. **virologically** adv. **virologist** n.

virtu /vərtōō/ n. (also **vertu**) **1** a knowledge of or expertise in the fine arts. **2** virtuosity. □ **article** (or **object**) **of virtu** an article interesting because of its workmanship, antiquity, rarity, etc. [It. *virtù* VIRTUE, virtu]

virtual /várchōōal/ adj. **1** that is such for practical purposes though not in name or according to strict definition (*is the virtual manager of the business*; *take this as a virtual promise*). **2** Optics relating to the points at which rays would meet if produced backward (*virtual focus*; *virtual image*). **3** Mech. relating to an infinitesimal displacement of a point in a system. **4** Computing not physically existing as such but made by software to appear to do so (*virtual memory*). □ **virtual reality** the generation by computer software of an image or environment that appears real to the senses. □□ **virtuality** /-álitee/ n. **virtually** adv. [ME f. med.L *virtualis* f. L *virtus* after LL *virtuosus*]
■ **1** effective, essential; practical, understood, accepted. □□ **virtually** essentially, effectively, practically, almost, to all intents and purposes, for all practical purposes, more or less, nearly, as good as, substantially, in effect, in essence.

virtue /várchōō/ n. **1** moral excellence; uprightness; goodness. **2** a particular form of this (*patience is a virtue*). **3** chastity, esp. of a woman. **4** a good quality (*has the virtue of being adjustable*). **5** efficacy; inherent power (*no virtue in such drugs*). **6** an angelic being of the seventh order of the celestial hierarchy (see ORDER *n.* 19). □ **by** (or **in**) **virtue of** on the strength or ground of (*got the job by virtue of his experience*). **make a virtue of necessity** derive some credit or benefit from an unwelcome obligation. □□ **virtueless** *adj.* [ME f. OF *vertu* f. L *virtus -tutis* f. *vir* man]

■ **1** morality, high-mindedness, honor, goodness, justness, righteousness, fairness, integrity, right-mindedness, honesty, probity, uprightness, rectitude, decency, worth, worthiness, nobility, character, respectability, virtuousness. **3** virginity, chastity, chasteness, honor, innocence, purity. **4** quality, credit, merit, strength, good point, strong point, advantage, asset. □ **by** (or **in**) **virtue of** by dint of, owing to, thanks to, by reason of, because of, on account of, on the strength of, on the grounds of.

virtuoso /vɜ́rchŏo-ő́sŏ, -zŏ́/ *n.* (*pl.* **virtuosi** /-see, -zee/ or **-os**) **1 a** a person highly skilled in the technique of a fine art, esp. music. **b** (*attrib.*) displaying the skills of a virtuoso. **2** a person with a special knowledge of or taste for works of art or virtu. □□ **virtuosic** /-ósik/ *adj.* **virtuosity** /-ósitee/ *n.* **virtuosoship** *n.* [It., = learned, skillful, f. LL (as VIRTU-OUS)]

■ **1 a** master, maestro, expert, genius, talent, prodigy, old hand, wizard, *colloq.* maven, whiz, whiz kid, esp. *Brit. colloq.* dab hand. **b** masterful, masterly, expert, talented, brilliant, dazzling, bravura, prodigious, excellent, superb, extraordinary, exceptional, superior, first-rate, superlative, matchless, peerless, sterling, marvelous, remarkable. □□ **virtuosity** (technical) skill, technique, ability, expertise, mastery, virtu, excellence, brilliance, craftsmanship, craft, flair, dash, élan, éclat, panache, pyrotechnics, showmanship, show, staginess, *sl.* razzle-dazzle.

virtuous /vɜ́rchŏo-əs/ *adj.* **1** possessing or showing moral rectitude. **2** chaste. □ **virtuous circle** a beneficial recurring cycle of cause and effect (cf. *vicious circle* (see CIRCLE *n.* 11)). □□ **virtuously** *adv.* **virtuousness** *n.* [ME f. OF *vertuous* f. LL *virtuosus* f. *virtus* VIRTUE]

■ **1** moral, honorable, ethical, honest, good, upstanding, high-principled, upright, righteous, right, pure, uncorrupted, incorruptible, blameless, irreproachable, unimpeachable, just, fair, right-minded, fair-minded, high-minded, scrupulous, trustworthy. **2** chaste, innocent, virginal, virgin, pure; decent, proper, unsullied, faithful, true, uncorrupted. □□ **virtuousness** see HONOR *n.* 2, 3.

virulent /víyələnt, vírə-/ *adj.* **1** strongly poisonous. **2** (of a disease) violent or malignant. **3** bitterly hostile (*virulent animosity*; *virulent abuse*). □□ **virulence** /-ləns/ *n.* **virulently** *adv.* [ME, orig. of a poisoned wound, f. L *virulentus* (as VIRUS)]

■ **1, 2** lethal, life-threatening, deadly, fatal, pernicious, septic, poisonous, toxic, baleful, noxious, dangerous, harmful, injurious, detrimental, deleterious, destructive, malignant, unhealthy, unwholesome. **3** vicious, venomous, bitter, spiteful, malignant, malign, malicious, malevolent, poisonous, splenetic, acrimonious, acerbic, acid, mordant, sarcastic, nasty, trenchant, caustic, antagonistic, hateful, hostile. □□ **virulence** virulency, poisonousness, venomousness, toxicity, noxiousness, deadliness, perniciousness, injuriousness, destructiveness, malignity, malignancy, violence, balefulness; acrimony, acrimoniousness, bitterness, acerbity, rancor, spleen, poison, venom, malevolence, maliciousness, malice, spite, hostility, resentment, antagonism, hatred.

virus /vírəs/ *n.* **1** a microscopic organism consisting mainly of nucleic acid in a protein coat, multiplying only in living cells and often causing diseases. **2** *Computing* = *computer virus.* **3** *archaic* a poison, a source of disease. **4** a harmful or corrupting influence. [L, = slimy liquid, poison]

Vis. *abbr.* **1** Viscount. **2** Viscountess.

visa /véezə/ *n. & v.* ● *n.* an endorsement on a passport, etc., showing that it has been found correct, esp. as allowing the holder to enter or leave a country. ● *v.tr.* (**visas, visaed**

/-zəd/, **visaing**) mark with a visa. [F f. L *visa* neut. pl. past part. of *vidēre* see]

visage /vízij/ *n. literary* a face; a countenance. □□ **visaged** *adj.* (also in *comb.*). [ME f. OF f. L *visus* sight (as VISA)]

■ see FACE *n.* 1.

vis-à-vis /véezaavée/ *prep., adv., & n.* ● *prep.* **1** in relation to. **2** opposite to. ● *adv.* facing one another. ● *n.* (*pl.* same) **1** a person or thing facing another, esp. in some dances. **2** a person occupying a corresponding position in another group. **3** a social partner. [F, = face to face, f. *vis* face f. L (as VISAGE)]

■ *prep.* **1** re, with reference to, regarding, with regard to. **2** see OPPOSITE *prep.* ● *adv.* see *face to face.*

Visc. *abbr.* **1** Viscount. **2** Viscountess.

viscacha /viskáachə/ *n.* (also **vizcacha** /viz-/) any S. American burrowing rodent of the genus *Lagidium*, having valuable fur. [Sp. f. Quechua (*h*)*uiscacha*]

viscera /vísərə/ *n.pl.* the interior organs in the great cavities of the body (e.g., brain, heart, liver), esp. in the abdomen (e.g., the intestines). [L, pl. of *viscus*: see VISCUS]

visceral /vísərəl/ *adj.* **1** of the viscera. **2** relating to inward feelings rather than conscious reasoning. □ **visceral nerve** a sympathetic nerve (see SYMPATHETIC *adj.* 9). □□ **viscerally** *adv.*

viscid /vísid/ *adj.* **1** glutinous; sticky. **2** semifluid. □□ **viscidity** /-síditee/ *n.* [LL *viscidus* f. L *viscum* birdlime]

■ **1** see STICKY *adj.* 2. **2** see THICK *adj.* 5a.

viscometer /viskómitər/ *n.* an instrument for measuring the viscosity of liquids. □□ **viscometric** /vískəmétrik/ *adj.* **viscometrically** /vískəmétrikəlee/ *adv.* **viscometry** *n.* [var. of *viscosimeter* (as VISCOSITY)]

viscose /vískōs/ *n.* **1** a form of cellulose in a highly viscous state suitable for drawing into yarn. **2** rayon made from this. [LL *viscosus* (as VISCOUS)]

viscosity /viskósitee/ *n.* (*pl.* **-ies**) **1** the quality or degree of being viscous. **2** *Physics* **a** (of a fluid) internal friction; the resistance to flow. **b** a quantity expressing this. □ **dynamic viscosity** a quantity measuring the force needed to overcome internal friction. □□ **viscosimeter** /-kəsimitər/ *n.* [ME f. OF *viscosité* or med.L *viscositas* (as VISCOUS)]

■ **1** see BODY *n.* 8.

viscount /víkownt/ *n.* a British nobleman ranking between an earl and a baron. □□ **viscountcy** /-kówntsee/ *n.* (*pl.* **-ies**). **viscountship** *n.* **viscounty** *n.* (*pl.* **-ies**). [ME f. AF *viscounte*, OF *vi(s)conte* f. med.L *vicecomes -mitis* (as VICE-, COUNT²)]

viscountess /víkowntis/ *n.* **1** a viscount's wife or widow. **2** a woman holding the rank of viscount in her own right.

viscous /vískəs/ *adj.* **1** glutinous; sticky. **2** semifluid. **3** *Physics* having a high viscosity; not flowing freely. □□ **viscously** *adv.* **viscousness** *n.* [ME f. AF *viscous* or LL *viscosus* (as VISCID)]

■ **1** see STICKY *adj.* 2. **2** see THICK *adj.* 5a.

viscus /vískəs/ *n.* (*pl.* **viscera** /vísərə/) (usu. in *pl.*) any of the soft internal organs of the body. [L]

vise /vīs/ *n. & v.* ● *n.* (esp. *Brit.* **vice**) an instrument, esp. attached to a workbench, with two movable jaws between which an object may be clamped so as to leave the hands free to work on it. ● *v.tr.* secure in a vise. □□ **viselike** *adj.* [ME, = winding stair, screw, f. OF *vis* f. L *vitis* vine].

Vishnu /víshnōō/ *n.* a Hindu god regarded by his worshipers as the supreme deity and savior, by others as the second member of a triad with Brahma and Siva. □□ **Vishnuism** *n.* **Vishnuite** *n. & adj.* [Skr. *Vishṇu*]

visibility /vízibilitee/ *n.* **1** the state of being visible. **2** the range or possibility of vision as determined by the conditions of light and atmosphere (*visibility was down to 50 yards*). [F *visibilité* or LL *visibilitas* f. L *visibilis*: see VISIBLE]

visible /vízibəl/ *adj.* **1 a** that can be seen by the eye. **b** (of

/.../ **pronunciation**	● **part of speech**
□ **phrases, idioms, and compounds**	
□□ **derivatives**	■ **synonym section**
cross-references appear in SMALL CAPITALS or *italics*	

light) within the range of wavelengths to which the eye is sensitive. **2** that can be perceived or ascertained; apparent; open (*has no visible means of support*; *spoke with visible impatience*). **3** (of exports, etc.) consisting of actual goods (cf. *invisible exports*). □ **the Church visible** the whole body of professed Christian believers. □□ **visibleness** *n.* **visibly** *adv.* [ME f. OF *visible* or L *visibilis* f. *vidēre vis-* see]

■ **1** seeable, perceivable, perceptible, discernible, detectable, discoverable, noticeable, unmistakable, clear, obvious, observable; visual. **2** obvious, conspicuous, evident, apparent, prominent, manifest, distinct, patent, well-defined, identifiable, overt, unconcealed, plain. □□ **visibly** see *outwardly* (OUTWARD).

Visigoth /vízigoth/ *n.* a West Goth, a member of the branch of the Goths who settled in France and Spain in the 5th c. and ruled much of Spain until 711. [LL *Visigothus*]

vision /vízhən/ *n.* & *v.* ● *n.* **1** the act or faculty of seeing, sight (*has impaired his vision*). **2 a** a thing or person seen in a dream or trance. **b** a supernatural or prophetic apparition. **3** a thing or idea perceived vividly in the imagination (*the romantic visions of youth*; *had visions of warm sandy beaches*). **4** imaginative insight. **5** statesmanlike foresight; sagacity in planning. **6** a person, etc., of unusual beauty. **7** what is seen on a television screen; television images collectively. ● *v.tr.* see or present in or as in a vision. □ **field of vision** all that comes into view when the eyes are turned in some direction. □□ **visional** *adj.* **visionless** *adj.* [ME f. OF f. L *visio -onis* (as VISIBLE)]

■ *n.* **1** eyesight, perception, sight. **2** phantom, apparition, chimera, delusion, hallucination, mirage, specter, eidolon, revenant, phantasm, materialization, illusion, ghost, wraith, *literary* shade, visitant. **3** view, perspective, perception, envisioning, visualization, envisaging, dream, idea, plan, scheme, conception, notion. **4, 5** farsightedness, understanding, perception, imagination, foresight, foresightedness, insight, sagacity. **6** sight for sore eyes, (welcome) sight, dream, picture. **7** image(s), picture(s).

visionary /vízhəneree/ *adj.* & *n.* ● *adj.* **1** informed or inspired by visions; indulging in fanciful theories. **2** existing in or characteristic of a vision or the imagination. **3** not practicable. ● *n.* (*pl.* **-ies**) a visionary person. □□ **visionariness** *n.*

■ *adj.* **1** unpractical, dreamy, idealistic, unrealistic, romantic, quixotic, Utopian; see also IMAGINATIVE 2. **2** dreamy, dreamlike, speculative, fanciful, unreal; see also IMAGINARY. **3** unpractical, impractical, unrealistic, idealistic, unworkable, Utopian. ● *n.* dreamer, idealist, romantic, fantast, fantasist, wishful thinker, Don Quixote, Utopian.

visit /vízit/ *v.* & *n.* ● *v.* (**visited, visiting**) **1 a** *tr.* (also *absol.*) go or come to see (a person, place, etc.) as an act of friendship or ceremony, on business or for a purpose, or from interest. **b** *tr.* go or come to see for the purpose of official inspection, supervision, consultation, or correction. **2** *tr.* reside temporarily with (a person) or at (a place). **3** *intr.* be a visitor. **4** *tr.* (of a disease, calamity, etc.) come upon; attack. **5** *tr. Bibl.* **a** (foll. by *with*) punish (a person). **b** (often foll. by *upon*) inflict punishment for (a sin). **6** *intr.* **a** (foll. by *with*) go to see (a person) esp. socially. **b** (usu. foll. by *with*) converse; chat. **7** *tr. archaic* (often foll. by *with*) comfort; bless (with salvation, etc.). ● *n.* **1 a** an act of visiting, a call on a person or at a place (*was on a visit to some friends*; *paid him a long visit*). **b** temporary residence with a person or at a place. **2** (foll. by *to*) an occasion of going to a doctor, dentist, etc. **3** a formal or official call for the purpose of inspection, etc. **4** a chat. □□ **visitable** *adj.* [ME f. OF *visiter* or L *visitare* go to see, frequent. of *visare* view f. *vidēre* vissee: (n.) perh. f. F *visite*]

■ *v.* **1** (go *or* come to) see, call (in *or* on *or* upon), look in on, stop by, pop in *or* by, descend on, stop in, *colloq.* drop by *or* in (on), look up, take in. **2** see STAY[1] *v.* 2. **4** afflict, attack, fall upon, come upon, assail, seize, scourge, descend upon, affect, *archaic or literary* smite,

poet. befall. **5 b** see INFLICT. ● *n.* **1** stay, call, sojourn, stop, stopover. **3** visitation.

visitant /vízit'nt/ *n.* & *adj.* ● *n.* **1** a visitor, esp. a supposedly supernatural one. **2** = VISITOR 2. ● *adj. archaic* or *poet.* visiting. [F *visitant* or L *visitare* (as VISIT)]

■ *n.* **1** see VISION *n.* 2.

visitation /vízitáyshən/ *n.* **1** an official visit of inspection, esp. a bishop's examination of a church in his diocese. **2** trouble or difficulty regarded as a divine punishment. **3** (**Visitation**) **a** the visit of the Virgin Mary to Elizabeth related in Luke 1:39–56. **b** the festival commemorating this on July 2. **4** *Brit. colloq.* an unduly protracted visit or social call. **5** the boarding of a vessel belonging to another nation to learn its character and purpose. **6** the instance of a parent using his or her visitation rights. □ **right of visitation** the right to conduct a visitation of a vessel, not including the right of search. **visitation rights** legal right of a noncustodial parent to visit or have temporary custody of his or her child. [ME f. OF *visitation* or LL *visitatio* (as VISIT)]

■ **1** visit, tour (of inspection). **2** affliction, ordeal, trial, punishment, disaster, catastrophe, cataclysm, calamity, tragedy, curse, scourge, blight, plague, pestilence.

visitatorial /vízitətáwreeəl/ *adj.* of an official visitor or visitation. [ult. f. L *visitare* (as VISIT)]

visiting /víziting/ *n.* & *adj.* ● *n.* paying a visit or visits. ● *attrib.adj.* (of an academic) spending some time at another institution (*a visiting professor*). □ **visiting card** a card with a person's name, etc., sent or left in lieu of a formal visit; calling card. **visiting fireman** (*pl.* **-men**) *sl.* a visitor given especially cordial treatment.

visitor /vízitər/ *n.* **1** a person who visits a person or place. **2** a migratory bird present in a locality for part of the year (*winter visitor*). **3** *Brit.* (in a college, etc.) an official with the right or duty of occasionally inspecting and reporting. □ **visitors' book** a book in which visitors to a hotel, church, embassy, etc., write their names and addresses and sometimes remarks. [ME f. AF *visitour*, OF *visiteur* (as VISIT)]

■ **1** caller, guest, company; tourist, sightseer, traveler, nonresident, foreigner, alien, migrant, visitant, esp. *Brit.* holidaymaker.

visitorial /vízitáwreeəl/ *adj.* of an official visitor or visitation.

visor /vízər/ *n.* (also esp. *Brit.* **vizor**) **1 a** a movable part of a helmet covering the face. **b** *hist.* a mask. **c** the projecting front part of a cap. **2** a shield (fixed or movable) to protect the eyes from unwanted light, esp. one at the top of a vehicle windshield. □□ **visored** *adj.* **visorless** *adj.* [ME f. AF *viser*, OF *visiere* f. *vis* face f. L *visus*: see VISAGE]

VISTA /vístə/ *abbr.* Volunteers in Service to America.

vista /vístə/ *n.* **1** a long, narrow view as between rows of trees. **2** a mental view of a long succession of remembered or anticipated events (*opened up new vistas to his ambition*). □□ **vistaed** *adj.* [It., = view, f. *visto* seen, past part. of *vedere* see f. L *vidēre*]

■ see VIEW *n.* 2a.

visual /vízhōōəl/ *adj.* & *n.* ● *adj.* of, concerned with, or used in seeing. ● *n.* (usu. in *pl.*) a visual image or display; a picture. □ **visual aid** a movie, model, etc., as an aid to learning. **visual angle** the angle formed at the eye by rays from the extremities of an object viewed. **visual display unit** esp. *Brit.* = *video display terminal.* **visual field** field of vision. **visual purple** = RHODOPSIN. **visual ray** *Optics* a line extended from an object to the eye. □□ **visuality** /vízhoo-álitee/ *n.* **visually** *adv.* [ME f. LL *visualis* f. L *visus* sight f. *vidēre* see]

■ *n.* see PICTURE *n.* 1a.

visualize /vízhōōəliz/ *v.tr.* **1** make visible, esp. to one's mind (a thing not visible to the eye). **2** make visible to the eye. □□ **visualizable** *adj.* **visualization** /-izáyshən/ *n.*

■ **1** see PICTURE *v.* 2.

vital /vít'l/ *adj.* & *n.* ● *adj.* **1** of, concerned with, or essential to organic life (*vital functions*). **2** essential to the existence of a thing or to the matter in hand (*a vital question*; *secrecy is vital*). **3** full of life or activity. **4** affecting life. **5** fatal to life or to success, etc. (*a vital error*). **6** *disp.* important. ● *n.* (in *pl.*) the body's vital organs, e.g., the heart and brain.

□ **vital capacity** the volume of air that can be expelled from the lungs after taking the deepest possible breath. **vital force 1** (in Bergson's philosophy) life force. **2** any mysterious vital principle. **vital power** the power to sustain life. **vital signs** pulse rate, rate of respiration, and body temperature considered as signs of life. **vital statistics 1** the number of births, marriages, deaths, etc. **2** *colloq.* the measurements of a woman's bust, waist, and hips. □□ **vitally** *adv.* [ME f. OF f. L *vitalis* f. *vita* life]

■ *adj.* **1** living, animate; life-giving, invigorating, quickening, animating, vitalizing, reviving, vivifying, revivifying, enlivening, rejuvenating. **2** imperative, essential, necessary, needed, requisite, required, indispensable, mandatory, compulsory, cardinal, fundamental, basic, critical, crucial, central, pivotal, life-and-death, key, paramount, main. **3** lively, full of life, vivacious, spirited, vigorous, dynamic, alive, animated, brisk, energetic, sprightly. **5** fatal, grave, serious. **6** see IMPORTANT 1. ● *n.* (*vitals*) see GUT *n.* 1, 2.

vitalism /ví'lizəm/ *n. Biol.* the doctrine that life originates in a vital principle distinct from chemical and other physical forces. □□ **vitalist** *n.* **vitalistic** *adj.* [F *vitalisme* or f. VITAL]

vitality /vītálitee/ *n.* **1** liveliness; animation. **2** the ability to sustain life; vital power. **3** (of an institution, language, etc.) the ability to endure and to perform its functions. [L *vitalitas* (as VITAL)]

■ **1** energy, vigor, power, intensity, force, liveliness, vivacity, vivaciousness, verve, animation, sparkle, spiritedness, joie de vivre, exuberance, go, zip, *colloq.* zing, pep, get-up-and-go, vim, *sl.* pizzazz, oomph. **2** life, life force, vigor, vital force, vital power. **3** stamina, hardiness, endurance, energy, strength, robustness.

vitalize /vít'līz/ *v.tr.* **1** endow with life. **2** infuse with vigor. □□ **vitalization** *n.*

■ stimulate, activate, arouse, vivify, animate, awaken, inspirit, invigorate, enliven, inspire, revive, rejuvenate, energize, fortify, reinvigorate, renew, refresh, charge (up), perk up, *colloq.* pep up.

vitally /vít'lee/ *adv.* essentially; indispensably.

vitamin /vítəmin/ *n.* any of a group of organic compounds essential in small amounts for many living organisms to maintain normal health and development. □ **vitamin A** = RETINOL. **vitamin B complex** (or **B vitamins**) any of a group of vitamins which, although not chemically related, are often found together in the same foods. **vitamin B$_1$** = THIAMINE. **vitamin B$_2$** = RIBOFLAVIN. **vitamin B$_6$** = PYRIDOXINE. **vitamin B$_{12}$** = CYANOCOBALAMIN. **vitamin C** = ASCORBIC ACID. **vitamin D** any of a group of vitamins found in liver and fish oils, essential for the absorption of calcium and the prevention of rickets in children and osteomalacia in adults. **vitamin D$_2$** = CALCIFEROL. **vitamin D$_3$** = CHOLECALCIFEROL. **vitamin E** = TOCOPHEROL. **vitamin K** any of a group of vitamins found mainly in green leaves and essential for the blood-clotting process. **vitamin M** = FOLIC ACID. [orig. *vitamine* f. L *vita* life + AMINE, because orig. thought to contain an amino acid]

vitaminize /vítəminiz/ *v.tr.* add vitamins to.

vitellary /vitéləree, vī-/ *adj.* of or relating to the vitellus.

vitelli *pl.* of VITELLUS.

vitellin /vitélin, vī-/ *n. Chem.* the chief protein constituent of the yolk of egg. [VITELLUS + -IN]

vitelline /vitélin, -leen, vī-/ *adj.* of the vitellus. □ **vitelline membrane** the yolk sac. [med.L *vitellinus* (as VITELLUS)]

vitellus /vitéləs, vī-/ *n.* (*pl.* **vitelli** /-lī/) **1** the yolk of an egg. **2** the contents of the ovum. [L, = yolk]

vitiate /vísheeayt/ *v.tr.* **1** impair the quality or efficiency of; corrupt; debase; contaminate. **2** make invalid or ineffectual. □□ **vitiation** /-sheeáyshən/ *n.* **vitiator** *n.* [L *vitiare* f. *vitium* VICE^1]

■ **1** spoil, ruin, harm, impair, mar, sully, contaminate, adulterate, weaken, degrade, downgrade, depreciate, diminish, depress, vulgarize, lower, reduce, undermine; debase, deprave, pervert, corrupt, defile, *archaic*

demoralize. **2** invalidate, destroy, delete, cancel, nullify, annul, revoke, void, abrogate, abolish, withdraw, quash, suppress. □□ **vitiation** see *impairment* (IMPAIR).

viticulture /vítikulchər/ *n.* the cultivation of grapevines; the science or study of this. □□ **viticultural** *adj.* **viticulturist** *n.* [L *vitis* vine + CULTURE]

vitreous /vítreeəs/ *adj.* **1** of, or of the nature of, glass. **2** like glass in hardness, brittleness, transparency, structure, etc. (*vitreous enamel*). □ **vitreous humor** (or **body**) *Anat.* a transparent jellylike tissue filling the eyeball. □□ **vitreousness** *n.* [L *vitreus* f. *vitrum* glass]

vitrescent /vitrésənt/ *adj.* tending to become glass. □□ **vitrescence** *n.*

vitriform /vítrifawrm/ *adj.* having the form or appearance of glass.

vitrify /vítrifī/ *v.tr. & intr.* (**-ies, -ied**) convert or be converted into glass or a glasslike substance, esp. by heat. □□ **vitrifaction** /-fákshən/ *n.* **vitrifiable** *adj.* **vitrification** /-fikáyshən/ *n.* [F *vitrifier* or med.L *vitrificare* (as VITREOUS)]

vitriol /vítreeōl, -əl/ *n.* **1** sulfuric acid or a sulfate, orig. one of glassy appearance. **2** caustic or hostile speech, criticism, or feeling. □ **copper vitriol** copper sulfate. **oil of vitriol** concentrated sulfuric acid. [ME f. OF *vitriol* or med.L *vitriolum* f. L *vitrum* glass]

■ **2** see GALL^1 1, 2.

vitriolic /vítreeólik/ *adj.* (of speech or criticism) caustic or hostile.

■ see *scathing* (SCATHE *v.* 2).

vitta /vítə/ *n.* (*pl.* **vittae** /-vitee/) **1** *Bot.* an oil tube in the fruit of some plants. **2** *Zool.* a stripe of color. □□ **vittate** *adj.* [L, = band, chaplet]

vituperate /vitōopərayt, -tyōō-, vi-/ *v.tr. & intr.* revile; abuse. □□ **vituperation** /-ráyshən/ *n.* **vituperative** /-rətiv, -ráytiv/ *adj.* **vituperator** *n.* [L *vituperare* f. *vitium* VICE^1]

■ berate, rate, reproach, revile, vilify, execrate, abuse, denounce, decry, deprecate, disparage, devalue, diminish, put down, run down, devaluate, depreciate, blame, inculpate, censure, find fault with, criticize, attack, assail, castigate, scold, reprimand, upbraid, rebuke, chasten, *archaic or literary* chide, *sl.* knock. □□ **vituperation** see ABUSE *n.* 2. **vituperative** abusive, calumniatory, calumnious, scurrilous, derogatory, belittling, depreciatory, depreciative, detractory, contemptuous, damning, denunciatory, denigrating, deprecatory, censorious, aspersive, defamatory, slanderous, libelous, castigatory, condemnatory, malign, scornful, withering, harsh, sardonic, sarcastic, biting, acid, contumelious, opprobrious, insulting.

viva^1 /vívə, veé-/ *n. & v. Brit. colloq.* ● *n.* = VIVA VOCE *n.* ● *v.tr.* (**vivas, vivaed** /-vəd/, **vivaing**) = VIVA VOCE *v.* [abbr.]

viva^2 /veévə/ *int. & n.* ● *int.* long live. ● *n.* a cry of this as a salute, etc. [It., 3rd sing. pres. subj. of *vivere* live f. L]

vivace /vivaáchay/ *adv. Mus.* in a lively brisk manner. [It. f. L (as VIVACIOUS)]

vivacious /vivávshəs/ *adj.* lively; sprightly; animated. □□ **vivaciously** *adv.* **vivaciousness** *n.* **vivacity** /vivásitee/ *n.* [L *vivax -acis* f. *vivere* live]

■ lively, spirited, sprightly, spry, energetic, animated, brisk, ebullient, effervescent, bubbly, gay, cheerful, happy, perky, jaunty, bouncy, lighthearted, sunny, merry, high-spirited, buoyant, *colloq.* peppy, full of pep, full of beans, zippy, chipper, *poet.* blithe. □□ **vivaciousness, vivacity** see VITALITY 1.

vivarium /vīváireeəm, vi-/ *n.* (*pl.* **vivaria** /-reeə/) a place artificially prepared for keeping animals in (nearly) their natural state. [L, = warren, fishpond, f. *vivus* living f. *vivere* live]

/.../ **pronunciation**	● **part of speech**
□ **phrases, idioms, and compounds**	
□□ **derivatives**	■ **synonym section**
cross-references appear in SMALL CAPITALS or *italics*	

vivat /víˈvat, veeˈvat/ *int.* & *n.* = VIVA². [L, 3rd sing. pres. subj. of *vivere* live]

viva voce /vīvə vōˈsee, vōˈchee, veeˈvə/ *adj.*, *adv.*, *n.*, & *v.*
● *adj.* oral. ● *adv.* orally. ● *n. Brit.* an oral examination for an academic qualification. ● *v.tr. Brit.* (**viva-voce**) (**-voces, -voceed, -voceing**) examine orally. [med.L, = with the living voice]
■ *adj.* see ORAL *adj.*

viverrid /vivérid, vī-/ *n.* & *adj.* ● *n.* any mammal of the family Viverridae, including civets, mongooses, and genets. ● *adj.* of or relating to this family. [L *viverra* ferret + -ID³]

vivid /vívid/ *adj.* **1** (of light or color) strong; intense; glaring (*a vivid flash of lightning*; *of a vivid green*). **2** (of a mental faculty, impression, or description) clear; lively; graphic (*has a vivid imagination*; *have a vivid recollection of the scene*). **3** (of a person) lively; vigorous. □□ **vividly** *adv.* **vividness** *n.* [L *vividus* f. *vivere* live]
■ **1** intense, strong, brilliant, fresh, bright, dazzling, rich, clear, colorful, bold, violent, glowing, lurid, glaring, *poet.* lucid. **2** clear, detailed, sharp, realistic, graphic, expressive, true to life, lifelike, distinct, powerful, strong, memorable, dramatic, striking; lively, prolific, fruitful, fertile, fecund, inventive, creative, active.

vivify /vívifī/ *v.tr.* (**-ies, -ied**) enliven; animate; make lively or living. □□ **vivification** /-fikáyshən/ *n.* [F *vivifier* f. LL *vivificare* f. L *vivus* living f. *vivere* live]
■ see ENLIVEN 1.

viviparous /vivípərəs, vī-/ *adj.* **1** *Zool.* bringing forth young alive, not hatching them by means of eggs (cf. OVIPAROUS). **2** *Bot.* producing bulbs or seeds that germinate while still attached to the parent plant. □□ **viviparity** /vívipáriteee/ *n.* **viviparously** *adv.* **viviparousness** *n.* [L *viviparus* f. *vivus*: see VIVIFY]

vivisect /vívisekt/ *v.tr.* perform vivisection on. [back-form. f. VIVISECTION]

vivisection /vívisékshən/ *n.* **1** dissection or other painful treatment of living animals for purposes of scientific research. **2** unduly detailed or ruthless criticism. □□ **vivisectional** *adj.* **vivisectionist** *n.* **vivisector** /-séktər/ *n.* [L *vivus* living (see VIVIFY), after *dissection* (as DISSECT)]

vixen /víksən/ *n.* **1** a female fox. **2** a spiteful or quarrelsome woman. □□ **vixenish** *adj.* **vixenly** *adj.* [ME *fixen* f. OE, fem. of FOX]
■ **2** see SHREW.

viz. /viz, or by substitution náymlee/ *adv.* (usu. introducing a gloss or explanation) namely; that is to say; in other words (*came to a firm conclusion, viz. that we were right*). [abbr. of VIDELICET, *z* being med.L symbol for abbr. of *-et*]
■ see NAMELY.

vizard /vízərd/ *n. archaic* a mask or disguise. [VISOR + -ARD]

vizcacha var. of VISCACHA.

vizier /vizéer, vízièr/ *n. hist.* a high official in some Muslim countries, esp. in Turkey under Ottoman rule. □□ **vizierate** /-rət/ *n.* **vizierial** /vizéereeəl/ *adj.* **viziership** *n.* [ult. f. Arab. *wazīr* caliph's chief counselor]

vizor var. of VISOR.

VJ *abbr. video jockey.*

Vlach /vlaak, vlak/ *n.* & *adj.* ● *n.* a member of a people chiefly inhabiting Romania and Moldova. ● *adj.* of or relating to this people. [Bulg. f. OSlav. *Vlachŭ* Romanian, etc., f. Gmc, = foreigner]

V.M.D. *abbr.* doctor of veterinary medicine. [L *Veterinariae Medicinae Doctor*]

V neck /veenék/ *n.* (often *attrib.*) **1** a neck of a sweater, etc., with straight sides meeting at an angle in the front to form a V. **2** a garment with this.

VO *abbr.* **1** very old (as an indication of a whiskey's or brandy's age). **2** (in the UK) Royal Victorian Order.

voc. *abbr.* **1** vocational. **2** vocative.

vocab. *abbr.* vocabulary.

vocable /vōˈkəbəl/ *n.* a word, esp. with reference to form rather than meaning. [F *vocable* or L *vocabulum* f. *vocare* call]

vocabulary /vōkábyələree/ *n.* (*pl.* **-ies**) **1** the (principal) words used in a language or a particular book or branch of science, etc., or by a particular author (*scientific vocabulary*; *the vocabulary of Shakespeare*). **2** a list of these, arranged alphabetically with definitions or translations. **3** the range of words known to an individual (*his vocabulary is limited*). **4** a set of artistic or stylistic forms or techniques, esp. a range of set movements in ballet, etc. [med.L *vocabularius, -um* (as VOCABLE)]
■ **1** see TERMINOLOGY.

vocal /vōˈkəl/ *adj.* & *n.* ● *adj.* **1** of or concerned with or uttered by the voice (*a vocal communication*). **2** expressing one's feelings freely in speech (*was very vocal about her rights*). **3** *Phonet.* voiced. **4** *poet.* (of trees, water, etc.) endowed with a voice or a similar faculty. **5** (of music) written for or produced by the voice with or without accompaniment (cf. INSTRUMENTAL). ● *n.* **1** (in *sing.* or *pl.*) the sung part of a musical composition. **2** a musical performance with singing. □ **vocal cords** folds of the lining membrane of the larynx near the opening of the glottis, with edges vibrating in the air stream to produce the voice. **vocal score** a musical score showing the voice parts in full. □□ **vocality** /vəkálitee/ *n.* **vocally** *adv.* [ME f. L *vocalis* (as VOICE)]
■ *adj.* **1** see ORAL *adj.*

vocalic /vōkálik/ *adj.* of or consisting of a vowel or vowels.

vocalism /vōˈkəlizəm/ *n.* **1** the use of the voice in speaking or singing. **2** a vowel sound or system.

vocalist /vōˈkəlist/ *n.* a singer, esp. of jazz or popular songs.
■ singer, soloist, choirboy, choir girl, choir member, chorus boy, chorus girl, chorus member, chorister, caroller, songster, minstrel, chorine; diva, prima donna, chanteuse; cantor, crooner.

vocalize /vōˈkəlīz/ *v.* **1** *tr.* **a** form (a sound) or utter (a word) with the voice. **b** make sonant (*f is vocalized into v*). **2** *intr.* utter a vocal sound. **3** *tr.* write (Hebrew, etc.) with vowel points. **4** *intr. Mus.* sing with several notes to one vowel. □□ **vocalization** *n.* **vocalizer** *n.*
■ **1a, 2** see ENUNCIATE 1.

vocation /vōkáyshən/ *n.* **1** a strong feeling of fitness for a particular career or occupation (in religious contexts regarded as a divine call). **2 a** a person's employment, esp. regarded as requiring dedication. **b** a trade or profession. [ME f. OF *vocation* or L *vocatio* f. *vocare* call]
■ **1** call, calling. **2** calling, mission, trade, métier, business, profession, occupation, career, employment, job, pursuit, work, line (of work), *colloq.* thing, *sl.* bag.

vocational /vōkáyshənəl/ *adj.* **1** of or relating to an occupation or employment. **2** (of education or training) directed at a particular occupation and its skills. □□ **vocationalism** *n.* **vocationalize** *v.tr.* **vocationally** *adv.*

vocative /vókətiv/ *n.* & *adj. Gram.* ● *n.* the case of nouns, pronouns, and adjectives used in addressing or invoking a person or thing. ● *adj.* of or in this case. [ME f. OF *vocatif -ive* or L *vocativus* f. *vocare* call]

vociferate /vōsífərayt/ *v.* **1** *tr.* utter (words, etc.) noisily. **2** *intr.* shout; bawl. □□ **vociferance** /-rəns/ *n.* **vociferant** /-rənt/ *adj.* & *n.* **vociferation** /-ráyshən/ *n.* **vociferator** *n.* [L *vociferari* f. *vox* voice + *ferre* bear]
■ see BAWL 1, SHOUT *v.*

vociferous /vōsífərəs/ *adj.* **1** (of a person, speech, etc.) noisy; clamorous. **2** insistently and forcibly expressing one's views. □□ **vociferously** *adv.* **vociferousness** *n.*
■ **1** see OBSTREPEROUS. **2** see INSISTENT 2. □□ **vociferously** see *warmly* (WARM).

vocoder /vōˈkōdər/ *n.* a synthesizer that produces sounds from an analysis of speech input. [VOICE + CODE]

vodka /vódkə/ *n.* an alcoholic spirit made orig. in Russia by distillation of rye, etc. [Russ., dimin. of *voda* water]

vogue /vōg/ *n.* **1** (prec. by *the*) the prevailing fashion. **2** popular use or currency (*has had a great vogue*). □ **in vogue** in fashion, generally current. **vogue word** a word currently fashionable. □□ **voguish** *adj.* [F f. It. *voga* rowing, fashion f. *vogare* row, go well]
■ **1** fashion, mode, style, look, trend, rage, craze, last word, dernier cri, (latest) thing, fad, latest. **2** popularity, favor, preference, acceptance, currency,

prevalence, fashionableness. □ **in vogue** see FASHIONABLE.

voice /voys/ *n. & v.* ● *n.* **1 a** sound formed in the larynx, etc., and uttered by the mouth, esp. human utterance in speaking, shouting, singing, etc. (*heard a voice*; *spoke in a low voice*). **b** the ability to produce this (*has lost her voice*). **2 a** the use of the voice; utterance, esp. in spoken or written words (esp. *give voice*). **b** an opinion so expressed. **c** the right to express an opinion (*I have no voice in the matter*). **d** an agency by which an opinion is expressed. **3** *Gram.* a form or set of forms of a verb showing the relation of the subject to the action (*active voice*; *passive voice*). **4** *Mus.* **a** a vocal part in a composition. **b** a constituent part in a fugue. **5** *Phonet.* sound uttered with resonance of the vocal cords, not with mere breath. **6** (usu. in *pl.*) the supposed utterance of an invisible guiding or directing spirit. ● *v.tr.* **1** give utterance to; express (*the letter voices our opinion*). **2** (esp. as **voiced** *adj.*) *Phonet.* utter with vibration of the vocal cords (e.g., *b, d, g, v, z*). **3** *Mus.* regulate the tone quality of (organ pipes). □ **in voice** (or **good voice**) in proper vocal condition for singing or speaking. **voice box** the larynx. **voice mail** an automatic telephone answering system that records messages from callers. **voice-over** narration in a movie, etc., not accompanied by a picture of the speaker. **voice vote** a vote taken by noting the relative strength of calls of *aye* and *no*. **with one voice** unanimously. □□ **-voiced** *adj.* **voicer** *n.* (in sense 3 of *v.*). [ME f. AF *voiz*, OF *vois* f. L *vox vocis*]

■ *n.* **2 a** speech, utterance, articulation, words, expression. **c** share, part, vote, participation, say, decision, option, turn. **d** spokesman, spokeswoman, spokesperson, representative, agent, agency, instrument; organ, medium, vehicle, forum, publication. ● *v.* **1** express, utter, articulate, enunciate, present, verbalize, put into words, give utterance *or* voice *or* expression *or* tongue *or* vent to, vocalize, communicate, convey, declare, state, assert, make known, reveal, disclose, raise, bring up, air, ventilate. □ **voice-over** see *narration* (NARRATE).

voiceful /vóysfŏŏl/ *adj. poet.* or *rhet.* **1** vocal. **2** sonorous.

voiceless /vóyslis/ *adj.* **1** dumb; mute; speechless. **2** *Phonet.* uttered without vibration of the vocal cords (e.g., *f, k, p, s, t*). □□ **voicelessly** *adv.* **voicelessness** *n.*

■ **1** see DUMB 1, 2.

voiceprint /vóysprint/ *n.* a visual record of speech, analyzed with respect to frequency, duration, and amplitude.

void /voyd/ *adj., n., & v.* ● *adj.* **1 a** empty, vacant. **b** (foll. by *of*) lacking; free from (*a style void of affectation*). **2** esp. *Law* (of a contract, deed, promise, etc.) invalid; not binding (*null and void*). **3** useless; ineffectual. **4** (often foll. by *in*) *Cards* (of a hand) having no cards in a given suit. **5** (of an office) vacant (esp. *fall void*). ● *n.* **1** an empty space; a vacuum (*vanished into the void*; *cannot fill the void made by death*). **2** an unfilled space in a wall or building. **3** (often foll. by *in*) *Cards* the absence of cards in a particular suit. ● *v.tr.* **1** render invalid. **2** (also *absol.*) excrete. □□ **voidable** *adj.* **voidness** *n.* [ME f. OF dial. *voide*, OF *vuide, vuit*, rel. to L *vacare* VACATE: v. partly f. AVOID, partly f. OF *voider*]

■ *adj.* **1 a** empty, vacant, unused, unutilized, blank, clear; bare, deserted. **b** (*void of*) devoid of, without, lacking, free from; destitute of, bereft of. **2** null and void, invalid, not (legally) binding, inoperative, unenforceable. **3** ineffectual, futile, ineffective, vain, unavailing, idle, useless, pointless, *archaic* bootless. **5** vacant, unoccupied, unfilled. ● *n.* **1** emptiness, vacantness, vacuum, blankness, nothingness, voidness, vacuity, hollowness; hole, space, niche, slot, opening, place, vacancy, gap. **2** gap, space, opening. ● *v.* **1** nullify, annul, cancel, delete, declare *or* render null and void, invalidate, quash, abandon, disestablish, neutralize, disenact, set *or* put aside, rescind, reverse, abnegate, abrogate, *Law* vacate, discharge. **2** evacuate, discharge, expel, emit, purge, clear, empty, drain, eject; excrete, urinate, defecate.

voidance /vóyd'ns/ *n.* **1** *Eccl.* a vacancy in a benefice. **2** the act or an instance of voiding; the state of being voided. [ME f. OF (as VOID)]

voided /vóydid/ *adj. Heraldry* (of a bearing) having the central area cut away so as to show the field.

voile /voyl, vwaal/ *n.* a thin, semitransparent dress material of cotton, wool, or silk. [F, = VEIL]

vol. *abbr.* **1** volume. **2** volcano. **3** volunteer.

volant /vólənt/ *adj.* **1** *Zool.* flying; able to fly. **2** *Heraldry* represented as flying. **3** *literary* nimble; rapid. [F f. *voler* f. L *volare* fly]

volar /vólər/ *adj. Anat.* of the palm or sole. [L *vola* hollow of hand or foot]

volatile /vólət'l, -tīl/ *adj. & n.* ● *adj.* **1** evaporating rapidly (*volatile salts*). **2** changeable; fickle. **3** lively; light-hearted. **4** apt to break out into violence. **5** transient. ● *n.* a volatile substance. □ **volatile oil** = *essential oil.* □□ **volatileness** *n.* **volatility** /-tílitee/ *n.* [OF *volatil* or L *volatilis* f. *volare* volat-fly]

■ *adj.* **1** vaporizing, evaporable, evaporative. **2** changeable, fickle, flighty, inconstant, erratic, restless, unstable, variable, mercurial, capricious, unpredictable, temperamental. **4** explosive, hair-trigger, sensitive, charged, eruptive, tense, tension-ridden. **5** see TRANSIENT *adj.* □□ **volatileness, volatility** see *inconstancy* (INCONSTANT).

volatilize /vólət'līz/ *v.* **1** *tr.* cause to evaporate. **2** *intr.* evaporate. □□ **volatilizable** *adj.* **volatilization** *n.*

vol-au-vent /váwlōvoN/ *n.* a (usu. small) round case of puff pastry filled with meat, fish, etc., and sauce. [F, lit. 'flight in the wind']

volcanic /volkánik/ *adj.* (also **vulcanic** /vul-/) of, like, or produced by a volcano. □ **volcanic bomb** a mass of ejected lava usu. rounded and sometimes hollow. **volcanic glass** obsidian. □□ **volcanically** *adv.* **volcanicity** /vólkənísitee/ *n.* [F *volcanique* f. *volcan* VOLCANO]

volcano /volkáynō/ *n.* (*pl.* **-oes**) **1** a mountain or hill having an opening or openings in the earth's crust through which lava, cinders, steam, gases, etc., are or have been expelled continuously or at intervals. **2 a** a state of things likely to cause a violent outburst. **b** a violent esp. suppressed feeling. [It. f. L *Volcanus* Vulcan, Roman god of fire]

volcanology /vólkənólǝjee/ *n.* (also **vulcanology** /vúl-/) the scientific study of volcanoes. □□ **volcanological** /-nǝlójikǝl/ *adj.* **volcanologist** *n.*

vole[1] /vōl/ *n.* any small ratlike or mouselike plant-eating rodent of the family Cricetidae. [orig. *vole-mouse* f. Norw. f. *voll* field + *mus* mouse]

vole[2] /vōl/ *n. archaic* the winning of all tricks at cards. [F f. *voler* fly f. L *volare*]

volet /vólay/ *n.* a panel or wing of a triptych. [F f. *voler* fly f. L *volare*]

volitant /vólit'nt/ *adj. Zool.* volant. [L *volitare* frequent. of *volare* fly]

volition /vǝlíshǝn/ *n.* **1** the exercise of the will. **2** the power of willing. □ **of** (or **by**) **one's own volition** voluntarily. □□ **volitional** *adj.* **volitionally** *adv.* **volitive** /vólitiv/ *adj.* [F *volition* or med.L *volitio* f. *volo* I wish]

■ **1** (free) will, choice, option, choosing, choice, discretion, preference. □ **of** (or **by**) **one's own volition** see *voluntarily* (VOLUNTARY). □□ **volitional** see VOLUNTARY *adj.* 1, 7.

volley /vólee/ *n. & v.* ● *n.* (*pl.* **-eys**) **1 a** the simultaneous discharge of a number of weapons. **b** the bullets, etc., discharged in a volley. **2** (usu. foll. by *of*) a noisy emission of oaths, etc., in quick succession. **3** *Tennis* the return of a ball in play before it touches the ground. **4** *Soccer* the kicking of a ball in play before it touches the ground. ● *v.* (**-eys, -eyed**) **1** *tr.* (also *absol.*) *Tennis & Soccer* return or send (a ball) by a volley. **2** *tr. & absol.* discharge (bullets, abuse, etc.)

/..../ **pronunciation**	● **part of speech**
□ **phrases, idioms, and compounds**	
□□ **derivatives**	■ **synonym section**
cross-references appear in SMALL CAPITALS or *italics*	

in a volley. **3** *intr.* (of bullets, etc.) fly in a volley. **4** *intr.* (of guns, etc.) sound together. **5** *intr.* make a sound like a volley of artillery. □□ **volleyer** *n.* [F *volée* ult. f. L *volare* fly]

■ *n.* **1** salvo, bombardment, barrage, cannonade, fusillade, discharge, hail, shower. **2** outpouring, torrent, flood, deluge, inundation, burst, storm, outbreak. ● *v.* **3** see HAIL¹ *v.* 2.

volleyball /vóleebawl/ *n.* a game for two teams of six hitting a large ball by hand over a net.

volplane /vólplayn/ *n.* & *v.* Aeron. ● *n.* a glide. ● *v.intr.* glide. [F *vol plané* f. *vol* flight + *plané* past part. of *planer* hover, rel. to PLANE¹]

vols. *abbr.* volumes.

volt¹ /vōlt/ *n.* the SI unit of electromotive force, the difference of potential that would carry one ampere of current against one ohm resistance. ¶ Abbr.: V. [A. *Volta*, It. physicist d. 1827]

volt² /vawlt, vōlt/ *n.* & *v.* ● *n.* **1** *Fencing* a quick movement to escape a thrust. **2** a sideways circular movement of a horse. ● *v.intr. Fencing* make a volt. [F f. It. *volta* turn, fem. past part. of *volgere* turn f. L *volvere* roll]

voltage /vóltij/ *n.* electromotive force or potential difference expressed in volts.

voltaic /voltáyik/ *adj. archaic* of electricity from a primary battery; galvanic (*voltaic battery*).

voltameter /vōltámitər/ *n.* an instrument for measuring an electric charge.

volte-face /vawltfaass/ *n.* **1** a complete reversal of position in argument or opinion. **2** the act or an instance of turning around. [F f. It. *voltafaccia*, ult. f. L *volvere* roll + *facies* appearance, face]

■ see *reversal* (REVERSE).

voltmeter /vōltmeetər/ *n.* an instrument for measuring electric potential in volts.

voluble /vólyəbəl/ *adj.* **1** speaking or spoken vehemently, incessantly, or fluently (*voluble spokesman; voluble excuses*). **2** *Bot.* twisting around a support; twining. □□ **volubility** *n.* **volubleness** *n.* **volubly** *adv.* [F *voluble* or L *volubilis* f. *volvere* roll]

■ **1** talkative, glib, fluent, loquacious, garrulous, chatty, profuse, gossipy, exuberant, long-winded, bombastic, windy, wordy, *colloq.* blessed with the gift of gab.

volume /vólyōōm/ *n.* **1 a** a set of sheets of paper, usu. printed, bound together and forming part or the whole of a work or comprising several works (*issued in three volumes; a library of 12,000 volumes*). **b** *hist.* a scroll of papyrus, etc., an ancient form of book. **2 a** solid content; bulk. **b** the space occupied by a gas or liquid. **c** (foll. by *of*) an amount or quantity (*large volume of business*). **3 a** quantity or power of sound. **b** fullness of tone. **4** (foll. by *of*) **a** a moving mass of water, etc. **b** (usu. in *pl.*) a wreath or coil or rounded mass of smoke, etc. □□ **volumed** *adj.* (also in *comb.*). [ME f. OF *volum(e)* f. L *volumen -minis* roll f. *volvere* to roll]

■ **1** book, tome. **2 a** mass, bulk, content. **b** capacity, size, dimensions, measure. **c** amount, quantity, supply, abundance, sum total, aggregate. **3** loudness.

volumetric /vólyōōmétrik/ *adj.* of or relating to measurement by volume. □□ **volumetrically** *adv.* [VOLUME + METRIC]

voluminous /vəlóōminəs/ *adj.* **1** large in volume; bulky. **2** (of drapery, etc.) loose and ample. **3** consisting of many volumes. **4** (of a writer) producing many books. □□ **voluminosity** /-nósitee/ *n.* **voluminously** *adv.* **voluminousness** *n.* [LL *voluminosus* (as VOLUME)]

■ **1** large, extensive, great, spacious, capacious, expansive, roomy, big, bulky, cavernous, oversize(d), outsize, massive, huge, immense, substantial, tremendous, enormous, gigantic, mammoth, vast. **2** ample, billowing, full, loose. **4** copious, prolific, productive.

voluntarism /vóləntərizəm/ *n.* **1** the principle of relying on voluntary action rather than compulsion. **2** *Philos.* the doctrine that the will is a fundamental or dominant factor in the individual or the universe. **3** *hist.* the doctrine that the church or schools should be independent of the government

and supported by voluntary contributions. □□ **voluntarist** *n.* [irreg. f. VOLUNTARY]

voluntary /vólənteree/ *adj.* & *n.* ● *adj.* **1** done, acting, or able to act of one's own free will; not constrained or compulsory; intentional (*a voluntary gift*). **2** unpaid (*voluntary work*). **3** (of an institution) supported by voluntary contributions. **4** *Brit.* (of a school) built by a voluntary institution but maintained by a local education authority. **5** brought about, produced, etc., by voluntary action. **6** (of a movement, muscle, or limb) controlled by the will. **7** (of a confession by a criminal) not prompted by a promise or threat. **8** *Law* (of a conveyance or disposition) made without return in money or other consideration. ● *n.* (*pl.* **-ies**) **1 a** an organ solo played before, during, or after a church service. **b** the music for this. **c** *archaic* an extempore performance esp. as a prelude to other music. **2** (in competitions) a special performance left to the performer's choice. **3** *hist.* a person who holds that the church or schools should be independent of the government and supported by voluntary contributions. □□ **voluntarily** *adv.* **voluntariness** *n.* [ME f. OF *voluntaire* or L *voluntarius* f. *voluntas* will]

■ *adj.* **1** free, elective, willing, spontaneous, unsolicited, unbidden, unasked, unprompted. **2** see UNPAID. **7** discretionary, discretional, unconstrained, intentional, willful, deliberate, conscious, intended, premeditated, planned, volitional, optional. □□ **voluntarily** freely, willingly, spontaneously, of *or* by one's own volition, of one's own accord *or* free will, on one's own (initiative *or* recognizance *or* responsibility), without prompting, without being prompted *or* asked, gratis, gratuitously; by choice, intentionally, purposely, on purpose, deliberately.

voluntaryism /vóləntereeizəm/ *n. hist.* = VOLUNTARISM 1, 3. □□ **voluntaryist** *n.*

volunteer /vólənteer/ *n.* & *v.* ● *n.* **1** a person who voluntarily undertakes a task or enters military or other service. **2** (usu. *attrib.*) a self-sown plant. ● *v.* **1** *tr.* (often foll. by *to* + infin.) undertake or offer (one's services, a remark or explanation, etc.) voluntarily. **2** *intr.* (often foll. by *for*) make a voluntary offer of one's services; be a volunteer. [F *volontaire* (as VOLUNTARY), assim. to -EER]

■ *v.* see OFFER *v.* 2, ENROLL 1.

voluptuary /vəlúpchōōeree/ *n.* & *adj.* ● *n.* (*pl.* **-ies**) a person given up to luxury and sensual pleasure. ● *adj.* concerned with luxury and sensual pleasure. [L *volupt(u)arius* (as VOLUPTUOUS)]

voluptuous /vəlúpchōōəs/ *adj.* **1** of, tending to, occupied with, or derived from, sensuous or sensual pleasure. **2** full of sexual promise, esp. through shapeliness or fullness. □□ **voluptuously** *adv.* **voluptuousness** *n.* [ME f. OF *voluptueux* or L *voluptuosus* f. *voluptas* pleasure]

■ **1** sensual, sensualistic, sensuous, luxurious, voluptuary, sybaritic(al), hedonist(ic), pleasure-seeking, pleasure-loving, luxury-loving, (self-)indulgent. **2** seductive, erotic, sexy, attractive, desirable, beautiful, tempting, inviting, appealing, enticing, alluring, ravishing, luscious, ripe, delicious, gorgeous; shapely, buxom, busty, well-proportioned, well-built, *colloq.* well-endowed, curvaceous. □□ **voluptuousness** see LUXURY 1.

volute /vəlōōt/ *n.* & *adj.* ● *n.* **1** *Archit.* a spiral scroll characteristic of Ionic capitals and also used in Corinthian and composite capitals. **2 a** any marine gastropod mollusk of the genus *Voluta.* **b** the spiral shell of this. ● *adj.* esp. *Bot.* rolled up. □□ **voluted** *adj.* [F *volute* or L *voluta* fem. past part. of *volvere* roll]

volution /vəlōōshən/ *n.* **1** a rolling motion. **2** a spiral turn. **3** a whorl of a spiral shell. **4** *Anat.* a convolution. [as VOLUTE, after REVOLUTION]

vomer /vómər/ *n. Anat.* the small thin bone separating the nostrils in humans and most vertebrates. [L, = plowshare]

vomit /vómit/ *v.* & *n.* ● *v.tr.* **1** (also *absol.*) eject (matter) from the stomach through the mouth. **2** (of a volcano, chimney, etc.) eject violently; belch (forth). ● *n.* **1** matter vomited from the stomach. **2** *archaic* an emetic. □□ **vomiter** *n.* [ME ult. f. L *vomere vomit-* or frequent. L *vomitare*]

■ *v.* **1** spew, bring up; regurgitate, gag, retch, heave, *colloq.* throw up, return (food), *Brit. colloq.* sick up, *sl.* puke, upchuck, barf, *Austral. sl.* chunder,. **2** eject, spew out *or* up, spit up, belch forth. ● *n.* **1** puke, *colloq.* throw-up, *Brit. colloq.* sick, *Austral. sl.* chunder.

vomitorium /vómitáwreeəm/ *n.* (*pl.* **vomitoria** /-reeə/) *Rom. Antiq.* a vomitory. [L; see VOMITORY]

vomitory /vómitawree/ *adj.* & *n.* ● *adj.* emetic. ● *n.* (*pl.* **-ies**) *Rom. Antiq.* each of a series of passages for entrance and exit in an amphitheater or theater. [L *vomitorius* (adj.), *-um* (n.) (as VOMIT)]

V-1 /veéwún/ *n. hist.* a type of German flying bomb used in World War II, esp. against England. [abbr. of G *Vergeltungswaffe* reprisal weapon]

voodoo /voõdoõ/ *n.* & *v.* ● *n.* **1** use of or belief in religious witchcraft, esp. as practiced in the W. Indies. **2** a person skilled in this. **3** a voodoo spell. ● *v.tr.* (**voodoos, voodooed**) affect by voodoo; bewitch. □□ **voodooism** *n.* **voodooist** *n.* [Dahomey *vodu*]

voracious /vawráyshəs, və-/ *adj.* **1** greedy in eating; ravenous. **2** very eager in some activity (*a voracious reader*). □□ **voraciously** *adv.* **voraciousness** *n.* **voracity** /vərásitee/ *n.* [L *vorax* f. *vorare* devour]

■ **1** insatiable, gluttonous, ravenous, ravening, rapacious, piggish, hoggish, predacious, devouring, greedy, avaricious, uncontrollable, uncontrolled, unquenchable, enormous, prodigious, *archaic or joc.* esurient, *literary or joc.* edacious. **2** thirsty, hungry, desirous, avid, eager, zealous, enthusiastic, fervent, fervid, ardent, earnest, passionate, devoted.

-vorous /vərəs/ *comb. form* forming adjectives meaning 'feeding on' (*carnivorous*). □□ **-vora** /vərə/ *comb. form* forming names of groups. **-vore** /vawr/ *comb. form* forming names of individuals. [L *-vorus* f. *vorare* devour]

vortex /váwrteks/ *n.* (*pl.* **vortices** /-tiseez or **vortexes**/) **1** a mass of whirling fluid, esp. a whirlpool or whirlwind. **2** any whirling motion or mass. **3** a system, occupation, pursuit, etc., viewed as swallowing up or engrossing those who approach it (*the vortex of society*). **4** *Physics* a portion of fluid whose particles have rotatory motion. □ **vortex ring** a vortex whose axis is a closed curve, e.g., a smoke ring. □□ **vortical** /-tikəl/ *adj.* **vortically** *adv.* **vorticity** /vortísitee/ *n.* **vorticose** /-tikós/ *adj.* **vorticular** /vawrtíkyələr/ *adj.* [L *vortex -icis* eddy, var. of VERTEX]

■ **1-3** see EDDY *n.*

vorticella /váwrtisélə/ *n.* any sedentary protozoan of the family Vorticellidae, consisting of a tubular stalk with a bell-shaped ciliated opening. [mod.L, dimin. of VORTEX]

vorticist /váwrtisist/ *n.* **1** *Art* a painter, writer, etc., of a school influenced by futurism and using the 'vortices' of modern civilization as a basis. **2** *Metaphysics* a person regarding the universe, with Descartes, as a plenum in which motion propagates itself in circles. □□ **vorticism** *n.*

votary /vótəree/ *n.* (*pl.* **-ies**; *fem.* **votaress**) (usu. foll. by *of*) **1** a person vowed to the service of God or a god or cult. **2** a devoted follower, adherent, or advocate of a person, system, occupation, etc. □□ **votarist** *n.* [L *vot-*: see VOTE]

vote /vót/ *n.* & *v.* ● *n.* **1** a formal expression of choice or opinion by means of a ballot, show of hands, etc., concerning a choice of candidate, approval of a motion or resolution, etc. (*let us take a vote on it*; *gave my vote to the independent candidate*). **2** (usu. prec. by *the*) the right to vote, esp. in a government election. **3** **a** an opinion expressed by a majority of votes. **b** *Brit.* money granted by a majority of votes. **4** the collective votes that are or may be given by or for a particular group (*will lose the Southern vote*; *the Conservative vote increased*). **5** a ticket, etc., used for recording a vote. ● *v.* **1** *intr.* (often foll. by *for*, *against*, or *to* + infin.) give a vote. **2** *tr.* **a** (often foll. by *that* + clause) enact or resolve by a majority of votes. **b** grant (a sum of money) by a majority of votes. **c** cause to be in a specified position by a majority of votes (*was voted off the committee*). **3** *tr. colloq.* pronounce or declare by general consent (*was voted a fail-*

ure). **4** *tr.* (often foll. by *that* + clause) *colloq.* announce one's proposal (*I vote that we all go home*). **5** *tr.* cast a ballot in accordance with (*vote your conscience*). □ **put to a** (or **the**) **vote** submit to a decision by voting. **vote down** defeat (a proposal, etc.) in a vote. **vote in** elect by votes. **vote of censure** = *vote of no confidence*. **vote of confidence** (or **no confidence**) a vote showing that the majority support (or do not support) the policy of the governing body, etc. **vote with one's feet** *colloq.* indicate an opinion by one's presence or absence. **voting machine** a machine for the automatic registering of votes. **voting stock** stock entitling the holder to a vote. □□ **votable** *adj.* **voteless** *adj.* [ME f. past part. stem *vot-* of L *vovēre* vow]

■ *n.* **1** ballot, election, poll, show of hands, referendum, plebiscite. **2** suffrage, franchise, right to vote; voice, say. **3** **a** opinion, preference, selection, choice. **4** voter(s), elector(s). **5** voting ballot, or *Brit.* ticket card *or* slip *or* paper. ● *v.* **1** cast one's vote, ballot, express *or* signify one's opinion, express *or* signify one's preference, express *or* signify one's desire; (*vote for*) choose, elect, select, pick, opt for, plump for, settle on, come out for, return; (*vote against*) come out against, veto, reject. **2 a** resolve, decide, pass, enact. **3** declare, pronounce, proclaim.

voter /vótər/ *n.* **1** a person with the right to vote at an election. **2** a person voting.

votive /vótiv/ *adj.* offered or consecrated in fulfillment of a vow (*votive offering*; *votive picture*). □ **votive Mass** *Eccl.* a Mass celebrated for a special purpose or occasion. [L *votivus* (as VOTE)]

vouch /vowch/ *v.* **1** *intr.* (foll. by *for*) answer for; be surety for (*will vouch for the truth of this*; *can vouch for him*; *could not vouch for his honesty*). **2** *tr. archaic* cite as an authority. **3** *tr. archaic* confirm or uphold (a statement) by evidence or assertion. [ME f. OF *vo(u)cher* summon, etc., ult. f. L *vocare* call]

■ **1** (*vouch for*) support, guarantee, be surety for, answer for, back (up), endorse, certify; uphold, sponsor, bear witness to, attest to.

voucher /vówchər/ *n.* **1** a document which can be exchanged for goods or services as a token of payment made or promised by the holder or another. **2** a document establishing the payment of money or the truth of accounts. **3** a person who vouches for a person, statement, etc. [AF *voucher* (as VOUCH) or f. VOUCH]

■ **1, 2** token, coupon; see also CHECK[1] *n.* 5.

vouchsafe /vówchsáyf/ *v.tr. formal* **1** condescend to give or grant (*vouchsafed me no answer*). **2** (foll. by *to* + infin.) condescend. [ME f. VOUCH in sense 'warrant' + SAFE]

■ **1** offer, give (up), yield, accord, supply, grant, impart, bestow, condescend to give, permit, allow, *archaic* deign to give, suffer. **2** see GRANT *v.* 1b.

voussoir /voõswaár/ *n.* each of the wedge-shaped or tapered stones forming an arch. [OF *vossoir*, etc. f. pop.L *volsorium* ult. f. L *volvere* roll]

vow /vow/ *n.* & *v.* ● *n.* **1** *Relig.* a solemn promise, esp. in the form of an oath to God or another deity or to a saint. **2** (in *pl.*) the promises by which a monk or nun is bound to poverty, chastity, and obedience. **3** a promise of fidelity (*lovers' vows*; *marriage vows*). **4** (usu. as **baptismal vows**) the promises given at baptism by the baptized person or by sponsors. ● *v.tr.* **1** promise solemnly (*vowed obedience*). **2** dedicate to a deity. **3** (also *absol.*) *archaic* declare solemnly. □ **under a vow** having made a vow. [ME f. AF *v(o)u*, OF *vo(u)*, f. L (as VOTE): (v.) f. OF *vouer*, in sense 2 partly f. AVOW]

■ *n.* oath, pledge, promise, agreement; (solemn) word (of honor). ● *v.* **1** swear, pledge, promise, assure,

---

/.../ **pronunciation**	● **part of speech**
□ **phrases, idioms, and compounds**	
□□ **derivatives**	■ **synonym section**
cross-references appear in SMALL CAPITALS or *italics*	

state, declare, give (one's) (solemn) word (of honor), *archaic* plight one's troth.

vowel /vówəl/ *n.* **1** a speech sound made with vibration of the vocal cords but without audible friction, more open than a consonant and capable of forming a syllable. **2** a letter or letters representing this, as *a, e, i, o, u, aw, ah.* □ **vowel gradation** = ABLAUT. **vowel mutation** = UMLAUT 2. **vowel point** each of a set of marks indicating vowels in Hebrew, etc. □□ **voweled** *adj.* (also in *comb.*). **vowelless** *adj.* **vowely** or **vowelly** *adv.* [ME f. OF *vouel, voiel* f. L *vocalis* (*littera*) VOCAL (letter)]

vowelize /vówəlīz/ *v.tr.* insert the vowels in (shorthand, Hebrew, etc.).

vox angelica /vóks anjélikə/ *n.* an organ stop with a soft tremulous tone. [LL, = angelic voice]

vox humana /vóks hyōōmáynə-, -máanə, -mánə/ *n.* an organ stop with a tone supposed to resemble a human voice. [L, = human voice]

vox pop /vóks póp/ *n. esp. Brit. Broadcasting colloq.* popular opinion as represented by informal comments from members of the public; statements or interviews of this kind. [abbr. of VOX POPULI]

vox populi /vóks pópyəlee, -lī/ *n.* public opinion, the general verdict, popular belief or rumor. [L, = the people's voice]

voyage /vóyij/ *n. & v.* ● *n.* **1** a journey, esp. a long one by water, air, or in space. **2** an account of this. ● *v.* **1** *intr.* make a voyage. **2** *tr.* traverse, esp. by water or air. □□ **voyageable** *adj.* **voyager** *n.* [ME f. AF & OF *veiage, voiage* f. L *viaticum*]

■ *n.* **1** see JOURNEY *n.* ● *v.* **1** see JOURNEY *v.* **2** see TRAVERSE *v.* **1.** □□ **voyager** see TRAVELER 1.

voyageur /vwaáyaazhŏr/ *n.* a Canadian boatman, esp. *hist.* one employed in transporting goods and passengers between trading posts. [F, = voyager (as VOYAGE)]

voyeur /vwaayŏr/ *n.* a person who obtains sexual gratification from observing others' sexual actions or organs. □□ **voyeurism** *n.* **voyeuristic** /-rístik/ *adj.* **voyeuristically** /-rístikəlee/ *adj.* [F f. *voir* see]

VP *abbr.* **1** vice president. **2** variable pitch. **3** verb phrase.

VR *abbr.* **1** Queen Victoria. **2** voltage regulator. [sense 1 f. L *Victoria Regina*]

VS *abbr.* veterinary surgeon.

vs. *abbr.* **1** versus. **2** verse.

V sign /vee sín/ *n.* **1** a sign of the letter V made with the first two fingers pointing up and the palm of the hand facing outward, as a symbol of victory. **2** *Brit.* a similar sign made with the back of the hand facing outward as a gesture of abuse, contempt, etc.

VSOP *abbr.* very special old pale (brandy).

VT *abbr.* Vermont (in official postal use).

Vt. *abbr.* Vermont.

VTO *abbr.* vertical takeoff.

VTOL /veétol/ *abbr.* vertical takeoff and landing.

V-2 /veétōō/ *n.* a type of German rocket-powered missile used in late World War II, esp. against England. [abbr. of G *Vergeltungswaffe* reprisal weapon]

vug /vug/ *n.* a rock cavity lined with crystals. □□ **vuggy** *adj.* **vugular** *adj.* [Corn. *vooga*]

vulcanic var. of VOLCANIC.

vulcanite /vúlkənīt/ *n.* a hard, black, vulcanized rubber, ebonite. [as VULCANIZE]

vulcanize /vúlkənīz/ *v.tr.* treat (rubber or rubberlike material) with sulfur, etc., esp. at a high temperature to increase its strength. □□ **vulcanizable** *adj.* **vulcanization** *n.* **vulcanizer** *n.* [*Vulcan*, Roman god of fire and metal-working]

vulcanology var. of VOLCANOLOGY.

Vulg. *abbr.* Vulgate.

vulgar /vúlgər/ *adj.* **1 a** of or characteristic of the common people; plebeian. **b** coarse in manners; low (*vulgar expres-*

sions; vulgar tastes). **2** in common use; generally prevalent (*vulgar errors*). □ **vulgar fraction** *Brit.* = *common fraction.* **Vulgar Latin** informal Latin of classical times. **the vulgar tongue** esp. *Brit.* the national or vernacular language, esp. formerly as opposed to Latin. □□ **vulgarly** *adv.* [ME f. L *vulgaris* f. *vulgus* common people]

■ **1 a** common, plebeian, uncultured, uncultivated, unrefined, low, lowbrow, low-class. **b** indelicate, boorish, inelegant, unladylike, ungentlemanly, gauche, uncouth, ill-bred, ill-mannered, uncivilized, barbarian, coarse, tasteless, ostentatious, ignoble; indecent, rude, crude, naughty, dirty, improper, impolite, off color, risqué, ribald, blue, low, indecorous, nasty, offensive, gross, lustful, obscene, lewd, lascivious, licentious, smutty, salacious, scatological, filthy, pornographic, *colloq.* tarty, flash, raunchy. **2** popular, vernacular, ordinary, everyday, general, homespun, common, commonplace, household, average.

vulgarian /vulgáireeən/ *n.* a vulgar (esp. rich) person.

vulgarism /vúlgərizəm/ *n.* **1** a word or expression in coarse or uneducated use. **2** an instance of coarse or uneducated behavior.

vulgarity /vulgáritee/ *n.* (*pl.* **-ies**) **1** the quality of being vulgar. **2** an instance of this.

■ **1** coarseness, lack of refinement *or* sophistication, crudeness, rudeness, indelicacy, tawdriness, baseness, unsophistication, gaucherie, gaucheness, ignobility; impropriety, ribaldry, lewdness, grossness, foulness, vileness, filthiness, obscenity, *colloq.* raunchiness.

vulgarize /vúlgərīz/ *v.tr.* **1** make (a person, manners, etc.) vulgar; infect with vulgarity. **2** spoil (a scene, sentiment, etc.) by making it too common, frequented, or well known. **3** popularize. □□ **vulgarization** *n.*

■ **1** see VITIATE 1.

Vulgate /vúlgayt, -gət/ *n.* **1 a** the Latin version of the Bible prepared mainly by St. Jerome in the late fourth century. **b** the official Roman Catholic Latin text as revised in 1592. **2** (**vulgate**) the traditionally accepted text of any author. **3** (**vulgate**) common or colloquial speech. [L *vulgata* (*editio* edition), fem. past part. of *vulgare* make public f. *vulgus*: see VULGAR]

vulnerable /vúlnərəbəl/ *adj.* **1** that may be wounded or harmed. **2** (foll. by *to*) exposed to damage by a weapon, criticism, etc. **3** *Bridge* having won one game toward rubber and therefore liable to higher penalties. □□ **vulnerability** *n.* **vulnerableness** *n.* **vulnerably** *adv.* [LL *vulnerabilis* f. L *vulnerare* to wound f. *vulnus -eris* wound]

■ **1** exposed, defenseless, weak, sensitive, unprotected, unguarded, unshielded, helpless, powerless, insecure. **2** (*vulnerable to*) see SUSCEPTIBLE 2a. □□ **vulnerability**, **vulnerableness** see FRAILTY 1, 2.

vulnerary /vúlnəreree/ *adj. & n.* ● *adj.* useful or used for the healing of wounds. ● *n.* (*pl.* **-ies**) a vulnerary drug, plant, etc. [L *vulnerarius* f. *vulnus*: see VULNERABLE]

vulpine /vúlpīn/ *adj.* **1** of or like a fox. **2** crafty; cunning. [L *vulpinus* f. *vulpes* fox]

vulture /vúlchər/ *n.* **1** any of various large birds of prey of the family Cathartidae or Accipitridae, with the head and neck more or less bare of feathers, feeding chiefly on carrion and reputed to gather with others in anticipation of a death. **2** a rapacious person. □□ **vulturine** /-rīn/ *adj.* **vulturish** *adj.* **vulturous** *adj.* [ME f. AF *vultur*, OF *voltour*, etc., f. L *vulturius*]

vulva /vúlvə/ *n.* (*pl.* **vulvas**) *Anat.* the external female genitals, esp. the external opening of the vagina. □□ **vulvar** *adj.* **vulvitis** /-vítis/ *n.* [L, = womb]

vv. *abbr.* **1** verses. **2** volumes. **3** violins.

vying *pres. part.* of VIE.

W¹ /dúbəlyōō/ *n.* (also **w**) (*pl.* **Ws** or **W's**) the twenty-third letter of the alphabet.

W² *abbr.* (also **W.**) **1** watt(s). **2** West; Western. **3** women's (size). **4** Welsh.

W³ *symb. Chem.* the element tungsten.

w. *abbr.* **1** warden. **2** wide(s). **3** with. **4** wife. **5** watt(s).

WA *abbr.* **1** Washington (state) (in official postal use). **2** Western Australia.

WAAC /wak/ *n. hist.* a member of the Women's Army Auxiliary Corps (*US* 1942–48 or *Brit.* 1917–19). [initials *WAAC*]

Wac /wak/ *n.* a member of the US Army's Women's Army Corps.

wack¹ /wak/ *n. sl.* a crazy person. [prob. back-form. f. WACKY]

wack² /wak/ *n. Brit. dial.* a familiar term of address. [perh. f. *wacker* Liverpudlian]

wacke /wákə/ *n. hist.* a grayish-green or brownish rock resulting from the decomposition of basaltic rock. [G f. MHG *wacke* large stone, OHG *wacko* pebble]

wacko /wákō/ *adj. & n.* (also **whacko**) *sl.* ● *adj.* crazy. ● *n.* (*pl.* **-os** or **-oes**) a crazy person. [WACKY + -o]

wacky /wákee/ *adj. & n.* (also **whacky**) *sl.* ● *adj.* (**-ier, -iest**) crazy. ● *n.* (*pl.* **-ies**) a crazy person. □□ **wackily** *adv.* **wackiness** *n.* [orig. dial., = left-handed, f. WHACK]

  ■ *adj.* see CRAZY 1.

wad /wod/ *n. & v.* ● *n.* **1** a lump or bundle of soft material used esp. to keep things apart or in place or to stuff up an opening. **2** a disk of felt, etc., keeping powder or shot in place in a gun. **3** a number of bills of currency or documents placed together. **4** *Brit. sl.* a bun, sandwich, etc. **5** (in *sing.* or *pl.*) a large quantity, esp. of money. ● *v.tr.* (**wadded, wadding**) **1** stop up (an aperture or a gun barrel) with a wad. **2** keep (powder, etc.) in place with a wad. **3** line or stuff (a garment or quilt, etc.) with wadding. **4** protect (a person, walls, etc.) with wadding. **5** press (cotton, etc.) into a wad or wadding. [perh. rel. to Du. *watten*, F *ouate* padding, cotton wool]

  ■ *n.* **1** pad, mass, lump, clod, ball, plug, chunk, hunk, block, pack, *Brit. colloq.* wodge. **3** roll, bundle, pocketful, heap, quantity, load, bankroll. **5** see MINT² *n.* 2 . ● *v.* **1** see STOP *v.* 7. **3** see PAD *v.* 1.

wadding /wóding/ *n.* **1** soft, pliable material of cotton or wool, etc., used to line or stuff garments, quilts, etc., or to pack fragile articles. **2** any material from which gun wads are made.

  ■ **1** padding, filling, stuffing.

waddle /wód'l/ *v. & n.* ● *v.intr.* walk with short steps and a swaying motion, like a stout, short-legged person or a bird with short legs set far apart (e.g., a duck or goose). ● *n.* a waddling gait. □□ **waddler** *n.* [perh. frequent. of WADE]

  ■ *v.* toddle, shuffle, wobble, totter, pad, duckwalk, *colloq.* waggle.

waddy /wódee/ *n.* (*pl.* **-ies**) **1** an Australian Aboriginal war club. **2** *Austral. & NZ* any club or stick. [Aboriginal, perh. f. WOOD]

wade /wayd/ *v. & n.* ● *v.* **1** *intr.* walk through water or some impeding medium, e.g., snow, mud, or sand. **2** *intr.* make one's way with difficulty or by force. **3** *intr.* (foll. by *through*) read (a book, etc.) in spite of its dullness, etc. **4** *intr.* (foll. by *into*) *colloq.* attack (a person or task) vigorously. **5** *tr.* ford (a stream, etc.) on foot. ● *n.* a spell of wading. □ **wade in** *colloq.* make a vigorous attack or intervention. **wading bird** any long-legged waterbird that wades. □□ **wadable** *adj.* (also **wadeable**). [OE *wadan* f. Gmc, = go (through)]

  ■ *v.* **1** paddle, splash, plod, trudge, squelch. **2** make one's way, trek, trudge, plow. **3** (*wade through*) plow through, work one's way through, plod through, hammer *or* pound away at, peg away at. **4** (*wade into*) attack, approach, get *or* set to work on, plunge *or* dive into, *Brit. sl.* get stuck into; lunge at. **5** ford, cross, traverse, walk across, make one's way across. □ **wade in** enter, get in, join in, attack, get *or* set to work, plunge in, dive in, *Brit. sl.* get stuck in.

wader /wáydər/ *n.* **1 a** a person who wades. **b** a wading bird, esp. any of various birds of the order Charadriiformes. **2** (in *pl.*) high waterproof boots, or a waterproof garment for the legs and body, worn in fishing, etc.

wadi /waádee/ *n.* (also **wady**) (*pl.* **wadis** or **wadies**) a rocky watercourse in N. Africa, etc., dry except in the rainy season. [Arab. *wādī*]

Waf /waf/ *n.* (in the US) a member of the Women in the Air Force.

wafer /wáyfər/ *n. & v.* ● *n.* **1** a very thin, light, crisp sweet cake, cookie, or biscuit. **2** a thin disk of unleavened bread used in the Eucharist. **3** *Brit.* a disk of red paper stuck on a legal document instead of a seal. **4** *Electronics* a very thin slice of a semiconductor crystal used as the substrate for solid-state circuitry. **5** *hist.* a small disk of dried paste formerly used for fastening letters, holding papers together, etc. ● *v.tr.* fasten or seal with a wafer. □ **wafer-thin** very thin. □□ **wafery** *adj.* [ME f. AF *wafre*, ONF *waufre*, OF *gaufre* (cf. GOFFER) f. MLG *wāfel* waffle: cf. WAFFLE²]

waffle¹ /wófəl/ *n. & v. colloq.* ● *n.* verbose but aimless, misleading, or ignorant talk or writing. ● *v.intr.* indulge in waffle. □□ **waffler** *n.* **waffly** *adj.* [orig. dial., frequent. of *waff* = yelp, yap (imit.)]

  ■ *n.* talk, palaver, verbiage, prattle, twaddle, blather, prolixity, wordiness, jabber, prevarication, evasiveness, *sl.* hot air. ● *v.* carry on, jabber (on), prattle (on), prate, blather (on *or* away), run on; equivocate, hedge, quibble, shuffle, tergiversate, hem and haw, prevaricate, beat around *or* about the bush; *colloq.* weasel, natter (on).

waffle² /wófəl/ *n.* a small, crisp batter cake with an indented lattice pattern. □ **waffle iron** a utensil, usu. of two shallow metal pans hinged together, for cooking waffles. [Du. *wafel*, *waefel* f. MLG *wāfel*: cf. WAFER]

waft /woft, waft/ *v. & n.* ● *v.tr. & intr.* convey or travel easily as through air or over water; sweep smoothly and lightly along. ● *n.* **1** (usu. foll. by *of*) a whiff or scent. **2** a transient sensation of peace, joy, etc. **3** (also **waif** /wayf/) *Naut.* a distress signal, e.g., an ensign rolled or knotted or a garment flown in the rigging. [orig. 'convoy (ship, etc.),' back-form.]

/.../ **pronunciation**	● **part of speech**
□ **phrases, idioms, and compounds**	
□□ **derivatives**	■ **synonym section**
cross-references appear in SMALL CAPITALS or *italics*	

f. obs. *waughter, wafter* armed convoy ship, f. Du. or LG *wachter* f. *wachten* to guard]

■ *v.* drift, float, blow, whiff, be borne *or* carried *or* conveyed *or* transported. ● *n.* **1** breath, suggestion, puff, whiff, scent, hint.

wag[1] /wag/ *v.* & *n.* ● *v.* (**wagged, wagging**) **1** *tr.* & *intr.* shake or wave rapidly or energetically to and fro. **2** *intr. archaic* (of the world, times, etc.) go along with varied fortune or characteristics. ● *n.* a single wagging motion (*with a wag of his tail*). □ **the tail wags the dog** the less or least important member of a society, section of a party, or part of a structure has control. **tongues** (or **beards** or **chins** or **jaws**) **wag** there is talk. [ME *waggen* f. root of OE *wagian* sway]

■ *v.* **1** wave, oscillate, fluctuate, sway, undulate, flutter, flap, flip, flicker, shake, vibrate, quiver, wiggle, nod, rock, dance, wobble, bob, waver, *colloq.* waggle. ● *n.* wave, oscillation, fluctuation, sway, undulation, flutter, flap, flip, flicker, shake, vibration, quiver, wiggle, nod, wobble, waver, *colloq.* waggle.

wag[2] /wag/ *n.* **1** a facetious person; a joker. **2** *Brit. sl.* a truant (*play the wag*). [prob. f. obs. *waghalter* one likely to be hanged (as WAG[1], HALTER)]

■ **1** comedian, wit, punster, pundit, joker, jester, comic, jokester, droll, merry-andrew, clown, *colloq.* card. **2** truant, absentee.

wage /wayj/ *n.* & *v.* ● *n.* **1** (in *sing.* or *pl.*) a fixed regular payment, usu. daily or weekly, made by an employer to an employee, esp. to a manual or unskilled worker (cf. SALARY). **2** (in *sing.* or *pl.*) requital (*the wages of sin is death*). **3** (in *pl.*) *Econ.* the part of total production that rewards labor rather than remunerating capital. ● *v.tr.* carry on (a war, conflict, or contest). □ **living wage** a wage that affords the means of normal subsistence. **wage earner** a person who works for wages. **wage slave** a person dependent on income from labor in conditions like slavery. [ME f. AF & ONF *wage*, OF *g(u)age*, f. Gmc, rel. to GAGE[1], WED]

■ *n.* **1** pay, compensation, emolument, remuneration, payment, fee, salary, stipend, recompense, reward, earnings, income; honorarium. **2** requital, return, reward, recompense. ● *v.* carry on, pursue, conduct, engage in, practice, prosecute with.

wager /wáyjər/ *n.* & *v.tr.* & *intr.* = BET. □ **wager of battle** *hist.* an ancient form of trial by personal combat between the parties or their champions. **wager of law** *hist.* a form of trial in which the defendant was required to produce witnesses who would swear to his or her innocence. [ME f. AF *wageure* f. *wager* (as WAGE)]

waggery /wágəree/ *n.* (*pl.* **-ies**) **1** waggish behavior, joking. **2** a waggish action or remark; a joke.

waggish /wágish/ *adj.* playful; facetious. □□ **waggishly** *adv.* **waggishness** *n.*

■ see COMIC *adj.* □□ **waggishness** see HUMOR *n.* 1a.

waggle /wágəl/ *v.* & *n. colloq.* ● *v.* **1** *intr.* & *tr.* wag. **2** *intr. Golf* swing the club head to and fro over the ball before playing a shot. ● *n.* a waggling motion. [WAG[1] + -LE[4]]

■ *v.* **1** see WAG[1] *v.* ● *n.* see WAG[1] *n.*

waggly /wáglee/ *adj.* unsteady.

Wagnerian /vaagneéreeən/ *adj.* & *n.* ● *adj.* of, relating to, or characteristic of the music dramas of Richard Wagner, German composer d. 1883, esp. with reference to their large scale. ● *n.* an admirer of Wagner or his music.

wagon /wágən/ *n.* (also *Brit.* **wagon**) **1 a** a four-wheeled vehicle for heavy loads, often with a removable tilt or cover. **b** a truck. **2** *Brit.* a railroad vehicle for goods, esp. a flatcar. **3** *Brit.* a cart for conveying tea, etc. **4** (in full **water wagon**) a vehicle for carrying water. **5** a light horse-drawn vehicle. **6** *colloq.* an automobile, esp. a station wagon. □ **on the wagon** (or *Brit.* **water wagon**) *sl.* teetotal. **wagon roof** (or **vault**) = *barrel vault.* [earlier *wagon, wag(h)en*, f. Du. *wag(h)en*, rel. to OE *wægn* WAIN]

wagoner /wágənər/ *n.* (also *Brit.* **waggoner**) the driver of a wagon. [Du. *wagenaar* (as WAGON)]

wagonette /wágənét/ *n.* (also *Brit.* **waggonette**) a four-

wheeled, horse-drawn pleasure vehicle, usu. open, with facing side seats.

wagon-lit /vágawnleé/ *n.* (*pl.* **wagons-lits** *pronunc.* same) a railroad sleeping car, esp. in continental Europe. [F]

wagtail /wágtayl/ *n.* any small bird of the genus *Motacilla* with a long tail in frequent motion.

Wahhabi /wəhaábee/ *n.* (also **Wahabi**) (*pl.* **-is**) a member of a sect of Muslim puritans following strictly the original words of the Koran. [Muhammad ibn Abd-el-*Wahhab*, founder in the 18th c.]

wahine /waaheénee/ *n.* **1** (in Polynesia and Hawaii) a woman or wife. **2** *sl.* a female surfer. [Maori]

wahoo[1] /wóhoō, wáw-/ *n.* any of several N. American shrubs or trees, as *Ulmus alata*, an elm tree.

wahoo[2] /wóhoō, wáw-/ *n.* a shrubby N. American tree, *Euonymus atropurpurea.*

wahoo[3] /wóhoō, wáw-/ *n.* a large mackerel, *Acanthocybium solanderi*, found in warm seas.

wahoo[4] /wóhoō, wáw-/ *int.* & *n.* an expression of exhilaration or enthusiasm.

wahwah var. of WA-WA.

waif /wayf/ *n.* **1** a homeless and helpless person, esp. an abandoned child. **2** an ownerless object or animal; a thing cast up by or drifting in the sea or brought by an unknown agency. **3** var. of WAFT *n.* 3. □ **waifs and strays** *Brit.* **1** homeless or neglected children. **2** odds and ends. □□ **waifish** *adj.* [ME f. AF *waif, weif*, ONF *gaif*, prob. of Scand. orig.]

■ see FOUNDLING.

wail /wayl/ *n.* & *v.* ● *n.* **1** a prolonged and plaintive loud, high-pitched cry of pain, grief, etc. **2** a sound like or suggestive of this. ● *v.* **1** *intr.* utter a wail. **2** *intr.* lament or complain persistently or bitterly. **3** *intr.* (of the wind, etc.) make a sound like a person wailing. **4** *tr. poet.* or *rhet.* bewail; wail over. □ **Wailing Wall** a high wall in Jerusalem said to stand on the site of Herod's temple, where Jews traditionally pray and lament on Fridays. □□ **wailer** *n.* **wailful** *adj. poet.* **wailingly** *adv.* [ME f. ON, rel. to WOE]

■ *n.* **1, 2** see CRY *n.* ● *v.* **1** see CRY *v.* 2a. **2** see COMPLAIN 1, LAMENT *v.* **3** howl, moan.

wain /wayn/ *n. archaic* **1** a wagon. **2** (prec. by *the*) = CHARLES'S WAIN. [OE *wæg(e)n, wæn*, f. Gmc, rel. to WAY, WEIGH[1]]

wainscot /wáynskət -skot, -skōt/ *n.* & *v.* ● *n.* **1** boarding or wooden paneling on the lower part of an interior wall. **2** *Brit. hist.* imported oak of fine quality. ● *v.tr.* line with wainscot. [ME f. MLG *wagenschot*, app. f. *wagen* WAGON + *schot* of uncert. meaning]

wainscoting /wáynskōting, -skot-, -skə-/ *n.* **1** a wainscot. **2** material for this.

wainwright /wáynrīt/ *n.* a wagon builder.

waist /wayst/ *n.* **1 a** the part of the human body below the ribs and above the hips, usu. of smaller circumference than these; the narrower middle part of the normal human figure. **b** the circumference of this. **2** a similar narrow part in the middle of a violin, hourglass, wasp, etc. **3 a** the part of a garment encircling or covering the waist. **b** the narrow middle part of a woman's dress, etc. **c** a blouse or bodice. **4** the middle part of a ship, between the forecastle and the quarterdeck. □ **waist-deep** (or **-high**) up to the waist (*waist-deep in water*). □□ **waisted** *adj.* (also in *comb.*). **waistless** *adj.* [ME *wast*, perh. f. OE f. the root of WAX[2]]

■ **1** see MIDDLE 2.

waistband /wáystband/ *n.* a strip of cloth forming the waist of a garment.

waistcloth /wáystklawth/ *n.* a loincloth.

waistcoat /wéskət, wáystkōt/ *n. Brit.* a close-fitting waist-length garment, without sleeves or collar but usu. buttoned, worn usu. over a shirt and often under a jacket; a vest.

waistline /wáystlīn/ *n.* the outline or the size of a person's body at the waist.

wait /wayt/ *v.* & *n.* ● *v.* **1** *intr.* **a** defer action or departure for a specified time or until some expected event occurs (*wait a minute; wait till I come; wait for a fine day*). **b** be expectant or on the watch (*waited to see what would happen*). **c** (foll. by *for*) refrain from going so fast that (a person) is left behind (*wait for me!*). **2** *tr.* await (an opportunity, one's turn, etc.). **3** *tr.* defer (an activity) until a person's arrival or until some expected event occurs. **4** *intr.* (usu. as **waiting** *n.*) *Brit.* park a vehicle for a short time at the side of a road, etc. (*no waiting*). **5** *intr.* **a** (in full **wait at** or **on table**) act as a waiter or as a servant with similar functions. **b** act as an attendant. **6** *intr.* (foll. by *on*, *upon*) **a** await the convenience of. **b** serve as an attendant to. **c** pay a respectful visit to. ● *n.* **1** a period of waiting (*had a long wait for the train*). **2** (usu. foll. by *for*) watching for an enemy; ambush (*lie in wait*; *lay wait*). **3** (in *pl.*) *Brit.* **a** archaic street singers of Christmas carols. **b** *hist.* official bands of musicians maintained by a city or town. □ **wait-a-bit** a plant with hooked thorns, etc., that catch the clothing. **wait and see** await the progress of events. **wait for it!** *Brit. colloq.* **1** do not begin before the proper moment. **2** used to create an interval of suspense before saying something unexpected or amusing. **wait on 1** act as a waiter, etc. **2** be patient; wait. **wait-staff** people who serve food to diners, as at a restaurant. **wait up** (often foll. by *for*) **1** not go to bed until a person arrives or an event happens. **2** slow down until a person catches up, etc. (*wait up, I'm coming with you*). **you wait!** used to imply a threat, warning, or promise. [ME f. ONF *waitier* f. Gmc, rel. to WAKE[1]]

■ *v.* **1 a** linger, hold on, stay, stop, remain, rest, pause, bide one's time, mark time, stand by, hang about or around, dally, cool one's heels, *archaic or literary* tarry, *colloq.* stick around, sit tight, stay put, hang on. **b** see *watch out* 1. **2** await, wait for. **3** defer, delay, postpone, shelve, put off, *colloq.* put on ice *or* the back burner. **6 b** (*wait on or upon*) serve, attend, minister to. ● *n.* **1** delay, pause, stay, holdup, interval, halt, stop, stoppage, break, hiatus, lacuna, gap, respite, rest (period), intermission, discontinuation, postponement, moratorium, recess.

waiter /wáytər/ *n.* **1** a person who serves at table in a hotel or restaurant, etc. **2** a person who waits for a time, event, or opportunity. **3** a tray or salver.

■ **1** boy, garçon, steward, attendant, *usu. derog.* flunky; head waiter, maître d'hôtel, host; sommelier, wine steward, wine waiter, cupbearer; *colloq.* carhop.

waiting /wáyting/ *n.* **1** in senses of WAIT *v.* **2 a** official attendance at court. **b** one's period of this. □ **waiting game** abstention from early action in a contest, etc., so as to act more effectively later. **waiting list** a list of people waiting for a thing not immediately available. **waiting room** a room provided for people to wait in, esp. by a doctor, dentist, etc., or at a railroad or bus station.

waitperson /wáytpərsən/ *n.* a waiter or waitress.

waitress /wáytris/ *n.* a woman who serves at table in a hotel or restaurant, etc.

■ hostess, stewardess; bunny (girl).

waive /wayv/ *v.tr.* refrain from insisting on or using (a right, claim, opportunity, legitimate plea, rule, etc.). [ME f. AF *weyver*, OF *gaiver* allow to become a WAIF, abandon]

■ give up, relinquish, renounce, resign, forsake, forgo, cede, sign away, surrender, abandon, disclaim, yield, dispense with, set *or* put aside; ignore, disregard, overlook.

waiver /wáyvər/ *n.* *Law* the act or an instance of waiving. [as WAIVE]

■ renunciation, relinquishment, cession, resignation, surrender, abandonment, deferral, remission.

wake[1] /wayk/ *v. & n.* ● *v.* (*past* **woke** /wōk/ or **waked**; *past part.* **woken** /wōkən/ or **waked**) **1** *intr.* & *tr.* (often foll. by *up*) cease or cause to cease to sleep. **2** *intr.* & *tr.* (often foll. by *up*) become or cause to become alert, attentive, or active (*needs something to wake him up*). **3** *intr.* (archaic except as **waking** *adj.* & *n.*) be awake (*in her waking hours*; *waking or sleeping*). **4** *tr.* disturb (silence or a place) with noise; make reecho. **5** *tr.* evoke (an echo). **6** *intr.* & *tr.* rise or raise from the dead. ● *n.* **1** a watch beside a corpse before burial; lamentation and (less often) merrymaking in connection with this. **2** (usu. in *pl.*) an annual holiday in (industrial) northern England. **3** *Brit. hist.* **a** a vigil commemorating the

dedication of a church. **b** a fair or merrymaking on this occasion. □ **be a wake-up** (often foll. by *to*) *Austral. sl.* be alert or aware. **wake-robin 1** an arum, esp. the cuckoopint. **2** any plant of the genus *Trillium*. □□ **waker** *n.* [OE *wacan* (recorded only in past *woc*), *wacian* (weak form), rel. to WATCH: sense 'vigil' perh. f. ON]

■ *v.* **1** awaken, awake, rouse, waken, bring around; stir, bestir oneself, become conscious, get up, rise, come to, get going. **2** awake, waken, awaken, reawaken, animate, stimulate, enliven, galvanize, fire, quicken, inspirit, inspire, activate, liven up, vivify, kindle, vitalize, stir, arouse, get a person going, bring to life. **5** see *call forth*. ● *n.* **1** vigil, watch.

wake[2] /wayk/ *n.* **1** the track left on the water's surface by a moving ship. **2** turbulent air left behind a moving aircraft, etc. □ **in the wake of** behind; following; as a result of; in imitation of. [prob. f. MLG f. ON *vōk* hole or opening in ice]

■ **1** track, trail, aftermath, path, backwash, wash, bow wave. **2** turbulence, track, trail, path. □ **in the wake of** following (on or upon), behind, after, subsequent to; as a result or consequence of, on account of, because of, owing to, by virtue of; in imitation of.

wakeful /wáykfŏŏl/ *adj.* **1** unable to sleep. **2** (of a night, etc.) passed with little or no sleep. **3** vigilant. □□ **wakefully** *adv.* **wakefulness** *n.*

■ **1** awake, sleepless, waking, unsleeping, restless, restive, insomniac. **2** sleepless, disturbed, restless. **3** watchful, (on the) alert, on the qui vive, sharp, attentive, vigilant, wary, cautious, observant, heedful, on the lookout.

waken /wáykən/ *v.tr.* & *intr.* make or become awake. [ON *vakna* f. Gmc, rel. to WAKE[1]]

■ see WAKE[1] *v.* 1, 2.

Walachian var. of WALLACHIAN.

Waldenses /woldénseez/ *n.pl.* a puritan religious sect orig. in S. France, now chiefly in Italy, the United States, and Uruguay, founded *c.*1170 and much persecuted. □□ **Waldensian** *adj.* & *n.* [med.L f. Peter *Waldo* of Lyons, founder]

wale /wayl/ *n.* & *v.* ● *n.* **1** = WEAL[1]. **2** a ridge on a woven fabric, e.g., corduroy. **3** *Naut.* a broad, thick timber along a ship's side. **4** a specially woven strong band around a woven basket. ● *v.tr.* provide or mark with wales; thrash; whip. □ **wale knot** a knot made at the end of a rope by intertwining strands to prevent unraveling or act as a stopper. [OE *walu* stripe, ridge]

walk /wawk/ *v. & n.* ● *v.* **1** *intr.* **a** (of a person or other biped) progress by lifting and setting down each foot in turn, never having both feet off the ground at once. **b** progress with similar movements (*walked on his hands*). **c** go with the gait usual except when speed is desired. **d** (of a quadruped) go with the slowest gait, always having at least two feet on the ground at once. **2** *intr.* **a** travel or go on foot. **b** take exercise in this way (*walks for two hours each day*). **3** *tr.* **a** perambulate; traverse on foot at walking speed; tread the floor or surface of. **b** traverse or cover (a specified distance) on foot (*walks five miles a day*). **4** *tr.* **a** cause to walk with one. **b** accompany in walking. **c** ride or lead (a horse, dog, etc.) at walking pace. **d** *Brit.* take charge of (a puppy) at walk (see sense 4 of *n.*). **5** *intr.* (of a ghost) appear. **6** *intr.* *Cricket* leave the wicket on being out. **7** *Baseball* **a** *intr.* reach first base on balls. **b** *tr.* allow to do this. **8** *intr.* archaic live in a specified manner; conduct oneself (*walk humbly*; *walk with God*). **9** *intr.* *sl.* be released from suspicion or from a charge. ● *n.* **1 a** an act of walking, the ordinary human gait (*go at a walk*). **b** the slowest gait of an animal. **c** a person's manner of walking (*know him by his walk*). **2 a** a taking a (usu. specified) time to walk a distance (*is only ten minutes' walk from here*; *it's quite a walk to the bus stop*). **b** an excursion on foot; a stroll or constitutional (*go for a walk*). **c** a journey on foot completed to earn money promised for a charity, etc. **3 a** a place, track, or route intended or suitable for walking; a promenade, colonnade, or footpath. **b** a person's favorite place or route for walking. **c** esp. *Brit.* the round of a mail carrier, peddler, etc. **4** esp. *Brit.* a farm, etc., where a hound puppy is sent to accustom it to various surroundings. **5** the place where a gamecock is kept. **6** a part of a forest under one keeper. □ **in a walk** without effort (*won in a walk*). **walk about** stroll. **walk all over** *colloq.* **1** defeat easily. **2** take advantage of. **walk away from 1** easily outdistance. **2** refuse to become involved with; fail to deal with. **3** survive (an accident, etc.) without serious injury. **walk away with** *colloq.* = *walk off with.* **walk the boards** = *tread the boards* (see TREAD). **walk in** (often foll. by *on*) enter or arrive, esp. unexpectedly or easily. **walk into 1** *colloq.* encounter through unwariness (*walked into the trap*). **2** *sl. archaic* attack forcefully. **3** *sl. archaic* eat heartily. **walk it 1** make a journey on foot; not ride. **2** *colloq.* achieve something (esp. a victory) easily. **walk off 1** depart (esp. abruptly). **2** get rid of the effects of (a meal, ailment, etc.) by walking (*walked off his anger*). **walk a person off his** or **her feet** (or **legs**) exhaust a person with walking. **walk off with** *colloq.* **1** steal. **2** win easily. **walk of life** an occupation, profession, or calling. **walk-on 1** (in full **walk-on part**) a minor, esp. nonspeaking, dramatic role. **2** the player of this. **walk on air** see AIR. **walk out 1** depart suddenly or angrily. **2** (usu. foll. by *with*) *Brit. archaic* go for walks in courtship. **3** cease work, esp. to go on strike. **walk out on** desert; abandon. **walk over 1** *colloq.* = *walk all over.* **2** (often *absol.*) traverse (a racecourse) without needing to hurry, because one has no opponents or only inferior ones. **walk the plank** see PLANK. **walk the streets 1** be a prostitute. **2** traverse the streets, esp. in search of work, etc. **walk tall** *colloq.* feel justifiable pride. **walk up!** *Brit.* a showman's invitation to a circus, etc. **walk-up** *adj.* (of a building) allowing access to the upper floors only by stairs. ● *n.* a walk-up building. **walk up to** approach (a person) for a talk, etc. **walk the wards** *Brit.* be a medical student. □□ **walkable** *adj.* [OE *wealcan* roll, toss, wander, f. Gmc]

■ *v.* **1, 2** advance, proceed, move, go, go *or* make one's way on foot, travel on foot, tread, step, perambulate, stalk, stride, tramp, stroll, amble, ramble, shamble, pad, shuffle, saunter, trudge, trek, wade, plod, slog, footslog, foot it, hike, parade, promenade, strut, swagger, prance, march, goose-step, pace, trip, sidle, tiptoe, flounce, stagger, lurch, limp, waddle, stamp, mince, slink, steal, prowl, skulk, sneak, creep, pussyfoot, go by shanks's mare *or* pony, ride by shanks's mare *or* pony, *colloq.* traipse, sashay, *literary or archaic* wend; *sl.* hoof it. **3 a** patrol, trace out, stalk, cover, traverse, prowl, wander, roam, rove, range about in *or* on, frequent. **b** see WALK *v.* 1, 2 above. **4** take, convoy, accompany, escort, go with; conduct, lead. ● *n.* **1** gait, step, pace, stride. **2 b** constitutional, stroll, perambulation, promenade, amble, ramble, saunter, turn, walkabout, wander; slog, footslog, tramp, trek, hike. **3 a** path, lane, pathway, walkway, alley, arcade, track, route, trail, footway, pavement, footpath, promenade, esplanade, boardwalk, sidewalk. **c** round, beat, circuit, route. □ **walk all over 1** see ROUT *v.* **walk off with 1** see STEAL *v.* 1. **2** see WIN *v.* 1. **walk of life** see SPHERE *n.* 4b. **walk out 1, 3** leave, depart, storm out; strike, go (out) on strike, walk off the job, protest, *Brit.* take industrial action. **walk out on** see DESERT¹ *v.* 2.

walkabout /wáwkəbowt/ *n.* **1** esp. *Brit.* an informal stroll among a crowd by a visiting dignitary. **2** a period of wandering in the bush by an Australian Aboriginal.

walkathon /wáwkəthon/ *n.* an organized fund-raising walk. [WALK, after MARATHON]

walker /wáwkər/ *n.* **1** a person or animal that walks. **2 a** a wheeled *or* footed framework in which a baby can learn to walk. **b** a usu. tubular metal frame with rubberized ferrules, used by disabled or elderly people to help them walk.

■ **1** see PEDESTRIAN *n.* 1.

walkie-talkie /wáwkeetáwkee/ *n.* a two-way radio carried on the person, esp. by police officers, etc.

walking /wáwking/ *n. & adj.* in senses of WALK *n.* □ **walking delegate** a labor union official who visits members and their employers for discussions. **walking dictionary** (or **encyclopedia**) *colloq.* a person having a wide general knowledge. **walking fern** any American evergreen fern of the genus *Camptosorus,* with fronds that root at the ends. **walking leaf** = *walking fern.* **walking papers** *colloq.* dismissal (*gave him his walking papers*). **walking stick 1** a stick carried when walking, esp. for extra support. **2** (also **walkingstick**) a stick insect, esp. *Diapheromera femorata.* **walking tour** esp. *Brit.* a pleasure journey on foot, esp. of several days. **walking wounded 1** (of soldiers, etc.) able to walk despite injuries; not bedridden. **2** *colloq.* a person or people having esp. mental or emotional difficulties.

■ **walking papers** see *dismissal* (DISMISS).

Walkman /wáwkmən/ *n.* (*pl.* **-mans**) *propr.* a type of small portable stereo equipment with headphones.

walkout /wáwkowt/ *n.* a sudden angry departure, esp. as a protest or strike.

■ see STRIKE *n.* 2.

walkover /wáwkōvər/ *n.* an easy victory or achievement.

■ see PUSHOVER.

walkway /wáwkway/ *n.* a passage or path for walking along, esp.: **1** a raised passageway connecting different sections of a building. **2** a wide path in a garden, etc.

■ see PATH 1.

wall /wawl/ *n. & v.* ● *n.* **1 a** a continuous and usu. vertical structure of usu. brick or stone, having little width in proportion to its length and height and esp. enclosing, protecting, or dividing a space or supporting a roof. **b** the surface of a wall, esp. inside a room (*hung the picture on the wall*). **2** anything like a wall in appearance or effect, esp.: **a** the steep side of a mountain. **b** a protection or obstacle (*a wall of steel bayonets; a wall of indifference*). **c** *Anat.* the outermost layer or enclosing membrane, etc., of an organ, structure, etc. **d** the outermost part of a hollow structure (*stomach wall*). **e** *Mining* rock enclosing a lode or seam. ● *v.tr.* **1** (esp. as **walled** *adj.*) surround or protect with a wall (*walled garden*). **2 a** (usu. foll. by *up, off*) block or seal (a space, etc.) with a wall. **b** (foll. by *up*) enclose (a person) within a sealed space (*walled them up in the dungeon*). □ **drive a person up the wall** *colloq.* **1** make a person angry; infuriate. **2** drive a person mad. **go to the wall** be defeated or ruined. **off the wall** *sl.* unorthodox; unconventional; crazy; outlandish. **up the wall** *colloq.* crazy or furious (*went up the wall when he heard*). **wall bar** one of a set of parallel bars, attached to the wall of a gymnasium, on which exercises are performed. **wall fern** an evergreen polypody, *Polypodium vulgare,* with very large leaves. **wall painting** a mural or fresco. **wall pepper** a succulent stonecrop, *Sedum acre,* with a pungent taste. **wall plate** timber laid in or on a wall to distribute the pressure of a girder, etc. **wall rocket** see ROCKET². **wall rue** a small fern, *Asplenium ruta-muraria,* with leaves like rue, growing on walls and rocks. **walls have ears** it is unsafe to speak openly, as there may be eavesdroppers. **wall-to-wall 1** (of a carpet) fitted to cover a whole room, etc. **2** *colloq.* profuse; ubiquitous (*wall-to-wall pop music*). □□ **walling** *n.* **wall-less** *adj.* [OE f. L *vallum* rampart f. *vallus* stake]

■ *n.* **1** barricade, fortification, bulwark, breastwork, parapet, embankment, dyke, rampart, palisade, stockade. **2** screen, partition, divider, enclosure, separator, bulkhead, barrier, obstruction, obstacle, impediment, block, fence, protection, defense. ● *v.* **2 a** block, seal, close, brick, enclose, fence, screen, partition. **b** (*wall up*) immure, imprison, shut up, lock up, confine. □ **drive a person up the wall 1** see IRRITATE 1. **2** drive a person crazy *or* insane *or* mad, madden, unhinge, dement, derange. **go to the wall** fail, collapse, be ruined, face ruin, go bankrupt, go under, lose everything, *colloq.* go broke, fold (up), go bust. **off the wall** see OFFBEAT *adj.* **up the wall** insane, mad, frantic, furious, out of one's mind, *colloq.* crazy, livid, around the bend, *sl.* off one's rocker *or* nut, *Brit. sl.* off one's chump; see also INSANE 1.

wallaby /wóləbee/ *n.* (*pl.* **-ies**) any of various marsupials of the family Macropodidae, smaller than kangaroos, and having large hind feet and long tails. □ **on the wallaby** (or **wallaby track**) *Austral.* vagrant; unemployed. [Aboriginal *wolabā*]

Wallachian /woláykeeən/ *adj.* & *n.* (also **Walachian**) ● *adj.* of the former Principality of Wallachia, now part of Romania. ● *n.* a native of Wallachia. [*Wallachia* (as VLACH)]

wallah /wólə/ *n.* orig. *Anglo-Ind.*, now esp. *Brit. sl.* **1** a person concerned with or in charge of a usu. specified thing, business, etc. (*asked the ticket wallah*). **2** a person doing a routine administrative job; a bureaucrat. [Hindi *-wālā* suffix = -ER¹]

wallaroo /wólərōō/ *n.* a large, brownish-black kangaroo, *Macropus robustus*. [Aboriginal *wolarū*]

wallboard /wáwlbawrd/ *n.* a type of wall covering made from wood pulp, plaster, etc.

wallet /wólit/ *n.* **1** a small flat esp. leather case for holding paper money, etc. **2** *archaic* a bag for carrying food, etc., on a journey, esp. as used by a pilgrim or beggar. [ME *walet*, prob. f. AF *walet* (unrecorded), perh. f. Gmc]
■ purse, billfold, *Brit.* pocketbook, notecase.

walleye /wáwli/ *n.* **1 a** an eye with a streaked or opaque white iris. **b** an eye squinting outwards. **2** (also **walleyed pike**) an American perch, *Stizostedion vitreum*, with large prominent eyes. □□ **walleyed** *adj.* [back-form. f. *wall-eyed*: ME f. ON *vagleygr* f. *vagl* (unrecorded: cf. Icel. *vagl* film over the eye) + *auga* EYE]

wallflower /wáwlflowr/ *n.* **1 a** a fragrant spring garden plant, *Cheiranthus cheiri*, with esp. brown, yellow, or dark-red clustered flowers. **b** any of various flowering plants of the genus *Cheiranthus* or *Erysimum*, growing wild on old walls. **2** *colloq.* a neglected or socially awkward person, esp. a woman sitting out at a dance for lack of partners.

Walloon /woolōōn/ *n.* & *adj.* ● *n.* **1** a member of a French-speaking people inhabiting S. and E. Belgium and neighboring France (see also FLEMING). **2** the French dialect spoken by this people. ● *adj.* of or concerning the Walloons or their language. [F *Wallon* f. med.L *Wallo -onis* f. Gmc: cf. WELSH]

wallop /wóləp/ *v.* & *n. sl.* ● *v.tr.* **1 a** thrash; beat. **b** hit hard. **2** (as **walloping** *adj.*) big; strapping; thumping (*a walloping profit*). ● *n.* **1** a heavy blow; a thump. **2** *Brit.* beer or any alcoholic drink. □□ **walloping** *n.* [earlier senses 'gallop,' 'boil,' f. ONF (*walop* n. f.) *waloper*, OF *galoper*: cf. GALLOP]
■ *v.* **1** see BEAT v. 1. **2** (**walloping**) see THUMPING.
● *n.* **1** see BLOW² 1.

walloper /wóləpər/ *n.* **1** a person or thing that wallops. **2** *Austral. sl.* a policeman.

wallow /wólō/ *v.* & *n.* ● *v.intr.* **1** (esp. of an animal) roll about in mud, sand, water, etc. **2** (usu. foll. by *in*) indulge in unrestrained sensuality, pleasure, misery, etc. (*wallows in nostalgia*). ● *n.* **1** the act or an instance of wallowing. **2 a** a place used by buffalo, etc., for wallowing. **b** the depression in the ground caused by this. □□ **wallower** *n.* [OE *walwian* roll f. Gmc]
■ *v.* **1** roll about *or* around, loll about *or* around, welter, writhe, tumble, splash, plash. **2** (*wallow in*) luxuriate in, bask in, revel in, glory in, indulge (oneself) in, give oneself up to, succumb to, take to, appreciate, fancy, enjoy, like, love, savor, *colloq.* get a kick from *or* out of; *sl.* get a buzz from *or* out of, *sl.* get a bang from.

wallpaper /wáwlpaypər/ *n.* & *v.* ● *n.* **1** paper sold in rolls for pasting on to interior walls as decoration. **2** esp. *Brit.* an unobtrusive background, esp. (usu. *derog.*) with ref. to sound, music, etc. ● *v.tr.* (often *absol.*) decorate with wallpaper.

Wall Street *n.* the U.S. financial world and investment market. [street in New York City where banks, the stock exchanges, etc., are situated]

wally /wólee/ *n.* (*pl.* **-ies**) *Brit. sl.* a foolish or inept person. [orig. uncert., perh. shortened form of *Walter*]

walnut /wáwlnut/ *n.* **1** any tree of the genus *Juglans*, having aromatic leaves and drooping catkins. **2** the nut of this tree containing an edible kernel in two half shells shaped like boats. **3** the timber of the walnut tree used in cabinetmaking. [OE *walh-hnutu* f. Gmc NUT]

Walpurgis Night /valpŏŏrgis/ *n.* the eve of May 1, when witches are alleged to meet on the Brocken mountain in Germany and hold revels with the Devil. [G *Walpurgisnacht* f. *Walpurgis* genit. of *Walpurga* Engl. woman saint (8th c.) + *Nacht* NIGHT]

walrus /wáwlrəs, wól-/ *n.* a large, amphibious, long-tusked arctic mammal, *Odobenus rosmarus*, related to the seal and sea lion. □ **walrus mustache** a long thick drooping mustache. [prob. f. Du. *walrus, -ros*, perh. by metath. after *walvisch* 'whale-fish' f. word repr. by OE *horschwæl* 'horse-whale']

waltz /wawlts, wawls/ *n.* & *v.* ● *n.* **1** a dance in triple time performed by couples who rotate and progress around the floor. **2** the usu. flowing and melodious music for this. ● *v.* **1** *intr.* dance a waltz. **2** *intr.* (often foll. by *in, out, round*, etc.) *colloq.* move lightly, casually, with deceptive ease, etc. (*waltzed in and took first prize*). **3** *tr.* move (a person) in or as if in a waltz, with ease (*was waltzed off to Paris*). □ **waltzer** *n.* [G *Walzer* f. *walzen* revolve]

wampum /wómpəm/ *n.* beads made from shells and strung together for use as money, decoration, or as aids to memory by N. American Indians. [Algonquian *wampumpeag* f. *wap* white + *umpe* string + *-ag* pl. suffix]

wan /won/ *adj.* **1** (of a person's complexion or appearance) pale; exhausted; weak; worn. **2** (of a star, etc., or its light) partly obscured; faint. **3** *archaic* (of night, water, etc.) dark; black. □□ **wanly** *adv.* **wanness** *n.* [OE *wann* dark, black, of unkn. orig.]
■ **1** white, sickly, pale, pallid, livid, pasty, peaky, ashen, bloodless, waxen, whey-faced, washed-out, sallow, colorless, deathly, ghostly, ghastly, cadaverous, exhausted, worn, weary, drawn, weak, feeble, faint, frail. **2** weak, feeble, faint.

wand /wond/ *n.* **1 a** a supposedly magic stick used in casting spells by a fairy, magician, etc. **b** a stick used by a magician for effect. **2** a slender rod carried or used as a marker in the ground. **3** a staff symbolizing some officials' authority. **4** *colloq.* a conductor's baton. **5** a handheld electronic device which can be passed over a bar code to read the data this represents. [ME prob. f. Gmc: cf. WEND, WIND²]
■ **1–4** baton, stick, staff, rod.

wander /wóndər/ *v.* & *n.* ● *v.* **1** *intr.* (often foll. by *in, off*, etc.) go about from place to place aimlessly. **2** *intr.* **a** (of a person, river, road, etc.) wind about; diverge; meander. **b** (of esp. a person) get lost; leave home; stray from a path, etc. **3** *intr.* talk or think incoherently; be inattentive or delirious. **4** *tr.* cover while wandering (*wanders the world*). ● *n.* the act or an instance of wandering (*went for a wander around the garden*). □ **Wandering Jew 1 a** a legendary person said to have been condemned by Christ to wander the earth until the second advent. **b** a person who never settles down. **2 a** a climbing plant, *Tradescantia albiflora*, with stemless variegated leaves. **b** a trailing plant, *Zebrina pendula*, with pink flowers. **wandering sailor** the moneywort. □□ **wanderer** *n.* **wandering** *n.* (esp. in *pl.*). [OE *wandrian* (as WEND)]
■ *v.* **1** walk, go, roam, rove, range, stray, ramble, stroll, saunter, knock about *or* around, travel, meander, drift, cruise, prowl, *colloq.* mooch, tootle; *sl.* mosey. **2 a** wind, meander, snake, zigzag, turn this way and that; diverge. **3** deviate, digress, turn, stray, drift, depart, go off at a tangent, lose one's train of thought, lapse, lose the thread; go off, become absentminded, go woolgathering, lose concentration *or* focus; *literary* divagate. ● *n.* see STROLL *n.* □□ **wanderer** see ROVER¹.
wandering see TRAVEL *n.* 1b.

/.../ **pronunciation**	● **part of speech**
□ **phrases, idioms, and compounds**	
□□ **derivatives**	■ **synonym section**
cross-references appear in SMALL CAPITALS or *italics*	

wanderlust /wóndərlust/ *n.* an eagerness for traveling or wandering. [G]

wanderoo /wondəro͞o/ *n.* a langur, *Semnopithecus vetulus*, of Sri Lanka. [Sinh. *wanderu* monkey]

wane /wayn/ *v.* & *n.* ● *v.intr.* **1** (of the moon) decrease in apparent size after the full moon (cf. WAX²). **2** decrease in power, vigor, importance, brilliance, size, etc.; decline. ● *n.* **1** the process of waning. **2** a defect of a plank, etc., that lacks square corners. □ **on the wane** waning; declining. □□ **waney** *adj.* (in sense 2 of *n.*). [OE *wanian* lessen f. Gmc]
■ *v.* decrease, diminish, grow less, lessen, dwindle, shrink, decline, die out, abate, ebb, subside, fade (away), dim, taper off, peter out, draw to a close, wind down, weaken. ● *n.* **1** decrease, diminution, lessening, dwindling, decline, abatement, ebb, subsidence, fading, tapering off, petering out, winding down, weakening, deterioration, degeneration. □ **on the wane** on the decrease *or* decline *or* ebb, diminishing, decreasing, declining, waning, abating, subsiding, fading, tapering off, petering out, winding down, weakening, deteriorating, degenerating.

wangle /wánggəl/ *v.* & *n.* *colloq.* ● *v.tr.* **1** (often *refl.*) to obtain (a favor, etc.) by scheming, etc. (*wangled himself a free trip*). **2** alter or fake (a report, etc.) to appear more favorable. ● *n.* the act or an instance of wangling. □□ **wangler** *n.* [19th-c. printers' sl.: orig. unkn.]
■ *v.* **1** scheme, plot, work out, contrive, maneuver, engineer, manage, pull off, *colloq.* fix, work, finagle, swing, *sl.* fiddle. **2** see FIDDLE *v.* 2b.

wank /wangk/ *v.* & *n.* esp. *Brit. coarse sl.* ¶ Usually considered a taboo word. ● *v.intr.* & *tr.* masturbate. ● *n.* an act of masturbating. [20th c.: orig. unkn.]

Wankel engine /wángkəl, váng-/ *n.* a rotary internal-combustion engine with a continuously rotated and eccentrically pivoted, nearly triangular shaft. [F. *Wankel*, Ger. engineer d. 1988]

wanker /wángkər/ *n. Brit. coarse sl.* ¶ Usually considered a taboo word. **1** a contemptible or ineffectual person. **2** a person who masturbates.

wannabe /wónəbee/ *n. sl.* **1** an avid fan who tries to emulate the person he or she admires. **2** anyone who would like to be someone or something else.

want /wont, wawnt/ *v.* & *n.* ● *v.* **1** *tr.* **a** (often foll. by *to* + infin.) desire; wish for possession of; need (*wants a toy train; wants it done immediately; wanted to leave; wanted him to leave*). **b** need or desire (a person, esp. sexually). **c** esp. *Brit.* require to be attended to in esp. a specified way (*the garden wants weeding*). **d** (foll. by *to* + infin.) *colloq.* ought; should; need (*you want to pull yourself together; you don't want to overdo it*). **2** *intr.* (usu. foll. by *for*) lack; be deficient (*wants for nothing*). **3** *tr.* be without or fall short by (esp. a specified amount or thing) (*the drawer wants a handle*). **4** *intr.* (foll. by *in, out*) *colloq.* desire to be in, out, etc. (*wants in on the deal*). **5** *tr.* (as **wanted** *adj.*) (of a suspected criminal, etc.) sought by the police. ● *n.* **1** (often foll. by *of*) **a** a lack, absence, or deficiency (*could not go for want of time; shows great want of judgment*). **b** poverty; need (*living in great want; in want of necessities*). **2 a** a desire for a thing, etc. (*meets a long-felt want*). **b** a thing so desired (*can supply your wants*). □ **do not want to** am unwilling to. **want ad** a classified newspaper advertisement, esp. for something sought. □□ **wanter** *n.* [ME f. ON *vant* neut. of *vanr* lacking = OE *wana*, formed as WANE]
■ *v.* **1 a** desire, crave, wish (for), long for, pine for, hope (for), fancy, covet, hanker after, lust after, hunger for *or* after, thirst for *or* after, yearn for, *colloq.* have a yen for. **c** need, require, call for, demand, be in want *or* need of, stand in want *or* need of. **d** ought, should, need, must. **2, 3** need, lack, miss, require, call for, demand, be deficient in, be in want *or* need of, stand in want *or* need of; be *or* fall short of. ● *n.* **1 a** need, lack, shortage, deficiency, dearth, scarcity, scarceness, insufficiency, scantiness, inadequacy, paucity; absence. **b** poverty, need, indigence, destitution, privation, pauperism, penury, neediness, impecuniousness.

2 a appetite, hunger, thirst, craving, desire, fancy, wish, aspiration, longing, yearning, hankering, demand, *colloq.* yen. **b** desire, fancy, wish, necessity, requirement, requisite, prerequisite.

wanting /wónting, wáwn-/ *adj.* **1** lacking (in quality or quantity); deficient; not equal to requirements (*wanting in judgment; the standard is sadly wanting*). **2** absent; not supplied nor provided. □ **be found wanting** fail to meet requirements.
■ **1** lacking, deficient, inadequate, not up to par *or* scratch *or* expectations, insufficient, leaving much to be desired, unsatisfactory, unsatisfying, disappointing, second-rate, inferior, poor, shabby, shoddy, flawed, faulty, imperfect, incomplete, unfinished, defective, patchy, impaired, unsound. **2** absent, missing, lacking, short (of), *colloq.* shy (of). □ **be found wanting** see FAIL *v.* 1, 2a.

wanton /wóntən/ *adj., n.,* & *v.* ● *adj.* **1** licentious; lewd; sexually promiscuous. **2** capricious; random; arbitrary; motiveless (*wanton destruction*). **3** luxuriant; unrestrained; unruly (*wanton extravagance; wanton behavior*). **4** *archaic* playful; sportive (*a wanton child*). ● *n.* *literary* an immoral or licentious person, esp. a woman. ● *v.intr. literary* **1** gambol; sport; move capriciously. **2** (foll. by *with*) behave licentiously. □□ **wantonly** *adv.* **wantonness** *n.* [ME *wantowen* (wan- UN-¹ + *towen* f. OE *togen* past part. of *tēon* discipline, rel. to TEAM)]
■ *adj.* **1** immoral, dissolute, profligate, dissipated, depraved, loose, promiscuous, shameless, lustful, licentious, lecherous, wild, fast, libidinous, lewd, lascivious, unchaste. **2** capricious, random, indiscriminate, whimsical, unjustified, unprovoked, uncalled-for, purposeless, aimless, groundless, motiveless, unmotivated, unjustifiable, arbitrary, gratuitous; reckless, rash, heedless, irresponsible, careless. **3** lavish, extravagant, luxuriant, luxurious; abandoned, unrestrained, undisciplined, ungoverned, ungovernable, unmanageable, outrageous, immoderate, intemperate, untempered. ● *n.* loose woman, prostitute, voluptuary, trollop, Jezebel, call girl, *archaic* harlot, *archaic or rhet.* strumpet, *colloq.* vamp, *derog.* whore, slut, *sl.* tart, hooker, *US sl.* working girl, *Brit. sl. derog.* slag; see also TART² *n.* ● *v.* **1** see SPORT *v.* 1. **2** (*wanton with*) see TRIFLE *v.* 2. □□ **wantonly** see FAST¹ *adv.* 5. **wantonness** see DISSIPATION 1.

wapentake /wópəntayk, wáp-/ *n. Brit. hist.* (in areas of England with a large Danish population) a division of a shire; a hundred. [OE *wǣpen(ge)tæc* f. ON *vápnatak* f. *vápn* weapon + *tak* taking f. *taka* TAKE: perh. with ref. to voting in assembly by show of weapons]

wapiti /wópitee/ *n.* (*pl.* **wapitis**) a N. American deer, *Cervus canadensis*. [Cree *wapitik* white deer]

war. *abbr.* warrent.

war /wawr/ *n.* & *v.* ● *n.* **1 a** armed hostilities esp. between nations; conflict (*war broke out; war zone*). **b** a specific conflict or the period of time during which such conflict exists (*was before the war*). **c** the suspension of international law, etc., during such a conflict. **2** (as **the war**) a war in progress or recently ended; the most recent major war. **3 a** hostility or contention between people, groups, etc. (*war of words*). **b** (often foll. by *on*) a sustained campaign against crime, disease, poverty, etc. ● *v.intr.* (**warred, warring**) **1** (as **warring** *adj.*) **a** rival; fighting (*warring factions*). **b** conflicting (*warring principles*). **2** make war. □ **art of war** strategy and tactics. **at war** (often foll. by *with*) engaged in a war. **go to war** declare or begin a war. **go to the wars** *archaic* serve as a soldier. **have been in the wars** *colloq.* appear injured, bruised, unkempt, etc. **war baby** a child, esp. illegitimate, born in wartime, esp. of a soldier father. **war bride** a woman who marries a serviceman met during a war. **war chest** funds for a war or any other campaign. **war cloud** a threatening international situation; an indication of impending conflict. **war correspondent** a correspondent reporting from a scene of war. **war crime** a crime violating the international laws of war. **war criminal** a person committing or sentenced for such crimes. **war cry 1** a phrase or name shouted to rally one's troops. **2** a party slogan, etc. **war dance** a dance performed by primitive peoples, etc., before a battle or to celebrate victory. **war department** a government office in charge of the army, etc. **war game 1** a military exercise testing or improving tactical knowledge, etc. **2** a battle, etc., conducted with toy soldiers. **war-gaming** the playing of war games. **war grave** the grave of a serviceman who died on active service, esp. one in a special cemetery, etc. **war of attrition** a war in which each side seeks to wear out the other over a long period. **war of the elements** *poet.* storms or natural catastrophes. **war of nerves** an attempt to wear down an opponent by psychological means. **war poet** a poet writing on war themes, esp. of the two world wars. **Wars of the Roses** *hist.* the 15th-c. civil wars in England between the houses of York and Lancaster, represented by white and red roses. **war-weary** (esp. of a population) exhausted and dispirited by war. **war widow** a woman whose husband has been killed in war. **war zone** an area in which a war takes place. [ME *werre* f. AF, ONF var. of OF *guerre*: cf. WORSE]

■ *n.* **1** warfare, combat, conflict, fighting, clash, hostilities, battle, action, struggle, engagement, encounter, strife, contention. **3 b** campaign, drive, crusade, battle, fight, attack, offensive, struggle. ● *v.* **1** (**warring**) see HOSTILE 1. **2** do battle, fight, struggle, (engage in) combat, make *or* wage war, take up arms, strive, campaign, tilt, cross swords, contend, *hist.* joust. □ **at war** fighting, battling, in combat, in conflict; in disagreement, in dispute, in contention, struggling, antagonistic, at daggers drawn. **war cry** see SLOGAN. **war game 1** see MANEUVER *n.* 2.

warb /wawrb/ *n. Austral. sl.* an idle, unkempt, or disreputable person. [20th c.: orig. unkn.]

warble[1] /wáwrbəl/ *v. & n.* ● *v.* **1** *intr. & tr.* sing in a gentle, trilling manner. **2** *tr.* **a** speak or utter in a warbling manner. **b** express in a song or verse (*warbled his love*). ● *n.* a warbled song or utterance. [ME f. ONF *werble(r)* f. Frank. *hwirbilōn* whirl, trill]

■ *v.* see SING *v.* 1, 2.

warble[2] /wáwrbəl/ *n.* **1** a hard lump on a horse's back caused by the galling of a saddle. **2 a** the larva of a warble fly beneath the skin of cattle, etc. **b** a tumor produced by this. □ **warble fly** any of various flies of the genus *Hypoderma*, infesting the skin of cattle and horses. [16th c.: orig. uncert.]

warbler /wáwrblər/ *n.* **1** any small, insect-eating songbird of the family Sylviidae, including the black cap, or, in N. America, Parulidae, including the wood warbler, whitethroat, and chiffchaff, not always remarkable for their song. **2** a person, bird, etc., that warbles.

ward /wawrd/ *n. & v.* ● *n.* **1** a separate room or division of a hospital, prison, etc. (*men's surgical ward*). **2 a** *Brit.* an administrative division of a constituency, usu. electing a councilor or councilors, etc. **b** a similar administrative division. **3 a** a minor under the care of a guardian appointed by the parents or a court. **b** (in full **ward of the court**) a minor or mentally deficient person placed under the protection of a court. **4** (in *pl.*) the corresponding notches and projections in a key and a lock. **5** *archaic* **a** the act of guarding or defending a place, etc. **b** the bailey of a castle. **c** a guardian's control; confinement; custody. ● *v.tr. archaic* guard; protect. □ **ward heeler** a party worker in elections, etc. **ward off 1** parry (a blow). **2** avert (danger, poverty, etc.). [OE *weard, weardian* f. Gmc: cf. GUARD]

■ *n.* **2** district, division, precinct, section, zone, quarter. **3** minor, dependant, charge, protégé(e). □ **ward off** parry, fend off, repel, avert, avoid, block, thwart, keep away *or* off, keep at bay *or* arm's length, stave off, check, repulse, chase away *or* off, forestall.

-ward /wərd/ *suffix* (also **-wards**) added to nouns of place or destination and to adverbs of direction and forming: **1** adverbs (usu. **-wards**) meaning 'toward the place, etc.' (*moving backward; set off homeward*). **2** adjectives (usu. **-ward**) meaning 'turned or tending toward' (*a downward look; an onward rush*). **3** (less commonly) nouns meaning 'the region

toward or about' (*look to the eastward*). [from or after OE *-weard* f. a Gmc root meaning 'turn']

warden /wáwrd'n/ *n.* **1** (usu. in *comb.*) a supervising official (*churchwarden; game warden*). **2 a** chief administrator of a prison. **b** *Brit.* a president or governor of a college, school, hospital, youth hostel, etc. □□ **wardenship** *n.* [ME f. AF & ONF *wardein* var. of OF *g(u)arden* GUARDIAN]

■ **1** see KEEPER.

warder /wáwrdər/ *n.* **1** *Brit.* (*fem.* **wardress**) a prison officer. **2** a guard. [ME f. AF *wardere, -our* f. ONF *warder*, OF *garder* to GUARD]

■ **1** see JAILER. **2** see GUARD *n.* 2.

wardrobe /wáwrdrōb/ *n.* **1** a large movable or built-in case with rails, shelves, hooks, etc., for storing clothes. **2** a person's entire stock of clothes. **3** the costume department or costumes of a theater, a movie company, etc. **4** a department of a royal household in charge of clothing. □ **wardrobe mistress** (or **master**) a person in charge of a theatrical or movie wardrobe. **wardrobe trunk** a trunk fitted with rails, shelves, etc., for use as a traveling wardrobe. [ME f. ONF *warderobe*, OF *garderobe* (as GUARD, ROBE)]

■ **1** closet, *Brit.* clothes-cupboard. **2** (collection *or* stock of) clothing *or* clothes *or formal* attire *or* apparel.

wardroom /wáwrdrōom, -rŏŏm/ *n.* a room in a warship for the use of commissioned officers.

-wards var. of -WARD.

wardship /wáwrdship/ *n.* **1** a guardian's care or tutelage (*under his wardship*). **2** the condition of being a ward.

■ **1** see CHARGE *n.* 3b.

ware[1] /wair/ *n.* **1** (esp. in *comb.*) things of the same kind, esp. ceramics, made usu. for sale (*chinaware; hardware*). **2** (usu. in *pl.*) **a** articles for sale (*displayed his wares*). **b** a person's skills, talents, etc. **3** ceramics, etc., of a specified material, factory, or kind (*Wedgwood ware; delftware*). [OE *waru* f. Gmc, perh. orig. = 'object of care,' rel. to WARE[3]]

■ **2** merchandise, goods, commodities, manufactures, produce, stock(-in-trade), supplies, lines, truck.

ware[2] /wair/ *v.tr.* (also esp. *Brit.* **'ware**) (esp. in hunting) look out for; avoid (usu. in *imper.*: *ware hounds!*). [OE *warian* f. Gmc (as WARE[3]), & f. ONF *warer*]

ware[3] /wair/ *predic.adj. poet.* aware. [OE *wær* f. Gmc: cf. WARD]

warehouse /wáirhows/ *n. & v.* ● *n.* **1** a building in which esp. retail goods are stored; a repository. **2** a wholesale or large retail store. ● *v.tr.* /also -howz/ store (esp. furniture or bonded goods) temporarily in a repository. □□ **warehouseman** *n.* (*pl.* **-men**).

■ *n.* **1** storehouse, store, storeroom, depository, repository, stockroom, depot, entrepôt, godown.

warfare /wáwrfair/ *n.* a state of war; campaigning or engaging in war (*chemical warfare*).

■ see WAR *n.* 1.

warfarin /wáwrfərin/ *n.* a water-soluble anticoagulant used esp. as a rat poison. [*W*isconsin *A*lumni *R*esearch *F*oundation + *-arin*, after COUMARIN]

warhead /wáwrhed/ *n.* the explosive head of a missile, torpedo, or similar weapon.

warhorse /wáwrhawrs/ *n.* **1** *hist.* a knight's or soldier's powerful horse. **2** *colloq.* a veteran soldier, politician, etc. **3** a song, play, etc., that has been performed to the point of triteness.

■ **2** see VETERAN 1.

warlike /wáwrlīk/ *adj.* **1** threatening war; hostile. **2** martial; soldierly. **3** of or for war; military (*warlike preparations*).

■ **1** combative, militant, belligerent, bellicose, aggressive, pugnacious, hostile, bloodthirsty; hawkish, militaristic, jingoistic, warmongering. **2** see MARTIAL 2. **3** military, martial.

/.../ **pronunciation**	● **part of speech**
□ **phrases, idioms, and compounds**	
□□ **derivatives**	■ **synonym section**
cross-references appear in SMALL CAPITALS or *italics*	

warlock /wáwrlok/ *n. archaic* a sorcerer or wizard. [OE *wǽr-loga* traitor f. *wǽr* covenant: *loga* rel. to LIE²]
■ see SORCERER.

warlord /wáwrlawrd/ *n.* a military commander or commander in chief.

warm /wawrm/ *adj., v.,* & *n.* ● *adj.* **1** of or at a fairly or comfortably high temperature. **2** (of clothes, etc.) affording warmth (*needs warm gloves*). **3 a** (of a person, action, feelings, etc.) sympathetic; cordial; friendly; loving (*a warm welcome; has a warm heart*). **b** enthusiastic; hearty (*was warm in her praise*). **4** animated; heated; excited; indignant (*the dispute grew warm*). **5** *colloq. iron.* dangerous, difficult, or hostile (*met a warm reception*). **6** *colloq.* **a** (of a participant in esp. a children's game of seeking) close to the object, etc., sought. **b** near to guessing or finding out a secret. **7** (of a color, light, etc.) reddish, pink, or yellowish, etc., suggestive of warmth. **8** *Hunting* (of a scent) fresh and strong. **9 a** (of a person's temperament) amorous; sexually demanding. **b** erotic; arousing. ● *v.* **1** *tr.* **a** make warm (*fire warms the room*). **b** excite; make cheerful (*warms the heart*). **2** *intr.* **a** (often foll. by *up*) warm oneself at a fire, etc. (*warmed himself up*). **b** (often foll. by *to*) become animated, enthusiastic, or sympathetic (*warmed to his subject*). ● *n.* **1** the act of warming; the state of being warmed (*gave it a warm; had a nice warm by the fire*). **2** the warmth of the atmosphere, etc. **3** *Brit. archaic* a warm garment, esp. an army greatcoat. □ **warm-blooded 1** (of an organism) having warm blood; mammalian (see HOMEOTHERM). **2** ardent; passionate. **warmed-up** (or **-over**) **1** (of food, etc.) reheated. **2** stale; secondhand. **warm front** an advancing mass of warm air. **warming pan** *hist.* a usu. brass container for live coals with a flat body and a long handle, used for warming a bed. **warm up 1** (of an athlete, performer, etc.) prepare for a contest, performance, etc., by practicing. **2** (of a room, etc.) become warmer. **3** (of a person) become enthusiastic, etc. **4** (of an engine, etc.) reach a temperature for efficient working. **5** reheat (food). **warm-up** *n.* a period of preparatory exercise for a contest or performance. **warm work** *Brit.* **1** work, etc., that makes one warm through exertion. **2** dangerous conflict, etc. □□ **warmer** *n.* (also in *comb.*). **warmish** *adj.* **warmly** *adv.* **warmness** *n.* **warmth** *n.* [OE *wearm* f. Gmc]
■ *adj.* **1** heated, tepid, lukewarm, warmish, cozy, comfortable, not uncomfortable, balmy. **3 a** amiable, friendly, cordial, affable, sympathetic, pleasant, genial, cheerful, kindly, hospitable; affectionate, tender, mellow, loving, amorous. **b** ardent, enthusiastic, hearty, wholehearted, earnest, eager, sincere. **4** passionate, impassioned, excited, animated, fervent, fervid, spirited, ardent, zealous, keen, eager, emotional, heated, intense, furious, stormy, turbulent, vigorous, violent, *joc.* lively; indignant, irritated, annoyed, vexed, angry, irate, testy, short-tempered, touchy, quick-tempered, irascible, irritable, hot under the collar, *colloq.* worked up, steamed up. **5** uncomfortable, awkward, difficult, unpleasant, strained, tense, dangerous; hostile, unfriendly, unsympathetic. **6** close *or* near (to making a discovery), about to make *or* on the brink of a discovery. ● *v.* **1 a** heat (up), warm up *or* over. **b** stir, move, excite, please, delight, gladden, make a person feel good, cheer (up), encourage, brighten. **2 b** (*warm to*) become less antagonistic *or* hostile to *or* toward(s), become enthusiastic *or* supportive of, become excited *or* animated about *or* over, be attracted *or* sympathetic to *or* toward(s), come to like *or* feel affection for. □ **warm-blooded 1** homeothermic, homeothermal. **2** passionate, ardent, fervid, hot-blooded, impetuous, randy. **warm up 1** see EXERCISE *v.* 3. **5** reheat, heat up, warm over, *Brit. colloq.* hot up. **warm-up** see EXERCISE *n.* 3. □□ **warmish** tepid, lukewarm. **warmly** cordially, amiably, amicably, solicitously, warmheartedly; affectionately, tenderly, fondly, lovingly; well, kindly; vigorously, intensely, fiercely, intensively, intently, energetically, doggedly, persistently, zealously, fervently, fervidly, hotly, ardently, enthusiastically, earnestly, eagerly, heartily;

heatedly, vehemently, vociferously, forcefully, feverishly, frantically, furiously, angrily, violently. **warmth** heat, warmness, hotness, torridness, torridity, fieriness, warm; cordiality, heartiness, friendliness, geniality, amiableness, kindliness, tenderness, affability, love; ardor, effusiveness, enthusiasm, zeal, excitedness, fervor, vehemence, vigor, ebullience, passion; irritation, indignation, annoyance.

warmhearted /wáwrmháartid/ *adj.* having a warm heart; kind; friendly. □□ **warmheartedly** *adv.* **warmheartedness** *n.*
■ see KIND². □□ **warmheartedly** see *warmly* (WARM). **warmheartedness** see KINDNESS 1.

warmonger /wáwrmunggər, -mong-/ *n.* a person who seeks to bring about or promote war. □□ **warmongering** *n.* & *adj.*
■ see AGGRESSOR. □□ **warmongering** (*adj.*) see BELLIGERENT *adj.* 1. (*n.*) see *jingoism* (JINGO).

warn /wawrn/ *v.tr.* **1** (also *absol.*) **a** (often foll. by *of*, or *that* + clause, or *to* + infin.) inform of danger, unknown circumstances, etc. (*warned them of the danger; warned her that she was being watched; warned him to expect a visit*). **b** (often foll. by *against*) inform (a person, etc.) about a specific danger, hostile person, etc. (*warned her against trusting him*). **2** (usu. with *neg.*) admonish; tell forcefully (*has been warned not to go*). **3** give (a person) cautionary notice regarding conduct, etc. (*shall not warn you again*). □ **warn off** esp. *Brit.* **1** tell (a person) to keep away (from). **2** prohibit from attending races, esp. at a specified course. □□ **warner** *n.* [OE *war(e)nian, wearnian* ult. f. Gmc: cf. WARE³]
■ **1, 2** caution, admonish, advise, notify, apprise, inform, give (fair) warning, alert, give (prior) notice, put a person on notice *or* guard *or* the alert, make a person aware (of), forewarn, tip off, counsel.

warning /wáwrning/ *n.* **1** in senses of WARN *v.* **2** anything that serves to warn; a hint or indication of difficulty, danger, etc. **3** *archaic* = NOTICE *n.* 3b. □ **warning coloration** *Biol.* conspicuous coloring that warns a predator, etc., against attacking. **warning track** (or **path**) *Baseball* dirt strip that borders the outfield just inside the fence. □□ **warningly** *adv.* [OE *war(e)nung*, etc. (as WARN, -ING¹)]
■ **1** caution, admonition, advice, counsel, caveat, word (to the wise), tip, notification, notice, tip-off; threat. **2** lesson, example; omen, sign, signal, indication, hint, augury, foretoken, portent, presage, premonition, foreshadowing, forewarning, prophecy, knell.

warp /wawrp/ *v.* & *n.* ● *v.* **1** *tr.* & *intr.* **a** make or become bent or twisted out of shape, esp. by the action of heat, damp, etc. **b** make or become perverted, bitter, or strange (*a warped sense of humor*). **2 a** *tr.* haul (a ship) by a rope attached to a fixed point. **b** *intr.* progress in this way. **3** *tr.* fertilize by flooding with warp. **4** *tr.* (foll. by *up*) choke (a channel) with an alluvial deposit, etc. **5** *tr.* arrange (threads) as a warp. ● *n.* **1 a** a state of being warped, esp. of shrunken or expanded lumber. **b** perversion, bitterness, etc., of the mind or character. **2** the threads stretched lengthwise in a loom to be crossed by the weft. **3** a rope used in towing or warping, or attached to a trawl net. **4** sediment, etc., left esp. on poor land by standing water. □□ **warpage** *n.* (esp. in sense 1a of *v.*). **warper** *n.* (in sense 5 of *v.*). [OE *weorpan* throw, *wearp* f. Gmc]
■ *v.* **1 a** twist, contort, distort, deform, bend out of shape, buckle, kink, curve, wrench, misshape. **b** pervert, corrupt, twist, distort. ● *n.* **1** twist, contortion, distortion, bias, deformity, deformation, bend, wrench, perversion, kink, idiosyncrasy, quirk, deviation.

warpaint /wáwrpaynt/ *n.* **1** paint used to adorn the body before battle, esp. by N. American Indians. **2** *colloq.* elaborate make-up.

warpath /wáwrpath/ *n.* **1** a warlike expedition of N. American Indians. **2** *colloq.* any hostile course or attitude (*is on the warpath again*).

warplane /wáwrplayn/ *n.* a military aircraft, esp. one armed for warfare.

warragal var. of WARRIGAL.

warrant /wáwrənt, wór-/ *n. & v.* ● *n.* **1 a** anything that authorizes a person or an action (*have no warrant for this*). **b** a person so authorizing (*I will be your warrant*). **2 a** a written authorization, money voucher, travel document, etc. (*a dividend warrant*). **b** a written authorization allowing police to search premises, arrest a suspect, etc. **3** a document authorizing counsel to represent the principal in a lawsuit (*warrant of attorney*). **4** a certificate of service rank held by a warrant officer. ● *v.tr.* **1** serve as a warrant for; justify (*nothing can warrant his behavior*). **2** guarantee or attest to esp. the genuineness of an article, the worth of a person, etc. □ **I** (or **I'll**) **warrant** I am certain; no doubt (*She'll be sorry, I'll warrant*). **warrant officer** an officer ranking between commissioned officers and NCOs. □□ **warranter** *n.* **warrantor** *n.* [ME f. ONF *warant*, var. of OF *guarant*, *-and* f. Frank. *werend* (unrecorded) f. *giwerēn* be surety for]

■ *n.* **1 a** authorization, sanction, reason, justification, approval, validation, license, right, certification, entitlement, grounds, cause, rationale, basis, assurance, carte blanche, guarantee, pledge, security, charter, warranty. **2** writ, order, affidavit, paper, document, credential, authority, entitlement, license, permit, voucher, summons, subpoena, mandate, decree, fiat, edict, ukase. ● *v.* **1** authorize, sanction, justify, explain, approve, verify, validate, permit, allow, provide *or* offer grounds for, provide *or* offer justification for, provide *or* offer cause for, provide *or* offer reason for, call for, necessitate, entitle, empower, excuse, license. **2** guarantee, attest to, promise, assure, ensure, insure, answer for, be answerable for, certify, vouch for, underwrite, back up, uphold, stand by *or* behind.

warrantable /wáwrəntəbəl, wór-/ *adj.* **1** able to be warranted. **2** (of a deer) old enough to be hunted (5 or 6 years). □□ **warrantableness** *n.* **warrantably** *adv.*

warrantee /wáwrəntee, wór-/ *n.* a person to whom a warranty is given.

warranty /wáwrəntee, wór-/ *n.* (*pl.* **-ies**) **1** an undertaking as to the ownership or quality of a thing sold, hired, etc., often accepting responsibility for defects or liability for repairs needed over a specified period. **2** (usu. foll. by *for* + verbal noun) an authority or justification. **3** an undertaking by an insured person of the truth of a statement or fulfillment of a condition. [ME f. AF *warantie*, var. of *garantie* (as WARRANT)]

■ **1** guarantee, assurance, promise, commitment, covenant, undertaking, agreement, pledge, bond. **2** see WARRANT *n.* 1a.

warren /wáwrən, wór-/ *n.* **1 a** a network of interconnecting rabbit burrows. **b** a piece of ground occupied by this. **2** a densely populated or labyrinthine building or district. **3** *hist.* an area of land on which game is preserved. [ME f. AF & ONF *warenne*, OF *garenne* game park f. Gmc]

warrigal /wáwrigəl/ *n. & adj.* (also **warragal**) *Austral.* ● *n.* **1** a dingo dog. **2** an untamed horse. ● *adj.* wild, untamed. [Aboriginal]

warring /wáwring/ *adj.* rival; antagonistic.

■ rival, antagonistic, competing, battling, contending; see also HOSTILE 1.

warrior /wáwreeər, wór-/ *n.* **1** a person experienced or distinguished in fighting. **2** a fighting person, esp. a man, esp. of primitive peoples. **3** (*attrib.*) martial (*a warrior nation*). [ME f. ONF *werreior*, etc., OF *guerreior*, etc., f. *werreier, guerreier* make WAR]

warship /wáwrship/ *n.* an armored ship used in war.

wart /wawrt/ *n.* **1** a small, hardish, roundish growth on the skin caused by a virus-induced abnormal growth of papillae and thickening of the epidermis. **2** a protuberance on the skin of an animal, surface of a plant, etc. **3** *colloq.* an objectionable person. □ **warts and all** *colloq.* with no attempt to conceal blemishes or inadequacies. □□ **warty** *adj.* [OE *wearte* f. Gmc]

warthog /wáwrt-hog/ *n.* an African wild pig of the genus *Phacochoerus*, with a large head and warty lumps on its face, and large curved tusks.

wartime /wáwrtim/ *n.* the period during which a war is waged.

wary /wáiree/ *adj.* (**warier, wariest**) **1** on one's guard; given to caution; circumspect. **2** (foll. by *of*) cautious; suspicious (*am wary of using elevators*). **3** showing or done with caution or suspicion (*a wary expression*). □□ **warily** *adv.* **wariness** *n.* [WARE[2] + -Y[1]]

■ cautious, careful, on (one's) guard, circumspect, guarded, prudent, apprehensive, chary, suspicious, distrustful, watchful, vigilant, on the qui vive, heedful, observant, on one's toes, *colloq.* cagey, wide awake; *sl.* leery. □□ **warily** see GINGERLY *adv.* **wariness** see SUSPICION 1.

was *1st* & *3rd sing. past* of BE.

Wash. *abbr.* Washington.

wash /wosh, wawsh/ *v. & n.* ● *v.* **1** *tr.* cleanse (oneself or a part of oneself, clothes, etc.) with liquid, esp. water. **2** *tr.* (foll. by *out, off, away*, etc.) remove (a stain or dirt, a surface, or some physical feature of the surface) in this way; eradicate all traces of. **3** *intr.* wash oneself or esp. one's hands and face. **4** *intr.* wash clothes, etc. **5** *intr.* (of fabric or dye) bear washing without damage. **6** *intr.* (foll. by *off, out*) (of a stain, etc.) be removed by washing. **7** *tr. poet.* moisten; water (*tear-washed eyes; a rose washed with dew*). **8** *tr.* (of a river, sea, etc.) touch (a country, coast, etc.) with its waters. **9** *tr.* (of moving liquid) carry along in a specified direction (*a wave washed him overboard; was washed up on the shore*). **10** *tr.* (also foll. by *away, out*) **a** scoop out (*the water had washed a channel*). **b** erode; denude (*sea-washed cliffs*). **11** *intr.* (foll. by *over, along*, etc.) sweep, move, or splash. **12** *tr.* sift (ore) by the action of water. **13** *tr.* **a** brush a thin coat of watery paint or ink over (paper in watercolor painting, etc., or a wall). **b** (foll. by *with*) coat (inferior metal) with gold, etc. ● *n.* **1 a** the act or an instance of washing; the process of being washed (*give them a good wash; only needed one wash*). **b** (prec. by *the*) treatment at a laundry, etc. (*sent them to the wash*). **2** a quantity of clothes for washing or just washed. **3** the visible or audible motion of agitated water or air, esp. due to the passage of a ship, etc., or aircraft. **4** a soil swept off by water; alluvium. **b** a sandbank exposed only at low tide. **5** kitchen slops and scraps given to pigs. **6 a** thin, weak, or inferior liquid food. **b** liquid food for animals. **7** a liquid to spread over a surface to cleanse, heal, or color. **8** a thin coating of watercolor, wall paint, or metal. **9** malt, etc., fermenting before distillation. **10** a lotion or cosmetic. □ **come out in the wash** *colloq.* be clarified, or (of contingent difficulties) be resolved or removed, in the course of time. **wash-and-wear** *adj.* (of a fabric or garment) easily and quickly laundered. **wash one's dirty linen in public** see LINEN. **wash down 1** wash completely (esp. a large surface or object). **2** (usu. foll. by *with*) accompany or follow (food) with a drink. **washed out 1** faded by washing. **2** pale. **3** *colloq.* limp; enfeebled. **washed up** *sl.* defeated, having failed. **wash one's hands** *euphem.* go to the lavatory. **wash one's hands of** renounce responsibility for. **wash out 1** clean the inside of (a thing) by washing. **2** clean (a garment, etc.) by brief washing. **3 a** rain out (an event, etc.). **b** *colloq.* cancel. **4** (of a flood, downpour, etc.) make a breach in (a road, etc.). **wash-out** *n.* **1** *colloq.* a fiasco; a complete failure. **2** a breach in a road, railroad track, etc., caused by flooding (see also WASHOUT). **wash up 1** *tr.* (also *absol.*) esp. *Brit.* wash (dishes, etc.) after use. **2** wash one's face and hands. **won't** (or **doesn't**) **wash** *colloq.* (of an argument, etc.) will not be (or is not) believed or accepted. [OE *wæscan*, etc., f. Gmc, rel. to WATER]

■ *v.* **1, 3** wash up, clean (up), bathe, shower, douche, douse, scrub (up), shampoo, soap up, lather, launder, scour, wash down, soak, rinse, flush, wet, wash out, irrigate, drench, sponge (off), *Brit.* bath, *colloq.*

/.../ **pronunciation**	● **part of speech**
□ **phrases, idioms, and compounds**	
□□ **derivatives**	■ **synonym section**
cross-references appear in SMALL CAPITALS or *italics*

perform one's ablutions, *usu. formal* cleanse, *literary* lave. **2** scrub off, clean off, rinse off, soak out, sponge off; wear away, remove, delete, erase, expunge, destroy, eradicate, obliterate, extinguish, blot out, wipe off *or* out. **9** remove, move, transport, carry, bear, convey, deliver, deposit, drive, sweep. **10 a** erode, cut *or* dig *or* wear *or* eat *or* dredge (away *or* out), excavate, scoop out, channel. **b** erode, denude, undermine, wear away. **11** splash, spatter, splatter, plash, dash, beat, pound, thrash, break, toss, surge, undulate, rush, run, lap, ripple, roll, flow, sweep. **12** decontaminate, purify, sift, filter, depurate. **13** overlay, film, coat, paint, glaze; plate. • *n.* **1** clean, scrub, scour, shampoo, bath, shower, sponge, sponge bath; laundering; *colloq.* ablutions, tub. **2** washing, laundry. **3** wave, wake, surge, backwash; flow, swell, welling, sweep, ebb and flow, undulation, rise and fall. **5** swill, pigswill, hogwash, pigwash, slop(s). **7, 10** lotion, rinse, liniment, salve, embrocation, emulsion; mouthwash, gargle; eyewash, collyrium. **8** coat, coating, film, overlay, glaze; plating. □ **wash down 1** see WASH *v.* 1, 3 above. **washed out 1** faded, bleached. **2** wan, pale, pallid, peaky, colorless, faded, lackluster, flat; blanched, bleached, etiolated. **3** exhausted, spent, tired, tired out, weary, worn out, fatigued, drained, enfeebled, enervated, knocked up, *colloq.* fagged (out), bone-tired, done in, all in, knocked out, bushed, tuckered out, pooped, *sl.* beat, *Brit. sl.* knackered. **washed up** finished, through, failed, defeated, done for, played out, over (and done with), *sl.* kaput. **wash one's hands of** stay or keep away from, disown, repudiate, turn one's back on, have nothing more *or* further to do with, get rid of, rid oneself of, desert, abandon, leave. **wash out 1, 2** see WASH *v.* 1, 3 above. **3 a** *Brit.* rain out, rain off. **wash-out 1** failure, disaster, débâcle, (total) loss, fiasco, disappointment, *Brit.* damp squib, *colloq.* lead balloon, *sl.* flop, dud. **won't** (or **doesn't**) **wash** won't hold up, won't stand up, won't stand the test of time, won't carry weight, won't bear scrutiny, won't prove true, won't make sense, won't be believable *or* credible, won't hold water.

washable /wóshəbəl, wáwsh-/ *adj.* that can be washed, esp. without damage. □□ **washability** /-bílitee/ *n.*

washateria var. of WASHETERIA.

washbasin /wóshbaysin, wáwsh-/ *n.* = WASHBOWL.

washboard /wóshbawrd, wáwsh-/ *n.* **1** a board of ribbed wood or a sheet of corrugated zinc on which clothes are scrubbed in washing. **2** this used as a percussion instrument, played with the fingers.

washbowl /wóshbōl, wáwsh-/ *n.* a bowl for washing one's hands, face, etc.

washcloth /wóshkloth, wáwsh-/ *n.* a cloth for washing the face or body.
■ facecloth, *Brit.* flannel.

washday /wóshday, wáwsh-/ *n.* a day on which clothes, etc., are washed.

washer /wóshər, wáwsh-/ *n.* **1 a** a person or thing that washes. **b** a washing machine. **2** a flat ring of rubber, metal, leather, etc., inserted at a joint to tighten it and prevent leakage. **3** a similar ring placed under the head of a screw, bolt, etc., or under a nut, to disperse its pressure. **4** *Austral.* a washcloth. □ **washer-up** (*pl.* **washers-up**) *Brit.* a person who washes dishes, etc.

washerwoman /wóshərwoomən, wáwsh-/ *n.* (*pl.* **-women**) (also **washwoman**) a woman whose occupation is washing clothes; a laundress.

washeteria /wóshətéereeə, wáwsh-/ *n.* (also **washateria**) = LAUNDROMAT.

washhouse /wóshhowss, wáwsh-/ *n.* a building where clothes, etc., are washed.

washing /wóshing, wáwsh-/ *n.* a quantity of clothes for washing or just washed. □ **washing machine** a machine for washing clothes and linen, etc. **washing soda** sodium carbonate, used dissolved in water for washing and cleaning.

washing-up *Brit.* **1** the process of washing dishes, etc., after use. **2** used dishes, etc., for washing.
■ laundry, clothes.

washland /wóshland, wáwsh-/ *n. Brit.* land periodically flooded by a stream.

washout /wóshowt wáwsh-/ *n. Geol.* a narrow river channel that cuts into preexisting sediments (see also *wash-out*).

washroom /wóshroom, -room, wáwsh-/ *n.* a room with washing and toilet facilities.
■ see TOILET 1.

washstand /wóshstand, wáwsh-/ *n.* a piece of furniture to hold a washbowl, pitcher, soap, etc.

washtub /wóshtub, wáwsh-/ *n.* a tub or vessel for washing or soaking clothes, etc.

washy /wóshee, wáwsh-/ *adj.* (**washier, washiest**) **1** (of liquid food) too watery or weak; insipid. **2** (of color) faded-looking; thin; faint. **3** (of a style, sentiment, etc.) lacking vigor or intensity. □□ **washily** *adv.* **washiness** *n.*

wasn't /wúzənt, wóz/ *contr.* was not.

WASP /wosp/ *n.* (also **Wasp**) *usu. derog.* a middle-class American white Protestant descended from early English settlers. □□ **Waspy** *adj.* [White Anglo-Saxon Protestant]

wasp /wosp/ *n.* **1** a stinging, often flesh-eating insect of the order Hymenoptera, esp. the common social wasp *Vespa vulgaris*, with black and yellow stripes and a very thin waist. **2** (in *comb.*) any of various insects resembling a wasp in some way (*wasp beetle*). □ **wasp waist** a very slender waist. **wasp-waisted** having a very slender waist. □□ **wasplike** *adj.* [OE *wæfs, wæps, wæsp,* f. WG: perh. rel. to WEAVE[1] (from the weblike form of its nest)]

waspish /wóspish/ *adj.* irritable; petulant; sharp in retort. □□ **waspishly** *adv.* **waspishness** *n.*
■ irascible, irritable, bad-tempered, foul-tempered, temperamental, testy, grouchy, sensitive, volatile, querulous, edgy, petulant, spiteful, peevish, cantankerous, curmudgeonly, cross, crabby, crabbed, crotchety, splenetic, grumpy, captious, crusty; cranky.

wassail /wósəl, wósayl, wosáyl/ *n. & v. archaic* • *n.* **1** a festive occasion; a drinking bout. **2** a kind of liquor drunk on such an occasion. • *v.intr.* make merry; celebrate with drinking, etc. □ **wassail bowl** (or **cup**) a bowl or cup from which healths were drunk, esp. on Christmas Eve and Twelfth Night. □□ **wassailer** *n.* [ME *wæs hæil*, etc., f. ON *ves heill*, corresp. to OE *wes hāl* 'be in health,' a form of salutation: cf. HALE[1]]

Wassermann test /wáasərmən/ *n.* a test for syphilis using the reaction of the patient's blood serum. [A. von *Wassermann*, Ger. pathologist d. 1925]

wast /wost, wəst/ *archaic* or *dial. 2nd sing. past* of BE.

wastage /wáystij/ *n.* **1** an amount wasted. **2** loss by use, wear, or leakage. **3** *Commerce* loss of employees other than by layoffs.
■ **1, 2** see LOSS 2.

waste /wayst/ *v., adj., & n.* • *v.* **1** *tr.* use to no purpose or for inadequate result or extravagantly (*waste time*). **2** *tr.* fail to use (esp. an opportunity). **3** *tr.* (often foll. by *on*) give (advice, etc.), utter (words, etc.), without effect. **4** *tr. & intr.* wear gradually away; make or become weak; wither. **5** *tr.* a ravage; devastate. **b** *sl.* murder; kill. **6** *tr.* treat as wasted or valueless. **7** *intr.* be expended without useful effect. • *adj.* **1** superfluous; no longer serving a purpose. **2** (of a district, etc.) not inhabited nor cultivated; desolate (*waste ground*). **3** presenting no features of interest. • *n.* **1** the act or an instance of wasting; extravagant or ineffectual use of an asset, of time, etc. **2** waste material or food; refuse; useless remains or by-products. **3** a waste region; a desert, etc. **4** the state of being used up; diminution by wear and tear. **5** *Law* damage to an estate caused by an act or by neglect, esp. by a tenant. **6** = *waste pipe*. □ **go** (or **run**) **to waste** be wasted. **lay waste** ravage; devastate. **waste one's breath** see BREATH. **waste not, want not** extravagance leads to poverty. **waste pipe** a pipe to carry off waste material, e.g., from a sink. **waste products** useless by-products of manufacture or of an organism or organisms. **waste words** see WORD.

□□ **wastable** *adj.* **wasteless** *adj.* [ME f. ONF *wast(e)*, var. of OF *g(u)ast(e)*, f. L *vastus*]

■ *v.* **1** squander, misuse, throw away, fritter away, misspend, dissipate, *colloq.* splurge; *sl.* blow. **2** see LOSE 9. **4** enervate, enfeeble, emaciate, gnaw, destroy, consume, debilitate, exhaust, disable; diminish, deteriorate, dwindle, decline, decay, atrophy, wither, shrink, weaken, become debilitated, fade, peak, become enervated *or* enfeebled *or* emaciated, regress, ebb, sink. **5 a** see DEVASTATE 1. **b** assassinate, murder, kill, *colloq.* do away with, *sl.* put away, rub out, ice; see also KILL¹ *v.* 1. ● *adj.* **1** extra, leftover, unused, superfluous; worthless, useless, unproductive, unusable, unsalvageable, unrecyclable, unprofitable. **2** barren, empty, uninhabited, unpopulated, uncultivated, unproductive, desert, desolate, wild. ● *n.* **1** extravagance, prodigality, wastefulness, squandering, indulgence, lavishness, profligacy, dissoluteness, improvidence, overindulgence; misuse, misapplication, dissipation, misemployment, abuse, neglect. **2** refuse, rubbish, garbage, dregs, debris, dross, leavings, scrap, sweepings, litter, slag, trash, *Austral.* mullock. **3** wasteland, desert, wilderness, barrens, wilds, emptiness, vastness. □ **lay waste** devastate, destroy, demolish, ruin, wreck, ravage, pillage, sack, plunder, loot, rob, strip, spoil, gut, ransack, wreak havoc (up)on, crush, raze, annihilate, *literary* despoil.

wastebasket /wáystbaskit/ *n.* a receptacle for wastepaper, etc.

wasteful /wáystfŏŏl/ *adj.* **1** extravagant. **2** causing or showing waste. □□ **wastefully** *adv.* **wastefulness** *n.*

■ extravagant, spendthrift, profligate, prodigal, lavish, improvident, unthrifty, uneconomical, thriftless, penny wise and pound foolish. □□ **wastefully** see *like water* (WATER). **wastefulness** see WASTE *n.* 1.

wasteland /wáystland/ *n.* **1** an unproductive or useless area of land. **2** a place or time considered spiritually or intellectually barren.

■ **1** rough ground, scrub, badlands, bomb site; see also WILD *n.*

wastepaper /wáystpaypər/ *n.* spoiled, valueless, or discarded paper. □ **wastepaper basket** = WASTEBASKET.

waster /wáystər/ *n.* **1** a wasteful person. **2** *colloq.* a wastrel.

■ **2** see LOAFER.

wastrel /wáystrəl/ *n.* **1** a wasteful or good-for-nothing person. **2** a waif; a neglected child.

■ **1** spendthrift, profligate, prodigal, big spender, squanderer; idler, layabout, malingerer, loafer, shirker, good-for-nothing, ne'er-do-well, drone, *colloq.* lazybones.

watch /woch/ *v. & n.* ● *v.* **1** *tr.* keep the eyes fixed on; look at attentively. **2** *tr.* **a** keep under observation; follow observantly. **b** monitor or consider carefully; pay attention to (*have to watch my weight*; *watched their progress with interest*). **3** *intr.* (often foll. by *for*) be in an alert state; be vigilant; take heed (*watch for the holes in the road*; *watch for an opportunity*). **4** *intr.* (foll. by *over*) look after; take care of. **5** *intr. archaic* remain awake for devotions, etc. ● *n.* **1** a small portable timepiece for carrying on one's person. **2** a state of alert or constant observation or attention. **3** *Naut.* **a** a four-hour period of duty. **b** (in full **starboard** or **port watch**) each of the halves, divided according to the position of the bunks, into which a ship's crew is divided to take alternate watches. **4** *hist.* a watchman or group of watchmen, esp. patrolling the streets at night. **5** a former division of the night. **6** a period of wakefulness at night. **7** *Sc. hist.* irregular Highland troops in the 18th c. □ **on the watch** waiting for an expected or feared occurrence. **set the watch** *Naut.* station sentinels, etc. **watch chain** a metal chain for securing a pocket watch. **watch crystal** a glass disk covering the dial of a watch. **watch glass** *Brit.* a glass disk used in a laboratory, etc., to hold material for use in experiments. **watch it** (or **oneself**) *colloq.* be careful. **watch night 1** the last night of the year. **2** a religious service held on this night. **watch one's step** proceed cautiously. **watch out 1** (often foll. by *for*) be on

one's guard. **2** as a warning of immediate danger. **watch spring** the mainspring of a watch. **watch strap** esp. *Brit.* = WATCHBAND. □□ **watchable** *adj.* **watcher** *n.* (also in *comb.*). [OE *wæcce* (n.), rel. to WAKE¹]

■ *v.* **1** observe, regard, look at, gaze at *or* on, take in, contemplate, eye, peer at; ogle, make eyes at. **2 a, 4** look after, tend, mind, keep an eye on, watch over, guard, care for, take care of, safeguard, protect, shield, keep safe, supervise, superintend; chaperon, accompany, attend; babysit, sit (with). **2 b** observe, note, notice, make *or* take note of, see, pay attention to, attend (to), follow, heed, take heed of, monitor, examine, inspect, scrutinize, pore over. **3** see *watch out* below; (*watch for*) watch out for, look for, be on the watch *or* lookout *or* alert for, guard against, keep an eye open for, be watchful for, note, take note *or* notice of, take heed of, be vigilant for *or* of, keep one's eyes open *or* peeled *or* skinned for, keep a (sharp) lookout for, be prepared *or* ready for, be careful of, await, wait for, keep a *or* one's weather eye open for, *disp.* anticipate. ● *n.* **1** clock, timepiece, pocket watch, wristwatch; chronometer. **2** vigil, surveillance, observation, lookout. **4** sentry, sentinel, (security) guard, lookout, (night) watchman, caretaker. □ **on the watch** on the alert, on the lookout, on (one's) guard, on the qui vive, alert, awake, observant, watchful, cautious, wary, vigilant, circumspect. **watch one's step** see STEP.

watch out 1 watch, look, look out, be on the watch *or* lookout *or* alert *or* qui vive, be on (one's) guard, keep an eye open, be watchful, take note *or* notice, take heed, be vigilant, keep one's eyes open *or* peeled *or* skinned, keep a (sharp) lookout, be prepared *or* ready, be careful, wait, keep a *or* one's weather eye open. □□ **watcher** see OBSERVER.

watchband /wóchband/ *n.* a strap or bracelet for fastening a watch on the wrist.

watchcase /wóchkays/ *n.* the outer, usu. metal case enclosing the works of a watch.

watchdog /wóchdawg, dog/ *n. & v.* ● *n.* **1** a dog kept to guard property, etc. **2** a person or body monitoring others' rights, behavior, etc. ● *v.tr.* (**-dogged**, **-dogging**) maintain surveillance over.

■ *n.* **1** guard dog. **2** see MONITOR *n.* 1.

watchful /wóchfŏŏl/ *adj.* **1** accustomed to watching. **2** on the watch. **3** showing vigilance. **4** *archaic* wakeful. □□ **watchfully** *adv.* **watchfulness** *n.*

■ **2, 3** see VIGILANT. □□ **watchfulness** see VIGILANCE.

watchmaker /wóchmaykər/ *n.* a person who makes and repairs watches and clocks. □□ **watchmaking** *n.*

watchman /wóchmən/ *n.* (*pl.* **-men**) **1** a person employed to look after an empty building, etc., at night. **2** *archaic* or *hist.* a member of a night watch.

■ (security) guard, sentinel, sentry, lookout, watch, night watchman, custodian, caretaker.

watchtower /wóchtower/ *n.* a tower from which observation can be kept.

watchword /wóchwərd/ *n.* **1** a phrase summarizing a guiding principle; a slogan. **2** *hist.* a military password.

■ see SLOGAN 1–3.

water /wáwtər, wót-/ *n. & v.* ● *n.* **1** a colorless, transparent, odorless, tasteless liquid compound of oxygen and hydrogen. ¶ Chem. formula: H_2O. **2** a liquid consisting chiefly of this and found in seas, lakes, and rivers, in rain, and in secretions of organisms. **3** an expanse of water; a sea, lake, river, etc. **4** (in *pl.*) part of a sea or river (*in Icelandic waters*). **5** (often as **the waters**) mineral water at a spa, etc. **6** the state of a tide (*high water*). **7** a solution of a specified substance in water (*lavender water*). **8** the quality of the transparency and brilliance of a gem, esp. a diamond. **9** *Finance*

/. . . / **pronunciation**	● **part of speech**
□ **phrases, idioms, and compounds**	
□□ **derivatives**	■ **synonym section**
cross-references appear in SMALL CAPITALS or *italics*	

an amount of nominal capital added by watering (see sense 10 of *v.*). **10** (*attrib.*) **a** found in or near water. **b** of, for, or worked by water. **c** involving, using, or yielding water. • *v.* **1** *tr.* sprinkle or soak with water. **2** *tr.* supply (a plant) with water. **3** *tr.* give water to (an animal) to drink. **4** *intr.* (of the mouth or eyes) secrete water as saliva or tears. **5** *tr.* (as **watered** *adj.*) (of silk, etc.) having irregular wavy glossy markings. **6** *tr.* adulterate (milk, beer, etc.) with water. **7** *tr.* (of a river, etc.) supply (a place) with water. **8** *intr.* (of an animal) go to a pool, etc., to drink. **9** *intr.* (of a ship, engine, etc., or the person in charge of it) take in a supply of water. **10** *tr. Finance* increase (a company's debt, or nominal capital) by the issue of new shares without a corresponding addition to assets. □ **by water** using a ship, etc., for travel or transport. **cast one's bread upon the waters** see BREAD. **like water** lavishly; profusely. **like water off a duck's back** see DUCK[1]. **make one's mouth water** cause one's saliva to flow; stimulate one's appetite or anticipation. **of the first water 1** (of a diamond) of the greatest brilliance and transparency. **2** of the finest quality or extreme degree. **on the water** on a ship, etc. **on the water wagon** *Brit.* see WAGON. **water bag** a bag of leather, canvas, etc., for holding water. **water bear** = TARDIGRADE *n.* **the Water Bearer** (or esp. *Brit.* **Carrier**) the zodiacal sign or constellation Aquarius. **water bed** a mattress of rubber or plastic, etc., filled with water. **water biscuit** (or **cracker**) an unsweetened cracker made from flour and water. **water blister** a blister containing a colorless fluid, not blood nor pus. **water boatman** any aquatic bug of the family Notonectidae or Corixidae, swimming with oarlike hind legs. **water brash** heartburn. **water buffalo** the common domestic E. Indian buffalo, *Bubalus arnee.* **water butt** a barrel used to catch rainwater. **water cannon** a device giving a powerful jet of water to disperse a crowd, etc. **water chestnut 1** an aquatic plant, *Trapa natans,* bearing an edible seed. **2 a** (in full **Chinese water chestnut**) a sedge, *Eleocharis tuberosa,* with rushlike leaves arising from a corm. **b** this corm used as food. **water clock** a clock measuring time by the flow of water. **water closet** a room or compartment equipped with a toilet bowl. **water-cooled** cooled by the circulation of water. **water cure** = HYDROPATHY. **water diviner** esp. *Brit.* a person who dowses (see DOWSE[1]) for water. **water down 1** dilute with water. **2** make less vivid, forceful, or horrifying. **water gate 1** a floodgate. **2** a gate giving access to a river, etc. **water gauge 1** a glass tube, etc., indicating the height of water in a reservoir, boiler, etc. **2** pressure expressed in terms of a head of water. **water glass 1** a solution of sodium or potassium silicate used for preserving eggs, as a vehicle for fresco painting, and for hardening artificial stone. **2** a tube with a glass bottom enabling objects under water to be observed. **3** a drinking glass. **water hammer** a knocking noise in a water pipe when a faucet is suddenly turned off. **water heater** a device for heating (esp. domestic) water. **water hemlock** a poisonous plant, *Cicuta maculata,* found in marshes, etc.: also called COWBANE. **water hole** a shallow depression in which water collects (esp. in the bed of a river otherwise dry). **water hyacinth** a tropical river weed, *Eichhornia crassipes.* **water ice** = SORBET. **water jump** a place where a horse in a steeplechase, etc., must jump over water. **water level 1 a** the surface of the water in a reservoir, etc. **b** the height of this. **2** *Brit.* = *water table.* **3** a level using water to determine the horizontal. **water lily** any aquatic plant of the family Nymphaeaceae, with broad flat floating leaves and large usu. cup-shaped floating flowers. **water main** the main pipe in a water-supply system. **water meadow** a meadow periodically flooded by a stream. **water meter** a device for measuring and recording the amount of water supplied to a house, etc. **water mill** a mill worked by a waterwheel. **water moccasin 1** a venomous snake, *Agkistrodon piscivorus,* found in wet or marshy areas of the southern US; a cottonmouth. **2** any of various harmless water snakes. **water nymph** a nymph regarded as inhabiting or presiding over water. **water of crystallization** water forming an essential part of the structure of some crystals. **water of life** *rhet.* spiritual enlightenment. **water ouzel** =

DIPPER 1. **water pepper** an aquatic herb, *Polygonum hydropiper*: also called *smartweed.* **water pipe 1** a pipe for conveying water. **2** a hookah. **water pistol** a toy pistol shooting a jet of water. **water plantain** any marsh plant of the genus *Alisma,* with plantainlike leaves. **water polo** a game played by swimmers, with a ball like a soccer ball. **water purslane** a creeping plant, *Lythrum portula,* growing in damp places. **water rail** a wading bird, *Rallus aquaticus,* frequenting marshes, etc. **water rat 1** any rodent of aquatic habits. **2** a muskrat. **3** *sl.* a waterfront vagrant or thug. **water-repellent** not easily penetrated by water. **water scorpion** any aquatic bug of the family Nepidae, living submerged and breathing through a bristlelike tubular tail. **water ski** (*pl.* **-skis**) each of a pair of skis for skimming the surface of the water when towed by a motorboat. **water softener** an apparatus or substance for softening hard water. **water-soluble** soluble in water. **water supply** the provision and storage of water, or the amount of water stored, for the use of a town, house, etc. **water table** a level below which the ground is saturated with water. **water torture** a form of torture in which the victim is exposed to the incessant dripping of water on the head, or the sound of dripping. **water tower** a tower with an elevated tank to give pressure for distributing water. **water under the bridge** past events accepted as past and irrevocable. **water vole** an aquatic vole, esp. *Arvicola amphibius*; a water rat. **water wings** inflated floats fixed on the arms of a person learning to swim. □□ **waterer** *n.* **waterless** *adj.* [OE *wæter* f. Gmc, rel. to WET]

■ *n.* **1, 2** H_2O, Adam's ale; distilled water, tap water, drinking water, rainwater, bottled water, spa water, still water, soda (water), effervescent water, fizzy water, mineral water; sea water, brine, salt water; ditchwater, dishwater, bathwater, heavy water, deuterium oxide. • *v.* **1** inundate, flood, drench, saturate, soak, douse, irrigate, besprinkle, hose, wet, shower, splash, spray, sprinkle, moisten, damp, dampen, bedew. **4** run, stream. **6** see *water down* 1 below. □ **like water** lavishly, extravagantly, freely, wastefully, profligately, openhandedly, liberally, excessively, copiously, profusely, unstintingly, unreservedly. **of the first water 2** of superior quality *or* grade, of excellent quality *or* grade, of first quality *or* grade, of top quality *or* grade, of A1 quality *or* grade, of the finest quality *or* grade, of the highest quality *or* grade, of the best quality *or* grade; first-grade, top-grade; of the worst *or* lowest *or* basest kind. **water closet** see TOILET 1. **water down 1** dilute, weaken, water, thin out, adulterate, cut, *colloq.* doctor. **2** mollify, modify, soften, tone down, qualify, moderate, soft-pedal. **water hole** watering hole, watering place, *Austral.* gnamma, claypan. **water main** see MAIN. *n.*[1] 1. **water pipe 1** see PIPE *n.* 1. □□ **waterless** see DRY *adj.* 1.

waterborne /wáwtərbawrn, wótər-/ *adj.* **1** (of goods, etc.) conveyed by or traveling on water. **2** (of a disease) communicated or propagated by contaminated water.

waterbuck /wáwtərbuk, wótər-/ *n.* (*pl.* same or **waterbucks**) any of various African antelopes of the genus *Kobus,* frequenting riverbanks.

waterbus /wáwtərbus, wótər-/ *n.* (*pl.* **-buses** or **-busses**) a boat carrying passengers on a regular run on a river, lake, etc.

watercolor /wáwtərkúlər, wótər-/ *n* (*Brit.* **watercolour**) **1** artists' paint made of pigment to be diluted with water and not oil. **2** a picture painted with this. **3** the art of painting with watercolors. □□ **watercolorist** *n.*
■ **2** aquarelle.

watercooler /wáwtərkoolər, wótər-/ *n.* a tank of cooled drinking water.

watercourse /wáwtərkawrs, wótər-/ *n.* **1** a brook, stream, or artificial water channel. **2** the bed along which this flows.
■ **1** see STREAM *n.* 1.

watercress /wáwtərkres, wótər-/ *n.* a hardy perennial cress, *Nasturtium officinale,* growing in running water, with pungent leaves used in salad.

waterfall /wáwtərfawl, wótər-/ n. a stream or river flowing over a precipice or down a steep hillside.
■ cascade, cataract, fall (s), *No. of Engl.* force; *Sc.* linn.

Waterford glass /wáwtərfərd, wótər-/ n. a clear, colorless flint glass. [*Waterford* in Ireland]

waterfowl /wáwtərfowl, wótər-/ n. (usu. collect. as *pl.*) birds frequenting water, esp. swimming game birds.

waterfront /wáwtərfrunt, wótər-/ n. the part of a town or city adjoining a river, lake, harbor, etc.

Watergate /wáwtərgayt, wótər-/ n. a political or commercial scandal on a large scale. [a building in Washington, DC, that in 1972 housed the national headquarters of the Democratic Party, the bugging and burglary of which by people connected with the Republican administration led to a national scandal and the resignation of President R. M. Nixon]

watering /wáwtəring, wótər-/ n. the act or an instance of supplying water or (of an animal) obtaining water. □ **watering can** a portable container with a long spout usu. ending in a perforated sprinkler, for watering plants. **watering hole 1** a pool of water from which animals regularly drink; = *water hole.* **2** *sl.* a bar. **watering place 1** = *watering hole.* **2** a spa or seaside resort. **3** a place where water is obtained. [OE *wæterung* (as WATER, -ING[1])]
■ □ **watering hole 2** see PUB 2.

waterline /wáwtərlin, wótər-/ n. **1** the line along which the surface of water touches a ship's side (marked on a ship for use in loading). **2** a linear watermark.

waterlogged /wáwtərlawgd, -logd, wótər-/ adj. **1** saturated with water. **2** (of a boat, etc.) hardly able to float from being saturated or filled with water. **3** (of ground) made useless by being saturated with water. [*waterlog* (v.), f. WATER + LOG[1], prob. orig. = 'reduce (a ship) to the condition of a log']
■ **1, 3** see *soaking n.* (SOAK).

Waterloo /wáwtərlōō, wótər-/ n. a decisive defeat or contest (*meet one's Waterloo*). [*Waterloo* in Belgium, where Napoleon was finally defeated in 1815]

waterman /wáwtərmən, wótər-/ n. (*pl.* -**men**) **1** a boatman plying for hire. **2** an oarsman as regards skill in keeping the boat balanced.

watermark /wáwtərmaark, wótər-/ n. & v. ● n. a faint design made in some paper during manufacture, visible when held against the light, identifying the maker, etc. ● v.tr. mark with this.

watermelon /wáwtərmelən, wótər-/ n. a large, smooth, green melon, *Citrullus lanatus,* with red pulp and watery juice.

waterpower /wáwtərpowr, wótər-/ n. **1** mechanical force derived from the weight or motion of water. **2** a fall in the level of a river, as a source of this force.

waterproof /wáwtərprōōf, wótər-/ adj., n., & v. ● adj. impervious to water. ● n. *Brit.* a waterproof garment or material. ● v.tr. make waterproof.
■ adj. watertight, sealed.

watershed /wáwtərshed, wótər-/ n. **1** a line of separation between waters flowing to different rivers, basins, or seas. **2** a turning point in affairs. [WATER + *shed* ridge of high ground (rel. to SHED[2]), after G *Wasserscheide*]
■ **2** see LANDMARK 2.

waterside /wáwtərsid, wótər-/ n. the margin of a sea, lake, or river.

water-ski /wáwtərskee, wótər-/ v.intr. (-**skis**, -**skied** /-skeed/; -**skiing**) travel on water skis. □□ **water-skier** n.

waterspout /wáwtərspowt, wótər-/ n. a gyrating column of water and spray formed by a whirlwind between sea and cloud.

watertight /wáwtərtit, wótər-/ adj. **1** (of a joint, container, vessel, etc.) closely fastened or fitted or made so as to prevent the passage of water. **2** (of an argument, etc.) unassailable.
■ **1** sealed, waterproof. **2** unassailable, impregnable, solid, airtight, flawless, faultless, incontrovertible; without loopholes.

waterway /wáwtərway, wótər-/ n. **1** a navigable channel. **2** a route for travel by water. **3** a thick plank at the outer edge of a deck along which a channel is hollowed for water to run off by.

waterweed /wáwtərweed, wótər-/ n. any of various aquatic plants, esp. of the genus *Elodea.*

waterwheel /wáwtərhweel, wótər-, -weel/ n. a wheel driven by water to work machinery, or to raise water.

waterworks /wáwtərwərks, wótər-/ n. **1** an establishment for managing a water supply. **2** *colloq.* the shedding of tears. **3** *Brit. colloq.* the urinary system.

watery /wáwtəree, wótər-/ adj. **1** containing too much water. **2** too thin in consistency. **3** of or consisting of water. **4** (of the eyes) suffused or running with water. **5** (of conversation, style, etc.) vapid; uninteresting. **6** (of color) pale. **7** (of the sun, moon, or sky) rainy-looking. □ **watery grave** the bottom of the sea as a place where a person lies drowned. □□ **wateriness** n. [OE *wæterig* (as WATER, -Y[1])]
■ **1** wet, swampy, boggy, marshy, aqueous, squelchy, squashy, squishy; soggy, moist, damp, humid. **2** weak, dilute(d), watered down, thin, liquid, runny, sloppy, wishy-washy. **4** weeping, teary, tearful, bleary, running, streaming, damp, moist, weepy, rheumy, *formal* lachrymose. **5** vapid, uninteresting, insipid, jejune, flat, dull, bland, tame. **6** pale, anemic, pallid, weak, feeble, washed-out, wishy-washy, colorless.

WATS /wots/ abbr. Wide-Area Telecommunications Service.

watt /wot/ n. the SI unit of power, equivalent to one joule per second, corresponding to the rate of energy in an electric circuit where the potential difference is one volt and the current one ampere. ¶ Symb.: **W.** □ **watt-hour** the energy used when one watt is applied for one hour. [J. *Watt,* Sc. engineer d. 1819]

wattage /wótij/ n. an amount of electrical power expressed in watts.

wattle[1] /wót'l/ n. & v. ● n. **1 a** interlaced rods and split rods as a material for making fences, walls, etc. **b** (in *sing.* or *pl.*) rods and twigs for this use. **2** an Australian acacia with long pliant branches, with bark used in tanning and golden flowers used as the national emblem. **3** *Brit. dial.* a wicker hurdle. ● v.tr. **1** make of wattle. **2** enclose or fill up with wattles. □ **wattle and daub** a network of rods and twigs plastered with mud or clay as a building material. [OE *watul,* of unkn. orig.]

wattle[2] /wót'l/ n. **1** a loose fleshy appendage on the head or throat of a turkey or other birds. **2** = BARB n. 3. □□ **wattled** adj. [16th c.: orig. unkn.]

wattmeter /wótmeetər/ n. a meter for measuring the amount of electricity in watts.

wave /wayv/ v. & n. ● v. **1 a** intr. (often foll. by *to*) move a hand, etc., to and fro in greeting or as a signal (*waved to me across the street*). **b** tr. move (a hand, etc.) in this way. **2 a** intr. show a sinuous or sweeping motion as of a flag, tree, or a wheat field in the wind; flutter; undulate. **b** tr. impart a waving motion to. **3** tr. brandish (a sword, etc.) as an encouragement to followers, etc. **4** tr. tell or direct (a person) by waving (*waved them away; waved them to follow*). **5** tr. express (a greeting, etc.) by waving (*waved good-bye to them*). **6** tr. give an undulating form to (hair, drawn lines, etc.); make wavy. **7** intr. (of hair, etc.) have such a form; be wavy. ● n. **1** a ridge of water between two depressions. **2** a long body of water curling into an arched form and breaking on the shore. **3** a thing compared to this, e.g., a body of persons in one of successive advancing groups. **4** a gesture of waving. **5 a** the process of waving the hair. **b** an undulating form produced in the hair by waving. **6 a** a temporary occurrence or increase of a condition, emotion, or influence (*a wave of enthusiasm*). **b** a specified period of widespread weather (*heat wave*). **7** *Physics* **a** the disturbance of the particles of a fluid medium to form ridges and troughs for the propagation or direction of motion, heat, light, sound, etc.,

without the advance of the particles. **b** a single curve in the course of this motion (see also *standing wave, traveling wave* (see TRAVEL)). **8** *Electr.* a similar variation of an electromagnetic field in the propagation of radiation through a medium or vacuum. **9** (in *pl.*; prec. by *the*) *poet.* the sea; water. □ **make waves** *colloq.* cause trouble. **wave aside** dismiss as intrusive or irrelevant. **wave equation** a differential equation expressing the properties of motion in waves. **wave front** *Physics* a surface containing points affected in the same way by a wave at a given time. **wave function** a function satisfying a wave equation and describing the properties of a wave. **wave mechanics** a method of analysis of the behavior esp. of atomic phenomena with particles represented by wave equations (see *quantum mechanics*). **wave number** *Physics* the number of waves in a unit distance. **wave theory** *hist.* the theory that light is propagated through the ether by a wave motion imparted to the ether by the molecular vibrations of the radiant body. □□ **waveless** *adj.* **wavelike** *adj. & adv.* [OE *wafian* (v.) f. Gmc: (n.) also alt. of ME *wawe, wage*]
■ *v.* **1 a** signal, sign, gesture, gesticulate. **2** undulate, billow, move to and fro, flap, flutter, quiver, flip-flop, swing, sway, ripple, oscillate, zigzag, fluctuate, shake; wag, whiffle, brandish, *colloq.* wigwag, wiggle, waggle. **3** see FLOURISH *v.* 4. **5** signal, sign, indicate, signify; gesture, gesticulate. ● *n.* **1, 2** swell, undulation, billow, sea, heave, roller, whitecap, white horse; ripple, wavelet, breaker, comber, boomer. **4** signal, sign, gesticulation, gesture. **6 a** surge, swell, welling up, groundswell, movement, flood, spurt, upsurge, uprising, current, tide. **b** spell. □ **wave aside** see DISMISS 4.

waveband /wáyvband/ *n.* a range of (esp. radio) wavelengths between certain limits.

waveform /wáyvfawrm/ *n. Physics* a curve showing the shape of a wave at a given time.

waveguide /wáyvgid/ *n. Electr.* a metal tube, etc., confining and conveying microwaves.

wavelength /wáyvlengkth, -length, -lenth/ *n.* **1** the distance between successive crests of a wave, esp. points in a sound wave or electromagnetic wave. ¶ Symb.: λ. **2** this as a distinctive feature of radio waves from a transmitter. **3** *colloq.* a particular mode or range of thinking and communicating (*we don't seem to be on the same wavelength*).
■ **3** (*be on the same wavelength with*) see SYMPATHIZE 1.

wavelet /wáyvlit/ *n.* a small wave on water.
■ see RIPPLE *n.*¹ 1.

waver /wáyvər/ *v.intr.* **1** be or become unsteady; falter; begin to give way. **2** be irresolute or undecided between different courses or opinions; be shaken in resolution or belief. **3** (of a light) flicker. □□ **waverer** *n.* **waveringly** *adv.* [ME f. ON *vafra* flicker f. Gmc, rel. to WAVE]
■ **1** see TEETER 1, FLUCTUATE . **2** see DOUBT *v.* 2, 3.

wavy /wáyvee/ *adj.* (**wavier, waviest**) (of a line or surface) having waves or alternate contrary curves (*wavy hair*). □□ **wavily** *adv.* **waviness** *n.*

wa-wa /waáwaa/ *n.* (also **wahwah**) *Mus.* an effect achieved on brass instruments by alternately applying and removing a mute and on an electric guitar by controlling the output from the amplifier with a pedal. [imit.]

wax¹ /waks/ *n. & v.* ● *n.* **1** a sticky, plastic, yellowish substance secreted by bees as the material of honeycomb cells; beeswax. **2** a white translucent material obtained from this by bleaching and purifying and used for candles, in modeling, as a basis of polishes, and for other purposes. **3** any similar substance, e.g., earwax. **4** *colloq.* **a** a phonograph record. **b** material for the manufacture of this. **5** (*attrib.*) made of wax. ● *v.tr.* **1** cover or treat with wax. **2** *colloq.* record for the phonograph. □ esp. *Brit.* **lost wax** = CIRE PERDUE.
wax bean a yellow-podded snap bean. **wax light** a taper or candle of wax. **wax myrtle** a tree, *Myrtus cerifera*, yielding wax and oil used for candles. **wax-painting** = ENCAUSTIC.
wax palm 1 a South American palm, *Ceroxylon alpinum*, with its stem coated in a mixture of resin and wax. **2** a car-

nauba. **wax paper** (also **waxed paper**) paper waterproofed with a layer of wax. □□ **waxer** *n.* [OE *wæx, weax* f. Gmc]

wax² /waks/ *v.intr.* **1** (of the moon between new and full) have a progressively larger part of its visible surface illuminated, increasing in apparent size. **2** become larger or stronger. **3** pass into a specified state or mood (*wax lyrical*). □ **wax and wane** undergo alternate increases and decreases. [OE *weaxan* f. Gmc]
■ **2** see GROW 1. **3** see BECOME 1.

wax³ /waks/ *n. Brit. sl.* a fit of anger. [19th c.: orig. uncert.: perh. f. WAX² *wroth*, etc.]

waxberry /wáksbəree/ *n.* (*pl.* **-ies**) **1** a wax myrtle. **2** the fruit of this.

waxbill /wáksbil/ *n.* any of various birds esp. of the family Estrildidae, with usu. red bills resembling the color of sealing wax.

waxcloth /wáksklawth, -kloth/ *n. Brit.* oilcloth.

waxen /wáksən/ *adj.* **1** having a smooth pale translucent surface as of wax. **2** able to receive impressions like wax; plastic. **3** *archaic* made of wax.

waxwing /wákswing/ *n.* any bird of the genus *Bombycilla*, with small tips like red sealing wax to some wing feathers.

waxwork /wákswərk/ *n.* **1 a** an object, esp. a lifelike dummy, modeled in wax. **b** the making of waxworks. **2** (in *pl.*) an exhibition of wax dummies.

waxy¹ /wáksee/ *adj.* (**waxier, waxiest**) resembling wax in consistency or in its surface. □□ **waxily** *adv.* **waxiness** *n.* [WAX¹ + -Y¹]
■ see GREASY 1, PLASTIC *adj.* 1a.

waxy² /wáksee/ *adj.* (**waxier, waxiest**) *Brit. sl.* angry; quick-tempered. [WAX³ + -Y¹]

way /way/ *n. & adv.* ● *n.* **1** a road, track, path, etc., for passing along. **2** a course or route for reaching a place, esp. the best one (*asked the way to Rockefeller Center*). **3** a place of passage into a building, through a door, etc. (*could not find the way out*). **4 a** a method or plan for attaining an object (*that is not the way to do it*). **b** the ability to obtain one's object (*has a way with him*). **5 a** a person's desired or chosen course of action. **b** a custom or manner of behaving; a personal peculiarity (*has a way of forgetting things; things had a way of going badly*). **6** a specific manner of life or procedure (*soon got into the way of it*). **7** the normal course of events (*that is always the way*). **8** a traveling distance; a length traversed or to be traversed (*is a long way away*). **9 a** an unimpeded opportunity of advance. **b** a space free of obstacles. **10** a region or ground over which advance is desired or natural. **11** advance in some direction; impetus; progress (*pushed my way through*). **12** movement of a ship, etc. (*gather way; lose way*). **13** the state of being engaged in movement from place to place; time spent in this (*met them on the way home; with songs to cheer the way*). **14** a specified direction (*step this way; which way are you going?*). **15** (in *pl.*) parts into which a thing is divided (*split it three ways*). **16** *Brit. colloq.* the scope or range of something (*want a few things in the stationery way*). **17** a person's line of occupation or business. **18** a specified condition or state (*things are in a bad way*). **19** a respect (*is useful in some ways*). **20 a** (in *pl.*) a structure of lumber, etc., down which a new ship is launched. **b** parallel rails, etc., as a track for the movement of a machine. ● *adv. colloq.* to a considerable extent; far (*you're way off the mark*). □ **across** (or **over**) **the way** opposite. **any way** = ANYWAY. **be on one's way** set off; depart. **by the way 1** incidentally; as a more or less irrelevant comment. **2** during a journey. **by way of 1** through; by means of. **2** as a substitute for or as a form of (*did it by way of apology*). **3** with the intention of (*asked by way of discovering the truth*). **come one's way** become available to one; become one's lot. **find a way** discover a means of obtaining one's object. **get** (or **have**) **one's way** (or **have it one's own way**, etc.) get what one wants; ensure one's wishes are met. **give way 1 a** make concessions. **b** fail to resist; yield. **2** (often foll. by *to*) concede precedence (to). **3** (of a structure, etc.) be dislodged or broken under a load; collapse. **4** (foll. by *to*) be superseded by. **5** (foll. by *to*) be overcome by (an emotion, etc.). **6** (of rowers) row hard. **go out of one's way** (often foll. by

to + infin.) make a special effort; act gratuitously or without compulsion (*went out of their way to help*). **go one's own way** act independently, esp. against contrary advice. **go one's way 1** leave; depart. **2** (of events, circumstances, etc.) be favorable to one. **go a person's way** accompany a person (*are you going my way?*). **have it both ways** see BOTH. **in its way** if regarded from a particular standpoint appropriate to it. **in no way** not at all; by no means. **in a way** in a certain respect but not altogether or completely. **in the** (or **one's**) **way** forming an obstacle or hindrance. **lead the way 1** act as guide or leader. **2** show how to do something. **look the other way 1** ignore what one should notice. **2** disregard an acquaintance, etc., whom one sees. **one way and another** taking various considerations into account. **one way or another** by some means. **on the** (or **one's**) **way 1** in the course of a journey, etc. **2** having progressed (*is well on the way to completion*); in the pipeline. **3** *colloq.* (of a child) conceived but not yet born. **on the way out** *colloq.* going down in status, estimation, or favor; going out of fashion. **the other way around** (or **about**) in an inverted or reversed position or direction. **out of the way 1** no longer an obstacle or hindrance. **2** disposed of; settled. **3** (of a person) imprisoned or killed. **4** uncommon; remarkable; seldom met with (*nothing out of the way*). **5** (of a place) remote; inaccessible. **out of one's way** not on one's intended route. **put a person in the way of** give a person the opportunity of. **way back** *colloq.* long ago. **Way of the Cross** the series of stations of the cross (see STATION). **way of life** the principles or habits governing all one's actions, etc. **way of thinking** one's customary opinion of matters. **way of the world** conduct no worse than is customary. **way-out** *colloq.* **1** unusual; eccentric. **2** avant-garde; progressive. **3** excellent; exciting. **ways and means 1** methods of achieving something. **2** methods of raising government revenue. **way station 1** a minor station on a railroad. **2** a point marking progress in a certain course of action, etc. [OE *weg* f. Gmc: (adv.) f. AWAY]
■ *n.* **1, 2** path, road, street, avenue, course, route, track, trail, channel, direction. **4 a** manner, method, mode, fashion, means, system, course (of action), strategy, plan, policy, procedure, approach, scheme, technique, practice, modus operandi, m.o. **b** knack, skill, ability, facility, art. **5 b** habit, custom, knack, behavior pattern, manner, approach, style, conduct, technique, nature, mores; idiosyncrasy, peculiarity, eccentricity, oddity, characteristic, personality, temperament, disposition, habit. **6** way of life, lifestyle, modus vivendi; see also ROUTINE *n.* 1. **8** distance, haul. **9** clearance, pathway, opening, space, room, avenue, scope, freedom, opportunity. **11** progress, passage, advance, headway. **12** speed, velocity, motion, (forward) movement, impetus, momentum. **13** see JOURNEY *n.* **18** condition, situation, state. **19** aspect, respect, particular, detail, point, sense, feature. □ **by the way 1** incidentally, by the by, parenthetically, in passing, en passant, apropos. **by way of 1** via, through, by means of. **2** (functioning) as, in (the) way of, in the capacity of, equivalent to, more or less, as a substitute for, as a form of, instead of, something like. **give way 1** yield, surrender, retreat, concede, withdraw, accede, defer, make concessions, acquiesce. **3** give, collapse, break (down), fail, cave in, fall (down), crumble, crumple, snap, disintegrate, go to pieces. **go out of one's way** see *make a point of* (POINT). **go one's way 1** see LEAVE¹ *v.* 1b, 3, 4. **lead the way 1** see GUIDE *v.* 1, 3. **2** see TEACH 1. **look the other way 1** turn a blind eye, turn a deaf ear, pay no attention, take no notice, turn one's back. **one way or another** see SOMEHOW. **on the** (or **one's**) **way 1** see *on the move* 2 (MOVE). **2** see *in the pipeline* (PIPELINE). **on the way out** see OBSOLESCENT. **the other way around** (or **about**) see VICE VERSA. **out of the way 2** disposed of, dealt with, settled, finished with, finalized. **4** see PECULIAR 1. **5** untraveled, unfrequented, isolated, outlying, secluded, inaccessible, distant, far-flung. **way back** see FORMERLY. **way of life** see CULTURE *n.* 2,

CUSTOM 1. **way of thinking** see OPINION 1, 3. **way-out 1** bizarre, mad, weird, crazy, strange, odd, peculiar, freakish, freaky, unusual, eccentric, queer, abnormal, offbeat, outrageous, wild, exotic, esoteric, far-out, *colloq.* kinky, *sl.* kooky, screwy, nutty, batty, flaky, screwball, off-the-wall. **2** avant-garde, advanced, original, innovative, unorthodox, unconventional, experimental, precedent-setting, progressive, exploratory, groundbreaking, trailblazing, far-out. **3** see SPLENDID 3.

-way /way/ *suffix* = -WAYS.

wayback /wáybak/ *n.* esp. *Austral.* = OUTBACK.

waybill /wáybil/ *n.* a list of goods being shipped on a vehicle.

wayfarer /wáyfairər/ *n.* a traveler, esp. on foot.
■ see TRAVELER 1.

wayfaring /wáyfairing/ *n.* traveling, esp. on foot. □ **wayfaring tree** a white-flowered European and Asian shrub, *Viburnum lantana*, common along roadsides, with berries turning from green through red to black.

waylay /waylay/ *v.tr.* (*past* and *past part.* **waylaid**) **1** lie in wait for. **2** stop to rob or interview. □□ **waylayer** *n.*
■ **1** ambush, lie in wait for, await, bushwhack. **2** hold up, detain, intercept, pounce upon *or* on, swoop down on *or* upon, set upon, attack, mug, seize, assault, assail, accost, *Austral.* & *NZ* bail up, *colloq.* buttonhole.

wayleave /wáyleev/ *n.* a right of way granted over another's property.

waymark /wáymaark/ *n.* *Brit.* a natural or artificial object as a guide to travelers, esp. walkers.

-ways /wayz/ *suffix* forming adjectives and adverbs of direction or manner (*sideways*) (cf. -WISE). [WAY + -´s]

wayside /wáysid/ *n.* **1** the side or margin of a road. **2** the land at the side of a road. □ **fall by the wayside** fail to continue in an endeavor or undertaking (after Luke 8:5).

wayward /wáywərd/ *adj.* **1** childishly self-willed or perverse; capricious. **2** unaccountable or freakish. □□ **waywardly** *adv.* **waywardness** *n.* [ME f. obs. *awayward* turned away f. AWAY + -WARD: cf. FROWARD]
■ see CAPRICIOUS, PERVERSE 2.

wayworn /wáywawrn/ *adj.* tired with travel.

Wb *abbr.* weber(s).

WC *abbr.* **1** *Brit.* water closet. **2** West Central (London postal district). **3** without charge.

we /wee/ *pron.* (*obj.* **us**; *poss.* **our**, **ours**) **1** (*pl.* of I²) used by and with reference to more than one person speaking or writing, or one such person and one or more associated persons. **2** used for or by a royal person in a proclamation, etc., and by a writer or editor in a formal context. **3** people in general (cf. ONE *pron.* 2). **4** *colloq.* = I² (*give us a chance*). **5** *colloq.* (often implying condescension) you (*how are we feeling today?*). [OE f. Gmc]

weak /week/ *adj.* **1** deficient in strength, power, or number; fragile; easily broken or bent or defeated. **2** deficient in vigor; sickly; feeble (*weak health*; *a weak imagination*). **3 a** deficient in resolution; easily led (*a weak character*). **b** (of an action or features) indicating a lack of resolution (*a weak surrender*; *a weak chin*). **4** unconvincing or logically deficient (*weak evidence*; *a weak argument*). **5** (of a mixed liquid or solution) watery; thin; dilute (*weak tea*). **6** (of a style, etc.) not vigorous nor well-knit; diffuse; slipshod. **7** (of a crew) short-handed. **8** (of a syllable, etc.) unstressed. **9** *Gram.* in Germanic languages: **a** (of a verb) forming inflections by the addition of a suffix to the stem. **b** (of a noun or adjective) belonging to a declension in which the stem originally ended in *-n* (opp. STRONG *adj.* 22). □ **weak ending** an unstressed syllable in a normally stressed place at the end of a verse line. **the weaker sex** *derog.* women. **weak grade** *Gram.* an unstressed ablaut form. **weak interaction** *Physics* the weakest form of interaction between elementary particles. **weak-**

/. . ./ pronunciation	● part of speech
□ phrases, idioms, and compounds	
□□ derivatives	■ synonym section
cross-references appear in SMALL CAPITALS or *italics*	

kneed *colloq.* lacking resolution. **weak-minded 1** mentally deficient. **2** lacking in resolution. **weak-mindedness** the state of being weak-minded. **weak moment** a time when one is unusually compliant or temptable. **weak point** (or **spot**) **1** a place where defenses are assailable. **2** a flaw in an argument or character or in resistance to temptation. □□ **weakish** *adj.* [ME f. ON *veikr* f. Gmc]

■ **1** feeble, frail, fragile, unsubstantial, insubstantial, flimsy, breakable, frangible, delicate, rickety, unsteady, unsound, decrepit, shaky, infirm; powerless, helpless, defenseless, unprotected, unguarded, unshielded, vulnerable, exposed; (*of visible or audible things*) faint, subdued, indistinct, wavering, faltering, unclear, muted; (*of visible things*) dim, poor, dull, pale, faded, vague, hazy, imperceptible, indiscernible, blurred, blurry, muzzy, ill-defined, flickering; (*of audible things*) low, soft, hushed, muffled, almost inaudible, stifled. **2** frail, feeble, infirm, debilitated, enervated, incapacitated, weedy, delicate, sickly, anemic, wasted, decrepit, puny, effete, worn out, tired, exhausted. **3 a** unassertive, retiring, namby-pamby, spineless, irresolute, impotent, powerless, ineffectual, ineffective, incompetent, feckless, inept, wishy-washy, weak-minded, timid, meek, craven, timorous, cowardly, pusillanimous, lily-livered, chickenhearted, fainthearted, *colloq.* chicken, weak-kneed, yellow. **4** feeble, lame, half-baked, poor, miserable, unconvincing, unpersuasive, empty, shallow, hollow, flimsy, tenuous, pathetic, pitiful, unbelievable, untenable. **5** see WATERY 2. **8** see UNACCENTED. □ **weak-kneed** see WEAK 3a above. **weak-minded 1** dim-witted, dull-witted, slow-witted, foolish, feebleminded, simple, simpleminded, softheaded, stupid, dull, moronic, imbecilic, *colloq.* dumb. **2** see WEAK 3a above. **weak-mindedness** see *stupidity* (STUPID). **weak point** (or **spot**) **2** see WEAKNESS 2.

weaken /wéekən/ *v.* **1** *tr.* & *intr.* make or become weak or weaker. **2** *intr.* relent; give way; succumb to temptation, etc. □□ **weakener** *n.*

■ **1** debilitate, enfeeble, enervate, emasculate, mitigate, moderate, deplete, diminish, lessen, depress, lower, reduce, sap, undermine, vitiate, erode, drain, exhaust, impoverish, impair, cripple, water (down), dilute, thin (out); fade, dwindle, decline, tire, droop, sink, sag, fail, give way, crumble, flag, abate, wane, ebb, subside. **2** give in, relent, acquiesce, give way, yield, accede, consent, agree, assent; soften, bend, ease up, let up, ease off, relax; succumb (to temptation), fall.

weakfish /wéekfish/ *n.* (*pl.* same or **-fishes**) a marine fish of the genus *Cynoscion*, used as food. [obs. Du. *weekvisch* f. *week* soft (formed as WEAK) + *visch* FISH[1]]

weakling /wéekling/ *n.* a feeble person or animal.

■ weed, runt, milksop, baby, mollycoddle, lightweight, namby-pamby, *colloq.* cream puff, sissy, loser, jellyfish, pushover, softy, wimp, schlemiel, *sl.* twerp, schnook.

weakly /wéeklee/ *adv.* & *adj.* ● *adv.* in a weak manner. ● *adj.* (**weaklier, weakliest**) sickly; not robust. □□ **weakliness** *n.*

■ *adj.* see PUNY 1, 2, UNHEALTHY 1.

weakness /wéeknis/ *n.* **1** the state or condition of being weak. **2** a weak point; a defect. **3** the inability to resist a particular temptation. **4** (foll. by *for*) a self-indulgent liking (*have a weakness for chocolate*).

■ **1** feebleness, frailty, fragility, delicacy, delicateness, flimsiness, vulnerability, infirmity, debility, decrepitude, puniness. **2** weak point *or* spot, foible, failing, fault, shortcoming, deficiency, flaw, Achilles heel, defect, imperfection, liability. **3** incapacity, irresolution, irresoluteness, impotence, powerlessness. **4** soft spot, fondness, affection, liking, preference, bent, leaning, inclination, fancy, penchant, predilection, proclivity, predisposition, partiality, appreciation, appetite, sweet tooth, taste, eye.

weal[1] /weel/ *n.* & *v.* ● *n.* a ridge raised on the flesh by a stroke of a rod or whip. ● *v.tr.* mark with a weal. [var. of WALE, infl. by obs. *wheal* suppurate]

■ *n.* see WELT *n.* 2.

weal[2] /weel/ *n. literary* welfare; prosperity; good fortune. [OE *wela* f. WG (as WELL[1])]

Weald /weeld/ *n.* (also **weald**) (prec. by *the*) *Brit.* a formerly wooded district including parts of Kent, Surrey, and East Sussex. □ **weald clay** beds of clay, sandstone, limestone, and ironstone, forming the top of Wealden strata, with abundant fossil remains. [OE, = *wald* WOLD]

wealth /welth/ *n.* **1** riches; abundant possessions; opulence. **2** the state of being rich. **3** (foll. by *of*) an abundance or profusion (*a wealth of new material*). **4** *archaic* welfare or prosperity. [ME *welthe*, f. WELL[1] or WEAL[2] + -TH[2], after *health*]

■ **1** affluence, riches, money, opulence, prosperity, property, possessions, holdings, substance, capital, assets, fortune, *colloq.* wherewithal, cash. **2** affluence, prosperity, opulence. **3** profusion, abundance, bounty, copiousness, fullness, store, cornucopia, richness, *literary* plenitude, *poet.* bounteousness, plenteousness.

wealthy /wélthee/ *adj.* (**wealthier, wealthiest**) having an abundance esp. of money. □□ **wealthily** *adv.* **wealthiness** *n.*

■ rich, affluent, well off, prosperous, well-to-do, opulent, comfortable, moneyed, in clover, *colloq.* in the money, on easy street, flush, filthy rich, rolling in it, well-heeled, *sl.* loaded, stinking (rich).

wean[1] /ween/ *v.tr.* **1** accustom (an infant or other young mammal) to food other than (esp. its mother's) milk. **2** (often foll. by *from*, *away from*) disengage (from a habit, etc.) by enforced discontinuance. [OE *wenian* accustom f. Gmc: cf. WONT]

wean[2] /ween/ *n. Sc.* a young child. [contr. of *wee ane* little one]

weaner /wéenər/ *n.* a young animal recently weaned.

weanling /wéenling/ *n.* a newly weaned child, etc.

weapon /wépən/ *n.* **1** a thing designed or used or usable for inflicting bodily harm (e.g., a gun or a knife). **2** a means employed for trying to gain the advantage in a conflict (*irony is a double-edged weapon*). □□ **weaponed** *adj.* (also in *comb.*). **weaponless** *adj.* [OE *wǣp(e)n* f. Gmc]

■ **2** see DEVICE 2, TOOL *n.* 2. □□ **weaponless** unarmed, unprotected, defenseless.

weaponry /wépənree/ *n.* weapons collectively.

wear[1] /wair/ *v.* & *n.* ● *v.* (*past* **wore** /wawr/; *past part.* **worn** /wawrn/) **1** *tr.* have on one's person as clothing or an ornament, etc. (*is wearing shorts*; *wears earrings*). **2** *tr.* be dressed habitually in (*wears green*). **3** *tr.* exhibit or present (a facial expression or appearance) (*wore a frown*; *the day wore a different aspect*). **4** *tr. Brit. colloq.* (usu. with *neg.*) tolerate; accept (*they won't wear that excuse*). **5** (often foll. by *away*, *down*) **a** *tr.* injure the surface of, or partly obliterate or alter, by rubbing, stress, or use. **b** *intr.* undergo such injury or change. **6** *tr.* & *intr.* (foll. by *off*, *away*) rub or be rubbed off. **7** *tr.* make (a hole, etc.) by constant rubbing or dripping, etc. **8** *tr.* (often foll. by *out*) exhaust; tire or be tired. **9** *tr.* (foll. by *down*) overcome by persistence. **10** *intr.* **a** remain for a specified time in working order or a presentable state; last long. **b** (foll. by *well*, *badly*, etc.) endure continued use or life. **11 a** *intr.* (of time) pass, esp. tediously. **b** *tr.* pass (time) gradually away. **12** *tr.* (of a ship) fly (a flag). ● *n.* **1** the act of wearing or the state of being worn (*suitable for informal wear*). **2** things worn; fashionable or suitable clothing (*sportswear*; *footwear*). **3** (in full **wear and tear**) damage sustained from continuous use. **4** the capacity for resisting wear and tear (*still a great deal of wear left in it*). □ **in wear** being regularly worn. **wear one's heart on one's sleeve** see HEART. **wear off** lose effectiveness or intensity. **wear out 1** use or be used until no longer usable. **2** tire or be tired out. **wear the pants** see PANTS. **wear thin** (of patience, excuses, etc.) begin to fail. **wear** (or **wear one's years**) **well** *colloq.* remain young-looking. □□ **wearable** *adj.* **wearability** /wáirəbílitee/ *n.* **wearer** *n.* **wearing** *adj.* **wearingly** *adv.* [OE *werian* f. Gmc]

■ *v.* **1, 2** be dressed *or* clothed in, dress in, be in, have on, sport. **3** display, show, exhibit, present, have, sport, adopt, assume. **5** wear down *or* away, damage, impair, harm, fray, chafe, rub, erode, abrade, corrode. **8** tire, fatigue, exhaust, debilitate, weary, enervate, drain, burden. **9** (*wear down*) see GRIND *v.* 3. **10** last, endure, survive, hold up, bear up, stand up. **11 a** drag, pass slowly, creep by *or* along, go by gradually *or* tediously. ● *n.* **1** wearing, use, utilization. **2** garb, clothing, clothes, dress, *colloq.* gear, *formal* attire, apparel. **3** wear and tear, attrition, deterioration, damage, fraying, chafing, abrasion, erosion, corrosion. □ **wear off** see SUBSIDE 1. **wear out 2** see WEAR *v.* 8 above.
□□ **wearing** tiring, exhausting, wearying, enervating, taxing, strenuous, burdensome, wearisome; irksome, tedious, vexing, annoying, irritating, exasperating.

wear² /wair/ *v.* (*past* and *past part.* **wore** /wawr/) **1** *tr.* bring (a ship) about by turning its head away from the wind. **2** *intr.* (of a ship) come about in this way (cf. TACK¹ *v.* 4a). [17th c.: orig. unkn.]

wearisome /weereesǝm/ *adj.* tedious; tiring by monotony or length. □□ **wearisomely** *adv.* **wearisomeness** *n.*
■ see TEDIOUS.

weary /weeree/ *adj.* & *v.* ● *adj.* (**wearier, weariest**) **1** unequal to or disinclined for further exertion or endurance; tired. **2** (foll. by *of*) dismayed at the continuing of; impatient of. **3** tiring or tedious. ● *v.* (**-ies, -ied**) **1** *tr.* & *intr.* make or grow weary. **2** *intr.* esp. *Sc.* long. □□ **weariless** *adj.* **wearily** *adv.* **weariness** *n.* **wearyingly** *adv.* [OE wērig, wǣrig f. WG]

■ *adj.* **1** tired, fatigued, exhausted, worn out, drained, spent, ready to drop, dog-tired, knocked up, *colloq.* fagged (out), all in, done in, dead (on one's feet), frazzled, dead beat, knocked out, shot, pooped, bushed, tuckered out, esp. *Brit. colloq.* whacked; *sl.* zonked (out). **2** bored, impatient, jaded, blasé, fed up, *colloq.* sick and tired, sick to death, *sl.* browned off. **3** boring, irksome, irritating, tedious, vexing, annoying, exasperating, burdensome, wearying, tiring, fatiguing, draining, taxing, wearisome. ● *v.* **1** exhaust, enervate, fatigue, tire, debilitate, drain, tax, wear *or* tire out; tire (of), be *or* become bored (with *or* by), be *or* become impatient (with), be *or* become jaded (with *or* by), be *or* become fed up (with), *colloq.* be *or* become sick and tired (of) *or* sick to death (of). □□ **weariness** see LETHARGY 2.

weasel /weezǝl/ *n.* & *v.* ● *n.* **1** a small, reddish-brown, flesh-eating mammal, *Mustela nivalis*, with a slender body, related to the stoat and ferret. **2** a stoat. **3** *colloq.* a deceitful or treacherous person. ● *v.intr.* **1** equivocate or quibble. **2** (foll. by *on, out*) default on an obligation. □ **weasel-faced** having thin sharp features. **weasel word** (usu. in *pl.*) a word that is intentionally ambiguous or misleading. □□ **weaselly** *adj.* [OE wesle, wesule f. WG]

■ *v.* **1** see EQUIVOCATE. **2** (*weasel out of*) see EVADE 1, 2.
□ **weasel word** (*weasel words*) flattery, humbug, blarney, *colloq.* soft soap, sweet talk.

weather /wethǝr/ *n.* & *v.* ● *n.* **1** the state of the atmosphere at a place and time as regards heat, cloudiness, dryness, sunshine, wind, and rain, etc. **2** (*attrib.*) *Naut.* windward (*on the weather side*). ● *v.* **1** *tr.* expose to or affect by atmospheric changes, esp. deliberately to dry, season, etc. (*weathered shingles*). **2 a** *tr.* (usu. in *passive*) discolor or partly disintegrate (rock or stones) by exposure to air. **b** *intr.* be discolored or worn in this way. **3** *tr.* make (boards or tiles) overlap downward to keep out rain, etc. **4** *tr.* **a** come safely through (a storm). **b** survive (a difficult period, etc.). **5** *tr.* (of a ship or its crew) get to the windward of (a cape, etc.). □ **keep a** (or **one's**) **weather eye open** be watchful. **make good** (or **bad**) **weather of it** *Naut.* (of a ship) behave well (or badly) in a storm. **make heavy weather of** *colloq.* exaggerate the difficulty or burden presented by (a problem, course of action, etc.). **under the weather** *colloq.* indisposed or out of sorts; drunk. **weather-beaten** affected by exposure to the weather. **weather-bound** unable to pro-

ceed owing to bad weather. **weather forecast** an analysis of the state of the weather with an assessment of likely developments over a certain time. **weather map** a diagram showing the state of the weather over a large area. **weather side** the side from which the wind is blowing (opp. *lee side*). **weather station** an observation post for recording meteorological data. **weather strip** (or **stripping**) a piece of material used to make a door or window proof against rain or wind. **weather-strip** install a weather strip. **weather vane** see VANE. [OE weder f. Gmc]

■ *n.* **1** (meteorological) condition(s), climate, the elements. ● *v.* **4** stand, survive, suffer, bear up against, endure, withstand, rise above, ride out, live through, come through, brave. □ **keep a** (or **one's**) **weather eye open** see *watch out*. **under the weather** ailing, ill, sickly, unwell, indisposed, out of sorts, off color, sick, poorly, *Brit. colloq.* seedy; see also DRUNK *adj.* 1.
weather-beaten dry, craggy, rugged, rough; tanned, brown, bronzed, sunburnt, suntanned.

weatherboard /wethǝrbawrd/ *n.* & *v.* ● *n. Brit.* clapboard; siding. ● *v.tr.* fit or supply with weatherboards. □□ **weatherboarding** *n.* **weatherboarded** *adj.*

weathercock /wethǝrkok/ *n.* **1** a weather vane (see VANE) in the form of a cock. **2** an inconstant person.

weatherglass /wethǝrglas/ *n.* a simple barometer or hygroscope.

weathering /wethǝring/ *n.* **1** the action of the weather on materials, etc., exposed to it. **2** exposure to adverse weather conditions (see WEATHER *v.* 1).
■ **1** see EROSION .

weatherly /wethǝrlee/ *adj. Naut.* **1** (of a ship) making little leeway. **2** capable of keeping close to the wind. □□ **weatherliness** *n.*

weatherman /wethǝrman/ *n.* (*pl.* **-men**) a meteorologist, esp. one who broadcasts a weather forecast.

weatherproof /wethǝrproof/ *adj.* & *v.* ● *adj.* resistant to the effects of bad weather, esp. rain. ● *v.tr.* make weatherproof. □□ **weatherproofed** *adj.*

weatherworn /wethǝrwawrn/ *adj.* damaged by exposure to weather.

weave¹ /weev/ *v.* & *n.* ● *v.* (*past* **wove** /wōv/; *past part.* **woven** /wōvǝn/ or **wove**) **1** *tr.* **a** form (fabric) by interlacing long threads in two directions. **b** form (thread) into fabric in this way. **2** *intr.* **a** make fabric in this way. **b** work at a loom. **3** *tr.* make (a basket or wreath, etc.) by interlacing rushes or flowers, etc. **4** *tr.* **a** (foll. by *into*) make (facts, etc.) into a story or connected whole. **b** make (a story) in this way. ● *n.* a style of weaving. [OE wefan f. Gmc]

■ *v.* **1 b** braid, plait, entwine, intertwine, interlace, interweave, crisscross, knit (together). **4 a** blend, combine, fuse, merge, unite, intermingle, mesh, splice, dovetail, join. **b** construct, make, contrive, build, create, fabricate, compose, spin, design.

weave² /weev/ *v.intr.* **1** move repeatedly from side to side; take an intricate course to avoid obstructions. **2** *colloq.* maneuver an aircraft in this way; take evasive action. □ **get weaving** *sl.* begin action; hurry. [prob. f. ME *weve*, var. of *waive* f. ON *veifa* WAVE]

■ **1** zigzag, crisscross, make one's way, wind, dodge, bob and weave, shift, *literary or archaic* wend one's way.
□ **get weaving** get started, get a move on, hurry (up), start, shake a leg, *colloq.* get cracking, *sl.* get one's ass in gear, *Brit. sl.* get *or* pull one's finger out, get a wiggle on.

weaver /weevǝr/ *n.* **1** a person whose occupation is weaving. **2** = WEAVERBIRD. □ **weaver's knot** (or **hitch**) a sheet bend (see SHEET²) used in weaving.

weaverbird /weevǝrbǝrd/ *n.* any tropical bird of the family Ploceidae, building elaborately woven nests.

/.../ **pronunciation**	● **part of speech**
□ **phrases, idioms, and compounds**	
□□ **derivatives**	■ **synonym section**
cross-references appear in SMALL CAPITALS or *italics*	

web /web/ *n. & v.* ● *n.* **1 a** a woven fabric. **b** an amount woven in one piece. **2** a complete structure or connected series (*a web of lies*). **3** a cobweb, gossamer, or a similar product of a spinning creature. **4 a** a membrane between the toes of a swimming animal or bird. **b** the vane of a bird's feather. **5 a** a large roll of paper used in a continuous printing process. **b** an endless wire mesh on rollers, on which this is made. **6** a thin, flat part connecting thicker or more solid parts in machinery, etc. ● *v.* (**webbed, webbing**) **1** *tr.* weave a web on. **2** *intr.* weave a web. □ **web-footed** having the toes connected by webs. **web-offset** offset printing on a web of paper. □□ **webbed** *adj.* [OE *web, webb* f. Gmc]
■ *n.* **2** net, network, mesh, entanglement, tangle, tissue, series. **3** spider's web, cobweb, gossamer; snare, trap.

webbing /wébing/ *n.* strong, narrow, closely woven fabric used for supporting upholstery, for belts, etc.

weber /wébər, váybər/ *n.* the SI unit of magnetic flux, causing the electromotive force of one volt in a circuit of one turn when generated or removed in one second. ¶ Abbr.: **Wb.** [W. E. *Weber*, Ger. physicist d. 1891]

webworm /wébwərm/ *n.* a gregarious caterpillar spinning a large web in which to sleep or to feed on enclosed foliage.

Wed. *abbr.* Wednesday.

wed /wed/ *v.* (**wedding;** *past* and *past part.* **wedded** or **wed**) **1** usu. *formal* or *literary* **a** *tr. & intr.* marry. **b** *tr.* join in marriage. **2** *tr.* unite (*wed efficiency to economy*). **3** *tr.* (as **wedded** *adj.*) of or in marriage (*wedded bliss*). **4** *tr.* (as **wedded** *adj.*) (foll. by *to*) obstinately attached or devoted (to a pursuit, etc.). [OE *weddian* to pledge f. Gmc]
■ **1** marry, get married, become husband and wife, say *or* take (one's) (marriage) vows, join in marriage, join *or* unite in holy wedlock, join *or* unite in holy matrimony, *archaic* espouse; lead down the aisle, lead to the altar, *archaic* wive; *colloq.* tie the knot, get hitched, get spliced. **2** combine, unite, ally, marry, blend, merge, join, mingle, intermingle, mix, intermix, amalgamate, compound, alloy, fuse, *literary* commingle. **3** (**wedded**) see *matrimonial* (MATRIMONY). **4** (*wedded to*) intimately attached *or* connected to, obstinately attached *or* connected to, enamored of, devoted to.

we'd /weed/ *contr.* **1** we had. **2** we should; we would.

wedding /wéding/ *n.* a marriage ceremony (considered by itself or with the associated celebrations). □ **wedding cake** a rich iced cake served at a wedding reception. **wedding day** the day or anniversary of a wedding. **wedding march** a march played at the entrance of the bride or the exit of the couple at a wedding. **wedding night** the night after a wedding (esp. with ref. to its consummation). **wedding ring** (or **band**) a ring worn by a married person. [OE *weddung* (as WED, -ING¹)]
■ marriage (ceremony), wedding ceremony, nuptials.

wedge¹ /wej/ *n. & v.* ● *n.* **1** a piece of wood or metal, etc., tapering to a sharp edge, that is driven between two objects or parts of an object to secure or separate them; a thing separating two people or groups of people. **2** anything resembling a wedge (*a wedge of cheese; troops formed a wedge*). **3** a golf club with a wedge-shaped head. **4 a** a wedge-shaped heel. **b** a shoe with this. ● *v.tr.* **1** tighten, secure, or fasten by means of a wedge (*wedged the door open*). **2** force open or apart with a wedge. **3** (foll. by *in, into*) pack or thrust (a thing or oneself) tightly in or into. □ **thin end of the wedge** esp. *Brit. colloq.* an action or procedure of little importance in itself, but likely to lead to more serious developments. **wedge-shaped 1** shaped like a solid wedge. **2** V-shaped. □□ **wedgelike** *adj.* **wedgewise** *adv.* [OE *wecg* f. Gmc]
■ *n.* **1** block, chock, cleat; separation, separator, division, partition, split, fissure, cleavage. **2** see SLAB *n.* **4 b** *colloq.* wedgie. ● *v.* **3** ram, jam, stuff, cram, crowd, force, squeeze, sandwich, pack, thrust.

wedge² /wej/ *v.tr. Pottery* prepare (clay) for use by cutting, kneading, and throwing down. [17th c.: orig. uncert.]

wedgie /wéjee/ *n. colloq.* **1** a shoe with an extended wedge-shaped heel. **2** the condition of having one's underwear, etc., wedged between one's buttocks.

Wedgwood /wéjwood/ *n. propr.* **1** ceramic ware made by J.

Wedgwood, Engl. potter d. 1795, and his successors, esp. a kind of fine stoneware usu. with a white cameo design. **2** the characteristic blue color of this stoneware.

wedlock /wédlok/ *n.* the married state. □ **born in** (or **out of**) **wedlock** born of married (or unmarried) parents. [OE *wedlāc* marriage vow f. *wed* pledge (rel. to WED) + *-lāc* suffix denoting action]
■ marriage, matrimony.

Wednesday /wénzday, -dee/ *n. & adv.* ● *n.* the fourth day of the week, following Tuesday. ● *adv. colloq.* **1** on Wednesday. **2** (**Wednesdays**) on Wednesdays; each Wednesday. [ME *wednesdei*, OE *wōdnesdæg* day of (the god) Odin]

Weds. *abbr.* Wednesday.

wee¹ /wee/ *adj.* (**weer** /wéeər/; **weest** /wéeist/) **1** esp. *Sc.* little; very small. **2** *colloq.* tiny; extremely small (*a wee bit*). [orig. Sc. noun, f. north.ME *wei* (small) quantity f. Anglian *wēg*: cf. WEY]
■ tiny, small, diminutive, little, minuscule, midget, minute, miniature, lilliputian, microscopic; unimportant, insignificant, trivial, puny; *colloq.* teeny (-weeny), teensy(-weensy); *colloq. usu. derog.* itty-bitty, itsy-bitsy.

wee² /wee/ *n. esp. Brit. sl.* = WEEWEE.

weed /weed/ *n. & v.* ● *n.* **1** a wild plant growing where it is not wanted. **2** a thin, weak-looking person or horse. **3** (prec. by *the*) *sl.* **a** marijuana. **b** tobacco. ● *v.* **1** *tr.* **a** clear (an area) of weeds. **b** remove unwanted parts from. **2** *tr.* (foll. by *out*) **a** sort out (inferior or unwanted parts, etc.) for removal. **b** rid (a quantity or company) of inferior or unwanted members, etc. **3** *intr.* cut off or uproot weeds. □ **weed-killer** a substance used to destroy weeds; herbicide. □□ **weeder** *n.* **weedless** *adj.* [OE *wēod*, of unkn. orig.]
■ *n.* **2** see DRIP *n.* 2, WEAKLING. ● *v.* **2** (*weed out*) exclude, eliminate, remove, rout out, root out; screen, sift, winnow, clarify, refine, purify, clean, purge, *usu. formal* cleanse.

weeds /weedz/ *n.pl.* (in full **widow's weeds**) *Brit. archaic* deep mourning worn by a widow. [OE *wǣd(e)* garment f. Gmc]

weedy /wéedee/ *adj.* (**weedier, weediest**) **1** having many weeds. **2** (esp. of a person) **a** weak; feeble; of poor stature. **b** very thin; lanky. □□ **weediness** *n.*

week /week/ *n.* **1** a period of seven days reckoned usu. from and to midnight on Saturday–Sunday. **2** a period of seven days reckoned from any point (*would like to stay for a week*). **3** the six days between Sundays. **4 a** the five days Monday to Friday. **b** a normal amount of work done in this period (*a 35-hour week*). **5** (in *pl.*) a long time; several weeks (*have not seen you for weeks; did it weeks ago*). **6** esp. *Brit.* (prec. by a specified day) a week after (that day) (*Tuesday week; tomorrow week*). [OE *wice* f. Gmc, prob. orig. = sequence]

weekday /wéekday/ *n.* a day other than Sunday or other than at a weekend (often *attrib.: a weekday afternoon*).

weekend /wéekénd/ *n. & v.* ● *n.* **1** the end of a week, esp. Saturday and Sunday. **2** this period extended slightly esp. for a vacation or visit, etc. (*going away for the weekend; a weekend cottage*). ● *v.intr.* spend a weekend (*decided to weekend in the country*).

weekender /wéekéndər/ *n.* **1** a person who spends weekends away from home. **2** a weekend traveling bag.

weeklong /wéeklawng, -long/ *adj.* lasting for a week.

weekly /wéeklee/ *adj., adv., & n.* ● *adj.* done, produced, or occurring once a week. ● *adv.* once a week; from week to week. ● *n.* (*pl.* **-ies**) a weekly newspaper or periodical.

ween /ween/ *v.tr. archaic* be of the opinion; think; suppose. [OE *wēnan* f. Gmc]

weeny /wéenee/ *adj.* (**weenier, weeniest**) *colloq.* tiny. □ **weenybopper** esp. *Brit.* a girl like a teenybopper but younger. [WEE¹ after *tiny, teeny*]

weep /weep/ *v. & n.* ● *v.* (*past* and *past part.* **wept** /wept/) **1** *intr.* shed tears. **2 a** *tr. &* (foll. by *for*) *intr.* shed tears for; bewail; lament over. **b** *tr.* utter or express with tears (*"Don't go," he wept; wept her thanks*). **3 a** *intr.* be covered with or send forth drops. **b** *intr. & tr.* come or send forth in drops; exude liquid (*weeping sore*). **4** *intr.* (as **weeping** *adj.*) (of a tree) having drooping branches (*weeping willow*). • *n.* a fit or spell of weeping. □ **weep out** esp. *Brit.* utter with tears. □□ **weepingly** *adv.* [OE *wēpan* f. Gmc (prob. imit.)]

■ *v.* **1, 2** cry, shed tears, bawl, blubber, sob, wail, keen, lament, mourn, moan, grieve, whine, whimper, mewl, snivel, *Brit. colloq.* grizzle, *literary* pule; (*weep for* or *over*) bemoan, bewail. **3** ooze, seep, exude, drip.

weeper /wéepər/ *n.* **1** a person who weeps, esp. *hist.* a hired mourner at a funeral. **2** a small image of a mourner on a monument. **3** (in *pl.*) *hist.* **a** a man's crepe hatband for funerals. **b** a widow's black crepe veil or white cuffs.

weepie /wéepee/ *n.* (also **weepy**) (*pl.* **-ies**) *colloq.* a sentimental or emotional motion picture, play, etc.; tearjerker.

weepy /wéepee/ *adj.* (**weepier, weepiest**) *colloq.* inclined to weep; tearful. □□ **weepily** *adv.* **weepiness** *n.*

■ see TEARFUL 1.

weever /wéevər/ *n.* any marine fish of the genus *Trachinus*, with sharp venomous dorsal spines. [perh. f. OF *wivre, guivre*, serpent, dragon, f. L *vipera* VIPER]

weevil /wéevil/ *n.* **1** any destructive beetle of the family Curculionidae, with its head extended into a beak or rostrum and feeding esp. on grain. **2** any insect damaging stored grain. □□ **weevily** *adj.* [ME f. MLG *wevel* f. Gmc]

weewee /wéewee/ *n.* & *v. sl.* • *n.* **1** the act or an instance of urinating. **2** urine. • *v.intr.* (**-wees, -weed, -weeing**) urinate. [20th c.: orig. unkn.]

■ *v.* see URINATE.

weft /weft/ *n.* **1 a** the threads woven across a warp to make fabric. **b** yarn for these. **c** a thing woven. **2** filling strips in basket weaving. [OE *weft(a)* f. Gmc: rel. to WEAVE[1]]

Wehrmacht /váirmaakht/ *n. hist.* the German armed forces, esp. the army, from 1921 to 1945. [G, = defensive force]

weigh[1] /way/ *v.* **1** *tr.* find the weight of. **2** *tr.* balance in the hands to guess at or as if to guess the weight of. **3** *tr.* (often foll. by *out*) **a** take a definite weight of; take a specified weight from a larger quantity. **b** distribute in exact amounts by weight. **4** *tr.* **a** estimate the relative importance, importance, or desirability of; consider with a view to choice, rejection, or preference (*weighed the consequences; weighed the merits of the candidates*). **b** (foll. by *with, against*) compare (one consideration with another). **5** *tr.* be equal to (a specified weight) (*weighs three pounds*). **6** *intr.* **a** have (esp. a specified) importance; exert an influence. **b** (foll. by *with*) be regarded as important by (*the point that weighs with me*). **7** *intr.* (often foll. by *on*) be heavy or burdensome (to); be depressing (to). □ **weigh anchor** see ANCHOR. **weigh down 1** bring or keep down by exerting weight. **2** be oppressive or burdensome to (*weighed down with worries*). **weigh in** (of a boxer before a contest, or a jockey after a race) be weighed. **weigh-in** *n.* the weighing of a boxer, etc., before a fight. **weigh into** *colloq.* attack (physically or verbally). **weigh in with** *colloq.* advance (an argument, etc.) assertively or boldly. **weigh up** *colloq.* form an estimate of; consider carefully. **weigh one's words** carefully choose the way one expresses something. □□ **weighable** *adj.* **weigher** *n.* [OE *wegan* f. Gmc, rel. to WAY]

■ **3** see MEASURE *v.* 6. **4 a** judge, estimate, assess, evaluate, value, gauge, determine; consider, ponder, contemplate, think over or about, mull over, turn over in the *or* one's mind, ruminate over *or* on, chew over, reflect on *or* upon, brood over, pore over, study, examine, *archaic* think on, *colloq.* weigh up. **b** see COMPARE *v.* 2. **5** weigh in at *or* out at, tip *or* turn the scales at. **6** matter, count, have (an) effect *or* influence, carry weight, be of value *or* account, *sl.* cut any ice. **7** (*weigh on*) lie heavy on, burden, depress, prey on, preoccupy, oppress, disturb, perturb, upset. □ **weigh down 1** see WEIGHT *v.* **2** burden, overburden, load, overload, encumber, tax, overtax, strain, trouble, afflict, worry, depress, oppress. **weigh into** see ATTACK *v.* 1, 3. **weigh up** see WEIGH[1] 4a above.

weigh[2] /way/ *n.* □ **under weigh** *disp.* = *under way*. [18th c.: from an erron. assoc. with *weigh anchor*]

weighbridge /wáybrij/ *n.* a platform scale for weighing ve-

hicles, usu. having a plate set into the road for vehicles to drive on to.

weight /wayt/ *n.* & *v.* • *n.* **1** *Physics* **a** the force experienced by a body as a result of the earth's gravitation (cf. MASS[1] *n.* 8). **b** any similar force with which a body tends to a center of attraction. **2** the heaviness of a body regarded as a property of it; its relative mass or the quantity of matter contained by it giving rise to a downward force (*is twice your weight; kept in position by its weight*). **3 a** the quantitative expression of a body's weight (*has a weight of three pounds*). **b** a scale of such weights (*troy weight*). **4** a body of a known weight for use in weighing. **5** a heavy body esp. used in a mechanism, etc. (*a clock worked by weights*). **6** a load or burden (*a weight off my mind*). **7 a** influence; importance (*carried weight with the public*). **b** preponderance (*the weight of evidence was against them*). **8** a heavy object thrown as an athletic exercise; = SHOT[1] 7. **9** the surface density of cloth, etc., as a measure of its suitability. • *v.tr.* **1 a** attach a weight to. **b** hold down with a weight or weights. **2** (foll. by *with*) impede or burden. **3** *Statistics* multiply the components of (an average) by factors to take account of their importance. **4** assign a handicap weight to (a horse). **5** treat (a fabric) with a mineral, etc., to make it seem stouter. □ **put on weight 1** increase one's weight. **2** get fat. **throw one's weight about** (or **around**) *colloq.* be unpleasantly self-assertive. **worth one's weight in gold** (of a person) exceedingly useful or helpful. [OE (*ge*)*wiht* f. Gmc: cf. WEIGH[1]]

■ *n.* **2, 3** heaviness, mass, tonnage, heft. **6** burden, load, millstone, onus, pressure, strain, encumbrance, albatross, cross. **7 a** influence, authority, power, substance, force, moment, importance, consequence, impact, persuasiveness, value, worth, *colloq.* clout. **b** mass, preponderance, bulk, *disp.* majority. • *v.* **1** load, charge, ballast, weigh down, weight down.

weightless /wáytlis/ *adj.* (of a body, esp. in an orbiting spacecraft, etc.) not apparently acted on by gravity. □□ **weightlessly** *adv.* **weightlessness** *n.*

weightlifting /wáytlifting/ *n.* the sport or exercise of lifting a heavy weight, esp. a barbell. □□ **weightlifter** *n.*

weighty /wáytee/ *adj.* (**weightier, weightiest**) **1** weighing much; heavy. **2** momentous; important. **3** (of utterances, etc.) deserving consideration; careful and serious. **4** influential; authoritative. □□ **weightily** *adv.* **weightiness** *n.*

■ **1** heavy, ponderous; massive, huge, bulky, substantial, ample, large, mammoth, colossal, immense, enormous, gigantic, prodigious; corpulent, fat, obese, adipose, hefty. **2** important, consequential, significant, momentous, grave, serious, crucial, portentous, thought-provoking, provocative. **3, 4** influential, convincing, persuasive, authoritative, impressive, telling, powerful, potent, leading; forceful. □□ **weightiness** see GRAVITY 3a.

Weimaraner /wímərdaanər, ví-/ *n.* a usu. gray dog of a variety of pointer used as a hunting dog. [G, f. *Weimar* in Germany, where it was developed]

weir /weer/ *n.* **1** a dam built across a river to raise the level of water upstream or regulate its flow. **2** an enclosure of stakes, etc., set in a stream as a trap for fish. [OE *wer* f. *werian* dam up]

weird /weerd/ *adj.* & *n.* • *adj.* **1** uncanny; supernatural. **2** *colloq.* strange; queer; incomprehensible. **3** *archaic* connected with fate. • *n.* esp. *Sc. archaic* fate; destiny. □ **the Weird Sisters 1** the Fates. **2** witches. □□ **weirdly** *adv.* **weirdness** *n.* [(earlier as noun) f. OE *wyrd* destiny f. Gmc]

■ *adj.* **1, 2** strange, odd, peculiar, bizarre, curious, incomprehensible, abnormal, unnatural, eerie, queer, grotesque, freakish, freaky, outlandish, far-out, uncanny, unearthly, otherworldly, supernatural,

---

/ . . . / **pronunciation**   • **part of speech**

□ **phrases, idioms, and compounds**

□□ **derivatives**   ■ **synonym section**

cross-references appear in SMALL CAPITALS or *italics*

preternatural, *colloq.* spooky, kinky, way-out, eldritch. □□ **weirdness** see ODDITY 3.

weirdie /weerdee/ *n.* (also **weirdy**) (*pl.* **-ies**) *colloq.* = WEIRDO.

weirdo /weerdō/ *n.* (*pl.* **-os**) *colloq.* an odd or eccentric person.
▪ eccentric, madman, madwoman, lunatic, psychotic, crank, *colloq.* crazy, weirdie, oddball, queer fish, freak, psycho, *sl.* nutcase, nut, crackpot, loony, *sl.* screwball, kook, *Brit. sl.* nutter.

Weismannism /vísmaanizəm/ *n.* the theory of heredity assuming continuity of germ plasm and nontransmission of acquired characteristics. [A. *Weismann,* Ger. biologist d. 1914]

weka /wékə/ *n.* any flightless New Zealand rail of the genus *Gallirallus.* [Maori: imit. of its cry]

Welch /welch, welsh/ var. of WELSH.

welch var. of WELSH.

welcome /wélkəm/ *n., int., v.,* & *adj.* ● *n.* the act or an instance of greeting or receiving (a person, idea, etc.) gladly; a kind or glad reception (*gave them a warm welcome*). ● *int.* expressing such a greeting (*welcome!; welcome home!*). ● *v.tr.* receive with a welcome (*welcomed them home; would welcome the opportunity*). ● *adj.* **1** that one receives with pleasure (*a welcome guest; welcome news*). **2** (foll. by *to,* or *to* + infin.) **a** cordially allowed or invited; released of obligation (*you are welcome to use my car*). **b** *iron.* gladly given (an unwelcome task, thing, etc.) (*here's my work and you are welcome to it*). □ **make welcome** receive hospitably. **you're** (or **you are**) **welcome** there is no need for thanks; your thanks are accepted. □□ **welcomely** *adv.* **welcomeness** *n.* **welcomer** *n.* **welcomingly** *adv.* [orig. OE *wilcuma* one whose coming is pleasing f. *wil-* desire, pleasure + *cuma* comer, with later change to *wel-* WELL[1] after OF *bien venu* or ON *velkominn*]
▪ *n.* reception, greeting, salutation, glad hand.
● *v.* greet, hail, meet, receive, accept, make welcome, offer hospitality to. ● *adj.* **1** accepted, acceptable, well-received, desirable, agreeable, gratifying, appreciated. **2 a** freely permitted *or* allowed, invited, entitled, suffered; (*be welcome*) may.

weld[1] /weld/ *v.* & *n.* ● *v.tr.* **1 a** hammer or press (pieces of iron or other metal usu. heated but not melted) into one piece. **b** join by fusion with an electric arc, etc. **c** form by welding into some article. **2** fashion (arguments, members of a group, etc.) into an effectual or homogeneous whole. ● *n.* a welded joint. □□ **weldable** *adj.* **weldability** /wéldəbílitee/ *n.* **welder** *n.* [alt. of WELL[2] *v.* in obs. sense 'melt or weld (heated metal),' prob. infl. by past part.]
▪ *v.* **1** fuse, attach, connect, link, join; solder, braze, cement, bond. **2** unite, combine, merge, fuse, connect, link, join, cement, bond, weave. ● *n.* seam, joint, juncture, union, commissure.

weld[2] /weld/ *n.* **1** a plant, *Reseda luteola,* yielding a yellow dye. **2** *hist.* this dye. [ME f. OE *w(e)alde* (unrecorded): cf. MDu. *woude,* MLG *walde*]

welfare /wélfair/ *n.* **1** well-being; happiness; health and prosperity (of a person or a community, etc.). **2 a** the maintenance of persons in such a condition esp. by statutory procedure or social effort. **b** financial support given for this purpose. □ **welfare state 1** a system whereby the government undertakes to protect the health and well-being of its citizens, esp. those in financial or social need, by means of grants, pensions, etc. **2** a country practicing this system. [ME f. WELL[1] + FARE]
▪ **1** benefit, good, advantage, well-being, prosperity, (good) fortune, profit, interest, (good) health, happiness, felicity. **2 b** see CHARITY 1b.

welfarism /wélfairizəm/ *n.* principles characteristic of a welfare state. □□ **welfarist** *n.*

welkin /wélkin/ *n. poet.* sky; the upper air. [OE *wolcen* cloud, sky]

well[1] /wel/ *adv., adj.,* & *int.* ● *adv.* (**better, best**) **1** in a satisfactory way (*you have worked well*). **2** in the right way (*well said; you did well to tell me*). **3** with some talent or dis-

tinction (*plays the piano well*). **4** in a kind way (*treated me well*). **5 a** thoroughly; carefully (*polish it well*). **b** intimately; closely (*knew them well*). **6** with heartiness or approval; favorably (*speak well of; the book was well reviewed*). **7** probably; reasonably; advisably (*you may well be right; you may well ask; we might well take the risk*). **8** to a considerable extent (*is well over forty*). **9** successfully; fortunately (*it turned out well*). **10** luckily; opportunely (*well met!*). **11** with a fortunate outcome; without disaster (*were well rid of them*). **12** profitably (*did well for themselves*). **13** comfortably; abundantly; liberally (*we live well here; the job pays well*). ● *adj.* (**better, best**) **1** (usu. *predic.*) in good health (*are you well?; was not a well person*). **2** (*predic.*) **a** in a satisfactory state or position (*all is well*). **b** advisable (*it would be well to inquire*). ● *int.* expressing surprise, resignation, insistence, etc., or resumption or continuation of talk, used esp. after a pause in speaking (*well, I never!; well, I suppose so; well, who was it?*). □ **as well 1** in addition; to an equal extent. **2** (also **just as well**) with equal reason; with no loss of advantage or need for regret (*may as well give up; it would be just as well to stop now*). **as well as** in addition to. **leave** (or **let**) **well alone** avoid needless change or disturbance. **take well** react calmly to (a thing, esp. bad news). **well-acquainted** (usu. foll. by *with*) familiar. **well-adjusted 1** in a good state of adjustment. **2** *Psychol.* mentally and emotionally stable. **well-advised** (usu. foll. by *to* + infin.) (of a person) prudent (*would be well-advised to wait*). **well-affected** (often foll. by *to, toward*) favorably disposed. **well and good** expressing dispassionate acceptance of a decision, etc. **well and truly** esp. *Brit.* decisively; completely. **well-appointed** having all the necessary equipment. **well aware** certainly aware (*well aware of the danger*). **well away 1** having made considerable progress. **2** *Brit. colloq.* fast asleep or drunk. **well-balanced 1** sane; sensible. **2** equally matched. **3** having a symmetrical or orderly arrangement of parts. **well-behaved** see BEHAVE. **well-being** a state of being well, healthy, contented, etc. **well-beloved** *adj.* dearly loved. ● *n.* (*pl.* same) a dearly loved person. **well-bred** having or showing good breeding or manners. **well-built 1** of good construction. **2** (of a person) big and strong and well-proportioned. **well-chosen** (of words, etc.) carefully selected for effect. **well-conditioned** in good physical or moral condition. **well-conducted** (of a meeting, etc.) properly organized and controlled. **well-connected** see CONNECTED. **well-covered** *Brit. colloq.* plump, corpulent. **well-defined** clearly indicated or determined. **well-deserved** rightfully merited or earned. **well-disposed** (often foll. by *toward*) having a good disposition or friendly feeling (for). **well-done 1** (of meat, etc.) thoroughly cooked. **2** (of a task, etc.) performed well (also as *int.*). **well-dressed** fashionably smart. **well-earned** fully deserved. **well-endowed 1** well provided with talent, etc. **2** *colloq.* sexually potent or attractive; having large sexual organs. **well-established** long-standing; familiar; traditional. **well-favored** good-looking. **well-fed** having or having had plenty to eat. **well-found** = *well-appointed*. **well-founded** (of suspicions, etc.) based on good evidence; having a foundation in fact or reason. **well-groomed** (of a person) with carefully tended hair, clothes, etc. **well-grounded 1** = *well-founded*. **2** having a good training in or knowledge of the groundwork of a subject. **well-heeled** *colloq.* wealthy. **well-hung** *colloq.* (of a man) having large genitals. **well-informed** having much knowledge or information about a subject. **well-intentioned** having or showing good intentions. **well-judged** esp. *Brit.* opportunely, skillfully, or discreetly done. **well-kept** kept in good order or condition. **well-knit** closely related; compact; not loosely constructed nor sprawling (*a well-knit family; a well-knit physique*). **well-known 1** known to many. **2** known thoroughly. **well-made 1** strongly or skillfully manufactured. **2** (of a person or animal) having a good build. **well-mannered** having good manners. **well-marked** distinct; easy to detect. **well-matched** see MATCH[1]. **well-meaning** (or **-meant**) well-intentioned (but ineffective or unwise). **well-off 1** having plenty of money. **2** in a fortunate situation or circumstances. **well-oiled** *colloq.* **1** drunk. **2** operating efficiently (*a well-*

oiled committee); **3** esp. *Brit.* (of a compliment, etc.) easily expressed through habitual use. **well-ordered** arranged in an orderly manner. **well-paid 1** (of a job) that pays well. **2** (of a person) amply rewarded for a job. **well-pleased** highly gratified or satisfied. **well-preserved** see PRESERVE. **well-read** knowledgeable through much reading. **well-received** welcomed; favorably received. **well-rounded 1** complete and symmetrical. **2** (of a phrase, etc.) complete and well expressed. **3** (of a person) having or showing a fully developed personality, ability, etc. **4** fleshy; plump. **well-spent** (esp. of money or time) used profitably. **well-spoken** articulate or refined in speech. **well-thought-of** having a good reputation; esteemed; respected. **well-thought-out** carefully devised. **well-thumbed** esp. *Brit.* bearing marks of frequent handling. **well-timed** opportune; timely. **well-to-do** prosperous. **well-tried** often tested with good results. **well-trodden** much frequented. **well-turned 1** (of a compliment, phrase, or verse) elegantly expressed. **2** (of a leg, ankle, etc.) elegantly shaped or displayed. **well-upholstered** see UPHOLSTER. **well-wisher** a person who wishes one well. **well-worn 1** much worn by use. **2** (of a phrase, etc.) trite; hackneyed. **well worth** certainly worth (*well worth a visit*; *well worth visiting*). ¶ A hyphen is normally used in combinations of *well-* when used attributively, but not when used predicatively, e.g., *a well-made coat* but *the coat is well made*. [OE *wel, well* prob. f. the same stem as WILL¹]
■ *adv.* **1** satisfactorily, sufficiently, adequately, agreeably, nicely, (well) enough, *colloq.* OK, okay. **2** appropriately, correctly, accurately, properly, proficiently, effectively. **3** skillfully, expertly, adeptly, proficiently, ably. **4** kindly, graciously, thoughtfully, considerately, hospitably, cordially, genially, humanely. **5 a** thoroughly, extensively, exhaustively, intensively, completely, through and through, carefully, painstakingly, sedulously, assiduously, scrupulously, meticulously. **b** intimately, closely, familiarly, personally; thoroughly, profoundly, soundly, fully, in detail, through and through, completely. **6** graciously, kindly, highly, favorably, glowingly, approvingly, warmly, genially, cordially, amiably, kindheartedly, warmheartedly, affectionately, lovingly. **7** likely, probably, in all probability, doubtless(ly), without doubt, not unexpectedly, indeed; reasonably, justifiably, rightly, justly, properly, understandably, advisably, advisedly. **8** far, by a long way, immeasurably, considerably, (very) much; far and away, definitely, positively, obviously, clearly, plainly, manifestly, evidently, unquestionably, decidedly, beyond (the shadow of a) doubt, indubitably, *Brit.* by a long chalk. **9** successfully, fortunately, happily, smoothly, famously, marvelously, wonderfully, fabulously, incredibly, splendidly, admirably, spectacularly, excellently, superbly, swimmingly. **10** luckily, opportunely, propitiously. **12** profitably, advantageously, favorably. **13** comfortably, luxuriously, prosperously, extravagantly, showily, pretentiously, ostentatiously, sumptuously, grandly, opulently; fairly, justly, suitably, properly, adequately, reasonably, fully, abundantly, generously, liberally, amply. ● *adj.* **1** healthy, fit, hale (and hearty), robust, vigorous, hearty, in good health, in fine *or* good fettle, in good shape, *colloq.* in the pink. **2 a** satisfactory, pleasing, agreeable, good, right, all right, fine, proper, in order, *colloq.* OK, okay. **b** see ADVISABLE. □ **as well 1** see *in addition* (ADDITION). **as well as** see *in addition to* (ADDITION). **take well** accept, resign oneself to, react good-naturedly *or* equably *or* coolly *or* serenely *or* calmly *or* soberly *or* unexcitedly *or* sedately to, receive *or* take good-naturedly *or* equably *or* coolly *or* serenely *or* calmly *or* soberly *or* unexcitedly *or* sedately. **well-acquainted** see FAMILIAR *adj.* 3; (*well-acquainted with*) see FAMILIAR *adj.* 2. **well-adjusted 2** see *well-balanced* 1 below. **well-advised** prudent, wise, sensible, intelligent, smart. **well and truly** see TRULY 5. **well-balanced 1** rational, sane, sensible, reasonable,

levelheaded, sober, sound, well-adjusted, stable, cool (headed), *colloq.* together. **2** evenly matched *or* balanced, equally matched *or* balanced, equal. **3** even, symmetric(al), harmonious, well-proportioned, orderly, well-ordered, well-disposed. **well-being** see WELFARE *n.* 1. **well-bred** well brought up, well-mannered, polite, decorous, mannerly, refined, courteous, cultivated, polished, cultured, gentlemanly, ladylike, elegant, suave, urbane, sophisticated, gracious, courtly, genteel, gallant, chivalrous. **well-built 1** see STRONG *adj.* 1. **2** see STURDY *adj.* 1. **well-chosen** see APPROPRIATE *adj.* **well-defined** see DISTINCT 2. **well-deserved** see JUST *adj.* 2. **well-disposed** (*well-disposed to*) see SYMPATHETIC *adj.* 5. **well-done 1** thoroughly cooked, cooked through and through, completely cooked. **2** properly done, first-class, first-rate, *colloq.* top-notch, tip-top. **well-dressed** see DAPPER 1. **well-earned** see DUE *adj.* 2, 3. **well-endowed 2** see VOLUPTUOUS 2. **well-established** long-standing, traditional, set, venerable, well-known, accepted, familiar, well-founded. **well-fed** plump, chunky, thickset, chubby, (well-)rounded, rotund, portly, stout, fleshy, overweight, adipose, fat, obese, gross, pudgy, esp. *Brit.* podgy. **well-founded** see SOLID *adj.* 6a. **well-groomed** neat, dapper, fastidious, tidy, trim, smart, chic, soigné(e), clean-cut, spruce, well-dressed, *archaic sl.* spiffing, *colloq.* natty, nifty, *sl.* spiffy. **well-grounded 2** (*well-grounded in*) see VERSED. **well-heeled** see WEALTHY. **well-informed** knowledgeable, learned, well-read, well-versed, well up, well-educated, lettered, literate, educated, enlightened, au courant, *au fait*, apprised, aware, *colloq.* in the know, wise, *sl.* hip. **well-intentioned** see KIND². **well-kept** see TIDY *adj.* 1. **well-knit** well-proportioned, compact; see ROBUST 1. **well-known 1** famous, noted, notable, celebrated, renowned, illustrious, legendary, famed, public, prominent, eminent, preeminent. **2** known, familiar, (well-)established, acknowledged, proverbial, customary, everyday. **well-made 1** see SOLID *adj.* 4, EXQUISITE *adj.* 1. **2** see STURDY *adj.* 1. **well-mannered** see COURTEOUS. **well-meaning** see KIND². **well-off 1** comfortable, wealthy, rich, affluent, prosperous, opulent, moneyed, well-to-do, *colloq.* flush, well-heeled, *sl.* loaded. **2** fortunate, lucky, blessed. **well-ordered** see SYSTEMATIC 1. **well-paid 1** see PROFITABLE 1. **well-pleased** see PROUD 1. **well-read** see KNOWLEDGEABLE. **well-received** popular, successful, celebrated, well-liked, favorite, favored; see also FASHIONABLE, WELCOME *adj.* 1. **well-rounded 4** see FULL¹ *adj.* 8. **well-spent** see FRUITFUL 2. **well-spoken** see ELOQUENT 1. **well-thought-of** admired, highly regarded, respected, reputable, venerated, esteemed, revered, looked-up-to, valued. **well-timed** timely, seasonable, opportune, auspicious, favorable, propitious, advantageous, beneficial. **well-to-do** see *well-off* 1 (WELL¹) above. **well-worn** see TIMEWORN.

well² /wel/ *n.* & *v.* ● *n.* **1** a shaft sunk into the ground to obtain water, oil, etc. **2** an enclosed space like a well shaft, e.g., in the middle of a building for stairs or an elevator, or for light or ventilation. **3** (foll. by *of*) a source, esp. a copious one (*a well of information*). **4 a** a mineral spring. **b** (in *pl.*) a spa. **5** = INKWELL. **6** *archaic* a water spring or fountain. **7** *Brit.* a railed space for lawyers, etc., in a court of law. **8** a depression for gravy, etc., in a dish or tray, or for a mat in the floor. **9** *Physics* a region of minimum potential, etc. ● *v.intr.* (foll. by *out, up*) spring as from a fountain; flow copiously. □ [OE *wella* (= OHG *wella* wave, ON *vella* boiling heat), *wellan* boil, melt f. Gmc]
■ *n.* **1** shaft, bore, borehole; gusher. **3** source, spring,

wellspring, fountain, mine, reservoir, supply, *poet.* fount. **4a, 6** wellspring, spring, fountain, wellhead, fountainhead, source, reservoir, *poet.* fount. ● *v.* flow, spring, surge, rise, stream, brim over, swell, start; gush, spurt, jet, spout.

we'll /weel, wil/ *contr.* we shall; we will.

wellborn /wélbáwrn/ *adj.* of wealthy or noble lineage.
■ see *upper-class* (UPPER¹).

wellhead /wélhed/ *n.* a source esp. of a spring or stream; a fountainhead.

Wellington /wélingtən/ *n.* (in full **Wellington boot**) *Brit.* a waterproof rubber or plastic boot usu. reaching the knee. [after the 1st Duke of *Wellington*, Brit. general and statesman d. 1852]

wellness /wélnəs/ *n.* the state or condition of being in good physical and mental health.

well-nigh /wélní/ *adv.* archaic or rhet. almost (*well-nigh impossible*).
■ see ALMOST.

Welsh /welsh/ *adj. & n.* ● *adj.* of or relating to Wales or its people or language. ● *n.* **1** the Celtic language of Wales. **2** (prec. by *the*; treated as *pl.*) the people of Wales. □ **Welsh corgi** see CORGI. **Welsh dresser** a type of dresser with open shelves above a cupboard. **Welsh harp** a harp with three rows of strings. **Welsh onion** a species of onion, *Allium fistulosum*, forming clusters of bulbs. **Welsh rabbit** (or **rarebit** by folk etymology) a dish of melted cheese, etc., on toast. [OE *Welisc*, *Wælisc*, etc., f. Gmc f. L *Volcae*, the name of a Celtic people]

welsh /welsh/ *v.intr.* (also **welch** /welch/) **1** (of a loser of a bet, esp. a bookmaker) decamp without paying. **2** evade an obligation. **3** (foll. by *on*) **a** fail to carry out a promise to (a person). **b** fail to honor (an obligation). □□ **welsher** *n.* [19th c.: orig. unkn.]
■ **3 b** (*welsh on*) see go back on (BACK). □□ **welsher** nonpayer, cheat, cheater, swindler, *sl.* deadbeat.

Welshman /wélshmən/ *n.* (*pl.* **-men**) a person who is Welsh by birth or descent; a resident of Wales.

Welshwoman /wélshwŏŏmən/ *n.* (*pl.* **-women**) a woman who is Welsh by birth or descent; a woman resident of Wales.

welt /welt/ *n. & v.* ● *n.* **1** a leather rim sewn around the edge of a shoe upper for the sole to be attached to. **2** = WEAL¹. **3** a ribbed or reinforced border of a garment; a trimming. **4** a heavy blow. ● *v.tr.* **1** provide with a welt. **2** rain welts on; thrash. [ME *welte*, *walt*, of unkn. orig.]
■ *n.* **2** bruise, contusion, bump, lump, ridge, scar, weal. **3** bead, ridge, seam, edge, wale, stripe, binding, trimming. ● *v.* **2** see BEAT *v.* 1.

Weltanschauung /véltaanshówŏŏng/ *n.* a particular philosophy or view of life; a conception of the world. [G f. *Welt* world + *Anschauung* perception]

welter¹ /wéltər/ *v. & n.* ● *v.intr.* **1** roll; wallow; be washed about. **2** (foll. by *in*) lie prostrate or be soaked or steeped in blood, etc. ● *n.* **1** a state of general confusion. **2** (foll. by *of*) a disorderly mixture or contrast of beliefs, policies, etc. [ME f. MDu., MLG *welteren*]
■ *v.* **1** roll (about), flounder, wallow. **2** (*welter in*) be soaked in, lie prostrate in; be sunk *or* involved in, be bogged down in, be entangled *or* ensnarled in. ● *n.* **2** mass, mess, jumble, tangle, confusion, mishmash, muddle, clutter, hodgepodge.

welter² /wéltər/ *n.* **1** a heavy rider or boxer. **2** *colloq.* a heavy blow. **3** *colloq.* a big person or thing. [19th c.: orig. unkn.]

welterweight /wéltərwayt/ *n.* **1** a weight in certain sports intermediate between lightweight and middleweight. **2** an athlete of this weight.

weltschmerz /véltshmairts/ *n.* a feeling of pessimism; an apathetic or vaguely yearning outlook on life. [G f. *Welt* world + *Schmerz* pain]

wen¹ /wen/ *n.* **1** a benign tumor on the skin, esp. of the scalp. **2** *Brit.* an outstandingly large or congested city. □ **the great wen** London. [OE *wen, wenn*, of unkn. orig.: cf. Du. *wen*, MLG *wene*, LG *wehne* tumor, wart]

wen² var. of WYNN.

wench /wench/ *n. & v.* ● *n.* **1** *joc.* a girl or young woman. **2** *archaic* a prostitute. ● *v.intr. archaic* (of a man) consort with prostitutes. □□ **wencher** *n.* [ME *wenche, wenchel* f. OE *wencel* child: cf. OE *wancol* weak, tottering]
■ *n.* **1** see GIRL 2.

Wend /wend/ *n.* a member of a Slavic people of N. Germany, now inhabiting E. Saxony. □□ **Wendic** *adj.* **Wendish** *adj.* [G *Wende* f. OHG *Winida*, of unkn. orig.]

wend /wend/ *v.tr. & intr. literary* or *archaic* go. □ **wend one's way** make one's way. [OE *wendan* turn f. Gmc, rel. to WIND²]

Wensleydale /wénzleedayl/ *n.* **1** a variety of white or blue cheese. **2 a** a sheep of a breed with long wool. **b** this breed. [*Wensleydale* in Yorkshire]

went *past* of GO¹.

wentletrap /wént'ltrap/ *n.* any marine snail of the genus *Clathrus*, with a spiral shell of many whorls. [Du. *wenteltrap* winding stair, spiral shell]

wept *past* of WEEP.

were *2nd sing. past, pl. past, and past subj.* of BE.

we're /weer/ *contr.* we are.

weren't /wərnt, wərənt/ *contr.* were not.

werewolf /wéerwŏŏlf, wáir-/ *n.* (also **werwolf** /wər-/) (*pl.* **-wolves**) a mythical being who at times changes from a person to a wolf. [OE *werewulf*: first element perh. f. OE *wer* man = L *vir*]

wert *archaic 2nd sing. past* of BE.

Wesleyan /wézleeən/ *adj. & n.* ● *adj.* of or relating to a Protestant denomination founded by the English evangelist John Wesley (d. 1791) (cf. METHODIST). ● *n.* a member of this denomination. □□ **Wesleyanism** *n.*

west /west/ *n., adj., & adv.* ● *n.* **1 a** the point of the horizon where the sun sets at the equinoxes (cardinal point 90° to the left of north). **b** the compass point corresponding to this. **c** the direction in which this lies. **2** (usu. **the West**) **a** European in contrast to Oriental civilization. **b** the non-Communist nations of Europe and N. America. **c** the western part of the late Roman Empire. **d** the western part of a country, town, etc., esp. the American West. **3** *Bridge* a player occupying the position designated "west". ● *adj.* **1** toward, at, near, or facing west. **2** coming from the west (*west wind*). ● *adv.* **1** toward, at, or near the west. **2** (foll. by *of*) further west than. □ **go west** *sl.* be killed or destroyed, etc.; die. **West Bank** a region west of the Jordan River assigned to Jordan in 1948 and occupied by Israel since 1967. **West Indian 1** a native or national of any island of the West Indies. **2** a person of West Indian descent. **West Indies** the islands of Central America, including Cuba and the Bahamas. **west-northwest** (or **southwest**) the direction or compass point midway between west and northwest (or southwest). **West Side** the western part of Manhattan in New York City. [OE f. Gmc]

westbound /wéstbownd/ *adj.* traveling or leading westward.

westering /wéstəring/ *adj.* (of the sun) nearing the west. [*wester* (v.) ME f. WEST]

westerly /wéstərlee/ *adj., adv., & n.* ● *adj. & adv.* **1** in a western position or direction. **2** (of a wind) blowing from the west. ● *n.* (*pl.* **-ies**) a wind blowing from the west. [*wester* (adj.) f. OE *westra* f. WEST]

western /wéstərn/ *adj. & n.* ● *adj.* **1** of or in the west; inhabiting the west. **2** lying or directed toward the west. **3** (**Western**) of or relating to the West (see WEST *n.* 2). ● *n.* a motion picture or novel about cowboys in western North America. □ **Western Church** the part of Christendom that has continued to derive its authority, doctrine, and ritual from the popes in Rome. **western hemisphere** the half of the earth containing the Americas. □□ **westernmost** *adj.* [OE *westerne* (as WEST, -ERN)]

Westerner /wéstərnər/ *n.* a native or inhabitant of the West.

westernize /wéstərnīz/ *v.tr.* (also **Westernize**) influence with or convert to the ideas and customs, etc., of the West. □□ **westernization** *n.* **westernizer** *n.*

westing /wésting/ *n.* *Naut.* the distance traveled or the angle of longitude measured westward from either a defined north–south grid line or a meridian.

Westminster /wéstminstər/ *n.* the Parliament at Westminster in London.

■ see PARLIAMENT 1a.

westward /wéstwərd/ *adj., adv.,* & *n.* ● *adj.* & *adv.* (also **westwards**) toward the west. ● *n.* a westward direction or region.

wet /wet/ *adj., v.,* & *n.* ● *adj.* (**wetter, wettest**) **1** soaked, covered, or dampened with water or other liquid (*a wet sponge*; *a wet surface*; *got my feet wet*). **2** (of the weather, etc.) rainy (*a wet day*). **3** (of paint, ink, etc.) not yet dried. **4** used with water (*wet shampoo*). **5** *Brit. colloq.* feeble; inept. **6** *Brit. Polit. colloq.* Conservative with liberal tendencies, esp. as regarded by right-wing Conservatives. **7** *sl.* (of a country, of legislation, etc.) allowing the free sale of alcoholic drink. **8** (of a baby or young child) incontinent (*is still wet at night*). ● *v.tr.* (**wetting**; *past* and *past part.* **wet** or **wetted**) **1** make wet. **2 a** urinate in or on (*wet the bed*). **b** *refl.* urinate involuntarily. ● *n.* **1** moisture; liquid that wets something. **2** rainy weather; a time of rain. **3** *Brit. colloq.* a feeble or inept person. **4** *Brit. Polit. colloq.* a Conservative with liberal tendencies (see sense 6 of *adj.*). **5** *Brit. colloq.* a drink. □ **wet the baby's head** *Brit. colloq.* celebrate its birth with a (usu. alcoholic) drink. **wet behind the ears** immature; inexperienced. **wet blanket** see BLANKET. **wet dock** a dock in which a ship can float. **wet dream** an erotic dream with involuntary ejaculation of semen. **wet fly** an artificial fly used under water by an angler. **wet look** a shiny surface given to clothing materials. **wet nurse** a woman employed to suckle another's child. **wet-nurse 1** act as a wet nurse to. **2** *colloq.* treat as if helpless. **wet pack** the therapeutic wrapping of the body in wet cloths, etc. **wet suit** a close-fitting rubber garment worn by skin divers, etc., to keep warm. **wet through** (or **to the skin**) with one's clothes soaked. **wetting agent** a substance that helps water, etc., to spread or penetrate. **wet one's whistle** *colloq.* drink. □□ **wetly** *adv.* **wetness** *n.* **wettable** *adj.* **wetting** *n.* **wettish** *adj.* [OE *wēt* (adj. & n.), *wǣtan* (v.), rel. to WATER: in ME replaced by past part. of the verb]

■ *adj.* **1** moist, moistened, damp, dampened, soaked, soaking, sopping, wringing, dripping, sodden, soggy, soppy, saturated, drenched, awash, waterlogged, watery; clammy, humid, dank. **2** rainy, raining, teeming, pouring, drizzling, showery. **3** tacky, sticky. **5** feeble, weak, irresolute, effete, namby-pamby, foolish, ineffectual, ineffective, weedy, inept, spineless, timorous, cowardly. ● *v.* **1** dampen, damp, moisten, saturate, drench, souse, douse, steep, immerse, submerge, dip, soak, water. ● *n.* **1** moisture, water, wetness, dampness, damp, humidity, liquid. **2** rain, wetness, drizzle, damp. **3** milksop, lightweight, weed, *colloq.* drip, loser, sissy, softy, wimp; *sl.* schnook. □ **wet behind the ears** see *inexperienced* (INEXPERIENCE). **wet nurse 1** see NURSE *v.* 2. **wet one's whistle** see DRINK *v.* 1. □□ **wetness** see PERSPIRATION, WET *n.* 1, 2 above.

wetback /wétbak/ *n. offens.* an illegal immigrant from Mexico to the US. [WET + BACK: from the practice of swimming the Rio Grande to reach the US]

wether /wéthər/ *n.* a castrated ram. [OE f. Gmc]

wetlands /wétləndz/ *n.pl.* swamps and other damp areas of land.

we've /weev/ *contr.* we have.

wey /way/ *n. Brit.* a former unit of weight or volume varying with different kinds of goods, often 256 pounds or 40 bushels. [OE *wǣg(e)* balance, weight f. Gmc, rel. to WEIGH[1]]

w.f. *abbr. Printing* wrong font.

whack /hwak, wak/ *v.* & *n. colloq.* ● *v.tr.* **1** strike or beat forcefully with a sharp blow. **2** (as **whacked** *adj.*) esp. *Brit.* = *whacked-out* ● *n.* **1** a sharp or resounding blow. **2** *Brit. sl.* a share. □ **have a whack at** *sl.* attempt. **out of whack** *sl.* out of order; malfunctioning. **whacked-out 1** tired out; exhausted. **2** under the influence of narcotics or alcohol. □□ **whacker** *n.* **whacking** *n.* [imit., or alt. of THWACK]

■ *v.* **1** see BEAT *v.* 1. **2** (**whacked**) see TIRED 1. ● *n.* **1** see BLOW[2] 1. □ **out of whack** see *out of order* 1 (ORDER).

whacking /hwáking, wák-/ *adj.* & *adv. Brit. colloq.* ● *adj.* very large. ● *adv.* very (*a whacking great skyscraper*).

whacko /hwákō, wák-/ *int., adj.,* & *n.* ● *int. Brit. sl.* expressing delight or enjoyment. ● *adj.* & *n.* var. of WACKO.

whacky var. of WACKY.

whale[1] /hwayl, wayl/ *n.* (*pl.* same or **whales**) any of the larger marine mammals of the order Cetacea, having a streamlined body and horizontal tail, and breathing through a blowhole on the head. □ **a whale of a** *colloq.* an exceedingly good or fine, etc. **whale oil** oil from the blubber of whales. **whale shark** a large tropical whalelike shark, *Rhincodon typus*, feeding close to the surface. [OE *hwæl*]

whale[2] /hwayl, wayl/ *v.tr. colloq.* beat; thrash. [var. of WALE]

whaleback /hwáylbak, wáyl-/ *n.* anything shaped like a whale's back.

whaleboat /hwáylbōt, wáyl-/ *n.* a double-bowed boat of a kind used in whaling.

whalebone /hwáylbōn, wáyl-/ *n.* an elastic horny substance growing in thin parallel plates in the upper jaw of some whales, used as stiffening, etc. □ **whalebone whale** a baleen whale.

whaler /hwáylər, wáyl-/ *n.* **1** a whaling ship or a seaman engaged in whaling. **2** an Australian shark of the genus *Carcharhinus*. **3** *Austral. sl.* a tramp.

whaling /hwáyling, wáyl-/ *n.* the practice or industry of hunting and killing whales, esp. for their oil or whalebone. □ **whaling master** the captain of a whaler.

wham /hwam, wam/ *int., n.,* & *v. colloq.* ● *int.* expressing the sound of a forcible impact. ● *n.* such a sound. ● *v.* (**whammed, whamming**) **1** *intr.* make such a sound or impact. **2** *tr.* strike forcibly. [imit.]

■ *int.* & *n.* see THUD *n.*

whammy /hwámee, wám-/ *n.* (*pl.* **-ies**) *colloq.* an evil or unlucky influence. [20th c.: orig. unkn.]

whang /hwang, wang/ *v.* & *n. colloq.* ● *v.* **1** *tr.* strike heavily and loudly; whack. **2** *intr.* (of a drum, etc.) sound under or as under a blow. ● *n.* a whanging sound or blow. [imit.]

whangee /hwanggée, wang-/ *n.* **1** a Chinese or Japanese bamboo of the genus *Phyllostachys*. **2** a cane made from this. [Chin. *huang* old bamboo sprouts]

wharf /hwawrf, wawrf/ *n.* & *v.* ● *n.* (*pl.* **wharves** /wawrvz/ or **wharfs**) a level quayside area to which a ship may be moved to load and unload. ● *v.tr.* **1** moor (a ship) at a wharf. **2** store (goods) on a wharf. [OE *hwearf*]

wharfage /hwáwrfij, wáwr-/ *n.* **1** accommodation at a wharf. **2** a fee for this.

wharfinger /hwáwrfinjər, wáwr-/ *n.* an owner or keeper of a wharf. [prob. ult. f. WHARFAGE]

wharves *pl.* of WHARF.

what /hwot, wot, hwut, wut/ *adj., pron.,* & *adv.* ● *interrog.adj.* **1** asking for a choice from an indefinite number or for a statement of amount, number, or kind (*what books have you read?*; *what news have you?*). **2** *colloq.* = WHICH *interrog.adj.* (*what book have you chosen?*). ● *adj.* (usu. in exclam.) how great or remarkable (*what luck!*). ● *rel.adj.* the or any … that (*will give you what help I can*). ● *pron.* (corresp. to the functions of the *adj.*) **1** what thing or things? (*what is your name?*; *I don't know what you mean*). **2** (asking for a remark to be repeated) = what did you say? **3** asking for confirmation or agreement of something not completely understood (*you did what?*; *what, you really mean it?*). **4** how much (*what you must have suffered!*). **5** (as *rel.pron.*) that or those which; a or the or any thing which (*what followed was worse*; *tell me what you think*). ● *adv.* to what extent (*what does it matter?*). □ **what about** what is the news or position or your opinion of (*what about me?*; *what about a game of tennis?*). **what-d'you-call-it** or **whatcha-macallit** or **what's-its-name** *colloq.* a substitute for a name not recalled. **what for** *colloq.* **1** for what reason? **2** a

---

severe reprimand (esp. *give a person what for*). **what have
you** *colloq.* (prec. by *or*) anything else similar. **what if? 1**
what would result, etc., if. **2** what would it matter if. **what
is more** and as an additional point; moreover. **what next?**
colloq. what more absurd, shocking, or surprising thing is
possible? **what not** (prec. by *and*) other similar things.
what of? what is the news concerning? **what of it?** why
should that be considered significant? **what's-his** (or **-its**)
-name = *what-d'you-call-it*. **what's what** *colloq.* what is
useful or important, etc. **what with** *colloq.* because of (usu.
several things). [OE *hwæt* f. Gmc]

■ □ **what for 2** see *a piece of one's mind*. **what is more**
see MOREOVER. **what's what** see ROPE *n.* 3a.

whate'er /hwotáir, wot-, hwut-, wut-/ *poet.* var. of WHAT-
EVER.

whatever /hwotévǝr, wot-, hwut, wut-/ *adj. & pron.* **1** =
WHAT (in relative uses) with the emphasis on indefiniteness
(*lend me whatever you can; whatever money you have*). **2**
though anything (*we are safe whatever happens*). **3** (with *neg.*
or *interrog.*) at all; of any kind (*there is no doubt whatever*). **4**
colloq. what at all or in any way (*whatever do you mean?*) □ **or
whatever** *colloq.* or anything similar.

whatnot /hwótnot, wót-, hwút-, wút-/ *n.* **1** an indefinite or
trivial thing. **2** a stand with shelves for small objects.

whatsit /hwótsit, wót-, hwút-, wút-/ *n.* *colloq.* a person or
thing whose name one cannot recall or does not know.

whatso /hwótsō, wót-, hwút-, wút-/ *adj. & pron. archaic* =
WHATEVER 1, 2. [ME, = WHAT + SO, f. OE *swā hwæt swā*]

whatsoe'er /hwótsō-áir, wót-, hwút-, wút-/ *poet.* var. of
WHATSOEVER.

whatsoever /hwótsō-évǝr, wót-, hwút-, wút-/ *adj. & pron.*
= WHATEVER 1–3.

whaup /hwawp, wawp/ *n.* esp. *Sc.* a curlew. [imit. of its cry]

wheal var. of WEAL[1].

wheat /hweet, weet/ *n.* **1** any cereal plant of the genus *Tri-
icum*, bearing dense four-sided seed spikes. **2** its grain, used
in making flour, etc. □ **separate the wheat from the chaff**
see CHAFF. **wheat belt** a region where wheat is the chief
agricultural product. **wheat germ** the embryo of the wheat
grain, extracted as a source of vitamins. [OE *hwǣte* f. Gmc,
rel. to WHITE]

wheatear /hwéeteer, wéet-/ *n.* any small migratory bird of
the genus *Oenanthe*, esp. with a white belly and rump. [app.
f. *wheatears* (WHITE, + ARSE)]

wheaten /hwéetǝn, wéet-/ *adj.* made of wheat.

wheatgrass /hwéetgras, wéet-/ *n.* a couch grass grown esp.
as forage.

Wheatstone bridge /hwéetstōn, wéet-/ *n.* an apparatus for
measuring electrical resistances by equalizing the potential
at two points of a circuit. [C. *Wheatstone*, Engl. physicist d.
1875]

whee /hwee, wee/ *int.* expressing delight or excitement.
[imit.]

wheedle /hwéedǝl, wéedǝl/ *v.tr.* **1** coax by flattery or en-
dearments. **2** (foll. by *out*) **a** get (a thing) out of a person
by wheedling. **b** cheat (a person) out of a thing by wheedling. □□ **wheedler** *n.* **wheedling** *adj.* **wheedlingly** *adv.*
[perh. f. G *wedeln* fawn, cringe f. *Wedel* tail]

■ **1** coax, cajole, inveigle, charm, beguile, persuade,
induce, talk around, *colloq.* butter up, sweet-talk,
sl. con.

wheel /hweel, weel/ *n. & v.* ● *n.* **1** a circular frame or disk
arranged to revolve on an axle and used to facilitate the
motion of a vehicle or for various mechanical purposes. **2** a
wheellike thing (*Catherine wheel; potter's wheel; steering
wheel*). **3** motion as of a wheel, esp. the movement of a line
of people with one end as a pivot. **4** a machine, etc., of which
a wheel is an essential part. **5** (in *pl.*) *sl.* a car. **6** *sl.* = big
wheel 2. **7** a set of short lines concluding a stanza. ● *v.* **1**
intr. & *tr.* **a** turn on an axis or pivot. **b** swing around in line
with one end as a pivot. **2 a** *intr.* (often foll. by *about, around,
round*) change direction or face another way. **b** *tr.* cause to
do this. **3** *tr.* push or pull (a wheeled thing esp. a wheelbarrow, bicycle, wheelchair, or stroller, or its load or occupant).
4 *intr.* go in circles or curves (*seagulls wheeling overhead*).

□ **at the wheel 1** driving a vehicle. **2** directing a ship. **3** in
control of affairs. **on wheels** (or **oiled wheels**) *Brit.*
smoothly. **wheel and deal** engage in political or commercial scheming. **wheel-back** *adj.* (of a chair) with a back
shaped like or containing the design of a wheel. **wheel lock
1** an old kind of gunlock having a steel wheel to rub against
flint, etc. **2** a gun with this. **wheel of fortune 1** luck. **2** a
gambling device that is spun and allowed to stop at random
to indicate the winner or the prize. **wheels within wheels**
Brit. **1** intricate machinery. **2** *colloq.* indirect or secret agencies. □□ **wheeled** *adj.* (also in *comb.*). **wheelless** *adj.* [OE
hwēol, hwēogol f. Gmc]

■ □ *n.* **1** disk, ring, circle, hoop, esp. *Math. & Biol.*
annulus. **3** see REVOLUTION 3, 4. **5** (*wheels*) see CAR 1.
● *v.* **1** see REVOLVE 1, 2. **2** spin, turn, veer, swivel,
pivot, swing, whirl. **4** circle, go around, gyrate. □ **at the
wheel 3** in control, in charge, in command, at the
helm, in the driver's seat, in the saddle; (*be at the
wheel*) be in charge *or* control *or* command, have the
whip hand, wear the trousers.

wheelbarrow /hwéelbarō, wéel-/ *n.* a small cart with one
wheel and two shafts for carrying garden loads, etc.

wheelbase /hwéelbays, wéel-/ *n.* the distance between the
front and rear axles of a vehicle.

wheelchair /hwéelchair, wéel-/ *n.* a chair on wheels for an
invalid or disabled person.

wheeler /hwéelǝr, wée-/ *n.* **1** (in *comb.*) a vehicle having a
specified number of wheels. **2** a wheelwright. **3** a horse harnessed next to the wheels and behind another. □ **wheeler-
dealer** *colloq.* a person who wheels and deals.

wheelhouse /hwéelhows, weel-/ *n.* = PILOTHOUSE.

wheelie /hwéelee, wée-/ *n.* *sl.* the stunt of riding a bicycle or
motor cycle for a short distance with the front wheel off the
ground.

wheelman /hwéelmǝn, wéel-/ *n.* **1** a driver of a wheeled vehicle, esp. a gateway car. **2** a helmsman.

wheelsman /hwéelzmǝn, wéel-/ *n.* (*pl.* **-men**) a helmsman.

wheelspin /hwéelspin, wéel-/ *n.* rotation of a vehicle's wheels
without traction.

wheelwright /hwéelrīt, wéel-/ *n.* a person who makes or
repairs esp. wooden wheels.

wheeze /hweez, weez/ *v. & n.* ● *v.* **1** *intr.* breathe with an
audible chesty whistling sound. **2** *tr.* (often foll. by *out*) utter
in this way. ● *n.* **1** a sound of wheezing. **2** *colloq.* **a** *Brit.* a
clever scheme. **b** an actor's interpolated joke, etc. **c** a catchphrase. □□ **wheezer** *n.* **wheezingly** *adv.* **wheezy** *adj.*
(**wheezier, wheeziest**). **wheezily** *adv.* **wheeziness** *n.*
[prob. f. ON *hvæsa* to hiss]

whelk[1] /hwelk, welk/ *n.* any predatory marine gastropod mollusk of the family Buccinidae, esp. the edible kind of the
genus *Baccinum*, having a spiral shell. [OE *wioloc, weoloc*, of
unkn. orig.: perh. infl. by WHELK[2]]

whelk[2] /hwelk, welk/ *n.* a pimple. [OE *hwylca* f. *hwelian* sup-
purate]

whelm /hwelm, welm/ *v.tr. poet.* **1** engulf; submerge. **2** crush
with weight; overwhelm. [OE *hwelman* (unrecorded) =
hwylfan overturn]

whelp /hwelp, welp/ *n. & v.* ● *n.* **1** a young dog; a puppy. **2**
archaic a cub. **3** an ill-mannered child or youth. **4** (esp. in
pl.) a projection on the barrel of a capstan or windlass.
● *v.tr.* (also *absol.*) **1** bring forth (a whelp or whelps). **2** *derog.*
(of a human mother) give birth to. **3** originate (an evil
scheme, etc.). [OE *hwelp*]

■ *n.* **1** pup, puppy. **3** see PUP *n.* 3.

when /hwen, wen/ *adv., conj., pron., & n.* ● *interrog.adv.* **1**
at what time? **2** on what occasion? **3** how soon? **4** how long
ago? ● *rel.adv.* (prec. by *time*, etc.) at or on which (*there are
times when I could cry*). ● *conj.* **1** at the or any time that; as
soon as (*come when you like; come when ready; when I was
your age*). **2** although; considering that (*why stand up when
you could sit down?*). **3** after which; and then; but just then
(*was nearly asleep when the bell rang*). ● *pron.* what time? (*till
when can you stay?; since when it has been better*). ● *n.* time,
occasion, date (*have finally decided on the where and when*).
[OE *hwanne, hwenne*]

whence /hwens, wens/ *adv. & conj. formal* ● *adv.* from what place? (*whence did they come?*). ● *conj.* **1** to the place from which (*return whence you came*). **2** (often prec. by *place*, etc.) from which (*the source whence these errors arise*). **3** and thence (*whence it follows that*). ¶ Use of *from whence* as in *the place from whence they came*, though common, is generally considered incorrect. [ME *whannes, whennes* f. *whanne, whenne* f. OE *hwanon(e)* whence, formed as WHEN + -S³: cf. THENCE]

whencesoever /hwéns-sō-évər, wéns-/ *adv. & conj. formal* from whatever place or source.

whene'er /hwenáir, wen-/ *poet.* var. of WHENEVER.

whenever /hwenévər, wen-/ *conj. & adv.* **1** at whatever time; on whatever occasion. **2** every time that. □ **or whenever** *colloq.* or at any similar time.

whensoe'er /hwénsō-áir, wén-/ *poet.* var. of WHENSOEVER.

whensoever /hwénsō-évər, wén-/ *conj. & adv. formal* = WHENEVER.

where /hwair, wair/ *adv., conj., pron., & n.* ● *interrog.adv.* **1** in or to what place or position? (*where is the milk?*; *where are you going?*). **2** in what direction or respect? (*where does the argument lead?*; *where does it concern us?*). **3** in what book, etc.?; from whom? (*where did you read that?*; *where did you hear that?*). **4** in what situation or condition? (*where does that leave us?*). ● *rel.adv.* (prec. by *place*, etc.) in or to which (*places where they meet*). ● *conj.* **1** in or to the or any place, direction, or respect in which (*go where you like*; *that is where you are wrong*; *delete where applicable*). **2** and there (*reached Albuquerque, where the car broke down*). ● *pron.* what place? (*where do you come from?*; *where are you going to?*). ● *n.* place; scene of something (see WHEN *n.*). [OE *hwǣr, hwār*]

whereabouts *adv. & n.* ● *adv.* /hwáirəbówts, wáir-/ where or approximately where? (*whereabouts are they?*; *show me whereabouts to look*). ● *n.* /hwáirəbowts, wáir-/ (as *sing.* or *pl.*) a person's or thing's location roughly defined.
■ *adv.* where, in or at or to what place, *archaic* whither.
● *n.* location, position, place, site, situation, address, locale.

whereafter /hwairáftər, wair/ *conj. formal* after which.

whereas /hwairáz, wair-/ *conj.* **1** in contrast or comparison with the fact that. **2** (esp. in legal preambles) taking into consideration the fact that.
■ **2** see SEEING *conj.*

whereat /hwairát, wair-/ *conj. archaic* **1** at which place or point. **2** for which reason.

whereby /hwairbí, wair-/ *conj.* by what or which means.

where'er /hwairáir, wair-/ *poet.* var. of WHEREVER.

wherefore /hwáirfawr, wáir-/ *adv. & n.* ● *adv. archaic* **1** for what reason? **2** for which reason. ● *n.* a reason (*the whys and wherefores*).
■ *adv.* **2** see THEREFORE.

wherefrom /hwairfrúm, -fróm, wair-/ *conj. archaic* from which; from where.

wherein /hwairín, wair-/ *conj. & adv. formal* ● *conj.* in what or which place or respect. ● *adv.* in what place or respect?

whereof /hwairúv, -óv, wair-/ *conj. & adv. formal* ● *conj.* of what or which (*the means whereof*). ● *adv.* of what?

whereon /hwairón, -áwn, wair-/ *conj. & adv. archaic* ● *conj.* on what or which. ● *adv.* on what?

wheresoe'er /hwáirsōáir, wáir-/ *poet.* var. of WHERESOEVER.

wheresoever /hwáirsō-évər, wáir-/ *conj. & adv. formal or literary* = WHEREVER.

whereto /hwairtóō, wair-/ *conj. & adv. formal* ● *conj.* to what or which. ● *adv.* to what?

whereupon /hwáirəpón, -páwn, wáir-/ *conj.* immediately after which.

wherever /hwairévər, wair-/ *adv. & conj.* ● *adv.* in or to whatever place. ● *conj.* in every place that. □ **or wherever** *colloq.* or in any similar place.

wherewithal /hwáirwithawl, -with-, wáir-/ *n. colloq.* money, etc., needed for a purpose (*has not the wherewithal to do it*).
■ see MONEY 3.

wherry /hwéree, wéree/ *n.* (*pl.* **-ies**) **1** a light row boat usu. for carrying passengers. **2** *Brit.* a large, light barge. [ME: orig. unkn.]

wherryman /hwéreemən, wér-/ *n.* (*pl.* **-men**) a person employed on a wherry.

whet /hwet, wet/ *v. & n.* ● *v.tr.* (**whetted, whetting**) **1** sharpen (a scythe or other tool) by grinding. **2** stimulate (the appetite or a desire, interest, etc.). ● *n.* **1** the act or an instance of whetting. **2** a small quantity stimulating one's appetite for more. □□ **whetter** *n.* (also in *comb.*). [OE *hwettan* f. Gmc]
■ *v.* **1** sharpen, hone, grind, file, put an edge on, strop. **2** pique, sharpen, awaken, arouse, stimulate, kindle, fire, increase, excite, enhance.

whether /hwéthər, wéth-/ *conj.* introducing the first or both of alternative possibilities (*I doubt whether it matters*; *I do not know whether they have arrived or not*). □ **whether or no** (or **not**) see NO². [OE *hwæther, hwether* f. Gmc]

whetstone /hwétstōn, wét-/ *n.* **1** a tapered stone used with water to sharpen curved tools, e.g., sickles, hooks (cf. OILSTONE). **2** a thing that sharpens the senses, etc.

whew /hwyōō/ *int.* expressing surprise, consternation, or relief. [imit.: cf. PHEW]

whey /hway, way/ *n.* the watery liquid left when milk forms curds. □ **whey-faced** pale esp. with fear. [OE *hwæg, hweg* f. LG]

which /hwich, wich/ *adj. & pron.* ● *interrog.adj.* asking for choice from a definite set of alternatives (*which John do you mean?*; *say which book you prefer*; *which way shall we go?*). ● *rel.adj.* being the one just referred to; and this or these (*ten years, during which time they admitted nothing*; *a word of advice, which action is within your power, will set things straight*). ● *interrog.pron.* **1** which person or persons (*which of you is responsible?*). **2** which thing or things (*say which you prefer*). ● *rel.pron.* (*poss.* **of which, whose** /hōōz/) **1** which thing or things, usu. introducing a clause not essential for identification (cf. THAT *pron.* 7) (*the house, which is empty, has been damaged*). **2** used in place of *that* after *in* or *that* (*there is the house in which I was born*; *that which you have just seen*). □ **which is which** a phrase used when two or more persons or things are difficult to distinguish from each other. [OE *hwilc* f. Gmc]

whichever /hwichévər, wich-/ *adj. & pron.* **1** any which (*take whichever you like*; *whichever one you like*). **2** no matter which (*whichever one wins, they both get a prize*).

whichsoever /hwíchsō-évər, wích-/ *adj. & pron. archaic* = WHICHEVER.

whidah var. of WHYDAH.

whiff /hwif, wif/ *n. & v.* ● *n.* **1** a puff or breath of air, smoke, etc. (*went outside for a whiff of fresh air*). **2** a smell (*caught the whiff of a cigar*). **3** (foll. by *of*) a trace or suggestion of scandal, etc. **4** *Brit.* a small cigar. **5** *Brit.* a minor discharge (of grapeshot, etc.). **6** *Brit.* a light, narrow outrigged scull. ● *v.* **1** *tr. & intr.* blow or puff lightly. **2** *intr. Brit.* smell (esp. unpleasant). **3** *tr.* get a slight smell of. **4** *intr. Baseball* strike out by swinging and missing on the third strike. **5** *tr. Baseball* strike out a batter in this way. [imit.]
■ *n.* **1** see BREATH 2a. **2** see SMELL *n.* 2. **3** see HINT *n.* 3.

whiffle /hwífəl, wíf-/ *v. & n.* ● *v.* **1** *intr. & tr.* (of the wind) blow lightly, shift about. **2** *intr.* be variable or evasive. **3** *intr.* (of a flame, leaves, etc.) flicker; flutter. **4** *intr.* make the sound of a light wind in breathing, etc. ● *n.* a slight movement of air. □□ **whiffler** *n.* [WHIFF + -LE⁴]

whiffletree /hwífəltree, wíf-/ *n.* a crossbar pivoted in the middle, to which the traces are attached in a cart, plow, etc. [var. of WHIPPLETREE]

whiffy /hwífee, wíf-/ *adj. Brit. colloq.* (**whiffier, whiffiest**) having an unpleasant smell.

Whig /hwig, wig/ *n. hist.* **1** *Polit.* a member of the British reforming and constitutional party that after 1688 sought the supremacy of Parliament and was eventually succeeded in the 19th c. by the Liberal Party (opp. TORY *n.* 2). **2** a 17th-

---

/.../ **pronunciation**	● **part of speech**
□ **phrases, idioms, and compounds**	
□□ **derivatives**	■ **synonym section**
cross-references appear in SMALL CAPITALS or *italics*	

c. Scottish Presbyterian. **3 a** a supporter of the American Revolution. **b** a member of an American political party in the 19th c., succeeded by the Republicans. □□ **Whiggery** n. **Whiggish** adj. **Whiggism** n. [prob. a shortening of Sc. *whiggamer, -more*, nickname of 17th-c. Sc. rebels, f. *whig* to drive + MARE¹]

while /hwīl, wīl/ n., conj., v., & adv. ● n. **1** a space of time, time spent in some action (*a long while ago; waited a while; all this while*). **2** (prec. by *the*) **a** during some other process. **b** *poet.* during the time that. **3** (prec. by *a*) for some time (*have not seen you a while*). ● conj. **1** during the time that; for as long as; at the same time as (*while I was away, the house was burgled; fell asleep while reading*). **2** in spite of the fact that; although; whereas (*while I want to believe it, I cannot*). ● v.tr. (foll. by *away*) pass (time, etc.) in a leisurely or interesting manner. ● rel.adv. (prec. by *time*, etc.) during which (*the summer while I was abroad*). □ **all the while** during the whole time (of use). **for a long while** for a long time past. **for a while** for some time. **a good** (or **great**) **while** a considerable time. **in a while** (or **little while**) soon; shortly. **worth while** (or **one's while**) worth the time or effort spent. [OE *hwīl* f. Gmc: (conj.) abbr. of OE *thā hwīle the*, ME *the while that*]
  ■ n. **1** see TIME n. 4, 6. ● conj. **2** see THOUGH conj. 1.
  ● v. (*while away*) see PASS¹ v. 12. □ **for a while** see *temporarily* (TEMPORARY). **in a while** (or **little while**) see SHORTLY 1.

whiles /hwīlz, wīlz/ conj. archaic = WHILE. [orig. in the adverbs *somewhiles, otherwhiles*]

whilom /hwīləm, wī-/ adv. & adj. archaic ● adv. formerly; once. ● adj. erstwhile (*my whilom friend*). [OE *hwīlum* dative pl. of *hwīl* WHILE]

whilst /hwīlst, wīlst/ adv. & conj. esp. Brit. while. [ME f. WHILES: cf. AGAINST]

whim /hwim, wim/ n. **1 a** a sudden fancy; a caprice. **b** capriciousness. **2** archaic a kind of windlass for raising ore or water from a mine. [17th c.: orig. unkn.]
  ■ **1 a** see FANCY n. 2.

whimbrel /hwímbrəl, wím-/ n. a small curlew, esp. *Numenius phaeopus.* [WHIMPER (imit.): cf. *dotterel*]

whimper /hwímpər, wím-/ v. & n. ● v. **1** intr. make feeble, querulous, or frightened sounds; cry and whine softly. **2** tr. utter whimperingly. ● n. **1** a whimpering sound. **2** a feeble note or tone (*the conference ended on a whimper*). □□ **whimperer** n. **whimperingly** adv. [imit., f. dial. *whimp*]
  ■ v. **1, 2** see CRY v. 2a, WEEP v. 1, 2. ● n. **1** see GROAN n.

whimsical /hwímzikəl, wím-/ adj. **1** capricious. **2** fantastic. **3** odd or quaint; fanciful; humorous. □□ **whimsicality** /-kálitee/ n. **whimsically** adv. **whimsicalness** n.
  ■ **1** capricious, erratic, eccentric, wavering, flighty, unsettled, fickle, mercurial, wavering, fluctuating, unpredictable, inconsistent, volatile, unsteady.
  2, 3 quaint, fey, fanciful, odd, curious, unusual, chimeric(al), queer, singular, peculiar, funny, humorous, fantastic(al), pixyish, playful, puckish, absurd, preposterous, offbeat.

whimsy /hwímzee, wím-/ n. (also **whimsey**) (pl. **-ies** or **-eys**) **1** a whim; a capricious notion or fancy. **2** capricious or quaint humor. [rel. to WHIM-WHAM: cf. *flimsy*]
  ■ **1** see FANCY n. 2.

whim-wham /hwímhwam, wímwam/ n. archaic **1** a toy or plaything. **2** = WHIM 1. [redupl.: orig. uncert.]

whin¹ /hwin, win/ n. esp. Brit. (in sing. or pl.) furze; gorse. [prob. Scand.: cf. Norw. *hvine*, Sw. *hven*]

whin² /hwin, win/ n. Brit. **1** hard dark esp. basaltic rock or stone. **2** a piece of this. [ME: orig. unkn.]

whinchat /hwínchat, wín-/ n. a small, brownish European songbird, *Saxicola rubetra.* [WHIN¹ + CHAT²]

whine /hwin, win/ n. & v. ● n. **1** a complaining, long-drawn wail as of a dog. **2** a similar shrill, prolonged sound. **3 a** a querulous tone. **b** an instance of feeble or undignified complaining. ● v. **1** intr. emit or utter a whine. **2** intr. complain in a querulous tone or in a feeble or undignified way. **3** tr. utter in a whining tone. □□ **whiner** n. **whiningly** adv. **whiny** adj. (**whinier, whiniest**). [OE *hwīnan*]

■ n. **1, 2** see HOWL n. 1. **3 b** see GRIPE n. 2. ● v. **1** see HOWL v. 1. **2** see MOAN v.

whinge /hwinj, winj/ v. & n. Brit. & Austral. colloq. ● v.intr. whine; grumble peevishly. ● n. a whining complaint; a peevish grumbling. □□ **whinger** n. **whingingly** adv. **whingy** adj. [OE *hwinsian* f. Gmc]
  ■ v. see GRIPE v. 1. ● n. see GRIPE n. 2.

whinny /hwínee, wín-/ n. & v. ● n. (pl. **-ies**) a gentle or joyful neigh. ● v.intr. (**-ies, -ied**) give a whinny. [imit.: cf. WHINE]

whinstone /hwínstōn, wín-/ n. Brit. = WHIN².

whip /hwip, wip/ n. & v. ● n. **1** a lash attached to a stick for urging on animals or punishing, etc. **2 a** a member of a political party in a legislative body appointed to control its party discipline and tactics, esp. ensuring attendance and voting in debates. **b** Brit. the whips' written notice requesting or requiring attendance for voting at a division, etc., variously underlined according to the degree of urgency (*three-line whip*). **c** (prec. by *the*) Brit. party discipline and instructions (*asked for the Labour whip*). **3** a dessert made with whipped cream, etc. **4** the action of beating cream, eggs, etc., into a froth. **5** = WHIPPER-IN. **6** a rope-and-pulley hoisting apparatus. ● v. (**whipped, whipping**) **1** tr. beat or urge on with a whip. **2** tr. beat (cream or eggs, etc.) into a froth. **3** tr. & intr. take or move suddenly, unexpectedly, or rapidly (*whipped away the tablecloth; whipped out a knife; whip off your coat; whipped behind the door*). **4** tr. Brit. sl. steal (*who's whipped my pen?*). **5** tr. sl. **a** excel. **b** defeat. **6** tr. bind with spirally wound twine. **7** tr. sew with overcast stitches. □ **whip graft** Hort. a graft with the tongue of the scion in a slot in the stock and vice versa. **whip hand 1** a hand that holds the whip (in riding, etc.). **2** (usu. prec. by *the*) the advantage or control in any situation. **whip in** bring (hounds) together. **whip on** urge into action. **whip scorpion** any arachnid of the order Uropygi, with a long, slender, taillike appendage, which secretes an irritating vapor. **whip snake** any of various long slender snakes of the family Colubridae. **whip up 1** excite or stir up (feeling, etc.). **2** gather; summon up. **3** prepare (a meal, etc.) hurriedly. □□ **whipless** adj. **whiplike** adj. **whipper** n. [ME (h)*wippen* (v.), prob. f. MLG & MDu. *wippen* swing, leap, dance]
  ■ n. **1** scourge, lash, rawhide, quirt, horsewhip, bullwhip, cane, birch, switch, thong, (riding) crop, kourbash, sjambok, pizzle, Bibl. scorpion, hist. cat-o'-nine-tails, rope's end, cat, knout. ● v. **1** beat, thrash, lash, flog, horsewhip, scourge, switch, cane, birch, flagellate, leather, wale, spank, strap, colloq. lambaste, sl. tan; castigate, chastise, punish, discipline. **2** beat, whisk, fluff up. **3** whisk, pull, jerk, snatch, colloq. yank; run, scamper, scoot, race, scurry, scramble, hurry, flit, rush, dash, dart, flash, zip, zoom, colloq. skedaddle. **5 a** see EXCEL 1. **b** trounce, defeat, beat, conquer, overwhelm, rout, overcome, overpower, thwart, check, worst, drub, batter, stop, outdo, destroy, smash, colloq. lick, best, murder, slaughter, kill, wipe the floor with, pulverize, cream, sl. clobber, ruin, squash. **6** bind, fasten, tie, Naut. seize. **7** overcast. □ **whip hand 2** see *predominance* (PREDOMINANT). **whip up 1** stir up, agitate, arouse, rouse, work up, kindle, fuel, inflame, excite, incite. **2** see *summon up*. **3** improvise, put together quickly or hurriedly, assemble quickly or hurriedly, prepare quickly or hurriedly, knock together, knock up, slap or throw together.

whipcord /hwípkawrd, wíp-/ n. **1** a tightly twisted cord such as is used for making whiplashes. **2** a close-woven worsted fabric.

whiplash /hwíplash, wíp-/ n. **1** the flexible end of a whip. **2** a blow with a whip. **3** = *whiplash injury*. □ **whiplash injury** an injury to the neck caused by a jerk of the head, esp. as in a motor vehicle accident.

whipper-in /hwipərín, wip-/ n. a huntsman's assistant who manages the hounds.

whippersnapper /hwípərsnapər, wíp-/ n. **1** a small child. **2** an insignificant but presumptuous or intrusive (esp. young) person. [perh. for *whipsnapper*, implying noise and unimportance]

■ **1** see CHILD 1a. **2** see PUP *n.* 3.

whippet /hwípit, wíp-/ *n.* a crossbred dog of the greyhound type used for racing. [prob. f. obs. *whippet* move briskly, f. *whip it*]

whipping /hwíping, wíp-/ *n.* **1** a beating, esp. with a whip. **2** cord wound around in binding. □ **whipping boy 1** a scapegoat. **2** *hist.* a boy educated with a young prince and punished instead of him. **whipping cream** cream suitable for whipping. **whipping post** *hist.* a post used for public whippings.

■ **1** beating, thrashing, lashing, flogging, horsewhipping, drubbing, scourging, switching, caning, birching, flagellation, spanking. **2** binding, tying, winding, fastening, *Naut.* seizing. □ **whipping boy 1** see SCAPEGOAT *n.*

whippletree /hwípəltree, wíp-/ *n.* = WHIFFLETREE. [app. f. WHIP + TREE]

whippoorwill /hwípərwil, wíp-/ *n.* an American nightjar, *Caprimulgus vociferus.* [imit. of its cry]

whippy /hwípee, wípee/ *adj.* (**whippier, whippiest**) flexible; springy. □□ **whippiness** *n.*

whipsaw /hwípsaw, wíp-/ *n.* & *v.* ● *n.* a saw with a narrow blade held at each end by a frame. ● *v.* (*past part.* **-sawn** or **-sawed**) **1** *tr.* cut with a whipsaw. **2** *sl.* a *tr.* cheat by joint action on two others. **b** *intr.* be cheated in this way.

whipstitch /hwípstich, wíp-/ *v.* & *n.* ● *v.tr.* sew with overcast stitches. ● *n.* a stitch made this way.

whipstock /hwípstok, wíp-/ *n.* the handle of a whip.

whir /hwər, wər/ *n.* & *v.* (also **whirr**) ● *n.* a continuous rapid buzzing or softly clicking sound as of a bird's wings or of cogwheels in constant motion. ● *v.intr.* (**whirred, whirring**) make this sound. [ME, prob. Scand.: cf. Da. *hvirre*, Norw. *kvirra*, perh. rel. to WHIRL]

■ *v.* see HUM[1] *v.* 1.

whirl /hwərl, wərl/ *v.* & *n.* ● *v.* **1** *tr.* & *intr.* swing around and around; revolve rapidly. **2** *tr.* & *intr.* (foll. by *away*) convey or go rapidly in a vehicle, etc. **3** *tr.* & *intr.* send or travel swiftly in an orbit or a curve. **4** *intr.* **a** (of the brain, senses, etc.) seem to spin around. **b** (of thoughts, etc.) be confused; follow each other in bewildering succession. ● *n.* **1** a whirling movement (*vanished in a whirl of dust*). **2** a state of intense activity (*the social whirl*). **3** a state of confusion (*my mind is in a whirl*). **4** *colloq.* an attempt (*give it a whirl*). □ **whirling dervish** see DERVISH. □□ **whirler** *n.* **whirlingly** *adv.* [ME: (v.) f. ON *hvirfla*: (n.) f. MLG & MDu. *wervel* spindle & ON *hvirfill* circle f. Gmc]

■ *v.* **1** see REVOLVE 1, 2. **4** see SWIRL *v.* ● *n.* **1** swirl, twist, roll, curl, twirl, spiral; see also EDDY *n.*, SPIN *n.* 1, 3. **2** see FLURRY *n.* 3. **3** see MUDDLE *n.* **4** see GO *n.*[1] 5.

whirligig /hwírligig, wərl-/ *n.* **1** a spinning or whirling toy. **2** a merry-go-round. **3** a revolving motion. **4** anything regarded as hectic or constantly changing (*the whirligig of time*). **5** any freshwater beetle of the family Gyrinidae that circles about on the surface. [ME f. WHIRL + obs. *gig* whipping-top]

whirlpool /hwərlpōōl, wərl-/ *n.* a powerful circular eddy in the sea, etc., often causing suction to its center.

■ maelstrom, vortex, eddy, whirl, swirl; waterspout.

whirlwind /hwərlwind, wərl-/ *n.* **1** a mass or column of air whirling rapidly around and around in a cylindrical or funnel shape over land or water. **2** a confused tumultuous process. **3** (*attrib.*) very rapid (*a whirlwind romance*). □ **reap the whirlwind** suffer worse results of a bad action.

■ **1** vortex, cyclone, typhoon, hurricane, tornado, dust devil, twister, *Austral.* willy-willy; waterspout. **2** confusion, tumult, turmoil, pandemonium, whirl, disorder, bedlam, chaos. **3** (*attrib.*) speedy, quick, swift, rapid, sudden, precipitous, precipitate, lightning, headlong, hasty, rash, impetuous.

whirlybird /hwərleebərd, wər-/ *n. colloq.* a helicopter.

whirr var. of WHIR.

whisht /hwisht/ *v.* (also **whist** /hwist/) esp. *Sc.* & *Ir. dial.* **1** *intr.* (esp. as *int.*) be quiet; hush. **2** *tr.* quieten. [imit.]

whisk /hwisk, wisk/ *v.* & *n.* ● *v.* **1** *tr.* **a** brush with a sweeping movement. **b** take with a sudden motion (*whisked the plate away*). **2** *tr.* whip (cream, eggs, etc.). **3** *tr.* & *intr.* convey or go (esp. out of sight) lightly or quickly (*whisked me off to the doctor; the mouse whisked into its hole*). **4** *tr.* wave or lightly brandish. ● *n.* **1** a whisking action or motion. **2** a utensil for whisking eggs or cream, etc. **3** a bunch of grass, twigs, bristles, etc., for removing dust or flies. [ME *wisk*, prob. Scand.: cf. ON *visk* wisp]

■ *v.* **1** sweep, brush. **2** whip, beat, fluff up, stir. **3** speed, rush, carry, whip, hasten, hustle, hurry; dart, flit, sweep. ● *n.* **1** sweep, wave, brush, flick. **2** beater, whip. **3** brush, fly whisk.

whisker /hwískər, wís-/ *n.* **1** (usu. in *pl.*) the hair growing on a man's face, esp. on the cheek. **2** each of the bristles on the face of a cat, etc. **3** *colloq.* a small distance (*within a whisker of*; *won by a whisker*). **4** a strong, hairlike crystal of metal, etc. □ **have** (or **have grown**) **whiskers** *colloq.* (esp. of a story, etc.) be very old. □□ **whiskered** *adj.* **whiskery** *adj.* [WHISK + -ER[1]]

whiskey /hwískee, wís-/ *n.* (also **whisky**) (*pl.* **-eys** or **-ies**) **1** an alcoholic liquor distilled esp. from grain, such as corn or malted barley. **2** a drink of this. [abbr. of obs. *whiskybae*, var. of USQUEBAUGH]

■ **1** Scotch, rye, bourbon, esp. *Ir.* & *Sc.* usquebaugh, bourbon, *colloq.* malt, firewater, hooch, *sl.* hard stuff, red-eye.

whisper /hwíspər, wís-/ *v.* & *n.* ● *v.* **1** *a intr.* speak very softly without vibration of the vocal cords. **b** *intr.* & *tr.* talk or say in a barely audible tone or in a secret or confidential way. **2** *intr.* speak privately or conspiratorially. **3** *intr.* (of leaves, wind, or water) rustle or murmur. ● *n.* **1** whispering speech (*talking in whispers*). **2** a whispering sound. **3** a thing whispered. **4** a rumor or piece of gossip. **5** a brief mention; a hint or suggestion. □ **it is whispered** there is a rumor.

whispering gallery a gallery esp. under a dome with acoustic properties so that a whisper may be heard around its entire circumference. □□ **whisperer** *n.* **whispering** *n.* [OE *hwisprian* f. Gmc]

■ *v.* **1** breathe, murmur, mutter, mumble, hiss, speak *or* say softly, speak *or* say under one's breath, sigh. **2** gossip, bruit about, noise abroad, murmur, insinuate, hint, rumor, disclose, divulge, reveal, breathe a word. **3** rustle, swish, sibilate, swoosh, whoosh, hiss, whisk. ● *n.* **1** murmur, undertone, hushed tone(s), *literary* susurration, susurrus. **2** swoosh, whoosh, whisk; see also RUSTLE *n.* **4** rumor, hearsay, gossip. **5** hint, suggestion, inkling, soupçon, suspicion. □□ **whispering** see MURMUR *n.* 1.

whist[1] /hwist, wist/ *n.* a card game usu. for four players, with the winning of tricks. □ **whist drive** *Brit.* a social occasion with the playing of progressive whist. [earlier *whisk*, perh. f. WHISK (with ref. to whisking away the tricks): perh. assoc. with WHIST[2]]

whist[2] var. of WHISHT.

whistle /hwísəl, wís-/ *n.* & *v.* ● *n.* **1** a clear shrill sound made by forcing breath through a small hole between nearly closed lips. **2** a similar sound made by a bird, the wind, a missile, etc. **3** an instrument used to produce such a sound. ● *v.* **1** *intr.* emit a whistle. **2** **a** *intr.* give a signal or express surprise or derision by whistling. **b** *tr.* (often foll. by *up*) summon or give a signal to (a dog, etc.) by whistling. **3** *tr.* (also *absol.*) produce (a tune) by whistling. **4** *intr.* (foll. by *for*) vainly seek or desire. □ **as clean** (or **clear** or **dry**) **as a whistle** very clean or clear or dry. **blow the whistle on** *colloq.* bring (an activity) to an end; inform on (those responsible). **whistle in the dark** pretend to be unafraid. **whistle-stop 1** a small, unimportant town on a railroad line. **2** a politician's brief pause for a campaign speech on

/.../ **pronunciation**	● **part of speech**
□ **phrases, idioms, and compounds**	
□□ **derivatives**	■ **synonym section**
cross-references appear in SMALL CAPITALS or *italics*	

tour. **3** (*attrib.*) with brief pauses (*a whistle-stop tour*). [OE (*h*)*wistlian* (v.), (*h*)*wistle* (n.) of imit. orig.: cf. ON *hvísla* whisper, MSw. *hvisla* whistle]

whistleblower /hwísəlblōər, wi-/ *n. colloq.* one who reports wrongdoing in a workplace or organization to authorities, the news media, etc.

whistler /hwíslər, wis-/ *n.* **1** any bird of the genus *Pachycephala*, with a whistling cry. **2** a kind of marmot.

Whit /hwit, wit/ *adj.* connected with, belonging to, or following Whitsunday.

whit /hwit, wit/ *n.* a particle; a least possible amount (*not a whit better*). □ **every whit** the whole; wholly. **no** (or **never a** or **not a**) **whit** not at all. [earlier *w*(*h*)*yt* app. alt. f. WIGHT in phr. *no wight*, etc.]

■ see PARTICLE 2.

white /hwīt, wīt/ *adj., n.,* & *v.* ● *adj.* **1** resembling a surface reflecting sunlight without absorbing any of the visible rays; of the color of milk or fresh snow. **2** approaching such a color; pale esp. in the face (*turned as white as a sheet*). **3** less dark than other things of the same kind. **4 a** of the human group having light-colored skin. **b** of or relating to white people. **5** albino (*white mouse*). **6 a** (of hair) having lost its color esp. in old age. **b** (of a person) white-haired. **7** *colloq.* innocent; untainted. **8** (in *comb.*) (of esp. animals) having some white on the body (*white-throated*). **9 a** (of a plant) having white flowers or pale-colored fruit, etc. (*white hyacinth*; *white cauliflower*). **b** (of a tree) having light-colored bark, etc. (*white ash*; *white poplar*). **10** (of wine) made from white grapes or dark grapes with the skins removed. **11** *Brit.* (of coffee) with milk or cream added. **12** transparent; colorless (*white glass*). **13** *hist.* counterrevolutionary or reactionary (*white guard*; *white army*). ● *n.* **1** a white color or pigment. **2 a** white clothes or material (*dressed in white*). **b** (in *pl.*) white garments as worn in tennis, etc. **3 a** (in a game or sport) a white piece, ball, etc. **b** the player using such pieces. **4** the white part or albumen around the yolk of an egg. **5** the visible part of the eyeball around the iris. **6** a member of a light-skinned race. **7** a white butterfly. **8** a blank space in printing. ● *v.tr. archaic* make white. □ **bleed white** drain (a person, country, etc.) of wealth, etc. **white admiral** a butterfly, *Limenitis camilla*, with a white band across its wings. **white ant** a termite. **white cell** (or **blood cell** or **corpuscle**) a leukocyte. **white Christmas** Christmas with snow on the ground. **white coal** water as a source of power. **white-collar** (of a worker) engaged in clerical or administrative rather than manual work. **white currant** a cultivar of red currant with pale edible berries. **whited sepulcher** see SEPULCHER. **white dwarf** a small, very dense star. **white elephant** a useless and troublesome possession or thing. **white ensign** see ENSIGN. **white feather** a symbol of cowardice (a white feather in the tail of a game bird being a mark of bad breeding). **white flag** a symbol of surrender or a period of truce. **white friar** (or **White Friar**) a Carmelite. **white frost** see FROST. **white goods 1** domestic linen. **2** large domestic electrical appliances. **white heat 1** the temperature at which metal emits white light. **2** a state of intense passion or activity. **white hope 1** a person expected to achieve much for a group, organization, etc. **2** a white athlete, esp. a boxer that supporters hope or expect will defeat a black champion. **white horses** whitecaps. **white-hot** at white heat. **White House** the official residence of the US president and offices of the executive branch of government in Washington. **white lead** a mixture of lead carbonate and hydrated lead oxide used as pigment. **white lie** a harmless or trivial untruth. **white light** colorless light, e.g., ordinary daylight. **white magic** magic used only for beneficent purposes. **white matter** the part of the brain and spinal cord consisting mainly of nerve fibers (see also *gray matter*). **white meat** poultry, veal, rabbit, and pork. **white metal** a white or silvery alloy. **white night** *Brit.* a sleepless night. **white noise** noise containing many frequencies with equal intensities. **white-out** a dense blizzard esp. in polar regions. **white paper** a government report giving information or proposals on an issue. **white pepper** see PEPPER. **white poplar** = ABELE. **white rose** the emblem of

Yorkshire, England or the House of York. **White Russian 1** a Belorussian. **2** a cocktail of vodka, coffee liqueur, and cream or milk. **white sale** a sale of household linen. **white sauce** a sauce of flour, melted butter, and milk or cream. **white slave** a woman tricked or forced into prostitution, usu. abroad. **white slavery** traffic in white slaves. **white sock** = STOCKING 3. **white sugar** purified sugar. **white tie** a man's white bow tie as part of full evening dress. **white vitriol** *Chem.* zinc sulfate. **white water** a shallow or foamy stretch of water. **white wedding** *Brit.* a wedding at which the bride wears a formal white wedding dress. **white whale** a northern cetacean, *Delphinapterus leucas*, white when adult: also called BELUGA. □□ **whitely** *adv.* **whiteness** *n.* **whitish** *adj.* [OE *hwīt* f. Gmc]

■ *adj.* **1** snow-white, snowy, chalk-white, chalky, ivory, creamy, milky, whitish, milk-white, oyster-white, off-white, lily-white; silver, hoary. **2** pale, pallid, pasty, wan, whey-faced, ashen, bloodless, drained, washed out, whitish, waxen, ghastly, ghostly, anemic, dead white, deathly white, cadaverous, corpse-like. **4** Caucasian, Caucasoid, light-skinned, fair-skinned, pale-complexioned. **7** innocent, pure, unsullied, untainted, stainless, unblemished, spotless, immaculate, virginal, virtuous, undefiled, chaste. **12** colorless, transparent, see-through, clear, pellucid. □ **white-collar** see CLERICAL 2. **white elephant** see LUMBER² *n.* 1, 2. **white horses** see WAVE *n.* 1, 2. **white-hot** see HOT *adj.* 1. **white lie** see FIB *n.* **white magic** see MAGIC *n.* 1. □□ **whitish** see WHITE *adj.* 2 above.

whitebait /hwítbayt, wít-/ *n.* (*pl.* same) **1** (usu. *pl.*) the small, silvery-white young of herrings and sprats esp. as food. **2** *NZ* a young inanga.

whitebeam /hwítbeem, wít-/ *n.* a rosaceous tree, *Sorbus aria*, having red berries and leaves with a white, downy underside.

whitecap /hwítkap, wít-/ *n.* a white-crested wave at sea.

whiteface /hwítfays, wít-/ *n.* the white makeup of an actor, etc.

whitefish /hwítfish, wít-/ *n.* (*pl.* same or **-fishes**) **1** any freshwater fish of the genus *Coregonus*, etc., of the trout family, and used esp. for food. **2** a marine fish, *Caulolatilus princeps*, of California used esp. for food. **3** *Brit.* any nonoily, pale-fleshed fish, e.g., plaice, cod, etc.

whitefly /hwítflī, wít-/ *n.* (*pl.* **-flies**) any small insect of the family Aleyrodidae, having wings covered with white powder and feeding on the sap of shrubs, crops, etc.

Whitehall /hwít-hawl, wít-/ *n.* **1** the British Government. **2** its offices or policy. [a street in London on which government offices are situated]

whitehead /hwít-hed, wít-/ *n. colloq.* a white or white-topped skin pustule.

■ see PIMPLE.

whiten /hwítən, wít-/ *v.tr.* & *intr.* make or become white. □□ **whitener** *n.* **whitening** *n.*

■ see BLEACH *v.*

whitesmith /hwítsmith, wít-/ *n.* **1** a worker in tin. **2** a polisher or finisher of metal goods.

whitethorn /hwít-thawrn, wít-/ *n.* the hawthorn.

whitethroat /hwít-thrōt, wít-/ *n.* any of several birds with a white patch on the throat, esp. the warbler *Sylvia communis* or the finch *Zonotrichia albicollis*.

whitewall /hwítwawl, wít-/ *n.* a tire having a white band encircling the outer sidewall.

whitewash /hwítwosh, -wawsh, wít-/ *n.* & *v.* ● *n.* **1** a solution of lime or of whiting and size for whitening walls, etc. **2** a means employed to conceal mistakes or faults in order to clear a person or institution of imputations. ● *v.tr.* **1** cover with whitewash. **2** attempt by concealment to clear the reputation of. **3** *Brit.* (in *passive*) (of an insolvent) get a fresh start by passage through a bankruptcy court. **4** defeat (an opponent) without allowing any opposing score. □□ **whitewasher** *n.*

■ *v.* **2** gloss over, cover up, sugarcoat, hide, camouflage, conceal, qualify, minimize, extenuate, diminish, play down, downplay, make light of, rationalize, excuse. **4** see SLAUGHTER *v.* 3.

whitewood /hwítwŏŏd, wít-/ *n.* **1** any of several trees with white or light-colored wood, esp. the tulip tree. **2** the wood from such trees.

whitey /hwítee, wí-/ *n.* (also **Whitey**) (*pl.* **-eys**) *sl. offens.* **1** a white person. **2** white people collectively.

whither /hwíthər, wíth-/ *adv. & conj. archaic* ● *adv.* **1** to what place, position, or state? **2** (prec. by *place*, etc.) to which (*the house whither we were walking*). ● *conj.* **1** to the or any place to which (*go whither you will*). **2** and thither (*we saw a house, whither we walked*). [OE *hwider* f. Gmc: cf. WHICH, HITHER, THITHER]
■ *adv.* **1** see WHEREABOUTS *adv.*

whithersoever /hwíthərsō-évər, wíth-/ *adj. & conj. archaic* to any place to which.

whiting[1] /hwíting, wí-/ *n.* a small, white-fleshed fish, *Merlangus merlangus*, used as food. [ME f. MDu. *wijting*, app. formed as WHITE + -ING[3]]

whiting[2] /hwíting, wí-/ *n.* ground chalk used in whitewashing, etc.

whitleather /hwítlethər, wít-/ *n.* tawed leather. [ME f. WHITE + LEATHER]

whitlow /hwítlō, wít-/ *n.* an inflammation near a fingernail or toenail. [ME *whitflaw, -flow*, app. = WHITE + FLAW[1] in the sense 'crack,' but perh. of LG orig.: cf. Du. *fijt*, LG *fīt* whitlow]

Whitsun /hwítsən, wít-/ *n. & adj.* ● *n.* = WHITSUNTIDE. ● *adj.* = WHIT. [ME, f. *Whitsun Day* = Whitsunday]

Whitsunday /hwítsúnday, wít-/ the seventh Sunday after Easter, commemorating the descent of the Holy Spirit at Pentecost (Acts 2). [OE *Hwīta Sunnandæg*, lit. white Sunday, prob. f. the white robes of the newly baptized at Pentecost]

Whitsuntide /hwítsəntīd, wít-/ *n.* the weekend or week including Whitsunday.

whittle /hwítəl, wítəl/ *v.* **1** *tr.* & (foll. by *at*) *intr.* pare (wood, etc.) with repeated slicing with a knife. **2** *tr.* (often foll. by *away, down*) reduce by repeated subtractions. [var. of ME *thwitel* long knife f. OE *thwītan* to cut off]
■ **1** pare (down *or* away), shave, trim, cut, carve, hew, shape. **2** pare, shave, cut, trim, reduce, diminish, erode, eat away at.

whity /hwítee, wí-/ *adj.* (also **whitey**) whitish; rather white (usu. in *comb.*: *whity-brown*) (cf. WHITEY).

whiz /hwiz, wiz/ *n. & v.* (also **whizz**) *colloq.* ● *n.* (*pl.* **whizzes**) **1** the sound made by the friction of a body moving through the air at great speed. **2** (also **wiz**) *colloq.* a person who is remarkable or skillful in some respect (*is a whiz at chess*). ● *v.intr.* (**whizzed, whizzing**) move with or make a whiz. □ **whiz kid** *colloq.* a brilliant or highly successful young person. [imit.: in sense 2 infl. by WIZARD]
■ *n.* **1** whoosh, swish, whistle. **2** see EXPERT *n.* ● *v.* see FLASH *v.* 4b. □ **whiz kid** see VIRTUOSO 1a.

whizbang /hwízbang, wíz-/ *n. & adj.* ● *n. colloq.* **1** a high-velocity shell from a small-caliber gun, whose passage is heard before the gun's report. **2** a jumping kind of firework. ● *adj.* **1** very rapid, rushed, etc. **2** extremely effective and successful.

WHO *abbr.* World Health Organization.

who /hōō/ *pron. (obj.* **whom** /hōōm/ *or colloq.* **who**; *poss.* **whose** /hōōz/) **1 a** what or which person or persons? (*who called?*; *you know who it was*; *whom* or *who did you see?*). ¶ In the last example *whom* is correct but *who* is common in less formal contexts. **b** what sort of person or persons? (*who am I to object?*). **2** (a person) that (*anyone who wishes can come*; *the woman whom you met*; *the man who you saw*). ¶ In the last two examples *whom* is correct but *who* is common in less formal contexts. **3** and or but he, she, they, etc. (*gave it to Tom, who sold it to Jim*). **4** *archaic* the or any person or persons that (*whom the gods love die young*). □ **as who should say** like a person who said; as though one said. **who-does-what** (of a dispute, etc.) about which group of workers should do a particular job. **who goes there?** see GO[1]. **who's who 1** who or what each person is (*know who's*

who). **2** a list or directory with facts about notable persons. [OE *hwā* f. Gmc: *whom* f. OE dative *hwām, hwǣm*: *whose* f. genit. *hwæs*]

whoa /wō/ *int.* used as a command to stop or slow a horse, etc. [var. of HO]

who'd /hōōd/ *contr.* **1** who had. **2** who would.

whodunit /hōōdúnit/ *n.* (also **whodunnit**) *colloq.* a story or play about the detection of a crime, etc., esp. murder. [= *who done* (illiterate for *did*) *it?*]
■ see MYSTERY[1] 5.

whoe'er /hōō-áir/ *poet.* var. of WHOEVER.

whoever /hōō-évər/ *pron. (obj.* **whomever** /hōōm-/ or *colloq.* **whoever**; *poss.* **whosever** /hōōz-/) **1** the or any person or persons who (*whoever comes is welcome*). **2** though anyone (*whoever else objects, I do not*; *whosever it is, I want it*). **3** *colloq.* (as an intensive) who ever; who at all (*whoever heard of such a thing?*).

whole /hōl/ *adj. & n.* ● *adj.* **1** in an uninjured, unbroken, intact, or undiminished state (*swallowed it whole*; *there is not a plate left whole*). **2** not less than; all there is of; entire; complete (*waited a whole year*; *tell the whole truth*; *the whole school knows*). **3** (of blood or milk, etc.) with no part removed. **4** (of a person) healthy; recovered from illness or injury. ● *n.* **1** a thing complete in itself. **2** all there is of a thing (*spent the whole of the summer by the ocean*). **3** (foll. by *of*) all members, inhabitants, etc., of (*the whole of Congress knows it*). □ **as a whole** as a unit; not as separate parts. **go (the) whole hog** see HOG. **on the whole** taking everything relevant into account; in general (*it was, on the whole, a good report*; *they behaved well on the whole*). **out of whole cloth** without fact; entirely fictitious. **whole-grain** made with or containing whole grains (*whole-grain bread*). **whole-life insurance** life insurance for which premiums are payable throughout the remaining life of the person insured. **whole lot** see LOT. **whole note** esp. *Mus.* a note having the time value of four quarter notes, and represented by a ring with no stem. **whole number** a number without fractions; an integer. **whole-tone scale** *Mus.* a scale consisting entirely of tones, with no semitones. **whole-wheat** made of wheat with none of the bran or germ removed. □□ **wholeness** *n.* [OE *hāl* f. Gmc]
■ *adj.* **1** entire, complete, full, total, intact, uncut, unbroken, undiminished, unabridged, unabbreviated, undivided; in one piece, unharmed, undamaged, unscathed, unimpaired, unhurt, uninjured. **2** complete, entire, full, total. **4** well, healthy, sound, fit, strong, recovered, healed. ● *n.* **1** ensemble, aggregate, composite; everything; *sl.* whole kit and caboodle. **2** all, entirety, (sum) total, totality, lot. □ **as a whole** see *at large* (LARGE *n.* 2). **on the whole** largely, mostly, usually, more often than not, for the most part, in general, generally, by and large, with few exceptions, all things considered, all in all, altogether, as a rule, chiefly, mainly, in the main, predominantly.
□□ **wholeness** see ENTIRETY 1.

wholefood /hōlfŏŏd/ *n. Brit.* food which has not been unnecessarily processed or refined.

wholehearted /hōlhaártid/ *adj.* **1** (of a person) completely devoted or committed. **2** (of an action, etc.) done with all possible effort, attention, or sincerity; thorough. □□ **wholeheartedly** *adv.* **wholeheartedness** *n.*
■ devoted, dedicated, committed, earnest, sincere, real, true, genuine, hearty, serious, enthusiastic, zealous, warm, fervent, ardent, spirited, eager, energetic; (*only of an action, etc.*) unqualified, unmitigated, unreserved, unequivocal, unconditional, complete, entire, thorough, unstinting, heartfelt. □□ **wholeheartedly** see SINCERELY. **wholeheartedness** see DEDICATION 1.

wholemeal /hōlmeel/ *n.* (usu. *attrib.*) *Brit.* = *whole-wheat*.

/.../ pronunciation	● part of speech
□ phrases, idioms, and compounds	
□□ derivatives	■ synonym section
cross-references appear in SMALL CAPITALS or *italics*	

wholesale /hṓlsayl/ *n., adj., adv.,* & *v.* ● *n.* the selling of things in large quantities to be retailed by others (cf. RETAIL). ● *adj.* & *adv.* **1** by wholesale; at a wholesale price (*can get it for you wholesale*). **2** on a large scale (*wholesale destruction occurred; was handing out samples wholesale*). ● *v.tr.* sell wholesale. □□ **wholesaler** *n.* [ME: orig. *by whole sale*] ■ *adj.* **2** see SWEEPING *adj.* 1.

wholesome /hṓlsəm/ *adj.* **1** promoting or indicating physical, mental, or moral health (*wholesome pursuits; a wholesome appearance*). **2** prudent (*wholesome respect*). □□ **wholesomely** *adv.* **wholesomeness** *n.* [ME, prob. f. OE (unrecorded) *hālsum* (as WHOLE, -SOME¹)] ■ **1** healthful, healthy, health-giving, nutritious, nourishing, beneficial, tonic, salubrious, strengthening, bracing, stimulating; moral, ethical, righteous, upright, honorable, decent, principled, proper, fit, *archaic* meet, salutary. **2** see SOUND² *adj.* 3.

wholism var. of HOLISM.

wholly /hṓlee/ *adv.* **1** entirely; without limitation nor diminution (*I am wholly at a loss*). **2** purely; exclusively (*a wholly bad example*). [ME, f. OE (unrecorded) *hāllīce* (as WHOLE, -LY²)] ■ **1** altogether, entirely, absolutely, quite, totally, thoroughly, completely, *in toto*, fully, in all respects, in every way, all in all, utterly, unqualifiedly, every inch, a *or* one hundred percent; lock, stock, and barrel; root and branch; bag and baggage; hook, line, and sinker; to the nth degree, *colloq.* (the) whole hog. **2** only, exclusively, solely, purely, categorically, unequivocally, unambiguously, explicitly.

whom *objective case* of WHO.

whomever *objective case* of WHOEVER.

whomso *archaic objective case* of WHOSO.

whomsoever *objective case* of WHOSOEVER.

whoop /hoop, hwoop, woop/ *n.* & *v.* (also **hoop**) ● *n.* **1** a loud cry of or as of excitement, etc. **2** a long, rasping, indrawn breath in whooping cough. ● *v.intr.* utter a whoop. □ **whooping cough** an infectious bacterial disease, esp. of children, with a series of short, violent coughs followed by a whoop. **whooping crane** a white N. American crane with a loud, whooping cry. **whoop it up** *colloq.* **1** engage in revelry. **2** make a stir. [ME: imit.] ■ *n.* **1** shout, shriek, yell, roar, bellow, hoot, (battle *or* war) cry, war whoop, outcry, scream, screech, squeal, yelp, yowl, howl, bark; cheer, hurrah, hurray; *colloq.* holler. ● *v.* shout, shriek, yell, roar, bellow, hoot, cry (out), scream, screech, squeal, yelp, yowl, howl, bark, *colloq.* holler; cheer, hurrah. □ **whoop it up 1** see REVEL *v.* 1.

whoopee /hwoopee, woop-, hwoo-, woo-/ *int.* & *n. colloq.* ● *int.* expressing exuberant joy. ● *n.* exuberant enjoyment or revelry. □ **make whoopee** *colloq.* **1** rejoice noisily or hilariously. **2** engage in sexual play. **whoopee cushion** a rubber cushion that when sat on makes a sound like the breaking of wind.

whooper /hoopər, hwoo-, woo-/ *n.* **1** one that whoops. **2** a whooping crane. **3** a whooper swan. □ **whooper swan** a swan, *Cygnus cygnus*, with a characteristic whooping sound in flight.

whoops /hwoops, woops/ *int. colloq.* expressing surprise or apology, esp. on making an obvious mistake. [var. of OOPS]

whoosh /hwoosh, woosh/ *v., n.,* & *int.* (also **woosh**) ● *v.intr.* & *tr.* move or cause to move with a rushing sound. ● *n.* a sudden movement accompanied by a rushing sound. ● *int.* an exclamation imitating this. [imit.] ■ *v.* see SWISH *v.* ● *n.* see SWISH *n.*

whop /hwop, wop/ *v.tr.* (**whopped, whopping**) *sl.* **1** thrash. **2** defeat; overcome. [ME: var. of dial. *wap*, of unkn. orig.]

whopper /hwopər, wóp-/ *n. sl.* **1** something big of its kind. **2** a great lie.

whopping /hwóping, wóp-/ *adj. sl.* very big (*a whopping lie; a whopping fish*). ■ huge, great, enormous, colossal, gigantic, immense, tremendous, prodigious, monstrous, mammoth,

massive; outrageous, extravagant, *colloq.* thumping, terrible, awful.

whore /hawr/ *n.* & *v.* ● *n.* **1** a prostitute. **2** *derog.* a promiscuous woman. ● *v.intr.* **1** (of a man) seek or chase after whores. **2** *archaic* (foll. by *after*) commit idolatry or iniquity. □□ **whoredom** *n.* **whorer** *n.* [OE *hōre* f. Gmc] ■ *n.* **1** see PROSTITUTE *n.* 1a. **2** slattern, sloven, trollop, *derog.* slut, jade, hussy, *Brit. sl.* slag.

whorehouse /hawrhows/ *n.* a brothel. ■ see BROTHEL.

whoremaster /háwrmastər/ *n. archaic* = WHOREMONGER.

whoremonger /háwrmunggər, -mong-/ *n. archaic* a sexually promiscuous man; a lecher.

whoreson /háwrsən/ *n. archaic* **1** a disliked person. **2** (*attrib.*) (of a person or thing) vile.

whorish /háwrish/ *adj.* of or like a whore. □□ **whorishly** *adv.* **whorishness** *n.*

whorl /hwawrl, wawrl, hwərl, wərl/ *n.* **1** a ring of leaves or other organs around a stem of a plant. **2** one turn of a spiral, esp. on a shell. **3** a complete circle in a fingerprint. **4** *archaic* a small wheel on a spindle steadying its motion. □□ **whorled** *adj.* [ME *wharwyl, whorwil*, app. var. of WHIRL: infl. by *wharve* (n.) = whorl of a spindle]

whortleberry /hwórtəlberee, wərt-/ *n.* (*pl.* **-ies**) a bilberry. [16th c.: dial. form of *hurtleberry*, ME, of unkn. orig.]

whose /hooz/ *pron.* & *adj.* ● *pron.* of or belonging to which person (*whose is this book?*). ● *adj.* of whom or which (*whose book is this?; the man, whose name was Tim; the house whose roof was damaged*).

whoseso *archaic poss.* of WHOSO.

whosesoever *poss.* of WHOSOEVER.

whosever /hoozévər/ *poss.* of WHOEVER.

whoso /hoosō/ *pron.* (*obj.* **whomso** /hoom-/; *poss.* **whoseso** /hooz-/) *archaic* = WHOEVER. [ME, = WHO + SO¹, f. OE *swā hwā swā*]

whosoever /hoosō-évər/ *pron.* (*obj.* **whomsoever** /hoom-/; *poss.* **whosesoever** /hooz-/) *archaic* = WHOEVER.

why /hwī, wī/ *adv., int.,* & *n.* ● *adv.* **1 a** for what reason or purpose (*why did you do it?; I do not know why you came*). **b** on what grounds (*why do you say that?*). **2** (*prec. by reason,* etc.) for which (*the reasons why I did it*). ● *int.* expressing: **1** surprised discovery or recognition (*why, it's you!*). **2** impatience (*why, of course I do!*). **3** reflection (*why, yes, I think so*). **4** objection (*why, what is wrong with it?*). ● *n.* (*pl.* **whys**) a reason or explanation (esp. *whys and wherefores*). □ **why so?** on what grounds?; for what reason or purpose? [OE *hwī, hwȳ* instr. of *hwæt* WHAT f. Gmc]

whydah /hwidə, wid-/ *n.* (also **whidah**) any small African weaverbird of the genus *Vidua*, the male having mainly black plumage and tail feathers of great length. [orig. *widow bird*, altered f. assoc. with *Whidah* (now Ouidah) in Benin]

WI *abbr.* **1** West Indies. **2** West Indian. **3** Wisconsin (in official postal use).

wich- var. of WYCH-.

Wichita /wíchitaw/ *n.* **1 a** a N. American people native to Kansas. **b** a member of this people. **2** the language of this people.

wick¹ /wik/ *n.* & *v.* ● *n.* **1** a strip or thread of fibrous or spongy material feeding a flame with fuel in a candle, lamp, etc. **2** *Surgery* a gauze strip inserted in a wound to drain it. ● *v.tr.* draw (moisture) away by capillary action. □ **dip one's wick** *coarse sl.* (of a man) have sexual intercourse. **get on a person's wick** *Brit. colloq.* annoy a person. [OE *wēoce, -wēoc* (cf. MDu. *wiecke*, MLG *wēke*), of unkn. orig.]

wick² /wik/ *n. Brit. dial.* exc. in compounds, e.g., *bailiwick*, and in place names, e.g., *Hampton Wick, Warwick* **1** *archaic* a town, hamlet, or district. **2** *Brit.* a dairy farm. [OE *wīc*, prob. f. Gmc f. L *vicus* street, village]

wicked /wíkid/ *adj.* (**wickeder, wickedest**) **1** sinful; iniquitous; given to or involving immorality. **2** spiteful; ill-tempered; intending or intended to give pain. **3** playfully malicious. **4** *colloq.* foul; very bad; formidable (*wicked weather; a wicked cough*). **5** *sl.* excellent; remarkable. □□ **wickedly** *adv.* **wickedness** *n.* [ME f. obs. *wick* (perh. adj. use of OE *wicca* wizard) + -ED¹ as in *wretched*]

■ **1** evil, bad, immoral, amoral, unprincipled, sinful, impious, irreligious, blasphemous, profane, sacrilegious, ungodly, godless, diabolic(al), satanic, Mephistophelian, demonic, demoniac(al), hellish, infernal, accursed, damnable, fiendish, ghoulish; depraved, dissolute, villainous, black-hearted, iniquitous, nefarious, horrible, horrid, hideous, heinous, beastly, base, low, vile, debased, degenerate, perverse, perverted, corrupt, foul, offensive, abominable, disgraceful, shameful, scandalous, dreadful, awful, gross, gruesome, grim, appalling, grisly, loathsome, lawless, unrepentant, unregenerate, incorrigible, criminal, felonious, knavish, terrible, egregious, execrable; dirty, pornographic, filthy, erotic, obscene, lewd, offensive, indecent, prurient, smutty, rude, taboo, blue, coarse, bawdy, vulgar, salacious, licentious, nasty, *colloq.* raunchy, *often joc.* rascally. **2** vicious, beastly, savage, cruel, nasty, bad, violent, mean, spiteful, ill-tempered, malicious, malignant, malevolent, vindictive. **3** naughty, mischievous, impish, sly, devilish, roguish, scampish, knavish, puckish, *often joc.* rascally; vexatious, exasperating, annoying, irritating, irksome, trying, galling, bothersome. **4** foul, offensive, pernicious, baleful, baneful, mephitic, disgusting, revolting, sickening, repulsive, repellent, objectionable, nauseous, nauseating, repugnant, rotten, pestilential, noxious, formidable, *sl.* stinking, dreadful. **5** expert, ingenious, superior, superb, superlative, excellent, outstanding, remarkable, masterful, masterly, skillful, deft, adept, *sl.* bad. □□ **wickedly** see BADLY 1.
wickedness see EVIL *n.* 2.

wicker /wíkər/ *n.* plaited twigs or osiers, etc., as material for chairs, baskets, mats, etc. [ME, f. E.Scand.: cf. Sw. *viker* willow, rel. to *vika* bend]

wickerwork /wíkərwərk/ *n.* **1** wicker. **2** things made of wicker.

wicket /wíkit/ *n.* **1** (in full **wicket door** or **gate**) a small door or gate esp. beside or in a larger one or closing the lower part only of a doorway. **2** an aperture in a door or wall usu. closed with a sliding panel. **3** a croquet hoop. **4** *Cricket* **a** a set of three stumps with the bails in position defended by a batsman. **b** the ground between two wickets. **c** the state of this (*a slow wicket*). **d** an instance of a batsman being got out (*bowler has taken four wickets*). **e** a pair of batsmen batting at the same time (*a third-wicket partnership*). □ **on a good** (or **sticky**) **wicket** *Brit. colloq.* in a favorable (or unfavorable) position. [ME f. AF & ONF *wiket*, OF *guichet*, of uncert. orig.]

wicketkeeper /wíkitkeepər/ *n. Cricket* the fielder stationed close behind a batsman's wicket.

wickiup /wíkeeup/ *n.* a Native American hut of a frame covered with grass, etc. [Fox *wikiyap*]

widdershins var. of WITHERSHINS.

wide /wīd/ *adj., adv.,* & *n.* ● *adj.* **1 a** measuring much or more than other things of the same kind across or from side to side. **b** considerable; more than is needed (*a wide margin*). **2** (following a measurement) in width (*a foot wide*). **3** extending far; embracing much; of great extent (*has a wide range; has wide experience; reached a wide public*). **4** not tight nor close nor restricted; loose. **5 a** free; liberal; unprejudiced (*takes wide views*). **b** not specialized; general. **6** open to the full extent (*staring with wide eyes*). **7 a** (foll. by *of*) not within a reasonable distance of. **b** at a considerable distance from a point or mark. **8** *Brit. sl.* shrewd; skilled in sharp practice (*wide boy*). **9** (in *comb.*) extending over the whole of (*nationwide*). ● *adv.* **1** widely. **2** to the full extent (*wide awake*). **3** far from the target, etc. (*is shooting wide*). ● *n.* **1** *Cricket* a ball judged to pass the wicket beyond the batsman's reach and so scoring a run. **2** (prec. by *the*) the wide world. □ **give a wide berth to** see BERTH. **wide-angle** (of a lens) having a short focal length and hence a field covering a wide angle. **wide awake 1** fully awake. **2** *colloq.* wary; knowing. **wide-eyed** surprised or naive. **wide of the mark** see MARK¹. **wide open** (often foll. by *to*) exposed or vulnerable (to attack, etc.). **wide-ranging** covering an extensive

range. **the wide world** all the world great as it is. □□ **wideness** *n.* **widish** *adj.* [OE *wīd* (adj.), *wīde* (adv.) f. Gmc]
■ *adj.* **1 a** spacious, roomy, ample, extensive, expansive, broad, vast. **b** considerable, substantial, sizable, major, big, large, extreme. **3** broad, extensive, comprehensive, encyclopedic, (all-)inclusive, all-embracing, all-encompassing, far-reaching, wide-ranging, widespread, sweeping. **4** full, ample, generous; see also LOOSE *adj.* 3 5. **6 a** broad, broad minded, free, liberal, tolerant, unprejudiced, latitudinarian. **b** general, nonspecialized, nonspecific, global, overall, universal, generalized. ● *adv.* **1** widely, far apart, stretched out. **2** all the way, as much as possible, fully, completely, to the utmost. **3** astray, afield, wide of the mark, off the mark, off (the) target, off course, not on target, to one side. □ **wide awake 1** see AWAKE *adj.* 1a. **2** see ALERT *adj.* 1. **wide-eyed** see *goggle-eyed*, GULLIBLE. **wide open** open, exposed, unprotected, undefended, unguarded, vulnerable. **wide-ranging** see EXTENSIVE 2. □□ **wideness** see WIDTH 1.

wideawake /wídəwáyk/ *n.* a soft felt hat with a low crown and wide brim.

widely /wídlee/ *adv.* **1** to a wide extent; far apart. **2** extensively (*widely read; widely distributed*). **3** by many people (*it is widely thought that*). **4** considerably; to a large degree (*holds a widely different view*).
■ **2** see *far and wide*. **3** extensively, thoroughly, universally, everywhere, generally, popularly, by many. **4** to a large *or* great extent, greatly, largely, very much, extremely, considerably, substantially.

widen /wíd'n/ *v.tr.* & *intr.* make or become wider. □□ **widener** *n.*
■ distend, dilate, open out, spread, stretch, enlarge, increase, expand; extend, broaden, supplement, add to, augment.

widespread /wídspréd/ *adj.* widely distributed or disseminated.
■ see EXTENSIVE 2.

widgeon /wíjən/ *n.* (also **wigeon**) a species of dabbling duck, esp. *Anas penelope* or *Anas americana*. [16th c.: orig. uncert.]

widget /wíjit/ *n. colloq.* any gadget or device. [perh. alt. of GADGET]
■ see GADGET.

widow /wídō/ *n.* & *v.* ● *n.* **1** a woman who has lost her husband by death and has not married again. **2** a woman whose husband is often away on or preoccupied with a specified activity (*golf widow; football widow*). **3** extra cards dealt separately and taken by the highest bidder. **4** *Printing* the short last line of a paragraph, esp. at the top of a page or column. ● *v.tr.* **1** make into a widow or widower. **2** (as **widowed** *adj.*) bereft by the death of a spouse (*my widowed mother*). **3** (foll. by *of*) deprive of. □ **widow bird** a whydah. **widow's cruse** an apparently small supply that proves or seems inexhaustible (see 1 Kgs. 17:10–16). **widow's mite** a small money contribution, esp. by one who is quite poor (see Mark 12:42). **widow's peak** a V-shaped growth of hair toward the center of the forehead. **widow's weeds** see WEEDS. [OE *widewe*, rel. to OHG *wituwa*, Skr. *vidhávā*, L *viduus* bereft, widowed, Gk *eitheos* unmarried man]

widower /wídōər/ *n.* a man who has lost his wife by death and has not married again.

widowhood /wídōhōōd/ *n.* the state or period of being a widow or widower.

width /width, witth, with/ *n.* **1** measurement or distance from side to side. **2** a large extent. **3** breadth or liberality of thought, views, etc. **4** a strip of material of full width as woven. □□ **widthways** *adv.* **widthwise** *adv.* [17th c. (as WIDE, -TH²) replacing *wideness*]
■ **1** breadth, wideness, compass, broadness, span;

/. . ./ **pronunciation**	● **part of speech**
□ **phrases, idioms, and compounds**	
□□ **derivatives**	■ **synonym section**
cross-references appear in SMALL CAPITALS or *italics*	

diameter, caliber, bore; measure; *Naut.* beam. **2** reach, scope, range, breadth, extent, extensiveness. **3** see BREADTH 4.

wield /weeld/ *v.tr.* **1** hold and use (a weapon or tool). **2** exert or command (power or authority, etc.). □□ **wielder** *n.* [OE *wealdan, wieldan* f. Gmc]
■ **1** flourish, swing, brandish, wave, handle, ply, use, employ. **2** exercise, employ, exert, command, use, utilize.

wieldy /weeldee/ *adj.* (**wieldier, wieldiest**) easily wielded, controlled, or handled.

wiener /weenər/ *n.* a frankfurter. [Ger. *Wiener wurst* Viennese sausage]

Wiener schnitzel /veenər shnítsəl/ *n.* a veal cutlet breaded, fried, and garnished. [G, = Viennese slice]

wife /wif/ *n.* (*pl.* **wives** /wivz/) **1** a married woman esp. in relation to her husband. **2** *archaic* a woman, esp. an old or uneducated one. **3** (in *comb.*) a woman engaged in a specified activity (*fishwife; housewife; midwife*). □ **have** (or **take**) **to wife** *archaic* marry (a woman). **wife swapping** *colloq.* exchanging wives for sexual relations. □□ **wifehood** *n.* **wifeless** *adj.* **wifelike** *adj.* **wifely** *adj.* **wifeliness** *n.* **wifish** *adj.* [OE *wif* woman: ult. orig. unkn.]
■ **1** mate, helpmate, spouse, bride, partner, *colloq.* better half, old lady *or* woman, *colloq. often derog.* little woman, *joc.* lady wife; *sl. or joc.* the missus.

wig[1] /wig/ *n.* an artificial head of hair esp. to conceal baldness or as a disguise, or worn by a judge or barrister or as period dress. □□ **wigged** *adj.* (also in *comb.*). **wigless** *adj.* [abbr. of PERIWIG: cf. WINKLE]

wig[2] /wig/ *v.tr.* (**wigged, wigging**) *Brit. colloq.* rebuke sharply; rate. [app. f. WIG[1] in sl. or colloq. sense 'rebuke' (19th c.)]

wigeon var. of WIDGEON.

wigging /wíging/ *n. Brit. colloq.* a reprimand.

wiggle /wígəl/ *v.* & *n. colloq.* ● *v.intr.* & *tr.* move or cause to move quickly from side to side, etc. ● *n.* an act of wiggling. □□ **wiggler** *n.* [ME f. MLG & MDu. *wiggelen*: cf. WAG[1], WAGGLE]
■ *v.* see WAG[1] *v.* 1. ● *n.* see WAG[1] *n.*

wiggly /wíglee/ *adj.* (**wigglier, wiggliest**) *colloq.* **1** showing wiggles. **2** having small irregular undulations.

wight /wīt/ *n. archaic* a person (*wretched wight*). [OE *wiht* = thing, creature, of unkn. orig.]

wigwag /wígwag/ *v.intr.* (**wigwagged, wigwagging**) *colloq.* **1** move lightly to and fro. **2** wave flags in this way in signaling. [redupl. f. WAG[1]]

wigwam /wígwom/ *n.* **1** a Native American hut or tent of skins, mats, or bark on poles. **2** a similar structure for children, etc. [Ojibwa *wigwaum*, Algonquian *wikiwam* their house]

wilco /wílkō/ *int. colloq.* expressing compliance or agreement, esp. acceptance of instructions received by radio. [abbr. of *will comply*]

wild /wīld/ *adj., adv.,* & *n.* ● *adj.* **1** (of an animal or plant) in its original natural state; not domesticated nor cultivated (esp. of species or varieties allied to others that are not wild). **2** not civilized; barbarous. **3** (of scenery, etc.) having a conspicuously desolate appearance. **4** unrestrained; disorderly; uncontrolled (*a wild youth; wild hair*). **5** tempestuous; violent (*a wild night*). **6 a** intensely eager; excited; frantic (*wild with excitement; wild delight*). **b** (of looks, appearance, etc.) indicating distraction. **c** (foll. by *about*) *colloq.* enthusiastically devoted to (a person or subject). **7** *colloq.* infuriated; angry (*makes me wild*). **8** haphazard; ill-aimed; rash (*a wild guess; a wild shot; a wild venture*). **9** (of a horse, game bird, etc.) shy; easily startled. **10** *colloq.* exciting; delightful. **11** (of a card) having any rank chosen by the player holding it (*the joker is wild*). ● *adv.* in a wild manner (*shooting wild*). ● *n.* **1** a wild tract. **2** a desert. □ **in the wild** in an uncultivated, etc., state. **in** (or **out in**) **the wilds** *colloq.* far from normal habitation. **run wild** grow or stray unchecked or undisciplined. **sow one's wild oats** see OAT. **wild-and-woolly** uncouth; lacking refinement. **wild boar** see BOAR. **wild card 1** see sense 11 *adj.* **2** *Computing* a character

that will match any character or sequence of characters in a file name, etc. **3** *Sports* an extra player or team chosen to enter a competition at the selectors' discretion. **wild-goose chase** a foolish or hopeless and unproductive quest. **wild horse 1** a horse not domesticated nor broken in. **2** (in *pl.*) *colloq.* even the most powerful influence, etc. (*wild horses would not drag the secret from me*). **wild hyacinth** = BLUEBELL 1. **wild rice** any tall grass of the genus *Zizania*, yielding edible grains. **wild silk 1** silk from wild silkworms. **2** an imitation of this from short silk fibers. **Wild West** the western US in a time of lawlessness in its early history. □□ **wildish** *adj.* **wildly** *adv.* **wildness** *n.* [OE *wilde* f. Gmc]
■ *adj.* **1** undomesticated, untamed, unbroken, savage, feral; natural, uncultivated. **2** savage, uncivilized, barbarous, primitive, rude, uncultured, uncultivated, brutish, barbaric, fierce, ferocious. **3** uncultivated, uninhabited, waste, desert, deserted, desolate, virgin, unpopulated, empty, trackless, barren, lifeless; rugged, rough. **4** uncontrolled, unrestricted, unrestrained, untrammeled, unbridled, unfettered, unshackled, free, unchecked, uninhibited, impetuous, unconventional, undisciplined, disobedient, insubordinate, obstreperous, self-willed, wayward, mutinous, rowdy(ish), boisterous, tumultuous, unruly, uproarious, chaotic; uncontrollable, unmanageable, ungovernable, intractable, unrestrainable; disordered, disorderly, disheveled, unkempt, untidy, tousled, windblown, messed-up, *colloq.* mussed-up. **5** tempestuous, turbulent, violent; see also STORMY 1, 2. **6 a, b** excited, eager, vehement, passionate, mad, maniac(al), crazed, crazy, frenzied, frantic, distracted, distraught, hysterical, raving, raging, demented, delirious, berserk. **c** enthusiastic, avid, eager, mad, excited, infatuated, passionate, *colloq.* crazy, dotty, nuts, esp. *Brit. colloq.* daft, *sl.* nutty, *Brit. sl.* potty. **7** see FURIOUS 1, 2. **8** haphazard, random, ill-aimed, absurd, crazy, irrational, unreasonable, unthinking, extravagant, fantastic, imprudent, foolish, foolhardy, ill-conceived, impractical, impracticable, unpractical, unworkable, ridiculous, reckless, rash, silly, giddy, flighty, madcap, outrageous, preposterous, offbeat, *colloq.* cockeyed. **10** see *thrilling* (THRILL). ● *n.* waste, wasteland, wilderness, desert; vastness, emptiness. □ **in** (or **out in**) **the wilds** in the backwoods, in the bush, *Brit.* in the back of beyond, esp. *Austral.* in the outback, *colloq.* in the middle of nowhere, in the sticks, *sl.* in the boondocks. **wild horse 1** bronco, *Austral.* brumby. □□ **wildly** see MADLY 2. **wildness** see NATURE 6, VIOLENCE 1.

wildcat /wíldkat/ *n.* & *adj.* ● *n.* **1** a hot-tempered or violent person. **2** any of various smallish cats, esp. the European *Felis sylvestris* or the N. American bobcat. **3** an exploratory oil well. ● *adj.* (*attrib.*) **1** reckless; financially unsound. **2** (of a strike) sudden and unofficial. □ **wildcat strike** an unauthorized strike by esp. union laborers.
■ *adj.* **1** see RECKLESS.

wildebeest /wíldəbeest, víl-/ *n.* = GNU. [Afrik. (as WILD, BEAST)]

wilder /wíldər/ *v.tr. archaic* **1** lead astray. **2** bewilder. [perh. based on WILDERNESS]

wilderness /wíldərnis/ *n.* **1** a desert; an uncultivated and uninhabited region. **2** part of a garden left with an uncultivated appearance. **3** (foll. by *of*) a confused assemblage of things. □ **in the wilderness** *Brit.* out of political office. **voice in the wilderness** an unheeded advocate of reform (see Matt. 3:3, etc.). [OE *wildēornes* f. *wild dēor* wild deer]
■ **1** see DESERT[2] *n.* **2** jungle.

wildfire /wíldfir/ *n. hist.* **1** a combustible liquid, esp. Greek fire, formerly used in warfare. **2** = WILL-O'-THE-WISP. □ **spread like wildfire** spread with great speed.

wildflower /wíldflowər, wíəld-, -flowr/ *n.* **1** any wild or uncultivated flowering plant. **2** the flower of such a plant.

wildfowl /wíldfowl/ *n.* (*pl.* same) a game bird, esp. an aquatic one.

wilding /wílding/ *n.* (also **wildling** /-ling/) **1** a plant sown by natural agency, esp. a wild crab apple. **2** the fruit of such a plant. [WILD + -ING³]

wildlife /wíldlīf/ *n.* wild animals collectively.

wildwood /wíldwŏŏd/ *n. poet.* uncultivated or unfrequented woodland.

wile /wīl/ *n. & v.* ● *n.* (usu. in *pl.*) a stratagem; a trick or cunning procedure. ● *v.tr.* (foll. by *away, into*, etc.) lure or entice. [ME *wīl*, perh. f. Scand. (ON *vél* craft)]
■ *n.* trick, stratagem, ruse, artifice, subterfuge, dodge, trap, snare, maneuver, contrivance, move, gambit, plot, scheme, machination, (little) game, *colloq.* ploy. ● *v.* see ENTICE.

wilful *Brit.* var. of WILLFUL.

wiliness see WILY.

will¹ /wil/ *v.aux. & tr.* (*3rd sing. present* **will**; *past* **would** /wŏŏd/) (foll. by infin. without *to*, or *absol.*; present and past only in use) **1** (in the 2nd and 3rd persons, and often in the 1st: see SHALL) expressing the future tense in statements, commands, or questions (*you will regret this; they will leave at once; will you go to the party?*). **2** (in the 1st person) expressing a wish or intention (*I will return soon*). ¶ For the other persons in senses 1, 2, see SHALL. **3** expressing desire, consent, or inclination (*will you have a sandwich?; come when you will; the door will not open*). **4** expressing ability or capacity (*the jar will hold a quart*). **5** expressing habitual or inevitable tendency (*accidents will happen; will sit there for hours*). **6** expressing probability or expectation (*that will be my wife*). □ **will do** *colloq.* expressing willingness to carry out a request. [OE *wyllan*, (unrecorded) *willan* f. Gmc: rel. to L *volo*]

will² /wil/ *n. & v.* ● *n.* **1** the faculty by which a person decides or is regarded as deciding on and initiating action (*the mind consists of the understanding and the will*). **2** control exercised by deliberate purpose over impulse; self-control; willpower (*has a strong will*). **3** a deliberate or fixed desire or intention (*a will to live*). **4** energy of intention; the power of effecting one's intentions or dominating others. **5** directions (usu. written) in legal form for the disposition of one's property after death (*make one's will*). **6** disposition toward others (*good will*). **7** *archaic* what one desires or ordains (*thy will be done*). ● *v.tr.* **1** have as the object of one's will; intend unconditionally (*what God wills; willed that we should succeed*). **2** (*absol.*) exercise willpower. **3** instigate or impel or compel by the exercise of willpower (*you can will yourself into contentment*). **4** bequeath by the terms of a will (*shall will my money to charity*). □ **at will 1** whenever one pleases. **2** *Law* able to be evicted without notice (*tenant at will*). **have one's will** obtain what one wants. **what is your will?** what do you wish done? **where there's a will there's a way** determination will overcome any obstacle. **a will of one's own** obstinacy; willfulness of character. **with the best will in the world** esp. *Brit.* however good one's intentions. **with a will** energetically or resolutely. □□ **willed** *adj.* (also in *comb.*). **willer** *n.* **will·less** *adj.* [OE *willa* f. Gmc]
■ *n.* **2** willpower, self-control, resolve, commitment, resolution, determination, volition, fortitude, *colloq.* guts. **3** desire, wish, longing, liking, inclination, disposition, intent, intention, resolve, commitment, resolution, determination. **4** drive, purposefulness, purpose, intent, intention, motivation. **5** (last will and) testament, last wishes. **6** disposition, attitude, feeling(s), intentions. **7** choice, wishes, desire, inclination. ● *v.* **1** want, desire, wish, choose, intend, command, order, ordain, require, see fit. **3** make, compel, force, instigate, impel. **4** leave, bequeath, hand down *or* on, pass on, transfer; *Law* devise. □ **at will 1** as *or* when one pleases, as *or* when one wishes, as *or* when one thinks fit(ting), at one's desire *or* whim *or* discretion, *formal* at one's pleasure.

willet /wílit/ *n.* (*pl.* same) a large N. American wader, *Catoptrophorus semipalmatus*. [*pill-will-willet*, imit. of its cry]

willful /wílfŏŏl/ *adj.* (*Brit.* **wilful**) **1** (of an action or state) intentional, deliberate (*willful murder; willful neglect; willful disobedience*). **2** (of a person) obstinate, headstrong. □□ **willfully** *adv.* **willfulness** *n.* [ME f. WILL² + -FUL]

■ **1** intentional, deliberate, voluntary, conscious, intended, purposeful, premeditated. **2** stubborn, headstrong, pigheaded, obstinate, mulish, inflexible, adamant, obdurate, intransigent, unyielding, self-willed, ungovernable, recalcitrant, unruly, immovable, intractable, dogged, determined, refractory, uncompromising, wayward, perverse, contrary. □□ **willfully** see *deliberately* (DELIBERATE). **willfulness** see *obstinacy* (OBSTINATE).

willies /wíleez/ *n.pl. colloq.* nervous discomfort (esp. *give* or *get the willies*). [19th c.: orig. unkn.]
■ see JITTER *n.*

willing /wíling/ *adj. & n.* ● *adj.* **1** ready to consent or undertake (*a willing ally; am willing to do it*). **2** given or done, etc., by a willing person (*willing hands; willing help*). ● *n.* cheerful intention (*show willing*). □□ **willingly** *adv.* **willingness** *n.*
■ *adj.* **1** agreeable, acquiescent, compliant, amenable, consenting, assenting, complaisant, ready, well-disposed, inclined, prepared, happy, content, pleased, delighted, enthusiastic, avid, eager, zealous, keen, game. □□ **willingly** readily, happily, contentedly, gladly, cheerfully, amenably, agreeably, freely, of one's own accord *or* free will, on one's own, ungrudgingly, by choice, voluntarily, unhesitatingly, nothing loath, eagerly, enthusiastically, zealously, avidly, at the drop of a hat.

will-o'-the-wisp /wíləthəwísp/ *n.* **1** a phosphorescent light seen on marshy ground, perhaps resulting from the combustion of gases; ignis fatuus. **2** an elusive person. **3** a delusive hope or plan. [orig. *Will with the wisp*: *wisp* = handful of (lighted) hay, etc.]
■ **3** see ILLUSION 4.

willow /wílō/ *n.* **1** a tree or shrub of the genus *Salix*, growing usu. near water in temperate climates, with small flowers borne on catkins, and pliant branches yielding osiers and wood for cricket bats, baskets, etc. **2** an item made of willow wood, esp. a cricket bat. □ **willow herb** any plant of the genus *Epilobium*, etc., esp. one with leaves like a willow and pale purple flowers. **willow pattern** a conventional design representing a Chinese scene, often with a willow tree, of blue on white porcelain, stoneware, or earthenware. **willow warbler** (or **wren**) a small woodland bird, *Phylloscopus trochilus*, with a tuneful song. [OE *welig*]

willowy /wílō-ee/ *adj.* **1** having or bordered by willows. **2** lithe and slender.
■ **2** lissome, pliant, lithe, flexible, supple, limber, loose-limbed; slim, slender, graceful, sylphlike, svelte, thin, long-limbed, clean(-limbed).

willpower /wílpowr/ *n.* control exercised by deliberate purpose over impulse; self-control (*overcame his shyness by willpower*).

willy-nilly /wíleenílee/ *adv. & adj.* ● *adv.* whether one likes it or not. ● *adj.* existing or occurring willy-nilly. [later spelling of *will I, nill I* I am willing, I am unwilling]
■ *adv.* whether one likes it or not, inevitably, necessarily, of necessity, one way or the other, *archaic* perforce, *colloq.* like it or not, so there, *literary* nolens volens. ● *adj.* necessary, unavoidable, inevitable, involuntary.

willy-willy /wíleewílee/ *n.* (*pl.* **-ies**) *Austral.* a cyclone or dust storm. [Aboriginal]

wilt¹ /wilt/ *v. & n.* ● *v.* **1** *intr.* (of a plant, leaf, or flower) wither; droop. **2** *intr.* (of a person) lose one's energy; flag; tire; droop. **3** *tr.* cause to wilt. ● *n.* a plant disease causing wilting. [orig. dial.: perh. alt. f. *wilk, welk*, of LG or Du. orig.]
■ *v.* **1** sag, droop, wither, shrink, shrivel (up *or* away), flop, diminish. **2** sag, droop, bow, weaken, sink, wane,

---

/.../ **pronunciation**	● **part of speech**
□ **phrases, idioms, and compounds**	
□□ **derivatives**	■ **synonym section**
cross-references appear in SMALL CAPITALS or *italics*	

wither, lose courage *or* nerve, flag, dwindle, languish, tire.

wilt² /wilt/ *archaic 2nd person sing.* of WILL¹.

Wilton /wiltən/ *n.* a kind of woven carpet with a thick pile. [*Wilton* in S. England]

wily /wīlee/ *adj.* (**wilier, wiliest**) full of wiles; crafty; cunning. □□ **wilily** *adv.* **wiliness** *n.*

■ shrewd, cunning, crafty, sly, artful, guileful, clever, foxy, vulpine, disingenuous, scheming, plotting, calculating, designing, sharp, canny, deceitful, deceiving, deceptive, treacherous, perfidious, false, double-dealing, dishonest, underhand(ed), tricky, smooth, slick, slippery, oily, unctuous, *colloq.* cagey, shifty, crooked, two-timing.

wimp /wimp/ *n. colloq.* a feeble or ineffectual person. □□ **wimpish** *adj.* **wimpishly** *adv.* **wimpishness** *n.* **wimpy** *adj.* [20th c.: orig. uncert.]

■ see DRIP *n.* 2.

wimple /wimpəl/ *n. & v.* ● *n.* a linen or silk headdress covering the neck and the sides of the face, formerly worn by women and still worn by some nuns. ● *v.tr. & intr.* arrange or fall in folds. [OE *wimpel*]

Wimshurst machine /wimzhərst/ *n.* a device for generating an electric charge by turning glass disks in opposite directions. [J. *Wimshurst*, Engl. engineer d. 1903]

win /win/ *v. & n.* ● *v.* (**winning**; *past* and *past part.* **won** /wun/) **1** *tr.* acquire or secure as a result of a fight, contest, bet, litigation, or some other effort (*won some money*; *won my admiration*). **2** *tr.* be victorious in (a fight, game, race, etc.). **3** *intr.* **a** be the victor; win a race or contest, etc. (*who won?*; *persevere, and you will win*). **b** (foll. by *through, free*, etc.) make one's way or become by successful effort. **4** *tr.* reach by effort (*win the summit*; *win the shore*). **5** *tr.* obtain (ore) from a mine. **6** *tr.* dry (hay, etc.) by exposure to the air. ● *n.* victory in a game or bet, etc. □ **win the day** be victorious in battle, argument, etc. **win over** persuade; gain the support of. **win one's spurs 1** *colloq.* gain distinction or fame. **2** *Brit. hist.* gain a knighthood. **win through** (or **out**) overcome obstacles. **you can't win** *colloq.* there is no way to succeed. **you can't win them** (or **'em**) **all** *colloq.* a resigned expression of consolation on failure. □□ **winnable** *adj.* [OE *winnan* toil, endure: cf. OHG *winnan*, ON *vinna*]

■ *v.* **1** gain, carry off *or* away, bear off *or* away, attain, acquire, get, obtain, secure, procure, receive, collect, net, earn, achieve, realize, pick up, glean, *colloq.* bag, walk off *or* away with. **2** finish first in, achieve first place in, triumph in, be victorious in, be the victor in, gain a victory in, prevail in, succeed in, carry off, take first prize in. **3 a** come (in *or* out) first, finish first, achieve first place, carry the day, carry off the palm, win the day, conquer, overcome, triumph, be victorious, be the victor, gain a victory, prevail, succeed, take first prize, *colloq.* bring home the bacon. **4** reach, attain, arrive at, get to, *colloq.* make it to. ● *n.* victory, conquest, triumph, success. □ **win over** influence, sway, incline, persuade, charm, prevail upon, convert, induce, bring around, gain the support of, convince.

wince¹ /wins/ *n. & v.* ● *n.* a start or involuntary shrinking movement showing pain or distress. ● *v.intr.* give a wince. □□ **wincer** *n.* **wincingly** *adv.* [ME f. OF *guenchir* turn aside: cf. WINCH, WINK]

■ *v.* see CRINGE *v.* 1.

wince² /wins/ *n. Brit.* var. of WINCH 4.

winch /winch/ *n. & v.* ● *n.* **1** the crank of a wheel or axle. **2** a windlass. **3** *Brit.* the reel of a fishing rod. **4** a roller for moving textile fabric through a dyeing vat. ● *v.tr.* lift with a winch. □□ **wincher** *n.* [OE *wince* f. Gmc: cf. WINCE¹]

Winchester /winchestər/ *n.* **1** *propr.* a breech-loading repeating rifle. **2** (in full **Winchester disk**) *Computing* a hermetically sealed data-storage device (so called because its original numerical designation corresponded to that of the rifle's caliber). [O. F. *Winchester* d. 1880, US manufacturer of the rifle]

wind¹ /wind/ *n. & v.* ● *n.* **1 a** air in more or less rapid natural

motion, esp. from an area of high pressure to one of low pressure. **b** a current of wind blowing from a specified direction or otherwise defined (*north wind*; *opposing wind*). **2 a** breath as needed in physical exertion or in speech. **b** the power of breathing without difficulty while running or making a similar continuous effort (*let me recover my wind*). **c** a spot below the center of the chest where a blow temporarily paralyzes breathing. **3** mere empty words; meaningless rhetoric. **4** gas generated in the bowels, etc., by indigestion; flatulence. **5 a** an artifically produced current of air, esp. for sounding an organ or other wind instrument. **b** air stored for use or used as a current. **c** the wind instruments of an orchestra collectively (*poor balance between wind and strings*). **6** a scent carried by the wind, indicating the presence or proximity of an animal, etc. ● *v.tr.* **1** exhaust the wind of by exertion or a blow. **2** renew the wind of by rest (*stopped to wind the horses*). **3** make breathe quickly and deeply by exercise. **4** *Brit.* make (a baby) bring up wind after feeding; burp. **5** detect the presence of by a scent. **6** /wīnd/ (*past* and *past part.* **winded** or **wound** /wownd/) *poet.* sound (a bugle or call) by blowing. □ **before the wind** helped by the wind's force. **between wind and water** at a vulnerable point. **close to** (or **near**) **the wind 1** sailing as nearly against the wind as is consistent with using its force. **2** *colloq.* verging on indecency or dishonesty. **get wind of 1** smell out. **2** begin to suspect; hear a rumor of. **get** (or **have**) **the wind up** *Brit. colloq.* be alarmed or frightened. **how** (or **which way**) **the wind blows** (or **lies**) **1** what is the state of opinion. **2** what developments are likely. **in the wind** happening or about to happen. **in the wind's eye** directly against the wind. **like the wind** swiftly. **off the wind** *Naut.* with the wind on the quarter. **on a wind** *Naut.* against a wind on either bow. **on the wind** (of a sound or scent) carried by the wind. **put the wind up** *Brit. colloq.* alarm or frighten. **take wind** *Brit.* be rumored; become known. **take the wind out of a person's sails** frustrate a person by anticipating an action or remark, etc. **throw caution to the wind** (or **winds**) not worry about taking risks; be reckless. **to the winds** (or **four winds**) **1** in all directions. **2** into a state of abandonment or neglect. **wind and weather** exposure to the effects of the elements. **wind band** a group of wind instruments as a band or section of an orchestra. **wind cone** = *wind sock.* **wind force** the force of the wind esp. as measured on the Beaufort, etc., scale. **wind gap** a dried-up former river valley through ridges or hills. **wind gauge 1** an anemometer. **2** an apparatus attached to the sights of a gun enabling allowance to be made for the wind in shooting. **3** a device showing the amount of wind in an organ. **wind instrument** a musical instrument in which sound is produced by a current of air, esp. the breath. **wind machine** a device for producing a blast of air or the sound of wind. **wind** (or **winds**) **of change** a force or influence for reform. **wind rose** a diagram of the relative frequency of wind directions at a place. **wind sail** a canvas funnel conveying air to the lower parts of a ship. **wind shear** a variation in wind velocity at right angles to the wind's direction. **wind sock** a canvas cylinder or cone on a mast to show the direction of the wind at an airfield, etc. **wind tunnel** a tunnellike device to produce an air stream past models of aircraft, etc., for the study of wind effects on them. □□ **windless** *adj.* [OE f. Gmc]

■ *n.* **1** breeze, *literary* zephyr; puff, gust, blast, squall, breath, draft, current (of air). **2a, b** breath, air, puff. **3** puffery, bombast, rodomontade, rhetoric, bluster, boasting, braggadocio, vain speech, blather, (idle *or* empty) talk, fustian, nonsense, twaddle, humbug, babble, gibberish, claptrap, *colloq.* gab, hogwash, esp. *Brit. colloq.* waffle, *sl.* hot air, hooey, rot, baloney. **4** gas, flatulence, windiness, flatus, borborygmus. **6** whiff, scent, smell, trace. ● *v.* **4** *Brit.* bring up the wind of, *colloq.* burp. □ **before the wind** downwind, *Naut.* off the wind. **get wind of 1** see SMELL *v.* 1. **2** hear of, learn of, come to know, pick up, be made *or* become aware of, gather, understand, hear tell of, *colloq.* hear on the grapevine. **get** (or **have**) **the wind up** take fright, become alarmed *or* frightened *or* afraid *or* apprehensive, panic. **in the wind** around, about, rumored, in the air, detectable, discernible, discoverable, imminent, impending, approaching, close (at hand), about to happen *or* take place *or* occur, afoot, in the offing, near, on the way, on *or* in the cards. **like the wind** see *swiftly* (SWIFT). **off the wind** before the wind, downwind. **on a wind** upwind, windward, *Naut.* to the wind, into (the teeth *or* eye of) the wind, in the wind's eye; close to *or* near the wind. **put the wind up** scare, frighten, alarm, unnerve, *colloq.* scare the pants off. **take the wind out of a person's sails** deflate *or* disconcert a person, destroy a person's advantage, ruin a person's superiority *or* supremacy *or* ascendancy. **wind sock** wind sleeve, wind cone. □□ **windless** see CALM *adj.* 1.

wind² /wind/ *v. & n.* ● *v.* (*past* and *past part.* **wound** /wownd/) **1** *intr.* go in a circular, spiral, curved, or crooked course (*a winding staircase*; *the path winds up the hill*). **2** *tr.* make (one's way) by such a course (*wind your way up to bed*; *wound their way into our affections*). **3** *tr.* wrap closely; surround with or as with a coil (*wound the blanket around me*; *wound my arms around the child*; *wound the child in my arms*). **4 a** *tr.* coil; provide with a coiled thread, etc. (*wind the ribbon onto the card*; *wound cotton on a reel*; *winding yarn into a ball*). **b** *intr.* coil; (of yarn, etc.) coil into a ball (*the vine winds around the pole*; *the yarn wound into a ball*). **5** *tr.* wind up (a clock, etc.). **6** *tr.* hoist or draw with a windlass, etc. (*wound the cable car up the mountain*). ● *n.* **1** a bend or turn in a course. **2** a single turn when winding. □ **wind down 1** lower by winding. **2** (of a mechanism) unwind. **3** (of a person) relax. **4** draw gradually to a close. **wind-down** *n. colloq.* a gradual lessening of excitement or reduction of activity. **wind off** unwind (string, wool, etc.). **wind around one's finger** see FINGER. **wind up 1** coil the whole of (a piece of string, etc.). **2** esp. *Brit.* tighten the coiling or coiled spring of (esp. a clock, etc.). **3 a** *colloq.* increase the tension or intensity of (*wound myself up to fever pitch*). **b** irritate or provoke (a person) to the point of anger. **4** bring to a conclusion; end (*wound up his speech*). **5** *Commerce* **a** arrange the affairs of and dissolve (a company). **b** (of a company) cease business and go into liquidation. **6** *colloq.* arrive finally; end in a specified state or circumstance (*you'll wind up in prison*; *wound up owing $100*). **7** *Baseball* (of a pitcher) carry out a windup. [OE *windan* f. Gmc, rel. to WANDER, WEND]

■ *v.* **1** turn, bend, twist, spiral, circle, snake, worm, twine, zigzag, slew, swerve, loop, coil, curve, meander, wander, ramble, veer. **3** wrap, fold, enfold, encircle, envelop. **4** reel, roll, spiral, turn, twist, curl, coil, wrap, twine, wreathe, twirl. **5** crank (up), wind up. ● *n.* **1** see TURN *n.* 2. **2** turn, revolution, rotation, twist, coil. □ **wind down 3** relax, become calm *or* tranquil, calm down, cool off *or* down, regain one's equilibrium *or* composure, ease up *or* off, take it easy, *colloq.* unwind, let one's hair down. **4** taper off, slow down, diminish, reduce, close down, slacken *or* slack off (on), ease (up on), decrease, cut back *or* down (on); wind up, close out. **wind up 3 a** excite, energize, stimulate, inspire, arouse, invigorate, stir up. **b** agitate, fluster, disconcert, ruffle, irritate, exasperate, annoy, anger, provoke, nettle, madden, *colloq.* rile, needle. **4** end, close, conclude, terminate, finish, bring to an end *or* a close *or* conclusion, wrap up. **5** close (down *or* up), finish (up), wrap up; dissolve, liquidate, settle. **6** end up, finish (up), land (up), land oneself, find oneself.

windage /windij/ *n.* **1** the friction of air against the moving part of a machine. **2 a** the effect of the wind in deflecting a missile. **b** an allowance for this. **3** the difference between the diameter of a gun's bore and its projectile, allowing the escape of gas.

windbag /windbag/ *n. colloq.* a person who talks a lot but says little of any value.

■ see *talker* (TALK).

windblown /windblōn/ *adj.* exposed to or blown about by the wind.

windbound /windbownd/ *adj.* unable to sail because of opposing winds.

windbreak /windbrayk/ *n.* a row of trees or a fence or wall, etc., serving to break the force of the winds.

windbreaker /windbraykər/ *n.* a kind of wind-resistant outer jacket with close-fitting neck, cuffs, and lower edge.

windburn /windbərn/ *n.* inflammation of the skin caused by exposure to the wind.

windcheater /windcheetər/ *n. Brit.* = WINDBREAKER.

windchill /windchil/ *n.* the cooling effect of wind blowing on a surface.

winder /windər/ *n.* a winding mechanism esp. of a clock or watch.

windfall /windfawl/ *n.* **1** an apple or other fruit blown to the ground by the wind. **2** a piece of unexpected good fortune, esp. a legacy.

■ **2** bonanza, godsend, stroke of (good) fortune, serendipitous find, boon, piece of (good) luck, jackpot, (lucky) strike.

windflower /windflowr/ *n.* an anemone.

windhover /windhuvər/ *n. Brit.* a kestrel.

winding /winding/ *n.* **1** in senses of WIND² *v.* **2** curved or sinuous motion or movement. **3 a** a thing that is wound around or coiled. **b** *Electr.* coils of wire as a conductor around an armature, etc. □ **winding-sheet** a sheet in which a corpse is wrapped for burial.

■ □ **winding-sheet** see SHROUD *n.* 1.

windjammer /windjamər/ *n.* **1** a merchant sailing ship. **2** a member of its crew.

windlass /windləs/ *n. & v.* ● *n.* a machine with a horizontal axle for hauling or hoisting. ● *v.tr.* hoist or haul with a windlass. [alt. (perh. by assoc. with dial. *windle* to wind) of obs. *windas* f. OF *guindas* f. ON *vindáss* f. *vinda* WIND² + *áss* pole]

windlestraw /windˈlstraw/ *n. archaic* an old dry stalk of grass. [OE *windelstrēaw* grass for plaiting f. *windel* basket (as WIND², -LE¹) + *strēaw* STRAW]

windmill /windmil/ *n.* **1** a mill worked by the action of the wind on its sails. **2** *Brit.* = PINWHEEL 1. □ **throw one's cap (or bonnet) over the windmill** esp. *Brit.* act recklessly or unconventionally. **tilt at (or fight) windmills** attack an imaginary enemy or grievance.

window /windō/ *n.* **1 a** an opening in a wall, roof, or vehicle, etc., usu. with glass in fixed, sliding, or hinged frames, to admit light or air, etc., and allow the occupants to see out. **b** the glass filling this opening (*have broken the window*). **2 a** space for display behind the front window of a shop. **3** an aperture in a wall, etc., through which customers are served in a bank, ticket office, etc. **4** an opportunity to observe or learn. **5** an opening or transparent part in an envelope to show an address. **6** a part of a computer monitor display selected to show a particular category or part of the data. **7 a** an interval during which atmospheric and astronomical circumstances are suitable for the launch of a spacecraft. **b** any interval or opportunity for action. **8** strips of metal foil dispersed in the air to obstruct radar detection. **9** a range of electromagnetic wavelengths for which a medium is transparent. □ **out of the window** *Brit. colloq.* no longer taken into account. **window box** a box placed on an outside windowsill for growing flowers. **window dressing 1** the art of arranging a display in a store window, etc. **2** an adroit presentation of facts, etc., to give a deceptively favorable impression. **window ledge** = WINDOWSILL. **window seat 1** a seat below a window, esp. in a bay or alcove. **2** a seat next to a window in an aircraft, train, etc. **window-shop (-shopped, -shopping)** look at goods displayed in store windows, usu. without buying anything. **window-shopper** a person who window-shops. **window tax** *Brit. hist.* a tax on windows or similar openings (abolished in 1851). **win-**

---

dow washer a person who is employed to clean windows. □□ **windowed** adj. (also in comb.). **windowless** adj. [ME f. ON *vindauga* (as WIND¹, EYE)]

windowing /wíndōing/ n. *Computing* the selection of part of a stored image for display or enlargement.

windowpane /wíndōpayn/ n. **1** a pane of glass in a window. **2** a tattersall.

windowsill /wíndōsil/ n. a sill below a window.

windpipe /wíndpīp/ n. the air passage from the throat to the lungs; the trachea.

windrow /wíndrō/ n. a line of raked hay, sheaves of grain, etc., for drying by the wind.

windscreen /wíndskreen/ n. *Brit.* = WINDSHIELD.

windshield /wíndsheeld/ n. a shield of glass at the front of a motor vehicle. □ **windshield wiper** a device consisting of a rubber blade on an arm, moving in an arc, for keeping a windshield clear of rain, etc.

Windsor /wínzər/ n. (usu. *attrib.*) denoting or relating to the British royal family since 1917. [*Windsor* in S. England, site of the royal residence at Windsor Castle]

Windsor chair n. a wooden dining chair with a semicircular back supported by upright rods.

windsurfing /wíndsərfing/ n. the sport of riding on water on a sailboard. □□ **windsurf** v.intr. **windsurfer** n.

windswept /wíndswept/ adj. exposed to or swept back by the wind.

■ disordered, disorderly, disheveled, unkempt, untidy, tousled, windblown, messed-up, *colloq.* mussed-up; see also BLEAK¹ 1.

windup /wíndup/ n. **1** a conclusion; a finish. **2** *Brit.* a state of anxiety; the provocation of this. **wound up** adj. (of a person) excited or tense or angry. **3** *Baseball* the motions made by a pitcher, esp. arm swinging, in preparation for releasing a pitch.

windward /wíndwərd/ adj., adv., & n. ● adj. & adv. on the side from which the wind is blowing (opp. LEEWARD). ● n. the windward region, side, or direction (*to windward*; *on the windward of*). □ **get to windward of 1** place oneself there to avoid the smell of. **2** gain an advantage over.

windy /wíndee/ adj. (**windier**, **windiest**) **1** stormy with wind (*a windy night*). **2** exposed to the wind; windswept (*a windy plain*). **3** generating or characterized by flatulence. **4** *colloq.* wordy; verbose; empty (*a windy speech*). **5** *Brit. colloq.* nervous; frightened. □□ **windily** adv. **windiness** n. [OE *windig* (as WIND¹, -Y¹)]

■ **1** blustery, blowing, blowy, breezy, gusting, gusty, wild, boisterous, rough, squally, stormy, tempestuous. **2** windswept, exposed, unprotected, bleak. **3** flatulent. **4** talkative, long-winded, garrulous, wordy, verbose, prolix, loquacious, rambling, voluble, fluent, effusive, glib, turgid, bombastic, pompous.

wine /wīn/ n. & v. ● n. **1** fermented grape juice as an alcoholic drink. **2** a fermented drink resembling this made from other fruits, etc., as specified (*elderberry wine*; *ginger wine*). **3** the dark-red color of red wine. ● v. **1** intr. drink wine. **2** tr. entertain to wine. □ **wine and dine** entertain to or have a meal with wine. **wine bar** a bar or small restaurant where wine is the main drink available. **wine bottle** a glass bottle for wine, the standard size holding 26 ⅔ fl. oz. or 75 cl. **wine box** a square carton of wine with a dispensing tap. **wine cellar 1** a cellar for storing wine. **2** the contents of this. **wine list** a list of wines available in a restaurant, etc. **wine steward** a waiter responsible for serving wine; sommelier. **wine vinegar** vinegar made from wine as distinct from malt. □□ **wineless** adj. [OE *wīn* f. Gmc f. L *vinum*]

wineberry /wínberee/ n. (pl. **-ies**) **1 a** a deciduous bristly shrub, *Rubus phoenicolasius*, from China and Japan, producing scarlet berries used in cookery. **b** this berry. **2** = MAKO².

winebibber /wínbibər/ n. a tippler or drunkard. □□ **winebibbing** n. & adj. [WINE + *bib* to tipple]

wineglass /wínglas/ n. **1** a glass for wine, usu. with a stem and foot. **2** the contents of this, a wineglassful.

wineglassful /wínglasfool/ n. (pl. **-fuls**) **1** the capacity of a wineglass, esp. of the size used for sherry, as a measure of liquid, about four tablespoons. **2** the contents of a wineglass.

winegrower /wíngrōər/ n. a cultivator of grapes for wine.

winepress /wínpres/ n. a press in which grapes are squeezed in making wine.

winery /wínəree/ n. (pl. **-ies**) an establishment where wine is made.

wineskin /wínskin/ n. a whole skin of a goat, etc., sewn up and used to hold wine.

winetasting /wíntaysting/ n. **1** judging the quality of wine by tasting it. **2** an occasion for this.

wing /wing/ n. & v. ● n. **1** each of the limbs or organs by which a bird, bat, or insect is able to fly. **2** a rigid horizontal winglike structure forming a supporting part of an aircraft. **3** part of a building, etc., which projects or is extended in a certain direction (*lived in the north wing*). **4 a** a forward player at either end of a line in soccer, hockey, etc. **b** the side part of a playing area. **5** (in *pl.*) the sides of a theater stage out of view of the audience. **6** a section of a political party in terms of the extremity of its views. **7** a flank of a battle array (*the cavalry were massed on the left wing*). **8** *Brit.* the fender of a motor vehicle. **9 a** an air-force unit of several squadrons or groups. **b** (in *pl.*) a pilot's badge in the air force, etc. (*get one's wings*). **10** *Anat.* & *Bot.* a lateral part or projection of an organ or structure. ● v. **1** intr. & tr. travel or traverse on wings or in an aircraft (*winging through the air*; *am winging my way home*). **2** tr. wound in a wing or an arm. **3** tr. equip with wings. **4** tr. enable to fly; send in flight (*fear winged my steps*; *winged an arrow toward them*). □ **give** (or **lend**) **wings to** speed up (a person or a thing). **on the wing** flying or in flight. **on a wing and a prayer** with only the slightest chance of success. **spread** (or **stretch**) **one's wings** develop one's powers fully. **take under one's wing** treat as a protégé. **take wing** fly away; soar. **waiting in the wings** holding oneself in readiness. **wing beat** one complete set of motions with a wing in flying. **wing case** the horny cover of an insect's wing. **wing chair** a chair with side pieces projecting forward at the top of a high back. **wing collar** a man's high, stiff collar with turned-down corners. **winged words** highly apposite or significant words. **wing game** *Brit.* game birds. **wing nut** a nut with projections for the fingers to turn it on a screw. **wing tip 1** the outer end of an aircraft's or a bird's wing. **2** a style of shoe with a pattern of perforations on the toe resembling extended bird wings. □□ **winged** adj. (also in comb.). **wingless** adj. **winglet** n. **winglike** adj. [ME pl. *wenge*, -en, -es f. ON *vængir*, pl. of *vængr*]

■ n. **6** faction, group, fringe movement, lobby. ● v. **1** see FLY¹ v. 1. **2** see WOUND¹ v. □ **take under one's wing** see PROVIDE 2b. **take wing** see FLY¹ v. 1.

wingding /wíngding/ n. *sl.* **1** a wild party. **2** a drug addict's real or feigned seizure. [20th c.: orig. unkn.]

winger /wíngər/ n. **1** a player on a wing in soccer, hockey, etc. **2** (in *comb.*) a member of a specified political wing (*left-winger*).

wingspan /wíngspan/ n. measurement right across the wings of a bird or aircraft.

wingspread /wíngspred/ n. = WINGSPAN.

wink /wingk/ v. & n. ● v. **1 a** tr. close and open (one eye or both eyes) quickly. **b** intr. close and open an eye. **2** intr. (often foll. by *at*) wink one eye as a signal of friendship or greeting or to convey a message to a person. **3** intr. (of a light, etc.) twinkle; shine or flash intermittently. ● n. **1** the act or an instance of winking, esp. as a signal, etc. **2** *colloq.* a brief moment of sleep (*didn't sleep a wink*). □ **as easy as winking** esp. *Brit. colloq.* very easy. **in a wink** very quickly. **wink at 1** purposely avoid seeing; pretend not to notice. **2** connive at (a wrongdoing, etc.). [OE *wincian* f. Gmc: cf. WINCE¹, WINCH]

■ v. **3** see TWINKLE v. □ **in a wink** see *rapidly* (RAPID). **wink at** see OVERLOOK v. 1.

winker /wíngkər/ n. **1** *Brit. colloq.* a flashing indicator light on a motor vehicle. **2** (usu. in *pl.*) a horse's blinker.

winkle /wíngkəl/ n. & v. ● n. see PERIWINKLE². ● v.tr. (foll. by *out*) esp. *Brit.* extract or eject (*winkled the information out of them*). □□ **winkler** n. [abbr. of PERIWINKLE²: cf. WIG¹]

■ *v.* (*winkle out*) see EXTRACT *v.* 2.

Winnebago /wínəbắgō/ *n.* **1 a** a N. American people native to Wisconsin. **b** a member of this people. **2** the language of this people.

winner /wínər/ *n.* **1** a person, racehorse, etc., that wins. **2** *colloq.* a successful or highly promising idea, enterprise, etc. (*the new scheme seemed a winner*).
■ **1** victor, champion, prizewinner, titleholder, conqueror, conquering hero, *colloq.* top dog, *literary* vanquisher, *sl.* champ. **2** see KNOCKOUT 4.

winning /wíning/ *adj.* & *n.* ● *adj.* **1** having or bringing victory or an advantage (*the winning entry; a winning basket*). **2** attractive; persuasive (*a winning smile; winning ways*). ● *n.* (in *pl.*) money won esp. in betting, etc. □ **winning post** a post marking the end of a race. □□ **winningly** *adv.* **winningness** *n.*
■ *adj.* **1** triumphant, conquering, victorious, successful. **2** engaging, attractive, appealing, alluring, captivating, endearing, prepossessing, winsome, bewitching, fetching, taking, persuasive, seductive, enchanting, pleasing, delightful, charming, amiable, friendly, pleasant, sweet. ● *n.* (*winnings*) see PRIZE¹ *n.* 2.

winnow /wínō/ *v.tr.* **1** blow (grain) free of chaff, etc., by an air current. **2** (foll. by *out*, *away*, *from*, etc.) get rid of (chaff, etc.) from grain. **3 a** sift; separate; clear of refuse or inferior specimens. **b** sift or examine (evidence for falsehood, etc.). **c** clear, sort, or weed out (rubbish, etc.). **4** *poet.* **a** fan (the air with wings). **b** flap (wings). **c** stir (the hair, etc.). □□ **winnower** *n.* (in senses 1, 2). [OE *windwian* (as WIND¹)]

wino /wínō/ *n.* (*pl.* **-os**) *sl.* a habitual excessive drinker of cheap wine; an alcoholic.
■ see ALCOHOLIC *n.*

winsome /wínsəm/ *adj.* (of a person, looks, or manner) winning; attractive; engaging. □□ **winsomely** *adv.* **winsomeness** *n.* [OE *wynsum* f. *wyn* JOY + -SOME¹]
■ see WINNING *adj.* 2.

winter /wíntər/ *n.* & *v.* ● *n.* **1** the coldest season of the year, in the N. hemisphere from December to February and in the S. hemisphere from June to August. **2** *Astron.* the period from the winter solstice to the vernal equinox. **3** a bleak or lifeless period or region, etc. (*nuclear winter*). **4** *poet.* a year (esp. of a person's age) (*a man of fifty winters*). **5** (*attrib.*) a characteristic of or suitable for winter (*winter light; winter clothes*). **b** (of fruit) ripening late or keeping until or during winter. **c** (of wheat or other crops) sown in autumn for harvesting the following year. ● *v.* **1** *intr.* (usu. foll. by *at*, *in*) pass the winter (*likes to winter in Florida*). **2** *tr.* keep or feed (plants, cattle) during winter. □ **winter aconite** see ACONITE 2. **winter cress** any bitter-tasting cress of the genus *Barbarea*, esp. *B. vulgaris*. **winter garden** a garden or conservatory of plants flourishing in winter. **winter jasmine** a jasmine, *Jasminum nudiflorum*, with yellow flowers. **winter quarters** a place where soldiers spend the winter. **winter sleep** hibernation. **winter solstice** see SOLSTICE. **winter sports** sports performed on snow or ice esp. in winter (e.g., skiing, hockey, and ice skating). □□ **winterer** *n.* **winterless** *adj.* **winterly** *adj.* [OE f. Gmc, prob. rel. to WET]

wintergreen /wíntərgreen/ *n.* any of several plants esp. of the genus *Pyrola* or *Gaultheria* remaining green through the winter.

winterize /wíntəriz/ *v.tr.* adapt for operation or use in cold weather. □□ **winterization** *n.*

wintertide /wíntərtid/ *n. poet.* = WINTERTIME.

wintertime /wíntərtim/ *n.* the season of winter.

wintry /wíntree/ *adj.* (also **wintery** /-təree/) (**wintrier, wintriest**) **1** characteristic of winter (*wintry weather; a wintry sun; a wintry landscape*). **2** (of a smile, greeting, etc.) lacking warmth or enthusiasm. □□ **wintrily** *adv.* **wintriness** *n.* [OE *wintrig*, or f. WINTER]
■ **1** icy, snowy, freezing, frozen, frosty, cold, frigid, bitter (cold), chilly, chilling, piercing, cutting, glacial, hyperborean, *colloq.* arctic, nippy, *literary* chill. **2** cold, frigid, chilly, cool, chilling, icy, frosty, glacial; forbidding, bleak, dismal, cheerless, dreary, harsh,

unfriendly, ugly, menacing, ominous, threatening, dark, uninviting.

winy /wínee/ *adj.* (**winier, winiest**) resembling wine in taste or appearance. □□ **wininess** *n.*

wipe /wíp/ *v.* & *n.* ● *v.tr.* **1** clean or dry the surface of by rubbing with the hands or a cloth, etc. **2** rub (a cloth) over a surface. **3** spread (a liquid, etc.) over a surface by rubbing. **4** (often foll. by *away*, *off*, etc.) **a** clear or remove by wiping (*wiped the mess off the table; wipe away your tears*). **b** remove or eliminate completely (*the village was wiped off the map*). **5 a** erase (data, a recording, etc., from a magnetic medium). **b** erase data from (the medium). **6** *Austral.* & *NZ sl.* reject or dismiss (a person or idea). ● *n.* **1** an act of wiping (*give the floor a wipe*). **2** a piece of disposable absorbent cloth, usu. treated with a cleansing agent, for wiping something clean (*antiseptic wipes*). □ **wipe down** clean (esp. a vertical surface) by wiping. **wipe a person's eye** *Brit. colloq.* get the better of a person. **wipe the floor with** *colloq.* inflict a humiliating defeat on. **wipe out 1 a** destroy; annihilate (*the whole population was wiped out*). **b** obliterate (*wiped it out of my memory*). **2** *sl.* murder. **3** clean the inside of. **4** *Brit.* avenge (an insult, etc.). **wiped out** *sl.* tired out, exhausted. **wipe the slate clean** see SLATE. **wipe up 1** take up (a liquid, etc.) by wiping. **2** *Brit.* dry (dishes, etc.). [OE *wipian*: cf. OHG *wifan* wind around, Goth. *weipan* crown: rel. to WHIP]
■ *v.* **1** wipe off *or* out *or* up, rub, clean (off *or* out *or* up), usu. *formal* cleanse; dry (off *or* out *or* up), dust (off), polish, mop (up), blot, swab, sponge (off *or* up). **3** spread, smear, rub, apply. **4 a** remove, clear, take off *or* away, get rid of. **b** remove, eliminate, get rid of. **5** see ERASE 1. ● *n.* **1** rub, clean, dust, mop, sponge, brush, sweep, polish. □ **wipe the floor with** see ROUT¹ *v.* **wipe off** annul, cancel, remove, erase, get rid of, write off. **wipe out 1 a** annihilate, destroy, massacre, kill (off), eradicate, exterminate, extirpate, root out, stamp out, dispose of, wipe off the face of the earth. **b** obliterate, remove, get rid of, efface, erase, delete, blot out, extinguish, expunge, eradicate, *literary* deracinate. **2** murder, kill (off), annihilate, massacre, dispose of, eliminate, exterminate, get rid of, wipe off the face of the earth, *colloq.* do away with, finish (off).

wipeout /wípowt/ *n.* **1** the obliteration of one radio signal by another. **2** an instance of destruction or annihilation. **3** *sl.* a fall from a surfboard.

wiper /wípər/ *n.* **1** = windshield wiper. **2** *Electr.* a moving contact. **3** a cam or tappet.

wire /wír/ *n.* & *v.* ● *n.* **1 a** a metal drawn out into the form of a thread or thin flexible rod. **b** a piece of this. **c** (*attrib.*) made of wire. **2** a length or quantity of wire used for fencing or to carry an electric current, etc. **3** a telegram or cablegram. ● *v.tr.* **1** provide, fasten, strengthen, etc., with wire. **2** (often foll. by *up*) *Electr.* install electrical circuits in (a building, piece of equipment, etc.). **3** *colloq.* telegraph (*wired me that they were coming*). **4** snare (an animal, etc.) with wire. **5** (usu. in *passive*) *Croquet* obstruct (a ball, shot, or player) by a hoop. □ **by wire** by telegraph. **get one's wires crossed** become confused and misunderstood. **wire brush 1** a brush with tough wire bristles for cleaning hard surfaces, esp. metal. **2** a brush with wire strands brushed against cymbals to produce a soft metallic sound. **wire cloth** cloth woven from wire. **wire cutter** a tool for cutting wire. **wire gauge 1** a gauge for measuring the diameter of wire, etc. **2** a standard series of sizes in which wire, etc., is made. **wire gauze** a stiff gauze woven from wire. **wire grass** any of various grasses with tough wiry stems. **wire netting** netting of wire twisted into meshes. **wire-puller** a politician, etc., who exerts a hidden influence. **wire-pulling** an instance of such. **wire rope** rope made by twisting wires together as

---

/.../ **pronunciation**	● **part of speech**
□ **phrases, idioms, and compounds**	
□□ **derivatives**	■ **synonym section**
cross-references appear in SMALL CAPITALS or *italics*	

strands. **wire service** a business that gathers news and distributes it to subscribers, usu. newspapers. **wire-walker** = tightrope walker (see TIGHTROPE). **wire wheel** a vehicle wheel with spokes of wire. **wire wool** *Brit.* = *steel wool.* □□ **wirer** *n.* [OE *wīr*]

■ *n.* **2** see CABLE *n.* 1. **3** see TELEGRAM. ● *v.* **3** see CABLE *v.* 3.

wiredraw /wírdraw/ *v.tr.* (*past* **-drew** /-drōō/; *past part.* **-drawn** /-drawn/) **1** draw (metal) out into wire. **2** elongate; protract unduly. **3** (esp. as **wiredrawn** *adj.*) refine or apply or press (an argument, etc.) with idle or excessive subtlety.

wirehaired /wírhaird/ *adj.* (esp. of a dog) having stiff or wiry hair.

wireless /wírlis/ *n. & adj.* ● *n.* **1** esp. *Brit.* **a** (in full **wireless set**) a radio receiving set. **b** the transmission and reception of radio signals. ¶ Now old-fashioned, esp. with ref. to broadcasting, and superseded by *radio*. **2** = *wireless telegraphy*. ● *adj.* lacking or not requiring wires. □ **wireless telegraphy** telegraphy using radio transmission.

■ *n.* **1 a** see RADIO *n.*

wireman /wírmən/ *n.* (*pl.* **-men**) **1** an installer or repairer of electric wires. **2** a journalist working for a telegraphic news agency. **3** a wiretapper.

wiretap /wírtap/ *v.* (**-tapped**, **-tapping**) **1** *intr.* connect a listening device to (a telephone or telegraph line, etc.) to listen to a call or transmission. **2** *tr.* obtain (information, etc.) by wiretapping. □□ **wiretapper** *n.* **wiretapping** *n.*

wireworm /wírwərm/ *n.* the larva of the click beetle causing damage to crop plants.

wiring /wíring/ *n.* **1** a system of wires providing electrical circuits. **2** the installation of this (*came to do the wiring*).

wiry /wíree/ *adj.* (**wirier**, **wiriest**) **1** tough and flexible as wire. **2** (of a person) thin and sinewy; untiring. **3** made of wire. □□ **wirily** *adv.* **wiriness** *n.*

■ **1** tough, flexible. **2** muscular, sinewy, lean, lank, spare, skinny, thin, strong, tough; untiring, tireless.

Wis. *abbr.* Wisconsin.

wis /wis/ *v.intr. archaic* know well. [orig. *I wis* = obs. *iwis* 'certainly' f. OE *gewis*, erron. taken as 'I know' and as pres. tense of *wist* (WIT²)]

Wisd. *abbr.* Wisdom of Solomon (Apocrypha).

wisdom /wízdəm/ *n.* **1** the state of being wise. **2** experience and knowledge together with the power of applying them critically or practically. **3** sagacity; prudence; common sense. **4** wise sayings, thoughts, etc., regarded collectively. □ **in his** (or **her**, etc.) **wisdom** usu. *iron.* thinking it would be best (*the committee in its wisdom decided to abandon the project*). **wisdom tooth** each of four hindmost molars not usu. cut before 20 years of age. [OE *wīsdōm* (as WISE¹, -DOM)]

■ **2, 3** sagacity, sageness, judgment, discernment, reason, prudence, judiciousness, (common) sense, insight, penetration, sapience, understanding, rationality, clear-sightedness, clearheadedness, perspicacity, perspicuity, percipience, perception, perceptiveness, intelligence, acuteness, acumen, astuteness, sharpness, shrewdness, longheadedness. **4** knowledge, learning, erudition, lore, scholarship, enlightenment.

wise¹ /wīz/ *adj. & v.* ● *adj.* **1 a** having experience and knowledge and judiciously applying them. **b** (of an action, behavior, etc.) determined by or showing or in harmony with such experience and knowledge. **2** sagacious; prudent; sensible; discreet. **3** having knowledge. **4** suggestive of wisdom (*with a wise nod of the head*). **5** *colloq.* **a** alert; crafty. **b** (often foll. by *to*) having (usu. confidential) information (about). ● *v.tr. & intr.* (foll. by *up*) *colloq.* put or get wise. □ **be** (or **get**) **wise to** *colloq.* become aware of. **no** (or **none the** or **not much**) **wiser** knowing no more than before. **put a person wise** (often foll. by *to*) *colloq.* inform a person (about). **wise guy 1** *colloq.* a know-it-all. **2** *sl.* a member of organized crime. **wise man** a wizard, esp. one of the Magi. **without anyone's being the wiser** undetected. □□ **wisely** *adv.* [OE *wīs* f. Gmc; see WIT²]

■ *adj.* **1** sage, sagacious, judicious, reasonable, commonsensical, prudent, sensible, insightful,

understanding, rational, sound, clear-sighted, clearheaded, discerning, perspicacious, perspicuous, percipient, perceptive, intelligent, acute, astute, sharp, shrewd, crafty, clever, bright, quick-witted, smart, brilliant, longheaded, brainy, *literary* sapient. **2** well-advised, advisable, judicious, sensible, sagacious, expedient, reasonable, sound, strategic, tactful, tactical, prudent, politic, discreet, diplomatic, well-thought-out, well-considered, proper, fitting, appropriate, *archaic* meet. **3** knowledgeable, learned, enlightened, informed, erudite; (well-)educated, knowing, well-read, well-versed, well-informed, lettered, scholarly. **4** knowing, shrewd, perceptive, understanding. **5 a** see FOXY 2, ALERT *adj.* 1. **b** aware, knowledgeable, informed, awake, *colloq.* in the know. ● *v.* see *be (or get) wise to*, *put a person wise* below. □ **be** (or **get**) **wise to** be or become aware of, be or become knowledgeable of or about, be or become informed of or about, be or become sensitive to, be on to, be or become awake to, wake up to, *colloq.* be in the know about, wise up about. **put a person wise** inform or advise or warn a person, put in the picture, *colloq.* wise up. **wise guy** wiseacre, *archaic usu. derog.* witling; *colloq.* know-it-all, smart aleck, smarty-pants, smarty, smart ass, *Brit. sl.* smart-arse.

wise² /wīz/ *n. archaic* way, manner, or degree (*in solemn wise*; *on this wise*). □ **in no wise** not at all. [OE *wīse* f. Gmc f. WIT²]

-wise /wīz/ *suffix* forming adjectives and adverbs of manner (*crosswise*; *clockwise*; *lengthwise*) or respect (*moneywise*) (cf. -WAYS). ¶ More fanciful phrase-based combinations, such as *employment-wise* (= as regards employment) are *colloq.*, and restricted to informal contexts. [as WISE²]

wiseacre /wízaykər/ *n.* a person who affects a wise manner; a wise guy. [MDu. *wijsseggher* soothsayer, prob. f. OHG *wīssago, wīzago*, assim. to WISE¹, ACRE]

■ see *wise guy* (WISE¹).

wisecrack /wízkrak/ *n. & v. colloq.* ● *n.* a smart pithy remark. ● *v.intr.* make a wisecrack. □□ **wisecracker** *n.*

■ *n.* joke, quip, rejoinder, witticism, pun, barb, jest, gag, gibe, *colloq.* dig. ● *v.* joke, quip, pun, gibe.

wisent /wéezənt/ *n.* the European bison, *Bison bonasus.* [G: cf. BISON]

wish /wish/ *v. & n.* ● *v.* **1** *intr.* (often foll. by *for*) have or express a desire or aspiration for (*wish for happiness*). **2** *tr.* (often foll. by *that* + clause, usu. with *that* omitted) have as a desire or aspiration (*I wish I could sing*; *I wished that I was dead*). **3** *tr.* want or demand, usu. so as to bring about what is wanted (*I wish to go*; *I wish you to do it*; *I wish it done*). **4** *tr.* express one's hopes for (*we wish you well*; *wish them no harm*; *wished us a pleasant journey*). **5** *tr.* (foll. by *on, upon*) *colloq.* foist on a person. ● *n.* **1 a** a desire, request, or aspiration. **b** an expression of this. **2** a thing desired (*got my wish*). □ **best** (or **good**) **wishes** hopes felt or expressed for another's happiness, etc. **wish fulfillment** a tendency for subconscious desire to be satisfied in fantasy. **wishing well** a well into which coins are dropped and a wish is made. □□ **wisher** *n.* (in sense 4 of *v.*); (also in *comb.*). [OE *wȳscan* f. OHG *wunsken* f. Gmc, ult. rel. to WEEN, WONT]

■ *v.* **1** yearn, long, hope, aspire, hanker, have a mind, (have a) fancy, care; (*wish for*) desire, want, crave, choose. **3** require, request, want, demand, order. **5** (*wish on*) foist or force or thrust or impose on, fob or palm off on. ● *n.* **1** desire, request, whim, want, need, aspiration, craving, longing, hankering, yearning, thirst, appetite, hunger, urge, itch, liking, passion, fondness, fancy, preference, predisposition, disposition, inclination, *colloq.* yen.

wishbone /wíshbōn/ *n.* **1** a forked bone between the neck and breast of a cooked bird: when broken between two people the longer portion entitles the holder to make a wish. **2** an object of similar shape.

wishful /wíshfŏŏl/ *adj.* **1** (often foll. by *to* + infin.) desiring; wishing. **2** having or expressing a wish. □ **wishful thinking**

belief founded on wishes rather than facts. □□ **wishfully**
adv. **wishfulness** *n.*
■ see DESIROUS 2.
wish-wash /wíshwosh, -wawsh/ *n.* **1** a weak or watery drink.
2 insipid talk or writing. [redupl. of WASH]
wishy-washy /wísheewóshee, -wáwshee/ *adj.* **1** feeble, insipid, or indecisive in quality or character. **2** (of tea, soup,
etc.) weak; watery; sloppy. [redupl. of WASHY]
■ **1** neither here nor there, undecided, indecisive,
irresolute, insipid, feeble, vapid, halfhearted, lukewarm,
namby-pamby, shilly-shallying, tergiversating,
vacillating, uncertain, of *or* having mixed feelings, in
two minds. **2** feeble, weak, watery, watered down, thin,
vapid, flat, bland, runny, sloppy, diluted, tasteless,
insipid, flavorless, stale.
wisp /wisp/ *n.* **1** a small, bundle or twist of straw, etc. **2** a
small separate quantity of smoke, hair, etc. **3** a small, thin
person, etc. **4** a flock (of snipe). □□ **wispy** *adj.* (**wispier,
wispiest**). **wispily** *adv.* **wispiness** *n.* [ME: orig. uncert.:
cf. WFris. *wisp*, and WHISK]
■ **2** streak, shred, scrap, strand, thread, snippet, tuft,
lock. □ **wispy** thin, streaky, flimsy, insubstantial,
gossamer.
wist *past* and *past part.* of WIT².
wisteria /wisteéreeə/ *n.* (also **wistaria** /-stáiriə/) any climbing plant of the genus *Wisteria*, with hanging racemes of
blue, purple, or white flowers. [C. *Wistar* (or *Wister*), Amer.
anatomist d. 1818]
wistful /wístfŏŏl/ *adj.* (of a person, looks, etc.) yearningly or
mournfully expectant, thoughtful, or wishful. □□ **wistfully**
adv. **wistfulness** *n.* [app. assim. of obs. *wistly* (*adv.*) intently
(cf. WHISHT) to *wishful*, with corresp. change of sense]
■ melancholy, mournful, sad, morose, sorrowful,
disconsolate, heartsick, forlorn, woeful, woebegone,
doleful, desirous, longing, yearning; thoughtful,
contemplative, pensive, absentminded, detached,
absorbed, in a brown study, preoccupied, meditating,
meditative, reflective, ruminating, ruminative, dreamy,
dreaming, daydreaming, musing.
wit¹ /wit/ *n.* **1** (in *sing.* or *pl.*) intelligence; quick understanding (*has quick wits; a nimble wit*). **2 a** the unexpected, quick,
and humorous combining or contrasting of ideas or expressions (*conversation sparkling with wit*). **b** the power of giving
intellectual pleasure by this. **3** a person possessing such a
power, esp. a cleverly humorous person. □ **at one's wit's**
(or **wits'**) **end** utterly at a loss or in despair. **have** (or **keep**)
one's wits about one be alert or vigilant or of lively intelligence. **live by one's wits** live by ingenious or crafty expedients, without a settled occupation. **out of one's wits**
mad; distracted. **set one's wits to** esp. *Brit.* argue with.
□□ **witted** *adj.* (in sense 1); (also in *comb.*). [OE *wit(t),
gewit(t)* f. Gmc]
■ **1** intelligence, brains, mind, (common) sense,
judgment, understanding, discernment, wisdom,
sagacity, insight, astuteness, cleverness, *sl.* savvy.
2 humor, drollery, levity, joking, repartee, raillery,
facetiousness, waggishness, badinage, banter,
jocularity, wordplay, paronomasia; amusement,
entertainment. **3** comedian, comedienne, humorist,
comic, wag, joker, jester, farceur, farceuse, punster,
madcap, zany; parodist, satirist, caricaturist; *colloq.*
card, character; *archaic usu. derog.* witling. □ **at one's
wit's** (or **wits'**) **end** see FRANTIC 2.
wit² /wit/ *v.tr.* & *intr.* (*1st* & *3rd sing. present* **wot** /wot/; *past*
and *past part.* **wist**) (often foll. by *of*) *archaic* know. □ **to wit**
that is to say; namely. [OE *witan* f. Gmc]
witch /wich/ *n.* & *v.* ● *n.* **1** a sorceress, esp. a woman supposed to have dealings with the devil or evil spirits. **2** an ugly
old woman; a hag. **3** a fascinating girl or woman. ● *v.tr.
archaic* **1** bewitch. **2** fascinate; charm; lure. □ **witch doctor**
a tribal magician of primitive people. **witch hazel 1** any
American shrub of the genus *Hamamelis*, with bark yielding
an astringent lotion. **2** this lotion, esp. from the leaves of *H.
virginiana*. **witches' Sabbath** a supposed general midnight
meeting of witches with the Devil. **witch-hunt 1** *hist.* a

search for and persecution of supposed witches. **2** a campaign directed against a particular group of those holding
unpopular or unorthodox views, esp. communists. **the
witching hour** midnight, when witches are supposedly active (after Shakesp. *Hamlet* III. ii. 377 *the witching time of
night*). □□ **witching** *adj.* **witchlike** *adj.* [OE *wicca* (masc.),
wicce (fem.), rel. to *wiccian* (v.) practice magic arts]
■ *n.* **1** sorceress, enchantress, sibyl, pythoness. **2** hag,
fury, crone, gorgon, ogress, Xanthippe, shrew, virago,
harridan, fishwife, termagant, *archaic* beldam, *colloq.*
battleaxe, *sl. derog.* old bag, *sl. offens.* bitch. ● *v.* **1, 2**
see BEWITCH. □ **witch doctor** see SORCERER.
witch- var. of WYCH-.
witchcraft /wíchkraft/ *n.* the use of magic; sorcery.
■ see *sorcery* (SORCERER).
witchery /wíchəree/ *n.* **1** witchcraft. **2** power exercised by
beauty or eloquence or the like.
■ **1** see *sorcery* (SORCERER). **2** see MAGIC *n.* 4.
witchetty /wíchətee/ *n.* (*pl.* **-ies**) *Austral.* a large white larva
of a beetle or moth, eaten as food by Aborigines. [Aborigi-
nal]
witenagemot /wít'nəgəmōt/ *n. hist.* an Anglo-Saxon national council or parliament. [OE *witena* genit. pl. of *wita*
wise man (as WIT²) + *gemōt* meeting: cf. MOOT]
with /with, with/ *prep.* expressing: **1** an instrument or means
used (*cut with a knife; can walk with assistance*). **2** association
or company (*lives with his mother; works with Shell; lamb with
mint sauce*). **3** cause or origin (*shiver with fear; in bed with
measles*). **4** possession; attribution (*the woman with dark hair;
a vase with handles*). **5** circumstances; accompanying conditions (*sleep with the window open; a vaction with all expenses
paid*). **6** manner adopted or displayed (*behaved with dignity;
spoke with vehemence; handle with care; won with ease*). **7**
agreement or harmony (*sympathize with; I believe with you
that it can be done*). **8** disagreement; antagonism; competition (*incompatible with; stop arguing with me*). **9** responsibility
or care for (*the decision rests with you; leave the child with me*).
10 material (*made with gold*). **11** addition or supply; possession of as a material, attribute, circumstance, etc. (*fill it
with water; threaten with dismissal; decorate with flowers*). **12**
reference or regard (*be patient with them; how are things with
you?; what do you want with me?; there's nothing wrong with
expressing one's opinion*). **13** relation or causative association
(*changes with the weather; keeps pace with the cost of living*).
14 an accepted circumstance or consideration (*with all your
faults, we like you*). □ **away** (or **in** or **out**, etc.) **with** (as *int.*)
take, send, or put (a person or thing) away, in, out, etc. **be
with a person 1** agree with and support a person. **2** *colloq.*
follow a person's meaning (*are you with me?*). **one with** part
of the same whole as. **with child** (or **young**) *literary* pregnant. **with it** *colloq.* **1** up to date; conversant with modern
ideas, etc. **2** alert and comprehending. **with-it** *adj. colloq.* in
step with the times, fashion, etc. **with that** thereupon. [OE,
prob. shortened f. a Gmc prep. corresp. to OE *wither*, OHG
widar against]
■ **2** BESIDE 1. □ **with it 1** see MODERN *adj.* **2** see ALERT *adj.*
withal /witháwl, with-/ *adv.* & *prep. archaic* ● *adv.* moreover; as well; at the same time. ● *prep.* (placed after its
expressed or omitted object) with (*what shall he fill his belly
withal?*). [ME f. WITH + ALL]
■ see *in addition* (ADDITION).
withdraw /withdráw, with-/ *v.* (*past* **withdrew** /-drŏŏ/; *past
part.* **withdrawn** /-dráwn/) **1** *tr.* pull or take aside or back
(*withdrew my hand*). **2** *tr.* discontinue; cancel; retract (*withdrew my support; the promise was later withdrawn*). **3** *tr.* remove; take away (*withdrew the child from school; withdrew
their troops*). **4** *tr.* take (money) out of an account. **5** *intr.*
retire or go away; move away or back. **6** *intr.* (as **withdrawn**
adj.) abnormally shy and unsociable; mentally detached.

┌───┐
│ /.../ **pronunciation**   ● **part of speech** │
│ □ **phrases, idioms, and compounds** │
│ □□ **derivatives**   ■ **synonym section** │
│ **cross-references** appear in SMALL CAPITALS or *italics* │
└───┘

□ **withdrawing room** *archaic* = DRAWING ROOM 1. □□ **with-drawer** *n.* [ME f. *with-* away (as WITH) + DRAW]

■ **1** draw back, retract, pull back *or* aside *or* away, take back *or* aside. **2** retract, recall, take back, cancel, discontinue, rescind, recant, disavow, disclaim, abjure, void, annul, go back on, back down (on). **3** remove, extract, take away *or* out, pull out; recall. **4** remove, take *or* get (out). **5** retire, retreat, go (away), repair, leave, depart, secede, absent oneself, beat a retreat, *colloq.* drop out, make oneself scarce; move away *or* back, back away *or* out, pull back *or* out, draw back, recoil, shrink back. **6** (**withdrawn**) reserved, detached, distant, remote, standoffish, aloof, shy, unsociable, antisocial, reclusive, diffident, bashful, timid, timorous, introverted, taciturn, reticent, silent, quiet, retiring, shrinking.

withdrawal /wiṯẖdráwǝl, with-/ *n.* **1** the act or an instance of withdrawing or being withdrawn. **2** a process of ceasing to take addictive drugs, often with an unpleasant physical reaction (*withdrawal symptoms*). **3** = *coitus interruptus*.

■ **1** extraction, removal; see also RETREAT *n.* 1a, 2, CANCELLATION, DENIAL 2.

withe /with, wiṯẖ, wiṯẖ/ *n.* a tough, flexible shoot esp. of willow or osier used for tying a bundle of wood, etc. [OE *withthe, withig* f. Gmc, rel. to WIRE]

wither /wiṯẖǝr/ *v.* **1** *tr.* & *intr.* (often foll. by *up*) make or become dry and shriveled (*withered flowers*). **2** *tr.* & *intr.* (often foll. by *away*) deprive of or lose vigor, vitality, freshness, or importance. **3** *intr.* decay; decline. **4** *tr.* **a** blight with scorn, etc. **b** (as **withering** *adj.*) scornful (*a withering look*). □□ **witheringly** *adv.* [ME, app. var. of WEATHER differentiated for certain senses]

■ **1** see SHRIVEL. **2, 3** see WASTE *v.* 4. **4 b** (**withering**) see SCORNFUL.

withers /wiṯẖǝrz/ *n.pl.* the ridge between a horse's shoulder blades. [shortening of (16th-c.) *widersome* (or *-sone*) f. *wider-, wither-* against (cf. WITH), as the part that resists the strain of the collar: second element obscure]

withershins /wiṯẖǝrshinz/ *adv.* (also **widdershins** /wid-/) esp. *Sc.* **1** in a direction contrary to the sun's course (considered as unlucky). **2** counterclockwise. [MLG *weddersins* f. MHG *widersinnes* f. *wider* against + *sin* direction]

withhold /with-hóld, with-/ *v.tr.* (*past* and *past part.* **-held** /-héld/) **1** (often foll. by *from*) hold back; restrain. **2** refuse to give, grant, or allow (*withhold one's consent; withhold the truth*). □□ **withholder** *n.* [ME f. *with-* away (as WITH) + HOLD¹]

■ **1** hold *or* keep back, deduct, retain, reserve; restrain, control, repress, suppress, check, hide, conceal. **2** refuse, deny, deprive (of), disallow.

within /wiṯẖín, with-/ *adv., prep.* & *n.* ● *adv. archaic* or *literary* **1** inside; to, at, or on the inside; internally. **2** indoors (*is anyone within?*). **3** in spirit (*make me pure within*). ● *prep.* **1** inside; enclosed or contained by. **2 a** not beyond or exceeding (*within one's means*). **b** not transgressing (*within the law; within reason*). **3** not further off than (*within three miles of a station; within shouting distance; within ten days*). ● *n.* the inside part of a place, building, etc. □ **within doors** esp. *Brit.* in or into a house. **within one's grasp** see GRASP. **within reach** (or **sight**) **of** near enough to be reached or seen. [OE *withinnan* on the inside (as WITH, *innan* (adv. & prep.) within, formed as IN)]

■ *adv.* see INSIDE *adv.* 1.

without /wiṯẖówt, with-/ *prep., adv., n.,* & *conj.* ● *prep.* **1** not having, feeling, or showing (*came without any money; without hesitation; without any emotion*). **2** with freedom from (*without fear; without embarrassment*). **3** in the absence of (*cannot live without you; the train left without us*). **4** with neglect or avoidance of (*do not leave without telling me*). ¶ Use as a *conj.*, as in *do not leave without you tell me*, is nonstandard. **5** *archaic* outside (*without the city wall*). ● *adv. archaic* or *literary* **1** outside (*seen from without*). **2** out of doors (*remained shivering without*). **3** in outward appearance (*rough without but kind within*). ● *n.* the outside part of a place, building, etc. ● *conj. dial.* unless (*the dog won't eat without*

you give him some meat) □ **without end** infinite; eternal. [OE *withūtan* (as WITH, *ūtan* from outside, formed as OUT)]

■ *prep.* **1** see EMPTY *adj.* 6. **2** see FREE *adj.* 4. ● *adv.* see OUTSIDE *adv.*

withstand /wiṯẖstánd, with-/ *v.* (*past* and *past part.* **-stood** /-sto͝od/) **1** *tr.* oppose; resist; hold out against (a person, force, etc.). **2** *intr.* make opposition; offer resistance. □□ **withstander** *n.* [OE *withstandan* f. *with-* against (as WITH) + STAND]

■ **1** resist, oppose, stand (up to), face, defy, confront, combat, grapple with, fight against, cope with, hold out against, bear up against, weather, suffer, survive, tolerate, take, bear, last through, endure, support, brave, *colloq.* stick.

withy /wiṯẖee/ *n.* (*pl.* **-ies**) esp. *Brit.* **1** a willow of any species. **2** a withe.

witless /wítlis/ *adj.* **1** lacking wits; foolish; stupid. **2** crazy. □□ **witlessly** *adv.* **witlessness** *n.* [OE *witlēas* (as WIT¹, -LESS)]

■ see FOOLISH.

witling /wítling/ *n. archaic* usu. *derog.* a person who fancies himself or herself as a wit.

witness /wítnis/ *n.* & *v.* ● *n.* **1** a person present at some event and able to give information about it (cf. EYEWITNESS). **2 a** a person giving sworn testimony. **b** a person attesting another's signature to a document. **3** (foll. by *to, of*) a person or thing whose existence, condition, etc., attests or proves something (*is a living witness to their generosity*). **4** testimony; evidence; confirmation. ● *v.* **1** *tr.* be a witness of (an event, etc.) (*did you witness the accident?*). **2** *tr.* be witness to the authenticity of (a document or signature). **3** *tr.* serve as evidence or an indication of. **4** *intr.* (foll. by *against, for, to*) give or serve as evidence. □ **bear witness to** (or **of**) **1** attest the truth of. **2** state one's belief in. **call to witness** appeal to for confirmation, etc. **witness-box** *Brit.* = *witness stand*. **witness stand** an enclosure in a court of law from which witnesses give evidence. [OE *witnes* (as WIT¹, -NESS)]

■ *n.* **1** observer, onlooker, spectator, viewer, eyewitness, bystander, watcher, looker-on. **2** *Law* deponent, testifier, corroborating witness, corroborator. **3** see MONUMENT 4. **4** see TESTIMONY 1, 2. ● *v.* **1** see, observe, watch, look on *or* at, view, mark, note, notice, take in, catch, *colloq.* spot, *literary* behold. **2** countersign, sign, certify, endorse, substantiate, validate, document, certificate, notarize. **3, 4** see *bear witness to* below. □ **bear witness to** (or **of**) **1** testify (to), attest (to), witness (to), be *or* give *or* provide *or* furnish *or* constitute evidence of *or* to, be *or* give *or* provide *or* furnish *or* constitute proof of *or* to, be *or* give *or* provide *or* furnish *or* constitute testimony of *or* to, verify, confirm, corroborate, show, prove, bear out. **2** avow, asseverate, confess, profess, declare, affirm, *archaic or rhet.* avouch, *formal* aver.

witter /wítǝr/ *v.intr.* (often foll. by *on*) *Brit. colloq.* speak tediously on trivial matters. [20th c.: prob. imit.]

■ see PRATTLE *v.*

witticism /wítisizǝm/ *n.* a witty remark. [coined by Dryden (1677) f. WITTY, after *criticism*]

■ pun, quip, play on words, paronomasia, bon mot, mot, jest, joke, epigram, clever remark, sally, gag, *colloq.* wisecrack, one-liner, *literary* conceit.

witting /wíting/ *adj.* **1** aware. **2** intentional. □□ **wittingly** *adv.* [ME f. WIT² + -ING²]

■ □□ **wittingly** see *deliberately* (DELIBERATE).

witty /wítee/ *adj.* (**wittier, wittiest**) **1** showing verbal wit. **2** characterized by wit or humor. □□ **wittily** *adv.* **wittiness** *n.* [OE *witig, wittig* (as WIT¹, -Y¹)]

■ ingenious, subtle, clever, quick-witted, sharp-witted, humorous, sarcastic, sardonic, piquant, epigrammatic, humorous, comic(al), facetious, amusing, jocular, waggish, droll, funny.

wivern var. of WYVERN.

wives *pl.* of WIFE.

wiz var. of WHIZ *n.* 2.

wizard /wízərd/ *n. & adj.* • *n.* **1** a sorcerer; a magician. **2** a person of remarkable powers, a genius. **3** a conjuror. • *adj. sl. Brit.* wonderful; excellent. □□ **wizardly** *adj.* **wizardry** *n.* [ME f. WISE[1] + -ARD]

■ *n.* **1, 3** see MAGICIAN 1. **2** see VIRTUOSO 1a. □□ **wizardry** see MAGIC *n.* 1, 2.

wizened /wízənd/ *adj.* (also **wizen**) (of a person or face, etc.) shriveled-looking. [past part. of *wizen* shrivel f. OE *wisnian* f. Gmc]

■ wrinkled, shrunken, shriveled (up), withered, gnarled, dried up, wilted, faded, wasted.

wk. *abbr.* **1** week. **2** work. **3** weak.

wks. *abbr.* weeks.

Wm. *abbr.* William.

WMO *abbr.* World Meteorological Organization.

WNW *abbr.* west-northwest.

WO *abbr.* warrant officer.

woad /wōd/ *n. hist.* **1** a cruciferous plant, *Isatis tinctoria*, yielding a blue dye now superseded by indigo. **2** the dye obtained from this. [OE *wād* f. Gmc]

wobbegong /wóbigong/ *n.* an Australian brown shark, *Orectolobus maculatus*, with buff patterned markings. [Aboriginal]

wobble /wóbəl/ *v. & n.* • *v.* **1 a** *intr.* sway or vibrate unsteadily from side to side. **b** *tr.* cause to do this. **2** *intr.* stand or go unsteadily; stagger. **3** *intr.* waver; vacillate; act inconsistently. **4** *intr.* (of the voice or sound) quaver; pulsate. • *n.* **1** a wobbling movement. **2** an instance of vacillation or pulsation. □□ **wobbler** *n.* [earlier *wabble*, corresp. to LG *wabbeln*, ON *vafla* waver f. Gmc: cf. WAVE, WAVER, -LE[4]]

■ *v.* **1** see SHAKE *v.* 1, 2, 5. **2** see STAGGER *v.* 1a. **4** see QUIVER[1] *v.* • *n.* see SHAKE *n.* 1.

wobbly /wóblee/ *adj.* (**wobblier, wobbliest**) **1** wobbling or tending to wobble. **2** wavy; undulating (*a wobbly line*). **3** unsteady; weak after illness (*feeling wobbly*). **4** wavering; vacillating; insecure (*the economy was wobbly*). □ **throw a wobbly** *Brit. sl.* have a fit of nerves. □□ **wobbliness** *n.*

■ see SHAKY.

wodge /woj/ *n. Brit. colloq.* a chunk or lump. [alt. of WEDGE[1]]

woe /wō/ *n. archaic* or *literary* **1** affliction; bitter grief; distress. **2** (in *pl.*) calamities; troubles. **3** *joc.* problems (*told me a tale of woe*). □ **woe betide** *Brit.* there will be unfortunate consequences for (*woe betide you if you are late*). **woe is me** an exclamation of distress. [OE *wā, wǣ* f. Gmc, a natural exclam. of lament]

■ **1** trouble, hardship, adversity, misery, anguish, tribulation, calamity, wretchedness, grief, unhappiness, desolation, melancholy, gloom, depression, sadness, disconsolateness, misfortune, affliction, sorrow, distress, suffering, *literary* dolor. **2** (*woes*) troubles, calamities, hardships, trials, tribulations, adversities, misfortunes, afflictions, problems.

woebegone /wóbigon, -gawn/ *adj.* dismal-looking. [WOE + *begone* = surrounded f. OE *begān* (as BE-, GO[1])]

■ troubled, miserable, anguished, wretched, griefstricken, unhappy, desolate, doleful, melancholy, melancholic, gloomy, mournful, sorrowful, depressed, dejected, sad, glum, crestfallen, chapfallen, lugubrious, downcast, disconsolate, dismal, unfortunate, afflicted, distressed, woeful, forlorn, downhearted, brokenhearted, heartbroken, disheartened, *archaic* star-crossed, *literary or joc.* dolorous.

woeful /wōfŏŏl/ *adj.* **1** sorrowful; afflicted with distress (*a woeful expression*). **2** causing sorrow or affliction. **3** very bad; wretched (*woeful ignorance*). □□ **woefully** *adv.* **woefulness** *n.*

■ **1** see SORROWFUL 1. **2** see PATHETIC 1. **3** see AWFUL 1a, b. □□ **woefully** see *painfully* (PAINFUL).

wog[1] /wog/ *n. sl. offens.* a foreigner, esp. a nonwhite one. [20th c.: orig. unkn.]

wog[2] /wog/ *n. Austral. sl.* an illness or infection. [20th c.: orig. unkn.]

wok /wok/ *n.* a bowl-shaped metal pan used in esp. Chinese cooking. [Cantonese]

woke *past* of WAKE[1].

woken *past part.* of WAKE[1].

wold /wōld/ *n.* a piece of high, open, uncultivated land. [OE *wald* f. Gmc, perh. rel. to WILD: cf. WEALD]

wolf /wŏŏlf/ *n. & v.* • *n.* (*pl.* **wolves** /wŏŏlvz/) **1** a wild, flesh-eating, tawny-gray mammal related to the dog, esp. *Canis lupus*, preying on rodents, mammals, etc., and hunting in packs. **2** *sl.* a man given to seducing women. **3** a rapacious or greedy person. **4** *Mus.* **a** a jarring sound from some notes in a bowed instrument. **b** an out-of-tune effect when playing certain chords on old organs (before the present 'equal temperament' was in use). • *v.tr.* (often foll. by *down*) devour (food) greedily. □ **cry wolf** raise repeated false alarms (so that a genuine one is disregarded). **have** (or **hold**) **a wolf by the ears** esp. *Brit.* be in a precarious position. **keep the wolf from the door** avert hunger or starvation. **lone wolf** a person who prefers to act alone. **throw to the wolves** sacrifice without compunction. **wolf cub 1** a young wolf. **2** *Brit.* the former name for a Cub Scout. **wolf in sheep's clothing** a hostile person who pretends friendship. **wolf pack** an attacking group of submarines or aircraft. **wolf spider** any ground-dwelling spider of the family Lycosidae, hunting instead of trapping its prey. **wolf whistle** a sexually admiring whistle by a man to a woman. □□ **wolfish** *adj.* **wolfishly** *adv.* **wolflike** *adj. & adv.* [OE *wulf* f. Gmc]

■ *v.* see DEVOUR 1.

wolffish /wŏŏlffish/ *n.* any large voracious blenny of the genus *Anarrhichas*.

wolfhound /wŏŏlfhownd/ *n.* a borzoi or other dog of a kind used orig. to hunt wolves.

wolfram /wŏŏlfrəm/ *n.* **1** tungsten. **2** tungsten ore; a native tungstate of iron and manganese. [G: perh. f. *Wolf* WOLF + *Rahm* cream, or MHG *rām* dirt, soot]

wolframite /wŏŏlfrəmīt/ *n.* = WOLFRAM 2.

wolfsbane /wŏŏlfsbayn/ *n.* an aconite, esp. *Aconitum lycoctonum*.

wolfskin /wŏŏlfskin/ *n.* **1** the skin of a wolf. **2** a mat, cloak, etc., made from this.

wolverine /wŏŏlvəreen/ *n.* a voracious carnivorous mammal, *Gulo gulo*, of the weasel family. [16th-c. *wolvering*, somehow derived f. *wolv-*, stem of WOLF]

wolves *pl.* of WOLF.

woman /wŏŏmən/ *n.* (*pl.* **women** /wímin/) **1** an adult human female. **2** the female sex; any or an average woman (*how does woman differ from man?*). **3** a wife or female sexual partner. **4** (prec. by *the*) emotions or characteristics traditionally associated with women (*brought out the woman in him*). **5** a man with characteristics traditionally associated with women. **6** (*attrib.*) female (*woman driver; women friends*). **7** (as second element in *comb.*) a woman of a specified nationality, profession, skill, etc. (*Englishwoman; horsewoman*). **8** *colloq.* a female domestic servant. **9** *archaic* or *hist.* a queen's, etc., female attendant ranking below lady (*woman of the bedchamber*). □ **woman of the streets** a prostitute. **women's lib** *colloq.* = *women's liberation.* **women's libber** *colloq.* a supporter of women's liberation. **women's liberation** the liberation of women from inequalities and subservient status in relation to men, and from attitudes causing these. **Women's Liberation** (or **Movement**) a movement campaigning for women's liberation. **women's rights** rights that promote a position of legal and social equality of women with men. □□ **womanless** *adj.* **womanlike** *adj.* [OE *wīfmon*, *-man* (as WIFE, MAN), a formation peculiar to English, the ancient word being WIFE]

■ **1** female, lady, miss, esp. *Sc. & No. of Engl.* or *poet.* lass, *archaic* gentlewoman, *archaic or literary* damsel, *archaic or poet.* maid, maiden, *archaic or sl.* dame, *colloq.* girl; lassie, *Brit. colloq.* popsy, *derog. offens.* baggage, *sl.* chick, gal, broad, moll, *sl. derog.* piece, piece of goods, heifer, *sl. offens.* (bit *or* piece of) skirt, *Austral. & NZ*

W
Z

sl. sheila, *Brit. sl.* bird. **2** womankind, womenkind, womenfolk, the fair sex, *derog.* the weaker sex.
3 wife, spouse, bride, ladylove, sweetheart, lady, girl, girlfriend, mistress, concubine, mate, helpmate, partner, lover, inamorata, paramour, *archaic* leman, *colloq.* sweetie, better half, old lady *or* woman, *colloq. often derog.* little woman, *joc.* lady wife, *sl. or joc.* the missus. **8** domestic, (domestic) help, housekeeper, maid, cleaning woman *or* lady, cleaner, maidservant, chambermaid, charwoman, *archaic* handmaid(en), *Brit. colloq.* char, daily. **9** attendant, lady-in-waiting.
□□ **womanlike** see FEMININE *adj.* 1.

womanhood /wŏomənhŏod/ *n.* **1** female maturity. **2** womanly instinct. **3** womankind.

womanish /wŏomǝnish/ *adj.* usu. *derog.* **1** (of a man) effeminate; unmanly. **2** suitable to or characteristic of a woman. □□ **womanishly** *adv.* **womanishness** *n.*
■ **1** see EFFEMINATE. **2** see FEMININE *adj.* 1.

womanize /wŏomǝnīz/ *v.* **1** *intr.* chase after women; philander. **2** *tr.* make womanish. □□ **womanizer** *n.*
■ **1** see PHILANDER. □□ **womanizer** see *philanderer* (PHILANDER).

womankind /wŏomǝnkīnd/ *n.* (also **womenkind** /wímin-/) women in general.

womanly /wŏomǝnlee/ *adj.* (of a woman) having or showing qualities traditionally associated with women; not masculine nor girlish. □□ **womanliness** *n.*
■ see FEMININE *adj.* 1.

womb /wŏom/ *n.* **1** the organ of conception and gestation in a woman and other female mammals; the uterus. **2** a place of origination and development. □□ **womblike** *adj.* [OE *wamb, womb*]

wombat /wómbat/ *n.* any burrowing, plant-eating Australian marsupial of the family Vombatidae, resembling a small bear, with short legs. [Aboriginal]

women *pl.* of WOMAN.

womenfolk /wíminfōk/ *n.* **1** women in general. **2** the women in a family.

womenkind var. of WOMANKIND.

won *past* and *past part.* of WIN.

wonder /wúndǝr/ *n.* & *v.* ● *n.* **1** an emotion excited by what is unexpected, unfamiliar, or inexplicable, esp. surprise mingled with admiration or curiosity, etc. **2** a strange or remarkable person or thing, specimen, event, etc. **3** (*attrib.*) having marvelous or amazing properties, etc. (*a wonder drug*). **4** a surprising thing (*it is a wonder you were not hurt*). ● *v.* **1** *intr.* (often foll. by *at*, or *to* + infin.) be filled with wonder or great surprise. **2** *tr.* (foll. by *that* + clause) be surprised to find. **3** *tr.* desire or be curious to know (*I wonder what the time is*). **4** *tr.* expressing a tentative inquiry (*I wonder whether you would mind?*). **5** *intr.* (foll. by *about*) ask oneself with puzzlement or doubt about; question (*wondered about the sense of the decision*). □ **I shouldn't wonder** *colloq.* I think it likely. **I wonder** I very much doubt it. **no** (or **small**) **wonder** (often foll. by *that* + clause) one cannot be surprised; one might have guessed; it is natural. **Seven Wonders of the World** seven buildings and monuments regarded in antiquity as specially remarkable. **wonder-struck** (or **-stricken**) reduced to silence by wonder. **wonders will** (or **will wonders**) **never cease** an exclamation of extreme (usu. agreeable) surprise. **wonder-worker** a person who performs wonders. **work** (or **do**) **wonders 1** do miracles. **2** succeed remarkably. □□ **wonderer** *n.* [OE *wundor, wundrian*, of unkn. orig.]
■ *n.* **1** awe, astonishment, admiration, amazement, wonderment, surprise, stupefaction, fascination, curiosity. **2** prodigy, phenomenon, spectacle, rarity, sight, curiosity, miracle, *colloq.* knockout, stunner. ● *v.* **1** marvel, goggle, gawk, gape, stare, be awed, be thunderstruck, be amazed, be astonished, be surprised. **3** ponder, meditate, think, theorize, conjecture, puzzle, query, question, inquire, be inquisitive, be curious, ask oneself, speculate, cudgel one's brains, *literary* marvel, muse. **5** (*wonder about*) ask oneself about, question,

doubt, puzzle over *or* about; question *or* doubt the sanity *or* reason *or* reasonableness of.

wonderful /wúndǝrfŏol/ *adj.* **1** very remarkable or admirable. **2** arousing wonder. □□ **wonderfully** *adv.* **wonderfulness** *n.* [OE *wunderfull* (as WONDER, -FUL)]
■ **1** see TERRIFIC 1b. **2** see STUNNING. □□ **wonderfully** see *beautifully* (BEAUTIFUL), WELL[1] *adv.* 9.

wondering /wúndǝring/ *adj.* filled with wonder; marveling (*their wondering gaze*). □□ **wonderingly** *adv.*

wonderland /wúndǝrland/ *n.* **1** a fairyland. **2** a land of surprises or marvels.

wonderment /wúndǝrmǝnt/ *n.* surprise; awe.
■ see WONDER *n.* 1.

wondrous /wúndrǝs/ *adj.* & *adv. poet.* ● *adj.* wonderful. ● *adv. archaic* or *literary* wonderfully (*wondrous kind*). □□ **wondrously** *adv.* **wondrousness** *n.* [alt. of obs. *wonders* (adj. & adv.), = genit. of WONDER (cf. -s[3]) after *marvelous*]

wonky /wóngkee/ *adj.* (**wonkier, wonkiest**) *Brit. sl.* **1** crooked. **2** loose; unsteady. **3** unreliable. □□ **wonkily** *adv.* **wonkiness** *n.* [fanciful formation]

wont /wōnt, wawnt, wunt/ *adj.*, *n.*, & *v.* ● *predic. adj. archaic* or *literary* (foll. by *to* + infin.) accustomed (*as we were wont to say*). ● *n. formal* or *joc.* what is customary; one's habit (*as is my wont*). ● *v.tr.* & *intr.* (*3rd sing. present* **wonts** or **wont**; *past* **wont** or **wonted**) *archaic* make or become accustomed. [OE *gewunod* past part. of *gewunian* f. *wunian* dwell]
■ *n.* see CUSTOM 1a.

won't /wōnt/ *contr.* will not.

wonted /wōntid, wáwn-, wún-/ *attrib.adj.* habitual; accustomed; usual.

woo /wŏo/ *v.tr.* (**woos, wooed**) **1** court; seek the hand or love of (a woman). **2** try to win (fame, fortune, etc.). **3** seek the favor or support of. **4** coax or importune. □□ **wooable** *adj.* **wooer** *n.* [OE *wōgian* (intr.), *āwōgian* (tr.), of unkn. orig.]
■ **1** see COURT *v.* 1b. **2** chase, follow, pursue, seek. **3** make advances to, ingratiate oneself with, pay court to, curry favor with, *sl.* suck up to, butter up, shine up to.

wood /wŏod/ *n.* **1 a** a hard fibrous material that forms the main substance of the trunk or branches of a tree or shrub. **b** this cut for lumber or for fuel, or for use in crafts, manufacture, etc. **2** (in *sing.* or *pl.*) growing trees densely occupying a tract of land. **3** (prec. by *the*) wooden storage, esp. a cask, for wine, etc. (*poured straight from the wood*). **4** a wooden-headed golf club. **5** = BOWL[2] *n.* 1. □ **out of the woods** (or **wood**) out of danger or difficulty. **wood alcohol** methanol. **wood anemone** a wild spring-flowering anemone, *Anemone nemorosa.* **wood engraver** a maker of wood engravings. **wood engraving 1** a relief cut on a block of wood sawn across the grain. **2** a print made from this. **3** the technique of making such reliefs and prints. **wood fiber** fiber obtained from wood esp. as material for paper. **wood grouse** = CAPERCAILLIE. **wood hyacinth** = BLUEBELL 1. **wood louse** any small terrestrial isopod crustacean of the genus *Oniscus*, etc., feeding on rotten wood, etc., and often able to roll into a ball. **wood mouse** any of various forest-dwelling mice. **wood nymph** a dryad or hamadryad. **wood pulp** wood fiber reduced chemically or mechanically to pulp as raw material for paper. **wood pigeon** a dove, *Columba palumbus*, having white patches like a ring round its neck. (Also called RINGDOVE). **wood screw** a metal male screw with a slotted head and sharp point. **wood sorrel** a small plant, *Oxalis acetosella*, with trifoliate leaves and white flowers streaked with purple. **wood spirit** crude methanol obtained from wood. **wood warbler 1** a European woodland bird, *Phylloscopus sibilatrix*, with a trilling song. **2** any American warbler of the family Parulidae. **wood-wool** *Brit.* fine pine, etc., shavings used as a surgical dressing or for packing. □□ **woodless** *adj.* [OE *wudu, wi(o)du* f. Gmc]
■ **2** (*wood* or *woods*) woodland, forest, copse, brake, grove, covert, thicket, brush, *Brit.* spinney; timber, trees.

woodbine /wŏodbīn/ *n.* **1** wild honeysuckle. **2** Virginia creeper.

woodblock /wŏŏdblok/ *n.* a block from which woodcuts are made.

woodchuck /wŏŏdchuk/ *n.* a reddish-brown and gray N. American marmot, *Marmota monax.* Also called GROUND-HOG. [Algonquian name: cf. Cree *wuchak, otchock*]

woodcock /wŏŏdkok/ *n.* (*pl.* same) any game bird of the genus *Scolopax,* inhabiting woodland.

woodcraft /wŏŏdkraft/ *n.* **1** skill in woodwork. **2** knowledge of woodland esp. in camping, scouting, etc.

woodcut /wŏŏdkut/ *n.* **1** a relief cut on a block of wood sawn along the grain. **2** a print made from this, esp. as an illustration in a book. **3** the technique of making such reliefs and prints.

woodcutter /wŏŏdkutər/ *n.* **1** a person who cuts wood. **2** a maker of woodcuts.

wooded /wŏŏdid/ *adj.* having woods or many trees.
■ sylvan, forested, afforested, tree-covered, woody, timbered, *literary* bosky.

wooden /wŏŏd'n/ *adj.* **1** made of wood. **2** like wood. **3 a** stiff, clumsy, or stilted; without animation or flexibility (*wooden movements; a wooden performance*). **b** expressionless (*a wooden stare*). □ **wooden horse** = *Trojan Horse.* **wooden spoon** esp. *Brit.* a booby prize (orig. a spoon given to the candidate coming last in the Cambridge University mathematical tripos). □□ **woodenly** *adv.* **woodenness** *n.*
■ **1** wood, woody, ligneous. **3 a** stiff, rigid, inflexible, artificial, clumsy, stilted, unnatural, awkward, ungainly, spiritless, unanimated, dead, lifeless, dry, passionless, unimpassioned, colorless, deadpan. **b** vacant, empty, expressionless, impassive, deadpan, poker-faced.

woodenhead /wŏŏd'nhed/ *n. colloq.* a stupid person.

woodenheaded /wŏŏd'nhedid/ *adj. colloq.* stupid. □□ **woodenheadedness** *n.*
■ wooden-headed unintelligent, blockheaded, stupid, dull, insensitive, slow-witted, dull-witted, obtuse, oafish, doltish, dim-witted, dunderheaded, *colloq.* thick.

woodland /wŏŏdlənd/ *n.* wooded country, woods (often *attrib.: woodland scenery*). □□ **woodlander** *n.*

woodlark /wŏŏdlaark/ *n.* a lark, *Lullula arborea.*

woodman /wŏŏdmən/ *n.* (*pl.* **-men**) **1** a forester. **2** a woodcutter.

woodnote /wŏŏdnōt/ *n.* (often in *pl.*) a natural or spontaneous note of a bird, etc.

woodpecker /wŏŏdpekər/ *n.* any bird of the family Picidae that climbs and taps tree trunks in search of insects.

woodpile /wŏŏdpil/ *n.* a pile of wood, esp. for fuel.

woodruff /wŏŏdruf/ *n.* a white-flowered plant of the genus *Galium,* esp. *G. odoratum* grown for the fragrance of its whorled leaves when dried or crushed.

woodshed /wŏŏdshed/ *n.* a shed where wood for fuel is stored. □ **something nasty in the woodshed** esp. *Brit. colloq.* a shocking or distasteful thing kept secret.

woodsman /wŏŏdzmən/ *n.* (*pl.* **-men**) **1** a person who lives in or is familiar with woodland. **2** a person skilled in woodcraft.

woodsy /wŏŏdzee/ *adj.* like or characteristic of woods. [irreg. f. WOOD + -Y¹]

woodwind /wŏŏdwind/ *n.* (often *attrib.*) **1** (*collect.*) the wind instruments of the orchestra that were (mostly) orig. made of wood, e.g., the flute and clarinet. **2** (usu. in *pl.*) an individual instrument of this kind or its player (*the woodwinds are out of tune*).

woodwork /wŏŏdwərk/ *n.* **1** the making of things in wood. **2** things made of wood, esp. the wooden parts of a building. □ **crawl** (or **come**) **out of the woodwork** *colloq.* (of something unwelcome) appear; become known. □□ **woodworker** *n.* **woodworking** *n.*

woodworm /wŏŏdwərm/ *n.* **1** the wood-boring larva of the furniture beetle. **2** the damaged condition of wood affected by this.

woody /wŏŏdee/ *adj.* (**woodier, woodiest**) **1** (of a region) wooded; abounding in woods. **2** like or of wood (*woody tissue*). □ **woody nightshade** see NIGHTSHADE. □□ **woodiness** *n.*
■ **1** see WOODED.

woodyard /wŏŏdyaard/ *n.* a yard where wood is used or stored.

woof¹ /wŏŏf/ *n.* & *v.* ● *n.* the gruff bark of a dog. ● *v.intr.* give a woof. [imit.]

woof² /wŏŏf, wŏŏf/ *n.* = WEFT. [OE ōwef, alt. of ōwebb (after wefan WEAVE¹), formed as A-², WEB: infl. by *warp*]

woofer /wŏŏfər/ *n.* a loudspeaker designed to reproduce low frequencies (cf. TWEETER). [WOOF¹ + -ER¹]

wool /wŏŏl/ *n.* **1** fine, soft, wavy hair from the fleece of sheep, goats, etc. **2 a** yarn produced from this hair. **b** cloth or clothing made from it. **3** any of various woollike substances (*steel wool*). **4** soft, short, underfur or down. **5** *colloq.* a person's hair, esp. when short and curly. □ **pull the wool over a person's eyes** deceive a person. **wool fat** lanolin. **wool stapler 1** a person who grades wool. **2** a wool dealer. □□ **woollike** *adj.* [OE *wull* f. Gmc]

woolen /wŏŏlən/ *adj.* & *n.* (also **woollen**) ● *adj.* made wholly or partly of wool, esp. from short fibers. ● *n.* **1** a fabric produced from wool. **2** (in *pl.*) woolen garments. [OE *wullen* (as WOOL, -EN²)]

woolfell /wŏŏlfel/ *n.* esp. *Brit.* = WOOLSKIN.

woolgathering /wŏŏlgathəring/ *n.* absent-mindedness; dreamy inattention.

woolgrower /wŏŏlgrōər/ *n.* a breeder of sheep for wool. □□ **woolgrowing** *n.*

woolly /wŏŏlee/ *adj.* & *n.* (also **wooly**) ● *adj.* (**woollier, woolliest**) **1** bearing or naturally covered with wool or woollike hair. **2** resembling or suggesting wool (*woolly clouds*). **3** (of a sound) indistinct. **4** (of thought) vague or confused. **5** *Bot.* downy. **6** lacking in definition, luminosity, or incisiveness. ● *n.* (*pl.* **-ies**) esp. *Brit. colloq.* a woolen garment, esp. a knitted undergarment. □ **woolly bear** a large hairy caterpillar, esp. of the tiger moth. □□ **woolliness** *n.*
■ *adj.* **1** fleecy, woolen, wool-bearing, laniferous, lanigerous, downy, fuzzy, furry, fluffy, shaggy, hairy, flocculent, flocky. **2** fleecy, fluffy, flocculent, flocky. **3, 4, 6** hazy, fuzzy, unclear, obscure(d), foggy, indistinct, confused, vague, cloudy, clouded, nebulous, ill-defined, imprecise.

woolpack /wŏŏlpak/ *n.* **1** a fleecy cumulus cloud. **2** *hist.* a bale of wool.

woolsack /wŏŏlsak/ *n.* **1** (in the UK) the Lord Chancellor's wool-stuffed seat in the House of Lords. **2** the position of Lord Chancellor.

woolshed /wŏŏlshed/ *n. Austral. & NZ* a large shed for shearing and baling wool.

woolskin /wŏŏlskin/ *n.* the skin of a sheep, etc., with the fleece still on.

woolsorter's disease /wŏŏlsawrtərz dizeez/ *n.* anthrax.

woomera /wŏŏmərə/ *n. Austral.* **1** an Aboriginal stick for throwing a dart or spear more forcibly. **2** a club used as a missile. [Aboriginal]

woop woop /wŏŏp wŏŏp/ *n. Austral. & NZ sl.* **1** a jocular name for a remote outback town or district. **2** (also **Woop Woop**) an imaginary remote place. [mock Aboriginal]

woosh var. of WHOOSH.

woozy /wŏŏzee/ *adj.* (**woozier, wooziest**) *colloq.* **1** dizzy or unsteady. **2** dazed or slightly drunk. **3** vague. □□ **woozily** *adv.* **wooziness** *n.* [19th c.: orig. unkn.]
■ **1** see DIZZY *adj.* 1a. **2** see TIGHT *adj.* 6.

wop /wop/ *n. sl. offens.* an Italian or other S. European. [20th c.: orig. uncert.: perh. f. It. *guappo* bold, showy, f. Sp. *guapo* dandy]

Worcestershire sauce /wŏŏstərsheer, -shər/ *n.* a pungent sauce first made in Worcester, England.

word /wərd/ *n.* & *v.* ● *n.* **1** a sound or combination of sounds forming a meaningful element of speech, usu. shown with a space on either side of it when written or printed, used as

---

/..../ **pronunciation**	● **part of speech**
□ **phrases, idioms, and compounds**	
□□ **derivatives**	■ **synonym section**
cross-references appear in SMALL CAPITALS or *italics*	

part (or occas. as the whole) of a sentence. **2** speech, esp. as distinct from action (*bold in word only*). **3** one's promise or assurance (*gave us their word*). **4** (in *sing.* or *pl.*) a thing said, a remark or conversation. **5** (in *pl.*) the text of a song or an actor's part. **6** (in *pl.*) angry talk (*they had words*). **7** news; intelligence; a message. **8** a command, password, or motto (*gave the word to begin*). **9** a basic unit of the expression of data in a computer. ● *v.tr.* put into words; select words to express (*how shall we word that?*). □ **at a word** as soon as requested. **be as good as** (or **better than**) **one's word** fulfill (or exceed) what one has promised. **break one's word** fail to do what one has promised. **have no words for** be unable to express. **have a word** (often foll. by *with*) speak briefly (to). **in other words** expressing the same thing differently. **in so many words** explicitly or bluntly. **in a** (or **one**) **word** briefly. **keep one's word** do what one has promised. **my** (or **upon my**) **word** an exclamation of surprise or consternation. **not the word for it** not an adequate or appropriate description. **of few words** taciturn. **of one's word** reliable in keeping promises (*a woman of her word*). **on** (or **upon**) **my word** a form of asseveration. **put into words** express in speech or writing. **take a person at his** or **her word** interpret a person's words literally or exactly. **take a person's word for it** believe a person's statement without investigation, etc. **too . . . for words** too . . . to be adequately described (*was too funny for words*). **waste words** talk in vain. **the Word** (or **Word of God**) the Bible. **word-blind** incapable of identifying written or printed words. **word blindness** this condition. **word-deaf** incapable of identifying spoken words. **word deafness** this condition. **word for word** in exactly the same or (of translation) corresponding words. **word game** a game involving the making or selection, etc., of words. **word of honor** an assurance given upon one's honor. **word of mouth** speech (only). **word-of-mouth** verbal, unwritten. **word order** the sequence of words in a sentence, esp. affecting meaning, etc. **word painting** a vivid description in writing. **word-perfect** knowing one's part, etc., by heart. **word picture** a piece of word painting. **word processor** a computer software program for electronically storing text entered from a keyboard, incorporating corrections, and providing a printout. **words fail me** an expression of disbelief, dismay, etc. **word square** a set of words of equal length written one under another to read the same down as across (e.g., *too old ode*). **a word to the wise** enough said; verbum sap. □□ **wordage** *n.* **wordless** *adj.* **wordlessly** *adv.* **wordlessness** *n.* [OE f. Gmc]

■ *n.* **1** name, term, designation, locution, expression, phrase, *formal* appellation. **3** promise, pledge, vow, oath, (solemn) word of honor, undertaking, parole, assurance, warrant, guarantee, warranty. **4** utterance, expression, declaration, statement, remark, comment, observation; (little) talk, (brief) conversation, chat, discussion, consultation, dialogue, huddle, parley, tête-à-tête, confabulation, conference, interview, powwow, *colloq.* chitchat, confab. **5** (*words*) lyrics, book, libretto, text, script, lines. **6** (*words*) quarrel, dispute, argument. **7** news, intelligence, information, facts, data, report, story, account, communiqué, bulletin, dispatch, advice, message, notice, notification, *colloq.* lowdown, info, *literary* tidings, *sl.* dope, poop. **8** command, order, decree, signal, direction, instruction, password, motto, *colloq.* high sign. ● *v.* put (forth), say, couch, express, phrase, utter, state, term, style, set forth. □ **break one's word** see RENEGE 1a. **have a word** speak, communicate, chat, converse, talk. **in a** (or **one**) **word** succinctly, briefly, in brief, in a few words, concisely, in short, in fine, in summary, in sum, in a nutshell, not to mince words, to make a long story short, when all is said and done, when it's all boiled down, in the final analysis, not to beat about the bush. **put into words** see EXPRESS¹ 1, 2. **the Word** (or **Word of God**) see SCRIPTURE 2a. **word for word** see VERBATIM. **word-of-mouth** see VERBAL *adj.* 2. □□ **wordless** see MUTE *adj.* 1–3. **wordlessly** see *silently* (SILENT).

wordbook /wə́rdbŏŏk/ *n.* a book with lists of words; a vocabulary or dictionary.

wording /wə́rding/ *n.* **1** a form of words used. **2** the way in which something is expressed.

■ phraseology, language, phrasing, expression, diction, terminology, choice of words, word choice.

wordplay /wə́rdplay/ *n.* use of words to witty effect, esp. by punning.

■ see WIT¹ 2.

wordsmith /wə́rdsmith/ *n.* a skilled user or maker of words.

■ see WRITER 1.

wordy /wə́rdee/ *adj.* (**wordier, wordiest**) **1** using or expressed in many or too many words; verbose. **2** consisting of words. □□ **wordily** *adv.* **wordiness** *n.* [OE *wordig* (as WORD, -Y¹)]

■ **1** verbose, prolix, rambling, long-winded, ponderous; pleonastic, redundant, repetitious; garrulous, windy, talkative, loquacious. □□ **wordiness** see RHETORIC 2.

wore¹ *past* of WEAR¹.

wore² *past* and *past part.* of WEAR².

work /wərk/ *n.* & *v.* ● *n.* **1** the application of mental or physical effort to a purpose; the use of energy. **2 a** a task to be undertaken. **b** the materials for this. **c** (prec. by *the*; foll. by *of*) a task occupying (no more than) a specified time (*the work of a moment*). **3** a thing done or made by work; the result of an action; an achievement; a thing made. **4** a person's employment or occupation, etc., esp. as a means of earning income (*looked for work*; *is out of work*). **5 a** a literary or musical composition. **b** (in *pl.*) all such by an author or composer, etc. **6** actions or experiences of a specified kind (*good work!*; *this is thirsty work*). **7 a** (in *comb.*) things or parts made of a specified material or with specified tools, etc. (*ironwork*; *needlework*). **b** *archaic* needlework. **8** (in *pl.*) the operative part of a clock or machine. **9** *Physics* the exertion of force overcoming resistance or producing molecular change (*convert heat into work*). **10** (in *pl.*) *colloq.* all that is available; everything needed. **11** (in *pl.*) operations of building or repair (*road works*). **12** (in *pl.*; often treated as *sing.*) esp. *Brit.* a place where manufacturing is carried on. **13** (usu. in *pl.*) *Theol.* a meritorious act. **14** (usu. in *pl.* or in *comb.*) a defensive structure (*earthworks*). **15** (in *comb.*) **a** ornamentation of a specified kind (*scrollwork*). **b** articles having this. ● *v.* (*past* and *past part.* **worked** or (esp. as *adj.*) **wrought**) **1** *intr.* (often foll. by *at, on*) do work; be engaged in bodily or mental activity. **2** *intr.* **a** be employed in certain work (*works in industry*; *works as a secretary*). **b** (foll. by *with*) be the coworker of (a person). **3** *intr.* (often foll. by *for*) make efforts; conduct a campaign (*works for peace*). **4** *intr.* (foll. by *in*) be a craftsman (in a material). **5** *intr.* operate or function, esp. effectively (*how does this machine work?*; *your idea will not work*). **6** *intr.* (of a part of a machine) run; revolve; go through regular motions. **7** *tr.* carry on, manage, or control (*cannot work the machine*). **8** *tr.* **a** put or keep in operation or at work; cause to toil (*this mine is no longer worked*; *works the staff very hard*). **b** cultivate (land). **9** *tr.* bring about; produce as a result (*worked miracles*). **10** *tr.* knead; hammer; bring to a desired shape or consistency. **11** *tr.* do, or make by, needlework, etc. **12** *tr.* & *intr.* (cause to) progress or penetrate, or make (one's way), gradually or with difficulty in a specified way (*worked our way through the crowd*; *worked the peg into the hole*). **13** *intr.* (foll. by *loose*, etc.) gradually become (loose, etc.) by constant movement. **14** *tr.* artificially excite (*worked themselves into a rage*). **15** *tr.* solve (an equation, etc.) by mathematics. **16** *tr.* **a** purchase with one's labor instead of money (*work one's passage*). **b** obtain by labor the money for (one's way through college, etc.). **17** *intr.* (foll. by *on, upon*) have influence. **18** *intr.* be in motion or agitated; cause agitation; ferment (*his features worked violently*; *the yeast began to work*). **19** *intr. Naut.* sail against the wind. □ **at work** in action or engaged in work. **give a person the works 1** *colloq.* give or tell a person everything. **2** *colloq.* treat a person harshly. **3** *sl.* kill a person. **have one's work cut out** be faced with a hard task. **in the works** *colloq.* in progress; in the pipeline.

in work *Brit.* **1** having a job. **2** = *in the works.* **out of work** unemployed. **set to work** begin or cause to begin operations. **work away** (or **on**) continue to work. **work camp 1** a camp at which community work is done esp. by young volunteers. **2** a prison camp. **work one's fingers to the bone** see BONE. **work in** find a place for. **work it** *colloq.* bring it about; achieve a desired result. **work of art** a fine picture, poem, or building, etc. **work off** get rid of by work or activity. **work out 1** solve (an equation, etc.) or find out (an amount) by calculation; resolve (a problem, etc.). **2** (foll. by *at*) be calculated (*the total works out at 230*). **3** give a definite result (*this sum will not work out*). **4** have a specified or satisfactory result (*the plan worked out well; glad the arrangement worked out*). **5** provide for the details of (*has worked out a plan*). **6** accomplish or attain with difficulty (*work out one's salvation*). **7** exhaust with work (*the mine is worked out*). **8** engage in physical exercise or training. **work over 1** examine thoroughly. **2** *colloq.* treat with violence. **work sheet 1** a paper for recording work done or in progress. **2** a paper listing questions or activities for students, etc., to work through. **work-shy** disinclined to work. **work-study program** a system of combining academic studies with related practical employment. **work to rule** esp. *Brit.* (esp. as a form of industrial action) follow official working rules exactly in order to reduce output and efficiency. **work-to-rule** esp. *Brit.* the act or an instance of working to rule. **work up 1** bring gradually to an efficient state. **2** (foll. by *to*) advance gradually to a climax. **3** elaborate or create by degrees; bring to a state of agitation. **4** mingle (ingredients) into a whole. **5** learn (a subject) by study. **work one's will** (foll. by *on, upon*) *archaic* accomplish one's purpose on (a person or thing). **work wonders** see WONDER. □□ **workless** *adj.* [OE *weorc*, etc., f. Gmc]

■ *n.* **1** labor, toil, effort, drudgery, exertion, industry, slog, *colloq.* grind, sweat, elbow grease, esp. *Brit. colloq.* fag, *literary* travail, *Brit. sl.* graft. **2** task, function, duty, service, assignment, job, project, charge, responsibility, chore, commission, undertaking, stint. **3** feat, achievement, creation, accomplishment, handiwork, workmanship, output, result, product, end product, production. **4** employment, business, occupation, vocation, calling, profession, trade, line, métier, career, livelihood, job, post, position, situation. **5** opus, *oeuvre*, production; composition, creation, piece, writing(s), masterwork, masterpiece, chef-d'œuvre, magnum opus. **8** (*works*) mechanism, machinery, action, workings, (moving *or* working) parts, guts, *colloq.* innards, insides; clockwork. **10** (*the works*) everything, the lot, everything but the kitchen sink, *colloq.* the whole shooting match, *sl.* the whole (kit and) caboodle, the whole shebang. **12** (*works*) plant, factory, workshop, shop, mill. ● *v.* **1** labor, toil, exert oneself, sweat, slave (away), peg away, slog (away), grind (away), fag, *archaic* moil, *colloq.* beaver, plug (away), *Brit. sl.* graft. **2 a** have a job, hold (down) a post or position, earn a living, be employed. **3** see STRIVE 1. **5** function, operate, run, go, perform; be effective, succeed. **7** control, manage, manipulate, maneuver, wield, ply, handle, operate, use, make use of, utilize, exploit, deal with, bring into play. **8 a** operate, use, employ, put to (good *or* effective) use; drive, exploit. **b** till, plow, farm, cultivate. **9** bring about, effect, accomplish, carry out *or* off, make, produce, achieve, engender, create, do, put through, execute, effectuate, implement, realize, *literary* beget. **10** knead, hammer, mold, form, fashion, shape; mix, stir, incorporate. **12** wade, plod, plow; maneuver, manipulate, guide, direct. **17** (*work on*) importune, press, pressurize, pressure; influence, persuade, wheedle, coax, act on, prevail upon, induce, dispose, urge. **18** see FERMENT *v.* 1, TWIST *v.* 1a, b. □ **give a person the works 2** give a person a thrashing *or* beating *or* drubbing *or* battering *or* flogging *or* lambasting, beat, thrash, *sl.* wallop. **in the works** in production, under way, being done, being planned, in

the pipeline, in the planning stage(s). **out of work** unemployed, idle, jobless, between engagements, unwaged, available, free, redundant, *colloq.* on *or* collecting unemployment, *Brit. colloq.* on the dole, *Brit. euphem.* resting. **work in** find time *or* space for, find a place for, include, insert, introduce, fit in, squeeze in, accommodate. **work of art** see MASTERPIECE 1. **work out 1** see SOLVE. **2** (*work out at*) equal, total (up to), tot up to, result in, amount to, come to. **4** go, develop, turn out, pan out, evolve; succeed, prosper, come out all right, prove satisfactory, go well, be effective. **5** formulate, work up, contrive, draw up, detail, plan, develop, devise, put together, elaborate, expand, enlarge (on). **8** exercise, do callisthenics, do aerobics, warm up, do setting-up exercises, jog, lift weights, train. **work over 2** see POUND[2] 1a, b. **work-to-rule** slowdown, *Brit.* go-slow, industrial action. **work up 1** prepare, (make *or* get) ready, whip into shape, develop, come up with, write up, put together, produce, turn out. **2** advance, ascend, rise (in a crescendo), move up *or* ahead *or* on. **3** excite, make excited, agitate, inflame, arouse, rouse, foment, stir, move, animate, incite, spur, fire (up), *colloq.* get a person (all) steamed *or* het up, *literary* enkindle. □□ **workless** see *out of work* above.

workable /wɔ́rkəbəl/ *adj.* **1** that can be worked or will work. **2** that is worth working; practicable; feasible (*a workable plan*). □□ **workability** (/-bílitee/) *n.* **workableness** *n.* **workably** *adv.*
■ **1** see OPERABLE. **2** see FEASIBLE 1.

workaday /wɔ́rkəday/ *adj.* **1** ordinary; everyday; practical. **2** fit for, used, or seen on workdays.
■ **1** see ORDINARY *adj.*

workaholic /wɔ̀rkəhólik/ *n. & adj. colloq.* (a person) addicted to working.

workbag /wɔ́rkbag/ *n.* a bag containing sewing materials, etc.

workbasket /wɔ́rkbaskit/ *n.* a basket containing sewing materials, etc.

workbench /wɔ́rkbench/ *n.* a bench for doing mechanical or practical work, esp. carpentry.

workbox /wɔ́rkboks/ *n.* a box for holding tools, materials for sewing, etc.

workday /wɔ́rkday/ *n.* a day on which work is usually done.

worker /wɔ́rkər/ *n.* **1** a person who works, esp. a manual or industrial employee. **2** a neuter or undeveloped female of various social insects, esp. a bee or ant, that does the basic work of its colony. □ **worker-priest** a French Roman Catholic or an Anglican priest who engages part-time in secular work.
■ **1** laborer, working man *or* woman, workman, hand, operative, operator, employee; artisan, craftsman, tradesman, mechanic; drudge, journeyman, white-collar worker, blue-collar worker, proletarian, breadwinner, wage earner.

workforce /wɔ́rkfawrs/ *n.* **1** the workers engaged or available in an industry, etc. **2** the number of such workers.
■ see STAFF[1] *n.* 2.

workhorse /wɔ́rkhawrs/ *n.* a horse, person, or machine that performs hard work.
■ see SLAVE *n.* 2.

workhouse /wɔ́rkhows/ *n.* **1** a house of correction for petty offenders. **2** *Brit. hist.* a public institution in which the destitute of a parish received board and lodging in return for work done; poorhouse.

working /wɔ́rking/ *adj. & n.* ● *adj.* **1** engaged in work, esp. in manual or industrial labor. **2** functioning or able to function. ● *n.* **1** the activity of work. **2** the act or manner of functioning of a thing. **3 a** a mine or quarry. **b** the part of this in which work is being or has been done (*a disused working*). □ **working capital** the capital actually used in a busi-

ness. **working class** the class of people who are employed for wages, esp. in manual or industrial work. **working-class** *adj.* of the working class. **working day** esp. *Brit.* **1** a workday. **2** the part of the day devoted to work. **working drawing** a drawing to scale, serving as a guide for construction or manufacture. **working girl 1** a young woman who works for a living. **2** *sl.* a prostitute. **working hours** hours normally devoted to work. **working hypothesis** a hypothesis used as a basis for action. **working knowledge** knowledge adequate to work with. **working lunch**, etc., a meal at which business is conducted. **working order** the condition in which a machine works (satisfactorily or as specified). **working-out 1** the calculation of results. **2** the elaboration of details. **working papers** documents that authorize (a person, esp. an alien or a minor) to be employed.
■ *adj.* **1** see BUSY *adj.* 3. **2** see FUNCTIONAL 1, ACTIVE *adj.* 2, 3. ● *n.* **3** see PIT¹ *n.* 1. □ **working-class** (*adj.*) see PLEBEIAN *adj.* 1.

workload /wŕklōd/ *n.* the amount of work to be done by an individual, etc.

workman /wŕkmən/ *n.* (*pl.* **-men**) **1** a person employed to do manual labor. **2** a person considered with regard to skill in a job (*a good workman*).
■ see WORKER.

workmanlike /wŕkmənlīk/ *adj.* characteristic of a good workman; showing practiced skill.
■ see YEOMANLY.

workmanship /wŕkmənship/ *n.* **1** the degree of skill in doing a task or of finish in the product made. **2** a thing made or created by a specified person, etc.
■ **1** craft, craftsmanship, artistry, art, technique, handiwork, skill, skillfulness, mastery, artisanship.

workmate /wŕkmayt/ *n. Brit.* a coworker.

workout /wŕkowt/ *n.* a session of physical exercise or training.
■ see EXERCISE *n.* 3.

workpeople /wŕkpeepəl/ *n.pl. Brit.* employees; workers.

workpiece /wŕkpees/ *n.* a thing worked on with a tool or machine.

workplace /wŕkplays/ *n.* a place at which a person works; an office, factory, etc.

workroom /wŕkrŏŏm, -rŏŏm/ *n.* a room for working in, esp. one equipped for a certain kind of work.

workshop /wŕkshop/ *n.* **1** a room or building in which goods are manufactured. **2 a** a meeting for concerted discussion or activity (*a dance workshop*). **b** the members of such a meeting.

workstation /wŕkstayshən/ *n.* **1** the location of a stage in a manufacturing process. **2** a computer terminal or the desk, etc., where this is located.

worktable /wŕktayb'l/ *n.* a table for working at, esp. with a sewing machine.

worktop /wŕktop/ *n.* esp. *Brit.* a flat surface for working on, esp. in a kitchen.

workwoman /wŕkwŏŏmən/ *n.* (*pl.* **-women**) a female worker or operative.

world /wərld/ *n.* **1 a** the earth, or a planetary body like it. **b** its countries and their inhabitants. **c** all people; the earth as known or in some particular respect. **2 a** the universe or all that exists; everything. **b** everything that exists outside oneself (*dead to the world*). **3 a** the time, state, or scene of human existence. **b** (*prec.* by *the, this*) mortal life. **4** secular interests and affairs. **5** human affairs; their course and conditions; active life (*how goes the world with you?*). **6** average, respectable, or fashionable people or their customs or opinions. **7** all that concerns or all who belong to a specified class, time, domain, or sphere of activity (*the medieval world; the world of baseball*). **8** (foll. by *of*) a vast amount (*that makes a world of difference*). **9** (*attrib.*) affecting many nations, of all nations (*world politics; a world champion*). □ **all the world and his wife** esp. *Brit.* **1** any large mixed gathering of people. **2** all with pretensions to fashion. **be worlds apart** differ greatly, esp. in nature or opinion. **bring into the world** give birth to or attend at the birth of. **carry the world before one** esp. *Brit.* have rapid and complete success. **come into the**

world be born. **for all the world** (foll. by *like, as if*) precisely (*looked for all the world as if they were real*). **get the best of both worlds** benefit from two incompatible sets of ideas, circumstances, etc. **in the world** of all; at all (used as an intensifier in questions) (*what in the world is it?*). **man** (or **woman**) **of the world** a person experienced and practical in human affairs. **the next** (or **other**) **world** life after death. **out of this world** *colloq.* extremely good, etc. (*the food was out of this world*). **see the world** travel widely; gain wide experience. **think the world of** have a very high regard for. **World Bank** *colloq.* the International Bank for Reconstruction and Development, an organization administering economic aid among member nations. **world-beater** a person or thing surpassing all others. **world-class** of a quality or standard regarded as high throughout the world. **World Cup** a competition among soccer or other sporting teams from various countries. **world-famous** known throughout the world. **the world, the flesh, and the devil** the various kinds of temptation. **world language 1** an artificial language for international use. **2** a language spoken in many countries. **the** (or **all the**) **world over** throughout the world. **world power** a nation having power and influence in world affairs. **the world's end** the farthest attainable point of travel. **World Series** the championship for U.S. major-league baseball teams. **world-shaking** of supreme importance. **the world to come** supposed life after death. **world war** a war involving many important nations (*First World War* or *World War I*; 1914–18; *Second World War* or *World War II*, 1939–45). **world-weariness** being worldweary. **world-weary** weary of the world and life on it. **world without end** for ever. [OE *w(e)orold, world* f. a Gmc root meaning 'age': rel. to OLD]
■ **1 a** earth, planet, sphere, globe. **c** humanity, mankind, people, the human race, society, the public, men, humankind, everybody, everyone, the world at large. **2 a** universe, cosmos, existence, creation, life; everything. **5** affairs, things, circumstances, events, life. **7** period, time, age, era, epoch, time(s); area, sphere, domain, community, clique, crowd, circle, fraternity, faction, set, coterie. □ **bring into the world** deliver, have, bear, give birth to, *colloq.* birth, *literary* beget. **for all the world** precisely, exactly, in all respects, in every respect, in every way, just. **out of this world** marvelous, wonderful, exceptional, unbelievable, incredible, excellent, superb, far-out, *colloq.* great, smashing, fantastic, fabulous, out of sight, magic; see also EXCELLENT.

worldline /wɔ́rldlīn/ *n. Physics* a curve in space-time joining the positions of a particle throughout its existence.

worldling /wɔ́rldling/ *n.* a worldly person.

worldly /wɔ́rldlee/ *adj.* (**worldlier, worldliest**) **1** temporal or earthly (*worldly goods*). **2** engrossed in temporal affairs, esp. the pursuit of wealth and pleasure. □ **worldly-minded** intent on worldly things. **worldly wisdom** prudence as regards one's own interests. **worldly-wise** having worldly wisdom. □□ **worldliness** *n.* [OE *woruldlic* (as WORLD, -LY¹)]
■ **1** mundane, earthly, terrestrial, temporal, physical, carnal, fleshly, corporeal, human, material; lay, nonspiritual, nonreligious, civic, secular, profane. **2** urbane, suave, sophisticated, cosmopolitan, worldly-wise, *colloq.* with it, *sl.* hip, hep, cool.

worldview /wɔ́rldvyŏŏ/ *n.* = WELTANSCHAUUNG.

worldwide /wɔ́rldwíd/ *adj. & adv.* ● *adj.* affecting, occurring in, or known in all parts of the world. ● *adv.* throughout the world.
■ *adj.* see GLOBAL 1.

worm /wərm/ *n. & v.* ● *n.* **1** any of various types of creeping or burrowing invertebrate animals with long, slender bodies and no limbs, esp. segmented in rings or parasitic in the intestines or tissues. **2** the long, slender larva of an insect, esp. in fruit or wood. **3** (in *pl.*) intestinal or other internal parasites. **4** a blindworm or slowworm. **5** a maggot supposed to eat dead bodies in the grave. **6** an insignificant or contemptible person. **7 a** the spiral part of a screw. **b** a short screw working in a worm gear. **8** the spiral pipe of a still in which the vapor is cooled and condensed. **9** the ligament under a dog's tongue. ● *v.* **1** *intr.* & *tr.* (often *refl.*) move with a crawling motion (*wormed through the bushes*; *wormed our way through the bushes*). **2** *intr.* & *refl.* (foll. by *into*) insinuate oneself into a person's favor, confidence, etc. **3** *tr.* (foll. by *out*) obtain (a secret, etc.) by cunning persistence (*managed to worm the truth out of them*). **4** *tr.* cut the worm of (a dog's tongue). **5** *tr.* rid (a plant or dog, etc.) of worms. **6** *tr. Naut.* make (a rope, etc.) smooth by winding thread between the strands. □ **can of worms** unwanted complications (*let's not open a can of worms*). **food for worms** a dead person. **worm-eaten 1 a** eaten into by worms. **b** rotten; decayed. **2** old and dilapidated. **worm-fishing** fishing with worms for bait. **worm gear** an arrangement of a toothed wheel worked by a revolving spiral. **worm's-eye view** a view as seen from below or from a humble position. **worm wheel** the wheel of a worm gear. **a** (or **even a**) **worm will turn** the meekest will resist or retaliate if pushed too far. □□ **wormer** *n.* **wormlike** *adj.* [OE *wyrm* f. Gmc]

■ *n.* **6** see WRETCH 2. ● *v.* **1** see SLITHER *v.* **2** (*worm oneself*) see INSINUATE 2a, b. **3** (*worm out*) see EXTRACT *v.* 2.

wormhole /wɔ́rmhōl/ *n.* a hole left by the passage of a worm.

wormseed /wɔ́rmseed/ *n.* **1** seed used to expel intestinal worms. **2** a plant, e.g., santonica, bearing this seed.

wormwood /wɔ́rmwŏŏd/ *n.* **1** any woody shrub of the genus *Artemisia*, with a bitter aromatic taste, used in the preparation of vermouth and absinthe and in medicine. **2** bitter mortification or a source of this. [ME, alt. f. obs. *wormod* f. OE *wormōd, wermōd*, after *worm, wood*: cf. VERMOUTH]

wormy /wɔ́rmee/ *adj.* (**wormier, wormiest**) **1** full of worms. **2** wormeaten. □□ **worminess** *n.*

worn /wawrn/ *past part.* of WEAR¹. ● *adj.* **1** damaged by use or wear. **2** looking tired and exhausted. **3** (in full **well-worn**) (of a joke, etc.) stale; often heard.

■ *adj.* **1** shabby, threadbare, tatty, tattered, ragged, frayed, dilapidated. **2** worn out, tired, fatigued, exhausted, spent, jaded, played out, haggard, drawn, shattered, the worse for wear, dog-tired, *colloq.* fagged (out), dead (on one's feet), frazzled, all in, done in, pooped, esp. *Brit. colloq.* whacked, *sl.* beat. **3** see BANAL.

worriment /wɔ́reement, wúr-/ *n.* **1** the act of worrying or state of being worried. **2** a cause of worry.

worrisome /wɔ́reesəm, wúr-/ *adj.* causing or apt to cause worry or distress. □□ **worrisomely** *adv.*

■ see TROUBLESOME 2.

worry /wɔ́ree, wúr-/ *v.* & *n.* ● *v.* (**-ies, -ied**) **1** *intr.* give way to anxiety or unease; allow one's mind to dwell on difficulty or troubles. **2** *tr.* harass; importune; be a trouble or anxiety to. **3** *tr.* **a** (of a dog, etc.) shake or pull about with the teeth. **b** attack repeatedly. **4** (as **worried** *adj.*) **a** uneasy; troubled in the mind. **b** suggesting worry (*a worried look*). ● *n.* (*pl.* **-ies**) **1** a thing that causes anxiety or disturbs a person's tranquillity. **2** a disturbed state of mind; anxiety; a worried state. **3** a dog's worrying of its quarry. □ **not to worry** *colloq.* there is no need to worry. **worry along** (or **through**) manage to advance by persistence in spite of obstacles. **worry beads** a string of beads manipulated with the fingers to occupy or calm oneself. **worry oneself** (usu. in *neg.*) take needless trouble. **worry out** obtain (the solution to a problem, etc.) by dogged effort. □□ **worriedly** *adv.* **worrier** *n.* **worryingly** *adv.* [OE *wyrgan* strangle f. WG]

■ *v.* **1** be anxious, be fearful, be apprehensive, be nervous *or* a bundle of nerves, be concerned, fret, brood, agonize, be distressed, be vexed, *colloq.* stew, bite *or* chew one's nails, go *or* get gray, get gray hair, sweat blood. **2** annoy, irk, pester, nettle, harry, harass, irritate, tease, bother, torment, trouble, perturb, vex, plague, provoke, importune, hector, badger, gall, get on a person's nerves, get *or* put a person's back up, *colloq.* peeve, hassle, needle. **4** (**worried**) fearful, apprehensive, anxious, distressed, nervous, uneasy, anguished, disquieted, agonized, agonizing, distraught, on edge, on tenterhooks, ill at ease, troubled, fretful, agitated, perturbed, upset, suffering. ● *n.* **1** concern,

care, responsibility; problem, bother, burden, trouble, tribulation, affliction, irritation, annoyance, vexation. **2** anguish, anxiety, uneasiness, unease, nervousness, distress, apprehension, disquiet, perturbation, agitation, upset, misgiving.

worrywart /wɔ́reewawrt, wúr-/ *n. colloq.* a person who habitually worries unduly.

worse /wərs/ *adj., adv.,* & *n.* ● *adj.* **1** more bad. **2** (*predic.*) in or into worse health or a worse condition (*is getting worse*; *is none the worse for it*). ● *adv.* more badly or more ill. ● *n.* **1** a worse thing or things (*you might do worse than accept*). **2** (*prec. by the*) a worse condition (*a change for the worse*). □ **none the worse** (often foll. by *for*) not adversely affected (by). **or worse** or as an even worse alternative. **the worse for drink** fairly drunk. **the worse for wear 1** damaged by use. **2** injured. **3** *joc.* drunk. **worse luck** see LUCK. **worse off** in a worse (esp. financial) position. [OE *wyrsa, wiersa* f. Gmc]

worsen /wɔ́rsən/ *v.tr.* & *intr.* make or become worse.

■ exacerbate, aggravate; weaken, deteriorate, decline, degenerate, decay, slip, sink, slide, fail, disintegrate, take a turn for the worse, get worse, go from bad to worse, *colloq.* go downhill.

worship /wɔ́rship/ *n.* & *v.* ● *n.* **1 a** homage or reverence paid to a deity, esp. in a formal service. **b** the acts, rites, or ceremonies of worship. **2** adoration or devotion comparable to religious homage shown toward a person or principle (*the worship of wealth*; *regarded them with worship in their eyes*). **3** *archaic* worthiness; merit; recognition given or due to these; honor and respect. ● *v.* (**worshiped, worshiping** or **worshipped, worshipping**) **1** *tr.* adore as divine; honor with religious rites. **2** *tr.* idolize or regard with adoration (*worships the ground she walks on*). **3** *intr.* attend public worship. **4** *intr.* be full of adoration. □ **Your** (or **His** or **Her**) **Worship** esp. *Brit.* a title of respect used to or of a mayor, certain magistrates, etc. □□ **worshiper** *n.* (or **worshipper**). [OE *weorthscipe* (as WORTH, -SHIP)]

■ *n.* **1, 2** veneration, reverence, adoration, devotion, homage, honor, respect, esteem, exaltation, praise, admiration, adulation, glorification, deification, idolatry. ● *v.* **1, 2** venerate, revere, reverence, extol, honor, hallow, exalt, praise, admire, adore, adulate, glorify, deify, idolize, be devoted to, pay homage to, bow down before, kneel before, put on a pedestal, *archaic* magnify.

worshipful /wɔ́rshipfŏŏl/ *adj.* **1** (usu. **Worshipful**) *Brit.* a title given to justices of the peace and to certain old companies or their officers, etc. **2** *archaic* entitled to honor or respect. **3** *archaic* imbued with a spirit of veneration. □□ **worshipfully** *adv.* **worshipfulness** *n.*

worst /wərst/ *adj., adv., n.,* & *v.* ● *adj.* most bad. ● *adv.* most badly. ● *n.* the worst part, event, circumstance, or possibility (*the worst of the storm is over*; *prepare for the worst*). ● *v.tr.* get the better of; defeat; outdo. □ **at its**, etc., **worst** in the worst state. **at worst** (or **the worst**) in the worst possible case. **do your worst** an expression of defiance. **get** (or **have**) **the worst of it** be defeated. **if worst comes to worst** if the worst happens. [OE *wierresta, wyrresta* (adj.), *wyrst, wyrrest* (adv.), f. Gmc]

■ *v.* see BEAT *v.* 3a.

worsted /wŏŏstid, wɔ́r-/ *n.* **1** a fine smooth yarn spun from combed long, stapled wool. **2** fabric made from this. [*Worste(a)d* in S. England]

wort /wərt, wawrt/ *n.* **1** *archaic* (except in names) a plant or herb (*liverwort*; *St. John's wort*). **2** the infusion of malt which after fermentation becomes beer. [OE *wyrt*: rel. to ROOT¹]

worth /wərth/ *adj.* & *n.* ● *predic.adj.* (governing a noun like a preposition) **1** of a value equivalent to (*is worth $50*; *is worth very little*). **2** such as to justify or repay; deserving;

bringing compensation for (*worth doing*; *not worth the trouble*). **3** possessing or having property amounting to (*is worth a million dollars*). ● *n.* **1** what a person or thing is worth; the (usu. specified) merit of (*of great worth*; *persons of worth*). **2** the equivalent of money in a commodity (*ten dollars' worth of gasoline*). □ **for all one is worth** *colloq.* with one's utmost efforts; without reserve. **for what it is worth** without a guarantee of its truth or value. **worth it** *colloq.* worth the time or effort spent. **worth one's salt** see SALT. **worth while** (or **one's while**) see WHILE. [OE *w(e)orth*]

■ *n.* **1** quality, merit, value, advantage, benefit, good, importance, significance, usefulness.

worthless /wə́rthlis/ *adj.* without value or merit. □□ **worthlessly** *adv.* **worthlessness** *n.*

■ valueless, unimportant, insignificant, inessential, unessential, dispensable, disposable, meaningless, paltry, trifling; pointless, silly, inane, vain, unavailing, useless, futile, fruitless, unproductive, unprofitable, *archaic* bootless; cheap, tawdry, poor, trashy, rubbishy, shabby, wretched, tinny, chintzy, *sl.* cheesy.

worthwhile /wə́rth-hwíl, -wíl/ *adj.* that is worth the time or effort spent; of value or importance. □□ **worthwhileness** *n.*

■ profitable, justifiable, productive, gainful, rewarding, fruitful, cost-effective, remunerative, beneficial, helpful, advantageous; useful, valuable, invaluable, important, good, worthy, desirable.

worthy /wə́rthee/ *adj. & n.* ● *adj.* (**worthier, worthiest**) **1** estimable; having some moral worth; deserving respect (*lived a worthy life*). **2** (of a person) entitled to (esp. condescending) recognition (*a worthy old couple*). **3 a** (foll. by *of* or *to* + infin.) deserving (*worthy of a mention*; *worthy to be remembered*). **b** (foll. by *of*) adequate or suitable to the dignity, etc., of (*in words worthy of the occasion*). ● *n.* (*pl.* **-ies**) **1** a worthy person. **2** a person of some distinction. **3** *joc.* a person. □□ **worthily** *adv.* **worthiness** *n.* [ME *wurthi*, etc. f. WORTH]

■ *adj.* **1** worthwhile, meritorious, praiseworthy, good, estimable, exemplary, creditable, commendable, laudable, honorable, upright, sterling, irreproachable, respectable. **3 a** deserving, meriting, qualified, fit. ● *n.* **2** dignitary, personage, notable, eminence, celebrity, luminary.

-worthy /wərthee/ *comb. form* forming adjectives meaning: **1** deserving of (*blameworthy*; *noteworthy*). **2** suitable or fit for (*newsworthy*; *roadworthy*).

wot see WIT².

wotcher /wóchər/ *int. Brit. sl.* a form of casual greeting. [corrupt. of *what cheer*]

would /wŏŏd, when unstressed wəd/ *v.aux.* (*3rd sing.* **would**) *past* of WILL¹, used esp.: **1** (in the 2nd and 3rd persons, and often in the 1st: see SHOULD). **a** in reported speech (*he said he would be home by evening*). **b** to express the conditional mood (*they would have been killed if they had gone*). **2** to express habitual action (*would wait for her every evening*). **3** to express a question or polite request (*would they like it?*; *would you come in, please?*). **4** to express probability (*I guess she would be over fifty by now*). **5** (foll. by *that* + clause) *literary* to express a wish (*would that you were here*). **6** to express consent (*they would not help*). □ **would-be** often *derog.* desiring or aspiring to be (*a would-be politician*). [OE *wolde*, past of *wyllan*: see WILL¹]

■ □ **would-be** professed; see also SELF-STYLED.

wouldn't /wŏŏd'nt/ *contr.* would not. □ **I wouldn't know** *colloq.* (as is to be expected) I do not know.

wouldst /wŏŏdst/ *archaic 2nd sing. past* of WOULD.

wound¹ /wŏŏnd/ *n. & v.* ● *n.* **1** an injury done to living tissue by a cut or blow, etc., esp. beyond the cutting or piercing of the skin. **2** an injury to a person's reputation or a pain inflicted on a person's feelings. **3** *poet.* the pangs of love. ● *v.tr.* inflict a wound on (*wounded soldiers*; *wounded feelings*). □□ **woundingly** *adv.* **woundless** *adj.* [OE *wund* (n.), *wundian* (v.)]

■ *n.* **1** damage, hurt, injury, trauma, traumatism; laceration, puncture, cut, gash, slash, lesion, bruise, contusion. **2** slight, damage, injury, harm, blow,

distress, mortification, torment, torture, anguish, pain, insult. ● *v.* harm, injure, hurt, traumatize, maim; cut, slash, gash, lacerate, slit, stab, shoot, wing; slight, distress, damage, mortify, insult, pain, grieve, offend, wrong.

wound² *past and past part.* of WIND² (cf. WIND¹ *v.* 6).

woundwort /wŏŏndwərt, -wawrt/ *n.* any of various plants esp. of the genus *Stachys*, formerly supposed to have healing properties.

wove¹ *past* of WEAVE¹.

wove² /wōv/ *adj.* (of paper) made on a wire-gauze mesh and so having a uniform unlined surface. [var. of *woven*, past part. of WEAVE¹]

woven *past part.* of WEAVE¹.

wow¹ /wow/ *int., n., & v.* ● *int.* expressing astonishment or admiration. ● *n. sl.* a sensational success. ● *v.tr. sl.* impress or excite greatly. [orig. Sc.: imit.]

wow² /wow/ *n.* a slow pitch fluctuation in sound reproduction, perceptible in long notes. [imit.]

wowser /wówzər/ *n. Austral. sl.* **1** a puritanical fanatic. **2** a spoilsport. **3** a teetotaler. [20th c.: orig. uncert.]

■ **1** see PURITAN *n.* 3. **2** see SPOILSPORT.

WP *abbr.* word processor; word processing.

w.p. *abbr.* **1** weather permitting. **2** *Baseball* wild pitch(es).

w.p.m. *abbr.* words per minute.

wrack /rak/ *n.* **1** seaweed cast up or growing on the shore. **2** destruction. **3** a wreck or wreckage. **4** = RACK². **5** = RACK⁵. [ME f. MDu. *wrak* or MLG *wra(c)k*, a parallel formation to OE *wrec*, rel. to *wrecan* WREAK: cf. WRECK, RACK⁵]

wraggle-taggle var. of RAGGLE-TAGGLE.

wraith /rayth/ *n.* **1** a ghost or apparition. **2** the spectral appearance of a living person supposed to portend that person's death. □□ **wraithlike** *adj.* [16th-c. Sc.: orig. unkn.]

■ see GHOST *n.* 1. □□ **wraithlike** see GHOSTLY.

wrangle /ránggəl/ *n. & v.* ● *n.* a noisy argument, altercation, or dispute. ● *v.* **1** *intr.* engage in a wrangle. **2** *tr.* herd (cattle). [ME, prob. f. LG or Du.: cf. LG *wrangelen*, frequent. of *wrangen* to struggle, rel. to WRING]

■ *n.* see ARGUMENT 1. ● *v.* **1** see ARGUE 1.

wrangler /rángglər/ *n.* **1** a person who wrangles. **2** a cowboy. **3** (at Cambridge University) a person placed in the first class of the mathematical tripos.

wrap /rap/ *v. & n.* ● *v.tr.* (**wrapped, wrapping**) **1** (often foll. by *up*) envelop in folded or soft encircling material (*wrap it up in paper*; *wrap up a package*). **2** (foll. by *around, about*) arrange or draw (a pliant covering) around (a person) (*wrapped the coat closer around me*). **3** (foll. by *around*) *sl.* crash (a vehicle) into a stationary object. ● *n.* **1** a shawl or scarf or other such addition to clothing; a wrapper. **2** material used for wrapping. □ **take the wraps off** disclose. **under wraps** in secrecy. **wrapped up in** engrossed or absorbed in. **wrap up 1** finish off; bring to completion (*wrapped up the deal in two days*). **2** put on warm clothes (*mind you wrap up well*). **3** (in *imper.*) *Brit. sl.* be quiet. [ME: orig. unkn.]

■ *v.* **1** swathe, swaddle, bind, cover, envelop, surround, shroud, enfold, fold, muffle, enclose, lag, sheathe, cocoon, encase, *literary* enshroud, enwrap; pack, package, do up, gift wrap. **2** twine, wind, entwine, coil. ● *n.* **1** stole, shawl, scarf, mantle, poncho, serape, wrapper, cloak, cape, coat. **2** wrapping, packaging, covering. □ **under wraps** see SECRET *adj.* 1. **wrapped up in** immersed in, submerged in, buried in, absorbed in, engrossed in, bound up in, involved in, occupied with *or* by *or* in, engaged in, dedicated to, devoted to. **wrap up 1** complete, conclude, finish, end, bring to a close, terminate, finalize, wind up, settle, tidy up. **3** be silent, be quiet, stop talking, *colloq.* hold your tongue, shut up, *sl.* shut your face, shut your trap, shut your mouth, button your lip.

wraparound /rápərownd/ *adj. & n.* ● *adj.* **1** (esp. of clothing) designed to wrap around. **2** curving or extending around at the edges. ● *n.* anything that wraps around.

wrappage /rápij/ *n.* a wrapping or wrappings.

wrapper /rápər/ *n.* **1** a cover for a candy, chocolate, etc. **2** a cover enclosing a newspaper or similar packet for mailing. **3** a paper cover of a book, usu. detachable. **4** a loose enveloping robe or gown. **5** a tobacco leaf of superior quality enclosing a cigar.

■ **1, 2** envelope, package, packing, wrapping, covering, jacket, case, casing, container. **3** cover, jacket, dustcover, dust jacket, sleeve, dust wrapper. **4** housecoat, robe, dressing gown, bathrobe, kimono, happi (coat), negligee, lounging robe, peignoir.

wrapping /ráping/ *n.* (esp. in *pl.*) material used to wrap; wraps; wrappers. □ **wrapping paper** strong or decorative paper for wrapping packages.

■ see WRAPPER 1, 2.

wrasse /ras/ *n.* any bright-colored marine fish of the family Labridae with thick lips and strong teeth. [Corn. *wrach*, var. of *gwrach*, = Welsh *gwrach*, lit. 'old woman']

wrath /rath, roth, rawth/ *n. literary* extreme anger. [OE *wrǣththu* f. *wrāth* WROTH]

■ see ANGER *n.*

wrathful /ráthfŏŏl, róth-, ráwth-/ *adj. literary* extremely angry. □□ **wrathfully** *adv.* **wrathfulness** *n.*

■ see ANGRY 1.

wrathy /ráthee, róth-, ráwthee/ *adj. esp. Brit.* = WRATHFUL.

wreak /reek/ *v.tr.* **1** (usu. foll. by *upon*) give play or satisfaction to; put in operation (vengeance or one's anger, etc.). **2** cause (damage, etc.) (*the hurricane wreaked havoc on the crops*). **3** *archaic* avenge (a wrong or wronged person). □□ **wreaker** *n.* [OE *wrecan* drive, avenge, etc., f. Gmc: cf. WRACK, WRECK, WRETCH]

■ **1** inflict, exercise, exert, carry out, bring (to bear), visit, effect, work, unleash, execute, impose, force, vent, let loose, loose.

wreath /reeth/ *n.* (*pl.* **wreaths** /reethz, reeths/) **1** flowers or leaves fastened in a ring esp. as an ornament for a person's head or a building or for laying on a grave, etc., as a mark of honor or respect. **2 a** a similar ring of soft twisted material such as silk. **b** *Heraldry* a representation of this below a crest. **3** a carved representation of a wreath. **4** (foll. by *of*) a curl or ring of smoke or cloud. **5** a light drifting mass of snow, etc. [OE *writha* f. weak grade of *wrīthan* WRITHE]

■ **1** see GARLAND *n.* 1.

wreathe /reeth/ *v.* **1** *tr.* encircle as, with, or like a wreath. **2** *tr.* (foll. by *around*) put (one's arms, etc.) around (a person, etc.). **3** *intr.* (of smoke, etc.) move in the shape of wreaths. **4** *tr.* form (flowers, silk, etc.) into a wreath. **5** *tr.* make (a garland). [partly back-form. f. archaic *wrethen* past part. of WRITHE; partly f. WREATH]

■ **1** see CIRCLE *v.* 2. **3** see TWINE *v.*

wreck /rek/ *n. & v.* ● *n.* **1** the destruction or disablement esp. of a ship. **2** a ship that has suffered a wreck (*the shores are strewn with wrecks*). **3** a greatly damaged or disabled building, thing, or person (*had become a physical and mental wreck*). **4** (foll. by *of*) a wretched remnant or disorganized set of remains. **5** *Law* goods, etc., cast up by the sea. ● *v.* **1** *tr.* cause the wreck of (a ship, etc.). **2** *tr.* completely ruin (hopes, chances, etc.). **3** *intr.* suffer a wreck. **4** *tr.* (as **wrecked** *adj.*) involved in a shipwreck (*wrecked sailors*). **5** *intr.* deal with wrecked vehicles, etc. [ME f. AF *wrec*, etc. (cf. VAREC) f. a Gmc root meaning 'to drive': cf. WREAK]

■ *n.* **1** destruction, loss, sinking, devastation, foundering, grounding, capsizal, capsizing, disabling, disablement, wreckage, wrecking; demolition, demolishing, leveling, tearing down, razing, pulling down, obliteration, ruin, ruining. **2** hulk, shipwreck, ruins. **3** mess, disaster, ruin(s); wrack. **4** remnant, remains, remainder, wreckage. **5** flotsam, jetsam. ● *v.* **1** sink, scuttle, shipwreck, run aground, founder, capsize; destroy, ruin, devastate, demolish, smash, shatter, spoil, dash (to pieces), reduce to nothing, annihilate, *Brit. sl.* scupper. **2** ruin, destroy, demolish, devastate, shatter, dash, spoil, annihilate, undermine, sabotage, *Austral.* euchre, *Brit. sl.* scupper.

wreckage /rékij/ *n.* **1** wrecked material. **2** the remnants of a wreck. **3** the action or process of wrecking.

■ **1, 2** debris, fragments, pieces, remains, flotsam, rubble, ruin(s), wrack. **3** see WRECK *n.* 1.

wrecker /rékər/ *n.* **1** a person or thing that wrecks or destroys. **2** esp. *hist.* a person on the shore who tries to bring about a shipwreck in order to plunder or profit by the wreckage. **3** a person employed in demolition, or in recovering a wrecked ship or its contents. **4** a person who breaks up damaged vehicles for spares and scrap. **5** a vehicle or train used in recovering a damaged one.

wren /ren/ *n.* any small, usu. brown, short-winged songbird of the family Troglodytidae, esp. *Troglodytes troglodytes* of Europe, having an erect tail. [OE *wrenna*, rel. to OHG *wrendo, wrendilo*, Icel. *rindill*]

wrench /rench/ *n. & v.* ● *n.* **1** a violent twist or oblique pull or act of tearing off. **2** an adjustable tool for gripping and turning nuts, etc. **3** an instance of painful uprooting or parting (*leaving home was a great wrench*). **4** *Physics* a combination of a couple with the force along its axis. ● *v.tr.* **1 a** twist or pull violently around or sideways. **b** injure (a limb, etc.) by undue straining; sprain. **2** (often foll. by *off, away,* etc.) pull off with a wrench. **3** seize or take forcibly. **4** distort (facts) to suit a theory, etc. [(earlier as verb:) OE *wrencan* twist]

■ *n.* **1** twist, jerk, pull, tug, rip, *colloq.* yank. **2** monkey wrench, *Brit.* spanner. ● *v.* **1 a** twist, jerk, force, pull, tug, tear, wring, rip, *colloq.* yank. **b** strain, sprain, overstrain, rack, esp. *Brit.* rick. **3** extract, wrest, wring, force, prize, pry. **4** distort, twist, pervert, slant, warp.

wrest /rest/ *v. & n.* ● *v.tr.* **1** force or wrench away from a person's grasp. **2** (foll. by *from*) obtain by effort or with difficulty. **3** distort into accordance with one's interests or views (*wrest the law to suit themselves*). ● *n. archaic* a key for tuning a harp or piano, etc. □ **wrest block** the part of a piano or harpsichord holding the wrest pins. **wrest pin** each of the pins to which the strings of a piano or harpsichord are attached. [OE *wrǣstan* f. Gmc, rel. to WRIST]

■ *v.* **1** see WRENCH *v.* 1a, 3, SNATCH *v.* 1, 3. **2** see EXTRACT *v.* 2.

wrestle /résəl/ *n. & v.* ● *n.* **1** a contest in which two opponents grapple and try to throw each other to the ground, esp. as an athletic sport under a code of rules. **2** a hard struggle. ● *v.* **1** *intr.* (often foll. by *with*) take part in a wrestle. **2** *tr.* fight (a person) in a wrestle (*wrestled his opponent to the ground*). **3** *intr.* (foll. by *with, against*) struggle; contend. **b** (foll. by *with*) do one's utmost to deal with (a task, difficulty, etc.). **4** *tr.* move with efforts as if wrestling. □□ **wrestler** *n.* **wrestling** *n.* [OE (unrecorded) *wrǣstlian*: cf. MLG *wrostelen*, OE *wraxlian*]

■ *n.* **1** see STRUGGLE *n.* 2. **2** fight, battle, tussle, effort, strain, struggle; see also LABOR *n.* 1. ● *v.* **1, 3** battle, fight, contend, tussle, struggle, grapple, strive, do battle.

wretch /rech/ *n.* **1** an unfortunate or pitiable person. **2** (often as a playful term of depreciation) a reprehensible or contemptible person. [OE *wrecca* f. Gmc]

■ **1** unfortunate, miserable creature, down-and-out, *colloq.* poor fellow or chap or beggar, poor devil, sad sack, *sl.* poor bastard or son of a bitch. **2** scoundrel, blackguard, worm, villain, cur, rogue, good-fornothing, knave, scalawag, *archaic* whoreson, *archaic or joc.* varlet, rapscallion, *often joc.* rascal, poet. *or archaic* caitiff, *colloq.* beast, dog, rat, swine, *colloq. or joc.* bounder, *Brit. colloq.* blighter, *sl.* bastard, bum, stinker, louse, scumbag, creep, esp. *Brit. sl.* rotter.

wretched /réchid/ *adj.* (**wretcheder, wretchedest**) **1** unhappy or miserable. **2** of bad quality or no merit; contemptible. **3** unsatisfactory or displeasing. □ **feel wretched 1** be unwell. **2** be much embarrassed. □□ **wretchedly** *adv.* **wretchedness** *n.* [ME, irreg. f. WRETCH + -ED¹: cf. WICKED]

■ **1** unhappy, sad, miserable, woebegone, woeful, dismal, downhearted, heartbroken, brokenhearted, heartsick, dejected, depressed, melancholic, melancholy, mournful, disconsolate, inconsolable, doleful, cheerless, crestfallen, joyless, desolate; pitiable, pathetic, sorry, pitiful, hapless, hopeless, unfortunate. **2** worthless, inferior, shabby, tawdry, trashy, rubbishy, poor, cheap; vile, shameful, scurvy, underhand(ed), treacherous, contemptible, despicable, base, low, mean, paltry, mean-spirited, detestable. **3** unsatisfactory, displeasing, miserable, atrocious, deplorable, unpleasant, disagreeable, *colloq.* awful, dreadful, lousy, terrible, *sl.* rotten; see also BAD *adj.* 1, REPULSIVE.

wriggle /rígəl/ *v. & n.* ● *v.* **1** *intr.* (of a worm, etc.) twist or turn its body with short, writhing movements. **2** *intr.* (of a person or animal) make wriggling motions. **3** *tr. & intr.* (foll. by *along,* etc.) move or go in this way (*wriggled into the corner*; *wriggled his hand into the hole*). **4** *tr.* make (one's way) by wriggling. **5** *intr.* practice evasion. ● *n.* an act of wriggling. □ **wriggle out of** *colloq.* avoid on a contrived pretext. □□ **wriggler** *n.* **wriggly** *adj.* [ME f. MLG *wriggelen* frequent. of *wriggen*]

■ *v.* **1–3** twist, squirm, snake, worm, writhe, slither, crawl; wobble, shake, tremble, quiver, jiggle, fidget, *colloq.* wiggle, waggle. ● *n.* wriggling, writhing, squirm, squirming, slither, slithering, shaking, trembling, quiver, quivering, shimmying, twisting, twist, *colloq.* wiggle, wiggling, waggle, waggling. □ **wriggle out of** get out of, escape, evade, avoid, back out of, weasel out of, *colloq.* duck (out of).

wright /rit/ *n.* a maker or builder (usu. in *comb.*: *playwright*; *shipwright*). [OE *wryhta,* *wyrhta* f. WG: cf. WORK]

wring /ring/ *v. & n.* ● *v.tr.* (*past* and *past part.* **wrung** /rung/) **1 a** squeeze tightly. **b** (often foll. by *out*) squeeze and twist esp. to remove liquid. **2** twist forcibly; break by twisting. **3** distress or torture. **4** extract by squeezing. **5** (foll. by *out,* *from*) obtain by pressure or importunity; extort. ● *n.* an act of wringing; a squeeze. □ **wring a person's hand** clasp it forcibly or press it with emotion. **wring one's hands** clasp them as a gesture of great distress. **wring the neck of** kill (a chicken, etc.) by twisting its neck. [OE *wringan,* rel. to WRONG]

■ *v.* **5** see EXTORT.

wringer /ríngər/ *n.* **1** a device for wringing water from washed clothes, etc. **2** a difficult ordeal (*that exam put me through the wringer*).

wringing /rínging/ *adj.* (in full **wringing wet**) so wet that water can be wrung out.

■ see WET *adj.* 1.

wrinkle /ríngkəl/ *n. & v.* ● *n.* **1** a slight crease or depression in the skin such as is produced by age. **2** a similar mark in another flexible surface. **3** *colloq.* a useful tip or clever expedient. ● *v.* **1** *tr.* make wrinkles in. **2** *intr.* form wrinkles; become marked with wrinkles. [orig. repr. OE *gewrinclod* sinuous]

■ *n.* **1** crow's-foot, dimple, crease, fold, line, furrow, crinkle, depression, corrugation, pucker, ridge. **2** crease, fold, line, furrow, crinkle, depression, corrugation, pucker, ridge. **3** dodge, device, ruse, scheme, tip, trick, expedient, idea, plan, plot, stunt, way, approach, technique, method, *colloq.* gimmick, ploy. ● *v.* **1** crease, fold, line, furrow, crinkle, corrugate, pucker, gather, ruck (up), crimp, screw up, rumple, crumple. **2** crease, fold, furrow, crinkle, pucker, ruck up, rumple, crumple.

wrinkly /ríngklee/ *adj. & n.* ● *adj.* (**wrinklier, wrinkliest**) having many wrinkles. ● *n.* (also **wrinklie**) (*pl.* **-ies**) *sl. offens.* an old or middle-aged person.

wrist /rist/ *n.* **1** the part connecting the hand with the forearm. **2** the corresponding part in an animal. **3** the part of a garment covering the wrist. **4 a** (in full **wrist-work**) the act or practice of working the hand without moving the arm. **b** the effect got in fencing, ball games, sleight of hand, etc., by this. **5** (in full **wrist pin**) *Mech.* a stud projecting from

a crank, etc., as an attachment for a connecting rod. □ **wrist-drop** the inability to extend the hand through paralysis of the forearm muscles. [OE f. Gmc, prob. f. a root rel. to WRITHE]

wristband /rístband / *n.* a band forming or concealing the end of a shirt sleeve; a cuff.

wristlet /rístlit / *n.* a band or ring worn on the wrist to strengthen or guard it or as an ornament, bracelet, handcuff, etc.

wristwatch /rístwoch / *n.* a small watch worn on a strap around the wrist.

wristy /rístee/ *adj.* (esp. of a shot in tennis, etc.) involving or characterized by movement of the wrist.

writ[1] /rit/ *n.* **1** a form of written command in the name of a sovereign, court, government, etc., to act or abstain from acting in some way. **2** (in the UK) a Crown document summoning a peer to Parliament or ordering the election of a member or members of Parliament. □ **serve a writ on** deliver a writ to (a person). [OE (as WRITE)]

■ see WARRANT *n.* 2.

writ[2] /rit/ *archaic past part.* of WRITE. □ **writ large** in magnified or emphasized form.

write /rit/ *v.* (*past* **wrote** /rōt/; *past part.* **written** /rít'n/) **1** *intr.* mark paper or some other surface by means of a pen, pencil, etc., with symbols, letters, or words. **2** *tr.* form or mark (such symbols, etc.). **3** *tr.* form or mark the symbols that represent or constitute (a word or sentence, or a document, etc.). **4** *tr.* fill or complete (a form, check, etc.) with writing. **5** *tr.* put (data) into a computer store. **6** *tr.* (esp. in *passive*) indicate (a quality or condition) by one's or its appearance (*guilt was written on his face*). **7** *tr.* compose (a text, article, novel, etc.) for written or printed reproduction or publication; put into literary, etc., form and set down in writing. **8** *intr.* be engaged in composing a text, article, etc. (*writes for the local newspaper*). **9** *intr.* (foll. by *to*) write and send a letter (to a recipient). **10** *tr. colloq.* write and send a letter to (a person) (*wrote him last week*). **11** *tr.* convey (news, information, etc.) by letter (*wrote that they would arrive next Friday*). **12** *tr.* state in written or printed form (*it is written that*). **13** *tr.* cause to be recorded. **14** *tr.* underwrite (an insurance policy). **15** *tr.* (foll. by *into, out of*) include or exclude (a character or episode) in a story by suitable changes of the text. **16** *tr. archaic* describe in writing. □ **nothing to write home about** *colloq.* of little interest or value. **write down 1** record or take note of in writing. **2** write as if for those considered inferior. **3** disparage in writing. **write-down** a reduction of the book value of (an asset, etc.). **write in 1** send a suggestion, query, etc., in writing to an organization, esp. a broadcasting station. **2** add (an extra name) on a list of candidates when voting. **write-in** *n.* an instance of writing in (see *write in* 2). **write off 1** write and send a letter. **2** cancel the record of (a bad debt, etc.); acknowledge the loss of or failure to recover (an asset). **3** damage (a vehicle, etc.) so badly that it cannot be repaired. **4** compose with facility. **5** dismiss as insignificant. **write-off** *n.* a thing written off, esp. a vehicle too badly damaged to be repaired. **write out 1** write in full or in finished form. **2** exhaust (oneself) by writing (*have written myself out*). **write up 1** write a full account of. **2** praise in writing. **3** make a report (of a person) esp. to cite a violation of rules, etc. **write-up** *n. colloq.* a written or published account; a review. □□ **writable** *adj.* [OE *wrītan* scratch, score, write, f. Gmc: orig. used of symbols inscribed with sharp tools on stone or wood]

■ **2** inscribe, pen, pencil, scribble, scrawl. **3, 4** pen, scribble, get off, dash off; inscribe, make out, draw up, draft, *formal or joc.* indite. **5** input, load. **7** compose, create, make up, compile, *disp.* author. **9** (*write to*) correspond with, send a letter *or* note *or* postcard *or* postal card to, communicate with. **10** see sense 9 above. □ **nothing to write home about** see UNDISTINGUISHED. **write down 1** register, list, catalog, note, make a note *or* notation of, record, transcribe, document, chronicle, report, set *or* jot *or* take down, note, put in writing, put in black and white. **3** decry, disparage, put down, minimize, make little of, play down, detract, belittle, *formal* derogate. **write off 2** delete, cancel, disregard, ignore, forgive, forget (about), annul, eradicate, erase. **write-up** see REPORT *n.* 2.

writer /rī́tər/ *n.* **1** a person who writes or has written something. **2** a person who writes books; an author. **3** *Brit.* a clerk, esp. in the navy or in government offices. **4** *Brit.* a scribe. □ **writer's block** (of a writer) a temporary inability to proceed with the composition of a novel, play, etc. **writer's cramp** a muscular spasm due to excessive writing. [OE *wrītere* (as WRITE)]

■ **1** author, wordsmith, hack, journalist, newsman, reporter, correspondent, (gossip) columnist, ghost writer, penny-a-liner, *colloq.* stringer, scribe, *colloq. derog.* pen pusher, pencil pusher, *often derog.* scribbler, *joc.* member of the fourth estate. **2** author, novelist, litterateur, man of letters, penman; essayist, poet, dramatist. **3, 4** scribe, copyist, scrivener, clerk, amanuensis, secretary.

writhe /rīth/ *v.* & *n.* ● *v.* **1** *intr.* twist or roll oneself about in or as if in acute pain. **2** *intr.* suffer severe mental discomfort or embarrassment (*writhed with shame*; *writhed at the thought of it*). **3** *tr.* twist (one's body, etc.) about. ● *n.* an act of writhing. [OE *wrīthan*, rel. to WREATHE]

■ *v.* **1, 3** wriggle, worm, squirm, wiggle, twist, flounder, fidget, shift. **2** see SQUIRM *v.* 2, SWEAT *v.* 2.

writing /rī́ting/ *n.* **1** a group or sequence of letters or symbols. **2** = HANDWRITING. **3** the art or profession of literary composition. **4** (usu. in *pl.*) a piece of literary work done; a book, article, etc. **5** (**Writings**) the Hagiographa. □ **in writing** in written form. **writing desk** a desk for writing at, esp. with compartments for papers, etc. **the writing on the wall** an ominously significant event, etc. (see Dan. 5:5, 25-8). **writing pad** a pad (see PAD¹ *n.* 2) of paper for writing on. **writing paper** paper for writing (esp. letters) on.

■ **1** notation, letters, characters, symbols, hieroglyphs, runes. **2** handwriting, longhand, penmanship, printing, script, calligraphy, chirography, *derog.* scrawl, scribble, *sl.* fist. **3** literature, belles lettres, letters, creative writing. **4** (literary) work(s) *or* text(s), composition(s), publication(s); prose, poetry, nonfiction, fiction; book, article, piece, critique, criticism, review, editorial, column, exposé, essay, poem, novel, novelette, drama, play, document, letter, correspondence, leading article, leader.

written *past part.* of WRITE.

wrong /rawng, rong/ *adj., adv., n.,* & *v.* ● *adj.* **1** mistaken; not true; in error (*gave a wrong answer*; *we were wrong to think that*). **2** unsuitable; less or least desirable (*the wrong road*; *a wrong decision*). **3** contrary to law or morality (*it is wrong to steal*). **4** amiss; out of order; in or into a bad or abnormal condition (*something wrong with my heart*; *my watch has gone wrong*). ● *adv.* (usually placed last) in a wrong manner or direction; with an incorrect result (*guessed wrong*; *told them wrong*). ● *n.* **1** what is morally wrong; a wrong action. **2** injustice; unjust action or treatment (*suffer wrong*). ● *v.tr.* **1** treat unjustly; do wrong to. **2** mistakenly attribute bad motives to; discredit. □ **do wrong** commit sin; transgress; offend. **do wrong to** malign or mistreat (a person). **get in wrong with** incur the dislike or disapproval of (a person). **get on the wrong side of** fall into disfavor with. **get wrong 1** misunderstand (a person, statement, etc.). **2** obtain an incorrect answer to. **get** (or **get hold of**) **the wrong end of the stick** misunderstand completely. **go down the wrong way** (of food) enter the windpipe instead of the esophagus. **go wrong 1** take the wrong path. **2** stop functioning properly. **3** depart from virtuous or suitable behavior. **in the wrong** responsible for a quarrel, mistake, or offense. **on the wrong side of 1** out of favor with (a person). **2** somewhat more than (a stated age). **wrong side** the worse or undesired or unusable side of something, esp. fabric. **wrong side out** inside out. **wrong way around** (or **round**) in the opposite or reverse of the normal or desirable

orientation or sequence, etc. □□ **wronger** *n.* **wrongly** *adv.* **wrongness** *n.* [OE *wrang* f. ON *rangr* awry, unjust, rel. to WRING]

■ *adj.* **1** mistaken, in error, erroneous, incorrect, inaccurate, imprecise, inexact, fallacious, untrue, askew, false, wide of the mark, *colloq.* off base, off (the) target, off the beam, out in left field. **2** incorrect, improper, unsuitable, inappropriate, inapt, unfitting, unacceptable, undesirable, incongruous, out of place; ill-considered, wrongheaded, imprudent, misguided, inexpedient, impolitic, injudicious, infelicitous. **3** improper, unjust, unfair, unethical, terrible, foul, awful, bad, immoral, sinful, evil, iniquitous, villainous, wicked, vile, diabolic(al), infernal, fiendish, corrupt, dishonest, reprehensible, abominable, dreadful, dishonorable, blameworthy, shameful, disgraceful, criminal, felonious, illegal, illicit, unlawful, illegitimate, indecorous, unseemly, unbecoming, out of order, out of line, *archaic* naughty, *colloq.* crooked, esp. *Brit. sl.* bent. **4** out of order, not working, faulty, abnormal, awry, amiss, defective, imperfect, unsound, flawed, deficient, *colloq.* out of sync. ● *adv.* awry, imperfectly, incorrectly, improperly, inappropriately, amiss, badly, wrongly. ● *n.* **1** see SIN¹ *n.* 1. **2** see GRIEVANCE. ● *v.* **1** abuse, mistreat, injure, misuse, maltreat, ill-use, ill-treat, impose upon, take advantage of, harm, damage, oppress. **2** discredit, asperse, malign, vilify, (be)smirch, (be)smear, sully, calumniate, slander, libel, dishonor. □ **do wrong** see TRANSGRESS. **do wrong to** see *ill-treat*. **get wrong 1** see MISUNDERSTAND. **get** (or **get hold of**) **the wrong end of the stick** see MISUNDERSTAND. **go wrong 2** fail, malfunction, break down, miscarry, backfire, fall through, come to grief, *colloq.* bust, conk out *sl.* flop, go kaput. **3** go astray, falter, fail, lapse, err, fall from grace, go to the bad, deteriorate, go downhill, backslide, regress, retrogress, *sl.* go to the dogs. **in the wrong** see *at fault* (FAULT). **wrong side** see REVERSE *n.* 5. **wrong side out** see *inside out.* □□ **wrongly** see ILL *adv.* 1.

wrongdoer /ráwngdŏŏər, róng-/ *n.* a person who behaves immorally or illegally. □□ **wrongdoing** *n.*

■ see *transgressor* (TRANSGRESS). □□ **wrongdoing** see *transgression* (TRANSGRESS).

wrongful /ráwngfŏŏl, róng-/ *adj.* **1** characterized by unfairness or injustice. **2** contrary to law. **3** (of a person) not entitled to the position, etc., occupied. □□ **wrongfully** *adv.* **wrongfulness** *n.*

■ **1** see GRIEVOUS 2, 3. **2** see ILLEGAL 2. □□ **wrongfully** see ILL *adv.* 1. **wrongfulness** see SIN¹ *n.* 1.

wrongheaded /ráwngheded, róng-/ *adj.* perverse and obstinate. □□ **wrongheadedly** *adv.* **wrongheadedness** *n.*

■ see PERVERSE 2,3.

wrote *past* of WRITE.

wroth /rawth, roth, rōth/ *predic.adj. archaic* angry. [OE *wrāth* f. Gmc]

■ see ANGRY 1.

wrought /rawt/ *archaic past* and *past part.* of WORK. ● *adj.* (of metals) beaten out or shaped by hammering. □ **wrought iron** a tough malleable form of iron suitable for forging or rolling, not cast.

wrung *past* and *past part.* of WRING.

wry /rī/ *adj.* (**wryer, wryest** or **wrier, wriest**) **1** distorted or turned to one side. **2** (of a face or smile, etc.) contorted in disgust, disappointment, or mockery. **3** (of humor) dry and mocking. □□ **wryly** *adv.* **wryness** *n.* [*wry* (v.) f. OE *wrīgian* tend, incline, in ME deviate, swerve, contort]

■ **1** distorted, contorted, twisted, lopsided, deformed, crooked, one-sided, askew, awry, bent, tilted, off-

/.../ **pronunciation**	● **part of speech**
□ **phrases, idioms, and compounds**	
□□ **derivatives**	■ **synonym section**
cross-references appear in SMALL CAPITALS or *italics*	

center. **2** contorted, distorted, twisted. **3** dry, droll, witty, sardonic, sarcastic, ironic(al), mocking, amusing; perverse, fey.

wryneck /rínek/ *n.* **1** = TORTICOLLIS. **2** any bird of the genus *Jynx* of the woodpecker family, able to turn its head over its shoulder.

WSW *abbr.* west-southwest.

wt. *abbr.* weight.

Wu /woō/ *n.* a dialect of Chinese spoken in the Kiangsu and Chekiang Provinces. [Chin.]

wunderkind /vŏōndərkind/ *n. colloq.* a person who achieves great success while relatively young. [G f. *Wunder* wonder + *Kind* child]

wurst /wərst, woōrst/ *n.* German or Austrian sausage. [G]

wuss /woōs/ *n. colloq.* a person seen as a coward or weakling. □□ **wussy** *adj.*

WV *abbr.* West Virginia (in official postal use).

W.Va. *abbr.* West Virginia.

WW *abbr.* World War (I, II).

WY *abbr.* Wyoming (in official postal use).

wych- /wich/ *comb. form* (also **wich-**, **witch-**) in names of trees with pliant branches. **wych elm** a species of European elm, *Ulmus glabra*. **wych hazel 1** var. of *witch hazel*. **2** = *wych elm*. [OE *wic(e)* app. f. a Gmc root meaning 'bend': rel. to WEAK]

wyn var. of WYNN.

wynd /wind/ *n. Sc.* a narrow street or alley. [ME, app. f. the stem of WIND²]

wynn /win/ *n.* (also **wyn** or **wen** /wen/) a runic letter in Old and Middle English, later replaced by *w*. [OE, var. of *wyn* joy (see WINSOME), used because it begins with this letter: cf. THORN 3]

Wyo. *abbr.* Wyoming.

WYSIWYG /wízeewig/ *adj.* (also **wysiwyg**) *Computing* denoting the representation of text onscreen in a form exactly corresponding to its appearance on a printout. [acronym of *what you see is what you get*]

wyvern /wívərn/ *n.* (also **wivern**) *Heraldry* a winged two-legged dragon with a barbed tail. [ME *wyver* f. OF *wivre*, *guivre* f. L *vipera*: for -n cf. BITTERN]

X¹ /eks/ *n.* (also **x**) (*pl.* **Xs** or **X's**) **1** the twenty-fourth letter of the alphabet. **2** (as a Roman numeral) ten. **3** (usu. **x**) *Algebra* the first unknown quantity. **4** *Geom.* the first coordinate. **5** an unknown or unspecified number or person, etc. **6** a cross-shaped symbol esp. used to indicate position (*X marks the spot*) or incorrectness or to symbolize a kiss or a vote, or as the signature of a person who cannot write.

X² *symb.* = *X-rated.* □ **X-rated** (of motion pictures, etc.) classified as suitable for adults only.

■ see BLUE¹ *adj.* 3.

-x /z/ *suffix* forming the plural of many nouns ending in *-u* taken from French (*beaux; tableaux*). [F]

xanthate /zánthayt/ *n.* any salt or ester of xanthic acid.

xanthic /zánthik/ *adj.* yellowish. □ **xanthic acid** any colorless unstable acid containing the -OCS₂H group. [Gk *xanthos* yellow]

Xanthippe /zanthípee, -típ-/ *n.* (also **Xantippe** /-típee/) a shrewish or ill-tempered woman or wife. [name of Socrates' wife]

■ see SHREW 2.

xanthoma /zanthṓmə/ *n.* (*pl.* **xanthomas** or **xanthomata** /-mətə/) *Med.* **1** a skin disease characterized by irregular yellow patches. **2** such a patch. [as XANTHIC + -OMA]

xanthophyll /zánthəfil/ *n.* any of various oxygen-containing carotenoids associated with chlorophyll, some of which cause the yellow color of leaves in the autumn. [as XANTHIC + Gk *phullon* leaf]

X chromosome /éks krṓməsōm/ *n.* a sex chromosome of which the number in female cells is twice that in male cells. [*X* as an arbitrary label + CHROMOSOME]

x.d. *abbr.* ex dividend.

Xe *symb. Chem.* the element xenon.

xebec /zéebek/ *n.* (also **zebec, zebeck**) a small, three-masted Mediterranean vessel with lateen and usu. some square sails. [alt. (after Sp. *xabeque*) of F *chebec* f. It. *sciabecco* f. Arab. *šabāk*]

xeno- /zénō, zée-/ *comb. form* **1 a** foreign. **b** a foreigner. **2** other. [Gk *xenos* strange, foreign, stranger]

xenogamy /zənógəmee/ *n. Bot.* cross-fertilization. □□ **xenogamous** *adj.*

xenolith /zénəlith, zéenə-/ *n. Geol.* an inclusion within an igneous rock mass, usu. derived from the immediately surrounding rock.

xenon /zénon, zée-/ *n. Chem.* a heavy, colorless, odorless inert gaseous element occurring in traces in the atmosphere and used in fluorescent lamps. ¶ Symb.: **Xe.** [Gk, neut. of *xenos* strange]

xenophobe /zénəfōb, zéenə-/ *n.* a person given to xenophobia.

xenophobia /zénəfṓbeeə, zéenə-/ *n.* a deep dislike of foreigners. □□ **xenophobic** *adj.*

■ see *intolerance* (INTOLERANT). □□ **xenophobic** see INHOSPITABLE 1.

xeranthemum /zeeránthiməm/ *n.* a composite plant of the genus *Xeranthemum,* with dry everlasting composite flowers. [mod.L f. Gk *xēros* dry + *anthemon* flower]

xeric /zérik, zée-/ *adj.* ECOL. having or characterized by dry conditions. [as XERO- + -IC]

xero- /zéerō/ *comb. form* dry. [Gk *xēros* dry]

xeroderma /zeerədɔ́rmə/ *n.* any of various diseases characterized by extreme dryness of the skin, esp. ichthyosis. [mod.L (as XERO-, Gk *derma* skin)]

xerography /zeerógrəfee/ *n.* a dry copying process in which black or colored powder adheres to parts of a surface remaining electrically charged after exposure of the surface to light from an image of the document to be copied. □□ **xerographic** /-rəgráfik/ *adj.* **xerographically** *adv.*

xerophilous /zeerófiləs/ *adj.* (of a plant) adapted to extremely dry conditions.

xerophyte /zéerəfit/ *n.* (also **xerophile** /-fil/) a plant able to grow in very dry conditions, e.g., in a desert.

Xerox /zéeroks/ *n. & v.* ● *n. propr.* **1** a machine for copying by xerography. **2** a copy made using this machine. ● *v.tr.* (**xerox**) reproduce by this process. [invented f. XEROGRAPHY]

■ *n.* **2** see DUPLICATE *n.* ● *v.* see DUPLICATE *v.*

Xhosa /kṓsə, -zə, káw-/ *n. & adj.* ● *n.* **1** (*pl.* same or **Xhosas**) a member of a Bantu people of Cape Province, South Africa. **2** the Bantu language of this people, similar to Zulu. ● *adj.* of or relating to this people or language. [native name]

xi /zi, sī, ksee/ *n.* the fourteenth letter of the Greek alphabet (Ξ, ξ). [Gk]

-xion /kshən/ *suffix* forming nouns (see -ION) from Latin participial stems ending in *-x-* (*fluxion*).

xiphisternum /zifistɔ́rnəm/ *n. Anat.* = *xiphoid process.* [as XIPHOID + STERNUM]

xiphoid /zifoyd/ *adj. Biol.* sword-shaped. □ **xiphoid process** the cartilaginous process at the lower end of the sternum. [Gk *xiphoeidēs* f. *xiphos* sword]

Xmas /krísməs, éksməs/ *n. colloq.* = CHRISTMAS. [abbr., with X for the initial chi of Gk *Khristos* Christ]

xoanon /zṓənon/ *n.* (*pl.* **xoana** /-nə/) *Gk Antiq.* a primitive usu. wooden image of a deity supposed to have fallen from heaven. [Gk f. *xeō* carve]

X ray /éksray/ *n. & v.* (also **x-ray**) ● *n.* **1** (in *pl.*) electromagnetic radiation of short wavelength, able to pass through opaque bodies. **2** an image made by the effect of X rays on a photographic plate, esp. showing the position of bones, etc., by their greater absorption of the rays. □ **X-ray astronomy** the branch of astronomy concerned with the X-ray emissions of celestial bodies. **X-ray crystallography** the study of crystals and their structure by means of the diffraction of X rays by the regularly spaced atoms of a crystalline material. **X-ray tube** a device for generating X rays by accelerating electrons to high energies and causing them to strike a metal target from which the X rays are emitted. **X-ray** *adj.* [transl. of G *x-Strahlen* (pl.) f. *Strahl* ray, so called because when discovered in 1895 the nature of the rays was unknown]

x-ray /éksray/ *v.tr.* (also **X-ray**) photograph, examine, or treat with X rays.

xylem /zíləm/ *n. Bot.* woody tissue (cf. PHLOEM). [Gk *xulon* wood]

xylene /zíleen/ *n. Chem.* one of three isomeric hydrocarbons

---

/.../ **pronunciation**	● **part of speech**
□ **phrases, idioms, and compounds**	
□□ **derivatives**	■ **synonym section**
cross-references appear in SMALL CAPITALS or *italics*	

1779

formed from benzene by the substitution of two methyl groups, obtained from wood, etc. [formed as XYLEM + -ENE]

xylo- /zílō/ *comb. form* wood. [Gk *xulon* wood]

xylocarp /zíləkaarp/ *n.* a hard woody fruit. □□ **xylocarpous** *adj.*

xylograph /zíləgraf/ *n.* a woodcut or wood engraving (esp. an early one).

xylography /zīlógrəfee/ *n.* **1** the (esp. early or primitive) practice of making woodcuts or wood engravings. **2** the use of woodblocks in printing.

xylophagous /zīlófəgəs/ *adj.* (of an insect or mollusk) eating, or boring into, wood.

xylophone /zíləfōn/ *n.* a musical instrument of wooden or metal bars graduated in length and struck with a small wooden hammer or hammers. □□ **xylophonic** /-fónik/ *adj.* **xylophonist** *n.* [Gk *xulon* wood + -PHONE]

xystus /zístəs/ *n.* (*pl.* **xysti** /-tī/) **1** a covered portico used by athletes in ancient Greece for exercise. **2** *Rom. Antiq.* a garden walk or terrace. [L f. Gk *xustos* smooth f. *xuō* scrape]

Yy

Y[1] /wī/ *n.* (also **y**) (*pl.* **Ys** or **Y's**) **1** the twenty-fifth letter of the alphabet. **2** (usu. **y**) *Algebra* the second unknown quantity. **3** *Geom.* the second coordinate. **4 a** a Y-shaped thing, esp. an arrangement of lines, piping, roads, etc. **b** a forked clamp or support.

Y[2] *abbr.* (also **Y.**) **1** yen. **2** yeomanry. **3** = YMCA, YWCA.

Y[3] *symb. Chem.* the element yttrium.

y. *abbr.* year(s).

y- /ee/ *prefix archaic* forming past participles, collective nouns, etc. (*yclept*). [OE ge- f. Gmc]

-y[1] /ee/ *suffix* forming adjectives: **1** from nouns and adjectives, meaning: **a** full of; having the quality of (*messy*; *icy*; *horsy*). **b** addicted to (*boozy*). **2** from verbs, meaning 'inclined to,' 'apt to' (*runny*; *sticky*). [from or after OE -ig f. Gmc]

-y[2] /ee/ *suffix* (also **-ey, -ie**) forming diminutive nouns, pet names, etc. (*granny*; *Sally*; *nightie*; *Mickey*). [ME (orig. Sc.)]

-y[3] /ee/ *suffix* forming nouns denoting: **1** state, condition, or quality (*courtesy*; *orthodoxy*; *modesty*). **2** an action or its result (*colloquy*; *remedy*; *subsidy*). [from or after F -ie f. L -ia, -ium, Gk -eia, -ia: cf. -ACY, -ERY, -GRAPHY, and others]

yabber /yábər/ *v.* & *n. Austral.* & *NZ colloq.* ● *v.intr.* & *tr.* talk. ● *n.* talk; conversation; language. [perh. f. an Aboriginal language]

yabby /yábee/ *n.* (*pl.* **-ies**) *Austral.* **1** a small freshwater crayfish, esp. of the genus *Cherax.* **2** a marine prawn, *Callianassa australiensis*, often used as bait. [Aboriginal]

yacht /yot/ *n.* & *v.* ● *n.* **1** a light sailing vessel, esp. equipped for racing. **2** a larger usu. power-driven vessel equipped for cruising. ● *v.intr.* race or cruise in a yacht. □ **yacht club** a club for yachtsmen and yachtswomen organized to promote yachting and boating. □□ **yachting** *n.* [early mod.Du. *jaghte* = *jaghtschip* fast pirate ship f. *jag(h)t* chase f. *jagen* to hunt + *schip* SHIP]
■ *n.* **1** see BOAT *n.* ● *v.* see CRUISE *v.*

yachtsman /yótsmən/ *n.* (*pl.* **-men**; *fem.* **yachtswoman**, *pl.* **-women**) a person who sails yachts.

yack /yak/ *n.* & *v.* (also **yackety-yack** /yákəteeyák/, **yak**) *sl. derog.* ● *n.* trivial or unduly persistent conversation. ● *v.intr.* engage in this. [imit.]
■ *n.* see JABBER *n.* ● *v.* see JABBER *v.* 1.

yager var. of JAEGER.

yah /yaa/ *int.* expressing derision or defiance. [imit.]

yahoo /yaáhōō/ *n.* a coarse, bestial person. [name of an imaginary race of brutish creatures in Swift's *Gulliver's Travels* (1726)]
■ see BARBARIAN *n.* 1.

Yahweh /yaáway, -we/ *n.* (also **Yahveh** /-vay, -ve/) the Hebrew name of God in the Old Testament. [Heb. *YHVH* with added vowels: see JEHOVAH]

Yahwist /yaáwist/ *n.* (also **Yahvist** /-vist/) the postulated author or authors of parts of the Hexateuch in which God is regularly named *Yahweh.*

yak /yak/ *n.* a long-haired, humped Tibetan ox, *Bos grunniens.* [Tibetan *gyag*]

y'all var. of *you-all.*

yam /yam/ *n.* **1 a** any tropical or subtropical climbing plant of the genus *Dioscorea.* **b** the edible starchy tuber of this. **2** a sweet potato. [Port. *inhame* or Sp. *iñame*, of unkn. orig.]

yammer /yámər/ *n.* & *v. colloq.* or *dial.* ● *n.* **1** a lament, wail, or grumble. **2** voluble talk. ● *v.intr.* **1** utter a yammer. **2** talk volubly. □□ **yammerer** *n.* [OE *geōmrian* f. *geōmor* sorrowful]
■ *v.* **1** see MOAN *v.* 2. **2** see YAP *v.* 2.

yang /yang/ *n.* (in Chinese philosophy) the active male principle of the universe (cf. YIN). [Chin.]

Yank /yangk/ *n.* esp. *Brit. colloq.* often *derog.* an inhabitant of the US; an American. [abbr.]

yank /yangk/ *v.* & *n. colloq.* ● *v.tr.* pull with a jerk. ● *n.* a sudden hard pull. [19th c.: orig. unkn.]
■ *v.* & *n.* jerk, jolt, tug, wrench, snatch, hitch.

Yankee /yángkee/ *n. colloq.* **1** often *derog.* = YANK. **2** an inhabitant of New England or one of the northern states. **3** *hist.* a federal Union soldier in the Civil War. **4** *Brit.* a type of bet on four or more horses to win (or be placed) in different races. **5** (*attrib.*) of or as of the Yankees. □ **Yankee Doodle 1** an American tune and song popularized during the American Revolution. **2** = YANKEE. [18th c.: orig. uncert.: perh. f. Du. *Janke* dimin. of *Jan* John attested (17th c.) as a nickname]

yap /yap/ *v.* & *n.* ● *v.intr.* (**yapped, yapping**) **1** bark shrilly or fussily. **2** *colloq.* talk noisily, foolishly, or complainingly. ● *n.* **1** a sound of yapping. **2** *sl.* the mouth. □□ **yapper** *n.* [imit.]
■ *v.* **1** bark, yelp. **2** gabble, babble, blather, chatter, jabber, tattle, prattle, prate, run on, *colloq.* natter, jaw, *colloq. or dial.* yammer, yatter (on), *Brit. colloq.* witter (on). ● *n.* **1** bark, yelp. **2** mouth, *sl.* trap, esp. *Brit. sl.* gob.

yapok /yápok/ *n.* = POSSUM 2. [*Oyapok, Oiapoque*, N. Brazilian river]

yapp /yap/ *n. Brit.* a form of bookbinding with a limp leather cover projecting to fold over the edges of the leaves. [name of a London bookseller *c.*1860, for whom it was first made]

Yarborough /yaárbərō, -burō, -bərə/ *n.* a whist or bridge hand with no card above a 9. [Earl of *Yarborough* (d. 1897), said to have betted against its occurrence]

yard[1] /yaard/ *n.* **1** a unit of linear measure equal to 3 feet (0.9144 meter). **2** this length of material (*a yard and a half of fabric*). **3** a square or cubic yard esp. (in building) of sand, etc. **4** a cylindrical spar tapering to each end slung across a mast for a sail to hang from. **5** (in *pl.*; foll. by *of*) *colloq.* a great length (*yards of spare wallpaper*). □ **by the yard** esp. *Brit.* at great length. **yard goods** = *piece goods.* **yard-of-ale** *Brit.* **1** a deep, slender beer glass, about a yard long and holding two to three pints. **2** the contents of this. [OE *gerd* f. WG]
■ **4** see SPAR[1].

yard[2] /yaard/ *n.* & *v.* ● *n.* **1** a piece of ground esp. attached to a building or used for a particular purpose. **2** the lawn and garden area of a house. ● *v.tr.* put (cattle) into a stockyard. [OE *geard* enclosure, region, f. Gmc: cf. GARDEN]
■ *n.* **1** see ENCLOSURE 2. **2** garden, backyard.

/.../ **pronunciation**	● **part of speech**
□ **phrases, idioms, and compounds**	
□□ **derivatives**	■ **synonym section**
cross-references appear in SMALL CAPITALS or *italics*	

yardage /yaárdij/ *n.* **1** a number of yards of material, etc. **2 a** the use of a stockyard, etc. **b** payment for this.
- ■ **1** see MEASUREMENT 2.

yardarm /yaárdaarm/ *n.* the outer extremity of a ship's yard.

yardbird /yaárdbərd/ *n. sl.* **1** a new military recruit. **2** a convict.

yardman /yaárdmən/ *n.* (*pl.* **-men**) *n.* **1** a person working in a railroad yard or lumberyard. **2** a gardener or a person who does various outdoor jobs.

yardmaster /yaárdmastər/ *n.* the manager of a railroad yard.

yardstick /yaárdstik/ *n.* **1** a standard used for comparison. **2** a measuring rod a yard long, usu. divided into inches, etc.
- ■ **1** measure, benchmark, criterion, standard, norm, gauge, basis, touchstone, scale, exemplar.

yarmulke /yaárməlkə, yaáməl-/ *n.* (also **yarmulka**) a skullcap worn by Jewish men. [Yiddish]

yarn /yaarn/ *n. & v.* ● *n.* **1** any spun thread, esp. for knitting, weaving, rope making, etc. **2** *colloq.* a long or rambling story or discourse. ● *v.intr. colloq.* tell yarns. [OE *gearn*]
- ■ *n.* **1** thread, fiber, strand. **2** tale, story, account, narrative, anecdote; tall tale, fable, fabrication, fiction, cock-and-bull story, *Brit. colloq.* fishing story, *sl.* whopper.

yarrow /yárō/ *n.* any perennial herb of the genus *Achillea*, esp. milfoil. [OE *gearwe*, of unkn. orig.]

yashmak /yaáshmaak, yáshmak/ *n.* a veil concealing the face except the eyes, worn by some Muslim women when in public. [Arab. *yaśmak*, Turk. *yaśmak*]

yataghan /yátəgan/ *n.* a sword without a guard and often with a double-curved blade, used in Muslim countries. [Turk. *yātāgan*]

yatter /yátər/ *v. & n. colloq.* or *dial.* ● *v.intr.* (often foll. by *on*) talk idly or incessantly; chatter. ● *n.* idle talk; incessant chatter. □□ **yattering** *n. & adj.*

yaw /yaw/ *v. & n.* ● *v.intr.* (of a ship or aircraft, etc.) move on the vertical axis; fail to hold a straight course; fall off; go unsteadily (esp. turning from side to side). ● *n.* the yawing of a ship, etc., from its course. [16th c.: orig. unkn.]
- ■ *v.* see TOSS *v.* 2.

yawl /yawl/ *n.* **1** a two-masted, fore-and-aft sailing vessel with the mizzenmast stepped far aft. **2** a small kind of fishing boat. **3** *hist.* a ship's jolly boat with four or six oars. [MLG *jolle* or Du. *jol*, of unkn. orig.: cf. JOLLY²]

yawn /yawn/ *v. & n.* ● *v.* **1** *intr.* (as a reflex) open the mouth wide and inhale esp. when sleepy or bored. **2** *intr.* (of a chasm, etc.) gape; be wide open. **3** *tr.* utter or say with a yawn. ● *n.* **1** an act of yawning. **2** *colloq.* a boring or tedious idea, activity, etc. □□ **yawner** *n.* **yawningly** *adv.* [OE *ginian, geonian*]

yawp /yawp/ *n. & v.* ● *n.* **1** a harsh or hoarse cry. **2** foolish talk. ● *v.intr.* utter these. □□ **yawper** *n.* [ME (imit.)]

yaws /yawz/ *n.pl.* (usu. treated as *sing.*) a contagious tropical skin disease with large red swellings. [17th c.: orig. unkn.]

Yb *symb. Chem.* the element ytterbium.

Y chromosome /wí-krŏməsōm/ *n.* a sex chromosome occurring only in male cells. [*Y* as an arbitrary label + CHROMOSOME]

yclept /iklépt/ *adj. archaic* or *joc.* called (by the name of). [OE *gecleopod* past part. of *cleopian* call f. Gmc]

yd. *abbr.* yard (measure).

yds. *abbr.* yards (measure).

ye¹ /yee/ *pron. archaic pl.* of THOU¹. □ **ye gods!** *joc.* an exclamation of astonishment. [OE *ge* f. Gmc]

ye² /yee/ *adj. pseudo-archaic* = THE (*ye olde tea shoppe*). [var. spelling f. the *y*-shaped letter THORN (representing *th*) in the 14th c.]

yea /yay/ *adv. & n. formal* ● *adv.* **1** yes. **2** indeed (*ready, yea eager*). ● *n.* the word 'yea.' □ **yea and nay** shilly-shally. **yeas and nays** affirmative and negative votes. [OE *gea, ge* f. Gmc]

yeah /yeə/ *adv. colloq.* yes. □ **oh yeah?** expressing incredulity. [casual pronunc. of YES]

yean /yeen/ *v.tr. & intr. archaic* bring forth (a lamb or kid). [perh. f. OE *geēanian* (unrecorded, as Y-, *ēanian* to lamb)]

yeanling /yeénling/ *n. archaic* a young lamb or kid.

year /yeer/ *n.* **1** (also **astronomical year, equinoctial year, natural year, solar year, tropical year**) the time occupied by the earth in one revolution around the sun, 365 days, 5 hours, 48 minutes, and 46 seconds in length (cf. *sidereal year*). **2** (also **calendar year, civil year**) the period of 365 days (**common year**) or 366 days (see *leap year*) from Jan. 1 to Dec. 31, used for reckoning time in ordinary affairs. **3 a** a period of the same length as this starting at any point (*four years ago*). **b** such a period in terms of a particular activity, etc., occupying its duration (*school year; tax year*). **4** (in *pl.*) age or time of life (*young for his years*). **5** (usu. in *pl.*) *colloq.* a very long time (*it took years to get served*). **6 a** a group of students entering college, etc., in the same academic year; a class. □ **in the year of Our Lord** (foll. by the year) in a specified year AD. **of the year** chosen as outstanding in a particular year (*sportsman of the year*). **a year and a day** the period specified in some legal matters to ensure the completion of a full year. **year in, year out** continually over a period of years. **year of grace** the year AD. **year-round** existing, etc., throughout the year. [OE *gē(a)r* f. Gmc]
- ■ **5** (*years*) see AGE *n.* 2a. **6** class, grade, *Brit.* form.

yearbook /yeérbook/ *n.* **1** an annual publication dealing with events or aspects of the (usu. preceding) year. **2** such a publication, usu. produced by a school's graduating class and featuring students, activities, sports, etc.
- ■ annual, annal, almanac.

yearling /yeérling/ *n. & adj.* ● *n.* **1** an animal between one and two years old. **2** a racehorse in the calendar year after the year of foaling. ● *adj.* **1** a year old; having existed or been such for a year (*a yearling heifer*). **2** esp. *Brit.* intended to terminate after one year (*yearling bonds*).

yearlong /yeérlóng/ *adj.* lasting a year or the whole year.

yearly /yeérlee/ *adj. & adv.* ● *adj.* **1** done, produced, or occurring once a year. **2** of or lasting a year. ● *adv.* once a year; from year to year. [OE *gēarlic, -lice* (as YEAR)]
- ■ *adj.* **1** annual, once-a-year. ● *adv.* annually, once a year, per year, per annum, by the year, each year; perennially, every year, year after year, year in (and) year out, regularly.

yearn /yərn/ *v.intr.* **1** (usu. foll. by *for, after*, or *to* + infin.) have a strong emotional longing. **2** (usu. foll. by *to, toward*) be filled with compassion or tenderness. □□ **yearner** *n.* **yearning** *n. & adj.* **yearningly** *adv.* [OE *giernan* f. a Gmc root meaning 'eager']
- ■ **1** long, pine, ache, hanker, itch, hunger, thirst, crave, have a craving, desire, wish, want, fancy, prefer.
- □□ **yearning** (*n.*) see LONGING *n.* (*adj.*) see DESIROUS 2.

yeast /yeest/ *n.* **1** a grayish-yellow fungous substance obtained esp. from fermenting malt liquors and used as a fermenting agent, to raise bread, etc. **2** any of various unicellular fungi in which vegetative reproduction takes place by budding or fission. □□ **yeastless** *adj.* **yeastlike** *adj.* [OE *gist, giest* (unrecorded): cf. MDu. *ghist*, MHG *jist*, ON *jöstr*]

yeasty /yeéstee/ *adj.* (**yeastier, yeastiest**) **1** frothy or tasting like yeast. **2** in a ferment. **3** working like yeast. **4** (of talk, etc.) light and superficial. □□ **yeastily** *adv.* **yeastiness** *n.*

yegg /yeg/ *n. sl.* a traveling burglar or safecracker. [20th c.: perh. a surname]

yell /yel/ *n. & v.* ● *n.* **1** a loud sharp cry of pain, anger, fright, encouragement, delight, etc. **2** a shout. **3** an organized cry, used esp. to support a sports team. **4** *Brit. sl.* an amusing person or thing. ● *v.tr. & intr.* utter with or make a yell. [OE *g(i)ellan* f. Gmc]
- ■ *n.* **1, 2** shout, scream, cry, bellow, bawl, howl, screech, yowl, roar, caterwaul, squall, yelp, *colloq.* holler.

yellow /yélō/ *adj., n., & v.* ● *adj.* **1** of the color between green and orange in the spectrum, of buttercups, lemons, egg yolks, or gold. **2** of the color of faded leaves, ripe wheat, etc. **3** having a yellow skin or complexion. **4** *colloq.* cowardly. **5** (of looks, feelings, etc.) jealous, envious, or suspicious. **6** (of newspapers, etc.) unscrupulously sensational. ● *n.* **1** a yellow color or pigment. **2** yellow clothes or material (*dressed in yellow*). **3 a** a yellow ball, piece, etc., in a game or sport. **b** the player using such pieces. **4** (usu. in *comb.*) a yellow moth or butterfly. **5** (in *pl.*) jaundice of horses, etc. **6** a peach disease with yellowed leaves. ● *v.tr.* & *intr.* make or become yellow. □ **yellow-bellied 1** *colloq.* cowardly. **2** (of a fish, bird, etc.) having yellow underparts. **yellow card** *Soccer* a card shown by the referee to a player being cautioned. **yellow fever** a tropical virus disease with fever and jaundice. **yellow flag 1** a flag displayed by a ship in quarantine. **2** an iridaceous plant, *Iris pseudacorus*, with slender sword-shaped leaves and yellow flowers. **yellow jack 1** = *yellow fever*. **2** = *yellow flag*. **yellow jacket 1** any of various wasps of the family Vespidae with yellow and black bands. **2** *sl.* a capsule of phenobarbital. **yellow metal** brass of 60 parts copper and 40 parts zinc. **Yellow Pages** (or **yellow pages**) a section of a telephone directory on yellow paper and listing business subscribers according to the goods or services they offer. **the yellow peril** *derog.* the political or military threat regarded as emanating from Asian peoples, esp. the Chinese. **yellow spot** the point of acutest vision in the retina. **yellow streak** *colloq.* a trait of cowardice. □□ **yellowish** *adj.* **yellowly** *adv.* **yellowness** *n.* **yellowy** *adj.* [OE *geolu, geolo* f. WG, rel. to GOLD]

■ *adj.* **4** see COWARDLY *adj.* □□ **yellowish** see GOLDEN 2.

yellowback /yélōbak/ *n.* a cheap novel, etc., in a yellow cover.

yellowbelly /yélōbélee/ *n.* **1** *colloq.* a coward. **2** any of various fish with yellow underparts.

yellowhammer /yélōhamər/ *n.* a bunting, *Emberiza citrinella*, of which the male has a yellow head, neck, and breast. [16th c.: orig. of *hammer* uncert.]

yelp /yelp/ *n.* & *v.* ● *n.* a sharp, shrill cry of or as of a dog in pain or excitement. ● *v.intr.* utter a yelp. □□ **yelper** *n.* [OE *gielp(an)* boast (imit.): cf. YAWP]

■ *n.* see HOWL *n.* 1. ● *v.* see HOWL *v.* 1.

yen[1] /yen/ *n.* (*pl.* same) the chief monetary unit of Japan. [Jap. f. Chin. *yuan* round, dollar]

yen[2] /yen/ *n.* & *v. colloq.* ● *n.* a longing or yearning. ● *v.intr.* (**yenned, yenning**) feel a longing. [Chin. dial.]

■ *n.* see LONGING *n.*

yeoman /yṓmən/ *n.* (*pl.* **-men**) **1** esp. *hist.* a man holding and cultivating a small landed estate. **2** *Brit. hist.* a person qualified by possessing free land of an annual value of 40 shillings to serve on juries, vote for the knight of the shire, etc. **3** *Brit.* a member of the yeomanry force. **4** *hist.* a servant in a royal or noble household. **5** *Brit.* (in full **yeoman of signals**) a petty officer in the navy, concerned with visual signaling. **6** in the US Navy, a petty officer performing clerical duties on board ship. □ **yeoman of the guard 1** a member of the British sovereign's bodyguard. **2** (in general use) a warder in the Tower of London. **yeoman** (or **yeoman's**) **service** efficient or useful help in need. [ME *yoman, yeman,* etc., prob. f. YOUNG + MAN]

■ **1** see FARMER.

yeomanly /yṓmənlee/ *adj.* **1** of the rank of yeoman. **2** characteristic of or befitting a yeoman; sturdy; reliable.

■ **2** workmanlike, useful, staunch, courageous, loyal, dedicated, faithful, steadfast, unswerving, unwavering, firm, sturdy, reliable, solid.

yeomanry /yṓmənree/ *n.* (*pl.* **-ies**) **1** a body of yeomen. **2** *Brit. hist.* a volunteer cavalry force raised from the yeoman class (1794–1908).

yep /yep/ *adv.* & *n.* (also **yup** /yup/) *colloq.* = YES. [corrupt.]

-yer /yər/ *suffix* var. of -IER esp. after *w* (*bowyer; lawyer*).

yerba maté /yérbə mátay/ *n.* = MATÉ. [Sp., = herb maté]

yes /yes/ *adv.* & *n.* ● *adv.* **1** equivalent to an affirmative sentence: the answer to your question is affirmative; it is as you say or as I have said; the statement, etc., made is correct; the request or command will be complied with; the negative statement, etc., made is not correct. **2** (in answer to a summons or address) an acknowledgment of one's presence. ● *n.* an utterance of the word *yes.* □ **say yes** grant a request or confirm a statement. **yes? 1** indeed? is that so? **2** what do you want? **yes and no** that is partly true and partly untrue. **yes-man** (*pl.* **-men**) *colloq.* a weakly acquiescent per-

son. [OE *gēse, gīse,* prob. f. *gīa sīe* may it be (*gīa* is unrecorded)]

■ *adv.* **1** *archaic* yea, *archaic* or *dial.* aye. **2** here, present, *colloq.* yeah, *US colloq.* yep. □ **yes-man** toady, sycophant, timeserver, hanger-on, lickspittle, truckler, courtier, spaniel, lapdog, *archaic* toadeater, *colloq.* bootlicker, jackal, *usu. derog.* flunky.

yester- /yéstər/ *comb. form poet.* or *archaic* of yesterday; that is the last past (*yester-eve*). [OE *geostran*]

yesterday /yéstərday/ *adv.* & *n.* ● *adv.* **1** on the day before today. **2** in the recent past. ● *n.* **1** the day before today. **2** the recent past. □ **yesterday morning** (or **afternoon,** etc.) in the morning (or afternoon, etc.) of yesterday. [OE *giestran dæg* (as YESTER-, DAY)]

■ *n.* **2** see PAST *n.* 1.

yesteryear /yéstəryeer/ *n. literary* **1** last year. **2** the recent past.

■ **2** see PAST *n.* 1.

yet /yet/ *adv.* & *conj.* ● *adv.* **1** as late as, or until, now or then (*there is yet time; your best work yet*). **2** (with *neg.* or *interrog.*) so soon as, or by, now or then (*it is not time yet; have you finished yet?*). **3** again; in addition (*more and yet more*). **4** in the remaining time available; before all is over (*I will do it yet*). **5** (foll. by *compar.*) even (*a yet more difficult task*). **6** nevertheless; and in spite of that; but for all that (*it is strange, and yet it is true*). ● *conj.* but at the same time; but nevertheless (*I won, yet what good has it done?*). □ **nor yet** esp. *Brit.* and also not (*won't listen to me nor yet to you*). [OE *gīet(a),* = OFris. *iēta,* of unkn. orig.]

■ *adv.* **1** still, even now, up to this time, up to now, till *or* until now, to this day. **2** as yet, (up) till *or* until now, up to now, so far, hitherto, to the present (time), *formal* thus far. **3, 5** even, still. **4** in the future, in time to come, later, eventually. **6** still, notwithstanding, anyway, anyhow, nonetheless, nevertheless, in spite of *or* despite everything, just *or* all the same, even so, after all, *colloq.* still and all. ● *conj.* still, but.

yeti /yétee/ *n.* = *abominable snowman.* [Tibetan]

yew /yōō/ *n.* **1** any dark-leaved evergreen coniferous tree of the genus *Taxus,* having seeds enclosed in a fleshy red aril, and often planted in landscaped settings. **2** its wood, used formerly as a material for bows and still in cabinetmaking. [OE *īw, ēow* f. Gmc]

Yggdrasil /ígdrəsil/ *n.* (in Scandinavian mythology) an ash tree whose roots and branches join heaven, earth, and hell. [ON *yg(g)drasill* f. *Yggr* Odin + *drasill* horse]

YHA *abbr.* Youth Hostels Association.

Yid /yid/ *n. sl. offens.* a Jew. [back-form. f. YIDDISH]

Yiddish /yídish/ *n.* & *adj.* ● *n.* a vernacular used by Jews in or from central and eastern Europe, orig. a German dialect with words from Hebrew and several modern languages. ● *adj.* of or relating to this language. [G *jüdisch* Jewish]

yield /yeeld/ *v.* & *n.* ● *v.* **1** *tr.* (also *absol.*) produce or return as a fruit, profit, or result (*the land yields crops; the land yields poorly; the investment yields 15%*). **2** *tr.* give up; surrender; concede; comply with a demand for (*yielded the fortress; yielded themselves prisoners*). **3** *intr.* (often foll. by *to*) a surrender; make submission. **b** give consent or change one's course of action in deference to; respond as required to (*yielded to persuasion*). **4** *intr.* (foll. by *to*) be inferior or confess inferiority to (*I yield to none in understanding the problem*). **5** *intr.* (foll. by *to*) give right of way to other traffic. **6** *intr.* allow another the right to speak in a debate, etc. ● *n.* an amount yielded or produced; an output or return. □ **yield point** *Physics* the stress beyond which a material becomes plastic. □□ **yielder** *n.* [OE *g(i)eldan* pay f. Gmc]

■ *v.* **1** produce, bear, supply, bring forth; earn, return, pay, bring in, generate, net. **2** give up, surrender, give over, hand in *or* over, abandon, relinquish, concede,

---

renounce, cede. **3 a** surrender, give up (the fight *or* struggle), give in, knuckle under, submit, cede, cry quits, throw in the towel *or* the sponge, capitulate, succumb, raise the white flag. **b** agree, consent, comply, concede, relent, assent, give way, accede, concur. ● *n.* crop, harvest, production, product; return, output, revenue, takings, gate, earnings, income, proceeds, profit, gain.

yielding /yéelding/ *adj.* **1** compliant, submissive. **2** (of a substance) able to bend; not stiff nor rigid. □□ **yieldingly** *adv.* **yieldingness** *n.*
■ **1** accommodating, docile, submissive, amenable, tractable, compliant, obedient, flexible, acquiescent, agreeable, obliging, manageable, manipulable. **2** pliant, flexible, pliable, soft, plastic, elastic, resilient, supple, springy, bouncy, spongy, rubbery, *archaic* flexile.

yin /yin/ *n.* (in Chinese philosophy) the passive female principle of the universe (cf. YANG). [Chin.]

yip /yip/ *v. & n.* ● *v.intr.* (**yipped, yipping**) = YELP *v.* ● *n.* = YELP *n.* [imit.]

yippee /yíppée/ *int.* expressing delight or excitement. [natural excl.]

yippie /yíppee/ *n.* a hippie associated with political activism, esp. as a member of a radical organization. [Youth International Party]

-yl /əl/ *suffix Chem.* forming nouns denoting a radical (*ethyl*; *hydroxyl*; *phenyl*).

ylang-ylang /éelaangéelaang/ *n.* (also **ilang-ilang**) **1** a Malayan tree, *Cananga odorata*, from the fragrant yellow flowers of which a perfume is distilled. **2** the perfume itself. [Tagalog *álang-ílang*]

YMCA *abbr.* Young Men's Christian Association.

YMHA *abbr.* Young Men's Hebrew Association.

-yne /īn/ *suffix Chem.* forming names of unsaturated compounds containing a triple bond (*ethyne* = acetylene).

yo /yō/ *int.* used to call attention, express affirmation, or greet informally.

yob /yob/ *n. Brit. sl.* a lout or hooligan. □□ **yobbish** *adj.* **yobbishly** *adv.* **yobbishness** *n.* [back sl. for BOY]
■ see HOODLUM 1.

yobbo /yóbō/ *n.* (*pl.* **-os**) *Brit. sl.* = YOB.

yod /yōd, yod/ *n.* **1** the tenth and smallest letter of the Hebrew alphabet. **2** its semivowel sound /y/. [Heb. *yōd* f. *yad* hand]

yodel /yōd'l/ *v. & n.* ● *v.tr. & intr.* sing with melodious inarticulate sounds and frequent changes between falsetto and the normal voice in the manner of the Swiss mountain-dwellers. ● *n.* a yodeling cry. □□ **yodeler** *n.* [G *jodeln*]
■ *v.* see SING *v.* 1, 2.

yoga /yōgə/ *n.* **1** a Hindu system of philosophic meditation and asceticism designed to effect reunion with the universal spirit. **2** = HATHA YOGA. □□ **yogic** /yōgik/ *adj.* [Hind. f. Skr., = union]

yogh /yog/ *n.* a Middle English letter used for certain values of *g* and *y*. [ME]

yogi /yōgee/ *n.* a person proficient in yoga. □□ **yogism** *n.* [Hind. f. YOGA]

yogurt /yōgərt/ *n.* (also **yoghurt**) a semisolid sourish food prepared from milk fermented by added bacteria. [Turk. *yoğurt*]

yo-heave-ho /yóheevhó/ *int. & n.* = heave-ho.

yo-ho /yōhō/ *int.* (also **yo-ho-ho** /yōhōhó/) **1** used to attract attention. **2** = YO-HEAVE-HO. [cf. YO-HEAVE-HO & HO]

yoicks /yoyks/ *int.* a cry used by foxhunters to urge on the hounds. [orig. unkn.: cf. *hyke* call to hounds, HEY¹]

yoke /yōk/ *n. & v.* ● *n.* **1** a wooden crosspiece fastened over the necks of two oxen, etc., and attached to the plow or wagon to be drawn. **2** (*pl.* same or **yokes**) a pair (of oxen, etc.). **3** an object like a yoke in form or function, e.g., a wooden shoulder-piece for carrying a pair of pails, the top section of a dress or skirt, etc., from which the rest hangs. **4** sway, dominion, or servitude, esp. when oppressive. **5** a bond of union, esp. that of marriage. **6** *Rom. Hist.* an uplifted yoke, or an arch of three spears symbolizing it, under which a defeated army was made to march. **7** *archaic* the amount

of land that one yoke of oxen could plow in a day. **8** a crossbar on which a bell swings. **9** the crossbar of a rudder to whose ends ropes are fastened. **10** a bar of soft iron between the poles of an electromagnet. ● *v.* **1** *tr.* put a yoke on. **2** *tr.* couple or unite (a pair). **3** *tr.* (foll. by *to*) link (one thing) to (another). **4** *intr.* match or work together. [OE *geoc* f. Gmc]
■ *n.* **2** see TEAM *n.* 2. **4** see SLAVERY 1. **5** bond, union, tie, link. ● *v.* **2** see COUPLE *v.* 1. **4** see TWIN *v.*

yokel /yōkəl/ *n.* a rustic; a country bumpkin. [perh. f. dial. *yokel* green woodpecker]
■ see RUSTIC *n.*

yolk¹ /yōk/ *n.* **1** the yellow internal part of an egg that nourishes the young before it hatches. **2** *Biol.* the corresponding part of any animal ovum. □ **yolk sac** a membrane enclosing the yolk of an egg. □□ **yolked** *adj.* (also in *comb.*). **yolkless** *adj.* **yolky** *adj.* [OE *geol(o)ca* f. *geolu* YELLOW]

yolk² /yōk/ *n.* = SUINT. [OE *eowoca* (unrecorded)]

Yom Kippur /yawm kípər, keepōōr, yōm, yom/ *n.* = *Day of Atonement* (see ATONEMENT). [Heb.]

yon /yon/ *adj., adv., & pron. literary & dial.* ● *adj. & adv.* yonder. ● *pron.* yonder person or thing. [OE *geon*]

yonder /yóndər/ *adv. & adj.* ● *adv.* over there; at some distance in that direction; in the place indicated by pointing, etc. ● *adj.* situated yonder. [ME: cf. OS *gendra*, Goth. *jaindrē*]

yoni /yōnee/ *n.* a symbol of the female genitals venerated by Hindus, etc. [Skr., = source, womb, female genitals]

yoo-hoo /yōōhōō/ *int.* used to attract a person's attention. [natural excl.]

yore /yawr/ *n. literary* □ **of yore** formerly; in or of old days. [OE *geāra*, *geāre*, etc., adv. forms of uncert. orig.]

Yorkist /yáwrkist/ *n. & adj.* ● *n. hist.* a follower of the House of York or of the White Rose party supporting it in England's Wars of the Roses (cf. LANCASTRIAN). ● *adj.* of or concerning the House of York.

Yorkshire pudding /yáwrksheer/ *n.* a pudding of baked unsweetened batter usu. eaten with roast beef. [*Yorkshire* in the No. of England]

Yorkshire terrier /yáwrksheer/ *n.* a small, long-haired, blue-gray and tan kind of terrier.

Yoruba /yáwrəbə/ *n.* **1** a member of a black African people inhabiting the west coast, esp. Nigeria. **2** the language of this people. [native name]

you /yōō/ *pron.* (*obj.* **you**; *poss.* **your, yours**) **1** used with reference to the person or persons addressed or one such person and one or more associated persons. **2** (as *int.* with a noun) in an exclamatory statement (*you fools!*). **3** (in general statements) one, a person, anyone, or everyone (*it's bad at first, but you get used to it*). □ **you-all** (often **y'all** esp. *Southern US colloq.* you (usu. more than one person). **you and yours** you together with your family, property, etc. **you-know-what** (or **-who**) something or someone unspecified but understood. [OE *ēow* accus. & dative of *gē* YE¹ f. WG: supplanting *ye* because of the more frequent use of the obj. case, and *thou* and *thee* as the more courteous form]

you'd /yōōd/ *contr.* **1** you had. **2** you would.

you'll /yōōl, yōol/ *contr.* you will; you shall.

young /yung/ *adj. & n.* ● *adj.* (**younger** /yúnggər/; **youngest** /yúnggist/) **1** not far advanced in life, development, or existence; not yet old. **2** immature or inexperienced. **3** felt in or characteristic of youth (*young love*; *young ambition*). **4** representing young people (*Young Republicans*; *young America*). **5** distinguishing a son from his father (*young Jones*). **6** (**younger**) **a** distinguishing one person from another of the same name (*the younger Davis*). **b** *Sc.* the heir of a landed commoner. ● *n.* (*collect.*) offspring, esp. of animals before or soon after birth. □ **with young** (of an animal) pregnant. **young blood** see BLOOD. **young fustic** see FUSTIC. **young hopeful** see HOPEFUL. **young idea** the child's mind. **young lady 1** a young, usu. unmarried woman. **2** a girlfriend or sweetheart. **young man 1** a young adult male. **2** a boyfriend or sweetheart. **Young Pretender** Charles Stuart (1720–80), grandson of James II and claimant to the British throne. **young thing** *archaic* or *colloq.* an indulgent term for a young person. **Young Turk 1** a member of a revolutionary party in Turkey in 1908. **2** a young person eager for radical change to the established order. **young turk** *offens.* a violent child or youth. **young 'un** *colloq.* a youngster. □□ **youngish** *adj.* **youngling** *n.* [OE *g(e)ong* f. Gmc]

■ *adj.* **1** youthful, teenage(d), adolescent, prepubescent, pubescent, juvenile, minor, junior, under age; new, developing, undeveloped. **2** immature, callow, green, inexperienced, unfledged, uninitiated, unsophisticated, childlike, innocent, naive. **3** childish, boyish, girlish, puerile, infantile, babyish, sophomoric. ● *n.* offspring, babies, little ones, progeny, litter, brood; children, small fry. □ **young lady 2, young man 2** see LOVE *n.* 4a, 5.

youngster /yúngstər/ *n.* a child or young person.
■ see YOUTH 4.

younker /yúngkər/ *n. archaic* = YOUNGSTER. [MDu. *jonckher* f. *jonc* YOUNG + *hēre* lord: cf. JUNKER]

your /yoŏr, yawr/ *poss.pron.* **1** of or belonging to you or yourself or yourselves (*your house; your own business*). **2** *colloq.* usu. *derog.* much talked of; well known (*none so fallible as your self-styled expert*). [OE *ēower* genit. of *gē* YE¹]

you're /yoŏr, yawr/ *contr.* you are.

yours /yoŏrz, yawrz/ *poss.pron.* **1** the one or ones belonging to or associated with you (*it is yours; yours are over there*). **2** your letter (*yours of the 10th*). **3** introducing a formula ending a letter (*yours ever; yours truly*). □ **of yours** of or belonging to you (*a friend of yours*).

yourself /yoŏrsélf, yawr-/ *pron.* (*pl.* **yourselves** /-sélvz/) **1 a** *emphat. form* of YOU. **b** *refl. form* of YOU. **2** in your normal state of body or mind (*are quite yourself again*). □ **be yourself** act in your normal, unconstrained manner. **how's yourself?** *sl.* how are you? (esp. after answering a similar inquiry).

youth /yoŏth/ *n.* (*pl.* **youths** /yoŏthz/) **1** the state of being young; the period between childhood and adult age. **2** the vigor or enthusiasm, inexperience, or other characteristic of this period. **3** an early stage of development, etc. **4** a young person (esp. male). **5** (*pl.*) young people collectively (*the youth of the country*). □ **youth center** (or **club**) a place or organization provided for young people's leisure activities. **youth hostel** a place where (esp. young) travelers can put up cheaply for the night. **youth hosteler** a user of a youth hostel. [OE *geoguth* f. Gmc, rel. to YOUNG]

■ **1** childhood, boyhood, girlhood, young manhood, young womanhood, prepubescence, pubescence, adolescence, teens, salad days; minority, immaturity. **3** infancy, beginning, start, emergence, dawn. **4** child, youngster, schoolchild, teenager, teen, minor, juvenile, adolescent, *colloq.* young 'un, kid; boy, schoolboy, stripling, young boy *or* man, lad, whippersnapper; *colloq.* (little) shaver; esp. *Sc.* & *No. of Engl. or poet.* lass, *colloq.* lassie. **5** children, youngsters, juveniles, adolescents, young people, young, *colloq.* kids.

youthful /yoŏthfŏol/ *adj.* **1** young, esp. in appearance or manner. **2** having the characteristics of youth (*youthful impatience*). **3** having the freshness or vigor of youth (*a youthful complexion*). □□ **youthfully** *adv.* **youthfulness** *n.*
■ **1** see YOUNG *adj.* 1. **2** see CHILDLIKE

you've /yoŏv, yoŏv/ *contr.* you have.

yowl /yowl/ *n.* & *v.* ● *n.* a loud, wailing cry of or as of a cat or dog in pain or distress. ● *v.intr.* utter a yowl. [imit.]
■ *n.* see HOWL *n.* 1. ● *v.* see HOWL *v.* 1.

yo-yo /yóyō/ *n.* & *v.* ● *n.* (*pl.* **yo-yos**) **1** *propr.* a toy consisting of a pair of disks with a deep groove between them in which string is attached and wound, and which can be spun alternately downward and upward by its weight and momentum as the string unwinds and rewinds. **2** a thing that repeatedly falls and rises again. ● *v.intr.* (**yo-yoes, yo-yoed, yo-yoing**) **1** play with a yo-yo. **2** move up and down; fluctuate. [20th c.: orig. unkn.]
■ *v.* **2** see FLUCTUATE.

yr. *abbr.* **1** year(s). **2** your. **3** younger.
yrs. *abbr.* **1** years. **2** yours.

ytterbium /itárbeeəm/ *n. Chem.* a silvery metallic element of the lanthanide series occurring naturally as various isotopes. ¶ Symb.: **Yb**. [mod.L f. *Ytterby* in Sweden]

yttrium /ítreeəm/ *n. Chem.* a grayish metallic element resembling the lanthanides, occurring naturally in uranium ores and used in making superconductors. ¶ Symb.: **Y**. [formed as YTTERBIUM]

yuan /yoŏ-aán, yö-/ *n.* (*pl.* same) the chief monetary unit of China. [Chin.: see YEN¹]

yucca /yúkə/ *n.* any American white-flowered liliaceous plant of the genus *Yucca*, with swordlike leaves. [Carib]

yuck /yuk/ *int.* & *n. sl.* ● *int.* an expression of strong distaste or disgust. ● *n.* something messy or repellent. [imit.]

yucky /yúkee/ *adj.* (**-ier, -iest**) *sl.* **1** messy; repellent. **2** sickly; sentimental.
■ **1** disgusting, repugnant, repellent, unappetizing, vomit-provoking, sickening, nauseous, nauseating, revolting, foul, mucky, messy, beastly, awful, esp. *Brit. sl.* grotty. **2** see SENTIMENTAL.

Yugoslav /yoŏgəslaav/ *n.* & *adj.* (also **Jugoslav**) *hist.* ● *n.* **1** a native or national of the former republic of Yugoslavia. **2** a person of Yugoslav descent. ● *adj.* of or relating to Yugoslavia or its people. □□ **Yugoslavian** *adj.* & *n.* [Austrian G *Jugoslav* f. Serb. *jugo-* f. *jug* south + SLAV]

yule /yoŏl/ *n.* (in full **yuletide**) *archaic* the Christmas festival. □ **Yule log 1** a large log burned in the hearth on Christmas Eve. **2** a log-shaped cake eaten at Christmas. [OE *gēol(a)*: cf. ON *jól*]

Yuma /yoŏmə/ *n.* **1 a** a N. American people native to Arizona. **b** a member of this people. **2** the language of this people.

yummy /yúmee/ *adj.* (**yummier, yummiest**) *colloq.* tasty; delicious. [YUM-YUM + -Y¹]
■ delicious, mouthwatering, luscious, appetizing, tasty, toothsome, savory, ambrosial, *colloq.* scrumptious, *literary* delectable.

yum-yum /yúmyúm/ *int.* expressing pleasure from eating or the prospect of eating. [natural excl.]

yup var. of YEP.

yuppie /yúpee/ *n.* & *adj.* (also **yuppy**; *pl.* **-ies**) *colloq.*, usu. *derog.* ● *n.* a young, middle-class professional person working in a city. ● *adj.* characteristic of a yuppie or yuppies. [young *urban* professional]

YWCA *abbr.* Young Women's Christian Association.
YWHA *abbr.* Young Women's Hebrew Association.

/.../ **pronunciation** ● **part of speech**
□ **phrases, idioms, and compounds**
□□ **derivatives** ■ **synonym section**
cross-references appear in SMALL CAPITALS or *italics*

Zz

Z /zee/ *n.* (also **z**) (*pl.* **Zs** or **Z's**) **1** the twenty-sixth letter of the alphabet. **2** (usu. **z**) *Algebra* the third unknown quantity. **3** *Geom.* the third coordinate. **4** *Chem.* atomic number.

zabaglione /záabaalyŏnee, -yáwne/ *n.* an Italian dessert of whipped and heated egg yolks, sugar, and (esp. Marsala) wine. [It.]

zaffer /záfər/ *n. Brit.* (**zaffre**) an impure cobalt oxide used as a blue pigment. [It. *zaffera* or F *safre*]

zag /zag/ *n. & v.* ● *n.* a sharp change of direction in a zigzag course. ● *v.intr.* (**zagged, zagging**) move in one of the two directions in a zigzag course. [ZIGZAG]

zany /záynee/ *adj. & n.* ● *adj.* (**zanier, zaniest**) comically idiotic; crazily ridiculous. ● *n.* **1** a buffoon or jester. **2** *hist.* an attendant clown awkwardly mimicking a chief clown in shows; a merry-andrew. □□ **zanily** *adv.* **zaniness** *n.* [F *zani* or It. *zan(n)i*, Venetian form of *Gianni, Giovanni* John]
■ *adj.* clownish, mad, wild, frolicsome, sportive, playful, gay, merry, slapstick, funny, comic(al), amusing, hilarious, absurd, nonsensical, ludicrous, ridiculous, silly, foolish, inane, madcap, idiotic, eccentric, *colloq.* crazy, *sl.* goofy, wacky, loony, crackpot, nutty, kooky. ● *n.* clown, comic, jester, fool, joker, buffoon, wag, comedian, merry-andrew, laughingstock, *sl.* nut, screwball.

zap /zap/ *v., n., & int. sl.* ● *v.* (**zapped, zapping**) **1** *tr.* **a** kill or destroy; deal a sudden blow to. **b** hit forcibly (*zapped the ball over the net*). **c** send an electric current, radiation, etc., through (someone or something). **2** *intr.* move quickly and vigorously. **3** *tr.* overwhelm emotionally. **4** *tr. Computing* erase or change (an item in a program). **5** *intr.* (foll. by *through*) fast-forward a videotape to skip a section. **6** *tr.* heat or cook (food) by microwave. **7** *tr.* change (television channels) by remote control. ● *n.* **1** energy; vigor. **2** a strong emotional effect. ● *int.* expressing the sound or impact of a bullet, ray gun, etc., or any sudden event. [imit.]
■ *v.* **1 a** destroy, kill, slaughter, annihilate, murder, assassinate, liquidate, erase, snuff out, shoot, electrocute, *colloq.* do away with, finish (off), *literary or joc.* slay, *sl.* knock off, bump off, rub out, hit, ice. **b** see HIT *v.* 1a. **2** see RUSH¹ *v.* 1. ● *n.* **1** see VIGOR 1.

zapateado /záapətayaádō, tháapaatayaáthō, saá-/ *n.* (*pl.* **-os**) **1** a flamenco dance with rhythmic stamping of the feet. **2** this technique or action. [Sp. f. *zapato* shoe]

zapper /zápər/ *n. colloq.* a hand-held remote-control device for changing television channels, adjusting volume, etc.

zappy /zápee/ *adj.* (**zappier, zappiest**) *colloq.* **1** lively; energetic. **2** striking.

zarape var. of SERAPE.

Zarathustrian var. of ZOROASTRIAN.

zareba /zəréebə/ *n.* (also **zariba**) **1** a hedged or palisaded enclosure for the protection of a camp or village in the Sudan, etc. **2** a restricting or confining influence. [Arab. *zarība* cattle pen]

zarzuela /zaarzwáylə, thaarthwáylə, saarswáy-/ *n.* a Spanish traditional form of musical comedy. [Sp.: app. f. a placename]

zeal /zeel/ *n.* **1** earnestness or fervor in advancing a cause or rendering service. **2** hearty and persistent endeavor. [ME *zele* f. eccl.L *zelus* f. Gk *zēlos*]
■ **1** see ENTHUSIASM 1. **2** diligence, persistence,

sedulousness, sedulity, tirelessness, indefatigability, perseverance.

zealot /zélət/ *n.* **1** an uncompromising or extreme partisan; a fanatic. **2** (**Zealot**) *hist.* a member of an ancient Jewish sect aiming at a world Jewish theocracy and resisting the Romans until AD 70. □□ **zealotry** *n.* [eccl.L *zelotes* f. Gk *zēlōtēs* (as ZEAL)]
■ **1** fanatic, extremist, partisan, radical, bigot, maniac, crank, militant. □□ **zealotry** fanaticism, extremism, radicalism, bigotry, militantism, militancy; single-mindedness, monomania, fervor, frenzy, hysteria, obsession, obsessiveness.

zealous /zéləs/ *adj.* full of zeal; enthusiastic. □□ **zealously** *adv.* **zealousness** *n.*
■ see ENTHUSIASTIC.

zebec (also **zebeck**) var. of XEBEC.

zebra /zeebrə/ *n.* **1** any of various African quadrupeds, esp. *Equus burchelli*, related to the ass and horse, with black and white stripes. **2** (*attrib.*) with alternate dark and pale stripes. □ **zebra crossing** *Brit.* a striped crosswalk where pedestrians have precedence over vehicles. □□ **zebrine** /-brin/ *adj.* [It. or Port. f. Congolese]

zebu /zeebōō/ *n.* a humped ox, *Bos indicus*, of India, E. Asia, and Africa. [F *zébu*, of unkn. orig.]

Zech. *abbr.* Zechariah (Old Testament).

zed /zed/ *n. Brit.* the letter Z. [F *zède* f. LL *zeta* f. Gk ZETA]

zedoary /zédōeree/ *n.* an aromatic, gingerlike substance made from the rootstock of E. Indian plants of the genus *Curcuma* and used in medicine, perfumery, and dyeing. [ME f. med.L *zedoarium* f. Pers. *zidwār*]

zee /zee/ *n.* the letter Z. [17th c.: var. of ZED]

Zeeman effect /záymən/ *n. Physics* the splitting of the spectrum line into several components by a magnetic field. [P. Zeeman, Du. physicist d. 1943]

zein /zée-in/ *n. Biochem.* the principal protein of corn. [*Zea* the generic name of corn + -IN]

Zeitgeist / tsítgīst, zít-/ *n.* **1** the spirit of the times. **2** the trend of thought and feeling in a period. [G f. *Zeit* time + *Geist* spirit]

Zen /zen/ *n.* a form of Mahayana Buddhism emphasizing the value of meditation and intuition. □□ **Zenist** *n.* (also **Zennist**). [Jap., = meditation]

zenana /zináanə/ *n.* the part of a house for the seclusion of women of high-caste families in India and Iran. [Hind. *zenāna* f. Pers. *zanāna* f. *zan* woman]

Zend /zend/ *n.* an interpretation of the Avesta, each Zend being part of the Zend-Avesta. □ **Zend-Avesta** the Zoroastrian sacred writings of the Avesta or text and Zend or commentary. [Pers. *zand* interpretation]

Zener cards /zéenər/ *n.* a set of 25 cards each with one of five different symbols, used in ESP research. [K. E. *Zener*, Amer. psychologist b. 1903]

zenith /zéenith/ *n.* **1** the part of the celestial sphere directly above an observer (opp. NADIR). **2** the highest point in one's fortunes; a time of great prosperity, etc. □ **zenith distance** an arc intercepted between a celestial body and its zenith; the complement of a body's altitude. [ME f. OF *cenit* or med.L *cenit* ult. f. Arab. *samt* (*ar-ra's*) path (over the head)]
■ **2** meridian, summit, acme, apex, vertex, apogee, high point, top, peak, pinnacle.

zenithal /zeˈenithəl/ adj. of or relating to a zenith. □ **zenithal projection** a projection of part of a globe on to a plane tangential to the center of the part, showing the correct directions of all points from the center.

zeolite /ˈzeˈəlit/ n. each of a number of minerals consisting mainly of hydrous silicates of calcium, sodium, and aluminum, able to act as cation exchangers. □□ **zeolitic** /-ˈlitik/ adj. [Sw. & G zeolit f. Gk zeō boil + -LITE (from their characteristic swelling and fusing under the blowpipe)]

Zeph. abbr. Zephaniah (Old Testament).

zephyr /ˈzéfər/ n. **1** literary a mild gentle wind or breeze. **2** a fine cotton fabric. **3** an athlete's thin gauzy jersey. [F zéphyr or L zephyrus f. Gk zephuros (god of the) west wind]
■ **1** see BREEZE[1] n. 1.

zeppelin /ˈzépəlin/ n. hist. a German large dirigible airship of the early 20th c., orig. for military use. [Count F. von Zeppelin, Ger. airman d. 1917, its first constructor]

zero /ˈzéˈerō/ n. & v. ● n. (pl. -os) **1 a** the figure 0; naught. **b** no quantity or number; nil. **2** a point on the scale of an instrument from which a positive or negative quantity is reckoned. **3** (attrib.) having a value of zero; no; not any (zero population growth). **4** (in full **zero hour**) **a** the hour at which a planned, esp. military, operation is timed to begin. **b** a crucial moment. **5** the lowest point; a nullity or nonentity. ● v.tr. (**-oes, -oed**) **1** adjust (an instrument, etc.) to zero point. **2** set the sights of (a gun) for firing. □ **zero in on 1** take aim at. **2** focus one's attention on. **zero option** a disarmament proposal for the total removal of certain types of weapons on both sides. **zero-sum** (of a game, political situation, etc.) in which whatever is gained by one side is lost by the other so that the net change is always zero. [F zéro or It. zero f. OSp. f. Arab. ṣifr CIPHER]
■ n. **1** nil, null, nothing, naught; cipher, goose egg, Cricket duck, archaic aught, naught, sl. nix, zilch. **5** (rock) bottom, nadir; nobody, nothing, nonentity, nullity, colloq. nebbish. □ **zero in on 2** focus on, pinpoint, fix on, home in on, concentrate on, bring to bear on.

zeroth /ˈzéˈerōth/ adj. immediately preceding what is regarded as 'first' in a series.

zest /zest/ n. **1** piquancy; a stimulating flavor or quality. **2 a** keen enjoyment or interest. **b** (often foll. by for) relish. **c** gusto (entered into it with zest). **3** a scraping of orange or lemon peel as flavoring. □□ **zestful** adj. **zestfully** adv. **zestfulness** n. **zestiness** n. **zesty** adj. (**zestier, zestiest**). [F zeste orange or lemon peel, of unkn. orig.]
■ **1** spice, relish, tang, pepper, ginger, piquancy, pungency, edge, bite, flavor, zip, colloq. zing, sl. pizzazz. **2** eagerness, zestfulness, exuberance, enjoyment, gusto, appetite, interest, enthusiasm, zeal, relish, hunger, thirst. **3** peel, rind. □□ **zestful** see ENERGETIC 1, 2, SPICY 1.

zeta /ˈzáytə, zéˈe-/ n. the sixth letter of the Greek alphabet (Z, ζ). [Gk zēta]

zeugma /ˈzóōgmə/ n. a figure of speech using a verb or adjective with two nouns, to one of which it is strictly applicable while the word appropriate to the other is not used (e.g., with weeping eyes and [sc. grieving] hearts) (cf. SYLLEPSIS). □□ **zeugmatic** /-mátik/ adj. [L f. Gk zeugma -atos f. zeugnumi to yoke, zugon yoke]

zibet /ˈzíbit/ n. **1** an Asian or Indian civet, Viverra zibetha. **2** its scent. [med.L zibethum: see CIVET]

zidovudine /zīˈdōvyōōdeˈen/ n. = AZT. [chem. name azidothymidine]

ziff /zif/ n. Austral. sl. a beard. [20th c.: orig. unkn.]

ziggurat /ˈzígərat/ n. a rectangular stepped tower in ancient Mesopotamia, surmounted by a temple. [Assyr. ziqquratu pinnacle]

zigzag /ˈzígzag/ n., adj., adv., & v. ● n. **1** a line or course having abrupt alternate right and left turns. **2** (often in pl.) each of these turns. ● adj. having the form of a zigzag; alternating right and left. ● adv. with a zigzag course. ● v.intr. (**zigzagged, zigzagging**) move in a zigzag course. □□ **zigzaggedly** adv. [F f. G zickzack]

■ n. **2** see TWIST n. 4. ● adj. see TORTUOUS 1. ● v. see WIND[2] v. 1.

zilch /zilch/ n. sl. nothing. [20th c.: orig. uncert.]
■ see ZERO n. 1.

zillah /ˈzílə/ n. an administrative district in India, containing several parganas. [Hind. ḍilah division]

zillion /ˈzílyən/ n. colloq. an indefinite large number. □□ **zillionth** adj. & n. [Z (perh. = unknown quantity) + MILLION]
■ (zillions) see LOT n. 1.

zinc /zingk/ n. Chem. a white metallic element occurring naturally as zinc blende, and used as a component of brass, in galvanizing sheet iron, in electric batteries, and in printing plates. ¶ Symb.: Zn. □ **flowers of zinc** = zinc oxide. **zinc blende** = SPHALERITE. **zinc chloride** a white crystalline deliquescent solid used as a preservative and flux. **zinc oxide** a powder used as a white pigment and in medicinal ointments. **zinc sulfate** a white, water-soluble compound used as a mordant. □□ **zinced** adj. [G Zink, of unkn. orig.]

zinco /ˈzíngkō/ n. & v. ● n. (pl. -os) = ZINCOGRAPH. ● v.tr. & intr. (**-oes, -oed**) = ZINCOGRAPH. [abbr.]

zincograph /ˈzíngkəgraf/ n. & v. ● n. **1** a zinc plate with a design etched in relief on it for printing from. **2** a print taken from this. ● v. **1** tr. & intr. etch on zinc. **2** tr. reproduce (a design) in this way. □□ **zincography** /-kógrəfee/ n.

zincotype /ˈzíngkətip/ n. = ZINCOGRAPH.

zing /zing/ n. & v. colloq. ● n. vigor; energy. ● v.intr. move swiftly or with a shrill sound. □□ **zingy** adj. (**zingier, zingiest**). [imit.]
■ n. see VIGOR 1.

zingaro /tseˈenggaarō/ n. (pl. **zingari** /-ree/; fem. **zingara** /-raa/) a gypsy. [It.]

zinger /ˈzíngər/ n. sl. **1** a witty retort. **2** an unexpected or startling announcement, etc. **3** an outstanding person or thing.

zinnia /ˈzíneeə/ n. a composite plant of the genus Zinnia, with showy rayed flowers of deep red and other colors. [J. G. Zinn, Ger. physician and botanist d. 1759]

Zion /ˈzíən/ n. (also **Sion** /ˈsíən/) **1** the hill of Jerusalem on which the city of David was built. **2 a** the Jewish people or religion. **b** the Christian church. **3** (in Christian thought) the kingdom of God in heaven. [OE f. eccl.L Sion f. Heb. ṣiyôn]

Zionism /ˈzíənizəm/ n. a movement (orig.) for the re-establishment and (now) the development of a Jewish nation in what is now Israel. □□ **Zionist** n.

zip /zip/ n. & v. ● n. **1** a light fast sound, as of a bullet passing through air. **2** energy; vigor. **3** Brit. **a** (in full **zip fastener**) = ZIPPER. **b** (attrib.) having a zipper (zip bag). ● v. (**zipped, zipping**) **1** tr. & intr. (often foll. by up) fasten with a zipper. **2** intr. move with zip or at high speed. [imit.]
■ n. **2** see ENERGY 1. ● v. **2** see STREAK v. 2.

zip code /zip/ n. (also **ZIP code**) a US system of postal codes consisting of five-digit or nine-digit numbers. [zone improvement plan]

zipper /ˈzípər/ n. & v. ● n. a fastening device of two flexible strips with interlocking projections closed or opened by pulling a slide along them. ● v.tr. (often foll. by up) fasten with a zipper. □□ **zippered** adj.

zippy /ˈzípee/ adj. (**zippier, zippiest**) colloq. **1** bright; fresh; lively. **2** fast; speedy. □□ **zippily** adv. **zippiness** n.
■ **1** see ENERGETIC 1, 2. **2** fast, quick, speedy.

zircon /ˈzárkon/ n. a zirconium silicate of which some translucent varieties are cut into gems (see HYACINTH 4, JARGON[2]). [G Zirkon: cf. JARGON[2]]

zirconium /zərˈkōneeəm/ n. Chem. a gray metallic element occurring naturally in zircon and used in various industrial applications. ¶ Symb.: Zr. [mod.L f. ZIRCON + -IUM]

zit /zit/ n. sl. a pimple. [20th c.: orig. unkn.]

zither /ˈzíthər/ n. a musical instrument consisting of a flat wooden sound box with numerous strings stretched across

---

/.../ **pronunciation**	● **part of speech**
□ **phrases, idioms, and compounds**	
□□ **derivatives**	■ **synonym section**
cross-references appear in SMALL CAPITALS or italics	

it, placed horizontally and played with the fingers and a plectrum. ▫▫ **zitherist** *n.* [G (as CITTERN)]

zizz /ziz/ *n.* & *v. Brit. colloq.* ● *n.* **1** a whizzing or buzzing sound. **2** a short sleep. ● *v.intr.* **1** make a whizzing sound. **2** doze or sleep. [imit.]

zloty /zláwtee/ *n.* (*pl.* same or **zlotys**) the chief monetary unit of Poland. [Pol., lit. 'golden']

Zn *symb. Chem.* the element zinc.

zodiac /zṓdeeak/ *n.* **1 a** a belt of the heavens limited by lines about 8° from the ecliptic on each side, including all apparent positions of the sun, moon, and planets as known to ancient astronomers, and divided into twelve equal parts (**signs of the zodiac**), each formerly containing the similarly named constellation but now by precession of the equinoxes coinciding with the constellation that bears the name of the preceding sign: Aries, Taurus, Gemini, Cancer, Leo, Virgo, Libra, Scorpio, Sagittarius, Capricorn(us), Aquarius, Pisces. **b** a diagram of these signs. **2** a complete cycle, circuit, or compass. [ME f. OF *zodiaque* f. L *zodiacus* f. Gk *zōidiakos* f. *zōidion* sculptured animal figure, dimin. of *zōion* animal]

zodiacal /zədíəkəl/ *adj.* of or in the zodiac. ▫ **zodiacal light** a luminous area of sky shaped like a tall triangle occasionally seen in the east before sunrise or in the west after sunset, esp. in the tropics. [F (as ZODIAC)]

zoetrope /zṓeetrōp/ *n. hist.* an optical toy in the form of a cylinder with a series of pictures on the inner surface which give an impression of continuous motion when viewed through slits with the cylinder rotating. [irreg. f. Gk *zōē* life + *-tropos* turning]

-zoic /zṓik/ *comb. form* **1** of or relating to animals. **2** *Geol.* (of rock, etc.) containing fossils; with traces of animal or plant life. [prob. back-form. f. AZOIC]

Zollner illusion /tsőlnər/ *n.* parallel lines made to appear not parallel by short oblique intersecting lines. [J. K. F. *Zöllner,* Ger. physicist d. 1882]

Zollverein /tsáwlfərin/ *n. hist.* a customs union, esp. of German states in the 19th c. [G]

zombie /zómbee/ *n.* **1** *colloq.* a dull or apathetic person. **2** a corpse said to be revived by witchcraft. [W.Afr. *zumbi* fetish]

zonation /zōnáyshən/ *n.* distribution in zones, esp. (*Ecol.*) of plants into zones characterized by the dominant species.

zonda /zóndə/ *n.* a hot, dusty north wind in Argentina. [Amer. Sp.]

zone /zōn/ *n.* & *v.* ● *n.* **1** an area having particular features, properties, purpose, or use (*danger zone; erogenous zone; smokeless zone*). **2** any well-defined region of more or less beltlike form. **3 a** an area between two exact or approximate concentric circles. **b** a part of the surface of a sphere enclosed between two parallel planes, or of a cone or cylinder, etc., between such planes cutting it perpendicularly to the axis. **4** (in full **time zone**) a range of longitudes where a common standard time is used. **5** *Geol.,* etc., a range between specified limits of depth, height, etc., esp. a section of strata distinguished by characteristic fossils. **6** *Geog.* any of five divisions of the earth bounded by circles parallel to the equator (see FRIGID, TEMPERATE, TORRID). **7** an encircling band or stripe distinguishable in color, texture, or character from the rest of the object encircled. **8** *archaic* a belt or girdle worn around the body. ● *v.tr.* **1** encircle as or with a zone. **2** arrange or distribute by zones. **3** assign as or to a particular area. ▫▫ **zonal** *adj.* **zoning** *n.* (in sense 3 of *v.*). [F *zone* or L *zona* girdle f. Gk *zōnē*]

■ *n.* **1, 2** area, quarter, district, region, sector, section, sphere, belt, territory, province, realm, domain, precinct, department, terrain, tract, stretch, circle, locality, locale, *joc.* bailiwick.

zonk /zongk/ *v.* & *n. sl.* ● *v.* **1** *tr.* hit or strike. **2** (foll. by *out*) **a** *tr.* overcome with sleep; intoxicate. **b** *intr.* fall heavily asleep. ● *n.* (often as *int.*) the sound of a blow or heavy impact. [imit.]

zonked /zongkt/ *adj. sl.* (often foll. by *out*) exhausted; intoxicated.

■ see WEARY *adj.* 1.

zoo /zōō/ *n.* a zoological garden. [abbr.]

■ zoological garden(s), menagerie, (safari *or* wildlife) park.

zoo- /zṓə/ *comb. form* of animals or animal life. [Gk *zōio-* f. *zōion* animal]

zoogeography /zṓəjee-ógrəfee/ *n.* the branch of zoology dealing with the geographical distribution of animals. ▫▫ **zoogeographic** /-jeeəgráfik/ *adj.* **zoogeographical** *adj.* **zoogeographically** *adv.*

zoography /zō-ógrəfee/ *n.* descriptive zoology.

zooid /zṓ-oyd/ *n.* **1** a more or less independent invertebrate organism arising by budding or fission. **2** a distinct member of an invertebrate colony. ▫▫ **zooidal** /-óyd'l/ *adj.* [formed as ZOO- + -OID]

zool. *abbr.* **1** zoological. **2** zoology.

zoolatry /zō-ólətree/ *n.* the worship of animals.

zoological /zṓəlójikəl/ *adj.* of or relating to zoology. ▫ **zoological garden** (or **gardens**) a public garden or park with a collection of animals for exhibition and study. ▫▫ **zoologically** *adv.*

zoology /zō-óləjee/ *n.* the scientific study of animals, esp. with reference to their structure, physiology, classification, and distribution. ▫▫ **zoologist** *n.* [mod.L *zoologia* (as ZOO-, -LOGY)]

zoom /zōōm/ *v.* & *n.* ● *v.* **1** *intr.* move quickly, esp. with a buzzing sound. **2 a** *intr.* cause an airplane to mount at high speed and a steep angle. **b** *tr.* cause (an airplane) to do this. **3 a** *intr.* (of a camera) close up rapidly from a long shot to a close-up. **b** *tr.* cause (a lens or camera) to do this. ● *n.* **1** an airplane's steep climb. **2** a zooming camera shot. ▫ **zoom lens** a lens allowing a camera to zoom by varying the focal length. [imit.]

■ *v.* **1** see SPEED *v.* 1.

zoomancy /zṓəmansee/ *n.* divination from the appearances or behavior of animals.

zoomorphic /zṓəmáwrfik/ *adj.* **1** dealing with or represented in animal forms. **2** having gods of animal form. ▫▫ **zoomorphism** *n.*

zoonosis /zṓənṓsis/ *n.* any of various diseases which can be transmitted to humans from animals. [ZOO- + Gk *nosos* disease]

zoophyte /zṓəfīt/ *n.* a plantlike animal, esp. a coral, sea anemone, or sponge. ▫▫ **zoophytic** /-fítik/ *adj.* [Gk *zōophuton* (as ZOO-, -PHYTE)]

zooplankton /zṓəplángktən/ *n.* plankton consisting of animals.

zoospore /zṓəspawr/ *n.* a spore of fungi, algae, etc. capable of motion. ▫▫ **zoosporic** /-spáwrik/ *adj.*

zootomy /zō-ótəmee/ *n.* the dissection or anatomy of animals.

zoot suit /zōōt/ *n. colloq.* a man's suit with a long, loose jacket and high-waisted, tapering pants. [rhyming on SUIT]

zori /záwree/ *n.* (*pl.* same or **zoris**) a Japanese straw or rubber, etc., sandal held on the foot by a thong between the first two toes. [Jap.]

zoril /záwril, zór-/ *n.* (also **zorille**) a flesh-eating African mammal, *Ictonyx striatus,* of the skunk and the weasel family. [F *zorille* f. Sp. *zorrilla* dimin. of *zorro* fox]

Zoroastrian /záwrō-ástreeən/ *adj.* & *n.* (also **Zarathustrian** /zárəthŏŏstreeən/) ● *adj.* of or relating to Zoroaster (or Zarathustra) or the dualistic religious system taught by him or his followers in the Zend-Avesta, based on the concept of a conflict between a spirit of light and good and a spirit of darkness and evil. ● *n.* a follower of Zoroaster. ▫▫ **Zoroastrianism** *n.* [L *Zoroastres* f. Gk *Zōroastrēs* f. Avestan *Zarathustra,* Persian founder of the religion in the 6th c. BC]

Zouave /zōō-aáv, zwaav/ *n.* a member of a French light-infantry corps originally formed of Algerians and retaining their oriental uniform. [F f. *Zouaoua,* name of a tribe]

zounds /zowndz/ *int. archaic* expressing surprise or indignation. [(*God*)'s *wounds* (i.e., those of Christ on the cross)]

ZPG *abbr.* zero population growth.

Zr *symb. Chem.* the element zirconium.

zucchetto /zōōkétō, tsōōkétō/ *n.* (*pl.* **-os**) a Roman Catholic ecclesiastic's skullcap, black for a priest, purple for a bishop, red for a cardinal, and white for a pope. [It. *zucchetta* dimin. of *zucca* gourd, head]

zucchini /zōōkeénee/ *n.* (*pl.* same or **zucchinis**) a green variety of smooth-skinned summer squash. [It., pl. of *zucchino* dimin. of *zucca* gourd]

zugzwang /tsŏŏktsvaang/ *n.* Chess an obligation to move in one's turn even when this must be disadvantageous. [G f. *Zug* move + *Zwang* compulsion]

Zulu /zōōlōō/ *n.* & *adj.* ● *n.* **1** a member of a black South African people orig. inhabiting Zululand and Natal. **2** the language of this people. ● *adj.* of or relating to this people or language. [native name]

Zuni /zōōnee/ *n.* (also **Zuñi** /zōōnyee/) **1 a** a N. American people native to New Mexico. **b** a member of this people. **2** the language of this people.

zwieback /zwíbak, -baak, zweé-, swí-, sweé-/ *n.* a kind of rusk or sweet cake toasted in slices. [G, = twice baked]

Zwinglian /zwíngleeən, tsvíng-/ *n.* & *adj.* ● *n.* a follower of the Swiss religious reformer U. Zwingli (d. 1531). ● *adj.* of or relating to Zwingli or his reforms.

zwitterion /tsvítərīən, zwít-/ *n.* a molecule or ion having separate positively and negatively charged groups. [G f. *Zwitter* a hybrid]

zygo- /zígō, zigō/ *comb. form* joining; pairing. [Gk *zugo-* f. *zugon* yoke]

zygodactyl /zígōdáktil, zígə-/ *adj.* & *n.* ● *adj.* (of a bird) having two toes pointing forward and two backward. ● *n.* such a bird. □□ **zygodactylous** *adj.*

zygoma /zigŏmə, zee-/ *n.* (*pl.* **zygomata** /-tə/) the bony arch of the cheek formed by connection of the zygomatic and temporal bones. [Gk *zugōma -atos* f. *zugon* yoke]

zygomatic /zígəmátik, zígə-/ *adj.* of or relating to the zygoma. □ **zygomatic arch** = ZYGOMA. **zygomatic bone** the bone that forms the prominent part of the cheek.

zygomorphic /zígəmáwrfik, zígə-/ *adj.* (also **zygomorphous** /-máwrfəs/) (of a flower) divisible into similar halves only by one plane of symmetry.

zygospore /zígəspawr, zígə-/ *n.* a thick-walled spore formed by certain fungi.

zygote /zígōt, zig-/ *n.* Biol. a cell formed by the union of two gametes. □□ **zygotic** /-gótik/ *adj.* **zygotically** /-gótikəlee/ *adv.* [Gk *zugōtos* yoked f. *zugoō* to yoke]

zymase /zímays/ *n.* the enzyme fraction in yeast which catalyzes the alcoholic fermentation of glucose. [F f. Gk *zumē* leaven]

zymology /zimóləjee/ *n.* Chem. the scientific study of fermentation. □□ **zymological** /-məlójikəl/ *adj.* **zymologist** *n.* [as ZYMASE + -LOGY]

zymosis /zimṓsis, zi-/ *n.* archaic fermentation. [mod.L f. Gk *zumōsis* (as ZYMASE)]

zymotic /zimótik, zi-/ *adj.* archaic of or relating to fermentation. □ **zymotic disease** archaic an epidemic, endemic, contagious, infectious, or sporadic disease regarded as caused by the multiplication of germs introduced from outside. [Gk *zumōtikos* (as ZYMOSIS)]

zymurgy /zímərjee/ *n.* the branch of applied chemistry dealing with the use of fermentation in brewing, etc. [Gk *zumē* leaven, after *metallurgy*]

/ . . . / pronunciation ● part of speech
□ phrases, idioms, and compounds
□□ derivatives ■ synonym section
cross-references appear in SMALL CAPITALS or *italics*

Appendices

Appendix 1 The History of English

1. Fifteen centuries of English cannot easily be summarized, so this account is intended to pick out features on the landscape of language rather than to describe the scene in detail. This may afford some perspective on the information given in the dictionary, and help to make more sense of the strange and often unpredictable ways in which words seem to behave.

Origins

2.1 English belongs to the Indo-European family of languages, a vast group with many branches, thought to be derived from a common ancestor-language called Proto-Indo-European. The words we use in English are derived from a wide range of sources, mostly within this family. The earliest sources are Germanic, Norse, and Romanic; later, they are the languages of Europe more generally; and most recently, with developments in such areas as medicine, electronics, computers, and communications, they have been worldwide.

2.2 It is difficult to be sure exactly what we mean by an "English" word. Most obviously, words are English if they can be traced back to the Anglo-Saxons, Germanic peoples who settled in Britain from the fifth century and eventually established several kingdoms together corresponding roughly to present-day England. From this time are derived many common words such as *eat, drink, speak, work, house, door, man, woman, husband, wife*. They displaced the Celtic peoples, whose speech survives in Scottish and Irish Gaelic, in Welsh, and in the local languages of two extremities of the British Isles, Manx (in the Isle of Man) and Cornish (in Cornwall, a county in southwestern England). Little Celtic influence remains in English, except in names of places such as *Brecon, Carlisle,* and *London,* and in many river names, such as *Avon, Thames,* and *Trent.* This fact may be attributed to a lack of cultural interaction, the Celts being forced back into the fringes of the British Isles by the Anglo-Saxon invaders.

3. Anglo-Saxon Britain continued to have contact with the Roman Empire, of which Britain had formerly been a part, and with Latin, which was the official language throughout the Empire and survived as a language of ritual (and for a time also of learning and communication) in the Western Christian Church. Christianity was brought to England with the mission of St. Augustine in AD 597. The Christianized Anglo-Saxons built churches and monasteries, and there were considerable advances in art and learning. At this time English was enriched by words from Latin, many of which are still in use, such as *angel, disciple, martyr,* and *shrine.* Other words came from Latin via the Germanic languages, for example *copper, mint* (in the sense of coinage), *pound, sack,* and *title,* and others were ultimately of oriental origin, for example *camel* and *pepper.*

4.1 The next important influence on the vocabulary of English came from the Danish and other Scandinavian invaders of the ninth and tenth centuries, collectively called Vikings. They occupied much of the eastern portion of England, and under Cnut (Canute) ruled the whole country for a time. The Danes had much more contact with the Anglo-Saxons than did the Celts, and their period of occupation has left its mark in the number of Scandinavian (Old Norse) words taken into English. Because Old Norse was also a Germanic language (of a different branch from English) many words were similar to the Anglo-Saxon ones, and it is difficult to establish the extent of the Old Norse influence. However, a number of Norse words are identifiable and are still in use, such as *call, take,* and *law,* names of parts of the body such as *leg,* and other basic words such as *egg, root,* and *window.* Many more Norse words are preserved in some dialects of eastern England, in English place-names ending in *-thwaite* and *-thorpe* (both meaning 'settlement') and in *-by* (*Grimsby, Rugby,* and so on), and in English street names ending in *-gate* (from the Old Norse *gata* meaning 'street') such as *Coppergate* in York.

4.2 In the Saxon kingdom of Wessex, King Alfred (871–99) and his successors did much to keep English alive by using it (rather than Latin) as the language of education and learning; by the tenth century there was a considerable amount of English prose and verse literature. Saxon and Danish kingdoms existed side by side for several generations, and there was much linguistic interaction. One very important effect on English was the gradual disappearance of many word-endings, or inflections, leading to a simpler grammar. This was partly because the stems of English and Norse words were often very close in form (for example, *stān* and *steinn,* meaning 'stone'), and only the inflections differed as an impediment to mutual understanding. So forms such as *stāne, stānes,* etc., began to be simplified and, eventually, eliminated. The process continued for hundreds of years into Middle English (see below).

The Norman Conquest

5. In 1066 William of Normandy defeated the English king, Harold, at the Battle of Hastings; he was crowned King of England on Christmas Day. The arrival of the French-speaking Normans as a ruling nobility brought a transforming Romance influence on the language. The Romance languages (chiefly French, Italian, Spanish, Portuguese, and Romanian) have their roots in the spoken or "vulgar" Latin that continued in use until about AD 600. For two hundred years after the Norman Conquest, French (in its regional Norman form) was the language of the aristocracy, the lawcourts, and the Church hierarchy in England. Gradually the Normans were integrated into English society, and by the reign of Henry II (1154–89) many of the aristocracy spoke English. During these years many French words were adopted into English. Some were connected with law and government, such as *justice, council,* and *tax,* and some were abstract terms such as *liberty, charity,* and *conflict.* The Normans also had an important effect on the spelling of English words. The combination of letters *cw-,* for example, was standardized in the Norman manner to *qu-,* so that *cwēn* became *queen* and *cwic* became *quik* (later *quick*).

6. This mixture of conquering peoples and their languages—Germanic, Scandinavian, and Romance—has had a decisive effect on the forms of words in modern English. The three elements make up the basic stock of English vocabulary, and different practices of putting sounds into writing are reflected in each. The different grammatical characteristics of each element can be seen in the structure and endings of many words. Many of the variable endings such as *-ant* and *-ent, -er* and *-or, -able* and *-ible* exist because the Latin words on which they are based belonged to different classes of verbs and nouns, each of which had a different ending. For example, *important* comes from the Latin verb *portare,* meaning 'to carry' (which belongs to one class or conjugation) while *repellent* comes from the Latin verb *pellere,* meaning 'to drive' (which belongs to another). *Capable* comes from a Latin word ending in *-abilis,* while *sensible* comes from one ending in *-ibilis,* and so on.

Middle English

7. Middle English, as the English of *c.*1100–1500 is called, emerged as the spoken and written form of the language under these influences. The use of French diminished, especially after King John (1199–1216) lost possession of Normandy in 1204, severing an important Anglo-French link. Many Anglo-Saxon words continued in use, while others disappeared altogether: for example, *niman* was replaced by the Old Norse (Scandinavian) *taka* (meaning 'take'), and the Old English *sige* was replaced by a word derived from Old French, *victory.* Other Old English words that disappeared are *ādl* (disease), *lof* (praise), and *lyft* (air: compare German *Luft*). Sometimes new and old words continued in use side by side, in some cases on a roughly equal footing, and in others with a distinction in

meaning (as with *doom* and *judgment,* and *stench* and *smell*). This has produced pairs of words which are both in use today, such as *shut* and *close,* and *buy* and *purchase,* in which the second word of each pair is Romance in origin. Sometimes an even larger overlap was produced, as when *commence* (from the French) was added to the existing Old English *begin* and *start.* (The original meaning of *start* was 'leap,' 'move suddenly,' which is still current though no longer the main sense.)

8. Hundreds of the Romance words were short simple words that would now be distinguished with difficulty from Old English words if their origin were not known: for example, *bar, cry, fool, mean, pity, stuff, touch,* and *tender.* Others, such as *commence* and *purchase,* have more formal connotations. The result was a mixture of types of words, a feature of modern English. For many meanings we now have a choice of less and more formal words, the more formal ones used only in very specific circumstances. For example, the words *vendor* is used instead of *seller* only in commercial contexts. Many technical words derived from or ultimately from Latin, such as *estop* and *usucaption,* survive only in legal contexts, to the great confusion of the layperson. These levels of formality are reflected in the dictionary's identification of usage level in particular cases as colloquial, formal, and so on.

Printing

9. There was much regional variation in the spelling and pronunciation of Middle English, although a good measure of uniformity was imposed by the development of printing from the fifteenth century. This uniformity was based as much on practical considerations of the printing process as on what seemed most "correct" or suitable. It became common practice, for example, to add a final *e* to words to fill a line of print. The printers—many of them foreign—used rules from their own languages, especially Dutch and Flemish, when setting English into type. William Caxton, the first English printer (1422–91), exercised an important but not always beneficial influence. The unnecessary insertion of *h* in *ghost,* for example, is due to Caxton (who learned the business of printing on the Continent), and the change had its effect on other words such as *ghastly* and (perhaps) *ghetto.* In general, Caxton used the form of English prevalent in the southeast of England, although the East Midland dialect was the more extensive. This choice, together with the importance of London as the English capital, gave the dialect of southeastern England a significance and influence that survives to the present day.

Pronunciation

10. At roughly the same time as the early development of printing, the pronunciation of English was also undergoing major changes. The main change, which began in the fourteenth century during the lifetime of the poet Chaucer (1340?–1400), was in the pronunciation of vowel sounds. The so-called "great vowel shift" resulted in the reduction of the number of words that are pronounced with the vowel sound in long vowels (*deed* as distinct from *dead*). It also affected the pronunciation of other vowels: the word *life,* for example, was once pronounced as we now pronounce *leaf,* and *name* was pronounced as two syllables to rhyme with *comma.* In many cases, as with *name,* the form of the word did not change; this accounts for many of the "silent" vowels at the ends of words. The result of these developments was a growing difference between what was spoken and what was written.

The Renaissance

11. The rediscovery in Europe of the culture and history of the ancient Greek and Roman worlds exercised a further Romanizing influence on English. This began at the end of the Middle Ages and blossomed in the European Renaissance of the fifteenth to seventeenth centuries. Scholarship flourished, and the language used by scholars and writers was Latin. During the Renaissance words such as *arena, dexterity, excision, genius, habitual, malignant, specimen,* and *stimulus* came into use in English. They are familiar and useful words but their Latin origins sometimes make them awkward to handle, as, for example, when we use *arena, genius,* and *stimulus* in the plural. There was also a tendency in the Renaissance to try to emphasize the Greek or Latin origins of words when writing them. This accounts for the *b* in *debt* (the earlier English word was *det*; in Latin it is *debitum*), the *l* in *fault* (earlier *faut*; the Latin source is *fallere*), the *s* in *isle* (earlier *ile*; *insula* in Latin), and the *p* in *receipt* (earlier *receit*; *recepta* in Latin). Some words that had gone out of use were reintroduced, usually with changed meanings, for example *artificial, disk* (originally the same as *dish*), and *fastidious.*

Later influences

12. The development of machines and technology from the eighteenth century onwards, followed by the electronic revolution of our own times, has also played a part in continuing the influence of Latin. New technical terms have come into use, and they have often been formed on Latin or Greek source-words because these can convey precise ideas in easily combinable forms, for example *bacteriology, microscope, radioactive,* and *semiconductor.* Combinations of Germanic elements are also used, as in *software, splashdown,* and *take-off.* This process has sometimes produced odd mixtures, such as *television,* which is half Greek and half Latin, and *microchip,* which is half Greek and half Germanic.

13.1 In recent times English speakers have come into contact with people from other parts of the world, through trade, international relations, and improved communications generally. This contact has produced a rich supply of new words. India, where the British first had major dealings in the seventeenth century, is the source of words such as *bungalow, jodhpurs,* and *khaki.* Examples from other parts of the world are *harem* and *mufti* (from Arabic), *bazaar* (from Persian), *kiosk* (from Turkish), and *anorak* (from Eskimo). From European countries we have acquired *balcony* (from Italian), *envelope* (from French), and *yacht* (from Dutch).

13.2 Thousands of such words, though not English in the Germanic sense, are regarded as fully absorbed into English. In addition, there are many unnaturalized words and phrases that are used in English contexts but are generally regarded as "foreign," and are conventionally printed in italics to distinguish them when used in an English context. Very many of these are French, for example *accouchement* (childbirth), *bagarre* (a scuffle), *bonhomie* (geniality), *flânerie* (idleness), and *rangé* (domesticated), but other languages are represented, as with *echt* (genuine) and *macht-politik* (power politics) from German, and *mañana* (tomorrow) from Spanish.

14.1 Usage often recognizes the difficulties of absorbing words from various sources by assimilating them into familiar forms. The word *picturesque,* which came into use in the eighteenth century, is a compromise between its French source *pittoresque* and the existing Middle English word *picture,* to which it is obviously related. The English word *cockroach* is a conversion of its Spanish source-word *cucaracha* into a pair of familiar words *cock* (a bird) and *roach* (a fish). Cockroaches have nothing to do with cocks or roaches, and the association is simply a matter of linguistic convenience.

14.2 Problems of inflection arise with words taken from other languages. The ending *-i* in particular is very unnatural in English, and usage varies between *-is* and *-ies* in the plural. A similar difficulty occurs with the many adopted nouns ending in *-o,* some of which come from the Italian (*solo*), some from

Spanish (*armadillo*), and some from Latin (*hero*); here usage varies between *-os* and *-oes*. Verbs often need special treatment, as *bivouac* (from French, and before that probably from Swiss German) which needs a *k* in the past tense (*bivouacked*, not *bivouaced* which might be mispronounced), and *ski* (from Norwegian) where usage allows both *ski'd* and *skied* as past forms.

Dictionaries

15.1 One obvious consequence of the development of printing in the fifteenth century was that it allowed the language to be recorded in glossaries and dictionaries, and this might be expected to have had a considerable effect on the way words were used and spelled. However, listing all the words in the language systematically in alphabetical order with their spellings and meanings is a relatively recent idea. There was nothing of the sort in Shakespeare's time, for example. In 1580, when Shakespeare was sixteen, a schoolmaster named William Bullokar published a manual for the "ease, speed, and perfect reading and writing of English," and he called for the writing of an English dictionary. Such a dictionary, the work of Robert Cawdrey (another schoolmaster), was not published until 1604. Like the dictionaries that followed in quick succession (including Bullokar's own *English Expositor*), its purpose was described as being for the understanding of "hard words." It was not until the eighteenth century that dictionaries systematically listed all the words in general use at the time regardless of how "easy" or "hard" they were; the most notable of these were compiled by Nathaniel Bailey (1721) and, especially, Samuel Johnson (1755). They were partly a response to a call, expressed by Swift, Pope, Addision, and other writers, for the language to be fixed and stabilized, and for the establishment of an English Academy to monitor it. None of these hopes as such were realized, but the dictionaries played an important role in settling the form and senses of English words. Noah Webster's American dictionaries set new standards for spelling and concision, starting with his edition of 1828.

15.2 The systematic investigation and recording of words in all their aspects and on a historical basis is first represented in the *Oxford English Dictionary*, begun by the Scottish schoolmaster James A. H. Murray in 1879. This describes historically the spelling, inflection, origin, and meaning of words, and is supported by citations from printed literature and other sources as evidence from Old English to the present day. A new edition integrating the original dictionary and its *Supplement* (1972–86) appeared in 1989. Because of its depth of scholarship, the *Oxford English Dictionary* forms a major basis of all English dictionaries produced since. Smaller desktop, college, and other abridged dictionaries that aim at recording the main vocabulary in current use began to appear early this century and in recent years the number has grown remarkably.

15.3 Dictionaries of current English, as distinct from historical dictionaries, generally record the language as it is being used at the time, and with usage constantly changing the distinction between "right" and "wrong" is sometimes difficult to establish. Unlike French, which is guided by the rulings of the *Académie Française*, English is not monitored by any single authority; established usage is the principal criterion. One result of this is that English tolerates many more alternative spellings than other languages. The alternatives are based on patterns of word formation and variation in the different languages through which they have passed before reaching ours.

15.4 It should also be remembered that dictionaries, such as this one, provide a selection, based on currency, of a recorded stock of over half a million words; that is to say, they represent about 15–20 percent of what is attested to exist by printed sources and other materials. Dictionaries therefore differ in the selection they make, beyond the core of vocabulary and idiom that can be expected to be found in any dictionary.

Dialect

16. Within the United States, regional forms and dialects, with varying accents and usage, have continued to exist since colonial days, although in recent times, especially with the emergence of mass communications, there has been some regularization. A special feature of a dialect is its vocabulary of words (often for everyday things) that are understood only locally. It is not possible in a small dictionary to treat this kind of vocabulary in any detail, but its influence can be seen in the origins of words that have achieved a more general currency, for example *boss-eyed* (from a dialect word *boss* meaning 'miss,' 'bungle'), *fad*, *scrounge* (from dialect *scrunge* meaning 'steal'), and *shoddy*. Far more information on dialect words is available in *The Dictionary of American Regional English* (ed. by F. Cassidy and J. Hall, 1985 and ff.), in the *Oxford English Dictionary*, and in numerous glossaries published by dialect societies.

English worldwide

17.1 Modern usage is greatly influenced by rapid worldwide communications, by newspapers and, in particular, by television and radio. The influence of American English, often regarded by the British as unsettling or harmful, has had a considerable effect on the vocabulary, idiom, and spelling of British English, and continues to do so. Among the many words and idioms in general use, usually without any awareness of or concern about their American origin, are *OK*, *to fall for*, *to fly off the handle*, *round trip*, and *to snoop*. American English often has more regular spellings, for example the use of *-er* for *-re* in words such as *theater*, the standardization of *-or* and *-our* to *-or* in words such as *harbor* (Brit. *harbour*), and the use of *-se* in forms such as *defense* and *license*, where British English either has *-ce* only or both forms (for example, a *practice* but *to practise*).

17.2 English is now used all over the world; as a result, there are many varieties of English, with varying accents, vocabulary, and usage, as in Southern Africa, India, Australia, New Zealand, Canada, and elsewhere. These varieties have an equal claim to be regarded as "English" and, although learners of English may look to British English as the center of an English-speaking world, or British and American English as the two poles of such a world, it is very important that dictionaries should take account of other varieties of English, especially as it affects that in use elsewhere. The process is a strengthening and enriching one, and is the mark of a living and flourishing language.

Further reading

18. Those who are interested in exploring further will find a host of books on the history and development of English. Good general accounts are A. C. Baugh and T. Cable, *A History of the English Language* (3rd ed., New Jersey and London, 1978) and B. M. H. Strang, *A History of English* (London, 1970). At a more popular level, and more up to date on recent trends, are R. W. Burchfield, *The English Language* (Oxford, 1985) and R. McCrum *et al.*, *The Story of English* (London, 1986). *The Oxford Companion to the English Language* (ed. T. McArthur, Oxford, 1992) contains much that will interest those who want to know more about the English of today and its place among the languages of the world.

Appendix 2 Some Points of English Usage

1 Meanings

The following words are often used wrongly or carelessly, or confused with other similar words.

adverse/averse

Adverse means 'unfavorable, opposed,' and is usually applied to situations and events, not people, e.g., *The new drug has adverse side effects.* **Averse** is related in origin and also has the sense of 'opposition,' but its use is best restricted to describing a person's attitude, e.g., *I would not be averse to the prospect of traveling with you.*

affect/effect

Both these words are both verbs and nouns, but only **effect** is common as a noun, usually meaning 'a result, consequence, impression, etc.,' e.g., *My father's strictness had no effect on my desire to learn.* As verbs they are used differently. **Affect** means 'to produce an effect upon,' e.g., *Smoking during pregnancy can affect a baby's development.* **Effect** means 'to bring about,' e.g., *Alterations were effected with some sympathy for the existing fabric.*

aggravate

This word is commonly used in informal contexts to mean 'to annoy or exasperate,' rather than 'to make worse or more serious'; this is considered incorrect by many people. An example of correct usage is *The psychological stress aggravates the horse's physical stress.*

alibi

The chief meaning of this word is 'evidence that when something took place one was elsewhere,' e.g., *He has no alibi for Wednesday afternoon.* It is also sometimes used informally to mean 'an excuse, pretext, or justification'; this is considered incorrect by many people.

all right/alright

Although found widely, **alright** remains non-standard, even where standard spelling is somewhat cumbersome, e.g., *I wanted to make sure it was all all right.*

all together/altogether

These variants are used in different contexts. **All together** means 'all at once' or 'all in one place or in one group,' e.g., *They came all together; We managed to get three bedrooms all together* (i.e., near each other). **Altogether** means 'in total,' e.g., *The hotel has twenty rooms altogether.*

alternate/alternative

These words should not be confused. In British English **alternate** means 'every other,' e.g., *There will be a dance on alternate Saturdays,* whereas **alternative** means 'available as another choice,' e.g., *an alternative route.* In American usage, however, **alternate** can be used to mean 'available as another choice.'

altogether see all together.

amend/emend

Amend, meaning 'to make improvements or corrections in,' is often confused with **emend,** a more technical word used in the context of textual correction. Examples of each are: *The Constitution was amended to limit presidential terms of office; The poems have been collected, arranged, and emended.*

anticipate

Anticipate in the sense 'expect, foresee' is well-established in informal use (e.g., *He anticipated a restless night*), but is regarded as incorrect by some people. The formal sense, 'deal with or use before the proper time,' is illustrated by the sentence *The specialist would find that the thesis he had been planning had already been anticipated.*

anyone/any one

Anyone is written as two words only to emphasize a numerical sense, e.g., *Any one of us can do it.* Otherwise it is written as one word (e.g., *Anyone who wants to can come*).

Arab/Arabian

Arab is now the usual term for a native of Arabia. **Arabian** is generally used as an adjective, especially in geographical contexts (e.g., *Arabian peninsula*).

averse see adverse.

baluster/banister

These words are sometimes confused. A **baluster** is usually part of a balustrade, whereas a **banister** supports the handrail of a staircase.

beg the question

This phrase is often used to mean (1) to evade a difficulty, or (2) to pose or invite the question (that . . .), instead of (3) to assume the truth of an argument or proposition to be proved. (1) and (2) are considered incorrect by many people.

born/borne

Born is used with reference to birth (e.g., *was born in Detroit*). **Borne,** meaning 'carried,' is used in the expression *borne by* followed by the name of the mother (e.g., *was borne by Mary*), as well as in other senses (e.g., *a litter borne by four slaves*).

censor/censure

Both these words are both verbs and nouns, but **censor** is used to mean 'to cut unacceptable parts out of a book, movie, etc.' or 'a person who does this,' while **censure** means 'to criticize harshly' or 'harsh criticism.'

chronic

This word is often used to mean 'habitual, inveterate,' e.g., *a chronic liar.* This use is considered to be incorrect by some people. The precise meaning of this word is 'persisting for a long time' and it is used chiefly of illnesses or other problems, e.g., *Over one million people in the US have chronic bronchitis.*

complacent/complaisant

Complacent means 'smugly self-satisfied,' e.g., *After four consecutive championships the team became complacent,* while **complaisant,** a much rarer word, means 'deferential, willing to please,' e.g., in *When released from the kennel, the dogs are very peaceful and complaisant.*

compose/comprise

Both these words can be used to mean 'to constitute or make up' but **compose** is preferred in this sense, e.g., *Citizens act as witnesses in the courts and finally may compose the jury.* **Comprise** is correctly used to mean 'to be composed of, consist of,' e.g., *Each crew comprises a commander, a gunner, and a driver.*

continual/continuous

Continual is used of something that happens very frequently, e.g., *There were continual interruptions,* whereas **continuous** is used of something that happens without pause, e.g., *There was a dull, continuous background noise.*

crucial

Crucial is used in formal contexts to mean 'decisive, critical,' e.g., *The first five years of a child's life are crucial.* Its use to mean 'very important,' as in *It is crucial not to forget your passport,* should be restricted to informal contexts.

decimate

The usual sense of this word is now 'destroy a large proportion of.' This use is considered inappropriate by purists because the original and literal sense is 'to kill or remove one in ten of.' In any case, this word should not be used to mean 'to defeat utterly.'

definite/definitive

Definitive in the sense '(of an answer, verdict, etc.) decisive, unconditional, final' is sometimes confused with **definite**. However, **definite** does not have the connotations of authority: *a definite no* is simply a firm refusal, whereas a *definitive no* is an authoritative judgment or decision that something is not the case.

deprecate/depreciate

Deprecate means 'to express disapproval of, to deplore,' e.g., *The establishment magazines began by deprecating the film's attitude towards terrorism,* while **depreciate** (apart from its financial senses) means 'to disparage or belittle,' e.g., *He was depreciating his own skills out of a strong sense of humility.*

dilemma

This word should be used with regard to situations in which a difficult choice has to be made between undesirable alternatives, as in *You see his dilemma? Whatever he did next, his wife would find out, divorce him, and get custody of the child.* Its use to mean simply 'a difficult situation' is considered incorrect by some people.

disinterested/uninterested

Disinterested is sometimes used in informal contexts to mean 'not interested or uninterested,' but this is widely regarded as incorrect. The proper meaning is 'impartial,' e.g., *I for one am making a disinterested search for information.* The use of the noun **disinterest** to mean 'a lack of interest' is also objected to, but it is rarely used in any other sense.

effect see affect.

emend see amend.

emotional/emotive

Although the senses of these two words overlap, **emotive** is more common in the sense 'arousing emotion,' e.g., *Drug use is an emotive issue,* and is not used at all to describe a person as being liable to excessive emotion.

enormity

This word is commonly used to mean 'great size,' e.g., *wilting under the enormity of the work,* but this is regarded as incorrect by some people. The original and preferred meaning is 'extreme wickedness,' as in *the enormity of the crime.*

exceptionable/exceptional

Exceptionable means 'open to objection,' e.g., *There was nothing exceptionable in her behavior,* and is usually found in negative contexts. It is sometimes confused with the much commoner word **exceptional** meaning 'unusual, outstanding.'

feasible

The correct meaning of this word is 'practicable' or 'possible,' e.g., *Walking at night was not feasible without the aid of a flashlight.* It should not be used to mean 'likely' or 'probable.'

flammable see inflammable.

flaunt/flout

These words are often confused because both suggest an element of arrogance or showing off. However, **flaunt** means 'to display ostentatiously,' e.g., *He liked to flaunt his wealth,* while **flout** means 'to express contempt for or disobey (laws, convention, etc),' e.g., *The fine is too low for those who flout the law continuously.*

-fuls/-s full

The combining form **-ful** is used to form nouns meaning 'the amount needed to fill,' e.g., *cupful, spoonful.* The plural form of such words is -s, (*cupfuls, spoonfuls,* etc.). *Three cups full* would denote the individual cups rather than a quantity regarded in terms of a cup used as a measure, and would be used in contexts such as *They brought us three cups full of water.*

fulsome

This word means 'excessive, cloying, or insincere,' but is often imprecisely used to mean 'generous,' as in the phrase *fulsome praise.*

hoi polloi

This phrase is usually preceded by *the,* e.g., *The hoi polloi grew weary and sat on the floor.* Strictly speaking, the *the* is unecessary because *hoi* means 'the' (in Greek).

hopefully

Some purists object to the use of this word as a sentence modifier, with the meaning 'it is to be hoped,' e.g., *Hopefully, all the details will be in this evening's newspapers.* However, this usage is not only very common but is long-established in English and in keeping with similar uses of other sentence-modifying adverbs such as *regrettably* and *frankly.*

impedance/impediment

Impedance is a specialized electrical term, while **impediment** is an everyday term meaning 'a hindrance or obstruction,' e.g., *He would have to write by hand but that was no impediment.*

imply see infer.

inchoate

This word means 'just begun or rudimentary, undeveloped,' e.g., *All was as yet in an inchoate state,* but it is often used incorrectly to mean 'chaotic' or 'incoherent.' The *ch* is pronounced hard, like *k.*

incredible/incredulous

The adjective **incredible** means 'unbelievable' or 'not convincing' and can be applied to a situation, statement, policy, or threat to a person, e.g, *I find this testimony incredible.* **Incredulous** means 'disinclined to believe; skeptical' and is usually applied to a person's attitude, e.g., *You shouldn't wonder that I'm incredulous after all your lies.*

infer/imply

Infer should be used to mean 'to deduce or conclude,' as in *We can infer from these studies that. . . .* Its use to mean 'to imply or suggest' is widely considered incorrect.

inflammable/flammable/non-flammable

Both **inflammable** and **flammable** mean 'easily set on fire or excited.' The opposite is **non-flammable.** Where there is a danger of **inflammable** being understood to mean the opposite, i.e., 'not easily set on fire,' **flammable** should be used to avoid confusion.

ingenious/ingenuous

These words are sometimes confused. **Ingenious** means 'clever, skillful, or resourceful,' e.g., *an ingenious device,* while **ingenuous** means 'artless' or 'frank,' e.g., *charmed by the ingenuous honesty of the child.*

intense/intensive

Intense is sometimes wrongly used instead of **intensive** to describe a course of study that covers a large amount of material in a short space of time.

interface

The use of **interface** to mean 'a place or means of interaction,' e.g., *Experts looked at the crucial interface between broadcasters and independents,* or as a verb meaning 'to interact,' e.g., *courses where business executives interface with nature at great expense,* is deplored by some people.

interment/internment

Interment means 'the burial of a corpse,' while **interment** means 'the confining of a prisoner, etc.'

irregardless see regardless.

latter

This word means 'the second-mentioned of two.' Its use to mean 'the last-mentioned of three or more' is common, but considered incorrect by some people since *latter* means 'later' rather than 'latest.' Last or last-mentioned is to be preferred where three or more things are involved.

laudable/laudatory

These words are sometimes confused. **Laudable** is the more common and means 'commendable' or 'praiseworthy,' e.g., *The foundation pursued a laudable charitable program that involved the foundation and maintenance of schools and hospitals.* **Laudatory** means 'expressing praise,' e.g., *The proposed legislation enjoyed a good reception—including a laudatory frontpage endorsement from the city's only daily newspaper.*

lay/lie

In standard English **lay** is a transitive verb and **lie** intransitive. The intransitive use of **lay**, as in *It gave him the opportunity of laying on the grass at lunchtime,* is best avoided. Similarly, the transitive use of **lie**, as in *Lie it on the table* is also avoided by careful speakers and writers. In the first example *laying* should be *lying* and in the second *lie* should be *lay*. These two verbs are often confused owing to their close similarity in form, including the fact that the past tense of *lie* is *lay*. A mnemonic using the traditional child's prayer *Now I lay me down to sleep* . . . serves as a reminder that lay is transitive (with direct object *me*).

leading question

This phrase means 'a question that prompts the answer wanted' and was originally a legal term. In weakened use it tends to mean 'an awkward, pointed, or loaded question,' or even 'principal question,' but these usages are considered incorrect by some people.

liable

This word is commonly used with *to* to mean 'likely to do something undesirable,' e.g., *Without his glasses he's liable to smash into a tree.* This usage is considered incorrect by some people. Correct usage is exemplified by the sentence *You could be liable for a heavy fine if you are at fault.*

lie see lay.

like

The use of **like** as a conjunction meaning 'as' or 'as if,' e.g., *I don't have a wealthy set of in-laws like you do; They sit up like they're begging for food,* is considered incorrect by some people.

locate

In formal English it is not acceptable to use **locate** to mean merely 'find,' e.g., *It drives him out of his mind when he can't locate something.* **Locate** is used more precisely to mean 'discover the exact place or position of,' e.g., *One club member was proposing to use an echo sounder to help locate fish in the lake.*

luxuriant/luxurious

These words are sometimes confused. **Luxuriant** means 'lush, profuse, or prolific,' e.g., *forests of dark luxuriant foliage; luxuriant black eyelashes.* **Luxurious,** a much commoner word, means 'supplied with luxuries, extremely comfortable,' e.g., *a luxurious hotel.*

masterful/masterly

These words overlap in meaning and are sometimes confused. Apart from meaning 'domineering,' **masterful** also means 'masterly' or 'very skillful.' However, **masterful** is generally used in this sense to describe a person, e.g., *He's just got a marginal talent that he's masterful at exploiting,* while **masterly** usually describes an achievement or action, e.g., *This was a masterly use of the backhand volley.*

mutual

This word is sometimes used with no sense of reciprocity, simply to mean 'common to two or more people,' as in *a mutual friend; a mutual interest.* Such use is considered incorrect by some people, for whom **common** is preferable.

non-flammable see inflammable.

off/off of

The use of **off of** to mean **off**, e.g., *He took the cup off of the table,* is non-standard and to be avoided.

perquisite/prerequisite

These words are sometimes confused. **Perquisite** usually means 'an extra benefit or privilege,' e.g., *There were no perquisites that came with the job, apart from one or two special privileges.* **Prerequisite** means 'something required as a precondition,' e.g., *A general education in the sciences is a prerequisite of professional medical training.*

plus

The use of **plus** as a conjunction meaning 'and furthermore,' e.g., *plus we will be pleased to give you personal financial advice,* is considered incorrect by many people.

prerequisite see perquisite.

prescribe/proscribe

These words are sometimes confused, but they are nearly opposite in meaning. **Prescribe** means 'to advise the use of' or 'impose authoritatively,' whereas **proscribe** means 'to reject, denounce, or ban.' Examples of each are as follows:

The teachers would prescribe topics to be dealt with.

The superintendent proscribed tabloid newspapers from all school libraries.

A dictatorial regime which both prescribes and proscribes literature.

prevaricate/procrastinate

Prevaricate means 'to act or speak evasively,' e.g., *When the teacher asked what I was reading, I knew I would have to prevaricate or risk a detention.* It is sometimes confused with **procrastinate,** which means 'to postpone or put off an action,' e.g., *He hesitates and procrastinates until the time for action is over.*

proscribe see prescribe.

protagonist

The correct meaning of this word is 'chief or leading person,' e.g., *The choreographer must create movements that display each protagonist's particular behavior and reactions.* However, it is also used, usually with *of* or *for*, to mean 'an advocate or champion of a cause etc.,' e.g., *. . . the flawed economics of the nuclear protagonists's case.*

refute/repudiate

Strictly speaking, **refute** means 'to prove (a person or statement) to be wrong,' e.g., *No amount of empirical research can either confirm or refute it.* However, it is also sometimes used to mean 'to deny or repudiate.' This usage is considered incorrect by some people.

regardless/irregardless

The latter word, with its illogical negative prefix, is widely heard, perhaps arising under the influence of such perfectly correct forms as *irrespective.* It is avoided by careful users of English.

scenario

The proper meaning of this word is 'an outline of a plot' or 'a postulated sequence of events.' It should not be used in standard English to mean 'situation,' e.g., *a nightmare scenario*.

Scotch/Scots/Scottish

In Scotland the terms **Scots** and **Scottish** are preferred to **Scotch** and they mean the same (e.g., *a Scots/Scottish accent, miner, farmer*, etc.) **Scotch** is used in various compound nouns such as *Scotch broth, egg, fir, mist, terrier*, and *whiskey*. Similarly, **Scotsman** and **Scotswoman** are preferred to **Scotchman** and **Scotchwoman**.

seasonable/seasonal

Seasonable means 'usual or suitable for the season' or 'opportune,' e.g., *Although seasonable, the weather was not suitable for picnics*. **Seasonal** means 'of, depending on, or varying with the season,' e.g., *Seasonal changes posed problems for mills situated on larger rivers*.

sensual/sensuous

These two words are of similar meaning and are often, therefore, confused. Both mean 'of the senses,' but **sensual** means 'of the senses as opposed to the intellect or spirit' and has sexual overtones while **sensuous** is used with regard to the senses aesthetically rather than physically. Examples illustrate this difference:

The smoke-filled barroom was alive with sensual music and dancing.

The interior of the hotel is a sensuous explosion of light, texture, and sound.

'til/till see until.

tortuous/torturous

These words sound similar but have different meanings. **Tortuous** means 'full of twists and turns' or 'devious; circuitous,' e.g., *Both paths have proved tortuous and are strewn with awkward boulders.*

Torturous is an adjective that is derived from *torture* and means 'involving torture; excruciating,' e.g., *I found the concert a torturous experience because of the loudness of the music.*

triumphal/truimphant

These words are sometimes confused. The more common, **triumphant**, means 'victorious' or 'exultant,' e.g., *She had chaired a difficult meeting through to its triumphant conclusion*, or *Rosie returned triumphant with the file that had been missing.*

Triumphal means 'used in or celebrating a triumph,' e.g., *The last element to be added was the magnificent triumphal arch*, or *The victorious troops marched in a triumphal ticker-tape parade.*

turbid/turgid

Turbid is used of a liquid or color to mean 'muddy; not clear,' or of literary style, etc., to mean 'confused,' e.g., *the turbid utterances and twisted language of Carlyle.*

Turgid means 'swollen, inflated, or enlarged' but is also often used to describe literary style that is pompous or bombastic, e.g., *Communications from corporate headquarters were largely turgid memos filled with bureaucratic lingo.*

unexceptionable see exceptionable.

unsociable/unsocial see antisocial.

until/till/'til

Until is more formal than **till**, and is more usual at the beginning of a sentence, e.g., *Until the 1920s it was quite unusual for women to wear short hair.*

'Til is considered incorrect in standard English and should be avoided.

venal/venial

These words are sometimes confused. **Venal** means 'corrupt, able to be bribed, or involving bribery,' e.g., *Their high court is venal and can take decades to decide a case.*

Venial is used among Christians to describe a certain type of sin and means 'pardonable, excusable, not mortal,' e.g., *The Reformation renounced purgatory as an intermediate stage in which those who had committed venial sins might earn their way into heaven.*

worth while/worthwhile

Worth while (two words) is used only predicatively, e.g., *Nobody had thought it worth while to call the police*, and means 'worth the time or effort spent.'

Worthwhile (one word) also has this meaning but can be used both predicatively and attributively, e.g., *Only in unusual circumstances would investment be worthwhile* (predicative), or *He was a worthwhile subject for the "cure"* (attributive). In addition, *worthwhile* has the sense 'of value or importance,' e.g., *It's great to be doing such a worthwhile job.*

2 Grammar

as

In the following sentences, formal usage requires the *subjective* case (*I, he, she, we, they*) because the pronoun would be the subject if a verb were supplied:

You are just as intelligent as he (in full, *as he is*)

He . . . might not have heard the motif so often as I (in full, *as I had*)

Informal usage permits *You are just as intelligent as* him.

Formal English uses the *objective* case (*me, him, her, us, them*) only when the pronoun would be the object if a verb were supplied:

I thought you preferred John to Mary, but I see that you like her just as much as him (which means . . . *just as much as you like him*).

collective nouns

Collective nouns are singular words that denote many individuals, e.g., *audience, government, orchestra, the clergy, the public.*

It is normal for collective nouns, being singular, to be followed by singular verbs and pronouns (*is, has, consists*, and *it* in the examples below):

The Government is *determined to beat inflation, as* it *has promised*

Their family is *huge: it consists of five boys and three girls*

The bourgeoisie is *despised for not being proletarian*

The singular verb and pronouns are preferable unless the collective is clearly and unmistakably used to refer to separate individuals rather than to a united body, e.g.

The Cabinet has made its *decision*, but

The Cabinet are resuming their places around the table with the president

The singular should always be used if the collective noun is qualified by a singular word like *this, that, every*, etc.:

This family is *divided*

Every team has *its chance to win*

● Do not mix singular and plural, as (wrongly) in

The congregation were *now dispersing. It tended to break up into small groups.*

comparison of adjectives and adverbs

The two ways of forming the comparative and superlative of adjectives and adverbs are:

(*a*) The addition of the comparative and superlative suffixes *-er* and *-est*. Monosyllabic adjectives and adverbs almost always require these suffixes, e.g., *big* (*bigger, biggest*), *soon* (*sooner, soonest*), and so normally do many adjectives of two syllables, e.g., *narrow* (*narrower, narrowest*), *silly* (*sillier, silliest*).

(*b*) The placing of the comparative and superlative adverbs *more* and *most* before the adjective or adverb. These are used with adjectives of three syllables or more (e.g., *difficult, memorable*), participles (e.g., *bored, boring*), many adjectives of two syllables (e.g., *afraid, awful, childish, harmless, static*), and adverbs ending in *-ly* (e.g., *highly, slowly*).

Adjectives with two syllables vary between the use of the suffixes and of the adverbs.

There are many that never take the suffixes, e.g.,

antique	breathless	futile
bizarre	constant	steadfast

There is also a large class that is acceptable with either, e.g.,

clever	handsome	solemn
common	pleasant	tranquil
cruel	polite	

The choice is largely a matter of style.

group possessive

The group possessive is the construction by which the ending *-'s* of the possessive case can be added to the last word of a noun phrase, which is regarded as a single unit, e.g.,

The king of Spain's daughter

John and Mary's baby

Somebody else's umbrella

A quarter of an hour's drive

Expressions like these are natural and acceptable.

-ics, nouns in

Nouns ending in *-ics* denoting subjects or disciplines are sometimes treated as singular and sometimes as plural. Examples are:

apologetics	genetics	optics
classics (as	linguistics	phonetics
a study)	mathematics	physics
dynamics	mechanics	politics
economics	metaphysics	statistics
electronics	obstetrics	tactics
ethics		

When used strictly as the name of a discipline they are treated as singular:

Psychometrics is unable to investigate the nature of intelligence

So also when the complement is singular:

Mathematics is his strong point

When used more loosely, to denote a manifestation of qualities, often accompanied by a possessive, they are treated as plural:

His politics were a mixture of fear, greed, and envy

I don't understand the mathematics of it, which are complicated

The acoustics in this hall are dreadful

So also when they denote a set of activities or pattern of behavior, as commonly with words like:

acrobactics	dramatics	heroics
athletics	gymnastics	hysterics

E.g., *The mental gymnastics required to believe this are beyond me.*

I or me, we or us, etc.

There is often confusion about which case of a personal pronoun to use when the pronoun stands alone or follows the verb *to be*.

1. When the personal pronoun stands alone, as when it forms the answer to a question, formal usage requires it to have the case it would have if the verb were supplied:

Who killed Cock Robin?—I (in full, *I killed him*)

Which of you did he approach?—Me (in full, *he approached me*)

Informal usage permits the objective case in both kinds of sentence, but this is not acceptable in formal style. It so happens that the subjective case often sounds stilted. It is then best to avoid the problem by providing the substitute verb *do*, or, if the preceding sentence contains an auxiliary, by repeating the auxiliary, e.g.

Who likes cooking?—I do

Who can cook?—I can

2. When a personal pronoun follows *it is, it was, it may be, it could have been*, etc., it should always have the subjective case:

Nobody could suspect that it was *she*

We are given no clues as to what it must have felt like to be he

Informal usage favors the objective case:

I thought it might have been him *at the door*

Don't tell me it's them *again!*

● This is not acceptable in formal usage.

When *who* or *whom* follows, the subjective case is obligatory in formal usage and quite usual informally:

It was I who painted the back door purple

The informal use of the objective case often sounds substandard:

It was her who would get into trouble

(For agreement between the personal pronoun antecedent and the verb in *It is I who* etc., see **I who, you who,** etc.)

In constructions that have the form *I am* + noun or noun phrase + *who*, the verb following *who* agrees with the noun (the antecedent of *who*) and is therefore always in the third person (singular or plural)

I am the sort of person who likes *peace and quiet*

You are the fourth of my colleagues who's told me that ('s = *has*, agreeing with *the fourth*)

I who, you who, etc.

The verb following a personal pronoun (*I, you, he*, etc.) + *who* should agree with the pronoun and should not be in the third person singular unless the third person singular pronoun precedes *who*:

I, who have no savings to speak of, had to pay for the work

This remains so even if the personal pronoun is in the objective case:

They made me, who have no savings at all, pay for the work (not *who has*)

When *it is* (*it was*, etc.) precedes *I who*, etc., the same rule applies: the verb agrees with the personal pronoun:

It's I who have done it

It could have been we who were mistaken

Informal usage sometimes permits the third person to be used (especially when the verb *to be* follows *who*):

You who's supposed to be so practical!

Is it me who's supposed to be keeping an eye on you?

● This is not acceptable in formal usage.

may or might

There is sometimes confusion about whether to use *may* or *might* with the perfect infinitive referring to a past event, e.g., *He may have done* or *He might have done*.

1. If uncertainty about the action or state denoted by the perfect infinitive remains, i.e., at the time of speaking or writing the truth of the event is still unknown, then either *may* or *might* is acceptable:

As they all wore so many different clothes of identically the same kind . . . there may *have been several more or several less*

For all we knew our complaint went unanswered, although of course they might *have tried to call us while we were out of town.*

2. If there is no longer uncertainty about the event, or the matter was never put to the test, and therefore the event did not in fact occur, use *might*:

If that had come ten days ago my whole life might *have been different*

You should not have let him come home alone; he might *have gotten lost*

● It is a common error to use *may* instead of *might* in these circumstances:

If they had not invaded, then eventually we may *have agreed to give them aid.*

I am grateful for his intervention without which they may *have remained in the refugee camp indefinitely*

Schoenberg may *never have gone atonal but for the break-up of his marriage*

In each of these sentences *might* should be substituted for *may*.

none (pronoun)

The pronoun *none* can be followed either by singular verb and singular pronouns, or by plural ones. Either is acceptable, although the plural tends to be more common.

Singular: *None of them was allowed to forget for a moment*

Plural: *None of the fountains ever* play

None of the authors expected their *books to become best-sellers*

shall and will

"*The horror of that moment," he said, "I* shall *never, never forget!" "You* will*, though," she replied, "if you don't make a memorandum of it."*

There is considerable confusion about when to use *shall* and *will*. Put simply, the traditional rule in standard English is:

1. In the first person, singular and plural.

(a) *I* shall*, we* shall express the simple future, e.g.,

I am not a manual worker and please God I never shall *be one*

In the following pages we shall *see good words . . . losing their edge*

(b) *I* will*, we* will express intention or determination on the part of the speaker (especially a promise made by him or her), e.g.,

I will *take you to see her tomorrow morning*

I will *no longer accept responsibility for the fruitless loss of life*

'I don't think we will *ask Mr. Fraser's opinion,' she said coldly*

2. For the second and third persons, singular and plural, the rule is exactly the converse.

(a) *You, he, she, it,* or *they* will express the simple future, e.g.,

Will it disturb you if I keep the lamp on for a bit?

Serapina will *last much longer than a car. She'll probably last longer than you* will

(b) *You, he, she, it,* or *they* shall express intention or determination on the part of the speaker or someone other than the actual subject of the verb, especially a promise made by the speaker to or about the subject, e.g.

Today you shall *be with me in Paradise*

One day you shall *know my full story*

Shall the common man be pushed back into the mud, or shall he not?

In informal usage, *I will* and *we will* are quite often used for the simple future, e.g.,

I will *be a different person after I finish my degree.*

More often the distinction is covered up by the contracted form *'ll*, e.g.,

I don't quite know when I'll get the time to write again

singular or plural

1. When subject and complement are different in number (i.e., one is singular, the other plural), the verb normally agrees with the subject, e.g.,

(Plural subject)

Their wages were *a mere pittance*

Liqueur chocolates are *our specialty*

The Biblical *The wages of sin* is *death* reflects an obsolete idiom by which *wages* took a singular verb.

(Singular subject)

What we need is *customers*

Our speciality is *liqueur chocolates*

2. A plural word or phrase used as a name, title, or quotation counts as singular, e.g.,

Sons and Lovers has *always been one of Lawrence's most popular novels*

3. A singular phrase (such as a prepositional phrase following the subject) that happens to end with a plural word should nevertheless be followed by a singular verb, e.g.,

Everyone except the French wants *(not* want*) Britain to join*

One in six has *(not* have*) this problem*

See also **-ics, -s plural or singular**

-s plural or singular

Some nouns, though they have the plural ending *-s*, are nevertheless usually treated as singular, taking singular verbs and pronouns referring back to them.

1. *News*

2. Diseases:

    measles   mumps   rickets   shingles

Measles and *rickets* can also be treated as ordinary plural nouns.

3. Games:

billiards	*dominoes*	*ninepins*
checkers	*fives*	*skittles*
darts		

4. Countries:

the Bahamas	*the Philippines*
the Netherlands	*the United States*

These are treated as singular when considered as a unit, which they commonly are in a political context, or when the complement is singular, e.g.,

The Philippines is *a predominantly agricultural country*

The United States has *withdrawn its ambassador*

The Bahamas and the Philippines are also the geographical names of the groups of islands that the two nations comprise, and in this use can be treated as plurals, e.g.,

The Bahamas were *settled by British subjects*

See also *-ics*.

we (with phrase following)

Expressions consisting of *we* or *us* followed by a qualifying word or phrase, e.g., *we Americans, us Americans,* are often misused with the wrong case of the first person plural pronoun. In fact the rules are exactly the same as for *we* or *us* standing alone.

If the expression is the subject, *we* should be used:

(Correct)   *Not always laughing as heartily as we Americans are supposed to do*

(Incorrect) *We all make mistakes, even us judges* (substitute *we judges*)

If the expression is the object or the complement of a preposition, *us* should be used:

(Correct)   *To us Americans, personal liberty is a vital principle.*

(Incorrect) *The president said some nice things about we reporters in the press corps.*

you and I or you and me

When a personal pronoun is linked by *and* or *or* to a noun or another pronoun there is often confusion about which case to put the pronoun in. In fact the rule is exactly as it would be for the pronoun standing alone.

1. If the two words linked by *and* or *or* constitute the subject, the pronoun should be in the subjective case, e.g.,

Only she *and her mother cared for the old house*

That's what we *would do, that is* John *and* I

Who could go?—Either you *or* he

The use of the objective case is quite common in informal speech, but it is non-standard, e.g. (examples from the speech of characters in novels),

Perhaps only her *and Mrs Natwick had stuck to the christened name*

That's how we *look at it,* me *and Martha*

Either Mary had to leave or me

2. If the two words linked by *and* or *or* constitute the object of the verb, or the complement of a preposition, the objective case should be used:

The afternoon would suit her *and John better*

It was time for Sebastian and me *to go down to the living room*

The use of the subjective case is very common informally. It probably arises from an exaggerated fear of the error indicated under 1 above.

● It remains, however, non-standard, e.g.,

It was this that set Charles and I *talking of old times*

Why is it that people like you and I *are so unpopular?*

Between you and I

This last expression is very commonly heard. *Between you and me* should always be substituted.

Appendix 3 Selected Proverbs

A

ABSENCE makes the heart grow fonder

He who is **ABSENT** is always in the wrong

ACCIDENTS will happen

There is no **ACCOUNTING** for tastes

ACTIONS speak louder than words

When **ADAM** delved and Eve span, who was then the gentleman?

ADVENTURES are to the adventurous

ADVERSITY makes strange bedfellows

AFTER a storm comes a calm

AFTER dinner rest a while, after supper walk a mile

ALL good things must come to an end

It takes **ALL** sorts to make a world

ALL things are possible with God

ALL things come to those who wait

ALL would live long, but none would be old

Good **AMERICANS** when they die go to Paris

ANY port in a storm

If **ANYTHING** can go wrong, it will

APPEARANCES are deceptive

APPETITE comes with eating

An **APPLE** a day keeps the doctor away

The **APPLE** never falls far from the tree

One bad **APPLE** spoils the barrel (or bunch)

APRIL showers brings May flowers

An **ARMY** marches on its stomach

ART is long and life is short

ASK a silly question and you get a silly answer

ASK no questions and hear no lies

B

A **BAD** excuse is better than none

BAD money drives out good

BAD news travels fast

A **BAD** penny always turns up

A **BAD** workman blames his tools

A **BARKING** dog never bites

BE what you would seem to be

BEAR and forbear

If you can't **BEAT** 'em, join 'em

BEAUTY is in the eye of the beholder

BEAUTY is only skin-deep

Where **BEES** are, there is honey

Set a **BEGGAR** on horseback, and he'll ride to the Devil

BEGGARS can't be choosers

BELIEVE nothing of what you hear, and only half of what you see

All's for the **BEST** in the best of all possible worlds

The **BEST** is the enemy of the good

The **BEST**-laid schemes of mice and men gang aft agley

The **BEST** of friends must part

The **BEST** of men are but men at best

The **BEST** things come in small packages

The **BEST** things in life are free

It is **BEST** to be on the safe side

BETTER be an old man's darling, than a young man's slave

BETTER be envied than pitied

BETTER safe than sorry

BETTER late than never

The **BETTER** the day, the better the deed

The devil you know is **BETTER** than the devil you don't know

It is **BETTER** to be born lucky than rich

It is **BETTER** to give than to receive

'Tis **BETTER** to have loved and lost, than never to have loved at all

It is **BETTER** to travel hopefully than to arrive

BETTER to wear out than to rust out

BEWARE Greeks bearing gifts

BIG fish eat little fish

BIG fleas have little fleas upon their backs to bite them, and little fleas have lesser fleas, and so *ad infinitum*

The **BIGGER** they are, the harder they fall

A **BIRD** in the hand is worth two in the bush

BIRDS in their little nests agree

BIRDS of a feather flock together

Little **BIRDS** that can sing and won't sing must be made to sing

BLESSED is he who expects nothing, for he shall never be disappointed

There's none so **BLIND** as those who will not see

When the **BLIND** lead the blind, both shall fall into the ditch

You can't get **BLOOD** from a stone

BLOOD is thicker than water

BLOOD will have blood

BLOOD will tell

BLUE are the hills that are far away

You can't tell (*or* judge) a **BOOK** by its cover

If you're **BORN** to be hanged then you'll never be drowned

Neither a **BORROWER** nor a lender be

You can take the **BOY** out of the country but you can't take the country out of the boy

Never send a **BOY** to do a man's job

BOYS will be boys

None but the **BRAVE** deserve the fair

BRAVE men lived before Agamemnon

The **BREAD** never falls but on its buttered side

What's **BRED** in the bone will come out in the flesh

BREVITY is the soul of wit

You cannot make **BRICKS** without straw

Happy is the **BRIDE** that the sun shines on

Always a **BRIDESMAID**, never a bride

If it ain't **BROKE**, don't fix it

A **BULLY** is always a coward

A **BURNT** child dreads the fire

The **BUSIEST** men have the most leisure

BUSINESS before pleasure

BUY in the cheapest market and sell in the dearest

Let the **BUYER** beware

The **BUYER** has need of a hundred eyes, the seller of but one

C

CAESAR's wife must be above suspicion

He who CAN, does; he who cannot, teaches

Where the CARCASS is, there shall the eagles be gathered to-gether

A CARPENTER is known by his chips

A CAT in gloves catches no mice

A CAT may look at a king

When the CAT's away, the mice will play

The CAT would eat fish, but would not wet her feet

It is easier to CATCH flies with honey than with vinegar

At night all CATS are gray

A CHAIN is no stronger than its weakest link

Don't CHANGE horses in mid-stream

A CHANGE is as good as a rest

CHARITY begins at home

CHARITY covers a multitude of sins

CHEATERS never prosper

Monday's CHILD is fair of face

The CHILD is the father of the man

CHILDREN and fools tell the truth

CHILDREN are certain cares, but uncertain comforts

CHILDREN should be seen and not heard

CIRCUMSTANCES alter cases

A CIVIL question deserves a civil answer

CIVILITY costs nothing

CLEANLINESS is next to godliness

Hasty CLIMBERS have sudden falls

A CLOSED mouth catches no flies

CLOTHES make the man

Every CLOUD has a silver lining

Every COCK will crow upon his own dunghill

COLD hands, warm heart

COMING events cast their shadows before

A man is known by the COMPANY he keeps

The COMPANY makes the feast

COMPARISONS are odious

He that COMPLIES against his will is of his own opinion still

CONFESS and be hanged

CONFESSION is good for the soul

CONSCIENCE makes cowards of us all

CONSTANT dropping wears away a stone

CORPORATIONS have neither bodies to be punished nor souls to be damned

COUNCILS of war never fight

Don't COUNT your chickens before they are hatched

In the COUNTRY of the blind, the one-eyed man is king

Happy is the COUNTRY which has no history

The COURSE of true love never did run smooth

Why buy a COW when milk is so cheap?

COWARDS die many times before their death

Give CREDIT where credit is due

Don't CROSS the bridge till you come to it

CROSSES are ladders that lead to heaven

Don't CRY before you're hurt

It is no use CRYING over spilled milk

What can't be CURED must be endured

CURIOSITY killed the cat

CURSES, like chickens, come home to roost

The CUSTOMER is always right

Don't CUT off your nose to spite your face

CUT your coat according to your cloth

D

They that DANCE must pay the fiddler

The DARKEST hour is just before the dawn

Let the DEAD bury the dead

DEAD men don't bite

DEAD men tell no tales

Blessed are the DEAD that the rain rains on

There's none so DEAF as those who will not hear

A DEAF husband and a blind wife are always a happy couple

DEATH is the great leveler

DEATH pays all debts

The best DEFENSE is a good offense

DELAYS are dangerous

DESPERATE diseases must have desperate remedies

The DEVIL can quote Scripture for his own ends

The DEVIL finds work for idle hands to do

Why should the DEVIL have all the best tunes?

The DEVIL is not so black as he is painted

The DEVIL looks after his own

The DEVIL's children have the Devil's luck

DEVIL take the hindmost

The DEVIL was sick, the Devil a saint would be; the Devil was well, the devil a saint was he!

DIAMOND cuts diamond

You can only DIE once

DIFFERENT strokes for different folks

The DIFFICULT is done at once, the impossible takes a little longer

DILIGENCE is the mother of good luck

Throw DIRT enough, and some will stick

DIRTY water will quench fire

DISCRETION is the better part of valor

DISTANCE lends enchantment to the view

DIVIDE and conquer

DO as I say, not as I do

DO as you would be done by

DO right and fear no man

DO not do that which you would not have known

DO unto others as you would they should do unto you

DOG does not eat dog

Every DOG has his day

Every DOG is allowed one bite

A DOG that will fetch a bone will carry a bone

DOGS bark, but the caravan goes on

What's DONE cannot be undone

A DOOR must either be shut or open

Whosoever **DRAWS** his sword against the prince must throw the scabbard away

DREAM of a funeral and you hear of a marriage

DREAMS go by contraries

He that **DRINKS** beer, thinks beer

A **DRIPPING** June sets all in tune

You can **DRIVE** out Nature with a pitchfork, but she keeps on coming back

A **DROWNING** man will clutch at a straw

E

EAGLES don't catch flies

The **EARLY** bird catches the worm

The **EARLY** man never borrows from the late man

EARLY to bed and early to rise, makes a man healthy, wealthy, and wise

EAST, west, home's best

EASY come, easy go

EASY does it

You are what you **EAT**

We must **EAT** a peck (or pound) of dirt before we die

He that would **EAT** the fruit must climb the tree

EAT to live, not live to eat

An **EGG** today is better than a hen tomorrow

Don't put all your **EGGS** in one basket

EMPTY sacks will never stand upright

EMPTY vessels make the most sound

The **END** crowns the work

The **END** justifies the means

ENGLAND is the paradise of women, the hell of horses, and the purgatory of servants

ENGLAND's difficulty is Ireland's opportunity

The **ENGLISH** are a nation of shopkeepers

One **ENGLISHMAN** can beat three Frenchmen

An **ENGLISHMAN**'s home is his castle

An **ENGLISHMAN**'s word is his bond

ENOUGH is as good as a feast

To **ERR** is human (to forgive divine)

EVERY little (bit) helps

EVERY man for himself

EVERY man for himself, and God for us all

EVERY man for himself, and the Devil take the hindmost

EVERY many has his price

EVERY man is the architect of his own fortune

EVERY man to his taste

What **EVERYBODY** says must be true

EVERYBODY's business is nobody's business

EVERYTHING has an end

Never do **EVIL** that good may come of it

Of two **EVILS** choose the less(er)

EXAMPLE is better than precept

The **EXCEPTION** proves the rule

There is an **EXCEPTION** to every rule

A fair **EXCHANGE** is no robbery

He who **EXCUSES**, accuses himself

What can you **EXPECT** from a pig but a grunt?

EXPERIENCE is the best teacher

EXPERIENCE is the father of wisdom

EXPERIENCE keeps a dear school (yet fools will learn in no other)

EXTREMES meet

What the **EYE** doesn't see, the heart doesn't grieve over

The **EYES** are the window of the soul

F

FACT is stranger than fiction

FACTS are stubborn things

FAINT heart never won fair lady

All's **FAIR** in love and war

FAIR play's a jewel

FAITH will move mountains

FAMILIARITY breeds contempt

The **FAMILY** that prays together stays together

Like **FATHER**, like son

A **FAULT** confessed is half redressed

FEED a cold and starve a fever

The **FEMALE** of the species is more deadly than the male

FIELDS have eyes, and woods have ears

FIGHT fire with fire

He who **FIGHTS** and runs away, may live to fight another day

FINDERS keepers (losers weepers)

FINE feathers make fine birds

FINGERS were made before forks

FIRE is a good servant but a bad master

FIRST come, first served

The **FIRST** duty of a soldier is obedience

FIRST impressions are the most lasting

It is the **FIRST** step that is difficult

FIRST things first

There is always a **FIRST** time

The **FISH** always stinks from the head downwards

FISH and guests stink after three days

There are as good **FISH** in the sea as ever came out of it

A **FOOL** and his money are soon parted

A **FOOL** at forty is a fool indeed

There's no **FOOL** like an old fool

A **FOOL** may give a wise man counsel

You can **FOOL** all the people some of the time and some of the people all the time, but you cannot fool all the people all the time

FOOLS ask questions that wise men cannot answer

FOOLS build houses and wise men live in them

FOOLS for luck

FOOLS rush in where angels fear to tread

FOREWARNED is forearmed

FORTUNE favors fools

FORTUNE favors the brave

FOUR eyes see more than two

There's no such thing as a **FREE** lunch

A **FRIEND** in need is a friend indeed

FULL cup, steady hand

Out of the **FULLNESS** of the heart the mouth speaks

One **FUNERAL** makes many

G

GARBAGE in, garbage out

In takes three **GENERATIONS** to make a gentleman

GENIUS is an infinite capacity for taking pains

Never look a **GIFT** horse in the mouth

GIVE and take is fair play

GIVE the Devil his due

He **GIVES** twice who gives quickly

Those who live in **GLASS** houses shouldn't throw stones

All that **GLITTERS** is not gold

GO abroad and you'll hear news of home

GO further and fare worse

You cannot serve **GOD** and Mammon

GOD helps them that help themselves

GOD made the country, and man made the town

GOD makes the back to the burden

GOD never sends mouths but He sends meat

GOD sends meat, but the Devil sends cooks

GOD's in his heaven; all's right with the world

GOD tempers the wind to the shorn lamb

Whom the **GODS** love die young

The **GODS** send nuts to those who have no teeth

Whom the **GODS** would destroy, they first make mad

He that **GOES** a-borrowing, goes a-sorrowing

What **GOES** around comes around

When the **GOING** gets tough, the tough get going

GOLD may be bought too dear

A **GOLDEN** key can open any door

If you can't be **GOOD**, be careful

A **GOOD** beginning makes a good ending

The **GOOD** die young

He is a **GOOD** dog who goes to church

GOOD fences make good neighbors

The **GOOD** is the enemy of the best

A **GOOD** Jack makes a good Jill

GOOD men are scarce

There's many a **GOOD** tune played on an old fiddle

One **GOOD** turn deserves another

What is **GOT** over the Devil's back is spent under his belly

While the **GRASS** grows, the steed starves

The **GRASS** is always greener on the other side of the fence

A **GREAT** book is a great evil

GREAT minds think alike

GREAT oaks from little acorns grow

The **GREATER** the sinner, the greater the saint

The **GREATER** the truth, the greater the libel

When **GREEK** meets Greek, then comes the tug of war

All is **GRIST** that comes to the mill

A **GUILTY** conscience needs no accuser

H

What you've never **HAD** you never miss

HALF a loaf is better than none (*or* no bread)

The **HALF** is better than the whole

One **HALF** of the world does not know how the other half lives

HALF the truth is often a whole lie

When all you have is a **HAMMER**, everything looks like a nail

One **HAND** for oneself and one for the ship

The **HAND** that rocks the cradle rules the world

One **HAND** washes the other

HANDSOME is as handsome does

One might as well be **HANGED** for a sheep as a lamb

HAPPY families are all alike

If you would be **HAPPY** for a week take a wife; if you would be happy for a month kill a pig; but if you would be happy all your life plant a garden

Call no man **HAPPY** till he dies

HARD words break no bones

HASTE is from the Devil

More **HASTE**, less speed

HASTE makes waste

Make **HASTE** slowly

What you **HAVE**, hold

You can't **HAVE** your cake and eat it too

If you don't like the **HEAT**, get out of the kitchen

HEAVEN helps those who help themselves

HEAVEN protects children, sailors, and drunken men

HELL hath no fury like a woman scorned

He who **HESITATES** is lost

Those who **HIDE** can find

HISTORY repeats itself

HOME is home though it's never so homely

HOME is where the heart is

(Be it ever so humble,) There's no place like **HOME**

HOMER sometimes nods

HONESTY is the best policy

HONEY catches more flies than vinegar

There is **HONOR** among thieves

HOPE deferred makes the heart sick

HOPE for the best and prepare for (*or* expect) the worst

HOPE is a good breakfast but a bad supper

HOPE springs eternal

If it were not for **HOPE**, the heart would break

You can take a **HORSE** to the water, but you can't make him drink

HORSES for courses

One **HOUR**'s sleep before midnight is worth two after

When **HOUSE** and land are gone and spent, then learning is most excellent

A **HOUSE** divided cannot stand

HUNGER drives the wolf out of the wood

HUNGER is the best sauce

The **HUSBAND** is always the last to know

Appendix 3

I

An **IDLE** brain is the Devil's workshop
IDLE people have the least leisure
IDLENESS is the root of all evil
Where **IGNORANCE** is bliss, 'tis folly to be wise
IGNORANCE of the law is no excuse (for breaking it)
It's an **ILL** bird that fouls its own nest
ILL gotten goods never thrive
It's **ILL** waiting for dead men's shoes
ILL weeds grow apace
It's an **ILL** wind that blows nobody any good
IMITATION is the sincerest form of flattery
IN for a penny, in for a pound

J

Every **JACK** has his Jill
JACK is as good as his master
JAM tomorrow and jam yesterday, but never jam today
JOVE but laughs at lovers' perjury
No one should be **JUDGE** in his own cause
JUDGE not, that ye be not judged
Be **JUST** before you're generous

K

Why **KEEP** a dog and bark yourself?
KEEP a thing seven years and you'll always find a use for it
KEEP no more cats than will catch mice
KEEP your shop and your shop will keep you
KILLING no murder
The **KING** can do no wrong
KINGS have long arms
KISSING goes by favor
To **KNOW** all is to forgive all
What you don't **KNOW** can't hurt you
KNOW thyself
You never **KNOW** what you can do till you try
KNOWLEDGE is power

L

The **LABORER** is worthy of his hire
Every **LAND** has its own law
The **LAST** drop makes the cup run over
It is the **LAST** straw that breaks the camel's back
LAUGH and the world laughs with you; weep and you weep alone
Let them **LAUGH** that win
He **LAUGHS** best who laughs last
He who **LAUGHS** last, laughs best (*or* longest)
One **LAW** for the rich and another for the poor
A man who is his own **LAWYER** has a fool for his client
LEAST said, soonest mended
There is nothing like **LEATHER**
LEND your money and lose your friend
The **LEOPARD** does not change his spots

LESS is more
LET well (enough) alone
A **LIAR** ought to have a good memory
If you **LIE** down with dogs, you will get up with fleas
LIFE begins at forty
LIFE isn't all beer and skittles
While (*or* Where) there's **LIFE** there's hope
LIGHTNING never strikes the same place twice
LIKE breeds like
LIKE will to like
Loose **LIPS** sink ships
LISTENERS never hear any good of themselves
There is no **LITTLE** enemy
A **LITTLE** knowledge is a dangerous thing
LITTLE leaks sink the ship
LITTLE pitchers have large (*or* big) ears
A **LITTLE** pot is soon hot
LITTLE strokes fell great oaks
LITTLE thieves are hanged, but great ones escape
LITTLE things please little minds
LIVE and learn
LIVE and let live
If you want to **LIVE** and thrive, let the spider run alive
A **LIVE** dog is better than a dead lion
They that **LIVE** longest, see most
He who **LIVES** by the sword dies by the sword
He that **LIVES** in hope dances to an ill tune
He **LIVES** long who lives well
The **LONGEST** way around is the shortest way home
LOOK before you leap
You cannot **LOSE** what you never had
One man's **LOSS** is another man's gain
There's no great **LOSS** without some gain
LOVE and a cough cannot be hid
He that falls in **LOVE** with himself will have no rivals
One cannot **LOVE** and be wise
LOVE begets love
LOVE is blind
LOVE laughs at locksmiths
LOVE makes the world go round
LOVE me, love my dog
LOVE will find a way
LOVE your neighbor, yet don't pull down your hedge
There is **LUCK** in leisure
There is **LUCK** in odd numbers
LUCKY at cards, unlucky in love

M

Dont' get **MAD**, get even
MAKE hay while the sun shines
As you **MAKE** your bed, so you must lie upon it
MAN cannot live by bread alone
Whatever **MAN** has done, man may do
A **MAN** is as old as he feels, and a woman as old as she looks

1806

MAN is the measure of all things

MAN proposes, God disposes

MAN's extremity is God's opportunity

The same **MAN** cannot be both a friend and a flatterer

MANNERS maketh man

There's **MANY** a slip 'twixt cup and lip

MANY are called but few are chosen

MANY complain of their memory, few of their judgment

MANY hands make light work

MARCH comes in like a lion, and goes out like a lamb

MARRIAGE is a lottery

There goes more to **MARRIAGE** than four bare legs in a bed

MARRIAGES are made in heaven

Never **MARRY** for money, but marry where money is

MARRY in haste and repent at leisure

Like **MASTER**, like man

There is **MEASURE** in all things

One man's **MEAT** is another man's poison

Do not **MEET** troubles half-way

MIGHT makes right

The **MILLS** of God grind slowly, yet they grind exceeding small

The age of **MIRACLES** is past

MISERY loves company

MISFORTUNES never come singly

A **MISS** is as good as a mile

You never **MISS** the water till the well runs dry

If you don't make **MISTAKES** you don't make anything

MODERATION in all things

MONEY has no smell

MONEY isn't everything

MONEY is power

(The love of) **MONEY** is the root of all evil

MONEY makes a man

MONEY makes money

MONEY talks

MORE people know Tom Fool than Tom Fool knows

The **MORE** the merrier

The **MORE** you get, the more you want

MORNING dreams come true

Like **MOTHER**, like daughter

If the **MOUNTAIN** will not come to Mahomet, Mahomet must go to the mountain

A **MOUSE** may help a lion

Out of the **MOUTHS** of babes—

MUCH cry and little wool

MUCH would have more

MURDER will out

What **MUST** be, must be

N

NATURE abhors a vacuum

The **NEARER** the bone, the sweeter the meat

The **NEARER** the church, the farther from God

NECESSITY is the mother of invention

NECESSITY knows no law

NECESSITY never made a good bargain

NEEDS must when the Devil drives

NEVER is a long time

NEVER say never

It is **NEVER** too late to learn

It is **NEVER** too late to mend

NEVER too old to learn

A **NEW** broom sweeps clean

You can't put **NEW** wine in old bottles

NIGHT brings counsel

NINE tailors make a man

NO man can serve two masters

NO man is a hero to his valet

NO news is good news

NO pain, no gain

A **NOD**'s as good as a wink to a blind horse

NOTHING comes of nothing

NOTHING for nothing

NOTHING is certain but death and taxes

NOTHING is certain but the unforeseen

There is **NOTHING** new under the sun

NOTHING is so popular as goodness

NOTHING so bad but it might have been worse

There is **NOTHING** so good for the inside of a man as the outside of a horse

NOTHING succeeds like success

NOTHING venture(d) nothing gain(ed)

O

Beware of an **OAK**, it draws the stroke; avoid an ash, it counts the flash; creep under the thorn, it can save you from harm

He that cannot **OBEY** cannot command

It is best to be **OFF** with the old love before you are on with the new

OFFENDERS never pardon

OLD habits die hard

You cannot put an **OLD** head on young shoulders

OLD sins cast long shadows

OLD soldiers never die, they just fade away

You cannot make an **OMELET** without breaking eggs

ONCE a—, always a—

ONCE bitten, twice shy

When **ONE** door shuts, another opens

ONE nail drives out another

ONE year's seeding makes seven years' weeding

The **OPERA** isn't over till the fat lady sings

OPPORTUNITY makes a thief

OPPORTUNITY never knocks twice at any man's door

OTHER times, other manners

An **OUNCE** of prevention is worth a pound of cure

OUT of sight, out of mind

P

It is the **PACE** that kills

Things **PAST** cannot be recalled

PATIENCE is a virtue

If you **PAY** peanuts, you get monkeys

He who **PAYS** the piper calls the tune

You **PAYS** your money and you takes your choice

You get what you **PAY** for

If you want **PEACE**, you must prepare for war

Do not throw **PEARLS** to swine

The **PEN** is mightier than the sword

Take care of the **PENNIES** and the dollars will take care of themselves

A **PENNY** saved is a penny earned

PENNY wise and pound foolish

PHYSICIAN, heal thyself

One **PICTURE** is worth ten thousand words

Every **PICTURE** tells a story

See a **PIN** (or penny) and pick it up, all the day you'll have good luck; see a pin (or penny) and let it lie, bad luck you'll have all the day

The **PITCHER** will go to the well once too often

PITY is akin to love

A **PLACE** for everything, and everything in its place

There's no **PLACE** like home

If you **PLAY** with fire you get burned

You can't **PLEASE** everyone

POLITICS makes strange bedfellows

It is a **POOR** dog that's not worth whistling for

It is a **POOR** heart that never rejoices

POSSESSION is nine points of the law

When **POVERTY** comes in at the door, love flies out of the window

POVERTY is no disgrace, but it is a great inconvenience

POVERTY is not a crime

POWER corrupts; absolute power corrupts absolutely

PRACTICE makes perfect

PRACTICE what you preach

PRIDE feels no pain

PRIDE goes before a fall

PROCRASTINATION is the thief of time

PROMISES, like piecrust, are made to be broken

The **PROOF** of the pudding is in the eating

A **PROPHET** is not without honor save in his own country

PROVIDENCE is always on the side of the big battalions

Any **PUBLICITY** is good publicity

It is easier to **PULL** down than to build up

PUNCTUALITY is the politeness of princes

To the **PURE** all things are pure

Never **PUT** off till tomorrow what you can do today

Q

QUITTERS never win and winners never quit

The **QUARREL** of lovers is the renewal of love

R

The **RACE** is not to the swift, nor the battle to the strong

RAIN before seven, fine before eleven

It never **RAINS** but it pours

It is easier to **RAISE** the Devil than to lay him

The heart has its **REASONS** that reason knows nothing of

RED sky at night, shepherd's (or sailor's) delight; red sky in the morning, shepherd's (or sailor's) warning

A **REED** before the wind lives on, while mighty oaks do fall

There is a **REMEDY** for everything except death

REVENGE is a dish best eaten cold

REVENGE is sweet

The **RICH** man has his ice in the summer and the poor man gets his in the winter

If you can't **RIDE** two horses at once, you shouldn't be in the circus

He who **RIDES** a tiger is afraid to dismount

A **RISING** tide lifts all boats

The **ROAD** to hell is paved with good intentions

All **ROADS** lead to Rome

A **ROLLING** stone gathers no moss

When in **ROME**, do as the Romans do

ROME was not built in a day

There is always **ROOM** at the top

Give a man **ROPE** enough and he will hang himself

The **ROTTEN** apple injures its neighbor

There is no **ROYAL** road to learning

You cannot **RUN** with the hare and hunt with the hounds

S

SAFE bind, safe find

There is **SAFETY** in numbers

Help you to **SALT**, help you to sorrow

What's **SAUCE** for the goose is sauce for the gander

SAVE us from our friends

SCRATCH a Russian and you find a Tartar

He that would go to **SEA** for pleasure, would go to hell for a pastime

The **SEA** refuses no river

SECOND thoughts are best

What you **SEE** is what you get

SEE no evil, hear no evil, speak no evil

Good **SEED** makes a good crop

SEEING is believing

SEEK and ye shall find

SELF-PRESERVATION is the first law of nature

If you would be well **SERVED**, serve yourself

From **SHIRTSLEEVES** to shirtsleeves in three generatons

If the **SHOE** fits, wear it

The **SHOEMAKER**'s child always goes barefoot

SHROUDS have no pockets

A **SHUT** mouth catches no flies

SILENCE is golden

SILENCE means consent

You can't make a **SILK** purse out of a sow's ear

SING before breakfast, cry before night

SIX hours' sleep for a man, seven for a woman, and eight for a fool

Let **SLEEPING** dogs lie

SLOW but sure

SMALL choice in rotten apples

SMALL is beautiful

Where there's SMOKE there's fire

A SOFT answer turneth away wrath

SOFTLY, softly, catchee monkey

If you're not part of the SOLUTION, you're part of the problem

You don't get SOMETHING for nothing

SOMETHING is better than nothing

SOMETHING old, something new, something borrowed, something blue

My SON is my son till he gets him a wife, but my daughter's my daughter all the days of her life

SOON ripe, soon rotten

The SOONER begun, the sooner done

A SOW may whistle, though it has an ill mouth for it

As you SOW, so you reap

They that SOW the wind shall reap the whirlwind

SPARE the rod and spoil the child

Never SPEAK ill of the dead

Everyone SPEAKS well of the bridge which carries him over

If you don't SPECULATE, you can't accumulate

SPEECH is silver, but silence is golden

What you SPEND, you have

It is not SPRING until you can plant your foot upon twelve daisies

The SQUEAKING wheel gets the grease

It is too late to shut the STABLE-door after the horse has bolted

One STEP at a time

It is easy to find a STICK to beat a dog

STICKS and stones may break my bones, but words (or names) will never hurt me

A STILL tongue makes a wise head

STILL waters run deep

A STITCH in time saves nine

STOLEN fruit is sweet

One STORY is good till another is told

STRAWS tell which way the wind blows

A STREAM cannot rise above its source

STRETCH your arm no further than your sleeve will reach

STRIKE while the iron is hot

The STYLE is the man

From the SUBLIME to the ridiculous is only a step

If at first you don't SUCCEED, try, try again

SUCCESS has many fathers, while failure is an orphan

Never give a SUCKER an even break

SUFFICIENT unto the day is the evil thereof

Never let the SUN go down on your anger

The SUN loses nothing by shining into a puddle

He who SUPS with the Devil should have a long spoon

One SWALLOW does not make a summer

From the SWEETEST wine, the tartest vinegar

T

TAKE the goods the gods provide

A TALE never loses in the telling

Never tell TALES out of school

TALK is cheap

TALK of the Devil, and he is bound to appear

TASTES differ

You can't TEACH an old dog new tricks

Don't TEACH your grandmother to suck eggs

TELL the truth and shame the Devil

Set (or It takes) a THIEF to catch a thief

When THIEVES fall out, honest men come by their own

If a THING's worth doing, it's worth doing well

When THINGS are at the worst they begin to mend

THINK first and speak afterwards

The THIRD time pays for all

The THIRD time's the charm

THOUGHT is free

THREATENED men live long

THREE may keep a secret, if two of them are dead

THRIFT is a great revenue

Don't THROW out your dirty water until you get in fresh

Don't THROW the baby out with the bathwater

There is a TIME and place for everything

TIME and tide wait for no man

TIME flies

Do not squander TIME, for that is the stuff life is made of

There is a TIME for everything

TIME is a great healer

TIME is money

No TIME like the present

TIME will tell

TIME works wonders

TIMES change and we with time

You may delay, but TIME will not

TOMORROW is another day

TOMORROW never comes

The TONGUE always returns to the sore tooth

TOO many cooks spoil the broth

You can have TOO much of a good thing

TRADE follows the flag

TRAVEL broadens the mind

He TRAVELS fastest who travels alone

As a TREE falls, so shall it lie

The TREE is known by its fruit

There are TRICKS in every trade

A TROUBLE shared is a trouble halved

Never TROUBLE trouble till trouble troubles you

Many a TRUE word is spoken in jest

Put your TRUST in God, and keep your powder dry

There is TRUTH in wine

TRUTH is stranger than fiction

TRUTH lies at the bottom of a well

TRUTH will out

TURNABOUT is fair play

As the TWIG is bent, so is the tree inclined

While TWO dogs are fighting for a bone, a third runs away with it

TWO heads are better than one

TWO is company, but three's a crowd

TWO of a trade never agree

If TWO ride on a horse, one must ride behind

There are TWO sides to every question

It takes TWO to make a bargain

It takes TWO to make a quarrel

It takes TWO to tango

TWO wrongs don't make a right

U

The UNEXPECTED always happens

UNION is strength

UNITED we stand, divided we fall

What goes UP must come down

V

VARIETY is the spice of life

VIRTUE is its own reward

The VOICE of the people is the voice of God

W

We must learn to WALK before we can run

WALLS have ears

WALNUTS and pears you plant for your heirs

If you WANT a thing done well, do it yourself

For WANT of a nail the shoe was lost; for want of a shoe the horse was lost; and for want of a horse the man was lost

One does not WASH one's dirty linen in public

WASTE not, want not

A WATCHED pot never boils

Don't go near the WATER until you learn how to swim

The WAY to a man's heart is through his stomach

There are more WAYS of killing a cat than choking it with cream

There are more WAYS of killing a dog than choking it with butter

There are more WAYS of killing a dog than hanging it

The WEAKEST go to the wall

One WEDDING brings another

WEDLOCK is a padlock

WELL begun is half done

WELL done is better than well said

All's WELL that ends well

When the WELL is dry we know the worth of water

A WILFUL man must have his way

WILFUL waste makes woeful want

Where there's a WILL, there's a way

He who WILLS the end, wills the means

You WIN a few, you lose a few

You can't WIN them all

When the WIND is in the east, 'tis neither good for man nor beast

In WINE there is truth

When the WINE is in, the wit is out

It is easy to be WISE after the event

It is a WISE child that knows its own father

The WISH is father to the thought

If WISHES were horses, beggars would ride

A WOMAN's place is in the home

A WOMAN's work is never done

WONDERS will never cease

Happy's the WOOING that is not long a-doing

Many go out for WOOL and come home shorn

A WORD to the wise is sufficient

All WORK and no play makes Jack a dull boy

WORK expands so as to fill the time available

It is not WORK that kills, but worry

If you won't WORK you shan't eat

Even a WORM will turn

The WORTH of a thing is what it will bring

Y

YOUNG folks think old folks to be fools, but old folks know young folks to be fools

A YOUNG man married is a young man marred

YOUNG men may die, but old men must die

YOUNG saint, old devil

YOUTH must be served

Appendix 4 Books of the Bible

Old Testament

Genesis (Gen.)
Exodus (Exod.)
Leviticus (Lev.)
Numbers (Num.)
Deuteronomy (Deut.)
Joshua (Josh.)
Judges (Judg.)
Ruth
First Book of Samuel (1 Sam.)
Second Book of Samuel (2 Sam.)
First Book of Kings (1 Kgs.)
Second Book of Kings (2 Kgs.)
First Book of Chronicles (1 Chr.)
Second Book of Chronicles (2 Chr.)

Ezra
Nehemiah (Neh.)
Esther
Job
Psalms (Ps.)
Proverbs (Prov.)
Ecclesiastes (Eccles.)
Song of Songs, Song of Solomon,
  Canticles (S. of S., Cant.)
Isaiah (Isa.)
Jeremiah (Jer.)
Lamentations (Lam.)
Ezekiel (Ezek.)

Daniel (Dan.)
Hosea (Hos.)
Joel
Amos
Obadiah (Obad.)
Jonah
Micah (Mic.)
Nahum (Nah.)
Habakkuk (Hab.)
Zephaniah (Zeph.)
Haggai (Hag.)
Zechariah (Zech.)
Malachi (Mal.)

Apocrypha

First Book of Esdras (1 Esd.)
Second Book of Esdras (2 Esd.)
Tobit
Judith
Rest of Esther (Rest of Esth.)
Wisdom of Solomon (Wisd.)

Ecclesiasticus, Wisdom of Jesus the
  Son of Sirach (Ecclus., Sir.)
Baruch
Song of the Three Children
  (S. of III Ch.)

Susanna (Sus.)
Bel and the Dragon (Bel & Dr.)
Prayer of Manasseh (Pr. of Man.)
First Book of Maccabees (1 Macc.)
Second Book of Maccabees (2 Macc.)

New Testament

Gospel according to St. Matthew
  (Matt.)
Gospel according to St. Mark (Mark)
Gospel according to St. Luke (Luke)
Gospel according to St. John (John)
Acts of the Apostles (Acts)
Epistle to the Romans (Rom.)
First Epistle to the Corinthians
  (1 Cor.)
Second Epistle to the Corinthians
  (2 Cor.)

Epistle to the Galatians (Gal.)
Epistle to the Ephesians (Eph.)
Epistle to the Philippians (Phil.)
Epistle to the Colossians (Col.)
First Epistle to the Thessalonians
  (1 Thess.)
Second Epistle to the Thessalonians
  (2 Thess.)
First Epistle to Timothy (1 Tim.)
Second Epistle to Timothy (2 Tim.)
Epistle to Titus (Tit.)

Epistle to Philemon (Philem.)
Epistle to the Hebrews (Heb.)
Epistle of James (Jas.)
First Epistle of Peter (1 Pet.)
Second Epistle of Peter (2 Pet.)
First Epistle of John (1 John)
Second Epistle of John (2 John)
Third Epistle of John (3 John)
Epistle of Jude (Jude)
Revelation, Apocalypse (Rev., Apoc.)

Appendix 5 Terms for Groups of Animals, etc.

Terms marked † belong to 15th-c. lists of "proper terms," notably that in the *Book of St Albans* attributed to Dame Juliana Barnes (1486). Many of these are fanciful or humorous terms which probably never had any real currency, but have been taken up by Joseph Strutt in *Sports and Pastimes of England* (1801) and by other antiquarian writers.

a †shrewdness of apes
a herd or †pace of asses
a †cete of badgers
a †sloth or †sleuth of bears
a hive of bees; a swarm, drift, or bike of bees
a flock, flight (*dial.*) parcel, pod (= small flock), †fleet, or †dissimulation of (small) birds; a volary of birds in an aviary
a sounder of wild boar
a †blush of boys
a herd or gang of buffalo
a †clowder or †glaring of cats; a †dowt (= ?do-out) or †destruction of wild cats
a herd, drove, (*dial.*) drift, or (*Austral.*) mob of cattle
a brood, (*dial.*) cletch or clutch, or †peep of chickens
a †chattering or †clattering of choughs
a †drunkship of cobblers
a †trag or †rake of colts
a †hastiness of cooks
a †covert of coots
a herd of cranes
a herd of curlew
a †cowardice of curs
a herd or mob of deer
a pack or kennel of dogs
a trip of dotterel
a flight, †dole, or †piteousness of doves
a raft, bunch, or †paddling of ducks on water; a team of wild ducks in flight
a fling of dunlins
a herd of elephants
a herd or gang of elk
a †business of ferrets
a charm or †chirm of finches
a shoal of fish; a run of fish in motion
a cloud of flies
a †stalk of foresters
a †skulk of foxes
a gaggle or (in the air) a skein, team, or wedge of geese
a herd of giraffes
a flock, herd, or (*dial.*) trip of goats
a pack or covey of grouse
a †husk or †down of hares
a cast of hawks let fly
an †observance of hermits
a †siege of herons
a stud or †haras of (breeding) horses; (*dial.*) a team of horses
a kennel, pack, cry, or †mute of hounds
a flight or swarm of insects
a mob or troop of kangaroos
a kindle of kittens
a bevy of ladies
a †desert of lapwing

an †exaltation or bevy of larks
a †leap of leopards
a pride of lions
a †tiding of magpies
a †sord or †sute (= suit) of mallard
a †richesse of martens
a †faith of merchants
a †labor of moles
a troop of monkeys
a †barren of mules
a †watch of nightingales
a †superfluity of nuns
a covey of partridges
a †muster of peacocks
a †malapertness (= impertinence) of peddlers
a rookery of penguins
a head or (*dial.*) nye of pheasants
a kit of pigeons flying together
a herd of pigs
a stand, wing, or †congregation of plovers
a rush or flight of pochards
a herd, pod, or school of porpoises
a †pity of prisoners
a covey of ptarmigan
a litter of pups
a bevy or drift of quail
a string of racehorses
an †unkindness of ravens
a bevy of roes
a parliament or †building of rooks
a hill of ruffs
a herd or rookery of seals; a pod (= small herd) of seals
a flock, herd, (*dial.*) drift or trip, or (*Austral.*) mob of sheep
a †dopping of sheldrake
a wisp or †walk of snipe
a †host of sparrows
a †murmuration of starlings
a flight of swallows
a game or herd of swans; a wedge of swans in the air
a herd of swine; a †sounder of tame swine, a †drift of wild swine
a †glozing (= fawning) of taverners
a †spring of teal
a bunch or knob of waterfowl
a school, herd, or gam of whales; a pod (= small school) of whales; a grind of bottle-nosed whales
a company or trip of widgeon
a bunch, trip, or plump of wildfowl; a knob (less than 30) of wildfowl
a pack or †trout of wolves
a gaggle of women (*derisive*)
a †fall of woodcock
a herd of wrens

Appendix 6 Signs and Symbols

1. General

&	and
&c.	et cetera (and so forth)
©	copyright(ed)
®	registered; of a trademark or service mark
†	death; died
℞	take (Latin *recipe*); used on prescriptions
#	1. number (before a figure)
	2. pound(s) (after a figure)
	3. space (in printing)
x	by, as in *an 8' × 12' room*
w/	with
w/o	without
§	section (of a text)
"	ditto marks; repeat the word or sign located in the line above
☣	poison
☢	radioactive; radiation

2. Science and mathematics

♂ □	male
♀ ○	female
+	1. plus
	2. positive (number or charge)
−	1. minus
	2. negative (number or charge)
±	plus or minus
× *or* · *or* ⋆	multiplied by
÷	divided by
=	equal to
≠	not equal to
>	greater than
<	less than
≥	greater than or equal to
≤	less than or equal to
≡	identical with
≈	approximately equal to
≅	congruent to (in geometry)
:	is to; the ratio of
!	factorial of
Σ	sum
π	pi; the ratio of the circumference of a circle to its diameter (3.14159265+)
∞	infinity
∴	therefore
∵	since
∥	parallel to
⊥	perpendicular to
√	radical sign; root
°	degree
′	1. minute(s) of arc
	2. foot, feet
″	1. second(s) of arc
	2. inch(es)
∅	empty set

3. Suits of playing cards

♠	spade	♦	diamond
♥	heart	♣	club

4. Commerce and finance

$	dollar(s)
¢	cent(s)
£	pound(s) sterling (UK)
p	(new) pence (UK)
¥	yen (Japan)
@	at the rate of
%	percent
DM	Deutsche mark (Germany)
F	franc (France)

5. Signs of the zodiac

Spring

♈	Aries the Ram
♉	Taurus, the Bull
♊ or Ⅱ	Gemini, the Twins

Summer

♋ or ♋	Cancer, the Crab
♌	Leo, the Lion
♍	Virgo, the Virgin

Autumn

♎	Libra, the Balance
♏	Scorpio, the Scorpion
♐ or ⚹	Sagittarius, the Archer

Winter

♑ or ♄	Capricorn, the Goat
♒	Aquarius, the Water Bearer
♓ or ♓	Pisces, the Fishes

6. Diacritical marks
(to distinguish sounds or values of letters)

´	acute (as in the French word *née*)
`	grave (as in the French word *père*)
~	tilde (as in the Spanish word *piñata*)
ˆ	circumflex (as in the word *rôle*)
‾	macron (as used in pronunciation: āge, īce, ūse)
˘	breve (as used in pronunciation: tăp, rĭp, fŏb)
¨	dieresis (as in the word *Noël*)
¸	cedilla (as in the word *façade*)

7. Arabic and Roman numerals

Arabic	Roman	Arabic	Roman
0		17	XVII
1	I	18	XVIII
2	II	19	XIX
3	III	20	XX
4	IV or IIII	30	XXX
5	V	40	XL
6	VI	50	L
7	VII	60	LX
8	VIII	70	LXX
9	IX or VIIII	80	LXXX
10	X	90	XC
11	XI	100	C
12	XII	400	CD
13	XIII	500	D
14	XIV	900	CM
15	XV	1,000	M
16	XVI	2,000	MM

Appendix 7 Geology

Fossil history

millions of years

Cenozoic Era
- Quaternary
  - Holocene
  - Pleistocene
- Tertiary 63 million years
  - Pliocene
  - Miocene
  - Oligocene
  - Eocene
  - Paleocene

Mesozoic Era
- Cretaceous 79 million years
- Jurassic 69 million years
- Triassic 35 million years

Paleozoic Era
- Permian 38 million years
- Carboniferous 74 million years
- Devonian 48 million years
- Silurian 30 million years
- Ordovician 67 million years
- Cambrian 85 million years

Pre-Cambrian 4 billion years

(note: all figures are approximate and are based on present evidence)

coelenterates (including corals), echinoderms, brachiopods, cephalopods, jawless fish (lampreys etc.), bony fish, cartilaginous fish (sharks, skates, rays, etc.), amphibians, reptiles, birds, mammals, genus *Homo* appears

(dinosaurs)

warm-blooded vertebrates

terrestrial vertebrates

trilobites, graptolites, bony-plated fish

vertebrates

table above

present
570
first multicellular animals (soft-bodied)
670 beginning of Cambrian—first animals with hard skeletons

1,900 first cells with nuclei

millions of years ago

first fossil microbes 3,100 first deposits indicating life
3,500
oldest known sedimentary rocks 3,700

4,600 origin of the Earth

Time-scale of events in the Earth's history

Appendix 8 Chemical Elements

Periodic Table of the Elements

IA	IIA	IIIB	IVB	VB	VIB	VIIB	VIII	VIII	VIII	IB	IIB	IIIA	IVA	VA	VIA	VIIA	O
1 H																	2 He
3 Li	4 Be											5 B	6 C	7 N	8 O	9 F	10 Ne
11 Na	12 Mg				Transitional metals							13 Al	14 Si	15 P	16 S	17 Cl	18 Ar
19 K	20 Ca	21 Sc	22 Ti	23 V	24 Cr	25 Mn	26 Fe	27 Co	28 Ni	29 Cu	30 Zn	31 Ga	32 Ge	33 As	34 Se	35 Br	36 Kr
37 Rb	38 Sr	39 Y	40 Zr	41 Nb	42 Mo	43 Tc	44 Ru	45 Rh	46 Pd	47 Ag	48 Cd	49 In	50 Sn	51 Sb	52 Te	53 I	54 Xe
55 Cs	56 Ba	*57 La	72 Hf	73 Ta	74 W	75 Re	76 Os	77 Ir	78 Pt	79 Au	80 Hg	81 Ti	82 Pb	83 Bi	84 Po	85 At	86 Rn
87 Fr	88 Ra	†89 Ac	104 Rf	105 Ha	106 Sg	107 Ns	108 Hs	109 Mt									

* Lanthanides	57 La	58 Ce	59 Pr	60 Nd	61 Pm	62 Sm	63 Eu	64 Gd	65 Tb	66 Dy	67 Ho	68 Er	69 Tm	70 Yb	71 Lu
† Actinides	89 Ac	90 Th	91 Pa	92 U	93 Np	94 Pu	95 Am	96 Cm	97 Bk	98 Cf	99 Es	100 Fm	101 Md	102 No	103 Lr

Element	Symbol	Element	Symbol	Element	Symbol	Element	Symbol
actinium	Ac	fermium	Fm	molybdenum	Mo	scandium	Sc
aluminum	Al	fluorine	F	neodymium	Nd	seaborgium[1]	Sg
americium	Am	francium	Fr	neon	Ne	selenium	Se
antimony	Sb	gadolinium	Gd	neptunium	Np	silicon	Si
argon	Ar	gallium	Ga	nickel	Ni	silver	Ag
arsenic	As	germanium	Ge	nielsbohrium[1]	Ns	sodium	Na
astatine	At	gold	Au	niobium	Nb	strontium	Sr
barium	Ba	hafnium	Hf	nitrogen	N	sulfur	S
berkelium	Bk	hahnium[1]	Ha	nobelium	No	tantalum	Ta
beryllium	Be	hassium[1]	Hs	osmium	Os	technetium	Tc
bismuth	Bi	helium	He	oxygen	O	tellurium	Te
boron	B	holmium	Ho	palladium	Pd	terbium	Tb
bromine	Br	hydrogen	H	phosphorus	P	thallium	Tl
cadmium	Cd	indium	In	platinum	Pt	thorium	Th
calcium	Ca	iodine	I	plutonium	Pu	thulium	Tm
californium	Cf	iridium	Ir	polonium	Po	tin	Sn
carbon	C	iron	Fe	potassium	K	titanium	Ti
cerium	Ce	krypton	Kr	praseodymium	Pr	tungsten	W
cesium	Cs	lanthanum	La	promethium	Pm	uranium	U
chlorine	Cl	lawrencium	Lr	protactinium	Pa	vanadium	V
chromium	Cr	lead	Pb	radium	Ra	xenon	Xe
cobalt	Co	lithium	Li	radon	Rn	ytterbium	Yb
copper	Cu	lutetium	Lu	rhenium	Re	yttrium	Y
curium	Cm	magnesium	Mg	rhodium	Rh	zinc	Zn
dysprosium	Dy	manganese	Mn	rubidium	Rb	zirconium	Zr
einsteinium	Es	meitnerium[1]	Mt	ruthenium	Ru		
erbium	Er	mendelevium	Md	rutherfordium[1]	Rf		
europium	Eu	mercury	Hg	samarium	Sm		

[1]Names formed systematically based on atomic numbers are preferred by the International Union of Pure and Applied Chemistry (IUPAC) for numbers from 104 onward. These names are formed on the numerical roots *nil* (= 0), *un* (= 1), *bi* (= 2), etc. (e.g., *unnilquadium* = 104, *unnilpentium* = 105, *unnilhexium* = 106, *unnilseptium* = 107, *unniloctium* = 108, *unnilnovium* = 109, etc.)

Appendix 9 Weights, Measures, Scientific Units, and Formulas

1. Standard weights and measures with metric equivalents

Linear measure

1 inch	= 25.4 millimeters exactly
1 foot = 12 inches	= 0.3048 meter exactly
1 yard = 3 feet	= 0.9144 meter exactly
= 36 inches	
1 (statute) mile = 1,760 yards	= 1.609 kilometers
= 5,280 feet	

Square measure

1 sq. inch	= 6.45 sq. centimeters
1 sq. foot = 144 sq. inches	= 9.29 sq. decimeters
1 sq. yard = 9 sq. feet	= 0.836 sq. meter
1 acre = 4,840 sq. yards	= 0.405 hectare
1 sq. mile = 640 acres	= 259 hectares

Cubic measure

1 cu. inch	= 16.4 cu. centimeters
1 cu. foot = 1.728 cu. inches	= 0.0283 cu. meter
1 cu. yard = 27 cu. feet	= 0.765 cu. meter

Capacity measure

Dry measure

1 pint = 33.60 cu. inches	= 0.550 liter
1 quart = 2 pints	= 1.101 liters
1 peck = 8 quarts	= 8.81 liters
1 bushel = 4 pecks	= 35.3 liters

Liquid measure

1 fluid ounce	= 29.573 milliliters
1 gill = 4 fluid ounces	= 118.294 milliliters
1 pint = 16 fluid ounces	= 0.473 liter
= 28.88 cu. inches	
1 quart = 2 pints	= 0.946 liter
1 gallon = 4 quarts	= 3.785 liters

Avoirdupois weight

1 grain	= 0.065 gram
1 dram	= 1.772 grams
1 ounce = 16 drams	= 28.35 grams
1 pound = 16 ounces	= 0.4536 kilograms
= 7,000 grains	(0.45359237 exactly)
1 stone (Brit.) = 14 pounds	= 6.35 kilograms
1 ton	= 2,000 pounds
1 hundred weight (US)	= 100 pounds
20 hundred weight (US)	= 2,000 pounds

2. Metric weights and measures with standard equivalents

Linear measure

1 millimeter (mm)	= 0.039 inch
1 centimeter (cm) = 10 mm	= 0.394 inch
1 decimeter (dm) = 10 cm	= 3.94 inches
1 meter (m) = 10 dm	= 1.094 yards
1 decameter = 10 m	= 10.94 yards
1 hectometer = 100 m	= 109.4 yards
1 kilometer (km) = 1,000 m	= 0.6214 mile

Square measure

1 sq. centimeter	= 0.155 sq. inch
1 sq. meter = 10,000 sq. cm	= 1.196 sq. yards
1 are = 100 sq. meters	= 119.6 sq. yards
1 hectare = 100 ares	= 2.471 acres
1 sq. kilometer	= 0.386 sq. mile
= 100 hectares	

Cubic measure

1 cu. centimeter	= 0.061 cu. inch
1 cu. meter	= 1.308 cu. yards
= 1,000,000 cu. cm	

Capacity measure

1 milliliter (ml)	= 0.034 fluid ounces
1 centiliter (cl) = 10 ml	= 0.34 fluid ounces
1 deciliter (dl) = 10 cl	= 3.38 fluid ounces
1 liter (l) = 10 dl	= 1.06 quarts
1 decaliter = 10 l	= 2.20 gallons
1 hectoliter = 100 l	= 2.75 bushels

Weight

1 milligram (mg)	= 0.015 grain
1 centigram (cg) = 10 mg	= 0.154 grain
1 decigram (dg) = 10 cg	= 1.543 grains
1 gram (g) = 10 dg	= 15.43 grains
1 decagram = 10 g	= 5.64 drams
1 hectogram = 100 g	= 3.527 ounces
1 kilogram (kg) = 1,000 g	= 2.205 pounds
1 ton (metric ton) = 1,000 kg	= 0.984 (long) ton

3. Metric prefixes

	Abbreviation or symbol	Factor
deca-	da	10
hecto-	h	10^2
kilo-	k	10^3
mega-	M	10^6
giga-	G	10^9
tera-	T	10^{12}
peta-	P	10^{15}
exa-	E	10^{18}
deci-	d	10^{-1}
centi-	c	10^{-2}
milli-	m	10^{-3}
micro-	μ	10^{-6}
nano-	n	10^{-9}
pico-	p	10^{-12}
femto-	f	10^{-15}
atto-	a	10^{-18}

4. Temperature

Fahrenheit: Water boils (under standard conditions) at 212° and freezes at 32°.

Celsius or Centigrade: Water boils at 100° and freezes at 0°.

Kelvin: Water boils at 373.15 K and freezes at 273.15 K.

Celsius	Fahrenheit
−17.8°	0°
−10°	14°
0°	32°
10°	50°
20°	68°
30°	86°
40°	104°
50°	122°
60°	140°
70°	158°
80°	176°
90°	194°
100°	212°

Fahrenheit	Celsius
0°	−17.8°
10°	−12.2°
20°	−6.6°
32°	0.0°
40°	3.5°
50°	10.0°
60°	15.5°
70°	21.1°
80°	26.6°
90°	32.2°
98.6°	37.0°
100°	37.6°
212°	100.0°

To convert Celsius into Fahrenheit: multiply by 9, divide by 5, and add 32.

To convert Fahrenheit into Celsius: subtract 32, multiply by 5, and divide by 9.

5. Scientific units

Base units

Physical quantity	Name	Abbreviation or symbol
length	meter	m
mass	kilogram	kg
time	second	s
electric current	ampere	A
temperature	kelvin	K
amount of substance	mole	mol
luminous intensity	candela	cd

Supplementary units

Physical quantity	Name	Abbreviation or symbol
plane angle	radian	rad
solid angle	steradian	sr

Derived units with special names

Physical quantity	Name	Abbreviation or symbol
frequency	hertz	Hz
energy	joule	J
force	newton	N
power	watt	W
pressure	pascal	Pa
electric charge	coulomb	C
electromotive force	volt	V
electric resistance	ohm	Ω
electric conductance	siemens	S
electric capacitance	farad	F
magnetic flux	weber	Wb
inductance	henry	H
magnetic flux density	tesla	T
luminous flux	lumen	lm
illumination	lux	lx

6. Formulas from geometry

The following symbols are used:
r: radius; h: altitude; b: base; a: side opposite base; C: circumference; A: area; S: surface area; B: area of base; V: volume

circle: $A = \pi r^2$; $C = 2\pi r$

triangle: $A = \frac{1}{2}bh$

rectangle and parallelogram: $A = bh$

trapezoid: $A = \frac{1}{2}(a + b)h$

right circular cylinder: $V = \pi r^2 h$; $S = 2\pi rh$

right circular cone: $V = \frac{1}{3}\pi r^2 h$; $S = \pi r\sqrt{r^2 + h^2}$

sphere: $V = \frac{4}{3}\pi r^3$; $S = 4\pi r^2$

prism (with parallel bases): $V = Bh$

pyramid: $V = \frac{1}{3}Bh$

Appendix 10 Musical Notation and the Orchestra

Values of notes and rests

notes   rests

1 whole note

equals

2 half notes

or

4 quarter notes

or

8 eighth notes

or

16 sixteenth notes

or

32 thirty-second notes

Some common symbols

treble or G clef   bass or F clef   C (alto) clef   C (tenor) clef   key signature   time signature   } staff

(position for middle C is shown for each clef)

sharp (single & double)   flat (single & double)   natural   staccato   legato   tie   dotted note (value increased by half)   fermata (hold)   repeat

The circle of fifths

C   a

F   d

G   e

Bb   g

D   b

Eb   c

A   f#

Ab   f

E   c#

Db   bb

Cb   ab

C#   a#

Gb   eb

B   g#

F#   d#

The circle of fifths, showing key signatures in treble and bass clefs for all major and minor keys. Major keys are indicated by capital letters; minor keys by lower-case letters. At the bottom of the circle the keys overlap, so that, for example, Db major is enharmonically equivalent to C# major.

Orchestral layout

Dynamics

<	*crescendo*	get louder
>	*diminuendo*	get quieter
ppp	*pianississimo*	very, very quiet
pp	*pianissimo*	very quiet
p	*piano*	quiet
mp	*mezzopiano*	moderately quiet
mf	*mezzoforte*	moderately loud
f	*forte*	loud
ff	*fortissimo*	very loud
fff	*fortississimo*	very, very loud
sf	*sforzando*	suddenly very loud

Tempo indicators

adagio	slow
largo	slow and dignified
andante	flowing, at a walking pace
allegro	quick and bright
allegretto	not as quick as allegro
vivace	fast and lively
presto	very quick
accelerando	getting faster
ritardando (rit.)	holding back
rallentando (rall.)	getting slower
rubato	flexible tempo

Interpretive indicators

cantabile	singing style		*legato*	smooth
dolce	soft and sweet		*staccato*	detached
espressivo	expressively			

1819

Appendix 11 Architecture

Classical

A Greek Doric temple

tympanum

metope   triglyph   cornice

pediment

entablature   frieze

                                                            architrave

column

stoa   naos   statue of   peristyle
                        goddess

Orders of architecture: Greek origin

abacus

volute

acanthus

shaft

base

Doric   Ionic   Corinthian

Structure

flying buttress

clerestory

triforium

spandrel

gargoyle

pier or pillar

aisle   nave

finial   crocket

buttress

pinnacle

clerestory

spire

steeple

tower

chancel

vestry   transept   nave   aisle   porch

Periods

(note: some churches include architectural details that are earlier or later than the main periods that they illustrate)

Windows

quatrefoil

cusp

embrasure or splay

Norman, 12th c.

lancet, early 13th c. (interior)

geometric bar tracery, late 13th c.

Decorated curvilinear tracery with ogee arch, 14th c.

Perpendicular tracery, 15th c.

Vaults

boss

corbel

groined vault

ribbed vault

fan vault

Hammer-beam roof

ridge-pole

hammer-beam

Appendix 12 Countries of the World

(Countries are given for linguistic information on the names in use; some dependent territories are included.)

country	person (name in general use)	related adjective (in general use)
Afghanistan	Afghan	Afghan
Albania	Albanian	Albanian
Algeria	Algerian	Algerian
America *see* United States of America		
American Samoa (*dependent territory*)	American Samoan	American Samoan
Andorra	Andorran	Andorran
Angola	Angolan	Angolan
Anguilla	Anguillan	Anguillan *or* Anguilla
Antigua and Barbuda	Antiguan; Barbudan	Antiguan; Barbudan
Argentina	Argentinian	Argentine *or* Argentinian
Armenia	Armenian	Armenian
Australia	Australian	Australian
Austria	Austrian	Austrian
Azerbaijan	Azerbaijani	Azerbaijani
the Bahamas	Bahamian	Bahamian
Bahrain	Bahraini	Bahraini *or* Bahrain
Bangladesh	Bangladeshi	Bangladeshi
Barbados	Barbadian	Barbadian
Belarus	Belarusian	Belarusian
Belgium	Belgian	Belgian
Belize	Belizean	Belizean
Benin	Beninese	Beninese
Bermuda (*dependent territory*)	Bermudan	Bermudan
Bhutan	Bhutanese	Bhutanese
Bolivia	Bolivian	Bolivian
Bosnia-Hercegovina	Bosnian-Hercegovinan	Bosnian, Hercegovinian
Botswana	Motswana, Batswana, *pl.*	
Brazil	Brazilian	Brazilian
Britain *see* Great Britain		
Brunei	Bruneian	Bruneian *or* Brunei
Bulgaria	Bulgarian	Bulgarian
Burkina Faso	Burkinabe	Burkinabe *or* Burkine
Burma (*now officially called* Myanmar)	Burmese	Burmese
Burundi	Burundian	Burundi
Cambodia (*also called* Kampuchea)	Cambodian	Cambodian
Cameroon	Cameroonian	Cameroonian
Canada	Canadian	Canadian
Cape Verde Islands	Cape Verdean	Cape Verdean
Cayman Islands (*dependent territory*)	Caymanian	Cayman Islands
Central African Republic	Central African	Central African
Chad	Chadian	Chadian
Chile	Chilean	Chilean
China	Chinese	Chinese
Colombia	Colombian	Colombian
Comoros	Comoran	Comoran
Congo	Congolese	Congolese *or* Congo

country	person (name in general use)	related adjective (in general use)
Costa Rica	Costa Rican	Costa Rican
Côte d'Ivoire (Ivory Coast)	Ivorian	Ivorian
Croatia	Croat	Croatian
Cuba	Cuban	Cuban
Cyprus	Cypriot	Cypriot *or* Cyprus
Czech Republic	Czech	Czech
Denmark	Dane	Danish
Djibouti	Djiboutian	Djiboutian
Dominica	Dominican	Dominican
Dominican Republic	Dominican	Dominican
Ecuador	Ecuadorean	Ecuadorean
Egypt	Egyptian	Egyptian
El Salvador	Salvadoran	Salvadoran
England	Englishman, Englishwoman	English
Equatorial Guinea	Equatorial Guinean *or* Equatoguinean	Equatorial Guinea *or* Equatoguinean
Eritrea	Eritrean	Eritrean
Estonia	Estonian	Estonian
Ethiopia	Ethiopian	Ethiopian
Falkland Islands (*dependent territory*)	Falkland Islander	Falkland Islands
Fiji	Fijian	Fijian
Finland	Finn	Finnish
France	Frenchman, Frenchwoman	French
Gabon	Gabonese	Gabonese
Gambia, The	Gambian	Gambian
Georgia	Georgian	Georgian
Germany	German	German
Ghana	Ghanaian	Ghanaian *or* Ghana
Gibraltar (*dependent territory*)	Gibraltarian	Gibraltar
Great Britain	Briton	British
Greece	Greek	Greek
Grenada	Grenadian	Grenadian
Guam (*dependent territory*)	Guamanian	Guamanian
Guatemala	Guatemalan	Guatemalan
Guinea	Guinean	Guinean
Guinea-Bissau	Guinea-Bissauan	Guinea-Bissauan
Guyana	Guyanese	Guyanese
Haiti	Haitian	Haitian
Holland *see* Netherlands		
Honduras	Honduran	Honduran
Hong Kong (*dependent territory*)	Inhabitant of Hong Kong	Hong Kong
Hungary	Hungarian	Hungarian
Iceland	Icelander	Icelandic
India	Indian	Indian
Indonesia	Indonesian	Indonesian
Iran	Iranian	Iranian
Iraq	Iraqi	Iraqi *or* Iraq

country	person (name in general use)	related adjective (in general use)
Ireland, Republic of	Irishman, Irishwoman	Irish
Israel	Israeli	Israeli or Israel
Italy	Italian	Italian
Ivory Coast see Côte d'Ivoire		
Jamaica	Jamaican	Jamaican
Japan	Japanese	Japanese
Jordan	Jordanian	Jordanian
Kampuchea see Cambodia		
Kazakhstan	Kazakhstani	Kazakhstani
Kenya	Kenyan	Kenyan
Kiribati	I-Kiribati	Kiribati
Korea, North	North Korean	North Korean
Korea, South	South Korean	South Korean
Kuwait	Kuwaiti	Kuwaiti
Kyrgyzstan	Kyrgyz	Kyrgyz
Laos	Lao or Laotian	Lao or Laotian
Latvia	Latvian	Latvian
Lebanon	Lebanese	Lebanese
Lesotho	Mosotho, Basotho, pl.	Basotho
Liberia	Liberian	Liberian
Libya	Libyan	Libyan
Liechtenstein	Lichtensteiner	Lichtenstein
Lithuania	Lithuanian	Lithuanian
Luxembourg	Luxembourger	Luxembourg
Macedonia, The Former Yugoslav Republic of	Macedonian	Macedonian
Madagascar	Malagasy	Malagasy
Malawi	Malawian	Malawian
Malaysia	Malaysian	Malaysian
Maldives	Maldivian	Maldivian
Mali	Malian	Malian
Malta	Maltese	Maltese
Marshall Islands	Marshallese	Marshallese
Mauritania	Mauritanian	Mauritanian
Mauritius	Mauritian	Mauritian
Mexico	Mexican	Mexican
Micronesia, Federated States of	Micronesian	Micronesian
Moldova	Moldavian or Moldovan	Moldovan
Monaco	Monegasque	Monegasque
Mongolia	Mongolian	Mongolian
Montenegro	Montenegrin	Montenegrin
Montserrat (dependent territory)	Montserratian	Monserrat
Morocco	Moroccan	Moroccan
Mozambique	Mozambican	Mozambican or Mozambique
Myanmar see Burma		
Namibia	Namibian	Namibian
Nauru	Nauruan	Nauruan
Nepal	Nepalese	Nepalese
Netherlands	Dutchman, Dutchwoman	Dutch or Netherlands
New Zealand	New Zealander	New Zealand
Nicaragua	Nicaraguan	Nicaraguan
Niger	Nigerien	Nigerien
Nigeria	Nigerian	Nigerian
Northern Ireland	Ulsterman, Ulsterwoman	Northern Irish or Northern Ireland
Norway	Norwegian	Norwegian
Oman	Omani	Omani or Oman
Pakistan	Pakistani	Pakistani
Palau	Palauan	Palauan
Panama	Panamanian	Panamanian
Papua New Guinea	Papua New Guinean	Papua New Guinean
Paraguay	Paraguayan	Payaguayan
Peru	Peruvian	Peruvian
Philippines	Filipino, Filipina	Philippine
Pitcairn Islands (dependent territory)	Pitcairn Islander	Pitcairn Islands
Poland	Pole	Polish
Portugal	Portuguese	Portuguese
Puerto Rico	Puerto Rican	Puerto Rican
Qatar	Qatari	Qatari or Qatar
Romania	Romanian	Romanian
Russia	Russian	Russian
Rwanda	Rwandan	Rwandan
Saint Helena (dependent territory)	St. Helenian	St. Helenian or St. Helena
Saint Kitts and Nevis	Kittsian; Nevisian	Kittsian; Nevisian; St. Kitts and Nevis
Saint Lucia	St. Lucian	St. Lucian or St. Lucia
Saint Vincent and the Grenadines	(Saint) Vincentian	(Saint) Vincentian
San Marino	Sammarinese	Sammarinese
São Tomé and Principe	São Toméan	São Toméan
Saudi Arabia	Saudi Arabian or Saudi	Saudi Arabian or Saudi
Scotland	Scot, Scotsman, Scotswoman	Scottish or Scots or Scotch (see SCOTCH in the dictionary)
Senegal	Senegalese	Senegalese
Serbia	Serb	Serbian
Seychelles	Seychellois	Seychelles
Sierra Leone	Sierra Leonean	Sierra Leonean
Singapore	Singaporean	Singapore
Slovakia	Slovak	Slovak
Slovenia	Slovene	Slovenian
Solomon Islands	Solomon Islander	Solomon Islands
Somalia	Somali	Somali
South Africa	South African	South African
Spain	Spaniard	Spanish
Sri Lanka	Sri Lankan	Sri Lankan or Sri Lanka
Sudan	Sudanese	Sudanese
Suriname	Surinamer	Surinamese
Swaziland	Swazi	Swazi
Sweden	Swede	Swedish
Switzerland	Swiss	Swiss
Syria	Syrian	Syrian
Taiwan	Taiwanese	Taiwanese
Tajikistan	Tajik	Tajik

country	person (*name in general use*)	related adjective (*in general use*)	country	person (*name in general use*)	related adjective (*in general use*)
Tanzania	Tanzanian	Tanzanian	Uruguay	Uruguayan	Uruguayan
Thailand	Thai	Thai	Uzbekistan	Uzbek	Uzbek
Togo	Togolese	Togolese			
Tonga	Tongan	Tongan	Vanuatu	Ni-Vanuatu	Ni-Vanuatu
Trinidad and Tobago	Trinidadian; Tobagonian	Trinidadian; Tobagonian *or* Tobagan	Vatican City	Vatican citizen	Vatican
			Venezuela	Venezuelan	Venezuelan
Tunisia	Tunisian	Tunisian	Vietnam	Vietnamese	Vietnamese
Turkey	Turk	Turkish	Virgin Islands	Virgin Islander	Virgin Islands
Turkmenistan	Turkmen	Turkmen			
Tuvalu	Tuvaluan	Tuvaluan	Wales	Welshman, Welshwoman	Welsh
			Western Samoa	Western Samoan	Western Samoan
Uganda	Ugandan	Ugandan *or* Uganda			
Ukraine	Ukrainian	Ukrainian	Yemen	Yemeni	Yemeni
United Arab Emirates	Emirian	Emirian	Yugoslavia	Yugoslav	Yugoslav
United Kingdom	Briton	British	Zaire	Zairean *or* Zairian	Zairean *or* Zairian
United States of America	American	American *or* United States	Zambia	Zambian	Zambian
			Zimbabwe	Zimbabwean	Zimbabwean *or* Zimbabwe

State (with official and postal abbreviations)	Capital	Nickname
Alabama (Ala., AL)	Montgomery	Yellowhammer State, Heart of Dixie, Cotton State
Alaska (Alas., AK)	Juneau	Great Land
Arizona (Ariz., AZ)	Phoenix	Grand Canyon State
Arkansas (Ark., AR)	Little Rock	Land of Opportunity
California (Calif., CA)	Sacramento	Golden State
Colorado (Col., CO)	Denver	Centennial State
Connecticut (Conn., CT)	Hartford	Constitution State, Nutmeg State
Delaware (Del., DE)	Dover	First State, Diamond State
Florida (Fla., FL)	Tallahassee	Sunshine State
Georgia (Ga., GA)	Atlanta	Empire State of the South, Peach State
Hawaii (HI)	Honolulu	The Aloha State
Idaho (Ida., ID)	Boise	Gem State
Illinois (Ill., IL)	Springfield	Prairie State
Indiana (Ind., IN)	Indianapolis	Hoosier State
Iowa (Ia., IA)	Des Moines	Hawkeye State
Kansas (Kan., KS)	Topeka	Sunflower State
Kentucky (Ky., KY)	Frankfort	Bluegrass State
Louisiana (La., LA)	Baton Rouge	Pelican State
Maine (Me., ME)	Augusta	Pine Tree State
Maryland (Md., MD)	Annapolis	Old Line State, Free State
Massachusetts (Mass., MA)	Boston	Bay State, Old Colony
Michigan (Mich., MI)	Lansing	Great Lake State, Wolverine State
Minnesota (Minn., MN)	St. Paul	North Star State, Gopher State
Mississippi (Miss., MS)	Jackson	Magnolia State
Missouri (Mo., MO)	Jefferson City	Show Me State
Montana (Mont., MT)	Helena	Treasure State
Nebraska (Nebr., NE)	Lincoln	Cornhusker State
Nevada (Nev., NV)	Carson City	Sagebrush State, Battleborn State, Silver State
New Hampshire (N.H., NH)	Concord	Granite State
New Jersey (N.J., NJ)	Trenton	Garden State
New Mexico (N. Mex., NM)	Santa Fe	Land of Enchantment
New York (N.Y., NY)	Albany	Empire State
North Carolina (N.C., NC)	Raleigh	Tar Heel State, Old North State
North Dakota (N.Dak., ND)	Bismarck	Peace Garden State
Ohio (O., OH)	Columbus	Buckeye State
Oklahoma (Okla., OK)	Oklahoma City	Sooner State
Oregon (Oreg., OR)	Salem	Beaver State
Pennsylvania (Pa., PA)	Harrisburg	Keystone State
Rhode Island (R.I., RI)	Providence	Little Rhody, Ocean State
South Carolina (S.C., SC)	Columbia	Palmetto State
South Dakota (S. Dak., SD)	Pierre	Coyote State, Sunshine State
Tennessee (Tenn., TN)	Nashville	Volunteer State
Texas (Tex., TX)	Austin	Lone Star State
Utah (Ut., UT)	Salt Lake City	Beehive State
Vermont (Vt., VT)	Montpelier	Green Mountain State
Virginia (Va., VA)	Richmond	Old Dominion
Washington (Wash., WA)	Olympia	Evergreen State
West Virginia (W. Va., WV)	Charleston	Mountain State
Wisconsin (Wis., WI)	Madison	Badger State
Wyoming (Wyo., WY)	Cheyenne	Equality State

Appendix 14 Presidents of the United States

Name and life span	Place of birth	Party	Term
1. George Washington 1732–99	Virginia	Federalist	1789–97
2. John Adams 1735–1826	Massachusetts	Federalist	1797–1801
3. Thomas Jefferson 1743–1826	Virginia	Democratic-Republican	1801–09
4. James Madison 1751–1836	Virginia	Democratic-Republican	1809–17
5. James Monroe 1758–1831	Virginia	Democratic-Republican	1817–25
6. John Quincy Adams 1767–1848	Massachusetts	Independent	1825–29
7. Andrew Jackson 1767–1845	South Carolina	Democrat	1829–37
8. Martin Van Buren 1782–1862	New York	Democrat	1837–41
9. William H. Harrison 1773–1841	Virginia	Whig	1841
10. John Tyler 1790–1862	Virginia	Whig, then Democrat	1841–45
11. James K. Polk 1795–1849	North Carolina	Democrat	1845–49
12. Zachary Taylor 1784–1850	Virginia	Whig	1849–50
13. Millard Fillmore 1800–74	New York	Whig	1850–53
14. Franklin Pierce 1804–69	New Hampshire	Democrat	1853–57
15. James Buchanan 1791–1868	Pennsylvania	Democrat	1857–61
16. Abraham Lincoln 1809–65	Kentucky	Republican	1861–65
17. Andrew Johnson 1808–75	North Carolina	Democrat	1865–69
18. Ulysses S. Grant 1822–85	Ohio	Republican	1869–77
19. Rutherford B. Hayes 1822–93	Ohio	Republican	1877–81
20. James A. Garfield 1831–81	Ohio	Republican	1881
21. Chester A. Arthur 1830–86	Vermont	Republican	1881–85
22. Grover Cleveland 1837–1908	New Jersey	Democrat	1885–89
23. Benjamin Harrison 1833–1901	Ohio	Republican	1889–93
24. Grover Cleveland (see above)	(see above)	Democrat	1893–97
25. William McKinley 1843–1901	Ohio	Republican	1897–1901
26. Theodore Roosevelt 1858–1919	New York	Republican	1901–09
27. William H. Taft 1857–1930	Ohio	Republican	1909–13
28. Woodrow Wilson 1856–1924	Virginia	Democrat	1913–21
29. Warren G. Harding 1865–1923	Ohio	Republican	1921–23
30. Calvin Coolidge 1872–1933	Vermont	Republican	1923–29
31. Herbert Hoover 1874–1964	Iowa	Republican	1929–33
32. Franklin D. Roosevelt 1882–1945	New York	Democrat	1933–45
33. Harry S Truman 1884–1972	Missouri	Democrat	1945–53
34. Dwight D. Eisenhower 1890–1969	Texas	Republican	1953–61
35. John F. Kennedy 1917–63	Massachusetts	Democrat	1961–63
36. Lyndon B. Johnson 1908–73	Texas	Democrat	1963–69
37. Richard M. Nixon 1913–94	California	Republican	1969–74
38. Gerald R. Ford 1913–	Nebraska	Republican	1974–77
39. James Earl Carter 1924–	Georgia	Democrat	1977–81
40. Ronald W. Reagan 1911–	Illinois	Republican	1981–89
41. George H. W. Bush 1924–	Massachusetts	Republican	1989–93
42. William J. Clinton 1946–	Arkansas	Democrat	1993–

Appendix 15 Leaders and Rulers

aga high-ranking official of the Ottoman Empire

archon chief magistrate of ancient Athens

Asantehene paramount chief of the Ashanti people of West Africa

ataman/hetman Cossack chief

ayatollah highest ranking religious leader of the Shiite branch of Islam

boy/beg provincial governor or other high official in the Ottoman Empire

cacique chief of a Native American tribe in Latin America; local political boss in Latin America

Caesar Roman emperor; any powerful or dictatorial leader

caliph ruler of a Muslim state

capo divisional leader in the Mafia

caudillo Spanish military dictator

chancellor chief government minister in some parliamentary systems; high university official

Chogyal ruler of Sikkim

collector chief administrative officer of a district of India during British rule

consul chief official or magistrate in the ancient Roman Republic, ruling in a pair

czar, tsar emperor of Russia in former times

Dalai Lama leader of Tibetan Buddhists

dey Turkish governor or commander in Algeria in former times

doge chief magistrate of the old republics of Venice and of Genoa

duce leader (Italian), esp. B. Mussolini

emir Muslim prince, chieftain, or governor in the Middle East

emperor ruler of an empire

fugleman political leader; formerly, a leader or demonstrator in military drill

Führer leader (German), esp. A. Hitler

Gauleiter district governor in Nazi Germany

governor chief executive officer of a U.S. state government

imam Muslim religious leader

kabaka former ruler of the Baganda people of Uganda

Kaiser Holy Roman emperor, Austro-Hungarian emperor, or German emperor

khan/cham medieval emperor or ruler in China or central Asia

khedive viceroy in Egypt during the period of Ottoman control

king male ruler of a monarchy

maharajah a ruling prince of India

mandarin senior civil servant in imperial China; any powerful and relatively independent official

mikado, Tenno emperor of Japan

Mogul Mongol ruler of India (1526–1857)

nawab Muslim prince or ruler in India in former times

nizam former ruler of Hyderabad

pasha former provincial governor in the Ottoman Empire

pharaoh hereditary sovereign in ancient Egypt

premier prime minister

president chief executive officer of a republic or corporation

prime minister leading government official or top cabinet official, esp. in parliamentary governments

queen female ruler of a monarchy, or wife of a king

sachem, sagamore Native American tribal chief in North America

satrap provincial governor in ancient Persia; any dictatorial minor ruler

shah former ruler of Iran

sheikh leader of an Arab tribe or village; Muslim religious leader

shogun Japanese military commander, especially any of those who effectively ruled Japan in former times

sovereign one exercising supreme, esp. hereditary power; monarch

stadholder chief magistrate or provincial governor in the Netherlands in former times

sultan ruler of a Muslim state, especially under the Ottoman Empire

suzerain feudal lord

Taoiseach prime minister of the Irish Republic

tetrarch any of four joint rulers, or ruler of a quarter of a region; prince enjoying limited power in the Roman Empire

tuchun military governor of a Chinese province in former times

viceroy governor of a country, colony, or the like, ruling in the name of his sovereign or government

vizier high-ranking official, such as provincial governor or chief minister, in Muslim countries, especially under the Ottoman Empire

Appendix 16 Alphabets

Braille

A	B	C	D	E
F	G	H	I	J
K	L	M	N	O
P	Q	R	S	T
U	V	W	X	Y
Z	and	for	of	the

Morse code

A	B	C	D	E
F	G	H	I	
J	K	L	M	N
O	P	Q	R	
S	T	U	V	W
X	Y	Z		

Manual alphabet

1828

Arabic

				Name	Translit.
ا	ا			'alif	'
ب	ب	ﺒ	ﺑ	bā'	b
ت	ت	ﺘ	ﺗ	tā'	t
ث	ث	ﺜ	ﺛ	thā'	th
ج	ج	ﺠ	ﺟ	jīm	j
ح	ح	ﺤ	ﺣ	ḥā'	ḥ
خ	خ	ﺨ	ﺧ	khā'	kh
د	ﺪ			dāl	d
ذ	ﺬ			dhāl	dh
ر	ﺮ			rā'	r
ز	ﺰ			zay	z
س	ﺲ	ﺴ	ﺳ	sīn	s
ش	ﺶ	ﺸ	ﺷ	shīn	sh
ص	ﺺ	ﺼ	ﺻ	ṣād	ṣ
ض	ﺾ	ﻀ	ﺿ	ḍād	ḍ
ط	ﻂ	ﻄ	ﻃ	ṭā'	ṭ
ظ	ﻆ	ﻈ	ﻇ	ẓā'	ẓ
ع	ﻊ	ﻌ	ﻋ	'ayn	'
غ	ﻎ	ﻐ	ﻏ	ghayn	gh
ف	ﻒ	ﻔ	ﻓ	fā'	f
ق	ﻖ	ﻘ	ﻗ	qāf	q
ك	ﻚ	ﻜ	ﻛ	kāf	k
ل	ﻞ	ﻠ	ﻟ	lām	l
م	ﻢ	ﻤ	ﻣ	mīm	m
ن	ﻦ	ﻨ	ﻧ	nūn	n
ه	ﻪ	ﻬ	ﻫ	hā'	h
و	ﻮ			wāw	w
ى	ﻯ	ﻴ	ﻳ	yā'	y

Hebrew

Letter	Name	Translit.
א	aleph	'
ב	beth	b, bh
ג	gimel	g, gh
ד	daleth	d, dh
ה	he	h
ו	waw	w
ז	zayin	z
ח	ḥeth	ḥ
ט	ṭeth	ṭ
י	yodh	y
כ ך	kaph	k, kh
ל	lamedh	l
מ ם	mem	m
נ ן	nun	n
ס	samekh	s
ע	'ayin	'
פ ף	pe	p, ph
צ ץ	ṣadhe	ṣ
ק	qoph	q
ר	resh	r
שׂ	śin	ś
שׁ	shin	sh
ת	taw	t, th

Greek

Letter	Name	Translit.
A α	alpha	a
B β	beta	b
Γ γ	gamma	g
Δ δ	delta	d
E ε	epsilon	e
Z ζ	zeta	z
H η	eta	ē
Θ θ	theta	th
I ι	iota	i
K κ	kappa	k
Λ λ	lambda	l
M μ	mu	m
N ν	nu	n
Ξ ξ	xi	x
O o	omicron	o
Π π	pi	p
P ρ	rho	r, rh
Σ σ ς	sigma	s
T τ	tau	t
Y υ	upsilon	u
Φ φ	phi	ph
X χ	chi	kh
Ψ ψ	psi	ps
Ω ω	omega	ō

Russian

Letter	Translit.
А а	a
Б б	b
В в	v
Г г	g
Д д	d
Е е	e
Ё ё	ë
Ж ж	zh
З з	z
И и	i
Й й	ĭ
К к	k
Л л	l
М м	m
Н н	n
О о	o
П п	p
Р р	r
С с	s
Т т	t
У у	u
Ф ф	f
Х х	kh
Ц ц	ts
Ч ч	ch
Ш ш	sh
Щ щ	shch
Ъ ъ	" ('hard sign')
Ы ы	y
Ь ь	' ('soft sign')
Э э	é
Ю ю	yu
Я я	ya